YEARBOOK OF THE UNITED NATIONS 2009

Volume 63

YEARBOOK OF THE UNITED NATIONS, 2009

Volume 63

The United Nations Department of Public Information is dedicated to communicating the ideals and work of the United Nations to the world; to interacting and partnering with diverse audiences; and to building support for peace, development, and human rights for all. Based on official documents, although not an official record, the *Yearbook of the United Nations* stands as the authoritative reference work on the Organization and an indispensable tool for anyone seeking information on the UN system.

The *Yearbook of the United Nations* is produced by the Yearbook Unit of the Publications and Editorial Section in the Outreach Division of the Department of Public Information.

Chief Editor: Orrin F. Summerell

Managing Editor: Edoardo Bellando

Senior Editors: Lawri Moore, Anthony Paterniti, John R. Sebesta, Vikram Sura

Associate Editors: Natalie Alexander, Udy Bell, Meghan Lynn, Shiyun Sang

Copy Editor: Sunita Chabra

Typesetter: Galina V. Brazhnikova

Researcher: Nilton Sperb

Administrative Assistant: Sheila Poinesette

Copy Coordinator: Melissa Gay

Editorial Assistant: Rosario Magno

Yearbook of the United Nations
Room S-927
United Nations
New York, New York 10017
United States of America

e-mail: **unyearbook@un.org**

All volumes of the *Yearbook of the United Nations* from the 1946–47 edition (Vol. 1) to the 2008 edition (Vol. 62) can be accessed in full online on the *Yearbook* website: **unyearbook.un.org**.

For more information on the United Nations, please visit the website of the Organization: **un.org**.

YEARBOOK OF THE UNITED NATIONS 2009

Volume 63

Department of Public Information
United Nations, New York

Yearbook of the United Nations, 2009
Volume 63

Published by the United Nations Department of Public Information
New York, New York 10017, United States of America

ISBN: 978-92-1-101275-0
eISBN: 978-92-1-056297-3
ISSN: 0082-8521
United Nations publication
Sales No. E.11.I.1 H

Jacket Design: Graphic Design Unit, United Nations, New York

Printed in the United States of America

Foreword

From the beginning, the guiding vision of the United Nations has been as broad as it has been profound: maintaining international peace and security; developing friendly relations among nations; and promoting social progress, better living standards and human rights. In 2009, we met significant challenges on all fronts, as we worked to protect lives while safeguarding our planet.

During the year, the United Nations addressed numerous conflict situations, mainly in Africa, as well as a major armed crisis in Gaza, while continuing to support post-conflict countries in sustaining peace and stability and rebuilding national institutions, as in Afghanistan and Iraq. Through Security Council resolution 1888(2009), which mandated peacekeeping missions to protect women and children from rampant sexual violence, the Organization deepened its commitment to mitigating the impact of armed conflict on civilians.

Throughout the world, the continuing economic and food security crises contributed to unrest and political instability, and threatened the resources required for progress towards the Millennium Development Goals (MDGs), even as substantial advances were made in fighting AIDS, tuberculosis, malaria and vaccine-preventable diseases. We acted to facilitate more effective international coordination, including reform of the international monetary and financial system, and sought to meet development needs for agreed MDG targets in such lagging areas as primary education, maternal health and basic infrastructure. We also framed these crises as opportunities to make needed changes by encouraging green growth and clean technologies.

The United Nations Climate Change Conference produced the Copenhagen Accord, in which Governments converged in defining the long-term goal of limiting the maximum global average temperature increase to no more than 2 degrees Celsius. There was no agreement, however, on how to achieve that goal in practical terms, leaving much work to be done.

The coordinated United Nations response to the pandemic influenza A(H1N1) outbreak in 2009 testified to our success in improving national and international response to global health challenges. The commencement of the functioning of the Special Tribunal for Lebanon during the year marked yet another important effort to advance the rule of law. Overall, the United Nations continued its efforts to protect human rights worldwide, as 182 States adopted the outcome document of the anti-racism Durban Review Conference.

In a significant development for the United Nations and the peoples it serves, the General Assembly supported the consolidation of four bodies working for the advancement of women into a new organization, UN-Women, and so further empowered the United Nations system to empower women everywhere.

As documented in this *Yearbook of the United Nations*, I called in 2009 for a spirit of renewed multilateralism recognizing the interconnections among the challenges confronting us; privileging the most vulnerable people; establishing multi-stakeholder coalitions; and strengthening the existing global multilateral architecture. These needs remain. Like the volumes that have come before it, this *Yearbook* represents our work through what we have done, what we advocate, and what we ourselves are called to do. It is our own witness to the history that is shaped by the efforts of the United Nations.

Ban Ki-moon
Secretary-General of the United Nations
New York, October 2013

Table of contents

Foreword   v

Table of contents   vii

About the 2009 edition of the *Yearbook*   xiv

Abbreviations commonly used in the *Yearbook*   xv

Explanatory note on documents   xvi

Report of the Secretary-General on the work of the Organization   3

Part One: Political and security questions

I. International peace and security   37

PROMOTION OF INTERNATIONAL PEACE AND SECURITY, 37: Maintenance of international peace and security, 37; Conflict prevention, 39; Peacemaking and peace-building, 43; Protection issues, 50; Special political missions, 63. THREATS TO INTERNATIONAL PEACE AND SECURITY, 66: International terrorism, 66. PEACEKEEPING OPERATIONS, 71: General aspects of UN peacekeeping, 74; Comprehensive review of peacekeeping, 78; Operations in 2009, 79; Roster of 2009 operations, 80; Financial and administrative aspects of peacekeeping operations, 82.

II. Africa   100

PROMOTION OF PEACE IN AFRICA, 103. CENTRAL AFRICA AND GREAT LAKES REGION, 116: Great Lakes region, 116; Democratic Republic of the Congo, 118; Burundi, 137; Central African Republic, 146; Chad and Central African Republic, 153; Uganda, 163; Rwanda, 165. WEST AFRICA, 166: Regional issues, 166; Côte d'Ivoire, 170; Liberia, 191; Sierra Leone, 206; Guinea-Bissau, 215; Cameroon–Nigeria, 226; Guinea, 228; Mauritania, 232. HORN OF AFRICA, 232: Sudan, 232; Chad–Sudan, 268; Somalia, 270; Djibouti and Eritrea, 297; Eritrea–Ethiopia, 302. NORTH AFRICA, 304: Western Sahara, 304. OTHER ISSUES, 310: Madagascar, 310; Mauritius–United Kingdom/France, 311.

III. Americas   312

CENTRAL AMERICA, 312: Guatemala, 312; Honduras, 314. HAITI, 318: Political and security situation, 318; Programme of support for Haiti, 325. MINUSTAH, 326. OTHER ISSUES, 329: Colombia, 329; Cuba–El Salvador, 329; Cuba–United States, 330; Cooperation between the United Nations and regional organizations, 331.

IV. Asia and the Pacific   332

AFGHANISTAN, 334: Situation in Afghanistan, 334; Sanctions, 353. IRAQ, 362: Situation in Iraq, 362; UN Assistance Mission for Iraq, 362; International Advisory and Monitoring Board, 372. IRAQ–KUWAIT, 375: Kuwaiti property and missing persons, 375; UN Compensation Commission and Fund, 376. TIMOR-LESTE, 376: United Nations Integrated Mission in Timor-Leste, 377; Financing of UN operations, 381. DEMOCRATIC PEOPLE'S REPUBLIC OF KOREA, 384. NEPAL, 388. IRAN, 394: IAEA reports, 394. OTHER ISSUES, 396: Myanmar, 396; Sri Lanka, 397; India–Pakistan, 398; Benazir Bhutto assassination inquiry, 398; The Philippines, 399; United Arab Emirates–Iran, 399.

V. Europe and the Mediterranean   400

BOSNIA AND HERZEGOVINA, 400: Implementation of Peace Agreement, 401; European Union missions in Bosnia and Herzegovina, 407. KOSOVO, 408: Political and security developments, 408; EULEX, 412; UNMIK, 412. THE FORMER YUGOSLAV REPUBLIC OF MACEDONIA, 414. GEORGIA, 414: Situation in Abkhazia, 415; UN Observer Mission in Georgia, 419. ARMENIA AND AZERBAIJAN, 421. ORGANIZATION FOR DEMOCRACY AND ECONOMIC DEVELOPMENT-GUAM, 422. CYPRUS, 422: Political and security developments, 423. OTHER ISSUES, 431: Strengthening of security and cooperation in the Mediterranean, 431; Cooperation with the Organization for Security and Cooperation in Europe, 432; Observer status, 432.

VI. Middle East   433

PEACE PROCESS, 433: Diplomatic efforts, 433; Occupied Palestinian Territory, 434. ISSUES RELATED TO PALESTINE, 458: General aspects, 458; Assistance to Palestinians, 462; UNRWA, 466. PEACEKEEPING OPERATIONS, 476: Lebanon, 476; Syrian Arab Republic, 488.

VII. Disarmament   495

UN MACHINERY, 495. UN ROLE IN DISARMAMENT, 499. NUCLEAR DISARMAMENT, 502: Comprehensive Nuclear-Test-Ban Treaty, 512; Advisory opinion of the International Court of Justice, 516; Prohibition of the use of nuclear weapons, 517. NON-PROLIFERATION ISSUES, 518: Non-proliferation treaty, 518; Non-proliferation of weapons of mass destruction, 520; Multilateralism in disarmament and non-proliferation, 523; International Atomic Energy Agency, 527; Radioactive waste, 532; Nuclear-weapon-free zones, 533. BACTERIOLOGICAL (BIOLOGICAL) AND CHEMICAL WEAPONS, 540: Bacteriological (biological) weapons, 540; Chemical weapons, 542. CONVENTIONAL WEAPONS, 544: Towards an arms trade treaty, 544; Small arms, 545, Convention on excessively injurious conventional weapons and Protocols, 550; Cluster munitions, 553; Anti-personnel mines, 553; Practical disarmament, 555; Transparency, 555. OTHER DISARMAMENT ISSUES, 560: Prevention of an arms race in outer space, 560; Observance of environmental norms, 562; Science and technology and disarmament, 563. STUDIES, RESEARCH AND TRAINING, 563. REGIONAL DISARMAMENT, 564: Central Africa Standing Advisory Committee, 567; Regional centres for peace and disarmament, 568.

VIII. Other political and security questions 573

GENERAL ASPECTS OF INTERNATIONAL SECURITY, 573: Support for democracies, 573. REGIONAL ASPECTS OF INTERNATIONAL PEACE AND SECURITY, 575: Indian Ocean, 575. DECOLONIZATION, 576: Decade for the Eradication of Colonialism, 576; Puerto Rico, 588; Territories under review, 588. PEACEFUL USES OF OUTER SPACE, 599: Implementation of UNISPACE III recommendations, 602; Scientific and Technical Subcommittee, 603; Legal Subcommittee, 606. EFFECTS OF ATOMIC RADIATION, 607. INFORMATION AND TELECOMMUNICATIONS IN INTERNATIONAL SECURITY, 609. INFORMATION, 610: UN public information, 610.

Part Two: Human rights

I. Promotion of human rights 623

UN MACHINERY, 623: Human Rights Council, 623; Office of the High Commissioner for Human Rights, 627. HUMAN RIGHTS INSTRUMENTS, 630: Convention against racial discrimination, 631; Covenant on Civil and Political Rights and Optional Protocols, 632; Covenant on Economic, Social and Cultural Rights and Optional Protocol, 632; Convention on elimination of discrimination against women and Optional Protocol, 635; Convention against torture, 635; Convention on the Rights of the Child, 636; Convention on migrant workers, 641; Convention on rights of persons with disabilities, 642; International Convention for protection from enforced disappearance, 643; Convention on genocide, 644; General aspects, 645. OTHER ACTIVITIES, 647: Strengthening action to promote human rights, 647; Human rights education, 653; International Year for People of African Descent, 655; Follow-up to 1993 World Conference, 655.

II. Protection of human rights 656

SPECIAL PROCEDURES, 656. CIVIL AND POLITICAL RIGHTS, 657: Racism and racial discrimination, 657; Human rights defenders, 666; Reprisals for cooperation with human rights bodies, 668; Protection of migrants, 668; Discrimination against minorities, 672; Religious intolerance, 673; Right to self-determination, 680; Rule of law, democracy and human rights, 685; Other issues, 689. ECONOMIC, SOCIAL AND CULTURAL RIGHTS, 702: Realizing economic, social and cultural rights, 702; Human Rights Council special session, 702; Right to development, 703; Social Forum, 716; Extreme poverty, 717; Right to food, 718; Right to adequate housing, 723; Cultural rights, 724; Right to education, 726; Environmental and scientific concerns, 727; Right to health, 729; Slavery and related issues, 731; Vulnerable groups, 733.

III. Human rights country situations 750

GENERAL ASPECTS, 750. AFRICA, 751: Burundi, 751; Democratic Republic of the Congo, 752; Liberia, 754; Sierra Leone, 755; Somalia, 756; Sudan, 757. AMERICAS, 758: Bolivia, 758; Colombia, 759; Guatemala, 760; Haiti, 761; Honduras, 761. ASIA, 762: Afghanistan, 762; Cambodia, 763; Democratic People's Republic of Korea, 764; Iran, 768; Myanmar, 771; Nepal, 777; Sri Lanka, 777. EUROPE AND THE MEDITERRANEAN, 778: Cyprus, 778; Georgia, 778. MIDDLE EAST, 780: Territories occupied by Israel, 780.

Part Three: Economic and social questions

I. **Development policy and international economic cooperation**   **791**

INTERNATIONAL ECONOMIC RELATIONS, 792: Development and international economic cooperation, 792; Sustainable development, 799; Eradication of poverty, 808; Science and technology for development, 813. ECONOMIC AND SOCIAL TRENDS, 827. DEVELOPMENT POLICY AND PUBLIC ADMINISTRATION, 828: Committee for Development Policy, 828; Public administration, 829. GROUPS OF COUNTRIES IN SPECIAL SITUATIONS, 831: Least developed countries, 832; Small island developing States, 837; Landlocked developing countries, 840.

II. **Operational activities for development**   **844**

SYSTEM-WIDE ACTIVITIES, 844. TECHNICAL COOPERATION THROUGH UNDP, 854: UNDP/UNFPA Executive Board, 854; UNDP operational activities, 856; Financial and administrative matters, 862. OTHER TECHNICAL COOPERATION, 867: Development Account, 867; UN activities, 868; UN Office for Partnerships, 868; UN Office for Project Services, 869; UN Volunteers, 873; Economic and technical cooperation among developing countries, 873; UN Capital Development Fund, 880.

III. **Humanitarian and special economic assistance**   **882**

HUMANITARIAN ASSISTANCE, 882: Coordination, 882; Resource mobilization, 888; White Helmets, 890; Mine clearance, 891; Humanitarian activities, 893. SPECIAL ECONOMIC ASSISTANCE, 899: African economic recovery and development, 899; Other economic assistance, 904. DISASTER RESPONSE, 907: International cooperation, 907; Disaster reduction, 908; Disaster assistance, 912.

IV. **International trade, finance and transport**   **916**

INTERNATIONAL TRADE, 916: Global trade activity, 916; Multilateral trading system, 917; Trade policy, 922; Trade promotion and facilitation, 923; Commodities, 925. FINANCE, 929: Financial policy, 929; Financing for development, 939; Other issues, 958. TRANSPORT, 959: Maritime transport, 959; Transport of dangerous goods, 960. UNCTAD INSTITUTIONAL AND ORGANIZATIONAL QUESTIONS, 963.

V. **Regional economic and social activities**   **966**

REGIONAL COOPERATION, 966. AFRICA, 968: Economic trends, 968; Activities in 2009, 969; Programme and organizational questions, 974. ASIA AND THE PACIFIC, 974: Economic trends, 975; Activities in 2009, 975; Programme and organizational questions, 980. EUROPE, 980: Economic trends, 981; Activities in 2009, 981; Housing and land management, 983; Programme and organizational questions, 984. LATIN AMERICA AND THE CARIBBEAN, 984: Economic trends, 984; Activities in 2009, 985. WESTERN ASIA, 989: Economic trends, 989; Activities in 2009, 989.

VI. **Energy, natural resources and cartography**   **993**

ENERGY AND NATURAL RESOURCES, 993: Natural resources, 998. CARTOGRAPHY, 1000.

VII. **Environment and human settlements**   **1002**

ENVIRONMENT, 1002: UN Environment Programme, 1002; Global Environment Facility, 1014; International conventions and mechanisms, 1015; Environmental activities, 1025. HUMAN SETTLEMENTS, 1038: Implementation of Habitat Agenda and strengthening of UN-Habitat, 1038; UN Human Settlements Programme, 1042.

VIII. **Population**   **1045**

FOLLOW-UP TO 1994 CONFERENCE ON POPULATION AND DEVELOPMENT, 1045: Implementation of Programme of Action, 1045. INTERNATIONAL MIGRATION AND DEVELOPMENT, 1047. UNITED NATIONS POPULATION FUND, 1048. OTHER POPULATION ACTIVITIES, 1054.

IX. **Social policy, crime prevention and human resources development**   **1057**

SOCIAL POLICY AND CULTURAL ISSUES, 1057: Social development, 1057; Persons with disabilities, 1067; Cultural development, 1070. CRIME PREVENTION AND CRIMINAL JUSTICE, 1080: Preparations for Twelfth (2010) United Nations Crime Congress, 1080; Commission on Crime Prevention and Criminal Justice, 1081; Crime prevention programme, 1083; Transnational organized crime, 1091; Strategies for crime prevention, 1096; UN standards and norms, 1103; Other crime prevention and criminal justice issues; 1106. HUMAN RESOURCES DEVELOPMENT, 1107; UN research and training institutes, 1109; International Year of Languages, 1113.

X. **Women**   **1114**

FOLLOW-UP TO THE FOURTH WORLD CONFERENCE ON WOMEN AND BEIJING+5, 1114: Critical areas of concern, 1119. UN MACHINERY, 1151: Convention on the elimination of discrimination against women, 1151; Commission on the Status of Women, 1154; UN Development Fund for Women (UNIFEM), 1157; International Research and Training Institute (INSTRAW), 1158.

XI. **Children, youth and ageing persons**   **1160**

CHILDREN, 1160: Follow-up to 2002 General Assembly special session on children, 1160; Guidelines for the Alternative Care of Children, 1161; United Nations Children's Fund, 1172. YOUTH, 1184. AGEING PERSONS, 1188: Follow-up to the Second World Assembly on Ageing (2002), 1188.

XII. **Refugees and displaced persons**   **1191**

OFFICE OF THE UNITED NATIONS HIGH COMMISSIONER FOR REFUGEES, 1192: Programme policy, 1192; Financial and administrative questions, 1198. REFUGEE PROTECTION AND ASSISTANCE, 1202: Protection issues, 1202; Assistance measures, 1204; Regional activities, 1206.

XIII. Health, food and nutrition 1216

Health, 1216: AIDS prevention and control, 1216; Non-communicable diseases, 1222; Tobacco, 1222; Malaria, 1222; Global public health, 1226; Road safety, 1229. Food and agriculture, 1230: Food aid, 1230; Food security, 1231. Nutrition, 1235: Standing Committee on Nutrition, 1235; UNU activities, 1235.

XIV. International drug control 1236

Cooperation against the world drug problem, 1236. Conventions, 1240: International Narcotics Control Board, 1241. World drug situation, 1242. UN action to combat drug abuse, 1251: UN Office on Drugs and Crime, 1251; Commission on Narcotic Drugs, 1253.

XV. Statistics 1257

Work of Statistical Commission, 1257: Economic statistics, 1258; Demographic and social statistics, 1261; Other statistical activities, 1263.

Part Four: Legal questions

I. International Court of Justice 1269

Judicial work of the Court, 1269: Contentious proceedings, 1269; Advisory proceedings, 1277. Other questions, 1277: Functioning and organization of the Court, 1277; Trust Fund to Assist States in the Settlement of Disputes, 1278.

II. International tribunals and court 1279

International Tribunal for the Former Yugoslavia, 1279: The Chambers, 1280; Office of the Prosecutor, 1285; The Registry, 1285; Financing, 1286. International Tribunal for Rwanda, 1288: The Chambers, 1288; Office of the Prosecutor, 1293; The Registry, 1294; Financing, 1294. Functioning of the Tribunals, 1296: Implementation of completion strategies, 1296. International Criminal Court, 1298: The Chambers, 1300.

III. International legal questions 1303

Legal aspects of international political relations, 1303: International Law Commission, 1303; International State relations and international law, 1308; Diplomatic relations, 1312; Treaties and agreements, 1312. Other international legal questions, 1314: Rule of law at the national and international levels, 1314; International economic law, 1315; International organizations and international law, 1321; Host country relations, 1327.

IV. Law of the sea 1330

UN Convention on the Law of the Sea, 1330: Institutions created by the Convention, 1344; Other developments related to the Convention, 1346; Division for Ocean Affairs and the Law of the Sea, 1363.

Part Five: Institutional, administrative and budgetary questions

I. United Nations restructuring and institutional matters   1367

RESTRUCTURING ISSUES, 1367: Programme of reform, 1367. INSTITUTIONAL MATTERS, 1373: Intergovernmental machinery, 1373. INSTITUTIONAL MACHINERY, 1374: General Assembly, 1374; Security Council, 1379; Economic and Social Council, 1380. COORDINATION, MONITORING AND COOPERATION, 1380: Institutional mechanisms, 1380; Other coordination matters, 1382. UN AND OTHER ORGANIZATIONS, 1383: Cooperation with organizations, 1383; Participation in UN work, 1384.

II. United Nations financing and programming   1388

FINANCIAL SITUATION, 1388. UN BUDGET, 1388: Budget for 2008–2009, 1388; Budget for 2010–2011, 1394. CONTRIBUTIONS, 1410: Assessments, 1410. ACCOUNTS AND AUDITING, 1415: Financial management practices, 1416; Review of UN administrative and financial functioning, 1416. PROGRAMME PLANNING, 1417: Programme performance, 1418.

III. Administrative and staff matters   1419

ADMINISTRATIVE MATTERS, 1419: Managerial reform and oversight, 1419. OTHER ADMINISTRATIVE MATTERS, 1427: Conference management, 1427; UN information systems, 1436; UN premises and property, 1442. STAFF MATTERS, 1452: Conditions of service, 1452; Staff safety and security, 1458; Other staff matters, 1463; UN Joint Staff Pension Fund, 1471; Travel-related matters, 1472; Administration of justice, 1472.

Appendices

I. Roster of the United Nations   1489

II. Charter of the United Nations and Statute of the International Court of Justice   1492

III. Structure of the United Nations   1510

IV. Agendas of United Nations principal organs in 2009   1523

V. United Nations information centres and services   1534

VI. Intergovernmental organizations related to the United Nations   1537

Indices

Subject index   1541

Index of resolutions and decisions   1574

Index of Security Council presidential statements   1577

About the 2009 edition of the *Yearbook*

This sixty-third volume of the *Yearbook of the United Nations* continues the tradition of providing the most comprehensive coverage available of the annual activities and concerns of the United Nations.

The present volume shows how the United Nations responded in 2009 to conflict situations and unconstitutional changes of government in different parts of the world, while supporting peacebuilding, democratic processes and economic development in numerous post-conflict countries. It also relates UN achievements in helping advance human rights, formulating development policy and facilitating international economic cooperation—especially with a view to mitigating the effects of the continuing global financial crisis—as well as in providing humanitarian assistance to those in need.

Readers can locate information contained in this volume by using the Table of contents, the Subject index, the Index of resolutions and decisions, and the Index of Security Council presidential statements. The volume also features six appendices: Appendix I comprises a current roster of Member States; Appendix II reproduces the Charter of the United Nations and the Statute of the International Court of Justice; Appendix III presents the structure of the principal organs of the United Nations; Appendix IV provides the agenda for each session of the principal organs in 2009; Appendix V gives the current addresses of United Nations information centres and services worldwide; and Appendix VI lists the current addresses of the specialized agencies and other related organizations of the UN system with their respective heads as of 2009.

Structure and scope of articles

The *Yearbook* is subject-oriented and divided into five parts covering political and security matters; human rights issues; economic and social questions; legal issues; and institutional, administrative and budgetary matters. Chapters present summaries of pertinent UN activities, including those of intergovernmental and expert bodies, as well as major reports, Secretariat activities and, in selected cases, the views of States in written communications.

Activities of UN bodies. All resolutions, decisions and other major activities of the principal organs and, on a selective basis, those of subsidiary bodies are either reproduced or summarized in the appropriate chapter. The texts of all resolutions and decisions of a substantive nature adopted in 2009 by the General Assembly, the Security Council and the Economic and Social Council are reproduced or summarized under the relevant topic. These texts are preceded by procedural details giving date of adoption, meeting number and vote totals (in favour–against–abstaining), if any, and an indication of their approval by a sessional or subsidiary body prior to final adoption. The texts are followed by details of any recorded or roll-call vote.

Major reports. Most reports of the Secretary-General in 2009, along with selected reports from other UN sources, such as seminars and working groups, are summarized.

Secretariat activities. The operational activities of the United Nations for development and humanitarian assistance in 2009 are described under the relevant topics. For major activities financed outside the UN regular budget, selected information is given on contributions and expenditures.

Views of States. Written communications sent to the United Nations by Member States and circulated as documents of the principal organs have been summarized, in selected cases, under the relevant topics. Substantive action by the Security Council has been analysed and brief reviews of the Council's deliberations given, particularly in cases where an issue was taken up but no resolution was adopted.

Multilateral treaties. Information on signatories and parties to multilateral treaties and conventions has been taken from the series *Multilateral Treaties Deposited with the Secretary-General* (ST/LEG/SER/E) (see **treaties.un.org**).

Terminology

Formal titles of bodies, organizational units, conventions, declarations and officials are given in full on first mention in each main section. They are also used in resolution/decision texts, as well as in the Subject index under the key word of the title. Short titles may be used in subsequent references.

Acknowledgements

The Yearbook Unit would like to express its appreciation to the following persons for their contribution to the *Yearbook of the United Nations, 2009*:

Contributing Editors/Writers: Luisa Balacco, Elizabeth Baldwin-Penn, Kathryn Gordon, Peter Jackson, Christine Koerner

Copy Editor: Alison M. Koppelman

Proofreaders: June Chesney, Judith Goss

Interns: Cate Attwood, Kelsey Keech, Janet Mason, Elsa Pietrucci, Yang Shen, Rebecca Wolf, Daniel Zugna

Indexer: Maria A. Sullivan

Abbreviations commonly used in the *Yearbook*

ACABQ	Advisory Committee on Administrative and Budgetary Questions
AU	African Union
BINUB	United Nations Integrated Office in Burundi
BONUCA	United Nations Peacebuilding Support Office in the Central African Republic
CARICOM	Caribbean Community
CEB	United Nations System Chief Executives Board for Coordination
CIS	Commonwealth of Independent States
CPC	Committee for Programme and Coordination
DPKO	Department of Peacekeeping Operations
DPRK	Democratic People's Republic of Korea
DRC	Democratic Republic of the Congo
ECA	Economic Commission for Africa
ECE	Economic Commission for Europe
ECLAC	Economic Commission for Latin America and the Caribbean
ECOWAS	Economic Community of West African States
ESCAP	Economic and Social Commission for Asia and the Pacific
ESCWA	Economic and Social Commission for Western Asia
EU	European Union
FAO	Food and Agriculture Organization of the United Nations
HIV/AIDS	human immunodeficiency virus/ acquired immunodeficiency syndrome
IAEA	International Atomic Energy Agency
ICAO	International Civil Aviation Organization
ICC	International Criminal Court
ICJ	International Court of Justice
ICRC	International Committee of the Red Cross
ICSC	International Civil Service Commission
ICTR	International Criminal Tribunal for Rwanda
ICTY	International Tribunal for the Former Yugoslavia
IDPs	internally displaced persons
IFAD	International Fund for Agricultural Development
IFC	International Finance Corporation
ILO	International Labour Organization
IMF	International Monetary Fund
IMO	International Maritime Organization
ITU	International Telecommunication Union
JIU	Joint Inspection Unit
LDC	least developed country
MDGs	Millennium Development Goals
MINURCAT	United Nations Mission in the Central African Republic and Chad
MINURSO	United Nations Mission for the Referendum in Western Sahara
MINUSTAH	United Nations Stabilization Force in Haiti
MONUC	United Nations Organization Mission in the Democratic Republic of the Congo
NEPAD	New Partnership for Africa's Development
NGO	non-governmental organization
NPT	Treaty on the Non-Proliferation of Nuclear Weapons
NSGT	Non-Self-Governing Territory
OAS	Organization of American States
OCHA	Office for the Coordination of Humanitarian Affairs
ODA	official development assistance
OECD	Organisation for Economic Co-operation and Development
OHCHR	Office of the United Nations High Commissioner for Human Rights
OIOS	Office of Internal Oversight Services
OSCE	Organization for Security and Cooperation in Europe
PA	Palestinian Authority
UNAIDS	Joint United Nations Programme on HIV/AIDS
UNAMA	United Nations Assistance Mission in Afghanistan
UNAMI	United Nations Assistance Mission for Iraq
UNAMID	African Union-United Nations Hybrid Operation in Darfur
UNCTAD	United Nations Conference on Trade and Development
UNDOF	United Nations Disengagement Observer Force
UNDP	United Nations Development Programme
UNEP	United Nations Environment Programme
UNESCO	United Nations Educational, Scientific and Cultural Organization
UNFICYP	United Nations Peacekeeping Force in Cyprus
UNFPA	United Nations Population Fund
UN-Habitat	United Nations Human Settlements Programme
UNHCR	Office of the United Nations High Commissioner for Refugees
UNICEF	United Nations Children's Fund
UNIDO	United Nations Industrial Development Organization
UNIFIL	United Nations Interim Force in Lebanon
UNIPSIL	United Nations Integrated Peacebuilding Office in Sierra Leone
UNMIK	United Nations Interim Administration Mission in Kosovo
UNMIL	United Nations Mission in Liberia
UNMIS	United Nations Mission in the Sudan
UNMIT	United Nations Integrated Mission in Timor-Leste
UNOCI	United Nations Operation in Côte d'Ivoire
UNODC	United Nations Office on Drugs and Crime
UNOGBIS	United Nations Peacebuilding Support Office in Guinea-Bissau
UNOMIG	United Nations Observer Mission in Georgia
UNOPS	United Nations Office for Project Services
UNOWA	Office of the Special Representative of the Secretary-General for West Africa
UNRWA	United Nations Relief and Works Agency for Palestine Refugees in the Near East
UNTSO	United Nations Truce Supervision Organization
WFP	World Food Programme
WHO	World Health Organization
WIPO	World Intellectual Property Organization
WMDs	weapons of mass destruction
WMO	World Meteorological Organization
WTO	World Trade Organization
YUN	Yearbook of the United Nations

Explanatory note on documents

The following principal United Nations official document symbols appear in this volume:

A/- refers to documents of the General Assembly, numbered in separate series by session. Thus, A/64/- refers to documents issued for consideration at the sixty-fourth session, beginning with A/64/1. Documents of special and emergency special sessions are identified as A/S and A/ES-, followed by the session number.

A/C.- refers to documents of the Assembly's Main Committees. For example, A/C.1/- identifies documents of the First Committee, A/C.6/- documents of the Sixth Committee. A/BUR/- refers to documents of the General Committee. A/AC.- documents are those of the Assembly's ad hoc bodies and A/CN.- of its commissions. For example, A/AC.105/- identifies documents of the Assembly's Committee on the Peaceful Uses of Outer Space, A/CN.4/- of its International Law Commission. Assembly resolutions and decisions since the thirty-first (1976) session have been identified by two Arabic numerals: the first indicates the session of adoption, the second the sequential number in the series. Resolutions are numbered consecutively from 1 at each session. Decisions since the fifty-seventh (2002) session are numbered consecutively from 401 for those concerned with elections and appointments and from 501 for all other decisions. Decisions of special and emergency special sessions are numbered consecutively from 11 for those concerned with elections and appointments and from 21 for all other decisions.

E/- refers to documents of the Economic and Social Council, numbered in separate series by year. Thus, E/2009/- refers to documents issued for consideration by the Council at its 2009 sessions, beginning with E/2009/1. E/AC.-, E/C.- and E/CN.-, followed by identifying numbers, refer to documents of the Council's subsidiary ad hoc bodies, committees and commissions. For example, E/CN.5/- refers to documents of the Council's Commission for Social Development, E/C.2/- to documents of its Committee on Non-Governmental Organizations. E/ICEF/- documents are those of the United Nations Children's Fund (UNICEF). Symbols for the Council's resolutions and decisions, since 1978, consist of two Arabic numerals: the first indicates the year of adoption and the second the sequential number in the series. There are two series: one for resolutions, beginning with 1 (resolution 2009/1), and one for decisions, beginning with 201 (decision 2009/201).

S/- refers to documents of the Security Council. Its resolutions are identified by consecutive numbers followed by the year of adoption in parentheses, beginning with resolution 1(1946).

ST/-, followed by symbols representing the issuing department or office, refers to documents of the United Nations Secretariat.

Documents of certain bodies bear special symbols, including the following:

CD/-	Conference on Disarmament
CERD/-	Committee on the Elimination of Racial Discrimination
DC/-	Disarmament Commission
DP/-	United Nations Development Programme
HSP/-	United Nations Human Settlements Programme
ITC/-	International Trade Centre
TD/-	United Nations Conference on Trade and Development
UNEP/-	United Nations Environment Programme

Many documents of the UN regional commissions bear special symbols, which are sometimes preceded by the following:

E/ECA/-	Economic Commission for Africa
E/ECE/-	Economic Commission for Europe
E/ECLAC/-	Economic Commission for Latin America and the Caribbean
E/ESCAP/-	Economic and Social Commission for Asia and the Pacific
E/ESCWA/-	Economic and Social Commission for Western Asia

Various other document symbols include the following:

L.- refers to documents of limited distribution, such as draft resolutions.

CONF.- refers to conference documents.

INF- refers to general information documents.

SR.- refers to summary records and is followed by a meeting number.

PV.- refers to verbatim records and is followed by a meeting number.

United Nations sales publications each carry a sales number with the following components separated by periods: a capital letter indicating the language(s) of the publication; two Arabic numerals indicating the year; a Roman numeral indicating the subject category; a capital letter indicating a subdivision of the category, if any; and an Arabic numeral indicating the number of the publication within the category. Examples: E.06.II.A.2; E/F/R.05.II.E.8; E.08.II.C.2.

All documents cited in the text in square brackets may be obtained through the website of the Official Document System of the United Nations: **documents. un.org**.

Report of the Secretary-General on the work of the Organization

Report of the Secretary-General on the work of the Organization

Following is the Secretary-General's report on the work of the Organization **[A/64/1]**, *dated 4 August 2009, submitted to the sixty-third session of the General Assembly. The Assembly took note of it on 6 October* (**decision 64/504**).

Chapter I

Introduction

1. Ten years into the new millennium, the scope and magnitude of the tectonic shifts that are shaping the emerging global landscape are coming into sharper relief. The accelerated globalization of recent decades has linked people's fates together in ways we could only have imagined when the United Nations was created 64 years ago.

2. In recent times, the world has experienced unprecedented prosperity, peace, convergence on an increasingly universal normative framework and, thanks to the expansion of global communication, a heightened sense of community. However, not everyone has benefited from these global developments. Indeed, some have been left behind.

3. Just as over the past few decades, lives around the globe have become increasingly intertwined, so today, as our world is wracked by crisis, globalization is uniting our destinies in unprecedented ways. This past year the shock waves from the economic crisis spread to all corners of the globe with devastating effects on the most vulnerable populations and countries. An ongoing crisis of food insecurity continues to ravage families and communities, with over 1 billion people now going to bed hungry every night. The influenza A(H1N1) pandemic, the first influenza pandemic in over 40 years, has reminded us that our most precious commodity—our health—is linked to that of every other individual on the planet. Looming over all these crises, and potentially dwarfing them, the climate crisis we face continues to unfold, with scientists warning that the changes to our planet and its people are happening faster, and with a more severe impact, than most of our models predicted even a year or two ago.

4. We stand on a precipice. And yet, we cannot lose our nerve, or let the multiple crises turn into a crisis of confidence of our peoples. This is the ultimate multilateral moment. We are seeing the convergence of complex challenges across a spectrum of issues that lie at the core of the United Nations mission. To meet these challenges will require a multilateral effort of immense magnitude—one that draws upon the strengths and contributions of all the countries of the world, as well as their citizens.

5. Twenty-first century multilateralism must build on the multilateral foundations of the previous century, but must also broaden and deepen them in dramatic new ways. There are five essential elements of a new multilateralism that can lead us through the current crisis-ridden landscape to a more bountiful, peaceful and sustainable future.

6. First, the new multilateralism must prioritize the provision of global public goods that counter those threats that are contagious across borders and that most directly link the destinies of all our peoples: we must deal with climate change; ensuring economic stability, food availability and prosperity for all; global health; disarmament and non-proliferation; and the struggle against terrorism.

7. Second, a new twenty-first century multilateralism must recognize the complex interconnections among the challenges that confront us, both the global goods issues and the ongoing challenges of national and regional conflicts, humanitarian disasters and the struggle for truly universal human rights. Solving the problems one by one is neither possible, nor efficient nor effective. An integrated approach must inform our every effort.

8. Third, it must privilege the most vulnerable people around the world and must deliver much-needed security, development and human rights for them. This is essential both on moral grounds, as solidarity is the glue which will keep our human family together, and on enlightened self-interest grounds. The systematic bias against the poor and most vulnerable in good times and bad is simply not sustainable. Twenty-first century globalization must be for all, and must in the first instance be premised on realization of the Millennium Development Goals.

9. Fourth, it must bring to bear a much broader and deeper set of forces to address the multiple crises, broadening our collective response to include at its core, not as add-ons, constituencies from the private sector, civil society and academia. Multi-stakeholder coalitions must become the norm and not the exception if we are to successfully address the challenges before us.

10. Fifth, our new multilateralism will need to adapt and strengthen the existing global multilateral architecture to address the challenges of the twenty-first century. This will mean drawing upon the strengths of all nations, particularly those that are rising with the new century. It will mean harnessing both power and principle. A choice between one or the other is a false one. It also means improving the channels and mechanisms that ensure that the voices of the weak and vulnerable are heard in key decision-making forums. The United Nations is uniquely positioned to marshal this effort.

11. Strengthening our multilateral institutional architecture will also require adapting our multilateral mechanisms to be significantly more robust, as well as faster, more flexible and responsive than they have ever been. This is due in part to the fact that the accelerated pace of life in our contemporary globalized world has shrunk our time horizons, requiring much faster decision-making, and in part to the fact that the alliances and cooperation necessary to achieve desired goals increasingly vary widely from issue area to issue area and change over time.

12. The United Nations can and should be the hub of the new multilateralism. The Organization must provide the platform to harmonize competing interests and views of how to solve the problems the world faces. The United Nations must also continue to develop its ability to deliver the required services to people all over the world, especially those most in need. Not only is this a natural vocation for a universal organization, it is also the comparative advantage of an organization that has global reach, draws upon the resources and strengths of all nations and is charged by its Member States to address the broad spectrum of security, development, humanitarian and human rights challenges.

13. The Organization is committed to adapting to the new realities of this millennium and as this report reveals, has already taken many proactive steps to do so. However, without the full engagement and support of Member States, the magnitude of the global changes under way will quickly overtake our capacities. But with the help and commitment of our Member States, the Organization can be the agent of transformation that helps the human family adjust and adapt to the tremors and tectonic shifts reshaping our world.

Chapter II
Delivering results for people most in need

14. As the financial and economic crisis threatens to drive nations to look inward, now more than ever, the United Nations has an important role to play in giving voice to the voiceless and meeting the needs of the most vulnerable.

15. There is no question that the economic crisis is affecting us all in developing and developed countries alike. The United Nations report *World economic situation and prospects as of mid-2009* (E/2009/73) foresees that the world economy will shrink by 2.6 per cent in 2009, the first negative global growth since the Second World War.

16. Notwithstanding the hardships faced in many parts of the developed world, the scenarios unfolding in many developing countries are grimmer. At least 60 developing countries are expected to face declining per capita income. Weak capacities for crisis mitigation in most developing countries further threaten to undermine efforts to address poverty, hunger and disease.

17. As the guardian of the global development and security agenda, the United Nations must play a key role in addressing these crises. It must use this historical moment to promote progress.

A. Development

18. In 2000, with the adoption of the Millennium Development Goals, the United Nations charted out an ambitious course for development. Today, that course is threatened by uncertainty. However, if the global community responds with unity and in a determined and coordinated fashion, we will be able to overcome this difficult period in the world's history and secure peace and prosperity for all.

1. The Millennium Development Goals and the other internationally agreed development goals

19. With economies contracting, the resources needed to ensure continued progress towards the Millennium Development Goals are in short supply these days. At the same time, the demand has never been greater. The Millennium Development Goals require our redoubled efforts from now till the target date of 2015. As detailed in the 2009 Millennium Development Goals Report, in areas where global investments have been scaled up—such as in efforts on AIDS, tuberculosis, malaria and vaccine-preventable diseases—we are seeing heartening progress. In areas where Millennium Development Goal investments are still lagging, such as primary education, maternal health, smallholder agriculture and basic infrastructure for the poor, the world is far behind in reaching its agreed targets.

20. Current projections suggest that overall poverty rates in the developing world will still fall in 2009, but at a much slower pace than before the downturn. For some countries, this may mean the difference between reaching or not reaching their poverty reduction target. According to the United Nations *World economic situation and prospects as of mid-2009*, this year 73 million to 103 million more people will remain in extreme poverty because of the current crisis. Without strong action to fight against hunger as outlined by the High-Level Task Force on the Global Food Security Crisis, the targets to reduce the prevalence of undernourished people and underweight children will not be achieved by 2015.

21. The world is getting closer to universal primary education, although too slowly to meet the 2015 target. Major breakthroughs have been achieved in sub-Saharan Africa, where enrolment increased by 15 per cent from 2000 to 2007, and Southern Asia, which gained 11 per cent over the same period. Still, 72 million children worldwide were denied the right to education in 2007. Over the past five years, more girls have been enrolled in all levels of education. But the target of eliminating gender disparities in primary and secondary education by 2005 was missed. By denying education to children today, we are sentencing them to a life of poverty and we are having an irreversible negative impact on the future development of their countries.

22. It is of great concern that the current economic crisis is likely to have a dramatic impact on gender equality and women's empowerment. In many developing parts of the world, women provide most of the workforce to the agricultural sector. Those who are able to secure paid jobs outside agriculture generally fail to access decent work. They tend to be overrepresented in part-time or seasonal employment where job security and benefits are not provided. In Oceania, Southern Asia and sub-Saharan Africa, this type of work accounts for more than 80 per cent of all women's jobs.

23. Historically, in many instances these patterns of employment make women most vulnerable to economic downturns. In poor households, particularly those where the main wage-earner is a woman, job loss has a devastating impact on the entire family. In economic downturns, the risk that women will become the victims of domestic violence also increases as unemployed husbands and fathers vent their frustrations at home. In order to accelerate efforts to protect women and reduce violence, the United Nations has initiated a campaign "Unite to End Violence against Women". The Organization urges Member States to support this effort.

24. Promoting and securing health is an ethical imperative and a foundation for prosperity, stabil-ity and poverty reduction. Health is at the heart of the Millennium Development Goals and a critical precondition for progress towards most other goals. Progress, however, has been mixed.

25. Despite a reduction in child mortality in all regions, deaths of children under five remain unacceptably high. Many countries, particularly in sub-Saharan Africa and Southern Asia, have made little or no progress at all towards agreed targets. The levels are highest in sub-Saharan Africa, where, in 2007, close to one in seven children died before his or her fifth birthday. Child mortality tends to be highest among rural and poor families where mothers lack a basic education. The leading causes of these deaths—pneumonia, diarrhoea, malaria and measles—are all preventable through cost-effective improvements in neonatal and maternal care and basic health services. With a relatively small investment we can reduce child mortality markedly.

26. Progress on Millennium Development Goal 5 (reducing maternal mortality rates) is abysmal. In 2005, more than half a million women died as a result of pregnancy-related complications. Ninety-nine per cent of these deaths occurred in the developing regions, with sub-Saharan Africa and Southern Asia accounting for 85 per cent of all maternal deaths. In order to address this unacceptable situation, we must mobilize a concerted campaign of Governments, international organizations, the private sector, philanthropists, civil society and average citizens. We cannot delay.

27. The gains in the prevention and treatment of HIV/AIDS, tuberculosis, malaria and other diseases, especially neglected tropical diseases, are encouraging. As a result of improvements in prevention programmes and wider provision of antiretroviral therapies, the number of people newly infected with HIV declined from 3 million in 2001 to 2.7 million in 2007 and the estimated number of AIDS deaths also appears to be declining (2 million in 2007).

28. Increased attention, coordination and funding are enabling countries to adopt more aggressive strategies against malaria. Evidence suggests that the rapid rise in the distribution of mosquito nets coupled with the large-scale expansion of prevention programmes, improved access to diagnosis and treatment and more effective antimalarial drugs have substantially reduced malaria cases and deaths.

29. Success in eradicating tuberculosis rests on early detection of new cases and effective treatment. To achieve the target of halving the world's 1990 prevalence and death rates by 2015, regions in Africa and major countries in Asia which are lagging behind will have to improve both the extent and timeliness of the diagnosis of active tuberculosis and increase the rate of successful treatment.

30. Reaching the environmental sustainability goals set for 2015 will require concerted effort. The extraordinary accomplishment of reducing consumption of ozone-depleting substances by 97 per cent in the 20 years since the Montreal Protocol was ratified, shows what can be achieved with sustained global cooperation and the integration of sustainable development principles into national policy frameworks. We must now shift the focus to reducing greenhouse gas emissions. The current economic crisis provides an opportunity to make needed changes by encouraging green growth and clean technologies. We must also preserve our forests and wildlife. We should be particularly concerned by the rising reports of species facing extinction in the developing world.

31. We must also address the impending global water shortage crisis. More than 1.2 billion people live under conditions of physical water scarcity. Northern Africa and Western Asia are under serious stress, as are some regions within large countries, especially in Asia. We must promote practices and invest in technologies designed to reduce water wastage and increase water reclamation.

32. At their 2005 Gleneagles summit meeting, leaders of the Group of Eight countries promised to increase annual global official development assistance flows by $50 billion (in 2004 terms) by 2010, and within this envelope, to more than double aid to Africa by increasing annual flows by $25 billion. To date, these pledges have not been met. Nevertheless, meeting earlier this year, the Group of Twenty and Group of Eight reaffirmed previous commitments to increase aid, including the Gleneagles commitments, and to help countries achieve the Millennium Development Goals. These and additional resources will be necessary if world leaders are to address the growing needs of low-income countries.

33. For our part, the United Nations system is developing a comprehensive system-wide crisis response in support of national development strategies and plans to put into place a Global Impact and Vulnerability Alert System that will track the impact of global crises on the poor and most vulnerable people. Concrete measures such as these over the rest of the year will be crucial if we are to weather the current crisis and continue to make timely progress towards the Millennium Development Goals.

2. The special needs of Africa

34. Over the past decade, Africa has achieved impressive rates of economic expansion and growth, reaching an average annual growth in gross domestic product of 5.9 per cent during 2004–2007. However, the global economic crisis could reverse these trends.

35. According to the *World economic situation and prospects as of mid-2009*, a sharp decline in Africa's average annual growth rate from 6 per cent during 2004–2008 to just 0.9 per cent is expected for 2009. Against this backdrop, unemployment and precarious employment are on the rise as lower export earnings and a decrease in government revenues are affecting all economic activity. In the absence of comprehensive social safety nets, this will severely impact people's livelihoods and thus endanger the timely achievement of the Millennium Development Goals.

36. Over the past year the United Nations system has been able to strengthen its support for the African development agenda in general and the New Partnership for Africa's Development in particular. In July 2008, the Millennium Development Goals Africa Steering Group, which brings together the leaders of the African Union Commission, the Africa Development Bank Group, the European Commission, the International Monetary Fund, the Islamic Development Bank Group, the Organization for Economic Cooperation and Development, the World Bank and the United Nations, launched at the eleventh African Union Summit a comprehensive and fully costed set of recommendations on the key actions the international system could take to support Africa's accelerated achievement of the Millennium Development Goals. The Organization is working steadfastly to see these recommendations financed and implemented. It has also made steady progress in improving the effectiveness and coherence of United Nations programme delivery in Cape Verde, Mozambique, Rwanda and the United Republic of Tanzania, where pilot joint programmes are being adopted.

37. Nevertheless, as the year progresses, there is a danger that deteriorating economic conditions will give rise to political tensions. We have already seen food riots in several African countries and a troubling re-emergence of unconstitutional changes of government. In Chad and Somalia, internal crises are reaching new levels of gravity, threatening to destabilize the region.

38. The international community must help Africa tackle the crisis. World leaders should adhere to the renewed commitments they made at the General Assembly's high-level meeting on Africa's development needs, held in September 2008, and through the adoption of the political declaration on Africa's development needs in Assembly resolution 63/1.

39. As part of Africa's growing architecture of institutions in peace and security, the African Peer Review Mechanism, the work of the African Union Peace and Security Council, the African Union's early warning system, the African Standby Force and the Pan-African Parliament are important. The steadily expanding strategic relationship between the United Nations and the African Union, particularly in the area of peacekeeping, is a positive development as is

the United Nations Security Council's decision to broaden the scope of its consideration of matters of peace and security to include violence against women and children, with special attention to Africa.

B. Peace and security

40. Unfortunately, in too many corners of the world, conflicts continue unabated and both State and non-State actors act with considerable disregard for civilians, often targeting women with particularly heinous crimes. Wherever possible, the United Nations is actively pursuing opportunities for peace. Over the past year the United Nations did have some success in improving the situation of those most-affected and needy populations. The global economic crisis added a new layer of complexity to our work by catalysing social unrest and political instability in many places.

1. Preventive diplomacy and support to peace processes

41. A key role of the United Nations is to assist national actors in resolving conflict at an early stage, and to help build national capacity to sustain peace and protect human rights. Without political settlements, the world will be left with festering conflicts which place a heavy burden on humanitarian delivery systems and on peacekeeping.

42. This past year, the Organization's engagement in preventive diplomacy and support to peace processes was extensive. Support was provided to the peace processes in the Democratic Republic of the Congo, Somalia, the Central African Republic and the Comoros. Following the elections, intensive diplomatic efforts took place in Zimbabwe under the overall mediation of the Southern African Development Community and South Africa. The Organization was also asked to support political processes in Kenya, Sierra Leone, Guinea-Bissau, Niger, Cameroon, Gabon, Equatorial Guinea and Madagascar. In all these cases, it offered political and technical support, often in cooperation with partners such as the African Union.

43. The Organization continues to support full-fledged negotiations in Cyprus and political dialogue and reconciliation in Iraq. In Nepal, the Organization provided assistance in the implementation of the comprehensive peace agreement. In Central Asia, it worked closely with all countries of the region to facilitate joint approaches to cross-border challenges, including terrorism, drug trafficking and organized crime, and the management of natural resources.

44. As part of recently intensified diplomatic efforts by the international community in the Middle East peace process, the good offices of the Secretary-General have continued. The need for the resumption of direct talks on a two-State solution and comprehensive regional peace was underscored by events such

as the major armed crisis in Gaza, discontinuation of Israeli-Palestinian negotiations undertaken in the Annapolis framework and limited progress towards Palestinian unity. In Lebanon, the Secretary-General's good offices were extended with a view to sustaining the relative calm that has prevailed in the post-election period.

45. The Organization looks forward to working further with Member States on investing in capacities to respond to crises quickly and effectively and to support peace processes more predictably and professionally.

2. Peacekeeping

46. The challenges that peacekeepers face today are unprecedented in scale, complexity, and risk level. Their engagement includes supporting political dialogue between parties, assisting national Governments to extend State authority, strengthening human rights and the rule of law, advising on security sector reform, supporting disarmament, demobilization and reintegration programmes and protecting civilians. The latter, in particular, is challenging the capacity of the Organization's peacekeeping missions to robustly implement authorized mandates.

47. The Department of Peacekeeping Operations, with the support of the Department of Field Support, currently manages 17 operations deployed across five continents. These operations comprise more than 117,000 deployed military, police and civilian personnel. The budget has risen to nearly $7.8 billion a year, at a time when available resources are in danger of shrinking.

48. On the ground, peacekeepers encounter a full spectrum of environments ranging from those where some form of conflict continues, to those where a fragile stability has been reached, to those where solid peace processes are in place and peacebuilding processes dominate.

49. Over the past year the United Nations peacekeeping presence in Chad, Darfur and the Democratic Republic of the Congo increased. In Chad, a United Nations peacekeeping mission successfully succeeded the military force deployed by the European Union in March. In Darfur, deployments increased allowing the mission to project its presence more effectively. Nevertheless, the mission continued to lack resources, including helicopters, critical to the effective implementation of its mandate. The United Nations Mission in the Sudan has continued to support the resolution of core issues of the Comprehensive Peace Agreement which promise to enhance the prospects for stability in the entire region.

50. In the Democratic Republic of the Congo, renewed fighting erupted at the end of August 2008. The Security Council approved in November the mis-

sion's request to deploy an additional 3,000 military and police to increase the flexibility and reaction capacity of the mission to meet emerging needs. While some of these additional capabilities were expected to begin deploying by July 2009, the deployment of other specialized capabilities remained uncertain.

51. A deteriorating security environment is also a primary concern for the United Nations presence in Afghanistan. The efforts of the United Nations mission have been focused on coordinating the international community's development assistance and providing support to national institutions, including their preparations for elections in August 2009.

52. In Somalia, the Organization pursued a carefully calibrated set of steps in support of the highly fragile peace process, as endorsed by the Security Council in resolutions 1863(2009) and 1872(2009). Preparedness plans are being drawn up in the event of a future decision by the Security Council to deploy a United Nations peacekeeping mission.

53. The past year saw relative stability and some progress towards a reduction of tensions in Lebanon. The United Nations peacekeeping mission focused its efforts on confidence-building and assisting securing stability.

54. In Burundi, Côte d'Ivoire, Haiti, Sierra Leone and Timor-Leste, peacekeepers are supporting peace consolidation processes, extension of the rule of law, national capacity-building on gender equality issues and the creation of an environment conducive to the development of a sustainable local economy.

55. Despite divergent political views in the Security Council on the situations in Georgia and in Kosovo, the missions carried out their mandates over the past year supported by concerted diplomatic efforts. Following an agreement in the Security Council, the United Nations Mission in Kosovo began the phased handover of the operational responsibility in the rule of law area to the European Union in December 2008. The mission in Georgia came to an end this June due to a lack of consensus among Security Council Members on mandate extension.

56. Over the last year, the Departments of Peacekeeping Operations and Field Support continued to evolve and adapt. Important organizational reforms are under way, including developing a standing police capacity in a strengthened Police Division, increasing capacity in the Office of Rule of Law and Security Institutions and in the Office of Military Affairs in the Department of Peacekeeping Operations, and developing the capacity of the Department of Field Support as a service provider. Notwithstanding these recent reforms, much work still remains to ensure that the United Nations can meet evolving demands.

57. United Nations peacekeeping is at a crossroads. The Organization needs a renewed global partnership with Member States and its partners within and outside the United Nations system to ensure that requests for United Nations peacekeeping are accompanied by active political strategies and political support to implement mandates, support for faster deployment, and adequately calibrated and optimally configured human and capital resources. This is essential if the Organization is to deliver results for a more secure world.

3. Peacebuilding

58. The recent report on peacebuilding in the immediate aftermath of conflict (A/63/881-S/2009/304) emphasized that peacebuilding is first and foremost a national process. In countries emerging from conflict, the needs of a country and its people are enormous. To seize the opportunities presented by the end of conflict, a timely, prioritized and adequately resourced response from national, regional and international actors is essential.

59. The report sets out a number of concrete proposals, including measures to improve not only the Organization's own response but also its ability to provide leadership to the wider international community during this period. Specifically, the report highlights the need to strengthen and support our leadership teams in the field, to promote strategic coherence from the earliest stage of the international response, to strengthen national capacity from the outset, to improve the international community's ability to provide rapid and predictable capacities, particularly in recurring priority areas, and to enhance the speed, flexibility and risk tolerance of post-conflict funding.

60. The evolving role of the Peacebuilding Commission, the Peacebuilding Fund and the Peacebuilding Support Office are closely linked to this agenda. Over the last year, Member States working through the Peacebuilding Commission have continued to provide support to nationally driven efforts to achieve sustainable peace in Burundi, the Central African Republic, Guinea-Bissau and Sierra Leone.

61. In the past year, the Peacebuilding Fund has provided funding assistance to a growing number of countries emerging from conflict. As of April 2009, with more than $309 million in deposits, the Fund had already allocated over $131 million to 12 countries for a total of 65 projects. These support national dialogue and conflict reconciliation initiatives, security and justice sector reform and demobilization and disarmament of former combatants. On 17 June 2009, the General Assembly approved revised terms of reference for the Fund which incorporate lessons learned from the operational experiences of the Fund over the last two years.

62. Despite all of this progress, additional efforts are needed to effectively meet the challenges of coun-

tries recovering from conflict and to close the gap in our institutional response to peacebuilding needs. Ensuring coherence among key national, regional and international actors will be essential for effective action.

C. Humanitarian affairs

63.   Throughout 2008, the United Nations continued its efforts to improve the timeliness and effectiveness of humanitarian assistance worldwide in response to the devastating effects of several large-scale natural disasters, worsening conflict situations and the global food crisis.

64.   In collaboration with Governments and other partners, the United Nations supported the humanitarian response to some 55 emergencies. The damage caused by Cyclone Nargis in Myanmar, conflict in Georgia, the repeated hurricanes in Haiti and Cuba, the cholera outbreak in Zimbabwe and drought in Ethiopia were among the crises calling for coordinated efforts.

65.   The year 2008 saw significant improvements within the international humanitarian system. The principles and approaches of the 2005–2006 humanitarian reform initiative which aimed to ensure a more rapid, predictable and accountable humanitarian response are now the standard way the United Nations system supports Governments and affected populations. The humanitarian architecture at the country level is now clearer: a Humanitarian Coordinator; a cluster (sector) lead agency for each of the main areas of humanitarian response; and an inclusive humanitarian country team which shapes overall strategic direction for the humanitarian response. The cluster approach—which establishes clear sector-based partnerships to address gaps and strengthen the effectiveness of humanitarian response—was implemented in 13 new countries, including 5 that experienced sudden-onset emergencies, bringing the total number of countries with Humanitarian or Resident Coordinators using the cluster approach to 33.

66.   With almost $12 billion in humanitarian spending registered globally, 2008 was a year of near-record resource mobilization. About half of this global humanitarian funding was provided to projects in United Nations consolidated appeals and flash appeals, covering approximately 70 per cent of the $7 billion in appeal requirements. This represented a 40 per cent increase in total funding over 2007.

67.   Thanks to concerted mobilization efforts, $453 million was contributed to the Central Emergency Response Fund and $406 million to country-level pooled funds, ensuring better coordination of funding. This represented a 22 per cent increase compared to pooled resources obtained in 2007. The Organization and its partners also worked hard to im-prove relationships on the ground, particularly with non-governmental organizations, in order to improve assistance to those most in need.

68.   Major challenges for some humanitarian work include growing humanitarian access problems, increasingly unsafe operating environments and decreasing respect for the basic humanitarian principles of humanity, independence, impartiality and neutrality. The challenges of providing timely and predictable humanitarian assistance will be intensified by the current global financial crisis. On the policy side, work on issues such as needs assessment, better impact evaluation and the transition from emergency relief must be intensified.

69.   The year 2008 also brought new insights into how humanitarian work might be shaped in the future. Emerging threats like the global food crisis and climate change placed additional strains on the international humanitarian system, demonstrating how factors other than the traditional triggers of humanitarian crisis can generate acute vulnerability. The degree to which these issues are reflected in the global agenda remains inadequate. These new challenges remind the United Nations system, and the humanitarian community as a whole, of the critical need to remain flexible and adapt constantly to changing circumstances.

D. Human rights, rule of law, genocide prevention and the responsibility to protect, and democracy and good governance

70.   History shows that economic crises often catalyse unhealthy trends in our societies and polities like chauvinism, racism, human rights violations and abrogation of the rule of law. For this reason and at this time, it is imperative that the United Nations make a special effort to promote respect for human rights and non-discrimination, support the further development of the rule of law globally, embrace genocide prevention and the responsibility to protect and renew its commitment and engagement to foster democracy and good governance. Protecting these rights is central to our mission to deliver to those most in need and is indispensable for our peace and development efforts to be sustainable.

1. Human rights

71.   Notwithstanding the enormous progress made in recent years in the field of human rights in developing new legal instruments and strengthening institutions, serious violations of human rights continue to be committed on a daily basis in numerous countries around the world. Celebrations for last year's sixtieth anniversary of the Universal Declaration of Human Rights revealed enormous popular enthusiasm for the ideals enshrined in the Declaration,

but also provided a reminder of the distance still to be covered before we can proclaim the rights of all to be truly protected.

72. The anniversary of the Declaration coincided with growing recognition of the relevance of human rights in crafting responses to a host of global challenges, including climate change, the food and financial crises and the HIV/AIDS pandemic.

73. Increasing economic hardship, exacerbated by the global economic crisis, has resulted in a rise in xenophobia and discrimination against migrants in many countries of the world. Nonetheless, the Organization's advocacy contributed to an increased number of Member States ratifying the International Convention on the Protection of the Rights of All Migrants and Members of Their Families and highlighted the human rights dimensions of migration.

74. Marginalization, disempowerment, racial discrimination and intolerance were also addressed at the Durban Review Conference in April 2009. Notwithstanding the tensions around the Conference, the outcome document does provide a basis for addressing racial discrimination globally and constructively addresses the crucial issue of incitement to racial and religious hatred. The Committee that monitors implementation of the International Convention on the Elimination of All Forms of Racial Discrimination has further enhanced and streamlined its early warning and urgent action procedure to address grave and urgent threats to racial groups and ethnic populations in different regions of the world.

75. The universal periodic review of the Human Rights Council, under which the human rights record of 80 countries has been reviewed to date, has put additional emphasis on national implementation by creating a review mechanism with broad participation. A range of recommendations adopted through the process is already being implemented by many reviewed States with the support of the United Nations country teams on the ground. These are important achievements, but the Human Rights Council can and must do more to address the many serious human rights situations around the world.

2. Rule of law

76. The past year was a historic one for the effort to combat impunity for serious international crimes, owing to the renewed commitment by some Member States to the rule of law. Yet, scores of victims of violations of international humanitarian and human rights law in many countries await justice.

77. The Organization continues to be the global centre for the promotion of the rule of law. Over 40 United Nations system entities conduct activities in more than 110 countries. Activities are vast and include the promotion and implementation of norms and standards in most fields of international law, supporting transitional justice, strengthening security and justice institutions and providing the rule of law in mediation processes (see A/63/64). The Organization includes judicial mechanisms, such as ad hoc tribunals, and supports other accountability mechanisms. This year marked the commencement of the functioning of the Special Tribunal for Lebanon. The Organization's rule of law activities also help address global challenges like international piracy; the United Nations Office on Drugs and Crime, for example, has been supporting Kenya and other East African countries in the prosecution of suspects involved in piracy off the coast of Somalia.

78. The arrangements to improve the coherence and quality of United Nations rule of law assistance are producing results. To provide overall policy direction, the Rule of Law Coordination and Resource Group has issued guidance notes on the United Nations approach to rule of law assistance, justice for children and United Nations assistance to constitution-making processes.

79. The Organization's dialogue with Member States to promote rule of law at the international level has borne fruit in terms of both moving the rule of law agenda forward and contributing to an emerging consensus on assistance policies and coordination among key stakeholders.

3. Genocide prevention and the responsibility to protect

80. The Secretary-General takes very seriously the responsibility of the United Nations system as a whole to prevent genocide and other mass atrocities. Over the past year, two Special Advisers to the Secretary-General who address these issues have made significant efforts to achieve greater progress towards the establishment of a system that will prevent and respond to such crimes. Both mandates operate on the basis of three pillars of responsibility: the State's responsibility for its populations, international support for the State, and timely and decisive response by the international community, in accordance with the Charter, when States manifestly fail to protect their populations from the specified crimes.

81. The office of the Special Adviser on the Prevention of Genocide has put in place a framework of analysis to help in determining situations that if not addressed urgently could result in mass violations of international humanitarian law, including genocide. This framework suggests areas where proactive efforts for early warning and prevention can be undertaken. It has been reviewed by experts from within the United Nations system. Using the framework, the office has analysed a number of country situations in Africa and Asia.

82. The office has established an information collection system and has instituted collaboration with partners within and outside the United Nations. It has increased its visibility through the creation of a website and other means, as general awareness is one of the tools available for the prevention of genocide. Finally, the Special Adviser has strengthened his outreach activities with regard to Member States, in particular the members of the Security Council, by briefing every incoming President and by holding meetings for the exchange of information.

83. The Special Adviser who focuses on the responsibility to protect has addressed the conceptual, institutional and political dimensions of rendering operational the principles contained in paragraphs 138 and 139 of the 2005 World Summit Outcome (General Assembly resolution 60/1). The report on implementing the responsibility to protect (A/63/677)—based on extensive research and wide consultations with Member States, United Nations departments, agencies and programmes, non-governmental organization representatives and independent experts—outlines an operational strategy for preventing genocide, war crimes, ethnic cleansing and crimes against humanity, as well as their incitement, and for responding in a timely and decisive manner, in accordance with the Charter, when they occur. In late July, the General Assembly held a three-day debate on the Secretary-General's report that demonstrated both broad support for the Secretary-General's three-pillared strategy for addressing the responsibility to protect, as well as the need for continuing consultations and deliberation on its various aspects.

84. To improve early warning and assessment capacity, as mandated by paragraph 138 of the World Summit Outcome, the Special Advisers are consolidating appropriate mechanisms for an inclusive process of collaboration within the United Nations system and with Member States.

4. Democracy and good governance

85. Democratic principles are woven throughout the normative fabric of the Organization and have been continually strengthened by the progressive adoption of international norms, standards and resolutions, as well as by ever greater operational activity in the area of democracy promotion.

86. In the past year, the Organization provided ongoing support to almost 50 Member States in conducting genuine and periodic elections across a range of peacekeeping, peacebuilding and development contexts. Examples included multiparty elections in Nepal, Sierra Leone, Zambia, Bangladesh, Honduras, Maldives and Guinea-Bissau. The Organization continued its extensive efforts to assist in the development of democratic institutions and good governance

worldwide. The use of information and communications technology and e-government contributed to enhancing transparency, accountability and public administration.

87. The Organization's efforts to support democracy worldwide have been strengthened through the grant-making United Nations Democracy Fund. Specifically targeting local non-governmental organizations, the Fund's projects aim to strengthen the voice of civil society, promote human rights and encourage the participation of all groups in democratic processes. To date, the Fund has received more than $90 million in contributions and supported 204 projects around the world in two funding rounds.

Chapter III
Securing global goods

88. The world has changed. Ties of commerce, communication and migration are binding us ever closer. At the same time we see the emergence of a set of global threats that are challenging all of our fates. Just as the issues have become more interdependent, so have we.

89. The United Nations is ideally situated for providing the global leadership needed to address these twenty-first-century challenges. As the only universal organization with a comprehensive mandate, it can catalyse action by its entire membership and can build innovative stakeholder partnerships needed for addressing the range and scope of the challenges on the international agenda today. Moreover, the Organization's Member States expect it to do so. It is for this reason that at the beginning of his tenure the Secretary-General announced that one of his key priorities would be to deliver on global goods. This past year, he has adhered to this commitment, spearheading major policy initiatives in climate change, global health, counter-terrorism, and disarmament and non-proliferation.

A. Climate change

90. In 2009—the year of climate change—Governments will convene in Copenhagen to negotiate and, hopefully, conclude a new global climate agreement. A strong, scientifically sound agreement in Copenhagen is essential for mitigating emissions, bolstering the adaptation potential of vulnerable countries and catalysing the lower-carbon green growth that will power a more sustainable global economy.

91. The Secretary-General has called climate change the defining challenge of our generation. It affects every sphere of activity, from energy and the economy to health, food, development and security. No issue better demonstrates the need for global solidarity. No issue is more fundamental to revitalizing the global economy and ensuring sustainable prosperity.

And no issue is more essential to our survival as a species. From the moment the Secretary-General took office, he sought to mobilize the political will needed to address this increasingly grave global threat. This year, leadership at the highest level, from each and every country, is urgently needed to protect the planet, save lives and build a more sustainable global economy.

92.　Last year's December meeting on climate change in Poznan, Poland, was an important milestone on the road from Bali to Copenhagen. Much remains to be done, however. While there are other forums for climate discussions, only the United Nations Framework Convention on Climate Change enjoys global legitimacy based on the principle of near-universal participation. It will continue to facilitate negotiations among all parties.

93.　Several elements require resolution to seal a deal in Copenhagen. At present, these include ambitious mitigation targets from industrialized countries; mitigation measures from the developing countries, beyond what they are already doing; increased financing, both for mitigation and adaptation, including incentives for reducing emissions from deforestation and degradation; equitable institutional and governance arrangements; and a framework for adaptation to assist those countries most vulnerable to the impacts of climate change.

94.　To further prospects for success in Copenhagen, the Secretary-General is organizing a high-level event on climate change for all Heads of State and Government at United Nations Headquarters on 22 September 2009. It will be the only international climate meeting before Copenhagen to bring together all the world's leaders, from the major emitters to the most vulnerable.

95.　Going forward, the United Nations system is committed to assisting Governments in the implementation of all existing and future climate change agreements. To that end, the Organization continues to draw upon an increasingly coherent and well-coordinated response from United Nations agencies, funds and programmes focused on adaptation, capacity-building, climate knowledge, prevention of deforestation and degradation and technology development and transfer, which is coordinated through the Chief Executives Board for Coordination.

96.　Numerous examples of inter-agency cooperation exist, including at the country level, where the Organization is delivering results for those most in need. One such initiative supports rainforest countries in reducing emissions caused by deforestation and degradation, while protecting indigenous livelihoods. Another helps developing countries strengthen their involvement in mitigation actions that advance sustainable development through the clean development mechanism of the Kyoto Protocol.

97.　The inter-agency climate change adaptation network supports developing countries with the information and technology needed to bolster community-based climate resilience measures. Disaster risk reduction efforts, another core element of adaptation policy, are helping create safer communities, both now and under the more extreme weather conditions of the future.

98.　Finally, the global green economy initiative, launched last year, provides policymakers with the timely analysis needed to help transform the economy in a lower-carbon direction. If it is fully implemented—and backed by an ambitious climate agreement in Copenhagen—lives and livelihoods can be saved and the world set on a safer, more sustainable course of green growth.

99.　Combating climate change is a moral imperative—and an economic opportunity. In addressing the climate challenge, we can help catalyse economic recovery, improve energy access and food security for the poor and strengthen our efforts to achieve the Millennium Development Goals. This year, we must join together to help realize the ultimate global good: protecting lives while protecting our planet, for this and future generations.

B.　Global health

100.　The Secretary-General has made advancing global health a core priority. In this interconnected world, illness and disease in one part of the world affect the well-being of people worldwide, either through direct or indirect channels. The influenza A(H1N1) outbreak reminded us that geography no longer guarantees immunity and that we can only protect ourselves if we come together and join forces. This is true for pandemics as well as the other global health challenges we face today.

101.　The United Nations system has been working to prepare and respond to the possibility of a pandemic. Over the past years, the system has initiated advance planning, encouraged transparency in sharing real-time information and intelligence on the progress of diseases, advocated for investment in strong public health systems and sought to forge strong partnerships between the private, public and voluntary sectors. These measures have dramatically improved our response capacity to new outbreaks and emerging diseases.

102.　The Organization has looked beyond the influenza outbreak to the more systemic problems underlying global health provision. These are closely linked to progress on development and the achievement of the Millennium Development Goals. A healthier world is a better world, a safer world and a more just world.

103. Central to this quest is the need to address maternal health, the Millennium Development Goal which lags behind the rest. Maternal health is a critical indicator of the health and prosperity of a nation. Women are central to building productive and social capital: they provide the labour force and the glue cementing communities together, and they frequently are responsible for caring for extended families which would otherwise be completely destitute.

104. Over the past few years, the Organization has seen important progress in the prevention and treatment of HIV/AIDS, tuberculosis and malaria. The multi-stakeholder partnerships that have been forged to address these diseases have proven to be effective. Ending malaria deaths, for example, may soon be a reality.

105. We must continue to address a host of diseases primarily affecting the world's poor in both the South and the North, particularly the neglected tropical diseases. We must also direct our attention to preventing and treating chronic diseases, especially heart disease, stroke, diabetes and cancer, which are the biggest killers worldwide. Without focusing on these threats to health, we will not be able to improve livelihoods and continue to expand healthy lifespans.

106. In the current economic crisis, there may be some temptation to cut budgets for health and reduce services available to the poor. This would be both morally wrong and economically counterproductive. Investment in health has huge positive implications for a country's economic and social well-being today and decades into the future.

107. Many of these themes have been picked up and further elaborated at the Economic and Social Council's 2009 Annual Ministerial Review on "Implementing the internationally agreed goals and commitments in regard to global public health". The Organization looks forward to continuing the dialogue to help fine-tune the strategies it is currently employing for a healthier world.

C. Countering terrorism

108. Addressing terrorism is one of the global challenges that must be met if we are to enjoy a future of peace, security and development. The General Assembly adopted resolution 60/288, the United Nations Global Counter-Terrorism Strategy, in September 2006 as a concrete plan to counter terrorism and the conditions conducive to its spread, while maintaining human rights imperatives. In September 2008, the Assembly renewed its commitment to the Strategy. Earnest efforts are needed at the national, regional, international and grass-roots levels to ensure the continued implementation of the Strategy in a comprehensive and integrated manner.

109. In September 2008, Member States urged the Secretary-General to make the necessary arrangements to institutionalize the United Nations Counter-Terrorism Implementation Task Force, a body established to ensure coordination and coherence in counter-terrorism efforts among various entities within the United Nations system (General Assembly resolution 62/272). In response to this request, the Secretary-General has relocated the base of operations of the Task Force to the Department of Political Affairs. A new, full-time Task Force Chair will be appointed who will continue to work in a coordinated fashion with Member States and with the member entities of the Task Force, including the Security Council's counter-terrorism-related bodies.

110. In assisting implementation of the Global Counter-Terrorism Strategy, the Task Force has identified cross-cutting areas of work where cooperation across Task Force entities can provide added value. At present, eight working groups are organized around these cross-cutting issues: *(a)* integrated assistance for countering terrorism; *(b)* preventing and resolving conflicts; *(c)* supporting and highlighting victims of terrorism; *(d)* preventing and responding to weapons of mass destruction attacks; *(e)* tackling the financing of terrorism; *(f)* countering the use of the Internet for terrorist purposes; *(g)* strengthening the protection of vulnerable targets; and *(h)* protecting human rights while countering terrorism. The Task Force briefed Member States on its work most recently in March 2009.

111. As part of this work, last year the Secretary-General convened an international symposium on supporting victims of terrorism that brought together victims, experts and representatives of Member States, regional organizations, civil society and the media. The symposium gave victims of terrorism a human face and provided a forum for sharing best practices and discussing concrete steps to assist them.

112. While the Task Force and United Nations system entities have a role to play, the greater part of Strategy implementation must be undertaken at the national, regional and grass-roots levels. As the Organization looks to the future, it anticipates increased efforts to expand and strengthen partnerships between Member States, the United Nations system, regional and subregional organizations and civil society.

D. Disarmament and non-proliferation

113. The world continues to face risks from the existence of weapons of mass destruction, especially nuclear weapons; their geographical spread; and their possible acquisition by non-State actors and terrorists. Moreover, despite certain achievements in the field of conventional arms, the destabilizing accumulation and proliferation of conventional arms still remains a serious security threat.

114. There is an encouraging growing momentum towards achieving the goal of a world free from nuclear weapons. This momentum has materialized in a variety of initiatives not just by civil society but by nuclear-weapon States and non-nuclear-weapon States alike. These efforts point the way to move from the divisions and paralysis of the past towards genuine dialogue and progress. The joint understanding for a follow-on agreement to the START Treaty resulting from the talks held in July in Moscow between President Barack Obama and President Dmitry Medvedev is particularly welcome. The new verifiable and legally binding agreement will contain significant reductions in the number of strategic nuclear warheads and delivery systems.

115. There are challenges that require urgent global action. The second nuclear test that the Democratic People's Republic of Korea conducted on 25 May 2009 was declared a clear and grave violation of relevant Security Council resolutions and the norm established by the Comprehensive Nuclear-Test-Ban Treaty. The event highlighted the urgency of the Treaty's entry into force.

116. Concerns remain about the nuclear programme of the Islamic Republic of Iran. Efforts to find a peaceful resolution of the outstanding issues must continue. The Islamic Republic of Iran has a responsibility to implement measures to establish confidence in the exclusively peaceful nature of its nuclear programme.

117. Last October, the Secretary-General outlined his five-point plan for disarmament. He encouraged nuclear-weapon States to make further cuts in their nuclear arsenals, underscored the need for new efforts to bring the Comprehensive Nuclear-Test-Ban Treaty into force, and emphasized that the Conference on Disarmament must begin negotiations on a fissile material treaty without preconditions. In May, the Conference on Disarmament was able to reach an agreement on its programme of work, ending the stalemate that has virtually paralysed the world's single multilateral negotiating body on disarmament for more than a decade.

118. The review process of the Treaty on the Non-Proliferation of Nuclear Weapons regained part of the ground lost in 2005 and there are expectations that the States parties will continue to build on the positive momentum towards a successful 2010 Review Conference.

119. In the area of conventional weapons, combating the illicit trade in small arms and light weapons remains one of the Organization's priorities. The Organization calls upon Member States to negotiate and adopt a legally binding treaty on the import, export and transfer of conventional arms on a non-discriminatory and transparent basis. The United Nations Regional Centres for Peace and Disarmament in Africa, Asia and the Pacific and Latin America and the Caribbean will continue to provide expertise and active support to build the capacity of States to fight the scourge of armed violence and eradicate illicit arms trafficking.

120. March 2009 marked the tenth anniversary of the entry into force of the Ottawa Convention on Landmines. The progress thus far has been remarkable in stigmatizing the use and banning the transfer of anti-personnel landmines, although much remains to be done to achieve the goal of a world free of them. The Organization will continue to support the new Convention on Cluster Munitions—opened for signature in Oslo in December 2008—to achieve its early entry into force. It also encourages the conclusion of negotiations on cluster munitions in the context of the Convention on Conventional Weapons as complementary and mutually reinforcing to the process leading to the Convention on Cluster Munitions.

121. The coming year is likely to provide a window of opportunity for tangible progress in the area of disarmament and non-proliferation. We must work together to maintain and reinvigorate effective disarmament and non-proliferation norms, so that stability and security can prevail both nationally and internationally.

Chapter IV
Creating a stronger United Nations

122. When the Secretary-General took office, he pledged that he would make reform a key priority. If the United Nations is to be successful in delivering to those most in need and addressing global challenges through the provision of global goods, it must improve and streamline its organizational functioning through improved accountability, transparency and efficiency. While current reforms are designed to optimize the Organization's performance, the full and active engagement and support of Member States is required to fulfil these expectations. Member States must align their demands on the Organization with a realistic assessment and subsequent provision of resources to attain the stated goals. We have much work ahead of us if we are to make the needed structural and policy improvements. Without these, we will not be able to be fully accountable to each other and to the global citizenry whom we serve.

A. The Secretariat, the intergovernmental machinery, system-wide coherence and cooperation with regional organizations

123. In order for the United Nations to function effectively, the Secretariat, the intergovernmental machinery and regional organizations must work seamlessly together. Over the past year, in collaboration with Member States, the Organization has been working hard to strengthen the core and build the connective tissue.

1. The Secretariat

124. If the Secretariat is to deliver results for those most in need, it must have a modern, efficient and nimble administration capable of supporting increasingly operational and field-based programmes. As part of proposed reforms, the Secretary-General launched a strategic workforce planning initiative designed to attract new talent and provide more mobility and career development opportunities for existing staff. In December 2008, the General Assembly agreed to replace the Organization's cumbersome contractual structure with a simplified framework and harmonize conditions of service across the Secretariat (resolution 63/250). The Assembly's decision to strengthen the development pillar of the Secretariat (resolution 63/260) is very welcome given currently overtaxed capacities.

125. Human resource reforms alone, however, are not enough to ensure timely and efficient delivery of results. The Secretariat's business processes must be streamlined and firmly rooted in a culture of client orientation. To this end, in December 2008 the General Assembly authorized the Enterprise Resource Planning project named "Umoja" that will redesign and integrate core administrative processes across the Secretariat and peacekeeping operations. A revised service delivery model, based on accepted best practices, will enhance the Organization's ability to fulfil its mandates more effectively by improving the way it delivers its finance, procurement, supply chain, logistics, central support and human resources services. In the meantime, it has already implemented a number of procurement reforms as well as the Lean Six Sigma capacity-building programme, which will support departments in implementing management reforms.

126. The global economic crisis poses a unique challenge this year to securing the funding required for the Secretariat to carry out its mandates. It has influenced budget proposals for the biennium 2010–2011 and has made reforming the budget process an even more pressing priority. The Organization is committed to strengthening the budget process. The Organization counts on the support of Member States to assist it in ensuring that there is a more timely discussion of the budget and that decision-making is focused on how resources are best spent to achieve results.

127. The Secretary-General is determined to develop a results-oriented culture at every level of the Organization, starting with senior management and cascading down to individual staff. This year for the first time, the assessment of each senior manager's performance in 2008 was published to demonstrate that achieving results and strengthening accountability and transparency are central to the Organization's management reform agenda.

128. Accountability was also strengthened through the introduction of a new system of administration of justice to handle internal disputes and disciplinary matters in the United Nations in a more efficient and professional manner. Two new tribunals, the United Nations Dispute Tribunal and the United Nations Appeals Tribunal, will provide a judicial review of cases where informal resolution has not been possible.

129. The capital master plan—the renovation of the Organization's Headquarters—is now well under way. This five-year project will modernize our facilities and result in a 50 per cent decrease in energy consumption compared to existing conditions. It will create a better work environment and should promote innovation and better performance.

2. Intergovernmental machinery

130. If the Secretariat serves as the heart, the various legislative and other bodies that make up the intergovernmental machinery function as the arteries and nerves, transporting the life blood and energy to the Organization. For the past year, in addition to their usual diverse activities, the General Assembly, the Security Council and the Economic and Social Council have had the additional challenge of responding to the global financial and economic crisis.

131. The General Assembly played an important role in promoting dialogue and raising public awareness through interactive thematic debates on the financial crisis and its impact on development and on energy efficiency and new and renewable energy sources. These debates have helped forge consensus among Member States on policy responses.

132. In order to provide more opportunity for direct exchange between the Secretariat and Member States and enhance transparency and accountability, the Secretary-General continued with the well-established practice of periodically briefing the General Assembly on his most recent activities.

133. In December 2008, the General Assembly decided to hold its comprehensive review of the United Nations system's operational activities for development every four years instead of triennially. This is a welcome development as it will give more time to the United Nations system to focus on implementing recommendations.

134. Intra-State conflicts, threats of terrorism, piracy and nuclear proliferation have dominated the Security Council's agenda. In an attempt to address these complex challenges, the Security Council has increasingly taken a multidimensional approach which emphasizes prevention, peacemaking, peacekeeping and peacebuilding as interdependent and complementary components.

135. Over the past year, the Secretariat has worked to facilitate a number of Security Council missions, engaged with Member States to enhance the effectiveness of the Council's subsidiary bodies and expert groups and assisted in orienting newly elected Council members. As part of an initiative to increase transparency and information exchange, the Secretariat has also continued to make progress on technical matters, including the wider and more user-friendly dissemination of information vital to Member State implementation of the Security Council's mandatory sanctions measures, as well as the provision of information on the Security Council's programme and activities to non-Council members.

136. The Organization is following with interest the efforts of the Security Council to collaborate with the General Assembly and the Economic and Social Council and to streamline its working methods. The Organization trusts that the Security Council will consolidate the gains that have been made and keep moving forward.

137. The Secretary-General views reform of the Security Council as part of the ongoing efforts to make this indispensable organ more broadly representative and efficient. He encourages all Member States to maintain the momentum and engage in a fruitful process of negotiation.

138. The Organization appreciates the contribution of the Economic and Social Council to advancing thinking on the global economic crisis and financing for development. The Council's high-level meeting with the Bretton Woods institutions, the World Trade Organization and the United Nations Conference on Trade and Development produced important inputs for the United Nations Conference on the World Financial and Economic Crisis and its Impact on Development convened in June 2009.

139. The Economic and Social Council has also provided important support to the global health agenda. In addition to a special event on "Philanthropy and the global health agenda", the Council has encouraged five country-led regional meetings on financing strategies for health care, promoting health literacy, addressing non-communicable diseases, fighting HIV/AIDS and promoting e-health. These contributed to the preparation of the 2009 Annual Ministerial Review on the theme of "Implementing the internationally agreed goals and commitments in regard to global public health".

3. System-wide coherence

140. The 2007 comprehensive policy review, General Assembly resolution 62/277 and ongoing informal consultations with Member States on system-wide coherence continue to guide our efforts to make the United Nations more coherent, efficient and effective at country, regional and global levels.

141. A bottom-up approach owned by national Governments is driving the progress that has been made to date in the "Delivering as one" pilot countries. Pilot countries are exhibiting greater Government ownership of United Nations development assistance at the country level; closer alignment of United Nations initiatives with national priorities owing to more coherent and simplified common country programming and joint budgetary frameworks; efficiency gains and cost savings thanks to increasingly streamlined and harmonized business practices; better access to the normative, substantive and technical expertise of non-resident agencies; and empowered leadership in the United Nations country team/resident coordinator system. The pilots clearly present an important achievement for United Nations reform and strengthening efforts.

142. The Chief Executives Board, through its three pillars focusing on policy coherence, management and harmonization of business practices and the provision of operational guidance and tools, is providing more coordinated support to countries. The work of the Co-Chairs for system-wide coherence has advanced the intergovernmental dialogue on funding, governance, gender equality and empowerment of women. These efforts, both within the United Nations family and through the intergovernmental process, provide us with the foundations for the Organization to work more effectively in meeting the complex development needs of Member States.

4. Cooperation with regional organizations

143. The unfolding financial and economic crisis has further emphasized the importance of and opportunities for building partnerships with regional organizations and leveraging joint resources.

144. Strengthening the United Nations partnership with the African Union within the framework of the Ten-Year Capacity-Building Programme is a high priority. The recommendations of the Prodi report (S/2008/813, annex) on practical ways to support African Union peacekeeping operations authorized by the United Nations will assist efforts to meet peace and security challenges on the continent. Desk-to-desk consultations between the Department of Political Affairs of the Secretariat and the African Union and collaboration with the Southern African Development Community and the Economic Community of West African States on building capacities in mediation and conflict prevention provide excellent opportunities for coordinating and strengthening our joint peacemaking and post-conflict peacebuilding efforts.

145. The past year's desk-to-desk dialogue between the United Nations and the Organization of the Islamic Conference, the League of Arab States and the Organization of American States, respectively, allowed valuable information-sharing and is building the basis for more in-depth collaboration.

146. In Asia, the Organization works closely with the Association of Southeast Asian Nations. Coordination and exchange of information with the Commonwealth and the Pacific Islands Forum increased proportionately to our engagement in Fiji during 2008 and early 2009.

147. The Organization has continued to develop cooperative ties with the European Union. This included annual desk-to-desk dialogue and ongoing discussions on capacity-building in mediation and security sector reform. We have continued our cooperation with the Organization for Security and Cooperation in Europe, including through the annual meeting on conflict prevention issues.

148. These examples point to a continuous deepening of our cooperation and partnership with regional bodies along a vast spectrum of activities and the Organization looks forward to continued collaboration.

B. Global constituencies

149. Expanding our partnerships with civil society, the business community and academia is of utmost importance if the Organization is to be at the cutting edge of innovation in both policy and operations. Over the past year, there have been a number of important initiatives that have served to deepen the Organization's engagement with these important global constituencies.

1. Strengthening partnerships with civil society

150. Collaboration between civil society and the United Nations was evident in the preparations for a discussion of financing for development last December. More than 250 civil society organizations and networks participated in the Follow-up International Conference on Financing for Development to Review the Implementation of the Monterrey Consensus in Doha, Qatar. The Doha Declaration on Financing for Development, adopted by the Conference, emphasizes the role of civil society organizations in the implementation of the conference outcome and reaffirms the need for their continued engagement in the follow-up process.

151. The Organization has been working with traditional and new media to reach millions of viewers and listeners around the world and to inform and engage world public opinion, public organizations and civil society groups to help shape public attitudes and expand support for multilateralism. The campaign "Know Your Rights 2008", developed by the United Nations Regional Information Centre in Brussels, highlighted 425 human rights-related projects from 55 countries in all continents. Over 116 million people participated worldwide in the United Nations campaign to "Stand Up and Take Action against Poverty" in 2008, up from 43 million in 2007. These demonstrations of solidarity are particularly relevant to younger audiences, who can help tip the balance in creating a global movement.

152. This year, the Organization launched a new initiative to engage civil society—the Academic Impact—which seeks to strengthen the links between the United Nations and institutions of higher learning across a number of diverse disciplines ranging from technology and medicine to education and the fine arts.

2. Engaging the business community

153. In the past year notable efforts were made at the institutional and operational levels to enhance engagement with the business community, despite an environment of global economic upheaval. For the first time, the United Nations hosted a private sector forum in conjunction with the annual debate of the General Assembly. At the forum, business leaders made important contributions to intergovernmental discussions on the Millennium Development Goals and food sustainability. The decision to hold this forum annually—with the upcoming meeting focused on climate change—marks a new phase in collaboration.

154. At the operational level, there has been a steady evolution in the capacity of the Organization to work with business. The launch of a new United Nations-business website in September will provide a markedly improved platform for proactive engagement. Additionally, the business community has worked to advance key issues through the United Nations Global Compact, which stands as the world's largest corporate citizenship initiative with 6,500 participants in more than 130 countries.

Chapter V
Conclusion

155. It is clear that, over the past two and a half years, the Organization and its Member States have begun to make structural and policy changes that will be crucial in defining the nature of multilateralism in this new century. The role of the United Nations in this new framework is gradually crystallizing.

156. The United Nations is emerging as a key partner in managing the consequences of

the economic crisis by identifying, protecting and advocating for the poorest and most vulnerable populations. The Organization is also showing a willingness to take on the hardest issues related to humanitarian assistance and peacekeeping in the hardest places. In order to respond to growing demands from our Member States, the Organization is building its mediation, conflict prevention and peacebuilding support capacities. In the area of human rights and rule of law, it is operationalizing the responsibility to protect and increasing its systemic capacity.

157.   In response to the emerging global threats that characterize the new environment, the Organization is adapting itself to ensure that it can deliver on a set of crucial global goods. In two years it has turned climate change into a leaders-level issue. It helped revive negotiations with the adoption of the Bali Road Map and is taking important steps towards sealing the deal in Copenhagen on an ambitious agreement consistent with the science. The coordinated United Nations response to the influenza A(H1N1) outbreak is testimony to the advances made over the past years in improving response to global health challenges at national and international levels. In the fight against terrorism, the Organization has secured full consensus on a global counter-terrorism strategy and catalysed its implementation.

158.   To meet these increasingly demanding and complex challenges, the Organization has initiated with Member States important steps to strengthen its accountability, efficiency and effectiveness. It will continue to build on the improvements it has made to deliver more within constrained resources on the mandates entrusted to the Organization.

159.   When generations look back at 2009, they are likely to recall it as a pivotal year, a year which signalled the end of several decades of global optimism and euphoria and the dawn of a new era of sobriety and realism in national and international affairs. A year when confidence in global prosperity and progress in achieving the Millennium Development Goals united with the acknowledgement of a sense of joint purpose. They will recall its multiple crises and complex challenges and the manner in which the global community tackled them. Let us hope that they also characterize this year as a turning point in history, where Governments and peoples around the world made a conscious decision to strengthen our international community and unite to address the world's problems through decisive action. Let us join together to make 2009 the year when we remade the world, restoring global hope and solidarity and renewing the foundation for international security and peace, sustainable development and human rights.

ANNEX

Millennium Development Goals, targets and indicators, 2009: statistical tables

GOAL 1
Eradicate extreme poverty and hunger

Target 1.A
Halve, between 1990 and 2015, the proportion of people whose income is less than one dollar a day

Indicator 1.1
Proportion of population living below $1.25 purchasing power parity (PPP) per day[a, b]
(Percentage)

	1990	1999	2005
Developing regions	45.5	32.9	26.6
Northern Africa	4.5	4.4	2.6
Sub-Saharan Africa	57.4	58.2	50.7
Latin America and the Caribbean	11.3	10.9	8.2
Caribbean	28.8	25.4	25.8
Latin America	10.5	10.2	7.4
Eastern Asia	60.1	35.6	15.9
Southern Asia	49.5	42.2	38.6
Southern Asia excluding India	44.6	35.3	30.7
South-Eastern Asia	39.2	35.3	18.9
Western Asia	2.2	4.1	5.8
Oceania	—	—	—
Commonwealth of Independent States	2.7	7.8	5.3
Commonwealth of Independent States, Asia	6.3	22.3	19.2
Commonwealth of Independent States, Europe	1.6	3.0	0.3
Transition countries in South-Eastern Europe	0.1	1.9	0.5
Least developed countries	63.3	60.4	53.4
Landlocked developing countries	49.1	50.7	42.8
Small island developing States	32.4	27.7	27.5

[a] High-income economies, as defined by the World Bank, are excluded.

[b] Estimates by the World Bank, April 2009.

Indicator 1.2
Poverty gap ratio[a, b]
(Percentage)

	1990	1999	2005
Developing regions	15.6	11.6	8.0
Northern Africa	0.8	0.8	0.5
Sub-Saharan Africa	26.2	25.7	20.6
Latin America and the Caribbean	3.9	3.8	2.8
Caribbean	13.4	12.7	12.8
Latin America	3.5	3.4	2.3
Eastern Asia	20.7	11.1	4.0
Southern Asia	14.5	11.2	9.8
Southern Asia excluding India	14.2	9.9	8.1
South-Eastern Asia	11.1	9.6	4.2
Western Asia	0.6	1.0	1.5
Oceania	—	—	—
Commonwealth of Independent States	0.9	2.5	1.5
Commonwealth of Independent States, Asia	2.1	7.5	5.4
Commonwealth of Independent States, Europe	0.5	0.8	0.1
Transition countries in South-Eastern Europe	0.0	0.5	0.2
Least developed countries	27.5	24.7	19.9

	1990	1999	2005
Landlocked developing countries	21.9	20.2	15.5
Small island developing States	14.4	12.3	11.9

[a] The poverty gap ratio measures the magnitude of poverty. It is the result of multiplying the proportion of people who live below the poverty line (at $1.25 PPP per day) by the difference between the poverty line and the average income of the population living under the poverty line.

[b] High-income economies, as defined by the World Bank, are excluded.

Indicator 1.3
Share of poorest quintile in national consumption
(Percentage)

	2005[a]
Northern Africa	6.1
Sub-Saharan Africa	3.6
Latin America and the Caribbean	2.9
Eastern Asia	4.3
Southern Asia	7.4
South-Eastern Asia	5.7
Western Asia	6.2
Commonwealth of Independent States	7.0
Transition countries in South-Eastern Europe	8.2

[a] High-income economies, as defined by the World Bank, are excluded.

Target 1.B
Achieve full and productive employment and decent work for all, including women and young people

Indicator 1.4
Growth rate of gross domestic product (GDP) per person employed
(a) Annual growth rate of GDP per person employed
(Percentage)

	1998	2008
World	1.0	2.1
Developing regions	0.7	4.5
Northern Africa	1.9	3.1
Sub-Saharan Africa	−0.7	2.3
Latin America and the Caribbean	−0.3	2.9
Eastern Asia	3.4	7.5
Southern Asia	3.4	4.3
South-Eastern Asia	−8.6	3.2
Western Asia	−0.4	2.2
Oceania	−5.5	3.4
Commonwealth of Independent States	−2.7	5.7
Commonwealth of Independent States, Asia . . .	0.5	4.5
Commonwealth of Independent States, Europe	−2.7	6.1
Developed regions	1.7	1.6
Transition countries in South-Eastern Europe . .	0.5	7.1
Least developed countries	1.0	3.7
Landlocked developing countries	−1.1	3.4
Small island developing States	−2.1	0.8

(b) GDP per person employed
(2005 United States dollars (PPP))

	1998	2008
World	17 203	21 449
Developing regions	7 597	11 201
Northern Africa	16 546	18 977
Sub-Saharan Africa	4 252	5 258
Latin America and the Caribbean	20 063	21 659

	1998	2008
Eastern Asia	5 307	11 097
Southern Asia	4 873	7 427
South-Eastern Asia	6 835	9 336
Western Asia	34 676	43 021
Oceania	5 645	5 434
Commonwealth of Independent States	12 547	22 191
Commonwealth of Independent States, Asia	6 354	11 897
Commonwealth of Independent States, Europe	14 264	25 563
Developed regions	60 181	71 301
Transition countries in South-Eastern Europe	14 267	24 971
Least developed countries	2 065	2 910
Landlocked developing countries	3 438	4 973
Small island developing States	18 320	23 528

Indicator 1.5
Employment-to-population ratio
(a) Total
(Percentage)

	1991	2000	2008
World	62.5	61.6	61.1
Developing regions	64.6	63.3	62.5
Northern Africa	42.7	42.3	45.1
Sub-Saharan Africa	64.4	64.0	64.3
Latin America and the Caribbean	55.0	58.5	61.3
Eastern Asia	74.8	73.7	71.3
Eastern Asia excluding China	60.1	59.1	60.2
Southern Asia	58.8	56.5	55.9
Southern Asia excluding India	58.2	55.9	57.5
South-Eastern Asia	67.8	66.5	65.8
Western Asia	48.3	46.2	44.5
Oceania	67.7	68.3	68.3
Commonwealth of Independent States	58.0	53.8	57.7
Commonwealth of Independent States, Asia	57.1	55.6	58.4
Commonwealth of Independent States, Europe	58.3	53.3	57.5
Developed regions	56.5	56.6	56.1
Transition countries in South-Eastern Europe	52.4	51.7	47.9
Least developed countries	70.7	69.2	69.1
Landlocked developing countries	65.9	65.8	67.8
Small island developing States	53.5	56.1	57.3

(b) Men, women and youth, 2008
(Percentage)

	Men	Women	Youth
World	73.0	49.3	44.4
Developing regions	75.5	49.2	45.1
Northern Africa	67.9	22.7	26.1
Sub-Saharan Africa	73.8	55.2	48.6
Latin America and the Caribbean	74.9	48.3	45.2
Eastern Asia	75.5	67.0	53.5
Eastern Asia excluding China	70.0	50.8	32.6
Southern Asia	77.3	33.3	41.1
Southern Asia excluding India	78.4	35.9	46.2
South-Eastern Asia	78.2	53.6	45.9
Western Asia	66.5	20.8	26.9
Oceania	72.8	63.9	53.1
Commonwealth of Independent States . . .	63.6	52.7	34.6
Commonwealth of Independent States, Asia	64.2	53.1	37.4
Commonwealth of Independent States, Europe	63.4	52.6	33.1

	Men	Women	Youth
Developed regions	63.6	48.9	42.9
Transition countries in South-Eastern Europe	54.7	41.6	25.3
Least developed countries	79.6	58.8	57.1
Landlocked developing countries	75.7	60.2	54.9
Small island developing States	69.7	45.3	40.7

Indicator 1.6
Proportion of employed people living below $1.25 (PPP) per day

	1991	2000	2008
World	43.3	31.4	18.0
Developing regions	56.3	39.5	22.2
Northern Africa	6.8	5.7	2.3
Sub-Saharan Africa	63.5	63.6	57.0
Latin America and the Caribbean	12.7	12.3	6.4
Eastern Asia	69.5	35.8	9.3
Eastern Asia excluding China	4.7	2.9	1.3
Southern Asia	62.0	52.6	34.0
Southern Asia excluding India	53.9	45.5	30.8
South-Eastern Asia	45.6	33.1	15.2
Western Asia	8.6	9.6	9.3
Oceania	49.1	40.3	33.5
Commonwealth of Independent States	4.5	7.5	4.8
Commonwealth of Independent States, Asia	15.8	25.7	19.2
Commonwealth of Independent States, Europe	1.7	2.2	0.1
Developed regions	0.4	0.3	0.2
Transition countries in South-Eastern Europe	23.0	16.9	9.8
Least developed countries	59.4	59.8	50.3
Landlocked developing countries	56.0	55.6	44.7
Small island developing States	16.7	18.6	18.5

Indicator 1.7
Proportion of own-account and contributing family workers in total employment
(a) Both sexes
(Percentage)

	1991	2000	2008
World	55.1	52.5	49.3
Developing regions	69.0	63.7	59.2
Northern Africa	34.4	32.2	31.5
Sub-Saharan Africa	81.0	78.7	75.2
Latin America and the Caribbean	35.4	32.4	31.9
Eastern Asia	69.6	59.8	52.9
Eastern Asia excluding China	36.5	35.7	30.8
Southern Asia	80.1	79.3	74.9
Southern Asia excluding India	72.6	71.0	67.7
South-Eastern Asia	69.0	65.0	60.6
Western Asia	43.5	33.3	28.1
Oceania	70.8	67.9	75.9
Commonwealth of Independent States	6.9	16.1	12.5
Commonwealth of Independent States, Asia	21.4	39.1	29.5
Commonwealth of Independent States, Europe	3.2	9.4	6.9
Developed regions	12.2	11.2	9.9
Transition countries in South-Eastern Europe	20.1	30.6	22.0
Least developed countries	87.3	84.8	81.2
Landlocked developing countries	69.6	74.7	71.0
Small island developing States	36.9	36.8	39.3

(b) Men
(Percentage)

	1991	2000	2008
World	52.5	50.8	47.9
Developing regions	64.4	60.4	56.2
Northern Africa	31.9	28.9	27.7
Sub-Saharan Africa	76.6	73.4	69.5
Latin America and the Caribbean	35.4	33.4	32.0
Eastern Asia	63.4	55.1	48.4
Eastern Asia excluding China	33.0	32.8	29.2
Southern Asia	76.3	76.0	71.7
Southern Asia excluding India	68.4	66.9	63.9
South-Eastern Asia	64.6	61.3	57.7
Western Asia	37.5	29.2	25.6
Oceania	66.0	62.7	69.4
Commonwealth of Independent States	7.1	15.7	12.8
Commonwealth of Independent States, Asia	19.8	37.0	28.7
Commonwealth of Independent States, Europe	3.7	9.4	7.4
Developed regions	12.1	11.8	11.2
Transition countries in South-Eastern Europe	17.5	29.4	22.5
Least developed countries	83.5	80.5	77.3
Landlocked developing countries	66.9	71.5	67.2
Small island developing States	36.4	37.9	40.7

(c) Women
(Percentage)

	1991	2000	2008
World	59.1	55.0	51.3
Developing regions	76.7	69.0	63.9
Northern Africa	43.8	43.0	42.7
Sub-Saharan Africa	87.0	85.8	82.6
Latin America and the Caribbean	35.3	30.5	31.6
Eastern Asia	77.3	65.5	58.2
Eastern Asia excluding China	41.8	39.8	32.9
Southern Asia	89.7	87.8	82.7
Southern Asia excluding India	83.2	81.2	76.3
South-Eastern Asia	75.2	70.1	64.8
Western Asia	63.5	47.7	37.0
Oceania	76.9	74.1	83.4
Commonwealth of Independent States	6.6	16.5	12.2
Commonwealth of Independent States, Asia	23.3	41.5	30.4
Commonwealth of Independent States, Europe	2.6	9.5	6.5
Developed regions	12.4	10.5	8.4
Transition countries in South-Eastern Europe	23.3	32.1	21.4
Least developed countries	92.6	90.9	86.5
Landlocked developing countries	73.0	78.7	75.6
Small island developing States	37.9	35.0	37.2

Target 1.C
Halve, between 1990 and 2015, the proportion of people who suffer from hunger

Indicator 1.8
Prevalence of underweight children under 5 years of age
(a) Total
(Percentage)

	1990	2007
Developing regions	31	26
Northern Africa	11	7
Sub-Saharan Africa	31	28
Latin America and the Caribbean	11	6

	1990	2007
Eastern Asia	17	7
Eastern Asia excluding China	12	6
Southern Asia	54	48
Southern Asia excluding India	67	48
South-Eastern Asia	37	25
Western Asia	14	14
Oceania	—	—

(b) By sex, 2000–2008
(Percentage)

	Boys	Girls	Boy-to-girl ratio
Developing regions	34	34	0.99
Northern Africa	—	—	—
Sub-Saharan Africa	28	27	1.06
Latin America and the Caribbean	—	—	—
Eastern Asia	—	—	—
Eastern Asia excluding China	22	21	1.06
Southern Asia	45	47	0.95
Southern Asia excluding India	41	42	0.98
South-Eastern Asia	25	25	0.99
Western Asia	14	14	1.00
Oceania	—	—	—
Commonwealth of Independent States	5	5	0.97
Commonwealth of Independent States, Asia	7	7	1.00
Commonwealth of Independent States, Europe	—	—	—
Transition countries of South-Eastern Europe	3	3	1.02

(c) By residence, 2000–2008
(Percentage)

	Rural	Urban
Developing regions	30	17
Northern Africa	8	5
Sub-Saharan Africa	30	19
Latin America and the Caribbean	12	5
Eastern Asia	9	2
Eastern Asia excluding China	6	7
Southern Asia	48	35
Southern Asia excluding India	37	44
South-Eastern Asia	26	21
Western Asia	18	7
Oceania	—	—
Commonwealth of Independent States	—	—
Commonwealth of Independent States, Asia	8	5
Transition countries of South-Eastern Europe	3	3

Indicator 1.9
Proportion of population below minimum level of dietary energy consumption

	1990–1992	2004–2006	2008
World	16	13	14
Developing regions	20	16	17
Northern Africa	<5	<5	<5
Sub-Saharan Africa	32	28	29
Latin America and the Caribbean	12	8	8
Eastern Asia	15	10	10
Eastern Asia excluding China	8	12	13
Southern Asia	24	22	21
Southern Asia excluding India	24	22	22
South-Eastern Asia	24	15	15
Western Asia	6	8	8
Oceania	12	13	15
Commonwealth of Independent States	6	<5	<5
Commonwealth of Independent States, Asia	15	11	9

	1990–1992	2004–2006	2008
Commonwealth of Independent States, Europe	<5	<5	<5
Developed regions	<5	<5	<5
Transition countries of South-Eastern Europe	5	<5	<5
Least developed countries	39	34	34
Landlocked developing countries	34	27	28
Small island developing States	23	21	21

GOAL 2
Achieve universal primary education

Target 2.A
Ensure that, by 2015, children everywhere, boys and girls alike, will be able to complete a full course of primary schooling

Indicator 2.1
Net enrolment ratio in primary education

(a) Total[a]

	1991	2000	2007
World	82.0	84.7	89.0
Developing regions	79.6	83.0	88.1
Northern Africa	82.8	91.3	95.6
Sub-Saharan Africa	53.5	58.5	73.5
Latin America and the Caribbean	86.7	94.3	94.9
Eastern Asia	98.0	99.1	95.2
Eastern Asia excluding China	—	97.3	97.3
Southern Asia	71.9	79.1	89.8
Southern Asia excluding India	—	66.3	79.4
South-Eastern Asia	95.6	94.3	94.1
Western Asia	80.4	84.8	88.2
Oceania	—	—	—
Commonwealth of Independent States	90.0	90.5	93.6
Commonwealth of Independent States, Asia	88.3	93.7	95.1
Commonwealth of Independent States, Europe	90.8	88.0	92.5
Developed regions	97.9	97.4	96.4
Least developed countries	53.0	58.7	76.0
Landlocked developing countries	53.7	63.1	77.4
Small island developing States	67.3	81.5	76.0

[a] Primary- and secondary-level enrolees per 100 children of primary-education enrolment age. Ratios correspond to school years ending in the years for which data are presented.

(b) By sex[a]

	1991 Boys	1991 Girls	2000 Boys	2000 Girls	2007 Boys	2007 Girls
World	87.2	76.7	87.3	82.3	90.3	87.7
Developing regions	85.7	73.3	86.2	79.6	89.6	86.5
Northern Africa	89.7	75.5	94.0	88.4	97.4	93.7
Sub-Saharan Africa	57.5	49.5	61.8	55.0	76.1	70.9
Latin America and the Caribbean	87.5	86.3	95.1	93.5	94.9	94.8
Eastern Asia	100.0	97.3	98.6	99.7	94.9	95.6
Eastern Asia excluding China	—	—	99.2	95.3	97.9	96.7
Southern Asia	85.7	57.0	85.7	71.9	91.7	87.8
Southern Asia excluding India	—	—	71.6	60.7	81.1	77.6
South-Eastern Asia	97.8	94.0	95.5	93.0	94.7	93.4
Western Asia	87.0	73.3	89.1	80.4	91.5	84.7
Oceania	—	—	—	—	—	—

	1991		2000		2007	
	Boys	Girls	Boys	Girls	Boys	Girls
Commonwealth of Independent States	90.2	89.8	90.8	90.2	93.8	93.4
Commonwealth of Independent States, Asia	88.6	88.0	93.7	93.6	96.0	94.2
Commonwealth of Independent States, Europe	91.0	90.6	88.5	87.5	92.2	92.9
Developed regions	97.7	98.1	97.5	97.4	96.1	96.8
Least developed countries..	58.6	47.2	62.3	55.0	78.0	74.0
Landlocked developing countries	58.2	49.2	67.6	58.6	80.1	74.7
Small island developing States	63.6	71.1	82.8	80.1	77.3	74.6

[a] Primary- and secondary-level enrolees per 100 children of primary-education enrolment age. Ratios correspond to school years ending in the years for which data are presented.

Indicator 2.2
Proportion of pupils starting grade 1 who reach last grade of primary school[a]

	1999			2007		
	Total	Boys	Girls	Total	Boys	Girls
World	81.7	84.4	78.8	87.3	89.2	85.3
Developing regions ..	78.9	82.2	75.5	85.8	88.0	83.4
Northern Africa ...	86.6	90.4	82.6	95.1	97.0	93.1
Sub-Saharan Africa	49.9	54.2	45.6	63.1	68.5	57.7
Latin America and the Caribbean ..	96.6	96.1	97.1	100.4	99.7	101.2
Eastern Asia	101.8	101.5	102.1	100.7	101.2	100.3
Eastern Asia excluding China	97.5	96.5	98.6	97.9	99.9	95.9
Southern Asia	66.9	73.4	60.0	80.6	83.0	78.0
Southern Asia excluding India	60.5	64.3	56.4	69.1	71.4	66.7
South-Eastern Asia	89.2	89.9	88.4	98.1	98.4	97.8
Western Asia	80.4	86.8	73.8	87.0	92.3	81.5
Oceania	—	—	—	—	—	—
Commonwealth of Independent States	95.9	96.3	95.5	96.6	96.9	96.3
Commonwealth of Independent States, Asia	95.6	95.9	95.2	98.6	99.5	97.7
Commonwealth of Independent States, Europe ..	96.1	96.5	95.6	95.1	95.0	95.3
Developed regions ..	99.2	98.6	99.9	98.6	97.9	99.2
Least developed countries	44.0	47.9	40.1	59.1	63.0	55.0
Landlocked developing countries	53.1	58.3	47.8	64.4	68.9	59.7
Small island developing States	73.9	73.9	74.0	74.5	74.8	74.1

[a] Primary completion rates correspond to school years ending in the years for which data are presented. The primary completion rate is calculated using the gross intake rate at the last grade of primary, which is defined as follows: "Total number of new entrants in the last grade of primary education, regardless of age, expressed as a percentage of the population of the theoretical entrance age to the last grade". (*Global Education Digest 2004: Comparing Education Statistics Across the World* (Montreal, Canada, United Nations Educational, Scientific and Cultural Organization (UNESCO) Institute for Statistics (UIS), 2004), annex B, p. 148).

Indicator 2.3
Literacy rate of 15–24 year-olds, women and men
(a) Total[a]
(Percentage who can both read and write)

	1985–1994	1995–2004	2005–2007
World	76.2	82.1	83.9
Developing regions	68.0	76.8	79.4
Northern Africa	48.6	60.9	67.8
Sub-Saharan Africa	53.7	59.5	62.2
Latin America and the Caribbean	86.6	89.7	91.0
Eastern Asia	79.1	91.4	93.6
Eastern Asia excluding China	99.1	99.0	99.0
Southern Asia	47.5	58.9	64.2
Southern Asia excluding India	45.6	52.9	59.3
South-Eastern Asia	85.1	90.2	91.4
Western Asia	75.8	82.2	83.8
Oceania	65.3	65.5	65.4
Commonwealth of Independent States ...	98.2	99.2	99.3
Commonwealth of Independent States, Asia	97.8	98.4	98.6
Commonwealth of Independent States, Europe	98.3	99.4	99.6
Developed regions	99.1	99.3	99.3
Least developed countries	46.1	53.4	56.6
Landlocked developing countries	55.7	60.3	62.9
Small island developing States	80.2	82.0	84.0

[a] The regional averages presented in this table are calculated using a weighted average of the latest available observed data point for each country or territory for the reference period. UNESCO Institute for Statistics estimates have been used for countries with missing data.

(b) By sex[a]
(Percentage who can both read and write)

	1985–1994		1995–2004		2005–2007	
	Men	Women	Men	Women	Men	Women
World	82.4	70.0	87.1	77.3	88.4	79.4
Developing regions	76.6	59.1	83.4	70.1	85.4	73.4
Northern Africa	61.4	35.7	72.3	49.5	77.3	58.3
Sub-Saharan Africa	63.1	45.0	68.9	50.8	71.1	53.8
Latin America and the Caribbean	87.7	85.6	90.5	89.0	91.7	90.3
Eastern Asia	87.8	70.1	95.4	87.3	96.6	90.5
Eastern Asia excluding China ...	99.3	98.8	99.3	98.7	99.3	98.7
Southern Asia	60.1	34.0	70.3	46.7	74.4	53.3
Southern Asia excluding India ...	55.9	34.7	61.7	43.8	67.9	50.3
South-Eastern Asia	90.1	80.4	93.3	87.3	94.2	88.7
Western Asia	85.4	65.5	90.0	73.9	91.1	75.9
Oceania	70.0	60.4	70.1	60.7	68.9	61.9
Commonwealth of Independent States	99.4	97.2	99.6	98.9	99.6	99.1
Commonwealth of Independent States, Asia	98.8	96.9	99.0	97.8	99.1	98.1
Commonwealth of Independent States, Europe	99.5	97.3	99.7	99.2	99.7	99.4
Developed regions	99.4	98.8	99.5	99.1	99.5	99.2
Least developed countries	56.1	36.6	63.0	44.2	65.8	47.8
Landlocked developing countries	62.4	49.3	68.2	53.0	70.9	55.4

	1985–1994		1995–2004		2005–2007	
	Men	Women	Men	Women	Men	Women
Small island developing States	81.9	78.6	83.5	80.6	84.6	83.4

[a] The regional averages presented in this table are calculated using a weighted average of the latest available observed data point for each country or territory for the reference period. UNESCO Institute for Statistics estimates have been used for countries with missing data.

GOAL 3
Promote gender equality and empower women

Target 3.A
Eliminate gender disparity in primary and secondary education, preferably by 2005, and in all levels of education no later than 2015

Indicator 3.1
Ratios of girls to boys in primary, secondary and tertiary education

(a)   Primary[a]

	1991	2000	2007
World	0.89	0.92	0.96
Developing regions	0.87	0.91	0.94
Northern Africa	0.82	0.91	0.94
Sub-Saharan Africa	0.83	0.85	0.90
Latin America and the Caribbean	0.99	0.97	0.97
Eastern Asia	0.94	1.01	0.99
Eastern Asia excluding China	1.00	0.96	0.98
Southern Asia	0.77	0.84	0.95
Southern Asia excluding India	0.77	0.83	0.95
South-Eastern Asia	0.97	0.97	0.98
Western Asia	0.82	0.88	0.91
Oceania	0.90	0.90	0.89
Commonwealth of Independent States	0.99	0.99	0.99
Commonwealth of Independent States, Asia	0.99	0.99	0.98
Commonwealth of Independent States, Europe	1.00	0.99	1.00
Developed regions	0.99	0.99	1.00
Least developed countries	0.79	0.86	0.92
Landlocked developing countries	0.82	0.83	0.90
Small island developing States	0.96	0.95	0.95

[a] Using gross enrolment ratios.

(b)   Secondary[a]

	1991	2000	2007
World	0.83	0.93	0.95
Developing regions	0.75	0.90	0.94
Northern Africa	0.79	0.95	0.98
Sub-Saharan Africa	0.76	0.81	0.79
Latin America and the Caribbean	1.01	1.06	1.07
Eastern Asia	0.78	0.97	1.01
Eastern Asia excluding China	0.99	1.01	0.97
Southern Asia	0.60	0.77	0.85
Southern Asia excluding India	0.63	0.91	0.92
South-Eastern Asia	0.90	0.98	1.03
Western Asia	0.69	0.80	0.84
Oceania	0.82	0.91	0.87
Commonwealth of Independent States ...	1.03	1.00	0.98
Commonwealth of Independent States, Asia	0.98	0.98	0.97
Commonwealth of Independent States, Europe	1.06	1.02	0.98
Developed regions	1.01	1.01	1.00

	1991	2000	2007
Least developed countries	0.58	0.82	0.81
Landlocked developing countries	0.85	0.87	0.84
Small island developing States	1.05	1.04	1.03

[a] Using gross enrolment ratios.

(c)   Tertiary[a]

	1991	2000	2007
World	—	0.95	1.08
Developing regions	—	0.77	0.96
Northern Africa	0.54	0.68	1.04
Sub-Saharan Africa	—	0.63	0.67
Latin America and the Caribbean	—	1.13	1.19
Eastern Asia	—	0.55	0.96
Eastern Asia excluding China	—	0.60	0.68
Southern Asia	—	0.67	0.77
Southern Asia excluding India	—	0.73	0.88
South-Eastern Asia	0.83	0.90	1.11
Western Asia	—	0.82	0.93
Oceania	—	0.68	0.85
Commonwealth of Independent States	1.16	1.21	1.29
Commonwealth of Independent States, Asia	1.04	0.91	1.07
Commonwealth of Independent States, Europe	1.20	1.27	1.33
Developed regions	1.07	1.20	1.29
Least developed countries	—	0.53	0.58
Landlocked developing countries	0.86	0.75	0.80
Small island developing States	—	1.21	1.55

[a] Using gross enrolment ratios.

Indicator 3.2
Share of women in wage employment in the non-agricultural sector
(Percentage of employees)

	1990	2000	2005	2007
World	35.3	37.6	38.6	39.0
Developing regions	31.5	33.5	34.3	34.7
Northern Africa	21.0	19.8	19.5	20.4
Sub-Saharan Africa	22.8	26.2	28.0	28.9
Latin America and the Caribbean	36.5	40.7	42.1	42.7
Eastern Asia	38.0	39.6	40.9	41.3
Eastern Asia excluding China	39.3	41.9	43.8	44.2
Southern Asia	13.4	17.2	18.3	18.8
Southern Asia excluding India	15.0	18.5	18.7	18.3
South-Eastern Asia	35.6	37.4	37.0	37.4
Western Asia	17.3	19.6	20.7	21.2
Oceania	32.8	35.1	35.6	35.8
Commonwealth of Independent States	49.5	50.2	51.0	51.1
Commonwealth of Independent States, Asia	45.4	45.5	46.2	46.2
Commonwealth of Independent States, Europe	50.3	51.2	52.1	52.1
Developed regions	43.4	45.4	46.4	46.5

Indicator 3.3
Proportion of seats held by women in national parliament[a]
(Percentage)

	1990	2000	2005	2009[b]
World	12.8	12.5	15.6	18.5
Developing regions	10.4	10.8	13.9	17.2
Northern Africa	2.6	2.1	5.4	8.3
Sub-Saharan Africa	7.2	9.1	14.2	18.1
Latin America and the Caribbean ..	11.9	14.8	19.0	22.2
Caribbean	22.1	19.9	26.0	29.4

	1990	2000	2005	2009[b]
Latin America	8.6	12.9	16.4	19.4
Eastern Asia	20.2	19.9	19.4	20.2
Eastern Asia excluding China	17.8	14.6	17.2	17.2
Southern Asia	5.7	6.7	8.6	16.7
Southern Asia excluding India ..	5.9	5.6	8.8	18.7
South-Eastern Asia	10.4	9.7	15.5	17.3
Western Asia	4.6	4.7	5.0	9.2
Oceania	1.2	3.4	3.0	2.5
Commonwealth of Independent States	—	7.3	10.2	14.1
Commonwealth of Independent States, Asia	—	7.1	9.9	14.0
Commonwealth of Independent States, Europe	—	7.5	10.5	14.1
Developed regions	16.3	17.5	20.9	22.9
Least developed countries...........	7.2	7.3	12.9	18.8
Landlocked developing countries	14.0	7.7	13.4	21.0
Small island developing States	15.2	13.1	17.8	20.9

[a] Single or lower house only.

[b] As of 31 January 2009.

GOAL 4
Reduce child mortality

Target 4.A
Reduce by two thirds, between 1990 and 2015, the under-five mortality rate

Indicator 4.1
Under-five mortality rate[a]

	1990	2000	2007
World	93	80	67
Developing regions	103	88	74
Northern Africa	83	48	35
Sub-Saharan Africa	183	164	145
Latin America and the Caribbean	54	33	24
Eastern Asia	45	36	22
Eastern Asia excluding China	31	28	27
Southern Asia	122	95	77
Southern Asia excluding India	134	105	88
South-Eastern Asia	77	46	34
Western Asia	67	46	34
Oceania	85	69	59
Commonwealth of Independent States	46	40	26
Commonwealth of Independent States, Asia	78	62	42
Commonwealth of Independent States, Europe	26	23	15
Developed regions	11	7	6
Transition countries of South-Eastern Europe	30	19	13

[a] Deaths of children before reaching age 5 per 1,000 live births.

Indicator 4.2
Infant mortality rate[a]

	1990	2000	2007
World	64	55	47
Developing regions	71	60	51
Northern Africa	62	39	30
Sub-Saharan Africa	107	98	88
Latin America and the Caribbean	43	28	21
Eastern Asia	36	29	19
Eastern Asia excluding China	24	22	21
Southern Asia	87	70	58

	1990	2000	2007
Southern Asia excluding India	97	77	66
South-Eastern Asia	53	35	26
Western Asia	52	36	28
Oceania	62	52	46
Commonwealth of Independent States	39	34	23
Commonwealth of Independent States, Asia	64	52	36
Commonwealth of Independent States, Europe	22	19	13
Developed regions	9	6	5
Transition countries of South-Eastern Europe	24	16	11

[a] Deaths of children under age 1 per 1,000 live births.

Indicator 4.3
Proportion of 1-year-old children immunized against measles[a]
(Percentage)

	1990	2000	2007
World	72	72	82
Developing regions	71	70	80
Northern Africa	84	93	96
Sub-Saharan Africa	56	55	73
Latin America and the Caribbean	76	92	93
Eastern Asia	98	85	94
Eastern Asia excluding China	95	88	95
Southern Asia	57	58	72
Southern Asia excluding India	60	68	84
South-Eastern Asia	70	80	84
Western Asia	79	87	87
Oceania	70	68	62
Commonwealth of Independent States	85	97	98
Commonwealth of Independent States, Asia	—	96	97
Commonwealth of Independent States, Europe	85	97	99
Developed regions	84	91	93
Transition countries of South-Eastern Europe	91	93	96

[a] Children aged 12–23 months who received at least one dose of measles vaccine.

GOAL 5
Improve maternal health

Target 5.A
Reduce by three quarters, between 1990 and 2015, the maternal mortality ratio

Indicator 5.1
Maternal mortality ratio[a, b]

	1990	2005
World	430	400
Developing regions	480	450
Northern Africa	250	160
Sub-Saharan Africa	920	900
Latin America and the Caribbean	180	130
Eastern Asia	95	50
Eastern Asia excluding China	—	170
Southern Asia	620	490
Southern Asia excluding India	—	570
South-Eastern Asia	450	300
Western Asia	190	160
Oceania	550	430
Commonwealth of Independent States	58	51
Developed regions	11	9

	1990	2005[b]
Least developed countries	900	870

[a] Maternal deaths per 100,000 live births.

[b] No new global or regional data are available. Data presented are from 2008 report (A/63/1).

Indicator 5.2
Proportion of births attended by skilled health personnel
(Percentage)

	Around 1990	Around 2007
World	58	64
Developing regions	53	61
Northern Africa	45	79
Sub-Saharan Africa	42	44
Latin America and the Caribbean[a]	70	87
Eastern Asia	94	98
Southern Asia	29	42
Southern Asia excluding India	15	30
South-Eastern Asia	46	68
Western Asia	62	77
Oceania	—	—
Commonwealth of Independent States	98	99
Commonwealth of Independent States, Asia ...	96	99
Commonwealth of Independent States, Europe	99	99
Developed regions	99	99
Transition countries of South-Eastern Europe	99	98

[a] For deliveries in health-care institutions only.

Target 5.B
Achieve, by 2015, universal access to reproductive health

Indicator 5.3
Contraceptive prevalence rate[a]
(Percentage)

	1990	2005
World	52.8	63.1
Developing regions	50.2	62.3
Northern Africa	44.0	60.5
Sub-Saharan Africa	12.0	21.5
Latin America and the Caribbean	62.0	71.8
Eastern Asia	77.5	86.4
Southern Asia	38.5	54.0
South-Eastern Asia	47.9	60.7
Western Asia	43.3	54.1
Oceania	—	28.8[b]
Commonwealth of Independent States	61.2[c]	66.6
Commonwealth of Independent States, Asia ...	54.5[c]	55.5
Commonwealth of Independent States, Europe	63.4	71.2
Developed regions	66.5	67.5
Transition countries of South-Eastern Europe ...	56.0	57.4
Least developed countries	16.1	30.2
Landlocked developing countries	22.6	33.9
Small island developing States	46.8	55.2

[a] Among women aged 15–49 who are married or in union.

[b] Data from 2000.

[c] Data from 1995.

Indicator 5.4
Adolescent birth rate[a]

	1990	2006
World	61.0	48.7
Developing regions	66.5	53.0
Northern Africa	42.9	28.1

	1990	2006
Sub-Saharan Africa	130.6	123.1
Latin America and the Caribbean	77.4	71.8
Eastern Asia	21.3	4.5
Eastern Asia excluding China	5.8	3.1
Southern Asia	90.1	52.0
South-Eastern Asia	50.4	44.4
Western Asia	63.6	51.1
Oceania	82.3	61.2
Commonwealth of Independent States	52.1	28.4
Commonwealth of Independent States, Asia ...	44.8	28.6
Commonwealth of Independent States, Europe	55.2	28.3
Developed regions	34.7	22.5
Transition countries of South-Eastern Europe	48.2	29.5
Least developed countries	129.3	120.5
Landlocked developing countries	104.5	105.2
Small island developing States	80.4	65.7

[a] Births per 1,000 women aged 15–19 years.

Indicator 5.5

Antenatal care coverage
(at least one visit and at least four visits)

(a) At least one visit[a]
(Percentage)

	Around 1990	Around 2006
World	64	79
Developing regions	64	79
Northern Africa	48	77
Sub-Saharan Africa	68	75
Latin America and the Caribbean	79	95
Eastern Asia	80	90
Southern Asia	48	70
Southern Asia excluding India	22	57
South-Eastern Asia	73	92
Western Asia	54	77
Oceania	—	—
Commonwealth of Independent States, Asia	90	96

[a] Proportion of women aged 15–49 years who received antenatal care during pregnancy from skilled health personnel, at least once.

(b) At least four visits[a]
(Percentage)

	2003–2008[b]
World	47
Developing regions	47
Northern Africa	56
Sub-Saharan Africa	42
Latin America and the Caribbean	83
Eastern Asia	—
Southern Asia	36
Southern Asia excluding India	34
South-Eastern Asia	74
Western Asia	—
Oceania	—

[a] Proportion of women aged 15–49 years who received antenatal care during pregnancy from skilled health personnel, at least four times.

[b] Data refer to the most recent year available during the period specified.

Indicator 5.6
Unmet need for family planning[a]
(Percentage)

	Around 1995	Around 2005
Developing regions	13.7	11.1
Northern Africa	16.3	10.4
Sub-Saharan Africa	25.2	24.2
Latin America and the Caribbean	12.5	10.5
Eastern Asia	3.5	2.3
Southern Asia	19.1	14.7
South-Eastern Asia	12.8	10.3
Western Asia	16.4	12.3
Commonwealth of Independent States, Asia	—	13.5[b]
Transition countries in South-Eastern Europe	14.7	15.0
Least developed countries	25.9	24.5
Landlocked developing countries	25.1	24.8

[a] Among married women of reproductive age (aged 15–49 years).

[b] Latest available data pertain, approximately, to 2000.

GOAL 6
Combat HIV/AIDS, malaria and other diseases

Target 6.A
Have halted by 2015 and begun to reverse the spread of HIV/AIDS

Indicator 6.1
HIV prevalence among population aged 15–24 years[a]
(Percentage)

	1990 Estimated adult (15–49) HIV prevalence	1990 Adults (15+) living with HIV who are women	2002 Estimated adult (15–49) HIV prevalence	2002 Adults (15+) living with HIV who are women	2007 Estimated adult (15–49) HIV prevalence	2007 Adults (15+) living with HIV who are women
Developing regions	0.3	51	1.0	57	0.9	58
Northern Africa	<0.1	20	<0.1	27	0.1	29
Sub-Saharan Africa	2.1	54	5.4	59	4.9	59
Latin America and the Caribbean	0.2	27	0.5	35	0.6	35
Eastern Asia	<0.1	19	0.1	26	0.1	28
Eastern Asia excluding China	<0.1	[b]	<0.1	23	<0.1	27
Southern Asia	<0.1	35	0.3	38	0.3	38
Southern Asia excluding India	<0.1	14	0.1	24	0.1	27
South-Eastern Asia	0.2	15	0.4	32	0.4	34
Western Asia	<0.1	41	0.1	46	0.1	47
Oceania	<0.1	27	0.4	36	1.3	39
Commonwealth of Independent States, Asia	<0.1	10	<0.1	21	0.1	25
Commonwealth of Independent States, Europe	<0.1	[b]	0.7	27	1.2	31
Developed regions	0.2	14	0.3	21	0.3	23

[a] No new global or regional data available. Data presented are from 2008 report (A/63/1).

[b] Data not available: epidemics in this region are recent and no data are available for earlier years.

Indicator 6.2
Condom use at last high-risk sex[a], 2000–2008[b]

	Women Number of countries covered by surveys	Women Percentage who used a condom at last high-risk sex	Men Number of countries covered by surveys	Men Percentage who used a condom at last high-risk sex
Sub-Saharan Africa	36	30	29	45
Latin America and the Caribbean	10	49	—	—
Southern Asia	1	22	2	38
Commonwealth of Independent States, Asia	—	—	3	49

[a] Proportion of young women and men aged 15–24 years reporting the use of a condom during sexual intercourse with a non-regular sexual partner in the last 12 months, among those who had such a partner in the last 12 months.

[b] Data refer to the most recent year available during the period specified.

Indicator 6.3
Proportion of population aged 15–24 years with comprehensive correct knowledge of HIV/AIDS[a], 2000–2008[b]
(Percentage)

	Women Number of countries covered by surveys	Women Percentage who have comprehensive knowledge	Men Number of countries covered by surveys	Men Percentage who have comprehensive knowledge
World	85	19	48	31[c]
Developing regions	67	19	41	31[c]
Northern Africa	3	8	—	—
Sub-Saharan Africa	38	24	30	30
Southern Asia	4	18	2	36
Southern Asia excluding India	11	3	—	—
South-Eastern Asia	5	18	4	17
Commonwealth of Independent States, Europe	11	28	—	—
Commonwealth of Independent States, Asia	8	20	3	7
Transition countries of South-Eastern Europe	7	18	2	5

[a] Proportion of young women and men aged 15–24 who correctly identify the two major ways of preventing the sexual transmission of HIV (using condoms and limiting sex to one faithful, uninfected partner), who reject two common local misconceptions and who know that a healthy-looking person can transmit the AIDS virus.

[b] Data refer to the most recent year available during the period specified.

[c] Excludes China.

Indicator 6.4
Ratio of school attendance of orphans to school attendance of non-orphans aged 10–14 years[a], 2000–2008[b]

	Number of countries with data	School attendance ratio
Developing regions	46	0.76
Sub-Saharan Africa	34	0.77
Southern Asia	2	0.73
South-Eastern Asia	3	0.84

[a] Ratio of the current school attendance rate of children aged 10–14 years both of whose biological parents have died, to the current school attendance rate of children aged 10–14 years both of whose parents are still alive and who currently live with at least one biological parent.

[b] Data refer to the most recent year available during the period specified.

Target 6.B

Achieve, by 2010, universal access to treatment for HIV/AIDS for all those who need it

Indicator 6.5

Proportion of population with advanced HIV infection with access to antiretroviral drugs[a, b]
(Percentage)

	2006	2007
Developing regions	22	31
Northern Africa	24	32
Sub-Saharan Africa	21	30
Latin America and the Caribbean	57	62
Eastern Asia	18	18
Eastern Asia excluding China	<1	<1
Southern Asia	10	16
South-Eastern Asia	32	44
Oceania	25	38
Commonwealth of Independent States	9	14
Commonwealth of Independent States, Asia	21	22
Commonwealth of Independent States, Europe	9	14
Developed regions	—	—
Least developed countries	20	31
Landlocked developing countries	23	32
Small island developing States	30	44

[a] Receiving antiretroviral therapy.

[b] No new global or regional data available. Data presented are from 2008 report (A/63/1).

Target 6.C

Have halted by 2015 and begun to reverse the incidence of malaria and other major diseases

Indicator 6.6

Incidence and death rates associated with malaria

(a) Incidence[a]

World	47
Northern Africa	0
Sub-Saharan Africa	278
Latin America and the Caribbean	5
Caribbean	9
Latin America	5
Eastern Asia	<0.5
Eastern Asia excluding China	1
Southern Asia	10
Southern Asia excluding India	11
South-Eastern Asia	14
Western Asia	2
Oceania	238
Commonwealth of Independent States, Asia	<0.5
Least developed countries	175
Landlocked developing countries	168
Small island developing States	102

[a] Number of new cases per 1,000 population, 2006, in malaria epidemic countries.

(b) Deaths[a]

	All ages	Children under 5
World	17	139
Northern Africa	0	0
Sub-Saharan Africa	107	574
Latin America and the Caribbean	<0.5	1
Caribbean	4	10
Latin America	<0.5	1
Eastern Asia	<0.5	<0.5
Eastern Asia excluding China	0	0
Southern Asia	1	5
Southern Asia excluding India	2	9
South-Eastern Asia	3	7
Western Asia	1	2
Oceania	43	126
Commonwealth of Independent States, Asia	<0.5	<0.5
Least developed countries	68	374
Landlocked developing countries	65	357
Small island developing States	26	113

[a] Number of deaths per 100,000 population, 2006, in malaria epidemic countries.

Indicator 6.7

Proportion of children under 5 sleeping under insecticide-treated bednets[a]
(Percentage)

Sub-Saharan Africa (28 countries)	20[b]

[a] 2006–2008.

[b] Data for a subset or 22 countries in sub-Saharan Africa with trend data showed that the use of insecticide-treated bednets among children increased from 2 per cent in 2000 to 20 per cent in 2006.

Indicator 6.8

Proportion of children under 5 with fever who are treated with appropriate antimalarial drugs[a]
(Percentage)

Sub-Saharan Africa (30 countries)	36
Southern Asia (4 countries)	7

[a] 2006–2008.

Indicator 6.9

Incidence, prevalence and death rates associated with tuberculosis

(a) Incidence
(Number of new cases per 100,000 population, excluding HIV-infected)

	1990	2000	2007
World	122	119	118
Developing regions	149	140	139
Northern Africa	60	48	42
Sub-Saharan Africa	150	204	234
Latin America and the Caribbean	84	55	44
Caribbean	90	76	74
Latin America	83	54	41
Eastern Asia	122	107	100
Southern Asia	172	161	160
South-Eastern Asia	277	228	202
Western Asia	55	42	38
Oceania	202	188	158
Commonwealth of Independent States	48	101	96
Commonwealth of Independent States, Asia	60	104	114
Commonwealth of Independent States, Europe	44	100	89
Developed regions	25	19	14
Transition countries of South-Eastern Europe	60	83	69

(b) Prevalence

(Number of existing cases per 100,000 population, excluding HIV-infected)

	1990	2000	2007
World	294	250	195
Developing regions	370	303	234
Northern Africa	65	50	43
Sub-Saharan Africa	333	389	421
Latin America and the Caribbean	128	77	56
Caribbean	151	116	101
Latin America	127	74	53
Eastern Asia	331	270	195
Southern Asia	543	415	268
South-Eastern Asia	459	333	265
Western Asia	93	61	51
Oceania	395	360	302
Commonwealth of Independent States	76	146	112
Commonwealth of Independent States, Asia	99	137	138
Commonwealth of Independent States, Europe	69	150	102
Developed regions	29	22	14
Transition countries of South-Eastern Europe	100	120	78

(c) Deaths

(Number of deaths per 100,000 population, excluding HIV-infected)

	1990	2000	2007
World	27	24	20
Developing regions	34	29	23
Northern Africa	6	4	3
Sub-Saharan Africa	38	44	48
Latin America and the Caribbean	11	7	6
Caribbean	20	16	14
Latin America	11	7	5
Eastern Asia	26	21	15
Southern Asia	44	39	27
South-Eastern Asia	66	45	30
Western Asia	8	6	6
Oceania	52	41	33
Commonwealth of Independent States	7	16	14
Commonwealth of Independent States, Asia	9	14	17
Commonwealth of Independent States, Europe	7	17	13
Developed regions	3	2	2
Transition countries of South-Eastern Europe	8	11	10

Indicator 6.10

Proportion of tuberculosis cases detected and cured under directly observed treatment short course

(a) New cases detected under directly observed treatment short course (DOTS)

(DOTS smear-positive case detection rate: percentage)

	2000	2007
World	28	63
Developing regions	29	63
Northern Africa	89	90
Sub-Saharan Africa	36	46
Latin America and the Caribbean	41	72
Eastern Asia	29	77
Southern Asia	14	67
South-Eastern Asia	39	75
Western Asia	36	54
Oceania	12	20

	2000	2007
Commonwealth of Independent States	12	51
Commonwealth of Independent States, Asia	36	53
Commonwealth of Independent States, Europe	4	50
Developed regions	22	56
Transition countries of South-Eastern Europe	13	83

(b) Patients successfully treated under directly observed treatment short course

(Percentage)

	2000	2006
World	82	85
Developing regions	82	85
Northern Africa	88	88
Sub-Saharan Africa	72	76
Latin America and the Caribbean	81	76
Eastern Asia	94	94
Southern Asia	83	87
South-Eastern Asia	86	89
Western Asia	80	85
Oceania	76	77
Commonwealth of Independent States	76	64
Commonwealth of Independent States, Asia	78	76
Commonwealth of Independent States, Europe	68	59
Developed regions	76	70
Transition countries of South-Eastern Europe	85	84

GOAL 7
Ensure environmental sustainability

Target 7.A
Integrate the principles of sustainable development into country policies and programmes and reverse the loss of environmental resources

Indicator 7.1
Proportion of land area covered by forest

(Percentage)

	1990	2000	2005
World	31.3	30.6	30.3
Northern Africa	1.3	1.5	1.5
Sub-Saharan Africa	29.2	27.3	26.5
Latin America and the Caribbean	49.9	47.2	46.0
Caribbean	23.4	24.9	26.1
Latin America	50.3	47.5	46.3
Eastern Asia	16.5	18.1	19.8
Eastern Asia excluding China	14.6	13.3	12.7
Southern Asia	14.0	14.3	14.2
Southern Asia excluding India	7.5	7.0	6.8
South-Eastern Asia	56.3	49.9	46.8
Western Asia	3.3	3.4	3.5
Oceania	68.3	65.0	63.4
Commonwealth of Independent States	38.6	38.7	38.6
Commonwealth of Independent States, Asia	3.9	3.9	3.9
Commonwealth of Independent States, Europe	46.6	46.7	46.7
Developed regions	30.4	30.7	30.8
Transition countries of South-Eastern Europe	29.6	29.8	30.4
Least developed countries	30.3	28.4	27.4
Landlocked developing countries	19.1	17.8	17.2
Small island developing States	64.4	36.1	62.5

Indicator 7.2

Carbon dioxide emissions, total, per capita and per \$1 GDP (PPP)

(a) Total[a]

(Millions of metric tons)

	1990	2000	2005	2006
World	21 899	24 055	28 013	28 704
Developing regions	6 803	9 731	13 107	13 817
Northern Africa	232	362	437	424
Sub-Saharan Africa	465	555	652	644
Latin America and the Caribbean	1 078	1 325	1 449	1 513
Caribbean	84	97	103	114
Latin America	994	1 228	1 346	1 399
Eastern Asia	2 940	3 980	6 235	6 714
Eastern Asia excluding China	525	574	610	611
Southern Asia	1 009	1 675	2 051	2 179
Southern Asia excluding India	319	489	627	668
South-Eastern Asia	427	778	1 045	1 046
Western Asia	646	1 049	1 227	1 286
Oceania	6	7	11	11
Commonwealth of Independent States	3 796	2 144	2 303	2 371
Commonwealth of Independent States, Asia[b]	499	330	387	410
Commonwealth of Independent States, Europe[b]	2 806	1 814	1 915	1 960
Developed regions	11 173	11 961	12 337	12 244
Least developed countries	62	111	152	156
Landlocked developing countries	51	403	462	487
Small island developing States	139	161	180	188
Annex I countries[c,d]	11 602	12 561	12 979	12 881

(b) Per capita

(Metric tons)

	1990	2000	2005	2006
World	4.1	3.9	4.3	4.4
Developing regions	1.7	2.0	2.5	2.6
Northern Africa	2.0	2.6	2.9	2.7
Sub-Saharan Africa	0.9	0.8	0.8	0.8
Latin America and the Caribbean	2.4	2.6	2.6	2.7
Caribbean	2.7	2.8	2.8	3.1
Latin America	2.4	2.5	2.6	2.7
Eastern Asia	2.4	2.9	4.5	4.8
Eastern Asia excluding China	7.4	7.2	7.5	7.5
Southern Asia	0.8	1.1	1.3	1.4
Southern Asia excluding India	1.0	1.2	1.4	1.4
South-Eastern Asia	1.0	1.5	1.9	1.9
Western Asia	4.7	5.9	6.3	6.4
Oceania	1.0	0.9	1.3	1.2
Commonwealth of Independent States	13.5	7.6	8.3	8.5
Commonwealth of Independent States, Asia[b]	7.3	4.6	5.2	5.5
Commonwealth of Independent States, Europe[b]	13.0	8.6	9.4	9.6
Developed regions	12.0	12.2	12.2	12.1
Least developed countries	0.1	0.2	0.2	0.2
Landlocked developing countries	0.2	1.2	1.2	1.3
Small island developing States	3.1	3.1	3.2	3.3
Annex I countries[c,d]	11.9	12.2	12.2	12.0

(c) Per \$1 GDP (PPP)

(Kilograms)

	1990	2000	2005	2006
World	0.54	0.50	0.49	0.48
Developing regions	0.64	0.58	0.60	0.59
Northern Africa	0.43	0.54	0.54	0.49
Sub-Saharan Africa	0.56	0.53	0.49	0.46
Latin America and the Caribbean	0.34	0.31	0.30	0.29
Caribbean	0.57	0.64	0.58	0.59
Latin America	0.34	0.30	0.29	0.29
Eastern Asia	1.46	0.89	0.93	0.91
Eastern Asia excluding China	0.46	0.48	0.41	0.38
Southern Asia	0.60	0.62	0.55	0.54
Southern Asia excluding India	0.49	0.51	0.49	0.50
South-Eastern Asia	0.42	0.46	0.48	0.46
Western Asia	0.51	0.59	0.55	0.53
Oceania	0.30	0.26	0.39	0.38
Commonwealth of Independent States[b]	1.54	1.26	0.98	0.93
Commonwealth of Independent States, Asia[b]	2.38	1.71	1.33	1.21
Commonwealth of Independent States, Europe[b]	1.45	1.20	0.93	0.89
Developed regions	0.49	0.41	0.39	0.37
Least developed countries	0.15	0.19	0.19	0.18
Landlocked developing countries	0.20	0.87	0.74	0.67
Small island developing States	0.57	0.44	0.42	0.40
Annex I countries[c,d]	0.51	0.43	0.40	0.38

[a] Total CO_2 emissions from fossil fuels include emissions from solid fuel consumption, liquid fuel consumption, gas fuel consumption, cement production and gas flaring (United States Carbon Dioxide Information Analysis Center).

[b] The 1990 column shows 1992 data.

[c] Based on the annual national emission inventories of annex I countries (with the exception of Belarus, the Russian Federation and Ukraine, which are included in the Commonwealth of Independent States) that report to the Conference of the Parties to the United Nations Framework Convention on Climate Change; non-annex I countries do not have annual reporting obligations.

[d] Excluding emissions/removals from land use, land-use change and forestry.

Indicator 7.3

Consumption of ozone-depleting substances

(Tons of ozone depletion potential)

	1990[a]	2000	2006
Developing regions	247 536	212 493	55 419
Northern Africa	6 203	8 129	1 972
Sub-Saharan Africa	23 449	9 561	1 295
Latin America and the Caribbean	76 048	31 087	7 386
Caribbean	2 177	1 669	272
Latin America	73 871	29 418	7 114
Eastern Asia	103 217	105 762	29 870
Eastern Asia excluding China	12 904	14 885	4 680
Southern Asia	3 338	28 161	4 408
Southern Asia excluding India	3 338	9 466	1 437
South-Eastern Asia	21 108	16 809	3 299
Western Asia	11 470	11 882	6 975
Oceania	47	129	33
Commonwealth of Independent States	139 454	27 585	1 672
Commonwealth of Independent States, Asia	2 738	928	175
Commonwealth of Independent States, Europe	136 716	26 657	1 497

	1990[a]	2000	2006
Developed regions	826 801	24 060	4 793
Transition countries of South-Eastern Europe	6 239	966	103
Least developed countries	1 461	4 764	1 178
Landlocked developing countries	3 354	2 386	468
Small island developing States	7 162	2 125	483

[a] For years prior to the entry into force of the reporting requirement for a group of substances, missing country consumption values have been estimated at the base year level. This applies to substances in annexes B, C and E, whose years of entry into force are 1992, 1992 and 1994, respectively.

Indicator 7.4
Proportion of fish stocks within safe biological limits
(Percentage)

	1990	2000	2006
Total	81	72	72
Fully exploited	50	47	52
Under- and moderately exploited	31	25	20

Indicator 7.5
Proportion of total water resources used[a], around 2000

(Percentage)

Developing regions	6.7
Northern Africa	77.5
Sub-Saharan Africa	2.2
Latin America and the Caribbean	1.4
Eastern Asia	21.4
Eastern Asia excluding China	15.4
Southern Asia	26.6
Southern Asia excluding India	19.5
South-Eastern Asia	4.5
Western Asia	47.5
Oceania	0.0
Commonwealth of Independent States	5.4
Developed regions	9.3
Transition countries of South-Eastern Europe	12.9
Least developed countries	3.5
Landlocked developing countries	8.2
Small island developing States	1.3

[a] Surface water and groundwater withdrawal as a proportion of total actual renewable water resources.

Target 7.B
Reduce biodiversity loss, achieving, by 2010, a significant reduction in the rate of loss

Indicator 7.6
Proportion of terrestrial and marine areas protected

(a) Terrestrial and marine[a]
(Percentage)

	Excluding undated protected areas			Including undated protected areas (total)
	1990	2000	2008	
World[b]	5.4	8.0	9.8	12.1
Developing regions	6.1	9.5	11.2	13.0
Northern Africa	2.1	3.1	3.4	3.7
Sub-Saharan Africa	8.4	8.9	9.4	11.5
Latin America and the Caribbean	7.3	14.4	18.8	21.0
Eastern Asia	7.0	9.9	10.9	14.0
Eastern Asia excluding China	3.9	11.9	11.9	11.9
Southern Asia	4.4	5.0	5.3	5.6
Southern Asia excluding India	4.6	5.5	6.1	6.5
South-Eastern Asia	2.6	5.3	6.0	7.5
Western Asia	3.7	17.8	17.8	17.9
Oceania	0.4	1.0	7.0	7.2
Commonwealth of Independent States	1.7	2.8	2.8	7.6
Developed regions	7.9	10.4	14.0	16.9
Least developed countries	8.7	9.4	10.7	12.0
Landlocked developing countries	8.0	9.4	10.5	11.4
Small island developing States	3.1	13.9	14.1	14.7

[a] Ratio of protected area (terrestrial and marine combined) to total territorial area.

[b] Including territories that are not considered in the calculations of regional aggregates.

(b) Terrestrial[a]
(Percentage)

	Excluding undated protected areas			Including undated protected areas (total)
	1990	2000	2008	
World[b]	5.9	8.4	9.4	12.0
Developing regions	7.1	11.0	12.6	14.6
Northern Africa	2.1	3.1	3.4	3.7
Sub-Saharan Africa	9.1	9.5	10.0	12.3
Latin America and the Caribbean	8.2	15.5	20.2	22.7
Eastern Asia	7.4	10.5	11.5	14.7
Eastern Asia excluding China	4.0	12.6	12.6	12.6
Southern Asia	4.6	5.3	5.6	5.9
Southern Asia excluding India	4.9	5.9	6.5	6.9
South-Eastern Asia	5.4	11.0	11.8	15.0
Western Asia	4.0	19.1	19.1	19.2
Oceania	1.8	2.9	2.9	3.3
Commonwealth of Independent States	1.7	2.6	2.6	7.7
Developed regions	8.2	9.7	10.2	13.5
Least developed countries	9.6	10.4	10.9	12.3
Landlocked developing countries	8.0	10.5	10.6	11.4
Small island developing States	5.4	26.5	26.7	27.4

[a] Ratio of terrestrial protected area to total surface area.

[b] Including territories that are not considered in the calculations of regional aggregates.

(c) Marine[a]
(Percentage)

	Excluding undated protected areas			Including undated protected areas (total)
	1990	2000	2008	
World[b]	2.4	5.6	12.3	12.8
Developing regions	0.6	2.2	3.1	3.4
Northern Africa	0.3	2.6	3.4	4.9
Sub-Saharan Africa	0.5	1.5	1.8	1.9
Latin America and the Caribbean	1.5	7.3	10.0	10.5
Eastern Asia	0.4	0.6	0.6	0.6
Eastern Asia excluding China	2.0	2.0	2.0	2.0
Southern Asia	1.2	1.3	1.3	1.3
Southern Asia excluding India	1.0	1.2	1.2	1.2
South-Eastern Asia	0.3	0.7	1.3	1.5
Western Asia	0.6	1.7	1.7	1.8
Oceania	0.1	0.5	8.0	8.1
Commonwealth of Independent States	2.3	5.6	5.6	5.9
Developed regions	6.6	13.9	33.1	34.2

	Excluding undated protected areas			Including undated protected areas (total)
	1990	2000	2008	
Least developed countries	0.4	1.0	9.0	9.0
Landlocked developing countries[c]	0.0	0.0	0.0	0.0
Small island developing States	0.9	1.7	1.9	2.3

[a] Ratio of marine protected area to total territorial waters.

[b] Includes territories that are not considered in the calculations of regional aggregates.

[c] Some landlocked developing countries have territorial water claims within inland seas.

Indicator 7.7

Proportion of species threatened with extinction[a]

(Percentage of species not expected to become extinct in the near future)

	Birds		Mammals	
	1994	2008	1996	2008
World	92.20	91.85	86.03	85.33
Developing regions	92.55	92.19	85.87	85.13
Northern Africa	97.60	97.12	90.18	89.82
Sub-Saharan Africa	93.75	93.60	86.76	86.59
Latin America and the Caribbean	93.10	92.95	87.09	86.56
Caribbean	96.01	95.93	89.81	89.94
Latin America	93.49	93.35	87.59	87.04
Eastern Asia	96.19	95.78	91.42	90.67
Southern Asia	95.99	95.52	86.92	86.21
South-Eastern Asia	93.40	92.66	84.27	82.59
Western Asia	97.60	96.99	92.95	92.50
Oceania	91.86	91.41	85.16	84.39
Commonwealth of Independent States	96.44	95.71	92.28	91.68
Developed regions	93.51	93.09	91.04	90.79

[a] International Union for Conservation of Nature (IUCN) Red List Index values for non-data deficient species.

Target 7.C

Halve, by 2015, the proportion of people without sustainable access to safe drinking water and basic sanitation

Indicator 7.8

Proportion of population using an improved drinking water source[a]

(Percentage)

	1990			2006		
	Total	Urban	Rural	Total	Urban	Rural
World	77	95	63	87	96	78
Developing regions	71	93	59	84	94	76
Northern Africa	88	95	82	92	96	87
Sub-Saharan Africa	49	82	35	58	81	46
Latin America and the Caribbean	84	94	61	92	97	73
Eastern Asia	68	97	55	88	98	81
Eastern Asia excluding China ...	—	98	—	—	98	—
Southern Asia	74	91	68	87	95	84
Southern Asia excluding India	82	95	77	83	91	78
South-Eastern Asia	73	92	64	86	92	81
Western Asia	86	95	70	90	95	80
Oceania	51	92	39	50	91	37
Commonwealth of Independent States	93	97	84	94	99	86

	1990			2006		
	Total	Urban	Rural	Total	Urban	Rural
Commonwealth of Independent States, Asia	87	95	80	88	98	79
Commonwealth of Independent States, Europe	95	98	87	97	99	91
Developed regions	98	100	95	99	100	97

[a] No new global or regional data available. Data presented are from 2008 report (A/63/1).

Indicator 7.9

Proportion of population using an improved sanitation facility[a]

(Percentage)

	1990			2006		
	Total	Urban	Rural	Total	Urban	Rural
World	54	78	36	62	79	45
Developing regions	41	66	28	53	71	39
Northern Africa	62	82	44	76	90	59
Sub-Saharan Africa	26	40	20	31	42	24
Latin America and the Caribbean	68	81	35	79	86	52
Eastern Asia	48	61	43	65	74	59
Southern Asia	21	53	10	33	57	23
Southern Asia excluding India	39	74	25	48	70	37
South-Eastern Asia	50	74	40	67	78	58
Western Asia	79	93	56	84	94	64
Oceania	52	80	44	52	80	43
Commonwealth of Independent States	90	95	81	89	94	81
Commonwealth of Independent States, Asia	95	97	93	93	95	92
Commonwealth of Independent States, Europe	89	94	77	88	94	75
Developed regions	99	100	96	99	100	96

[a] No new global or regional data available. Data presented are from 2008 report (A/63/1).

Target 7.D

By 2020, to have achieved a significant improvement in the lives of at least 100 million slum-dwellers

Indicator 7.10

Proportion of urban population living in slums[a]

(Percentage)

	1990	2000	2005
Developing regions	46.3	39.4	35.7
Northern Africa	36.2	20.3	14.5
Sub-Saharan Africa	71.5	65.8	62.2
Latin America and the Caribbean	33.7	29.2	27.0
Eastern Asia	43.7	37.4	36.5
Southern Asia	57.2	45.8	42.9
South-Eastern Asia	49.5	39.6	34.2
Western Asia	22.5	20.6	25.8
Oceania	—	—	24.1

[a] Represented by the urban population living in households with at least one of the four characteristics: lack of access to improved drinking water, lack of access to improved sanitation, overcrowding (three or more persons per room) and dwellings made of non-durable material. Half of pit latrines are considered improved sanitation. These new figures are not comparable to previously published estimates where all households using pit latrine were considered slum households.

GOAL 8
Develop a global partnership for development

Target 8.A
Develop further an open, rule-based, predictable, non-discriminatory trading and financial system

Includes a commitment to good governance, development and poverty reduction—both nationally and internationally

Target 8.B
Address the special needs of the least developed countries

Includes: tariff- and quota-free access for the least developed countries' exports; enhanced programme of debt relief for heavily indebted poor countries (HIPC) and cancellation of official bilateral debt; and more generous official development assistance (ODA) for countries committed to poverty reduction

Target 8.C
Address the special needs of landlocked developing countries and small island developing States (through the Programme of Action for the Sustainable Development of Small Island Developing States and the outcome of the twenty-second special session of the General Assembly)

Target 8.D
Deal comprehensively with the debt problems of developing countries through national and international measures in order to make debt sustainable in the long term

Official development assistance (ODA)

Indicator 8.1
Net ODA, total and to the least developed countries, as a percentage of Organization for Economic Cooperation and Development/Development Assistance Committee donors' gross national income

(a) **Annual total assistance**[a]
(Billions of United States dollars)

	1990	2002	2003	2004	2005	2006	2007	2008[b]
All developing countries	52.7	58.3	69.1	79.4	107.1	104.4	103.5	119.8
Least developed countries	15.1	15.8	22.4	23.4	24.6	30.0	32.0	—

[a] Including non-ODA debt forgiveness but excluding forgiveness of debt for military purposes.

[b] Preliminary data.

(b) **Share of OECD/DAC donors' gross national income**
(Percentage)

	1990	2002	2003	2004	2005	2006	2007	2008[a]
All developing countries	0.33	0.23	0.25	0.26	0.33	0.31	0.28	0.30
Least developed countries	0.09	0.06	0.08	0.08	0.08	0.09	0.09	—

[a] Preliminary data.

Indicator 8.2
Proportion of total bilateral, sector-allocable ODA of OECD/DAC donors to basic social services (basic education, primary health care, nutrition, safe water and sanitation)

	1998	2000	2002	2004	2007
Percentage	10.7	14.1	18.0	15.9	19.2
Billions of United States dollars	3.0	4.3	5.6	7.7	12.3

Indicator 8.3
Proportion of bilateral official development assistance of OECD/DAC donors that is untied[a]

	1990	2003	2004	2005	2006	2007
Percentage	67.6	91.8	91.3	92.3	89.0	84.6
Billions of United States dollars	16.3	30.1	30.8	48.9	62.2	60.2

[a] Based on only about 40 per cent of total ODA commitments from OECD/DAC countries, as it excludes technical cooperation and administrative costs, as well as all ODA from Austria, Luxembourg, New Zealand and the United States of America, which do not report the tying status of their ODA.

Indicator 8.4
ODA received in landlocked developing countries as a proportion of their gross national incomes

	1990	2003	2004	2005	2006	2007
Percentage	6.3	8.1	7.8	7.1	6.3	5.6
Billions of United States dollars	7.0	12.0	13.9	14.7	16.5	18.7

Indicator 8.5
ODA received in small island developing States as a proportion of their gross national incomes

	1990	2003	2004	2005	2006	2007
Percentage	2.7	2.7	2.8	2.7	2.7	3.0
Billions of United States dollars	2.1	1.8	2.1	2.5	2.6	3.2

Market access

Indicator 8.6
Proportion of total developed country imports (by value and excluding arms) from developing countries and least developed countries, admitted free of duty
(Percentage)

	1996	1998	2000	2003	2007[a]
(a) *Excluding arms*					
Developing countries[a]	53	54	63	71	83
Least developed countries	68	81	75	81	89
(b) *Excluding arms and oil*					
Developing countries[a]	54	54	65	71	79
Northern Africa	20	18	26	63	95
Sub-Saharan Africa	88	89	83	90	93
Latin America and the Caribbean	58	58	58	92	95
Latin America	74	77	82	90	93
Eastern Asia	35	35	52	60	68
Southern Asia	41	42	46	54	64
South-Eastern Asia	60	58	76	75	79
Western Asia	45	46	56	57	94
Oceania	82	84	79	81	89
Commonwealth of Independent States	59	59	59	84	89
Least developed countries	78	78	70	78	80

[a] Includes Commonwealth of Independent States countries.

Indicator 8.7

**Average tariffs imposed by developed countries
on agricultural products and textiles and clothing
from developing countries**
(Percentage)

		1996	2000	2003	2005	2007
(a)	*Agricultural goods*					
	Developing countries	10.4	9.2	9.4	8.8	8.4
	Least developed countries	3.9	3.7	2.8	3.1	2.1
(b)	*Textiles*					
	Developing countries..........	7.3	6.5	5.8	5.3	5.0
	Least developed countries.....	4.6	4.1	3.5	3.2	3.1
(c)	*Clothing*					
	Developing countries	11.4	10.8	9.6	8.3	8.2
	Least developed countries	8.1	7.8	7.0	6.4	6.4

Indicator 8.8

**Agricultural support estimate for OECD countries
as a percentage of their gross domestic product**

	1990	2003	2004	2005	2006	2007[a]
Percentage	2.03	1.17	1.13	1.05	0.97	0.89
Billions of United States dollars	322	351	381	376	363	365

[a] Preliminary data.

Indicator 8.9

**Proportion of ODA provided
to help build trade capacity[a]**

	2001	2003	2005	2007
Trade policy and regulations and trade-related adjustment[b]	1.0	0.8	0.8	0.8
Economic infrastructure....................	21.5	14.8	17.2	13.1
Building productive capacity	16.0	13.4	12.8	13.3

[a] Aid-for-trade proxies as a percentage of bilateral sector-allocable ODA.

[b] Reporting of trade-related adjustment data commenced in 2007. Only Canada and the European Community reported.

Debt sustainability

Indicator 8.10

**Total number of countries that have reached
their HIPC decision points and number
that have reached their HIPC completion points**
(cumulative)

	2000[a]	2009[b]
Reached completion point............................	1	24
Reached decision point but not completion point.....	21	11
Yet to be considered for decision point	13	6
Total eligible countries	**35**	**41**

[a] As of December 2000; including only countries that are heavily indebted poor countries (HIPC) in 2009.

[b] As of March 2009.

Indicator 8.11

**Debt relief committed under HIPC
and Multilateral Debt Relief initiatives[a]**
(Billions of United States dollars, cumulative)

	2000	2009
To countries that reached decision or completion point	30	77

[a] Expressed in end-2007 net present value terms; commitment status as of March 2009.

Indicator 8.12

**Debt service as a percentage of exports of goods and
services[a, b]**

	1990	1995	2000	2007
Developing regions	19.7	14.4	12.6	4.1
Northern Africa	39.9	22.7	15.4	7.2
Sub-Saharan Africa	17.6	10.4	9.4	4.2
Latin America and the Caribbean	20.6	18.7	21.8	8.0
Caribbean	16.8	10.8	8.0	11.9
Latin America	20.7	19.0	22.2	7.9
Eastern Asia	10.6	9.0	5.1	0.6
Southern Asia	17.7	26.9	13.7	7.4
Southern Asia excluding India	9.3	22.3	11.5	7.4
South-Eastern Asia	16.7	7.9	6.5	3.3
Western Asia	27.8	22.3	17.6	11.8
Oceania	14.0	7.8	5.9	4.1
Commonwealth of Independent States ...	0.6[c]	6.1	8.1	2.2
Commonwealth of Independent States, Asia	0.6[c]	3.8	8.4	1.4
Commonwealth of Independent States, Europe	0.6[c]	6.2	8.1	2.3
Transition countries of South-Eastern Europe	9.7	11.7	11.8	4.2
Least developed countries	16.8	13.4	11.6	6.8
Landlocked developing countries	14.9	7.3	8.6	2.0
Small island developing States	13.7	9.5	8.7	11.2

[a] Debt service as a proportion of exports of goods and services and net income from abroad.

[b] Including countries reporting to the World Bank Debtor Reporting System. Aggregates are based on available data and, for some years, might exclude countries that do not have data on exports of goods and services and net income from abroad.

[c] Data for 1993.

Target 8.E

**In cooperation with pharmaceutical companies,
provide access to affordable, essential drugs in
developing countries**

Indicator 8.13

**Proportion of population with access to affordable essential
drugs on a sustainable basis**
(no global or regional data are available)

Target 8.F

**In cooperation with the private sector, make available
the benefits of new technologies, especially
information and communications**

Indicator 8.14

Number of fixed telephone lines per 100 population

	1990	2000	2007
World	9.8	16.0	19.0
Developing regions	2.3	8.0	13.3
Northern Africa	2.8	7.2	12.1
Sub-Saharan Africa	1.0	1.4	1.5
Latin America and the Caribbean	6.3	14.6	17.9
Caribbean	7.1	11.6	10.9
Latin America	6.2	14.9	18.4
Eastern Asia	2.4	13.7	28.5
Eastern Asia excluding China	24.9	43.0	40.2
Southern Asia	0.7	3.3	4.4
Southern Asia excluding India	1.1	3.5	7.1
South-Eastern Asia	1.3	4.8	11.3

	1990	2000	2007
Western Asia	9.6	17.5	17.6
Oceania	3.3	5.2	5.0
Commonwealth of Independent States	12.4	18.5	25.4
Commonwealth of Independent States, Asia	7.9	8.8	11.6
Commonwealth of Independent States, Europe	13.9	21.8	30.6
Developed regions	42.4	55.1	47.6
Transition countries of South-Eastern Europe	13.1	21.1	24.1
Least developed countries	0.3	0.5	0.9
Landlocked developing countries	2.4	2.7	3.6
Small island developing States	8.0	13.2	12.1

Indicator 8.15
Cellular subscribers per 100 population

	1995	2000	2007
World	1.6	12.1	50.3
Developing regions	0.4	5.5	38.6
Northern Africa	<0.05	2.8	57.3
Sub-Saharan Africa	0.1	1.7	22.9
Latin America and the Caribbean	0.8	12.2	67.0
Caribbean	1.2	6.6	42.9
Latin America	0.8	12.6	68.9
Eastern Asia	0.5	9.9	43.8
Eastern Asia excluding China	3.4	50.2	76.2
Southern Asia	<0.05	0.4	23.0
Southern Asia excluding India	<0.05	0.5	30.6
South-Eastern Asia	0.7	4.3	48.2
Western Asia	0.9	14.6	71.8
Oceania	0.2	2.4	16.2
Commonwealth of Independent States	<0.05	1.8	93.4
Commonwealth of Independent States, Asia	<0.05	1.3	42.4
Commonwealth of Independent States, Europe	0.1	2.0	112.5
Developed regions	7.8	47.8	100.0

	1995	2000	2007
Transition countries of South-Eastern Europe	0.1	8.9	94.7
Least developed countries[a]	<0.05	0.3	14.5
Landlocked developing countries	<0.05	1.0	18.2
Small island developing States	1.5	10.5	44.4

[a] The 1995 column shows 1996 data.

Indicator 8.16
Internet users per 100 population

	1995	2000	2007
World	0.7	6.5	20.6
Developing regions	0.1	2.1	12.7
Northern Africa	<0.05	0.8	14.4
Sub-Saharan Africa	0.1	0.5	3.7
Latin America and the Caribbean	0.1	3.9	25.7
Caribbean	0.1	2.9	18.3
Latin America	0.1	4.0	26.3
Eastern Asia	0.1	3.6	18.7
Eastern Asia excluding China	0.9	27.1	53.3
Southern Asia	<0.05	0.5	6.9
Southern Asia excluding India[a]	<0.05	0.3	7.0
South-Eastern Asia	0.1	2.4	11.8
Western Asia	0.1	3.9	15.7
Oceania	<0.05	1.9	5.7
Commonwealth of Independent States	0.1	1.4	17.8
Commonwealth of Independent States, Asia[a]	<0.05	0.5	7.8
Commonwealth of Independent States, Europe	0.1	1.7	21.5
Developed regions	3.9	29.9	63.5
Transition countries of South-Eastern Europe	0.1	3.4	23.4
Least developed countries[b]	<0.05	0.1	1.5
Landlocked developing countries[a]	<0.05	0.3	3.5
Small island developing States	0.2	5.0	19.1

[a] The 1995 column shows 1996 data.
[b] The 1995 column shows 1998 data.

SOURCES: United Nations Inter-Agency and Expert Group on Millennium Development Goals Indicators and MDG Indicators Database (http://mdgs.un.org).

NOTES: Except where indicated, regional groupings are based on United Nations geographical regions, with some modifications necessary to create, to the extent possible, homogeneous groups of countries for analysis and presentation. The regional composition adopted for 2009 reporting on MDG indicators is available at http://mdgs.un.org, under "Data".

Commonwealth of Independent States (CIS) comprises Belarus, Republic of Moldova, Russian Federation and Ukraine in Europe, and Armenia, Azerbaijan, Georgia, Kazakhstan, Kyrgyzstan, Tajikistan, Turkmenistan and Uzbekistan in Asia.

Where shown, "Developed regions" comprises Europe (except CIS countries), Australia, Canada, Japan, New Zealand and the United States of America. In the tables, developed regions always include transition countries in Europe.

PART ONE

Political and security questions

Chapter I

International peace and security

The year 2009 brought new challenges for international peace and security, as the United Nations worked to address several conflict situations, mainly in Africa, and further incidents of international terrorism, while supporting the efforts of post-conflict countries to sustain peace and stability, rebuild national institutions and restore economic development. The Security Council took forward the reform of peacekeeping operations and debated ways to strengthen collective security, stressing the role of mediation in settling disputes. It also reviewed measures to ensure the protection of civilians in armed conflict and met regularly with troop-contributing countries with respect to ongoing peacekeeping operations. The Peacebuilding Commission enhanced its efforts in support of countries emerging from conflict, including through its country configurations relating to Burundi, the Central African Republic, Guinea-Bissau and Sierra Leone. During the year, the United Nations maintained 12 political and peacebuilding missions and offices.

The United Nations Observer Mission in Georgia ceased to exist on 15 June, after the Russian Federation vetoed a technical roll-over for the mission. At the end of 2009, there were 15 peacekeeping operations, served by 119,577 uniformed and civilian personnel.

The scale and frequency of international terrorist acts continued, resulting in the deaths of hundreds of innocent civilians and injuries to many others. In addition to Afghanistan, Pakistan and Iraq, areas affected included Iran, Indonesia and Somalia. A suicide bomb attack in Islamabad on 5 October killed five World Food Programme staff members, and a Taliban attack in Kabul on 28 October killed five UN staff members. The Council issued statements condemning those attacks as unacceptable and unjustifiable. The General Assembly in December requested that the Secretary-General provide the resources necessary to finalize the institutionalization of the Counter-Terrorism Implementation Task Force, in order to ensure coordination and coherence in the counter-terrorism efforts of the UN system.

During the year, the Council also issued statements on mediation and dispute settlement, post-conflict peacebuilding, civilians in armed conflict and the conduct of peacekeeping operations. In November, it adopted a resolution on the protection of civilians in armed conflict, in which it demanded that parties to a conflict comply with their obligations under international humanitarian, human rights and refugee law, urging them to take all measures required to respect the civilian population. By a resolution on conflict diamonds, the General Assembly reaffirmed its support for the Kimberley Process Certification Scheme and for the Kimberley Process as a whole. By a resolution on the Peacebuilding Fund, it affirmed the respective roles of the General Assembly, the Peacebuilding Commission and the independent Advisory Group to provide policy guidance on the use of the Fund to maximize its impact and improve its functioning. The Assembly also adopted texts on a comprehensive review of peacekeeping operations in all their aspects, the peacekeeping support account, the scale of assessments for apportioning the expenses of peacekeeping operations, rates of reimbursement to troop-contributing countries, the financing of the United Nations Logistics Base at Brindisi, criminal accountability of UN officials and experts on missions, and the responsibility to protect.

Regarding the financial position of UN peacekeeping operations, expenditures rose by 13.6 per cent, from \$6,265.8 million to \$7,120.6 million for the 2008/09 financial year. The increase was mainly due to the expansion of the African Union-United Nations Hybrid Operation in Darfur, the United Nations Mission in the Central African Republic and Chad and the United Nations Organization Mission in the Democratic Republic of the Congo. Unpaid assessed contributions decreased by 5 per cent to \$967.5 million.

Promotion of international peace and security

Maintenance of international peace and security

Security sector reform

Special Committee on Peacekeeping Operations consideration. During its 2009 substantive session (New York, 23 February–20 March) [A/63/19], the Special Committee said that UN assistance for security sector reform through peacekeeping missions should be undertaken at the request of the host country. In post-conflict countries, such reform was normally a long-term process, rooted in the needs and conditions of the country concerned. Its sustainability depended on national ownership and the sustained support of the international community, including bilateral donors. The United Nations and the international community should avoid imposing external models of security sector reform and concentrate on strengthening the host country's capacity to develop, manage and implement such reform through inclusive consultation processes at all stages of the transition from peacekeeping to peacebuilding and sustainable development.

The Special Committee stressed that security sector reform must take place within a broad framework of the rule of law and should contribute to the overall strengthening of UN rule of law activities in peacekeeping operations. It recognized the need for a holistic and coherent UN approach, and acknowledged the principal role of the Department of Peacekeeping Operations (DPKO) in supporting such reform activities in peacekeeping missions. The establishment of an effective, professional and accountable national security sector was a critical element in the transition from UN peacekeeping to sustainable peace and development, including economic recovery. The Committee encouraged DPKO's continued assistance and advice to UN peacekeeping and special political missions. It reiterated the importance of incorporating gender perspectives in security sector reform programmes, and stressed the need to establish a security sector reform unit in the DPKO Office of Rule of Law and Security Institutions.

Mediation and settlement of disputes

Report of Secretary-General. Pursuant to presidential statement S/PRST/2008/36 [YUN 2008, p. 40], the Secretary-General, in April, submitted a report on enhancing mediation and its support activities [S/2009/189] that examined the challenges faced by the United Nations and its partners in providing professional mediation assistance to parties in conflict. It described the need for experienced and knowledgeable mediators and support teams, with women adequately represented, and sufficient resources to provide assistance at an early stage to help parties design and pursue processes that would address the root causes of their conflicts, overcome obstacles blocking progress, and achieve agreements leading to sustainable peace. It discussed the importance of building local, national and regional capacity for mediation and the need for coherent partnership between the United Nations, regional and subregional organizations, States and nongovernmental organizations (NGOs). It stated that the new Mediation Support Unit in the Department of Political Affairs had, by late 2008, supported 18 ongoing or new peace processes. The cost-effectiveness of mediation in the resolution of disputes was highlighted.

Among its recommendations, the report emphasized the need for early UN engagement to strengthen conflict prevention and resolution; increasing support for mediators; developing the next generation of UN mediators; and integrating mediation support into UN field operations.

Security Council consideration. On 21 April [meeting 6108], the Council held an open debate on mediation and settlement of disputes and on the report of the Secretary-General. The Council was briefed by the Under-Secretary-General for Political Affairs, B. Lynn Pascoe, on the establishment of the Mediation Support Unit and a reserve pool of expert mediators; the importance of working with Member States, regional organizations and NGOs in efforts to mediate; and support activities for mediators in the planning and management of peace processes. More than 40 speakers addressed the day-long debate.

SECURITY COUNCIL ACTION

On 21 April [meeting 6108], following consultations among Security Council members, the President made statement **S/PRST/2009/8** on behalf of the Council:

The Security Council recalls the statement by its President of 23 September 2008 and takes note of the report of the Secretary-General on enhancing mediation and its support activities, as well as the recommendations contained therein.

The Council, in accordance with the Charter of the United Nations and as the organ with the primary responsibility for the maintenance of international peace and security, underscores its intention to remain engaged in all stages of the conflict cycle, including in support of mediation, and expresses its readiness to explore further ways and means to reinforce the promotion of mediation as an important means for the pacific settlement of disputes, wherever possible before they evolve into violence.

The Council recognizes the importance of mediation, to be launched in the earliest possible phases of conflicts as well as in the implementation phases of signed peace agreements, and underlines the need to design mediation processes that address the root causes of conflicts and contribute to peacebuilding, in order to ensure sustainable peace.

The Council stresses that the principal responsibility for the peaceful settlement of disputes rests with the parties to the conflict and that it is only through their full participation and genuine commitment to resolve the conflict, including its underlying causes, that peace can be achieved and sustained. In this regard, the Council underlines the importance of building national and local capacity for mediation.

The Council emphasizes the importance of the actions undertaken by the Secretary-General in promoting mediation and in the pacific settlement of disputes, and welcomes the continued efforts of the Department of Political Affairs of the Secretariat, in particular through the Mediation Support Unit, to respond to emerging and existing crises. It underscores that mediation support efforts should be responsive to the demands of fast-moving peace processes.

The Council recalls the important contribution of Member States, regional and subregional organizations, civil society and other stakeholders to the pacific settlement of disputes. The Council welcomes the efforts made by regional and subregional organizations to enhance their mediation role, and appreciates the efforts of the Secretary-General to continue to assist them in this regard.

The Council urges the Secretariat to work with all partners to ensure the availability of well-trained, experienced and geographically diverse mediation experts at all levels to ensure the timely and highest quality support to mediation efforts, and it urges those possessing cadres of mediation experts to cooperate with the Secretariat in this endeavour.

The Council further requests the Secretary-General to work in partnership with Member States, regional and subregional organizations and other relevant partners in a coordinated and mutually complementary manner when cooperating in a mediation process.

The Council notes with concern the very low numbers of women in formal roles in mediation processes, and stresses the need to ensure that women are appropriately appointed at decision-making levels, as high-level mediators, and within the composition of the mediators' teams in line with resolutions 1325(2000) and 1820(2008). It reiterates its call to the Secretary-General and the heads of regional and subregional organizations to take the appropriate measures to that end.

The Council requests the Secretary-General to keep it informed of the action undertaken by him in promoting and supporting mediation and the pacific settlement of disputes, ensuring coherence with the ongoing efforts to strengthen peacebuilding and peacekeeping.

United Nations and regional organizations

Security Council consideration. On 18 March [meeting 6092], the Security Council held a high-level debate on peace and security in Africa, during which it discussed the report [YUN 2008, p. 111] of the panel led by Romano Prodi containing recommendations on strengthening cooperation between the African Union (AU) and the United Nations. In statement **S/PRST/2009/3** (see p. 105), the Council emphasized the importance of establishing more effective strategic relationships between the AU and the United Nations, and encouraged further efforts in that direction.

On 26 October [meeting 6206], after having considered peace and security in Africa, the Council adopted statement **S/PRST/2009/26** on cooperation with regional organizations, in particular the AU, in maintaining international peace and security (see p. 109). The Council welcomed the intention of the UN Secretariat and the AU Commission to set up a joint task force on peace and security to review immediate and long-term strategic and operational issues.

Conflict prevention

The General Assembly, by **decision 63/563** of 14 September, deferred consideration of the item entitled "Prevention of armed conflict" and included it in the draft agenda of its sixty-fourth (2009) session. On 24 December, the Assembly, by **decision 64/549**, decided that the item "Prevention of armed conflict" would remain for consideration during its resumed sixty-fourth (2010) session.

Conflict diamonds

Kimberley Process. The Kimberley Process [YUN 2000, p. 76], at its seventh annual session (Swakopmund, Namibia, 2–5 November) continued its work relating to the Kimberley Process Certification Scheme (KPCS), which was established in 2003 [YUN 2003, p. 55] to stop the trade in conflict diamonds from fuelling armed conflict, protect the legitimate diamond industry and ensure implementation of UN resolutions on trade in conflict diamonds. As at 5 November, KPCS had 49 members. In accordance with General Assembly resolution 63/134 [YUN 2008, p. 45], Namibia, on 8 December, transmitted to the Secretary-General the 2009 Kimberley Process report [A/64/559] in its capacity as Chair of KPCS.

Since the inception of KPCS, there had been a dramatic improvement in the security situation in several diamond-producing countries to which the Process contributed significantly, the report stated. With regard to concerns relating to diamond smuggling, illicit trade activities and human rights violations in the Marange diamond fields in Zimbabwe, a joint workplan was formulated at the 2009 plenary to improve security at access control points and enhance security of processing and storage areas. In accordance with Security Council resolution 1842(2008) [YUN 2008, p. 194], KPCS had maintained close cooperation with the United Nations Group of Experts on Côte d'Ivoire. The KPCS Working Group on Monitoring continued to use satellite monitoring technology to monitor illicit rough diamonds production. In 2008–2009, Belgium funded the footprinting of the Kimberley Process data project, which aimed at improving the quality of the statistical analysis data in order to quickly identify statistical anomalies, and develop an adequate statistical filtering methodology, as well as a regional analysis of statistical data for West Africa, Central Africa and South America so as to enhance implementation of the Kimberley Process in those regions.

A new Kimberley Process rough diamond statistics system was launched as a means of containing the flow of conflict diamonds into the legitimate market and as a regular source of information on KPCS implementation. The system had built-in security measures to implement quality edit checks and controls to ensure data consistency during the data entry phase. Stressing that technical assistance from participants and organizations remained key to enhancing Kimberley Process implementation, the report noted, for example, that the European Community provided technical advisers to Liberia to help that country comply with recommendations made by the Kimberley Process review teams after their visits there in 2008 and 2009.

The Working Group of Diamond Experts had been tasked by the Moscow Resolution (2005) and the Brussels Initiative (2007) to calculate the possible diamond production of Côte d'Ivoire on a yearly basis for two diamondiferous regions in the north. It had also been tasked with studying the characteristics of diamonds produced in West Africa, and assisting with their identification by developing footprints for the different diamond productions, in order to stop Côte d'Ivoire diamonds from being mixed with other productions. In follow-up to the Moscow Resolution/Brussels Initiative, the production estimates of Côte d'Ivoire had been partly based on satellite imagery. During 2009, the World Diamond Council trained staff to take digital photographs of all rough diamond exports in order to depict their origin, pending the production of footprints by the Working Group.

Although the Kimberley Process had made significant strides, it still faced daunting challenges. Participants had occasionally been confronted with the appearance of fraudulent Kimberley Process certificates, which in itself posed a threat and a challenge for the Process. Increases in Internet sales and postal shipments had become a concern, as it had proved difficult to track and reconcile rough diamond shipments via the Internet or postal service. As for its next session, Israel, the Vice-Chair for 2009, would succeed Namibia as Kimberley Process Chair, with effect from 1 January 2010, and the Democratic Republic of the Congo would serve as Vice-Chair in 2010.

(On the Security Council Committee established pursuant to resolution 1572(2004) [YUN 2004, p. 187], which monitored the embargo on the import of rough diamonds from Côte d'Ivoire, and its Expert Group, see p. 184.)

GENERAL ASSEMBLY ACTION

On 11 December [meeting 63], the General Assembly adopted **resolution 64/109** [draft: A/63/L.26 & Add.1] without vote [agenda item 12].

The role of diamonds in fuelling conflict: breaking the link between the illicit transaction of rough diamonds and armed conflict as a contribution to prevention and settlement of conflicts

The General Assembly,

Recognizing that the trade in conflict diamonds continues to be a matter of serious international concern, which can be directly linked to the fuelling of armed conflict, the activities of rebel movements aimed at undermining or overthrowing legitimate Governments and the illicit traffic in and proliferation of armaments, especially small arms and light weapons,

Recognizing also the devastating impact of conflicts fuelled by the trade in conflict diamonds on the peace, safety and security of people in affected countries, and the systematic and gross human rights violations that have been perpetrated in such conflicts,

Noting the negative impact of such conflicts on regional stability and the obligations placed upon States by the Charter of the United Nations regarding the maintenance of international peace and security,

Recognizing that continued action to curb the trade in conflict diamonds is imperative,

Noting with appreciation that the Kimberley Process, as an international initiative of the Governments of participant States, has pursued its deliberations on an inclusive basis involving concerned stakeholders, including producing, exporting and importing States, the diamond industry and civil society, as well as applicant States and international organizations,

Recalling that the elimination of conflict diamonds from legitimate trade is the primary objective of the Kimberley Process,

Calling for the consistent implementation of commitments made by Kimberley Process participant States,

Acknowledging that the diamond sector is an important catalyst for achieving poverty reduction and meeting the requirements of the Millennium Development Goals in many producing countries, particularly in developing countries,

Bearing in mind the positive benefits of the legitimate diamond trade to producing countries, and underlining the need for continued international action to prevent the problem of conflict diamonds from negatively affecting the trade in legitimate diamonds, which makes a critical contribution to the economies of many of the producing, exporting and importing States, especially developing States,

Noting that the vast majority of rough diamonds produced in the world are from legitimate sources,

Recalling the Charter and all the relevant resolutions of the Security Council related to conflict diamonds, and determined to contribute to and support the implementation of the measures provided for in those resolutions,

Recalling also Security Council resolution 1459(2003) of 28 January 2003, in which the Council strongly supported the Kimberley Process Certification Scheme as a valuable contribution against trafficking in conflict diamonds,

Welcoming the important contribution of the Kimberley Process, which was initiated by African diamond-producing countries,

Noting with satisfaction that the implementation of the Kimberley Process Certification Scheme continues to have a positive impact in reducing the opportunity for conflict diamonds to play a role in fuelling armed conflict and would help to protect legitimate trade and ensure the effective implementation of the relevant resolutions on trade in conflict diamonds,

Acknowledging that lessons learned from the Kimberley Process are useful for the work of the Peacebuilding Commission in its consideration of the countries included in its agenda, as appropriate,

Recalling its resolutions 55/56 of 1 December 2000, 56/263 of 13 March 2002, 57/302 of 15 April 2003, 58/290 of 14 April 2004, 59/144 of 15 December 2004, 60/182 of 20 December 2005, 61/28 of 4 December 2006, 62/11 of 26 November 2007 and 63/134 of 11 December 2008, in which it called for the development and implementation as well as a periodic review of proposals for a simple, effective and pragmatic international certification scheme for rough diamonds,

Welcoming, in this regard, the implementation of the Kimberley Process Certification Scheme in such a way as not to impede the legitimate trade in diamonds or impose an undue burden on Governments or industry, particularly smaller producers, nor hinder the development of the diamond industry,

Welcoming also the decision of forty-nine Kimberley Process Participants, representing seventy-five countries, including the twenty-seven members of the European Union represented by the European Commission, to address the problem of conflict diamonds by participating in the Process and implementing the Kimberley Process Certification Scheme,

Noting the consensual outcomes of the plenary meeting of the Kimberley Process, held in Swakopmund, Namibia, from 2 to 5 November 2009,

Welcoming the important contribution in fulfilling the purposes of the Kimberley Process that has been made and continues to be made by civil society and the diamond industry, in particular the World Diamond Council which represents all aspects of the diamond industry, to assist international efforts to stop the trade in conflict diamonds,

Welcoming also the voluntary self-regulation initiatives for the diamond industry announced by the World Diamond Council, and recognizing that a system of such voluntary self-regulation contributes, as described in the Interlaken Declaration of 5 November 2002 on the Kimberley Process Certification Scheme for Rough Diamonds, to ensuring the effectiveness of national systems of internal control for rough diamonds,

Recognizing that State sovereignty should be fully respected and that the principles of equality, mutual benefits and consensus should be adhered to,

Recognizing also that the Kimberley Process Certification Scheme, which came into effect on 1 January 2003, will be credible only if all Participants have requisite national legislation coupled with effective and credible internal systems of control designed to eliminate the presence of conflict diamonds in the chain of producing, exporting and importing rough diamonds within their own territories, while taking into account that differences in production methods and trading practices, as well as differences in institutional controls thereof, may require different approaches to meeting minimum standards,

Welcoming the efforts of the Kimberley Process to continue elaborating new rules and procedural norms to regulate the activities of its working bodies, Participants and observers, and to enhance the effectiveness of the Kimberley Process Certification Scheme,

1. *Reaffirms its strong and continuing support* for the Kimberley Process Certification Scheme and the Kimberley Process as a whole;

2. *Recognizes* that the Kimberley Process Certification Scheme can help to ensure the effective implementation of relevant resolutions of the Security Council containing sanctions on the trade in conflict diamonds and act as a mechanism for the prevention of future conflicts, and calls for the full implementation of existing Council measures targeting the illicit trade in rough diamonds, particularly conflict diamonds which play a role in fuelling conflict;

3. *Welcomes* the admission of new Participants to the Kimberley Process;

4. *Recognizes* the important contributions that the international efforts to address the problem of conflict diamonds, including the Kimberley Process Certification Scheme, have made to the settlement of conflicts and the consolidation of peace in Angola, Liberia and Sierra Leone;

5. *Notes* the efforts, including the creation of a team of technical experts, to strengthen import confirmation requirements and examine the compliance of cross-border Internet sales with Kimberley Process Certification Scheme requirements;

6. *Also notes* the decision of the General Council of the World Trade Organization of 15 May 2003 granting a waiver with respect to the measures taken to implement the Kimberley Process Certification Scheme, effective from 1 January 2003 to 31 December 2006, and the decision of the General Council of 17 November 2006 granting an extension of the waiver until 31 December 2012;

7. *Takes note* of the report of the Chair of the Kimberley Process submitted pursuant to General Assembly resolution 63/134, and congratulates the participating Governments, the regional economic integration organization, the diamond industry and civil society organizations involved in the Process for contributing to the development, implementation and monitoring of the Kimberley Process Certification Scheme;

8. *Welcomes* the efforts of the Kimberley Process Participants to fully implement the Kimberley Process Certification Scheme, and stresses the need to implement the minimum requirements and additional recommended measures established by the Kimberley Process and the intention to increase the efficiency of internal controls;

9. *Acknowledges* the progress made by Kimberley Process working groups, Participants and observers during 2009 in fulfilling the objectives set by the Chair to strengthen implementation of the peer review system, increase the transparency and accuracy of statistics, promote research into the traceability of diamonds, promote inclusiveness by broadening the level of involvement by Governments, industry and civil society in the Kimberley Process Certification Scheme, foster a sense of ownership by Participants, improve information and communication

flows and enhance the capacity of the Certification Scheme to respond to emerging challenges;

10. *Stresses* that the widest possible participation in the Kimberley Process Certification Scheme is essential, and encourages all Member States to contribute to the work of the Kimberley Process by seeking membership, participating actively in the Certification Scheme and complying with its undertakings, and welcomes the increased involvement of civil society organizations, in particular those from producer countries, in the Process;

11. *Recognizes* the importance of the Kimberley Process continuing to articulate and improve rules and procedures to further enhance the effectiveness of the Kimberley Process Certification Scheme, and notes with satisfaction the systematization of the work of the Process with respect to developing transparent and uniform rules and procedures and improving the mechanism for consultations and coordination within the Process;

12. *Welcomes* the adoption of new guidelines pertaining to implementation and enforcement in order to enhance the capacity of the Kimberley Process and provide guidance to national authorities to address specific enforcement issues such as fraudulent certificates, shipments of suspicious origin and the exchange of information in cases of infringement;

13. *Notes with appreciation* the willingness of the Kimberley Process to support and provide technical assistance to those Participants experiencing temporary difficulties in complying with the requirements of the Kimberley Process Certification Scheme;

14. *Notes* the adoption by the Swakopmund plenary meeting of the decision on the sharing of information on the Kimberley Process with the United Nations and on the participation of observers in the Process;

15. *Welcomes* the establishment of a scientific subgroup on characterization and identification of rough diamonds to improve the current footprinting work that is being done by the Kimberley Process on rough diamonds from Côte d'Ivoire;

16. *Notes with appreciation* the continued cooperation of the Kimberley Process with the United Nations on the issue of diamonds from Côte d'Ivoire and the continued monitoring of the situation in that country on the basis of the reports of the United Nations Group of Experts on Côte d'Ivoire, originally established by the Security Council in its resolution 1584(2005) of 1 February 2005, and through liaison with Côte d'Ivoire, and encourages continued cooperation between the Process and the United Nations in addressing this issue, with the ultimate objective of meeting the preconditions for the lifting of United Nations sanctions on the trade in rough diamonds from Côte d'Ivoire;

17. *Acknowledges* the adoption by the plenary meeting of the Kimberley Process of a plan to strengthen the internal controls of Guinea and to assess that country's production capacity, welcomes the commitment of Liberia to host a regional meeting to foster further regional cooperation in rough diamond controls, and appreciates the continued efforts of Ghana to strengthen internal controls and prevent the infiltration of illicit Ivorian diamonds into the legitimate trade;

18. *Notes with satisfaction* the development of a new Kimberley Process rough diamond statistics website with enhanced security measures and controls, welcomes the progress made towards the collection and submission of complete and accurate statistical reports on the production of and trade in rough diamonds, and encourages all the Process Participants to continue to enhance the quality of data and respond promptly to the process of analysis of the data;

19. *Also notes with satisfaction* the footprint work conducted by the Kimberley Process Working Group of Diamond Experts with respect to Côte d'Ivoire, Ghana, Guinea, Liberia, Togo and the Marange diamond fields in Zimbabwe;

20. *Notes with appreciation* the progress achieved under the action plan by the artisanal and alluvial diamond-producing countries and the sharing of information on the impact of the global financial crisis, namely the economic and social consequences and their impact on internal controls;

21. *Calls upon* all Kimberley Process Participants to implement internal controls in diamond trading and manufacturing centres as part of their own internal controls for ensuring adequate Government oversight over the trade in rough diamonds;

22. *Notes with appreciation* the assistance and capacity-building efforts extended by various donors, and encourages other donors to provide financial and technical expertise and organizational support to Kimberley Process Participants, in particular new Participants, to help them to develop tighter monitoring and control measures;

23. *Acknowledges with great appreciation* the important contribution that Namibia, as Chair of the Kimberley Process in 2009, has made to the efforts to curb the trade in conflict diamonds, and takes note that the Process has selected Israel as Chair and the Democratic Republic of the Congo as Vice-Chair of the Process for 2010;

24. *Requests* the Chair of the Kimberley Process to submit to the General Assembly at its sixty-fifth session a report on the implementation of the Process;

25. *Decides* to include in the provisional agenda of its sixty-fifth session the item entitled "The role of diamonds in fuelling conflict".

Implementation of 1970 Declaration

The General Assembly, by **decision 64/513** of 2 December, included in the provisional agenda of its sixty-sixth (2011) session the item entitled "Review of the implementation of the Declaration on the Strengthening of International Security" [YUN 1970, p. 105].

Climate change and security

General Assembly action. On 3 June, the General Assembly adopted **resolution 63/281** on climate change and its possible security implications (see p. 1026). The Assembly invited the relevant UN organs to intensify their efforts in considering and addressing climate change, including its possible security implications.

Proliferation of nuclear weapons

The Security Council, by **resolution 1887(2009)** of 24 September (see p. 525), reaffirmed its support for the Treaty on the Non-Proliferation of Nuclear Weapons, calling on States that were not parties to accede to it. The Council demanded that parties involved in major challenges to the non-proliferation regime comply fully with their obligations and find early negotiated solutions to those issues.

The Council urged States to curb the export of nuclear-related material to countries that had terminated their compliance with the International Atomic Energy Agency safeguards agreements. It also called upon States to refrain from conducting nuclear test explosions and to ratify the Comprehensive Nuclear-Test-Ban Treaty in order to bring it into force.

Peacemaking and peacebuilding

Post-conflict peacebuilding

Post-conflict stabilization

Pursuant to presidential statement S/PRST/2008/16 [YUN 2008, p. 52], the Secretary-General in June issued a report [A/63/881-S/2009/304] on peacebuilding in the immediate aftermath of conflict, defined as the first two years after the end of a main conflict, which focused on the challenges that post-conflict countries and the international community faced in that period. Reflecting on past peacebuilding experience, the report underscored the imperative of national ownership, highlighting the unique challenges arising from early post-conflict situations. The report stated that the threats to peace were often greatest during the early post-conflict phase, but so too were the opportunities to set virtuous cycles in motion. That early phase offered a window of opportunity to provide basic security, deliver peace dividends, shore up confidence in the political process, and strengthen national capacity to lead peacebuilding efforts. If countries developed a vision and strategy that succeeded in addressing those objectives early on, it substantially increased the chances for sustainable peace and reduced the risk of relapse into conflict, but those early opportunities had often been missed. The report identified several recurring priorities that related to those core objectives, and for which international assistance was frequently requested. Seizing the window of opportunity required that international actors were, at a minimum, capable of responding coherently, rapidly and effectively to support those priorities.

The report described UN efforts to enhance the efficiency and effectiveness of its post-conflict response. It identified systemic challenges related to differing mandates, governance structures and financing arrangements across diverse UN entities, which prevented the Organization from making deeper reforms. The report set out an agenda to strengthen the UN post-conflict response and to facilitate an earlier, more coherent international response. That agenda included stronger, more effective and better supported UN leadership teams on the ground; early agreement on priorities and alignment of resources behind them; and strengthening UN support for national ownership and capacity development. It also included rationalizing and enhancing the UN system's capacity to provide knowledge, expertise and personnel to meet the most urgent peacebuilding needs, in concert with partners who had a comparative advantage in particular areas, as well as assisting countries to identify and draw on the most relevant capacities globally.

Finally, the report considered the critical role of the Peacebuilding Commission in supporting post-conflict countries and made suggestions to Member States on how the Commission could strengthen its advisory role in the early post-conflict period.

The General Assembly, by **decision 63/571** of 14 September, deferred consideration of the report until its sixty-fourth (2009) session under the items entitled "Report of the Peacebuilding Commission" and "Report of the Secretary-General on the Peacebuilding Fund".

Security Council consideration. On 22 July, the Council held an open debate [meeting 6165] on post-conflict peacebuilding, presided over by Uganda's Minister for Foreign Affairs, Sam K. Kutesa. The Secretary-General presented his report, emphasizing that peacebuilding entailed much more than ending war; it was about putting into place the institutions and trust that would carry people forward into a peaceful future. Chile, as Chairperson of the Peacebuilding Commission, said that the Commission would support Governments in managing the difficult process of establishing clear and attainable peacebuilding priorities, working closely with UN country staff to ensure coordination and avoid duplication. The Director of the Bureau for Crisis Prevention and Recovery of the United Nations Development Programme (UNDP) said that effective and quick peacebuilding action was essential if countries emerging from conflict were to succeed in meeting the Millennium Development Goals. The Director of the Fragile and Conflict-Affected Countries Group of the World Bank stressed the need for financial accountability to maintain long-term predictable financial support, adding that often the highest priority in the aftermath of conflict was personal security, justice and ending impunity. Forty speakers addressed the day-long debate.

On 22 July [meeting 6165], following consultations among Security Council members, the President made statement **S/PRST/2009/23** on behalf of the Council:

The Security Council recalls the statement by its President of 20 May 2008, and emphasizes the critical importance of post-conflict peacebuilding as the foundation for building sustainable peace and development in the aftermath of conflict.

The Council welcomes the report of the Secretary-General on peacebuilding in the immediate aftermath of conflict as an important contribution towards a more effective and coherent international response to post-conflict peacebuilding. The Council also welcomes the strong commitment of the Secretary-General, expressed in the report, to improve the peacebuilding efforts of the United Nations, and urges him to pursue these objectives.

The Council emphasizes the importance of national ownership and the need for national authorities to take responsibility as soon as possible for re-establishing the institutions of government, restoring the rule of law, revitalizing the economy, reforming the security sector, providing basic services and other key peacebuilding needs. The Council underscores the vital role of the United Nations in assisting national authorities to develop an early strategy, in close consultation with international partners, to address these priorities, and encourages international partners to align their financial, technical and political support behind this strategy.

The Council stresses the need, in countries emerging from conflict, to draw upon and develop existing national capacities at the earliest possible stage, and the importance of rapidly deployable civilian expertise to help to achieve this, including, where appropriate, relevant expertise from the region. The Council welcomes, in this regard, the recommendation of the Secretary-General for a review to be undertaken to analyse how the United Nations and the international community can help to broaden and deepen the pool of civilian experts, giving particular attention to mobilizing capacities from developing countries and especially women.

The Council recognizes that post-conflict situations require from the outset experienced and skilled leadership on the ground with effective support teams, and requests the United Nations to increase its efforts in this regard. The Council welcomes the efforts of the Secretary-General to enhance the authority and accountability of senior United Nations representatives in carrying out their duties and responsibilities.

The Council emphasizes the need for the United Nations system to strengthen strategic partnerships with the World Bank and other international financial institutions, and to complete by the end of 2009 the clarification of roles and responsibilities for key peacebuilding needs and to keep these under regular review, so that the appropriate expertise is generated to achieve a timely and predictable response.

The Council recalls its resolution 1645(2005) and recognizes the important role of the Peacebuilding Commission in promoting and supporting an integrated and coherent approach to peacebuilding, welcomes the progress it has achieved, calls upon it to further enhance its advisory role and support for countries on its agenda and looks forward to the recommendations of the 2010 review of the Commission's founding resolutions on how its role can continue to be enhanced.

The Council recognizes the critical importance of rapid, flexible and predictable funding for post-conflict peacebuilding. The Council urges Member States to help to achieve this, building on the recommendations contained in the report of the Secretary-General and, in particular, increasing the impact of the Peacebuilding Fund, improving donor practices to make funding faster and more flexible and making use of in-country multi-donor trust funds, which are designed to accommodate the funding requirements of donors.

The Council reaffirms that ending impunity is essential if a society recovering from conflict is to come to terms with past abuses committed against civilians affected by armed conflict and to prevent such abuses in the future. The Council notes that justice and reconciliation mechanisms can promote not only individual responsibility for serious crimes, but also peace, truth, reconciliation and the rights of victims.

The Council, in accordance with its resolutions 1325(2000) and 1820(2008), underlines the key role that women and young persons can play in re-establishing the fabric of society and stresses the need for their involvement in the development and implementation of post-conflict strategies in order to take account of their perspectives and needs.

The Council reaffirms the role of regional and subregional organizations in the prevention, management and resolution of conflicts in accordance with Chapter VIII of the Charter of the United Nations, and the need to strengthen their capacity in post-conflict peacebuilding.

The Council recognizes the importance of launching peacebuilding assistance at the earliest possible stage. The Council affirms the importance of early consideration of peacebuilding in its own deliberations and of ensuring coherence between peacemaking, peacekeeping, peacebuilding and development to achieve an early and effective response to post-conflict situations. The Council will strive to apply this integrated approach and requests the Secretary-General to intensify his efforts in this regard.

The Council invites the Secretary-General to report within twelve months to the Council and the General Assembly on progress achieved in fulfilling his agenda for action to improve the peacebuilding efforts of the United Nations, taking into consideration the views of the Peacebuilding Commission.

Disarmament, demobilization and reintegration

Special Committee on Peacekeeping Operations consideration. The Special Committee on Peacekeeping Operations, at its 2009 substantive session (New York, 23 February–20 March) [A/63/19] stressed that disarmament, demobilization and reintegration programmes were crucial components of peacekeeping operations, and that their success depended upon the political will and concerted effort of all parties.

It was crucial, therefore, that disarmament, demobilization and reintegration (DDR) were firmly established within a political process and that all actors were prepared for a multi-year programme. The Special Committee recognized that the DDR process was an evolving field and that its programmes could be tailored to specific contexts. It stressed that the civilian reintegration of ex-combatants posed particular challenges, requiring concerted efforts to help jump-start the economy in order to create employment opportunities for ex-combatants and the wider community. The Special Committee welcomed the support provided to field missions by the DPKO Disarmament, Demobilization and Reintegration Section and reiterated the importance of close partnership with Governments, other UN actors, the World Bank, donors, partners, regional arrangements and non-governmental agencies in the design and implementation of DDR programmes.

Rule of law

Special Committee on Peacekeeping Operations consideration. The Special Committee [A/63/19] recognized that creating and sustaining stability in the aftermath of conflict required that the causes of the conflict be addressed and that rule of law capacities be assessed, restored and enhanced from the beginning of a peacekeeping operation. It reiterated the need for greater clarity and specificity in UN peacekeeping mandates on rule of law issues and requested that DPKO continue to ensure that rule of law and transitional justice were integrated into the planning of peacekeeping operations. The Special Committee welcomed the progress made in assessing lessons learned and options for rule of law strategies for ongoing and future peacekeeping operations. It called upon DPKO to ensure cooperation and coordination among UN actors in order to ensure a holistic and coherent approach to the rule of law.

The Special Committee, following the recent establishment of the DPKO Office of Rule of Law and Security Institutions, re`quested that DPKO include in its next annual report an assessment on how the creation of that Office had contributed to closer coherence and synergies among its own sections and between other UN actors to deliver rule of law mandates more effectively. It recognized the importance of holistic and integrated rule of law assistance being provided to host countries from the very outset of the establishment of new peacekeeping missions.

Other peacebuilding issues

Special Committee on Peacekeeping Operations consideration. The Special Committee [A/63/19] reaffirmed the need for DPKO to plan and conduct UN peacekeeping activities in such a manner as to facilitate post-conflict peacebuilding, the prevention of recurrence of armed conflicts and progress towards sustainable peace and development. The Special Committee underlined the importance of coordination among DPKO, the Department of Political Affairs, the Peacebuilding Support Office, UN funds, programmes and agencies and non-UN partners in peacebuilding efforts. The Special Committee underlined the need to formulate peacebuilding strategies and programmes that were integrated with host-nation strategies and programmes to ensure national ownership, and recommended that DPKO explore opportunities for partnerships in post-conflict situations with international financial institutions and regional arrangements.

The Special Committee underlined the role of the Peacebuilding Commission in developing integrated peacebuilding strategies and marshalling resources for their implementation, ensuring fulfilment of mutual commitments on the part of stakeholders, enhancing coordination on the ground and promoting dialogue on cross-cutting issues. The Special Committee welcomed the efforts by DPKO and the Peacebuilding Support Office to ensure that lessons learned in the transition from UN peacekeeping operations to integrated peacebuilding offices were captured, and noted the importance of those lessons being taken into consideration in other transitional processes. It also recognized the need to support Governments in the delivery of critical recovery and peacebuilding requirements in immediate post-conflict environments.

Peacebuilding Commission

In accordance with Security Council resolutions 1645(2005) and 1646(2005) [YUN 2005, p. 94] and General Assembly resolution 60/180 [ibid.], the Peacebuilding Commission in September reported [A/64/341-S/2009/444] on its work during its third session, from 23 June 2008 to 30 June 2009. During its first three years, the Commission consolidated its core advisory role and demonstrated increasing support for the countries on its agenda—Burundi, the Central African Republic, Guinea-Bissau and Sierra Leone. It held that the role of its Organizational Committee needed to be reassessed, given the need for overall strategic vision and guidance for the Commission's work.

The Commission had gained valuable experience through engagement with the countries on its agenda, which would continue to inform its work, its interpretation of its advisory role and the implementation of its mandates. The Commission's continuous engagement with a wide range of partners, within and beyond the United Nations, had helped in maximizing its outreach and fostered a greater understanding of the Commission's work among its partners. Those partnerships would add to the Commission's repertoire of knowledge and expertise, which would facilitate the discharge of its mandate.

The Commission's Working Group on Lessons Learned provided an informal platform for the Peacebuilding Commission to draw on the expertise of practitioners from within and outside the UN system, as well as from countries with experience in post-conflict peacebuilding, on critical peacebuilding priorities in the countries on the Commission's agenda. In five meetings held between 20 October 2008 and 28 May 2009, it focused on lessons learned and good practices associated with the role of the United Nations in rule of law assistance; regional approaches to disarmament, demobilization and reintegration in the Great Lakes region of Africa; the development of national capacity after conflict; the coordination of the Commission with regional and subregional organizations; and sustainable community-based reintegration in post-conflict situations.

The Commission continued to work towards building and strengthening partnerships, at the Headquarters and country levels, and with bilateral and multilateral partners—including donors, international financial institutions and regional and subregional organizations. The report stated that the Commission would also encourage closer cooperation with regional processes, including the African Peer Review Mechanism of the New Partnership for Africa's Development. National, regional and international partners needed to be fully engaged in the development, monitoring and implementation of the common strategic framework for peacebuilding at the country level if a country was to have access to and make the most efficient use of the support it needed for peacebuilding. The Commission would continue to work in close collaboration with the international financial institutions, particularly in the areas of strengthening the functions of the State and promoting economic recovery.

Discussions in the Commission focused on how it could build on or make use of existing in-country assessments, strategy-setting processes and plans in countries on its agenda, in order to ensure that peacebuilding priorities received attention and support without generating high transaction costs for the national partners. The Commission also began to explore the possibility of diversifying the forms of its engagement with countries on its agenda, including through a multitiered approach. With respect to resource mobilization, the Commission recognized that rapid and flexible funding was critical for successful peacebuilding. It addressed the challenges associated with the mobilization of resources, including through advocacy at Headquarters and in capitals, while also exploring ways of engaging non-traditional partners, the diaspora, private foundations and the private sector in order to supplement the flow of official development assistance and to foster employment creation and economic recovery and growth.

The Commission noted the limited awareness about its role, the evolving concept of peacebuilding, and how the international community could best support peacebuilding, especially in the countries on its agenda. There was little awareness and much confusion about the Commission's role and links with the Peacebuilding Fund. The Commission decided to explore outreach initiatives, such as the appointment of goodwill ambassadors, the establishment of a group of friends for peacebuilding, and the convening of an annual high-level peacebuilding forum. It would also encourage outreach activities by its Chairs, members and the senior-most UN representatives in the field in support of peacebuilding priorities.

Security Council consideration. On 25 November, during an open debate on post-conflict peacebuilding [meeting 6224], the Council invited the Chair of the Peacebuilding Commission to introduce the report of the Commission on its third session (see above). It welcomed the strengthening of the Commission's coordination and cooperation with relevant stakeholders within and outside the UN system. Council members extended their support for the strengthening of interaction between the Council and the Commission and underlined their commitment to refining the Commission's work by constructively contributing to its 2010 review.

(For activities of the Peacebuilding Commission in Burundi, the Central African Republic, Guinea-Bissau and Sierra Leone, see PART ONE, Chapter II.)

Organizational Committee

At its 7 January meeting [PBC/3/OC/SR.2], the Peacebuilding Commission's Organizational Committee considered employment and income-generation and private sector development in post-conflict countries. It elected the Chairperson and Vice-Chairperson of the Commission, as well as the Chairpersons of its country-specific configurations on Burundi, the Central African Republic, Guinea-Bissau and Sierra Leone, as well as the Chairperson of its Working Group on Lessons Learned. At its 25 February meeting [PBC/3/OC/SR.3], it elected the Chairperson of its country-specific configuration on Sierra Leone, to replace the newly elected Chairperson, who had relinquished his position. At its fourth meeting, on 29 June [PBC/3/OC/SR.4], the Committee elected the Chairperson of its country-specific configuration on Burundi, to replace the recently elected Chairperson, who was relinquishing his position.

At its 13 July meeting [PBC/3/OC/SR.5], the Committee considered the report of the Secretary-General on peacebuilding in the immediate aftermath of conflict [A/63/881-S/2009/304]. It heard a statement by the Secretary-General, who said that the challenges facing countries emerging from conflict were enormous.

First, the Secretary-General said, there was a need for national ownership in order to anchor peacebuilding at the country level. Second, Member States expected the United Nations to be poised and ready to lead the international community; the report therefore called for the creation of a senior-level mechanism to ensure that the right leadership and support teams were in place as early as possible. Third, effective peacebuilding required input from all parts of the UN system: peacemaking, peacekeeping, peacebuilding and recovery must happen together. Coordination was therefore crucial to success and fragmentation must be avoided.

Fourth, national and international actors needed to align behind and provide financial support for a common strategic vision with realistic priorities. In some cases, such efforts had taken years; in most cases, they had never taken place. He therefore called on the international community to take the swift action required. Fifth, there was a need for predictable and credible delivery. He would therefore be asking Member States to help the United Nations build its capacity to respond rapidly to the most urgent needs in order to protect civilians and strengthen the rule of law, support political processes, help restore basic services and Government functions, and revitalize the economy.

At its 4 September meeting [PBC/3/OC/SR.6], the Committee adopted the draft report of the Peacebuilding Commission on its third session, heard remarks by Judy Cheng-Hopkins, the Assistant Secretary-General for Peacebuilding Support, and closed its third session. The Assistant Secretary-General said that peacebuilding consisted of three building blocks, held together by the cement of national ownership: firstly, the essential role of government in such areas as security, political reconciliation, the rule of law and justice; secondly, the provision of basic services, including health care, education and basic infrastructure, to restore a sense of normality to the population following the end of conflict; and, thirdly, the creation of livelihoods, both to give hope to ordinary people—the "peace dividend"—and to enable the demobilization of soldiers, which was an essential but challenging aspect of peacebuilding.

The most important component of the new peacebuilding architecture was the Peacebuilding Commission, she said. The functioning of the second component of the new architecture—the Peacebuilding Fund—had been revised so that instead of three funding windows it now had two, consisting of an immediate response facility to prevent flare-ups of conflict and a peacebuilding and recovery facility, which depended on an integrated-plan approach. Lastly, the Peacebuilding Support Office, the third component of the new architecture, would strive to perform an even better support and facilitation role.

Organizational Committee membership

Security Council. In a 6 January letter [A/63/799-S/2009/168], the Security Council informed the Secretary-General that, following informal consultations, the Council had selected Burkina Faso and Mexico as the two elected members of the Council to participate in the Organizational Committee for a one-year term, until the end of 2009.

In a 31 December letter [S/2009/683], the Council informed the General Assembly President that, following consultations, it had designated Gabon and Mexico, two of its elected members, to serve as members of the Organizational Committee for a one-year term, until the end of 2010.

Economic and Social Council. On 15 December [E/2009/99], the Economic and Social Council elected Australia, Brazil and Egypt to the Organizational Committee for a term beginning on 1 January 2010 and expiring on 31 December 2010 to fill vacancies arising from the expiration of the terms of Algeria, El Salvador and Luxembourg (**decision 2009/201 F**).

Peacebuilding Fund

In response to General Assembly resolution 63/282 (see p. 49), the Secretary-General in August submitted an annual report [A/64/217-S/2009/419] on the Peacebuilding Fund, established in 2006 [YUN 2006, p. 58] as a mechanism for extending critical support at the early stages of a peace process. The report reviewed the Fund's operations and activities from 1 July 2008 to 30 June 2009. As at 30 June, the Fund was active in 12 countries, contributing to building the foundations for peace in countries emerging from conflict or helping post-conflict countries to prevent a relapse into conflict. Recent evaluations and performance reports submitted by recipient organizations confirmed that early notable results had been achieved during the Fund's initial two years and that it had the potential to fill a unique peacebuilding niche. The evaluations also identified management and operational challenges, which were being addressed in part through a revision of the Fund's terms of reference (see below) and in part through management improvements instituted by the Peacebuilding Support Office. The revised terms of reference were endorsed by the General Assembly on 17 June (see p. 49), and gave impetus for a broad revision of the Fund's operational and procedural guidelines.

The financial situation of the Peacebuilding Fund from its inception to 30 June 2009 reflected robust growth. As at 30 June, the Fund's portfolio stood at $312.9 million (up $44 million from June 2008), with deposits of $309.6 million (an increase of $71 million from June 2008). With 45 donors, the Fund enjoyed one of the broadest donor bases of any multi-donor trust fund administered by the United Nations, with 18 countries contributing more than once to the Fund. The 10 largest contributors were Sweden, the United Kingdom, Norway, the Netherlands, Japan, Canada, Ireland, Spain, Germany and Denmark. Out of programmable funds of $309.6 million (those received in the trust fund account), $141.3 million was allocated to peacebuilding activities in 12 countries, four of which were on the Peacebuilding Commission's agenda. Five countries not on its agenda were declared eligible for Fund support by the Secretary-General and had received it, while nine country situations drew on emergency funding, some also receiving support under priority plan funding. While the Fund's position was solid, the global financial crisis might have an adverse impact on future funding, and that had to be taken into account when Fund allocations were being programmed and when Fund-supported projects were looking for additional funding.

Addressing the four countries on the Commission's agenda (window I), the report stated that 4 of the 18 projects approved in Burundi had been completed and all but one were expected to be closed by year's end. During the previous 12 months, implementation had improved and the delivery rate against the total budget of $35 million reached 75 per cent at the end of June. The Peacebuilding Support Office had quickly released additional emergency funding for demobilizing and reintegrating Forces Nationales de Libération (FNL) combatants, resulting in the registration of more than 5,000 of the 11,000 adults associated with FNL. They were issued return kits, paid the first instalment of return assistance and transported to their home communities. Support under the Fund complemented other efforts that enabled some 3,500 FNL elements to be assimilated into the military and police.

Peacebuilding in the Central African Republic continued to face challenges in building on the momentum created by the national political dialogue in late 2008. Initial funding for demobilization activities of $4 million—40 per cent of the Fund envelope—was used to start up that exercise, while additional appeals were made to the international community for support to disarmament, demobilization and reintegration activities. The priority plan funded 11 projects in the areas of demobilization and reintegration (60 per cent of the envelope); governance and rule of law, primarily to support human rights and women's networks (14 per cent); and revitalization of communities affected by conflict (26 per cent).

In Guinea-Bissau, significant political and military tension caused disruptions in three Fund projects; however, meetings of the Guinea-Bissau configuration, coupled with numerous UN country support visits, enabled continuous engagement and tracking of projects—including a professional training and employment programme for 500 youth; enhancement of police capacity and prison security to combat drug trafficking and organized crime; and public tenders for rehabilitating 10 military barracks.

In March, Sierra Leone saw the worst political violence since the end of the civil war in 2002. An inter-party dialogue facilitated by the United Nations Integrated Peacebuilding Office in Sierra Leone (UNIPSIL) brought the two main parties to the negotiating table, leading to a joint communiqué. The quick application of contingency funds provided for setting up a commission of inquiry to investigate allegations of sexual violence during the disturbances, as well as for rehabilitating the damaged offices of one of the political parties. Two projects prepared by UNIPSIL and approved by the Peacebuilding Support Office in May in support of the joint communiqué aimed at improving police control and techniques for riot control and fostering national political dialogue and reconciliation. Notable results included improved outreach of the National Human Rights Commission, increased awareness of the recently passed Gender and Child Rights Act, and a sharp reduction in the backlog of detainees awaiting trial, with 90 per cent of 600 cases cleared.

The report also reviewed activities in support of countries declared eligible for funding by the Secretary-General under window II—Comoros, Côte d'Ivoire, the Democratic Republic of the Congo, Guinea, Liberia and Nepal. As for emergency funding under window III, assistance was provided for 9 one-off projects of less than $1 million. That facility had proven to be a flexible and responsive instrument that enabled the Secretary-General to respond quickly to imminent threats to peace, while demonstrating the Fund's risk-taking capabilities. Nearly all the emergency projects, however, experienced implementation delays due to local circumstances that affected quick delivery. Requests for extending projects or for additional funding were received from Burundi, the Central African Republic, Côte d'Ivoire, Haiti and Kenya. During the reporting period, two new emergency projects were approved for Sierra Leone, and one each for Burundi and Timor-Leste.

Addressing lessons learned, the report found that the start-up phase of activities in a country was one of the most critical and labour-intensive periods for the UN country team and its national partners. It was therefore essential to ensure greater focus on start-up support to address weak planning, programming and implementation capacity. Synergy between the Fund and the Commission had improved, but there was scope for better calibrating that engagement. More attention must be given to the role of the joint steering committees and to ensuring that they were able to play their role to the fullest. Finally, the tensions inherent in the concept underlying the Fund and the competing demands and expectations required a strong strategic communications strategy at both the field and global levels.

According to the report, the way ahead included establishment of full fund management capacity within the Peacebuilding Support Office to improve global and country-level support, in particular during the critical start-up phase of Fund activities in each country; the establishment of a robust accountability framework to respond to the information and oversight requirements of the Fund's donors; improved synergy with the Peacebuilding Commission; using the Fund to improve UN cooperation and collaboration on peacebuilding to strengthen the system's ability to support countries emerging from conflict; and expanding the Fund's operations to strategically assist more countries requiring urgent peacebuilding support.

Revised terms of reference. In April [A/63/818], the Secretary-General submitted to the General Assembly revised terms of reference for the Peacebuilding Fund, following up on an earlier report [YUN 2006, p. 57] in which he had laid out terms of reference and indicated that they should be reviewed no later than two years after their adoption, following consultations with the Advisory Group and the outcome of an independent evaluation. The revised terms of reference annexed to the report emerged from that process.

The revision had been guided by two broad objectives. The first was to enhance the Fund's capacity to serve as a flexible, responsive and focused resource for peacebuilding support—including through rationalizing and simplifying the Fund's structure and architecture. The second objective was to maximize the synergy between the Peacebuilding Commission and the Fund through enhanced consultation and dialogue. The Peacebuilding Support Office would review Fund guidance documents in cooperation with the UNDP Multi-donor Trust Fund Office, as well as with the Advisory Group, donors, recipient UN organizations and country-level stakeholders. The UNDP Multi-donor Trust Fund Office would continue to serve as the Peacebuilding Fund's administrative agent, with primary responsibility for maintaining its accounts. The Fund itself would be managed in accordance with UNDP regulations, rules, directives and procedures. To enhance accountability and clarify roles and responsibilities, arrangements detailing the relationship between the Head of the Peacebuilding Support Office and the UNDP Multi-donor Trust Fund Office would be reviewed so as to reflect the provisions of the revised terms of reference.

As set out in the revised terms of reference, the Peacebuilding Support Office would conduct regular briefings on the Fund's performance with Member States, the Peacebuilding Commission and donors, while a proposed annual meeting would enable stakeholders to review Fund performance, results and emerging lessons. That event would also provide an opportunity to regularly replenish the Fund. It was the Secretary-General's view that the revised terms of reference would contribute to improving the Fund's efficiency and effectiveness in stabilizing countries emerging from conflict, in addressing critical gaps immediately following the signing of peace agreements, and in strengthening national capacities to pursue peacebuilding programmes. Fund resources, combined with the efforts of the Peacebuilding Commission, would help to ensure that post-conflict countries would benefit from sustained international attention and support. Member States were encouraged to continue providing regular voluntary contributions.

GENERAL ASSEMBLY ACTION

On 17 June [meeting 90], the General Assembly adopted **resolution 63/282** [draft: A/63/L.72 & Add.1] without vote [agenda item 101].

The Peacebuilding Fund

The General Assembly,

Recalling its resolution 60/180 and Security Council resolution 1645(2005) of 20 December 2005, as well as its resolution 60/287 of 8 September 2006,

1. *Takes note* of the arrangements for the revision of the terms of reference for the Peacebuilding Fund as contained in the report of the Secretary-General and the revised terms of reference for the Fund contained in the annex thereto;

2. *Notes* that the broad objectives of the revision of the terms of reference for the Peacebuilding Fund are to enhance the capacity of the Fund to serve as a flexible, responsive and focused resource for peacebuilding support and to enhance and maximize the synergy between the Peacebuilding Commission and the Fund;

3. *Affirms* the respective roles of the General Assembly, the Peacebuilding Commission and the independent Advisory Group to provide policy guidance on the use of the Fund to maximize its impact and improve its functioning;

4. *Welcomes* the contributions and financial pledges made to the Fund, and emphasizes the necessity of sustained contributions in order to enhance the capacity of the Fund to provide the predictable and catalytic resources needed to launch post-conflict peacebuilding activities;

5. *Urges* all Member States to consider making voluntary contributions to the Fund;

6. *Requests* the Secretary-General to submit an annual report to the General Assembly on the operation and activities of the Fund;

7. *Also requests* the Secretary-General to include in his annual report on the operation and activities of the Fund to be submitted to the General Assembly at its sixty-sixth session the findings and recommendations from the next comprehensive independent evaluation;

8. *Decides* to include in the provisional agenda of its sixty-fourth session the item entitled "Report of the Secretary-General on the Peacebuilding Fund".

Protection issues

Responsibility to protect

Report of Secretary-General. Following up on paragraphs 138 and 139 of the 2005 World Summit Outcome [YUN 2005, p. 62], the Secretary-General, in January, submitted a report [A/63/677] on implementing the responsibility to protect. The report responded to a cardinal challenge posed in those paragraphs of the World Summit Outcome: operationalizing the responsibility to protect. The Heads of State and Government had unanimously affirmed at the Summit that "each individual State has the responsibility to protect its populations from genocide, war crimes, ethnic cleansing and crimes against humanity". They had agreed as well that the international community should assist States in exercising that responsibility and in building their protection capacities. When a State nevertheless was "manifestly failing" to protect its population from genocide, war crimes, ethnic cleansing or crimes against humanity, they had confirmed that the international community was prepared to take collective action in a "timely and decisive manner" through the Security Council and in accordance with the UN Charter. The report underscored that the best way to discourage States or groups of States from misusing the responsibility to protect for inappropriate purposes would be to develop fully the UN strategy, standards, processes, tools and practices for the responsibility to protect.

The report outlined a three-pillar strategy for advancing the agenda mandated by the Heads of State and Government. Those pillars were the protection responsibilities of the State, international assistance and capacity-building, and timely and decisive response. The strategy stressed the value of prevention and, when it failed, of early and flexible response tailored to the circumstances of each case. The report provided examples of policies and practices that were contributing, or could contribute, to advancing goals relating to the responsibility to protect under each of the pillars.

Addressing the way forward, the report set out points that the General Assembly might wish to consider as part of its "continuing consideration" mandate under paragraph 139 of the Summit Outcome. Some preliminary ideas on early warning and assessment, as called for in paragraph 138 of the Summit Outcome, were set out in an annex. The report also presented policy ideas that might merit further consideration by Member States, although the Secretary-General did not request the Assembly to take action on them.

General Assembly debate (July). The General Assembly held a four-day debate (21, 23, 24 and 28 July) on the responsibility to protect and the Secretary-General's report. The President of the General Assembly, the Secretary-General, the High Commissioner for Human Rights, delegates from 94 States as well as experts addressed the debate and engaged in an informal interactive dialogue [A/63/PV.96-101 & Corr.].

In his closing remarks on 28 July, General Assembly President Miguel d'Escoto Brockmann (Nicaragua) said that the majority of States felt that any action under Chapter VII of the UN Charter must be in conformity with the Charter and international law, considered on a case-by-case basis. Any coercion must take place under the collective security provisions of the Charter, and only in cases posing an immediate threat to international peace and security. Some States had expressed concern that the United Nations should not take the enormous leap to make the responsibility to protect operational as presently formulated, voicing doubts that the global community could respond to massive Government failure to protect populations without falling back on double standards. Recent "disastrous" interventions had given developing countries reason to fear that laudable motives could be misused to justify interventions against weaker States. Keeping those concerns in mind, Member States were unified in their conviction that the international community could no longer remain silent in the face of genocide, ethnic cleansing, war crimes and crimes against humanity. Most States also favoured an approach that focused on finding ways to prevent such crises and on dealing with their root causes.

GENERAL ASSEMBLY ACTION

On 14 September [meeting 105], the General Assembly adopted **resolution 63/308** [draft: A/63/L.80/Rev.1 & Add.1] without vote [agenda items 44 & 107], as orally revised.

The responsibility to protect

The General Assembly,

Reaffirming its respect for the principles and purposes of the Charter of the United Nations,

Recalling the 2005 World Summit Outcome, especially paragraphs 138 and 139 thereof,

1. *Takes note* of the report of the Secretary-General and of the timely and productive debate organized by the President of the General Assembly on the responsibility to protect, held on 21, 23, 24 and 28 July 2009, with full participation by Member States;

2. *Decides* to continue its consideration of the responsibility to protect.

Protection of civilians in armed conflict

Security Council consideration (January). On 14 January [meeting 6066], the Security Council held a day-long debate on the protection of civilians in armed conflict.

John Holmes, Under-Secretary-General for Humanitarian Affairs and Emergency Relief Co-ordinator, said that the debate was taking place in the shadow of the conflict in the Gaza Strip between Israeli forces and Hamas militants, and the Council's focus should be on the conduct of hostilities and the need for strict compliance with international humanitarian law. The situation in southern Israel and Gaza was pressing and desperate. Civilians in southern Israel had long lived under the constant threat of rocket and mortar attacks by Palestinian militants. Considering the number of rockets and mortars fired, civilian casualties had been limited, but the frequent and indiscriminate nature of the attacks inflicted severe psychological suffering. While those attacks were contrary to international law and must cease, Israel's response must itself comply with international humanitarian law.

In the conduct of military operations, Mr. Holmes said, constant care must be taken to spare civilian populations from the effects of hostilities. For those launching attacks, that included doing everything feasible to verify that the objectives were neither civilians nor civilian objects and refraining from indiscriminate attacks. For those in defence, it meant removing civilians and civilian objects from the vicinity of military objectives and avoiding locating military objectives within or near densely populated areas. Looking at what had been happening in Gaza in the past three weeks, neither Israel nor Hamas had come close to respecting those rules.

Other situations raised profound concerns over the degree of respect for those rules and for international humanitarian law. A catastrophic situation had unfolded in August 2008 around Goma, in the eastern Democratic Republic of the Congo, where civilians had found themselves in the worst of all worlds: subject to attacks, displacement, sexual violence and forced recruitment perpetrated by advancing rebel forces; and to acts of violence, rape and looting carried out by members of the armed forces and rebel militias. Civilians were at risk in southern Sudan, Somalia, Afghanistan and Sri Lanka. If the international community was serious about sparing civilian lives, obtaining access to those in need and ensuring the safety of humanitarian workers, humanitarian actors must have sustained dialogue with all parties to conflict, be it the Taliban, Hamas or Al-Shabaab. It was simply not sufficient to oppose such engagement for fear that it would confer a degree of recognition on those groups.

Representatives of 45 Member States addressed the ensuing debate.

At the end of the debate, Mr. Holmes gave the latest figures regarding Palestinian casualties and injured in Gaza, as provided by the Palestinian Ministry of Health: 1,013 dead, including 322 children and 76 women.

SECURITY COUNCIL ACTION

On 14 January [meeting 6066], following consultations among Security Council members, the President made statement **S/PRST/2009/1** on behalf of the Council:

The Security Council reaffirms its commitment to the full and effective implementation of its resolutions on the protection of civilians in armed conflict and recalls previous statements on the issue made by its President.

The Council remains committed to addressing the impact of armed conflict on civilians. The Council expresses its deepest concern that civilians continue to account for the majority of victims of acts of violence committed by parties to armed conflict, including as a result of deliberate targeting, indiscriminate and excessive use of force, use of civilians as human shields and of sexual and gender-based violence, as well as all other acts that violate applicable international law. The Council condemns all violations of international law, including international humanitarian law, human rights law and refugee law, committed against civilians in situations of armed conflict. The Council demands that all relevant parties immediately put an end to such practices. The Council reaffirms in this regard that parties to armed conflict bear the primary responsibility to take all feasible steps to ensure the protection of affected civilians and to meet their basic needs, including by giving attention to the specific needs of women and children.

The Council recalls the obligations of all States to ensure respect for international humanitarian law, including the four Geneva Conventions of 12 August 1949, and once again emphasizes the responsibility of States to comply with their obligations to end impunity and to prosecute those responsible for war crimes, genocide, crimes against humanity or other serious violations of international humanitarian law.

The Council recognizes the needs of civilians under foreign occupation and stresses further, in this regard, the responsibilities of the occupying Power.

The Council condemns terrorism in all its forms and manifestations, however and by whomever committed.

The Council underlines the importance of safe and unhindered access of humanitarian personnel and of the timely, safe and unhindered passage of essential relief goods, to provide assistance to civilians in armed conflict in accordance with applicable international law. The Council stresses the importance of upholding and respecting the humanitarian principles of humanity, neutrality, impartiality and independence.

Recalling that on 15 March 2002, the Council first adopted the aide-memoire annexed to the statement by its President as a means to facilitate its consideration of issues pertaining to the protection of civilians and recalling further that in the statements by its President of 20 December 2002 and 15 December 2003, the Council expressed its willingness to update the aide-memoire regularly in order to reflect emerging trends in the protection of civilians in armed conflict, the Council adopts the updated aide-memoire contained in the annex to the present statement by its President.

The Council reiterates the importance of the aide-memoire as a practical tool that provides a basis for improved analysis and diagnosis of key protection issues, particularly during deliberations on peacekeeping mandates, and stresses the need to implement the approaches set out therein on a more regular and consistent basis, taking into account the particular circumstances of each conflict situation, and undertakes to remain actively seized of the matter.

ANNEX

Protection of civilians in armed conflict

Aide-memoire

For the consideration of issues pertaining to the protection of civilians in armed conflict

Enhancing the protection of civilians in armed conflict is at the core of the work of the Security Council for the maintenance of peace and security. In order to facilitate the Council's consideration of protection of civilians concerns in a given context, including at the time of the establishment or renewal of peacekeeping mandates, in June 2001 members of the Council suggested that an aide-memoire, listing the relevant issues, be drafted in cooperation with the Council. On 15 March 2002, the Council adopted the aide-memoire as a practical guide for its consideration of issues pertaining to the protection of civilians and agreed to review and update its contents periodically. It was subsequently updated and adopted as an annex to the presidential statement of 15 December 2003.

This is the third edition of the aide-memoire and is based on the previous deliberations of the Council on the protection of civilians, including resolutions 1265(1999), 1296(2000), 1674(2006) and 1738(2006). It is the result of consultation between the Council and the Office for the Coordination of Humanitarian Affairs, as well as between the Office and concerned United Nations departments and agencies, and other relevant humanitarian organizations.

The aide-memoire is intended to facilitate the Council's consideration of issues relevant to the protection of civilians in armed conflict. To this end, it highlights primary objectives for Council action; offers, on the basis of the Council's past practice, specific issues for consideration in meeting those objectives; and provides, in the addendum, a selection of agreed language from Council resolutions and presidential statements that refer to such concerns.

Bearing in mind that each peacekeeping mandate has to be elaborated on a case-by-case basis, the aide-memoire is not intended as a blueprint for action. The relevance and practicality of the various measures described has to be considered and adapted to the specific conditions in each situation.

Most frequently, civilians are caught in circumstances of dire need where a peacekeeping operation has not been established. Such situations may require urgent attention by the Council. The present aide-memoire may, therefore, also provide guidance in circumstances where the Council may wish to consider action outside the scope of a peacekeeping operation.

I. General protection concerns pertaining to the conflict-affected population

A. Protection of, and assistance to, the conflict-affected population

Parties to armed conflict to take the necessary measures to protect and meet the basic needs of the conflict-affected population

Issues for consideration:

— Stress the responsibility of parties to armed conflict to respect, protect and meet the basic needs of civilian populations within their effective control.

— Condemn, and call for the immediate cessation of, acts of violence or abuses committed against civilians in situations of armed conflict in violation of applicable international humanitarian law and human rights law.

— Call for strict compliance by parties to armed conflict with applicable international humanitarian law and human rights law, including with regard to:

  • The prohibition against violence to life and person, in particular murder, mutilation, cruel treatment and torture; enforced disappearances; outrages upon personal dignity; rape, sexual slavery, enforced prostitution, forced pregnancy, enforced sterilization, and any other form of sexual violence.

  • The prohibition against arbitrary deprivation of liberty; corporal punishment; collective punishment; and the passing of sentences and the carrying out of executions without previous judgment pronounced by a regularly constituted court, affording all judicial guarantees which are generally recognized as indispensable.

  • The prohibition against the taking of hostages.

  • The prohibition against ordering the displacement of the civilian population for reasons related to the conflict, unless the security of the civilians involved or imperative military reasons so demand.

  • The prohibition against the recruitment or the active use of children in hostilities by parties to armed conflict in violation of applicable international law.

  • The prohibition against slavery and the slave trade in all their forms and uncompensated or abusive forced labour.

  • The prohibition against wilfully impeding relief supplies as provided for under international humanitarian law.

  • The prohibition of persecution on political, religious, racial or gender grounds.

  • The prohibition of any adverse distinction in the application of international humanitarian law and human rights law based on race, colour, sex, language, religion or belief, political or other opinion, national or social origin, wealth, birth or other status.

  • The obligation to respect and protect, to whichever party they belong, the wounded and sick, to take all possible measures, particularly after an engagement, to search for and collect the wounded and sick and to provide, to the fullest extent practicable and with the least possible delay, the medical care and attention required by their condition without distinction on any grounds other than medical ones.

—Mandate United Nations peacekeeping and other relevant missions authorized by the Security Council, where appropriate and on a case-by-case basis, to contribute to the protection of the civilian population, particularly those under imminent threat of physical danger, within their zones of operation. In doing so, request:

• The development of clear guidelines/directives as to what missions can do to protect civilians.

• That the protection of civilians is prioritized in decisions about the use of available capacity and resources, including information and intelligence resources, in the implementation of mandates.

—Request that reports of the Secretary-General on country-specific situations include the protection of civilians as a specific aspect of the report; and request the development of mission-specific strategies and plans of action, in consultation with United Nations country teams, for enhancing the protection of civilians that take into account the needs of different population groups, including internally displaced persons and refugees, women, children, older persons and persons with disabilities.

—Request troop- and police-contributing countries to ensure the provision of appropriate training to heighten the awareness and responsiveness to protection concerns of their personnel participating in United Nations peacekeeping and other relevant missions authorized by the Security Council to protect civilians.

—Urge relevant regional and/or subregional bodies to develop and implement policies, activities and advocacy for the benefit of civilians affected by armed conflict.

B. Displacement

Parties to armed conflict and other relevant actors to refrain from, and take the necessary measures to prevent and respond to, the displacement of the civilian population

Issues for consideration:

—Condemn, and call for the immediate cessation of, displacement in violation of applicable international humanitarian law and human rights law.

—Call for strict compliance by parties to armed conflict with applicable international humanitarian law, human rights law and refugee law, including with regard to:

• The prohibition against deportation, forcible transfer or displacement of the civilian population, in whole or in part, unless the security of the civilians concerned or imperative military reasons so demand.

• The obligation, in case of displacement, to ensure to the greatest practicable extent that the civilians concerned are received under satisfactory conditions of shelter, hygiene, health, safety and nutrition and that members of the same family are not

separated, and that basic needs are met during displacement.

• The right to freedom of movement and to leave one's country and seek asylum.

• The right to non-refoulement under the Convention relating to the Status of Refugees, the protection of which does not extend to any person with respect to whom there are serious reasons for considering that she or he has been guilty of acts contrary to the purposes and principles of the United Nations.

—Underline the primary responsibility of States to respect and maintain the security and civilian character of camps for refugees and internally displaced persons, including disarming armed elements, separating combatants, curbing the flow of small arms in camps and preventing recruitment by armed groups in and around camps.

—Mandate United Nations peacekeeping and other relevant missions authorized by the Security Council to take all feasible measures to ensure security in and around such camps and for their inhabitants.

—Request that reports of the Secretary-General on country-specific situations include the protection of displaced persons as a specific aspect of the report.

—Urge relevant regional and/or subregional bodies to develop and implement policies, activities and advocacy for the benefit of internally displaced persons and refugees.

Safe, voluntary and dignified return and reintegration of refugees and internally displaced persons

Issues for consideration:

—Call for strict compliance by parties to armed conflict with applicable international humanitarian law, refugee law and human rights law, including with regard to:

• Respect for the right of refugees and displaced persons to voluntary return in safety and dignity to their homes.

• Respect for the property rights of refugees and displaced persons, without adverse distinction on the basis of gender, age or other status.

—Affirm in relevant resolutions the right of refugees and displaced persons to voluntary, safe and dignified return to their homes.

—Call upon all parties concerned to create the conditions conducive to allowing voluntary, safe, dignified and sustainable return, inter alia, by concluding agreements and/or adopting measures designed to facilitate return, and by promoting favourable conditions for the reconstruction and economic and social development of areas of return.

—Call upon all parties concerned to ensure non-discriminatory treatment of returning refugees and internally displaced persons.

—Call upon all parties concerned to ensure the participation of refugees and internally displaced persons and inclusion of their needs, including their right to voluntary, safe and dignified return and reintegration, in all peace processes, peace agreements and post-conflict recovery and reconstruction planning and programmes.

—Encourage United Nations peacekeeping and other relevant missions authorized by the Security Council, as appropriate and on a case-by-case basis, to support domestic mechanisms for addressing housing, land and property issues or their establishment by national authorities.

—Encourage United Nations peacekeeping and other relevant missions authorized by the Security Council, as appropriate and on a case-by-case basis, to prevent the illegal appropriation and confiscation of land and property belonging to refugees and internally displaced persons and to ensure the protection of returning refugees and internally displaced persons.

C. Humanitarian access and safety and security of humanitarian workers

Parties to armed conflict to agree to and facilitate relief operations that are humanitarian and impartial in character and to allow and facilitate rapid and unimpeded passage of relief consignments, equipment and personnel

Issues for consideration:

—Condemn, and call for the immediate removal of, impediments to humanitarian access in violation of applicable international humanitarian law.

—Call for strict compliance by parties to armed conflict with applicable international humanitarian law, including:

- The prohibition against using starvation of civilians as a method of warfare by depriving them of objects indispensable to their survival, including willfully impeding relief supplies as provided for under applicable international humanitarian law.
- Agreeing to relief actions which are humanitarian and impartial in character and conducted without any adverse distinction.

—Call for strict compliance by parties to armed conflict and third States with their obligations under applicable international humanitarian law to allow and facilitate the rapid and unimpeded passage of relief consignments, equipment and personnel subject to their right to prescribe technical arrangements, including search, under which such passage is permitted.

—Mandate United Nations peacekeeping and other relevant missions authorized by the Security Council, where appropriate and as requested, to facilitate the provision of humanitarian assistance.

Parties to armed conflict to respect and protect humanitarian workers and facilities

Issues for consideration:

—Condemn, and call for the immediate cessation of, attacks deliberately targeting humanitarian workers.

—Call for strict compliance by parties to armed conflict with applicable international humanitarian law, including the duty to respect and protect relief personnel and installations, material, units and vehicles involved in humanitarian assistance.

—Mandate United Nations peacekeeping and other relevant missions authorized by the Security Council to contribute, as requested and within capabilities, to the creation of the necessary security conditions for the provision of humanitarian assistance.

—Encourage the Secretary-General to bring to the attention of the Security Council situations in which humanitarian assistance is denied as a consequence of violence directed against humanitarian personnel and facilities.

—Request that States include key provisions of the Convention on the Safety of United Nations and Associated Personnel and the Optional Protocol thereto, such as those regarding the prevention of attacks against members of United Nations operations, the criminalization of such attacks and the prosecution or extradition of offenders, in future as well as, if necessary, in existing status-of-forces, status-of-mission and host country agreements negotiated with the United Nations.

D. Conduct of hostilities

Parties to armed conflict to take all feasible precautions to spare civilians from the effects of hostilities

Issues for consideration:

—Condemn, and call for the immediate cessation of, all acts of violence or abuses committed against civilians in violation of applicable international humanitarian law and human rights law.

—Call for strict compliance by parties to armed conflict with applicable international humanitarian law, including the prohibitions against:

- Directing attacks against the civilian population or against individual civilians not directly taking part in hostilities.
- Directing attacks against civilian objects.
- Launching an attack that is indiscriminate, i.e., of a nature to strike military objectives and civilians or civilian objects without distinction.
- Launching an attack which may be expected to cause incidental loss of life or injury to civilians or damage to civilian objects or a combination thereof which would be excessive in relation to the concrete and direct military advantage anticipated.
- Directing attacks against personnel, installations, material, units or vehicles involved in a humanitarian assistance or peacekeeping mission in accordance with the Charter of the United Nations, as long as they are entitled to the protection given to civilians or civilian objects under international humanitarian law.
- Utilizing the presence of a civilian or other protected person to render certain points, areas or military forces immune from military operations.
- Rape and other forms of sexual violence.
- Directing attacks against buildings dedicated to religion, education, art, science or charitable purposes, historical monuments, hospitals and places where the sick and wounded are collected, provided they are not military objectives.
- Directing attacks against buildings, material, medical units and transport, and personnel using the distinctive emblems of the Geneva Conventions in conformity with international law.
- Destroying or seizing the property of the adversary unless required by military necessity.

- Using starvation of civilians as a method of warfare by depriving them of objects indispensable to their survival, including wilfully impeding relief supplies as provided for under applicable international humanitarian law.
—Request regular reporting by United Nations peacekeeping and other relevant missions authorized by the Security Council on concrete steps taken to ensure the protection of the civilian population in the conduct of hostilities and on measures to ensure accountability for violations of applicable international humanitarian law.

E.   Small arms and light weapons, mines and explosive remnants of war

Protection of the civilian population through the control of, and reduction in the availability of, illicit small arms and light weapons

Issues for consideration:
—Request States and regional and subregional organizations to adopt measures to curb and reduce illicit trafficking in small arms and light weapons, such as voluntary collection and destruction; effective stockpile management; arms embargoes; sanctions; and legal measures against corporate actors, individuals and entities involved in such activities.
—Encourage strengthened practical cooperation between United Nations peacekeeping and other relevant missions authorized by the Security Council aimed at monitoring and preventing the cross-border movement of small arms and light weapons.
—Mandate United Nations peacekeeping and other relevant missions authorized by the Security Council to collect and dispose of or secure illicit and/or surplus small arms and light weapons as well as surplus ammunition stockpiles.
—Consider imposing arms embargoes and other measures aimed at preventing the sale or supply of arms and related materiel of all types to parties to armed conflict that commit violations of applicable international law.
—Encourage strengthened practical cooperation among relevant sanctions monitoring groups of the Security Council peacekeeping and other relevant missions authorized by the Council and States.
—Request the establishment of a baseline arms inventory as well as arms marking and registration systems in situations where a United Nations arms embargo coincides with disarmament, demobilization and reintegration efforts.

Protection of the civilian population through the marking, clearance, removal or destruction of mines and explosive remnants of war, including cluster munition remnants

Issues for consideration:
—Call upon parties to armed conflict, after the cessation of active hostilities and as soon as feasible, to mark, clear, remove or destroy mines and explosive remnants of war (ERW) in affected territories under their control, prioritizing areas affected by mines and

ERW which are assessed to pose serious humanitarian risk.
—Call upon parties to armed conflict to record and retain information on the use of mines and explosive ordnance or the abandonment of explosive ordnance, to facilitate rapid marking and clearance, removal or destruction of mines and ERW and risk education, and to provide the relevant information to the party in control of, and civilian populations in, the territory.
—Call upon parties to armed conflict to take all feasible precautions in the territory under their control affected by mines and ERW to protect the civilian population, in particular children, including issuing warnings, undertaking risk education, marking, fencing and monitoring territory affected by mines and ERW.
—Call upon parties to armed conflict to protect United Nations peacekeeping and other relevant missions authorized by the Security Council, as well as humanitarian organizations, from the effects of mines and ERW and to make available information on the location of mines and ERW that they are aware of in the territory where the mission/organizations are or will be operating.
—Call upon parties to armed conflict, States and other relevant actors to provide technical, financial, material or human resources assistance to facilitate the marking, clearance, removal or destruction of mines and ERW.
—Call upon parties to armed conflict, States and other relevant actors to provide assistance for the care, rehabilitation and economic and social reintegration of victims of ERW and their families and communities.

F.   Compliance, accountability and the rule of law

Compliance by parties to armed conflict with applicable international humanitarian law and human rights law

Issues for consideration:
—Call upon parties to armed conflict to take appropriate measures to respect and ensure respect for international humanitarian law and human rights law, including by:
  - Enforcing appropriate military disciplinary measures and upholding the principle of command responsibility.
  - Training troops on applicable international humanitarian law and human rights law.
  - Vetting armed and security forces to ensure that personnel have a reliably attested record of not having been involved in violations of international humanitarian law or human rights law.
—Consider applying targeted and graduated measures against parties to armed conflict that commit violations of applicable international humanitarian law and human rights law.

Accountability for persons suspected of genocide, crimes against humanity, war crimes or serious violations of human rights law

Issues for consideration:

—Stress the importance of ending impunity for criminal violations of applicable international humanitarian law and human rights law as part of a comprehensive approach to seeking sustainable peace, justice, truth and national reconciliation.

—Call upon States to comply with their obligations to investigate, search for, prosecute or extradite persons suspected of committing genocide, war crimes, crimes against humanity or other serious violations of human rights law.

—Stress the need for the exclusion of, and reject any form of, or endorsement of, amnesty for genocide, crimes against humanity, war crimes or other serious violations of human rights in conflict resolution processes and ensure that no such amnesty previously granted is a bar to prosecution before any United Nations-created or assisted court.

—Mandate United Nations peacekeeping and other relevant missions authorized by the Security Council to promote, in cooperation with relevant States, the establishment of effective arrangements for investigating and prosecuting violations of international humanitarian law or other serious violations of human rights law.

—Request the cooperation of States and United Nations peacekeeping and other relevant missions authorized by the Security Council in the apprehension and surrender of alleged perpetrators of genocide, crimes against humanity, war crimes or other serious violations of human rights law.

—Consider the establishment, in situations where local judicial mechanisms are overwhelmed, of ad hoc judicial mechanisms at the national or international level to investigate and prosecute war crimes and serious violations of human rights law.

—Consider the referral of situations involving genocide, crimes against humanity or war crimes to the International Criminal Court.

Protection of civilians through the restoration and enforcement of the rule of law

Issues for consideration:

—Call upon States to ensure equal protection under the law and equal access to justice for victims of violations of international humanitarian law and human rights law, including women and children, and to take the necessary measures to ensure the protection of victims and witnesses.

—Mandate United Nations peacekeeping and other relevant missions authorized by the Security Council to support restoration of the rule of law, including the provision of assistance in monitoring, restructuring and reforming the justice sector.

—Request the rapid deployment of qualified and well-trained international civilian police, justice and corrections experts as a component of United Nations peacekeeping and other relevant missions authorized by the Security Council.

—Call upon States and regional and subregional organizations to provide technical assistance for local police, judiciary and penitentiaries (e.g., mentoring, legislative drafting).

Build confidence and enhance stability by promoting truth and reconciliation mechanisms

Issues for consideration:

—Mandate the establishment of appropriate, locally adapted mechanisms for truth and reconciliation (e.g., technical assistance, funding, reintegration of civilians within communities).

—Request, where appropriate, the establishment by the Secretary-General of commissions of inquiry and similar measures with regard to situations involving genocide, war crimes, crimes against humanity or serious violations of human rights law.

G.   Media and information

Protection of journalists, other media professionals and associated personnel

Issues for consideration:

—Condemn, and call for the immediate cessation of, attacks against journalists, media professionals and associated personnel operating in situations of armed conflict.

—Call for compliance by parties to armed conflict with applicable international humanitarian law and respect for the civilian status of journalists, media professionals and associated personnel as well as their equipment and installations.

—Demand that States take all necessary steps to prosecute those responsible for attacks against journalists, media professionals and associated personnel in violation of applicable international humanitarian law.

Counter occurrences of speech used to incite violence

Issues for consideration:

—Condemn, and call for the immediate cessation of, incitements to violence against civilians in situations of armed conflict.

—Demand that States bring to justice individuals who incite or otherwise cause such violence.

—Impose targeted and graduated measures in response to media broadcasts inciting genocide, crimes against humanity, war crimes or other serious violations of human rights law.

—Mandate United Nations peacekeeping and other relevant missions authorized by the Security Council to promote the establishment of media monitoring mechanisms to ensure effective monitoring, reporting and documenting of any incidents, origins and contents that incite "hate media".

Promote and support accurate management of information on the conflict

Issues for consideration:

—Urge parties to armed conflict to respect the professional independence of journalists, media professionals and associated personnel.

—Encourage United Nations peacekeeping and other relevant missions authorized by the Security Council to include a mass-media component that can disseminate information about international humanitarian law and human rights law while also giving objective information about the activities of the United Nations.

—Request relevant actors to provide technical assistance to States in drafting and enforcing anti-hate speech legislation.

II. Specific protection concerns arising from Security Council discussions on children affected by armed conflict

Parties to armed conflict to take the necessary measures to meet the specific protection, health, education and assistance needs of children

Issues for consideration:

—Condemn, and call for the immediate cessation of, violations and abuses committed against children in situations of armed conflict, including the recruitment or active use in hostilities of children by parties to armed conflict in violation of applicable international law; the killing or maiming of children; rape and other grave sexual abuse of children; abduction of children; attacks against schools or hospitals; and denial of humanitarian access for children.

—Call for strict compliance by parties to armed conflict with applicable international humanitarian law and human rights law relating to children affected by armed conflict.

—Call upon relevant parties to develop and implement concrete time-bound action plans to halt recruitment and use of children, in close collaboration with United Nations peacekeeping missions, United Nations country teams and the Special Representative of the Secretary-General for Children and Armed Conflict.

—Call upon all parties concerned to implement the recommendations of the Security Council Working Group on Children and Armed Conflict.

—Include specific provisions for the protection of children in the mandates of United Nations peacekeeping and other relevant missions authorized by the Security Council.

—Request that reports of the Secretary-General on country-specific situations include the protection of children as a specific aspect of the report.

—Call upon all parties concerned to ensure that the protection, rights and well-being of children affected by armed conflict are specifically integrated into peace processes, peace agreements and post-conflict recovery and reconstruction planning and programmes, including measures for family tracing and reunification, the rehabilitation and reintegration of separated children, and the release and rein-

tegration of children associated with armed forces and groups.

—Urge States, United Nations entities, regional and subregional organizations and other concerned parties to take appropriate measures to control illicit subregional and cross-border activities harmful to children, as well as other violations and abuses committed against children in situations of armed conflict in violation of applicable international law.

—Urge relevant regional and/or subregional bodies to develop and implement policies, activities and advocacy for the benefit of children affected by armed conflict.

III. Specific protection concerns arising from Security Council discussions on women affected by armed conflict

Parties to armed conflict and other relevant actors to refrain from, and take the necessary measures to prevent and respond to, sexual violence

Issues for consideration:

—Condemn, and call for the immediate cessation of, acts of sexual violence committed in the context of, and associated with, armed conflict.

—Call for strict compliance by parties to armed conflict with the rules of international humanitarian law and human rights law prohibiting rape, sexual slavery, enforced prostitution, forced pregnancy, enforced sterilization or any other form of sexual violence.

—Call upon parties to armed conflict to take appropriate measures to refrain from, prevent and protect all persons from all forms of sexual violence, including by:

• Enforcing appropriate military disciplinary measures and upholding the principle of command responsibility.

• Training troops on the categorical prohibition of all forms of sexual violence.

• Debunking myths that fuel sexual violence.

• Vetting armed and security forces to ensure that personnel have a reliably attested record of not having been involved in the perpetration of rape and other forms of sexual violence.

• Evacuating to safety civilians under imminent threat of sexual violence.

—Request that reports of the Secretary-General on country-specific situations include sexual violence as a specific aspect of the report, including, to the extent possible, disaggregated data as to gender and age of victims; and request the development of mission-specific strategies and plans of action for preventing and responding to sexual violence, as part of a broader protection of civilians strategy.

—Urge relevant regional and/or subregional bodies to develop and implement policies, activities and advocacy for the benefit of civilians affected by sexual violence.

—Request troop- and police-contributing countries to deploy higher numbers of women peacekeepers or police, and to ensure the provision of appropriate training to their personnel participating in United Nations peacekeeping and other relevant missions on the protection of civilians, including women and children, and the prevention of sexual violence in conflict and post-conflict situations.

Parties to armed conflict to take the necessary measures to meet the specific protection, health and assistance needs of women and girls

Issues for consideration:

—Condemn, and call for the immediate cessation of, violations and abuses committed against women and girls in situations of armed conflict.

—Call for strict compliance by parties to armed conflict with applicable international humanitarian law and human rights law relating to the protection of women and girls affected by armed conflict.

—Call upon all parties concerned to ensure that the protection, rights and well-being of women and girls affected by armed conflict are specifically integrated into all peace processes, peace agreements and post-conflict recovery and reconstruction planning and programmes.

—Include specific provisions for the protection of women and girls in the mandates of United Nations peacekeeping and other relevant missions authorized by the Security Council.

—Request that reports of the Secretary-General on country-specific situations include the protection of women and girls as a specific aspect of the report.

—Urge relevant regional and/or subregional bodies to develop and implement policies, activities and advocacy for the benefit of women and girls affected by armed conflict.

Equal participation and full involvement of women in the prevention and resolution of armed conflict

Issues for consideration:

—Urge States, United Nations entities, regional and subregional organizations and other concerned parties to ensure increased representation of women at all decision-making levels in national, regional and international institutions and mechanisms for the prevention, management and resolution of conflict.

—Call upon all actors involved in negotiating and implementing peace agreements to adopt a gender perspective, including by considering:

• The needs of women and girls during repatriation and resettlement and for rehabilitation, reintegration and post-conflict reconstruction.

• Measures that support local women's peace initiatives and indigenous processes for conflict resolution, and that involve women in the implementation mechanisms of peace agreements.

• Measures that ensure the protection of, and respect for, the human rights of women and girls, particularly as they relate to the constitution, the electoral system, the police and the judiciary.

—Urge the Secretary-General and his Special Envoys to ensure the participation of women in discussions pertinent to the prevention and resolution of conflict, the maintenance of peace and security, and post-conflict peacebuilding, and encourage all parties to such talks to facilitate the equal and full participation of women at all decision-making levels.

—Ensure that Security Council missions take into account gender considerations and the rights of women and girls, including through consultation with local and international women's groups.

—Urge troop- and police-contributing countries to expand the role, numbers and contribution of women in United Nations operations, and especially among military observers and civilian police.

Sexual exploitation and abuse

Issues for consideration:

—Urge humanitarian and development organizations to take appropriate action to prevent sexual exploitation and abuse by their personnel, including predeployment and in-theatre awareness training and, in the case of United Nations actors, to promote and ensure compliance, including by civilian staff of United Nations peacekeeping and other relevant missions, with the Secretary-General's bulletin on special measures for protection from sexual exploitation and sexual abuse.

—Urge troop- and police-contributing countries to take appropriate action to prevent sexual exploitation and abuse by their personnel, including predeployment and in-theatre awareness training to promote and ensure compliance with the Secretary-General's bulletin on special measures for protection from sexual exploitation and sexual abuse.

—Urge troop- and police-contributing countries to ensure full accountability in cases of sexual exploitation and abuse involving their personnel and to report to the Secretary-General on action taken.

An addendum to the statement provided a selection of agreed language.

Report of Secretary-General. In response to presidential statement S/PRST/2008/18 [YUN 2008, p. 795], the Secretary-General, in May, submitted a report [S/2009/277] on the protection of civilians in armed conflict, in which he noted that, since the subject had been placed on the Council's agenda 10 years earlier [YUN 1999, p. 647], further efforts to strengthen the protection of civilians remained crucial as actions on the ground had not matched the progress in words and the development of international norms and standards. Common to old and new conflicts alike were persistent and sometimes appalling levels of human suffering owing to the fundamental failure of parties to respect their obligations to protect civilians. That failure demanded a reinvigorated commitment by the Security Council, Member States and the United Nations to the protection of civilians and the promotion of respect for the principles of international humanitarian law, human rights law and refugee law on which the concept was founded. That commitment required determined action to meet five core challenges: enhancing compliance with international law by parties to conflict, particularly in the conduct of hostilities; enhancing compliance with the law by non-State armed groups; enhancing protection through more effective and better resourced peacekeeping; enhancing humanitarian access; and enhancing accountability for violations of the law.

To promote systematic compliance with the law, the Council should use all available opportunities to condemn violations and demand compliance by parties with their obligations; publicly threaten and, if necessary, apply targeted measures against the leadership of parties that consistently defied those demands and routinely violated their obligations to respect civilians; and systematically request reports on violations and consider mandating commissions of inquiry—including with a view to identifying those responsible and either prosecuting them or referring the situation to the International Criminal Court (ICC).

Among measures to enhance compliance by non-State armed groups, a first useful step might be to convene an "Arria formula" meeting to discuss the experience of United Nations and non-governmental actors in working with such armed groups, and to identify additional measures that the Council and Member States could take to improve compliance. The inclusion of protection activities within the mandates of UN peacekeeping and other missions had been a significant development in the Council's efforts to improve protection on the ground. To that end, more missions were beginning to develop mission-specific protection strategies and action plans.

With respect to humanitarian access, the Council should consistently call for the immediate removal of impediments to humanitarian access that violated international humanitarian law, requesting strict compliance by all parties with their obligations to allow and facilitate the rapid and unimpeded passage of relief consignments, equipment and personnel. The Council was also urged to address attacks and other violations against humanitarian workers, including the application of targeted measures against individuals responsible for such attacks and the referral of grave instances to the ICC.

To enhance accountability, Member States should prosecute those suspected of genocide, crimes against humanity and war crimes, provide training to combatants on international humanitarian law and human rights law and adopt legislation to prosecute persons suspected of genocide, crimes against humanity, war crimes and other serious violations of human rights law. The Council was urged to insist that Member States cooperate fully with the ICC and enforce such cooperation through targeted measures.

The Secretary-General concluded that the last 10 years had provided a tantalizing sense of the potential of the protection of civilians agenda. The task was to take the necessary steps to fully realize that potential and meet the five core challenges identified in the report. The recommendations of the report were premised on the need to enhance compliance and accountability in conflict—compliance by all parties with the applicable law and the demands of the Security Council, and accountability for those individuals and parties that failed to comply. The Council had the tools required to take forward the recommendations of the report. In practice, that entailed consistent application of the aide-memoire on the protection of civilians annexed to presidential statement S/PRST/2009/1; regular meetings of the Security Council Expert Group on the Protection of Civilians prior to establishing or renewing peacekeeping mandates; consistent condemnation of violations of the law by all parties to conflict, without exception; ensuring of compliance through targeted measures, commissions of inquiry and referral of situations to the ICC; and timely deployment of peacekeeping missions or additional temporary capacity with robust protection mandates.

Security Council consideration (June). On 26 June, the Council held a day-long debate [meeting 6151] to discuss the Secretary-General's report, hearing a briefing by Mr. Holmes, the Under-Secretary-General for Humanitarian Affairs and Emergency Relief Coordinator, who gave a detailed account of the sufferings of millions of civilians trapped in armed conflict or forced into flight. He said that, despite progress in the past 10 years, particularly with respect to the Council's involvement, the situation on the ground remained largely unchanged. Civilians continued to bear the brunt of the armed conflicts, and much greater efforts were required to enhance compliance with the applicable laws and accountability on the part of those who failed to do so.

During the ensuing debate, in which more than 40 delegations participated, speakers stressed the need for all parties to conflict to respect international humanitarian law and provide safe and unhindered access for humanitarian aid.

Security Council consideration (November). On 11 November [meeting 6216], the Security Council held a day-long meeting on the protection of civilians in armed conflict. The Council had before it a concept paper [S/2009/567] submitted by Austria.

Opening the discussion, the Secretary-General welcomed the prominent place that the protection of civilians had assumed on the Council's agenda, noting, however, that much remained to be done to effectively protect civilians in all conflicts. Appalling levels of human suffering pointed to a fundamental failure of the parties to respect their obligations to protect civilians. Such a failure demanded a reinvigorated commitment to the principles of international law on the part of the Security Council, Member States and the United Nations.

Under-Secretary-General for Humanitarian Affairs Holmes deplored the gap between the rules of international humanitarian law and their application, as well as the gap between the protection mandates of some peacekeeping missions and the subsequent reality. It was crucial to develop operational guidance for that purpose, based on the understanding that protection involved a broad range of activities, from the return of refugees to strengthening the host State's ability to protect its own population. The Council needed a consistent approach to accountability issues, encouraging States to give top priority to the protection of civilians and calling them to account when they did not, on the basis of the facts rather than political convenience.

Deputy High Commissioner for Human Rights Kyung-wha Kang said that the authority of international law and the obligations of the parties to conflict could not be replaced by more amorphous notions of protection, or by less obligatory notions of charitable action. Where conflict entailed abuse of human rights, the international community must act to identify the facts and apply the law. Law without enforcement was of little moment to would-be perpetrators, and the Council should ensure accountability for perpetrators of war crimes, crimes against humanity and other gross violations.

Representatives of 56 Member States addressed the ensuing debate.

SECURITY COUNCIL ACTION

On 11 November [meeting 6216], the Security Council unanimously adopted **resolution 1894(2009)**. The draft [S/2009/582] was submitted by Austria, Azerbaijan, Belgium, Benin, Burkina Faso, Canada, Costa Rica, Croatia, Cyprus, the Czech Republic, Estonia, Finland, France, Germany, Greece, Italy, Japan, Liechtenstein, Lithuania, Luxembourg, Mexico, Moldova, the Netherlands, Norway, Slovakia, Slovenia, Sweden, Switzerland, the United Kingdom, the United Republic of Tanzania and the United States.

The Security Council,

Reaffirming its commitment to the continuing and full implementation, in a mutually reinforcing manner, of resolutions 1265(1999) of 17 September 1999, 1296(2000) of 19 April 2000, 1325(2000) of 31 October 2000, 1612(2005) of 26 July 2005, 1674(2006) of 28 April 2006, 1738(2006) of 23 December 2006, 1820(2008) of 19 June 2008, 1882(2009) of 4 August 2009, 1888(2009) of 30 September 2009 and 1889(2009) of 5 October 2009, and all relevant statements by its President,

Reaffirming its commitment also to the purposes of the Charter of the United Nations as set out in Article 1, paragraphs 1 to 4, and to the principles of the Charter as set out in Article 2, paragraphs 1 to 7, including its commitment to the principles of the political independence, sovereign equality and territorial integrity of all States, and respect for the sovereignty of all States,

Noting that 2009 marks the tenth anniversary of the progressive consideration by the Security Council of the protection of civilians in armed conflict as a thematic issue, and acknowledging the enduring need for the Council and Member States to strengthen further the protection of civilians in armed conflict,

Noting also that 2009 also marks the sixtieth anniversary of the Geneva Conventions of 1949, which, together with the Additional Protocols thereto, constitute the basis for the legal framework for the protection of civilians in armed conflict,

Recognizing that States bear the primary responsibility to respect and ensure the human rights of their citizens, as well as all individuals within their territory, as provided for by relevant international law,

Reaffirming that parties to armed conflict bear the primary responsibility to take all feasible steps to ensure the protection of civilians,

Reaffirming also the relevant provisions of the 2005 World Summit Outcome regarding the protection of civilians in armed conflict, including paragraphs 138 and 139 thereof regarding the responsibility to protect populations from genocide, war crimes, ethnic cleansing and crimes against humanity,

Reiterating its deep regret that civilians continue to account for the vast majority of casualties in situations of armed conflict,

Stressing the particular impact that armed conflict has on women and children, including as refugees and internally displaced persons, as well as on other civilians who may have specific vulnerabilities, including persons with disabilities and older persons, and stressing the protection and assistance needs of all affected civilian populations,

Noting the adoption on 23 October 2009 of the African Union Convention for the Protection and Assistance of Internally Displaced Persons in Africa,

Noting with grave concern the severity and prevalence of constraints on humanitarian access, as well as the frequency and gravity of attacks against humanitarian personnel and objects and the significant implications of such attacks for humanitarian operations,

Recognizing the need for States in or emerging from armed conflict to restore or build accountable security institutions and independent national judicial systems,

Recalling the inclusion of war crimes, crimes against humanity and genocide in the statutes of the ad hoc international criminal tribunals and the Rome Statute of the International Criminal Court, and emphasizing in this regard the principle of complementarity,

Recognizing the importance of reparations programmes in response to serious violations of international humanitarian law and gross human rights violations,

Recognizing also the importance of empowering vulnerable civilians through education and training as a means to support efforts to halt and prevent abuses committed against civilians in situations of armed conflict,

Recognizing further the valuable contribution to the protection of children in armed conflict of the Special Representative of the Secretary-General for Children and Armed Conflict and the Security Council Working Group on Children and Armed Conflict, including the conclusions and recommendations of the Working Group issued in line with resolution 1612(2005), and recalling resolution 1882(2009), which aims to strengthen the protection of children in situations of armed conflict,

Recalling its decision, in resolution 1888(2009), to address violence against women and children in situations of armed conflict by requesting the Secretary-General to appoint a special representative and to identify and take the appropriate measures to deploy rapidly a team of experts to situations of particular concern with respect to sexual violence in armed conflict,

Noting the practice of briefings by the Office for the Coordination of Humanitarian Affairs of the Secretariat to members of the Council on behalf of the United Nations humanitarian community, through both formal and informal channels,

Taking note of the report of the Secretary-General of 29 May 2009 on the protection of civilians in armed conflict and the annex thereto, on constraints on humanitarian access, in which the core challenges to the effective protection of civilians are identified, namely, enhancing compliance with international law, enhancing compliance by non-State armed groups with their obligations under international law, enhancing protection through more effective and better resourced United Nations peacekeeping and other relevant missions, enhancing humanitarian access, and enhancing accountability for violations,

Welcoming the proposals, conclusions and recommendations on the protection of civilians included in the report of the Special Committee on Peacekeeping Operations and its Working Group and the important work conducted by the Security Council Working Group on Peacekeeping Operations, including its efforts aimed at enhancing the implementation of protection mandates,

Recalling the statement by its President of 5 August 2009, and welcoming ongoing efforts to strengthen United Nations peacekeeping,

Noting that United Nations peacekeeping missions constitute one of several means at the disposal of the United Nations to protect civilians in situations of armed conflict,

1. *Demands* that parties to armed conflict comply strictly with the obligations applicable to them under international humanitarian, human rights and refugee law, and implement all relevant decisions of the Security Council, and in this regard urges them to take all measures required to respect and protect the civilian population and meet its basic needs;

2. *Reiterates its condemnation in the strongest terms* of attacks in situations of armed conflict directed against civilians as such and other protected persons or objects as well as indiscriminate or disproportionate attacks and the utilization of the presence of civilians to render certain

points, areas or military forces immune from military operations, as flagrant violations of international humanitarian law, and demands that all parties immediately put an end to such practices;

3. *Notes* that the deliberate targeting of civilians as such and other protected persons, and the commission of systematic, flagrant and widespread violations of applicable international humanitarian and human rights law in situations of armed conflict may constitute a threat to international peace and security, and reaffirms in this regard its readiness to consider such situations and, where necessary, to adopt appropriate steps;

4. *Reiterates its willingness* to respond to situations of armed conflict where civilians are being targeted or humanitarian assistance to civilians is being deliberately obstructed, including through the consideration of appropriate measures at the disposal of the Council in accordance with the Charter of the United Nations;

5. *Reiterates its call upon* States that have not already done so to consider signing, ratifying or acceding to the relevant instruments of international humanitarian, human rights and refugee law, and to take appropriate legislative, judicial and administrative measures to implement their obligations under those instruments;

6. *Demands* that all States and parties to armed conflict fully implement all relevant decisions of the Council and in this regard cooperate fully with United Nations peacekeeping missions and country teams in the follow-up to and implementation of those decisions;

7. *Calls upon* all parties concerned:

(a) To ensure the widest possible dissemination of information about international humanitarian, human rights and refugee law;

(b) To provide training for public officials, members of armed forces and armed groups, personnel associated with armed forces, civilian police and law enforcement personnel, and members of the judicial and legal professions, and to raise awareness among civil society and the civilian population on relevant international humanitarian, human rights and refugee law, as well as on the protection, special needs and human rights of women and children in conflict situations, to achieve full and effective compliance;

(c) To ensure that orders and instructions issued to armed forces and other relevant actors are in compliance with applicable international law, and that they are observed, inter alia, by establishing effective disciplinary procedures, central to which must be the strict adherence to the principle of command responsibility to support compliance with international humanitarian law;

(d) To seek, where appropriate, support from United Nations peacekeeping and other relevant missions, as well as United Nations country teams and the International Committee of the Red Cross and, where appropriate, other members of the International Red Cross and Red Crescent Movement, on training and awareness-raising on international humanitarian, human rights and refugee law;

8. *Emphasizes* the importance of addressing in its country-specific deliberations the compliance of parties to armed conflict with international humanitarian, human rights and refugee law, notes the range of existing methods used, on a case-by-case basis, for gathering information on alleged violations of applicable international law relating to

the protection of civilians, and underlines the importance in this regard of receiving information that is timely, objective, accurate and reliable;

9. *Considers* the possibility, to this end, of using the International Humanitarian Fact-Finding Commission established by article 90 of Additional Protocol I to the Geneva Conventions;

10. *Affirms its strong opposition* to impunity for serious violations of international humanitarian law and human rights law, and emphasizes in this context the responsibility of States to comply with their relevant obligations to end impunity and to thoroughly investigate and prosecute persons responsible for war crimes, genocide, crimes against humanity or other serious violations of international humanitarian law in order to prevent violations, avoid their recurrence and seek sustainable peace, justice, truth and reconciliation;

11. *Recalls* that accountability for such serious crimes must be ensured by taking measures at the national level and by enhancing international cooperation in support of national mechanisms, draws attention to the full range of justice and reconciliation mechanisms to be considered, including national, international and "mixed" criminal courts and tribunals, and truth and reconciliation commissions, as well as national reparation programmes for victims and institutional reforms, and underlines the role of the Council in ending impunity;

12. *Reaffirms* the role of the Council in promoting an environment that is conducive to the facilitation of humanitarian access to those in need;

13. *Stresses* the importance for all, within the framework of humanitarian assistance, of upholding and respecting the humanitarian principles of humanity, neutrality, impartiality and independence;

14. *Also stresses* the importance for all parties to armed conflict to cooperate with humanitarian personnel in order to allow and facilitate access to civilian populations affected by armed conflict;

15. *Expresses its intention:*

(a) To call upon parties to armed conflict to comply with the obligations applicable to them under international humanitarian law to take all steps required to protect civilians and to facilitate the rapid and unimpeded passage of relief consignments, equipment and personnel;

(b) To mandate United Nations peacekeeping and other relevant missions, where appropriate, to assist in creating conditions conducive to safe, timely and unimpeded humanitarian assistance;

16. *Also expresses its intention:*

(a) To consistently condemn and call for the immediate cessation of all acts of violence and other forms of intimidation deliberately directed against humanitarian personnel;

(b) To call upon parties to armed conflict to comply with the obligations applicable to them under international humanitarian law to respect and protect humanitarian personnel and consignments used for humanitarian relief operations;

(c) To take appropriate steps in response to deliberate attacks against humanitarian personnel;

17. *Invites* the Secretary-General to continue the systematic monitoring and analysis of constraints on humanitarian access, to include, as appropriate, observations and recommendations in his briefings and country-specific reports to the Council;

18. *Recalls its determination* to upgrade the strategic oversight of peacekeeping operations, mindful of the important role that peacekeeping operations play for the protection of civilians, reaffirms its support for the efforts made by the Secretary-General to review peacekeeping operations and to provide enhanced planning and support, and renews its encouragement to deepen those efforts, in partnership with troop- and police-contributing countries and other relevant stakeholders;

19. *Reaffirms* its practice of ensuring that mandates of United Nations peacekeeping and other relevant missions include, where appropriate and on a case-by-case basis, provisions regarding the protection of civilians, stresses that mandated protection activities must be given priority in decisions about the use of available capacity and resources, including information and intelligence resources, in the implementation of mandates, and recognizes that the protection of civilians when and as mandated requires a coordinated response from all relevant mission components;

20. *Reaffirms also* the importance of entrusting peacekeeping and other relevant missions that are tasked with the protection of civilians with clear, credible and achievable mandates, based on accurate and reliable information on the situation on the ground and a realistic assessment of threats against civilians and missions, made in consultation with all relevant stakeholders, further reaffirms the importance of a greater awareness in the Council of the resource and field support implications of its decisions, and stresses the necessity of ensuring the execution of the aforementioned mandates to protect civilians in the field;

21. *Recognizes* the necessity of taking into account the protection needs of civilians, in particular women and children, in situations of armed conflict, in the early phase of mandate drafting and throughout the life cycle of United Nations peacekeeping and other relevant missions, and in this regard underlines the importance of engagement with the countries concerned and of close consultation with the Secretariat, troop- and police-contributing countries and other relevant actors;

22. *Recognizes also* the need for comprehensive operational guidance on the tasks and responsibilities of peacekeeping missions in the implementation of protection of civilians mandates, and requests the Secretary-General to develop, in close consultation with Member States, including troop- and police-contributing countries, and other relevant actors, an operational concept for the protection of civilians and to report back on progress made;

23. *Requests* the Secretary-General, in consultation with relevant actors, to ensure that peacekeeping missions with protection of civilians mandates, in keeping with the strategic plans that guide their deployment, conduct mission-wide planning, predeployment training and senior leadership training on the protection of civilians, and requests troop- and police-contributing countries to ensure the provision of appropriate training of their personnel

participating in United Nations peacekeeping and other relevant missions to heighten the awareness of and responsiveness to protection concerns, including training on HIV/AIDS and zero tolerance of sexual exploitation and abuse in United Nations peacekeeping missions;

24. *Also requests* the Secretary-General to ensure that all relevant peacekeeping missions with protection mandates incorporate comprehensive protection strategies into the overall mission implementation plans and contingency plans which include assessments of potential threats and options for crisis response and risk mitigation and establish priorities, actions and clear roles and responsibilities under the leadership and coordination of the Special Representative of the Secretary-General, with the full involvement of all relevant actors and in consultation with United Nations country teams;

25. *Further requests* the Secretary-General to ensure that United Nations missions provide local communities with adequate information with regard to the role of the mission and, in this regard, ensure coordination between a United Nations mission and relevant humanitarian agencies;

26. *Takes note* of practical measures taken by ongoing peacekeeping missions and United Nations country teams to enhance the protection of civilians in the field, and requests the Secretary-General to include best practices in his next report on protection of civilians to the Council;

27. *Reaffirms* its practice of requiring benchmarks, as and where appropriate, to measure and review progress made in the implementation of peacekeeping mandates, and stresses the importance of including indicators of progress regarding the protection of civilians in such benchmarks for relevant missions;

28. *Emphasizes* the need for a comprehensive approach to facilitate the implementation of protection mandates by promoting economic growth, good governance, democracy, the rule of law and respect for and protection of human rights, and in this regard urges the cooperation of Member States and underlines the importance of a coherent, comprehensive and coordinated approach by the principal organs of the United Nations, cooperating with one another and within their respective mandates;

29. *Notes* that the excessive accumulation and destabilizing effect of small arms and light weapons pose a considerable impediment to the provision of humanitarian assistance and have the potential to exacerbate and prolong conflicts, endanger civilians and undermine security and the confidence required for a return to peace and stability, calls upon parties to armed conflict to take all feasible precautions to protect the civilian population, including children, from the effects of landmines and other explosive remnants of war, and in this regard encourages the international community to support country efforts in clearing landmines and other explosive remnants of war and to provide assistance for the care, rehabilitation and economic and social reintegration of victims, including persons with disabilities;

30. *Reiterates* the importance of the aide-memoire on the protection of civilians in armed conflict as a practical tool that provides a basis for improved analysis and diagnosis of key protection issues, particularly during delibera-

tions on peacekeeping mandates, and stresses the need to implement the approaches set out therein on a more regular and consistent basis, taking into account the particular circumstances of each conflict situation;

31. *Recognizes* the important role of the Secretary-General in providing timely information to the Council on the protection of civilians in armed conflict, in particular through thematic and country-specific reports and through briefings;

32. *Requests* the Secretary-General to include in his reports to the Council on country-specific situations more comprehensive and detailed information relating to the protection of civilians in armed conflict, including on protection-related incidents and actions taken by parties to armed conflict to implement their obligations to respect and protect the civilian population, including information specific to the protection needs of refugees, internally displaced persons, women, children and other vulnerable groups;

33. *Also requests* the Secretary-General to develop guidance for United Nations peacekeeping and other relevant missions on reporting on the protection of civilians in armed conflict with a view to streamlining reporting and enhancing monitoring and oversight by the Council of the implementation of protection mandates of United Nations peacekeeping and other missions;

34. *Stresses* the importance of consultation and cooperation between the United Nations, the International Committee of the Red Cross and other relevant organizations, including regional organizations, to improve the protection of civilians in armed conflict;

35. *Requests* the Secretary-General to submit his next report on the protection of civilians in armed conflict by November 2010;

36. *Decides* to remain seized of the matter.

Special political missions

OIOS audit of management of special political missions

Pursuant to General Assembly resolution 63/261 [YUN 2008, p. 49], the Office of Internal Oversight Services (OIOS) conducted an audit of the management of special political missions by the Department of Political Affairs (DPA) as a follow-up to its previous report [YUN 2006, p. 63]. In its August report [A/64/294], OIOS noted that the main objective of the audit was to determine whether the recommendations contained in its previous report had been implemented, and to assess mitigating controls in place to address some high-risk areas that were identified by the OIOS risk assessment, as well as similar assessments conducted by DPA and the Board of Auditors. Those high-risk areas included internal governance and accountability mechanisms; strategic planning and management; and backstopping of special political missions and the Department's coordination strategy with partners. The audit also considered findings and recommendations from other oios audits and evaluations of special political missions. Of the 15 recommendations made in the previous oios audit, six had been implemented, seven were in progress and two had been closed without implementation, as they had been overtaken by the establishment of the Department of Field Support (dfs).

The audit found that the revision of dpko's mandate to reflect its responsibilities for directing the substantive operations of special political missions was nearing completion. The development of a support strategy and service-level agreement between dpa and dfs for providing administrative support to special political missions was still in progress; hence, the Organization was exposed to the risk of unclear responsibilities. The development of policies and standard processes and guidelines as a tool for equipping the dpa desk officers to backstop special political missions was also still in progress, and dpa needed to develop standard operating procedures for the start-up planning for such missions to facilitate the deployment of new missions. The oios recommendations about improving the quality of the budgets of special political missions had been implemented; however, the control of dpa over the preparation of the budgets of such missions could be improved.

The audit found that dpa did not have a proper performance management system to measure and monitor how effectively the regional divisions and their staff were managing special political missions, the responsibilities of regional divisions and their staff had not been clearly defined, and the development of accountability mechanisms for heads of dpa-led special political missions had not been finalized.

From 1999 to 2009, the budgets of special political missions increased almost tenfold, from $47.5 million to $461.2 million—a threefold increase without the budgets for the United Nations Assistance Mission in Afghanistan (unama) and the United Nations Assistance Mission for Iraq (unami)—but there was no corresponding increase in the overall budget of dpa. Oios also found that the budget of dpa did not distinguish the requirements for managing special political missions from those for other Department activities. As regards large special political missions such as unami, when the Department is, exceptionally, assigned the lead role, it should propose to the General Assembly an appropriate mechanism to use mission posts at Headquarters to ensure that it had stable and adequate capacity for providing backstopping services.

Dpa had made some progress in implementing the oios recommendations, the report concluded, but more needed to be done to ensure effective and efficient backstopping of special political missions.

Roster of 2009 political missions and offices

On 1 January 2009, 12 UN political missions and offices were in operation: 6 in Africa, 4 in Asia and the Pacific and 2 in the Middle East. On 21 December, the Security Council welcomed the establishment of the United Nations Integrated Peacebuilding Office in the Central African Republic (binuca) on 1 January 2010 for a period of one year, to succeed the United Nations Peacebuilding Office in the Central African Republic (bonuca). On 26 June 2009, the Council extended the mandate of the United Nations Peacebuilding Support Office in Guinea-Bissau (unogbis) until 31 December, and requested that the Secretary-General establish a United Nations Integrated Peacebuilding Office in Guinea-Bissau (uniogbis) to succeed unogbis for an initial 12-month period, beginning on 1 January 2010. Thus, 12 missions and offices were in operation at the end of the year.

Also in Africa, the Council, on 16 January, welcomed the Secretary-General's proposal [YUN 2008, p. 285] to establish within the United Nations Political Office for Somalia (unpos) a dedicated capacity that would include expertise in police and military training, planning for future disarmament, demobilization and reintegration activities and security sector reform activities, as well as rule of law and correction components. The Council extended the mandate of the United Nations Integrated Peacebuilding Office in Sierra Leone (unipsil) until 30 September 2010, and the United Nations Integrated Office in Burundi (binub) until 31 December 2010.

With regard to Asia and the Pacific, the Council renewed the mandate of the United Nations Mission in Nepal (unmin) to 23 January 2010, unama until 23 March 2010 and unami until 31 December 2010. In the Democratic People's Republic of Korea, the United Nations Command continued to implement the maintenance of the 1953 Armistice Agreement [YUN 1953, p. 136].

(For the financing of UN political and peacebuilding missions, see PART FIVE, Chapter II.)

UNPOS

United Nations Political Office for Somalia
Established: 15 April 1995.

Mandate: To monitor the situation in Somalia and keep the Security Council informed, particularly about developments affecting the humanitarian and security situations, repatriation of refugees and impacts on neighbouring countries.

Special Representative of the Secretary-General: Ahmedou Ould-Abdallah (Mauritania).

Strength: 43 international civilian staff, 15 local civilian staff.

UNOGBIS

United Nations Peacebuilding Support Office in Guinea-Bissau

Established: 3 March 1999.

Ended: December 2009. Succeeded by the United Nations Integrated Peacebuilding Office in Guinea-Bissau (UNIOGBIS).

Mandate: To support efforts to consolidate constitutional rule, enhance political dialogue and promote national reconciliation, respect for the rule of law and human rights; assist in strengthening the capacity of national institutions; and support security sector reform.

Representative of the Secretary-General: Joseph Mutaboba (Rwanda).

Strength: 12 international civilian staff, 13 local civilian staff, 2 military advisers, 1 police adviser.

UNSCO

Office of the United Nations Special Coordinator for the Middle East

Established: 1 October 1999.

Mandate: To act as the focal point for the United Nations contribution to the peace process and to enhance UN humanitarian and development assistance.

Special Coordinator for the Middle East Peace Process and Personal Representative of the Secretary-General to the Palestine Liberation Organization and the Palestinian Authority: Robert H. Serry (Netherlands).

Strength: 29 international civilian staff, 26 local civilian staff.

BONUCA

United Nations Peacebuilding Office in the Central African Republic

Established: 15 February 2000.

Ended: December 2009. Succeeded by the United Nations Integrated Peacebuilding Office in the Central African Republic (BINUCA).

Mandate: To support efforts to consolidate peace and promote national reconstruction and economic recovery.

Representative of the Secretary-General: Sahle-Work Zewde (Ethiopia).

Strength: 24 international civilian staff, 53 local civilian staff, 5 military advisers, 6 police, 3 UN volunteers.

UNSCOL

Office of the United Nations Special Coordinator for Lebanon (formerly known as the Office of the Personal Representative of the Secretary-General for Southern Lebanon)

Established: 16 February 2007.

Mandate: To represent the Secretary-General politically and coordinate UN work in Lebanon.

Special Coordinator for Lebanon: Michael C. Williams (United Kingdom).

Strength: 20 international civilian staff, 51 local civilian staff.

UNOWA

Office of the Special Representative of the Secretary-General for West Africa

Established: 29 November 2001.

Mandate: To enhance the contribution of the United Nations towards the achievement of peace and security priorities in West Africa.

Special Representative of the Secretary-General: Said Djinnit (Algeria).

Strength: 13 international civilian staff, 10 local civilian staff, 4 military advisers.

UNAMA

United Nations Assistance Mission in Afghanistan

Established: 28 March 2002.

Mandate: To fulfil the tasks and responsibilities entrusted to the United Nations in the Bonn Agreement; promote national reconciliation and rapprochement; manage UN humanitarian relief, recovery and reconstruction activities; and assist in the promotion of the political process.

Special Representative of the Secretary-General: Kai Eide (Norway).

Strength: 339 international civilian staff, 1,298 local civilian staff, 17 military observers, 3 police, 53 UN volunteers.

UNAMI

United Nations Assistance Mission for Iraq

Established: 14 August 2003.

Mandate: To advise, support and assist the Government and the Independent High Electoral Commission on the development of processes for holding elections and referenda, as well as to promote political facilitation, regional dialogue, human rights, and reconstruction and development.

Special Representative of the Secretary-General: Ad Melkert (Netherlands).

Strength (staff based in Iraq, Jordan and Kuwait): 321 international civilian staff, 456 local civilian staff, 221 troops, 11 military observers.

UNIPSIL

United Nations Integrated Peacebuilding Office in Sierra Leone

Established: 1 October 2008.

Mandate: To provide political support for resolving tensions and threats of potential conflict; monitor and promote human rights, democratic institutions and the rule of law, including efforts to counter transnational organized crime and drug trafficking; consolidate good governance reforms, with a focus on anti-corruption instruments; support decentralization, reviewing the 1991 Constitution and the enactment of legislation; and support the work of the Peacebuilding Commission, the implementation of the Sierra Leone Cooperation Framework and projects supported by the Peacebuilding Fund.

Executive Representative of the Secretary-General: Michael von der Schulenburg (Germany).

Strength: 29 international civilian staff, 29 local civilian staff.

BINUB

United Nations Integrated Office in Burundi

Established: 1 January 2007.

Mandate: To support the Government in its efforts towards long-term peace and stability, focusing on peace consolidation and democratic governance; disarmament, demobilization and reintegration; security sector reform; promotion and protection of human rights and measures to end impunity; and donor and UN agency coordination.

Executive Representative of the Secretary-General: Youssef Mahmoud (Tunisia).

Strength: 125 international civilian staff, 239 local civilian staff, 5 military observers, 10 police, 50 UN volunteers.

UNMIN

United Nations Mission in Nepal

Established: 23 January 2007.

Mandate: To support the peace process by: monitoring the management of arms and armed personnel of the Nepal Army and the Maoist Army; assisting the parties, through a Joint Monitoring Coordinating Committee, in implementing the agreement on the management of arms and armed personnel; assisting in the monitoring of ceasefire agreements; and providing technical assistance to the Election Commission.

Representative of the Secretary-General: Karin Landgren (Sweden).

Strength: 48 international civilian staff, 119 local civilian staff, 72 military observers, 19 UN volunteers.

UNRCCA

United Nations Regional Centre for Preventive Diplomacy for Central Asia

Established: 10 December 2007.

Mandate: To liaise with Governments of the region and other parties on preventive diplomacy issues; monitor and analyse the situation on the ground and provide the Secretary-General with information related to conflict prevention; facilitate coordination and information exchange with regional organizations; and support the efforts of regional coordinators and the UN system in promoting an integrated approach to preventive development and humanitarian assistance.

Special Representative of the Secretary-General: Miroslav Jenča (Slovakia).

Strength: 7 international civilian staff, 13 local civilian staff.

Threats to international peace and security

International terrorism

Global Counter-Terrorism Strategy

The Secretary-General in 2005 established the Counter-Terrorism Implementation Task Force [YUN 2005, p. 77] to bring together key UN system actors and their partners dealing with counter-terrorism issues.

The General Assembly in 2006, by resolution 60/288 [YUN 2006, p. 66], adopted the Global Counter-Terrorism Strategy—a common strategic approach to fight terrorism worldwide. The Strategy welcomed the Secretary-General's intention to institutionalize the Task Force within the Secretariat in order to ensure overall coordination and coherence in the UN system's counter-terrorism efforts.

On 24 December, by resolution 64/235, the Assembly requested the Secretary-General to provide the resources necessary to institutionalize the Task Force.

GENERAL ASSEMBLY ACTION

On 24 December [meeting 68], the General Assembly adopted **resolution 64/235** [draft: A/64/L.27 & Add.1] without vote [agenda item 115].

Institutionalization of the Counter-Terrorism Implementation Task Force

The General Assembly,

Recalling the United Nations Global Counter-Terrorism Strategy, contained in its resolution 60/288 of 8 September

2006, and the first review of the Strategy, contained in its resolution 62/272 of 5 September 2008,

Requests the Secretary-General to provide the resources necessary to finalize the institutionalization of the Counter-Terrorism Implementation Task Force without delay in order to ensure overall coordination and coherence in the counterterrorism efforts of the United Nations system.

Terrorist attacks in 2009

In 2009, terrorist attacks continued worldwide, resulting in the deaths of hundreds of innocent civilians and injuries to many others. Those attacks were condemned by the Security Council, Member States and the Secretary-General, who called for increased efforts to combat the threat they posed to international peace and security.

Afghanistan

On 11 February [SG/SM/12095], the Secretary-General condemned the acts of terrorism that had occurred on the same day against Government buildings in Kabul, which took the lives of at least 20 innocent civilians and injured many more. The Security Council condemned the attacks in a press statement [SC/9593], noting that the Taliban had claimed responsibility and reiterating that no terrorist act could reverse the path towards peace, democracy and reconstruction in Afghanistan.

On 1 April [SG/SM/12161], the Secretary-General said that he was appalled and saddened by suicide attacks that had occurred on the same day at the Provincial Office near the United Nations Office in Kandahar City, in which two people were reportedly killed and a large number of civilians injured, including one staff member of UNAMA.

On 17 August [SG/SM/12415], the Secretary-General condemned the suicide car bomb attack that had occurred on the same day in a central area of Kabul, in which seven people were reportedly killed and a large number of civilians were injured, including one UN staff member. He expressed concern at the indiscriminate violence days before the presidential and provincial elections scheduled for 20 August.

On 26 August [SG/SM/12425], the Secretary-General expressed shock and dismay regarding the attack that took place in Kandahar the previous evening, causing the death of over 40 civilians and injuring more than 80 others. On the same day the Council members condemned the attack in a press statement [SC/9735], underlining the need to bring perpetrators, organizers, financiers and sponsors of those acts of terrorism to justice.

On 8 October [SG/SM/12529], the Secretary-General condemned the senseless attack that had occurred on the same day in Kabul in the vicinity of the Indian Embassy and the Afghan Ministry of the Interior, which reportedly killed 17 and injured 80 more. On the same day the Council, in a press statement [SC/9763], condemned the terrorist suicide attack, which caused numerous deaths and injuries, including among Afghan civilians and the Embassy's security personnel, also noting that the Taliban had claimed responsibility for the attacks.

On 28 October [SG/SM/12570], the Secretary-General expressed shock and outrage at the cowardly attack on a guest house in central Kabul that had occurred on the same day, which killed five UN staff members and injured a number of others. He condemned the despicable and brutal killing, for which the Taliban claimed responsibility in an apparent effort to disrupt the second round of the presidential election. The Security Council, in a press statement [SC/9778], condemned the terrorist attack, which caused deaths and injuries among UN staff and members of the Afghan National Security Forces.

SECURITY COUNCIL ACTION

On 29 October [meeting 6211], following consultations among Security Council members, the President made statement **S/PRST/2009/28** on behalf of the Council:

> The Security Council expresses its strong condemnation of the terrorist attack in Kabul on 28 October 2009 and offers its condolences to the Secretary-General and the families of the victims.
>
> The Council condemns in the strongest terms the Taliban, who claimed responsibility for the attack and continue to attempt to destabilize the country.
>
> The Council expresses its strong support for the Secretary-General, his Special Representative for Afghanistan and all United Nations personnel in fulfilling their difficult but important tasks, further expresses solidarity with United Nations staff on the ground, and commends the determination of the United Nations not to be deterred by the tragic incident and to carry on its mission in Afghanistan.
>
> The Council stresses the need to ensure the security of United Nations staff and its support to this end. The Council expresses its support for the measures already taken by the Secretary-General in this regard and looks forward to the further detailed proposals from him.
>
> The Council expresses its solidarity with the people of Afghanistan and its support for the upcoming runoff presidential elections, which should be carried out as scheduled with the continued support of the United Nations.
>
> The Council renews its commitment to assisting Afghanistan on its path towards peace, democracy and reconstruction.

Indonesia

The Secretary-General, in a 17 July press statement [SG/SM/12371], condemned the bombings that occurred on the same day in two hotels in Jakarta.

SECURITY COUNCIL ACTION

On 17 July [meeting 6164], following consultations among Security Council members, the President made statement **S/PRST/2009/22** on behalf of the Council:

> The Security Council condemns in the strongest terms the terrorist attacks that occurred in Jakarta on 17 July 2009, causing numerous deaths and injuries. It expresses its deep sympathy and condolences to the victims of these heinous acts of terrorism and to their families, and to the people and Government of Indonesia.
>
> The Council underlines the need to bring the perpetrators, organizers, financers and sponsors of these reprehensible acts of terrorism to justice, and affirms its confidence in the Government of Indonesia, and urges all States, in accordance with their obligations under international law and relevant Council resolutions, to cooperate actively with the Indonesian authorities in this regard.
>
> The Council reaffirms that terrorism in all its forms and manifestations constitutes one of the most serious threats to international peace and security, and that any acts of terrorism are criminal and unjustifiable, regardless of their motivation, wherever, whenever and by whomsoever committed.
>
> The Council further reaffirms the need to combat by all means, in accordance with the Charter of the United Nations, threats to international peace and security caused by terrorist acts. The Council reminds States that they must ensure that measures taken to combat terrorism comply with all their obligations under international law, in particular international human rights, refugee and humanitarian law.
>
> The Council reiterates its determination to combat all forms of terrorism, in accordance with its responsibilities under the Charter.

Iraq

On 13 February [SG/SM/12101], the Secretary-General said that he was appalled by the suicide bomb attack that had occurred on the same day against Shia pilgrims near Baghdad and similar attacks targeting innocent civilians in the past days, which left dozens dead and wounded, including many women and children.

In a 25 April press statement [SC/9643], the Security Council condemned the terrorist attacks in Baghdad and Diyala on 23 and 24 April, which caused numerous deaths and injuries.

On 29 June [SG/SM/12341], the Secretary-General condemned the attacks and assassinations in Baghdad, Kirkuk and Anbar in recent days that killed and wounded a large number of Iraqis.

On 31 July [SG/SM/12392], the Secretary-General condemned the bomb attacks on five Shia mosques that had occurred on the same day in Baghdad, which left dozens dead and wounded, stressing that attacks against places of worship could not be justified by any political or religious cause. Noting that those attacks appeared to be aimed at provoking sectarian strife and undermining stability, he appealed to the Iraqi people to remain steadfast in their efforts to resolve differences through dialogue and achieve national reconciliation.

In a 19 August press statement [SC/9733], Council members condemned the series of terrorist attacks that occurred on that day in Baghdad, which caused numerous deaths and injuries and damage, including at the Ministry of Foreign of Affairs, other Government ministries and diplomatic missions.

On 26 October [SG/SM/12563], the Secretary-General said that he was shocked and saddened at the double car bombing attacks that had occurred on 25 October near the Iraqi Ministry of Justice and the Baghdad Provincial Governorate Building in central Baghdad, in which hundreds were killed and wounded. He condemned those senseless and indiscriminate acts of violence that targeted the innocent and aimed to disrupt Iraq's recovery. The Security Council condemned the attacks in a 25 October press statement [SC/9775].

On 16 November, by statement **S/PRST/2009/30** (see p. 370), the Council underlined its condemnation of the series of terrorist attacks that occurred on 19 August and 25 October 2009 in Baghdad, which caused numerous deaths, injuries and damage, including to Government institutions.

On 9 December [SC/9810], the Security Council condemned the series of terrorist attacks that occurred on 8 December in Baghdad, causing numerous deaths and injuries and damage.

Iran

On 29 May [SG/SM/12281], the Secretary-General condemned the previous day's bomb attack in a mosque in the city of Zahedan, which reportedly killed at least 20 people and wounded many others.

On 19 October [SG/SM/12553], the Secretary-General condemned the previous day's terrorist attacks in the Sistan-Baluchistan province, which resulted in the death of a large number of people and many injured. On 20 October [SC/9770], in a press statement, the Security Council condemned that deadly terrorist attack in the border city of Pishin, causing at least 57 deaths and 150 injuries.

Pakistan

On 2 February [SG/SM/12083], the Secretary-General condemned the attack that had occurred on the same day on two workers of the Office of the United Nations High Commissioner for Refugees (UNHCR) in Quetta, in which one refugee worker was killed and another abducted.

On 5 June [SG/SM/12292], the Secretary-General condemned the bomb attack that had occurred on the same day in a mosque in the Upper Dir district, which reportedly killed at least 30 people; he reiterated his rejection of such indiscriminate and reprehensible acts of violence.

On 16 July [SG/SM/12368], the Secretary-General said that he was shocked and saddened by the killing that had occurred on the same day of a senior UNHCR national staff member, Zill-e-Usman, in the Katcha Garhi camp for displaced people near Peshawar. He condemned the brutal attack on humanitarian personnel working for the well-being of the Pakistani people, in which, in addition, one camp guard was killed and a UN national staff member and a camp guard were injured.

On 18 September [SG/SM/12462], the Secretary-General condemned the suicide car bomb attack that had occurred on the same day at a village market in north-west Pakistan, which reportedly killed more than 30 people and injured dozens.

On 5 October [SG/SM/12516], the Secretary-General condemned the unjustifiable attack that had occurred on the same day at the Office of the World Food Programme (WFP) in Islamabad—a terrible tragedy for the United Nations and the whole humanitarian community in Pakistan. Five WFP staff members were killed in that attack.

On 28 October [SG/SM/12572], the Secretary-General condemned the bomb attack that had occurred on the same day at a market in Peshawar, reportedly killing more than 80 people, many of them women, and injuring more than 160. No cause could justify such inhuman and indiscriminate violence.

Somalia

On 17 September [SG/SM/12457], the Secretary-General expressed shock and outrage by the reported suicide attack that had occurred on the same day against the African Union Mission in Somalia (AMISOM) Force Headquarters in Mogadishu, which reportedly killed or wounded a number of AMISOM troops, including at the command level. He condemned the attack on those who were there to help foster peace.

On 3 December [SG/SM/12653], the Secretary-General condemned the suicide attack that had occurred on the same day at a graduation ceremony of medical students in Mogadishu. Reports indicated that at least 15 Somalis had lost their lives, among them three cabinet ministers of the Transitional Federal Government, graduating students and journalists; another minister was severely wounded.

SECURITY COUNCIL ACTION

On 3 December [meeting 6229], following consultations among Security Council members, the President made statement **S/PRST/2009/31** on behalf of the Council:

> The Security Council condemns in the strongest terms the terrorist attack on 3 December 2009 in Mogadishu at a graduation ceremony for Somali medical students at Benadir University, which resulted in the death of innocent civilians and the Somali Ministers of Health, Higher Education and Education. This was a criminal attack on people dedicated to building a peaceful, stable and prosperous future for the people of Somalia.
>
> The Council expresses its deepest sympathy and condolences to the families of those killed and to those injured in the attack, as well as to the Transitional Federal Government and the people of Somalia.
>
> The Council urges that a thorough investigation be conducted and that the perpetrators of this attack be brought swiftly to justice.
>
> The Council underlines its determination to continue to support the people of Somalia in their quest for peace and reconciliation, and the Transitional Federal Government as the legitimate authority in Somalia, and reiterates its full support for the Djibouti peace process, which provides a framework for reaching a lasting political solution in Somalia.
>
> The Council reaffirms its demand that all opposition groups immediately end attacks, put down their arms, renounce violence and join reconciliation efforts. The Council further calls upon all parties to abide by their obligations under international humanitarian law, in particular to respect the security of civilians, humanitarian workers and personnel of the African Union Mission in Somalia.
>
> The Council welcomes the work of the Mission in supporting the casualties of the attack and their relatives. It reiterates its strong support for the Mission and expresses its continued appreciation for the commitment of troops by the Governments of Uganda and Burundi.
>
> The Council reaffirms that Somalia's long-term security rests with the effective development by the Transitional Federal Government of the National Security Force and the Somali Police Force, within the framework of the Djibouti Agreement and in line with a national security strategy. The Council urges the international community to support the Somali security institutions, in coordination with the Mission, including through training and equipment.

Measures to eliminate international terrorism

In 2009, the United Nations strengthened its efforts to combat and eliminate international terrorism. The General Assembly, having considered the Secretary-General's report [A/64/161 & Add.1] on measures to eliminate international terrorism, the report of the Ad Hoc Committee established by General Assembly resolution 51/210 [A/64/37] and the oral report at the Assembly's sixty-fourth session [A/C.6/64/SR.14] of the Chairperson of the Working Group established by the Sixth (Legal) Committee, requested, by its **resolution 64/118** of 16 December (see p. 1309), that the Terrorism Prevention Branch of the United Nations Office on Drugs and Crime (UNODC) continue enhancing UN capabilities in preventing terrorism. It recognized, in the context of the United Nations Global Counter-Terrorism Strategy [YUN 2006, p. 66] and Security Council resolution 1373(2001) [YUN 2001, p. 61], the Branch's role in assisting States in becoming parties to and implementing the international conventions and protocols relating to terrorism and in strengthening international cooperation mechanisms in criminal matters related to terrorism.

In **resolution 64/38** of 2 December on measures to prevent terrorists from acquiring weapons of mass destruction (see p. 522), the Assembly urged Member States to strengthen measures to prevent terrorists from acquiring such weapons, their means of delivery, and materials and technologies related to their manufacture.

In **resolution 64/177** of 18 December (see p. 1100), on technical assistance for implementing the international conventions and protocols related to terrorism, the Assembly urged Member States to strengthen international cooperation in order to prevent and combat terrorism, including by entering into bilateral and multilateral treaties on extradition and mutual legal assistance.

Communications. During 2009, communications related to terrorism were submitted by Cuba [A/64/534-S/2009/593], Iran [A/63/695-S/2009/53, A/64/481] and the Republic of Korea [A/63/811-S/2009/179].

On 19 February [A/63/739-S/2009/114], New Zealand, on behalf of members of the Pacific Islands Forum based in New York, transmitted the conclusions of the regional consultation workshop on measures for the legislative implementation of the legal regime against terrorism in the Pacific region and related technical assistance delivery (Suva, Fiji, 2–3 June 2008).

On 4 May [A/63/844-S/2009/237], Kenya transmitted the outcome document of the subregional workshop on the preparation of responses to the Security Council

Committees dealing with counter-terrorism (Nairobi, 11–13 November 2008), hosted by Kenya and organized by the Terrorism Prevention Branch of UNODC, in cooperation with the experts of the Committees.

Counter-Terrorism Committee

In 2009, the Committee established pursuant to Council resolution 1373(2001), known as the Counter-Terrorism Committee (CTC), held 18 formal meetings and 5 informal meetings. The CTC Chairman submitted on 3 February and 27 July its work programmes for the periods from 1 January to 30 June [S/2009/71] and 1 July to 31 December [S/2009/389]. CTC was assisted in its work by the Counter-Terrorism Committee Executive Directorate (CTED).

On 5 October [S/2009/506], the Security Council announced that it had elected Ranko Vilović (Croatia) as Chairman of CTC for the period ending 31 December. On 11 December [S/2009/655], the Secretary-General informed the Security Council of his intention to extend the appointment of Mike Smith (Australia) as CTED Executive Director until 31 December 2010. On 16 December [S/2009/656], the Council took note of that intention.

Report of CTC Acting Chairman (May). Reporting to the Security Council on 26 May [meeting 6128], the CTC Acting Chairman said that stocktaking had allowed CTC to enhance its regular dialogue with Member States and identify areas where the implementation of resolution 1373(2001) was still inadequate. The Committee had continued to organize visits to Member States as a fundamental component of its activities for the effective monitoring of the implementation of resolution 1373(2001). Along with comprehensive visits, CTED's revised organizational plan envisaged a more flexible approach by allowing shorter visits focused on one or two aspects of the concerned State's counter-terrorism regime. The plan also laid out the basis for regional visits and for missions that would examine examples of good practice, as well as vulnerabilities.

The Executive Directorate had compiled a technical guide to the implementation of resolution 1373(2001), covering such areas as terrorist financing; border security, arms trafficking and law enforcement; general legal issues, including legislation, extradition, and mutual legal assistance; and human rights aspects of counter-terrorism in the context of resolution 1373(2001).

Interim review (June). Pursuant to resolution 1805(2008) [YUN 2008, p. 71], by which the Security Council had decided to conduct an interim review of CTED, the CTC Acting Chairman, in June, submitted a report [S/2009/289] prepared for that review. The report concluded that the Executive Directorate had provided the Committee with valuable support and fulfilled the tasks assigned to it. The Committee welcomed the achievements of the Executive Directorate over the 14 months since the adoption of resolution 1805(2008), in particular in deepening its dialogue with Member States in all regions, developing a more proactive strategy to facilitate technical assistance and becoming more engaged with its partner organizations. The Committee recognized that the Executive Directorate had become more consistent in its assessments and was working across all regions in a more harmonized and focused way, and encouraged it to strengthen its capacity to deliver on that crucial aspect of its mandate.

The Security Council conducted the interim review of the work of CTED on 11 June [A/64/2]. It expressed its appreciation for the work undertaken by the Executive Directorate and supported the content of the report of the CTC Acting Chairman.

Report of CTC Chairman (November). The Chairman of the Committee briefed the Security Council on 13 November [meeting 6217], informing it about the adoption of the interim review of the Executive Directorate, the finalization of the preliminary implementation assessments and the related stocktaking process, as well as about visits to and dialogue with Member States. As for implementation of resolution 1624(2005) [YUN 2005, p. 102], 104 Member States had submitted reports on their implementation of the resolution. The Committee had encouraged those States that had not yet done so to submit the relevant information; it had also encouraged Member States to become parties to and implement the 16 international counter-terrorism instruments.

Implementation of resolution 1373(2001). Resolution 1373(2001) set out a comprehensive agenda of counter-terrorism activities, including steps aimed at bringing to justice perpetrators of terrorist acts as well as those who harboured, aided and supported them. It required States to cooperate on a wide range of counter-terrorism issues and to report to the Committee on their implementation of the resolution. As at 31 July [A/64/2], the Committee had received 711 reports from Member States and other entities. It had also received 100 reports from Member States pursuant to resolution 1624(2005) which called on States to combat terrorism, including prohibiting by law and preventing incitement to commit terrorist acts.

On 3 December, the CTC Chairman submitted the second report of CTC on the implementation of resolution 1373(2001) [S/2009/620], focusing on counter-terrorism legislation, counter-financing of terrorism, law enforcement, border control and international cooperation. The report assessed the implementation of resolution 1373(2001) in regions and subregions, drew conclusions about progress in its implementation and provided recommendations for future action by the Committee.

Reports of States. Between March and December, the CTC Chairman transmitted to the Council President reports submitted by Member States on action they had taken or planned to take to implement resolutions 1373(2001) and 1624(2005) [S/2009/133, S/2009/134, S/2009/448, S/2009/474, S/2009/498, S/2009/617, S/2009/618].

Nuclear and radiological terrorism

The General Conference of the International Atomic Energy Agency, at its fifty-third session (Vienna, 14–18 September), adopted resolution GC(53)/RES/11 on nuclear security, including measures to protect against nuclear and radiological terrorism, in which it called upon Member States to provide the necessary support to international efforts to enhance nuclear security through bilateral, regional and international arrangements. It called upon States parties to the Convention on the Physical Protection of Nuclear Material to work towards its universal adherence, to accelerate the ratification of the amendment to the Convention expanding its scope and to act for the early entry into force of that amendment. It encouraged them to act in accordance with the object and purpose of the amendment until such time as it entered into force, and encouraged States that had not done so to adhere to the Convention and the amendment as soon as possible. The amendment would make it legally binding for States parties to protect nuclear facilities and material in peaceful domestic use, storage and transport; it provided for expanded State cooperation regarding rapid measures to locate and recover stolen or smuggled nuclear material, mitigate any radiological consequences of sabotage, and prevent and combat related offences.

Peacekeeping operations

In 2009, the General Assembly and the Security Council continued to oversee the management and operation of UN peacekeeping missions. The Council addressed key issues pertaining to the overall conduct of those operations and reviewed the individual mandates of several ongoing operations. The Assembly took action on a number of financial and administrative matters.

The Department of Peacekeeping Operations (DPKO) continued to implement the recommendations of the Special Committee on Peacekeeping Operations, whose mandate was to review the whole question of peacekeeping operations in all their aspects.

Security Council consideration (January). On 23 January [meeting 6075], the Council held a debate on peacekeeping operations, following an informal seminar on 22 January organized by France and the United Kingdom. The two countries also issued a non-paper on peacekeeping.

The Under-Secretary-General for Peacekeeping Operations, Alain Le Roy, said that peacekeeping operations were more numerous and widely spread than at any time in UN history, with mandates that were both more complex and more robust than ever. UN peacekeeping was clearly overstretched, both operationally and politically. With 18 operations deployed in five continents and with 78,000 military, 11,500 police and 23,500 civilians deployed, the operational challenge of maintaining full support to all missions and mounting new ones was far beyond what the Brahimi reforms had envisaged. At the same time, many missions carried out mandates that represented much more than the deployment of uniformed personnel, being fundamentally political operations supporting complex transitions to peace within deeply divided countries. To ensure that UN peacekeeping remained a viable and indeed a stronger instrument, it was necessary to begin finding new potential contributors to peacekeeping. To deploy at high pace into remote territories, innovative ways should be found to draw on support which only Member States could provide. On-hand capacities were needed to reinforce missions if a crisis erupted. In missions where the United Nations had stabilized the peace process but where lack of peacebuilding investment was threatening gains, critical resources needed to flow to shore up peacekeeping. There was a need for a "political surge"—for intensifying political efforts to support peace processes or to help realize peace where it had not been realized.

The Under-Secretary-General for Field Support, Susana Malcorra, said that her Department was supporting 16 peacekeeping missions and 18 special political missions, and administered more than 22,000 staff members. It operated and maintained more than 250 medical facilities, 300 aircraft, 18,000 vehicles and 40,000 computers. The creation of the Department of Field Support (DFS) had led to greater clarity of purpose and improved focus on service delivery in the field, becoming "field-centric". Among the challenges, she listed finding a more strategic approach to doing its business; exploring new, more efficient ways of working; doing it "right and fast"; partnering with Member States, UN entities, regional organizations and civil society in meeting the support challenge; and finding a regulatory framework that was strong yet agile, prudent yet reasonable. To address those concerns, her Department was developing a support strategy that would include regional support

hubs rather than attempting to recreate a full support structure in each and every mission.

Other speakers included the Head of the United Nations Stabilization Mission in Haiti, Hédi Annabi; representatives of major troop contributors (India, Pakistan, Jordan, Uruguay); and representatives of the European Union (EU), the African Union (AU) and the Non-Aligned Movement (NAM). Participants welcomed the Franco-British initiative to address the challenges of peacekeeping, and stressed the need to reinforce dialogue among the main actors, particularly with troop-contributing countries, at all stages of the preparation, conduct and evaluation of operations.

Communication. On 23 February [S/2009/112], France and the United Kingdom transmitted to the Security Council an updated version of the United Kingdom-France non-paper on peacekeeping, which was revised to take account of the discussion at the informal seminar on 22 January and the Council debate on 23 January.

Security Council consideration (June). On 29 June [meeting 6153], the Council held a day-long debate on the reform of peacekeeping operations, with the participation of major troop- and police-contributing countries and including the EU, the AU and NAM. The Under-Secretaries-General for Peacekeeping Operations and Field Support briefed the Council on their joint review of the UN peacekeeping system and its expected outcome, in the form of a non-paper entitled "A new partnership agenda: charting a new horizon for United Nations peacekeeping".

The Under-Secretary-General for Peacekeeping Operations said that the theme of the meeting—the relationship between the Council and the police- and troop-contributing countries—reflected the fact that UN peacekeeping was a global partnership that brought together the Council, with its legal and political authority, with the Member States. In the current global environment, financial constraints required a review of the basic models of peacekeeping. The costs, troop numbers and capability requirements could not all continue to rise indefinitely.

DPKO and DFS were working jointly on New Horizon, an initiative to help form a new partnership agenda for peacekeeping. The initiative focused on critical peacekeeping tasks and functions requiring a renewed consensus on issues such as the role of peacekeepers in civilian protection; measures to improve mission design, resourcing and deployment; proposals on assessing and building the capacities needed for future peacekeeping; and a strategy to create a stronger, more flexible support system.

The Under-Secretary-General for Field Support noted that the past decade had seen several useful innovations, including the creation of the Strategic Deployment Stocks that allowed the United Nations to equip and supply missions more quickly, and the establishment of a Peacekeeping Reserve Fund allowing for commitment authority of up to $50 million in advance of a Security Council mandate. There was a need for a lighter mission footprint, faster turnaround and greater use of local staff and local suppliers. One way to build capability and performance was to invest more in technology-driven solutions, such as better information analysis, improved communications and higher-performing equipment.

In the debate that followed, in which 35 delegations spoke, many Member States underlined their support for reform initiatives, as well as the need to strengthen coordination and cooperation among the Security Council, the troop- and police-contributing countries and the Secretariat.

Security Council consideration (August). The Council on 5 August held a day-long debate on peacekeeping [meeting 6178] attended by some 20 force and police commanders of UN peacekeeping missions. Opening the debate, Council President John Sawers (United Kingdom) said that in January the United Kingdom and France had launched an initiative that sought to ensure that the Council could play its part to best effect. In the early stages, the focus had been on strategic oversight of peacekeeping, seeking to ensure that mandates were credible, measurable and achievable. The Council had also sought ways to improve information-sharing and consultations with countries contributing troops and police.

The Under-Secretaries-General for Peacekeeping Operations and for Field Support briefed the Council on the non-paper entitled "A new partnership agenda: charting a new horizon for United Nations peacekeeping", the result of their joint review of the UN peacekeeping system. The Under-Secretary-General for Peacekeeping Operations outlined the recommendations contained in the non-paper, which was part of the New Horizon process to reinvigorate the peacekeeping partnership. The document highlighted the importance of enhanced information-sharing, consultations and communication and effective planning, which depended upon peacekeeping partners indicating clearly and early on where and how they might be able to assist in establishing an operation. The non-paper also examined ways to improve management and oversight, while highlighting the need to strengthen command-and-control systems at every level, including through more robust accountability frameworks.

The Under-Secretary-General for Field Support said that one of the key enablers of the New Horizon initiative would be the support strategy, the overarching goal of which was to provide improved support services with quality, speed and efficiency. DFS would develop options, outline opportunities to improve and

present sound business plans to support the decision process.

In the debate that followed, participants stressed the necessity of a comprehensive reform agenda, featuring all aspects of the peacekeeping machinery, including the political-strategic, administrative, financial and operational aspects.

SECURITY COUNCIL ACTION

On 5 August [meeting 6178], following consultations among Security Council members, the President made statement **S/PRST/2009/24** on behalf of the Council:

The Security Council reaffirms the recommendations made in its resolutions 1327(2000) and 1353(2001) and in the statements by its President of 3 May and 4 November 1994, 28 March 1996, 31 January 2001 and 17 May 2004 and the note by its President of 14 January 2002 and confirms its intention to strengthen further efforts to implement fully those recommendations. The Council recalls, in particular, from the statement by its President of 3 May 1994, the appropriate factors that should be taken into account when the establishment of a new peacekeeping operation is under consideration.

The Council believes that United Nations peacekeeping is a unique global partnership that draws together the contributions and commitment of the entire United Nations system. The Council is committed to strengthening this partnership. The Council recognizes the important work conducted by the Special Committee on Peacekeeping Operations of the General Assembly, the Security Council Working Group on Peacekeeping Operations, the Fifth Committee of the Assembly and the Secretariat to ensure that peacekeeping efforts provide the best possible results.

The Council has endeavoured in the past six months to improve its dialogue with the Secretariat and with troop- and police-contributing countries on the collective oversight of peacekeeping operations and to develop the following practices:

(i) Regular dialogue with the Secretariat on the general challenges of peacekeeping;

(ii) Efforts to deepen consultations with troop- and police-contributing countries, including through the Working Group on Peacekeeping Operations and the debates organized on 23 January and 29 June 2009;

(iii) Organization of political-military meetings on specific operations to improve the shared analysis of operational challenges;

(iv) Encouraging regular updating of planning documents by the Secretariat to ensure consistency with mandates;

(v) Improved monitoring and evaluation, through the use of benchmarks, as and where appropriate, that enable progress to be charted against a comprehensive and integrated strategy.

The Council has identified several areas where further reflection is required to improve the preparation, planning, monitoring and evaluation, and completion of peacekeeping operations:

  (i) Ensuring that mandates for peacekeeping operations are clear, credible and achievable and matched by appropriate resources. The Council stresses the need regularly to assess, in consultation with other stakeholders, the strength, mandate and composition of peacekeeping operations with a view to making the necessary adjustments where appropriate, according to progress achieved or changing circumstances on the ground;

  (ii) Better information-sharing, particularly on the military operational challenges, through, inter alia, systematic consultation by the Secretariat with Member States in advance of the deployment of a technical assessment mission on its objectives and broad parameters, and debriefing on its main findings on its return. The Council encourages the practice of holding meetings between Council members and the Secretariat at the political-military expert level prior to discussion of mandate renewals. The Council recognizes the need to improve its access to military advice, and intends to pursue its work on mechanisms to that effect. The Council will continue to review the role of the Military Staff Committee;

  (iii) The Council intends to increase its interaction with the Secretariat in the early phase of mandate drafting and throughout mission deployment on the military, police, justice, rule of law and peacebuilding dimensions of an operation;

  (iv) Earlier and more meaningful engagement with troop- and police-contributing countries before the renewal or modification of the mandate of a peacekeeping operation. The Council welcomes practical suggestions to deepen such consultations. It recognizes that, through their experience and expertise, troop- and police-contributing countries can greatly contribute to effective planning, decision-making and deployment of peacekeeping operations. In this regard, the Council welcomes the interim report of its Working Group on Peacekeeping Operations and encourages the Working Group to continue to address the issue of cooperation with troop- and police-contributing countries and other stakeholders. The Council commits to making progress on this issue and to reviewing its progress in 2010;

  (v) Greater awareness in the Council of the resource and field support implications of its decisions. The Council requests that, where a new peacekeeping mission is proposed, or where significant change to a mandate is envisaged, an estimate of the resource implications for the mission be provided to it;

  (vi) Enhanced awareness in the Council of the strategic challenges faced across peacekeeping operations. The Council welcomes the briefings to that effect received from the Department of Peacekeeping Operations and the Department of Field Support of the Secretariat since January 2009, which should continue on a regular basis.

The Council recognizes the need to weigh the full range of responses when addressing a situation which may endanger international peace and security, and to deploy United Nations peacekeeping missions only as an accompaniment, not as an alternative, to a political strategy. The Council recognizes the importance of mobilizing and maintaining the political and operational support of all stakeholders.

The Council recognizes the urgent need to increase the pool of available troop and police contributors and welcomes efforts of Member States to coordinate bilateral assistance to them. The Council supports efforts to improve cooperation and coordination throughout the life of a mission with relevant regional and subregional organizations and other partners. The Council recognizes the priority of strengthening the capacity of the African Union, and the role of regional and subregional organizations, in maintaining international peace and security in accordance with Chapter VIII of the Charter of the United Nations.

The Council welcomes efforts by the Secretariat to review peacekeeping operations and to provide enhanced planning and support, and encourages the Secretariat to deepen those efforts. In this regard, the Council takes note of the assessments and recommendations provided in the non-paper entitled 'A new partnership agenda: charting a new horizon for United Nations peacekeeping' and the support strategy contained therein, and intends to give them careful consideration.

The Council recognizes that further debate is required among Member States, including in the Special Committee on Peacekeeping Operations, to develop a wider consensus on a range of issues, including the robust approach to peacekeeping and the implementation of protection of civilians mandates. The Council reaffirms the relevant provisions of its resolution 1674(2006) and in this regard looks forward to reviewing the implementation of protection of civilians mandates later in 2009.

The Council recalls the statement by its President of 22 July 2009 on post-conflict peacebuilding and, in particular, re-emphasizes the need for coherence between, and integration of, peacemaking, peacekeeping, peacebuilding and development to achieve an effective response to post-conflict situations from the outset. The Council requests the Secretary-General to provide in his reports on specific missions an indication of progress towards achieving a coordinated United Nations approach in-country and, in particular, on critical gaps to achieving peacebuilding objectives alongside the mission.

The Council remains committed to improving further the overall performance of United Nations peacekeeping and will conduct a further review in early 2010.

General aspects of UN peacekeeping

Strengthening operational capacity

In July, *A New Partnership Agenda: Charting a New Horizon for United Nations Peacekeeping*, developed by DPKO and DFS, was released to UN Member States and peacekeeping partners as part of a process aimed at assessing the major policy dilemmas facing UN peacekeeping, as well as to reinvigorate the dialogue on possible solutions.

The Special Committee on Peacekeeping Operations, at its 2009 substantive session [A/63/19], encouraged the two Departments to engage with troop-contributing countries in the development of the New Horizon initiative and looked forward for close interaction between the Secretariat and Member States. Having discussed extensively the concerns about the use of military utility helicopters in peacekeeping missions, the Special Committee requested that the Secretary-General submit to the General Assembly, before the end of 2009, a report on the current status and developments in the area of aviation safety in UN peacekeeping, including administrative and safety arrangements related to the management and use of military utility helicopters in peacekeeping missions.

Noting the sustained increase of the police dimension in a number of missions, the Special Committee stressed the importance of maintaining an appropriate support capacity at Headquarters to ensure an adequate level of oversight and guidance to the field. It called upon the Secretariat to continue its efforts in developing standard operating guidelines and procedures and guidelines for UN policing. It also took note of the report of the informal open-ended working group on enhanced rapidly deployable capacities [A/AC.121/2009/1], which agreed that the concept was currently not viable, given the lack of appropriate financial arrangements and support from Member States. The Special Committee invited the Secretariat to explore other possibilities until its next session, in order to make the necessary capacities available for UN peacekeeping missions in crisis. It also reiterated the need for the full implementation of the integrated mission planning process.

Strategies for complex peacekeeping operations

The Special Committee on Peacekeeping Operations [A/63/19] stressed that peacekeeping operations needed to be complemented with activities aimed at improving the living conditions of the affected populations, including quick implementation of highly effective and visible projects that helped to create jobs and deliver basic social services in the post-conflict phase. The Special Committee gave particular attention to issues relating to peacebuilding and the Peacebuilding Commission; disarmament, demobilization and reintegration; security sector reform; the rule of law; gender and peacekeeping; children and peacekeeping; and HIV/AIDS and other health-related issues.

The Special Committee welcomed the implementation of quick-impact projects by peacekeeping opera-

tions, which made an important contribution to the implementation of mandates by addressing the immediate needs of local populations and building support for peacekeeping missions, their mandates and the peace processes. It also stressed the importance of the effective and full implementation of other mandated tasks, such as support to the restoration and extension of State authority, support to political processes and protection of civilians under imminent threat of violence.

Safety and security

The Special Committee on Peacekeeping Operations [A/63/19] expressed its concern about the precarious security environment prevailing in many peacekeeping missions, calling on the Secretariat to give utmost priority to enhancing the safety and security of UN and associated personnel. Noting that some deployed troop formations were being stretched to cover geographic areas that exceeded their capacities, the Special Committee urged DPKO to ensure that peacekeeping personnel were deployed in accordance with agreed concepts of operation and deployment arrangements. It requested that the Secretariat present a thorough screening and verification policy before hiring local security personnel, including background checks on any criminal and human rights violations of the candidates, as well as links to security companies.

The Special Committee underlined the importance of adequate measures to ensure the safety and security of military and police officers, especially unarmed military observers. Concerned at the loss of lives as a result of the negligence and incompetence of medical staff, it emphasized the responsibility of the United Nations to ensure that medical personnel assigned in mission areas were qualified to provide immediate and proper medical attention to peacekeepers, and to hold them accountable. The Special Committee welcomed progress made in developing the Joint Operations Centres and Joint Mission Analysis Centres in DPKO-led field missions, and looked forward to completion of the draft guidelines on the Joint Mission Analysis Centres before its 2010 session.

Conduct and discipline

The Special Committee on Peacekeeping Operations [A/63/19] reaffirmed the need to ensure that all peacekeeping personnel function in a manner that preserved the image, credibility, impartiality and integrity of the United Nations. It emphasized that the same standards of conduct must be applied to all categories of UN peacekeeping personnel. Violations of those standards would result in appropriate action within the authority of the

Secretary-General, while criminal and disciplinary responsibility in respect of members of national contingents would depend on the national law of the Member State concerned. It reiterated that troop-contributing countries bore the primary responsibility for maintaining discipline among their contingents deployed in peacekeeping missions.

The Special Committee took note of the Secretary-General's 2007 report on strengthening investigations [YUN 2007, p. 1473] and looked forward to the outcome of the General Assembly's deliberations on it. In June, the Assembly, by **resolution 63/287** (see p. 84), endorsed the principle of restructuring the Investigation Division of the Office of Internal Oversight Services (OIOS). It requested that OIOS undertake a three-year pilot project involving investigation centres based in New York, Nairobi, and Vienna.

Sexual exploitation and abuse in UN peacekeeping operations

Report of Secretary-General. Pursuant to General Assembly resolution 57/306 [YUN 2003, p. 1237], the Secretary-General, in February, submitted a report [A/63/720] on special measures for protection from sexual exploitation and sexual abuse, presenting data on allegations of sexual exploitation and abuse in the UN system during 2008. There were 83 allegations of abuse involving personnel of DPKO and DFS, marking a decrease from 2006 (357) and 2007 (127). Of that number, 34 were considered "egregious" forms of sexual exploitation and abuse, namely sexual exploitation and abuse of minors, including rape. Eighty out of 83 cases had been investigated. Of those involving military personnel, 58 cases had been substantiated; among civilian personnel, 4 cases; and among police and corrections personnel, 8 cases. DPKO and DFS had communicated the results of those investigations to the relevant troop- or police-contributing countries and the individuals were repatriated and barred from future peacekeeping operations. The decrease in the number of allegations could be attributed to increased training and awareness-raising, but a change in how data was being collected in the past few years might also have contributed to the lower number. Nevertheless, there had been an increase in the number of allegations that had been substantiated, particularly allegations involving minors. That situation would be monitored closely. The report also described progress made in enforcing UN standards of conduct related to sexual exploitation and abuse.

On 30 June, the General Assembly deferred consideration of the Secretary-General's report until its sixty-fourth session (**decision 63/550 C**).

Special Committee on Peacekeeping Operations consideration. The Special Committee [A/63/19] un-derlined the gravity of all acts of sexual and gender-based violence, including sexual exploitation and abuse, and stressed the importance of addressing the needs of victims. The Special Committee recognized the work undertaken by gender advisers in the field and by the DPKO gender trainer. Underlining the need to finalize and implement the gender training strategy, the Special Committee looked forward to working with the Secretary-General in developing and implementing training programmes for all peacekeeping personnel to help them better prevent, recognize and respond to sexual violence and other forms of violence against women and girls.

The Special Committee underlined the importance of implementing the policy of zero tolerance of sexual exploitation and abuse in UN peacekeeping operations, and welcomed progress made towards the elimination and prevention of misconduct, including sexual exploitation and abuse. However, while noting the continuing decline in the number of allegations of sexual exploitation and abuse, the Special Committee regretted that the number of the most egregious allegations had not gone down. It reiterated its suggestion for disaggregating such data according to the type of serious misconduct alleged, to permit a deeper analysis. The Special Committee also welcomed the adoption of General Assembly resolution 62/214 [YUN 2007, p. 1519] containing the United Nations Comprehensive Strategy on Assistance and Support to Victims of Sexual Exploitation and Abuse by United Nations Staff and Related Personnel.

Report of Secretary-General. Pursuant to resolution 62/214, the Secretary-General in July reported [A/64/176] on action taken to implement the Comprehensive Strategy, which sought to ensure that victims of sexual exploitation and abuse by UN staff and related personnel received appropriate and timely assistance and support in the form of medical care, legal services, support for psychological and social care and immediate material care, including food, clothing and shelter. He reviewed the approach adopted to implement the Strategy, discussed ongoing activities at country and agency levels, identified challenges and lessons learned and provided recommendations on the way forward.

Cooperation with troop-contributing countries

The Special Committee on Peacekeeping Operations [A/63/19] stressed the need to enhance the relationship between those who planned, mandated and managed UN peacekeeping operations and those who implemented the operations' mandates, with troop-contributing countries involved early and fully in all aspects and stages of those operations. To enhance transparency and effectiveness, the Special Committee urged the Secretariat to circulate in a timely manner the reports of the Secretary-General on specific UN peacekeeping operations and to organize regular meetings with troop- and police-contributing countries prior to Security Council consultations. It requested that the Secretariat produce predeployment threat assessments and make them available to potential troop-contributing countries, and that the Secretariat call for a meeting of troop- and police-contributing countries in all cases of an emergency situation or in the event of a serious incident.

The Special Committee urged the Secretariat to consult with the troop-contributing countries when planning any change in the tasks, mission-specific rules of engagement, operational concepts or command and control structure which would have an impact on the personnel, equipment, training and logistics requirements, so as to enable those countries to give their advice in the planning process and to ensure that their troops had the capacity to meet the new demands. The Secretariat was requested to establish a web-based access for troop- and police-contributing countries to relevant reports, documents, standard operating procedures, directives, guidelines, policies and briefing materials.

Cooperation with regional organizations

At its 2009 substantive session [A/63/19], the Special Committee on Peacekeeping Operations reaffirmed the important contribution that regional arrangements and agencies could make to peacekeeping, in accordance with Chapter VIII of the UN Charter. It welcomed positive developments in the field of cooperation with regional arrangements or agencies and encouraged the Secretariat to further strengthen those linkages, such as the one with the African Union (AU). In that regard, it emphasized the importance of implementing the joint action plan for UN support to the AU in peacekeeping in the short, medium and long terms, and the 10-year plan for capacity-building.

Women in peacekeeping

With respect to gender and peacekeeping, the Special Committee on Peacekeeping Operations [A/63/19] emphasized the importance of full and effective implementation of Security Council resolutions 1325(2000) [YUN 2000, p. 1113] and 1820(2008) [YUN 2008, p. 1265] on women and peace and security and of all General Assembly resolutions on the elimination of all forms of violence against women. It underlined the gravity of acts of sexual and gender-based violence, and looked forward to working with the Secretary-General in developing and implementing training programmes to help UN peacekeeping personnel to better prevent, recognize and respond

to sexual violence and other violence against women and girls.

The Special Committee acknowledged the important role of women in the prevention and resolution of conflicts and in peacebuilding, and stressed the importance of their equal participation and full involvement in all peace and security efforts. It urged DPKO to continue to develop a comprehensive strategy to increase the participation of women in all aspects and at all levels of UN peacekeeping operations, and to continue to support the implementation and promotion of gender perspectives in peacekeeping activities. It reiterated its concern at the low proportion of women among UN peacekeeping staff at Headquarters and in the field, and encouraged Member States to increase the participation of women among uniformed personnel at all levels.

On 30 September, the Security Council, in **resolution 1888(2009)** (see p. 1137), on women and peace and security requested the Secretary-General to continue to implement the policy of zero tolerance of sexual exploitation and abuse in UN peacekeeping operations, also urging troop- and police-contributing countries to provide awareness training and to ensure accountability in cases of such conduct by their personnel.

On 5 October, the Council, in **resolution 1889(2009)** (see p. 1141), called for a wide range of measures to improve the participation of women at all stages of peace processes.

Security Council Working Group on Peacekeeping Operations

In July, the Chairman of the Security Council Working Group on Peacekeeping Operations submitted to the Council its interim report [S/2009/398], covering its work since the beginning of the year. Since 2002 [YUN 2002, p. 61], the Working Group had been convening joint meetings with troop-contributing countries as a means of promoting closer dialogue among Council members, troop-contributing countries, the Secretariat and significant stakeholders on issues pertaining to peacekeeping operations. In meetings on 25 February, 29 April, 9 and 19 June, and 17 July, the Working Group discussed the formulation of mandates, including protection of civilians; prioritization and streamlining of mandates; resources, including capacity-building; inter-mission cooperation; gaps between mandates and their implementation; and mission planning throughout the whole cycle of the mission.

On 17 December, the Working Group Chairman submitted to the Council a report of the Working Group [S/2009/659] on the enhancement of cooperation with troop-contributing countries, police-contributing countries and other stakeholders. The report summarized the discussion held at four meetings in November and December, with the participation of 30 countries and organizations.

Oversight activities

The Office of Internal Oversight Services (OIOS) reported in February [A/63/302 (Part II)] on its peace-keeping oversight activities in 2008. The Office issued 199 oversight reports related to peace operations, which accounted for 43 per cent of all OIOS recommendations for the year. They underscored the need for the United Nations to develop a formal internal control framework to ensure that risks were managed consistently and systematically through focused control processes across the Organization. In 2008, 87 out of the 162 audits in the workplan were completed in various focus areas—including financial management; strategic management and governance; safety and security; the management of human resources, information technology, logistics, procurement and contracts, programmes and projects, and properties and facilities. For 14 audits, the field work was completed and the draft reports were being prepared; the field work was in an advanced stage for 22 other audits; 14 audits were in the planning stage; and 10 were carry-overs to 2009.

During 2008, the Investigations Division received 336 reports of possible misconduct regarding peace operations, comprising 54 per cent of all reports made to OIOS that year. Additionally, the then Procurement Task Force received 17 reports of misconduct regarding peacekeeping matters. That reflected a decrease of 133 reports (28 per cent) of possible misconduct in peace operation-related activities from the previous year. Similarly, the intake on matters relating to sexual exploitation and abuse declined by 44 reports (35 per cent). While those numbers underscored the need for stronger efforts to prevent misconduct, particularly sexual exploitation and abuse, the decline in allegations reflected positively on the concerted efforts of the Organization following the report of the adviser to the Secretary-General on a comprehensive strategy to eliminate future sexual exploitation and abuse in UN peacekeeping operations [YUN 2005, p. 119]. Some of those efforts included alternative reporting mechanisms for prohibited conduct and enhanced local outreach programmes.

A sampling of OIOS findings revealed that the United Nations Operation in Côte d'Ivoire had generally been able to ensure a secure and stable environment in the country, with a majority of Ivorians appreciating the role of the peacekeeping force in ending the conflict and contributing to stability and security. In the United Nations Mission in the Sudan (UNMIS), OIOS substantiated reports that a national staff member had abducted and sexually assaulted a local minor; the matter was pending with the Office of Human

Resources Management. In the United Nations Organization Mission in the Democratic Republic of the Congo (MONUC), OIOS substantiated reports that a senior military observer had improperly assisted a licensed civilian diamond prospector and others involved in diamond exploration—a matter in which a high-ranking member of a national military contingent was also implicated but who had been repatriated before the commencement of the investigation. Pursuant to OIOS recommendations, DFS had referred the case to the concerned Member State for appropriate action, but had received no response.

An audit of the management of expendable inventory found that the United Nations Mission in Liberia (UNMIL) had not established adequate controls over such inventory, valued at $60 million as at 30 June 2008; UNMIL agreed with the OIOS recommendations and issued guidelines on inventory management which had been implemented as at December 2008. In an audit of the supply of food rations and combat ration packs in MONUC, OIOS found that the contractor had failed to maintain critical stock levels for some items as required by contract; DFS stated that the contractor had been penalized proportionally for the non-delivery of reserves and lack of the required warehouse space. OIOS also found delays in replacing repatriated MONUC police officers, thus reducing the operational capacity of the police and posing the risk of programmed activities not being implemented effectively; the Mission accepted the OIOS recommendation that it coordinate with DPKO to ensure timely replacements. In addition, it found that MONUC's information technology-related standard operating procedures, administrative instructions and other policies and procedures were largely incomplete or outdated. MONUC accepted the OIOS recommendation that it update its information technology policies and procedures and ensure their continuous update.

On 30 June, the General Assembly deferred consideration of the report until its sixty-fourth session (**decision 63/550 C**).

Comprehensive review of peacekeeping

Special Committee on Peacekeeping Operations

As requested by the General Assembly in resolution 62/273 [YUN 2008, p. 82], the Special Committee on Peacekeeping Operations and its Working Group continued their comprehensive review of the whole question of peacekeeping operations in all their aspects.

The Special Committee held its 2009 substantive session from 23 February to 20 March [A/63/19]. It discussed guiding principles, definitions and implementation of mandates, restructuring of peace-keeping, safety and security, conduct and discipline, strengthening operational capacity, strategies for complex peacekeeping operations, cooperation with troop-contributing countries, cooperation with regional arrangements, enhancement of African peacekeeping capabilities, best practices, training, personnel issues and financial matters.

As requested by the Special Committee, the Secretary-General in December reported [A/64/573 & Add.1] on the implementation of the recommendations contained in the report of the Special Committee. He outlined progress made in implementing those recommendations and in restructuring and strengthening UN peacekeeping. He outlined four priority building blocks for future effectiveness: guidance on critical tasks; mobilizing and building the capabilities necessary for high performance in the field; adapting the UN support system to enable performance and the effective use of resources; and stronger planning, management and oversight of missions.

GENERAL ASSEMBLY ACTION

On 8 May [meeting 82], the General Assembly, on the recommendation of the Fourth (Special Political and Decolonization) Committee [A/63/402/Add.1], adopted **resolution 63/280** without vote [agenda item 31].

Comprehensive review of the whole question of peacekeeping operations in all their aspects

The General Assembly,

Recalling its resolution 2006(XIX) of 18 February 1965 and all other relevant resolutions,

Recalling in particular its resolution 62/273 of 11 September 2008,

Affirming that the efforts of the United Nations in the peaceful settlement of disputes, including through its peacekeeping operations, are indispensable,

Convinced of the need for the United Nations to continue to improve its capabilities in the field of peacekeeping and to enhance the effective and efficient deployment of its peacekeeping operations,

Considering the contribution that all States Members of the United Nations make to peacekeeping,

Noting the widespread interest in contributing to the work of the Special Committee on Peacekeeping Operations expressed by Member States, in particular troop-contributing countries,

Bearing in mind the continuous necessity of preserving the efficiency and strengthening the effectiveness of the work of the Special Committee,

1. *Welcomes* the report of the Special Committee on Peacekeeping Operations;

2. *Endorses* the proposals, recommendations and conclusions of the Special Committee, contained in paragraphs 16 to 180 of its report;

3. *Urges* Member States, the Secretariat and relevant organs of the United Nations to take all necessary steps to implement the proposals, recommendations and conclusions of the Special Committee;

4. *Reiterates* that those Member States that become personnel contributors to the United Nations peacekeeping operations in years to come or participate in the future in the Special Committee for three consecutive years as observers shall, upon request in writing to the Chairman of the Special Committee, become members at the following session of the Special Committee;

5. *Decides* that the Special Committee, in accordance with its mandate, shall continue its efforts for a comprehensive review of the whole question of peacekeeping operations in all their aspects and shall review the implementation of its previous proposals and consider any new proposals so as to enhance the capacity of the United Nations to fulfil its responsibilities in this field;

6. *Requests* the Special Committee to submit a report on its work to the General Assembly at its sixty-fourth session;

7. *Decides* to include in the provisional agenda of its sixty-fourth session the item entitled "Comprehensive review of the whole question of peacekeeping operations in all their aspects".

On 10 December, the Assembly, by **decision 64/519**, took note of the report of the Fourth Committee on the comprehensive review of peacekeeping operations [A/64/407].

Operations in 2009

As at 1 January 2009, there were 16 peacekeeping missions in operation—7 in Africa, 1 in the Americas, 2 in Asia, 3 in Europe and the Mediterranean and 3 in the Middle East. During the year, one mission ended, the United Nations Observer Mission in Georgia, bringing the total number of missions in operation at year's end to 15.

Africa

In Africa, the Security Council extended the mandates of the United Nations Mission for the Referendum in Western Sahara (MINURSO) until 30 April 2010; the United Nations Mission in Liberia (UNMIL) until 30 September 2010; the United Nations Mission in the Sudan (UNMIS) until 30 April 2010; the United Nations Organization Mission in the Democratic Republic of the Congo (MONUC) until 31 May 2010; the African Union-United Nations Hybrid Operation in Darfur (UNAMID) until 31 July 2010; and the United Nations Mission in the Central African Republic and Chad (MINURCAT) until 15 March 2010. By Security Council resolution 1861(2009) of 14 January, the mandate of MINURCAT was expanded to assume responsibility for the tasks of the European

Union Force (EUFOR), whose mandate expired on 15 March, regarding protection of civilians, facilitation of delivery of humanitarian aid and protection of UN personnel and facilities. The Council twice renewed the mandate of the United Nations Operation in Côte d'Ivoire (UNOCI)—first, until 31 July 2009, and second, until 31 January 2010.

Americas

In the Americas, the Security Council extended the mandate of the United Nations Stabilization Mission in Haiti (MINUSTAH) until 15 October 2010.

Asia

In Asia, the United Nations Military Observer Group in India and Pakistan (UNMOGIP), established in 1949, continued to monitor the ceasefire in Jammu and Kashmir. The Security Council extended the mandate of the United Nations Integrated Mission in Timor-Leste (UNMIT) until 26 February 2010. It extended the authorization of the International Security Assistance Force in Afghanistan to 13 October 2010.

Europe and the Mediterranean

In Europe and the Mediterranean, the Security Council extended the mandate of the United Nations Observer Mission in Georgia (UNOMIG) to 15 June, when a draft resolution that would have extended its mandate for two weeks to allow divergent views to coalesce around a new security regime was vetoed by the Russian Federation. UNOMIG thus ceased to exist at midnight on the same day. The Council extended the United Nations Peacekeeping Force in Cyprus (UNFICYP) twice—to 15 December 2009 and to 15 June 2010. The United Nations Interim Administration Mission in Kosovo (UNMIK), Serbia, remained in place. On 18 November, the Council authorized the Member States acting through or in cooperation with the European Union (EU) to establish, for a further 12 month-period, a multinational stabilization force, EUFOR, in Bosnia and Herzegovina.

Middle East

Three long-standing operations continued in the Middle East. The United Nations Truce Supervision Organization (UNTSO) continued to monitor ceasefires, supervise armistice agreements and assist other peacekeeping operations in the region. The Security Council extended the mandate of the United Nations Disengagement Observer Force (UNDOF) to 31 December 2009, and that of the United Nations Interim Force in Lebanon (UNIFIL) to 31 August 2010.

Roster of 2009 operations

UNTSO

United Nations Truce Supervision Organization
Established: May 1948.
Mandate: To monitor ceasefires, supervise armistice agreements and assist other peacekeeping operations in the region.
Strength: 151 military observers.

UNMOGIP

United Nations Military Observer Group in India and Pakistan
Established: January 1949.
Mandate: To supervise the ceasefire between India and Pakistan in Jammu and Kashmir.
Strength: 43 military observers.

UNFICYP

United Nations Peacekeeping Force in Cyprus
Established: March 1964.
Mandate: To prevent the recurrence of fighting between the two Cypriot communities and to contribute to the maintenance and restoration of law and order and a return to normal conditions.
Strength: 855 troops, 66 police.

UNDOF

United Nations Disengagement Observer Force
Established: June 1974.
Mandate: To supervise the ceasefire between Israel and the Syrian Arab Republic and the disengagement of Israeli and Syrian forces in the Golan Heights.
Strength: 1,043 troops.

UNIFIL

United Nations Interim Force in Lebanon
Established: March 1978.
Mandate: To restore peace and security and assist the Lebanese Government in ensuring the return of its effective authority in the area; expanded in 2006 to include monitoring the cessation of hostilities between Hizbullah and Israel [YUN 2006, p. 584], supporting the deployment of the Lebanese Armed Forces throughout southern Lebanon, helping to ensure humanitarian access to civilian populations and the return of displaced persons, and assisting the Government in securing its borders to prevent the entry of unauthorized arms or materiel.
Strength: 11,862 troops.

MINURSO

United Nations Mission for the Referendum in Western Sahara

Established: April 1991.

Mandate: To monitor and verify the implementation of a settlement plan for Western Sahara and assist in the holding of a referendum in the Territory.

Strength: 27 troops, 199 military observers, 6 police.

UNOMIG

United Nations Observer Mission in Georgia

Established: August 1993.

Mandate: To verify compliance with a ceasefire agreement between the parties to the conflict in Georgia and investigate ceasefire violations; expanded in 1994 [YUN 1994, p. 584] to include monitoring the implementation of an agreement on a ceasefire and separation of forces and observing the operation of a multinational peacekeeping force.

Ended: June 2009.

UNMIK

United Nations Interim Administration Mission in Kosovo

Established: June 1999.

Mandate: To promote the establishment of substantial autonomy and self-government in Kosovo, perform basic civilian administrative functions, organize and oversee the development of provisional institutions, facilitate a political process to determine Kosovo's future status, support reconstruction of key infrastructure, maintain civil law and order, protect human rights and assure the return of refugees and displaced persons.

Strength: 9 military observers, 8 police.

MONUC

United Nations Organization Mission in the Democratic Republic of the Congo

Established: November 1999.

Mandate: To establish contacts with the signatories to the Ceasefire Agreement, provide technical assistance in the implementation of the Agreement, provide information on security conditions, plan for the observation of the ceasefire, facilitate the delivery of humanitarian assistance and assist in the protection of human rights; expanded in 2007 [YUN 2007, p. 119] to include assisting the Government in establishing a stable security environment and supporting the strengthening of democratic institutions and the rule of law.

Strength: 18,646 troops, 705 military observers, 1,158 civilian police.

UNMIL

United Nations Mission in Liberia

Established: September 2003.

Mandate: To support the implementation of the ceasefire agreement and the peace process; protect UN staff, facilities and civilians; support humanitarian and human rights activities; and assist in national security reform, including national police training and formation of a new, restructured military.

Strength: 9,505 troops, 118 military observers, 1,324 police.

UNOCI

United Nations Operation in Côte d'Ivoire

Established: April 2004.

Mandate: To monitor the implementation of the 3 May 2003 comprehensive ceasefire agreement and the movement of armed groups; assist in disarmament, demobilization, reintegration, repatriation and resettlement; protect UN personnel, institutions and civilians; support humanitarian assistance; support implementation of the peace process; assist in the promotion of human rights, public information, and law and order. The mandate was expanded in 2007 [YUN 2007, p. 170] to include assisting in disarming and dismantling militias; identifying the population and organizing elections; reforming the security sector; monitoring the arms embargo; and supporting the redeployment of State administration.

Strength: 7,202 troops, 189 military observers, 1,145 police.

MINUSTAH

United Nations Stabilization Mission in Haiti

Established: June 2004.

Mandate: To provide support in ensuring a secure and stable environment; support the constitutional and political process; assist in maintaining the rule of law, public safety and public order; promote and protect human rights; and support the political process, promoting an inclusive political dialogue and national reconciliation.

Strength: 7,032 troops, 2,025 police.

UNMIS

United Nations Mission in the Sudan

Established: March 2005.

Mandate: To support the implementation of the 9 January 2005 Comprehensive Peace Agreement between the Government of the Sudan and the Sudan People's Liberation Movement/Army; facilitate and coordinate humanitarian assistance and the return of refugees and internally displaced persons; assist with demining; and protect and promote human rights. The mandate was expanded in 2006 [YUN 2006, p. 282] to support implementation of the May 2006 Darfur Peace Agreement and the 2004 N'djamena Agreement on Humanitarian Ceasefire on the Conflict in Darfur.

Strength: 9,093 troops, 476 military observers, 693 police.

UNMIT

United Nations Integrated Mission in Timor-Leste

Established: August 2006.

Mandate: To support the Government of Timor-Leste in consolidating stability; enhancing a culture of democratic governance; facilitating political dialogue; conducting the 2007 electoral process; establishing a continuous presence in the three border districts, alongside UN police officers; reviewing the role and needs of the security sector; building the capacity of State and Government institutions and strengthening capacity and mechanisms for monitoring, promoting and protecting human rights; and promoting justice and reconciliation.

Strength: 35 military observers, 1,517 police.

UNAMID

African Union-United Nations Hybrid Operation in Darfur

Established: July 2007.

Mandate: To contribute to the protection of civilians, contribute to security for humanitarian assistance, monitor and verify implementation of agreements, assist an inclusive political process, contribute to the promotion of human rights and the rule of law, and monitor and report on the situation along the borders with Chad and the Central African Republic.

Strength: 15,114 troops, 260 military observers, 4,575 police.

MINURCAT

United Nations Mission in the Central African Republic and Chad

Established: September 2007.

Mandate: To select, train, advise and facilitate support to elements of the Police tchadienne pour la protection humanitaire; contribute to the creation of a more secure environment; exchange information on threats to humanitarian activities in the region; contribute to the monitoring, promotion and protection of human rights; support the strengthening of the capacity of the Governments of Chad and the Central African Republic, and civil society, through training in international human rights standards and efforts to end the recruitment and use of children by armed groups; and assist Chad and the Central African Republic in promoting the rule of law. In 2009, its mandate was expanded to include protection of civilians, facilitation of delivery of humanitarian aid, protection of UN personnel and facilities and creation of conditions for the return of refugees.

Strength: 2,489 troops, 24 military observers, 264 police.

Financial and administrative aspects of peacekeeping operations

The General Assembly considered a number of issues related to financial and administrative aspects of UN peacekeeping operations, including the financial performance of UN peacekeeping operations, the support account for peacekeeping operations, funds for closed missions, financial reports and audited financial statements, apportionment of costs, reimbursements to Member States for contingent-owned equipment, management and financing of the United Nations Logistics Base at Brindisi, Italy, restructuring, UN police capacities, personnel matters, criminal accountability of UN staff and experts on mission, welfare and recreational needs of peacekeeping staff, death and disability, and training.

Financing

Expenditures for UN peacekeeping operations from 1 July 2008 to 30 June 2009 [A/64/5 (Vol. II)] rose by 13.6 per cent, from $6,265.8 million in the previous fiscal year to $7,120.6 million. The increase, which was mainly due to the expansion of UNAMID, MINURCAT and MONUC and support for the American Union Mission in Somalia (AMISOM), was partially offset by the reduced expenditures for UNMIL, the closure of the United Nations Mission in Ethiopia and Eritrea (UNMEE) and the drawdown of UNMIK. Total assessments rose by 5.0 per cent, from $6,722.5 million to $7,060.5 million, while unpaid assessments pertaining to active peacekeeping missions decreased by 5.0 per cent, from $1,018.9 million to $967.5 million. Unpaid assessments for closed missions decreased marginally, from $557.6 million to $542.6 million. Therefore, the overall level of unpaid assessments decreased from $1,576.5 million to $1,510.1 million.

Available cash for active peacekeeping missions as at 30 June totalled $2,096.6 million, while liabilities reached $2,764.9 million. For closed missions, available cash totalled $440.2 million, while liabilities amounted to $395.2 million. Closed missions with cash surpluses remained the only available lending source for active missions. During the reporting period, the United Nations Peace Forces provided loans of $164.0 million, to UNFICYP ($3.0 million), MINURSO ($21.0 million), UNOMIG ($6.0 million), UNMIK ($32.0 million), UNMIL ($10.0 million), UNOCI ($46.0 million), MINUSTAH ($38.0 million) and UNMIT ($8.0 million). Total loans outstanding amounted to $28.6 million.

Notes of Secretary-General. In January [A/C.5/63/21], the Secretary-General, further to the information provided in 2008 [YUN 2008, p. 86] on approved resources for peacekeeping operations for 1 July 2008 to 30 June 2009, including requirements for the United Nations Logistics Base (UNLB) at Brindisi and the support account for peacekeeping operations, provided information on further financing actions taken by the General Assembly at the main part of its sixty-third session in respect of UNMEE and the support account for peacekeeping operations, for a total of $7,038,517,100.

In May [A/C.5/63/23], the Secretary-General provided information reflecting financing actions taken by the Assembly during the first part of its resumed sixty-third session in respect of MINURCAT, UNMIS and AMISOM, which brought the total to $7,310,003,400.

In May [A/C.5/63/24], in accordance with General Assembly resolution 49/233 A [YUN 1994, p. 1338], the Secretary-General submitted to the Fifth (Administrative and Budgetary) Committee information on the proposed budgetary requirements of each peacekeeping operation, including budget levels for UNLB and the support account for peacekeeping operations, for 1 July 2009 to 30 June 2010, by category, with the aggregate total resource requirements amounting to $8,180,297,800.

In June [A/C.5/63/25], the Secretary-General submitted to the Fifth Committee a note reflecting the resources to be approved by the Assembly in respect of each peacekeeping mission, including the prorated shares of the support account for peacekeeping operations and UNLB.

In August [A/C.5/63/26], the Secretary-General submitted information on approved resources for peacekeeping operations for 1 July 2009 to 30 June 2010, including requirements for UNLB and the support account for peacekeeping operations, amounting to $7,769,979,100.

Financial performance

In January [A/63/696], the Secretary-General submitted an overview report on the financing of UN peacekeeping operations: budget performance for the period from 1 July 2007 to 30 June 2008 and the budget for 1 July 2009 to 30 June 2010. During the former period, total expenditure amounted to $6,276.6 million, against an approved budget of $6,770.7 million, exclusive of voluntary contributions in kind. The budget for peacekeeping operations for the latter period was estimated at $8,185.2 million. In March [A/63/784], the Secretary-General provided additional information in response to the recommendations of the Board of Auditors contained in its report [A/63/5 (Vol. II)] on UN peacekeeping operations for the period ended 30 June 2008 [YUN 2008, p. 86].

The Advisory Committee on Administrative and Budgetary Questions (ACABQ), reporting in April [A/63/746] on administrative and budgetary aspects of the financing of peacekeeping operations, addressed matters arising from the reports of the Secretary-General on peacekeeping operations, including reference to recommendations or observations of the Board of Auditors. It commented on general issues arising from the report of the Board of Auditors on the accounts of the UN peacekeeping operations for the financial period ended 30 June 2008. ACABQ also provided its observations and recommendations on reports addressing other peacekeeping matters.

On 30 June, the General Assembly deferred consideration of the Secretary-General's report and the related ACABQ report until its sixty-fourth session (**decision 63/550 C**).

Peacekeeping support account

In February [A/63/698 & Add.1], the Secretary-General submitted the performance report on the budget of the support account for peacekeeping operations for the period from 1 July 2007 to 30 June 2008. Expenditures for the period amounted to $222,450,800, against approved resources of $230,509,900, resulting in unutilized resources totalling $8,059,100. That unencumbered balance was attributable to underexpenditure in respect of post and non-post resources, in particular under facilities and infrastructure, offset by additional requirements under the other supplies, services and equipment class of expenditures.

The Secretary-General recommended that the General Assembly apply the unencumbered balance of $8,059,100 and the total amount of $6,997,200—comprising interest income ($3,248,500), other income ($245,900) and cancellation of prior-period obligations ($3,502,800)—to the support account requirements for the period from July 2009 through June 2010.

In March [A/63/767 & Corr.1], the Secretary-General submitted the budget for the support account for peacekeeping operations for the period from 1 July 2009 to 30 June 2010, amounting to $324,447,100. It provided for 1,362 posts, comprising 1,180 continuing posts and 182 new posts.

The Independent Audit Advisory Committee in February [A/63/703] submitted its comments on the proposed OIOS budget under the support account for peacekeeping operations for 1 July 2009 to 30 June 2010.

In May [A/63/841], ACABQ provided its observations and recommendations on the Secretary-General's report on strengthening the capacity of the United Nations to manage and sustain peacekeeping operations (see below), the performance report on the budget of the support account for peacekeeping operations for 1 July 2007 to 30 June 2008 (see above) and the proposed budget for the support account for peacekeeping operations from 1 July 2009 to 30 June 2010 (see above). It recommended approval of 106 of the 182 posts proposed by the Secretary-General in his March report. Its recommendations involved reductions totalling $19,817,800 gross ($17,913,100 net), as detailed in the report. Accordingly, it recommended that the Assembly approve staffing and non-staffing resources of $304,629,300 gross ($276,422,900 net) for the support account from July 2009 through June 2010.

With regard to a proposal in the Secretary-General's February report on the performance report for the period from 1 July 2007 to 30 June 2008 (see above), the Advisory Committee recommended that the Assembly apply the total amount of $15,056,300, comprising the unencumbered balance of $8,059,100 in respect of the financial period from July 2007 through June 2008, and the total amount of $6,997,200, comprising interest income ($3,248,500), other income ($245,900) and cancellation of prior-period obligations ($3,502,800), to the support account requirements for the period from July 2009 to June 2010.

General Assembly consideration. On 30 June, the Assembly had before it the reports of the Secretary-General on the financing of the support account for peacekeeping operations [A/63/698 & Add.1 & A/63/767 & Corr.1] and on strengthening the UN capacity to manage and sustain peacekeeping operations [A/63/702 & Corr.1]; the reports of the Independent Audit Advisory Committee on the proposed OIOS budget under the support account for peacekeeping operations for the period from 1 July 2009 to 30 June 2010 [A/63/703] and on vacant posts in OIOS

[A/63/737]; the OIOS report on the audit of the Secretariat's structure for managing and sustaining peacekeeping operations [A/63/837]; and the related ACABQ report [A/63/841].

GENERAL ASSEMBLY ACTION

On 30 June [meeting 93], the General Assembly, on the recommendation of the Fifth Committee [A/63/894], adopted **resolution 63/287** without vote [agenda item 132].

Support account for peacekeeping operations

The General Assembly,

Recalling its resolutions 45/258 of 3 May 1991, 47/218 A of 23 December 1992, 48/226 A of 23 December 1993, 55/238 of 23 December 2000, 56/241 of 24 December 2001, 56/293 of 27 June 2002, 57/318 of 18 June 2003, 58/298 of 18 June 2004, 59/301 of 22 June 2005, 60/268 of 30 June 2006, 61/245 and 61/246 of 22 December 2006, 61/256 of 15 March 2007, 61/279 of 29 June 2007 and 62/ of 20 June 2008, its decisions 48/489 of 8 July 1994, 49/469 of 23 December 1994 and 50/473 of 23 December 1995 and its other relevant resolutions,

Having considered the reports of the Secretary-General on the financing of the support account for peacekeeping operations and on strengthening the capacity of the United Nations to manage and sustain peacekeeping operations, the reports of the Independent Audit Advisory Committee on the proposed budget for the Office of Internal Oversight Services under the support account for peacekeeping operations for the period from 1 July 2009 to 30 June 2010 and on vacant posts in the Office, the report of the Office of Internal Oversight Services on the audit of the Secretariat's structure for managing and sustaining peacekeeping operations and the related report of the Advisory Committee on Administrative and Budgetary Questions,

Recognizing the importance of the United Nations being able to respond and deploy rapidly to a peacekeeping operation upon adoption of a relevant resolution of the Security Council, within thirty days for traditional peacekeeping operations and ninety days for complex peacekeeping operations,

Recognizing also the need for adequate support during all phases of peacekeeping operations, including the liquidation and termination phases,

Mindful that the level of the support account should broadly correspond to the mandate, number, size and complexity of peacekeeping missions,

Attaching great importance to the provision of adequate resources for peacekeeping operations and their backstopping as well as for all priority activities of the Organization, in particular activities in the area of development, and underlining the need for genuine and meaningful partnership between the Security Council, the troop-contributing Governments and other Member States,

1. *Takes note* of the reports of the Secretary-General on the financing of the support account for peacekeeping operations and on strengthening the capacity of the United Nations to manage and sustain peacekeeping operations,

the reports of the Independent Audit Advisory Committee on the proposed budget for the Office of Internal Oversight Services under the support account for peacekeeping operations for the period from 1 July 2009 to 30 June 2010 and on vacant posts in the Office and the report of the Office of Internal Oversight Services on the audit of the Secretariat's structure for managing and sustaining peacekeeping operations;

2.   *Reaffirms* its role in carrying out a thorough analysis and approval of human and financial resources and policies with a view to ensuring the full, effective and efficient implementation of all mandated programmes and activities and the implementation of policies in this regard;

3.   *Also reaffirms* that the Fifth Committee is the appropriate Main Committee of the General Assembly entrusted with responsibility for administrative and budgetary matters;

4.   *Further reaffirms* rule 153 of its rules of procedure;

5.   *Reaffirms* that the support account funds shall be used for the sole purpose of financing human resources and non-human resource requirements for backstopping and supporting peacekeeping operations at Headquarters, and that any changes in this limitation require the prior approval of the General Assembly;

6.   *Also reaffirms* the need for adequate funding for the backstopping of peacekeeping operations, as well as the need for full justification for that funding in support account budget submissions;

7.   *Further reaffirms* the need for effective and efficient administration and financial management of peacekeeping operations, and urges the Secretary-General to continue to identify measures to increase the productivity and efficiency of the support account;

8.   *Reiterates* that the delegation of authority on the part of the Secretary-General should be in order to facilitate the better management of the Organization, but stresses that the overall responsibility for management of the Organization rests with the Secretary-General as the Chief Administrative Officer;

9.   *Affirms* the need for the Secretary-General to ensure that the delegation of authority to the Department of Peacekeeping Operations, the Department of Field Support and field missions is in strict compliance with relevant resolutions and decisions, as well as relevant rules and procedures of the General Assembly on this matter;

10.   *Stresses* that heads of departments report to and are accountable to the Secretary-General;

11.   *Requests* the Secretary-General, when submitting his budget proposals, to include details of the full annual cost of posts for the subsequent budget;

12.   *Also requests* the Secretary-General to ensure the full implementation of the relevant provisions of General Assembly resolutions 59/296 of 22 June 2005, 60/266 of 30 June 2006 and 61/276 of 29 June 2007 and other relevant resolutions;

13.   *Notes* that the overall benefits of the restructuring of the Department of Peacekeeping Operations and the Department of Field Support, remain yet to be fully assessed, and, in this regard, requests the Secretary-General to continue to make every effort to strengthen the capacity of the Organization to manage and sustain peacekeeping operations in the face of their surge in volume and complexity;

14.   *Reiterates* that the Secretary-General should address systemic issues that hamper good management of the Organization, including by improving work processes and procedures, and, in that context, stresses that structural change is no substitute for managerial improvement;

15.   *Stresses* the need for the Secretary-General to ensure a strategic and coherent vision when undertaking reform initiatives, and, in this context, emphasizes that any new proposal for reform should fully take into account ongoing and past management reforms;

16.   *Emphasizes* the importance of preserving the unity of command in missions at all levels, as well as a coherence in policy and strategy and clear command structures in the field and up to and including Headquarters;

17.   *Also emphasizes* the importance of interaction and coordination with troop-contributing countries;

18.   *Further emphasizes* the need to ensure the safety and security of United Nations personnel;

19.   *Takes note* of the report of the Office of Internal Oversight Services, and urges the Secretary-General to ensure the full implementation of the recommendations therein;

20.   *Also takes note* of the observations and recommendations contained in the report of the Independent Audit Advisory Committee on vacant posts in the Office of Internal Oversight Services, and requests the Secretary-General to fill the vacancies in the Office, in accordance with the existing relevant provisions governing recruitment in the United Nations and the provisions of the present resolution;

21.   *Requests* the Secretary-General to entrust the Office of Internal Oversight Services to implement the recommendations of the Independent Audit Advisory Committee contained in paragraphs 22 to 29 and 33 to 35 of its report;

22.   *Stresses*, in this regard, the importance for the Office of Internal Oversight Services, in its reports on investigations of fraud and corruption in the Organization, to define and make a clear differentiation between the actual value of financial loss to the Organization, if any, and other findings that may not have direct financial implication and the total number and value of contracts investigated, in order to convey an accurate perception of the value of financial loss;

23.   *Reiterates* the importance of strengthened accountability in the Organization and of ensuring greater accountability of the Secretary-General to Member States, inter alia, for the effective and efficient implementation of legislative mandates and the use of human and financial resources;

24.   *Reiterates its regret* at the delay in the response of the Secretary-General to its outstanding requests in its resolutions 59/288 of 13 April 2005, 61/246 of 22 December 2006, 61/276 of 29 June 2007 and 62/269 of 20 June 2008, and urges him, as a matter of priority, to submit a report on procurement governance and other issues, as requested in resolutions 61/246, 61/276 and 62/269, with full justification of the reasons for the delay;

25.   *Endorses* the conclusions and recommendations contained in the report of the Advisory Committee on

Administrative and Budgetary Questions, subject to the provisions of the present resolution;

26. *Notes* the observation of the Board of Auditors that there is no defined formula to show the relationship between the level and complexity of peacekeeping operations and the level of the support account, and, in this regard, emphasizes the need to develop a sound approach for determining the proposed support account staffing requirements, so that Member States can make fully informed decisions on resources;

27. *Requests* the Secretary-General to review the level of the support account on a regular basis, taking into consideration the number, size and complexity of peacekeeping operations;

28. *Takes note* of paragraph 45 of the report of the Advisory Committee, and requests the Secretary-General, taking into account the relevant legislative mandates, to include, in his rejustification of the totality of support account staffing requirements, inter alia, information on and an analysis of the following:

(a) The lead agency, entity, department and/or offices for major strands of activity and the scope of their respective responsibilities;

(b) Comprehensive assessment of the evolution of the support account;

(c) Related human resources funded from the regular budget and other sources of funding, including in other departments of the United Nations Secretariat, resources in field missions and, where relevant, the specialized agencies and funds and programmes;

(d) Impact of the requested resources on the improvement to the administrative and financial management of peacekeeping operations;

(e) All functions covered by the proposed resources other than that of backstopping peacekeeping operations;

(f) The impact of information and communications technology initiatives, including related business process improvements, on the enhancement of productivity and on the level of resources requested;

(g) The outcome of business process improvements;

(h) Lessons learned from recent experience of operating the support account, including on the conversion of general temporary assistance positions;

29. *Recalls* section I, paragraph 6, of resolution 55/238, paragraph 11 of resolution 56/241, paragraph 19 of resolution 61/279, and paragraph 22 of resolution 62/250, and requests the Secretary-General to make further concrete efforts to ensure proper representation of troop-contributing countries in the Department of Peacekeeping Operations and the Department of Field Support, taking into account their contribution to United Nations peacekeeping;

30. *Reiterates* section III, paragraph 10, of resolution 63/250, and invites the Secretary-General, when appointing officials at the D-1 and D-2 levels in the Departments of the Secretariat that provide backstopping and/or policy guidance to field missions, to fully consider the relevant field experience of the candidates, as one of the highly desirable appointment criteria;

31. *Recalls* its resolution 63/280 of 8 May 2009 and decides to establish the Security Sector Reform Unit in the Office of Rule of Law and Security Institutions;

32. *Also recalls* paragraph 17 of resolution 60/268, and reiterates its request to the Secretary-General to entrust to the Office of Internal Oversight Services the task of refining the methodology for allocating resident auditors, taking also into account the risks and complexity of the operation of individual peacekeeping operations, and to report thereon to the General Assembly;

33. *Stresses* that the due process rights afforded to staff under investigation have to withstand review by the system of the administration of justice, including in the context of the establishment of the new system;

34. *Notes with serious concern* the decision to advertise vacancies for positions not approved by the General Assembly, and stresses the need for vacancy announcements to be made in accordance with existing relevant provisions governing recruitment in the United Nations and that any changes involving administrative and financial implications shall be subject to the review and approval of the Assembly in accordance with established procedures;

35. *Decides* to maintain, for the financial period from 1 July 2009 to 30 June 2010, the funding mechanism for the support account used in the current period, from 1 July 2008 to 30 June 2009, as approved in paragraph 3 of its resolution 50/221 B of 7 June 1996;

36. *Takes note* of paragraph 175 of the report of the Advisory Committee;

37. *Decides* not to introduce the proposed structure based on the hub approach at this stage, and decides to designate, as a pilot project, centres of investigation in Nairobi, Vienna and New York from 1 July 2009 to 30 June 2012;

38. *Recognizes* the value of resident investigators, and decides to maintain resident investigations staff presence in some peacekeeping operations, pending its consideration of the comprehensive report referred to in paragraph 40 below;

39. *Requests* the Secretary-General to submit a preliminary report on the status of implementation of the pilot project at the second part of its resumed sixty-fifth session;

40. *Also requests* the Secretary-General to submit to the General Assembly for consideration, in the context of the 2012/13 support account budget, after full consultations with all relevant stakeholders, integrating in particular the comments and observations of field missions, a comprehensive report on the pilot project, with a view to deciding on a restructuring of the Investigations Division of the Office of Internal Oversight Services, including:

(a) A complete qualitative analysis of the implementation of the three-year pilot project, including the lessons learned;

(b) A clear and transparent presentation of the existing structure and the pilot project structure and their respective coverage of field missions;

(c) A comprehensive cost-benefit analysis, including of the effectiveness and efficiency of the structure of the pilot project based on accurate assumptions, including an analysis of the long-term trend of investigations in field missions;

(d) Fully justified rationale for all deployments of investigations staff and resources and the ability of the Office of Internal Oversight Services to respond to changing caseload requirements;

(e) Complete and updated information on the current staffing, vacancy rate and caseload;

41. *Requests* the Advisory Committee on Administrative and Budgetary Questions to request the Board of Auditors to conduct an audit of the implementation of the pilot project for the period of 1 July 2009 to 30 June 2012, without prejudice to the role of the Independent Audit Advisory Committee, and to report thereon separately to the General Assembly at the second part of its resumed sixty-sixth session;

Financial performance report for the period from 1 July 2007 to 30 June 2008

42. *Takes note* of the report of the Secretary-General on the financial performance of the support account for peacekeeping operations for the period from 1 July 2007 to 30 June 2008;

Budget estimates for the financial period from 1 July 2009 to 30 June 2010

43. *Approves* the support account requirements in the amount of 294,030,900 United States dollars for the financial period from 1 July 2009 to 30 June 2010, including 1,182 continuing posts, and 63 new temporary posts contained in annex I to the present resolution, and 83 continuing and 60 new general temporary assistance positions contained in annex II, as well as their related post and non-post requirements;

Financing of the budget estimates

44. *Decides* that the requirements for the support account for peacekeeping operations for the financial period from 1 July 2009 to 30 June 2010 shall be financed as follows:

(a) The unencumbered balance and other income in the total amount of 15,056,300 dollars in respect of the financial period ended 30 June 2008, to be applied to the resources required for the financial period from 1 July 2009 to 30 June 2010;

(b) The amount of 7,322,600 dollars representing the excess of the authorized level of the Peacekeeping Reserve Fund in respect of the financial period ended 30 June 2008, to be applied to the resources required for the financial period from 1 July 2009 to 30 June 2010;

(c) The amount of 62,800 dollars representing the excess of the appropriation for the support account requirements in respect of the financial period ended 30 June 2007, to be applied to the resources required for the financial period from 1 July 2009 to 30 June 2010;

(d) The balance of 271,589,200 dollars to be prorated among the budgets of the active peacekeeping operations for the financial period from 1 July 2009 to 30 June 2010;

(e) The estimated staff assessment income of 28,273,500 dollars, comprising the amount of 27,486,900 dollars for the financial period from 1 July 2009 to 30 June 2010 and the increase of 786,600 dollars in respect of the financial period ended 30 June 2008, to be set off against the balance referred to in subparagraph (d) above, to be prorated among the budgets of the individual active peacekeeping operations.

ANNEX I

Support account posts to be established for the period from 1 July 2009 to 30 June 2010

Organizational unit		Number of posts	Post level
Department of Peacekeeping Operations			
Office of Operations	GTA conversion	1	1 P-5
Office of Rule of Law and Security Institutions	New	20	1 D-1, 1 P-5, 10 P-4, 6 P-3, 2 GS (OL)
	GTA conversion	1	P-3
Subtotal		22	
Department of Field Support			
Office of the Under-Secretary-General	New	1	1 GS (PL)
Field Budget and Finance Division	New	2	2 P-4
Field Personnel Division	GTA conversion	2	2 P-3
Logistics Support Division	New	7	3 P-4, 3 P-3, 1 GS (PL)
	Reclassification		1 P-3 to P-4
	GTA conversion	1	1 GS (OL)
Subtotal		13	
Department of Management			
Office of Programme Planning, Budget and Accounts	New	2	1 P-4, 1 GS (OL)
	GTA conversion	4	1 P-4, 3 P-3
	Reclassification		1 P-3 to P-4; 1 P-4 to P-5
Office of Human Resources Management	New	11	1 P-4, 5 P-3, 1 P-2, 1 GS (PL), 3 GS (OL)
	GTA conversion	3	2 P-4, 1 GS (OL)
Office of Central Support Services	New	3	1 P-4, 2 P-3
Subtotal		23	
Office of Internal Oversight Services			
Inspection and Evaluation Division	New	1	1 P-4
Internal Audit Division	New	1	1 P-5
Subtotal		2	
Office of Legal Affairs	New	2	1 P-5, 1 P-4
Subtotal		2	
Office of the United Nations Ombudsman	New	1	1 P-5
Subtotal		1	
TOTAL		63	1D-1, 5 P-5, 23 P-4, 22 P-3, 1 P-2, 3 GS (PL), 8 GS (OL)

Abbreviations: GS (OL), General Service (Other Level); GS (PL), General Service (Principal Level); GTA (General Temporary Assistance).

ANNEX II

Support account general temporary assistance positions to be established for the period from 1 July 2009 to 30 June 2010

Organizational unit		Number of positions	Position level
Department of Peacekeeping Operations			
Office of Operations	Continuation	2	1 P-4, 1 GS (OL)
Office of Rule of Law and Security Institutions	New	1	1 P-3
Policy, Evaluation and Training Division	Continuation	8	1 P-5, 3 P-4, 3 P-3, 1 GS (OL)
	Subtotal	11	
Department of Field Support			
Field Personnel Division	Continuation	6	4 P-3, 2 GS (OL)
	New	13	11 P-3, 2 GS (OL)
Field Budget and Finance Division	Continuation	1	1 P-4
Logistics Support Division	Continuation	2	2 P-3
	New	1	1 P-3
	Subtotal	23	
Department of Management			
Office of the Under-Secretary-General	New	2	1 P-4, 1 GS (OL)
Office of Programme Planning, Budget and Accounts	Continuation	14	5 P-4, 4 P-3, 1 P-2, 4 GS (OL)
Office of Human Resources Management*	New	22	4 P-4, 4 P-3, 2 P-2, 12 GS (OL)
Office of Central Support Services	Continuation	3	3 GS (OL)
	New	4	3 P-3, 1 P-2
	Subtotal	45	
Office of Internal Oversight Services			
Investigations Division	Continuation	2	NEW YORK: 1 P-3, 1 GS (OL)
	New	7	NEW YORK: 1 P-5, 3 P-4, 1 P-3, 2 GS (OL)
	Continuation	14	VIENNA: 1 D-1, 1 P-5, 2 P-4, 7 P-3, 2 GS (OL), 1 GS (PL)
	New	6	NAIROBI: 1 D-1, 1 P-5, 1 P-4, 1 P-3, 2 GS (OL)
	Continuation	10	NAIROBI: 3 P-4, 5 P-3, 2 GS (OL)
	Continuation	12	MONUC: 1 P-4, 1 P-3, 1 NGS UNMIL: 1 P-4, 2 P-3, 1 NGS UNMIS: 1 P-4, 2 P-3 MINUSTAH: 1 P-4 UNOCI: 1 P-4
	Subtotal	51	
Office of Legal Affairs	New	1	1 P-4
	Subtotal	1	
Ethics Office	Continuation	2	1 P-3, 1 GS (OL)
	Subtotal	2	
Office of Information and Communications Technology	Continuation	7	5 P-3, 2 GS (OL)
	New	3	1 P-5, 2 P-3
	Subtotal	10	
	TOTAL	**143**	

Note: General temporary assistance positions equivalent to 2,018,900 dollars (before the application of the approved vacancy rates).

Abbreviations: GS (OL), General Service (Other Level); GS (PL), General Service (Principal Level); NGS (National General Service).

Funds for closed missions

A Secretary-General's report [A/63/581] updated the information on the financial position of 21 closed peacekeeping missions as at 30 June 2008. The net cash surplus in the accounts of 16 closed missions available for credit to Member States as at that date amounted to $186,297,000. That amount did not include loans totalling $37,816,000 owed by two closed missions—the United Nations Support Mission in Haiti/United Nations Transition Mission in Haiti/United Nations Civilian Police Mission in Haiti ($7,366,000) and the United Nations Mission in the Central African Republic ($3,450,000)—and by two active peacekeeping missions—MINURSO ($14,000,000) and UNMIK ($13,000,000)—which remained unpaid. Five of the 21 closed missions reflected cash deficits totalling $86,712,000, owing to outstanding payments of assessed contributions. The Secretary-General recommended that the General Assembly approve retention of the cash balance of $186,297,000 available in 16 closed peacekeeping missions, in the light of the experience with respect to cash requirements of the Organization during the 2007/08 and 2008/09 financial periods.

In May [A/63/856], ACABQ provided its comments on the Secretary-General's report. With respect to the disposition of the $186,297,000, it cited regulation 5.3 of the United Nations Financial Regulations and Rules, which provided that appropriations should remain available for 12 months following the end of the financial period to which they related, to the extent that they were required to discharge obligations in respect of goods supplied and services rendered in the financial period, and to liquidate any other outstanding legal obligation of the financial period. The regulation also stated that the balance of the appropriations should be surrendered. The Advisory Committee reiterated its view that it was for the General Assembly to decide on the disposition of such balances.

On 30 June, the General Assembly deferred consideration of the Secretary-General's and ACABQ reports until its sixty-fourth session (**decision 63/550 C**).

Also on 30 June, by **decision 63/557**, the Assembly decided to return two thirds of the credits available in the account of the United Nations Iraq-Kuwait Observation Mission to the Government of Kuwait in the amount of $996,800. It also decided to continue to consider the updated financial position of closed peacekeeping missions during its sixty-fourth (2009) session.

Accounts and auditing

At its resumed sixty-third (2009) session, the General Assembly considered the financial report and audited financial statements for UN peacekeeping operations for the period from 1 July 2007 to 30 June

2008 [A/63/5 (Vol. II)], the Secretary-General's report on the recommendations of the Board of Auditors [A/63/784] and the related ACABQ report [A/63/746] (see p. 83).

(see p. 83).

GENERAL ASSEMBLY ACTION

On 30 June [meeting 93], the General Assembly, on the recommendation of the Fifth Committee [A/63/637/Add.1] adopted **resolution 63/246 B** without vote [agenda item 116].

Financial reports and audited financial statements, and reports of the Board of Auditors

The General Assembly,

Recalling its resolutions 62/223 B of 20 June 2008 and 63/246 A of 24 December 2008,

Having considered the financial report and audited financial statements for the twelve-month period from 1 July 2007 to 30 June 2008 and the report of the Board of Auditors on the United Nations peacekeeping operations, the report of the Advisory Committee on Administrative and Budgetary Questions on the report of the Board of Auditors on the accounts of the United Nations peacekeeping operations for the financial period ended 30 June 2008 and the report of the Secretary-General on the implementation of the recommendations of the Board of Auditors concerning the United Nations peacekeeping operations for the financial period ended 30 June 2008,

1. *Accepts* the audited financial statements of the United Nations peacekeeping operations for the period from 1 July 2007 to 30 June 2008;

2. *Takes note* of the observations and endorses the recommendations contained in the report of the Board of Auditors;

3. *Reiterates* that the issue of outstanding assessed contributions is a policy matter of the General Assembly, and urges all Member States to make every possible effort to ensure the payment of their assessed contributions in full and on time;

4. *Takes note* of the observations and endorses the recommendations contained in the report of the Advisory Committee on Administrative and Budgetary Questions;

5. *Commends* the Board of Auditors for the quality of its report and the streamlined format thereof;

6. *Takes note* of the report of the Secretary-General on the implementation of the recommendations of the Board of Auditors concerning the United Nations peacekeeping operations for the financial period ended 30 June 2008;

7. *Requests* the Secretary-General to ensure the full implementation of the recommendations of the Board of Auditors, including those relating to expendable and non-expendable property, and the related recommendations of the Advisory Committee in a prompt and timely manner, subject to the provisions of the present resolution;

8. *Also requests* the Secretary-General to continue to indicate an expected time frame for the implementation of the recommendations of the Board of Auditors and the priorities for their implementation, including the office holders to be held accountable and measures taken in that regard;

9. *Further requests* the Secretary-General to provide, in the next report on the implementation of the recommendations of the Board of Auditors concerning the United Nations peacekeeping operations, a full explanation for the delays in the implementation of all outstanding recommendations of the Board, the root causes of the recurring issues and the measures to be taken.

Apportionment of costs

Report of Secretary-General. The Secretary-General reported in September [A/64/220] on the scale of assessments for the apportionment of the expenses of UN peacekeeping operations. He recalled that in its resolution 55/235 [YUN 2000, p. 102], the General Assembly had adopted a new system of adjustments of the scale of assessments for the regular budget to be used in fixing rates of assessment applicable to peacekeeping operations. That system was based on assigning each Member State to one of 10 levels, using its average per capita gross national product during the period 1993–1998 and other criteria.

Also in resolution 55/235, the Assembly requested the Secretary-General to update the composition of the levels on a triennial basis, in conjunction with the reviews of the scale of assessments for the regular budget, and to report thereon to the Assembly. By the same resolution, the Assembly decided that the structure of contribution levels to be implemented from 1 July 2001 would be reviewed after nine years. By its resolution 61/243 [YUN 2006, p. 1629], the Assembly decided to carry out the review at its sixty-fourth session and requested the Secretary-General to report on the updating of the composition of levels of contribution for peacekeeping operations for the period from 2010 to 2012. The report responded to that request and provided information on updating the composition of those levels. It provided information on changes in the peacekeeping levels of Member States based on average per capita gross national income during the 2002–2007 period. Those were based on the data used by the Committee on Contributions in reviewing the scale of assessments for the 2010–2012 period, which would be considered by the Assembly during its sixty-fourth session.

Until the General Assembly adopted a new scale, it would not be possible to determine the corresponding rates of assessment for peacekeeping. Further, any adjustments to the structure of contribution levels for peacekeeping operations, as might be decided by the Assembly, would also need to be taken into account in determining the rates of assessment for peacekeeping. For illustrative purposes, however, on the basis of the current structure of contributions levels, an annex showed the peacekeeping rates of assessment corresponding to the scale of assessments for the 2010–2012 period included in the report of the Committee on Contributions [A/64/11].

GENERAL ASSEMBLY ACTION

On 24 December [meeting 68], the General Assembly, on the recommendation of the Fifth Committee [A/64/595], adopted **resolution 64/249** without vote [agenda item 145].

Scale of assessments for the apportionment of the expenses of United Nations peacekeeping operations

The General Assembly,

Recalling its resolutions 55/235 and 55/236 of 23 December 2000, 58/256 of 23 December 2003 and 61/243 of 22 December 2006,

Recalling also its request to the Secretary-General, in paragraph 15 of resolution 55/235, to update the composition of the levels of contribution of Member States for peacekeeping operations described in the resolution on a triennial basis, in conjunction with the regular budget scale of assessment reviews, in accordance with the criteria established in the resolution, and to report thereon to the General Assembly,

Recalling further its decision, in paragraph 16 of resolution 55/235, to review the structure of levels of contribution for peacekeeping operations after nine years,

Reaffirming the principles set out in its resolutions 1874(S-IV) of 27 June 1963, 3101(XXVIII) of 11 December 1973 and 55/235,

Having considered the report of the Secretary-General on the implementation of resolutions 55/235 and 55/236,

1. *Takes note* of the report of the Secretary-General and of the updated composition of levels of contribution for peacekeeping operations for the period 2010 to 2012 contained therein;

2. *Reaffirms* the following general principles underlying the financing of United Nations peacekeeping operations:

(a) The financing of such operations is the collective responsibility of all States Members of the United Nations and, accordingly, the costs of peacekeeping operations are expenses of the Organization to be borne by Member States in accordance with Article 17, paragraph 2, of the Charter of the United Nations;

(b) In order to meet the expenditures caused by such operations, a different procedure is required from that applied to meet expenditures under the regular budget of the United Nations;

(c) Whereas the economically more developed countries are in a position to make relatively larger contributions to peacekeeping operations, the economically less developed countries have a relatively limited capacity to contribute towards peacekeeping operations involving heavy expenditures;

(d) The special responsibilities of the permanent members of the Security Council for the maintenance of peace and security should be borne in mind in connection with their contributions to the financing of peace and security operations;

(e) Where circumstances warrant, the General Assembly should give special consideration to the situation of any Member States which are victims of, and those which are otherwise involved in, the events or actions leading to a peacekeeping operation;

3. *Also reaffirms* that assessment rates for the financing of peacekeeping operations should be based on the scale of assessments for the regular budget of the United Nations, with an appropriate and transparent system of adjustments based on the levels of Member States, consistent with the principles outlined above;

4. *Further reaffirms* that the permanent members of the Security Council should form a separate level and that, consistent with their special responsibilities for the maintenance of peace and security, they should be assessed at a higher rate than for the regular budget;

5. *Affirms* that all discounts resulting from adjustments to the regular budget assessment rates of Member States in levels C through J shall be borne on a pro rata basis by the permanent members of the Security Council;

6. *Reaffirms* that the least developed countries should be placed in a separate level and receive the highest rate of discount available under the scale;

7. *Also reaffirms* that the statistical data used for setting the rates of assessment for peacekeeping should be the same as the data used in preparing the regular budget scale of assessments, subject to the provisions of the present resolution;

8. *Further reaffirms* the decision to create levels of discount to facilitate automatic, predictable movement between categories on the basis of the per capita gross national income of Member States;

9. *Decides* that, as from 1 January 2010, the rates of assessment for peacekeeping should be based on the ten levels of contribution and parameters set forth in the table below, subject to the provisions of the present resolution:

Level	Criteria	Threshold in US dollars (2010–2012)	Discount (per cent)
A	Permanent members of the Security Council	Not applicable	Premium
B	All Member States, except those covered below and level A	Not applicable	0
C	As listed in the annex to General Assembly resolution 55/235	Not applicable	7.5
D	Member States with per capita gross national income less than 2 times the average for all Member States (except level A, C and J contributors)	Under 13,416	20
E	Member States with per capita gross national income less than 1.8 times the average for all Member States (except level A, C and J contributors)	Under 12,074	40
F	Member States with per capita gross national income less than 1.6 times the average for all Member States (except level A, C and J contributors)	Under 10,733	60
G	Member States with per capita gross national income less than 1.4 times the average for all Member States (except level A, C and J contributors)	Under 9,391	70
H	Member States with per capita gross national income less than 1.2 times the average for all Member States (except level A, C and J contributors)	Under 8,050	80 (or 70 on a voluntary basis)[a]
I	Member States with per capita gross national income less than the average for all Member States (except level A, C and J contributors)	Under 6,708	80
J	Least developed countries (except level A and C contributors)	Not applicable	90

[a] Member States in level H have a discount of 70 per cent.

10. *Reaffirms* that Member States will be assigned to the lowest level of contribution with the highest discount for which they are eligible, unless they indicate a decision to move to a higher level;

11. *Also reaffirms* that for purposes of determining the eligibility of Member States for contribution in particular levels during the 2010–2012 scale period, the average per capita gross national income of all Member States will be 6,708 United States dollars and the per capita gross national income of Member States will be the average of 2002 to 2007 figures;

12. *Further reaffirms* that transition periods of two years will apply to countries moving up by two levels, and that transition periods of three years will apply to countries moving up by three or more levels without prejudice to paragraph 10 above;

13. *Reaffirms* that transitions as specified above will occur in equal increments over the transition period as designated above;

14. *Endorses* the updated composition of levels to be applied in adjusting regular budget scale rates to establish Member States' rates of assessment for peacekeeping operations for the period from 2010 to 2012, subject to the provisions of the present resolution;

15. *Requests* the Secretary-General to continue updating the composition of the levels described above on a triennial basis, in conjunction with the regular budget scale of assessment reviews, in accordance with the criteria established above, and to report thereon to the General Assembly;

16. *Recognizes* the concerns raised by Member States, including Bahrain and the Bahamas, regarding the structure of the levels of the scale of assessments for the apportionment of the expenses of United Nations peacekeeping operations;

17. *Also recognizes* the need to review the structure of the levels of the scale of assessments for the apportionment of the expenses of United Nations peacekeeping operations;

18. *Desires* to address the issues referred to above in an effective and expeditious manner;

19. *Decides* to review the structure of the levels of the scale of assessments for the apportionment of the expenses of United Nations peacekeeping operations with a view to a decision, if agreed, no later than at its sixty-seventh session.

Also on 24 December, the General Assembly decided that the agenda item on the scale of assessments for the apportionment of the expenses of UN peacekeeping operations would remain for consideration during its resumed sixty-fourth (2010) session (**decision 64/549**).

New rates of assessment. On 31 December [A/64/220/Add.1], following the adoption, by **resolution 64/248** (see p. 1412), of a new scale of assessments for the regular budget for the period 2010–2012 and the endorsement, by resolution 64/249 (see above), of the updated composition of levels for the period 2010–2012, the Secretary-General set out effective rates of assessment for peacekeeping for 2010–2012.

Reimbursement issues

Reimbursement for contingent-owned equipment

During its 2009 substantive session [A/63/19], the Special Committee on Peacekeeping Operations emphasized the importance of effective and transparent inspections of contingent-owned equipment. It acknowledged that troop costs had not been reviewed since 2002 and looked forward to the recommendations the Fifth Committee would make on that matter.

Report of Secretary-General. In January, the Secretary-General submitted a report [A/63/697] on the review of the methodology for rates of reimbursement to troop-contributing countries, pursuant to General Assembly resolution 62/252 [YUN 2008, p. 93]. The rate of reimbursement for troop costs, unchanged since 1 January 2002, included $1,028 for basic pay and allowance, a $303 specialists' allowance (payable for 10 per cent of infantry contingents and formed police units and for 25 per cent of support contingents), and a $73 allowance for personal clothing, gear, equipment and personal weapons and ammunition. The proposed methodology for rates of reimbursement to troop-contributing countries, described in a 2006 report [YUN 2006, p. 101], was resubmitted for consideration and approval by the Assembly.

The Secretary-General suggested that data and views on the daily allowance be collected through questionnaires to force commanders and to randomly selected peacekeepers. As for recreational leave allowance, contingent personnel could earn leave at 2.5 days per month, for a total of 15 days during a six-month assignment, but were entitled only to a recreational leave allowance of $10.50 per day for a maximum of seven days. The 2008 Working Group on Contingent-Owned Equipment had recommended [YUN 2008, p. 93] an increase in recreational leave allowance from 7 to 15 days for each six-month tour of duty for members of military contingents/formed police units.

The Secretary-General recommended that the Assembly approve the proposed methodology for the rates of reimbursement; the proposed rate of exchange reference date for the conversion of collected cost data from national currencies to United States dollars; the conduct of the first survey in 2009 and proposed periodicity thereafter; the proposed field questionnaires to collect data on the daily allowance for troops; and the increase in the number of days of recreational leave allowance for members of the military contingents and formed police units from 7 to 15.

ACABQ report. In April [A/63/746], ACABQ noted the Secretary-General's intention to provide valid, reliable and comprehensive data, which would constitute an improved basis for informed decision-making by the General Assembly and would be more transparent. The Committee further noted that the application of the methodology could lead to a change in the current applicable rates of reimbursement. It did not object to the Secretary-General's proposals.

GENERAL ASSEMBLY ACTION

On 30 June [meeting 93], the General Assembly, on the recommendation of the Fifth Committee [A/63/894], adopted **resolution 63/285** without vote [agenda item 132].

Rates of reimbursement to troop-contributing countries

The General Assembly,

Recalling its resolution 62/252 of 20 June 2008,

Recalling also its resolutions 55/274 of 14 June 2001 and 59/298 of 22 June 2005,

Having considered the updated report of the Secretary-General on the review of the methodology for rates of reimbursement to troop-contributing countries and the related report of the Advisory Committee on Administrative and Budgetary Questions,

1. *Takes note* of the updated report of the Secretary-General on the review of the methodology for rates of reimbursement to troop-contributing countries;

2. *Endorses* the recommendations contained in the report of the Advisory Committee on Administrative and Budgetary Questions, subject to the provisions of the present resolution, and requests the Secretary-General to ensure their full implementation;

3. *Decides* that the cost of any equipment purchased in a foreign currency by a troop-contributing country as well as the salary of any troop paid in a foreign currency may be reported in that currency;

4. *Also decides* to approve the increase in the number of days of recreational leave allowance paid to members of the military contingents and formed police units from seven to fifteen.

Management of peacekeeping assets

United Nations Logistics Base

The General Assembly, at its resumed sixty-third (2009) session, considered the performance report on the budget of the United Nations Logistics Base (UNLB) at Brindisi, Italy, for the period from 1 July 2007 to 30 June 2008 [A/63/626]. Expenditure totalled $40,201,500 gross ($37,198,600 net) against an appropriation of $40,379,600 gross ($37,687,200 net), resulting in an unencumbered balance of $178,100.

The value of strategic deployment stock activities for the period from 1 July 2007 to 30 June 2008 amounted to $132.4 million, including a $55.2 million rollover from the prior-period fund balance and $77.2 million corresponding to the shipment of strategic deployment stocks at replacement values to peacekeeping and special political missions.

The amount of $81.2 million was rolled over into the 2008/09 fund balance. The Secretary-General requested that the Assembly decide on the treatment of the unencumbered balance, as well as of other income for the period amounting to $3,031,700 from interest income ($2,571,000), other/miscellaneous income ($27,300) and cancellation of prior-period obligations ($433,400).

The Assembly also considered the proposed UNLB budget for 1 July 2009 to 30 June 2010 [A/63/824 & Corr.1], amounting to $68,240,300 and providing for 151 international staff and 268 national staff.

In June [A/63/746/Add.17], ACABQ evaluated the Secretary-General's proposed budget. Addressing the Fifth Committee on 4 June [A/C.5/63/SR.52], ACABQ Chair Susan McLurg recommended against approval of a number of the proposed staffing changes; the related reduction would amount to $9,888,100.

GENERAL ASSEMBLY ACTION

On 30 June [meeting 93], the General Assembly, on the recommendation of the Fifth Committee [A/63/894], adopted **resolution 63/286** without vote [agenda item 132].

Financing of the United Nations Logistics Base at Brindisi, Italy

The General Assembly,

Recalling section XIV of its resolution 49/233 A of 23 December 1994 and its resolution 62/231 of 22 December 2007,

Recalling also its decision 50/500 of 17 September 1996 on the financing of the United Nations Logistics Base at Brindisi, Italy, and its subsequent resolutions thereon, the latest of which was resolution 62/251 of 20 June 2008,

Recalling further its resolution 56/292 of 27 June 2002 concerning the establishment of the strategic deployment stocks and its subsequent resolutions on the status of the implementation of the strategic deployment stocks, the latest of which was resolution 62/251,

Having considered the reports of the Secretary-General on the financing of the United Nations Logistics Base, the related report of the Advisory Committee on Administrative and Budgetary Questions, and the oral statement of the Chairman of the Advisory Committee,

Reiterating the importance of establishing an accurate inventory of assets,

1. *Notes with appreciation* the facilities provided by the Government of Italy to the United Nations Logistics Base at Brindisi, Italy;

2. *Endorses* the conclusions and recommendations contained in the report of the Advisory Committee on Administrative and Budgetary Questions and the oral statement of the Chairman of the Advisory Committee, subject to the provisions of the present resolution, and requests the Secretary-General to ensure their full implementation;

3. *Recalls* paragraphs 9 and 13 of the report of the Advisory Committee, and requests the Secretary-General to ensure that indicators of achievement reflect more fully the scope of functions and services provided by the United Nations Logistics Base to peacekeeping operations and other field missions;

4. *Requests* the Secretary-General to take measures to expedite receipt and inspection procedures on strategic deployment stocks shipped from the United Nations Logistics Base and to report thereon in the context of the next budget submission;

5. *Welcomes* the intention of the Secretary-General to submit proposals to the General Assembly on a global support strategy for United Nations peacekeeping operations as referred to in paragraph 24 of the report of the Advisory Committee, and requests the Secretary-General to ensure that his proposals include a thorough cost-benefit analysis;

6. *Recalls* paragraph 51 of the report of the Advisory Committee, and decides to relocate the Standing Police Capacity to the United Nations Logistics Base;

7. *Requests* the Secretary-General to ensure the full implementation of the relevant provisions of its resolutions 59/296 of 22 June 2005, 60/266 of 30 June 2006 and 61/276 of 29 June 2007, as well as other relevant resolutions;

Financial performance report for the period from 1 July 2007 to 30 June 2008

8. *Takes note* of the report of the Secretary-General on the financial performance of the United Nations Logistics Base for the period from 1 July 2007 to 30 June 2008;

Budget estimates for the period from 1 July 2009 to 30 June 2010

9. *Approves* the cost estimates for the United Nations Logistics Base amounting to 57,954,100 United States dollars for the period from 1 July 2009 to 30 June 2010;

Financing of the budget estimates

10. *Decides* that the requirements for the United Nations Logistics Base for the period from 1 July 2009 to 30 June 2010 shall be financed as follows:

(a) The unencumbered balance and other income in the total amount of 3,209,800 dollars in respect of the financial period ended 30 June 2008 to be applied against the resources required for the period from 1 July 2009 to 30 June 2010;

(b) The balance of 54,744,300 dollars to be prorated among the budgets of the active peacekeeping operations for the period from 1 July 2009 to 30 June 2010;

(c) The estimated staff assessment income of 5,404,400 dollars, comprising the amount of 5,093,900 dollars for the period from 1 July 2009 to 30 June 2010 and the increase of 310,500 dollars in respect of the period from 1 July 2007 to 30 June 2008, to be offset against the balance referred to in subparagraph (b) above, to be prorated among the budgets of the individual active peacekeeping operations;

11. *Also decides* to consider at its sixty-fourth session the question of the financing of the United Nations Logistics Base at Brindisi, Italy.

Restructuring issues

Special Committee on Peacekeeping Operations consideration. The Special Committee [A/63/19] noted the increase in complex peacekeeping operations, and that the Security Council had mandated peacekeeping operations that included activities beyond the traditional tasks of monitoring and reporting. It therefore stressed the need for DPKO and DFS to be efficiently structured and adequately staffed. Noting that a number of senior posts within DFS were unfilled, it recommended action to fill all vacancies in both Departments.

The Special Committee reiterated the importance of preserving unity of command in missions at all levels, as well as coherence in policy and strategy and clear command structures—in the field and at Headquarters. It requested that the Secretary-General ensure a clear chain of command, accountability, coordination and maintenance of adequate checks and balances. It stressed that the success of the restructuring hinged upon the principles of unity of command and integration of efforts at all levels, in the field and at Headquarters. Noting that the integrated operational teams had yet to function effectively and efficiently, it requested that attention be given to improving communication with Member States.

Report of Secretary-General. In accordance with paragraph 67 of General Assembly resolution 61/279 [YUN 2007, p. 97], which called for a comprehensive review of the impact of the new structure of DPKO and DFS in the implementation of mission mandates and on the efficiency and effectiveness of programme delivery, the Secretary-General, in February, submitted a report [A/63/702 & Corr.1] on strengthening the UN capacity to manage peacekeeping operations, which set the context of restructuring, outlined the progress and initial impact of the restructuring effort and described ongoing challenges for UN peacekeeping.

The report stated that in the 18 months following the adoption of resolution 61/279 concerning the restructuring, significant strategic and operational benefits had been realized. The most noticeable impact of the restructuring had been the creation of consolidated, dedicated areas of expertise in the areas of rule of law and field support. The establishment of the DPKO Office of Rule of Law and Security Institutions had allowed a more balanced, comprehensive support to the related elements within the 18 peacekeeping operations and special political missions under the responsibility of DPKO. In forming DFS, the role of mission support had been elevated and was now rightly positioned as a "strategic enabler" in the delivery of peacekeeping and political mandates to those operations, including 16 missions for which the Department of Political Affairs (DPA) had lead responsibility. Overall, unity of command had been preserved, greater integration of effort achieved, guidance to the field enhanced, and improvements to administrative and management processes realized.

New, more complex and urgent mandates continued to strain the Organization, the report stated. With the growth in the authorized strength of peacekeeping personnel by over 30 per cent and the establishment of two highly complex operations in Chad and the Central African Republic, as well as in Darfur, the operational demands on the two Departments had continued to grow. As a result, the effort to deliver new, larger and more diverse field operations had often conflicted with the capability of the Departments to engage in strategic planning and to organize in a more effective and efficient manner. A similar situation had occurred in respect of the establishment of the integrated operational teams, which had achieved varying measures of success.

DFS was developing a comprehensive support strategy to pursue innovative ways of working while increasing accountability. Refinements were also being made to the integrated operational team concept. Other areas identified for further reform included an improved division of labour within DPA and strengthened rule of law capacities. Implementation of General Assembly resolution 63/250 [YUN 2008, p. 1616] on human resources management would strengthen the Organization's capability to attract and retain highly qualified staff for UN field operations.

The reform agenda set by Member States to strengthen DPA and DFS was achieving clear benefits. The Departments would conduct a comprehensive analysis of the challenges and opportunities for peacekeeping, with a view to identifying approaches and to articulating strategic and policy goals to minimize risk, optimize partnerships and maximize effectiveness in mounting and sustaining UN operations.

In May [A/63/841], ACABQ submitted its comments on the Secretary-General's report.

OIOS report. Pursuant to Assembly resolution 61/279, OIOS conducted an audit of the Secretariat's structure for managing and sustaining peacekeeping operations. Reporting to the Assembly in April [A/63/837], OIOS stated that the main objective of the audit was to assess whether the organizational roles, responsibilities, reporting lines and other governance and accountability mechanisms in the Secretariat's new structure for peacekeeping were adequately defined. To that end, it reviewed roles of the heads of missions, DPKO, DFS, DPA, the Department of Management and other entities involved in peacekeeping.

Among its main findings, OIOS held that the new structure would allow DPKO to focus on substantive peacekeeping issues, but it was too early to determine whether the new structure was operating effectively and efficiently. Similarly, the roles and accountabilities of DFS and each mission's support component in providing support to missions were yet to be clearly defined. OIOS had made recommendations to address those issues, and the concerned departments had accepted them.

UN police capacities

Special Committee on Peacekeeping Operations consideration. The Special Committee [A/63/19] noted the sustained increase of the police dimension in a number of missions and stressed the importance of maintaining an appropriate support capacity at Headquarters to ensure an adequate level of oversight and guidance to the field. Noting the review of the DPKO Police Division carried out since its previous report, the Committee acknowledged the gaps in the capacities of the Division and stressed the importance of addressing them in a timely manner. The Special Committee called upon the Secretariat to continue developing standard operating guidelines and procedures for UN policing, including for formed police units, in consultation with Member States. It recognized the need to recruit qualified personnel for police components of UN peacekeeping operations, and encouraged the Secretariat to improve procedures and guidance, in cooperation with contributing countries, for timely, effective and transparent evaluation and recruitment of candidates.

Personnel matters

The Special Committee on Peacekeeping Operations [A/63/19] recognized the efforts made by DPKO and DFS with regard to balanced recruiting of staff. It urged the Secretary-General to ensure a fair representation of troop-contributing countries when selecting personnel for such staff positions, and acknowledged the progress made by the Secretariat in ensuring a better representation of troop-contributing countries, in particular developing countries, in regard to senior mission leadership appointments. The Special Committee expressed concern at the continuing low proportion of women in the Secretariat, in particular women from developing countries, especially at the senior levels. It stressed that, in the recruitment process, women from certain countries, in particular developing countries, should be accorded equal opportunities, in conformity with relevant resolutions. The Special Committee requested that the Secretary-General ensure equitable representation of Member States at the senior and policymaking levels of the Secretariat, especially those with inadequate representation at those levels.

Concerned about the high number of vacancies in peacekeeping missions, the Special Committee requested that the Secretariat accelerate the recruitment of personnel, including senior mission leadership. It requested that the Secretary-General swiftly implement the decisions on contractual arrangements and harmonization of conditions of service as a means of dealing with the high vacancy issue. It also requested that he continue to ensure greater use of national staff in peacekeeping operations.

The Special Committee acknowledged that the interaction of UN military, police and civilian personnel with the local population was necessary for the efficiency and success of peacekeeping operations, and that language skills should constitute an important element of selection and training. It therefore urged DPKO and DFS to recruit staff and experts on mission with language skills that were relevant to the mission area where they were to be deployed. Good command of the official language in the country should also be taken into account.

Criminal accountability of UN staff and experts on mission

Report of Secretary-General. Pursuant to General Assembly resolution 63/119 [YUN 2008, p. 98], the Secretary-General, in July, submitted a report [A/64/183 & Add.1] on the criminal accountability of UN officials and experts on mission that provided information from Governments on the extent to which their laws established jurisdiction over serious crimes committed by their nationals while serving as UN officials or experts on mission, as well as information on cooperation among States and with the United Nations in the exchange of information and the facilitation of investigations and prosecution. The report also detailed recent Secretariat activities, including bringing credible allegations to the attention of the concerned State and providing training on UN standards of conduct before deployment and during a mission.

Working Group consideration. On 23 October [A/C.6/64/SR.14], Maria Telalian (Greece), Chairperson of the Working Group on criminal accountability of United Nations officials and experts on mission [YUN 2008, p. 98], briefed the General Assembly Sixth Committee on the activities of the Working Group, which met on 13 and 15 October. Participants had exchanged views mainly on the question of whether it was timely and appropriate to start negotiations on a draft international convention on criminal accountability, as proposed by the Group of Legal Experts [YUN 2006, p. 109].

Some delegations held that a binding legal instrument would constitute a solid legal basis for establishing criminal jurisdiction by the State of nationality of the alleged offender, so as to eliminate potential jurisdictional gaps, and for enhancing cooperation among States and between States and the United Nations. Adoption of a convention would give a strong political signal that criminal conduct by UN officials or experts on mission would not be tolerated. Other delegations considered it premature to discuss a draft convention, as further information and study were needed to understand the nature and extent of the problem—including potential jurisdictional gaps or obstacles to cooperation—and to assess whether a convention would be an appropriate response. Some felt that efforts should focus on implementing the measures adopted in Assembly resolutions 62/63 [YUN 2007, p. 102] and 63/119, in particular the improvement by individual States of their own legislation, as well as enhanced cooperation among States. Others suggested adapting the model status-of-forces agreements and status-of-mission agreements to specific situations, by focusing on the elaboration of jurisdictional clauses and provisions aimed at strengthening cooperation in the prosecution of serious crimes committed by UN officials and experts on mission. Informal consultations had also begun on the elaboration of a draft resolution that would reaffirm the need to implement the short-term measures envisaged in those resolutions.

On 16 December [meeting 64], the General Assembly, on the recommendation of the Sixth Committee [A/64/446], adopted **resolution 64/110** without vote [agenda item 78].

Criminal accountability of United Nations officials and experts on mission

The General Assembly,

Recalling its resolution 59/281 of 29 March 2005, in which it endorsed the recommendation of the Special Committee on Peacekeeping Operations that the Secretary-General make available to the United Nations membership a comprehensive report on the issue of sexual exploitation and abuse in United Nations peacekeeping operations,

Recalling also that the Secretary-General, on 24 March 2005, transmitted to the President of the General Assembly a report of his Adviser concerning sexual exploitation and abuse by United Nations peacekeeping personnel,

Recalling further its resolution 59/300 of 22 June 2005, in which it endorsed the recommendation of the Special Committee on Peacekeeping Operations that a group of legal experts be established to provide advice on the best way to proceed so as to ensure that the original intent of the Charter of the United Nations can be achieved, namely that United Nations staff and experts on mission would never be effectively exempt from the consequences of criminal acts committed at their duty station, nor unjustly penalized without due process,

Recognizing the valuable contribution of United Nations officials and experts on mission towards the fulfilment of the principles and purposes of the Charter,

Reaffirming the need to promote and ensure respect for the principles and rules of international law,

Reaffirming also that the present resolution is without prejudice to the privileges and immunities of United Nations officials and experts on mission and the United Nations under international law,

Reaffirming further the obligation of United Nations officials and experts on mission to respect the national laws of the host State, as well as the right of the host State to exercise, where applicable, its criminal jurisdiction, in accordance with the relevant rules of international law and agreements governing operations of United Nations missions,

Deeply concerned by reports of criminal conduct, and conscious that such conduct, if not investigated and, as appropriate, prosecuted, would create the negative impression that United Nations officials and experts on mission operate with impunity,

Reaffirming the need to ensure that all United Nations officials and experts on mission function in a manner that preserves the image, credibility, impartiality and integrity of the United Nations,

Emphasizing that crimes committed by such persons are unacceptable and have a detrimental effect on the fulfilment of the mandate of the United Nations, in particular with respect to the relations between the United Nations and the local population in the host country,

Conscious of the importance of protecting the rights of victims of criminal conduct, as well as of ensuring adequate protection for witnesses, and recalling the adoption of its resolution 62/214 of 21 December 2007 on the United Nations Comprehensive Strategy on Assistance and Support to Victims of Sexual Exploitation and Abuse by United Nations Staff and Related Personnel,

Emphasizing the need to enhance international cooperation to ensure the criminal accountability of United Nations officials and experts on mission,

Recalling its resolution 61/29 of 4 December 2006, by which it established the Ad Hoc Committee on criminal accountability of United Nations officials and experts on mission,

Having considered the report of the Group of Legal Experts established by the Secretary-General pursuant to its resolution 59/3006 and the report of the Ad Hoc Committee, as well as the note by the Secretariat and the reports of the Secretary-General on criminal accountability of United Nations officials and experts on mission,

Recalling its resolutions 62/63 of 6 December 2007 and 63/119 of 11 December 2008,

Convinced of the need for the United Nations and its Member States to urgently take strong and effective steps to ensure criminal accountability of United Nations officials and experts on mission in the interest of justice,

1. *Expresses its appreciation* for the work done by the Working Group of the Sixth Committee on criminal accountability of United Nations officials and experts on mission;

2. *Strongly urges* States to take all appropriate measures to ensure that crimes by United Nations officials and experts on mission do not go unpunished and that the perpetrators of such crimes are brought to justice, without prejudice to the privileges and immunities of such persons and the United Nations under international law, and in accordance with international human rights standards, including due process;

3. *Strongly urges* all States to consider establishing to the extent that they have not yet done so jurisdiction, particularly over crimes of a serious nature, as known in their existing domestic criminal laws, committed by their nationals while serving as United Nations officials or experts on mission, at least where the conduct as defined in the law of the State establishing jurisdiction also constitutes a crime under the laws of the host State;

4. *Encourages* all States to cooperate with each other and with the United Nations in the exchange of information and in facilitating the conduct of investigations and, as appropriate, prosecution of United Nations officials and experts on mission who are alleged to have committed crimes of a serious nature, in accordance with their domestic laws and applicable United Nations rules and regulations, fully respecting due process rights, as well as to consider strengthening the capacities of their national authorities to investigate and prosecute such crimes;

5. *Also encourages* all States:

(a) To afford each other assistance in connection with criminal investigations or criminal or extradition proceedings in respect of crimes of a serious nature committed by United Nations officials and experts on mission, including assistance in obtaining evidence at their disposal, in accordance with their domestic law or any treaties or other arrangements on extradition and mutual legal assistance that may exist between them;

(b) In accordance with their domestic law, to explore ways and means of facilitating the possible use of information and material obtained from the United Nations for purposes of criminal proceedings initiated in their territory for the prosecution of crimes of a serious nature committed by United Nations officials and experts on mission, bearing in mind due process considerations;

(c) In accordance with their domestic law, to provide effective protection for victims of, witnesses to, and others who provide information in relation to, crimes of a serious nature alleged to have been committed by United Nations officials and experts on mission and to facilitate access by victims to victim assistance programmes, without prejudice to the rights of the alleged offender, including those relating to due process;

(d) In accordance with their domestic law, to explore ways and means of responding adequately to requests by host States for support and assistance in order to enhance their capacity to conduct effective investigations in respect of crimes of a serious nature alleged to have been committed by United Nations officials and experts on mission;

6. *Requests* the Secretariat to continue to ensure that requests to Member States seeking personnel to serve as experts on mission make States aware of the expectation that persons who serve in that capacity should meet high standards in their conduct and behaviour and be aware that certain conduct may amount to a crime for which they may be held accountable;

7. *Urges* the Secretary-General to continue to take such other practical measures as are within his authority to strengthen existing training on United Nations standards of conduct, including through predeployment and

in-mission induction training for United Nations officials and experts on mission;

8. *Decides*, bearing in mind its resolutions 62/63 and 63/119, that the consideration of the report of the Group of Legal Experts, in particular its legal aspects, taking into account the views of Member States and the information contained in the note by the Secretariat, shall be continued during its sixty-seventh session in the framework of a working group of the Sixth Committee;

9. *Requests* the Secretary-General to bring credible allegations that reveal that a crime may have been committed by United Nations officials or experts on mission to the attention of the States against whose nationals such allegations are made and to request from those States an indication of the status of their efforts to investigate and, as appropriate, prosecute crimes of a serious nature, as well as the types of appropriate assistance that States may wish to receive from the Secretariat for the purposes of such investigations and prosecutions;

10. *Requests* the United Nations, when its investigations into allegations suggest that crimes of a serious nature may have been committed by United Nations officials or experts on mission, to consider any appropriate measures that may facilitate the possible use of information and material for purposes of criminal proceedings initiated by States, bearing in mind due process considerations;

11. *Encourages* the United Nations, when allegations against United Nations officials or experts on mission are determined by a United Nations administrative investigation to be unfounded, to take appropriate measures, in the interests of the Organization, to restore the credibility and reputation of such officials and experts on mission;

12. *Urges* the United Nations to continue cooperating with States exercising jurisdiction in order to provide them, within the framework of the relevant rules of international law and agreements governing activities of the United Nations, with information and material for purposes of criminal proceedings initiated by States;

13. *Emphasizes* that the United Nations, in accordance with the applicable rules of the Organization, should take no action that would retaliate against or intimidate United Nations officials and experts on mission who report allegations concerning crimes of a serious nature committed by United Nations officials and experts on mission;

14. *Takes note with appreciation* of the information provided by Governments in response to its resolutions 62/63 and 63/119, and urges Governments to continue taking the measures necessary for the implementation of those resolutions, including their provisions addressing the establishment of jurisdiction, particularly over crimes of a serious nature, as known in their existing domestic criminal laws, committed by their nationals while serving as United Nations officials or experts on mission, as well as cooperation among States;

15. *Reiterates its request* to the Secretary-General to report to the General Assembly at its sixty-fifth session on the implementation of the present resolution, in particular with respect to paragraphs 3, 5 and 9 above, as well as any practical problems in its implementation, on the basis of information received from Governments and the Secretariat;

16. *Requests* the Secretary-General to include in his report information on the number and types of credible allegations and any actions taken by the United Nations and its Member States regarding crimes of a serious nature committed by United Nations officials and experts on mission;

17. *Also requests* the Secretary-General to include in his report information on how the United Nations might support Member States, at their request, in the development of domestic criminal law relevant to crimes of a serious nature committed by their nationals while serving as United Nations officials or experts on mission;

18. *Decides* to include in the provisional agenda of its sixty-fifth session the item entitled "Criminal accountability of United Nations officials and experts on mission".

Welfare and recreational needs

The Special Committee [A/63/19] reaffirmed the importance of welfare and recreation for peacekeeping personnel, including non-contingent personnel, bearing in mind that it contributed to strengthening morale and discipline. It believed that the provision of facilities related to welfare and recreation should be prioritized during the establishment of peacekeeping missions. The Special Committee reaffirmed the important role of troop- and police-contributing countries in the welfare and recreation of contingent personnel.

Pursuant to the request of the Special Committee at its 2008 session, which was endorsed by the General Assembly in its resolution 62/273 [YUN 2008, p. 82], the Secretary-General, in January, submitted a report on the welfare and recreation needs of all categories of personnel and detailed implications [A/63/675 & Corr.1]. The report reviewed the practices of mission welfare and recreation programmes, and described the status of the measures that were under consideration or under way. DFS had conducted two surveys to assess the state of welfare and recreation in the field, which identified a variety of issues on the need to improve the quality of the environment in which UN personnel worked and lived. The Secretary-General proposed measures to address those issues, and presented indicative resource projections for establishing minimum welfare and recreation kits.

The Secretariat had taken measures to improve the welfare of all categories of peacekeeping personnel, which addressed commissaries and utilities and travel for leave and recreational purposes. Specific measures applicable to UN police officers and military observers included compensatory time-off policy. Measures applicable to military contingents and formed police units addressed annual leave, adequate access to communication, leave centres within or outside the mission area and minimum recreation facilities. The Secretary-General invited the Assembly to take note of those measures and to approve the establishment of minimum welfare and recreation standards.

The report concluded that strengthened welfare programmes would add to the well-being of all personnel and enhance the morale and efficiency of peacekeepers. A minimum standard of welfare and recreation throughout missions would promote adherence to codes of conduct and discipline by alleviating adverse conditions. It would also help to reduce the level of staff turnover and foster a shared sense of purpose among the personnel serving the United Nations.

On 7 April, the General Assembly deferred consideration of the Secretary-General's report until its sixty-fourth session (**decision 63/550 C**).

Death and disability

The Special Committee [A/63/19] expressed concern that the UN death and disability claims process for peacekeeping personnel was overly cumbersome, lengthy and lacking in transparency. It also noted that discrepancies existed between the compensation benefits provided to experts on mission and those provided to members of contingents. The Special Committee in that context recalled section X of General Assembly resolution 61/276 [YUN 2007, p. 81], on death and disability claims, and requested that the Secretary-General ensure its implementation.

Training

Report of Secretary-General. Pursuant to General Assembly resolution 60/266 [YUN 2006, p. 89], the Secretary-General, in January, reported [A/63/680] on the progress of training in peacekeeping, reviewing the key findings of a peacekeeping training needs assessment and the training strategy that had been implemented to meet priority needs. The report reviewed the roles and responsibilities of the various offices and sections, both at Headquarters and in the field. It described the training initiatives being undertaken throughout DPKO and DFS, and examined the resources required as well as the methods and localities for peacekeeping training.

While much work had been done to improve training, further work was needed to finalize and implement a new training strategy, the Secretary-General said. Peacekeeping personnel were increasingly required to operate in complex, changing and challenging conditions, which required that the United Nations deploy personnel able to perform a variety of tasks across different functional areas, often in difficult environments and with limited resources. A strategic training needs assessment undertaken in the first half of 2008 by the Integrated Training Service—a shared resource that supported DPKO, DFS, peacekeeping missions and Member States—examined the three main phases of peacekeeping training: prior to

deployment to a mission; on arrival at a mission or at Headquarters; and throughout a peacekeeping assignment.

Accordingly, a new UN peacekeeping training strategy was developed and approved in May 2008, with a view to creating a training system that met the needs of modern, complex peacekeeping operations. The strategy redefined the role that each office should play vis-à-vis field missions, Headquarters and Member States, to maximize comparative advantage, expertise and value. It aimed to enable peacekeeping personnel to meet evolving challenges, perform their specialist functions in an effective, professional and integrated manner, and demonstrate the core UN values and competencies.

As UN peacekeeping was an ongoing, long-term effort, effective training must be linked to career development and the establishment of a cadre of peacekeeping professionals, the Secretary-General said. The United Nations had made considerable progress in developing and implementing peacekeeping training. Predeployment, induction and ongoing training were steadily improving and continued progress could be expected. Nevertheless, the Organization must be realistic about what could be achieved. While the new training strategy established clear goals and mechanisms, limited resources meant that not all training needs could be met. Member States and training partners were therefore encouraged to continue to support the two Departments in those efforts.

On 7 April, the General Assembly deferred consideration of the Secretary-General's report until its sixty-fourth session (**decision 63/550 C**).

Special Committee on Peacekeeping Operations consideration. The Special Committee [A/63/19] reaffirmed the need to ensure that all personnel selected for peacekeeping missions had the required professional background, expertise and training, and recalled the shared responsibility of the Member States and the Secretariat concerning the training of personnel to be deployed in UN peacekeeping operations. It took note of the development by DPKO of its UN peacekeeping training strategy. It also took note of the ongoing work of the Integrated Training Service concerning the development of a set of minimum training standards and training modules. It welcomed the updating of training material with information on the prevention of sexual exploitation and abuse and on HIV/AIDS.

Acknowledging that the complex and multidimensional nature of peacekeeping demanded expertise and experience that most Member States could not muster on a continuous basis, the Special Committee encouraged cooperation in peacekeeping training among Member States, including through the provision of training opportunities and assistance to new and emerging troop-contributing countries. It expressed support for the efforts of Member States and regional arrangements to enhance the capacity of peacekeeping personnel at peacekeeping training centres. It expressed support for the efforts of DPKO in providing those peacekeeping training centres, as well as national training focal points, with guidance on training.

Looking forward to further improvement of the standardized training modules for potential senior mission leaders, the Special Committee renewed its call for the finalization of training standards and guidelines for formed police units, as well as the finalization of specialized training modules for police. It welcomed the first standardized UN police predeployment training curriculum and mission-specific training, and noted the recent predeployment mission-specific training that was conducted in partnership

with the Secretariat and Member States, which resulted in an increase from 10 to 70 per cent of newly deployed police personnel receiving predeployment training. It stressed the importance of maintaining an appropriate support and guidance capacity at UN Headquarters to ensure oversight and guidance to the field and to complement the work of the Integrated Training Service.

The Special Committee welcomed the integrated distance learning programmes provided to the peacekeeping missions by the Peace Operations Training Institute, and urged DPKO and the Institute to work together to promote the e-learning programmes. It underlined that training and awareness-raising in regard to misconduct were among the key elements in ensuring the orderly conduct of UN personnel, a matter in which troop- and police-contributing countries and the Secretariat played important roles.

Chapter II

Africa

In 2009, the United Nations maintained its commitment to promoting peace, stability and development in Africa through six United Nations political and peacebuilding missions and seven peacekeeping operations. The Organization faced daunting challenges in helping the countries in conflict situations and those in transition to post-conflict peacebuilding in Central Africa and the Great Lakes region, West Africa and the Horn of Africa return to peace, stability and prosperity. Many countries faced the complex task of bringing rebel groups to the negotiating table, concluding disarmament, demobilization and reintegration programmes for ex-combatants, promoting national reconciliation and creating the conditions for economic and social development.

The Office of the Special Adviser on Africa and the Office of the Special Representative of the Secretary-General for West Africa (UNOWA) brought a regional perspective to issues facing the continent, promoted conflict prevention and raised awareness about subregional problems. The United Nations worked closely with international actors and the African Union (AU), the Economic Community of West African States, the Economic Community of Central African States and other regional organizations to assist Governments in improving security, ensuring humanitarian access, energizing peace processes and promoting development. The United Nations continued to monitor Security Council-sanctioned arms embargoes in the Democratic Republic of the Congo (DRC), the Darfur region of western Sudan and Somalia.

The United Nations Peacebuilding Commission contributed to post-conflict stabilization in Burundi, the Central African Republic, Guinea-Bissau and Sierra Leone. As at 30 June, the Peacebuilding Fund had received $309.6 million from 45 donors.

In May, a Security Council mission visited the DRC, Ethiopia, Liberia and Rwanda to promote peace and reconciliation.

Central Africa and the Great Lakes region saw significant progress in efforts to restore the region to peace and stability, notably the agreements reached between the DRC with Rwanda and with rebel groups; concerted efforts in Burundi to implement the 2006 Comprehensive Ceasefire Agreement and the 2008 Bujumbura Declaration; and implementation in the Central African Republic of the recommendations of the 2008 inclusive dialogue. However, renewed hostilities by rebel groups operating in the border areas of the Central African Republic, Chad and the Western Darfur region of the Sudan, as well as the continued activities of the Lord's Resistance Army (LRA) out of Uganda, threatened the efforts of the United Nations and the international community to restore peace, stability and development to the region. In December, the Secretary-General informed the Security Council of his intention to establish the United Nations Office for Central Africa in Libreville, Gabon, to cooperate with African regional organizations to promote peace and stability in the subregion.

In the DRC, efforts intensified to implement the 2007 Nairobi communiqué for ending the threat to peace and security. On 23 March, the Government and armed rebel groups signed a peace agreement. As a result, the United Nations Organization Mission in the Democratic Republic of the Congo (MONUC) was able to scale down its operations in the western part of the country and transfer them to the eastern part, where the security situation remained volatile. The Presidents of the DRC and Rwanda, at a bilateral summit meeting in Goma on 6 August, pledged to start a new era in relations between the two countries and agreed on a range of bilateral accords, including a re-launch of the DRC-Rwanda Joint Permanent Commission. The DRC and Rwanda, and later the DRC assisted by MONUC, launched campaigns to oust the rebel movement Forces démocratiques de libération du Rwanda from Congolese territory.

In Burundi, the last rebel movement, the Forces nationales de libération (FLN), disarmed and transformed itself into a political party, thus concluding the last stage of the peace process. The Government established the National Independent Electoral Commission and preparations began for holding elections in 2010. In the light of that progress, the mandate of the South African Facilitator ended, the Office of the Facilitation closed and the AU Special Task Force withdrew. Progress was also made in disarming and demobilizing former FLN combatants.

Despite significant challenges, the Central African Republic made positive steps forward. A broad-based Government was established and the committees for implementing the various aspects of the December 2008 recommendations were established. Progress was made in the preparations for holding elections in 2010, and in the disarmament, demobilization and reintegration of former combatants. To support the promising peacebuilding opportunities, the Secretary-General proposed establishing a United Nations Integrated Peacebuilding Office in the Central African Republic.

In March, the United Nations Mission in the Central African Republic and Chad (MINURCAT) took over security responsibilities from the European Union force (EUFOR), adding a large military component to its operations. EUFOR troops were re-hatted while troops from other countries arrived to take up duties.

LRA did not fulfil its commitments under the 2008 Final Peace Agreement and continued its attacks on civilians, causing death, abductions and the displacement of thousands of civilians. The Government of Uganda and LRA representatives were yet to sign the final peace agreement. On 30 June, the Secretary-General suspended the mission of the Special Envoy for the LRA-affected areas, Joaquim Alberto Chissano, and closed his office in Kampala, as the Special Envoy had achieved the main objectives of his mandate. He would, however, be available if a signing ceremony of the final peace agreement was arranged.

In Rwanda, the United Nations continued the programme of information and outreach entitled "The Rwanda Genocide and the United Nations" to mobilize civil society for Rwanda genocide victim remembrance and education in order to help prevent future acts of genocide. In December, the General Assembly adopted a resolution on assistance to survivors of the 1994 genocide, particularly orphans, widows and victims of sexual violence, and extended the mandate of the outreach programme.

In West Africa, the year 2009 witnessed an overall improvement in the peace and security situation, despite some reversals. The region continued to face debilitating factors, including food insecurity, climate change and corruption. UNOWA coordinated UN political and developmental assistance to the subregion and guided countries in their quest for consolidation of peace. Among the issues addressed by UNOWA, weakness in governance and the rule of law remained major concerns, and security threats increased, including organized crime and terrorist activities. Social, economic and humanitarian challenges remained— the international financial crisis, drought and floods, food insecurity, high population growth and high unemployment rates, notably among the young. West African economies continued to grow, but at a slower pace. Wealth was concentrated in a few individuals while living conditions for the majority deteriorated. Some progress was made in democratization, with some countries, such as Mali and Senegal, holding transparent, free and fair elections. At the same time there was a resurgence of unconstitutional changes of government, compounded by the impunity of perpetrators.

In Côte d'Ivoire, the focus of the international community was to proceed with the implementation of the 2007 Ouagadougou Political Agreement and its supplementary accords, which called for creating a transitional Government, merging the forces of the opposing sides through an integrated command centre, and replacing the zone separating north and south with a "green line", to be monitored by the United Nations Operation in Côte d'Ivoire (UNOCI). In 2009, UNOCI worked with the Government to organize presidential elections postponed from 2008 until 29 November 2009. The mission provided technical and logistical support to the national commission responsible for elections. Substantial progress was made in identification and registration of voters and the validation of candidates running for President. However, because of delays in preparations, the elections were again postponed and rescheduled for February/March 2010. Nevertheless, work continued and remained on track for elections and implementation of the Agreement. Progress was more limited in other areas—in implementing the supplementary agreement on disarmament, reunification of defence and security forces, restoration of State authority to all areas of the country, and reunification of the treasury. In October, the Security Council renewed for another year the arms, travel and diamond sanctions imposed on Côte d'Ivoire.

The Government of Liberia continued its efforts to improve governance and security, consolidate State authority, manage natural resources, address human rights issues and build a better economy. It was assisted in those endeavours by the United Nations Mission in Liberia, which began to implement the third stage of the drawdown in October by reducing its forces by 2,029 soldiers to a strength of 8,202 military personnel. In 2009, the Government focused on reform of the security sector, in particular the national police and armed forces, which needed assistance in improving training and management capabilities. The Government also worked on drafting legislation in preparation for elections scheduled for 2011. The Truth and Reconciliation Commission completed its work and issued a final report in June. Three months later, the legislature decided not to take action on the Commission's recommendations until 2010. In December, the Security Council renewed the arms embargo imposed on Liberia and the travel ban and assets freeze against certain individuals for another year.

In Sierra Leone, the Government continued to develop strategies and activities aimed at peace consolidation and economic recovery, based on the President's Agenda for Change, a three-year plan issued in tandem with the Joint Vision of the United Nations Family for Sierra Leone, the plan for coordinating assistance from UN agencies and programmes. The Government was assisted in its efforts by the United Nations Integrated Peacebuilding Office in Sierra Leone. The Peacebuilding Commission continued its engagement with the country, focusing on maintaining progress in peacebuilding efforts and broadening the donor base. The peace consolidation process was briefly interrupted by political violence in March, which was ended with the signing on 2 April of a joint communiqué reaffirming the path towards peace and stability. The Special Court for Sierra Leone neared the conclusion of its trials of those bearing the greatest responsibility for serious violations of humanitarian laws committed in the country since 1996. By the end of 2009, only one trial remained ongoing—that of former Liberian President Charles Taylor.

The situation in Guinea-Bissau remained tense due to four assassinations during 2009, including in March of the President and the Chief of the General Staff. Those events, however, did not crush the Government's efforts to consolidate peace, organize presidential elections, reform the security sector and combat drug trafficking and organized crime. In those efforts, the Government was assisted by the United Nations Peacebuilding Support Office in Guinea-Bissau (UNOGBIS). As provided for by the Constitution, presidential elections were held in June and July, resulting in the election of Malam Bacai Sanha. In June, the Security Council extended the mandate of UNOGBIS until the end of the year, to be succeeded by a United Nations Integrated Peacebuilding Office in Guinea-Bissau (UNIOGBIS) with a smaller staff. The Peacebuilding Commission continued its engagement in Guinea-Bissau, focusing on the peace process, in particular on security sector reform and preparations for the presidential elections.

Cameroon and Nigeria continued to cooperate to advance implementation of the 2002 ruling of the International Court of Justice on their land and maritime boundary through the Cameroon-Nigeria Mixed Commission. In 2009, the joint technical team of surveyors resumed work on delineating the land boundary, and by the end of the year, some 1,420 kilometres of the total length of 1,950 kilometres had been surveyed. The Mixed Commission focused on the emplacement of the first permanent border demarcation pillars on the ground, which began in mid-November.

Guinea faced a period of uncertainty and tension following the death in December 2008 of President Lansana Conté and the coup led by the National Council for Democracy and Development (CNDD), a military junta. Once it seized power, CNDD sus-

pended governmental institutions and the Constitution while claiming that it would hand over power to a civilian president after elections in 2009, which were subsequently postponed. Opposition parties organized a rally on 28 September 2009, which quickly turned violent, leaving 156 dead. At the urging of the international community, the Secretary-General established a Commission of Inquiry to investigate the circumstances, which issued its report in December. Meanwhile, the international mediation process continued throughout the year; however, there was little progress in narrowing the gap in positions between CNDD and the coalition of opposition groups.

Following the overthrow of the President of Mauritania in 2008, UNOWA joined international efforts to assist the country in re-establishing constitutional order. The situation improved markedly in 2009 with presidential elections held in July that were declared free and fair by international observers.

The Organization strove to achieve a lasting peace in the Horn of Africa. As southern Sudan experienced an unusually violent and politically unstable year, the United Nations Mission in the Sudan (UNMIS) continued to support the resolution of core issues of the 2005 Comprehensive Peace Agreement (CPA), which promised to enhance the prospects for stability in the entire region. UNMIS responded swiftly to a number of violent outbreaks and, in February, it helped launch the Sudan Disarmament, Demobilization and Reintegration programme. Preparations for national elections, to be held in accordance with the CPA and planned for April 2010, dominated much of the political environment. Voter registration began on 1 November in most of the country and was concluded on 7 December, with approximately 16.5 million voters out of an estimated 20 million registered. The political landscape was affected by the arrest warrant against Sudanese President Omar Al-Bashir issued by the International Criminal Court on 4 March, to which the Sudanese Government responded by expelling 13 international non-governmental organizations (NGOs) from the Darfur region and shutting down three local NGOs. The humanitarian situation in southern Sudan continued to deteriorate, resulting in the death of an estimated 2,500 people and the displacement of 359,000 during the year.

The African Union-United Nations Hybrid Operation in Darfur (UNAMID) encountered successes, obstacles and tragedies amid a delicate peace as it closed out its second year. The costliest UN peacekeeping mission and its second-largest in personnel was tasked with helping bring peace to Darfur, which had endured one of the world's worst humanitarian crises in recent years. Increased deployment allowed UNAMID to project its presence more effectively, but it continued to lack resources, including helicopters, critical to the effective implementation of its mandate.

Regional peace efforts remained stalled as a result of continued tension between Chad and the Sudan. On 3 May, Chad and the Sudan signed an agreement in Doha, Qatar, pledging to refrain from the use of force and to cease providing support to opposition armed groups. However, on 4 May, a rebel group made an incursion in eastern Chad, clashing with Government forces. On 5 May, Chad accused the Sudan of sending armed elements into eastern Chad, thus breaching the Doha agreement. The Sudan denied the accusation, stating that it remained committed to the agreement. Relations between Chad and the Sudan remained tense during the rest of the year.

In Somalia, the Organization pursued a carefully calibrated set of steps in support of the fragile peace process, as endorsed by the Security Council in resolutions 1863(2009) and 1872(2009). Preparedness plans were drawn up in the event of a decision by the Security Council to deploy a UN peacekeeping mission as a follow-on force to the African Union Mission in Somalia (AMISOM). Meanwhile, the installation of a new Government, together with the withdrawal of the Ethiopian forces in mid-January—reconciliation measures laid out in the 2008 Djibouti Peace Agreement—were positive indicators for the direction of the peace process. The United Nations Political Office for Somalia, together with its regional and international partners, worked to advance the implementation of the Djibouti Agreement, while the newly established United Nations Support Office for the African Union Mission in Somalia (UNSOA) was mandated to deliver a support package to AMISOM similar to that of a UN peacekeeping mission. The Contact Group on Piracy off the Coast of Somalia was set up in January to combat the increasingly daring and sophisticated attacks against maritime vessels, and the Djibouti Code of Conduct, adopted by the International Maritime Organization in January, was signed by 10 States of the region. The Security Council in December imposed arms and travel sanctions on Eritrea for supporting insurgents trying to topple the Somali Government, extended the arms embargo on Somalia and expanded the mandate of the Monitoring Group overseeing implementation and violations of the embargo. The Council called on Member States, including Eritrea, to support the Djibouti peace process and reconciliation efforts by the Somali Government.

The Council in January urged Djibouti and Eritrea to resolve peacefully their ongoing border dispute. In December, the Council demanded that Eritrea withdraw its forces from the disputed area and engage in diplomatic efforts to settle the border issue.

Negotiations towards a lasting political solution to the question of Western Sahara continued, but the two parties to the dispute concerning the Territory—Morocco and the Frente Polisario para la Liberación de Saguía el-Hamra y de Río de Oro (Frente Polisario)—remained far apart on ways to achieve that goal. The United Nations Mission for the Referendum in Western Sahara (MINURSO) monitored compliance with the 1991 ceasefire between the parties. The Security Council in April extended MINURSO's mandate for another year, until 30 April 2010.

Promotion of peace in Africa

In 2009, the United Nations continued to identify and address the root causes of conflict in Africa and ways to promote sustainable peace and development on the continent. The Security Council considered the relationship between the United Nations and regional organizations, in particular the African Union (AU), in conflict prevention and resolution; Africa's peacekeeping capacity; the resurgence of coups d'état; and drug trafficking as a threat to peace and security in Africa. In addition, the Council conducted a mission from 14 to 21 May to the AU, Rwanda and the Democratic Republic of the Congo, and Liberia. The New York-based Office of the Special Adviser on Africa, headed by Cheick Sidi Diarra (Mali), continued to promote international support for Africa's development and security, including through the New Partnership for Africa's Development (NEPAD) [YUN 2001, p. 900], and to assist the Secretary-General in improving the coordination of UN system support to Africa.

Conflict prevention and resolution

AU special session. On 15 September [S/2009/461], the AU forwarded to the Security Council the outcome documents adopted by the AU Assembly of Heads of State and Government at its special session on the consideration and resolution of conflicts in Africa (Tripoli, Libyan Arab Jamahiriya, 30–31 August). At the session, Heads of State and Government reviewed the state of peace and security on the continent and proposed steps to hasten the attainment of a conflict-free Africa. While noting progress made in achieving peace between African nations, participants expressed concern at the resurgence of unconstitutional changes of Government; the emerging trend of election-related violence and conflicts; the threats posed by terrorism, drug trafficking, transnational organized crime, piracy and illicit exploitation of natural resources to fuel conflicts; and the persistence of border disputes and conflicts. Of equal concern was the issue of climate change and its consequences—food insecurity, scarce water resources, damage to coastal infrastructure and cities, reduced agricultural yields and environmentally-induced migration. Participants declared the year 2010 as the Year of Peace and Security in Africa, and requested that the AU Commission Chairperson prepare a programme that would identify steps to promote peace, security and stability.

Working Group. The Security Council on 15 December agreed that the Ad Hoc Working Group on Conflict Prevention and Resolution in Africa, initially established in March 2002 [YUN 2002, p. 93] for a one-year period, would continue its work until 31 December 2010 [S/2009/650].

On 30 December, the Chairman of the Working Group reported [S/2009/681] on its activities for 2009, having convened four times throughout the year. On 17 March, the Group met to consult on its activities and work programme for 2009. On 18 May, Uganda, in its capacity as Chairman of the Working Group, co-led a Security Council mission to the AU in Addis Ababa. The meetings with the AU reviewed the situations in Somalia and the Sudan, the resurgence of unconstitutional changes of Governments and the financing of peacekeeping operations in Africa. On 18 June, the Group adopted a programme of work that included informal and thematic meetings, workshops and forums; review of the situation in West Africa, including the impact of increasing drug trafficking; addressing ways to improve the working methods, cooperation and consultative process between the Council and the AU Peace and Security Council; reviewing how the United Nations, working with the AU, could implement conflict prevention and resolution strategies in Africa; and discussing how to address the needs of African countries emerging from conflict. On the same day, Said Djinnit, the Head of the United Nations Office for West Africa, gave a briefing on the situation in the region, the impact of drug trafficking and the risk of relapse posed to countries that were previously in conflict. On 9 December, the Working Group heard a briefing by Patrick Hayford, Director of the Office of the Special Adviser on Africa, on how the needs of African countries emerging from conflict could be addressed by assisting them in laying the foundations for sustainable peace and development.

General Assembly action. On 2 December, by **resolution 64/61** (see p. 567) on the activities of the United Nations Standing Advisory Committee on Security Questions in Central Africa, the Assembly encouraged the States members of the Standing Advisory Committee to render the early-warning mechanisms for central Africa fully operational. The Secretary-General had established the Standing Committee in 1992 [YUN 1992, p. 72] to encourage arms limitation, disarmament, non-proliferation and development in the subregion.

Resurgence of coups d'état

AU action. The AU Assembly, at its twelfth ordinary session (Addis Ababa, Ethiopia, 1–3 February) [A/63/848], adopted a decision [Assembly/AU/Dec.220 (XII)] on the resurgence of coups d'état in Africa. Expressing concern over such resurgence, the Assembly condemned the coups d'état that took place in 2008 in Mauritania and Guinea, as well as an attempted coup d'état in Guinea-Bissau; supported decisions taken by the AU Peace and Security Council on those three countries; reiterated the commitment of the AU to the related provisions of its Constitutive Act, the Protocol relating to the establishment of the Peace and Security Council, the 1999 Algiers Declaration and the 2000 Lomé Declaration on Unconstitutional Changes of Government; urged member States to sign and ratify the African Charter on Democracy, Elections and Governance; requested that the AU Commission Chairperson submit recommendations for preventive measures; and requested that the AU's partners lend support to the decisions made by the Peace and Security Council and other AU organs on unconstitutional changes of government.

SECURITY COUNCIL ACTION

On 5 May [meeting 6118], following consultations among Security Council members, the President made statement **S/PRST/2009/11** on behalf of the Council:

> The Security Council expresses its deep concern over the resurgence of unconstitutional changes of government in a few African countries. The Council expresses its concern at the possible violence that may accompany such events, as well as the negative impact on the economic and social welfare of the people and the development of affected countries. The Council stresses the importance of expeditiously restoring constitutional order, including through open and transparent elections.
>
> The Council reiterates its primary responsibility for the maintenance of international peace and security and recalls that cooperation with regional and subregional organizations, consistent with Chapter VIII of the Charter of the United Nations, can improve collective security.
>
> The Council welcomes the continuing important efforts of the African Union and subregional organizations, consistent with Council resolutions and decisions, to settle conflicts and promote human rights, democracy, the rule of law and constitutional order in Africa.
>
> The Council also welcomes the decision of the Assembly of the African Union at its twelfth ordinary session, held from 1 to 3 February 2009, in which it expressed the African Union's concern and condemnation of the resurgence of coups d'état, which it concluded not only constitute a dangerous political downturn and a serious setback to the democratic processes, but could also pose a threat to the peace, security and stability of the continent.
>
> The Council further welcomes preventive measures undertaken by the African Union and subregional organizations against unconstitutional changes of government.

Relationship between the United Nations and regional organizations

Cooperation between the AU and UN system

On 18 March [meeting 6092], the Security Council considered the relationship between the United Nations and regional organizations, in particular the AU, in maintaining international peace and security. The Council had before it the report of the AU-UN panel on modalities for support to AU peacekeeping operations [YUN 2008, p. 111]. The Secretary-General said that many of the challenges facing the AU resulted from difficulties in securing the necessary resources to support the deployment of peacekeeping operations. The Panel's recommendations had far-reaching implications. Its proposal on assessed contributions, in particular, must be considered by the requisite UN legislative bodies and processes. The Secretary-General said that the development of the African Peace and Security Architecture was crucial to an effective long-term approach to conflict prevention and resolution. That would require sustained international support, including that of the European Union, and many bilateral partnerships. The strategic relationship between the United Nations and the AU was at the heart of that evolving framework and had the potential to affect millions of people in Africa.

Presenting the report, the Chairman of the panel, Romano Prodi (Italy), stressed the responsibility of regional actors to address issues of peace and security in their own regions, and emphasized that peace in Africa could not be achieved through the deployment of military force alone, and that all Member States must be committed to the process. He underlined the need for a shared vision, based on long-term partnerships underpinned by credible institutional capabilities requiring resources and contributions, while ownership must belong to Africa. The AU Commissioner for Peace and Security, Ramtane Lamamra, stressed that peacekeeping in Africa was a shared responsibility requiring boldness, harmonization of efforts and cohesiveness. The Minister for Foreign Affairs of South Africa, Nkosazana Dlamini Zuma, and the Chairperson of the AU Peace and Security Council, Édouard Aho-Glélé, as well as 30 other delegations, addressed the meeting.

SECURITY COUNCIL ACTION

On 18 March [meeting 6092], following consultations among Security Council members, the President made statement **S/PRST/2009/3** on behalf of the Council:

The Security Council reiterates its primary responsibility for the maintenance of international peace and security and recalls that cooperation with regional and subregional organizations in matters relating to the maintenance of peace and security and consistent with Chapter VIII of the Charter of the United Nations, can improve collective security.

The Council recalls its previous relevant resolutions and statements which underscore the importance of developing effective partnerships between the United Nations and regional organizations, in particular the African Union, in accordance with the Charter and the relevant statutes of the regional organizations, in particular the African Union.

The Council welcomes the continuing important efforts of the African Union to settle conflicts on the African continent, and expresses its support for peace initiatives conducted by the African Union.

The Council reaffirms its resolution 1809(2008), in which it recognizes the need to enhance the predictability, sustainability and flexibility of financing for regional organizations when they undertake peacekeeping under a United Nations mandate.

The Council recognizes that regional organizations have the responsibility to secure human, financial, logistical and other resources for their organizations.

The Council underscores the importance of supporting and improving, in a sustained way, the capacity of the African Union, and welcomes recent developments regarding cooperation between the United Nations, the African Union and international partners, including the enhancement of the African Union capacities.

The Council welcomes the efforts of the African Union-United Nations panel in producing a report on modalities to support African Union peacekeeping operations. The Council notes with interest the report of the panel.

The Council requests the Secretary-General to submit a report, no later than 18 September 2009, on practical ways to provide effective support for the African Union when it undertakes peacekeeping operations authorized by the United Nations, that includes a detailed assessment of the recommendations contained in the report of the African Union-United Nations panel, in particular those on financing, as well as on the establishment of a joint African Union-United Nations team.

The Council further requests the Secretary-General to take into account in his report the lessons learned from past and current African Union peacekeeping efforts, in particular the African Union-United Nations Hybrid Operation in Darfur (UNAMID), and the efforts to provide a logistical support package for the African Union Mission in Somalia and the establishment of the trust fund called for in Council resolution 1863(2009).

The Council underlines the importance of implementing the Ten-Year Capacity Building Programme for the African Union on peace and security, in particular the operationalization of the African Standby Force and the Continental Early Warning System. The Council stresses its support for ongoing efforts to strengthen the African Peace and Security Architecture and reiterates its call for the international community, particularly donors, to fulfil their commitments in the 2005 World Summit Outcome.

The Council emphasizes the importance of establishing more effective strategic relationships between the United Nations Security Council and the African

Union Peace and Security Council and between the United Nations Secretariat and the African Union Commission, and encourages further joint efforts in this direction focusing on issues of mutual interest. The Security Council calls upon the Secretariat and the African Union Commission to further collaborate on issues of mutual interest, including by developing a list of the military, technical, logistical and administrative capacities that need developing, supporting regular follow-up missions, experience-sharing, staff exchanges, and in financial and logistical areas.

The Council expresses its intention to further consider this issue following the report of the Secretary-General.

Report of Secretary-General. In September [A/64/359-S/2009/470], pursuant to presidential statement S/PRST/2009/3 (see above), the Secretary-General reported on support to au peacekeeping operations authorized by the United Nations. The report addressed the strategic partnership between the United Nations and the au; financing for au-led, UN-authorized peacekeeping operations; and building institutional capacity for peacekeeping operations. The Secretary-General underscored the importance of a close strategic partnership between the United Nations and the au and elaborated on the mechanisms and processes that should be put in place to enhance their partnership. It assessed the mechanisms available to improve the predictability, sustainability and flexibility of financing UN-authorized peacekeeping operations. It detailed the gaps in the au capacity to plan, manage, deploy and liquidate peacekeeping operations and proposed measures by which the United Nations could assist in building that capacity. It also summarized the long-term peacekeeping objective of the au embodied in the African Standby Force, underlining that many of the challenges that applied to the immediate peacekeeping demands of the au would remain relevant in operationalizing the Standby Force.

In his closing observations, the Secretary-General highlighted the increasingly active role played by regional organizations in supporting the Security Council, under Chapter VIII of the UN Charter, in carrying out its responsibilities in the maintenance of peace and security, as well as his commitment to supporting the au as it fulfilled its potential as a partner of the United Nations. He welcomed the decision of the au to increase the allotment of the regular budget to the au Peace Fund, which would be especially important in addressing the challenges that the au might face in financing the African Standby Force and other peacekeeping operations. While emphasizing the requirement for the provision of sustainable and predictable resources to ensure the success of au peacekeeping operations authorized by the United Nations, he said that ultimately, it would be the responsibility of au member States to provide the necessary resources. When peacekeeping was determined the best course of action to address a conflict in Africa, it was essential that the United Nations and the au work together to build consensus and support for the operation and to align mandates with objectives and resources. At the same time, it was important to recall that peacekeeping was part of a political solution, not an alternative, and that efforts must be made in parallel to enhance preventive diplomacy, early warning, and conflict resolution and mediation.

GENERAL ASSEMBLY ACTION

On 14 September [meeting 105], the General Assembly adopted **resolution 63/310** [draft: A/63/L.101 & Add.1] without vote [agenda item 114 *(a)*].

**Cooperation between the United Nations
and the African Union**

The General Assembly,

Having considered the report of the Secretary-General on cooperation between the United Nations and regional and other organizations,

Recalling the provisions of Chapter VIII of the Charter of the United Nations, as well as its resolutions 55/218 of 21 December 2000, 56/48 of 7 December 2001, 57/48 of 21 November 2002, 59/213 of 20 December 2004 and 61/296 of 17 September 2007,

Recalling also the principles enshrined in the Constitutive Act of the African Union adopted in 2000 in Lomé,

Recalling further the decisions and declarations adopted by the Assembly of the African Union at all its ordinary and extraordinary sessions,

Welcoming the adoption of the framework for the ten-year capacity-building programme for the African Union set out in the declaration on enhancing United Nations-African Union cooperation, signed in Addis Ababa on 16 November 2006 by the Secretary-General and the Chairperson of the African Union Commission, which highlights the key areas for cooperation between the African Union and the United Nations,

Acknowledging the decision of the African Union Peace and Security Council at its sixty-eighth meeting, held on 14 December 2006, on the establishment of a coordination and consultation mechanism between the African Union Peace and Security Council and the United Nations Security Council, welcoming the June 2007 agreement to hold joint meetings at least once a year, and taking note of the third consultative meeting held in July 2009 in Addis Ababa,

Recalling the adoption of the African Union Non-Aggression and Common Defence Pact at the fourth ordinary session of the Assembly of the African Union, as an instrument to reinforce cooperation among States members of the African Union in the areas of defence and security and which, in particular, can contribute to the work of the African Union Peace and Security Council and its cooperation with the United Nations,

Welcoming, while taking into account the role of the General Assembly, the statements by the President of the Security Council of 19 November 2004 on the institutional relationship with the African Union, of 28 March 2007 on the relationship between the United Nations and regional organizations, in particular the African Union, in the maintenance of international peace and security, and of 18 March 2009 on peace and security in Africa, as well as Security Council resolution 1809(2008) of 16 April 2008,

Welcoming also the efforts to enhance cooperation between the peace and security structures of the United Nations and the African Union in the realm of conflict prevention and resolution, crisis management, peacekeeping and post-conflict peacebuilding in Africa, including efforts to implement the African Union Framework for Post-conflict Reconstruction and Development,

Acknowledging the significant contribution of the African Union towards the prevention and combating of terrorism, and noting the centrality of the international partnership and cooperation between the African Union, the relevant United Nations organs and the wider international community in the global fight against terrorism,

Recognizing the need to enhance the strategic relationship between the United Nations and the African Union, as a basis for a more effective partnership embodying the principles of mutual respect when addressing issues of mutual concern,

Welcoming the efforts of the African Union and the United Nations, together with other international partners, to provide effective support for peacekeeping missions undertaken in accordance with Chapter VIII of the Charter by regional organizations, in particular the African Union, with reference to start-up funding, equipment, logistics and long-term capacity-building, as reflected in Security Council resolution 1809(2008),

Bearing in mind the United Nations Declaration on the New Partnership for Africa's Development, and various relevant resolutions adopted since 2002,

Recognizing the pivotal need to bring Africa into the mainstream of the global economy and to strengthen the global partnership to address the special development needs of Africa, particularly the eradication of poverty, and in this regard, welcoming the political declaration adopted on 22 September 2008 on the occasion of the high-level meeting on the theme "Africa's development needs: state of implementation of various commitments, challenges and the way forward", and the importance of its implementation and the responsibilities of the States members of the African Union and the United Nations in this regard, as well as the implementation of the New Partnership for Africa's Development,

Stressing the need for extending the scope of cooperation between the United Nations and the African Union in the area of combating the illegal exploitation of natural resources in Africa,

Emphasizing the importance of the effective, coordinated and integrated implementation of the United Nations Millennium Declaration, the Doha Development Agenda, the Monterrey Consensus of the International Conference on Financing for Development, the Doha Declaration on Financing for Development, the Plan of Implementation of the World Summit on Sustainable Development ("Johannesburg Plan of Implementation") and the 2005 World Summit Outcome,

Emphasizing also the importance of the 1995 World Summit for Social Development, at which the Copenhagen Declaration on Social Development was adopted, and the 1995 Fourth World Conference on Women, and stressing to all Member States the importance of the full and effective implementation of the Beijing Declaration and Platform for Action, the Programme of Action of the International Conference on Population and Development and the outcome of the twenty-third special session of the General Assembly,

Recalling the African Union Convention on Preventing and Combating Corruption and the Protocol to the African Charter on Human and People's Rights on the Rights of Women in Africa, adopted in Maputo on 11 July 2003,

Recommitting to improving the effectiveness of development assistance, including the fundamental principles of ownership, alignment, harmonization, managing for results and mutual accountability, calling for a continuing dialogue to improve the effectiveness of aid, including the full implementation of the Accra Agenda for Action by countries and organizations that commit to it,

Acknowledging the contribution of the United Nations Liaison Office at Addis Ababa in strengthening coordination and cooperation between the United Nations and the African Union, as well as the need to consolidate it so as to enhance its performance in view of the expanding scope of cooperation between the United Nations and the African Union,

Convinced that strengthening cooperation between the United Nations and the African Union will contribute to the advancement of the principles of the Charter of the United Nations, the principles of the Constitutive Act of the African Union and the development of Africa,

1. *Takes note with appreciation* of the report of the Secretary-General, calls for the implementation of the declaration on enhancing United Nations-African Union cooperation: framework for the ten-year capacity-building programme for the African Union, and in this regard requests the Secretary-General to continue to take appropriate measures to strengthen the capacity of the United Nations Secretariat and to implement its mandate with respect to meeting the special needs of Africa, in accordance with the established United Nations procedures;

2. *Recalls* the primary responsibility of the Security Council in the maintenance of international peace and security, and requests the United Nations system to intensify its assistance to the African Union, as appropriate, in strengthening the institutional and operational capacity of its Peace and Security Council, and in coordinating with other international partners when needed;

3. *Emphasizes* the need to pursue the ongoing measures to improve the effectiveness and efficiency of United Nations and African Union cooperation, recommends the continued improvement of the field presence of the United Nations Secretariat at the headquarters of the African Union, recognizing the need to ensure an appropriate level of representation at the United Nations Liaison Office at Addis Ababa commensurate with the increasing political integration of the African Union, the responsibilities for implementing all aspects of the ten-year capacity-building programme, coordinating the United Nations system in existing and emerging areas of cooperation in peace and

security and political and humanitarian affairs, in order to enhance the strategic and operational partnership between the United Nations and the African Union and its subregions;

4. *Recognizes* the need to enhance the predictability, sustainability and flexibility of financing for regional organizations when they undertake peacekeeping under a United Nations mandate, and looks forward to the report to be submitted by the Secretary-General pursuant to the statement by the President of the Security Council of 18 March 2009;

5. *Stresses* the urgent need for the United Nations and the African Union to develop close cooperation and concrete programmes aimed at addressing the problems posed by illicit trafficking in small arms and light weapons and anti-personnel mines, within the framework of the relevant declarations and resolutions adopted by the two organizations;

6. *Calls upon* the United Nations system, the African Union and the international community to intensify their cooperation in the global fight against terrorism through the implementation of the relevant international and regional treaties and protocols and, in particular, the African Plan of Action adopted in Algiers on 14 September 2002, as well as their support for the operation of the African Centre for Studies and Research on Terrorism inaugurated in Algiers in October 2004;

7. *Calls upon* the United Nations system to intensify its efforts, in collaboration with the African Union, in combating the illegal exploitation of natural resources, particularly in conflict areas, in accordance with relevant resolutions and decisions of the United Nations and the African Union;

8. *Also calls upon* the United Nations system to support the African Union and its member States in their efforts to implement the internationally agreed development goals, including the Millennium Development Goals;

9. *Stresses* the need for closer cooperation and coordination between the United Nations system and the African Union, in accordance with the Cooperation Agreement as well as other relevant memorandums of understanding between the two organizations, particularly in the implementation of the commitments contained in the United Nations Millennium Declaration and the 2005 World Summit Outcome and as regards achieving the internationally agreed development goals, including the Millennium Development Goals, at the national, subregional and regional levels;

10. *Encourages* the deepening of collaboration between the African Union, recalling its Framework for Post-conflict Reconstruction and Development, and the Peacebuilding Commission on enhancing international support for African countries on the agenda of the Commission, and reiterates the need for enhanced coordination and consultations between the Commission and the African Union on assistance for countries emerging from conflict;

11. *Invites* the Secretary-General to request all relevant United Nations agencies, funds and programmes to intensify their efforts to support cooperation with the African Union, including through the implementation of the protocols to the Constitutive Act of the African Union and the Treaty establishing the African Economic Community, and to assist in harmonizing the programmes of the Afri-

can Union with those of the African regional economic communities with a view to enhancing regional economic cooperation and integration;

12. *Encourages* the United Nations and the African Union to pursue joint initiatives for partnerships in Africa through, inter alia, the United Nations Office for Partnerships and the Global Compact;

13. *Encourages* the United Nations system to effectively support the efforts of the African Union by urging the international community to strive for the successful and timely completion of the Doha round of trade negotiations, including negotiations aimed at substantial improvements in areas such as trade-related measures, including market access and regional economic integration, to promote sustainable growth in Africa;

14. *Invites* the United Nations system to enhance its support for African countries in their efforts to implement the Johannesburg Plan of Implementation;

15. *Encourages* the United Nations to take special measures to address the challenges of poverty eradication through the United Nations funds, programmes and agencies, noting the importance of addressing, inter alia, debt cancellation, enhanced official development assistance, increases in flows of foreign direct investment and voluntary transfer of technology, the World Food Programme, the agriculture partnership to combat hunger, universal primary education initiatives, gender equality programmes, improved maternal health programmes, and HIV/AIDS education;

16. *Calls upon* the United Nations system to accelerate the implementation of the Plan of Action contained in the document entitled "A world fit for children", adopted on 10 May 2002 at the twenty-seventh special session of the General Assembly on children, and to provide assistance, as appropriate, to the African Union and its member States in this regard, welcomes the ongoing efforts of the African Union to ensure the protection of the rights of children, and recalls in this regard the adoption of the Call for accelerated action on the implementation of the Plan of Action towards Africa Fit for Children (2008–2012);

17. *Calls upon* the United Nations system and the African Union to develop a coherent and effective strategy, including through joint programmes and activities, for the promotion and protection of human rights in Africa, within the framework of the implementation of regional and international treaties, resolutions and plans of action adopted by the two organizations;

18. *Urges* the United Nations system to increase its support for Africa in the implementation of the declaration of the extraordinary summit meeting of the Assembly of Heads of State and Government of the Organization of African Unity on HIV/AIDS, malaria, tuberculosis and other related infectious diseases, held in Abuja in April 2001, and the Declaration of Commitment on HIV/AIDS so as to arrest the spread of these diseases, inter alia, through sound capacity-building in human resources;

19. *Also urges* the United Nations system to continue to implement General Assembly resolutions 58/149 of 22 December 2003 and 63/149 of 18 December 2008, on assistance to refugees, returnees and displaced persons in Africa, and effectively to support African countries in their efforts to incorporate the problems of refugees into national and regional development plans;

20. *Requests* the United Nations system to cooperate with the African Union and its member States in the implementation of appropriate policies for the promotion of the culture of democracy, good governance, respect for human rights and the rule of law and the strengthening of democratic institutions;

21. *Calls upon* the Secretary-General and the international community to fulfil the commitments they undertook during the high-level event on the Millennium Development Goals, held in New York on 25 September 2008;

22. *Welcomes and supports* the ongoing efforts of the African Union to support gender equality, the empowerment of women and social development, and recalls in this regard the declaration of the African Women's Decade by the Assembly of the African Union in February 2009, and the African Union Gender Policy, the Social Policy Framework for Africa and the Windhoek Declaration on Social Development, as adopted by the Executive Council of the African Union in January 2009;

23. *Recalls* its resolution 63/250 of 24 December 2008 on human resources management, and urges the Secretary-General to encourage the United Nations system, within existing rules and regulations, to work towards ensuring the effective and equitable representation of African men and women at senior and policy levels at the respective headquarters of its organizations and in their regional fields of operation;

24. *Calls upon* the Secretary-General and the Chairperson of the African Union Commission, working in collaboration, to review every two years the progress made in the cooperation between the two organizations, and requests the Secretary-General to include the results of the review in his next report;

25. *Requests* the Secretary-General to report to the General Assembly at its sixty-fifth session on the implementation of the present resolution.

AU press statement. On 19 October [S/2009/541], the AU transmitted to the Security Council a press statement adopted by the AU Peace and Security Council at its 206th meeting (Addis Ababa, 15 October), concerning the funding of AU-led peace support operations and cooperation between the AU and the United Nations. Following an exchange of views on those issues in light of the Secretary-General's September report, the AU Peace and Security Council expressed the readiness of the AU to continue working with the United Nations towards ensuring predictable, sustainable and flexible funding for AU-led peace support operations through assessed contributions.

Security Council consideration. On 26 October [meeting 6206], the Council considered the Secretary-General's September report. Alain Le Roy, the Under-Secretary-General for Peacekeeping Operations, said that the enhanced peacekeeping role of the AU and of African regional economic communities was a major and welcome development, noting that they were able to deploy quickly, with limited resources when the situation on the ground had needed a robust intervention, and often before international consensus

had time to be built. If the international community really wished to assist them in addressing conflicts, it must support more actively the strengthening of an African peacekeeping capacity. That could include training of African troop contributors, providing financial contributions to sustain peacekeeping operations and demonstrating the political will necessary to resolve conflicts. AU peacekeeping was entirely dependent on the same small pool of donors, with little flexibility, sustainability or predictability in its stream of resources, affecting the AU's ability to plan missions and pay troop-contributing countries. Such constraints could invalidate planning and put a mission at the risk of failure. If the international community requested that the AU bear the brunt of its initial response to a crisis, it had an obligation to support it in ensuring that its response was credible.

The AU agreed that funding for UN-authorized peacekeeping operations remained a central concern for the organization, and it was clear that the most viable option was to make use of UN assessed contributions. Such funding would enable the Council to utilize local comparative advantages in tackling threats to international peace and security. The AU had demonstrated a renewed willingness to shoulder its share of responsibility for the maintenance of peace and security with the support of international partners. In August, the AU had decided to increase the percentage of its regular budget transferred to the Peace Fund.

Twenty delegations addressed the ensuing debate.

SECURITY COUNCIL ACTION

On 26 October [meeting 6206], following consultations among Security Council members, the President made statement **S/PRST/2009/26** on behalf of the Council:

The Security Council recalls its previous relevant resolutions and the statements by its President which underscore the importance of developing effective partnerships between the United Nations and regional organizations, in particular the African Union, in accordance with the Charter of the United Nations and the relevant statutes of the regional organizations.

The Council reiterates its primary responsibility under the Charter for the maintenance of international peace and security, and recalls that cooperation with regional and subregional organizations in matters relating to the maintenance of international peace and security, and consistent with Chapter VIII of the Charter, can improve collective security.

The Council welcomes the continuing important efforts and enhanced peacekeeping role of the African Union and its subregional organizations, consistent with Council resolutions and decisions, to prevent, mediate and settle conflicts on the African continent.

The Council reaffirms its resolution 1809(2008), in which it recognizes the need to enhance the predictability, sustainability and flexibility of financing for regional organizations when they undertake peacekeeping under United Nations authorization.

The Council reiterates that regional organizations have the responsibility to secure human, financial, logistical and other resources for their organizations, including through contributions by their members and support from donors. The Council commends the support extended by donors to the African Peace and Security Architecture through specific mechanisms, including the African Peace Facility.

The Council recalls the statement by its President of 18 March 2009, in which it requested the Secretary-General to submit a report on practical ways to provide effective support for the African Union when it undertakes peacekeeping operations authorized by the United Nations, that includes a detailed assessment of the recommendations contained in the report of the African Union-United Nations panel on modalities for support to African Union peacekeeping operations, in particular those on financing, as well as on the establishment of a joint African Union-United Nations team. The Council notes that the aforementioned report is an important contribution to the overall efforts to enhance the capacity of the African Union in undertaking peacekeeping operations.

The Council takes note with appreciation of the report of the Secretary-General on support to African Union peacekeeping operations authorized by the United Nations.

The Council reiterates the importance of establishing a more effective strategic relationship between the United Nations Security Council and the African Union Peace and Security Council and between the United Nations Secretariat and the African Union Commission. The Security Council encourages further enhancement of regular interaction, coordination and consultation between the United Nations and the African Union on matters of mutual interest. The Council notes the ongoing efforts of the Secretariat and the Commission in this regard.

The Council underlines the importance of expediting the implementation, in close consultation with other international partners, of the 2006 United Nations-African Union Ten-Year Capacity-Building Programme for the African Union focusing mainly on peace and security, in particular the operationalization of the African Standby Force and the Continental Early Warning System. The Council supports the ongoing efforts to strengthen the African Peace and Security Architecture and reiterates its call for the international community, particularly donors, to fulfil their commitments as endorsed in the 2005 World Summit Outcome.

The Council recognizes that, in deploying peacekeeping operations authorized by the Council, the African Union is contributing towards the maintenance of international peace and security, in a manner consistent with the provisions of Chapter VIII of the Charter.

The Council notes the assessment of the options for financing African Union peacekeeping operations authorized by the Council outlined in the report of the Secretary-General and expresses its intention to keep all options under consideration.

The Council notes that the African Union needs to enhance its institutional capacity to enable it to effectively plan, manage and deploy peacekeeping operations. The Council, in this regard, calls upon the African Union, in the context of developing its Strategic Plan for 2009–2012, to develop a long-term, comprehensive capacity-building road map in consultation with the United Nations and other international partners.

The Council underlines the need for the United Nations and the African Union to study the lessons learned from the light and heavy support packages for the African Union Mission in the Sudan, the logistics package for the African Union Mission in Somalia, as well as collaboration relating to the African Union-United Nations Hybrid Operation in Darfur and the United Nations Support Office for the African Union Mission in Somalia in close consultation with other international partners.

The Council welcomes the intention of the United Nations Secretariat and the African Union Commission to set up a joint task force on peace and security to review immediate and long-term strategic and operational issues.

The Council requests the Secretary-General to update the Council by 26 April 2010 and to submit a progress report no later than 26 October 2010.

Security Council mission to Africa

On 12 May [S/2009/243], the Security Council President informed the Secretary-General that the Council would send a mission to Africa from 14 to 21 May. The mission would travel to Ethiopia, Rwanda, the Democratic Republic of the Congo (DRC) and Liberia. John Sawers (United Kingdom) and Ruhakana Rugunda (Uganda) would co-lead the Ethiopia (Addis Ababa) and Rwanda (Kigali) segments; Jean-Maurice Ripert (France) would lead the DRC (Goma and Kinshasa) segment; and Susan Rice (United States) would lead the Liberia (Monrovia) segment.

The four mission leaders briefed the Council about the mission on 28 May [meeting 6131].

Mission report. The mission report [S/2009/303] to the Council on 11 June had three sections, covering the Council's visits to the AU, Rwanda and the DRC, and Liberia. Each section offered recommendations to the Council, the parties involved and the international community.

Meeting with the AU in Addis Ababa, the Council discussed issues facing the organization. Regarding Somalia, the members of the Council were concerned at the precariousness of the situation. While the political situation had been evolving positively, there had been a series of negative developments on the security front; a large number of civilians had been killed and insurgent forces were reportedly regrouping. While the African Union Mission in Somalia (AMISOM) had a strong mandate, it lacked the capabilities to respond robustly.

In the Sudan, there were continued challenges with the implementation of the Comprehensive Peace Agreement and with the situation in Darfur, where a number of international non-governmental organizations (NGOs) had been expelled. The Sudan was entering a critical phase, with elections planned in 2010 and a referendum in 2011. Concerning relations between Chad and the Sudan, there were outbreaks of renewed conflict between rebel groups and the Chadian Government. Unconstitutional changes of government across Africa were a concern, especially with the violence that might accompany such events. With the economic crisis and the achievement of the Millennium Development Goals at risk, it was unrealistic to expect that African nations finance major peacekeeping operations in Africa.

The Council members recommended that the Security Council continue to work closely with the AU Peace and Security Council; that the Security Council remain seized of the deteriorating situation in Somalia and consider further measures to strengthen AMISOM; and that the Council, working closely with the AU, encourage Sudanese parties to overcome any obstacles to the implementation of the Comprehensive Peace Agreement and continue to provide support to the Joint AU-UN mediation in Darfur.

The Council's mission to Rwanda and the DRC took place following major developments that had re-shaped the security and political landscape in eastern DRC and the Great Lakes region. The Governments of the DRC, Rwanda and Uganda had agreed to work together to address the threat of armed groups in eastern DRC. The Council members voiced support for the improved relations between the DRC and Rwanda, including with respect to stemming the illegal trafficking of natural resources, in order to guarantee the stabilization of the Great Lakes region. In the DRC, the mission emphasized the importance of protecting civilians, including with respect to sexual violence and children associated with armed groups, as well as combating impunity and ensuring respect for human rights. The Council members emphasized the responsibility of the Government in that regard, also noting the need to reform the security sector.

Governments in the region were encouraged to build on the positive momentum created by their recent improved relations, including through the Economic Community of the Great Lakes Countries. Co-Facilitators were encouraged to deepen efforts with the leadership of the countries of the region to enhance cooperation in security and economic development.

The Government of the DRC was advised to commit the resources necessary to ensure the payment of soldiers' salaries and their sustenance. The DRC national army should ensure the separation of children from armed groups and set up vetting mechanisms to prevent the integration of elements that had been involved in gross human rights violations. The Government should continue to disburse its share of resources and take legislative measures to ensure that local elections were held in a timely manner. The Government was advised to undertake reform of the security sector as a matter of priority. Concerning the rule of law and sexual and gender-based violence, the Government should address confirmed human rights abuses by soldiers of the national army and build on steps taken to address the prevalence of sexual violence throughout the country. The Governments of the region were advised to bring an end to the illegal exploitation and trade of natural resources.

The mission to Liberia came after significant progress had been achieved in consolidating peace and stability. Liberia had reached the decision point under the enhanced Heavily Indebted Poor Countries Initiative, and the Government had finalized its first national poverty reduction strategy following broad-based consultations. However, the economic recovery started from extremely low levels, and poverty and unemployment levels remained high, resulting in mounting criticism of the lack of a visible peace dividend. Prevailing peace and stability remained fragile, and the problem of limited capacity of national security institutions was compounded by shortfalls in the justice and corrections systems. Civil unrest could erupt from several sources, including idle former combatants, unemployed youth, former armed forces and police personnel who were retrenched and had not found alternative livelihood, mob violence, and persisting land and ethnic disputes. In addition, a number of ongoing processes—including the final report of the Truth and Reconciliation Commission, the trial against former President Charles Taylor, and the presidential and legislative elections in 2011—could generate tensions, and many Liberians were vulnerable to incidents of armed robbery, sexual and gender-based violence and other violent crimes. The fragility of relative peace was exacerbated by continued instability in the subregion, particularly the uncertain prospect of elections in Guinea and Côte d'Ivoire later in 2009, and tensions between the two main political parties in Sierra Leone. Drug trafficking in the subregion was an additional challenge.

The Council recommended that the Government of Liberia step up efforts to build its military and police capacity to be able to assume full security responsibilities once the United Nations Mission in Liberia (UNMIL) completed its mandate. Acknowledging the impact of the international financial crisis, it was noted that donors should continue to provide support to ensure that the Government's Poverty Reduction Strategy was adequately financed, and that the Government should continue to support small and medium-size enterprises. Welcoming the Government's commitment to combat sexual violence, it was recommended that it redouble efforts to address that critical issue. Unmil was encouraged to continue to focus on building the capacity of Liberian counterparts, in particular within the security sector.

Office of the Special Adviser on Africa

In 2009, the Office of the Special Adviser on Africa (osaa), established by General Assembly resolution 57/7 [YUN 2002, p. 910], continued to enhance international support for Africa's development and security through its advocacy and analytical work; assist the Secretary-General in improving coherence and coordination of UN system support to Africa; and facilitate global intergovernmental deliberations on Africa, in particular relating to nepad [YUN 2001, p. 900]. Among other activities, the Office organized, in cooperation with other Advocacy Cluster members of the Regional Consultative Mechanism, a Regional Media Dialogue on nepad (The Vaal, South Africa, 19–20 February) with the participation of senior media experts from Africa; an expert group meeting on Africa's cooperation with new and emerging development partners (Addis Ababa, 10–11 February); an expert group meeting on African perspectives on international terrorism (Addis Ababa, 3–4 June); and, together with the United Nations University and the Office of the High Representative for the Least Developed Countries, Landlocked Developing Countries and Small Island Developing States, a panel discussion on recovering from the global crisis: towards an action plan for Africa and the least developed countries (New York, 25 June).

African peacekeeping capacity

The Special Committee on Peacekeeping Operations, at its 2009 substantive session (New York, 23 February–20 March) [A/63/19], discussed the enhancement of African peacekeeping capacities. It underlined the need for a strategic relationship between the United Nations and the au in the context of peacekeeping operations and emphasized the importance of increasing the au capacity in the areas of conflict prevention, mediation and peacekeeping. It emphasized the importance of implementing the joint action plan for United Nations support to the au in peacekeeping in the short-, medium- and long-terms, and the 10-year plan for capacity-building. It requested that the multidisciplinary au peacekeeping support team continue to serve as a coordinating point for all issues in the Department of Peacekeeping Operations related to cooperation with the au. It underlined the need to address the au peacekeeping requirements at the continental level, taking into consideration the report prepared by the au-UN panel on

modalities for support to au peacekeeping operations [YUN 2008, p. 111], and recommended the enhancement of an effective partnership to improve African peacekeeping operations. The Committee reaffirmed the need to strengthen training and logistics, which would enhance deployment of UN peacekeeping missions in Africa and ensure cost-effectiveness.

Implementation of Secretary-General's 1998 recommendations on promotion of peace

In 2009, the General Assembly continued its consideration of the item on the implementation of the recommendations contained in the 1998 report on causes of conflict and promotion of durable peace and sustainable development in Africa [YUN 1998, p. 66].

GENERAL ASSEMBLY ACTION

On 23 July [meeting 97], the General Assembly adopted **resolution 63/304** [draft: A/63/L.61/Rev.1 & Add.1] without vote [agenda item 57 *(b)*].

Implementation of the recommendations contained in the report of the Secretary-General on the causes of conflict and the promotion of durable peace and sustainable development in Africa

The General Assembly,

Recalling the report of the Open-ended Ad Hoc Working Group on the Causes of Conflict and the Promotion of Durable Peace and Sustainable Development in Africa, its resolution 53/92 of 7 December 1998 and subsequent annual resolutions, including resolutions 60/223 of 23 December 2005, 61/230 of 22 December 2006 and 62/275 of 11 September 2008, as well as its resolutions 62/179 of 19 December 2007 on the New Partnership for Africa's Development and 59/213 of 20 December 2004 on cooperation between the United Nations and the African Union,

Recalling also in this context Security Council resolutions 1809(2008) of 16 April 2008 on peace and security in Africa, 1325(2000) of 31 October 2000 and 1820(2008) of 19 June 2008 on women and peace and security, 1366(2001) of 30 August 2001 on the role of the Council in the prevention of armed conflicts, 1612(2005) of 26 July 2005 on children and armed conflict, 1625(2005) of 14 September 2005 on strengthening the effectiveness of the Council's role in conflict prevention, particularly in Africa, and 1631(2005) of 17 October 2005 on cooperation between the United Nations and regional and subregional organizations in maintaining international peace and security,

Recalling further the 2005 World Summit Outcome, through which world leaders reaffirmed their commitment to addressing the special needs of Africa, and its resolution 60/265 of 30 June 2006,

Reaffirming the political declaration on Africa's development needs adopted at the high-level meeting on Africa's development needs on 22 September 2008,

Recognizing that development, peace, security and human rights are interlinked and mutually reinforcing,

Stressing that the responsibility for peace and security in Africa, including the capacity to address the root causes of conflict and to resolve conflicts in a peaceful manner, lies primarily with African countries, while recognizing the need for support from the international community and the United Nations, taking into account the responsibilities of the United Nations in this regard, according to the Charter,

Recognizing, in particular, the importance of strengthening the capacity of the African Union and subregional organizations to address the causes of conflict in Africa,

Noting that despite the positive trends and advances in obtaining durable peace in Africa, the conditions required for sustainable development have yet to be consolidated throughout the continent and that there is therefore an urgent need to continue developing African human and institutional capacities, particularly in countries emerging from conflict,

Noting also that conflict prevention and the consolidation of peace would benefit from the coordinated, sustained and integrated efforts of the United Nations system and Member States and regional and subregional organizations, as well as international and regional financial institutions,

Reaffirming the need to strengthen the synergy between Africa's economic and social development programmes and its peace and security agenda,

Underlining the need to address the negative implications of the illegal exploitation of natural resources in all its aspects for peace, security and development in Africa, and condemning illicit trade in natural resources that fuels armed conflict, and the illicit trade in and proliferation of arms, especially small arms and light weapons,

Reaffirming the importance of the Peacebuilding Commission as a dedicated mechanism to address, within its existing mandate and in an integrated manner, the special needs of countries emerging from conflict towards recovery, reintegration and reconstruction and to assist them in laying the foundation for peace and sustainable development, taking into consideration the principle of national ownership,

1. *Takes note* of the progress report of the Secretary-General on the implementation of the recommendations contained in his report on the causes of conflict and the promotion of durable peace and sustainable development in Africa, and welcomes recent institutional developments in addressing such causes and other efforts in conflict prevention, peacemaking, peacekeeping and peacebuilding undertaken by African countries, African regional organizations and the United Nations system;

2. *Welcomes* the progress made, in particular by the African Union and subregional organizations, in the prevention, management and resolution of conflict and in post-conflict peacebuilding in a number of African countries, and calls for intensified efforts and a coordinated approach between national Governments, the African Union, subregional organizations, the United Nations system and partners with a view to achieving further progress towards the goal of a conflict-free Africa;

3. *Also welcomes* the ongoing efforts of the African Union and subregional organizations to strengthen their peacekeeping capacity and to take the lead in peacekeeping operations on the continent, in accordance with Chapter VIII of the Charter of the United Nations and in close coordination with the United Nations, through the Peace and Security Council of the African Union, as well as ongoing efforts to develop a continental early warning system, response capacity, such as the African Standby Force, and enhanced mediation capacity, including through the Panel of the Wise;

4. *Calls upon* the United Nations system and Member States to support the peace consolidation mechanisms and processes, including the Panel of the Wise, the African Union Post-Conflict Reconstruction and Development Framework and the early warning system, as well as the operationalization of the African Standby Force;

5. *Calls upon* Member States to support relevant United Nations bodies, including the Peacebuilding Commission, and to assist post-conflict countries, at their request, in achieving a smooth transition from relief to development;

6. *Stresses* the importance of creating an environment conducive to national reconciliation and social and economic recovery in countries emerging from conflict;

7. *Invites* the United Nations and the donor community to increase efforts to support ongoing regional efforts to build African mediation and negotiation capacity;

8. *Calls upon* the United Nations system and Member States to support the African Union in its effort to effectively integrate training in international humanitarian law and international human rights law, with particular emphasis on the rights of women and children, in the training of civilian and military personnel of national standby contingents at both the operational and tactical levels, as set out in article 13 of the Protocol Relating to the Establishment of the Peace and Security Council of the African Union;

9. *Recognizes* that international and regional efforts to prevent conflict and consolidate peace in Africa should be channelled towards the sustainable development of Africa and the human and institutional capacity-building of African countries and organizations, particularly in priority areas identified at the continental level;

10. *Recalls* the signing of the declaration on enhancing cooperation between the United Nations and the African Union in Addis Ababa on 16 November 2006 and the ongoing efforts in this regard, and underlines the importance of the implementation of the ten-year capacity-building programme for the African Union, focusing mainly on peace and security, in particular the operationalization of the African Standby Force, urges all stakeholders to support the full implementation of the ten-year capacity-building programme, and requests the Secretary-General to include in his next annual report on the implementation of the recommendations contained in his 1998 report a detailed account of the progress achieved in this regard;

11. *Stresses* the critical importance of a regional approach to conflict prevention, in particular with respect to cross-border issues such as disarmament, demobilization and reintegration programmes, the prevention of illegal exploitation of natural resources and trafficking in high-value commodities and the illicit trade in small arms and light weapons in all its aspects, and emphasizes in this regard the central role of the African Union and subregional organizations in addressing such issues;

12. *Notes with concern* that violence against women and children everywhere continues and often increases, even as

armed conflicts draw to an end, urges further progress in the implementation of policies and guidelines relating to the protection of and assistance to women and children in conflict and post-conflict situations, and notes the adoption by the Security Council of its resolution 1820(2008) on women and peace and security;

13. *Also notes with concern* the tragic plight of children in conflict situations in Africa, in particular the phenomenon of child soldiers, as well as other grave violations against children, and stresses the need for the protection of children in armed conflicts, post-conflict counselling, rehabilitation and education, with due regard for the relevant resolutions of the General Assembly and the Security Council;

14. *Calls for* the enhancement of the role of women in conflict prevention, conflict resolution and post-conflict peacebuilding, consistent with Security Council resolutions 1325(2000) and 1820(2008);

15. *Welcomes* the ongoing efforts of the African Union to ensure the protection of the rights of women in conflict and post-conflict situations, recalls in this regard the adoption and entry into force of the Protocol to the African Charter on Human and Peoples' Rights on the Rights of Women in Africa (2003), the Solemn Declaration on Gender Equality in Africa (2004) and the African Union Gender Policy (2009), as well as the Southern African Development Community Protocol on Gender and Development (2008), stresses the significance of those instruments for all countries in Africa in strengthening the role of women in peace and conflict prevention on the continent, and strongly urges the United Nations and all parties to redouble their efforts and support in this regard;

16. *Calls for* the safeguarding of the principle of refugee protection and the resolution of the plight of refugees, including through support for efforts aimed at addressing the causes of refugee movement and bringing about the safe and sustainable return and reintegration of those populations;

17. *Welcomes* African-led initiatives to strengthen political, economic and corporate governance, such as the African Peer Review Mechanism, encourages even more African countries to join this process, and calls upon the United Nations system and Member States to assist African Member States and regional and subregional organizations in their efforts to enhance good governance, including the promotion of the rule of law and the holding of free and fair elections;

18. *Recognizes* the role of the Peacebuilding Commission in ensuring that national ownership of the peacebuilding process in countries emerging from conflict is observed and that nationally identified priorities are at the core of international and regional efforts in post-conflict peacebuilding in the countries under consideration, notes the important steps taken by the Commission in engaging with Sierra Leone, Burundi, Guinea-Bissau and the Central African Republic through integrated peacebuilding strategies, calls for sustained regional and international commitment to the implementation of those strategies and their design process, recalls the adoption of the Sierra Leone Peacebuilding Cooperation Framework and the Strategic Frameworks for Peacebuilding in Burundi and in Guinea-Bissau, and calls for their implementation;

19. *Takes note* of the conclusions of the expert group meeting on "Promoting partnerships in support of African Peer Review Mechanism implementation", held in Ethiopia in November 2007, and invites the United Nations system and Member States to take those conclusions into account in support of good governance in Africa;

20. *Calls upon* the United Nations system and invites Member States to assist African countries emerging from conflict in their efforts to build national capacities of governance, including the rehabilitation of the security sector, the disarmament, demobilization and reintegration of ex-combatants, provision for the safe return of internally displaced persons and refugees, the launch of income-generation activities, particularly for youth and women, and the delivery of basic public services;

21. *Stresses* the importance of effectively addressing challenges that continue to hamper the achievement of peace, stability and sustainable development on the continent, inter alia, the food, fuel and financial crises, the increased prevalence of infectious diseases such as HIV/AIDS, the effects of global warming and climate change, the extremely high rates of youth unemployment, human trafficking, massive displacements of people, the illegal exploitation of natural resources, the illicit trade in small arms and light weapons, the emergence of terrorist networks and the increased activity of transnational organized crime, including drug trafficking, and in this regard encourages the United Nations system and Member States to assist African countries in effectively addressing these challenges;

22. *Calls upon* the United Nations system and Member States, as well as bilateral and multilateral partners, to deliver expeditiously on commitments and to ensure the full and speedy implementation of the provisions of the political declaration on Africa's development needs;

23. *Encourages* African Governments to strengthen structures and policies to create an environment conducive to attracting foreign direct investment, calls upon African Member States and regional and subregional organizations to assist the African countries concerned, at their request, by enhancing their capacity to devise and improve their national natural resources and public revenue management structures, and in this regard invites the international community to assist in that process by providing adequate financial and technical assistance, as well as by renewing its commitment to efforts aimed at combating the illegal exploitation of the natural resources of those countries in conformity with international law;

24. *Requests* the Secretary-General to submit to the General Assembly at its sixty-fifth session a report on the outcome of the review of the recommendations contained in his 1998 report, focusing on new and emerging challenges and persistent obstacles, as well as innovative solutions, gains and accomplishments, in the attainment of durable peace and sustainable development in Africa, with due regard for the complexities of the transition from fragile peace to long-term sustainable development that many African countries are undergoing;

25. *Decides* to continue to monitor the implementation of the recommendations contained in the 1998 report of the Secretary-General;

26. *Requests* the Secretary-General to submit to the General Assembly at its sixty-fourth session a progress report on the implementation of the present resolution.

Report of Secretary-General. In response to General Assembly resolution 63/304 (see above), the Secretary-General in August submitted a report [A/64/210] on the implementation of the recommendations contained in the 1998 report on causes of conflict and promotion of durable peace and sustainable development in Africa [YUN 1998, p. 66]. The report indicated that, in the previous year, progress in achieving lasting peace and security had been mixed, and drew attention to post-election violence in Kenya in 2008, the escalation of acts of piracy in the Horn of Africa, instances of non-constitutional changes in Guinea, Madagascar and Mauritania, the resumption of warfare in some regions and the perpetuation of violence in others, such as in Darfur. African organizations had shown their resolve to settle post-electoral disputes, conduct conflict management and mediation efforts and take a firm stance on leaders emerging from military coups d'état by excluding them and their countries until the return to constitutional order. Despite vulnerabilities and the destabilizing effects of the economic and financial crisis, Africa appeared to be on a positive, although uneven, path to growth. However, there was a need to ensure that cyclical violence, destabilizing economic crises or deviations from the rule of law did not undermine the progress achieved. The Secretary-General observed that the evolution that had taken place in the continent and in the international community in the decade since the 1998 recommendations necessitated a fresh look at those recommendations, focusing on new and emerging challenges and persistent obstacles to the attainment of peace and sustainable development in Africa.

Drug trafficking as a threat to peace and security

Security Council consideration. On 8 December [meeting 6233], the Security Council held an open debate on drug trafficking as a threat to international security on the basis of a concept paper [S/2009/615] submitted by Burkina Faso on 30 November. According to the concept paper, the situation in African countries was of particular concern due to the impact of drug trafficking on socio-economic development; the link between drug trafficking, financing of conflict, organized transnational crime, illicit arms trafficking and money-laundering; and the continuous increase in the volume of trafficking, production and consumption.

SECURITY COUNCIL ACTION

On 8 December [meeting 6233], following consultations among Security Council members, the President made statement **S/PRST/2009/32** on behalf of the Council:

The Security Council reaffirms its primary responsibility for the maintenance of international peace and security in accordance with the Charter of the United Nations.

The Council notes with concern the serious threats posed, in some cases, by drug trafficking and related transnational organized crime to international security in different regions of the world, including in Africa. The increasing link, in some cases, between drug trafficking and the financing of terrorism is also a source of growing concern.

The Council stresses the importance of strengthening transregional and international cooperation on the basis of a common and shared responsibility to counter the world drug problem and related criminal activities, and in support of relevant national, subregional and regional organizations and mechanisms, including with a view to strengthening the rule of law.

The Council recognizes the importance of the actions undertaken by the General Assembly, the Economic and Social Council, the Commission on Narcotic Drugs, the United Nations Office on Drugs and Crime and other relevant United Nations organs and agencies in facing numerous security risks caused by drug trafficking in many countries and regions, including in Africa. The Security Council encourages them to undertake further actions in this regard.

The Council stresses the need to reinforce the coordination of United Nations actions, including cooperation with the International Criminal Police Organization (INTERPOL), in order to enhance the effectiveness of international efforts in the fight against drug trafficking at the national, regional and international levels to tackle this global challenge in a more comprehensive manner, in accordance with the principle of common and shared responsibility.

The Council reaffirms and commends in that regard the important work of the United Nations Office on Drugs and Crime, in collaboration with the relevant United Nations entities, and emphasizes the need for adequate capacities to support national efforts.

The Council invites the Secretary-General to consider mainstreaming the issue of drug trafficking as a factor in conflict prevention strategies, conflict analysis, integrated mission assessment and planning and peacebuilding support.

The Council encourages States to comply with their obligations to combat drug trafficking and other forms of transnational organized crime, to consider acceding to relevant international conventions, in particular the three United Nations drug conventions and to investigate and prosecute, as appropriate, persons and entities responsible for drug trafficking and related crimes consistent with international human rights and due process standards.

The Council recognizes the important contribution of States and regional and subregional organizations in tackling drug trafficking in all its aspects, and encourages them to share best practices, as well as information about illicit drug trafficking networks.

The Council also recognizes the important contribution of civil society and other stakeholders in tackling drug trafficking in a comprehensive manner.

The Council calls upon the international community and the United Nations system to strengthen their cooperation with regional and subregional organizations in the fight against drug trafficking, including in Africa.

The Council calls upon the Secretary-General to provide, as appropriate, more information on drug trafficking and related issues where it risks threatening or exacerbating an existing threat to international peace and security.

Speaking after the statement, the Secretary-General said that the international community should pursue those who ran trafficking operations and thwart them with the full force of the law and international resolve. He said that the framework for international cooperation was built around strong, UN-backed legal instruments, with the assistance of the United Nations Office on Drugs and Crime (UNODC) and other organizations. However, not all States had become parties to the instruments, which needed to be implemented more effectively. Cooperation among Governments was lagging behind cooperation among organized crime networks. To counter the global threat, States must share intelligence, carry out joint operations, build capacity and provide mutual legal assistance.

UNODC Executive Director Antonio Maria Costa said that Africa was facing a severe and complex drug problem—not only trafficking but also production and consumption. Serious consequences in terms of health, development and security were inevitable. The recent discovery of laboratories in Guinea showed that West Africa was also becoming a producer of synthetic drugs—amphetamines—and of crystal cocaine, refined from pasta basica. In East Africa, 30 to 35 tons of Afghan heroin were being imported, causing a dramatic increase in heroin addiction and spreading HIV/AIDS in the slums of Mombasa and Nairobi, Kenya's two main cities. The two streams of illicit drugs—heroin into eastern Africa and cocaine into western Africa—were meeting in the Sahara, creating new trafficking routes of unprecedented scale across Chad, Mali and Niger. Drugs were enriching not only organized crime but also terrorists and other anti-Government forces. To counter that threat, national capacity must be strengthened and information-sharing promoted. He urged the creation of a trans-Saharan crime monitoring network to improve information, monitor suspicious activity, exchange evidence, facilitate legal cooperation and strengthen regional efforts.

Thirty-four delegations addressed the ensuing debate, stressing their concern over the threats to international security caused by drug trafficking and other transnational organized crime and the increasing link between drug trafficking and the financing of terrorism. They underlined the necessity of strengthening transregional and international cooperation as well as the coordination of UN actions, including cooperation with INTERPOL.

Central Africa and Great Lakes region

Great Lakes region

Third International Conference on Great Lakes Region

On 10 August, the third summit meeting of the International Conference on the Great Lakes Region was held in Lusaka, Zambia. The event was attended by the Heads of State of Kenya, Uganda, the United Republic of Tanzania and Zambia, as well as by high-level officials from Burundi, the Central African Republic, the DRC and Rwanda. Summit participants were briefed by the Co-Facilitators, former President Olusegun Obasanjo of Nigeria and former President Benjamin Mkapa of Tanzania, on the situation in eastern DRC. It was proposed to convene an extraordinary summit on the Great Lakes region to discuss the Co-Facilitators report. Participants decided that regular summit meetings of the International Conference on the Great Lakes Region would be held on 15 December every two years.

Special Envoy on Great Lakes region

Reports of Special Envoy (January–November). On 15 January, the Special Envoy of the Secretary-General on the Great Lakes region, Mr. Obasanjo, reported to the Security Council during its consideration of the situation in the Great Lakes region [meeting 6067] that the Nairobi dialogue between the Government of the DRC and the leadership of the Congrès national pour la défense du people (CNDP), begun in November 2008 [YUN 2008, p. 119], resumed on 6 January 2009. At a 8 January meeting with the Special Envoy, DRC President Joseph Kabila and Rwandan President Paul Kagame reported significant improvement in the relationship between the two countries. In line with the 2007 Nairobi communiqué [YUN 2007, p. 127], both countries agreed on a military plan to put pressure on the former Rwandan Army forces (ex-FAR)/Interahamwe, known as the Forces démocratiques de libération du Rwanda (FDLR). On 12 January, the parties agreed to the last three documents that together laid the ground rules for substantive discussions to follow. One of those documents, the terms of reference, reflected a common understanding on the outcome of the Nairobi dialogue, which was "to conclude a comprehensive agreement incorporating the *Actes d'engagement* signed in Goma [YUN 2008, p. 120] and their modalities of implementation through a framework to be agreed by the parties". However, despite the parties' re-engagement in discussions towards a joint cessation of hostilities declaration, there were reports and rumours of a web of plans and counter-plans and of deals within deals, once more slowing down the momentum of the dialogue. Both sides remained intransigent. In the circumstance, the Special Envoy called for a brief recess in the dialogue. He noted that any cessation of hostilities would need to be undergirded by an effective independent monitoring mechanism. In the meantime, he pleaded with both parties to accept that the United Nations Organization Mission in the Democratic Republic of the Congo (MONUC) monitor and verify the cessation of hostilities declarations currently in place.

During the Council's consideration of the situation in the Great Lakes region on 9 November [meeting 6215], the Special Envoy reported that the situation had been dramatically transformed. The humanitarian situation had greatly improved. Many internally displaced persons (IDPs) were returning to their homes. CNDP no longer existed as a politico-military organization. The threat to regional peace posed by the armed groups, in particular FDLR, had been considerably reduced, and there had been a notable warming in regional relations. The Nairobi dialogue laid the groundwork for the signature of the 23 March peace agreements between the Congolese Government, CNDP and the other armed groups (see p. 120), as well as the decision of the two countries to take decisive military action against FDLR on Congolese soil. Several provisions of that agreement had been or were about to be implemented.

The Special Envoy noted that the success recorded was due in large part to the coming together of the heads of State of the region and to the resolve of Presidents Kabila and Kagame to improve their relationship. The fruits of that rapprochement had been seen in the joint operation against FDLR, the historic meeting between Presidents Kabila and Kagame, the economic cooperation on joint energy, and the restoration of diplomatic relations and exchange of ambassadors. During a 17 October meeting, President Kabila spoke confidently of the steadily improving relations with Rwanda and Uganda and the good relations with Angola and Burundi. The Special Envoy and the Co-Facilitator, Mr. Mkapa, informed President Kabila of their intention to take a step back from an active role in the peace process in the eastern part of the DRC and the Great Lakes region, while national and regional leaders implemented measures to strengthen peace, cooperation and development. As part of his exit strategy, the Special Envoy said that he had again written to President Kabila, urging action to accelerate implementation of the 23 March Agreements, and would submit a final report to the African Union (AU) leaders at their regular summit in January 2010. To provide assistance in the case of a new crisis, he was working with the United Nations to re-tool his support office in Nairobi into a small,

dedicated post, which would continue to liaise with the secretariat of the International Conference on the Great Lakes Region, assess the implementation of the 23 March Agreements, monitor efforts to counter the violence of the residual foreign armed groups and monitor the consolidation of the regional rapprochement and actions to sustain peace. To address the underlying causes of recurring crisis, he recommended an umbrella approach bringing together the United Nations, the AU, the International Conference on the Great Lakes Region and international development partners in an effort to strengthen governance institutions in the DRC.

Special Adviser on the Prevention of Genocide

In March [S/2009/151], the Secretary-General forwarded to the Security Council the report of his Special Adviser on the Prevention of Genocide, Francis Deng, on his mission to the Great Lakes region (22 November–5 December 2008) with respect to the situation in the DRC. The Adviser said that the root causes of the conflict in the eastern part of the DRC were primarily political and economic and not related to identity. However, extreme ethnic polarization and hatred had become associated with that conflict. The Special Adviser believed that the risk of ethnic targeting in North Kivu was much higher than other potential causes of genocide. References to genocide having occurred in the past or allegedly going on were used to predict that genocide might occur again, in particular against the Tutsi, who were popularly viewed as the principal perpetrators of mass atrocities. The likelihood of ethnically motivated killings by armed groups and the escalation of genocidal hysteria among the civilian populations were factors that had to be addressed. The regional dimensions of such a prospect also had to be taken into account. The report recommended enhancing protection of the civilian populations; shifting the focus from military action to political engagement and the search for peaceful solutions; building the Government's capacity for democratic governance and the rule of law, with justice for all groups; fostering inter-ethnic reconciliation; encouraging regional cooperation; and continuing the cooperation between the AU and the United Nations in supporting the DRC and the regional initiatives.

Establishment of UN Office for Central Africa

On 11 December [S/2009/697], the Secretary-General informed the Security Council that, following a request in 2008 by the Heads of State and Government of the Economic Community of Central African States (ECCAS), he intended to establish the United Nations Office for Central Africa in Libreville, Gabon, to be led by a Special Representative of the Secretary-General. The Office would cooperate with ECCAS, the Central African Economic and Monetary Community, the International Conference on the Great Lakes Region, the Economic Community of the Great Lakes Countries and other key partners and assist them in their promotion of peace and stability in the Central African subregion; carry out good offices and special assignments in countries of the subregion, including in the areas of conflict prevention and peacebuilding; enhance linkages in the work of the United Nations and other partners in the subregion, with a view to promoting an integrated subregional approach and facilitating coordination and information exchange; and report to Headquarters on significant subregional developments.

Standing Advisory Committee on Security Questions

At its twenty-eighth (Libreville, Gabon, 4–8 May) [A/64/85-S/2009/288] and twenty-ninth (N'Djamena, Chad, 9–13 November) [A/64/638-S/2010/54] ministerial meetings, the 11-member United Nations Standing Advisory Committee on Security Questions in Central Africa reviewed the geopolitical situation in the region, including political and institutional developments, internal and cross-border security, and issues related to governance and the humanitarian and human rights situation. The Committee noted that, since its last meeting [YUN 2008, p. 646], there had been sharply contrasting developments in the geopolitical and security situation in Central Africa, with notable progress in consolidation of democratic processes and the smooth functioning of institutions. On the other hand, the subregion was confronted with a number of situations of concern on the level of security.

The General Assembly, in **resolution 64/61** of 2 December (see p. 567), reaffirmed its support for efforts to promote confidence-building measures in order to ease tensions and conflicts in Central Africa and to further peace, stability and development; and welcomed the adoption by the Committee on 8 May of the Code of Conduct for the Defence and Security Forces in Central Africa and the major strides made in drafting a legal instrument on the control of small arms and light weapons in Central Africa.

(For information on the Committee's review of the promotion of disarmament and arms limitation in Central Africa and the Secretary-General's report on the Committee's activities, see p. 567).

Democratic Republic of the Congo

In 2009 the situation in the Democratic Republic of the Congo (DRC) continued to present complex challenges, despite developments that significantly re-shaped the political and military landscape. In January, the leader of CNDP, Bosco Ntaganda, announced that CNDP and the Government had reached an agreement on the immediate cessation of hostilities, the participation of CNDP in the operations against FDLR on the basis of the DRC-Rwanda joint plan and the immediate integration of CNDP combatants into the Armed Forces of the Democratic Republic of the Congo (FARDC). That allowed the Secretary-General to revise the concept of operations and terms of engagement of the United Nations Organization Mission in the Democratic Republic of the Congo (MONUC), with a stress on the protection of civilians and with a focus on eastern DRC, as the security situation in the western part of the country improved. Various MONUC tasks in the western part were handed over to the UN country team. Those events were followed, on 23 March, by the signing of peace agreements between the Government and CNDP, paving the way for the integration of the Congolese armed groups into FARDC and the establishment of the Independent Electoral Commission to prepare for elections in 2010. Military operations conducted by FARDC in eastern DRC, with MONUC support, dislodged foreign and residual Congolese armed groups from their strongholds and enabled the Government to extend its control into previously inaccessible areas, including in important economic zones. However, the overall situation in the east, especially in the Kivus and in parts of Orientale province, remained fragile. Despite the enhanced and innovative measures taken by MONUC to protect civilians, the operations took a heavy toll on civilians, who were displaced and subjected to reprisal attacks by retreating armed groups. Furthermore, the actions of undisciplined and recently integrated FARDC elements seeking to settle old ethnic scores resulted in serious violations of international humanitarian law, including killings of civilians, forcing MONUC to redefine its relationship with FARDC. In December, the Security Council requested MONUC to continue its coordination of operations with FARDC, with the protection of civilians as a priority.

Follow-up to resolutions 1843(2008) and 1856(2008)

Communications. On 27 January [S/2009/52], the Secretary-General informed the Security Council that, despite the Organization's efforts to generate the additional resources for MONUC required by resolutions 1843(2008) [YUN 2008, p. 128] and 1856(2008) [ibid., p. 130], troop-contributing countries had not been as receptive as hoped. In all, 49 troop contributors and 12 potential contributors had been asked to provide the Mission with the additional troops and resources authorized. A few countries had made offers and the Secretariat would assess the expressions of interest most closely matching the Mission's resource requirements. However, more than two months after the adoption of resolution 1843(2008), no formal offers had been made in response to those requests. The Secretary-General was especially concerned about the lack of formal offers of special forces' companies, and there had been no commitments or expressions of interest regarding the remaining air assets or the deployment of the 200 military training instructors/advisers needed—resources that were essential for the Mission's mobility and rapid reaction. The Secretary-General renewed his appeal to troop- and police-contributing countries with the necessary capacities to enable the Mission to discharge its mandate.

On 19 February [S/2009/105], the Secretary-General informed the Council that, as requested by the Council in resolution 1856(2008), the Department of Peacekeeping Operations (DPKO) and MONUC had revised the Mission's concept of operations and rules of engagement to meet the requirements of the Mission's robust mandate, as outlined in that resolution. While highlighting the priority of protecting civilians, the revised concept of operations made it clear that the main area of focus was in eastern DRC, and took into account tasks arising from the provisions of the Goma and Nairobi frameworks, with flexibility to enable MONUC to react robustly to the evolving realities on the ground.

The rules of engagement were also extensively reviewed and critical aspects amended, including with regard to fire support, air-to-ground engagements, collateral damage and levels of authorization for the use of specific weapons systems. The revision clarified and removed restrictive clauses on the terms for the use of force during the conduct of military operations, as outlined in the revised concept of operations.

Technical Assessment Mission. In response to a Council's request in resolution 1856(2008), the Assistant Secretary-General for Peacekeeping Operations, Edmond Mulet, led a technical assessment mission to the DRC (23 February–6 March) to develop with MONUC a strategic plan with appropriate benchmarks for tracking progress on the implementation of activities mandated under that resolution. The plan would take into account the gradual concentration of the Mission's efforts in the east and the progressive handover of certain civilian tasks to the UN country team and other partners. However, the mission determined that the resources of the UN country team in the west were limited in terms of personnel and programmes, and that the country team and other partners would not be in a position to take over all of the tasks carried out by MONUC. Nevertheless, a carefully managed transition would allow for a drawdown of MONUC presences in the west over the next 6 to 24 months and the scaling up of the programmes and presence of the UN country team and interna-

tional partners, depending on donor interest and the ability of the country team to refocus and expand its resources. While the potential for instability in the west remained, there were no major security threats posed by armed groups. That would allow for a rapid scaling down of the remaining MONUC military elements, while sufficient UN police capacity would be maintained for the mentoring, training and coaching of the national police. MONUC staffing levels in the west would gradually decrease, while that of the UN country team would increase. After the MONUC drawdown from the western provinces, static military and police capacities and a mobile military and police response capacity should remain to protect UN personnel and property, together with a residual presence for the transition phase, consisting of small, multidisciplinary joint teams in specific provinces to work on peace consolidation with provincial authorities and the UN country team.

To address the issue of the remaining foreign armed group elements, the mission recommended that MONUC develop a multidisciplinary campaign plan. As future needs arose, surge MONUC support arrangements to facilitate the influx of repatriated persons should be activated. MONUC should downsize its military presence in areas of low-level violence, such as the western part of the DRC and Katanga, and redeploy those assets in the Kivus and Haut Uélé. The reconfiguration envisaged the redeployment of one of the two battalions from the west to the Ituri brigade to enhance operations in Haut Uélé, and the consolidation of the Benin battalion in northern Katanga to support operations in the Kivus. The majority of the military observers would be redeployed from the west and Katanga to the Kivu and Ituri brigades to conduct liaison-related tasks, and could supplement the joint protection teams. The force's posture should be consolidated and reoriented to allow for a more mobile and robust presence in key areas of threat, concentrated in the Kivus and Haut Uélé. A special task force should be established to manage operations for disrupting the military capability of illegal armed groups.

Political and security developments

Security Council consideration. On 17 February [meeting 6083], John Holmes, the Under-Secretary-General for Humanitarian Affairs and Emergency Relief Coordinator, reported on his visit the previous week to the eastern and northern provinces of the DRC. He said that the deteriorating stability in several areas over the past six months, renewed fighting between various rebel groups, principally CNDP and FARDC in the Kivus, the resurgence of armed groups and subsequent clashes with FARDC in Ituri district, and new vicious attacks by the Lord's Resistance Army (LRA) in Province Orientale had left many hundreds dead, provoked the displacement of a further half-million people and worsened the already dire humanitarian situation. In North Kivu, some 250,000 people had been displaced since August 2008, adding to the longstanding North Kivu caseload of more than 800,000. Perceptions of insecurity had heightened in some areas due to the current offensive against FDLR, and the presence of FARDC in some areas was far from reassuring, given their own dreadful indiscipline and violence during the CNDP offensive. Continuing and improved humanitarian assistance remained essential to relieve the suffering in the Kivus and in Orientale province but was not enough to enable the people there to rebuild their lives. The authority and capacity of the central and local authorities had to be rebuilt at every level. The international community could help to achieve that, including through the stabilization strategy being pursued by MONUC together with the United Nations and donor partners.

The Under-Secretary-General said that the humanitarian needs throughout the DRC were substantial, including the western provinces, and not only in the conflict areas: 76 per cent of the population was undernourished and chronically subject to food insecurity; 54 per cent had no access to clean water. Malaria, cholera, plague and the Ebola virus further weakened already vulnerable people. The 2009 Humanitarian Action Plan (see p. 894) estimated that some $831 million was needed to cover humanitarian needs, an increase of 11 per cent from the previous year.

Report of Secretary-General (March). Reporting [S/2009/160] on MONUC in March pursuant to Security Council resolution 1856(2008), the Secretary-General said that, following the December 2008 agreement on a joint military plan to address the presence of FDLR forces in the eastern part of the DRC [YUN 2008, p. 134], Bosco Ntaganda, the then Chief of Staff of CNDP, announced that he had replaced Laurent Nkunda as leader of the group on 5 January. The arrest warrant for Mr. Ntaganda issued by the International Criminal Court in 2006 for alleged crimes committed in Ituri in 2002 and 2003 was unsealed in 2008 [ibid., p. 1428]. On 16 January, Mr. Ntaganda announced that CNDP and the DRC Government had reached an agreement on the immediate cessation of hostilities; the participation of CNDP in the operation against FDLR on the basis of the DRC-Rwanda joint plan; and the immediate integration of CNDP combatants into FARDC. On the same day, the Coalition des patriotes résistants congolais (PARECD) issued a statement on a cessation of hostilities, which was followed by similar statements by most other Congolese armed groups in North Kivu. On 22 January, Congolese authorities announced that Mr. Nkunda had been arrested in Rwanda. On 26 January, FARDC began the accelerated integration of CNDP and other armed groups into its

ranks. On 4 February, CNDP reaffirmed the end of hostilities, announced its transformation into a political movement and called for the resumption of talks with the Government, the granting of amnesty for its members and the establishment of a new ministry for internal security and intercommunity relations. Separately, at a meeting of the bilateral "Four plus Four" Commission (6–7 February), the DRC and Rwanda agreed to establish a technical team to elaborate the modalities for the extradition of Mr. Nkunda to the DRC.

The joint FARDC-Rwandan Defence Forces operation against FDLR began on 20 January, when an estimated 3,500 to 4,000 Rwandan troops crossed the border north of Goma into the DRC. During the month-long joint operation, as many as seven FARDC integrated brigades and three Rwandan battalions proceeded along three main axes in North Kivu: Goma-Rutshuru-Ishasha, Rutshuru-Tongo-Pinga and Sake-Masisi-Hombo. The operation, which was confined to North Kivu, was aimed at neutralizing FDLR, including through the targeting of its economic interests. The start of the joint operation prompted the issuance, on 5 February, of a statement by FDLR President Ignace Murwanashyaka calling for direct political negotiations with Rwanda and a peaceful resolution of the conflict. MONUC did not participate in the operation, but reached agreement with the joint forces that it would review tactical-level operations against FDLR to ensure that they included the protection of civilians as a key element. The joint operation succeeded in dislodging FDLR elements from most of their strongholds in Rutshuru, Lubero and Masisi territories and deprived FDLR of important sources of revenue from checkpoints and "market taxes". The operation, which resulted in the return of more than 6,000 Rwandans from the DRC, concluded on 25 February. MONUC assisted FARDC in planning follow-up operations against FDLR aimed at protecting civilians and pursuing the neutralization of FDLR by preventing it from reoccupying former positions and cutting its lines of economic sustenance. MONUC also provided logistical and fire support to FARDC in the context of that operation. While some Government ministers and members of political parties welcomed the joint operation with Rwanda, others criticized the secrecy in which the joint plan was developed, as well as the operation itself.

23 March Agreements. The Secretary-General's Special Envoy on 27 and 28 February met with the delegations of the Government and CNDP, who shared with him a draft peace agreement. Talks on the agreement began in Goma on 18 March and led to the signing of an agreement between the Government and CNDP in Goma on 23 March. The agreement provided for the conversion of CNDP into a political party and the release of political prisoners; specified mechanisms to facilitate local and national reconciliation, including the creation of a community policing mechanism; and contained commitments to reform the police and the army and secure the return of refugees and internally displaced persons. At the signing ceremony, similar agreements were signed between the Government and representatives of various remaining armed groups in the Kivus.

Security Council consideration. On 9 April [meeting 6104], the Special Representative of the Secretary-General and Head of MONUC, Alan Doss, told the Council that the prospect for ending the main conflict, which had dominated the situation in the Kivus for almost two years, had created real hope that a lasting solution would finally be achieved. The first concrete results were encouraging. A large portion of the two most affected territories, Rutshuru and Masisi, were more secure, and State authority was being re-established there. FDLR had been pushed back from several zones in North Kivu and there was a significant increase in voluntary repatriation. Displaced persons were beginning to return home and the Government had launched an initiative to accelerate rehabilitation programmes in order to build peace in the Kivus. However, the integration process and ongoing operations against FDLR were encountering considerable difficulties. Furthermore, tensions existed at the national level following debates on joint operations with the Rwandan and Ugandan armies, and at the local level, where changing alliances had raised concerns, in particular in terms of land disputes, which the return of more than 1 million displaced persons could provoke. MONUC deployed more than 90 per cent of its troops to the east and thinned out considerably its civilian presence in many of the western provinces. However, the handover of tasks envisioned in resolution 1856(2008) was hampered by the fact that UN agencies were largely concentrated in the east. An effective hand-over, as recommended by the technical assessment mission, required the rebalancing of the presence and resources of UN agencies. A strategic workplan with benchmarks for guiding the transfer of functions and the eventual drawdown of MONUC's presence was being developed. The Special Representative hoped that the strengthened security situation in the east would allow MONUC to gradually reduce its presence throughout the country and to prepare its departure.

Security Council action. On the same day, the Security Council, in a press statement [SC/9633], welcomed the 23 March Agreements between the Congolese Government and CNDP and commended the role played by the Special Envoy of the Secretary-General, Mr. Obasanjo, and the Co-Facilitator, Mr. Mkapa. The Council noted the progress made in integrating the Congolese armed groups into FARDC and stressed the importance of security sector reform. It expressed support to operations jointly planned and conducted by FARDC and MONUC against FDLR, LRA and other armed groups, and commended the Secretary-General's efforts to reconfigure MONUC in order to improve its efficiency, mobility and capacity to protect civilians.

Implementation of 23 March Agreements. A national follow-up committee, comprising five members for each signatory, was established on 30 April to oversee the implementation of the Agreements. Three subcommittees were established and were composed of, respectively, the Government and CNDP; the Government and North Kivu armed groups; and the Government and South Kivu armed groups. The follow-up committee, at its first session (4–27 May), adopted a revised implementation timetable for the Agreements covering a three-month period. At the same time, CNDP representatives expressed concern at the slow pace of implementation of their agreement with the Government, including the release of political prisoners and the integration of their elements into national political processes and institutions. On 6 May, the Parliament adopted the amnesty law foreseen in the Agreements, which President Kabila promulgated the following day. Despite calls from some opposition members to broaden its geographical scope, the law only applied to acts of war and crimes committed in North and South Kivu. On the basis of the Agreements, some CNDP administrative elements were deployed in Rutshuru and Masisi territories alongside State officials as part of the integration of CNDP elements into the provincial administration and political structures.

The accelerated integration of CNDP and other Congolese armed groups into FARDC ended on 18 April. During the closing ceremony in Goma, nine former armed groups, including representatives from CNDP and from PARECO Mayi-Mayi groups, signed a declaration stating that their elements had been either integrated into the national army or voluntarily demobilized; that the existence of armed groups in North Kivu had ended; and that recalcitrant elements would be considered as armed bandits. According to FARDC, 12,074 elements were integrated into the army in North Kivu as a result of the accelerated integration process. However, the unstructured way in which it was done, including the lack of a vetting process, led to delays in the payment of salaries, disparate levels of training and the lack of barracks, equipment and adequate means of sustaining the considerably increased numbers. Some FARDC units continued to prey on the populations, and in some areas ex-CNDP integrated elements continued to erect roadblocks and charge illegal taxes. Reports of desertions also increased.

On 4 May, seven Mayi-Mayi groups that were signatories to the 23 March Agreements threatened to withdraw their integration into FARDC, citing differences over the nomination of representatives to the national follow-up committee. Some of the groups also expressed discontent with the distribution of ranks within FARDC and the preference given to CNDP. Pockets of recalcitrant Mayi-Mayi and PARECO elements also resisted integration, in particular in Walikale and Masisi territories.

Following repeated concerns expressed by CNDP and other Congolese armed groups regarding the slow pace of implementation of the 23 March Agreements, and at the request of the Special Envoy of the Secretary-General, the national follow-up committee held its second session (Goma, 5–7 August) together with representatives of the international follow-up committee. Agreement was reached for the Government to release some 400 political prisoners on the basis of the Amnesty Law. The list of prisoners was reviewed by the Government and MONUC, and it was decided that those whose crimes were not covered by the Amnesty Law would continue to be detained. In addition, it was agreed to establish sub-committees to address the needs of the war-wounded, widows and orphans and the issue of military ranks and returnees. MONUC was requested to assist the Government in training the former armed groups for integration into the national police. However, a number of outstanding issues remained. The former armed groups expressed concern over the lack of appropriate rules of engagement and procedures within the national follow-up committee; the continued incarceration of some political prisoners; the ranks for ex-armed elements in FARDC; the lack of Government assistance to the CNDP war-wounded; and expectations regarding political and administrative tenures at the national and provincial levels. The Government, for its part, expressed concern regarding the continuation of parallel territorial administration arrangements by CNDP elements in some parts of North Kivu, and indicated that some demands related to army posts and the integration into national political and civil life might be unrealistic.

Mechanisms for assisting the war-wounded, widows and orphans were established. However, key provisions of the 23 March Agreements, including the integration of elements from the armed groups into national political life, were not implemented. In addition, there were delays in establishing community reconciliation initiatives and support structures for returning IDPs and refugees. On 10 November, CNDP President Désiré Kamanzi announced his resignation, citing concerns regarding the Government's delay in implementing the Agreements.

Security Council mission to eastern DRC. As part of its mission to Africa (14–21 May) [S/2009/303] (see p. 110), a Security Council mission visited the eastern DRC. Among its recommendation to the Council, the mission stated that Special Envoy Obasanjo and Co-Facilitator Mpaka should continue

to follow-up on the 23 March Agreements through the international follow-up committee in order to encourage the signatories to implement their commitments in full. The Government should commit the resources necessary to ensure the payment of soldiers' salaries and their sustenance, including with respect to newly integrated elements from CNDP and other armed groups; take legislative measures to ensure that local elections were held in a timely manner; and embark on security sector reform.

Report of Secretary-General (June). In his June report [S/2009/335] on MONUC, the Secretary-General stated that the security situation remained volatile and the humanitarian situation had deteriorated. Military operations against foreign armed groups and the remaining Congolese armed groups continued, but the targeting of civilians by those groups contributed to additional population displacements and human rights abuses, including sexual violence. There was no improvement in the socio-economic situation, and the financial crisis facing the country made stabilization and peacebuilding efforts more difficult. Meanwhile, progress was achieved in preparations for local elections, but observers continued to express concern at the limited progress in reforming governance, curbing corruption and combating human rights abuses.

On 2 March, FARDC, with MONUC support, began operations against FDLR in North Kivu. FARDC succeeded in reoccupying and retaining control of strategic locations from which FDLR elements had been dislodged during the DRC-Rwanda joint military operations in January and February. FARDC also dislodged FDLR from some mining areas in Walikale, Lubero and Shabunda, and conducted military operations in Virunga National Park, pushing back and eliminating FDLR units. MONUC carried out joint planning with FARDC and provided logistical support. In addition, since March, 624 FDLR combatants had voluntarily participated in the MONUC disarmament, demobilization, repatriation, reintegration and resettlement process.

In South Kivu, limited operations were launched in early June. The humanitarian contingency and protection plans for South Kivu were updated to minimize the humanitarian impact of the operations. In response, FDLR reportedly imposed restrictions on movements of civilians in areas surrounding their strongholds and attacked FARDC in the Bunyakiri area. There was limited progress in integrating the South Kivu armed groups into FARDC. As at 16 June, only 829 armed group elements were registered at the Luberizi and Kalehe cantonment centres. None of the approximately 150 Forces républicaines fédéralistes elements and very few of the Yakutumba Mayi-Mayi had moved to the cantonment centres. However, the number of candidates for integration or demobilization was expected to increase with the opening of a third South Kivu cantonment centre.

In Orientale province, FARDC and MONUC on 26 March signed a joint directive to launch an operation aimed at containing the threat of LRA. FARDC expanded its presence in the province to 6,300 soldiers and MONUC reinforced its deployment to the forward operating base in Dungu. Nevertheless, LRA reprisal attacks against civilians continued, including killings, abductions and pillaging, leading to significant population displacements. In Ituri, FARDC, with logistical support from MONUC, launched on 12 April an operation in southern Irumu and succeeded in recapturing more than 10 villages controlled by the rebels. However, reports indicated that undisciplined elements of FARDC and the national police had been harassing and committing abuses against the local population. On 19 May, the Ituri District Commissioner established a multi-ethnic committee to negotiate with the rebels. MONUC held a meeting with 20 Kinshasa-based Ituri political leaders and encouraged their involvement to end the conflict in southern Irumu.

Some progress was made in the area of institutional reform. The Parliament adopted laws on the delimitation of the country's maritime boundaries and the law on amnesty for armed groups in the Kivus. However, legislation pertaining to the local elections and the reform of the national police remained pending.

Meanwhile, the humanitarian situation in eastern DRC continued to deteriorate. Since January, more than half a million people had been displaced from their homes or temporary shelters for IDPs, owing mainly to the confrontations between FARDC and FDLR in the Kivus. On a more positive note, some 350,000 IDPs had returned to their homes in North Kivu, mainly in Masisi and Rutshuru territories.

MONUC continued to transfer its presences in the west to the eastern part of the country. It began a mapping exercise to identify capacities in the Western provinces, the conditions for the progressive handover of operations to the UN country team and a transition timetable.

Activities continued in support of the stabilization and reconstruction plan for areas emerging from armed conflict. Rehabilitation work on the six priority axes continued, and construction and rehabilitation of administrative and justice/penitentiary buildings began in June. Under the UN security and stabilization support strategy, MONUC would assist the Government's law enforcement and mine inspection agencies to deploy in resource-rich areas in order to bring mines under the control of armed groups within State control. The second phase of the national programme for disarmament, demobilization and reintegration was launched on 23 April, targeting the remaining caseloads of 97,600 combatants. However, the Government had excluded some 10,000 Republican Guard members from the process. President Kabila

and the National Defence Council approved the revised army reform plan announced on 4 February, which was being reviewed by the Parliament. In the meantime, an interim emergency reform plan had been developed, highlighting immediate and short-term priorities for defence sector reform. The terms of reference for a national coordination body to guide the defence sector reform process had been approved by the Minister of Defence and were being reviewed by the President.

Some progress was made in the preparations for local elections. The Independent Electoral Commission presented a revised budget of $163 million, which was endorsed by the Government and its international development partners on 24 March. On 28 March, the Commission published the timetable for the update of the voter register, which began on 7 June in Kinshasa. The second phase for the rest of the country was to begin on 2 August, and polling in the first quarter of 2010. A major concern continued to be the legal framework for the elections. The Commission had yet to receive an authoritative list of the territorial entities that would become the electoral constituencies.

The Secretary-General, noting the impact of military operations on the civilian population, requested MONUC and the United Nations High Commissioner for Refugees to develop a UN system-wide concept on the protection of civilians in the DRC encompassing security, humanitarian and human rights dimensions in order to reconcile the priority focus of MONUC on protecting civilians with its mandate to support FARDC operations. He also recognized that the military option alone could not resolve the question of the armed groups in the east, and requested MONUC to develop a multidimensional approach to address the presence of FDLR, in close collaboration with the Governments of the DRC and Rwanda, his Special Envoy for the Great Lakes Region and other partners.

Security Council action. The Security Council on 10 July [meeting 6159] considered the Secretary-General's report, which was presented by his Special Representative. Following the briefing, the Council, by a press statement [SC/9703], encouraged MONUC to continue monitoring the performance and conduct of FARDC units involved in joint operations against armed groups. The Council expressed concern over the renewed activity of illegal armed groups and condemned the targeted attacks against the civilian population by those groups, in particular FDLR and LRA. It expressed concern over continued reports of massive human rights violations, widespread sexual violence and recruitment and use of children by those groups, as well as some elements of the national security forces. Stressing that fighting impunity was an integral part of the much-needed reform of the security sector, the Council welcomed steps taken by the authorities to address the issue of impunity within the national security forces, including the announcement on 5 July of a "zero-tolerance policy" against criminal acts and misconduct in the armed forces. It encouraged the authorities to continue taking steps in that regard and called for an effective vetting mechanism within the national security forces.

Communication. The AU, in the Plan of Action of the Tripoli Declaration on the Elimination of Conflicts in Africa and the Promotion of Sustainable Peace, adopted at its special session on that issue (Tripoli, Libyan Arab Jamahiriya, 30–31 August) [S/2009/461], called for immediate and concrete steps to support the DRC for the full implementation of the 23 March Agreements.

Report of Secretary-General (September). In his September report on MONUC activities [S/2009/472], the Secretary-General stated that FARDC-led military operations against FDLR were extended in North Kivu into Lubero and Walikale territories, and began in South Kivu on 12 July. By the end of August, MONUC assessed that three main pockets of several hundred FDLR combatants remained in the perimeter area between Masisi and Walikale and in southern Lubero territories. In South Kivu, those operations resulted in some important success, as FARDC gained control of much of Kalehe, Kabare and Shabunda territories after years of FDLR domination. On 28 July, FARDC succeeded in dislodging FDLR from Kashindaba, its main headquarters in South Kivu, and, in August, challenged FDLR strongholds in Walungu, Mwenga and Sange and around Uvira. On 20 August, FARDC successfully concluded operations to clear FDLR from the Kahuzi-Biega National Park, as well as Tchivanga and Nindja areas in Kabare territory.

On 31 August, the Chiefs of Defence of Burundi, the DRC and Rwanda, and senior MONUC military representatives met in Goma to evaluate the progress of the operations. The Chiefs of Defence agreed that, in North Kivu and the northern part of South Kivu, the operations had succeeded in dismantling FDLR strongholds and neutralizing a considerable number of its elements, although pockets of FDLR elements continued to operate in small groups. The FDLR command and control, logistics, and administrative and political structures in both Kivus had been disrupted. In terms of next steps, the Chiefs of Defence agreed that operations should continue in order to dismantle FDLR bases in Fizi territory, South Kivu. MONUC agreed to enhance disarmament, demobilization, repatriation, reintegration and resettlement efforts in forward positions and to reinforce its presence along Lake Tanganyika to prevent a possible retreat of FDLR elements into Burundi.

Despite those achievements, the military operations were accompanied by FDLR reprisal attacks,

as well as some exactions against civilians by FARDC elements, leading to significant population displacements. FDLR intensified attacks on civilians from its strongholds in the areas of Mwenga, Sange-Uvira and Hombo throughout July. On 12 July, it also attacked the MONUC base at Mwenga, South Kivu. In addition, an increasing number of attacks involving remnant Congolese armed groups were reported, including against a FARDC camp at Mpama near the Bisiye mine on 12 August.

In Orientale province, FARDC led operations against LRA, supported by intelligence teams from the Uganda defence forces. As a result, 111 LRA elements were reportedly killed and another 65 arrested. Nonetheless, LRA attacks against civilians increased, with a reported 74 attacks across Haut and Bas Uélé resulting in 65 deaths and 152 abductions of civilians between 1 July and 31 August. In Ituri, FARDC regained control of three militia bases in Janda, Pkoma and Matalatala.

On 31 July, the Independent Electoral Commission announced the postponement of the voter registration update in the provinces beyond Kinshasa because of delays in the revision of the list of territorial entities, which had been approved by provincial assemblies in only four of the ten provinces. On 4 August, the voter registration process in Kinshasa was extended until 20 August, owing to limited turnout. Delays in the disbursement of Government funds also hampered the work of the Commission. Those factors were likely to delay local elections beyond the first quarter of 2010.

Security Council consideration. During the Security Council's consideration of the Secretary-General's report on 16 October [meeting 6203], the Special Representative said that resolution 1856(2008) listed 41 tasks, which had given MONUC considerable flexibility in a rapidly changing environment. However, it also generated many demands and high expectations that needed to be rationalized. The preparation of an integrated strategic framework provided an opportunity to reflect on how that might be done. The framework—a joint undertaking of MONUC and the UN country team—would outline the key challenges facing the DRC and indicate how the United Nations might assist the country, taking account of the Government's priorities and the Council's directives.

Report of Secretary-General (December). In his December report on MONUC [S/2009/623], the Secretary-General said that the overall situation in the east, especially in the Kivus and in parts of Orientale province, remained fragile. Military operations conducted by FARDC in eastern DRC, with MONUC support, continued to dislodge foreign and residual Congolese armed groups from their strongholds and enabled the Government to extend its control into previously inaccessible areas, including important economic zones. Monuc also supported efforts to extend State authority, including through the deployment of national police elements to areas from which FDLR had been dislodged. Despite the enhanced and innovative measures taken by monuc to protect civilians, the operations took a heavy toll on civilians, who were displaced and subjected to reprisal attacks by retreating armed groups. Furthermore, the actions of undisciplined and recently integrated FARDC elements seeking to settle old ethnic scores resulted in serious violations of international humanitarian law, including killings of civilians.

To address FARDC indiscipline, monuc developed a policy setting out the conditions under which the Mission could support FARDC units, which was transmitted to the Government and entered into effect in November. The policy specified that monuc would not participate in or support operations with FARDC units if there were substantial grounds for believing that there was a real risk that such units would violate international humanitarian, human rights or refugee law. On the basis of the policy, monuc would intervene with the FARDC command if the Mission had reason to believe that elements of a unit receiving its support was committing grave violations, and would suspend support for a unit if FARDC took no action against those responsible or if the elements of the unit continued to commit violations. Monuc military and human rights components would closely monitor FARDC conduct and the application of the policy. Furthermore, the Secretary-General decided to send a mission to the DRC, led by DPKO, to assess the policy and related issues. On 1 November, monuc suspended its logistical support for one FARDC unit suspected of having committed major human rights violations.

Monuc and a number of international nongovernmental organizations (NGOS) reported alleged or confirmed massacres and gross human rights violations committed by FARDC elements against civilian populations. As a result, human rights organizations and some components of the UN system called for an immediate end to the operation in the Kivus and for the withdrawal of monuc support for FARDC, as that support could not be reconciled with the Mission's mandate of protecting civilians, and put the Mission in a difficult position that might expose it to charges of association with serious violations of international humanitarian law committed by FARDC elements.

On 6 October, Ildephonse Nizeyimana, an indictee of the International Criminal Tribunal for Rwanda, was arrested in Uganda and transferred to the Tribunal (see p. 1288). On 17 November, the German police arrested FDLR President Ignace Murwanashyaka and his deputy, Straton Musoni, in Germany on charges of membership in a foreign terrorist organization and for war crimes and crimes against humanity committed in eastern DRC.

On 30 October, despite appeals by several human rights organizations and other international partners encouraging the Congolese Government to arrest Bosco Ntaganda, against whom the International Criminal Court had issued an arrest warrant for crimes allegedly committed in Ituri in 2002 and 2003, the Government reiterated its position ruling out his arrest and transfer to the Court at that stage. The Government stated again that Mr. Ntaganda did not exercise command functions within FARDC, including in the context of the operation in the Kivus, despite reports to the contrary. Monuc made it clear to the Government that there would be significant legal obstacles to its participation in or support of an operation in which Mr. Ntaganda were to play a prominent role.

On 1 November, monuc suspended its support for a FARDC unit found to have targeted and killed at least 62 civilians, including women and children, between May and September in the Lukweti area of North Kivu. Investigations conducted by human rights organizations indicated that as many as 270 civilians might have been killed over that period. A UN system-wide strategy on the protection of civilians was developed to coordinate responses to that priority.

Monuc and FARDC developed an updated joint operations directive for the next phase of the operations against FDLR, under which the military operations would concentrate on a "clear, hold and build" strategy. That implied a shift to limited, jointly planned military operations focusing on clearing identified areas in which FDLR elements were attempting to regroup and on the group's remaining leadership; holding the cleared key areas; and assisting the Congolese authorities in establishing civilian State authority in areas from which FDLR had been dislodged, including building institutional capacities and infrastructure under the UN security and stabilization support strategy.

Important progress was achieved in support of the Government's Stabilization and Reconstruction Plan for War-Affected Areas. In South Kivu, the United Nations Development Programme (UNDP) and the International Organization for Migration continued to rehabilitate accommodation facilities in order to garrison approximately 3,000 FARDC elements at Camp Saio. In addition, more than 30 State buildings, including police stations, courts, prisons and local administrative offices, were under construction in the Kivus and Ituri, with completion expected in early 2010. Road and bridge rehabilitation efforts continued, including the completion of the rehabilitation of the Ituri I bridge and the commencement of work on the Bukavu-Shabunda road by the United Nations

Office for Project Services and MONUC military engineering contingents. On 22 October, the steering committee for the Stabilization and Reconstruction Plan for War-Affected Areas launched joint coordination structures and approved the priority plan for the DRC, which would determine the allocation of the $20 million from the Peacebuilding Fund.

MONUC and the UN country team began developing an Integrated Strategic Framework for the UN system in the DRC. The Framework would include a shared vision of the Organization's objectives and a set of agreed results, timelines and responsibilities for tasks critical to the consolidation of peace. In preparation of the Framework, senior UN system managers held a workshop (Kinshasa, 3 September) during which they defined common objectives and priorities for 2010–2012. The workshop was followed by the establishment of technical working groups organized around thematic pillars, involving MONUC and the UN country team.

In September, the Independent Electoral Commission completed the voter registration update in Kinshasa and issued approximately 1.4 million new voter cards. On 25 November, the Government confirmed its commitment to holding local elections before general elections and indicated that a timetable would be issued before 10 December. However, accumulated delays made it unlikely that local elections could be held before the end of 2010.

The Secretary-General, in recognition of the realities in the DRC, stated that MONUC and the Secretariat would discuss with the DRC the direction and configuration of the Mission and he would present to the Security Council, in April 2010, recommendations to that effect. Meanwhile, he recommended that the Mission's mandate be extended until 30 June 2010 to permit the completion of those discussions. On the basis of recommendations to be submitted in his April report, the Security Council would conduct a more careful review of MONUC with a view to developing, in June 2010, a new mandate, including its military drawdown.

Security Council consideration. On 16 December [meeting 6244], during the consideration of the Secretary-General's report on MONUC, the Special Representative observed that the Council was aware of the dilemma faced by MONUC, which was inherent in the mandate that enjoined it to give priority to the protection of civilians, while at the same time working with FARDC, which included elements that had been responsible for human rights violations, to disarm groups, such as FDLR, that had been a threat to the people of eastern Congo for over a decade. There was no easy answer to that dilemma and MONUC was looking to the Council for guidance in that respect.

SECURITY COUNCIL ACTION

On 23 December [meeting 6253], the Security Council unanimously adopted **resolution 1906(2009)**. The draft [S/2009/663] was submitted by France.

The Security Council,

Recalling its previous resolutions, in particular resolutions 1843(2008) of 20 November 2008, 1856(2008) of 22 December 2008 and 1896(2009) of 30 November 2009, and the statements by its President concerning the Democratic Republic of the Congo,

Reaffirming its commitment to the sovereignty, territorial integrity and political independence of the Democratic Republic of the Congo,

Stressing the primary responsibility of the Government of the Democratic Republic of the Congo for ensuring security in its territory and protecting its civilians with respect for the rule of law, human rights and international humanitarian law, and stressing also the importance of urgently undertaking comprehensive and lasting security sector reform and of permanently disarming, demobilizing, resettling or repatriating, as appropriate, and reintegrating Congolese and foreign armed groups for the long-term stabilization of the Democratic Republic of the Congo, and of the contribution made by international partners in this field,

Calling upon all parties to armed conflict in the Great Lakes region to comply with the obligations applicable to them under international humanitarian law to take all required steps to protect civilians and to facilitate the rapid and unimpeded passage of relief consignments, equipment and personnel,

Encouraging the countries of the Great Lakes region to maintain a high level of commitment to jointly promote peace and stability in the region, and welcoming the recent improvements in the relations between the Governments of the Democratic Republic of the Congo and Rwanda, Uganda and Burundi,

Stressing that the Goma and Nairobi processes as well as the agreements of 23 March 2009 are the appropriate framework for stabilizing the situation in the eastern part of the Democratic Republic of the Congo, and urging all parties to fully abide by and implement those agreements,

Deeply concerned that some militias and armed groups in the eastern part of the Democratic Republic of the Congo have not yet laid down their arms and continue to prey on the population,

Expressing its extreme concern at the deteriorating humanitarian and human rights situation and the continued impunity of those responsible for human rights abuses and other atrocities, condemning, in particular, the targeted attacks against the civilian population, widespread sexual violence, recruitment and use of child soldiers and extrajudicial executions, stressing the urgent need for the Government of the Democratic Republic of the Congo, in cooperation with the United Nations Organization Mission in the Democratic Republic of the Congo and other relevant actors, to end violations of human rights and international humanitarian law, and to bring the perpetrators to justice, and calling upon Member States to assist in this regard and to continue to provide medical, humanitarian and other assistance to victims,

Calling upon all parties concerned to create the conditions conducive to a voluntary, safe, dignified and sustainable return of refugees and internally displaced persons,

Welcoming the commitments made by the Government of the Democratic Republic of the Congo to hold accountable those responsible for atrocities in the country, noting the cooperation of the Government with the International Criminal Court, and stressing the importance of actively seeking to hold accountable those responsible for war crimes and crimes against humanity in the country,

Recalling its resolutions 1325(2000) of 31 October 2000, 1820(2008) of 19 June 2008, 1888(2009) of 30 September 2009 and 1889(2009) of 5 October 2009 on women and peace and security, its resolution 1502(2003) of 26 August 2003 on the protection of United Nations personnel, associated personnel and humanitarian personnel in conflict zones, its resolutions 1674(2006) of 28 April 2006 and 1894(2009) of 11 November 2009 on the protection of civilians in armed conflict and its resolutions 1612(2005) of 26 July 2005 and 1882(2009) of 4 August 2009 on children and armed conflict, and recalling also the conclusions of the Security Council Working Group on Children and Armed Conflict pertaining to parties to the armed conflict in the Democratic Republic of the Congo,

Emphasizing that the linkage between the illicit exploitation of and trade in natural resources and the proliferation of and trafficking in arms is one of the major factors fuelling and exacerbating conflicts in the Great Lakes region, particularly in the Democratic Republic of the Congo, urging all States, particularly those in the region, to implement fully the measures set out in its resolution 1896(2009), and reiterating its determination to continue to closely monitor the implementation of and compliance with the measures set out in resolution 1896(2009),

Underscoring the long-term, sustainable efforts needed from the Government of the Democratic Republic of the Congo to provide a calendar for local, general and presidential elections, with full respect for the provisions of the Constitution, to consolidate democracy and promote the rule of law, democratic governance, recovery and development, with the support of its international partners,

Expressing its full support for the Mission, condemning all attacks against United Nations peacekeepers and humanitarian personnel, regardless of the perpetrators, and emphasizing that those responsible for such attacks must be brought to justice,

Taking note of the thirtieth regular report of the Secretary-General on the Mission, of 4 December 2009, and of the recommendations contained therein,

Determining that the situation in the Democratic Republic of the Congo continues to pose a threat to international peace and security in the region,

Acting under Chapter VII of the Charter of the United Nations,

1. *Decides* to extend the deployment of the United Nations Organization Mission in the Democratic Republic of the Congo until 31 May 2010, with the intention to extend it further at that date for twelve months, authorizes the continuation until that date of up to 19,815 military personnel, 760 military observers, 391 police personnel and 1,050 personnel of formed police units, and stresses its intention to consider in the subsequent resolution assessing and adjusting the mandate and to remain strongly committed to contributing to the long-term stability of the Democratic Republic of the Congo;

2. *Requests* the Secretary-General to conduct a strategic review of the situation in the Democratic Republic of the Congo and the progress of the Mission towards achieving its mandate, taking into account the Integrated Strategic Framework for the United Nations presence in the country, to further develop the existing benchmarks for this purpose, to determine, in close cooperation with the Government of the Democratic Republic of the Congo and troop- and police-contributing countries of the Mission, the modalities of a reconfiguration of the mandate of the Mission, in particular the critical tasks that need to be accomplished before the Mission can envisage its drawdown without triggering a relapse into instability, and to report to the Security Council with recommendations by 1 April 2010;

3. *Urges* the Government of the Democratic Republic of the Congo to establish sustainable peace in the eastern part of the country, to effectively protect the civilian population, to develop sustainable security sector institutions which fully respect the rule of law, and to ensure respect for human rights and the fight against impunity by strengthening the capacity of the judicial and correctional systems;

4. *Recognizes* the interrelated nature of the effective protection of civilians, the reduction and removal of the threat of armed groups, and comprehensive and sustainable security sector reform, and underlines that efforts made in each of these key areas contribute significantly and with complementarity both to the aim of improving the humanitarian situation and to the strategic objective of peace and stability in the Democratic Republic of the Congo;

5. *Decides* that, from the adoption of the present resolution, the Mission, working in close cooperation with the Government of the Democratic Republic of the Congo, shall have the following mandate, in order of priority:

(*a*) To ensure the effective protection of civilians, humanitarian personnel and United Nations personnel and facilities, in accordance with paragraphs 3 (*a*) to (*e*) and 4 (*c*) of resolution 1856(2008) and paragraphs 7 to 18 below;

(*b*) To carry out enhanced activities of disarmament, demobilization and reintegration of Congolese armed groups and of disarmament, demobilization, repatriation, resettlement and reintegration of foreign armed groups, including as set out in paragraphs 19 to 28 below and paragraphs 3 (*n*) to (*p*) of resolution 1856(2008);

(*c*) To support the security sector reform led by the Government of the Democratic Republic of the Congo, including as set out in paragraphs 29 to 38 below;

6. *Authorizes* the Mission to use all necessary means, within the limits of its capacity and in the areas where its units are deployed, to carry out the tasks of its mandate listed in paragraphs 3 (*a*) to (*e*) of resolution 1856(2008) and paragraphs 9, 20, 21 and 24 below;

Protection of civilians, including humanitarian personnel and human rights defenders, and United Nations personnel and facilities

7.   *Emphasizes* that the protection of civilians, as described in paragraph 5 *(a)* above, must be given priority in decisions about the use of available capacity and resources, over any of the other tasks described in paragraphs 5 *(b)* and *(c)* above;

8.   *Recalls* that the protection of civilians requires a coordinated response from all relevant Mission components, and encourages the Mission to enhance interaction, under the authority of the Special Representative of the Secretary-General for the Democratic Republic of the Congo, between its civil and military components at all levels and humanitarian actors, in order to consolidate expertise on the protection of civilians;

9.   *Requests* the Mission to build on best practices and extend successful protection measures piloted in North Kivu, in particular the establishment of joint protection teams, early warning centres, communications liaisons with local villages and other measures, to other areas, particularly South Kivu;

10.   *Demands* that all armed groups, in particular the Forces democratiques de libération du Rwanda and the Lord's Resistance Army, immediately cease all forms of violence and human rights abuse against the civilian population in the Democratic Republic of the Congo, in particular gender-based violence, including rape and other forms of sexual abuse;

11.   *Demands also* that the Government of the Democratic Republic of the Congo, in furtherance of resolution 1888(2009), immediately take appropriate measures to protect civilians, including women and children, from violations of international humanitarian law and human rights abuses, including all forms of sexual violence, urges the Government to ensure the full implementation of its "zero-tolerance policy" with respect to discipline and human rights violations, including sexual and gender-based violence, committed by elements of the Armed Forces of the Democratic Republic of the Congo, and further urges that all reports of such violations be thoroughly investigated, with the support of the Mission, and that all those responsible be brought to justice through a robust and independent process;

12.   *Requests* the Secretary-General to continue to fully investigate the allegations of sexual exploitation and abuse by civilian and military personnel of the Mission, and to take the appropriate measures set out in the Secretary-General's bulletin on special measures for protection from sexual exploitation and sexual abuse;

13.   *Also requests* the Secretary-General to ensure that technical support is provided, in predeployment and in theatre, to troop- and police-contributing countries of the Mission, to include guidance and training for military and police personnel on the protection of civilians from imminent threat and appropriate responses, including on human rights, sexual violence and gender issues;

14.   *Encourages* the Mission to enhance its interaction with the civilian population to raise awareness and understanding about its mandate and activities and to collect reliable information on violations of international humanitarian law and human rights abuses perpetrated against civilians;

15.   *Demands* that all armed groups, in particular the Forces democratiques de libération du Rwanda and the Lord's Resistance Army, immediately stop recruiting and using children and release all children associated with them, and calls upon the Government of the Democratic Republic of the Congo to continue to work with the Mission, the monitoring and reporting mechanism and other relevant actors to finalize the elaboration of an action plan to release children present in the Armed Forces of the Democratic Republic of the Congo and to prevent further recruitment;

16.   *Calls upon* the Governments of the Great Lakes region to coordinate their efforts to address the threat posed by the Lord's Resistance Army and strongly encourages enhanced regular information-sharing about the Lord's Resistance Army, in this respect, with the United Nations Organization Mission in the Democratic Republic of the Congo and other United Nations missions in the areas where the Lord's Resistance Army is threatening the population, and requests the Secretary-General to enhance cooperation and information-sharing between United Nations missions in the region on all issues related to regional security threats;

17.   *Calls upon* the States in the region to ensure that any military actions against armed groups are carried out in accordance with international humanitarian, human rights and refugee law and that they take appropriate measures to protect civilians and reduce the impact of military actions upon the civilian population, including through regular contacts with and early warning of the civilian population on potential attacks;

18.   *Requests* the Special Representative to identify women's protection advisers among the gender advisers and human rights protection units of the Mission in line with its comprehensive strategy against sexual violence;

Disarmament, demobilization and reintegration of Congolese armed groups and disarmament, demobilization, repatriation, resettlement and reintegration of foreign armed groups

19.   *Demands* that all armed groups, in particular the Forces democratiques de libération du Rwanda, the Lord's Resistance Army and other foreign armed groups, immediately lay down their arms, and demands further that the Congolese armed groups present themselves without any further delay or preconditions to the Congolese authorities and the Mission for disarmament, demobilization and reintegration, and that the foreign armed groups similarly present themselves to the Congolese authorities and the Mission for disarmament, demobilization, repatriation, resettlement and reintegration;

20.   *Underlines* that the Mission shall deter any attempt at the use of force to threaten the Goma and Nairobi processes from any armed group, particularly in the eastern part of the Democratic Republic of the Congo, and undertake all operations necessary to prevent attacks on civilians and disrupt the military capability of armed groups that continue to use violence in that area;

21.   *Requests* the Mission, working in close cooperation with the Government of the Democratic Republic of the Congo, to continue its coordination of operations with the brigades of the Armed Forces of the Democratic Republic of the Congo deployed in the eastern part of the Democratic Republic of the Congo, premised on the protection of civil-

ians as a priority and on operations being jointly planned with these brigades, and in accordance with its policy paper referred to in paragraph 23 below, with a view to:

(a) Disarming foreign and Congolese armed groups in targeted areas in order to ensure their participation in the disarmament, demobilization, repatriation, resettlement and reintegration and disarmament, demobilization and reintegration process;

(b) Holding the territories cleared of armed groups in order to ensure the protection of civilian populations;

(c) Helping the Government of the Democratic Republic of the Congo to restore its authority in these territories, in particular in the eastern part of the Democratic Republic of the Congo, areas freed from armed groups and key mining areas;

(d) Carrying out enhanced efforts to prevent the provision of support to armed groups, including support derived from illicit economic activities and illicit trade in natural resources;

22. *Reiterates*, consistent with paragraphs 3 *(g)* and 14 of resolution 1856(2008), that the support of the Mission to military operations against foreign and Congolese armed groups led by the Armed Forces of the Democratic Republic of the Congo is strictly conditioned on compliance by the Armed Forces with international humanitarian, human rights and refugee law and on an effective joint planning of these operations, decides that the military leadership of the Mission shall confirm, prior to providing any support to such operations, that sufficient joint planning has been undertaken, especially regarding the protection of the civilian population, calls upon the Mission to intercede with the Armed Forces command if elements of a unit of the Armed Forces receiving support from the Mission are suspected of having committed grave violations of such laws, and, if the situation persists, calls upon the Mission to withdraw support from those units of the Armed Forces;

23. *Notes*, in this regard, the development by the Mission of a policy paper setting out the conditions under which the Mission can provide support to units of the Armed Forces of the Democratic Republic of the Congo, and requests the Secretary-General to establish an appropriate mechanism to regularly assess the implementation of this policy;

24. *Urges* the Mission, in close cooperation with other partners, including the World Bank and the United Nations Development Programme, to contribute further to the implementation of the disarmament, demobilization and reintegration of Congolese combatants and their dependents, with particular attention to children, by monitoring the disarmament process and providing, as appropriate, security in some sensitive locations, as well as by supporting reintegration efforts pursued by the Congolese authorities in cooperation with the United Nations country team and bilateral and multilateral partners;

25. *Also urges* the Mission to enhance its support to the voluntary demobilization and repatriation of disarmed foreign combatants and their dependents, and calls upon the Governments of the Democratic Republic of the Congo and the neighbouring States to remain engaged in this process;

26. *Urges* the Governments of the Democratic Republic of the Congo and Rwanda to work together and to agree on a clear set of end-state objectives on the Forces democra-

tiques de libération du Rwanda, within the framework of a multidimensional approach;

27. *Urges* all States to take appropriate legal action against leaders of the Forces democratiques de libération du Rwanda residing in their countries, including through effective implementation of the sanctions regime established by resolution 1533(2004) of 12 March 2004 and renewed by resolution 1896(2009);

28. *Also urges* all States, especially those in the region, to take appropriate steps to end the illicit trade in natural resources, including, if necessary, through judicial means, and, where necessary, to report to the Council, and urges the Mission, in accordance with paragraph 3 *(j)* of resolution 1856(2008), to consolidate and assess, jointly with the Government of the Democratic Republic of the Congo, the pilot project of bringing together all State services in five trading counters in North and South Kivu in order to improve the traceability of mineral products;

Support for security sector reform

29. *Reiterates* the primary responsibility of the Government of the Democratic Republic of the Congo regarding the reform of the security sector, and encourages the Government, working in cooperation with the Mission and other international partners, to build a core, well-vetted, multi-ethnic force, whose size, composition and structure should be developed by the Government, with the support of the Mission, with a view to strengthening the capacity, discipline and professionalism of the Armed Forces of the Democratic Republic of the Congo;

30. *Requests* the Mission, in cooperation with the Congolese authorities, to coordinate the efforts of the international community, including all bilateral and multilateral actors working in this field, on security sector reform issues, and calls upon all Member States and international organizations to fully cooperate with the Mission in this regard;

31. *Further requests* the Mission to provide military training, including in the area of human rights, international humanitarian law, child protection and the prevention of gender-based and sexual violence, to the Armed Forces of the Democratic Republic of the Congo, including to the integrated brigades deployed in the eastern part of the Democratic Republic of the Congo, as part of broader international efforts to support security sector reform;

32. *Reiterates its call upon* the Congolese authorities, with the support of the Mission, to establish an effective vetting mechanism, in accordance with international standards, for the Armed Forces of the Democratic Republic of the Congo and the national security forces, to ensure the exclusion of those persons associated with violations of international humanitarian law and human rights abuses and to trigger the judicial process against such persons where appropriate;

33. *Encourages* the Government of the Democratic Republic of the Congo, with the support of the Mission, to ensure that armed groups newly integrated into the Armed Forces of the Democratic Republic of the Congo are deployed throughout the country and not restricted to their regions of origin;

34. *Urges* the Government of the Democratic Republic of the Congo to expeditiously adopt legislation related to the reform of the Armed Forces of the Democratic Republic

of the Congo, the High Defence Council and the status of the military personnel of the Armed Forces by the Parliament, as well as the legislation on police reform, also urges the Government to ensure progress in their implementation within the time frame of the present resolution, and urges further the adoption of a comprehensive national strategy for the security sector on the whole territory;

35. *Requests* that the Government of the Democratic Republic of the Congo, with the support of the Mission and other international partners, ensure appropriate conditions for the Armed Forces of the Democratic Republic of the Congo, including attributing ranks to the newly integrated elements, ensuring salary payments and equipment and providing barracks;

36. *Calls upon* all the parties to the agreements of 23 March 2009 to fulfil their commitments and accelerate the implementation of all aspects of the agreements, and requests the Mission to assist in this regard by helping with the integration of the armed groups and the establishment of mechanisms for resolving local disputes as foreseen in those agreements;

37. *Recommends* that the Government of the Democratic Republic of the Congo, in particular through the Armed Forces of the Democratic Republic of the Congo and the Congolese National Police, working in cooperation with the Mission, pursue its efforts to maintain a comprehensive and accurate database containing all available information on the weapons and ammunition in their custody;

38. *Demands* that all parties cooperate fully with the operations of the Mission and that they ensure the security of, and unhindered and immediate access for, United Nations and associated personnel in carrying out their mandate, throughout the territory of the Democratic Republic of the Congo, and requests the Secretary-General to report without delay any failure to comply with these demands;

39. *Requests* the Mission and the United Nations country team to continue their support to extend State authority in the Democratic Republic of the Congo, in particular within the framework of the Government's Stabilization and Reconstruction Plan and the United Nations Security and Stabilization Support Strategy, with a particular emphasis on strengthening democratic institutions and building effective rule of law capacity, including justice and corrections;

40. *Requests* the Secretary-General to provide a briefing on the implementation of the system-wide protection strategy and a progress report on the Integrated Strategic Framework to the Security Council and troop- and police-contributing countries by 16 February 2010;

41. *Also requests* the Secretary-General to provide a full report on the situation in the Democratic Republic of the Congo and on the activities of the Mission by 1 April 2010, in order to prepare the strategic review as set out in paragraph 2 of the present resolution, and requests that this full report include:

(a) Specific information on the challenges of the Mission's role in the protection of civilians, an assessment of existing protection mechanisms, in particular the measures described in paragraphs 8, 9, 11, 12 and 13 of the present resolution, and an assessment of special measures for protection from sexual violence;

(b) An assessment of the implementation of the policy paper setting out the conditions of support by the Mission to the Armed Forces of the Democratic Republic of the Congo as described in paragraphs 22 and 23 of the present resolution;

(c) Information on the further deployment and use of the additional capabilities authorized by resolution 1843(2008);

(d) An assessment of the progress in the security sector reform, including the effectiveness of the training measures set out in paragraph 31 of the present resolution;

42. *Commends* the contribution of troop- and police-contributing countries and donors to the Mission, and calls upon Member States to pledge and contribute the remaining helicopters, air capabilities, intelligence assets and other force enablers required for the Mission;

43. *Requests* the Secretary-General to ensure that the concept of operations and rules of engagement of the Mission are regularly updated to bring them fully in line with the provisions of the present resolution and to report on this to the Council and troop-contributing countries;

44. *Also requests* the Secretary-General, through his Special Representative, to continue to coordinate all the activities of the United Nations system in the Democratic Republic of the Congo;

45. *Decides* to remain actively seized of the matter.

Year-end developments. In a later report [S/2010/164], the Secretary-General informed the Security Council that FARDC on 31 December announced the conclusion of operation against FDLR in North and South Kivu. In accordance with the MONUC policy regarding support to FARDC, MONUC and FARDC signed a joint operational directive on 17 December. Meanwhile, investigations carried out by MONUC confirmed that a massacre had occurred at Mabanga ya Talo on the night of 14–15 December, in which more than 100 people had been killed, reportedly by LRA. Further investigations were required to verify the exact numbers.

On the political front, the Parliament on 15 December adopted laws aimed at improving the business environment and reconsidered the national budget for 2010, including salary allocations for the armed forces and police services. A Joint Commission was established to harmonize outstanding differences between the National Assembly and the Senate regarding the draft law on the National Independent Electoral Commission responsible for the conduct of the general elections.

In 2009, 3,751 FDLR elements were repatriated to Rwanda. That repatriation rate was three times that achieved in 2008. In addition, MONUC received 433 Congolese members of FDLR who had yet to benefit from a disarmament, demobilization and reintegration programme. On 25–26 November, the national strategy on sexual and gender-based violence was launched in Kinshasa with the support of MONUC and the UN country team. The strategy included priority elements identified in the operational plan for the implementation of the UN comprehensive strategy to address sexual violence in the eastern DRC. In addition, in line with the five pillars outlined in the comprehensive strategy, five thematic working groups were established.

Children and armed conflict

In March, as requested in resolution 1612(2005) [YUN 2005, p. 863], the Secretary-General submitted to the Security Council a report [A/63/785-S/2009/158 & Corr.1] on children and armed conflict, which contained information on the DRC. From September 2007 to December 2008, MONUC documented 554 children, including 26 girls, who were newly recruited. Some 1,098 children, including 48 girls, were documented to have separated from or escaped from armed groups. Although systematic recruitment of children by FARDC had ceased in accordance with its military policy and applicable international laws, children continued to be integrated into the force through the brassage process, owing to the lack of proper screening. The release of children within FARDC had been frequently obstructed, and some FARDC commanders had denied access to brassage centres to child protection partners seeking to identify and separate children. The presence of children continued to be reported in remaining non-integrated FARDC brigades, particularly in the Kivus. Widespread sexual violence remained a concern, with a majority of the perpetrators being elements of armed groups, but also including FARDC soldiers and national police officers. Recent events, such as the splitting of CNDP, the detention of Laurent Nkunda by the Rwandan Government and the joint military operations by FARDC and Rwandan forces against FDLR, carried significant implications for children, in terms of the increased risk of children being used in military operations or killed or injured in hostilities, as well as the demobilization of children within CNDP and other armed groups.

The Security Council, in presidential statement **S/PRST/2009/9** of 29 April (see p. 737), invited the Secretary General to strengthen efforts to bring the monitoring and reporting mechanism to its full capacity in order to allow for prompt advocacy and effective response to all violations and abuses committed against children.

The Security Council took action on the Secretary General's report in **resolution 1882(2009)** of 4 August (see p. 739).

In August [S/2009/437], the Chairman of the Security Council Working Group on Children and Armed Conflict, following the Group's meeting on 1 July, forwarded to the Secretary-General its conclusions [S/AC.51/2009/3] on the parties to the armed conflict in the DRC. The Chairman welcomed the initiatives taken by MONUC in partnership with the United Nations Children's Fund (UNICEF) to improve child protection, raise awareness and change behaviours regarding violations and abuses committed against children; the launch of regional child protection working groups; the development of an accelerated common action plan to combat sexual and gender-based violence and the appointment of a senior adviser and coordinator on sexual violence; and the provision of technical support, advice and training to military prosecutors and military judicial police inspectors on the investigation and prosecution of violations and abuses committed against children. He invited the Secretary-General to request UNDP, UNICEF and other UN entities, in close cooperation with the DRC, to continue to address socio-economic issues, the welfare of children affected by armed conflict, and to strengthen the education system, including in conflict-affected areas; as well as to address the long-term effects of armed conflict on children. MONUC should share information with the Group of Experts on the DRC established pursuant to resolution 1533(2004) [YUN 2004, p. 137], especially on the support received by armed groups on recruitment and use of children and on the targeting of women and children in situations of armed conflict.

Arms embargo

The Security Council Committee on the DRC, established pursuant to resolution 1533(2004) [YUN 2004, p. 137] to review and monitor the arms embargo on armed groups imposed by resolution 1493(2003) [YUN 2003, p. 130], reported [S/2009/667] on its activities in 2009, during which it held six informal meetings. In October, by resolution 1896(2009) (see p. 132), the Council extended the arms embargo until 30 November 2010. In accordance with resolution 1807(2008) [YUN 2008, p. 136], the Committee received 10 notifications from States in advance of the shipment of arms or related materiel for the DRC, or the provision of assistance, advice or training to military activities in the DRC. The Committee received reports from 15 States on their implementation of the sanctions imposed by resolution 1857(2008) [ibid., p. 141].

Group of Experts

The Group of Experts on the DRC, established pursuant to Security Council resolution 1533(2004) to gather and analyse information on flows of arms and related materiel as well as networks operating in violation of the measures imposed by paragraph 20 of resolution 1493(2003), submitted during the year an interim report [S/2009/253] and a final report [S/2009/603].

As requested by resolutions 1799(2008) [YUN 2008, p. 136] and 1807(2008), respectively, the Secretary-General, on 13 February [S/2009/93], reappointed three new experts to constitute the Group for a period ending on 30 November.

Reports of Group of Experts. As requested by Council resolution 1857(2008), the Security Council Committee on the DRC in May submitted to the Council the interim report [S/2009/253] of the Working Group, which drew attention to the continued presence of children in the ranks of the recently integrated FARDC brigades in North Kivu, as well as to human rights abuses committed by former commanders of armed groups integrated in FARDC. That made a compelling argument for establishing a vetting mechanism that would make it possible to screen the human rights records of FARDC military commanders. Such an initiative was indispensable for a sustainable integration process, and would strengthen the capacity of the Government to extend State authority in eastern DRC. The Group highlighted other concerns on the issue of military integration, notably the maintenance of parallel command structures operated by former senior CNDP officers who had been integrated into FARDC. It also noted that several armed groups in South Kivu had not joined the integration process, including some Mai-Mai militias. The Group was also monitoring the situation in north-eastern DRC, after it received verified reports of hundreds of civilian casualties and abductions at the hands of LRA since December 2008. The Group had obtained information that arms and ammunition were transported to FARDC from the Sudan on two occasions. It had been in contact with two Belgian companies, Traxys and Trademet, which had been named in its previous report [YUN 2008, p. 140] as consumers of minerals originating from businesses controlled by FDLR and CNDP, and was awaiting for replies from those companies concerning due diligence. The Group recommended that the Government implement a vetting mechanism to screen the human rights records of FARDC officers within the wider context of security sector reform; that the Government undertake a review of the mining legislation to improve transparency in the trade of minerals mined in the DRC; and that States exporting military equipment to the DRC notify the Committee of their exports.

In November [S/2009/603], the Committee submitted to the Council the final report of the Working Group, in accordance with resolutions 1533(2004) and 1857(2008). The report concluded that military operations against FDLR had failed to dismantle the organization's political and military structures in eastern DRC. FDLR continued to benefit from residual but significant support from FARDC top commanders, especially in South Kivu, and had sealed strategic alliances with other armed groups in North and South Kivu. External support networks—for instance in Burundi and the United Republic of Tanzania—had been used to counteract the effects of the FARDC military operations. FDLR had a far-reaching international diaspora network involved in the day-to-day running of the movement, the coordination of military operations and arms trafficking and the management of financial activities. The report presented two case studies on the involvement of individuals linked to faith-based organizations.

FDLR's exploitation of gold and cassiterite in the Kivus continued to deliver millions of dollars into the FDLR coffers, the report said. FDLR gold networks were tightly intertwined with trading networks operating within Burundi and Uganda, as well as the United Arab Emirates. End buyers of cassiterite included corporations based in Malaysia and the United Kingdom. The report analysed the integration of non-State armed groups into FARDC through the rapid integration process in January, as well as prior to and during the FARDC-Rwandan force joint operations. In that context, the CNDP officer class, in particular General Bosco Ntaganda, continued to retain heavy weapons in spite of its integration into FARDC and still controlled revenue-generating activities and parallel local administrations. The Group also presented documentary evidence showing that General Ntaganda continued to act as the deputy operational commander of the FARDC operations in the Kivus. CNDP military officers deployed as part of FARDC operations profited from their deployment in mineral-rich areas and from direct involvement in the supply of minerals to exporting houses in North and South Kivu, some of which also supplied international companies. The Group conclusively documented irregular deliveries of arms to the DRC from the Democratic People's Republic of Korea and the Sudan, as well as deliveries of trucks and aircraft to FARDC.

In response to the reports, the Security Council extended the arms embargo and related sanctions until 30 November 2010.

SECURITY COUNCIL ACTION

On 30 November, [meeting 6225], the Security Council unanimously adopted **resolution 1896(2009)**. The draft [S/2009/604] was submitted by France.

The Security Council,

Recalling its previous resolutions, in particular resolutions 1804(2008) of 13 March 2008, 1807(2008) of 31 March 2008 and 1857(2008) of 22 December 2008, and the statements by its President concerning the Democratic Republic of the Congo,

Reaffirming its commitment to the sovereignty, territorial integrity and political independence of the Democratic Republic of the Congo as well as all States in the region,

Taking note of the interim and final reports of the Group of Experts on the Democratic Republic of the Congo ("the Group of Experts") established pursuant to resolution 1771(2007) of 10 August 2007, whose mandate was extended pursuant to resolutions 1807(2008) and 1857(2008), and of the recommendations contained therein,

Reiterating its serious concern regarding the presence of armed groups and militias in the eastern part of the Democratic Republic of the Congo, particularly in the provinces of North and South Kivu, Ituri and Orientale Province, which perpetuates a climate of insecurity in the whole region,

Demanding that all armed groups, in particular the Forces democratiques de libération du Rwanda and the Lord's Resistance Army, immediately lay down their arms and cease their attacks against the civilian population, demanding also that all the parties to the agreements of 23 March 2009 respect the ceasefire and implement their commitments effectively and in good faith,

Expressing its concern about the support received by armed groups operating in the eastern part of the Democratic Republic of the Congo from regional and international networks,

Welcoming the commitments of the Democratic Republic of the Congo and the countries of the Great Lakes region to jointly promote peace and stability in the region, and reiterating the importance of the Government of the Democratic Republic of the Congo and all Governments, particularly those in the region, taking effective steps to ensure that there is no support, in and from their territories, for the armed groups in the eastern part of the Democratic Republic of the Congo,

Noting with great concern the persistence of human rights and humanitarian law violations against civilians in the eastern part of the Democratic Republic of the Congo, including the killing and displacement of significant numbers of civilians, the recruitment and use of child soldiers and widespread sexual violence, stressing that the perpetrators must be brought to justice, reiterating its firm condemnation of all violations of human rights and international humanitarian law in the country, and recalling all its relevant resolutions on women and peace and security, on children and armed conflict and on the protection of civilians in armed conflict,

Stressing the primary responsibility of the Government of the Democratic Republic of the Congo for ensuring security in its territory and protecting its civilians with respect for the rule of law, human rights and international humanitarian law,

Stressing also the need to fight impunity as an integral part of the much-needed comprehensive reform of the security sector, and strongly encouraging the Government of the Democratic Republic of the Congo to implement its "zero-tolerance policy" against criminal acts and misconduct in the armed forces,

Encouraging the Government of the Democratic Republic of the Congo to take concrete measures to reform the justice sector and implement the penitentiary system reform action plan, in order to ensure a fair and credible system against impunity,

Recalling its resolution 1502(2003) of 26 August 2003 on the protection of United Nations personnel, associated personnel and humanitarian personnel in conflict zones,

Condemning the continuing illicit flow of weapons within and into the Democratic Republic of the Congo in violation of resolutions 1533(2004) of 12 March 2004, 1807(2008) and 1857(2008), declaring its determination to continue to monitor closely the implementation of the arms embargo and other measures set out in its resolutions concerning the Democratic Republic of the Congo, and stressing the obligation of all States to abide by the notification requirements set out in paragraph 5 of resolution 1807(2008),

Recognizing the linkage between the illegal exploitation of natural resources, illicit trade in such resources and the proliferation of and trafficking in arms as one of the major factors fuelling and exacerbating conflicts in the Great Lakes region of Africa,

Welcoming the announcement by the Department of Peacekeeping Operations of the Secretariat of its intention to develop guidelines to enhance cooperation and information-sharing between the United Nations peacekeeping missions and the Security Council sanctions committee expert panels,

Determining that the situation in the Democratic Republic of the Congo continues to constitute a threat to international peace and security in the region,

Acting under Chapter VII of the Charter of the United Nations,

1. *Decides* to renew until 30 November 2010 the measures on arms imposed by paragraph 1 of resolution 1807(2008), and reaffirms the provisions of paragraphs 2, 3 and 5 of that resolution;

2. *Decides also* to renew, for the period specified in paragraph 1 above, the measures on transport imposed by paragraphs 6 and 8 of resolution 1807(2008), and reaffirms the provisions of paragraph 7 of that resolution;

3. *Decides further* to renew, for the period specified in paragraph 1 above, the financial and travel measures imposed by paragraphs 9 and 11 of resolution 1807(2008), and reaffirms the provisions of paragraphs 10 and 12 of that resolution regarding the individuals and entities referred to in paragraph 4 of resolution 1857(2008);

4. *Decides* to expand the mandate of the Security Council Committee as set out in paragraph 8 of resolution 1533(2004), expanded upon in paragraph 18 of resolution 1596(2005) of 18 April 2005, paragraph 4 of resolution 1649(2005) of 21 December 2005 and paragraph 14 of resolution 1698(2006) of 31 July 2006, and reaffirmed in paragraph 15 of resolution 1807(2008) and paragraphs 6 and 25 of resolution 1857(2008), to include the following tasks:

(a) To promulgate guidelines, taking into account paragraphs 17 to 24 of resolution 1857(2008), within six months of the date of adoption of the present resolution, in order to facilitate the implementation of the measures imposed by the present resolution, and to keep them under active review as may be necessary;

(b) To hold regular consultations with concerned Member States in order to ensure full implementation of the measures set forth in the present resolution;

(c) To specify the necessary information that Member States should provide in order to fulfil the notification requirement set out in paragraph 5 of resolution 1807(2008) and to circulate this among Member States;

5. *Calls upon* all States, particularly those in the region and those in which individuals and entities designated pursuant to paragraph 3 of the present resolution are based, to implement fully the measures specified in the present resolution and to cooperate fully with the Committee in carrying out its mandate, and further calls upon those Member States that have not previously done so to report to the Committee, within forty-five days of the date of adoption of the present resolution, on the actions they have taken to implement the measures imposed by paragraphs 1 to 3 above;

6. *Requests* the Secretary-General to extend, for a period expiring on 30 November 2010, the mandate of the Group of Experts established pursuant to resolution 1533(2004) and renewed by subsequent resolutions, and requests the Group of Experts to fulfil its mandate as set out in paragraph 18 of resolution 1807(2008) and expanded by paragraphs 9 and 10 of resolution 1857(2008), and to report to the Council in writing, through the Committee, by 21 May 2010 and again before 20 October 2010;

7. *Decides* that the mandate of the Group of Experts referred to in paragraph 6 above shall also include the task of producing, taking into account paragraph 4 *(g)* of resolution 1857(2008), drawing, inter alia, on its reports and taking advantage of work done in other forums, recommendations to the Committee for guidelines for the exercise of due diligence by the importers, processing industries and consumers of mineral products regarding the purchase, sourcing (including steps to be taken to ascertain the origin of mineral products), acquisition and processing of mineral products from the Democratic Republic of the Congo;

8. *Requests* the Group of Experts to focus its activities in North and South Kivu, Ituri and Orientale Province, as well as on regional and international networks providing support to armed groups operating in the eastern part of the Democratic Republic of the Congo;

9. *Recommends* the Government of the Democratic Republic of the Congo to promote stockpile security, accountability and management of arms and ammunition as an urgent priority, and to implement a national weapons marking programme in line with the standards established by the Nairobi Protocol for the Prevention, Control and Reduction of Small Arms and Light Weapons in the Great Lakes Region and the Horn of Africa and the Regional Centre on Small Arms;

10. *Requests* the Governments of the Democratic Republic of the Congo and of all States, particularly those in the region, the United Nations Organization Mission in the Democratic Republic of the Congo and the Group of Experts to cooperate intensively, including by exchanging information regarding arms shipments, trading routes and strategic mines known to be controlled or used by armed groups, flights from the Great Lakes region to the Democratic Republic of the Congo and from the Democratic Republic of the Congo to the Great Lakes region, the illegal exploitation of and trafficking in natural resources, and activities of individuals and entities designated by the Committee pursuant to paragraph 4 of resolution 1857(2008);

11. *Requests in particular* that the Mission share all relevant information with the Group of Experts, especially information on the recruitment and use of children and on the targeting of women and children in situations of armed conflict;

12. *Further demands* that all parties and all States ensure cooperation with the Group of Experts by individuals and entities within their jurisdiction or under their control, and in this regard requests all States to identify a focal point to the Committee in order to enhance cooperation and information-sharing with the Group of Experts;

13. *Reiterates its demand*, expressed in paragraph 21 of resolution 1807(2008) and reaffirmed in paragraph 14 of resolution 1857(2008), that all parties and all States, particularly those in the region, cooperate fully with the work of the Group of Experts and that they ensure the safety of its members, and unhindered and immediate access, in particular to persons, documents and sites that the Group of Experts deems relevant to the execution of its mandate;

14. *Calls upon* Member States to take measures to ensure that importers, processing industries and consumers of Congolese mineral products under their jurisdiction exercise due diligence on their suppliers and on the origin of the minerals they purchase;

15. *Also calls upon* Member States to cooperate fully with the Group of Experts in respect of its mandate under paragraph 7 of the present resolution to develop recommendations for the Committee for guidelines for the exercise of due diligence, in particular by providing details of any relevant national guidelines, licensing requirements or legislation relating to trading in mineral products;

16. *Recommends* that importers and processing industries adopt policies and practices, as well as codes of conduct, to prevent indirect support to armed groups in the Democratic Republic of the Congo through the exploitation of and trafficking in natural resources;

17. *Also recommends* that Member States, particularly those in the Great Lakes region, regularly publish full import and export statistics for gold, cassiterite, coltan and wolframite;

18. *Urges* the donor community to consider providing increased technical or other assistance and support to strengthen the institutional capacity of the mining, law enforcement and border control agencies and institutions of the Democratic Republic of the Congo;

19. *Encourages* Member States to submit to the Committee, for inclusion on its list of designees, individuals or entities that meet the criteria set out in paragraph 4 of resolution 1857(2008), as well as any entities owned or controlled, directly or indirectly, by the submitted individuals or entities, or individuals or entities acting on behalf of or at the direction of the submitted entities;

20. *Reiterates* the provisions on listing individuals and entities by Member States as set out in paragraphs 17 to 20 of resolution 1857(2008), on de-listing individuals and entities as set out in paragraphs 22 to 24 of resolution 1857(2008), and on the role of the Focal Point, as set out in resolution 1730(2006) of 19 December 2006;

21. *Decides* that, when appropriate and no later than 30 November 2010, it shall review the measures set forth in the present resolution, with a view to adjusting them, as appropriate, in the light of the security situation in the Democratic Republic of the Congo, in particular progress in security sector reform, including the integration of the armed forces and the reform of the national police, and in disarming, demobilizing, repatriating, resettling and reintegrating, as appropriate, Congolese and foreign armed groups;

22. *Decides also* to remain actively seized of the matter.

Communication. On 9 December [S/2009/657], the United Republic of Tanzania denied what it called "erroneous conclusions" contained in the Group of Experts on the DRC report that illegal shipments of arms to FDLR was done with its knowledge.

MONUC

The United Nations Organization Mission in the Democratic Republic of the Congo (MONUC), established by Security Council resolution 1279(1999) [YUN 1999, p. 92], continued to discharge its mandate, as enhanced by Council resolutions 1565(2004) [YUN 2004, p. 129], 1756(2007) [YUN 2007, p. 119] and 1856(2008) [YUN 2008, p. 130]. MONUC, headquartered in the DRC capital, Kinshasa, was headed by Alan Doss (United Kingdom), the Special Representative of the Secretary-General for the DRC.

Sexual exploitation and abuse. In the context of its peace operations oversight, the Office of Internal Oversight Services (OIOS) [A/64/326 (Part II)] found prima facie evidence that some peacekeepers from a troop-contributing country had, between December 2007 and April 2009, sexually exploited and abused minors from several displaced persons camps. Three members from a MONUC military contingent were reported to have sexually abused a minor. Two MONUC teams concluded that the claims were unsubstantiated. OIOS assessed that under the circumstances there would be little value in conducting further investigations, and advised the Department of Field Support that there should be enhanced collaboration between MONUC and OIOS in the implementation of investigative operating protocols and best practices for addressing serious misconduct.

Financing

In June, the General Assembly considered the performance report [A/63/563] on the MONUC budget for the period 1 July 2007 to 30 June 2008, which showed expenditures of $1,071,488,800 against an appropriation of $1,112,739,500, leaving an unencumbered balance of $41,250,700. The Assembly also had before it the proposed budget [A/63/806] for MONUC for the period from 1 July 2009 to 30 June 2010, amounting to $1,423,169,600. The Advisory Committee on Administrative and Budgetary Questions (ACABQ) recommended [A/63/746/Add.16] that the unencumbered balance be credited to Member States in a manner to be determined by the Assembly. Consequential reductions arising from the Committee's recommendations as a result of the costing analysis would be communicated to the Assembly by the Committee Chairman.

The ACABQ Chairman told the Fifth (Administrative and Budgetary) Committee on 3 June [A/C.5/63/SR.51]

that ACABQ's recommendations, which included the application of a higher delayed deployment factor for military and police personnel, a higher vacancy rate for international staff and a reduction of $50 million in operating costs, would entail an overall reduction of $66,818,200 in the Mission's budget for the period from 1 July 2009 to 30 June 2010.

GENERAL ASSEMBLY ACTION

On 30 June [meeting 93], the General Assembly, on the recommendation of the Fifth Committee [A/63/898], adopted **resolution 63/291** without vote [agenda item 136].

Financing of the United Nations Organization Mission in the Democratic Republic of the Congo

The General Assembly,

Having considered the reports of the Secretary-General on the financing of the United Nations Organization Mission in the Democratic Republic of the Congo, the related report of the Advisory Committee on Administrative and Budgetary Questions, and the oral statement by the Chairman of the Advisory Committee on Administrative and Budgetary Questions,

Recalling Security Council resolutions 1258(1999) of 6 August 1999 and 1279(1999) of 30 November 1999 regarding, respectively, the deployment to the region of the Democratic Republic of the Congo of military liaison personnel and the establishment of the United Nations Organization Mission in the Democratic Republic of the Congo, and the subsequent resolutions by which the Council extended the mandate of the Mission, the latest of which were resolution 1843(2008) of 20 November 2008, by which the Council authorized a temporary increase of the authorized military strength of the Mission by up to 2,785 military personnel and the strength of its formed police unit by up to 300 personnel, and resolution 1856(2008) of 22 December 2008, by which the Council extended the deployment of the Mission until 31 December 2009 and authorized the continuation until that date of up to 19,815 military personnel, 760 military observers, 391 police personnel and 1,050 personnel of formed police units,

Recalling also its resolution 54/260A of 7 April 2000 on the financing of the Mission and its subsequent resolutions thereon, the latest of which was resolution 62/256 of 20 June 2008,

Recalling further its resolution 58/315 of 1 July 2004,

Reaffirming the general principles underlying the financing of United Nations peacekeeping operations, as stated in General Assembly resolutions 1874(S-IV) of 27 June 1963, 3101(XXVIII) of 11 December 1973 and 55/235 of 23 December 2000,

Noting with appreciation that voluntary contributions have been made to the Mission,

Mindful of the fact that it is essential to provide the Mission with the financial resources necessary to enable it to fulfil its responsibilities under the relevant resolutions of the Security Council,

1. *Requests* the Secretary-General to entrust the Head of Mission with the task of formulating future budget proposals in full accordance with the provisions of General Assembly resolutions 59/296 of 22 June 2005, 60/266 of 30 June 2006 and 61/276 of 29 June 2007, as well as other relevant resolutions;

2. *Takes note* of the status of contributions to the United Nations Organization Mission in the Democratic Republic of the Congo as at 30 April 2009, including the contributions outstanding in the amount of 274.0 million United States dollars, representing some 4 per cent of the total assessed contributions, notes with concern that only forty-two Member States have paid their assessed contributions in full, and urges all other Member States, in particular those in arrears, to ensure payment of their outstanding assessed contributions;

3. *Expresses its appreciation* to those Member States which have paid their assessed contributions in full, and urges all other Member States to make every possible effort to ensure payment of their assessed contributions to the Mission in full;

4. *Expresses concern* at the financial situation with regard to peacekeeping activities, in particular as regards the reimbursements to troop contributors that bear additional burdens owing to overdue payments by Member States of their assessments;

5. *Also expresses concern* at the delay experienced by the Secretary-General in deploying and providing adequate resources to some recent peacekeeping missions, in particular those in Africa;

6. *Emphasizes* that all future and existing peacekeeping missions shall be given equal and non-discriminatory treatment in respect of financial and administrative arrangements;

7. *Also emphasizes* that all peacekeeping missions shall be provided with adequate resources for the effective and efficient discharge of their respective mandates;

8. *Reiterates its request* to the Secretary-General to make the fullest possible use of facilities and equipment at the United Nations Logistics Base at Brindisi, Italy, in order to minimize the costs of procurement for the Mission;

9. *Acknowledges with appreciation* that the use of the logistics hub at Entebbe, Uganda, has been cost-effective and has resulted in savings for the United Nations, and welcomes the expansion of the logistics hub to provide logistical support to peacekeeping operations in the region and to contribute further to their enhanced efficiency and responsiveness, taking into account the ongoing efforts in this regard;

10. *Requests* the Secretary-General to ensure that proposed peacekeeping budgets are based on the relevant legislative mandates;

11. *Endorses* the conclusions and recommendations contained in the report of the Advisory Committee on Administrative and Budgetary Questions, and the oral statement by the Chairman of the Advisory Committee on Administrative and Budgetary Questions, subject to the provisions of the present resolution, and requests the Secretary-General to ensure their full implementation;

12. *Takes note* of paragraphs 48 and 49 of the report of the Advisory Committee, and decides to approve 16 general temporary assistance positions for the Office of the Special

Envoy of the Secretary-General for the Great Lakes Region for six months;

13. *Also takes note* of paragraph 69 of the report of the Advisory Committee;

14. *Requests* the Secretary-General to ensure the full implementation of the relevant provisions of resolutions 59/296, 60/266 and 61/276;

15. *Also requests* the Secretary-General to take all necessary action to ensure that the Mission is administered with a maximum of efficiency and economy;

16. *Further requests* the Secretary-General, in order to reduce the cost of employing General Service staff, to continue efforts to recruit local staff for the Mission against General Service posts, commensurate with the requirements of the Mission;

Financial performance report for the period from 1 July 2007 to 30 June 2008

17. *Takes note* of the report of the Secretary-General on the financial performance of the Mission for the period from 1 July 2007 to 30 June 2008;

Budget estimates for the period from 1 July 2009 to 30 June 2010

18. *Decides* to appropriate to the Special Account for the United Nations Organization Mission in the Democratic Republic of the Congo the amount of 1,405,912,000 dollars for the period from 1 July 2009 to 30 June 2010, inclusive of 1,346,584,600 dollars for the maintenance of the Mission, 49,374,900 dollars for the support account for peacekeeping operations and 9,952,500 dollars for the United Nations Logistics Base;

Financing of the appropriation

19. *Also decides* to apportion among Member States the amount of 702,956,000 dollars for the period from 1 July to 31 December 2009, in accordance with the levels updated in General Assembly resolution 61/243 of 22 December 2006, and taking into account the scale of assessments for 2009, as set out in Assembly resolution 61/237 of 22 December 2006;

20. *Further decides* that, in accordance with the provisions of its resolution 973(X) of 15 December 1955, there shall be set off against the apportionment among Member States, as provided for in paragraph 19 above, their respective share in the Tax Equalization Fund of the amount of 16,179,450 dollars, comprising the estimated staff assessment income of 13,118,150 dollars approved for the Mission, the prorated share of 2,570,050 dollars of the estimated staff assessment income approved for the support account and the prorated share of 491,250 dollars of the estimated staff assessment income approved for the United Nations Logistics Base;

21. *Decides* to apportion among Member States the amount of 702,956,000 dollars for the period from 1 January to 30 June 2010 at a monthly rate of 117,159,333 dollars, in accordance with the levels updated in resolution 61/243, and taking into account the scale of assessments for 2010, subject to a decision of the Security Council to extend the mandate of the Mission;

22. *Also decides* that, in accordance with the provisions of its resolution 973(X), there shall be set off against the ap-

portionment among Member States, as provided for in paragraph 21 above, their respective share in the Tax Equalization Fund of the amount of 16,179,450 dollars, comprising the estimated staff assessment income of 13,118,150 dollars approved for the Mission, the prorated share of 2,570,050 dollars of the estimated staff assessment income approved for the support account and the prorated share of 491,250 dollars of the estimated staff assessment income approved for the United Nations Logistics Base;

23. *Further decides* that, for Member States that have fulfilled their financial obligations to the Mission, there shall be set off against their apportionment, as provided for in paragraph 19 above, their respective share of the unencumbered balance and other income in the total amount of 69,974,500 dollars in respect of the financial period ended 30 June 2008, in accordance with the levels updated in resolution 61/243, and taking into account the scale of assessments for 2008, as set out in resolution 61/237;

24. *Decides* that, for Member States that have not fulfilled their financial obligations to the Mission, there shall be set off against their outstanding obligations their respective share of the unencumbered balance and other income in the total amount of 69,974,500 dollars in respect of the financial period ended 30 June 2008, in accordance with the scheme set out in paragraph 23 above;

25. *Also decides* that the decrease of 330,100 dollars in the estimated staff assessment income in respect of the financial period ended 30 June 2008 shall be set off against the credits from the amount of 69,974,500 dollars referred to in paragraphs 23 and 24 above;

26. *Emphasizes* that no peacekeeping mission shall be financed by borrowing funds from other active peacekeeping missions;

27. *Encourages* the Secretary-General to continue to take additional measures to ensure the safety and security of all personnel participating in the Mission under the auspices of the United Nations, bearing in mind paragraphs 5 and 6 of Security Council resolution 1502(2003) of 26 August 2003;

28. *Invites* voluntary contributions to the Mission in cash and in the form of services and supplies acceptable to the Secretary-General, to be administered, as appropriate, in accordance with the procedure and practices established by the General Assembly;

29. *Decides* to include in the provisional agenda of its sixty-fourth session the item entitled "Financing of the United Nations Organization Mission in the Democratic Republic of the Congo".

On 24 December, by **decision 64/549**, the Assembly decided that the agenda item on MONUC financing would remain for consideration during its resumed sixty-fourth (2010) session.

Burundi

In 2009, the peace process in Burundi made significant progress, despite some residual tasks and challenges. The parties made concerted efforts to implement the 2006 Comprehensive Ceasefire Agreement [YUN 2006, p. 153] and the December 2008 Bujum-bura Declaration [YUN 2008, p. 150] on disarmament. The Forces nationales de libération (FNL), the last rebel movement, disarmed and transformed itself into a political party, thus concluding the last stage of the peace process and paving the way for its members to be appointed to civil service positions. The Government established the National Independent Electoral Commission and preparations began for the holding of elections in 2010. In the light of that progress, the mandate of the South African Facilitator ended, the Office of the Facilitation closed and the African Union (AU) Special Task Force withdrew. Significant progress was also made in the disarmament and demobilization of former FNL combatants, with World Bank financial support. A UN technical assessment mission visited Burundi in March and made recommendations to the Security Council for supporting Burundi in consolidating peace, strengthening its institutions and promoting its economic and social development.

Political and security developments

Report of Secretary-General (May). In his fifth report [S/2009/270] on the United Nations Integrated Office in Burundi (BINUB), submitted pursuant to Security Council resolution 1858(2008) [YUN 2008, p. 150], the Secretary-General stated that, following the breakthrough in the peace process in December 2008 [ibid.], the FNL leadership, in line with the 2008 Bujumbura Declaration, on 4 January consulted its members on changing the group's name in line with the legal requirements for political party accreditation. On 9 January, FNL Chairperson Agathon Rwasa announced the change of name from "Parti pour la libération du peuple hutu-Forces nationales de libération" (PALIPEHUTU-FNL) to "FNL", thereby removing the ethnic reference that had blocked progress in the peace process. Early in January, the Government and FNL resolved another outstanding issue by agreeing to use the 2004–2005 arms-to-combatant ratios as a platform for discussions on the disarmament and integration of FNL. The Government authorized the release of 247 FNL prisoners and, by 15 January, the Joint Verification and Monitoring Mechanism had supervised the release of 118 of them. FNL however insisted that the Ministry of Justice had agreed to release 422 prisoners in October 2008. In February, the Ministry indicated that the issue was under review.

The South African Facilitator, Charles Nqakula, convened a meeting of the two parties and the Group of Special Envoys for Burundi (Bujumbura, 16–17 January) to review progress made in the peace process and to discuss outstanding issues. The Facilitator reported that the close protection team of the AU Special Task Force would continue to provide security to the FNL senior leadership until the end of the year and that the mandates of the Facilitation and the AU

Special Task Force would be extended. The meeting culminated in the Bujumbura Declaration reflecting the respective time-bound commitments of the Government and FNL regarding: the beginning of the disarmament, demobilization and reintegration process by 30 January; the release of remaining FNL prisoners by 21 January; the separation and release of children associated with FNL combatants by 30 January; and the submission of an application to the Ministry of the Interior for the political accreditation of FNL. FNL submitted its application for registration as a political party on 30 January, but the Government stated that it would be registered only after the separation of its political and military wings. In mid-March, following meetings with President Pierre Nkurunziza and the FNL Chairperson, the Facilitator called for the commencement of the assembly and disarmament of FNL combatants. The assembly of FNL began as a first wave of 3,475 elements voluntarily disarmed and was transported to the Rubira assembly area on 16 March. At a meeting of the Political Directorate in Pretoria, South Africa, the national parties agreed that 3,500 FNL elements would be integrated into the security and defence forces, 5,000 would be demobilized and 11,000 granted subsidies to help them return to their communities. It was also agreed that FNL would be accredited as a political party upon the surrendering of its weapons to the AU Special Task Force. At the same meeting, it was proposed that a Partnership for Peace in Burundi should be established as a successor structure to the Office of the Facilitation, to monitor the completion of the peace process and help ensure the sustainability of the gains achieved. The structure would include the Political Directorate, the secretariat of the International Conference on the Great Lakes Region, the Group of Special Envoys on Burundi, the Peacebuilding Commission and BINUB.

A decisive step forward in the peace process was taken when the FNL Chairperson disarmed and registered for demobilization at a public ceremony on 18 April. On 21 April, FNL combatants in pre-assembly areas surrendered outstanding weapons to the AU Special Task Force. On the same day, the FNL disarmament was certified by the Facilitation, and the Ministry of the Interior accredited FNL as the forty-second political party in Burundi. To support the disarmament, demobilization and reintegration of FNL following the closure of the World Bank's Multi-country Demobilization and Reintegration Programme on 31 December 2008, a new three-part configuration was established, led and supported by multiple actors, including the United Nations Development Programme (UNDP) and other international partners. UN agencies laid the groundwork for the longer-term socio-economic reintegration of former FNL combatants through a pilot project funded by the Peacebuilding Fund, which supported both the re-

integration of conflict-affected populations in several provinces and the reinforcement of State capacities.

In accordance with the December 2008 decree [YUN 2008, p. 150] setting out the organization and mandate of the Electoral Commission, the President on 20 January convened an extraordinary parliamentary session to approve the list of the five selected members of the Commission. Neither chamber of Parliament endorsed the President's list. After consultations with the main political parties, he presented a new list, which was approved by Parliament on 13 February. On 4 March, the President issued a new decree on the organization and mandate of the Electoral Commission, modifying the provisions that were of concern for the political opposition. A further decree appointing the five members of the Commission approved by Parliament was issued on 13 March.

The security situation improved, especially in the north-western provinces, as advances were made in the peace process. Accordingly, the UN security phase was adjusted from phase IV to III in Bujumbura Rural and Bubanza Provinces, thus bringing the entire country under security phase III. Criminal activities perpetrated by alleged FNL elements, former combatants, members of the security forces and unidentified armed individuals persisted, however, throughout the country.

Assistant Secretary-General for Peacekeeping Operations, Edmond Mulet, led a multidisciplinary technical assessment mission to Burundi from 2 to 12 March. The mission noted the breakthroughs in the peace process and the encouraging developments with regard to preparations for the 2010 elections. However, it assessed that the situation remained fragile and the consolidation of peace and security faced challenges, which were compounded by the increasingly difficult socioeconomic situation. The mission recommended that BINUB should shift focus and reconfigure capacities to balance the implementation of the political and strategic elements of its mandate with a more selective involvement in project execution. Project activities should focus on the political dialogue, enhancing confidence in the electoral process, conflict prevention, human rights, transitional justice, civilian disarmament and security sector reform. BINUB should continue to use its facilitation mandate for political dialogue and conflict prevention, as well as play a more proactive and strategic role in areas critical to peace consolidation. It should carry out its mandate through its good offices and the empowerment of national actors. With the UN system in Burundi, it should support the Government in increasing its coordination capacity and strengthening its leadership of specific coordination mechanisms; increase its support for the Executive Representative of the Secretary-General in his role as UN system Resident Coordinator; and prioritize support for socio-economic reintegration.

Security Council consideration. On 9 June [meeting 6138], the Secretary-General's Executive Representative and Head of BINUB, Youssef Mahmoud, in presenting the Secretary-General's report, added that in early June, the Government nominated around 24 FNL leaders to senior civil service positions, including ambassadorial posts and governorships. The FNL Chair was appointed director of the National Institute for Social Security. The South African Facilitation ended its mission on 31 May; 100 elements from the AU Special Task Force VIP Protection Unit would, however, remain in Burundi until 31 December, to continue protecting FNL leaders while training a newly created joint FNL-Government protection police unit. As to the nature of the UN presence beyond 2009, the Secretary-General intended to consult with the Government and submit recommendations in his next report to the Council.

Security Council action. The Council on the same day, by a press statement [SC/9676], urged all Burundian parties to address the remaining challenges, in particular the completion of the disarmament, demobilization and reintegration process. The Council welcomed the creation of the Partnership for Peace and the appointment of the National Independent Electoral Commission. It also expressed support for the recommendations of the UN multidisciplinary technical assessment mission and encouraged the Government to pursue efforts regarding the remaining peace challenges.

Report of Secretary-General (November). In his November report [S/2009/611], the Secretary-General said that the successor mechanism to the South African Facilitation, the Partnership for Peace in Burundi, established on 27 May to monitor challenges to the peace process, including helping foster FNL's transformation into a political party and its full integration into civilian and security institutions, mobilizing regional States and the international community and proposing corrective measures, was chaired by South African Ambassador Dumisani Kumalo. BINUB served as its secretariat. The first meeting of the Partnership for Peace (Bujumbura, 13 July) reviewed progress in FNL accreditation as a political party and the integration and training of 3,500 ex-FNL combatants into the national army and police. In a communiqué, the Partnership for Peace urged the parties to fill the outstanding nine positions allocated to FNL and to accelerate the demobilization of 5,000 ex-combatants of PALIPEHUTU-FNL, as well as the disengagement of 11,000 adults associated with the former rebel movement. It also called for the release of remaining former PALIPEHUTU-FNL prisoners. The Partnership was scheduled to meet at the end of November to discuss the way forward when its mandate expired at the end of December.

Concerning the 2010 presidential, legislative and local elections, the National Independent Electoral Commission was operational and the legislative framework was in place. On 29 May, international partners established a mechanism to coordinate international assistance for the elections. The Consultative Strategic Committee, chaired by Executive Representative of the Secretary-General, served as a forum for defining strategic guidelines for international assistance and for promoting an exchange of views and information among national and international stakeholders to ensure the smooth conduct of the electoral process. The Technical Coordination Committee, chaired by the UNDP Country Director, coordinated international technical, logistical and financial assistance through the National Independent Electoral Commission and oversaw the management of the fund established by UNDP. The Minister of the Interior, on 8 June, accredited the Mouvement pour la solidarité et la démocratie as a political party, bringing the number of registered parties to 43.

At the request of President Nkurunziza, a needs assessment mission visited Burundi (6–14 July) to appraise the status of the electoral preparations in order to develop recommendations on UN electoral assistance. The mission determined that conditions were generally propitious for the holding of credible elections as the National Independent Electoral Commission enjoyed the trust of all and was perceived as impartial and independent. Nevertheless, the mission recommended that a UN electoral support programme, managed by the UNDP Office in Burundi, be established to provide technical expertise and support in the planning and implementation of electoral operations; the National Independent Electoral Commission establish a cell to advise the Commission on election-related security matters; sustained support continue to be given to the Government to address challenges critical to ensuring long-term stability, including the sustainable reintegration of returnees and former combatants, the alleviation of extreme poverty and further improvements in security, human rights, justice and governance; BINUB provide logistical support to the Commission at crucial phases of the electoral process; and its transportation and air assets be strengthened to allow the Mission to provide such support. On 3 September [S/2009/445], the Secretary-General informed the Security Council of the findings and recommendations of the electoral needs assessment mission.

The National Independent Electoral Commission, in cooperation with the United Nations, made progress in preparing a nationwide civic education campaign, launched by President Nkurunziza on 4 September. Also on that date, the Minister of the Interior announced the establishment of an electoral department within that Ministry. In response to opposition concern that that could lead to political interference in the Commission's activities, the Minister gave public assurances that the Commission would remain in charge of the organization of the elections. On 5 November, the Commission appointed the members of the 17 independent provincial electoral commissions. On 18 September, the Minister of External Relations and International Cooperation and the UNDP Country Director signed a project document outlining priority areas in the electoral process that needed international support. In other developments, the Parliament adopted a number of laws, among them the law on the National Commission for Land and Other Assets, the law on small arms and light weapons control, and the revised electoral code, which was promulgated on 19 September.

Although the peace process was progressing relatively well, some strains were apparent within FNL. An FNL "extraordinary congress" (Bujumbura, 4 October) decided to remove FNL Chairperson Rwasa. Mr. Rwasa condemned the holding of the "congress". On 20 October, the Minister of the Interior distanced himself from the outcome of the "extraordinary congress" and recognized Mr. Rwasa as the legitimate FNL leader. On 7 October, the Government established by decree the Permanent Forum for Dialogue among accredited political parties, aimed at strengthening the party system and promoting dialogue on national issues.

Significant progress was registered in the disarmament and demobilization of former FNL combatants. The World Bank approved a $15 million grant to the Government to support demobilization. Subsequently, the Technical Coordination Team processed 4,950 FNL ex-combatants and 1,556 FNL dissidents. The AU took over the responsibilities for monitoring the process and reporting to the Political Directorate. The last assembly area and the Gitega demobilization centre were officially closed on 10 and 15 August, respectively. Meanwhile, the Government started payment of the second installment of return indemnity to demobilized ex-combatants in their communities. The process to assist some 11,000 adults associated with FNL combatants was completed on 27 October. To strengthen community reinsertion in the provinces with the highest concentration of adults associated with FNL, UNDP launched the Community Reconstruction Service, in coordination with the Government and international partners, aimed at creating job opportunities to reconstruct community infrastructure and to support other community needs.

The Secretary-General said that much had been achieved in Burundi, yet the situation remained fragile. Burundi had to be assisted to ensure that the gains achieved were consolidated before, during and after the 2010 elections, so that the country could continue on the path of national reconciliation, democratic and accountable governance and development. He recom-

mended that the BINUB mandate be renewed for an additional year when it expired on 31 December.

Security Council consideration. On 10 December [meeting 6236], the Executive Representative of the Secretary-General reported to the Security Council that, on 20 November, the South African Facilitator, Mr. Nqakula, presented his final report on the Burundi peace process to the leaders of the Regional Initiative for Peace in Arusha, United Republic of Tanzania. On 30 November, the Partnership for Peace held its third formal meeting in Bujumbura and decided, as part of its exit strategy, to entrust the close protection of FNL leaders to a joint Government-FNL unit to be selected from the national defence and security forces. Work had begun to put the joint unit in place, with the help of BINUB and the outgoing Special Task Force. Other residual tasks of the peace process discussed at the 30 November meeting included the assignment of the remaining Government posts to FNL and the release of additional political and war prisoners, to be finalized by the Government and FNL. The FNL general congress, held on 29 November, confirmed its Chairperson, Mr. Rwasa, as party leader and designated him the FNL presidential candidate for the 2010 elections.

SECURITY COUNCIL ACTION

On 17 December [meeting 6245], the Security Council unanimously adopted **resolution 1902(2009)**. The draft [S/2009/652] was submitted by France.

The Security Council,

Recalling its resolutions and the statements by its President on Burundi, in particular resolutions 1719(2006) of 25 October 2006, 1791(2007) of 19 December 2007 and 1858(2008) of 22 December 2008,

Reaffirming its strong commitment to the sovereignty, independence, territorial integrity and unity of Burundi,

Reaffirming the importance of the Declaration of the Summit of the Heads of State and Government of the Great Lakes Region on the Burundi Peace Process, which took place in Bujumbura on 4 December 2008, and the agreements reached between the Government of Burundi and the Parti pour la libération du peuple hutu-Forces nationales de libération,

Paying tribute to the Regional Peace Initiative on Burundi, the South African Facilitation, the Partnership for Peace in Burundi, the African Union and the Political Directorate for their sustained engagement in support of Burundi's peace consolidation efforts,

Welcoming the progress achieved by Burundi in key peace consolidation areas, as well as in addressing the remaining challenges, in particular the transformation of the Parti pour la libération du peuple hutu-Forces nationales de libération into a political party, the Forces nationales de libération, nominating leaders of the Forces nationales de libération to civil service positions, strengthening good governance, ensuring the sustainability of the disarmament, demobilization and reintegration process, and taking forward the reform of the security sector,

Commending the Government of Burundi and the political parties for the consensus achieved in nominating the members of the Independent National Electoral Commission and the consensual adoption of the revised electoral code, welcoming the decision of the Government to provide a legal framework for the Permanent Forum for Dialogue among parties, and recalling the importance of the elections scheduled for 2010 being prepared and conducted in a free, fair and peaceful environment,

Emphasizing the need for the United Nations system and the international community to maintain their support for peace consolidation and long-term development in Burundi, and welcoming in this regard the holding of the Consultative Group meeting of donors in Paris on 26 and 27 October 2009, and the twin mechanism put in place to coordinate international assistance for the elections,

Welcoming the continued engagement of the Peacebuilding Commission in Burundi and the recent visit of the Chair of the Burundi configuration of the Commission, and taking note of the July 2009 biannual review of progress in the implementation of the Strategic Framework for Peacebuilding in Burundi and of the briefing by the Chair of the Burundi configuration of the Commission on 10 December 2009,

Recognizing the importance of transitional justice in promoting lasting reconciliation among all the people of Burundi, and welcoming the process of national consultations on the establishment of transitional justice mechanisms, in accordance with the Arusha Agreement of 2000 and Security Council resolution 1606(2005) of 20 June 2005,

Noting with concern the continuing human rights violations and restrictions on civil liberties, including restrictions on the freedom of assembly and expression of the political opposition and representatives of civil society, and expressing equal concern about the reports of violence perpetuated by youth groups associated with some political parties,

Encouraging the Government of Burundi to continue its efforts to fight impunity and to bring to expeditious conclusion cases of human rights violations, including killings,

Recalling its resolutions 1325(2000) of 31 October 2000, 1820(2008) of 19 June 2008, 1888(2009) of 30 September 2009 and 1889(2009) of 5 October 2009 on women and peace and security, its resolutions 1674(2006) of 28 April 2006 and 1894(2009) of 11 November 2009 on the protection of civilians in armed conflict and its resolutions 1612(2005) of 26 July 2005 and 1882(2009) of 4 August 2009 on children and armed conflict,

Having considered the sixth report of the Secretary-General on the United Nations Integrated Office in Burundi,

1. *Decides* to extend until 31 December 2010 the mandate of the United Nations Integrated Office in Burundi, as set out in resolution 1719(2006) and renewed in resolutions 1791(2007) and 1858(2008);

2. *Encourages* the Government of Burundi and the Forces nationales de libération to make every effort to achieve the implementation of the agreements of 4 December 2008, calls upon all parties to desist from any action that may foster the resumption of tensions, and encourages them to resolve outstanding issues in the spirit of reconciliation and dialogue enshrined in the Constitution of Burundi;

3. *Acknowledges* the contribution brought to peacebuilding in Burundi by the Regional Peace Initiative on Burundi, the South African Facilitation, the Political Directorate and the Partnership for Peace in Burundi until 2009, and encourages the Regional Peace Initiative leaders, the African Union and other international partners to remain actively engaged on the ground to ensure that the implementation of the Declaration of 4 December 2008 is irreversible and to consolidate the peace process;

4. *Reiterates its request* for the Secretary-General, in particular through the United Nations Integrated Office in Burundi, to play a robust political role in support of all facets of the peace process, in full coordination with subregional, regional and international partners;

5. *Decides* that the United Nations Integrated Office in Burundi, working in close cooperation with the Government of Burundi, shall pay particular attention to supporting the electoral process, democratic governance, the consolidation of peace, sustainable reintegration and gender issues;

6. *Recognizes* the primary responsibility of the Government of Burundi and its national partners to create propitious conditions for the elections in 2010, urges the Government to take the measures necessary to create an environment conducive to the holding of free, fair and peaceful elections in 2010, and encourages the Government and the political parties to remain engaged in dialogue, in particular through the Permanent Forum for Dialogue;

7. *Urges* the Government of Burundi and the political parties to continue their efforts to preserve the independence and credibility of the Independent National Electoral Commission;

8. *Supports* the launch in September 2009 by President Nkurunziza of a nationwide civic education campaign for the elections, and encourages the pursuit of civic education activities throughout the electoral process;

9. *Welcomes* the United Nations readiness to assist in the electoral process, and requests the United Nations Integrated Office in Burundi to be prepared to provide, within its existing resources and if required, logistical support to the Independent National Electoral Commission at crucial phases of the electoral process;

10. *Reiterates its request* to the Executive Representative of the Secretary-General for Burundi to facilitate and promote dialogue among national and international stakeholders, in particular in the context of the upcoming elections, while continuing to support their efforts to sustain peace and stability;

11. *Encourages* the Government of Burundi, the Peacebuilding Commission and Burundi's national and international partners to honour the commitments they have made under the Strategic Framework for Peacebuilding in Burundi, and requests the Commission, with support from the United Nations Integrated Office in Burundi, to continue to assist the Government in laying the foundations for sustainable peace and security, reintegration and long-term development in Burundi and in mobilizing the resources needed to achieve these aims, including for the coming elections;

12. *Encourages* the Government of Burundi to pursue its efforts regarding peace consolidation challenges, in particular democratic governance, security reforms, land

tenure, justice and the protection of human rights, with a special focus on women's and children's rights;

13. *Also encourages* the Government of Burundi, with the support of the United Nations Integrated Office in Burundi and other international partners, to step up its efforts to pursue the structural reforms aimed at improving political, economic and administrative governance, with continued focus on the fight against corruption, and encourages, in particular, the implementation of the comprehensive public administration reform programme;

14. *Underscores* the importance of security sector reform, and urges all international partners, together with the United Nations Integrated Office in Burundi, to support the efforts of the Government of Burundi to professionalize and enhance the capacity of the national security services and the police, in particular in the fields of training in human rights and sexual and gender-based violence;

15. *Encourages* the Government of Burundi, in collaboration with all international partners, including the United Nations Integrated Office in Burundi, the United Nations Development Programme and the World Bank, to complete the disarmament and demobilization process and the strategy for the sustainable socio-economic reintegration of demobilized soldiers, former combatants, returning refugees, the displaced and other vulnerable groups affected by the conflict, particularly women and children, and urges international partners, particularly the Peacebuilding Commission, to stand ready to support this;

16. *Welcomes* the progress made by the Tripartite Commission comprising Burundi, the Office of the United Nations High Commissioner for Refugees and the United Republic of Tanzania towards achieving dignified durable solutions for refugees living in the United Republic of Tanzania, and encourages a sustained effort with regard to the residual Burundi refugee caseload;

17. *Encourages* the Government of Burundi, with the support of the United Nations Integrated Office in Burundi and other partners, to continue the national consultations on transitional justice with a view to their timely completion and the publication of the final report, and to ensure that the results of those consultations form the basis for the establishment of transitional justice mechanisms;

18. *Calls upon* the Government of Burundi to pursue its efforts to broaden respect for and protection of human rights, including through the establishment of a credible National Independent Human Rights Commission, in conformity with the Paris Principles outlined in the annex to General Assembly resolution 48/134 of 20 December 1993, and further encourages the Government to end impunity and to take the measures necessary to ensure that its citizens fully enjoy their civil, political, social, economic and cultural rights without fear or intimidation, as enshrined in the Constitution of Burundi and provided for in international human rights instruments, including those ratified by Burundi;

19. *Expresses, in particular, its concern* at the continuing sexual and gender-based violence, and urges the Government of Burundi to continue to take the necessary steps to prevent further violations and to ensure that those responsible are brought to justice;

20. *Welcomes* the release of all children by armed groups, emphasizes the need for their sustainable reinte-

gration and reinsertion, welcomes in this regard the programme launched by the World Bank in this field, and urges the Government of Burundi, with the support of the United Nations Integrated Office in Burundi, the United Nations Children's Fund and other members of the Country Task Force on Monitoring and Reporting Grave Child Rights Violations, to fight impunity for violators of children's rights;

21. *Urges* the United Nations Integrated Office in Burundi to strengthen current provisions for cooperation with the United Nations Organization Mission in the Democratic Republic of the Congo, within the limits of their respective capacities and current mandates, in cooperation with the Governments of Burundi and the Democratic Republic of the Congo, as appropriate;

22. *Requests* the Secretary-General to provide to the Security Council a briefing on the electoral process in May 2010 and a full report on the implementation of the mandate of the United Nations Integrated Office in Burundi in November 2010, and requests the Secretary-General to incorporate in that report a detailed review of the extent to which the benchmarks set forth in the addendum of 14 August 2006 to his report of 21 June 2006 have been met, and, following consultations with the Government of Burundi, to provide recommendations on what changes need to be made to the direction and composition of the United Nations presence in Burundi, including recommendations on a revised time frame for the transition to a more development-focused presence;

23. *Decides* to remain actively seized of the matter.

Year-end developments. A later report [S/2010/608] of the Secretary-General said that the National Independent Electoral Commission on 15 December set out an electoral calendar for five elections in 2010: communal (24 May), presidential (28 June), National Assembly (23 July), senatorial (28 July) and *collinaires* (7 September). A national civilian disarmament campaign in October, supported by BINUB, saw the mass collection of firearms, grenades, ordnance and ammunition. National consultations on establishing transitional justice mechanisms were completed nationwide in December.

Peacebuilding Commission

Review of Strategic Framework. In February, the Peacebuilding Commission considered the second progress report [PBC/3/BDI/2] reviewing developments in the implementation of the Strategic Framework for Peacebuilding in Burundi [YUN 2007, p. 52]. The report analysed trends and reviewed progress and challenges in the areas of governance, the Comprehensive Ceasefire Agreement, the security sector, justice, the promotion of human rights, action to combat impunity, land issues and economic recovery. It assessed mutual commitments of all parties and the coordination of assistance. The report showed that considerable progress had been made in the peacebuilding process as a result of the support of the Government, civil society, the United Nations and other international partners. Despite such progress, all stakeholders needed to continue to pay attention to the remaining challenges, which were becoming increasingly complex owing to social and political developments. The Commission made recommendations for consolidating achievements and fostering progress.

In its conclusions of the second biannual review [PBC/3BDI/3], the Commission welcomed the progress made in implementing the Strategic Framework and the financial support provided by multilateral and bilateral partners. It requested the Peacebuilding Support Office to present a strategic assessment of the impact of the Peacebuilding Commission in support of peacebuilding in Burundi. It recommended that the Government: ensure an environment conducive to the holding of free, fair and peaceful elections in 2010; take further action to fight corruption; ensure the release of FNL prisoners and children associated with FNL, as well as the disarmament, demobilization and reintegration of FNL combatants, the registration of FNL as a political party, its integration into national institutions and into the army and police; prepare a national plan for security sector reform; increase efforts to broaden the respect for human rights and enforce the rule of law; finalize and implement the strategy for socio-economic reintegration of former FNL combatants, demobilized soldiers, ex-combatants, the displaced and other vulnerable groups; and implement the land tenure policy paper and put in place mechanisms to coordinate land dispute resolutions. International partners should continue to monitor and support implementation of the Comprehensive Ceasefire Agreement and the follow-up to the Bujumbura Declaration; provide financial and technical support to the implementation of the Ceasefire Agreement; and support the implementation of the Government's priorities. For its part, the Commission would advocate for and follow up on the implementation of its conclusions; advocate for support for activities relating to the Strategic Framework; and support the implementation of the peace process.

The third progress report on the implementation of the Strategic Framework [PBC/3/BDI/5], which was submitted to the Peacebuilding Commission at its third session in July, described the overall progress, trends and challenges confronting all stakeholders, particularly the Government, with regard to the Commission February recommendations, and presented recommendations and lines of action. In each of the priority sectors, key messages were formulated for the attention of stakeholders over the next six months.

The Commission in July, in its conclusions of the third biannual review [PBC/3/BDI/6], noted that the peace process had entered a new phase and welcomed

the progress achieved in disarmament and demobilization, the establishment of the Partnership for Peace in Burundi, progress in preparing for the 2010 elections, the beginning of the national consultations on transitional justice and progress in other areas of the Strategic Framework. Among its recommendations, the Government was requested to provide the National Independent Electoral Commission with the resources required to fulfil its mandate and preserve its independence; promote dialogue and political space for all; respect civil and political rights, in particular the rights of political parties to hold meetings and other activities in compliance with the law; and ensure equal access to the media. It should also speed up efforts to combat corruption by expediting the settlement of cases before the courts, including the conclusion of pending cases. The Government should work with the Partnership for Peace in monitoring the peace process and addressing any challenges that might arise, particularly from the disarmament, demobilization and reintegration process; and continue to improve overall security and build the capacity of the security forces, in particular the police. It should conclude the national consultations on the establishment of the transitional justice mechanisms scheduled to be completed by December so as to ensure their establishment in order to address accountability for past crimes and reconciliation; finalize and start implementing the long-term strategy for community-based socio-economic reintegration of former FNL combatants, children formerly associated with demobilized soldiers, returnees, internally displaced people and other vulnerable groups; finalize and adopt laws relating to inheritance and matrimonial regimes containing provisions relating to women's access to land; support the National Commission on Land and Other Assets and implement the national land policy; seek to achieve the minimum 30 per cent female representation in the Government and the Parliament; and promote women's integration in the political process and their participation in the upcoming elections.

The Commission and international partners should provide, in response to request by the Government, resources, including financial resources, and ensure coordinated monitoring of the electoral process; support the finalization of the national plan for security sector reform and its implementation; maintain the level of financial contributions and provide additional resources to help Burundi face the challenges of the global financial, economic and food crisis; help the Government to make effective use of those resources; provide strategic support to the upcoming review of the Poverty Reduction Strategy Paper and related resource mobilization efforts; and use that review for policy dialogue with the Government on the opportunities to harmonize the Strategy Paper and the Strategic Framework.

Reporting on its third session (23 June 2008–30 June 2009) [A/64/341-S/2009/444], the Commission stated that there had been crucial developments in the peace process and peacebuilding efforts. In its third year of engagement with Burundi, the Commission focused on supporting those efforts, with emphasis on ensuring the durability of the peace gains and making them amenable to the country's socio-economic development needs.

The Chair of the Burundi configuration visited Burundi in May to follow up on progress and mutual commitments made in the implementation of the Strategic Framework. The Chair concluded that the peacebuilding process had entered a new phase; however, the completion of the disarmament, demobilization and reintegration process and the preparation of a long-term socio-economic reintegration strategy would require support from the Commission. The national elections scheduled for 2010 presented an opportunity to consolidate peace and democracy.

On 17 December, the Security Council, in resolution 1902(2009) (see p. 140), took note of the July biannual review of progress in the implementation of the Strategic Framework for Peacebuilding in Burundi.

(For further information on the Peacebuilding Commission, see p. 45.)

Children and armed conflict

The Secretary-General, in his March report on children and armed conflict [A/63/785-S/2009/158], reported on the situation in Burundi. He stated that PALIPEHUTU-FNL, led by Agathon Rwasa, continued to recruit and use children. The Bujumbura Declaration agreed upon in January (see p. 138) set out deadlines on critical aspects of the peace process, including the unconditional separation of all children associated with FNL by 30 January. However, FNL failed to meet that deadline. It subsequently assured the Government and the international community of its willingness to release the children associated with the movement, but made the release conditional on the start of the disarmament, demobilization and reintegration process for all its combatants and the integration of its members into security institutions. Despite repeated pledges and agreements, FNL did not cooperate on the issue.

Sexual violence against children continued to be a concern, with most of the victims being girls. Perpetrators included members of the national police, the national defence forces, FNL and alleged FNL dissidents, although most of the cases were perpetrated by civilians in an environment of insecurity and impunity. The adoption of the revised Penal Code

by the National Assembly and by the Senate with amendments that strengthened the sentencing of perpetrators of sexual violence against children was welcomed.

The Security Council, in presidential statement **S/PRST/2009/9** of 29 April (see p. 737), invited the Secretary General to strengthen efforts to bring the monitoring and reporting mechanism to its full capacity in order to allow for prompt advocacy and effective response to all violations and abuses committed against children.

The Council also took action on the Secretary-General's report in **resolution 1882(2009)** of 4 August (see p. 739).

In September [S/2009/450], the Secretary-General submitted a report on children and armed conflict in Burundi, pursuant to Security Council resolution 1612(2005) [YUN 2005, p. 863], covering the period from September 2007 to June 2009. The report noted that cases of rape and sexual violence, abduction and detention of children, and child recruitment by FNL increased during that period before the release of all children identified as associated with their forces in April. It emphasized that, despite improvements in security, a climate of impunity for violators of the rights of children persisted. The Secretary-General commended the Government for progress made on issues addressed in his previous reports, including the demobilization and reintegration of children associated with FNL and alleged FNL dissidents, improvement in the training of security forces, and ensuring protection and access to justice of victims of sexual and gender-based violence. He encouraged the Government to consider the protection of children in the application of transitional justice mechanisms and in all provisions of security sector reform, and to facilitate the adoption of an integrated child protection system. The Government should also fully reintegrate all children from armed groups, and relevant authorities should act to redress impunity for crimes against children through the rigorous investigation and prosecution of such cases.

Welcoming the commitment of the Government to address the problem, the Security Council Working Group on Children and Armed Conflict, in conclusions adopted on 12 October [S/AC.51/2009/6], noted that, as at August, there were no further known cases of children associated with armed groups in Burundi and that the community and family reintegration of children formerly associated with armed groups had started. However, despite those achievements, much more remained to be done in addressing impunity for violations and abuses committed against children. The Working Group addressed recommendations to the Government and the Secretary-General.

BINUB

The United Nations Integrated Office in Burundi (BINUB), established by Security Council resolution 1719(2006) [YUN 2006, p. 153] to support the Government in its efforts towards long-term peace and stability and coordinate the work of UN agencies in the country, focused on peace consolidation and democratic governance; disarmament, demobilization and reintegration of ex-combatants; security sector reform; promotion and protection of human rights; measures to end impunity through a truth and reconciliation commission and special tribunal; and donor and UN agency coordination. Headquartered in the capital, Bujumbura, BINUB was headed by the Secretary-General's Executive Representative for Burundi, Youssef Mahmoud (Tunisia).

Financing

In December, the General Assembly considered the Secretary-General's October reports [A/64/349/Add.3] on proposed requirements for special political missions, good offices and other political initiatives authorized by the General Assembly and/or the Security Council, which included resource requirements for BINUB totalling $46,258,000 for 2010, an increase of $8,359,600 over the 2009 requirements, and the related ACABQ report [A/64/7/Add.13]. On 24 December, in section VI of **resolution 64/245** (see p. 1407), the Assembly endorsed ACABQ's recommendations and approved the resource requirements, including those for BINUB.

ONUB

The United Nations Operation in Burundi (ONUB), established in 2004 by Security Council resolution 1545(2004) [YUN 2004, p. 145], concluded its mandate on 31 December 2006 [YUN 2006, p. 157] and was replaced by BINUB on 1 January 2007.

Financing

The Secretary-General, in a report on the financing of ONUB [A/63/551], provided details on the final disposition of its assets, with an inventory value of $59,152,442 as at 3 November 2008. Group I assets ($51,336,469) were transferred to BINUB, other missions or the United Nations Logistics Base at Brindisi; Group II assets ($4,735,622) were donated to the Government of Burundi or sold to UN agencies, other organizations, private companies and individuals; Group III assets ($3,080,351) were written off.

ACABQ, in its report on the subject [A/63/773], recommended that the Secretary-General provide a fuller explanation of the final disposition of assets in future reports, including the residual value of all group assets.

On 30 June [meeting 93], the General Assembly, on the recommendation of the Fifth Committee [A/63/895], adopted **resolution 63/288** without vote [agenda item 133].

Financing of the United Nations Operation in Burundi

The General Assembly,

Having considered the report of the Secretary-General on the financing of the United Nations Operation in Burundi and the related report of the Advisory Committee on Administrative and Budgetary Questions,

Recalling Security Council resolution 1545(2004) of 21 May 2004, by which the Council authorized, for an initial period of six months as from 1 June 2004, with the intention to renew it for further periods, the deployment of a peacekeeping operation called the United Nations Operation in Burundi, and the subsequent resolutions by which the Council extended the mandate of the Operation, the last of which was resolution 1692(2006) of 30 June 2006, by which the Council extended the mandate of the Operation until 31 December 2006,

Recalling also its resolution 58/312 of 18 June 2004 on the financing of the Operation and its subsequent resolutions thereon, the latest of which was resolution 62/253 of 20 June 2008,

Reaffirming the general principles underlying the financing of United Nations peacekeeping operations, as stated in General Assembly resolutions 1874(S-IV) of 27 June 1963, 3101(XXVIII) of 11 December 1973 and 55/235 of 23 December 2000,

1. *Takes note* of the status of contributions to the United Nations Operation in Burundi as at 31 March 2009, including the credits in the amount of 49.4 million United States dollars;

2. *Endorses* the conclusions and recommendations contained in the report of the Advisory Committee on Administrative and Budgetary Questions, and requests the Secretary-General to ensure their full implementation;

Disposition of assets

3. *Takes note* of the report of the Secretary-General on the financing of the United Nations Operation in Burundi;

4. *Encourages* Member States that are owed credits for the closed peacekeeping mission accounts to apply those credits to any accounts where they have outstanding assessed contributions;

5. *Urges* all Member States to make every possible effort to ensure the payment of their assessed contributions in full;

6. *Decides* to include in the provisional agenda of its sixty-fourth session the item entitled "Financing of the United Nations Operation in Burundi".

On 24 December, by **decision 64/549**, the Assembly decided that the agenda item on ONUB financing would remain for consideration during its resumed sixty-fourth (2010) session.

Central African Republic

In 2009, despite significant remaining challenges, particularly the re-emergence of rebel groups in the northern part of the country, the Central African Republic made important steps forward, heightening expectations that the country was entering a new phase of peace and stability. Significant efforts were made to implement the recommendations of the December 2008 inclusive political dialogue [YUN 2008, p. 157]. A broad-based Government was established in January and the committees for implementing the various aspects of those recommendations were established. Progress was made in the preparations for holding elections in 2010, including the creation of the Independent Electoral Commission. Some advances were also made in disarmament, demobilization and reintegration, but the process remained largely delayed. To support the promising peacebuilding opportunities arising from the inclusive political dialogue and the involvement of the Peacebuilding Commission, the Security Council welcomed the Secretary-General's proposals for establishing, from 1 January 2010, the United Nations Integrated Peacebuilding Office in the Central African Republic (BINUCA) to succeed the United Nations Peacebuilding Support Office in the Central African Republic (BONUCA), and the Commission's adoption of the Strategic Framework for Peacebuilding in the Central African Republic.

Establishment of United Nations Integrated Peacebuilding Office in the Central African Republic (BINUCA)

On 3 March [S/2009/128], the Secretary-General informed the Security Council that, in keeping with his decision to establish an integrated UN presence in the Central African Republic [YUN 2008, p. 158] following the December 2008 inclusive political dialogue, he proposed that the mandate of the UN presence would include: assisting national and local efforts in implementing the dialogue outcomes, in particular through support for governance reforms and electoral processes; assisting in disarmament, demobilization and reintegration and in activities promoting the rule of law; supporting efforts to restore State authority in the provinces, enhance national human rights capacity and promote respect for human rights and the rule of law; supporting the work of the Peacebuilding Commission, the implementation of the Strategic Framework for Peacebuilding and projects supported through the Peacebuilding Fund; and supporting the United Nations Mission in the Central African Republic and Chad. The integrated office would be headed by a Special Representative of the Secretary-General. The integrated presence would succeed BONUCA initially until 31 December 2009. Should the

Council extend its mandate in 2010, full financial requirements would be presented to the General Assembly in the 2010 budget proposal. In the meantime, the integrated office would be operational within the 2009 budget allocation.

Security Council consideration. During the Security Council's consideration of the Secretary-General's proposals on 10 March [meeting 6091], the Special Representative of the Secretary-General and Head of BONUCA, François Lonseny Fall, and the Chair of the Central African configuration of the Peacebuilding Commission briefed the Council on the situation in the country. Mr. Fall provided additional information on the conclusions reached at the December 2008 dialogue. He said that the agreements included the commitment to hold municipal, legislative and presidential elections in 2009 and 2010; the revision of the electoral code; the conduct of independent audits of revenue-generating State institutions; the establishment of mechanisms to promote permanent dialogue among the country's political and social actors; the implementation of security sector reform; the restructuring of the armed forces; a disarmament, demobilization and reintegration programme; combating the proliferation of small arms; the introduction of measures to identify and indemnify victims of past conflicts; the implementation of the poverty reduction strategy for 2008–2011; the reform of public finances; the reform of the management of natural resources; and the development of national human resources.

He also informed the Council that, on 30 January, the Economic and Monetary Community of Central Africa (CEMAC) had pledged 8 billion CFA francs to finance disarmament, demobilization and reintegration activities.

SECURITY COUNCIL ACTION

On 7 April [meeting 6102], following consultations among Security Council members, the President made statement **S/PRST/2009/5** on behalf of the Council:

> The Security Council welcomes the recent progress towards implementing the recommendations of the inclusive political dialogue, held in Bangui from 8 to 20 December 2008. It reiterates its full support for this process, as an effective framework to foster national reconciliation and stability in the Central African Republic. The Council calls upon all parties to sustain the momentum created by the dialogue and the spirit of compromise and cooperation that enabled its successful holding.
>
> The Council demands that all armed groups which have not yet done so, particularly those recently operating in the northern Central African Republic, cease violence immediately. It calls upon all parties to respect and implement the comprehensive peace agreement signed at Libreville on 21 June 2008 and their earlier commitments contained in the Sirte agreement of 2 February 2007 and the Birao agreement of 13 April 2007. It in-

vites countries in the region to support efforts to bring all groups into the peace process.

The Council calls upon all armed groups to immediately cease the recruitment and use of children and release all children associated with them. The Council calls upon all parties, as a matter of priority, to develop and implement, in close collaboration with the United Nations Integrated Peacebuilding Office in the Central African Republic, action plans within the framework of Council resolutions 1539(2004) and 1612(2005).

The Council stresses the urgency and imperative necessity of carrying out the disarmament, demobilization and reintegration process. It calls upon all parties in the Central African Republic to work with determination to that end. The Council welcomes the pledge made by the Central African Economic and Monetary Community on 30 January 2009 to contribute to funding the disarmament, demobilization and reintegration process, and calls upon the international community to provide timely and adequate support to the process.

The Council calls upon the Government of the Central African Republic and all political stakeholders to ensure the timely, effective and transparent preparation of the 2009 and 2010 municipal, legislative and presidential elections.

The Council welcomes the recommendation of the Secretary-General, in his letter dated 3 March 2009, to establish a United Nations Integrated Peacebuilding Office in the Central African Republic to succeed the current United Nations Peacebuilding Support Office. It notes with satisfaction that the United Nations Integrated Peacebuilding Office will perform the following tasks:

(a) To assist national and local efforts in implementing the dialogue outcomes, in particular through support for governance reforms and electoral processes;

(b) To assist in the successful completion of the disarmament, demobilization and reintegration process and the reform of security sector institutions, and support activities to promote the rule of law;

(c) To support efforts to restore State authority in the provinces;

(d) To support efforts to enhance national human rights capacity and promote respect for human rights and the rule of law, justice and accountability;

(e) To closely coordinate with and support the work of the Peacebuilding Commission, as well as the implementation of the Strategic Framework for Peacebuilding in the Central African Republic and projects supported through the Peacebuilding Fund;

(f) To exchange information and analysis with the United Nations Mission in the Central African Republic and Chad on emerging threats to peace and security in the region.

The Council also requests the Secretary-General to ensure that the integrated office undertakes the following additional task:

(g) To help to ensure that child protection is properly addressed in the implementation of the comprehensive peace agreement and the disarmament, demobilization and reintegration process, including by supporting the monitoring and reporting mechanism established according to resolutions 1539(2004) and 1612(2005).

The Council requests the Secretary-General to ensure that the smooth transition to the new integrated office takes place as soon as possible, including through the early deployment of the new Special Representative and Deputy Special Representative. The Council further requests the Secretary-General to inform it in his next report on the structure and strength of the new office, bearing in mind that resources for special political missions are limited.

The Council welcomes the support provided by the Peacebuilding Commission to the Central African Republic, looks forward to the finalization of the Strategic Framework for Peacebuilding, and calls upon the donor community to work with the Commission to identify sectors that are critical for long-term stability and development in the Central African Republic and to intensify their support in those sectors.

Appointment of Special Representative. On 26 May [S/2009/279], the Secretary General informed the Security Council of his intention to appoint Sahle-Work Zewde (Ethiopia) as his new Special Representative in the Central African Republic and Head of BONUCA, which was to be succeeded by BINUCA. The Council took note of the Secretary-General's intention on 29 May [S/2009/280].

Transition arrangements. The Secretary-General reported in June [S/2009/309] that the plan for the transition from BONUCA to BINUCA comprised three phases: the completion of the preparatory work to ensure a seamless transition on 1 January 2010, including finalization of the budget, the recruitment of staff, the pre-positioning of facilities and other administrative support and development of implementation plans for each of the integrated programmes; the end of BONUCA operations on 31 December 2009 and administrative liquidation from 1 January to 30 June 2010, while BINUCA would start operation on 1 January 2010; and completion of the activities envisaged under the integrated strategic framework, subject to developments on the ground.

BINUCA's staffing strength would include the Special Representative and Deputy Special Representative, 63 international civilian staff, 2 military advisers and 2 civilian police advisers, as well as 14 national officers and 7 United Nations Volunteers.

Political and security developments

Report of Secretary-General (June). In his report [S/2009/309] on the situation in the Central African Republic and on BONUCA activities, submitted in response to Security Council presidential statement S/PRST/2001/25 [YUN 2001, p. 156], the Secretary-General said that the slow pace of implementation of the recommendations of the inclusive political dialogue demonstrated the difficulty of maintaining the momentum created. On 28 January, President François Bozizé established a broad-based Government, as recommended during the dialogue, whose composition was criticized by the opposition and some political-military groups. The Union des forces vives de la nation (UFVN), the main democratic opposition alliance, refused to participate. As recommended by the dialogue, the Follow-up Committee on the implementation of the recommendations of the dialogue, the Steering Committee on Disarmament, Demobilization and Reintegration and the High Court of Justice were set up. The dialogue Follow-up Committee met monthly to review progress in implementing the recommendations of the dialogue. At its meeting in Bangui of 18 and 19 May, the Committee regretted the slow pace of implementation of the recommendations and complained about the lack of adequate logistical and financial resources to carry out its functions. The Steering Committee on Disarmament, Demobilization and Reintegration made progress in advancing the disarmament, demobilization and reintegration programme: essential programme documentation was completed and a list of 7,902 potential beneficiaries was submitted by the four political-military groups. Regarding elections, the Minister for Territorial Administration and Decentralization on 12 May inaugurated a broad-based ad hoc Committee to review the electoral code in preparation for the 2010 legislative and presidential elections. Once the draft electoral code was agreed upon, the text would be submitted for adoption by Parliament, to be followed by the establishment of the independent electoral commission. Reflecting the mistrust on the electoral issue, the main opposition parties declared that they would not accept the postponement of the 2010 polls. On 21 May, the Prime Minister reaffirmed the Government's intention to make the necessary budget allocations for the elections.

Although the Security Council, in presidential statement S/PRST/2009/5 of 7 April (see p. 146), had demanded that all armed groups, in particular those in the north, cease violence immediately, the activities of three rebel groups, the Mouvement des libérateurs centrafricains pour la justice (MLCJ), the Front démocratique du peuple centrafricain (FDPC) and the Convergence des patriotes centrafricains pour la justice et la paix (CPJP), raised the most concern. The leaders of the three parties turned to rebellion because of the alleged Government failure to fully implement the recommendations of the dialogue. They claimed, in particular, that the Government set up in January by President Bozizé was not sufficiently broad-based. The Secretary-General said that he had encouraged diplomatic and political efforts to end the rebellion and persuade the leaders to embrace the peace process. To that end, President Bozizé sought the assistance of the Libyan leader and AU Chairperson, Colonel Muammar Qaddafi, who reaffirmed his support for efforts to find peaceful and lasting solutions to the ongoing instability in the north. MLCJ leader Abakar Sabone informed BONUCA of his readiness to end his movement's rebellion, join the peace process and submit to disarmament, demobilization and reintegration. He returned to Bangui on 31 May. The President reportedly held discussions with FDPC leader Abdoulaye Miskine with a view to facilitating his return to Bangui to join the peace process. CPJP leader Charles Massi was reportedly arrested and detained by Chad, which intended to put him on trial for attempted destabilization and alleged violation of that country's territorial integrity.

While the security situation in Bangui and its surrounding area remained relatively calm, violence continued in the northern provinces. In some cases, rebel groups reportedly carried out attacks, often withdrawing after being confronted by Government troops or local self-defence fighters. Violent attacks against civilians sometimes ensued, in the form of reprisals, for perceived collaboration with rebel groups. In other cases, violence was the result of criminal activity, inter-communal confrontations and external incursions.

In the area of the rule of law, the High Court of Justice was established on 12 May. The Court would mainly deal with cases of accusation of high treason and other acts of serious misconduct involving Cabinet ministers, Members of Parliament and the Head of State. The Government agreed to set up a national human rights commission and sought to restore discipline within the armed forces. In April, the Permanent Military Tribunal prosecuted 22 junior military officers accused of human rights violations. However, the problem of impunity at higher levels of the military hierarchy remained largely unaddressed.

The Secretary-General observed that there was a sense that the country had turned over a new page and was looking increasingly towards a more hopeful future despite the many challenges remaining. To help prevent a relapse, it would be important to build on the emerging momentum by taking steps to end rebellion and insecurity through disarmament, demobilization and reintegration and security sector reform, ensure that the 2010 national elections took place in a timely, peaceful and credible manner, end impunity and corruption, promote respect for human rights and the rule of law, and improve the living conditions and quality of life of the population.

The imminent establishment of BINUCA would help to ensure a better coordinated and more coherent framework to optimize UN system assistance. He therefore recommended that the Security Council approve BINUCA's proposed structure and mandate for an initial period of one year, following which he would seek resources for its funding from the General Assembly.

Security Council consideration. On 22 June [meeting 6147], the Council was briefed on the situation in the country by the Under-Secretary-General for Political Affairs, B. Lynn Pascoe; the Chairperson of the Central African Republic configuration of the Peacebuilding Commission; and the representative of the Central African Republic. The Under-Secretary-General stated that the best way to address the multi-faceted problems besetting the country was through the implementation of the Strategic Framework for Peacebuilding. He added that, while there were important efforts to implement the recommendations of the 2008 inclusive political dialogue, activities of violent rebels were undermining the peacebuilding framework and bringing about increased insecurity.

Report of Secretary-General (December). In his December report on the Central African Republic and BONUCA [S/2009/627], the Secretary-General indicated that the Dialogue Follow-up Committee, at its third quarterly meeting (Bangui, 5–6 October), regretted the slow pace of implementation of the recommendations of the dialogue, and deplored the non-implementation of key political recommendations relating to the separation of powers, the establishment of a permanent dialogue mechanism and an end to the practice of Government officials holding multiple functions. To help promote national reconciliation, President Bozizé on 27 August appointed the former Archbishop of Bangui, Paulin Pomodimo, as the National Mediator to replace Abel Nguende Goumba, who died on 11 May. Mr. Pomodimo met with the political opposition and the Government to find peaceful solutions to the country's political problems. In another development, the Government dismissed Saifee Durbar, a controversial businessman who had been named Deputy Minister for Foreign Affairs in January. Mr. Durbar had previously claimed diplomatic immunity in order to escape judicial prosecution in London and Paris. On 3 August, President Bozizé promulgated into law the text of the electoral code which the Constitutional Court had ruled on 30 July as containing anti-constitutional provisions. On 27 August, the President signed a decree, based on the disputed electoral code, establishing the Independent Electoral Commission. Those actions led the opposition UFVN and other parties to suspend participation in the Independent Electoral Commission and to request the Constitutional Court to annul the electoral code. The Constitutional Court, in a 26 September decision, requested the Government to respect the Court's 30 July judgement. Subsequently, President Bozizé agreed to remove the contentious provisions from the electoral code and to promulgate a new code on 2 October. The following day, he signed a decree establishing the Independent Electoral Commission and, on 8 October, another decree appointing the 30 members of the Commission, drawn from the six groups that had participated in the inclusive political dialogue. On 12 October, Joseph Binguimale was elected President of the Commission.

On 22 September, the National Assembly adopted the supplementary budget for the remainder of 2009, which included 1 billion CFA francs ($2,296,000) for funding the elections. That was seen as an important step in the electoral process, as the opposition had earlier interpreted the non-inclusion of provisions for elections in the 2009 budget as a demonstration of the Government's lack of intention to hold the elections in 2010. At the Government's request, the Secretary-General dispatched an electoral needs assessment mission to Bangui from 29 October to 12 November. The mission underscored the need to mobilize resources to operationalize the Independent Electoral Commission and to put in place the complex structures and operations needed for the conduct of credible elections. The mission recommended that the United Nations provide electoral assistance to the country to create the conditions for the organization of peaceful and transparent elections. On the basis of the mission's recommendations, UNDP prepared a UN electoral assistance package. Among potential candidates in the forthcoming polls, much attention was given to the candidacy of former President Ange-Félix Patassé, who returned to Bangui on 30 October after six years in exile. At a meeting with President Bozizé in Bangui on 9 November, Mr. Patassé reaffirmed his intention to contest the presidential elections. President Bozizé, for his part, had yet to announce his candidacy.

The first phase of the sensitization campaign prior to disarmament, demobilization and reintegration, launched by President Bozizé on 13 August, was conducted from 26 August to 4 September. The opportunity was also used to promote reconciliation between former rebels and local Government officials in former rebel-occupied territories, leading to the removal of illegal roadblocks that had been put in place by rebel groups. Meanwhile, the Steering Committee on Disarmament, Demobilization and Reintegration continued preparations for the full implementation of the disarmament, demobilization and reintegration programme. On 17 September, the Technical Committee revised the programme's calendar and budget, estimated at some $27 million. A UNDP support team visited Bangui from 24 September to 1 October to finalize the verification methodology for the lists of ex-combatants, as well as the document guiding the disarmament, demobilization and reintegration process. All former rebel groups had submitted their lists of combatants by April, except for MLCJ.

Most rebel groups were participating in the peace process, except CPJP, led by Charles Massi. The Government initiated dialogue with the CPJP military leadership, in the hope of persuading the group to join the peace process. Similarly, following the signing of a peace agreement with the leader of FDPC, Abdoulaye Miskine, in July, about 21 former FDPC fighters returned to Bangui to join the peace process. However, since returning to Bangui some rebel groups faced internal crises, and some senior members of MLCJ formed a new movement, the Mouvement national du salut de la patrie (MNSP), led by Hassan Ousman. Likewise, elements of FDPC, led by Gazzam Betty, broke away from the FDPC leader, Abdoulaye Miskine, who had announced his intention to withdraw from the peace process.

The political and security situation in the Vakaga region near the borders with Chad and the Sudan was calm but unpredictable, in the wake of recurrent inter-ethnic conflict between the Kara and Goula ethnic groups in the town of Birao. Tension also grew between the Kara and Haoussa ethnic groups. As part of the strategy to enhance the operational capacity of the armed forces, a round table on security sector reform was organized in Bangui on 29 October to define strategies for addressing the security challenges. The meeting did not, however, yield any concrete pledges in support of the security sector reform process.

On 27 and 28 August, the Chairperson of the Peacebuilding Commission undertook a mission to the country to follow up with the national authorities and members of the international community on a number of issues relating to the peacebuilding process, including disarmament, demobilization and reintegration and security sector reform, preparations for the 2010 general elections, and progress in the development hubs project. Regarding the development hubs project, the Chairperson noted that preparations were ongoing, but that communities, particularly those that had suffered the most from the violence, were increasingly concerned at the slow pace of implementation of the project. He also expressed concern that only about one quarter of the total estimated budget for peacebuilding projects had been mobilized. He urged the Government to indicate the technical and financial support it expected from the international community in support of peacebuilding efforts.

The Secretary-General urged the Government to ensure free movement and security for all actors, particularly those belonging to opposition parties, to allow them to carry out their electoral campaigns without intimidation or harassment. He urged the presidential candidates and their supporters to put national interest above narrow political or personal gain and to show civic responsibility and respect for the rights of others so as to contribute to a peaceful environment before, during and after the elections. He also called for efforts to disarm the other armed groups, including the self-defence groups, the Kara, Goula and Rounga ethnic militias, who were not covered by the disarmament, demobilization and reintegration programme.

Security Council consideration. On 15 December [meeting 6240], the Secretary-General's Special Representative and Head of BONUCA, Ms. Zewde, and the Chair of the Central African Republic configuration of the Peacebuilding Commission, Jan Grauls, briefed the Security Council on the situation in the country.

SECURITY COUNCIL ACTION

On 21 December [meeting 6250], following consultations among Security Council members, the President made statement **S/PRST/2009/35** on behalf of the Council:

The Security Council welcomes ongoing efforts aimed at national reconciliation in the Central African Republic based on the Libreville comprehensive peace agreement of 21 June 2008 and the commitments contained in the Sirte agreement of 2 February 2007 and the Birao agreement of 13 April 2007. The Council encourages the Government of the Central African Republic to continue to ensure that the recommendations of the inclusive political dialogue of December 2008 are expeditiously and fully implemented.

The Council reiterates its call upon the Government of the Central African Republic to strengthen and accelerate efforts to reform security sector institutions, which is a crucial element for the peacebuilding process in the Central African Republic and for addressing widespread impunity and increasing respect for human rights. It also reiterates its call upon the Government to carry out without delay a transparent and accountable disarmament, demobilization and reintegration process and ensure the completion of disarmament and demobilization before the 2010 elections. In these efforts, transparent funding and coordination of reintegration programmes are critical to the long-term success of the programme. The Council encourages the international community, including the United Nations Integrated Peacebuilding Office in the Central African Republic, to provide timely and adequate support to the process.

The Council strongly condemns the ongoing attacks by the Lord's Resistance Army in the Central African Republic and calls for the countries of the region and the United Nations missions to coordinate and enhance information-sharing regarding the threat posed by the Lord's Resistance Army to the population.

The Council demands that the Government of the Central African Republic and all political stakeholders ensure free, fair, transparent and credible preparation and conduct of the 2010 elections, and that the elections take place within the time frame set by the Constitution. The Council calls upon the Government, the United Nations and other stakeholders to support timely preparation of the elections with adequate resources.

The Council welcomes the establishment of the United Nations Integrated Peacebuilding Office in the Central African Republic on 1 January 2010 for the period of one year. The Council urges the Special Representative of the Secretary-General for the Central African Republic to take all necessary steps so that the Office will be fully operational as soon as possible after 1 January 2010, in accordance with its mandate as set out in the statement by its President of 7 April 2009. The Council confirms its full support for the efforts of the Special Representative, Ms. Sahle-Work Zewde, in this regard. The support of the Office, together with the United Nations country team, to national and local efforts to consolidate peace, enhance governance and complete the disarmament, demobilization and reintegration process is crucial and needed.

The Council also requests the Secretary-General to propose in his next report a set of clear and measurable benchmarks to guide the progress of the mission and enable the United Nations Integrated Peacebuilding Office in the Central African Republic to evaluate its progress against its mandate.

The Council welcomes the support provided by the Peacebuilding Commission to the Central African Republic, and reiterates its call upon the donor community to enhance its support to sectors identified as critical for sustainable peace and development in the Central African Republic, as set out in the Strategic Framework for Peacebuilding in the Central African Republic developed by the Commission.

Year-end developments. In a later report [S/2010/295], the Secretary-General said that the Disarmament, Demobilization and Reintegration Steering Committee on 17 December adopted a road map setting the beginning of disarmament and demobilization for February and March 2010. As recommended by the October/November electoral needs assessment mission (see above), the Steering Committee on Elections was established on 22 December, to be chaired by the Secretary-General's Special Representative. Also in December, the leader of the former rebel movement, MNSP, Hassan Ousman, disappeared from his premises at the Bangui base of the Mission for the Consolidation of Peace in the Central African Republic, a subregional peacekeeping force. His whereabouts were unknown.

A delegation of the Peacebuilding Commission visited the country from 3 to 10 December in the context of the first biannual review of the strategic framework for peacebuilding. The mission concluded that the key challenges for 2010 were the implementation of the disarmament, demobilization and reintegration process and the organization of presidential and legislative elections. While the disarmament, demobilization and reintegration process was technically ready to start, political and security challenges continued to hamper its launch. The mission stressed that the responsibility for completing the process lay with national authorities.

The mission noted that while the Government had demonstrated ownership in implementing short-term commitments in the field of security sector reform, the security sector reform round table held in October had not yielded the expected outcome in terms of funding. The Commission encouraged the Government to streamline the list of projects submitted to the round table and to adapt them to the country's peacebuilding context. Recognizing the efforts made by the Government in preparation for the 2010 elections, the mission expressed concern over human rights abuses and the weak capacity of the Independent Electoral Commission to organize free, fair and credible elections within the constitutional timelines.

BINUCA

The United Nations Integrated Peacebuilding Office in the Central African Republic (BINUCA), set up in accordance with Security Council presidential statement S/PRST/2009/5 (see p. 146), would succeed, as at 1 January 2010, the United Nations Peacebuilding Support Office in the Central African Republic (BONUCA). The mandate of BINUCA included assisting efforts in implementing the outcomes of the December 2008 inclusive political dialogue. BINUCA was headed by the Secretary-General's Special Representative, Sahle-Work Zewde (Ethiopia).

Financing

In October [A/64/349 & Add.3], the Secretary-General submitted resource requirements for BINUCA for 2010 in the amount of $17,991,600, within the context of his overall financing proposals for the 27 special political missions, which were endorsed by ACABQ in its observations and recommendations thereon [A/64/7/Add.13].

The General Assembly approved those requirements in section VI of **resolution 64/245** of 24 December (see p. 1407).

Peacebuilding Commission

On 20 January [PBC/3/CAF/4], the Chair of the Peacebuilding Commission configuration on the Central African Republic indicated that the configuration planned to assist the authorities in implementing the recommendations of the December 2008 inclusive political dialogue and to work with the Government and other stakeholders to draft a strategic framework for peacebuilding. From 22 January to 5 February, a delegation from the Peacebuilding Support Office visited the country to facilitate consultations among national and international stakeholders in preparation for the development of the country's strategy document.

In a 9 March statement [PBC/3/CAF/5], the Chair expressed the concern of the Commission at the resurgence of violence in the north, resulting in insecurity and the additional displacement of thousands of civilians. The Commission encouraged all parties to implement the recommendations of the dialogue in the spirit of national reconciliation and called upon all politico-military groups, in particular FDPC, to sign and adhere to the Libreville Comprehensive Peace Agreement [YUN 2008, p. 156]. The Commission urged restraint on all parties, stressed the need to avoid retaliatory attacks and encouraged a response to the needs of displaced civilians. It believed that the most urgent action required to maintain the momentum of the inclusive political dialogue was the finalization and implementation of a disarmament, demobilization and reintegration programme, which could not be finalized without complete lists of combatants of each of the politico-military groups. The initial 25 February deadline for the completion of the lists had already been postponed to 16 March, and no further delays should be entertained. With regard to the funding of the disarmament, demobilization and reintegration process, the Commission stood ready to advocate for contributions from international partners to the UNDP trust fund. The Commission called upon the Government and UNDP to finalize arrangements for the transfer of the 8 billion CFA francs pledged by the Central African Economic and Monetary Community in Libreville on 30 January for disarmament, demobilization and reintegration activities (see p. 146).

The Strategic Framework for Peacebuilding in the Central African Republic 2009–2011 [PBC/3/CAF/7], drafted in cooperation with national and international stakeholders, set the ground for long-term engagement between the country and the Peacebuilding Commission. Under the Framework, priority activities in the security sector aimed at improving the distribution of national security forces in the country, as well as their training and equipment. In the area of governance and the rule of law, it was proposed to establish an environment favouring the organization of credible and transparent elections; take steps to strengthen and better monitor institutions; strengthen human rights protection; foster a culture of peace, democracy and national reconciliation; promote fair justice for all; and fight impunity. The "development poles" project represented a national strategy aimed at organizing the economy around regional growth engines that would spread out over a radius of 50 to 100 kilometres. Each pole will be surrounded by sets of activities aimed at rehabilitating and reconstructing a set of community services. The goal was to support initiatives aimed at restoring administrative services and favouring improved availability and access on the part of citizens to basic social services and infrastructure. The development poles would also contribute to the return and reintegration of refugees and displaced persons. Those initiatives sought to strengthen the contribution of regional economic spaces to the establishment and equitable distribution of assets.

The Commission adopted the Strategic Framework on 6 May [A/64/341-S/2009/444]. Subsequently,

the Chair of the Central African Republic configuration undertook a mission to Bangui to present the Strategic Framework document to all national stakeholders, with a view to strengthening national ownership of the strategy and beginning its implementation. The Chair also directed his effort at increasing international attention to the situation in the country, mobilizing resources for implementing the Strategic Framework and supporting coordination among stakeholders. The country benefited from two allocations from the Peacebuilding Fund: one was made under the Fund's emergency window to support the inclusive political dialogue; the other, of $10 million, was made through the Fund's second window, out of which $4 million was for launching the disarmament, demobilization and reintegration programme.

Report of Commission mission. Reporting in December [PBC/4/CAF/1] on its mission to the country (3–10 December), the Peacebuilding Commission said that implementation of the recommendations of the inclusive political dialogue was slow, despite some achievements. Developments in security sector reform were encouraging, with the Government demonstrating real ownership in implementing short-term commitments. The Government had agreed on a security sector reform strategy with the international community. In that regard, the Peacebuilding Commission would organize a donor round table in 2010 to mobilize resources for 24 projects amounting to $102 million.

Disarmament, demobilization and reintegration continued to be hampered by political and security challenges. The finalization of a cooperation agreement with the Economic Community of Central African States removed the last remaining stumbling block.

Notable progress was achieved in the lead-up to the 2010 elections, including the revision of the electoral code and the establishment of the Independent Electoral Commission. Much remained to be done, notably in human rights and the management of natural resources. Capacity had to be strengthened at all levels, particularly as the Government resumed its functions throughout the country. The adoption of the revised mining code represented another setback to the transparent management of natural resources and the equitable distribution of related state incomes, despite the country's adherence to the Extractive Industries Transparency Initiative. The development poles project had yet to start in earnest, although the mapping of the specific needs for each pole had been completed. The Government needed to take ownership of the project; infrastructure reconstruction, particularly of the road network through public employment programmes, would contribute to the success of the project.

(For further information on the Peacebuilding Commission, see p. 45.)

Children and armed conflict

In February [S/2009/66], the Secretary-General submitted a report on children and armed conflict in the Central African Republic, which focused on grave violations perpetrated against children and identified parties to the conflict, both State and non-State actors, who had committed such abuses. It highlighted the fact that children had been consistently recruited and used by non-State armed groups, including Government-backed self-defence militias. All parties to the conflict had perpetrated rapes and other grave sexual violence. Non-State armed groups and bandits, especially in the north-west, had used abductions as a means of recruiting children and to threaten and extort ransom from the population. The report acknowledged the challenges in addressing grave violations against children and outlined recommendations to put an end to those violations.

The Working Group on Children and Armed Conflict, at its meeting on 24 February [S/AC.51/2009/2], considered the Secretary-General's report and adopted recommendations addressed to the Government, the Secretary-General, the Security Council and the Peacebuilding Commission.

In a further report issued in March [A/63/785-S/2009/158], the Secretary-General expressed concern at the incidence of rape and sexual violence against children by armed elements. Cases of rape and sexual violence and of abduction, killing and maiming of children had also been attributed to criminal gangs, the zaraguinas. He noted patterns of displacement that were unique to the country and could be distinguished in two categories. In the first case, persons left their villages in an organized manner and stayed in the bush for a few days. Such "preventive" displacement or coping strategy was usually provoked by rumours of movements of armed forces and groups or zaraguinas. In the second case, displacement was a reaction to unexpected attacks on villages by armed forces and groups or zaraguinas, and populations typically had no time to organize their escape and left without any basic necessities. They might hide in the bush, move from one village to the other, or end up in the internally displaced persons camp of Kabo (central north). In that unpredictable context, children were particularly vulnerable, given the possibility of being left behind or suffering violations such as abduction and recruitment, killing, maiming or sexual violence.

The Security Council, in presidential statement **S/PRST/2009/9** of 29 April (see p. 737), invited the Secretary General to strengthen efforts to bring the monitoring and reporting mechanism to its full capacity in order to allow for prompt advocacy and effective response to all violations and abuses committed against children.

The Council also took action on the Secretary-General's March report in **resolution 1882(2009)** of 4 August (see p. 739).

On 12 August [S/2009/436], the Security Council forwarded to the Secretary-General a letter of the same date by the Chairman of the Security Council Working Group on Children and Armed Conflict, established pursuant to Council resolution 1612(2005) [YUN 2005, p. 863]. The Chairman, in follow-up to the recommendations of the Working Group (see above), invited the Secretary-General to continue strengthening the Task Force on Monitoring and Reporting; to liaise with national institutions, as well as NGOs and civil society networks, to ensure collaboration and coordination of child protection activities; to ensure, given the regional dimension of the crisis involving the Central African Republic, Chad and the Sudan and the implications for children, better information exchange and closer cooperation among UN country teams and peacekeeping missions on child protection issues; and to take note of the framework of collaboration being piloted between the UNICEF Child Protection Sections in the Central African Republic and Chad.

Chad and Central African Republic

In 2009, UN operations in Chad and the Central African Republic entered a new phase. The Security Council in January authorized the deployment of a military component of the United Nations Mission in the Central African Republic and Chad (MINURCAT) and the transfer of authority on 15 March from the European Union-led military force (EUFOR) in Chad and the Central African Republic to MINURCAT. The Council also expanded the Mission's mandate to include, among other tasks, the security and protection of civilians and UN personnel and property and support to regional peace efforts.

As requested by the Council, the Secretary-General in July submitted a strategic workplan towards a MINURCAT exit strategy.

Political and security developments

Acting on the Secretary-General's recommendation contained in his December 2008 report on MINURCAT [YUN 2008, p. 166], the Security Council on 14 January 2009, by resolution 1861(2009) (see below), extended the mission's mandate until 15 March 2010. It authorized the deployment of a military component in follow up to EUFOR in Chad and the Central African Republic, and decided that the transfer of authority between EUFOR and the MINURCAT military component would take place on 15 March.

SECURITY COUNCIL ACTION

On 14 January [meeting 6064], the Security Council unanimously adopted **resolution 1861(2009)**. The draft [S/2009/29] was submitted by France.

The Security Council,

Recalling its resolutions and the statements by its President concerning Chad, the Central African Republic and the subregion, including resolutions 1778(2007) of 25 September 2007 and 1834(2008) of 24 September 2008, and its resolution 1769(2007) of 31 July 2007,

Reaffirming its commitment to the sovereignty, unity, territorial integrity and political independence of Chad and the Central African Republic, and to the cause of peace in the region,

Reiterating its concern at the humanitarian and security repercussions in eastern Chad and the north-eastern Central African Republic of the ongoing violence in Darfur,

Deeply concerned at armed activities and banditry in eastern Chad, the north-eastern Central African Republic and western Sudan, which threaten the security of the civilian population, the conduct of humanitarian operations in those areas and the stability of those countries, and which result in serious violations of human rights and international humanitarian law,

Welcoming the recent resumption of diplomatic relations between the Governments of Chad and the Sudan and the efforts of the Government of the Libyan Arab Jamahiriya to promote it, and stressing that a further improvement of relations between the Sudan, Chad and the Central African Republic will contribute to long-term peace and stability in the region,

Stressing that a proper settlement of the Darfur issue, the full implementation of the Sirte and Libreville agreements and the efforts at national political dialogue in Chad and the Central African Republic will contribute to long-term peace and stability in the region and to the voluntary, secure and sustainable return of refugees and internally displaced persons,

Reiterating its full support for the efforts of the Secretary-General, the African Union and regional actors to find solutions to the armed conflicts in the region,

Reaffirming that any attempt at destabilization through violent means or seizing power by force is unacceptable,

Reaffirming also its resolutions 1325(2000) of 31 October 2000 and 1820(2008) of 19 June 2008 on women and peace and security, its resolution 1502(2003) of 26 August 2003 on the protection of humanitarian and United Nations personnel and its resolution 1674(2006) of 28 April 2006 on the protection of civilians in armed conflict,

Reaffirming further its resolution 1612(2005) of 26 July 2005 on children and armed conflict, taking note of the report of the Secretary-General on children and armed conflict in Chad and the recommendations contained therein, and recalling the conclusions regarding Chad adopted by its Working Group on Children and Armed Conflict, as approved by the Council,

Recognizing that the Governments of Chad and the Central African Republic bear primary responsibility for ensuring the security of civilians in their territories,

Bearing in mind the Convention relating to the Status of Refugees of 28 July 1951 and the Protocol thereto, of 31 January 1967, along with the Organization of African Unity Convention governing the specific aspects of refugee problems in Africa of 10 September 1969,

Emphasizing the need to respect international refugee law, preserve the civilian and humanitarian nature of refugee camps and internally displaced persons sites and prevent any recruitment of individuals, including children, which might be carried out in or around the camps and sites by armed groups,

Recalling its authorization under resolution 1778(2007) of a multidimensional presence in the regions of eastern Chad and the north-eastern Central African Republic indicated in paragraph 37 of the report of the Secretary-General of 10 August 2007 (hereinafter referred to as "eastern Chad and the north-eastern Central African Republic"),

Commending the deployment by the European Union of an operation (EUFOR Chad/Central African Republic) to support the United Nations Mission in the Central African Republic and Chad, and recalling that the mandate of EUFOR Chad/Central African Republic runs until 15 March 2009,

Welcoming the ongoing selection and training by the Mission of police and gendarmerie officers of the Détachement intégré de sécurité, and stressing the need to expedite the deployment of the Détachement intégré de sécurité,

Having examined the report of the Secretary-General of 4 December 2008 (hereinafter referred to as "the report of the Secretary-General") and the recommendations contained therein on the arrangements for following up EUFOR Chad/Central African Republic at the end of its mandate,

Welcoming the letter dated 6 January 2009 from the President of Chad and the letter dated 5 December 2008 from the President of the Central African Republic regarding the deployment of a military component of the Mission in both countries to follow up EUFOR Chad/Central African Republic at the end of its mandate,

Determining that the situation in the region of the border between the Sudan, Chad and the Central African Republic constitutes a threat to international peace and security,

1. *Decides* to extend for a period of twelve months, in accordance with paragraphs 2 to 7 below, the multidimensional presence in Chad and the military presence in the Central African Republic intended to help to create the security conditions conducive to a voluntary, secure and sustainable return of refugees and displaced persons, inter alia, by contributing to the protection of refugees, displaced persons and civilians in danger, by facilitating the provision of humanitarian assistance in eastern Chad and the north-eastern Central African Republic and by creating favourable conditions for the reconstruction and economic and social development of those areas;

2. *Also decides*, for that purpose, to extend until 15 March 2010 the mandate of the United Nations Mission in the Central African Republic and Chad, as set out in paragraphs 6 and 7 below;

3. *Authorizes* the deployment of a military component of the Mission to follow up EUFOR Chad/Central African Republic in both Chad and the Central African Republic at the end of its mandate, welcomes the concept of operations proposed in paragraphs 57 to 61 and in option 2 in paragraph 62 of the report of the Secretary-General of 4 December 2008, and decides that the transfer of author-

ity between EUFOR Chad/Central African Republic and the military component of the Mission shall take place on 15 March 2009;

4. *Decides* that the Mission shall include a maximum of 300 police officers, 25 military liaison officers, 5,200 military personnel and an appropriate number of civilian personnel;

5. *Recalls* that in paragraph 5 of resolution 1778(2007), it endorsed the police concept referred to in the report of the Secretary-General of 10 August 2007, including the provisions regarding the establishment of the Police tchadienne pour la protection humanitaire, now the Détachement intégré de sécurité, which is dedicated exclusively to maintaining law and order in refugee camps, sites with concentrations of internally displaced persons and key towns in neighbouring areas and to assisting in securing humanitarian activities in eastern Chad;

6. *Decides* that the Mission shall have the following mandate in eastern Chad and the north-eastern Central African Republic, in liaison with the United Nations country team and, as appropriate, in liaison with the United Nations Peacebuilding Support Office in the Central African Republic and without prejudice to the mandate of the Office:

Security and protection of civilians

(a) To select, train, advise and facilitate support to elements of the Détachement intégré de sécurité referred to in paragraph 5 above;

(b) To liaise with the national army, the gendarmerie and police forces, the nomad national guard, the judicial authorities and prison officials in Chad and the Central African Republic to contribute to the creation of a more secure environment, combating in particular the problems of banditry and criminality;

(c) To liaise with the Government of Chad and the Office of the United Nations High Commissioner for Refugees in support of their efforts to relocate refugee camps which are in close proximity to the border, and to provide to the Office of the High Commissioner, on availability and on a cost-reimbursable basis, logistical assistance for that purpose;

(d) To liaise with the Government of the Sudan, the African Union-United Nations Hybrid Operation in Darfur (UNAMID), the United Nations Peacebuilding Support Office in the Central African Republic, the multinational force of the Economic Community of Central African States in the Central African Republic and the Community of Sahel-Saharan States to exchange information on threats to humanitarian activities in the region;

(e) To support the initiatives of national and local authorities in Chad to resolve local tensions and promote local reconciliation efforts, in order to enhance the environment for the return of internally displaced persons;

Human rights and the rule of law

(f) To contribute to the monitoring and to the promotion and protection of human rights in Chad, with particular attention to sexual and gender-based violence, and to recommend action to the competent authorities with a view to fighting impunity;

(g) To support, within its capabilities, efforts aimed at strengthening the capacity of the Government of Chad and civil society through training in international human rights standards, and efforts to put an end to the recruitment and use of children by armed groups;

(h) To assist the Government of Chad in the promotion of the rule of law, including through support for an independent judiciary and a strengthened legal system, in close coordination with United Nations agencies;

Regional peace support

(i) To continue to play a role as observer, with UNAMID, in the Contact Group that was established under the Dakar Agreement of 13 March 2008 to monitor its implementation and assist, as necessary, the Governments of Chad, the Sudan and the Central African Republic to build good-neighbourly relations;

7. Acting under Chapter VII of the Charter of the United Nations,

(a) *Decides* that the Mission shall be authorized to take all necessary measures, within its capabilities and its area of operations in eastern Chad, to fulfil the following functions, in liaison with the Government of Chad:

    (i) To contribute to protecting civilians in danger, particularly refugees and internally displaced persons;

    (ii) To facilitate the delivery of humanitarian aid and the free movement of humanitarian personnel by helping to improve security in the area of operations;

    (iii) To protect United Nations personnel, facilities, installations and equipment and to ensure the security and freedom of movement of its staff and United Nations and associated personnel;

(b) *Decides also* that the Mission shall be authorized to take all necessary measures, within its capabilities and its area of operations in the north-eastern Central African Republic, to fulfil the following functions, by establishing a permanent military presence in Birao and in liaison with the Government of the Central African Republic:

    (i) To contribute to the creation of a more secure environment;

    (ii) To execute operations of a limited character in order to extract civilians and humanitarian workers in danger;

    (iii) To protect United Nations personnel, facilities, installations and equipment and to ensure the security and freedom of movement of its staff and United Nations and associated personnel;

(c) *Notes* the agreements entered into by the Secretary-General and the Governments of Chad and the Central African Republic on the status of the Mission, of 21 March 2008 and 21 November 2008 respectively, requests the Secretary-General and both Governments to conclude, prior to 15 March 2009, amendments to those agreements to ensure that they fully cover the Mission, including its military component authorized by the present resolution, taking into account General Assembly resolution 59/47 of 2 December 2004 on the scope of legal protection under the Convention on the Safety of United Nations and Associated Personnel, Assembly resolution 60/42 of 8 December 2005 on the Optional Protocol to the Convention and Assembly resolution 63/138 of 11 December 2008 on the safety and security of humanitarian personnel and the protection of United Nations personnel, and decides that the model status-of-forces agreement of 9 October 1990 shall apply provisionally to supplement the existing agreements pending their amendment;

8. *Requests* the Secretary-General and the Governments of Chad and the Central African Republic to cooperate closely throughout the period of deployment of the Mission;

9. *Recalls* that it authorized the European Union operation, after 15 March 2009, to take all appropriate measures to achieve an orderly disengagement, by means including the fulfilment of the functions indicated in paragraph 6 *(a)* of resolution 1778(2007), within the limits of its residual capacity;

10. *Requests* the European Union and the Secretary-General to continue to cooperate closely throughout the period of deployment of the European Union operation, until its complete disengagement;

11. *Underscores* the importance that the military concept of operations and rules of engagement be fully in line with the provisions of the present resolution, and requests the Secretary-General to report on them to the Security Council and troop-contributing countries;

12. *Encourages* the Governments of Chad and the Central African Republic to continue to cooperate with the United Nations and the European Union to facilitate the smooth transition from EUFOR Chad/Central African Republic to the United Nations military component, including the handover of all sites and infrastructure established by EUFOR Chad/Central African Republic to the United Nations follow-on presence;

13. *Calls upon* the Government of Chad, and the Mission according to its mandate, to expedite and complete the selection, training and deployment of the Détachement intégré de sécurité;

14. *Encourages* Member States to contribute the necessary force requirements for the Mission, in particular the helicopters, reconnaissance elements, engineers, logistics and medical facilities;

15. *Urges* all Member States, particularly the States bordering Chad and the Central African Republic, to facilitate the delivery to Chad and the Central African Republic freely, without obstacles or delay, of all personnel, equipment, provisions, supplies and other goods, including vehicles and spare parts, intended for the Mission, and the European Union operation until its complete disengagement;

16. *Invites* donors to continue to contribute to the Mission trust fund, established to support the Détachement intégré de sécurité;

17. *Exhorts* the donor community to sustain its efforts to address the humanitarian, reconstruction and development needs of Chad and the Central African Republic;

18. *Calls upon* all parties to cooperate fully in the deployment and operations of the Mission, and the European Union operation until its complete disengagement, including by guaranteeing the security and freedom of movement of their personnel and associated personnel;

19. *Encourages* the respective Governments of the Sudan, Chad and the Central African Republic to ensure that their territories are not used to undermine the sovereignty of others, to cooperate actively with a view to implementing the Dakar Agreement of 13 March 2008 and previ-

ous agreements, and to cooperate with a view to putting an end to the activities of armed groups in the region and their attempts to seize power by force, and welcomes the role played in particular by the Dakar Agreement Contact Group, the Governments of the Libyan Arab Jamahiriya and the Republic of the Congo as African Union mediators, as well as the African Union and the United Nations, including through the Special Representative of the Secretary-General for the Central African Republic and Chad and Head of the Mission, in support of the Dakar process;

20. *Demands* that armed groups cease violence immediately, and urges all parties in Chad and the Central African Republic, respectively, to respect and implement the Sirte Agreement of 25 October 2007 and the comprehensive peace agreement signed at Libreville on 21 June 2008;

21. *Encourages* the authorities and political stakeholders in Chad and the Central African Republic to continue to pursue their efforts at national dialogue, with respect for the constitutional frameworks, welcomes the holding of the inclusive political dialogue in the Central African Republic, with the support of the dialogue Chair, Mr. Pierre Buyoya, and the regional peace facilitator, President Omar Bongo Ondimba of Gabon, and the conclusion of the inclusive political dialogue that calls for a government gathering the entities participating in the dialogue, emphasizes also the importance of the political agreement for the reinforcement of the democratic process signed at N'Djamena on 13 August 2007, and encourages the parties to proceed with its implementation, in particular with a view to holding early elections;

22. *Reaffirms* the obligation of all parties to implement fully the rules and principles of international humanitarian law, particularly those regarding the protection of humanitarian personnel, and furthermore requests all the parties involved to provide humanitarian personnel with immediate, free and unimpeded access to all persons in need of assistance, in accordance with applicable international law;

23. *Encourages* efforts by the Mission and the United Nations country team, including through the appointment of child protection advisers, to prevent the recruitment of refugees and children and to maintain the civilian nature of refugee camps and internally displaced persons sites, in coordination with the Détachement intégré de sécurité and the humanitarian community;

24. *Takes note* of the measures already undertaken by the authorities of Chad to put an end to the recruitment and use of children by armed groups, encourages them to pursue their cooperation with United Nations bodies in this regard, particularly the United Nations Children's Fund, and calls upon all the parties involved to ensure that children are protected;

25. *Endorses* the benchmarks presented in paragraph 70 of the report of the Secretary-General of 4 December 2008 towards the exit strategy of the Mission, and stresses in particular the following:

(a) Voluntary return and resettlement in secure and sustainable conditions of a critical mass of internally displaced persons;

(b) Demilitarization of refugee and internally displaced persons camps as evidenced by a decrease in arms, violence and human rights abuses;

(c) Improvement in the capacity of Chadian authorities in eastern Chad, including national law enforcement agencies, the judiciary and the prison system, to provide the necessary security for refugees, internally displaced persons, civilians and humanitarian workers, with respect for international human rights standards;

26. *Stresses* that an improved capacity of the Government of the Central African Republic to exercise its authority in the north-eastern part of the country is also critical to the fulfilment of the objectives of the Mission as set out in paragraph 1 above, and calls upon the Government of the Central African Republic, Member States, the United Nations Peacebuilding Support Office in the Central African Republic, United Nations agencies and the Peacebuilding Commission to provide the necessary support to the reform of the security sector in the Central African Republic;

27. *Also stresses* that improved cooperation between the Sudan, Chad and the Central African Republic with a view to putting an end to the activities of armed groups in the region is also critical to the restoration of peace and security in eastern Chad and the north-eastern Central African Republic;

28. *Requests* the Secretary-General to continue to report regularly, and at least every three months, on the security and humanitarian situation, including movements of refugees and internally displaced persons, in eastern Chad, the north-eastern Central African Republic and the region, on progress in the implementation of the relevant agreements, on progress towards the fulfilment of the benchmarks in paragraphs 25 and 26 above, and on the implementation of the mandate of the Mission, and to provide to the Council, with the same regularity, a specific update on the military situation;

29. *Also requests* the Secretary-General to inform the Council in his upcoming reports on the development of a strategic workplan containing indicative timelines to measure and track progress on the implementation of the benchmarks in paragraphs 25 and 26 above, with a view to meeting them by 15 March 2011;

30. *Stresses* that it will take duly into account progress against those benchmarks when considering the possible renewal of the mandate of the Mission beyond 15 March 2010;

31. *Decides* to remain actively seized of the matter.

Deployment of MINURCAT. The Secretary-General reported [S/2009/199] that MINURCAT engaged the Governments of Chad and the Central African Republic to put in place the legal and administrative arrangements for the deployment of a UN force. On 13 February, MINURCAT and the Government of Chad signed a memorandum of understanding providing for the transfer of EUFOR sites and infrastructure to MINURCAT, upon their transfer from EUFOR to the Government on 15 March. On 3 and 18 March, MINURCAT submitted to Chad and the Central African Republic, respectively, draft amendments to the Status of Mission Agreements. In accordance with Security Council resolution 1861(2009) (see p. 154), the model status of forces agreement was in force in both countries to supplement existing agreements pending their amendment. On 27 February, MINURCAT and EUFOR agreed on the technical arrangement for the handover of the operation, covering operational issues, force protection, information-sharing, as well as command, control and coordination during the transitional period. The United Nations would provide support for the EUFOR phased withdrawal. Also in accordance with Council resolution 1861(2009), EUFOR transferred its military authority to the newly constituted military component of MINURCAT on 15 March. As at 31 March, the MINURCAT force strength was 2,079 troops out of the authorized strength of 5,200. The build-up of the force would be phased, and was expected to reach full strength by the end of the year. The Secretariat had not received commitments for all the force requirements, especially for a signals unit and for logistic support and engineering elements, and had only received pledges for 6 of the 18 military helicopters.

Appointment. On 27 February [S/2009/121], the Secretary-General indicated his intention to appoint Major General Elhadji Mouhamedou Kandji as MINURCAT Force Commander, following the transfer of authority from EUFOR to MINURCAT on 15 March. The Security Council took note of the Secretary-General's intention on 3 March [S/2009/122].

Security Council action. The Council on 17 March held consultations on the situation in Chad, the Central African Republic and the subregion. On the same day, by a press statement [SC/9614], the Council welcomed the successful transfer of authority on 15 March between EUFOR and MINURCAT, and commended the European Union (EU) for the deployment of EUFOR Chad/the Central African Republic, the support it provided to UN activities and its contribution to the delivery of humanitarian assistance and the security and stability in its area of operations. The Council took note of the completion of the deployment of the Détachement Intégré de Sécurité (DIS), which was a critical element of the multidimensional presence deployed in Chad to contribute to the protection of refugees from Darfur, IDPs and other vulnerable civilians in regions affected by the Darfur crisis, and encouraged donors to provide funding for the DIS trust fund.

The Council recalled its demand that all armed groups in Chad and the Central African Republic renounce violence and respect and implement the Sirte Agreement [YUN 2007, p. 156] and the Libreville Agreement [YUN 2008, p. 156], and encouraged the authorities and political stakeholders to pursue their efforts of national dialogue, in the framework of the 13 August 2007 N'Djamena Agreement [YUN 2007, p. 152] and of the conclusions of the December 2008 inclusive political dialogue held in Bangui [YUN 2008, p. 157].

Report of Secretary-General (April). In his April report on MINURCAT [S/2009/199], the Secretary-General said that armed opposition groups in Chad had reasserted their intention to mobilize against Chadian President Idriss Déby. On 18 January, following a lull in the fighting and five months of negotiations, seven of the groups signed a manifesto establishing a new coalition, the Union des forces de la résistance (UFR), which included the Rassemblement des forces pour le changement (RFC), the Union des forces pour le changement et la démocratie, the Union des forces pour la démocratie et le développement-fondamentale, the Conseil démocratique révolutionnaire, the Front populaire pour la renaissance nationale, the Front pour le salut de la République and the Union des forces pour la démocratie et le développement. On the same day, the Union démocratique tchadienne also joined under a separate protocol. On 23 January, RFC leader Timan Erdimi was appointed to head UFR. On 20 March, UFR appointed its military command, with Tahir Odji as Force Commander. Only one Chadian opposition group remained outside the coalition. Little progress was made in implementing the agreement of 13 August 2007 between the Government of Chad and the political opposition [YUN 2007, p. 155]. Increases in the cost of living, combined with austerity measures introduced by the Government in January and February, resulted in significant social tensions, particularly in N'Djamena. On 23 March, the President reshuffled the Cabinet. While responsibilities for the key ministries were unchanged and the four ministers from the Coalition of Political Parties for the Defence of the Constitution remained in their posts, former rebel leader Yaya Dillo, who had joined the Government after the failed rebel attack of February 2008 [YUN 2008, p. 160], was removed from his post as Minister of Mines and Energy.

As to the security situation, several armed attacks against civilians were recorded in eastern Chad. The prevailing insecurity and uncontrolled circulation of small arms accounted for many such incidents, while others resulted from tensions between local communities. In particular, tensions between the Zaghawa and the Tama communities in the Birak area (Wadi Fira region) were of concern. At least 42 incidents against humanitarian workers were recorded in eastern Chad between January and March, mainly office and compound break-ins and carjackings. In March, four attacks against three international humanitarian organizations took place in the Ouaddai and Sila regions. As a result, an NGO suspended its water and sanitation activities in Koukou, Kerfi and Louboutiqué and relocated its staff, while another suspended its activities in Goz Beida. On 7 April, in Abéché, a soldier serving under EUFOR shot dead two EUFOR soldiers and a MINURCAT soldier, and later in the day, a Chadian civilian. On 9 April, the soldier was arrested

by Chadian authorities. Chadian armed opposition groups continued to consolidate their forces in West Darfur, near El Geneina. Meanwhile, the Chadian armed forces strengthened their positions in eastern Chad in anticipation of a possible rebel offensive. On 24 March, the Chadian Minister for External Relations, Moussa Faki, convened an urgent meeting with the diplomatic community in N'Djamena and warned diplomats of an imminent threat of rebel attack. While tensions remained high, no cross-border attacks were reported.

Within the MINURCAT area of operations in the north-eastern Central African Republic, the security situation remained relatively calm. However, insecurity resulting from clashes between Government forces and rebels in the north led to population displacements into Chad. In response to the proliferation of armed groups moving inside the border region of the northern Central African Republic, the Chadian armed forces reinforced their troops along Chad's southern border.

Eastern Chad continued to face a humanitarian crisis. Following high-level advocacy by MINURCAT with local and national authorities and improvements in security, humanitarian aid workers returned to the Sila region in January. The provision of humanitarian assistance also resumed in the Am Nabak refugee camp in February, after being suspended following an attack by armed elements in 2008. From mid-January, clashes between rebel factions and Government forces in northern Central African Republic resulted in a new and continuing influx of refugees from the north-eastern Central African Republic into the Salamat region of Chad, bringing the number of refugees receiving humanitarian aid in Chad to approximately 320,000.

As at 31 March, 240 UN police officers were deployed in Chad. On 7 February, with the graduation of 246 DIS officers, MINURCAT completed the training of the 850-strong DIS. As at 27 March, 667 DIS officers were deployed to 6 DIS stations and 12 posts throughout eastern Chad. Since their initial deployment in October 2008, DIS officers had conducted day and night patrols to maintain law and order in sites of refugee and IDPS concentration and neighbouring areas. They had arrested 81 individuals suspected of involvement in serious crimes, searched more than 800 vehicles and secured over 900 humanitarian aid convoys. MINURCAT faced logistical challenges in the installation of DIS infrastructure and support to its operations. The construction of police stations, police posts and accommodation was not completed due to difficulties in identifying a suitable contractor and the shortage of skilled labour. As a result, MINURCAT agreed to pay DIS members housing allowances while they lived in temporary accommodations. MINURCAT developed a tracking system for the cases of individuals arrested or detained by DIS. From 15 January to 8 February 2009, MINURCAT trained 206 DIS officers on the criminal code, judicial organization and investigation techniques.

The Secretary-General observed that it would be important to consider changing DIS from a donor-supported initiative to one financed by the Government of Chad, in accordance with the benchmarks for the withdrawal of MINURCAT endorsed by the Security Council in resolution 1861(2009). That would be a focus of the upcoming comprehensive assessment of the DIS concept. It was also important that MINURCAT reach its full strength and operating capability as soon as possible. The Secretary-General urged Member States to provide the missing force personnel and enablers, particularly night-capable military helicopters. He would present a strategic workplan in his next report to the Council, incorporating the findings and recommendations of the forthcoming comprehensive assessment of DIS. He expressed concern at the impasse in the implementation of the 13 August 2007 agreement between the Government and the political opposition regarding the electoral law, and urged both sides to overcome their differences and arrive at a mutually acceptable arrangement. The Secretary-General offered his good offices to facilitate reconciliation.

Communication. On 21 April [S/2009/214], the EU Secretary-General and High Representative for the Common Foreign and Security Policy transmitted to the Security Council two reports on the activities of EUFOR in Chad and the Central African Republic covering the periods form 15 March to 15 September 2008 and 15 September 2008 to March 2009. The latter report stated that EUFOR had set the conditions for a successful transition to MINURCAT. The EUFOR presence had had a tangible effect on improving overall security in the region, but the unpredictable political environment would make MINURCAT mission challenging.

Security Council consideration. On 24 April [meeting 6111], the Council was briefed on the situation in Chad, the Central African Republic and the subregion by the Assistant Secretary-General for Peacekeeping Operations, Edmond Mulet.

Report of Secretary-General (July). In July [S/2009/359], the Secretary-General reported that in Chad some progress was made in implementing the 13 August 2007 agreement between the Government and the political opposition. On 28 May, representatives of the Comité de suivi et d'appui, established to follow up on the implementation of the agreement, reached a consensus on two draft laws on the status of the opposition and the political parties' charter. They also agreed on a decree enacting the implementation modalities of the laws on the electoral code and the National Independent Electoral Commission. The

laws were approved by the Council of Ministers on 4 June and were tabled for discussion during an extraordinary session of the National Assembly, which began on 25 June.

In the aftermath of the fighting between Chadian forces and armed opposition groups in May, the continued proliferation of light weapons and unexploded ordnance left on the ground further increased security risks. Crimes against humanitarian personnel and their compounds and vehicles, incidents of road banditry and attacks against civilians were reported, including 32 cases of carjacking. Three DIS personnel were killed by gunfire, two during attacks on the DIS sites in Farchana and Goz Amer on 14 April and 13 May, and another during a carjacking chase at Am Nabak on 17 June.

As at 30 June, MINURCAT strength stood at 2,424 personnel, 46 per cent of its authorized strength. In response to the Security Council's request in resolution 1861(2009) (see p. 154), the Secretary-General annexed to his report a strategic workplan to track progress in implementing benchmarks towards an exit strategy for MINURCAT [YUN 2008, p. 167]. The plan outlined several indicators and related activities for each of the benchmarks. The exit strategy depended, in particular, on developing the capacity of Chadian law enforcement agencies to protect civilians and humanitarian actors with minimal international support. The plan contained a new benchmark on peace and security in the subregion, which provided an important element of context. The threat to the security of civilians in eastern Chad and the necessity to protect them was likely to remain as long as tensions on the Chad-Sudan border persisted and the potential for fighting between respective rebels and government forces in Chad and Darfur remained high. In addition, the curtailment or management of local conflicts between ethnic groups in eastern Chad was a precondition for the return of many internally displaced persons. The establishment of stability in the MINURCAT area of operations would require sustained efforts by the Government of Chad, neighbouring States and the international community to resolve the causes of armed conflict.

Security Council consideration. On 28 July [meeting 6172], the Secretary-General's Special Representative and Head of MINURCAT, Victor da Silva Angelo, briefed the Council on the situation in Chad, the Central African Republic and the subregion.

Report of Secretary-General (October). In October [S/2009/535], the Secretary-General reported that the Government of Chad and the political opposition made some progress in implementing the 13 August 2007 agreement. The population census was completed on 30 June, and the data, a precondition for voter registration and constituency delimitation, were released on 13 October. The results were accepted by the parties to the 13 August agreement as a basis for planning for the elections. In addition, the Government and opposition parties agreed on the names of the 30 members of the National Independent Electoral Commission, who were appointed by presidential decree on 13 July. On 16 July, the Secretary-General of the Teachers' Union, Gami Ngarmajal, was designated Head of the Electoral Commission. Also 16 July, the National Assembly adopted new legislation on political parties, and on 24 July, a law outlining the relations between political parties and their elected members, which included a ban on the latter from changing membership of a party during an electoral mandate. The law was promulgated by President Déby on 31 August. Implementation of Chapter 4 of the 13 August agreement on the demilitarization and depoliticization of the administration and reform of the judiciary and armed forces was slow. In addition, the ruling party and the opposition had yet to agree on the modalities of the voter registration process. At the request of the Electoral Commission, the United Nations dispatched a needs assessment mission to N'Djamena from 29 August to 8 September. On 25 July, the Government of Chad and the Mouvement national, a coalition of three Chadian rebel groups led by Ahmat Hassaballah Soubiane, signed a peace agreement in Tripoli, Libyan Arab Jamahiriya. The agreement, sponsored by Libya, provided for an end to hostilities, the return of the Mouvement national to Chad, the integration of its fighters into the army or civil service and the participation of the movement into political life. During August and September, approximately 1,500 combatants associated with Chadian armed groups reportedly relinquished their arms and returned to Chad. However, the UFR coalition, which had attacked Chadian territory on 4 May, remained outside the framework of any peace agreement. On 19 August, the former President of Chad, Goukouny Weddeye, returned to N'Djamena after 20 years in exile in Algeria. Following a meeting with President Déby, he announced that he had no political ambitions and would hold talks with all stakeholders, including opposition leaders and representatives of civil society, to promote peace in the country.

The security situation in eastern Chad improved, owing in part to the rainy season, which hampered road movements, halted cross-border incursions and contributed to a significant decline in banditry and other security incidents. Meanwhile, enhanced coordination between the United Nations, DIS and the national police and gendarmerie contributed to an increase in police operations in eastern Chad.

In the Central African Republic, MINURCAT conducted extensive patrols of Birao and its vicinity to reassure the local population and assist the civilian authorities. The force also extended its radius and pro-

jected presence in Sam Ouandja, in the Haute-Kotto department. On 15 September, Operation Scorpion was launched in Sam Ouandja to provide security to World Food Programme operations, as well as for personnel of the Office of the United Nations High Commissioner for Refugees and of NGOs.

Humanitarian organizations continued to respond to the crisis in eastern Chad, providing aid to 254,000 Sudanese refugees in 12 camps, 70,000 Central African Republic refugees in 11 camps, and 171,000 internally displaced persons in 38 sites, as well as approximately 150,000 members of the host population affected by conflict. As the MINURCAT force expanded, its military activities contributed to the enhancement of a security umbrella and the development of a more integrated response to the security situation. However, criminality continued to constrain humanitarian space in eastern Chad. Since the beginning of the year, 192 attacks on humanitarians had been reported.

Security Council consideration. On 22 October [meeting 6204], the Assistant Secretary-General for Peacekeeping Operations, Mr. Mulet, briefed the Security Council on the situation in Chad, the Central African Republic and the subregion.

Further report of Secretary-General. In a later report [S/2010/217], the Secretary-General said that the security situation in the MINURCAT area of operations in north-eastern Central African Republic remained unstable. Two international NGO workers were kidnapped in Birao on 22 November. On 22 and 23 December, unidentified armed elements attacked Ouanda-Djalle and Sam Ouandja (200 kilometres south of Birao), forcing residents to flee. On 14 December MINURCAT deployed a military detachment to Sam Ouandja to deter violence against civilians.

MINURCAT supported the Government of Chad in its efforts to raise awareness about ending violence against women and children. The Government on 17 October launched a national sensitization campaign on the theme "Unite to End Violence against Women", with the support of the Mission. The campaign ran through December.

MINURCAT

The mandate of the United Nations Mission in the Central African Republic and Chad (MINURCAT), established by Security Council resolution 1778(2007) [YUN 2007, p. 153] to help create the security conditions for the return of refugees and displaced persons, and favourable conditions for reconstruction and development, was expanded in January by the Council in resolution 1861(2009) (see p. 154) to include activities related to the security and protection of civilians, human rights and the rule of law and regional peace support, as well as create a secure environment in the Central African Republic, extract civilians and humanitarian workers in danger and protect UN personnel and facilities.

Its authorized strength was 300 police officers, 25 military liaison officers and 5,200 military personnel, in addition to civilian personnel. Major General El-hadji Mouhamedou Kandji (Senegal) was appointed Force Commander in March, following the transfer of authority from EUFOR to MINURCAT.

MINURCAT financing

In February [A/63/727], the Secretary-General requested commitment authority for the period from 1 July 2008 to 30 June 2009 in the amount of $140,731,900, including $49,868,400 previously authorized by ACABQ, to facilitate the transfer of authority from EUFOR to the United Nations, in addition to the $301,124,200 already appropriated for MINURCAT for that period by Assembly resolution 62/223 B [YUN 2008, p. 168].

In March [A/63/768], ACABQ recommended that the Assembly authorize the Secretary-General to enter into commitment for the amount requested.

GENERAL ASSEMBLY ACTION

On 7 April [meeting 79], the General Assembly, on the recommendation of the Fifth Committee [A/63/788], adopted **resolution 63/274 A** without vote [agenda item 149].

Financing of the United Nations Mission in the Central African Republic and Chad

The General Assembly,

Having considered the note by the Secretary-General on the financing arrangements for the United Nations Mission in the Central African Republic and Chad for the period from 1 July 2008 to 30 June 2009 and the related report of the Advisory Committee on Administrative and Budgetary Questions,

Recalling Security Council resolution 1861(2009) of 14 January 2009, in which the Council extended the mandate of the Mission until 15 March 2010, authorized the deployment of a military component of the Mission to follow up the European Union-led military force in both Chad and the Central African Republic at the end of its mandate, decided that the transfer of authority between the European Union-led military force and the military component of the Mission would take place on 15 March 2009, and also decided that the Mission should include a maximum of 300 police officers, 25 military liaison officers, 5,200 military personnel, and an appropriate number of civilian personnel,

1. *Endorses* the conclusions and recommendations contained in the report of the Advisory Committee on Administrative and Budgetary Questions, subject to the provisions of the present resolution, and requests the Secretary-General to ensure their full implementation;

Budget estimates for the period from 1 July 2008 to 30 June 2009

2. *Authorizes* the Secretary-General to enter into commitments for the United Nations Mission in the Central African Republic and Chad for the period from 1 July 2008 to 30 June 2009 in a total amount not exceeding 139,671,300 United States dollars, inclusive of the amount of 49,868,400 dollars previously authorized by the Advisory Committee under the terms of section IV of General Assembly resolution 49/233 A of 23 December 1994, and in addition to the amount of 301,124,200 dollars already appropriated for the maintenance of the Mission for the period from 1 July 2008 to 30 June 2009 under the terms of Assembly resolution 62/233 B of 20 June 2008;

Financing of the commitment authority

3. *Decides* to apportion among Member States the amount of 139,671,300 dollars for the period from 1 July 2008 to 30 June 2009, in accordance with the levels updated in General Assembly resolution 61/243 of 22 December 2006, and taking into account the scale of assessments for 2008 and 2009, as set out in its resolution 61/237 of 22 December 2006;

4. *Also decides* to keep under review during its sixty-third session the item entitled "Financing of the United Nations Mission in the Central African Republic and Chad".

The Secretary-General also submitted the financial performance report for MINURCAT for the period from 1 July 2007 to 30 June 2008 [A/63/565], totalling expenditures of $165,183,700 and an unencumbered balance of $17,260,300. He also submitted the budget for MINURCAT [A/63/817] for the period from 1 July 2009 to 30 June 2010, in the amount of $768,190,100. ACABQ, in its conclusions and recommendations on both reports [A/63/746/Add.13], recommended that the unencumbered balance, as well as other adjustments, be credited to Member States as determined by the Assembly. The results of the costing of the proposed 2009–2010 budget would be communicated to the Assembly.

On 29 June [A/C.5/63/SR.50], the ACABQ Chairman recommended reductions for 2009–2010 amounting to $128,465,900.

GENERAL ASSEMBLY ACTION

On 30 June [meeting 93], the General Assembly, on the recommendation of the Fifth Committee [A/63/788/Add.1], adopted **resolution 63/274 B** without vote [agenda item 149].

The General Assembly,

Having considered the reports of the Secretary-General on the financing of the United Nations Mission in the Central African Republic and Chad, the related report of the Advisory Committee on Administrative and Budgetary Questions and the oral statement by the Chairman of the Advisory Committee on Administrative and Budgetary Questions,

Recalling Security Council resolution 1778(2007) of 25 September 2007, by which the Council established in Chad and the Central African Republic a multidimensional presence, including a United Nations Mission in the Central African Republic and Chad, and the subsequent resolutions by which the Council extended the mandate of the Mission, the latest of which was resolution 1861(2009) of 14 January 2009, by which the Council decided to extend the mandate of the Mission until 15 March 2010 and authorized the deployment of a military component of the Mission,

Recalling also its resolution 62/233 A of 22 December 2007 on the financing of the United Nations Mission in the Central African Republic and Chad and its subsequent resolutions thereon, the latest of which was resolution 63/274 A of 7 April 2009,

Reaffirming the general principles underlying the financing of United Nations peacekeeping operations, as stated in General Assembly resolutions 1874(S-IV) of 27 June 1963, 3101(XXVIII) of 11 December 1973 and 55/235 of 23 December 2000,

Mindful of the fact that it is essential to provide the Mission with the financial resources necessary to enable it to fulfil its responsibilities under the relevant resolutions of the Security Council,

Noting with appreciation that voluntary contributions have been made to the Mission,

1. _Requests_ the Secretary-General to entrust the Head of Mission with the task of formulating future budget proposals, in full accordance with the provisions of General Assembly resolutions 59/296 of 22 June 2005, 60/266 of 30 June 2006, 61/276 of 29 June 2007 and other relevant resolutions;

2. _Takes note_ of the status of contributions to the United Nations Mission in the Central African Republic and Chad as at 30 April 2009, including the contributions outstanding in the amount of 66.4 million United States dollars, representing some 14 per cent of the total assessed contributions, notes with concern that only thirty-eight Member States have paid their assessed contributions in full, and urges all other Member States, in particular those in arrears, to ensure payment of their outstanding assessed contributions;

3. _Expresses its appreciation_ to those Member States which have paid their assessed contributions in full, and urges all other Member States to make every possible effort to ensure payment of their assessed contributions to the Mission in full;

4. _Expresses concern_ at the financial situation with regard to peacekeeping activities, in particular as regards the reimbursements to troop contributors that bear additional burdens owing to overdue payments by Member States of their assessments;

5. _Also expresses concern_ at the delay experienced by the Secretary-General in deploying and providing adequate resources to some recent peacekeeping missions, in particular those in Africa;

6. _Emphasizes_ that all future and existing peacekeeping missions shall be given equal and non-discriminatory treatment in respect of financial and administrative arrangements;

7. _Also emphasizes_ that all peacekeeping missions shall be provided with adequate resources for the effective and efficient discharge of their respective mandates;

8. _Reiterates its request_ to the Secretary-General to make the fullest possible use of the facilities and equipment at the United Nations Logistics Base at Brindisi, Italy, in order to minimize the costs of procurement for the Mission;

9. _Acknowledges with appreciation_ that the use of the logistics hub at Entebbe, Uganda, has been cost-effective and has resulted in savings for the United Nations, and welcomes the expansion of the logistics hub to provide logistical support to peacekeeping operations in the region and to contribute further to their enhanced efficiency and responsiveness, taking into account ongoing efforts in this regard;

10. _Requests_ the Secretary-General to ensure that proposed peacekeeping budgets are based on the relevant legislative mandates;

11. _Endorses_ the conclusions and recommendations contained in the report of the Advisory Committee on Administrative and Budgetary Questions and the oral statement by the Chairman of the Advisory Committee, subject to the provisions of the present resolution, and requests the Secretary-General to ensure their full implementation;

12. _Takes note_ of paragraphs 24, 31, 44, 46, 49 and 60 of the report of the Advisory Committee;

13. _Decides_ to reclassify the post of Chief of Staff in the Office of the Special Representative of the Secretary-General from the D-1 to the D-2 level;

14. _Takes note_ of paragraph 41 of the report of the Advisory Committee, and recognizes that improvement of national airport infrastructure is the responsibility of the host country, where possible;

15. _Welcomes_ the dispatch of a Tiger Team to the Mission, which considerably expedited the recruitment of national and international staff, and requests the Secretary-General to continue his efforts in this regard;

16. _Commends_ the initiative of the Mission to prepare a water production and conservation policy, and requests the Secretary-General, in this regard, to ensure that lessons learned are shared with other operations in similar situations;

17. _Also commends_ the Mission for its efforts to assist in increasing the number of female officers in the Détachement intégré de sécurité, and requests the Secretary-General to ensure continued efforts in this regard;

18. _Reaffirms_ section XX of resolution 61/276, and encourages the United Nations Mission in the Central African Republic and Chad and other United Nations missions in the region to continue, where possible, the efforts to achieve greater synergies, while bearing in mind that individual missions are responsible for the preparation and implementation of their own budgets and for controlling their own assets and logistical operations;

19. _Requests_ the Secretary-General to ensure the full implementation of the relevant provisions of resolutions 59/296, 60/266 and 61/276;

20. _Also requests_ the Secretary-General to take all necessary action to ensure that the Mission is administered with a maximum of efficiency and economy;

21. _Further requests_ the Secretary-General, in order to reduce the cost of employing General Service staff, to con-

tinue efforts to recruit local staff for the Mission against General Service posts, commensurate with the requirements of the Mission;

Financial performance report for the period from 1 July 2007 to 30 June 2008

22. *Takes note* of the report of the Secretary-General on the financial performance of the Mission for the period from 1 July 2007 to 30 June 2008;

Budget estimates for the period from 1 July 2009 to 30 June 2010

23. *Decides* to appropriate to the Special Account for the United Nations Mission in the Central African Republic and Chad the amount of 721,167,400 dollars for the period from 1 July 2009 to 30 June 2010, inclusive of 690,753,100 dollars for the maintenance of the Mission, 25,312,100 dollars for the support account for peacekeeping operations and 5,102,200 dollars for the United Nations Logistics Base;

Financing of the appropriation

24. *Also decides* to apportion among Member States the amount of 509,857,584 dollars for the period from 1 July 2009 to 15 March 2010, in accordance with the levels updated in General Assembly resolution 61/243 of 22 December 2006, and taking into account the scale of assessments for 2009, as set out in its resolution 61/237 of 22 December 2006, and for 2010;

25. *Further decides* that, in accordance with the provisions of resolution 973(X) of 15 December 1955, there shall be set off against the apportionment among Member States, as provided for in paragraph 24 above, their respective share in the Tax Equalization Fund of the amount of 7,379,117 dollars, comprising the estimated staff assessment income of 5,160,026 dollars approved for the Mission, the prorated share of 1,862,981 dollars of the estimated staff assessment income approved for the support account and the prorated share of 356,110 dollars of the estimated staff assessment income approved for the United Nations Logistics Base;

26. *Decides* to apportion among Member States the amount of 211,309,816 dollars for the period from 16 March to 30 June 2010 at a monthly rate of 60,097,283 dollars, taking into account the scale of assessments for 2010, subject to a decision of the Security Council to extend the mandate of the Mission;

27. *Also decides* that, in accordance with the provisions of resolution 973(X), there shall be set off against the apportionment among Member States, as provided for in paragraph 26 above, their respective share in the Tax Equalization Fund of 3,058,283 dollars, comprising the estimated staff assessment income of 2,138,574 dollars approved for the Mission, the prorated share of 772,119 dollars of the estimated staff assessment income approved for the support account and the prorated share of 147,590 dollars of the estimated staff assessment income approved for the United Nations Logistics Base;

28. *Further decides* that, for Member States that have fulfilled their financial obligations to the Mission, there shall be set off against their apportionment, as provided for in paragraph 24 above, their respective share of the unencumbered balance and other income in the total amount of 18,647,300 dollars in respect of the financial period ended 30 June 2008, in accordance with the levels updated in General Assembly resolution 61/243, and taking into account the scale of assessments for 2008, as set out in its resolution 61/237;

29. *Decides* that, for Member States that have not fulfilled their financial obligations to the Mission, there shall be set off against their outstanding obligations their respective share of the unencumbered balance and other income in the total amount of 18,647,300 dollars in respect of the financial period ended 30 June 2008, in accordance with the scheme set out in paragraph 28 above;

30. *Also decides* that the decrease of 1,537,800 dollars in the estimated staff assessment income in respect of the financial period ended 30 June 2008 shall be set off against the credits from the amount of 18,647,300 dollars referred to in paragraphs 28 and 29 above;

31. *Emphasizes* that no peacekeeping mission shall be financed by borrowing funds from other active peacekeeping missions;

32. *Encourages* the Secretary-General to continue to take additional measures to ensure the safety and security of all personnel participating in the Mission under the auspices of the United Nations, bearing in mind paragraphs 5 and 6 of Security Council resolution 1502(2003) of 26 August 2003;

33. *Invites* voluntary contributions to the Mission in cash and in the form of services and supplies acceptable to the Secretary-General, to be administered, as appropriate, in accordance with the procedure and practices established by the General Assembly;

34. *Decides* to include in the provisional agenda of its sixty-fourth session the item entitled "Financing of the United Nations Mission in the Central African Republic and Chad".

In December [A/64/556], the Secretary-General submitted the performance report for MINURCAT for the period from 1 July 2008 to 30 June 2009, which showed expenditures of $424,073,000 and an unencumbered balance of $16,722,500.

The Assembly, by **decision 64/549** of 24 December, decided that the item on the financing of MINURCAT would remain for consideration during the Assembly's resumed sixty-fourth (2010) session.

Uganda

Security Council action. On 16 January, in consultations of the whole, the Council was briefed by the Under-Secretary-General for Humanitarian Affairs and Emergency Relief Coordinator, John Holmes, on the humanitarian consequences of the joint operation by the DRC, Uganda and the Sudan against the Lord's Resistance Army (LRA). The Council, in a press statement [SC/9576], condemned the attacks carried out by LRA resulting in over 500 dead and over 400 abducted, as well as the displacement of over 104,000 people. The Council expressed concern at the scale of those atrocities and emphasized that those responsible had to be brought to justice. It also expressed concern that the Council's previous calls for LRA to cease its attacks and recruitment and use of children, and to release all women, children and non-combatants, had not been heeded. The Council demanded that LRA cease all attacks on civilians and urged LRA to surrender, assemble and disarm, as required by the final peace agreement [YUN 2008, p. 169].

End of mandate of Special Envoy. On 26 May [S/2009/281], the Secretary-General informed the Security Council that his Special Envoy for the LRA-affected areas, Joaquim Alberto Chissano, had achieved the main objectives of his mandate [YUN 2006, p. 171]. Under his facilitation and the mediation of the Government of Southern Sudan, Uganda and LRA had concluded their negotiations with the signing of agreements on all substantive agenda items by March 2008 [YUN 2008, p. 169]. However, due to the failure of LRA leader Joseph Kony to honour his commitments, the Government of Uganda and LRA representatives were yet to sign the final peace agreement they had initialled. The Secretary-General agreed with the Special Envoy that the onus lay with Mr. Kony to sign the final peace agreement. The Secretary-General declared his intention to suspend the Special Envoy's assignment as at 30 June and to close on the same date the office in Kampala established to support his activities. The Special Envoy would attend on his behalf any ceremony arranged for the signing of the final peace agreement. On 29 May [S/2009/282], the Council took note of the Secretary-General's intention.

Security Council action. On 17 November, the Under-Secretary-General for Political Affairs, B. Lynn Pascoe, briefed the Council on the situation in the areas affected by LRA. He said that the problem posed by LRA could be solved only by a well-coordinated approach that included the countries in the region and the relevant UN peacekeeping missions. On the same day the Council, in a press statement [SC/9791], condemned the continuing attacks carried out by LRA in the Central African Republic, the Democratic Republic of the Congo and the Sudan, which had resulted in the death, abduction and displacement of thousands of civilians. The Council expressed concern at the threat that LRA posed to the civilian population, the conduct of humanitarian operations and regional stability. It commended the States in the region for their increased cooperation, welcomed their joint efforts to address the threat posed by LRA and encouraged them to cooperate with the United Nations and share information with UN operations in the region to ensure the protection of civilians, in particular women and children. The Council reiterated its demand that LRA cease all attacks on civilians and urged it to surrender, assemble and disarm, as required by the final peace agreement.

Children and armed conflict

In response to Security Council resolution 1612(2005) [YUN 2005, p. 863], the Secretary-General in September submitted a report [S/2009/462] on children and armed conflict in Uganda covering the period from December 2008 to June 2009. The Ugandan defence forces and its auxiliary forces, the local defence units, had been removed from the annexes to the Secretary-General's report on children and armed conflict [A/63/785-S/2009/158], which listed parties that recruited or used children in situations of armed conflict. That de-listing followed the signing in January 2009 of an action plan in line with Council resolutions 1539(2004) [YUN 2004, p. 787] and 1612(2005) between Uganda and the United Nations country-level task force on monitoring and reporting. The Secretary-General outlined the implementation of that action plan and the follow-up activities to the conclusions and recommendations of the Security Council Working Group on Children and Armed Conflict with regard to Uganda [YUN 2008, p. 852]. The Government had agreed that the task force on monitoring and reporting could carry out verification visits in facilities of the Ugandan defence forces in northern Uganda. A round of visits had been carried out and another was planned for later in the year. The report said that the cooperation with the Government had been effective and had allowed the United Nations and its partners to verify that no more children were present in the ranks of the Ugandan defence forces or its auxiliary forces, and that no cases of recruitment or use of children had been reported since August 2007.

The report showed that LRA remained very active in the region, despite the fact that no military activity had been reported on Ugandan territory since the signing of the Cessation of Hostilities Agreement in August 2006 [YUN 2006, p. 170]. Violent incidents of killing and maiming of children, abductions, recruitment and grave sexual violence were regularly reported in the Central African Republic, the DRC, and southern Sudan. The report emphasized the regional dimension of LRA activities and how United Nations actors and country-level task forces on monitoring and reporting were working on regional coordination for information-sharing, data collection and the repatriation of abducted children to their countries of origin.

The Secretary-General encouraged the Working Group to visit Uganda and the region to assess the impact of its work and to review the regional impact of violent LRA activities on children there. He urged LRA to engage with UN country teams in the region for the immediate release of all children associated with its forces, and asked his Special Representative for Children and Armed Conflict to devise an advocacy and contact group to effect that release. The

Secretary-General encouraged UN task forces on monitoring and reporting and UN missions in the region to report in a more coordinated manner on LRA abuses. He urged the Government of Uganda to prioritize the protection of children in its military actions against LRA elements, either on Ugandan territory or in joint operations in neighbouring countries.

On 12 October [S/AC.51/2010/1], the Working Group on Children and Armed Conflict welcomed the Secretary-General's report and its recommendations. It condemned all violations and abuses committed against children by LRA in contravention of international law, involving the recruitment and use of child soldiers, killing and maiming, rape and other sexual violence and abductions in the Central African Republic, the DRC, southern Sudan and Uganda. The Working Group would monitor compliance with Council resolutions until there was complete release of children associated with LRA and no more patterns of abuses against children.

Rwanda

In 2009, the United Nations continued the activities of the programme of information and outreach entitled "The Rwanda Genocide and the United Nations", established by General Assembly resolution 60/225 [YUN 2005, p. 216] "to mobilize civil society for Rwanda genocide victim remembrance and education in order to help prevent future acts of genocide". In December, the General Assembly adopted a resolution on assistance to survivors of the 1994 genocide, particularly orphans, widows and victims of sexual violence, and extended the mandate of the outreach programme.

Report of Secretary-General. In response to Assembly resolution 62/96 [YUN 2007, p. 163], the Secretary-General in August submitted a report [A/64/313] on assistance to survivors of the 1994 genocide in Rwanda, particularly orphans, widows and victims of sexual violence, which analysed the challenges to the delivery of relief and rehabilitation assistance by the United Nations and its partners to the survivors. According to the report, 15 years after those tragic events, the country was slowly recovering and on the path to a more promising future. Overall, Rwanda's economic performance continued to be on track. The Government had shown strong commitment to national reconciliation and consolidation of peace through demobilization and reintegration of ex-combatants. The democratization effort focused on a decentralized and inclusive administration representing all segments of the population, including marginalized communities, political parties and academia. As a result, remarkable progress had been made in peace and stability through the strengthening of democratic institutions and processes. How-

ever, Rwanda was confronted with many challenges in its pursuit of development, including high population density (368 persons per square kilometre), limited access of the population to safe water and energy, poor infrastructure, high reliance on subsistence and limited participation of the private sector in the economy. The genocide and the surge in HIV/AIDS cases had left Rwanda with one of the world's highest proportions of child-headed households. In education, the main challenge was to accommodate the increasing number of primary school pupils while improving quality. Access to economic and social services by genocide survivors remained limited, as evidenced by the low school enrolment rate of the children of genocide survivors. Most of the survivors' families lacked access to adequate housing and safe water, and suffered from discrimination in accessing bank credit as well as economic opportunities. The Ubudehe programme, a governmental programme of collective action that enforced the tradition of mutual assistance to create income-generating opportunities, was not effectively addressing those challenges. Moreover, the right to security of the genocide survivors was threatened and there was a lingering genocide ideology. To address those challenges, the Government, with the support of the donor community and the United Nations, was striving to sustain achievements made in the social sectors in the past 15 years. Efforts were being made to modernize the agriculture sector by introducing irrigation systems, to invest in infrastructure and human capacity in order to create a climate conducive to investment, and to capitalize on opportunities offered by the East African Community, which Rwanda had recently joined. The Government was trying to revise and streamline investment regulations to create additional stimuli for private-sector development. The Government continued to implement an ambitious reform programme for poverty reduction. The UN country team had developed a programme aimed at addressing access to economic and social rights by genocide survivors and at enhancing their political participation.

The Secretary-General observed that, despite the remarkable progress in peace and stability made by Rwanda since 1994, which had translated into improved economic performance, the country still faced enormous challenges to sustain those gains. Continued UN support in priority areas to consolidate democratic governance and improve productivity was critical. The second United Nations Development Assistance Framework (2008–2012), which was the basic reference for UN system support, focused on governance, health, education, environment and natural resources management, sustainable growth and social protection. Supporting groups to build sustainable micro-, small and medium enterprises and other income-generating activities through capacity-building, microcredit and access to markets remained a priority for self-sufficiency and poverty alleviation. Support to special initiatives to address the needs of those who had experienced physical injuries that had resulted in mental or physical disabilities was critical, as was support for ageing genocide survivors.

GENERAL ASSEMBLY ACTION

On 22 December [meeting 67], the General Assembly adopted **resolution 64/226** [draft: A/64/L.40 & Add.1] without vote [agenda item 71].

Assistance to survivors of the 1994 genocide in Rwanda, particularly orphans, widows and victims of sexual violence

The General Assembly,

Guided by the Charter of the United Nations and the Universal Declaration of Human Rights,

Recalling the findings and recommendations of the independent inquiry commissioned by the Secretary-General, with the approval of the Security Council, into the actions of the United Nations during the 1994 genocide in Rwanda,

Recalling also the 2005 World Summit Outcome, particularly its recognition that all individuals, in particular vulnerable people, are entitled to freedom from fear and freedom from want, with an equal opportunity to enjoy all their rights and fully develop their human potential,

Recalling further its resolution 59/137 of 10 December 2004, in which it requested the Secretary-General to encourage relevant agencies, funds and programmes of the United Nations system to continue to work with the Government of Rwanda to develop and implement programmes aimed at supporting vulnerable groups that continue to suffer from the effects of the 1994 genocide,

Welcoming the report of the Secretary-General,

Recalling its resolution 60/225 of 23 December 2005, in which it urged Member States to develop educational programmes on the lessons of the genocide in Rwanda, and also requested the Secretary-General to establish a programme of outreach for Rwanda genocide victim remembrance and education, in order to prevent future acts of genocide,

Recognizing the numerous difficulties faced by survivors of the 1994 genocide in Rwanda, particularly the orphans, widows and victims of sexual violence, who are poorer and more vulnerable as a result of the genocide, especially the many victims of sexual violence who have contracted HIV and have since either died or become seriously ill with AIDS,

Recognizing also Security Council resolution 1503(2003) of 28 August 2003, in which the Council called upon the International Criminal Tribunal for Rwanda to take all possible measures to complete all trial activities by the end of 2008 and all of its work in 2010,

Firmly convinced of the necessity of restoring the dignity of the survivors of the 1994 genocide in Rwanda, which would help to promote reconciliation and healing in Rwanda,

Commending the tremendous efforts of the Government and people of Rwanda and civil society organizations, as well as international efforts, to provide support for restoring the dignity of the survivors, including the allocation by the Government of Rwanda of 5 per cent of its national budget every year to support genocide survivors and the Diaspora One Dollar Campaign for Genocide Survivors,

1. *Requests* the Secretary-General to continue to encourage the relevant agencies, funds and programmes of the United Nations system to implement resolution 59/137 expeditiously, inter alia, by providing assistance in the areas of education for orphans, medical care and treatment for victims of sexual violence, including HIV-positive victims, trauma and psychological counselling, and skills training and microcredit programmes aimed at promoting self-sufficiency and alleviating poverty;

2. *Calls upon* Member States and the United Nations system to urgently implement the conclusions and recommendations contained in the report of the Secretary-General;

3. *Requests* the Secretary-General to continue the activities of the programme of outreach entitled "The Rwanda Genocide and the United Nations" aimed at Rwanda genocide victim remembrance and education, in order to help to prevent future acts of genocide;

4. *Notes* the importance of residual issues, including witness protection and victim support, the archives of the International Criminal Tribunal for Rwanda and judicial issues and capacity-building for the Rwandan judiciary, and underlines the need for increased and sustained attention to these issues;

5. *Requests* the Secretary-General, in consultation with the Government of Rwanda, to encourage the relevant agencies, funds and programmes of the United Nations system to take appropriate steps to support, in particular, efforts to enhance judicial capacity-building and victim support in Rwanda;

6. *Also requests* the Secretary-General, in view of the critical situation of the survivors of the 1994 genocide in Rwanda and the International Criminal Tribunal for Rwanda completion strategy, to take all necessary and practicable measures for the implementation of the present resolution and to report thereon to the General Assembly, at its sixty-sixth session, with concrete recommendations on support for survivors of the Rwandan genocide of 1994;

7. *Decides* to include in the provisional agenda of its sixty-sixth session the item entitled "Assistance to survivors of the 1994 genocide in Rwanda, particularly orphans, widows and victims of sexual violence".

West Africa

Regional issues

Peace and security situation in West Africa

Report of Secretary-General (June). Responding to the Security Council's request to report on the fulfilment of the revised mandate of the United Nations Office for West Africa (UNOWA) every six months [YUN 2007, p. 168], the Secretary-General in June submitted a report [S/2009/332] covering the period from 1 January to 30 June 2009 and following up on his previous report [YUN 2008, p. 173]. The overall peace and security situation in West Africa continued to improve, despite some debilitating factors, including food insecurity and the global financial crisis. Among issues addressed by UNOWA, governance and the rule of law remained fragile, and security threats increased, including organized crime, terrorist activities and climate change. West African economies continued to grow, albeit at a slower pace. Wealth generally remained concentrated within a small number of individuals, while living conditions for the majority were rapidly deteriorating. Gains in the economy were countered in part by the global financial crisis. Among its effects was a significant reduction in remittances from West African migrant workers. Remittances received in Guinea-Bissau in 2008 were 18 per cent lower than in 2007; in Senegal, the International Monetary Fund (IMF) forecasted a 28 per cent decline in remittances in 2009. Widespread poverty, rapid urbanization, high rates of population growth and overdependence on rain-fed agriculture contributed to food insecurity. Epidemics posed a challenge in the region, which was facing the worst meningitis epidemic recorded in the past five years. Drug trafficking and cross-border organized crime remained threats to security; however, growing international engagement was beginning to yield results, including a decline in seizures of narcotics. Threats to security in the Gulf of Guinea included human smuggling, oil bunkering, proliferation of small arms and light weapons, piracy, and terrorist activities in the Sahel, in particular activities of criminal networks and terrorist groups related to Al-Qaida.

Progress in democratization was noted in transparent, free and fair elections, as in Mali and Senegal. Nevertheless, the resurgence of unconstitutional changes of Government was a concern, as expressed by the Security Council in its statement S/PRST/2009/11 (see p. 104); that was compounded by the impunity of perpetrators in the military and security establishment. Most unconstitutional or violent changes of government in early 2009 occurred in the subregion.

Despite some positive developments, the Secretary-General remained concerned by the continued fragility of the progress made. Continued engagement of financial and development institutions was needed to mitigate the adverse effects of the decline in economic growth and other destabilizing factors. Despite advances in governance and rule of law, the subregion was confronted with many setbacks. Efforts of regional and subregional organizations, notably the African Union (AU) and the Economic Community of West African States (ECOWAS), to reject and prevent unconstitutional changes of government deserved

support. UNOWA's role had proved useful in building synergies among UN bodies and in providing a forum for West Africans to define their goals within the overall objective of supporting peace and stability in the subregion. ECOWAS and the Mano River Union were endeavouring to address vulnerabilities and UNOWA would maintain its close working relationship with them, in particular in the areas of good governance, human security, human rights, gender and the rule of law. It would also continue to address the scourge of drug trafficking and organized crime. UNOWA could further facilitate ongoing efforts if strengthened with a small police capacity with specialist expertise.

Security Council consideration. On 21 January [meeting 6073] and 7 July [meeting 6157], the Security Council considered the issue of peace consolidation in West Africa and the related reports of the Secretary-General.

SECURITY COUNCIL ACTION

On 10 July [meeting 6160], following consultations among Security Council members, the President made statement **S/PRST/2009/20** on behalf of the Council:

The Security Council notes with satisfaction continued progress in the overall peace and security situation in West Africa. The Council especially welcomes positive developments in the areas of post-conflict recovery and peacebuilding, as well as improvements in governance and the rule of law.

The Council, however, notes with deep concern the resurgence of unconstitutional changes of government and undemocratic seizures of power and, recalling the statement by its President of 5 May 2009, stresses again the importance of expeditiously restoring constitutional order, including through open and transparent elections.

The Council reiterates its primary responsibility for the maintenance of international peace and security and recalls that cooperation with regional and subregional organizations, consistent with Chapter VIII of the Charter of the United Nations, can improve collective security.

The Council welcomes the continuing important efforts of the Economic Community of West African States, in synergy with the African Union, the United Nations and the wider international community, consistent with Council resolutions and decisions, to settle conflicts and promote human rights, democracy, the rule of law and constitutional order in West Africa.

The Council also expresses its concern over the fact that the progress achieved remains fragile. The Council is concerned, in particular, by growing or emerging threats to security in West Africa, notably terrorist activities in the Sahel band, maritime insecurity in the Gulf of Guinea and illicit drug trafficking, which pose a threat to regional stability with possible impact on international security.

The Council reaffirms the importance of addressing illicit drug trafficking and criminal activities by an approach of shared responsibility, and encourages the efforts by West African States to combat illicit drug trafficking and organized crime, especially through the Economic Community of West African States regional action plan on illicit drug trafficking and organized crime. The Council welcomes West African States' continued leadership in implementing the regional action plan and the role of the United Nations Office for West Africa in support of the implementation of the regional action plan, and takes note of the proposal to strengthen its capacity.

The Council also commends the joint action of the United Nations Office on Drugs and Crime, the United Nations Office for West Africa, the Department of Peacekeeping Operations and the Department of Political Affairs of the Secretariat and the International Criminal Police Organization (INTERPOL) to help to implement the Economic Community of West African States regional plan of action on illicit drug trafficking and organized crime, and underlines the importance of their continuing to strengthen their partnership on these issues. It also commends national and international partners, such as the European Union, for their support to the Economic Community of West African States in the fight against drug trafficking in West Africa.

The Council stresses the importance of taking into account a comprehensive strategy of conflict resolution and crisis prevention while addressing cross-border issues and regional challenges. The Council supports the regional efforts to curb the proliferation of small arms and light weapons and to achieve security sector reform.

The Council expresses its concern at the impact of the global economic crisis on West African economies, since the region is already confronted with development challenges such as rising food insecurity, climate change adaptation and mitigation, and youth unemployment. The Council encourages the continued engagement of financial institutions and development partners to mitigate the adverse effects of the decline in economic growth and other destabilizing factors in West Africa.

The Council recognizes and commends the important role played by the Special Representative of the Secretary-General for West Africa and the United Nations Office for West Africa in promoting and strengthening a regional and integrated approach to cross-border issues, as well as helping to consolidate peace and security, democracy and the rule of law, and requests the Secretary-General, through his Special Representative, to continue to develop further the active cooperation existing between the United Nations and regional and subregional organizations.

Report of Secretary-General (December). In a December report [S/2009/682] covering the second half of 2009, the Secretary-General said that West Africa had continued to make progress in a number of areas, but challenges such as climate change, criminal activities, weaknesses in governance and in managing the security sector undermined progress. A number of countries continued to face political crises, and some economic and humanitarian challenges had escalated. Floods had directly affected 800,000 people and resulted in 195 deaths. Drought, coastal erosion and the spread of tropical and vector-borne diseases, includ-

ing the outbreak of dengue fever in Cape Verde that affected more than 20,000 people, were also effects of climate change. Food insecurity and malnutrition persisted: despite some assistance, 16.9 million children were suffering from chronic malnutrition and more than 5 million from acute malnutrition. Drought and flooding had affected food production. On 4 December, the relief community launched in Dakar the 2010 Consolidated Humanitarian Appeal for West Africa, the sixth regional humanitarian appeal since 2003, for $368 million.

With support from the United Nations and the international community, ECOWAS made progress in tackling drug trafficking and organized crime, starting with the recruitment of a special adviser on drugs and crime. The discovery of clandestine laboratories and seizures of cocaine and ecstasy processing equipment in the subregion showed that drug cartels were not only using West Africa as a transit point, but might be developing on-site capacities for narcotics production. The recent discovery of a cargo plane in northern Mali suspected of having carried narcotics was an indication of destabilizing trends.

Difficulties remained in the area of governance, with a number of West African countries affected by political crises resulting from contested electoral process or unconstitutional changes of government. Preparations for the presidential election in Togo, scheduled for February 2010, were marred by disputes between the political parties over the electoral process. The political and constitutional crisis in Niger undermined the progress achieved in democratic governance and rule of law. In Côte d'Ivoire, the election date for November 2009 was missed. The political situation in Guinea deteriorated in late 2009 with gross violations of human rights. The Secretary-General's Special Representative would continue to use his good offices to mobilize support for maintaining constitutional order and the rule of law.

UNOWA

Activities

During the year, UNOWA activities, covered in the Secretary-General's reports [S/2009/39, S/2009/682], focused on building synergies among UN entities in the subregion; cooperating with regional and subregional partners; restoring democratic rule and the rule of law in countries where governance was under threat; assisting countries in cross-border issues including drug trafficking, organized crime, cross-border security and the security situation in the Sahel; promoting youth unemployment, human rights and gender equality; and assisting the Cameroon-Nigeria Mixed Commission (see p. 226).

The Office, headed by the Secretary-General's Special Representative for West Africa, Said Djinnit, organized meetings of heads of UN agencies in Dakar, Senegal, on 9 January and 23 April to exchange information on political and security issues, including food security, the impact of the global financial crisis, specific countries of concern (Guinea-Bissau, Guinea, Mauritania, Togo) and other matters, such as aviation safety. UNOWA collaborated with regional and subregional partners, in particular ECOWAS and the AU, in dealing with crisis situations. It engaged in international efforts aimed at restoring democratic rule in countries that had undergone military coups or where democratic processes were under threat; in particular, it supported efforts to create conditions conducive to the holding of elections in Côte d'Ivoire, Guinea, Guinea-Bissau, Mauritania, Niger and Togo.

On 20 and 21 July, the Secretary-General's Special Representative, the President of the ECOWAS Commission and the AU Special Envoy undertook a mission to Niger to consult with national stakeholders and to express concern over the constitutional crisis in the country. The mission expressed concern about President Mamadou Tandja's unilateral agenda, including his initiative to hold a constitutional referendum and plans to complete major development projects. The referendum was held on 4 August, endorsing the President's proposals. UNOWA also closely monitored the evolving situation in Togo, including preparations for the February 2010 presidential election and the recommendations of the workshop on the role of the security sector in electoral processes (Lomé, 12 May), in consultation with the Mediator for Togo, Burkina Faso's President Blaise Compaoré, ECOWAS, Togolese stakeholders and the UN country team. From 7 to 15 September, a UN electoral needs assessment mission was dispatched to Lomé to assess the pre-electoral environment and make recommendations for possible UN assistance in organizing the election. The opposition raised concerns about the process, specifically the revision of the voters' list, the need for two rounds of voting rather than one as planned, the method chosen to secure voting ballots, and access to State media. UNOWA consulted with ECOWAS and the UN country team on the establishment of a local mechanism for mediation to assist in building trust among Togolese stakeholders during the electoral process.

UNOWA held a consultative meeting on 2 September with UN regional offices and other UN entities based in Dakar to review the situations in those countries, in particular as they related to unconstitutional changes of government, the security sector, drug trafficking and organized crime. In efforts to combat drug trafficking and organized crime, UNOWA enhanced cooperation with the United Nations Office on Drugs and Crime (UNODC), supporting ECOWAS in the implementation of its regional action plan on drug trafficking, and seeking to strengthen its own capacity to play a role in combating the scourge. With UNODC guidance, the West Africa Coast Initiative, aimed at establishing transnational crime units in four pilot countries (Côte d'Ivoire, Guinea-Bissau, Liberia, Sierra Leone), was launched to strengthen national law enforcement and intelligence-gathering capacities.

In the area of security and defence, UNOWA participated in a seminar on terrorism (Abidjan, 6–9 February) and gave presentations on the United Nations and terrorism, security threats, bomb alerts and demining. The seventeenth high-level meeting of heads of UN peace missions in West Africa, organized by UNOWA (Dakar, 27 October), reviewed developments in the subregion, with emphasis on the situation in Guinea and its cross-border implications. The Office followed developments and liaised with international partners on the security situation in the Sahel, in particular activities of criminal networks and terrorist groups related to Al-Qaida, especially in the light of the abduction of the Secretary-General's Special Envoy for Niger, Robert Fowler, and others. On 12 and 13 March, the Secretary-General's Special Representative held discussions in Niamey with Niger officials on the upcoming local, legislative and presidential elections and the situation in the northern part of the country. UNOWA facilitated the establishment on 28 and 29 April of a subregional working group on women, peace and security which adopted its terms of reference and a workplan for 2009–2010 and organized a workshop on the issue (Abidjan, 26–28 July). In addition, the Office: convened an expert meeting on political crises and human rights in West Africa (19–21 October); co-organized the launching of the campaign to end violence against women (November); held a training-of-trainers session in human rights-based approaches to programming for representatives of UN country teams in West Africa (1–5 December); and convened a meeting of senior officers from UN peace missions and other offices on enhancing the exchange of information and identifying possible joint action for 2010 to strengthen peace and security in the subregion (6–7 December).

Financing

In a report issued in October [A/64/349/Add.3] dealing with estimated requirements for special political missions grouped under thematic cluster III (UN offices, peacebuilding offices, integrated offices and commissions), the Secretary-General proposed resource requirements for UNOWA in the amount of $6,966,100 for 2010, which ACABQ recommended for approval [A/64/7/Add.13].

On 24 December, in section VI of **resolution 64/245** (see p. 1407), the General Assembly endorsed the recommendations of ACABQ and approved the budgets for the 26 special political missions, including UNOWA, under section 3, Political affairs, of the proposed programme budget for the biennium 2010–2011.

Côte d'Ivoire

In 2009, the United Nations, in cooperation with the Economic Community of West African States (ECOWAS), the African Union (AU) and the international community, continued to support Government efforts to move the peace process forward in Côte d'Ivoire through implementation of the 2007 Ouagadougou Political Agreement and its supplementary accords [YUN 2007, pp. 174 & 184]. The United Nations Operation in Côte d'Ivoire (UNOCI) worked with the Government in efforts to organize presidential elections postponed in 2008 to 29 November 2009 and provided logistical support to the Independent Electoral Commission. Substantial progress was made in identification of voters and other election-related tasks provided for in the Agreement, including the publication of the provisional electoral list, the launch of the appeals process concerning the list, and the validation of candidates for the presidential election. However, on 11 November, the Commission announced that the first round of the presidential election would be postponed again as a result of delays incurred in preparing and publishing the provisional electoral list. It also announced a timeline for further stages of preparations for the election, which was scheduled for February/March 2010. Despite the postponement, the electoral process remained on track and preparations continued.

Progress in implementing the fourth supplementary agreement to the Ouagadougou Agreement—which related to disarmament, reunification of defence and security forces, restoration of State authority to all areas of the country and reunification of the treasury—remained limited. However, in November President Laurent Gbagbo signed several decrees related to the reunification of the defence and security forces, which were expected to contribute to enhancing the security of the electoral process.

The Panel of Experts continued to monitor implementation of the arms, travel and diamond sanctions imposed on Côte d'Ivoire. In October, the Security Council renewed those sanctions through 2010.

Political and security developments

In 2009, the United Nations sought further implementation of the 2007 Ouagadougou Political Agreement, its supplementary agreements and resolution 1721(2006) [YUN 2006, p. 197], which provided a road map for the transition period leading to elections. The lifting of the Green Line, which replaced the zone of confidence that had separated troops of the National Armed Forces of Côte d'Ivoire—deployed by the Government in the south of the country—from those of the rebel movement known as Forces nouvelles—remained in effect under the control of the Integrated Command Centre (CCI) [YUN 2007, pp. 175 & 182], a joint force established to merge the national defence and security forces and the Forces nouvelles and to implement the military and security aspects of the Agreement. UNOCI, with a force of some 8,000 troops at the beginning of the year, carried out its revised mandate [YUN 2007, p. 170], with the support of the French Licorne forces.

The overall security situation remained generally stable and the freedom of movement of people, goods and services throughout the country contributed to improving the security situation. Other factors, however, such as the existence of armed militias and violent youth groups, the incomplete cantonment of former combatants of the Forces nouvelles, the inability of the Government to pay all expected allowances for former combatants, and the continued control by the Forces nouvelles commanders of local administration in the north, contributed to the fragility of the situation.

Report of Secretary-General (January). The Secretary-General, in a January report on UNOCI [S/2009/21] submitted pursuant to Council resolution 1826(2008) [YUN 2008, p. 184], said that progress in regrouping and demobilizing former combatants of the Forces nouvelles and in dismantling militias had been slow. The fourth supplementary agreement to the Ouagadougou Agreement, signed in December 2008 [YUN 2008, p. 189], provided for the disarmament of Forces nouvelles former combatants and pro-Government militias at least two months before elections, with payment of a demobilization package to those declared eligible by CCI, but the institutions in charge of reintegrating former combatants and militias faced financial and logistical constraints. State administration was not fully functional in the north, owing to the reluctance of Force nouvelles commanders to relinquish control. All parties remained committed to hold elections as early as possible in 2009. They stressed the need to ensure that the necessary conditions for a credible and transparent electoral process were met before determining a date for the presidential election. UNOCI was ready to assist the Independent Electoral Commission in developing an integrated master plan for conducting elections and to provide technical and logistical assistance to the Commission and those involved in the electoral process. UNOCI and the UN assessment mission sent to Côte d'Ivoire in December 2008 agreed that the UNOCI force could be reduced to 7,450 troop personnel and that it should be positioned in fewer but more concentrated positions. It also proposed benchmarks for a more substantial drawdown of the force following successful elections: completion of disarmament, demobilization and reintegration of former combatants and dismantling of militias; security sector reform; and restoration of State authority throughout the country. The mission noted that most of the key processes under the Agreement, including the electoral process, remained plagued by funding gaps, and that this jeopardized the progress made.

Significant progress had been made in implementing the Agreement, the Secretary-General said, but much remained to be done. To safeguard the gains achieved by the parties, it would be necessary to address the technical and logistical delays that led to the postponement of the presidential elections previously scheduled for November 2008, and he called on the Independent Electoral Commission to set a new realistic electoral timetable. Considering the developments in the country, he recommended that the UNOCI mandate be extended for six months, until 31 July 2009, that its troop level be reduced by one battalion (from 8,115 to 7,450 troop personnel) and that the force's posture and configuration be adjusted.

SECURITY COUNCIL ACTION

On 27 January [meeting 6076], the Security Council unanimously adopted **resolution 1865(2009)**. The draft [S/2009/49] was submitted by France.

The Security Council,

Recalling its previous resolutions, in particular resolutions 1739(2007) of 10 January 2007, 1765(2007) of 16 July 2007, 1795(2008) of 15 January 2008, 1826(2008) of 29 July 2008 and 1842(2008) of 29 October 2008 relating to the situation in Côte d'Ivoire, and resolution 1836(2008) of 29 September 2008 on the situation in Liberia,

Recalling also the statements by its President relating to the situation in Côte d'Ivoire and in particular that, in the statement of 7 November 2008, it noted that the delays that had occurred since the launch of the identification and voter registration processes had proven greater than expected and expressed its deep concern about a possible third consecutive delay of the presidential elections since the signing of the Ouagadougou Political Agreement,

Reaffirming its strong commitment to the sovereignty, independence, territorial integrity and unity of Côte d'Ivoire, and recalling the importance of the principles of good-neighbourliness, non-interference and regional cooperation,

Recalling that it endorsed the Ouagadougou Political Agreement, signed by President Laurent Gbagbo and Mr. Guillaume Soro in Ouagadougou on 4 March 2007, and the first three supplementary agreements, as recommended by the African Union,

Expressing again its appreciation to President Blaise Compaoré of Burkina Faso ("the Facilitator") for his continued efforts to support the peace process in Côte d'Ivoire, in particular through the follow-up mechanisms of the Ouagadougou Political Agreement, commending and encouraging the continued efforts of the African Union and the Economic Community of West African States to promote peace and stability in Côte d'Ivoire, and reiterating its full support for them,

Stressing again the importance of the international consultative organ participating in the meetings of the Evaluation and Monitoring Committee, as an observer,

Reiterating its strong condemnation of any attempt to destabilize the peace process by force, and expressing its intention to examine without delay the situation after any such attempt, on the basis of a report by the Secretary-General,

Having taken note of the report of the Secretary-General of 8 January 2009,

Recalling its resolution 1674(2006) of 28 April 2006 on the protection of civilians in armed conflict, and condemning all violations of international humanitarian law,

Noting with concern, in spite of the sustained improvement in the overall human rights situation, the persistence of cases of human rights violations against civilians in different parts of the country, including numerous acts of sexual violence, stressing that the perpetrators must be brought to justice, and reiterating its firm condemnation of all violations of human rights and international humanitarian law in Côte d'Ivoire,

Recalling its resolution 1612(2005) of 26 July 2005 on children and armed conflict and the subsequent conclusions of the Security Council Working Group on Children and Armed Conflict pertaining to parties to the armed conflict in Côte d'Ivoire, and expressing its deep concern that children continue to suffer from various forms of violence,

Recalling also its resolutions 1325(2000) of 31 October 2000 and 1820(2008) of 19 June 2008 on women and peace and security, condemning any sexual violence, stressing again the importance of the equal participation and full involvement of women in all efforts for the maintenance of peace and promotion of peace and security and the need to increase their role in decision-making with regard to conflict prevention and resolution, and encouraging the Secretary-General to mainstream a gender perspective in the implementation of the mandate of the United Nations Operation in Côte d'Ivoire,

Emphasizing the importance of the continuing support of the United Nations system and the international community for strengthening the capacity of the Government of Côte d'Ivoire and of the electoral bodies to organize the electoral process,

Determining that the situation in Côte d'Ivoire continues to pose a threat to international peace and security in the region,

Acting under Chapter VII of the Charter of the United Nations,

Supporting the Ouagadougou political process

1.   *Welcomes* the progress of the operations of identification of the population and of registration of voters, and calls upon the Ivorian parties to continue to take immediately and as a priority the concrete steps necessary to complete these operations before the end of February 2009;

2. *Notes with deep concern* that the presidential elections scheduled for 30 November 2008 have been postponed, pursuant to the communiqué of 10 November 2008 of the Permanent Consultative Framework established by the Ouagadougou Political Agreement;

3. *Urges* the Ivorian political actors to find without delay an agreement on a new and realistic time frame leading quickly to free, open, fair and transparent elections, recalls that this time frame should elaborate some key stages, such as the publication of the provisional and final versions of the electoral list, the production and distribution of identity and voter cards and the date of the presidential elections, and again urges the President of the Independent Electoral Commission to share publicly such a timeline, as requested in the statement by the President of the Security Council of 7 November 2008 and pursuant to the communiqué of the Permanent Consultative Framework mentioned in paragraph 2 above;

4. *Expresses its intention*, in this regard, to examine as soon as possible the new time frame referred to in paragraph 3 above, which will bind the Ivorian political actors and reflect their level of political commitment towards free, open, fair and transparent elections, and reiterates its determination to bring its full support to a credible electoral process in Côte d'Ivoire;

5. *Encourages* the Government of Côte d'Ivoire to make available to the Ivorian institutions involved in the electoral process the necessary resources, and encourages the international community to continue their support to the electoral process, including by providing, with the agreement of the Ivorian authorities, electoral observation capacity and related technical assistance;

6. *Welcomes* the signing on 22 December 2008 by President Laurent Gbagbo and Mr. Guillaume Soro, under the facilitation of President Blaise Compaoré of Burkina Faso, of the fourth supplementary agreement to the Ouagadougou Political Agreement;

7. *Takes note* of the delays that have occurred in the implementation of the fourth supplementary agreement referred to in paragraph 6 above, and urges the Ivorian parties, pursuant to this agreement, to make progress, including in order to create a secure environment for the holding of elections, in the disarmament and dismantling of militias, the cantonment and disarmament, demobilization and reintegration programme, the unification and restructuring of the defence and security forces and the restoration of State authority throughout the country;

8. *Urges* the Ivorian parties to implement the processes mentioned in paragraph 7 above in accordance with internationally agreed standards, and calls upon the international donors to continue to provide their support to them, as appropriate;

9. *Recalls* that it is fully prepared to impose targeted measures pursuant to paragraph 16 of resolution 1842(2008), including against persons who are determined to be a threat to the peace and national reconciliation process in Côte d'Ivoire, and recalls further that, pursuant to paragraph 6 of the above-mentioned resolution, any threat to the electoral process in Côte d'Ivoire, in particular any attack or obstruction of the action of the Independent Electoral Commission in charge of the organization of the elections or the action of the operators mentioned in para-graphs 1.3.3 and 2.1.1 of the Ouagadougou Political Agreement, shall constitute a threat to the peace and national reconciliation process for the purposes of paragraph 9 and 11 of resolution 1572(2004) of 15 November 2004;

10. *Again urges* the political parties to comply fully with the Code of Good Conduct for Elections which they signed under the auspices of the Secretary-General, and, in particular, urges the Ivorian authorities to allow equitable access to public media;

11. *Calls upon* all parties concerned to ensure that the protection of women and children is addressed in the implementation of the Ouagadougou Political Agreement as well as in the post-conflict reconstruction and recovery phases, including continued monitoring and reporting of the situation of women and children, and that all reported abuses are investigated and those responsible brought to justice;

12. *Calls upon* all Ivorian parties to take appropriate measures to refrain from, prevent and protect civilians from all forms of sexual violence, which could include enforcing appropriate military disciplinary measures, upholding the principle of command responsibility, and training troops on the categorical prohibition of all forms of sexual violence;

13. *Stresses* the importance of an inclusive participation of Ivorian civil society in the electoral process of ensuring equal protection of and respect for the human rights of every Ivorian as they relate to the electoral system, and, in particular, of removing obstacles and challenges to women's participation and full involvement in public life;

14. *Urges* the signatories to the Ouagadougou Political Agreement to take the steps necessary to protect vulnerable civilian populations, including by guaranteeing the voluntary return, reinstallation, reintegration and security of displaced persons, with the support of the United Nations system, and to fulfil in this regard their commitments in accordance with the Agreement and their obligations under international humanitarian law;

Renewing the mandates of the United Nations Operation in Côte d'Ivoire and of the French forces supporting it

15. *Decides* to renew the mandates of the United Nations Operation in Côte d'Ivoire and of the French forces supporting it, as determined in resolution 1739(2007), until 31 July 2009, in particular to support the organization in Côte d'Ivoire of free, open, fair and transparent elections;

16. *Endorses* the recommendations contained in paragraphs 46 and 61 of the report of the Secretary-General of 8 January 2009, and decides to reduce the level of authorized military personnel from 8,115 to 7,450;

17. *Requests* the United Nations Operation in Côte d'Ivoire, within its existing resources, to support actively the full implementation of the Ouagadougou Political Agreement and its supplementary agreements, including the fourth supplementary agreement, and, in particular, to continue to contribute to bringing the security needed by the peace process, including by supporting the disarmament, demobilization and reintegration programme and the disarmament and dismantling of militias, and by the electoral process, and to provide technical and logistical support to the Independent Electoral Commission for the preparation and the holding of the elections;

18. *Endorses*, to this end, taking into consideration the progress achieved by the Ivorian parties in the implementation of the peace process and of the electoral process, as well as the remaining challenges, the recommendations on the posture and configuration of the United Nations Operation in Côte d'Ivoire contained in paragraphs 48 to 54 and in paragraph 61 of the report of the Secretary-General of 8 January 2009;

19. *Also endorses* the benchmarks proposed by the Secretary-General in paragraph 47 of his report of 8 January 2009 for a possible further drawdown, requests the Secretary-General to monitor progress on their achievement, encourages him to continue to refine and update these benchmarks and to report to the Council, and expresses its intention to review these benchmarks before 31 July 2009;

20. *Reiterates its full support* for the efforts of the Special Representative of the Secretary-General for Côte d'Ivoire, recalls that he shall certify that all stages of the electoral process provide all the necessary guarantees for the holding of open, free, fair and transparent presidential and legislative elections in accordance with international standards, requests the United Nations Operation in Côte d'Ivoire to continue to sensitize actively the Ivorian population to this certification role, and reaffirms its support to the five-criteria framework elaborated by the Special Representative and referred to in the report of the Secretary-General of 15 April 2008;

21. *Recalls* that the publication of the electoral list is a crucial step in the electoral process, calls upon the Independent Electoral Commission, the technical operators, the authorities of Côte d'Ivoire and the political parties to redouble their efforts in this regard, and requests the Special Representative of the Secretary-General to certify it explicitly;

22. *Commends* the Facilitator for continuing to support the process to settle the crisis in Côte d'Ivoire, and requests the United Nations Operation in Côte d'Ivoire to continue to assist him and his Special Representative in Abidjan in the conduct of the facilitation, including by helping the Facilitator, as appropriate and upon his request, to carry out his arbitration role according to the provisions of paragraph 8.1 of the Ouagadougou Political Agreement and paragraphs 8 and 9 of the third supplementary agreement;

23. *Reaffirms its intention*, as expressed in resolution 1836(2008), to authorize the Secretary-General to redeploy troops, as may be needed, between the United Nations Mission in Liberia and the United Nations Operation in Côte d'Ivoire on a temporary basis and in accordance with the provisions of resolution 1609(2005) of 24 June 2005, as recommended by the Secretary-General in paragraphs 52 and 62 of his report of 8 January 2009;

24. *Underscores* the importance of the military concept of operations and rules of engagement being regularly updated and fully in line with the provisions of the present resolution, in particular paragraphs 16 and 18 above, and requests the Secretary-General to report on them to the Council and troop-contributing countries;

25. *Requests* the United Nations Operation in Côte d'Ivoire to continue to contribute, pursuant to paragraph 2 (*k*) of resolution 1739(2008), to the promotion and protection of human rights in Côte d'Ivoire, with special attention to violence committed against children and women, and to continue to support the efforts that all parties should undertake pursuant to paragraph 12 above, and further requests the Secretary-General to continue to include in his reports to the Council relevant information on progress in this area;

26. *Requests* the Secretary-General to continue to take the necessary measures to ensure full compliance in the United Nations Operation in Côte d'Ivoire with the United Nations zero-tolerance policy on sexual exploitation and abuse and to keep the Council informed, and urges troop-contributing countries to take appropriate preventive action, including predeployment awareness training, and other action to ensure full accountability in cases of such conduct involving their personnel;

27. *Also requests* the Secretary-General to keep the Council regularly informed, at least every three months, of the situation on the ground, including a specific update on the security situation, and of the preparation of the electoral process, including the process of establishment of the electoral list;

28. *Further requests* the Secretary-General to inform the Council in his upcoming reports on the development of a strategic workplan containing indicative timelines to measure and track progress on the implementation of the benchmarks referred to in paragraph 19 above;

29. *Expresses its intention* to review by 31 July 2009 the mandates of the United Nations Operation in Côte d'Ivoire and of the French forces supporting it, the level of troops of the United Nations Operation in Côte d'Ivoire and the benchmarks referred to in paragraph 19 above, in the light of the progress achieved in the electoral process and in the implementation of the key steps of the peace process, and requests the Secretary-General to provide to the Council a report to this end, three weeks before that date;

30. *Decides* to remain actively seized of the matter.

Report of Secretary-General (April). In his April report on UNOCI [S/2009/196], the Secretary-General said that the security situation had remained stable, with largely unhindered freedom of movement of people, goods and services, although several incidents highlighted the fragility of the security situation. Violent clashes between student groups frequently disrupted public order. Identification agents on strike in several areas seized sensitive voter registration materials, including data collected during identification and voter registration operations. The continued presence of armed militias, the incomplete disarmament of former combatants of the Forces nouvelles, the proliferation of small arms and difficulties in moving towards the reunification of security forces and the restoration of State authority had the potential to adversely affect the peace process. Strikes in several public services disrupted the functioning of State administration and delivery of basic services. On 23 March, Innocent Anaky Kobena, the leader of the opposition party Mouvement des forces de l'avenir, urged the overthrow of President Gbagbo, following which he was briefly detained.

Since the signing of the Ouagadougou Political Agreement in 2007, progress had been made towards restoring normalcy in Côte d'Ivoire, including the end of hostilities; the removal of the zone of confidence that had physically divided the country; the restoration of the free movement of people and goods; the ongoing process to identify and register voters; the improvement of the human rights situation; sustained dialogue among the main political leaders; the gradual return to the north of State officials displaced during the conflict; the rebounding of the economy; and technical preparations for the elections. Two more processes were now needed to restore normalcy—reunification and elections—and a plan for those processes was set forth in the fourth supplementary agreement; however, the parties had not been able to meet the deadlines set for completing that plan. The Secretary-General's Special Representative had engaged with key leaders to discuss ways to advance the peace process, and he had consulted with the Facilitator, President Blaise Compaoré of Burkina Faso, who remained committed to helping the peace process with a view to holding elections in 2009. Discussions were continuing among the parties on ways to overcome obstacles and work towards reunification of the country. The cci had established a joint working group to review proposals on modalities for reunification. Uneven progress was made in efforts to restore State authority throughout the country, including the fiscal, customs and judicial administration; consequently the Forces nouvelles commanders remained, de facto, in control of the local administration. Nearly all judges and prosecutors were nominated and redeployed to the north, but the redeployment of court clerks and penitentiary personnel was not completed. No further major progress was made in disarming Forces nouvelles combatants. As at 31 March, 5.9 million Ivorians had been identified and registered as voters at 10,730 registration centres. On 29 March, the Independent Electoral Commission announced the postponement of the registration of Ivorians abroad to an unspecified date owing to financial constraints.

As at 31 March, unoci's military strength stood at 8,024 personnel, comprising 7,745 troops, 187 military observers and 92 staff officers, including 102 women. Pursuant to Security Council resolution 1865(2009), plans were made for the withdrawal of one battalion, scheduled for June, which would leave the troop level at 7,450. The police strength stood at 1,112 personnel, comprising 362 UN police officers and 750 personnel in six police units, of whom 18 were female officers. In addition to its election assistance and monitoring of the military and political situation, unoci carried out activities to incorporate gender aspects in recruitment practices and integrate female personnel in the police force, to monitor and report on human rights abuses, to include hiv/aids awareness in its programmes, to investigate allegations of sexual exploitation and abuse committed by unoci personnel, to expand its outreach through public information, and to ensure the security of its personnel. The French Licorne force was in a drawdown process, due to be completed in June, which would reduce the force from 1,800 to 900 personnel.

About 76,670 internally displaced persons had voluntarily returned to their areas of origin. Land disputes and a weak social fabric posed threats to the return and resettlement of the remaining internally displaced in the west. Critical humanitarian needs, requiring $37 million, faced funding shortfalls. Intercommunity tensions, mainly in the west, and social unrest persisted. Insecurity, in particular in the west and north as well as in the former zone of confidence, resulted in human rights violations, including extortions, armed attacks against civilians, rape and killings.

The Secretary-General expressed regret that the implementation of key elements of the fourth supplementary agreement had stalled, and he called on the signatories to find ways to overcome obstacles to reunification. He welcomed the initiatives by President Compaoré, President Gbagbo and Prime Minister Guillaume Soro to intensify consultations with the parties, and urged all stakeholders to agree on arrangements, including a realistic timeline, to achieve the reunification and restoration of State authority, with focus on integrating Force nouvelles into the new army, the completion of disarmament, demobilization and reintegration of former combatants, the dismantling of militias and the transfer of authority from the Forces nouvelles zone commanders to the *corps préfectoral* (local authorities).

Indicators for peace process. In an annex to his report, the Secretary-General, in response to Council resolution 1865(2009), provided indicators under each of the four benchmarks he had proposed for completion of the peace process—disarmament, demobilization and reintegration of former combatants; holding of elections; restoration of State authority; and commencement of security sector reform. He pointed out that the parties had full ownership of the peace process and the prerogative to set timelines for implementing the remaining tasks under the Ouagadougou Agreement, and unoci had no control over the pace of the process. In addition, Côte d'Ivoire controlled the financing of key aspects of the peace process, including restoration of State authority, the electoral process, the disarmament of former combatants and the dismantling of the militias; therefore the indicators were to be considered as tentative and were expected to evolve.

Security Council consideration. At a meeting on 28 April [meeting 6113] to consider the Secretary-General's report, the Security Council heard a briefing by the Special Representative and Head of UNOCI, Choi Young-Jin, who said that at the outset of 2009, the momentum for an early election had weakened considerably. Since the signing of the fourth supplementary agreement to the Ouagadougou Agreement, the priority between elections and reunification had reversed, with the de facto reunification now to take place before the elections, including the transfer of authority from zone commanders to préfets, the centralization of the treasury, the completion of the integration of Forces nouvelles elements into the military and other services, and a payment to each ex-combatant. Any new electoral timeline would be predicated on the progress of the reunification process. Unfortunately, critical elements of the reunification were not progressing as envisioned. Deadlines had repeatedly been missed. Positive developments included a return to normalcy of daily life, including commercial activities, the fact that no major incident had occurred in the identification process, and financial support provided to the country by the World Bank and IMF.

Communication. On 19 February [S/2009/101], Burkina Faso forwarded the communiqué of the sixth meeting of the Evaluation and Monitoring Committee of the Ouagadougou Political Agreement, adopted three days earlier. The Committee members reviewed the results of the identification and voter registration operation, under which 4,520,948 people—or 52.2 per cent of the target population of 8,663,149—had been registered and urged the Independent Electoral Commission to produce a realistic timeline for the electoral process.

Permanent Consultative Framework meeting (May). The Permanent Consultative Framework of the Ouagadougou Political Agreement held its fifth meeting on 18 May, under the auspices of the Facilitator of the inter-Ivorian Direct Dialogue, President Compaoré. In a press statement [S/2009/257], the Facilitator welcomed the scheduling of the first round of the presidential election for 29 November and called for the conclusion of the voter registration operation by 30 June. He thanked the international community for its financial and technical support which had helped to achieve progress in the peace process and put the country's economic programmes back on track. The members of the Framework—President Gbagbo, Prime Minister Soro, Henri Koran Bédié, President of the Parti démocratique de Côte d'Ivoire-Rassemblement Démocrate Africain, and Alassane Dramane Ouattara, President of the Rassemblement des républicains—discussed issues relating to the completion of the identification and voter registration operations, the implementation of the electoral

timetable and a security plan for the electoral process, as well as the financing of the crisis recovery process.

The Framework welcomed the plan to deploy CCI joint police and gendarmerie units, launched on 5 May, and the reinstatement of judges and court officers. It noted the continuing obstacles to the free movement of persons and goods as a result of the proliferation of road blocks and extortion. In view of the elections, the Framework invited the Government and the regulatory bodies, specifically the National Council for Broadcast Communication and the National Press Council, to abide by the principle of equitable access by political parties to the media and of fair and balanced reporting.

On 29 May [meeting 6133], following consultations among Security Council members, the President made statement **S/PRST/2009/16** on behalf of the Council:

> The Security Council welcomes the communiqué of 18 May 2009 of the Permanent Consultative Framework of the Ouagadougou Political Agreement, which provides a comprehensive electoral time frame leading to the first round of the presidential elections in Côte d'Ivoire on 29 November 2009. It stresses that this time frame has been endorsed by all the main Ivorian political actors, as requested in the statement by the President of the Security Council of 7 November 2008 and in resolution 1865(2009).
>
> The Council underlines the importance of the effective implementation of each of the five stages leading to the elections, as referred to in the report of the Secretary-General of 13 April 2009, namely: (1) the publication of the provisional voters list at the end of voter registration operations, (2) the publication of the final voters list, (3) the production of identification and voter cards, (4) the distribution of identification and voter cards and (5) the electoral campaigning period.
>
> The Council, consistent with its resolution 1865(2009), underlines that this time line binds the Ivorian political actors and that the way it will be implemented will reflect their level of political commitment towards the holding of free, fair, open and transparent elections in a secure environment. The Council urges the Ivorian political actors to meet their commitments in full and without further delay. It again urges the political actors in particular to comply fully with the Code of Good Conduct for Elections that they signed under the auspices of the Secretary-General on 24 April 2008.
>
> The Council reaffirms its full support for the Special Representative of the Secretary-General for Côte d'Ivoire and to the United Nations Operation in Côte d'Ivoire, and recalls that the Special Representative of the Secretary-General shall certify that all stages of the electoral process provide all the necessary guarantees for the holding of free, fair, open and transparent presidential and legislative elections in accordance with international standards, consistent with paragraph 20 of resolution 1865(2009). It takes note of the request by

the Ivorian parties that the Special Representative of the Secretary-General make known and explain to all Ivorian stakeholders the content and modus operandi of the five-criteria framework referred to in the report of the Secretary-General of 15 April 2008 and in resolution 1865(2009).

The Council reiterates its full support for the Facilitator, and calls upon the Ivorian political actors to continue to cooperate fully with him, in particular in this critical phase of the peace process.

The Council expresses the hope that the announcement of the electoral time frame will give a new impetus to the implementation of the Ouagadougou Political Agreement and its supplementary agreements. It takes note of the ceremony of transfer of authority held in Bouaké on 26 May 2009 as a positive development and again urges the Ivorian parties to continue to make progress.

The Council reiterates its determination to bring its full support to a credible electoral process in Côte d'Ivoire. To this end, it requests the Secretary-General to keep it closely and regularly informed of the progress made by the parties in the implementation of each of the key stages of the electoral time frame.

Report of Secretary-General (July). In his July report on UNOCI [S/2009/344], the Secretary-General said that to promote implementation of the Ouagadougou Agreement, the Under-Secretary-General for Peacekeeping Operations, Alain Le Roy, visited Côte d'Ivoire and Burkina Faso from 10 to 14 June to consult national and international stakeholders. All his interlocutors—including President Compaoré, President Gbagbo, Prime Minister Soro and the leaders of the opposition—reiterated their commitment to hold elections on 29 November. Progress in implementing the fourth supplementary agreement remained limited. However, an encouraging development was the ceremony in Bouaké on 26 May for launching the transfer of authority from the Forces nouvelles zone commanders in the north to the *corps préfectoral*. Further work was required to develop the operational capacity of the *corps préfectoral* and the redeployed local administration structures, including the judiciary, fiscal authorities and law enforcement agencies. Plans were made for the deployment of mixed brigades, but those elements already formed did not yet have the capacity to provide security. Progress on reunification of the fiscal administration was very limited. Positive developments were the disbursal of redeployment allowances to some civil servants in northern and western regions and progress in re-establishing judiciary and justice institutions in the north.

Disarmament and reintegration of former combatants and militias remained stalled. While agreement had been made on the payment for each demobilized combatant, there was no clarity on availability of funds or payment modalities. UNOCI, in collaboration with the United Nations Development Programme (UNDP) and the Peacebuilding Fund, was supporting the reintegration process through 510 microprojects benefiting 2,768 ex-combatants and others. The CCI and the national programme for reinsertion and community rehabilitation completed the profiling and registration of 37,436 government militias in May.

By the end of June, the Independent Electoral Commission had not yet produced a detailed timeline for key aspects of the electoral process, other than the date for the presidential election. Outstanding issues included the publication of the provisional and final lists of voters, the production and distribution of identification and voters' cards, and the electoral campaign period. As at 1 July, when registration was officially completed, some 6.4 million Ivorians had been identified and registered.

UNOCI military strength stood at 7,854 personnel as at 1 July, against an authorized strength of 7,450. In early June, the French Licorne completed the reduction of its force by 50 per cent, retaining some 900 troops. UNOCI and the United Nations Mission in Liberia (UNMIL) continued to cooperate on cross-border security issues. The Inter-Mission Force Commanders Conference (Abidjan, 8 May) reviewed contingency plans for possible reinforcement of UNOCI by UNMIL for a limited period, starting 30 days prior to elections. UNOCI police strength stood at 1,183 against an authorized ceiling of 1,200. The police component continued to provide advice and training to the national police and gendarmerie and assistance to national security authorities in the redeployment of personnel to northern areas.

Security incidents included armed robberies, killings, armed attacks, abductions and rape of women and girls, theft and extortion of money, particularly in the west and north of the country. The upsurge in tensions in the west remained a concern and had slowed the pace of return of internally displaced persons (IDPs).

While approximately 77,860 IDPs, out of some 120,000, had returned to their areas of origin, land disputes and a weak social fabric posed a threat to the pace of further returns. The Office of the United Nations High Commissioner for Refugees (UNHCR) worked with local authorities and traditional leaders to find solutions to the causes of conflict and to promote IDPs' return. UNHCR deployed 23 monitors to monitor tensions and to prevent or respond to conflicts through interventions with local authorities and partners. UNOCI disseminated information and raised awareness of basic human rights norms and principles at the grass-roots level. Other issues of concern and activity were women's rights, child protection, HIV/AIDS training and counselling, financial support for the peace process, media monitoring, and conduct, discipline and security of UNOCI personnel.

The Secretary-General recommended that the UNOCI mandate be extended by six months, through 31 January 2010. Should the Security Council agree to extend the mandate, the cost of maintaining it for six months would be limited to the amounts approved by the General Assembly. Welcoming the announcement of 29 November as the date for presidential elections, the Secretary-General looked forward to the publication of a timeline for completion of the remaining preparatory tasks, including the publication of voter lists. The reunification issue would likely remain a key challenge after the elections. Another failure to hold elections would test the credibility of the peace process, he said, while the holding of free, fair and transparent elections could provide a basis for devising an exit strategy for UNOCI.

Extension of UNOCI mandate

The Security Council, at a meeting on 23 July [meeting 6168], considered the Secretary-General's July report (see above) and heard a statement by his Special Representative and Head of UNOCI, Mr. Choi. He remarked that despite probable delays in both the elections and the reunification process, solid achievements had been made in the electoral process, including the mobile court operation and the identification and voter registration operation. All major protagonists appeared to have accepted the end of the voter registration on 30 June, and a climate of peace and stability prevailed. The major impediments to respecting the date for presidential elections were technical, managerial and planning aspects. A public electoral timeline with detailed stages would be an important remedy to the problem.

At a further meeting on the issue, the Council extended UNOCI's mandate for six months (see below) [meeting 6174].

SECURITY COUNCIL ACTION

On 30 July [meeting 6174], the Security Council unanimously adopted **resolution 1880(2009)**. The draft [S/2009/390] was submitted by France.

The Security Council,

Recalling its previous resolutions, in particular resolutions 1528(2004) of 27 February 2004, 1721(2006) of 1 November 2006, 1739(2007) of 10 January 2007, 1765(2007) of 16 July 2007, 1795(2008) of 15 January 2008, 1826(2008) of 29 July 2008, 1842(2008) of 29 October 2008 and 1865(2009) of 27 January 2009, and the statements by its President relating to the situation in Côte d'Ivoire, and its resolution 1836(2008) of 29 September 2008 on the situation in Liberia,

Reaffirming its strong commitment to the sovereignty, independence, territorial integrity and unity of Côte d'Ivoire, and recalling the importance of the principles of good-neighbourliness, non-interference and regional cooperation,

Recalling that it endorsed the agreement signed by President Laurent Gbagbo and Mr. Guillaume Soro in Ouagadougou on 4 March 2007 ("the Ouagadougou Political Agreement"), and that it welcomed the four subsequent supplementary agreements,

Recalling in particular that, in resolution 1721(2006), it notably endorsed the decision of the Peace and Security Council of the African Union on the mandate of the Head of State, and recalling further that in the statement by its President of 28 March 2007, it endorsed the Ouagadougou Political Agreement, including chapter V thereof, on the institutional framework for implementation, and that the Agreement provided for a period of ten months for the holding of the presidential elections,

Expressing again its appreciation to President Blaise Compaoré of Burkina Faso ("the Facilitator") for his continued efforts to support the peace process in Côte d'Ivoire, in particular through the follow-up mechanisms of the Ouagadougou Political Agreement, commending and encouraging the continued efforts of the African Union and the Economic Community of West African States to promote peace and stability in Côte d'Ivoire, and reiterating its full support for them,

Stressing again the importance of the international consultative organ participating in the meetings of the Evaluation and Monitoring Committee, as an observer,

Stressing the need for the Security Council to pursue a rigorous, strategic approach to peacekeeping deployments,

Reiterating its strong condemnation of any attempt to destabilize the peace process by force, and expressing its intention to examine without delay the situation after any such attempt, on the basis of a report by the Secretary-General,

Having taken note of the report of the Secretary-General of 7 July 2009,

Recalling its resolution 1674(2006) of 28 April 2006 on the protection of civilians in armed conflict, noting with concern, in spite of the sustained improvement in the overall human rights situation, the persistence of human rights violations against civilians in different parts of the country, including numerous acts of sexual violence, stressing that the perpetrators must be brought to justice, and reiterating its firm condemnation of all violations of human rights and international humanitarian law in Côte d'Ivoire,

Recalling also its resolution 1612(2005) of 26 July 2005 on children and armed conflict and the subsequent conclusions of the Security Council Working Group on Children and Armed Conflict pertaining to parties to the armed conflict in Côte d'Ivoire, and expressing its deep concern that children continue to suffer from various forms of violence,

Recalling further its resolutions 1325(2000) of 31 October 2000 and 1820(2008) of 19 June 2008 on women and peace and security, condemning any sexual violence, stressing again the importance of the equal participation and full involvement of women in all efforts for the maintenance of peace and promotion of peace and security and the need to increase their role in decision-making with regard to conflict prevention and resolution, and encouraging the Secretary-General to mainstream a gender perspective in the implementation of the mandate of the United Nations Operation in Côte d'Ivoire,

Determining that the situation in Côte d'Ivoire continues to pose a threat to international peace and security in the region,

Acting under Chapter VII of the Charter of the United Nations,

Supporting the Ouagadougou political process

1. *Recalls* that, in the statement by its President of 29 May 2009, it welcomed the new electoral timeline endorsed in Ouagadougou by all the main Ivorian political actors and leading to the first round of the presidential elections on 29 November 2009, and underlines that the Ivorian political actors are bound to respect this timeline to demonstrate their political commitment towards the holding of free, fair, open and transparent elections;

2. *Reiterates its determination* to bring its full support to a credible electoral process for the presidential and legislative elections in Côte d'Ivoire, and expresses its conviction that any postponement of the presidential elections of 29 November 2009 would be inconsistent with a credible process and with the Ouagadougou Political Agreement as endorsed by the Security Council;

3. *Welcomes* the successful completion of the registration of voters;

4. *Recalls* that, in its resolution 1865(2009), it requested the President of the Independent Electoral Commission to share publicly the details of the time frame, and takes note of the dates he has provided for the five stages leading to the elections of 29 November 2009;

5. *Reiterates* that the publication of the electoral list is a crucial step in the electoral process, looks forward to the publication of the provisional voters list before the end of August 2009, and urges the Ivorian actors to meet their commitments in full and without delay;

6. *Expresses its determination* to follow closely the publication of the provisional and final electoral lists, encourages the Facilitator and the Special Representative of the Secretary-General for Côte d'Ivoire to inform it without delay of any difficulty that may put the electoral time frame at risk, expresses its intention to examine any such situation without delay, and requests the Special Representative of the Secretary-General to certify the voters list explicitly;

7. *Reiterates* that the Special Representative of the Secretary-General shall certify that all stages of the electoral process provide all the necessary guarantees for the holding of open, free, fair and transparent presidential and legislative elections in accordance with international standards, and reaffirms its full support to the Special Representative of the Secretary-General in his certification role;

8. *Stresses* that it will base its assessment of the electoral process on the certification that will be prepared by the Special Representative of the Secretary-General consistent with the five-criteria framework referred to in the report of the Secretary-General of 15 April 2008 and after inclusive contacts with all stakeholders in Côte d'Ivoire, including civil society;

9. *Stresses also* the importance of an inclusive participation of Ivorian civil society in the electoral process, of ensuring equal protection of and respect for the human rights of every Ivorian as they relate to the electoral system, and, in particular, respect for freedom of opinion and expression, and of removing obstacles and challenges to women's participation and full involvement in public life;

10. *Urges* the Government of Côte d'Ivoire to provide the operators involved in the electoral process with the necessary support, and encourages the international community to continue their support to the electoral process, including by providing, with the agreement of the Ivorian authorities, electoral observation capacity and related technical assistance;

11. *Recalls* that it is fully prepared to impose targeted measures pursuant to paragraph 16 of resolution 1842(2008), including against persons who are determined to be a threat to the peace and national reconciliation process in Côte d'Ivoire, and recalls further that, pursuant to paragraph 6 of the above-mentioned resolution, any threat to the electoral process in Côte d'Ivoire, in particular any attack or obstruction of the action of the Independent Electoral Commission in charge of the organization of the elections or the action of the operators mentioned in paragraphs 1.3.3 and 2.1.1 of the Ouagadougou Political Agreement, shall constitute a threat to the peace and national reconciliation process for the purposes of paragraphs 9 and 11 of resolution 1572(2004) of 15 November 2004;

12. *Again urges* the political parties to comply fully with the Code of Good Conduct for Elections which they signed under the auspices of the Secretary-General, and, in particular, urges the Ivorian authorities to allow equitable access to public media;

13. *Takes note again* of the ceremony of transfer of authority, held in Bouaké on 26 May 2009, as a positive development, urges the Ivorian parties to make further progress to advance the reunification and disarmament processes, and encourages the international donors to continue to provide their support to them, as appropriate;

14. *Calls upon* all parties concerned to ensure that the protection of women and children is addressed in the implementation of the Ouagadougou Political Agreement as well as in the post-conflict reconstruction and recovery phases, including continued monitoring and reporting of the situation of women and children, and that all reported abuses are investigated and those responsible brought to justice;

15. *Calls upon* all Ivorian parties to take appropriate measures to refrain from, prevent and protect civilians from all forms of sexual violence, which could include enforcing appropriate military disciplinary measures, upholding the principle of command responsibility, and training troops on the categorical prohibition of all forms of sexual violence;

16. *Recalls* the recommendation of its Working Group on Children and Armed Conflict that a national action plan to address sexual violence in Côte d'Ivoire be adopted, welcomes the steps taken so far and urges the Government of Côte d'Ivoire, with the support of the United Nations Operation in Côte d'Ivoire and other relevant actors, to finalize and implement it, welcomes also the programme of action, signed by the Forces nouvelles in January 2009, to combat sexual violence in the areas within their control, pursuant to the above-mentioned recommendations, as well as the communiqué issued by four militia groups indicating their willingness to combat sexual violence, and calls upon all relevant parties, with the continued support

of the United Nations Operation in Côte d'Ivoire, to work together to implement their commitments;

17. *Urges* the signatories to the Ouagadougou Political Agreement to take the steps necessary to protect vulnerable civilian populations, including by guaranteeing the voluntary return, reinstallation, reintegration and security of displaced persons, including by addressing land tenure issues, with the support of the United Nations system, and to fulfil in this regard their commitments in accordance with the Agreement and their obligations under international law;

18. *Welcomes* the progress made in the identification process, which is key to the long-term stability of Côte d'Ivoire, and calls upon the Ivorian parties to continue the identification operations, including after the elections;

Renewing the mandate of the United Nations Operation in Côte d'Ivoire

19. *Decides* to renew the mandate of the United Nations Operation in Côte d'Ivoire, as determined in resolution 1739(2007), until 31 January 2010, in particular to support the organization in Côte d'Ivoire of free, open, fair and transparent elections, within the electoral time frame referred to in paragraph 1 above;

20. *Requests* the United Nations Operation in Côte d'Ivoire, within its existing resources and mandate, to support actively the parties in the full implementation of the remaining tasks under the Ouagadougou Political Agreement and its supplementary agreements, in particular those that are essential to the holding of free, fair, open and transparent presidential elections on 29 November 2009, and to continue to support the disarmament, demobilization and reintegration programme and the disarmament and dismantling of militias, and to provide technical and logistical support to the Independent Electoral Commission for the preparation and the holding of the elections in a secure environment;

21. *Requests* the Secretary-General to continue to monitor progress in the achievement of the benchmarks referred to in annex I to his report of 7 July 2009, encourages him to continue to refine and update them and to report to the Council, and expresses its intention to review these benchmarks in full before 15 October 2009, taking into account, in particular, the progress of the electoral process;

22. *Reiterates its full support* to the efforts of the Special Representative of the Secretary-General, and requests the United Nations Operation in Côte d'Ivoire to continue to actively sensitize the Ivorian population to his certification role;

23. *Commends* the Facilitator for continuing to support the process to settle the crisis in Côte d'Ivoire, and requests the United Nations Operation in Côte d'Ivoire to continue to assist him and his Special Representative in Abidjan in the conduct of the facilitation, including by helping the Facilitator, as appropriate and upon his request, to carry out his arbitration role according to the provisions of paragraph 8.1 of the Ouagadougou Political Agreement and paragraphs 8 and 9 of the third supplementary agreement;

24. *Reaffirms its intention*, as expressed in resolution 1836(2008), to authorize the Secretary-General to redeploy troops, as may be needed, between the United Nations Mission in Liberia and the United Nations Operation in Côte d'Ivoire on a temporary basis and in accordance with the provisions of resolution 1609(2005) of 24 June 2005, as recommended by the Secretary-General in paragraph 25 of his report of 7 July 2009, and calls upon troop-contributing countries to support the efforts of the Secretary-General in that regard;

25. *Underscores* the importance of updating the military concept of operations and rules of engagement before 30 September 2009, and requests the Secretary-General to report thereon to the Council and troop-contributing countries;

26. *Requests* the United Nations Operation in Côte d'Ivoire to continue to contribute, pursuant to paragraph 2 *(k)* of resolution 1739(2007), to the promotion and protection of human rights in Côte d'Ivoire, with special attention to violence committed against children and women, to monitor and help to investigate human rights violations with a view to ending impunity, and to continue to support the efforts that all parties should undertake pursuant to paragraphs 15 and 16 above, and further requests the Secretary-General to continue to include in his reports to the Council relevant information on progress in this area;

27. *Also requests* the United Nations Operation in Côte d'Ivoire, in this context, to also continue to contribute, pursuant to paragraph 2 *(m)* of resolution 1739(2007), to assisting the Government of Côte d'Ivoire in restoring a civilian policing presence throughout Côte d'Ivoire, and to advise the Government on the restructuring of the internal security services, and in re-establishing the authority of the judiciary and the rule of law throughout Côte d'Ivoire;

28. *Stresses* the need for the United Nations Operation in Côte d'Ivoire and humanitarian agencies to continue to work closely together, in relation to areas of tension and areas of return of displaced persons, and to exchange information on possible outbreaks of violence and other threats against civilians in order to respond thereto in a timely and appropriate manner;

29. *Requests* the Secretary-General to continue to take the measures necessary to ensure full compliance in the United Nations Operation in Côte d'Ivoire with the United Nations zero-tolerance policy on sexual exploitation and abuse and to keep the Council informed, and urges troop-contributing countries to take appropriate preventive action, including predeployment awareness training, and other action to ensure full accountability in cases of such conduct involving their personnel;

30. *Decides* to extend until 31 January 2010 the authorization it provided to the French forces in order to support the United Nations Operation in Côte d'Ivoire, within the limits of their deployment and their capabilities;

31. *Expresses its intention* to review the situation as well as, as appropriate, the mandate of the United Nations Operation in Côte d'Ivoire, subject to the progress of the electoral process and, in particular, to the establishment of the electoral list and in any case no later than 15 October 2009, requests the Secretary-General to inform the Council in early September 2009 of the publication of the provisional electoral list, and further requests the Secretary-General to provide to the Council a midterm report, by the end of September 2009, on the situation on the ground, including a specific update on the security situation, and on the preparation of the electoral process;

32. *Requests* the Secretary-General to inform the Council in his upcoming reports on the development of his strategic workplan containing indicative timelines to measure and track progress on the implementation of the benchmarks referred to in paragraph 21 above;

33. *Expresses its intention* to review by 31 January 2010 the mandate of the United Nations Operation in Côte d'Ivoire and the authorization provided to the French forces supporting it, the level of troops of the United Nations Operation in Côte d'Ivoire and the benchmarks referred to in paragraph 21 above, in the light of the progress achieved in the electoral process and in the implementation of the key steps of the peace process, and requests the Secretary-General to provide to the Council a report to this end, three weeks before that date;

34. *Decides* to remain actively seized of the matter.

Election preparations

The Secretary-General, in a 4 September letter [S/2009/446] to the Security Council, provided an update on the preparation of the provisional electoral list for the presidential election. The Independent Electoral Commission, which was responsible for preparing that list by 29 August with support from other national technical bodies, as well as a contracted international private company from France (Sagem), had missed that deadline. In a statement issued on 19 August, the Independent Electoral Commission had expressed concern about delays in key steps required to prepare the list: that the National Commission for the Supervision of Identification (CNSI) had not designated representatives to the committees charged with arbitration of identification and voter registration data; that the CCI had not provided security for all the coordination centres where the data was processed; and that the Government had yet to disburse the remaining funds required for the electoral process. Subsequently, the Prime Minister's office indicated that there would be a two-week delay in publishing the provisional electoral list.

On 25 August the Government had adopted legal texts on the electoral process, including: decree 2009/270 which regularized the duration of the concluded voter registration operations, carried out between 15 September 2008 and 30 June 2009, by extending the deadline for the voter registration process; ordinance 2009/268 which compressed the time for displaying the provisional electoral list from three months to 30 days prior to the elections; and ordinance 2009/269 which compressed the time for completing the distribution of voter cards from two weeks to eight days prior to the elections. On 1 September, the Independent Electoral Commission and CNSI started arbitrating identification and voter registration data in the coordination centres. As at 2 September, 40 of the 70 coordination centres had completed processing voter registration data. UNOCI

was working with international partners to resolve funding issues, and with national authorities to address the obstacles to the deployment of the mixed brigades that were charged with providing security to the coordination centres and the electoral process.

Following the completion of the identification and voter registration operations on 30 June, the Independent Electoral Commission announced that 6,552,694 people had registered, including 38,496 who had registered in 23 foreign countries. On 23 July, the Independent Electoral Commission published the following timeline for the remaining stages of the electoral process: the publication of the provisional electoral list on 29 August; the publication of the final electoral list following the conclusion of the appeals process between 15 and 21 October; the production of identification and voter cards by 20 October; the distribution of those cards by 26 November; and the electoral campaign period from 13 to 27 November. UNOCI, with UNDP assistance, continued to provide assistance to the electoral process, including procurement of electoral materials and preparations to help transport those materials.

Report of Secretary-General (September). In his September report on UNOCI [S/2009/495], the Secretary-General said that the security situation showed sustained improvement; however, the crime rate remained high in most parts of the country, in particular in the west. The situation remained fragile given the unresolved aspects of the peace process, including the incomplete disarmament of Forces nouvelles elements and dismantling of pro-Government militias, the inability of CCI to fully deploy the mixed brigades, the unresolved issues related to the reunification of the security forces and the slow pace of the re-establishment of rule-of-law institutions in the west and in the north.

Significant progress was made in implementing key aspects of the Ouagadougou Agreement, including completion of the identification and voter registration operations on 30 June, and the beginning of the compilation of the provisional electoral list. The deadlines for completing the latter were missed, however. Progress in other areas had remained slow, in particular the implementation of the fourth supplementary agreement, which addressed security issues and the reunification of the country. The Facilitator, President Compaoré, convened the Evaluation and Monitoring Committee on 9 August to review progress in implementing the Ouagadougou Agreements. Participants from both sides agreed that the remaining security-related issues should be resolved, in particular the harmonization of the ranks of the 5,000 personnel from Forces nouvelles who should join the national army, the cantonment of those elements, the deployment by CCI of 8,000 personnel (4,000 from the Forces nouvelles and 4,000 from the national police and gendarmerie) in mixed brigades, and the centralization of the treasury. As at 14 September, of the expected 8,000 personnel, only 601, from both sides, had been deployed. In addition the deployed brigades, whose main task was to provide security for the electoral process, still lacked the capacities and resources for carrying out that responsibility. Meanwhile, the cantonment of the 5,000 Forces nouvelles elements had stalled, owing in part to the lack of a legal framework governing the integration process and the absence of adequate facilities. Following the ceremony to transfer authority from the Forces nouvelles zone commanders to the *corps préfectoral* in May, the prefects started taking administrative decisions in the northern areas controlled by the Forces nouvelles. However, the authority of the prefects to enforce administrative decisions and maintain public order was hampered by the absence of CCI operational units. Uneven progress was made in the redeployment of the judiciary to the north due to the lack of magistrates. With regard to customs and tax offices, the Forces nouvelles continued to collect taxes in the north and had requested the inclusion of Forces nouvelles-affiliated personnel in all fiscal and financial services, including customs, treasury and tax offices.

The national programme for reinsertion and community rehabilitation, in collaboration with CCI, continued to review the preliminary list of 37,451 profiled pro-Government militias. It was expected that 25,000 people would be on the final list of militia personnel eligible for reintegration support. However, the final list of eligible militia personnel remained incomplete, due mainly to the unavailability of the $1,000 demobilization allowance for each ex-combatant and militia member. UNOCI, UNDP and the Peacebuilding Fund provided short-term assistance for some of them through micro-projects.

As at 22 September, the UNOCI military strength stood at 7,218 personnel, against an authorized ceiling of 7,450, and the police strength stood at 1,180. The force conducted exercises to test the readiness of its rapid-response capability. The UNOCI military concept of operations and rules of engagement were updated to align them with the new posture of the force, as requested by the Security Council in resolution 1880(2009) (see p. 177). The mission continued its activities in other fields, namely humanitarian assistance, human rights, women's rights, child protection, HIV/AIDS, economic recovery, financial support to the peace process, media monitoring, personnel conduct and discipline, and safety and security of personnel.

The Secretary-General welcomed the completion of the identification and voter registration operation as a major step towards securing lasting peace, considering that the identification of the population was one of the issues at the core of the crisis that had divided the country. The main challenge was to hold free, fair and transparent elections, which required publication of the provisional electoral list and resolving any disputes emanating from the list. The decrees passed by the Government to compress the time frame showed a determination on the part of the authorities to conduct the elections as scheduled. The Secretary-General warned that the uncompleted tasks could create risks for the election if they were not carefully managed, and he urged the parties to sustain a spirit of compromise in doing so.

SECURITY COUNCIL ACTION

On 29 September [meeting 6193], following consultations among Security Council members, the President made statement **S/PRST/2009/25** on behalf of the Council:

The Security Council reiterates its full support for the Ouagadougou political process and the electoral timeline endorsed by all the main Ivorian political actors, leading to the first round of open, free, fair and transparent presidential elections on 29 November 2009. It commends the Facilitator, President Blaise Compaoré of Burkina Faso, for his continued efforts to support the peace process in Côte d'Ivoire.

The Council further reiterates its determination to bring its full support to a credible electoral process and highlights the importance of an inclusive participation of Ivorian civil society. It stresses that, to this end, it has extended the mandate and has maintained the troop level of the United Nations Operation in Côte d'Ivoire in its resolution 1880(2009). It further stresses that it expressed in that resolution its intention to authorize the Secretary-General to redeploy troops, as may be needed, between the United Nations Mission in Liberia and the United Nations Operation in Côte d'Ivoire.

The Council expresses its concern at the delay in the publication of the provisional voters list, and highlights that further delays in the publication of the voters list may put at risk the timeline for open, free, fair and transparent presidential elections.

The Council reiterates that the Ivorian political actors are bound to respect the electoral timeline. It urges all Ivorian actors to comply fully with their commitments, in order for the voters list to be published as soon as possible within the framework of a transparent and inclusive process. It recalls that the Special Representative of the Secretary-General for Côte d'Ivoire shall certify the voters list explicitly.

The Council will review the situation by 15 October 2009. It expresses its intention to react as appropriate, consistent with resolution 1880(2009), towards those who would block the progress of the electoral process.

The Council further expresses its intention to start considering the future direction of the United Nations Operation in Côte d'Ivoire by reviewing its mandate and benchmarks for a possible drawdown of the operation by 15 October 2009, in particular in the light of the progress of the electoral process.

Postponement of presidential election

Permanent Consultative Framework meeting (December). The Permanent Consultative Framework of the Ouagadougou Political Agreement held its sixth meeting (Ouagadougou, 3 December) and in a statement transmitted to the Security Council [S/2009/626] noted the postponement of the presidential election. At the time of the meeting, the provisional electoral list consisted of 6,384,253 voter registrations, of which 5,300,586 had been confirmed; 1,083,667 applicants had been requested to clarify their status. Those individuals were waiting for their cases to be resolved under the complaint procedure. Prime Minister Soro presented a report evaluating implementation of the Ouagadougou Agreement and the fourth supplementary agreement. The Framework members welcomed the progress in the identification and voter registration exercise, the Constitutional Council's confirmation of the 14 candidates for the presidential election, the issuance of the provisional electoral list and the opening of a 38-day period for lodging complaints.

The Framework noted that there had been delays in following the electoral timetable; that for technical and financial reasons, it had not been possible to hold the presidential election on 29 November; and that important tasks (preparation of the electoral list and issuance of identity and voter registration cards) had yet to be carried out. Consequently, the members endorsed the following stages and timeline: December 2009—handling of complaints regarding the provisional electoral list; January 2010—preparation and issuance of the final electoral list, the lists of persons authorized to vote at each polling station, voter registration cards and national identity cards; February 2010—issuance of voter registration and national identity cards and electoral campaign; late February-early March 2010—first round of the presidential election.

The Framework stressed the importance of equitable access to the media for political parties and candidates. It encouraged the Secretary-General's Special Representative to continue to fulfil his mandate to certify the electoral process in cooperation with all concerned parties, including the Office of the Facilitator. While noting the signing by the President on 16 November of decrees concerning reunification of the army, the Framework encouraged the signatories to the Ouagadougou Agreement to settle the remaining military issues. The Framework called on all parties to respect the Codes of Good Conduct, particularly those of the political parties and the media. To finance the remaining activities of the crisis recovery process, the members urged the Government to release to the Independent Electoral Commission the remainder of the latter's 2009 budget and to provide it with an advance on its 2010 budget by 15 January 2010.

SECURITY COUNCIL ACTION

On 8 December [meeting 6234], following consultations among Security Council members, the President made statement **S/PRST/2009/33** on behalf of the Council:

The Security Council notes with concern the postponement of the first round of the presidential elections, scheduled for 29 November 2009 in the communiqué of 18 May 2009 of the Permanent Consultative Framework of the Ouagadougou Political Agreement, which was endorsed by all the main Ivorian political actors.

The Council welcomes the positive steps taken by the Ivorian actors, in particular the publication of the provisional voters list and the list of candidates. It further welcomes the communiqué of 3 December 2009 of the Permanent Consultative Framework. It commends the Facilitator, President Blaise Compaoré of Burkina Faso, for his continued efforts to support the peace process in Côte d'Ivoire.

The Council notes that the Permanent Consultative Framework considered, on the basis of a presentation by the Independent Electoral Commission, that the postponement of the elections was due to technical and financial constraints and that the first round of the presidential elections would be organized by the end of February or the beginning of March 2010. It urges the Ivorian actors to address the remaining tasks and to hold open, free, fair and transparent presidential elections in accordance with international standards at the earliest possible date.

The Council notes again that the publication of a final voters list certified by the Special Representative of the Secretary-General for Côte d'Ivoire is crucial for the holding of open, free, fair and transparent presidential elections. It urges the Ivorian stakeholders to meet their commitments to support the elections and to facilitate this process without delay, in particular during the 38-day phase during which the provisional list can be challenged before local independent electoral commissions and courts. It again urges the Ivorian authorities to allow equitable access to public media, consistent with the Code of Good Conduct for Elections. It reiterates its intention to react as appropriate, consistent with its resolution 1880(2009), towards those who would block the progress of the electoral process.

The Council welcomes the signing by President Laurent Gbagbo on 17 November 2009 of several military rules and regulations, including seven decrees. It urges the Ivorian parties to make further concrete progress, before and after the elections, to advance the reunification and disarmament processes.

The Council recalls that it will review the mandate and the troop level of the United Nations Operation in Côte d'Ivoire by 31 January 2010. It reiterates its determination to bring its full support to a credible electoral process in Côte d'Ivoire. The Council requests the Secretary-General to provide to it, in the report referred to in resolution 1880(2009), options for the future direction of the United Nations Operation in Côte d'Ivoire, in particular in the light of the publication of the final voters list and of a credible electoral time frame, including preliminary indications on timing, benchmarks and modalities for a possible drawdown of the Operation.

Year-end developments

The Secretary-General reported [S/2010/15] that the security situation at the end of the year was stable, despite an upsurge in armed robberies and other crime, particularly in the west. Attacks by armed bandits resulted in 16 deaths. Clashes between two rival student groups in September disrupted school registration activities and led to material damage. Despite the postponement of the first round of the presidential election, progress was made in identification and election-related tasks provided for in the Ouagadougou Agreement, including the publication of the provisional electoral list, the launch of the appeals process and the validation of all major candidates for the election. Progress in implementing the fourth supplementary agreement, dealing with disarmament and reunification of the country, remained limited. However, on 16 November, President Gbagbo signed several decrees related to the reunification of the defence and security forces, which were expected to enhance the security of the electoral process.

Following examination and cross-checking of data concerning voters, the Independent Electoral Commission announced on 8 November that 5,300,586 people had been confirmed on the provisional electoral list, and 1,033,985 remained to be confirmed. On 11 November, the Commission announced that the first round of the presidential election would be postponed as a result of the delays incurred in preparing and publishing the provisional electoral list. The publication of that list was eventually completed on 23 November and endorsed by the Special Representative. The appeals process, launched on 24 November, was expected to be completed in early January 2010. Unoci assisted in distributing the provisional electoral list to all local electoral commissions through logistical support provided to the Independent Electoral Commission. The mission also supported transportation of electoral materials from Abidjan port to Commission warehouses and stepped up efforts to coordinate election observation activities. The Constitutional Council of Côte d'Ivoire validated 14 of the 20 candidates for the president election, including the candidatures of the two main opposition leaders, Mr. Bédié and Mr. Ouattara, and the current President, Mr. Gbagbo. Political parties conducted information activities in a generally calm environment. On 3 December, the Permanent Consultative Framework endorsed the new timeline for the remaining stages of the electoral process. The Secretary-General recommended that the Security Council extend the UNOCI mandate for six months, through 31 July 2010.

The national programme for reintegration of former combatants reported the number of demobilized fighters as 16,081. It was estimated that an additional 12,000 Forces nouvelles elements were yet to be demobilized. Of those already demobilized, only a few had received reintegration assistance. Meanwhile, no progress was made in dismantling pro-Government militias. In the Secretary-General's view, it was important to continue the programme of micro-projects offering assistance to former combatants, militias, youth and women affected by the conflict as a stop-gap measure. By year's end, 526 micro-projects had benefited 3,483 people.

The reunification of the defence and security forces had been hampered by prolonged negotiations on the harmonization of the ranks of Forces nouvelles personnel and by continued capacity constraints of the CCI, which was created to implement all security-related provisions of the Ouagadougou Agreement. On 16 November, President Gbagbo signed several decrees on harmonization of the ranks of Forces nouvelles elements, including the promotion of several high-ranking officers. Other decrees clarified the status of 3,400 Forces nouvelles personnel who were expected to help secure the electoral process and provided for the incorporation into the gendarmerie of 300 out of the 600 Forces nouvelles security auxiliaries trained by UNOCI in 2006. While the six mixed brigades established along the former zone of confidence continued to operate despite financial and logistical challenges, the deployment of 600 mixed security personnel to Bouaké and Abidjan to secure the elections was temporarily suspended. According to the Ivorian military, only 2,000 of the planned 8,000 would be deployed two weeks prior to the elections. On 11 December, a mixed brigade with 100 elements was inaugurated, marking the launch of the installation process of police stations and mixed brigades with 1,000 elements in 10 other cities in central, northern and western areas. Forces nouvelles elements serving in those mixed brigades had not received their salaries.

State officials in the north continued to experience difficulties in exercising their full authority in view of the uneven deployment of operational units from the CCI and despite the ceremonial transfer of authority from the Forces nouvelles zone commanders to the *corps préfectoral*. Meanwhile, the process to redeploy State officials continued at a slow pace. Progress towards the reunification of the State treasury remained limited. Despite efforts by the State to resume revenue collection in the north, the Forces nouvelles continued to collect taxes and customs revenues and to staff border crossings. Some progress was made towards re-establishing the judiciary and justice institutions in the north. All 11 courts had reopened, although the courts in Bouaké and Korhogo continued to lack the required personnel to be fully operational. As a result, criminal cases remained largely unprosecuted. Of the 11 prison facilities in the north, only five were operational; they were operated by the Forces nouvelles pending the redeployment of Ivorian staff. The international community continued to support the peace efforts through financial contributions to funds administered by UNDP. In 2009, those funds contributed $38.6 million for that purpose.

As at 31 December, the UNOCI military strength was 7,391 personnel, against a ceiling of 7,450 authorized by the Council, and the police strength was 1,138. The French Licorne strength remained at 900.

The incidence of serious but isolated human rights violations remained high: 126 attacks by armed individuals resulted in 16 deaths, with only 10 arrests made by the local police. In both the north and south, elements of the defence and security forces subjected civilians to excessive use of force, abduction, illegal arrest and detention, ill-treatment, racketeering and unlawful interference with private property. UNOCI continued to raise awareness about human rights norms and principles through sensitization activities, and it continued activities in women's rights and gender-based violence, child protection, HIV/AIDS, malnutrition and media monitoring.

Children and armed conflict

The Secretary-General, as requested by the Security Council in 2008 [YUN 2008, p. 850], reported in March on children and armed conflict [A/63/785-S/2009/158]. Concerning developments in Côte d'Ivoire, he reported that there was no substantiated evidence of use of child soldiers by armed forces or groups during the reporting period (September 2007–December 2008). In February 2008, UNOCI had received allegations against militia groups in the west, which were investigated and disproved. The leadership of the groups allowed full access by the United Nations for verification. Following that, the militia groups issued a communiqué condemning the use of child soldiers. Similar cooperation was extended by Forces de défense et de sécurité des Forces nouvelles (FDS-FN).

Rape and other sexual violence, as well as other grave violations against children, were prevalent throughout Côte d'Ivoire and were perpetrated with impunity by individuals and groups, who took advantage of the lack of rule of law. The situation was more serious in areas under FDS-FN control in the north. The Ministry of Family, Women and Social Welfare requested UNOCI to submit a draft proposal to the Government on the creation of a national commission for children affected by armed conflict. A separate proposal on the establishment of a national action plan to combat sexual violence was submitted at the Government's request in September 2008. The proposals were under the Government's review. The leadership of FDS-FN also developed a programme of action against sexual violence, signed on 19 January 2009, in response to the request of the Security Coun-

cil Working Group on Children and Armed Conflict. It included elements of prevention, addressing impunity and providing witness protection and assistance to victims of sexual violence.

Sanctions

Sanctions committee. The Security Council Committee established pursuant to resolution 1572(2004) [YUN 2004, p. 187] concerning Côte d'Ivoire continued to monitor implementation of the arms embargo, travel restrictions and assets freeze on designated individuals and entities, and the ban on the import of all rough diamonds from Côte d'Ivoire. Those sanctions were renewed by resolutions 1643(2005) [YUN 2005, p. 251], 1782(2007) [YUN 2007, p. 188] and 1842(2008) [YUN 2008, p. 194].

In January [S/2009/5], the Secretary-General informed the Security Council of his appointment of a fifth expert to serve on the Group of Experts overseeing implementation of the sanctions, until 31 October. In December [S/2009/646], the Secretary-General, referring to Council resolution 1893(2009) (see p. 186), noted the Council's decision to extend the mandate of the Group of Experts until 31 October 2010 and therefore appointed five experts for that period.

In a report on its 2009 activities [S/2009/689], the Committee remarked that the primary responsibility for implementing the measures imposed by the Security Council rested with Member States. In monitoring the measures, the Committee benefited from information provided by the Group of Experts, UNOCI and other sources. The Committee held seven informal consultations during the year. It received a request on 27 April from Côte d'Ivoire for the delisting of one of the listed individuals, but did not reach a consensus to remove the individual from the list. On 22 July, Côte d'Ivoire requested two exemptions to the arms embargo; however, the Committee lacked the proper documentation for approval. During the year, the Committee considered 10 monthly arms embargo and media monitoring reports as well as five quarterly human rights reports (three from 2009 and two from 2008), all prepared by UNOCI.

Report of Group of Experts (April). In accordance with resolution 1842(2008), the Group of Experts monitoring the implementation of the sanctions concerning Côte d'Ivoire, in a midterm report issued in April [S/2009/188], reviewed cooperation with stakeholders, monitoring of the embargo, verification of the air fleet capacity, military assistance to Côte d'Ivoire, violations of the arms embargo, financing of the Government and Forces nouvelles, the diamond embargo, customs, and individual sanctions. The Group believed that several years of north-south polarization had introduced new political and economic tensions into the crisis. The north of the country was fractured into several politico-military commands, which competed for control over natural resources and commerce. Elements within the Government and the Forces nouvelles operated powerful economic networks and, despite the arms embargo, remained sufficiently armed to engage in sustained armed hostilities.

In regard to the arms embargo, the Group expressed concern with the continued refusal of the Ivorian authorities to allow it unhindered access to equipment, sites and installations without notice, and the lack of training on conducting inspections on the part of many UNOCI monitors. It acquired evidence that suggested a consistent pattern of violations of the arms embargo. Several arms investigations were ongoing. Reported arms and ammunition requirements for the police appeared to far exceed requirements. There was evidence of illegal smuggling from Guinea to the Lac Buyo region. Concerning the Ivorian air fleet, the Group reported that the Government had leased two helicopters from a South African company, and it advised the company that the use of the aircraft for military purposes constituted a violation of the embargo. The Group learned of the existence of unsupervised airstrips in western Côte d'Ivoire, near Liberia. Recognizing the potential for the trade in diamonds to fuel armed conflict in Côte d'Ivoire, the Group endeavoured to identify persons and entities involved in, facilitating, and benefiting from the Ivorian diamond trade. Various reports confirmed the existence of previously unreported mining activities in three locations, currently under the Group's investigation, and that diamonds from Côte d'Ivoire continued to be exported to international markets in violation of the embargo. The Group concluded that deficiencies in the country's customs infrastructure posed risks in terms of potential breaches of the arms embargo.

Among its recommendations, the Group called for a permanent arms expert within UNOCI. It advised States to remain vigilant to the possibility that arms and related materiel might be retransferred in violation of the arms embargo. The Group urged Ivorian financial and banking institutions to improve transparency and accountability with regard to accounts and revenues and to provide copies of their 2009 budgets, and international and Ivorian financial institutions to share information to better monitor and enforce the assets freeze on sanctioned individuals and to combat money-laundering. It recommended international standardization of rough diamond origin determination methodologies, such as by the Kimberley Process Working Group Diamond Experts. The Group believed it was imperative to conduct a geological survey of the diamond-mining capacities of the country.

Report of Group of Experts (October). In October, the Chairman of the Security Council Committee established pursuant to resolution 1572(2004) transmitted to the Council President the final 2009 report of the Group of Experts on Côte d'Ivoire [S/2009/521], in accordance with resolution 1842(2008). The Group noted that the Government's primary security concern was not necessarily the Forces nouvelles, but rather the containment of political opposition in the south, potentially violent, which could prompt it to increase its import of arms and related materiel in the near future. Northern Côte d'Ivoire bore more resemblance to a warlord economy than to a functioning government administration. Largely independent military "zone commanders" of the Forces nouvelles controlled and exploited natural resources, including cocoa, cotton, timber, gold and diamonds, providing both motive and means to sustain territorial control in the north.

The Group identified seven cases in which the Government and the Forces nouvelles had imported arms and related materiel banned by sanctions; of those, it found that two cases constituted breaches of the arms embargo. It identified two cases of importation of ammunition apparently destined for the civilian market in Côte d'Ivoire. It found systematic transfers of weapons and ammunition to the Forces nouvelles-controlled north of the country, possibly linked to cocoa smuggling. Elements within the Forces nouvelles were rearming and had acquired related military materiel, including communications equipment, vehicles adapted to military uses and military apparel.

Concerning finance, the Group highlighted the fact that the Government controlled the world's largest share (40 per cent) of cocoa production. Its management of cocoa revenues remained opaque, and the Group noted suspicious cases linking the Government's cocoa revenues to the purchase of military materiel. Ten Forces nouvelles zone commanders controlled the world's seventh largest cocoa producing region and benefited from large-scale cocoa smuggling. They also levied taxes on a range of other natural resources and road commerce. The Group observed intensified diamond mining in the north, and pointed out that the development of new mining technologies created a market-driven imperative to export Ivorian rough diamonds in contravention of the sanctions regime. The absence of effective border controls in Burkina Faso and Mali allowed the rough diamond trade in Côte d'Ivoire to extend into those countries. An unexplained rise in Guinea's exports of rough diamonds, and its weak system of internal controls, suggested that there was a high risk that Ivorian diamonds might be illegally exported through Guinea. The Group expressed similar concerns with regard to Liberia.

In the area of customs, the Group noted that the Government had not yet introduced the necessary regulatory measures to prevent the import or export of items prohibited by the sanctions regime. The Forces nouvelles had not established a functioning customs regime in the territories under its control. In connection with the individual sanctions, the Group determined that two of the three individuals subject to the assets freeze and the travel bans had continued to access and accrue revenues despite the sanctions imposed on them.

Among its recommendations, the Group called on the Government to allow the Group of Experts and UNOCI access to all sites and military installations, and urged the Force nouvelles leadership to ensure that zone commanders allowed them access to all arms and related materiel. It called on Member States to notify the Committee in advance of exports of security-related materiel to Côte d'Ivoire. The Group recommended that both parties increase transparency and disclosure of sources of revenue. Concerning diamonds, it recommended that the Ministry of Mines and Energy, in conjunction with the Forces nouvelles, take immediate control of rough diamond mining sites and re-establish its administration, monitoring and regulation of all diamond mining activities. It called on the Kimberley Process and its participants to take measures to prevent the import of rough diamonds from Côte d'Ivoire. The Group recommended that UNOCI create a monitoring unit, jointly composed of UNOCI and Ivorian customs personnel, to assist in monitoring the arms embargo. It recommended that Member States, in particular Côte d'Ivoire and neighbouring States, enforce the asset freeze and travel ban imposed on the three sanctioned individuals.

SECURITY COUNCIL ACTION

On 29 October [meeting 6209], the Security Council unanimously adopted **resolution 1893(2009)**. The draft [S/2009/560] was submitted by France.

The Security Council,

Recalling its previous resolutions and the statements by its President relating to the situation in Côte d'Ivoire, in particular resolutions 1842(2008) of 29 October 2008 and 1880(2009) of 30 July 2009,

Reaffirming its strong commitment to the sovereignty, independence, territorial integrity and unity of Côte d'Ivoire, and recalling the importance of the principles of good-neighbourliness, non-interference and regional cooperation,

Taking note of the report of the Secretary-General of 29 September 2009 and of the reports of the Group of Experts on Côte d'Ivoire transmitted on 8 April and 7 October 2009,

Emphasizing the continued contribution to Côte d'Ivoire's stability, in particular in the context of the planned presidential elections, of the measures imposed by resolutions 1572(2004) of 15 November 2004 and 1643(2005) of 15 December 2005,

Noting again with concern, in spite of the sustained improvement in the overall human rights situation, the persistence of reported human rights and humanitarian law violations against civilians in different parts of the country, including numerous acts of sexual violence, stressing that the perpetrators must be brought to justice, reiterating its firm condemnation of all violations of human rights and international humanitarian law in Côte d'Ivoire, and recalling its resolutions 1325(2000) of 31 October 2000, 1820(2008) of 19 June 2008, 1888(2009) of 30 September 2009 and 1889(2009) of 5 October 2009 on women and peace and security, its resolutions 1612(2005) of 26 July 2005 and 1882(2009) of 4 August 2009 on children and armed conflict and its resolution 1674(2006) of 28 April 2006 on the protection of civilians in armed conflict,

Determining that the situation in Côte d'Ivoire continues to pose a threat to international peace and security in the region,

Acting under Chapter VII of the Charter of the United Nations,

1. *Decides* to renew until 31 October 2010 the measures on arms and the financial and travel measures imposed by paragraphs 7 to 12 of resolution 1572(2004) and the measures preventing the importation by any State of all rough diamonds from Côte d'Ivoire imposed by paragraph 6 of resolution 1643(2005);

2. *Decides also* to review the measures renewed in paragraph 1 above in the light of the progress achieved in the electoral process and in the implementation of the key steps of the peace process, as referred to in resolution 1880(2009), by the end of the period mentioned in paragraph 1 above, and decides further to carry out during the period mentioned in paragraph 1 above:

(a) A review of the measures renewed in paragraph 1 above no later than three months after the holding of open, free, fair and transparent presidential elections in accordance with international standards, with a view to possibly modifying the sanctions regime; or

(b) A midterm review no later than 30 April 2010 if no review has been scheduled on the basis of paragraph 2 (a) of the present resolution at that date;

3. *Calls upon* the Ivorian parties to the Ouagadougou Political Agreement and all States, in particular those in the subregion, to fully implement the measures renewed in paragraph 1 above, including, as appropriate, by making the necessary rules and regulations, calls upon the United Nations Operation in Côte d'Ivoire to bring its full support, in particular, to the implementation of the measures on arms renewed in paragraph 1 above, within its capacities and its mandate, as determined in resolution 1739(2007) of 10 January 2007 and renewed in resolution 1880(2009), and calls upon the French forces to support the United Nations Operation in Côte d'Ivoire in this regard, within the limits of their deployment and their capabilities;

4. *Again reiterates its demand*, in particular, that the Ivorian authorities take the necessary measures to put an immediate end to any violation of measures imposed by paragraph 11 of resolution 1572(2004), including those violations mentioned by the Group of Experts on Côte d'Ivoire in its reports of 21 September 2007, 8 October 2008 and 7 October 2009;

5. *Demands* that the Ivorian parties to the Ouagadougou Political Agreement, in particular the Ivorian authorities, provide unhindered access, particularly to the Group of Experts first established pursuant to paragraph 7 of reso-

lution 1584(2005) of 1 February 2005, to equipment, sites and installations referred to in paragraph 2 *(a)* of resolution 1584(2005) and to all weapons, ammunition and related materiel, regardless of location, when appropriate without notice and including those under the control of Republican Guard units, and demands further that they provide access under the same conditions to the United Nations Operation in Côte d'Ivoire in order to enable it to carry out its mandate, and to the French forces supporting it, as set out in resolutions 1739(2007) and 1880(2009);

6. *Reiterates* that any threat to the electoral process in Côte d'Ivoire, in particular any attack on or obstruction of the action of the Independent Electoral Commission in charge of the organization of the elections or the action of the operators mentioned in paragraphs 1.3.3 and 2.1.1 of the Ouagadougou Political Agreement shall constitute a threat to the peace and national reconciliation process for the purposes of paragraphs 9 and 11 of resolution 1572(2004);

7. *Reiterates also* that any serious obstacle to the freedom of movement of the United Nations Operation in Côte d'Ivoire or the French forces supporting it, or any attack or obstruction of the action of the United Nations Operation in Côte d'Ivoire, the French forces, the Special Representative of the Secretary-General for Côte d'Ivoire, the Facilitator mentioned in paragraph 23 of resolution 1880(2009) or his Special Representative in Côte d'Ivoire shall constitute a threat to the peace and national reconciliation process for the purposes of paragraphs 9 and 11 of resolution 1572(2004);

8. *Requests* the Secretary-General and the Government of France to report to the Security Council immediately, through the Security Council Committee established pursuant to resolution 1572(2004), any serious obstacle to the freedom of movement of the United Nations Operation in Côte d'Ivoire or the French forces supporting it, including the names of those responsible, and requests the Secretary-General and the Facilitator to report to the Council immediately, through the Committee, any attack or obstruction of their action or the action of the Special Representatives mentioned in paragraph 7 above;

9. *Requests* all States concerned, in particular those in the subregion, to cooperate fully with the Committee, and authorizes the Committee to request whatever further information it may consider necessary;

10. *Decides* to extend the mandate of the Group of Experts as set out in paragraph 7 of resolution 1727(2006) of 15 December 2006 until 31 October 2010, and requests the Secretary-General to take the necessary administrative measures;

11. *Decides also* that the report referred to in paragraph 7 *(e)* of resolution 1727(2006) may include, as appropriate, any information and recommendations relevant to the possible additional designation by the Committee of the individuals and entities described in paragraphs 9 and 11 of resolution 1572(2004);

12. *Requests* the Group of Experts to provide a midterm report to the Committee by 15 April 2010 and to submit a final written report to the Council, through the Committee, fifteen days before the end of its mandated period, on the implementation of the measures imposed by paragraphs 7, 9 and 11 of resolution 1572(2004) and paragraph 6 of resolution 1643(2005), as well as recom-mendations in this regard, and also requests the Group of Experts to include in its report specific information on persons who deny it access to weapons, ammunition and related materiel;

13. *Requests* the Secretary-General to communicate, as appropriate, to the Council, through the Committee, information gathered by the United Nations Operation in Côte d'Ivoire and, where possible, reviewed by the Group of Experts, concerning the supply of arms and related materiel to Côte d'Ivoire;

14. *Requests* the Government of France to communicate, as appropriate, to the Council, through the Committee, information gathered by the French forces and, where possible, reviewed by the Group of Experts, concerning the supply of arms and related materiel to Côte d'Ivoire;

15. *Requests* the Kimberley Process to communicate, as appropriate, to the Council, through the Committee, information which, where possible, has been reviewed by the Group of Experts, concerning the production and illicit export of diamonds from Côte d'Ivoire;

16. *Decides* that the measures imposed by paragraph 6 of resolution 1643(2005) shall not apply to an import that will be used solely for the purposes of scientific research and analysis to facilitate the development of specific technical information concerning Ivorian diamond production, provided that the research is coordinated by the Kimberley Process and approved on a case-by-case basis by the Committee;

17. *Decides also* that a request made in accordance with paragraph 16 above shall be submitted to the Committee jointly by the Kimberley Process and the importing Member State, and decides further that, where the Committee has approved an exemption pursuant to this paragraph, the importing Member State shall notify the Committee of the results of the study and share the results, without delay, with the Group of Experts to assist it in its investigations;

18. *Urges* all States, relevant United Nations bodies and other organizations and interested parties, including the Kimberley Process, to cooperate fully with the Committee, the Group of Experts, the United Nations Operation in Côte d'Ivoire and the French forces, in particular by supplying any information at their disposal on possible violations of the measures imposed by paragraphs 7, 9 and 11 of resolution 1572(2004) and paragraph 6 of resolution 1643(2005) and reiterated in paragraph 1 above;

19. *Urges*, in this context, that all Ivorian parties and all States, particularly those in the region, ensure:

—The safety of the members of the Group of Experts;

—Unhindered access by the Group of Experts, in particular to persons, documents and sites, in order for the Group of Experts to execute its mandate;

20. *Underlines* that it is fully prepared to impose targeted measures against persons to be designated by the Committee who are determined to be, among other things:

(a) A threat to the peace and national reconciliation process in Côte d'Ivoire, in particular by blocking the implementation of the peace process as referred to in the Ouagadougou Political Agreement;

(b) Attacking or obstructing the action of the United Nations Operation in Côte d'Ivoire, the French forces supporting it, the Special Representative of the Secretary-

General, the Facilitator, or his Special Representative in Côte d'Ivoire;

(c) Responsible for obstacles to the freedom of movement of the United Nations Operation in Côte d'Ivoire and the French forces supporting it;

(d) Responsible for serious violations of human rights and international humanitarian law committed in Côte d'Ivoire;

(e) Publicly inciting hatred and violence;

(f) Acting in violation of the measures imposed by paragraph 7 of resolution 1572(2004);

21. *Decides* to remain actively seized of the matter.

UNOCI

The United Nations Operation in Côte d'Ivoire (UNOCI) was established in 2004 by Security Council resolution 1528(2004) [YUN 2004, p. 173] to replace the United Nations Mission in Côte d'Ivoire and ECOWAS forces. Its mandate was to monitor the ceasefire and the movement of armed groups; assist in disarmament, demobilization, reintegration, repatriation and resettlement; protect UN personnel and civilians; support implementation of the peace process; and provide assistance in the monitoring of human rights, public information and law and order. The UNOCI mandate was revised in 2007 [YUN 2007, p. 170] to include supporting the work of the Integrated Command Centre (CCI), monitoring the cessation of hostilities and movement of armed groups, and providing other security-related assistance. Unoci was supported by the French Licorne forces. Headquartered in Abidjan, UNOCI was Headed by the Special Representative of the Secretary-General, Choi Young-Jin (Republic of Korea).

The Council, by resolution 1865(2009) (see p. 171), renewed the mandate of UNOCI until 31 July 2009, and by resolution 1880(2009) (see p. 177), it renewed the mandate until 31 January 2010. During 2009, the Secretary-General submitted reports to the Council on developments in Côte d'Ivoire and UNOCI activities in January [S/2009/21], April [S/2009/196], July [S/2009/344] and September [S/2009/495], with a later report covering the end of the year [S/2010/15].

In addition to political, security, human rights and humanitarian activities, the reports covered personnel conduct and discipline matters. Unoci, in cooperation with the Office of Internal Oversight Services (OIOS), continued to investigate allegations of misconduct by UNOCI personnel and recommended disciplinary action where allegations were substantiated. Early in the year, the United Nations and troop-contributing countries completed investigations into serious allegations of sexual exploitation and abuse committed by personnel of UNOCI contingents previously stationed in Bouaké and Logoualé. The findings were shared with the concerned troop-contributing countries for

appropriate action. In October, UNOCI received reports of allegations of sexual exploitation and abuse committed by some members of one of its military contingents that might have occurred in 2006 and appeared to involve minors. The mission immediately dispatched an assessment team to the area where the allegations reportedly occurred and apprised OIOS of the matter. The authorities of the concerned troop-contributing country were informed and were requested to investigate. The personnel allegedly involved had returned to their home country on regular rotation. Meanwhile, UNOCI implemented additional measures to enforce compliance with the zero-tolerance policy regarding sexual exploitation and abuse.

Communication. By a letter transmitted by the Secretary-General to the Security Council on 29 December [S/2009/694], President Gbagbo of Côte d'Ivoire and President Compaoré of Burkina Faso proposed the deployment, for a three-month period, of a military unit of up to 500 troops from Burkina Faso to Côte d'Ivoire as part of UNOCI in order to reinforce the general security arrangements for the Ivorian presidential elections that were expected to be held by March 2010. Such redeployment required the authorization of the Council. In his September report on UNOCI, the Secretary-General had mentioned his intention to request the Council's authorization for the temporary redeployment of one infantry company and two helicopters from UNMIL to Côte d'Ivoire; should the deployment of a contingent from Burkina Faso be feasible and acceptable to the Security Council, it would no longer be necessary to redeploy an infantry company from UNMIL.

Appointment. On 8 December [S/2009/637], the Secretary-General informed the Security Council that, following consultations, he intended to appoint Major General Abdul Hafiz (Bangladesh) as Operation Force Commander of UNOCI with effect from 1 January 2010; he would replace Major General Fernand Marcel Amoussou (Benin), whose tour of duty would end on 31 December 2009. The Council took note of the appointment on 10 December [S/2009/638]. After further consultations with President Gbagbo, the Secretary-General, on 18 December [S/2009/672] informed the Council that the appointment would not take effect until 1 April 2010 and that the tour of duty of the current Force Commander would be extended until 31 March 2010. The Council took note on 24 December [S/2009/673].

Report of OIOS. OIOS, in a February report [A/63/713], presented a programme evaluation of UNOCI's performance and achievement of results. The objective of the report was to determine the relevance, efficiency, effectiveness and impact of the mission in relation to its mandated objectives, as stipulated in Security Council resolutions 1528(2004), 1609(2005),

1795(2008) [YUN 2008, p. 176] and 1826(2008) [YUN 2008, p. 184]. OIOS observed substantial progress with regard to the mandated elements over which the mission had direct operational control, whereas limited progress was achieved in regard to the mandated tasks where the Ivorians were in the lead and UNOCI played a supporting role. Many of the targets established by Council resolutions and the political accords signed by the parties, such as elections and disarmament, had either not been achieved or postponed. Progress had been made in some cross-cutting issues such as gender mainstreaming and child protection. In the view of OIOS, the Ouagadougou Agreement, while addressing key issues that hindered the peace process, had resulted in some contradiction with the UNOCI mandate and had added a degree of ambiguity to the mission's role. While the Council continued to renew all previous mandates, it also requested UNOCI to limit its role to supporting implementation of the Agreement, while the Ivorian parties assumed the lead role.

OIOS identified several critical issues. It believed that UNOCI strategic planning needed strengthening. The mission's implementation plan was not updated regularly, resulting in inadequate guidance for mission priorities, and it lacked an exit strategy that addressed consolidation, drawdown and withdrawal. The organization of elections risked being compromised by logistical and technical problems, including the identification and registration of voters and insufficient financial resources. The limited progress in disarmament, demobilization and reintegration, and the absence of a formal mechanism for coordinating security sector reform, posed risks to the peace process. While some progress had been made in disarmament and reintegration through micro-projects, there did not appear to be a formal needs assessment to determine actual requirements and preferences of beneficiaries. Overall coordination with regional partners needed strengthening. There was a threat of violence erupting during and after the elections that endangered the safety of UN personnel and institutions and that needed to be closely managed. OIOS recommended that UNOCI: review operational guidelines, particularly with regard to the protection of civilians; seek guidance from the Department of Peacekeeping Operations (DPKO) on its post-Agreement role; review and update its strategic planning; undertake strategic planning for consolidation, gradual drawdown and eventual exit with appropriate benchmarks to begin a handover; strengthen its planning to support disarmament, demobilization and reintegration activities; strengthen the capacity of the CCI to support those activities; work with development agencies and partners to optimize the effectiveness of reintegration programmes; develop an overarching security sector reform framework; and strengthen coordination with regional missions.

Financing

In June, at its resumed sixty-third (2009) session, the General Assembly considered the Secretary-General's financial performance report on the budget of UNOCI for the period from 1 July 2007 to 30 June 2008 [A/63/610] and the proposed budget from 1 July 2009 to 30 June 2010 [A/63/724], the related ACABQ report [A/63/746/Add.7] and the OIOS report on the programme evaluation of the performance and achievement of results by UNOCI [A/63/713] (see above). The 2007/08 budget showed actual expenditure at $465,272,000 against an appropriation of $470,856,100. The proposed UNOCI budget for the period from 1 July 2009 to 30 June 2010 amounted to $505,799,500 (gross), which provided for the deployment of 7,250 military contingent personnel, 200 military observers, 450 UN police officers, 750 formed police units personnel, 479 international staff, 723 national staff, 301 UN Volunteers, 8 Government-provided personnel, 5 international temporary positions and 7 national temporary positions. ACABQ recommended that the 2009/10 budget be reduced to $496,307,600. The General Assembly took action on the recommendations in resolution 63/289 (see below).

GENERAL ASSEMBLY ACTION

On 30 June [meeting 93], the General Assembly, on the recommendation of the Fifth Committee [A/63/896], adopted **resolution 63/289** without vote [agenda item 134].

Financing of the United Nations Operation in Côte d'Ivoire

The General Assembly,

Having considered the reports of the Secretary-General on the financing of the United Nations Operation in Côte d'Ivoire, the related report of the Advisory Committee on Administrative and Budgetary Questions and the report of the Office of Internal Oversight Services on the programme evaluation of the performance and the achievement of results by the United Nations Operation in Côte d'Ivoire,

Recalling Security Council resolution 1528(2004) of 27 February 2004, by which the Council established the United Nations Operation in Côte d'Ivoire for an initial period of twelve months as from 4 April 2004, and the subsequent resolutions by which the Council extended the mandate of the Operation, the latest of which was resolution 1865(2009) of 27 January 2009, by which the Council extended the mandate of the Operation until 31 July 2009,

Recalling also its resolution 58/310 of 18 June 2004 on the financing of the Operation and its subsequent resolutions thereon, the latest of which was resolution 62/254 of 20 June 2008,

Reaffirming the general principles underlying the financing of United Nations peacekeeping operations, as stated in General Assembly resolutions 1874(S-IV) of 27 June 1963, 3101(XXVIII) of 11 December 1973 and 55/235 of 23 December 2000,

Mindful of the fact that it is essential to provide the Operation with the financial resources necessary to enable it to fulfil its responsibilities under the relevant resolutions of the Security Council,

1. *Requests* the Secretary-General to entrust the Head of Mission with the task of formulating future budget proposals in full accordance with the provisions of General Assembly resolutions 59/296 of 22 June 2005, 60/266 of 30 June 2006 and 61/276 of 29 June 2007, as well as other relevant resolutions;

2. *Takes note* of the status of contributions to the United Nations Operation in Côte d'Ivoire as at 30 April 2009, including the contributions outstanding in the amount of 132.2 million United States dollars, representing some 6 per cent of the total assessed contributions, notes with concern that only forty-nine Member States have paid their assessed contributions in full, and urges all other Member States, in particular those in arrears, to ensure payment of their outstanding assessed contributions;

3. *Expresses its appreciation* to those Member States which have paid their assessed contributions in full, and urges all other Member States to make every possible effort to ensure payment of their assessed contributions to the Operation in full;

4. *Expresses concern* at the financial situation with regard to peacekeeping activities, in particular as regards the reimbursements to troop contributors that bear additional burdens owing to overdue payments by Member States of their assessments;

5. *Also expresses concern* at the delay experienced by the Secretary-General in deploying and providing adequate resources to some recent peacekeeping missions, in particular those in Africa;

6. *Emphasizes* that all future and existing peacekeeping missions shall be given equal and non-discriminatory treatment in respect of financial and administrative arrangements;

7. *Also emphasizes* that all peacekeeping missions shall be provided with adequate resources for the effective and efficient discharge of their respective mandates;

8. *Reiterates its request* to the Secretary-General to make the fullest possible use of facilities and equipment at the United Nations Logistics Base at Brindisi, Italy, in order to minimize the costs of procurement for the Operation;

9. *Requests* the Secretary-General to give consideration to making the fullest possible use of the facilities at the logistics hub at Entebbe, Uganda;

10. *Also requests* the Secretary-General to ensure that proposed peacekeeping budgets are based on the relevant legislative mandates;

11. *Endorses* the conclusions and recommendations contained in the report of the Advisory Committee on Administrative and Budgetary Questions, subject to the provisions of the present resolution, and requests the Secretary-General to ensure their full implementation;

12. *Takes note* of paragraph 10 of the report of the Advisory Committee;

13. *Requests* the Secretary-General to ensure the full implementation of the relevant provisions of resolutions 59/296, 60/266 and 61/276;

14. *Also requests* the Secretary-General to take all action necessary to ensure that the Operation is administered with a maximum of efficiency and economy;

15. *Further requests* the Secretary-General, in order to reduce the cost of employing General Service staff, to continue efforts to recruit local staff for the Operation against General Service posts, commensurate with the requirements of the Operation;

16. *Takes note* of the report of the Office of Internal Oversight Services on the programme evaluation of the performance and the achievement of results by the Operation, and requests the Secretary-General to ensure the full implementation of the recommendations therein;

17. *Expresses concern* at the comments of the Office of Internal Oversight Services contained in paragraphs 14, 31 and 32 of its report;

Financial performance report for the period from 1 July 2007 to 30 June 2008

18. *Takes note* of the report of the Secretary-General on the financial performance of the Operation for the period from 1 July 2007 to 30 June 2008;

Budget estimates for the period from 1 July 2009 to 30 June 2010

19. *Decides* to appropriate to the Special Account for the United Nations Operation in Côte d'Ivoire the amount of 513,442,600 dollars for the period from 1 July 2009 to 30 June 2010, inclusive of the amount of 491,774,100 dollars for the maintenance of the Operation, 18,033,500 dollars for the support account for peacekeeping operations and 3,635,000 dollars for the United Nations Logistics Base;

Financing of the appropriation

20. *Also decides* to apportion among Member States the amount of 42,786,883 dollars for the period from 1 to 31 July 2009 in accordance with the levels updated in General Assembly resolution 61/243 of 22 December 2006, and taking into account the scale of assessments for 2009, as set out in Assembly resolution 61/237 of 22 December 2006;

21. *Further decides* that, in accordance with the provisions of its resolution 973(X) of 15 December 1955, there shall be set off against the apportionment among Member States, as provided for in paragraph 20 above, their respective share in the Tax Equalization Fund of 990,333 dollars, comprising the estimated staff assessment income of 803,992 dollars approved for the Operation, the prorated share of 156,441 dollars of the estimated staff assessment income approved for the support account and the prorated share of 29,900 dollars of the estimated staff assessment income approved for the United Nations Logistics Base;

22. *Decides* to apportion among Member States the amount of 470,655,717 dollars for the period from 1 August 2009 to 30 June 2010, at a monthly rate of 42,786,883 dollars, in accordance with the levels updated in resolution 61/243, and taking into account the scale of assessments for 2009, as set out in resolution 61/237, and for 2010, subject to a decision of the Security Council to extend the mandate of the Operation;

23. *Also decides* that, in accordance with the provisions of its resolution 973(X), there shall be set off against the apportionment among Member States, as provided for

in paragraph 22 above, their respective share in the Tax Equalization Fund of 10,893,667 dollars, comprising the estimated staff assessment income of 8,843,908 dollars approved for the Operation, the prorated share of 1,720,859 dollars of the estimated staff assessment income approved for the support account and the prorated share of 328,900 dollars of the estimated staff assessment income approved for the United Nations Logistics Base;

24. *Further decides* that, for Member States that have fulfilled their financial obligations to the Operation, there shall be set off against their apportionment, as provided for in paragraph 20 above, their respective share of the unencumbered balance and other income in the total amount of 19.5 million dollars in respect of the financial period ended 30 June 2008, in accordance with the levels updated in resolution 61/243, and taking into account the scale of assessments for 2008, as set out in resolution 61/237;

25. *Decides* that, for Member States that have not fulfilled their financial obligations to the Operation, there shall be set off against their outstanding obligations their respective share of the unencumbered balance and other income in the total amount of 19.5 million dollars in respect of the financial period ended 30 June 2008, in accordance with the scheme set out in paragraph 24 above;

26. *Also decides* that the decrease of 156,100 dollars in the estimated staff assessment income in respect of the financial period ended 30 June 2008 shall be set off against the credits from the amount of 19.5 million dollars referred to in paragraphs 24 and 25 above;

27. *Emphasizes* that no peacekeeping mission shall be financed by borrowing funds from other active peacekeeping missions;

28. *Encourages* the Secretary-General to continue to take additional measures to ensure the safety and security of all personnel participating in the Operation under the auspices of the United Nations, bearing in mind paragraphs 5 and 6 of Security Council resolution 1502(2003) of 26 August 2003;

29. *Invites* voluntary contributions to the Operation in cash and in the form of services and supplies acceptable to the Secretary-General, to be administered, as appropriate, in accordance with the procedure and practices established by the General Assembly;

30. *Decides* to include in the provisional agenda of its sixty-fourth session the item entitled "Financing of the United Nations Operation in Côte d'Ivoire".

On 24 December, the General Assembly decided that the agenda item on the financing of UNOCI would remain for consideration during its sixty-fourth (2010) session (**decision 64/549**).

Liberia

The Government of Liberia continued its efforts in 2009 to improve governance and security, consolidate State authority, manage natural resources, address human rights issues, and build a better economy. Assistance in those goals was provided by the United Nations Mission in Liberia (UNMIL) and other international and regional organizations. The Government began implementing its first national poverty reduction strategy. Under that strategy, special attention was paid to reform of rule-of-law institutions and the security sector, in particular the Liberian National Police and the Armed Forces of Liberia, both of which needed assistance for upgrading training and management capabilities. Those reforms were proposed against a background of continued tensions between ethnic groups and communities. The Government drafted several constitutional amendments on elections, in preparation for and conduct of the elections scheduled for 2011. The Truth and Reconciliation Commission submitted its final report to the legislature and the President in June, and three months later the legislature decided not to take action on the Commission's recommendations until 2010. The public remained divided on the main issues raised in the report, and debate focused on whether the leaders of the warring factions and others reportedly responsible for atrocities should be prosecuted.

In August, the Security Council approved the Secretary-General's recommendation to implement the third stage of UNMIL's drawdown, beginning in October, by repatriating 2,029 military personnel, leaving the military strength at 8,202 personnel, of whom 250 would be based at the Special Court for Sierra Leone.

The Panel of Experts established to assess implementation of the arms embargo imposed on Liberia, as well as the travel ban and assets freeze of a number of individuals, reviewed applications for exemptions and investigated possible violations. In December, the Security Council renewed the arms embargo and restrictions against listed individuals for another 12 months.

Political and security developments

Report of Secretary-General (February). In his eighteenth progress report on UNMIL [S/2009/86], submitted pursuant to Security Council resolution 1836(2008) [YUN 2008, p. 201], the Secretary-General said that the relationship between the legislative and executive branches had continued to improve, allowing for the adoption of several key legislative bills, particularly those on defence and corruption. The National Elections Commission submitted to the Legislature a number of constitutional amendments, which dealt with election procedures in preparation for elections in 2011. A comprehensive plan for the preparation and conduct of the elections, including the required financial and technical support, had yet to be developed. In February, President Ellen Johnson-Sirleaf appointed a constitutional reform task force to oversee political and legal reform. Although the Government had undertaken some reconciliation initiatives, tensions between ethnic groups and communities remained a concern, especially given the recent escalation of disputes over land and natural resources. The security situation continued to be fragile, with continued law and order incidents such as armed robbery, mob violence, rape and attacks on police officers.

To improve the economic situation, the Government focused on deliverables under the four poverty reduction strategy pillars: security, economic recovery, rule of law, and infrastructure and basic services. Gross domestic product (GDP) was estimated at $871 million in 2008, with a per capita GDP of $221. Owing to the rising food and fuel prices, the trade deficit doubled during 2008 and the inflation rate peaked at 22 per cent in October. The humanitarian situation continued to improve, although remote communities often lived in precarious circumstances with limited basic services.

Following the completion of the national security strategy, an implementation matrix, covering all security and law enforcement agencies, was finalized and approved as the road map for security sector reform. Among the identified challenges were capacity deficits, dependence on donor funding and the need to establish county security coordination mechanisms. Training for the new armed forces, particularly development of the command and control structure, continued with international support. Progress was made in reform and strengthening of the national police, in particular the formulation of a five-year police strategic plan. Training and infrastructure development continued; however, the achievement of full operational capability remained a challenge due to infrastructure limitations and insufficient funding. The appointment of 10 legally qualified county attorneys had improved the quality of prosecutions, but the absence of public defenders had reduced their impact. Promotion of human rights remained limited, and harmful traditional practices, including trials by ordeal, ritual killings and female genital mutilation, were widely practiced. There had been some progress in consolidating State authority, with an increased presence of public officials throughout the country, the renovation of a majority of county administrative buildings, and the strengthening of coordination and monitoring structures. The reach of State authority, however, remained limited, especially in remote areas. President Johnson-Sirleaf stressed the importance of governance reforms, in particular the need to fight corruption.

Among efforts to manage natural resources, the Government adhered to the Kimberley Process Certification Scheme for diamonds, although challenges remained owing to poor infrastructure and inadequate security and administrative coverage in mining areas. Progress was made in establishing a mining cadastral system and in drafting a new mineral exploration regulation, aimed at improving State control over mining

areas. The Forestry Development Authority awarded the first three forestry management contracts, encompassing 235,876 hectares for a period of 25 years.

As directed by Council resolution 1836(2008), UNMIL began its drawdown of troops, reducing its troop strength to 10,231 by 31 March by withdrawing 1,460. UNMIL continued to provide security for the Special Court for Sierra Leone and had taken over administrative and logistical support to the Court following the completion of the mandate of the United Nations Integrated Office in Sierra Leone (UNIOSIL) on 30 September 2008 [ibid., p. 218]. The mission's police strength stood at 1,226. UNMIL monitored progress towards meeting the drawdown benchmarks, as proposed by the Secretary-General in his March 2008 report [ibid., p. 200], using them as a tool to prioritize and monitor work in support of national priorities.

The Secretary-General urged international partners to support Liberia during that crucial phase, especially with financial assistance for activities under the poverty reduction strategy. He noted that challenges remained in meeting core security and rule of law benchmarks. While the finalization of the national police strategic plan was a significant step forward, it needed to be matched by progress in strengthening judicial and correctional institutions. Likewise, challenges remained in developing the national army to ensure that it reached full operational capability. Following the finalization of the first volume of the report of the Truth and Reconciliation Commission, which focused on the root causes of the conflict, the Government needed to implement the Commission's recommendations. In view of the remaining challenges, in particular security issues and uncertainty in the subregion, the Secretary-General recommended that no further adjustment be made to UNMIL military and police components. A technical assessment mission led by DPKO would be sent to Liberia to develop a mission drawdown and eventual withdrawal plan.

Technical assessment mission

The Secretary-General, in response to the Security Council's request in resolution 1836(2008) for recommendations on further adjustments to the military and police components of UNMIL, sent a technical assessment mission to Liberia from 26 April to 6 May and summarized its findings in a June special report [S/2009/299]. Led by DPKO, the mission consulted a number of Liberian and international stakeholders and visited six counties. All interlocutors advised the mission that an objective assessment of progress made in consolidating peace must be placed in the context of the significant challenges inherited by the Government when it came into office in 2006 and of the state in which UNMIL found Liberia at the end of the conflict in 2003. They recalled that at the end of the

14-year-long civil war, Liberia was a failed State, with three warring factions controlling different parts of Monrovia and the interior. The limited infrastructure lay in ruins, a third of the population had been displaced, and the public sector had collapsed. The national army and police had disintegrated into factions; the justice system had broken down; and criminal economic exchange, dominated by illegal exploitation of natural resources, was thriving. They stressed that consolidation of peace would require that institutions be built from scratch in order to be free of corruption, inclusive and able to provide services to the entire population.

Notwithstanding those conditions, the mission found that peace consolidation efforts had made progress in many areas and that the Government had made strides in implementing its recovery programme. Key achievements included: the expansion of access to health-care services; free and compulsory primary education; measures to meet the preconditions for lifting sanctions on timber and diamond exports; and the implementation of a programme which reduced revenue leakages in State-owned enterprises. The value of the country's exports rose from $131 million in 2005 to $260 million in 2008.

Many of the mission's interlocutors said that the existing stability could not be sustained without a significant UNMIL presence and cautioned against a hasty drawdown. They pointed to many contentious issues that could become destabilizing factors—the political and economic marginalization of the indigenous majority, rampant corruption, land disputes, ethnic divisions and the concentration of State services in Monrovia. The dysfunctional justice system perpetrated a culture of settling disputes through mob violence. All stakeholders characterized the 2011 elections as a milestone that would test the sustainability of the peace and the capacity of the security, electoral and rule-of-law institutions. A number of election-related issues, including the composition of the National Elections Commission, were already creating political tensions. The interlocutors recommended that the conduct of free and fair elections be among the core benchmarks guiding the drawdown and that UNMIL maintain a significant troop level through the elections. It was expected that the national authorities would require substantial assistance from the United Nations and, to that end, the Department of Political Affairs and UNDP dispatched an electoral needs assessment mission in May. The situation in the subregion presented major security risks for Liberia, in particular the estimated 2,000 Liberian combatants associated with pro-Government militias in western Côte d'Ivoire and an undetermined number of Liberian elements associated with the Forces nouvelles in northern Côte d'Ivoire.

In addition, the situations in Guinea and Sierra Leone were sources of concern.

The Secretary-General reviewed progress in attaining his benchmarks on peace consolidation—basic training of 3,500 national police officers; completion of police operating procedures; formation of a 500-strong police Emergency Response Unit; equipping of police personnel and their deployment to the counties; finalization of the national security strategy and implementation throughout the country; training and operationalization of the first and second battalions of the armed forces; and restoration of State authority throughout the country. Training of the 2,000-member armed forces, led by the United States, was making progress. ECOWAS provided officers to fill the leadership gap in the new army. The basic training of some 3,500 police officers was completed in 2007, but their full operational capability was beset with challenges. Stakeholders described the force as ineffectual, and identified chief problems as poor conditions of service, ineffective management, and inadequate transport, communications equipment and infrastructure. Relations between the police and their communities remained poor and the credibility of the police was affected by indiscipline, corrupt practices and abuses of the population, as well as inability to maintain law and order or respond effectively to crime. The development of the 500-strong Emergency Response Unit had made progress, although it was still only marginally operational. Overall, there was a need to put the police development project back on track. Given the plethora of security agencies created by previous regimes, the need to streamline those agencies and repeal security-related legislation was identified as a security priority. However, the draft enabling legislation, or Omnibus Act, had not yet been submitted to the legislature. The emphasis on restructuring the army and police without commensurate assistance for the justice and corrections systems had created bottlenecks in the rule-of-law sector.

When the national disarmament, demobilization and reintegration programme closed in April, all 101,495 demobilized former combatants were offered the opportunity to participate in a reintegration project. However, some 5,000 did not come forward to participate. Many interlocutors expressed to the mission their doubts that the ex-fighters had successfully integrated into their communities, and the mission found that a longer-term effort was required to transform the violent mindset of ex-combatants. In addition, State authority had expanded to some of the counties, but the overall capacity of State officials to deliver services to rural communities remained extremely limited.

The mission determined that the uneven progress towards achieving the core benchmarks, coupled with the fragility of the peace, justified maintaining the strategy of gradual consolidation, drawdown and withdrawal approved by the Security Council in resolution 1712(2006) [YUN 2006, p. 218]. Having started with drawdowns in September 2008 and March 2009, UNMIL stood at an authorized strength of 10,231 troops, reduced from 15,250, and a police authorized strength of 1,375 personnel. The mission made recommendations for the third stage of the drawdown: a reduction of 2,029 troops (two infantry battalions and 365 additional military personnel) to be repatriated between October 2009 and May 2010, accompanied by repatriation of combat equipment and consolidation of bases; no further reduction would be made to the UNMIL police component, and further reductions would be linked to progress in deploying a competent national police; UNMIL would adjust its civilian component to adapt to evolving priorities; it would maintain the current capability of its military and civilian logistical and support resources; and its continued presence would be required at key strategic UN locations until a security assessment was completed. At the conclusion of the third drawdown, UNMIL would have 7,952 troops and maintain that strength throughout the electoral period. In anticipation of the withdrawal of the peacekeeping mission after the 2011 elections, UNMIL had started planning an exit strategy and handover of security responsibilities to the Government. According to the Secretary-General, once the national army and police were operational, Liberia would need continued assistance to sustain them and to develop judicial and corrections systems. He urged the Security Council to approve the plan for the third stage of the UNMIL drawdown.

Security Council mission

The Security Council, on 12 May [S/2009/243], informed the Secretary-General of its decision to send a mission to Africa from 14 to 21 May. In Liberia, the mission would review progress in implementing the UNMIL mandate, in particular progress made in meeting the benchmarks outlined in the Secretary-General's eighteen progress report (see above), and assess the logistic constraints affecting UNMIL, the operational capacity of the national police, the training of the armed forces and other national security institutions.

In its June report [S/2009/303], the mission said that the visit, its first since 2004, came after significant progress had been achieved in consolidating peace and stability. Since the Government of President Johnson-Sirleaf came into office in 2006, significant progress had been made in establishing a macroeconomic framework; Liberia had reached the decision point under the enhanced Heavily Indebted Poor Countries Initiative; and the Government had finalized its first national poverty reduction strategy following broad-based consultations.

Nevertheless, poverty and unemployment remained high, and the global economic crisis had had a negative impact on recovery. Consequently, the prevailing peace and stability remained extremely fragile. A number of ongoing processes—including the final report of the Truth and Reconciliation Commission, the trial against former President Charles Taylor, and the presidential and legislative elections in 2011—could generate tensions. At the regional level, the mission noted that while political relations between the countries of the Mano River Union (Guinea, Liberia, Sierra Leone) were sound, the porous borders and the situation in Guinea were potential threats to Liberia, along with the presence of groups of Liberian former combatants along the borders, particularly in western Côte d'Ivoire. According to the President, a large portion of the population remained accustomed to violence. The President outlined the Government's poverty reduction strategy, which revolved around four pillars: peace and security; economic development; governance and rule of law; and infrastructure and basic services. The protracted war had led to a lack of trust in national institutions and a massive brain drain, which had weakened and factionalized the civil service. The Government was therefore trying to attract Liberians to return from abroad to help with reconstruction. Another key issue that needed to be addressed was property rights and land claims. In that regard, there were plans to establish a national land commission.

The members of the Council recommended that the Government step up efforts to build its military and police capacity to be able to assume full security responsibilities once UNMIL completed its mandate. At the same time, the Council confirmed that there would be no precipitous withdrawal of UNMIL. The Council called on donors to continue to provide support to ensure that the poverty reduction strategy was adequately financed, and on the Government to support small and medium-size enterprises. The Government should continue efforts to encourage the Liberian diaspora to return to help build their country, and redouble efforts to combat sexual violence. UNMIL should continue to support the authorities in consolidating peace, and should seek to ensure that the identified benchmarks were met within the expected timelines. UNMIL should also continue to focus on building the capacity of the Liberian counterparts, in particular within the security sector.

Truth and Reconciliation Commission

In a report issued in August [S/2009/411], the Secretary-General said that since February, political activity had been dominated by events related to the work of the Truth and Reconciliation Commission. After holding consultations throughout the country, the Commission convened a national reconciliation conference in June, bringing together some 500 delegates from all 15 counties and the diaspora. On 30 June, the Commission concluded its mandate and submitted a final report to the legislature and the President. In the report, the Commission outlined the root causes of the Liberian conflict, stated that all factions had committed egregious violations of domestic and international criminal law, international human rights law and international humanitarian law, and made recommendations on accountability, reparations and amnesty, as well as reforms. The recommendations included the establishment of an extraordinary criminal tribunal to prosecute those having committed gross violations of human rights and economic crimes. Eight leaders of the warring factions, including former President Taylor, as well as 98 individuals identified as "most notorious perpetrators", were among those recommended for prosecution. Thirty-six persons were identified as being responsible for war crimes and crimes against humanity, but were not recommended for prosecution because they had spoken truthfully before the Commission and expressed remorse. The Commission also identified 50 individuals as financiers or supporters of the warring factions whom the Commission recommended be subject to public sanctions and be barred from public office for 30 years. That list included President Johnson-Sirleaf and other members of the Government.

Reactions to the report were mixed. Two Commissioners issued dissenting reports, stating that the recommendations would not further national reconciliation. Six of the former faction leaders recommended for prosecution gave a joint press conference to reject the recommendations, saying that they contravened the immunity signed into law by then-President Taylor in 2003, as well as the letter and spirit of the 2003 Comprehensive Peace Agreement [YUN 2003, p. 192]. Nearly 60 civil society organizations issued a joint statement welcoming the report. The International Contact Group on Liberia released a statement urging the Government to establish the Independent National Commission on Human Rights, which was mandated to oversee implementation of the recommendations of the Commission.

The 2005 Truth and Reconciliation Commission Act required that all of the Commission's recommendations be implemented and that the President report on implementation to the legislature on a quarterly basis. On 27 July, President Johnson-Sirleaf assured the nation that she would work with all stakeholders to implement the recommendations where the report lived up to its mandate and mission.

In September, the legislature decided not to take action on the recommendations until January 2010, according to the Secretary-General's later report [S/2010/88]. On 1 December 2009, the Commission issued the final report with 10 of its 12 appendices completed. That report expanded on the recommendations for the "Palava Hut" mechanism—a traditional conflict resolution mechanism presided over by a committee of members of integrity in the community, where perpetrators could publicly request forgiveness. The Commission recommended that an appearance before such a committee could lead to a reduction or waiver of an individual's public sanction. President Johnson-Sirleaf welcomed the report and said that a strategy was being planned for implementation, balancing the need for national reconciliation, peace and justice. Liberian society was deeply divided on the main issues.

Electoral needs assessment mission

On 10 February, the Liberian National Elections Commission requested the United Nations to deploy a needs assessment mission to Liberia to evaluate the Commission's needs in preparing for and conducting voter registration in 2009, ahead of presidential and legislative elections in October 2011. As the Secretary-General reported in August [S/2009/411], the Under-Secretary-General for Political Affairs deployed such a mission from 18 to 27 May. That mission, in cooperation with UNDP and UNMIL, consulted stakeholders and made recommendations. It remarked that early clarity on the electoral legal framework was needed to avoid delays in election preparations, including boundary delimitation and voter registration. Protracted debates had delayed adoption of the Threshold Bill, which was essential to begin to delineate electoral constituencies, and election law needed reform.

The needs assessment mission recommended, in view of political and social tensions that could impede elections, that all stakeholders should facilitate constructive dialogue while also establishing mechanisms for early warning and dispute resolution. Given the primary responsibility of Liberian institutions for organizing and conducting the 2011 elections, the mission determined that building local capacities should be the primary focus of international electoral assistance. UNMIL should provide logistical support for the elections to cover gaps in national capacities. While the conduct of elections had been added to the list of UNMIL's drawdown benchmarks, UNMIL was not mandated to provide electoral assistance. The needs assessment mission recommended that the UNMIL mandate be revised to include election-related tasks in support of national institutions, including logistical support. It also recommended that UNMIL support institutions and political parties in creating an environment conducive to peaceful elections. Recommendations called for: medium- and long-term capacity-building in operations and planning, boundary delimitation, voter registration and results management, civic and voter education, logistics and procurement, as well as advice in legal affairs and external relations. International financial and technical assistance would be required for conducting the electoral process.

Further developments

Report of Secretary-General (August). In his nineteenth UNMIL progress report issued in August [S/2009/411], the Secretary-General said that the political landscape had changed during the period under review. A new Senate President pro tempore was elected on 26 March, ending a leadership dispute that had hampered the legislature in 2008. The legislature had adopted important legislation, including a law establishing a commission to mediate land disputes. Also, the legislature passed the national budget for 2009–2010 in record time. Political parties formed new alliances. However, political party structures remained organizationally weak and centred largely on personalities rather than political programmes. Among its reconciliation initiatives, the Government addressed the contentious issue of land reform by measures such as its endorsement of the recommendations of a special commission established to mediate land disputes in Nimba County.

The Under-Secretary-General for Peacekeeping Operations visited Liberia from 14 to 17 June to take stock of UNMIL operations, and he confirmed the findings of the technical assessment mission, particularly the fragility of the prevailing peace, the need to expedite the development of security institutions and the rule of law sector, and the importance of political dialogue and reconciliation. The security situation was still fragile, marked by law and order incidents, including rape and armed robbery. Communal and mob violence continued, often emanating from tensions over land disputes. UNMIL continued to monitor security challenges related to ex-combatants, whose residual organizational capacity and command structures were contributing factors in the escalation of security incidents. In July, the President closed the national disarmament, demobilization, rehabilitation and reintegration programme, which had disarmed and demobilized more than 101,000 ex-combatants and provided reintegration assistance to 90,000 others since 2003.

The Government continued to implement its poverty reduction strategy and make economic reforms. The economic situation improved somewhat, with a growth rate of nearly 5 per cent in 2009, down from 7.1 per cent in 2008, while inflation dropped to 7 per cent in May, from its peak of 27 per cent in August 2008. The human rights situation improved, although the weakness of rule of law institutions, economic insecurity, and limited access to social services posed challenges for human rights protection. The Government began developing a national human rights action plan and established a steering committee to oversee the process. The Independent National Commission on Human Rights had not yet been constituted, though the act establishing it was signed in 2005 and amended in 2009.

UNMIL started a process with the Ministry of Defence and the armed forces for training and mentoring the new army. The national police was finalizing procedures, including standard operating procedures for police stations and a policy on professional standards. Improvements were noted in the police's capacity to investigate and resolve violent crimes in Monrovia. Effective State authority beyond Monrovia remained limited because of absenteeism of public officials and a lack of logistical support. The issue of governance was the subject of an executive order signed by the President on 11 June, establishing a Law Reform Commission expected to reform and develop Liberia's laws, ensure consistency within the law and propose a law reform framework. The Anti-Corruption Commission began investigations into two major corruption cases. Regarding natural resources management, the legislature approved the first three forestry management contracts, which would allow large-scale logging operations to begin. In July, the legislature approved a concession agreement with Malaysia for the production of rubber and palm oil.

The Secretary-General observed that Liberia had reached a critical moment with the release of the report of the Truth and Reconciliation Commission. The Liberian people should be afforded the opportunity to consider the Commission's recommendations and determine for themselves how best to implement them. The Secretary-General commended the Government for taking steps to address some of the challenges identified in his June special report (see p. 192), including by appointing new leadership for the national police and increasing its budget. Security sector reform would require strengthening other rule of law institutions, including corrections and the judiciary. The Government would require international assistance for its armed forces and its security sector.

The Secretary-General was also encouraged by some progress on the poverty reduction strategy, in particular that a stronger mechanism for monitoring the implementation of the strategy had been put in place under the Liberia Reconstruction and Development Committee, and that the improved working relationship between the legislative and executive branches had allowed for the adoption of key legislation related to the strategy. Regarding the elections of 2011, the Secretary-General concurred with the needs assessment mission's recommendation that UNMIL be mandated to fulfil some electoral assistance tasks, including logistical support, coordination of international electoral assistance, and facilitating the creation of a positive climate for peaceful elections. Recalling his recommendations made in his special report for the third stage of UNMIL drawdown and for the conduct of elections to be added to the list of the Mission's drawdown benchmarks, the Secretary-General requested that the Security-Council approve the recommendations and extend the UNMIL mandate for one year, until 30 September 2010.

SECURITY COUNCIL ACTION

On 15 September [meeting 6188], the Security Council unanimously adopted **resolution 1885(2009)**. The draft [S/2009/455] was prepared in consultations among Council members.

The Security Council,

Recalling its resolutions and the statements by its President concerning the situation in Liberia and the subregion, in particular resolutions 1509(2003) of 19 September 2003, 1626(2005) of 19 September 2005 and 1836(2008) of 29 September 2008,

Welcoming the report of the Secretary-General of 10 August 2009, as well as his special report of 10 June 2009, and taking note of the recommendations contained in both reports,

Welcoming also the efforts of the Government of Liberia to further national reconciliation and economic recovery, and to combat corruption and promote efficiency and good governance, in particular steps taken with regard to strengthening Government control over natural resources and to address the important issue of land reform,

Taking note of the conclusion of the work of the Truth and Reconciliation Commission, which provides an important opportunity for the people of Liberia to move the national reconciliation agenda forward and engage in a constructive national dialogue on the root causes of the Liberian conflict,

Recognizing that lasting stability in Liberia and the subregion will require well-functioning and sustainable security and rule of law sectors, and noting the continuing progress being made in developing and professionalizing the Armed Forces of Liberia and the Liberia National Police,

Recalling the benchmarks for the drawdown phase of the United Nations Mission in Liberia, including core benchmarks on the Liberia National Police and the national security strategy, and noting with concern those areas where progress is still slow,

Recognizing the significant challenges that remain across all sectors, including continuing problems with violent crime,

Welcoming the efforts of the Secretary-General to keep all peacekeeping operations, including the Mission, under close review, and stressing the need for the Security Council to pursue a rigorous, strategic approach to peacekeeping deployments, consistent with the statement by its President of 5 August 2009 on United Nations peacekeeping operations,

Expressing its appreciation for the continuing support of the international community, the Economic Community of West African States and the African Union,

Noting with concern the threats to subregional stability, including to Liberia, in particular those posed by drug trafficking, organized crime and illicit arms,

Commending the work of the Mission, under the leadership of the Special Representative of the Secretary-General

for Liberia, for its continuing and significant contribution to maintaining peace and stability in Liberia, and welcoming the close cooperation between the Mission and the United Nations Operation in Côte d'Ivoire, as well as with neighbouring Governments, in coordinating security activities in the border areas in the subregion,

Taking note of the conclusions of the needs assessment mission that evaluated the requirements of the Liberian National Elections Commission to prepare for and conduct the October 2011 general presidential and legislative elections, and stressing that the responsibility for the preparation and conduct of the elections rests with the Liberian authorities, with the support of the international community,

Welcoming the progress achieved on the benchmarks laid down in the reports of the Secretary-General of 12 September 2006, 8 August 2007 and 19 March 2008,

Recalling its resolutions 1325(2000) of 31 October 2000 and 1820(2008) of 19 June 2008 on women and peace and security, and condemning any sexual violence, further welcoming the continuing efforts of the Mission, in close cooperation with the Government of Liberia, to promote and protect the rights of civilians, in particular women and children, noting with appreciation that the Government strategy for the implementation of resolution 1325(2000) is in place, recognizing the challenges that remain in addressing the serious issues of gender-based violence and sexual exploitation and abuse, and calling upon Member States to increase support to the Government in its efforts,

Encouraging the Liberian authorities to expedite their efforts to constitute the Independent National Commission on Human Rights,

Reiterating the continuing need for support by the Mission for the security of the Special Court for Sierra Leone, subject to periodic review as the work of the Court progresses,

Determining that the situation in Liberia continues to constitute a threat to international peace and security in the region,

Acting under Chapter VII of the Charter of the United Nations,

1. *Decides* that the mandate of the United Nations Mission in Liberia shall be extended until 30 September 2010;

2. *Authorizes* the Mission to assist the Government of Liberia with the 2011 general presidential and legislative elections by providing logistical support, particularly to facilitate access to remote areas, coordinating international electoral assistance and supporting Liberian institutions and political parties in creating an atmosphere conducive to the conduct of peaceful elections;

3. *Calls upon* the Liberian authorities to ensure that the outstanding issues regarding the electoral legal framework, including the delineation of constituencies and proposed constitutional amendments, are finalized to facilitate adequate preparations for the elections;

4. *Endorses* the recommendation of the Secretary-General that the conduct of free and fair, conflict-free elections be a core benchmark for the future drawdown of the Mission;

5. *Reaffirms its intention* to authorize the Secretary-General to redeploy troops, as may be needed, between the Mission and the United Nations Operation in Côte d'Ivoire

on a temporary basis, in accordance with the provisions of resolution 1609(2005) of 24 June 2005, and calls upon troop-contributing countries to support the efforts of the Secretary-General in this regard;

6. *Endorses* the recommendation of the Secretary-General in his special report of 10 June 2009 to implement the third stage of the drawdown of the Mission from October 2009 to May 2010, repatriating 2,029 military personnel, 3 attack helicopters and 72 armoured personnel carriers, leaving the military strength of the Mission at 8,202 personnel, including 7,952 troops in Liberia and 250 at the Special Court for Sierra Leone, and keeping the Mission police component at its current authorized strength;

7. *Requests* the Secretary-General, following consultations with the Government of Liberia, to develop and submit to the Security Council a strategic integrated plan to coordinate activity towards the achievement of benchmarks, and, recalling the statements by its President of 22 July and 5 August 2009, which emphasized the need for coherence between, and integration of, peacemaking, peacekeeping, peacebuilding and development to achieve an effective response to post-conflict situations, requests the Secretary-General to provide in his reports an indication of progress towards achieving a coordinated United Nations approach in Liberia and, in particular, on critical gaps to achieving peacebuilding objectives;

8. *Underscores* the importance of the military concept of operations and rules of engagement being regularly updated and fully in line with the provisions of the present resolution, and requests the Secretary-General to report on them to the Council and troop-contributing countries;

9. *Requests* the Secretary-General to continue to monitor progress on core benchmarks, in particular on progress on preparations for the 2011 elections, and on the progress made towards building the capability of the Liberia National Police, and to report regularly on that progress to the Council;

10. *Calls upon* the Government of Liberia, in coordination with the Mission, the United Nations country team and international partners, to redouble efforts to develop national security and rule of law institutions that are fully and independently operational, and to this end encourages coordinated progress on the implementation of all security and justice development plans, including the Liberia National Police strategic plan referred to in paragraph 29 of the report of the Secretary-General of 10 August 2009;

11. *Requests* the Secretary-General to keep the Council regularly informed of the situation on the ground and to provide by 15 August 2010 a report on the issues addressed in paragraphs 2 and 9 above;

12. *Decides* to remain seized of the matter.

Year-end developments

The Secretary-General reported [S/2010/88] that in September the legislature concluded the fourth session of its six-year tenure. A number of critical legislative instruments were adopted during the session. However, election-related amendments to the Constitution, which would greatly facilitate the 2011 elections, had not yet been adopted.

The security situation had improved, with reports of armed robbery having decreased by half from September to the end of the year. The high number of reported rapes remained a concern, especially given that the majority of cases involved victims under the age of 15. Lack of public confidence in the justice system continued to fuel mob violence. Tensions between the armed forces and other security agencies continued. Armed forces soldiers assaulted national police officers in October, November and December. Members of the armed forces were also involved in assaults on citizens.

The global financial crisis continued to affect the economy, particularly in the rubber sector, resulting in decreased exports, increased rural unemployment and delays in foreign investment. Growth in gross domestic product fell from 7.1 per cent in 2008 to a projected 4.6 per cent for 2009. The rate of inflation stood at 7.6 per cent at the end of 2009, increasing from 6.8 per cent in the first quarter, due to increased costs of imported goods.

Security agencies made some progress in meeting the goals set under the security pillar of the poverty reduction strategy. The new county security mechanism was launched in December to enhance security policy coordination at the county level. The two battalions of the armed forces completed the United States Army Training and Evaluation Programme in September and December, marking the conclusion of the initial training phase of the new army. Unmil began joint training with specialized units of the armed forces, such as engineering, military police and headquarters personnel. The national police finalized its policy on professional standards, which would improve the quality of investigations into police misconduct. The legal, judicial and corrections sectors continued to confront deficiencies in human capacity, infrastructure and equipment.

Government efforts to consolidate State authority throughout the country continued. The Cabinet approved the decentralized and local governance policy in November. However, the devolution of political, fiscal and administrative powers was not expected to follow soon. In September, the reform of the civil service was strengthened by the launch of eight internal reform committees to oversee institutional reforms, including pay and grade reforms. Management of natural resources remained weak. Both the Kimberley Process review mission report completed in October and the report of the Panel of Experts on Liberia presented in December noted that implementation of the Kimberley Process Certification Scheme had not progressed sufficiently. Weaknesses in the Government's control of diamond mining and trade, as well as its control over mining areas, were raised as concerns.

In November, the Government adopted several strategies and policies to ensure implementation of the poverty reduction strategy.

UNMIL continued to work with the Government in a number of cross-cutting issues—public information, HIV/AIDS awareness and prevention, gender mainstreaming and women's empowerment, personnel conduct and discipline, and security and safety of UN personnel. In accordance with Security Council resolution 1885(2009), the mission was conducting the third stage of its drawdown.

Sanctions

The Security Council received three reports on the implementation of sanctions imposed on Liberia, pursuant to Council resolutions 1521(2003) [YUN 2003, p. 208] and 1792(2007) [YUN 2007, p. 206], which banned arms and related materiel, as well as international travel by and assets freeze on individuals who constituted a threat to the peace in Liberia and the subregion. Financial sanctions were also imposed on former Liberian President Charles Taylor, his immediate family and senior officials of the former Taylor regime by resolution 1532(2004) [YUN 2004, p. 204]. The Council terminated sanctions on timber in 2006 by resolution 1689(2006) [YUN 2006, p. 226] and on diamonds in 2007 by resolution 1753(2007) [YUN 2007, p. 202]. By resolution 1854(2008) [YUN 2008, p. 210], the Council asked the Panel of Experts on Liberia (see below) to assess implementation of forestry legislation passed by the legislature in 2006 and to assess compliance by Liberia with the Kimberley Process Certification Scheme.

Appointments. On 20 January [S/2009/47], the Secretary-General, as requested by the Council in resolution 1854(2008), informed it that he had reappointed two members of the Panel of Experts [YUN 2008, p. 206]. On 24 February [S/2009/109], he informed the Council of his appointment of the third expert.

The Council, after consultations among its members, announced on 17 March [S/2009/182] that the members had elected the Chairman of the Security Council Committee established pursuant to resolution 1521(2003) that dealt with travel and asset bans—Abdurrahman Mohamed Shalgham (Libyan Arab Jamahiriya). Turkey and Uganda would continue to serve as Vice-Chairmen for the year.

Implementation of sanctions regime

Report of Expert Panel (June). In June, the Chairman of the Security Council Committee established pursuant to resolution 1521(2003) concerning Liberia transmitted to the Council a report [S/2009/290] of the Panel of Experts reviewing the export of diamonds, forestry management, the travel ban on designated individuals, the freeze on assets of certain individuals and entities, and the arms embargo. UNMIL provided assistance in logistics and information sharing.

Liberia had been a participant in the Kimberley Process since 2007, joining the regime that required certificates for diamond shipment, internal controls for exporting and importing rough diamonds, and recording and reporting statistics. Between 1 January and 30 April, the Government authorized the export of over 2,500 carats of rough diamonds valued at almost $1.99 million, earning the Government over $59,000 in royalties. Exports had decreased significantly since 2008, when the Government netted $296,000 in royalties, although the average value per carat had increased. Sixteen licenses for diamond exporting were valid at the end of February. Recommendations were made to improve implementation of the system of internal controls, including the revision and expansion of the Government Diamond Office procedures manual. An individual arrested for impersonating an authority of the Government diamond export authorizing agency was indicted in March, although his whereabouts were unknown. Three assistant ministers of the Ministry of Lands, Mines and Energy were dismissed during the reporting period on allegations of corruption. Liberia submitted to the Kimberley Process its annual report for 2008 by 31 March 2009, as required.

At the time of the Panel's report, there were 64 companies pre-qualified to bid on logging concessions. The first three forest management contracts were amended to include the original annual bid premium payment and were signed by the President; they were awaiting final ratification by the legislature as of 5 May. For the next four forest management contracts, the Forestry Development Authority (FDA) approved the sales contracts, having made improvements to the bid documents that clarified technical and financial requirements and provided clearer guidance to the bid evaluation panel. Only one company had started logging and the sector was unlikely to provide significant revenues in the current fiscal year. The FDA had begun discussing the need to revise the National Forestry Reform Law, which constituted, along with FDA regulations, the framework for forest management. In the three years since the lifting of sanctions on the import of timber from Liberia, there had been no legal export of timber from commercial logging concessions. The Panel was examining developments in relation to the process for awarding forest resources licenses (timber sales contracts and forest management contracts) and overall progress towards restarting commercial logging. Given delays in restarting commercial logging, discussions emerged in Liberia about the need to revise laws and regulations.

The Security Council Committee established pursuant to resolution 1521(2003) concerning Liberia had de-listed two persons—former Minister of Lands, Mines and Energy Jenkins Dunbar and Gus Kouvenhoven—from both the travel ban and assets freeze lists since its previous report in December 2008. The Panel had confirmed that seven designated individuals had been in touch with former Liberian President Taylor since his incarceration. The former President's son, Charles "Chuckie" Taylor, Jr., was sentenced to 97 years for his convictions in a Miami Federal Court for torture, firearms and conspiracy; he was appealing his conviction. The trial of the former President by the Special Court for Sierra Leone was ongoing. The Panel investigated allegations of unapproved travel by individuals subject to the Council's travel restrictions. The Government had issued at least four passports, including diplomatic passports, to listed individuals. Immigration officials at the Liberian-Sierra Leone border were not in possession of the travel ban list during a Panel visit on 12 May. In addition, the Panel had undertaken investigations to assess the impact and effectiveness of the Council's assets freeze measures. The Panel had written to a number of Member States to request access to bank records and other information as part of the ongoing tracing exercise to determine where monies had gone. The Panel collected data on the assets of designated individuals in Liberia and provided that information to the Government for action. It was still uncertain as to whether the Government would act to implement the assets freeze measures, despite assurances to the Panel that the Ministry of Justice thought the legal framework existed.

Regarding the arms embargo, the Panel held consultations with relevant stakeholders in Liberia, Sierra Leone and the United States to discuss the arms embargo and the status of exemptions granted by the Committee. During the period covered by the report, the Panel had not found any concrete evidence of major violations or attempted violations of the arms embargo.

Among its recommendations, the Panel urged Liberia to strengthen its internal controls for diamond mining and trading and to continue collaboration with the Kimberley Process and neighbouring countries to ensure that rough diamonds from Côte d'Ivoire did not enter Liberia and be exported as Liberian diamonds. Given the difficulty of obtaining information on some individuals, the Panel recommended that the Committee develop a plan for updating the publicly available information on individuals and communicate with the Panel. It considered that implementation of the travel ban could improve though collaboration with organizations such as INTERPOL. The Panel recommended that the UNMIL firearm inspection team start conducting regular inspections of the weapons, ammunition and related materiel imported under exemption to the arms embargo for training and equipping the Liberian armed forces. It called for a national registry of small arms and light weapons to ensure effective monitoring of imports.

Report of Expert Panel (December). On 11 December, the Sanctions Committee Chairman transmitted the report of the Panel of Experts [S/2009/640] to the Security Council. Concerning diamond exports, the Government had issued 48 Kimberley Process certificates in the first nine months of 2009 authorizing the export of 18,000 carats of rough diamonds valued at $7.4 million. The volume of exports for the first three quarters of 2009 was low in comparison with the same period of 2008, during which diamonds totalling 42,475 carats were exported. However, the average value per carat had increased from $210 per carat to $410. Since 2007, the Government had issued 132 Kimberley Process certificates authorizing the export of 86,745 carats valued at $19.95 million. The Panel found that while the Government was in compliance with some requirements of the Kimberley Process Certification Scheme, it was not in compliance with regard to the maintenance and sharing of data. The Panel concluded that the Government was in danger of non-compliance in other areas. Of most concern were indications of abuses of the system of internal controls, mounting evidence of the presence of regional trading networks and the potential infiltration of sanctioned Ivorian diamonds into Liberian exports. The political will to implement the Kimberley Process Certification Scheme had diminished, at least within the Ministry of Lands, Mines and Energy.

The legislature ratified and the President signed into law seven acts confirming the awarding of seven forest management contracts between late May and late September. As at 12 November, only two companies with forest management contracts had paid all of their required fees, with a third making a partial payment; four companies had not made any payment. The Panel found numerous breaches of basic processes and criteria relating to the awarding of concessions. Companies had challenged the awarding of three of the four most recent forest management contracts. A Supreme Court justice denied their petitions without explanation. In terms of transparency, the FDA was not making any documents and information available on the Internet as required by law. The Panel had been unable to ascertain the existence of a forest management stakeholders list, another legal requirement. On a positive note, the legislature passed the Community Rights Law with respect to forest lands, and the FDA vetted a comprehensive law on wildlife conservation.

Among designated individuals mentioned in the report, Charles Taylor testified in his own defence at his trial before the Special Court for Sierra Leone, held in The Hague from mid-July to early November. Victor Bout remained in jail in Thailand pending an appeal on the United States request for his extradition. Aziz Nassour in 2004 was convicted in absentia in Antwerp, Belgium, to eight years for his involvement in diamond smuggling from West Africa to the Antwerp diamond market and was the subject of a Belgian arrest warrant issued in 2006. Leonid Minin might be in Italy and was under investigation for involvement in Russian organized crime. Benoni Urey was appointed acting Mayor of Careysburg, Montserrado County, by the President. The Panel confirmed that Cyril Allen violated the travel ban by travelling to Ghana in early October. Neither Edwin M. Snowe nor Jewell Howard Taylor had complied with the conditions of waivers granted to them by the Sanctions Committee. Further clarification was required to explain Mr. Snowe's travel to Ghana from Abidjan on Emirates Airways. The Panel had been informed of allegations that Samih Ossaily had travelled from Belgium to the Democratic Republic of the Congo, but had not been able to confirm those claims. The effectiveness of the sanctions imposed through the freezing of assets and economic resources of designated individuals and entities continued to be low. The Government had not made any movement to freeze assets. The Panel had new evidence indicating that financial benefits were realized by non-designated individuals as a result of links to several designated individuals and that both designated and related individuals had considerable financial resources. Those sums were significantly greater than the aggregate asset amounts disclosed as having been frozen by Members States.

The Panel did not find any concrete evidence of major actual or attempted violations of the arms embargo. The capacity of the Government to control weapons and to provide security to its citizens remained low, which was of concern given the volatile regional situation in Guinea and Côte d'Ivoire. In June, Liberia completed its internal process of ratification of the ECOWAS Convention on Small Arms and Light Weapons, Their Ammunition and Other Related Materials, but it had not yet deposited its instrument of ratification with the ECOWAS secretariat.

The Panel recommended that the Government and concerned partners, including UNMIL, reconstitute the Presidential Task Force on Diamonds and review implementation challenges and reasons for the lack of progress. The Panel also recommended that the Task Force review options for transitioning to a diamond board or a broader precious minerals board (to include gold) with broad stakeholder involvement. It recommended that the Government improve its implementation of the Kimberley Process review, report periodically to the Chair of the Process and share its information database. It also recommended that the Government conduct investigations into the regional

trading network and the potential infiltration of Ivorian diamonds into Liberia and neighbouring countries. It proposed that the FDA review its operational policies and practices, especially regarding commercial logging operations; alternatively, the Government could improve implementation of requirements for allocating commercial concessions. The Panel also recommended that donors agree on benchmarks to gauge progress in implementing the National Forestry Reform Law.

The Panel recommended that the Security Council maintain the travel ban and asset freeze until after the 2011 elections and the conclusion of the trial of Charles Taylor. The Sanctions Committee was urged to consider carefully each request for de-listing with regard to the implications for Liberia and the subregion in the period prior to the 2011 elections and the conclusion of the trial of Charles Taylor. The Panel recommended that the Committee review its procedures for issuing and verifying adherence to travel ban waivers.

Regarding the arms embargo, the Panel recommended setting up a working group comprising UNMIL, the Liberian National Commission on Small Arms, the ministries in charge of security personnel and the United States Embassy to support Liberia in complying with the ECOWAS Convention requirements that would enable States to identify and trace illicit small arms and light weapons. UNMIL should maintain a strict and regular regime of firearms inspections in the security sector institutions throughout 2010. The Panel also proposed ways to improve collection of data on weapons, both those of the Government and those acquired by rebel groups.

SECURITY COUNCIL ACTION

On 17 December [meeting 6246], the Security Council unanimously adopted **resolution 1903(2009)**. The draft [S/2009/648] was submitted by the United States.

The Security Council,

Recalling its previous resolutions and the statements by its President on the situation in Liberia and West Africa,

Welcoming the sustained progress made by the Government of Liberia since January 2006 in rebuilding Liberia for the benefit of all Liberians, with the support of the international community,

Recalling its decision not to renew the measures in paragraph 10 of resolution 1521(2003) of 22 December 2003 regarding round logs and timber products originating in Liberia, and stressing that Liberia's progress in the timber sector must continue with the effective implementation and enforcement of the National Forestry Reform Law signed into law on 5 October 2006, and other new legislation related to revenue transparency (the Liberia Extractive Industries Transparency Initiative Act) and resolution of land and tenure rights (the Community Rights Law with respect to Forest Lands and the Lands Commission Act),

Recalling also its decision to terminate the measures in paragraph 6 of resolution 1521(2003) regarding diamonds, welcoming the Government of Liberia's participation and leadership at the regional and international levels in the Kimberley Process, noting the findings of the Panel of Experts on Liberia re-established pursuant to resolution 1854(2008) of 19 December 2008 concerning diamonds, in particular those findings regarding domestic implementation of the Kimberley Process Certification Scheme, noting Liberia's minimum implementation of the necessary internal controls and other requirements of the Certification Scheme, and stressing the need for the Government to redouble its commitment and efforts to ensure the effectiveness of these controls,

Recalling further the statement by its President of 25 June 2007 recognizing the role of voluntary initiatives aimed at improving revenue transparency, such as the Extractive Industries Transparency Initiative, and, taking note of General Assembly resolution 62/274 of 11 September 2008 on strengthening transparency in industries, recognizing Liberia's achievement of Initiative-compliant status, supporting Liberia's decision to take part in other extractive industry transparency initiatives, and encouraging Liberia's continued progress in improving revenue transparency,

Stressing the continuing importance of the United Nations Mission in Liberia in improving security throughout Liberia and helping the Government of Liberia to establish its authority throughout the country, particularly in the regions producing diamonds, timber and other natural resources, and border areas,

Taking note of the report of the Panel of Experts on Liberia, including on the issues of diamonds, timber, targeted sanctions, and arms and security, submitted on 11 December 2009,

Having reviewed the measures imposed by paragraphs 2 and 4 of resolution 1521(2003) and paragraph 1 of resolution 1532(2004) of 12 March 2004 and the progress made towards meeting the conditions set out in paragraph 5 of resolution 1521(2003), noting the cooperation of the Government of Liberia with the Mission in weapons marking, and concluding that insufficient progress has been made towards that end,

Underlining its determination to support the Government of Liberia in its efforts to meet the conditions of resolution 1521(2003), and encouraging all stakeholders, including donors, to support the Government in its efforts,

Welcoming the announcement by the Department of Peacekeeping Operations of the Secretariat of provisional guidelines on cooperation and information-sharing between the United Nations peacekeeping missions and the Security Council sanctions committees' expert panels,

Determining that, despite significant progress having been made in Liberia, the situation there continues to constitute a threat to international peace and security in the region,

Acting under Chapter VII of the Charter of the United Nations,

1. *Decides* to renew the measures on travel imposed by paragraph 4 of resolution 1521(2003) for a period of twelve months from the date of adoption of the present resolution;

2. *Recalls* that the measures imposed by paragraph 1 of resolution 1532(2004) remain in force, notes with serious concern the findings of the Panel of Experts on Liberia on the lack of progress with regard to the implementation of the financial measures imposed by paragraph 1 of resolution 1532(2004), and demands that the Government of Liberia make all necessary efforts to fulfil its obligations;

3. *Decides* that the measures on arms, previously imposed by paragraph 2 of resolution 1521(2003) and modified by paragraphs 1 and 2 of resolution 1683(2006) of 13 June 2006 and by paragraph 1 *(b)* of resolution 1731(2006) of 20 December 2006, are replaced by those in paragraph 4 below, and shall not apply to the supply, sale or transfer of arms and related materiel and the provision of any assistance, advice or training related to military activities to the Government of Liberia for the period set forth in paragraph 4 below;

4. *Decides also* that all States shall take the measures necessary to prevent the direct or indirect supply, sale or transfer, from their territories or by their nationals, or using their flag vessels or aircraft, of arms and any related materiel and the provision of any assistance, advice or training related to military activities, including financing and financial assistance, to all non-governmental entities and individuals operating in the territory of Liberia for a period of twelve months from the date of adoption of the present resolution;

5. *Decides further* that the measures in paragraph 4 above shall not apply to:

(a) Supplies of arms and related materiel as well as technical training and assistance intended solely for the support of or use by the United Nations Mission in Liberia;

(b) Protective clothing, including flak jackets and military helmets, temporarily exported to Liberia by United Nations personnel, representatives of the media and humanitarian and development workers and associated personnel for their personal use only;

(c) Other supplies of non-lethal military equipment intended solely for humanitarian or protective use and related technical assistance and training, as notified in advance to the Security Council Committee established pursuant to paragraph 21 of resolution 1521(2003) (hereinafter "the Committee") in accordance with paragraph 6 below;

6. *Decides* that, for the period set forth in paragraph 4 above, all States shall notify in advance to the Committee any shipment of arms and related materiel to the Government of Liberia, or any provision of assistance, advice or training related to military activities for the Government, except those referred to in paragraphs 5 *(a)* and *(b)* above, and stresses the importance of such notifications containing all relevant information, including, where applicable, the type and quantity of weapons and ammunitions delivered, the end-user, the proposed date of delivery and the itinerary of shipments; and reiterates that the Government shall subsequently mark the weapons and ammunition, maintain a registry of them and formally notify the Committee that these steps have been taken;

7. *Reconfirms its intention* to review the measures imposed by paragraph 1 of resolution 1532(2004) at least once a year, and directs the Committee, in coordination with the relevant designating States and with the assistance of the Panel of Experts, to update, as necessary, the publicly available reasons for listing for entries on the travel ban and assets freeze lists as well as the Committee's guidelines;

8. *Decides* to review any of the above measures at the request of the Government of Liberia, once the Government reports to the Council that the conditions set out in resolution 1521(2003) for terminating the measures have been met and provides the Council with information to justify its assessment;

9. *Decides also* to extend the mandate of the Panel of Experts appointed pursuant to paragraph 4 of resolution 1854(2008) for a further period, until 20 December 2010, to undertake the following tasks:

(a) To conduct two follow-up assessment missions to Liberia and neighbouring States, in order to investigate and compile a midterm report and a final report on the implementation, and any violations, of the measures imposed by paragraphs 4 and 6 above and resolution 1521(2003), as amended by paragraphs 3 and 4 above, including any information relevant to the designation by the Committee of the individuals described in paragraph 4 (a) of resolution 1521(2003) and paragraph 1 of resolution 1532(2004), and including the various sources of financing, such as from natural resources, for the illicit trade in arms;

(b) To assess the impact and effectiveness of the measures imposed by paragraph 1 of resolution 1532(2004), including, in particular, with respect to the assets of former President Charles Taylor;

(c) To identify and make recommendations regarding areas where the capacity of Liberia and the States in the region can be strengthened to facilitate the implementation of the measures imposed by paragraph 4 of resolution 1521(2003) and paragraph 1 of resolution 1532(2004);

(d) Within the context of Liberia's evolving legal framework, to assess the extent to which forestry and other natural resources are contributing to peace, security and development rather than to instability and to what extent relevant legislation (the National Forestry Reform Law, the Lands Commission Act, the Community Rights Law with respect to Forest Lands and the Liberia Extractive Industries Transparency Initiative Act) is contributing to this transition;

(e) To assess the compliance of the Government of Liberia with the Kimberley Process Certification Scheme, and to coordinate with the Kimberley Process in assessing compliance;

(f) To provide a midterm report to the Council, through the Committee, by 1 June 2010 and a final report to the Council, through the Committee, by 20 December 2010 on all the issues listed in the present paragraph, and to provide informal updates to the Committee, as appropriate, before those dates, especially on progress in the timber sector since the lifting of the measures imposed by paragraph 10 of resolution 1521(2003) in June 2006, and in the diamond sector since the lifting of the measures imposed by paragraph 6 of resolution 1521(2003) in April 2007;

(g) To cooperate actively with other relevant groups of experts, in particular the Group of Experts on Côte d'Ivoire re-established by paragraph 10 of resolution 1893(2009) of 29 October 2009, and with the Kimberley Process Certification Scheme;

(h) To assist the Committee in updating the publicly available reasons for listing for entries on the travel ban and assets freeze lists;

(i) To assess the impact of paragraphs 3 and 4 above, specifically the effect on the stability and security of Liberia;

10. *Requests* the Secretary-General to reappoint the Panel of Experts and to make the necessary financial and security arrangements to support the work of the Panel;

11. *Calls upon* all States and the Government of Liberia to cooperate fully with the Panel of Experts in all aspects of its mandate;

12. *Reiterates* the importance of continuing assistance by the Mission to the Government of Liberia, the Committee and the Panel of Experts, within its capabilities and areas of deployment, and, without prejudice to its mandate, continuing to carry out its tasks set forth in previous resolutions, including resolution 1683(2006);

13. *Urges* the Government of Liberia to implement the recommendations of the 2009 Kimberley Process review team to strengthen internal controls over diamond mining and exports;

14. *Encourages* the Kimberley Process to continue to cooperate with the Panel of Experts and to report on developments regarding implementation by Liberia of the Kimberley Process Certification Scheme;

15. *Decides* to remain actively seized of the matter.

Security Council Committee. The Security Council Committee established pursuant to resolution 1521(2003) concerning Liberia submitted a report [S/2009/691] on its 2009 activities on 31 December. The Committee considered requests for exemptions to the sanctions against Liberia. During the year, it approved requests for exceptions to the arms embargo: to enable members of the Liberian armed forces to participate in training courses offered by the United States Government; to enable the United States Government to provide training and equipment to the Liberian Ministry of Defence; to allow the United States Government to ship equipment needed for planned training activities for the Liberian Special Security Service; and to permit the United States Government to provide equipment to the Liberian armed forces. The Committee received one notification about shipment of arms, as required, from the United Kingdom. In addition, it received three communications from UNMIL transmitting reports on the Mission's inspections of inventories of weapons and ammunition. The Committee considered ten requests for travel-ban waivers, of which six were granted. It approved one notification from the Netherlands regarding its intention to authorize access to frozen funds in accordance with resolution 1532(2004).

The Committee reported that during 2009 it received de-listing requests with regard to 11 individuals from its travel-ban list (and assets-freeze list, where applicable). Of those, two were received from Member States and nine were submitted through the focal point process. The Committee agreed to de-list two individuals—Talal Eldine and Ali Kleilat. The Committee did not consider eight of the nine de-listing requests received through the focal point since the designating State did not support those requests. The Committee observed that the removal of the two individuals from the lists was illustrative of the trend towards the conditioned removal of sanctions related to Liberia, which began with the end of the prohibition on timber imports from Liberia in 2006 and on rough diamond imports from Liberia in 2007.

UNMIL

The United Nations Mission in Liberia (UNMIL), established by Security Council resolution 1509(2003) [YUN 2003, p. 194], was mandated to support the implementation of the 2003 Agreement on Ceasefire and Cessation of Hostilities [ibid., p. 189] and the peace process; protect UN staff, facilities and civilians; support humanitarian and human rights activities; and assist in national security reform, including national police training and the formation of a new, restructured military. By resolution 1638(2005) [YUN 2005, p. 267], the Council enhanced the mandate to include the apprehension and detention of former President Taylor in the event of his return to Liberia, as well as his transfer to the Special Court for Sierra Leone. By resolution 1750(2007) [YUN 2007, p. 194], the Council decided that the Mission's mandate should include the provision of administrative and related support and security, on a cost-reimbursable basis, for activities conducted in Liberia by the Special Court for Sierra Leone with the consent of the Government. By resolution 1885(2009) (see p. 197), the Council approved the Secretary-General's recommendation to implement the third stage of UNMIL's drawdown, beginning in October, repatriating 2,029 military personnel, 3 helicopters and 72 armoured personnel carriers, leaving the military strength at 8,202 personnel, of whom 250 would be based at the Special Court for Sierra Leone, and keeping the UNMIL police component at its current authorized strength of 1,375 officers.

On 28 December [S/2009/679], the Secretary-General informed the Security Council of the security needs for the Special Court for Sierra Leone, which had been provided by UNMIL with a contingent of up to 250, as authorized by the Council. Two recent developments—the transfer on 31 October of the eight prisoners convicted by the Court to Rwanda, where they would serve out their sentences, and the transfer on 16 November of the Court's detention facilities to Sierra Leone—had led to a reassessment of security needs. The Secretary-General recommended maintaining the military guard force assigned to the Court until its work was completed in 2011. However, in view of the reduction in threats, he recommended that the strength of the guard force be reduced by 100 soldiers, leaving a 150-strong military company, including support personnel, to secure the Court's fa-

cilities. The Council, on 30 December [S/2009/680], took note of the Secretary-General's intention.

During the year, the Secretary-General issued three progress reports on developments in Liberia and UNMIL activities (see above). UNMIL continued to be headed by the Special Representative of the Secretary-General for Liberia, Ellen Margrethe Løj (Denmark), and maintained its headquarters at Monrovia, the capital.

Appointments. In an exchange of letters with the Security Council President on 19 October [S/2009/546] and 22 October [S/2009/547], the Secretary-General appointed Lieutenant General Sikander Afzal (Pakistan) as Force Commander of UNMIL, to replace Lieutenant General A.T.M. Zahirul Alam (Bangladesh), whose tour of duty ended on 19 October.

Financing

In June, at its resumed sixty-third (2009) session, the General Assembly considered the performance report on the UNMIL budget for 1 July 2007 to 30 June 2008 [A/63/588 & Corr.1], showing actual expenditures amounting to $649,521,900 against an appropriation of $688,383,400, and the proposed budget for 1 July 2009 to 30 June 2010 [A/63/734] in the amount of $593,488,800, together with the related ACABQ report [A/63/746/Add.8]. The proposed budget provided for the deployment of 133 military observers, 9,635 military contingent personnel, 470 UN police officers, 845 formed police unit personnel, 546 international staff, 1,038 national staff, 237 United Nations Volunteers and 32 Government-provided personnel. ACABQ made suggestions for savings and recommended approving the proposed budget for 2009/2010 in the amount of $574,797,700.

GENERAL ASSEMBLY ACTION

On 30 June [meeting 93], the General Assembly, on the recommendation of the Fifth Committee [A/63/903], adopted **resolution 63/296** without vote [agenda item 143].

Financing of the United Nations Mission in Liberia

The General Assembly,

Having considered the reports of the Secretary-General on the financing of the United Nations Mission in Liberia and the related report of the Advisory Committee on Administrative and Budgetary Questions,

Recalling Security Council resolution 1497(2003) of 1 August 2003, by which the Council declared its readiness to establish a United Nations stabilization force to support the transitional government and to assist in the implementation of a comprehensive peace agreement in Liberia,

Recalling also Security Council resolution 1509(2003) of 19 September 2003, by which the Council decided to establish the United Nations Mission in Liberia for a period of twelve months, and the subsequent resolutions by which the Council extended the mandate of the Mission, the latest of which was resolution 1836(2008) of 29 September 2008, by which the Council extended the mandate of the Mission until 30 September 2009,

Recalling further its resolution 58/315 of 1 July 2004,

Recalling its resolution 58/261 A of 23 December 2003 on the financing of the Mission and its subsequent resolutions thereon, the latest of which was resolution 62/263 of 20 June 2008,

Reaffirming the general principles underlying the financing of United Nations peacekeeping operations, as stated in General Assembly resolutions 1874(S-IV) of 27 June 1963, 3101(XXVIII) of 11 December 1973 and 55/235 of 23 December 2000,

Noting with appreciation that voluntary contributions have been made to the Mission,

Mindful of the fact that it is essential to provide the Mission with the financial resources necessary to enable it to fulfil its responsibilities under the relevant resolutions of the Security Council,

1. *Requests* the Secretary-General to entrust the Head of Mission with the task of formulating future budget proposals in full accordance with the provisions of General Assembly resolutions 59/296 of 22 June 2005, 60/266 of 30 June 2006 and 61/276 of 29 June 2007, as well as other relevant resolutions;

2. *Takes note* of the status of contributions to the United Nations Mission in Liberia as at 30 April 2009, including the contributions outstanding in the amount of 96.6 million United States dollars, representing some 2 per cent of the total assessed contributions, notes with concern that only sixty-seven Member States have paid their assessed contributions in full, and urges all other Member States, in particular those in arrears, to ensure payment of their outstanding assessed contributions;

3. *Expresses its appreciation* to those Member States which have paid their assessed contributions in full, and urges all other Member States to make every possible effort to ensure payment of their assessed contributions to the Mission in full;

4. *Expresses concern* at the financial situation with regard to peacekeeping activities, in particular as regards the reimbursements to troop contributors that bear additional burdens owing to overdue payments by Member States of their assessments;

5. *Also expresses concern* at the delay experienced by the Secretary-General in deploying and providing adequate resources to some recent peacekeeping missions, in particular those in Africa;

6. *Emphasizes* that all future and existing peacekeeping missions shall be given equal and non-discriminatory treatment in respect of financial and administrative arrangements;

7. *Also emphasizes* that all peacekeeping missions shall be provided with adequate resources for the effective and efficient discharge of their respective mandates;

8. *Reiterates its request* to the Secretary-General to make the fullest possible use of facilities and equipment at the United Nations Logistics Base at Brindisi, Italy, in order to minimize the costs of procurement for the Mission;

9. *Requests* the Secretary-General to give consideration to making the fullest possible use of facilities at the logistics hub at Entebbe, Uganda;

10. *Also requests* the Secretary-General to ensure that proposed peacekeeping budgets are based on the relevant legislative mandates;

11. *Endorses* the conclusions and recommendations contained in the report of the Advisory Committee on Administrative and Budgetary Questions, subject to the provisions of the present resolution, and requests the Secretary-General to ensure their full implementation;

12. *Recalls* paragraph 40 of the report of the Advisory Committee, and requests the Secretary-General to enhance his efforts to carry out the approved quick-impact projects in a timely manner, while addressing the underlying issues hampering implementation at the Mission;

13. *Also recalls* paragraph 19 of the report of the Advisory Committee, and encourages the Secretary-General to improve the presentation of the needs for personnel in order to have a clear view of the new posts proposed;

14. *Takes note* of paragraph 36 of the report of the Advisory Committee;

15. *Stresses* the importance of maintaining experienced staff during the drawdown period of the Mission and of expanding the skills of all staff, including national staff;

16. *Recalls* paragraph 44 of the report of the Advisory Committee, and requests the Secretary-General to continue to make efforts to implement all planned activities, especially those related to national capacity-building;

17. *Requests* the Secretary-General to keep the staffing structure of the Mission under review and to report to the General Assembly about possible post reductions, in particular for the support activities, in the context of the budget for the period 2010/11;

18. *Welcomes* the efforts of the Mission with regard to environmental issues;

19. *Requests* the Secretary-General to ensure the full implementation of the relevant provisions of resolutions 59/296, 60/266 and 61/276;

20. *Also requests* the Secretary-General to take all action necessary to ensure that the Mission is administered with a maximum of efficiency and economy;

21. *Further requests* the Secretary-General, in order to reduce the cost of employing General Service staff, to continue efforts to recruit local staff for the Mission against General Service posts, commensurate with the requirements of the Mission;

Financial performance report for the period from 1 July 2007 to 30 June 2008

22. *Takes note* of the report of the Secretary-General on the financial performance of the Mission for the period from 1 July 2007 to 30 June 2008;

Budget estimates for the period from 1 July 2009 to 30 June 2010

23. *Decides* to appropriate to the Special Account for the United Nations Mission in Liberia the amount of 585,682,100 dollars for the period from 1 July 2009 to 30 June 2010, inclusive of 560,978,700 dollars for the maintenance of the Mission, 20,559,300 dollars for the support account for peacekeeping operations and 4,144,100 dollars for the United Nations Logistics Base;

Financing of the appropriation

24. *Also decides* to apportion among Member States the amount of 146,420,525 dollars for the period from 1 July to 30 September 2009, in accordance with the levels updated in General Assembly resolution 61/243 of 22 December 2006, and taking into account the scale of assessments for 2009, as set out in Assembly resolution 61/237 of 22 December 2006;

25. *Further decides* that, in accordance with the provisions of General Assembly resolution 973(X) of 15 December 1955, there shall be set off against the apportionment among Member States, as provided for in paragraph 24 above, their respective share in the Tax Equalization Fund of 3,419,800 dollars, comprising the estimated staff assessment income of 2,782,450 dollars approved for the Mission, the prorated share of 535,075 dollars of the estimated staff assessment income approved for the support account and the prorated share of 102,275 dollars of the estimated staff assessment income approved for the United Nations Logistics Base;

26. *Decides* to apportion among Member States the amount of 439,261,575 dollars for the period from 1 October 2009 to 30 June 2010, at a monthly rate of 48,806,842 dollars, in accordance with the levels updated in resolution 61/243, and taking into account the scale of assessments for 2009, as set out in resolution 61/237, and for 2010, subject to a decision of the Security Council to extend the mandate of the Mission;

27. *Also decides* that, in accordance with the provisions of resolution 973(X), there shall be set off against the apportionment among Member States, as provided for in paragraph 26 above, their respective share in the Tax Equalization Fund of 10,259,400 dollars, comprising the estimated staff assessment income of 8,347,350 dollars approved for the Mission, the prorated share of 1,605,225 dollars of the estimated staff assessment income approved for the support account and the prorated share of 306,825 dollars of the estimated staff assessment income approved for the United Nations Logistics Base;

28. *Further decides* that, for Member States that have fulfilled their financial obligations to the Mission, there shall be set off against their apportionment, as provided for in paragraph 24 above, their respective share of the unencumbered balance and other income in the total amount of 54,157,100 dollars in respect of the financial period ended 30 June 2008, in accordance with the levels updated in resolution 61/243, and taking into account the scale of assessments for 2008, as set out in resolution 61/237;

29. *Decides* that, for Member States that have not fulfilled their financial obligations to the Mission, there shall be set off against their outstanding obligations their respective share of the unencumbered balance and other income in the total amount of 54,157,100 dollars in respect of the financial period ended 30 June 2008, in accordance with the scheme set out in paragraph 28 above;

30. *Also decides* that the decrease of 758,400 dollars in the estimated staff assessment income in respect of the financial period ended 30 June 2008 shall be set off against the credits from the amount of 54,157,100 dollars referred to in paragraphs 28 and 29 above;

31. *Emphasizes* that no peacekeeping mission shall be financed by borrowing funds from other active peacekeeping missions;

32. *Encourages* the Secretary-General to continue to take additional measures to ensure the safety and security of all personnel participating in the Mission under the auspices of the United Nations, bearing in mind paragraphs 5 and 6 of Security Council resolution 1502(2003) of 26 August 2003;

33. *Invites* voluntary contributions to the Mission in cash and in the form of services and supplies acceptable to the Secretary-General, to be administered, as appropriate, in accordance with the procedure and practices established by the General Assembly;

34. *Decides* to include in the provisional agenda of its sixty-fourth session the item entitled "Financing of the United Nations Mission in Liberia".

On 24 December, the General Assembly decided that the agenda item on the financing of UNMIL would remain for consideration during its sixty-fourth (2010) session (**decision 64/549**).

Sierra Leone

In 2009, the Government of Sierra Leone continued to develop strategies and carry out activities aimed at peace consolidation and economic recovery. Its plans and actions were based on President Ernest Bai Koroma's Agenda for Change, which laid out the basic policies and priorities of the Government over the next three years and set out the foundation for peacebuilding in Sierra Leone. The Agenda was issued in 2008 in tandem with the Joint Vision of the United Nations Family for Sierra Leone, the UN plan for sustaining those priorities through support provided by multiple UN bodies, in particular its peacebuilding mission.

The peace consolidation process was briefly interrupted in March by an outbreak of political violence and intolerance that underlined the fragile nature of the nascent democratic process. A concerted effort on the part of President Koroma and senior party leaders brought about an end to the violence with the signing on 2 April of a joint communiqué, resulting in a return to the path towards democracy, peace and stability.

The Government was assisted in its efforts by the newly established United Nations Integrated Peacebuilding Office in Sierra Leone (UNIPSIL), the successor to the peacekeeping mission in the country. UNIPSIL and the Government endeavoured to implement the Joint Vision, which brought together the political mandate of UNIPSIL with the development and humanitarian mandates of UN agencies, funds and programmes. It defined the contribution of the UN system in implementing the President's Agenda for Change and the Sierra Leone poverty reduction strategy.

The Peacebuilding Commission, during its third year of engagement with Sierra Leone, focused on maintaining progress in peacebuilding efforts, broadening the donor base, and supporting activities in priority areas. At its High-level Special Session on Sierra Leone, which articulated a roadmap for the Commission's continued engagement with the country, the Commission called on the parties to continue to implement the 2 April communiqué. The Commission recognized the Joint Vision for Sierra Leone as an innovative approach to peacebuilding and the mobilization of financial resources for its implementation.

The Special Court for Sierra Leone neared the conclusion of its trials of those bearing the greatest responsibility for serious violations of international and national humanitarian laws committed in the country since 1996. By the end of 2009, only one trial remained under way—that of former Liberian President Charles Taylor. The trial of three men who were leaders of opposition forces, which was concluded in 2008, reached its final stage with the Appeals Chamber upholding the sentences handed down by the Trial Court.

Political and security developments

Report of Secretary-General (January). The transition from the United Nations Integrated Office in Sierra Leone (UNIOSIL) to the United Nations Integrated Peacebuilding Office in Sierra Leone (UNIPSIL), which took effect on 1 October 2008 [YUN 2008, p. 215], proceeded as planned, according to the Secretary-General in his first report on the new Office released in January 2009 [S/2009/59]. That transition culminated with the adoption of the Joint Vision of the United Nations Family for Sierra Leone, a strategic framework that outlined common priority areas as well as joint operational and logistical arrangements for UN organizations. The Joint Vision focused on providing support to the Government in constitutional reform, building police capacity, tackling corruption, illicit drug trafficking and organized crime, as well as addressing youth unemployment and preparing for elections in 2012. UNIPSIL, with a strength of 73, was headed by the Secretary-General's Executive Representative in Sierra Leone, Michael von der Schulenburg. The Office's five substantive sections dealt with political affairs and peace consolidation, human rights and rule of law, democratic institutions, police and security, and strategic planning.

While the political situation remained stable since the transition, there was a climate of distrust between the former ruling Sierra Leone People's Party (SLPP), currently the opposition party, and the All Peoples' Congress (APC), currently in power. The Government made the fight against corruption a key element of its reform platform. UNIPSIL maintained close contacts with the political parties and emphasized the need for dialogue and national cohesion following national and local elections that witnessed ethnic and regional

divides. The Government sought to focus national attention on the massive development challenges. The Yenga border dispute between Guinea and Sierra Leone remained unresolved, yet continued to be the subject of diplomatic discussions. The economic performance in 2008 was mixed. Real growth in GDP reached 6 per cent, but there was a slowdown in mining activities. The third review of the performance of Sierra Leone under a four-year arrangement related to the IMF Poverty Reduction and Growth Facility was completed in December 2008. Subsequently, the IMF approved $16.1 million to augment the country's foreign reserve position to cope with the global financial crisis. The security situation remained calm. Of immediate concern, however, was the increasing use of Sierra Leone as a trans-shipment point for trafficking illegal narcotics from South America to Europe, and piracy in coastal waters.

On 10 January, the National Electoral Commission, with UN support, conducted two parliamentary by-elections in the western urban area in Freetown and in Pujehun District, in the south. The elections were judged by observers to have been credible and peaceful. UNIPSIL provided input in developing policing standards for the police. Support was also provided in setting out operating procedures on intervention of illegal drug trafficking and for security in territorial waters, preparation of draft legislation establishing the new broadcast service in accordance with international standards, launching the national Human Rights Commission, recruiting magistrates, and training police prosecutors and investigators on human rights issues. The Agenda for Change identified the Government's main priorities as enhancing the supply of electricity; promoting economic growth, in particular through agriculture and fisheries; improving infrastructure; and improving health, education and other social services. The continued threat of corruption was identified as a major source of concern. The Joint Vision was developed as a means of coordinating and promoting support for priorities, in particular in implementing the Agenda and the country's poverty reduction strategy. The Peacebuilding Commission also provided development assistance (see p. 211).

Report of Secretary-General (May). In his second report on UNIPSIL, issued in May [S/2009/267], the Secretary-General said that Sierra Leone had experienced a sudden and worrying outbreak of political violence and intolerance that underlined the fragile nature of the nascent democratic process. However, largely as a result of the determination of President Koroma and the commitment of senior political party leaders of APC and SLPP, a new round of conflict was prevented and the situation returned to calm. Clashes had broken out from 9 to 12 March in the run-up to local council by-elections in Pujehun District, and later in Freetown. On 16 March, the SLPP headquarters in Freetown was attacked by riotous crowds; the building was ransacked, a number of SLPP supporters were injured and there were allegations of women being raped and sexually assaulted. The police appeared overwhelmed and ill-equipped to deal with the incidents. Radio stations owned by political parties apparently contributed to the atmosphere of political intolerance and their broadcast facilities were closed. The Executive Representative intervened in support of the authorities to help end the violence. Immediately after the violent episodes, UNIPSIL started a dialogue between the two major parties in consultation with the President and members of the diplomatic corps, and as a result, the two parties' leaders signed a joint communiqué on 2 April. The third largest political party, the People's Movement for Democratic Change (PMDC), subsequently indicated that it would adhere to the agreements in the communiqué.

The joint communiqué called for an end to all acts of political intolerance and violence; the recognition by the Government and the opposition of their respective roles and responsibilities; and the establishment of independent mechanisms to investigate the incidents of political violence and the alleged acts of rape and sexual violence. In addition, the President committed to consulting with the opposition on senior appointments to national institutions. More significantly, the communiqué called for strengthening of and bipartisan respect for State institutions, including the police, the judiciary, the National Electoral Commission, the Political Parties Registration Commission and the National Human Rights Commission. The communiqué stressed the bipartisan consensus on the need to work together to integrate ex-combatants, to disband militant youth groups and to overcome any hostilities among party youth wings. It underscored the potential dangers posed by political party radio stations, and the need for an independent national public broadcaster where all points of view were aired. The implementation of the communiqué would require international support. The Government pursued its attitudinal change campaign to promote a sense of civic duty and accountability. The security situation returned to calm by the end of March. The police began prosecuting a number of persons associated with the incident of 16 March at the SLPP offices in Freetown. The Government indicated on 30 March that its discussions with Guinea on the Yenga border dispute had not proceeded as planned. The withdrawal of Guinean armed forces from Yenga and efforts to resolve the border dispute were complicated by issues of command and control.

While a positive trend towards respect for human rights continued, harmful traditional practices undermined the rights of women and girls. The World Health Organization estimated that nearly 94 per cent of all girls were involuntarily subjected to female genital mutilation before the age of 18 years. Seven years after the end of the civil war, the Government finally put in place the machinery for implementing the reparations programme as recommended by the Truth and Reconciliation Commission. In early 2009, the Government registered about 16,500 war victims who had some entitlements to repatriation. Because of limited funds, only some of the immediate needs of victims could be addressed.

Progress on the planned constitutional review had stalled. The Government had made no pronouncements on how it would deal with the constitutional review report submitted to President Koroma. The United Nations remained committed to assisting the process by providing advisory and technical services to the Constitutional Review Commission. Following the suspension of the two main radio stations in the wake of the political violence, the Cabinet approved draft legislation for creating an autonomous independent public broadcasting corporation. The broadcasting reform process was supported by UNIPSIL.

UNIPSIL and the UN country team completed the documents for the Joint Vision, including political and developmental benchmarks for the peacebuilding efforts of the UN system, and a summary of all projects and programmes that would be implemented under the Joint Vision. The Mission and the country team developed benchmarks for each of the five priority areas of their Joint Vision to provide a clear focus and indicators of achievement for their political and developmental activities. As part of the Joint Vision strategy, two regional field offices were established and plans were made for six more to enable UN agencies, programmes and funds as well as other development partners to have greater outreach and to provide logistical support.

The Peacebuilding Fund's funding envelope of $35 million would be fully utilized by the end of June: $32.7 million had been allocated for 14 projects (11 active and 3 closed) and $2.2 million for 6 projects in the pipeline. It was expected that all 20 projects would be implemented by the end of 2009.

The Secretary-General remarked that the outbreak of political violence served as a wake-up call for the Government and people of Sierra Leone on the critical challenges that required urgent attention, and as a reminder for the international community of the importance of its continued support for the peace consolidation process.

Report of Secretary-General (September). In his third report on UNIPSIL, issued in September [S/2009/438], the Secretary-General said that the political situation had remained calm. In the spirit of the joint communiqué of 2 April, the major political parties continued interactions under the framework of the dialogue forums organized by the Political Parties Registration Commission, with the support of the United Nations. A Joint Communiqué Adherence Committee, co-chaired by the Political Parties Registration Commission and UNIPSIL, was established on 29 April. In addition to APC and SLPP, the membership included the police, the National Commission for Democracy and the Inter-Religious Council of Sierra Leone. The joint communiqué not only called for a cessation of violence, but also provided a framework for developing bi-party consensus on youth issues, illicit drug trafficking and strengthening democratic institutions. President Koroma established a Commission of Inquiry to investigate the allegations of rape and sexual violence reported during the 16 March attack on the SLPP offices in Freetown. Several inter-party dialogues aimed at fostering political tolerance and non-violence were held in Freetown and the provinces. The dialogues were organized by the Political Parties Registration Commission, with support from UNIPSIL and UNDP. Each of the three major political parties had held their conventions. While SLPP and PMDC had not yet chosen their candidates for the 2012 elections, APC nominated President Koroma as the party's presidential candidate.

The Independent Media Commission on 8 July announced that the licenses of the political party radio stations owned by APC and SLPP would be withdrawn. Meanwhile, the Sierra Leone Broadcasting Corporation Act 2009 was passed by Parliament but had not been signed by the President. It would provide for the transformation of the state-owned Sierra Leone Broadcasting Service into an independent national broadcaster.

On 13 and 14 July, President Koroma paid an official visit to Guinea where he met the leader of Guinea, Captain Moussa Dadis Camara. The two heads of State discussed the Yenga border dispute and reiterated their commitment to the peaceful resolution of the matter. They agreed to reactivate the joint technical team established earlier to address the border dispute. Those talks opened on 31 July, focusing on the use of the Mona River as the boundary between the two countries and on the demilitarization of the Yenga area. UNIPSIL contributed logistical support to the talks.

The economic situation worsened somewhat in 2009 with real growth in GDP projected to be 4 per cent, a 1.5 per cent decrease from the previous year. The recent 25 per cent depreciation of the local currency against the major currencies had caused a massive rise in consumer prices. At the same time, export earnings declined about 27 per cent since 2008. Falling world prices for diamonds had resulted in a decline of revenue. The total value of diamond exports fell by 49 per cent, or around $70 million. Foreign direct investment, including remittances from Sierra Leoneans abroad, was projected to fall about 25 per cent in 2009 over the previous year's peak of $69 million.

Implementation of the Agenda for Change continued to be supported by the United Nations Joint Vision for consolidating peace, stimulating economic growth, creating employment, especially for youth, fighting organized crime, impeding corruption and making progress towards the Millennium Development Goals. The UN country team moved to develop programmes and inter-agency agreements for common services and to establish a multi-donor trust fund.

The Political Parties Registration Commission mediated an intra-party dispute between two factions of PMDC just before the party held its national conference on 24 July. The National Electoral Commission conducted a local council by-election in the Dwarzak constituency in Freetown. Following the passage by Parliament of a Chieftaincy Bill, which clarified the responsibility of the National Electoral Commission in the conduct of chieftaincy elections, the Commission announced that elections would be held in November to fill about 40 paramount chieftaincy vacancies. The Independent Media Commission continued to assert itself in regulating the print and broadcast media. The Government took actions to address impunity, including by restoring military justice through the re-establishment of a court martial board of the armed forces. A legal aid programme was established to provide assistance to vulnerable groups. The National Human Rights Commission established regional offices in all of the country's three provinces. With support from the United Nations, the implementation of the reparations programme, as recommended by the Truth and Reconciliation Commission, made progress. The programme had registered 28,000 war victims and conducted symbolic reparations in 18 chiefdoms. The Anti-Corruption Commission, in collaboration with Parliament, began developing a code of conduct for parliamentarians and a similar initiative was under consideration for local government officials. In addition to corruption, high youth unemployment and trafficking in illicit drugs continued to pose challenges to the consolidation of peace.

As the first fully integrated mission led by the Department of Political Affairs, UNIPSIL's success or failures would contribute to determining the functions of future peacebuilding missions, the Secretary-General observed. The UN system in Sierra Leone had developed a new approach to peacebuilding, with a fully integrated peacebuilding strategy, the Joint Vision. The main aim of that approach was to provide more focused and effective assistance to the Government and people of Sierra Leone. In the Joint Vision, UNIPSIL and the UN country team agreed to work together on five priority areas and to implement co-operatively 21 programmes, guided by a set of joint benchmarks. They also put into place a system for joint programming and programme evaluation, as well as operational integration. UNIPSIL was a much leaner and more cost-effective peacebuilding office in comparison with previous peacekeeping missions in Sierra Leone.

The Secretary-General remarked that the completion of the much awaited constitutional reform process was long overdue. To expedite the process, he called on the Government to establish a participatory consultation mechanism to enable wider input by civil society and other national stakeholders. UNIPSIL was ready to provide technical support. The mission had made steady progress in implementing its mandate to support the Government's efforts to consolidate peace and to ensure an integrated UN approach to peacebuilding. In view of the many challenges remaining, he recommended to the Security Council that it extend the UNIPSIL mandate for one year, until 30 September 2010.

Security Council consideration. The Security Council considered the situation in Sierra Leone on 9 February [meeting 6080], 8 June [meeting 6137] and 14 September [meeting 6187].

SECURITY COUNCIL ACTION

On 15 September [meeting 6189], the Security Council unanimously adopted **resolution 1886(2009)**. The draft [S/2009/456] was prepared in consultations among Council members.

The Security Council,

Recalling its previous resolutions and the statements by its President concerning the situation in Sierra Leone, in particular resolution 1829(2008) of 4 August 2008,

Commending the valuable contribution that the United Nations Integrated Peacebuilding Office in Sierra Leone has made to peacebuilding efforts and to the peace, security and development of the country,

Welcoming the report of the Secretary-General of 1 September 2009 and his recommendation that the mandate of the United Nations Integrated Peacebuilding Office in Sierra Leone be extended for a period of one year, until 30 September 2010, with a view to providing continued peacebuilding assistance to the Government of Sierra Leone,

Emphasizing the importance of continued integrated support of the United Nations system and the international community for the long-term peace, security and development of Sierra Leone, particularly through the strengthening of the capacity of the Government of Sierra Leone,

Welcoming the Agenda for Change of the Government of Sierra Leone as the core strategic document for the country for the period until the end of 2012, and calling upon all international partners to align their assistance with the priorities outlined in the Agenda for Change,

Commending the United Nations Integrated Peacebuilding Office in Sierra Leone and the United Nations country team for articulating a new and innovative approach to peacebuilding in the United Nations joint vision document, welcoming the integration of the political mandate of the Office with the development and humanitarian mandates of the United Nations country team, and encouraging all United Nations entities in Sierra Leone to continue to implement the joint vision strategy,

Welcoming the political parties' joint communiqué of 2 April 2009 and its contribution towards the immediate cessation of the political violence in Sierra Leone, and calling upon all political parties and other relevant actors to adhere to its provisions and ensure its implementation,

Reiterating its appreciation for the work of the Peacebuilding Commission, and welcoming the outcome of the High-level Special Session on Sierra Leone held by the Commission on 10 June 2009, which articulated a road map for the continued engagement of the Commission with Sierra Leone in alignment with the Agenda for Change of the Government of Sierra Leone,

Reiterating its appreciation also for the work of the Special Court for Sierra Leone, stressing the importance of the trial of former President of Liberia Charles Taylor by the Court, as well as effective outreach on the trial at the local level, welcoming the progress made in other trials, reiterating its expectation that the Court will finish its work as soon as possible, and calling upon Member States to contribute to the Court,

Welcoming the role played by the Economic Community of West African States, and encouraging the States members of the Mano River Union and other regional organizations to continue promoting regional peace and security,

1. *Decides* to extend the mandate of the United Nations Integrated Peacebuilding Office in Sierra Leone, as set out in resolution 1829(2008), until 30 September 2010;

2. *Emphasizes* the importance for the United Nations Integrated Peacebuilding Office in Sierra Leone of achieving, jointly with the United Nations country team, the objectives of the joint vision within their respective mandates and, in particular, focusing on providing support to the Government of Sierra Leone in its efforts regarding constitutional reform, building police capacity, tackling corruption, illicit drug trafficking and organized crime, as well as addressing youth unemployment, supporting the preparations for the 2012 elections, and assisting the work of the Peacebuilding Commission and the Peacebuilding Fund;

3. *Encourages* the Executive Representative of the Secretary-General for Sierra Leone to pursue his action to enhance the integration and effectiveness of United Nations efforts on the ground in support of the implementation of the joint vision for Sierra Leone and of the recovery and development priorities of the Government and people of Sierra Leone;

4. *Calls upon* the Secretary-General to develop a set of benchmarks for the transition of the United Nations Integrated Peacebuilding Office in Sierra Leone into a United Nations country team presence, taking into account those already agreed upon by the Government of Sierra Leone and the United Nations in the joint vision for Sierra Leone, and the particular challenges involved in preparing for the 2012 elections, to keep them under active review, and regularly report on progress to the Security Council;

5. *Emphasizes* that the Government of Sierra Leone bears primary responsibility for peacebuilding, security and long-term development in the country, and encourages the Government to continue the implementation of the Agenda for Change, the Peacebuilding Commission to follow actively developments and mobilize international support as needed, and existing as well as potential new international donors to provide support to the Government;

6. *Calls upon* the Government of Sierra Leone, the United Nations Integrated Peacebuilding Office in Sierra Leone and all other stakeholders in the country to increase their efforts to promote good governance, including through continued measures to combat corruption, improve accountability, promote the development of the private sector to generate wealth and employment opportunities, intensify efforts against drug trafficking, strengthen the judiciary and promote human rights, including by implementing the recommendations of the Truth and Reconciliation Commission and sustaining support to the National Human Rights Commission;

7. *Emphasizes* the important role of women in the prevention and resolution of conflicts and in peacebuilding, as recognized in resolutions 1325(2000) of 31 October 2000 and 1820(2008) of 19 June 2008, underlines that a gender perspective should be taken into account in implementing all aspects of the mandate of the United Nations Integrated Peacebuilding Office in Sierra Leone, and encourages the Office to work with the Government of Sierra Leone in this regard;

8. *Requests* that the Secretary-General keep the Council informed every six months of progress made in the implementation of the mandate of the United Nations Integrated Peacebuilding Office in Sierra Leone and the present resolution;

9. *Decides* to remain actively seized of the matter.

Year-end developments. The Secretary-General reported that overall, the security situation was calm at the end of the year [S/2010/135], despite a rise in armed robberies. Following the passage of the Chieftaincy Act, 37 paramount chieftaincy elections were held—a significant development given the role traditional authorities played in local administration. The Act provided an improved legal framework for the elections, and the elections marked the continuing development of democratic tendencies in the country. The Commission of Inquiry established pursuant to the joint communiqué of 2 April completed its investigation of alleged acts of rape and sexual violence reported to have occurred during attacks on the SLPP offices in Freetown on 16 March. The Commission stated that after a thorough consideration of testimonies, there was no evidence to sustain the allegations of rape. However, it found that the victims had been subjected to physical mistreatment that constituted a breach of their human rights. On 29 September, President Koroma appointed an Independent Review Panel, as stipulated in the joint communiqué, to inquire into the causes of the political violence in March. In December, UNIPSIL, in collaboration with UNDP and the Political

Parties Registration Commission, organized intra-party retreats for SLPP, APC and PMDC. The retreats focused on leadership training for senior members of the parties. Despite those initiatives, the relationship between the ruling party and the main opposition party was characterized by mistrust and suspicion.

In the second half of the year, there was a sudden rise in armed robberies. To address the problem, on 10 October the President invoked the Military Assistance to Civil Power Act, which legally enabled the armed forces to work jointly with the police, and their efforts greatly reduced the crime rate. UNIPSIL, with support from the Government, UNDP and the Peacebuilding Fund, developed a strategy aimed at strengthening the cohesion between the police and the armed forces. A training package for over 7,500 soldiers and police officers was formulated in the areas of strategic communication, attitudinal change and discipline. With regard to relations with neighbouring countries, Sierra Leone and Guinea maintained cooperative ties. They conducted joint border patrols and discussed common security concerns.

Sierra Leone and its development partners held the sixth Consultative Group meeting (London, 18–19 November), with the aim to increase assistance to the country and to broaden the donor support base. The meeting endorsed both the United Nations multi-donor trust fund, which focused on capacity-building, and the World Bank multi-donor trust fund, which focused on infrastructure. With international support, the Government made efforts to decentralize government, and in November the Ministry of Internal Affairs, Local Government and Rural Development launched the performance assessment results system for local councils, which was intended to enhance the accountability of councils to their constituents. The Ministry of Finance and Economic Development trained internal auditors of the 19 local councils.

Human rights organizations remained concerned about the increase in sexual and gender-based violence. UNIPSIL supported activities to enhance the capacity of the National Human Rights Commission and, in collaboration with UNDP, organized a workshop in September for members of the parliamentary Human Rights Committee on human rights, gender and access to justice. In December, UNIPSIL and UNDP facilitated a dialogue forum for civil society and parliamentarians. UNIPSIL and other UN agencies continued to support the Government in confronting corruption, drug trafficking and youth unemployment.

Peacebuilding Commission

The Peacebuilding Commission, reporting in September on its third session (23 June 2008–30 June 2009) [A/64/341-S/2009/444], said that during its third year of engagement with Sierra Leone it had focused on three primary objectives: maintaining attention and reviewing progress in peacebuilding efforts; broadening the donor base and enhancing the coherence of international assistance; and supporting new or improving existing activities in priority areas. In addition to formal six-monthly review meetings, the Chair of the Sierra Leone configuration convened consultations with representatives of the private sector, philanthropic foundations and international financial institutions to mobilize support for peace consolidation. In a 6 April statement, the Commission welcomed the adoption by the political parties of the joint communiqué developed following the political violence in March. The Commission commended the Government and opposition leaders on reaching agreement on critical issues, including the role of the ruling and opposition parties and the strengthening of democratic institutions.

As a follow-up to the joint communiqué, the Chair of the Sierra Leone configuration undertook a fact-finding mission to the country from 20 to 24 April. While highlighting Sierra Leone's continued progress towards peace consolidation, the Chair noted that the country's impressive democratic and peacebuilding gains were still fragile and required sustained international support. The visit also provided an opportunity to prepare for the Commission's High-level Special Session on Sierra Leone.

High-level Special Session. The Peacebuilding Commission's High-level Special Session on Sierra Leone (New York, 10 June) focused on providing political support for the implementation of the parties' communiqué; endorsing the Government's Agenda for Change as the core strategy guiding all development efforts; supporting the Joint Vision for Sierra Leone as an innovative approach to peacebuilding and mobilizing financial resources for its implementation; and enhancing the coordination and coherence of international support for peace consolidation efforts.

The Special Session adopted an outcome document [PBC/3/SLE/6] which established the basis for a new and lighter form of engagement with Sierra Leone, and which aligned the Commission's work with the peacebuilding priorities identified in the Agenda for Change—namely good governance and the rule of law, and combating illicit drug trafficking and youth unemployment. The Commission agreed to hold six-monthly review meetings to monitor progress in priorities of the Agenda for Change, focus international attention on priorities requiring additional action, provide recommendations on ways to overcome challenges, and mobilize support for the Agenda.

The Special Session underscored that Sierra Leone had made impressive progress towards peace, security and democratic governance since the end of its decade-long civil war in 2002, but continued na-

tional leadership and sustained international support remained critical to overcoming the root causes of the conflict and to addressing threats to the consolidation of peace. The Commission commended the parties for their 2 April joint communiqué and for the steps of reconciliation and dialogue undertaken since then, urged stakeholders to implement the communiqué in both letter and spirit, and welcomed the allocation of $1.8 million from the Peacebuilding Fund to support implementation of the joint communiqué agreements.

Welcoming the Government's Agenda for Change—the second poverty reduction strategy for Sierra Leone—the Commission took note of its emphasis on economic growth and the prioritization of agriculture, energy and the development of road infrastructure. It welcomed the Joint Vision for Sierra Leone and commended UNIPSIL and the UN country team for articulating that new and innovative approach to peacebuilding. The Commission endorsed the integration of the political mandate of UNIPSIL with the development and humanitarian mandates of the 17 UN agencies that worked in Sierra Leone and formed the UN country team. Moreover, it congratulated UNIPSIL and the UN country team on taking a common approach to jointly managing regional field offices, promoting an effective outreach initiative, operating a strategic office and managing a number of support services. In that context, the Commission appealed to its member States to provide the necessary financial resources for funding Joint Vision projects.

Participation in Sierra Leone configuration. By a letter of 27 February from the Chairperson of the Peacebuilding Commission [PBC/3/OC/16], the International Organization for Migration was invited to participate in the Commission's country-specific configuration on Sierra Leone.

(For further information on the Peacebuilding Commission, see p. 45.)

Sanctions

The Security Council Committee established pursuant to resolution 1132(1997) [YUN 1997, p. 135] concerning Sierra Leone submitted a report [S/2009/690] covering its 2009 activities in monitoring and implementing the 1998 embargo on the sale or supply of arms to non-governmental forces in Sierra Leone and the travel ban on leading members of the former military junta in Sierra Leone and of the Revolutionary United Front (RUF), imposed by resolution 1171(1998) [YUN 1998, p. 169]. During 2009, the Committee carried out its work through written procedures, holding no formal meetings or informal consultations. The Committee received seven notifications of exports of arms and related materiel to Sierra Leone.

On 14 August, Canada forwarded to the United Nations two letters dated 13 and 14 August, from the Acting Registrar and the President of the Special Court for Sierra Leone, respectively. Both letters contained a request to the Committee to grant a waiver of the travel restrictions imposed by resolution 1171(1998) to allow for the transfer to Rwanda of three listed individuals who had been convicted by the Special Court for Sierra Leone (Messrs. Brima Bazzy Kamara, Alex Tamba Brima, Santigie Borbor Kanu) for the enforcement of their sentences. On 26 August, the Chairman informed Canada that the Committee had no objection. In regard to a request of Rwanda to allow for the transfer to Rwanda of two listed individuals who had been convicted by the Special Court (Messrs. Morris Kallon and Issa H. Sesay) for the enforcement of their sentences, the Chairman, on 28 October, informed Rwanda that the Committee had acceded to the waiver of travel restrictions. In letters dated 27 and 29 October, the Acting Registrar of the Special Court provided the Committee with information in connection with the transfer of those five listed individuals. On 4 November, the Acting Registrar informed the Chairman that the five individuals had been transferred to Rwanda on 31 October for the enforcement of their sentences.

During the year, no violations or alleged violations of the sanctions regime were brought to the attention of the Committee. In light of the Government's 2008 suggestion regarding the review of the notification requirements for the delivery of arms or related materiel to Sierra Leone, the Chairman encouraged members of the Committee and the Security Council to continue consultations to determine the appropriate time to streamline the legal basis for sanctions in Sierra Leone and to possibly terminate the measures at a time Council members deemed appropriate.

Communication. On 30 July [S/2009/397], the Committee Chairman informed the Security Council of notifications received from the United Kingdom and the United States about military supplies sent to assist the armed forces of Sierra Leone.

UNIPSIL

The United Nations Integrated Peacebuilding Office in Sierra Leone (UNIPSIL) was established on 1 October 2008 by Security Council resolution 1829(2008) [YUN 2008, p. 215] as the successor mission to the United Nations Integrated Office in Sierra Leone (UNIOSIL), with a reduced military contingent and a mandate focused on strengthening governmental capacities. Its mandate included assisting the Government in: providing political support to national and local efforts for identifying and resolving tensions and threats of conflict; monitoring and promoting human rights, democratic institutions and the rule of law; consolidating good

governance reforms, with a focus on anti-corruption efforts; reviewing the 1991 Constitution and key legislation; strengthening the justice sector, Parliament and key governance institutions; promoting the effective functioning of local government; supporting the Peacebuilding Cooperation Framework, the work of the Peacebuilding Commission and projects of the Peacebuilding Fund; coordinating strategy and programmes among the UN agencies in Sierra Leone; and cooperating with other peace operations in the subregion to promote regional peace.

In an effort to consolidate its operations following the closure of UNIOSIL, UNIPSIL moved to a new and smaller location in Freetown, resulting in savings in rent and operating costs.

Appointment. On 5 January [S/2009/17], the Secretary-General informed the Council of his appointment of Michael von der Schulenburg (Germany), the Acting Executive Representative since 2008, as his Executive Representative for UNIPSIL. He would also serve as the Resident Representative of UNDP and the United Nations Resident Coordinator. The Council took note of the appointment on 8 January [S/2009/18].

Financing

In an October report [A/64/349/Add.3] providing budget estimates for 2010 in respect of special political missions and other offices grouped under thematic cluster III (UN offices, peacebuilding offices, integrated offices and commissions), the Secretary-General proposed resource requirements for UNIPSIL in the amount of $16,934,500, which ACABQ recommended to the General Assembly for approval [A/64/7/Add.13].

On 24 December, in section VI of **resolution 64/245** (see p. 1407), the Assembly endorsed the recommendations of ACABQ and approved the budgets for 26 special political missions and other offices, including the UNIPSIL budget, under section 3, Political affairs, of the programme budget for the 2010–2011 biennium.

Financing of UNAMSIL

In January [A/63/681], the Secretary-General issued the final performance report of the United Nations Mission in Sierra Leone (UNAMSIL), which included information on the assets, outstanding liabilities and fund balance as at 30 June 2008 in respect of the United Nations Observer Mission in Sierra Leone (UNOMSIL) and UNAMSIL. The cash balance was reported as $15,149,000, and uncollected assessments and other receivables at $7,248,000, bringing the total fund balance to $22,397,000. ACABQ [A/63/746/

Add.1], in comments on the final performance report, requested the Secretary-General to provide an update on the status of the collection of assessments and other receivables to the Assembly. As proposed by the Secretary-General, ACABQ recommended that the Assembly agree that the cash balance of $15,149,000 be credited to Member States.

The mandate of UNOMSIL ended on 13 December 1999 and that of UNAMSIL on 31 December 2005.

GENERAL ASSEMBLY ACTION

On 30 June [meeting 93], the General Assembly, on the recommendation of the Fifth Committee [A/63/906], adopted **resolution 63/299** without vote [agenda item 145].

Financing of the United Nations Mission in Sierra Leone

The General Assembly,

Having considered the report of the Secretary-General on the final performance of the United Nations Mission in Sierra Leone and the related report of the Advisory Committee on Administrative and Budgetary Questions,

1. *Takes note* of the status of contributions to the United Nations Observer Mission in Sierra Leone and the United Nations Mission in Sierra Leone as at 30 April 2009, including the credits in the amount of 44.9 million United States dollars;

2. *Endorses* the conclusions and recommendations contained in the report of the Advisory Committee on Administrative and Budgetary Questions, subject to the provisions of the present resolution, and requests the Secretary-General to ensure their full implementation;

3. *Takes note* of the report of the Secretary-General on the final performance of the United Nations Mission in Sierra Leone;

4. *Decides* that Member States that have fulfilled their financial obligations to the Mission shall be credited with their respective share of the net cash available in the Special Account for the United Nations Mission in Sierra Leone in the amount of 15,633,000 dollars as at 30 April 2009, in accordance with the levels updated in General Assembly resolution 58/256 of 23 December 2003, and taking into account the scale of assessments for 2006, as set out in Assembly resolution 58/1 B of 23 December 2003;

5. *Encourages* Member States that are owed credits referred to in paragraph 4 above to apply those credits to any accounts where they have outstanding assessed contributions;

6. *Urges* all Member States to make every possible effort to ensure payment of their assessed contributions in full;

7. *Decides* that, for Member States that have not fulfilled their financial obligations to the Mission, their respective share of the net cash available in the Special Account for the Mission in the amount of 15,633,000 dollars as at 30 April 2009 shall be set off against their outstanding obligations, in accordance with the scheme set out in paragraph 4 above;

8. *Also decides* that updated information on the financial position of the Mission shall be included in the report on the updated position of closed peacekeeping missions, to be considered by the General Assembly at its sixty-fourth session under the item entitled "Administrative and budgetary aspects of the financing of the United Nations peacekeeping operations";

9. *Further decides* to delete from its agenda the item entitled "Financing of the United Nations Mission in Sierra Leone".

Special Court for Sierra Leone

The Special Court for Sierra Leone, jointly established by the Government of Sierra Leone and the United Nations in 2002 [YUN 2002, p. 164] pursuant to Security Council resolution 1315(2000) [YUN 2000, p. 205], continued in 2009 to try those bearing the greatest responsibility for violations of international humanitarian and Sierra Leonean laws committed in the territory of Sierra Leone since November 1996. Except for the ongoing trial of Charles Taylor, the former President of Liberia, at The Hague, the Court concluded its trials in 2009.

In the case of *Prosecutor v. Charles Ghankay Taylor*, the Prosecution, having called 91 witnesses, completed presentation of evidence in January and closed its case on 27 February. Trial Chamber II dismissed a defence motion for a judgment on acquittal, ruling that there was evidence capable of sustaining a conviction on all 11 counts of the indictment. On 13 July, the defence opened its case, with Mr. Taylor giving evidence in his own defence. The case continued throughout the year.

In the case of *Prosecutor v. Issa Hassan Sesay, Morris Kallon and Augustine Gbao* (the RUF trial), the Special Court, on 8 April, following their conviction on 25 February for crimes against humanity and other serious violations of international humanitarian law during the civil war in Sierra Leone, sentenced former interim leader Issa Hassan Sesay, former commander Morris Kallon and former senior commander Augustine Gbao, all of the erstwhile RUF, to 52, 40 and 25 years' imprisonment, respectively [S/2009/267]. The three were convicted of acts of terrorism, collective punishments, extermination, murder as a crime against humanity, murder as a war crime, rape, sexual slavery, forced marriage as an inhumane act, outrages upon personal dignity, mutilations, physical violence as a crime against humanity, enslavement as a crime against humanity, pillage, intentionally directing attacks against UNAMSIL peacekeepers, and murder in relation to UNAMSIL peacekeepers. Messrs. Sesay and Kallon were also found guilty of the crime of using children to participate in hostilities. Each of them and the Prosecution filed notices of appeal on 28 April. The Appeals Chamber of the Court, on 26 October, revised the sentences imposed by the Trial Chamber on some of the counts, but upheld the total terms of imprisonment imposed on each of the accused [S/2010/135].

On 13 August and 26 October, the Court designated Rwanda as the State where convicted persons would serve their sentences. The convicts were transferred to Mpanga prison in Kigali on 31 October to serve the remainder of their sentences.

The Management Committee of the Court in July approved the updated completion strategy of its work, setting February 2011 as the expected completion date of its judicial activities. In anticipation of the Court's concluding its work, attention was placed on planning for its residual functions—its legal and practical obligations that continued beyond the completion of all trials and appeals proceedings. The Outreach and Public Affairs Section of the Court continued to publicize the Court's activities throughout Sierra Leone and to the people of the subregion, and increasingly in Liberia. As the Court neared the completion of its mandate, it continued downsizing its personnel.

The President of the Special Court, Justice Renate Winter, and the Prosecutor, Stephen Rapp, briefed the Security Council on the work of the Court on 16 July [meeting 6163].

Guinea-Bissau

In 2009, the United Nations Peacebuilding Support Office in Guinea-Bissau (UNOGBIS) assisted the Government in its efforts to consolidate peace, organize presidential elections, promote governmental cohesion and effectiveness, reform the security sector, and combat drug trafficking and organized crime. The climate remained tense, particularly between the political and military leadership, despite the relative calm in the military situation. Twice during the year, assassinations temporarily halted the progress in the path to consolidation of peace. On 1 and 2 March, the Chief of the General Staff, General Batista Tagme Na Waie, and President João Bernado Vieira were killed, and a new interim Government was formed, led by the Speaker of the National Assembly, Raimundo Pereira, in keeping with the Constitution. The situation within the military remained fragile and was characterized by distrust between different services, and the security situation deteriorated.

As provided for in the Constitution, presidential elections were held on 28 June, with a run-off between the two leading candidates on 26 July. The elections occurred without major incident, and Malam Bacai Sanha, the candidate of the governing African Party for the Independence of Guinea and Cape Verde, won the election, defeating former President Mohamed Yalá, the candidate of the Social Renewal Party (PRS).

President Sanha expressed the wish to open a new chapter in the country's political life on the basis of dialogue, stability and the rule of law.

In June, the Security Council extended the mandate of UNOGBIS until the end of the year, after which it would be succeeded by a United Nations Integrated Peacebuilding Office in Guinea-Bissau (UNIOGBIS). The new Office, with a greatly reduced staff, was mandated to strengthen national capacities to maintain constitutional order, public security and the rule of law; support law enforcement and criminal justice systems; support political dialogue and national reconciliation; provide strategic and technical support to the Government in security sector reform; and assist in national efforts to combat drug trafficking and organized crime.

The Guinea-Bissau configuration of the Peacebuilding Commission continued its engagement with the country and maintained its commitment to the peace process, focusing in particular on security sector reform and preparations for the presidential elections.

Political and security developments

Report of Secretary-General (March). Early 2009 was a period characterized by growing tensions within the political and military leadership, according to the Secretary-General's March report on developments in the country and on the activities of the United Nations Peacebuilding Support Office in Guinea-Bissau (UNOGBIS) [S/2009/169]. Those tensions and a degradation of the security and governance structures culminated in the assassinations of the President, João Bernardo Vieira, and the Chief of the General Staff, General Batista Tagme Na Waie. Prior to that event, political tensions had increased due to, among other events, the attack on 23 November 2008 on the President's residence [YUN 2008, p. 226]. The Prime Minister, Carlos Gomes, Jr., met on 11 February 2009 with military leaders to discuss security sector reform, the drug problem and the possible return of Rear Admiral Bubo Na Tchuto, who had fled to the Gambia following his arrest for involvement in an alleged coup attempt in August 2008.

Prior to the assassinations, the country had taken modest steps to improve its democratic and governance direction. In January, Prime Minister Gomes and the cabinet—all members of the ruling African Party for the Independence of Guinea and Cape Verde (PAIGC)—were sworn in. That party unanimously approved the draft Government Programme and passed a motion of confidence in the Prime Minister on 15 February. The five priority challenges identified in the Programme were: promoting good governance and consolidating democracy and the rule of law; ensuring political stability and social cohesion; reforming and modernizing the State; ensuring economic growth; and re-establishing the internal and external reputation of the State. The Programme also provided for an overhaul of the defence sector through appropriate legislation and called for local elections to be held by the end of 2010. Under the Programme, adopted on 18 March, reform of the security sector would continue and the programme to combat drug trafficking and organized crime would be implemented. Although there were no major drug seizures in early 2009, reliable sources indicated the use of Guinea-Bissau for trans-shipping large consignments of cocaine from Latin America to markets in Europe and emerging markets in Africa and Asia.

The economic situation remained fragile and the country had severe cash flow difficulties. The Government faced arrears of four months' salary for civil servants and owed debts to regional and local commercial banks. IMF decided to extend the emergency post-conflict assistance programme, which ran for 2008, until the end of June 2009. An IMF mission visited the country from 17 February to 3 March to discuss the programme in 2009 and work with the Government on a 2009 budget based on realistic assumptions regarding revenue and donor support. African Development Bank sanctions were suspended until 2010 and disbursements for current projects and funds, amounting to approximately $3 million, resumed. The EU, the World Bank, France, Portugal and Spain began discussions with the Government, with a view to setting up a mechanism for the framing and monitoring of future budget support. The World Bank granted Guinea-Bissau $5 million to finance a mechanism to assist the most vulnerable populations and help small farmers increase agricultural production. The European Commission was providing 6 million euros for emergency aid in agriculture. The Secretary-General urged the international partners of Guinea-Bissau, in particular ECOWAS and the EU, to enhance their support for security sector reform in cooperation with UNOGBIS, and to support the Government by providing assistance in organizing elections and implementing economic reforms.

Assassinations of President and Chief of Staff

On the evening of 1 March, a bomb explosion killed the Chief of the General Staff, General Tagme Na Waie, and destroyed part of his headquarters. Early the next morning, machine-gun fire, pistols and rocket-propelled grenades exploded in the vicinity of the residence of President Vieira. It was later confirmed that assailants had taken over the residence and assassinated the President. Following the assassination of General Tagme, the General Staff established a Commission of Military Chiefs to manage the crisis and to control military personnel. The spokesman

of the Commission, Navy Commander José Zamora Induta, released a statement informing the nation that General Tagme and three of his escorts had died in an explosion caused by a bomb set by unknown individuals, and that a "group of unidentified citizens" had attacked the residence of President Vieira in the early hours of 2 March and had shot him dead. The statement reaffirmed the armed forces' commitment to remaining subordinate to the civilian authorities and their allegiance to their constitutional duties. At an extraordinary meeting of the Council of Ministers on 2 March, the Government established a Commission of Inquiry to look into the assassinations. On 3 March, the Speaker of the National Assembly, Raimundo Pereira, was sworn in as interim President, in keeping with the Constitution which mandated the election of a new president within 60 days. The Prime Minister informed the Secretary-General's Representative that the Commission of Inquiry needed human and financial assistance from the United Nations to carry out its mission efficiently.

The Secretary-General, in a statement of 2 March [SG/SM/12121], expressed shock and dismay over the incidents. The Community of Portuguese-speaking Countries, ECOWAS and Angola sent delegations to explore measures that could be taken to stabilize the country. In his March report [S/2009/169], the Secretary-General acknowledged efforts by the national authorities to investigate the assassinations and called for a credible and transparent process. He stressed the importance for the State to ascertain the facts behind the November 2008 attack [YUN 2008, p. 226] and the two assassinations of March 2009, in order to end impunity in the country, uphold the rule of law and maintain the integrity of the State. It was also important that the defendants receive a fair hearing. The two assassinations underscored the need to implement the reforms of the justice, defence and security sectors.

SECURITY COUNCIL ACTION

On 3 March [meeting 6089], following consultations among Security Council members, the President made statement **S/PRST/2009/2** on behalf of the Council:

The Security Council condemns in the strongest terms the assassinations of the President of Guinea-Bissau, Mr. João Bernardo Vieira, and the Chief of Staff of the armed forces, General Tagme Na Waie, on 1 and 2 March 2009. It expresses its deep sympathy and condolences to the families of the victims and to the people and Government of Guinea-Bissau.

The Council calls upon the Government of Guinea-Bissau to bring to justice those responsible for these violent acts. It calls upon the Government, the political leaders, the armed forces and the people of Guinea-Bissau to remain calm, exercise restraint, maintain stability and constitutional order and respect the rule of law and the democratic process. It also urges all parties to resolve their disputes through political and peaceful means within the framework of the democratic institutions and opposes any attempt to change the government through unconstitutional means.

The Council welcomes in this regard the statements condemning the incidents by the Secretary-General of the United Nations, the African Union, the Economic Community of West African States, the European Union and other members of the international community, and calls upon all to assist in preserving the constitutional order in Guinea-Bissau and to continue to support peace-building efforts in the country.

The Council reaffirms its commitment to support the efforts of the Government and people of Guinea-Bissau to consolidate democratic institutions, peace and stability in that country.

The Council shall remain seized of developments in Guinea-Bissau.

Communication. On 3 March [S/2009/120], Portugal transmitted to the Security Council the statement of the Community of Portuguese-speaking Countries (CPLP) on Guinea-Bissau, in which the Community condemned the assassination of the President and the Chief of Staff and expressed its intention to send, in the next few days, a political mission to Bissau for consultations with the Guinea-Bissau institutions to promote internal dialogue.

Security Council consideration. On 8 April [meeting 6103], the Council was briefed by the Secretary-General's Representative and Head of UNOGBIS, Joseph Mutaboba, who stressed the need for security sector reforms in the country.

SECURITY COUNCIL ACTION

On 9 April [meeting 6105], following consultations among Security Council members, the President made statement **S/PRST/2009/6** on behalf of the Council:

The Security Council recalls its previous statements on Guinea-Bissau, and takes note of the latest report of the Secretary-General on developments in Guinea-Bissau and on the activities of the United Nations Peacebuilding Support Office in Guinea-Bissau. The Council reaffirms its support for the continuing efforts to consolidate peace in that country.

The Council welcomes the swearing-in as interim President of Guinea-Bissau of Mr. Raimundo Pereira and notes with satisfaction the commitment of the new authorities to maintain constitutional order following the assassinations of the President of Guinea-Bissau, Mr. João Bernardo Vieira, and of the Chief of Staff of the armed forces, General Tagme Na Waie, and to deepen national consensus on the transition and the electoral process.

The Council also welcomes the convening of the presidential elections for 28 June 2009, and urges the Government of Guinea-Bissau and all political actors to create the best conditions for the holding of free, fair, transparent and credible presidential elections. It welcomes the assistance already provided by bilateral and multilateral partners to support the electoral budget, and calls upon the donors to continue to provide technical and financial assistance for the electoral process.

The Council takes note of the final communiqué of the 26th meeting of the Economic Community of West African States Mediation and Security Council expressing the need to deploy military and police contingents to ensure the protection of the republican institutions and the authorities, as well as the electoral process in Guinea-Bissau. In this regard, the Security Council invites the Economic Community of West African States to work in coordination with the Government of Guinea-Bissau.

The Council condemns recent cases of arbitrary detention, armed attacks and intimidation, and demands full protection of the human rights and fundamental freedoms of the people of Guinea-Bissau. It urges the armed forces leadership to ensure that its commitment to abide by the civilian authorities and respect constitutional order is fully honoured.

The Council stresses the importance of national reconciliation and the fight against impunity in Guinea-Bissau, and calls upon the international community to support the commission of inquiry established to investigate the assassinations of the President and of the Chief of Staff of the armed forces.

The Council reiterates the importance of security sector reform in Guinea-Bissau and, in this regard, urges the international partners to continue to support the implementation of the quick-impact projects. It welcomes the convening of a round table on Guinea-Bissau's security sector reform with a view to following up the coordination and the implementation of the identified projects and programmes on security sector reform, to be held in Praia on 20 April 2009.

The Council remains seriously concerned by the growth in illegal drug trafficking as well as transnational organized crime in Guinea-Bissau and in the subregion. It commends the joint action of the United Nations Office on Drugs and Crime, the Department of Political Affairs of the Secretariat/United Nations Office for West Africa, the Department of Peacekeeping Operations of the Secretariat and the International Criminal Police Organization (INTERPOL) to help to implement the Economic Community of West African States plan of action against drug trafficking. It calls upon the international community to continue to support the implementation of the Guinea-Bissau anti-narcotics operational plan, as well as of the Economic Community of West African States plan of action.

The Council calls upon the international community to provide timely and adequate support for the implementation of the Strategic Framework for Peacebuilding in Guinea-Bissau adopted by the Peacebuilding Commission. It looks forward to a sustainable mobilization of resources for economic reconstruction and peace consolidation in Guinea-Bissau.

The Council reiterates the importance of the regional dimension in the resolution of the problems faced by Guinea-Bissau and, in this regard, welcomes the role of the African Union, the Economic Community of West African States, the Community of Portuguese-speaking Countries and the European Union in the peacebuilding process.

The Council commends the Representative of the Secretary-General in Guinea-Bissau and the staff of the United Nations Peacebuilding Support Office in Guinea-Bissau, as well as the United Nations country team and the Guinea-Bissau configuration of the Peacebuilding Commission for their contribution to peace, democracy and the rule of law in Guinea-Bissau. The Council reiterates that it looks forward to receiving recommendations from the Secretary-General on how the United Nations presence in Guinea-Bissau should be reconfigured to support peacebuilding more effectively.

Killing of political leaders. The Security Council, by a press statement of 9 June [SC/9677], condemned the killing in Guinea-Bissau on 5 June of Baciro Dabó, one of the candidates in the presidential elections of 28 June, and Helder Proença, a former Minister of Defence, and two of his bodyguards. The Council called on the Government, the political leaders, the armed forces and the people of Guinea-Bissau to exercise restraint, maintain stability and constitutional order, and respect the rule of law and the democratic process.

On 9 June [S/2009/298], Portugal forwarded to the Security Council a communiqué issued by the Presidency of CPLP, which condemned the assassinations and called for a rigorous inquiry into the facts, as well as respect for the constitutional order in the lead-up to national elections.

Further developments

Report of Secretary-General (June). In his June report on developments in Guinea-Bissau and UNOGBIS activities [S/2009/302], the Secretary-General said that the period under review was marked by the political and military crisis that followed the assassinations of the President and the Chief of the General Staff and preparations for the presidential elections to be held on 28 June. Following the March assassinations, there followed a period of calm; however, that was disrupted when the Minister of Territorial Administration and candidate in the presidential elections, Baciro Dabó, was killed by armed men in military uniform at his residence. Another leading parliamentarian from PAIGC and two others in his car were killed in a car ambush at approximately the same time. According to the State intelligence services, both were allegedly resisting arrest and, together with eight other people, including four members of Parliament, were accused of involvement in a coup attempt. Those assassinations were condemned by the international community.

Interim President Pereira on 31 March issued a decree setting 28 June as the date for the presidential elections. The Government requested UN support for the elections; UNDP immediately provided assistance to the national authorities in mobilizing funds and deployed a team of technical experts to the National Electoral Commission and the Technical Electoral Support Office. That assistance included civic education and training for polling station officials. The Government presented a budget of $5 million, which envisaged a first round and a possible run-off, but did not include security costs, amounting to $700,000. The Commission requested that UNOGBIS coordinate the activities of the international observers. The EU confirmed that it would deploy an electoral observation mission. Having reviewed candidates' applications, the Supreme Court published a final list validating 13 applications.

The twenty-sixth ministerial-level meeting of the ECOWAS Mediation and Security Council (Bissau, 19 March) recommended that ECOWAS mobilize international support, including from the United Nations, for the preventive deployment of the military and police to ensure the protection of State institutions, Government officials and the electoral process. It recommended immediate steps to implement the ECOWAS plan of action against drug trafficking, using Guinea-Bissau as one of the pilot countries. The Council addressed the issue of impunity and called for the creation of an international commission of inquiry into events in the country since August 2008, when Rear Admiral Bubo Na Tchuto allegedly carried out a coup attempt [YUN 2008, p. 224]. The CPLP Council of Ministers, meeting in Praia, Cape Verde, on 25 March, supported the establishment of an international commission of inquiry. It endorsed the ECOWAS proposal on preventive security deployment, if it was requested by Guinea-Bissau, coordinated by the AU and undertaken under a UN mandate. However, on 1 April, the Minister of Social Communication and Spokesperson of the Government denied that the Government had made any request for such a deployment and said that what was needed was international support for security sector reform. Subsequently, a donor round-table on security sector reform was held in Praia.

The situation within the military remained fragile and was characterized by distrust. A number of military officers and civilians were arrested in connection with a parallel investigation launched by the military into the assassination of General Tagme. On several occasions, the new military leadership accused unnamed politicians of attempting to incite the lower ranks against them. The Defence and Security Reconciliation Commission embarked on its sixth round of consultations since its inception in 2005 with defence and security personnel in Bissau and the regions to discuss the events of 1 and 2 March, the role of the defence and security forces in democracy, and collaboration between defence and security personnel. UNOGBIS, in cooperation with the Government, organized five one-day workshops throughout the country to validate the national survey on small arms and light weapons. Public security deteriorated in Bissau during the reporting period, and 21 political parties called on the Government to resign because of its inability to protect citizens and institutions. As decided by the ECOWAS Mediation and Security Council on 19 March, a donor round table on restructuring and modernizing the defence and security sector was organized by CPLP, ECOWAS, UNOGBIS and the Governments of Guinea-Bissau and Cape Verde in Praia on 20 April to promote security sector reform. The round table, among its recommendations, called for setting up a pension fund, creating a police academy and strengthening institutional capacity to provide special security for democratic institutions and their representatives. With regard to the fight against drug trafficking and organized crime, the conference highlighted the commitment of the police to cooperate with the international community. It stressed the regional dimension of drug trafficking and the need for both a national and an international response. The Prime Minister commended the efforts of the United Nations Office on Drugs and Crime (UNODC) to combat drug trafficking and organized crime, and he requested UNODC to design a police academy and a high-security prison in Bissau.

The fiscal and economic situation was extremely difficult. The Government faced major challenges in repaying sizeable domestic arrears, including three months of civil service salary arrears from 2008 and two months currently. Following an IMF mission to Bissau from 17 February to 3 March, the Government agreed to control spending, increase revenue collection and improve transparency and governance. It was estimated that Guinea-Bissau would need budgetary support of $44 million in 2009. Assuming that it met benchmarks under the emergency post-conflict assistance programme, the Government hoped to move to a Poverty Reduction and Growth Facility arrangement with IMF later in 2009. The economic situation was affected by the depressed price of cashews on the international market. Social tensions over food prices had lessened, owing in particular to controls on basic food and fuel prices. The Government's inability to pay civil service salaries was a source of social tension, which led to a wave of strikes in the health and education sectors that limited access to basic social services. In addition to a chronic lack of power, the capital city of Bissau suffered from severe water shortages owing to a lack of power to operate pumping equipment.

Proposal for UNIOGBIS

The Secretary-General, in his June report on Guinea-Bissau [S/2009/302], recalled that in December 2008, the Security Council had noted the need to establish an integrated UN office in Guinea-Bissau

[YUN 2008, p. 230], as recommended in the statement made by the Council President on 15 October 2008 [ibid., p. 225]. An inter-agency technical assessment mission was sent to the country from 21 to 30 April to discuss peace consolidation and to develop proposals for establishing an integrated UN presence. Following consultations, the Secretary-General proposed that UNOGBIS be succeeded in January 2010 by the United Nations Integrated Peacebuilding Office in Guinea-Bissau (UNIOGBIS) for an initial period of one year. He proposed that UNIOGBIS be mandated to assist the Government in: collaborating with the Peacebuilding Commission in its engagement with the country; strengthening the capacity of national institutions to maintain constitutional order and respect for the rule of law; establishing effective law enforcement and criminal justice systems; supporting an inclusive political dialogue and a national reconciliation process; providing strategic and technical support in the security sector reform strategy; combating human trafficking, drug trafficking and organized crime; promoting, protecting and monitoring human rights; mainstreaming a gender perspective into peacebuilding; curbing the proliferation of small arms; enhancing cooperation with the AU, ECOWAS, CPLP, the EU and other partners in contributing to stabilization; and helping in mobilizing international assistance.

It was proposed that UNIOGBIS be headed by a Special Representative, who would report to the Secretary-General through the Department of Political Affairs, and have a staffing strength of a deputy, 38 professional staff, 37 security officers, 16 UN police, 37 support staff and 5 UN Volunteers. There would be four substantive sections—political affairs, human rights and gender, security sector reform, and public information. Each section would work with the UN country team. UNIOGBIS would have an expanded police role, with a focus on issues related to the reform, restructuring and rebuilding of the police and other law enforcement agencies.

Security Council consideration. On 23 June [meeting 6149], the Council was briefed by the Secretary-General's Representative, who said that the challenges in the country were enormous, adding that, although the Government and the people of Guinea-Bissau had the primary responsibility to address them, the international community should provide much-needed support for reforms in the justice, public administration, defence and security sectors and, most urgently, for the conduct of peaceful presidential elections.

SECURITY COUNCIL ACTION

On 26 June [meeting 6152], the Security Council unanimously adopted **resolution 1876(2009)**. The draft [S/2009/327] was submitted by Burkina Faso.

The Security Council,

Recalling its previous resolutions and the statements by its President concerning the situation in Guinea-Bissau, as well as the letter dated 22 December 2008 from its President to the Secretary-General,

Expressing its deep concern at the resurgence of political violence, in particular the political assassinations in Guinea-Bissau,

Stressing the fact that such developments demonstrate the fragility of the political situation and jeopardize the efforts to restore peace and stability, as well as the rule of law in Guinea-Bissau,

Stressing also the importance of the upcoming presidential elections in Guinea-Bissau of 28 June 2009 and the need to have free, fair and transparent elections as a crucial and necessary step towards the full return to constitutional order, the consolidation of democracy and national reconciliation,

Underlining the need for everyone to respect the results of the elections, and calling upon all stakeholders to contribute to a peaceful environment during and after the elections,

Reaffirming that the Government of Guinea-Bissau and all stakeholders must remain committed to security sector reform, the promotion of the rule of law and the fight against impunity and illicit drug trafficking,

Stressing the importance of security sector reform, and reiterating the continued support of the United Nations and the international community for the long-term security and development of Guinea-Bissau, particularly in the fields of security sector reform, justice, and building the capacity of the Government to fight against illicit drug trafficking,

Reiterating the importance of regional and subregional cooperation in addressing the challenges faced by Guinea-Bissau,

Recalling the adoption on 1 October 2008 of the Strategic Framework for Peacebuilding in Guinea-Bissau, and encouraging the Government of Guinea-Bissau to continue its close engagement with the Peacebuilding Commission towards its accelerated implementation,

Noting that the situation in Guinea-Bissau continues to be extremely fragile, in particular as a result of increased drug trafficking and organized crime that could pose a threat to regional stability and should also be addressed by an approach of shared responsibility,

Stressing its concern about human trafficking, especially that of children outside the country,

Reaffirming its full commitment to the consolidation of peace and stability in Guinea-Bissau,

1. *Decides* to extend the mandate of the United Nations Peacebuilding Support Office in Guinea-Bissau until 31 December 2009;

2. *Welcomes* the report of the Secretary-General of 10 June 2009 on developments in Guinea-Bissau and on the activities of the United Nations Peacebuilding Support Office in that country, and takes note of the recommendations contained therein;

3. *Requests* the Secretary-General to establish a United Nations Integrated Peacebuilding Office in Guinea-Bissau to succeed the United Nations Peacebuilding Support Office in Guinea-Bissau, as recommended by him in his report, for an initial period of twelve months, beginning on 1 January 2010, with the following key tasks:

(a) Assisting the Peacebuilding Commission in its work in addressing critical peacebuilding needs in Guinea-Bissau;

(b) Strengthening the capacities of national institutions in order to maintain constitutional order, public security and full respect for the rule of law;

(c) Supporting national authorities to establish effective and efficient police and law enforcement and criminal justice systems;

(d) Supporting an inclusive political dialogue and national reconciliation process;

(e) Providing strategic and technical support and assistance to the Government of Guinea-Bissau in developing and coordinating the implementation of security sector reform;

(f) Assisting national authorities to combat drug trafficking and organized crime, as well as human trafficking, especially child trafficking;

(g) Supporting the national efforts to curb the proliferation of small arms and light weapons;

(h) Undertaking human rights promotion, protection and monitoring activities and supporting the institutionalization of respect for the rule of law;

(i) Mainstreaming a gender perspective into peacebuilding, in line with Security Council resolutions 1325(2000) of 31 October 2000 and 1820(2008) of 19 June 2008;

(j) Enhancing cooperation with the African Union, the Economic Community of West African States, the Community of Portuguese-speaking Countries, the European Union and other partners in their efforts to contribute to the stabilization of Guinea-Bissau;

(k) Helping in the mobilization of international assistance;

4. *Underlines* the need for appropriate expertise to ensure that the United Nations Integrated Peacebuilding Office in Guinea-Bissau effectively and efficiently implements its mandate;

5. *Underlines also* the importance of establishing a fully integrated office with effective coordination of strategies and programmes between the United Nations agencies, funds and programmes, between the United Nations and international donors, and between the integrated office, the Economic Community of West African States and other United Nations missions in the subregion, and requests the Secretary-General to take the necessary measures with the United Nations Peacebuilding Support Office in Guinea-Bissau to ensure a smooth transition between the Peacebuilding Support Office and the new integrated office;

6. *Requests* the Secretary-General to develop a strategic workplan with appropriate benchmarks to measure and track progress on the implementation of the mandate described in paragraph 3 above and to report on its implementation in accordance with paragraph 14 below;

7. *Calls upon* the Government and all political stakeholders of Guinea-Bissau to work together in order to set up the best conditions for national reconciliation and to consolidate peace and security throughout Guinea-Bissau;

8. *Urges* all members of the armed forces, including their leaders, to abide by civilian rule and to refrain from any interference in political issues, and to guarantee the security of the national institutions, as well as the population in general, and calls for the full protection and respect of human rights;

9. *Urges* Guinea-Bissau's political leaders to refrain from involving the military in politics, and requests them to use legal and peaceful means to solve their differences;

10. *Calls upon* the Government of Guinea-Bissau to conduct credible and transparent investigations into the political assassinations in March and June 2009, and to bring to justice those responsible for these acts, and also calls upon the international community to support those investigations;

11. *Requests in particular* the Secretary-General, in consultation with the African Union, the Economic Community of West African States and the Community of Portuguese-speaking Countries, to assist the Government of Guinea-Bissau in carrying out a credible investigation process;

12. *Takes note* of the initiatives undertaken by regional organizations for ensuring the protection of the national institutions and the authorities;

13. *Requests* the Secretary-General, through his Special Representative for Guinea-Bissau and the United Nations Integrated Peacebuilding Office in Guinea-Bissau, to assist the Government of Guinea-Bissau for effective coordination of the support provided by the international community to security sector reform in Guinea-Bissau, taking into account the work already undertaken by the European Union and other international actors in this area;

14. *Also requests* the Secretary-General to keep the Council regularly informed every four months on progress in establishing the United Nations Integrated Peacebuilding Office in Guinea-Bissau, with the first report due by 31 October 2009, and thereafter in the implementation of the present resolution;

15. *Decides* to remain actively seized of the matter.

Presidential elections

The presidential elections, held on 28 June, with a run-off between the two leading candidates on 26 July, passed without major incident, the Secretary-General reported in October [S/2009/552]. Malam Bacai Sanha, the candidate of the governing PAIGC party, won the election, defeating former President Mohamed Yalá, the PRS candidate. Raimundo Pereira, who had served as Interim President since March, resumed his mandate as the Speaker of the National Assembly.

Out of the 13 presidential candidates, only 11 participated in the presidential elections on 28 June. The campaigning period was generally peaceful, although an escalation in negative attacks during the final days of the campaign was observed. The results were not contested and were judged by international observers as free, fair and transparent. The voter and civic education campaigns prior to the run-off election focused on reducing voter abstention.

UNDP supported the Government in planning, resource mobilization and the coordination of donors' support for the elections. An innovation was the involvement of civil society organizations, together with the National Electoral Commission, in the conceptualization, planning and implementation of the civic education activities. The National Electoral Commission, with UNDP assistance, organized a national meeting to map out a strategy for the civic education campaign, which resulted in the establishment of a coordination group of civil society organizations working with the Commission/UNDP team. In addition to providing funds, UNDP mobilized and channelled contributions from regional organizations and a number of countries. UNOGBIS coordinated the activities of international election observers, with technical assistance from Canada, and the activities of regional election observation missions. In partnership with the Faculty of Law of Bissau, UNOGBIS organized a seminar on the electoral law with a focus on the voting process (16–17 June), attended by 22 representatives of the campaign management teams of the 11 candidates and 7 journalists.

Further developments

Report of Secretary-General (October). In his report on developments in Guinea-Bissau and UNOGBIS activities [S/2009/552], the Secretary-General said that the tense atmosphere following the 5 June assassinations had slowly given way to the return of normalcy. On 22 June, interim President Pereira and interim Chief of General Staff Induta attended the meeting of ECOWAS Heads of State and Government in Abuja. The summit issued a communiqué urging all stakeholders, especially the security forces, to take all measures to guarantee a climate of peace conducive to free, transparent and credible elections. The summit commended the decision by the President of Nigeria to provide financial assistance of $3.5 million to cover three months of salary arrears of the armed forces and provide vehicles and communications equipment to them. The payment of salary arrears contributed to creating the necessary conditions for the military to secure the elections and play a neutral role. The Government deployed 4,000 personnel nationwide under its security plan for elections. President Sanha confirmed the appointment of Navy Captain Induta as Chief of General Staff of the Armed Forces.

The National Assembly began preparing for the convening of a national conference on the theme "Conflicts in Guinea-Bissau: causes, prevention, resolution and consequences". It was envisaged that a series of regional conferences would culminate in a national conference to identify the causes of conflicts in the country, the contradictions between State and non-State institutions and conflict prevention mechanisms and strategies. The conferences would involve civil society organizations, the justice and security sectors, veterans, faith organizations, women, youth and the media.

On 13 July, the media reported incidents allegedly related to drug trafficking along the border between Guinea-Bissau and Guinea. The Guinea-Bissau authorities subsequently increased the level of security alertness on the border. The armed forces stressed that troops were not involved in any of the incidents, nor was there a military threat to the country. On 6 August, the Prime Minister and Minister of Defence visited Guinea to discuss border issues. The Minister of Natural Resources, on 29 September, expressed concerns over developments in Guinea and stated that Guinea-Bissau was working on a contingency response plan, especially for a possible influx of Guineans seeking refuge in Guinea-Bissau.

Security sector reform in Guinea-Bissau was discussed at the ECOWAS summit, in particular the need to send a joint team of experts of ECOWAS and the West African Economic and Monetary Union to assess the needs in that area and in financial stability. A draft pension fund proposal, developed with EU support, was presented in August to the armed forces leadership and the Government. In October, the Council of Ministers approved a six-month extension of the mandate of the EU mission established to support security sector reform, which had submitted to the Government a number of proposed laws and organizational documents in the areas of military, police and public prosecution.

A downward trend over several months in cocaine trafficking through West Africa was reported. However, the identification of laboratories producing cocaine, heroin and ecstasy in Guinea raised concerns that this exposed Guinea-Bissau to criminal groups' activities. In May, investigators from the judicial police anti-drug unit documented a network involved in producing false travel documents with the assistance of accomplices working in public administration, and the smuggling of migrants. Judicial police officers trained by UNODC, with the support of Brazil, the EU and Portugal, increased their presence and intervention. UNODC held a workshop on international cooperation mechanisms in the fight against drugs and organized crime and sent a legal expert to assist in prison system reform, training of public officials, legal counselling and implementation of international legal standards.

The economic and fiscal situation remained fragile, but there were encouraging signs. Economic growth was predicted to decline by 0.4 per cent, less than the initial forecast of 1.3 per cent, largely owing to record exports of cashew nuts, the main export crop. The Government was up to date with civil service salaries,

although it owed three months of salary arrears from 2008. National revenue increased by 12.2 per cent in the first half of 2009 as a result of better revenue collection. However, the disbursement of financial support from international partners was delayed, and only $12.24 million out of the $44 million pledged was disbursed as of early August. The World Bank approved an $8 million grant to Guinea-Bissau to better implement its poverty reduction strategy. IMF approved in June a third emergency post-conflict assistance programme of approximately $2.74 million. It noted that recent progress on structural reforms to strengthen fiscal management was encouraging and demonstrated that the authorities had the capacity to implement the proposed programme. The African Development Bank made grants for projects to develop governmental capacity. UNOGBIS continued to assist the Government in other areas, including elimination of discrimination against women, rule of law, human rights protection, and mission staff security.

Noting the record abstention rate for the presidential elections, the Secretary-General urged political leaders to foster dialogue and accountability towards their constituents, in order to reinforce democracy and regain citizens' confidence in their Government. He noted that the new President and Government had reaffirmed their commitment to hold investigations into the political assassinations, which, when completed, would assist in combating impunity and contribute to justice and national reconciliation.

Security Council consideration. Briefing the Council on 5 November [meeting 6212], Antonio Maria Costa, Executive Director of UNODC, said that West Africa, and especially Guinea-Bissau, served for the transfer of drugs, in particular cocaine, from Latin America to Europe. As Europe's craving for cocaine persisted, the Government needed greater assistance in interception activities. The most serious negative development had been the discovery of sites containing large amounts of chemicals used to refine cocaine and manufacture ecstasy, meaning that West Africa was on the verge of becoming a source of drugs and that organized crime was growing indigenous roots. Guinea-Bissau was particularly vulnerable to such developments because of its poor judicial system, uncontrolled sea and airspace and open land borders. UNODC was doing its utmost to help, along with its partners, in establishing a Transnational Crime Unit in the country, supporting criminal justice capacity-building and security sector reform and helping to establish a national police academy.

SECURITY COUNCIL ACTION

On 5 November [meeting 6213], following consultations among Security Council members, the President made statement **S/PRST/2009/29** on behalf of the Council:

The Security Council recalls its previous statements and resolutions on Guinea-Bissau, and takes note of the latest report of the Secretary-General on developments in Guinea-Bissau and on the activities of the United Nations Peacebuilding Support Office in Guinea-Bissau. The Council reaffirms its support for the continuing efforts to consolidate peace in that country.

The Council welcomes the peaceful presidential elections that were held on 28 June and 26 July 2009, and the inauguration of President Malam Bacai Sanha on 8 September 2009. It also takes note of the commitment by the President to combat impunity, foster national reconciliation and achieve socio-economic development. The Council reiterates that the human rights and fundamental freedoms of the people of Guinea-Bissau must be fully protected. It again urges the armed forces of Guinea-Bissau to ensure that their commitment to abide by the civilian authorities and respect constitutional order is fully honoured.

The Council also takes note of the plans of the National Assembly to convene a national conference on the theme 'Conflicts in Guinea-Bissau: causes, prevention, resolution and consequences', and underscores the need to conduct an inclusive political dialogue process aimed at ensuring national reconciliation in the country.

The Council reiterates the importance of consolidating democracy, security, the rule of law, national reconciliation and the fight against impunity to ensure sustainable peace in Guinea-Bissau. In this regard, it takes note of the ongoing consultations between the United Nations, the African Union, the Economic Community of West African States and the Community of Portuguese-speaking Countries to assist the Government of Guinea-Bissau, at its request, in carrying out a credible, thorough and expeditious investigation, in accordance with international standards, into the political assassinations of March and June 2009. The Council calls upon the Government to expedite this process, and calls upon the above-mentioned organizations and the international community as a whole to bring their support to this end.

The Council underlines the challenges faced by the Government of Guinea-Bissau, in particular to ensure that the security sector is effective, professional and accountable. In this regard, the Council emphasizes the necessity of pursuing and implementing an effective and comprehensive national strategy for security sector reform, to be supported by the international partners. The Council reiterates its request to the Secretary-General, through his Special Representative for Guinea-Bissau and the United Nations Integrated Peacebuilding Office in Guinea-Bissau, for effective coordination of the support provided by the international community to security sector reform in Guinea-Bissau, taking into account the work already undertaken by the European Union and other international actors in this area.

The Council urges the Government of Guinea-Bissau to take the necessary actions within the framework of the Guinea-Bissau anti-narcotics operational plan and the Economic Community of West African States plan of action against drug trafficking and organized crime in West Africa. The Council further notes that the situation in Guinea-Bissau continues to be extremely fragile, in particular as a result of increased drug trafficking and organized crime that could pose a threat to regional stability, and should be addressed by an approach of shared responsibility. In this context, the Council welcomes the progress in implementing the West Africa Coast Initiative involving the Economic Community of West African States, commends the action of the United Nations Office on Drugs and Crime, the Department of Peacekeeping Operations and the Department of Political Affairs of the Secretariat and the International Criminal Police Organization (INTERPOL) in support of the fight against organized crime and drug trafficking in West Africa, and calls upon the international partners to continue supporting this partnership and the efforts of the national authorities to strengthen activities on policing and internal security, including law enforcement and border control, as part of the security sector reform process.

The Council calls upon the international community to provide timely and adequate support for the implementation of the Strategic Framework for Peacebuilding in Guinea-Bissau, adopted by the Peacebuilding Commission on 1 October 2008, including that of the quick-impact projects. The Council takes note of the importance of building synergies among the donors. It further takes note of the preparations for the first review of the Strategic Framework for Peacebuilding and looks forward to its finalization. The Council reiterates its support for the work of the Guinea-Bissau configuration of the Commission.

The Council welcomes the ongoing planning for the transition of the United Nations Peacebuilding Support Office in Guinea-Bissau to the United Nations Integrated Peacebuilding Office in Guinea-Bissau on 1 January 2010, and looks forward to the timely development of an Integrated Strategic Framework, including a strategic workplan with appropriate benchmarks to measure and track progress on the implementation of the mandate of the new Office.

The Council reiterates the importance of the regional dimension in the resolution of the problems faced by Guinea-Bissau and in this regard welcomes the role of the Economic Community of West African States, the African Union, the Community of Portuguese-speaking Countries and the European Union in the peacebuilding process in that country.

Year-end developments

The last months of 2009 were relatively calm as the new Government began to implement its programme, according to the Secretary-General in a later report [S/2010/106]. President Sanha issued two decrees on 28 October changing the structure of the Government and appointing a new cabinet that was streamlined from 21 ministers to 18. At the opening of the 2009–2010 legislative session on 3 November, he called for a comprehensive reform of the State and its institutions, revision of the Constitution and the establishment of a council of traditional leaders. The President appointed as Prosecutor General Amine Saad, who opened an investigation into the alleged involvement of senior officials of the Ministry of

Fisheries in corrupt practices, illegal concessions of fishing licenses and financial mismanagement. On 23 November, the National Assembly discussed a report supposedly prepared and made public by the Military Information and Security Division of the armed forces which claimed that certain parliamentarians from PAIGC posed a risk to internal stability and warned that internal divisions within the party could poison relations between the Prime Minister and the President. Parliamentarians voiced concern about the role of military intelligence in politics. On 7 December, the National Assembly approved the 2010 State budget.

Regional security issues were addressed at a meeting on border issues between Guinea-Bissau and Senegal (Bissau, 23 October). The meeting was prompted by renewed fighting in the Senegalese region of Casamance and the reported displacement of border markers along the demarcation line between the two countries. Both countries agreed to revive a joint cooperation commission and, among other measures, to create a joint commission to survey the demarcation line and ensure that the border markers were in place. On 25 November, the Minister of Defence launched a pilot project for collecting and destroying small arms and light weapons in Bairro Militar, the largest suburb in Bissau, with assistance from the United Nations and ECOWAS.

In the area of security sector reform, the Council of Ministers in December approved key draft legal instruments prepared with the assistance of the EU mission, including a draft bill on such reform and a decree on a pension fund for defence sector personnel. At the same time, the Ministries of Interior and Defence agreed on creating a 1,700-member new entity, with military status and police functions, called the "Guarda Nacional". A number of meetings on security sector reform were held between Guinea-Bissau officials and representatives of the international partners providing support in that area, in particular UNOGBIS, the EU, the AU and ECOWAS. A Portuguese technical cooperation mission in October provided basic training to 60 officers from the Public Order Police and to 160 officers from the Judiciary Police.

The economic and fiscal situation showed some gains in the last quarter of 2009. Although the economic growth rate fell by 0.4 per cent compared to 2008, that was offset by the record volume of cashew exports and improved performance in the construction sector, contributing to an annual growth of 2.9 per cent of GDP in 2009. The improvement of fiscal policy execution allowed the Government to keep up with the payment of salaries, primarily from internal revenues. At the end of 2009, the country received significant support from key international partners, amounting to $68 million.

Peacebuilding Commission

Report of Peacebuilding Commission. The Peacebuilding Commission, reporting in September on its third session (23 June 2008–30 June 2009) [A/64/341-S/2009/444], reviewed the work of its Guinea-Bissau configuration. The Commission said that in the latter part of 2008, the first year of its engagement with Guinea-Bissau, it focused on finalizing the Strategic Framework for Peacebuilding in Guinea-Bissau and supporting the organization of legislative elections, both of which were achieved that year [YUN 2008, p. 229].

The Guinea-Bissau configuration of the Commission continued its engagement with the country throughout 2009, following the constitution of the new Government on 7 January. The Guinea-Bissau National Steering Committee for Peacebuilding, the primary point of contact for the Commission's engagement with national stakeholders, was reconstituted in February. Following the assassinations of President Vieira and General Tagme in March, the Chair of the configuration, Maria Luiza Ribeiro Viotti (Brazil), issued a statement [PBC/3/GNB/5] in which she condemned those acts and encouraged all stakeholders to maintain their commitment to peace consolidation. In particular, she encouraged the international community to support the preparations of the presidential elections, in accordance with the Constitution. The configuration also focused on security sector reform, connecting with the Government on 25 March via video link. On 15 April, the configuration convened an informal meeting on security sector reform to highlight ongoing initiatives and review collaboration among the actors, in preparation for the conference on security sector reform (Praia, Cape Verde, 20 April) at which the Chair represented the Commission. On 11 May, the Chair presented her findings from her April fact-finding visit to Guinea-Bissau at an informal meeting of the configuration. The meeting was apprised of the recommendations of the Integrated Task Force Technical Assessment Mission that visited Guinea-Bissau from 21 to 30 April, and was briefed by IMF and the World Bank on their engagement with the country.

Following the assassinations of two politicians, the configuration issued a statement on 16 June [PBC/3/GNB/6] condemning the killings and reiterating its continued support to the consolidation of peace. On 22 June, the configuration convened an informal meeting to hear briefings by the Under-Secretary-General for Political Affairs, B. Lynn Pascoe, on his recent visit to Guinea-Bissau, and by the Secretary-General's Representative, Mr. Mutaboba, on the political developments in the country. Based on those discussions, the Chair briefed the Security Council on 23 June [meeting 6149] on the way forward and the areas in which the Commission could provide support, such as national reconciliation, security sector reform, youth employment and the fight against illicit drug trafficking. The Commission reinforced its call to the international financial institutions, in particular IMF and the World Bank, to apply flexible measures and to increase funding for the socio-economic needs of the country, which were critical to peacebuilding.

Peacebuilding Fund. A project on professional training and youth employment supported by the Peacebuilding Fund provided training to 400 young people in the areas of electricity, civil construction, auto repair, refrigeration and air conditioning, sewing, business start-ups and management. Construction work to rehabilitate prisons began in two towns in July. In an August report on the activities of the Peacebuilding Fund from 1 July 2008 to 30 June 2009 [A/64/217-S/2009/419], the Secretary-General said that 39 per cent of projects planned for that period had been implemented, at a cost of $6 million. That period was characterized by significant political and military tension, causing disruption to three ongoing Fund projects.

Peacebuilding Strategic Framework (December). In December, the Peacebuilding Commission issued its first progress report [PBC/4/GNB/1] on implementation of the Peacebuilding Strategic Framework for Guinea-Bissau, which was adopted by the Commission and the Government on 1 October 2008 [YUN 208, p. 229]. Initially scheduled for the first quarter of 2009, it was delayed following assassinations in March and June. A year after the adoption of the Strategic Framework, the list of priorities the Government had identified in 2008 remained generally valid. They included elections and ensuring institution-building for the National Electoral Commission; measures to jump-start the economy and rehabilitate infrastructure, particularly in the energy sector; security and defence sector reform; strengthening the justice sector, consolidating the rule of law and combating drug-trafficking; public administration reform and modernization; and social questions critical for peacebuilding. The performance of Guinea-Bissau public finances had improved remarkably during 2009, particularly since the Government had regularized its salary arrears and current-accounts management through budgetary support provided by long-term partners. At the infrastructural level, the inauguration of the São Vicente Bridge, half way between Bissau and the northern border with Senegal, had facilitated automobile circulation along a major highway axis. Many steps had been taken towards implementing the strategic document for restructuring and modernizing the security sector, but reform had not progressed quickly, particularly with regard to the security forces. There had been significant efforts to contribute to the

administration of justice and consolidate the rule of law by strengthening institutional capacity.

Despite an increase by the Government in the number of health-care professionals at the local level, the health sector remained largely dependent on international aid, with more than 90 per cent of the ministry budget derived from international contributions. Nevertheless, Guinea-Bissau did not experience an outbreak of cholera in 2009 (as it did in 2008), partly thanks to public awareness campaigns and improved access to potable water. The crisis of the education sector was evident in 2008/2009, when difficulties related to salary payments led to a long strike by teachers. There were three major subregional threats to peacebuilding: rekindling of separatist activities in the Senegalese region of Casamance, north of Guinea-Bissau; political and social instability in Guinea; and trafficking of persons, small arms and drugs.

The report concluded that, given the specificities of Guinea-Bissau and the difficulties that different partners were facing in implementing projects, the Government and Commission should conduct annual rather than six-monthly reviews of the implementation of both parties' commitments. It offered conclusions and recommendations on a variety of questions, including: elections and institutional support for the National Electoral Commission; measures to jump-start the economy and rehabilitate infrastructure, particularly in the energy sector; security and defence sector reform; strengthening the justice sector, consolidating the rule of law and combating drug trafficking; public administration reform and modernization; and social questions critical for peacebuilding.

An addendum [PBC/4/GNB/1/Add.1] outlined the implementation of the commitments of the Peacebuilding Commission and the international community in table form, following each commitment with its current status and the next steps in implementation.

Participation in Guinea-Bissau configuration. By letters from the Chairperson or Acting Chairperson of the Peacebuilding Commission, the following were invited to participate, at their request, in all future meetings of the configuration: on 7 January, Brazil and Ghana [PBC/3/OC/9 & PBC/3/OC/10]; and on 20 January, Angola [PBC/3/OC/13].

UNOGBIS

The United Nations Peacebuilding Support Office in Guinea-Bissau (UNOGBIS), a political mission established in 1999 by decision of the Secretary-General and supported by Security Council resolution 1233(1999) [YUN 1999, p. 140], was extended until 31 December 2009 by Security Council resolution 1876(2009). Its mandate was revised by resolution 1580(2004) [YUN 2004, p. 229] in the face of intensified political turmoil and uncertainty, and in 2007

[YUN 2007, p. 230] to allow the Office to contribute to mobilizing international support for national efforts to eliminate drug trafficking.

On 27 January [S/2009/55], the Secretary-General informed the Security Council of his intention to appoint Joseph Mutaboba (Rwanda) as Representative for Guinea-Bissau and Head of UNOGBIS, to replace Shola Omoregie (Nigeria). On 30 January [S/2009/56], the Council took note of the intention.

During 2009, the Secretary-General submitted reports on developments in Guinea-Bissau and UNOGBIS in March [S/2009/169], June [S/2009/302] and October [S/2009/552], with a later report covering the end of the year [S/2010/106].

Financing

In an October report [A/64/349/Add.3] dealing with estimated requirements for 2010 for special political missions grouped under thematic cluster III (UN offices, peacebuilding support offices, integrated offices and commissions), which emanated from Security Council decisions, including requirements for the follow-on missions such as the transition of UNOGBIS to UNIOGBIS, the Secretary-General proposed resource requirements for UNOGBIS in the amount of $19,016,600 for 2010, which ACABQ recommended for approval [A/64/7/Add.13].

On 24 December, in section VI of **resolution 64/245** (see p. 1407), the Assembly endorsed the recommendations of ACABQ and approved the budgets for 26 special political missions, including the UNOGBIS budget, under section 3, Political affairs, of the programme budget for the 2010–2011 biennium.

Cameroon–Nigeria

In 2009, Cameroon and Nigeria continued to cooperate in implementing the 2002 ruling of the International Court of Justice (ICJ) [YUN 2002, p. 1265] on the land and maritime boundary between the two countries through the Cameroon-Nigeria Mixed Commission. The Commission at its twenty-fifth session (Yaoundé, Cameroon, 8–9 October) focused on the emplacement of the first permanent border demarcation pillars on the ground, which started in mid-November. A ceremony to mark the start of the pillar emplacement was held on 14 December. The joint technical team of surveyors resumed the field assessment on 12 November; by the end of the year, Cameroon and Nigeria had agreed on a total distance of 1,192 kilometres of the boundary. Regarding the maritime boundary, whose delineation had been completed in 2007, Cameroon and Nigeria were working on a framework agreement for cross-border cooperation.

The Follow-up Committee tasked with monitoring implementation of the 2006 Greentree Agreement continued to meet. In October, it considered the report of UN observers following their visit to the "zone" in the Bakassi peninsula and reviewed security-related cooperation between the parties.

Cameroon-Nigeria Mixed Commission

The Cameroon-Nigeria Mixed Commission—the mechanism established by the Secretary-General in 2002 at the request of the Presidents of Cameroon and Nigeria to facilitate the implementation of the ICJ ruling of 10 October 2002 on the border dispute between them [YUN 2003, p. 8]—was chaired by the Special Representative of the Secretary-General for West Africa, Said Djinnit (Algeria). The Commission was responsible for the demarcation of the land and maritime boundaries between the two countries; the withdrawal of civil administration, military and police forces and a transfer of authority in relevant areas along the boundary; the demilitarization of the Bakassi peninsula; the protection of the rights of the affected populations; the development of projects to promote joint economic ventures and cross-border cooperation; and the reactivation of the five-member Lake Chad Basin Commission (Cameroon, Central African Republic, Chad, Niger, Nigeria), created in 1964 for the regulation and planning of the uses of the Lake and other natural resources of the conventional basin. In 2007, all four sections of the ICJ ruling—comprising the withdrawal and transfer of authority in the Lake Chad area in December 2003, the withdrawal and transfer of authority along the land border in July 2004, the agreement on the modalities of withdrawal and transfer of authority in the Bakassi peninsula in June 2006, and the agreement on the delineation of the maritime boundary in May 2007—were resolved to the satisfaction of the two countries [YUN 2007, p. 232]. The transfer of authority from Nigeria to Cameroon was completed in a final handover ceremony in Calabar, Nigeria, on 14 August 2008 [YUN 2008, p. 231]. A UN team based in Dakar, Senegal, provided technical and logistical support to the Commission and its subsidiary bodies. The United Nations Office for West Africa (UNOWA) also provided support to the work of the Commission.

The Mixed Commission in 2009 continued its work on the delimitation and demarcation process along the boundary. The Commission resumed the field assessment of the land boundary; by the end of the year, the total length of assessed boundary was approximately 1,420 kilometres, out of the 1,950 kilometre-long boundary. In November, construction of permanent cement boundary pillars began along the boundary, providing Cameroon and Nigeria with the first tangible evidence of the land demarcation process.

Activities

The Special Representative of the Secretary-General for West Africa, Mr. Djinnit, continued to support the activities of the Cameroon-Nigeria Mixed Commission in his capacity as its Chairman, in particular the delimitation and demarcation process along the border. The Secretary-General described those activities in his January [S/2009/39], June [S/2009/332] and December [S/2009/682] reports on UNOWA. The United Nations continued to provide support for the demarcation of the boundary, foster cross-border cooperation and work with the communities in the affected areas to build a stable and prosperous future. UNOWA assisted demarcation and civilian observer teams of the Commission with human resources, logistical and administrative support. It also assisted the Follow-up Committee established by the 2006 Greentree Agreement [YUN 2006, p. 252] to monitor implementation of the agreement. During a visit to Abuja, Nigeria, on 23 February, the Special Representative worked with the parties to remove obstacles to the convening of the twenty-fourth session of the Commission. His efforts resulted in the resumption of the field assessment of the land boundary and an agreement to hold the twenty-fourth session of the Commission on 11 and 12 June. The Follow-up Committee also met in New York on 16 June.

By mid-June, 832 kilometres out of the 1,950 kilometres of the land boundary had been assessed and agreed upon by the parties. At the twenty-fourth session of the Commission, the parties demonstrated their willingness to strengthen cross-border cooperation, including by engaging more actively in sensitization efforts and community development projects targeting affected populations along the border and in Bakassi.

Communications. On 30 November [S/2009/642], the Secretary-General informed the Security Council of the latest progress made by the Commission. In the course of 2009, the Commission continued to facilitate the implementation of the ICJ decision, including helping to maintain dialogue and communication between the two countries. Concerning demarcation of the land boundary, the Commission expected to complete two field assessments along the boundary by the end of 2009, amounting to a total assessed boundary of approximately 1,420 kilometres. Concerning physical demarcation, the majority of preliminary mapping and preliminary large-scale mapping through satellite imagery was completed, as was the contract which established a geodetic network for the "as-built" survey of constructed pillars and the subsequent final mapping.

Of particular significance was the start in November of construction of permanent cement boundary pillars along the boundary—the end result of complex technical preparatory work. The project allowed for the construction of up to 60 primary and 640 secondary boundary pillars at locations and to specifications defined by the Mixed Commission. The project, implemented by the United Nations Office of Project Services, was divided into three segments, the first of which covered some 700 kilometres from Lake Chad to the Benue River and was scheduled for completion by March 2010.

Reports by UN civilian observers monitoring the border situation concluded that the prevailing situation continued to be peaceful. In 2009, the Mixed Commission continued to support the formulation of confidence-building measures to guarantee the security and welfare of affected populations and to promote initiatives to build trust between the two Governments and their peoples.

The Follow-up Committee continued its work under its new Chairman, Mr. Djinnit, who was appointed by the Secretary-General on 21 May to replace Sir Kieran Prendergast. The meetings of the Committee (New York, 16 June; Geneva 22–23 October) allowed for agreement on activities to be conducted in the "zone" during the transitional five-year period (August 2008–August 2013) during which the Greentree Agreement provided for special legal protection to be granted to Nigerian residents. Those discussions also allowed for the resumption of observer visits to Bakassi in October and for renewed cooperation between Cameroon and Nigeria on security matters.

The Secretary-General outlined plans for the Mixed Commission, providing a schedule for future activities, including the completion of the remaining length of the land boundary field assessment in 2011 and boundary pillar emplacement by 2012. At the request of Cameroon and Nigeria, the Commission would continue to provide technical and legal guidance to the parties in 2010, and UN civilian observers would continue to monitor the situation of affected populations in the Lake Chad area, along the land boundary and in the Bakassi Peninsula. In addition, the United Nations would continue to advise the parties on confidence-building measures and projects. Key areas for cooperation included food security, education, health, water and basic infrastructure. Given the cost-effectiveness of the mission and the remaining tasks to advance implementation of the ICJ ruling, the Secretary-General intended to seek resources from the regular budget for the Commission for 2010.

The Security Council on 14 December [S/2009/643] noted the Secretary-General's intention. It also urged the members of the Mixed Commission to work with international donors to seek further voluntary contributions.

Financing

In an October report [A/64/349/Add.3] dealing with estimated requirements for special political missions grouped under thematic cluster III (United Nations offices, peacebuilding offices, integrated offices and commissions), the Secretary-General proposed resource requirements for the Mixed Commission in the amount of $8,930,100 for 2010, which ACABQ recommended for approval [A/64/7/Add.13].

On 24 December, in section VI of **resolution 64/245** (see p. 1407), the Assembly endorsed the recommendations of ACABQ and approved the budgets of 26 Special political missions, including the Commission's budget, under section 3, Political affairs, of the programme budget for the 2010–2011 biennium.

Guinea

Following the death on 22 December 2008 of the long-serving President of Guinea, General Lansana Conté and the coup d'état by a military junta, the United Nations joined other international organizations in attempting to lead the country on the road to a return to democracy and constitutional order. In 2009, the Secretary-General's Special Representative for West Africa coordinated UN efforts in that regard, participating in several sessions of the International Contact Group on Guinea.

On 23 December 2008, Captain Moussa Dadis Camara became President, suspending governmental institutions and the Constitution and creating with his fellow officers a National Council for Democracy and Development (CNDD). The new leadership claimed that it was willing to hand over power to a civilian president after elections in 2009, which it later postponed, and that President Camara and the Prime Minister would not participate in the elections. However, tension rose as speculation mounted on whether President Camara and CNDD would stand for the legislative and presidential elections. Opposition movements organized a rally on 28 September 2009 which quickly turned violent when elements of the security forces opened fire on the crowds and committed gross human rights violations. The international community condemned the action and requested the Secretary-General to establish an international Commission of Inquiry to investigate the matter. Having received the cooperation of the Government, the Secretary-General dispatched the Commission to carry out a thorough investigation, to report on its findings and to make recommendations. The international mediation process continued throughout 2009, but the consultations bringing together CNDD and the "forces vives" coalition of opposition groups revealed a wide gap in positions. General Sekouba Konaté acted as interim President in the absence of President Camara,

who was flown to Morocco for medical care after an attempted assassination on 3 December.

Alongside the mediation process, UNOWA worked with the UN country team in Guinea to develop support programmes, including project proposals for conflict prevention, justice and security sector reform in the lead-up to elections.

Political and security developments

International Contact Group on Guinea. On 11 March [S/2009/140], Burkina Faso forwarded to the Security Council the final communiqué of the first session of the International Contact Group on Guinea (ICG-G). The Group, established at the consultative meeting on the situation in Guinea (Addis Ababa, 30 January), held its first session in Conakry, Guinea's capital, on 16 and 17 February. The session was attended by the AU, ECOWAS, the United Nations, the International Organization of la Francophonie, the EU, the Mano River Union, the Organization of the Islamic Conference, the Community of Sahelo-Saharan States and the World Bank. Other participants included Angola, as President of the AU Peace and Security Council, and Nigeria, as ECOWAS Chairman; African members (Burkina Faso, Libyan Arab Jamahiriya) and permanent members (China, France, Russian Federation, United Kingdom, United States) of the Security Council; and Spain. At the opening ceremony, the Prime Minister of Guinea, Kabine Komara, highlighted the progress made by the Government and expressed the hope that the Group would make appropriate recommendations for the successful conduct of the transition of Government. The Group took note of the announcement made by the Head of State and the CNDD Chairman regarding the establishment of a transition period comprised of four stages: establishment of transition institutions; Truth, Justice and Reconciliation Commission activities; adoption of constitutional reforms; and publication of the laws on the electoral process. The CNDD Chairman reiterated that the Prime Minister, members of CNDD and the Government would not run in the next elections. The Group expressed the hope that the dialogue between CNDD and stakeholders would yield results so that a timetable might be established for holding elections by the end of 2009.

After noting the improved security situation, the Group expressed concern about the arbitrary arrests and extrajudicial detentions, as well as the increasingly high number of roadblocks. It expressed its conviction that the holding of free, fair and transparent elections in 2009 would bolster political stability and consolidate democracy. It called for joint assessment missions in Guinea to evaluate the situation, and it urged CNDD and the Government to contribute to the establishment of the rule of law and respect for human rights. In addition, the Group shared the concerns of CNDD and urged the authorities to work with international organizations to combat drug and human trafficking and the proliferation of small arms and light weapons.

On 5 August [S/2009/422], Guinea forwarded the final communiqué of the fifth meeting of ICG-G (Conakry, 16–17 July). The Group noted with concern the delays in implementing the transition timetable and called on the authorities to rectify those matters. Urging CNDD and the Government to step up the fight against impunity, it noted the repeated acts of violence and extortion committed by armed personnel in uniform against businessmen and civilians, as well as the violations of the freedom of expression and the freedom of movement of political parties. Further meetings were held on 3 and 4 September in Conakry, on 22 September in New York, on 12 October in Abuja and on 13 December in Ouagadougou.

Communication. Guinea, in a letter of 4 August [S/2009/421] to the Secretary-General, said that Captain Camara, President and Commander-in-Chief, held a meeting in Conakry in July with representatives of political parties, trade unions and civil society. The meeting agreed to create an ad hoc committee to conduct a midterm review of the transition process and make proposals for its completion. The President subsequently established a joint committee with representatives of the Government, CNDD, political parties, trade unions and civil society.

Outbreak of violence

In mid-August, with the President declining to rule out his possible candidacy in the 2010 presidential elections, the police and gendarmerie gathered intelligence on the opposition's reactions and learned of a demonstration planned for 28 September. On that day, the police and gendarmerie turned out in force at the site of the demonstration, according to the Commission of Inquiry established later by the Secretary-General [S/2009/693] (see p. 230), and clashes broke out between security forces and demonstrators at several locations. The security forces used tear gas and clubs and fired shots into the air while demonstrators threw stones, attacked a police station and set fires. The most serious violence occurred at the stadium complex at Dixinn, where demonstrators were killed by gunfire, or stabbed or beaten to death, and those seeking to escape were killed by members of a commando regiment known as the "red berets", gendarmes and other forces, or were suffocated or trampled in stampedes. Rapes and other acts of sexual violence were committed almost immediately after the red berets entered the stadium. Women were taken by red berets from the stadium and from the Ratoma medical centre, and held as sex slaves for several days in different loca-

tions. Red berets attacked political leaders, several of whom were seriously injured. After several hours, the violence abated and some of the demonstrators began leaving their hideouts. The Commission of Inquiry confirmed 156 persons killed or disappeared, as well as 109 cases of rape or other acts of sexual violence.

Meeting in Addis Ababa on 15 October, the AU Peace and Security Council, by a press statement forwarded to the Security Council [S/2009/541], condemned the killings and acts of violence against unarmed civilians and the raping of women by armed units under the authority of CNDD. The Council endorsed the communiqué of the eighth session of the ICG-G (Abuja, 12 October), in particular the invitation to the Secretary-General, in conjunction with ECOWAS and the AU, to establish an International Commission of Inquiry to investigate the 28 September events, so that those responsible would be brought to justice. In addition, the Council reiterated its decision of 17 September to impose sanctions against the CNDD President and other individuals, if they did not confirm that they would not run in the presidential elections. At a summit meeting on 29 October in Abuja, the AU Council adopted a decision on Guinea, which it forwarded to the Security Council on the same day [S/2009/568], reiterating those positions.

The ECOWAS extraordinary summit of Heads of State and Government (Abuja, 17 October) mandated Burkina Faso's President Blaise Compaoré with securing the establishment of a new transitional authority; ensuring that the CNDD Chairman and members as well as the Prime Minister would not be candidates in the forthcoming elections; and developing benchmarks for the transition. The summit directed the ECOWAS Commission to work with the AU on a regime of sanctions against those obstructing the transitional agenda and to design a security sector reform programme for Guinea.

SECURITY COUNCIL ACTION

On 28 October [meeting 6207], following consultations among Security Council members, the President made statement **S/PRST/2009/27** on behalf of the Council:

> The Security Council remains deeply concerned by the situation in Guinea, which might pose a risk to regional peace and security following the killings that occurred in Conakry on 28 September 2009, when members of the army opened fire on civilians attending a rally. It strongly condemns the violence that reportedly caused more than 150 deaths and hundreds of wounded and other blatant violations of human rights, including numerous rapes and sexual crimes against women, as well as the arbitrary arrest of peaceful demonstrators and opposition party leaders.
>
> The Council reiterates the need for the national authorities to fight against impunity, bring the perpetrators

to justice, uphold the rule of law, including respect for basic human rights, and release all the individuals who are being denied due process under the law.

The Council welcomes the public statements by the International Contact Group on Guinea, the Economic Community of West African States and the African Union, in particular the communiqué issued by the Peace and Security Council of the African Union at its meeting held on 15 October 2009 and the communiqué issued by the Economic Community of West African States at its summit held on 17 October 2009. It welcomes the mediation undertaken by President Blaise Compaoré of Burkina Faso, including his efforts to create a more conducive and secure environment in Guinea, and calls upon the international community to support his action.

The Security Council welcomes the statement of the Economic Community of West African States summit supporting the decision of the Secretary-General to establish an international commission of inquiry to investigate the events of 28 September 2009, in order to ascertain the facts that took place, to identify the perpetrators with a view to ensuring that those responsible for violations are held accountable and to make recommendations to him. The Council takes note of the fact that the authorities of Guinea have officially committed to support the work of the international commission of inquiry in secure conditions.

The Council welcomes further the statement of the Economic Community of West African States summit stressing the importance of the establishment of a new transitional authority that would ensure credible, free and fair elections, of ensuring that the Chairman and members of the Conseil national pour la démocratie et le développement, the Prime Minister and those who hold high office in the new transitional authority will not be candidates in the forthcoming presidential elections, and of setting up benchmarks in the transition timetable. The Council calls for the elections to be organized as scheduled in 2010.

The Council further recalls, in this context, its resolution 1888(2009), in which it urged the Secretary-General, Member States and the heads of regional organizations to take measures to increase the representation of women in mediation processes and decision-making processes with regard to conflict resolution and peacebuilding.

The Council takes note of the decisions taken by the Peace and Security Council of the African Union on 17 September and 15 October 2009 regarding the imposition of targeted sanctions against the President of the Conseil national pour la démocratie et le développement and other individuals. It also takes note of the decision of the Economic Community of West African States to impose an arms embargo on Guinea. It notes further that the Peace and Security Council will meet at the level of Heads of State on 29 October 2009.

The Security Council expresses its intention to follow the situation closely. It requests the Secretary-General to update it, as appropriate, on the situation on the ground, the potential implications for the subregion, the international investigation of the killings of 28 September 2009 and the measures taken by the Economic Community of West African States and by the African Union.

Commission of Inquiry

The Secretary-General informed the Security Council on 28 October [S/2009/556] of his decision to establish an international Commission of Inquiry to investigate the killings, injuries and alleged gross human rights violations that took place on 28 September, in response to appeals from Member States, including Guinea, and members of ECOWAS, the AU and the Security Council. On 16 October, he sent an exploratory mission to Guinea and the subregion to assess the willingness of the Government to cooperate with the Commission, which was well received. The Commission would be mandated to establish the facts and circumstances of the 28 September events and related aftermath, qualify the crimes perpetrated, determine responsibilities, and, where possible, identify those responsible. It would also make recommendations, in particular on accountability measures.

The Commission became operational on 18 November and conducted its investigation from 25 November to 4 December. Its final report, submitted to the Council on 18 December [S/2009/693], described the violations committed on 28 September and qualified the nature of the crimes. The Commission interviewed 687 witnesses, victims and relatives of victims, as well as officials from clinics and hospitals that treated the injured. It verified the identity of 156 persons who were killed or disappeared; 67 victims whose bodies were recovered and buried by their families; 40 other persons who were seen dead in the stadium or in morgues but whose bodies had not been found; and 49 other identified persons who were seen in the stadium but whose fate was unknown. It confirmed 109 cases of rape and other sexual violence, as well as hundreds of cases of torture or cruel, inhuman or degrading treatment. The report gave a thorough description of the events of that day and days following, and provided details of the perpetrators. The Commission also described the reaction of the Government to the events and the explanations of the authorities on how and why the police took action. In general, the Commission found those explanations inconsistent with the Commission's findings in a number of respects. The treatment of the wounded and dead after the events demonstrated, contrary to the statements by the authorities, serious deficiencies, even behaviour, that, taken together with other acts, seemed deliberately designed to conceal the evidence of what had occurred. The events as described in the report constituted serious human rights violations under the conventions guaranteeing basic human rights that were signed by Guinea, as well as crimes against humanity, because they were of a widespread and systematic nature directed against the civilian population in pursuit of a strategy aimed at quelling political opposition.

The Commission considered that the red berets, the members of the National Gendarmerie and the units under Commander Moussa Thégboro Camara, the police and the militia were presumed to be individually responsible from a criminal standpoint, having had knowledge of the general and systematic attack against the civilian population. The State was responsible for violations committed by soldiers, gendarmes and police officers, as well as for the violations committed by militias who cooperated with the security forces. Members of the red berets committed the bulk of the murders, sexual violence and other crimes. The Special Services, generally known as "Thégboro's gendarmes" (from the name of the Minister in charge of those Services), also committed murders, sexual violence and torture against civilians. The National Gendarmerie, known as "green berets", played a role in the violations, as did the national police. The Commission was able to confirm the participation of militias in the violations; however, it was unable to confirm the identity or nationality of the militiamen. The determination of individual criminal responsibility lay exclusively with a court of law. However, the Commission was obliged to identify, where possible, the perpetrators of the crimes, whether directly or indirectly responsible. It concluded that there were reasonable grounds to suspect individual criminal responsibility on the part of: Captain Moussa Dadis Camara, President of Guinea; Lieutenant Aboubacar Chérif Diakité (alias Toumba), commander of the President's personal security detail and his aide-de-camp; and Commander Moussa Thégboro Camara, whose unit played a central role in the organized attack on civilian demonstrators. The Commission saw sufficient reason to conclude that the latter bore direct criminal responsibility for the commission of the crimes. Other persons were also mentioned for their lesser roles in the events.

In order to prevent any worsening of the situation, the Commission called for: the Security Council to remain seized of the situation, with all the political and legal consequences which that implied; and the Office of the United Nations High Commissioner for Human Rights to monitor the situation, at least in 2010, during which the country was likely to remain unstable, by an appropriately significant presence, to serve as a deterrent to potential violators of international law. In order to address internal institutional weaknesses, it recommended: that the most competent national and international bodies consider measures to streamline the military system through the introduction of a unified command structure, stricter discipline, promotion on the basis of merit and not on ethnic affiliation, a higher sense of duty, and respect for life and for the obligations of military personnel; that the United Nations and the international community call upon the Government to reform the judicial system with a view to putting an end to impunity; and that Guinea undertake to seek the truth so as to shed light on its painful past since its accession to independence, thereby contributing to national reconciliation. Guinea was urged to shed light on the 28 September events, prosecute those responsible, provide compensation to the victims and provide the families concerned with all relevant information on the cases of disappeared persons.

Where there was a strong presumption that crimes against humanity were committed, the cases against the individuals concerned should be referred to the International Criminal Court. The families of deceased persons should receive adequate compensation and the injured should receive reparations. In order to assist the Government in making reparations, the international community was encouraged to offer assistance. The Commission noted the targeted sanctions imposed by ECOWAS, the AU, the EU and the United States against the individuals presumed to be directly or indirectly responsible; it recommended that the measures should be extended to cover the individuals named in the report. It also recommended that the Government fulfil its obligations to protect victims and witnesses.

Further developments

From 3 to 11 November, President Compaoré held consultations with the "forces vives" coalition of opposition groups and CNDD representatives in Ouagadougou in the presence of UN and AU representatives, the Secretary-General reported [S/2009/682]. Those consultations revealed a wide gap between the positions of the two sides, especially the role of CNDD in the transition and the eligibility of Captain Camara to stand for elections. The written proposals submitted by President Compaoré to the parties on 18 November were rejected by the forces vives on the grounds that they did not take into account either their key concerns or those expressed by the international community.

The situation was further complicated by the attempted assassination of Mr. Camara by his aide de camp, Aboubacar Toumba Diakité, on 3 December, leading to further violence and human rights violations by security forces. On 5 December, the forces vives condemned the assassination attempt and called for CNDD to step down and to establish a transitional authority. General Konaté continued to act as the interim Head of State and leader of CNDD. He made a public statement warning that the army would no longer tolerate rogue elements within its ranks and called for reform of the army. On 10 December, both the forces vives and CNDD reaffirmed their commitment to the mediation process.

Mauritania

In 2009, the United Nations and other international organizations, in particular UNOWA, sought to assist Mauritania in returning to constitutional order following the overthrow of President Sidi Mohamed Ould Cheikh Abdallahi by General Mohamed Ould Abdel Aziz in a coup on 6 August 2008 [YUN 2008, p. 231].

The AU Peace and Security Council, in a communiqué adopted on 5 February 2009 and forwarded to the UN Security Council five days later [S/2009/85], imposed sanctions, effective that day, against Mauritania, pursuant to the 2000 Lomé Declaration and the Protocol Relating to the Establishment of the Peace and Security Council on Unconstitutional Changes of Government. The measures included visa denials, travel restrictions and freezing of assets on all individuals whose activities sought to maintain the unconstitutional status quo in Mauritania.

The situation improved later in 2009, as described by the Secretary-General in his December report on UNOWA activities [S/2009/682]. Following the signing of the Dakar Framework Agreement on 4 June, presidential elections were held on 18 July and were declared free and fair by international observers. The high-level panel appointed by the Secretary-General to follow the electoral process confirmed that General Aziz was declared the winner, and the Special Representative for West Africa attended his inauguration on 5 August. On 10 September, the International Contact Group on Mauritania, including the Special Representative, met in Nouakchott to review progress since the signing of the Dakar Framework Agreement, to assess remaining tasks and to redefine its role in the light of the return to constitutional order. The Contact Group urged the parties to engage in an inclusive political dialogue in line with the Agreement and encouraged the Government to be more proactive and to show leadership in that respect. The Group decided to transform itself into an ad hoc mechanism that would support consolidation of the democratic process and the mobilization of financial and economic assistance to the country.

Horn of Africa

Sudan

Operating in an unusually violent and politically unstable environment, the United Nations Mission in the Sudan (UNMIS) in 2009 undertook a new, proactive approach to peacekeeping, enabling further progress towards implementation of the 2005 Comprehensive Peace Agreement (CPA) [YUN 2005, p. 301] between the Sudan People's Liberation Movement/Army (SPLM/A) and the Government of National Unity, although significant tests still lay ahead, among them on elections, on developing effective security in the border areas, on the results of the national census, and on the referendum on national unity due in January 2011.

During the year, UNMIS helped launch the much-awaited Sudan Disarmament, Demobilization and Reintegration (DDR) programme, which began on 10 February in the Blue Nile State capital of Ed Damazin; reintegration commenced six weeks later. Similar programmes were later unveiled in other states. As at 31 December, 18,731 former combatants and members of special needs groups had been demobilized in the Sudan and had received their reinsertion packages for three months, and 1,741 former combatants in Southern Sudan and 7,149 in the Three Areas (Abyei, Blue Nile and Southern Kordofan) had received reintegration counselling. UNDP started contracting reintegration services for approximately 7,000 former combatants in Southern Sudan and 4,000 former combatants in Northern Sudan.

UNMIS moved quickly to defuse tensions in the aftermath of violent clashes in several hotspots in the southern region of the country. As inter-tribal turmoil escalated in southern Sudan, the Mission implemented a stabilization programme in Jonglei State that sharply curtailed fighting in one of the country's most turbulent corners. UNMIS achieved significant headway in its support of milestones of the CPA, such as voter registration, police training, child protection and the disputed boundaries of the oil-rich area of Abyei.

In the lead-up to the elections of April 2010, the Mission's electoral assistance division provided technical help and logistical support to the National Elections Commission (NEC), the Southern Sudan High Committee and the 25 state-level high committees. The division played a vital support role in the run-up to the voter registration process, which began in nearly all state capitals across the country on 1 November.

In one of the few positive political developments in 2009, the National Congress Party (NCP) and SPLM accepted the 22 July ruling by the Permanent Court of Arbitration in The Hague on the Abyei boundary dispute, rendered pursuant to the 2008 Abyei Road Map Agreement [YUN 2008, p. 238]. A boundary committee was subsequently appointed, but its work proceeded extremely slowly.

The annual Misseriya migration into disputed areas inhabited by Dinka Ngok communities went off relatively peacefully. UNMIS supported the convening of meetings among Dinka Ngok, Misseriya leaders and government officials in the aftermath of the arbitration court's ruling on Abyei.

Marauding bands of gunmen belonging to the Lord's Resistance Army (LRA) continued to terrorize communities living near southern Sudan's border with the Democratic Republic of the Congo and the Central African Republic. However, the scale and frequency of LRA attacks declined as the year proceeded, and its gunmen broke into small, isolated groups with little ability to mount serious raids deep inside Sudanese territory.

As well as by rising tensions between the country's two leading political parties, the political landscape was affected by the arrest warrant against President Omar Al-Bashir issued by the International Criminal Court (ICC) on 4 March (see p. 1300). The Sudanese Government responded by expelling 13 international non-governmental organizations (NGOs) from the Darfur region and shutting down three local NGOs.

The results of the 2008 national census [YUN 2008, p. 239] and the resultant allocation of National Assembly seats were not accepted by all political actors. Continued bickering between the NCP and SPLM stalled efforts in the National Assembly to approve enabling legislation for the southern Sudan and Abyei referendums, slated for January 2011. In an effort to prompt CPA partners to consider various post-referendums scenarios they might have to deal with in order to ensure a peaceful implementation of the agreement, UNMIS held a symposium in November on the future of the country.

In April, the Security Council renewed the UNMIS mandate and requested the Mission to help the parties to conclude the demarcation of the 1956 North-South border and to assist in promoting the rule of law.

Political and security developments

Report of Secretary-General (January). In his report of 30 January on the Sudan [S/2009/61], submitted pursuant to Council resolution 1590(2005) [YUN 2005, p. 304] and covering developments since his October 2008 report [YUN 2008, p. 239], the Secretary-General said that with little over two years of the interim period remaining, the CPA had reached a critical juncture. Daunting challenges lay ahead and key benchmarks—including census results, elections, border demarcations, disarmament, demobilization and reintegration, and preparations for referendums and popular consultations—needed to be achieved within a tight timeframe. The parties' political will, determination and decisive action would be required to consolidate achievements made since 2005, complete the interim period securely and prepare for a peaceful referendum as well as post-referendum stability. However, the relationship among the parties remained fragile and was affected by uncertainties, in particular regarding the 2011 referendum.

Southern Sudanese self-determination was a complex issue with profound implications for security in the Sudan and in the region, the Secretary-General continued, calling on the parties to begin preparations for referendums and their possible results. He welcomed their request for close involvement of his Special Representative and urged them to begin dialogue about wealth-sharing in the post-2011 period.

As the parties to the CPA were yet to present to the people of Southern Sudan a convincing case for unity, the Secretary-General called on them to use the remaining two years to explore all options available to make unity attractive. That would have to include the generation of a visible peace dividend, and the population, particularly in the south and the border areas, needed to see tangible benefits from the Agreement, including the provision of basic public services.

Insecurity continued to plague parts of the country where banditry, tribal clashes and militia activities remained a concern, the Secretary-General observed. The abundance of small arms, local dissatisfaction, a lack of economic prospects and the presence of spoilers could form a dangerous constellation. Tribal conflicts bore the inherent danger of escalation, and land rights, migration issues and peaceful tribal co-existence needed to be addressed. Providing security throughout the Sudan was a precondition for the well-being of the people and economic development.

The Joint Integrated Units (JIUs), composed of members of the Sudanese Armed Forces (SAF) and the Sudan People's Liberation Army (SPLA), a pillar of the security architecture of the Sudan and an important symbol of national unity, were facing many political, logistical and operational hurdles and were not fully functioning as intended in the CPA. The Secretary-General welcomed the efforts of the Ceasefire Political Commission and the Joint Defence Board to address the outstanding issues.

The Secretary-General welcomed the progress made in implementing the 2008 Abyei Road Map Agreement [YUN 2008, p. 238] and called on the Abyei Area Administration to assume its full responsibilities and demonstrate leadership and on the parties to the CPA to provide all necessary financial and political support. At the same time, he was concerned about the renewed flare-up of violent clashes, for the second time in eight months. He urged the Government of the Sudan to remove all restrictions on the freedom of movement of UNMIS throughout the Three Areas in order to restore the Mission's situational awareness and its ability to defuse conflicts.

Momentum in the DDR programme needed to be maintained, the Secretary-General stated. An early start of demobilization in the Three Areas would do much to build confidence and show tangible progress. At the same time, it was important that the parties begin discussions on the proportional downsizing of the forces on both sides. The international donor community could contribute significantly by making early and generous commitments to DDR, and he was grateful for Japan's leadership in that regard.

The Secretary-General urged the parties to expedite the demarcation of the North-South border. The Ad Hoc Technical Border Committee had delayed the release of its report; those delays would inevitably affect the preparations of the elections and the implementation of other CPA benchmarks. The Darfur crisis complicated the Sudan's political and military dynamics, taxing the parties' capacity to adapt to the changes required by the CPA. The possibility of military spillover, particularly into Southern Kordofan, were of concern, while other cross-cutting issues, including the census and elections, demanded coordinated efforts and the pursuit of a strategic approach. Increased insecurity in Southern Sudan related to the faltering LRA peace talks was a further concern.

In anticipation of a possible action by the ICC against President Al-Bashir (see p. 1300), the National Assembly had taken steps to amend the criminal code so as to allow prosecution of crimes within the Court's jurisdiction in national courts. High-level government officials reiterated their refusal to recognize the Court's jurisdiction in the Sudan or to extradite any Sudanese national to The Hague. Meanwhile, SPLM and nine Southern political parties urged the NCP to engage with the ICC and avoid a confrontational approach.

The ICC's actions had a major impact on political dynamics and diverted much attention at a time when outstanding issues related to the CPA required the parties' cooperation. While encouraged by the assurance of continued Government support, the Secretary-General was concerned about remarks suggesting that the Government might redefine its relationship with UNMIS should an arrest warrant be issued against the President. He called on the Government to fulfil its obligations to ensure the safety of UN staff and nationals of UN Member States. He expected both parties to remain committed to all aspects of the CPA and relevant Security Council resolutions, including cooperation with UNMIS.

Communication. On 6 February [S/2009/78], the Sudan requested the Security Council to retain on the list of matters of which it was seized the item entitled "Letter dated 20 February 1958 from the representative of the Sudan addressed to the Secretary-General (S/3963)" [YUN 1958, p. 83], which dealt with the issue of the Sudan-Egypt border.

Security Council consideration. On 20 March [meeting 6096], the Council considered the Secretary-General's reports and heard a statement by Rashid Khalikov, Director of the Office for the Coordination

of Humanitarian Affairs, on the humanitarian situation in northern Sudan following the suspension of the operations of three national NGOs and the expulsion of 13 international NGOs.

Communication. On 15 April [S/2009/207], the Sudan transmitted a progress report detailing achievements regarding the different aspects of the implementation of the CPA as at 9 April.

Report of Secretary-General (April). In a 17 April report [S/2009/211] submitted pursuant to Council resolution 1590(2005) [YUN 2005, p. 304], the Secretary-General assessed the overall situation since his 30 January report and reviewed the activities of UNMIS through 7 April. He reported that the overall security situation remained fragile and unpredictable. Several incidents of significant violence marked the reporting period in addition to ongoing tribal conflicts and heightened tensions following the announcement on 4 March of the ICC arrest warrant for President Al-Bashir, after which the Government expelled 13 international NGOs and closed down three national NGOs.

On 24 February, fighting erupted in Malakal, Upper Nile State, between the SAF and the SPLA elements of the JIU. An estimated 62 people were killed and 94 wounded. The situation was contained by swift action taken jointly by the parties to the CPA and UNMIS.

The DDR programme was achieving positive momentum that should lead to further confidence-building and progress in implementing the CPA. The Secretary-General welcomed the NEC's announcement of a proposed electoral timeline, its efforts to establish operational infrastructure and its request to UNMIS for assistance, and pledged the full support of the Organization. The United Nations also remained committed to assist in the conduct of referendums in 2011 in Southern Sudan and Abyei. The Secretary-General called for the necessary preparations for popular consultations to be carried out by elected state legislators in Southern Kordofan and Blue Nile States. UNMIS stood ready to support the two parties in honouring their commitment to "make unity attractive" and urged them to explore every available option in pursuing that goal in the limited time remaining.

SECURITY COUNCIL ACTION

On 30 April [meeting 6116], the Security Council unanimously adopted **resolution 1870(2009)**. The draft [S/2009/225] was submitted by the United States.

The Security Council,

Recalling all its resolutions and the statements by its President concerning the situation in the Sudan,

Reaffirming its resolution 1674(2006) of 28 April 2006 on the protection of civilians in armed conflict, in which it reaffirms, inter alia, the relevant provisions of the 2005 World Summit Outcome, its resolution 1612(2005) of

26 July 2005 on children and armed conflict, its resolution 1502(2003) of 26 August 2003 on the protection of humanitarian and United Nations personnel and its resolutions 1325(2000) of 31 October 2000 and 1820(2008) of 19 June 2008 on women and peace and security,

Taking note of the report of the Secretary-General of 30 January 2009 on the Sudan, the report of the Secretary-General of 10 February 2009 on children and armed conflict in the Sudan, including his recommendations, and the report of the Secretary-General of 29 August 2007 on children and armed conflict in the Sudan, and recalling the conclusions on parties to the armed conflict in the Sudan endorsed by the Security Council Working Group on Children and Armed Conflict,

Reaffirming its commitment to the sovereignty, unity, independence and territorial integrity of the Sudan and to the cause of peace throughout the region,

Commending the work of the United Nations Mission in the Sudan in support of the Comprehensive Peace Agreement of 9 January 2005, and commending the continuing commitment of troop- and police-contributing countries in support of the Mission,

Stressing its firm commitment to the cause of peace and stability throughout the Sudan and the region, noting the importance of the full implementation of the Comprehensive Peace Agreement, and recognizing that the Agreement has reached a critical stage,

Encouraging all parties to continue to take positive action in order to consolidate and build upon the achievements since 2005, and reaffirming the invaluable support of the Mission for these efforts,

Condemning all acts and forms of violence perpetrated by any party that prevent or hinder peace and stability in the Sudan and the region, and deploring its effect, in particular, on women and children,

Stressing the importance of providing humanitarian assistance to the civilian populations throughout the Sudan, in particular in the Three Areas after the events of 4 and 5 March 2009, and for the implementation of the Comprehensive Peace Agreement, and taking note of the joint assessment being conducted in the Three Areas and the need for continued cooperation between the Government of the Sudan, the United Nations and humanitarian organizations,

Commending the continuing work of the Assessment and Evaluation Commission,

Recalling the commitment of the international community to support the Comprehensive Peace Agreement process, including through development assistance, and urging donors to support the implementation of the Agreement and to honour all pledges of financial and material support,

Recalling also the importance of free and fair elections, including the planned national elections, for national reconciliation, the consolidation of democracy and the restoration of peace and stability,

Noting with deep concern the inability to reach agreement on the funding of the Abyei Interim Administration, thereby preventing it from reducing political instability and insecurity in the Abyei region,

Welcoming the increased cooperation among the United Nations Mission in the Sudan, the United Nations Organization Mission in the Democratic Republic of the Congo, the African Union-United Nations Hybrid Operation in Darfur (UNAMID) and the United Nations Mission in the Central African Republic and Chad, and looking forward to the sharing of information among them to help to counter regional threats such as the Lord's Resistance Army,

Determining that the situation in the Sudan continues to constitute a threat to international peace and security,

1. *Decides* to extend the mandate of the United Nations Mission in the Sudan until 30 April 2010, with the intention to renew it for further periods as may be required;

2. *Requests* the Secretary-General to report to the Security Council every three months on the implementation of the mandate of the Mission, progress on the implementation of the Comprehensive Peace Agreement, and respect for the ceasefire, and to provide an assessment and recommendations on measures that the Mission might take to further support elections and advance the peace process;

3. *Welcomes* the military capability review conducted into the deployment of the Mission, stresses the importance of appropriate and flexible deployment of the Mission in order to address the most likely points of conflict, in particular in areas where civilians are under threat of violence, and requests regular reviews of deployment and implementation of recommendations to ensure that the force is best placed to support the implementation of the Comprehensive Peace Agreement;

4. *Stresses* the importance of full and expeditious implementation of all elements of the Comprehensive Peace Agreement, and implementation of the Abyei road map, agreements on Darfur and the Eastern Sudan Peace Agreement of 14 October 2006, and calls upon all parties to respect and abide by their commitments to these agreements without delay;

5. *Welcomes* the sustained commitment of the parties to work together in the Government of National Unity, and urges the continued cooperation of the National Congress Party and the Sudan People's Liberation Movement in carrying out their responsibilities in further implementing the Comprehensive Peace Agreement;

6. *Stresses* the critical role of the Assessment and Evaluation Commission in overseeing and reporting on the implementation of the Comprehensive Peace Agreement, and urges all parties to cooperate fully with the Commission and implement its recommendations;

7. *Calls for* all parties to cooperate with full and unrestricted access to the Mission in monitoring and verification of the Abyei region, without prejudice to the final agreement on the Abyei boundaries, and urges the Mission, consistent with its current mandate and within its means and capabilities, to consult with the parties and to deploy, as appropriate, sufficient personnel to the Abyei region to improve conflict prevention efforts and security to the civilian population;

8. *Welcomes* the agreement by the parties to submit the Abyei boundary dispute to the Abyei Arbitration Tribunal at the Permanent Court of Arbitration for resolution, calls upon the parties to abide by and implement the decision of the Tribunal on the final settlement of the Abyei boundary dispute, urges the parties to reach agreement on providing the funding of the Abyei Interim Administration in accordance with the Comprehensive Peace Agreement, and urges

all parties to redeploy their military forces away from the disputed border of 1 January 1956;

9. *Also welcomes* the completion of the enumeration phase and technical analysis of the national census, expresses its concern about the delay in announcing the results, and urges the parties to reach agreement expeditiously on the 2008 national census results in a way that does not increase tensions;

10. *Urges* all Sudanese parties to continue to demonstrate their full commitment to the democratic process by preparing expeditiously for the conduct of peaceful, transparent and credible elections in February 2010 as recommended by the National Electoral Commission;

11. *Requests* the Mission, consistent with its mandate and within its current capabilities, to support the National Electoral Commission in preparing for credible national elections, including through the provision of assistance and advice, as required, with security preparations and coordinating United Nations election support efforts in close collaboration with the United Nations Development Programme, and ensuring that the efforts of the Mission are complementary to those of the international community and the parties to the Comprehensive Peace Agreement, and urges the international community to provide technical and material assistance, including electoral observation capacity as requested by the Government of National Unity, to support credible elections;

12. *Recalls* the provision in the Comprehensive Peace Agreement for referendums, including the responsibility of the parties to pursue efforts to make unity attractive, and, reaffirming the support of the Mission for these efforts, requests that the Mission be prepared to provide assistance to the parties, if requested, to support preparations for a referendum in 2011;

13. *Expresses its concern* for the health and welfare of the civilian populations in the Sudan, calls upon the parties to the Comprehensive Peace Agreement and the communiqué signed by the United Nations and the Government of National Unity in Khartoum on 28 March 2007 to support, protect and facilitate all humanitarian operations and personnel in the Sudan, and urges the Government of the Sudan to continue working with the United Nations to support the three-track approach delineated by the Secretary-General to ensure the continuity of humanitarian assistance;

14. *Requests* the Mission to make full use of its current mandate and capabilities to provide security to the civilian population, humanitarian and development actors and United Nations personnel under imminent threat of violence, as stated in resolution 1590(2005) of 24 March 2005, stresses that this mandate includes the protection of refugees, displaced persons and returnees, and emphasizes, in particular, the need for the Mission to make full use of its current mandate and capabilities with regard to the activities of militias and armed groups such as the Lord's Resistance Army in the Sudan, as stated in resolution 1663(2006) of 24 March 2006;

15. *Deplores* the persistent localized conflict and violence and its effect on civilians, especially within Southern Sudan, and the continuing potential for violence, and calls upon the Mission to strengthen its conflict management capacity by completing, as soon as possible, its integrated strategy to support local tribal conflict resolution mechanisms in order to maximize the protection of civilians; welcomes the development of a comprehensive strategy on the protection of civilians and encourages the Mission to continue and complete its work on the strategy in a timely manner; and again calls upon the Mission, consistent with its current mandate and capabilities, to proactively conduct patrols in areas at high risk of localized conflict;

16. *Notes* that conflict in one area of the Sudan affects conflict in other areas of the Sudan and in the region, and therefore urges the Mission, consistent with its current mandate, to cooperate closely with all United Nations entities operating in the region, including the African Union-United Nations Joint Mediation Support Team and other stakeholders, so that the implementation of the mandates of these bodies supports the overall objective of peace in the Sudan and the region;

17. *Requests* the Mission, acting within its current mandate and within its current means and capabilities, to provide technical and logistical support to the Ad hoc Technical Border Committee, as requested, to help the parties to urgently conclude the process of demarcation of the north/south border of 1956, in accordance with the Comprehensive Peace Agreement;

18. *Stresses* the important role of the Joint Integrated Units for the full implementation of the Comprehensive Peace Agreement, calls upon the Joint Defence Board to exercise command, control and management of the Joint Integrated Units, requests the Mission to explore ways to support Sudanese efforts to build the capabilities of the Joint Integrated Units, and urges donors to offer support, both materiel and training, coordinated by the Mission in consultation with the Joint Defence Board, to enable the full establishment and operational effectiveness of Joint Integrated Units and Joint Integrated Police Units as soon as possible;

19. *Encourages* the Mission, consistent with its mandate, and within authorized levels of civilian police, to continue efforts to assist the parties to the Comprehensive Peace Agreement in promoting the rule of law and restructuring the police and corrections services throughout the Sudan, and to assist in the training of civilian police and corrections officers;

20. *Encourages* the parties to undertake a prioritized roll-out of disarmament, demobilization and reintegration in all states, and requests the Mission to work closely with the Sudanese Armed Forces and the Sudan People's Liberation Army to assist in voluntary disarmament and weapons collection and destruction efforts in implementation of disarmament, demobilization and reintegration under the Comprehensive Peace Agreement;

21. *Further urges* donors to respond to calls for assistance to the disarmament, demobilization and reintegration process, in particular the reintegration phase, and calls upon donors to honour their obligations and pledges made at the Oslo donors' conferences of 2005 and 2008;

22. *Requests* the Mission, consistent with its mandate and in coordination with the relevant parties and taking into account the need to pay particular attention to the protection, release and reintegration of children recruited to and participating with armed forces and armed groups, to increase its support for the National Disarmament, Demo-

bilization and Reintegration Coordination Council and the Northern and Southern Sudan Disarmament, Demobilization and Reintegration Commissions, with special emphasis on reintegrating such children with their families, and to monitor the reintegration process;

23. *Welcomes* the continuing organized return of internally displaced persons and refugees to the Three Areas and Southern Sudan, and encourages the promotion of efforts, including the provision of necessary resources to the Office of the United Nations High Commissioner for Refugees and implementing partners, to ensure that such returns are voluntary and sustainable; and requests the Mission, within its current mandate, capabilities and areas of deployment, to coordinate with partners to facilitate sustainable returns, including by helping to establish and maintain the necessary security conditions;

24. *Calls upon* the Government of National Unity to cooperate fully with all the United Nations operations within its territory in the implementation of their mandates;

25. *Reiterates its concern* over the restrictions and impediments placed on Mission personnel and materiel, and the adverse impact that such restrictions and impediments have on the ability of the Mission to perform its mandate effectively and on the ability of the humanitarian community to reach affected persons; and in this regard calls for all parties to cooperate fully with the Mission and to facilitate the performance of its mandate, and to abide by their obligations under international humanitarian law;

26. *Stresses* the importance of achievable and realistic targets against which the progress of United Nations peacekeeping operations can be measured; in this regard, requests the Secretary-General to develop benchmarks for measuring and tracking progress in the implementation of the mandate of the Mission; and further requests the Secretary-General to include in his next quarterly report an assessment of progress made against these benchmarks, as well as any consequent recommendations regarding the configuration of the Mission;

27. *Underscores* the importance of the military concept of operations and rules of engagement being regularly updated and fully in line with the provisions of the mandate of the Mission under relevant Council resolutions, and requests the Secretary-General to report on them to the Council and troop-contributing countries and to provide the Council, with the same regularity as referred to in paragraph 2 above, with a specific update on the security situation;

28. *Requests* the Secretary-General to continue to take the measures necessary to ensure full compliance by the Mission with the United Nations zero-tolerance policy on sexual exploitation and abuse and to keep the Council fully informed, and urges troop-contributing countries to take appropriate preventive action, including predeployment awareness training, and other action to ensure full accountability in cases of such conduct involving their personnel;

29. *Decides* to remain actively seized of the matter.

Communication. On 18 June [S/2009/317], the Sudan informed the Security Council that on 6 and 11 June, hostile airplanes had violated Sudanese airspace and that it reserved its right to respond decisively to such provocations.

Report of Secretary-General (July). In a report of 14 July [S/2009/357], submitted pursuant to Council resolution 1590(2005), the Secretary-General said that the security situation in Southern Sudan had deteriorated as long-simmering local conflicts escalated into waves of violence, at times triggering vicious cycles of attack. Preparations for the elections began to dominate the political scene after NEC announced February 2010 as the polling date. The National Congress Party (NCP) and the Sudan People's Liberation Movement (SPLM), as well as most other political parties, accepted the timetable. On 1 July, the Commission released a revised timetable, with polling to take place in April 2010.

Despite SPLM reservations, the National Security Bill was tabled for debate in Parliament, and on 8 June, the Parliament passed the Press and Printed Material Bill. Opposition parties and observers remained concerned that the Bill gave the Presidency and Press Council excessive control over the media.

The finalization of the draft Referendum Act on the 2011 referendums remained behind schedule. With voter registration for the referendum scheduled to take place in July 2010, enactment of the Act and the concurrent establishment of the Referendum Commission were urgently required.

On 23 April, NCP and SPLM concluded their final submissions in the Abyei boundaries dispute to the Permanent Court of Arbitration in The Hague. Both parties assured UNMIS that they were committed to implementing the Court decision, expected by 22 July. In the meantime, the security situation in Abyei remained volatile. Alleged violations of the 2008 Abyei Road Map Agreement [YUN 2008, p. 238] included the presence of mobile and armed Oil Field Protection Police in the Road Map Area, as well as the presence of heavily armed militia. Freedom of movement for UNMIS was generally granted, with the exception of the Akur area where SPLA denied access. The issue was taken up in the Ceasefire Joint Monitoring Commission and referred to the Ceasefire Political Commission for clarification. UNMIS movements north of the Road Map Area remained restricted, denying the Mission awareness with regard to deployment of forces by both sides just outside the Road Map Area, and affecting its ability to take action to prevent any escalation.

Slow progress was made in the deployment of the Joint Integrated Police Units. The Unit in Abyei comprised 155 personnel from the north and 179 from the south.

The Secretary-General observed that the centrality of the CPA was acknowledged by all participants of the Forum for Supporters of the Agreement (Washington, D.C., 23 June), hosted by the United States. The United Nations would continue to support the parties and stood ready to help, but the parties themselves had to engage in meaningful dialogue and reach agreement on outstanding issues. As the Permanent Court of Arbitration prepared to render its decision, the situation in Abyei required immediate attention. While UNMIS was undertaking contingency planning, it was the responsibility of the parties to ensure that peace was maintained. The parties' commitment to accept and carry out the Court's decision would have to be translated into orders to the security apparatus and to the local leaders and communities. Abyei needed a functional civilian administration and the United Nations stood ready to assist.

Escalating inter-tribal violence in Southern Sudan was a threat to the stability of the Sudan as a whole. Civilian disarmament needed to be implemented equitably; UNMIS was working with the Southern Sudan Government to stress a comprehensive approach to community security. The limited capacity of the institutions of the Government of Southern Sudan remained a concern: despite repeated incidents resulting in significant loss of life and continued insecurity, no visible steps had been taken to strengthen the capacity of local authorities and the security apparatus to deter conflicts. The components of the Malakal Joint Integrated Unit that were involved in the 24 February clashes, during which fighting had erupted between the Unit's SAF and SPLA elements, needed to be relocated; the Secretary-General urged the Joint Defence Board and other authorities to ensure that the JIUs did not remain a source of instability.

Delays in the preparations for the 2011 referendums were worrisome, with the Sudan Referendum Act two years behind schedule, and there was a need for a functioning institutional and legal framework. The debate on unity and secession remained a zero-sum game and the Secretary-General urged the parties to initiate dialogue in order to reach agreements for the post-2011 period, irrespectively of the referendum results.

Demarcation of the 1-1-56 north-south border, which would geographically define Southern Sudan and the southern bounds of the Abyei Area, was another key provision of the CPA in need of attention. Uncertainty on the issue affected preparations for the referendum. The United Nations stood ready to support the parties with technical and logistical assistance in the delineation and demarcation process.

The Secretary-General was encouraged by the positive developments in the joint efforts of the Government and the United Nations and its partners to narrow the humanitarian gap in the aftermath of the 4 March expulsions of international NGOs, but assistance levels remained insufficient in some areas. Humanitarian assistance was only a temporary measure: the parties needed to reach durable political solutions so that a transition towards recovery and development could occur.

Encouraged by the momentum in demobilizing ex-combatants, the Secretary-General hoped that this might serve to inspire progress in other areas of implementation of the CPA; he called for sustained international funding for that vital component of disarmament, demobilization and reintegration.

Communication. On 15 July [S/2009/368], the Sudan transmitted to the Security Council a progress report on the implementation of the CPA as at 10 June which, according to the Sudan, reflected remarkable progress.

Report of Secretary-General (October). In a 21 October report [S/2009/545], submitted pursuant to Council resolution 1590(2005), the Secretary-General said that the security situation in Southern Sudan remained unstable, particularly in Jonglei, Upper Nile and Lake States, where as many as 54 clashes resulted in the deaths of at least 316 people during the reporting period. In addition to the inter-tribal violence, a clash in Bentiu, Unity State, on 2 October between SPLA soldiers left 18 soldiers and 3 civilians dead and 40 people wounded. UNMIS received reports of LRA attacks in Western Equatoria State, in particular near food distribution sites. After an attack on 12 August on Ezo town (120 kilometres north-west of Yambio), during which 17 people were reportedly abducted, 29 international UN and NGO staff were relocated and UN operations temporarily suspended. In response to banditry incidents and criminality in the Central and Eastern Equatoria States of Southern Sudan, a policy of armed escorts for staff movement was established as from 31 August. In Babanusa, Southern Kordofan, the Justice and Equality Movement (JEM) and SAF reportedly clashed on 2 August, resulting in casualties on both sides.

Delays in the implementation of key CPA benchmarks continued to be a concern. In addition to outstanding issues with respect to election preparations, NCP and SPLM had not reached final agreement on the Referendum Act, which was now 27 months behind schedule.

The decision on the Abyei boundary dispute, announced on 22 July by the Permanent Court of Arbitration, was accepted fully by both SPLM and NCP, clearing the way for further progress in implementing the Abyei Protocol. During the seventh Southern Sudan Governors' Forum (Juba, 10–15 August), the Permanent Court of Arbitration award was discussed together with the financial crisis, elections and referendums. Forum members were unanimous in their call for civilians in Southern Sudan to be disarmed, forcibly if necessary, by SPLM. On 5 September, the National Umma Party (NUP) and SPLM signed a Declaration of Principles outlining their common views on issues including democratic transformation, elections, the referendum, census results and Darfur.

From 26 to 30 September, approximately 20 political opposition parties met in Juba to discuss key national issues, including the census, elections, reconciliation and development, and stressed the importance of the Government's implementing democratic reforms ahead of the elections. The tripartite mechanism, which was led by the United States Special Envoy to the Sudan and involving NCP and SPLM, and which provided an opportunity for the parties to recommit to the deadlines set out in the CPA, met several times in Khartoum and Juba.

With regard to the implementation of the CPA, the Presidency appointed a Boundary Demarcation Committee and reappointed the Abyei Area Administration and Council. UNMIS provided the parties with a base map and offered logistical support for the demarcation. However, the Committee's work was significantly delayed owing to disagreements between its northern and southern members, which also affected military redeployment and the conduct of elections and referendums. The Court's decision placed the Higlig oilfields outside the Abyei Area. SPLM accepted that aspect of the decision, but challenged the course of the 1 January 1956 border, arguing that Higlig fell within Unity State in the South; the strategic importance of the Higlig oilfields might further complicate the border demarcation, the Secretary-General said, also noting that the Misseriya leadership expressed concern about its future status under the decision. The Joint Integrated Unit in Abyei lacked the resources and support needed to secure the Abyei area and the Diffra oilfields, while the Abyei Administration was still in the process of recruiting a local police force to replace the Joint Integrated Police Unit. Financial support to the Abyei Administration was still outstanding, but recently the Ministry of Finance had approved $10 million for building 21 kilometres of roads within Abyei town. The end of the rainy season in October might lead to an increase in Dinka Ngok and Misseriya returns to the Abyei Area, which could result in further disputes and create a potential for conflict. UNMIS and UNDP facilitated a Dinka-Misseriya peace conference (Abyei Town, 1 July), which adopted a resolution laying the foundation for reconciliation and acknowledging UNMIS' role in fostering inter-tribal reconciliation. Following the decision of the Permanent Court of Arbitration, Dinka Ngok and Misseriya leaders met with senior NCP and SPLM leaders to find ways to promote peaceful coexistence.

In Southern Kordofan, the parties committed themselves to the integration of political, administrative, social, economic and security structures before 31 October. On 8 September, the Governor of Southern Kordofan State dissolved the local government and appointed new ministers, advisers and commissioners. UNMIS worked closely with the recently established Reconciliation and Peaceful Coexistence Mechanism,

a body composed of tribal and local government authorities, to address long-standing conflicts between the tribes. A reconciliation conference held in August between the Angolo and Korongo Nuba tribes was attended by 600 people representing SPLA, SAF and native administration leaders. In Blue Nile State, the integration of SPLM/A personnel into the Sudanese national police was successfully completed. UNMIS continued to assist the parties in defining the local population's concerns in the implementation of the CPA and in addressing shortcomings. SPLA redeployment from Blue Nile and Southern Kordofan States was said to stand at 27.6 per cent, a figure the parties failed to agree on, while SAF redeployment from the South was at 100 per cent, not including Blue Nile and Southern Kordofan.

The Joint Integrated Unit strength was 82.6 per cent of the mandated 39,639 troops. On 24 August, the Ceasefire Joint Monitoring Commission and the Unit commanders agreed that final verification of Unit strength would be conducted by 15 November. UNMIS was conducting a quality assessment of the Units, focusing on bringing levels of cohesion up to the required standards.

Total oil revenue of the Sudan from January to June was $787.01 million, of which the shares of the Government of National Unity and the Government of Southern Sudan stood at $422.15 million and $364.86 million, respectively. In August, the Government of National Unity paid back approximately $52 million to the Government of Southern Sudan deducted unilaterally for the national elections process, and all the revenue arrears owed to the Government of Southern Sudan for the first half of the year had been settled as well. The 2 per cent share allotted to local Dinka Ngok and Misseriya, in accordance with the Abyei Protocol, continued to be transferred to separate accounts under the Abyei Area Administration and the Government of Southern Kordofan State, and in August the Ministry of Finance released 20 million Sudanese pounds to the Dinka Ngok.

On 19 August, parties to the CPA agreed to ask the Government of National Unity to request the International Monetary Fund (IMF) to review the implementation of the two banking systems under the Central Bank, but as at 1 October no such request had yet been made. The National Civil Service Commission, established to ensure adequate representation of the South in the National Civil Service, announced that only 1,000 positions in the Government of National Unity had been filled by southerners, about half of what was mandated under the CPA.

In Eastern Sudan, the political and security situation remained calm. The High Joint Committee, tasked with monitoring the Eastern Sudan Peace Agreement, held its sixth meeting on 11 August, focusing on funding and the work of the Eastern Sudan Reconstruction and Development Fund. Of the $600 million stipulated under the Agreement, only $85 million had been transferred to the Fund and disbursed to all three eastern states for recovery and development projects.

In implementing its mandate, UNMIS maintained constant dialogue with the Sudanese political leadership and key Sudanese and international stakeholders in the peace process. With insecurity increasing in Jonglei and Upper Nile States, the Mission collaborated with the Government of Southern Sudan and the state governments to implement the Jonglei Stabilization Plan with a view to enhancing civilian protection. UNMIS supported the Southern Sudan Peace Commission's efforts to begin the peacebuilding process in Jonglei State, and was supporting reconciliation between the Shilluk and Dinka in Upper Nile State. The Mission also worked with the 10 Southern states and the Government of Southern Sudan to monitor civilian disarmament initiatives. Preparations for the reintegration of demobilized persons in the Three Areas and Southern Sudan were ongoing.

Internally displaced person (IDP) and refugee returns continued at a steady rate, although reduced with the onset of heavy rains. Since the signing of the CPA, well over 1.9 million IDPS were estimated to have returned to their places of origin, particularly in the Three Areas and Southern Sudan, and refugee returns reached a total of 327,984. It was estimated that more than 2.4 million Sudanese, including spontaneous and organized returns, had reached their home areas in Northern and Southern Sudan by the end of July.

In Southern Sudan, the humanitarian situation had deteriorated sharply and inter-tribal violence and LRA attacks had resulted in the displacement of approximately 250,000 people. In Upper Nile, Eastern Equatoria, Warrap, Jonglei and Northern Bahr El Ghazal the situation had been made worse by high cereal and low livestock prices and poor rainfall, with as many as 1.5 million people facing severe food insecurity. A budgetary crisis in Southern Sudan, the result of falling oil prices and global economic downturn, hampered transition from humanitarian to early-recovery programming. UN agencies issued an emergency action plan to address the food gap, requiring an additional $57,155,456.

UNMIS and the Advisory Council for Human Rights of the Government of the Sudan co-chaired the third meeting of the Human Rights Forum (Khartoum, 20 August), at which UNMIS raised concerns about the lack of progress on human rights issues, while the Council presented its position on the pending appointment by the United Nations Human Rights Council of an independent expert on the human rights situation in the Sudan (see p. 758). The Press and Printed Materials Act came into force in Northern Sudan in July, while new media laws for Southern Sudan were pending approval.

UNMIS monitored and supported the legislative reform process, including drafting of the Referendum Bill and the Southern Sudan Police Bill, which was passed by the Southern Sudan Legislative Assembly in October. As part of the Jonglei Stabilization Plan, UNMIS and UNDP completed an analysis of rule-of-law institutions in Jonglei State.

LRA continued to abduct children in Southern Sudan, despite military operations against it, and more than 200 children abducted during inter-tribal violence in Jonglei State since January had not been returned to their families. UNMIS and the United Nations Children's Fund (UNICEF) were working to secure the signing of an action plan by armed forces for the release and reintegration of children.

Since the beginning of its activities, UNMIS mine action teams had opened 33,686 kilometres of road, cleared 54,170,814 square metres of land, destroyed 18,911 mines and 834,463 items of unexploded ordnance and provided mine-risk education to 2,832,710 people.

The Secretary-General observed that while some progress had been made in implementing the CPA, important benchmarks had not been reached. Resolving the key outstanding issues—most notably elections and the referendums—would require deep commitment and extraordinary efforts by the parties. The key to implementing the Agreement remained the relationship between NCP and SPLM. The Secretary-General encouraged the international community to intensify its engagement with the parties and other key stakeholders and to take into consideration the link between progress in implementing the CPA and the Darfur peace process. He welcomed the involvement of the Special Envoys in implementing the CPA and the progress made in the tripartite mechanism involving the United States, NCP and SPLM. He warned that potential for conflict in Abyei remained; continued stability would require the parties to address the demarcation of the Abyei Area, the formation of the Abyei Referendum Commission, the funding of the Abyei Area Administration, the realization of peace dividends and the return of the displaced population.

The Secretary-General expressed concern that the Joint Integrated Units could not fulfil their functions as foreseen in the CPA, in particular with respect to neutrality, security and acting as a symbol of unity; the Units had sometimes themselves been the source of conflict. He was also concerned that the dispute over the use of the census results threatened the success of the electoral process; coming to an agreement on how to proceed with elections would allow the parties to give the requisite attention to preparations for the 2011 referendums. Concerted efforts had to be made to ensure the participation in the elections of all groups, especially IDPs and the populations in Darfur and Eastern and Southern Sudan. The timeline of the referendums in Southern Sudan and Abyei being at stake, the Secretary-General urged the parties to pass the required bills and engage in discussions about the post-referendum arrangements, irrespective of the outcome. Similarly, progress had to be made on the popular consultation process in Southern Kordofan and Blue Nile States.

Concerned about the targeting of unarmed civilians during tribal attacks and reports of widespread proliferation of arms, the Secretary-General called on the Government of Southern Sudan to strengthen efforts to end recurring violence and bring those responsible to justice. The lack of a resolution on the outstanding issues impeding the work of the Border Commission carried wide-ranging ramifications for the implementation of the CPA. He appealed to the international community and the parties to ensure adequate funding for all components of the DDR programme.

Annexed to the report were revised benchmarks and indicators of progress for 2009–2011 in the implementation of the CPA.

Year-end developments

Report of Secretary-General. According to a later report [S/2010/31], the security situation remained calm in the North, with the exception of incidents in Darfur. In the South, there were numerous clashes and attacks, mainly in Upper Nile, Unity and Jonglei States, as well as the triangle between Jonglei, Central Equatoria and Lakes States. The security situation in Bentiu remained tense following fighting on 2 October between forces commanded by Governor Taban Deng Gai and the Second-in-Command of SPLA, General Paulino Matiep. In order to reduce tension, UNMIS airlifted between 17 and 23 October 297 SPLA troops loyal to General Matiep to Juba. Continuing tensions led to the temporary occupation of the SPLM political bureau in Bentiu by a parallel SPLM state leadership on 2 October.

The seasonal north-south migration was relatively peaceful. Misseriya cattle herders moved into the Abyei Area without any significant incident, although reports of armed Misseriya groups without cattle persisted. UNMIS patrols and Abyei demarcation teams encountered Misseriya camps in the northern part of the area and were informed by the inhabitants that they would forcefully obstruct any attempt to demarcate the border. The Misseriya did not attempt to block UNMIS movement within the Abyei area.

LRA continued to threaten local security in southwestern communities, launching attacks on villages in Western Equatoria State, reportedly killing 25 and abducting 23 persons. SPLA freed 46 IDPs abducted from a camp in Western Bahr El Ghazal after an attack blamed on LRA left three policemen dead.

Tensions between NCP and SPLM escalated, although agreement on some key issues was reached. Citing a lack of progress on critical legislation and reforms, SPLM on 19 October withdrew its delegation from the National Assembly, which continued its session without addressing the legislation at the heart of the dispute. In early November, SPLM and NCP agreed to discuss the major remaining legislative issues, including the Southern Sudan Referendum Bill, the Abyei Referendum Bill, the National Intelligence and Security Services Bill, the Popular Consultations Bill and the treatment of the disputed census results in the 2010 elections. Following the arrest of a number of key SPLM and opposition figures on 7 December during a peaceful demonstration in front of the National Assembly, several demonstrations in the South turned violent and protesters burnt down an NCP office in Warrap State. The CPA parties took steps to calm the situation, including direct meetings between Government of National Unity President Al-Bashir and Government of Southern Sudan President Kiir. On 13 December, the parties announced that they had reached an agreement on legislative issues. The national security legislation was passed on 20 December, although without the support of SPLM or the opposition parties. Legislation governing the referendum in the South was finally passed on 29 December in a form that met SPLM concerns. Legislation enabling the holding of a referendum on the future of Abyei was passed on 30 December.

The parties to the CPA increasingly acknowledged the need to prepare for the post-referendum period and discussed the need to lay the groundwork for a peaceful separation while continuing efforts to make unity attractive.

Southern Sudanese opposition figures continued to accuse SPLM of attempting to suppress opposition parties, in particular the new SPLM-Democratic Change party founded by former Foreign Minister Lam Akol. On 9 November, the Government of Southern Sudan issued an order to the Southern governors instructing them not to obstruct the activities of any political party "except the so-called SPLM-DC". Mr. Akol appealed the order under the Interim National Constitution and on 3 December announced that the Constitutional Court had granted his appeal.

Little progress was made on implementing the Permanent Court of Arbitration decision on Abyei, and opposition to the decision had hardened among some elements of the Misseriya, while misunderstandings, misinterpretations and false rumours had increased tension throughout the area. Resulting security concerns, including armed obstruction of the work of the demarcation team, blocked efforts to demarcate the Abyei Area border and represented a continuing threat to the civilian population and intercommunal relations. The parties reported progress in the Technical Ad Hoc Border Committee, but procedural and substantive disagreements continued to delay its final report, expected to define the uncontested areas of the North-South border and specify those areas on which the Committee could not reach agreement and which would require a political decision from the Presidency. Unmis assisted the Committee through specialized training.

Security incidents involving political or ethnic violence in Southern Kordofan decreased. The Abu Junok (Nuba) and Um Sileem (Misseriya) signed a peace accord on 5 October, ending a three-year conflict. The Nuba Katla and Wali also finalized a peace agreement on 12 November. New state-level institutional arrangements, including the Council of Elders ("Wise Men") played a significant role. The Southern Kordofan State government made significant progress in incorporating the 1,708 splm civil servants into its political and administrative structures. The passage of national legislation enabling the holding of popular consultations in Southern Kordofan and Blue Nile States on 30 December was an important step forward in the implementation of the cpa.

The parties accepted figures on the redeployment of saf and spla in the 108th Cease Fire Joint Monitoring Commission on 16 November, according to which saf had redeployed 100 per cent of its forces from Southern Sudan, while spla had reached a 33.7 per cent redeployment from Northern Sudan of the stated strength of 59,168. The figures did not reflect the redeployment on the ground claimed by spla, much of which had occurred outside the scope of the cpa monitoring and verification instruments. A political agreement would be necessary, the Secretary-General said, to resolve those redeployments, including 9,599 "voluntarily demobilized" spla troops in Southern Kordofan and Blue Nile States and 32,814 otherwise unaccounted for spla troops.

Joint integration stood at 82.6 per cent of the mandated strength of 39,639 troops, unchanged since April. There had been no reports of significant security incidents related to jius, although they remained a source of tension in some areas. Agreement to rotate the Malakal Joint Integrated Unit out of the area after the February clashes between the Unit's saf and spla elements had not been implemented.

Key economic challenges that required attention, particularly in advance of the post-2011 wealth-sharing discussions, were foreign reserves management, inadequate Southern Sudanese customs author-ities and stalled land reforms. The parties contested control of the Bank of Southern Sudan's foreign reserves. The revenue from the Higlig oilfields remained a contentious issue.

No progress was reported in implementing the outstanding provisions of the power-sharing protocol to the 2006 Eastern Sudan Peace Agreement [YUN 2006, p. 264], which included increasing Eastern Sudanese representation in the national civil service and appointing local Eastern Front representatives throughout Red Sea, Kassala and Gedaref States. The Eastern Front appeared to have been split into several smaller political parties along tribal lines in the run-up to the elections, further undermining the implementation of the Agreement. By November, the Government of National Unity had transferred $110 million of the agreed-upon $600 million to the Eastern Sudan Recovery and Development Fund.

Significant progress had been made since the ddr programme had started in February. As at 31 December, 18,731 former combatants and members of special needs groups in the Sudan had been demobilized and had received their reinsertion packages for three months, and 1,741 former combatants in Southern Sudan and 7,149 in the Three Areas had received reintegration counselling. Unmis carried out an independent assessment of the registration and verification procedures of the demobilization process. The results were presented in a November report that highlighted some gaps in the process.

Returns of idps increased towards the end of the rainy season. By mid-year, more than 170,000 idps were estimated to have returned to Southern Sudan, including 11,000 assisted returnees, and just under 32,000 refugees were repatriated, mostly from Uganda. Cumulative spontaneous returns were estimated to have reached approximately 2 million people, while total organized and assisted returns of refugees and idps topped 263,850. Approximately 1,700 individuals returned to nine locations in the Abyei area during November.

In Southern Sudan, the humanitarian situation continued to deteriorate. An estimated 2,500 people had died and 359,000 had been displaced since January as a result of intertribal conflict and lra-related violence. More than 1.5 million people were receiving emergency food assistance.

The Government of National Unity took some steps to further human rights, although significant progress in the overall human rights situation remained to be achieved. As at December, 119 children had been pardoned by the President and released from detention in connection with the May 2008 Omdurman attacks [YUN 2008, p. 236]. The National Assembly passed a Child Rights Act, and on 20 December gave final approval to the National Intelligence and Security

Services Bill, despite opposition from SPLM and opposition parties. The Bill was contrary to the role of those services as set out in the CPA. UNMIS continued to receive complaints from political parties of violations of political rights associated with the electoral process. Progress had been slow in the South in establishing and strengthening the capacity of government institutions to prevent or mitigate the escalation of violence and to prevent impunity. Women continued to suffer from discrimination, harmful traditional practices and gender violence. Also of concern was the lack of progress in appointing commissioners to the Independent Human Rights Commission, an important CPA benchmark. The low-level of enjoyment of economic and social rights represented a major threat to peace, security and stability, and forcible evictions continued to affect IDPs and vulnerable communities. UNMIS provided support to the legislative reform process and the implementation of the rule of law, and was developing a strategy and security concept for the protection of civilians.

Electoral process

In accordance with the CPA and the Interim National Constitution, general elections at all levels of Government in the Sudan were to be completed by the end of the fourth year of the interim period, that is, by July 2009. On 2 April, the National Elections Commission (NEC) announced that the national executive and legislative elections envisaged by the CPA would be held in February 2010. On 1 July, the Commission released a modified timetable according to which the elections were scheduled for April 2010. By resolution 1769(2007) [YUN 2007, p. 251], the Security Council mandated UNAMID to ensure the implementation of all peace agreements in the Sudan, particularly with regard to the national provisions of those agreements. In keeping with a request by Southern Sudan of August 2008 [YUN 2008, p. 241], the United Nations was to provide support to the electoral administration and planning process and the preparation of a reliable voters' list. On 19 February 2009, the NEC Chairman forwarded a request to the Secretary-General's Special Representative for support with electoral material; logistics and operational planning; electoral awareness; training of electoral staff, capacity-building and advisory support; and coordination of international assistance to the electoral process.

The Government of National Unity and the National Assembly took important steps towards the holding of elections, including the adoption of the National Elections Act, the establishment of the NEC, the appointment of State and Southern Sudan-level High Committees, the establishment of the Political Parties Affairs Council and the registration of political parties. The parties to the CPA, a number of political parties and civil society actors expressed their commitment to the holding of elections as stipulated under the Agreement. Members of the SPLM voiced concern over the legislative framework, the results of the 2008 census and their impact on representation in the National Assembly, as well as the impact of the unresolved North-South border delimitation on constituency delimitation. Opposition parties and civil society organizations based in Khartoum and Juba stressed that their participation in the elections would be contingent on the guarantee of basic political freedoms and freedom of movement. In Darfur, opposition parties and civil society organizations actors called on the Government to ensure the freedom of movement, assembly, association and speech required to ensure a free and fair process, and IDP leaders stated that peace, security, compensation and IDP return should come before the holding of elections; they also voiced the fear that voter registration of IDPs in camps would be tantamount to relinquishing their lands.

Communication. On 16 July [S/2009/374], the Sudan transmitted to the Security Council explanatory notes on the work of the NEC and the modified timeframe for the elections.

Reports of Secretary-General. On 28 July, pursuant to Council resolution 1870(2009) (see p. 234), the Secretary-General reported [S/2009/391] on elections in the Sudan. He said that, further to a request of the NEC Chairman, the United Nations dispatched a multidisciplinary mission—comprising representatives of the Departments of Peacekeeping Operations, Political Affairs, Safety and Security, as well as UNDP—to the Sudan from 28 April to 8 May to assess the conditions for the conduct of electoral activities; the activities and plans of international donors to provide technical and financial assistance; and the extent to which UN assistance might contribute to the electoral process.

In accordance with the National Elections Act, the NEC on 18 June established the Southern Sudan High Committee and one high committee in each of the 25 States. The NEC had since delegated to the Southern Sudan High Committee primary responsibility for supervising the election of the President of the Government of Southern Sudan and of the Southern Sudan Legislative Assembly, in coordination with it and the State High Committees in the south. On 18 June, members of the High Committees were sworn in and began their work.

The Political Parties Affairs Council, established in November 2008 [YUN 2008, p. 241], was preparing, with UNMIS support, public information materials on the registration process and the Political Parties Act adopted by the National Assembly in 2007 [YUN 2007, p. 236]. The Council requested further UNMIS support in conflict management training and in developing a code of ethics for political parties. The number of registered parties totalled 71.

In May, the NEC created two committees to help coordinate international assistance and to address issues of mutual concern. The Policy Committee, co-chaired by the Commission and the Special Representative, focused on electoral issues of a political nature, while the Technical Committee, co-chaired by the Commission and the UNMIS Chief Electoral Affairs Officer, addressed technical electoral issues. The Commission had begun the process of constituency delimitation and reviewed drafts of voter registration forms with UNMIS electoral experts. UNMIS provided technical assistance to the Commission, the Southern Sudan High Committee and 10 State committees in the south and was preparing to support the 15 northern State committees. Nevertheless, the Commission had not completed the operational plan for the conduct and organization of the elections, on the basis of which its original electoral budget of $1.1 billion was to be reviewed, and the Southern Sudan High Committee and State committees were not fully operational and lacked sufficient financing, logistics and staff.

The modified elections timetable released by the Commission on 1 July foresaw the start of polling on 5 April and the announcements of the results on 12 April 2010. The revised timeline allowed for more electoral preparations to take place during the dry season, although some would still need to be carried out during the rainy season in the south. The delimitation of geographical constituencies would begin on 10 June and the final draft of constituency boundaries would be prepared by 12 September. Voter registration was to begin on 1 November, with the final list of registered voters to be published on 5 January 2010. The nomination of candidates was to begin on 6 January and their final list would be published by 2 February. The electoral campaign was to be conducted from 4 February to 4 April 2010. No provision was made for the date of possible run-off elections for the President of the Republic and the President of the Government of Southern Sudan.

On 21 May and 6 June, respectively, the census results for northern Sudan and Southern Sudan were announced. The results showed that the 10 States of Southern Sudan had just over 21 per cent of the total Sudanese population of 39 million. In accordance with the CPA and the Interim National Constitution, National Assembly seats were to be allocated on the basis of the census results. On 15 June, the NEC announced the allocation of those seats, with Southern Sudan receiving 22 per cent and northern Sudan 78 per cent. In accordance with the CPA and based on the 1986 census, in the period leading up to the

elections, 34 per cent of the seats were allocated to Southern Sudan and 66 per cent to northern Sudan.

The Southern Sudan Legislative Assembly on 17 June rejected the determination of Southern Sudan seats in the National Assembly. The census results were also rejected by the major Darfur movements and a number of political parties, as some communities were not covered and some IDP camps boycotted the exercise.

The NEC indicated that it had begun delimitating constituency boundaries on 10 June and reviewed the preliminary report on draft constituency boundaries for 18 States in mid-July. The process was moving slowly in the Southern States as the task of drawing up more than 740 State geographical constituencies was a difficult challenge for the State High Committees, many of which lacked office space, communications and transportation. The NEC had requested international assistance for the exercise. The delimitation of constituencies also required agreement on the use of the census results and the delimitation of the North-South border. In the absence of the latter, the NEC would base preliminary constituency delimitation on the border of 1 January 1956, and constituency delimitation would be adjusted once the border was delimited.

UNMIS was leading UN electoral assistance efforts, which were focused on the provision of advisory and technical support to the Commission. It also took a leadership role with the Commission in ensuring the coherence of international donor assistance. Under the 2009–2010 budget, UNMIS had an authorized strength of 141 electoral staff, of whom nearly 100 were already deployed in Khartoum (UNMIS headquarters), Juba (Regional Office), the 10 State capitals of Southern Sudan, and El Fasher (Darfur).

UNMIS was helping the Commission to finalize its operational plan for voter registration. Complementing UNMIS' role, UNDP supported capacity-building and institutional development. The initial UNDP budget for support to the Commission, not including the costs of polling, was $42.6 million until the end of 2010, whereas contributions received only amounted to approximately $7 million. It was expected that once the NEC finalized the electoral plan, additional requirements might be as high as $100 million. The United States Agency for International Development was providing the largest portfolio to support the electoral process, in the amount of $95 million.

The Secretary-General expressed concern that elections preparations remained seriously behind schedule and that basic steps had yet to be taken. Most importantly, the Government of National Unity, the National Assembly and the Government of Southern Sudan had to provide a free and fair electoral environment, guaranteeing basic political freedoms, including freedom of assembly, speech and the press, as provided for under the CPA and the Interim National Constitution. Concrete steps also needed to be taken towards a comprehensive peace agreement between the Government of National Unity and the Darfur movements addressing the concerns of IDPS in Darfur: that included a cessation of hostilities, progress towards compensation, land rights and redressing marginalization. Differences with regard to the use of the census results needed to be resolved, and significant voter education was required. The NEC needed to ensure an inclusive process by addressing the constraints relating to the registration of IDPS, refugees and those without necessary papers, and had to engage more effectively with donors and technical experts in order to ensure that the operational aspects were carried out in a timely manner; in that regard, the Commission should finalize the elections operational plan and review its initial $1.1 billion budget accordingly.

With regard to the referendum to be held in 2011 in Southern Sudan and Abyei, the Secretary-General stated that no matter the outcome, north and south Sudan had to discuss without delay the measures necessary to ensure peaceful coexistence; he intended to deploy to UNMIS a number of experts to work with the parties in addressing the numerous challenges related to the process.

The elections to be held in April 2010 could provide an important opportunity to strengthen national reconciliation and democratic transformation. Yet, as elections could also be divisive, the Secretary-General was concerned about the tensions and violence, particularly in Darfur, areas of Southern Sudan and the Three Areas. The Government of National Unity, the Government of Southern Sudan and local actors had to ensure that contingency measures and outreach were undertaken early to ease tensions and deter potential spoilers. Solving the political and operational challenges of the elections would require greater political will to compromise and reach agreement than the parties to the CPA and the Darfur movements had recently shown. Nevertheless, the elections could begin a process of national healing, reconciliation and political transformation that could only strengthen the CPA and the Darfur peace process.

On 3 August [S/2009/391/Add.1], the Secretary-General informed the Security Council that the financial implications for the support of the elections were estimated at $46.6 million, which provided for the deployment of 100 additional UN police officers and 127 civilian personnel, as well as for the deployment of 5 additional helicopters effective 1 October 2009 for three months and 16 helicopters effective 1 March 2010 for two months.

In his October report on UNMIS [S/2009/545], the Secretary-General said that constituency delimita-tion began in late June and all preliminary reports were submitted by the end of July and distributed to the political parties in August. By the deadline of 14 September, the NEC had received more than 500 objections to the constituency delimitation, which it planned to review by the end of November.

The Commission continued to have limited capacity, and the absence of an operational plan and corresponding budget remained a challenge. For participation in the elections, 76 political parties, including NCP, which formally endorsed President Al-Bashir, had registered with the Political Parties Affairs Council as at 31 August, with as many as 20 applications pending. UNMIS urged the Council to establish a clear deadline for applications. The voter registration plan had been finalized, with registration due to begin on 1 November. but registration of IDPS continued to be an important issue.

Approximately 93 per cent of the UNMIS electoral assistance staff for 2008–2009 had been recruited, and more than 160 UN police master trainers, police trainers and five language assistants had been trained in election security duties, but the Government had not formalized a request for 100 additional police officers to assist during the elections. UNMIS was establishing a seven-person team to cover preparations for the 2011 referendums.

According to a later report of the Secretary-General [S/2010/31], preparations for the 2010 national elections continued to dominate much of the political environment. In the absence of what they considered to be a conducive environment for the elections, SPLM and the northern opposition parties maintained the threat of a possible electoral boycott. Nevertheless, voter registration began on 1 November in most parts of the country and was concluded on 7 December. As at 16 December, the NEC reported the registration of approximately 16.5 million voters out of an estimated 20 million, including 71 per cent of the estimated electorate in the north (including Darfur). The turnout was significantly higher than expected; UNMIS received reports of irregularities, including the improper use of government resources, registration of military units outside their home constituencies, and registration of more than 100 per cent of estimated eligible voters in several states. UNMIS encouraged the NEC to address those irregularities and raised its concerns about the political environment with both parties to the CPA. Following the conclusion of the constituency delimitation process, the Commission upheld 400 of the 885 objections filed by the 14 September deadline and published its final constituency delimitation plan on 6 October. On 28 October, the Supreme Court accepted 4 of the 58 legal challenges to the plan filed after publication and the Commission modified the plan accordingly.

A Policy Committee, jointly chaired by the NEC and the Secretary-General's Special Representative, was established to provide recommendations on the delivery of credible and transparent elections.

Children and armed conflict

Report of Secretary-General. Pursuant to Security Council resolution 1612(2005) [YUN 2005, p. 863], the Secretary-General in February submitted his third report [S/2009/84] on children and armed conflict in the Sudan, covering the period from 1 August 2007 to 30 December 2008. The report focused on grave violations perpetrated against children and identified State and non-State parties responsible for such violations. The report highlighted that all parties to the conflict continued to recruit and use children, that rape and sexual violence continued to be systematic and widespread and that children and women in an around refugee camps and IDPs' settlements were especially vulnerable. It documented alarming levels of attacks against humanitarian personnel, particularly in Darfur. The report noted some limited progress in establishing child protection dialogue with parties to the conflict and highlighted initiatives by the Government of National Unity and the Government of Southern Sudan, such as adoption of legislation for child protection, establishment of child protection modalities in the national police and focus on children in the disarmament, demobilization and reintegration process. The report outlined recommendations to address grave violations, facilitate the implementation of child protection commitments and foster coordination among stakeholders.

Having examined the Secretary-General's report on 24 February, the Security Council Working Group on Children and Armed Conflict in December submitted its conclusions on children in the armed conflict in the Sudan [S/AC.51/2009/5]. The Group recommended that the Security Council President address letters to the Government of National Unity, the Security Council, the Secretary-General and donors. The Group issued a statement condemning the recruitment and use of children, their killing and maiming, rape and other sexual violence. It condemned the use of a large number of children by JEM in its May 2008 attack on Omdurman [YUN 2008, p. 236] and urged all parties to end targeting the civilian population, including children; release all children within their ranks; end and prevent rape and other sexual violence and bring those responsible to justice; and allow full and secure access for humanitarian assistance to children. The Group emphasized that the full implementation of an action plan in line with relevant Security Council resolutions was a prerequisite for a party to be de-listed from the annexes

to the reports of the Secretary-General on children and armed conflict. The Group would monitor compliance with resolution 1612(2005) and further steps would be considered against armed groups that did not abide by their obligations.

The Secretary-General's Special Representative for Children and Armed Conflict visited the Sudan (15–23 November) and called on the Government to adopt a national strategy to combat sexual violence against children. She met with the leadership of several Darfur armed movements, including SLA-Free Will, SLA-Mother and JEM-Peace Wing, who agreed to begin a dialogue with the United Nations concerning action plans to end the use of child soldiers. The SAF leadership, too, agreed to consider adopting an action plan, extended to pro-Government militia groups in Darfur. SLA Minni Minawi (SLA/MM) agreed to unhindered verification by the United Nations of its military camps and areas of concentration. The Government of National Unity Minister for Justice committed not to execute children under the age of 18; UNMIS and UNAMID child protection staff would follow up on that commitment and see if access would be granted to six children associated with JEM currently on death row.

UNMIS

The United Nations Mission in the Sudan (UNMIS), established by Security Council resolution 1590(2005) [YUN 2005, p. 304], continued to support implementation of the Comprehensive Peace Agreement signed by the Government of the Sudan and SPLM/A; facilitate and coordinate the voluntary return of refugees and IDPs, and humanitarian assistance; assist with demining; and protect and promote human rights. UNMIS was headed by the Special Representative of the Secretary-General in the Sudan, Ashraf Jehangir Qazi (Pakistan). In April, the Council extended the UNMIS mandate until 30 April 2010.

As at 31 December, 9,569 of the authorized 10,000 military personnel were deployed, including 476 military observers, 200 staff officers and 8,893 troops. Of its mandated police strength of 715, UNMIS had deployed 98 per cent to 25 team sites as at 24 November.

Financing

On 11 March [A/63/756], the Secretary-General submitted a note on UNMIS financing arrangements from 1 July 2008 to 30 June 2009, recommending the appropriation of an additional $56,173,100 for maintaining UNMIS during that period above the $820,720,600 already appropriated by the General Assembly in 2008 [YUN 2008, p. 243]. On 19 March [A/63/777], the Advisory Committee on Administrative and Budgetary Questions (ACABQ) endorsed that recommendation.

GENERAL ASSEMBLY ACTION

On 7 April [meeting 79], the General Assembly, on the recommendation of the Fifth Committee [A/63/787], adopted **resolution 63/273 A** without vote [agenda item 146].

Financing of the United Nations Mission in the Sudan

The General Assembly,

Having considered the note by the Secretary-General on the financing arrangements for the United Nations Mission in the Sudan for the period from 1 July 2008 to 30 June 2009 and the related report of the Advisory Committee on Administrative and Budgetary Questions,

Recalling Security Council resolution 1812(2008) of 30 April 2008, in which the Council decided to extend the mandate of the Mission until 30 April 2009,

Recalling also its resolution 62/267 of 20 June 2008 on the financing of the Mission,

1. *Endorses* the conclusions and recommendations contained in the report of the Advisory Committee on Administrative and Budgetary Questions, and requests the Secretary-General to ensure their full implementation;

Budget estimates for the period from 1 July 2008 to 30 June 2009

2. *Decides* to appropriate to the Special Account for the United Nations Mission in the Sudan the amount of 56,173,100 United States dollars for the maintenance of the Mission for the period from 1 July 2008 to 30 June 2009, in addition to the amount of 820,720,600 dollars already appropriated for the maintenance of the Mission for the period from 1 July 2008 to 30 June 2009 under the terms of its resolution 62/267;

Financing of the appropriation

3. *Also decides*, taking into account the amount of 715,642,666 dollars already apportioned under the terms of its resolution 62/267 for the period from 1 July 2008 to 30 April 2009, to apportion among Member States the additional amount of 42,129,825 dollars for the period from 1 July 2008 to 30 April 2009, in accordance with the levels updated in General Assembly resolution 61/243 of 22 December 2006, and taking into account the scale of assessments for 2008 and 2009, as set out in its resolution 61/237 of 22 December 2006;

4. *Further decides* that, in accordance with the provisions of its resolution 973(X) of 15 December 1955, there shall be set off against the apportionment among Member States, as provided for in paragraph 3 above, their respective share in the Tax Equalization Fund of 973,833 dollars, representing the increase in the estimated staff assessment income approved for the Mission for the period from 1 July 2008 to 30 April 2009;

5. *Decides*, taking into account the amount of 143,128,534 dollars already apportioned under the terms of its resolution 62/267 for the period from 1 May to 30 June 2009, to apportion among Member States the additional amount of 8,425,965 dollars at a monthly rate of 4,212,982 dollars for the period from 1 May to 30 June 2009, in accordance with the levels updated in General As-

sembly resolution 61/243, and taking into account the scale of assessments for 2009, as set out in its resolution 61/237, subject to a decision of the Security Council to extend the mandate of the Mission;

6. *Also decides* that, in accordance with the provisions of its resolution 973(X), there shall be set off against the apportionment among Member States, as provided for in paragraph 5 above, their respective share in the Tax Equalization Fund of 194,767 dollars, representing the increase in the estimated staff assessment income approved for the Mission for the period from 1 May to 30 June 2009;

7. *Further decides* to keep under review during its sixty-third session the item entitled "Financing of the United Nations Mission in the Sudan".

On 24 April [A/63/746/Add.5], ACABQ considered the Secretary-General's performance report on the UNMIS budget from 1 July 2007 to 30 June 2008 [A/63/604] and the proposed budget from 1 July 2009 to 30 June 2010 [A/63/714]. The Committee recommended that for the earlier period, the unencumbered balance of $25,817,700, as well as other income or adjustments amounting to $56,381,400, be credited to Member States, and that the Assembly appropriate $951,666,000 for maintaining the Mission from 1 July 2009 to 30 June 2010.

GENERAL ASSEMBLY ACTION

On 30 June [meeting 93], the General Assembly, on the recommendation of the Fifth Committee [A/63/787/Add.1], adopted **resolution 63/273 B** without vote [agenda item 146].

Financing of the United Nations Mission in the Sudan

The General Assembly,

Having considered the reports of the Secretary-General on the financing of the United Nations Mission in the Sudan and the related report of the Advisory Committee on Administrative and Budgetary Questions,

Recalling Security Council resolution 1590(2005) of 24 March 2005, by which the Council established the United Nations Mission in the Sudan for an initial period of six months as from 24 March 2005, and the subsequent resolutions by which the Council extended the mandate of the Mission, the latest of which was resolution 1870(2009) of 30 April 2009, by which the Council extended the mandate of the Mission until 30 April 2010,

Recalling also its resolution 59/292 of 21 April 2005 on the financing of the Mission and its subsequent resolutions thereon, the latest of which was resolution 63/273 A of 7 April 2009,

Recalling further its resolution 58/315 of 1 July 2004,

Reaffirming the general principles underlying the financing of United Nations peacekeeping operations, as stated in General Assembly resolutions 1874(S-IV) of 27 June 1963, 3101(XXVIII) of 11 December 1973 and 55/235 of 23 December 2000,

Noting with appreciation that voluntary contributions have been made to the Trust Fund in Support of the Peace Process in the Sudan,

Mindful of the fact that it is essential to provide the Mission with the financial resources necessary to enable it to fulfil its responsibilities under the relevant resolutions of the Security Council,

1. *Requests* the Secretary-General to entrust the Head of Mission with the task of formulating future budget proposals in full accordance with the provisions of General Assembly resolutions 59/296 of 22 June 2005, 60/266 of 30 June 2006 and 61/276 of 29 June 2007, as well as other relevant resolutions;

2. *Takes note* of the status of contributions to the United Nations Mission in the Sudan as at 30 April 2009, including the contributions outstanding in the amount of 65.5 million United States dollars, representing some 2 per cent of the total assessed contributions, notes with concern that only seventy-nine Member States have paid their assessed contributions in full, and urges all other Member States, in particular those in arrears, to ensure payment of their outstanding assessed contributions;

3. *Expresses its appreciation* to those Member States which have paid their assessed contributions in full, and urges all other Member States to make every possible effort to ensure payment of their assessed contributions to the Mission in full;

4. *Expresses concern* at the financial situation with regard to peacekeeping activities, in particular as regards the reimbursements to troop contributors that bear additional burdens owing to overdue payments by Member States of their assessments;

5. *Also expresses concern* at the delay experienced by the Secretary-General in deploying and providing adequate resources to some recent peacekeeping missions, in particular those in Africa;

6. *Emphasizes* that all future and existing peacekeeping missions shall be given equal and non-discriminatory treatment in respect of financial and administrative arrangements;

7. *Also emphasizes* that all peacekeeping missions shall be provided with adequate resources for the effective and efficient discharge of their respective mandates;

8. *Reiterates its request* to the Secretary-General to make the fullest possible use of facilities and equipment at the United Nations Logistics Base at Brindisi, Italy, in order to minimize the costs of procurement for the Mission;

9. *Acknowledges with appreciation* that the use of the logistics hub at Entebbe, Uganda, has been cost-effective and has resulted in savings for the United Nations, and welcomes the expansion of the logistics hub to provide logistical support to peacekeeping operations in the region and to contribute further to their enhanced efficiency and responsiveness, taking into account the ongoing efforts in this regard;

10. *Requests* the Secretary-General to ensure that proposed peacekeeping budgets are based on the relevant legislative mandates;

11. *Endorses* the conclusions and recommendations contained in the report of the Advisory Committee on Administrative and Budgetary Questions, subject to the provisions of the present resolution, and requests the Secretary-General to ensure their full implementation;

12. *Takes note* of paragraph 35 *(b)* of the report of the Advisory Committee, and decides to approve the post of Chief Operations Officer at the P-5 level for the Joint Operations Centre;

13. *Also takes note* of paragraph 35 *(c)* of the report of the Advisory Committee, and decides to establish the post of Programme Officer at the P-3 level in the Office of the Force Commander;

14. *Further takes note* of paragraph 35 *(d)* of the report of the Advisory Committee, and decides to establish the post of Senior Security Sector Reform Officer at the P-5 level in the Rule of Law, Judicial System and Prison Advisory Section;

15. *Takes note* of paragraph 35 *(h)* (ii) of the report of the Advisory Committee, and decides to establish the post of Field Service Security Officer (internal audit) and 10 posts of Field Service Security Officer (risk assessment) in the Safety and Security Section;

16. *Also takes note* of paragraphs 35 *(g)* and *(k)* of the report of the Advisory Committee, and decides to establish the 187 disarmament, demobilization and reintegration-related posts and positions, and to apply a 50 per cent vacancy factor to the new international posts, comprising 20 posts at the P-3 level and 18 Field Service posts, for the period 2009/10;

17. *Further takes note* of paragraph 51 of the report of the Advisory Committee;

18. *Reaffirms* section XX of resolution 61/276, and encourages the Secretary-General, where feasible, to enhance regional and inter-mission cooperation with a view to achieving greater synergies in the use of the resources of the Organization and the implementation of mandates of the missions, while bearing in mind that individual missions are responsible for the preparation and implementation of their own budgets and for controlling their own assets and logistical operations;

19. *Requests* the Secretary-General to ensure that future budget submissions contain sufficient information, explanation and justification of the proposed resource requirements relating to operational costs in order to allow Member States to take well-informed decisions;

20. *Also requests* the Secretary-General to ensure the full implementation of the relevant provisions of resolutions 59/296, 60/266 and 61/276;

21. *Further requests* the Secretary-General to take all necessary action to ensure that the Mission is administered with a maximum of efficiency and economy;

22. *Requests* the Secretary-General, in order to reduce the cost of employing General Service staff, to continue efforts to recruit local staff for the Mission against General Service posts, commensurate with the requirements of the Mission;

Financial performance report for the period from 1 July 2007 to 30 June 2008

23. *Takes note* of the report of the Secretary-General on the financial performance of the Mission for the period from 1 July 2007 to 30 June 2008;

Budget estimates for the period from 1 July 2009 to 30 June 2010

24. *Decides* to appropriate to the Special Account for the United Nations Mission in the Sudan the amount of 1,000,577,700 dollars for the period from 1 July 2009 to 30 June 2010, inclusive of 958,350,200 dollars for the maintenance of the Mission, 35,143,600 dollars for the support account for peacekeeping operations and 7,083,900 dollars for the United Nations Logistics Base;

Financing of the appropriation

25. *Also decides* to apportion among Member States the amount of 833,814,750 dollars for the period from 1 July 2009 to 30 April 2010, in accordance with the levels updated in General Assembly resolution 61/243 of 22 December 2006, and taking into account the scale of assessments for 2009, as set out in its resolution 61/237 of 22 December 2006, and for 2010;

26. *Further decides* that, in accordance with the provisions of its resolution 973(X) of 15 December 1955, there shall be set off against the apportionment among Member States, as provided for in paragraph 25 above, their respective share in the Tax Equalization Fund of 22,145,833 dollars, comprising the estimated staff assessment income of 18,514,333 dollars approved for the Mission, the prorated share of 3,048,750 dollars of the estimated staff assessment income approved for the support account and the prorated share of 582,750 dollars of the estimated staff assessment income approved for the United Nations Logistics Base;

27. *Decides* to apportion among Member States the amount of 166,762,950 dollars for the period from 1 May to 30 June 2010, at a monthly rate of 83,381,475 dollars, taking into account the scale of assessments for 2010, subject to a decision of the Security Council to extend the mandate of the Mission;

28. *Also decides* that, in accordance with the provisions of its resolution 973(X), there shall be set off against the apportionment among Member States, as provided for in paragraph 27 above, their respective share in the Tax Equalization Fund of 4,429,167 dollars, comprising the estimated staff assessment income of 3,702,867 dollars approved for the Mission, the prorated share of 609,750 dollars of the estimated staff assessment income approved for the support account and the prorated share of 116,550 dollars of the estimated staff assessment income approved for the United Nations Logistics Base;

29. *Further decides* that, for Member States that have fulfilled their financial obligations to the Mission, there shall be set off against their apportionment, as provided for in paragraph 25 above, their respective share of the unencumbered balance and other income in the total amount of 82,199,100 dollars in respect of the financial period ended 30 June 2008, in accordance with the levels updated in its resolution 61/243, and taking into account the scale of assessments for 2008, as set out in its resolution 61/237;

30. *Decides* that, for Member States that have not fulfilled their financial obligations to the Mission, there shall be set off against their outstanding obligations their respective share of the unencumbered balance and other income in the total amount of 82,199,100 dollars in respect of the financial period ended 30 June 2008, in accordance with the scheme set out in paragraph 29 above;

31. *Also decides* that the increase of 2,348,600 dollars in the estimated staff assessment income in respect of the financial period ended 30 June 2008 shall be added to the credits from the amount of 82,199,100 dollars referred to in paragraphs 29 and 30 above;

32. *Emphasizes* that no peacekeeping mission shall be financed by borrowing funds from other active peacekeeping missions;

33. *Encourages* the Secretary-General to continue to take additional measures to ensure the safety and security of all personnel participating in the Mission under the auspices of the United Nations, bearing in mind paragraphs 5 and 6 of Security Council resolution 1502(2003) of 26 August 2003;

34. *Invites* voluntary contributions to the Mission in cash and in the form of services and supplies acceptable to the Secretary-General, to be administered, as appropriate, in accordance with the procedure and practices established by the General Assembly;

35. *Decides* to include in the provisional agenda of its sixty-fourth session the item entitled "Financing of the United Nations Mission in the Sudan".

The Assembly, by **decision 64/549** of 24 December, decided that the agenda item on UNMIS financing would remain for consideration during its resumed sixty-fourth (2010) session.

Darfur

The security situation in the Darfur region of the Sudan deteriorated dramatically and violence escalated even as the deployment of the African Union-United Nations Hybrid Operation in Darfur (UNAMID) continued. Two years into its mandate, UNAMID had made significant progress towards full deployment and was now focused on its tasks of protecting civilians and facilitating humanitarian delivery. UNAMID encouraged greater dialogue between local Sudanese authorities and IDPs, provided round-the-clock security patrols at IDP camps and contributed to a substantial reduction in the levels of violence and the number of those affected by violence. Other UNAMID initiatives included enhancement of the Government and the police to address human rights violations and inadequacies in the local judicial services, as well as the establishment of a UNAMID gender crimes special investigation unit to monitor and report on investigations of crimes committed against women and children. However, kidnappings and confrontations, tribal clashes, banditry and attacks against peacekeepers made it increasingly difficult for the Mission to conduct its work.

The humanitarian obstacles confronting UNAMID worsened following the 4 March decision by the International Criminal Court (ICC) to indict President Omar Al-Bashir. The Sudan retaliated immediately by expelling 13 international NGOs and shutting down three national NGOs; that led to

UNAMID, UN agencies and other partners spending much of the year trying to fill the gaps in the delivery of humanitarian services.

On the political front, the year started on a promising note as the Government of National Unity and JEM agreed to AU/UN-mediated talks in Doha, Qatar. On 17 February, the parties reached an "Agreement of Good Will and Confidence-Building for the Settlement of the Problem in Darfur", which Qatar transmitted to the Security Council on 18 February [S/2009/100]. The Agreement was signed under the auspices of Qatar and the AU-UN Joint Chief Mediator and within the framework of the Afro-Arab initiative on peace in Darfur.

Regrettably, the parties did not fully implement the Agreement. In mid-November, the AU-UN Mediation made notable progress by bringing together a diverse group of Darfur civil society in Doha to arrive at a consensus on critical issues such as security arrangements, wealth-sharing and power-sharing.

While the Sudan Liberation Army/Abdul Wahid (SLA/AW) and other factions remained outside the talks, efforts continued to have them agree on a common platform in anticipation of joining the Government of National Unity/JEM talks. Egypt, the Libyan Arab Jamahiriya and the United States complemented those efforts by working to reunify some of the smaller movements. The AU High-level Panel on Darfur, headed by former South African President Thabo Mbeki, also made a significant contribution to international efforts to find a solution to the crisis.

In the light of progress in the political process, recovery partners began discussions on medium- and long-term planning. However, challenges remained, including military confrontations between the Government of the Sudan and armed elements, attacks on UNAMID and humanitarian convoys, and armed attempts to prevent UNAMID from patrolling. The most serious impediment to sustainable peace continued to be the failure of some parties to fully engage in the peace process.

SLA/AW and JEM boycotted voter registration for the April 2010 general elections and called on their supporters in the IDP camps to do the same, but did not direct major violence or attacks at the exercise.

UNAMID's first Joint Special Representative, Rodolphe Adada (Congo), and its first Force Commander, General Martin Luther Agwai (Nigeria), completed their tours of duty in August. Police Commissioner Michael Fryer (South Africa) and Deputy Police Commissioner Elizabeth Muwanga (Uganda) finished their tour of duty on 20 December. As at 1 September, Lieutenant General Patrick Nyamvumba (Rwanda) took up the post of Force Commander and Deputy Joint Special Representative Henry Anyidoho (Ghana) assumed the functions

of Joint Special Representative ad interim. Ibrahim Gambari (Nigeria) was appointed Joint Special Representative effective 1 January 2010.

Political and security developments

Since the signing of the 17 February Doha Goodwill Agreement, the process of negotiations between the Government of National Unity and the armed movements slowed, due to a crisis of confidence between the principal belligerents, as well as differences that undermined the cohesion of the movements. The joint AU-UN Mediation intensified its efforts with JEM of Khalil Ibrahim, as well as with the Sudan Liberation Movement (SLM) of Abdul Wahid Al-Nur. The Mediation aimed at uniting the positions of those two movements, and those of the other movements of Darfur. Reunification efforts of the movements were supported by the Libyan Arab Jamahiriya and the United States.

On 18 November in Doha, the Mediation, in partnership with Qatar, launched the Darfur peace talks in the presence of representatives of all Darfur communities, as well as of women's groups, youth and IDPs. Representatives of the Government of National Unity and the armed movements also attended. The aims of the talks were to find a comprehensive resolution of the underlying causes of the crisis, to overcome inter-communal hatreds caused by war, and to accelerate socio-economic development by addressing the central issues, including the reintegration of IDPs and refugees; the promotion of human rights and security; the fight against poverty and marginalization; the end of military hostilities and political and security arrangements; the 2010 elections and democratic good governance; the resolution of land disputes; and compensation, reconciliation and justice, including an end to impunity.

Report of Secretary-General (February). The Secretary-General, in a report of 10 February on UNAMID deployment [S/2009/83], submitted pursuant to Council resolution 1828(2008) [YUN 2008, p. 252], noted that the security situation across Darfur had deteriorated dramatically between December 2008 and January 2009. The unilateral ceasefire announced by President Al-Bashir on 12 November 2008 [YUN 2008, p. 257] had not taken hold. Of major concern had been the military offensives by armed movements, especially JEM, and counter-attacks by SAF, which included aerial bombardments. There had been fighting within several armed movements, and tribal clashed over natural resources engulfed Southern Darfur on a scale not seen since early 2008.

In light of the escalating violence, the Joint African Union-United Nations Chief Mediator for Darfur, Djibrill Yipènè Bassolé, had been leading AU-UN efforts towards a cessation of hostilities.

On 31 January and 1 February, Sudanese authorities informed UNAMID that they believed that JEM intended to initiate larger-scale hostilities in Southern Darfur and that SAF would therefore use "all means possible" to dislodge JEM from the area. They called on UNAMID to relocate personnel out of the Muhajeria team site to another location, in order to prevent any unnecessary loss of life similar to the 2007 attack on the African Union Mission in the Sudan at Haskanita [YUN 2007, p. 255]. Government officials made it clear that they viewed the area of Muhajeria as vital to the security of Southern Darfur and Kordofan. Intense diplomatic efforts, including a meeting of the Secretary-General with President Al-Bashir, were undertaken to convince the Government and JEM to stand down. In response to UN calls to exercise maximum restraint and abide by existing agreements, including with respect to the safety and security of AU-UN personnel, the Government assured that restraint would be exercised and UNAMID would not be asked to depart from Muhajeria. Following similarly intense engagement with the JEM leadership, JEM withdrew its forces 50 to 60 kilometres outside of Muhajeria by 3 February. On the same day, a UNAMID delegation that aimed to assess the security situation and UNAMID reinforcements needs was prevented by government security officials from travelling to Muhajeria, in breach of the 2008 status-of-forces agreement [YUN 2008, p. 246], which guaranteed UNAMID unrestricted freedom of movement throughout Darfur.

Tribal fighting, arising from long-standing disputes over land jurisdiction and local authority, remained a key destabilizing factor in a context of the proliferation of firearms, the absence of law and order, and precarious economic conditions. Continued violence increased the vulnerability of civilians, while additional population displacements increased the number of people depending on life-saving assistance. As a result of the violence, humanitarian organizations had to reduce movements by road and rely increasingly on air assets. Among positive developments, most of Darfur received sufficient rainfall, allowing more people to farm.

Progress in the political process was impeded by JEM military action, resumption of aerial bombardments by the Government and the sense that all concerned were waiting for the ICC decision regarding the Prosecutor's application for an arrest warrant against President Al-Bashir. The position of the main parties had not changed. SLA/AW continued to reject dialogue with the Government. JEM claimed to be ready for direct negotiations, but its actions on the ground, in particular its 15 January attack on SLA/MM in Muhajeria, signalled its focus on military action. In addition, JEM continued to reject the inclusion of other movements in the peace talks. Fighting between Government forces and SLA/MM in Graida could jeopard-

ize the security and political arrangements between them, the Secretary-General warned.

On 21 January, President Al-Bashir issued decrees establishing three committees to deal with fundamental issues related to the Darfur conflict, namely to assess the administrative structure of Darfur states, to follow up on reconciliation conferences, and on native administration. The recommendation of the Sudan People's Forum, launched by the President in October 2008 [YUN 2008, p. 257], had yet to be taken forward by the Government in direct negotiations with the armed movements, and some of the parties that participated in the Forum's inaugural meeting had since expressed their concern regarding the initiative's credibility. Prospects for participation in the Forum of the Popular Congress Party were undermined with the arrest of its leader, Hassan Al-Turabi, on 15 January, following his remarks in support of the ICC process against President Al-Bashir.

Meeting in Doha on 14 January, the ad hoc Afro-Arab ministerial committee on resolving the Darfur crisis endorsed efforts to facilitate the resumption of the peace talks and called for discussions with the Security Council on suspending all Darfur ICC cases in the interest of the peace process.

The Tripartite Committee on UNAMID, consisting of the Government of the Sudan, the AU and the United Nations, held its third periodic consultation on 19 January in Addis Ababa. Participants signed a memorandum of understanding enabling UNAMID to make more effective use of Sudanese airport infrastructure. UNAMID continued to face restrictions on its freedom of movement, and staff members were increasingly victims of carjacking.

With limited capability at its disposal, UNAMID had nevertheless made a difference on the ground, the Secretary-General observed. An important requirement would be to consolidate the capabilities of the troops on the ground; the provision of outstanding equipment, in particular military helicopter assets, remained critical. The latest security developments highlighted the fundamental challenges that UNAMID faced while operating in an environment where the parties showed no intent to give up the use of force. In the meantime, UNAMID continued to balance the dual priorities of continuing with deployment while minimizing risk to personnel in a phase IV security environment.

As the fundamental responsibility for making progress rested with the parties, the Sudan and the armed rebel movements must cease hostilities and engage in dialogue under the auspices of the AU-UN mediation. The Government must demonstrate its seriousness with respect to the outcomes of the Sudan People's Forum by taking concrete action, and it was critical for regional stability and lasting peace in Darfur that

Chad and the Sudan improve relations. In the aftermath of the violence in Muhajeria, it was clear that the parties did not have the will or capacity to transcend the conflict alone. The Secretary-General called on Member States with influence over the parties to support Joint Chief Mediator Bassolé's efforts towards a negotiated solution.

Report of Secretary-General (April). In a 14 April report [S/2009/201] on UNAMID, covering the situation in February and March, the Secretary-General said that the 17 February Agreement between the Sudan and JEM was a preliminary document that established the two parties' commitment to create an environment conducive to substantive talks. It called for the two parties to refrain from harassing IDPS, guarantee the smooth flow of humanitarian aid and exchange prisoners. It also committed them to finalize a more substantive framework agreement. On 15 March, five rebel groups (SLM-Unity, SLM-Khamees, the United Revolutionary Force Front, SLM-Juba and JEM-Azraq) signed the "Tripoli Charter", an agreement to create a unified front and participate in the peace negotiations. They committed themselves to participating in the Doha process and were working with the AU-UN mediation and Qatar towards holding talks with the Sudan. On 20 March, JEM announced that it intended to suspend participation in the Doha process until the Sudan reversed its decision to expel and dissolve 16 NGOs. One of the three committees established by presidential decree on 21 January, overseeing the review of the number of Darfur states, had begun its work and had held consultations with stakeholders in Darfur on 27 and 28 March. UNAMID continued to engage local stakeholders on issues related to reconciliation and conflict resolution in the context of the Darfur-Darfur Dialogue and Consultation mechanism.

Notwithstanding the positive political steps by the Government and JEM, an alarming number of clashes took place between them and UNAMID received numerous reports of aerial bombardment of JEM positions by Government forces. Since the beginning of March, Government forces had been carrying out a large military build-up in the area of Al Mallam, east of Jebel Marra, a stronghold of SLA/AW now under Government control. The Government had reportedly concentrated its forces around Dobo Al Umdah and Dobo Madrassa, blocking all entry points to the Jebel Marra Mountains in Northern Darfur.

Tribal clashes continued despite UNAMID-facilitated reconciliation efforts, and the security situation along the Chad-Sudan border remained tense.

For the United Nations, the security level in Darfur remained at phase IV, with 62 security incidents during the reporting period and random carjacking and banditry posing the greatest risk to UN personnel.

UNAMID was also deliberately attacked on three separate occasions.

Humanitarian assistance efforts faced challenges as a consequence of increased insecurity in the areas of Muhajeriya and Graida in Southern Darfur in early February and the expulsion of 13 international and suspensions of three national NGOs on 4 March. Since 4 February, large numbers of people, mostly from the Zaghawa tribe, moved from Muhajeriya and surrounding villages, as well as from rural areas between Muhajeriya and Shaeria. Some 36,000 IDPs from Southern Darfur arrived in the greater El Fasher area, in particular at Zam Zam camp, severely straining the surrounding environment. UNAMID provided protection patrols and water supplies to Zam Zam on a nearly daily basis, and UN entities and NGOs complemented Government efforts to provide food, medicines and tents. Humanitarian access to some areas of Darfur affected by fighting had been restricted. In February, after reports of aerial bombardments and with tens of thousands on the move in Shaeria locality, the Government did not provide flight clearance to various interagency assessment missions in Southern Darfur. Access to eastern Jebel Marra was also consistently denied. Government forces imposed restrictions on UNAMID's freedom of movement, on security grounds, before and after military engagements with rebel groups.

UNAMID continued to expand its Community Policing Initiative: it operated 58 community policing centres in or adjacent to IDP camps and conducted training courses for the Sudanese police, for the movements police and for community policing volunteers in IDP camps across Darfur. It assisted IDPs in identifying ways and means of improving the lives of women and children and to document incidents of sexual and gender-based violence. UNAMID also established 24 additional quick-impact projects, bringing their number to 142. It delivered education on explosive remnants of war and mine risk to 6,446 people, destroyed 115 items of explosive remnants of war, assessed 50 villages and surveyed more than 200 kilometres of road. On 25 February, the Mine Action Office was informed that it did not have the mandate to work in Southern Darfur; from 2 March, all mine action activities throughout Darfur were suspended until further instruction from the Ministry of Humanitarian Affairs.

On 19 February, the Sudan transmitted to the Security Council the agreed outcomes of the Tripartite Committee meeting on 18 February, focusing on air operations, railways, visas, and UNAMID vehicles for the Sudanese police during convoy protection [S/2009/104]. On 31 March, the Tripartite Committee met again to discuss those and other issues [S/2009/173]. The Government agreed to a bridging solution while the final approval for the UNAMID broadcasting licenses was finalized. With respect to the assets of the international NGOs whose licenses were revoked, the Government agreed that UNAMID would safeguard equipment and materials until a solution was reached.

The situation was dominated by the 4 March decision of the Pre-Trial Chamber I of the ICC to issue an arrest warrant for President Al-Bashir, for two counts of war crimes and five counts of crimes against humanity (see p. 1300). The Secretary-General trusted that the Government would address the issues in a manner consistent with Council resolution 1593(2005) [YUN 2005, p. 324]. He reiterated the determination of the United Nations to continue to conduct its mediation, peacekeeping, humanitarian, human rights and development activities in the Sudan, and called on the Government to cooperate while fulfilling its obligations to ensure the safety and security of the civilian population, UN personnel and property and UN implementing partners. He considered the decision to expel or dissolve 16 NGOs an extremely negative development and called on the Government to re-establish trust and mutual confidence with the humanitarian community. He was concerned about the impact of that action on UNAMID's work, as a significant disruption in providing humanitarian assistance would increase tensions among IDPs, complicating UNAMID's ability to perform its protection mandate.

In Muhajeriya, the clashes and intensive aerial bombardments in early February required the relocation of all unarmed UNAMID personnel to Nyala, while UNAMID military sought to provide protection to the affected population; at one point, as many as 10,000 individuals gathered around the UNAMID camp. UNAMID had been unable to visit locations to assess the impact of the bombardments on the civilian population as a result of the insecurity due to continued clashes between the Government and the movements, recurrent tribal fighting and the build-up of forces along the Chad-Sudan border, as well as attacks on UN and associated personnel, highlighted by the killing of a UN peacekeeper and the kidnapping of five Médecins Sans Frontières-Belgium staff in March. Those developments highlighted the challenges UNAMID faced in an environment where the parties showed no intent to give up the use for force.

Security Council consideration. On 27 April [meeting 6112], the Council considered the Secretary-General's report and was briefed by Rodolphe Adada, Joint AU-UN Special Representative for Darfur and head of UNAMID, who provided an overview of the state of affairs, progress and the obstacles encountered.

Report of Secretary-General (June). In his 9 June report on UNAMID deployment [S/2009/297], the Secretary-General said that negotiations between the Government and JEM resumed and were concluded on 12 May with an agreement to pursue the implementation of the 17 February Agreement. The two sides reiterated their commitment to the peace process and reaffirmed their attachment to Doha as the venue for negotiations. They exchanged lists of their respective detainees and agreed to set up a committee with the participation of the Mediation to verify the lists with a view to accelerating the release of prisoners. They also discussed the humanitarian situation as well as requirements for a cessation of hostilities. On 27 May, JEM and the Government returned to Doha to build on the 17 February Agreement, discuss the military situation and work towards addressing outstanding issues such as prisoner exchange and cessation of hostilities.

In early April, 21 senior Sudanese Liberation Army-Unity and United Resistance Front commanders joined JEM, including Suleiman Jamous, Adam Bakhit and Adam Ali Shogar. The "Tripoli group", comprised of five rebel movements, confirmed its willingness to participate in the peace process and met with the Mediation in Doha on 29 April. At a meeting in Switzerland, SLA/AW confirmed its position that negotiations with the Government could not take place until preconditions were met, including disarmament of the pro-Government militias, removal of new settlers from the land of IDPs and a cessation of offensive military actions.

Following high-level negotiations in Doha, Chad and the Sudan on 3 May signed the Doha Agreement as a step towards the normalization of bilateral relations. Despite the Agreement, there was increased fighting along the border, an incursion by Chadian forces into Western Darfur, and clashes in Western Darfur between JEM and SLA/MM supported by SAF.

The AU High-level Panel on Darfur, led by former South African President Mbeki, visited Darfur in April and May to consult with civil society, political parties, rebel movements and IDP groups. The Panel was mandated by the AU Peace and Security Council to submit proposals to address issues of accountability for serious crimes, for expediting the peace process in Darfur and for reconciling warring parties in the region.

The humanitarian situation in Darfur was centred around efforts to cope with the expulsions and dissolution of 16 NGOs in Northern Sudan in March. After the expulsions and following incidents of hostage-taking and criminal attacks, the humanitarian community had significantly reduced its presence in remote field locations. By 1 June, the international humanitarian presence in Southern and Western Darfur was approximately 64 per cent of pre-4 March levels. In Northern Darfur, the aid community was confined to El Fasher owing to the situation of insecurity. The pre-expulsion standards of delivery had yet to be restored and the health sector remained an area of concern. The situation in the Zam Zam IDP camp continued to be serious as the camp had exceeded its capacity to provide adequate services. UNAMID transported 45,000 litres of water per day to the camp and provided daily escorts for agencies and staff. It provided 24-hour protection of four warehouses previously managed by an expelled NGO and 67 vehicles belonging to UN partners and NGOs.

The Sudanese Government had taken steps towards facilitating humanitarian assistance in Darfur and expanded the membership of the High-level Committee to include more ministries from the Government of National Unity and the international community.

UN, security phase IV remained in effect throughout Darfur as 143 security incidents affecting UN staff were recorded during the reporting period, including increasingly violent cases of carjacking. UNAMID continued to face restrictions of its freedom of movement, mainly by the Government of the Sudan, as well as obstructions to the implementation of quick-impact projects and detention of national staff. During the reporting period, UNAMID documented 17 cases of arbitrary and illegal arrests and detentions by government security forces. It also documented five cases of threats and harassment of human rights workers, national UNAMID staff, international NGOs and civil society. It continued to receive allegations of rape and physical assaults against women and girls.

UNAMID conducted 20 training courses for local police and supported traditional conflict resolution between leaders at the Dourti IDP camp and the neighbouring Umm Al-Qura Arab community. UNAMID engagement produced positive signs of willingness to negotiate the conflict between the Massalit community and local nomads in Masteri, Western Darfur. On 12 May, the National Intelligence and Security Service terminated a UNAMID-organized workshop at the University of Zalingei, Western Darfur, on the role of native administration in peace, conflict resolution and reconciliation, despite proper registration with local authorities.

Since 2 March, all mine operations continued to be suspended, and the issue was addressed during the 31 March meeting of the Tripartite Committee. In letters to the Sudanese Government, UNAMID and the Under-Secretary-General for Peacekeeping Operations requested that the mine action teams resume operations in order to fulfil UNAMID's mandate and protect the civilian population.

As at 26 May, UNAMID's military strength stood at 13,455. With the planned deployment of a Thai infantry battalion in October, all 18 UNAMID battalions were expected to be deployed to Darfur by year's end.

UNAMID police personnel numbered 2,877, while civilian personnel stood at 3,497.

The Secretary-General expressed concern at continued military engagements between JEM and both SLA/MM and the Government of the Sudan in Northern Darfur. He called on both parties to suspend military action and address the issues in the second round of talks that began in Doha on 27 May. The challenges with respect to UNAMID's freedom of movement and ability to implement its mandate—the obstruction of patrolling activities, the detention of quick-impact projects implementing partners, the confiscation of project funds, the detention and apparent mistreatment of UNAMID national staff, and the slow pace with which visas were issued—signalled a negative trend with regard to the Government's cooperation with UNAMID and had to be reversed.

Regarding the ongoing Darfur-related cases before the ICC, the Secretary-General took note of the voluntary appearance before the Court on 18 May of the commander of the United Resistance Front in Darfur, Bahr Idriss Abu Garda, in response to charges of war crimes committed on 29 September 2007 [YUN 2007, p. 255] at the Haskanita base of the African Union Mission in the Sudan.

As the main parties to the Darfur conflict continued to choose violence over compromise and demonstrated a lack of will or capacity to solve the conflict alone, the Secretary-General called on all parties, and the States with influence over them, to work with the Joint Chief Mediator towards a negotiated solution.

Report of Secretary-General (July). In a 13 July report [S/2009/352], the Secretary-General, in anticipation of the Security Council's discussions on the renewal of UNAMID's mandate which would expire on 31 July, covered key developments during the month of June, rather than the typical 60-day period.

The Government of the Sudan and JEM met in Doha from 27 May to 18 June to discuss the implementation of the 17 February Agreement. The parties discussed ways to move the peace process forward, particularly with respect to an exchange of prisoners, cessation of hostilities and a framework agreement that would define the areas to be discussed during comprehensive negotiations. JEM insisted that the Government release all its prisoners before initiating discussion on a framework agreement and cessation of hostilities, while the Government insisted on agreeing to a cessation of hostilities before any prisoner exchange. Meanwhile, on 9 June, a criminal court in Khartoum sentenced an additional 12 JEM members to death for their involvement in the May 2008 attacks on Omdurman [YUN 2008, p. 236], bringing the number of death sentences for JEM members to 103. The talks were suspended on 18 June to allow the parties to undertake internal consultations. The

Mediation continued to work with both parties in anticipation of reconvening in Doha in late July. On 29 June, the Mediation met with leaders of Darfurian armed movements in Tripoli to discuss the Doha negotiations and work towards their participation in the resolution of the Darfur crisis; the movements declared themselves ready to engage in dialogue with the Government, and the Mediator would propose a date for such consultations in cooperation with the Libyan and Qatari authorities.

The AU High-level Panel on Darfur visited Darfur for the third time from 15 to 26 June, meeting with civil society, tribal leaders, IDPs and rebel groups, as well as with President Al-Bashir and other senior government officials, and JEM members in Khartoum prisons.

Following JEM attacks on positions near Umm Baru in mid-May, there had been no significant military operations, although SAF maintained an increased presence and military patrolling activities in the areas of Kornoi, Tine and Umm Baru in Northern Darfur. On 29 June, a group of 20 to 25 unknown armed men attacked a UNAMID formed police unit convoy in El Geneina, firing several shots and injuring the commander. There were nine incidents of carjacking reported in Darfur during the review period.

Humanitarian assistance sought to address the consequences of the 4 March expulsions of and dissolution of NGOs. Joint efforts by the Government of the Sudan, the United Nations and the remaining NGOs had helped to narrow the gap in aid delivery, but concerns remained about quality and standard.

From 1 to 30 June, UNAMID military conducted 635 confidence-building patrols, 1,356 escort patrols, 282 night patrols and 16 investigation patrols covering 1,364 villages. UNAMID police carried out 2,795 patrols inside IDP camps and 1,139 outside the camps, and assisted in building a community policing centre in Tawila, Northern Darfur, bringing the number of completed centres to four, out of an authorized 83.

As at 30 June, 201 quick-impact projects in education, health and sanitation had been approved and were in various stages of implementation; 39 of them had been completed, 36 of them in Northern Darfur. On 16 June, the National Intelligence and Security Service released $77,000 allocated to quick-impact project funds it had confiscated in May in Zalingei, Western Darfur.

UNAMID carried out 28 human rights monitoring missions, documenting 13 cases of arbitrary and illegal arrest and detention. On 10 June, the Government of the Sudan instructed all prisons in Northern Darfur to permit UNAMID correction officers access. UNAMID continued to receive reports of rape and physical assaults against women and girls.

On 9 June, the UNAMID voluntary returns working group, led by the Deputy Joint Special Representative,

travelled to Donki Dreisa and Muhagiriya in Southern Darfur, where some 1,500 residents were reported to have returned to their homes. On 17 June, the team visited Seraf Jidad in Western Darfur, where the inhabitants of approximately 2,100 households had reportedly returned to their homes.

UNAMID dedicated considerable energies to developing modalities for collaboration with the Government of the Sudan. Of particular concern was the speed with which visas were issued to UNAMID personnel. There continued to be instances where Khartoum-based decisions to support UNAMID work were not implemented locally, especially concerning freedom of movement of personnel and customs clearances. On the whole, there had been considerable improvement in the quality of Government cooperation, and the tripartite mechanism had become an effective tool for ensuring that operational impediments were addressed.

The Mission's priority would continue to be the protection of civilians and facilitation of humanitarian assistance. However, the environment in which UNAMID worked had changed in significant ways as large-scale violence stretching over a wide territory and for lengthy periods had become infrequent. Many IDP camps, some five years old, were now entrenched, while small-scale but consistent spontaneous returns were occurring in some locations. Nevertheless, the situation for civilians remained troubling, with 2.6 million IDPs unable to return to their homes, some 4.7 million Darfurians in need of assistance, and banditry and sexual violence continuing.

Taking into accounts the many complex challenges facing Darfur, the Secretary-General recommended an extension of UNAMID's mandate for a further 12 months.

Communication. In a 21 July letter [S/2009/388], the Libyan Arab Jamahiriya transmitted to the Security Council the communiqué on the situation in Darfur adopted by the AU Peace and Security Council on 21 July.

SECURITY COUNCIL ACTION

The Security Council met on 24 July [meeting 6170] to consider the Secretary-General's June and July reports. On 30 July [meeting 6175], the Council unanimously adopted **resolution 1881(2009)**. The draft [S/2009/392] was submitted by the United Kingdom.

The Security Council,

Reaffirming all its previous resolutions and the statements by its President concerning the situation in the Sudan,

Reaffirming its strong commitment to the sovereignty, unity, independence and territorial integrity of the Sudan and its determination to work with the Government of the Sudan, in full respect of its sovereignty, to assist in tackling the various challenges in the Sudan,

Recalling its resolution 1674(2006) of 28 April 2006 on the protection of civilians in armed conflict, in which it reaffirms, inter alia, the relevant provisions of the 2005 World Summit Outcome, its resolution 1612(2005) of 26 July 2005 on children and armed conflict, its resolution 1502(2003) of 26 August 2003 on the protection of humanitarian and United Nations personnel and its resolutions 1325(2000) of 31 October 2000 and 1820(2008) of 19 June 2008 on women and peace and security,

Taking note of the report of the Secretary-General of 10 February 2009 on children and armed conflict in the Sudan, including his recommendations, and the report of the Secretary-General of 29 August 2007 on children and armed conflict in the Sudan, and recalling the conclusions on parties to the armed conflict in the Sudan endorsed by the Security Council Working Group on Children and Armed Conflict,

Welcoming the important role of the African Union,

Welcoming also the report of the Secretary-General of 13 July 2009 on the African Union-United Nations Hybrid Operation in Darfur (UNAMID),

Stressing the need for the Council to pursue a rigorous, strategic approach to peacekeeping deployments,

Expressing its concern, two years after the adoption of its resolution 1769(2007) of 31 July 2007, at the continued seriousness of the security situation and deterioration of the humanitarian situation in Darfur and at the recurring attacks on the civilian population, reiterating its condemnation of all violations of human rights and international humanitarian law in Darfur, calling upon all parties to comply with their obligations under international humanitarian and human rights law, emphasizing the need to bring to justice the perpetrators of such crimes, and urging the Government of the Sudan to comply with its obligations in this respect,

Reaffirming its concern over the negative effect of the ongoing violence in Darfur on the stability of the Sudan as a whole as well as the region, noting with concern the negative effect of ongoing tensions between the Governments of the Sudan and Chad, reiterating that a reduction in these tensions and rebel activity in both countries must be addressed to achieve long-term peace in Darfur and in the region, and encouraging the Sudan and Chad to engage constructively with the Dakar Contact Group and the international community,

Expressing its strong commitment and determination to promote and support the political process in Darfur and the efforts of the Joint African Union-United Nations Chief Mediator for Darfur, and deploring the fact that some groups continue to refuse to join the political process,

Determining that the situation in the Sudan constitutes a threat to international peace and security,

1. *Decides* to extend the mandate of the African Union-United Nations Hybrid Operation in Darfur (UNAMID) as set out in resolution 1769(2007) for a further twelve months, until 31 July 2010;

2. *Underlines* the need for UNAMID to make full use of its mandate and capabilities, particularly with regard to *(a)* the protection of civilians across Darfur, and *(b)* ensuring safe, timely and unhindered humanitarian access, the safety and security of humanitarian personnel and the protection of humanitarian convoys;

3. *Commends* the contribution of troop- and police-contributing countries and donors to UNAMID; calls upon States Members of the United Nations to pledge and contribute the remaining helicopter, aerial reconnaissance, ground transport, medical and logistical units and other force enablers required; underlines the need for capable battalions effectively able to carry out UNAMID's mandated tasks; in this regard requests the continuing assistance of donors in ensuring that battalions are suitably trained and equipped; and further requests UNAMID to examine how it could maximize the use of its capabilities in Darfur;

4. *Welcomes* the improvement in the Government of the Sudan's cooperation with UNAMID, commends the credible work of the Tripartite Commission, calls upon all parties in Darfur to remove all obstacles to the full and expeditious deployment of UNAMID and the proper discharge of its mandate, including by ensuring its security and freedom of movement; and in this regard calls upon the Government of the Sudan to comply with the status-of-forces agreement fully and without delay, in particular the timely provision of visas for UNAMID personnel and of flight and equipment clearances;

5. *Reiterates its condemnation* of previous attacks on UNAMID by armed groups, underlines that any attack or threat on UNAMID is unacceptable, demands that there be no recurrence of such attacks, and stresses the need to enhance the safety and security of UNAMID personnel;

6. *Stresses* the importance of achievable and realistic targets against which the progress of United Nations peacekeeping operations can be measured, and in this regard requests the Secretary-General, following consultations with the African Union:

(a) To submit, for the consideration of the Security Council, a strategic workplan containing benchmarks to measure and track progress being made by UNAMID in implementing its mandate;

(b) To include in his next report an assessment of progress made against these benchmarks, as well as consequent recommendations regarding the mandate and configuration of UNAMID; and

(c) To report to the Council every ninety days thereafter on progress made towards implementing the mandate of UNAMID across Darfur, as well as on progress on the political process, on the security and humanitarian situation and on compliance by all parties with their international obligations;

7. *Demands* that all parties to the conflict in Darfur immediately end violence and attacks on civilians, peacekeepers and humanitarian personnel, and comply with their obligations under human rights and international humanitarian law; calls for an immediate cessation of hostilities and for all parties to commit themselves to a sustained and permanent ceasefire; requests the Secretary-General to consult with relevant parties with a view to developing a more effective ceasefire monitoring mechanism; and underlines the need for UNAMID to report on major instances of violence which undermine the parties' full and constructive efforts towards peace;

8. *Reiterates* that there can be no military solution to the conflict in Darfur and that an inclusive political settlement and the successful deployment of UNAMID are essential to re-establishing peace; reaffirms its full support

for the African Union-United Nations-led political process for Darfur and the work of the Joint African Union-United Nations Chief Mediator for Darfur, Mr. Djibrill Yipènè Bassolé; demands that all parties to the conflict, including all rebel groups, immediately engage fully and constructively in the peace process without preconditions, including by entering into talks under the mediation of Mr. Bassolé with a view to finalizing a framework agreement; welcomes the work of Qatar and the Libyan Arab Jamahiriya in this regard and the support of other countries in the region; calls upon UNAMID to support the Joint Chief Mediator and the African Union-United Nations Joint Mediation Support Team; and underlines the need for the engagement of civil society, including women and women-led organizations, community groups and tribal leaders, in order to create a conducive environment for peace and security through constructive and open dialogue;

9. *Calls upon* the Sudan and Chad to abide by their obligations under the Doha Agreement of 3 May 2009, the Dakar Agreement of 13 March 2008 and previous bilateral agreements; and reaffirms the need for both countries to engage constructively with the Dakar Contact Group with a view to normalizing relations, ceasing support for armed groups, strengthening actions to combat arms trafficking in the region, establishing effective joint border monitoring, and cooperating through diplomatic means to establish peace and stability in Darfur and the wider region;

10. *Notes* that conflict in one area of the Sudan affects other areas of the Sudan and the wider region, and urges UNAMID to coordinate closely with other United Nations missions in the region, including the United Nations Mission in the Sudan and the United Nations Mission in the Central African Republic and Chad;

11. *Requests* UNAMID, consistent with its current capabilities and mandate, to assist and complement the efforts of the United Nations Mission in the Sudan in preparing for credible national elections through the provision of advice and assistance where required;

12. *Expresses its serious concern* at the continued deterioration of the humanitarian situation in Darfur, calls for the full implementation of the joint communiqué between the Government of the Sudan and the United Nations on the facilitation of humanitarian activities in Darfur, and demands that the Government of the Sudan, all militias, armed groups and all other stakeholders ensure the full, safe and unhindered access of humanitarian organizations and relief personnel and the delivery of humanitarian assistance to populations in need;

13. *Demands* that all parties to the conflict in Darfur create the conditions conducive to allowing the voluntary, safe, dignified and sustainable return of refugees and internally displaced persons;

14. *Demands also* that the parties to the conflict immediately take appropriate measures to protect civilians, including women and children, from all forms of sexual violence, in line with resolution 1820(2008); and requests the Secretary-General to develop a comprehensive strategy for providing protection to women and girls from sexual violence and gender-based violence and to ensure that the relevant provisions of resolutions 1325(2000) and 1820(2008) are implemented by UNAMID, and to include information on this in his reporting to the Council;

15. *Requests* the Secretary-General to ensure *(a)* continued monitoring and reporting, as part of the reports referred to in paragraph 6 above, of the situation of children and *(b)* continued dialogue with the parties to the conflict towards the preparation of time-bound action plans to end the recruitment and use of child soldiers and other violations of international humanitarian law against children;

16. *Decides* to remain seized of the matter.

Further developments

Communications. On 29 October [S/2009/568], the AU transmitted the decision adopted on that day by the AU Peace and Security Council endorsing the report of the AU High-level Panel on Darfur. On 17 November, the Secretary-General submitted the Panel's report [S/2009/599] to the Council.

Report of Secretary-General (November). On 16 November, the Secretary-General, in accordance with Council resolution 1881(2009) (see above), reported [S/2009/592] on UNAMID activities from July through October, which included a proposal for a strategic workplan with benchmarks to track progress made by the Mission in implementing its mandate.

Military activities by the parties to the conflict continued as the Sudanese Government exerted pressure on JEM and SLA/AW. The ongoing violence, which included aerial bombardment, and freedom of movement continued to be a concern for UNAMID and UN agencies. Access to IDP camps was frequently denied.

UN security phase IV remained in effect throughout Darfur, with the exceptions of the towns of El Fasher, Nyala and Zalingei, where security was lowered to phase III on 10 August. Two international UN-AMID staff members were being held in captivity in an unknown location since being forcefully taken from their home in Zalingei, Western Darfur, on 29 August. Three international members of NGOs had been kidnapped during the reporting period. UNAMID personnel were attacked on four occasions, resulting in the death of one peacekeeper.

The Mediation continued its consultations with the armed groups and the Government, but efforts to resume peace negotiations were unsuccessful as both SLA/AW and JEM refused to engage in substantive discussions with the Government. In the meantime, efforts led by Egypt, the Libyan Arab Jamahiriya and the United States to facilitate unification of smaller movements—primarily splinter groups from SLA/AW and JEM—led to the creation of two coalitions of groups in Addis Ababa and Tripoli. However, those groups had yet to resolve their leadership differences. Modalities to resume peace talks were discussed at several high-level international meetings. During consultations with the Sudanese parties and international partners, the Mediation worked to consolidate the emerging consensus that Darfur's adequate participation and representation in the April 2010 elections would be greatly facilitated by the conclusion of a political settlement that complemented the CPA.

At a workshop in Doha in October, the Mediation discussed with experts from the United Nations, the AU, the League of Arab States (LAS), UNMIS, UNAMID and international partners the design and content of the civil society consultation process. The Mediation would work with the Government of the Sudan and armed movements to create the political space for such consultation.

The AU High-level Panel on Darfur visited Darfur for the fourth and final round of consultations. The AU Peace and Security Council endorsed its report on 29 October.

UNAMID continued to support the UNMIS Electoral Affairs Division regarding national elections scheduled for April 2010. Few Darfur movements had registered as political parties and the only party conducting any election-related campaigns was the National Congress Party of President Al-Bashir, which had held conventions in all three Darfur States.

Malnutrition increased and health and sanitation conditions deteriorated. On 5 August, the High-level Committee on humanitarian affairs, comprising senior Sudanese government officials, representatives of the diplomatic community, regional organizations and NGOs, endorsed the creation of a mechanism to verify the voluntary return of IDPs, as well as to ensure the safety and security in return areas. The UN Resident Coordinator and Humanitarian Coordinator submitted a proposal for a joint monitoring mechanism for returns, to which the Government had yet to respond as at 19 October.

As a result of the sixth meeting (Khartoum, 12 July) [S/2009/356] of the Tripartite Mechanism on peace-building initiatives in Darfur, agreement was reached to locate the Ethiopian tactical helicopter unit in Nyala airport. No progress was made on obtaining a radio frequency for UNAMID.

UNAMID continued to prioritize its protection activities and efforts to facilitate humanitarian delivery. It took significant steps towards expanding its patrolling activities, maintaining a continuous presence in IDP camps, and enhancing the capacity of the Government and the police to address human rights violations, in particular sexual and gender-based violence. Several expansions of UNAMID protection activities, such as long-range patrols and night patrols, took place. Of the 83 mandated community policing centres, 59 had been made operational. On 22 July, UNAMID established the Gender Crimes Special Investigation Unit to address cases of rape. The Darfur Child Disarmament, Demobilization and Reintegration Programme, implemented in collaboration with the Darfur Security Arrangements Implementation

Commission and UNICEF, began in July; under the programme, 2,000 registered children associated with Darfur movements were to be released. During the reporting period, 144 children associated with the SLA/Free Will faction were released in Northern Darfur, and plans were under way to start the programme in Southern Darfur.

The Darfur-Darfur Dialogue and Consultation held discussions with women representatives in Northern and Southern Darfur, as well as with youth representatives, to build consensus around six issues of common concern: land and natural resources, security, identity, recovery and development, administration and democracy, and reconciliation.

UNAMID explored ways of increasing outreach to the general population in the absence of radio stations, working with mobile telephone companies to disseminate peace messages. It delivered risk education on unexploded ordnance to 5,393 people, destroyed 98 unexploded ordnance items, conducted general explosive hazard assessments in 52 villages and assessed 438 kilometres of road. Scheduled mine-related operations resumed at full capacity on 1 October.

UNAMID carried out 40 human rights-monitoring field missions, documenting and investigating 61 cases of violations involving 94 victims; 72 victims of sexual and gender-based violence, including 10 minors; 36 killings; 12 cases of injury by shootings; and 3 assaults on UNAMID national staff. Four UNAMID national staff and two individual contractors were reportedly harassed, threatened or arrested by the National Intelligence and Security Services. UNAMID investigated 37 pre-trial detention cases, involving 72 people. Human rights concerns were taken up with the authorities, resulting in the release of 28 people, while 44 remained in custody. UNAMID continued efforts to gain access to two JEM soldiers in Government custody in Khartoum, who had been injured in fighting near Umm Barru, Northern Darfur, in late May, to verify whether they were treated in accordance with international humanitarian law.

To address inadequacies in judicial services across Darfur, UNAMID, in collaboration with other UN entities, obtained consent to work with the Government to set up mobile courts. The first training session on human rights and prison management was held for 30 staff of six prison facilities in Northern Darfur in August. UNAMID concluded an assessment of the juvenile justice system in Western Darfur and was helping to set up a dedicated juvenile court. UNAMID quick-impact projects initiative continued with the approval of 117 new projects in the areas of health, education, water and sanitation, agriculture, income generation, women's empowerment, and shelter.

As UNAMID neared two years in Darfur, the Secretary-General observed, it was focusing on its tasks of humanitarian protection and facilitation of humanitarian delivery. Challenges remained, including increased threats to international staff, ongoing military activities between Chad and the Sudan and within Darfur, limitations on the freedom of movement and access for UNAMID and humanitarian personnel, and a failure of the parties to the conflict to commit to a settlement. The four kidnapping incidents of international NGO staff that had occurred since March and the recent kidnapping of two UNAMID staff in Zalingei on 29 August represented an alarming development.

The Secretary-General was also concerned at the reports of ongoing fighting between the Government and rebel groups, which put civilian lives at risk and demonstrated that the parties had not fully committed to a political solution. The repeated incidents of government officials preventing UNAMID patrols access violated the Status of Forces Agreement and impeded the Mission's capacity to implement its mandate. He urged the Government to ensure that UNAMID and humanitarian personnel were granted full access to affected areas.

The political process had reached a critical juncture. Despite the efforts of the key States and the Joint Chief Mediator, the movements had not shown themselves ready to unify and engage in substantive discussions. The Government had declared its readiness to engage in the process, but its military operations continued. The Mediation's increasing focus on civil society reflected the lack of readiness on the part of the movements and the Government, as well as an understanding that the people of Darfur must be represented in any future peace agreement.

The Mediation's efforts to reflect the views of the people of Darfur in the peace process offered an opportunity to maximize the participation of Darfurians in the upcoming elections. The elections had to be a credible step towards meaningful participation of Darfur at the national level in the Sudan, and concerted efforts had to be made to ensure that all groups in Darfur, especially the IDPs, were able to participate.

The Secretary-General's report included a set of benchmarks and indicators for measuring progress towards the achievement of UNAMID's mandate: the achievement of a comprehensive political solution; the establishment of a secure and stable environment; the enhancement of the rule of law; and a stabilized humanitarian situation.

Security Council consideration (November, December). The Security Council met on 30 November [meeting 6227] to consider the Secretary-General's report. Edmond Mulet, Assistant-Secretary-General for Peacekeeping Operations, noted that a number of Darfur groups, including IDPS, JEM and SLA/Abdul Wahid, continued to express concerns about the holding of elections before the conclusion of a peace agreement, and the start of the elections

registration on 1 November had led to heightened tension in some areas. Mr. Bassolé, the Chief Mediator, said that the refusal of some armed movements to take part in political dialogue and the persistent divisions between others should not be allowed to block the establishment of peace. The Mediation would submit to the belligerent parties for approval the solutions emerging through consensus from all of Darfur's communities. With the genuine popular support of the Darfur people and international assistance, it would be possible to make significant progress towards durable social peace.

On 21 December [meeting 6251], the Council was briefed on the report of the AU High-level Panel on Darfur. Welcoming the report, the Secretary-General said that the Panel members had clearly articulated the links between the crisis in Darfur and broader efforts to implement the CPA. Following the briefing, the Council, by a press statement [SC/9831], agreed with the report that the causes and consequences of the conflict had yet to be addressed, reiterated its call for all parties to fully commit to and participate in peace talks, and called for the Government of the Sudan and other parties in the Sudan and the region to work with President Mbeki and his colleagues.

Year-end developments. In a later report on UNAMID [S/2010/50], the Secretary-General assessed the Mission's progress against the benchmarks of his 16 November report. Two years into its mandate, UNAMID had made significant progress towards full deployment. The seventh tripartite coordination mechanism meeting (Khartoum, 16 November) was attended by the Government of the Sudan, the AU, DPKO, the Department of Field Support and UNAMID. Participants agreed that, as UNAMID reached near-full deployment, the focus of the Mission and the tripartite meetings would shift towards effective employment of troops and police, in particular with regard to the Mission's freedom of movement and measures to reduce criminality and enhance security for UN personnel.

The Darfur Mediation continued its intensive interaction with the parties and with regional and international stakeholders, and engaged with the Government of the Sudan to encourage the implementation of measures to improve the security situation for civilians and to create a climate of trust. In that context, the Government played a constructive role in facilitating the civil society forum (Doha, 17–20 November) in support of the peace process. On 18 November, the Mediation and Qatar began a round of peace talks with all major Darfur communities.

Voter registration was undertaken without major security incidents. In collaboration with local authorities, the NEC established registration centres in five IDP camps in Northern Darfur, four in Southern Darfur and six in Western Darfur. Displaced persons from camps in which registration centres were not located had the option of registering in nearby centres. According to official NEC results, 2,433,920 Darfurians registered—approximately 67 per cent of the voting population according to the 2008 census.

Despite the high turnout, voter registration did not proceed without difficulties as the continued retention of emergency laws restricted freedom of expression, association and assembly. Additional constraints included inadequate civic and voter education, an insufficient number of registration centres, allegations of improper use of State resources and the failure to register domestic observer groups. On 9 November, Khalil Ibrahim, Chairman of JEM, and Ibrahim Al-Helwu, spokesperson of SLA/Abdul Wahid, called on the people of Darfur to boycott the electoral process on the grounds that a comprehensive peace had not been achieved. As a result of the boycott and direct threats to registration officials, voter registration was not conducted in areas controlled by the two movements. Groups sympathetic to the two movements also boycotted the process in other areas of Darfur.

The security situation in certain areas was marked by intermittent military operations between SAF and armed movements. Increasing intercommunal violence and banditry were also of concern, putting civilians at risk and resulting in displacement. Two of the most severe attacks were carried out against Negea, 35 kilometres north-east of Khor Abeche, on 18 November and 23 December, during which 18 civilians were killed, villages burnt and property looted.

Although the redeployment, as a confidence-building measure, of Chadian armed opposition group elements from the border in Western Darfur to areas around Saya and Mellit in Northern Darfur was a welcome development, there were indications that Chadian rebels had contributed to increased insecurity in the areas to which they had been relocated. Locals complained of harassment and human rights abuses by those elements.

Despite the continued absence of an agreed policy framework for the disarmament, demobilization and reintegration of ex-combatants in Darfur, the Government of the Sudan organized a discharge exercise for more than 300 former combatants in El Fasher, Northern Darfur, from 22 to 24 November. While that was a unilateral initiative not linked to any formal programme, UNAMID provided logistical support, including security, transport and health services.

Access restrictions for UNAMID were of concern, and UNAMID personnel were attacked on several occasions. In incidents on 4 and 5 December, five UNAMID peacekeepers were killed and three injured. In a positive development, two UNAMID international staff members who had been held in captivity for 107 days were released without harm on 13 December.

As part of its efforts to address gender-based violence, UNAMID and UN agencies organized between 24 November and 10 December events in connection with the annual international campaign "16 Days of Activism against Gender Violence", including training workshops for lawyers and prison officials.

On 29 October, the Wali of Western Darfur issued a decree establishing a State Human Rights Forum, to be assisted by UNAMID. The Mission also held meetings on human rights concerns with the Government of the Sudan and with government authorities at State level.

UNAMID continued to assist Sudanese prison management, conducted training programmes for 125 Government police and trained 144 movement police personnel. It conducted election security training for 4,625 Government police and 1,400 police recruits and facilitated the construction of four training centres.

The humanitarian workplan for the Sudan was launched in November as part of the 2010 consolidated appeals process. Total distribution of non-food items in 2009 served 586,464 households; more than 20 national and international organizations supported the distribution efforts under UN coordination. During November and December, the World Food Programme and cooperating partners distributed food to approximately 4.2 million people throughout Darfur. The joint verification mechanism for the return of IDPs, established by the High-level Committee in October, was inaugurated on 6 December with the International Organization for Migration and the United Nations High Commissioner for Refugees as the lead organizations. As at December, 262 quick-impact projects had been approved by UNAMID and were in various stages of implementation: 60 per cent of the projects provided support in education and the remaining projects addressed needs in the areas of water, sanitation, health, environment, shelter, agriculture, women's empowerment and income generation.

Despite those developments, a comprehensive and sustainable solution to the humanitarian situation in Darfur had yet to be achieved and conditions conducive to the voluntary return of the more than 2 million displaced persons had not yet been established. Sustaining the presence of the humanitarian community in remote rural areas continued to be a major challenge, particularly in the light of the security situation in some parts, the abduction of humanitarian workers and the obstruction of humanitarian assessment and field missions.

Activities of ICC Prosecutor

Communications. On 10 February [S/2009/99], Cuba transmitted to the Security Council the position agreed on by the Fifteenth Ministerial Conference of the Non-Aligned Movement (NAM) in July 2008 on the application submitted by the ICC Prosecutor against the President of the Sudan, as well as statements on the matter by the AU, LAS and the Organization of the Islamic Conference (OIC), expressing concern that the ICC actions could undermine the ongoing efforts aimed at facilitating the resolution of the conflict in Darfur and the promotion of peace and reconciliation in the Sudan. On 25 February [S/2009/117], Cuba, representing NAM, Oman for the Group of Arab States, Senegal for the Group of African States, and Uganda as Chairman of the OIC Group of States, requested the Council to take measures to defer the ICC-initiated process, to ensure that the peace efforts and the Joint Chief Mediation were not jeopardized and the situation not further inflamed. The Libyan Arab Jamahiriya, on 6 March [S/2009/144], transmitted a communiqué of the 175th meeting of the AU Peace and Security Council (Addis Ababa, 5 March) reaffirming that the ICC process and the Pre-Trial Chamber's decision had the potential to undermine those efforts. Similar views were expressed in a 16 March letter by LAS [S/2009/148] and in a communiqué of the International Muslim Women's Union, transmitted by the Sudan on 25 March [S/2009/162]. Participants in a High-level consultative meeting on Darfur (Khartoum, 17–18 May)—the Sudan, the AU, LAS and OIC—called [S/2009/259] on the Security Council to heed the previous requests regarding the ICC decision on the President of the Sudan; they agreed to combine efforts and intensify contacts with other international and regional groupings to realize that objective.

Briefing by ICC Prosecutor (June). In his briefing to the Security Council on 5 June [meeting 6135], the ICC Prosecutor, Luis Moreno-Ocampo, reported that his Office had impartially collected evidence on massive crimes committed in Darfur, relying on information provided by many actors, including the Government of the Sudan, and on the testimonies of more than 130 witnesses in over 18 countries. In the first case, the Court investigated the massive killings of civilians during 2003–2005, which led to the displacement of 4 million people; the evidence revealed the role of the Minister of State for the Interior, Ahmad Harun, as the coordinator of massive crimes against civilians not participating in the conflict, and the role of Janjaweed militia leader Ali Kushayb in specific attacks. In the second case, the Court covered the same massive crimes against villagers and the continuing crimes against displaced persons in the camps. The evidence showed the role played by President Al-Bashir beginning in 2003, when he ordered the operations against civilians in the villages, through 2005, when he appointed Ahmed Haroun as the Minister of State for Humanitarian Affairs and organized the strangulation of the displaced com-

munities, denying them any meaningful assistance, preventing their return, forcing the United Nations and others to set up the world's largest humanitarian operation and yet obstructing each step of their work.

On 4 March 2009, Pre-Trial Chamber I issued an arrest warrant for five counts of crimes against humanity, including extermination, rapes and killings, and two counts of war crimes against President Al-Bashir. By a two to one vote, the Judges rejected the three genocide charges; the Office appealed and the Pre-Trial Chamber had yet to decide to grant leave to appeal on that topic. The Judges retained the charge of extermination as a crime against humanity. The only difference between extermination and genocide was the latter's requirement that an intention to eliminate a specific group had to be demonstrated, but extermination, before the eyes of the international community, had been happening since at least 2004, with 2.5 million victims so far.

On 7 May, Pre-Trial Chamber I issued a first summons for Bahr Idriss Abu Garda, President of the United Resistance Front (URF), in relation to the Haskanita attacks in September 2007, which had caused the death of 12 AU peacekeepers and left thousands of people without protection [YUN 2007, p. 255]; he appeared in The Hague on 18 May.

The Court had investigated the crimes committed in Darfur over the past six years and had identified six individuals most responsible. Three arrest warrants and one summons had been issued and the Judge's decision on two remaining individuals in the Haskanita case was pending. The hearing for the confirmation of the charges against Mr. Abu Garda was scheduled for 12 October. The arrest warrant concerning President Al-Bashir had been sent to the Sudanese authorities and the Government of the Sudan had the responsibility to arrest him, their legal obligation stemming from the UN Charter and resolution 1593(2005) [YUN 2005, p. 324] by which the Council established the Government's duty to cooperate with the Court. The Government also had the duty to arrest Mr. Harun and Mr. Kushayb, for both of whom the ICC had issued arrest warrants [YUN 2007, p. 259]. The designation of Mr. Harun as Governor of South Kordofan contravened Security Council resolutions. In July 2008, a few days after the Prosecutor had submitted to the Judges an application for an arrest warrant against President Al-Bashir, the Council adopted resolution 1828(2008), which again emphasized the need to bring to justice the perpetrators of such crimes and urged the Government to comply with its obligations.

There were no national proceedings in the Sudan in relation to the massive crimes investigated by the Court. Over the previous six years, the Sudan had tried and completed only seven cases, with no connection to the campaign of crimes coordinated by

Mr. Harun, perpetrated by Mr. Kushayb and others and ordered by President Al-Bashir. The Arab League had been pushing successfully for the adoption of a criminal code in the Sudan that included Rome Statute crimes. The other promises, including the investigation and prosecution of individuals responsible for crimes, no matter what their level or rank, made by the Government of the Sudan to LAS Secretary-General Amre Moussa the past July, could, if fulfilled, help turn the tide in terms of impunity in Darfur. The ICC was a court of last resort, complementary to the national judiciary. Should regional organizations succeed in promoting national accounting mechanisms for the victims of other crimes and stop new abuses, the ICC would not need to intervene further.

Briefing by ICC Prosecutor (December). Briefing the Security Council on 4 December [meeting 6230], the ICC Prosecutor said that there had been positive developments since his June briefing. Judicial proceedings were progressing, cooperation with the AU, LAS and other international bodies had been fruitful, and States and international organizations had maintained consistent support for the execution of the Council's arrest warrants. On 19 November, rebel leader Bahr Abu Garda, the URF President, was the first person to appear in the Court in relation to Darfur crimes. At the initiative of the LAS Secretary-General, international crimes had been included in the Sudanese penal code.

Efforts had converged to encourage the Sudan to respect its responsibilities as a UN Member State, to put an end to crimes and to arrest the persons sought by the Court. During the General Assembly debate in October, 56 States emphasized the importance of cooperation with the Court, including in relation to the arrests. As a consequence, President Al-Bashir, at risk of being arrested, had not travelled to attend the UN General Assembly or high-level events on the territory of States parties (Nigeria, South Africa, Uganda, Venezuela) or other international meetings. That was a way to ensure his marginalization and arrest and would send a clear message.

However, the Sudan refused to cooperate with the Court and crimes continued, in non-compliance with Security Council decisions. President Al-Bashir refused to appear in Court and to appoint a lawyer to represent his position. He also refused to arrest Mr. Kushayb and Mr. Harun. Instead, over the past six months, the President had used the State apparatus to conduct a diplomatic, political and communications campaign against the Court and endeavoured to shift international attention to other pressing issues, such as the conflict with the South. The President was willing to exacerbate such conflict, if it could divert attention from the crimes in Darfur and his responsibility for them.

The Prosecutor said that he would need the Council's full support to ensure that the focus remained on the need to arrest President Al-Bashir and other individuals sought by the Court, and on the need to end the continuing crimes in Darfur. As recently as last week, on 25 November, there were reports of Janjaweed militia attacks against two villages in Northern Darfur, in which civilians were captured, villagers beaten and property looted.

The Prosecutor informed the Council that his Office was reviewing information in four main areas. The first was acts affecting displaced persons, as on 10 November, the Humanitarian Aid Commissioner announced that the Sudanese Government would close the camps for displaced persons by early 2010, without guarantees of access to food and water and without guarantees of security; any forced return of displaced persons in those conditions could constitute a new crime within ICC jurisdiction. The second area was acts against civilians in the camps, including rape, by the forces of President Al-Bashir. Thirdly, the Court was monitoring the use of child soldiers, which was a crime under its jurisdiction. Fourthly, ICC's investigation into the case of President Al-Bashir demonstrated that he used the State apparatus not only to commit massive crimes but also to conceal them, and the Prosecutor's Office was considering the criminal responsibility of Sudanese officials who denied and concealed crimes; they did not benefit from any immunity under the Rome Statute. On 4 March, the ICC Judges had ruled that President Al-Bashir's policy against 2.5 million Sudanese citizens in the camps constituted extermination, as a crime against humanity; the Appeals Chamber was considering whether the charge of genocide should be added.

Instead of stopping the crimes, President Al-Bashir was stopping information about the crimes. The decision to expel humanitarian workers and silence others by threats of expulsion, or the attempts at restricting the freedom of movement of UNAMID were part of a policy to reduce the international community's monitoring capacity. By placing impediments on the movements of peacekeepers, the Government breached the Status of Forces Agreement of UNAMID, which was the last international presence able to keep a protective eye on camps and rural areas and to report on rapes and sexual violence.

Sanctions

The Security Council, by resolution 1556(2004) [YUN 2004, p. 240], imposed an arms embargo on all non-governmental entities and individuals, including the Janjaweed, operating in Darfur. By resolution 1591(2005) [YUN 2005, p. 319], the Council imposed a travel ban and assets freeze, and established a Committee to oversee implementation of the sanctions against individuals to be designated by the Committee. The Secretary-General was requested to appoint a Panel of Experts for six months to assist the work of the Council and the Committee. The Panel, established in June 2005 [ibid., p. 322], was mandated to assist the Committee in monitoring implementation of the arms embargo and sanctions; make recommendations to the Committee on possible Council actions; and provide information on individuals who impeded the peace process, committed violations of international law, or were responsible for offensive military overflights.

Extension of Panel of Experts. In October, the Security Council extended until 15 October 2010 the mandate of the Panel of Experts and requested it to submit during 2010 an interim report and a final report with findings and recommendations. The Panel's mandate had been previously extended by resolutions 1651(2005) [YUN 2005, p. 322], 1665(2006) [YUN 2006, p. 294], 1713(2006) [ibid., p. 295], 1779(2007) [YUN 2007, p. 261] and 1841(2008) [YUN 2008, p. 262].

SECURITY COUNCIL ACTION

On 13 October [meeting 6199], the Security Council unanimously adopted **resolution 1891(2009)**. The draft [S/2009/528] was submitted by the United States.

The Security Council,

Recalling its previous resolutions and the statements by its President concerning the Sudan,

Reaffirming its commitment to the sovereignty, unity, independence and territorial integrity of the Sudan, and recalling the importance of the principles of good-neighbourliness, non-interference and cooperation in the relations among States in the region,

Stressing again its firm commitment to the cause of peace throughout the Sudan, full implementation of the Comprehensive Peace Agreement of 9 January 2005 and, bearing in mind the Darfur Peace Agreement, completion of the political process and an end to the violence and abuses in Darfur,

Reiterating the importance of promoting a political process to restore peace and stability in Darfur, and strongly urging those parties that have not yet agreed to participate in negotiations to do so immediately and all parties to the conflict to engage fully and constructively in the process and to cooperate with the Joint African Union-United Nations Chief Mediator for Darfur, Mr. Djibril Yipènè Bassolé,

Reiterating also the need for a lasting political solution and sustained security in Darfur, and deploring the fact that the Darfur Peace Agreement has not been fully implemented by the signatories and has not been signed by all parties to the conflict in Darfur,

Noting with deep concern the ongoing violence, impunity and consequent deterioration of the humanitarian aid situation and humanitarian access to populations in need, reiterating its deep concern about the security of civilians and humanitarian aid workers, and calling upon all parties in Darfur to cease offensive actions immediately and to refrain from further violent attacks,

Demanding that the parties to the conflict exercise restraint and cease military action of all kinds,

Demanding also an immediate and complete cessation by all parties to armed conflict of all acts of sexual violence against civilians, in line with resolution 1888(2009) of 30 September 2009, recruitment and use of children, in line with resolutions 1612(2005) of 26 July 2005 and 1882(2009) of 4 August 2009, and indiscriminate attacks against civilians,

Commending the efforts of, and reiterating its full support for, the Joint African Union-United Nations Chief Mediator, the United Nations Secretary-General, the League of Arab States and the leaders of the region to promote peace and stability in Darfur, looking forward to the full and effective deployment of the African Union-United Nations Hybrid Operation in Darfur, and expressing its strong support for the political process under the African Union-United Nations-led mediation,

Welcoming the announcement by the Department of Peacekeeping Operations of the Secretariat of its intention to develop guidelines to enhance cooperation and information-sharing between United Nations peacekeeping missions and the expert panels of the Security Council sanctions committees,

Recalling the midterm report of 30 April 2009 of the Panel of Experts on the Sudan, which was appointed by the Secretary-General pursuant to paragraph 3 *(b)* of resolution 1591(2005) of 29 March 2005 and whose mandate was extended by subsequent resolutions, taking note of the final report of the Panel, and expressing its intention to study, through the Security Council Committee established pursuant to paragraph 3 *(a)* of resolution 1591(2005) (hereinafter "the Committee"), the recommendations of the Panel and to consider appropriate next steps,

Expressing concern over the obstacles that have been imposed on the work of the Panel of Experts during the course of its last mandate, including obstacles to freedom of movement,

Emphasizing the need to respect the provisions of the Charter of the United Nations concerning privileges and immunities and the Convention on the Privileges and Immunities of the United Nations, as applicable to United Nations operations and persons engaged in such operations,

Determining that the situation in the Sudan continues to constitute a threat to international peace and security in the region,

Acting under Chapter VII of the Charter,

1. *Decides* to extend until 15 October 2010 the mandate of the Panel of Experts on the Sudan originally appointed pursuant to resolution 1591(2005), which was previously extended by resolutions 1651(2005) of 21 December 2005, 1665(2006) of 29 March 2006, 1713(2006) of 29 September 2006, 1779(2007) of 28 September 2007 and 1841(2008) of 15 October 2008, and requests the Secretary-General to take the necessary administrative measures;

2. *Requests* the Panel of Experts to provide, no later than 31 March 2010, a midterm briefing on its work and, no later than ninety days after the adoption of the present resolution, an interim report to the Committee, and a final

report to the Security Council, no later than thirty days prior to the termination of its mandate, with its findings and recommendations;

3. *Also requests* the Panel of Experts to coordinate its activities, as appropriate, with the operations of the African Union-United Nations Hybrid Operation in Darfur and with international efforts to promote the political process in Darfur, and to assess in its interim and final reports progress towards reducing violations by all parties of the measures imposed by paragraphs 7 and 8 of resolution 1556(2004) of 30 July 2004 and paragraph 7 of resolution 1591(2005) and progress towards removing impediments to the political process, threats to stability in Darfur and the region and other violations of the above-mentioned resolutions;

4. *Urges* all States, relevant United Nations bodies, the African Union and other interested parties to cooperate fully with the Committee and the Panel of Experts, in particular by supplying any information at their disposal on the implementation of the measures imposed by resolutions 1556(2004) and 1591(2005);

5. *Encourages* all States, in particular those in the region, to report to the Committee on the actions they have taken to implement the measures imposed by resolutions 1556(2004) and 1591(2005);

6. *Reaffirms* the mandate of the Committee to encourage dialogue with interested Member States, in particular those in the region, including by inviting representatives of such States to meet with the Committee to discuss the implementation of the measures;

7. *Decides* to remain actively seized of the matter.

Report of Panel of Experts. On 27 October [S/2009/562], the Chairman of the Security Council Committee established pursuant to resolution 1591(2005) transmitted to the Council the final report of the Panel of Experts in response to resolution 1841(2008).

The Panel reported that almost all sides in the Darfur conflict had failed in their obligations to comply with Security Council sanctions and to cooperate with the monitoring efforts of the Panel. Most of the major armed actors had continued to exercise their military options, violate the arms embargo and international humanitarian and human rights law, and impede the peace process. The Darfurian population continued to be affected by attacks and counter-attacks involving most of the armed movements, which frequently led to disproportionate use of force by the Sudanese armed forces and their auxiliary forces, and resulted in killings, injuries and displacements. The women of Darfur continued to suffer from all forms of gender-based violence. The Government of the Sudan continued to move military equipment and supplies into the Darfur region without seeking the prior approval of the Sanctions Committee, as required under resolution 1591(2005); it contended that it was complying with the CPA when it redeployed eight battalions to Darfur and sought UN assistance to transfer an additional four battalions. Among the armed movements, JEM was the most active violator of the arms embargo.

Concerning the travel ban and assets freeze, the Panel had received no replies to its requests to Chad and the Sudan about the implementation of those measures.

The Sudanese Government had failed to take action with regard to: facilitating international relief for the humanitarian disaster by means of a moratorium on all restrictions that might hinder the provision of humanitarian assistance and access to the affected populations; advancing independent investigation of violations of human rights and humanitarian law; establishing security conditions for the protection of the civilian population and humanitarian actors; seeking approval for the transfer of troops and military materiel into Darfur; disarming all the Janjaweed militias and bringing to justice Janjaweed leaders and their associates who had incited and carried out human rights and international humanitarian law violations and other atrocities. The Panel stressed the need for an intensified effort by the Security Council and the Sanctions Committee to secure the cooperation of the Government. As part of such effort, the Panel recommended that the Government be requested to report bimonthly to the Committee on its movements of troops and military materiel into and out of Darfur; on the identity and size of Darfurian tribes that had to be disarmed, and to what degree they were being disarmed and reintegrated; on achievements in or requirements for enhancing the protection of all Darfurians located within the territory under the control of the Government; and on achievements or requirements for the prevention of gender-based violence.

The Panel determined that the overwhelming majority of violent incidents in Darfur had been the result of cross-border military and rebel activities, and that the tensions between Chad and the Sudan caused increasing instability in the region. The Panel recommended that the Security Council explore ways to assist the cross-border monitoring activities of the Dakar Contact Group established to follow up on and implement the 2008 Dakar Agreement between Chad and the Sudan [YUN 2008, p. 268], including by expanding the mandate of UNAMID, providing it with the necessary resources and taking into account the issues of command and control.

The Panel found that certain dual-use products and services offered by arms and ammunition manufacturers, manufacturers of 4x4 vehicles and heavy trucks, air and sea transportation companies, communication services and website providers could affect the ability of the belligerents to perpetrate violence and should be addressed by the Security Council. It recommended that the Council include in future resolutions a call on the private sector to enhance its business conduct guidelines to better promote peace and security in Darfur and other areas of conflict.

Appointment of experts. On 14 December [S/2009/639], the Secretary-General informed the Security Council that, in accordance with resolution 1891(2009), he had appointed four persons to serve on the Panel of Experts until 15 October 2010; a fifth expert would be proposed shortly.

Report of Sanctions Committee. Pursuant to resolution 1591(2005), the Sanctions Committee reported to the Security Council [S/2010/16] on its activities in 2009. In addition, the Chairman, during informal consultations of the whole on 10 March, 19 June, 15 September and 15 December, delivered four 90-day reports on the Committee's activities.

The Committee held eight informal consultations during the year. On 27 January, it heard an interim briefing by the Panel of Experts, and on 3 March, it discussed a progress report by the Panel. Given the non-issuance of a visa by the Government of the Sudan to the arms expert and subsequent lack of UN security clearance owing to security conditions on the ground, the Panel had been unable to visit the Sudan. Thus, it travelled to Chad to pursue secondary priorities of its mandate. On 28 April the Committee exchanged views with the AU-UN Joint Special Representative for Darfur and Head of UNAMID.

On 26 May, the Committee discussed the midterm report of the Panel of Experts, submitted on 30 April and updated on 25 May. The Panel had been able to travel to the Sudan, although without the arms expert, who had not received a visa and who subsequently resigned. The Panel made two recommendations, related to information-sharing between peacekeeping operations and the Panel, and to security clearance for the Panel. On 8 July, the Committee heard an oral progress report by the Panel. On 29 July, the Chairman wrote to a Member State requesting information on behalf of the Panel and asking to facilitate a possible visit by the Panel. The Member State provided information on 6 and 26 August. On 6 and 20 October, respectively, the Panel heard an oral presentation on its final report, as well as on the confidential annex to that report. The Committee discussed the recommendations of the report and agreed to take action on one of them.

While some members of the Committee shared the Panel's assessments of violations and alleged violations of the sanctions regime, others pointed to what they perceived as a "disconnect" between the Panel's reporting of the security situation on the ground and the reports of other bodies, such as UNAMID, which had recorded a decrease in the level of violence. One member expressed concern that the Panel's findings might adversely affect the political process, while others confirmed the need for the Panel's independent presence on the ground.

On 7 December, DPKO briefed the Committee on the provisional guidelines for peacekeeping missions in support of Security Council panels. Those guidelines outlined the support to be provided by the relevant missions in information-sharing, logistics/administrative support and security. The idea of such guidelines had originated in the midterm report of the Panel, following which the Council, by resolution 1891(2009), welcomed DPKO's announcement of the preparation of such a document.

The Committee did not receive requests to remove the names of individuals on the consolidated travel-ban and assets-freeze lists or for exemptions to the targeted sanctions.

UNAMID

The African Union-United Nations Hybrid Operation in Darfur (UNAMID) was established in 2007 by Security Council resolution 1769(2007) [YUN 2007, p. 251] as the first AU-UN hybrid operation. It incorporated the African Union Mission in the Sudan, which had been deployed in Darfur since 2004. The core mandate of UNAMID was to protect civilians, while other tasks included contributing to security for humanitarian assistance, monitoring the implementation of agreements, assisting the political process, promoting human rights and the rule of law, and monitoring the situation along the Sudan's border with Chad (see p. 268) and the Central African Republic.

By resolution 1881(2009) (see p. 255), the Security Council extended UNAMID's mandate for another 12 months.

At the end of 2009, UNAMID military personnel stood at 15,374, out of a total authorized strength of 19,555. UNAMID police numbered 4,575 personnel and the civilian component stood at 3,984.

Appointments. On 22 July [S/2009/382], the Secretary-General informed the Council that he agreed with the appointment by the Chairperson of the AU Commission of Lieutenant General Patrick Nyamvumba (Rwanda) as UNAMID Force Commander with effect from 1 September, succeeding General Martin Luther Agwai (Nigeria) who had served as Force Commander since the establishment of the Mission. The Council took note of the agreement on 24 July [S/2009/383].

On 1 December [S/2009/621], the Secretary-General informed the Council that, following consultations with the Chairperson of the AU Commission, it was their intention to appoint Ibrahim Gambari (Nigeria) as Joint Special Representative for UNAMID with effect from 1 January 2010, to succeed Rodolphe Adada (Congo), who had served in that position from the establishment of the Mission until July 2009. The Council took note of that intention on 3 December [S/2009/622].

OIOS audit

OIOS report. On 2 January [A/63/668], the Office of Internal Oversight Services (OIOS) presented a report on the audit of the use of extraordinary measures for UNAMID, which was conducted from February to May 2008 pursuant to General Assembly resolution 62/232 A [YUN 2007, p. 263]. The Secretary-General had authorized such measures to allow flexibility in administrative policies and procedures in order to expedite and facilitate the deployment of the Mission. Of the 17 measures, six were meant to attract civilian personnel and expedite their deployment to UNAMID, two to facilitate the deployment of military personnel, and nine to enable the procurement of goods and services for the support infrastructure. OIOS found that while some conditions in UNAMID appeared to have justified the waiving of certain administrative requirements, not all of the approved measures were needed to achieve the operational goals. The measures pertaining to human resources did not significantly contribute to expediting recruitment and deployment of staff. The authorization to waive competitive biddings for the $250 million contract awarded to Pacific Architects and Engineers (PAE) for the provision of multifunction logistics services did not remove the Secretariat's responsibility to address accountability for the high level of financial and reputation risks created for the United Nations through that decision. OIOS identified serious weaknesses in the PAE contract and the lack of proper monitoring by UNAMID; it made recommendations to address those weaknesses and strengthen the internal control system, noting that certain corrective action had been taken after the audit. Overall, OIOS determined that the extraordinary measures had a limited impact on UNAMID deployment and had exposed the United Nations to significant financial and reputation risks.

Note of Secretary-General. The Secretary-General on 30 January [A/63/668/Add.1] provided comments and clarifications on the points made by OIOS. He noted that the major risk faced by the Secretariat in implementing the Security Council mandate for UNAMID was that failure to provide extensive facilities on the ground would have caused the Mission to fail; the choice of a sole-source contract solution brought within it risks, but those were judged less onerous than the risk of failing to provide facilities.

ACABQ comments. In its April report [A/63/746/Add.4] on the proposed UNAMID budget for the period from 1 July 2009 to 30 June 2010 (see below), ACABQ recognized the difficulties faced by UNAMID in its start-up phase in a challenging environment, but emphasized that it should take measures to implement the recommendations of the Board of Auditors [A/63/5(Vol. II)] and report on progress in the context of the next budget submission.

On 30 June, by resolution 63/258 B (see below), the General Assembly, taking note of the OIOS report and the Secretary-General's comments, requested him to ensure full implementation of the OIOS recommendations.

Financing

In February [A/63/717], the Secretary-General submitted budget proposals for UNAMID for the period from 1 July 2009 to 30 June 2010, in the amount of $1,789,411,200. The budget provided for the deployment of 240 military observers, 19,315 military personnel, 3,772 UN police officers, 2,660 formed police units personnel, 1,548 international staff and 3,437 national staff. The Secretary-General recommended an assessment of $149,117,600 for the period from 1 to 31 July 2009, and an assessment of $1,640,293,600 at a monthly rate of $149,117,600 should the Security Council decide to continue UNAMID's mandate.

ACABQ in April [A/63/746/Add.4] proposed a reduction of $168,684,100 in the UNAMID budget, taking into account the recommendations of the Board of Auditors [A/63/5(Vol. II)], in particular those concerning defects and delays in the procurement and the management of non-expendable property, as well as those concerning the sole source contract signed with a vendor for logistics services.

GENERAL ASSEMBLY ACTION

On 30 June [meeting 93], the General Assembly, on the recommendation of the Fifth Committee [A/63/647/Add.1], adopted **resolution 63/258 B** without vote [agenda item 148].

Financing of the African Union-United Nations Hybrid Operation in Darfur

The General Assembly,

Having considered the report of the Secretary-General on the financing of the African Union-United Nations Hybrid Operation in Darfur and the related report of the Advisory Committee on Administrative and Budgetary Questions, the report of the Office of Internal Oversight Services on the audit of the use of extraordinary measures for the African Union-United Nations Hybrid Operation in Darfur and the related note by the Secretary-General,

Recalling Security Council resolution 1769(2007) of 31 July 2007, by which the Council established the African Union-United Nations Hybrid Operation in Darfur for an initial period of twelve months as from 31 July 2007, and Council resolution 1828(2008) of 31 July 2008, by which the Council extended the mandate of the Operation until 31 July 2009,

Recalling also its resolution 62/232 A of 22 December 2007 on the financing of the Operation and its subsequent resolutions thereon, the latest of which was resolution 63/258 A of 24 December 2008,

Reaffirming the general principles underlying the financing of United Nations peacekeeping operations, as stated in its resolutions 1874(S-IV) of 27 June 1963, 3101(XXVIII) of 11 December 1973 and 55/235 of 23 December 2000,

Mindful of the fact that it is essential to provide the Operation with the necessary financial resources to enable it to fulfil its responsibilities under the relevant resolutions of the Security Council,

Noting the hybrid nature of the Operation, and in that regard stressing the importance of ensuring full coordination of efforts between the African Union and the United Nations at the strategic level, unity of command at the operational level and clear delegation of authority and accountability lines,

1. *Requests* the Secretary-General to entrust the Head of Operation with the task of formulating future budget proposals in full accordance with the provisions of General Assembly resolutions 59/296 of 22 June 2005, 60/266 of 30 June 2006 and 61/276 of 29 June 2007, as well as other relevant resolutions;

2. *Takes note* of the status of contributions to the African Union-United Nations Hybrid Operation in Darfur as at 30 April 2009, including the contributions outstanding in the amount of 200.0 million United States dollars, representing some 8 per cent of the total assessed contributions, notes with concern that only thirty-seven Member States have paid their assessed contributions in full, and urges all other Member States, in particular those in arrears, to ensure payment of their outstanding assessed contributions;

3. *Expresses its appreciation* to those Member States which have paid their assessed contributions in full, and urges all other Member States to make every possible effort to ensure payment of their assessed contributions to the Operation in full;

4. *Expresses concern* at the financial situation with regard to peacekeeping activities, in particular as regards the reimbursements to troop contributors that bear additional burdens owing to overdue payments by Member States of their assessments;

5. *Also expresses concern* at the delay experienced by the Secretary-General in deploying and providing adequate resources to some recent peacekeeping missions, in particular those in Africa;

6. *Emphasizes* that all future and existing peacekeeping missions shall be given equal and non-discriminatory treatment in respect of financial and administrative arrangements;

7. *Also emphasizes* that all peacekeeping missions shall be provided with adequate resources for the effective and efficient discharge of their respective mandates;

8. *Reiterates its request* to the Secretary-General to make the fullest possible use of facilities and equipment at the United Nations Logistics Base at Brindisi, Italy, in order to minimize the costs of procurement for the Operation;

9. *Acknowledges with appreciation* that the use of the logistics hub in Entebbe, Uganda, has been cost-effective and has resulted in savings for the United Nations, and welcomes the expansion of the logistics hub to provide logistical support to peacekeeping operations in the region and to contribute further to their enhanced efficiency and responsiveness, taking into account the ongoing efforts in this regard;

10. *Requests* the Secretary-General to ensure that proposed peacekeeping budgets are based on the relevant legislative mandates;

11. *Endorses* the conclusions and recommendations contained in the report of the Advisory Committee on Administrative and Budgetary Questions, subject to the provisions of the present resolution, and requests the Secretary-General to ensure their full implementation;

12. *Takes note* of paragraph 52 of the report of the Advisory Committee on Administrative and Budgetary Questions;

13. *Requests* the Secretary-General to take steps to ensure that all personnel adhere fully to the security procedures in place;

14. *Reaffirms* section XX of resolution 61/276, and encourages the Secretary-General, where feasible, to enhance regional and inter-mission cooperation with a view to achieving greater synergies in the use of the resources of the Organization and the implementation of the mandates of the missions, while bearing in mind that individual missions are responsible for the preparation and implementation of their own budgets and for controlling their own assets and logistical operations;

15. *Requests* the Secretary-General to ensure the full implementation of the relevant provisions of its resolutions 59/296, 60/266 and 61/276;

16. *Also requests* the Secretary-General to take all action necessary to ensure that the Operation is administered with a maximum of efficiency and economy;

17. *Further requests* the Secretary-General to ensure that future budget submissions contain sufficient information, explanation and justification of the proposed resource requirements relating to operational costs in order to allow Member States to take well-informed decisions;

18. *Requests* the Secretary-General to ensure that the activities of the Child Protection Unit are carried out in an integrated manner and that its resource requirements are appropriately reflected in the next budget submission;

19. *Also requests* the Secretary-General, in order to reduce the cost of employing General Service staff, to continue efforts to recruit local staff for the Operation against General Service posts, commensurate with the requirements of the Operation;

20. *Takes note* of the report of the Office of Internal Oversight Services and the comments of the Secretary-General thereon, and requests the Secretary-General to ensure the full implementation of the recommendations;

21. *Stresses* the importance of strengthened accountability in the Organization and of ensuring greater accountability of the Secretary-General to Member States, inter alia, for the effective and efficient implementation of legislative mandates on procurement and the related use of financial and human resources, as well as the provision of necessary information on procurement-related matters to enable Member States to make well-informed decisions;

22. *Requests* the Secretary-General to ensure that all procurement projects for the Organization are in full compliance with relevant resolutions;

23. *Also requests* the Secretary-General to ensure that lessons learned from the previous application of flexibility in administrative procedures are fully taken into account and to report thereon in the performance report on the Operation;

24. *Further requests*, in this regard, the Independent Audit Advisory Committee, in accordance with its terms of reference, to advise the General Assembly on measures to ensure the compliance of management with the audit and recommendations of the Office of Internal Oversight Services;

**Budget report for the period
from 1 July 2009 to 30 June 2010**

25. *Decides* to appropriate to the Special Account for the African Union-United Nations Hybrid Operation in Darfur the amount of 1,669,397,800 dollars for the period from 1 July 2009 to 30 June 2010, inclusive of 1,598,942,200 dollars for the maintenance of the Operation, 58,636,200 dollars for the support account for peacekeeping operations and 11,819,400 dollars for the United Nations Logistics Base;

Financing of the appropriation

26. *Also decides* to apportion among Member States the amount of 139,116,483 dollars for the period from 1 to 31 July 2009, in accordance with the levels updated in General Assembly resolution 61/243 of 22 December 2006, and taking into account the scale of assessments for 2009, as set out in its resolution 61/237 of 22 December 2006;

27. *Further decides* that, in accordance with the provisions of its resolution 973(X) of 15 December 1955, there shall be set off against the apportionment among Member States, as provided for in paragraph 26 above, their respective share in the Tax Equalization Fund of 2,694,308 dollars, comprising the estimated staff assessment income of 2,088,358 dollars approved for the Operation, the prorated share of 508,700 dollars of the estimated staff assessment income approved for the support account and the prorated share of 97,250 dollars of the estimated staff assessment income approved for the United Nations Logistics Base;

28. *Decides* to apportion among Member States the amount of 1,530,281,317 dollars for the period from 1 August 2009 to 30 June 2010, at a monthly rate of 139,116,483 dollars, in accordance with the levels updated in resolution 61/243, and taking into account the scale of assessments for 2009, as set out in resolution 61/237, and for 2010, subject to a decision of the Security Council to extend the mandate of the Operation;

29. *Also decides* that, in accordance with the provisions of its resolution 973(X), there shall be set off against the apportionment among Member States, as provided for in paragraph 28 above, their respective share in the Tax Equalization Fund of 29,637,392 dollars, comprising the estimated staff assessment income of 22,971,942 dollars approved for the Operation, the prorated share of 5,595,700 dollars of the estimated staff assessment income approved for the support account and the prorated share of 1,069,750 dollars of the estimated staff assessment income approved for the United Nations Logistics Base;

30. *Emphasizes* that no peacekeeping mission shall be financed by borrowing funds from other active peacekeeping missions;

31. *Encourages* the Secretary-General to continue to take additional measures to ensure the safety and security of all personnel participating in the Operation under the auspices of the United Nations, bearing in mind paragraphs 5 and 6 of Security Council resolution 1502(2003) of 26 August 2003;

32. *Invites* voluntary contributions to the Operation in cash and in the form of services and supplies acceptable to the Secretary-General, to be administered, as appropriate, in accordance with the procedure and practices established by the General Assembly;

33. *Decides* to include in the provisional agenda of its sixty-fourth session the item entitled "Financing of the African Union-United Nations Hybrid Operation in Darfur".

The Assembly, by **decision 64/549** of 24 December decided that the agenda item on UNAMID financing would remain for consideration during its sixty-fourth (2010) session.

Chad–Sudan

In 2009, tensions between the Sudan and Chad remained high and the security situation along the Chad-Sudan border continued to be unpredictable. No progress was made in implementing the Dakar Agreement of 13 March 2008 [YUN 2008, p. 160]. On 3 May in Doha, Qatar, both Governments signed a new agreement under the aegis of Qatar, committing themselves to normalize relations and deny support, in their respective territories, to rebel groups. However, on 4 May, a rebel group made an incursion in eastern Chad, clashing with Government forces. On 5 May, Chad accused the Sudan of sending armed elements into eastern Chad, thus breaching the Doha agreement. The Sudan denied the accusation, stating that it remained committed to the agreement. Chad requested a meeting of the Security Council, which on 8 May called on both countries to respect and implement their commitments in the Doha and previous agreements. Nevertheless, relations between Chad and the Sudan deteriorated further.

Political and security developments

Security Council action. The Security Council on 14 January, by resolution 1861(2009) (see p. 154), encouraged the Central African Republic, Chad and the Sudan to ensure that their territories were not used to undermine the sovereignty of others, to implement the Dakar Agreement and previous agreements, and to cooperate with a view to putting an end to the activities of armed groups in the region and their attempts to seize power by force. The Council welcomed the role played by the Dakar Agreement Contact Group formed under the Dakar Agreement, the Libyan Arab Jamahiriya and the Congo as AU mediators, as well as the AU and the United Nations.

Political developments. However, no progress was made in implementing the Dakar Agreement. The seventh meeting of the Dakar Contact Group, scheduled to take place on 15 February in Khartoum, was delayed until later in the month and then postponed indefinitely. The Sudan subsequently expressed its willingness for the Contact Group to meet in Khartoum before the end of April. However, the situation remained tense as the two Governments continued to accuse each other of supporting armed opposition groups within their territories. On 5 March, the Emir of Qatar, Hamad Ben Kalifa Al-Thani, met with Chadian President Idriss Déby Itno in N'Djamena and offered to provide assistance towards improving relations between Chad and the Sudan, including financial assistance for the deployment of the peace and security force endorsed by the Dakar Agreement. On 3 May, Chad and the Sudan signed a new bilateral agreement in Doha [S/2009/249], pledging to refrain from the use of force against each other, to cease providing support to armed opposition groups and to create an environment conducive to the implementation of previous agreements.

Renewed attacks by armed groups. On 4 May, Chadian armed opposition groups operating under the UFR coalition launched an attack on Chadian territory, with the stated aim of overthrowing the Government and establishing a transitional authority. On 5 May [S/2009/231], Chad accused the Sudan of sending armed elements into eastern Chad, thus breaching the Doha agreement. The Sudan denied the accusation, stating that it remained committed to the agreement. The AU Peace and Security Council [S/2009/242] condemned the attack on 8 May and appealed for the cessation of hostilities.

On 6 May [S/2009/232], Chad requested the convening of a meeting of the Security Council to discuss the attack by the Sudan against Chad, which it said was threatening the peace and security of the subregion and of Chad in particular.

On 8 May [meeting 6121], Dmitry Titov, Officer-in-Charge of DPKO, briefing the Security Council on the situation, reported that, on 26 April, DPKO received unconfirmed reports, including through the United Nations Mission in the Central African Republic and Chad (MINURCAT), of skirmishes between the Chadian security forces and small groups of UFR rebels in eastern Chad. It later received unconfirmed reports of air strikes conducted on 1 and 2 May by the Chadian armed forces on rebel positions near the border with the Sudan. On 4 May, the Secretary-General expressed concern over the build-up and movement of army and rebel forces and called on Chad and the Sudan to immediately ease tensions. The following day, MINURCAT confirmed that the Chadian armed forces were conducting air strikes against a rebel column in

eastern Chad in the area south of Goz Beida. Reports indicated the existence of three main rebel columns: two had moved into eastern Chad and the third remained in a static position across the border. As the situation intensified, the Secretary-General on 6 May expressed his concern and called for respect of the humanitarian character of UN operations and those of UN non-governmental partners in eastern Chad. On 6 and 7 May, MINURCAT reported air strikes targeting one of the rebel columns located south of Goz Beida. Reports were also received of heavy ground engagement between the Chadian army and UFR rebels north of Goz Beida. Meanwhile, the second rebel column was reported to have moved southward to the area of Tissi, near the border with the Central African Republic, and then moved westward towards Am Timan. The deteriorating security situation in eastern Chad prompted humanitarian actors, including three UN agencies and 11 international NGOs, to relocate non-essential staff. The United Nations suspended all activities in several regions of eastern Chad, owing to movement of armed opposition groups in those areas.

SECURITY COUNCIL ACTION

On 8 May [meeting 6122], following consultations among Security Council members, the President made statement **S/PRST/2009/13** on behalf of the Council:

> The Security Council condemns the renewed military incursions in eastern Chad of Chadian armed groups coming from outside.
>
> The Council stresses that any attempt at destabilization of Chad by force is unacceptable. It recalls the terms of the statements by its President of 4 February and 16 June 2008. It reiterates its commitment to the sovereignty, unity, territorial integrity and political independence of Chad. It demands that rebel armed groups cease violence immediately and calls upon all parties to re-engage in dialogue within the framework of the Sirte Agreement of 25 October 2007.
>
> The Council calls upon the Sudan and Chad to respect and fully implement their mutual commitments, in particular in the Doha Agreement of 3 May 2009 and the Dakar Agreement of 13 March 2008, and to engage constructively with the Dakar Agreement Contact Group and the good offices of the Libyan Arab Jamahiriya and Qatar, to normalize their relations, to cooperate to put an end to cross-border activities of armed groups and to strengthen actions to combat illicit arms trafficking in the region, including through the establishment of an effective joint border monitoring. The Council expresses its concern at the external support received by Chadian armed groups, as reported by the Secretary-General.
>
> The Council expresses deep concern at the direct threat the activity of armed groups poses for the safety of the civilian population and the conduct of humanitarian operations. It reiterates its full support for the United Nations Mission in the Central African Republic and Chad, which is mandated to contribute to protecting vulnerable

civilians, including refugees and internally displaced persons, to protect United Nations and associated personnel and to facilitate the delivery of humanitarian assistance.

The Council calls upon all parties to abide by their obligations under international humanitarian law, in particular to respect the security of civilians, including women and children, humanitarian workers and United Nations personnel.

The Council encourages the Chadian authorities in promoting political dialogue, with respect for the constitutional framework, as initiated in the agreement of 13 August 2007.

In July, the Secretary-General reported [S/2009/359] that relations between Chad and the Sudan deteriorated further in the aftermath of the 4 May attack, as both Governments accused each other of supporting rival armed opposition groups. On 13 May, 10,000 people protested in N'Djamena against what was perceived to be an attempt by the Government of the Sudan to destabilize the Government of Chad. On 15 and 16 May, the Chadian air force carried out three raids against Chadian rebels in the area of Mukjar, south of El Geneina in Western Darfur. The Sudan denounced the attacks and stressed its right to respond [S/2009/255]. On 17 May, Chad announced that it had withdrawn its forces after destroying seven rebel bases located as far as 40 kilometres inside Sudanese territory. On 28 and 29 May, reports were received of bombings, allegedly by Sudanese aircraft, in the area of Bahai in eastern Chad. Against that backdrop, no progress was made in implementing the 3 May Doha agreement or the 2008 Dakar agreement. On 25 May, following a meeting with Ahmed bin Abdullah Al-Mahmoud, State Minister for Foreign Affairs of Qatar, President Déby reiterated his readiness to respond positively to Qatar's efforts to end the tension. The previous day, Sudan's President Al-Bashir had also expressed his support for those efforts. The Libyan leader, Colonel Muammar Qadhafi, met separately, on 29 and 30 May, with both Presidents to encourage them to pursue a diplomatic solution.

During the fighting in May, some 22 Government soldiers and 225 rebels were killed and more than 200 rebels captured, including Mahamat Hamouda Bechir, deputy commander of the UFR military wing. The remaining combatants were pushed back to the Sudan, while the third column, which had reached the area around Mangeigne, withdrew and took refuge in Western Darfur.

Communications. On 13 July [S/2009/355], 16 July [S/2009/369] and 3 August [S/2009/400], the Sudan complained about aggressive acts by Chad, allegations which Chad refuted on 6 August [S/2009/408].

Further developments. In October, the Secretary-General reported [S/2009/535] that tensions between Chad and the Sudan remained high and no progress was made towards implementing the Dakar or Doha

commitments. Clashes took place between Chadian and Sudanese armed forces in July and August. On 16 July, reports were received that bombs dropped by Chadian aircraft struck locations in the vicinity of Umm Dukhum, a town in Western Darfur close to the Chadian border. The United Nations was not able to verify those reports. Efforts by Egypt, Libya and Qatar to bring both Governments together continued.

Somalia

Insecurity throughout Somalia remained widespread during the year, despite some progress in implementing the 2008 Djibouti Peace Agreement [YUN 2008, p. 281] that laid out the framework for political cooperation between the Transitional Federal Government and the Alliance for the Re-liberation of Somalia (ARS). The withdrawal of the Ethiopian forces in mid-January, the election of Sheikh Sharif Sheikh Ahmed as President on 30 January and the installation of a new Government at the end of February—reconciliation measures laid out in the Agreement—were positive indicators for the direction of the peace process.

The Transitional Federal Government, however, faced numerous challenges as well as threats from Somali extremists, mainly Al-Shabaab and Hizbul Islam, aided and abetted by foreign fighters, including an attempted coup d'état in May and two deadly attacks carried out by suicide bombers in February and September, killing Burundian and Ugandan peacekeepers as well as others. With the support of the African Union Mission in Somalia (AMISOM), the Government managed to hold strategic positions and government installations in Mogadishu. The Security Council in January expressed its intent to establish a UN peacekeeping operation in Somalia as a follow-on force to AMISOM and in May authorized the extension of AMISOM until 31 January 2010.

The Special Representative of the Secretary-General, Ahmedou Ould-Abdallah, who was leading the United Nations Political Office for Somalia (UNPOS) in consolidating the peace process, advocated for stronger diplomatic support and increased financial backing from regional Governments and the international community to strengthen security. In April, donors pledged more than $200 million at a UN-European Union-sponsored conference (Brussels, 23 April) for the support of Somali security institutions and AMISOM.

Implementation of the peace process gained momentum in August with a conference on "Addressing impunity: towards justice and reconciliation", facilitated by UNPOS, and diplomatic efforts including on the part of the United States, in support of the Government.

Off its shores, high-profile pirate attacks involving large ransoms and increasingly sophisticated equipment continued to focus attention on Somalia. Spurred by Council resolutions to expand measures to counter those attacks, the international community increased anti-piracy efforts, making it riskier for pirate ships to run the gauntlet of naval patrols and managing to reduce the number of successful incidents. The Special Representative maintained that the only durable solution to piracy and overall instability in Somalia was to address its root causes through effective governance, economic development, rule of law and security institutions—all pillars within the framework of the Djibouti Agreement. UNPOS, together with its regional and international partners, continued its work in advancing the implementation of the Agreement.

Political and security developments

The Transitional Federal Government continued to consolidate and expand its support base on three fronts. It intensified efforts to expand its base among the main opposition groups in Mogadishu, consolidated cooperation with the Ahlu Sunna Wal Jama'a (ASWJ) faction and began an in-depth review of its relationship with the "Puntland" regional authorities. On 21 June, the Government signed a cooperation agreement with ASWJ, and on 23 August, a cooperation agreement with the "Puntland" authorities. The political situation in the autonomous region of "Puntland" remained generally calm, despite violent incidents linked to inter-clan fighting, along with abductions and assassinations.

An increasing number of elements from the armed opposition renounced violence and opted to work in partnership with the Government; that included the defection of Mohamed Faruq and Ali Hassan Gheddi, two senior Al-Shabaab operatives, together with some 550 fighters, indicating growing divisions within Al-Shabaab. In a sign of improved functionality, the Government was working on a stabilization programme and the Parliament reconvened on 21 December, after being unable to meet for four months due to the absence from Somalia of several members of Parliament.

In "Somaliland", tension escalated in early September after the National Electoral Commission (NEC) announced a postponement of the presidential election scheduled for 27 September—the fifth deferral of the ballot initially planned for April 2008. The resulting tension eased with the one-month extension of the terms of the President and Vice-President and with the signing on 30 September of a memorandum of understanding between the ruling party, the United People's Democratic Party, and the two opposition parties, the Kulmiye and the

Justice and Welfare Party, which outlined the steps to be taken towards the holding of the presidential elections.

The constitution-making process gathered pace in mid-October with the reconstitution of the Independent Federal Constitutional Commission and the doubling of its membership, including six women commissioners. The International Contact Group (ICG) on Somalia, under the chairmanship of the Special Representative, continued to mobilize support of the reconciliation process. At the Group's meeting in Saudi Arabia on 17 December, the Government presented its strategy for 2010 on reconciliation and outreach; security; holding of an international conference on recovery and reconstruction; and coordination mechanisms between the Government and the international community. The Group reiterated that the Djibouti process remained the framework within which all international efforts should be undertaken, and agreed to hold an international conference on recovery and reconstruction, as specified in the Djibouti Agreement. President Sharif made several visits abroad as part of his efforts to generate financial resources and to brief on his efforts to bring peace and stability. He also held meetings with the Somali diaspora in the United States. In his address to the General Assembly on 25 September [A/64/PV.7], he renewed his appeal for assistance to the Transitional Federal Government and outlined the priorities of his Government: improving security, promoting reconciliation and facilitating the delivery of humanitarian assistance.

SECURITY COUNCIL ACTION

On 16 January [meeting 6068], the Security Council unanimously adopted **resolution 1863(2009)**. The draft [S/2009/37] was submitted by Burkina Faso, Burundi, Italy, the Libyan Arab Jamahiriya, Turkey, Uganda and the United States.

The Security Council,

Recalling its previous resolutions concerning the situation in Somalia, in particular resolutions 733(1992) of 23 January 1992, 751(1992) of 24 April 1992, 1356(2001) of 19 June 2001, 1425(2002) of 22 July 2002, 1519(2003) of 16 December 2003, 1725(2006) of 6 December 2006, 1744(2007) of 20 February 2007, 1772(2007) of 20 August 2007, 1801(2008) of 20 February 2008, 1811(2008) of 29 April 2008, 1814(2008) of 15 May 2008, 1831(2008) of 19 August 2008 and 1844(2008) of 20 November 2008, and the statements by its President, in particular those of 13 July 2006, 22 December 2006, 30 April 2007, 14 June 2007, 19 December 2007 and 4 September 2008,

Reiterating its commitment to a comprehensive and lasting settlement of the situation in Somalia,

Reaffirming its respect for the sovereignty, territorial integrity, political independence and unity of Somalia,

Further reaffirming that the Djibouti peace agreement represents the basis for a resolution of the conflict in Somalia, and stressing the importance of broad-based and representative institutions reached through a political process ultimately inclusive of all,

Welcoming the guiding principles agreed upon by the parties to the Djibouti peace agreement on 25 November 2008, in particular the establishment of a Unity Government and an inclusive Parliament,

Recognizing the need for all parties to contribute to an enhanced political process, calling upon the Somali parties to the Djibouti peace agreement to fulfil their obligations set out therein, and taking note of the request from the parties for United Nations authorization and deployment of an international stabilization force,

Welcoming the contribution of the African Union Mission in Somalia to lasting peace and stability in Somalia, expressing its appreciation for the continued commitment of the Governments of Uganda and Burundi in Somalia, condemning any hostilities towards the Mission, and stressing the importance of re-establishment, training and retention of Somali security forces,

Welcoming also the proposal of the Secretary-General for a partnership between the Somali parties, the United Nations, the Mission and other international partners to develop a programme of assistance to build Somali security capacity,

Reiterating its serious concern at the worsening humanitarian situation in Somalia, and calling upon all Member States to contribute to current and future consolidated humanitarian appeals,

Recognizing that serious crimes have been committed against civilians in the ongoing conflict in Somalia, and reaffirming the importance of the fight against impunity,

Noting the statement and five-point communiqué of the African Union, of 10 and 22 December 2008 respectively, whereby the Peace and Security Council of the African Union calls for an interim stabilization force in anticipation of a United Nations peacekeeping operation in Somalia in order to take over from the Mission and support the long-term stabilization and reconstruction of that country,

Determining that the situation in Somalia constitutes a threat to international peace and security in the region,

Acting under Chapter VII of the Charter of the United Nations,

1. *Welcomes* the decision of the African Union that the African Union Mission in Somalia will remain in Somalia until 16 March 2009, and requests the African Union to maintain the deployment of the Mission in Somalia and to reinforce that deployment to help to achieve the Mission's originally mandated troop strength of 8,000 troops, thereby enhancing the capability of the Mission to carry out its mandate and protect key installations in Mogadishu, including the airport, the seaport and other strategic areas;

2. *Decides* to renew for up to six months from the date of the present resolution the authorization of member States of the African Union to maintain a mission in Somalia, which shall be authorized to take all necessary measures to carry out the mandate set out in paragraph 9 of resolution 1772(2007); and underlines, in particular, that the Mission is authorized to take all necessary measures to provide security for key infrastructure and to contribute, as may be requested and within its capabilities and existing mandate, to the creation of the necessary security conditions for the provision of humanitarian assistance;

3. *Calls upon* the Somali parties and other stakeholders to uphold the principles of the Djibouti peace agreement, to cease hostilities, to ensure without delay unhindered humanitarian access and assistance to the Somali people, to terminate all acts of armed confrontation, to reach agreement on permanent ceasefire mechanisms, and to use the Joint Security Committee to resolve disputes over military issues; and requests the Secretary-General to report on ways to improve the implementation of the Djibouti peace agreement, including the option of an international peace conference to include local, regional and international actors;

4. *Expresses its intent* to establish a United Nations peacekeeping operation in Somalia as a follow-on force to the Mission, subject to a further decision of the Security Council by 1 June 2009;

5. *Requests* the Secretary-General to submit a report for a United Nations peacekeeping operation by 15 April 2009, to include developments in the situation in Somalia, progress towards the full deployment and strengthening of the Mission with a view to transition to a United Nations peacekeeping operation, progress in the political process and security conditions on the ground, in order to inform the Council of his assessment in advance of the decision referred to in paragraph 4 above and with a view to speedy deployment;

6. *Also requests* the Secretary-General, in that report, to develop recommendations on the mandate of such a United Nations peacekeeping operation, taking into account the following tasks in Mogadishu and its environs:

(a) To facilitate humanitarian assistance and improve humanitarian access, including by securing key humanitarian infrastructure and maintaining liaison with all parties to the Djibouti peace agreement and related subsequent agreements, and to facilitate delivery of humanitarian assistance to internally displaced persons, children and other affected persons;

(b) To assist with the free movement, safe passage and protection of those involved in the political process, to provide security for key political infrastructure and to protect and assist the institutions of a future Unity Government to help them to carry out their functions;

(c) To monitor, within its capabilities, the implementation of the cessation of hostilities under the Djibouti peace agreement, as well as any subsequent ceasefire arrangements and joint security arrangements agreed through the Joint Security Committee, to liaise with the Committee and provide technical assistance in the implementation of its functions, including in the investigation of ceasefire violations, and to support the monitoring of illegal weapons traffic by informing the Monitoring Group of any related information;

(d) To ensure the security and freedom of movement of United Nations personnel and to protect its personnel, facilities, installations, equipment and mission;

(e) To assist, in conjunction with regional and international donor partners and other interested parties, in supporting the effective re-establishment, training and retention of inclusive Somali security forces, including military, police and judiciary;

7. *Affirms* that the provisions set out in paragraphs 11 and 12 of resolution 1772(2007) shall continue to apply;

8.   *Requests* the Secretary-General to establish a trust fund to provide financial support to the Mission until a United Nations peacekeeping operation is deployed and to assist in the re-establishment, training and retention of all-inclusive Somali security forces as provided for in paragraph 4 *(c)* of resolution 1744(2007); also requests the Secretary-General to hold a donors conference to solicit contributions to this trust fund as soon as possible; requests the African Union, in consultation with the Secretary-General, to submit budgetary requests to this trust fund; and calls upon Member States to contribute to the trust fund, while noting that the existence of the trust fund does not preclude the conclusion of direct bilateral arrangements in support of the Mission;

9.   *Stresses* the need to create the conditions for the Special Representative of the Secretary-General for Somalia to continue to make progress on the political process;

10.   *Welcomes* the recommendations on strengthening the Mission contained in the letter dated 19 December 2008 from the Secretary-General to the President of the Security Council; recalls that the Council bears primary responsibility for the maintenance of international peace and security and that cooperation with regional and subregional organizations can improve collective security; further recalls that in resolution 1772(2007) it called for planning for possible deployment of a United Nations peacekeeping operation replacing the Mission and that in resolution 1744(2007) it noted that the Mission was intended to contribute to an initial stabilization phase evolving into a possible United Nations operation; welcomes in this regard the proposal of the Secretary-General for immediate in-kind enhancement of the Mission through the transfer of assets following the liquidation of the United Nations Mission in Ethiopia and Eritrea; and requests the Secretary-General, in order for the forces of the Mission to be incorporated into a United Nations peacekeeping operation, to provide a United Nations logistical support package to the Mission, including equipment and services, as described in paragraphs 7 and 8 of his proposal, but not including transfer of funds to the Mission, until 1 June 2009 or until the decision referred to in paragraph 4 above, whichever is earlier;

11.   *Requests* the Secretary-General to oversee the assistance referred to in paragraph 10 above, and further requests the Secretary-General to report no later than 30 January 2009 on the precise equipment and services being provided and to report to the Council at thirty-day intervals thereafter on progress in the deployment of such goods and services;

12.   *Requests* the Mission to ensure that all equipment and services provided by the United Nations pursuant to the present resolution are used in a transparent and effective manner for the purposes intended, and further requests the Mission to report to the Secretary-General on the usage of such equipment and services in a manner to be detailed in a memorandum of understanding between the United Nations and the African Union based on appropriate internal control procedures;

13.   *Requests* the Secretary-General to lend his support to African Union force generation efforts, to continue to support African Union planning and deployment preparations through the Secretariat's Planners team in Addis Ababa and to continue planning, in close cooperation with the African Union, for force generation and logistical, administrative, financial and other arrangements necessary to transition from the Mission to a United Nations peacekeeping operation;

14.   *Calls upon* Member States to contribute personnel, equipment and other resources to the Mission, and encourages Member States to cooperate closely with the African Union, the United Nations, troop-contributing countries and other donors to this end;

15.   *Calls upon* all parties to cooperate fully in the deployment and operations of the Mission, in particular by guaranteeing the safety, security and freedom of movement of African Union and United Nations personnel as well as associated personnel throughout Somalia, and to comply fully with their obligations under international law, including international humanitarian, human rights and refugee law;

16.   *Requests* the Secretary-General, through his Special Representative, to coordinate all activities of the United Nations system in Somalia, to provide good offices and political support for the efforts to establish lasting peace and stability in Somalia and to mobilize resources and support from the international community for both the immediate recovery and the long-term economic development of Somalia; decides that the United Nations Political Office for Somalia and the United Nations country team shall continue to promote lasting peace and stability in Somalia through the implementation of the Djibouti peace agreement and to facilitate coordination of international support to these efforts; and requests the Secretary-General to conduct immediate contingency planning for the deployment of United Nations offices and agencies into Somalia;

17.   *Demands* that all States in the region refrain from any action that might exacerbate instability in Somalia or the Horn of Africa region, and reiterates its intention to take measures against those who seek to prevent or block a peaceful political process, or those who threaten participants in the political process by force, or those who undermine stability in Somalia or the region;

18.   *Calls upon* Member States to contribute to current and future consolidated humanitarian appeals;

19.   *Reaffirms* its resolutions 1325(2000) of 31 October 2000 and 1820(2008) of 19 June 2008 on women and peace and security, and its resolutions 1674(2006) of 28 April 2006 and 1738(2006) of 23 December 2006 on the protection of civilians in armed conflict, and stresses the responsibility of all parties and armed groups in Somalia to take appropriate steps to protect the civilian population in the country, consistent with international humanitarian, human rights and refugee law, in particular by avoiding any indiscriminate or excessive use of force in populated areas;

20.   *Also reaffirms* its resolutions 1539(2004) of 22 April 2004 and 1612(2005) of 26 July 2005 on children and armed conflict, and recalls the subsequent conclusions of the Security Council Working Group on Children and Armed Conflict pertaining to parties to the armed conflict in Somalia;

21.   *Calls upon* the Somali parties to make further progress on establishing joint Transitional Security Forces, which ultimately would assume full responsibility for providing security in Somalia;

22.   *Requests* the Secretary-General to advise urgently on the implementation of his plans to assist the Transitional Federal Government and the Alliance for the Re-liberation of Somalia in developing and coordinating, through his Special Representative, in conjunction with the United Nations Development Programme, other international donors, Member States and the Mission, as appropriate, a coherent strategy and package for command and control, training and equipment to build Somalia's joint Transitional Security Forces and Police to an anticipated strength of some 15,000 personnel, as envisaged in his letter dated 19 December 2008 and in line with the recommendations of the Joint Security Committee of the Transitional Federal Government/Alliance for the Re-liberation of Somalia, as well as rule of law and correctional facilities, and other key areas identified by the Somali parties; and calls upon Member States to contribute to this package;

23.   *Calls upon* Member States, in response to the Secretary-General's letter dated 19 December 2008, to support strengthening and building capacity of the Somali government at the federal, state and local levels, particularly in the areas of institutional development, human resources development, public finance management and accountability processes and support to service delivery;

24.   *Welcomes* the Secretary-General's proposal of 19 December 2008 to establish within the United Nations Political Office for Somalia a dedicated capacity that would include expertise in police and military training, planning for future disarmament, demobilization and reintegration activities and security sector reform activities, as well as a rule of law and corrections component;

25.   *Decides* to remain actively seized of the matter.

Communication. On 30 January [S/2009/60], the Secretary-General informed the Security Council that to assist in building the Somali security and rule-of-law institutions established under the Djibouti peace process, the Secretariat had deployed a technical assistance mission, jointly led by UNPOS and DPKO, to assess the logistical, security and other operational conditions in Somalia, as well as the support capacity of AMISOM. The assessment revealed that the support AMISOM had been receiving was very basic and AMISOM was highly dependent on donor funding, which added a high degree of uncertainty. To meet the needs of the full AMISOM deployment of 8,000 authorized troops, efforts would focus on the establishment of more comprehensive support solutions; new support solutions under Council resolution 1863(2009) would comply with UN standards and be capable of rapid expansion to meet the needs of a full UN peacekeeping deployment, should one be authorized by the Council. The Department of Field Support was identifying fast-track measures. The logistics support package formed only one part of the assistance required to enable AMISOM to remain in place and build up its troop strength to its authorized level of 8,000. Subject to budgetary approval by the General Assembly in March, the United Nations would begin to deliver quick wins and elements of logistical support in the second quarter of 2009.

The mission's recommendations were aimed at enhancing the capacity of UNPOS to support the Djibouti process, coordinate with UNDP and assist in developing the security sector, human rights, justice and corrections, disarmament, demobilization and re-integration, and mine action. They also reflected the assistance required from bilateral partners in developing transitional security institutions.

Election of interim President. The Security Council, by a press statement of 3 February [SC/9588], welcomed the election by the Transitional Federal Parliament on 30 January of Sheikh Sharif Sheikh Ahmed as President of Somalia. The Council called upon the President to constitute a Government of National Unity at the earliest possible date.

Report of Secretary-General (March). Pursuant to presidential statement S/PRST/2001/30 [YUN 2001, p. 210], the Secretary-General in March submitted a report [S/2009/132] on the situation in Somalia, covering developments since his November 2008 report [YUN 2008, p. 282], with particular focus on progress made in the Djibouti peace process.

Following the resignation of President Abdullahi Yusuf Ahmed in December 2008 [ibid., p. 285], the Speaker of Parliament assumed the presidency in an acting capacity and on 12 January 2009 announced the formation of a Parliamentary Committee for the Presidential Election. On 26 January, the Transitional Federal Parliament voted in favour of an expansion by 275 seats, with 200 seats allocated to ARS and the remaining 75 reserved for members of civil society, businesspeople, women, the diaspora and opposition groups. On 27 January, the Parliament amended the Transitional Federal Charter in order to extend its mandate until August 2011. On 30 January, after two rounds of voting in Djibouti, the expanded Parliament elected the ARS Chairman, Sheikh Sharif Sheikh Ahmed, as the country's new interim President. On 13 February, the President appointed Omar Abdirashid Ali Sharmarke as the new Prime Minister. On 20 February, the Prime Minister announced the formation of a 36-member Cabinet, which Parliament endorsed on 21 February. On 23 February, President Ahmed returned to Mogadishu.

After the withdrawal of Ethiopian forces from Mogadishu in mid-January, in fulfilment of the 2008 ceasefire agreement [YUN 2008, p. 283], the Government and ARS, in a joint statement, called on the United Nations to deploy peacekeepers to Somalia. Following the Ethiopian withdrawal, traditional leaders of the Mudulood, the dominant Hawiye sub-clan in Mogadishu, reportedly warned that they would not tolerate the continuation of the insurgency. The elders and religious leaders urged residents to bury their differences and work towards peace, and women's groups in Mogadishu were said to have added their voice to the elders' appeal against attacking AMISOM troops. Meanwhile, the Al-Shabaab insurgent group, which opposed the Djibouti process, had taken control of Baidoa. The fall of Baidoa and the seizure of the Parliament building was a setback for the newly expanded Parliament. Al-Shabaab did not, however, overrun the country following the Ethiopian withdrawal as had been feared. A number of new militias, which were either clan- or religion-based, such as Al-Sunna wa-al-Jamaa, had emerged and were opposing Al-Shabaab, which reportedly commanded little popular support. Nevertheless, Al-Shabaab had vowed to continue with the insurgency and reiterated its opposition to the peace process.

The withdrawal of Ethiopian troops put further pressure on AMISOM, which continued to provide security at vital installations, including the airport, the seaport and the presidential palace. However, AMISOM would not be able to expand its area of operations or fully execute its mandate until it was strengthened in line with Council resolution 1863(2009), the Secretary-General said, and it was likely to remain the focus of insurgent attacks by Al-Shabaab.

On 8 January, "Puntland" elected as its new President Abdirahman Muhammad Farole, who, in a letter of 22 January to the Special Representative, reaffirmed the support of "Puntland" for any "legitimate, meaningful and representative reconciliation of the Somali people" and pledged to work with the new Administration of President Ahmed.

The security situation remained volatile as insurgent forces gained control over additional towns and territory, although they increasingly faced armed resistance from clans and local militias. Reports of civilians killed in crossfire increased and insurgent attacks against AMISOM intensified following the Ethiopian withdrawal; during the deadliest of them, on 22 February, 11 Burundian peacekeepers were killed and others injured. Beyond Mogadishu, insurgent forces consolidated their presence in the Lower Shabelle region and expanded further into the Bay and Gedo regions. Al-Shabaab forces were said to have been expelled from most towns in the Galgaduud region.

Given the continuing attacks against humanitarian workers, the United Nations was forced to reduce personnel and programme activity. In January, two World Food Programme (WFP) staff members were murdered in separate incidents, increasing to eight the number of UN staff members killed in the past 12 months. One UN staff member remained in captivity after having been taken hostage in June 2008. Nevertheless, the United Nations continued to provide support for institutional development and capacity-building, which was consolidated into a comprehensive framework launched in January, focusing on policy and law-making; budget-making and public finance management; human resources development; and infrastructure support.

The expansion of Parliament and subsequent peaceful election of Sheikh Sharif Sheikh Ahmed as the new interim President was clear testimony to the commitment of the parties to move forward with national reconciliation, the Secretary-General observed. The President had already stated his intention to reach out to other groups opposed to the Djibouti process. The human rights situation continued to be precarious, having a negative impact on the lives of civilians.

The proposed support to AMISOM and assistance in building security and rule-of-law institutions, together with the efforts of the Special Representative on the political front and the activities of the UN country team, constituted key elements of a comprehensive UN strategy to address the crisis, whose main objectives were: to enable AMISOM to sustain its operation, attain its authorized full strength of 8,000 troops and 270 police personnel and bring its contingents up to UN standards; to give AMISOM and the Somali security institutions the capacity to create a minimum level of security that would enable the Djibouti peace process and UNPOS to relocate to Somalia; to create an environment that mitigated the risks facing the UN country team and other humanitarian actors; and to promote respect for human rights. As requested by resolution 1863(2009), the Secretary-General intended to provide further recommendations on the deployment of a peacekeeping operation by 15 April.

Security Council consideration (March). On 20 March [meeting 6095], the Security Council met to consider the Secretary-General's report. Speaking before the Council, the Special Representative called for a 100-day assistance programme focusing on employment, renovation of infrastructure and humanitarian assistance, with simultaneous assistance to governance, security and development. Now that State legitimacy was established and the legality of new institutions recognized regionally, internationally and by the vast majority of Somalis, and the President, the Speaker, the Prime Minister, the Cabinet and Parliament were back in Mogadishu, the new seriousness of purpose invited the international community to back the progress being made through practical actions including immediate support for the new authorities; diplomatic and financial assistance to AMISOM; unhindered delivery of humanitarian assistance; dealing with the matter of individuals on the Security Council sanctions list; addressing impunity; and fighting piracy off the Somali coast.

Somalia said that over the past four weeks, the Government had taken five essential actions to lay the foundations for its programme of peace and reconciliation: the immediate and irreversible assumption of the seat of government in Mogadishu; the integration

of forces of the Government and ARS into the Joint
Security Force; the mobilization of the Somali people
in support of the peace process; the re-establishment
of the authority of the State and the rule of law in the
economy; and the re-establishment of dialogue with
the international community. Somalia welcomed the
commitment to establish a UN peacekeeping force
and confirmed that a number of benchmarks detailed
in the Secretary-General's report were already in place.

Report of Secretary-General (April). Pursuant to
Security Council resolution 1863(2009), the Secretary-
General, in a report of 16 April [S/2009/210], said that
the security situation remained extremely volatile and
unpredictable, as the realignment of armed factions
and groups continued. In some areas, popular support
for the insurgency seemed to be waning, but insurgent
attacks continued and reports of a new influx of foreign fighters allied to radical groups were of concern.
Insurgent attacks against AMISOM were becoming
more coordinated and lethal. Attacks also continued
against government officials; on 26 March, a roadside
bomb explosion struck the vehicle of the new Interior
Minister, killing one bodyguard and two civilians;
on 16 March, in Wajid, 280 kilometres north-west of
Mogadishu, four UN staff members were abducted,
but later released unharmed. In a memorandum to
the Prime Minister, traditional leaders recommended
that no additional AMISOM troops be deployed, that
AMISOM depart within 120 days and that no UN
troops enter Somalia.

Al-Shabaab and allied insurgent factions continued
to control large parts of south and central Somalia, although the popularity of Al-Shabaab appeared weakened, since two pillars of its political platform had
been removed by the withdrawal of Ethiopian forces
and the decision of the new Government on 10 March
to institute sharia law.

Popular resistance to the insurgency was more
frequently reported, but Al-Shabaab forces defeated
government forces in the northern town of Xuddur.
On 20 March, the leader of ARS (Asmara), Sheikh
Hassan Aweys, rejected the call, made in a recorded
statement by Osama bin Laden, for Somalis to topple
the Government.

UN activities in Somalia were scaled up, with international staff increased from 50 to 85, while national
staff reached approximately 800. Several critical programmes in Mogadishu were maintained by a small
number of national staff, but there was no international UN staff in the capital. International staff had
begun to return to Jawhar and to conduct missions
to Beledweyne, but a further significant expansion of
UN activities would necessitate more robust security
arrangements. Missions by UN international staff,
suspended in June 2008, resumed, although their
frequency and duration remained limited.

Owing to the combined effects of drought, conflict,
inflation and continued lack of access, the humanitarian crisis was deepening, with some 3.25 million
people in need of assistance. The human rights situation remained precarious, particularly with regard
to security, and civilians continued to risk death and
injury as a result of fighting between different groups
and the use of explosive devices. Attempted assassinations continued, targeting clerics and journalists,
among others. Grave violations against children and
women included the recruitment and use of children,
killing and maiming, indiscriminate or excessive use
of force, and rape and other forms of violence. Arbitrary arrests and detentions, and executions following
proceedings by Islamic courts, had been documented.
The reconciliation efforts initiated by the President
and the Government, while attracting concrete support from the population, had also brought about
counteractions, including increased attacks and attempts at political destabilization.

The political progress and opportunities for peace
deserved the international community's generous
and sustained support, the Secretary-General said.
While the deployment of a multidimensional UN
peacekeeping operation should remain the goal, he
recommended an incremental, three-phased approach
to addressing the ongoing security challenge: first, by
supporting the establishment of security institutions
and strengthening AMISOM; secondly, by establishing
a UN "light footprint" in Somalia; and thirdly, by
deploying, at an appropriate time, a UN peacekeeping operation.

To sustain its reconciliation efforts and extend its
authority on the ground, the Government required
international support and needed to be able to show to
the population the benefits of supporting the process,
including the creation of livelihoods, the provision of
basic services, the establishment of a more effective
revenue stream, and the rebuilding of its institutions
and infrastructure.

Communication. On 17 April [S/2009/213],
Eritrea transmitted a press statement affirming that
Governments fabricated or installed externally under
various labels of "transition" outside the due process
of law and contrary to the wishes of the Somali people
could not be imbued with legitimacy and recognition
as the duly constituted Government of a sovereign
Somalia. It was the right of, and incumbent upon,
the whole Somali people to determine the issues of
"Somaliland", "Puntland" or other lands by exercising their free will. That could not be usurped by any
other party, and the United Nations and the Security
Council did not have the authority or responsibility to
recognize and accept those dispersed "lands" outside,
or against the will of, the Somali people.

Security Council consideration. The Security Council met on 13 May [meeting 6124] to discuss the Secretary-General's 16 April report. Addressing the Council, the Under-Secretary-General for Political Affairs, B. Lynn Pascoe, said that despite the heavy fighting of the past few days, as Sheikh Hassan Dahir Aweys, with the help of Al-Shabaab fighters and international fighters, attempted to overthrow the Government, there were new reasons for hope as the peace process, facilitated by the Special Representative, produced a broad-based Government that enjoyed the support of large segments of the population and States members of the Intergovernmental Authority on Development (IGAD). The new Government was reaching out to opposition groups to forge national reconciliation. In order to assist Somalia to consolidate its still fragile peace process and lay the foundation for sustainable peace, reconstruction and development, the Secretary-General had elaborated a political strategy aimed at importing the peace process from Djibouti to Somalia; assisting the Transitional Federal Government to enhance the dialogue with opposition forces and build a critical mass in supporting the peace process; and consolidating the Transitional Federal Institutions. The success of the Brussels donor conference gave ground for hope; it was imperative that assistance reached the Government and AMISOM quickly in order to limit the ability of hardliners to threaten the efforts to build a Somali State.

SECURITY COUNCIL ACTION

On 15 May [meeting 6125], following consultations among Security Council members, the President made statement **S/PRST/2009/15** on behalf of the Council:

The Security Council reiterates its previous resolutions and the statements by its President on Somalia, in particular its resolution 1863(2009), which reaffirmed the Djibouti peace agreement as representing the basis for a lasting resolution of the conflict in Somalia.

The Council reaffirms its support for the Transitional Federal Government as the legitimate authority in Somalia under the Transitional Federal Charter and condemns the recent renewal in fighting led by Al-Shabaab and other extremists, which constitutes an attempt to remove that legitimate authority by force. The Council demands that opposition groups immediately end their offensive, put down their arms, renounce violence and join reconciliation efforts.

The Council urges the international community to provide its full support to the Transitional Federal Government in order to strengthen the National Security Force and the Somalia Police Force, reiterates its support for the African Union Mission in Somalia, expresses its appreciation for the contribution of troops by the Governments of Burundi and Uganda, and condemns any hostilities towards the Mission.

The Council expresses its concern at the loss of life and the worsening humanitarian situation arising out of the renewed fighting, and calls upon all parties to abide by their obligations under international humanitarian law, in particular to respect the security of civilians, humanitarian workers and Mission personnel.

The Council also expresses its concern over reports that Eritrea has supplied arms to those opposing the Transitional Federal Government of Somalia in breach of the United Nations arms embargo, and calls upon the sanctions monitoring group to investigate.

The Council reiterates its support for the political process outlined in the Transitional Federal Charter, which provides a framework for reaching a lasting political solution in Somalia. The ongoing attempts to take power by force can only delay the political process and prolong the suffering of the Somali people.

Communications. On 19 May [S/2009/256], Eritrea categorically rejected what it called unsubstantiated accusations against it in paragraph five of S/PRST/2009/15. Ethiopia's invasion of Somalia at the beginning of 2007, with the Security Council's endorsement, to prop up the previous "Transitional Government", had entailed two years of chaos and mayhem; "Transitional Governments" periodically hatched outside Somalia had never survived the test of time in spite of huge external military and financial support, which had further added fuel to the simmering conflicts.

On 20 May [S/2009/260], Ethiopia brought to the Council's attention a communiqué of the thirty-third extraordinary session of the IGAD Council of Ministers on the security and political situation in Somalia, which condemned Eritrea for its support to "criminal elements" in Somalia and called upon the Council to impose sanctions on Eritrea. IGAD's call for action against Eritrea was endorsed on 22 May in a communiqué by the AU Peace and Security Council.

Extension of AMISOM authorization

The Security Council on 26 May authorized AU members to maintain AMISOM until 31 January 2010.

SECURITY COUNCIL ACTION

On 26 May [meeting 6127], the Security Council unanimously adopted **resolution 1872(2009)**. The draft [S/2009/266] was submitted by the United Kingdom.

The Security Council,

Recalling all its previous resolutions and the statements by its President concerning the situation in Somalia,

Recalling also its resolutions 1325(2000) of 31 October 2000 and 1820(2008) of 19 June 2008 on women and peace and security, its resolutions 1674(2006) of 28 April 2006 and 1738(2006) of 23 December 2006 on the protection of civilians in armed conflict and its resolutions 1539(2004) of 22 April 2004 and 1612(2005) of 26 July 2005 on children and armed conflict,

Reaffirming its respect for the sovereignty, territorial integrity, political independence and unity of Somalia,

Reiterating its commitment to a comprehensive and lasting settlement of the situation in Somalia,

Further reaffirming that the Djibouti agreement represents the basis for a resolution of the conflict in Somalia, and stressing the importance of broad-based and representative institutions reached through a political process ultimately inclusive of all,

Welcoming in this regard the election by the Transitional Federal Parliament of Sheikh Sharif Sheikh Ahmed as President of Somalia, the subsequent appointment of a new Unity Cabinet under the Transitional Federal Government, and its relocation to Mogadishu,

Commending the contribution of the African Union Mission in Somalia to lasting peace and stability in Somalia, expressing its appreciation for the continued commitment of troops to the Mission by the Governments of Uganda and Burundi, and condemning any hostilities towards the Mission and the Transitional Federal Government,

Commending the Special Representative of the Secretary-General for Somalia, Mr. Ahmedou Ould-Abdallah, and reaffirming its strong support for his efforts,

Stressing the importance of the re-establishment, training, equipping and retention of Somali security forces, which is vital for the long-term stability of Somalia, and welcoming President Sheikh Sharif Sheikh Ahmed's focus on peace through strengthening of the security sector, as his Government's leading priority,

Reiterating its serious concern at the renewed fighting in Somalia, and reaffirming its support for the Transitional Federal Government,

Reiterating its serious concern also at the worsening humanitarian situation in Somalia, and calling upon all Member States to contribute to current and future consolidated humanitarian appeals,

Recognizing the commitment of the Transitional Federal Government to address the humanitarian situation in Somalia, and encouraging it to continue to work with the United Nations to build the capacity of its institutions to this end,

Expressing its concern that serious crimes, in particular killing and maiming, have been committed against civilians and humanitarian staff in the ongoing conflict in Somalia, and reaffirming the importance of the fight against impunity,

Recalling its resolution 1844(2008) of 20 November 2008 imposing measures against those individuals or entities who have been designated as engaging in or providing support for acts that threaten the peace, security or stability of Somalia, acting in violation of the arms embargo or obstructing humanitarian assistance to Somalia,

Recognizing that the ongoing instability in Somalia contributes to the problem of piracy and armed robbery at sea off the coast of Somalia, stressing the need for a comprehensive response by the international community to tackle piracy and its underlying causes, and welcoming the efforts of the Contact Group on Piracy off the Coast of Somalia, States and international and regional organizations,

Welcoming the report of the Secretary-General and the recommendations contained therein for continued action

on the political, security and recovery tracks by the Transitional Federal Government with the support of the international community,

Determining that the situation in Somalia constitutes a threat to international peace and security in the region,

Acting under Chapter VII of the Charter of the United Nations,

1. *Calls upon* all Somali parties to support the Djibouti agreement, and welcomes in this regard President Sheikh Sharif Sheikh Ahmed's call for all opposition groups to support this process;

2. *Requests* the Secretary-General, through his Special Representative for Somalia, to work with the international community to continue to facilitate reconciliation;

3. *Also requests* the Secretary-General to include in his next report recommendations on ways to strengthen the Djibouti peace process;

4. *Underlines* the crucial importance of all parties taking appropriate measures to ensure, without delay, unhindered humanitarian access and assistance to the Somali people;

5. *Condemns* the recent resurgence in fighting, and calls for the end of all hostilities, acts of armed confrontation and efforts to undermine the Transitional Federal Government;

6. *Emphasizes* that Somalia's long-term security rests with the effective development by the Transitional Federal Government of the National Security Force and the Somalia Police Force, within the framework of the Djibouti agreement and in line with a national security strategy;

7. *Welcomes* the International Conference in support of the Somali Security Institutions and the African Union Mission in Somalia, held in Brussels on 23 April 2009;

8. *Urges* Member States and regional and international organizations to contribute generously to the United Nations trust fund for the Somali security institutions, and to offer technical assistance for the training and equipping of the Somali security forces, consistent with paragraphs 11 *(b)* and 12 of resolution 1772(2007) of 20 August 2007;

9. *Requests* the Secretary-General to continue to assist the Transitional Federal Government in developing the transitional security institutions, including the Somalia Police Force and the National Security Force, and further requests the Secretary-General to support the Transitional Federal Government in developing a national security strategy, including plans for combating illicit arms trafficking, disarmament, demobilization and reintegration, and justice and corrections capacities;

10. *Calls upon* the Transitional Federal Government to develop, in the context of the national security strategy outlined above, the legal and policy framework for the operation of its security forces, including governance, vetting and oversight mechanisms, ensuring respect for the rule of law and the protection of human rights;

11. *Recalls* its statement of intent regarding the establishment of a United Nations peacekeeping operation as expressed in resolution 1863(2009) of 16 January 2009;

12. *Notes* that any decision to deploy such an operation would take into account, inter alia, the conditions set out in the report of the Secretary-General;

13. *Requests* the Secretary-General to take the steps identified in his report in paragraphs 82 to 86, subject to the conditions set out in his report, and to report on progress by 30 September 2009, and again by 31 December 2009; and expresses its intention to review the situation;

14. *Affirms* that the measures imposed by paragraph 5 of resolution 733(1992) of 23 January 1992 and further elaborated upon in paragraphs 1 and 2 of resolution 1425(2002) of 22 July 2002 shall not apply to supplies and technical assistance provided in accordance with paragraph 11 *(b)* of resolution 1772(2007) to the Transitional Federal Government for the purposes of the development of its security sector institutions, consistent with the Djibouti peace process and subject to the notification procedure set out in paragraph 12 of resolution 1772(2007);

15. *Requests* the African Union to maintain and enhance the deployment of the African Union Mission in Somalia in order to carry out its mandate as set out in paragraph 9 of resolution 1772(2007), welcomes its efforts to protect the airport, seaport and other strategic areas in Mogadishu, and encourages it to continue to assist the Transitional Federal Government in the establishment of the National Security Force and the Somalia Police Force;

16. *Decides* to authorize the member States of the African Union to maintain the Mission until 31 January 2010 to carry out its existing mandate;

17. *Requests* the Secretary-General to continue to provide a logistical support package for the Mission comprising equipment and services but not including the transfer of funds, as described in his letter dated 30 January 2009 to the President of the Security Council, to the Mission, until 31 January 2010; and further requests the Secretary-General to include in the reports requested in paragraph 13 above an update on the deployment of this package;

18. *Requests* the Mission to ensure that all equipment and services provided under the support package are used in a transparent and effective manner for their designated purposes, and further requests the African Union to report to the Secretary-General on the usage of such equipment and services in accordance with the memorandum of understanding to be established between the United Nations and the African Union based on appropriate internal control procedures;

19. *Requests* the Secretary-General to continue to provide technical and expert advice to the African Union in the planning and deployment of the Mission through the existing United Nations planning team in Addis Ababa;

20. *Urges* Member States and regional and international organizations to contribute generously to the United Nations trust fund for the Mission, while noting that the existence of the trust fund does not preclude the conclusion of direct bilateral arrangements in support of the Mission;

21. *Requests* the Secretary-General, through his Special Representative and the United Nations Political Office for Somalia, to coordinate effectively and develop an integrated approach to all activities of the United Nations system in Somalia, to provide good offices and political support for the efforts to establish lasting peace and stability in Somalia

and to mobilize resources and support from the international community for both the immediate recovery and the long-term economic development of Somalia;

22. *Also requests* the Secretary-General, through his Special Representative and the United Nations Political Office for Somalia, to work with the Transitional Federal Government to develop its capacity to address human rights issues and to support the Justice and Reconciliation Working Group to counter impunity;

23. *Further requests* the Secretary-General to expedite the proposed deployment of elements of the United Nations Political Office for Somalia and other United Nations offices and agencies, including the United Nations Support Office for the African Union Mission in Somalia, to Mogadishu consistent with the security conditions, as outlined in his report;

24. *Decides* to remain actively seized of the matter.

Declaration of state of emergency

In early May, intense fighting flared up again between insurgent groups and government forces, particularly in Mogadishu, taking a severe toll on the civilian population and displacing more than 200,000. Targeted killings by insurgent groups culminated in the assassination on 18 June of the Minister of National Security, Omar Hashi Aden; more than 30 others were killed in the attack. On 22 June, the Government declared a state of emergency, following a Cabinet meeting that concluded that the increased attacks posed a serious threat to the country.

The AU, at is thirteenth summit (Sirte, Libyan Arab Jamahiriya, 1–3 July) [Assembly/AU/Dec.252(XIII)], called on the Security Council to impose sanctions against all foreign actors, both within and outside the region, especially Eritrea, providing support to the armed groups engaged in destabilizing Somalia and undermining the peace and reconciliation efforts.

Security Council consideration. On 9 July [meeting 6158], the Security Council met to consider the situation in Somalia which, according to the Under-Secretary-General for Political Affairs, Mr. Pascoe, remained very fragile as the Government continued to face intense pressure from insurgent forces, backed by foreign fighters, who sought to seize power. While the Government attempted to win the hearts and minds of the people and to project a moderate vision of Islam in keeping with Somali culture, Al-Shabaab appeared to have intensified its strategy of coercion and intimidation, using targeted assassinations of clan elders and government officials and harsh punishments for seemingly minor offences.

SECURITY COUNCIL ACTION

On 9 July [meeting 6158], following consultations among Security Council members, the President made statement **S/PRST/2009/19** on behalf of the Council.

The Security Council reiterates its previous resolutions and the statements by its President on Somalia, in particular its resolution 1872(2009), in which it reaffirmed the Djibouti agreement as the basis for a resolution of the conflict in Somalia.

The Council reiterates its support for the Djibouti peace process outlined in the Transitional Federal Charter, which provides a framework for reaching a lasting political solution in Somalia. The Council reaffirms its support for the Transitional Federal Government as the legitimate authority in Somalia under the Transitional Federal Charter and notes the declaration on 22 June 2009 of a state of emergency as a result of the recent renewal in fighting led by Al-Shabaab and other violent opposition groups, which constitutes an attempt to remove that legitimate authority by force. The Council also reiterates its support for the Special Representative of the Secretary-General for Somalia, Mr. Ahmedou Ould-Abdallah, for his efforts towards advancing the political process in Somalia.

The Council condemns the recent attacks on the Transitional Federal Government and the civilian population by armed groups and foreign fighters who undermine peace and stability in Somalia. The Council reaffirms its demand of 15 May 2009 that violent opposition groups immediately end their offensive, put down their arms, renounce violence and join reconciliation efforts. The Council condemns the flow of foreign fighters into Somalia.

The Council deplores the loss of life in Somalia and the deteriorating humanitarian situation, which has resulted in increased flows of refugees and internally displaced persons, threatening stability in the region. The Council calls upon all parties to abide by their obligations under international humanitarian law, in particular to respect the security of civilians, humanitarian workers and personnel of the African Union Mission in Somalia.

The Council reaffirms that Somalia's long-term security rests with the effective development by the Transitional Federal Government of the National Security Force and the Somalia Police Force, within the framework of the Djibouti agreement and in line with a national security strategy, and urges the international community to support the Somali security institutions, including through training and equipping.

The Council commends the contribution of the Mission to lasting peace and stability in Somalia, expresses its continued appreciation for the commitment of troops to the Mission by the Governments of Uganda and Burundi, and condemns any hostilities towards the Mission. In this context the Council welcomes the decision of the African Union at its summit, held in Sirte, Libyan Arab Jamahiriya, on 3 July 2009, to increase the strength of the Mission to its mandated troop levels and its call for member States of the African Union to provide the necessary military and police personnel.

The Council takes note of the decision of the African Union at its summit in Sirte calling upon the Council to impose sanctions against those, including Eritrea, providing support to the armed groups engaged in undermining peace and reconciliation in Somalia and regional stability. The Council is deeply concerned in this regard and will consider expeditiously what action to take against any party undermining the Djibouti peace process, based on all available evidence, including that submitted to the Monitoring Group and the Committee established pursuant to resolution 751(1992).

Further developments

Following their unsuccessful assaults against the Government in May and June, insurgents led by Al-Shabaab and Hizbul Islam reinforced their ranks with militia outside Mogadishu and foreign fighters. In the second week of July, those groups launched a full-scale attack on key strategic positions, aimed at dislodging the Transitional Federal Government. Fighting raged for several days, culminating in fierce battles on 12 July. Insurgents came within 300 metres of the presidential palace and attempted to take over key locations, including the old seaport, which would have allowed them to control access to Mogadishu port. Government forces, supported by AMISOM, forced the insurgents to retreat.

Report of Secretary-General (July). In a report of 20 July [S/2009/373] covering developments since 16 April, the Secretary-General said that President Ahmed and the unity Government continued to engage with opposition groups still outside the Djibouti reconciliation process and held consultations with influential clan leaders, elders and Islamic clerics in efforts to broaden domestic support for the stabilization of the country. In the midst of the fighting, the Government signed a declaration with ASWJ on 21 June, by which the parties agreed to cooperate in the political, security, humanitarian and development areas. A former official of the Hizbul Islam, Sheikh Yusuf Mohamed Siad Inda'ade, was earlier included in the unity Government as Minister of State for Defence.

Despite increasing attacks on the Government, the Cabinet and Parliament continued to hold sessions in Mogadishu. President Ahmed visited a number of countries in Africa and Europe, appealing for support to enable his Government to resolve the security situation. He attended the thirteenth AU summit in July, which endorsed the call by IGAD and the AU Peace and Security Council for sanctions on Eritrea for aiding the insurgents and called on the United Nations to impose a sea blockade and a no-fly zone to stop the flow of weapons and other supplies to the insurgents. The ICG on Somalia, at its fifteenth meeting (Rome, 9–10 June), welcomed the efforts of President Ahmed to build a Government of national unity. UNPOS officials continued to make visits to Somalia, in solidarity with the Government.

Insurgent groups, such as Al-Shabaab, were alleged to extort money from private companies and recruit young people, including child soldiers, to join the fight against the Government. Al-Shabaab confirmed the presence of foreign fighters within its ranks and stated openly that it was working with Al-Qaida in Mogadishu to remove the Government. On 17 May, Al-Shabaab forces took control of Jowhar town and looted the UNICEF compound, the main hub for providing services and supplies to south-central Somalia; as at 7 July, the compound remained occupied by militia and inaccessible to UNICEF staff, with country-wide humanitarian implications.

As a consequence of the intensified fighting, the worsening drought country-wide and growing insecurity in most parts of south-central Somalia, the humanitarian situation deteriorated. At least 3.2 million people—43 per cent of the country's population—would require humanitarian assistance and livelihood support through September.

Attacks against humanitarian workers continued, with six workers killed during the first five months of 2009 and seven kidnapped. Sixteen humanitarian workers abducted in 2008 [YUN 2008, p. 285] remained in captivity. In June 2009, Médecins Sans Frontières announced that it would pull out of the Bakool region. Six journalists were killed in Mogadishu since January, four of whom appeared to be victims of targeted assassinations.

In parts of south-central Somalia, extreme interpretations of sharia law by insurgent groups led to allegations of violations of the right to life and physical integrity; summary executions, including beheadings, floggings, amputations, arbitrary arrests, restrictions on freedom of movement and violations of women's rights were reported. Concerns were raised about cases in "Puntland"—where the authorities continued to express their commitment to human rights—in which the death penalty was imposed in circumstances where the judicial process was considered unfair.

AMISOM played an important role in stabilizing the security situation in Mogadishu. As at 30 June, its strength in Mogadishu stood at 4,300 troops, or 54 per cent of the authorized strength of 8,000. With the arrival of its Police Commissioner in Mogadishu on 18 June, AMISOM had started the deployment of its police component; out of a mandated 270 police personnel, including trainers, advisors and mentors, 89 had been recruited and would be deployed to Mogadishu to begin the training of the 10,000 members of the all-inclusive Somalia Police Force. The police training task force, led jointly by UNDP and AMISOM, which reported to the UNPOS-led security sector technical working group, was developing a programme of training, mentoring and advice for the Somali police. Training for new police officers from south-central Somalia started on 13 July in "Puntland".

The United Nations supported institutional development and capacity-building under the Somali Institutional Development Project launched in January, which focused on capacity development of civil servants and on technical assistance in policy and law-making, budget-making and public-finance management, human resource development and infrastructure.

The security situation precluded progress in developing the transitional security institutions and a national security strategy. UNPOS, in collaboration with the UN country team and the donor community, and with DPKO support, worked with the Government towards revitalizing the Joint Security Committee—a key interface between the Government and the international community on all security-related issues. The registration of the Somali National Security Force had started.

The Police Advisory Committee, comprising parliamentarians, clan elders, journalists, business representatives and the Association of Women, continued to operate in Mogadishu, monitoring the situation of detainees following a 2008 Amnesty International report documenting gross human rights violations allegedly committed by government forces.

The Secretary-General was concerned about attempts to use force and violence to topple the Government, at a time when it was making concrete progress towards fulfilling its transitional agenda, which the population had increasingly welcomed. Every effort must be made to assist the Government and enable it to exercise its authority countrywide for the sake of the Somali people. The United Nations was working on the provision of logistics support to AMISOM.

Communication. On 20 July [S/2009/376], Ethiopia transmitted a letter of its Ministry of Foreign Affairs as IGAD Chairperson and the communiqué of the thirty-third extraordinary session of the IGAD Council of Ministers on the security and political situation in the subregion, in particular Somalia.

Security Council consideration (July). On 29 July [meeting 6173], the Security Council met to consider the Secretary-General's report. Briefing the Council, the Special Representative stated that despite multiple constraints, the Government was resisting and repelling multiple attempts to overthrow it and seize power illegally by force. It had made significant progress in training, equipping and paying its security forces. In continuation of its open-door policy, the Government welcomed members of the opposition; those who failed to join the peace process would miss an opportunity to contribute to rebuilding the country. The Government still required immediate political and financial support, and the authorities in "Puntland" and "Somaliland" needed resources to ensure that stability endured. Immediate support had to be extended to AMISOM, and support for IGAD and the AU in their decisions on Somalia would be most helpful. The time had come for the United Nations to show that it was serious about moving the Special Representative's office to Somalia; the establishment of a green zone would facilitate that process. The Council must continue to provide support against piracy.

Report of Secretary-General (October). In a report of 2 October [S/2009/503], the Secretary-General said that the Government continued efforts to consolidate its authority, particularly with respect to the security sector. On 23 July, it created a commission for security and pacification, tasked with reforming the security forces and all law enforcement agencies. On the same day, it announced the appointment of Abdullahi Mohamed Alim as Minister of National Security, to replace the assassinated Omar Hashi Aden. On 19 August, President Ahmed announced a reshuffle of his cabinet, as part of an internal reorganization aimed at improving the Government's coherence and ability to deliver services. The United Nations and other members of the international community continued to assist the Government with capacity-building.

The Transitional Federal Parliament continued to meet in Mogadishu. Since the expulsion of seven parliamentarians in July and warnings by the Speaker of Parliament that he would take disciplinary action against those who failed to attend its sessions, most parliamentarians residing outside Somalia had returned to the country. In an address on 27 July, President Sharif urged parliamentarians to remain united and focused on defending the country against foreign aggression and terrorism. On 19 August, the Parliament endorsed the President's decision of 22 June to declare a three-month state of emergency.

Armed opposition groups continued to resist the Government's calls to join an inclusive administration. The cooperation agreement signed between the Government and ASWJ on 21 June constituted an encouraging departure from that trend. However, Al-Shabaab and Hizbul Islam, the two main extremist groups that included foreign combatants and were supported by Al-Qaeda, remained outside the peace process.

On 22 August, rejecting the President's ceasefire call, elements of Hizbul Islam in the Gedo region announced that they had joined forces with Al-Shabaab, allegedly in response to the cooperation between the Government and its allies in the region. In addition to the threat posed by the insurgents, Somalia was plagued by the activities of unscrupulous domestic and external spoilers who, taking advantage of the prevailing lawlessness, had taken control of seaports and airstrips from where they supplied East Africa with a variety of contraband. They also illegally exported commodities such as charcoal and livestock and engaged in human and drug trafficking; the port of Kismayo remained the main entry point for weapons and logistics to the insurgents.

At the request of the Prime Minister, the United Nations was working closely with the authorities to revitalize and refocus the High-level Committee, especially in respect of policy coordination and the implementation of the Djibouti Agreement. The Committee, currently chaired by the United Nations, dealt with issues such as the drafting of a new constitution, justice and reconciliation, the management of the humanitarian crisis and the mobilization of popular support to the Djibouti Agreement.

Regional organizations continued to support the peace process, as did the United States, which issued a stern warning that it would take action against Eritrea if it did not cease supporting Al-Shabaab insurgents. Kenya reaffirmed its support for Somalia as well.

Under an agreement signed on 23 August, the Government and the "Puntland" Administration agreed to set up joint committees to enhance cooperation. In "Somaliland", tensions continued over the conduct of the elections previously scheduled for 27 September as opposition parties, civil society and the legislature rejected the decision made by the NEC to hold elections without a voters' roll. On 30 August, the Parliament established a committee composed of representatives of the three main political parties to undertake mediation efforts; in parallel, mediation efforts by regional and international actors were ongoing to bring the parties to an agreement.

The defeat in Mogadishu on 12 July was a setback for the insurgency, apparently undermining its cohesiveness and command authority. AMISOM demonstrated its ability to protect government installations and strategic positions against sustained attack; however, neither the government forces nor the insurgents had been able to consolidate control over contested territory. In early September, disparate militia still controlled most neighbourhoods in Mogadishu and the adjoining Banadir district, and fighting was reported almost daily, causing an estimated 20 to 50 fatalities per week. Many civilians continued to be killed in cross-fire and in long-range artillery and mortar attacks. On 16 August and 11 September, insurgent mortars attacked supply vessels contracted by the newly established United Nations Support Office for AMISOM (UNSOA) while in Mogadishu port, resulting in the death of 5 and 17 civilians, respectively. Another vessel contracted by UNSOA was attacked by pirates near Mogadishu on 27 August, but evaded capture.

The Government and AMISOM were continuously targeted, including through ambushes and coordinated attacks against strategic locations. They remained vulnerable to asymmetric attacks, as demonstrated by the attack against AMISOM on 17 September, when two vehicles carrying explosives drove into the AMISOM-controlled area at the Mogadishu airport and were detonated at the AMISOM Force headquarters and a building used by a contracted supply company. At least 21 people were confirmed killed, including 17 AMISOM soldiers.

Beyond Mogadishu, the security situation deteriorated markedly, with Government and allied militia challenging insurgent forces for control over strategically important towns in southern and central Somalia. In August, Al-Shabaab and Hizbul Islam forces were temporarily driven from the towns of Beledweyne and Bulobaarde in the Hiraan region and some insurgent strongholds in the Gedo region. However, the insurgents were able to retake many of those locations. In late August, Ethiopian forces reportedly crossed the border into Hiraan region and briefly entered Beledweyne to dislodge the insurgents. The overall security situation in southern and central Somalia had become more volatile, increasingly affecting humanitarian operations. Apparent supply shortages among insurgents led to a rise in criminal activities, and the risk of hostage-taking for international staff had significantly increased: 13 aid workers remained in captivity and a further nine had been killed since January, and on 20 July, Al-Shabaab militia looted UN compounds in Baidoa and Wajid. In late August, several NGO compounds were raided and on 16 August, Al-Shabaab militia again attacked the WFP compound in Wajid. As security assurances provided by insurgent leaders in southern and central Somalia became increasingly unreliable, UN international staff had to be relocated, while critical humanitarian operations continued with national staff and NGO partners.

The systematic looting of aid workers' compounds made it increasingly difficult for humanitarian operators to fulfil their mandate, particularly in the southern and central regions. In August, the latest UN food security assessment calculated that some 3.7 million people, or 50 per cent of the population of Somalia, were in need of livelihood and humanitarian support, up from 3.2 million in January. Most of them were concentrated in areas controlled by armed groups in southern and central Somalia.

Impunity for human rights abuses prevailed throughout the country. Reports continued about the illegal recruitment by armed groups of children under 18, and about executions, amputations and other abuses by extremist groups in the name of sharia law. In areas controlled by Al-Shabaab, women risked punishment, including detention, for refusing to wear appropriate clothing. Radio stations and other news media faced threats and intimidation. Insecurity continued to hamper the reconstruction of the justice and corrections sector.

In a welcome development, the designation of the Minster of Women's Development as high-level focal point for human rights facilitated capacity-building.

"Puntland" authorities also made commitments to greater respect for human rights and requested UN support. In "Somaliland", the annulment of the voters list had a negative impact on the human rights situation, especially on freedom of expression and the right to peaceful assembly. In late August, the police reportedly used excessive force against demonstrators in several towns. An independent television and radio station were closed down for having reported on inter-clan fighting related to a land dispute allegedly involving "Somaliland" authorities.

Regarding the implementation of the incremental approach laid out in his April report, the Secretary-General said that under the first phase of the approach, the United Nations had pursued its activities through its teams and offices based outside Somalia, as well as partners in the country, and more frequent missions by international UN staff to Mogadishu, Hargeisa and other accessible areas. Despite adverse security conditions, a cycle of missions had been established to carry out specific tasks and facilitate interaction with the Government, AMISOM and other partners. Critical humanitarian and other UN programmes continued in most regions, with 700 to 800 national staff and 60 to 80 international staff deployed throughout the country, including "Puntland" and" Somaliland". Planning was ongoing for the implementation of the second phase, which called for the deployment of a "light footprint" UN presence in Mogadishu, but the permanent assignment of UN international staff required downgrading the security phase from level V to level IV, which in turn depended on a significant improvement in security conditions.

The Special Representative continued his work with the international community to facilitate reconciliation and consolidate the peace process. Under his leadership, UNPOS, together with UN agencies, funds and programmes, continued to work towards the key objectives on the political track, including building governance capacity and incorporating human rights in all aspects of the peace process.

Following General Assembly approval of a $139 million budget for support to AU and AMISOM in June (see p. 294), the Department of Field Support, through UNSOA, started the delivery of the support package to AMISOM. Activities included establishing a secure strategic communications network and providing strategic equipment, including armoured vehicles. The memorandum of understanding between the AU and the United Nations, defining respective responsibilities and obligations in support of AMISOM, was signed on 12 July. The UN planning team in Addis Ababa continued to provide planning and operational support in respect of AMISOM deployment and operations. The United Nations Mine Action Service continued to build AMISOM capacity in explosive ordnance disposal.

The United Nations assisted the Government in developing the transitional security institutions, while also working towards the national security strategy called for in Council resolution 1872(2009) (see p. 277). While the focus remained on the short-term needs of the national security and police, significant progress was made towards coordinating international assistance and building consensus on the basis for a policy framework. UNPOS also continued to build up its security sector capacity.

On 25 July and 12 August, respectively, Somalia's Joint Security Committee held its first and second meeting in Mogadishu, attended by UNPOS and AMISOM. The Government, assisted by AMISOM, began restructuring its forces under unified command. Training and development of the police continued in all three regions of Somalia.

Despite restricted access and narrowing humanitarian space, the United Nations and its partners continued to provide assistance to those in need; since April, the United Nations had delivered a monthly average of 35,600 metric tons of food aid to over 2 million Somalis affected by drought and conflict. On 15 August, the United Nations conducted a mission into the Afgooye corridor, home to an estimated 500,000 IDPs, holding talks with armed groups to agree on security arrangements and communication links. On 7 September, a humanitarian mission was conducted into Mogadishu for a rapid assessment of the situation in the IDP settlements and the services provided through two major hospitals. Across the country, the United Nations provided capacity-building of civil servants and local government, developing policies and legislative frameworks for public administration and establishing effective systems for public financial management.

The Secretary-General observed that the Government had successfully weathered threats to its existence from extremist forces and garnered substantial domestic and international support. While many challenges remained, there was some encouraging progress towards fostering national reconciliation and sustaining dialogue between the Government and the opposition groups; building capacity for local governance; drafting the Constitution; integrating human rights into the peace process; and building a national security apparatus. Sustained international support would constitute a key contribution towards delivering administrative and basic services and managing the transition. There was a need for concurrent capacity-building of legal, judicial and correctional institutions, parliament and the civil service.

The Secretary-General was concerned about the worsening humanitarian crisis and criminal activities, including drug trafficking and arms smuggling, resulting in some individuals accumulating significant wealth and acting as spoilers to the peace process. Lack of adequate funding for priority humanitarian and recovery programmes was a matter of concern, and the Secretary-General urged Member States to support the consolidated appeals process and the United Nations Transition Plan for Somalia for 2008–2009. DPKO, in consultation with the AU, would further develop and refine contingency plans that would allow for the eventual transition from AMISOM to a UN peacekeeping operation.

Security Council consideration (October). Briefing the Security Council on 8 October [meeting 6197], Craig Boyd, Director of UNSOA, noted that resolution 1863(2009) had endorsed the Secretary-General's proposed strategy, including the provision of a UN support package for AMISOM and the strengthening of Somalia's security sector. Resolution 1872(2009) had reinforced the need for the continuation of that approach and the provision of logistics support. The support continued to be provided in an integrated manner, which combined voluntary contributions to UN trust funds, direct bilateral support to the Government and AMISOM, and the UN support package to AMISOM funded through assessed contributions.

Terrorist attack in Mogadishu

On 3 December, a terrorist attack was launched during a graduation ceremony for medical students at a hotel in Mogadishu: at least 23 people were killed, including the Ministers of Health, Higher Education and Education, as well as graduating students and journalists. Faculty members, parliamentarians and family members of the students were wounded.

Security Council action. On the same day, the Council held emergency consultations, and by statement **S/PRST/2009/31** (see p. 69), condemned the attack, which killed and injured innocent civilians. The Council urged that a thorough investigation be conducted and that the perpetrators be brought swiftly to justice; demanded that opposition groups end attacks immediately, put down their arms and join the reconciliation efforts; reiterated its support for the Djibouti peace process; and reaffirmed that Somalia's long-term security rested with the effective development by the Transitional Federal Government of the National Security Force and the Somali Police Force.

Year-end developments

Report of Secretary-General. In a later report [S/2009/684], the Secretary-General said that the Government continued to consolidate and expand its support base on three fronts. Firstly, the Government intensified efforts to expand its support base among the main opposition groups in Mogadishu; secondly, the cooperation between the Government and ASWJ was consolidated; and thirdly, the Government began an in-depth review of its relationship with the "Puntland" regional authorities. An increasing number of elements from the armed opposition renounced violence and opted to work for peace in partnership with the Government; that included the defection of Mohamed Faruq and Ali Hassan Gheddi, two senior Al-Shabaab operatives, together with some 550 fighters, indicating growing divisions within Al-Shabaab. However, the Government lacked adequate and regular resources to assist those defecting from insurgent groups. By 30 November, it had received $5.6 million out of the $58 million pledged in Brussels in April.

Further to the cooperation agreement signed between the Government and ASWJ on 21 June, the two were exploring modalities for implementing political and military cooperation, including power-sharing. The Special Representative was supporting the implementation of the cooperation agreement signed on 23 August between the Government and "Puntland" authorities, which covered political and security cooperation, notably in the area of counter-piracy.

The Government was working on a stabilization programme based on political, social and development priorities. The Parliament reconvened on 21 December, after being unable to meet for four months due to the absence from Somalia of several of its members. The cabinet approved the appointment of Mohamed Omar Farah as Chief Judge of the Supreme Court and the replacement of the senior military and police leadership in an attempt to shore up the security apparatus. Colonel Mohamed Gelle Kahiye was appointed as the new military commander, and General Ali Mohammed Hassan took command of the police.

The political situation in the autonomous region of "Puntland" remained generally calm, despite violent incidents linked to inter-clan fighting, along with abductions and assassinations. The "Puntland" authorities launched a programme aimed at accelerating prosecutions of suspected pirates.

The constitution-making process gathered pace in mid-October with the reconstitution of the Independent Federal Constitutional Commission and the doubling of its membership to 30, including six women commissioners.

The ICG on Somalia continued to mobilize support for the reconciliation process. At a meeting in Jeddah, Saudi Arabia, on 17 December, the Group reiterated that the Djibouti process remained the framework for all international efforts.

Insecurity remained widespread. In October, on two separate occasions, insurgent groups launched mortar attacks on the aircraft transporting President Sharif. Tension in Mogadishu between Al-Shabaab and Hizbul Islam led to increased clashes between the two groups. Clashes in Mogadishu restricted the ability of the international community to fully implement humanitarian programmes. In Bay and Bakool, Al-Shabaab continued to prevent the return of a UN presence, insisting that a memorandum of understanding be signed and that registration fees, amounting to several thousand dollars for each UN agency, be paid prior to re-entry. While Mogadishu remained the focus of the insurgency, fighting occurred in other parts of the country, especially in Beledweyne and Kismayo, as well as in Gedo and Bakool region. The northern regions of Galgaduud and Mudug remained tense, with numerous clashes between rival armed groups. Tensions between the regional authorities of "Puntland" and "Somaliland" continued. "Puntland" had become increasingly unstable as a result of several violent incidents, including assassinations. Efforts by the "Puntland" authorities to improve security suffered a setback when a senior judge and a member of Parliament were assassinated on the same day by unknown gunmen. The judge was known for having handed down strong sentences to Al-Shabaab members, human traffickers and pirates.

In Kismayo, fighting continued between Al-Shabaab and Hizbul Islam over control of the region. A series of targeted assassinations carried out by the two rival groups claimed the lives of several senior Hizbul Islam and Al-Shabaab members. Those assassinations appeared to have triggered the re-emergence of clan-based warlordism oriented towards economic gain, rather than ideology or strategy.

The humanitarian situation remained dire, with over 3.6 million, or nearly 50 per cent of the total population, requiring humanitarian assistance or livelihood support into 2010. The presence of hard-line Al-Shabaab elements, hostile to humanitarian organizations, resulted in a further shrinking of humanitarian space. Despite the increased needs, humanitarian funding dropped significantly; at the end of November, the 2009 Somalia consolidated appeals process was 60 per cent funded, with $512 million having been received out of the $851 million required. The United Nations by July had mobilized $117 million for recovery and development across Somalia. On 3 December, the 2010 Somalia consolidated appeals process was launched in Nairobi for $689 million.

Armed groups, including Al-Shabaab, continued to attack the Government and AMISOM from areas frequented by civilians. Particularly disturbing were increasing reports of gender-based violence in IDP settlements, particularly in "Puntland" and "Somaliland". Armed groups in southern and central Somalia continued to violate women's rights. Journalists were subjected to threats and short-term arbitrary detentions, and nine journalists were murdered during the year. Those abuses resulted in the closure of three radio stations and caused many journalists to flee the country. Hundreds of children were wounded, killed or maimed as a direct result of the conflict. In southern and central Somalia, children were exposed to recruitment into armed forces by all parties.

The United Nations continued to pursue the activities outlined in Security Council resolution 1872(2009), constituting a three-phased incremental approach implemented through AMISOM and international, national and local partners. At the end of November, critical humanitarian and other UN programmes continued in most regions, with 775 national and 57 international staff deployed throughout the country, including in "Puntland" and "Somaliland". Despite difficult security conditions, frequent visits to Mogadishu were made to enable UN staff to monitor operations and provide support to the Government and AMISOM.

The Special Representative maintained close contact with IGAD members, the AU Commission and other regional leaders, seeking political support for implementing the Djibouti Agreement. The High-level Committee was relaunched on 23 October, in a new format bringing together the Government and the international community; its expanded membership included UNPOS, AMISOM, troop-contributing countries and other members of the international community. The Committee would address areas of cooperation and prioritize the transitional tasks assigned to the Government.

AMISOM continued to play a significant role but was constrained by a variety of pressures, especially with regard to force generation and the provision of equipment. Deployment remained at around six battalions, or 65 per cent of the mandated strength. Logistic constraints had delayed the planned deployment of one additional battalion each from Uganda and Burundi, together with 400 troops from Djibouti. Although the AMISOM police component was evacuated from Mogadishu following the 17 September suicide attack on Mission headquarters, the unit continued pre-deployment training for 61 AU police in Ghana and Kenya. UNSOA continued to provide AMISOM with the logistical support package, including rations, fresh food, medical supplies and fuel.

In spite of the challenging environment and incessant attacks on the Government, the implementation of the Djibouti Agreement generally remained on track, the Secretary-General observed. The Somali leadership had demonstrated its commitment to ensuring the success of the peace process, notably by relocating its federal institutions to Mogadishu. A coordinated effort between the Government and the international community was required in 2010 to generate the necessary political and security conditions for the completion of the transition by 2011.

The Government needed to cement agreements and alliances with Somali partners inside the country. The AU, IGAD and AMISOM troop-contributing countries played a critical role in stabilizing Somalia. The training of professional security forces was a crucial element in the implementation of the Djibouti Agreement.

The three-phased incremental approach remained valid. Planning for the UN "light footprint", while subject to delays owing to the security situation in Mogadishu, continued. With UNPOS' current mandate ending in December 2009, the Secretary-General invited the Security Council to reauthorize the mandated activities for 2010–2011.

Piracy

During the first part of the year, an exponential increase in activity by pirates was reported in the Gulf of Aden and the Somali Basin. A reported 61 incidents took place in the first quarter of 2009, compared to six in the same period in 2008. From the beginning of the year through early June, there were 29 successful hijackings in the region. In January, one in every six hijackings was successful, that figure falling to one in every 13 in March as a result of effective patrolling of the seas, the escorting of groups of vessels registered with the Maritime Security Centre (Horn of Africa) along a transit corridor, and to a lesser degree, incidents of bad weather. The deployment of warships by the North Atlantic Treaty Organization (NATO) and Operation Atalanta of the European Union, together with initiatives by individual countries, had a positive impact as the international maritime presence off the Somali coast made it more costly for pirates to operate in the area. However, as a result of the military presence, pirates employed more daring tactics, operating further seawards, towards the Seychelles, and using more sophisticated weaponry. While no hijacking attacks were successful in the Gulf of Aden since July, pirates attacked ships, some of them as far away as 1,000 nautical miles off the Somali coast.

An outcome of Security Council resolution 1851(2008) [YUN 2008, p. 292], the Contact Group on Piracy off the Coast of Somalia was established on 14 January to act as a common point of contact among States, regional and international organizations on all aspects of combating piracy and armed robbery at sea off Somalia's coast. The Contact Group increased military-to-military cooperation, in addition to military and civilian cooperation. It started to harmonize regional capacity-building and facilitated the enhancement of the shipping industry's self-awareness and other capabilities for vessels passing through the region. In concert with the International Maritime Organization (IMO), flag States and those with significant numbers of mariners, as well as those involved in the maritime industry, were encouraged to redouble training efforts on internationally recognized best management practices to avoid, deter or delay pirate attacks. The Contact Group, which met in plenary on 17 March, 29 May and 10 September, was supported by four working groups: Working Group 1, chaired by the United Kingdom, examined activities related to military and operational coordination, information-sharing and the establishment of a regional coordination centre; Working Group 2, on legal issues, was chaired by Denmark; Working Group 3, on strengthening shipping self-awareness and other capabilities, was chaired by the United States; and Working Group 4, chaired by Egypt, dealt with diplomatic and public information efforts. Workings groups 1 and 2 met in November to undertake a needs assessment in order to develop a framework of regional counter-piracy capacity.

On 30 November, by resolution 1897(2009) (see p. 289), the Council renewed for 12 months the authorization given to States and regional organizations cooperating with the Transitional Federal Government to repress acts of piracy and armed robbery off the coast of Somalia.

Communication. On 4 February [S/2009/80], the United States informed the Security Council that on 14 January, 24 States and 5 regional and international organizations had met in New York and formed the Contact Group on Piracy off the Coast of Somalia, in response to the Council's call to establish an international cooperation mechanism to act as a common point of contact on all aspects of combating such piracy. The Group, at its first meeting, decided to keep the Council regularly informed of its activities and decisions.

Report of Secretary-General (March). Pursuant to Security Council resolution 1846(2008) [YUN 2008, p. 290], the Secretary-General on 16 March submitted a report [S/2009/146] which studied the piracy situation and examined the political, legal and operational activities by Member States, regional organizations, the United Nations and its partners in the fight against piracy off the coast of Somalia. The report suggested measures for the long-term security of international navigation off the coast of Somalia, including seaborne humanitarian deliveries, and outlined the role the United Nations could play. During the reporting period, there was an increase in the number of Member States undertaking maritime military operations off the coast of Somalia.

Of the 293 incidents of piracy or armed robbery at sea recorded by the International Maritime Bureau for 2008, 111 occurred off the coast of Somalia, representing an annual increase of nearly 200 per cent in the critical trade corridor linking the Suez Canal and the Indian Ocean. The most prominent pirate militias had their roots in the fishing communities of the Somali coast, especially in north-eastern and central Somalia, and their organization reflected Somali clan-based social structures. There were two main piracy networks—in "Puntland", where the most important pirate group was located in the Eyl district, and in the southern Mudug region. By the end of 2008, the "Eyl Group" was holding hostage six vessels and their crew and was estimated to have earned approximately $30 million in ransom payments. The "Mudug piracy network", operating from Xarardheere, held four ships from September 2008 to February 2009. Some of those groups rivalled established Somali authorities in terms of their military capabilities and resource bases. There were increasing reports of complicity by members of the "Puntland" administration in piracy activities, but the leadership appeared to be taking a more robust approach against piracy.

The general and complete arms embargo on Somalia, established by Security Council resolution 733(1992) [YUN 1992, p. 199], had been persistently and flagrantly violated over the past 16 years, contributing to the ready access to arms and ammunition by pirates; understanding the relationship between the growth of piracy and the non-enforcement of the arms embargo was crucial. The Monitoring Group on Somalia, in its December 2008 report, highlighted the overlap between piracy, contraband and arms trafficking across the Gulf of Aden. The Group noted that leading figures in piracy syndicates were responsible for arms embargo violations and recommended that they be considered for targeted sanctions; resolution 1844(2008) [YUN 2008, p. 297] provided a real opportunity for those who violated the arms embargo to be brought to account. Coordinated international efforts against piracy would generate an enduring effect if coupled with the interdiction of arms trafficking and the imposition of targeted sanctions against key pirate leaders and their sponsors. Reducing the availability of arms to pirates by implementing targeted individual sanctions and by adhering to exemption procedures under Council resolutions would serve to remedy the lack of accountability that had reinforced the crime of piracy.

The UNPOS focal point collated and shared naval information related to anti-piracy activities. The UN Secretariat, through its assistance to the Security Council and the General Assembly, its capacity-building and humanitarian assistance and its provision of advice and information, was playing an important role in the repression of piracy off the coast of Somalia.

The Secretary-General stressed the need to tackle the problem with a multifaceted approach to ensure that the political process, AMISOM peacekeeping efforts, the strengthening of law enforcement institutions and capacity-building initiatives worked in tandem, and that the humanitarian assistance efforts of WFP and others continued to address the needs of highly vulnerable people. The issue would be resolved only through an integrated approach that addressed the conflict, lack of governance and absence of sustainable livelihoods on land. The building of the capacity of local and regional players would be a determining factor in implementing durable solutions. To address the lack of sustainability that had led to impunity, the international community should implement the existing international legal framework and strengthen the regional and national legal framework to facilitate the apprehension and prosecution of those suspected of having committed piracy and armed robbery.

Communications. On 14 May [S/2009/251], Somalia informed the Security Council that Iran had decided to dispatch two naval vessels to the region off the coast of Somalia and the Gulf of Aden, in order to protect and escort ships related to Iran or Iranian citizens and shipping companies and to assist foreign vessels requesting help; they were expected to arrive on 15 May and were initially supposed to stay until 21 October.

On 14 October [S/2009/550], the United States informed the Security Council that it cooperated with the Transitional Federal Government in the fight against piracy and armed robbery. The United States anticipated the need for a continuation of the authorities that enabled action against piracy, as reflected in paragraph 10 of resolution 1846(2008) and paragraph 6 of resolution 1851(2008), specified for a 12-month period ending on 2 December.

On 15 October [S/2009/549], France informed the Council of the progress of actions it had undertaken in the exercise of the authority provided in paragraph 10 of resolution 1846(2008).

On 3 November [S/2009/569], the Secretary-General transmitted to the Council a report on the EU naval operation off the coast of Somalia from 12 December 2008 to 1 October 2009.

Report of Secretary-General (November). Reporting on the situation on 13 November [S/2009/590] pursuant to Security Council resolution 1846(2008), the Secretary-General said that from 1 January to 30 September, 34 ships were hijacked and more than 450 seafarers were taken hostage. As at 27 October, eight ships and 178 seafarers were being held hostage. The locus of activities shifted from the Gulf of Aden to the western Indian Ocean and, more recently, closer to the Seychelles, largely as a result of successful naval action. Increasingly, smaller ships, such as fishing vessels and pleasure craft, were being targeted.

International efforts to provide coherence to and support for international and regional initiatives against piracy intensified through the Contact Group on Pi-

racy Off the Coast of Somalia and other initiatives. The combined efforts of the international naval forces had reduced incidents in the region. Three multinational maritime coalitions had been contributing to the fight against piracy since the adoption of resolution 1846(2008): the EU Naval Force Operation Atalanta; NATO, using standing forces; and the United States-led Combined Maritime Forces. In addition, several Member States acted independently, some coordinating their efforts with the multinational coalitions.

The Djibouti Code of Conduct, adopted at a meeting convened by IMO on 29 January [C 102/14] and signed by 10 States of the region, was a central instrument in developing regional capacity to combat piracy, and the International Criminal Police Organization (INTERPOL) was working with national and regional police agencies, UN entities and the Contact Group to address the capacity needs of the police and enhance cooperation.

In addition to training and technical assistance to the Somali coast guard, the Government requested assistance for providing livelihoods in the coastal communities concerned in terms of educational and training facilities and cold storage facilities for fish catches. On 23 August, representatives of the Government and "Puntland" agreed to cooperate on means of fighting piracy, to establish a centre for the Somali marine forces and training facilities in "Puntland" for the Somali armed forces, and to provide logistics and material support. On 9 September, the Government and Djibouti agreed to accelerate the establishment of the planned Djibouti anti-piracy training and information centre and to train the Somali maritime security forces. In "Puntland", the authorities succeeded in launching limited activities to thwart, curb or investigate piracy: 110 people suspected of piracy were reported to be detained. The "Somaliland" coast guard was successfully interdicting and capturing piracy suspects and exchanging information with the international naval forces off the Somali coast. The authorities made efforts to improve security in the port of Berbera, with assistance from Norway.

The Secretary-General noted that four of five shipments to AMISOM had been attacked, in addition to attacks against a UN shipment of military equipment to AMISOM on 12 February. The United Nations remained committed to addressing the problem of piracy and armed robbery; the United Nations Integrated Task Force for Somalia had established a sub-working group, chaired by the Department of Political Affairs, to coordinate the various counter-piracy activities of UN departments, programmes and specialized agencies.

Member States had developed complex and comprehensive military naval operations and corresponding coordination mechanisms, the Secretary-General observed. The various military operations necessitated a lead role and coordination arrangements that went beyond the operational capacity and resources of the UN Secretariat. One of the ways to ensure the long-term security of international navigation off the Somali coast was through a concerted effort to stabilize the situation ashore; currently, however, the expanding maritime presence was playing a critical role in stabilizing the situation at sea. Any measures to combat piracy would require an integrated approach comprising the development of the rule of law and security institutions; the strengthening of capacity on land of the Transitional Federal Institutions and AMISOM; local and national capacity-building of legal and maritime institutions in Somalia and the region; the investigation and prosecution of those suspected of acts of piracy; strict compliance with Security Council arms embargoes; and development efforts to empower local communities to create sustainable livelihoods.

Efforts that contributed to the security of the Somali ports had demonstrated a tangible counter-piracy effect. Piracy was a symptom of a wider problem ashore. To address the root cause of piracy, it was crucial for the Somali authorities to provide sustainable livelihoods to their people and re-establish their security institutions and the rule of law. Corruption, human trafficking and the smuggling of illegal commodities needed to be eliminated, including by prosecuting officials.

SECURITY COUNCIL ACTION

On 30 November [meeting 6226], the Council unanimously adopted **resolution 1897(2009)**. The draft [S/2009/607] was submitted by 29 States.

The Security Council,

Recalling its previous resolutions concerning the situation in Somalia, especially resolutions 1814(2008) of 15 May 2008, 1816(2008) of 2 June 2008, 1838(2008) of 7 October 2008, 1844(2008) of 20 November 2008, 1846(2008) of 2 December 2008 and 1851(2008) of 16 December 2008,

Continuing to be gravely concerned by the ongoing threat that piracy and armed robbery at sea against vessels pose to the prompt, safe and effective delivery of humanitarian aid to Somalia and the region, to international navigation and the safety of commercial maritime routes and to other vulnerable ships, including fishing activities in conformity with international law, and the extended range of the piracy threat into the western Indian Ocean,

Reaffirming its respect for the sovereignty, territorial integrity, political independence and unity of Somalia, including Somalia's rights with respect to offshore natural resources, including fisheries, in accordance with international law,

Further reaffirming that international law, as reflected in the United Nations Convention on the Law of the Sea of 10 December 1982, sets out the legal framework applicable to combating piracy and armed robbery at sea, as well as other ocean activities,

Again taking into account the crisis situation in Somalia, and the limited capacity of the Transitional Federal Government to interdict or, upon interdiction, to prosecute pirates or to patrol or secure the waters off the coast of Somalia, including the international sea lanes and Somalia's territorial waters,

Noting the several requests of the Transitional Federal Government for international assistance to counter piracy off the coast of Somalia, including the letters dated 2 and 6 November 2009 from the Permanent Representative of Somalia to the United Nations expressing the appreciation of the Transitional Federal Government to the Security Council for its assistance, expressing the willingness of the Transitional Federal Government to consider working with other States and regional organizations to combat piracy and armed robbery at sea off the coast of Somalia, and requesting that the provisions of resolutions 1846(2008) and 1851(2008) be renewed for an additional twelve months,

Commending the efforts of the European Union operation Atalanta, which the European Union is committed to extending until December 2010, the North Atlantic Treaty Organization operations Allied Protector and Ocean Shield, the Combined Maritime Forces' Combined Task Force 151 and other States acting in a national capacity in cooperation with the Transitional Federal Government and each other to suppress piracy and to protect vulnerable ships transiting through the waters off the coast of Somalia,

Noting with concern that the continuing limited capacity and domestic legislation to facilitate the custody and prosecution of suspected pirates after their capture has hindered more robust international action against the pirates off the coast of Somalia, and in some cases has led to pirates being released without facing justice, regardless of whether there is sufficient evidence to support prosecution, reiterating that, consistent with the provisions of the United Nations Convention on the Law of the Sea concerning the repression of piracy, the Convention for the Suppression of Unlawful Acts against the Safety of Maritime Navigation of 10 March 1988 provides for parties to create criminal offences, establish jurisdiction and accept delivery of persons responsible for or suspected of seizing or exercising control over a ship by force or threat thereof or any other form of intimidation, and stressing the need for States to criminalize piracy under their domestic law and to favourably consider the prosecution, in appropriate cases, of suspected pirates, consistent with applicable international law,

Commending the efforts of Kenya to prosecute suspected pirates in its national courts, and noting with appreciation the assistance being provided by the United Nations Office on Drugs and Crime and other international organizations and donors, in coordination with the Contact Group on Piracy off the Coast of Somalia, to support Kenya, Somalia and other States in the region, including Seychelles and Yemen, to take steps to prosecute or incarcerate in a third State after prosecution elsewhere captured pirates, consistent with applicable international human rights law,

Noting the ongoing efforts within the Contact Group on Piracy off the Coast of Somalia to explore possible additional mechanisms to effectively prosecute persons suspected of piracy and armed robbery at sea off the coast of Somalia,

Noting with appreciation the ongoing efforts of the United Nations Office on Drugs and Crime and the United Nations Development Programme to support efforts to enhance the capacity of the corrections system in Somalia, including regional authorities, to incarcerate convicted pirates, consistent with applicable international human rights law,

Welcoming the adoption of the Code of Conduct concerning the Repression of Piracy and Armed Robbery against Ships in the Western Indian Ocean and the Gulf of Aden (Djibouti Code of Conduct), and the establishment of the International Maritime Organization Djibouti Code Trust Fund (a multi-donor trust fund initiated by Japan), as well as the international trust fund supporting initiatives of the Contact Group on Piracy off the Coast of Somalia, and recognizing the efforts of signatory States to develop the appropriate regulatory and legislative frameworks to combat piracy, enhance their capacity to patrol the waters of the region, interdict suspect vessels and prosecute suspected pirates,

Emphasizing that peace and stability within Somalia, the strengthening of State institutions, economic and social development and respect for human rights and the rule of law are necessary to create the conditions for a durable eradication of piracy and armed robbery at sea off the coast of Somalia, and further emphasizing that Somalia's long-term security rests with the effective development by the Transitional Federal Government of the National Security Force and the Somali Police Force, within the framework of the Djibouti Agreement and in line with a national security strategy,

Determining that the incidents of piracy and armed robbery at sea off the coast of Somalia exacerbate the situation in Somalia, which continues to constitute a threat to international peace and security in the region,

Acting under Chapter VII of the Charter of the United Nations,

1. *Reiterates* that it condemns and deplores all acts of piracy and armed robbery against vessels in the waters off the coast of Somalia;

2. *Notes again with concern* the findings contained in the report of the Monitoring Group on Somalia of 20 November 2008 that escalating ransom payments and the lack of enforcement of the arms embargo established by resolution 733(1992) of 23 January 1992 are fuelling the growth of piracy off the coast of Somalia, and calls upon all States to fully cooperate with the Monitoring Group;

3. *Renews its call upon* States and regional organizations that have the capacity to do so to take part in the fight against piracy and armed robbery at sea off the coast of Somalia, in particular, consistent with the present resolution and international law, by deploying naval vessels, arms and military aircraft and through seizures and disposition of boats, vessels, arms and other related equipment used in the commission of piracy and armed robbery at sea off the coast of Somalia, or for which there are reasonable grounds for suspecting such use;

4. *Commends* the work of the Contact Group on Piracy off the Coast of Somalia to facilitate coordination in order to deter acts of piracy and armed robbery at sea off the coast of Somalia, in cooperation with the International Maritime Organization, flag States and the Transitional Federal Government, and urges States and international organizations to continue to support those efforts;

5. *Acknowledges* Somalia's rights with respect to offshore natural resources, including fisheries, in accordance with international law, and calls upon States and interested organizations, including the International Maritime Organization, to provide technical assistance to Somalia, including regional authorities, and nearby coastal States upon their request, to enhance their capacity to ensure coastal and maritime security, including combating piracy and armed robbery at sea off the Somali and nearby coastlines, and stresses the importance of coordination in this regard through the Contact Group on Piracy off the Coast of Somalia;

6. *Invites* all States and regional organizations fighting piracy off the coast of Somalia to conclude special agreements or arrangements with countries willing to take custody of pirates in order to embark law enforcement officials ("shipriders") from the latter countries, in particular countries in the region, to facilitate the investigation and prosecution of persons detained as a result of operations conducted under the present resolution for acts of piracy and armed robbery at sea off the coast of Somalia, provided that the advance consent of the Transitional Federal Government is obtained for the exercise of third State jurisdiction by shipriders in Somali territorial waters and that such agreements or arrangements do not prejudice the effective implementation of the Convention for the Suppression of Unlawful Acts against the Safety of Maritime Navigation;

7. *Encourages* Member States to continue to cooperate with the Transitional Federal Government in the fight against piracy and armed robbery at sea, notes the primary role of the Transitional Federal Government in the fight against piracy and armed robbery at sea, and decides to renew, for a period of twelve months from the date of the present resolution, the authorizations as set out in paragraph 10 of resolution 1846(2008) and paragraph 6 of resolution 1851(2008) granted to States and regional organizations cooperating with the Transitional Federal Government in the fight against piracy and armed robbery at sea off the coast of Somalia, for which advance notification has been provided by the Transitional Federal Government to the Secretary-General;

8. *Affirms* that the authorizations renewed in the present resolution apply only with respect to the situation in Somalia and shall not affect the rights, obligations or responsibilities of Member States under international law, including any rights or obligations under the United Nations Convention on the Law of the Sea, with respect to any other situation, and underscores, in particular, that the present resolution shall not be considered as establishing customary international law, and affirms further that such authorizations have been renewed only following receipt of the letters dated 2 and 6 November 2009 conveying the consent of the Transitional Federal Government;

9. *Affirms also* that the measures imposed by paragraph 5 of resolution 733(1992) and further elaborated upon in paragraphs 1 and 2 of resolution 1425(2002) of 22 July 2002 do not apply to weapons and military equipment destined for the sole use of Member States and regional organizations undertaking measures in accordance with paragraph 7 above or to supplies of technical assistance to Somalia solely for the purposes set out in paragraph 5

above, which have been exempted from those measures in accordance with the procedure set out in paragraphs 11 *(b)* and 12 of resolution 1772(2007) of 20 August 2007;

10.   *Requests* that cooperating States take appropriate steps to ensure that the activities they undertake pursuant to the authorizations in paragraph 7 above do not have the practical effect of denying or impairing the right of innocent passage to the ships of any third State;

11.   *Calls upon* Member States to assist Somalia, at the request of the Transitional Federal Government and with notification to the Secretary-General, to strengthen capacity in Somalia, including regional authorities, to bring to justice those who are using Somali territory to plan, facilitate or undertake criminal acts of piracy and armed robbery at sea, and stresses that any measures undertaken pursuant to the present paragraph shall be consistent with applicable international human rights law;

12.   *Calls upon* all States, and in particular flag, port and coastal States, States of the nationality of victims and perpetrators of piracy and armed robbery, and other States with relevant jurisdiction under international law and national legislation to cooperate in determining jurisdiction and in the investigation and prosecution of persons responsible for acts of piracy and armed robbery off the coast of Somalia, consistent with applicable international law, including international human rights law, to ensure that all pirates handed over to judicial authorities are subject to a judicial process and to render assistance by, among other actions, providing disposition and logistics assistance with respect to persons under their jurisdiction and control, such as victims and witnesses and persons detained as a result of operations conducted under the present resolution;

13.   *Commends*, in this context, the decision of the Contact Group on Piracy off the Coast of Somalia to establish an international trust fund to support its initiatives, and encourages donors to contribute to it;

14.   *Urges* States parties to the United Nations Convention on the Law of the Sea and the Convention for the Suppression of Unlawful Acts against the Safety of Maritime Navigation to fully implement their relevant obligations under those Conventions and customary international law and to cooperate with the United Nations Office on Drugs and Crime, the International Maritime Organization, other States and other international organizations to build judicial capacity for the successful prosecution of persons suspected of piracy and armed robbery at sea off the coast of Somalia;

15.   *Welcomes* the revisions by the International Maritime Organization to its recommendations and guidance on preventing and suppressing piracy and armed robbery against ships, and urges States, in collaboration with the shipping and insurance industries, and the International Maritime Organization, to continue to develop and implement avoidance, evasion and defensive best practices and advisories to take when under attack or when sailing in the waters off the coast of Somalia, and further urges States to make their citizens and vessels available for forensic investigation, as appropriate, at the first port of call immediately following an act or attempted act of piracy or armed robbery at sea or release from captivity;

16.   *Requests* States and regional organizations cooperating with the Transitional Federal Government to inform the Security Council and the Secretary-General within nine months of the progress of actions undertaken in the exercise of the authorizations provided in paragraph 7 above, and further requests all States contributing through the Contact Group on Piracy off the Coast of Somalia to the fight against piracy off the coast of Somalia, including Somalia and other States in the region, to report by the same deadline on their efforts to establish jurisdiction and cooperation in the investigation and prosecution of piracy;

17.   *Requests* the Secretary-General to report to the Council within eleven months of the adoption of the present resolution on the implementation of the resolution and on the situation with respect to piracy and armed robbery at sea off the coast of Somalia;

18.   *Requests* the Secretary-General of the International Maritime Organization to brief the Council, on the basis of cases brought to his attention by the agreement of all affected coastal States, and duly taking into account the existing bilateral and regional cooperative arrangements, on the situation with respect to piracy and armed robbery;

19.   *Expresses its intention* to review the situation and to consider, as appropriate, renewing the authorizations provided in paragraph 7 above for additional periods upon the request of the Transitional Federal Government;

20.   *Decides* to remain seized of the matter.

Children and armed conflict

According to a March report [A/63/785-S/2009/158 & Corr.1] by the Secretary-General on children and armed conflict, approximately 1,300 children had been recruited into Government forces, the remnants of the Islamic Courts Union, Al-Shabaab and clan-based armed groups throughout central and southern Somalia, particularly in and around Mogadishu. As noted in a later report [S/2010/577], recruitment became more systematic during 2009. Although the total number of children being recruited and used in conflict was unknown, estimates suggested that several hundred children were in the forces of the Government or its associated militias, and several thousand among the insurgent groups. They were trained in basic arms techniques as well as more sophisticated skills such as assassination, intelligence collection, use of improvised explosive devices and suicide missions. In March alone, Al-Shabaab reportedly recruited 600 children, and in September, AMISOM gained information related to the deployment of 270 children within Mogadishu. Aswj reportedly recruited hundreds of children, mostly within the Hiraan and Galgaduud regions. The Government was said to recruit children between the ages of 14 and 18 years; some of them were sent to what was officially called a "rehabilitation centre" in Mogadishu, a training base for children who had previously fought for other armed groups.

Displacement, abandonment, neglect, orphanhood and destitution made children particularly vulnerable to recruitment. Children were typically recruited from schools and madrasas and from IDP settlements in Somalia and refugee camps in Kenya. Children as young as 11 were used by insurgent groups and were paid between $3 and $35 per operation. While recruitment of girls was rare and generally regarded as socially unacceptable, girls were enlisted for cooking and cleaning and for marriage to young combatants, as well as to transport detonators, receive weapons, provide logistics support and collect intelligence.

United Nations Political Office for Somalia

Since its establishment in 1995 [YUN 1995, p. 402], the United Nations Political Office for Somalia (unpos), headed by Ahmedou Ould-Abdallah (Mauritania), assisted the Secretary-General to advance the cause of peace and reconciliation through its contacts with Somali and subregional leaders, civil society organizations and States and organizations concerned about the Somali crisis. Unpos was also closely monitoring the situation in the country and encouraging the Government and other parties to engage in an inclusive dialogue. Unpos activities included political, disarmament, demobilization, reintegration, economic stabilization and human rights activities, and preparation for its relocation to Somalia. Unpos was also responsible for coordinating on the ground UN and international efforts to combat piracy off the Somali coast. It was a member of the anti-piracy coordination centre in Nairobi and a platform for interaction between UN Headquarters and UN agencies on the ground.

Communications. On 15 December [S/2009/664], the Secretary-General informed the Council of his intention to let unpos during the 2010–2011 biennium continue to: assist efforts to strengthen the Transitional Federal Institutions; guide international efforts to re-establish Somalia's security apparatus; coordinate UN political, security, electoral, humanitarian, recovery and development support; coordinate UN and international anti-piracy efforts; and support the regional authorities of "Puntland" and "Somaliland" in maintaining stability. Unpos would also work with UN Headquarters on updating the contingency planning for the possible deployment of a UN peacekeeping mission. The Council took note of the Secretary-General's intention on 21 December [S/2009/665].

Financing

Budget for 2009

In March [A/63/346/Add.6], the Secretary-General set out revised resource requirements for unpos in 2009, amounting to $12,795,500 net ($13,655,600 gross), a reduction of $2,464,600 compared to the appropriations for 2008, due to the inability to relocate to Somalia, resulting in lower requirements for

transportation, communications and information technology equipment. Based on actual 2008 expenditures of $10,158,300, it was estimated that a balance of $6,647,300 was available under the appropriation for the 2008–2009 biennium; accordingly, the net additional requirements for unpos for 2009 would amount to $6,148,000.

Acabq, in March [A/63/779], noted that the proposal for unpos had not been updated to reflect the most recent political development, including measures related to the implementation of Security Council resolution 1863(2009). The Committee was informed that the Secretary-General intended to submit revised budget proposals to the General Assembly at the second part of its resumed sixty-third session. Rather than consider the current proposal and a prospective update separately, acabq recommended that the Assembly take no action on the current proposal, with the exception of the proposals for additional security staff, pending submission of an updated proposal.

On 7 April, the Assembly, in section IV of **resolution 63/268** (see p. 1391), requested the Secretary-General to submit a revised budget proposal for unpos for 2009, for consideration during the second part of its resumed sixty-third (2009) session.

In May [A/63/346/Add.7], the Secretary-General set out the proposed revised unpos budget for 2009, in the amount of $16,004,100 net ($16,987,300 gross). Taking into account already appropriated amounts as well as actual expenditures incurred in 2008, the net additional appropriations amounted to $9,362,700 under section 3, Political affairs, and $983,200 under section 35, Staff assessment, to be offset by the same amount under income section 1, Income from staff assessment, of the 2008–2009 programme budget.

In June [A/63/868], acabq called for efforts to rationalize functions in order to avoid overlap and duplication of activities and resources and to attain greater efficiency and savings, in particular between unpos and unsoa. It recommended approval of the revised unpos budget as proposed by the Secretary-General, subject to its observations and recommendations.

The General Assembly, by **resolution 63/283** of 30 June (see p. 1393), approved the revised unpos budget in the amount of $16,178,500 gross ($15,262,300 net).

Resource requirements for 2010

In a 27 October report [A/64/349] providing estimates of special political missions, good offices and other political initiatives authorized by the Assembly and/or the Council, the Secretary-General submitted requirements for unpos in 2010 in the amount of $17,029,500. The 2010 estimates were detailed in another October report [A/64/349/Add.3] summarizing resource requirements for 10 political missions grouped under the thematic cluster of UN offices, peacebuilding offices, integrated offices and commissions.

The Advisory Committee in December [A/64/7/Add.13] recommended approval by the General Assembly of the resources requested by the Secretary-General, subject to its observations and recommendations.

The General Assembly, in section VI of **resolution 64/245** of 24 December (see p. 1407), endorsed ACABQ's recommendations and approved the budgets for the 26 political missions, including UNPOS, totalling $569,526,500.

African Union Mission in Somalia

The African Union Mission in Somalia (AMISOM) was authorized in 2007 [YUN 2007, p. 268] by the AU Peace and Security Council to support the Transitional Federal Institutions in their efforts to stabilize the country, facilitate the provision of humanitarian assistance and create conditions conducive to stabilization, reconstruction and development. By resolution 1744(2007) [ibid., p. 269], the Security Council approved the Mission's mandate, which was renewed every six months. The Council, by resolutions 1863(2009) (see p. 271) and 1872(2009) (see p. 277), authorized the AU to maintain AMISOM for another six month-period each. As at October 2009, AMISOM's military strength stood at about 5,200 troops, or 65 per cent of the full mandated force of 8,000.

Financing

By resolution 1863(2009) of 16 January, the Security Council requested the Secretary-General to provide UN logistical support to AMISOM in order for the AMISOM forces to be incorporated into a possible UN peacekeeping operation.

In March [A/63/758], the Secretary-General requested General Assembly authorization to enter into commitments for the period from 1 May 2007 to 30 June 2009 in the amount of $80,906,900, inclusive of $50,000,000 previously authorized by ACABQ, in connection with the financing of logistics support for AMISOM and other activities related to a future UN peacekeeping operation.

ACABQ, in March [A/63/780], concurred with the Secretary-General's request, bearing in mind its own observations and recommendations regarding, among others, a trust fund for AMISOM until the deployment of a UN peacekeeping operation, the proposed support office, a memorandum of understanding between the AU and the United Nations, procurement, staffing and accommodation.

On 7 April [meeting 79], the General Assembly, on the recommendation of the Fifth Committee [A/63/789], adopted **resolution 63/275 A** without vote [agenda item 157].

Financing of the activities arising from Security Council resolution 1863(2009)

The General Assembly,

Having considered the report of the Secretary-General on the financing of support for the African Union Mission in Somalia for the period from 1 July 2008 to 30 June 2009 and the related report of the Advisory Committee on Administrative and Budgetary Questions,

Recalling Security Council resolution 1863(2009) of 16 January 2009, in which the Council expressed its intent to establish a United Nations peacekeeping operation in Somalia as a follow-on force to the African Union Mission in Somalia, subject to a further decision of the Council by 1 June 2009, and requested the Secretary-General, in order for the forces of the Mission to be incorporated into a United Nations peacekeeping operation, to provide a United Nations logistical support package to the Mission, including equipment and services,

Recognizing that the costs of this support to the African Union Mission in Somalia are expenses of the Organization to be borne by Member States in accordance with Article 17, paragraph 2, of the Charter of the United Nations,

Recalling that, in its resolution 1863(2009), the Security Council requested the Secretary-General to submit a report on a United Nations peacekeeping operation in Somalia by 15 April 2009,

1. *Requests* the Secretary-General to make the fullest possible use of facilities and equipment at the United Nations Logistics Base at Brindisi, Italy, in order to minimize the costs of procurement for the logistical support package;

2. *Endorses* the conclusions and recommendations contained in the report of the Advisory Committee on Administrative and Budgetary Questions, subject to the provisions of the present resolution, and requests the Secretary-General to ensure their full implementation;

3. *Requests* the Secretary-General to take appropriate measures to ensure effectiveness, efficiency and transparency with regard to the use of United Nations resources, bearing in mind the specific nature of the support package;

Estimates for the period from 1 May 2007 to 30 June 2009

4. *Authorizes* the Secretary-General to establish a special account for the support provided to the African Union Mission in Somalia, for the purpose of accounting for the income received and the expenditure incurred;

5. *Also authorizes* the Secretary-General to enter into commitments for the support of the African Union Mission in Somalia for the period from 1 May 2007 to 30 June 2009 in a total amount not exceeding 77,790,900 United States dollars, inclusive of the amount of 50 million dollars previously authorized by the Advisory Committee under the terms of section IV of General Assembly resolution 49/233 A of 23 December 1994, which comprises the

amount of 2,149,000 dollars for the period from 1 May 2007 to 30 June 2008 and the amount of 47,851,000 dollars for the period from 1 July 2008 to 30 June 2009;

Financing of the commitment authority

6. *Decides* to apportion among Member States the amount of 2,149,000 dollars for the period from 1 May 2007 to 30 June 2008, in accordance with the levels updated in General Assembly resolution 61/243 of 22 December 2006, and taking into account the scale of assessments for 2007 and 2008, as set out in its resolution 61/237 of 22 December 2006;

7. *Also decides* that, in accordance with the provisions of its resolution 973(X) of 15 December 1955, there shall be set off against the apportionment among Member States, as provided for in paragraph 6 above, their respective share in the Tax Equalization Fund of 290,387 dollars, representing the estimated staff assessment income approved for the period from 1 May 2007 to 30 June 2008;

8. *Further decides* to apportion among Member States the amount of 69,338,401 dollars for the period from 1 July 2008 to 31 May 2009, in accordance with the levels updated in General Assembly resolution 61/243, and taking into account the scale of assessments for 2008 and 2009, as set out in its resolution 61/237;

9. *Decides* that, in accordance with the provisions of its resolution 973(X), there shall be set off against the apportionment among Member States, as provided for in paragraph 8 above, their respective share in the Tax Equalization Fund of 239,250 dollars, representing the estimated staff assessment income approved for the period from 1 July 2008 to 31 May 2009;

10. *Also decides* to apportion among Member States the amount of 6,303,499 dollars for the period from 1 to 30 June 2009, in accordance with the levels updated in General Assembly resolution 61/243, and taking into account the scale of assessments for 2008 and 2009, as set out in its resolution 61/237, subject to a decision of the Security Council to extend the mandate;

11. *Further decides* that, in accordance with the provisions of its resolution 973(X), there shall be set off against the apportionment among Member States, as provided for in paragraph 10 above, their respective share in the Tax Equalization Fund of 21,750 dollars, representing the estimated staff assessment income approved for the period from 1 to 30 June 2009, subject to a decision of the Security Council to extend the mandate;

12. *Invites* voluntary contributions to the United Nations Trust Fund established to support the African Union Mission in Somalia;

13. *Decides* to keep under review during its sixty-third session the item entitled "Financing of activities arising from Security Council resolution 1863(2009)".

In a report of 3 June [A/63/867], the Secretary-General stated that the continued presence of AMISOM in Mogadishu remained critical if security conditions were to be improved and maintained while Somali security forces were re-established, and pending a decision by the Security Council on the establishment of a UN peacekeeping operation. Without logistics support from the United Nations and donor assistance for

its other requirements, AMISOM would not achieve its mandated strength of 8,000 troops and 270 civilian police or establish effective peacekeeping operations. He requested General Assembly authorization to enter into commitments in the amount of $185,673,700 for the period from 1 July to 31 December 2009.

The Advisory Committee, in a report of 4 June [A/63/874], recommended that the Assembly authorize commitments in the amount of $124,000,000 for the period from 1 July to 31 December 2009. The Committee stressed that its recommendation in no way prejudged the position it might take on the structure, number and level of posts or on other resources intended for the provision of support to AMISOM or a future UN peacekeeping operation in Somalia.

GENERAL ASSEMBLY ACTION

On 30 June [meeting 93], on the recommendation of the Fifth Committee [A/63/789/Add.1], the General Assembly adopted **resolution 63/275 B** without vote [agenda item 157].

Financing of the activities arising from Security Council resolution 1863(2009)

The General Assembly,

Having considered the report of the Secretary-General on the financing of support of the African Union Mission in Somalia for the period from 1 July to 31 December 2009 and the related report of the Advisory Committee on Administrative and Budgetary Questions,

Recalling Security Council resolution 1863(2009) of 16 January 2009, by which the Council expressed its intent to establish a United Nations peacekeeping operation in Somalia as a follow-on force to the African Union Mission in Somalia, subject to its further decision by 1 June 2009, and requested the Secretary-General, in order for the forces of the Mission to be incorporated into a United Nations peacekeeping operation, to provide a United Nations logistical support package to the Mission, including equipment and services,

Recalling also Security Council resolution 1872(2009) of 26 May 2009, in which the Council requested the Secretary-General to continue to provide a logistical support package for the African Union Mission in Somalia until 31 January 2010,

Recalling further its resolution 63/275 A of 7 April 2009 on the financing of activities arising from Security Council resolution 1863(2009),

Reaffirming the general principles underlying the financing of United Nations peacekeeping operations, as stated in General Assembly resolutions 1874(S-IV) of 27 June 1963, 3101(XXVIII) of 11 December 1973 and 55/235 of 23 December 2000,

Noting with appreciation that voluntary contributions have been made to the United Nations Trust Fund established to support the African Union Mission in Somalia,

1. *Requests* the Secretary-General to make the fullest possible use of the facilities and equipment at the United Nations Logistics Base at Brindisi, Italy, in order to mini-

mize the costs of procurement for the logistical support package;

2. *Acknowledges with appreciation* that the use of the logistics hub at Entebbe, Uganda, has been cost-effective and has resulted in savings for the United Nations, and welcomes the expansion of the logistics hub to provide logistical support to peacekeeping operations in the region and to contribute further to their enhanced efficiency and responsiveness, taking into account the ongoing efforts in this regard;

3. *Requests* the Secretary-General to ensure that proposed peacekeeping budgets are based on relevant legislative mandates;

4. *Endorses* the conclusions and recommendations contained in the report of the Advisory Committee on Administrative and Budgetary Questions, subject to the provisions of the present resolution, and requests the Secretary-General to ensure their full implementation;

5. *Requests* the Secretary-General to take appropriate measures to ensure effectiveness, efficiency and transparency with regard to the use of United Nations resources, bearing in mind the specific nature of the support package;

**Estimates for the period
from 1 July to 31 December 2009**

6. *Takes note* of paragraph 20 of the report of the Advisory Committee on Administrative and Budgetary Questions;

7. *Authorizes* the Secretary-General to enter into commitments for the support of the African Union Mission in Somalia for the period from 1 July to 31 December 2009 in a total amount not exceeding 138,802,500 United States dollars;

8. *Requests* the Secretary-General to submit a full 2009/10 budget in a timely manner, with a view to taking a decision thereon no later than 31 October 2009;

Financing of the commitment authority

9. *Decides* to apportion among Member States the amount of 138,802,500 dollars for the period from 1 July to 31 December 2009, in accordance with the levels updated in General Assembly resolution 61/243 of 22 December 2006, and taking into account the scale of assessments for 2009, as set out in its resolution 61/237 of 22 December 2006;

10. *Also decides* that, in accordance with the provisions of its resolution 973(X) of 15 December 1955, there shall be set off against the apportionment among Member States, as provided for in paragraph 9 above, their respective share in the Tax Equalization Fund of 1,347,800 dollars, representing the estimated staff assessment income approved for the period from 1 July to 31 December 2009;

**Estimates for the support account for
peacekeeping operations and the United Nations
Logistics Base for the period from 1 July 2009 to
30 June 2010**

11. *Further decides* to appropriate to the Special Account for the support of the African Union Mission in Somalia the amount of 6,102,400 dollars for the period from 1 July 2009 to 30 June 2010, comprising 5,078,700 dollars for the support account for peacekeeping op-

erations and 1,023,700 dollars for the United Nations Logistics Base;

Financing of the appropriation

12. *Decides* to apportion among Member States the amount of 6,102,400 dollars, in accordance with the levels updated in resolution 61/243, and taking into account the scale of assessments for 2009, as set out in resolution 61/237, and the scale of assessments for 2010;

13. *Also decides* that, in accordance with the provisions of its resolution 973(X), there shall be set off against the apportionment among Member States, as provided for in paragraph 12 above, their respective share in the Tax Equalization Fund of 629,700 dollars, comprising the prorated share of 528,700 dollars of the estimated staff assessment income approved for the support account and the prorated share of 101,000 dollars of the estimated staff assessment income approved for the United Nations Logistics Base;

14. *Invites* voluntary contributions to the Trust Fund in Support of the African Union Mission to Somalia;

15. *Decides* to include in the provisional agenda of its sixty-fourth session the item entitled "Financing of activities arising from Security Council resolution 1863(2009)".

In September [A/64/465], the Secretary-General submitted the budget for the financing of support to AMISOM for the period from 1 July 2009 to 30 June 2010, amounting to $225,439,100, inclusive of budgeted voluntary contributions in kind in the amount of $1,059,100. The budget provided for the deployment of 176 international and 104 national staff in support of an authorized AMISOM strength of 8,000 military personnel and 270 police officers.

In October [A/64/509], ACABQ recommended a reduction of $9,800,000 in the proposed budget and an appropriation of $214,580,000.

GENERAL ASSEMBLY ACTION

On 10 December [meeting 62], the General Assembly, on the recommendation of the Fifth Committee [A/64/553], adopted **resolution 64/107** without vote [agenda item 163].

**Financing of support of the
African Union Mission in Somalia**

The General Assembly,

Having considered the report of the Secretary-General on the financing of support of the African Union Mission in Somalia for the period from 1 July 2009 to 30 June 2010 and the related report of the Advisory Committee on Administrative and Budgetary Questions,

Recalling Security Council resolution 1863(2009) of 16 January 2009, by which the Council expressed its intent to establish a United Nations peacekeeping operation in Somalia as a follow-on force to the African Union Mission in Somalia, subject to its further decision by 1 June 2009, and requested the Secretary-General, in order for the forces of the Mission to be incorporated into a United Nations peacekeeping operation, to provide a United Nations logistical support package to the Mission, including equipment and services,

Recalling also Security Council resolution 1872(2009) of 26 May 2009, by which the Council requested the Secretary-General to continue to provide a logistical support package to the African Union Mission in Somalia until 31 January 2010,

Recalling further its resolution 63/275 B of 30 June 2009 on the financing of the activities arising from Security Council resolution 1863(2009),

Reaffirming the general principles underlying the financing of United Nations peacekeeping operations, as stated in General Assembly resolutions 1874(S-IV) of 27 June 1963, 3101(XXVIII) of 11 December 1973 and 55/235 of 23 December 2000,

Noting with appreciation that voluntary contributions have been made to the United Nations Trust Fund established to support the African Union Mission in Somalia,

1. *Requests* the Secretary-General to make the fullest possible use of facilities and equipment at the United Nations Logistics Base at Brindisi, Italy, in order to minimize the costs of procurement for the logistical support package;

2. *Acknowledges with appreciation* that the use of the logistics hub at Entebbe, Uganda, has been cost-effective and has resulted in savings for the United Nations, and welcomes the expansion of the logistics hub to provide logistical support to peacekeeping operations in the region and to contribute further to their enhanced efficiency and responsiveness, taking into account the ongoing efforts in this regard;

3. *Endorses* the conclusions and recommendations contained in the report of the Advisory Committee on Administrative and Budgetary Questions, subject to the provisions of the present resolution, and requests the Secretary-General to ensure their full implementation;

4. *Requests* the Secretary-General to take appropriate measures to ensure effectiveness, efficiency and transparency with regard to the use of United Nations resources, bearing in mind the specific nature of the support package;

5. *Encourages* the Secretary-General to expedite the construction of facilities as set out in paragraph 124 of his report;

**Expenditure for the period
from 1 July 2008 to 30 June 2009**

6. *Takes note* of the expenditure report for the period from 1 July 2008 to 30 June 2009;

7. *Decides* to appropriate to the Special Account for the support provided to the African Union Mission in Somalia the amount of 75,641,900 United States dollars for the period from 1 July 2008 to 30 June 2009 previously authorized under the terms of General Assembly resolution 63/275 A of 7 April 2009;

**Estimates for the period
from 1 July 2009 to 30 June 2010**

8. *Also decides* to appropriate to the Special Account for the support provided to the African Union Mission in Somalia the amount of 213,580,000 dollars for the period from 1 July 2009 to 30 June 2010, inclusive of the amount of 138,802,500 dollars previously authorized under the terms of General Assembly resolution 63/275 B, and in addition to the amount of 6,102,400 dollars previously appropriated under the terms of resolution 63/275 B;

**Financing of the appropriation for the period
from 1 July 2009 to 30 June 2010**

9. *Further decides*, taking into account the amount of 138,802,500 dollars previously apportioned under the terms of resolution 63/275 B, to apportion among Member States the additional amount of 12,462,917 dollars for the period from 1 to 31 January 2010, in accordance with the levels updated in General Assembly resolution 61/243 of 22 December 2006, and taking into account the scale of assessments for 2010;

10. *Decides* that, in accordance with the provisions of its resolution 973(X) of 15 December 1955, there shall be set off against the apportionment among Member States, as provided for in paragraph 9 above, their respective share in the Tax Equalization Fund of 168,483 dollars, representing the additional staff assessment income for the period from 1 to 31 January 2010;

11. *Also decides* to apportion among Member States the amount of 62,314,583 dollars for the period 1 February to 30 June 2010 at a monthly rate of 12,462,917 dollars, taking into account the scale of assessments for 2010, subject to a decision of the Security Council to extend the mandate;

12. *Further decides* that, in accordance with the provisions of its resolution 973(X), there shall be set off against the apportionment among Member States, as provided for in paragraph 11 above, their respective share in the Tax Equalization Fund of 842,417 dollars;

13. *Decides* that, for Member States that have fulfilled their financial obligations to the entity, there shall be set off against their apportionment, as provided for in paragraph 9 above, their respective share of the unencumbered balance and other income in the total amount of 3,721,100 dollars in respect of the financial period ended 30 June 2009, in accordance with the levels updated in General Assembly resolution 61/243 and taking into account the scale of assessments for 2009, as set out in its resolution 61/237 of 22 December 2006;

14. *Also decides* that, for Member States that have not fulfilled their financial obligations to the entity, there shall be set off against their outstanding obligations their respective share of the unencumbered balance and other income in the total amount of 3,721,100 dollars in respect of the financial period ended 30 June 2009, in accordance with the scheme set out in paragraph 13 above;

15. *Further decides* that the increase of 258,000 dollars in the estimated staff assessment income in respect of the financial period ended 30 June 2009 shall be added to the credits from the amount of 3,721,100 dollars referred to in paragraphs 13 and 14 above;

16. *Invites* voluntary contributions to the United Nations Trust Fund established to support the African Union Mission in Somalia;

17. *Decides* to keep under review during its sixty-fourth session the item entitled "Financing of the activities arising from Security Council resolution 1863(2009)".

Sanctions

The Security Council, by resolution 733(1992) [YUN 1992, p. 199], imposed a general and complete arms embargo on Somalia, and by resolution

751(1992) [ibid., p. 202] established a Committee to oversee the embargo. Subsequently, in resolutions 1356(2001) [YUN 2001, p. 212], 1425(2002) [YUN 2002, p. 206], 1744(2007) [YUN 2007, p. 269] and 1772(2007) [ibid., p. 276], the Council outlined certain extensions to the embargo and further elaborated the scope of the measures.

By resolution 1844(2008) [YUN 2008, p. 297], the Council reaffirmed the general and complete arms embargo and by resolution 1853(2008) [ibid., p. 301], it extended the mandate of the Monitoring Group investigating the implementation and violations of the embargo for a 12-month period, with the addition of a fifth expert.

Speaking on 25 September at the General Assembly's general debate [A/64/PV.7], President Ahmed urged the Council to reconsider the matter of the arms embargo.

Appointments. On 6 March [S/2009/136] and 31 March [S/2009/172], the Secretary-General informed the Security Council of the five experts whom he had appointed to the Monitoring Group.

Communication. On 16 June [S/2009/312], Eritrea reaffirmed that it was not sending arms and ammunition to any party in Somalia and had not violated the arms embargo, contrary to accusations.

Security Council consideration. In resolution 1907(2009) of 23 December (see p. 299), the Council reiterated that all Member States, including Eritrea, should comply with the arms embargo. It demanded that Eritrea cease all efforts to destabilize or overthrow the Transitional Federal Government and cease arming, training and equipping armed groups that aimed to destabilize the region. The Council expanded the mandate of the Monitoring Group to undertake the additional tasks stipulated in the resolution.

Speaking during the Council debate [meeting 6254], Somalia said that it supported the resolution as a very positive step towards resolving the situation of insecurity in the Horn of Africa. Eritrea had been a major negative factor in the prolongation of the conflict in Somalia. The Transitional Federal Government had repeatedly shown its willingness to enter into dialogue with Eritrea with a view to resolving all differences and to persuading the latter to desist from meddling in Somalia's affairs, to no avail. Among Eritrea's hostile activities against Somalia during the past two decades were: giving refuge and safe haven to known terrorists, rebels, spoilers and human rights violators; providing financing and facilitating the flow of arms and resources to terrorist elements in Somalia; providing economic, political, moral and propaganda support to the armed insurgents; blatantly sabotaging peace efforts and reconciliation; and frustrating

government efforts towards stabilization, rehabilitation and reconstruction.

Committee on sanctions. The Committee on sanctions met four times during 2009 [S/2010/14] in informal consultations. On 17 February, the Committee approved a note to all Member States drawing their attention to the various provisions of Council resolution 1844(2008), and on 11 May, it adopted revised guidelines for the conduct of its work to facilitate implementation of that resolution. On 8 and 15 July, the Monitoring Group submitted, at the Committee's request, a draft list of individuals and entities who had violated the measures implemented by Member States in accordance with Council resolutions 733(1992) and 1844(2008), inside and outside Somalia, and their supporters. On 24 September, the Committee addressed a note to Member States drawing their attention to the measures in resolution 1844(2008), in particular to the procedure for exemptions to the arms embargo and to the Monitoring Group's mandate. On 2 October, the Committee addressed letters to Eritrea, Ethiopia, Kenya, Somalia, the United Arab Emirates and Yemen, as well as to the AU Commissioner for Peace and Security. On 16 November, the Committee Chairman briefed the Security Council in connection with its activities and regarding the review of measures to implement the sanctions. On 11 December, by a press release, the Committee deplored acts of intimidation and interference with the Monitoring Group's work and urged Member States to cooperate with the Group's investigation and to provide the necessary assistance to ensure that its activities continued unhindered.

During the year, the Committee approved two requests for exemptions from the arms embargo for non-lethal military equipment and 11 requests for exemptions pursuant to paragraph 11 *(b)* of Council resolution 1772(2007). The Committee did not approve one request for an exemption pursuant to paragraph 11 *(b)* of that same resolution, and in that connection, the Chairman on 18 June sent a letter to the Security Council Committee established pursuant to resolution 1737(2006) [YUN 2006, p. 436], which dealt with sanctions against Iran.

The Committee during the year received reports from 25 Member States on measures they had taken to implement the sanctions. Those reports were listed in an appendix.

Djibouti and Eritrea

In 2009, the border dispute between Djibouti and Eritrea on Ras Doumeira and Doumeira Island continued. The Security Council in January urged both countries to resolve their dispute peacefully. In December, the Council reiterated its demand that Eritrea withdraw its forces and ensure that no military presence or activity was pursued in the area where the conflict occurred—Ras Doumeira and Doumeira Island. The Council demanded that Eritrea acknowledge its border dispute with Djibouti, engage in diplomatic efforts to settle the border issue and cooperate with the Secretary-General's good offices. The Council imposed an arms embargo and targeted sanctions on Eritrea.

Communication. On 12 January [S/2009/28], Eritrea expressed concern at attempts by Security Council members to adopt a resolution in relation to a question "Djibouti-Eritrea" on the basis of unfounded accusations against Eritrea. For the fourth time, Eritrea was falling victim to political intrigues of major Powers by manufacturing a "Djibouti-Eritrea border conflict". The condemnation of Eritrea in June 2008 [YUN 2008, p. 316], followed by the dispatch of a fact-finding mission [ibid., p. 317], clearly demonstrated that certain Council members were bent on pursuing national interests with little or no regard to the facts on the ground and to the maintenance of regional peace and security. Eritrea had not occupied any land belonging to Djibouti and could not accept a resolution that demanded the "withdrawal of its forces" from its own territory.

SECURITY COUNCIL ACTION

On 14 January [meeting 6065], the Security Council unanimously adopted **resolution 1862(2009)**. The draft [S/2009/25] was submitted by France.

The Security Council,

Affirming its strong commitment to the sovereignty, independence, territorial integrity and unity of both Djibouti and Eritrea, and recalling the importance of the principles of good-neighbourliness, non-interference and regional cooperation,

Recalling that in the statement by its President of 12 June 2008, it condemned Eritrea's military action against Djibouti in Ras Doumeira and Doumeira Island and called upon the two parties to show maximum restraint and withdraw forces to the status quo ante,

Taking note of the letter dated 11 September 2008 from the Secretary-General to the President of the Security Council, in which he transmitted the report of the fact-finding mission that he sent following the meeting of the Council held on 24 June 2008,

Expressing its deep concern that, as mentioned in the report of the fact-finding mission referred to above, Eritrea has not withdrawn its forces to the status quo ante, as called for by the Council in the statement by its President of 12 June 2008,

Reiterating its serious concern at the absence of dialogue between the two parties and at the refusal of Eritrea so far to engage in dialogue, to accept bilateral contacts, mediation or facilitation efforts by subregional or regional organizations or to respond positively to the efforts of the Secretary-General,

Noting that Djibouti has withdrawn its forces to the status quo ante and has cooperated fully with the fact-finding mission mentioned above, as well as with other missions sent by subregional and regional organizations,

Taking note of the first visit to Asmara, since the conflict of June 2008, of the Chairperson of the African Union Commission in October 2008,

Expressing its deep concern about the continuing tense border dispute between Djibouti and Eritrea and over the possible impact of the grave and unstable security situation in the Doumeira area on subregional stability and security after the serious incidents of 10 June 2008, which led to dozens of dead and wounded,

1. *Urges* Djibouti and Eritrea to resolve their border dispute peacefully, as a matter of priority and in a manner consistent with international law, and emphasizes that it is the primary responsibility of the parties to set up the appropriate diplomatic and legal framework to this end;

2. *Reiterates its appreciation* for the efforts of the Secretary-General, the African Union and the League of Arab States to engage both parties, encourages them to strengthen their efforts in this regard, and also encourages regional and subregional organizations as well as Member States that are in a position to do so to provide their assistance to this end;

3. *Welcomes* the offer of good offices made by the Secretary-General, deeply regrets that Eritrea has continuously refused to grant visas to the members of the fact-finding mission mentioned above or to receive any envoy of the Secretary-General, and welcomes the continued readiness of the Secretary-General to send a fact-finding mission or an envoy to Eritrea;

4. *Also welcomes* the fact that Djibouti has withdrawn its forces to the status quo ante, as called for by the Security Council in the statement by its President of 12 June 2008 and as established by the fact-finding mission, and condemns the refusal of Eritrea to do so;

5. *Demands* that Eritrea:

    (i) Withdraw its forces and all their equipment to the positions of the status quo ante, and ensure that no military presence or activity is being pursued in the area where the conflict occurred in Ras Doumeira and Doumeira Island in June 2008;

    (ii) Acknowledge its border dispute with Djibouti in Ras Doumeira and Doumeira Island, engage actively in dialogue to defuse the tension and engage also in diplomatic efforts leading to a mutually acceptable settlement of the border issue;

    (iii) Abide by its international obligations as a Member of the United Nations, respect the principles mentioned in Article 2, paragraphs 3, 4 and 5, and Article 33 of the Charter of the United Nations, and cooperate fully with the Secretary-General, in particular through his proposal of good offices mentioned in paragraph 3 above;

6. *Also demands* that Eritrea comply immediately with paragraph 5 above and, in any case, no later than five weeks after the adoption of the present resolution;

7. *Requests* the Secretary-General to provide to the Council a report on the evolution of the situation, on compliance by both parties with their obligations, and on his contacts with both parties and, as appropriate, with the

African Union and other relevant regional organizations, no later than six weeks after the adoption of the present resolution;

8. *Decides* to review the situation six weeks from the adoption of the present resolution, on the basis of the report mentioned in paragraph 7 above, with a view to taking, as appropriate, a further decision;

9. *Decides also* to remain actively seized of the matter.

Communications. The Secretary-General, on 30 March [S/2009/163], reported to the Security Council that in a statement of 15 January, Eritrea had rejected resolution 1862(2009) (see above) characterizing it as ill-considered, unbalanced and unnecessary. In its efforts to implement the resolution, the UN Secretariat held discussions with representatives of Eritrea and Djibouti, as well as the AU. Efforts to discuss the matter further with IGAD had been hampered by the suspension of Eritrea's membership in IGAD in April 2007. The AU summit (Addis Ababa, 26 January–3 February) presented an opportunity to discuss the matter with AU officials and other Member States. At a meeting on 2 February in Addis Ababa, the President of Djibouti, Ismail Omar Guelleh, informed the Secretary-General of the tense situation between Djibouti and Eritrea, as the latter had refused both mediation and direct negotiations. The President reiterated that mediation and strong international pressure were necessary to persuade Eritrea to comply with resolution 1862(2009). Meetings with Eritrean officials did not take place in the margins of the AU summit. However, in January 2009, a senior UN official held encouraging discussions with government officials in Asmara; despite that diplomatic overture, attempts to send a fact-finding mission to Eritrea had not received a positive response. In addition, the Secretary-General's continuing efforts to engage the Eritrean Government by dispatching a high-level official to Eritrea and the region had yet to produce results. The situation, though calm, remained tense and there was no information that Eritrea had complied with paragraph 5 of resolution 1862(2009). Eritrea insisted that it had not occupied any land belonging to Djibouti and could not accept a demand that it withdraw its forces from its own territory. The Secretariat remained in contact with both countries, as well as with regional organizations. The Secretary-General would pursue those contacts to assess how the Secretariat could best assist the two parties and the region in implementing resolution 1862(2009).

On 6 April [S/2009/180], Djibouti said that almost a year had passed since Eritrea had illegally occupied Ras Doumeira and Doumeira Island. Eritrea should not be allowed to disregard the Council decision with impunity. Urgent implementation of the resolution was expected and the Council should be able to make an appropriate decision. On 23 April [S/2009/217], Dji-

bouti reported that since adoption of the resolution, several regional organizations had taken decisions with respect to implementation of resolution 1862(2009): IGAD (27 January); AU Assembly (1–3 February); League of Arab States (30 and 31 March); and Organization of the Islamic Conference (15 February). Their latest positions showed a growing convergence on the need to effect an appropriate decision without further delay. On 19 June [S/2009/319], Djibouti requested that action regarding implementation of resolution 1862(2009) by Eritrea be taken as soon as possible.

Sanctions

The AU, at is thirteenth summit (Sirte, Libyan Arab Jamahiriya, 1–3 July) [Assembly/AU/Dec.252(XIII)], called on the Security Council to impose sanctions against all foreign actors, both within and outside the region, especially Eritrea, providing support to the armed groups engaged in destabilizing Somalia and undermining the peace and reconciliation efforts and regional stability. It urged Eritrea to comply with AU and Security Council demands on the border crisis.

Communications. On 23 November [S/2009/602], Eritrea noted that a draft resolution, based on unfounded assumptions, was being circulated to Security Council members, supposedly to bring peace and stability to the Horn of Africa, but whose sole purpose was to impose sanctions on Eritrea. A durable solution in Somalia, Eritrea said, required the participation of all key Somali actors in an inclusive political process. The final and binding demarcation decision that was awarded by the Eritrea-Ethiopia Boundary Commission [YUN 2006, p. 324] could not remain shelved if peace and stability were to take root in the region. The matter was at the heart of the turbulent situation in the Horn of Africa, including the difficult relations between Djibouti and Eritrea. The Council should not ignore the real issue behind many conflicts in the region and should ensure that Ethiopia abides by treaty obligations and international law and withdraws its troops from sovereign Eritrean territories that it illegally occupied.

On 15 December [S/2009/658], Eritrea charged that the draft resolution tabled in the Council had no factual or legal justification. The draft resolution was tabled by Uganda, but the main architect of that resolution was the United States, whose unprovoked hostility towards Eritrea predated and transcended any recent developments.

SECURITY COUNCIL ACTION

On 23 December [meeting 6254], the Security Council adopted **resolution 1907(2009)** by vote (13-1-1). The draft [S/2009/654] was submitted by Uganda.

The Security Council,

Recalling its previous resolutions and the statements by its President concerning the situation in Somalia and the border dispute between Djibouti and Eritrea, in particular resolutions 751(1992) of 24 April 1992, 1844(2008) of 20 November 2008 and 1862(2009) of 14 January 2009, and the statements by its President of 12 June 2008 and 15 May and 9 July 2009,

Reaffirming its respect for the sovereignty, territorial integrity and political independence and unity of Somalia, Djibouti and Eritrea, respectively,

Expressing the importance of resolving the border dispute between Djibouti and Eritrea,

Reaffirming that the Djibouti agreement and peace process represent the basis for a resolution of the conflict in Somalia, and further reaffirming its support for the Transitional Federal Government,

Noting the decision adopted at the thirteenth Assembly of the African Union, held in Sirte, Libyan Arab Jamahiriya, from 1 to 3 July 2009, calling upon the Security Council to impose sanctions against foreign actors, both within and outside the region, especially Eritrea, providing support to the armed groups engaged in destabilization activities in Somalia and undermining the peace and reconciliation efforts as well as regional stability,

Noting also the decision of the thirteenth Assembly of the African Union expressing its grave concern at the total absence of progress regarding the implementation by Eritrea of, inter alia, resolution 1862(2009) regarding the border dispute between Djibouti and Eritrea,

Expressing its grave concern at the findings of the Monitoring Group on Somalia re-established by resolution 1853(2008) of 19 December 2008, as outlined in its report of 10 December 2008, that Eritrea has provided political, financial and logistical support to armed groups engaged in undermining peace and reconciliation in Somalia and regional stability,

Condemning all armed attacks on Transitional Federal Government officials and institutions, the civilian population, humanitarian workers and the personnel of the African Union Mission in Somalia,

Expressing its grave concern at Eritrea's rejection of the Djibouti agreement, as noted in the letter dated 19 May 2009 from the Permanent Representative of Eritrea to the United Nations addressed to the President of the Security Council,

Recalling its resolution 1844(2008), in which it decided to impose measures against individuals or entities designated as engaging in or providing support to acts that threaten peace, security and stability in Somalia, acting in violation of the arms embargo or obstructing the flow of humanitarian assistance to Somalia,

Expressing its appreciation of the contribution of the African Union Mission in Somalia to the stability of Somalia, and further expressing its appreciation for the continued commitment to the Mission by the Governments of Burundi and Uganda,

Reiterating its intention to take measures against those who seek to prevent or block the Djibouti peace process,

Expressing its deep concern that Eritrea has not withdrawn its forces to the status quo ante, as called for by the Council in its resolution 1862(2009) and the statement by its President of 12 June 2008,

Reiterating its serious concern at the refusal of Eritrea so far to engage in dialogue with Djibouti, or to accept bilateral contacts, mediation or facilitation efforts by subregional or regional organizations or to respond positively to the efforts of the Secretary-General,

Taking note of the letter dated 30 March 2009 from the Secretary-General to the President of the Security Council and the subsequent briefings by the Secretariat on the Djibouti-Eritrea conflict,

Noting that Djibouti has withdrawn its forces to the status quo ante and cooperated fully with all concerned, including the United Nations fact-finding mission and the good offices of the Secretary-General,

Determining that Eritrea's actions undermining peace and reconciliation in Somalia as well as the dispute between Djibouti and Eritrea constitute a threat to international peace and security,

Acting under Chapter VII of the Charter of the United Nations,

1. *Reiterates* that all Member States, including Eritrea, shall comply fully with the terms of the arms embargo imposed by paragraph 5 of resolution 733(1992) of 23 January 1992, as elaborated upon and amended by resolutions 1356(2001) of 19 June 2001, 1425(2002) of 22 July 2002, 1725(2006) of 6 December 2006, 1744(2007) of 20 February 2007 and 1772(2007) of 20 August 2007 on Somalia, and the provisions of resolution 1844(2008);

2. *Calls upon* all Member States, including Eritrea, to support the Djibouti peace process and support reconciliation efforts by the Transitional Federal Government in Somalia, and demands that Eritrea cease all efforts to destabilize or overthrow, directly or indirectly, the Transitional Federal Government;

3. *Reiterates its demand* that Eritrea immediately comply with resolution 1862(2009) and:

    (i) Withdraw its forces and all their equipment to the positions of the status quo ante, and ensure that no military presence or activity is being pursued in the area where the conflict occurred in Ras Doumeira and Doumeira Island in June 2008;

    (ii) Acknowledge its border dispute with Djibouti in Ras Doumeira and Doumeira Island, engage actively in dialogue to defuse the tension and engage also in diplomatic efforts leading to a mutually acceptable settlement of the border issue;

    (iii) Abide by its international obligations as a Member of the United Nations, respect the principles mentioned in Article 2, paragraphs 3, 4 and 5, and Article 33 of the Charter of the United Nations, and cooperate fully with the Secretary-General, in particular through his proposal of good offices mentioned in paragraph 3 of resolution 1862(2009);

4. *Demands* that Eritrea make available information pertaining to Djiboutian combatants missing in action since the clashes of 10 to 12 June 2008 so that those concerned may ascertain the presence and condition of Djiboutian prisoners of war;

5. *Decides* that all Member States shall immediately take the measures necessary to prevent the sale or supply to Eritrea, by their nationals or from their territories or using their flag vessels or aircraft, of arms and related materiel of all types, including weapons and ammunition, military vehicles and equipment, paramilitary equipment

and spare parts for the aforementioned, and technical assistance, training, and financial and other assistance related to military activities or to the provision, manufacture, maintenance or use of these items, whether or not originating in their territories;

6. *Decides also* that Eritrea shall not supply, sell or transfer directly or indirectly from its territory or by its nationals or using its flag vessels or aircraft any arms or related materiel, and that all Member States shall prohibit the procurement of the items, training and assistance described in paragraph 5 above from Eritrea by their nationals, or using their flag vessels or aircraft, whether or not originating in the territory of Eritrea;

7. *Calls upon* all Member States to inspect, in their territories, including seaports and airports, in accordance with their national authorities and legislation, and consistent with international law, all cargo to and from Somalia and Eritrea, if the State concerned has information that provides reasonable grounds to believe the cargo contains items, the supply, transfer or export of which is prohibited by paragraphs 5 and 6 of the present resolution or the general and complete arms embargo to Somalia established pursuant to paragraph 5 of resolution 733(1992) and elaborated upon and amended by subsequent resolutions for the purpose of ensuring strict implementation of those provisions;

8. . *Decides* to authorize all Member States to, and that all Member States shall, upon discovery of items prohibited by paragraphs 5 and 6 of the present resolution, seize and dispose of (either by destroying or rendering inoperable) items, the supply, sale, transfer or export of which is prohibited by paragraphs 5 and 6 of the present resolution, and decides further that all Member States shall cooperate in such efforts;

9. *Requires* any Member State, when it finds items, the supply, sale, transfer or export of which is prohibited by paragraphs 5 and 6 of the present resolution, to submit promptly a report to the Security Council Committee established pursuant to resolution 751(1992) and expanded by resolution 1844(2008) (hereinafter "the Committee") containing relevant details, including the steps taken to seize and dispose of the items;

10. *Decides* that all Member States shall take the measures necessary to prevent the entry into or transit through their territories of individuals designated by the Committee pursuant to the criteria in paragraph 15 below, provided that nothing in the present paragraph shall oblige a State to refuse entry into its territory to its own nationals;

11. *Decides also* that the measures imposed by paragraph 10 above shall not apply:

(a) Where the Committee determines on a case-by-case basis that such travel is justified on the grounds of humanitarian need, including religious obligation; or

(b) Where the Committee determines on a case-by-case basis that an exemption would otherwise further the objectives of peace and stability in the region;

12. *Decides further* that all Member States shall take the measures necessary to prevent the direct or indirect supply, sale or transfer by their nationals or from their territories or using their flag vessels or aircraft of arms and related materiel of all types, including weapons and ammunition, military vehicles and equipment, paramilitary equipment

and spare parts for the aforementioned and the direct or indirect supply of technical assistance or training, and financial and other assistance, including investment, brokering or other financial services, related to military activities or to the supply, sale, transfer, manufacture, maintenance or use of weapons and military equipment to the individuals or entities designated by the Committee pursuant to paragraph 15 below;

13. *Decides* that all Member States shall freeze without delay the funds, other financial assets and economic resources which are on their territories on the date of adoption of the present resolution or at any time thereafter that are owned or controlled, directly or indirectly, by the entities and individuals designated by the Committee pursuant to paragraph 15 below, or by individuals or entities acting on their behalf or at their direction, and decides further that all Member States shall ensure that no funds, financial assets or economic resources are made available by their nationals or by any individuals or entities within their territories to or for the benefit of such individuals or entities;

14. *Decides also* that the measures imposed by paragraph 13 above do not apply to funds, other financial assets or economic resources that have been determined by relevant Member States:

(a) To be necessary for basic expenses, including payment for foodstuffs, rent or mortgage, medicines and medical treatment, taxes, insurance premiums and public utility charges or exclusively for payment of reasonable professional fees and reimbursement of incurred expenses associated with the provision of legal services, or fees or service charges, in accordance with national laws, for routine holding or maintenance of frozen funds, other financial assets and economic resources, after notification by the relevant Member State to the Committee of the intention to authorize, where appropriate, access to such funds, other financial assets or economic resources and in the absence of a negative decision by the Committee within three working days of such notification;

(b) To be necessary for extraordinary expenses, provided that such determination has been notified by the relevant Member State(s) to the Committee and has been approved by the Committee; or

(c) To be the subject of a judicial, administrative or arbitral lien or judgment, in which case the funds, other financial assets and economic resources may be used to satisfy that lien or judgment, provided that the lien or judgment was entered into prior to the date of the present resolution, is not for the benefit of a person or entity designated pursuant to paragraph 15 below and has been notified by the relevant Member State(s) to the Committee;

15. *Decides further* that the provisions of paragraph 10 above shall apply to individuals, including but not limited to the Eritrean political and military leadership, and that the provisions of paragraphs 12 and 13 above shall apply to individuals and entities, including but not limited to the Eritrean political and military leadership, governmental and parastatal entities, and entities privately owned by Eritrean nationals living within or outside of Eritrean territory, designated by the Committee as:

(a) Violating the measures established by paragraphs 5 and 6 above;

(b) Providing support from Eritrea to armed opposition groups which aim to destabilize the region;

(c) Obstructing the implementation of resolution 1862(2009) concerning Djibouti;

(d) Harbouring, financing, facilitating, supporting, organizing, training or inciting individuals or groups to perpetrate acts of violence or terrorist acts against other States or their citizens in the region;

(e) Obstructing the investigations or work of the Monitoring Group on Somalia;

16. *Demands* that all Member States, in particular Eritrea, cease arming, training and equipping armed groups and their members, including Al-Shabaab, that aim to destabilize the region or incite violence and civil strife in Djibouti;

17. *Demands also* that Eritrea cease facilitating travel and other forms of financial support to individuals or entities designated by the Committee and other sanctions committees, in particular the Security Council Committee established pursuant to resolution 1267(1999), in line with the provisions set out in the relevant resolutions;

18. *Decides* to further expand the mandate of the Committee to undertake the additional tasks:

(a) To monitor, with the support of the Monitoring Group, the implementation of the measures imposed in paragraphs 5, 6, 8, 10, 12 and 13 above;

(b) To designate those individuals or entities subject to the measures imposed by paragraphs 10, 12 and 13 above, pursuant to criteria set forth in paragraph 15 above;

(c) To consider and decide upon requests for the exemptions set out in paragraphs 11 and 14 above;

(d) To update its guidelines to reflect its additional tasks;

19. *Decides also* to further expand the mandate of the Monitoring Group re-established by resolution 1853(2008) to monitor and report on the implementation of the measures imposed in the present resolution and undertake the tasks outlined below, and requests the Secretary-General to make appropriate arrangements for additional resources and personnel so that the expanded Monitoring Group may continue to carry out its mandate, and in addition:

(a) Assist the Committee in monitoring the implementation of the measures imposed in paragraphs 5, 6, 8, 10, 12 and 13 above, including by reporting any information on violations;

(b) Consider any information relevant to the implementation of paragraphs 16 and 17 above that should be brought to the attention of the Committee;

(c) Include in its reports to the Security Council any information relevant to the designation by the Committee of the individuals and entities described in paragraph 15 above;

(d) Coordinate as appropriate with panels of experts of other sanctions committees in pursuit of these tasks;

20. *Calls upon* all Member States to report to the Council within one hundred and twenty days of the adoption of the present resolution on steps that they have taken to implement the measures outlined in paragraphs 5, 6, 10, 12 and 13 above;

21. *Affirms* that it shall keep Eritrea's actions under review and that it shall be prepared to adjust the measures,

including through their strengthening, modification or lifting, in the light of Eritrea's compliance with the provisions of the present resolution;

22. *Requests* the Secretary-General to report within one hundred and eighty days on Eritrea's compliance with the provisions of the present resolution;

23. *Decides* to remain actively seized of the matter.

VOTE ON RESOLUTION 1907(2009):

In favour: Austria, Burkina Faso, Costa Rica, Croatia, France, Japan, Mexico, Russian Federation, Turkey, Uganda, United Kingdom, United States, Viet Nam.

Against: Libyan Arab Jamahiriya.

Abstaining: China.

Communication. Eritrea, on 23 December [S/2009/666], called the resolution shameful and imposing on it unjustifiable measures. The resolution recommended punitive measures against Eritrea on account of the United States-fabricated "border dispute with Djibouti". For seven years, since the Eritrea-Ethiopia Boundary Commission in 2002 [YUN 2002, p. 90] gave its binding award in the border dispute between Eritrea and Ethiopia, the Council had refused to ensure respect for that decision. That had encouraged Ethiopia to continue its occupation of Badme and other sovereign Eritrean lands.

Eritrea–Ethiopia

UNMEE

The mandate of the United Nations Mission in Ethiopia and Eritrea (UNMEE), established by the Security Council in its resolutions 1312(2000) [YUN 2000, p. 174] and 1320(2000) [ibid., p. 176], was terminated by Council resolution 1827(2008) [YUN 2008, p. 310] effective 31 July 2008.

Following the termination of its mandate, UNMEE on 1 August 2008 began its administrative liquidation, including the disposition of its assets. On the recommendation of the Secretary-General, supported by ACABQ, the General Assembly in April 2009 approved the donation of certain UNMEE assets to Ethiopia and to AMISOM.

Financing

Disposition of assets

In February [A/63/728], the Secretary-General provided details on the proposed donation of the assets of UNMEE to the Governments of Ethiopia and Eritrea and the AU. The inventory value of the Mission's assets proposed for donation to Eritrea and Ethiopia amounted to $7,480,600, representing 13.3 per cent of the total UNMEE assets inventory value of $56,218,700. The proposed donation to the AU of assets with inventory value of $6,911,400, representing 12.3 per cent of the total UNMEE assets inventory value, would enable the AU to enhance the operational capabilities of AMISOM.

ACABQ, in March [A/63/761], did not object to the course of action proposed by the Secretary-General. Introducing the report in the Fifth Committee, the ACABQ Vice-Chairman, on 17 March [A/C.5/63/SR.34], said that after the assets proposed for donation had been placed in temporary custody of the Governments of Ethiopia and Eritrea and the AU, Eritrea had informed the Advisory Committee that the donation had not been accepted by the communities concerned and that the United Nations should make the necessary arrangements for shipping out all its remaining assets from Eritrea. Since UNMEE had finalized the field liquidation process and repatriated its staff, it was not in a position to recover the assets and intended to leave them in situ.

On 7 April, by **decision 63/554**, the General Assembly approved the donation of UNMEE assets with an inventory value of $1,398,500 and corresponding residual value of $421,800 to the Government of Ethiopia, and the donation of assets with an inventory value of $6,911,400 and corresponding residual value of $1,967,900 to the AU in support of AMISOM.

Financial performance

At its resumed sixty-third session, the General Assembly considered the Secretary-General's performance report on the UNMEE budget for the period from 1 July 2007 to 30 June 2008 [A/63/562] and the related ACABQ report of 26 May [A/63/746/Add.12]. Appropriations for 2007/2008 totalled $113,483,400, while expenditures amounted to $106,085,200, resulting in an unencumbered balance of $7,398,200, while other income amounted $10,213,200; unencumbered balance and other income totalled $17,611,400. As at 30 April 2009, a total of $1,332,814,000 had been assessed on Member States in respect of UNMEE since its inception. Payments received amounted to $1,315,364,000, leaving an outstanding balance of $17,450,000. Taking into account liabilities and credits due to Member States, UNMEE had a cash shortfall of $14,736,400.

GENERAL ASSEMBLY ACTION

On 30 June [meeting 93], the General Assembly, on the recommendation of the Fifth Committee [A/63/646/Add.2], adopted **resolution 63/257 B** without vote [agenda item 139].

Financing of the United Nations Mission in Ethiopia and Eritrea

The General Assembly,

Having considered the report of the Secretary-General on the financing of the United Nations Mission in Ethiopia

and Eritrea and the related report of the Advisory Committee on Administrative and Budgetary Questions,

Recalling Security Council resolution 1312(2000) of 31 July 2000, by which the Council established the United Nations Mission in Ethiopia and Eritrea, and the subsequent resolutions by which the Council extended the mandate of the Mission, the last of which was resolution 1798(2008) of 30 January 2008, by which the Council extended the mandate of the Mission until 31 July 2008,

Recalling also Security Council resolution 1827(2008) of 30 July 2008, by which the Council terminated the mandate of the Mission effective 31 July 2008,

Recalling further its resolution 55/237 of 23 December 2000 on the financing of the Mission and its subsequent resolutions thereon, the latest of which was resolution 63/257 A of 24 December 2008,

Noting with appreciation that voluntary contributions have been made to the Mission,

1. *Takes note* of the status of contributions to the United Nations Mission in Ethiopia and Eritrea as at 30 April 2009, including the contributions outstanding in the amount of 17.5 million United States dollars, representing some 1 per cent of the total assessed contributions, notes with concern that only fifty-six Member States have paid their assessed contributions in full, and urges all other Member States, in particular those in arrears, to ensure payment of their outstanding assessed contributions;

2. *Expresses its appreciation* to those Member States which have paid their assessed contributions in full, and urges all other Member States to make every possible effort to ensure payment of their assessed contributions to the Mission in full;

3. *Endorses* the conclusions and recommendations contained in the report of the Advisory Committee on Administrative and Budgetary Questions, subject to the provisions of the present resolution, and requests the Secretary-General to ensure their full implementation;

Financial performance report for the period from 1 July 2007 to 30 June 2008

4. *Takes note* of the report of the Secretary-General on the financial performance of the Mission for the period from 1 July 2007 to 30 June 2008;

5. *Also takes note* of the unencumbered balance and other income in the Special Account for the United Nations Mission in Ethiopia and Eritrea in the amount of 17,611,400 dollars in respect of the financial period ended 30 June 2008;

6. *Decides* that Member States that have fulfilled their financial obligations to the Mission shall be credited with their respective share of the net cash available in the Special Account for the Mission in the amount of 2,875,000 dollars as at 30 April 2009 from the unencumbered balance and other income in the amount of 17,611,400 dollars in respect of the financial period ended 30 June 2008, in accordance with the levels updated in its resolution 61/243 of 22 December 2006, and taking into account the scale of assessments for 2008, as set out in its resolution 61/237 of 22 December 2006;

7. *Encourages* Member States that are owed credits referred to in paragraph 6 above to apply those credits to any accounts where they have outstanding assessed contributions;

8. *Decides* that, for Member States that have not fulfilled their financial obligations to the Mission, there shall be set off against their outstanding obligations their respective share of the net cash available in the Special Account for the Mission in the amount of 2,875,000 dollars as at 30 April 2009 from the unencumbered balance and other income in the amount of 17,611,400 dollars in respect of the financial period ended 30 June 2008, in accordance with the scheme set out in paragraph 6 above;

9. *Also decides* to defer until its sixty-fourth session a decision on the treatment of the balance of 14,736,400 dollars, and requests the Secretary-General to report to it at the second part of its resumed sixty-fourth session on the updated financial position of the Mission;

10. *Further decides* to include in the provisional agenda of its sixty-fourth session the item entitled "Financing of the United Nations Mission in Ethiopia and Eritrea".

The General Assembly, by **decision 64/549** of 24 December, retained the item on UNMEE financing for consideration during its resumed sixty-fourth (2010) session.

North Africa

Western Sahara

In 2009, negotiations towards a lasting political solution to the question of Western Sahara continued. Although the two parties to the dispute concerning the Territory—Morocco and the Frente Polisario para la Liberación de Saguía el-Hamra y de Río de Oro (Frente Polisario)—in August held talks with the Secretary-General's Personal Envoy for Western Sahara, they remained far apart on ways to achieve a solution. While Morocco remained committed to its autonomy proposal as presented in the negotiations held under UN auspices, Frente Polisario reiterated its position that the Saharan people should decide their future by means of a free referendum.

The United Nations Mission for the Referendum in Western Sahara (MINURSO), established by Security Council resolution 690(1991) [YUN 1991, p. 794], continued to monitor compliance with the 1991 formal ceasefire [ibid., p. 796] between the parties. Military Agreement No. 1, which MINURSO signed separately with the parties [YUN 1998, p. 194], remained the basic legal instrument governing the ceasefire monitoring of the five parts into which, for operational purposes, the disputed territory of Western Sahara was divided: one 5-kilometre-wide buffer strip to the east and south of the berm—the defensive sand wall built by the Royal Moroccan Army (RMA) between 1981 and 1987 across Western Sahara extending from the north-east corner to the south-west, near the Mauritanian border; two restricted areas, one 25 kilometres wide east of the berm and the other 30 kilometres wide west of it; and two areas with limited restrictions that encompassed the remainder of the Territory.

In January, following consultations with the parties, the Secretary-General appointed Christopher Ross to succeed Peter van Walsum as his Personal Envoy for Western Sahara. In November, Hany Abdel-Aziz was appointed Special Representative and Head of MINURSO. In March, the Personal Envoy began consultations in New York on the holding of one or more informal meetings of the parties and neighbouring States to prepare for a fifth round of negotiations.

The Security Council in April extended the mandate of MINURSO for another 12 months.

Political and security developments

Appointment. On 6 January [S/2009/19], the Secretary-General informed the Security Council that he intended to appoint Christopher Ross (United States) as his Personal Envoy for Western Sahara, succeeding Peter van Walsum (The Netherlands), who had served in that position from 2005 until August 2008. The Council took note of that intention on 8 January [S/2009/20].

Communications. On 10 April [S/2009/197], Morocco charged that on the same day, a group of 1,400 persons, setting out from Algerian territory and including foreigners and armed Polisario soldiers, came within 100 metres of the M.18 base of operations of the Berm for the Mahbès subsector. Some Polisario elements, armed with personal weapons and mine detectors, flanked the demonstrators, uprooted barbed wire and removed mines from the berm. A number of demonstrators were injured by a mine explosion. The operation, perpetrated in plain view of MINURSO observers, clearly violated Military Agreement No. 1 [YUN 1998, p. 194] and was an attempt by Algeria and Polisario to undermine UN efforts to relaunch the negotiation process. Morocco would continue to ensure that its territorial integrity and national unity were respected, and it reserved the right to take all measures necessary to put an end to such acts.

On 9 April [A/63/871-S/2009/198], Namibia transmitted a letter from Frente Polisario alleging systematic plunder of Western Sahara's natural resources by Morocco and foreign interests. As reaffirmed by General Assembly resolution 63/102 [YUN 2008, p. 665], the Saharawi people had the exclusive right to their natural resources and the Frente Polisario, as their internationally recognized representative, reserved the right to prevent and seek reparation in respect of any unauthorized activities. It was the responsibility of the Security Council to call a halt to the illegal plunder of those resources, which undermined efforts at confidence-building and progress towards a peaceful solution providing for the self-determination of the people of Western Sahara.

Report of Secretary-General. In a report of 13 April [S/2009/200 & Corr.1], submitted pursuant to Security Council resolution 1813(2008) [YUN 2008, p. 321], the Secretary-General reviewed the situation concerning Western Sahara, covering developments since his April 2008 report [ibid., p. 320]. The Territory remained largely calm. Frente Polisario on 27 February marked the thirty-third anniversary of the proclamation of the "Sahrawi Arab Democratic Republic".

On 22 January, Frente Polisario declared an exclusive economic zone for Western Sahara, which would extend 200 nautical miles from the coast of the Territory. The Secretary-General of Frente Polisario, Mohamed Abdelaziz, said in a statement that the declaration was based on the right of the people of Western Sahara to self-determination and to permanent sovereignty over their natural resources; he called on the European Union (EU) to suspend its 2005 fisheries agreement with Morocco.

The new Personal Envoy held consultations with the parties, as well as with Algeria, Mauritania and other interested countries. He visited the region from 17 to 28 February for in-depth consultations on the current positions of the parties and on ways to move the negotiations into a more intensive and substantive phase. Subsequently, he informed the Secretary-General that all of his interlocutors confirmed their commitment to cooperating with the United Nations with a view to reaching a solution to the issue of Western Sahara as a prerequisite for the stability, integration and development of the region and for the return of the Western Saharan refugees to normal life. The positions of the parties had not changed since the fourth round of negotiations in March 2008 [YUN 2008, p. 319] and remained far apart on ways to achieve a just, lasting and mutually acceptable political solution that would provide for the self-determination of the people of Western Sahara, as called for by the Security Council.

Violations of Military Agreement No. 1 by both parties decreased, and the parties imposed significantly fewer restrictions on the freedom of movement of MINURSO military observers. MINURSO recorded 11 new violations of the agreement by RMA, a slight decrease from the 14 recorded between April 2007 and 2008, and 7 new violations by Frente Polisario, a significant decrease compared to 22 recorded during the same 2007–2008 period. Violations by RMA included the construction of living accommodations and administrative buildings in the Mahbas and Oum Dreyga subsectors without MINURSO authorization, movement of a logistics convoy and of troops and equipment without prior notification, incursion into the buffer strip, and diversion of the original path of two segments of a trench. Frente Polisario violated the agreement by incursions in the buffer strip, con-

centration of military forces in Tifariti on the occasion of the commemoration of its thirty-fifth anniversary, and the establishment of a new observation post in the restricted area close to Agwanit, without authorization by MINURSO.

During the reporting period, RMA complained to MINURSO about 10 demonstrations by Frente Polisario inside the buffer strip, a heavily mined area; however, Military Agreement No. 1 did not pertain to civilian activities and, therefore, did not prohibit civilians from entering the strip. During the same time, Frente Polisario submitted four allegations against RMA, pertaining to small and heavy weapons fire near the berm, the alleged entry of RMA soldiers into the buffer strip and alleged reinforcement of the berm.

The Office of the United Nations High Commissioner for Refugees (UNHCR) and the World Food Programme continued to provide assistance and protection to the Western Saharan refugees in the camps near Tindouf, in partnership with the World Health Organization and several international and local organizations. UNHCR, with logistical support from MINURSO, continued to implement confidence-building measures in cooperation with the parties, facilitating family visits and providing free-of-charge telephone service between refugees in the Tindouf camps and their relatives in the Territory. Since the beginning of the programme in November 2004 [YUN 2004 p. 275], some 7,858 persons had participated in family visits.

Taking into account the latest consultations held by his Personal Envoy, the Secretary-General recommended that the Security Council reiterate its call on the parties to negotiate in good faith and without preconditions, and to show political will to enter into substantive discussions and ensure the success of the negotiations. He welcomed the parties' efforts to clear the Territory of mines and unexploded ordnance and was pleased with the progress achieved. The human dimension of the conflict, including the plight of the Western Saharan refugees, was a continuing concern. With regard to human rights, the Secretary-General called on the parties to respect the rights of the people of Western Sahara in the Territory and the refugee camps.

SECURITY COUNCIL ACTION

On 30 April [meeting 6117], the Security Council unanimously adopted **resolution 1871(2009)**. The draft [S/2009/224, orally amended] was submitted by France, the Russian Federation, Spain, the United Kingdom and the United States.

The Security Council,

Recalling all its previous resolutions on Western Sahara,

Reaffirming its strong support for the efforts of the Secretary-General and his Personal Envoy for Western

Sahara to implement resolutions 1754(2007) of 30 April 2007, 1783(2007) of 31 October 2007 and 1813(2008) of 30 April 2008,

Reaffirming its commitment to assist the parties to achieve a just, lasting and mutually acceptable political solution which will provide for the self-determination of the people of Western Sahara in the context of arrangements consistent with the principles and purposes of the Charter of the United Nations, and noting the role and responsibilities of the parties in this respect,

Reiterating its call upon the parties and States of the region to continue to cooperate fully with the United Nations and with each other to end the current impasse and to achieve progress towards a political solution,

Taking note of the proposal presented by Morocco to the Secretary-General on 11 April 2007 and welcoming serious and credible Moroccan efforts to move the process forward towards resolution, and also taking note of the proposal presented by the Frente Popular para la Liberación de Saguía el-Hamra y de Río de Oro to the Secretary-General on 10 April 2007,

Taking note also of the four rounds of negotiations held under the auspices of the Secretary-General, and welcoming the progress made by the parties to enter into direct negotiations,

Stressing the importance of making progress on the human dimension of the conflict as a means to promote transparency and mutual confidence through constructive dialogue and humanitarian confidence-building measures,

Welcoming in this context the agreement of the parties, expressed in the communiqué of the Personal Envoy of the Secretary-General of 18 March 2008, to explore the establishment of family visits by land, which would be in addition to the existing programme by air, and encouraging them to do so in cooperation with the United Nations High Commissioner for Refugees,

Welcoming also the commitment of the parties to continue the process of negotiations through United Nations-sponsored talks,

Noting the view of the Secretary-General that the consolidation of the status quo is not an acceptable outcome of the current process of negotiations, and noting further that progress in the negotiations will have a positive impact on the quality of life of the people of Western Sahara in all its aspects,

Welcoming the appointment of the Personal Envoy of the Secretary-General, Mr. Christopher Ross, and also welcoming his recent visit to the region and ongoing consultations with the parties,

Having considered the report of the Secretary-General of 13 April 2009,

1. *Reaffirms* the need for full respect of the military agreements reached with the United Nations Mission for the Referendum in Western Sahara with regard to the ceasefire;

2. *Welcomes* the parties' agreement with the suggestion of the Personal Envoy of the Secretary-General for Western Sahara to hold small, informal talks in preparation for a fifth round of negotiations, and recalls its endorsement of the recommendation in the previous report of the Secretary-General that realism and a spirit of compromise by the parties are essential to achieve progress in negotiations;

3. *Calls upon* the parties to continue to show political will and work in an atmosphere propitious for dialogue in order to enter into a more intensive and substantive phase of negotiations, thus ensuring the implementation of resolutions 1754(2007), 1783(2007) and 1813(2008) and the success of negotiations, and affirms its strong support for the commitment of the Secretary-General and his Personal Envoy towards a solution to the question of Western Sahara in this context;

4. *Also calls upon* the parties to continue negotiations under the auspices of the Secretary-General without preconditions and in good faith, taking into account the efforts made since 2006 and subsequent developments, with a view to achieving a just, lasting and mutually acceptable political solution which will provide for the self-determination of the people of Western Sahara in the context of arrangements consistent with the principles and purposes of the Charter of the United Nations, and notes the role and responsibilities of the parties in this respect;

5. *Invites* Member States to lend appropriate assistance to these talks;

6. *Requests* the Secretary-General to keep the Security Council informed on a regular basis of the status and progress of these negotiations under his auspices, and expresses its intention to meet to receive and discuss his report;

7. *Also requests* the Secretary-General to provide a report on the situation in Western Sahara well before the end of the mandate period;

8. *Urges* Member States to provide voluntary contributions to fund confidence-building measures that allow for increased contact between separated family members, especially family visits, as well as other confidence-building measures that may be agreed between the parties;

9. *Decides* to extend the mandate of the Mission until 30 April 2010;

10. *Requests* the Secretary-General to continue to take the measures necessary to ensure full compliance in the Mission with the United Nations zero-tolerance policy on sexual exploitation and abuse and to keep the Council informed, and urges troop-contributing countries to take appropriate preventive action, including predeployment awareness training, and other action to ensure full accountability in cases of such conduct involving their personnel;

11. *Decides* to remain seized of the matter.

Further developments. In a later report [S/2010/175], the Secretary-General noted that on 6 November, King Mohammed VI of Morocco proposed a five-point plan towards "regionalization", to be focused initially on the part of Western Sahara controlled by Morocco, and reaffirmed Morocco's commitment to its autonomy proposal. The Secretary-General of Frente Polisario, Mr. Abdelaziz, on 9 November reiterated his position that the Saharan people should decide their future by means of a free referendum.

An informal meeting of the parties and neighbouring States (Dürnstein, Austria, 9–10 August) achieved its principal objective of re-establishing the atmosphere of mutual respect and dialogue that had reigned at the beginning of the January 2008 negotiations in Manhasset, New York, United States [YUN 2008, p. 319], but had collapsed in the course of successive rounds. The parties concurred that a long-standing agreement to explore the road option in the context of an expansion of family visits between Western Sahara and the refugee camps should be implemented, and they agreed to consider in a positive spirit confidence-building measures that the High Commissioner for Refugees had proposed and others that the Personal Envoy might put forth. For the first time since 2004 [YUN 2004, p. 277], Algeria participated in the process at the ministerial level; it stated that it was ready to work with the parties on anything to which they agreed as regards confidence-building measures and human rights issues.

After the Dürnstein meeting, the Personal Envoy consulted regularly with the parties and determined that progress on the core substantive issues was most likely to emerge at a further informal meeting rather than at an immediate fifth round of formal negotiations. In September, during the sixty-fourth General Assembly session, the Secretary-General met separately with President Abdelaziz Bouteflika of Algeria and the Minister for Foreign Affairs of Morocco, Taïb Fassi-Fihri. Both expressed their continued commitment to the negotiating process and their support for the efforts of the Personal Envoy. Further consultations with the parties opened the way to serious engagement with respect to their proposals of April 2007 [YUN 2007, p. 296]. On that basis, the Personal Envoy proposed that a second informal meeting be held in November or December. However, beginning in October, a series of events made it increasingly impossible to meet on the proposed dates. Each party engaged in actions that the other deemed provocative and destructive of the positive atmosphere that had emerged in Dürnstein, and each questioned the good faith of the other. The Personal Envoy, as did other international actors, found himself operating in crisis-management mode to prevent the situation from deteriorating any further.

GENERAL ASSEMBLY ACTION

The General Assembly in December examined the Secretary-General's July report [A/64/185] summarizing his 1 July 2008 to 30 June 2009 reports to the Security Council on the question of Western Sahara and the relevant chapter of the 2009 report of the Special Committee on Decolonization [A/64/23].

On 10 December [meeting 62], the Assembly, on the recommendation of the Fourth (Special Political and Decolonization) Committee [A/64/413], adopted **resolution 64/101** without vote [agenda item 39].

Question of Western Sahara

The General Assembly,

Having considered in depth the question of Western Sahara,

Reaffirming the inalienable right of all peoples to self-determination and independence, in accordance with the principles set forth in the Charter of the United Nations and General Assembly resolution 1514(XV) of 14 December 1960 containing the Declaration on the Granting of Independence to Colonial Countries and Peoples,

Recognizing that all available options for self-determination of the Territories are valid as long as they are in accordance with the freely expressed wishes of the people concerned and in conformity with the clearly defined principles contained in General Assembly resolutions 1514(XV) of 14 December 1960 and 1541(XV) of 15 December 1960 and other resolutions of the Assembly,

Recalling its resolution 63/105 of 5 December 2008,

Recalling also all resolutions of the General Assembly and the Security Council on the question of Western Sahara,

Recalling further Security Council resolutions 658(1990) of 27 June 1990, 690(1991) of 29 April 1991, 1359(2001) of 29 June 2001, 1429(2002) of 30 July 2002, 1495(2003) of 31 July 2003, 1541(2004) of 29 April 2004, 1570(2004) of 28 October 2004, 1598(2005) of 28 April 2005, 1634(2005) of 28 October 2005, 1675(2006) of 28 April 2006 and 1720(2006) of 31 October 2006,

Underlining the adoption of Security Council resolutions 1754(2007) on 30 April 2007, 1783(2007) on 31 October 2007, 1813(2008) on 30 April 2008 and 1871(2009) on 30 April 2009,

Expressing its satisfaction that the parties have met on 18 and 19 June 2007, on 10 and 11 August 2007, from 7 to 9 January 2008 and from 16 to 18 March 2008 under the auspices of the Personal Envoy of the Secretary-General and in the presence of the neighbouring countries and that they have agreed to continue the negotiations,

Welcoming the appointment of Mr. Christopher Ross as the Personal Envoy of the Secretary-General for Western Sahara,

Expressing its satisfaction at the holding of an informal meeting convened by the Personal Envoy of the Secretary-General on 10 and 11 August 2009 in Dürnstein, Austria, to prepare for the fifth round of negotiations,

Calling upon all the parties and the States of the region to cooperate fully with the Secretary-General and his Personal Envoy and with each other,

Reaffirming the responsibility of the United Nations towards the people of Western Sahara,

Welcoming, in this regard, the efforts of the Secretary-General and his Personal Envoy in search of a mutually acceptable political solution to the dispute, which will provide for the self-determination of the people of Western Sahara,

Having examined the relevant chapter of the report of the Special Committee on the Situation with regard to the Implementation of the Declaration on the Granting of Independence to Colonial Countries and Peoples,

Having also examined the report of the Secretary-General,

1. *Takes note* of the report of the Secretary-General;

2. *Supports* the process of negotiations initiated by Security Council resolution 1754(2007) and further sus-

tained by Council resolutions 1783(2007), 1813(2008) and 1871(2009), with a view to achieving a just, lasting and mutually acceptable political solution, which will provide for the self-determination of the people of Western Sahara; and commends the efforts undertaken by the Secretary-General and his Personal Envoy in this respect;

3. *Welcomes* the commitment of the parties to continue to show political will and work in an atmosphere propitious for dialogue, in order to enter into a more intensive phase of negotiations, in good faith and without preconditions, taking note of efforts and developments since 2006, thus ensuring implementation of Security Council resolutions 1754(2007), 1783(2007), 1813(2008) and 1871(2009) and the success of negotiations;

4. *Also welcomes* the ongoing negotiations between the parties held on 18 and 19 June 2007, on 10 and 11 August 2007, from 7 to 9 January 2008 and from 16 to 18 March 2008 in the presence of the neighbouring countries under the auspices of the United Nations;

5. *Calls upon* the parties to cooperate with the International Committee of the Red Cross, and calls upon them to abide by their obligations under international humanitarian law;

6. *Requests* the Special Committee on the Situation with regard to the Implementation of the Declaration on the Granting of Independence to Colonial Countries and Peoples to continue to consider the situation in Western Sahara and to report thereon to the General Assembly at its sixty-fifth session;

7. *Invites* the Secretary-General to submit to the General Assembly at its sixty-fifth session a report on the implementation of the present resolution.

MINURSO

The United Nations Mission for the Referendum in Western Sahara (MINURSO), established by Security Council resolution 690(1991) [YUN 1991, p. 794], was mandated to help the Council achieve a just, lasting and mutually acceptable political solution that would provide for the self-determination of the people of Western Sahara. The Council extended the Mission's mandate for another 12 months, until 30 April 2010.

MINURSO continued to monitor compliance with the formal ceasefire between Frente Polisario and Morocco. Military Agreement No. 1, which MINURSO signed separately with the parties [YUN 1998, p. 194], remained the basic legal instrument governing the ceasefire monitoring of the disputed Territory of Western Sahara. The Mission's military observers carried out monitoring through a combination of ground and air patrols and observation posts, and through inspections of larger-than-company-size military units. Bilateral military agreements Nos. 2 and 3 [YUN 1999, p. 180], committing both parties to cooperating with MINURSO in the exchange of mine-related information, marking of mined areas and destruction of mines and unexploded ordnance, remained in force. Joint mine action efforts, aimed at diminishing the

threat posed by mines and unexploded ordnance, greatly improved the quality and scope of data collection regarding contamination by explosive remnants of war. Improvements to the safety and security of UN personnel working in contaminated areas were achieved. Nevertheless, 15 mine accidents, resulting in two fatalities and 23 injuries, were reported in 2009. During the year, Landmine Action, an international NGO contracted by the United Nations, cleared 2.9 million square metres of land of cluster munitions and unexploded ordnance.

At the end of 2009, MINURSO numbered 505 personnel: 199 military observers, 27 troops, 6 civilian police, 97 international and 157 local civilians, and 19 UN Volunteers. The Mission maintained its headquarters in Laayoune, Western Sahara, where the Office of the Special Representative and the Office of the Force Commander were located, and operated in 11 locations (Laayoune, Tindouf and nine military observer team sites—four on the Moroccan-controlled side and five on the Frente Polisario side).

Appointment. On 6 October [S/2009/526], the Secretary-General informed the Security Council of his intention to appoint Hany Abdel-Aziz (Egypt) as his Special Representative for Western Sahara and Head of MINURSO, with immediate effect, succeeding Julian Harston (United Kingdom). The Council took note of the Secretary-General's intention on 8 October [S/2009/527].

Financing

A performance report by the Secretary-General on the MINURSO budget for the period from 1 July 2007 to 30 June 2008 [A/63/608] showed appropriations of $46,075,800 and an unencumbered balance of $555,500, as well as other income/adjustments of $1,167,900. In March [A/63/757], the Secretary-General submitted cost estimates for MINURSO from 1 July 2009 to 30 June 2010, in the amount of $57,407,200, inclusive of voluntary budgeted contributions in kind amounting to $3,048,900.

In June [A/63/746/Add.15], ACABQ recommended that the unencumbered balance, as well as other income adjustments of $1,167,900, be credited to Member States. For the maintenance of MINURSO from 1 July 2009 to 30 June 2010, it recommended that the General Assembly appropriate $54,046,600.

The Assembly, on 30 June, appropriated $55,877,200 for the Mission for the period from 1 July 2009 to 30 June 2010.

GENERAL ASSEMBLY ACTION

On 30 June [meeting 93], the General Assembly, on the recommendation of the Fifth Committee [A/63/907], adopted **resolution 63/300** without vote [agenda item 147].

Financing of the United Nations Mission for the Referendum in Western Sahara

The General Assembly,

Having considered the reports of the Secretary-General on the financing of the United Nations Mission for the Referendum in Western Sahara and the related report of the Advisory Committee on Administrative and Budgetary Questions,

Recalling Security Council resolution 690(1991) of 29 April 1991, by which the Council established the United Nations Mission for the Referendum in Western Sahara, and the subsequent resolutions by which the Council extended the mandate of the Mission, the latest of which was resolution 1871(2009) of 30 April 2009, by which the Council extended the mandate of the Mission until 30 April 2010,

Recalling also its resolution 45/266 of 17 May 1991 on the financing of the Mission and its subsequent resolutions and decisions thereon, the latest of which was resolution 62/268 of 20 June 2008,

Reaffirming the general principles underlying the financing of United Nations peacekeeping operations, as stated in General Assembly resolutions 1874(S-IV) of 27 June 1963, 3101(XXVIII) of 11 December 1973 and 55/235 of 23 December 2000,

Noting with appreciation that voluntary contributions have been made to the Mission,

Mindful of the fact that it is essential to provide the Mission with the financial resources necessary to enable it to fulfil its responsibilities under the relevant resolutions of the Security Council,

1. *Requests* the Secretary-General to entrust the Head of Mission with the task of formulating future budget proposals in full accordance with the provisions of General Assembly resolutions 59/296 of 22 June 2005, 60/266 of 30 June 2006 and 61/276 of 29 June 2007, as well as other relevant resolutions;

2. *Takes note* of the status of contributions to the United Nations Mission for the Referendum in Western Sahara as at 30 April 2009, including the contributions outstanding in the amount of 46.1 million United States dollars, representing some 6 per cent of the total assessed contributions, notes with concern that only eighty-six Member States have paid their assessed contributions in full, and urges all other Member States, in particular those in arrears, to ensure payment of their outstanding assessed contributions;

3. *Expresses its appreciation* to those Member States which have paid their assessed contributions in full, and urges all other Member States to make every possible effort to ensure payment of their assessed contributions to the Mission in full;

4. *Expresses concern* at the financial situation with regard to peacekeeping activities, in particular as regards the reimbursements to troop contributors that bear additional burdens owing to overdue payments by Member States of their assessments;

5. *Also expresses concern* at the delay experienced by the Secretary-General in deploying and providing adequate resources to some recent peacekeeping missions, in particular those in Africa;

6. *Emphasizes* that all future and existing peacekeeping missions shall be given equal and non-discriminatory treatment in respect of financial and administrative arrangements;

7. *Also emphasizes* that all peacekeeping missions shall be provided with adequate resources for the effective and efficient discharge of their respective mandates;

8. *Reiterates its request* to the Secretary-General to make the fullest possible use of facilities and equipment at the United Nations Logistics Base at Brindisi, Italy, in order to minimize the costs of procurement for the Mission;

9. *Requests* the Secretary-General to ensure that proposed peacekeeping budgets are based on the relevant legislative mandates;

10. *Endorses* the conclusions and recommendations contained in the report of the Advisory Committee on Administrative and Budgetary Questions, subject to the provisions of the present resolution, and requests the Secretary-General to ensure their full implementation;

11. *Takes note* of paragraph 35 of the report of the Advisory Committee;

12. *Requests* the Secretary-General to ensure the full implementation of the relevant provisions of resolutions 59/296, 60/266 and 61/276;

13. *Also requests* the Secretary-General to take all action necessary to ensure that the Mission is administered with a maximum of efficiency and economy;

14. *Further requests* the Secretary-General, in order to reduce the cost of employing General Service staff, to continue efforts to recruit local staff for the Mission against General Service posts, commensurate with the requirements of the Mission;

Financial performance report for the period from 1 July 2007 to 30 June 2008

15. *Takes note* of the report of the Secretary-General on the financial performance of the Mission for the period from 1 July 2007 to 30 June 2008;

Budget estimates for the period from 1 July 2009 to 30 June 2010

16. *Decides* to appropriate to the Special Account for the United Nations Mission for the Referendum in Western Sahara the amount of 55,877,200 dollars for the period from 1 July 2009 to 30 June 2010, inclusive of 53,527,600 dollars for the maintenance of the Mission, 1,955,400 dollars for the support account for peacekeeping operations and 394,200 dollars for the United Nations Logistics Base;

Financing of the appropriation for the period from 1 July 2009 to 30 June 2010

17. *Also decides* to apportion among Member States the amount of 46,564,333 dollars for the period from 1 July 2009 to 30 April 2010, in accordance with the levels updated in General Assembly resolution 61/243 of 22 December 2006, and taking into account the scale of assessments for 2009, as set out in Assembly resolution 61/237 of 22 December 2006, and for 2010;

18. *Further decides* that, in accordance with the provisions of General Assembly resolution 973(X) of 15 December 1955, there shall be set off against the apportionment

among Member States, as provided for in paragraph 17 above, their respective share in the Tax Equalization Fund of 2,026,000 dollars, comprising the estimated staff assessment income of 1,823,917 dollars approved for the Mission, the prorated share of 169,583 dollars of the estimated staff assessment income approved for the support account and the prorated share of 32,500 dollars of the estimated staff assessment income approved for the United Nations Logistics Base;

19. *Decides* to apportion among Member States the amount of 9,312,867 dollars for the period from 1 May to 30 June 2010, at a monthly rate of 4,656,433 dollars, in accordance with the levels updated in resolution 61/243, and taking into account the scale of assessments for 2010, subject to a decision of the Security Council to extend the mandate of the Mission;

20. *Also decides* that, in accordance with the provisions of resolution 973(X), there shall be set off against the apportionment among Member States, as provided for in paragraph 19 above, their respective share in the Tax Equalization Fund of 405,200 dollars, comprising the estimated staff assessment income of 364,783 dollars approved for the Mission, the prorated share of 33,917 dollars of the estimated staff assessment income approved for the support account and the prorated share of 6,500 dollars of the estimated staff assessment income approved for the United Nations Logistics Base;

21. *Further decides* that, for Member States that have fulfilled their financial obligations to the Mission, there shall be set off against their apportionment, as provided for in paragraph 17 above, their respective share of the unencumbered balance and other income in the total amount of 1,723,400 dollars in respect of the financial period ended 30 June 2008, in accordance with the levels updated in resolution 61/243, and taking into account the scale of assessments for 2008, as set out in resolution 61/237;

22. *Decides* that, for Member States that have not fulfilled their financial obligations to the Mission, there shall be set off against their outstanding obligations their respective share of the unencumbered balance and other income in the total amount of 1,723,400 dollars in respect of the financial period ended 30 June 2008, in accordance with the scheme set out in paragraph 21 above;

23. *Also decides* that the increase of 151,600 dollars in the estimated staff assessment income in respect of the financial period ended 30 June 2008 shall be added to the credits from the amount of 1,723,400 dollars referred to in paragraphs 21 and 22 above;

24. *Emphasizes* that no peacekeeping mission shall be financed by borrowing funds from other active peacekeeping missions;

25. *Encourages* the Secretary-General to continue to take additional measures to ensure the safety and security of all personnel participating in the Mission under the auspices of the United Nations, bearing in mind paragraphs 5 and 6 of Security Council resolution 1502(2003) of 26 August 2003;

26. *Invites* voluntary contributions to the Mission in cash and in the form of services and supplies acceptable to the Secretary-General, to be administered, as appropriate, in accordance with the procedure and practices established by the General Assembly;

27. *Decides* to include in the provisional agenda of its sixty-fourth session the item entitled "Financing of the United Nations Mission for the Referendum in Western Sahara".

The Assembly, by **decision 64/549** of 24 December, decided that the agenda item on MINURSO financing would remain for consideration during its resumed sixty-fourth (2010) session.

Other issues

Madagascar

On 17 March [SG/SM/12138], the Secretary-General expressed concern about the developments in Madagascar. Taking note of the resignation of President Marc Ravalomanana on that day, he urged all parties to act responsibly to ensure stability and a smooth transition through democratic means. He called on all concerned, particularly the police and the army, to ensure the security of the population and work towards a non-violent resolution of the crisis.

On 20 March [S/2009/166], the Libyan Arab Jamahiriya transmitted a decision on the situation in Madagascar, adopted by the AU Peace and Security Council on the same date, condemning the change of Government—which it called unconstitutional—that conferred the office of President of the Republic to Andry Rajoelina following the resignation of President Ravalomanana under pressure from the civilian opposition and the armed forces. The Council suspended Madagascar from participating in AU activities until the restoration of the constitutional order.

On 10 August [SG/SM/12407], the Secretary-General welcomed the signing in Maputo on 9 August of agreements for resolving the political crisis. Congratulating the four leaders—Andry Rajoelina, Marc Ravalomanana, Didier Ratsiraka and Albert Zafy—for committing to a peaceful transition under a Government of National Unity, he urged them to quickly agree on its composition and on the establishment of transitional institutions leading to credible elections and the restoration of democracy and the rule of law.

On 15 September [S/2009/460], the AU transmitted a press statement issued by the AU Peace and Security Council on 10 September expressing concern at the rise of tension in Madagascar following the unilateral decision by the de facto authorities to establish what was termed a Government of National Unity without the participation of other political movements. The AU Council called on the parties to continue inclusive dialogue for a consensual distribution of posts of responsibility within the transitional institutions.

On 7 November [SG/SM/12591], the Secretary-General welcomed the agreement reached by the four Malagasy leaders in Addis Ababa for the establishment of a power-sharing administration. He urged them to speedily inaugurate the Government of National Unity and to put in place the transitional institutions foreseen in the Maputo agreements.

Mauritius–United Kingdom/France

Addressing the General Assembly on 25 September during the general debate [A/64/PV.7], Mauritius reaffirmed its sovereignty over the Chagos Archipelago, including Diego Garcia, which the United Kingdom had excised from the territory of Mauritius prior to its independence, in disregard of Assembly resolutions 1514(XV) [YUN 1960, p. 49] and 2066(XX) [YUN 1965, p. 587]. Mauritius said that it had consistently urged the United Kingdom to engage in a meaningful dialogue for the early return of the Archipelago; it was pleased to inform the Assembly that two rounds of talks had been held with the United Kingdom during 2009 and hoped that Mauritius would be able to exercise sovereignty over the Archipelago, including Diego Garcia, in the near future. In addition, the Government of Mauritius and the French authorities were in the process of addressing the issue of Tromelin and were discussing the modalities of co-managing the island, pending the settlement of the sovereignty issue which had to be resolved.

On 28 September [A/64/480], the United Kingdom, in the exercise of the right of reply, maintained that the British Indian Ocean Territory was British and had been since 1814. It did not recognize Mauritius' sovereignty claim. However, the British Government recognized Mauritius as the only State that had the right to assert a claim of sovereignty when the United Kingdom relinquished its own sovereignty. The Territory would be ceded when no longer required for defence purposes. The United Kingdom remained open to discussions regarding arrangements governing the Territory or its future; when the time came for the Territory to be ceded it would liaise closely with Mauritius. During recent meetings, British and Mauritian officials had discussed the latest legal and policy developments relating to the British Indian Ocean Territory and had set out their respective positions on sovereignty. The United Kingdom also set out its need to abide by its treaty obligations with the United States and its ongoing need of the Territory for defence purposes. There was mutual discussion of fishing rights, the environment, the continental shelf and future visits to the Territory by Chagossians.

Chapter III

Americas

During 2009, the United Nations continued to advance the cause of lasting peace, human rights, good governance and the rule of law in the Americas. In Guatemala, the International Commission against Impunity continued to implement its mandate. In September, the Secretary-General provided the General Assembly with an update on the activities of the Commission, and the UN role in the implementation of its mandate.

In Honduras, following a June coup d'état against President José Manuel Zelaya Rosales, the United Nations, along with the international community, sought a diplomatic solution to the crisis. Both the General Assembly and the Security Council convened meetings on the issue. In October, the Tegucigalpa-San José Accord was signed, which established the Government of National Unity and Reconciliation, and elections in November resulted in Porfirio Lobo Sosa being selected as the country's next President.

In Haiti, there were indications of a new readiness among the political leadership to work together. Key legislation was adopted, senatorial elections were conducted in April and June, and by year's end, preparations were under way for future elections. That collaboration, on the other hand, remained fragile. Jean-Max Bellerive was sworn in as Prime Minister in November following a vote of censure against the incumbent. A Security Council mission to the country found that gains were achieved in four of the five benchmarks for the consolidation of stability in Haiti: political dialogue and elections; extension of State authority; strengthening of security; and rule of law and human rights. Social and economic development, however, suffered a marked deterioration. The United Nations Stabilization Mission in Haiti continued to implement its mandate, including assisting the Haitian National Police in upholding the rule of law and enhancing police capacity. Widespread poverty and unemployment continued to pose a threat to stability. In May, the Secretary-General appointed former United States President William J. Clinton as United Nations Special Envoy for Haiti.

In other developments in the region, the General Assembly again called on States to refrain from promulgating laws and measures such as the ongoing embargo against Cuba by the United States.

Central America

In 2009, Central America further consolidated peace and built democratic and equitable societies upon the foundation developed in years of successful UN peacemaking efforts. The United Nations continued to assist the region through development programming, the good offices of the Secretary-General and other means. In that connection, the Organization continued its support of the International Commission against Impunity in Guatemala, and in the aftermath of the coup d'état in Honduras in June, convened meetings of the General Assembly and the Security Council to address the crisis.

Communications. On 24 April [A/63/835], Nicaragua transmitted to the Secretary-General the text of the Declaration of the Heads of State and Government of the Central American Integration System (SICA) on the meeting between the Presidents of the Isthmus and United States President Barack Obama, which outlined key priorities for an agenda of dialogue and cooperation between SICA countries and the United States. On 21 May [A/63/864], Nicaragua transmitted the text of the Declaration adopted at the special meeting of SICA (Managua, Nicaragua, 20 May).

On 30 October [A/64/530], Argentina and Slovakia transmitted to the Secretary-General the Co-Chairs' statement on the International Workshop on Contributing to the United Nations Approach to Security Sector Reform: Insights from Latin America and the Caribbean (Buenos Aires, Argentina, 28–29 September), which was attended by over 100 participants from 26 countries. The workshop was organized in the context of the ongoing UN debate on security sector reform.

On 24 December, by **decision 64/549,** the General Assembly decided that the agenda item entitled "The situation in Central America: progress in fashioning a region of peace, freedom, democracy and development" would remain for consideration at its resumed sixty-fourth (2010) session.

Guatemala

International Commission against Impunity

Five years after the ending of the mandate of the United Nations Verification Mission in Guatemala in 2004 [YUN 2004, p. 287], the country continued to build upon the foundation created in previous years. In 2009, the International Commission against Impunity in Guatemala (CICIG), established in 2007 [YUN 2007, p. 308] with the concurrent entry into force of the 2006 agreement between the country and the United Nations [YUN 2006, p. 870], continued to implement its mandate. Under the terms of the agreement, which set up the Commission as an independent, non-UN organ, the main CICIG objective was to assist, strengthen and support State institutions responsible for investigating and prosecuting crimes allegedly committed by illegal security forces and clandestine security organizations, and other criminal conduct related to those entities.

Extension of CICIG mandate. As the CICIG mandate would expire on 4 September, in a letter dated 24 March, the Guatemalan Minister for Foreign Affairs requested that the Secretary-General agree to extend the Commission's mandate for an additional two-year period. On 15 April, the Secretary-General confirmed the extension until 4 September 2011, which was ratified by the Guatemalan Congress on 16 July 2009.

Communication. On 21 May [A/63/863], Nicaragua transmitted to the Secretary-General the text of the Special Declaration on Guatemala adopted by SICA at its special meeting on 20 May. The Declaration condemned the crimes and violence against citizens that had recently taken place in Guatemala and noted that the Government had requested CICIG to launch an investigation into those events.

Report of Secretary-General. Pursuant to General Assembly resolution 63/19 [YUN 2008, p. 333], the Secretary-General transmitted a September report [A/64/370] on the activities of CICIG, which provided information on its key substantive tasks: criminal investigations and involvement in prosecutions, legal reform proposals and technical assistance. The Commission made significant progress in those areas, as well as in raising awareness among the Guatemalan population of the need to end impunity. On investigations and casework, the Commission and its Special Prosecutor's Office achieved results in a number of investigations in collaboration with the Public Prosecutor's Office and the National Civilian Police. High-level cases against the former head of the Crimes against Life Unit of the Public Prosecutor's Office and the former President of the country had placed the Commission in the public spotlight, underscoring that investigations and accountability were feasible in Guatemala, even when powerful interests were at stake. To date, the Commission had been accepted as a complementary prosecutor in nine cases.

On legal reform, the Commission recommended the adoption of public policies that would enable the eradication of clandestine security organizations and prevent their re-emergence. The submission of two sets of legal reform proposals in October 2008 and June 2009 resulted in congressional approval of four legislative initiatives and new laws on: arms and ammunition; strengthening criminal prosecutions; and criminal justice in high-risk proceedings; and a reformed law against organized crime. In the area of expert assistance, the Commission provided technical support in restructuring the national witness protection programme, including the training of 48 police academy graduates, and worked with the Public Prosecutor's Office on the terms of the new witness protection regulation, which was adopted by the Office in May.

In other activities, the Commission helped identify staff in the Public Prosecutor's Office and in the National Civilian Police who were obstructing progress in investigations and legal proceedings, supported the approval of a Law on Nominating Committees to render the process for the appointment of Supreme Court and Appellate Court judges more transparent, which was approved in May, and made proposals that contributed to the signing of a National Agreement for the Advancement of Security and Justice in Guatemala. The Agreement defined a long-term policy to combat crime and was based on a wide political consensus to make the fight against crime a State priority. The Commission also signed a cooperation agreement in February with the United Nations Children's Fund to conduct studies on children and adolescents with regard to crimes committed against them in the context of the activities of illegal security forces and clandestine security organizations. Along with receiving a high level of international support, the Commission received in July the expression of support for its work by 35 civil society organizations in Guatemala.

Despite those achievements, the Commission faced a number of obstacles, including challenges contesting its legal ability to participate in investigations and prosecutions involving the "law of *amparo*"; frequent personnel changes within Government justice and security institutions; the operational challenges arising from the Commission's status as a non-UN body; and security for the Commission's staff, as well as judges, prosecutors and witnesses, particularly with regard to investigations related to the activities of powerful criminal networks. In addition, some judges appeared to be subject to external influence to the detriment of justice. The Commission emphasized the need to create specialized courts located in Guatemala City to provide greater security for judges and ensure impartial decisions. The UN Secretariat and the Government were discussing ways to resolve the challenges faced by the Commission. The report also outlined the Commission's main objectives during the next year.

On 28 October [meeting 28], the General Assembly adopted **resolution 64/7** [draft: A/64/L.6 & Add.1] without vote [agenda item 20].

International Commission against Impunity in Guatemala

The General Assembly,

Recalling its relevant resolutions on the situation in Central America, and particularly resolution 63/19 of 10 November 2008 regarding the activities of the International Commission against Impunity in Guatemala,

Bearing in mind the Agreement between the United Nations and the State of Guatemala on the establishment of an International Commission against Impunity in Guatemala, which was signed on 12 December 2006, was approved by the Guatemalan Congress on 1 August 2007 and entered into force on 4 September 2007 for an initial period of two years,

Noting that, in accordance with article 14 of the Agreement, the mandate of the Commission was extended for an additional two years, starting 4 September 2009, through an exchange of letters between the Government of Guatemala and the Secretary-General on 20 March 2009 and 15 April 2009 and approved by the Guatemalan Congress on 16 July 2009,

Bearing in mind that the Commission has carried out its activities through voluntary contributions of Member States and other donors from the international community and plans to do so in the future,

Noting that the Government of Guatemala has provided additional budgetary allotments to State institutions to support their work in collaboration with the Commission,

Convinced that, pursuant to Articles 55 and 56 of the Charter, the United Nations promotes respect for human rights and fundamental freedoms for all and that Member States pledge themselves to take action in cooperation with the Organization for the achievement of that purpose,

1. *Takes note* of the report of the Secretary-General regarding the current state and activities of the International Commission against Impunity in Guatemala, which describes the important progress achieved as well as the significant operational challenges that result from the present status of the Commission as a non-United Nations body;

2. *Requests* the Secretary-General to undertake with the Government of Guatemala the steps necessary to address these operational challenges and to enhance the role that the United Nations plays in providing effective and efficient assistance to the Commission within the framework of its founding agreement signed on 12 December 2006;

3. *Calls upon* the Government of Guatemala to continue providing all the support necessary to consolidate the achievements and overcome the challenges outlined in the report of the Secretary-General;

4. *Also calls upon* the Government of Guatemala to persist in and redouble its efforts to strengthen the institutions that buttress the rule of law and the defence of human rights, and commends it for its commitment to combat impunity;

5. *Expresses its appreciation* to those Member States and other donors that have supported the Commission, through voluntary contributions, financial and in kind, and urges them to continue their support;

6. *Requests* the Secretary-General to periodically keep the General Assembly apprised of the work of the Commission and the implementation of the present resolution.

Honduras

Coup d'état against President. On 28 June, in the early hours of the morning, the residence of the Honduran President, José Manuel Zelaya Rosales, was invaded by the Honduran armed forces who arrested and expelled the President from the country, forcing him into exile in Costa Rica. The coup d'état was the first in the region since the end of the cold war and interrupted democratic rule in Honduras some five months before presidential elections were scheduled to be held in November.

In a 28 June note verbale [S/2009/329] to the Security Council, Honduras transmitted a statement on the democratic and Constitutional breaking in the country that was addressed to the international community, calling on it to demand respect for and the physical integrity of President Zelaya and his family, re-establish the President in the full exercise of his constitutional functions and reject any intent to substitute the President. It also indicated that the attempt to replace President Zelaya with the President of the National Congress, Roberto Micheletti, was not only illegal, but also an attempt to legitimize the coup d'état.

In a 28 June press statement [SG/SM/12340], the Secretary-General condemned President Zelaya's arrest and urged for the reinstatement of the democratically elected representatives and respect for human rights, including safeguards for the security of the President, members of his family and his Government. He also welcomed the diplomatic efforts of the Organization of American States (OAS), whose Permanent Council had held a special meeting that morning. The OAS Council adopted a resolution condemning the coup d'état and decided, among other action, to convene a special session of the OAS General Assembly on 30 June to take whatever decisions it deemed appropriate.

International community response. In a 29 June letter [A/63/911] to the Secretary-General, Venezuela transmitted the texts of two communiqués issued by the Bolivarian Alliance for the Americas (ALBA), formerly known as the Bolivarian Alternative for the Americas. In the first communiqué, dated 28 June, ALBA condemned the coup d'état staged by the Honduran armed forces; called for an immediate return to the rule of law and the reinstatement of President Zelaya; demanded that the Minister of Foreign Affairs, Patricia Rodas, be immediately released; and requested the UN General Assembly to convene a meeting immediately to consider the breakdown of constitutional order in Honduras. The second communiqué, dated three days earlier (25 June), drew the international community's attention to the coup d'état being staged against President Zelaya in order to prevent the holding of a democratic public consultation to establish whether the people agreed to the convening of a constituent assembly.

In letters dated 29 June, Cuba, as the Chair of the Coordinating Bureau of the Non-Aligned Movement (NAM), transmitted a 28 June communiqué [A/63/913] and a 29 June communiqué [A/63/912] condemning the coup d'état against President Zelaya and other violence that had taken place and calling for the reinstatement of the rule of law and of the President.

General Assembly consideration. On 29 June [A/63/PV.91], the Assembly considered the situation in Honduras under the agenda item "The situation in Central America: progress in fashioning a region of peace, freedom, democracy and development". Honduras stated that the constitutional order in the country had been broken by conservative forces due to the notion of consulting the Honduran people in a non-binding referendum to take place on a Sunday in June, in order to determine whether they agreed to a change in the general elections scheduled for November and whether a constituent national assembly was to be established to ascertain whether the Honduran people wanted to improve the structure of the Constitution. The call for the referendum to seek the opinion of the Honduran people did not violate the Constitution or the law, nor did it deviate from the President's power to call for plebiscites, referendums or any other action that sought to determine the will of the people.

Acknowledging that ALBA, SICA, the European Union, the Rio Group and the Governments of 10 States had condemned the coup d'état, Honduras called on the General Assembly to do the same and call for the country's President to be reinstated. During the deliberations, statements condemning the coup d'état were made on behalf of the Caribbean Community (CARICOM), the Group of Arab States, NAM, OAS and the Union of South American Nations, as well as those supporting OAS efforts to address the situation. Mexico indicated that Honduran Foreign Affairs Minister Rodas, who had been detained by the Honduran armed forces, had arrived in Mexico on 28 June.

On 30 June [A/63/PV.93], in his address to the Assembly, President Zelaya said that a number of charges had been levelled against him in Honduras, but no one had put him on trial, called him to the stand in his own defence, or indicated what his error or crime was. He stated that the law on the participation of citizens stipulated that Honduran citizens

had the right to request the Government to examine questions of general interest that involved or affected them. Pursuant to that law, he had received some 400,000 requests from individuals who had asked to be consulted on possible constitutional reforms. He had begun the process of launching a poll that was not binding, State-sanctioned or coercive, and would be similar to surveys carried out to take the public temperature, gauge trends and find out what people were thinking. The survey question was "Do you wish to see a fourth ballot box used in the next elections?" The fourth ballot box would be used for questions of national interest, such as citizen participation, through a possible constituent assembly, in the next Government.

President Zelaya stated that although he would not be there for those elections and would be leaving office, he had wished to leave behind a legacy of reform; to leave the people engaged in participation with full rights and newly empowered by those rights. He described the events leading up to his subsequent arrest and expulsion from the country, including the refusal of the armed forces to distribute the survey materials; the uprising of the people in support of the survey and the decision to move forward with the process; his march with 1,000 citizens to take back the electoral materials from the Honduran air force; the 27 June arrival of 37 observer countries, including from OAS, to observe the polling process; his television and radio broadcasts explaining the referendum; and a meeting with exit pollsters only a few hours before his arrest on 28 June. He also briefed the Assembly on the political and security situation in the country in the aftermath of his arrest.

GENERAL ASSEMBLY ACTION

On 30 June [meeting 93], the General Assembly adopted **resolution 63/301** [draft: A/63/L.74 & Add.1, orally revised] without vote [agenda item 20].

Situation in Honduras: democracy breakdown

The General Assembly,

Deeply concerned by the coup d'état that took place in the Republic of Honduras on 28 June 2009,

Deeply concerned also by the acts of violence against diplomatic personnel and accredited officials in the Republic of Honduras in violation of the 1961 Vienna Convention on Diplomatic Relations,

Recalling the principles and purposes of the Charter of the United Nations, international law and conventions on international peace and security,

Gravely concerned by the breakdown in the constitutional and democratic order that has led to the endangerment of security, democracy and the rule of law, which has jeopardized the security of Honduran and foreign citizens,

1. *Condemns* the coup d'état in the Republic of Honduras that has interrupted the democratic and constitutional order and the legitimate exercise of power in Honduras, and resulted in the removal of the democratically elected President of that country, Mr. José Manuel Zelaya Rosales;

2. *Demands* the immediate and unconditional restoration of the legitimate and Constitutional Government of the President of the Republic of Honduras, Mr. José Manuel Zelaya Rosales, and of the legally constituted authority in Honduras, in order for him to fulfil the mandate for which he was democratically elected by the Honduran people;

3. *Decides* to call firmly and unequivocally upon all States to recognize no Government other than that of the Constitutional President, Mr. José Manuel Zelaya Rosales;

4. *Expresses its firm support* for the regional efforts being undertaken pursuant to Chapter VIII of the Charter of the United Nations to resolve the political crisis in Honduras;

5. *Requests* the Secretary-General to inform the General Assembly in a timely manner of the evolving situation in the country.

OAS special session. The OAS General Assembly convened its thirty-seventh special session (Washington, D.C., 30 June–4 July) as a result of the political crisis in Honduras. On 1 July, OAS adopted a resolution condemning the coup d'état; demanding the immediate return of the President to his constitutional functions; declaring that no Government arising from the unconstitutional interruption would be recognized; and instructing the OAS Secretary-General to undertake diplomatic initiatives to restore democracy and the rule of law and reinstate President Zelaya. If those initiatives proved unsuccessful within 72 hours, OAS would invoke article 21 of the Inter-American Democratic Charter to suspend the membership of Honduras.

Between 1 and 3 July, the OAS Secretary-General held consultations with, among others, the President of the Honduran Supreme Court of Justice, the Cardinal Primate of Honduras, two former Presidents of Honduras and presidential candidates for the November elections from the Liberal Party, the National Party and the Popular Bloc. Neither the de facto Government nor the Supreme Court was disposed to change the course of action taken, with the Court indicating that there had been a pattern of illegality in President Zelaya's earlier conduct, which led to allegedly legal proceedings against him, carried out under a mantle of secrecy whereby they justified not having informed the President. The process had given rise to arrest warrants which the armed forces executed on the morning of 28 June. However, no explanation was provided as to how that procedure had resulted in violence and President Zelaya's expulsion from the country. The Court concluded that the arrest warrant was still in force and would be executed if President Zelaya returned.

The OAS Secretary-General informed the Supreme Court that the events of 28 June constituted an interruption of the legitimate institutional democratic order and that if the rule of law was not restored, OAS would apply article 21. The de facto regime remained firm in its position and after the departure of the OAS delegation, announced its withdrawal from OAS. On 4 July, OAS adopted a resolution suspending the right of Honduras to participate in OAS.

Communication. In a 6 July letter [A/63/920] to the Secretary-General, Cuba, as Chairman of the NAM Coordinating Bureau, stated that the Permanent Representative of Honduras had received notice that he had been dismissed from his post by the de facto Government. Annexed to the letter was a 6 July communiqué issued by NAM condemning the brutal use of force on 5 July by the Honduran army against unarmed civilians who were peacefully demonstrating and had gathered in support of the return of President Zelaya. As a result of the army opening fire with tear gas and live bullets, innocent persons were killed or injured. NAM further condemned the de facto Government's impeding, on the same day, the landing of the plane transporting President Zelaya, the UN General Assembly President and other officials in Tegucigalpa, the capital of Honduras. NAM also informed that the regime refused to comply with Assembly resolution 63/301 and ignored diplomatic efforts and initiatives to restore democracy and the rule of law.

Mediation efforts. In a 13 July press statement [SG/SM/12365], the UN Secretary-General expressed his support for the mediation efforts of President Óscar Árias (Costa Rica) to resolve the political crisis. He offered technical assistance for the mediation and agreed to work together with President Árias to help the parties reach an agreement.

On 14 July [A/63/928], Portugal, as President of the Community of Democracies, transmitted to the UN Secretary-General the text of the declaration adopted at its fifth ministerial meeting (Lisbon, Portugal, 12 July), which expressed support for the mediation led by President Árias, as well as by OAS and other regional efforts, and called on all actors to facilitate those efforts.

In a 17 July letter [A/63/930] to the UN Secretary-General, Honduras stated that despite intense international and regional efforts, the regime continued to refuse to restore constitutional and democratic order, and advised that measures be taken to ensure that no communication from those who carried out the coup d'état was accepted by any Secretariat official or UN system entity.

Security and human rights concerns

In a letter dated 22 September [S/2009/487] to the Security Council, Brazil stated that President Zelaya had entered Honduras by his own means and taken shelter in the Brazilian Embassy in Tegucigalpa. However, following a 21 September note (annexed to the letter) from the de facto authorities, Brazil expressed concern for the President's safety, and the security and physical integrity of the Embassy premises and personnel. The note alleged that Mr. Zelaya was a fugitive from Honduran justice and the fact that the Embassy had condoned the issuance from its premises of public phone calls for political mobilization by Mr. Zelaya was a violation of international law, rendering the mission and its Government responsible for any violence those acts might incite, either within or outside the mission. Brazil requested that an urgent meeting of the Council be convened to prevent any action that might further aggravate the situation.

In identical letters dated 23 September [A/64/374-S/2009/491] to the General Assembly and Council, Mexico, as President of the Rio Group, transmitted a 22 September statement issued by the Group, which supported the peaceful return of President Zelaya to Honduras and condemned both the acts of violence carried out by the de facto Government in the vicinity of the Brazilian mission on that date, and acts of intimidation against the mission. It urged that the inviolability of the Embassy be secured in compliance with the 1961 Vienna Convention on Diplomatic Relations [YUN 1961, p. 512] and demanded that the de facto authorities put an end to acts of repression against the civilian population and to the violations of the human rights of all Honduran citizens.

Suspension of UN technical assistance. On 23 September [SG/SM/12482], the Secretary-General decided to suspend temporarily the UN technical assistance to the Supreme Electoral Tribunal of Honduras for the November elections, as he did not believe that conditions were in place for holding credible elections that would advance peace and stability. The United Nations was concerned about the situation in the country, including allegations of human rights violations. He urged adherence to international human rights treaties and conventions ratified by Honduras and respect for the inviolability of Brazil's Embassy. In support of regional efforts to end the crisis, he joined oas and regional leaders in calling for a consensual agreement and urged all political actors to find common ground through peaceful dialogue.

Security Council consideration. On 25 September [meeting 6192], the Brazilian Minister of Foreign Affairs informed the Council of the situation at its Embassy in Tegucigalpa and called on the Council to ensure the security of the mission and the safety of President Zelaya. He expressed concern that those who had perpetrated the coup d'état might threaten the inviolability of the Embassy in order to arrest the President forcefully and in that regard, described actions taken by the de facto authorities, including a bailiff sent with a warrant to search the premises and treatment that implied the Embassy had ceased to enjoy diplomatic status. Since the President's arrival on 21 September, the Embassy had been virtually under siege, with electricity, water supply and phone connections cut off and cell phone communications hampered. Access to food had been restricted and movement of official Embassy vehicles curtailed. Such actions were a breach of the Vienna Convention and the recent ruling by the oas Inter-American Commission on Human Rights that the de facto Government must not threaten the safety of the President or anyone sheltered at the Brazilian mission. Brazil rejected all threats against its Embassy and against those under its protection, and expressed its support for dialogue based on relevant oas resolutions and the mediation efforts made by President Árias.

Further developments

Tegucigalpa-San José Accord. On 30 October, following a process of political dialogue, including the "Guaymuras Dialogue" in search of a peaceful and negotiated solution to the crisis, representatives of both the deposed President Zelaya Government and the de facto Micheletti Government signed the Tegucigalpa-San José Accord in Tegucigalpa. The Accord led to the establishment and installation of the Government of National Unity and Reconciliation in Honduras no later than 5 November and consisting of representatives of various political parties and social organizations. It also included agreements on the general elections and the transfer of Government; the armed forces and national police; the refusal to convene a National Constituent Assembly or redraft the Constitution in areas that could not be amended; the establishment of a Verification and Truth Commissions; the normalization of relations between Honduras and the international community; the appropriate decision by the National Congress with regard to reversing the status of the executive power to the situation prior to 28 June until the conclusion of the incumbent Government on 27 January 2010; and a schedule for compliance with the agreements of the Accord. Although a public signing ceremony would take place on 2 November, the Accord entered into force immediately.

In a 30 October press statement [SG/SM/12579], the Secretary-General, with regard to news from Tegucigalpa that an agreement had been reached between President Zelaya and the de facto authorities to resolve the political crisis, expressed the hope that Honduras was on a path to the full restoration of democratic, constitutional rule.

Communication. In identical notes verbales dated 15 November [A/64/537] to the UN Secretary-General and the General Assembly President, Honduras transmitted a 14 November letter from President Zelaya addressed to United States President Barack Obama, alleging that Mr. Micheletti "had broken the Agreement" and had stated that he would "form a unity government without Zelaya". President Zelaya expressed surprise to hear that State Department officials had changed their position and interpreted the Accord unilaterally, stating that the United States would recognize the elections with or without his reinstatement. He said that the Accord was a single 12-point agreement to be implemented fully and simultaneously, not as two separate agreements. Therefore, the Tegucigalpa-San José Accord was null and void because of the de facto Government's non-compliance. President Zelaya also raised objections to the elections scheduled for November, as they were to have been conducted within a legal framework and with international support, including from oas and the United Nations. In the absence of those political conditions, a free and transparent result could not be guaranteed. He noted that the new position of United States Government officials sidestepped the original aim of the San José dialogue and said that the electoral process was illegal because it covered up the military coup d'état and the de facto situation in Honduras. He reaffirmed his decision not to accept any agreement to return to the Presidency that would make him complicit in the coup d'état.

Year-end developments. In identical notes dated 11 December [A/64/565] to the UN Secretary-General and Assembly President, Honduras transmitted a letter from the Minister for Foreign Affairs addressed to the Secretary-General, as well as three official documents: the Guaymuras Dialogue–Tegucigalpa-San José Accord; the statement by the Supreme Electoral Tribunal; and the 2 December communiqué of the Honduran National Congress. The letter summarized progress made since the signing of the Accord on 30 October. General elections for presidential, parliamentary, congressional and municipal seats took place on 29 November, without incident and in an atmosphere of total freedom, with the presence of 494 international observers from 38 countries and 4,126 national observers. The five legally registered political parties took part in the process. Porfirio Lobo Sosa of the National Party, the party in opposition to the incumbent Government, was the winning candidate for the Presidency. All elected authorities would serve four-year terms.

On 2 December, the National Congress, by a vote of 111 in favour and 14 against, rejected the reinstatement of Mr. Zelaya to the presidency of the Republic, reaffirmed its support for the constitutional succession that brought Mr. Micheletti to the presi-dency and approved his continuance in the office of President. President-elect Lobo would take office on 27 January 2010. Referring to section 7 of the Accord on the normalization of relations, Honduras urged the UN Secretary-General to initiate the process of normalizing relations between the United Nations and its specialized agencies and Honduras, including the accreditation of the representatives of Honduras at the Secretariat.

Haiti

Political and security situation

During 2009, a new readiness among the Haitian political leadership to work together resulted in advances in a number of areas, including the adoption of legislation, holding of elections and pursuit of inclusive dialogue on major issues facing the country. In March, a Security Council mission to Haiti, among other activity, assessed implementation of the five benchmarks and the level of cooperation and coordination in each aspect of the mandate of the United Nations Stabilization Mission in Haiti (MINUSTAH). The Mission continued to provide support to the Haitian Government in border management and other security aspects, and to enhance the capacity of the Haitian National Police (HNP). In October, MINUS-TAH forces were reconfigured to meet the requirements on the ground. The deterioration of social and economic development was a concern.

National dialogue, capacity-building and elections

Report of Secretary-General (March). In his March report [S/2009/129], the Secretary-General said there were indications of a new readiness among the Haitian political leadership to work together, in particular in response to the crisis created by hurricanes and tropical storms in late 2008 and by renewed tensions related to the upcoming senatorial elections. President René Préval called for national unity to build peace and foster long-term development. In his New Year's address, he indicated that rebuilding the country's infrastructure and developing a national dialogue were his key priorities for 2009. Within the Senate, the sitting bureau was extended for an additional year without vote after none of the new candidates for the bureau presidency was able to secure a majority. Several attempts to convene a Senate session in January and February were unsuccessful, since a quorum (16 senators) could not be reached.

On 6 January, the Provisional Electoral Council issued a list of 33 political parties authorized to compete in the senatorial elections, and on 23 January, at the close of registration, 105 candidates had registered, with candidates from Lespwa, Fanmi Lavalas and Union running in all 10 departments. On 5 February, the Council published a list of 65 validated candidates while disqualifying 40 candidates from participating in Senate elections, including all representatives of the Fanmi Lavalas party, which was questioned by national and international actors in view of its potential impact on the credibility of the electoral process. The Council provided for a further one-week period to receive complaints from the rejected candidates, after which it published a revised list of 78 approved candidates. All Fanmi Lavalas candidates remained excluded on the basis that the party had failed to submit a single consolidated slate of candidates authorized by its formal leader, former President Jean-Bertrand Aristide. The update to the voter roll by the Haitian National Identification Office, with OAS support, resulted in the registration of more than 580,000 new voters as at February, bringing the total number of eligible voters to 4,119,600.

On institutional support and strengthening of the State, the adoption by the Senate and Chamber of Deputies of enhanced internal rules opened the way for the adoption of a statute on parliamentary staff, together with administrative and financial regulations that could improve the functioning of the legislature. In an effort to promote transparency, the Parliament's expenses for 2008 were published in January 2009 on the legislature's website and in local newspapers. MINUSTAH supported a programme to provide standardized training on public finance, protocol and ethics within all communes that was scheduled to be completed by July. The Mission also worked to support the Ministry of the Interior to undertake its functions in mandate-related areas such as border control and local administration. Security in the country remained generally calm, with a decline in some criminal activities, in particular kidnappings. Persistent poverty and youth unemployment had created an environment vulnerable to civil unrest and renewed gang activity, and the situation remained fragile, with violence increasing steadily. MINUSTAH troops and police continued to help mitigate security concerns and maintain political stability to help promote public order. The Mission also continued support in maritime patrolling and border patrol operations; enhancement of the capacity of HNP; and certification and vetting activities in 8 of the 10 departments of Haiti.

In other developments, on 19 February, President Préval officially launched a follow-up commission on the reform of the judiciary. Some progress also took place in initiatives to enhance corrections capacity, with bilateral support. However, the prison population continued to expand: as at 12 February, some 8,202 inmates were held in the country's 17 prisons.

The Secretary-General observed that incremental advances had been achieved in four of the five benchmarks: political dialogue and elections; extension of State authority; strengthening of security; and rule of law and human rights. In the fifth area, social and economic development, there had been a marked deterioration in terms of the daily living conditions faced by the majority of the Haitian people, with 78 per cent of the population living on \$2 or less per day. Continued engagement by the authorities and enhanced international community support would be critical to recover ground that had been lost and to secure and build on the gains achieved.

Security Council mission to Haiti

On 10 March [S/2009/139], the President of the Security Council informed the Secretary-General that the Council had decided to send a mission to Haiti from 11 to 14 March, headed by Jorge Urbina (Costa Rica). The mission would, among other things, assess the status of implementation of Council resolution 1840(2008) [YUN 2008, p. 340]; review progress achieved by the Government in the areas of security, border management, institutional support and governance, rule of law, human rights and economic and social development; assess the level of MINUSTAH cooperation and coordination in each aspect of its mandate; and reaffirm the Council's support for the Government and people of Haiti to rebuild their country, consolidate peace and stability, and promote recovery and development.

Report of Security Council mission. In the report on its activities [S/2009/175], the mission stated that it had met with a wide range of stakeholders, including the President and Prime Minister and a number of ministers, officials of the Provisional Electoral Council, the HNP Director-General, leaders of political parties, representatives of the private sector and civil society, senior MINUSTAH officials, the UN country team and members of the Core Group established pursuant to Council resolution 1542(2004) [YUN 2004, p. 294]. The report summarized the main challenges facing Haiti, which included: security, political dialogue and the elections, extension of State authority, the rule of law and human rights, humanitarian relief, and social and economic development.

Significant progress had been made in security due to the gradual strengthening of HNP. MINUSTAH and HNP had contributed to the dismantling of armed gangs responsible for much of the violence in the country, yet the overall security situation remained fragile. Poverty and youth unemployment created an environment of civil unrest. Sixty-four demonstrations were reported in February, while drug trafficking and border security were also of concern. The mission was of the view that the continued presence of MINUSTAH troops and police remained critical to the maintenance of a secure and stable environment. Although the political climate had improved considerably since the establishment of an elected Government in 2006 [YUN 2006, p. 348], Haiti's democratic institutions continued to be undermined by divisions within Haitian society and ongoing political tensions between contending factions. Relations between the executive branch and the Parliament remained fraught. The Provisional Electoral Council's decision not to accept any Fanmi Lavalas candidates (see p. 319) raised questions about the inclusiveness of the forthcoming April senatorial elections. The mission was encouraged by the commitment of Fanmi Lavalas leaders to use only legal means to seek a reversal of the Council's decision, and by signs of willingness on the part of the Government, Parliament, political parties, the private sector and civil society to hold a dialogue on issues of critical importance to the future of the country. President Préval and Electoral Council magistrates informed the mission that eight electoral processes would be spread out over the forthcoming 36 months.

Despite MINUSTAH efforts to help enhance institutional capacity, both the central Government and local administration continued to suffer from limited capacity to deliver basic services, with health and education services being the weakest. Positive developments included a significant increase in the collection of revenue by customs, and efforts by the Government, with assistance from MINUSTAH and other stakeholders, to prepare and update a number of key policy texts related to border management. On the rule of law and human rights, steps had been taken towards HNP professionalization, the enhancement of HNP institutional capacity and the development of key infrastructure. Support provided to HNP by MINUSTAH in collaboration with UN agencies and bilateral partners had boosted public confidence in the police. However, even with the gains achieved over the previous five years, HNP still lacked the capacity to address the array of threats to Haiti's stability, and in particular organized crime and drug trafficking. Some progress had been made towards the implementation of the three fundamental laws on the independence of the judiciary, such as the inauguration of the School for Magistrates on 12 March. Other areas to be addressed included implementation of the national plan for justice reform, the establishment of the Superior Council for the Judiciary, the situation within Haiti's prisons of extreme overcrowding in inadequate facilities, and the limitations on economic, social and cultural rights. On the humanitarian situation, progress was made in the area of disaster prevention and risk reduction, but food security remained one of the greatest concerns in the country, as well as difficulties in the farming sector. Three million people were moderately or extremely food insecure—nearly a third of the population. The mission concluded its report with observations on the main challenges facing Haiti, regional cooperation, the UN role in the country and the eventual drawdown of MINUSTAH.

On 19 March [meeting 6093], Mr. Urbina briefed the Security Council on the mission's findings.

Security Council consideration (April). On 6 April [meeting 6101], the Special Representative and Head of MINUSTAH, Hédi Annabi, briefed the Council on the situation in Haiti. He underscored the high level of international commitment to the stabilization process in the country, noting that it built upon the visits to Haiti on 9 and 10 March by the Secretary-General and former United States President William Clinton, and the Security Council mission from 11 to 14 March. Although socio-economic issues were not the core work of a peacekeeping operation, it remained clear that in Haiti, the promotion of security and development were closely linked. Estimated damage of $1 billion from the 2008 hurricanes was compounded by the global financial crisis. Assistance was needed in three broad areas: humanitarian relief, early recovery and longer-term development. He urged the international community to make a further effort towards the stabilization process at the 14 April 2009 donor conference on Haiti to be hosted by the Inter-American Development Bank in Washington, D.C.

SECURITY COUNCIL ACTION

On 6 April [meeting 6101], following consultations among Security Council members, the President made statement **S/PRST/2009/4** on behalf of the Council:

> The Security Council welcomes the progress achieved so far in critical areas for the consolidation of Haiti's stability, namely political dialogue, extension of State authority, including border management, strengthening of security, and rule of law and human rights.
>
> The Council notes with concern the challenges in the area of social and economic development, as there has been a marked deterioration in the living standards of the vast majority of Haitians. The Council reiterates the need for security to be accompanied by social and economic development as a way for Haiti to achieve lasting stability. In this regard, the Council calls upon the United Nations Stabilization Mission in Haiti and the United Nations country team to enhance further their coordination with the Government of Haiti and international and regional partners, while bearing in mind the ownership and primary responsibility of the Government and people of Haiti.
>
> The Council recognizes the vital importance of the high-level donor conference on Haiti to be hosted by the Inter-American Development Bank in Washington, D.C., on 14 April 2009. The Council welcomes the valuable continuing support of donors and urges them to make available the additional technical and financial assistance required by the Government of Haiti to meet the country's immediate humanitarian, early recovery and

reconstruction needs, while laying the foundations for sustainable economic and social development.

The Council urges the institutions of Haiti to intensify their efforts to meet the basic needs of the Haitian population, and to work together to promote dialogue, the rule of law and good governance.

The Council reaffirms the need for the upcoming elections for the renewal of one third of the Senate to be inclusive, free and fair. The Council calls upon all political actors in Haiti to ensure that the elections are held in a peaceful atmosphere.

The Council reiterates its strong support for the Mission and the Special Representative of the Secretary-General for Haiti, for their efforts to improve stability and governance in Haiti, while emphasizing the need for the Mission to continue to adjust to changing circumstances on the ground, and expresses its appreciation to all Member States who support the stabilization process, in particular the troop- and police-contributing countries.

Further political and security developments

Senatorial elections. The elections held in April and June to fill 12 vacancies in the Senate represented the first elections held since the 2006 electoral cycle [YUN 2006, p. 345], and the first to be organized by the new Provisional Electoral Council, with technical, logistical and security support from MINUSTAH. While conditions were generally peaceful during the first round of elections on 19 April 2009, a series of violent incidents led to the closure of voting centres in the Artibonite Department and the cancellation of the vote in the Centre Department. The second round of elections in the nine departments other than the Centre Department was held on 21 June, without significant disruptions. A review of the April elections conducted jointly by HNP and MINUSTAH helped to develop an enhanced security strategy for the second round. National and international observers generally expressed satisfaction with the technical aspects of the electoral process. The rerun of the first round of elections in the Centre Department was expected to be held once the authorities took action on the basis of the Electoral Council investigation. The election results were published on 24 July. Representatives of Lespwa won 6 out of 11 seats, while a single seat was won by representatives of Fusion, Konba, Standard Bearer in Action and Organization of the Struggling People, and a candidate who ran as an independent. The low level of voter turnout countrywide—11.3 per cent in April and 10.9 per cent in June—raised concerns about the degree of public engagement in the political process. The reversal of the results in the South Department and allegations of vote tampering in the Petite Rivière region of the Artibonite Department also prompted controversy within the Electoral Council.

Appointment of Special Envoy. In a 19 May press statement [SG/A/1185], the Secretary-General announced the appointment of former United States President William Clinton to the position of United Nations Special Envoy for Haiti. In that capacity, President Clinton would assist the Government of Haiti and its people in their efforts to create new jobs, improve the delivery of basic services and infrastructure, strengthen disaster recovery and preparedness, attract private sector investment and garner greater international support.

Report of Secretary-General (September). In September [S/2009/439], the Secretary-General said that increased political cooperation had permitted progress in a number of areas, including the holding of senatorial elections, the adoption of key legislation and the pursuit of an inclusive dialogue on major issues. However, that collaboration remained fragile, with a potential for renewed tensions and conflict among and within the governing institutions. In order for the 11 successful electoral candidates to assume their functions in the Senate (see above), the Constitution required validation by their peers. A number of sitting Senators had threatened not to validate the elected candidates until allegations of electoral tampering had been clarified, while others had threatened to block the validation process owing to the exclusion of the Fanmi Lavalas party in the elections. Meanwhile, a number of electoral exercises lay ahead, including the rerun for the senatorial elections in the Centre Department and elections for all members of the Chamber of Deputies and for one third of the Senate whose terms would expire on 12 January 2010. It remained unclear whether those elections would be held before the end of 2009. The next presidential elections would be held on 28 November 2010.

Efforts continued to strengthen national and local institutional capacity. MINUSTAH provided support to the Parliament, which adopted several measures aimed at enhancing its performance, including the appointment on 9 July of a Secretary-General of the Chamber of Deputies. With technical assistance from MINUSTAH, the Government prepared an integrated border management plan and a draft customs code. Construction of expanded border facilities at Ouanaminthe and Malpasse was completed and the upgrading of the customs data system, the physical improvement of the border crossing points, and the intensification of patrols by security forces contributed to increased customs revenue. As at 19 August, 128 quick-impact projects had been launched to provide basic public services, construct or rehabilitate public infrastructure, and provide income-generating activities.

The security environment remained calm, although fragile. Potential threats to stability included the risk of resumed activity by gangs, criminals and other armed groups; corruption and violence associated with illegal trafficking; and large-scale civil unrest. Demonstrations that had begun in Port-au-Prince in June, where students took to the streets to express academic grievances, were subsequently joined by protesters in favour of the proposed minimum wage increase, and appeared to have been infiltrated by external, violent elements. MINUSTAH security components continued to play a critical role in maintaining a stable and secure environment, providing HNP support in responding to civil disorder and other threats, regular patrolling throughout the country, and border management support through maritime, air and land patrols. MINUSTAH operations in Cité Soleil and in Martissant resulted in the arrest of a number of gang leaders, and joint HNP/MINUSTAH operations contributed to a decline in reported kidnappings. MINUSTAH also continued to enhance HNP professionalism, develop its institutional capacity and facilitate the establishment of necessary infrastructure. As at 18 August, HNP numbered some 9,715 officers, which included a group of 468 new officers who graduated on that day as members of the twenty-first promotion. Another 1,500 candidates for the twenty-second promotion would begin their training within the coming months.

On the consolidation plan for Haiti, while there had been some advances in the past year and the progress indicators proposed in 2008 [YUN 2008, p. 339] remained valid, some adjustments were warranted by specific developments in the five benchmark areas. The benchmarks and revised indicators for progress for 2009–2011 were annexed to the report.

The Secretary-General observed that five years into the stabilization process, the gains achieved remained fragile. Continued commitment by the Haitian leadership and its people, the United Nations and the international community was critical for the consolidation of stability. Further efforts to curb corruption and impunity were also needed, including effective follow-up to the violent incidents during the 19 April elections. As MINUSTAH security components and technical expertise remained vital to the process, he recommended the extension of the MINUSTAH mandate for an additional year, until 15 October 2010. With regard to the ongoing review of MINUSTAH forces, he recommended a reduction of the military component by some 120 troops down to 6,940 personnel, and an increase of 120 officers bringing the police component to 2,211 personnel.

Security Council consideration (September). On 9 September [meeting 6186], the Special Envoy for Haiti briefed the Council on the six areas of his mandate, which included implementation of the Government's recovery programme. He urged all who had made commitments during April's high-level donor conference to fund them as soon as possible.

2 x 9 Mechanism on Haiti. On 2 October [S/2009/509], Argentina transmitted to the Security Council a joint communiqué of the 2 x 9 Mechanism on Haiti [YUN 2008, p. 339], which brought together the Latin American countries contributing military and police personnel to MINUSTAH. The Mechanism supported the recommendations of the Secretary-General's September report (see p. 321) and the report of the Ad Hoc Advisory Group (see p. 325).

SECURITY COUNCIL ACTION

On 13 October [meeting 6200], the Security Council unanimously adopted **resolution 1892(2009)**. The draft [S/2009/530] was submitted by 21 Member States.

The Security Council,

Reaffirming its previous resolutions on Haiti, in particular resolutions 1542(2004) of 30 April 2004, 1576(2004) of 29 November 2004, 1608(2005) of 22 June 2005, 1658(2006) of 14 February 2006, 1702(2006) of 15 August 2006, 1743(2007) of 15 February 2007, 1780(2007) of 15 October 2007 and 1840(2008) of 14 October 2008,

Reaffirming its strong commitment to the sovereignty, independence, territorial integrity and unity of Haiti, welcoming the progress achieved so far in critical areas for the consolidation of Haiti's stability, reaffirming its support to the Government of Haiti, and welcoming its contribution to political stability and the consolidation of democracy in Haiti,

Welcoming the recent progress made towards enhanced governance, including through the election of new Senators with the support of the United Nations Stabilization Mission in Haiti and other stakeholders and towards the adoption of the constitutional reform, stressing the importance of establishing credible, competent, transparent and accountable governance and encouraging the Government of Haiti to further strengthen State institutions, and emphasizing the need to continue international efforts to reinforce the capacities of the Government and its State institutions,

Encouraging the Government of Haiti and all the other relevant Haitian actors to strengthen democratic dialogue and forge the widest and most inclusive consensus possible, recognizing that leadership and constant political will of the Government among the relevant Haitian actors is needed to strengthen governance and national capacities to address the highest-priority issues in its national agenda,

Emphasizing the need for increased efforts to support the participation of women in the political process,

Emphasizing also the role of regional organizations in the ongoing process of stabilization and reconstruction in Haiti, calling upon the Mission to continue to work closely with the Organization of American States and the Caribbean Community, and taking note of the joint communiqué issued by the 2 x 9 Mechanism on Haiti on 28 September 2009,

Recognizing the interconnected nature of the challenges in Haiti, reaffirming that sustainable progress on security, the rule of law and institutional reform, national reconciliation and development is mutually reinforcing, and welcoming the continuing efforts of the Government of Haiti and the international community to address these challenges,

Reiterating the need for security to be accompanied by social and economic development as a way for Haiti to achieve lasting stability,

Recognizing that respect for human rights, due process, addressing the issue of criminality and putting an end to impunity are essential to ensuring the rule of law and security in Haiti,

Commending the Mission for continuing to assist the Government of Haiti to ensure a secure and stable environment, expressing its gratitude to the personnel of the Mission and to their countries, and paying tribute to those injured or killed in the line of duty,

Acknowledging some improvements in the security situation in the last year, but noting that the security situation remains fragile,

Acknowledging also the continued support of the Organization of American States to modernizing the Haitian voter registry, and calling upon the Haitian authorities, with the continued support of the Mission and the international community, to establish permanent and effective electoral institutions and to hold elections consistent with Haiti's constitutional and legal requirements,

Calling upon the Government of Haiti, in coordination with the international community, to continue to advance security sector reform, in particular as called for in the Haitian National Police Reform Plan adopted by the Government,

Underlining the need to accelerate the steps taken towards strengthening the judicial system in accordance with the national justice reform plan, including judicial institution modernization and improvement in the access to justice,

Supporting the initial recommendations of the Consultative Commission on Prolonged Pretrial Detention, and stressing the need to address the situation of the majority of Haitian prisoners,

Recognizing the devastation that has been suffered by the people of Haiti during the previous hurricane seasons, acknowledging the challenges faced by the Government of Haiti in responding to the humanitarian and other needs of its people, welcoming the efforts undertaken by the Haitian authorities and the contribution of the international community in this regard, and stressing the importance for future actions in this regard to be fully coordinated among donors and partners of Haiti, with the Government as well as within the United Nations system,

Recognizing also that external economic impacts such as the food, fuel, financial and economic crises continue to pose a significant threat to the overall process of stabilization in Haiti,

Welcoming the appointment of the former President of the United States of America, Mr. William J. Clinton, as the United Nations Special Envoy for Haiti,

Underlining the need for the quick implementation of highly effective and visible labour-intensive projects that help to create jobs and deliver basic social services that contribute to increased support of the Mission by the Haitian population,

Recognizing the importance of long-term commitment of international donors and partners of Haiti, and encouraging them to continue strengthening their assistance in a coordinated way, aligned to Haitian national priorities,

Underlining the need for the Government of Haiti and the Parliament to work together in devising a legislative and regulatory environment to generate economic activity and create jobs with a view to promoting growth and reducing poverty,

Welcoming the report of the Secretary-General of 1 September 2009,

Taking note of the report of the Ad Hoc Advisory Group on Haiti of the Economic and Social Council,

Welcoming the efforts of the Secretary-General to keep peacekeeping operations, including the Mission, under review, and stressing the need for the Security Council to pursue a strategic approach to peacekeeping deployments in partnership with troop- and police-contributing countries and other relevant stakeholders, consistent with the statement by its President of 5 August 2009 on United Nations peacekeeping operations,

Recalling the statements by its President of 22 July and 5 August 2009, which emphasized the need for coherence between, and integration of, peacemaking, peacekeeping, peacebuilding and development to achieve an effective response to post-conflict situations, and stressing the need for the Secretary-General to provide in his reports an indication of progress towards achieving a coordinated United Nations approach in Haiti and, in particular, on critical gaps to achieving peacebuilding objectives,

Determining that the situation in Haiti continues to constitute a threat to international peace and security in the region, despite the progress achieved thus far,

Acting under Chapter VII of the Charter of the United Nations, as described in section I of paragraph 7 of resolution 1542(2004),

1. *Decides* to extend the mandate of the United Nations Stabilization Mission in Haiti, as contained in resolutions 1542(2004), 1608(2005), 1702(2006), 1743(2007), 1780(2007) and 1840(2008), until 15 October 2010, with the intention of further renewal;

2. *Endorses* the recommendation made by the Secretary-General in paragraphs 26 and 27 of his report to maintain the current Mission overall force levels until the planned substantial increase of the Haitian National Police capacity allows for a reassessment of the situation, while adjusting its force configuration to better meet current requirements on the ground;

3. *Decides*, therefore, that the Mission shall consist of a military component of up to 6,940 troops of all ranks and of a police component of up to 2,211 police;

4. *Recognizes* the ownership and primary responsibility of the Government and the people of Haiti over all aspects of the country's stabilization, recognizes the role of the Mission in supporting the efforts of the Government in this regard, and encourages the Government to continue to take full advantage of international support to enhance its capacity, with a view to the eventual resumption of full responsibility;

5. *Stresses* the need for coordination among all international actors on the ground;

6. *Expresses its full support* for the Special Representative of the Secretary-General for Haiti, notably in his efforts related to improving stability and governance in close co-

operation with the Government of Haiti, and reaffirms his authority in the coordination and conduct of all activities of United Nations agencies, funds and programmes in Haiti;

7.   *Also expresses its full support* for the United Nations Special Envoy for Haiti, former President of the United States of America William J. Clinton, notably in his efforts to assist the Government and people of Haiti in creating new jobs, improving the delivery of basic services and infrastructure, strengthening disaster recovery and preparedness, attracting private sector investment and garnering greater international support;

8.   *Reaffirms its call upon* the Mission to support the political process under way in Haiti, including through the good offices of the Special Representative, and, in cooperation with the Government of Haiti, to promote an all-inclusive political dialogue and national reconciliation, and to provide logistical and security assistance for the upcoming elections of 2010 in order to ensure that the democratically elected political institutions can continue carrying forward the reform work laid down in the National Growth and Poverty Reduction Strategy Paper;

9.   *Welcomes* the continuing contribution of the Mission to the efforts of the Government of Haiti to build institutional capacity at all levels, and calls upon the Mission, consistent with its mandate, to continue such support to strengthen self-sustaining State institutions, especially outside Port-au-Prince, including through the provision of specialized expertise to key ministries and institutions;

10.   *Requests* that the Mission continue its support of the Haitian National Police as deemed necessary to ensure security in Haiti, encourages the Mission and the Government of Haiti to continue to undertake coordinated deterrent actions to further decrease the level of crime and violence, including through improved and enhanced implementation of the Haitian National Police Reform Plan, and requests the Mission, consistent with its mandate, to remain engaged in assisting the Government to reform and restructure the National Police, notably by supporting the monitoring, mentoring, training and vetting of police personnel and the strengthening of institutional and operational capacities, consistent with its overall strategy to progressively transfer geographical and functional responsibility for conventional law and order duties to its Haitian counterparts in accordance with the Reform Plan;

11.   *Invites* Member States, including neighbouring and regional States, in coordination with the Mission, to strengthen their engagement with the Government of Haiti to address cross-border illicit trafficking in persons, in particular children, and trafficking in drugs and arms and other illegal activities, and to contribute to strengthening the capacity of the Haitian National Police in these areas, including through the provision by the Mission of technical expertise in support of efforts to implement an integrated border management approach, with emphasis on State capacity-building, and underlines the need for coordinated international support for Government efforts in this area;

12.   *Recognizes* the need for the Mission to continue its efforts to patrol along maritime and land border areas in support of border security activities by the Haitian National Police, and encourages the Mission to continue discussions with the Government of Haiti and Member States to assess the threats along Haiti's land and maritime borders;

13.   *Requests* the United Nations country team, and calls upon all actors, to complement security and development operations undertaken by the Government of Haiti with the support of the Mission with activities aimed at effectively improving the living conditions of the concerned populations and protecting the rights of children, and requests the Mission to continue to implement quick-impact projects;

14.   *Condemns* any attack against personnel or facilities of the Mission, and demands that no acts of intimidation or violence be directed against United Nations and associated personnel or facilities or other actors engaged in humanitarian, development or peacekeeping work;

15.   *Welcomes* the steps taken towards the reform of rule of law institutions, requests the Mission to continue to provide necessary support in this regard, and encourages the Haitian authorities to take full advantage of that support, notably in modernizing key legislation and in the implementation of the justice reform plan, to take the necessary steps, including nominations, that will allow superior judicial institutions to function adequately and to address the issue of prolonged pretrial detentions and prison overcrowding, with special regard to children;

16.   *Encourages* the implementation of the strategic plan of the National Prison Administration, and requests the Mission to remain engaged in supporting the mentoring and training of corrections personnel and the strengthening of institutional and operational capacities;

17.   *Requests* the Mission to continue to pursue its community violence reduction approach, including through support to the National Commission on Disarmament, Dismantlement and Reintegration and concentrating its efforts on labour-intensive projects, the development of a weapons registry, the revision of current laws on importation and possession of arms, the reform of the weapons permit system and the development and implementation of a national community policing doctrine;

18.   *Reaffirms* the human rights mandate of the Mission, calls upon the Haitian authorities to continue their efforts to promote and protect human rights, and calls upon the Mission to continue to provide human rights training to the Haitian National Police and other relevant institutions, including the correctional services;

19.   *Strongly condemns* the grave violations against children affected by armed violence, as well as widespread rape and other sexual abuse of women and girls, and requests the Mission and the United Nations country team, in close cooperation with the Government of Haiti, to continue to promote and protect the rights of women and children as set out in Security Council resolutions 1325(2000) of 31 October 2000, 1612(2005) of 26 July 2005, 1820(2008) of 19 June 2008, 1882(2009) of 4 August 2009, 1888(2009) of 30 September 2009 and 1889(2009) of 5 October 2009;

20.   *Requests* the Secretary-General to continue to take the measures necessary to ensure full compliance of all Mission personnel with the United Nations zero-tolerance policy on sexual exploitation and abuse, and to keep the Council informed, and urges troop- and police-contributing countries to ensure that acts involving their personnel are properly investigated and punished;

21.   *Calls upon* the Mission and the United Nations country team to further enhance their coordination and,

in concert with the Government of Haiti and international partners, help to ensure greater efficiency in the implementation of the National Growth and Poverty Reduction Strategy Paper in order to achieve progress in the area of socio-economic development, which was recognized as essential for the stability of Haiti in the consolidation plan of the Secretary-General, and address urgent development problems;

22. *Welcomes* the important work done by the Mission in support of urgent needs in Haiti, and encourages the Mission, within its mandate, to make full use of existing means and capabilities, including its engineers, with a view to further enhancing stability in the country;

23. *Also welcomes* the progress made by the Mission in its communications and public outreach strategy, and requests it to continue these activities;

24. *Further welcomes* the work done by the Secretary-General to develop five benchmarks and indicators to measure progress being made towards the consolidation of stability in Haiti, and requests the Secretary-General to continue updating the consolidation plan, including by refining those benchmarks and indicators of progress, in consultation with the Government of Haiti, taking into account the National Growth and Poverty Reduction Strategy Paper, as appropriate, and to inform the Council accordingly in his reports;

25. *Requests* the Secretary-General to report to the Council on the implementation of the mandate of the Mission semi-annually and no later than forty-five days prior to its expiration;

26. *Also requests* the Secretary-General to include in his reports a comprehensive assessment of threats to security in Haiti, judicial sector reform, correctional system reform, and counter-narcotics capacity, taking into account a review of the activities and the composition of the Mission, its coordination with the United Nations country team and other development actors and the need for poverty eradication and sustainable development in Haiti, and to propose, as appropriate, options to reconfigure the composition of the Mission;

27. *Underscores* the importance of the planning documents for the military and police components, such as the concept of operations and rules of engagement, being regularly updated, as appropriate, and in line with the provisions of all relevant Council resolutions, and requests the Secretary-General to report on them to the Council and troop- and police-contributing countries;

28. *Decides* to remain seized of the matter.

Year-end developments. In a later report [S/2010/200 & Corr.1], the Secretary-General said that progress had been made towards legislative, presidential and municipal elections to be held in 2010. On 14 September 2009, both legislative Chambers approved a proposition in favour of constitutional amendments that, if ratified, would simplify the electoral calendar and improve the investment climate, including by providing for dual citizenship for the diaspora. Prime Minister Jean-Max Bellerive was sworn in on 12 November, replacing former incumbent Michèle Pierre-Louis after a vote of censure against her

Government. As at late November, 69 political parties and alliances had registered with the Provisional Electoral Council in anticipation of the February 2010 elections. Of those, the Council approved 53, excluding, among others, Eskamp, Fanmi Lavalas, Konba and Union. Two new parties had emerged: Inité (Unity), President René Préval's platform, and Alternative Patriotique pour le Progrès (Patriotic Alternative for Progress), a coalition that included Fusion, the Organization of the Struggling People and Konfederasyon Inité Democratik, and emerged as the principal opposition party.

Programme of support for Haiti

Ad Hoc Advisory Group. The Ad Hoc Advisory Group on Haiti, mandated by Economic and Social Council decision 2004/322 [YUN 2004, p. 939] to follow and advise on the long-term development of the country, submitted a June report [E/2009/105], based on the findings of the Group's visit to Haiti from 4 to 7 May. The terms of reference of the visit concerned development planning and aid coordination; institutional capacity-building; and economic and social development. The Group noted that since the beginning of the year, Haiti had received a high level of international attention and commitments of support and that the third conference on Haiti's economic and social development (Washington, D.C., 14 April) benefited from that momentum. Some $378 million was pledged in response to the plan presented to the Government. The UN system elaborated the United Nations Development Assistance Framework for 2009–2011, which offered a common programming framework to all UN entities in Haiti and linked that collective action to the national strategy for growth and poverty reduction.

The report also discussed the continued weakness of State institutions, the concomitant risk of donor impatience and fatigue and the fact that long-term planning efforts were often overshadowed by the need to find immediate solutions to acute problems. As at early May, the flash appeal organized by the Office for the Coordination of Humanitarian Affairs was 50.3 per cent funded. A renewed momentum in favour of the private sector was cited as an underutilized economic strategy that could play a greater role. The Group was encouraged, in particular, with Government efforts to implement the National Growth and Poverty Reduction Strategy Paper and make it central to the Washington D.C. conference in April through its plan for economic recovery and the document "Haiti: a new paradigm". The report concluded with nine recommendations aimed at improving the economic and social situation and the impact of development support.

On 20 April, the Economic and Social Council appointed the Permanent Representative of Peru to the United Nations as an additional member of the Ad Hoc Advisory Group on Haiti (**decision 2009/211**).

Communications. On 10 April [E/2009/52], Mexico transmitted to the Secretary-General a statement by the States members of the Rio Group and CARICOM entitled "Towards a new paradigm of cooperation", issued on 8 April in preparation for the 14 April conference on Haiti's economic and social development. The statement urged donors and other cooperation partners to increase their support to the country and reaffirmed their support of MINUSTAH's work.

On 1 October [E/2009/117], El Salvador informed the Council of its intention to join the Ad Hoc Advisory Group on Haiti. On 15 December, the Council appointed the Permanent Representative of El Salvador to the United Nations as an additional member of the Ad Hoc Advisory Group on Haiti (**decision 2009/267**).

The Economic and Social Council, in **resolution 2009/4** of 23 July (see p. 904), extended the Group's mandate until July 2010. The Council also welcomed the nomination of a United Nations Special Envoy for Haiti (see p. 321).

MINUSTAH

In 2009, the United Nations Stabilization Mission in Haiti (MINUSTAH), established by Security Council resolution 1542(2004) [YUN 2004, p. 294], maintained its focus on ensuring a secure and stable environment, supporting the electoral process and reform of rule-of-law structures, strengthening State institutions, providing humanitarian and development assistance, and protecting and promoting human rights. Based in Port-au-Prince, MINUSTAH continued to be headed by the Secretary-General's Special Representative for Haiti, Hédi Annabi (Tunisia), and Major General Carlos Alberto dos Santos Cruz (Brazil) remained in his role as Force Commander through March. By resolution 1892(2009), the Council extended MINUSTAH's mandate to 15 October 2010.

Appointment. On 26 March [S/2009/164], the Secretary-General informed the Security Council of his intention to appoint Major General Floriano Peixoto Vieira Neto (Brazil) to the post of Force Commander of MINUSTAH, replacing Major General Santos Cruz, of which the Council took note on 30 March [S/2009/165].

Plane crash. On 9 October, a UN flight in Haiti affiliated with MINUSTAH and carrying 11 passengers and crew members, crashed. In a 10 October press statement [SC/9764], the Security Council expressed distress and shock at the deadly crash.

MINUSTAH activities

During 2009, the Secretary-General reported to the Security Council on MINUSTAH activities and developments in Haiti for the periods from 27 August 2008 to 27 February 2009 [S/2009/129] and 28 February to August 2009 [S/2009/439]. Activities for the remainder of the year were covered in a later report [S/2010/200 & Corr.1]. In addition to political and security aspects, the reports summarized MINUSTAH activities dealing with human rights; child protection; the humanitarian and development situation; gender issues; reform of rule-of-law structures; the consolidation plan; strengthening of the State; the conduct and discipline of UN personnel; and Mission support.

Human Rights. Overcrowding and inhumane conditions in the prisons and police holding cells remained the most frequent violations of political and civil rights, while lynching continued to be a widespread phenomenon throughout the country. MINUSTAH and the Office of the United Nations High Commissioner for Human Rights (OHCHR) conducted a campaign on the right to safe drinking water jointly with the Ministry of Public Works, the United Nations Children's Fund (UNICEF) and the United Nations Development Programme (UNDP). At the local level, MINUSTAH and OHCHR involved national and international non-governmental organizations in implementing water purification, distribution or management projects. Widespread poverty and unemployment, combined with a lack of access to acceptable and affordable food, housing, education and health care and the ongoing deterioration in the environment continued to pose a threat to individual rights and to national stability.

Child protection. The overall threat to children's rights from armed violence continued to diminish, with a significant reduction in kidnapping of children. However, children continued to suffer from criminal acts. Minors were reported to be the victims of 22 kidnappings and 84 rape cases, while internal and cross-border child trafficking for sexual or economic exploitation and inter-country adoption remained a matter of concern. MINUSTAH sought to safeguard the rights of children within the justice system and continued efforts to ensure that the cases of those in prolonged pretrial detention were heard by appropriately prepared judges, and that, where possible, they were immediately released after trial. In support of those efforts, UNICEF provided free legal assistance.

Humanitarian situation. One year after the 2008 hurricanes [YUN 2008, p. 345], the grave socioeconomic situation continued to pose a direct threat to the country's stability. Food insecurity was affecting 1.9 million Haitians and social safety nets remained virtually non-existent. Basic social services such as education, were almost entirely run by non-

State actors and the private sector. The Government presented a national preparedness strategy for the hurricane season, while capacity-building for the country's civil protection directorate continued, with support from UNDP, the World Bank and the European Commission. Operational arrangements were also in place for joint emergency response activities by MINUSTAH and the UN country team. The World Food Programme pre-positioned food in strategically located warehouses and the World Health Organization distributed medical supplies and other equipment to strengthen the response capacity of the Ministry of Health. MINUSTAH provided training on issues related to human immunodeficiency virus and acquired immunodeficiency syndrome (HIV/AIDS) to Mission personnel, members of the National Police, community leaders and representatives of civil society.

Development. Upon the invitation of the Government, the Director of the Earth Institute and the Secretary-General's Special Adviser on the Millennium Development Goals (MDGs) visited Haiti from 14 to 17 July to review the development priorities of the country and explore ways to advance their implementation. The United Nations Special Envoy for Haiti played a critical role in mobilizing public and private investment, while fostering the commitment of State institutions and national actors to work together to improve the lives of Haitian people. On 9 August, the Special Envory announced that he would lead an international trade mission of private investors to Haiti in October. Although the economic growth rate was forecast to rise to 2 per cent during 2009 and 2010, compared with 1.2 per cent in 2008, that rate would barely keep pace with the projected population growth of 2.4 per cent.

Gender. MINUSTAH continued efforts to support women's participation in the political process. During the year, the Mission conducted training sessions on leadership and women's political participation for 44 leaders, including three men and five of the seven women who were competing for seats in the Senate. Efforts to tackle sexual violence, however, continued to suffer from weaknesses in the rule-of-law system. MINUSTAH supported the implementation of the National Plan of Action to combat violence against women, and implemented a country-wide sensitization programme for representatives of civil society organizations, including 148 women and 62 men.

Other activities. In addition to routine tasks, key Mission support activities included radio and television programming; logistical assistance for the senatorial elections in April and June; construction of MINUSTAH facilities to support border patrol activities; and the provision of multimedia centres. MINUSTAH activities continued to be guided by progress in implementing the consolidation plan for Haiti, which comprised indicators in five broad benchmark areas.

Financing of MINUSTAH

In June, the General Assembly considered the performance report [A/63/549 & Corr.1] on the MINUSTAH budget for the period from 1 July 2007 to 30 June 2008, which showed expenditures of $534,068,200 against a total appropriation of $535,372,800, leaving an unencumbered balance of $1,304,600 and other income and adjustments amounting to $17,720,800. The Assembly also had before it the proposed MINUSTAH budget for the period from 1 July 2009 to 30 June 2010 [A/63/709], which amounted to $618,624,000 gross, and provided for the deployment of 7,060 military personnel, 951 UN police officers, 1,140 formed police personnel, 24 Government-provided personnel, 552 international staff, 1,293 national staff and 231 UN Volunteers, including temporary positions.

The Advisory Committee on Administrative and Budgetary Questions [A/63/746/Add.10] identified reductions totalling $3,298,700 and recommended that the Assembly appropriate $615,325,300 for the 2009–2010 budget period, and that the unencumbered balance and amount resulting from other income and adjustments for the 2007–2008 budget period be credited to Member States in a manner to be determined by the Assembly.

GENERAL ASSEMBLY ACTION

On 30 June [meeting 93], the General Assembly, on the recommendation of the Fifth (Administrative and Budgetary) Committee [A/63/901], adopted **resolution 63/294** without vote [agenda item 141].

Financing of the United Nations Stabilization Mission in Haiti

The General Assembly,

Having considered the reports of the Secretary-General on the financing of the United Nations Stabilization Mission in Haiti and the related report of the Advisory Committee on Administrative and Budgetary Questions,

Recalling Security Council resolution 1529(2004) of 29 February 2004, by which the Council declared its readiness to establish a United Nations stabilization force to support continuation of a peaceful and constitutional political process and the maintenance of a secure and stable environment in Haiti,

Recalling also Security Council resolution 1542(2004) of 30 April 2004, by which the Council decided to establish the United Nations Stabilization Mission in Haiti for an initial period of six months, and the subsequent resolutions by which the Council extended the mandate of the Mission, the latest of which was resolution 1840(2008) of 14 October 2008, by which the Council extended the mandate of the Mission until 15 October 2009,

Recalling further its resolution 58/315 of 1 July 2004,

Recalling its resolution 58/311 of 18 June 2004 on the financing of the Mission and its subsequent resolutions thereon, the latest of which was resolution 62/261 of 20 June 2008,

Reaffirming the general principles underlying the financing of United Nations peacekeeping operations, as stated in General Assembly resolutions 1874(S-IV) of 27 June 1963, 3101(XXVIII) of 11 December 1973 and 55/235 of 23 December 2000,

Mindful of the fact that it is essential to provide the Mission with the financial resources necessary to enable it to fulfil its responsibilities under the relevant resolutions of the Security Council,

1. *Requests* the Secretary-General to entrust the Head of Mission with the task of formulating future budget proposals in full accordance with the provisions of General Assembly resolutions 59/296 of 22 June 2005, 60/266 of 30 June 2006 and 61/276 of 29 June 2007, as well as other relevant resolutions;

2. *Takes note* of the status of contributions to the United Nations Stabilization Mission in Haiti as at 30 April 2009, including the contributions outstanding in the amount of 132.8 million United States dollars, representing some 6 per cent of the total assessed contributions, notes with concern that only sixty-six Member States have paid their assessed contributions in full, and urges all other Member States, in particular those in arrears, to ensure payment of their outstanding assessed contributions;

3. *Expresses its appreciation* to those Member States which have paid their assessed contributions in full, and urges all other Member States to make every possible effort to ensure payment of their assessed contributions to the Mission in full;

4. *Expresses concern* at the financial situation with regard to peacekeeping activities, in particular as regards the reimbursements to troop contributors that bear additional burdens owing to overdue payments by Member States of their assessments;

5. *Also expresses concern* at the delay experienced by the Secretary-General in deploying and providing adequate resources to some recent peacekeeping missions, in particular those in Africa;

6. *Emphasizes* that all future and existing peacekeeping missions shall be given equal and non-discriminatory treatment in respect of financial and administrative arrangements;

7. *Also emphasizes* that all peacekeeping missions shall be provided with adequate resources for the effective and efficient discharge of their respective mandates;

8. *Reiterates its request* to the Secretary-General to make the fullest possible use of the facilities and equipment at the United Nations Logistics Base at Brindisi, Italy, in order to minimize the costs of procurement for the Mission;

9. *Requests* the Secretary-General to ensure that proposed peacekeeping budgets are based on the relevant legislative mandates;

10. *Endorses* the conclusions and recommendations contained in the report of the Advisory Committee on Administrative and Budgetary Questions, subject to the provisions of the present resolution, and requests the Secretary-General to ensure their full implementation;

11. *Takes note* of paragraph 41 of the report of the Advisory Committee, and emphasizes the importance of providing appropriate training for national staff, as it contributes to building national capacity;

12. *Also takes note* of paragraphs 32 and 47 of the report of the Advisory Committee;

13. *Requests* the Secretary-General to ensure the full implementation of the relevant provisions of resolutions 59/296, 60/266 and 61/276;

14. *Also requests* the Secretary-General to take all action necessary to ensure that the Mission is administered with a maximum of efficiency and economy;

15. *Further requests* the Secretary-General, in order to reduce the cost of employing General Service staff, to continue efforts to recruit local staff for the Mission against General Service posts, commensurate with the requirements of the Mission;

16. *Stresses* the importance of hiring Haitian nationals against national posts in the Mission, taking into account the need to promote national capacity-building and in order to bring to the Mission experience and knowledge of the local culture, language, traditions and institutions, and in this regard requests the Secretary-General to ensure accurate and timely posting of vacancy announcements for national staff on the Mission website;

17. *Decides* to allocate up to 3 million dollars for quick-impact projects for the period from 1 July 2009 to 30 June 2010;

18. *Requests* the Secretary-General to strengthen the coordination between the Mission, the United Nations country team and other United Nations entities, including in addressing the root causes of unexpected emergencies, such as the unrest generated by the food crisis in Haiti;

Financial performance report for the period from 1 July 2007 to 30 June 2008

19. *Takes note* of the report of the Secretary-General on the financial performance of the Mission for the period from 1 July 2007 to 30 June 2008;

Budget estimates for the period from 1 July 2009 to 30 June 2010

20. *Decides* to appropriate to the Special Account for the United Nations Stabilization Mission in Haiti the amount of 638,706,400 dollars for the period from 1 July 2009 to 30 June 2010, inclusive of 611,751,200 dollars for the maintenance of the Mission, 22,433,300 dollars for the support account for peacekeeping operations and 4,521,900 dollars for the United Nations Logistics Base;

Financing of the appropriation

21. *Also decides* to apportion among Member States the amount of 186,289,366 dollars for the period from 1 July to 15 October 2009, in accordance with the levels updated in General Assembly resolution 61/243 of 22 December 2006, and taking into account the scale of assessments for 2009, as set out in Assembly resolution 61/237 of 22 December 2006;

22. *Further decides* that, in accordance with the provisions of its resolution 973(X) of 15 December 1955, there shall be set off against the apportionment among Member States, as provided for in paragraph 21 above, their respective share in the Tax Equalization Fund of 4,914,321 dollars, comprising the estimated staff assessment income of 4,102,960 dollars approved for the Mission, the prorated

share of 681,161 dollars of the estimated staff assessment income approved for the support account and the prorated share of 130,200 dollars of the estimated staff assessment income approved for the United Nations Logistics Base;

23. *Decides* to apportion among Member States the amount of 452,417,034 dollars for the period from 16 October 2009 to 30 June 2010 at a monthly rate of 53,225,533 dollars, in accordance with the levels updated in resolution 61/243, and taking into account the scale of assessments for 2009, as set out in resolution 61/237, and for 2010, subject to a decision of the Security Council to extend the mandate of the Mission;

24. *Also decides* that, in accordance with the provisions of its resolution 973(X), there shall be set off against the apportionment among Member States, as provided for in paragraph 23 above, their respective share in the Tax Equalization Fund of 11,934,779 dollars, comprising the estimated staff assessment income of 9,964,340 dollars approved for the Mission, the prorated share of 1,654,239 dollars of the estimated staff assessment income approved for the support account and the prorated share of 316,200 dollars of the estimated staff assessment income approved for the United Nations Logistics Base;

25. *Further decides* that, for Member States that have fulfilled their financial obligations to the Mission, there shall be set off against their apportionment, as provided for in paragraph 21 above, their respective share of the unencumbered balance and other income in the total amount of 19,025,400 dollars in respect of the financial period ended 30 June 2008, in accordance with the levels updated in resolution 61/243, and taking into account the scale of assessments for 2008, as set out in resolution 61/237;

26. *Decides* that, for Member States that have not fulfilled their financial obligations to the Mission, there shall be set off against their outstanding obligations their respective share of the unencumbered balance and other income in the total amount of 19,025,400 dollars in respect of the financial period ended 30 June 2008, in accordance with the scheme set out in paragraph 25 above;

27. *Also decides* that the increase in the estimated staff assessment income of 44,300 dollars in respect of the financial period ended 30 June 2008 shall be added to the credits from the amount of 19,025,400 dollars referred to in paragraphs 25 and 26 above;

28. *Emphasizes* that no peacekeeping mission shall be financed by borrowing funds from other active peacekeeping missions;

29. *Encourages* the Secretary-General to continue to take additional measures to ensure the safety and security of all personnel participating in the Mission under the auspices of the United Nations, bearing in mind paragraphs 5 and 6 of Security Council resolution 1502(2003) of 26 August 2003;

30. *Invites* voluntary contributions to the Mission in cash and in the form of services and supplies acceptable to the Secretary-General, to be administered, as appropriate, in accordance with the procedure and practices established by the General Assembly;

31. *Decides* to include in the provisional agenda of its sixty-fourth session the item entitled "Financing of the United Nations Stabilization Mission in Haiti".

On 24 December, by **decision 64/549** the General Assembly decided that the item on financing of MINUSTAH would remain for consideration at its resumed sixty-fourth (2010) session.

Other issues

Colombia

Colombia–Venezuela. On 3 December [S/2009/608], Venezuela transmitted a note dated 23 November from the Foreign Affairs Minister that expressed concern about Colombia's armed conflict and the threat to international peace and security that it posed in the region. The note indicated that the intensification of hostilities between the Colombian armed forces and irregular armed groups in the country had had a negative impact on neighbouring countries, resulting in paramilitarism, drug trafficking and other crimes, such as kidnappings and paid assassinations. Venezuela had been a victim of the Colombian conflict, which in recent years had worsened, allegedly as a result of the war policy of the Colombian Government. Venezuela requested that the issue of Colombia's armed conflict be included in the agenda of the Security Council.

Children and armed conflict

In response to Security Council resolution 1612(2005) [YUN 2005, p. 863], the Secretary-General submitted an August report [S/2009/434] on children and armed conflict in Colombia, which covered developments in 2008. The report provided information on grave violations against children, such as killing and maiming, the recruitment and use of children in armed forces and groups, abduction of children, sexual violence against children, attacks on schools and hospitals, and denial of humanitarian access to children. It stressed the priority of combating impunity for those violations, acknowledged Government efforts and progress made in the protection of children, and made a series of recommendations to strengthen actions for the protection of children affected by armed conflict in the country.

Cuba–El Salvador

On 3 August [A/63/937], El Salvador transmitted to the Secretary-General a letter dated 17 July from its Foreign Affairs Minister, indicating that within the framework of the inauguration of President Carlos Mauricio Funes Cartagena on 1 June, the Governments of El Salvador and Cuba had decided to announce the restoration of full diplomatic relations between their countries. Annexed to the letter was a copy of the joint communiqué (San Salvador, El Salvador, 1 June) on the restoration of full diplomatic relations signed by the Foreign Ministers of the two States.

Cuba–United States

In response to General Assembly resolution 63/7 [YUN 2008, p. 349], the Secretary-General submitted a June report [A/64/97] on information received as at 30 July 2009 from 121 States, the European Union and 25 UN bodies and specialized agencies on the implementation of that resolution. The text of the resolution had called on States to refrain from the unilateral application of economic and trade measures against other States, and urged them to repeal or invalidate such measures.

GENERAL ASSEMBLY ACTION

On 28 October [meeting 27], the General Assembly adopted **resolution 64/6** [draft: A/64/L.4] by recorded vote (187-3-2) [agenda item 19].

Necessity of ending the economic, commercial and financial embargo imposed by the United States of America against Cuba

The General Assembly,

Determined to encourage strict compliance with the purposes and principles enshrined in the Charter of the United Nations,

Reaffirming, among other principles, the sovereign equality of States, non-intervention and non-interference in their internal affairs and freedom of international trade and navigation, which are also enshrined in many international legal instruments,

Recalling the statements of the Heads of State and Government at the Ibero-American Summits concerning the need to eliminate unilateral application of economic and trade measures by one State against another that affect the free flow of international trade,

Concerned about the continued promulgation and application by Member States of laws and regulations, such as that promulgated on 12 March 1996 known as "the Helms-Burton Act", the extraterritorial effects of which affect the sovereignty of other States, the legitimate interests of entities or persons under their jurisdiction and the freedom of trade and navigation,

Taking note of declarations and resolutions of different intergovernmental forums, bodies and Governments that express the rejection by the international community and public opinion of the promulgation and application of measures of the kind referred to above,

Recalling its resolutions 47/19 of 24 November 1992, 48/16 of 3 November 1993, 49/9 of 26 October 1994, 50/10 of 2 November 1995, 51/17 of 12 November 1996, 52/10 of 5 November 1997, 53/4 of 14 October 1998, 54/21

of 9 November 1999, 55/20 of 9 November 2000, 56/9 of 27 November 2001, 57/11 of 12 November 2002, 58/7 of 4 November 2003, 59/11 of 28 October 2004, 60/12 of 8 November 2005, 61/11 of 8 November 2006, 62/3 of 30 October 2007 and 63/7 of 29 October 2008,

Concerned that, since the adoption of its resolutions 47/19, 48/16, 49/9, 50/10, 51/17, 52/10, 53/4, 54/21, 55/20, 56/9, 57/11, 58/7, 59/11, 60/12, 61/11, 62/3 and 63/7, further measures of that nature aimed at strengthening and extending the economic, commercial and financial embargo against Cuba continue to be promulgated and applied, and concerned also about the adverse effects of such measures on the Cuban people and on Cuban nationals living in other countries,

1. *Takes note* of the report of the Secretary-General on the implementation of resolution 63/7;

2. *Reiterates its call upon* all States to refrain from promulgating and applying laws and measures of the kind referred to in the preamble to the present resolution, in conformity with their obligations under the Charter of the United Nations and international law, which, inter alia, reaffirm the freedom of trade and navigation;

3. *Once again urges* States that have and continue to apply such laws and measures to take the necessary steps to repeal or invalidate them as soon as possible in accordance with their legal regime;

4. *Requests* the Secretary-General, in consultation with the appropriate organs and agencies of the United Nations system, to prepare a report on the implementation of the present resolution in the light of the purposes and principles of the Charter and international law and to submit it to the General Assembly at its sixty-fifth session;

5. *Decides* to include in the provisional agenda of its sixty-fifth session the item entitled "Necessity of ending the economic, commercial and financial embargo imposed by the United States of America against Cuba".

RECORDED VOTE ON RESOLUTION 64/6:

In favour: Afghanistan, Albania, Algeria, Andorra, Angola, Antigua and Barbuda, Argentina, Armenia, Australia, Austria, Azerbaijan, Bahamas, Bahrain, Bangladesh, Barbados, Belarus, Belgium, Belize, Benin, Bhutan, Bolivia, Bosnia and Herzegovina, Botswana, Brazil, Brunei Darussalam, Bulgaria, Burkina Faso, Burundi, Cambodia, Cameroon, Canada, Cape Verde, Central African Republic, Chad, Chile, China, Colombia, Comoros, Congo, Costa Rica, Côte d'Ivoire, Croatia, Cuba, Cyprus, Czech Republic, Democratic People's Republic of Korea, Democratic Republic of the Congo, Denmark, Djibouti, Dominica, Dominican Republic, Ecuador, Egypt, El Salvador, Equatorial Guinea, Eritrea, Estonia, Ethiopia, Fiji, Finland, France, Gabon, Gambia, Georgia, Germany, Ghana, Greece, Grenada, Guatemala, Guinea, Guinea-Bissau, Guyana, Haiti, Honduras, Hungary, Iceland, India, Indonesia, Iran, Iraq, Ireland, Italy, Jamaica, Japan, Jordan, Kazakhstan, Kenya, Kiribati, Kuwait, Kyrgyzstan, Lao People's Democratic Republic, Latvia, Lebanon, Lesotho, Liberia, Libyan Arab Jamahiriya, Liechtenstein, Lithuania, Luxembourg, Madagascar, Malawi, Malaysia, Maldives, Mali, Malta, Mauritania, Mauritius, Mexico, Moldova, Monaco, Mongolia, Montenegro, Morocco, Mozambique, Myanmar, Namibia, Nauru, Nepal, Netherlands, New Zealand, Nicaragua, Niger, Nigeria, Norway, Oman, Pakistan, Panama, Papua New Guinea, Paraguay, Peru, Philippines,

Poland, Portugal, Qatar, Republic of Korea, Romania, Russian Federation, Rwanda, Saint Kitts and Nevis, Saint Lucia, Saint Vincent and the Grenadines, Samoa, San Marino, Sao Tome and Principe, Saudi Arabia, Senegal, Serbia, Seychelles, Sierra Leone, Singapore, Slovakia, Slovenia, Solomon Islands, Somalia, South Africa, Spain, Sri Lanka, Sudan, Suriname, Swaziland, Sweden, Switzerland, Syrian Arab Republic, Tajikistan, Thailand, The former Yugoslav Republic of Macedonia, Timor-Leste, Togo, Tonga, Trinidad and Tobago, Tunisia, Turkey, Turkmenistan, Tuvalu, Uganda, Ukraine, United Arab Emirates, United Kingdom, United Republic of Tanzania, Uruguay, Uzbekistan, Vanuatu, Venezuela, Viet Nam, Yemen, Zambia, Zimbabwe.

Against: Israel, Palau, United States.

Abstaining: Marshall Islands, Micronesia.

Communications. On 24 July [A/63/967-S/2009/515], Egypt transmitted to the Secretary-General a Non-Aligned Movement (NAM) Special Declaration, which urged an end to the United States embargo against Cuba. On 19 October [A/64/499], Cuba transmitted the Final Declaration of the Sixth Forum of Cuban Civil Society against the Embargo and the Annexation (Havana, 16 October). Other communications from Cuba addressed the treatment of prisoners held in the United States, including a spouse seeking a visa to visit her incarcerated husband [A/63/945]; the release from prison in the United States of an alleged terrorist, Santiago Álvarez Fernández-Magriña [A/64/534-S/2009/593]; and a request for items to be retained on the list of matters of which the Security Council was seized [S/2009/70].

Cooperation between the United Nations and regional organizations

Caribbean Community

On 3 April [A/63/810-S/2009/185], the Secretary-General transmitted the joint statement adopted by the participants of the Fifth General Meeting between the United Nations and the Caribbean Community (CARICOM) at UN Headquarters (New York, 9–10 February), which reviewed actions taken following the Fourth General Meeting [YUN 2007, p. 322] and discussed various issues, including a proposal for establishing a regional strategic framework for planning and monitoring collaboration between the United Nations and CARICOM; sustainable development and CARICOM efforts to develop and implement a common environment and natural resources framework to protect the Caribbean Sea and promote sustainable fisheries; UNDP's support to CARICOM in promoting energy efficiency and in developing the institutional capacity of CARICOM member States; the high percentage of the Caribbean population under the age of 24 and the needs of adolescents and youth; the CARICOM proposal to establish a special rapporteur on gender-based violence; and the establishment of the Caribbean regional strategic framework on HIV/AIDS. The meeting identified areas for attention under the regional strategic framework and agreed that it should reflect a three- to five-year perspective, rather than be limited to the two-year intervals of the UN-CARICOM General Meetings.

Chapter IV

Asia and the Pacific

In 2009, the United Nations continued to address political and security challenges in Asia and the Pacific in its efforts to restore peace and stability and to promote economic and social development.

In Afghanistan, the security situation continued to deteriorate in 2009 and attacks on UN staff forced UN operations, including the United Nations Assistance Mission in Afghanistan (UNAMA), to relocate some staff outside of the country temporarily. A Taliban attack on 28 October against a guest house in Kabul, in which over 30 UN personnel resided, killed five staff members and wounded five. Taliban attacks against UN personnel or premises included improvised explosive device attacks against UN vehicles in Uruzgan and Kunduz in May and June, respectively, and four rocket attacks against UN premises in Herat.

Other terrorist actions targeted government facilities, causing many deaths and injuries, and affecting innocent civilians. Those actions included an attack on 11 February and the suicide attack on 8 October outside the Indian embassy in Kabul.

UNAMA, headed by Kai Eide, continued to coordinate international humanitarian and development activities, foster political dialogue and help the Government build institutions. In March, the Security Council extended UNAMA's mandate by another year. In May, UNAMA opened two new offices, in Tirin Kot and Sari Pul. For much of the year, the Mission continued its work in support of the presidential and provincial council elections, which were held on 20 August. When a subsequent recount showed that neither of the two leading presidential candidates—Hamid Karzai and Abdullah Abdullah—had received over 50 per cent of the vote, a second round became necessary. When Mr. Abdullah's conditions for that round were rejected, he withdrew his participation, and President Karzai was inaugurated for a second term.

The International Security Assistance Force (ISAF), a multinational force established by the Council in 2001 and led by the North Atlantic Treaty Organization (NATO), continued to assist the Government in maintaining security. The Council extended ISAF's authorization until October 2010.

In December, the Security Council adopted resolution 1904(2009) on the threats to international peace and security caused by terrorist acts, outlining sanctions to be taken with respect to Al-Qaida, Osama bin Laden and the Taliban, and other individuals, groups, undertakings and entities associated with them. Those included preventing their entry into or transit through the territories of Member States, freezing their funds and other financial assets or economic resources, and preventing the direct or indirect supply, sale or transfer to them of arms and related materiel.

In Iraq, although 2009 saw an improvement in the overall security situation, there was a spike in indiscriminate and violent mass attacks, causing high civilian casualties. A wave of suicide bombings culminated in a coordinated series of four bomb blasts across Iraq in March and nearly 20 suicide bombings in April. By the end of July, incident levels remained high in northern Iraq as armed groups continued attempts to exploit tensions. Incident levels remained relatively low across southern Iraq, as the security forces continued to discover weapons and ammunition caches. On 19 August and 25 October, coordinated attacks targeted key government institutions in Baghdad, in the most significant attacks since the withdrawal of multinational forces from Iraqi cities at the end of June under the bilateral security agreement between Iraq and the United States.

On 17 August, the Independent High Electoral Commission announced the certified results of the Kurdistan regional elections of 25 July, with incumbent President Masoud Barzani winning with a clear majority. With UN assistance, the parties reached agreement on key amendments to the Election Law, which was adopted as revised on 6 December. Two days later, there were five coordinated bombings across Baghdad, resulting in the death of more than 100 Iraqis and injuring many more. The following day, Prime Minister Nuri Kamel al-Maliki, in his capacity as Commander-in-Chief of the Armed Forces, replaced the Chief of the Baghdad Operations Command. On 13 December, the Presidency Council announced that national parliamentary elections would be held on 7 March 2010.

The United Nations Assistance Mission for Iraq (UNAMI) advised the Government on developing civil and social services, fostered human rights protection and legal reforms, and contributed to the coordination of development and reconstruction. In July, Ad Melkert was appointed as the Secretary-General's Special Representative for Iraq and Head of UNAMI, succeeding Staffan de Mistura, who had completed his 18-month tenure on 30 June. In August, by resolution 1883(2009), the Council extended UNAMI's mandate for another year.

The United Nations continued following up on issues relating to Iraq's 1990 invasion of Kuwait— including the repatriation of the remains of Kuwaiti and third-country nationals, the return of Kuwaiti property and compensation for losses and damage.

On 30 August, Timor-Leste marked the tenth anniversary of the popular consultation that led to its independence. The United Nations Integrated Mission in Timor-Leste (UNMIT) continued to assist the country in reforming the security sector, strengthening the rule of law, promoting economic and social development and fostering democratic governance, and on 26 February the Security Council, by resolution 1867(2009), extended its mandate for another year. In accordance with that resolution, Prime Minister Kay Rala Xanana Gusmão and the Secretary-General's Special Representative reached agreement in May on the respective roles and responsibilities of the Polícia Nacional de Timor-Leste and UNMIT police.

The security situation remained calm. As of August, all 65 camps for internally displaced persons in Dili and Baucau had been closed, with some 3,000 internally displaced remaining in transitional shelters. Elections for local authorities on 9 October had high turnout and were generally peaceful. However, human rights violations by members of the security services continued to be reported—in particular ill-treatment and excessive use of force and intimidation.

With effect from 28 December, Ameerah Haq became the Secretary-General's Special Representative for Timor-Leste and Head of UNMIT, succeeding Atul Khare, who completed his assignment on 10 December.

The year was a challenging one with respect to the Democratic People's Republic of Korea's (DPRK) nuclear programme. In April, the country launched a long-range rocket with the official aim of placing a satellite in orbit. The Security Council condemned the launch and demanded that the DPRK not conduct any further launch. In June, the Council, by resolution 1874(2009), condemned a 25 May underground nuclear test by the DPRK, citing it as a violation of resolution 1718(2006), which imposed sanctions against the country after its nuclear test in October 2006. In July, the DPRK launched several missiles, in violation of resolutions 1718(2006) and 1874(2009), and the Council called on the country to comply with those resolutions. In September, the DPRK stated that it was continuing its nuclear weapons programme.

The peace process in Nepal, which had raised hopes after a peace agreement in 2006 and democratic elections in 2008, stalled in 2009 when relations between the party of the former Maoist insurgents and the other major political parties deteriorated. The Prime Minister resigned in May, and the Maoist party went on to block Parliament and hold numerous street protests and strikes throughout the rest of the year.

One of the unfulfilled provisions of the peace process was the rehabilitation or integration into the government security forces of some 19,000 Maoist army personnel who had remained cantoned in camps since the end of the civil war. The ex-combatants were to have been discharged after completion of a verification process, but the army had resisted integrating them.

Karin Landgren, Representative of the Secretary-General in Nepal and Head of United Nations Mission in Nepal (UNMIN), carried out continuous quiet diplomacy throughout the year. On 16 December, the Government, the Maoist party and the United Nations signed an action plan for the discharge of Maoist army personnel disqualified in the UNMIN-led verification process in 2007. The plan was to be monitored by an UNMIN-led team.

In November, the Board of Governors of the International Atomic Energy Agency (IAEA) urged Iran to comply with its obligations under the relevant Security Council resolutions and its own requirements. Those included immediate suspension of construction of a new pilot enrichment plant at Qom, the resolution of all outstanding issues concerning its nuclear programme and full compliance with its nuclear safeguards obligations. By year's end, IAEA reported that Iran had not provided the necessary cooperation to permit it to confirm that all nuclear material in Iran was being used in peaceful activities. Iran maintained that its peaceful nuclear programmes posed no threats to other States and that according to IAEA, there had never been any diversion in its peaceful nuclear activities.

The Secretary-General's Special Adviser on Myanmar visited the country in January, followed by the Special Rapporteur on human rights in Myanmar in mid-February. The Secretary-General visited the country in July, but his request to meet with the General Secretary of the National League for Democracy, Aung San Suu Kyi, was denied. In December, the General Assembly, by resolution 64/238, called on the Government to release all prisoners of conscience, undertake a genuine dialogue with Ms. Suu Kyi and other concerned parties, and take the necessary steps towards a free, fair, transparent and inclusive electoral process.

In Sri Lanka, fighting intensified between the Government and the Liberation Tigers of Tamil Eelam (LTTE). The Secretary-General in January expressed concern about 250,000 civilians caught in the area of fighting and called on both parties to ensure their protection. In May, the Security Council expressed concern over reports of hundreds of civilian casualties in the north-east. Visiting Sri Lanka in May, after the Government declared that its military operation against LTTE had ended, the Secretary-General stressed the importance of accountability for addressing violations of humanitarian and human rights law. In November, the Secretary-General welcomed the release of over half of the internally displaced persons from camps in the north and called on the Government to prioritize the return of internally displaced persons.

Also during the year, the Council established a three-member Commission of Inquiry into the 2007 assassination of the former Prime Minister of Pakistan, Mohtarma Benazir Bhutto. It later extended the Commission's mandate to 31 March 2010.

Afghanistan

Situation in Afghanistan

In 2009, the international community continued to assist the Government of Afghanistan in laying the foundation for peace and stability and the restoration of economic and social development, through support provided by the United Nations Assistance Mission in Afghanistan (UNAMA), under the direction of the Special Representative of the Secretary-General and Head of Mission, and the International Security Assistance Force (ISAF), led by the North Atlantic Treaty Organization (NATO).

The Secretary-General submitted four progress reports to the General Assembly and the Security Council, in March [A/63/751-S/2009/135], June [A/63/892-S/2009/323], September [A/64/364-S/2009/475] and December [A/64/613-S/2009/674], on the situation in Afghanistan and on UNAMA activities, as well as a later report including information relating to 2009 [A/64/705-S/2010/127].

ISAF activities were reported to the Council by the NATO Secretary-General through the UN Secretary-General [S/2009/283, S/2010/35, S/2010/353]. The Council, by resolution 1868(2009) (see p. 335), extended the UNAMA mandate until 23 March 2010, and by resolution 1890(2009) (see p. 352) it extended the ISAF authorization until 13 October 2010. Kai Eide (Norway) continued to serve as the Secretary-General's Special Representative for Afghanistan and Head of UNAMA.

Attacks in Kabul. In a press statement of 11 February [SC/9593], the Security Council members condemned that day's terrorist attacks on government facilities in Kabul, causing numerous deaths and injuries. Council members noted that the Taliban claimed responsibility for the attack and underlined the need to bring the perpetrators, organizers, financiers and sponsors to justice. They reiterated their concern at the threat to the population, national security forces, international military and international assistance efforts

posed by the Taliban, Al-Qaida, illegal armed groups, criminals and those involved in the narcotics trade. No terrorist act could reverse the path towards peace, democracy and reconstruction, which was supported by the people and the Government of Afghanistan and the international community.

Report of Secretary-General (March). In a 10 March report [A/63/751-S/2009/135], the Secretary-General said that at stake over the next six months was the relegitimization of the Government's authority through credible elections for the presidency and provincial councils. Voter registration was completed, and on 19 January, the Independent Electoral Commission presented international donors with a budget of some $220 million for election costs. On the regional level, President Asif Ali Zardari of Pakistan on 9 January made his first visit to Afghanistan, where he met with President Hamid Karzai, which enabled the resumption of such initiatives as the Peace Jirga process.

The year 2008 had been Afghanistan's most violent since 2001, and the situation was not expected to improve before the summer. Nevertheless, an integrated approach was being piloted to ensure a more coherent and effective use of civilian and military resources. The Afghan National Army consisted of five corps of two to four brigades each, which served as regional commands mirroring the ISAF Regional Command structure, but 10 provinces remained without a permanent presence.

The Mine Action Programme for Afghanistan continued to make progress towards the goals outlined in the Afghanistan Compact [YUN 2006, p. 363]. Community-based demining projects in Helmand, Kunar and Uruzgan focused on marginalized communities with limited infrastructure or support, aiming to bring socio-economic and stability dividends into the south and east of the country. Nevertheless, an estimated 2,082 communities remained contaminated by mines, and an additional $53 million was needed in 2009 to reach the Compact's benchmarks.

The Afghan-United Nations Office on Drugs and Crime *Afghanistan Opium Winter Rapid Assessment* report in February projected a possible further decrease in opium cultivation in 2009, resulting from a decrease in the main poppy cultivation areas of the south-west and south, and a possible increase in the number of poppy-free provinces to 22. Opium cultivation was mainly confined to the most unstable provinces in the south and south-west: Farah, Helmand, Kandahar, Nimroz, Uruzgan, Daikundi and Zabul.

Afghanistan continued to face human rights challenges linked to weak governance, entrenched impunity, lack of attention to transitional justice, extreme poverty and discriminatory laws and practices, in particular against women and girls. Freedom of expression remained precarious, with continued reports of intimidation of journalists by State and non-State actors. Resumed implementation of the death penalty was disquieting given manifest deficiencies in due process and fair trial guarantees.

In support of UNAMA's expanded and sharpened mandate, the General Assembly had increased its budget by 91.5 per cent, increasing the number of its staff and providing for the opening of four additional provincial offices—in Ghazni, Sari Pul, Helmand and Farah. By the end of the year, UNAMA was expected to have 15 provincial and 8 regional offices, in addition to its liaison offices in Islamabad and Tehran, which supported activities of a regional dimension.

Security Council consideration (March). Briefing the Council on 19 March [meeting 6094], Kai Eide, the Secretary-General's Special Representative, reported that the security situation had continued to deteriorate. The results of Government and international aid efforts had fallen short of popular expectations as Afghans suffered the effects of drought and a global rise in food prices. He urged the international community to support efforts to bolster the national police, promote agriculture and support the private sector in order to combat corruption, the funding of insurgents, and food insecurity. The representative of Afghanistan also made a statement.

SECURITY COUNCIL ACTION

On 23 March [meeting 6098], the Security Council unanimously adopted **resolution 1868(2009)**. The draft [S/2009/152] was submitted by Japan.

The Security Council,

Recalling its previous resolutions on Afghanistan, in particular resolution 1806(2008) of 20 March 2008, in which it extended until 23 March 2009 the mandate of the United Nations Assistance Mission in Afghanistan as established by resolution 1662(2006) of 23 March 2006, and resolution 1659(2006) of 15 February 2006, in which it endorsed the Afghanistan Compact, and recalling also the report of the Security Council mission to Afghanistan from 21 to 28 November 2008,

Reaffirming its strong commitment to the sovereignty, independence, territorial integrity and national unity of Afghanistan,

Stressing the importance of a comprehensive approach to address the situation in Afghanistan, and recognizing that there is no purely military solution to ensure the stability of Afghanistan,

Reaffirming its continued support for the Government and people of Afghanistan as they rebuild their country, strengthen the foundations of sustainable peace and constitutional democracy and assume their rightful place in the community of nations,

Reaffirming in this context its support for the implementation, under the ownership of the Afghan people, of the Afghanistan Compact, the Afghanistan National Development Strategy and the National Drug Control Strategy,

and noting that sustained and coordinated efforts by all relevant actors are required to consolidate progress made towards their implementation and to overcome continuing challenges,

Recalling that the Afghanistan Compact is based on a partnership between the Government of Afghanistan and the international community, based on the desire of the parties for Afghanistan to progressively assume responsibility for its own development and security, and with a central and impartial coordinating role for the United Nations,

Stressing the central and impartial role that the United Nations continues to play in promoting peace and stability in Afghanistan by leading the efforts of the international community, including, jointly with the Government of Afghanistan, the coordination and monitoring of efforts in implementing the Afghanistan Compact, and expressing its appreciation and strong support for the ongoing efforts of the Secretary-General, his Special Representative for Afghanistan and the women and men of the Mission,

Welcoming the continued commitment of the international community to support the stability and development of Afghanistan, and also welcoming in this regard international initiatives, including the special conference on Afghanistan under the aegis of the Shanghai Cooperation Organization, to be held in Moscow on 27 March 2009, the international conference on Afghanistan, to be held in The Hague on 31 March 2009 and the outreach session of the Ministerial Meeting of the Group of Eight, to be held in Trieste, Italy, on 26 and 27 June 2009,

Welcoming also ongoing efforts to ensure an orderly, open, fair and democratic process that preserves stability and security through the election period, underscoring the challenges that the Afghan Independent Electoral Commission is successfully confronting, and welcoming the announcement by the Commission of the holding of presidential and provincial council elections in August 2009,

Recognizing once again the interconnected nature of the challenges in Afghanistan, reaffirming that sustainable progress on security, governance and development, as well as the cross-cutting issue of counter-narcotics, is mutually reinforcing, and welcoming the continuing efforts of the Government of Afghanistan and the international community to address these challenges through a comprehensive approach,

Stressing the importance of a comprehensive approach in addressing the challenges in Afghanistan, noting in this context the synergies in the objectives of the Mission and of the International Security Assistance Force, and stressing the need for strengthened cooperation, coordination and mutual support, taking due account of their respective designated responsibilities,

Stressing also the need to urgently address the humanitarian situation by improving the reach, quality and quantity of humanitarian aid, by ensuring efficient, effective and timely coordination and delivery of humanitarian assistance through enhanced coordination among the United Nations agencies, funds and programmes under the authority of the Special Representative and between the United Nations and other donors, and through the expansion and strengthening of the United Nations humanitarian presence in the provinces, where it is most needed,

Condemning the increasing attacks against humanitarian workers, and underlining the need for all parties to ensure safe and unhindered access of all humanitarian actors, including United Nations staff and associated personnel, and comply fully with applicable international humanitarian law,

Reiterating its concern about the security situation in Afghanistan, in particular the increased violent and terrorist activities by the Taliban, Al-Qaida, illegal armed groups, criminals and those involved in the narcotics trade, and the increasingly strong links between terrorism activities and illicit drugs, resulting in threats to the local population, including children, national security forces and international military and civilian personnel,

Expressing its serious concern over the harmful consequences of violent and terrorist activities by the Taliban, Al-Qaida and other extremist groups on the capacity of the Government of Afghanistan to guarantee the rule of law, to provide security and basic services to the Afghan people and to ensure the improvement and protection of their human rights and fundamental freedoms,

Recognizing the increased threats posed by the Taliban, Al-Qaida and other extremist groups as well as the challenges related to the efforts to address such threats,

Recalling its resolutions 1674(2006) of 28 April 2006 and 1738(2006) of 23 December 2006 on the protection of civilians in armed conflict, expressing its concern at the high number of civilian casualties, as stated in the recent report of the Secretary-General on the situation in Afghanistan, reiterating its call for all feasible steps to be taken to ensure the protection of civilians, and calling for compliance with international humanitarian and human rights law as applicable,

Expressing its concern at the serious threat that anti-personnel mines, remnants of war and improvised explosive devices may pose to the civilian population, and stressing the need to refrain from the use of weapons and devices prohibited by international law,

Welcoming the declaration addressed to the International Narcotics Control Board by the Government of Afghanistan that there is no legal use for acetic anhydride in Afghanistan for the time being and that producing and exporting countries should abstain from authorizing the export of this substance to Afghanistan without a request from the Government of Afghanistan, and encouraging, pursuant to resolution 1817(2008) of 11 June 2008, Member States to increase their cooperation with the Board, notably by complying fully with the provisions of article 12 of the United Nations Convention against Illicit Traffic in Narcotic Drugs and Psychotropic Substances of 1988,

Recalling the importance of the Kabul Declaration on Good-neighbourly Relations of 22 December 2002, looking forward to the Third Regional Economic Cooperation Conference on Afghanistan, to be held in Islamabad on 13 and 14 May 2009, and stressing the crucial importance of advancing regional cooperation as an effective means to promote security, governance and development in Afghanistan,

Expressing its support for the Afghan-Pakistani Peace Jirga process,

Recalling its resolutions 1265(1999) of 17 September 1999, 1296(2000) of 19 April 2000, 1674(2006) and 1738(2006) on the protection of civilians in armed conflict, its resolutions 1325(2000) of 31 October 2000 and 1820(2008) of 19 June 2008 on women and peace and security, and its resolution 1612(2005) of 26 July 2005 on children and armed conflict, and taking note of the report of the Secretary-General on children and armed conflict in Afghanistan,

1. *Welcomes* the report of the Secretary-General of 10 March 2009;

2. *Expresses its appreciation* for the United Nations long-term commitment to work with the Government and people of Afghanistan, and reiterates its full support for the work of the United Nations Assistance Mission in Afghanistan and the Special Representative of the Secretary-General for Afghanistan;

3. *Decides* to extend the mandate of the Mission, as defined in resolutions 1662(2006), 1746(2007) of 23 March 2007 and 1806(2008), until 23 March 2010;

4. *Decides also* that the Mission and the Special Representative, within their mandate and guided by the principle of reinforcing Afghan ownership and leadership, shall continue to lead the international civilian efforts, in accordance with their priorities as laid down in paragraph 4 of resolution 1806(2008), namely:

(a) To promote, as co-chair of the Joint Coordination and Monitoring Board, more coherent support by the international community to the Government of Afghanistan and the adherence to the principles of aid effectiveness enumerated in the Afghanistan Compact, including through mobilization of resources, coordination of the assistance provided by international donors and organizations and direction of the contributions of United Nations agencies, funds and programmes, in particular for counter-narcotics, reconstruction and development activities;

(b) To strengthen cooperation with the International Security Assistance Force at all levels and throughout the country, in accordance with their existing mandates, in order to improve civil-military coordination, to facilitate the timely exchange of information and to ensure coherence between the activities of national and international security forces and of civilian actors in support of an Afghan-led development and stabilization process, including through engagement with provincial reconstruction teams and engagement with non-governmental organizations;

(c) Through a strengthened and expanded presence throughout the country, to provide political outreach, promote at the local level the implementation of the Afghanistan Compact, the Afghanistan National Development Strategy and the National Drug Control Strategy, and facilitate inclusion in and understanding of the policies of the Government of Afghanistan;

(d) To provide good offices to support, if requested by the Government of Afghanistan, the implementation of Afghan-led reconciliation programmes, within the framework of the Afghan Constitution and with full respect for the implementation of measures introduced by the Security Council in its resolution 1267(1999) of 15 October 1999 and other relevant resolutions of the Council;

(e) To support and strengthen efforts to improve governance and the rule of law and to combat corruption at the local and national levels, and to promote development initiatives at the local level with a view to helping to bring

the benefits of peace and deliver services in a timely and sustainable manner;

(f) To play a central coordinating role to facilitate the delivery of humanitarian assistance in accordance with humanitarian principles and with a view to building the capacity of the Government of Afghanistan, including by providing effective support to national and local authorities in assisting and protecting internally displaced persons and to creating conditions conducive to the voluntary, safe, dignified and sustainable return of refugees and internally displaced persons;

(g) To continue, with the support of the Office of the United Nations High Commissioner for Human Rights, to cooperate with the Afghan Independent Human Rights Commission, to cooperate also with relevant international and local non-governmental organizations, to monitor the situation of civilians, to coordinate efforts to ensure their protection and to assist in the full implementation of the fundamental freedoms and human rights provisions of the Afghan Constitution and international treaties to which Afghanistan is a State party, in particular those regarding the full enjoyment by women of their human rights;

(h) To support, at the request of the Afghan authorities, preparations for the crucial upcoming presidential elections, in particular through the Afghan Independent Electoral Commission, by providing technical assistance, coordinating other international donors, agencies and organizations providing assistance and channelling existing and additional funds earmarked to support the process;

(i) To support regional cooperation to work towards a stable and prosperous Afghanistan;

5. *Calls upon* all Afghan and international parties to coordinate with the Mission in the implementation of its mandate and in efforts to promote the security and freedom of movement of United Nations and associated personnel throughout the country;

6. *Stresses* the importance of strengthening and expanding the presence of the Mission and other United Nations agencies, funds and programmes in the provinces, encourages the Secretary-General to continue his current efforts to take the measures necessary to address the security issues associated with such strengthening and expansion, and underlines the authority of the Special Representative in the coordination of all activities of United Nations agencies, funds and programmes in Afghanistan;

7. *Underscores* the importance of the upcoming presidential and provincial council elections for Afghanistan's democratic development, calls for all efforts to be made to ensure the credibility, safety and security of the elections, recognizes the key role of the Mission, at the request of the Government of Afghanistan, in supporting the electoral process, and calls upon members of the international community to provide the necessary assistance to these ends;

8. *Calls upon* the Government of Afghanistan, and the international community and international organizations, to implement the Afghanistan Compact and the annexes thereto in full, and stresses in this context the importance of meeting the benchmarks and timelines of the Compact for progress on security, governance, the rule of law and human rights, and economic and social development, as well as the cross-cutting issue of counter-narcotics;

9. *Reaffirms* the central role played by the Joint Coordination and Monitoring Board in coordinating, facilitating and monitoring the implementation of the Afghanistan Compact, and calls upon all relevant actors to cooperate with the Board in this regard;

10. *Calls upon* international donors and organizations and the Government of Afghanistan to adhere to their commitments made at the International Conference in Support of Afghanistan, held in Paris on 12 June 2008, and reiterates the importance of further efforts in improving aid coordination and effectiveness, including by ensuring transparency and combating corruption;

11. *Calls upon* the Government of Afghanistan, with the assistance of the international community, including the International Security Assistance Force and the Operation Enduring Freedom coalition, in accordance with their respective designated responsibilities as they evolve, to continue to address the threat to the security and stability of Afghanistan posed by the Taliban, Al-Qaida, illegal armed groups, criminals and those involved in the narcotics trade;

12. *Condemns in the strongest terms* all attacks, including improvised explosive device attacks, suicide attacks and abductions, targeting civilians and Afghan and international forces and their deleterious effect on the stabilization, reconstruction and development efforts in Afghanistan, and condemns further the use by the Taliban and other extremist groups of civilians as human shields;

13. *Welcomes* the achievements to date in the implementation of the Mine Action Programme for Afghanistan, and encourages the Government of Afghanistan, with the support of the United Nations and all the relevant actors, to continue its efforts towards the removal of anti-personnel landmines, anti-tank landmines and explosive remnants of war in order to reduce the threats posed to human life and peace and security in the country;

14. *Recognizes* the efforts made by the Force and other international forces to minimize the risk of civilian casualties, and calls upon them to continue to make robust efforts in this regard, notably by the continuous review of tactics and procedures and the conduct of after-action reviews and investigations in cooperation with the Government of Afghanistan in cases where civilian casualties have occurred and when the Government finds these joint investigations appropriate;

15. *Emphasizes* the importance of ensuring access for relevant organizations, as applicable, to all prisons and places of detention in Afghanistan, and calls for full respect for relevant international law, including humanitarian law and human rights law;

16. *Expresses its strong concern* about the recruitment and use of children by Taliban forces in Afghanistan as well as the killing and maiming of children as a result of the conflict, reiterates its strong condemnation of the recruitment and use of child soldiers in violation of applicable international law and all other violations and abuses committed against children in situations of armed conflict, in particular attacks against schools, calls for those responsible to be brought to justice, stresses the importance of implementing Council resolution 1612(2005) in this context, and requests the Secretary-General to strengthen the child protection component of the Mission, in particular through the appointment of child protection advisers;

17. *Reiterates* the importance of increasing, within a comprehensive framework, the functionality, professionalism and accountability of the Afghan security sector through training, mentoring and empowerment efforts, in order to accelerate progress towards the goal of self-sufficient and ethnically balanced Afghan security forces providing security and ensuring the rule of law throughout the country;

18. *Welcomes*, in this context, the continued progress in the development of the Afghan National Army and its improved ability to plan and undertake operations, and encourages sustained training efforts, including through the operational mentoring and liaison teams, and advice in developing a sustainable defence planning process as well as assistance in defence reform initiatives;

19. *Takes note with appreciation* of the recent serious efforts of the Afghan authorities to enhance the capabilities of the Afghan National Police, calls for further efforts towards that goal, including through the Focused District Development programme, and stresses the importance, in this context, of international assistance through financial support and the provision of trainers and mentors, including the contribution of the European Union through the European Union Police Mission in Afghanistan;

20. *Welcomes* the progress in the implementation by the Government of Afghanistan of the programme of disbandment of illegal armed groups, and calls for accelerated efforts for further progress, with support from the international community;

21. *Takes note* of the recent progress in addressing opium production, remains concerned at the serious harm that opium cultivation, production and trafficking continue to cause to the security, development and governance of Afghanistan as well as to the region and internationally, calls upon the Government of Afghanistan, with the assistance of the international community, to accelerate the implementation of the National Drug Control Strategy, including through alternative livelihood programmes, and to mainstream counter-narcotics throughout national programmes, and encourages additional international support for the four priorities identified in the Strategy;

22. *Calls upon* States to strengthen international and regional cooperation to counter the threat to the international community posed by the illicit production of and trafficking in drugs originating in Afghanistan, including through border management cooperation in drug control and cooperation for the fight against the illicit trafficking in drugs and precursors and against money-laundering linked to such trafficking, taking into account the outcome of the Second Ministerial Conference on Drug Trafficking Routes from Afghanistan, organized by the Government of the Russian Federation in cooperation with the United Nations Office on Drugs and Crime and held in Moscow from 26 to 28 June 2006, within the framework of the Paris Pact initiative, and in this regard calls for full implementation of Council resolution 1817(2008);

23. *Welcomes* the launch of the National Justice Programme, and reiterates the importance of its full, sequenced, timely and coordinated implementation by all the relevant Afghan institutions and other actors with a view to accelerating the establishment of a fair and transparent justice system, eliminating impunity and contributing to the affirmation of the rule of law throughout the country;

24. *Stresses*, in this context, the importance of further progress in the reconstruction and reform of the prison sector in Afghanistan, in order to improve respect for the rule of law and human rights therein;

25. *Notes with strong concern* the effects of widespread corruption on security, good governance, counter-narcotics efforts and economic development, and urges the Government of Afghanistan, with the assistance of the international community, to vigorously lead the fight against corruption and to enhance its efforts to establish a more effective, accountable and transparent administration;

26. *Encourages* all Afghan institutions, including the executive and legislative branches, to work in a spirit of cooperation, calls upon the Government of Afghanistan to pursue continued legislative and public administration reform in order to ensure good governance, full representation and accountability at both the national and the subnational levels, and stresses the need for further international efforts to provide technical assistance in this area;

27. *Encourages* the international community to assist the Government of Afghanistan in making capacity-building and human resources development a cross-cutting priority;

28. *Calls for* full respect for human rights and fundamental freedoms and international humanitarian law throughout Afghanistan, notes with concern the increasing restrictions on freedom of the media, commends the Afghan Independent Human Rights Commission for its courageous efforts to monitor respect for human rights in Afghanistan as well as to foster and protect those rights and to promote the emergence of a pluralistic civil society, and stresses the importance of full cooperation with the Commission by all relevant actors;

29. *Recognizes* the significant progress achieved on gender equality in Afghanistan in recent years, strongly condemns continuing forms of discrimination and violence against women and girls, in particular violence aimed at preventing girls from attending school, stresses the importance of implementing Council resolutions 1325(2000) and 1820(2008), and requests the Secretary-General to continue to include in his reports to the Council relevant information on the process of integration of women into the political, economic and social life of Afghanistan;

30. *Welcomes* the efforts of the Government of Afghanistan to promote dialogue with those elements in opposition to the Government who are ready to renounce violence, denounce terrorism and accept the Afghan Constitution, and calls for enhanced efforts to ensure the full implementation of the Action Plan on Peace, Justice and Reconciliation in accordance with the Afghanistan Compact, without prejudice to the implementation of measures introduced by the Council in its resolution 1267(1999) and other relevant resolutions of the Council;

31. *Also welcomes* the cooperation of the Government of Afghanistan and the Mission with the Security Council Committee established pursuant to resolution 1267(1999) in the implementation of resolution 1822(2008) of 30 June 2008, including by identifying individuals and entities participating in the financing or support of acts or activities of Al-Qaida and the Taliban using proceeds derived from illicit cultivation and production of and trafficking

in narcotic drugs and their precursors, and encourages the continuation of such cooperation;

32. *Further welcomes* ongoing efforts by the Government of Afghanistan and its neighbouring and regional partners to foster trust and cooperation with each other, as well as recent cooperation initiatives developed by the countries concerned and regional organizations, including the Second Trilateral Summit of Afghanistan, Pakistan and Turkey, held in Istanbul, Turkey, on 5 December 2008, and the ministerial meeting held in La Celle-Saint-Cloud, France, on 14 December 2008, and stresses the importance of increasing cooperation between Afghanistan and the partners against the Taliban, Al-Qaida and other extremist groups, in promoting peace and prosperity in Afghanistan and in fostering cooperation in the economic and development sectors as a means to achieve the full integration of Afghanistan into regional dynamics and the global economy;

33. *Calls for* the strengthening of the process of regional economic cooperation, including measures to facilitate regional trade, to increase foreign investments and to develop infrastructure, noting Afghanistan's historical role as a land bridge in Asia;

34. *Recognizes* the importance of the voluntary, safe, orderly return and sustainable reintegration of the remaining Afghan refugees for the stability of the country and the region, and calls for continued and enhanced international assistance in this regard;

35. *Affirms* the importance of the voluntary, safe, orderly return and sustainable reintegration of internally displaced persons;

36. *Requests* the Secretary-General to report to the Council every three months on developments in Afghanistan, and to develop, for inclusion in his next report, benchmarks for measuring and tracking progress in the implementation of the mandate of the Mission and priorities as set out in paragraph 4 of the present resolution, and calls upon all actors concerned to cooperate with the Mission in this process;

37. *Decides* to remain actively seized of the matter.

Appointment of Deputy Special Representative. On 25 March, the Secretary-General announced [SG/A/1178] the appointment of Peter Galbraith (United States) as his Deputy Special Representative for UNAMA, responsible for political issues, including continuing electoral and parliamentary matters, and issues related to peace and stability, security sector reform and human rights.

Communications. On 6 May [S/2009/235], Afghanistan informed the Security Council that it had decided to stop the import of the chemical precursor acetic anhydride—a substance used to process heroin. That decision had been communicated to the International Narcotics Control Board.

On 27 May [S/2009/275], Iran transmitted to the Security Council the text of the Tehran Declaration, issued at the end of the first meeting on trilateral cooperation between the Heads of State of Afghanistan, Iran and Pakistan (Tehran, 24 May).

Report of Secretary-General (June). In a 23 June report [A/63/892-S/2009/323], covering the period since 10 March, the Secretary-General said that 80 countries and organizations met in a strong political manifestation of support for Afghanistan at the International Conference on Afghanistan: a Comprehensive Strategy in a Regional Context (The Hague, 31 March), co-chaired by the United Nations, Afghanistan and the Netherlands. In May, UNAMA opened two new offices, in Tirin Kot and Sari Pul. Preparations for the 20 August elections accelerated, and there had been continued progress in key areas, including agriculture, private sector development and capacity-building, donor coordination, and expansion of the National Army and National Police. Apart from improvement in some areas, notably Kabul and its neighbouring provinces, the security situation continued to deteriorate.

The candidate nomination process was held between 25 April and 8 May. The final list of candidates was released on 13 June, and included 41 presidential candidates and 3,178 provincial council candidates. The election campaign period began on 16 June. Controversies that dominated the political debate in early 2009 had been resolved with the active participation of the Secretary-General's Special Representative. On 9 June, the Electoral Complaints Commission announced that 57 candidates, including two presidential contenders, had been disqualified from running in the elections for not meeting the eligibility criteria. The European Union decided to send an election observation mission and the Organization for Security and Cooperation in Europe an election support team.

The overall number of security incidents continued to rise, with May figures exceeding 1,000 for the first time since 2001. The free movement of unarmed civil servants was adversely affected by the intensified fighting and the increased campaign of intimidation and assassination. Attacks on the United Nations included ambush of a UN convoy north of Herat on 3 February; detonation of an improvised explosive device against a marked UN armoured vehicle in the city of Tirin Kot, Uruzgan province, on 5 May; and an attack on 8 June on the compound of the Food and Agriculture Organization of the United Nations (FAO) in Kunduz.

Following the Paris Conference [YUN 2008, p. 361], UNAMA had participated in identifying the sectors of agriculture, energy, private-sector development, capacity-building, and higher education and vocational training as essential for Afghanistan's long-term economic growth. Encouraging progress had been made in some of those areas. A new Comprehensive Agricultural and Rural Development Facility aimed to reduce the threat of poppy production by increasing incentives for the cultivation of licit crops. The

Ministry of the Interior was taking serious steps to fight corruption, enhance administrative accountability and improve leadership and merit-based appointments in the National Police. On 10 June, UNAMA launched a local procurement campaign to encourage the international community to buy Afghan products and reduce reliance on more expensive imports.

Several conferences on regional cooperation had taken place over the previous six months, including in Brussels, Islamabad, Paris and Tehran. In the bilateral dialogue between Afghanistan and Pakistan, a number of meetings had taken place between the two Presidents and key ministers, including in Ankara, Turkey, on 1 April and in Washington, D.C., on 6 May.

UNAMA recorded 800 civilian casualties between January and May, mostly in the south, south-east and eastern regions of the country—a 24 per cent increase over the same period in 2008. According to UNAMA figures, 55 per cent of those deaths were caused by anti-government elements and 33 per cent by international and Afghan forces, with the remaining 12 per cent unattributed. The use of improvised explosive devices by the insurgency, which by their nature were indiscriminate, had increased. In the humanitarian sphere, heavy rains and flash floods had destroyed houses and property across many regions, inundating more than 17,000 acres of farmland, killing over 10,000 head of livestock and destroying bridges and roads. UN agencies, non-governmental organizations and other partners worked closely with local authorities to provide assistance.

Security Council consideration (June). Briefing the Council on 30 June [meeting 6154], the Secretary-General's Special Representative stressed the importance of the upcoming presidential and provincial council elections in August. This reflected an increased emphasis on civilian efforts, a focus on subnational governance and the better alignment of international efforts.

SECURITY COUNCIL ACTION

On 15 July [meeting 6162], following consultations among Security Council members, the President made statement **S/PRST/2009/21** on behalf of the Council:

The Security Council welcomes the Afghan-led preparations for the upcoming presidential and provincial council elections and stresses the importance that the elections be free, fair, transparent, credible, secure and inclusive. The Council also calls upon the people of Afghanistan to exercise their vote in this historic opportunity for all Afghans to make their voices heard. The Council calls upon all parties concerned to adhere to the fundamental principles laid down in the electoral law and all other relevant regulations, the presidential decree on non-interference in election affairs, and the

guidelines issued by the Special Representative of the Secretary-General for Afghanistan to ensure a credible electoral process. It reaffirms the primary responsibility of the Government of Afghanistan and the Afghan Independent Electoral Commission to set the necessary conditions for elections, with the active support of the international community. The Council welcomes the intention of international partners, including the European Union and the Organization for Security and Cooperation in Europe, to send electoral observation missions and support teams at the request of the Government of Afghanistan. The Council stresses the importance of a secure environment for conducting elections, condemns those who resort to violence to obstruct the electoral process, and, while recognizing the ongoing efforts of the Government, encourages its additional efforts, with the assistance of the International Security Assistance Force, to ensure security during the electoral period.

The Council welcomes the strengthened commitment that the international community has shown recently in various forums, including those in Moscow, The Hague, Ankara, Strasbourg/Kehl, Washington, D.C., Islamabad, Tehran, Yekaterinburg and Trieste, to help the Government of Afghanistan to build a stable and prosperous Afghanistan well integrated in its region.

The Council emphasizes the central role of the United Nations Assistance Mission in Afghanistan and the Special Representative in leading and coordinating the international civilian efforts in Afghanistan and notes the expectation expressed at the Hague conference for the expansion of the presence of the Mission. In this regard, the Council expresses its support for the intention of the Secretary-General to further strengthen the Mission in 2009 and invites the Secretary-General to provide further details of his proposals.

The Council welcomes the progress achieved by the Government of Afghanistan in implementing the Afghanistan Compact and the Afghanistan National Development Strategy during the period covered by the latest report of the Secretary-General, encourages the Government to undertake enhanced efforts in addressing issues in the areas of security, governance, the rule of law and human rights, including gender equality, and economic and social development, as well as the cross-cutting issue of counter-narcotics, and calls upon the international community to continue to support the efforts of the Government, including provision of humanitarian assistance, in this regard. The Council recalls the priorities identified at the Paris conference and reaffirmed at the Hague conference, and emphasizes the importance of providing sufficient support needed for progress in these priority areas.

The Council takes note of the status of the work of developing benchmarks for measuring and tracking progress in the implementation of the mandate and priorities of the Mission and expresses its hope that the work will be completed through consultation with all actors concerned and that finalized benchmarks will be included in the next report of the Secretary-General.

Security Council statement on elections. In a 20 August press statement [SC/9734], Council members welcomed the holding of presidential and provincial council elections on that day. Looking forward to the announcement of the final results by the Independent Electoral Commission, Council members called on those involved to continue cooperating with all Afghan electoral institutions.

Attack in Kandahar. On 26 August, in a press statement [SC/9735], Council members condemned the terrorist attack in Kandahar on 25 August, which caused numerous deaths and injuries.

Report of Secretary-General (September). In a 22 September report [A/64/364-S/2009/475], the Secretary-General said that presidential and provincial council elections had been held on 20 August but the Independent Election Commission could not certify the results until all complaints had been adjudicated by the Electoral Complaints Commission, which received 433 complaints during the campaign period that ended on 18 August. The voting had been marred by irregularities, and a campaign of intimidation by the Taliban had stifled turnout, particularly in the south. The increased intensity of insurgency operations in the week before the election included a vehicle-borne suicide bombing near the ISAF base in Kabul City on 15 August, which killed at least 7 and wounded 70.

The Electoral Complaints Commission received 2,842 complaints, and on 8 September it ordered the Independent Election Commission to conduct an audit and a recount at polling stations where there were indicators of serious irregularities. Alleged irregularities included ballot box stuffing, premature closing of centres, opening of unauthorized centres, underage voting, multiple voting, proxy voting, campaigning by candidate agents inside polling centres and complaints by candidates about their agents not being permitted to enter and observe the voting. One safeguard of the electoral process was the presence of observers and candidate agents at the polling centres. The Independent Election Commission accredited 169,709 candidate agents for provincial council candidates and 92,897 agents for presidential candidates. The Free and Fair Election Foundation of Afghanistan reported that it had deployed over 7,000 domestic observers in all 34 provinces.

Since the future Afghan State must be founded on solid institutions staffed with competent officials selected and promoted on the basis of merit, training Afghans who served or wished to serve in Government was as important as retaining qualified staff. UNAMA had supported the development of a standard curriculum across the five common civil service functions of accounting, procurement, human resources, project management and policy development. Unfortunately, implementation of anti-corruption initiatives had lacked urgency and enforcement, causing a general mistrust in their effectiveness.

Insecurity continued to be the single greatest factor impeding progress. The tactics of the insurgency, which had evolved in their complexity, continued to rely on asymmetric tactics, the avoidance of force-to-force encounters, targeting representatives of State institutions and international organizations and a disregard for human life. There had been some 898 incidents in the first seven months of 2009, compared with 677 during that period in 2008. Incidents involving improvised explosive devices increased by 60 per cent, to an average of more than eight per day. The National Army continued to recruit and train faster than expected, with troop strength reaching 93,000 in July—5,000 more than projected.

Opium cultivation had decreased by 22 per cent since January, from 157,000 to 123,000 hectares. The country now had 20 opium-free provinces, compared to 18 in 2008 and none in 2004, with a sharp, one-third reduction in Helmand province. Renewed attention had been given to arresting high-level operators in the opium economy, dismantling drug trafficking networks and interrupting the flow of precursor chemicals into the country.

In support of the Afghan National Development Strategy, the Secretary-General's Special Representative in June challenged the international community to increase by at least 10 per cent the amount of goods and services they procured locally. The United Nations had led by example, increasing its overall procurement from local sources. Unfortunately, pledges and contributions to the Afghan Reconstruction Trust Fund were almost $50 million less than in 2008. The Government had increased its focus on the need for a dialogue with its northern neighbours on transborder water management.

Much attention, both by the international arena and by Afghanistan, had focused on the rights of women. A UN report issued in July examined factors contributing to a rising trend of threats and attacks against women in public life and sexual abuse of women and girls. A culture of impunity for rape partly accounted for the deep-rooted nature of the problem. On 19 July, President Karzai signed the law on the elimination of violence against women, criminalizing sexual violence, including rape, forced and underage marriage, forced labour and prostitution.

Meanwhile, the Mission recorded 1,500 civilian casualties between January and August, with August being the deadliest month since the beginning of 2009. Humanitarian workers were increasingly subject to intimidation, robberies, abduction and assassination, with the Afghan National Safety Office reporting 75 such incidents in the first six months of 2009 alone.

UN-supported mine action activities contributed to the removal of some 80,000 anti-personnel landmines, 900 anti-tank mines and 2.5 million explosive remnants of war during the past 12 months, and provided mine risk education to more than 750,000 men, women, girls and boys. The number of casualties in 2009 had dropped to under 50 victims per month, the lowest level in over 10 years. As for UNAMA, its estimated budget for 2010 would increase by some 70 per cent over 2009, to cover its planned future expansion and strengthening as called for in Security Council resolution 1868(2009) (see p. 335).

Security Council consideration (September). Briefing the Council on 29 September [meeting 6194], the Special Representative, Mr. Eide, called on the future Afghan President to appoint a Government that would intensify the struggle against corruption, strengthen respect for the rule of law, end the culture of impunity and promote social and economic justice. Afghanistan's Foreign Minister, Rangin Dadfar Spanta, also spoke on his country's elections, and stressed the need for a long-term assistance strategy focused on stabilization, humanitarian concerns, reconstruction and development. He said that UNAMA was well positioned to play a leading role in assisting Afghanistan in shaping its future.

Attack on Indian embassy. On 8 October, Security Council members, in a press statement [SC/9763], condemned that day's terrorist suicide attack that occurred outside the Indian embassy in Kabul, causing numerous deaths and injuries, including among Afghan civilians and the embassy's security personnel. Noting that the Taliban had claimed responsibility for the attack, Council members underlined the need to bring the perpetrators, organizers, financiers and sponsors of that act to justice.

Killing of UN personnel. On 28 October, the Secretary-General reported [A/64/613-S/2009/674] that five UN personnel were killed and five wounded in an early morning attack against a guest house in Kabul, in which over 30 UN personnel resided. Only the "truly heroic" acts of UN security personnel who lived in the guest house, two of whom were killed in the line of duty, prevented further casualties.

The Secretary-General issued a statement [SG/SM/12570] expressing shock and outrage. The Security Council, in a press statement [SC/9778], condemned the attack, which caused deaths and injuries among UN staff and members of the Afghan National Security Forces.

Expressing its strong condemnation, the Council, in presidential statement **S/PRST/2009/28** of 29 October (see p. 67), condemned the Taliban, who claimed responsibility for the attack, expressed solidarity with UN staff on the ground and stressed the need to ensure their security. The Council expressed its solidarity with the Afghan people and its support for the upcoming run-off presidential elections, which

should be carried out as scheduled with the continued support of the United Nations.

Security Council statement on elections. In a 6 November press statement [SC/9784], Council members acknowledged the conclusion of the electoral process following the decision of the Independent Electoral Commission to declare Mr. Karzai President. Looking forward to working with President Karzai and his new Administration, Council members stressed the need for a government-led renewed and inclusive political process.

GENERAL ASSEMBLY ACTION

On 9 November [meeting 40], the General Assembly adopted **resolution 64/11** [draft: A/64/L.8 & Add.1] without vote [agenda item 17].

The situation in Afghanistan

The General Assembly,

Recalling its resolution 63/18 of 10 November 2008 and all its previous relevant resolutions,

Recalling also all relevant Security Council resolutions and statements by the President of the Council on the situation in Afghanistan, in particular resolutions 1659(2006) of 15 February 2006, 1817(2008) of 11 June 2008, 1868(2009) of 23 March 2009 and 1890(2009) of 8 October 2009, as well as the statements by the President of the Council of 11 July 2008 and 15 July 2009,

Reaffirming its strong commitment to the sovereignty, independence, territorial integrity and national unity of Afghanistan, and respecting its multicultural, multi-ethnic and historical heritage,

Welcoming the first elections in Afghanistan run entirely under the responsibility of the Afghan authorities with the support of the international community, applauding the courage of the Afghan people for their active engagement in the electoral process and participation in the election despite the security threats and incidents caused by the Taliban, Al-Qaida and other illegal armed groups and those involved in the narcotics trade, welcoming the efforts of the relevant institutions to address irregularities identified by the electoral institutions in Afghanistan and to ensure a credible and legitimate process in accordance with the Afghan electoral law and within the framework of the Afghan Constitution, urging all political actors to respect the rule of law and to continue to take responsibility for the stability and unity of Afghanistan, and stressing the need for the new Government of Afghanistan to build a renewed relationship of trust with its citizens by achieving concrete and visible results,

Reaffirming its continued support for the implementation of the Afghanistan Compact of 31 January 2006, which provides the framework for the partnership between the Government of Afghanistan and the international community, as well as of the Declaration of the International Conference in Support of Afghanistan, held in Paris on 12 June 2008, and recalling in this regard the spirit and the provisions of the Bonn Agreement of 5 December 2001 and the Berlin Declaration of 1 April 2004, including the annexes thereto,

Recognizing once again the interconnected nature of the challenges in Afghanistan, reaffirming that sustainable progress on security, governance, human rights, the rule of law and development, as well as on the cross-cutting theme of counter-narcotics, is mutually reinforcing, and welcoming the continuing efforts of the Government of Afghanistan and the international community to address these challenges in a coherent manner,

Reiterating the urgent need to tackle the challenges in Afghanistan, in particular the increased violent criminal and terrorist activities by the Taliban, Al-Qaida, illegal armed groups and those involved in the narcotics trade, in particular in the south and east, the development of Afghan Government institutions, including at the subnational level, the strengthening of the rule of law and democratic processes, the fight against corruption, the acceleration of justice sector reform, the promotion of national reconciliation, without prejudice to the fulfilment of the measures introduced by the Security Council in resolution 1267(1999) of 15 October 1999 and other relevant resolutions, an Afghan-led transitional justice process, the safe and voluntary return of Afghan refugees and internally displaced persons in an orderly and dignified manner, the promotion and protection of human rights and the advancement of economic and social development,

Condemning in the strongest terms all attacks, including improvised explosive device attacks, suicide attacks and abductions, targeting civilians and Afghan and international forces and their deleterious effect on the stabilization, reconstruction and development efforts in Afghanistan, and condemning further the use by the Taliban, Al-Qaida and other extremist and criminal groups of civilians as human shields,

Deeply concerned about the recent increase in violence in Afghanistan, in particular in the south and east, and recognizing the increased threats posed by the Taliban, Al-Qaida and other extremist and criminal groups, as well as the challenges related to the efforts to address such threats,

Expressing its serious concern about the high number of civilian casualties, noting recent relevant statements by Afghan authorities and high-ranking United Nations officials in this regard, recalling that the Taliban, Al-Qaida and other extremist and criminal groups are responsible for the significant majority of the civilian casualties in Afghanistan, and calling for compliance with international humanitarian and human rights law and for all appropriate measures to be taken to ensure the protection of civilians,

Recognizing additional efforts made by the International Security Assistance Force and other international forces to ensure the protection of the civilian population, and calling upon them to continue to make enhanced efforts in this regard, notably through the continuous review of tactics and procedures and the conduct of after-action reviews and investigations in cooperation with the Government of Afghanistan in cases where civilian casualties have occurred and when the Government finds these joint investigations appropriate,

Noting the importance of the national Government being inclusive and representative of the ethnic diversity of the country and ensuring also the full and equal participation of women,

1. *Stresses* the central and impartial role of the United Nations in promoting peace and stability in Afghanistan, expresses its appreciation and strong support for all efforts of the Secretary-General and his Special Representative in this regard, and welcomes the leading role of the United Nations Assistance Mission in Afghanistan in the coordination of the international civilian effort, guided by the principle of reinforcing Afghan ownership and leadership;

2. *Welcomes* the reports of the Secretary-General and the recommendations contained therein;

3. *Reaffirms* that the Afghanistan Compact, including the annexes thereto, remains the agreed basis for the work of both Afghanistan and the international community, stresses the need for an intensive dialogue with the Government of Afghanistan aimed at renewing the Afghanistan Compact in 2010 in accordance with the increasing ownership and responsibility of the Government, and reiterates in this regard its appreciation for the Afghanistan National Development Strategy;

4. *Welcomes*, in this context, the support expressed by the Secretary-General for the convening of an international conference on Afghanistan in cooperation with the new Government of Afghanistan;

5. *Expresses its strong concern* about the security situation in Afghanistan, stresses the need to continue to address the threat to the security and stability of Afghanistan caused by increased violent and terrorist activity by the Taliban, Al-Qaida and other extremist and criminal groups, including those involved in the narcotics trade, and strongly condemns all acts of violence and intimidation committed in Afghanistan, in particular in the south and east, including suicide attacks;

6. *Expresses deep regret*, in this regard, at the resulting loss of life and physical harm inflicted upon Afghan civilians and civilians of other nationalities, including the personnel of Afghan and international agencies and all other humanitarian workers and the diplomatic corps, as well as the personnel of the Afghan National Security Forces, the International Security Assistance Force and the Operation Enduring Freedom coalition, and pays homage to all those who have lost their lives;

7. *Stresses* the need for the Government of Afghanistan and the international community to continue to work closely together in countering the challenges of terrorist attacks by the Taliban, Al-Qaida and other extremist and criminal groups, which are threatening the democratic process as well as the reconstruction and economic development of Afghanistan, reiterates in this regard its call for the full implementation of measures introduced in relevant Security Council resolutions, in particular resolution 1267(1999), and calls upon all Member States to deny these groups any form of sanctuary or financial, material and political support;

8. *Notes with concern* that the security situation is causing some organizations to cease or curtail their humanitarian and development work in some parts of Afghanistan;

9. *Stresses* the importance of the provision of sufficient security, welcomes the presence of the International Security Assistance Force throughout Afghanistan, and calls upon Member States to continue contributing personnel, equip-

ment and other resources to the Force and to further develop the provincial reconstruction teams in close coordination with the Government of Afghanistan and the Mission;

10. *Notes*, in the context of the comprehensive approach, the synergies in the objectives of the Mission and of the International Security Assistance Force;

11. *Also notes* that the responsibility for providing security and law and order throughout the country resides with the Government of Afghanistan supported by the International Security Assistance Force and the Operation Enduring Freedom coalition, and recognizes the institutional progress achieved in this respect and the continued coordination between the Force and the coalition;

12. *Stresses* the importance of further extending central government authority, including the presence of Afghan security forces, to all provinces of Afghanistan;

13. *Calls upon* the Government of Afghanistan, with the assistance of the international community, including through the Operation Enduring Freedom coalition and the International Security Assistance Force, in accordance with their respective designated responsibilities, to continue to address the threat to the security and stability of Afghanistan;

14. *Commends* the Afghan National Security Forces, the International Security Assistance Force and the Operation Enduring Freedom coalition for their efforts to improve security conditions in Afghanistan;

15. *Welcomes* the continued development of the Afghan National Army and the Afghan National Police, recognizes the international support provided, calls for intensified Afghan and international efforts to modernize and strengthen both institutions and related Government departments, with particular attention to the Afghan National Police, expresses its appreciation for the assistance provided by international partners, acknowledges the continued deployment of the European Union Police Mission in Afghanistan, the support provided by the North Atlantic Treaty Organization, in particular through the establishment of its training mission in Afghanistan, the planned European Gendarmerie Force contribution to that mission, as well as other bilateral training programmes, encourages further coordination where appropriate, and welcomes the focused district development and in-district reform programmes;

16. *Acknowledges*, in this context, that the Afghan National Army and the Afghan National Police require additional support to enhance their capability and professionalism, including through the provision of increased training and mentoring, more modern equipment and infrastructure, and continued salary support;

17. *Urges* the Afghan authorities, with the support of the international community, to take all possible steps to ensure the safety, security and free movement of all United Nations, development and humanitarian personnel and their safe and unhindered access to all affected populations and to protect the property of the United Nations and of development or humanitarian organizations;

18. *Also urges* the Afghan authorities to make every effort, in accordance with General Assembly resolution 60/123 of 15 December 2005, to bring to justice the perpetrators of attacks;

19. *Stresses* the importance of advancing the full implementation of the programme of disbandment of illegal armed groups, throughout the country, under Afghan ownership, while ensuring coordination and coherence with other relevant efforts, including security sector reform, community development, counter-narcotics, district-level development and Afghan-led initiatives to ensure that entities and individuals do not illegally participate in the political process, in particular in forthcoming elections, in accordance with adopted laws and regulations in Afghanistan, and calls for adequate support in order for the Ministry of the Interior to increasingly assume its leading role in implementing the programme of disbandment of illegal armed groups;

20. *Welcomes* the commitment of the Government of Afghanistan to stand firm on the disbandment of illegal armed groups and to work actively at the national, provincial and local levels to advance this commitment, stresses in this regard the importance of all efforts to create sufficient legal income-earning opportunities, and calls for continued international support for these efforts;

21. *Remains deeply concerned* about the problem of millions of anti-personnel landmines and explosive remnants of war, which constitute a great danger to the population and a major obstacle to the resumption of economic activities and to recovery and reconstruction efforts;

22. *Welcomes* the progress achieved through the Mine Action Programme for Afghanistan, supports the Government of Afghanistan in its efforts to meet its responsibilities under the Convention on the Prohibition of the Use, Stockpiling, Production and Transfer of Anti-personnel Mines and on Their Destruction, to cooperate fully with the Mine Action Programme coordinated by the United Nations and to eliminate all known or new stocks of anti-personnel landmines, and acknowledges the need for continued assistance from the international community in this regard;

23. *Stresses* that regional cooperation constitutes an effective means to promote security and development in Afghanistan, encourages in this regard improved relations and closer cooperation between Afghanistan and its neighbours, and welcomes in this context the Third Regional Economic Cooperation Conference on Afghanistan, held in Islamabad on 13 and 14 May 2009, as well as efforts made by regional organizations;

24. *Pledges its continued support*, after the successful completion of the political transition, to the Government and people of Afghanistan as they rebuild their country, strengthen the foundations of a constitutional democracy and resume their rightful place in the community of nations;

25. *Recalls* the constitutional guarantee of human rights and fundamental freedoms for all Afghans as a significant political achievement, and stresses the need to fully implement the human rights provisions of the Afghan Constitution, in accordance with obligations under applicable international law, including those regarding the full enjoyment by women and children of their human rights;

26. *Calls for* full respect of the human rights and fundamental freedoms of all, without discrimination of any kind, including on the basis of gender, ethnicity or religion, in accordance with obligations under the Afghan Constitution and international law;

27. *Acknowledges and encourages* the efforts made by the Government of Afghanistan in this respect, and expresses its concern at the harmful consequences of violent and terrorist activities by the Taliban, Al-Qaida and other extremist and criminal groups for the enjoyment of human rights and for the capacity of the Government to ensure human rights and fundamental freedoms for all Afghans;

28. *Recalls* Security Council resolutions 1674(2006) of 28 April 2006 and 1738(2006) of 23 December 2006, as well as the statement by the President of the Council of 14 January 2009, on the protection of civilians in armed conflict, expresses its concern at the high number of civilian casualties, including women and children, notes that the Taliban, Al-Qaida and other extremist and criminal groups are responsible for the significant majority of civilian casualties, reiterates its call for all feasible steps to be taken to ensure the protection of civilians, and calls for additional appropriate steps in this regard and for full compliance with international humanitarian and human rights law;

29. *Recognizes* the importance of holding free, fair, credible, secure and inclusive elections as crucial steps towards consolidating democracy for all Afghans, as identified in the Afghanistan Compact, stresses the responsibility of the Afghan authorities in this regard and the need for timely and orderly preparation of the forthcoming elections, calls upon the international community to continue to provide financial and technical assistance, recalls the leading role of the United Nations Assistance Mission in Afghanistan in coordinating these efforts, encourages international partners, including the European Union and the Organization for Security and Cooperation in Europe, to send electoral observation missions and support teams at the request of the Government of Afghanistan, and calls upon the international community to continue to provide support to the Government to ensure the security of the elections;

30. *Welcomes* the steps taken by the Government of Afghanistan on justice sector reform, stresses the need for further accelerated progress towards the establishment of a fair, transparent and effective justice system as an important step towards the goals of strengthening the Government, providing security and ensuring the rule of law throughout the country, and urges the international community to continue to support the efforts of the Government in these areas in a coordinated manner;

31. *Urges* all concerned bodies, in this regard, to implement the National Justice Programme in a timely manner, and stresses the importance of improving security as well as legal rights and services for the Afghan people;

32. *Acknowledges* the progress made by the Government of Afghanistan and the international community towards devoting adequate resources to the reconstruction and reform of the prison sector in order to improve respect for the rule of law and human rights therein, while reducing physical and mental health risks to inmates;

33. *Emphasizes* the importance of ensuring access for relevant organizations to all prisons in Afghanistan, and calls for full respect for relevant international law, including humanitarian law and human rights law, where applicable, including with regard to minors in detention;

34. *Notes with concern* reports of continued violations of human rights and international humanitarian law, including violent or discriminatory practices, violations committed against persons belonging to ethnic and religious minorities, as well as violations committed against women and children, in particular girls, stresses the need to promote tolerance and religious freedom, as guaranteed by the Afghan Constitution, emphasizes the necessity of investigating allegations of current and past violations, and stresses the importance of facilitating the provision of efficient and effective remedies to the victims and of bringing the perpetrators to justice in accordance with national and international law;

35. *Commends* the Government of Afghanistan for the submission of its first universal periodic review report to the Human Rights Council in 2009, and encourages the timely implementation of the recommendations addressed therein;

36. *Stresses* the need to ensure respect for the right to freedom of expression and the right to freedom of thought, conscience or belief, as enshrined in the Afghan Constitution, welcomes in this regard the new mass media law as important progress, while noting with concern the growing intimidation and violence targeting Afghan journalists and challenges to the independence of the media, condemns cases of the abduction and even killing of journalists by terrorist as well as extremist and criminal groups, and urges that harassment and attacks on journalists be investigated by the Afghan authorities and that those responsible be brought to justice;

37. *Reiterates* the important role of the Afghan Independent Human Rights Commission in the promotion and protection of human rights and fundamental freedoms, stresses the need to expand its range of operation in all parts of Afghanistan in accordance with the Afghan Constitution, encourages the Government of Afghanistan to take increasing responsibility for the core funding of the Commission, and calls upon the international community for continued support in this regard;

38. *Calls for* the full implementation by the Government of Afghanistan of the Action Plan on Peace, Justice and Reconciliation, encourages the implementation of Government-led reintegration, reconciliation and transitional justice processes aimed at reintegrating those ready to renounce violence, denounce terrorism, accept the Afghan Constitution and commit themselves to working constructively for peace, stability and development, within the framework of the Constitution, without prejudice to the implementation of measures introduced by the Security Council in resolution 1267(1999), and recalls other relevant resolutions in this regard;

39. *Recalls* Security Council resolutions 1325(2000) of 31 October 2000, 1820(2008) of 19 June 2008, 1888(2009) of 30 September 2009 and 1889(2009) of 5 October 2009 on women and peace and security, commends the efforts of the Government of Afghanistan to mainstream gender issues and to protect and promote the equal rights of women and men as guaranteed, inter alia, by virtue of its ratification of the Convention on the Elimination of All Forms of Discrimination against Women and by the Afghan Constitution, and reiterates the continued importance of the full and equal participation of women in all spheres of Afghan life and of equality before the law and equal access to legal counsel without discrimination of any kind;

40. *Reiterates*, in view of legislation recently adopted, the continued importance of upholding international obli-

gations for the advancement of women's rights, as enshrined in the Afghan Constitution, welcomes the presidential decree regarding the law on the elimination of violence against women and calls for its timely implementation, and appreciates the preparation by the Government of Afghanistan for reporting to the Committee on the Elimination of Discrimination against Women in 2010;

41. *Strongly condemns* incidents of discrimination and violence against women and girls, in particular if directed against women activists and women prominent in public life, wherever they occur in Afghanistan, including killings, maimings and "honour killings" in certain parts of the country;

42. *Welcomes* the creation of a special fund for the protection of women at risk, set up by the United Nations Development Fund for Women with the support of the Office of the United Nations High Commissioner for Refugees;

43. *Also welcomes* the implementation of the National Action Plan for Women in Afghanistan and the significant efforts by the Government of Afghanistan to counter discrimination, urges the Government to actively involve all elements of Afghan society, in particular women, in the development and implementation of relief, rehabilitation, recovery and reconstruction programmes, and encourages the collection and use of statistical data on a sex-disaggregated basis to provide information on gender-based violence and to accurately track the progress of the full integration of women into the political, economic and social life of Afghanistan;

44. *Further welcomes* the achievements and stresses the need for continued progress in gender equality, in accordance with obligations under international law, and in the empowerment of women in Afghan politics, which will help to consolidate durable peace and national stability in Afghanistan, while noting the need to promote the empowerment of women also at the subnational level, to facilitate the access of women to employment and to ensure female literacy, professional training and entrepreneurship, and calls upon the international community to continue to support Afghan institutions in this regard;

45. *Stresses* the need to ensure respect for the human rights and fundamental freedoms of children in Afghanistan, welcomes the submission of the initial report of Afghanistan to the Committee on the Rights of the Child, and recalls the need for the full implementation of the Convention on the Rights of the Child and the two Optional Protocols thereto by all States parties, as well as of Security Council resolutions 1612(2005) of 26 July 2005 and 1882(2009) of 4 August 2009 on children and armed conflict;

46. *Expresses its concern*, in this regard, about the ongoing recruitment and use of children by illegal armed and terrorist groups in Afghanistan, as described in the report of the Secretary-General on children and armed conflict in Afghanistan of 10 November 2008, stresses the importance of ending the use of children contrary to international law, and welcomes the progress achieved by and the firm commitment of the Government of Afghanistan in this regard, including the strong condemnation of any exploitation of children;

47. *Welcomes* the adoption by the Government of Afghanistan of the National Plan of Action on Combating Child Trafficking, also welcomes initiatives to pass legislation on human trafficking, guided by the Protocol to Prevent, Suppress and Punish Trafficking in Persons, Especially Women and Children, supplementing the United Nations Convention against Transnational Organized Crime, and stresses the importance of considering becoming a party to the Protocol;

48. *Urges* the Government of Afghanistan to continue to effectively reform the public administration sector in order to implement the rule of law and to ensure good governance and accountability at both the national and subnational levels, and stresses the importance of meeting the respective benchmarks of the Afghanistan Compact, with the support of the international community;

49. *Welcomes* the appointment of officials to the Senior Appointments Panel, and encourages the Government of Afghanistan to make active use of this panel, as agreed upon in the Afghanistan Compact, thus enhancing efficiency and transparency in the appointment of senior officials;

50. *Encourages* the international community, including all donor nations, to assist the Government of Afghanistan in making capacity-building and human resources development a cross-cutting priority and to align with efforts by the Government, including the work of the Independent Administrative Reform and Civil Service Commission, to build administrative capacity at the national and subnational levels;

51. *Welcomes* the ratification by Afghanistan of the United Nations Convention against Corruption, calls for further progress by the Government of Afghanistan in pursuing its efforts to establish a more effective, accountable and transparent administration at national, provincial and local levels of Government leading the fight against corruption in accordance with the Afghanistan Compact, and notes with deep concern the effects of corruption with regard to security, good governance, the combating of the narcotics industry and economic development;

52. *Applauds* recent efforts to improve subnational governance and administration in Afghanistan through the Independent Directorate of Local Governance, underscores the importance of more visible, accountable and capable subnational institutions and actors in reducing the political space for insurgents, calls upon Afghan authorities and the international community to actively support the work of the Directorate, strongly encourages the Government of Afghanistan to approve and implement the Subnational Governance Policy to strengthen the roles of subnational institutions and allocate more resources and authority to provincial government, and looks forward to the development of a robust implementation plan;

53. *Urges* the Government of Afghanistan to address, with the assistance of the international community, the question of claims for land property through a comprehensive land titling programme, including formal registration of all property and improved security of property rights, and welcomes the steps already taken by the Government in this regard;

54. *Welcomes* the Afghanistan National Development Strategy and the first annual progress report thereon, as well as further efforts by the Government of Afghanistan to achieve the Millennium Development Goals;

55. *Also welcomes* the continuing and growing ownership of rehabilitation, reconstruction and development efforts by the Government of Afghanistan, and emphasizes the crucial need to achieve ownership in all fields of governance and to improve institutional capabilities, including at the subnational level, in order to use aid more effectively;

56. *Stresses* the need for a continued strong international commitment to humanitarian assistance and for programmes, under the ownership of the Government of Afghanistan, of recovery, rehabilitation, reconstruction and development, while expressing its appreciation to the United Nations system and to all States and international and non-governmental organizations whose international and local staff continue to respond positively to the humanitarian, transition and development needs of Afghanistan despite increasing security concerns and difficulties of access in certain areas;

57. *Expresses its appreciation* for the humanitarian and development assistance work of the international community in the reconstruction and development of Afghanistan, recognizes the necessity for further improvement in the living conditions of the Afghan people, and emphasizes the need to strengthen and support the capacity of the Government of Afghanistan to deliver basic social services, in particular education and public health services, and to promote development;

58. *Urges* the Government of Afghanistan to enhance efforts to reform key service delivery sectors, such as energy and drinking water supply, as preconditions for progress in social and economic development, commends the Government for its efforts to date to increase revenues and taxes collected to reach fiscal sustainability, and urges continued commitment to revenue generation;

59. *Expresses its appreciation* for the work of the provincial reconstruction teams;

60. *Urgently appeals* to all States, the United Nations system and international and non-governmental organizations to continue to provide, in close coordination with the Government of Afghanistan and in accordance with its national development strategy, all possible and necessary humanitarian, recovery, reconstruction, development, financial, educational, technical and material assistance for Afghanistan, and recalls in this regard the leading role of the Mission in coordinating international efforts;

61. *Urges* the international community, in accordance with the Afghanistan Compact, to increase the proportion of donor assistance channelled directly to the core budget, as agreed bilaterally between the Government of Afghanistan and each donor, as well as through other more predictable core budget funding modalities in which the Government participates, such as the Afghanistan Reconstruction Trust Fund and the Law and Order Trust Fund;

62. *Invites* all States and intergovernmental and non-governmental organizations providing assistance to Afghanistan to focus on institution-building in a coordinated manner and to ensure that such work complements and contributes to the development of an economy characterized by sound macroeconomic policies, the development of a financial sector that provides services, inter alia, to micro-enterprises, small and medium-sized enterprises and households, transparent business regulations and accountability;

63. *Encourages* the international community and the corporate sector to support the Afghan economy as a measure for long-term stability and to explore possibilities for increased investments and enhanced local procurements;

64. *Urgently encourages* all States as well as intergovernmental and non-governmental organizations to expand agricultural cooperation with Afghanistan, within the National Agricultural Development Framework and in line with the Afghanistan National Development Strategy;

65. *Welcomes* all efforts to increase regional economic cooperation, and recognizes the important role of the Economic Cooperation Organization and the South Asian Association for Regional Cooperation in promoting Afghanistan's development;

66. *Calls for* the strengthening of the process of regional economic cooperation, including measures to facilitate regional trade and transit, increase foreign investments and develop infrastructure, including energy supply and integrated border management, noting Afghanistan's historical role as a land bridge in Asia;

67. *Reiterates* the necessity of providing Afghan children, especially Afghan girls, with educational and health facilities in all parts of the country, welcomes progress achieved in the sector of public education, recalls the National Education Strategic Plan as a promising basis for further achievements, and reiterates further the need to provide vocational training for adolescents;

68. *Recognizes* the special needs of girls, strongly condemns terrorist attacks on educational facilities, especially on those for Afghan girls, and encourages the Government of Afghanistan, with the assistance of the international community, to expand those facilities, train professional staff and promote full and equal access to them by all members of Afghan society, including in remote areas;

69. *Welcomes* the continuous return of refugees and internally displaced persons, in a voluntary and sustainable manner, while noting with concern that conditions in parts of Afghanistan are not yet conducive to safe and sustainable return to some places of origin;

70. *Expresses its appreciation* to those Governments that continue to host Afghan refugees, acknowledging the huge burden they have so far shouldered in this regard, and reminds the host countries and the international community of their obligations under international refugee law with respect to the protection of refugees, the principle of voluntary return and the right to seek asylum and to ensure unhindered access for humanitarian relief agencies in order to provide protection and assistance to the refugees;

71. *Urges* the Government of Afghanistan, acting with the support of the international community, to continue to strengthen its efforts to create the conditions for the voluntary, safe, dignified and sustainable return and reintegration of the remaining Afghan refugees and internally displaced persons;

72. *Notes*, in this regard, the continued constructive work between the countries of the region, as well as the tripartite agreements between the Office of the United Nations High Commissioner for Refugees, the Government of Afghanistan and the Governments of countries hosting refugees from Afghanistan, in particular Pakistan and the Islamic Republic of Iran;

73. *Calls for* the provision of continued international assistance to the large numbers of Afghan refugees and internally displaced persons to facilitate their voluntary, safe, dignified and orderly return and sustainable reintegration into society so as to contribute to the stability of the entire country;

74. *Recognizes* that underdevelopment and lack of capacity increase the vulnerability of Afghanistan to natural disasters and harsh climate conditions, and in this regard urges the Government of Afghanistan, with the support of the international community, to increase its efforts aimed at strengthening disaster risk reduction at the national and subnational levels and at modernizing the agricultural sector and strengthening its agricultural production, thereby reducing Afghanistan's vulnerability to adverse external conditions such as drought, flooding and other natural disasters;

75. *Commends* the swift and successful relief efforts by the Government of Afghanistan and donors during last year's food crisis, but continues to express its concern at the overall humanitarian situation, stresses the continued need for food assistance, and calls for continued international support for and the early fulfilment, before the approaching winter, of the funding target of the Afghanistan Humanitarian Action Plan;

76. *Welcomes* the growing number of poppy-free provinces and other continued positive developments in fighting drug production in Afghanistan, as reported by the United Nations Office on Drugs and Crime in the *Afghanistan Opium Survey 2009*, released on 2 September 2009, but reiterates its deep concern about the continued cultivation and production of narcotic drugs in Afghanistan, mainly concentrated in areas where the Taliban, Al-Qaida and other extremist and criminal groups are particularly active, as well as the ongoing drug trafficking, and stresses the need for more coordinated and resolute efforts by the Government of Afghanistan, supported by the international community, to fight this menace;

77. *Stresses* the importance of a comprehensive approach in addressing the drug problem of Afghanistan, which, to be effective, must be integrated into the wider context of efforts carried out in the areas of security, governance, the rule of law and human rights, and economic and social development, and stresses that the development of alternative livelihood programmes is of key importance in the success of the counter-narcotics efforts in Afghanistan;

78. *Notes with great concern* the increasingly strong nexus between the drug trade and terrorist activities by the Taliban, Al-Qaida and other extremist and criminal groups, which pose a serious threat to security, the rule of law and development in Afghanistan, and stresses the importance of the implementation of all relevant Security Council resolutions in this regard, including resolution 1735(2006) of 22 December 2006;

79. *Calls upon* all Member States to further intensify their efforts to reduce the demand for drugs in their respective countries and globally in order to contribute to the sustainability of the elimination of illicit cultivation in Afghanistan;

80. *Stresses* the need to prevent trafficking in and diversion of chemical precursors used in the illicit manufacturing of drugs, including heroin for illicit use, in Afghanistan,

and calls for the full implementation of Security Council resolution 1817(2008) in this regard;

81. *Urges* the Government of Afghanistan, supported by the international community, to work to mainstream counter-narcotics throughout all the national programmes and to ensure that counter-narcotics is a fundamental part of the comprehensive approach, as well as to increase its efforts against opium cultivation and drug trafficking in accordance with the balanced eight-pillar plan of the Afghan National Drug Control Strategy;

82. *Commends* the efforts of the Government of Afghanistan in this regard, as well as the efforts to implement the National Drug Control Strategy, including the Prioritized Implementation Plan, urges the Government and the international community to take decisive action, in particular to stop the processing of and trade in drugs, by pursuing the concrete steps set out in the Strategy and in the Afghanistan Compact and through initiatives such as the Good Performers Initiative established to provide incentives for governors to reduce cultivation in their provinces, and encourages the Afghan authorities to work at the provincial level on elaborating counter-narcotics implementation plans;

83. *Calls upon* the international community to assist the Government of Afghanistan in implementing its National Drug Control Strategy, aimed at eliminating the cultivation, production and consumption of and trafficking in illicit drugs, including through increased support for Afghan law enforcement and criminal justice agencies, agricultural and rural development, demand reduction, the elimination of illicit crops, increased public awareness, the building of the capacity of drug control institutions and care and treatment centres for drug addicts and the creation of alternative livelihoods for farmers, and reiterates its call upon the international community to channel counter-narcotics funding through the Government to the extent possible;

84. *Urges* the Government of Afghanistan, assisted by the international community, to promote the development of sustainable livelihoods in the formal production sector, as well as in other sectors, and to improve access to reasonable and sustainable credit and financing in rural areas, thus improving substantially the lives, health and security of the people, particularly in rural areas;

85. *Supports* the fight against the illicit trafficking in drugs from and precursors to Afghanistan and neighbouring States and countries along trafficking routes, including increased cooperation among them in strengthening anti-narcotic controls and the monitoring of the international trade in chemical precursors, and takes note of the establishment of the Central Asian Regional Information and Coordination Centre in Almaty on 22 March 2009;

86. *Calls upon* States to strengthen international and regional cooperation to counter the increasing threat to the international community posed by the illicit production of drugs in Afghanistan and trafficking in drugs, recognizes the progress achieved by relevant initiatives within the framework of the Paris Pact, the Tehran agreement on a triangular initiative by Afghanistan, the Islamic Republic of Iran and Pakistan and the third Trilateral Summit of Afghanistan, Pakistan and Turkey, and stresses the importance of further progress in the implementation of these initiatives;

87. *Pays homage* to all those who have innocently lost their lives in the fight against drug traffickers, in particular members of the security forces of Afghanistan and its neighbours;

88. *Welcomes* initiatives to promote border management cooperation in drug control, including the financial dimension, between Afghanistan and its neighbours, and emphasizes the importance of pursuing such cooperation, especially through bilateral arrangements and those launched by the Collective Security Treaty Organization;

89. *Stresses* the importance of further, effective cooperative support by relevant international and regional actors, including the United Nations and the International Security Assistance Force, within its designated responsibilities, to Afghan-led sustained efforts to address the threat posed by the illicit production of and trafficking in drugs, and welcomes in this regard the regional programme on Afghanistan and neighbouring countries of the United Nations Office on Drugs and Crime;

90. *Expresses its appreciation* for the work of the Mission as mandated by the Security Council in resolution 1868(2009), and stresses the continued importance of the central and impartial role played by the Mission in promoting and coordinating a more coherent international engagement;

91. *Welcomes* the ongoing extension of the presence of the Mission into additional provinces, which thus ensures that the United Nations fulfils its essential coordinating role, and encourages the Mission to consolidate its presence and to continue its expansion throughout the country, in particular in the south, security conditions permitting;

92. *Stresses* the need to ensure that the Mission is adequately resourced to fulfil its mandate;

93. *Acknowledges* the central role played by the Joint Coordination and Monitoring Board in facilitating and monitoring the implementation of the Afghanistan Compact, stresses that the role of the Board is to support Afghanistan by, inter alia, coordinating international assistance and reconstruction programmes, and welcomes further efforts to provide appropriate guidance and promote a more coherent international engagement;

94. *Commends* the continuing efforts of the signatories of the Kabul Declaration on Good-neighbourly Relations of 22 December 2002 to implement their commitments under the Declaration, and furthermore calls upon all other States to respect and support the implementation of those provisions and to promote regional stability;

95. *Welcomes and encourages* further efforts by the Government of Afghanistan and its neighbouring partners to foster trust and cooperation with each other, and looks forward, where appropriate, to increasing cooperation between Afghanistan, all its neighbouring and regional partners, and regional organizations against the Taliban, Al-Qaida and other extremist and criminal groups and in promoting peace and prosperity in Afghanistan, in the region and beyond;

96. *Welcomes* ongoing efforts by the Government of Afghanistan and its neighbouring and regional partners to foster trust and cooperation with each other, as well as recent cooperation initiatives developed by the countries concerned and regional organizations, including the ministerial meeting in La Celle-Saint-Cloud, France, in December 2008, the trilateral summits of Afghanistan, Pakistan and Turkey in Ankara in April 2009, of Afghanistan, Pakistan and the United States of America in May 2009, of Afghanistan, Pakistan and the Islamic Republic of Iran in May 2009 and of Afghanistan, Pakistan and Tajikistan in June 2009 and the quadrilateral summit of Afghanistan, Pakistan, Tajikistan and the Russian Federation, also in June 2009, as well as efforts made by the Shanghai Cooperation Organization and initiatives within the framework of the Dubai Process to promote the country's stability and development; these efforts are essential to foster cooperation in the economic and development sectors as a means to achieve the full integration of Afghanistan into the regional and global economy;

97. *Appreciates* the continued commitment of the international community to supporting the stability and development of Afghanistan, recalls the additional international support as pledged, welcomes the special conference on Afghanistan held under the aegis of the Shanghai Cooperation Organization in Moscow on 27 March 2009 and the International Conference on Afghanistan held in The Hague on 31 March 2009, and welcomes the relations between the Organization for Security and Cooperation in Europe and Afghanistan;

98. *Welcomes* the outreach session of the meeting of Group of Eight Ministers for Foreign Affairs held in Trieste, Italy, on 26 and 27 June 2009, and encourages the Group of Eight countries to continue to stimulate and support cooperation between Afghanistan and its neighbours through mutual consultation and agreement, including on development projects in areas such as repatriation of refugees, border management and economic development;

99. *Appreciates* the efforts of the members of the Tripartite Commission, namely Afghanistan, Pakistan and the International Security Assistance Force, to continue to address cross-border activities and to broaden their cooperation;

100. *Emphasizes* the need to maintain, strengthen and review civil-military relations among international actors, as appropriate, at all levels in order to ensure complementarity of action based on the different mandates and comparative advantages of the humanitarian, development, law enforcement and military actors present in Afghanistan, bearing in mind the central and impartial coordinating role of the United Nations;

101. *Requests* the Secretary-General to report to the General Assembly every three months during its sixty-fourth session on developments in Afghanistan, as well as on the progress made in the implementation of the present resolution;

102. *Decides* to include in the provisional agenda of its sixty-fifth session the item entitled "The situation in Afghanistan".

Recall of Deputy Special Representative. On 30 September, the Secretary-General announced [SG/SM/12508] his decision to recall Deputy Special Representative Galbraith from Afghanistan and end his appointment. The decision was in the best interest of the Mission.

Report of Secretary-General (December). In a 28 December report [A/64/613-S/2009/674], the Secretary-General, reviewing the situation in Afghanistan since 22 September, said that the controversial 2009 elections had undermined confidence in Afghanistan's leadership and affected international support for engagement there. However, it had ultimately yielded a result that was acceptable to Afghans and respected Afghanistan's laws and institutions. Following a recount order of 8 September of the Electoral Complaints Commission, his Special Representative had engaged in more than two weeks of intense dialogue with that body and the Independent Electoral Commission to forge an agreement on how to implement the order and address the suspected fraud in the 20 August presidential election. On 24 September, the two bodies agreed that the best modality for implementing the order was to audit suspect ballots through statistical sampling. While leading presidential candidates Hamid Karzai and Abdullah Abdullah welcomed the audit in principle, they both had concerns with how it would be administered. On 19 October, the Electoral Complaints Commission announced that it had completed its work on the presidential elections. The preliminary results showed that no candidate had obtained over 50 per cent of the vote, thereby triggering the need for a second round.

On 26 October, Dr. Abdullah announced a set of conditions for his participation in the second round, including the dismissal of the Independent Electoral Commission Chairman, the removal of additional election officials, governors and police chiefs and the suspension of three cabinet members. Both the Commission and President Karzai rejected the conditions. On 1 November, Dr. Abdullah announced that he would not participate in a second round and that he would not join any Government coalition, but would continue to work in the interest of the Afghan people. On 2 November, the Secretary-General visited Afghanistan, where he met with President Karzai and Dr. Abdullah and noted the need to bring the electoral process to a conclusion in a legal and timely manner. On the same day, the Independent Electoral Commission declared Hamid Karzai, the sole candidate in the run-off election, as the President-elect for a second five-year term. On 19 November, Mr. Karzai was inaugurated as President.

The security situation had worsened over the reporting period, with an average of 1,244 incidents per month in the third quarter of 2009. UNAMA recorded 784 conflict-related civilian casualties between August and October 2009, up 12 per cent from the same period in 2008. The deteriorating security environment also had an impact on the delivery of aid, with attacks on the aid community becoming a near daily occurrence. There was a return of suicide attacks in Kabul, where the deployment of an additional 5,000 policemen in the nine square kilometres forming the centre of Kabul (the "Ring of Steel") provided only limited relief.

In the areas of donor coordination and aid effectiveness, UNAMA was stretching its limited resources to support the Government's refocusing and restructuring efforts, to assist Ministries in developing and executing new programmes and to coordinate donor support. Polio remained a major health concern, with 24 confirmed polio cases reported from January to October, mainly in the south. Repatriation of Afghans from neighbouring countries was considerably lower than in 2008. Following the 28 October attack on a guest house in Kabul where UN staff resided, a decision was taken to temporarily relocate some UN personnel within Afghanistan as well as to other duty stations, pending the identification of secure premises.

According to a subsequent report by the Secretary-General [A/64/705-S/2010/127], the Independent Electoral Commission between 12 November and 26 December certified the provincial council election results for all 34 provinces, regarding the election of 418 provincial council members, of which 122 were women, to 420 seats. During the second half of 2009, the Government increased its collection of revenue by an estimated 65 per cent, and saw an increase in foreign direct investment. The year 2009 was the most volatile since the fall of the Taliban in 2001, averaging 960 security incidents per month, compared with 741 in 2008.

Children and armed conflict

In a report on children and armed conflict issued in March [A/63/785-S/2009/158 & Corr.1] pursuant to presidential statement S/PRST/2008/6 [YUN 2008, p. 850], the Secretary-General said that allegations of recruitment of children by armed groups, including those associated with the Taliban, had been received from all regions of Afghanistan, particularly from the south, south-east and east. An UNAMA study documented cases of children being used by the Taliban to carry out suicide attacks. There were concerns that, due to inadequate age-verification procedures in National Police recruitment processes, children had been found in its ranks. Children had been captured, arrested and detained by Afghan law enforcement agencies and international military forces because of their alleged association with armed groups, and there was evidence of children being ill-treated, detained for long periods by the National Directorate of Security and prevented access to legal assistance, in contravention of the provisions of the Afghan Juvenile Code and international standards on juvenile justice.

Reports of child casualties due to the conflict had been received from all across Afghanistan, and children were caught between opposing sides in the conflict in the southern and eastern regions. Children had also been victims of asymmetric attacks, which included suicide bombings, vehicle-borne improvised explosive devices, body-borne improvised explosive devices, and attacks by anti-government elements, including the Taliban, in the north-east, west and central regions. Reports of children being sexually abused and exploited by members of armed forces and groups had also been documented. The Secretary-General stated that Taliban forces had also been responsible for the killing and maiming of children, attacks on schools and hospitals and the denial of humanitarian access to children.

The Security Council on 27 August transmitted to the Secretary-General a letter [S/2009/435] from the Chairman of the Security Council Working Group on Children and Armed Conflict based on the Working Group's conclusions on Afghanistan adopted on 1 July [S/AC.51/2009/1].

UNAMA

The United Nations Assistance Mission in Afghanistan (UNAMA) was established by Security Council resolution 1401(2002) [YUN 2002, p. 264] to promote, among other things, national reconciliation and the responsibilities entrusted to the United Nations under the 2001 Bonn Agreement [YUN 2001, p. 263]. It comprised the Office of the Special Representative, two substantive pillars—one political (Pillar I) and one on relief, recovery and reconstruction (Pillar II)—and an administrative component. UNAMA was headquartered in Kabul, with regional offices in Bamyan, Gardez, Herat, Jalalabad, Kabul, Kandahar, Kunduz and Mazar-e-Sharif, and provincial offices in Badakhshan, Badghis, Daikundi, Faryab, Ghor, Khost, Kunar, Nimroz, Sari Pul, Tirin Kot and Zabul. UNAMA was headed by the Special Representative of the Secretary-General, Kai Eide (Norway). By resolution 1868(2009) (see p. 335), the Security Council extended the UNAMA mandate until 23 March 2010.

UNAMA financing

In October [A/64/349/Add.4], the Secretary-General outlined proposed resource requirements for UNAMA from 1 January to 31 December 2010, totalling $241,944,300 net ($256,579,500 gross). In December [A/64/7/Add.13], the Advisory Committee on Administrative and Budgetary Questions (ACABQ) recommended approval of those figures.

On 24 December, the General Assembly, by section VI of **resolution 64/245** (see p. 1407), approved that amount as part of the $569,526,500 budget for

the 26 special political missions authorized by the General Assembly and/or the Security Council.

International Security Assistance Force

During 2009, the Secretary-General transmitted to the Security Council, in accordance with Council resolutions 1386(2001) [YUN 2001, p. 267] and 1510(2003) [YUN 2003, p. 310], a report from the International Security Assistance Force (ISAF) on its activities for the period from 1 August 2008 to 31 January 2009 [S/2009/283]. Subsequent reports covered ISAF activities from 1 August to 31 October 2009 [S/2010/35]; and 1 November 2009 to 31 January 2010 [S/2010/353]. Throughout the year, ISAF continued to assist the Afghan Government in accordance with relevant Security Council resolutions.

As at 2 February, ISAF had 57,249 personnel from 26 NATO countries and 15 non-NATO countries. Between 1 August 2008 and 31 January 2009, ISAF suffered 777 casualties—113 killed in action and 664 wounded in action. ISAF security operations emphasized ensuring freedom of movement, particularly along the ring road, building the capacity of the Afghan National Security Forces, and assisting the Government with voter registration. Combined operations with the National Security Forces included moving critical electricity-generation equipment to the Kajaki dam.

As at 31 October, ISAF had 80,123 personnel from 28 NATO nations and 14 non-NATO nations. During the quarter ending 31 October, ISAF suffered 1,446 casualties—170 killed in action, 1,260 wounded in action and 16 non-battle-related deaths. On 23 October, the NATO defence ministers adopted four key priorities: to improve protection of the Afghan people; to build the capacity of the Afghan National Security Forces and facilitate their lead role in security; to facilitate governance and development; and to engage with Afghanistan's regional neighbours, especially Pakistan.

Communication. In a letter of 31 March [A/63/805-S/2009/177], the Russian Federation transmitted to the Secretary-General the texts of documents adopted on 27 March at the Special Conference on Afghanistan, held in Moscow under the auspices of the Shanghai Cooperation Organization (SCO): the Declaration of the Conference and the Plan of Action of the SCO member States and Afghanistan on combating terrorism, illicit drug trafficking and organized crime. The Declaration welcomed the fact that ISAF, in cooperation with the Afghan Government, had joined the fight against drug production and proliferation in Afghanistan, and supported its wide-ranging participation in multilateral efforts in that area.

Letter from Afghanistan. In a 20 September letter [S/2009/522], Afghan Foreign Minister Rangin

Dadfar Spanta expressed appreciation for the role played by ISAF in his country and welcomed the proposed continuation of its operations.

Extension of ISAF mandate

On 8 October [meeting 6198], the Security Council unanimously adopted **resolution 1890(2009)**. The draft [S/2009/523] was submitted by Japan.

The Security Council,

Reaffirming its previous resolutions on Afghanistan, in particular resolutions 1386(2001) of 20 December 2001, 1510(2003) of 13 October 2003, 1833(2008) of 22 September 2008 and 1868(2009) of 23 March 2009,

Reaffirming also its resolutions 1267(1999) of 15 October 1999, 1368(2001) of 12 September 2001, 1373(2001) of 28 September 2001 and 1822(2008) of 30 June 2008, and reiterating its support for international efforts to root out terrorism in accordance with the Charter of the United Nations,

Recalling its resolutions 1265(1999) of 17 September 1999, 1296(2000) of 19 April 2000, 1674(2006) of 28 April 2006 and 1738(2006) of 23 December 2006 on the protection of civilians in armed conflict, its resolutions 1325(2000) of 31 October 2000, 1820(2008) of 19 June 2008, 1888(2009) of 30 September 2009 and 1889(2009) of 5 October 2009 on women and peace and security and its resolutions 1612(2005) of 26 July 2005 and 1882(2009) of 4 August 2009 on children and armed conflict,

Reaffirming its strong commitment to the sovereignty, independence, territorial integrity and national unity of Afghanistan,

Recognizing that the responsibility for providing security and law and order throughout the country resides with the Afghan authorities, stressing the role of the International Security Assistance Force in assisting the Government of Afghanistan to improve the security situation, and welcoming the cooperation of the Government with the Force,

Recognizing once again the interconnected nature of the challenges in Afghanistan, reaffirming that sustainable progress on security, governance and development, as well as the cross-cutting issue of counter-narcotics, is mutually reinforcing, and welcoming the continuing efforts of the Government of Afghanistan and the international community to address these challenges through a comprehensive approach,

Stressing, in this context, the need for further efforts by the Government of Afghanistan to fight corruption, promote transparency and increase its accountability,

Stressing also the central and impartial role that the United Nations continues to play in promoting peace and stability in Afghanistan by leading the efforts of the international community, noting in this context the synergies in the objectives of the United Nations Assistance Mission in Afghanistan and of the International Security Assistance Force, and stressing the need for strengthened cooperation, coordination and mutual support, taking due account of their respective designated responsibilities,

Expressing its strong concern about the security situation in Afghanistan, in particular the increased violent and terrorist activities by the Taliban, Al-Qaida, illegal armed groups, criminals and those involved in the narcotics trade, and the increasingly strong links between terrorism activities and illicit drugs, resulting in threats to the local population, including children, national security forces and international military and civilian personnel,

Encouraging the International Security Assistance Force to further effectively support, within its designated responsibilities, Afghan-led sustained efforts to address, in cooperation with relevant international and regional actors, the threat posed by the illicit production of and trafficking in drugs, and recognizing the important role played by the United Nations Office on Drugs and Crime in fighting the negative impact of drug production and trade on security and stability in the region,

Expressing its concern over the harmful consequences of violent and terrorist activities by the Taliban, Al-Qaida and other extremist groups on the capacity of the Government of Afghanistan to guarantee the rule of law, to provide security and basic services to the Afghan people and to ensure the full enjoyment of their human rights and fundamental freedoms,

Reiterating its support for the continuing endeavours of the Government of Afghanistan, with the assistance of the international community, including the International Security Assistance Force and the Operation Enduring Freedom coalition, to improve the security situation and to continue to address the threat posed by the Taliban, Al-Qaida and other extremist groups, and stressing in this context the need for sustained international efforts, including those of the Force and the coalition,

Condemning in the strongest terms all attacks, including improvised explosive device attacks, suicide attacks and abductions, targeting civilians and Afghan and international forces and their deleterious effect on the stabilization, reconstruction and development efforts in Afghanistan, and condemning further the use by the Taliban, Al-Qaida and other extremist groups of civilians as human shields,

Recognizing the increased threats posed by the Taliban, Al-Qaida and other extremist groups as well as the challenges related to the efforts to address such threats,

Expressing its serious concern about the high number of civilian casualties, and calling for compliance with international humanitarian and human rights law and for all appropriate measures to be taken to ensure the protection of civilians,

Recognizing additional efforts made by the International Security Assistance Force and other international forces to minimize the risk of civilian casualties, welcoming their intention to undertake continued enhanced efforts in this regard, including the increased focus on protecting the Afghan population as a central element of the mission, and noting the importance of conducting continuous reviews of tactics and procedures and after-action reviews and investigations in cooperation with the Government of Afghanistan in cases where civilian casualties have occurred and when the Government finds these joint investigations appropriate,

Acknowledging the progress made in security sector reform, welcoming support provided by the international partners in this regard, in particular the establishment of the North Atlantic Treaty Organization Training Mission–Afghanistan, the planned European Gendarmerie Force contribution to this mission and assistance extended to the Afghan National Police, including through the European Union Police Mission in Afghanistan, and stressing the need for Afghanistan, together with international donors, to further strengthen the Afghan National Army and the Afghan National Police and increase its efforts in the disbandment of illegal armed groups and counter-narcotics,

Stressing, in this context, the importance of further progress by the Government of Afghanistan in ending impunity and strengthening judicial institutions, the rule of law and respect for human rights within Afghanistan, including for women and girls, and in the reconstruction and reform of the prison sector in Afghanistan,

Reiterating its call upon all Afghan parties and groups to engage constructively in peaceful political dialogue within the framework of the Afghan Constitution, to work together with international donors for the socio-economic development of the country and to avoid resorting to violence, including through the use of illegal armed groups, and encouraging the implementation of the reintegration and reconciliation programmes led by the Government of Afghanistan within the framework of the Afghan Constitution and with full respect for the implementation of measures introduced by the Security Council in resolution 1267(1999) and other relevant resolutions of the Council,

Noting the leading role played by the Afghan authorities in organizing the 2009 presidential and provincial council elections, and the support of the United Nations and the International Security Assistance Force, and recognizing the need for timely and orderly preparations for the 2010 elections and for international support in this regard,

Recognizing the importance of the contribution of neighbouring and regional partners, as well as regional organizations, to the stabilization of Afghanistan, stressing the crucial importance of advancing regional cooperation as an effective means to promote security, governance and development in Afghanistan, and welcoming the regional efforts in this regard,

Welcoming the continued coordination between the International Security Assistance Force and the Operation Enduring Freedom coalition, and the cooperation established between the Force and the European Union presence in Afghanistan,

Expressing its appreciation for the leadership provided by the North Atlantic Treaty Organization and for the contributions of many nations to the International Security Assistance Force and to the Operation Enduring Freedom coalition, including its maritime interdiction component, which operates within the framework of the counter-terrorism operations in Afghanistan and in accordance with the applicable rules of international law,

Determining that the situation in Afghanistan still constitutes a threat to international peace and security,

Determined to ensure the full implementation of the mandate of the International Security Assistance Force, in coordination with the Government of Afghanistan,

Acting, for these reasons, under Chapter VII of the Charter,

1. *Decides* to extend the authorization of the International Security Assistance Force, as defined in resolutions 1386(2001) and 1510(2003), for a period of twelve months beyond 13 October 2009;

2. *Authorizes* the Member States participating in the International Security Assistance Force to take all measures necessary to fulfil its mandate;

3. *Recognizes* the need to further strengthen the International Security Assistance Force to meet all its operational requirements, and in this regard calls upon Member States to contribute personnel, equipment and other resources to the Force;

4. *Stresses* the importance of increasing, within a comprehensive framework, the functionality, professionalism and accountability of the Afghan security sector, encourages the International Security Assistance Force and other partners to sustain their efforts, as resources permit, to train, mentor and empower the Afghan national security forces in order to accelerate progress towards the goal of self-sufficient, accountable and ethnically balanced Afghan security forces providing security and ensuring the rule of law throughout the country, welcomes the increasing leadership role played by the Afghan authorities in security responsibilities throughout the country, and stresses the importance of supporting the planned expansion of the Afghan National Army and the Afghan National Police;

5. *Calls upon* the International Security Assistance Force to continue to work in close consultation with the Government of Afghanistan and the Special Representative of the Secretary-General for Afghanistan as well as with the Operation Enduring Freedom coalition in the implementation of the mandate of the Force;

6. *Requests* the leadership of the International Security Assistance Force to keep the Security Council regularly informed, through the Secretary-General, on the implementation of its mandate, including through the provision of quarterly reports;

7. *Decides* to remain actively seized of the matter.

Sanctions

UN sanctions-related activities were guided by the measures adopted by Security Council resolution 1822(2008) [YUN 2008, p. 377] and previous resolutions against Osama bin Laden, Al-Qaida, the Taliban, their associates and associated entities, which further refined the financial measures, travel ban and arms embargo imposed on those persons identified in the consolidated list created pursuant to resolution 1267(1999) [YUN 1999, p. 265]. The Al-Qaida and Taliban Sanctions Committee, established pursuant to resolution 1267(1999), oversaw the implementation of those measures. The Committee was assisted by an Analytical Support and Sanctions Monitoring Team.

On 29 January [S/2009/54], the Secretary-General informed the Council that he had appointed an expert to the Monitoring Team for the period ending 31 December, to replace the expert who stepped down on 30 October 2008. On 22 April [S/2009/219], he reported that he had appointed another expert through 31 December 2009, to succeed the expert whose term had ended on 31 December 2008.

Sanctions Committee activities

On 30 December, the Al-Qaida and Taliban Sanctions Committee submitted a report [S/2009/676] covering its activities in 2009. During the year, the Committee held 2 formal meeting and 25 informal meetings. Following consultations among Security Council members, the Council elected the Bureau of the Committee for 2009, which consisted of Thomas Mayr-Harting (Austria) as Chairman, with Burkina Faso and the Russian Federation providing the two Vice-Chairmen.

A priority of the Committee was reviewing the 488 names on the consolidated list of individuals and entities subject to sanctions measures as at 30 June 2008. Pursuant to resolution 1822(2008), the Committee was to consider an annual review of individuals reported to be deceased; and to conduct an annual review of all names on the consolidated list that had not been reviewed in three or more years.

Since May 2009, the Committee had considered 84 names on the consolidated list, confirming 56 listings as appropriate and removing 9 names, with the reviews of 19 names awaiting further information. The list was updated 22 times during 2009; by the end of the year, 503 individuals and entities were inscribed on it.

During 2009, the Committee continued to respond to requests from relevant authorities seeking its assistance in confirming the identity of certain individuals or entities for the purpose of implementing the sanctions measures. Mindful that the Council provided for exemptions to the assets freeze, including for humanitarian purposes, the Committee continued to consider notifications and requests for exemptions submitted pursuant to resolution 1452(2002) [YUN 2002, p. 280], receiving 17 such communications from States in 2009.

The Sanctions Committee Chairman briefed the Security Council on its work over the previous six months on 26 May [meeting 6128] and 13 November [meeting 6217]. The text of those statements was subsequently made available on the Committee's website.

Communications. Reports on their compliance with the sanctions regime were submitted to the Committee by Saint Vincent and the Grenadines on 12 March [S/AC.37/2009/(1455)/1], Antigua and Barbuda on 25 August [S/AC.37/2009/(1455)/5], Togo on 19 October [S/AC.37/2009/(1455)/2], Saint Lucia on 3 December [S/AC.37/2009/(1455)/3] and Nigeria on 4 December [S/AC.37/2009/(1455)/4].

Monitoring Team

The Analytical Support and Sanctions Monitoring Team (the Monitoring Team), established by Security Council resolution 1526(2004) [YUN 2004, p. 332]

and most recently extended by resolution 1822(2008) [YUN 2008, p. 377] had the mandate of collating, assessing, monitoring, reporting on and making recommendations on the implementation of measures imposed by that resolution.

Report of Monitoring Team (February). In accordance with resolution 1822(2008), the Sanctions Committee Chairman on 11 May transmitted to the Security Council the Monitoring Team's ninth report [S/2009/245], dated 28 February and covering the period from April 2008 through February 2009. It stated that resolution 1822(2008) had added significantly to the fairness and transparency of the procedures followed by the Sanctions Committee. The threat from Al-Qaida and the Taliban was firmly focused on South Asia. On both sides of the Afghanistan/Pakistan border, the authorities faced an increasing challenge, tied mainly to the various Taliban groups, which defied a purely military solution. Nevertheless, the Security Council and the Committee had to ensure that the sanctions regime had the maximum impact by inhibiting the capabilities of the Taliban and Al-Qaida worldwide. That would require further work on the consolidated list and effective application of the new procedures introduced by resolution 1822(2008), as well as more committed implementation and greater engagement by Member States.

In the 11 months ending February 2009, the Monitoring Team visited 19 States. It maintained close cooperation with international and regional organizations, and participated in 28 international and regional conferences to promote a better understanding of the sanctions regime and the work of the Committee. It also worked closely with the Counter-Terrorism Committee Executive Directorate (see p. 70) and the expert group supporting the Committee established pursuant to Security Council resolution 1540(2004) [YUN 2004, p. 544] to publicize their distinct but related mandates.

On 17 August, the Sanctions Committee Chairman submitted a report [S/2009/427] containing the Committee's position on the recommendations made in the Monitoring Team's ninth report. Those recommendations addressed an array of issues concerning the consolidated list, the assets freeze, the travel ban, the arms embargo, activities of the Monitoring Team and reporting by Member States.

Report of Monitoring Team (July). On 28 September, the Sanctions Committee Chairman transmitted to the Security Council the Monitoring Team's tenth report [S/2009/502], concerning Al-Qaida and the Taliban and associated individuals and entities, dated 31 July. It stated that since the Team began its work in March 2004, Al-Qaida, even more than the Taliban, had to adapt to relentless pressure from international, regional and national bodies worldwide. Although it remained a threat, Al-Qaida had been weakened. Increasingly, its future depended on what happened to the groups of fighters loosely known as the Taliban, who had carved out space on either side of the Pakistan-Afghanistan border.

The sanctions regime could become a more useful tool in splitting Al-Qaida from the Taliban and in promoting divisions within the Taliban through a more flexible use of its listing and de-listing procedures. The list must be a credible expression of the main elements of the threat and allow accurate identification of listed persons. With the help of many Member States, the list continued to improve, but still contained vague or dated entries. A more succinct list, coupled with a new format making it easier to use, would reinvigorate the sanctions regime and encourage its greater use.

The sanctions measures themselves were effective but underutilized, the report stated. The assets freeze was a key tool in limiting the ability of Al-Qaida, the Taliban and their associates to mount attacks, but those groups still managed to collect and spend large amounts of money. The Team proposed that more work be undertaken on understanding and undermining the nexus between drug trafficking and terrorism, as well as on the role played by alternative remittance systems and non-profit organizations.

The Team visited 9 States between March and July; one visit was made jointly with the Counter-Terrorism Committee Executive Directorate. Since March 2004, the Team had visited 85 Member States, and both the Committee and the Team attached great importance to such direct engagement with national authorities. The Committee had received reports from all but 36 States.

SECURITY COUNCIL ACTION

On 17 December [meeting 6247], the Security Council unanimously adopted **resolution 1904(2009)**. The draft [S/2009/647] was submitted by Austria, Burkina Faso, Croatia, France, Mexico, Turkey, the United Kingdom and the United States.

The Security Council,

Recalling its resolutions 1267(1999) of 15 October 1999, 1333(2000) of 19 December 2000, 1363(2001) of 30 July 2001, 1373(2001) of 28 September 2001, 1390(2002) of 16 January 2002, 1452(2002) of 20 December 2002, 1455(2003) of 17 January 2003, 1526(2004) of 30 January 2004, 1566(2004) of 8 October 2004, 1617(2005) of 29 July 2005, 1624(2005) of 14 September 2005, 1699(2006) of 8 August 2006, 1730(2006) of 19 December 2006, 1735(2006) of 22 December 2006 and 1822(2008) of 30 June 2008, and the relevant statements by its President,

Reaffirming that terrorism in all its forms and manifestations constitutes one of the most serious threats to peace and security and that any acts of terrorism are criminal and unjustifiable regardless of their motivations, whenever and by whomsoever committed, and reiterating its unequivocal condemnation of Al-Qaida, Osama bin Laden and the Taliban, and other individuals, groups, undertakings and entities associated with them, for ongoing and multiple criminal terrorist acts aimed at causing the death of innocent civilians and other victims, and the destruction of property and greatly undermining stability,

Reaffirming also the need to combat by all means, in accordance with the Charter of the United Nations and international law, including applicable international human rights, refugee and humanitarian law, threats to international peace and security caused by terrorist acts, and stressing in this regard the important role that the United Nations plays in leading and coordinating this effort,

Expressing its concern at the increase in incidents of kidnapping and hostage-taking by individuals, groups, undertakings and entities associated with Al-Qaida, Osama bin Laden or the Taliban with the aim of raising funds or gaining political concessions,

Reiterating its support for the fight against the illicit production of and trafficking in drugs from, and chemical precursors to, Afghanistan, in neighbouring countries, countries on trafficking routes, drug destination countries and precursor-producing countries,

Stressing that terrorism can only be defeated by a sustained and comprehensive approach involving the active participation and collaboration of all States and international and regional organizations to impede, impair, isolate and incapacitate the terrorist threat,

Emphasizing that sanctions are an important tool under the Charter in the maintenance and restoration of international peace and security, and stressing in this regard the need for robust implementation of the measures in paragraph 1 of the present resolution as a significant tool in combating terrorist activity,

Urging all Member States to participate actively in maintaining and updating the list created pursuant to resolutions 1267(1999) and 1333(2000) ("the Consolidated List") by contributing additional information pertinent to current listings, by submitting de-listing requests when appropriate, and by identifying and nominating for listing additional individuals, groups, undertakings and entities which should be subject to the measures referred to in paragraph 1 of the present resolution,

Taking note of challenges, both legal and otherwise, to the measures implemented by Member States under paragraph 1 of the present resolution, welcoming improvements to the procedures of the Security Council Committee established pursuant to resolution 1267(1999) and the quality of the Consolidated List, and expressing its intention to continue efforts to ensure that procedures are fair and clear,

Reiterating that the measures referred to in paragraph 1 of the present resolution are preventative in nature and are not reliant upon criminal standards set out under national law,

Recalling the adoption by the General Assembly on 8 September 2006 of the United Nations Global Counter-Terrorism Strategy and the creation of the Counter-Terrorism Implementation Task Force to ensure overall coordination and coherence in the counter-terrorism efforts of the United Nations system,

Welcoming the continuing cooperation between the Committee and the International Criminal Police Organization (INTERPOL), the United Nations Office on Drugs and Crime, in particular on technical assistance and capacity-building, and all other United Nations bodies, and encouraging further engagement with the Counter-Terrorism Implementation Task Force to ensure overall coordination and coherence in the counter-terrorism efforts of the United Nations system,

Noting with concern the continued threat posed to international peace and security, ten years after the adoption of resolution 1267(1999), by Al-Qaida, Osama bin Laden and the Taliban, and other individuals, groups, undertakings and entities associated with them, and reaffirming its resolve to address all aspects of that threat,

Acting under Chapter VII of the Charter,

Measures

1. *Decides* that all States shall take the following measures, as previously imposed by paragraph 4 *(b)* of resolution 1267(1999), paragraph 8 *(c)* of resolution 1333(2000) and paragraphs 1 and 2 of resolution 1390(2002), with respect to Al-Qaida, Osama bin Laden and the Taliban, and other individuals, groups, undertakings and entities associated with them, as referred to in the list created pursuant to resolutions 1267(1999) and 1333(2000) ("the Consolidated List"):

(a) Freeze without delay the funds and other financial assets or economic resources of those individuals, groups, undertakings and entities, including funds derived from property owned or controlled, directly or indirectly, by them or by persons acting on their behalf or at their direction, and ensure that neither these nor any other funds, financial assets or economic resources are made available, directly or indirectly, for the benefit of such persons by their nationals or by persons within their territories;

(b) Prevent the entry into or transit through their territories of those individuals, provided that nothing in the present paragraph shall oblige any State to deny entry into or require the departure from its territories of its own nationals and that the present paragraph shall not apply where entry or transit is necessary for the fulfilment of a judicial process, or the Security Council Committee established pursuant to resolution 1267(1999) determines on a case-by-case basis only that entry or transit is justified;

(c) Prevent the direct or indirect supply, sale or transfer to those individuals, groups, undertakings and entities, from their territories or by their nationals outside their territories, or using their flag vessels or aircraft, of arms and related materiel of all types, including weapons and ammunition, military vehicles and equipment, paramilitary equipment, and spare parts for the aforementioned, and technical advice, assistance or training related to military activities;

2. *Reaffirms* that acts or activities indicating that an individual, group, undertaking or entity is associated with Al-Qaida, Osama bin Laden or the Taliban include:

(a) Participating in the financing, planning, facilitating, preparing or perpetrating of acts or activities by, in conjunction with, under the name of, on behalf of, or in support of;

(b) Supplying, selling or transferring arms and related materiel to;

(c) Recruiting for; or

(d) Otherwise supporting acts or activities of Al-Qaida, Osama bin Laden or the Taliban, or any cell, affiliate, splinter group or derivative thereof;

3. *Further reaffirms* that any undertaking or entity owned or controlled, directly or indirectly, by, or otherwise supporting, such an individual, group, undertaking or entity associated with Al-Qaida, Osama bin Laden or the Taliban shall be eligible for designation;

4. *Confirms* that the requirements in paragraph 1 *(a)* above apply to financial and economic resources of every kind, including but not limited to those used for the provision of Internet hosting or related services, used for the support of Al-Qaida, Osama bin Laden or the Taliban, and other individuals, groups, undertakings or entities associated with them;

5. *Confirms also* that the requirements in paragraph 1 *(a)* above shall also apply to the payment of ransoms to individuals, groups, undertakings or entities on the Consolidated List;

6. *Decides* that Member States may permit the addition to accounts frozen pursuant to the provisions of paragraph 1 above of any payment in favour of listed individuals, groups, undertakings or entities, provided that any such payments continue to be subject to the provisions in paragraph 1 above and are frozen;

7. *Encourages* Member States to make use of the provisions regarding available exemptions to the measures in paragraph 1 *(a)* above as set out in paragraphs 1 and 2 of resolution 1452(2002), as amended by resolution 1735(2006), and directs the Committee to review the procedures for exemptions as set out in the Committee guidelines to facilitate their use by Member States and to continue to ensure that humanitarian exemptions are granted expeditiously and transparently;

Listing

8. *Encourages* all Member States to submit to the Committee for inclusion in the Consolidated List names of individuals, groups, undertakings and entities participating, by any means, in the financing or support of acts or activities of Al-Qaida, Osama bin Laden or the Taliban, and other individuals, groups, undertakings and entities associated with them, as described in paragraph 2 of resolution 1617(2005) and reaffirmed in paragraph 2 above, and further encourages Member States to appoint a national contact point concerning entries on the Consolidated List;

9. *Notes* that such means of financing or support include but are not limited to the use of proceeds derived from illicit cultivation and production of and trafficking in narcotic drugs originating particularly in Afghanistan, and their precursors;

10. *Reiterates its call for* continued cooperation between the Committee and the Government of Afghanistan and the United Nations Assistance Mission in Afghanistan, including by identifying individuals and entities participating in the financing or support of acts or activities of Al-Qaida and the Taliban as described in paragraph 30 of resolution 1806(2008) of 20 March 2008;

11. *Reaffirms* that, when proposing names to the Committee for inclusion in the Consolidated List, Member States shall act in accordance with paragraph 5 of resolution 1735(2006) and paragraph 12 of resolution 1822(2008) and provide a detailed statement of case, and decides further that the statement of case shall be releasable, upon request, except for the parts that a Member State identifies as being confidential to the Committee, and may be used to develop the narrative summary of reasons for listing described in paragraph 14 below;

12. *Encourages* Member States proposing a new designation, as well as Member States that have proposed names for inclusion in the Consolidated List before the adoption of the present resolution, to specify whether the Committee may make known, upon request from a Member State, the status of the Member State as a designating State;

13. *Calls upon* Member States, when proposing names to the Committee for inclusion in the Consolidated List, to use the new standard form for listing, once it is adopted and placed on the Committee website, and requests that they provide the Committee with as much relevant information as possible on the proposed name, in particular sufficient identifying information to allow for the accurate and positive identification of individuals, groups, undertakings and entities, and directs the Committee to update, as necessary, the standard form for listing in accordance with the provisions of the present resolution;

14. *Directs* the Committee, with the assistance of the Analytical Support and Sanctions Monitoring Team and in coordination with the relevant designating States, to make accessible on the Committee website, at the same time that a name is added to the Consolidated List, a narrative summary of reasons for listing for the corresponding entry or entries, and further directs the Committee, with the assistance of the Monitoring Team and in coordination with the relevant designating States, to continue its efforts to make accessible on the Committee website narrative summaries of reasons for listing for entries that were added to the Consolidated List before the date of adoption of resolution 1822(2008);

15. *Encourages* Member States and relevant international organizations to inform the Committee of any relevant court decisions and proceedings so that the Committee can consider them when it reviews a corresponding listing or updates a narrative summary of reasons for listing;

16. *Calls upon* all members of the Committee and the Monitoring Team to share with the Committee any information they may have available regarding a listing request from a Member State so that this information may help to inform the decision of the Committee on designation and provide additional material for the narrative summary of reasons for listing described in paragraph 14 above;

17. *Directs* the Committee to amend its guidelines to extend the period of time for members of the Committee to verify that names proposed for listing merit inclusion in the Consolidated List and include adequate identifying information to ensure full implementation of the measures, with exceptions, at the discretion of the Chair of the Committee, for emergency and time-sensitive listings, and notes that listing requests may be placed on the agenda of the Committee upon request of a member of the Committee;

18. *Decides* that the Secretariat shall, after publication but within three working days after a name is added to the Consolidated List, notify the permanent mission of the country or countries where the individual or entity is believed to be located and, in the case of individuals, the country of which the person is a national (to the extent this information is known), in accordance with paragraph 10 of resolution 1735(2006), and requests the Secretariat to publish on the Committee website all relevant publicly releasable information, including the narrative summary of reasons for listing, immediately after a name is added to the Consolidated List;

19. *Reaffirms* the provisions in paragraph 17 of resolution 1822(2008) regarding the requirement that Member States take all possible measures, in accordance with their domestic laws and practices, to notify or inform in a timely manner the listed individual or entity of the designation and to include with this notification the narrative summary of reasons for listing, a description of the effects of designation, as provided in the relevant resolutions, the procedures of the Committee for considering de-listing requests, including the possibility of submitting such a request to the Ombudsperson in accordance with paragraphs 20 and 21 below and annex II to the present resolution, and the provisions of resolution 1452(2002) regarding available exemptions;

De-listing/Ombudsperson

20. *Decides* that, when considering de-listing requests, the Committee shall be assisted by an Office of the Ombudsperson, to be established for an initial period of eighteen months from the date of adoption of the present resolution, and requests the Secretary-General, in close consultation with the Committee, to appoint an eminent individual of high moral character, impartiality and integrity with high qualifications and experience in relevant fields, such as legal, human rights, counter-terrorism and sanctions, to be the Ombudsperson, with the mandate outlined in annex II to the present resolution, and further decides that the Ombudsperson shall perform these tasks in an independent and impartial manner and shall neither seek nor receive instructions from any Government;

21. *Decides also* that, after the appointment of the Ombudsperson, the Office of the Ombudsperson shall receive requests from individuals and entities seeking to be removed from the Consolidated List, in accordance with the procedures outlined in annex II to the present resolution, and that, after the appointment of the Ombudsperson, the Focal Point mechanism established in resolution 1730(2006) shall no longer receive such requests, and notes that the Focal Point shall continue to receive requests from individuals and entities seeking to be removed from other sanctions lists;

22. *Directs* the Committee to continue to work, in accordance with its guidelines, to consider de-listing requests of Member States for the removal from the Consolidated List of members and/or associates of Al-Qaida, Osama bin Laden or the Taliban who no longer meet the criteria established in the relevant resolutions, which shall be placed on the agenda of the Committee upon request of a member of the Committee;

23. *Encourages* States to submit de-listing requests for individuals that are officially confirmed to be dead, particu-

larly where no assets are identified, and for entities that have ceased to exist, while at the same time taking all reasonable measures to ensure that the assets that had belonged to these individuals or entities have not been or will not be transferred or distributed to other entities or individuals on the Consolidated List;

24.   *Encourages* Member States, when unfreezing the assets of a deceased individual or defunct entity as a result of a de-listing, to recall the obligations set forth in resolution 1373(2001) and, in particular, to prevent unfrozen assets from being used for terrorist purposes;

25.   *Encourages* the Committee to give due consideration to the opinions of the designating State(s) and State(s) of residence, nationality or incorporation when considering de-listing requests, and calls upon members of the Committee to make every effort to provide their reasons for objecting to such de-listing requests;

26.   *Requests* the Monitoring Team, upon conclusion of the review pursuant to paragraph 25 of resolution 1822(2008), to circulate to the Committee every six months a list of individuals on the Consolidated List who are reportedly deceased, along with an assessment of relevant information, such as the certification of death, and to the extent possible, the status and location of frozen assets and the names of any individuals or entities who would be in a position to receive any unfrozen assets, directs the Committee to review these listings to decide whether they remain appropriate, and encourages the Committee to remove listings of deceased individuals where credible information regarding death is available;

27.   *Decides* that the Secretariat shall, within three working days after a name is removed from the Consolidated List, notify the permanent mission of the country or countries where the individual or entity is believed to be located and, in the case of individuals, the country of which the person is a national (to the extent this information is known), and demands that States receiving such notification take measures, in accordance with their domestic laws and practices, to notify or inform the concerned individual or entity of the de-listing in a timely manner;

Review and maintenance of the Consolidated List

28.   *Encourages* all Member States, in particular designating States and States of residence or nationality, to submit to the Committee additional identifying and other information, along with supporting documentation, on listed individuals, groups, undertakings and entities, including updates on the operating status of listed entities, groups and undertakings, the movement, incarceration or death of listed individuals and other significant events, as such information becomes available;

29.   *Welcomes* the significant progress made by the Committee in its review of all names on the Consolidated List pursuant to paragraph 25 of resolution 1822(2008), directs the Committee to complete this review by 30 June 2010, and requests that all States concerned respond to requests from the Committee for information relevant to this review no later than 1 March 2010;

30.   *Requests* the Monitoring Team to submit a report to the Committee by 30 July 2010 on the outcome of the review described in paragraph 25 of resolution 1822(2008) and the efforts made by the Committee, Member States and the Monitoring Team to conduct the review;

31.   *Also requests* the Monitoring Team, upon conclusion of the review described in paragraph 25 of resolution 1822(2008), to circulate to the Committee annually a list of individuals and entities on the Consolidated List whose entries lack identifiers necessary to ensure effective implementation of the measures imposed upon them, and directs the Committee to review these listings to decide whether they remain appropriate;

32.   *Further directs* the Committee, upon completion of the review described in paragraph 25 of resolution 1822(2008), to conduct an annual review of all names on the Consolidated List that have not been reviewed in three or more years, in which the relevant names are circulated to the designating States and States of residence and/or citizenship, where known, pursuant to the procedures set forth in the Committee guidelines, in order to ensure that the Consolidated List is as updated and accurate as possible and to confirm that listing remains appropriate, and notes that the consideration by the Committee of a de-listing request after the date of adoption of the present resolution, pursuant to the procedures set out in annex II to the present resolution, should be considered equivalent to a review of that listing;

Measures—implementation

33.   *Reiterates* the importance of all States identifying, and if necessary introducing, adequate procedures to implement fully all aspects of the measures described in paragraph 1 above;

34.   *Encourages* the Committee to continue to ensure that fair and clear procedures exist for placing individuals and entities on the Consolidated List and for removing them, as well as for granting humanitarian exemptions, and directs the Committee to keep its guidelines under active review in support of these objectives;

35.   *Directs* the Committee, as a matter of priority, to review its guidelines with respect to the provisions of the present resolution, in particular paragraphs 7, 13, 14, 17, 18, 22, 23, 34 and 41;

36.   *Encourages* Member States and relevant international organizations to send representatives to meet with the Committee for more in-depth discussion of relevant issues, and welcomes voluntary briefings by interested Member States on their efforts to implement the measures referred to in paragraph 1 above, including particular challenges that hinder full implementation of the measures;

37.   *Requests* the Committee to report to the Council on its findings regarding implementation efforts by Member States, and to identify and recommend steps necessary to improve implementation;

38.   *Directs* the Committee to identify possible cases of non-compliance with the measures pursuant to paragraph 1 above and to determine the appropriate course of action on each case, and requests the Chair of the Committee, in periodic reports to the Council pursuant to paragraph 46 below, to provide progress reports on the work of the Committee on this issue;

39.   *Urges* all Member States, in their implementation of the measures set out in paragraph 1 above, to ensure that

fraudulent, counterfeit, stolen and lost passports and other travel documents are invalidated and removed from circulation, in accordance with domestic laws and practices, as soon as possible, and to share information on those documents with other Member States through the INTERPOL database;

40. *Encourages* Member States to share with the private sector, in accordance with their domestic laws and practices, information in their national databases related to fraudulent, counterfeit, stolen and lost identity or travel documents pertaining to their own jurisdictions and, if a listed party is found to be using a false identity, including to secure credit or fraudulent travel documents, to provide the Committee with information in this regard;

41. *Directs* the Committee to amend its guidelines to ensure that no matter is left pending before the Committee for a period longer than six months, unless the Committee determines on a case-by-case basis that extraordinary circumstances require additional time for consideration, and further directs any member of the Committee that has requested more time to consider a proposal to provide updates after three months of progress in resolving all pending matters;

42. *Also directs* the Committee to conduct a comprehensive review of all issues pending before the Committee as of the date of adoption of the present resolution, and further urges the Committee and its members to resolve all such pending issues, to the extent possible, by 31 December 2010;

Coordination and outreach

43. *Reiterates* the need to enhance ongoing cooperation between the Security Council Committee established pursuant to resolution 1267(1999), the Security Council Committee established pursuant to resolution 1373(2001) concerning counter-terrorism (the Counter-Terrorism Committee) and the Security Council Committee established pursuant to resolution 1540(2004), as well as their respective groups of experts, including through, as appropriate, enhanced information-sharing, and coordination on visits to countries within their respective mandates, on facilitating and monitoring technical assistance, on relations with international and regional organizations and agencies and on other issues of relevance to all three Committees, expresses its intention to provide guidance to the Committees on areas of common interest in order better to coordinate their efforts and facilitate such cooperation, and requests the Secretary-General to make the necessary arrangements for the groups of experts to be co-located as soon as possible;

44. *Encourages* the Monitoring Team and the United Nations Office on Drugs and Crime to continue their joint activities, in cooperation with the Counter-Terrorism Committee Executive Directorate and the experts of the Committee established pursuant to resolution 1540(2004), to assist Member States in their efforts to comply with their obligations under the relevant resolutions, including by organizing regional and subregional workshops;

45. *Requests* the Committee established pursuant to resolution 1267(1999) to consider, where and when appropriate, visits to selected countries by the Chair and/or members of the Committee to enhance the full and effective implementation of the measures referred to in paragraph 1 above, with a view to encouraging States to comply fully with the present resolution and resolutions 1267(1999), 1333(2000), 1390(2002), 1455(2003), 1526(2004), 1617(2005), 1735(2006) and 1822(2008);

46. *Also requests* the Committee to report orally, through its Chair, at least every one hundred and eighty days to the Council on the state of the overall work of the Committee and the Monitoring Team and, as appropriate, in conjunction with the reports of the Chairs of the Counter-Terrorism Committee and the Committee established pursuant to resolution 1540(2004), including briefings for all interested Member States;

Monitoring Team

47. *Decides*, in order to assist the Committee established pursuant to resolution 1267(1999) in fulfilling its mandate, as well as to support the Ombudsperson, to extend the mandate of the current New York-based Monitoring Team, established pursuant to paragraph 7 of resolution 1526(2004), for a further period of eighteen months, under the direction of the Committee, with the responsibilities outlined in annex I to the present resolution, and requests the Secretary-General to make the necessary arrangements to this effect;

Reviews

48. *Decides also* to review the measures described in paragraph 1 above with a view to their possible further strengthening in eighteen months, or sooner if necessary;

49. *Decides further* to remain actively seized of the matter.

ANNEX I

In accordance with paragraph 47 of this resolution, the Monitoring Team shall operate under the direction of the Security Council Committee established pursuant to resolution 1267(1999) and shall have the following responsibilities:

(a) To submit, in writing, two comprehensive, independent reports to the Committee, the first by 30 July 2010, in accordance with paragraph 30 above, and the second by 22 February 2011, on implementation by Member States of the measures referred to in paragraph 1 of this resolution, including specific recommendations for improved implementation of the measures and possible new measures;

(b) To assist the Ombudsperson in carrying out his or her mandate as specified in annex II of this resolution;

(c) To assist the Committee in regularly reviewing names on the Consolidated List, including by undertaking travel and contact with Member States, with a view to developing the Committee's record of the facts and circumstances relating to a listing;

(d) To analyse reports submitted pursuant to paragraph 6 of resolution 1455(2003), the checklists submitted pursuant to paragraph 10 of resolution 1617(2005) and other information submitted by Member States to the Committee, as instructed by the Committee;

(e) To assist the Committee in following up on requests to Member States for information, including with respect to implementation of the measures referred to in paragraph 1 of this resolution;

(f) To submit a comprehensive programme of work to the Committee for its review and approval, as necessary, in which the Monitoring Team should detail the activities envisaged in order to fulfil its responsibilities, including proposed travel, based on close coordination with the Counter-Terrorism Committee Executive Directorate and the group of experts of the Committee established pursuant to resolution 1540(2004) to avoid duplication and reinforce synergies;

(g) To work closely and share information with the Counter-Terrorism Committee Executive Directorate and the group of experts of the Committee established pursuant to resolution 1540(2004) to identify areas of convergence and overlap and to help to facilitate concrete coordination, including in the area of reporting, among the three Committees;

(h) To participate actively in and support all relevant activities under the United Nations Global Counter-Terrorism Strategy, including within the Counter-Terrorism Implementation Task Force established to ensure overall coordination and coherence in the counter-terrorism efforts of the United Nations system, in particular through its relevant working groups;

(i) To assist the Committee established pursuant to resolution 1267(1999) with its analysis of non-compliance with the measures referred to in paragraph 1 of this resolution by collating information collected from Member States and submitting case studies, both on its own initiative and upon the Committee's request, to the Committee for its review;

(j) To present to the Committee recommendations which could be used by Member States to assist them with the implementation of the measures referred to in paragraph 1 of this resolution and in preparing proposed additions to the Consolidated List;

(k) To assist the Committee in its consideration of proposals for listing, including by compiling and circulating to the Committee information relevant to the proposed listing, and preparing a draft narrative summary, referred to in paragraph 14 of this resolution;

(l) To bring to the attention of the Committee new or noteworthy circumstances that may warrant a de-listing, such as publicly reported information on a deceased individual;

(m) To consult with Member States in advance of travel to selected Member States, based on its programme of work as approved by the Committee;

(n) To coordinate and cooperate with the national counter-terrorism focal point or similar coordinating body in the country of the visit, where appropriate;

(o) To encourage Member States to submit names and additional identifying information for inclusion in the Consolidated List, as instructed by the Committee;

(p) To present to the Committee additional identifying and other information to assist the Committee in its efforts to keep the Consolidated List as updated and accurate as possible;

(q) To study and report to the Committee on the changing nature of the threat of Al-Qaida and the Taliban and the best measures to confront it, including by developing a dialogue with relevant scholars and academic bodies, in consultation with the Committee;

(r) To collate, assess, monitor and report on and make recommendations regarding implementation of the meas-

ures, including implementation of the measure in paragraph 1 *(a)* of this resolution as it pertains to preventing the criminal misuse of the Internet by Al-Qaida, Osama bin Laden and the Taliban, and other individuals, groups, undertakings and entities associated with them; to pursue case studies, as appropriate; and to explore in depth any other relevant issues as directed by the Committee;

(s) To consult with Member States and other relevant organizations, including through regular dialogue with representatives in New York and in capitals, taking into account their comments, especially regarding any issues that might be contained in the reports of the Monitoring Team referred to in paragraph *(a)* of this annex;

(t) To consult with Member States' intelligence and security services, including through regional forums, in order to facilitate the sharing of information and to strengthen enforcement of the measures;

(u) To consult with relevant representatives of the private sector, including financial institutions, to learn about the practical implementation of the assets freeze and to develop recommendations for the strengthening of that measure;

(v) To work with relevant international and regional organizations in order to promote awareness of, and compliance with, the measures;

(w) To work with INTERPOL and Member States to obtain photographs of listed individuals for possible inclusion in INTERPOL Special Notices;

(x) To assist other subsidiary bodies of the Security Council, and their expert panels, upon request, with enhancing their cooperation with INTERPOL, referred to in resolution 1699(2006);

(y) To report to the Committee, on a regular basis or when the Committee so requests, through oral and/or written briefings on the work of the Monitoring Team, including its visits to Member States and its activities;

(z) Any other responsibility identified by the Committee.

ANNEX II

In accordance with paragraph 20 of this resolution, the Office of the Ombudsperson shall be authorized to carry out the following tasks upon receipt of a de-listing request submitted by, or on behalf of, an individual, group, undertaking or entity on the Consolidated List ("the petitioner"):

Information-gathering (two months)

1. Upon receipt of a de-listing request, the Ombudsperson shall:

(a) Acknowledge to the petitioner the receipt of the de-listing request;

(b) Inform the petitioner of the general procedure for processing de-listing requests;

(c) Answer specific questions from the petitioner about Committee procedures;

(d) Inform the petitioner in case the petition fails to properly address the original designation criteria, as set forth in paragraph 2 of this resolution, and return it to the petitioner for his or her consideration; and

(e) Verify if the request is a new request or a repeated request and, if it is a repeated request to the Ombudsperson

and it does not contain any additional information, return it to the petitioner for his or her consideration.

2.   For de-listing petitions not returned to the petitioner, the Ombudsperson shall immediately forward the de-listing request to the members of the Committee, designating State(s), State(s) of residence and nationality or incorporation, relevant United Nations bodies and any other States deemed relevant by the Ombudsperson. The Ombudsperson shall ask these States or relevant United Nations bodies to provide, within two months, any appropriate additional information relevant to the de-listing request. The Ombudsperson may engage in dialogue with these States to determine:

(a)   The opinions of these States on whether the de-listing request should be granted; and

(b)   Information, questions or requests for clarifications that these States would like to be communicated to the petitioner regarding the de-listing request, including any information or steps that might be taken by a petitioner to clarify the de-listing request.

3.   The Ombudsperson shall also immediately forward the de-listing request to the Monitoring Team, which shall provide to the Ombudsperson, within two months:

(a)   All information available to the Monitoring Team that is relevant to the de-listing request, including court decisions and proceedings, news reports and information that States or relevant international organizations have previously shared with the Committee or the Monitoring Team;

(b)   Fact-based assessments of the information provided by the petitioner that is relevant to the de-listing request; and

(c)   Questions or requests for clarifications that the Monitoring Team would like asked of the petitioner regarding the de-listing request.

4.   At the end of this two-month period of information-gathering, the Ombudsperson shall present a written update to the Committee on progress to date, including details regarding which States have supplied information. The Ombudsperson may extend this period once for up to two months if he or she assesses that more time is required for information-gathering, giving due consideration to requests by Member States for additional time to provide information.

Dialogue (two months)

5.   Upon completion of the information-gathering period, the Ombudsperson shall facilitate a two-month period of engagement, which may include dialogue with the petitioner. Giving due consideration to requests for additional time, the Ombudsperson may extend this period once for up to two months if he or she assesses that more time is required for engagement and the drafting of the comprehensive report described in paragraph 7 below.

6.   During this period of engagement, the Ombudsperson:

(a)   May ask the petitioner questions or request additional information or clarifications that may help the Committee's consideration of the request, including any questions or information requests received from relevant States, the Committee and the Monitoring Team;

(b)   Shall forward replies from the petitioner back to relevant States, the Committee and the Monitoring Team and follow up with the petitioner in connection with incomplete responses by the petitioner; and

(c)   Shall coordinate with States, the Committee and the Monitoring Team regarding any further inquiries of, or response to, the petitioner.

7.   Upon completion of the period of engagement described above, the Ombudsperson, with the help of the Monitoring Team, shall draft and circulate to the Committee a comprehensive report that will exclusively:

(a)   Summarize and, as appropriate, specify the sources of, all information available to the Ombudsperson that is relevant to the de-listing request. The report shall respect confidential elements of Member States' communications with the Ombudsperson;

(b)   Describe the activities of the Ombudsperson with respect to this de-listing request, including dialogue with the petitioner; and

(c)   Based on an analysis of all the information available to the Ombudsperson and the observations of the Ombudsperson, lay out for the Committee the principal arguments concerning the de-listing request.

Committee discussion and decision (two months)

8.   After the Committee has had thirty days to review the comprehensive report, the Chair of the Committee shall place the de-listing request on the agenda of the Committee for consideration.

9.   When the Committee considers the de-listing request, the Ombudsperson, aided by the Monitoring Team, as appropriate, shall present the comprehensive report in person and answer Committee members' questions regarding the request.

10.   After the Committee's consideration, the Committee shall decide whether to approve the de-listing request through its normal decision-making procedures.

11.   If the Committee decides to grant the de-listing request, then the Committee shall inform the Ombudsperson of this decision. The Ombudsperson shall then inform the petitioner of this decision and the listing shall be removed from the Consolidated List.

12.   If the Committee decides to reject the de-listing request, then the Committee shall convey to the Ombudsperson its decision, including, as appropriate, explanatory comments, any further relevant information about the decision of the Committee, and an updated narrative summary of reasons for listing.

13.   After the Committee has informed the Ombudsperson that the Committee has rejected a de-listing request, then the Ombudsperson shall send to the petitioner, with an advance copy sent to the Committee, within fifteen days, a letter that:

(a)   Communicates the decision of the Committee for continued listing;

(b)   Describes, to the extent possible and drawing upon the comprehensive report of the Ombudsperson, the process and the publicly releasable factual information gathered by the Ombudsperson; and

(c)   Forwards from the Committee all information about the decision provided to the Ombudsperson pursuant to paragraph 12 above.

14.   In all communications with the petitioner, the Ombudsperson shall respect the confidentiality of Committee deliberations and confidential communications between the Ombudsperson and Member States.

Other tasks of the Office of the Ombudsperson

15. In addition to the tasks specified above, the Ombudsperson shall:

(a) Distribute publicly releasable information about Committee procedures, including Committee guidelines, fact sheets and other documents prepared by the Committee, to anyone who requests such information;

(b) Where their address is known, notify individuals or entities about the status of their listing, after the Secretariat has officially notified the permanent mission of the State or States, pursuant to paragraph 18 of this resolution; and

(c) Submit biannual reports summarizing the activities of the Ombudsperson to the Security Council.

Other communications

During 2009, the Security Council received a range of communications relating to the situation in Afghanistan. Those included a joint statement of 1 April by the Presidents of the Russian Federation and the United States [A/63/814-S/2009/192]; a statement of 6 May by the State Duma of the Russian Federation on the growing threat to international security posed by the spread of narcotic drugs from Afghanistan [A/63/865-S/2009/273]; the 14 June Declaration by the Heads of States members of the Collective Security Treaty Organization [A/63/916-S/2009/342]; the Yekaterinburg Declaration of the Heads of member States of the Shanghai Cooperation Organization (Yekaterinburg, Russian Federation, 15–16 June) [A/63/924 & A/63/931-S/2009/372]; a summary of the discussions and of the documents adopted by the Group of Eight Summit (L'Aquila, Italy, 8–10 July) [A/63/927-S/2009/358]; the Final Document of the Fifteenth Summit Conference of the Movement of Non-Aligned Countries (Sharm el-Sheikh, Egypt, 11–16 July) [A/63/965-S/2009/514]; the statement of 26 August by the Community of Democracies Convening Group on the elections in Afghanistan [A/63/954]; the Final Communiqué of the Annual Coordination Meeting of Ministers for Foreign Affairs of the States members of the Organization of the Islamic Conference (New York, 25 September) [A/64/614-S/2009/677]; and the Nakhchivan Declaration signed by the Presidents of Azerbaijan, Kazakhstan, Kyrgyzstan and Turkey at the Ninth Summit of the Heads of the Turkic-speaking Countries (Nakhchivan City, Azerbaijan, 3 October) [A/64/522-S/2009/580].

Iraq

Situation in Iraq

In 2009, the United Nations, through the Secretary-General's Special Representative for Iraq and the United Nations Assistance Mission for Iraq (UNAMI), continued to assist the country in its transition to democratic governance and in promoting reconstruction and reconciliation. On 30 June, Staffan de Mistura (Sweden) completed his assignment as Special Representative and in July was succeeded by Ad Melkert (Netherlands). On 7 August, by resolution 1883(2009) (see p. 367), the Security Council extended UNAMI's mandate until 7 August 2010. On 21 December, by resolution 1905(2009) (see p. 372), the Council extended until 31 December 2010 the arrangements for the deposit of oil revenues into the Development Fund for Iraq and for its monitoring by the International Advisory and Monitoring Board.

UN Assistance Mission for Iraq

UNAMI, established by Security Council resolution 1500(2003) [YUN 2003, p. 346], continued to support the Secretary-General in fulfilling his mandate under Council resolution 1483(2003) [ibid., p. 338], as extended by resolution 1546(2004) [YUN 2004, p. 348]. The Secretary-General's Special Representative and Head of UNAMI and his substantive, security and administrative support staff were based in Baghdad, with regional offices in Arbil, Basra and Kirkuk.

During the year, the Secretary-General submitted four reports on UNAMI activities [S/2009/102, S/2009/284, S/2009/393, S/2009/585].

Provincial elections (January). The Security Council, in a press statement of 3 February [SC/9587], welcomed the holding of provincial elections in Iraq on 31 January. Expressing its appreciation to Iraq's Independent High Electoral Commission, the Council looked forward to the announcement of the Commission certifying the election results.

Report of Secretary-General (February). In his report on UNAMI activities [S/2009/102], submitted in response to resolution 1830(2008) [YUN 2008, p. 387] and summarizing developments since his November 2008 report [ibid., p. 388], the Secretary-General said that the successful holding of provincial elections on 31 January signified an encouraging accomplishment for Iraq. Millions of Iraqis had exercised their right to vote in an environment largely free of violence, in the first fully Iraqi-led and Iraqi-owned electoral process. On 6 February, he had paid his second visit to Iraq to commend its people, Government and the Independent High Electoral Commission on the conduct of the elections, and to offer the continued support of the United Nations. The implementation phase of the United States-Iraq bilateral security agreement [YUN 2008, p. 389] began on 1 January, and the handover process, including transfer of control of Baghdad's international zone, had been proceeding without major incident.

Unami continued giving priority attention to Iraq's disputed internal boundaries, working with the parliamentary committee set up according to Iraq's provincial elections law. The committee was tasked with determining a power-sharing formula before provincial elections were held in the Kirkuk Governorate; assessing the issue of property disputes; and considering demographic issues with UN technical assistance. On 2 February, unami facilitated the first trip of the committee's seven members to Kirkuk. Since that visit, the committee had begun to meet in Baghdad in the presence of unami. Unami also continued to provide support to the Government in its relations with neighbouring countries, and representation from the neighbouring countries was steadily increasing in Baghdad.

With respect to the 31 January elections, preliminary estimates pointed to a voter turnout of 51 per cent of the approximately 15 million eligible voters, which compared favourably with subnational election turnouts in other countries. Iraqi men and women from all communities had participated. Special procedures were put in place in advance of the election to enable the participation in the electoral process of some 600,000 police officers and military personnel who would be on duty on the polling day, as well as hospital patients and detainees. The Independent High Electoral Commission had recruited and trained more than 260,000 staff to work in more than 7,000 polling centres and 42,000 polling stations throughout the country—including polling stations to allow approximately 63,000 internally displaced persons to vote by absentee ballot for their governorate of origin.

A sharp decline in oil prices signalled a difficult budget year. The lack of private-sector growth was likely to add to those challenges, particularly for Iraq's labour force. The 2009 consolidated appeal for Iraq and the subregion, launched in November 2008, brought together humanitarian organizations from 12 countries to support Iraqis. It aimed at providing relief for those most vulnerable inside Iraq, including returnee families; supporting Iraqi refugees in safety and dignity until return was possible; and offering a platform for dialogue between Iraq and its neighbours on issues of common concern. The final appeal requested $192 million for activities inside Iraq and $355 million for activities outside Iraq, the latter to be coordinated by the Office of the United Nations High Commissioner for Refugees (unhcr).

In recent months, Iraq had witnessed gradual stabilization and further improvements in security conditions, with a lower number of violent, high-visibility, mass-casualty attacks by militias, insurgents and criminal gangs. Nonetheless, indiscriminate attacks by roadside, car or suicide bombs were almost a daily occurrence. A troubling aspect was the frequent use of women, and occasionally even children, as suicide bombers. In the weeks leading up to the January provincial elections, some killings of political candidates and electoral workers were recorded. Targeted killings or other types of attacks against journalists, educators, parliamentarians, humanitarian workers, judges, lawyers and members of minorities remained a worrying feature. In the Kurdistan region, journalists were subject to violent attacks, threats and lawsuits. The overall situation of detainees countrywide, including the Kurdistan region, remained of great concern. Many had been deprived of their liberty for months or even years, often in poor conditions, without access to defence counsel or without being formally charged with a crime or brought before a judge.

In addition to the $5 million approved by the General Assembly for work on the design of the unami integrated headquarters in Baghdad, which remained essential for the continued delivery of the Mission's mandate, the Prime Minister, Nuri Kamel al-Maliki, had confirmed his cabinet's decision to allocate $25 million towards the compound, which was a welcome development. Construction of new accommodation and office buildings in the Arbil regional office were well advanced, allowing staff permanently deployed to the office to move from prefabricated accommodation to the new building. The new logistical facilities at the Baghdad International Airport were also nearing completion.

Following the passage of the bilateral security agreement between the Governments of Iraq and the United States, the Iraqi Security Forces had assumed authority over the security environment in the international zone. Although the transfer of responsibilities would be gradual, the overall reduction in the role of the multinational force could begin to have an impact on the logistical and security resources available to support UN operations over the next six months. In the northern provinces of the Kurdish regional government, the security environment remained stable. Turkey had reportedly withdrawn a significant number of ground forces from the border areas of Dahuk and Arbil, but sporadic aerial bombardment continued. Most often, those attacks did not hit populated areas.

Security Council consideration (February). Briefing the Council on 26 February [meeting 6087], the Secretary-General's Special Representative, Mr. de Mistura, said that Iraq had taken a significant step forward with its provincial elections on 31 January, and highlighted the increasing capability of the Iraqi security forces over recent months and the improvement of the security situation. The representative of Iraq presented the views of the Government on the Secretary-General's report.

Attacks in Baghdad and Diyala. In a 25 April press statement [SC/9643], the Security Council condemned the terrorist attacks in Baghdad and Diyala on 23 and 24 April, which caused numerous deaths and injuries. The Council reaffirmed its support for the Government and its determination to combat all forms of terrorism.

Report of Secretary-General (June). In his report on UNAMI activities [S/2009/284], submitted in response to resolution 1830(2008), the Secretary-General summarized developments since his February report. He said that the release of governorate election results on 26 March had set in motion the process of the formation of provincial councils in the 14 governorates where elections took place in January. Muthanna was the last governorate to form its provincial council, with its new governor selected on 30 April. UNAMI continued its support for the Independent High Electoral Commission in preparation for a series of upcoming electoral activities, starting with the regional presidential and parliamentary elections in the Kurdistan region scheduled for 25 July, and culminating in the Council of Representatives elections in all 18 governorates at the end of 2009 or early in 2010.

On 6 March, Prime Minister al-Maliki had renewed calls for national reconciliation, including the need for outreach to former Baath Party cadres and officials. Sunni Vice-President Tariq al-Hashemi stressed that the reconciliation process required time and entailed incentives, including the possibility of more powers through constitutional amendments for the Sunni constituency to overcome years of mistrust. The reconciliation process remained delicate. Tensions flared on 28 March when a prominent Awakening Council leader in central Baghdad was arrested for allegedly having been involved in sectarian violence. Ayad al-Samarrai, a Tawafuq nominee and Vice-President al-Hashemi's deputy in the Iraqi Islamic Party, was elected the new Speaker of Parliament on 19 April, bringing to a close a four-month political impasse that followed the resignation of the previous Speaker in December 2008.

Although the overall security situation had improved, there had been a spike in indiscriminate and violent mass attacks, causing unacceptably high civilian casualties. A new wave of suicide bombings culminated in a coordinated series of four bomb blasts across Iraq on 23 March leaving at least 32 people dead and scores wounded. There were nearly 20 suicide bombings in April, with 355 Iraqis killed, making it the deadliest month in 2009. More than 80 Iranian pilgrims were also reportedly killed during the same month. On 20 May, a car bomb in northwest Baghdad killed 40 people and injured more than 70, followed the next day by a series of bombings in

Baghdad and Kirkuk that killed at least 23 people and injured many more.

The activities of UNAMI and the Special Representative had focused with renewed urgency on the disputed internal boundaries, with a view to promoting political dialogue between the Government and the Kurdistan regional government. UNAMI had prepared 15 reports on districts in four governorates across northern Iraq, from the border with the Syrian Arab Republic to the border with Iran. Analytical rather than prescriptive, the reports made no specific suggestions regarding the future administrative jurisdiction of those areas. A discussion paper on the status of the disputed city of Kirkuk offered four options, all of which used the Constitution as the starting point, treated the governorate as a single entity and required a political agreement among the parties over a transitional period, which could then be endorsed by way of a confirmatory referendum. UNAMI also continued to support the parliamentary committee on Kirkuk set up according to article 23 of the provincial elections law.

The reporting period witnessed a number of high-level visits to Iraq, which served to further strengthen bilateral contacts between Iraq and its neighbours. UNAMI was engaged in discussing ways of advancing the regional integration of Iraq, including by incorporating regional engagement into the new priorities of the International Compact with Iraq [YUN 2006, p. 391]. To facilitate dialogue on unresolved constitutional issues, the Mission's Office of Constitutional Support held a round-table discussion with Iraqi policymakers on 7 and 8 April to consider hydrocarbon management in the context of a federal system; a similar round table was organized in Erbil, with a broader pool of participants.

Some $1.3 billion, channelled through the International Reconstruction Fund Facility for Iraq to the United Nations, had delivered tangible, physical goods which improved the lives of the beneficiaries, despite an often difficult operating environment. The closure of the Facility for Iraq to new contributions, agreed at the eighth meeting of its Donor Committee in February, marked the start of a transition for UN assistance in Iraq. Contributions to the Facility would cease as at 30 June, with no new projects approved beyond 31 December and no new contractual commitments after 2010. Iraq would now enter a new phase of bilateral international assistance. To facilitate that process, UN agencies, funds and programmes decided to embark on a full United Nations Development Assistance Framework (UNDAF) for Iraq from 2011 to 2014, an approach endorsed by the Government in April.

Despite a spike in violence, Iraq continued to see displaced families returning at a steady pace, with the number of families that had returned since early

2008 reaching nearly 50,000, most of which had been internally displaced. Emergency relief operations by the United Nations and its partners continued to address disease outbreaks, food insecurity and chronic deprivation. UN assistance included the provision of food assistance to some 630,000 internally displaced persons countrywide by the World Food Programme (WFP). The World Health Organization received more than $1 million from the Central Emergency Response Fund to mobilize an emergency immunization campaign, in conjunction with the United Nations Children's Fund (UNICEF), to contain the continuing measles outbreak in five governorates. UNICEF also provided emergency assistance to 68 of the country's most vulnerable subdistricts, which were home to 1.6 million people, addressing access to water, sanitation, health care, education and psychosocial support.

UNAMI remained concerned about continuing deficiencies in the administration of justice and the rule-of-law sector—particularly the practice of relying heavily on confessions in criminal trial proceedings and harsh interrogation procedures that might amount, in some cases, to torture. In addition, UNAMI received credible information that some detainees were rearrested by Iraqi authorities immediately upon their release from detention facilities controlled by the multinational force. Honour-related killings and other forms of violence against women continued to be reported as accidents, attempts at suicide or suicide. UNAMI engaged members of the Government and national civil society organizations in raising awareness of women's rights and provided support to initiatives aimed at eradicating violence against women.

In line with the bilateral security agreement, the United States military had begun to withdraw from a number of bases and joint security stations across the country, and the Iraqi Security Forces were increasingly taking over security responsibilities. Overall, Kurdistan regional government areas remained stable, thereby allowing a more expansive programme of outreach activities by UNAMI and the UN country team. However, there was still a threat of militant elements infiltrating from other regions. Insurgent activity in Anbar province was concentrated along the Ramadi-Fallujah corridor, with isolated incidents reported in the vicinity of Al-Qaim (border area) and Hit. Incident levels remained low across southern Iraq, with the exception of two suicide attacks on pilgrims travelling to Karbala in February, and two car bomb attacks in the northern area of Al-Hillah.

Security Council consideration (June). Briefing the Council on 18 June [meeting 6145] prior to the completion of his assignment on 30 June, the Special Representative reviewed recent developments, stressing the improvements in the security situation as well as the continued need to work towards na-

tional reconciliation. He also recounted the activities of UNAMI, with emphasis on its study regarding the disputed internal administrative boundaries and its continued assistance to the Iraqi people and Government in preparation for the upcoming elections. At the end of the meeting, in which the representative of Iraq also participated, the Council adopted a presidential statement.

SECURITY COUNCIL ACTION

On 18 June [meeting 6145], following consultations among Security Council members, the President made statement **S/PRST/2009/17** on behalf of the Council:

The Security Council reaffirms its commitment to the independence, sovereignty, unity and territorial integrity of Iraq, and emphasizes the importance of the stability and security of Iraq for its people, the region and the international community.

The Council commends the important efforts made by the Government of Iraq to strengthen democracy and the rule of law, to improve security and public order and to combat terrorism and sectarian violence across the country, and reiterates its support to the people and the Government of Iraq in their efforts to build a secure, stable, united and democratic country, based on the rule of law and respect for human rights.

The Council reaffirms its full support for the United Nations Assistance Mission for Iraq in advising, supporting and assisting the people and Government of Iraq to strengthen democratic institutions, advance inclusive political dialogue and national reconciliation, facilitate regional dialogue, aid vulnerable groups, strengthen gender equality, promote the protection of human rights, including through the work of the Independent High Commission for Human Rights, and promote judicial and legal reform.

The Council encourages the continued work of the Mission, in coordination with the Government of Iraq, to help to create conditions conducive to the voluntary, safe, dignified and sustainable return of Iraqi refugees and internally displaced persons, and welcomes further attention to this issue by all concerned.

The Council underscores the important role of the Mission in supporting the people and Government of Iraq to promote dialogue, ease tension and develop a just and fair solution for the nation's disputed internal boundaries, and calls upon all the relevant parties to participate in an inclusive dialogue to this end.

The Council emphasizes the efforts of the Mission to assist the Government of Iraq and the Independent High Electoral Commission in the development of processes for holding elections. The Council strongly endorses the continued assistance of the Mission to the people and Government of Iraq in preparation for the upcoming elections.

The Council congratulates Mr. Staffan de Mistura, the departing Special Representative of the Secretary-General for Iraq, on his strong leadership of the Mission, and expresses deep gratitude to all the United Nations staff in Iraq for their courageous and tireless efforts.

New Special Representative. On 6 July [S/2009/346], the Secretary-General informed the Security Council that he intended to appoint Ad Melkert (Netherlands) as his Special Representative for Iraq and Head of UNAMI, to succeed Mr. de Mistura (Sweden), who had completed his assignment on 30 June. The Council took note of that intention on 8 July [S/2009/347].

Reports of Secretary-General (July). In his 30 July report on UNAMI operations [S/2009/393], the Secretary-General said that Iraq was once again entering a crucial period, highlighted by its increased responsibility for the security of the country and important national elections planned for January 2010. While an increase in violence had been anticipated during the redeployment of the United States military from cities on 30 June, a relative calm was achieved, and the Iraq security forces had succeeded in assuming security responsibilities in critical parts of the country. It was also encouraging that national institutions—especially the Independent High Electoral Commission—had developed their own expertise in implementing election activities. Most recently, elections had been conducted successfully in the Kurdistan region without incident. The challenge now was to maintain the transparency and independence of the Electoral Commission while establishing a strong platform from which to ensure that there was acceptance of the election results.

On 10 June, UNAMI launched the High-level Task Force to advance dialogue between senior representatives of the Government and the Kurdistan regional government on the UNAMI reports on disputed internal boundaries. The relationship between the Federal Government in Baghdad and the leadership of the Iraqi Kurdistan region was a matter of concern, and tensions had also arisen between Kurdish security forces and non-Kurdish communities in areas outside the Kurdistan region. In the light of the adoption of the draft Kurdistan regional constitution, which laid claim to areas under discussion in the Task Force, the Secretary-General called for an end to provocative statements, including those that prejudged in any way the future of areas such as Kirkuk, and to any unilateral actions that the other side would be likely to see as hostile in intent.

UNAMI and the Council of Representatives conducted a high-level conference (Baghdad, 14–15 June) on hydrocarbon revenue-sharing and water resource management, an area in which legislation was being held up because of disagreement between Baghdad and Arbil on definitive allocations of revenue to the Kurdistan regional government and on the financing of national infrastructure projects. There was more ground for consensus in the water-sharing discussions, given the common interest among all Iraqis in securing greater access to transboundary water flows from Iran, Syria and Turkey, especially during the current prolonged period of water shortage in Iraq.

The voter registration update for Iraqi Kurdistan, monitored by over 5,563 Iraqi observers and political party representatives, was deemed successful, and for the first time, the Electoral Commission managed the entire process. On 25 July, the people of the Kurdistan region turned out in large numbers to exercise their right to elect new regional representatives and the President of the region in an orderly environment that was notably free of violence.

The Secretary-General welcomed Iraq's decision to embark on a comprehensive, five-year National Development Plan 2010–2014, the first step of which was launched in June. Efforts to redefine the direction of the International Compact with Iraq and tailor it more strategically to Iraq's emerging context had also moved forward, and the Government had undertaken to work with international partners in defining benchmarks to be achieved. As a first step towards establishing the UNDAF 2011–2014—which would be the primary tool to ensure that the UN system could adapt to the evolving needs of Iraq, both structurally and substantively—the common country assessment was launched on 22 June in Baghdad, at the largest joint Government-UN event to be held in Iraq since 2003.

The humanitarian situation remained precarious, mainly because of insecurity and the difficulties of accessing those most in need. The combined requirements of the 2009 consolidated appeals process for Iraq and the region now totalled $650 million, including more than $341 million designated to assist the estimated 1.7 million Iraqis who had sought refuge in the neighbouring countries and beyond. The requirements for pillar 1 of the 2009 appeals process, which addressed the needs of vulnerable Iraqis inside the country, had increased by over a third to $308 million. UNAMI continued to collaborate closely with UNHCR in supporting the authorities with the return of refugees and internally displaced persons.

With drought expected to reduce wheat production by 35 per cent and exacerbate poverty levels, FAO conducted the construction and maintenance of 120 micro-irrigation schemes, while the United Nations Office for Project Services rehabilitated the water distribution systems in Arbil Governorate, improving water quality for 30,000 people. Preparations for the Iraq Population and Housing Census continued, with the support of the United Nations Population Fund. On 1 July, the United Nations Development Programme (UNDP) and UNICEF jointly launched a report reviewing progress made in mine action since entry into force in 2008 of the Ottawa Landmine Convention, and the United Nations Office on Drugs and

Crime (UNODC) was working to design more effective countermeasures for a national anti-corruption strategy.

UNAMI was organizing training for 25 civil society organizations on elements of human rights monitoring and was supporting a UNODC project to review anti-terrorism legislation in the context of international human rights standards. There were 31 executions during the reporting period despite the calls by UNAMI, the Office of the United Nations High Commissioner for Human Rights and other international organizations to the Government to institute a moratorium on the death penalty while undertaking an investigation into all allegations of abuse of authority in detention and reviewing the criminal legislation and procedures in the light of international standards and Iraq's obligations under international law.

In Baghdad, the targeting of political figures continued, including the assassination, on 12 June, of Harith al-Ubaidi, the parliamentary leader of the largest Sunni political bloc. Early in July, the apparent orchestration of a series of attacks on Christian churches using explosive devices was reported in Baghdad and Mosul, leaving at least four dead and dozens wounded, including children. Incident levels remained high in northern Iraq as armed opposition groups continued attempts to exploit tension, especially within the disputed territories, but incident levels across southern Iraq remained relatively low. Overall, the evolving nature of the security environment posed significant challenges in safeguarding UN personnel and assets.

On 30 June, Staffan de Mistura completed his 18-month tenure as the Secretary-General's Special Representative; Ad Melkert was appointed to fill that position on 9 July.

Security Council consideration (August). On 4 August [meeting 6177], the Council reviewed the Secretary-General's quarterly report [S/2009/393], hearing a briefing by Mr. Melkert. The new Special Representative said that the time had come to place economic and social conditions up front. With one third of Iraq's youth unemployed, a significant budget deficit combined with debt service and compensation obligations, drought and agricultural under-performance, as well as the reluctance of investors, there was a strong case for joining forces to invest in the productivity and social cohesion of the country. Eventually, progress should not only be measured at the level of political authorities, but also be tangible for Iraqis in their jobs, schools, hospitals and homes.

The representative of Iraq also addressed the Council.

Extension of UNAMI mandate

In a 29 July letter to the Security Council [S/2009/395], Iraqi Foreign Minister Hoshyar Zebari conveyed his Government's wish that UNAMI's mandate be extended for a 12-month period. The Government looked forward to a more effective role for UNAMI with the return to Iraq of the UN specialized agencies, funds and programmes and their direct and valuable contribution to its reconstruction.

SECURITY COUNCIL ACTION

On 7 August [meeting 6179], the Security Council unanimously adopted **resolution 1883(2009)**. The draft [S/2009/406] was submitted by the United Kingdom and the United States.

The Security Council,

Recalling all its previous relevant resolutions on Iraq, in particular resolutions 1500(2003) of 14 August 2003, 1546(2004) of 8 June 2004, 1557(2004) of 12 August 2004, 1619(2005) of 11 August 2005, 1700(2006) of 10 August 2006, 1770(2007) of 10 August 2007 and 1830(2008) of 7 August 2008,

Reaffirming the independence, sovereignty, unity and territorial integrity of Iraq,

Emphasizing the importance of the stability and security of Iraq for the people of Iraq, the region and the international community,

Commending the important efforts made by the Government of Iraq to strengthen democracy and the rule of law, to improve security and public order and to combat terrorism and sectarian violence across the country, and reiterating its support for the people and Government of Iraq in their efforts to build a secure, stable, federal, united and democratic nation, based on the rule of law and respect for human rights,

Welcoming improvements in the security situation in Iraq achieved through concerted political and security efforts, and stressing that challenges to security in Iraq still exist and that improvements need to be sustained through meaningful political dialogue and national unity,

Underscoring the need for all communities in Iraq to participate in the political process and an inclusive political dialogue, to refrain from statements and actions which could aggravate tensions, to reach a comprehensive solution on the distribution of resources, and to develop a just and fair solution for the nation's disputed internal boundaries and work towards national unity,

Reaffirming the importance of the United Nations, in particular the United Nations Assistance Mission for Iraq, in advising, supporting and assisting the people and Government of Iraq to strengthen democratic institutions, advance inclusive political dialogue and national reconciliation, facilitate regional dialogue, aid vulnerable groups, including refugees and internally displaced persons, strengthen gender equality, promote the protection of human rights, and promote judicial and legal reform, and emphasizing the importance of the United Nations, in particular the Mission, prioritizing advice, support and assistance to the people and Government of Iraq to achieve these goals,

Emphasizing the efforts of the Mission to assist the Independent High Electoral Commission and the Government of Iraq in the development of processes for holding successful Iraqi provincial elections in January 2009 and Kurdistan Regional Government elections in July 2009, and towards Iraqi national parliamentary elections in January 2010, and stressing the importance of the transparency, impartiality and independence of the Commission,

Expressing concern about human rights challenges in Iraq, stressing the importance of addressing those challenges, and in this regard urging the Government of Iraq to consider additional steps to support the Independent High Commission for Human Rights,

Expressing concern also about the humanitarian issues confronting the Iraqi people, and stressing the need to continue a coordinated response and to provide adequate resources to address those issues,

Underscoring the sovereignty of the Government of Iraq, reaffirming that all parties should continue to take all feasible steps and develop modalities to ensure the protection of affected civilians, including children, women and members of religious and ethnic minority groups, and should create conditions conducive to the voluntary, safe, dignified and sustainable return of refugees and internally displaced persons, welcoming commitments of the Government for the relief of internally displaced persons, encouraging continued efforts for internally displaced persons and refugees, and noting the important role of the Office of the United Nations High Commissioner for Refugees, based on its mandate, in providing advice and support to the Government, in coordination with the Mission,

Stressing the importance of implementing Security Council resolution 1882(2009) of 4 August 2009, including through the appointment of child protection advisers in the Mission, as appropriate,

Urging all those concerned, as set forth in international humanitarian law, including the Geneva Conventions of 1949 and the Regulations annexed to the Hague Convention IV of 1907, to allow full unimpeded access by humanitarian personnel to all people in need of assistance and to make available, as far as possible, all facilities necessary for their operations, and to promote the safety, security and freedom of movement of humanitarian personnel and United Nations and associated personnel and their assets,

Thanking Mr. Staffan de Mistura, former Special Representative of the Secretary-General for Iraq, for his service and strong leadership of the Mission,

Welcoming the appointment by the Secretary-General on 7 July 2009 of Mr. Ad Melkert as the new Special Representative for Iraq,

Expressing deep gratitude to all United Nations staff in Iraq for their courageous and tireless efforts,

1.   *Decides* to extend the mandate of the United Nations Assistance Mission for Iraq for a period of twelve months from the date of the present resolution;

2.   *Decides also* that the Special Representative of the Secretary-General for Iraq and the Mission, at the request of the Government of Iraq, and taking into account the letter dated 29 July 2009 from the Minister for Foreign Affairs of Iraq to the Secretary-General, shall continue to pursue their expanded mandate as stipulated in resolutions 1770(2007) and 1830(2008);

3.   *Recognizes* that the security of United Nations personnel is essential for the Mission to carry out its work for the benefit of the people of Iraq, and calls upon the Government of Iraq and other Member States to continue to provide security and logistical support to the United Nations presence in Iraq;

4.   *Welcomes* the contributions of Member States in providing the Mission with the financial, logistical and security resources and support that it needs to fulfil its mission, and calls upon Member States to continue to provide the Mission with these resources and support;

5.   *Expresses its intention* to review the mandate of the Mission in twelve months or sooner, if requested by the Government of Iraq;

6.   *Requests* the Secretary-General to report to the Security Council on a quarterly basis on the progress made towards the fulfilment of all the responsibilities of the Mission;

7.   *Decides* to remain seized of the matter.

Terrorist attacks. In a 19 August press statement [SC/9733], Security Council members condemned that day's series of terrorist attacks that caused numerous deaths, injuries and damage, including at the Ministry of Foreign of Affairs, other Government ministries and diplomatic missions. Noting that such tragedy had occurred on the sixth anniversary of the bombing of the UN Baghdad headquarters [YUN 2003, p. 346] that killed 22 people, including Sergio Vieira de Mello, the United Nations coordinator for Iraq, the Council reiterated its support for the humanitarian work of the United Nations and its staff in Iraq. The Council underlined the need to bring perpetrators, organizers, financiers and sponsors of those acts of terrorism to justice, and urged all States to cooperate with Iraqi authorities in that regard.

In a 26 October press statement [SC/9775], Council members condemned the series of terrorist attacks that had occurred on 25 October in Baghdad, causing numerous deaths, injuries and damage, including at the Ministry of Justice and the Baghdad governorate building.

Letter from Iraq. On 3 November, the Secretary-General transmitted to the Security Council a letter [S/2009/573] from Iraqi Foreign Minister Hoshyar Zebari, who referred to the Prime Minister's letter of 30 August on the terrorist attack of 19 August in Baghdad, which had targeted Government institutions, as well as to his letter of 25 September, which conveyed Iraq's desire for a high-level international envoy to be dispatched to assess the extent of foreign involvement in terrorist acts committed in Iraq and their impact on its stability and security.

Before the Council was able to take any practical measure in response to that request, he said, Baghdad had once again been the target of two simultaneous terrorist attacks on 25 October. The attacks, which killed and injured a large number of innocent civilians, had targeted Government institutions in the same manner as the previous attacks—confirming Iraq's view that they were intended to paralyse the

State and its institutions and to abort the democratic political process under way. His country therefore repeated its request for a high-level international envoy to be appointed to assess the extent of foreign involvement in terrorist acts committed in Iraq, since organized attacks of such size and complexity could not have been planned, funded and executed without significant support from outside parties. He called for that matter to be brought to the Council's attention as soon as possible, so that appropriate action to deter terrorism and its sponsors might be taken.

Report of Secretary-General (November). In a report on UNAMI's activities [S/2009/585] submitted in response to resolution 1883(2009), the Secretary-General said that on 17 August, the Independent High Electoral Commission had announced the certified results of the Kurdistan regional elections of 25 July, with incumbent President Masoud Barzani winning the election with a clear majority of ballots cast. The Iraqi Kurdistan Parliament nominated Iraq's Deputy Prime Minister, Barham Saleh, to serve as Prime Minister of the Kurdistan regional government, and he was appointed by President Barzani on 30 September to serve in that role. A cabinet was also formed with considerably fewer ministers than in the past, owing to a consolidation of regional government ministries.

After intense negotiations, and with technical assistance from UNAMI, the Council of Representatives reached agreement on amendments to the Electoral Law on 8 November—paving the way for the holding of elections in January 2010, as stipulated by the Constitutional Court. Those amendments included increasing the number of seats from 275 to 323, changing the electoral system to an open list, special measures for minority groups and an agreement on holding elections in Kirkuk.

To ensure a credible and accepted national election process, a programme to update the voter registry took place between 22 August and 30 September. Over 1.5 million Iraqis visited one of 1,082 voter registration centres to verify their data or add their names to the voter list, and the Commission was processing approximately 40,000 data forms per day in the data entry centre in Baghdad. The Commission had distributed almost 18 million voter information cards, informing voters where to cast their ballots. It had also accredited 187 domestic observer groups and the agents of 78 political entities, covering over 25,000 observers.

The Secretary-General's new Special Representative assumed his duties in Baghdad on 21 August, focusing on the promotion of political dialogue between the Government and the Kurdistan regional government on outstanding issues, and on preparations for the national elections. Senior advisers to the Iraqi Prime Minister and the President of the Kurdistan regional government continued to meet regularly, under UNAMI auspices, through the High-Level Task Force, to discuss the UNAMI reports on disputed internal boundaries.

On 19 August and 25 October, coordinated attacks had targeted key government institutions in Baghdad, including the Ministries of Foreign Affairs, Finance and Justice and the office of Baghdad's provincial council, resulting in the deaths of several hundred and the injury of many more. In response to requests from Iraq's Foreign Minister on 25 September and 28 October to appoint a high-level official to assess the attacks, the Secretary-General sent a team to Iraq led by Assistant Secretary-General Oscar Fernandez-Taranco to conduct preliminary consultations.

On the regional level, Iraq's Prime Minister visited Syria on 17 August and met with its President, in a move that both countries hailed as historic. The first ministerial meeting of the High-Level Strategic Cooperation Council between Iraq and Turkey was held in Istanbul on 17 September. To address the deterioration of the water situation in Iraq, the Ministers of Water of Iraq, Syria and Turkey met in Ankara on 3 September, when Turkey announced that it would increase the flow of water to Iraq and Syria.

The Government's efforts to chart a clear and strategic development trajectory through the National Development Plan 2010–2014 were nearly complete. At the Government's request, the UN country team had provided detailed comments on 12 sectoral analysis papers intended to form the foundation of the Plan and would provide further technical support. The United Nations viewed the Plan as the guiding document for its future effort in Iraq. In addition to its support for capacity-building and policy formation at the national level, the United Nations aimed to be more creative in meeting local needs by supporting job creation, better services and civic participation for all vulnerable groups in areas with high levels of return.

Preparations to hold the population and housing census in October had been postponed to October 2010, owing to technical and political challenges. On a positive note, and following advocacy efforts by the United Nations—particularly UNDP and UNICEF—the civilian demining activities that had been suspended since December 2008 resumed during the reporting period.

Funding for humanitarian action and early recovery was still greatly needed. Pillar 1 of the 2009 consolidated appeal process for Iraq was currently 44 per cent funded ($134,837,848 from the revised midyear requirement of $308,794,656), leaving many sectors critically underfunded, especially agriculture and mine action. Support was still needed to tackle Iraq's drought and desertification crisis, with rainfall remaining at 50 per cent below normal levels, river flows low, and Iraq generating only two thirds of the 10 million cubic metres of potable water required per day.

The establishment of an Independent High Commission for Human Rights continued to move forward, with the support of UNAMI. The UNAMI Human Rights Office continued to work to build the capacity of both civil society and the Government to ensure compliance with UN mechanisms for reporting on human rights—in particular, for preparation of the universal periodic review submission to the Human Rights Council. The UNAMI Human Rights Office had also continued to visit prisons nationwide to assess the situation of detainees and their conditions in order to build a human rights-based training programme for prison management.

Security Council consideration (November). On 16 November [meeting 6218], the Council reviewed the Secretary-General's quarterly report [S/2009/585], hearing a briefing by his Special Representative for Iraq, who said that the coming period should lay the foundation for Iraq's return to the league of middle-income countries, in conjunction with a jump in social development that was within reach if business initiatives were to thrive and oil revenues were spent wisely. The representative of Iraq also addressed the Council.

SECURITY COUNCIL ACTION

Also on 16 November [meeting 6219], following consultations among Security Council members, the President made statement **S/PRST/2009/30** on its behalf:

The Security Council reaffirms its commitment to the independence, sovereignty, unity and territorial integrity of Iraq, and emphasizes the importance of the stability and security of Iraq for its people, the region and the international community.

The Council reaffirms its full support for the Special Representative of the Secretary-General for Iraq, Mr. Ad Melkert, and the United Nations Assistance Mission for Iraq in advising, supporting and assisting the people and Government of Iraq to strengthen democratic institutions, advance inclusive political dialogue and national reconciliation, facilitate regional dialogue, aid vulnerable groups, strengthen gender equality, promote the protection of human rights, including through the work of the Independent High Commission for Human Rights, promote the protection of children and promote judicial and legal reform.

The Council encourages the continued work of the Mission, in coordination with the Government of Iraq, to help to create conditions conducive to the voluntary, safe, dignified and sustainable return of Iraqi refugees

and internally displaced persons, and welcomes further attention to this issue by all concerned.

The Council underscores the important role of the Mission in supporting the people and Government of Iraq in promoting dialogue, easing tension and developing a just and fair solution for the nation's disputed internal boundaries, and calls upon all the relevant parties to participate in an inclusive dialogue to this end.

The Council welcomes the agreement reached on 8 November 2009 in the Iraqi Council of Representatives on amendments to the electoral law of Iraq, which will allow for parliamentary elections to take place in January 2010, as stipulated by the Constitutional Court of Iraq. The Council emphasizes the efforts of the Mission to assist the Government of Iraq and the Independent High Electoral Commission in the development of processes for holding elections. The Council strongly endorses the continued assistance of the Mission to the people and Government of Iraq in preparation for the Iraqi national parliamentary elections planned for January 2010. The Council endorses the appeal by the Secretary-General to all political blocs and their leaders in Iraq to demonstrate true statesmanship during the election campaign and participate in a spirit of national unity.

The Council underlines its condemnation in the strongest terms of the series of terrorist attacks that occurred on 19 August and 25 October 2009 in Baghdad, which caused numerous deaths and injuries and damage, including to Iraqi Government institutions. The Council reiterates its deep condolences to the families of the victims and reaffirms its support for the people and the Government of Iraq, and its commitment to Iraq's security. The Council reaffirms the need to combat threats to international peace and security caused by terrorist acts by all means, in accordance with the Charter of the United Nations, ensuring that measures taken to combat terrorism fully comply with all obligations under international law, in particular international human rights, refugee and humanitarian law.

The Council welcomes the recent visit of United Nations officials to Iraq for preliminary consultations related to Iraq's security and sovereignty. The Council encourages the efforts of the Secretary-General in this regard, including the possibility of facilitating technical assistance through the Counter-Terrorism Committee Executive Directorate.

Baghdad bombings. On 8 December, the Security Council President issued a press statement [SC/9810] in which Council members condemned that day's series of terrorist attacks in Baghdad, which caused numerous deaths, injuries and damage.

Report of Secretary-General. In a later report [S/2010/76], the Secretary-General reviewed developments through the end of 2009. He said that the period had witnessed intense negotiations and a protracted debate within the Council of Representatives over amendments to the 2005 Election Law, which were required for the forthcoming national elections. On 18 November, Vice-President al-Hashemi vetoed several amendments which had been adopted by the

Council of Representatives on 8 November, on the grounds that the seat distribution formula and population data used to determine the total number of seats for the Council of Representatives, as well as their distribution per governorate, were discriminating against out-of-country voters.

Through its technical advice and mediation efforts, including the good offices of the Secretary-General's Special Representative, UNAMI helped the parties reach an agreement on key amendments to the Election Law. As a result, the revised law was adopted on 6 December by the Council of Representatives, and subsequently approved by the Presidency Council. On 13 December, the Presidency Council announced that the date for national elections would be 7 March 2010. The final decision apportioned the total number of seats in the Council of Representatives on the basis of 2005 population figures obtained from the Ministry of Trade, while accommodating a population growth of 2.8 per cent annually across all governorates. It called for the future parliament to comprise 325 seats—up from the previous 275—of which 310 were general seats and 15 were compensatory, with reserved quotas for component groups.

On 8 December, a few days after the adoption of the revised Election Law, there were five coordinated bombings across Baghdad, which struck a courthouse, two colleges, a mosque and a bank, resulting in the death of more than 100 people and injuring many more. The following day, 9 December, Prime Minister al-Maliki, in his capacity as Commander-in-Chief of the Armed Forces, replaced the Chief of the Baghdad Operations Command.

On 8 November, the Special Representative paid his second visit to Erbil and Sulaymaniyah to discuss outstanding issues between the Federal Government in Baghdad and the Kurdistan regional government. In November, the Kirkuk Provincial Council adopted measures recommended by UNAMI for the improved resolution of property disputes and formed a local committee to implement the recommendations. On 18 December, the Government requested the immediate withdrawal of Iranian forces that had reportedly deployed in the vicinity of the disputed Al-Fakkah oil field. Following an official letter of protest on 30 December, Iran and Iraq agreed to meet to reach a common understanding on the precise location of the border. On 23 November, the Council of Representatives amended its National Investment Law to allow foreigners to own land for housing projects, speed up the process of applying for investment licences, and clarify federal and provincial powers with regard to investors.

From 5 to 7 November, the Government led a conference in Erbil to review strategic priorities for the National Development Plan with national and international stakeholders. The United Nations participated in the conference to ensure the complementary alignment of the development frameworks of the Government and the United Nations. An UNDAF strategic planning retreat (15–17 November) identified priority areas to guide UN contributions to Iraq's national development priorities from 2011 to 2014. The Donor Committee of the International Reconstruction Fund Facility for Iraq met in Baghdad on 8 November, where the United Nations Development Group Iraq Trust Fund reported total donor deposits of $1.35 billion, with $1.25 billion approved and transferred for 165 projects and a fund balance of $135.63 million. The Donor Committee extended the deadline for programming the remaining funds to 30 June 2010.

The Iraq Humanitarian Action Plan was launched at the end of December as a joint humanitarian strategy for 2010. It was not accompanied by detailed project proposals, but instead aimed to facilitate fundraising of the estimated $193 million needed for humanitarian operations. On 14 December, UNAMI issued its latest human rights report, covering the period from 1 January to 30 June: issues of concern included the administration of justice, the situation in prisons and violence against women.

Appointment. On 23 December [SG/A/1211], the Secretary-General appointed Jerzy Skuratowicz (Poland) as his Deputy Special Representative for Iraq to head the UNAMI political, electoral and constitutional support component, replacing Andrew Gilmour (United Kingdom).

UNAMI financing

On 21 October [A/64/349/Add.5], the Secretary-General submitted the proposed resource requirements for UNAMI for the period from 1 January to 31 December 2010, totalling $158,989,300 net ($168,118,600 gross).

In December [A/64/7/Add.13], ACABQ recommended that the General Assembly approve the resources requested by the Secretary-General, subject to its observations and recommendations.

On 24 December, the General Assembly, by section VI of **resolution 64/245** (see p. 1407), approved that amount as part of the $569,526,500 budget for the 26 special political missions authorized by the General Assembly and/or the Security Council.

UN integrated compound

In section X of its resolution 63/263 [YUN 2008, p. 1548], the General Assembly had approved a commitment authority for $5 million for UNAMI in 2009 to undertake design work in connection with the construction of the UN integrated compound in Baghdad. However, the Secretary-General reported [A/64/349/Add.5] that new developments and the fast-evolving security situation had required repeated reviews of all planning requirements.

In March, the United States announced its intention to draw down its military presence to between 35,000 to 55,000 troops by 2011. Assurances were received that security arrangements for the UN presence would continue to be provided until the end of 2011, allowing UNAMI to revise its planning assumptions. On 19 August, a series of bomb attacks on the Ministries of Foreign Affairs and Finance left over 100 people killed and nearly 1,200 people wounded. Since the beginning of 2009, there had also been 24 indirect fire attacks, consisting of 38 rocket/mortar rounds, on the international zone, resulting in casualties and structural damage to facilities.

After a careful review, the conclusion was reached that the best approach would be to build an integrated compound that included a single hardened structure for common areas and a series of smaller "pre-engineered buildings" for office and living accommodation, to be completed by the end of 2011. Proposals from bidders were due on 20 November, and the earliest that a contract could be signed was 31 January 2010.

As a result, the timeline for submitting a comprehensive report to the Assembly had changed, and the report would be submitted during the resumed part of its sixty-fourth session. Since no obligations had been or would be made in 2009 against the commitment authority of $5 million approved for the biennium 2008–2009, it was proposed that a similar commitment authority be provided for the biennium 2010–2011.

In its review of the proposed financing of UNAMI [A/64/7/Add.13], ACABQ concurred with the Secretary-General's proposal and recommended that the Assembly approve a commitment authority of up to $5 million for the biennium 2010–2011, to undertake design work in connection with the construction of the UN integrated compound.

The General Assembly, in its **resolution 64/245** (see p. 1406), approved that commitment authority of up to $5 million under section 33 of the programme budget for the biennium 2010–2011. By section VI of that resolution, it requested that the Secretary-General submit updated comprehensive financial requirements for the construction of the compound for consideration at the main part of the Assembly's sixty-fifth (2011) session.

International Advisory and Monitoring Board

The International Advisory and Monitoring Board (IAMB), established by Security Council resolution 1483(2003) [YUN 2003, p. 338] to ensure that the Development Fund for Iraq was used in a transparent manner for the benefit of the Iraqi people and that the export sales of petroleum products and natural gas from Iraq were consistent with international market best practices, continued to oversee the auditing of the Fund.

In accordance with paragraph 3 of Council resolution 1859(2008) [YUN 2008, p. 393], the Secretary-General reported to the Council on 24 August [S/2009/430] on the activities of the Fund and of the Board. From the Fund's inception to the end of 2008, $165.1 billion had been deposited in it from the export sales of oil and oil products, $10.4 billion had been deposited from the balance of the oil-for-food funds held under escrow by the United Nations, and a further $1.5 billion had been deposited as proceeds from frozen assets.

Since 2006, the Iraqi Committee of Financial Experts had been working alongside the Board and had taken over the monitoring of the Fund on expiration of the Board's mandate. During 2009, the Committee's representative had briefed IAMB regularly on its activities to enable a smooth handover of oversight responsibility from the Board by the end of the year. Those activities included beginning the appointment process for the 2009 auditor as part of its action plan for the year. The Board agreed that the 2009 audit should cover the period from 1 January to 31 December, with an interim audit for the period 1 January to 30 June.

In April, the United Nations Controller, Jun Yamazaki—the Secretary-General's designated representative on the Board—briefed the Council on the activities of the Development Fund for Iraq and the Advisory Board.

SECURITY COUNCIL ACTION

On 21 December [meeting 6249], the Security Council unanimously adopted **resolution 1905(2009)**. The draft [S/2009/660] was submitted by Japan, Uganda, the United Kingdom and the United States.

The Security Council,

Taking note of the letter dated 13 December 2009 from the Prime Minister of Iraq to the President of the Security Council, which is annexed to the present resolution,

Recognizing the positive developments in Iraq and that the situation now existing in Iraq is significantly different from that which existed at the time of the adoption of resolution 661(1990) on 6 August 1990, also recognizing that Iraqi institutions are strengthening, and further recognizing the importance of Iraq achieving international standing equal to that which it held prior to the adoption of resolution 661(1990),

Recognizing also that the letter from the Prime Minister of Iraq also reaffirms the commitment by the Government of Iraq to resolve the debts and settle the claims inherited from the previous regime, and to continue to address those debts and claims until they are resolved or settled, and requests the continued assistance of the international community, as the Government works to complete this process,

Recognizing further the significant role of the Development Fund for Iraq and the International Advisory and Monitoring Board and the provisions of paragraph 22 of resolution 1483(2003) of 22 May 2003 in helping the Government of Iraq to ensure that Iraq's resources are being used transparently and accountably for the benefit of the Iraqi people, and recognizing also the need for Iraq to transition during 2010 to successor arrangements for the Development Fund and the Board, to include the Committee of Financial Experts,

Acting under Chapter VII of the Charter of the United Nations,

1. *Decides* to provide an extension, until 31 December 2010, of the arrangements established in paragraph 20 of resolution 1483(2003) for the deposit into the Development Fund for Iraq of proceeds from export sales of petroleum, petroleum products and natural gas and the arrangements referred to in paragraph 12 of resolution 1483(2003) and paragraph 24 of resolution 1546(2004) of 8 June 2004 for the monitoring of the Development Fund by the International Advisory and Monitoring Board, and further decides that, subject to the exception provided for in paragraph 27 of resolution 1546(2004), the provisions of paragraph 22 of resolution 1483(2003) shall continue to apply until that date, including with respect to funds, financial assets and economic resources described in paragraph 23 of that resolution;

2. *Decides also* that the provisions in paragraph 1 above for the deposit of proceeds into the Development Fund for Iraq and for the role of the International Advisory and Monitoring Board and the provisions of paragraph 22 of resolution 1483(2003) shall be reviewed at the request of the Government of Iraq or no later than 15 June 2010;

3. *Requests* the Secretary-General to provide written reports to the Security Council on a quarterly basis, the first report to be no later than 1 April 2010, to include details on progress made in strengthening the financial and administrative oversight of the current Development Fund for Iraq, as well as the legal issues and options to be considered to implement successor arrangements and an assessment of progress by the Government of Iraq in preparing for the successor arrangements for the Development Fund;

4. *Calls upon* the Government of Iraq to put in place the necessary action plan and timeline by 1 April 2010 and to ensure the timely and effective transition by 31 December 2010 to a post-Development Fund mechanism which takes into account the Stand-By Arrangement requirements of the International Monetary Fund and includes external auditing arrangements and enables Iraq to meet its obligations as established in the provisions of paragraph 21 of resolution 1483(2003);

5. *Requests* the Government of Iraq, through the head of the Committee of Financial Experts, to report to the Council on a quarterly basis, the first report to be no later than 1 April 2010, to provide an action plan and timeline for the transition from the Development Fund for Iraq and details on the progress made in strengthening the financial and administrative oversight of the current Development Fund, with subsequent quarterly reports to provide an assessment of progress against the action plan and oversight improvements;

6. *Decides* to remain actively seized of the matter.

ANNEX

Letter dated 13 December 2009 from Mr. Nuri Kamel al-Maliki, Prime Minister of Iraq, to the President of the Security Council

I refer to my letter dated 7 December 2008 addressed to the President of the Security Council, in which I made it clear that Iraq is committed to finding a satisfactory solution to the problem of the debts and claims that it inherited from the previous regime. In that letter, I expressed the wish of the Government of Iraq that the temporary assistance provided by the international community should continue, in order to permit that goal to be achieved. I also made it clear that the Government of Iraq recognizes that the Development Fund for Iraq plays an important role in ensuring that oil and gas revenues are employed in the best interests of the Iraqi people, and that the International Advisory and Monitoring Board helps to ensure that those resources are managed in a transparent and responsible fashion. In 2010, the Government of Iraq will make appropriate arrangements for the Development Fund for Iraq and the International Advisory and Monitoring Board, with a view to ensuring that oil revenue continues to be used fairly and in the interests of the Iraqi people. Such arrangements will be in keeping with the Constitution and with international best practices with respect to transparency, accountability and integrity. Here I should like to affirm that in 2009, the Government of Iraq made great progress in settling the above-mentioned debts and claims, including by concluding agreements on the reduction of sovereign debt and other bilateral agreements concerning certain claims.

During the remainder of 2009 and in 2010, we will take action to recover the international financial standing of Iraq while at the same time managing oil and gas revenues in order to benefit the people of Iraq.

Those goals cannot be achieved without the continued assistance of the international community by means of the adoption of a Security Council resolution whereby the conditions and arrangements provided for in resolution 1859(2008) are extended. That resolution concerned the extension of the mandates of the Development Fund for Iraq and the International Advisory and Monitoring Board for a period of 12 months. A review of the new extension should be conducted before 15 June 2010 at the request of the Government of Iraq.

I should be grateful if you would circulate this letter to the members of the Security Council as soon as possible and include it as an annex to the resolution currently being drafted on the extension of the mandates referred to above.

Security Council Committee
established pursuant to resolution 1518(2003)

On 22 December [S/2009/671], the Chairman of the Security Council Committee established pursuant to resolution 1518(2003) [YUN 2003, p. 362] submitted to the Council the Committee's annual report for 2009. The Committee was established to identify, in accordance with paragraphs 19 and 23 of resolution 1483(2003) [ibid., p. 338], individuals and entities associated with the former Iraqi regime whose funds, other financial assets and economic resources should be frozen and transferred to the Development Fund for Iraq. At year's end, the Committee's list of individuals contained 89 names; its list of entities contained 208 names.

Several issues brought to the Committee's attention in 2007 remained pending in 2009. The Chairman had undertaken consultations with the relevant Committee members with a view to resolving those outstanding matters, which he hoped could be achieved early in 2010. The assets-freeze and transfer lists of individuals and entities were available at the Committee's website.

United Nations Iraq Account

Following the termination of all activities under the oil-for-food programme [YUN 2003, p. 366], the United Nations retained responsibility for the administration and execution of letters of credit issued under the programme by the bank holding the United Nations Iraq Account, Banque Nationale de Paris Paribas, for purchasing humanitarian supplies for the south/centre of Iraq, until such letters were executed or expired, in accordance with Security Council resolution 1483(2003) [ibid., p. 338].

On 25 July 2008 [YUN 2008, p. 396], the Secretary-General had informed the Council about further arrangements for the termination of the operations related to the letters of credit issued against the United Nations Iraq Account under resolution 1483(2003). On 1 May 2009 [S/2009/230], the Secretary-General informed the Council about the status of the remaining activity relating to the operations of the letters of credit as at 31 March. Since July 2008, the number of outstanding letters of credit had been reduced from 147, worth some $495 million, to 92, worth approximately $313 million. As at 31 March, the United Nations Iraq Account contained $872 million, of which some $314 million was held in the cash collateral portion of the Account for expired letters of credit to cover the amount of claims of delivery made by suppliers, and $558 million in the non-collateral portion of the Account.

Pursuant to Security Council resolution 1483(2003), 3,009 contracts, with associated letters of credit valued at approximately $8 billion, were considered essential for the reconstruction and/or humanitarian needs of the Iraqi people. Out of those 3,009 letters of credit corresponding to prioritized contracts, only 92 letters of credit with an approximate value of $313 million remained outstanding. A total of $10.42 billion had been transferred from the United Nations Iraq Account to the Development Fund for Iraq, pursuant to Council resolution 1483(2003), including some $9.9 billion transferred from the humanitarian branch of the programme.

The Secretary-General noted that the United Nations had obtained no indemnification from the Iraqi Government on the funds transferred to the Development Fund for Iraq, as highlighted in his letter to the Council of 10 July 2006 [YUN 2006, p. 410].

(For information on the follow-up to the recommendations of the Independent Inquiry Committee into the United Nations Oil-for-Food Programme, see p. 1427.)

Board of Auditors report

On 18 June, the Secretary-General transmitted to the Security Council the report of the Board of Auditors [S/2009/314] on the financial statements of the United Nations escrow (Iraq) accounts for the year ended 31 December 2008. Those financial statements reflected the transactions covering the fifth year of the phase-down operations following the termination of the oil-for-food programme in November 2003 pursuant to Council resolution 1483(2003). The number of letters of credit had been reduced during 2008 from 210 to 95. However, the liquidation remained hampered by the delay in the issuance of authentication documents by the Iraqi Government despite the repeated calls of the Security Council and the Secretary-General.

In 2008, total income was $37.7 million and total expenditure was $24.3 million. Total expenditure for humanitarian activities of $18.5 million included $17.09 million relating to currency exchange adjustments and $1.41 million relating to the purchase of humanitarian supplies and spare parts. From the inception of the oil-for-food programme up to 31 December 2008, total expenditures for the purchase of humanitarian supplies and oil spares amounted to $43.91 billion.

Total cash resources (cash and term deposits and cash pool) at year's end amounted to $954.14 million, a 22 per cent decrease from $1.22 billion as at the end of 2006. Despite the decline, the cash resources of the "Humanitarian activities in Iraq" account, amounting to $928.63 million, were still sufficient to cover the $346.56 million of current and prior-year unliquidated obligations arising from approved contracts for humanitarian supplies and oil spares.

Also at year's end, the total reserves and fund balances of the "Humanitarian activities in Iraq" account and the "Administrative and operational costs" account amounted to $608.8 million. Of that amount, $2.5 million represented reserves for end-of-service and post-retirement benefits, $206.2 million stood for other reserves for any unanticipated claims from suppliers and expected administrative costs during liquidation, and the remaining $400.3 million was cumulative surplus.

The Board made two recommendations based on its audit: that the Administration settle the outstanding accounts payable and receivable of the United Nations Monitoring, Verification and Inspection Commission and transfer all remaining unencumbered funds to the Development Fund for Iraq in accordance with Council resolution 1762(2007) [YUN 2007, p. 356]; and that it keep the matter of transferring the unencumbered funds to the Development Fund for Iraq under review.

Iraq–Kuwait

Kuwaiti property and missing persons

By April 2009, Gennady Tarasov (Russian Federation) had served a full year as the new High-level Coordinator for the issue of missing Kuwaiti and third-country nationals and the repatriation of Kuwaiti property seized by Iraq during its occupation of Kuwait, which arose in August 1990 [YUN 1990, p. 189]. The Coordinator, whose mandate had been established by Security Council resolution 1284(1999) [YUN 1999, p. 230], briefed the Council in April [SC/9637] and October [SC/9772].

In a letter of 10 March to the Security Council [S/2009/143], the Foreign Minister of Iraq said that his country did not believe that the High-level Coordinator's mandate should remain open-ended and that the Security Council should remain seized of those matters. Iraq desired the ending of the mandate, which it said would not affect Iraq's continuing cooperation with Kuwait on the bilateral level or in the framework of the work of the Tripartite Commission.

In a 24 March letter [S/2009/178], the Foreign Minister of Kuwait, noting that the fate of only 236 of a total of 605 missing persons had been uncovered, said that the Coordinator's mandate should continue in tandem with the work of the Tripartite Commission and its Technical Subcommittee until the terms of all those mandates were fulfilled.

On 8 April [S/2009/190], in a 12-month progress report to the Council, the Secretary-General said that

Iraq and Kuwait would eventually need to agree on a mutually acceptable arrangement for resolving the issue and bring it to the Council. Noting the ongoing improvement in the bilateral relations between Iraq and Kuwait, attested to by official public declarations on both sides, he again stressed the need to translate political statements of goodwill into actions. To that end, he proposed introducing a confidence- and cooperation-building period lasting until June 2010, during which every effort should be made by all concerned to resolve those issues. In a press statement of 16 April [SC/9637], the Council expressed support for that proposal.

On 14 April [S/2009/203], Kuwait stated that it attached particular importance to determining the fate and finding the remains of Kuwaiti and third-country missing persons. The mandate of the Coordinator should continue, and Kuwait supported the Secretary-General's proposal that the mandate be extended to June 2010, provided that the Council considered the issue and took appropriate action.

On 21 May [S/2009/262], the Secretary-General said that the activities undertaken to fulfil the mandate of the Coordinator had led to expenditures of $183,400 from 25 April 2008 to 24 April 2009, which were provided through transfers from the Iraq escrow account. He took note of the agreement by Council members [SC/9637] to finance continuation of the Coordinator's activities for a six-month period, with the possibility of further extension. Given the need to intensify the activities of the Coordinator and his support staff, it would be necessary to allocate resources of $202,400 to finance those activities until 31 October. The funds could be earmarked from the operating reserves and fund balance of the 2.2 per cent part of the escrow account intended for administrative and operational costs. Should the Council agree, the funds would be transferred within the escrow account and made available to the Department of Political Affairs, which backstopped the Coordinator's activities. The Council took note of the Secretary-General's proposals on 22 May [S/2009/263].

On 8 July [S/2009/350], Iraq informed the Security Council that on 24 June it had handed over to the Kuwaiti authorities 24 boxes containing 2,121,166 dinars of old Kuwaiti currency, postage stamps and travel cheques belonging to the Kuwaiti Central Bank.

In an October report [S/2009/539] on Iraq's compliance since April with its obligations regarding those issues, the Secretary-General said that the confidence- and cooperation-building process, during its first six months, had given indications of movement with respect to the issue of missing Kuwaiti and third-country nationals. Nevertheless, progress remained fragile. He therefore recommended that the Council extend the financing of the Coordinator's mandate until June 2010. The Council on 22 October agreed to finance those activities for a further eight-month period [SC/9772].

In a 29 December letter [S/2009/685], the Secretary-General said that the mandated activities for the Coordinator and his staff had led to expenditures of $337,657 from 25 April 2008 to 31 October 2009, provided through transfers from the Iraq escrow account. Given the need to intensify those activities, it would be necessary to allocate resources of $251,400 to finance them through 30 June 2010. Should the Council agree, those funds could be earmarked from the operating reserves and fund balance of the 2.2 per cent part of the escrow account and would be transferred and made available to the Department of Political Affairs.

UN Compensation Commission and Fund

The United Nations Compensation Commission, established in 1991 [YUN 1991, p. 195] for the resolution and payment of claims against Iraq for losses and damages resulting from its 1990 invasion and occupation of Kuwait [YUN 1990, p. 189], continued in 2009 to expedite the settlement of claims through the United Nations Compensation Fund, which was established at the same time as the Commission. Under Council resolution 1483(2003) [YUN 2003, p. 338], the Fund received 5 per cent of the proceeds generated by export sales of Iraqi petroleum, petroleum products and natural gas.

The Commission on 29 January paid out $460.8 million to Kuwait and Saudi Arabia for distribution to 12 claimants; $300 million on 29 April to Kuwait for distribution to 10 claimants; $430 million on 29 July to Kuwait for distribution to 10 claimants; and $610 million on 29 October to Kuwait for distribution to 10 claimants. That payment brought the overall amount of compensation made available by the Commission for successful claims of individuals, corporations, Governments and international organizations to $28.2 billion.

Governing Council. The Commission's Governing Council held two sessions in Geneva during the year—the sixty-seventh (28–29 April) [S/2009/226] and sixty-eighth (10 and 12 November) [S/2009/594]—at which it considered reports on the activities of the Commission, the distribution by Governments and international organizations of payments to claimants, the transparency of the distribution process and the return of undistributed funds. The Commission adopted a decision on withholdings and the administration of funds [S/AC.26/Dec.266(2009)] and one on the payment mechanism and payment of remaining claims [S/AC.26/Dec.267(2009)].

The Council also took note of the activities of the Board of Auditors pertaining to the Commission and noted that the annual report of the Office of Internal Oversight Services to the General Assembly confirmed that the Commission had implemented all of the Office's audit recommendations.

Oversight activities

The Office of Internal Oversight Services (OIOS), in an August report on its activities for the period 1 July 2008–30 June 2009 [A/64/326 (Part I) & Corr.1], stated that the Compensation Commission continued to disburse award payments and monitor environmental projects being undertaken by claimant Governments with funds awarded for environmental damages. As at 31 May, the operations of the Commission had been downsized to four staff members, including the Executive Head. The follow-up programme for environmental awards had two professional staff with four more under recruitment.

In its audit of claims payments from July 2007 to December 2008, the Office found that the Commission had adequate control mechanisms to ensure that award and payment records as well as reports were accurate, properly documented and compliant with Governing Council decisions and United Nations Financial Regulations and Rules. As at 30 June, the Commission had paid $27 billion, for which most Governments and other submitting entities had fully complied with the Governing Council's distribution reporting requirements.

However, Governments and other submitting entities had yet to submit audit certificates relating to $34 million of awards disbursed to them. As audit certificates were intended to provide additional assurance that payments had been distributed to the claimants, OIOS recommended, and the Commission agreed, that its efforts to pursue the outstanding certificates should be continued. That was the only outstanding OIOS recommendation to the Commission.

On 24 December, the General Assembly decided that the agenda item on the "Consequences of the Iraqi occupation of and aggression against Kuwait" would remain for consideration during its resumed sixty-fourth (2010) session (**decision 64/549**).

Timor-Leste

The United Nations Integrated Mission in Timor-Leste (UNMIT), established by Security Council resolution 1704(2006) [YUN 2006, p. 422], continued to carry out its mandate to assist the Government in consolidating stability, enhancing democratic governance and facilitating political dialogue. It also provided support to the national police; helped to strengthen the country's human rights capacity; and cooperated with UN bodies and their partners in peacebuilding and capacity-building. The Mission was headed through 10 December by Atul Khare (India), who also served as the Secretary-General's Special Representative for Timor-Leste. His successor, Ameerah Haq (Bangladesh), was appointed effective 28 December.

United Nations Integrated Mission in Timor-Leste

Report of Secretary-General (January). Pursuant to Security Council resolution 1802(2008) [YUN 2008, p. 401], the Secretary-General submitted a 4 February report [S/2009/72] on major developments in Timor-Leste and on the activities of UNMIT since his previous report [YUN 2008, p. 403]. As at 20 January, UNMIT consisted of a civilian component comprising 340 international staff (122 women), 874 national staff (158 women), 1,510 police officers (74 women) and 31 military liaison and staff officers (2 women). The UN country team consisted of 254 international staff (111 women) and 508 national staff (133 women).

There was no change in the UNMIT police strength, with 1,510 officers (74 women) as at 20 January. Of those, 923 officers (including 140 in the Malaysian formed police unit, 139 in the Portuguese formed police unit and 36 in the Pakistani formed police unit) were deployed in Dili, the capital, and 587 to other districts, including 139 in the Bangladeshi formed police unit and 102 in the Pakistani formed police unit. They continued to perform the mandated task of interim law enforcement, while supporting training, institutional development and strengthening of the national police, the Polícia Nacional de Timor-Leste. The security situation remained generally calm—attributable in part to proactive policing strategies adopted by the police but also to UNMIT engagement with key political stakeholders. The presence and activities of UNMIT military liaison officers in the border districts had contributed to the stability of the security situation there.

UNMIT investigations into cases of serious human rights violations committed in 1999 [YUN 1999, p. 288] continued under the supervision of and in close collaboration with the Office of the Prosecutor-General. Investigations began in five new districts, in addition to the four where investigations were ongoing. UNMIT had completed investigations into 35 out of 396 outstanding cases and submitted final investigation reports to the Office of the Prosecutor-General. An additional 38 other cases were under investigation.

As at 20 January, 16,500 internally displaced families had registered for assistance under the Government's National Recovery Strategy. Fifty-four camps in Dili and Baucau (out of 63) had closed and the number of families benefiting from the recovery package reached 11,335. There were no major outbreaks of violence or serious resistance affecting the overall return process.

Security Council consideration (February). On 19 February [meeting 6085], the Council held an open debate on the situation in Timor-Leste in the presence of the Secretary-General, who introduced his report of 4 February. He said that remarkable progress had been made, including the settlement between the petitioners and the Government and the return home of most internally displaced persons. One of the main priorities in the year ahead should be developing the security sector, and a major step would be the gradual resumption of policing responsibilities by the national police.

The President of Timor-Leste, José Ramos-Horta, conveyed his gratitude for the support of the United Nations and reported on progress in the country. He noted that incidents, including assaults and homicides, had dropped significantly since 2007, and that in spite of the international financial crisis, the country's economy would be able to maintain two-digit growth in 2009.

The Special Representative of the Secretary-General also addressed the Council.

SECURITY COUNCIL ACTION

On 26 February [meeting 6086], the Security Council unanimously adopted **resolution 1867(2009)**. The draft [S/2009/111] was submitted by Australia, France, Japan, Malaysia, New Zealand, Portugal, Turkey, the United Kingdom and the United States.

The Security Council,

Reaffirming all its previous resolutions and the statements by its President on the situation in Timor-Leste, in particular resolutions 1599(2005) of 28 April 2005, 1677(2006) of 12 May 2006, 1690(2006) of 20 June 2006, 1703(2006) of 18 August 2006, 1704(2006) of 25 August 2006, 1745(2007) of 22 February 2007 and 1802(2008) of 25 February 2008,

Welcoming the report of the Secretary-General of 4 February 2009,

Reaffirming its full commitment to the sovereignty, independence, territorial integrity and national unity of Timor-Leste and the promotion of long-term stability in the country,

Welcoming the improvements in the political and security situation in Timor-Leste, which has recovered from the 2006 crisis and the events of 11 February 2008, and noting that the current political and security situation, although generally calm, remains fragile,

Welcoming also the six-week nationwide weapons collection campaign sponsored by the Government of Timor-Leste with the support of the United Nations Integrated Mission in Timor-Leste and the international security forces, which ended on 31 August 2008, and the destruction of the collected weapons on United Nations Day of that year,

Commending the political leadership and State institutions of Timor-Leste for restoring and securing stability, and welcoming the return of a significant number of internally displaced persons and the disbandment of the "petitioners" group, while recognizing the importance of additional measures to achieve meaningful reconciliation and their reintegration into their respective communities,

Reiterating its call upon the leadership and other stakeholders in Timor-Leste to continue to pursue peaceful dialogue and to avoid violent means to resolve differences,

Welcoming the efforts of the political leadership of Timor-Leste to create opportunities for all the political parties to make contributions to issues of national interest,

Reaffirming the need for respect for the independence of the judiciary and its responsibility, welcoming the conviction of the leaders of Timor-Leste of the need for justice and their determination to act against impunity, and in this regard acknowledging the serious resource constraints of the judicial system and encouraging the leadership of Timor-Leste to continue efforts to establish accountability for serious criminal offences committed during the 2006 crisis as recommended by the Independent Special Commission of Inquiry for Timor-Leste,

Recalling its previous statements on the need to implement fully the "Arrangement on the Restoration and Maintenance of Public Security in Timor-Leste and Assistance to the Reform, Restructuring and Rebuilding of the Timorese National Police and the Ministry of the Interior", concluded between the Government of Timor-Leste and the Mission on 1 December 2006, and in this regard, stressing the need for constructive engagement between Mission police and the National Police with a view to developing the capacity and capability of the National Police,

Expressing its full support for the role of the international security forces in assisting the Government of Timor-Leste and the Mission in the restoration and maintenance of law and stability, in response to the requests of the Government,

Expressing concern at the increase in poverty among the Timorese population, as indicated in the report of the Secretary-General, and underlining the importance of continued support for the socio-economic development of Timor-Leste,

Recalling that, while the manifestations of the current challenges in Timor-Leste are political and institutional in nature, poverty and its associated deprivations also contribute to these challenges, paying tribute to Timor-Leste's bilateral and multilateral partners for their invaluable assistance, particularly with regard to institutional capacity-building and social and economic development, and recognizing the progress being made in the development of many aspects of governance in Timor-Leste,

Reaffirming its resolutions 1325(2000) of 31 October 2000 and 1820(2008) of 19 June 2008 on women and peace and security, and its resolution 1502(2003) of 26 August 2003 on the protection of humanitarian and United Nations personnel, and welcoming the cooperation of the

Mission with other United Nations partners to support the efforts of the Government of Timor-Leste to develop a national gender equality policy and strategy,

Recognizing the important role that the Mission continues to play in promoting peace, stability and development in Timor-Leste, and expressing its appreciation for the efforts of the Mission and the United Nations country team, under the leadership of the Special Representative of the Secretary-General for Timor-Leste,

1. *Decides* to extend the mandate of the United Nations Integrated Mission in Timor-Leste until 26 February 2010 at the current authorized levels;

2. *Urges* all parties in Timor-Leste, in particular political leaders, to continue to work together and engage in political dialogue and consolidate peace, democracy, the rule of law, sustainable social and economic development, advancement of protection of human rights and national reconciliation in the country, and reaffirms its full support for the continued efforts of the Special Representative of the Secretary-General for Timor-Leste aimed at addressing critical political and security-related issues facing the country, including enhancing a culture of democratic governance, through inclusive and collaborative processes, including the expanded High-level Coordination Committee and the Trilateral Coordination Forum;

3. *Requests* the Mission to extend the necessary support, within its current mandate, for local elections currently planned for 2009, responding to the request of the Government of Timor-Leste, and encourages the international community to assist in this process;

4. *Reaffirms* the continued importance of the review and reform of the security sector in Timor-Leste, in particular the need to delineate roles and responsibilities between the Falintil-Forças de Defesa de Timor-Leste and the National Police of Timor-Leste, to strengthen legal frameworks and to enhance civilian oversight and accountability mechanisms of both security institutions, and requests the Mission to continue to support the Government of Timor-Leste in these efforts;

5. *Supports* the gradual resumption of policing responsibilities by the National Police of Timor-Leste, beginning in 2009, through a phased approach, while emphasizing that the National Police must meet the criteria mutually agreed between the Government of Timor-Leste and the Mission, as set out in paragraph 21 of the report of the Secretary-General, to guarantee the readiness of the National Police for the resumption of such responsibilities in any given district or unit, requests the Government and the Mission to cooperate with each other to implement the resumption process, and requests the Mission to continue to ensure, through the presence of the Mission police component and the provision of support to the National Police, the maintenance of public security in Timor-Leste, which includes interim law enforcement and public security until the National Police is fully reconstituted;

6. *Underscores* the need for the concept of operations and rules of engagement to be regularly updated as necessary and to be fully in line with the provisions of the present resolution, and requests the Secretary-General to report on them to the Security Council and troop- and police-contributing countries within ninety days of the adoption of the present resolution;

7. *Requests* the Mission, working with partners, to intensify its efforts to assist with further training, mentoring, institutional development and strengthening of the National Police of Timor-Leste with a view to enhancing its effectiveness, including with respect to addressing the special needs of women;

8. *Reaffirms* the importance of ongoing efforts to achieve accountability and justice, and underlines the importance of the implementation by the Government of Timor-Leste of the recommendations contained in the report of the Independent Special Commission of Inquiry for Timor-Leste of 2 October 2006, including paragraphs 225 to 228 thereof;

9. *Underlines* the importance of a coordinated approach to the justice sector reform, based on needs assessment, and the ongoing need to increase Timorese ownership and strengthen national capacity in judicial line functions, including the training and specialization of national lawyers and judges;

10. *Emphasizes* the need for sustained support of the international community to Timor-Leste to develop and strengthen its institutions and further build capacities in the justice sector;

11. *Requests* the Mission to continue its efforts, adjusting them as necessary to enhance the effectiveness of the judiciary, in assisting the Government of Timor-Leste in carrying out the proceedings recommended by the Commission of Inquiry;

12. *Calls upon* the Mission to continue to support the Government of Timor-Leste in its efforts to coordinate donor cooperation in areas of institutional capacity-building;

13. *Takes note* of the Timor-Leste National Recovery Strategy and the declaration by the Government of Timor-Leste of 2009 as the year of infrastructure, rural development and human resources capacity development, and in this regard calls upon the Mission to continue to cooperate and coordinate with the United Nations agencies, funds and programmes, as well as all relevant partners, to support the Government and relevant institutions in designing poverty reduction, promotion of sustainable livelihood and economic growth policies;

14. *Encourages* the Government of Timor-Leste to strengthen peacebuilding perspectives in such areas as integration of internally displaced persons, employment and empowerment, especially focusing on rural areas and youth, as well as local socio-economic development, including agricultural activities;

15. *Requests* the Mission to fully take into account gender considerations as set out in resolutions 1325(2000) and 1820(2008) as a cross-cutting issue throughout its mandate, and further requests the Secretary-General to include in his reporting to the Council progress on gender mainstreaming throughout the Mission and all other aspects relating to the situation of women and girls, especially on the need to protect them from gender-based violence, detailing special measures to protect women and girls from such violence;

16. *Requests* the Secretary-General to continue to take the measures necessary to ensure full compliance by the Mission with the United Nations zero-tolerance policy on sexual exploitation and abuse and to keep the Council informed, and urges those countries contributing troops and police to take appropriate preventive action and to ensure full accountability in cases of such conduct involving their personnel;

17. *Also requests* the Secretary-General to keep the Council regularly informed of the developments on the ground, including those related to preparations for the planned local elections, and on the implementation of the present resolution, including, in particular, progress on the transfer of policing responsibilities from the Mission to the National Police of Timor-Leste, and to submit to the Council, no later than 30 September 2009, a report reviewing, inter alia, the resumption of policing responsibilities by the National Police, and, no later than 1 February 2010, a report which includes possible adjustments in the mandate and strength of the Mission;

18. *Welcomes* the work undertaken by the Secretary-General and the Government of Timor-Leste to develop a medium-term strategy and establish benchmarks for measuring and tracking progress in Timor-Leste and assessing the level and form of United Nations support while keeping the benchmarks under active review, and underlines the importance of ownership of the strategy by the leaders and people of Timor-Leste in this process;

19. *Decides* to remain seized of the matter.

Policing agreement. In a 20 May letter to the Security Council [S/2009/261], requested by the Council in its resolution 1867(2009) (see p. 377), the Secretary-General said that the Council had not made any changes to the roles and tasks of the UNMIT military liaison group, so no adjustments were required to the military concept of operations. The concept of operations of the police component, however, had been carefully reviewed by the Department of Peacekeeping Operations and the Mission to meet the requirements of the mandate as outlined in that resolution.

Noting that the resolution supported the gradual resumption of policing responsibility by the national police through a phased approach, he said that Prime Minister Kay Rala Xanana Gusmão and the Special Representative had concluded an agreement on 13 May providing a basic framework for the resumption process and the respective roles and responsibilities of the national police and UNMIT police, in accordance with previous agreements and further to resolution 1867(2009) and his report of 4 February.

In line with that agreement, a revised concept of operations for the UNMIT police component was being prepared and was close to being finalized. The rules of engagement for the police component did not require any revisions at that time, as the UNMIT police would continue to have significant responsibilities for interim law enforcement until the national police had been fully reconstituted.

Security Council consideration (May). On 27 May, the Council held a private meeting [meeting 6129] with the troop-contributing countries to UNMIT, which were briefed by the Deputy Special Representative of the Secretary-General, Takahisa Kawakami, on issues relating to the concept of operations and rules of engagement for the UNMIT military liaison group and police component.

Report of Secretary-General (October). Pursuant to Security Council resolution 1867(2009), the Secretary-General, on 2 October, reported [S/2009/504] on major developments in Timor-Leste and UNMIT's activities since 4 February. As at 31 August, UNMIT consisted of a civilian component comprising 363 international staff (127 women); 888 national staff (170 women); 1,560 police officers (61 women); and 33 military liaison and staff officers (1 woman). The UN country team consisted of 260 international staff (110 women) and 481 national staff (121 women).

The reporting period was marked by a historical milestone, with the celebration on 30 August of the tenth anniversary of the popular consultation [YUN 1999, p. 280] that led to independence. The security situation remained calm, with substantial progress made in addressing the situation of internally displaced persons, a major public reminder of the 2006 crisis [YUN 2006, p. 415]. As at 22 August, all 65 camps for internally displaced persons in Dili and Baucau had officially been closed without significant incident, while some 3,000 internally displaced remained in transitional shelters as at 31 August. On 13 July, trial proceedings commenced against Gastão Salsinha, an associate of the late Military Police Commander of the armed forces, Alfredo Reinado, and 27 co-defendants accused of involvement in the 11 February 2008 attacks on President Ramos-Horta and Prime Minister Xanana Gusmão [YUN 2008, p. 400]. On 14 May, the gradual, phased resumption of primary policing responsibilities by the national police began in Lautém District, as agreed between the Government and UNMIT.

All political parties continued to demonstrate respect for State institutions, and on 17 March, President Ramos-Horta made an appeal to strengthen political debate and to turn it into a tool for consensus-building. Dialogue and reconciliation efforts also continued at the local level, as government dialogue teams, established with UNDP support, facilitated 45 preparatory meetings, leading to 16 community dialogue meetings as at 31 August. The teams supported mediations in 392 cases—focused primarily on the reintegration of internally displaced persons—of which 231 were resolved. As requested by Council resolution 1867(2009), UNMIT extended support, including the deployment of 62 United Nations Volunteers, for the preparation of local (village) elections to be held on 9 October. On 27 August, the six-day nomination period concluded with the registration of 1,168 village council candidate lists totalling close to 27,000 candidates.

There was no change in the UNMIT police strength, with 1,560 officers (61 women) as at 31 August. The security situation remained generally calm, owing in part to proactive policing strategies and UNMIT leadership's engagement with key political stakeholders. There had been further progress in the registration, screening and certification programme for the national police, with 2,897 officers (557 women)—92 per cent of the service—fully certified as at 31 August. The remaining 259 officers (18 women) faced pending criminal and/or disciplinary proceedings.

Human rights violations by members of the security services continued to be reported—in particular ill-treatment and excessive use of force and intimidation. Some limited progress had been made towards holding accountable those responsible for criminal acts and human rights violations during the 2006 crisis, including the funding, by the Office of the United Nations High Commissioner for Human Rights, of an international prosecutor to work on those cases. As at 31 August, final judgement had been rendered in two cases involving convictions against seven persons; five trials were under way; and 13 cases were under investigation.

There had been progress in meeting targets for the national priorities that constituted the international compact for Timor-Leste. More than 60 per cent of the targets set for the first and second quarters of 2009 were met or were well under way towards completion. The International Monetary Fund estimated that the country's non-oil gross domestic product (GDP) had increased by 12.8 per cent in 2008, and that its real non-oil GDP would grow by 7.2 per cent in 2009 and 7.9 per cent in 2010. In support of the Millennium Development Goals, the Government was taking measures to improve basic education, health and nutrition, and child protection. UNMIT, for its part, had continued to make steady progress towards achieving the benchmarks in its four mandated priority areas: review and reform of the security sector; strengthening of the rule of law; promoting a culture of democratic governance and dialogue; and economic and social development.

Security Council consideration (October). On 23 October [meeting 6205], the Council was briefed by outgoing Special Representative Atul Khare, who said that the stable security situation over the review period was encouraging. Nevertheless, continued international assistance was required to ensure long-term stability. Timor-Leste's Deputy Prime Minister, José Luís Guterres, who spoke on his country's institutional progress, also emphasized the need to invest in its social and economic development to ensure sustainable peace and stability.

New Special Representative. On 25 November [S/2009/612], the Secretary-General informed the Security Council of his intention to appoint Ameerah Haq (Bangladesh) as his Special Representative for Timor-Leste and Head of UNMIT, effective 28 December, to succeed Atul Khare (India), who would complete his assignment on 10 December. The Council took note of that intention on 1 December [S/2009/613].

Later developments

Report of Secretary-General. In a later report [S/2010/85], which covered developments in the last three months of 2009, the Secretary-General said that political developments had been generally indicative of continuing stability. Elections for local authorities, which were not based on political party affiliation, were held on 9 October, with voters casting ballots for chiefs and councils of the country's 442 villages. The election campaign from 30 September to 6 October and the voting were conducted in a generally peaceful atmosphere. Participation was high, with 67.75 per cent of registered voters casting ballots. The results saw only marginal gains in women's representation at the village level despite the advocacy efforts of President Ramos-Horta and the Secretary-General's Special Representative, with the number of women elected as village chiefs increasing slightly from 7 to 11.

Political parties demonstrated continued respect for democratic processes even when addressing contentious issues, and the security situation remained stable. An independent comprehensive needs assessment of the justice sector, containing 144 recommendations, was completed on 14 October and distributed to national counterparts and other major stakeholders. The Prosecutor-General reported that during 2009, 4,502 cases had been dealt with—some 3,362 in Dili—of which 1,230 had been sent to court, and the number of pending cases had continued to decline. As at 31 December, there were 4,981 pending cases nationwide, a large percentage of which were domestic violence cases. There was also an increasing number of new cases—3,976—indicating that while confidence in the formal justice system remained a challenge, the public was more willing to pursue cases.

The United Nations continued to advocate for enhanced measures to address the needs of women and the high incidence of gender-based violence. UNMIT and the UN country team supported efforts to increase general awareness that domestic violence was a public crime under the new Penal Code, including through an advocacy campaign launched on National Women's Day on 3 November. UNMIT also supported a 16-day campaign to end violence against women, which was launched on 25 November by Deputy Prime Minister Guterres.

Financing of UN operations

In 2009, the General Assembly considered the financing of the United Nations Integrated Mission in Timor-Leste (UNMIT) and the United Nations Mission in East Timor (UNAMET).

UNMIT was established by Security Council resolution 1704(2006) [YUN 2006, p. 422] to support the Government in consolidating stability, enhancing a culture of democratic governance and facilitating political dialogue; ensure the maintenance of public security; assist the Government in reviewing the role and needs of the security sector; strengthen capacity for promoting human rights, justice and reconciliation; and assist in implementing the Secretary-General's recommendations on justice and reconciliation.

UNAMET was established by Council resolution 1246(1999) [YUN 1999, p. 283] to conduct the 1999 popular consultation to ascertain the East Timorese people's will on the future status of East Timor [ibid., p. 288].

UNAMET

On 14 September, by **decision 63/567**, the General Assembly deferred consideration of the financing of UNAMET and included the item in the agenda of its sixty-fourth (2009) session. On 24 December, it decided that the item would remain for consideration during its resumed sixty-fourth (2010) session (**decision 64/549**).

UNMIT

The Secretary-General submitted to the General Assembly a report on the financial performance of UNMIT for the period from 1 July 2007 to 30 June 2008 [A/63/607], with expenditures amounting to $162,633,400. It was followed by a 6 February report [A/63/710] to the Assembly on the UNMIT budget for the period from 1 July 2009 to 30 June 2010, totalling $210,610,000.

On 23 April, ACABQ issued its report [A/63/746/Add.3] on UNMIT's financial performance report for the period from 1 July 2007 to 30 June 2008, and its proposed budget for the period from 1 July 2009 to 30 June 2010. With respect to the period from 1 July 2007 to 30 June 2008, ACABQ recommended that the unencumbered balance of $6,962,900, as well as other income and adjustments in the amount of $7,514,600, be credited to Member States in a manner to be determined by the Assembly. It further recommended that, should the Security Council extend the mandate of UNMIT beyond 26 February 2010, the Assembly appropriate $202,474,338—a reduction of $8,135,662 in the Secretary-General's proposed budget—for the maintenance of the Mission for the period from 1 July 2009 to 30 June 2010.

On 18 May [A/63/710/Add.1], the Secretary-General noted that since his previous budget recommendation, the Council, on 26 February, by resolution

1867(2009) (see p. 377), had requested that UNMIT extend support for the local elections, for which preparations were to begin in May, with the elections to be completed in April 2010. The Assembly should therefore take note of the resource requirements of $3,073,200 for support of the local elections.

The Secretary-General on 31 December submitted to the Assembly a performance report [A/64/617] on UNMIT for the period from 1 July 2008 to 30 June 2009.

GENERAL ASSEMBLY ACTION

On 30 June [meeting 93], the General Assembly, on the recommendation of the Fifth (Administrative and Budgetary) Committee [A/63/899], adopted **resolution 63/292** without vote [agenda item 138].

Financing of the United Nations Integrated Mission in Timor-Leste

The General Assembly,

Having considered the reports of the Secretary-General on the financing of the United Nations Integrated Mission in Timor-Leste, the related report of the Advisory Committee on Administrative and Budgetary Questions, and the oral statement by the Chairman of the Advisory Committee on Administrative and Budgetary Questions,

Recalling Security Council resolution 1704(2006) of 25 August 2006, by which the Council decided to establish a follow-on mission in Timor-Leste, the United Nations Integrated Mission in Timor-Leste, for an initial period of six months, with the intention to renew it for further periods, and the subsequent resolutions by which the Council extended the mandate of the Mission, the latest of which was resolution 1867(2009) of 26 February 2009, by which the Council extended the mandate of the Mission until 26 February 2010,

Recalling also its resolutions 61/249 A of 22 December 2006 and 61/249 B of 2 April 2007 on the financing of the Mission, and its subsequent resolutions thereon, the latest of which was resolution 62/258 of 20 June 2008,

Reaffirming the general principles underlying the financing of United Nations peacekeeping operations, as stated in General Assembly resolutions 1874(S-IV) of 27 June 1963, 3101(XXVIII) of 11 December 1973 and 55/235 of 23 December 2000,

Mindful of the fact that it is essential to provide the Mission with the financial resources necessary to enable it to fulfil its responsibilities under the relevant resolutions of the Security Council,

1. *Requests* the Secretary-General to entrust the Head of Mission with the task of formulating future budget proposals in full accordance with the provisions of General Assembly resolutions 59/296 of 22 June 2005, 60/266 of 30 June 2006 and 61/276 of 29 June 2007, as well as other relevant resolutions;

2. *Takes note* of the status of contributions to the United Nations Integrated Mission in Timor-Leste as at 30 April 2009, including the contributions outstanding in the amount of 42.2 million United States dollars, repre-

senting some 8 per cent of the total assessed contributions, notes with concern that only thirty-five Member States have paid their assessed contributions in full, and urges all other Member States, in particular those in arrears, to ensure payment of their outstanding assessed contributions;

3. *Expresses its appreciation* to those Member States which have paid their assessed contributions in full, and urges all other Member States to make every possible effort to ensure payment of their assessed contributions to the Mission in full;

4. *Expresses concern* at the financial situation with regard to peacekeeping activities, in particular as regards the reimbursements to troop contributors that bear additional burdens owing to overdue payments by Member States of their assessments;

5. *Also expresses concern* at the delay experienced by the Secretary-General in deploying and providing adequate resources to some recent peacekeeping missions, in particular those in Africa;

6. *Emphasizes* that all future and existing peacekeeping missions shall be given equal and non-discriminatory treatment in respect of financial and administrative arrangements;

7. *Also emphasizes* that all peacekeeping missions shall be provided with adequate resources for the effective and efficient discharge of their respective mandates;

8. *Reiterates its request* to the Secretary-General to make the fullest possible use of facilities and equipment at the United Nations Logistics Base at Brindisi, Italy, in order to minimize the costs of procurement for the Mission;

9. *Requests* the Secretary-General to ensure that proposed peacekeeping budgets are based on the relevant legislative mandates;

10. *Endorses* the conclusions and recommendations contained in the report of the Advisory Committee on Administrative and Budgetary Questions, and the oral statement by the Chairman of the Advisory Committee on Administrative and Budgetary Questions, subject to the provisions of the present resolution, and requests the Secretary-General to ensure their full implementation;

11. *Takes note* of paragraph 19 of the report of the Advisory Committee;

12. *Also takes note* of paragraph 26 of the report of the Advisory Committee;

13. *Further takes note* of paragraph 33 of the report of the Advisory Committee, and decides to approve the establishment of posts and United Nations Volunteer positions as proposed in paragraphs 59 to 87 of the report of the Secretary-General, except for one Field Service post for a CarLog/FuelLog Supervisor, four United Nations Volunteer positions for English Language Teachers, two national General Service posts for Administrative Assistants and nine national General Service posts for Security Assistants;

14. *Takes note* of paragraph 36 of the report of the Advisory Committee;

15. *Also takes note* of paragraph 40 of the report of the Advisory Committee;

16. *Requests* the Secretary-General to ensure that the Mission provides all the necessary support for the local elections planned for 2009 in Timor-Leste, as mandated by the Security Council in its resolution 1867(2009), and, in this regard, decides to approve the resource requirements

of 3,073,200 dollars for the support of local elections in Timor-Leste;

17. *Also requests* the Secretary-General to ensure the full implementation of relevant provisions of resolutions 59/296, 60/266 and 61/276;

18. *Further requests* the Secretary-General to take all necessary action to ensure that the Mission is administered with a maximum of efficiency and economy;

19. *Requests* the Secretary-General, in order to reduce the cost of employing General Service staff, to continue efforts to recruit local staff for the Mission against General Service posts, commensurate with the requirements of the Mission;

20. *Also requests* the Secretary-General to continue to take the steps necessary to facilitate the acceleration of the recruitment process and improve incumbency levels in the Mission;

21. *Welcomes* the introduction in July 2008 of the new database, the misconduct tracking system, to record and track allegations of misconduct aimed at having a more accurate recording of all complaints and allegations received by the Mission, notes the increased number of allegations of serious and minor misconduct, and requests the Secretary-General to ensure that the necessary measures are being taken in order to address this situation;

**Financial performance report for the period
from 1 July 2007 to 30 June 2008**

22. *Takes note* of the report of the Secretary-General on the financial performance of the Mission for the period from 1 July 2007 to 30 June 2008;

**Budget estimates for the period
from 1 July 2009 to 30 June 2010**

23. *Decides* to appropriate to the Special Account for the United Nations Integrated Mission in Timor-Leste the amount of 215,011,500 dollars for the period from 1 July 2009 to 30 June 2010, inclusive of 205,939,400 dollars for the maintenance of the Mission, 7,550,200 dollars for the support account for peacekeeping operations and 1,521,900 dollars for the United Nations Logistics Base;

**Financing of the appropriation for the period
from 1 July 2009 to 30 June 2010**

24. *Also decides* to apportion among Member States the amount of 142,061,175 dollars for the period from 1 July 2009 to 26 February 2010, in accordance with the levels updated in General Assembly resolution 61/243 of 22 December 2006, and taking into account the scale of assessments for 2009, as set out in Assembly resolution 61/237 of 22 December 2006, and for 2010;

25. *Further decides* that, in accordance with the provisions of its resolution 973(X) of 15 December 1955, there shall be set off against the apportionment among Member States, as provided for in paragraph 24 above, their respective share in the Tax Equalization Fund of 5,746,230 dollars, comprising the estimated staff assessment income of 5,127,605 dollars approved for the Mission, the prorated share of 519,320 dollars of the estimated staff assessment income approved for the support account and the prorated share of 99,305 dollars of the estimated staff assessment income approved for the United Nations Logistics Base;

26. *Decides* to apportion among Member States the amount of 72,950,325 dollars for the period from 27 February to 30 June 2010 at a monthly rate of 17,917,625 dollars, in accordance with the levels updated in resolution 61/243, and taking into account the scale of assessments for 2010, subject to a decision of the Security Council to extend the mandate of the Mission;

27. *Also decides* that, in accordance with the provisions of its resolution 973(X), there shall be set off against the apportionment among Member States, as provided for in paragraph 26 above, their respective share in the Tax Equalization Fund of 2,950,770 dollars, comprising the estimated staff assessment income of 2,633,095 dollars approved for the Mission, the prorated share of 266,680 dollars of the estimated staff assessment income approved for the support account and the prorated share of 50,995 dollars of the estimated staff assessment income approved for the United Nations Logistics Base;

28. *Further decides* that, for Member States that have fulfilled their financial obligations to the Mission, there shall be set off against their apportionment, as provided for in paragraph 24 above, their respective share of the unencumbered balance and other income in the total amount of 14,477,500 dollars in respect of the financial period ended 30 June 2008, in accordance with the levels updated in General Assembly resolution 61/243, and taking into account the scale of assessments for 2008, as set out in its resolution 61/237;

29. *Decides* that, for Member States that have not fulfilled their financial obligations to the Mission, there shall be set off against their outstanding obligations their respective share of the unencumbered balance and other income in the total amount of 14,477,500 dollars in respect of the financial period ended 30 June 2008, in accordance with the scheme set out in paragraph 28 above;

30. *Also decides* that the decrease of 761,200 dollars in the estimated staff assessment income in respect of the financial period ended 30 June 2008 shall be set off against the credits from the amount of 14,477,500 dollars referred to in paragraphs 28 and 29 above;

31. *Emphasizes* that no peacekeeping mission shall be financed by borrowing funds from other active peacekeeping missions;

32. *Encourages* the Secretary-General to continue to take additional measures to ensure the safety and security of all personnel participating in the Mission under the auspices of the United Nations, bearing in mind paragraphs 5 and 6 of Security Council resolution 1502(2003) of 26 August 2003;

33. *Invites* voluntary contributions to the Mission in cash and in the form of services and supplies acceptable to the Secretary-General, to be administered, as appropriate, in accordance with the procedure and practices established by the General Assembly;

34. *Decides* to include in the provisional agenda of its sixty-fourth session the item entitled "Financing of the United Nations Integrated Mission in Timor-Leste".

On 24 December, the General Assembly decided that the agenda item on the financing of UNMIT would remain for consideration during its sixty-fourth (2010) session (**decision 64/549**).

Democratic People's Republic of Korea

On 5 April, the Democratic People's Republic of Korea (DPRK) launched a long-range rocket with the stated aim of placing a satellite in orbit. On the same day [S/2009/176], Japan requested a meeting of the Security Council to consider the launch.

Statement by Secretary-General. On the same day [SG/SM/12171], the Secretary-General regretted that, against strong international appeal, the DPRK had gone ahead with its launch. Given the volatility in the region, as well as a stalemate in interaction among the concerned parties, such a launch was not conducive to efforts to promote dialogue, regional peace and stability. He urged the DPRK to comply with relevant Security Council resolutions, and all countries concerned to focus on ways to build confidence and restore dialogue, including the early resumption of the six-party talks (China, DPRK, Japan, Republic of Korea, Russian Federation, United States) aimed at the denuclearization of the Korean peninsula.

SECURITY COUNCIL ACTION

On 13 April [meeting 6106], following consultations among Security Council members, the President made statement **S/PRST/2009/7** on behalf of the Council:

> The Security Council bears in mind the importance of maintaining peace and stability on the Korean peninsula and in north-east Asia as a whole. The Council condemns the 5 April 2009 (local time) launch by the Democratic People's Republic of Korea, which is in contravention of Council resolution 1718(2006).
>
> The Council reiterates that the Democratic People's Republic of Korea must comply fully with its obligations under resolution 1718(2006).
>
> The Council demands that the Democratic People's Republic of Korea not conduct any further launch.
>
> The Council also calls upon all Member States to comply fully with their obligations under resolution 1718(2006).
>
> The Council agrees to adjust the measures imposed by paragraph 8 of resolution 1718(2006) through the designation of entities and goods, and directs the Security Council Committee established pursuant to resolution 1718(2006) to undertake its tasks to this effect and to report to the Council by 24 April 2009, and further agrees that, if the Committee has not acted, then the Council will complete action to adjust the measures by 30 April 2009.
>
> The Council supports the Six-Party Talks, calls for their early resumption, and urges all the participants to intensify their efforts for the full implementation of the joint statement issued on 19 September 2005 by China, the Democratic People's Republic of Korea, Japan, the Republic of Korea, the Russian Federation and the United States of America and their subsequent consensus documents, with a view to achieving the verifiable denuclearization of the Korean peninsula in a peaceful manner and to maintaining peace and stability on the Korean peninsula and in north-east Asia.

> The Council expresses its desire for a peaceful and diplomatic solution to the situation and welcomes efforts by Council members as well as other Member States to facilitate a peaceful and comprehensive solution through dialogue.
>
> The Council will remain actively seized of the matter.

Communication. On 14 April [S/2009/205], the United States transmitted to the Security Council a list of items, materials, equipment, goods and technology related to ballistic missile-related programmes that updated the list contained in a 2006 document [YUN 2006, p. 444] and might be useful for discussions related to presidential statement S/PRST/2009/7.

Sanctions Committee report. As requested by that presidential statement, on 24 April the Chairman of the Security Council Committee established by resolution 1718(2006) [ibid.] to oversee sanctions measures relating to the DPRK (Sanctions Committee) submitted its report [S/2009/222], which designated new entities and goods subject to sanctions.

Security Council consideration. On 25 May, the DPRK announced that it had conducted an underground nuclear test. On the same day, Japan requested that a Council meeting be convened to consider the announcement [S/2009/271]. By resolution 1874(2009) of 12 June (see below), the Council condemned the test and demanded that the DPRK not conduct any further nuclear test or any launch using ballistic missile technology. The Council introduced financial measures; established new cargo inspection provisions; imposed additional restrictions on the supply to, and export from, the DPRK of arms and related materiel; directed the Sanctions Committee to designate additional goods, entities and individuals; and established a Panel of Experts to help the Committee monitor and improve implementation of the relevant measures.

SECURITY COUNCIL ACTION

On 12 June [meeting 6141], the Security Council unanimously adopted **resolution 1874(2009)**. The draft [S/2009/301] was submitted by France, Japan, the Republic of Korea, the United Kingdom and the United States.

The Security Council,

Recalling its previous relevant resolutions, including resolutions 825(1993) of 11 May 1993, 1540(2004) of 28 April 2004, 1695(2006) of 15 July 2006 and, in particular, resolution 1718(2006) of 14 October 2006, as well as the statements by its President of 6 October 2006 and 13 April 2009,

Reaffirming that the proliferation of nuclear, chemical and biological weapons, as well as their means of delivery, constitutes a threat to international peace and security,

Expressing the gravest concern at the nuclear test conducted by the Democratic People's Republic of Korea on 25 May 2009 (local time) in violation of resolution 1718(2006), and at the challenge such a test constitutes to the Treaty on the Non-Proliferation of Nuclear Weapons and to international efforts aimed at strengthening the global regime of non-proliferation of nuclear weapons towards the 2010 Review Conference of the Parties to the Treaty, and the danger it poses to peace and stability in the region and beyond,

Stressing its collective support for the Treaty and commitment to strengthen the Treaty in all its aspects, and global efforts towards nuclear non-proliferation and nuclear disarmament, and recalling that the Democratic People's Republic of Korea cannot have the status of a nuclear-weapon State in accordance with the Treaty in any case,

Deploring the announcement by the Democratic People's Republic of Korea of withdrawal from the Treaty and its pursuit of nuclear weapons,

Underlining once again the importance that the Democratic People's Republic of Korea respond to other security and humanitarian concerns of the international community,

Underlining that measures imposed by the present resolution are not intended to have adverse humanitarian consequences for the civilian population of the Democratic People's Republic of Korea,

Expressing the gravest concern that the nuclear test and missile activities carried out by the Democratic People's Republic of Korea have further generated increased tension in the region and beyond, and determining that there continues to exist a clear threat to international peace and security,

Reaffirming the importance that all Member States uphold the purposes and principles of the Charter of the United Nations,

Acting under Chapter VII of the Charter, and taking measures under Article 41 thereof,

1. *Condemns in the strongest terms* the nuclear test conducted by the Democratic People's Republic of Korea on 25 May 2009 (local time) in violation and flagrant disregard of relevant Security Council resolutions, in particular resolutions 1695(2006) and 1718(2006), and the statement by its President of 13 April 2009,

2. *Demands* that the Democratic People's Republic of Korea not conduct any further nuclear test or any launch using ballistic missile technology;

3. *Decides* that the Democratic People's Republic of Korea shall suspend all activities related to its ballistic missile programme and in this context re-establish its pre-existing commitments to a moratorium on missile launches;

4. *Demands* that the Democratic People's Republic of Korea immediately comply fully with its obligations under relevant Council resolutions, in particular resolution 1718(2006);

5. *Demands also* that the Democratic People's Republic of Korea immediately retract its announcement of withdrawal from the Treaty on the Non-Proliferation of Nuclear Weapons;

6. *Demands further* that the Democratic People's Republic of Korea return at an early date to the Treaty and International Atomic Energy Agency safeguards, bearing in mind the rights and obligations of States parties to the Treaty, and underlines the need for all States parties to the Treaty to continue to comply with their Treaty obligations;

7. *Calls upon* all Member States to implement their obligations pursuant to resolution 1718(2006), including with respect to designations made by the Security Council Committee established pursuant to resolution 1718(2006) ("the Committee") pursuant to the statement by its President of 13 April 2009;

8. *Decides* that the Democratic People's Republic of Korea shall abandon all nuclear weapons and existing nuclear programmes in a complete, verifiable and irreversible manner and immediately cease all related activities, shall act strictly in accordance with the obligations applicable to parties under the Treaty and the terms and conditions of the International Atomic Energy Agency safeguards agreement and shall provide the Agency transparency measures extending beyond these requirements, including such access to individuals, documentation, equipment and facilities as may be required and deemed necessary by the Agency;

9. *Decides also* that the measures in paragraph 8 *(b)* of resolution 1718(2006) shall also apply to all arms and related materiel, as well as to financial transactions, technical training, advice, services or assistance related to the provision, manufacture, maintenance or use of such arms or materiel;

10. *Decides further* that the measures in paragraph 8 *(a)* of resolution 1718(2006) shall also apply to all arms and related materiel, as well as to financial transactions, technical training, advice, services or assistance related to the provision, manufacture, maintenance or use of such arms, except for small arms and light weapons and their related materiel, and calls upon States to exercise vigilance over the direct or indirect supply, sale or transfer to the Democratic People's Republic of Korea of small arms or light weapons, and further decides that States shall notify the Committee at least five days prior to selling, supplying or transferring small arms or light weapons to the Democratic People's Republic of Korea;

11. *Calls upon* all States to inspect, in accordance with their national authorities and legislation, and consistent with international law, all cargo to and from the Democratic People's Republic of Korea, in their territory, including seaports and airports, if the State concerned has information that provides reasonable grounds to believe the cargo contains items, the supply, sale, transfer or export of which is prohibited by paragraph 8 *(a)*, 8 *(b)* or 8 *(c)* of resolution 1718(2006) or by paragraph 9 or 10 of the present resolution, for the purpose of ensuring strict implementation of those provisions;

12. *Calls upon* all Member States to inspect vessels, with the consent of the flag State, on the high seas, if they have information that provides reasonable grounds to believe that the cargo of such vessels contains items, the supply, sale, transfer or export of which is prohibited by paragraph 8 *(a)*, 8 *(b)* or 8 *(c)* of resolution 1718(2006) or by paragraph 9 or 10 of the present resolution, for the purpose of ensuring strict implementation of those provisions;

13. *Calls upon* all States to cooperate with inspections pursuant to paragraphs 11 and 12 above, and, if the flag State does not consent to inspection on the high seas, decides that the flag State shall direct the vessel to proceed to an appropriate and convenient port for the required inspection by the local authorities pursuant to paragraph 11 above;

14. *Decides* to authorize all Member States to, and that all Member States shall, seize and dispose of items, the supply, sale, transfer or export of which is prohibited by paragraph 8 *(a)*, 8 *(b)* or 8 *(c)* of resolution 1718(2006)

or by paragraph 9 or 10 of the present resolution, that are identified in inspections pursuant to paragraph 11, 12 or 13 above in a manner that is not inconsistent with their obligations under applicable Council resolutions, including resolution 1540(2004), as well as any obligations of parties to the Treaty on the Non-Proliferation of Nuclear Weapons, the Convention on the Prohibition of the Development, Production, Stockpiling and Use of Chemical Weapons and on Their Destruction of 13 January 1993 and the Convention on the Prohibition of the Development, Production and Stockpiling of Bacteriological (Biological) and Toxin Weapons and on Their Destruction of 10 April 1972, and decides further that all States shall cooperate in such efforts;

15. *Requires* any Member State, when it undertakes an inspection pursuant to paragraph 11, 12 or 13 above, or seizes and disposes of cargo pursuant to paragraph 14 above, to submit promptly reports containing relevant details to the Committee on the inspection, seizure and disposal;

16. *Also requires* any Member State, when it does not receive the cooperation of a flag State pursuant to paragraph 12 or 13 above, to submit promptly to the Committee a report containing relevant details;

17. *Decides* that Member States shall prohibit the provision by their nationals or from their territory of bunkering services, such as the provision of fuel or supplies, or other servicing of vessels, to vessels of the Democratic People's Republic of Korea if they have information that provides reasonable grounds to believe they are carrying items, the supply, sale, transfer or export of which is prohibited by paragraph 8 *(a)*, 8 *(b)* or 8 *(c)* of resolution 1718(2006) or by paragraph 9 or 10 of the present resolution, unless the provision of such services is necessary for humanitarian purposes or until such time as the cargo has been inspected, and seized and disposed of if necessary, and underlines that the present paragraph is not intended to affect legal economic activities;

18. *Calls upon* Member States, in addition to implementing their obligations pursuant to paragraphs 8 *(d)* and *(e)* of resolution 1718(2006), to prevent the provision of financial services or the transfer to, through or from their territory, or to or by their nationals or entities organized under their laws (including branches abroad), or persons or financial institutions in their territory, of any financial or other assets or resources that could contribute to the Democratic People's Republic of Korea's nuclear-related, ballistic missile-related or other weapons of mass destruction-related programmes or activities, including by freezing any financial or other assets or resources on their territories or that hereafter come within their territories, or that are subject to their jurisdiction or that hereafter become subject to their jurisdiction, that are associated with such programmes or activities and applying enhanced monitoring to prevent all such transactions in accordance with their national authorities and legislation;

19. *Calls upon* all Member States and international financial and credit institutions not to enter into new commitments for grants, financial assistance or concessional loans to the Democratic People's Republic of Korea, except for humanitarian and development purposes directly addressing the needs of the civilian population or the promotion of denuclearization, and also calls upon States to exercise enhanced vigilance with a view to reducing current commitments;

20. *Calls upon* all Member States not to provide public financial support for trade with the Democratic People's Republic of Korea (including the granting of export credits, guarantees or insurance to their nationals or entities involved in such trade) where such financial support could contribute to the Democratic People's Republic of Korea's nuclear-related, ballistic missile-related or other weapons of mass destruction-related programmes or activities;

21. *Emphasizes* that all Member States should comply with the provisions of paragraphs 8 *(a)* (iii) and 8 *(d)* of resolution 1718(2006) without prejudice to the activities of the diplomatic missions in the Democratic People's Republic of Korea pursuant to the Vienna Convention on Diplomatic Relations;

22. *Calls upon* all Member States to report to the Council within forty-five days of the adoption of the present resolution and thereafter upon request by the Committee on concrete measures they have taken in order to implement effectively the provisions of paragraph 8 of resolution 1718(2006) as well as paragraphs 9 and 10 of the present resolution, as well as financial measures set out in paragraphs 18, 19 and 20 of the present resolution;

23. *Decides* that the measures set out in paragraphs 8 *(a)*, 8 *(b)* and 8 *(c)* of resolution 1718(2006) shall also apply to the items listed in INFCIRC/254/Rev.9/Part 1 and INFCIRC/254/Rev.7/Part 2;

24. *Decides also* to adjust the measures imposed by paragraph 8 of resolution 1718(2006) and the present resolution, including through the designation of entities, goods and individuals, and directs the Committee to undertake its tasks to this effect and to report to the Council within thirty days of the adoption of the present resolution, and further decides that, if the Committee has not acted, then the Council will complete action to adjust the measures within seven days of receiving that report;

25. *Decides further* that the Committee shall intensify its efforts to promote the full implementation of resolution 1718(2006), the statement by its President of 13 April 2009 and the present resolution, through a work programme covering compliance, investigations, outreach, dialogue, assistance and cooperation, to be submitted to the Council by 15 July 2009, and that it shall also receive and consider reports from Member States pursuant to paragraphs 10, 15, 16 and 22 of the present resolution;

26. *Requests* the Secretary-General to create for an initial period of one year, in consultation with the Committee, a group of up to seven experts ("the Panel of Experts"), acting under the direction of the Committee to carry out the following tasks: *(a)* assist the Committee in carrying out its mandate as specified in resolution 1718(2006) and the functions specified in paragraph 25 of the present resolution; *(b)* gather, examine and analyse information from States, relevant United Nations bodies and other interested parties regarding the implementation of the measures imposed in resolution 1718(2006) and in the present resolution, in particular incidents of non-compliance; *(c)* make recommendations on actions the Council, or the Committee or Member States, may consider to improve the implementation of the measures imposed in resolution 1718(2006) and in the present resolution; and *(d)* provide

an interim report on its work to the Council no later than ninety days after the adoption of the present resolution, and a final report to the Council no later than thirty days prior to the termination of its mandate, with its findings and recommendations;

27. *Urges* all States, relevant United Nations bodies and other interested parties to cooperate fully with the Committee and the Panel of Experts, in particular by supplying any information at their disposal on the implementation of the measures imposed by resolution 1718(2006) and the present resolution;

28. *Calls upon* all Member States to exercise vigilance and prevent specialized teaching or training of nationals of the Democratic People's Republic of Korea within their territories or by their nationals, in disciplines which could contribute to the Democratic People's Republic of Korea's proliferation-sensitive nuclear activities and the development of nuclear weapon delivery systems;

29. *Calls upon* the Democratic People's Republic of Korea to join the Comprehensive Nuclear-Test-Ban Treaty at the earliest date;

30. *Supports* peaceful dialogue, calls upon the Democratic People's Republic of Korea to return immediately to the Six-Party Talks without precondition, and urges all the participants to intensify their efforts for the full and expeditious implementation of the joint statement issued on 19 September 2005 and the joint documents issued on 13 February and 3 October 2007 by China, the Democratic People's Republic of Korea, Japan, the Republic of Korea, the Russian Federation and the United States of America, with a view to achieving the verifiable denuclearization of the Korean peninsula and to maintaining peace and stability on the Korean peninsula and in north-east Asia;

31. *Expresses its commitment* to a peaceful, diplomatic and political solution to the situation, and welcomes efforts by Council members as well as other Member States to facilitate a peaceful and comprehensive solution through dialogue and to refrain from any actions that might aggravate tensions;

32. *Affirms* that it shall keep the actions of the Democratic People's Republic of Korea under continuous review and that it shall be prepared to review the appropriateness of the measures contained in paragraph 8 of resolution 1718(2006) and relevant paragraphs of the present resolution, including the strengthening, modification, suspension or lifting of the measures, as may be needed at that time in the light of compliance by the Democratic People's Republic of Korea with relevant provisions of resolution 1718(2006) and the present resolution;

33. *Underlines* that further decisions will be required, should additional measures be necessary;

34. *Decides* to remain actively seized of the matter.

Sanctions Committee report. Pursuant to that resolution, the Sanctions Committee in July transmitted to the Security Council its report [S/2009/364], conveying its decision to designate additional entities, goods and individuals subject to the provisions of resolutions 1718(2006) and 1874(2009).

Security Council consideration. On 6 July [A/64/2], the Council held informal consultations following the firing on 4 July of several missiles by the DPRK. Council members expressed their concern and condemned the firing of those missiles, in yet another violation of relevant Council resolutions, and called on the DPRK to comply with its international obligations as specified in those resolutions.

Panel of experts. Pursuant to resolution 1874(2009), the Secretary-General in August informed the Council [S/2009/416] that he had appointed seven experts for the Panel of Experts that would support the Sanctions Committee's work. In October [S/2009/555], the Secretary-General informed the Council that he had appointed a new member of the Panel to replace an expert who was unable to assume her functions.

Statement by Secretary-General. The Secretary-General on 29 August [SG/SM/12429] welcomed the agreement between the DPRK and the Republic of Korea to resume cross-border family reunions in September for hundreds of Korean families separated since the Korean War. He was also pleased that the DPRK authorities had released, on 29 August, four crew members of a Republic of Korea fishing vessel who had been detained after accidentally crossing into northern waters.

Communication. By a 3 September letter to the Security Council [S/2009/443], the DPRK rejected the validity of sanctions imposed against it and stated that it would not respond to requests for information made by the Sanctions Committee. The DPRK stated that it was continuing to weaponize plutonium, and that experimental uranium enrichment had been successfully conducted "to enter into the completion phase". The country was prepared for both dialogue and sanctions. If some permanent members of the Security Council wished to put sanctions before dialogue, the DPRK would respond by bolstering its nuclear deterrence first, before meeting them in a dialogue.

Sanctions Committee report. Reporting to the Security Council on the activities of the Sanctions Committee in 2009 [S/2010/28], the Committee Chairman said that during the reporting period, 47 Member States reported to the Committee on the steps they had taken to implement provisions of resolutions 1718(2006) and 1874(2009), including financial measures set out in resolution 1874(2009). The Committee also received four separate reports of alleged violations in which the reporting States requested that the relevant information be treated as confidential. All four reported cases were being examined by the Committee and would continue to be investigated with the support and technical expertise of the Committee's Panel of Experts. A list of the reports of Member States, excluding those which had requested confidentiality, was annexed to the report and was accessible on the Committee's website.

Nepal

The United Nations Mission in Nepal (UNMIN), established in 2007 [YUN 2007, p. 385], continued to assist the country in its transition to peace following a decade of armed conflict. Headed until 6 February by Ian Martin (United Kingdom), the Secretary-General's Personal Representative in Nepal, and then by the Secretary-General's Representative in Nepal, Karin Landgren (Sweden), the Mission helped build confidence in the peace process, including through its arms monitoring responsibilities. Unarmed UN arms monitors were deployed in the Maoist army cantonment and satellite sites around the country, as well as at the Nepal Army arms storage depot in Kathmandu. The Security Council extended the Mission's mandate on 23 January and 23 July, the last time until 23 January 2010.

Report of Secretary-General (January). On 2 January [S/2009/1], the Secretary-General reported on the peace process in Nepal and UNMIN's activities since 24 October 2008 [YUN 2008, p. 419]. He said that the peace process remained fragile: critical agreements on the reintegration of former Maoist combatants were still lacking, and the country would continue to need UN assistance. It was regrettable that the political parties had failed to reach agreement regarding the Special Committee to supervise, integrate and rehabilitate Maoist army personnel so that it could begin its work. That was an indication of the wider tensions among the political parties, which could imperil the completion of the peace process and the drafting of the Constitution. An exit strategy for UNMIN required decisions regarding the future of those in the Maoist army cantonments, and that issue should be addressed through the agreed process—the Special Committee. An advisory team that visited the country in December 2008 found that all the Nepalese interlocutors were looking to the United Nations to play a role in assisting the Special Committee once it was functioning, and believed that the world body had an important role during the process of integration and rehabilitation. The United Nations could not immediately terminate the support it had been providing through UNMIN, as requested by the Government [ibid., p. 420], nor could the United Nations be expected to maintain indefinitely the monitoring of arms and armed personnel while the process for deciding the future of the former combatants was further delayed. The Secretary-General recommended a six-month extension of UNMIN, with further downsizing from 23 January. He proposed that the number of arms monitors contributed by Member States should be retained at the strength of 73, but that most of the 18 remaining civilian posts which had been filled by retired military officers should be abolished as at 23 January. The

Political Affairs Office would be further reduced, and other substantive posts eliminated, reducing substantive posts by one third. The support services would be substantially reduced and remaining functions increasingly performed by national staff; international support posts would be approximately halved. With the further downsizing, UNMIN would be headed by a representative instead of a special representative of the Secretary-General.

Security Council consideration (January). In his last briefing to the Security Council as the Secretary-General's Personal Representative, on 16 January [meeting 6069], Mr. Martin said that one need for change to which no political party and neither army was yet truly committed was the need to end impunity. He noted that in the three and a half years he had been in the country, not a single perpetrator of a major human rights violation, whether committed during the armed conflict or after, had been properly brought to justice. Although the parties had committed in 2006 to investigate disappearances, only now was Parliament about to consider legislation to set up a commission to do so.

SECURITY COUNCIL ACTION

On 23 January [meeting 6074], the Security Council unanimously adopted **resolution 1864(2009)**. The draft [S/2009/46] was submitted by the United Kingdom.

The Security Council,

Recalling its resolutions 1740(2007) of 23 January 2007, 1796(2008) of 23 January 2008 and 1825(2008) of 23 July 2008,

Reaffirming the sovereignty, territorial integrity and political independence of Nepal and its ownership of the implementation of the Comprehensive Peace Agreement and subsequent agreements,

Recalling the signing on 21 November 2006 by the Government of Nepal and the Communist Party of Nepal (Maoist) of the Comprehensive Peace Agreement, and the stated commitment of both parties to find a permanent and sustainable peace, and commending the steps taken to date to implement the Agreement,

Acknowledging the strong desire of the Nepalese people for peace and the restoration of democracy and the importance in this respect of the implementation of the Comprehensive Peace Agreement and subsequent agreements by the relevant parties,

Expressing its continued readiness to support the peace process in Nepal in the timely and effective implementation of the Comprehensive Peace Agreement and subsequent agreements, in particular the agreement of 25 June 2008, as requested by the Government of Nepal,

Welcoming the successful conclusion of the Constituent Assembly elections on 10 April 2008, and the progress made by the parties since the formation of the Assembly in working towards a democratic government, including the decision made at the first session of the Assembly to establish Nepal as a federal democratic republic,

Welcoming also the formation of a democratically elected government and institutions in Nepal,

Welcoming further the establishment of the Special Committee for the supervision, integration and rehabilitation of the Maoist army personnel, and calling upon the Government of Nepal and all political parties to work together to ensure the effective working of the Committee and to complete the integration and rehabilitation of the Maoist army personnel,

Echoing the call by the Secretary-General for all parties in Nepal to move forward swiftly in the implementation of the agreements reached, noting the assessment of the Secretary-General that the United Nations Mission in Nepal will be well placed to assist in the management of arms and armed personnel in accordance with the agreement of 25 June 2008 between the political parties, and recognizing the willingness of the Mission to assist the parties in this, as requested, in order to achieve a durable solution,

Welcoming the report of the Secretary-General of 2 January 2009 on the Mission, in accordance with his mandate,

Welcoming also the completion of the two phases of the verification process and continuing assistance with the management of arms and armed personnel of both sides in accordance with resolution 1740(2007) and in line with the provisions of the Comprehensive Peace Agreement, noting the importance of a durable long-term solution in helping to create the conditions for the completion of the activities of the Mission, noting also in this regard the need to address outstanding issues, particularly the release of minors in cantonment sites, welcoming the commitment by the Government of Nepal to discharge minors without further delay, and calling upon the Government to implement this commitment as soon as possible and for continued reporting on this issue as required under resolution 1612(2005) of 26 July 2005,

Noting with appreciation that, with the successful holding of the Constituent Assembly elections, some of the elements of the mandate relating to the Mission as set out in resolution 1740(2007) have already been accomplished,

Taking note of the letter dated 12 December 2008 from the Government of Nepal to the Secretary-General, in which it recognizes the contribution of the Mission and requests an extension of the Mission on a smaller scale to carry out the remainder of the mandate for six months, and further taking note of the intention of the Government with regard to the termination of the monitoring requirements of the Mission by the end of this six-month period,

Recognizing the need to pay special attention to the needs of women, children and traditionally marginalized groups in the peace process, as mentioned in the Comprehensive Peace Agreement and in resolution 1325(2000) of 31 October 2000,

Recognizing also that civil society can play an important role in democratic transition and conflict prevention,

Expressing its appreciation for the contribution of the Special Representative of the Secretary-General in Nepal and the efforts of his team in the Mission and the United Nations country team, including the Office of the United Nations High Commissioner for Human Rights, which is monitoring human rights at the request of the Government of Nepal, and stressing the need for coordination

and complementarity of efforts between the Mission and all the United Nations actors in the Mission area, particularly in order to ensure continuity, as the mandate comes to an end,

1. *Decides*, in line with the request of the Government of Nepal and the recommendations of the Secretary-General, to renew the mandate of the United Nations Mission in Nepal, as established under resolution 1740(2007), until 23 July 2009, taking into account the completion of some elements of the mandate, and the ongoing work on the monitoring of the management of arms and armed personnel in line with the agreement of 25 June 2008 between the political parties, which will support the completion of the peace process;

2. *Calls upon* all parties to take full advantage of the expertise and readiness of the Mission, within its mandate, to support the peace process to facilitate the completion of outstanding aspects of the mandate of the Mission;

3. *Concurs* with the view of the Secretary-General that the current monitoring arrangements cannot be maintained indefinitely, and underlines the need for the Government of Nepal to consider necessary measures to reduce the monitoring requirements of the Mission;

4. *Endorses* the recommendations of the Secretary-General for a phased, gradual drawdown and withdrawal of Mission staff, including arms monitors, as proposed in paragraphs 62 and 63 of his report;

5. *Requests* the Secretary-General to keep the Security Council informed of progress towards the implementation of the present resolution and to submit a report on this and the implications for the Mission, with a view to further downsizing of the Mission, no later than 30 April 2009;

6. *Calls upon* the Government of Nepal to continue to take the decisions necessary to create conditions conducive to the completion of the activities of the Mission by the end of the current mandate, including through the implementation of the agreement of 25 June 2008, in order to facilitate the withdrawal of the Mission from Nepal;

7. *Welcomes* the progress achieved so far, and calls upon all political parties in Nepal to expedite the peace process and to continue to work together in a spirit of cooperation, consensus and compromise in order to continue the transition to a durable long-term solution to enable the country to move to a peaceful, democratic and more prosperous future;

8. *Requests* the parties in Nepal to take the necessary steps to promote the safety, security and freedom of movement of Mission and associated personnel in executing the tasks defined in the mandate;

9. *Decides* to remain seized of the matter.

Appointment of Representative. On 27 January [S/2009/57], the Secretary-General informed the Security Council that he intended to appoint Karin Landgren (Sweden) as his Representative in Nepal and Head of UNMIN. The Council took note of that intention on 30 January [S/2009/58].

Report of Secretary-General (April). By his 24 April report [S/2009/221] on the peace process and UNMIN's activities since 2 January, the Secretary-General said that on 13 January, the Communist

Party of Nepal (Maoist) (CPN(M)) merged with the Communist Party of Nepal-Unity Centre (Masal), as the Unified Communist Party of Nepal-Maoist (UCPN-M). Coordination committees were formed to strengthen cooperation between UCPN-M and its major governing coalition partner, the Communist Party of Nepal-Unified Marxist-Leninist, and among the four political parties in the Maoist-led coalition Government. Nevertheless, those relations remained fractious, marked by public acrimony and weak consultation on major decisions.

The Constituent Assembly had made some progress on the Constitution-drafting process, which was to be completed by May 2010. The main challenges would be reaching agreement on the form of governance and the new federal structure of the country. The Special Committee to supervise, integrate and rehabilitate Maoist army personnel met for the first time on 16 January, and on 11 February requested that the Government proceed with the discharge from the cantonments and rehabilitation of the 4,008 Maoist army personnel who were disqualified during the UNMIN verification process, including the 2,973 who were minors in May 2006.

Upon the departure on 6 February of Ian Martin, the Secretary-General's Special Representative since the establishment of UNMIN in 2006, Karin Landgren took up her responsibilities as the Secretary-General's Representative. On 1 April, the Mission was downsized to 275 personnel from the previous authorized strength of 396. The United Nations High Commissioner for Human Rights, Navanethem Pillay, visited Nepal from 18 to 22 March, where she found progress in human rights since the end of the conflict. However, the general climate of impunity for violations remained a matter of concern, and progress towards judicial accountability had yet to be observed.

In January, the UN country team and international partners released a humanitarian transition appeal for 2009 for $115 million, focused on the needs of the food-insecure population, refugees and the residual needs from the 2008 floods. As at 10 April, it had been 44 per cent funded, primarily in the food assistance component. The United Nations Peace Fund for Nepal continued to support key aspects of the peace process, including the discharge and reintegration of disqualified Maoist army personnel and a programme for youth employment in selected districts.

The Government was preparing for the National Development Forum scheduled for mid-May, which would provide an opportunity for it to present a new two-year development strategy to the international community. In line with Government planning processes, the UN country team requested approval from the Government for a two-year extension, until 2012, of the United Nations Development Assistance Framework.

Security Council consideration (May). On 5 May, Ms. Landgren, the Secretary-General's Representative in Nepal, briefed the Council [meeting 6119] about developments in the country, including the political standoff that had led to the resignation of Prime Minister Pushpa Kamal Dahal "Prachanda" on 4 May. The representative of Nepal also addressed the Council.

SECURITY COUNCIL ACTION

On 5 May [meeting 6119], following consultations among Security Council members, the President made statement **S/PRST/2009/12** on behalf of the Council:

The Security Council expresses its concern about the current political crisis in Nepal, and underscores the urgent need for the Government of Nepal and all political parties to continue to work together in a spirit of compromise. The Council notes the steps taken so far in the implementation of the peace process and recalls its full support for that process.

The Council reaffirms its full support for the United Nations Mission in Nepal and recalls resolution 1864(2009) calling upon the Government of Nepal to continue to take the decisions necessary to create conditions conducive to completion of the activities of the Mission by the end of the current mandate, including through the work of the Special and Technical Committees for the supervision, integration and rehabilitation of Maoist army combatants.

The Council recalls the commitment by the Government of Nepal to discharge minors from the cantonment sites and calls upon the Government to implement this commitment in accordance with international law.

Report of Secretary-General (July). By his report of 13 July [S/2009/351], the Secretary-General said the modest progress witnessed in some aspects of the peace process during the first quarter of 2009 had stalled against a backdrop of mistrust and a further deterioration of relations among key stakeholders, notably between UCPN-M and the other major parties and between UCPN-M and the Nepal Army. That crisis led on 4 May to the resignation of Prime Minister Prachanda, following the action taken by President Ram Baran Yadav to reverse the cabinet decision of the previous day to dismiss the Chief of Army Staff, General Rookmangud Katawal. On 23 May, Madhav Kumar Nepal, a senior leader of the Communist Party of Nepal-Unified Marxist-Leninist (UML), was elected Prime Minister. He had since formed a new coalition Government with the support of 21 other political parties but without the participation of the Maoists.

The Special Committee set up to supervise, integrate and rehabilitate Maoist army personnel remained inactive, and no progress was made with regard to the discharge of disqualified Maoist army personnel. The Constituent Assembly made further progress on its central task of drafting the new Constitution, albeit with delays due in part to the uncertain political situation. Significant challenges remained, however, owing to fundamental differences on such issues as the new federal structure, the system of government and the allocation of resources.

As at 1 June, 253 of the authorized 275 UNMIN personnel were assigned to the Mission. Of 193 civilian personnel, 30 per cent were women, including 44 per cent of the 52 substantive staff and 24 per cent of the 141 administrative staff. The Child Protection Unit continued to support the work of the Mission in planning for the discharge and rehabilitation of the 2,973 Maoist army personnel who were disqualified as minors but who remained at the cantonment sites. The security situation was affected by the frequent strikes and protests of various groups across the country. Programme delivery by the United Nations and partners was disrupted due to the protests. A national monitoring group reported in late June that there had been 500 shutdowns in the previous six months.

The frequency of human rights violations committed by State actors remained generally unchanged, and no progress had been made towards fulfilling the commitments made by the previous Government and the leaders of the political parties to end impunity and ensure that the perpetrators of human rights violations and abuses, both past and present, were held to account. Human rights defenders continued to face significant challenges in carrying out their activities, particularly in the Tarai districts, where they were sometimes targeted by armed groups.

Recent political developments, including demonstrations and strikes by ethnic and political groups, had delayed UN service delivery. Delivery of food assistance to more than 325,000 highly food-insecure people, including flood victims and Bhutanese refugees, was delayed by 10 days in May. The 2008/2009 winter drought was the worst on record, resulting in a shortfall in wheat and barley production of 14 and 17 per cent, respectively, which would affect 1.5 million people in the central and far western regions, with 707,000 individuals requiring immediate food assistance. Nearly 70 per cent of households affected by the drought were already experiencing food shortages owing to the 17 per cent increase in food prices over the previous year. The United Nations and partners estimated that an additional $30 million was required to provide humanitarian support to the drought-affected populations. Meanwhile, the global financial crisis continued to reduce demand for migrant labour, and the insecurity in Nepal had limited investment, job creation and exports.

Communication. On 14 July [S/2009/360], the Secretary-General transmitted to the Security Council a letter of 7 July from Nepal requesting a six-month extension of UNMIN's mandate from 23 July, the date of its expiration.

SECURITY COUNCIL ACTION

On 23 July [meeting 6167], the Security Council unanimously adopted **resolution 1879(2009)**. The draft [S/2009/377] was submitted by the United Kingdom.

The Security Council,

Recalling its resolutions 1740(2007) of 23 January 2007, 1796(2008) of 23 January 2008, 1825(2008) of 23 July 2008 and 1864(2009) of 23 January 2009, and the statement by its President of 5 May 2009,

Reaffirming the sovereignty, territorial integrity and political independence of Nepal and its ownership of the implementation of the Comprehensive Peace Agreement and subsequent agreements,

Recalling the signing on 21 November 2006 by the Government of Nepal and the Communist Party of Nepal (Maoist) of the Comprehensive Peace Agreement, and the stated commitment of both parties to find a permanent and sustainable peace, and commending the steps taken to date to implement the Agreement,

Acknowledging the strong desire of the Nepalese people for peace and the restoration of democracy and the importance in this respect of the implementation of the Comprehensive Peace Agreement and subsequent agreements by the relevant parties,

Expressing its continued readiness to support the peace process in Nepal in the timely and effective implementation of the Comprehensive Peace Agreement and subsequent agreements, in particular the agreement of 25 June 2008, as requested by the Government of Nepal,

Welcoming the progress the Constituent Assembly has since made towards writing a new democratic constitution of Nepal within the stipulated time frame since the successful conclusion of the Assembly elections on 10 April 2008,

Noting with concern recent developments, and encouraging renewed and sustained efforts to create a unified approach among the political parties, including through the proposal for a high-level consultative mechanism as a forum for discussion on critical peace process issues,

Calling upon the Government of Nepal and all political parties to work together to ensure the early reconstitution and effective working of the Special Committee for the supervision, integration and rehabilitation of the Maoist army personnel, drawing upon the support of the Technical Committee,

Echoing the call by the Secretary-General for all parties in Nepal to move forward swiftly in the implementation of the agreements reached, noting the assessment of the Secretary-General that the United Nations Mission in Nepal will be well placed to assist in the management of arms and armed personnel in accordance with the agreement of 25 June 2008 between the political parties, and recognizing the willingness of the Mission to assist the parties in this, as requested, in order to achieve a durable solution,

Welcoming the report of the Secretary-General of 13 July 2009 on the Mission,

Recalling the completion of the two phases of the verification process, and welcoming continuing assistance with the management of arms and armed personnel of both sides in accordance with resolution 1740(2007) and in line with the provisions of the Comprehensive Peace Agreement, noting the importance of a durable long-term solution in helping to create the conditions for the completion of the activities of the Mission, noting also in this regard the need to address outstanding issues without further delay, welcoming in this regard the decision by the Government of Nepal and the Unified Communist Party of Nepal (Maoist) formally to launch the discharge and rehabilitation process for the disqualified Maoist army personnel, including minors, and calling upon all political parties to implement this process fully and expeditiously and for continued reporting on this issue as required under resolution 1612(2005) of 26 July 2005,

Recalling that, with the successful holding of the Constituent Assembly elections, some of the elements of the mandate of the Mission as set out in resolution 1740(2007) have already been accomplished,

Welcoming the action plan which the Government of Nepal has committed to prepare, the implementation of which will facilitate the withdrawal of the Mission from Nepal,

Taking note of the letter dated 7 July 2009 from the Government of Nepal to the Secretary-General, in which it recognizes the contribution of the Mission and requests an extension of the mandate of the Mission for six months, and further taking note of the commitments of the Government to reconstitute the Special Committee, strengthened with the support of the Ministry of Peace and Reconstruction, and also for beginning the process of integration and rehabilitation of the Maoist army personnel,

Recognizing the need to pay special attention to the needs and the role of women, children and traditionally marginalized groups in the peace process, as mentioned in the Comprehensive Peace Agreement and in resolution 1325(2000) of 31 October 2000,

Recognizing also the need to address impunity and to promote and protect human rights by building the capacity of independent national institutions,

Recognizing further that civil society can play an important role in democratic transition and conflict prevention,

Expressing its appreciation for the contribution of the Representative of the Secretary-General in Nepal and the efforts of her team in the Mission and the United Nations country team, including the Office of the United Nations High Commissioner for Human Rights, which is monitoring human rights at the request of the Government of Nepal, and stressing the need for coordination and complementarity of efforts between the Mission and all the United Nations actors in the Mission area, particularly in order to ensure continuity, as the mandate comes to an end,

1.   *Decides*, in line with the request of the Government of Nepal and the recommendations of the Secretary-General, to renew the mandate of the United Nations Mission in Nepal, as established under resolution 1740(2007), until 23 January 2010, taking into account the completion of some elements of the mandate, and the ongoing work on the monitoring of the management of arms and armed personnel in line with the agreement of 25 June 2008 between the political parties, which will support the completion of the peace process;

2.   *Calls upon* all parties to take full advantage of the expertise and readiness of the Mission, within its mandate, to support the peace process to facilitate the completion of outstanding aspects of the mandate of the Mission by 23 January 2010;

3.   *Concurs* with the view of the Secretary-General that the current monitoring arrangements were conceived as temporary measures, rather than long-term solutions, and cannot be maintained indefinitely, and underlines the need for the Government of Nepal to consider necessary measures to end the present monitoring arrangements;

4.   *Requests* the Secretary-General to report to the Security Council by 30 October 2009 on the implementation of the present resolution and progress in creating the conditions conducive to the completion of the activities of the Mission by the end of the current mandate, including the implementation of commitments made in the letter dated 7 July 2009 from the Government of Nepal to the Secretary-General;

5.   *Calls upon* the Government of Nepal to continue to take the decisions necessary to create conditions conducive to the completion of the activities of the Mission by the end of the current mandate, including through the implementation of the agreement of 25 June 2008, in order to facilitate the withdrawal of the Mission from Nepal;

6.   *Welcomes* the progress achieved so far, and calls upon all political parties in Nepal to expedite the peace process and to work together in a spirit of cooperation, consensus and compromise in order to continue the transition to a durable long-term solution to enable the country to move to a peaceful, democratic and more prosperous future;

7.   *Requests* the parties in Nepal to take the steps necessary to promote the safety, security and freedom of movement of Mission and associated personnel in executing the tasks defined in the mandate;

8.   *Decides* to remain seized of the matter.

Report of Secretary-General (October). By a 26 October report [S/2009/553], the Secretary-General said that the stalemate among the political parties that had held up progress in the peace process remained unresolved, although renewed efforts were being made to break the deadlock. The Special Committee to supervise, integrate and rehabilitate Maoist army personnel resumed its work in September, and the discharge and rehabilitation of the disqualified Maoist army personnel, including those determined by the 2007 verification process to be minors, was relaunched on 11 October.

The Constituent Assembly faced repeated delays in drafting the new Constitution, leading to growing public speculation and concern that the May 2010 promulgation deadline would not be met. Public security remained a matter of concern, especially in the Tarai, where armed groups continued to operate in a climate of impunity, and in some hill districts in the eastern and mid-western regions. The Government held two rounds of talks with five Tarai armed groups in August and September, which ended inconclusively.

As at 16 October, 261 of the 278 authorized personnel were assigned to UNMIN. Of 191 civilian personnel, 30 per cent were women. During the reporting period, UNMIN conducted a review of its arms monitoring arrangement and highlighted the need for the Nepal Army and the Maoist army to confirm the number of their respective personnel and increase cooperation with UNMIN on the notification of troop movements. UNMIN arms monitors witnessed salary payments for August and September to verified Maoist army personnel at the cantonment sites. In September, the Government increased the official death toll in the decade-long (1996–2006) Maoist insurgency by more than 3,000 to 16,278.

On 17 August, UNDP launched the *Nepal National Human Development Report 2009*. It also launched a five-year Livelihood Recovery for Peace programme during the reporting period, targeting 300,000 households in three Tarai districts. The United Nations Peace Fund for Nepal released a further $2.1 million to UNDP, UNICEF and UNFPA to prepare for the discharge and rehabilitation of disqualified Maoist army personnel. It also released $2 million to the Office of the United Nations High Commissioner for Human Rights to begin a transitional justice programme to support the truth and reconciliation commission and the commission of inquiry on disappearances.

A combination of drought and high food prices increased the number of food-insecure people to 3.4 million, and WFP added another 700,000 people to its beneficiary caseload, bringing the number of people receiving food assistance to more than 2 million.

Security Council consideration (November). On 6 November, the Secretary-General's Representative in Nepal, Ms. Landgren, briefed the Council [meeting 6214] about developments in the country, stating that while limited progress had been made in the peace process, overall it had faced protracted deadlock, with the added risk of confrontation.

Report of Secretary-General. In a later report [S/2010/17], the Secretary-General reviewed the situation since 26 October. He said that the tensions, deep differences and mistrust among the parties to the peace process had persisted. The Special Committee had not made headway in its work, but important progress was achieved in November, with the announcement by UCPN-M that it would proceed quickly with the discharge of all its personnel disqualified through the UNMIN-led verification of the Maoist army in 2007. On 16 December, further significant movement was made with the signing of an action plan by the Government, UCPN-M and the United Nations for the discharge and rehabilitation of those disqualified as minors. Meanwhile, the Con-

stituent Assembly had made slow progress on drafting the Constitution, which was to be promulgated by 28 May 2010.

UCPN-M-led protests calling for "civilian supremacy" disrupted daily life and the functioning of Government offices around the country. On the first day of a nationwide general strike held from 20 to 22 December, a major clash occurred between Maoist demonstrators and the security forces in Kathmandu, during which 75 people were reported injured, several seriously. Friction between youth wings of the political parties had continued, with violent clashes between cadres of the UML-affiliated Youth Force and the Young Communist League of UCPN-M in the eastern and mid-western regions in November and December, resulting in injuries on both sides.

As at 7 December, 264 of the authorized 278 personnel were serving in UNMIN. Out of 192 civilian personnel, 31 per cent were women. There was no substantial progress in addressing impunity and ensuring accountability for human rights violations committed during or after the conflict. Development activities were affected by the political stalemate, in part due to the disruptions caused by the Maoist protest programmes, and an additional 300,000 Nepalese were facing food insecurity because of the poor summer crop harvest, bringing the total number to 3.7 million. The United Nations Mine Action Team would soon begin the final phase of its work in support of Government efforts to meet its commitment to clear all remaining minefields. The United Nations Peace Fund for Nepal released $500,000, which partly met the funding requirements for that final phase of the Team's work.

UNMIN financing

On 26 October [A/64/349/Add.3], the Secretary-General estimated UNMIN's resource requirements for 2010 at $16,742,900. In an 11 December report [A/64/7/Add.13], ACABQ said that, in view of the anticipated expiration of the Mission's mandate, the Advisory Committee recommended that the proposed resources for safety issues and staff development related to official travel be reduced from $396,100 to $325,000. For the same reason, it recommended against the proposed provision of $259,800 for the replacement of equipment.

On 24 December, the General Assembly, by section VI of **resolution 64/245** (see p. 1407), approved the amount proposed by the Secretary-General as part of the $569,526,500 budget for the 26 special political missions authorized by the General Assembly and/or the Security Council.

Iran

In 2009, the United Nations continued to address Iran's nuclear programme and the sanctions it imposed and reinforced by resolutions 1737(2006) [YUN 2006, p. 436], 1747(2007) [YUN 2007, p. 374], 1803(2008) [YUN 2008, p. 409] and 1835(2008) [ibid., p. 414]. Meanwhile, a Committee established pursuant to resolution 1737(2006) continued overseeing implementation of the sanctions regime.

The International Atomic Energy Agency (IAEA) reported that during 2009, Iran had not implemented the Additional Protocol to Iran's Safeguards Agreement or the relevant resolutions of the Security Council and the IAEA Board of Governors. It had also failed to provide the necessary cooperation to permit the Agency to confirm that all nuclear material in Iran was being used in peaceful activities. Iran maintained that its nuclear programme was peaceful, as demonstrated by IAEA reports, and that it would never try to acquire nuclear weapons.

IAEA reports

During 2009, the Council had before it a number of reports by the IAEA Board of Governors on Iran's implementation of the Non-Proliferation Treaty Safeguards Agreement and relevant Security Council resolutions. Each one stated that the Agency had been able to continue its activities to verify the non-diversion of declared nuclear material, while elaborating on that process and the difficulties encountered.

IAEA report (February). IAEA's 19 February report [GOV/2009/8] on developments since 19 November 2008 [YUN 2008, p. 414] stated that in January, the Agency had again requested access to carry out a design information verification at the Iran Nuclear Research Reactor (IR-40) at Arak but Iran had refused, which had made it difficult for the Agency to report further on its construction, as requested by the Council. The Agency had also not received a positive reply in connection with its requests dating back to February 2008 and earlier to meet with Iranian authorities in Tehran, at the earliest possible opportunity, to resolve outstanding issues with respect to possible military dimensions to Iran's nuclear programme.

Security Council consideration (March). On 10 March [meeting 6090], Yukio Takasu (Japan), Chairman of the Security Council Committee established pursuant to Council resolution 1737(2006), briefed the Council on its activities from 11 December 2008 to 10 March 2009. He emphasized that, during the reporting period, the Committee had received a number of reports and exchanged letters and notifications

with States concerning their implementation of the sanctions, and informed the Council of the IAEA report on its programme during the technical cooperation cycle 2009–2011.

IAEA report (June). IAEA's 5 June report [GOV/2009/35] on developments since its February report stated that Iran had continued to refuse to permit the Agency to carry out design information verification at IR-40, and had not suspended its enrichment-related activities or its work on heavy water–related projects as required by the Security Council. On 23 May, the Agency conducted an inspection at the Fuel Manufacturing Plant, where it noted that, with the exception of the final quality control testing area, the process line for the production of fuel assemblies for the heavy water reactor fuel had been completed, and that one fuel assembly had been assembled from previously produced fuel rods. In a letter of 29 May, the Agency reiterated its request to meet with relevant Iranian authorities at the earliest possible opportunity to address the outstanding issues relating to possible military dimensions of Iran's nuclear programme.

Security Council consideration (June). On 15 June [meeting 6142], Mr. Takasu briefed the Council on Committee activities since 11 March, and drew attention to a request by the Committee for information from two Member States regarding a transfer of materiel that constituted a violation of paragraph 5 of resolution 1747(2007).

IAEA report (August). IAEA's report of 28 August [GOV/2009/55] stated that on 19 June, the Agency requested Iran to update the Design Information Questionnaire for the Fuel Manufacturing Plant and IR-40 to reflect the design features of the fuel assembly verified by the Agency during its inspection in May. On 21 August, Iran submitted an updated Questionnaire for the Fuel Manufacturing Plant, which the Agency was reviewing. On 17 August, Iran, following repeated requests, provided the Agency with access to the reactor facility at Arak, at which time it was able to carry out a design information verification. The Agency verified that the construction of IR-40 was ongoing, and that no reactor vessel was yet present.

The operator stated that the reactor vessel was still being manufactured, and that it would be installed in 2011. The facility at its current stage of construction conformed to the design information provided by Iran as at 24 January 2007. However, Iran still needed to provide updated and more detailed design information, in particular about the nuclear fuel characteristics, fuel handling and transfer equipment, and the nuclear material accountancy and control system. The Agency had continued using satellite imagery to monitor the status of the Heavy Water Production Plant, which seemed not to have been operating since the last report.

IAEA report (November). In its 16 November report [GOV/2009/74], the Agency stated that while Iran had recently submitted preliminary design information on the Darkhovin reactor, it continued to assert that it was not bound by the revised Code 3.1 of the Subsidiary Arrangements General Part to which it had agreed in 2003, and which it had ceased to implement in March 2007.

Iran had also informed the Agency about the construction of a new pilot enrichment plant at Qom. However, its failure to inform the Agency of the decision to construct, or to authorize construction of, a new facility as soon as such a decision was taken, and to submit information as the design was developed, was inconsistent with its obligations under the Subsidiary Arrangements to its Safeguards Agreement.

Moreover, Iran's delay in submitting such information did not contribute to the building of confidence, and while the plant corresponded to the design information provided, Iran's explanation about its purpose and the chronology of its design and construction required further clarification. Further, Iran had not suspended its enrichment-related activities or its work on heavy water-related projects, as required by the Security Council.

IAEA resolution. The Secretary-General on 7 December [S/2009/633] forwarded to the Council a resolution adopted on 27 November by the IAEA Board of Governors, in which the Board urged Iran to comply fully and without delay with its obligations under the relevant Council resolutions and to meet the requirements of the Board of Governors, including by suspending immediately construction at Qom. It further urged Iran to engage with the Agency on the resolution of all outstanding issues concerning its nuclear programme, comply fully with its safeguards obligations, apply the modified Code 3.1 and implement and ratify promptly the Additional Protocol.

The Board urged Iran to provide the Agency with the requested clarifications regarding the purpose of the enrichment plant at Qom and the chronology of its design and construction. It called on Iran to confirm that it had not taken a decision to construct, or authorize construction of, any other nuclear facility which had not yet been declared to the Agency, and requested that the IAEA Director General continue his efforts to implement the Safeguards Agreement, resolve the outstanding issues and implement the relevant Security Council resolutions.

IAEA report. A later IAEA report [GOV/2010/10], covering developments from 16 November to the end of 2009, affirmed that while the Agency continued to verify the non-diversion of declared nuclear material in Iran, the country had not provided the necessary cooperation to permit IAEA to confirm that all nuclear material in Iran was being used in peaceful activities.

Sanctions Committee report. On 31 December, the Sanctions Committee Chairman reported [S/2009/688] to the Security Council on its activities in 2009. By year's end, the Committee had received 91 reports pursuant to resolution 1737(2006), 78 reports pursuant to resolution 1747(2007) and 67 reports pursuant to resolution 1803(2008). The list of those reports was appended to the Committee's report.

During the year, the Committee received two notifications from a Member State of the supply of non-prohibited items relevant to the construction of the nuclear power plant in Bushehr, Iran, and received five notifications from a Member State of exemptions to the freeze for transactions made prior to the sanctions. It also received reports of three violations of paragraph 5 of resolution 1747(2007), which imposed an export ban on arms and related materiel on Iran, which it studied carefully.

In the first instance, the Committee received a letter dated 3 February from a Member State regarding the presence of suspicious cargo, originating from Iran and destined for another State. The carrying vessel was redirected to an anchorage in the territorial waters of the reporting State where two on-board inspections were conducted. According to that State, the cargo contained arms-related materiel. Following the receipt of guidance from the Committee, as sought by the State, the suspicious cargo was offloaded, further inspected and, ultimately, retained and stored by the State. In the second instance, the State reported that in line with its international obligations, it had retained, unloaded and stored cargo, originating from Iran and destined for another State, containing arms-related materiel, and would ensure that the items were neither allowed to reach their intended destination nor returned to their place of origin.

In the third instance, the vessel carrying the suspicious cargo, originating from Iran and destined for another State, was boarded by the navy of the reporting State, which conducted an on-board inspection and determined that the cargo contained arms-related materiel. The State reported that, in line with its international obligations, it had unloaded, retained and stored the cargo and would ensure that the items were neither allowed to reach their intended destination nor returned to their place of origin. The Committee invited the two States involved in the transfer of the arms-related materiel to provide additional information and an explanation for the transactions. The reported State of origin had not replied. The reported State of destination stated that it had found no record that one of the vessels was destined for one of its ports and that it was investigating the matter. The flag State of the other vessel subsequently submitted documentation confirming that the vessel had been carrying arms-related materiel originating from Iran.

Communication. In a letter of 5 November [S/2009/574] to the Council and the Secretary-General, Israel alleged violations of the sanctions regime.

Iran's position. During 2009, Iran sent communications to the Security Council on the non-proliferation and sanctions regime and related matters. In communications dated 26 February [S/2009/116], 10 March [S/2009/137], 1 April [S/2009/174], 15 June [S/2009/311], 24 September [S/2009/488] and 6 October [S/2009/520], Iran reiterated the peaceful character of its nuclear programme, as attested by IAEA reports. Iran submitted related communications on 14 April [S/2009/202], 21 September [S/2009/480], 16 October [S/2009/540], 2 December [S/2009/634] and 10 December [A/64/569-S/2009/649].

Other issues

Myanmar

Visit by Special Representative. On 30 January [SG/SM/12077], the Secretary-General announced that his Special Adviser, Ibrahim Gambari, would begin on 31 January a four-day visit to Myanmar, at the invitation of the Government. The Secretary-General had asked his Special Adviser to visit Myanmar to continue his consultations with the Government and other parties, in the implementation of the good offices mandate entrusted to him by the General Assembly.

During his four-day visit, Mr. Gambari met with Government officials and opposition and other political parties, including with the detained General Secretary of the National League for Democracy, Daw Aung San Suu Kyi.

Security Council consideration (February). On 20 February [A/64/2], in consultations of the whole, Mr. Gambari briefed the Council on the results of his visit.

Security Council statement (May). In a 22 May press statement [SC/9662], the Council reiterated the importance of releasing all political prisoners. It also reiterated the need for the Government to create the necessary conditions for a genuine dialogue with Ms. Suu Kyi and all concerned parties and ethnic groups, in order to achieve an inclusive national reconciliation.

The Secretary-General, in a statement [SG/SM/12351] issued during his second visit (3–4 July) to Myanmar in just over a year, said that he had met with representatives of registered political parties and with those armed groups that had chosen to observe a ceasefire, encouraging them, respectively, to honour their com-

mitments to the democratic process and peace. Nonetheless, the Government had the primary responsibility to move the country towards its stated goals of national reconciliation and democracy. Myanmar's human rights record remained a matter of concern. All political prisoners, including Ms. Suu Kyi, should be released. The Secretary-General had met Senior General Than Shwe, pressing for a visit to Ms. Suu Kyi, and was disappointed that he had refused. The country had to embark on a process of genuine dialogue that included all concerned parties, all ethnic groups and all minorities.

It was time for Myanmar to unleash its economic potential, the Secretary-General added. Myanmar sat in the middle of Asia's economic miracle. Harnessing Myanmar to the rapid advances taking place around it was the surest way to raise living standards. The Government must take advantage of the opportunities that the international community was prepared to offer to the people of Myanmar.

Security Council consideration (July). On 13 July [meeting 6161], the Secretary-General briefed the Council on the situation in Myanmar following his visit to the country. He made proposals focused on three outstanding concerns: the release of all political prisoners, including Ms. Suu Kyi; the resumption of substantive dialogue; and the creation of conditions conducive to the holding of credible elections in 2010. He proposed that the senior leadership of Myanmar enhance its cooperation with the United Nations to address the country's pressing development needs through a broad-based process involving all sectors of society. He also made clear that the international community expected the Government to deliver on its promise to make the 2010 elections inclusive, free and fair, and to take the necessary steps on his proposal in the near future.

The Council also heard a statement by the representative of Myanmar, who communicated his Government's priorities, which included handing over State power to a civilian government after the 2010 elections, as well as laying a good foundation for social and economic development.

Security Council statement (August). On 11 August, Ms. Suu Kyi was convicted of violating state security laws after an uninvited United States citizen in May gained access to her home; she was sentenced to a further 18 months of house arrest. By a press statement of 13 August [SC/9731], the Council expressed concern at the conviction and sentencing of Ms. Suu Kyi and its political impact. The Council urged the Government to create the necessary conditions for a genuine dialogue with Ms. Suu Kyi and all concerned parties and ethnic groups in order to achieve an inclusive national reconciliation.

General Assembly action (December). On 24 December, the Assembly adopted **resolution 64/238** (see p. 774), by which it called on the Government to release all prisoners of conscience; undertake a genuine dialogue with Ms. Suu Kyi and all other concerned parties and ethnic groups; ensure a free, fair, transparent and inclusive electoral process; allow a full, transparent, effective, impartial and independent investigation into all reports of human rights violations and bring to justice those responsible in order to end impunity for such crimes; ensure the independence and impartiality of the judiciary; and allow human rights defenders to pursue their activities unhindered and ensure their safety, security and freedom of movement.

Children and armed conflict

In June, pursuant to resolution 1612(2005) [YUN 2005, p. 863], the Secretary-General reported [S/2009/278] on the situation of children and armed conflict in Myanmar during the period from 1 October 2007 to 31 March 2009. According to the report, there had been several positive initiatives undertaken and measures purportedly implemented by the Government to prevent and halt the recruitment and use of children, but the country task force on monitoring and reporting had been unable to verify many of the outcomes of those initiatives. The country task force had received numerous credible reports concerning the recruitment and use of children by some Government military units of the Tatmadaw Kyi, Myanmar's national army. Reports indicated that orphans were often targeted for recruitment into the military. According to the International Labour Organization, in most cases, underage recruits went through the full formal recruitment process and were required to undertake some four and one-half months of training before being sent to their duty station.

According to the Landmine Monitor initiative, both Government troops and non-State armed groups continued to use anti-personnel mines in 2007 and 2008 to restrict the movement of people, hinder the movement of troops or mark areas of operations. Villagers and internally displaced persons, including children, in locations along the eastern border areas continued to suffer threats to their lives because of such mines. Owing to limited access to the contested and ceasefire areas of the country, the country task force was unable to obtain more information on cases of rape and sexual violence against children by parties to the conflict.

Among its recommendations, the report urged the Government to prevent the recruitment of children and to demobilize all children who participated in any capacity in its armed forces. The Government was urged to redress the prevailing culture of impunity, to investigate all incidents of recruitment and use of children, and to prosecute persons responsible for such acts. The Government should continue its education and awareness-raising activities for the Tatmadaw Kyi, particularly regional commanders, military recruiters and active service personnel of various ranks in all military training schools, directing military personnel to refuse the recruitment of children. They should also be instructed on the investigation, prosecution and disciplinary actions that would be undertaken for recruitment in contravention of international law, national law and Military Defence Council directives.

The report stressed the need for the Governments concerned to facilitate dialogue between the United Nations and the Karen National Union and Karenni National Progressive Party for the purposes of signing an action plan in accordance with Security Council resolutions 1539(2004) [YUN 2004, p. 787] and 1612(2005), following their initial deeds of commitment.

Sri Lanka

Statements by Secretary-General. On 26 January [SG/SM/12066], the Secretary-General expressed concern about the safety of civilians caught in intensified fighting in the Vanni region of Sri Lanka between the Government and the Liberation Tigers of Tamil Eelam (LTTE). He called on both parties to ensure the protection and well-being of civilians, and to allow the movement of 250,000 civilians in the area of fighting to safe areas.

On 5 March [SG/SM/12126] the Secretary-General expressed concern over the deteriorating situation for civilians trapped in the north; deplored the mounting death toll of civilians, including children; and stressed the need to bring the conflict to a speedy end without further loss of civilian life.

On 3 April [SG/SM/12166], the Secretary-General called upon LTTE to allow civilians to leave the conflict area and reminded the Government of its responsibility to protect civilians and to avoid the use of heavy weapons in areas where there were civilians.

Security Council statement. In a 13 May press statement [SC/9659], Security Council members expressed concern over the worsening humanitarian crisis in north-east Sri Lanka, in particular the reports of hundreds of civilian casualties, and called for action by all parties to ensure the safety of civilians. The Council condemned LTTE for its acts of terrorism over many years and for its continued use of civilians as human shields, and acknowledged the legitimate right of the Government to combat terrorism.

The Council demanded that LTTE lay down its arms and allow the tens of thousands of civilians in the conflict zone to leave. It expressed concern at the reports of continued use of heavy calibre weapons in areas with high concentrations of civilians, and expected the Government to fulfil its commitment in that regard. The Council called on the Government to take further steps to facilitate the evacuation of the trapped civilians, and reiterated its support for the personal involvement of the Secretary-General.

Joint statement. At the conclusion of the Secretary-General's visit to Sri Lanka (22–23 May), the Secretary-General and the Government issued a joint statement [SG/1251]. During his visit, the statement said, the Secretary-General held talks with President Mahinda Rajapaksa, the Foreign Minister and other senior leaders, also consulting other stakeholders, members of international humanitarian agencies and civil society. The Secretary-General visited the internally displaced persons sites at Vavuniya and overflew the conflict area near Mullaitivu that was the scene of the conflict.

The President and the Secretary-General agreed that, following the end of operations against the LTTE, the Government faced many immediate and long-term challenges relating to issues of relief, rehabilitation, resettlement and reconciliation. While addressing those issues, the new situation offered opportunities for long-term development of the north and for re-establishing democratic institutions and electoral politics after two and a half decades. The Government expressed its commitment to ensure the economic and political empowerment of the people of the north through its programmes. The President and the Secretary-General agreed that addressing the aspirations and grievances of all communities and working towards a lasting political solution was fundamental to ensuring long-term socio-economic development.

Sri Lanka reiterated its commitment to the promotion and protection of human rights. The Secretary-General underlined the importance of an accountability process for addressing violations of international humanitarian and human rights law.

Statement by Secretary-General. On 21 November [SG/SM/12622], the Secretary-General welcomed the Government's decision to grant increased freedom of movement to internally displaced persons residing in camps in northern Sri Lanka. He also welcomed the release of over half of the internally displaced persons from the camps, and encouraged the Government to continue to prioritize the return of internally displaced persons.

Children and armed conflict

Pursuant to Security Council resolution 1612(2005) [YUN 2005, p. 863], the Secretary-General in June submitted a report on children and armed conflict in Sri Lanka [S/2009/325] covering the period from 15 September 2007 to 31 January 2009. The report described incidents and trends of grave violations of children's rights by State and non-State actors. It emphasized that despite some limited progress and the release of children by LTTE and some efforts on the part of the Tamil Makkal Viduthalai Pulikal (TMVP), trends of child recruitment continued to be a source of concern. The killing and maiming of children also remained worrisome, especially in the context of the fighting and attacks, which had a direct impact on the civilian population. The provision of humanitarian assistance to affected children in the conflict zones was increasingly difficult. Limited progress had been registered with regard to dialogue with armed groups for action plans to stop the recruitment and use of children. Though LTTE had not achieved the requirements of a bona fide action plan throughout, TMVP had prepared an action plan in conjunction with the UN country team and the Government. However, concrete steps towards the complete release of children and their reintegration remained to be fully taken. Allegations of other armed groups engaging in recruitment, especially in internally displaced persons camps in the north, needed to be monitored and action taken to halt abuses. The report concluded with recommendations to be addressed by all parties to the conflict.

India–Pakistan

The United Nations Military Observer Group in India and Pakistan continued in 2009 to monitor the situation in Jammu and Kashmir.

In a 5 May letter to the Security Council [S/2009/233], the Secretary-General said that Denmark was withdrawing its participation in providing observers for the Mission, which comprised Chile, Croatia, Denmark, Finland, Italy, the Republic of Korea, Sweden and Uruguay. Having completed the necessary consultations, he proposed adding the Philippines to the list of contributors. The Council took note of the Secretary-General's intention on 7 May [S/2009/234].

Benazir Bhutto assassination inquiry

In a letter of 2 February to the Security Council [S/2009/67], the Secretary-General expressed his wish to accede to a request by Pakistan to establish an international commission in connection with the assassination, on 27 December 2007, of the former Prime Minister of Pakistan, Mohtarma Benazir Bhutto [YUN 2007, p. 63], by establishing a three-member Commission of Inquiry. Draft terms of reference for the proposed commission were annexed to his letter. The Council took note of the Secretary-General's intention on 3 February [S/2009/68].

In a letter dated 30 December [S/2010/7], the Secretary-General informed the Council that he had received from the Head of the Commission, Ambassador Heraldo Muñoz (Chile), a request to extend the conclusion of the Commission's mandate from 31 December 2009 to 31 March 2010, to enable it to complete its inquiry and prepare its report. The Secretary-General had agreed to that request, and the additional period would be funded by the existing voluntary contributions made by Member States. Pakistan had agreed to that extension.

The Philippines

Children and armed conflict

The second report of the Secretary-General on children and armed conflict in the Philippines [S/2010/36], submitted pursuant to Security Council resolution 1612(2005) [YUN 2005, p. 863], covered the period from 1 December 2007 to 30 November 2009 and gave an account of the grave violations of child rights committed in armed conflict situations. Cases covered in the report included developments involving the four major actors: the armed forces and the paramilitary Citizen Armed Force Geographical Unit; the Moro Islamic Liberation Front; the National Democratic Front of the Philippines—the New People's Army; and the Abu Sayyaf Group. The report also presented the progress made since the first country report [YUN 2008, p. 425], including the development of an action plan with the Moro Islamic Liberation Front and the challenges encountered.

The report presented recommendations for protecting children in conflict-affected areas, including the need for resources for implementing the monitoring and reporting mechanism initiatives, with special focus on the development and implementation of action plans.

United Arab Emirates–Iran

Greater Tunb, Lesser Tunb and Abu Musa

On 9 February [S/2009/89], the United Arab Emirates requested that the Security Council retain on its agenda for 2009 the item entitled "Letter dated 3 December 1971 from the Permanent Representatives of Algeria, Iraq, the Libyan Arab Republic and the People's Democratic Republic of Yemen to the United Nations addressed to the President of the Security Council" [YUN 1971, p. 209] concerning Iran's occupation of "the Greater Tunb, the Lesser Tunb and Abu Musa, three islands belonging to the United Arab Emirates", until such time as the dispute was resolved by peaceful means through direct negotiations or through the International Court of Justice.

The League of Arab States, in communications transmitted on 11 March [S/2009/145], 14 April [S/2009/206] and 14 September [S/2009/467], informed the Security Council of the adoption of two resolutions and one decision denouncing the Iranian Government's consolidation of its occupation of the three islands, and affirming the sovereignty of the United Arab Emirates over them. The League also resolved to inform the Secretary-General and the Council President of the importance of the Security Council's remaining seized of the issue until Iran ended its occupation of the islands and the United Arab Emirates regained its sovereignty over them.

In a letter of 9 April [S/2009/195] referring to letters from the Arab League, Iran said that the islands were an integral and eternal part of the Iranian territory and rejected any claims to the contrary. By a letter of 21 December [A/64/606], Iran drew attention to a report of the Secretary-General [A/64/118] in which he cited the United Arab Emirates' claim regarding those three islands which, Iran stated, were an integral part of Iranian territory; any claim to the contrary was unacceptable.

Chapter V

Europe and the Mediterranean

The restoration of peace and stability in the post-conflict countries in the European and Mediterranean region advanced in 2009, as efforts to re-establish their institutions and social and economic infrastructure continued. A number of issues remained unresolved, however, and in some of the countries the peace process was seriously challenged.

The international community, led by the European Union (EU), continued to assist Bosnia and Herzegovina to move towards full integration into Europe through the EU Stabilization and Association Process. The Parliamentary Assembly's adoption in March of the Brcko amendment, which ensured the Brcko District access to the Bosnia and Herzegovina Constitutional Court, was the first constitutional change since the 1995 Dayton Peace Agreement was signed. The country also issued its first biometric passports in October. Progress on the reform agenda was limited, however, due to anti-Dayton rhetoric challenging the sovereignty and constitutional order of the country.

In Kosovo, developments continued to be shaped by its declaration of independence in February 2008 and the entry into force of the Kosovo Constitution in June. In April 2009, the European Union Rule of Law Mission in Kosovo reached its full operational capacity, while reconfiguration of the United Nations Interim Administration Mission in Kosovo was completed in July. The UN position on Kosovo's status remained status-neutral. As of 15 December, Kosovo was recognized by 64 States.

Although representatives of the former Yugoslav Republic of Macedonia (FYROM) and Greece met twice in 2009 under UN auspices, with a view to reaching an agreement on the name of the State of FYROM, the issue remained unresolved at year's end.

The Georgian-Abkhaz peace process continued to be affected by the August 2008 war in South Ossetia and its aftermath, as well as Georgian-Russian relations. One of the five rounds of international discussions held in Geneva during the year resulted in an agreement addressing security issues on the ground. As the Security Council was unable to reach agreement on a future security regime that included activities of a UN mission, however, the mandate of the United Nations Observer Mission in Georgia was terminated effective 16 June 2009.

In March, the Secretary-General reported on the situation in the occupied territories of Azerbaijan. The Organization for Security and Cooperation in Europe Minsk Group continued to mediate negotiations on the Nagorno-Karabakh conflict, yet the issue remained unresolved.

The situation in Cyprus continued to improve, and efforts were focused on assisting the two sides in implementing the 8 July 2006 Set of Principles and Decision. Full-fledged negotiations between the Greek Cypriot and Turkish Cypriot sides continued under UN auspices, with progress achieved in the areas of governance and power-sharing, the economy and EU matters. The United Nations Peacekeeping Force in Cyprus continued to cooperate with the two communities, to facilitate projects benefiting Greek and Turkish Cypriots in the buffer zone and to advance the goal of restoring normal conditions and humanitarian functions on the island.

Bosnia and Herzegovina

During 2009, efforts to assist the two entities comprising the Republic of Bosnia and Herzegovina—the Federation of Bosnia and Herzegovina (where mainly Bosnian Muslims (Bosniacs) and Bosnian Croats resided) and the Republika Srpska (where mostly Bosnian Serbs resided)—in implementing the 1995 General Framework Agreement for Peace in Bosnia and Herzegovina and the annexes thereto (the Peace Agreement) [YUN 1995, pp. 544 & 551] were directed by the European Union (EU). Those efforts were accomplished through the activities of the Office of the High Representative for the Implementation of the Peace Agreement on Bosnia and Herzegovina (OHR), responsible for the Agreement's civilian aspects [YUN 1996, p. 293]; the European Union Police Mission in Bosnia and Herzegovina, responsible for helping develop sustainable policing arrangements; and the EU Force (EUFOR) mission, responsible for the Agreement's military aspects, which were transferred to it by the North Atlantic Treaty Organization (NATO) in 2004 [YUN 2004, p. 401]. The Peace Implementation Council (PIC) and its Steering Board continued to monitor and facilitate the Agreement's implementation.

During the year, the High Representative reported on the progress made in the implementation process and related political developments in the country in the context of his mission implementation plan, which set out a number of core tasks to be accomplished [YUN 2003, p. 401]. Bosnia and Herzegovina made progress with the adoption of the Brcko amendment in March, which ensured the Brcko District access to the Bosnia and Herzegovina Constitutional Court, and was the first change to the Constitution since 1995. It also issued the country's first biometric passports in October. Despite those achievements, limited progress was made on the reform agenda owing to political rhetoric challenging the sovereignty, territorial integrity and constitutional order of Bosnia and Herzegovina, as well as challenges to the authority of the High Representative and the Steering Board.

In November 2009, the Security Council extended the mandate of EUFOR for a further twelve-month period (see p. 405).

Implementation of Peace Agreement

Civilian aspects

The civilian aspects of the 1995 Peace Agreement entailed a broad range of activities, including the provision of humanitarian aid and resources for infrastructure rehabilitation, the establishment of political and constitutional institutions, the promotion of respect for human rights and the holding of free and fair elections [YUN 1995, p. 547]. The High Representative for Bosnia and Herzegovina, who chaired the PIC Steering Board and other key implementation bodies, was the final authority with regard to implementing the civilian aspects of the Peace Agreement [YUN 1996, p. 293].

Office of High Representative

Reports of High Representative. On 13 March, PIC appointed Valentin Inzko (Austria) to succeed Miroslav Lajčák (Slovakia) as the High Representative for Bosnia and Herzegovina, which was welcomed by the Security Council on 25 March in resolution 1869(2009) (see below). The new High Representative reported to the Council, through the Secretary-General, on the peace implementation process for the periods 1 November 2008 to 30 April 2009 [S/2009/246], 1 May to 31 October [S/2009/588] and 1 November to 30 April 2010 [S/2010/235]. The Council considered those reports on 28 May [meeting 6130] and 23 November [meeting 6222]. (For details on the reports, see below.)

OHR-EUSR transition. In 2009, while some gains were achieved in the remaining objectives and conditions for a transition from OHR to an EU Special Representative (EUSR) presence, progress was limited. In November, the PIC Steering Board determined that the Office would remain in place until the "5 plus 2" agenda was achieved (see p. 402).

On 25 March [meeting 6099], the Security Council unanimously adopted **resolution 1869(2009)**. The draft [S/2009/154] was submitted by Austria, Croatia, France, Germany, Italy, the Russian Federation, Turkey, the United Kingdom and the United States.

The Security Council,
Recalling all its previous relevant resolutions,
Recalling also the General Framework Agreement for Peace in Bosnia and Herzegovina and the annexes thereto (collectively the "Peace Agreement"), and the conclusions of the Peace Implementation Conferences held in Bonn, Germany, on 9 and 10 December 1997, in Madrid on 15 and 16 December 1998 and in Brussels on 23 and 24 May 2000, the declarations made by the Steering Board of the Peace Implementation Council on 27 February and 20 November 2008, as well as the statement made by the Steering Board on 13 March 2009,

1. *Welcomes and agrees* to the designation by the Steering Board of the Peace Implementation Council on 13 March 2009 of Mr. Valentin Inzko as High Representative for Bosnia and Herzegovina in succession to Mr. Miroslav Lajčák;

2. *Pays tribute* to the efforts of Mr. Lajčák in his work as High Representative;

3. *Reaffirms* the importance it attaches to the role of the High Representative in pursuing the implementation of the General Framework Agreement for Peace in Bosnia and Herzegovina and the annexes thereto (collectively the "Peace Agreement") and giving guidance to and coordinating the activities of the civilian organizations and agencies involved in assisting the parties to implement the Peace Agreement;

4. *Reaffirms also* the final authority of the High Representative in theatre regarding the interpretation of annex 10 on civilian implementation of the Peace Agreement;

5. *Takes note* of the declarations of the Steering Board of the Peace Implementation Council of 27 February and 20 November 2008 regarding fulfilment of the five objectives and two conditions required for a transition from the Office of the High Representative to an Office of the European Union Special Representative in Bosnia and Herzegovina;

6. *Decides* to remain seized of the matter.

Political situation and other developments

The High Representative, briefing the Security Council on 28 May [meeting 6130], said that some progress had been made towards the objective of making Bosnia and Herzegovina a peaceful, viable State; the country remained stable and the physical environment was secure. However, the State was not yet fully viable, and its role and competencies were contested by some of its political leaders.

In May, he reported [S/2009/246] that discussions following the signing of the Prud Agreement in November 2008 [YUN 2008, p. 429] resulted in the passage of the 2009 State budget in January and an agreement that led to the 26 March adoption by the Bosnia and

Herzegovina Parliamentary Assembly of the Brcko amendment. The amendment ensured the Brcko District access to the Bosnia and Herzegovina Constitutional Court. Despite those achievements, limited progress was made on the Bosnia and Herzegovina reform agenda. Divisive and nationalist, anti-Dayton rhetoric challenging the sovereignty, territorial integrity and constitutional order of Bosnia and Herzegovina, as well as challenges to the authority of the High Representative and the PIC Steering Board, continued to occur. Of particular note were attacks by the Republika Srpska Government against State institutions, competencies and laws. In March, the Steering Board recognized the progress made towards the "5 plus 2" agenda, the five objectives (resolution of State property, resolution of defence property, completion of the Brcko Final Award, fiscal sustainability, entrenchment of the rule of law) and two general conditions (signing of the Stabilization and Association Agreement and a positive assessment of the situation by the Steering Board) set by PIC in 2008 for the transition of OHR to EUSR [ibid.]. It also expressed concern about the prevailing political situation.

In November [S/2009/588], the High Representative said that progress had been achieved in the area of visa liberalization with the signing of an agreement on the electronic exchange of data between registers of police bodies and prosecutors' offices; the issuance of the first biometric passports in October; and the adoption by the House of Representatives of the Law on the Agency for the Prevention of Corruption and the Coordination of the Fight against Corruption, with passage by the House of Peoples pending. However, ongoing attacks against State institutions, competencies and laws, mainly by the Republika Srpska Government, and challenges to the authority of the High Representative and PIC Steering Board hampered progress. On 20 June and 18 September, the High Representative issued decisions, respectively, to annul the conclusions of the Republika Srpska National Assembly on transfers of constitutional competencies, which called into question the constitutional basis and legality of State competencies; and to prevent an imminent move by the Republika Srpska authorities to illegally dismantle the State electricity transmission company Elektroprijenos Bosnia and Herzegovina. In addition, due to the Republika Srpska's refusal to meet its remaining obligations under the Brcko Final Award and its attempts to assert authority in the Brcko District, the District Supervisor suspended preparations for the closure of his office and reserved the right to refer Republika Srpska non-compliance to the Arbitral Tribunal. As the parties failed to build on the success of the Brcko amendment to the Constitution adopted in March, or to engage in any meaningful dialogue on constitutional reform, they were also unable to launch a parliament-led constitutional reform process. In October, the EU and the United States initiated a high-level political dialogue (the "Butmir process") aiming to break the political stalemate and facilitate reforms needed for the country's Euro-Atlantic perspective and institutional capacity.

In a later report [S/2010/235], the High Representative indicated that the negotiations ended in November without a breakthrough. In other efforts, OHR began an inventory of State property in September, which was completed and turned over to State-level, entity and Brcko District governments in December; however, the relevant authorities had yet to start discussions on allocation of the property. Limited progress was made on the question of immovable defence property as political leaders remained divided on the matter. Consequently, none of the remaining three objectives on the "5 plus 2" agenda (apportionment of State property, apportionment of defence property and completion of the Brcko Final Award) was fully met in 2009. In November, the PIC Steering Board stated that until the domestic authorities delivered fully on the agenda, OHR would remain in place to exercise its mandate under the Peace Agreement.

Civil affairs

In May, the High Representative reported [S/2009/246] that despite a proclaimed commitment to the EU agenda, the State institutions made inadequate progress in relation to EU reforms during the reporting period. The Bosnia and Herzegovina Council of Ministers adopted only six EU reform laws and made limited progress on EU requirements. The State and entities continued to adopt legislation in an uncoordinated manner, and the lack of coordination on the part of the Republika Srpska in regard to the European integration process with State-level and other authorities was of particular concern. In April, the European Commission addressed the Bosnia and Herzegovina Parliamentary Assembly, noting a number of outstanding issues and referring to six outstanding laws, as well as the implementation of police reform laws, five of which had been blocked in parliament because of opposition from Republika Srpska parties. Bosnia and Herzegovina authorities took steps to establish the new State-level police bodies.

In his November report [S/2009/588], the High Representative indicated that more than one year after the elections, the City of Mostar still did not have a mayor and the parties had failed to negotiate seriously. In July, the city was gripped by widespread strikes and work stoppages, which prompted the High Representative to enact a temporary financing decision. On 30 October, he imposed a decision compelling the Mostar City Council to hold a Council session within 30 days to elect a mayor by secret ballot. He later reported [S/2010/235] that by December, the Council had proved unable to either elect a mayor or pass the 2009 budget. On 14 December, with support from the PIC Steering Board, the High Representative issued a decision enacting amendments to the Statute of the City of Mostar, which resulted in the election of a mayor and the adoption of a city budget on 18 December. He also used his executive powers, with PIC Steering Board support, to extend the mandates of international judges and prosecutors working in State-level judicial institutions in the War Crimes Divisions of the State Court and the Prosecutor's Office of Bosnia and Herzegovina that were to expire in late December (see below). The Republika Srpska Government and National Assembly rejected those decisions and called for a referendum on the High Representative's powers. In November, the High Representative issued decisions lifting bans on persons previously barred from being a candidate for elections or from holding any executive office at any level because of earlier obstruction of the General Framework Agreement for Peace.

Judicial reform

In 2009, implementation of both the National Justice Sector Reform Strategy and the National War Crimes Prosecution Strategy, adopted, respectively, in June and December 2008 [YUN 2008, p. 430], was marked by stagnation. Moreover, blockage by the Republika Srpska of the extension requested by the Bosnia and Herzegovina Court President and the Chief Prosecutor of the mandates of the international judges and prosecutors working in the State Court and Prosecutor's Office highlighted the continuing fragility of earlier justice sector reforms.

Although a Supervisory Board had been set up to monitor implementation of the National War Crimes Prosecution Strategy, performance lagged far behind the goals it outlined. The only visible progress achieved on the Strategy—the first comprehensive policy document for dealing with the war crimes caseload facing Bosnia and Herzegovina—was the adoption by the Council of Ministers of two amendments to the Criminal Procedural Code. However, the Parliamentary Assembly had yet to enact them. The lack of a central database with exact information on war crimes cases made further implementation of the Strategy nearly impossible. Following a request from the Board for assistance, OHR wrote to all prosecutors' offices urging them to cooperate in speeding up data collection from lower-level jurisdictions. Meanwhile, the State-wide Justice Sector Reform Strategy also fared poorly. Although implementation working groups were established in January, the process was hampered by the limited participation of the Republika Srpska Ministry of Justice and by the weak contribution of the Federation's Ministry of Justice.

A ministerial conference in May concluded that implementation rates had averaged less than 20 per cent over the preceding five months, and between 40 and 50 per cent of projects had registered no progress at all. By year's end, only 30 per cent of the requirements of the Strategy had been met. A technical secretariat was established to assist the Bosnia and Herzegovina Ministry of Justice to meet its coordination role. The Ministry also signed a memorandum of understanding with five civil society associations to reinforce their monitoring of the implementation of the Strategy.

On other rule of law issues, following the failure by the Bosnia and Herzegovina Parliamentary Assembly to adopt the required amendments requested by the Court and the Prosecutor's Office, as well as the International Tribunal for the Former Yugoslavia, on 14 December, the High Representative enacted amendments to the Law on the Court of Bosnia and Herzegovina and to the Law on the Prosecutor's Office. The presence of international judges and prosecutors working on war crimes cases in the State-level judicial institutions was thereby extended for a further three-year period. The High Representative's decision did not cover the extension of the mandates of international judges and prosecutors in the organized crime, economic crime and corruption departments; it was agreed that internationals might serve as advisers in those sectors. OHR also convened an international donors' meeting in December to address the departure of a number of international prosecutors, judges and legal assistants whose contracts had expired earlier in the year. Other problems affecting the judiciary were the ongoing failure to appoint three judges to the Federation Constitutional Court, which prevented the Court from ruling on vital national interest cases; and expenditure cuts required by the country's International Monetery Fund (IMF) standby arrangement that affected the salaries of judges and prosecutors.

Economic reforms

Economic indicators in the first half of 2009 demonstrated the adverse impact of the global economic crisis on Bosnia and Herzegovina. To mitigate those effects, the Bosnia and Herzegovina Fiscal Council [YUN 2008, p. 430] and IMF agreed in May to a three-year, €1.2 billion standby arrangement, which was approved by the IMF Executive Board on 8 July with the first tranche of funds being released on 10 July. Agreement within the Governing Board of the Indirect Taxation Authority facilitated the 18 June adoption of the Bosnia and Herzegovina Law on Excises and accompanying implementation legislation ensuring a boost in annual indirect tax revenues. On 24 November, the Governing Board agreed on a temporary methodology for the allocation of road toll tax revenues, unblocking over €28 million from the Single

Account. Since the issue of assets received by Bosnia and Herzegovina as a consequence of the post-Yugoslav succession agreement remained unresolved as at the 15 September deadline set by the PIC Steering Board, OHR issued on 18 September a decision enacting the Law on the Distribution, Purpose and Use of Financial Assets Obtained under Annex C to the Agreement on Succession Issues, which addressed the distribution of succession assets in a systematic manner; established exact allocation shares for the State, entities and Brcko; and established a method of rebalancing the assets allocated in April in line with the allocation shares. In the energy sector, operations of Elektroprijenos Bosnia and Herzegovina continued to deteriorate as a result of actions taken by Republika Srpska authorities and their representatives in the firm. On 18 September, OHR issued a second decision ensuring the continuity of the Elektroprijenos electric transmission operations.

Public administration reform

Due to concerns about amendments to the State law on the civil service that could reverse long-standing efforts to establish a merit-based, politically independent civil service, as well as undermine the State-level Civil Service Agency, a February intervention by the Acting High Representative led the parliamentary committee discussing the amendments to make the changes necessary to safeguard the core principles underlying the civil service system. The Bosnia and Herzegovina Parliamentary Assembly adopted the amendments at the end of April. As at July, the 2006 Public Administration Reform Strategy and the action plan [YUN 2006, p. 456] had been only partially (36 per cent) implemented. Meanwhile, severe delays in appointing directors and other key personnel to State-level institutions—owing to disagreement between the leading political parties on how to distribute the positions—affected the performance of the public administration. The appointments of more than 10 Directors were pending at the State level. On 23 December, the Republika Srpska National Assembly adopted legislation abolishing the institution of the Republika Srpska Ombudsman, clearing the last major obstacle for the Bosnia and Herzegovina Ombudsman's Office to become fully operational.

Media development

Media development and reform progressed slowly and was hampered by setbacks, including a deterioration of media freedoms at the beginning of the year. Between January and April, the Free Media Helpline of the Bosnia and Herzegovina Union of Journalists registered a 20 per cent increase of verbal assaults, direct physical attacks, death threats and other violations of journalists' rights compared with 2008. The little cooperation that existed between local media organizations responsible for media freedom had diminished. On 29 April 2009, the Radio Televizija Republike Srpske, the Republika Srpska public broadcaster and the Republika Srpska daily newspaper *Glas Srpski* walked out of the association of Bosnia and Herzegovina journalists, announcing the establishment of a separate, Republika Srpska-only association of journalists. Reform of the public broadcasting system (PBS) proceeded slowly, with many elements of the State-level PBS legislation adopted in 2005 [YUN 2005, p. 462] not yet implemented. The PBS System Board, finally inaugurated on 11 August, had yet to adopt a statute or register the PBS corporation. Meanwhile, the Communications Regulatory Agency, responsible for regulating the telecommunications and electronic media sectors, remained in a difficult position due to the continuing blockade of appointments both to its council and of its general director.

Relations with other countries

Relations between Bosnia and Herzegovina and its immediate neighbours, Croatia, Montenegro and Serbia, remained relatively stable, despite some political arguments among the leaders and small, unresolved border issues. Croatia and Serbia remained the most important trading partners of Bosnia and Herzegovina. The potential threat to that trade represented by the Parliamentary Assembly's adoption of protectionist legislation in June was averted in September when the Constitutional Court ruled that the legislation was unconstitutional. Meanwhile, the dispute with Croatia over its construction of a bridge from the Dalmatian mainland to the Peljesac peninsula that could imperil Bosnia and Herzegovina's access to the sea was put on hold when Croatia was forced, for fiscal reasons, to suspend construction during the summer. The most serious blow to good relations with Serbia was the September conviction by a court in Belgrade of Ilija Jurišić, a Bosnia and Herzegovina citizen sentenced to 12 years' imprisonment for his alleged part in ordering an attack by Tuzla Civil Defence units on a retreating Yugoslav People's Army convoy in May 1992. The verdict inflamed passions and underscored the need to improve regional cooperation and clarify jurisdictional responsibilities when it came to processing war crime cases.

Brcko District

On 26 March, two positive developments brought the Brcko District nearer to the point where closure of the supervisory regime was possible: the adoption by the Bosnia and Herzegovina Parliamentary Assembly of an amendment to the Bosnia and Herzegovina Constitution giving the Brcko District access to the Bosnia and Herzegovina Constitutional Court; and the formation of a new "concentration government" representing all political parties and constituent peoples. The amendment came into effect on 5 April. However, the entities and the State failed to resolve by the 15 September deadline the remaining issues specified in the PIC Steering Board's March communiqué regarding the Brcko District, including the settlement of mutual debts with the entities; the possibility for District residents to choose, declare or change their entity citizenship; the District's legal inclusion in the regulatory framework of the Bosnia and Herzegovina electricity market; and the District's right to share in the apportionment of ex-Yugoslav succession funds. The High Representative resorted to his executive powers and enacted the requisite legislation on 18 September. At that point, the only requirement for the State and entities was to publish the decisions in their respective official gazettes, thereby putting them into effect. Although the State, the Federation and the Brcko District complied with the High Representative's decisions, the Republika Srpska Government and Assembly rejected them. Consequently, the Brcko District Supervisor was unable to recommend the closure of his office.

SECURITY COUNCIL ACTION

On 18 November [meeting 6220], the Security Council unanimously adopted **resolution 1895(2009)**. The draft [S/2009/591] was submitted by Austria, Croatia, France, Germany, Italy, the Russian Federation, Turkey, the United Kingdom and the United States.

The Security Council,

Recalling all its previous relevant resolutions concerning the conflicts in the former Yugoslavia and the relevant statements by its President, including resolutions 1031(1995) of 15 December 1995, 1088(1996) of 12 December 1996, 1423(2002) of 12 July 2002, 1491(2003) of 11 July 2003, 1551(2004) of 9 July 2004, 1575(2004) of 22 November 2004, 1639(2005) of 21 November 2005, 1722(2006) of 21 November 2006, 1764(2007) of 29 June 2007, 1785(2007) of 21 November 2007, 1845(2008) of 20 November 2008 and 1869(2009) of 25 March 2009,

Reaffirming its commitment to the political settlement of the conflicts in the former Yugoslavia, preserving the sovereignty and territorial integrity of all States there within their internationally recognized borders,

Emphasizing its full support for the continued role in Bosnia and Herzegovina of the High Representative for Bosnia and Herzegovina,

Underlining its commitment to support the implementation of the General Framework Agreement for Peace in Bosnia and Herzegovina and the annexes thereto (collectively the "Peace Agreement"), as well as the relevant decisions of the Peace Implementation Council,

Recalling all the agreements concerning the status of forces referred to in appendix B to annex 1-A of the Peace Agreement, and reminding the parties of their obligation to continue to comply therewith,

Recalling also the provisions of its resolution 1551(2004) concerning the provisional application of the status-of-forces agreements contained in appendix B to annex 1-A of the Peace Agreement,

Emphasizing its appreciation to the High Representative, the Commander and personnel of the multinational stabilization force (the European Union Force), the Senior Military Representative and personnel of the North Atlantic Treaty Organization Headquarters Sarajevo, the Organization for Security and Cooperation in Europe, the European Union and the personnel of other international organizations and agencies in Bosnia and Herzegovina for their contributions to the implementation of the Peace Agreement,

Emphasizing that a comprehensive and coordinated return of refugees and displaced persons throughout the region continues to be crucial to lasting peace,

Recalling the declarations of the ministerial meetings of the Peace Implementation Council,

Recognizing that full implementation of the Peace Agreement is not yet complete, while paying tribute to the achievements of the authorities at State and entity level in Bosnia and Herzegovina and of the international community in the fourteen years since the signing of the Peace Agreement,

Emphasizing the importance of Bosnia and Herzegovina's progress towards Euro-Atlantic integration on the basis of the Peace Agreement, while recognizing the importance of Bosnia and Herzegovina's transition to a functional, reform-oriented, modern and democratic European country,

Taking note of the reports of the High Representative, including his latest report, of 6 November 2009,

Determined to promote the peaceful resolution of the conflicts in accordance with the purposes and principles of the Charter of the United Nations,

Recalling the relevant principles contained in the Convention on the Safety of United Nations and Associated Personnel of 9 December 1994 and the statement by its President on 9 February 2000,

Welcoming and encouraging efforts by the United Nations to sensitize peacekeeping personnel in the prevention and control of HIV/AIDS and other communicable diseases in all its peacekeeping operations,

Taking note of the conclusions of the Ministers for Foreign Affairs and Ministers of Defence of the European Union at their joint meeting held on 18 May 2009, in which they welcomed the positive contribution of the European Union Force to the safe and secure environment in Bosnia and Herzegovina, and added that the European Union Force continued to provide reassurance and remained ready to respond to possible security challenges throughout the country, and the conclusions of the Ministers for Foreign Affairs and Ministers of Defence of the European Union at their joint meeting held on 17 November 2009,

Recalling the letters between the European Union and the North Atlantic Treaty Organization sent to the Security Council on 19 November 2004 on how those organizations will cooperate together in Bosnia and Herzegovina in which both organizations recognize that the European Union Force will have the main peace stabilization role under the military aspects of the Peace Agreement,

Recalling also the confirmation by the Presidency of Bosnia and Herzegovina, on behalf of Bosnia and Herzegovina, including its constituent entities, of the arrangements for the European Union Force and the North Atlantic Treaty Organization Headquarters presence,

Welcoming the increased engagement of the European Union in Bosnia and Herzegovina and the continued engagement of the North Atlantic Treaty Organization,

Reiterating once again its calls upon the authorities in Bosnia and Herzegovina to implement in full their undertakings, as also confirmed in the declaration by the Steering Board of the Peace Implementation Council of 30 June 2009, and recognizing, in particular, the need to find a solution on State and defence property,

Welcoming the progress achieved by Bosnia and Herzegovina on some European Partnership priorities, towards implementing the Interim Agreement and towards fulfilling the visa liberalization road map requirements, and calling upon the authorities in Bosnia and Herzegovina to strengthen and step up their efforts to complete the urgent reforms highlighted by the European Commission in its progress report of 14 October 2009 to implement the European Partnership and to prepare to meet obligations under the Interim Agreement and, in due course, the Stabilization and Association Agreement,

Determining that the situation in the region continues to constitute a threat to international peace and security,

Acting under Chapter VII of the Charter of the United Nations,

1. *Reaffirms once again its support* for the General Framework Agreement for Peace in Bosnia and Herzegovina and the annexes thereto (collectively the "Peace Agreement"), as well as for the Dayton Agreement on Implementing the Federation of Bosnia and Herzegovina of 10 November 1995, and calls upon the parties to comply strictly with their obligations under those Agreements;

2. *Reiterates* that the primary responsibility for the further successful implementation of the Peace Agreement lies with the authorities in Bosnia and Herzegovina themselves and that the continued willingness of the international community and major donors to assume the political, military and economic burden of implementation and reconstruction efforts will be determined by the compliance and active participation by all the authorities in Bosnia and Herzegovina in implementing the Peace Agreement and rebuilding a civil society, in particular in full cooperation with the International Tribunal for the Prosecution of Persons Responsible for Serious Violations of International Humanitarian Law Committed in the Territory of the Former Yugoslavia since 1991, in strengthening joint institutions, which foster the building of a fully functioning self-sustaining State able to integrate itself into the European structures, and in facilitating returns of refugees and displaced persons;

3. *Reminds* the parties once again that, in accordance with the Peace Agreement, they have committed themselves to cooperate fully with all entities involved in the implementation of this peace settlement, as described in the Peace Agreement, or which are otherwise authorized by the Security Council, including the International Tribunal for the Former Yugoslavia, as it carries out its responsibilities for dispensing justice impartially, and underlines that full cooperation by States and entities with the Tribunal includes, inter alia, the surrender for trial or apprehension of all persons indicted by the Tribunal and the provision of information to assist in Tribunal investigations;

4. *Emphasizes its full support* for the continued role of the High Representative for Bosnia and Herzegovina in monitoring the implementation of the Peace Agreement and giving guidance to and coordinating the activities of the civilian organizations and agencies involved in assisting the parties to implement the Peace Agreement, and reaffirms that, under annex 10 of the Peace Agreement, the High Representative is the final authority in theatre regarding the interpretation of civilian implementation of the Peace Agreement and that, in case of dispute, he may give his interpretation and make recommendations, and make binding decisions as he judges necessary on issues as elaborated by the Peace Implementation Council in Bonn, Germany, on 9 and 10 December 1997;

5. *Expresses its support* for the declarations of the ministerial meetings of the Peace Implementation Council;

6. *Reaffirms* its intention to keep implementation of the Peace Agreement and the situation in Bosnia and Herzegovina under close review, taking into account the reports submitted pursuant to paragraphs 18 and 21 below, and any recommendations those reports might include, and its readiness to consider the imposition of measures if any party fails significantly to meet its obligations under the Peace Agreement;

7. *Recalls* the support of the authorities of Bosnia and Herzegovina for the European Union Force and the continued North Atlantic Treaty Organization presence and their confirmation that both are the legal successors to the Stabilization Force for the fulfilment of their missions for the purposes of the Peace Agreement, its annexes and appendices and relevant Security Council resolutions and can take such actions as are required, including the use of force, to ensure compliance with annexes 1-A and 2 of the Peace Agreement and relevant Council resolutions;

8. *Pays tribute* to those Member States which participated in the multinational stabilization force (the European Union Force), and in the continued North Atlantic Treaty Organization presence, established in accordance with its resolution 1575(2004) and extended by its resolutions 1639(2005), 1722(2006), 1785(2007) and 1845(2008), and welcomes their willingness to assist the parties to the Peace Agreement by continuing to deploy a multinational stabilization force (the European Union Force) and by maintaining a continued North Atlantic Treaty Organization presence;

9. *Welcomes* the intention of the European Union to maintain a European Union military operation to Bosnia and Herzegovina from November 2009;

10. *Authorizes* the Member States acting through or in cooperation with the European Union to establish for a further period of twelve months, starting from the date of the adoption of the present resolution, a multinational stabilization force (the European Union Force) as a legal successor to the Stabilization Force under unified command and control, which will fulfil its missions in relation to the implementation of annexes 1-A and 2 of the Peace Agreement in cooperation with the North Atlantic Treaty Organization Headquarters presence in accordance with the arrangements agreed between the North Atlantic Treaty Organization and the European Union as communicated

to the Security Council in their letters of 19 November 2004, which recognize that the European Union Force will have the main peace stabilization role under the military aspects of the Peace Agreement;

11. *Welcomes* the decision of the North Atlantic Treaty Organization to continue to maintain a presence in Bosnia and Herzegovina in the form of a North Atlantic Treaty Organization Headquarters in order to continue to assist in implementing the Peace Agreement in conjunction with the European Union Force, and authorizes the Member States acting through or in cooperation with the North Atlantic Treaty Organization to continue to maintain a North Atlantic Treaty Organization Headquarters as a legal successor to the Stabilization Force under unified command and control, which will fulfil its missions in relation to the implementation of annexes 1-A and 2 of the Peace Agreement in cooperation with the European Union Force in accordance with the arrangements agreed between the North Atlantic Treaty Organization and the European Union as communicated to the Security Council in their letters of 19 November 2004, which recognize that the European Union Force will have the main peace stabilization role under the military aspects of the Peace Agreement;

12. *Reaffirms* that the Peace Agreement and the provisions of its previous relevant resolutions shall apply to and in respect of both the European Union Force and the North Atlantic Treaty Organization presence as they have applied to and in respect of the Stabilization Force and that, therefore, references in the Peace Agreement, in particular in annex 1-A and the appendices thereto, and in relevant resolutions to the Implementation Force and/or the Stabilization Force, the North Atlantic Treaty Organization and the North Atlantic Council shall be read as applying, as appropriate, to the North Atlantic Treaty Organization presence, the European Union Force, the European Union and the Political and Security Committee and Council of the European Union respectively;

13. *Expresses its intention* to consider the terms of further authorization as necessary in the light of developments in the implementation of the Peace Agreement and the situation in Bosnia and Herzegovina;

14. *Authorizes* the Member States acting under paragraphs 10 and 11 above to take all necessary measures to effect the implementation of and to ensure compliance with annexes 1-A and 2 of the Peace Agreement, stresses that the parties shall continue to be held equally responsible for the compliance with those annexes and shall be equally subject to such enforcement action by the European Union Force and the North Atlantic Treaty Organization presence as may be necessary to ensure the implementation of those annexes and the protection of the European Union Force and the North Atlantic Treaty Organization presence;

15. *Authorizes* Member States to take all necessary measures, at the request of either the European Union Force or the North Atlantic Treaty Organization Headquarters, in defence of the European Union Force or the North Atlantic Treaty Organization presence respectively, and to assist both organizations in carrying out their missions, and recognizes the right of both the European Union Force and the North Atlantic Treaty Organization presence to take all necessary measures to defend themselves from attack or threat of attack;

16. *Authorizes* the Member States acting under paragraphs 10 and 11 above, in accordance with annex 1-A of the Peace Agreement, to take all necessary measures to ensure compliance with the rules and procedures governing command and control of airspace over Bosnia and Herzegovina with respect to all civilian and military air traffic;

17. *Demands* that the parties respect the security and freedom of movement of the European Union Force, the North Atlantic Treaty Organization presence and other international personnel;

18. *Requests* the Member States acting through or in cooperation with the European Union and the Member States acting through or in cooperation with the North Atlantic Treaty Organization to report to the Security Council on the activity of the European Union Force and the North Atlantic Treaty Organization Headquarters presence respectively, through the appropriate channels and at least at three-monthly intervals;

19. *Invites* all States, in particular those in the region, to continue to provide appropriate support and facilities, including transit facilities, for the Member States acting under paragraphs 10 and 11 above;

20. *Reiterates its appreciation* for the deployment by the European Union of its Police Mission to Bosnia and Herzegovina since 1 January 2003;

21. *Requests* the Secretary-General to continue to submit to the Security Council reports of the High Representative, in accordance with annex 10 of the Peace Agreement and the conclusions of the Peace Implementation Conference held in London on 4 and 5 December 1996, and later Peace Implementation Conferences, on the implementation of the Peace Agreement and, in particular, on compliance by the parties with their commitments under that Agreement;

22. *Decides* to remain seized of the matter.

Communications. On 1 December [S/2009/616], Turkey transmitted to the Security Council the final report of the meeting of the Organization of the Islamic Conference (OIC) Contact Group on Bosnia and Herzegovina (Istanbul, 9 November). In a letter [A/64/614-S/2009/677] dated 15 December to the Secretary-General, Syria, in its capacity as Chair of the OIC Group, submitted the Final Communiqué of the OIC Annual Coordination Meeting of Ministers for Foreign Affairs (New York, 25 September), which expressed its commitment to acting in solidarity with Bosnia and Herzegovina in its ongoing efforts towards ensuring an efficient state structure in the country.

European Union missions in Bosnia and Herzegovina

EUPM

The European Union Police Mission (EUPM), which was established as part of a broader rule of law approach and welcomed by the Security Council in presidential statement S/PRST/2002/33 [YUN 2002, p. 363], became operational on 1 January 2003. In 2009, the Mission continued to focus on supporting the fight against organized crime and assisted in coordinating the policing aspects of efforts to combat major and organized crime. In coordination with OHR and the EU Special Representative, EUPM continued to support police reform by monitoring and assessing the implementation of the police reform legislation adopted in 2008 [YUN 2008, p. 434]; promoting implementation of the new legislation; and encouraging the harmonization of existing laws. Their joint efforts also focused on harmonizing entity, cantonal and Brcko District police legislation; and developing proposals on reforming State-level legislation covering the State Investigation and Protection Agency and the Border Police.

EUFOR

The EU Force (EUFOR) mission in Bosnia and Herzegovina executed the military aspects of the Peace Agreement as specified in annexes 1-A and 2, which were transferred to it by NATO in 2004 [YUN 2004, p. 401]. Its activities in 2009 were described in five reports, covering the periods from 1 December 2008 to 28 February 2009 [S/2009/418], 1 March to 31 May [S/2009/354], 1 June to 31 August [S/2009/525], 1 September to 30 November [S/2010/113] and 1 December 2009 to 28 February 2010 [S/2010/510], submitted by the EU High Representative for the Common Foreign and Security Policy in accordance with various Security Council resolutions.

EUFOR continued to provide deterrence, ensure compliance in relation to the responsibilities specified in the Peace Agreement and contribute to maintaining a safe and secure environment. It provided support to law-enforcement agencies in fighting organized crime in close cooperation with the EU Police Mission, and to the International Tribunal for the Former Yugoslavia in the search for persons indicted for war crimes. As at 30 November, the force of some 2,000 EUFOR troops was concentrated in Sarajevo, with liaison and observation teams deployed throughout Bosnia and Herzegovina.

In the area of joint military affairs tasks, the law on civilian movement control (control of the movement of weapons and military equipment by Bosnia and Herzegovina contractors) came into force on 15 July. On 19 November, EUFOR handed that responsibility—the last task in the area of joint military affairs—to the Bosnia and Herzegovina authorities. EUFOR continued to monitor, mentor and advise in order to enhance the self-sustainability of the Bosnia and Herzegovina capabilities. In that context, EUFOR monitored some 1,300 joint military affairs activities by the Bosnia and Herzegovina authorities between September and November. EUFOR and the Armed Forces of Bosnia and Herzegovina continued to conduct combined training.

On 18 May, the EU Council approved the concept for a possible evolution of EUFOR towards a non-executive capacity-building and training operation. On 17 November, the EU Council assessed the political and security situation in the country; welcomed progress with preparatory planning work for the possible future evolution of EUFOR; and reiterated that a decision on that issue would need to take political developments into account, including the future role of the EU Special Representative.

Kosovo

In 2009, the United Nations Interim Administration Mission in Kosovo (UNMIK) faced challenges in fulfilling its mandate as envisaged in Security Council resolution 1244(1999) [YUN 1999, p. 353] owing to Kosovo's declaration of independence in February 2008 [YUN 2008, p. 437], the entry into force of the Kosovo Constitution on 15 June [ibid., p. 439], and the deployment of the EU Rule of Law Mission in Kosovo (EULEX) throughout Kosovo in December [ibid., p. 442]. Serbia condemned Kosovo's declaration of independence and maintained that action by Kosovo's Provisional Institutions of Self-Government violated resolution 1244(1999), which reaffirmed Serbia's sovereignty and territorial integrity, including Kosovo and Metohija. As at 15 December 2009, Kosovo was recognized by 64 States. The UN position on Kosovo's status was of status neutrality. During the year, the Secretary-General exercised the authority vested in him by resolution 1244(1999) to make adjustments to the presence, profile and priorities of the Mission as a result of changing circumstances on the ground. The Mission's strategic goal remained the promotion of security, stability and respect for human rights in Kosovo and in the region. The Organization for Security and Co-operation in Europe (OSCE) and EULEX played increasingly important roles that complemented UNMIK, within the framework of resolution 1244(1999).

In response to General Assembly resolution 63/3 [YUN 2008, p. 1404], the International Court of Justice (ICJ) held public hearings in December on the request for an advisory opinion on the question of the *Accordance with International Law of the Unilateral Declaration of Independence by the Provisional Institutions of Self-Government of Kosovo* (see p. 1277).

Political and security developments

Report of Secretary-General (March). In March [S/2009/149], the Secretary-General said that the Kosovo authorities continued to act on the basis of the Constitution of the Republic of Kosovo, which entered into force in June 2008 [YUN 2008,

p. 439], some three months after Kosovo declared its independence [ibid., p. 437]. In December, the Assembly of Kosovo had passed laws on the Constitutional Court, on the Foreign Service and on the Consular Service of Diplomatic and Consular Missions in Kosovo, which made no reference to the powers of the UN Special Representative for Kosovo under Security Council resolution 1244(1999) [YUN 1999, p. 353] or to the 2001 Constitutional Framework for Provisional Self-Government [YUN 2001, p. 352]. In accordance with Security Council presidential statement S/PRST/2008/44 [YUN 2008, p. 442] and the Secretary-General's November 2008 report [ibid., p. 441], the Government of Serbia and a majority of Kosovo Serbs had accepted the deployment of EU-LEX on the condition that it would operate under the overall authority of the United Nations and within its status-neutral framework. As of March 2009, some 2,493 staff members were working for EULEX. Meanwhile, the accelerated reconfiguration of UNMIK was being implemented in consultation with the main stakeholders on the ground, including the review and handover of UNMIK files to EULEX and the drawdown of UNMIK rule-of-law personnel.

On 17 February, celebrations organized in Pristina—the capital of Kosovo—and at the municipal level, on the one-year anniversary of Kosovo's declaration of independence took place without incident. On the same date, in Zveçan/Zvečan municipality in northern Kosovo, over 80 Serbian opposition lawmakers from the Serbian Parliament joined delegates from the Assembly of the Association of Serb Municipalities and approved a declaration affirming the constitutional status of Kosovo and Metohija within the Republic of Serbia and rejecting all unilateral and separatist activities of the provisional institutions in Pristina. In line with Belgrade's official policy, Kosovo Serbs continued to reject the authority of Kosovo institutions derived from the Kosovo Constitution, although increasing numbers were applying for Kosovo identity cards, driver's licences and other Kosovo documentation that facilitated their ability to live, work and move about freely in Kosovo. In the north, four municipal structures in Kosovo Serb-majority areas continued to function on the basis of Serbia's law on local self-governance. The reluctance of the Kosovo Serb community to participate in the new framework on local governance adopted by the Kosovo authorities hindered the creation of Kosovo Serb-majority municipalities and progress in decentralization throughout Kosovo.

The overall security situation remained stable, except for a series of incidents that occurred in the region of Mitrovicë/Mitrovica. Following the launch of the Kosovo Security Force (KSF) on 21 January, which rendered the Kosovo Protection Corps non-operational [YUN 2000, p. 364], UNMIK took appropriate measures, including abolishing the post of the Coordinator of the Corps. NATO, which had overseen the establishment and operations of the Security Force, announced that it would consist of 2,500 active members and 800 reservists. Serbia protested against the establishment of the Security Force.

UNMIK reconfiguration. Following the assumption by EULEX of operational responsibility in the area of rule of law in December, UNMIK personnel began transferring policing, judicial and customs-related responsibilities/functions to EULEX. As at 9 March 2009, all except 55 of 1,582 UNMIK police personnel on the ground on 1 December 2008 had been repatriated or assumed functions with EULEX police. The drawdown of UNMIK personnel was expected to be concluded before the start of the 2009–2010 budget cycle. The reconfigured Mission would maintain a small field presence, in particular in Mitrovicë/Mitrovica, that would focus on minority issues, including minority representation, returns and freedom of movement, as well as issues relating to the protection, preservation and reconstruction of cultural heritage in Kosovo. The office in Skopje advised on and provided evaluations of political developments in its area of responsibility. UNMIK would continue working towards the advancement of regional stability and prosperity, based on its continued mandate under resolution 1244(1999), in coordination with OSCE and the Kosovo Force (KFOR), and in cooperation with authorities in Pristina and Belgrade. Its main functions included monitoring and reporting, facilitation of external representation, facilitation of dialogue between Pristina and Belgrade, and activities related to the practical arrangements on the six points referred to in the Secretary-General's June [YUN 2008, p. 438] and November [ibid., p. 441] 2008 reports. As EULEX would perform the full range of rule of law operations, the UNMIK rule of law component would be replaced by a small police and justice liaison office with residual functions.

Report of Secretary-General (June). The Secretary-General reported in June [S/2009/300] that the reconfiguration and downsizing of UNMIK was close to finalization. On 6 April, EULEX assumed full operational capability and as at 31 May, mission staff numbered 2,569 (1,651 international and 918 local employees). The handover of case files from UNMIK to EULEX was completed, and the two missions exchanged information and coordinated on issues of mutual concern on a regular basis. Although Kosovo authorities maintained minimal contact with Special Representative Lamberto Zannier (Italy), and practical cooperation between UNMIK representatives and Kosovo officials continued, the Kosovo authorities—acting on the basis of the Kosovo Constitution and the assertion that resolution 1244(1999) was no longer relevant—

made a series of public statements requesting UNMIK to conclude its mission. The Special Representative and international stakeholders encouraged Pristina to take a more constructive stance towards UNMIK engagement. He also continued, together with the United Nations Office in Belgrade and UNMIK and EULEX experts, substantial technical discussions with Belgrade officials, with EULEX leading technical discussion on issues related to its role and activities in the areas of justice, police and customs, within the framework of resolution 1244(1999). The Belgrade authorities were keen to discuss arrangements in those areas, while Kosovo authorities remained reluctant to engage. Some progress was made in implementing solutions on the protection of Serbian cultural heritage in Kosovo.

In other developments, the Secretary-General said that municipal elections were expected to take place in October or November 2009. Following the entry into force of the Kosovo Constitution, Kosovo authorities had begun to assume full responsibility for the Central Elections Commission and its secretariat, but there was concern over the capacity of the local institutions to manage an electoral process. Despite the appointment of a new chairperson in May, the Commission continued to face serious challenges in terms of its proper management and functioning, owing to its increasing politicization, political deadlocks and limited professional capacities. OSCE, which had, as a part of UNMIK, been in charge of organizing Kosovo elections since the establishment of an international presence there in 1999, continued its regular capacity-building activities for the Commission, and the OSCE secretariat provided daily advice. Meanwhile, municipalities in the north continued to operate largely separately from the rest of Kosovo, and Northern Serb leaders maintained their non-acceptance of any institutions or symbols of Kosovo authorities. UNMIK continued to lend its good offices to all communities in northern Kosovo and to provide links with institutions in Pristina when required.

The overall security situation remained relatively calm. A series of incidents in the Kroi i Vitakut/Brdjani suburb of Mitrovicë/Mitrovica, where Kosovo Albanian residents started rebuilding their houses, which had been destroyed in 1999, led to daily protests by Kosovo Serbs. The Kosovo Police, EULEX and KFOR took action to protect the construction sites from demonstrators and continued to monitor the situation after an agreement was facilitated between the two sides that entailed the rebuilding of Kosovo Albanian homes and the building of Kosovo Serbs homes on parcels of land in the same area. Training by NATO of the newly established KSF continued. As over 90 per cent of the members of the Kosovo Protection Corps applied to join the Force, the UNMIK

Office of the Protection Corps would cease operations on 15 June.

In the justice sector, meetings with the Serbian authorities were held in Belgrade on 8 April, with the participation of UNMIK and EULEX representatives. Discussions focused on the reintroduction of local judges and prosecutors to the Mitrovicë/Mitrovica courthouse. Some progress was achieved in forming a commission composed of local staff to inventory the active case material stored in the courthouse. During the reporting period, UNMIK handed over to EULEX all remaining active cases with the exception of one ongoing criminal case and four proceedings of the Special Chamber of the Supreme Court in Kosovo. On other judicial matters, the ICJ received written statements by 36 UN Member States, as well as Kosovo authorities, on the question of whether Kosovo's declaration of independence was in accordance with international law (see p. 1277).

Report of Secretary-General (September). In September, the Secretary-General [S/2009/497] reported that as at 1 July, UNMIK had successfully concluded its reconfiguration, reached its authorized strength of 510 personnel, and moved into a new phase characterized by a focus on facilitating practical cooperation between communities, as well as between the authorities in Pristina and Belgrade. The UNMIK Office for Community Support and Facilitation was tasked with monitoring, reporting and facilitation functions, and with residual external representation and economic coordination functions. UNMIK and EULEX regularly exchanged information and coordinated at all levels, including through the UNMIK Rule of Law Liaison Office. OSCE and EULEX played increasingly important roles that complemented those of UNMIK. EULEX experts continued to take the lead in technical discussions with the Serbian authorities in the rule of law area.

Special Representative Zannier operated against a complex political background. Decision-making by the authorities in Pristina and Belgrade was influenced by concerns over how the ICJ might interpret their actions in considering the request of the General Assembly for an advisory opinion on whether Kosovo's declaration of independence was in accordance with international law. Authorities in Belgrade adopted a pragmatic approach to resolving some of the pending matters, while Pristina authorities remained unprepared to engage unless they could deal with their Belgrade counterparts directly as equals. The three Kosovo Serb-majority municipalities in the north functioned with few links to the authorities in Pristina, and the political leadership in northern Kosovo continued to consider UNMIK and KFOR as the only legitimate international presence under resolution 1244(1999).

On elections and decentralization, the Kosovo authorities announced on 16 June that municipal elections would be held on 15 November and called on the Central Election Commission to begin preparations for their organization. The electoral operations would be conducted by the Commission. OSCE would provide support in managing elections-related issues and planning electoral operations, but would have no role in the monitoring, observation and counting process. It would also be the first time that UNMIK was not expected to certify the election results since its deployment in 1999. On 28 June, the Assembly of the Association of Serbian Municipalities called on Serbian political parties to oppose the participation of Kosovo Serbs in the elections and appealed to Serbian institutions and the Serbian Orthodox Church to boycott them. In July, the Serbian Government declared that conditions for the participation of Kosovo Serbs in the elections did not exist and that the elections were not in line with resolution 1244(1999). On 16 August, local by-elections organized by the Serbian authorities took place in two Kosovo Serb-majority areas, Graçanicë/Gračanica (Pristina region) and Gorazhdec/Goraždevac (Pejë/Peć region). While the Kosovo authorities did not try to obstruct the by-elections, maintaining that they had no legal bearing and were invalid, opposition members and civil society representatives viewed the elections as an aggression by Serbia. Voter turnout was low, at around 20 per cent, due in part to the much lower turnout of internally displaced persons voting at polling stations.

The security situation remained calm, yet fragile in the north. UNMIK continued its mediation between the Kosovo Albanian and Kosovo Serb communities, including by defusing tensions surrounding the Kroi i Vitakut/Brdjani reconstruction activities, in co-operation with EULEX and KFOR. The Secretary-General urged all sides to adopt constructive policies in dealing with sensitive inter-ethnic issues and observed that in the light of ongoing tensions in northern Kosovo, EULEX and KFOR remained critical to security and stability. In other developments, the mid-August announcement of a possible EULEX-Serbian Ministry of the Interior agreement on police cooperation was met with resistance by the Kosovo authorities, who maintained that signing such agreements was their exclusive responsibility. On 26 August, some 60 activists of Self-Determination (Vetëvendosje), an ethnic Albanian nationalist group, vandalized 26 EULEX vehicles in Pristina in protest of the protocol. Other acts of vandalism against EULEX vehicles and some UN vehicles occurred in the ensuing days. On 14 September, three days after the agreement was signed, a demonstration against the agreement was organized in Pristina by 23 local non-governmental organizations (NGOs), with some 1,000 demonstrators calling for the withdrawal of EULEX from Kosovo.

ICJ advisory opinion request. On 14 September, following a request by Serbia [A/63/PV.105] that the agenda item on "Request for an advisory opinion of ICJ on whether the unilateral declaration of independence of Kosovo is in accordance with international law" be included in the draft agenda of its sixty-fourth (2009) session, the General Assembly approved the request (**decision 63/570**). On 24 December, the Assembly decided that the agenda item would remain for consideration during its resumed sixty-fourth (2010) session (**decision 64/549**).

Year-end developments. In a later report [S/2010/5], the Secretary-General said that the municipal and mayoral elections organized by Kosovo authorities on 15 November, which took place without major incident, marked an important step in the decentralization process. The elections were held in 36 municipalities—six more than in the local election held in November 2007—and were monitored by some 23,000 observers, including 600 international observers, who found that they adhered to democratic standards, despite some irregularities. Elections for the envisaged new municipalities in northern Mitrovicë/Mitrovica and Partesh/Parteš were postponed, due to lack of progress in gaining support for decentralization in those areas. Although Belgrade authorities had stated that the elections were not in line with resolution 1244(1999) and did not call on Kosovo Serbs to vote, the Serbian President made it clear that the Government would not stigmatize Kosovo Serbs who chose to participate. On 29 November, Serbia organized by-elections in the northernmost municipality in Kosovo, Leposaviq/Leposavić. The Kosovo authorities stated that they would not recognize those elections. On the other hand, the 15 November elections organized by the Kosovo authorities had no real political impact on the north, with virtually no turnout of Kosovo Serbs there. The UNMIK Office in Mitrovicë/Mitrovica continued to function as a go-between for Kosovo Serb municipal leaders and the Kosovo Albanian community in the north. UNMIK also served as the bridge between EULEX and local political leaders. Although the tension between Kosovo Albanians and Kosovo Serbs had significantly decreased in the northern Kosovo community of Kroi i Vitakut/Brdjani, the situation in the north remained fragile, with inter-ethnic incidents occurring in northern Mitrovicë/Mitrovica.

ICJ held public hearings from 1 to 11 December on whether Kosovo's unilateral declaration of independence was in accordance with international law. In addition to Serbia and Kosovo, representatives of 27 States, including all 5 permanent members of the Security Council, participated in the hearings. As at 15 December, Kosovo was recognized by 64 States.

The Secretary-General further reported [S/2010/169] that the election results for the second round of mayoral elections, organized by the Kosovo authorities and held on 13 December, were certified in 18 municipalities on 24 December. On 21 December, the President of Slovenia, Danilo Türk, became the first Head of State to visit Pristina since the Kosovo authorities declared independence.

Communication. On 1 April [A/63/820-S/2009/208], the Russian Federation transmitted a statement adopted by the State Duma of the Federal Assembly on 20 March supporting the policy adopted by the Serbian leadership in the search for a legal resolution to the conflict.

EULEX

The European Union Rule of Law Mission in Kosovo (EULEX), established to undertake an enhanced operational role in the rule-of-law area, with a focus on policing, justice and customs [YUN 2008, p. 441], was deployed throughout Kosovo in December 2008 [ibid., p. 442] and became fully operational in April 2009. EULEX operated under the overall authority and within the status-neutral framework of the United Nations, and submitted reports to it on a regular basis. On the occasion of the Mission's first anniversary in December, Kosovo President Fatmir Sejdiu and Prime Minister Hashim Thaçi commented on the work of EULEX during its first year of operations; the Prime Minister expressed confidence in the Mission's success. Meetings of the Joint Rule of Law Coordination Board, co-chaired by the Head of EULEX and the Deputy Prime Minister, took place on a monthly basis, and working groups were set up to coordinate the consultations. UNMIK and EULEX staff worked together in the UNMIK International Criminal Police Organization Office. On 24 December, EULEX was invited for the first time to take part in a Joint Implementation Committee meeting at the Serbian Border Police headquarters in Kuršumlija, Serbia.

The reports of the EU High Representative for the Common Foreign and Security Policy to the UN Secretary-General on EULEX activities were annexed to the UN Secretary-General's reports to the Security Council on UNMIK [S/2009/149, S/2009/300, S/2009/497, S/2010/5 and S/2010/169].

UNMIK

The United Nations Interim Administration Mission in Kosovo (UNMIK), established in 1999 [YUN 1999, p. 357] to facilitate a political process to determine Kosovo's political future, comprised five components: interim administration, institution-building, economic reconstruction, humanitarian affairs, and police and justice. Following Kosovo's declaration of independence in February 2008 [YUN 2008, p. 437]

and the deployment of EULEX throughout Kosovo in 2009, the profile and size of UNMIK was gradually reconfigured in accordance with changing circumstances on the ground. As at 1 July, the Mission reached its authorized strength of 510 personnel. The strategic goal of UNMIK remained the promotion of security, stability and respect for human rights in Kosovo and in the region through engagement with all communities in Kosovo, as well as with Pristina and Belgrade and with regional and international actors. UNMIK was headed by the Special Representative of the Secretary-General, Lamberto Zannier (Italy).

Financing

In June, the General Assembly considered the financial performance report for UNMIK for the period from 1 July 2007 to 30 June 2008 [A/63/569], the proposed budget for 1 July 2009 to 30 June 2010 [A/63/803 & Corr.1] and the related report of the Advisory Committee on Administrative and Budgetary Questions (ACABQ) [A/63/746/Add.14].

GENERAL ASSEMBLY ACTION

On 30 June [meeting 93], the General Assembly, on the recommendation of the Fifth (Administrative and Budgetary) Committee [A/63/902], adopted **resolution 63/295** without vote [agenda item 142].

Financing of the United Nations Interim Administration Mission in Kosovo

The General Assembly,

Having considered the reports of the Secretary-General on the financing of the United Nations Interim Administration Mission in Kosovo and the related report of the Advisory Committee on Administrative and Budgetary Questions,

Recalling Security Council resolution 1244(1999) of 10 June 1999 regarding the establishment of the United Nations Interim Administration Mission in Kosovo,

Recalling also its resolution 53/241 of 28 July 1999 on the financing of the Mission and its subsequent resolutions thereon, the latest of which was resolution 62/262 of 20 June 2008,

Acknowledging the complexity of the Mission,

Reaffirming the general principles underlying the financing of United Nations peacekeeping operations, as stated in General Assembly resolutions 1874(S-IV) of 27 June 1963, 3101(XXVIII) of 11 December 1973 and 55/235 of 23 December 2000,

Mindful of the fact that it is essential to provide the Mission with the financial resources necessary to enable it to fulfil its responsibilities under the relevant resolution of the Security Council,

Mindful also of the need to ensure coordination and cooperation with the European Union Rule of Law Mission in Kosovo,

1. *Requests* the Secretary-General to entrust the Head of Mission with the task of formulating future budget proposals in full accordance with the provisions of General Assembly resolutions 59/296 of 22 June 2005, 60/266 of 30 June 2006 and 61/276 of 29 June 2007, as well as other relevant resolutions;

2. *Takes note* of the status of contributions to the United Nations Interim Administration Mission in Kosovo as at 30 April 2009, including the contributions outstanding in the amount of 62.7 million United States dollars, representing some 2 per cent of the total assessed contributions, notes with concern that only eighty-eight Member States have paid their assessed contributions in full, and urges all other Member States, in particular those in arrears, to ensure payment of their outstanding assessed contributions;

3. *Expresses its appreciation* to those Member States which have paid their assessed contributions in full, and urges all other Member States to make every possible effort to ensure payment of their assessed contributions to the Mission in full;

4. *Expresses concern* at the financial situation with regard to peacekeeping activities, in particular as regards the reimbursements to troop contributors that bear additional burdens owing to overdue payments by Member States of their assessments;

5. *Also expresses concern* at the delay experienced by the Secretary-General in deploying and providing adequate resources to some recent peacekeeping missions, in particular those in Africa;

6. *Emphasizes* that all future and existing peacekeeping missions shall be given equal and non-discriminatory treatment in respect of financial and administrative arrangements;

7. *Also emphasizes* that all peacekeeping missions shall be provided with adequate resources for the effective and efficient discharge of their respective mandates;

8. *Reiterates its request* to the Secretary-General to make the fullest possible use of facilities and equipment at the United Nations Logistics Base at Brindisi, Italy, in order to minimize the costs of procurement for the Mission;

9. *Requests* the Secretary-General to ensure that proposed peacekeeping budgets are based on the relevant legislative mandates;

10. *Endorses* the conclusions and recommendations contained in the report of the Advisory Committee on Administrative and Budgetary Questions, subject to the provisions of the present resolution, and requests the Secretary-General to ensure their full implementation;

11. *Decides* to create three positions at the P-5, P-4 and P-3 levels in the Office of the Special Representative of the Secretary-General, to be funded under general temporary assistance and accommodated within the level of the approved budget;

12. *Takes note* of paragraph 35 of the report of the Advisory Committee;

13. *Requests* the Secretary-General to ensure the full implementation of the relevant provisions of resolutions 59/296, 60/266 and 61/276;

14. *Also requests* the Secretary-General to take all action necessary to ensure that the Mission is administered with a maximum of efficiency and economy;

15. *Further requests* the Secretary-General, in order to reduce the cost of employing General Service staff, to continue efforts to recruit local staff for the Mission against General Service posts, commensurate with the requirements of the Mission;

Financial performance report for the period from 1 July 2007 to 30 June 2008

16. *Takes note* of the report of the Secretary-General on the financial performance of the Mission for the period from 1 July 2007 to 30 June 2008;

Budget estimates for the period from 1 July 2009 to 30 June 2010

17. *Decides* to appropriate to the Special Account for the United Nations Interim Administration Mission in Kosovo the amount of 48,864,900 dollars for the period from 1 July 2009 to 30 June 2010, inclusive of 46,809,000 dollars for the maintenance of the Mission, 1,711,000 dollars for the support account for peacekeeping operations and 344,900 dollars for the United Nations Logistics Base;

Financing of the appropriation

18. *Also decides* to apportion among Member States the amount of 48,864,900 dollars, in accordance with the levels updated in General Assembly resolution 61/243 of 22 December 2006, and taking into account the scale of assessments for 2009, as set out in Assembly resolution 61/237 of 22 December 2006, and for 2010;

19. *Further decides* that, in accordance with the provisions of General Assembly resolution 973(X) of 15 December 1955, there shall be set off against the apportionment among Member States, as provided for in paragraph 18 above, their respective share in the Tax Equalization Fund in the amount of 4,204,600 dollars, comprising the estimated staff assessment income of 3,992,400 dollars approved for the Mission, the prorated share of 178,100 dollars of the estimated staff assessment income approved for the support account and the prorated share of 34,100 dollars of the estimated staff assessment income approved for the United Nations Logistics Base;

20. *Decides* that, for Member States that have fulfilled their financial obligations to the Mission, there shall be set off against their apportionment, as provided for in paragraph 18 above, their respective share of the unencumbered balance and other income in the total amount of 5,413,700 dollars in respect of the financial period ended 30 June 2008, in accordance with the levels updated in resolution 61/243, and taking into account the scale of assessments for 2008, as set out in resolution 61/237;

21. *Also decides* that, for Member States that have not fulfilled their financial obligations to the Mission, there shall be set off against their outstanding obligations their respective share of the unencumbered balance and other income in the total amount of 5,413,700 dollars in respect of the financial period ended 30 June 2008, in accordance with the scheme set out in paragraph 20 above;

22. *Further decides* that the increase of 317,000 dollars in the estimated staff assessment income in respect of the financial period ended 30 June 2008 shall be added to the credits from the amount of 5,413,700 dollars referred to in paragraphs 20 and 21 above;

23. *Emphasizes* that no peacekeeping mission shall be financed by borrowing funds from other active peacekeeping missions;

24. *Encourages* the Secretary-General to continue to take additional measures to ensure the safety and security of all personnel participating in the Mission under the auspices of the United Nations, bearing in mind paragraphs 5 and 6 of Security Council resolution 1502(2003) of 26 August 2003;

25. *Invites* voluntary contributions to the Mission in cash and in the form of services and supplies acceptable to the Secretary-General, to be administered, as appropriate, in accordance with the procedure and practices established by the General Assembly;

26. *Decides* to include in the provisional agenda of its sixty-fourth session the item entitled "Financing of the United Nations Interim Administration Mission in Kosovo".

In December, the Secretary-General submitted the performance report for UNMIK for the period 1 July 2008 to 30 June 2009 [A/64/604].

On 24 December, the Assembly decided that the agenda item on UNMIK financing would remain for consideration during its resumed sixty-fourth (2010) session (**decision 64/549**).

KFOR

In accordance with Security Council resolution 1244(1999) [YUN 1999, p. 353], the Secretary-General transmitted to the Council reports on the activities during 2009 of the Kosovo Force (KFOR), also known as Operation Joint Guard, covering the periods from 1 January to 31 March, 1 April to 30 June and 1 July to 30 September [S/2010/77], and 1 October to 31 December [S/2010/197]. As at 31 December, the Force, which operated under NATO leadership, comprised 11,600 troops, including 1,800 troops from non-NATO countries.

KFOR units continued to focus on maintaining a safe and secure environment and freedom of movement throughout Kosovo; preventing non-compliant-group activities; deterring outbreaks of violence by supporting the Kosovo Police and EULEX; and standing ready to assist them in a third responder position upon request. KFOR also conducted high-visibility operations throughout Kosovo to deter any possible attempt at destabilization.

The former Yugoslav Republic of Macedonia

Relations with Greece

In accordance with the 1995 Interim Accord on the normalization of relations between the former Yugoslav Republic of Macedonia (FYROM) and Greece

[YUN 1995, p. 599], representatives of both countries met twice during 2009 (11 February and 22 June), under the auspices of the Secretary-General. The countries exchanged views in the context of article 5 of the Accord, which provided for the continuation of negotiations towards reaching agreement on their differences, as described in Security Council resolutions 817(1993) [YUN 1993, p. 208] and 845(1993) [ibid., p. 209], concerning the name of the State of FYROM. Representatives of both countries also held separate meetings with the Secretary-General's Personal Envoy in July and November. The issue remained unresolved at year's end.

Communications. During the year, letters from Greece and from FYROM to the Secretary-General or General Assembly President dealt with relations between the two States [A/63/712-S/2009/82, A/63/772-S/2009/150, A/63/869-S/2009/285, A/63/934-S/2009/381, A/64/468 and A/64/500].

Georgia

In 2009, efforts to move the Georgian-Abkhaz peace process forward based on the 2001 Basic Principles for the Distribution of Competences between Tbilisi (Georgia's Government) and Sukhumi (the Abkhaz leadership) [YUN 2001, p. 386]—the framework for negotiations on the status of Abkhazia as a sovereign entity within the State of Georgia—continued to be affected by the 2008 war in South Ossetia [YUN 2008, p. 454] and its aftermath, as well as Georgian-Russian relations. The Russian Federation recognized Abkhazia and South Ossetia as independent States, while Georgia declared them territories occupied by the Russian Federation. In accordance with the six-point agreement of 12 August 2008 and implementing measures of 8 September, international discussions were held in Geneva. In February 2009, Georgia, the Russian Federation, the United States, and the Abkhaz and South Ossetian representatives participated in a discussion that resulted in the agreement on "Proposals for joint incident prevention and response mechanisms", which aimed to address security issues on the ground. Four subsequent rounds of talks were held during the year.

Despite the new challenges, the United Nations Observer Mission in Georgia (UNOMIG) continued to carry out its patrolling, observation and liaison activities as at 7 August 2008 and prior to the war in South Ossetia. However, as the context in which the UN Mission carried out that mandate—as defined by Security Council resolution 937(1994) [YUN 1994, p. 584]—had changed considerably, the Mission's role was reviewed. Although the Secretary-General submitted recommendations in May on a future security regime, which included activities of a UN mission, the Security Council was unable to reach an agreement and the UNOMIG mandate was terminated on 15 June 2009.

Situation in Abkhazia

Political developments and UN Mission activities

Report of Secretary-General (February). In a February report on the situation in Abkhazia [S/2009/69 & Corr.1], the Secretary-General stated that developments such as the recognition by the Russian Federation of Abkhazia's independence on 26 August 2008 [YUN 2008, p. 456], Georgia's withdrawal from the 1994 Moscow Agreement on a Ceasefire and Separation of Forces [YUN 1994, p. 583] on 29 August 2008 [YUN 2008, p. 456], and the termination of the mandate of the Collective Peacekeeping Forces of the Commonwealth of Independent States (CIS) on 10 October 2008 [YUN 2008, p. 457], had considerably affected the context in which UNOMIG carried out its mandated tasks as defined by Security Council resolution 937(1994) [YUN 1994, p. 584] and subsequent resolutions. The overall security situation in the Mission's area of responsibility remained tense, with a considerable number of security incidents involving casualties on both sides. On the Abkhaz-controlled side, Russian Federation forces had taken over previous positions of the CIS peacekeeping force and constructed new fortified positions in the zone of conflict. Abkhaz heavy weapons and military personnel had also been introduced into the zone. At the same time, Georgian Ministry of Internal Affairs personnel had established new positions and deployed light armoured vehicles in the security zone. Both sides had largely continued to respect limitations that were in place under the Moscow Agreement. Also of concern were the burdens experienced by local populations, including restrictions on their freedom of movement across the ceasefire line. In accordance with the six-point agreement of 12 August 2008 [YUN 2008, p. 456] and implementing measures of 8 September [ibid., p. 457], the UN Mission continued to carry out patrolling and other tasks mandated to UNOMIG as at 7 August 2008. Notwithstanding the new challenges, the UN Mission carried out those functions, on both sides of the ceasefire line, without major impediments.

Persistent tensions in Georgian-Russian relations continued to affect the overall situation in the region. Georgia maintained that Abkhazia and South Ossetia were territories occupied by the Russian Federation. It restricted access to those territories and prohibited economic and financial activities that did not comply with Georgian law. The Russian Federation, on the other hand, made references to the "new realities"

created after the August 2008 developments—specifically the recognition of Abkhazia and South Ossetia by the Russian Federation—and based the presence of Russian armed forces there on the Russian-Abkhaz and Russian-South Ossetian treaties on friendship, cooperation and mutual assistance [YUN 2008, p. 458]. It also planned to establish military bases and deploy some 3,700 troops. In accordance with the August 2008 six-point agreement and 8 September 2008 implementing measures, three rounds of international discussions co-chaired by the Secretary-General's Special Representative, together with EU and OSCE representatives, were held in Geneva in 2008 [ibid.]. A fourth round of discussions was scheduled for 17 and 18 February 2009. Although the Geneva discussions on security and stability had made some progress, the Secretary-General observed that they had yet to deliver tangible results. Discussions undertaken by his Special Representative with the parties and international stakeholders on the future role of the UN Mission had confirmed support for a continued UN presence, but had also identified considerable differences as to the nature and scope of its mandate.

In the absence of a renewed agreement on a comprehensive security regime, the Secretary-General recommended measures for consideration by the parties as a basis for a discussion on an effective security regime, which included strict observation of the ceasefire on land, at sea and in the air; a security zone on both sides of the ceasefire line where the presence of armed forces and equipment would not be allowed; a ban on overflights by military aircraft and unmanned aerial vehicles in the zone and additional zones; advanced notification of any changes in the deployment of armed personnel and equipment in the zones; and designation by each party of authorized representatives to liaise on a regular basis with a view to exchanging information and resolving incidents. Due to the precarious security situation and to contribute to the well-being of local populations, the Secretary-General also proposed that the Council endorse the continued presence of a UN mission, retaining the current mission's configuration and deployment. The mission's tasks would include, among other activities, patrolling its area of responsibility (the former zone of conflict), liaising with all parties to resolve incidents and ensure freedom of movement across the ceasefire line for local populations, monitoring parties' adherence to any elements of a security regime endorsed by the Council, contributing to improving the humanitarian situation, assisting the parties in the further development of a mutually agreed, comprehensive security regime and assisting law enforcement agencies on both sides of the ceasefire line.

UN Mission extension. On 13 February, in resolution 1866(2009), the Security Council extended the mandate of the UN Mission for a new period terminating on 15 June, and expressed its intention to out-line elements of a future UN presence in the region by that date, taking into account the recommendations in the Secretary-General's forthcoming report, the Geneva discussions and developments on the ground.

SECURITY COUNCIL ACTION

On 13 February [meeting 6082], the Security Council unanimously adopted **resolution 1866(2009)**. The draft [S/2009/88] was prepared in consultations among Council members.

The Security Council,

Recalling its previous resolutions, including resolutions 1808(2008) of 15 April 2008 and 1839(2008) of 9 October 2008,

Having considered the report of the Secretary-General of 3 February 2009,

Welcoming the six-point agreement of 12 August 2008 and subsequent implementing measures of 8 September 2008,

Taking note of the Geneva discussions which commenced on 15 October 2008, and encouraging the participants to reach practical results,

Underlining the importance of the peaceful resolution of disputes,

1. *Recalls* the arrangements entered into under the agreements of 12 August and 8 September 2008;

2. *Calls for* the provisions that were set out in para-graph 2 *(a)* of the Agreement on a Ceasefire and Separa-tion of Forces signed at Moscow on 14 May 1994 to be re-spected, pending consultations and agreement on a revised security regime, taking note of the recommendations on the security regime contained in the report of the Secretary-General of 3 February 2009;

3. *Underlines* the need to refrain from the use of force or from any act of ethnic discrimination against persons, groups of persons or institutions, and to ensure, without distinction, the security of persons, the right of persons to freedom of movement and the protection of the property of refugees and displaced persons;

4. *Calls for* facilitating and refraining from placing any impediment to humanitarian assistance to persons affected by the conflict, including refugees and internally displaced persons, and further calls for facilitating their voluntary, safe, dignified and unhindered return;

5. *Also calls for* the intensification of efforts to address the issue of regional security and stability and the issue of refugees and internally displaced persons, through the discussions currently under way in Geneva, and requests the Secretary-General, through his Special Representative for Georgia, to continue to fully support this process and to report on progress thereon;

6. *Requests* the Secretary-General to report to the Security Council on the implementation of the present resolution and on the situation on the ground and the ac-tivities of the United Nations mission, including recom-mendations on future activities, by 15 May 2009;

7. *Expresses its intention* to outline the elements of a future United Nations presence in the region by 15 June 2009, taking into account the recommendations to be con-tained in the report of the Secretary-General referred to in paragraph 6 above, the Geneva discussions and develop-ments on the ground;

8. *Decides* to extend the mandate of the United Nations mission for a new period terminating on 15 June 2009;

9. *Decides also* to remain actively seized of the matter.

Gali sector

In the Gali sector security and restricted-weapons zones, UNOMIG continued to observe the presence of Abkhaz military personnel and heavy military equipment, including a rotation of the heavy mili-tary equipment introduced in the zone of conflict by the Russian forces in August 2008 and the estab-lishment of a new position in the restricted-weapons zone near Ilori village south of the Ochamchira train-ing area. On 10 February 2009, two consecutive ex-plosions occurred on a road routinely used by UN patrols between Zeni and Tagiloni villages in the security zone. On 4 March, Russian forces denied a UN patrol access through a Russian position near Lekukhona village in the security zone. The Mission also observed on several occasions Russian military helicopters overflying the security zone close to the ceasefire line. On 30 March, UNOMIG observed an armed Abkhaz naval patrol vessel, anchored approxi-mately 700 metres offshore in waters adjacent to the security zone—the first Abkhaz navy vessel to be sighted in the area since August 2008. UNOMIG regu-larly conveyed to the representatives of the Russian Federation forces that the presence of military person-nel and heavy military equipment in the security and restricted-weapons zones was inconsistent with Secu-rity Council resolution 1866(2009). The UN police continued to liaise with local law enforcement agen-cies in the Gali, Ochamchira and Tkvarcheli districts. It also conducted 18 training courses in forensics, police management, police tactics and other policing skills. In other efforts, the UN police conducted a training programme in drug abuse awareness for 366 schoolchildren and organized an international round-table discussion on traffic safety.

Zugdidi sector and Kodori valley

While the situation in the Zugdidi sector in Janu-ary was tense and characterized by exchanges of fire along the ceasefire line, including 15 reported explo-sions near the village of Orsantia that UNOMIG as-sessed were caused by grenades, the situation from February on was generally calm. The Georgian Min-istry of Internal Affairs maintained approximately 250 personnel at 15 observation posts and their head-quarters in the security zone. It continued to deploy "Cobra" light armoured vehicles to patrol the cease-fire line. The Mission brought to the attention of the Georgian side that the deployment of those vehicles was inconsistent with resolution 1866(2009). The UN police continued to liaise and conduct joint patrols with the Georgian police regularly and to visit law enforcement facilities. It organized 45 training courses in police tactics, forensics and other policing skills; its also arranged training in drug abuse awareness for 1,475 schoolchildren in the Zugdidi district and held a 6 April round-table discussion with the participation of local and international NGOs in the framework of the project. In carrying out the operational aspects of its mandate, the Mission maintained regular contacts with the Georgian authorities and with the EU monitoring mission.

Following the conduct of four 1-day patrols to the Kodori Valley in February, March and April to observe the security and humanitarian situation, the Mission assessed the overall situation as calm. The Abkhaz side continued to maintain control of the Kodori valley with the support of Russian forces. The Mission's human rights officers participated in two patrols and noted the absence of school services but the availability of basic medical services in the valley.

Georgian–Russian relations

Report of Secretary-General (May). The Secretary-General reported [S/2009/254] that his Special Representative, together with EU and OSCE representatives, co-chaired the fourth round of discussions (Geneva, 17–18 February), in which Georgia, the Russian Federation, the United States and the Abkhaz and South Ossetian representatives participated. The participants agreed on "Proposals for joint incident prevention and response mechanisms", which envisaged regular meetings between officials responsible for security and public order and representatives of international organizations with the purpose of addressing security issues on the ground. On humanitarian issues, they agreed to focus efforts on facilitating the voluntary and safe return of refugees and internally displaced persons (IDPs). The Abkhaz side insisted that the meetings within the mechanism in which it would participate be held after 15 June, following the decision by the Security Council on a future UN presence. It also suggested that the meetings be chaired by the United Nations. On 23 April, the first meeting within the mechanism relating to South Ossetia was convened in Ergneti, Georgia, with the participation of the Georgian and South Ossetian sides, as well as representatives of the Russian Ministry of Defence, OSCE and the EU.

Following a period of relative stability along the ceasefire line in February and March, the situation on the ground changed on 9 April when the Georgian opposition started demonstrations against the Government, resulting in the introduction of additional Russian forces, including heavy military equipment, into the Mission's area of responsibility.

The Georgian side continued to protest against Russian plans to establish military bases in Abkhazia and South Ossetia. It called on the international community to stop the Russian military build-up, induce the Russian side to withdraw troops from the Georgian territory pursuant to the 12 August 2008 ceasefire agreement and reverse the recognition by the Russian Federation of Abkhazia and South Ossetia. Russian officials reiterated that the military bases were established on the basis of agreements with the Abkhaz and South Ossetian leaderships and claimed that there was increased military presence and activity by the Georgian side. On 30 April, the "Agreement between the Russian Federation and the Republic of Abkhazia on joint efforts in protection of the state border of the Republic of Abkhazia" and the "Agreement between the Russian Federation and the Republic of South Ossetia on joint efforts in protection of the state border of the Republic of South Ossetia" were signed in Moscow. The agreements were effective for five years, with the possibility of a five-year extension. The Georgian authorities called the signing of the documents a violation of the 12 August 2008 ceasefire agreement.

The Special Representative engaged with the Georgian and Abkhaz sides and key international stakeholders in discussions on a possible revised security regime as a core element of a future UN presence. The Secretary-General, during his discussions in Moscow on 26 and 27 March, also emphasized the need for an agreement on a credible security regime as the basis for a future UN mission. In May, he observed that the security situation in the Mission's area of responsibility remained fragile, with a continued threat of incidents, including from mines and improvised explosive devices. The local population, in particular in the Gali district, remained in a precarious situation, with limitations on its freedom of movement across the ceasefire line. In addition, the ceasefire regime—the key foundation for the separation of forces and stabilization—had continued to erode. Heavy military equipment and military personnel remained in the Mission's area of responsibility, despite the call in resolution 1866(2009) that the provisions in the Moscow Agreement be respected. The Secretary-General concluded that an agreement on a revised security regime was essential for long-term stabilization and a viable UN role. On the basis of consultations with the parties and international stakeholders, he made a series of recommendations on a future security regime.

Security Council consideration (June). On 15 June [meeting 6143], the Security Council considered a draft resolution [S/2009/310] extending the mandate of the UN Mission until 30 June. The Council also had before it two letters dated 10 June from Georgia. The first [S/2009/305] transmitted a document regarding violations by the Russian Federation of the six-point ceasefire agreement; and the second [S/2009/306] transmitted a statement by the Georgian Ministry of Foreign Affairs on the military actions in the Tskhinvali Region in August 2008. With regard to the draft resolution, the Russian Federation stated that the earlier mandate of UNOMIG had ceased to exist in August 2008 and there was no point in extending the Mission, as it was built on old realities. In the context of the new political and legal conditions, the majority of the old terms and terminology used in the international documents could not be applied. Moreover, the draft resolution affirmed Georgia's territorial integrity, while denying Abkhazia as a State, and the inclusion of a reference to Security Council resolution 1808(2008) [YUN 2008, p. 450] did not reflect the new military and political position of States in the region. Following the vote (10-1-4), the draft resolution was not adopted, owing to the negative vote of the Russian Federation, a permanent member of the Council. Four members abstained (China, Libya, Uganda, Viet Nam).

Termination of UNOMIG. On 15 June [SG/SM/12315], the Secretary-General, took note of the lack of agreement within the Security Council on the future activities of a UN stabilization mission. In accordance with the outcome, he would instruct his Special Representative to take measures to cease UNOMIG operations effective 16 June and consult with his senior advisers and the Special Representative on the immediate next steps.

Geneva talks. In accordance with the 12 August 2008 ceasefire agreement and 8 September 2008 implementing measures, international discussions co-chaired by the United Nations, the EU and OSCE continued to be held throughout 2009, including the fifth (18 May), sixth (1 July), seventh (17 September) and eighth (11 November) rounds. On 18 November, Georgia transmitted a statement [A/64/541-S/2009/600] of its Foreign Affairs Ministry on the eighth round of talks, which discussed the issues of security and stability and the return of refugees and IDPs. Participants also reviewed the report of the Independent International Fact-Finding Mission on the Conflict in Georgia (Tagliavini report). The ninth round of talks would be held on 28 January 2010.

Communications. On 5 August, Georgia transmitted [A/63/936-S/2009/409] a statement condemning the entry of Russian President Dmitry Medvedev into the Georgian occupied territory as an illegal crossing of the Georgian State border.

On 7 August, the Russian Federation transmitted [A/63/938-S/2009/413] a statement marking the one-year anniversary of the events in South Ossetia and stating that the presence of Russian troops and border guards under the bilateral agreements with Abkhazia and South Ossetia was legitimate.

Georgia transmitted on 10 August [A/63/953] the "Report by the Government of Georgia on the aggression by the Russian Federation against Georgia", covering the period from 1989 to October 2008; and on 17 December 2009 [A/64/585-S/2009/661] a statement condemning the 12 December presidential elections in Abkhazia as illegal. Georgia also transmitted letters regarding shootings, military and gang attacks, breaches of the six-point ceasefire agreement, the illegal use of its resources, air space and sea, and other violations of its sovereignty on 22 January [A/63/688-S/2009/48], 3 March [A/63/750-S/2009/127], 4 June [A/63/879], 11 June [A/63/885-S/2009/308], 17 July [A/63/932-S/2009/371], 1 September [A/63/955-S/2009/441], 8 December [A/64/560-S/2009/630] and 29 December [A/64/618-S/2010/6].

Human rights and humanitarian situation

The UN Mission's Human Rights Office in Abkhazia continued to implement its programme for the promotion and protection of human rights and to provide support to local NGOs. The Office conducted visits to detention facilities to monitor court proceedings and provided advisory services to the local population on the Abkhaz-controlled side of the ceasefire line. It also followed up on individual cases involving the right to physical integrity; the right to the security and safety of the person; equal treatment and non-discrimination; and the right to access health services, as well as on cases of alleged extortion. The Office facilitated the Assisting Communities Together project, which offered grants to local NGOs for human rights education and training at the grass-roots level.

On humanitarian and rehabilitation activities, the Mission contributed donations to schools, dispensaries, maternity clinics and residences of displaced persons. It also offered English classes to the local communities on both sides of the ceasefire line. In March, the Mission completed the renovation of the Gali hospital. The United Nations High Commissioner for Refugees began verifying and screening over 650 applications for its shelter rehabilitation programme and assisted a new project to rehabilitate 100 houses. The World Food Programme served 11,600 beneficiaries through its food-for-work programmes in the Gali, Tkvarcheli and Ochamchira districts. In April, the United Nations Children's Fund began a programme to improve access to health care for women and children and to promote the social inclusion of children with disabilities in the Gali district.

IDPs and refugees. On 9 September, the General Assembly adopted **resolution 63/307** (see p. 779) on the status of internally displaced persons (IDPs) and refugees from Abkhazia and South Ossetia, which recognized the right of return of all refugees and

IDPs, regardless of their ethnicity, to Abkhazia and South Ossetia; emphasized the need for unimpeded access for humanitarian activities to IDPs, refugees and other persons in conflict-affected areas in Georgia; and called upon the participants in the Geneva discussions to take steps to ensure respect for human rights and create security conditions conducive to the voluntary and safe return of IDPs and refugees to their places of origin.

UN Observer Mission in Georgia

The United Nations Observer Mission in Georgia (UNOMIG) was established by Security Council resolution 858(1993) [YUN 1993, p. 509]. It monitored compliance with the 1994 Moscow Agreement [YUN 1994, p. 583] and fulfilled other tasks as mandated by Council resolution 937(1994) [ibid., p. 584] and subsequent resolutions. In accordance with the 12 August 2008 six-point ceasefire agreement [YUN 2008, p. 456] and 8 September 2008 implementing measures [ibid., p. 457], during 2009, the Mission carried out the mandated UNOMIG functions as of 7 August 2008 and prior to the 2008 war in South Ossetia. On 13 February 2009, the Council extended the Mission's mandate until 15 June 2009 (see p. 416). However, on that date, Council members were unable to agree on the future activities of a UN stabilization mission and the UNOMIG mandate was terminated effective 16 June 2009.

UNOMIG's main headquarters was located in Sukhumi (Abkhazia, Georgia), with a liaison office in the Georgian capital of Tbilisi, and the team bases and sector headquarters in the Gali and Zugdidi sectors. A team in the Kodori Valley was manned by observers operating from Sukhumi.

As at 30 April, Mission strength stood at 129 military observers and 16 police advisers. Johan Verbeke (Belgium) continued to lead the Mission as the Secretary-General's Special Representative for Georgia and Head of the Mission. He was assisted by the Chief Military Observer, Major General Anwar Hussain (Bangladesh).

Financing

In June, the General Assembly had before it the Secretary-General's report on the UNOMIG budget for the period from 1 July 2009 to 30 June 2010 [A/63/684] and the related ACABQ report [A/63/746/Add.6]. In December, the Assembly also considered the reports of the Secretary-General on the revised UNOMIG budget for the period 1 July 2009 to 30 June 2010 [A/64/464] and the UNOMIG performance report for the period 1 July 2008 to 30 June 2009 [A/64/463], as well as the related ACABQ report [A/64/529].

On 30 June [meeting 93], the General Assembly, on the recommendation of the Fifth Committee [A/63/900], adopted **resolution 63/293** without vote [agenda item 140].

Financing of the United Nations Observer Mission in Georgia

The General Assembly,

Having considered the reports of the Secretary-General on the financing of the United Nations Observer Mission in Georgia and the related report of the Advisory Committee on Administrative and Budgetary Questions,

Recalling Security Council resolution 854(1993) of 6 August 1993, by which the Council approved the deployment of an advance team of up to ten United Nations military observers for a period of three months and the incorporation of the advance team into a United Nations observer mission if such a mission was formally established by the Council,

Recalling also Security Council resolution 858(1993) of 24 August 1993, by which the Council established the United Nations Observer Mission in Georgia, and the subsequent resolutions by which the Council extended the mandate of the Observer Mission, the last of which was resolution 1866(2009) of 13 February 2009,

Recalling further its decision 48/475 A of 23 December 1993 on the financing of the Observer Mission and its subsequent resolutions and decisions thereon, the latest of which was resolution 62/260 of 20 June 2008,

Reaffirming the general principles underlying the financing of United Nations peacekeeping operations, as stated in General Assembly resolutions 1874(S-IV) of 27 June 1963, 3101(XXVIII) of 11 December 1973 and 55/235 of 23 December 2000,

Mindful of the fact that it is essential to provide the Observer Mission with the financial resources necessary to enable it to complete its administrative liquidation,

1. *Takes note* of the status of contributions to the United Nations Observer Mission in Georgia as at 30 April 2009, including the contributions outstanding in the amount of 14.2 million United States dollars, representing some 4 per cent of the total assessed contributions, notes with concern that only seventy-four Member States have paid their assessed contributions in full, and urges all other Member States, in particular those in arrears, to ensure payment of their outstanding assessed contributions;

2. *Expresses its appreciation* to those Member States which have paid their assessed contributions in full, and urges all other Member States to make every possible effort to ensure payment of their assessed contributions to the Observer Mission in full;

3. *Takes note* of the report of the Advisory Committee on Administrative and Budgetary Questions;

4. *Requests* the Secretary-General to take all action necessary to ensure that the administrative liquidation of the Observer Mission is administered with a maximum of efficiency and economy;

5. *Also requests* the Secretary-General to submit the administrative liquidation budget for the Observer Mission to the General Assembly at the main part of its sixty-fourth session for consideration;

**Financial performance report for the period
from 1 July 2007 to 30 June 2008**

6. *Takes note* of the report of the Secretary-General on the financial performance of the Observer Mission for the period from 1 July 2007 to 30 June 2008;

**Budget estimates for the period
from 1 July to 31 December 2009**

7. *Decides* to appropriate to the Special Account for the United Nations Observer Mission in Georgia the amount of 15 million dollars for the administrative liquidation of the Observer Mission for the period from 1 July to 31 December 2009;

Financing of the appropriation

8. *Also decides* to apportion among Member States the amount of 10 million dollars for the period from 1 July to 31 December 2009, in accordance with the levels updated in General Assembly resolution 61/243 of 22 December 2006, and taking into account the scale of assessments for 2009, as set out in Assembly resolution 61/237 of 22 December 2006;

**Estimates for the support account
for peacekeeping operations and the
United Nations Logistics Base at Brindisi, Italy,
for the period from 1 July 2009 to 30 June 2010**

9. *Further decides* to appropriate to the Special Account the amount of 652,700 dollars for the period from 1 July 2009 to 30 June 2010, comprising 543,200 dollars for the support account for peacekeeping operations and 109,500 dollars for the United Nations Logistics Base at Brindisi, Italy;

10. *Decides* to apportion among Member States the amount of 652,700 dollars for the period from 1 July 2009 to 30 June 2010, in accordance with the levels updated in resolution 61/243, and taking into account the scale of assessments for 2009, as set out in resolution 61/237, and for 2010;

11. *Also decides* that, in accordance with the provisions of its resolution 973(X) of 15 December 1955, there shall be set off against the apportionment among Member States, as provided for in paragraph 10 above, their respective share in the Tax Equalization Fund of 67,400 dollars, comprising the prorated share of 56,600 dollars of the estimated staff assessment income approved for the support account and the prorated share of 10,800 dollars of the estimated staff assessment income approved for the United Nations Logistics Base;

12. *Further decides* that, for Member States that have fulfilled their financial obligations to the Observer Mission, there shall be set off against their apportionment, as provided for in paragraph 8 above, their respective share of the unencumbered balance and other income in the amount of 3,560,400 dollars in respect of the financial period ended 30 June 2008, in accordance with the levels updated in resolution 61/243, and taking into account the scale of assessments for 2008, as set out in resolution 61/237;

13. *Decides* that, for Member States that have not fulfilled their financial obligations to the Observer Mission, there shall be set off against their outstanding obligations their respective share of the unencumbered balance and other income in the total amount of 3,560,400 dollars in respect of the financial period ended 30 June 2008, in accordance with the scheme set out in paragraph 12 above;

14. *Also decides* that the decrease of 164,500 dollars in the estimated staff assessment income in respect of the financial period ended 30 June 2008 shall be set off against the credits from the amount of 3,560,400 dollars referred to in paragraphs 12 and 13 above;

15. *Encourages* the Secretary-General to continue to take additional measures to ensure the safety and security of all personnel participating in the Observer Mission under the auspices of the United Nations, bearing in mind paragraphs 5 and 6 of Security Council resolution 1502(2003) of 26 August 2003;

16. *Decides* to include in the provisional agenda of its sixty-fourth session the item entitled "Financing of the United Nations Observer Mission in Georgia".

On 22 December [meeting 67], the Assembly, on the recommendation of the Fifth Committee [A/64/552], adopted **resolution 64/234** without vote [agenda item 154].

Financing of the United Nations
Observer Mission in Georgia

The General Assembly,

Having considered the reports of the Secretary-General on the financing of the United Nations Observer Mission in Georgia and the related report of the Advisory Committee on Administrative and Budgetary Questions,

Recalling Security Council resolution 854(1993) of 6 August 1993, by which the Council approved the deployment of an advance team of up to ten United Nations military observers for a period of three months and the incorporation of the advance team into a United Nations observer mission if such a mission was formally established by the Council,

Recalling also Security Council resolution 858(1993) of 24 August 1993, by which the Council established the United Nations Observer Mission in Georgia, and the subsequent resolutions by which the Council extended the mandate of the Observer Mission, the last of which was resolution 1866(2009) of 13 February 2009,

Recalling further its decision 48/475 A of 23 December 1993 on the financing of the Observer Mission and its subsequent resolutions and decisions thereon, the latest of which was resolution 63/293 of 30 June 2009,

Reaffirming the general principles underlying the financing of United Nations peacekeeping operations, as stated in General Assembly resolutions 1874(S-IV) of 27 June 1963, 3101(XXVIII) of 11 December 1973 and 55/235 of 23 December 2000,

Mindful of the fact that it is essential to provide the Observer Mission with the financial resources necessary to enable it to complete its administrative liquidation,

1. *Takes note* of the status of contributions to the United Nations Observer Mission in Georgia as at 30 September 2009, including the contributions outstanding in the amount of 8.9 million United States dollars, representing some 2 per cent of the total assessed contributions, notes with concern that only thirty-seven Member States have paid their assessed contributions in full, and urges all other Member States, in particular those in arrears, to ensure payment of their outstanding assessed contributions;

2. *Expresses its appreciation* to those Member States which have paid their assessed contributions in full, and urges all other Member States to make every possible effort to ensure payment of their assessed contributions to the Observer Mission in full;

3. *Endorses* the conclusions and recommendations contained in the report of the Advisory Committee on Administrative and Budgetary Questions, and requests the Secretary-General to ensure their full implementation;

4. *Requests* the Secretary-General to take all action necessary to ensure that the administrative liquidation of the Observer Mission is administered with a maximum of efficiency and economy;

Financial performance report for the period from 1 July 2008 to 30 June 2009

5. *Takes note* of the report of the Secretary-General on the financial performance of the Observer Mission for the period from 1 July 2008 to 30 June 2009;

6. *Decides* to reduce the appropriation of 36,084,000 dollars approved for the Mission for the period from 1 July 2008 to 30 June 2009 under the terms of its resolution 62/260 of 20 June 2008 by the amount of 501,985 dollars, to 35,582,015 dollars;

7. *Also decides* to apportion among Member States the amount of 934,857 dollars, representing the difference between the amount of 33,047,358 dollars already apportioned by the General Assembly for the maintenance of the Mission and the actual expenditure of 33,982,215 dollars for the period from 1 July 2008 to 30 June 2009;

8. *Further decides* that, in accordance with the provisions of its resolution 973(X) of 15 December 1955, there shall be set off against the apportionment among Member States, as provided for in paragraph 7 above, their respective share in the Tax Equalization Fund of the estimated staff assessment income of 200,345 dollars, representing the difference between the amount of 2,313,129 dollars already assessed for the maintenance of the Mission and the actual expenditure of 2,513,474 dollars for the period from 1 July 2008 to 30 June 2009;

9. *Decides* to apportion among Member States the total amount of 66,658 dollars, comprising 58,108 dollars for the support account for peacekeeping operations and 8,550 dollars for the United Nations Logistics Base at Brindisi, Italy, remaining to be apportioned by the General Assembly for the period from 16 to 30 June 2009, taking into account the amount of 1,599,800 dollars already appropriated for the period from 1 July 2008 to 30 June 2009 under the terms of General Assembly resolution 62/260, comprising 1,394,600 dollars for the support account for peacekeeping operations and 205,200 dollars for the United Nations Logistics Base;

10. *Also decides* that, in accordance with the provisions of its resolution 973(X), there shall be set off against the apportionment among Member States, as provided for in paragraph 9 above, their respective share in the Tax Equalization Fund of 6,258 dollars, comprising the prorated share of 5,583 dollars of the estimated staff assessment income approved for the support account and the prorated share of 675 dollars of the estimated staff assessment income approved for the United Nations Logistics Base;

Revised budget estimates for the period from 1 July 2009 to 30 June 2010

11. *Further decides* to reduce the appropriation of 15 million dollars approved by the General Assembly under the terms of resolution 63/293 for the administrative liquidation of the Mission for the period from 1 July to 31 December 2009 to the amount of 10,946,000 dollars for the period from 1 July to 31 October 2009;

Financing of the appropriation

12. *Decides* to apportion among Member States the amount of 946,000 dollars for the period from 1 July to 31 October 2009, taking into account the amount of 10 million dollars already apportioned by the General Assembly under the terms of resolution 63/293, in accordance with the levels updated in Assembly resolution 61/243 of 22 December 2006, and taking into account the scale of assessments for 2009, as set out in Assembly resolution 61/237 of 22 December 2006;

13. *Also decides* that, in accordance with the provisions of its resolution 973(X), there shall be set off against the apportionment among Member States, as provided for in paragraph 12 above, their respective share in the Tax Equalization Fund of 933,500 dollars of the estimated staff assessment income approved for the Observer Mission;

14. *Further decides* that, for Member States that have fulfilled their financial obligations to the Observer Mission, there shall be set off against their apportionment, as provided for in paragraph 12 above, their respective share of other income in the total amount of 821,900 dollars in respect of the financial period ended 30 June 2009, in accordance with the levels updated in resolution 61/243, and taking into account the scale of assessments for 2009, as set out in resolution 61/237;

15. *Decides* that, for Member States that have not fulfilled their financial obligations to the Observer Mission, there shall be set off against their outstanding obligations their respective share of other income in the total amount of 821,900 dollars in respect of the financial period ended 30 June 2009, in accordance with the scheme set out in paragraph 14 above;

16. *Also decides* to keep under review during its sixty-fourth session the item entitled "Financing of the United Nations Observer Mission in Georgia".

On 24 December, the Assembly decided that the agenda item on UNOMIG financing would remain for consideration during its resumed sixty-fourth (2010) session (**decision 64/549**).

Armenia and Azerbaijan

In 2009, Armenia and Azerbaijan maintained their positions with regard to the Nagorno-Karabakh region of Azerbaijan, which had erupted in conflict in 1992 [YUN 1992, p. 388], followed by a ceasefire agreement in May 1994 [YUN 1994, p. 577]. Both sides addressed communications regarding the conflict to the

Secretary-General. The Organization for Security and Cooperation in Europe (osce) Minsk Group (France, Russian Federation, United States) continued to mediate the dispute between Armenia and Azerbaijan. The issue remained unresolved at year's end.

Report of Secretary-General. In accordance with General Assembly resolution 62/243 [YUN 2008, p. 461], the Secretary-General submitted a March report [A/63/804 & Corr.1] on the situation in the occupied territories of Azerbaijan. The report contained the replies received as at 10 February from the 3 Co-Chair countries of the osce Minsk Group (France, Russian Federation and United States), 12 Member States (Armenia, Azerbaijan, Belarus, Indonesia, Kazakhstan, Malaysia, Mexico, Pakistan, Slovakia, Sudan, Turkey, Ukraine), and the 2008 osce Chairman-in-Office (Finland) to notes verbales dated 15 and 24 September 2008, which invited Member States to contribute information for the preparation of the report. Replies were subsequently received from Iraq and Jordan [A/63/804/Add.1].

In the osce Minsk Group reply, the United States explained the Group's vote against resolution 62/243; took note of the Moscow Declaration [YUN 2008, p. 462] signed by the Presidents of Armenia, Azerbaijan and the Russian Federation on 2 November 2008, in which they reaffirmed the importance of continuing the mediation efforts of the Group's Co-Chairmen; and transmitted the statement addressed to the osce Permanent Council on 6 November 2008 outlining their activities relating to the Nagorno-Karabakh during the preceding year.

On 14 September 2009, the General Assembly deferred consideration of the agenda item on the situation in the occupied territories of Azerbaijan until its sixty-fourth (2009) session (**decision 63/569**).

Ongoing negotiations. Negotiations on the Nagorno-Karabakh conflict continued during the year, with meetings being convened under the aegis of the osce Minsk Group. Presidents Ilham Aliyev (Azerbaijan) and Serzh Sar-kisyan (Armenia) met on 28 January, on the margins of the World Economic Forum, and on 4 June, in Saint Petersburg, Russia. Armenia transmitted the texts of the statements by the Co-Chairs of the osce Minsk Group concerning the ongoing negotiations on 20 February [A/63/733] and 9 June [A/63/880]. At the meeting between the two Presidents held on 22 November in Munich, the sides achieved some progress in drawing their positions closer on several issues. In addition, in the framework of the seventeenth osce Ministerial Council (Athens, 1–2 December), the Council adopted a statement on the Armenia-Azerbaijan conflict.

Communications. Azerbaijan on 23 January transmitted to the Secretary-General [A/63/692-

S/2009/51] a report that discussed the international legal responsibilities of Armenia as an occupier of Azerbaijani territory; on 17 February [A/63/730-S/2009/103], supplementary documentation in response to the request for information on resolution 62/243 (see above); and on 6 July [A/63/917-S/2009/343], the press release on the Congress of the Azerbaijani Community of the Nagorno-Karabakh held on 5 June. Azerbaijan also transmitted letters on 11 September [A/63/963-S/2009/457], 30 September [A/64/475-S/2009/508], 12 October [A/64/491-S/2009/533], 30 October [A/64/514-S/2009/575], 30 November [A/64/546-S/2009/619] and 23 December [A/64/608-S/2009/670] regarding position statements, as well as ceasefire violations, bellicose rhetoric and other action taken by Armenia that challenged efforts to resolve the conflict. Armenia on 23 March transmitted to the Secretary-General [A/63/781-S/2009/156] the text of a memorandum refuting allegations, statements and reports made by Azerbaijan; and on 17 November [A/64/539-S/2009/596] a letter also refuting anti-Armenian documents disseminated by Azerbaijan.

On 24 December, the General Assembly decided that the agenda item would remain for consideration during its resumed sixty-fourth (2010) session (**decision 64/549**).

Organization for Democracy and Economic Development-GUAM

The Organization for Democracy and Economic Development-GUAM (Azerbaijan, Georgia, Moldova, Ukraine), a regional cooperation organization established by the Kyiv Declaration in 2006 [YUN 2006, p. 486] was headquartered in Kyiv, Ukraine. As for conflict settlement, GUAM emphasized respect for sovereignty, territorial integrity and the inviolability of the internationally recognized borders of those States.

On 24 December, the General Assembly decided that the agenda item on the protracted conflicts in the GUAM area and their implications for international peace, security and development would remain for consideration during its resumed sixty-fourth (2010) session (**decision 64/549**).

Cyprus

During 2009, the United Nations continued efforts through the Secretary-General's good offices to help resolve the Cyprus problem. The Secretary-General's Special Adviser on Cyprus, with support from the Special Representative, assisted the two sides in implementing the 8 July 2006 Set of Principles and a Decision [YUN 2006, p. 487], which included commitment to the unification of Cyprus based on a bizonal, bicommunal federation and political equality, and an agreement to meet regularly on issues affecting the day-to-day life of the Cypriot people. The Greek Cypriot and Turkish Cypriot leaders continued negotiations under UN auspices and in April agreed to implement 4 of the 23 confidence-building measures aimed at improving the daily life of Cypriots across the entire island. In April and May, the Security Council welcomed the progress made in the negotiations. In August, the leaders completed the first phase of the discussion of all six chapters: governance and power-sharing, property, EU-related matters, economic matters, territory, and security and guarantees. The pace of the meetings increased during the second phase, which began in September, and on 21 December the leaders issued a joint statement confirming their decision to hold negotiations in January 2010.

The United Nations Peacekeeping Force in Cyprus (UNFICYP) continued to cooperate with its UN partners and local actors to facilitate projects benefiting both Greek and Turkish Cypriots in and outside the buffer zone and to promote confidence-building measures between them. In December, the Council extended the UNFICYP mandate until 15 June 2010.

Political and security developments

Good offices mission

During the year, the Special Adviser on Cyprus, as the principal person responsible for the Secretary-General's good offices on the Cyprus problem, continued efforts to assist the parties in the conduct of full-fledged negotiations aimed at reaching a comprehensive settlement. He was supported by the Secretary-General's Special Representative and Head of UNFICYP, who served as his deputy on issues relating to the good offices. The Secretary-General described UN mediation efforts during 2009 in reports to the Security Council of 15 May [S/2009/248], 30 November [S/2009/610] and 11 May 2010 [S/2010/238].

As at 10 May, the Secretary-General reported that the Greek and Turkish Cypriot leaders had maintained a steady pace of almost 1 meeting per week, and since December 2008, they had held 18 meetings, bringing the number of meetings since the negotiation process was launched on 3 September [YUN 2008, p. 464] to 27. All of the meetings, which revolved around governance and power-sharing arrangements, property issues, EU matters and, partially, economic matters, took place in the presence of Special Adviser Alexander Downer (Australia) or Special Representative Tayé-Brook Zerihoun (Ethiopia), or both. In parallel to the negotiations, four of the seven technical committees established by the leaders in March 2008

[ibid.] continued to meet, namely, those on crime and criminal matters, cultural heritage, health matters, and the environment. On 14 April 2009, the leaders agreed to implement 4 of the 23 confidence-building measures identified by the technical committees, which were aimed at improving the daily life of Cypriots across the entire island. On 30 April, in presidential statement S/PRST/2009/10 (see below), the Security Council welcomed the progress achieved by the parties and reiterated its support for the negotiation process.

SECURITY COUNCIL ACTION

On 30 April [meeting 6115], following consultations among Security Council members, the President made **statement S/PRST/2009/10** on behalf of the Council:

The Security Council commends the Greek Cypriot and Turkish Cypriot leaders for the political leadership they have shown and warmly welcomes the progress made so far in the fully fledged negotiations, and the leaders' joint statements.

The Council strongly urges the leaders to increase the momentum of the negotiations to ensure the full exploitation of this opportunity to reach a comprehensive settlement based on a bicommunal, bizonal federation with political equality as set out in the relevant Council resolutions.

The Council emphasizes the importance of all parties engaging fully, flexibly and constructively and looks forward to decisive progress in the negotiations in the near future.

The Council recognizes that a solution requires the support of both sides and will require the approval of both communities in separate and simultaneous referendums. In this context, the Council fully supports the Secretary-General's good offices mission and encourages the Special Adviser to the Secretary-General on Cyprus to continue to offer the leaders any support they need to achieve a settlement.

The Council reiterates its full support for the process and underlines the benefits that reunification will bring to the island.

In May, the leaders publicly committed, through the Special Representative, to intensify their efforts further, not least through additional meetings at the level of their representatives. Topics remaining to be addressed in the first reading or review of negotiation issues related to security and guarantees and territory.

In August, the leaders completed the first phase of the discussion of all six chapters: governance and power-sharing, property, EU-related matters, economic matters, territory, and security and guarantees. Steady progress was made during the talks, with the leaders reaching agreement on a number of issues and gaining a better understanding of each other's position on the remaining issues. Considerable convergence was achieved in the areas of governance and power-sharing, the economy and EU matters. As the question of how power would be shared between the communities was at the heart of the debate in all chapters, the area of governance was considered to be among the most pivotal. The second phase of the discussion commenced on 11 September, and as agreed, the leaders began by focusing on governance and, in particular, on the election of the executive, federal competencies and external relations. The leaders increased the pace of the talks, deciding to meet twice a week from October onwards. As at 25 November, five meetings had been devoted to governance and power-sharing issues. Although both sides had introduced bridging proposals, convergence had yet to be achieved. The sides also established an expert group on treaties to discuss the process whereby they would jointly decide which treaties would be applicable to a united Cyprus. Meanwhile, since returning to the discussion of property in late October, the leaders had held five meetings on the subject and tasked their representatives with preparing the groundwork for fuller discussions on the issue. On 21 December, the leaders issued a joint statement reconfirming their earlier decision to hold intensive rounds of negotiations in January 2010, with the aim of reaching further convergence on governance and power-sharing, the economy and EU matters, as well as continuing discussion on the property issue.

Beyond his immediate office, the Special Adviser engaged several international experts to advise him on some of the more complex issues being discussed in the negotiations, such as governance and power-sharing, and property. The experts also met with their counterparts from the negotiating teams of both sides on their specific issues of focus. In October, as part of the EU commitment to provide technical support to the settlement process, the European Commission appointed an official to act as a liaison between the Commission and the good offices mission in Cyprus. On confidence-building measures, the four technical committees met regularly and made steady progress. The crime and criminal matters committee established a joint contact room for the exchange and provision of timely information on those topics; the cultural heritage committee established an advisory board for the preservation, physical protection and restoration of the immovable cultural heritage of Cyprus; the health committee began to implement the measure concerning the passage of ambulances through crossing points in cases of emergency; and the environment committee focused on the implementation of a joint awareness campaign aimed at saving water. On 26 June, the leaders decided to open a seventh crossing point between the communities and through the buffer zone to the northwest of the island, linking the villages of Limnitis/Yeşilirmak, in the north, and Kato Pyrgos, in the south. In November, the Secretary-General observed that while nearly two

dozen measures had been agreed upon during the preparatory phase of the talks, little progress had been made in their implementation, and urged the parties to make greater efforts to implement them.

Incidents and position statements

Communications. Throughout 2009, the Secretary-General received letters from the Government of Cyprus and from Turkish Cypriot authorities containing charges and countercharges, protests and accusations, and explanations of positions regarding the question of Cyprus. Letters from the "Turkish Republic of Northern Cyprus" were transmitted by Turkey. In communications dated between 10 February and 18 December, Cyprus reported violations of the international air traffic regulations and the national airspace or the maritime space of Cyprus by Turkish military aircraft [A/63/711-S/2009/81, A/63/813-S/2009/187, A/63/875-S/2009/291, A/63/878-S/2009/294, A/63/939-S/2009/417, A/64/488-S/2009/529, A/64/607-S/2009/668]. The "Turkish Republic of Northern Cyprus" refuted the allegations, stating that the flights mentioned took place within the sovereign airspace of the "Turkish Republic of Northern Cyprus" [A/63/742-S/2009/115, A/63/887-S/2009/313, A/63/948-S/2009/428, A/64/498-S/2009/543, A/64/639-S/2010/60].

On 17 April [A/63/828-S/2009/216], Turkey transmitted a letter from the "Turkish Republic of Northern Cyprus" conveying a 14 April letter from President Mehmet Ali Talat, which referred to prospective talks between the Greek Cypriot administration and Israel regarding the delimitation of maritime jurisdiction areas in the Eastern Mediterranean, as well as a preliminary deal reached between the Greek Cypriot administration and an energy company for drilling in an exclusive economic zone of Cyprus. He stated that the Greek Cypriot side's activities before a comprehensive settlement was achieved were aimed at violating the rights and interests of the Turkish Cypriot people, who had equal rights and say over the natural resources and the sea areas of the island of Cyprus.

In other communications, Cyprus transmitted position statements on 5 June [S/2009/296] and 25 September [A/64/467]. In reply, Turkey transmitted statements from the "Turkish Republic of Northern Cyprus" on 19 June [A/63/888-S/2009/321] and 21 October [A/64/502]. A further communication conveying a letter from President Talat was transmitted on 9 November [A/64/523-S/2009/581].

Nakhchivan Declaration. On 9 November [A/64/522-S/2009/580], Azerbaijan, Kazakhstan, Kyrgyzstan and Turkey transmitted to the Secretary-General the Nakhchivan Declaration and the Nakhchivan Agreement on the Establishment of the Cooperation Council of Turkic-speaking States, signed at the Ninth Summit of the Heads of the Turkic-speaking Countries (Nakhchivan City, Azerbaijan, 3 October). The Declaration supported, among other issues, the ongoing settlement negotiations between the two sides in Cyprus and lifting the isolation of the Turkish Cypriots.

OIC meeting. On 15 December [A/64/614-S/2009/677], Syria, in its capacity as Chair of the Organization of the Islamic Conference (OIC) Group in New York, transmitted the Final Communiqué of the OIC Annual Coordination Meeting of Ministers for Foreign Affairs (New York, 25 September). The Meeting expressed its support for the cause of the Muslim Turkish people of Cyprus and welcomed the commencement of the full-fledged negotiations in Cyprus.

On 24 December, the General Assembly decided that the agenda item on the question of Cyprus would remain for consideration during its resumed sixty-fourth (2010) session (**decision 64/549**).

UNFICYP

The United Nations Peacekeeping Force in Cyprus (UNFICYP), established in 1964 [YUN 1964, p. 165], continued in 2009 to monitor the ceasefire lines between the Turkish and Turkish Cypriot forces on the northern side and the Cypriot National Guard on the southern side of the island; to maintain the military status quo and prevent recurrence of fighting; and to undertake humanitarian and economic activities.

During 2009, Tayé-Brook Zerihoun (Ethiopia) continued to serve as the Secretary-General's Special Representative in Cyprus and Head of the Mission. As of 31 October, UNFICYP, under the command of Rear Admiral Mario Sánchez Debernardi (Peru), comprised 858 troops and 69 civilian police.

Activities

Report of Secretary-General (May). In May, the Secretary-General reported [S/2009/248] that the situation in the buffer zone remained stable and that the opposing forces had cooperated well with UNFICYP. Total military violations and other incidents during the reporting period amounted to 276, a 22 per cent decrease from the previous period. Typical violations were minor in nature and had little effect on the stability of the ceasefire lines. UNFICYP submitted a package of military confidence-building measures to both opposing forces. The Greek Cypriot National Guard responded by nominating a designated committee on confidence-building measures to work with UNFICYP. It was hoped that the Turkish Forces would follow with similar steps. Meanwhile, the Turkish Forces had increased restrictions on UNFICYP movements. Since 1 January, there had been 43 such incidents in the north, including preventing

UNFICYP personnel from crossing at Turkish Cypriot checkpoints and escorting them out of the northern part of the island. Further to those incidents, routes continued to be denied on the Karpas peninsula and tight controls were imposed on access to, as well as the conduct of operations within, the fenced area of Varosha. Positions established by the opposing forces in the Dherinia area that violated the status quo remained in place. On demining the buffer zone, the Cyprus Mine Action Centre continued to manage mine clearance operations. By the end of April, 21 of the 26 minefields agreed for clearance in 2008 [YUN 2008, p. 465] had been cleared. Discussions continued with a view to obtaining the agreement of the Turkish Forces on the clearance of 12 additional mined areas.

Cypriots from both sides sought UNFICYP assistance in facilitating day-to-day issues arising from the division of the island, including on educational matters, medical evacuations and the transfer of deceased individuals, as well as on commemorative, religious and sociocultural gatherings. The Mission facilitated 65 bicommunal events, bringing together more than 4,000 people from both communities. During the reporting period, UNFICYP recorded some 873,700 crossings through the buffer zone, with 210,950 through the Ledra Street crossing point. Regular meetings between Greek Cypriot and Turkish Cypriot political party leaders and representatives continued to be held at the Ledra Palace Hotel under the auspices of the Embassy of Slovakia. UNFICYP also delivered humanitarian assistance to Greek Cypriots and Maronites living in the northern part of the island; assisted Turkish Cypriots living in the south in obtaining identity documents, housing, welfare services, medical care, employment and education; and authorized 18 requests from both communities to use the buffer zone for various civilian activities. It also continued efforts to assist in maintaining good relations between the Greek Cypriot and Turkish Cypriot communities in the mixed village of Pyla in the buffer zone. The technical committee on crime and criminal matters, which was facilitated by the UN police, agreed to open a joint communications room staffed by representatives from both sides to exchange information and provide timely intelligence—the first formal arrangement of this type between the two sides.

As UNFICYP continued to play a vital role on the island, the Secretary-General recommended that the Security Council extend the Mission's mandate until 15 December 2009.

SECURITY COUNCIL ACTION

On 29 May [meeting 6132], the Security Council adopted **resolution 1873(2009)** by vote (14-1-0). The draft [S/2009/276] was submitted by China, France, the Russian Federation, the United Kingdom and the United States.

The Security Council,

Welcoming the report of the Secretary-General of 15 May 2009 on the United Nations operation in Cyprus,

Noting that the Government of Cyprus has agreed that, in view of the prevailing conditions on the island, it is necessary to keep the United Nations Peacekeeping Force in Cyprus beyond 15 June 2009,

Echoing the Secretary-General's firm belief that the responsibility for finding a solution lies first and foremost with the Cypriots themselves, stressing that there now exists a rare opportunity to make decisive progress, and reaffirming the primary role of the United Nations in assisting the parties to bring the Cyprus conflict and division of the island to a comprehensive and durable settlement,

Commending the Greek Cypriot and Turkish Cypriot leaders for the political leadership they have shown, and warmly welcoming the progress made so far in the fully fledged negotiations, and the leaders' joint statements,

Strongly urging the leaders to increase the momentum of the negotiations to ensure the full exploitation of this opportunity to reach a comprehensive settlement based on a bicommunal, bizonal federation with political equality, as set out in the relevant Security Council resolutions,

Emphasizing the importance attached by the international community to all parties engaging fully, flexibly and constructively in the negotiations, and looking forward to decisive progress in those negotiations in the near future,

Welcoming the intention of the Secretary-General to keep the Council informed of further development and progress,

Welcoming also the implementation of some of the confidence-building measures announced by the leaders, and calling for a renewed effort to implement the remaining measures and for agreement on and implementation of further steps to build trust between the communities,

Reaffirming the importance of continued crossings of the Green Line by Cypriots, encouraging the opening by mutual agreement of other crossing points, noting the commitment in the leaders' joint statements to pursue the opening of the Limnitis/Yeşilirmak crossing point, encouraging implementation of the commitment to a second phase of the restoration of the Ledra Street crossing, and in this context urging the leaders to make every effort to implement those measures,

Convinced of the many important benefits for all Cypriots that would flow from a comprehensive and durable Cyprus settlement, and encouraging both sides clearly to explain these benefits, as well as the need for increased flexibility and compromise in order to secure them, to both communities well in advance of any eventual referendums,

Highlighting the supportive role that the international community will continue to play in helping the Greek Cypriot and Turkish Cypriot leaders to exploit fully the current opportunity,

Taking note of the assessment of the Secretary-General that the security situation on the island and along the Green Line remains stable, welcoming the decrease in the overall number of incidents involving the two sides, and urging all sides to avoid any action, including restrictions on the movements of the Force as noted in the report of the Secretary-General, which could lead to an increase in tension, undermine the good progress achieved so far or damage the goodwill on the island,

Recalling the Secretary-General's firm belief that the situation in the buffer zone would be improved if both sides accepted the 1989 aide-memoire used by the United Nations,

Welcoming the progress made in proceeding with demining activities, and looking forward to the clearance of the remaining minefields,

Welcoming also the progress and continuation of the important activities of the Committee on Missing Persons in Cyprus, echoing the Secretary-General's call for every possible action to be taken to speed up the exhumation process, and trusting that this process will promote reconciliation between the communities,

Agreeing that active participation of civil society groups is essential to the political process and can contribute to making any future settlement sustainable, welcoming all efforts to promote bicommunal contacts and events, including on the part of all United Nations bodies on the island, and urging the two sides to promote the active engagement of civil society and the encouragement of cooperation between economic and commercial bodies and to remove all obstacles to such contacts,

Stressing the need for the Council to pursue a rigorous, strategic approach to peacekeeping deployments,

Welcoming the intention of the Secretary-General to keep all peacekeeping operations, including those of the Force, under close review, and noting the importance of contingency planning in relation to the settlement, including recommendations, as appropriate, for further adjustments to the mandate, force levels and concept of operations of the Force, taking into account developments on the ground and the views of the parties,

Welcoming also the continued efforts of Mr. Alexander Downer as the Special Adviser to the Secretary-General on Cyprus with a mandate to assist the parties in the conduct of fully fledged negotiations aimed at reaching a comprehensive settlement,

Echoing the Secretary-General's gratitude to the Government of Cyprus and the Government of Greece for their voluntary contributions to the funding of the Force, and his request for further voluntary contributions from other countries and organizations,

Welcoming and encouraging efforts by the United Nations to sensitize peacekeeping personnel in the prevention and control of HIV/AIDS and other communicable diseases in all its peacekeeping operations,

1.   *Welcomes* the analysis of developments on the ground over the last six months in the report of the Secretary-General in accordance with his mandate;

2.   *Welcomes also* the progress made so far in the fully fledged negotiations, and the prospect of further progress in the near future towards a comprehensive and durable settlement that this has created;

3.   *Urges* full exploitation of this opportunity, including by intensifying the momentum of negotiations, improving the current atmosphere of trust and goodwill and engaging in the process in a constructive and open manner;

4.   *Urges also* the implementation of confidence-building measures, and looks forward to agreement on and implementation of further such steps, including the opening of other crossing points;

5. *Reaffirms* all its relevant resolutions on Cyprus, in particular resolution 1251(1999) of 29 June 1999 and subsequent resolutions;

6. *Expresses its full support* for the United Nations Peacekeeping Force in Cyprus, and decides to extend its mandate for a further period ending 15 December 2009;

7. *Calls upon* both sides to continue to engage, as a matter of urgency and while respecting the mandate of the Force, in consultations with the Force on the demarcation of the buffer zone, and on the United Nations 1989 aide-memoire, with a view to reaching early agreement on outstanding issues;

8. *Calls upon* the Turkish Cypriot side and Turkish forces to restore in Strovilia the military status quo which existed there prior to 30 June 2000;

9. *Requests* the Secretary-General to submit a report on implementation of the present resolution, including on contingency planning in relation to the settlement, by 1 December 2009 and to keep the Security Council updated on events as necessary;

10. *Welcomes* the efforts being undertaken by the Force to implement the Secretary-General's zero-tolerance policy on sexual exploitation and abuse and to ensure full compliance of its personnel with the United Nations code of conduct, requests the Secretary-General to continue to take all necessary action in this regard and to keep the Council informed, and urges troop-contributing countries to take appropriate preventive action, including conducting predeployment awareness training, and to take disciplinary action and other action to ensure full accountability in cases of such conduct involving their personnel;

11. *Decides* to remain seized of the matter.

VOTE ON RESOLUTION 1873(2009):

In favour: Austria, Burkina Faso, China, Costa Rica, Croatia, France, Japan, Libyan Arab Jamahiriya, Mexico, Russian Federation, Uganda, United Kingdom, United States, Viet Nam.

Against: Turkey.

Abstaining: None.

Report of Secretary-General (November). In November the Secretary-General reported [S/2009/609] that the situation in the buffer zone remained stable and that the UNFICYP military chain of command maintained good relationships with their counterparts from both of the opposing forces. Military violations during the reporting period reflected a reduction in violations by the Turkish Forces following the positive approach they had taken in the previous months. For the second successive year, both the National Guard and the Turkish Forces announced the cancellation of their major annual exercises, "Nikiforos" and "Toros", respectively—an important confidence-building measure. However, despite a significant relaxation of restrictions on the movement of UNFICYP military personnel, the continued restriction on the movement of locally employed UN civilian personnel imposed by the Turkish Forces remained a concern. The number Greek Cypriot National Guard violations would have been markedly reduced if not for incidents of bayonet fixing by soldiers in observation posts along the buffer zone. In June, the National

Guard was responsible for an overmanning violation that resulted in two UNFICYP mobile patrols being threatened with weapons and detained. The prompt intervention of the respective Military Observation and Liaison Officers led to the immediate release of the UNFICYP personnel. Positions established by the opposing forces in the Dherinia area, in violation of the status quo, remained in place. The Turkish Forces retained the checkpoint in the Laroujina pocket; conducted regular inspections of the liaison post at Strovilia; repeatedly overmanned the position in violation of the military status quo in the area; and continued to impose tight controls on UN operations in the fenced area of Varosha. UNFICYP also mobilized its Mobile Force Reserve and the Force Military Police Unit in support of some 50 meetings held between the two leaders at the premises of the good offices mission in the United Nations Protected Area. While demining in the buffer zone progressed, with 57 of the 72 minefields cleared, a civilian contractor of the Mine Action Centre was killed in a demining accident on 28 October. A list of the remaining 15 minefields was submitted to the National Guard and Turkish Forces requesting their release for clearance.

UNFICYP efforts to restore normal conditions in the buffer zone and deliver humanitarian assistance to the communities continued. On 26 June, the Greek Cypriot and Turkish Cypriot leaders agreed on opening a buffer zone crossing at Limnitis/Yeşilirmak. A first trial crossing by ambulances from both sides was facilitated by UNFICYP on 6 August. UNFICYP facilitated 89 bicommunal events in which 4,472 people from both communities participated. The Mission also conducted 63 humanitarian convoys and visits to 364 Greek Cypriots and 131 Maronites in the north; authorized 28 projects in the buffer zone; and facilitated 17 religious and commemorative events on the island. Following an agreement reached by the two sides within the Technical Committee on Health, a mechanism was established to facilitate medical evacuations across the buffer zone on humanitarian grounds. On contingency planning in relation to a settlement, the Secretary-General observed that while considerable progress had been achieved in the Cyprus talks, the two sides had not yet considered in depth the UN role in support of the settlement. It was, therefore, too early to identify the parameters of UN involvement in the context of a possible solution. He recommended that the Council extend the UNFICYP mandate until 15 June 2010.

SECURITY COUNCIL ACTION

On 14 December [meeting 6239], the Security Council adopted **resolution 1898(2009)** by vote (14-1-0). The draft [S/2009/641] was submitted by China, France, the Russian Federation, the United Kingdom and the United States.

The Security Council,

Welcoming the report of the Secretary-General of 25 November 2009 on the United Nations operation in Cyprus and his report of 30 November 2009 on his mission of good offices in Cyprus,

Noting that the Government of Cyprus has agreed that, in view of the prevailing conditions on the island, it is necessary to keep the United Nations Peacekeeping Force in Cyprus beyond 15 December 2009,

Echoing the Secretary-General's firm belief that the responsibility for finding a solution lies first and foremost with the Cypriots themselves, stressing that there now exists a rare opportunity to make decisive progress in a timely fashion, and reaffirming the primary role of the United Nations in assisting the parties to bring the Cyprus conflict and division of the island to a comprehensive and durable settlement,

Commending the Greek Cypriot and Turkish Cypriot leaders for the political leadership they have shown, and warmly welcoming the progress made so far in the fully fledged negotiations, and the leaders' joint statements,

Strongly urging the leaders to increase the momentum of the negotiations to ensure the full exploitation of this opportunity to reach a comprehensive settlement based on a bicommunal, bizonal federation with political equality, as set out in the relevant Security Council resolutions,

Emphasizing the importance that the international community attaches to all parties engaging fully, flexibly and constructively in the negotiations, and looking forward to decisive progress in those negotiations in the near future,

Welcoming the intention of the Secretary-General to keep the Council informed of further developments and progress,

Welcoming also the implementation of some of the confidence-building measures announced by the leaders, and calling for a renewed effort to implement the remaining measures and for agreement on and implementation of further steps to build trust between the communities,

Reaffirming the importance of continued crossings of the Green Line by Cypriots, encouraging the opening by mutual agreement of other crossing points, welcoming the leaders' agreement to open the Limnitis/Yeşilirmak crossing point and the successful first trial crossing of ambulances from both sides, and urging implementation of the second phase of the restoration of the Ledra Street crossing,

Convinced of the many important benefits for all Cypriots that would flow from a comprehensive and durable Cyprus settlement, and encouraging both sides clearly to explain these benefits, as well as the need for increased flexibility and compromise in order to secure them, to both communities well in advance of any eventual referendums,

Highlighting the supportive role that the international community will continue to play in helping the Greek Cypriot and Turkish Cypriot leaders to exploit fully the current opportunity,

Taking note of the assessment of the Secretary-General that the security situation on the island and along the Green Line remains stable, and urging all sides to avoid any action which could lead to an increase in tension, undermine the good progress achieved so far or damage the goodwill on the island,

Recalling the Secretary-General's firm belief that the situation in the buffer zone would be improved if both sides accepted the 1989 aide-memoire used by the United Nations,

Welcoming the progress made in proceeding with demining activities, looking forward to the clearance of the remaining minefields, and regretting the tragic death on 28 October 2009 of a civilian contractor working for the Mine Action Centre,

Welcoming also the progress and continuation of the important activities of the Committee on Missing Persons in Cyprus, and trusting that this process will promote reconciliation between the communities,

Agreeing that active participation of civil society groups is essential to the political process and can contribute to making any future settlement sustainable, welcoming all efforts to promote bicommunal contacts and events, including on the part of all United Nations bodies on the island, and urging the two sides to promote the active engagement of civil society and the encouragement of cooperation between economic and commercial bodies and to remove all obstacles to such contacts,

Stressing the need for the Council to pursue a rigorous, strategic approach to peacekeeping deployments,

Welcoming the intention of the Secretary-General to keep all peacekeeping operations, including those of the Force, under close review, and noting the importance of contingency planning in relation to the settlement, including recommendations, as appropriate, for further adjustments to the mandate, force levels and concept of operations of the Force, taking into account developments on the ground and the views of the parties,

Welcoming also the continued efforts of Mr. Alexander Downer as the Special Adviser to the Secretary-General on Cyprus with a mandate to assist the parties in the conduct of fully fledged negotiations aimed at reaching a comprehensive settlement,

Echoing the Secretary-General's gratitude to the Government of Cyprus and the Government of Greece for their voluntary contributions to the funding of the Force, and his request for further voluntary contributions from other countries and organizations,

Welcoming and encouraging efforts by the United Nations to sensitize peacekeeping personnel in the prevention and control of HIV/AIDS and other communicable diseases in all its peacekeeping operations,

1. *Welcomes* the analysis of developments on the ground over the last six months in the reports of the Secretary-General, in accordance with his mandate;

2. *Welcomes also* the progress made so far in the fully fledged negotiations, and the prospect of further progress in the near future towards a comprehensive and durable settlement that this has created;

3. *Urges* full exploitation of this opportunity, including by intensifying the momentum of the negotiations, improving the current atmosphere of trust and goodwill and engaging in the process in a constructive and open manner;

4. *Urges also* the implementation of confidence-building measures, and looks forward to agreement on and implementation of further such steps, including the opening of other crossing points;

5. *Reaffirms* all its relevant resolutions on Cyprus, in particular resolution 1251(1999) of 29 June 1999 and subsequent resolutions;

6. *Expresses its full support* for the United Nations Peacekeeping Force in Cyprus, and decides to extend its mandate for a further period ending 15 June 2010;

7. *Calls upon* both sides to continue to engage, as a matter of urgency and while respecting the mandate of the Force, in consultations with the Force on the demarcation of the buffer zone, and on the United Nations 1989 aide-memoire, with a view to reaching early agreement on outstanding issues;

8. *Calls upon* the Turkish Cypriot side and Turkish forces to restore in Strovilia the military status quo which existed there prior to 30 June 2000;

9. *Requests* the Secretary-General to submit a report on the implementation of the present resolution, including on contingency planning in relation to the settlement, by 1 June 2010 and to keep the Security Council updated on events as necessary;

10. *Welcomes* the efforts being undertaken by the Force to implement the Secretary-General's zero-tolerance policy on sexual exploitation and abuse and to ensure full compliance of its personnel with the United Nations code of conduct, requests the Secretary-General to continue to take all necessary action in this regard and to keep the Council informed, and urges troop-contributing countries to take appropriate preventive action, including conducting pre-deployment awareness training, and to take disciplinary action and other action to ensure full accountability in cases of such conduct involving their personnel;

11. *Decides* to remain seized of the matter.

VOTE ON RESOLUTION 1898(2009):

In favour: Austria, Burkina Faso, China, Costa Rica, Croatia, France, Japan, Libyan Arab Jamahiriya, Mexico, Russian Federation, Uganda, United Kingdom, United States, Viet Nam.

Against: Turkey.

Abstaining: None.

Financing

In June, the General Assembly considered the Secretary-General's report on UNFICYP's financial performance for the period from 1 July 2007 to 30 June 2008 [A/63/536], the proposed UNFICYP budget for the period from 1 July 2009 to 30 June 2010 [A/63/693] and the related ACABQ report [A/63/746/Add.9].

GENERAL ASSEMBLY ACTION

On 30 June [meeting 93], the General Assembly, on the recommendation of the Fifth Committee [A/63/897], adopted **resolution 63/290** without vote [agenda item 135].

**Financing of the United Nations
Peacekeeping Force in Cyprus**

The General Assembly,

Having considered the reports of the Secretary-General on the financing of the United Nations Peacekeeping Force in Cyprus and the related report of the Advisory Committee on Administrative and Budgetary Questions,

Recalling Security Council resolution 186(1964) of 4 March 1964, regarding the establishment of the United Nations Peacekeeping Force in Cyprus, and the subsequent resolutions by which the Council extended the mandate of the Force, the latest of which was resolution 1873(2009) of 29 May 2009, by which the Council extended the mandate of the Force until 15 December 2009,

Recalling also its resolution 47/236 of 14 September 1993 on the financing of the Force and its subsequent resolutions and decisions thereon, the latest of which was resolution 62/255 of 20 June 2008,

Reaffirming the general principles underlying the financing of United Nations peacekeeping operations, as stated in General Assembly resolutions 1874(S-IV) of 27 June 1963, 3101(XXVIII) of 11 December 1973 and 55/235 of 23 December 2000,

Noting with appreciation that voluntary contributions have been made to the Force by certain Governments,

Noting that voluntary contributions were insufficient to cover all the costs of the Force, including those incurred by troop-contributing Governments prior to 16 June 1993, and regretting the absence of an adequate response to appeals for voluntary contributions, including that contained in the letter dated 17 May 1994 from the Secretary-General to all Member States,

Mindful of the fact that it is essential to provide the Force with the financial resources necessary to enable it to fulfil its responsibilities under the relevant resolutions of the Security Council,

Acknowledging paragraph 31 of the report of the Advisory Committee on Administrative and Budgetary Questions,

1. *Requests* the Secretary-General to entrust the Head of Mission with the task of formulating future budget proposals in full accordance with the provisions of General Assembly resolutions 59/296 of 22 June 2005, 60/266 of 30 June 2006 and 61/276 of 29 June 2007, as well as other relevant resolutions;

2. *Takes note* of the status of contributions to the United Nations Peacekeeping Force in Cyprus as at 30 April 2009, including the contributions outstanding in the amount of 16.6 million United States dollars, representing some 5 per cent of the total assessed contributions, notes with concern that only forty-eight Member States have paid their assessed contributions in full, and urges all other Member States, in particular those in arrears, to ensure payment of their outstanding assessed contributions;

3. *Expresses its appreciation* to those Member States which have paid their assessed contributions in full, and urges all other Member States to make every possible effort to ensure payment of their assessed contributions to the Force in full;

4. *Expresses concern* at the financial situation with regard to peacekeeping activities, in particular as regards the reimbursements to troop contributors that bear additional burdens owing to overdue payments by Member States of their assessments;

5. *Also expresses concern* at the delay experienced by the Secretary-General in deploying and providing adequate resources to some recent peacekeeping missions, in particular those in Africa;

6. *Emphasizes* that all future and existing peacekeeping missions shall be given equal and non-discriminatory

treatment in respect of financial and administrative arrangements;

7. *Also emphasizes* that all peacekeeping missions shall be provided with adequate resources for the effective and efficient discharge of their respective mandates;

8. *Reiterates its request* to the Secretary-General to make the fullest possible use of the facilities and equipment at the United Nations Logistics Base at Brindisi, Italy, in order to minimize the costs of procurement for the Force;

9. *Requests* the Secretary-General to ensure that proposed peacekeeping budgets are based on the relevant legislative mandates;

10. *Endorses* the conclusions and recommendations contained in the report of the Advisory Committee on Administrative and Budgetary Questions, subject to the provisions of the present resolution, and requests the Secretary-General to ensure their full implementation;

11. *Notes* the reduction in rotation travel costs, and requests the Secretary-General to continue his efforts to increase efficiency gains in this regard;

12. *Takes note* of paragraph 38 of the report of the Advisory Committee;

13. *Welcomes* the progress which has been made so far by the host Government and the Force regarding the renovation of the accommodation of military contingent personnel as well as other personnel of the Force, and requests the Secretary-General to continue making every effort, in coordination with the host Government, to ensure that the renovations are completed as scheduled, without delay, and to report thereon in the context of the next budget submission;

14. *Requests* the Secretary-General to ensure the full implementation of the relevant provisions of resolutions 59/296, 60/266 and 61/276;

15. *Also requests* the Secretary-General to take all action necessary to ensure that the Force is administered with a maximum of efficiency and economy;

16. *Further requests* the Secretary-General, in order to reduce the cost of employing General Service staff, to continue efforts to recruit local staff for the Force against General Service posts, commensurate with the requirements of the Force;

Financial performance report for the period from 1 July 2007 to 30 June 2008

17. *Takes note* of the report of the Secretary-General on the financial performance of the Force for the period from 1 July 2007 to 30 June 2008;

Budget estimates for the period from 1 July 2009 to 30 June 2010

18. *Decides* to appropriate to the Special Account for the United Nations Peacekeeping Force in Cyprus the amount of 56,794,900 dollars for the period from 1 July 2009 to 30 June 2010, inclusive of 54,412,700 dollars for the maintenance of the Force, 1,982,600 dollars for the support account for peacekeeping operations and 399,600 dollars for the United Nations Logistics Base;

Financing of the appropriation

19. *Notes with appreciation* that a one-third share of the net appropriation, equivalent to 18,074,373 dollars, will be funded through voluntary contributions from the Government of Cyprus and the amount of 6.5 million dollars from the Government of Greece;

20. *Decides* to apportion among Member States the amount of 32,220,527 dollars at a monthly rate of 2,685,044 dollars, in accordance with the levels updated in General Assembly resolution 61/243 of 22 December 2006, and taking into account the scale of assessments for 2009, as set out in Assembly resolution 61/237 of 22 December 2006, and for 2010, subject to a decision of the Security Council to extend the mandate of the Force;

21. *Also decides* that, in accordance with the provisions of its resolution 973(X) of 15 December 1955, there shall be set off against the apportionment among Member States, as provided for in paragraph 20 above, their respective share in the Tax Equalization Fund of 2,517,500 dollars, comprising the estimated staff assessment income of 2,271,700 dollars approved for the Force, the prorated share of 206,400 dollars of the estimated staff assessment income approved for the support account and the prorated share of 39,400 dollars of the estimated staff assessment income approved for the United Nations Logistics Base;

22. *Further decides* that, for Member States that have fulfilled their financial obligations to the Force, there shall be set off against their apportionment, as provided for in paragraph 20 above, their respective share of the unencumbered balance and other income in the amount of 704,903 dollars for the financial period ended 30 June 2008, in accordance with the levels updated in resolution 61/243, and taking into account the scale of assessments for 2008, as set out in resolution 61/237;

23. *Decides* that, for Member States that have not fulfilled their financial obligations to the Force, there shall be set off against their outstanding obligations, their respective share of the unencumbered balance and other income in the amount of 704,903 dollars in respect of the financial period ended 30 June 2008, in accordance with the scheme set out in paragraph 22 above;

24. *Also decides*, that the increase in the estimated staff assessment income of 214,000 dollars in respect of the financial period ended 30 June 2008 shall be added to the credits from the amount of 704,903 dollars referred to in paragraphs 22 and 23 above;

25. *Further decides*, taking into account its voluntary contribution for the financial period ended 30 June 2008, that one third of other income in the amount of 436,090 dollars in respect of the financial period ended 30 June 2008 shall be returned to the Government of Cyprus;

26. *Decides*, taking into account its voluntary contribution for the financial period ended 30 June 2008, that the prorated share of other income in the amount of 169,307 dollars in respect of the financial period ended 30 June 2008 shall be returned to the Government of Greece;

27. *Also decides* to continue to maintain as separate the account established for the Force for the period prior to 16 June 1993, invites Member States to make voluntary contributions to that account, and requests the Secretary-General to continue his efforts in appealing for voluntary contributions to the account;

28. *Emphasizes* that no peacekeeping mission shall be financed by borrowing funds from other active peacekeeping missions;

29. *Encourages* the Secretary-General to continue to take additional measures to ensure the safety and security of all personnel participating in the Force under the auspices of the United Nations, bearing in mind paragraphs 5 and 6 of Security Council resolution 1502(2003) of 26 August 2003;

30. *Invites* voluntary contributions to the Force in cash and in the form of services and supplies acceptable to the Secretary-General, to be administered, as appropriate, in accordance with the procedure and practices established by the General Assembly;

31. *Decides* to include in the provisional agenda of its sixty-fourth session the item entitled "Financing of the United Nations Peacekeeping Force in Cyprus".

On 24 December, the General Assembly decided that the agenda item on UNFICYP financing would remain for consideration during its resumed sixty-fourth (2010) session (**decision 64/549**).

Other issues

SEECP meeting. On 12 June [A/63/886], Moldova transmitted to the Secretary-General the texts of the Chisinau joint statement of the Heads of State and Government of the South-East European Cooperation Process and of the Chisinau Declaration adopted at its twelfth meeting (Chisinau, Moldova, 2–5 June). The participants expressed their determination in forging partnership for European integration, development and prosperity and strengthening of rule of law; and reconfirmed that regional cooperation and good neighbourly relations in South-East Europe were prerequisites for advancement of the countries towards European and Euro-Atlantic integration, and for consolidation and ensuring stability and security in the region.

Strengthening of security and cooperation in the Mediterranean

In response to General Assembly resolution 63/86 [YUN 2008, p. 471], the Secretary-General submitted a July report with a later addendum [A/64/119 & Add.1] containing replies received from Lebanon, Netherlands, Panama, Poland, Spain and Ukraine to his 23 February note verbale requesting the views of States on ways to strengthen security and cooperation in the Mediterranean region.

GENERAL ASSEMBLY ACTION

On 2 December [meeting 55], the General Assembly, on the recommendation of the First (Disarmament and International Security) Committee [A/64/396], adopted **resolution 64/68** without vote [agenda item 101].

Strengthening of security and cooperation in the Mediterranean region

The General Assembly,

Recalling its previous resolutions on the subject, including resolution 63/86 of 2 December 2008,

Reaffirming the primary role of the Mediterranean countries in strengthening and promoting peace, security and cooperation in the Mediterranean region,

Welcoming the efforts deployed by the Euro-Mediterranean countries to strengthen their cooperation in combating terrorism, in particular by the adoption of the Euro-Mediterranean Code of Conduct on Countering Terrorism by the Euro-Mediterranean Summit, held in Barcelona, Spain, on 27 and 28 November 2005,

Bearing in mind all the previous declarations and commitments, as well as all the initiatives taken by the riparian countries at the recent summits, ministerial meetings and various forums concerning the question of the Mediterranean region,

Welcoming, in this regard, the adoption on 13 July 2008 of the Joint Declaration of the Paris Summit, which launched a reinforced partnership, "the Barcelona Process: Union for the Mediterranean", and the common political will to revive efforts to transform the Mediterranean into an area of peace, democracy, cooperation and prosperity,

Welcoming also the entry into force of the African Nuclear-Weapon-Free Zone Treaty (Treaty of Pelindaba) as a contribution to the strengthening of peace and security both regionally and internationally,

Recognizing the indivisible character of security in the Mediterranean and that the enhancement of cooperation among Mediterranean countries with a view to promoting the economic and social development of all peoples of the region will contribute significantly to stability, peace and security in the region,

Recognizing also the efforts made so far and the determination of the Mediterranean countries to intensify the process of dialogue and consultations with a view to resolving the problems existing in the Mediterranean region and to eliminating the causes of tension and the consequent threat to peace and security, and their growing awareness of the need for further joint efforts to strengthen economic, social, cultural and environmental cooperation in the region,

Recognizing further that prospects for closer Euro-Mediterranean cooperation in all spheres can be enhanced by positive developments worldwide, in particular in Europe, in the Maghreb and in the Middle East,

Reaffirming the responsibility of all States to contribute to the stability and prosperity of the Mediterranean region and their commitment to respecting the purposes and principles of the Charter of the United Nations as well as the provisions of the Declaration on Principles of International Law concerning Friendly Relations and Cooperation among States in accordance with the Charter of the United Nations,

Noting the peace negotiations in the Middle East, which should be of a comprehensive nature and represent an appropriate framework for the peaceful settlement of contentious issues in the region,

Expressing its concern at the persistent tension and continuing military activities in parts of the Mediterranean that hinder efforts to strengthen security and cooperation in the region,

Taking note of the report of the Secretary-General,

1. *Reaffirms* that security in the Mediterranean is closely linked to European security as well as to international peace and security;

2. *Expresses its satisfaction* at the continuing efforts by Mediterranean countries to contribute actively to the elimination of all causes of tension in the region and to the promotion of just and lasting solutions to the persistent problems of the region through peaceful means, thus ensuring the withdrawal of foreign forces of occupation and respecting the sovereignty, independence and territorial integrity of all countries of the Mediterranean and the right of peoples to self-determination, and therefore calls for full adherence to the principles of non-interference, non-intervention, non-use of force or threat of use of force and the inadmissibility of the acquisition of territory by force, in accordance with the Charter and the relevant resolutions of the United Nations;

3. *Commends* the Mediterranean countries for their efforts in meeting common challenges through coordinated overall responses, based on a spirit of multilateral partnership, towards the general objective of turning the Mediterranean basin into an area of dialogue, exchanges and cooperation, guaranteeing peace, stability and prosperity, encourages them to strengthen such efforts through, inter alia, a lasting multilateral and action-oriented cooperative dialogue among States of the region, and recognizes the role of the United Nations in promoting regional and international peace and security;

4. *Recognizes* that the elimination of the economic and social disparities in levels of development and other obstacles as well as respect and greater understanding among cultures in the Mediterranean area will contribute to enhancing peace, security and cooperation among Mediterranean countries through the existing forums;

5. *Calls upon* all States of the Mediterranean region that have not yet done so to adhere to all the multilaterally negotiated legal instruments related to the field of disarmament and non-proliferation, thus creating the conditions necessary for strengthening peace and cooperation in the region;

6. *Encourages* all States of the region to favour the conditions necessary for strengthening the confidence-building measures among them by promoting genuine openness and transparency on all military matters, by participating, inter alia, in the United Nations system for the standardized reporting of military expenditures and by providing accurate data and information to the United Nations Register of Conventional Arms;

7. *Encourages* the Mediterranean countries to strengthen further their cooperation in combating terrorism in all its forms and manifestations, including the pos-

sible resort by terrorists to weapons of mass destruction, taking into account the relevant resolutions of the United Nations, and in combating international crime and illicit arms transfers and illicit drug production, consumption and trafficking, which pose a serious threat to peace, security and stability in the region and therefore to the improvement of the current political, economic and social situation and which jeopardize friendly relations among States, hinder the development of international cooperation and result in the destruction of human rights, fundamental freedoms and the democratic basis of pluralistic society;

8. *Requests* the Secretary-General to submit a report on means to strengthen security and cooperation in the Mediterranean region;

9. *Decides* to include in the provisional agenda of its sixty-fifth session the item entitled "Strengthening of security and cooperation in the Mediterranean region".

Cooperation with the Organization for Security and Cooperation in Europe

On 27 February [meeting 6088], the Chairperson-in-Office of the Organization for Security and Cooperation in Europe (OSCE), Dora Bakoyannis, briefed the Security Council about the work of OSCE and outlined its 2009 priorities, which included, among others: strengthening OSCE in the field, in particular a more comprehensive OSCE presence in Georgia; addressing humanitarian issues in the region; restructuring the international presence in Kosovo; taking OSCE further in border security and policing in Afghanistan; playing a key role in the fight against terrorism; examining cross-dimensional aspects of the migration phenomenon; and maintaining the highest standards for OSCE election observation activities. In addition to those key issues, many of which were common to the agendas of both organizations, she highlighted potential areas of OSCE-UN cooperation, such as new avenues for cooperation in Central Asia, strengthening of the thematic area of the rule of law, and dialogue and exchange of experience with the UN system on gender equality. She concluded that it was vital to strengthen further the OSCE-UN partnership.

Observer status

On 16 December, the General Assembly granted observer status to the Parliamentary Assembly of the Mediterranean (**resolution 64/124**) (see p. 1386) in the work of the Assembly.

Chapter VI

Middle East

The crisis in the Gaza Strip in early 2009 prompted renewed efforts towards peace and stability in the Middle East. "Operation Cast Lead", launched by Israel in response to indiscriminate Palestinian rocket and mortar attacks on southern Israel, worsened the humanitarian situation in Hamas-controlled Gaza and strengthened the blockade—now into its third year—enforced since Hamas won elections and formed the government in 2007. The Israeli air and infantry assault on Gaza led to massive damage to infrastructure, including to United Nations facilities, and hundreds of civilians died, mostly Palestinians.

The Security Council, by resolution 1860(2009) of 8 January, requested an immediate ceasefire leading to the withdrawal of Israeli forces from Gaza. The General Assembly resumed the tenth emergency special session to consider the crisis, while the Secretary-General visited the region to deliver the message that the fighting must stop and the parties must fully implement the Council resolution. The Quartet of the European Union, the Russian Federation, the United Nations and the United States urged a durable resolution to the crisis while addressing Israel's legitimate security concerns. The Human Rights Council established the United Nations Fact-Finding Mission on the Gaza Conflict, led by Justice Richard Goldstone of South Africa, which submitted its report in September.

The Mission noted that while Israel maintained that its Gaza operations were an act of self-defence, the Mission considered the operations to have been directed, at least in part, at the people of Gaza as a whole. The Mission considered whether the series of acts that deprived Palestinians in the Gaza Strip of their means of sustenance, employment, housing and water, freedom of movement and their right to leave and enter their own country, and limited access to courts of law and effective remedies, could amount to persecution, a crime against humanity. The Mission also concluded that Palestinian rocket and mortar attacks that did not discriminate between Israeli civilian and military targets would constitute war crimes and might amount to crimes against humanity.

The General Assembly in November called on Israel and the Palestinian side to investigate the serious violations of international humanitarian and human rights law reported by the Fact-Finding Mission.

The Security Council held around 20 meetings throughout the year to deliberate on the situation in the Middle East, including the Palestinian question. The Special Committee to Investigate Israeli Practices Affecting the Human Rights of the Palestinian People and Other Arabs of the Occupied Territories urged Member States and the Council to ensure implementation of the 2004 advisory opinion of the International Court of Justice on the legal consequences of the construction of the wall in the Occupied Palestinian Territory. A report by the Economic and Social Commission for Western Asia concluded that the Israeli closure system remained a primary cause of poverty and humanitarian crisis in the Territory, and restricted Palestinian access to natural resources. Another report by the United Nations Conference on Trade and Development concluded that the closures had deepened Palestinian economic dependence on Israel, with the share of Israel in Palestinian trade rising from 63 per cent in 1999 to 79 per cent in 2008. The United Nations Relief and Works Agency for Palestine Refugees in the Near East continued its critical humanitarian and economic assistance, despite movement restrictions and threats to its staff.

The Special Tribunal for Lebanon set up to investigate and prosecute the perpetrators of the 2005 assassination of former Lebanese Prime Minister Rafik Hariri and 22 others began operations in March, taking over from the United Nations International Independent Investigation Commission. The mandate of the United Nations Interim Force in Lebanon (UNIFIL) was extended for 12 more months, while it worked with the Lebanese armed forces to consolidate security in southern Lebanon and prevent non-state militias from attacking Israel. Also during the year, the mandate of the United Nations Disengagement Observer Force (UNDOF) in the Golan Heights was renewed twice. The United Nations Truce Supervision Organization continued to assist UNIFIL and UNDOF by providing unarmed military observers to supervise armistice agreements, ceasefires and related tasks.

Peace process

Diplomatic efforts

In 2009, diplomatic developments and events on the ground underscored the importance of a peaceful settlement of the question of Palestine. The year witnessed the discontinuation of Israeli-Palestinian negotiations undertaken within the framework of the Annapolis process [YUN 2007, p. 445], a destructive conflict in Gaza and southern Israel and a deepening internal divide despite efforts towards Palestinian unity. At the same time, the international community renewed its efforts to achieve the vision of two States living side by side in peace and security.

Representatives of the Middle East Quartet (European Union, Russian Federation, United Nations, United States), which continued to assist peace negotiations, met in June and September, joined by Quartet Representative Tony Blair, former Prime Minister of the United Kingdom.

The Security Council discussed the situation in the Middle East, including the Palestine question, at meetings held on 6 and 7 January [meeting 6061], 8 January [meeting 6063], 21 January [meeting 6072], 27 January [meeting 6077], 18 February [meeting 6084], 25 March [meeting 6100], 20 April [meeting 6107], 7 May [meeting 6120], 11 May [meeting 6123], 23 June [meeting 6150], 27 July [meeting 6171], 19 August [meeting 6182], 27 August [meeting 6183], 17 September [meeting 6190], 14 October [meeting 6201], 24 November [meeting 6223] and 17 December [meeting 6248]. During those meetings, the Council was briefed by Secretariat officials on the peace process and developments in the Occupied Palestinian Territory, especially the precarious situation in the Gaza Strip.

On 21 September, United States President Barack Obama hosted a meeting in New York with Israeli Prime Minister Benjamin Netanyahu and Palestinian President Mahmoud Abbas on the margins of the General Assembly. It was the first meeting between Palestinian and Israeli leaders since 2008.

Occupied Palestinian Territory

Political and security situation

Crisis in Gaza

At the outset of 2009, the Gaza Strip was a site of violent conflict, with Israel's "Operation Cast Lead" starting on 27 December 2008 [YUN 2008, p. 492] and lasting until 18 January 2009.

Communications. On 2 January [A/ES-10/431-S/2009/3], Palestine informed the Secretary-General and the Security Council that Israel was pressing on with the deadly and destructive military campaign it had launched six days earlier against the Palestinian civilian population in Gaza. Despite the international outcry and condemnation and despite the vast human suffering and humanitarian catastrophe, Israel continued its lethal military assaults against a defenceless civilian population.

On 4 January [S/2009/6], Israel informed the Secretary-General and the Security Council that on 3 January the Israeli Defense Forces had begun implementing the second stage of the military operation in the Gaza Strip, which included a ground campaign. That stage was intended to destroy the terrorist infrastructure of Hamas and to take control of rocket launching areas used by the terrorist organizations in Gaza, as part of the military operation that Israel had begun eight days earlier to protect civilians in Southern Israel.

Other communications were submitted by Palestine [A/ES-10/432-S/2009/4; A/ES-10/433-S/2009/8], Qatar [A/63/672-S/2009/7], Cuba, on behalf of the Non-Aligned Movement [S/2009/15; A/63/676], and Egypt [S/2009/14].

Security Council consideration. On 8 January [meeting 6063], the Council adopted resolution 1860(2009), in which it condemned violence against civilians and called for an immediate ceasefire leading to the withdrawal of Israeli forces from Gaza, as well as the unimpeded provision of humanitarian assistance.

SECURITY COUNCIL ACTION

On 8 January [meeting 6063], the Security Council adopted **resolution 1860(2009)** by vote (14-0-1). The draft [S/2009/23] was submitted by the United Kingdom.

The Security Council,

Recalling all its relevant resolutions, including resolutions 242(1967) of 22 November 1967, 338(1973) of 22 October 1973, 1397(2002) of 12 March 2002, 1515(2003) of 19 November 2003 and 1850(2008) of 16 December 2008,

Stressing that the Gaza Strip constitutes an integral part of the territory occupied in 1967 and will be a part of the Palestinian State,

Emphasizing the importance of the safety and well-being of all civilians,

Expressing grave concern at the escalation of violence and the deterioration of the situation, in particular the resulting heavy civilian casualties since the refusal to extend the period of calm, and emphasizing that the Palestinian and Israeli civilian populations must be protected,

Expressing grave concern also at the deepening humanitarian crisis in Gaza,

Emphasizing the need to ensure sustained and regular flow of goods and people through the Gaza crossings,

Recognizing the vital role played by the United Nations Relief and Works Agency for Palestine Refugees in the Near East in providing humanitarian and economic assistance within Gaza,

Recalling that a lasting solution to the Israeli-Palestinian conflict can only be achieved by peaceful means,

Reaffirming the right of all States in the region to live in peace within secure and internationally recognized borders,

1. *Stresses* the urgency of and calls for an immediate, durable and fully respected ceasefire, leading to the full withdrawal of Israeli forces from Gaza;

2.   *Calls for* the unimpeded provision and distribution throughout Gaza of humanitarian assistance, including food, fuel and medical treatment;

3.   *Welcomes* the initiatives aimed at creating and opening humanitarian corridors and other mechanisms for the sustained delivery of humanitarian aid;

4.   *Calls upon* Member States to support international efforts to alleviate the humanitarian and economic situation in Gaza, including through urgently needed additional contributions to the United Nations Relief and Works Agency for Palestine Refugees in the Near East and through the Ad Hoc Liaison Committee;

5.   *Condemns* all violence and hostilities directed against civilians and all acts of terrorism;

6.   *Calls upon* Member States to intensify efforts to provide arrangements and guarantees in Gaza in order to sustain a durable ceasefire and calm, including to prevent illicit trafficking in arms and ammunition and to ensure the sustained reopening of the crossing points on the basis of the Agreement on Movement and Access of 15 November 2005 between the Palestinian Authority and Israel, and in this regard welcomes the Egyptian initiative and other regional and international efforts that are under way;

7.   *Encourages* tangible steps towards intra-Palestinian reconciliation, including in support of mediation efforts of Egypt and the League of Arab States as expressed in the resolution of 26 November 2008, and consistent with Security Council resolution 1850(2008) and other relevant resolutions;

8.   *Calls for* renewed and urgent efforts by the parties and the international community to achieve a comprehensive peace based on the vision of a region where two democratic States, Israel and Palestine, live side by side in peace with secure and recognized borders, as envisaged in resolution 1850(2008), and recalls also the importance of the Arab Peace Initiative;

9.   *Welcomes* the Quartet's consideration, in consultation with the parties, of an international meeting in Moscow in 2009;

10.   *Decides* to remain seized of the matter.

VOTE ON RESOLUTION 1860(2009):

In favour: Austria, Burkina Faso, China, Costa Rica, Croatia, France, Japan, Libyan Arab Jamahiriya, Mexico, Russian Federation, Turkey, Uganda, United Kingdom, Viet Nam.

Against: None.

Abstaining: United States.

Emergency special session

In accordance with General Assembly resolution ES-10/15 [YUN 2004, p. 465] and at the requests of Indonesia [A/ES-10/440], Malaysia [A/ES-10/434], the Syrian Arab Republic [A/ES-10/441] and Venezuela [A/ES-10/436], the Assembly President on 15 January resumed the tenth emergency special session of the General Assembly—concerning illegal Israeli actions in occupied East Jerusalem and the rest of the Occupied Palestinian Territory—to consider the crisis in the Gaza Strip. Israel on 14 January [A/ES-10/439] demanded the cancellation of the meeting, stating

that the reconvening of the special session represented a violation of the UN Charter, as the Security Council was already addressing the situation in southern Israel and the Gaza Strip. On 16 January, the Assembly decided by recorded vote (112-10-20) (**decision ES-10/202**) to vote on the proposal submitted by Egypt [A/ES.10/L.21/Rev.1].

GENERAL ASSEMBLY ACTION

On 16 January [meeting 36], the General Assembly adopted **resolution ES-10/18** [draft: A/ES-10/L.21/Rev.1] by recorded vote (142-4-8) [agenda item 5].

General Assembly resolution supporting the immediate ceasefire according to Security Council resolution 1860(2009)

The General Assembly,

Reaffirming the permanent responsibility of the United Nations with regard to the question of Palestine until it is solved in all its aspects, in accordance with international law,

Recalling the relevant rules and principles of international law, including international humanitarian and human rights law, particularly the Fourth Geneva Convention relative to the Protection of Civilian Persons in Time of War, of 12 August 1949, which is applicable to the Occupied Palestinian Territory, including East Jerusalem,

Expressing grave concern about the developments on the ground since the adoption of Security Council resolution 1860(2009) on 8 January 2009, especially following the intensified military operations in the Gaza Strip, causing heavy casualties among civilians, including children and women, and the shelling of United Nations headquarters, hospitals, media premises and public infrastructure, and emphasizing that the Palestinian and Israeli civilian populations must be protected and that their suffering must end,

Convinced that achieving a just, lasting and comprehensive settlement of the question of Palestine, the core of the Arab-Israeli conflict, is imperative for the attainment of comprehensive, just and lasting peace and stability in the Middle East,

1.   *Demands* full respect for Security Council resolution 1860(2009), including its urgent call for an immediate, durable and fully respected ceasefire, leading to the full withdrawal of Israeli forces from the Gaza Strip, and its call for the unimpeded provision and distribution throughout the Gaza Strip of humanitarian assistance, including food, fuel and medical treatment;

2.   *Calls upon* all parties to exert all efforts to ensure, in cooperation with the Security Council, full and urgent compliance with resolution 1860(2009);

3.   *Expresses its support* for international and regional initiatives and efforts under way and for the mission undertaken by the Secretary-General of the United Nations;

4.   *Expresses its support* for the extraordinary efforts by the United Nations agencies, particularly the United Nations Relief and Works Agency for Palestine Refugees in the Near East, to provide emergency relief, medical and other humanitarian assistance to the Palestinian civilian population in the Gaza Strip;

5. *Calls upon* all Member States to urgently extend the necessary support to international and regional efforts aimed at alleviating the critical humanitarian and economic situation in the Gaza Strip, and emphasizes in this regard the need to ensure the sustained opening of border crossings for the free movement of persons and goods into and out of the Gaza Strip, in accordance with the Agreement on Movement and Access of 15 November 2005;

6. *Decides* to adjourn the tenth emergency special session temporarily and to authorize the President of the General Assembly at its most recent session to resume its meeting upon request from Member States.

RECORDED VOTE ON RESOLUTION ES-10/18:

In favour: Afghanistan, Albania, Algeria, Andorra, Angola, Argentina, Armenia, Austria, Azerbaijan, Bahamas, Bahrain, Bangladesh, Barbados, Belarus, Belgium, Belize, Benin, Bhutan, Bolivia, Bosnia and Herzegovina, Botswana, Brazil, Brunei Darussalam, Bulgaria, Burkina Faso, Burundi, Cambodia, Chile, China, Colombia, Comoros, Congo, Costa Rica, Croatia, Cuba, Cyprus, Czech Republic, Democratic People's Republic of Korea, Denmark, Egypt, El Salvador, Eritrea, Estonia, Ethiopia, Finland, France, Gambia, Germany, Greece, Grenada, Guatemala, Guinea, Guyana, Haiti, Honduras, Hungary, Iceland, India, Iraq, Ireland, Italy, Jamaica, Japan, Jordan, Kazakhstan, Kenya, Kuwait, Lao People's Democratic Republic, Latvia, Lebanon, Lesotho, Libyan Arab Jamahiriya, Liechtenstein, Lithuania, Luxembourg, Madagascar, Malaysia, Maldives, Mali, Malta, Mauritania, Mauritius, Mexico, Moldova, Monaco, Mongolia, Montenegro, Morocco, Mozambique, Myanmar, Namibia, Nepal, Netherlands, New Zealand, Niger, Norway, Oman, Pakistan, Panama, Papua New Guinea, Peru, Poland, Portugal, Qatar, Republic of Korea, Romania, Russian Federation, Saint Lucia, Saint Vincent and the Grenadines, San Marino, Saudi Arabia, Senegal, Serbia, Sierra Leone, Singapore, Slovakia, Slovenia, Solomon Islands, South Africa, Spain, Sri Lanka, Swaziland, Sweden, Switzerland, Tajikistan, Thailand, The former Yugoslav Republic of Macedonia, Togo, Trinidad and Tobago, Tunisia, Turkey, Uganda, Ukraine, United Arab Emirates, United Kingdom, United Republic of Tanzania, Uruguay, Uzbekistan, Viet Nam, Yemen, Zambia, Zimbabwe.

Against: Israel, Nauru, United States, Venezuela.

Abstaining: Australia, Canada, Côte d'Ivoire, Ecuador, Indonesia, Iran, Nigeria, Syrian Arab Republic.

Security Council action. On 21 January, following a briefing by the Secretary-General on his visit to the Middle East (14–20 January), the Council, by a press statement [SC/9580], welcomed the ceasefire in Gaza and the efforts of international and regional partners—in particular the Egyptian initiative—in helping bring it about. The Council emphasized the need for the ceasefire to be durable and fully respected, and for arrangements and guarantees to prevent illicit trafficking in arms and ammunition to Gaza and to ensure the reopening of the crossing points.

Communications. Communications on the situation in Gaza were submitted by Cuba [S/2009/33; A/63/678; A/63/679-S/2009/36], on behalf of the Non-Aligned Movement, Israel [S/2009/32], Palestine [A/ES-10/442-S/2009/40; A/ES-10/445-S/2009/65;

A/ES-10/470-S/2009/605], Malaysia [A/ES-10/443; A/ES-10/444], the Dominican Republic [A/ES-10/447], Qatar [A/63/691-S/2009/50; S/2009/12], Egypt [A/ES-10/446; A/63/705-S/2009/73] and Pakistan [A/63/718-S/2009/95].

On 3 March [A/63/748-S/2009/123; A/ES-10/450], Egypt transmitted the Conclusions by the Chair of the International Conference in Support of the Palestinian Economy for the Reconstruction of Gaza (Sharm el-Sheikh, Egypt, 2 March). The conference led to pledges of about $4.5 billion for Gaza's reconstruction.

Security Council consideration. On 27 January [meeting 6077], the Council was briefed on the situation in Gaza by the Under-Secretary-General for Humanitarian Affairs and Emergency Relief Coordinator, John Holmes, and the Commissioner-General of the United Nations Relief and Works Agency for Palestine Refugees in the Near East (UNRWA), Karen AbuZayd. Both expressed concern about the humanitarian situation and stressed the importance of free access for humanitarian aid.

On 18 February [meeting 6084], the Council was briefed by the Special Coordinator for the Middle East Peace Process, Robert Serry. He reported that a number of issues, including the humanitarian situation in Gaza, Palestinian reconciliation and the new political situation in Israel following elections, needed to be addressed for the peace process to advance, and emphasized the importance of a durable ceasefire as called for in resolution 1860(2009).

On 25 March [meeting 6100], the Council was briefed by the Under-Secretary-General for Political Affairs, B. Lynn Pascoe, who said that two months after ceasefires were declared in Gaza there was a worrying situation of impasse and uncertainty. Despite international engagement and support, little progress had been made on the key issues outlined in resolution 1860(2009). He stressed the importance of the international community and the Quartet in helping to stabilize Gaza and reinvigorate the peace process. On Lebanon, he said that the killing on 23 March by a roadside bomb of the Deputy Representative in Lebanon of the Palestine Liberation Organization had shattered the prevailing relative calm in the country. Twenty-six Member States and Palestine took part in the ensuing debate.

On 11 May [meeting 6123], the Council held a ministerial-level meeting chaired by the Russian Minister for Foreign Affairs, Sergey V. Lavrov. The Secretary-General stressed the need to generate momentum in the Israeli-Palestinian talks, warning that the situation could worsen easily without fresh efforts by both sides as well as the international community. He pointed out that, following the inconclusive results of the previous year's negotiations and the bloodshed in Gaza, the past three months had witnessed almost no progress on the two key resolutions—1850(2008) [YUN 2008, p. 491] and 1860(2009). The challenge was to begin implementing transformative changes on the ground, and to kick-start a renewed and irreversible drive to achieve an Israeli-Palestinian agreement.

SECURITY COUNCIL ACTION

On 11 May [meeting 6123], following consultations among Security Council members, the President made statement **S/PRST/2009/14** on behalf of the Council:

> The Security Council stresses the urgency of reaching comprehensive peace in the Middle East. Vigorous diplomatic action is needed to attain the goal set by the international community—lasting peace in the region, based on an enduring commitment to mutual recognition, freedom from violence, incitement and terror, and the two-State solution, building upon previous agreements and obligations.
>
> In this context, the Council recalls all its previous resolutions on the Middle East, in particular resolutions 242(1967), 338(1973), 1397(2002), 1515(2003), 1850(2008) and 1860(2009), and the Madrid principles, and notes the importance of the 2002 Arab Peace Initiative.
>
> The Council encourages the ongoing work of the Quartet to support the parties in their efforts to achieve a comprehensive, just and lasting peace in the Middle East.
>
> The Council reiterates its commitment to the irreversibility of the bilateral negotiations built upon previous agreements and obligations. The Council reiterates its call for renewed and urgent efforts by the parties and the international community to achieve a comprehensive, just and lasting peace in the Middle East, based on the vision of a region where two democratic States, Israel and Palestine, live side by side in peace within secure and recognized borders.
>
> The Council further calls upon the parties to fulfil their obligations under the performance-based road map to a permanent two-State solution to the Israeli-Palestinian conflict, refraining from any steps that could undermine confidence or prejudice the outcome of negotiations on all core issues.
>
> The Council calls upon all States and international organizations to support the Palestinian government that is committed to the Quartet principles and the Arab Peace Initiative and respects the commitments of the Palestine Liberation Organization, and the Council encourages tangible steps towards intra-Palestinian reconciliation, including in support of Egypt's efforts, on this basis. It calls for assistance to help develop the Palestinian economy, to maximize the resources available to the Palestinian Authority and to build Palestinian institutions.
>
> The Council supports the proposal of the Russian Federation to convene, in consultation with the Quartet and the parties, an international conference on the Middle East peace process in Moscow in 2009.

Security Council consideration. On 23 June [meeting 6150], the Council was briefed by the Special Coordinator for the Middle East Peace Process. He reported that international diplomatic efforts were under way to reinvigorate the peace process for a two-State solution, and underlined the importance of re-activating the regional tracks alongside a rejuvenated Israeli-Palestinian track. He emphasized the negative repercussions of the unresolved crisis in Gaza for efforts to advance the peace process. With regard to Lebanon, he noted that the parliamentary elections had been held on 7 June in an atmosphere of calm and that a climate of dialogue and cooperation had prevailed since then.

Quartet meeting. Meeting in Trieste, Italy, on 26 June [SG/2152], the Quartet affirmed its determination to seek a comprehensive resolution of the Arab-Israeli conflict. The Quartet underscored that the only viable solution to the conflict would be one that ended the occupation that began in 1967 and fulfilled the aspirations of both parties for independent homelands through two States for two peoples. The Quartet urged Israel to freeze all settlement activity, including natural growth; to dismantle outposts erected since March 2001; and to refrain from provocative actions in East Jerusalem. Both sides needed to stop incitement and violence against civilians. Noting the detrimental effect of Palestinian political divisions, the Quartet called on all Palestinians to commit themselves to non-violence, recognition of Israel, and acceptance of previous agreements and obligations. The Quartet expressed support for the mediation efforts of Egypt and the Arab League for Palestinian reconciliation.

The Quartet discussed Gaza, agreeing that the situation was unsustainable and not in the interests of any party. It reiterated the urgency of reaching a durable solution through the implementation of Council resolution 1860(2009). The Quartet called for a complete halt to all violence, as well as for preventing illicit arms and ammunition trafficking into Gaza, and for the reopening of all crossing points to ensure regular flow of people and goods. It called on those holding the abducted Israeli soldier Gilad Shalit to release him without delay. The Quartet welcomed plans by Israel to promote Palestinian economic development, and declared its readiness to work closely with Israel, the Palestinian government and international donors to achieve sustainable economic development.

Security Council consideration. On 27 July [meeting 6171], the Council was briefed by the Assistant Secretary-General for Political Affairs, Oscar Fernandez-Taranco, who outlined international efforts to create conditions under which negotiations could resume, including the Quartet meeting of 26 June. He emphasized that Council resolution 1860(2009) remained the main framework for a way forward in Gaza. He called for a positive response to the Secretary-General's proposal for the entry of materials needed to complete construction of housing, health and education facilities suspended since 2007 as a means to kick-start recovery in Gaza. Following the briefing, statements were made by Israel, Palestine, Council members and 23 other States.

Quartet meeting. Meeting in New York on 24 September [SG/2155], the Quartet noted recent meetings between United States President Obama, Israeli Prime Minister Netanyahu and Palestinian President Abbas as significant steps toward a resolution of the Arab-Israeli conflict. The Quartet welcomed the Palestinian Authority's (PA) plan for constructing the institutions of the Palestinian State within 24 months as a demonstration of its commitment to an independent State providing opportunity, justice and security for the Palestinian people and being a responsible neighbour to all States in the region. Economic growth in the West Bank had improved significantly and initial ministerial contact between Israel and the PA on economic issues was welcomed. The Quartet noted further steps by Israel to promote change on the ground and encouraged it to redouble those efforts, in particular concerning free movement of Palestinian people and goods.

The Quartet stressed the urgency of a durable resolution to the Gaza crisis and called for a solution addressing Israel's legitimate security concerns; promoting the reunification of Gaza and the West Bank under the legitimate PA; and facilitating the opening of crossings to allow for flow of humanitarian aid, commercial goods and persons to and from Gaza. Recognizing the significance of the Arab Peace Initiative [YUN 2002, p. 419], the Quartet urged regional Governments to support the resumption of bilateral negotiations, enter into a structured dialogue on issues of common concern and take steps to normalize regional relations.

Security Council consideration. On 14 October [meeting 6201], the Council was briefed by the Under-Secretary-General for Political Affairs, who said that political efforts to resolve the Arab-Israeli conflict had continued but there had been no significant progress on the ground. He confirmed the Secretary-General's support for the work of the Fact-Finding Mission on the Gaza Conflict (see p. 783) and his call for credible national investigations into the conduct of the conflict, which was echoed by a number of delegations that addressed the Council after the briefing. Speakers stressed the need to address the continuing grave humanitarian situation in the Gaza Strip, including the need for the long-overdue reconstruction process to commence.

Communications. On 2 October [S/2009/493] and 1 December [S/2009/614], Israel brought to the attention of the Secretary-General and the Security Council several incidents of rocket and mortar attacks emanating from the Hamas-controlled Gaza Strip.

Independent Fact-Finding Committee on Gaza

Following allegations of war crimes and violations of international humanitarian law during Operation Cast Lead from 27 December 2008 to 18 January 2009, the League of Arab States sent an Independent Fact-Finding Committee to the Gaza Strip, resulting in a report submitted to the Security Council on 12 May [S/2009/244]. The Committee, headed by John Dugard of South Africa, visited Gaza from 22 to 27 February, in addition to holding meetings with international organizations (NGOs), non-governmental organizations and victims of the conflict.

The Committee found that more than 1,400 Palestinians had been killed, including at least 850 civilians, and approximately 5,000 wounded as a result of operations of the Israel Defence Forces (IDF). Four Israeli civilians had been killed and 182 wounded by Palestinian rockets, while 10 Israeli soldiers had been killed (three by friendly fire) and 148 wounded. Buildings and property in the area had been destroyed or seriously damaged. The report concluded that IDF's operations could not be justified as self-defence and that war crimes were committed by both sides.

Board of Inquiry

On 4 May [A/63/855-S/2009/250], the Secretary-General submitted a letter to the Security Council describing his establishment of a United Nations Headquarters Board of Inquiry to investigate nine incidents that occurred during the course of the Gaza conflict in which UN personnel, premises and operations were affected, and summarizing the Board's findings and recommendations. Ian Martin of the United Kingdom was appointed head of the Board, which convened on 11 February and submitted its report to the Secretary-General on 21 April.

Following investigations, the Board determined that six of the nine incidents were conclusively caused by IDF. In one further incident, the Board concluded that damage to a UN vehicle was caused by IDF firing. In one incident, the Board concluded that damage to UN premises was caused by a Palestinian faction, most likely Hamas. In another incident, the Board was unable to reach any conclusions as to the cause.

The Board noted that UN premises were inviolable, and observed that UN personnel and all civilians within UN premises, as well as civilians in the immediate vicinity of those premises and elsewhere, were to be protected in accordance with international humanitarian law. The Board concluded that IDF actions involved varying degrees of negligence or recklessness with regard to UN premises and the safety of UN staff and other civilians within those premises. The Board recommended that accountability for injuries, deaths and damages, as well as acknowledgement of false claims, come from the responsible parties. It also recommended commendation for the courageous actions of UNRWA staff, and that further investigations be undertaken.

Fact-Finding Mission

The Human Rights Council in April established the United Nations Fact-Finding Mission on the Gaza Conflict (see p. 783), led by Justice Richard Goldstone of South Africa, to investigate possible violations of international human rights law and humanitarian law. From the facts gathered, the Mission found [A/HRC/12/48] that the Israeli armed forces in Gaza committed war crimes and breaches of the Fourth Geneva Convention, and that some of their actions might constitute crimes against humanity. The Mission also concluded that Palestinian rocket and mortar attacks that did not discriminate between Israeli civilian and military targets would constitute war crimes and might amount to crimes against humanity.

The General Assembly, in **resolution 64/10** of 5 November (see p. 785), called on the Government of Israel and the Palestinian side to undertake independent and credible investigations, within a three-month period, into the serious violations of international humanitarian and international human rights law reported by the United Nations Fact-Finding Mission.

(On the human rights aspects of the conflict in Gaza, see PART TWO, Chapter III).

Peaceful settlement of the question of Palestine

Report of Secretary-General. In a 15 September report [A/64/351-S/2009/464], submitted in accordance with General Assembly resolution 63/29 [YUN 2008, p. 494] and covering the period from September 2008 to August 2009, the Secretary-General provided his observations on the state of the Israeli-Palestinian conflict and on international efforts to move the peace process forward, as well as the views of the Security Council and the concerned parties on the question of Palestine.

For the Council, the goal of achieving a peaceful settlement remained one of the major challenges facing the international community. The Council considered the situation in Palestine every month under the agenda item "The situation in the Middle East, including the question of Palestine", with briefings followed by open Council meetings or consultations among Council members.

In a note of 30 April to the parties concerned, the Secretary-General sought the positions of Egypt, Israel, Jordan, Lebanon and the Syrian Arab Republic, as well as the Palestine Liberation Organization (PLO), regarding any steps they had taken to imple-

ment resolution 63/29. Replies were received from Israel and the PLO.

A 20 July note from Israel recalled that Israel had voted against the resolution, as it had on similar resolutions, which it considered one-sided. It was noted that, despite continuing Israeli-Palestinian dialogue during 2008, Hamas had launched over 3,100 rockets and mortars against Israel. Over 300 rockets and mortars had hit Israel between 21 December and 27 December, leaving it with no choice but to act to protect its civilians with Operation Cast Lead. During the operation, 571 rockets and 205 mortars landed in Israel. Notwithstanding the enduring campaign against Israeli civilians, Israel remained committed to humanitarian principles, allowing humanitarian aid into Gaza during Operation Cast Lead. Israeli authorities had authorized a major easing of security restrictions in the West Bank, including the dismantling of two thirds of the checkpoints and the taking down of roughly 140 roadblocks. The Israeli Government had urged Palestinians to nurture peaceful coexistence with Israel and had repeatedly extended an open invitation to launch peace talks with the PA.

A 26 June note from Palestine expressed the urgency of ending tragedy and injustice inflicted upon the Palestinian people. From Palestine's perspective, the role of the United Nations remained central for the promotion of a peaceful settlement. Palestine stressed that Israel's violation of its legal obligations and UN resolutions should not continue to be tolerated. Since the adoption of resolution 63/29, there had been a dramatic deterioration of the situation in the Occupied Palestinian Territory. Israel's colonization was felt to be contradictory to the objective of the peace process—achievement of the two-State solution of an independent State of Palestine living alongside Israel in peace and security, and on the basis of the 1967 borders. Palestine's commitment to a peace process was reaffirmed.

The Secretary-General observed that the past year had witnessed the discontinuation of Israeli-Palestinian negotiations undertaken within the framework of the Annapolis process [YUN 2007, p. 445], as well as a destructive conflict in Gaza and southern Israel, a deepening internal divide despite efforts toward Palestinian unity and the formation of a new Israeli Government. Rocket fire from Gaza into southern Israel and Israeli air strikes had accelerated throughout December 2008, and violence had escalated sharply with the commencement of Operation Cast Lead. The conflict further escalated on 3 January 2009, when IDF launched a major ground offensive into Gaza. The weeks that followed were marked by intense fighting, high numbers of civilian casualties and extensive damage to the civilian infrastructure in Gaza.

Following the adoption of resolution 1860(2009) on 8 January, the Secretary-General undertook an extended mission to the region to deliver the message that the fighting must stop and the resolution must be fully respected and implemented. Major military operations ended on 18 January with the declaration of unilateral ceasefires by the Israeli cabinet and Hamas. After January, violence in Gaza decreased significantly, but sporadic firing from both sides continued, underscoring the fragility of the situation. On 4 May, a summary of the Board of Inquiry's report, found that in seven incidents, the death, injuries and damages were caused by military actions of IDF, using munitions launched from the air or fired from the ground. The Secretary-General supported the United Nations Fact-Finding Mission on the Gaza Conflict led by Justice Goldstone and the mediation efforts to secure the release of Israeli Corporal Gilad Shalit in exchange for some of the 11,000 Palestinian prisoners held in Israeli jails. He regretted that three years after his capture, neither the International Committee of the Red Cross nor any other international body had been granted access to Corporal Shalit.

In the past 12 months, Egypt had convened six rounds of reconciliation talks between Fatah, Hamas and other Palestinian groups. Regrettably, the talks had only yielded limited progress. A key achievement was the beginning of Palestinian self-empowerment, with the fiscal, development planning and security reforms in the West Bank under the leadership of President Abbas and Prime Minister Salam Fayyad. That positive momentum must not be imperilled by the financial crisis facing the PA. The Israeli system of creating physical obstacles to movement in the West Bank and imposing elaborate permit requirements on Palestinians had continued, including for movement in and around East Jerusalem. However, recent measures by Israel to ease movement restrictions around Nablus, Jericho, Qalqiliya and Ramallah were welcomed.

Israeli actions in support of settlers in the heart of East Jerusalem were a matter of concern. Contrary to the 9 July 2004 advisory opinion of the International Court of Justice (ICJ) [YUN 2004, p. 452], the Security Barrier deviated significantly from the 1967 Green Line into the Occupied Palestinian Territory in the West Bank and restricted Palestinian access to East Jerusalem, key social services and agricultural land. The Quartet continued its valuable practice of consulting with the League of Arab States, and the League's renewed commitment to pursue a just and comprehensive regional peace in accordance with the Arab Peace Initiative, as expressed in its ministerial communiqué of 24 June 2009, was welcomed.

Communication. On 24 July [A/63/969-S/2009/517], Egypt, as Chair of the Coordinating Bureau of the Non-Aligned Movement (NAM), transmitted the NAM Heads of State and Government Declaration on Palestine adopted by the Fifteenth Summit of NAM (Sharm el-Sheikh, Egypt, 11–16 July).

GENERAL ASSEMBLY ACTION

On 2 December [meeting 54], the General Assembly adopted **resolution 64/19** [draft: A/64/L.23 & Add.1] by recorded vote (164-7-4) [agenda item 16].

Peaceful settlement of the question of Palestine

The General Assembly,

Recalling its relevant resolutions, including those adopted at its tenth emergency special session,

Recalling also its resolution 58/292 of 6 May 2004,

Recalling further relevant Security Council resolutions, including resolutions 242(1967) of 22 November 1967, 338(1973) of 22 October 1973, 1397(2002) of 12 March 2002, 1515(2003) of 19 November 2003, 1544(2004) of 19 May 2004 and 1850(2008) of 16 December 2008,

Welcoming the affirmation by the Security Council of the vision of a region where two States, Israel and Palestine, live side by side within secure and recognized borders,

Noting with concern that it has been more than sixty years since the adoption of its resolution 181(II) of 29 November 1947 and forty-two years since the occupation of Palestinian territory, including East Jerusalem, in 1967,

Having considered the report of the Secretary-General submitted pursuant to the request made in its resolution 63/29 of 26 November 2008,

Reaffirming the permanent responsibility of the United Nations with regard to the question of Palestine until the question is resolved in all its aspects in accordance with international law,

Recalling the advisory opinion rendered on 9 July 2004 by the International Court of Justice on the *Legal Consequences of the Construction of a Wall in the Occupied Palestinian Territory*, and recalling also its resolutions ES-10/15 of 20 July 2004 and ES-10/17 of 15 December 2006,

Convinced that achieving a just, lasting and comprehensive settlement of the question of Palestine, the core of the Arab-Israeli conflict, is imperative for the attainment of comprehensive and lasting peace and stability in the Middle East,

Aware that the principle of equal rights and self-determination of peoples is among the purposes and principles enshrined in the Charter of the United Nations,

Affirming the principle of the inadmissibility of the acquisition of territory by war,

Recalling its resolution 2625(XXV) of 24 October 1970,

Reaffirming the illegality of the Israeli settlements in the Palestinian territory occupied since 1967, including East Jerusalem,

Stressing the detrimental impact of Israeli settlement policies, decisions and activities on efforts to resume the peace process and achieve peace in the Middle East,

Reaffirming the illegality of Israeli actions aimed at changing the status of Jerusalem, including measures such as the so-called E-1 plan and all other unilateral measures aimed at altering the character, status and demographic composition of the city and of the Territory as a whole,

Reaffirming also that the construction by Israel, the occupying Power, of a wall in the Occupied Palestinian Territory, including in and around East Jerusalem, and its associated regime are contrary to international law,

Expressing deep concern about the continuing Israeli policy of closures and severe restrictions on the movement of persons and goods, including medical and humanitarian personnel and goods, via the imposition of prolonged closures and severe economic and movement restrictions that in effect amount to a blockade, crossing closures, checkpoints and a permit regime throughout the Occupied Palestinian Territory, including East Jerusalem, and the consequent negative impact on the socio-economic situation of the Palestinian people, which remains that of a dire humanitarian crisis, as well as on efforts aimed at rehabilitating and developing the damaged Palestinian economy and on the contiguity of the Territory,

Recalling the mutual recognition between the Government of the State of Israel and the Palestine Liberation Organization, the representative of the Palestinian people, and the need for full compliance with the agreements concluded between the two sides,

Recalling also the endorsement by the Security Council, in resolution 1515(2003), of the Quartet road map to a permanent two-State solution to the Israeli-Palestinian conflict and the call in Council resolution 1850(2008) for the parties to fulfil their obligations under the road map, as affirmed in the Israeli-Palestinian Joint Understanding reached at the international conference held in Annapolis, United States of America, on 27 November 2007, and to refrain from any steps that could undermine confidence or prejudice the outcome of negotiations,

Noting the Israeli withdrawal in 2005 from the Gaza Strip and parts of the northern West Bank and the dismantlement of the settlements therein as a step towards the implementation of the road map,

Recalling the Arab Peace Initiative adopted by the Council of the League of Arab States at its fourteenth session, held in Beirut on 27 and 28 March 2002,

Expressing support for the agreed principles for bilateral negotiations, as affirmed by the parties at the Annapolis conference, aimed at concluding a peace treaty resolving all outstanding issues, including all core issues, without exception, for the achievement of a just, lasting and peaceful settlement of the Israeli-Palestinian conflict and ultimately of the Arab-Israeli conflict as a whole for the realization of a comprehensive peace in the Middle East,

Expressing support also for the convening of an international conference in Moscow, as envisioned by the Security Council in resolution 1850(2008), for the advancement and acceleration of a resumed peace process,

Noting the important contribution to the peace process of the United Nations Special Coordinator for the Middle East Peace Process and Personal Representative of the Secretary-General to the Palestine Liberation Organization and the Palestinian Authority, including within the framework of the activities of the Quartet,

Welcoming the reconvening of the Ad Hoc Liaison Committee for the Coordination of the International Assistance to Palestinians, under the chairmanship of Norway, at United Nations Headquarters on 22 September 2009, affirming the importance of continued follow-up and fulfilment of pledges made at the International Conference in Support of the Palestinian Economy for the Reconstruction of Gaza, held in Sharm el-Sheikh, Egypt, on 2 March 2009, for the provision of emergency assistance and support for reconstruction and economic recovery in the Gaza Strip and alleviation of the socio-economic and humanitarian crisis being faced by the Palestinian people, and acknowledging the contribution of the Palestinian-European Mechanism for the Management of Socio-Economic Aid of the European Commission in this regard,

Recognizing the efforts being undertaken by the Palestinian Authority, with international support, to rebuild, reform and strengthen its damaged institutions, emphasizing the need to preserve and develop the Palestinian institutions and infrastructure, and welcoming in this regard the Palestinian Authority's plan for constructing the institutions of a Palestinian State within a twenty-four-month period as a demonstration of its serious commitment to an independent State that provides opportunity, justice and security for the Palestinian people and is a responsible neighbour to all States in the region,

Welcoming the efforts and progress made in the security sector by the Palestinian Authority, calling upon the parties to continue cooperation that benefits both Palestinians and Israelis, in particular by promoting security and building confidence, and expressing the hope that such progress will be extended to all major population centres,

Reiterating its concern over the negative developments that have continued to occur in the Occupied Palestinian Territory, including East Jerusalem, including the large number of deaths and injuries, mostly among Palestinian civilians, the acts of violence and brutality committed against Palestinian civilians by Israeli settlers in the West Bank, the widespread destruction of public and private Palestinian property and infrastructure, the internal displacement of civilians and the serious deterioration of the socio-economic and humanitarian conditions of the Palestinian people,

Expressing grave concern, in particular, over the crisis in the Gaza Strip as a result of the continuing prolonged Israeli closures and severe economic and movement restrictions that in effect amount to a blockade and the military operations in the Gaza Strip between December 2008 and January 2009, which caused extensive loss of life and injury, particularly among Palestinian civilians, including children and women, widespread damage and destruction to Palestinian homes, properties, vital infrastructure, public institutions, including hospitals and schools, and United Nations facilities, and internal displacement of civilians,

Stressing the need for the full implementation by all parties of Security Council resolution 1860(2009) of 8 January 2009 and General Assembly resolution ES-10/18 of 16 January 2009,

Expressing concern over continuing military actions in the Occupied Palestinian Territory, including raids and arrest campaigns, and over the continued imposition of hundreds of checkpoints and obstacles to movement in and around Palestinian population centres by the Israeli occupying forces, and emphasizing in this regard the need for the implementation by both sides of the Sharm el-Sheikh understandings,

Emphasizing the importance of the safety, protection and well-being of all civilians in the whole Middle East region, and condemning all acts of violence and terror against civilians on both sides,

Expressing concern over the unlawful takeover of Palestinian Authority institutions in the Gaza Strip in June 2007, and calling for the restoration of the situation to that which existed prior to June 2007 and for the continuation of the serious efforts being exerted by Egypt, the League of Arab States and other concerned parties for the promotion of dialogue towards reconciliation and the restoration of Palestinian national unity,

Stressing the urgent need for sustained and active international involvement, including by the Quartet, to support both parties in resuming, advancing and accelerating the peace process negotiations for the achievement of a just, lasting and comprehensive peace settlement, on the basis of United Nations resolutions, the road map and the Arab Peace Initiative,

Acknowledging the efforts being undertaken by civil society to promote a peaceful settlement of the question of Palestine,

Recalling the findings by the International Court of Justice, in its advisory opinion, including on the urgent necessity for the United Nations as a whole to redouble its efforts to bring the Israeli-Palestinian conflict, which continues to pose a threat to international peace and security, to a speedy conclusion, thereby establishing a just and lasting peace in the region,

Affirming once again the right of all States in the region to live in peace within secure and internationally recognized borders,

1. *Reaffirms* the necessity of achieving a peaceful settlement of the question of Palestine, the core of the Arab-Israeli conflict, in all its aspects, and of intensifying all efforts towards that end;

2. *Also reaffirms* its full support for the Middle East peace process, based on the relevant United Nations resolutions, the terms of reference of the Madrid Conference, including the principle of land for peace, the Arab Peace Initiative adopted by the Council of the League of Arab States at its fourteenth session and the Quartet road map to a permanent two-State solution to the Israeli-Palestinian conflict, and for the existing agreements between the Israeli and Palestinian sides, stresses the necessity for the establishment of a comprehensive, just and lasting peace in the Middle East, and welcomes in this regard the ongoing efforts of the Quartet and of the League of Arab States;

3. *Encourages* continued serious regional and international efforts to follow up and promote the Arab Peace Initiative, including by the Ministerial Committee formed at the Riyadh summit in March 2007;

4. *Urges* the parties to undertake, with the support of the Quartet and the international community, immediate and concrete steps in follow-up to the Israeli-Palestinian Joint Understanding reached at the international conference held in Annapolis, United States of America, on 27 November 2007, including through the resumption of active and serious bilateral negotiations;

5. *Encourages*, in this regard, the convening of an international conference in Moscow, as envisioned by the Security Council in resolution 1850(2008), for the advancement and acceleration of a resumed peace process;

6. *Calls upon* both parties to act on their previous agreements and obligations, in particular adherence to the road map, irrespective of reciprocity, in order to create the conditions necessary for the resumption of negotiations in the near term;

7. *Calls upon* the parties themselves, with the support of the Quartet and other interested parties, to exert all efforts necessary to halt the deterioration of the situation and to reverse all unilateral and unlawful measures taken on the ground since 28 September 2000;

8. *Underscores* the need for the parties to take confidence-building measures aimed at improving the situation on the ground, promoting stability and fostering the peace process, including the need for the further release of prisoners;

9. *Stresses* the need for a speedy end to the reoccupation of Palestinian population centres, inter alia, by easing movement and access, including through the removal of checkpoints and other obstructions to movement, and the need for respect and preservation of the territorial unity, contiguity and integrity of all of the Occupied Palestinian Territory, including East Jerusalem;

10. *Also stresses* the need for an immediate and complete cessation of all acts of violence, including military attacks, destruction and acts of terror;

11. *Reiterates its demand* for the full implementation of Security Council resolution 1860(2009);

12. *Reiterates* the need for the full implementation by both parties of the Agreement on Movement and Access and of the Agreed Principles for the Rafah Crossing, of 15 November 2005, and the need, specifically, to allow for the sustained opening of all crossings into and out of the Gaza Strip for humanitarian supplies, movement and access, as well as for commercial flows and all necessary construction materials, which are essential for alleviating the dire humanitarian crisis, improving the living conditions of the Palestinian people and promoting the recovery of the Palestinian economy;

13. *Stresses*, in this regard, the urgent necessity for the advancement of reconstruction in the Gaza Strip, including through the completion of numerous suspended projects managed by the United Nations, according to the proposal of the Secretary-General, and the commencement of United Nations-led civilian reconstruction activities;

14. *Calls upon* Israel, the occupying Power, to comply strictly with its obligations under international law, including international humanitarian law, and to cease all of its measures that are contrary to international law and unilateral actions in the Occupied Palestinian Territory, including East Jerusalem, that are aimed at altering the character, status and demographic composition of the Territory, including via the de facto annexation of land, and thus at prejudging the final outcome of peace negotiations;

15. *Reiterates its demand* for the complete cessation of all Israeli settlement activities in the Occupied Palestinian Territory, including East Jerusalem, and in the occupied Syrian Golan, and calls for the full implementation of the relevant Security Council resolutions;

16.   *Calls for* the cessation of all provocations, including by Israeli settlers, in East Jerusalem, including in and around religious sites;

17.   *Demands*, accordingly, that Israel, the occupying Power, comply with its legal obligations under international law, as mentioned in the advisory opinion rendered on 9 July 2004 by the International Court of Justice and as demanded in General Assembly resolutions ES-10/13 of 21 October 2003 and ES-10/15, and, inter alia, that it immediately cease its construction of the wall in the Occupied Palestinian Territory, including East Jerusalem, and calls upon all States Members of the United Nations to comply with their legal obligations, as mentioned in the advisory opinion;

18.   *Reaffirms its commitment*, in accordance with international law, to the two-State solution of Israel and Palestine, living side by side in peace and security within recognized borders, based on the pre-1967 borders;

19.   *Stresses* the need for:

(a)   The withdrawal of Israel from the Palestinian territory occupied since 1967, including East Jerusalem;

(b)   The realization of the inalienable rights of the Palestinian people, primarily the right to self-determination and the right to their independent State;

20.   *Also stresses* the need for a just resolution of the problem of Palestine refugees in conformity with its resolution 194(III) of 11 December 1948;

21.   *Calls upon* the parties to resume and accelerate direct peace negotiations towards the conclusion of a final peaceful settlement on the basis of relevant United Nations resolutions, especially of the Security Council, the terms of reference of the Madrid Conference, the road map and the Arab Peace Initiative;

22.   *Urges* Member States to expedite the provision of economic, humanitarian and technical assistance to the Palestinian people and the Palestinian Authority during this critical period in order to help to alleviate the humanitarian crisis being faced by the Palestinian people, particularly in the Gaza Strip, to rehabilitate the Palestinian economy and infrastructure and to support the rebuilding, restructuring and reform of Palestinian institutions and Palestinian State-building efforts;

23.   *Encourages*, in this regard, the continuing efforts of the Quartet's Special Representative, Mr. Tony Blair, to strengthen Palestinian institutions, promote Palestinian economic development and mobilize international donor support;

24.   *Requests* the Secretary-General to continue his efforts with the parties concerned, and in consultation with the Security Council, towards the attainment of a peaceful settlement of the question of Palestine and the promotion of peace in the region and to submit to the General Assembly at its sixty-fifth session a report on these efforts and on developments on this matter.

RECORDED VOTE ON RESOLUTION 64/19:

In favour: Afghanistan, Albania, Algeria, Andorra, Angola, Argentina, Armenia, Austria, Azerbaijan, Bahamas, Bahrain, Bangladesh, Barbados, Belarus, Belgium, Belize, Benin, Bhutan, Bolivia, Bosnia and Herzegovina, Botswana, Brazil, Brunei Darussalam, Bulgaria, Burundi, Cambodia, Cape Verde, Chad, Chile, China, Colombia, Comoros, Costa Rica, Côte d'Ivoire, Croatia, Cuba, Cyprus, Czech Republic, Democratic People's Republic of Korea, Democratic Republic of the Congo, Denmark, Djibouti, Dominica, Dominican Republic, Ecuador, Egypt, El Salvador, Eritrea, Estonia, Ethiopia, Finland, France, Gabon, Gambia, Georgia, Germany, Ghana, Greece, Guatemala, Guinea, Guinea-Bissau, Guyana, Haiti, Hungary, Iceland, India, Indonesia, Iran, Iraq, Ireland, Italy, Jamaica, Japan, Jordan, Kazakhstan, Kenya, Kuwait, Kyrgyzstan, Lao People's Democratic Republic, Latvia, Lebanon, Lesotho, Liberia, Libyan Arab Jamahiriya, Liechtenstein, Lithuania, Luxembourg, Madagascar, Malaysia, Maldives, Mali, Malta, Mauritania, Mauritius, Mexico, Moldova, Monaco, Mongolia, Montenegro, Morocco, Mozambique, Myanmar, Namibia, Nepal, Netherlands, New Zealand, Nicaragua, Niger, Nigeria, Norway, Oman, Pakistan, Papua New Guinea, Paraguay, Peru, Philippines, Poland, Portugal, Qatar, Republic of Korea, Romania, Russian Federation, Saint Lucia, Saint Vincent and the Grenadines, Samoa, San Marino, Saudi Arabia, Senegal, Serbia, Sierra Leone, Singapore, Slovakia, Slovenia, Solomon Islands, Somalia, South Africa, Spain, Sri Lanka, Sudan, Suriname, Swaziland, Sweden, Switzerland, Syrian Arab Republic, Tajikistan, Thailand, The former Yugoslav Republic of Macedonia, Togo, Trinidad and Tobago, Tunisia, Turkey, Turkmenistan, Uganda, Ukraine, United Arab Emirates, United Kingdom, United Republic of Tanzania, Uruguay, Uzbekistan, Venezuela, Viet Nam, Yemen, Zambia, Zimbabwe.

Against: Australia, Israel, Marshall Islands, Micronesia, Nauru, Palau, United States.

Abstaining: Cameroon, Canada, Fiji, Tonga.

In **resolution 64/150** of 18 December (see p. 681), the General Assembly reaffirmed the right of the Palestinian people to self-determination, including the right to their independent State of Palestine. By **decision 64/549** of 24 December, the Assembly decided that the agenda items on the situation in the Middle East and on the question of Palestine would remain for consideration during its resumed (2010) sixty-fourth session.

Israeli settlements

The issue of Israeli settlements in the West Bank, including in East Jerusalem, remained central to the question of the Occupied Palestinian Territory, as it did to the peace negotiations. The road map and the Annapolis joint statement committed Israel to dismantle all settlement outposts erected since 2001 and to freeze, consistent with the 2001 report of the Sharm el-Sheikh Fact-Finding Committee (Mitchell Report) [YUN 2001, p. 409], all settlement activity including natural growth.

Communications. Throughout the year, Palestine [A/ES-10/448-S/2009/98; A/ES-10/449-S/2009/113; A/ES-10/451-S/2009/130; A/ES-10/452-S/2009/194; A/ES-10/453-S/2009/209; A/ES-10/454-S/2009/228; A/ES-10/457-S/2009/269; A/ES-10/458-S/2009/338; A/ES-10/459-S/2009/401; A/ES-10/461-S/2009/453; A/ES-10/462-S/2009/494; A/ES-10/464-S/2009/513; A/ES-10/466-S/2009/534; A/ES-10/468-S/2009/565; A/ES-10/469-S/2009/598; A/ES-10/471-S/2009/662;

A/ES-10/473-S/2010/1], Egypt [A/ES-10/463; A/64/473-S/2009/507] on behalf of the Non-Aligned Movement, the Syrian Arab Republic [A/ES-10/465] on behalf of the Organization of the Islamic Conference, Yemen [S/2009/125] on behalf of the Arab Group in New York, as well as the Chairman of the Committee on the Exercise of the Inalienable Rights of the Palestinian People [A/63/861-S/2009/265; A/ES-10/456], brought to the attention of the Secretary-General and the Security Council the ongoing construction and expansion of Israeli settlements in the Occupied Palestinian Territory, especially in and around East Jerusalem.

The Special Rapporteur on the situation of human rights in the Palestinian territory [A/64/328] (see p. 782) also dealt with the issue of Israeli settlements and their impact on the enjoyment of human rights by the Palestinians.

Report of Secretary-General. In response to General Assembly resolution 63/97 [YUN 2008, p. 499], the Secretary-General in November submitted a report [A/64/516], prepared by the Office of the United Nations High Commissioner for Human Rights (OHCHR), on the implementation of that resolution, covering the period from September 2008 to August 2009 and focusing on the continuation of Israeli settlement activities in the occupied Arab territories as well as violence by Israeli settlers. Under phase I of the road map, Israel had committed to freezing all settlement activity from March 2001, consistent with the Mitchell Report, which stated that Israel should freeze all settlement activity, including the "natural growth" of existing settlements, and that the kind of security cooperation desired by Israel could not for long coexist with settlement activity.

According to the Office for the Coordination of Humanitarian Affairs (OCHA), about 485,800 settlers were residing in 121 settlements in the West Bank by the end of 2008, including 195,000 in 12 settlements in East Jerusalem. In addition to settlements, there were around 100 "outposts" throughout the West Bank. Outposts were settlements not authorized by the Israeli Government and were therefore illegal under Israeli law, in addition to being illegal under international law.

OCHA reported that settler-related incidents continued in 2009. Palestinians injured by settlers remained at the high level of 2008, with 269 settler-related incidents as at September 2009, 41 of which resulted in the injury of 108 Palestinians. As at December 2008, approximately half of all Palestinian injuries from settler violence were suffered by women and children.

In addition to having approved the expansion of settlements in East Jerusalem, Israel had implemented other policies the result of which was to change the demography of East Jerusalem. In particular, urban planning policies, the dispensing of building permits and the demolition of homes built without permits had a discriminatory impact on Palestinian residents of East Jerusalem.

The International Committee of the Red Cross estimated that the Israeli population in the occupied Syrian Golan was between 17,000 and 21,000, living in some 40 settlements. Since the occupation of the Syrian Golan in 1967, Israel had continued its settlement expansion, despite renewed resolutions to desist from doing so.

The report recommended that Israel should abide by international legal obligations and its pre-existing commitments, as stated in the road map, as well as the calls of the international community, namely, to dismantle settlement outposts erected since March 2001 and to freeze all settlement activity, including natural growth, including in occupied East Jerusalem. Israel should take action to halt attacks by Israeli settlers against the civilian population of the occupied territory, investigate settler violence and provide redress to victims. Israel should also ensure that the labour rights of Palestinian workers in settlements, including the right to form and join trade unions, were respected, and it should cease to exploit natural resources, including water, in the Occupied Palestinian Territory.

GENERAL ASSEMBLY ACTION

On 10 December [meeting 62], the General Assembly, on the recommendation of the Fourth Committee [A/64/406], adopted **resolution 64/93** by recorded vote (167-7-3) [agenda item 32].

Israeli settlements in the Occupied Palestinian Territory, including East Jerusalem, and the occupied Syrian Golan

The General Assembly,

Guided by the principles of the Charter of the United Nations, and affirming the inadmissibility of the acquisition of territory by force,

Recalling its relevant resolutions, including resolution 63/97 of 5 December 2008, as well as those resolutions adopted at its tenth emergency special session,

Recalling also the relevant resolutions of the Security Council, including resolutions 242(1967) of 22 November 1967, 446(1979) of 22 March 1979, 465(1980) of 1 March 1980, 476(1980) of 30 June 1980, 478(1980) of 20 August 1980, 497(1981) of 17 December 1981 and 904(1994) of 18 March 1994,

Reaffirming the applicability of the Geneva Convention relative to the Protection of Civilian Persons in Time of War, of 12 August 1949, to the Occupied Palestinian Territory, including East Jerusalem, and to the occupied Syrian Golan,

Considering that the transfer by the occupying Power of parts of its own civilian population into the territory it occupies constitutes a breach of the Fourth Geneva Convention and relevant provisions of customary law, including those codified in Additional Protocol I to the four Geneva Conventions,

Recalling the advisory opinion rendered on 9 July 2004 by the International Court of Justice on the *Legal Consequences of the Construction of a Wall in the Occupied Palestinian Territory*, and recalling also General Assembly resolutions ES-10/15 of 20 July 2004 and ES-10/17 of 15 December 2006,

Noting that the International Court of Justice concluded that "the Israeli settlements in the Occupied Palestinian Territory (including East Jerusalem) have been established in breach of international law",

Taking note of the recent report of the Special Rapporteur of the Human Rights Council on the situation of human rights in the Palestinian territories occupied by Israel since 1967,

Recalling the Declaration of Principles on Interim Self-Government Arrangements of 13 September 1993 and the subsequent implementation agreements between the Palestinian and Israeli sides,

Recalling also the Quartet road map to a permanent two-State solution to the Israeli-Palestinian conflict, and noting specifically its call for a freeze on all settlement activity, including so-called "natural growth", and the dismantlement of all settlement outposts erected since March 2001,

Aware that Israeli settlement activities involve, inter alia, the transfer of nationals of the occupying Power into the occupied territories, the confiscation of land, the exploitation of natural resources and other actions against the Palestinian civilian population that are contrary to international law,

Bearing in mind the detrimental impact of Israeli settlement policies, decisions and activities on efforts to resume the peace process and to achieve peace in the Middle East,

Expressing grave concern about the continuation by Israel, the occupying Power, of settlement activities in the Occupied Palestinian Territory, in violation of international humanitarian law, relevant United Nations resolutions and the agreements reached between the parties, and concerned particularly about Israel's construction and expansion of settlements in and around occupied East Jerusalem, including its so-called E-1 plan that aims to connect its illegal settlements around and further isolate occupied East Jerusalem, the continuing demolition of Palestinian homes and eviction of Palestinian families from the city, and intensifying settlement activities in the Jordan Valley,

Expressing grave concern also about the continuing unlawful construction by Israel of the wall inside the Occupied Palestinian Territory, including in and around East Jerusalem, and expressing its concern in particular about the route of the wall in departure from the Armistice Line of 1949, which is causing humanitarian hardship and a serious decline of socioeconomic conditions for the Palestinian people, is fragmenting the territorial contiguity of the Territory, and could prejudge future negotiations and make the two-State solution physically impossible to implement,

Deeply concerned that the wall's route has been traced in such a way as to include the great majority of the Israeli settlements in the Occupied Palestinian Territory, including East Jerusalem,

Deploring settlement activities in the Occupied Palestinian Territory, including East Jerusalem, and in the occupied Syrian Golan and any activities involving the confiscation of land, the disruption of the livelihood of protected persons and the de facto annexation of land,

Recalling the need to end all acts of violence, including acts of terror, provocation, incitement and destruction,

Gravely concerned about the rising incidents of violence, harassment, provocation and incitement by illegal armed Israeli settlers in the Occupied Palestinian Territory, including East Jerusalem, against Palestinian civilians and their properties and agricultural lands,

Noting the Israeli withdrawal from within the Gaza Strip and parts of the northern West Bank and the importance of the dismantlement of the settlements therein as a step towards the implementation of the road map,

Taking note of the relevant reports of the Secretary-General,

Taking note also of the special meeting of the Security Council convened on 26 September 2008,

1.   *Reaffirms* that the Israeli settlements in the Palestinian territory, including East Jerusalem, and in the occupied Syrian Golan are illegal and an obstacle to peace and economic and social development;

2.   *Calls upon* Israel to accept the de jure applicability of the Geneva Convention relative to the Protection of Civilian Persons in Time of War, of 12 August 1949, to the Occupied Palestinian Territory, including East Jerusalem, and to the occupied Syrian Golan and to abide scrupulously by the provisions of the Convention, in particular article 49;

3.   *Also calls upon* Israel, the occupying Power, to comply strictly with its obligations under international law, including international humanitarian law, with respect to the alteration of the character, status and demographic composition of the Occupied Palestinian Territory, including East Jerusalem;

4.   *Reiterates its demand* for the immediate and complete cessation of all Israeli settlement activities in all of the Occupied Palestinian Territory, including East Jerusalem, and in the occupied Syrian Golan, and calls in this regard for the full implementation of the relevant resolutions of the Security Council, including resolution 465(1980);

5.   *Demands* that Israel, the occupying Power, comply with its legal obligations, as mentioned in the advisory opinion rendered on 9 July 2004 by the International Court of Justice;

6.   *Reiterates its call* for the prevention of all acts of violence and harassment by Israeli settlers, especially against Palestinian civilians and their properties and agricultural lands, and stresses the need for the implementation of Security Council resolution 904(1994), in which the Council called upon Israel, the occupying Power, to continue to take and implement measures, including confiscation of arms, aimed at preventing illegal acts of violence by Israeli settlers, and called for measures to be taken to guarantee the safety and protection of the Palestinian civilians in the occupied territory;

7.   *Requests* the Secretary-General to report to the General Assembly at its sixty-fifth session on the implementation of the present resolution.

RECORDED VOTE ON RESOLUTION 64/93:

In favour: Afghanistan, Albania, Algeria, Andorra, Angola, Antigua and Barbuda, Argentina, Armenia, Australia, Austria, Azerbaijan, Bahamas, Bahrain, Bangladesh, Barbados, Belarus, Belgium, Belize, Benin, Bhutan, Bolivia, Bosnia and Herzegovina, Botswana, Brazil, Brunei Darussalam, Bulgaria, Burkina Faso, Burundi, Canada, Cape Verde, Chile, China, Colombia, Comoros, Congo, Costa Rica, Croatia, Cuba, Cyprus, Czech Republic, Democratic People's Republic of Korea, Denmark, Djibouti, Dominica, Dominican Republic, Ecuador, Egypt, El Salvador, Eritrea, Estonia, Ethiopia, Fiji, Finland, France, Gambia, Georgia, Germany, Ghana, Greece, Grenada, Guatemala, Guinea, Guinea-Bissau, Guyana, Honduras, Hungary, Iceland, India, Indonesia, Iran, Iraq, Ireland, Italy, Jamaica, Japan, Jordan, Kazakhstan, Kenya, Kuwait, Kyrgyzstan, Lao People's Democratic Republic, Latvia, Lebanon, Lesotho, Liberia, Libyan Arab Jamahiriya, Liechtenstein, Lithuania, Luxembourg, Madagascar, Malawi, Malaysia, Maldives, Mali, Malta, Mauritania, Mauritius, Mexico, Moldova, Monaco, Mongolia, Montenegro, Morocco, Mozambique, Myanmar, Namibia, Nepal, Netherlands, New Zealand, Nicaragua, Niger, Nigeria, Norway, Oman, Pakistan, Papua New Guinea, Paraguay, Peru, Philippines, Poland, Portugal, Qatar, Republic of Korea, Romania, Russian Federation, Saint Lucia, Saint Vincent and the Grenadines, Samoa, San Marino, Saudi Arabia, Senegal, Serbia, Sierra Leone, Singapore, Slovakia, Slovenia, Solomon Islands, Somalia, South Africa, Spain, Sri Lanka, Sudan, Suriname, Swaziland, Sweden, Switzerland, Syrian Arab Republic, Tajikistan, Thailand, The former Yugoslav Republic of Macedonia, Timor-Leste, Togo, Trinidad and Tobago, Tunisia, Turkey, Turkmenistan, Ukraine, United Arab Emirates, United Kingdom, United Republic of Tanzania, Uruguay, Uzbekistan, Venezuela, Viet Nam, Yemen, Zambia, Zimbabwe.

Against: Israel, Marshall Islands, Micronesia, Nauru, Palau, Panama, United States.

Abstaining: Cameroon, Côte d'Ivoire, Vanuatu.

Jerusalem

Report of Secretary-General. On 10 September [A/64/343], the Secretary-General reported that nine Member States (Colombia, Cuba, the Democratic People's Republic of Korea, Jordan, Mexico, Nicaragua, Qatar, the Sudan, the Syrian Arab Republic) had replied to his request for information on steps taken or envisaged to implement General Assembly resolution 63/30 [YUN 2008, p. 501] on Jerusalem. The resolution stressed that a comprehensive, just and lasting solution to the question of Jerusalem should take into account the legitimate concerns of both the Palestinian and Israeli sides and should include internationally guaranteed provisions to ensure the freedom of religion and of conscience of its inhabitants, as well as free and unhindered access to the holy places by the people of all religions and nationalities.

GENERAL ASSEMBLY ACTION

On 2 December [meeting 54], the General Assembly adopted **resolution 64/20** [draft: A/64/L.24 & Add.1] by recorded vote (163-7-5) [agenda item 15].

Jerusalem

The General Assembly,

Recalling its resolution 181(II) of 29 November 1947, in particular its provisions regarding the City of Jerusalem,

Recalling also its resolution 36/120 E of 10 December 1981 and all its subsequent relevant resolutions, including resolution 56/31 of 3 December 2001, in which it, inter alia, determined that all legislative and administrative measures and actions taken by Israel, the occupying Power, which have altered or purported to alter the character and status of the Holy City of Jerusalem, in particular the so-called "Basic Law" on Jerusalem and the proclamation of Jerusalem as the capital of Israel, were null and void and must be rescinded forthwith,

Recalling further the Security Council resolutions relevant to Jerusalem, including resolution 478(1980) of 20 August 1980, in which the Council, inter alia, decided not to recognize the "Basic Law" on Jerusalem,

Recalling the advisory opinion rendered on 9 July 2004 by the International Court of Justice on the *Legal Consequences of the Construction of a Wall in the Occupied Palestinian Territory*, and recalling its resolution ES-10/15 of 20 July 2004,

Expressing its grave concern about any action taken by any body, governmental or non-governmental, in violation of the above-mentioned resolutions,

Expressing its grave concern also, in particular about the continuation by Israel, the occupying Power, of illegal settlement activities, including the so-called E-1 plan, its construction of the wall in and around East Jerusalem, its restrictions on access to and residence in East Jerusalem and the further isolation of the city from the rest of the Occupied Palestinian Territory, which are having a detrimental effect on the lives of Palestinians and could prejudge a final status agreement on Jerusalem,

Expressing its grave concern further about the continuing Israeli demolition of Palestinian homes and the eviction of numerous Palestinian families from East Jerusalem neighbourhoods, as well as other acts of provocation and incitement, including by Israeli settlers, in the city,

Expressing its concern about the Israeli excavations undertaken in the Old City of Jerusalem, including in and around religious sites,

Reaffirming that the international community, through the United Nations, has a legitimate interest in the question of the City of Jerusalem and in the protection of the unique spiritual, religious and cultural dimensions of the city, as foreseen in relevant United Nations resolutions on this matter,

Having considered the report of the Secretary-General on the situation in the Middle East,

1. *Reiterates its determination* that any actions taken by Israel, the occupying Power, to impose its laws, jurisdiction and administration on the Holy City of Jerusalem are illegal and therefore null and void and have no validity whatsoever, and calls upon Israel to immediately cease all such illegal and unilateral measures;

2. *Stresses* that a comprehensive, just and lasting solution to the question of the City of Jerusalem should take into account the legitimate concerns of both the Palestinian and Israeli sides and should include internationally guaranteed provisions to ensure the freedom of religion and of

conscience of its inhabitants, as well as permanent, free and unhindered access to the holy places by the people of all religions and nationalities;

3. *Requests* the Secretary-General to report to the General Assembly at its sixty-fifth session on the implementation of the present resolution.

RECORDED VOTE ON RESOLUTION 64/20:

In favour: Afghanistan, Albania, Algeria, Andorra, Angola, Argentina, Armenia, Austria, Azerbaijan, Bahamas, Bahrain, Bangladesh, Barbados, Belarus, Belgium, Belize, Benin, Bhutan, Bolivia, Bosnia and Herzegovina, Botswana, Brazil, Brunei Darussalam, Bulgaria, Burundi, Cambodia, Canada, Cape Verde, Chad, Chile, China, Colombia, Comoros, Costa Rica, Croatia, Cuba, Cyprus, Czech Republic, Democratic People's Republic of Korea, Denmark, Djibouti, Dominica, Dominican Republic, Ecuador, Egypt, El Salvador, Eritrea, Estonia, Ethiopia, Finland, France, Gabon, Gambia, Georgia, Germany, Ghana, Greece, Guatemala, Guinea, Guinea-Bissau, Guyana, Haiti, Hungary, Iceland, India, Indonesia, Iran, Iraq, Ireland, Italy, Jamaica, Japan, Jordan, Kazakhstan, Kenya, Kuwait, Kyrgyzstan, Lao People's Democratic Republic, Latvia, Lebanon, Lesotho, Liberia, Libyan Arab Jamahiriya, Liechtenstein, Lithuania, Luxembourg, Madagascar, Malaysia, Maldives, Mali, Malta, Mauritania, Mauritius, Mexico, Moldova, Monaco, Mongolia, Montenegro, Morocco, Mozambique, Myanmar, Namibia, Nepal, Netherlands, New Zealand, Nicaragua, Niger, Nigeria, Norway, Oman, Pakistan, Papua New Guinea, Paraguay, Peru, Philippines, Poland, Portugal, Qatar, Republic of Korea, Romania, Russian Federation, Saint Lucia, Saint Vincent and the Grenadines, Samoa, San Marino, Saudi Arabia, Senegal, Serbia, Sierra Leone, Singapore, Slovakia, Slovenia, Solomon Islands, Somalia, South Africa, Spain, Sri Lanka, Sudan, Suriname, Swaziland, Sweden, Switzerland, Syrian Arab Republic, Tajikistan, Thailand, The former Yugoslav Republic of Macedonia, Togo, Trinidad and Tobago, Tunisia, Turkey, Turkmenistan, Uganda, Ukraine, United Arab Emirates, United Kingdom, United Republic of Tanzania, Uruguay, Uzbekistan, Venezuela, Viet Nam, Yemen, Zambia, Zimbabwe.

Against: Israel, Marshall Islands, Micronesia, Nauru, Palau, Panama, United States.

Abstaining: Australia, Cameroon, Côte d'Ivoire, Fiji, Tonga.

Other aspects

Special Committee to Investigate Israeli Practices Affecting Human Rights

As requested by General Assembly resolution 63/95 [YUN 2008, p. 507], the Special Committee to Investigate Israeli Practices Affecting the Human Rights of the Palestinian People and Other Arabs of the Occupied Territories (Special Committee on Israeli Practices), established by Assembly resolution 2443(XXIII) [YUN 1968, p. 555], reported for the forty-first time [A/64/339] on events and the human rights situation in the territories it considered occupied by Israel—the Syrian Arab Golan (see p. 488) and the occupied Palestinian territory of the West Bank, East Jerusalem and the Gaza Strip. The report was based on information gathered during the Special Committee's mission to Egypt (3–7 August), Jordan (7–11 August) and the

Syrian Arab Republic (11–13 August), where it heard the testimony of 33 witnesses. As in previous years, the Committee was unable to visit the occupied territories, having again received no authorization from Israel to do so.

The Special Committee noted that Israel continued to engage in practices and policies that were discriminatory against the Palestinian and Arab populations and that such conduct contravened Israel's obligations under international human rights and humanitarian laws. The Special Committee called on Israel to comply with the resolutions of the General Assembly and the Human Rights Council, in addition to the 2004 ICJ advisory opinion on the legal consequences of the construction of a wall in the Occupied Palestinian Territory [YUN 2004, p. 452].

The Special Committee was similarly concerned that the situation in the Gaza Strip had reached the level of a humanitarian catastrophe, particularly in terms of the inadequate availability of medicine and medical treatment and of construction and building materials. It urged the Security Council and Member States to ensure implementation of the ICJ Advisory Opinion and Assembly resolution ES-10/15, adopted at the tenth emergency special session on Palestine [YUN 2004, p. 465], requesting Israel to dismantle the segments of the separation wall and make reparations for the damage arising from its construction.

The Special Committee requested the High Contracting Parties to the Fourth Geneva Convention to take concrete measures in respect of their obligations to ensure respect for the Convention by Israel. For its part, the PA should abide by the relevant provisions of human rights law and international humanitarian law, and should aim to resolve the human rights and humanitarian crisis facing the Occupied Palestinian Territory and to fully restore the rule of law in areas under its control. The Special Committee urged civil society groups and diplomatic, academic and research institutions to use their influence to make widely known the serious human rights and humanitarian situation in the occupied territories, including in the occupied Syrian Golan. It encouraged the efforts of Israeli NGOs made on behalf of Palestinian human rights, and considered that the work of those organizations should receive greater recognition from Israeli civil society and Israeli institutions.

Report of Secretary-General. On 6 November [A/64/517], the Secretary-General submitted a report on the implementation of Assembly resolution 63/98 [YUN 2008, p. 505] on Israeli practices affecting the human rights of the Palestinian people in the Occupied Palestinian Territory, including East Jerusalem, covering the period from September 2008 to August 2009, on the basis of material submitted by OHCHR and drawing largely on information made available by OCHA.

The report addressed the humanitarian and human rights situation in the Occupied Palestinian Territory.

As at August 2009, the blockade of the Gaza Strip entered its third year. In September 2007, subsequent to the Hamas takeover of governmental functions in the Gaza Strip in June 2007, Israel declared Gaza a "hostile territory", closing its borders to exports, severely restricting imports and imposing a travel ban to and from Gaza. Following the expiration of the Egyptian-brokered truce between Israel and the Hamas-led government on 19 December 2008, Israel launched Operation Cast Lead on 27 December. The human rights and humanitarian situation, which was already acute prior to the launch of the operation, deteriorated further.

The Secretary-General recommended that Israel should end the blockade of Gaza, which was having a negative impact on the humanitarian and human rights situation of the civilian population. In particular, Israel should allow unimpeded access to Gaza for humanitarian aid and the non-humanitarian goods needed for reconstruction, and address immediately the water, sanitation and environmental crisis in Gaza.

All parties to the conflict should abide scrupulously by their obligations under international human rights and humanitarian law. All allegations of violations must be investigated by credible, independent and transparent accountability mechanisms. Equally crucial was upholding the right of victims to reparation.

Israel should take steps to facilitate freedom of movement for Palestinians in the West Bank. In accordance with the ICJ opinion, it should immediately cease construction of the wall and dismantle portions already built in occupied territory. Israel should also issue viable zoning plans and a less cumbersome process for issuing building permits in a non-discriminatory manner for all in East Jerusalem and other places in the West Bank. Until such time, the evictions and demolitions of Palestinian homes should cease. Victims of forced evictions should be afforded the possibility of redress. Punitive demolitions should cease.

Israel, as the occupying power, should ensure that the rights of children were respected, should address concerns with regard to the arrest and detention of Palestinian children, and should ensure that such detentions be conducted in compliance with international human rights law, with due respect of the vulnerability of children. Israel should refrain from discriminating between Israeli and Palestinian children with regard to the age of criminal responsibility and ensure that alternative measures to detention were explored and that detention was used only as a last resort.

The General Assembly and the international community should promote the implementation of the decisions, resolutions and recommendations of the Assembly, the Security Council, the ICJ and UN human rights mechanisms.

Report of Special Rapporteur. By a 25 August note [A/64/328], the Secretary-General transmitted the report of the Special Rapporteur on the situation of human rights in the Palestinian territories occupied since 1967, Richard Falk, covering the period from December 2008 to July 2009 (see p. 782).

(For information on the right of the Palestinian people to self-determination, see p. 681, and on the human rights situation in the Territories occupied by Israel, see p. 786.)

UN Register of Damage. On 30 April [A/ES-10/455], in accordance with Assembly resolution ES-10/17 [YUN 2006, p. 529], the Secretary-General transmitted to the General Assembly a progress report from the Board of the United Nations Register of Damage Caused by the Construction of the Wall in the Occupied Palestinian Territory. At its first substantive meeting (Vienna, 15–19 December 2008), the Board reviewed the first 30 claim forms, translated from Arabic into English, processed through the Register's electronic database and reviewed by its staff. The Board decided to include in the Register losses set out in each of those forms, signifying the beginning of existence of the Register. Israel maintained its well-known position of not cooperating with the Office of the Register and considered that any claims in relation to damage caused by the construction of the wall should be addressed through the existing Israeli mechanism. At the same time, on a practical level, the Office of the Register had not experienced any difficulties in carrying out its activities as outlined in resolution ES-10/17.

Since the Office of the Register was located at Vienna, the main operational challenge to the implementation of its mandate was outreach and claim intake activities in the Occupied Palestinian Territory, including in and around East Jerusalem. Consequently, a team of a few locally recruited claim intakers and an internationally recruited project manager was set up by the United Nations Office for Project Services in Ramallah at the request of the Office of the Register. At its second meeting (Vienna, 6–9 April 2009), the Board reviewed an additional 240 claim forms and decided to include losses set out in each of them in the Register, except for two claim forms where none of the losses met the eligibility criteria.

Communication. On 13 August [A/ES-10/460-S/2009/420], Palestine brought to the attention of the Secretary-General and the Security Council a memorandum from the Palestinian National Committee for the Register of Damage on the fifth anniversary of the 2004 ICJ advisory opinion on the legal consequences of the construction of a wall in the Occupied Palestinian Territory [YUN 2004, p. 452].

On 10 December [meeting 62], the General Assembly, on the recommendation of the Fourth (Special Political and Decolonization) Committee [A/64/406], adopted **resolution 64/94** by recorded vote (162-9-5) [agenda item 32].

Israeli practices affecting the human rights of the Palestinian people in the Occupied Palestinian Territory, including East Jerusalem

The General Assembly,

Recalling the Universal Declaration of Human Rights,

Recalling also the International Covenant on Civil and Political Rights, the International Covenant on Economic, Social and Cultural Rights and the Convention on the Rights of the Child, and affirming that these human rights instruments must be respected in the Occupied Palestinian Territory, including East Jerusalem,

Reaffirming its relevant resolutions, including resolution 63/98 of 5 December 2008, as well as those adopted at its tenth emergency special session,

Recalling the relevant resolutions of the Commission on Human Rights and the Human Rights Council,

Recalling also the relevant resolutions of the Security Council, and stressing the need for their implementation,

Having considered the report of the Special Committee to Investigate Israeli Practices Affecting the Human Rights of the Palestinian People and Other Arabs of the Occupied Territories and the report of the Secretary-General,

Taking note of the recent reports of the Special Rapporteur of the Human Rights Council on the situation of human rights in the Palestinian territories occupied since 1967,

Recalling the advisory opinion rendered on 9 July 2004 by the International Court of Justice, and recalling also General Assembly resolutions ES-10/15 of 20 July 2004 and ES-10/17 of 15 December 2006,

Noting in particular the Court's reply, including that the construction of the wall being built by Israel, the occupying Power, in the Occupied Palestinian Territory, including in and around East Jerusalem, and its associated regime are contrary to international law,

Aware of the responsibility of the international community to promote human rights and ensure respect for international law, and recalling in this regard its resolution 2625(XXV) of 24 October 1970,

Reaffirming the principle of the inadmissibility of the acquisition of territory by force,

Reaffirming also the applicability of the Geneva Convention relative to the Protection of Civilian Persons in Time of War, of 12 August 1949, to the Occupied Palestinian Territory, including East Jerusalem, and other Arab territories occupied by Israel since 1967,

Reaffirming further the obligation of the States parties to the Fourth Geneva Convention under articles 146, 147 and 148 with regard to penal sanctions, grave breaches and responsibilities of the High Contracting Parties,

Reaffirming that all States have the right and the duty to take actions in conformity with international law and international humanitarian law to counter deadly acts of violence against their civilian population in order to protect the lives of their citizens,

Stressing the need for full compliance with the Israeli-Palestinian agreements reached within the context of the Middle East peace process, including the Sharm el-Sheikh understandings, and the implementation of the Quartet road map to a permanent two-State solution to the Israeli-Palestinian conflict,

Stressing also the need for the full implementation of the Agreement on Movement and Access and the Agreed Principles for the Rafah Crossing, both of 15 November 2005, to allow for the freedom of movement of the Palestinian civilian population within and into and out of the Gaza Strip,

Expressing grave concern about the continuing systematic violation of the human rights of the Palestinian people by Israel, the occupying Power, including that arising from the excessive use of force, the use of collective punishment, the closure of areas, the confiscation of land, the establishment and expansion of settlements, the construction of a wall in the Occupied Palestinian Territory in departure from the Armistice Line of 1949, the destruction of property and infrastructure, and all other actions by it designed to change the legal status, geographical nature and demographic composition of the Occupied Palestinian Territory, including East Jerusalem,

Gravely concerned about the military actions that have been carried out since 28 September 2000 and that have led to thousands of deaths among Palestinian civilians, including hundreds of children, and tens of thousands of injuries,

Gravely concerned in particular about the continuing deterioration in the humanitarian and security situation in the Gaza Strip, including that resulting from the prolonged closures and severe economic and movement restrictions that in effect amount to a blockade and the military operations between December 2008 and January 2009, which caused extensive loss of life and injury, particularly among Palestinian civilians, including children and women; widespread destruction and damage to Palestinian homes, properties, vital infrastructure and public institutions, including hospitals, schools and United Nations facilities; and the internal displacement of civilians, as well as from the firing of rockets into Israel,

Stressing the need for the full implementation by all parties of Security Council resolution 1860(2009) of 8 January 2009 and General Assembly resolution ES-10/18 of 16 January 2009,

Gravely concerned by reports regarding serious human rights violations and grave breaches of international humanitarian law committed during the military operations in the Gaza Strip between December 2008 and January 2009, including the findings in the summary by the Secretary-General of the report of the Board of Inquiry and in the report of the United Nations Fact-Finding Mission on the Gaza Conflict, and stressing the necessity for serious follow-up by all parties to the recommendations addressed to them towards ensuring accountability and justice,

Expressing deep concern about the short- and long-term detrimental impact of such widespread destruction and the impeding of the reconstruction process by Israel, the occupying Power, on the human rights situation and on the socio-economic and humanitarian conditions of the Palestinian civilian population,

Expressing deep concern also about the Israeli policy of closures, severe restrictions, and a permit regime that obstruct the freedom of movement of persons and goods, including medical and humanitarian personnel and goods, throughout the Occupied Palestinian Territory, including East Jerusalem, and about the consequent violation of the human rights of the Palestinian people and the negative impact on their socio-economic situation, which remains that of a dire humanitarian crisis, particularly in the Gaza Strip,

Concerned in particular about the continued establishment of Israeli checkpoints in the Occupied Palestinian Territory, including East Jerusalem, and the transformation of several of these checkpoints into structures akin to permanent border crossings inside the Occupied Palestinian Territory, which are severely impairing the territorial contiguity of the Territory and undermining efforts and aid aimed at rehabilitating and developing the Palestinian economy, adversely affecting other aspects of the socio-economic conditions of the Palestinian people,

Expressing deep concern that thousands of Palestinians, including hundreds of children and women, continue to be held in Israeli prisons or detention centres under harsh conditions that impair their well-being, and expressing concern about the ill-treatment and harassment of any Palestinian prisoners and all reports of torture,

Convinced of the need for an international presence to monitor the situation, to contribute to ending the violence and protecting the Palestinian civilian population and to help the parties implement the agreements reached, and, in this regard, recalling the positive contribution of the Temporary International Presence in Hebron,

Emphasizing the right of all people in the region to the enjoyment of human rights as enshrined in the international human rights covenants,

1. *Reiterates* that all measures and actions taken by Israel, the occupying Power, in the Occupied Palestinian Territory, including East Jerusalem, in violation of the relevant provisions of the Geneva Convention relative to the Protection of Civilian Persons in Time of War, of 12 August 1949, and contrary to the relevant resolutions of the Security Council, are illegal and have no validity;

2. *Demands* that Israel, the occupying Power, cease all practices and actions that violate the human rights of the Palestinian people, including the killing and injury of civilians, and that it respect human rights law and comply with its legal obligations in this regard;

3. *Also demands* that Israel, the occupying Power, comply fully with the provisions of the Fourth Geneva Convention of 1949 and cease immediately all measures and actions taken in violation and in breach of the Convention, including all of its settlement activities and the construction of the wall in the Occupied Palestinian Territory, including in and around East Jerusalem, which, inter alia, gravely and detrimentally impact the human rights of the Palestinian people;

4. *Condemns* all acts of violence, including all acts of terror, provocation, incitement and destruction, especially the excessive use of force by the Israeli occupying forces against Palestinian civilians, particularly in the Gaza Strip in the recent period, which have caused extensive loss of life and vast numbers of injuries, including among children, massive damage and destruction to homes, properties, vital infrastructure and public institutions, including hospitals, schools and United Nations facilities, and agricultural lands, and internal displacement of civilians;

5. *Expresses grave concern* at the firing of rockets against Israeli civilian areas resulting in loss of life and injury;

6. *Reiterates its demand* for the full implementation of Security Council resolution 1860(2009);

7. *Calls upon* Israel, the occupying Power, to comply strictly with its obligations under international law, including international humanitarian law, with respect to the alteration of the character, status and demographic composition of the Occupied Palestinian Territory, including East Jerusalem;

8. *Demands* that Israel, the occupying Power, comply with its legal obligations under international law, as mentioned in the advisory opinion rendered on 9 July 2004 by the International Court of Justice and as demanded in resolutions ES-10/15 of 20 July 2004 and ES-10/13 of 21 October 2003, and that it immediately cease the construction of the wall in the Occupied Palestinian Territory, including in and around East Jerusalem, dismantle forthwith the structure situated therein, repeal or render ineffective all legislative and regulatory acts relating thereto, and make reparation for all damage caused by the construction of the wall, which has gravely impacted the human rights and the socio-economic living conditions of the Palestinian people;

9. *Reiterates* the need for respect for the territorial unity, contiguity and integrity of all of the Occupied Palestinian Territory and for guarantees of the freedom of movement of persons and goods within the Palestinian territory, including movement into and from East Jerusalem, into and from the Gaza Strip, and to and from the outside world;

10. *Calls upon* Israel, the occupying Power, to cease its imposition of prolonged closures and economic and movement restrictions, including those amounting to a blockade on the Gaza Strip, and, in this regard, to fully implement the Agreement on Movement and Access and the Agreed Principles for the Rafah Crossing, both of 15 November 2005;

11. *Urges* Member States to continue to provide emergency assistance to the Palestinian people to alleviate the financial crisis and the dire socio-economic and humanitarian situation, particularly in the Gaza Strip;

12. *Emphasizes* the need to preserve and develop the Palestinian institutions and infrastructure for the provision of vital public services to the Palestinian civilian population and the promotion of human rights, including civil, political, economic, social and cultural rights;

13. *Requests* the Secretary-General to report to the General Assembly at its sixty-fifth session on the implementation of the present resolution.

RECORDED VOTE ON RESOLUTION 64/94:

In favour: Afghanistan, Albania, Algeria, Andorra, Angola, Antigua and Barbuda, Argentina, Armenia, Austria, Azerbaijan, Bahamas, Bahrain, Bangladesh, Barbados, Belarus, Belgium, Belize, Benin, Bhutan, Bolivia, Bosnia and Herzegovina, Botswana, Brazil, Brunei Darussalam, Bulgaria, Burundi, Cape Verde, Chile, China, Colombia, Comoros, Congo, Costa Rica, Croatia, Cuba, Cyprus, Czech Republic, Democratic People's Republic of Korea, Denmark, Djibouti, Dominica, Dominican Republic, Ecuador, Egypt, El Salvador, Eritrea, Estonia, Ethiopia, Finland, France, Gambia, Georgia, Germany, Ghana, Greece, Grenada, Guatemala, Guinea, Guinea-Bissau, Guyana, Honduras, Hungary, Iceland, India, Indonesia, Iran, Iraq, Ireland, Italy, Jamaica, Japan, Jordan, Kazakhstan, Kenya, Kuwait,

Kyrgyzstan, Lao People's Democratic Republic, Latvia, Lebanon, Lesotho, Libyan Arab Jamahiriya, Liechtenstein, Lithuania, Luxembourg, Madagascar, Malawi, Malaysia, Maldives, Mali, Malta, Mauritania, Mauritius, Mexico, Moldova, Monaco, Mongolia, Montenegro, Morocco, Mozambique, Myanmar, Namibia, Nepal, Netherlands, New Zealand, Nicaragua, Niger, Nigeria, Norway, Oman, Pakistan, Papua New Guinea, Paraguay, Peru, Philippines, Poland, Portugal, Qatar, Republic of Korea, Romania, Russian Federation, Saint Lucia, Saint Vincent and the Grenadines, Samoa, San Marino, Saudi Arabia, Senegal, Serbia, Sierra Leone, Singapore, Slovakia, Slovenia, Solomon Islands, Somalia, South Africa, Spain, Sri Lanka, Sudan, Suriname, Swaziland, Sweden, Switzerland, Syrian Arab Republic, Tajikistan, Thailand, The former Yugoslav Republic of Macedonia, Timor-Leste, Togo, Trinidad and Tobago, Tunisia, Turkey, Turkmenistan, Ukraine, United Arab Emirates, United Kingdom, United Republic of Tanzania, Uruguay, Uzbekistan, Venezuela, Viet Nam, Yemen, Zambia, Zimbabwe.

Against: Australia, Canada, Israel, Marshall Islands, Micronesia, Nauru, Palau, Panama, United States.

Abstaining: Cameroon, Côte d'Ivoire, Fiji, Liberia, Vanuatu.

Work of Special Committee

Report of Secretary-General. On 8 September [A/64/340], the Secretary-General reported to the General Assembly on the implementation of its resolution 63/95 [YUN 2008, p. 507] as it concerned the work of the Special Committee and that of the United Nations Department of Public Information (DPI) in support of the Committee's efforts from August 2008 to July 2009. The Special Committee was supported by various UN agencies in the implementation of its mandate, specifically OHCHR and the United Nations Resident Coordinators in Egypt, Jordan and the Syrian Arab Republic in the organization of a mission and by offering in situ support. DPI continued to disseminate information on the Special Committee's work through various means, ensuring that such information was available to global audiences in the six official UN languages. The Department held its annual training programme for 10 Palestinian journalists (Washington, D.C., and Geneva, 27 October–5 December 2008). The travelling version of "The Question of Palestine and the United Nations" exhibit, which addressed the issue of human rights in the Occupied Palestinian Territory, was produced in Arabic, English and Spanish. The Spanish version was exhibited at the United Nations Latin American and Caribbean Meeting in Support of Israeli-Palestinian Peace and at the United Nations Public Forum in Support of Israeli-Palestinian Peace, both held in Santiago, Chile (11–13 December 2008).

GENERAL ASSEMBLY ACTION

On 10 December [meeting 62], the General Assembly, on the recommendation of the Fourth Committee [A/64/406], adopted **resolution 64/91** by recorded vote (92-9-74) [agenda item 32].

Work of the Special Committee to Investigate Israeli Practices Affecting the Human Rights of the Palestinian People and Other Arabs of the Occupied Territories

The General Assembly,

Guided by the purposes and principles of the Charter of the United Nations,

Guided also by international humanitarian law, in particular the Geneva Convention relative to the Protection of Civilian Persons in Time of War of 12 August 1949, as well as international standards of human rights, in particular the Universal Declaration of Human Rights and the International Covenants on Human Rights,

Recalling its relevant resolutions, including resolutions 2443(XXIII) of 19 December 1968 and 63/95 of 5 December 2008, and the relevant resolutions of the Commission on Human Rights and the Human Rights Council, including the resolution adopted by the Council at its twelfth special session on 16 October 2009,

Recalling also the relevant resolutions of the Security Council,

Taking into account the advisory opinion rendered on 9 July 2004 by the International Court of Justice on the *Legal Consequences of the Construction of a Wall in the Occupied Palestinian Territory*, and recalling in this regard General Assembly resolution ES-10/15 of 20 July 2004,

Convinced that occupation itself represents a gross and grave violation of human rights,

Gravely concerned about the continuing detrimental impact of the events that have taken place since 28 September 2000, including the excessive use of force by the Israeli occupying forces against Palestinian civilians, resulting in thousands of deaths and injuries, the widespread destruction of property and vital infrastructure, the internal displacement of civilians, the imposition of collective punishment measures, particularly against the civilian population in the Gaza Strip, and the detention and imprisonment of thousands of Palestinians,

Gravely concerned in particular by reports regarding serious human rights violations and grave breaches of international humanitarian law committed during the military operations in the Gaza Strip between December 2008 and January 2009, including the findings in the summary by the Secretary-General of the report of the Board of Inquiry and in the report of the United Nations Fact-Finding Mission on the Gaza Conflict, and stressing the necessity for serious follow-up by all parties to the recommendations addressed to them towards ensuring accountability and justice,

Having considered the report of the Special Committee to Investigate Israeli Practices Affecting the Human Rights of the Palestinian People and Other Arabs of the Occupied Territories and the relevant reports of the Secretary-General,

Recalling the Declaration of Principles on Interim Self-Government Arrangements of 13 September 1993 and the subsequent implementation agreements between the Palestinian and Israeli sides,

Stressing the urgency of bringing a complete end to the Israeli occupation that began in 1967 and thus an end to the violation of the human rights of the Palestinian people, and recalling in this regard its resolution 58/292 of 6 May 2004,

1. *Commends* the Special Committee to Investigate Israeli Practices Affecting the Human Rights of the Palestinian People and Other Arabs of the Occupied Territories for its efforts in performing the tasks assigned to it by the General Assembly and for its impartiality;

2. *Reiterates its demand* that Israel, the occupying Power, cooperate, in accordance with its obligations as a State Member of the United Nations, with the Special Committee in implementing its mandate;

3. *Deplores* those policies and practices of Israel that violate the human rights of the Palestinian people and other Arabs of the occupied territories, as reflected in the report of the Special Committee covering the reporting period;

4. *Expresses grave concern* about the critical situation in the Occupied Palestinian Territory, including East Jerusalem, particularly in the Gaza Strip, as a result of unlawful Israeli practices and measures, and especially condemns and calls for the immediate cessation of all illegal Israeli settlement activities and the construction of the wall, as well as the excessive and indiscriminate use of force against the civilian population, the destruction and confiscation of properties, measures of collective punishment, and the detention and imprisonment of thousands of civilians;

5. *Requests* the Special Committee, pending complete termination of the Israeli occupation, to continue to investigate Israeli policies and practices in the Occupied Palestinian Territory, including East Jerusalem, and other Arab territories occupied by Israel since 1967, especially Israeli violations of the Geneva Convention relative to the Protection of Civilian Persons in Time of War of 12 August 1949, and to consult, as appropriate, with the International Committee of the Red Cross according to its regulations in order to ensure that the welfare and human rights of the peoples of the occupied territories are safeguarded and to report to the Secretary-General as soon as possible and whenever the need arises thereafter;

6. *Also requests* the Special Committee to submit regularly to the Secretary-General periodic reports on the current situation in the Occupied Palestinian Territory, including East Jerusalem;

7. *Further requests* the Special Committee to continue to investigate the treatment of the thousands of prisoners and detainees in the Occupied Palestinian Territory, including East Jerusalem, and other Arab territories occupied by Israel since 1967;

8. *Requests* the Secretary-General:

(a) To provide the Special Committee with all necessary facilities, including those required for its visits to the occupied territories, so that it may investigate the Israeli policies and practices referred to in the present resolution;

(b) To continue to make available such staff as may be necessary to assist the Special Committee in the performance of its tasks;

(c) To circulate regularly to Member States the periodic reports mentioned in paragraph 6 above;

(d) To ensure the widest circulation of the reports of the Special Committee and of information regarding its activities and findings, by all means available, through the Department of Public Information of the Secretariat and, where necessary, to reprint those reports of the Special Committee that are no longer available;

(e) To report to the General Assembly at its sixty-fifth session on the tasks entrusted to him in the present resolution;

9. *Decides* to include in the provisional agenda of its sixty-fifth session the item entitled "Report of the Special Committee to Investigate Israeli Practices Affecting the Human Rights of the Palestinian People and Other Arabs of the Occupied Territories".

RECORDED VOTE ON RESOLUTION 64/91:

In favour: Afghanistan, Algeria, Angola, Antigua and Barbuda, Armenia, Azerbaijan, Bahrain, Bangladesh, Barbados, Belarus, Belize, Benin, Bhutan, Bolivia, Brazil, Brunei Darussalam, Chile, China, Comoros, Congo, Cuba, Democratic People's Republic of Korea, Djibouti, Dominica, Dominican Republic, Ecuador, Egypt, Eritrea, Gambia, Ghana, Grenada, Guinea, Guinea-Bissau, Guyana, India, Indonesia, Iran, Iraq, Jamaica, Jordan, Kenya, Kuwait, Kyrgyzstan, Lao People's Democratic Republic, Lebanon, Lesotho, Libyan Arab Jamahiriya, Malawi, Malaysia, Maldives, Mali, Mauritania, Mauritius, Morocco, Mozambique, Myanmar, Namibia, Nepal, Nicaragua, Niger, Nigeria, Oman, Pakistan, Qatar, Saint Lucia, Saint Vincent and the Grenadines, Saudi Arabia, Senegal, Sierra Leone, Singapore, Solomon Islands, Somalia, South Africa, Sri Lanka, Sudan, Suriname, Swaziland, Syrian Arab Republic, Tajikistan, Togo, Trinidad and Tobago, Tunisia, Turkey, Turkmenistan, United Arab Emirates, United Republic of Tanzania, Uzbekistan, Venezuela, Viet Nam, Yemen, Zambia, Zimbabwe.

Against: Australia, Canada, Israel, Marshall Islands, Micronesia, Nauru, Palau, Panama, United States.

Abstaining: Albania, Andorra, Argentina, Austria, Bahamas, Belgium, Bosnia and Herzegovina, Botswana, Bulgaria, Burundi, Cameroon, Colombia, Costa Rica, Côte d'Ivoire, Croatia, Cyprus, Czech Republic, Denmark, El Salvador, Estonia, Ethiopia, Fiji, Finland, France, Georgia, Germany, Greece, Guatemala, Honduras, Hungary, Iceland, Ireland, Italy, Japan, Kazakhstan, Latvia, Liberia, Liechtenstein, Lithuania, Luxembourg, Malta, Mexico, Moldova, Monaco, Mongolia, Montenegro, Netherlands, New Zealand, Norway, Papua New Guinea, Paraguay, Peru, Philippines, Poland, Portugal, Republic of Korea, Romania, Russian Federation, Samoa, San Marino, Serbia, Slovakia, Slovenia, Spain, Sweden, Switzerland, Thailand, The former Yugoslav Republic of Macedonia, Timor-Leste, Tonga, Ukraine, United Kingdom, Uruguay, Vanuatu.

Economic and social situation

ESCWA report. By a 7 May note [A/64/77-E/2009/13], the Secretary-General submitted a report on the economic and social repercussions of the Israeli occupation on the living conditions of the Palestinian people in the Occupied Palestinian Territory, including East Jerusalem, and of the Arab population in the occupied Syrian Golan, prepared by the Economic and Social Commission for Western Asia (ESCWA), in accordance with Economic and Social Council resolution 2008/31 [YUN 2008, p. 509] and Assembly resolution 63/201 [ibid., p. 511].

The report noted that the occupation of Palestinian territory, including East Jerusalem, the use of arbitrary detention, the disproportionate use of force, house demolitions, severe mobility restrictions, lack of building permits and closure policies continued to intensify the economic and social hardship in the Occupied Palestinian Territory. Internal Palestinian conflict had also continued to cause casualties and disrupted the delivery of essential services to the population. Attacks by Palestinian militants and the launching of rockets into Israeli cities from the Gaza Strip continued in 2008, as did Israeli military operations. The blockade imposed by Israel on the Gaza Strip led to rapidly deteriorating conditions, a near collapse of the private sector and shortages of essentials such as food, electricity and fuel. The Israeli closure system remained a primary cause of poverty and humanitarian crisis in the Territory and restricted Palestinian access to natural resources, including land, basic social services, employment, markets and social and religious networks. Nevertheless, the PA managed to make some progress in areas such as security, public financial management, local public infrastructure and health and education services. While both the Security Council and the General Assembly had declared that Israel's decision to annex the Golan was null and void, Israel had continued its expansion of settlements and its curtailment of the rights of the Syrian residents of the occupied Syrian Golan.

The Economic and Social Council took note of the report by **decision 2009/263** of 31 July.

ECONOMIC AND SOCIAL COUNCIL ACTION

On 31 July [meeting 45], the Economic and Social Council adopted **resolution 2009/34** [draft: E/2009/L.42] by roll-call vote (25-5-17) [agenda item 11].

Economic and social repercussions of the Israeli occupation on the living conditions of the Palestinian people in the Occupied Palestinian Territory, including East Jerusalem, and the Arab population in the occupied Syrian Golan

The Economic and Social Council,

Recalling General Assembly resolution 63/201 of 19 December 2008,

Recalling also its resolution 2008/31 of 25 July 2008,

Guided by the principles of the Charter of the United Nations affirming the inadmissibility of the acquisition of territory by force, and recalling relevant Security Council resolutions, including resolutions 242(1967) of 22 November 1967, 252(1968) of 21 May 1968, 338(1973) of 22 October 1973, 465(1980) of 1 March 1980 and 497(1981) of 17 December 1981,

Recalling the resolutions of the tenth emergency special session of the General Assembly, including resolutions ES-10/13 of 21 October 2003, ES-10/14 of 8 December 2003, ES-10/15 of 20 July 2004 and ES-10/17 of 15 December 2006,

Reaffirming the applicability of the Geneva Convention relative to the Protection of Civilian Persons in Time of War, of 12 August 1949, to the Occupied Palestinian Territory, including East Jerusalem, and to other Arab territories occupied by Israel since 1967,

Recalling the International Covenant on Civil and Political Rights, the International Covenant on Economic, Social and Cultural Rights and the Convention on the Rights of the Child, and affirming that these human rights instruments must be respected in the Occupied Palestinian Territory, including East Jerusalem, as well as in the occupied Syrian Golan,

Stressing the importance of the revival of the Middle East peace process on the basis of Security Council resolutions 242(1967), 338(1973), 425(1978) of 19 March 1978, 1397(2002) of 12 March 2002, 1515(2003) of 19 November 2003, 1544(2004) of 19 May 2004 and 1850(2008) of 16 December 2008, the principle of land for peace and the Arab Peace Initiative, as affirmed at the twenty-first session of the Council of the League of Arab States, held at summit level in Doha on 30 March 2009, as well as compliance with the agreements reached between the Government of Israel and the Palestine Liberation Organization, the representative of the Palestinian people,

Reaffirming the principle of the permanent sovereignty of peoples under foreign occupation over their natural resources, and expressing concern in this regard about the exploitation of natural resources by Israel, the occupying Power, in the Occupied Palestinian Territory, including East Jerusalem, and in the occupied Syrian Golan,

Convinced that the Israeli occupation has gravely impeded the efforts to achieve sustainable development and a sound economic environment in the Occupied Palestinian Territory, including East Jerusalem, and in the occupied Syrian Golan, and expressing grave concern about the consequent deterioration of economic and living conditions,

Gravely concerned, in this regard, about Israel's continuation of settlement activities and other related measures in the Occupied Palestinian Territory, particularly in and around occupied East Jerusalem, as well as in the occupied Syrian Golan, in violation of international humanitarian law and relevant United Nations resolutions,

Gravely concerned also by the serious repercussions on the economic and social conditions of the Palestinian people caused by Israel's construction of the wall and its associated regime inside the Occupied Palestinian Territory, including in and around East Jerusalem, and the resulting violation of their economic and social rights, including the right to work, to health, to education, to property and to an adequate standard of living,

Recalling, in this regard, the advisory opinion rendered on 9 July 2004 by the International Court of Justice on the *Legal Consequences of the Construction of a Wall in the Occupied Palestinian Territory* and General Assembly resolution ES-10/15, and stressing the need to comply with the obligations mentioned therein,

Expressing grave concern at the extensive destruction by Israel, the occupying Power, of properties, including homes, economic institutions, agricultural lands and orchards in the Occupied Palestinian Territory, including East Jerusalem, and, in particular, in connection with its construction of the wall, contrary to international law, in the Occupied Palestinian Territory, including in and around East Jerusalem,

Expressing grave concern also over the continued policy of home demolitions and displacement of the population in and around occupied East Jerusalem in particular, as well as over measures to further isolate the city from its natural Palestinian environs, including through the accelerated construction of settlements, the construction of the wall and the imposition of checkpoints, which have seriously exacerbated the already dire socio-economic situation being faced by the Palestinian population,

Expressing grave concern further about continuing Israeli military operations and the continuing Israeli policy of closures and severe restrictions on the movement of persons and goods, including humanitarian personnel and food, medical, fuel and other essential supplies, via the imposition of crossing closures, checkpoints and a permit regime throughout the Occupied Palestinian Territory, including East Jerusalem, and the consequent negative impact on the socio-economic situation of the Palestinian people, which remains that of dire humanitarian crisis, particularly in the Gaza Strip, where grave hardships continue to mount as a result of Israel's imposition of a blockade and siege as collective punishment of the entire civilian population,

Deploring the Israeli military aggression against the Gaza Strip that was launched on 27 December 2008, which caused heavy casualties among civilians, including hundreds of children and women, and widespread damage to homes, vital infrastructure, hospitals, schools and several United Nations facilities, gravely impacting the provision of vital health and social services to Palestinian women and their families, and in this regard calling for the expeditious commencement of the reconstruction process in the Gaza Strip with the assistance of donor countries, including the disbursement of funds pledged at the International Conference in Support of the Palestinian Economy for the Reconstruction of Gaza, held in Sharm el-Sheikh, Egypt, on 2 March 2009,

Gravely concerned by various reports of the United Nations and the specialized agencies regarding the almost total aid dependency caused by prolonged border closures, the inordinate rates of unemployment, the widespread poverty and the severe humanitarian hardships, including food insecurity and rising health-related problems, including high levels of malnutrition, among the Palestinian people, especially children, in the Occupied Palestinian Territory, including East Jerusalem,

Expressing grave concern at the increasing number of deaths and injuries among civilians, including children and women, and emphasizing that the Palestinian civilian population must be protected in accordance with international humanitarian law,

Emphasizing the importance of the safety and well-being of all civilians, and calling for the cessation of all acts of violence, including all acts of terror, provocation, incitement and destruction, and all firing of rockets,

Conscious of the urgent need for the reconstruction and development of the economic and social infrastructure of the Occupied Palestinian Territory, including East Jerusalem, as well as the urgent need to address the dire humanitarian crisis facing the Palestinian people,

Commending the important work being done by the United Nations, the specialized agencies and the donor community in support of the economic and social development of the Palestinian people, as well as the assistance being provided in the humanitarian field,

Recognizing the efforts being undertaken by the Palestinian Authority, with international support, to rebuild, reform and strengthen its damaged institutions and promote good governance, and emphasizing the need to preserve the Palestinian institutions and infrastructure and to ameliorate economic and social conditions,

Stressing the importance of national unity among the Palestinian people, and emphasizing the need for the respect and preservation of the territorial integrity and unity of the Occupied Palestinian Territory, including East Jerusalem,

Calling upon both parties to fulfil their obligations under the road map in cooperation with the Quartet,

1. *Calls for* the lifting of all mobility restrictions imposed on the Palestinian people, including those arising from ongoing Israeli military operations and the multilayered closures system, and also calls for other urgent measures to be taken to alleviate the desperate humanitarian situation in the Occupied Palestinian Territory, especially in the Gaza Strip;

2. *Stresses* the need to preserve the national unity and the territorial integrity of the Occupied Palestinian Territory, including East Jerusalem, and to guarantee the freedom of movement of persons and goods throughout the Occupied Palestinian Territory, including East Jerusalem, as well as to and from the outside world;

3. *Demands* that Israel comply with the Protocol on Economic Relations between the Government of Israel and the Palestine Liberation Organization, signed in Paris on 29 April 1994;

4. *Calls upon* Israel to restore and replace civilian properties, vital infrastructure, agricultural lands and governmental institutions that have been damaged or destroyed as a result of its military operations in the Occupied Palestinian Territory;

5. *Reiterates* the call for the full implementation of the Agreement on Movement and Access of 15 November 2005, particularly the urgent and uninterrupted reopening of all crossings into the Gaza Strip, including the Rafah and Karni crossings, which is crucial to ensuring the passage of foodstuffs and essential supplies, including construction materials and adequate fuel supplies, as well as the unhindered access of the United Nations and related agencies to and within the Occupied Palestinian Territory;

6. *Calls upon* all parties to respect the rules of international humanitarian law and to refrain from violence against the civilian population, in accordance with the Geneva Convention relative to the Protection of Civilian Persons in Time of War, of 12 August 1949;

7. *Reaffirms* the inalienable right of the Palestinian people and the Arab population of the occupied Syrian Golan to all their natural and economic resources, and calls upon Israel, the occupying Power, not to exploit, endanger or cause loss or depletion of these resources;

8. *Calls upon* Israel, the occupying Power, to cease its destruction of homes and properties, economic institutions and agricultural lands and orchards in the Occupied Palestinian Territory, including East Jerusalem, as well as in the occupied Syrian Golan;

9. *Also calls upon* Israel, the occupying Power, to end immediately its exploitation of natural resources, including water and mining resources, and to cease the dumping of all kinds of waste materials in the Occupied Palestinian Territory, including East Jerusalem, and in the occupied Syrian Golan, activities which gravely threaten their natural resources, namely, their water and land resources, and present a serious environmental hazard and health threat to their civilian populations, and also calls upon Israel, the occupying Power, to remove all obstacles that obstruct the implementation of critical environmental projects, including the sewage treatment plants in the Gaza Strip;

10. *Reaffirms* that the construction and expansion of Israeli settlements and related infrastructure in the Occupied Palestinian Territory, including East Jerusalem, and the occupied Syrian Golan are illegal and constitute a major obstacle to economic and social development, and calls for the full cessation of all settlement and settlement-related activity, including all measures aimed at advancing the illegal settlement campaign, in compliance with relevant Security Council resolutions and international law, including the Geneva Convention relative to the Protection of Civilian Persons in Time of War;

11. *Also reaffirms* that Israel's ongoing construction of the wall in the Occupied Palestinian Territory, including in and around East Jerusalem, is contrary to international law and is isolating East Jerusalem, fragmenting the West Bank and seriously debilitating the economic and social development of the Palestinian people, and calls in this regard for full compliance with the legal obligations mentioned in the advisory opinion rendered on 9 July 2004 by the International Court of Justice and in General Assembly resolution ES-10/15;

12. *Calls upon* Israel to comply with the provisions of the Geneva Convention relative to the Protection of Civilian Persons in Time of War and to facilitate the visits of Syrian citizens of the occupied Syrian Golan whose family members reside in their mother homeland, the Syrian Arab Republic, via the Qunaitra entrance;

13. *Emphasizes* the importance of the work of United Nations organizations and agencies and of the United Nations Special Coordinator for the Middle East Peace Process and Personal Representative of the Secretary-General to the Palestine Liberation Organization and the Palestinian Authority;

14. *Reiterates* the importance of the revival of the peace process on the basis of Security Council resolutions 242(1967), 338(1973), 425(1978), 1397(2002), 1515(2003), 1544(2004) and 1850(2008), the Madrid Conference, the principle of land for peace and the Arab Peace Initiative, as well as compliance with the agreements reached between the Government of Israel and the Palestine Liberation Organization, the representative of the Palestinian people, in order to pave the way for the establishment of an independent Palestinian State and the achievement of a just, lasting and comprehensive peace settlement;

15. *Requests* the Secretary-General to submit to the General Assembly at its sixty-fourth session, through the Economic and Social Council, a report on the implementation of the present resolution and to continue to include in the report of the United Nations Special Coordinator an update on the living conditions of the Palestinian people, in collaboration with relevant United Nations agencies;

16. *Decides* to include the item entitled "Economic and social repercussions of the Israeli occupation on the living conditions of the Palestinian people in the Occupied Palestinian Territory, including East Jerusalem, and the Arab population in the occupied Syrian Golan" in the agenda of its substantive session of 2010.

ROLL-CALL VOTE ON RESOLUTION 2009/34:

In favour: Algeria, Barbados, Belarus, Bolivia, Brazil, China, El Salvador, Guatemala, India, Indonesia, Iraq, Malaysia, Mauritius, Morocco, Mozambique, Namibia, Pakistan, Peru, Philippines, Russian Federation, Saint Lucia, Saudi Arabia, Sudan, Uruguay, Venezuela.

Against: Canada, Germany, Netherlands, Poland, United States.

Abstaining: Côte d'Ivoire, Estonia, France, Greece, Japan, Kazakhstan, Liechtenstein, Luxembourg, Malawi, Moldova, New Zealand, Norway, Portugal, Republic of Korea, Romania, Sweden, United Kingdom.

GENERAL ASSEMBLY ACTION

On 21 December [meeting 66], the General Assembly, on the recommendation of the Second (Economic and Financial) Committee [A/64/416], adopted **resolution 64/185** by recorded vote (165-8-7) [agenda item 40].

Permanent sovereignty of the Palestinian people in the Occupied Palestinian Territory, including East Jerusalem, and of the Arab population in the occupied Syrian Golan over their natural resources

The General Assembly,

Recalling its resolution 63/201 of 19 December 2008, and taking note of Economic and Social Council resolution 2009/34 of 31 July 2009,

Recalling also its resolutions 58/292 of 6 May 2004 and 59/251 of 22 December 2004,

Reaffirming the principle of the permanent sovereignty of peoples under foreign occupation over their natural resources,

Guided by the principles of the Charter of the United Nations, affirming the inadmissibility of the acquisition of territory by force, and recalling relevant Security Council resolutions, including resolutions 242(1967) of 22 November 1967, 465(1980) of 1 March 1980 and 497(1981) of 17 December 1981,

Recalling its resolution 2625(XXV) of 24 October 1970,

Reaffirming the applicability of the Geneva Convention relative to the Protection of Civilian Persons in Time of War, of 12 August 1949, to the Occupied Palestinian Territory, including East Jerusalem, and other Arab territories occupied by Israel since 1967,

Recalling, in this regard, the International Covenant on Civil and Political Rights and the International Covenant on Economic, Social and Cultural Rights, and affirming that these human rights instruments must be respected in the Occupied Palestinian Territory, including East Jerusalem, as well as in the occupied Syrian Golan,

Recalling also the advisory opinion rendered on 9 July 2004 by the International Court of Justice on the *Legal Consequences of the Construction of a Wall in the Occupied Palestinian Territory*, and recalling further its resolutions ES-10/15 of 20 July 2004 and ES-10/17 of 15 December 2006,

Expressing its concern at the exploitation by Israel, the occupying Power, of the natural resources of the Occupied Palestinian Territory, including East Jerusalem, and other Arab territories occupied by Israel since 1967,

Expressing its grave concern at the extensive destruction by Israel, the occupying Power, of agricultural land and orchards in the Occupied Palestinian Territory, including the uprooting of a vast number of fruit-bearing trees and the destruction of farms and greenhouses,

Expressing its concern at the widespread destruction caused by Israel, the occupying Power, to vital infrastructure, including water pipelines and sewage networks, in the Occupied Palestinian Territory, in particular in the Gaza Strip in the recent period, which, inter alia, pollutes the environment and negatively affects the water supply and other natural resources of the Palestinian people,

Taking note, in this regard, of the recent report by the United Nations Environment Programme regarding the grave environmental situation in the Gaza Strip, and stressing the need for follow-up to the recommendations therein,

Aware of the detrimental impact of the Israeli settlements on Palestinian and other Arab natural resources, especially as a result of the confiscation of land and the forced diversion of water resources, and of the dire socio-economic consequences in this regard,

Aware also of the detrimental impact on Palestinian natural resources being caused by the unlawful construction of the wall by Israel, the occupying Power, in the Occupied Palestinian Territory, including in and around East Jerusalem, and of its grave effect as well on the economic and social conditions of the Palestinian people,

Reaffirming the need for the resumption and advancement of negotiations within the Middle East peace process, on the basis of Security Council resolutions 242(1967), 338(1973) of 22 October 1973, 425(1978) of 19 March 1978 and 1397(2002) of 12 March 2002, the principle of land for peace, the Arab Peace Initiative, and the Quartet performance-based road map to a permanent two-State solution to the Israeli-Palestinian conflict, as endorsed by the Security Council in its resolution 1515(2003) of 19 November 2003 and supported by the Council in its resolution 1850(2008) of 16 December 2008, for the achievement of a final settlement on all tracks,

Noting the Israeli withdrawal from within the Gaza Strip and parts of the northern West Bank and the importance of the dismantlement of settlements therein in the context of the road map,

Stressing the need for respect and preservation of the territorial unity, contiguity and integrity of all of the Occupied Palestinian Territory, including East Jerusalem,

Recalling the need to end all acts of violence, including acts of terror, provocation, incitement and destruction,

Taking note of the note by the Secretary-General transmitting the report prepared by the Economic and Social Commission for Western Asia on the economic and social repercussions of the Israeli occupation on the living conditions of the Palestinian people in the Occupied Palestinian Territory, including East Jerusalem, and of the Arab population in the occupied Syrian Golan,

1. *Reaffirms* the inalienable rights of the Palestinian people and the population of the occupied Syrian Golan over their natural resources, including land and water;

2. *Demands* that Israel, the occupying Power, cease the exploitation, damage, cause of loss or depletion of, or endangerment of the natural resources in the Occupied Palestinian Territory, including East Jerusalem, and in the occupied Syrian Golan;

3. *Recognizes* the right of the Palestinian people to claim restitution as a result of any exploitation, damage, loss or depletion, or endangerment of their natural resources resulting from illegal measures taken by Israel, the occupying Power, in the Occupied Palestinian Territory, including East Jerusalem, and expresses the hope that this issue will be dealt with in the framework of the final status negotiations between the Palestinian and Israeli sides;

4. *Stresses* that the wall being constructed by Israel in the Occupied Palestinian Territory, including in and around East Jerusalem, is contrary to international law and is seriously depriving the Palestinian people of their natural resources, and calls in this regard for full compliance with the legal obligations mentioned in the 9 July 2004 advisory opinion of the International Court of Justice and in resolution ES-10/15;

5. *Calls upon* Israel, the occupying Power, to comply strictly with its obligations under international law, including international humanitarian law, with respect to the alteration of the character and status of the Occupied Palestinian Territory, including East Jerusalem;

6. *Also calls upon* Israel, the occupying Power, to cease all actions harming the environment, including the dumping of all kinds of waste materials in the Occupied Palestinian Territory, including East Jerusalem, and in the occupied Syrian Golan, which gravely threaten their natural resources, namely water and land resources, and which pose an environmental, sanitation and health threat to the civilian populations;

7. *Further calls upon* Israel to cease its destruction of vital infrastructure, including water pipelines and sewage networks, which, inter alia, has a negative impact on the natural resources of the Palestinian people;

8. *Requests* the Secretary-General to report to it at its sixty-fifth session on the implementation of the present resolution, and decides to include in the provisional agenda of its sixty-fifth session the item entitled "Permanent sovereignty of the Palestinian people in the Occupied Palestinian Territory, including East Jerusalem, and of the Arab population in the occupied Syrian Golan over their natural resources".

RECORDED VOTE ON RESOLUTION 64/185:

In favour: Afghanistan, Albania, Algeria, Andorra, Angola, Antigua and Barbuda, Argentina, Armenia, Austria, Azerbaijan, Bahamas, Bahrain, Bangladesh, Barbados, Belarus, Belgium, Belize, Benin, Bhutan, Bolivia, Bosnia and Herzegovina, Brazil, Brunei Darussalam, Bulgaria, Burkina Faso, Burundi, Cambodia, Cape Verde, Central African Republic, Chad, Chile, China, Colombia, Comoros, Congo, Costa Rica, Croatia, Cuba, Cyprus, Czech Republic, Democratic People's Republic of Korea, Denmark, Djibouti, Dominica, Dominican Republic, Ecuador, Egypt, El Salvador, Eritrea, Estonia,

Ethiopia, Finland, France, Gabon, Georgia, Germany, Ghana, Greece, Grenada, Guatemala, Guinea, Guinea-Bissau, Guyana, Haiti, Hungary, Iceland, India, Indonesia, Iran, Iraq, Ireland, Italy, Jamaica, Japan, Jordan, Kazakhstan, Kenya, Kuwait, Kyrgyzstan, Lao People's Democratic Republic, Latvia, Lebanon, Lesotho, Libyan Arab Jamahiriya, Liechtenstein, Lithuania, Luxembourg, Madagascar, Malawi, Malaysia, Maldives, Mali, Malta, Mauritania, Mauritius, Mexico, Moldova, Monaco, Mongolia, Montenegro, Morocco, Mozambique, Myanmar, Namibia, Nepal, Netherlands, New Zealand, Nicaragua, Niger, Nigeria, Norway, Oman, Pakistan, Paraguay, Peru, Philippines, Poland, Portugal, Qatar, Republic of Korea, Romania, Russian Federation, Rwanda, Saint Lucia, Saint Vincent and the Grenadines, Samoa, San Marino, Saudi Arabia, Senegal, Serbia, Singapore, Slovakia, Slovenia, Solomon Islands, Somalia, South Africa, Spain, Sri Lanka, Sudan, Suriname, Swaziland, Sweden, Switzerland, Syrian Arab Republic, Thailand, The former Yugoslav Republic of Macedonia, Timor-Leste, Togo, Trinidad and Tobago, Tunisia, Turkey, Turkmenistan, Uganda, Ukraine, United Arab Emirates, United Kingdom, United Republic of Tanzania, Uruguay, Uzbekistan, Venezuela, Viet Nam, Yemen, Zambia, Zimbabwe.

Against: Australia, Canada, Israel, Marshall Islands, Micronesia, Nauru, Palau, United States.

Abstaining: Cameroon, Côte d'Ivoire, Fiji, Panama, Papua New Guinea, Tonga, Tuvalu.

Fourth Geneva Convention

The applicability of the 1949 Geneva Convention relative to the Protection of Civilian Persons in Time of War (Fourth Geneva Convention) to the Israeli-occupied territories was reaffirmed during the year by the General Assembly and several other United Nations bodies, including the Special Committee on Israeli Practices.

Report of Secretary-General. In a 27 August report [A/64/332], the Secretary-General informed the General Assembly that Israel had not replied to his request for information on steps taken or envisaged to implement Assembly resolution 63/96 [YUN 2008, p. 513] demanding that Israel accept the de jure applicability of the Fourth Geneva Convention to the Occupied Palestinian Territory, including East Jerusalem, and other Arab territories occupied since 1967, and that it comply scrupulously with its provisions. The Secretary-General had drawn the attention of all High Contracting Parties to the Convention to paragraph 3 of resolution 63/96, calling on them to ensure Israel's respect for the Convention's provisions. Five Member States (Colombia, Egypt, Qatar, Syria, Venezuela) had replied to his request for information on steps taken to implement the resolution.

GENERAL ASSEMBLY ACTION

On 10 December [meeting 62], the General Assembly, on the recommendation of the Fourth Committee [A/64/406], adopted **resolution 64/92** by recorded vote (168-6-4) [agenda item 32].

Applicability of the Geneva Convention relative to the Protection of Civilian Persons in Time of War, of 12 August 1949, to the Occupied Palestinian Territory, including East Jerusalem, and the other occupied Arab territories

The General Assembly,

Recalling its relevant resolutions, including its resolution 63/96 of 5 December 2008,

Bearing in mind the relevant resolutions of the Security Council,

Recalling the Regulations annexed to The Hague Convention IV of 1907, the Geneva Convention relative to the Protection of Civilian Persons in Time of War, of 12 August 1949, and relevant provisions of customary law, including those codified in Additional Protocol I to the four Geneva Conventions,

Having considered the report of the Special Committee to Investigate Israeli Practices Affecting the Human Rights of the Palestinian People and Other Arabs of the Occupied Territories and the relevant reports of the Secretary-General,

Considering that the promotion of respect for the obligations arising from the Charter of the United Nations and other instruments and rules of international law is among the basic purposes and principles of the United Nations,

Recalling the advisory opinion rendered on 9 July 2004 by the International Court of Justice, and also recalling General Assembly resolution ES-10/15 of 20 July 2004,

Noting in particular the Court's reply, including that the Fourth Geneva Convention is applicable in the Occupied Palestinian Territory, including East Jerusalem, and that Israel is in breach of several of the provisions of the Convention,

Recalling the Conference of High Contracting Parties to the Fourth Geneva Convention on measures to enforce the Convention in the Occupied Palestinian Territory, including East Jerusalem, held on 15 July 1999, as well as the Declaration adopted by the reconvened Conference on 5 December 2001 and the need for the parties to follow up the implementation of the Declaration,

Welcoming and encouraging the initiatives by States parties to the Convention, both individually and collectively, according to article 1 common to the four Geneva Conventions, aimed at ensuring respect for the Convention, as well as the efforts of the depositary State of the Geneva Conventions in this regard,

Stressing that Israel, the occupying Power, should comply strictly with its obligations under international law, including international humanitarian law,

1. *Reaffirms* that the Geneva Convention relative to the Protection of Civilian Persons in Time of War, of 12 August 1949, is applicable to the Occupied Palestinian Territory, including East Jerusalem, and other Arab territories occupied by Israel since 1967;

2. *Demands* that Israel accept the de jure applicability of the Convention in the Occupied Palestinian Territory, including East Jerusalem, and other Arab territories occupied by Israel since 1967, and that it comply scrupulously with the provisions of the Convention;

3. *Calls upon* all High Contracting Parties to the Convention, in accordance with article 1 common to the

four Geneva Conventions and as mentioned in the advisory opinion of the International Court of Justice of 9 July 2004, to continue to exert all efforts to ensure respect for its provisions by Israel, the occupying Power, in the Occupied Palestinian Territory, including East Jerusalem, and other Arab territories occupied by Israel since 1967;

4. *Reiterates* the need for speedy implementation of the relevant recommendations contained in the resolutions adopted by the General Assembly at its tenth emergency special session, including resolution ES-10/15, with regard to ensuring respect by Israel, the occupying Power, for the provisions of the Convention;

5. *Requests* the Secretary-General to report to the General Assembly at its sixty-fifth session on the implementation of the present resolution.

RECORDED VOTE ON RESOLUTION 64/92:

In favour: Afghanistan, Albania, Algeria, Andorra, Angola, Antigua and Barbuda, Argentina, Armenia, Australia, Austria, Azerbaijan, Bahamas, Bahrain, Bangladesh, Barbados, Belarus, Belgium, Belize, Benin, Bhutan, Bolivia, Bosnia and Herzegovina, Botswana, Brazil, Brunei Darussalam, Bulgaria, Burkina Faso, Burundi, Canada, Cape Verde, Chile, China, Colombia, Comoros, Congo, Costa Rica, Croatia, Cuba, Cyprus, Czech Republic, Democratic People's Republic of Korea, Denmark, Djibouti, Dominica, Dominican Republic, Ecuador, Egypt, El Salvador, Eritrea, Estonia, Ethiopia, Finland, France, Gambia, Georgia, Germany, Ghana, Greece, Grenada, Guatemala, Guinea, Guinea-Bissau, Guyana, Honduras, Hungary, Iceland, India, Indonesia, Iran, Iraq, Ireland, Italy, Jamaica, Japan, Jordan, Kazakhstan, Kenya, Kuwait, Kyrgyzstan, Lao People's Democratic Republic, Latvia, Lebanon, Lesotho, Liberia, Libyan Arab Jamahiriya, Liechtenstein, Lithuania, Luxembourg, Madagascar, Malawi, Malaysia, Maldives, Mali, Malta, Mauritania, Mauritius, Mexico, Moldova, Monaco, Mongolia, Montenegro, Morocco, Mozambique, Myanmar, Namibia, Nepal, Netherlands, New Zealand, Nicaragua, Niger, Nigeria, Norway, Oman, Pakistan, Panama, Papua New Guinea, Paraguay, Peru, Philippines, Poland, Portugal, Qatar, Republic of Korea, Romania, Russian Federation, Saint Lucia, Saint Vincent and the Grenadines, Samoa, San Marino, Saudi Arabia, Senegal, Serbia, Sierra Leone, Singapore, Slovakia, Slovenia, Solomon Islands, Somalia, South Africa, Spain, Sri Lanka, Sudan, Suriname, Swaziland, Sweden, Switzerland, Syrian Arab Republic, Tajikistan, Thailand, The former Yugoslav Republic of Macedonia, Timor-Leste, Togo, Tonga, Trinidad and Tobago, Tunisia, Turkey, Turkmenistan, Ukraine, United Arab Emirates, United Kingdom, United Republic of Tanzania, Uruguay, Uzbekistan, Venezuela, Viet Nam, Yemen, Zambia, Zimbabwe.

Against: Israel, Marshall Islands, Micronesia, Nauru, Palau, United States.

Abstaining: Cameroon, Côte d'Ivoire, Fiji, Vanuatu.

Issues related to Palestine

General aspects

In 2009 the General Assembly, the Committee on the Exercise of the Inalienable Rights of the Palestinian People and other bodies addressed issues related to Palestine, while several UN programmes and

agencies provided assistance to the Palestinian people. The International Day of Solidarity with the Palestinian People, celebrated annually on 29 November in accordance with Assembly resolution 32/40 B [YUN 1977, p. 304], was observed at Headquarters and at the United Nations Offices at Geneva and Vienna.

Committee on Palestinian Rights

As mandated by General Assembly resolution 63/26 [YUN 2008, p. 516], the Committee on the Exercise of the Inalienable Rights of the Palestinian People (Committee on Palestinian Rights) reviewed and reported on the Palestine question and made suggestions to the Assembly and the Security Council. It continued to mobilize the international community in support of the Palestinian people, in cooperation with UN bodies, Governments, intergovernmental and civil society organizations and others. The Committee's report to the Assembly [A/64/35] covered the period from 7 October 2008 to 6 October 2009.

The Committee condemned the Israeli military offensive in the Gaza Strip in December 2008 and January 2009, denounced the firing of rockets and mortar rounds by Palestinian militants from Gaza and expressed dismay at the continued Israeli blockade of the Gaza Strip.

The Committee was concerned over Israel's ongoing settlement activity and reiterated that the presence of settlements in the Occupied Palestinian Territory, including East Jerusalem, was illegal under international law. The Committee denounced the continued construction of the wall in the Territory, including in East Jerusalem. Five years after the ICJ issued its landmark 2004 advisory opinion confirming the illegality of the construction of the wall on Palestinian land, the ruling had remained unheeded. The Committee called for the resumption of the permanent status negotiations between Israel and the Palestinians. It was concerned that the divisions among the Palestinian factions profoundly affected the legitimate Palestinian national interests and aspirations for statehood and peace and called for efforts to reconcile their positions. The Committee commended civil society organizations for their support of the Palestinian people. It lauded the courageous advocacy actions of numerous activists, including parliamentarians, who participated in demonstrations against the wall, provided assistance to Gaza and kept their home constituencies informed about the harsh realities of life under occupation.

Throughout the year, the Committee continued to raise awareness of the question of Palestine and support for the rights of the Palestinian people and the peaceful settlement of the question of Palestine through the following international meetings and conferences: United Nations Seminar on Assistance to the Palestinian People (Cairo, Egypt, 10–11 March); United Nations International Meeting in Support of Israeli-Palestinian Peace (Nicosia, Cyprus, 6–7 May); Consultations of the Committee delegation with parliamentarians and other experts participating in the United Nations International Meeting in Support of Israeli-Palestinian Peace (Nicosia, 8 May); United Nations Asian and Pacific Meeting on the Question of Palestine (Jakarta, Indonesia, 8–9 June); United Nations Public Forum in Support of the Palestinian People (Jakarta, 10 June); United Nations International Meeting on the Question of Palestine (Geneva, 22–23 July); Consultations of the Committee delegation with civil society organizations (Geneva, 24 July).

GENERAL ASSEMBLY ACTION

On 2 December [meeting 54], the General Assembly adopted **resolution 64/16** [draft: A/64/L.20 & Add.1] by recorded vote (109-8-55) [agenda item 16].

Committee on the Exercise of the Inalienable Rights of the Palestinian People

The General Assembly,

Recalling its resolutions 181(II) of 29 November 1947, 194(III) of 11 December 1948, 3236(XXIX) of 22 November 1974, 3375(XXX) and 3376(XXX) of 10 November 1975, 31/20 of 24 November 1976 and all its subsequent relevant resolutions, including those adopted at its emergency special sessions and its resolution 63/26 of 26 November 2008,

Recalling also its resolution 58/292 of 6 May 2004,

Having considered the report of the Committee on the Exercise of the Inalienable Rights of the Palestinian People,

Recalling the mutual recognition between the Government of the State of Israel and the Palestine Liberation Organization, the representative of the Palestinian people, as well as the existing agreements between the two sides and the need for full compliance with those agreements,

Recalling also the Quartet road map to a permanent two-State solution to the Israeli-Palestinian conflict, endorsed by the Security Council in resolution 1515(2003) of 19 November 2003,

Recalling further the Arab Peace Initiative adopted by the Council of the League of Arab States at its fourteenth session, held in Beirut on 27 and 28 March 2002,

Recalling the advisory opinion rendered on 9 July 2004 by the International Court of Justice on the *Legal Consequences of the Construction of a Wall in the Occupied Palestinian Territory*, and recalling also its resolutions ES-10/15 of 20 July 2004 and ES-10/17 of 15 December 2006,

Reaffirming that the United Nations has a permanent responsibility towards the question of Palestine until the question is resolved in all its aspects in a satisfactory manner in accordance with international legitimacy,

1. *Expresses its appreciation* to the Committee on the Exercise of the Inalienable Rights of the Palestinian People for its efforts in performing the tasks assigned to it by the General Assembly, and takes note of its annual report, including the conclusions and valuable recommendations contained in chapter VII thereof;

2. *Requests* the Committee to continue to exert all efforts to promote the realization of the inalienable rights of the Palestinian people, including their right to self-determination, to support the Middle East peace process and to mobilize international support for and assistance to the Palestinian people, and authorizes the Committee to make such adjustments in its approved programme of work as it may consider appropriate and necessary in the light of developments and to report thereon to the General Assembly at its sixty-fifth session and thereafter;

3. *Also requests* the Committee to continue to keep under review the situation relating to the question of Palestine and to report and make suggestions to the General Assembly, the Security Council or the Secretary-General, as appropriate;

4. *Further requests* the Committee to continue to extend its cooperation and support to Palestinian and other civil society organizations and to continue to involve additional civil society organizations and parliamentarians in its work in order to mobilize international solidarity and support for the Palestinian people, particularly during this critical period of humanitarian hardship and financial crisis, with the overall aim of promoting the achievement by the Palestinian people of its inalienable rights and a just, lasting and peaceful settlement of the question of Palestine, the core of the Arab-Israeli conflict, on the basis of the relevant United Nations resolutions, the terms of reference of the Madrid Conference, including the principle of land for peace, the Arab Peace Initiative and the Quartet road map;

5. *Requests* the United Nations Conciliation Commission for Palestine, established under General Assembly resolution 194(III), and other United Nations bodies associated with the question of Palestine to continue to cooperate fully with the Committee and to make available to it, at its request, the relevant information and documentation which they have at their disposal;

6. *Invites* all Governments and organizations to extend their cooperation to the Committee in the performance of its tasks;

7. *Requests* the Secretary-General to circulate the report of the Committee to all the competent bodies of the United Nations, and urges them to take the necessary action, as appropriate;

8. *Also requests* the Secretary-General to continue to provide the Committee with all the necessary facilities for the performance of its tasks.

RECORDED VOTE ON RESOLUTION 64/16:

In favour: Afghanistan, Albania, Algeria, Angola, Argentina, Armenia, Azerbaijan, Bahamas, Bahrain, Bangladesh, Barbados, Belarus, Belize, Bhutan, Bolivia, Botswana, Brazil, Brunei Darussalam, Burkina Faso, Burundi, Cambodia, Cape Verde, Chile, China, Comoros, Costa Rica, Côte d'Ivoire, Cuba, Cyprus, Democratic People's Republic of Korea, Democratic Republic of the Congo, Djibouti, Dominica, Dominican Republic, Ecuador, Egypt, Eritrea, Ethiopia, Gabon, Gambia, Ghana, Guinea, Guinea-Bissau, Guyana, Haiti, India, Indonesia, Iran, Iraq, Jamaica, Jordan, Kazakhstan, Kenya, Kuwait, Kyrgyzstan, Lao People's Democratic Republic, Lebanon, Lesotho, Liberia,

Libyan Arab Jamahiriya, Malaysia, Maldives, Mali, Malta, Mauritania, Mauritius, Mexico, Morocco, Mozambique, Myanmar, Namibia, Nepal, Nicaragua, Niger, Nigeria, Oman, Pakistan, Panama, Paraguay, Philippines, Qatar, Saint Lucia, Saint Vincent and the Grenadines, Saudi Arabia, Senegal, Sierra Leone, Singapore, Solomon Islands, Somalia, South Africa, Sri Lanka, Sudan, Suriname, Swaziland, Syrian Arab Republic, Tajikistan, Thailand, Togo, Trinidad and Tobago, Tunisia, Turkey, Turkmenistan, Uganda, United Arab Emirates, Uzbekistan, Venezuela, Viet Nam, Zambia, Zimbabwe.

Against: Australia, Canada, Israel, Marshall Islands, Micronesia, Nauru, Palau, United States.

Abstaining: Andorra, Austria, Belgium, Benin, Bosnia and Herzegovina, Bulgaria, Cameroon, Colombia, Croatia, Czech Republic, Denmark, El Salvador, Estonia, Fiji, Finland, France, Georgia, Germany, Greece, Guatemala, Hungary, Iceland, Ireland, Italy, Japan, Latvia, Liechtenstein, Lithuania, Luxembourg, Moldova, Monaco, Montenegro, Netherlands, New Zealand, Norway, Papua New Guinea, Peru, Poland, Portugal, Republic of Korea, Romania, Russian Federation, Samoa, San Marino, Serbia, Slovakia, Slovenia, Spain, Sweden, Switzerland, The former Yugoslav Republic of Macedonia, Tonga, Ukraine, United Kingdom, Uruguay.

Division for Palestinian Rights

Under the guidance of the Committee on Palestinian Rights, the Division for Palestinian Rights of the UN Secretariat carried out research, and monitored and disseminated information related to the Palestine question. The Division responded to requests for information and issued a number of publications, such as reports of international meetings and conferences organized under the Committee's auspices. It administered, maintained and expanded the United Nations Information System on the Question of Palestine (UNISPAL) and the "Question of Palestine" website on the UN home page. The Division conducted the annual training programme for PA staff and organized the observance of the International Day of Solidarity with the Palestinian People (29 November). The Committee, in its annual report [A/64/35], requested the Division to continue its work.

GENERAL ASSEMBLY ACTION

On 2 December [meeting 54], the General Assembly adopted **resolution 64/17** [draft: A/64/L.21 & Add.1] by recorded vote (112-9-54) [agenda item 16].

Division for Palestinian Rights of the Secretariat

The General Assembly,

Having considered the report of the Committee on the Exercise of the Inalienable Rights of the Palestinian People,

Taking note, in particular, of the relevant information contained in chapter V.B of that report,

Recalling its resolution 32/40 B of 2 December 1977 and all its subsequent relevant resolutions, including its resolution 63/27 of 26 November 2008,

1. *Notes with appreciation* the action taken by the Secretary-General in compliance with its resolution 63/27;

2. *Considers* that, by assisting the Committee on the Exercise of the Inalienable Rights of the Palestinian People in the implementation of its mandate, the Division for Palestinian Rights of the Secretariat continues to make a useful and constructive contribution to raising international awareness of the question of Palestine and to generating international support for the rights of the Palestinian people and a peaceful settlement of the question of Palestine;

3. *Requests* the Secretary-General to continue to provide the Division with the necessary resources and to ensure that it continues to carry out its programme of work as detailed in relevant earlier resolutions, in consultation with the Committee on the Exercise of the Inalienable Rights of the Palestinian People and under its guidance, including the monitoring of developments relevant to the question of Palestine, the organization of international meetings and conferences in various regions with the participation of all sectors of the international community, liaison and cooperation with civil society and parliamentarians, the further development and expansion of the "Question of Palestine" website and the documents collection of the United Nations Information System on the Question of Palestine, the preparation and widest possible dissemination of publications and information materials on various aspects of the question of Palestine and the further development and enhancement of the annual training programme for staff of the Palestinian Authority in contribution to Palestinian capacity-building efforts;

4. *Also requests* the Secretary-General to ensure the continued cooperation of the Department of Public Information and other units of the Secretariat in enabling the Division to perform its tasks and in covering adequately the various aspects of the question of Palestine;

5. *Invites* all Governments and organizations to extend their cooperation to the Division in the performance of its tasks;

6. *Requests* the Division, as part of the observance of the International Day of Solidarity with the Palestinian People on 29 November, to continue to organize, under the guidance of the Committee on the Exercise of the Inalienable Rights of the Palestinian People, an annual exhibit on Palestinian rights or a cultural event in cooperation with the Permanent Observer Mission of Palestine to the United Nations, and encourages Member States to continue to give the widest support and publicity to the observance of the Day of Solidarity.

RECORDED VOTE ON RESOLUTION 64/17:

In favour: Afghanistan, Albania, Algeria, Angola, Argentina, Azerbaijan, Bahamas, Bahrain, Bangladesh, Barbados, Belarus, Belize, Bhutan, Bolivia, Botswana, Brazil, Brunei Darussalam, Burkina Faso, Burundi, Cambodia, Cape Verde, Chad, Chile, China, Comoros, Costa Rica, Côte d'Ivoire, Cuba, Cyprus, Democratic People's Republic of Korea, Democratic Republic of the Congo, Djibouti, Dominica, Dominican Republic, Ecuador, Egypt, Eritrea, Ethiopia, Gabon, Gambia, Ghana, Guinea, Guinea-Bissau, Guyana, Haiti, India, Indonesia, Iran, Iraq, Jamaica, Jordan, Kazakhstan, Kenya, Kuwait, Kyrgyzstan, Lao People's Democratic Republic, Lebanon, Lesotho, Liberia, Libyan Arab Jamahiriya, Malaysia, Maldives, Mali, Malta, Mauritania, Mauritius, Mexico, Morocco, Mozambique, Myanmar, Namibia, Nepal, Nicaragua, Niger, Nigeria, Oman, Pakistan, Panama, Paraguay, Philippines, Qatar, Saint Lucia, Saint Vincent and the Grenadines, Saudi Arabia, Senegal, Sierra Leone, Singapore, Solomon Islands, Somalia, South Africa, Sri Lanka, Sudan, Suriname, Swaziland, Syrian Arab Republic, Tajikistan, Thailand, Togo, Trinidad and Tobago, Tunisia, Turkey, Turkmenistan, Uganda, United Arab Emirates, United Republic of Tanzania, Uruguay, Uzbekistan, Venezuela, Viet Nam, Yemen, Zambia, Zimbabwe.

Against: Australia, Canada, Israel, Marshall Islands, Micronesia, Nauru, New Zealand, Palau, United States.

Abstaining: Andorra, Armenia, Austria, Belgium, Benin, Bosnia and Herzegovina, Bulgaria, Cameroon, Colombia, Croatia, Czech Republic, Denmark, El Salvador, Estonia, Fiji, Finland, France, Georgia, Germany, Greece, Guatemala, Hungary, Iceland, Ireland, Italy, Japan, Latvia, Liechtenstein, Lithuania, Luxembourg, Moldova, Monaco, Montenegro, Netherlands, Norway, Papua New Guinea, Peru, Poland, Portugal, Republic of Korea, Romania, Russian Federation, Samoa, San Marino, Serbia, Slovakia, Slovenia, Spain, Sweden, Switzerland, The former Yugoslav Republic of Macedonia, Tonga, Ukraine, United Kingdom.

Special information programme

As requested by General Assembly resolution 63/28 [YUN 2008, p. 518], DPI continued its special information programme on the Palestine question, which included the organization of the annual training programme for Palestinian journalists and two international media seminars on peace in the Middle East (Vienna, 2–3 December 2008 and Rio de Janeiro, Brazil, 27–28 July 2009). A smaller-scale version of the exhibit "The Question of Palestine and the United Nations" was produced in Arabic, English and Spanish. The UN Dag Hammarskjöld Library continued to digitize documents for the UNISPAL document collection and the network of United Nations Information Centres and offices organized outreach activities, including in connection with the International Day of Solidarity with the Palestinian People on 29 November.

GENERAL ASSEMBLY ACTION

On 2 December [meeting 54], the General Assembly adopted **resolution 64/18** [draft: A/64/L.22 & Add.1] by recorded vote (162-8-5) [agenda item 16].

Special information programme on the question of Palestine of the Department of Public Information of the Secretariat

The General Assembly,

Having considered the report of the Committee on the Exercise of the Inalienable Rights of the Palestinian People,

Taking note, in particular, of the information contained in chapter VI of that report,

Recalling its resolution 63/28 of 26 November 2008,

Convinced that the worldwide dissemination of accurate and comprehensive information and the role of civil society

organizations and institutions remain of vital importance in heightening awareness of and support for the inalienable rights of the Palestinian people and the efforts to achieve a just, lasting and peaceful settlement of the question of Palestine,

Recalling the mutual recognition between the Government of the State of Israel and the Palestine Liberation Organization, the representative of the Palestinian people, as well as the existing agreements between the two sides,

Recalling also the Quartet road map to a permanent two-State solution to the Israeli-Palestinian conflict,

Recalling further the Arab Peace Initiative adopted by the Council of the League of Arab States at its fourteenth session, held in Beirut on 27 and 28 March 2002,

Recalling the advisory opinion rendered on 9 July 2004 by the International Court of Justice on the *Legal Consequences of the Construction of a Wall in the Occupied Palestinian Territory,*

Reaffirming that the United Nations has a permanent responsibility towards the question of Palestine until the question is resolved in all its aspects in a satisfactory manner in accordance with international legitimacy,

Expressing the hope that the Department of Public Information of the Secretariat, in its programme for 2010–2011, will continue to examine ways to foster and encourage the contribution of the media in support of the peace process between the Palestinian and Israeli sides,

1. *Notes with appreciation* the action taken by the Department of Public Information of the Secretariat in compliance with resolution 63/28;

2. *Considers* that the special information programme on the question of Palestine of the Department is very useful in raising the awareness of the international community concerning the question of Palestine and the situation in the Middle East and that the programme is contributing effectively to an atmosphere conducive to dialogue and supportive of the peace process;

3. *Requests* the Department, in full cooperation and coordination with the Committee on the Exercise of the Inalienable Rights of the Palestinian People, to continue, with the necessary flexibility as may be required by developments affecting the question of Palestine, its special information programme for 2010–2011, in particular:

(a) To disseminate information on all the activities of the United Nations system relating to the question of Palestine and the peace process, including reports on the work carried out by the relevant United Nations organizations, as well as on the efforts of the Secretary-General and his Special Envoy vis-à-vis the peace process;

(b) To continue to issue and update publications and audio-visual materials on the various aspects of the question of Palestine in all fields, including materials concerning the relevant recent developments in that regard, in particular the efforts to achieve a peaceful settlement of the question of Palestine;

(c) To expand its collection of audio-visual material on the question of Palestine, to continue the production and preservation of such material and to update, on a periodic basis, the public exhibit on the question of Palestine displayed in the General Assembly building as well as at United Nations headquarters in Geneva and Vienna;

(d) To organize and promote fact-finding news missions for journalists to the Occupied Palestinian Territory, including East Jerusalem, and Israel;

(e) To organize international, regional and national seminars or encounters for journalists aimed in particular at sensitizing public opinion to the question of Palestine and the peace process and at enhancing dialogue and understanding between Palestinians and Israelis for the promotion of a peaceful settlement to the Israeli-Palestinian conflict;

(f) To continue to provide assistance to the Palestinian people in the field of media development, in particular to strengthen the annual training programme for Palestinian broadcasters and journalists;

4. *Encourages* the Department to formulate ways for the media and representatives of civil society to engage in open and positive discussions to explore means for encouraging people-to-people dialogue and promoting peace and mutual understanding in the region.

RECORDED VOTE ON RESOLUTION 64/18:

In favour: Afghanistan, Albania, Algeria, Andorra, Angola, Argentina, Armenia, Austria, Azerbaijan, Bahrain, Bangladesh, Barbados, Belarus, Belgium, Belize, Bhutan, Bolivia, Bosnia and Herzegovina, Botswana, Brazil, Brunei Darussalam, Bulgaria, Burkina Faso, Burundi, Cambodia, Cape Verde, Chad, Chile, China, Colombia, Comoros, Costa Rica, Côte d'Ivoire, Croatia, Cuba, Cyprus, Czech Republic, Democratic People's Republic of Korea, Democratic Republic of the Congo, Denmark, Djibouti, Dominica, Dominican Republic, Ecuador, Egypt, El Salvador, Eritrea, Estonia, Ethiopia, Finland, France, Gabon, Gambia, Georgia, Germany, Ghana, Greece, Guatemala, Guinea, Guinea-Bissau, Guyana, Haiti, Hungary, Iceland, India, Indonesia, Iran, Iraq, Ireland, Italy, Jamaica, Japan, Jordan, Kazakhstan, Kenya, Kuwait, Kyrgyzstan, Lao People's Democratic Republic, Latvia, Lebanon, Lesotho, Liberia, Libyan Arab Jamahiriya, Liechtenstein, Lithuania, Luxembourg, Malaysia, Maldives, Mali, Malta, Mauritania, Mauritius, Mexico, Moldova, Monaco, Mongolia, Montenegro, Morocco, Mozambique, Myanmar, Namibia, Nepal, Netherlands, New Zealand, Nicaragua, Niger, Nigeria, Norway, Oman, Pakistan, Panama, Paraguay, Peru, Philippines, Poland, Portugal, Qatar, Republic of Korea, Romania, Russian Federation, Saint Lucia, Saint Vincent and the Grenadines, Samoa, San Marino, Saudi Arabia, Senegal, Serbia, Sierra Leone, Singapore, Slovakia, Slovenia, Solomon Islands, Somalia, South Africa, Spain, Sri Lanka, Sudan, Suriname, Swaziland, Sweden, Switzerland, Syrian Arab Republic, Tajikistan, Thailand, The former Yugoslav Republic of Macedonia, Togo, Trinidad and Tobago, Tunisia, Turkey, Turkmenistan, Uganda, Ukraine, United Arab Emirates, United Kingdom, United Republic of Tanzania, Uruguay, Uzbekistan, Venezuela, Viet Nam, Yemen, Zambia, Zimbabwe.

Against: Australia, Canada, Israel, Marshall Islands, Micronesia, Nauru, Palau, United States.

Abstaining: Benin, Cameroon, Fiji, Papua New Guinea, Tonga.

Assistance to Palestinians

UN activities

In response to General Assembly resolution 63/140 [YUN 2008, p. 521], the Secretary-General in May reported [A/64/78-E/2009/66] on United Nations and other assistance to the Palestinian people from May 2008 to April 2009. The report reviewed the work of UN agencies, in cooperation with the PA and donors, to assist the Palestinian people and institutions.

The overall economic and political situation was challenging, the report said. Increased isolation, internal Palestinian divisions and armed conflict led to substantial economic and humanitarian deterioration in the Gaza Strip, where Hamas continued its control. In the West Bank, although Israeli restrictions on movement decreased in some locations, the number of obstacles remained overall the same. Settlements and outposts had expanded and house demolitions had increased, in particular in East Jerusalem.

Overall humanitarian conditions deteriorated, with increased unemployment and poverty, especially in Gaza, as a result of continued closure. The 2008 unemployment rate was estimated to be 40 per cent in Gaza and 19 per cent in the West Bank, up from an average of 30 per cent and 18 per cent in 2007.

Gaza's established crossings remained closed for most of 2008, talks on intra-Palestinian reconciliation were inconclusive and there was no significant progress in negotiations between Israel and the Palestine Liberation Organization. In the West Bank, closures, settlement activity and house demolitions continued. Those factors posed significant challenges to the economic revival of the Occupied Palestinian Territory and to an effective response to humanitarian needs.

The economic situation in Gaza deteriorated markedly during the reporting period, owing mainly to its increased isolation and the crisis of December 2008–January 2009. The restrictions on the entry of cash into Gaza decreased depositors' confidence in banks and further reduced the ability of the population to meet its basic needs. Most UN projects were halted owing to the lack of materials. It became increasingly difficult to carry out humanitarian operations, and in November 2008 the Israeli authorities further restricted access of aid workers as well as delivery of commercial and humanitarian goods into Gaza. The already fragile situation deteriorated following Operation Cast Lead, which resulted in extensive destruction of and damage to homes and the public infrastructure, as well as some UN and government facilities.

No progress was made on the targets of the 2005 Agreement on Movement and Access, including the construction of the seaport or airport and the link between Gaza and the West Bank. Medical referrals for Gaza's residents to travel for outside treatment continued to require permits issued by the Israeli authorities.

The Erez crossing point, the only passage for movement of people between Gaza and the West Bank via Israel, remained virtually closed after June 2007, except for representatives of foreign media, who were denied access in November 2008, and international aid organizations. Karni, the main crossing point for goods, continued to be closed as from June 2007, except for the conveyor belt. The Rafah crossing also remained officially closed, although a few hundred Palestinians, mainly persons seeking medical care, students and pilgrims, were able to cross each month for specific purposes.

Barrier construction within the Occupied Palestinian Territory in deviation from the Green Line continued despite the 2004 ICJ advisory opinion and General Assembly resolution ES-10/17 of 15 December 2006. As of August 2008, 57.2 per cent (415 kilometres) of the planned route of the barrier (725 kilometres) had been completed, and 62 kilometres were under construction.

UN agencies and programmes continued to fulfil their responsibilities and mandates to the best of their abilities. They adjusted to a situation characterized by a continued political split between the Gaza Strip and the West Bank and the isolation of Gaza. As a result of Operation Cast Lead, a Gaza Flash Appeal was launched on 2 February, immediately after the ceasefire went into effect. A donors' conference (Sharm el-Sheikh, Egypt, 2 March) was organized to help rebuild Gaza, which resulted in pledges of approximately $4.5 billion.

The United Nations Relief and Works Agency for Palestine Refugees in the Near East (UNRWA) continued to provide free education to over 250,000 pupils in 315 elementary and preparatory schools in the West Bank and Gaza. The United Nations Educational, Scientific and Cultural Organization launched a technical assistance programme worth €3.4 million to establish national systems and operational frameworks to implement the Palestinian five-year education plan. The United Nations Children's Fund (UNICEF) and UNRWA developed a joint pilot programme for child-friendly schools, providing an additional opportunity for six government and four UNRWA schools to develop the child-friendly school concept. The United Nations Development Programme provided support to the Ministry of Education and Higher Education through a $7.5 million grant for the construction of four new schools, the rehabilitation of 12 schools and the provision of information and telecommunications equipment to 200 schools. With the support of the World Health Organization (WHO), the Palestinian health ministry prepared the 2008–2010 National Strategic Health Plan. The United Nations thematic group on HIV/AIDS started an $11 million project to combat HIV in the Occupied Palestinian Territory.

During Operation Cast Lead, UNRWA's critical operations, including food distribution and health-care services, continued to the extent possible, with around 1,000 of the Agency's 10,000 Palestinian staff in Gaza working throughout the crisis.

The Office of the United Nations Special Coordinator for the Middle East Peace Process continued to coordinate UN assistance to the Palestinian people and represented the United Nations at coordination forums.

The Economic and Social Council, by **decision 2009/261** of 31 July, took note of the Secretary-General's report.

UNCTAD assistance to Palestinians

At its fifty-sixth session (Geneva, 14–25 September and 12 October) [TD/B/56/11 & Corr.1], the Trade and Development Board of the United Nations Conference on Trade and Development (UNCTAD) considered an UNCTAD secretariat report on assistance to the Palestinian people [TD/B/56/3]. The report stated that in the 25 years that UNCTAD had been monitoring and investigating the performance of the economy of the Occupied Palestinian Territory and the policy environment affecting it, 2009 represented, without a doubt, an all-time low.

In particular, the devastation visited upon the occupied Gaza Strip and its economy had plunged its 1.5 million inhabitants into depths of poverty and disintegration unknown for generations. The blockade endured by Gaza had isolated it from the rest of the Territory and the world. As a result, real gross domestic product (GDP) was estimated to have grown by only 2 per cent in 2008, leading to a 1.2 per cent decline in per capita GDP. The cumulative effect was a 34 per cent drop in real per capita GDP between 2000 and 2008.

Agricultural development had been thwarted by the loss since 1967 of 40 per cent of West Bank land to settlements and related infrastructure. The Separation Barrier resulted in the confiscation of about one fifth of the West Bank's most fertile farmland, the destruction of infrastructures and limited access to water resources. Farmers had restricted access to their land. The barrier had forced 3,551 enterprises out of business and disrupted the road and water networks of 171 villages.

Closures had deepened Palestinian economic dependence on Israel, with the share of Israel in Palestinian trade rising from 63 per cent in 1999 to 79 per cent in 2008. The trade deficit with Israel as a percentage of GDP was estimated to have increased from 38 per cent in 1999 to 56 per cent in 2008. In close cooperation with the PA, UNCTAD assistance to the Palestinian people sought to support reform and development efforts within four clusters: trade policies and strategies; trade facilitation and logistics; finance and development; and enterprise, investment and competition policy.

Progress was achieved in implementing the United Nations Development Account project on promoting subregional growth-oriented policies towards achieving Millennium Development Goals 1 and 8 in the Occupied Palestinian Territory and five other Arab countries. By October 2008, the UNCTAD secretariat had completed the establishment of the Palestinian Shippers' Council, a private-sector institution engaged in facilitating trade. Coordination was ongoing with the Palestinian Ministry of National Economy to support the PA's efforts to integrate into the multilateral trading system.

GENERAL ASSEMBLY ACTION

On 16 December [meeting 64], the General Assembly adopted **resolution 64/125** [draft: A/64/L.35 & Add.1] without vote [agenda item 70 *(b)*].

Assistance to the Palestinian people

The General Assembly,

Recalling its resolution 63/140 of 11 December 2008, as well as its previous resolutions on the question,

Recalling also the signing of the Declaration of Principles on Interim Self-Government Arrangements in Washington, D.C., on 13 September 1993, by the Government of the State of Israel and the Palestine Liberation Organization, the representative of the Palestinian people, and the subsequent implementation agreements concluded by the two sides,

Recalling further all relevant international law, including humanitarian and human rights law, and, in particular, the International Covenant on Civil and Political Rights, the International Covenant on Economic, Social and Cultural Rights, the Convention on the Rights of the Child and the Convention on the Elimination of All Forms of Discrimination against Women,

Gravely concerned at the deterioration in the living conditions of the Palestinian people, in particular women and children, throughout the occupied Palestinian territory, which constitutes a mounting humanitarian crisis,

Conscious of the urgent need for improvement in the economic and social infrastructure of the occupied territory,

Welcoming, in this context, the development of projects, notably on infrastructure, to revive the Palestinian economy and improve the living conditions of the Palestinian people, stressing the need to create the appropriate conditions to facilitate the implementation of these projects, and noting the contribution of partners in the region and of the international community,

Aware that development is difficult under occupation and is best promoted in circumstances of peace and stability,

Noting the great economic and social challenges facing the Palestinian people and their leadership,

Emphasizing the importance of the safety and well-being of all people, in particular women and children, in the whole Middle East region,

Deeply concerned about the negative impact, including the health and psychological consequences, of violence on the present and future well-being of children in the region,

Conscious of the urgent necessity for international assistance to the Palestinian people, taking into account the Palestinian priorities,

Expressing grave concern about the humanitarian situation in Gaza, and underlining the importance of emergency and humanitarian assistance,

Welcoming the results of the Conference to Support Middle East Peace, convened in Washington, D.C., on 1 October 1993, the establishment of the Ad Hoc Liaison Committee for the Coordination of the International Assistance to Palestinians and the work being done by the World Bank as its secretariat and the establishment of the Consultative Group, as well as all follow-up meetings and international mechanisms established to provide assistance to the Palestinian people,

Underlining the importance of the International Conference in Support of the Palestinian Economy for the Reconstruction of Gaza, held in Sharm el-Sheikh, Egypt, on 2 March 2009, in addressing the immediate humanitarian situation in Gaza and in mobilizing donors to provide financial and political support for the Palestinian Authority in order to alleviate the socio-economic and humanitarian situation being faced by the Palestinian people,

Recalling the International Donors' Conference for the Palestinian State, held in Paris on 17 December 2007, the Berlin Conference in Support of Palestinian Civil Security and the Rule of Law, held on 24 June 2008, and the Palestine Investment Conference, held in Bethlehem from 21 to 23 May 2008,

Welcoming the meetings of the Ad Hoc Liaison Committee for the Coordination of the International Assistance to Palestinians, held in Oslo on 7 and 8 May 2009 and in New York on 22 September 2009,

Welcoming also the resumption of activities of the Joint Liaison Committee, which provides a forum in which economic policy and practical matters related to donor assistance are discussed with the Palestinian Authority,

Welcoming further the work of the Palestinian Authority to implement the Palestinian Reform and Development Plan 2008–2010, and stressing the need for continued international support for the Plan,

Stressing the need for the full engagement of the United Nations in the process of building Palestinian institutions and in providing broad assistance to the Palestinian people,

Welcoming recent steps to ease the restrictions on movement and access in the West Bank, while stressing the need for further steps to be taken in this regard, and recognizing that such steps would improve living conditions and the situation on the ground and could promote Palestinian economic development,

Welcoming also the action of the Special Representative of the Quartet, Mr. Tony Blair, charged with developing, with the Government of the Palestinian Authority, a multi-year agenda to strengthen institutions, promote economic development and mobilize international funds,

Stressing the urgency of reaching a durable solution to the crisis in Gaza through the full implementation of Security Council resolution 1860(2009) of 8 January 2009,

Stressing also the importance of the regular opening of the crossings for the movement of persons and goods, for both humanitarian and commercial flows,

Noting the active participation of the United Nations Special Coordinator for the Middle East Peace Process and Personal Representative of the Secretary-General to the Palestine Liberation Organization and the Palestinian Authority in the activities of the Special Envoys of the Quartet,

Welcoming the endorsement by the Security Council, in resolution 1515(2003) of 19 November 2003, of the performance-based road map to a permanent two-State solution to the Israeli-Palestinian conflict, and stressing the need for its implementation and compliance with its provisions,

Noting the Israeli withdrawal from the Gaza Strip in 2005 and from parts of the northern West Bank as a step towards implementation of the road map,

Commending the continuous efforts by the Administration of the United States of America in pursuing vigorously a two-State solution, noting the commitment of the Quartet to remain actively involved, and welcoming steps towards the relaunching of direct, bilateral negotiations as part of a comprehensive resolution of the Arab-Israeli conflict, on the basis of relevant Security Council resolutions and the terms of reference of the Madrid Conference, in order to ensure a political solution, with two States— Israel and an independent, democratic and viable Palestinian State—living side by side in peace and security,

Having considered the report of the Secretary-General,

Expressing grave concern about the continuation of the tragic and violent events that have led to many deaths and injuries, including among children and women,

1. *Takes note* of the report of the Secretary-General;

2. *Expresses its appreciation* to the Secretary-General for his rapid response and efforts regarding assistance to the Palestinian people;

3. *Also expresses its appreciation* to the Member States, United Nations bodies and intergovernmental, regional and non-governmental organizations that have provided and continue to provide assistance to the Palestinian people;

4. *Stresses* the importance of the work of the United Nations Special Coordinator for the Middle East Peace Process and Personal Representative of the Secretary-General to the Palestine Liberation Organization and the Palestinian Authority and of the steps taken under the auspices of the Secretary-General to ensure the achievement of a coordinated mechanism for United Nations activities throughout the occupied territories;

5. *Urges* Member States, international financial institutions of the United Nations system, intergovernmental and non-governmental organizations and regional and interregional organizations to extend, as rapidly and as generously as possible, economic and social assistance to the Palestinian people, in close cooperation with the Palestine Liberation Organization and through official Palestinian institutions;

6. *Welcomes*, in this regard, the meeting of the Ad Hoc Liaison Committee for the Coordination of the International Assistance to Palestinians and the outcome of the International Conference in Support of the Palestinian Economy for the Reconstruction of Gaza, held in Sharm el-Sheikh, Egypt, on 2 March 2009, at which donors pledged approximately 4.5 billion United States dollars to support the needs of the Palestinian people;

7. *Recalls* the International Donors' Conference for the Palestinian State, held in Paris on 17 December 2007, the Berlin Conference in Support of Palestinian Civil Security and the Rule of Law, held on 24 June 2008, and the Palestine Investment Conference, held in Bethlehem from 21 to 23 May 2008;

8. *Stresses* the importance of following up on the results of the International Conference in Support of the Palestinian Economy for the Reconstruction of Gaza;

9. *Calls upon* donors that have not yet converted their budget support pledges into disbursements to transfer funds as soon as possible, encourages all donors to increase their direct assistance to the Palestinian Authority in accordance with its government programme in order to enable it to build a viable and prosperous Palestinian State, underlines the need for equitable burden-sharing by donors in this effort, and encourages donors to consider aligning funding cycles with the Palestinian Authority's national budget cycle;

10. *Calls upon* relevant organizations and agencies of the United Nations system to intensify their assistance in response to the urgent needs of the Palestinian people in accordance with priorities set forth by the Palestinian side;

11. *Expresses its appreciation* for the work of the United Nations Relief and Works Agency for Palestine Refugees in the Near East, and recognizes the vital role of the Agency in providing humanitarian assistance to the Palestinian people, particularly in the Gaza Strip;

12. *Calls upon* the international community to provide urgently needed assistance and services in an effort to alleviate the dire humanitarian situation being faced by Palestinian women, children and their families and to help in the reconstruction of relevant Palestinian institutions;

13. *Stresses* the role that all funding instruments, including the European Commission's Palestinian-European Mechanism for the Management of Socio-Economic Aid and the World Bank trust fund, have been playing in directly assisting the Palestinian people;

14. *Urges* Member States to open their markets to exports of Palestinian products on the most favourable terms, consistent with appropriate trading rules, and to implement fully existing trade and cooperation agreements;

15. *Calls upon* the international donor community to expedite the delivery of pledged assistance to the Palestinian people to meet their urgent needs;

16. *Stresses*, in this context, the importance of ensuring free humanitarian access to the Palestinian people and the free movement of persons and goods;

17. *Also stresses* the need for the full implementation by both parties of the Agreement on Movement and Access and of the Agreed Principles for the Rafah Crossing, of 15 November 2005, to allow for the freedom of movement of the Palestinian civilian population, as well as for imports and exports, within and into and out of the Gaza Strip;

18. *Further stresses* the need to ensure the safety and security of humanitarian personnel, premises, facilities, equipment, vehicles and supplies, as well as the need to ensure safe and unhindered access by humanitarian personnel and delivery of supplies and equipment, in order to allow such personnel to efficiently perform their task of assisting affected civilian populations;

19. *Urges* the international donor community, United Nations agencies and organizations and non-governmental organizations to extend to the Palestinian people, as rapidly as possible, emergency economic assistance and humanitarian assistance, particularly in the Gaza Strip, to counter the impact of the current crisis;

20. *Stresses* the need for the continued implementation of the Paris Protocol on Economic Relations of 29 April 1994, fifth annex to the Israeli-Palestinian Interim Agreement on the West Bank and the Gaza Strip, signed in Washington, D.C., on 28 September 1995, including with regard to the full, prompt and regular transfer of Palestinian indirect tax revenues;

21. *Requests* the Secretary-General to submit a report to the General Assembly at its sixty-fifth session, through the Economic and Social Council, on the implementation of the present resolution, containing:

(a) An assessment of the assistance actually received by the Palestinian people;

(b) An assessment of the needs still unmet and specific proposals for responding effectively to them;

22. *Decides* to include in the provisional agenda of its sixty-fifth session the sub-item entitled "Assistance to the Palestinian people".

UNRWA

The United Nations Relief and Works Agency for Palestine Refugees in the Near East (UNRWA) continued to provide vital education, health, relief and social services, and micro-finance to an ever-growing refugee population in the Gaza Strip, the West Bank, Jordan, Lebanon and the Syrian Arab Republic.

Report of Commissioner-General. In his report on the work of the Agency in 2009 [A/65/13], the UNRWA Commissioner-General said that the closure of the Gaza Strip's borders had entered its fourth year. It affected every aspect of the public and private life of the 1.5 million people in the Gaza Strip, over half of whom were children, and caused human misery on a massive scale. For example, 80 per cent of the population was dependent on UN food assistance; 90 per cent of the water was unsafe to drink by WHO standards; and 95 per cent of the private sector businesses had closed down.

During Operation Cast Lead (see p. 434), from 27 December 2008 to 19 January 2009, UNRWA provided shelter in its schools to some 50,000 displaced people in the Gaza Strip. NGOs placed the number of persons killed between 1,387 and 1,417. The Gaza authorities reported 1,444 fatalities. The Government of Israel provided a figure of 1,166. Among the Palestinians killed, it had been estimated that between 310 and 350 were children; 5,015 Palestinians were reportedly wounded, including 11 UNRWA personnel while on duty at Agency premises; and 13 Israelis were killed. About 60,000 homes, belonging to refugees and non-refugees, were damaged or destroyed, as were hundreds of industrial facilities and businesses.

The level of conflict in the Gaza Strip dropped off steeply after 19 January, with a monthly average of 5 Palestinians killed and 12 injured from February to December. During the same period, one Israeli soldier was killed.

In the aftermath of the conflict, UNRWA increased its emergency food aid rolls from 550,000 to 900,000 refugees and provided financial support to families whose homes were destroyed or sustained damage. Of the 60,000 homes destroyed or damaged in the operation, 46,500 were refugee shelters.

Following the conflict, 76.7 per cent of households in the Gaza Strip were found to suffer from food insecurity or be vulnerable to it. Initial estimates put the economy's direct and indirect losses at approximately $4 billion, including an estimated $1 billion in costs associated with cushioning the conflict's humanitarian impact. The blockade of the Gaza Strip resulted in most basic materials for humanitarian and development interventions being denied entry, prompting delays and suspension of vital programmes, as well as the development of an economy serviced by several hundred tunnels under the Gaza-Egypt border. Up to 80 million litres of raw sewage were estimated to be pumped into the sea off the Gaza Strip each day, posing major environmental and health risks to the Mediterranean region. Average per capita consumption of water in Gaza was 91 litres per day, below the 100–150 litres per capita per day that the WHO saw as necessary.

In the West Bank, including in East Jerusalem, the occupation and associated regime of closures, separated road networks, house demolitions, land confiscation, settlement expansion, curfews and military operations continued to have an adverse effect on the Palestinian population. Communities in Area C of the West Bank and Palestinian refugees in East Jerusalem were particularly vulnerable, as were those living between the barrier and the Green Line. In East Jerusalem, there had been 80 house demolitions leading to the displacement of 300 people, including 149 children. The trauma of ongoing dispossession and the repeated displacement of refugees since 1948 could not be overemphasized.

Construction of new sections of the barrier continued to be largely frozen. With the exception of East Jerusalem, restrictions on movement were eased for Palestinians travelling between the main West Bank urban centres, following the removal of a number of checkpoints and roadblocks and improved checkpoint procedures.

In the West Bank, 21 Palestinians (including 7 minors) and 4 Israelis (including 1 minor) were killed, and 937 Palestinians (including 238 minors) and 117 Israelis (including 1 minor) were injured as a direct consequence of the conflict and occupation, including in military operations, artillery shelling, search and arrest campaigns, demonstrations, targeted killing, settler violence and Palestinian attacks on Israelis. Unrwa recorded 350 military incursions in the 19 West Bank camps, during which 2 refugees (both minors) were killed, 102 were injured (including 12 minors) and 371 were detained. Settler violence increased. While 2008 saw 363 incidents of settlers involved in hostile acts against Palestinians and/or their property (in itself a 118 per cent increase on 2007), 464 such incidents took place in 2009.

In Lebanon, the lack of employment rights remained a key obstacle to the well-being of Palestinian refugees. Major security incidents between Palestinian factions were relatively few, and escalated tensions between Lebanon and Israel in the second half of 2009 did not lead to any casualties. In the Syrian Arab Republic and Jordan, the Palestinian refugees continued to benefit from stable political environments.

Staff security remained a concern. The Agency noted that the local Unrwa employees were the only UN staff members in the area who did not receive hazard pay, and reiterated its calls for that to be addressed.

Unrwa concluded its three-year management reform initiative begun in August 2006. Israeli authorities, raising security concerns, continued to restrict the freedom of movement of Unrwa personnel in the Occupied Palestinian Territory, in violation of the UN Charter, the 1946 Convention on the Privileges and Immunities of the United Nations, relevant UN resolutions and the 1967 Comay-Michelmore Agreement, by which Israel was obligated to "facilitate the task of Unrwa to the best of its ability, subject only to regulations or arrangements which may be necessitated by considerations of military security". The Israeli authorities maintained that the restrictions were necessary to protect Israel against terrorist threats. Evidence was not available to the Agency, however, to indicate that measures concerning Agency staff and movement were other than matters of police or administrative convenience.

Advisory Commission. In its comments on the Agency's 2009 report, transmitted by its Chairman [A/65/13], the Unrwa Advisory Commission commended the Agency for continuing to deliver its programmes and services to all Palestinian refugees and for its vital role in contributing to regional stability. The Commission was concerned about the loss of life and the hardships endured by the majority of the Palestinian refugees in the West Bank and Gaza Strip. The restrictions on access to the Gaza Strip, along with periods of violence, had deepened the economic and social crisis, and led to even greater demand for Unrwa's services.

The Commission urged that access be permitted for all goods necessary for the Agency to carry out its humanitarian and development activities, including currency and construction materials. It expressed concern about attacks and threats against Unrwa facilities and staff by all parties and regretted that the separation barrier, closures, curfews and other restrictions on movement imposed by the Israeli authorities had led to further hardship. The Commission called upon the General Assembly to examine the direct taxation levied and additional restrictions imposed by Israel on Agency containers passing through Gaza crossings and to consider, in its resolution on Unrwa's operations, calling for reimbursement of those charges by the Israeli authorities.

The Commission was concerned about the long-term structural underfunding of the Agency, noting that, as in the previous year, Unrwa faced difficulties in reaching a funding level sufficient to maintain adequate service delivery. The Agency's appeal for $456.7 million, which was its largest to date, reflecting, in part, the impact of the conflict in the Gaza Strip, had received only $324 million. The Commission called for full support for the rebuilding of the Nahr El-Bared camp in Lebanon and for relief assistance to those displaced following its destruction in 2007 [YUN 2007, p. 472]. The Commission welcomed the medium-term strategy, the introduction of field and headquarters implementation plans and reforms of Unrwa's programmatic activities.

Report of Conciliation Commission. The United Nations Conciliation Commission for Palestine, established by General Assembly resolution 194(III) [YUN 1948–49, p. 203] to facilitate the repatriation, resettlement and economic and social rehabilitation of the refugees and the payment of compensation, in its sixty-third report [A/64/174], covering the period from 1 September 2008 to 31 August 2009, submitted in accordance with Assembly resolution 63/91 [YUN 2008, p. 524], noted the submission of its 2008 report [ibid.] and observed that it had nothing further to report.

By **decision 63/558** of 11 August, the Assembly decided to reschedule the high-level meeting commemorating the sixtieth anniversary of Unrwa to 24 September to ensure the participation of Member States at the ministerial level.

Communication. On 1 October [A/C.4/64/7] Israel, in a letter to the Secretary-General, complained that it was barred from speaking at the high-level event to mark Unrwa's sixtieth anniversary on 24 September, despite support by a vast majority of the event's steering committee, including Unrwa itself and many States. The consensus was broken by a clear political agenda of two member States on the event's steering committee, as well as an Observer Mission. Israel enclosed in its letter the intervention it would have delivered at the event.

GENERAL ASSEMBLY ACTION

On 10 December [meeting 62], the General Assembly, on the recommendation of the Fourth Committee [A/64/405], adopted **resolution 64/87** by recorded vote (168-1-7) [agenda item 31].

Assistance to Palestine refugees

The General Assembly,

Recalling its resolution 194(III) of 11 December 1948 and all its subsequent resolutions on the question, including resolution 63/91 of 5 December 2008,

Recalling also its resolution 302(IV) of 8 December 1949, by which, inter alia, it established the United Nations Relief and Works Agency for Palestine Refugees in the Near East,

Recalling further the relevant resolutions of the Security Council,

Aware of the fact that, for more than six decades, the Palestine refugees have suffered from the loss of their homes, lands and means of livelihood,

Affirming the imperative of resolving the problem of the Palestine refugees for the achievement of justice and for the achievement of lasting peace in the region,

Acknowledging the essential role that the United Nations Relief and Works Agency for Palestine Refugees in the Near East has played for sixty years since its establishment in ameliorating the plight of the Palestine refugees through the provision of education, health, relief and social services and ongoing work in the areas of camp infrastructure, microfinance, protection and emergency assistance,

Taking note of the report of the Commissioner-General of the United Nations Relief and Works Agency for Palestine Refugees in the Near East covering the period from 1 January to 31 December 2008,

Aware of the continuing needs of the Palestine refugees throughout all the fields of operation, namely, Jordan, Lebanon, the Syrian Arab Republic and the Occupied Palestinian Territory,

Expressing grave concern at the especially difficult situation of the Palestine refugees under occupation, including with regard to their safety, well-being and socio-economic living conditions,

Expressing grave concern in particular at the critical humanitarian situation and socio-economic conditions of the Palestine refugees in the Gaza Strip, and underlining the importance of emergency and humanitarian assistance and urgent reconstruction efforts,

Noting the signing of the Declaration of Principles on Interim Self-Government Arrangements on 13 September 1993 by the Government of Israel and the Palestine Liberation Organization and the subsequent implementation agreements,

1.   *Notes with regret* that repatriation or compensation of the refugees, as provided for in paragraph 11 of General Assembly resolution 194(III), has not yet been effected, and that, therefore, the situation of the Palestine refugees continues to be a matter of grave concern and the Palestine refugees continue to require assistance to meet basic health, education and living needs;

2.   *Also notes with regret* that the United Nations Conciliation Commission for Palestine has been unable to find a means of achieving progress in the implementation of paragraph 11 of General Assembly resolution 194(III), and

reiterates its request to the Conciliation Commission to continue exerting efforts towards the implementation of that paragraph and to report to the Assembly as appropriate, but no later than 1 September 2010;

3.   *Affirms* the necessity for the continuation of the work of the United Nations Relief and Works Agency for Palestine Refugees in the Near East and the importance of its unimpeded operation and its provision of services for the well-being and human development of the Palestine refugees and for the stability of the region, pending the just resolution of the question of the Palestine refugees;

4.   *Calls upon* all donors to continue to make the most generous efforts possible to meet the anticipated needs of the United Nations Relief and Works Agency for Palestine Refugees in the Near East, including with regard to increased expenditures arising from the continuing deterioration of the socio-economic and humanitarian situation in the region, particularly in the Occupied Palestinian Territory, and those mentioned in recent emergency appeals;

5.   *Commends* the United Nations Relief and Works Agency for Palestine Refugees in the Near East for its provision of vital assistance to the Palestine refugees and its role as a stabilizing factor in the region and the tireless efforts of the staff of the Agency in carrying out its mandate, and welcomes in this regard the high-level event of the General Assembly commemorating the sixtieth anniversary of the establishment of the Agency, on 24 September 2009.

RECORDED VOTE ON RESOLUTION 64/87:

In favour: Afghanistan, Albania, Algeria, Andorra, Angola, Antigua and Barbuda, Argentina, Armenia, Australia, Austria, Azerbaijan, Bahamas, Bahrain, Bangladesh, Barbados, Belarus, Belgium, Belize, Benin, Bhutan, Bolivia, Bosnia and Herzegovina, Botswana, Brazil, Brunei Darussalam, Bulgaria, Burkina Faso, Burundi, Canada, Cape Verde, Chile, China, Colombia, Comoros, Congo, Costa Rica, Côte d'Ivoire, Croatia, Cuba, Cyprus, Czech Republic, Democratic People's Republic of Korea, Denmark, Djibouti, Dominica, Dominican Republic, Ecuador, Egypt, El Salvador, Eritrea, Estonia, Ethiopia, Finland, France, Gambia, Georgia, Germany, Ghana, Greece, Grenada, Guatemala, Guinea, Guinea-Bissau, Guyana, Honduras, Hungary, Iceland, India, Indonesia, Iran, Iraq, Ireland, Italy, Jamaica, Japan, Jordan, Kazakhstan, Kenya, Kuwait, Kyrgyzstan, Lao People's Democratic Republic, Latvia, Lebanon, Lesotho, Liberia, Libyan Arab Jamahiriya, Liechtenstein, Lithuania, Luxembourg, Madagascar, Malawi, Malaysia, Maldives, Mali, Malta, Mauritania, Mauritius, Mexico, Moldova, Monaco, Mongolia, Montenegro, Morocco, Mozambique, Myanmar, Namibia, Nepal, Netherlands, New Zealand, Nicaragua, Niger, Nigeria, Norway, Oman, Pakistan, Panama, Papua New Guinea, Paraguay, Peru, Philippines, Poland, Portugal, Qatar, Republic of Korea, Romania, Russian Federation, Saint Lucia, Saint Vincent and the Grenadines, Samoa, San Marino, Saudi Arabia, Senegal, Serbia, Sierra Leone, Singapore, Slovakia, Slovenia, Solomon Islands, South Africa, Spain, Sri Lanka, Sudan, Suriname, Swaziland, Sweden, Switzerland, Syrian Arab Republic, Tajikistan, Thailand, The former Yugoslav Republic of Macedonia, Timor-Leste, Togo, Tonga, Trinidad and Tobago, Tunisia, Turkey, Turkmenistan, Ukraine, United Arab Emirates, United Kingdom, United Republic of Tanzania, Uruguay, Uzbekistan, Venezuela, Viet Nam, Yemen, Zambia, Zimbabwe.

Against: Israel.

Abstaining: Cameroon, Fiji, Marshall Islands, Micronesia, Nauru, United States, Vanuatu.

The Assembly, also on 10 December [meeting 62], and on the recommendation of the Fourth Committee [A/64/405], adopted **resolution 64/89** by recorded vote (167-6-4) [agenda item 31].

Operations of the United Nations Relief and Works Agency for Palestine Refugees in the Near East

The General Assembly,

Recalling its resolutions 194(III) of 11 December 1948, 212(III) of 19 November 1948, 302(IV) of 8 December 1949 and all subsequent related resolutions, including its resolution 63/93 of 5 December 2008,

Recalling also the relevant resolutions of the Security Council,

Having considered the report of the Commissioner-General of the United Nations Relief and Works Agency for Palestine Refugees in the Near East covering the period from 1 January to 31 December 2008,

Taking note of the letter dated 10 June 2009 from the Chair of the Advisory Commission of the United Nations Relief and Works Agency for Palestine Refugees in the Near East addressed to the Commissioner-General,

Deeply concerned about the critical financial situation of the Agency, as well as its rising expenditures resulting from the deterioration of the socio-economic and humanitarian conditions in the region and their significant negative impact on the provision of necessary Agency services to the Palestine refugees, including its emergency-related and development programmes,

Recalling Articles 100, 104 and 105 of the Charter of the United Nations and the Convention on the Privileges and Immunities of the United Nations,

Recalling also the Convention on the Safety of United Nations and Associated Personnel,

Affirming the applicability of the Geneva Convention relative to the Protection of Civilian Persons in Time of War, of 12 August 1949, to the Palestinian territory occupied since 1967, including East Jerusalem,

Aware of the continuing needs of the Palestine refugees throughout the Occupied Palestinian Territory and in the other fields of operation, namely, Jordan, Lebanon and the Syrian Arab Republic,

Gravely concerned about the extremely difficult living conditions being faced by the Palestine refugees in the Occupied Palestinian Territory, including East Jerusalem, particularly in the refugee camps in the Gaza Strip, as a result of the continuing prolonged Israeli closures and severe economic and movement restrictions that in effect amount to a blockade and the military operations in the Gaza Strip between December 2008 and January 2009, which caused extensive loss of life and injury, particularly among Palestinian civilians, including children and women; widespread damage and destruction to Palestinian homes, properties, vital infrastructure and public institutions, including hospitals, schools and United Nations facilities; and internal displacement of civilians,

Commending the extraordinary efforts by the Agency to provide emergency relief, medical, food, shelter and other humanitarian assistance to needy and displaced families in the Gaza Strip,

Recalling, in this regard, its resolution ES-10/18 of 16 January 2009 and Security Council resolution 1860(2009) of 8 January 2009,

Expressing regret over the continued suspension of the Agency's efforts to repair and rebuild thousands of damaged or destroyed refugee shelters due to the continued prohibition of the import of essential construction materials into the Gaza Strip by Israel,

Stressing the urgent need for reconstruction to begin in the Gaza Strip, including through the completion of numerous suspended projects managed by the Agency, according to the proposal of the Secretary-General, and the commencement of United Nations-led civilian reconstruction activities,

Welcoming, in this regard, the International Conference in Support of the Palestinian Economy for the Reconstruction of Gaza, held in Sharm el-Sheikh, Egypt, on 2 March 2009, and urging the disbursement of pledges to accelerate the reconstruction process,

Taking note of the Agency's continuing efforts to assist those refugees affected and displaced by the crisis in the Nahr el-Bared refugee camp in northern Lebanon, and welcoming the efforts of the Government of Lebanon and the international community to support the rebuilding by the Agency of the Nahr el-Bared camp,

Aware of the valuable work done by the Agency in providing protection to the Palestinian people, in particular Palestine refugees,

Gravely concerned about the endangerment of the safety of the Agency's staff and about the damage and destruction caused to the facilities of the Agency, in particular as a result of the military operations in the Gaza Strip during the reporting period,

Deploring the extensive damage and destruction of Agency facilities in the Gaza Strip caused during the military operations between December 2008 and January 2009, including to schools where civilians were sheltered and the Agency's main compound and warehouse, as reported in the summary by the Secretary-General of the report of the Board of Inquiry and in the report of the United Nations Fact-finding Mission on the Gaza Conflict,

Deploring also, in this regard, the breaches of the inviolability of United Nations premises, the failure to accord the property and assets of the Organization immunity from any form of interference and the failure to protect United Nations personnel, premises and property,

Deploring further the killing and injury of Agency staff members by the Israeli occupying forces in the Occupied Palestinian Territory since September 2000,

Deploring the killing and wounding of refugee children in the Agency schools by the Israeli occupying forces,

Expressing deep concern about the gravely negative impact of the continuing prolonged closures and severe restrictions on the movement of persons and goods, which in effect amount to a blockade in the Gaza Strip, and the construction of the wall, contrary to international law, in the Occupied Palestinian Territory, including in and around East Jerusalem, on the socio-economic situation of the Palestine refugees,

Deeply concerned about the continuing imposition of restrictions on the freedom of movement and access of the Agency's staff, vehicles and goods, and the injury, harassment and intimidation of the Agency's staff, which undermine and obstruct the work of the Agency, including its ability to provide essential basic and emergency services,

Aware of the agreement between the Agency and the Government of Israel,

Taking note of the agreement reached on 24 June 1994, embodied in an exchange of letters between the Agency and the Palestine Liberation Organization,

1. *Reaffirms* that the effective functioning of the United Nations Relief and Works Agency for Palestine Refugees in the Near East remains essential in all fields of operation;

2. *Expresses its appreciation* to the Commissioner-General of the United Nations Relief and Works Agency for Palestine Refugees in the Near East, as well as to all of the staff of the Agency, for their tireless efforts and valuable work, particularly in the light of the difficult conditions and dangerous circumstances faced during the past year, and, on the occasion of her impending retirement, expresses its appreciation to Commissioner-General Karen Koning AbuZayd for her nine years of dedicated service to the Palestine refugees;

3. *Expresses special commendation* to the Agency on the occasion of the sixtieth anniversary of its establishment;

4. *Expresses its appreciation* to the Advisory Commission of the United Nations Relief and Works Agency for Palestine Refugees in the Near East, and requests it to continue its efforts and to keep the General Assembly informed of its activities;

5. *Takes note with appreciation* of the two reports of the Working Group on the Financing of the United Nations Relief and Works Agency for Palestine Refugees in the Near East and the efforts of the Working Group to assist in ensuring the financial security of the Agency, and requests the Secretary-General to provide the necessary services and assistance to the Working Group for the conduct of its work;

6. *Commends* the Agency's six-year Medium-Term Strategy, commencing in January 2010, and the continuing efforts of the Commissioner-General to increase the budgetary transparency and efficiency of the Agency, as reflected in the Agency's programme budget for the biennium 2010–2011 and its comprehensive, three-year organizational development plan;

7. *Requests* the Secretary-General to support the institutional strengthening of the Agency through the provision of sufficient financial resources from the regular budget of the United Nations;

8. *Endorses* the conclusions in the report of the extraordinary meeting of the Working Group on the Financing of the United Nations Relief and Works Agency for Palestine Refugees in the Near East, in particular its request that the Secretary-General provide a report on the strengthening of the management capacity of the Agency to the relevant bodies of the General Assembly at the earliest possible date;

9. *Also endorses* the efforts of the Commissioner-General to continue to provide humanitarian assistance, as far as practicable, on an emergency basis, and as a temporary measure, to persons in the area who are internally displaced and in serious need of continued assistance as a result of recent crises in the Occupied Palestinian Territory and Lebanon;

10. *Welcomes* the pledges made at the International Donor Conference for the Recovery and Reconstruction of the Nahr el-Bared Palestine Refugee Camp and Conflict-affected Areas of Northern Lebanon, held in Vienna on 23 June 2008, and urges all parties to expedite the reconstruction of the camp to alleviate the ongoing suffering of the displaced persons;

11. *Acknowledges* the important support provided by the host Governments to the Agency in the discharge of its duties;

12. *Encourages* the Agency, in close cooperation with other relevant United Nations entities, to continue making progress in addressing the needs and rights of children and women in its operations in accordance with the Convention on the Rights of the Child and the Convention on the Elimination of All Forms of Discrimination against Women, respectively;

13. *Expresses concern* about the relocation of the international staff of the Agency from its headquarters in Gaza City and the disruption of operations at the headquarters due to the deterioration and instability of the situation on the ground;

14. *Calls upon* Israel, the occupying Power, to comply fully with the provisions of the Geneva Convention relative to the Protection of Civilian Persons in Time of War, of 12 August 1949;

15. *Also calls upon* Israel to abide by Articles 100, 104 and 105 of the Charter of the United Nations and the Convention on the Privileges and Immunities of the United Nations in order to ensure the safety of the personnel of the Agency, the protection of its institutions and the safeguarding of the security of its facilities in the Occupied Palestinian Territory, including East Jerusalem;

16. *Urges* the Government of Israel to speedily compensate the Agency for damage and destruction to its property and facilities resulting from actions by the Israeli side, including as a result of the military operations in the Gaza Strip between December 2008 and January 2009, and to expeditiously reimburse the Agency for all transit charges incurred and other financial losses sustained as a result of delays and restrictions on movement and access imposed by Israel;

17. *Calls upon* Israel particularly to cease obstructing the movement and access of the staff, vehicles and supplies of the Agency and to cease the levying of extra fees and charges, which affect the Agency's operations detrimentally;

18. *Also calls upon* Israel to cease its obstruction of the import of necessary construction materials and supplies for the reconstruction and repair of damaged or destroyed Agency facilities and for the implementation of suspended civilian infrastructure projects in refugee camps in the Gaza Strip;

19. *Requests* the Commissioner-General to proceed with the issuance of identification cards for Palestine refugees and their descendants in the Occupied Palestinian Territory;

20. *Notes with appreciation* the progress made by the Agency in the modernization of its archives through the Palestine Refugee Records Project, and encourages the Commissioner-General to finalize the project as rapidly as possible and to report on the progress made to the General Assembly at its sixty-fifth session;

21. *Notes* the success of the Agency's microfinance and microenterprise programmes, and calls upon the Agency, in close cooperation with the relevant agencies, to continue to contribute to the development of the economic and social stability of the Palestine refugees in all fields of operation;

22. *Reiterates its appeals* to all States, specialized agencies and non-governmental organizations to continue and to augment the special allocations for grants and scholarships for higher education to Palestine refugees in addition to their contributions to the regular budget of the Agency and to contribute to the establishment of vocational training centres for Palestine refugees, and requests the Agency to act as the recipient and trustee for the special allocations for grants and scholarships;

23. *Urges* all States, specialized agencies and nongovernmental organizations to continue and to increase their contributions to the Agency so as to ease the ongoing financial constraints, especially with respect to the Agency's regular budget deficit, noting that financial shortfalls have been exacerbated by the current humanitarian situation on the ground that has resulted in rising expenditures, in particular with regard to emergency services, and to support the Agency's valuable and necessary work in assisting the Palestine refugees in all fields of operation.

RECORDED VOTE ON RESOLUTION 64/89:

In favour: Afghanistan, Albania, Algeria, Andorra, Angola, Antigua and Barbuda, Argentina, Armenia, Australia, Austria, Azerbaijan, Bahamas, Bahrain, Bangladesh, Barbados, Belarus, Belgium, Belize, Benin, Bhutan, Bolivia, Bosnia and Herzegovina, Botswana, Brazil, Brunei Darussalam, Bulgaria, Burkina Faso, Burundi, Cape Verde, Chile, China, Colombia, Comoros, Congo, Costa Rica, Côte d'Ivoire, Croatia, Cuba, Cyprus, Czech Republic, Democratic People's Republic of Korea, Denmark, Djibouti, Dominica, Dominican Republic, Ecuador, Egypt, El Salvador, Eritrea, Estonia, Ethiopia, Finland, France, Gambia, Georgia, Germany, Ghana, Greece, Grenada, Guatemala, Guinea, Guinea-Bissau, Guyana, Honduras, Hungary, Iceland, India, Indonesia, Iran, Iraq, Ireland, Italy, Jamaica, Japan, Jordan, Kazakhstan, Kenya, Kuwait, Kyrgyzstan, Lao People's Democratic Republic, Latvia, Lebanon, Lesotho, Liberia, Libyan Arab Jamahiriya, Liechtenstein, Lithuania, Luxembourg, Madagascar, Malawi, Malaysia, Maldives, Mali, Malta, Mauritania, Mauritius, Mexico, Moldova, Monaco, Mongolia, Montenegro, Morocco, Mozambique, Myanmar, Namibia, Nepal, Netherlands, New Zealand, Nicaragua, Niger, Nigeria, Norway, Oman, Pakistan, Panama, Papua New Guinea, Paraguay, Peru, Philippines, Poland, Portugal, Qatar, Republic of Korea, Romania, Russian Federation, Saint Lucia, Saint Vincent and the Grenadines, Samoa, San Marino, Saudi Arabia, Senegal, Serbia, Sierra Leone, Singapore, Slovakia, Slovenia, Solomon Islands, South Africa, Spain, Sri Lanka, Sudan, Suriname, Swaziland, Sweden, Switzerland, Syrian Arab Republic, Tajikistan, Thailand, The former Yugoslav Republic of Macedonia, Timor-Leste, Togo, Tonga, Trinidad and Tobago, Tunisia, Turkey, Turkmenistan, Ukraine, United Arab Emirates, United Kingdom, United Republic of Tanzania, Uruguay, Uzbekistan, Venezuela, Viet Nam, Yemen, Zambia, Zimbabwe.

Against: Israel, Marshall Islands, Micronesia, Nauru, Palau, United States.

Abstaining: Cameroon, Canada, Fiji, Vanuatu.

UNRWA financing

In 2009, UNRWA expended $881.6 million, against a budget of $1,198.5 million, on its regular budget, projects and emergency appeal activities. The largest component was an expenditure of $514.7 million under the regular budget, accounting for 58.4 per cent of total expenditure. Emergency activities and projects accounted for 31.1 per cent and 10.5 per cent, respectively. In the West Bank and Gaza alone, UNRWA estimated the financial cost of meeting the emergency needs of refugees at $456.7 million. By the end of the year, total confirmed pledges to the Agency's emergency appeal stood at $324 million, or 71 per cent of total needs. The self-supporting microfinance department made up less than 1 per cent of total expenditure. Education remained the largest programme, accounting for 59 per cent of the regular budget, followed by health (17 per cent), and relief and social services (12 per cent). The unfunded portion of $33.9 million resulted from a difference between a needs-based budget and the donor contributions. The shortfall necessitated the adoption of stringent austerity measures throughout the Agency.

Working Group. The Working Group on the Financing of UNRWA held two meetings in 2009. In its report to the General Assembly on its meeting on 25 June [A/64/115], the Working Group drew attention to the fact that the real value of UNRWA's funding arrangements agreed upon by the Assembly in 1974 had declined over the past 35 years and was no longer in line with the Agency's needs; and that many senior management posts at UNRWA were undergraded. The Working Group welcomed the Agency's organizational development that led to a management transformation and expressed concern that those achievements could be reversed if adequate additional resources from the UN regular budget were not provided. The Working Group recommended that the Assembly review the basis for its decision in its resolution 3331(XXIX) B to provide funding to the Agency for international posts so as to enable it to meet demands from stakeholders and the Assembly itself; and called on the Secretary-General to provide a report on strengthening the Agency's management capacity.

Reporting to the General Assembly on its meeting of 9 November [A/64/519], the Working Group noted that the UNRWA regular budget for the biennium 2008–2009 amounted to $1,093.2 million, of which the cash component was $541.8 million for 2008 and $545.6 million for 2009. In mid-2008, the Agency revised the cash component of its regular budget for that year to $546.4 million to cover unbudgeted additional costs, including salary increases, resulting, inter alia, from the global food and energy crises. The funding gap for 2008 was $97.1 million, as the Agency's regular budget income for 2008 amounted to

$449.3 million ($430 million in donor contributions, and $19.3 million in transfers from the UN budget to cover the costs related to 119 international posts). As at 14 September, the anticipated funding gap for the Agency's budget for 2009 was $84 million.

The Working Group expressed concern about the large scale of the Gaza reconstruction and rehabilitation requirements following Operation Cast Lead. In the light of the constraints imposed by inadequate physical facilities on the Agency's ability to deliver quality services, recurrent project budget deficits would adversely affect regular services for the refugees. The Working Group was informed that the UNRWA $1.7 billion budget for the 2010–2011 biennium, excluding projects, had been endorsed by the Advisory Committee on Administrative and Budgetary Questions (ACABQ). The Working Group noted the Agency's concerns about the effects of understaffing on its ability to meet the demands of all stakeholders: donors, host authorities and the refugees themselves.

The Working Group noted that the 2008–2009 budget was seriously underfunded and expressed concern about the large funding gap anticipated for the Agency's 2009 regular budget. It reiterated that it was the responsibility of the international community to ensure that UNRWA services were maintained at an acceptable level and that funding kept pace with the changing needs of the refugee population.

Displaced persons

In an August report [A/64/323], submitted in compliance with General Assembly resolution 63/92 [YUN 2008, p. 528], which called for the accelerated return of all persons displaced as a result of the June 1967 and subsequent hostilities to their homes in the territories occupied by Israel, the Secretary-General said that, based on information obtained from the UNRWA Commissioner-General for the period from 1 July 2008 to 30 June 2009, 1,162 refugees registered with the Agency had returned to the West Bank and 901 to the Gaza Strip from places outside the Occupied Palestinian Territory. The number of displaced registered refugees known by the Agency to have returned since June 1967 was about 32,626. The Agency was unable to estimate the total number of displaced inhabitants who had returned. It kept records only of registered refugees and even those records, particularly with respect to the location of registered refugees, might be incomplete.

On 30 April, the Secretary-General sought information from Member States on action taken or envisaged to implement resolution 63/92. In a note of 5 August, Israel reaffirmed its intention to continue facilitating UNRWA's extension of vital humanitarian services, but remained concerned about the political motivation of resolution 63/92 and similar resolutions, as they did not reflect the reality on the ground. Israel favoured consolidating UNRWA resolutions and removing extraneous political language. It urged the Secretary-General and the Agency to consider ways in which the United Nations could enhance the manner in which it advanced the welfare of the Palestinian people.

GENERAL ASSEMBLY ACTION

On 10 December [meeting 62], the General Assembly, on the recommendation of the Fourth Committee [A/64/405], adopted **resolution 64/88** by recorded vote (166-7-4) [agenda item 31].

Persons displaced as a result of the June 1967 and subsequent hostilities

The General Assembly,

Recalling its resolutions 2252(ES-V) of 4 July 1967, 2341 B (XXII) of 19 December 1967 and all subsequent related resolutions,

Recalling also Security Council resolutions 237(1967) of 14 June 1967 and 259(1968) of 27 September 1968,

Taking note of the report of the Secretary-General submitted in pursuance of its resolution 63/92 of 5 December 2008,

Taking note also of the report of the Commissioner-General of the United Nations Relief and Works Agency for Palestine Refugees in the Near East covering the period from 1 January to 31 December 2008,

Concerned about the continuing human suffering resulting from the June 1967 and subsequent hostilities,

Taking note of the relevant provisions of the Declaration of Principles on Interim Self-Government Arrangements of 13 September 1993 with regard to the modalities for the admission of persons displaced in 1967, and concerned that the process agreed upon has not yet been effected,

1. *Reaffirms* the right of all persons displaced as a result of the June 1967 and subsequent hostilities to return to their homes or former places of residence in the territories occupied by Israel since 1967;

2. *Expresses deep concern* that the mechanism agreed upon by the parties in article XII of the Declaration of Principles on Interim Self-Government Arrangements of 13 September 1993 on the return of displaced persons has not been complied with, and stresses the necessity for an accelerated return of displaced persons;

3. *Endorses*, in the meanwhile, the efforts of the Commissioner-General of the United Nations Relief and Works Agency for Palestine Refugees in the Near East to continue to provide humanitarian assistance, as far as practicable, on an emergency basis, and as a temporary measure, to persons in the area who are currently displaced and in serious need of continued assistance as a result of the June 1967 and subsequent hostilities;

4. *Strongly appeals* to all Governments and to organizations and individuals to contribute generously to the Agency and to the other intergovernmental and non-governmental organizations concerned, for the above-mentioned purposes;

5. *Requests* the Secretary-General, after consulting with the Commissioner-General, to report to the General Assembly before its sixty-fifth session on the progress made with regard to the implementation of the present resolution.

RECORDED VOTE ON RESOLUTION 64/88:

In favour: Afghanistan, Albania, Algeria, Andorra, Angola, Antigua and Barbuda, Argentina, Armenia, Australia, Austria, Azerbaijan, Bahamas, Bahrain, Bangladesh, Barbados, Belarus, Belgium, Belize, Benin, Bhutan, Bolivia, Bosnia and Herzegovina, Botswana, Brazil, Brunei Darussalam, Bulgaria, Burkina Faso, Burundi, Cape Verde, Chile, China, Colombia, Comoros, Congo, Costa Rica, Côte d'Ivoire, Croatia, Cuba, Cyprus, Czech Republic, Democratic People's Republic of Korea, Denmark, Djibouti, Dominica, Dominican Republic, Ecuador, Egypt, El Salvador, Eritrea, Estonia, Ethiopia, Finland, France, Gambia, Georgia, Germany, Ghana, Greece, Grenada, Guatemala, Guinea, Guinea-Bissau, Guyana, Honduras, Hungary, Iceland, India, Indonesia, Iran, Iraq, Ireland, Italy, Jamaica, Japan, Jordan, Kazakhstan, Kenya, Kuwait, Kyrgyzstan, Lao People's Democratic Republic, Latvia, Lebanon, Lesotho, Liberia, Libyan Arab Jamahiriya, Liechtenstein, Lithuania, Luxembourg, Madagascar, Malawi, Malaysia, Maldives, Mali, Malta, Mauritania, Mauritius, Mexico, Moldova, Monaco, Mongolia, Montenegro, Morocco, Mozambique, Myanmar, Namibia, Nepal, Netherlands, New Zealand, Nicaragua, Niger, Nigeria, Norway, Oman, Pakistan, Papua New Guinea, Paraguay, Peru, Philippines, Poland, Portugal, Qatar, Republic of Korea, Romania, Russian Federation, Saint Lucia, Saint Vincent and the Grenadines, Samoa, San Marino, Saudi Arabia, Senegal, Serbia, Sierra Leone, Singapore, Slovakia, Slovenia, Solomon Islands, South Africa, Spain, Sri Lanka, Sudan, Suriname, Swaziland, Sweden, Switzerland, Syrian Arab Republic, Tajikistan, Thailand, The former Yugoslav Republic of Macedonia, Timor-Leste, Togo, Tonga, Trinidad and Tobago, Tunisia, Turkey, Turkmenistan, Ukraine, United Arab Emirates, United Kingdom, United Republic of Tanzania, Uruguay, Uzbekistan, Venezuela, Viet Nam, Yemen, Zambia, Zimbabwe.

Against: Israel, Marshall Islands, Micronesia, Nauru, Palau, Panama, United States.

Abstaining: Cameroon, Canada, Fiji, Vanuatu.

Palestinian women

Report of Secretary-General. In a report to the 2009 session of the Commission on the Status of Women [E/CN.6/2009/5], submitted in accordance with Economic and Social Council resolution 2008/11 [YUN 2008, p. 514], the Secretary-General summarized the situation of Palestinian women and reviewed UN assistance to them between October 2007 and September 2008, with particular reference to education and training; health; employment and entrepreneurship; women's human rights; violence against women; and humanitarian assistance.

Despite efforts to bring about a peaceful settlement, the crisis in the Territory continued with negative social and economic impacts on the Palestinian people, including on women and girls. Approximately 345 people were killed between the beginning of 2008 and 21 April 2008, 89 per cent of them in the Gaza Strip, including 31 women and 80 children. Internal conflict in the Territory compounded existing hardships.

After the Hamas takeover of Gaza, additional restrictions on the movement of goods and people into the Gaza Strip led to deteriorating conditions. Isolation of the Gaza Strip had a dramatic impact on women and children. The movement of women and girls continued to be restricted by closures, checkpoints and roadblocks, which limited their access to health care, employment and education. Pregnant women had difficulties accessing health services for antenatal care and safe delivery. Sixty-nine pregnant women were forced to give birth at Israeli military checkpoints; 39 babies and five women died as a result.

In July 2008, it was reported that 77 Palestinian female security prisoners—persons convicted of offences against State security—were held in Israeli prisons and detention centres. Approximately 25 per cent of Palestinian female prisoners suffered from treatable illnesses, including excessive weight loss, general weakness, anaemia and iron deficiency owing to poor quality food and the lack of essential nutrients. In addition, they were exposed to harsh treatment from male and female prison officers, with no regard for their condition or their special needs in pregnancy.

Although girls outnumbered boys in primary and secondary enrolment for the academic year 2007/2008 (548,781 women versus 548,314 men), the female dropout rate continued to surpass the male dropout rate at the secondary level—3.8 per cent versus 3 per cent. The dropouts were attributed to early marriage, the economic situation and travel restrictions. There were few safe spaces for Palestinian girls to go, and most of the 300 youth clubs across the Territory lacked funding and were poorly managed and equipped. Adolescence was often compromised by household demands and early marriage.

Incidents of violence against women, including domestic violence, continued during the period under review. Rates of domestic violence had risen since the beginning of the second intifada in 2000, with men using women as outlets for their anger, frustration and powerlessness. The majority of married (61.7 per cent) and unmarried (53.3 per cent) women were exposed to psychological violence.

The percentage of women in decision-making positions remained low. According to the Palestinian Central Bureau of Statistics, women accounted for 12.6 per cent of the members of the Legislative Council, 7.4 per cent of ambassadors, 11.2 per cent of judges and 12.1 per cent of general prosecutors.

Since improving the situation of Palestinian women was linked to the achievement of lasting peace, the report recommended undertaking renewed peace efforts, with women participating fully in all conflict resolution and peacebuilding in the region.

ECONOMIC AND SOCIAL COUNCIL ACTION

On 28 July [meeting 40], the Economic and Social Council, on the recommendation of the Commission on the Status of Women [E/2009/27], adopted **resolution 2009/14** by roll-call vote (23-5-16) [agenda item 14 *(a)*].

Situation of and assistance to Palestinian women

The Economic and Social Council,

Having considered with appreciation the report of the Secretary-General,

Recalling the Nairobi Forward-looking Strategies for the Advancement of Women, in particular paragraph 260 concerning Palestinian women and children, the Beijing Platform for Action, adopted at the Fourth World Conference on Women, and the outcomes of the twenty-third special session of the General Assembly, entitled "Women 2000: gender equality, development and peace for the twenty-first century",

Recalling also its resolution 2008/11 of 23 July 2008 and other relevant United Nations resolutions, including General Assembly resolution 57/337 of 3 July 2003 on the prevention of armed conflict and Security Council resolution 1325(2000) of 31 October 2000 on women and peace and security,

Reaffirming the important role of women in the prevention and resolution of conflicts and in peacebuilding, and stressing the importance of their equal participation and involvement in all efforts for the maintenance and promotion of peace and security and the need to increase their role in decision-making with regard to conflict prevention and resolution,

Recalling the Declaration on the Elimination of Violence against Women as it concerns the protection of civilian populations,

Recalling also the International Covenant on Civil and Political Rights, the International Covenant on Economic, Social and Cultural Rights and the Convention on the Rights of the Child, and reaffirming that these human rights instruments must be respected in the Occupied Palestinian Territory, including East Jerusalem,

Expressing grave concern over the increased difficulties being faced by Palestinian women and girls living under Israeli occupation, including the sharp increase in poverty, soaring unemployment, increased food insecurity, incidents of domestic violence and declining health, education and living standards, including the rising incidence of trauma and decline in their psychological well-being, and expressing grave concern also about the deepening humanitarian crisis and rising insecurity and instability on the ground in the Occupied Palestinian Territory, in particular in the Gaza Strip,

Deploring the deteriorating economic and social conditions of Palestinian women and girls in the Occupied Palestinian Territory, including East Jerusalem, and the systematic violation of their human rights resulting from the severe impact of ongoing illegal Israeli practices, including the continued imposition of closures and restrictions on the movement of persons and goods, which have detrimentally affected their right to health care, including access by pregnant women to health services for antenatal care and safe delivery, education, employment, development and freedom of movement,

Deploring also the intensified Israeli military operations in the Gaza Strip, which have caused heavy casualties among civilians, many of them children and women, and widespread damage to homes, United Nations schools and facilities, hospitals and public infrastructure, gravely impacting the provision of vital health and social services to Palestinian women and their families, and emphasizing that the civilian population must be protected,

Stressing the importance of providing assistance, especially emergency assistance, to alleviate the dire socio-economic and humanitarian situation being faced by Palestinian women and their families,

Emphasizing the importance of increasing the role of women in decision-making with regard to conflict prevention and the peaceful resolution of conflicts as part of efforts to ensure the safety and well-being of all women in the region,

Affirming the importance of exploring means to address the situation of and assistance to Palestinian women in the resolutions of the sixty-fourth session of the General Assembly under the relevant agenda items,

1. *Urges* the international community to continue to give special attention to the promotion and protection of the human rights of Palestinian women and girls and to intensify its measures for improving the difficult conditions being faced by Palestinian women and their families living under Israeli occupation;

2. *Reaffirms* that the Israeli occupation remains a major obstacle for Palestinian women in terms of their advancement, their self-reliance and their integration into the development of their society, and stresses the importance of efforts to increase their role in decision-making with regard to conflict prevention and resolution and to ensure their equal participation and involvement in all efforts for the maintenance and promotion of peace and security;

3. *Demands* that Israel, the occupying Power, comply fully with the provisions and principles of the Universal Declaration of Human Rights, the Regulations annexed to the Hague Convention IV of 1907, the Geneva Convention relative to the Protection of Civilian Persons in Time of War, of 12 August 1949, and all other relevant rules, principles and instruments of international law, including the international human rights covenants, in order to protect the rights of Palestinian women and their families;

4. *Calls upon* Israel to facilitate the return of all refugees and displaced Palestinian women and children to their homes and properties, in compliance with the relevant United Nations resolutions;

5. *Calls upon* the international community to continue to provide urgently needed assistance, especially emergency assistance, and services in an effort to alleviate the dire humanitarian crisis being faced by Palestinian women and their families and to help in the reconstruction of relevant Palestinian institutions, integrating a gender perspective into all international assistance programmes;

6. *Requests* the Commission on the Status of Women to continue to monitor and take action with regard to the implementation of the Nairobi Forward-looking Strategies for the Advancement of Women, in particular paragraph

260 concerning Palestinian women and children, the Beijing Platform for Action and the outcomes of the twenty-third special session of the General Assembly, entitled "Women 2000: gender equality, development and peace for the twenty-first century";

7. *Requests* the Secretary-General to continue to review the situation, to assist Palestinian women by all available means, including those set out in his report, and to submit to the Commission on the Status of Women at its fifty-fourth session a report, including information provided by the Economic and Social Commission for Western Asia, on the progress made in the implementation of the present resolution.

ROLL-CALL VOTE ON RESOLUTION 2009/14:

In favour: Algeria, Barbados, Bolivia, Brazil, China, El Salvador, Guatemala, India, Indonesia, Iraq, Kazakhstan, Malaysia, Morocco, Namibia, Pakistan, Peru, Philippines, Russian Federation, Saint Lucia, Saudi Arabia, Sudan, Uruguay, Venezuela.

Against: Canada, Netherlands, New Zealand, United Kingdom, United States.

Abstaining: Côte d'Ivoire, Estonia, France, Germany, Greece, Japan, Liechtenstein, Luxembourg, Malawi, Moldova, Norway, Poland, Portugal, Republic of Korea, Romania, Sweden.

Property rights

In response to General Assembly resolution 63/94 [YUN 2008, p. 529], the Secretary-General submitted an August report [A/64/324] on Palestine refugees' properties and their revenues. Only one Member State (Israel) had replied to his note requesting information from Israel and Member States on action taken or envisaged in relation to the implementation of resolutions 63/91 to 63/94 [ibid., pp. 524, 525, 528, 529]. In a 5 August note, Israel reiterated its support for the humanitarian activities of UNRWA; it would continue to facilitate the Agency's extension of vital humanitarian services to Palestinians, but remained concerned about the political motivation of those resolutions, as they did not reflect the reality on the ground. Israel favoured consolidating UNRWA resolutions and removing extraneous political language. It urged the Secretary-General and the Agency to consider ways in which the United Nations could enhance the manner in which it advanced the welfare of the Palestinian people.

GENERAL ASSEMBLY ACTION

On 10 December [meeting 62], the General Assembly, on the recommendation of the Fourth Committee [A/64/405], adopted **resolution 64/90** by recorded vote (168-6-3) [agenda item 31].

Palestine refugees' properties and their revenues

The General Assembly,

Recalling its resolutions 194(III) of 11 December 1948 and 36/146 C of 16 December 1981 and all its subsequent resolutions on the question,

Taking note of the report of the Secretary-General submitted pursuant to its resolution 63/94 of 5 December 2008, as well as that of the United Nations Conciliation Commission for Palestine for the period from 1 September 2008 to 31 August 2009,

Recalling that the Universal Declaration of Human Rights and the principles of international law uphold the principle that no one shall be arbitrarily deprived of his or her property,

Recalling in particular its resolution 394(V) of 14 December 1950, in which it directed the Conciliation Commission, in consultation with the parties concerned, to prescribe measures for the protection of the rights, property and interests of the Palestine refugees,

Noting the completion of the programme of identification and evaluation of Arab property, as announced by the Conciliation Commission in its twenty-second progress report, and the fact that the Land Office had a schedule of Arab owners and a file of documents defining the location, area and other particulars of Arab property,

Expressing its appreciation for the preservation and modernization of the existing records, including the land records, of the Conciliation Commission and the importance of such records for a just resolution of the plight of the Palestine refugees in conformity with resolution 194(III),

Recalling that, in the framework of the Middle East peace process, the Palestine Liberation Organization and the Government of Israel agreed, in the Declaration of Principles on Interim Self-Government Arrangements of 13 September 1993, to commence negotiations on permanent status issues, including the important issue of the refugees,

1. *Reaffirms* that the Palestine refugees are entitled to their property and to the income derived therefrom, in conformity with the principles of equity and justice;

2. *Requests* the Secretary-General to take all appropriate steps, in consultation with the United Nations Conciliation Commission for Palestine, for the protection of Arab property, assets and property rights in Israel;

3. *Calls once again upon* Israel to render all facilities and assistance to the Secretary-General in the implementation of the present resolution;

4. *Calls upon* all the parties concerned to provide the Secretary-General with any pertinent information in their possession concerning Arab property, assets and property rights in Israel that would assist him in the implementation of the present resolution;

5. *Urges* the Palestinian and Israeli sides, as agreed between them, to deal with the important issue of Palestine refugees' properties and their revenues within the framework of the final status negotiations of the Middle East peace process;

6. *Requests* the Secretary-General to report to the General Assembly at its sixty-fifth session on the implementation of the present resolution.

RECORDED VOTE ON RESOLUTION 64/90:

In favour: Afghanistan, Albania, Algeria, Andorra, Angola, Antigua and Barbuda, Argentina, Armenia, Australia, Austria, Azerbaijan, Bahamas, Bahrain, Bangladesh, Barbados, Belarus, Belgium, Belize, Benin, Bhutan, Bolivia, Bosnia and Herzegovina, Botswana, Brazil, Brunei Darussalam, Bulgaria, Burkina Faso, Burundi, Canada, Cape Verde, Chile, China, Colombia,

Comoros, Congo, Costa Rica, Côte d'Ivoire, Croatia, Cuba, Cyprus, Czech Republic, Democratic People's Republic of Korea, Denmark, Djibouti, Dominica, Dominican Republic, Ecuador, Egypt, El Salvador, Eritrea, Estonia, Ethiopia, Finland, France, Gambia, Georgia, Germany, Ghana, Greece, Grenada, Guatemala, Guinea, Guinea-Bissau, Guyana, Honduras, Hungary, Iceland, India, Indonesia, Iran, Iraq, Ireland, Italy, Jamaica, Japan, Jordan, Kazakhstan, Kenya, Kuwait, Kyrgyzstan, Lao People's Democratic Republic, Latvia, Lebanon, Lesotho, Liberia, Libyan Arab Jamahiriya, Liechtenstein, Lithuania, Luxembourg, Madagascar, Malawi, Malaysia, Maldives, Mali, Malta, Mauritania, Mauritius, Mexico, Moldova, Monaco, Mongolia, Montenegro, Morocco, Mozambique, Myanmar, Namibia, Nepal, Netherlands, New Zealand, Nicaragua, Niger, Nigeria, Norway, Oman, Pakistan, Panama, Papua New Guinea, Paraguay, Peru, Philippines, Poland, Portugal, Qatar, Republic of Korea, Romania, Russian Federation, Saint Lucia, Saint Vincent and the Grenadines, Samoa, San Marino, Saudi Arabia, Senegal, Serbia, Sierra Leone, Singapore, Slovakia, Slovenia, Solomon Islands, Somalia, South Africa, Spain, Sri Lanka, Sudan, Suriname, Swaziland, Sweden, Switzerland, Syrian Arab Republic, Tajikistan, Thailand, The former Yugoslav Republic of Macedonia, Togo, Tonga, Trinidad and Tobago, Tunisia, Turkey, Turkmenistan, Ukraine, United Arab Emirates, United Kingdom, United Republic of Tanzania, Uruguay, Uzbekistan, Venezuela, Viet Nam, Yemen, Zambia, Zimbabwe.

Against: Israel, Marshall Islands, Micronesia, Nauru, Palau, United States.

Abstaining: Cameroon, Fiji, Vanuatu.

Peacekeeping operations

In 2009, the United Nations Truce Supervision Organization (UNTSO), originally set up to monitor the ceasefire called for by Security Council resolution S/801 of 29 May 1948 [YUN 1947–48, p. 427] in the newly partitioned Palestine, continued its work. UNTSO unarmed military observers fulfilled evolving mandates—from supervising the four armistice agreements between Israel and its neighbours (Egypt, Jordan, Lebanon, the Syrian Arab Republic) to monitoring other ceasefires, as well as performing additional tasks. During the year, UNTSO personnel worked with the two other peacekeeping forces in the Middle East: the United Nations Disengagement Observer Force (UNDOF) in the Golan Heights and the United Nations Interim Force in Lebanon (UNIFIL).

Communications. On 9 January [S/2009/34], the Secretary-General informed the Security Council of his intention to appoint Major General Robert Mood (Norway) as the Head of Mission and Chief of Staff of UNTSO. The Council took note of that intention on 14 January [S/2009/35].

General Assembly action. By **decision 64/549** of 24 December, the Assembly decided that the agenda item on the financing of the UN peacekeeping forces in the Middle East would remain for consideration at its resumed sixty-fourth (2010) session.

Lebanon

Political and security developments

The political and security situation in Lebanon had improved markedly, the Secretary-General reported in April [S/2009/218]: the commitments made in the 2008 Doha Agreement [YUN 2008, p. 532] on the election of a new President had been either fully implemented or meaningfully acted upon, and political divisions between the majority March 14th Alliance and opposition March 8th Alliance had not led to paralysis, although there had been occasional tensions. The President, Michel Sleiman, had worked tirelessly to forge national unity. There had been notable steps towards the normalization of ties between Lebanon and the Syrian Arab Republic, including the establishment of embassies and the exchange of visits of senior Government officials. Positive regional developments had contributed to stability, in particular in the context of the Arab reconciliation efforts initiated by King Abdullah Bin Abdulaziz Al Saud at the Arab League Economic Summit held in Kuwait in January.

Parliamentary elections were held on 7 June, the Secretary-General said [S/2009/542], characterized by the highest voter turnout in the history of Lebanon and heralded as a success, with international and local observers deeming them to have been free and fair, despite some shortfalls and minor security incidents. Candidates belonging to the 14 March Alliance won 71 seats and candidates from the 8 March Alliance won 57 seats. President Sleiman called on Member of Parliament Saad Hariri to form a Government.

On 23 September, Syrian President Bashar Al-Assad travelled to Jeddah, Saudi Arabia, on the occasion of the inauguration of the King Abdullah University of Science and Technology, on the margins of which he met with the Saudi monarch. On 7 October, King Abdullah undertook his first visit to Syria since his accession to the throne in 2005 for a summit with the Syrian President. On 8 October, the two leaders released separate statements calling for the formation of a national unity Government in Lebanon.

On 9 November, President Sleiman and Prime Minister-Designate Hariri signed the decree forming a national unity Government [S/2010/193]. The new Government consisted of 30 ministers, 15 from the parliamentary majority, 10 from the opposition and 5 from a share allocated to the President.

On 12 November, President Sleiman made a short visit to Syria and met with Syrian President Al-Assad. The two Presidents agreed to work together to promote pan-Arab unity and to stabilize the situation in the region, also agreeing to further cooperation between their countries. On 19 December, the Prime Minister made his first visit to Damascus, where he met President Al-Assad for extensive talks. That was the first visit of a Lebanese Prime Minister since the brief trip by Fuad Siniora in 2005. Rhetoric on both sides emphasized the turning of a new page, and the summit marked a milestone in the normalization of relations between the two countries.

Security Council consideration. The Security Council considered the situation in Lebanon, including UNIFIL and the implementation of Council resolutions 1559(2004) [YUN 2004, p. 506] and 1701(2006) [YUN 2006, p. 583], on 7 May [meeting 6120] and 27 August [meeting 6183]. During the year, the Council expressed support for the role that UNIFIL continued to play in contributing to peace and stability in southern Lebanon. It reaffirmed its support for the sovereignty and territorial integrity of Lebanon. It welcomed the reconvening of the National Dialogue under the auspices of President Sleiman, and called for the early accomplishment of a national defence strategy. It underlined its concern over all violations of resolution 1701(2006). The Council urged all parties to adhere to the Doha Agreement and transcend sectarian interests. It welcomed the establishment of full diplomatic relations between Lebanon and the Syrian Arab Republic. Council members expressed their concern about security incidents in southern Lebanon and urged the parties to investigate acts of violence, tackle outstanding disputes and avoid any action that might destabilize the situation.

On 7 May [meeting 6120], the Council was briefed by the Special Envoy of the Secretary-General, Terje Roed-Larsen, who noted that the domestic, political and security situation had improved markedly, creating a favourable environment for strengthening sovereignty, political independence and Government control throughout the country. He stressed that the parties must continue to adhere to the Doha Agreement, including the commitment to refrain from using weapons to settle political disputes. The Special Envoy noted the lack of progress towards the disbanding and disarming of Lebanese and non-Lebanese militias, observed that the United Nations had no means to independently verify reports about the illegal transfer of weapons across the Syrian border into Lebanon, and expressed concern at the continuation of Israeli overflights of Lebanese territory.

On 8 July, the Council held informal consultations and was briefed by the Special Coordinator for Lebanon, who highlighted the parliamentary elections held on 7 June, the designation of Saad Hariri as Prime Minister and the process towards the formation of a new government. He reported on the establishment of full diplomatic relations between Lebanon and Syria, and noted that the next step to be taken would be the delineation of the border.

On 27 August [meeting 6183], in **resolution 1884(2009)** (see p. 483), the Council extended the mandate of UNIFIL for a further 12-month period, in accordance with the request of the Government of Lebanon. The Council called on all parties to fully respect the cessation of hostilities and the Blue Line—the provisional border drawn by the United Nations following the withdrawal of Israeli troops from southern Lebanon in 2000 [YUN 2000, p. 465]—and to cooperate fully with UNIFIL, and to work towards a permanent ceasefire and a long-term solution.

The Special Tribunal for Lebanon, established to investigate the 2005 bombing in Beirut that killed former Prime Minister Rafiq Hariri and 22 others, began operations at The Hague on 1 March.

Michael C. Williams (United Kingdom), appointed in 2008, continued to serve as the Secretary-General's Special Coordinator for Lebanon and head of the Beirut-based Office of the United Nations Special Coordinator for Lebanon.

On 21 December, the General Assembly adopted **resolution 64/195** (see p. 1011) on the oil slick on Lebanese shores that resulted from Israeli military action in 2006.

Communications. In communications received throughout the year, Lebanon reported on Israeli acts of aggression by air, land and sea, and violations of the Blue Line, and consequently, of Lebanese sovereignty and territorial integrity [A/63/682-S/2009/41; A/63/683-S/2009/42; A/63/687-S/2009/45; A/63/706-S/2009/74; A/63/707-S/2009/75; A/63/708-S/2009/76; A/63/738-S/2009/110; A/63/762-S/2009/141; A/63/763-S/2009/142; A/63/776-S/2009/155; A/63/808-S/2009/183; A/63/809-S/2009/184; A/63/827-S/2009/215; A/63/849-S/2009/238; A/63/850-S/2009/239; A/63/862-S/2009/268; A/63/877-S/2009/292; A/63/876-S/2009/293; A/63/889-S/2009/322; A/63/921-S/2009/348; A/63/922-S/2009/349; A/63/943-S/2009/414; A/63/944-S/2009/415; A/63/961-S/2009/452; A/63/962-S/2009/451; A/64/362-S/2009/479; A/64/492-S/2009/536; A/64/520-S/2009/578; A/64/521-S/2009/579; A/64/544-S/2009/606; A/64/563-S/2009/635; A/64/564-S/2009/636].

On 25 March 2009 [A/63/783-S/2009/157], Palestine, in identical letters to the Secretary-General and the Security Council, brought to their attention the assassination of General Kamal Naji of the Palestine Liberation Organization in Lebanon and the investigation undertaken by Lebanese authorities.

Implementation of resolution 1559(2004)

The Secretary-General submitted his ninth and tenth semi-annual reports on the implementation of Security Council resolution 1559(2004) [YUN 2004, p. 506], which called for strict respect of the sovereignty, territorial integrity, unity and political independence of Lebanon under the sole and exclusive authority of the Government, the withdrawal of all remaining foreign forces from Lebanon, and the disbanding and disarmament of all Lebanese and non-Lebanese militias.

Communication. On 10 March [A/63/760], the Syrian Arab Republic drew the attention of the Secretary-General to the proposed review of the logical framework of the budget for the Special Envoy of the Secretary-General for the implementation of Council resolution 1559(2004), which expanded the mandate of the Special Envoy to include elements of the provisions of Council resolution 1701(2006). Some achievement indicators of the logical framework that was proposed for review [A/63/346/Add.1] went beyond the role of the Secretariat in a manner that was contrary to the commitments set forth in the UN Charter, particularly Article 2, which prohibited any intervention by the Organization in the domestic jurisdiction of any State. The issues of diplomatic relations and the demarcation of borders between Lebanon and Syria were bilateral matters to be resolved by agreement between the two Governments. It was difficult to understand why the logical framework should ignore Israel's ongoing occupation of parts of southern Lebanon, its continued breaches of Lebanese airspace and its threat to UN forces in southern Lebanon, despite the fact that they all constituted a threat to, and a genuine violation of, Lebanon's sovereignty, independence and territorial integrity and were therefore an ongoing violation by Israel of resolution 1559(2004). Syria stated that, by withdrawing its military forces and the related security apparatus, it had implemented all the obligations incumbent on it under resolution 1559(2004) as of April 2005. The continued evocation of the name of Syria in the context of interpretations of the resolution were unacceptable and not in keeping with the UN Charter.

Report of Secretary-General (April). In his ninth semi-annual, report on the implementation of resolution 1559(2004) [S/2009/218], the Secretary-General stated that since 21 May 2008, when the Doha Agreement was adopted [YUN 2008, p. 532], and considering the level of tension and violence that prevailed in Lebanon prior to it, the implementation of the agreement had been particularly smooth. Since the election of President Sleiman [ibid., p. 533], Lebanon had witnessed its longest period of domestic stability since the adoption of resolution 1559(2004). However, occasional security incidents highlighted the proliferation of weapons and armed groups that continued to operate in Lebanon and whose existence was a violation of the resolution and a threat to the stability of the country and the region. The disbanding and disarming of Lebanese and non-Lebanese militias was a necessary element to the consolidation of Lebanon as a sovereign and democratic state;

it should be effected through an inclusive political dialogue that addressed the political interests of all Lebanese, and ultimately confirmed the sole political and military authority of the Government. The security incidents in and around Palestinian camps were of concern. While security cooperation between the Lebanese authorities and Palestinian factions had improved, more needed to be done to contain violence. The Lebanese authorities had to take the necessary measures, consistent with the decisions of the National Dialogue, to dismantle the paramilitary infrastructure outside refugee camps of the Damascus-headquartered Popular Front for the Liberation of Palestine-General Command (PFLP-GC) and Fatah al-Intifadah; Syria had a particular responsibility to aid the Lebanese authorities in those efforts.

Hizbullah was called upon to cease any militant activities outside Lebanon and to complete its transformation into a solely Lebanese political party, as required by the Taif Agreement [YUN 1989, p. 203]. The overall gains of the National Dialogue had remained limited. On the fourth anniversary of the withdrawal of Syrian troops from Lebanon, relations between Lebanon and Syria had improved markedly and entered a new phase with the establishment of diplomatic relations. The Secretary-General praised Presidents Al-Assad and Sleiman for their leadership and noted that he looked forward to the outcome of the work of the joint committee tasked with delineating the border between the two countries, as called for in resolution 1680(2006) [YUN 2006, p. 571].

Report of Secretary-General (October). On 21 October, the Secretary-General, in his tenth semi-annual report [S/2009/542] on the implementation of Council resolution 1559(2004), stated that Lebanese leaders had heeded his calls and seized the opportunity of the parliamentary election in June to show their commitment to democracy and to the sovereignty and political independence of their country. The threats posed by the existence of militias outside State control, especially Hizbullah's vast paramilitary infrastructure, could not be overstated. Disbanding and disarming militias was of vital importance to strengthen Lebanon's democracy and sovereignty. The Secretary-General called upon the leaders of Hizbullah to complete the transformation of the group into a solely Lebanese political party. The National Dialogue had served as a key mechanism to calm the political situation and represented an inclusive platform to address the key issue of disarmament of militias. The Secretary-General expressed concern at the continued presence of paramilitary infrastructure outside refugee camps by the Damascus-headquartered PFLP-GC and Fatah al-Intifada, in particular along the Syrian-Lebanese border, as well as at the security incidents in and around Palestinian camps. Security cooperation between the Lebanese authorities and Palestinian factions had improved, but more needed to be done to contain violence that could spill over into surrounding areas. The work of the outgoing Lebanese Government to improve the living conditions in refugee camps was commendable. The resumption of efforts by Syria and Lebanon to delineate their common border would be of mutual benefit, and the Secretary-General encouraged them to begin the process, consistent with resolution 1680(2006).

Communications. The Syrian Arab Republic, commenting on the Secretary-General's reports in identical letters to the Secretary-General and the Security Council dated 4 May [S/2009/227] and 2 November [S/2009/572], stated that it was no longer acceptable for the Secretary-General to introduce Syria into his reports on the implementation of resolution 1559(2004) after it had met all the obligations under the resolution by withdrawing its military forces and intelligence apparatus from Lebanese territory. The Secretariat once again mixed elements of Council resolutions 1559(2004), 1680(2006) and 1701(2006). Such mixing went beyond the mandates of the Special Envoy and was unjustified. It also provided Israel with a pretext for not abiding by the provisions of resolution 1559(2004) and other resolutions. Any outstanding provisions of the resolution were a Lebanese matter and had nothing to do with Syria. It would have been more useful if the reports had cited Israel as the party that had not implemented the resolution. Moreover, Israel continued to violate the sovereignty of Lebanon by air, land and sea. Implementation of the outstanding provisions of the resolution required the Security Council to bring pressure to bear on Israel in order to compel it to withdraw from the Lebanese territory it continued to occupy, including the Shab'a Farms, the Kafr Shuba hills and the northern part of the village of Ghajar, and to cease its violations of Lebanese sovereignty. The demarcation of the Syrian-Lebanese border was a bilateral matter and a sovereign prerogative of the two countries in which no party had the right to interfere.

Implementation of resolution 1701(2006) and UNIFIL activities

Resolution 1701(2006) [YUN 2006, p. 583], which was approved by both the Lebanese and the Israeli Governments, brought about a ceasefire, effective 14 August 2006, between Israel and Hizbullah after a month-long conflict that caused hundreds of civilian deaths and major infrastructure damage throughout Lebanon. By the same resolution, the Council expanded the mandate of UNIFIL to undertake substantial new tasks, in addition to those mandated under resolutions 425(1978) [YUN 1978, p. 312] and 426(1978) [ibid.], and authorized an increase in

the Force's strength from 2,000 to a maximum of 15,000 troops. The Secretary-General updated the Security Council on the implementation of resolution 1701(2006) in three periodic reports during the year.

UNIFIL was established by Council resolution 425(1978), following Israel's invasion of Lebanon [YUN 1978, p. 296]. The Force was originally entrusted with confirming the withdrawal of Israeli forces, restoring international peace and security, and assisting Lebanon in regaining authority in southern Lebanon. Following a second invasion in 1982 [YUN 1982, p. 428], the Council, in resolution 511(1982) [ibid., p. 450], authorized the Force to carry out the additional task of providing protection and humanitarian assistance to the local population. Following the withdrawal of Israeli forces from Lebanon in 2000 [YUN 2000, p. 465], UNIFIL was reinforced in order to monitor those territories previously occupied by Israeli forces, to prevent the recurrence of fighting and to create conditions for the restoration of Lebanese authority in the area.

On 6 August [S/2009/407], the Secretary-General recommended that the Council renew UNIFIL's mandate for a further 12 months, as requested by the Prime Minister of Lebanon in a letter of 4 July.

On 7 December [S/2009/628], the Secretary-General informed the Council of his intention to appoint Major General Alberto Asarta Cuevas (Spain) as Head of Mission and UNIFIL Force Commander. The Council took note of that intention on 9 December [S/2009/629].

Communications. On 8 January [S/2009/27], Israel informed the Secretary-General and the Security Council that on that day three Katyusha rockets were fired from Lebanese territory into Israel, striking the area of Nahariya and wounding two elderly women. The attack represented a violation of Security Council resolution 1701(2006) and proved that terrorist groups remained active in southern Lebanon and that weapons continued to be smuggled into Lebanese territory. The Lebanese Government must take all necessary action to implement resolution 1701(2006).

On 14 January [S/2009/38], Israel informed the Secretary-General and the Council that on that day three of four Katyusha rockets fired from Lebanese territory struck Kiryat Shmona in Israel. The Lebanese Government and its military were responsible for ensuring that Lebanese territory was not used for hostile activities against Israel and for taking all measures to implement resolution 1701(2006). The attack came as UNIFIL forces on the same day dismantled three Grad-type rockets shortly before they were to be launched at Israel. UNIFIL had to ensure that its area of operation remained free of armed personnel, assets and weapons other than those of the Government of Lebanon and UNIFIL.

On 15 January [A/63/685-S/2009/43], Lebanon drew the attention of the Secretary-General and the Security Council to incidents on 8 and 14 January, when Israeli forces bombarded Lebanese territories with mortars in violation of the Blue Line and resolution 1701(2006). Lebanon denounced the unilateral Israeli actions as violating its sovereignty and undermining the mandate of UNIFIL, even as Israel claimed that its violations were a response to rocket fire from Lebanon. On 14 January, a Joint Investigation Committee consisting of the Lebanese Armed Forces (LAF) and UNIFIL was established to investigate the firing of an unknown number of rockets from Lebanese territory towards the Occupied Territories. The investigation concluded that two Grad missiles were fired from Lebanese territory, and that due to the failure of one missile and a malfunction in the other, both missiles landed inside Lebanese territory and did not reach the Occupied Territories. The investigation also concluded that, shortly after the incident, Israel fired fifteen 155-mm shells towards Lebanese territory, targeting the launching and impact sites of the two missiles inside Lebanese territory. That unjustifiable Israeli targeting took place despite the fact that no missiles reached the Occupied Territories.

On 13 February [A/63/721-S/2009/97], Lebanon, in a position paper covering the period from 5 November 2008 to 1 February 2009, reported that Israeli forces had committed 627 air, 81 maritime and 49 land violations. The Israeli Government and high military officials had continued to threaten to bombard Lebanon, be it publicly or in the tripartite meetings in Naqoura, not sparing any civilian infrastructure or public institution, under the pretext of alleged arms stocking and transfer. The threats were in contradiction with Israel's obligation to refrain from any unilateral act and to report any alleged transfer of arms or stockpiling to UNIFIL so that the necessary verification with LAF could proceed. Despite all the mechanisms established by UNIFIL bilaterally and through the tripartite meetings, the Israel Defense Forces (IDF) had continued to resort to unilateral actions along the Blue Line. As to the marking of the Blue Line, Lebanon reiterated the agreement in the tripartite meeting to enhance the process and speed it up, knowing that IDF continued to put up hurdles to the marking exercise. Despite all efforts made by UNIFIL to facilitate the withdrawal of Israel from the northern part of Ghajar, IDF continued to occupy the area in contravention with resolution 1701(2006). The continued Israeli occupation of the Shab'a Farms constituted a threat to stability and security along the border and was a violation of Council resolution 425(1978). Israel still refused to supply the United Nations with the full strike data of the cluster bombs it showered Lebanon with in 2006.

Report of Secretary-General (March). In his ninth report [S/2009/119] on the implementation of res-

olution 1701(2006), issued on 3 March, the Secretary-General noted that tension along the Blue Line increased substantially as a result of two rocket attacks at the time of the hostilities in Gaza. Those attacks and the return fire strained the security and liaison arrangements established under the resolution, endangered the cessation of hostilities agreement and constituted the most serious challenge for the parties and UNIFIL since the adoption of the resolution.

The Secretary-General condemned the firing of rockets from southern Lebanon towards Israel, which constituted violations of the resolution. Those hostile activities were carried out from within the area between the Litani River and the Blue Line—an area that should be free of any unauthorized armed personnel, assets and weapons as stipulated in the resolution. It was a cause of concern that the 8 and 14 January rocket attacks were launched from sites close to populated areas, including a school occupied by students at the time, putting innocent civilians at risk. The Lebanese authorities had the primary responsibility to ensure that there were no unauthorized armed personnel, assets or weapons in the area between the Litani River and the Blue Line. UNIFIL supported LAF in that endeavour.

The Secretary-General acknowledged the quick increase of LAF troops in the south during the period of heightened tensions in the UNIFIL area of operations, as well as the significant expansion of common operational activities with UNIFIL. In partnership with LAF, and with the strong commitment and contributions of troop and maritime contributors, UNIFIL had laid a foundation towards achieving a permanent ceasefire. But that could not be sustained indefinitely and the window of opportunity provided by the UNIFIL deployment should be seized. In accordance with its obligations under the resolution, Israel must complete its withdrawal from southern Lebanon and end its occupation of the northern part of the village of Ghajar and the adjacent area north of the Blue Line. There had been encouraging developments at a meeting held by the United Nations Special Coordinator and UNIFIL Force Commander with Israeli officials on 8 February to discuss the implementation of the UNIFIL proposal for Ghajar.

The Secretary-General called upon Israel to immediately cease all overflights of Lebanese territory, as they violated Lebanese sovereignty and the resolution and undermined the credibility of UNIFIL and LAF. He remained concerned about Israel's failure to provide the technical strike data on the type, quantity and coordinates of the sub-munitions fired during the 2006 conflict [YUN 2006, p. 574]. That information was important for speeding up the clearance operations and reducing the number of casualties among civilians and mine-clearance experts. The continued presence of the PFLP-GC and Fatah al-Intifada military bases in

Lebanon and the threat they posed to Lebanon's stability was a cause for concern. He called on Lebanon to dismantle those bases, as agreed upon in the National Dialogue, and on Syria, which had influence on those groups, to support efforts in that regard. He regretted the unwillingness of Syria to engage on the issue, as conveyed to the United Nations Special Coordinator by senior officials in Damascus on 11 February.

The Secretary-General would continue his diplomatic efforts aimed at resolving the issue of the Shab'a Farms area, in accordance with the resolution and in spite of the lack of willingness of both Israel and Syria to resolve the issue. He commended Lebanon for the initial steps it had taken to design a comprehensive border strategy, as called for by the report of the Lebanon Independent Border Assessment Team II [YUN 2008, p. 543]. About Palestinian refugees in Lebanon, he noted that, without prejudice to the settlement of the refugee question in the context of a comprehensive peace agreement, it was imperative that progress be made in taking steps, including new legislation, to improve the conditions of refugees.

Communications. On 7 April [A/63/815-S/2009/191], Lebanon pointed to the risk posed by landmines and cluster munitions and unexploded ordnance left by Israeli forces, which would take years to clear. In the final 72 hours of the war in 2006, Israel had dropped 4 million cluster bombs all across South Lebanon after the adoption of resolution 1701(2006). Since then, 337 people, 34 of whom were children, had been killed or maimed by unexploded bombs.

On 20 May [A/63/860-S/2009/264] and 2 June [A/63/870-S/2009/287], Lebanon listed Israeli violations of resolution 1701(2006) in the form of spying networks inside Lebanon that constituted a violation of its sovereignty. In a position paper of 11 June [A/63/882-S/2009/307], Lebanon listed 388 air, 48 land and 77 maritime Israeli violations of the Blue Line between February and May.

Report of Secretary-General (June). On 29 June, the Secretary-General submitted his tenth report [S/2009/330] on the implementation of resolution 1701(2006). He noted that almost three years after the resolution was adopted, it remained the best available blueprint for the parties to move from the current state of cessation of hostilities towards a permanent ceasefire and a long-term solution. While the cessation of hostilities between Israel and Lebanon continued to hold, progress in other areas had been slower than expected and, in some cases, non-existent.

The Secretary-General reiterated that UNIFIL's cooperation with LAF had helped to establish a new strategic environment and to restore stability in southern Lebanon. That was achieved as a result of the significant deployment of troops and maritime assets, involving substantial financial resources and based on the strong commitment of many troop-contributing countries, which could not be sustained indefinitely. The Lebanese authorities had the primary responsibility to ensure that there were no unauthorized armed personnel, assets or weapons in the area between the Litani River and the Blue Line. UNIFIL supported LAF in that endeavour.

The Secretary-General was pleased that the parties continued to make progress, in cooperation with UNIFIL, to visibly mark the Blue Line in order to reduce inadvertent violations and build confidence. The handing over by Israel to UNIFIL on 12 May of technical strike data for the cluster bombs, which the United Nations had requested repeatedly since the cessation of hostilities in August 2006, was a positive development. However, the Secretary-General expressed concern at the allegations by Lebanon that Israeli spy cells had been operating in the country and that IDF helped alleged spies to cross from Lebanon into Israel through the Blue Line, which, if proved, could endanger the fragile cessation of hostilities.

The continued presence of armed groups in Lebanon operating outside Government control was a cause for concern, as was the threat to Lebanon's sovereignty from the presence of PFLP-GC and Fatah al-Intifada military bases. The Secretary-General called upon Lebanon to dismantle those bases, as agreed by the National Dialogue. Efforts to delineate and demarcate the Lebanese/Syrian border should not be delayed. He would continue his diplomatic efforts aimed at resolving the issue of the Shab'a Farms area, in accordance with the resolution. He encouraged Israel and Syria to respond to the provisional definition of the Shab'a Farms area that he had provided based on the best available information.

Member States should fulfil their obligations by respecting the arms embargo imposed on Lebanon—a fundamental aspect of the resolution and an important element for domestic and regional stability. In that connection, Lebanon's efforts to control its northern border through the Common Border Force and to deploy a second Common Border Force to the eastern border were welcomed. Progress needed to be made regarding measures aimed at improving the living conditions of Palestinian refugees in Lebanon, including the reconstruction of the Nahr al-Bared refugee camp.

Communications. On 16 July [S/2009/365], Israel brought to the attention of the Secretary-General and the Security Council a series of explosions on 14 July that ripped through an abandoned house in Khirbat Silim, a Shiite village in Lebanon. The house in question was a Hizbullah arms cache of rockets, mortars, artillery shells, grenades and additional ammunition which had been brought to the area following the 2006 conflict. The smuggling and presence of such weapons was in contravention of resolution

1701(2006), Israel said. The incident verified Israel's repeated claims since the adoption of the resolution that Hizbullah continued to build its military infrastructure throughout Lebanon, including south of the Litani river. In the aftermath of the explosions, a UN spokesperson confirmed that civilians had attempted to hamper the investigation by UNIFIL. Other credible reports noted that LAF had delayed the deployment of UNIFIL to conduct an investigation into the incident. Both Israel and reports in the Lebanese press suggested that Hizbullah operatives had used that delay to remove evidence of their illicit activity before UNIFIL was permitted to inspect the area.

On 20 July [S/2009/375], Israel drew attention to two additional violations. During the first incident, on 17 July, 15 Lebanese civilians crossed the Blue Line near a UNIFIL position adjacent to the Shuba village, penetrated 175 metres into Israeli territory and planted Hizbullah and Lebanese flags, subsequently returning into Lebanese territory. During the incident, UNIFIL did not take any action to prevent the crossing into Israeli territory. Israel called upon Lebanon to exercise its authority and prevent such violations of the Blue Line that endangered the stability along the border. The Secretary-General was called upon to exercise his influence and to ensure that UNIFIL would prevent any future incidents. Another incident took place in Khirbat Silim on 18 July, when 14 UNIFIL peacekeepers were injured by so-called Lebanese "civilians" after attempting to search a suspicious house. That episode—in the same place where an arms cache of the terrorist organization Hizbullah exploded on 14 July—verified that Hizbullah consistently obstructed the implementation of the resolution by building new military infrastructure south of the Litani River, and by preventing UNIFIL from fulfilling its mandate, including by using civilians in a violent manner to obstruct UNIFIL's mission.

Responding to Israel's allegations on 22 July [A/63/933-S/2009/379], Lebanon noted that a joint investigation by LAF and UNIFIL began two days after the explosion, since the site was not safe to approach on the day after the explosion. Despite the danger, LAF remained at the site on the day after the explosion and a LAF soldier was injured by a secondary explosion in the area near the building. That refuted the false Israeli allegations that LAF had deliberately delayed UNIFIL deployment at the explosion site and the start of the investigation. Upon investigation, it became evident that the cause of the explosion had been a fire that broke out in the unfinished non-residential building. It was concluded that the munitions and weapons were left over from the July 2006 war because: the items found included 100-mm Israeli tank shells with Hebrew writing; all weapons and munitions at the site were of types used during the July 2006 war; and there was ammunition for 130-mm artillery, which

the resistance did not possess, but which was used by the Lahad militia that collaborated with Israel prior to the 2000 liberation. On 19 July, LAF received information from the UNIFIL command concerning the possible removal of the munitions from the site of the explosion to another location in Khirbat Silim and requested the coordinates of the new location, which consisted of three houses under construction and one inhabited house. UNIFIL forces were then called in to review the results of the search and enter the location, accompanied by LAF. Two UNIFIL patrols arrived at the location, while other UNIFIL patrols went to other locations in the village. Because of a lapse in coordination, one UNIFIL unit attempted to enter one of the houses without a LAF escort. Taken by surprise, some women and girls screamed, after which some youths threw stones at the force, injuring a UNIFIL soldier. As a result, the situation deteriorated, and the locals began to pelt UNIFIL troops with stones, hitting several of them.

Letter from Secretary-General. On 6 August [S/2009/407] the Secretary-General requested the Council to consider renewing the UNIFIL mandate for one year, as requested by the Lebanese Prime Minister in a letter of 4 July. The Secretary-General noted that a serious breach was discovered on 14 July when a series of explosions occurred near Khirbat Silim. Preliminary investigations by UNIFIL in coordination with LAF indicated that the explosions were caused by the deflagration of ammunition present in the building, in which a large quantity of weapons and ammunition was stored. There was no evidence to suggest that those weapons and ammunition had been smuggled into the UNIFIL area of operations since the adoption of resolution 1701(2006). There were indications that suggested that the depot was under the control of Hizbullah, and that, in contrast to weapons and ammunition previously discovered by UNIFIL and LAF, it was not abandoned but actively maintained. Some of the individuals present on 15 July at the site of the explosions were identified to UNIFIL as belonging to Hizbullah. On 15 and 18 July, civilians attempted to obstruct UNIFIL's freedom of movement. Stone-throwing on 18 July injured UNIFIL peacekeepers. The Secretary-General expressed concern at the attempts to obstruct UNIFIL's freedom of movement, which the Lebanese authorities must ensure within the Force's area of operations.

In another incident on 17 July, approximately 30 civilians approached the Blue Line and several members of the group walked across it near UN position 4–31, in the vicinity of Kafr Shouba. The civilians were protesting against IDF construction works just south of the Blue Line, in the Shab'a farms area. The Lebanese authorities had the primary responsibility to ensure that there were no unauthorized armed personnel, assets or weapons in the area between the Blue Line and the Litani River.

IDF continued their occupation of part of the village of Ghajar and an adjacent area, in violation of resolution 1701(2006). Israel must withdraw IDF forces from the area and cease its air violations, which contributed to tension and continued unabated. Ground violations of the Blue Line should stop; inadvertent crossings could be reduced by accelerating progress on visibly marking the Blue Line.

SECURITY COUNCIL ACTION

On 27 August [meeting 6183], the Security Council unanimously adopted **resolution 1884(2009)**. The draft [S/2009/431] was submitted by Belgium, Croatia, France, Italy, Spain, the United Kingdom and the United States.

The Security Council,

Recalling all its previous resolutions on Lebanon, in particular resolutions 425(1978) and 426(1978) of 19 March 1978, 1559(2004) of 2 September 2004, 1680(2006) of 17 May 2006, 1701(2006) of 11 August 2006, 1773(2007) of 24 August 2007 and 1832(2008) of 27 August 2008, as well as the statements by its President on the situation in Lebanon,

Responding to the request of the Government of Lebanon to extend the mandate of the United Nations Interim Force in Lebanon for a new period of one year, without amendment, presented in a letter dated 4 July 2009 from the Minister for Foreign Affairs of Lebanon to the Secretary-General, and welcoming the letter dated 6 August 2009 from the Secretary-General to the President of the Security Council recommending this extension,

Reaffirming its commitment to the full implementation of all provisions of resolution 1701(2006), and aware of its responsibilities to help to secure a permanent ceasefire and a long-term solution as envisioned in the resolution,

Calling upon all parties concerned to strengthen their efforts to implement all provisions of resolution 1701(2006),

Expressing deep concern at all violations in connection with resolution 1701(2006), in particular the latest serious violations highlighted in the Secretary-General's letter dated 6 August 2009, emphasizing the importance of the establishment between the Blue Line and the Litani River of an area free of any armed personnel, assets and weapons other than those of the Government of Lebanon and the Force, and, to that end, encouraging further coordination between the Force and the Lebanese Armed Forces,

Calling upon all parties concerned to respect the Blue Line in its entirety, including through Ghajar, and encouraging the parties to coordinate further with the Force to visibly mark the Blue Line,

Recalling the relevant principles contained in the Convention on the Safety of United Nations and Associated Personnel,

Commending the active role and dedication of the personnel of the Force, notably its Commander, expressing its strong appreciation to Member States that contribute to the Force, and underlining the necessity that the Force have at its disposal all means and equipment necessary to carry out its mandate,

Recalling the request of the Government of Lebanon to deploy an international force to assist it to exercise its authority throughout the territory, and reaffirming the authority of the Force to take all necessary action, in areas of operations of its forces and as it deems within its capabilities, to ensure that its area of operations is not utilized for hostile activities of any kind and to resist attempts by forceful means to prevent it from discharging its mandate,

Welcoming the efforts of the Secretary-General to keep all peacekeeping operations, including the Force, under close review and stressing the need for the Council to pursue a rigorous, strategic approach to peacekeeping deployments,

Calling upon Member States to assist the Lebanese Armed Forces as needed to enable them to perform their duties, in line with resolution 1701(2006),

Determining that the situation in Lebanon continues to constitute a threat to international peace and security,

1. *Decides* to extend the present mandate of the United Nations Interim Force in Lebanon until 31 August 2010;

2. *Commends* the positive role of the Force, whose deployment together with the Lebanese Armed Forces has helped to establish a new strategic environment in southern Lebanon, welcomes the expansion of coordinated activities between the Force and the Lebanese Armed Forces, and encourages further enhancement of this cooperation;

3. *Strongly calls upon* all parties concerned to respect the cessation of hostilities and the Blue Line in its entirety, to cooperate fully with the United Nations and the Force and to abide scrupulously by their obligation to respect the safety of the Force and other United Nations personnel, including by avoiding any course of action which endangers United Nations personnel and by ensuring that the Force is accorded full freedom of movement within its area of operations;

4. *Urges* all parties to cooperate fully with the Security Council and the Secretary-General to achieve a permanent ceasefire and a long-term solution as envisioned in resolution 1701(2006), and emphasizes the need for greater progress in this regard;

5. *Welcomes* the efforts being undertaken by the Force to implement the Secretary-General's zero-tolerance policy on sexual exploitation and abuse and to ensure full compliance of its personnel with the United Nations code of conduct, requests the Secretary-General to continue to take all necessary action in this regard and to keep the Council informed, and urges troop-contributing countries to take preventive and disciplinary action to ensure that such acts are properly investigated and punished in cases involving their personnel;

6. *Requests* the Secretary-General to continue to report to the Council on the implementation of resolution 1701(2006) every four months, or at any time as he deems appropriate;

7. *Welcomes*, in this regard, receiving as soon as possible the conclusions of the review of the operational capacity of the Force, including its force structure, assets and requirements, that will be conducted during the coming months, as referred to in the Secretary-General's letter dated 6 August 2009, in an effort to ensure, in accordance with peacekeeping good practice, that the assets and resources of the mission are configured most appropriately to fulfil its mandated tasks;

8. *Stresses* the importance of, and the need to achieve, a comprehensive, just and lasting peace in the Middle East, based on all its relevant resolutions, including resolutions 242(1967) of 22 November 1967, 338(1973) of 22 October 1973 and 1515(2003) of 19 November 2003;

9. *Decides* to remain actively seized of the matter.

Communications. On 11 September, Israel reported [S/2009/454] about the firing on that day of three Katyusha rockets from Lebanese territory towards Israel. At least one landed near the city of Nahariya in northern Israel, with Israel exercising its right to self-defence under article 51 of the UN Charter.

On 14 September [A/63/964-S/2009/458], Lebanon reported that on 11 September IDF showered the outskirts of the town of Klaele in South Lebanon with around twelve 155-mm shells. Israel said that the shelling came in response to the launching of two Grad missiles from the same area and on the same day. Later in the evening, Israel jammed the telephone signal in South Lebanon and disrupted the telecommunications in the concerned areas. Immediately after the missile launch, LAF and UNIFIL jointly investigated the incident.

On 13 October [S/2009/532], Israel referred to an explosion in a civilian structure serving as an arms storage facility belonging to Hizbullah in the Lebanese village of Tayr Filsi, south of the Litani River. In the aftermath of the explosion, Hizbullah operatives sealed off the area and used two trucks to remove evidence from the scene to the nearby village of Deir Qanoun. On 26 October [S/2009/563], Israel stated that on that day, a 107 millimetre rocket was fired from Lebanon and struck the area of Kiryat Shmona in northern Israel. The rocket landed in an open area and no injuries or serious damage had been reported. In response, and in exercise of Israel's right to self-defence, IDF fired artillery shells at the source of the rocket launch.

On 19 October [A/64/496-S/2009/544], Lebanon transmitted to the Secretary-General and the Security-Council a position paper listing 370 air, 62 maritime and 69 land violations by Israel between 22 May and 30 September. The spying networks discovered over the last months, which were operating on Lebanese territory to the benefit of Israel, were a flagrant violation of resolution 1701(2006). The explosion of 17 October in the Houla region demonstrated that Israel had been planting spying devices in south Lebanon. On that day, Israel detonated two of them from a distance, and it continued its hostile activities when Israeli aircraft flew over LAF while the latter were working at dismantling the devices. The continued Israeli occupation of the Kafr Shuba hills and the Lebanese Shab'a Farms constituted a threat to security along the border and was a violation of Council

resolution 425(1978). The delayed Israeli submission of the data on the locations of unexploded ordnance, including the cluster bombs that it dropped and that landed indiscriminately in civilian areas, had caused the death and injury of over 340 people, 34 of whom were children. Most of the information received from Israel was already known as a result of the casualties themselves and three years of reconnaissance, survey and clearance operations. LAF and the Lebanese security agencies had not reported any incidents of arms smuggling since the previous report of the Secretary-General on the implementation of resolution 1701(2006).

Report of Secretary-General (November). On 2 November, the Secretary-General submitted his eleventh report [S/2009/566] on the implementation of resolution 1701(2006). He noted that the situation in the area of operations of UNIFIL remained generally stable and the cessation of hostilities between Israel and Lebanon continued to hold. Nevertheless, serious incidents and violations of the resolution had occurred, both across the Blue Line and in the area between the Blue Line and the Litani River. Of particular concern was the firing of rockets on 11 September and 27 October—the fourth and fifth such attacks in 2009 against Israel from Lebanese soil—and the arms and ammunitions depot that were discovered in Khirbat Silim, as well as the incidents in Tayr Falsay and the Houla area in October, which were under investigation.

The Secretary-General condemned the attacks on UNIFIL personnel by Lebanese civilians that resulted in injuries to peacekeepers and damage to their vehicles, and reiterated his concern regarding attempts to obstruct UNIFIL's freedom of movement. LAF continued to act with commitment and resolve, especially during times of heightened tension. The presence of armed groups in Lebanon operating outside State control continued to pose a challenge to the ability of the State to exercise its full sovereignty and control over its territory. Progress in delineating and demarcating the border between Lebanon and Syria was important for improved border control, and the Secretary-General encouraged the two Governments to pursue their bilateral efforts in that regard. The arms embargo imposed on Lebanon by resolution 1701(2006), of which it was a fundamental aspect, remained an essential factor in maintaining domestic and regional stability. The Secretary-General welcomed the steps taken by Lebanon to improve the control and management of its borders. Additional work needed to be done by the future Government to improve the living conditions of Palestinian refugees in Lebanon. Notwithstanding considerable international support, the task of reconstructing the destroyed Nahr al-Bared camp in northern Lebanon remained challenging. The discovery of archaeological remains on the site resulted in a further delay to the work, provoking Palestinian fears that reconstruction could be at risk. He commended Lebanon for its commitment to rebuild the camp.

Communications. The Syrian Arab Republic stated its position on the Secretary-General's reports by letters of 8 July [S/2009/345] and 10 November [S/2009/583]. Syria was astonished that the Secretary-General and his special representative should drag the country's name into the reports, because the country was not involved in the resolution and only Israel and Lebanon were concerned with its implementation. With regard to the delineation and determination of the Syro-Lebanese borders, Syria reiterated that the issue concerned Syria and Lebanon alone. The process of determining the border in the Shab'a Farms was difficult because of the Israeli occupation of those territories; that section could not be mapped until Israel had withdrawn. The Palestinian presence in Lebanon, both within and beyond the Palestinian camps, was a purely Lebanese-Palestinian issue that was governed by the Cairo Agreement signed by Lebanon and the Palestine Liberation Organization in 1969; Syria had nothing to do with the matter. Syria was astonished by the position of the Secretary-General with regard to the spy networks, which he described as "alleged", albeit 14 arrested Lebanese nationals had been brought before the court on charges of collaborating with Israel in blatant violation of the resolution. Israeli claims about arms smuggling across the Syrian-Lebanese border were fabrications disproven by senior Lebanese officials, and reports of the Lebanon Independent Border Assessment Team [YUN 2008, p. 543] had confirmed that no such activities occurred.

On 5 November [S/2009/574], Israel drew the attention of the Secretary-General and the Security Council to a cargo vessel, the *Francop*, sailing on 4 November under the flag of Antigua and Barbuda en route to Syria via the intended port of Beirut, as well as other ports, bearing 36 containers with hundreds of tons of a wide range of weaponry, including rockets, missiles, mortars, grenades and small arms and light weapons. The weapons—concealed, wrapped and declared as civilian cargo in the ship's manifest—were hidden among hundreds of other containers aboard the ship, which originated from Iran. The intended route of the *Francop,* coupled with the types of weaponry found on board, raised concerns that the incident constituted a violation of resolutions 1701(2006) and 1373(2001) [YUN 2001, p. 61]. That breach was only the latest in a series of violations by Iran documented and examined by the Committee established pursuant to resolution 1737(2006) [YUN 2006, p. 436], including the transfer of weapons aboard the *Monchegorsk* (January 2009) and the *Hansa India* (October 2009), both of which were carrying weapons en route from Iran

to Syria. Iran's national shipping company, referenced in resolution 1803(2008) [YUN 2008, p. 409], had been repeatedly found to be involved in transporting weapons and other banned items in violation of Council resolutions.

UNIFIL financing

The General Assembly had before it the performance report on UNIFIL's budget for the period 1 July 2007 to 30 June 2008 [A/63/520] which showed expenditures amounting to $591,589,000, out of an appropriation of $713,586,800, leaving an unencumbered balance of $121,997,800, as well as the Secretary-General's report on UNIFIL's budget for the period from 1 July 2009 to 30 June 2010 [A/63/689 & Corr.1], amounting to $646,580,400 and providing for the deployment of 15,000 military personnel, 412 international staff and 833 national staff, including temporary positions.

ACABQ in May [A/63/746/Add.11] recommended that the unencumbered balance of $121,997,800 as well as other income and adjustments in the amount of $32,293,700 for the period ended 30 June 2008 be credited to Member States in a manner to be determined by the General Assembly, and that the proposed budget from 1 July 2009 to 30 June 2010 be reduced to $609,763,000 in view of reduced resources for naval transportation, facilities and infrastructure, contingent-owned equipment, requirements for civilian and military personnel and a revised average fuel cost.

GENERAL ASSEMBLY ACTION

On 30 June [meeting 93], the General Assembly, on the recommendation of the Fifth (Administrative and Budgetary) Committee [A/63/905], adopted **resolution 63/298** by recorded vote (134-2-0) [agenda item 144 *(b)*].

Financing of the United Nations Interim Force in Lebanon

The General Assembly,

Having considered the reports of the Secretary-General on the financing of the United Nations Interim Force in Lebanon and the related report of the Advisory Committee on Administrative and Budgetary Questions,

Recalling Security Council resolution 425(1978) of 19 March 1978 regarding the establishment of the United Nations Interim Force in Lebanon and the subsequent resolutions by which the Council extended the mandate of the Force, the latest of which was resolution 1832(2008) of 27 August 2008, by which the Council extended the mandate of the Force until 31 August 2009,

Recalling also its resolution S-8/2 of 21 April 1978 on the financing of the Force and its subsequent resolutions thereon, the latest of which was resolution 62/265 of 20 June 2008,

Reaffirming its resolutions 51/233 of 13 June 1997, 52/237 of 26 June 1998, 53/227 of 8 June 1999, 54/267 of 15 June 2000, 55/180 A of 19 December 2000, 55/180 B of 14 June 2001, 56/214 A of 21 December 2001, 56/214 B of 27 June 2002, 57/325 of 18 June 2003, 58/307 of 18 June 2004, 59/307 of 22 June 2005, 60/278 of 30 June 2006, 61/250 A of 22 December 2006, 61/250 B of 2 April 2007, 61/250 C of 29 June 2007 and 62/265 of 20 June 2008,

Reaffirming also the general principles underlying the financing of United Nations peacekeeping operations, as stated in General Assembly resolutions 1874(S-IV) of 27 June 1963, 3101(XXVIII) of 11 December 1973 and 55/235 of 23 December 2000,

Noting with appreciation that voluntary contributions have been made to the Force,

Mindful of the fact that it is essential to provide the Force with the financial resources necessary to enable it to fulfil its responsibilities under the relevant resolutions of the Security Council,

1. *Requests* the Secretary-General to entrust the Head of the United Nations Interim Force in Lebanon with the task of formulating future budget proposals in full accordance with the provisions of General Assembly resolutions 59/296 of 22 June 2005, 60/266 of 30 June 2006 and 61/276 of 29 June 2007, as well as other relevant resolutions;

2. *Takes note* of the status of contributions to the Force as at 30 April 2009, including the contributions outstanding in the amount of 115.8 million United States dollars, representing some 2 per cent of the total assessed contributions, notes with concern that only seventy-five Member States have paid their assessed contributions in full, and urges all other Member States, in particular those in arrears, to ensure payment of their outstanding assessed contributions;

3. *Expresses its appreciation* to those Member States which have paid their assessed contributions in full, and urges all other Member States to make every possible effort to ensure payment of their assessed contributions to the Force in full;

4. *Expresses deep concern* that Israel did not comply with resolutions 51/233, 52/237, 53/227, 54/267, 55/180 A, 55/180 B, 56/214 A, 56/214 B, 57/325, 58/307, 59/307, 60/278, 61/250 A, 61/250 B, 61/250 C and 62/265;

5. *Stresses once again* that Israel should strictly abide by resolutions 51/233, 52/237, 53/227, 54/267, 55/180 A, 55/180 B, 56/214 A, 56/214 B, 57/325, 58/307, 59/307, 60/278, 61/250 A, 61/250 B, 61/250 C and 62/265;

6. *Expresses concern* at the financial situation with regard to peacekeeping activities, in particular as regards the reimbursements to troop contributors that bear additional burdens owing to overdue payments by Member States of their assessments;

7. *Also expresses concern* at the delay experienced by the Secretary-General in deploying and providing adequate resources to some recent peacekeeping missions, in particular those in Africa;

8. *Emphasizes* that all future and existing peacekeeping missions shall be given equal and non-discriminatory treatment in respect of financial and administrative arrangements;

9. *Also emphasizes* that all peacekeeping missions shall be provided with adequate resources for the effective and efficient discharge of their respective mandates;

10. *Reiterates its request* to the Secretary-General to make the fullest possible use of facilities and equipment at the United Nations Logistics Base at Brindisi, Italy, in order to minimize the costs of procurement for the Force;

11. *Requests* the Secretary-General to ensure that proposed peacekeeping budgets are based on the relevant legislative mandates;

12. *Endorses* the conclusions and recommendations contained in the report of the Advisory Committee on Administrative and Budgetary Questions, and requests the Secretary-General to ensure their full implementation;

13. *Recalls* paragraph 10 of General Assembly resolution 62/264 of 20 June 2008 and paragraph 12 of resolution 62/265, and decides not to endorse the recommendation contained in paragraph 16 of the report of the Advisory Committee;

14. *Takes note* of paragraph 29 of the report of the Advisory Committee;

15. *Decides* to apply a vacancy factor of 18 per cent for both international and national staff of the Force;

16. *Requests* the Secretary-General to ensure the full implementation of the relevant provisions of resolutions 59/296, 60/266 and 61/276;

17. *Also requests* the Secretary-General to take all action necessary to ensure that the Force is administered with a maximum of efficiency and economy;

18. *Further requests* the Secretary-General, in order to reduce the cost of employing General Service staff, to continue efforts to recruit local staff for the Force against General Service posts, commensurate with the requirements of the Force;

19. *Reiterates its request* to the Secretary-General to take the measures necessary to ensure the full implementation of paragraph 8 of resolution 51/233, paragraph 5 of resolution 52/237, paragraph 11 of resolution 53/227, paragraph 14 of resolution 54/267, paragraph 14 of resolution 55/180 A, paragraph 15 of resolution 55/180 B, paragraph 13 of resolution 56/214 A, paragraph 13 of resolution 56/214 B, paragraph 14 of resolution 57/325, paragraph 13 of resolution 58/307, paragraph 13 of resolution 59/307, paragraph 17 of resolution 60/278, paragraph 21 of resolution 61/250 A, paragraph 20 of resolution 61/250 B, paragraph 20 of resolution 61/250 C and paragraph 21 of resolution 62/265, stresses once again that Israel shall pay the amount of 1,117,005 dollars resulting from the incident at Qana on 18 April 1996, and requests the Secretary-General to report on this matter to the General Assembly at its sixty-fourth session;

Financial performance report for the period from 1 July 2007 to 30 June 2008

20. *Takes note* of the report of the Secretary-General on the financial performance of the Force for the period from 1 July 2007 to 30 June 2008;

Budget estimates for the period from 1 July 2009 to 30 June 2010

21. *Decides* to appropriate to the Special Account for the United Nations Interim Force in Lebanon the amount of 615,775,300 dollars for the period from 1 July 2009

to 30 June 2010, inclusive of 589,799,200 dollars for the maintenance of the Force, 21,618,500 dollars for the support account for peacekeeping operations and 4,357,600 dollars for the United Nations Logistics Base;

Financing of the appropriation

22. *Also decides* to apportion among Member States the amount of 102,629,217 dollars for the period from 1 July to 31 August 2009, in accordance with the levels updated in General Assembly resolution 61/243 of 22 December 2006, and taking into account the scale of assessments for 2009, as set out in Assembly resolution 61/237 of 22 December 2006;

23. *Further decides* that, in accordance with the provisions of General Assembly resolution 973(X) of 15 December 1955, there shall be set off against the apportionment among Member States, as provided for in paragraph 22 above, their respective share in the Tax Equalization Fund in the amount of 2,263,183 dollars, comprising the estimated staff assessment income of 1,816,400 dollars approved for the Force, the prorated share of 375,100 dollars of the estimated staff assessment income approved for the support account and the prorated share of 71,683 dollars of the estimated staff assessment income approved for the United Nations Logistics Base;

24. *Decides* to apportion among Member States the amount of 513,146,083 dollars for the period from 1 September 2009 to 30 June 2010 at a monthly rate of 51,314,608 dollars, in accordance with the levels updated in resolution 61/243, and taking into account the scale of assessments for 2009, as set out in resolution 61/237, and for 2010, subject to a decision of the Security Council to extend the mandate of the Force;

25. *Also decides* that, in accordance with the provisions of resolution 973(X), there shall be set off against the apportionment among Member States, as provided for in paragraph 24 above, their respective share in the Tax Equalization Fund in the amount of 11,315,917 dollars, comprising the estimated staff assessment income of 9,082,000 dollars approved for the Force, the prorated share of 1,875,500 dollars of the estimated staff assessment income approved for the support account and the prorated share of 358,417 dollars of the estimated staff assessment income approved for the United Nations Logistics Base;

26. *Further decides* that, for Member States that have fulfilled their financial obligations to the Force, there shall be set off against their apportionment, as provided for in paragraph 22 above, their respective share of the unencumbered balance and other income in the total amount of 154,291,500 dollars in respect of the financial period ended 30 June 2008, in accordance with the levels updated in resolution 61/243, and taking into account the scale of assessments for 2008, as set out in resolution 61/237;

27. *Decides* that, for Member States that have not fulfilled their financial obligations to the Force, there shall be set off against their outstanding obligations their respective share of the unencumbered balance and other income in the total amount of 154,291,500 dollars in respect of the financial period ended 30 June 2008, in accordance with the scheme set out in paragraph 26 above;

28. *Also decides* that the decrease of 2,703,200 dollars in the estimated staff assessment income in respect of the financial period ended 30 June 2008 shall be set off against

the credits from the amount of 154,291,500 dollars referred to in paragraphs 26 and 27 above;

29. *Emphasizes* that no peacekeeping mission shall be financed by borrowing funds from other active peacekeeping missions;

30. *Encourages* the Secretary-General to continue to take additional measures to ensure the safety and security of all personnel participating in the Force under the auspices of the United Nations, bearing in mind paragraphs 5 and 6 of Security Council resolution 1502(2003) of 26 August 2003;

31. *Invites* voluntary contributions to the Force in cash and in the form of services and supplies acceptable to the Secretary-General, to be administered, as appropriate, in accordance with the procedure and practices established by the General Assembly;

32. *Decides* to include in the provisional agenda of its sixty-fourth session, under the item entitled "Financing of the United Nations peacekeeping forces in the Middle East", the sub-item entitled "United Nations Interim Force in Lebanon".

RECORDED VOTE ON RESOLUTION 63/298:

In favour: Afghanistan, Albania, Algeria, Andorra, Antigua and Barbuda, Argentina, Armenia, Australia, Austria, Bahrain, Bangladesh, Belarus, Belgium, Benin, Bosnia and Herzegovina, Botswana, Brazil, Brunei Darussalam, Bulgaria, Burkina Faso, Burundi, Cameroon, Canada, Cape Verde, Chile, China, Congo, Costa Rica, Côte d'Ivoire, Croatia, Cuba, Cyprus, Czech Republic, Democratic People's Republic of Korea, Denmark, Djibouti, Dominican Republic, Ecuador, Egypt, El Salvador, Equatorial Guinea, Eritrea, Estonia, Finland, France, Gabon, Georgia, Germany, Ghana, Greece, Guatemala, Guinea, Guyana, Haiti, Hungary, Iceland, India, Indonesia, Iran, Iraq, Ireland, Italy, Jamaica, Japan, Jordan, Kazakhstan, Kenya, Kuwait, Kyrgyzstan, Lao People's Democratic Republic, Latvia, Liberia, Libyan Arab Jamahiriya, Liechtenstein, Lithuania, Luxembourg, Malaysia, Maldives, Mali, Malta, Mauritania, Mauritius, Mexico, Moldova, Monaco, Mongolia, Montenegro, Morocco, Myanmar, Netherlands, New Zealand, Nicaragua, Niger, Nigeria, Norway, Oman, Pakistan, Panama, Paraguay, Peru, Philippines, Poland, Portugal, Qatar, Republic of Korea, Romania, Russian Federation, Saint Lucia, Saint Vincent and the Grenadines, San Marino, Saudi Arabia, Senegal, Serbia, Singapore, Slovakia, Slovenia, Solomon Islands, South Africa, Sri Lanka, Sweden, Switzerland, Syrian Arab Republic, Tajikistan, Thailand, Togo, Tunisia, Ukraine, United Kingdom, Uruguay, Venezuela, Viet Nam, Yemen, Zambia, Zimbabwe.

Against: Israel, United States.
Abstaining: None.

Special Tribunal for Lebanon

The mandate of the United Nations International Independent Investigation Commission (UNIIIC), established by the Security Council in 2005 [YUN 2005, p. 553] to assist the Lebanese authorities in investigating the terrorist bombing in Beirut on 14 February 2005 that killed former Lebanese Prime Minister Rafiq Hariri and 22 others, ended on 28 February 2009 [YUN 2008, p. 550]. Its successor, the Special Tribunal for Lebanon, created in 2007 to investigate and prosecute the perpetrators of the bombing and related cases [YUN 2007, p. 506], started operations on 1 March.

Report of Secretary-General. Pursuant to Council resolution 1757(2007) [YUN 2007, p. 506], the Secretary-General on 24 February submitted his fourth report [S/2009/106] on the establishment of the Special Tribunal, describing the steps taken, in coordination with the Government of Lebanon, to establish the Tribunal. On 17 December 2008, following consultation by the UN Legal Counsel with the Prime Minister of Lebanon, Fouad Siniora, and with the UNIIIC Commissioner, Daniel Bellemare (Canada), the Secretary-General decided that the Tribunal would commence functioning on 1 March 2009. The Tribunal was located in The Hague. Mr. Bellemare would serve as Prosecutor. Arrangements for the transition from UNIIIC to the Special Tribunal were under way.

Security Council action. On 3 March, by a press statement [SC/9606], the Security Council welcomed the commencement of the functioning of the Special Tribunal on 1 March as an important step by Lebanon and the international community to bring to justice those responsible for the assassinations and to end impunity in Lebanon. The Council recalled its resolution 1852(2008) [YUN 2008, p. 550] which underlined the importance of full cooperation of Member States with the Office of the Prosecutor to enable effective investigations and prosecutions.

Report by President of Special Tribunal. On 14 September, the President of the Tribunal, Antonio Cassese (Italy), presented a report entitled "The STL six months on: a bird's eye view" to the Tribunal's Management Committee. The report reviewed the activities of the Tribunal in the six months since its establishment, including the activities carried out by its four organs: Chambers, Registry, Office of the Prosecutor and Defence Office. The Registry had worked towards the establishment of practical infrastructures and the recruitment of staff. The Judges had approved several legal documents for the functioning of the Tribunal. The Prosecutor had stepped up his investigations. The Head of the Defence Office had had intense contacts with the Lebanese bar associations and Lebanese lawyers. The Government of Lebanon had lent unreserved cooperation with the organs of the Tribunal. Lebanon had deferred jurisdiction and the Pre-Trial Judge had issued various orders on the four Lebanese Generals detained in Beirut in connection with the Hariri case. The Pre-Trial Judge ordered the release of the four Generals on 29 April because of lack of sufficient evidence to justify their detention. President Cassese reiterated that the Tribunal intended to dispense justice free from any political or ideological fetter and based on the full respect of the rights of victims and defendants.

Communication. On 15 September [S/2009/469], the Syrian Arab Republic brought to the attention of the Security Council the release after four years of four Lebanese military officers by the Pre-Trial Judge of the Special Tribunal for Lebanon and the subsequent media statements by one of them. The statements made it clear that the goal of UNIIIC had been to implicate Syria in the assassination of Prime Minister Hariri.

Syrian Arab Republic

The Golan Heights in the Syrian Arab Republic, occupied since 1967, was effectively annexed when Israel extended its laws, jurisdiction and administration to the territory in 1981 [YUN 1981, p. 309]. The General Assembly demanded once again that Israel withdraw from all the occupied Syrian Golan to the line of 4 June 1967, in implementation of the relevant Security Council resolutions, and that the two countries resume talks. UNDOF continued to supervise the ceasefire between Israel and Syria in the Golan Heights and to ensure the separation of militaries. The Mission's mandate was extended twice during the year.

Special Committee on Israeli Practices. The Special Committee to Investigate Israeli Practices Affecting the Human Rights of the Palestinian People and other Arabs of the Occupied Territories conducted a mission to Syria from 11 to 13 August [A/64/339]. The Committee reported that it visited the Syrian Golan and heard the testimony of six witnesses pertaining to the situation in the occupied Golan. Regrettably, the Committee was unable to visit the occupied Golan as it received no response from the Israeli Government to its request.

The Committee heard testimony on the planned expansion of Israeli Jewish settlements in the Golan that currently comprised about 20,000 settlers living in 33 settlements that were built on the ruins of Syrian villages and towns. Prior to the occupation of 1967, the population of the Golan was 138,000 people in over 312 towns and villages. With the start of the occupation, 131,000 people were reported to have fled to Syria. Currently, there were only five Syrian villages with a population of 20,000 in the northern Golan.

The Special Committee was informed that the number of settlers might continue to increase as a result of a policy that aimed to attract at least 100 new Israeli Jewish settlers each year. The Committee was alerted to the unequal distribution of water in the occupied Golan, where, according to witnesses, settlers received unlimited quantities at a minimal cost, while Arab farmers were charged double for limited quantities.

The Special Committee was informed that the Arab residents of the occupied Golan faced difficulties in finding adequate employment. Following a strike in protest of the Israeli annexation of the Syrian Golan in 1981, a number of Syrians lost their jobs and had been unable to regain meaningful employment.

The Syrian Ministry of Foreign Affairs, in its report to the Special Committee, noted its concern on the imposition of an Israeli curriculum on Arab schools, as well as the lack of investment in Arab educational facilities leading to chronic overcrowding and dilapidated institutions. The Ministry also informed the Special Committee of the minefields that continued to limit the movement of many Syrian citizens in the occupied territory and caused numerous casualties, including among children.

The Special Committee expressed concern about the adverse effects on many separated families, who shared their distress during the field mission.

Reports of Secretary-General. On 10 September [A/64/343], the Secretary-General reported that as at 31 August, Colombia, Cuba, the Democratic People's Republic of Korea, Jordan, Mexico, Nicaragua, Qatar, the Sudan and Syria had replied on their implementation of General Assembly resolution 63/31 [YUN 2008, p. 552]. The resolution demanded that Israel withdraw from all the occupied Syrian Golan to the line of 4 June 1967 in implementation of the relevant Security Council resolutions.

In his 16 September report on the occupied Syrian Golan [A/64/354], responding to Assembly resolution 63/99 [YUN 2008, p. 553], the Secretary-General stated that no reply had been received from Israel in response to his request for information on steps taken or to be taken concerning the implementation of the relevant provisions of the resolution, which dealt with Israeli policies in the occupied Syrian territory. The Secretary-General also noted that Colombia, Egypt, Qatar, Syria and Venezuela had replied to his note that drew attention to paragraph 6 of resolution 63/99, which called upon all Member States not to recognize any of the Israeli legislative and administrative measures and actions in the occupied Syrian Golan.

(On related action by the Human Rights Council, see PART TWO, Chapter III).

GENERAL ASSEMBLY ACTION

On 2 December [meeting 54], the General Assembly adopted **resolution 64/21** [draft: A/64/L.25 & Add.1] by recorded vote (116-7-51) [agenda item 15].

The Syrian Golan

The General Assembly,

Having considered the item entitled "The situation in the Middle East",

Taking note of the report of the Secretary-General on the situation in the Middle East,

Recalling Security Council resolution 497(1981) of 17 December 1981,

Reaffirming the fundamental principle of the inadmissibility of the acquisition of territory by force, in accordance with international law and the Charter of the United Nations,

Reaffirming once more the applicability of the Geneva Convention relative to the Protection of Civilian Persons in Time of War, of 12 August 1949, to the occupied Syrian Golan,

Deeply concerned that Israel has not withdrawn from the Syrian Golan, which has been under occupation since 1967, contrary to the relevant Security Council and General Assembly resolutions,

Stressing the illegality of the Israeli settlement construction and other activities in the occupied Syrian Golan since 1967,

Noting with satisfaction the convening in Madrid on 30 October 1991 of the Peace Conference on the Middle East, on the basis of Security Council resolutions 242(1967) of 22 November 1967, 338(1973) of 22 October 1973 and 425(1978) of 19 March 1978 and the formula of land for peace,

Expressing grave concern over the halt in the peace process on the Syrian track, and expressing the hope that peace talks will soon resume from the point they had reached,

1.   *Declares* that Israel has failed so far to comply with Security Council resolution 497(1981);

2.   *Also declares* that the Israeli decision of 14 December 1981 to impose its laws, jurisdiction and administration on the occupied Syrian Golan is null and void and has no validity whatsoever, as confirmed by the Security Council in resolution 497(1981), and calls upon Israel to rescind it;

3.   *Reaffirms its determination* that all relevant provisions of the Regulations annexed to the Hague Convention of 1907 and the Geneva Convention relative to the Protection of Civilian Persons in Time of War continue to apply to the Syrian territory occupied by Israel since 1967, and calls upon the parties thereto to respect and ensure respect for their obligations under those instruments in all circumstances;

4.   *Determines once more* that the continued occupation of the Syrian Golan and its de facto annexation constitute a stumbling block in the way of a just, comprehensive and lasting peace in the region;

5.   *Calls upon* Israel to resume the talks on the Syrian and Lebanese tracks and to respect the commitments and undertakings reached during the previous talks;

6.   *Demands once more* that Israel withdraw from all the occupied Syrian Golan to the line of 4 June 1967 in implementation of the relevant Security Council resolutions;

7.   *Calls upon* all the parties concerned, the co-sponsors of the peace process and the entire international community to exert all the efforts necessary to ensure the resumption of the peace process and its success by implementing Security Council resolutions 242(1967) and 338(1973);

8.   *Requests* the Secretary-General to report to the General Assembly at its sixty-fifth session on the implementation of the present resolution.

RECORDED VOTE ON RESOLUTION 64/21:

In favour: Afghanistan, Algeria, Angola, Argentina, Armenia, Azerbaijan, Bahamas, Bahrain, Bangladesh, Barbados, Belarus, Belize, Benin, Bhutan, Bolivia, Botswana, Brazil, Brunei Darussalam, Burkina Faso, Cambodia, Cape Verde, Chad, Chile, China, Colombia, Comoros, Costa Rica, Cuba, Cyprus, Democratic People's Republic of Korea, Djibouti, Dominica, Dominican Republic, Ecuador, Egypt, El Salvador, Eritrea, Ethiopia, Gabon, Gambia, Ghana, Guatemala, Guinea, Guinea-Bissau, Guyana, Haiti, India, Indonesia, Iran, Iraq, Jamaica, Jordan, Kazakhstan, Kenya, Kuwait, Kyrgyzstan, Lao People's Democratic Republic, Lebanon, Lesotho, Liberia, Libyan Arab Jamahiriya, Madagascar, Malaysia, Maldives, Mali, Mauritania, Mauritius, Mexico, Mongolia, Morocco, Mozambique, Myanmar, Namibia, Nepal, Nicaragua, Niger, Nigeria, Oman, Pakistan, Papua New Guinea, Paraguay, Peru, Philippines, Qatar, Russian Federation, Saint Lucia, Saint Vincent and the Grenadines, Saudi Arabia, Senegal, Sierra Leone, Singapore, Solomon Islands, Somalia, South Africa, Sri Lanka, Sudan, Suriname, Swaziland, Syrian Arab Republic, Tajikistan, Thailand, Togo, Trinidad and Tobago, Tunisia, Turkey, Turkmenistan, Uganda, United Arab Emirates, United Republic of Tanzania, Uruguay, Uzbekistan, Venezuela, Viet Nam, Yemen, Zambia, Zimbabwe.

Against: Canada, Israel, Marshall Islands, Micronesia, Nauru, Palau, United States.

Abstaining: Albania, Andorra, Australia, Austria, Belgium, Bulgaria, Cameroon, Côte d'Ivoire, Croatia, Czech Republic, Denmark, Estonia, Fiji, Finland, France, Georgia, Germany, Greece, Hungary, Iceland, Ireland, Italy, Japan, Latvia, Liechtenstein, Lithuania, Luxembourg, Malta, Moldova, Monaco, Montenegro, Netherlands, New Zealand, Norway, Panama, Poland, Portugal, Republic of Korea, Romania, Samoa, San Marino, Serbia, Slovakia, Slovenia, Spain, Sweden, Switzerland, The former Yugoslav Republic of Macedonia, Tonga, Ukraine, United Kingdom.

On 10 December [meeting 62], the General Assembly, on the recommendation of the Fourth Committee [A/64/406], adopted **resolution 64/95** by recorded vote (166-1-11) [agenda item 32].

The occupied Syrian Golan

The General Assembly,

Having considered the report of the Special Committee to Investigate Israeli Practices Affecting the Human Rights of the Palestinian People and Other Arabs of the Occupied Territories,

Deeply concerned that the Syrian Golan, occupied since 1967, has been under continued Israeli military occupation,

Recalling Security Council resolution 497(1981) of 17 December 1981,

Recalling also its previous relevant resolutions, the most recent of which was resolution 63/99 of 5 December 2008,

Having considered the report of the Secretary-General submitted in pursuance of resolution 63/99,

Recalling its previous relevant resolutions in which, inter alia, it called upon Israel to put an end to its occupation of the Arab territories,

Reaffirming once more the illegality of the decision of 14 December 1981 taken by Israel to impose its laws, jurisdiction and administration on the occupied Syrian Golan, which has resulted in the effective annexation of that territory,

Reaffirming that the acquisition of territory by force is inadmissible under international law, including the Charter of the United Nations,

Reaffirming also the applicability of the Geneva Convention relative to the Protection of Civilian Persons in Time of War, of 12 August 1949, to the occupied Syrian Golan,

Bearing in mind Security Council resolution 237(1967) of 14 June 1967,

Welcoming the convening at Madrid of the Peace Conference on the Middle East on the basis of Security Council resolutions 242(1967) of 22 November 1967 and 338(1973) of 22 October 1973 aimed at the realization of a just, comprehensive and lasting peace, and expressing grave concern about the stalling of the peace process on all tracks,

1. *Calls upon* Israel, the occupying Power, to comply with the relevant resolutions on the occupied Syrian Golan, in particular Security Council resolution 497(1981), in which the Council, inter alia, decided that the Israeli decision to impose its laws, jurisdiction and administration on the occupied Syrian Golan was null and void and without international legal effect and demanded that Israel, the occupying Power, rescind forthwith its decision;

2. *Also calls upon* Israel to desist from changing the physical character, demographic composition, institutional structure and legal status of the occupied Syrian Golan and in particular to desist from the establishment of settlements;

3. *Determines* that all legislative and administrative measures and actions taken or to be taken by Israel, the occupying Power, that purport to alter the character and legal status of the occupied Syrian Golan are null and void, constitute a flagrant violation of international law and of the Geneva Convention relative to the Protection of Civilian Persons in Time of War, of 12 August 1949, and have no legal effect;

4. *Calls upon* Israel to desist from imposing Israeli citizenship and Israeli identity cards on the Syrian citizens in the occupied Syrian Golan, and from its repressive measures against the population of the occupied Syrian Golan;

5. *Deplores* the violations by Israel of the Geneva Convention relative to the Protection of Civilian Persons in Time of War, of 12 August 1949;

6. *Calls once again upon* Member States not to recognize any of the legislative or administrative measures and actions referred to above;

7. *Requests* the Secretary-General to report to the General Assembly at its sixty-fifth session on the implementation of the present resolution.

RECORDED VOTE ON RESOLUTION 64/95:

In favour: Afghanistan, Albania, Algeria, Andorra, Angola, Antigua and Barbuda, Argentina, Armenia, Australia, Austria, Azerbaijan, Bahamas, Bahrain, Bangladesh, Barbados, Belarus, Belgium, Belize, Benin, Bhutan, Bolivia, Bosnia and Herzegovina, Botswana, Brazil, Brunei Darussalam, Bulgaria, Burkina Faso, Burundi, Canada, Cape Verde, Chile, China, Colombia, Comoros, Congo, Costa Rica, Croatia, Cuba, Cyprus, Czech Republic, Democratic People's Republic of Korea, Denmark, Djibouti, Dominica, Dominican Republic, Ecuador, Egypt, El Salvador, Eritrea, Estonia, Ethiopia, Finland, France,

Gambia, Georgia, Germany, Ghana, Greece, Grenada, Guatemala, Guinea, Guinea-Bissau, Guyana, Honduras, Hungary, Iceland, India, Indonesia, Iran, Iraq, Ireland, Italy, Jamaica, Japan, Jordan, Kazakhstan, Kenya, Kuwait, Kyrgyzstan, Lao People's Democratic Republic, Latvia, Lebanon, Lesotho, Liberia, Libyan Arab Jamahiriya, Liechtenstein, Lithuania, Luxembourg, Madagascar, Malawi, Malaysia, Maldives, Mali, Malta, Mauritania, Mauritius, Mexico, Moldova, Monaco, Mongolia, Montenegro, Morocco, Mozambique, Myanmar, Namibia, Nepal, Netherlands, New Zealand, Nicaragua, Niger, Nigeria, Norway, Oman, Pakistan, Papua New Guinea, Paraguay, Peru, Philippines, Poland, Portugal, Qatar, Republic of Korea, Romania, Russian Federation, Saint Lucia, Saint Vincent and the Grenadines, Samoa, San Marino, Saudi Arabia, Senegal, Serbia, Sierra Leone, Singapore, Slovakia, Slovenia, Solomon Islands, Somalia, South Africa, Spain, Sri Lanka, Sudan, Suriname, Swaziland, Sweden, Switzerland, Syrian Arab Republic, Tajikistan, Thailand, The former Yugoslav Republic of Macedonia, Timor-Leste, Togo, Trinidad and Tobago, Tunisia, Turkey, Turkmenistan, Ukraine, United Arab Emirates, United Kingdom, United Republic of Tanzania, Uruguay, Uzbekistan, Venezuela, Viet Nam, Yemen, Zambia, Zimbabwe.

Against: Israel.

Abstaining: Cameroon, Côte d'Ivoire, Fiji, Marshall Islands, Micronesia, Nauru, Palau, Panama, Tonga, United States, Vanuatu.

UNDOF

The mandate of the United Nations Disengagement Observer Force (UNDOF), established by Security Council resolution 350(1974) [YUN 1974, p. 205] to supervise the observance of the ceasefire between Israel and the Syrian Arab Republic in the Golan Heights and ensure the separation of their forces, was renewed twice in 2009, in June and December, each time for a six-month period.

UNDOF maintained an area of separation some 75 kilometres long and varying in width between 12.5 kilometres in the centre to less than 200 metres in the extreme south. The area of separation was inhabited and policed by the Syrian authorities, and no military forces other than UNDOF were permitted within it. As at 10 November, UNDOF comprised 1,040 troops from seven Member States assisted by 75 UNTSO military observers.

Reports of Secretary-General. The Secretary-General reported to the Security Council on UNDOF activities between 1 January and 30 June [S/2009/295] and 1 July and 31 December 2009 [S/2009/597]. Both reports noted that the UNDOF area of operations remained generally quiet. The Force supervised the area of separation by means of fixed positions and patrols, and carried out inspections of equipment and force levels in the areas of limitation. As in the past, both sides denied inspection teams access to some of their positions and imposed restrictions on the Force's freedom of movement. UNDOF continued to adapt its operation posture to the ongoing IDF training in the area

of limitation on the Alpha side and Syrian civilian settlement growth in the proximity to the ceasefire line in the area of separation. Both sides continued to build new and renovate existing defensive positions in the respective areas of limitations. Israeli customs officials continued to operate periodically at the IDF post at the UNDOF crossing gate between the Israeli-occupied Golan and Syria.

The Force also assisted the International Committee of the Red Cross with the passage of persons through the area of separation. In the area of operation, especially in the area of separation, mines continued to pose a threat to UNDOF personnel and local inhabitants. Owing to the long-term presence of the mines and the deterioration of their detonation systems, the threat had increased. UNDOF continued to carry out operational mine clearance, and remained available to support UNICEF in activities to promote mine awareness among the civilian population. The Force Commander and his staff maintained close contact with the military authorities of both sides, and both parties generally cooperated with UNDOF in the execution of its tasks.

The situation in the Middle East was tense and likely to remain so, unless and until a comprehensive settlement could be reached. The Secretary-General hoped that determined efforts would be made by all concerned to tackle the Middle East problem in all its aspects, with a view to arriving at a just and durable peace settlement, as called for by Council resolution 338(1973) [YUN 1973, p. 213]. In that context, he encouraged the parties to resume the indirect peace talks initiated under the auspices of Turkey, aimed at a comprehensive peace in accordance with the Madrid Conference terms of reference [YUN 1991, p. 221].

Stating that he considered UNDOF's continued presence in the area essential, the Secretary-General, with the agreement of both Israel and Syria, recommended in June that its mandate be extended until 30 December 2009, and in November, until 30 June 2010.

SECURITY COUNCIL ACTION

On 23 June [meeting 6148], the Security Council unanimously adopted **resolution 1875(2009)**. The draft [S/2009/320] was prepared in consultations among Council members.

The Security Council,

Having considered the report of the Secretary-General of 8 June 2009 on the United Nations Disengagement Observer Force, and reaffirming its resolution 1308(2000) of 17 July 2000,

1. *Calls upon* the parties concerned to implement immediately its resolution 338(1973) of 22 October 1973;

2. *Welcomes* the efforts being undertaken by the United Nations Disengagement Observer Force to im-

plement the Secretary-General's zero-tolerance policy on sexual exploitation and abuse and to ensure full compliance of its personnel with the United Nations code of conduct, requests the Secretary-General to continue to take all necessary action in this regard and to keep the Security Council informed, and urges troop-contributing countries to take preventive and disciplinary action to ensure that such acts are properly investigated and punished in cases involving their personnel;

3. *Decides* to renew the mandate of the Force for a period of six months, that is, until 31 December 2009;

4. *Requests* the Secretary-General to submit, at the end of this period, a report on developments in the situation and the measures taken to implement resolution 338(1973).

On 16 December [meeting 6241], the Security Council unanimously adopted **resolution 1899(2009)**. The draft [S/2009/651] was prepared in consultations among Council members.

The Security Council,

Having considered the report of the Secretary-General of 18 November 2009 on the United Nations Disengagement Observer Force, and reaffirming its resolution 1308(2000) of 17 July 2000,

1. *Calls upon* the parties concerned to implement immediately its resolution 338(1973) of 22 October 1973;

2. *Welcomes* the efforts being undertaken by the United Nations Disengagement Observer Force to implement the Secretary-General's zero-tolerance policy on sexual exploitation and abuse and to ensure full compliance of its personnel with the United Nations code of conduct, requests the Secretary-General to continue to take all necessary action in this regard and to keep the Security Council informed, and urges troop-contributing countries to take preventive and disciplinary action to ensure that such acts are properly investigated and punished in cases involving their personnel;

3. *Decides* to renew the mandate of the Force for a period of six months, that is, until 30 June 2010;

4. *Requests* the Secretary-General to submit, at the end of this period, a report on developments in the situation and the measures taken to implement resolution 338(1973).

After the adoption of each resolution, the President, following consultations among Council members made identical statements, **S/PRST/2009/18** [meeting 6148] on 23 June, and **S/PRST/2009/34** [meeting 6241] on 16 December, on behalf of the Council:

In connection with the resolution just adopted on the renewal of the mandate of the United Nations Disengagement Observer Force, I have been authorized to make the following complementary statement on behalf of the Security Council:

As is known, the report of the Secretary-General on the United Nations Disengagement Observer Force states in paragraph 11: "... the situation in the Middle East is tense and is likely to remain so, unless and until a comprehensive settlement covering all aspects of the Middle East problem can be reached". That statement of the Secretary-General reflects the view of the Security Council.

UNDOF financing

The General Assembly had before it the performance report of the Secretary-General on the UNDOF budget for the period from 1 July 2007 to 30 June 2008 [A/63/521], which showed expenditures amounting to $42,179,700 gross ($40,990,100 net) against an appropriation of $39,662,500 gross ($38,551,900 net), as well as the Secretary-General's report on the UNDOF budget for the period from 1 July 2009 to 30 June 2010 [A/63/686 & Corr.2], amounting to $45,369,600 and providing for the deployment of 1,047 military contingent personnel and 48 international and 108 national staff. It also had before it the related ACABQ report [A/63/746/Add.2], recommending to the Assembly a reduction of $113,600 and an appropriation of $45,256,000.

GENERAL ASSEMBLY ACTION

On 30 June [meeting 93], the General Assembly, on the recommendation of the Fifth Committee [A/63/904], adopted **resolution 63/297** without vote [agenda item 144 *(a)*].

Financing of the United Nations Disengagement Observer Force

The General Assembly,

Having considered the reports of the Secretary-General on the financing of the United Nations Disengagement Observer Force and the related report of the Advisory Committee on Administrative and Budgetary Questions,

Recalling Security Council resolution 350(1974) of 31 May 1974 regarding the establishment of the United Nations Disengagement Observer Force and the subsequent resolutions by which the Council extended the mandate of the Force, the latest of which was resolution 1848(2008) of 12 December 2008,

Recalling also its resolution 3211 B(XXIX) of 29 November 1974 on the financing of the United Nations Emergency Force and of the United Nations Disengagement Observer Force and its subsequent resolutions thereon, the latest of which was resolution 62/264 of 20 June 2008,

Reaffirming the general principles underlying the financing of United Nations peacekeeping operations, as stated in General Assembly resolutions 1874(S-IV) of 27 June 1963, 3101(XXVIII) of 11 December 1973 and 55/235 of 23 December 2000,

Mindful of the fact that it is essential to provide the Force with the financial resources necessary to enable it to fulfil its responsibilities under the relevant resolutions of the Security Council,

1. *Requests* the Secretary-General to entrust the Head of Mission with the task of formulating future budget proposals in full accordance with the provisions of General Assembly resolutions 59/296 of 22 June 2005, 60/266 of 30 June 2006 and 61/276 of 29 June 2007, as well as other relevant resolutions;

2. *Takes note* of the status of contributions to the United Nations Disengagement Observer Force as at 30 April 2009, including the contributions outstanding in the amount of 17.0 million United States dollars, representing some 1 per cent of the total assessed contributions, notes with concern that only forty-five Member States have paid their assessed contributions in full, and urges all other Member States, in particular those in arrears, to ensure payment of their outstanding assessed contributions;

3. *Expresses its appreciation* to those Member States which have paid their assessed contributions in full, and urges all other Member States to make every possible effort to ensure payment of their assessed contributions to the Force in full;

4. *Expresses concern* at the financial situation with regard to peacekeeping activities, in particular as regards the reimbursements to troop contributors that bear additional burdens owing to overdue payments by Member States of their assessments;

5. *Also expresses concern* at the delay experienced by the Secretary-General in deploying and providing adequate resources to some recent peacekeeping missions, in particular those in Africa;

6. *Emphasizes* that all future and existing peacekeeping missions shall be given equal and non-discriminatory treatment in respect of financial and administrative arrangements;

7. *Also emphasizes* that all peacekeeping missions shall be provided with adequate resources for the effective and efficient discharge of their respective mandates;

8. *Reiterates its request* to the Secretary-General to make the fullest possible use of facilities and equipment at the United Nations Logistics Base at Brindisi, Italy, in order to minimize the costs of procurement for the Force;

9. *Requests* the Secretary-General to ensure that proposed peacekeeping budgets are based on the relevant legislative mandates;

10. *Endorses* the conclusions and recommendations contained in the report of the Advisory Committee on Administrative and Budgetary Questions, subject to the provisions of the present resolution, and requests the Secretary-General to ensure their full implementation;

11. *Recalls* paragraph 10 of resolution 62/264 and paragraph 12 of General Assembly resolution 62/265 of 20 June 2008, and decides not to endorse the recommendation contained in paragraph 32 of the report of the Advisory Committee;

12. *Takes note* of paragraph 31 of the report of the Advisory Committee;

13. *Requests* the Secretary-General to ensure the full implementation of the relevant provisions of resolutions 59/296, 60/266 and 61/276;

14. *Also requests* the Secretary-General to take all action necessary to ensure that the Force is administered with a maximum of efficiency and economy;

15. *Further requests* the Secretary-General, in order to reduce the cost of employing General Service staff, to continue efforts to recruit local staff for the Force against General Service posts, commensurate with the requirements of the Force;

Financial performance report for the period from 1 July 2007 to 30 June 2008

16. *Takes note* of the report of the Secretary-General on the financial performance of the Force for the period from 1 July 2007 to 30 June 2008;

17. *Decides* to appropriate to the Special Account for the United Nations Disengagement Observer Force the amount of 2,517,200 dollars for the maintenance of the Force for the period from 1 July 2007 to 30 June 2008, in addition to the amount of 41,586,600 dollars already appropriated for the Force for the same period under the terms of General Assembly resolution 61/287 of 29 June 2007;

Financing of the additional appropriation for the period from 1 July 2007 to 30 June 2008

18. *Also decides*, taking into account the amount of 41,586,600 dollars already apportioned under the terms of resolution 61/287, to apportion among Member States the additional amount of 2,517,200 dollars for the maintenance of the Force for the period from 1 July 2007 to 30 June 2008, in accordance with the levels updated in General Assembly resolution 61/243 of 22 December 2006, and taking into account the scale of assessments for 2007 and 2008, as set out in Assembly resolution 61/237 of 22 December 2006;

19. *Further decides* that, in accordance with the provisions of General Assembly resolution 973(X) of 15 December 1955, there shall be set off against the apportionment among Member States, as provided for in paragraph 18 above, their respective share in the Tax Equalization Fund in the amount of 79,000 dollars, representing the additional staff assessment income for the Force for the period from 1 July 2007 to 30 June 2008;

Budget estimates for the period from 1 July 2009 to 30 June 2010

20. *Decides* to appropriate to the Special Account for the United Nations Disengagement Observer Force the amount of 47,020,300 dollars for the period from 1 July 2009 to 30 June 2010, inclusive of 45,029,700 dollars for the maintenance of the Force, 1,656,700 dollars for the support account for peacekeeping operations and 333,900 dollars for the United Nations Logistics Base;

Financing of the appropriation

21. *Also decides* to apportion among Member States the amount of 47,020,300 dollars at a monthly rate of 3,918,358 dollars, in accordance with the levels updated in resolution 61/243, and taking into account the scale of assessments for 2009, as set out in resolution 61/237, and for 2010, subject to a decision of the Security Council to extend the mandate of the Force;

22. *Further decides* that, in accordance with the provisions of resolution 973(X), there shall be set off against the apportionment among Member States, as provided for in paragraph 21 above, their respective share in the Tax Equalization Fund in the amount of 1,543,400 dollars, comprising the estimated staff assessment income of 1,338,000 dollars approved for the Force for the period from 1 July 2009 to 30 June 2010, the prorated share of 172,500 dollars of the estimated staff assessment income approved for the

support account and the prorated share of 32,900 dollars of the estimated staff assessment income approved for the United Nations Logistics Base;

23.   *Decides* that, for Member States that have fulfilled their financial obligations to the Force, there shall be set off against their apportionment, as provided for in paragraph 21 above, their respective share of other income in the total amount of 2,076,200 dollars in respect of the financial period ended 30 June 2008, in accordance with the levels updated in resolution 61/243, and taking into account the scale of assessments for 2008, as set out in resolution 61/237;

24.   *Also decides* that, for Member States that have not fulfilled their financial obligations to the Force, there shall be set off against their outstanding obligations their respective share of other income in the total amount of 2,076,200 dollars in respect of the financial period ended 30 June 2008, in accordance with the scheme set out in paragraph 23 above;

25.   *Emphasizes* that no peacekeeping mission shall be financed by borrowing funds from other active peacekeeping missions;

26.   *Encourages* the Secretary-General to continue to take additional measures to ensure the safety and security of all personnel participating in the Force under the auspices of the United Nations, bearing in mind paragraphs 5 and 6 of Security Council resolution 1502(2003) of 26 August 2003;

27.   *Invites* voluntary contributions to the Force in cash and in the form of services and supplies acceptable to the Secretary-General, to be administered, as appropriate, in accordance with the procedure and practices established by the General Assembly;

28.   *Decides* to include in the provisional agenda of its sixty-fourth session, under the item entitled "Financing of the United Nations peacekeeping forces in the Middle East", the sub-item entitled "United Nations Disengagement Observer Force".

Chapter VII

Disarmament

The Conference on Disarmament, the principal United Nations negotiating forum on the issue, in 2009 overcame years of deadlock and agreed on an agenda jump-starting its work, as the Russian Federation and the United States, the two largest nuclear-weapon powers, committed themselves to disarmament in accordance with their obligations under the Treaty on the Non-Proliferation of Nuclear Weapons (NPT). However, as the year progressed, the Conference was unable to implement its agenda, revealing rifts among Member States on nuclear issues. The Disarmament Commission, which started a fresh three-year cycle, also agreed on a work programme aimed at achieving consensus on nuclear disarmament and non-proliferation, declaring a fourth disarmament decade and developing confidence-building measures in conventional weapons. However, progress was small, as seen also in a related postponement by the General Assembly of a decision to convene a fourth special session on disarmament.

United States President Barack Obama in September chaired the Security Council's first summit on nuclear disarmament, attended by 13 heads of State and Government who called on NPT parties to comply fully with their obligations and on countries outside the Treaty to accede to it. The summit also called for a ban on nuclear testing and fissile material production. However, multilateral negotiations in both areas were sluggish. Though three more countries ratified the Comprehensive Nuclear-Test-Ban Treaty (CTBT), bringing the parties to 151, nine States held back ratifications, preventing the Treaty's entry into force. Meanwhile, the Democratic People's Republic of Korea—a CTBT non-signatory—conducted a second underground nuclear test in violation of Council resolution 1718(2006). The International Atomic Energy Agency continued its efforts to verify the peaceful nature of Iran's nuclear programme and investigated allegations of a destroyed nuclear reactor in the Syrian Arab Republic. While negotiations on the scope of a treaty banning production of fissile material and verification measures were no longer controversial, national security concerns stalled progress, as delegations faced the question whether a treaty should cover existing stockpiles.

The entry into force of the central Asian and African nuclear-weapon-free zones spurred non-proliferation in those regions, while discussions on establishing a similar zone free of nuclear weapons in the Middle East made little headway. The three regional centres for peace and disarmament continued to fulfil their mandates despite budgetary constraints.

On conventional weapons, the General Assembly decided to meet in 2012 to begin work on a treaty to reinforce licit trade and stamp down illicit trade in small arms.

The year marked the tenth anniversary of the Convention banning anti-personnel mines, and countries agreed on the Cartagena Declaration—a shared commitment for a mine-free world. By the end of the year, the Convention on Cluster Munitions was four ratifications short for entry into force. Three more States either ratified or acceded to the chemical weapons Convention, but in a climate of concern that the final extended deadline of 29 April 2012 for destruction of all categories of chemical weapons in the world might not be met.

The Advisory Board on Disarmament Matters discussed cyberwarfare, noting that in the area of dual use it shared similarities with biological and chemical warfare. The Secretary-General issued his first report on promoting development through the reduction and prevention of armed violence. He said that young men were most often the perpetrators and victims of armed violence—which was the consequence of underdevelopment—while women, girls and boys suffered most from acute forms of sexual violence.

To enhance public awareness about the effects of nuclear weapon test explosions and the need for their cessation, the General Assembly declared 29 August the International Day against Nuclear Tests.

UN machinery

Disarmament issues before the United Nations were considered mainly through the Security Council, the General Assembly and its First (Disarmament and International Security) Committee, the Disarmament Commission (a deliberative body) and the Conference on Disarmament (a multilateral negotiating forum meeting in Geneva). The Organization also maintained efforts to engage civil society organizations concerned with disarmament issues.

The United Nations Office for Disarmament Affairs provided substantive and organizational support to UN bodies, fostered disarmament measures and disseminated impartial and up-to-date information.

The General Assembly, by **decision 64/549** of 24 December, decided that the agenda item on general and complete disarmament would remain for consideration during its resumed sixty-fourth (2010) session.

Advancing the disarmament agenda

In his annual report on the work of the Organization [A/64/1], the Secretary-General noted that the world continued to face the twin risks from weapons of mass destruction (WMDs), especially nuclear weapons, their geographical spread, and possible acquisition by non-State actors and terrorists; and from the destabilizing accumulation and proliferation of conventional arms, which remained a security threat.

The momentum towards a world free from nuclear weapons had materialized in a variety of initiatives, including by civil society, nuclear-weapon and non-nuclear-weapon States alike, but chiefly by the joint understanding for a follow-on agreement to the Treaty on the Reduction and Limitation of Strategic Offensive Arms (START I) resulting from the talks held in July in Moscow between President Barack Obama of the United States and President Dmitry Medvedev of the Russian Federation.

The second nuclear test conducted by the Democratic People's Republic of Korea on 25 May (see p. 384) required global action and highlighted the need for the entry into force of the Comprehensive Nuclear-Test-Ban Treaty (see p. 512). The Secretary-General also expressed concerns about the nuclear programme of Iran (see p. 394), which had a responsibility to establish confidence in the programme's exclusively peaceful nature.

In May, the Conference on Disarmament (see p. 498) reached an agreement on its programme of work, ending the stalemate that had virtually paralysed the world's single multilateral negotiating body on disarmament for more than a decade.

In the area of conventional weapons, combating the illicit trade in small arms and light weapons remained one of the priorities of the Organization, and the Secretary-General called on Member States to negotiate and adopt a legally binding treaty on the import, export and transfer of conventional arms. After the success of the Mine-Ban Convention (see p. 553), the United Nations supported efforts for the entry into force of the new Convention on Cluster Munitions [ibid.], which had opened for signature in Oslo, Norway, in December 2008.

UN Office for Disarmament Affairs

Since its establishment in 2007 [YUN 2007, p. 524], the United Nations Office for Disarmament Affairs (UNODA) provided support for norm-setting in the area of disarmament through the work of the General Assembly and its First Committee, the Disarmament Commission, the Conference on Disarmament and other bodies. It fostered disarmament measures, encouraged regional disarmament efforts and provided information on multilateral disarmament issues and activities. The Office reinforced the advocacy potential of the Organization in the field of disarmament and non-proliferation, for example through the sixty-second Department of Public Information/Non-Governmental Organizations Annual Conference (Mexico City, 9–11 September), which addressed the theme "For Peace and Development: Disarm Now" (see p. 564), and the launch of the "WMD-WeMust-Disarm" campaign [ibid.] in support of nuclear disarmament. Under the leadership of the High Representative for Disarmament Affairs, the Office enhanced its engagement and cooperation with Member States, intergovernmental organizations and civil society.

UNODA carried out activities in support of multilateral efforts on disarmament and the non-proliferation of WMDs, in particular nuclear weapons, as well as in support of conventional disarmament, especially with regard to major weapons systems, small arms and light weapons, landmines and cluster munitions. Through its regional centres for Africa, Asia and the Pacific, and Latin America and the Caribbean, the Office contributed to generating a more active involvement in disarmament and non-proliferation issues of regional and subregional stakeholders.

An important area of UNODA activities involved information dissemination, including raising public awareness of disarmament and non-proliferation issues, and maintaining close liaison with the United Nations Institute for Disarmament Research, other research and educational institutions outside the United Nations, and non-governmental organizations (NGOs). In accordance with General Assembly resolution 61/95 [YUN 2006, p. 679], UNODA issued its flagship publication, *The United Nations Disarmament Yearbook* [Sales No. E.10.IX.1], in hard copy and on the UNODA website, continued the production of its quarterly e-publication, *UNODA Update*, and published four *Occasional Papers*.

Fourth special session devoted to disarmament

As in previous years, no progress was made in 2009 towards the convening of a fourth special session devoted to disarmament. Previously, the General Assembly had held three special sessions devoted to the subject—in 1978, 1982 and 1988. Only the first special session succeeded in producing a final document. The Assembly had been calling for a fourth special session since 1996 [YUN 1996, p. 447]. In 2002 it established a Working Group [YUN 2002, p. 487] to discuss the agenda and the possibility of establishing a preparatory committee for a fourth session. In 2006 [YUN 2006, p. 611], the Assembly established an open-ended group to consider objectives and agenda, including the possible establishment of a preparatory committee.

By resolution 62/29 [YUN 2007, p. 526], the Assembly mandated the reconvening of the Working Group and requested it to submit a report, including possible substantive recommendations, to the Assembly's sixty-second session. However, as the Group did not convene its organizational or substantive sessions during the year, the Assembly in 2008 decided [YUN 2008, p. 561] to continue work on convening the Group as soon as possible. With no related resolution adopted during its sixty-third session, the Assembly, by **decision 64/515** of 2 December, included the item on convening the fourth special session in the provisional agenda of its sixty-fifth (2010) session.

Disarmament Commission

The Disarmament Commission, comprising all UN Member States, in 2009 was able to agree on a substantive agenda, but not on recommendations for achieving nuclear disarmament and non-proliferation, nor on elements of a draft declaration of the 2010s as the fourth disarmament decade. The Commission held 12 plenary meetings in the first session (New York, 13 April–1 May) [A/64/42] of its new three-year cycle of deliberations. The main agenda items were recommendations for achieving the objective of nuclear disarmament and non-proliferation of nuclear weapons, addressed by the Commission's Working Group I; elements of a draft declaration of the 2010s as the fourth disarmament decade, addressed by its Working Group II; and practical confidence-building measures in the field of conventional weapons, which was to be taken up upon the conclusion of the work of Working Group II on the elements of the draft declaration. Working Group I had six meetings from 22 to 29 April, holding extensive discussions on its agenda items. Working Group II held nine meetings between 20 and 30 April, exchanging views on a non-paper of the Chairman [A/CN.10/2009/WG.II/CRP.1], which was later revised twice to reflect the views and proposals expressed by delegations [A/CN.10/2009/WG.II/CRP.1/Rev.1 & 2]. Working Group II decided to continue the consideration of the revised non-paper at the Commission's 2010 session. At its final meeting on 1 May, the Commission adopted its 2009 report to the General Assembly.

GENERAL ASSEMBLY ACTION

On 2 December [meeting 55], the General Assembly, on the recommendation of the First Committee [A/64/393], adopted **resolution 64/65** without vote [agenda item 98 *(b)*].

Report of the Disarmament Commission

The General Assembly,

Having considered the report of the Disarmament Commission,

Recalling its resolutions 47/54 A of 9 December 1992, 47/54 G of 8 April 1993, 48/77 A of 16 December 1993, 49/77 A of 15 December 1994, 50/72 D of 12 December 1995, 51/47 B of 10 December 1996, 52/40 B of 9 December 1997, 53/79 A of 4 December 1998, 54/56 A of 1 December 1999, 55/35 C of 20 November 2000, 56/26 A of 29 November 2001, 57/95 of 22 November 2002, 58/67 of 8 December 2003, 59/105 of 3 December 2004, 60/91 of 8 December 2005, 61/98 of 6 December 2006, 62/54 of 5 December 2007 and 63/83 of 2 December 2008,

Considering the role that the Disarmament Commission has been called upon to play and the contribution that it should make in examining and submitting recommendations on various problems in the field of disarmament and in the promotion of the implementation of the relevant decisions adopted by the General Assembly at its tenth special session,

1. *Takes note* of the report of the Disarmament Commission;

2. *Reaffirms* the validity of its decision 52/492 of 8 September 1998, concerning the efficient functioning of the Disarmament Commission;

3. *Recalls* its resolution 61/98, by which it adopted additional measures for improving the effectiveness of the Commission's methods of work;

4. *Reaffirms* the mandate of the Disarmament Commission as the specialized, deliberative body within the United Nations multilateral disarmament machinery that allows for in-depth deliberations on specific disarmament issues, leading to the submission of concrete recommendations on those issues;

5. *Also reaffirms* the importance of further enhancing the dialogue and cooperation among the First Committee, the Disarmament Commission and the Conference on Disarmament;

6. *Requests* the Disarmament Commission to continue its work in accordance with its mandate, as set forth in paragraph 118 of the Final Document of the Tenth Special Session of the General Assembly, and with paragraph 3 of Assembly resolution 37/78 H of 9 December 1982, and to that end to make every effort to achieve specific recommendations on the items on its agenda, taking into account the adopted "Ways and means to enhance the functioning of the Disarmament Commission";

7. *Recommends* that the Disarmament Commission continue the consideration of the following items at its substantive session of 2010:

(a) Recommendations for achieving the objective of nuclear disarmament and non-proliferation of nuclear weapons;

(b) Elements of a draft declaration of the 2010s as the fourth disarmament decade;

(c) Practical confidence-building measures in the field of conventional weapons. This item will be taken up upon the conclusion of the preparation of the elements of a draft declaration of the 2010s as the fourth disarmament decade, preferably by 2010 and in any case no later than 2011;

8. *Requests* the Disarmament Commission to meet for a period not exceeding three weeks during 2010, namely from 29 March to 16 April, and to submit a substantive report to the General Assembly at its sixty-fifth session;

9. *Requests* the Secretary-General to transmit to the Disarmament Commission the annual report of the Conference on Disarmament, together with all the official records of the sixty-fourth session of the General Assembly relating to disarmament matters, and to render all assistance that the Commission may require for implementing the present resolution;

10. *Also requests* the Secretary-General to ensure full provision to the Disarmament Commission and its subsidiary bodies of interpretation and translation facilities in the official languages and to assign, as a matter of priority, all the necessary resources and services, including verbatim records, to that end;

11. *Decides* to include in the provisional agenda of its sixty-fifth session the item entitled "Report of the Disarmament Commission".

Conference on Disarmament

The Conference on Disarmament, the Organization's sole multilateral disarmament negotiating body, held 45 formal and 20 informal plenary meetings in a three-part session in 2009 (Geneva, 19 January–27 March, 18 May–3 July, 3 August–18 September) [A/64/27].

As in previous years, the Conference's agenda included the cessation of the nuclear arms race and nuclear disarmament; prevention of nuclear war; prevention of an arms race in outer space; effective international arrangements to assure non-nuclear-weapon States against the use or threat of use of nuclear weapons; new types of WMDs and new systems of such weapons; a comprehensive programme of disarmament; and transparency in armaments.

The Secretary-General addressed the Conference at its meeting of 19 May [CD/PV.1135], referring to the new momentum for disarmament provided by a number of initiatives by States and their leaders, as well as to his five-point proposal [YUN 2008, p. 565] to revitalize the international disarmament agenda. He urged the Conference to seize the opportunity to move the disarmament agenda forward and called on the Conference to play its proper role as the world's single multilateral negotiation body on disarmament. To facilitate the work of the Conference, the 2009 Presidents appointed seven Coordinators who chaired informal meetings on the agenda items and reported

to the Presidents on their results, which were transmitted to the Secretary-General of the Conference.

On 29 May, the Conference ended its decade-long stalemate by adopting a programme of work [CD/1864] that provided for negotiations on a treaty to prohibit the production of fissile material for use in nuclear weapons or other explosive devices and allowed for substantive discussions on three other priority issues—assurances to non-nuclear-weapon States against the threat or use of nuclear weapons, prevention of an arms race in outer space and nuclear disarmament. The Conference, however, failed to achieve consensus on modalities for implementing the work programme and was thus unable to progress further during the remainder of its 2009 session.

On 13 March [CD/1859], the Russian Federation transmitted to the Conference the statement by its President on the conclusion of an agreement with the United States to succeed START I. On 27 March [CD/1860], France transmitted a letter concerning the visit to the former military facilities at Pierrelatte and Marcoule. On 20 April [CD/1861, CD/1862], the Russian Federation and the United States transmitted the Joint Statement by President Medvedev and President Obama regarding negotiations on further reductions in strategic offensive arms, made in London on 1 April. On 13 July [CD/1868], Italy transmitted the "L'Aquila statement on non-proliferation" adopted by the heads of State and Government of G8 member countries during the G8 Summit (L'Aquila, Italy, 8 July). On 16 July [CD/1869], the United States and the Russian Federation transmitted the "Joint Understanding for further reductions and limitations of Strategic Offensive Arms", signed by Presidents Obama and Medvedev in Moscow on 6 July. On 12 August [CD/1871], Pakistan transmitted a press release issued by its Ministry of Foreign Affairs entitled "Pakistan subscribes to the goals of nuclear disarmament and non-proliferation". On 25 August [CD/1875], Egypt transmitted the introduction and the section on disarmament and international security of the Final Document of the XV Summit of Heads of State and Government of the Non-Aligned Movement (Sharm el-Sheikh, Egypt, 11–16 July). On 16 September [CD/1878], Canada, Japan and the Netherlands transmitted the "draft for discussion prepared by the International Panel on Fissile Materials: A treaty banning the production of fissile materials for nuclear weapons or other nuclear explosive devices, with article-by-article explanations", of 2 September.

GENERAL ASSEMBLY ACTION

On 2 December [meeting 55], the General Assembly, on the recommendation of the First Committee [A/64/393], adopted **resolution 64/64** without vote [agenda item 98 *(a)*].

Report of the Conference on Disarmament

The General Assembly,

Having considered the report of the Conference on Disarmament,

Convinced that the Conference on Disarmament, as the sole multilateral disarmament negotiating forum of the international community, has the primary role in substantive negotiations on priority questions of disarmament,

Recognizing the address by the Secretary-General of the United Nations, as well as the addresses by Ministers for Foreign Affairs and other high-level officials in the Conference on Disarmament, as expressions of support for the endeavours of the Conference and its role as the sole multilateral disarmament negotiating forum,

Recognizing also the need to conduct multilateral negotiations with the aim of reaching agreement on concrete issues,

Recalling, in this respect, that the Conference on Disarmament has a number of urgent and important issues for negotiation,

Considering that the present international climate should give additional impetus to multilateral negotiations with the aim of reaching concrete agreements,

Acknowledging the support of the United Nations Security Council summit on nuclear non-proliferation and nuclear disarmament, held on 24 September 2009, for the work of the Conference on Disarmament,

Bearing in mind the decision of the Conference on Disarmament of 29 May 2009 to establish four working groups and appoint three special coordinators, including one working group under agenda item 1 entitled "Cessation of the nuclear arms race and nuclear disarmament", which shall negotiate a treaty banning the production of fissile material for nuclear weapons or other nuclear explosive devices, on the basis of the report of the Special Coordinator of 1995 and the mandate contained therein, without prescribing or precluding any outcome of discussions in the other three working groups, with a view to enabling future compromise and including the possibility of future negotiations under any agenda item, thus upholding the nature of the Conference,

Appreciating the continued cooperation among the States members of the Conference on Disarmament as well as the six successive Presidents of the Conference at its 2009 session,

Recognizing the importance of continuing consultations on the question of the expansion of the membership of the Conference on Disarmament,

Taking note of significant contributions made during the 2009 session to promote substantive discussions on issues on the agenda, as well as of discussions held on other issues that could also be relevant to the current international security environment,

Welcoming the enhanced engagement between civil society and the Conference on Disarmament at its 2009 session according to decisions taken by the Conference,

Stressing the urgent need for the Conference on Disarmament to commence its substantive work at the beginning of its 2010 session,

1. *Reaffirms* the role of the Conference on Disarmament as the sole multilateral disarmament negotiating forum of the international community;

2. *Welcomes* the consensus adoption of a programme of work for the 2009 session of the Conference on Disarmament, including the establishment of four working groups and the appointment of three special coordinators;

3. *Takes note* of the active discussions held on the implementation of the programme of work at the 2009 session of the Conference on Disarmament, as duly reflected in the report and the records of the plenary meetings;

4. *Welcomes* the decision of the Conference on Disarmament to request the current President and the incoming President to conduct consultations during the intersessional period and, if possible, make recommendations, taking into account all relevant proposals, past, present and future, including those submitted as documents of the Conference on Disarmament, views presented and discussions held, and to endeavour to keep the membership of the Conference informed, as appropriate, of their consultations;

5. *Requests* all States members of the Conference on Disarmament to cooperate with the current President and successive Presidents in their efforts to guide the Conference to the early commencement of substantive work, including negotiations, in its 2010 session;

6. *Requests* the Secretary-General to continue to ensure and strengthen, if needed, the provision to the Conference on Disarmament of all necessary administrative, substantive and conference support services;

7. *Requests* the Conference on Disarmament to submit a report on its work to the General Assembly at its sixty-fifth session;

8. *Decides* to include in the provisional agenda of its sixty-fifth session the item entitled "Report of the Conference on Disarmament".

UN role in disarmament

Disarmament and development

Pursuant to General Assembly resolution 63/52 [YUN 2008, p. 634], the Secretary-General in July reported [A/64/153] on trends to further strengthen within the United Nations the relationship between disarmament and development. The report contained information received from Cuba, Lebanon, Panama, the Philippines and Qatar on measures and efforts to devote part of the resources made available by the implementation of disarmament and arms limitation agreements to economic and social development. The Secretary-General noted that some examples of the UN focus on disarmament and development included the broad approach to the issue of small arms which he presented to the Security Council in 2008 [YUN 2008, p. 613]; the emphasis on a comprehensive approach in mine action; and the support by the United Nations to the Convention on Cluster Munitions [ibid., p. 623]. Member States themselves were giving increased attention to the relationship between disarmament and development within the UN framework. Earlier in the year, they embarked on discussions on a possible arms trade treaty (see p. 544). The Council in 2008 held a debate on collective security and armament regulation that led to a presidential statement [ibid., p. 592] on the Council's concern at increasing global military expenditure. The Council urged States to devote as many resources as possible to economic and social development, in particular to the fight against poverty and the achievement of the Millennium Development Goals. Member States since 1981 had been providing information on their military spending through the Standardized Instrument for Reporting Military Expenditures. Another example of the increased attention to the relationship between disarmament and development within the United Nations, the Secretary-General noted, was Assembly resolution 63/23, on "Promoting development through the reduction and prevention of armed violence" [ibid., p. 635]. Those developments illustrated the commitment of the United Nations to promote an interrelated perspective on disarmament and development, in accordance with the action programme of the 1987 International Conference on the Relationship between Disarmament and Development [YUN 1987, p. 82].

GENERAL ASSEMBLY ACTION

On 2 December [meeting 55], the General Assembly, on the recommendation of the First Committee [A/64/391], adopted **resolution 64/32** without vote [agenda item 96 *(o)*].

Relationship between disarmament and development

The General Assembly,

Recalling that the Charter of the United Nations envisages the establishment and maintenance of international peace and security with the least diversion for armaments of the world's human and economic resources,

Recalling also the provisions of the Final Document of the Tenth Special Session of the General Assembly concerning the relationship between disarmament and development, as well as the adoption on 11 September 1987 of the Final Document of the International Conference on the Relationship between Disarmament and Development,

Recalling further its resolutions 49/75 J of 15 December 1994, 50/70 G of 12 December 1995, 51/45 D of 10 December 1996, 52/38 D of 9 December 1997, 53/77 K of 4 December 1998, 54/54 T of 1 December 1999, 55/33 L of 20 November 2000, 56/24 E of 29 November 2001, 57/65 of 22 November 2002, 59/78 of 3 December 2004, 60/61 of 8 December 2005, 61/64 of 6 December 2006, 62/48 of 5 December 2007 and 63/52 of 2 December 2008, and its decision 58/520 of 8 December 2003,

Bearing in mind the Final Document of the Twelfth Conference of Heads of State or Government of Non-Aligned Countries, held in Durban, South Africa, from 29 August to 3 September 1998, and the Final Document of the Thirteenth Ministerial Conference of the Movement of Non-Aligned Countries, held in Cartagena, Colombia, on 8 and 9 April 2000,

Mindful of the changes in international relations that have taken place since the adoption on 11 September 1987 of the Final Document of the International Conference on the Relationship between Disarmament and Development, including the development agenda that has emerged over the past decade,

Bearing in mind the new challenges for the international community in the field of development, poverty eradication and the elimination of the diseases that afflict humanity,

Stressing the importance of the symbiotic relationship between disarmament and development and the important role of security in this connection, and concerned at increasing global military expenditure, which could otherwise be spent on development needs,

Recalling the report of the Group of Governmental Experts on the relationship between disarmament and development and its reappraisal of this significant issue in the current international context,

Bearing in mind the importance of following up on the implementation of the action programme adopted at the 1987 International Conference on the Relationship between Disarmament and Development,

1. *Stresses* the central role of the United Nations in the disarmament-development relationship, and requests the Secretary-General to strengthen further the role of the Organization in this field, in particular the high-level Steering Group on Disarmament and Development, in order to ensure continued and effective coordination and close cooperation between the relevant United Nations departments, agencies and sub-agencies;

2. *Requests* the Secretary-General to continue to take action, through appropriate organs and within available resources, for the implementation of the action programme adopted at the 1987 International Conference on the Relationship between Disarmament and Development;

3. *Urges* the international community to devote part of the resources made available by the implementation of disarmament and arms limitation agreements to economic and social development, with a view to reducing the ever-widening gap between developed and developing countries;

4. *Encourages* the international community to achieve the Millennium Development Goals and to make reference to the contribution that disarmament could provide in meeting them when it reviews its progress towards this purpose in 2010, as well as to make greater efforts to integrate disarmament, humanitarian and development activities;

5. *Encourages* the relevant regional and subregional organizations and institutions, non-governmental organizations and research institutes to incorporate issues related to the relationship between disarmament and development in their agendas and, in this regard, to take into account the report of the Group of Governmental Experts on the relationship between disarmament and development;

6. *Reiterates its invitation* to Member States to provide the Secretary-General with information regarding measures and efforts to devote part of the resources made available by the implementation of disarmament and arms limitation agreements to economic and social development, with a view to reducing the ever-widening gap between developed and developing countries;

7. *Requests* the Secretary-General to report to the General Assembly at its sixty-fifth session on the implementation of the present resolution, including the information provided by Member States pursuant to paragraph 6 above;

8. *Decides* to include in the provisional agenda of its sixty-fifth session the item entitled "Relationship between disarmament and development".

Promoting development through reduction of armed violence

In accordance with General Assembly resolution 63/23 [YUN 2008, p. 635], the Secretary-General, following consultations with Member States, UN agencies, funds and programmes and the three UN regional centres for peace and disarmament (see p. 568), reported in August [A/64/228] on the relation between armed violence and development.

The report said that the risk factors and effects of armed violence were often similar, with young men making up the majority of perpetrators and victims of such violence. In some armed conflicts, women, girls and boys suffered from acute forms of sexual violence. Weak institutions, systemic inequalities, exclusion of minority groups, unequal gender relations, limited education opportunities, persistent unemployment, organized crime and illicit markets, as well as the availability of firearms, alcohol and drugs, shaped the onset, duration and severity of armed violence. The report stressed the need to tackle the risks and effects of armed violence and underdevelopment. That included implementing conventions and agreements associated with armed violence and development; improving the effectiveness of prevention and reduction policies through investment in the production, analysis and use of evidence; strengthening capacities to diagnose, articulate strategies and implement programmes; developing measurable goals, targets and indicators for armed violence prevention and reduction; building partnerships within the UN system and with regional organizations, national authorities and civil society; increasing resources for prevention and reduction; and fostering greater international action.

Advisory Board on Disarmament Matters

The Advisory Board on Disarmament Matters, which advised the Secretary-General and served as the Board of Trustees of the United Nations Institute for Disarmament Research (UNIDIR), held its fifty-first and fifty-second sessions (New York, 18–20 February; Geneva, 1–3 July) [A/64/286], discussing cyberwarfare and its impact on international security and ways to strengthen nuclear verification, including the role of the United Nations. At its July session, the Board also discussed "Conceptual issues leading up to the 2010 NPT Review Conference", in view of developments in the field of nuclear disarmament and non-proliferation prior to the 2010 NPT Review Conference.

On cyberwarfare and its impact on international security, the Board's deliberations showed that cyberwarfare remained a complex issue that had a significant impact on national, international and human security; while qualitatively different from biological or chemical weapons, in particular in the area of dual use, it shared similarities with them. The Board debated whether cyberwarfare was a disarmament/arms control issue or a law enforcement issue. Some members were of the view that cyberwarfare should be addressed within the context of arms control rather than disarmament. The Board discussed the need to distinguish between hostile and non-hostile cyberactors, but several members stressed that Governments should not infringe upon civil liberties in their efforts to prevent cyberattacks. The Board also discussed the creation of social norms in cyberspace, but doubts were expressed as to whether such norm-setting would be possible in view of the gap in information technology capabilities among States. The Board recommended that the Secretary-General raise awareness among Governments and the general public of the emerging risks and threats related to cyberwarfare.

With regard to strengthening verification, including the role of the United Nations, the Board stressed that, in order for verification processes to be successful, they should be perceived as independent by all countries. Some Board members stressed that verification mechanisms were worthless if there were no ways to act against potential violators. Members emphasized the importance of taking into account the difference between making a deliberate choice for non-compliance and the lack of capability for compliance by a State. In connection with the verification of a fissile material cut-off treaty, many members said that it was important to address the meaning and scope of the treaty; which multilateral institution should undertake the verification; whether there should be separate international instruments for verification or whether internationally verifiable measures should be included in the basic instrument; and the costs involved. Mention was made of the need for such a verification system to be legally binding. The Board recommended that the Secretary-General encourage Member States to provide feedback on all verification studies for lessons learned, and for a better understanding that a "one-size-fits-all" approach in the field of verification could be counterproductive. The Board also felt that, although the United Nations had primary responsibility in dealing with international peace and security, it could consider a role for regional organizations in verification matters.

On conceptual issues leading up to the 2010 NPT Review Conference, the Board in July recommended that the Secretary-General continue to provide his strong support for the positive political momentum in bilateral and multilateral nuclear disarmament and non-proliferation through diplomatic channels and public statements, and encourage States to ratify the Additional Protocols of the International Atomic Energy Agency. The Board also recommended that, given new developments since the Secretary-General's proposed five-point plan, he might consider advancing an updated version of the plan.

In its capacity as the UNIDIR Board of Trustees, the Advisory Board adopted the Institute's 2009 programme and budget and approved for submission to the General Assembly the report of the Institute's Director on activities from August 2008 to July 2009, as well as the proposed programme of work and budget for 2009–2010. The Board also recommended the granting of a continuing support for UNIDIR from the UN regular budget for the biennium 2010–2011.

Multilateral disarmament agreements

As at 31 December, the following number of States had become parties to the multilateral arms regulation and disarmament agreements listed below (in chronological order, with the years in which they were initially signed or opened for signature).

(Geneva) Protocol for the Prohibition of the Use in War of Asphyxiating, Poisonous or Other Gases, and of Bacteriological Methods of Warfare (1925): 137 parties (two new parties)

The Antarctic Treaty (1959): 47 parties

Treaty Banning Nuclear Weapons Tests in the Atmosphere, in Outer Space and under Water (1963): 125 parties

Treaty on Principles Governing the Activities of States in the Exploration and Use of Outer Space, including the Moon and Other Celestial Bodies (1967) [YUN 1966, p. 41, GA res. 2222(XXI), annex]: 105 parties

Treaty for the Prohibition of Nuclear Weapons in Latin America and the Caribbean (Treaty of Tlatelolco) (1967): 33 parties

Treaty on the Non-Proliferation of Nuclear Weapons (1968) [YUN 1968, p. 17, GA res. 2373(XXII), annex]: 190 parties

Treaty on the Prohibition of the Emplacement of Nuclear Weapons and Other Weapons of Mass Destruction on the Sea-Bed and the Ocean Floor and in the Subsoil Thereof (1971) [YUN 1970, p. 18, GA res. 2660(XXV), annex]: 97 parties

Convention on the Prohibition of the Development, Production and Stockpiling of Bacteriological (Biological) and Toxin Weapons and on Their Destruction (1972) [YUN 1971, p. 19, GA res. 2826(XXV), annex]: 163 parties

Convention on the Prohibition of Military or Any Other Hostile Use of Environmental Modification Techniques (1977) [YUN 1976, p. 45, GA res. 31/72, annex]: 73 parties

Agreement Governing the Activities of States on the Moon and Other Celestial Bodies (1979) [YUN 1979, p. 111, GA res. 34/68, annex]: 13 parties

Convention on Prohibitions or Restrictions on the Use of Certain Conventional Weapons Which May Be Deemed to Be Excessively Injurious or to Have Indiscriminate Effects (1981): 111 parties (three new parties)

South Pacific Nuclear Free Zone Treaty (Treaty of Rarotonga) (1985): 13 parties

Treaty on Conventional Armed Forces in Europe (CFE Treaty) (1990): 30 parties

Treaty on Open Skies (1992): 34 parties (one new party)

Convention on the Prohibition of the Development, Production, Stockpiling and Use of Chemical Weapons and on Their Destruction (1993): 188 parties (three new parties)

Treaty on the Southeast Asia Nuclear-Weapon-Free Zone (Bangkok Treaty) (1995): 10 parties

African Nuclear-Weapon-Free Zone Treaty (Pelindaba Treaty) (1996): 29 parties (three new parties)

Comprehensive Nuclear-Test-Ban Treaty (1996): 151 parties (three new parties)

Inter-American Convention against the Illicit Manufacturing of and Trafficking in Firearms, Ammunition, Explosives, and Other Related Materials (1997): 30 parties (one new party)

Convention on the Prohibition of the Use, Stockpiling, Production and Transfer of Anti-Personnel Mines and on Their Destruction (Mine-Ban Convention, formerly known as Ottawa Convention) (1997): 156 parties

Inter-American Convention on Transparency in Conventional Weapons Acquisitions (1999): 13 parties (one new party)

Agreement on Adaptation of the CFE Treaty (1999): 4 parties

Treaty on a Nuclear-Weapon-Free Zone in Central Asia (2006): 5 parties (three new parties)

Convention on Cluster Munitions (2008): 26 parties (22 new parties)

[*United Nations Disarmament Yearbook*, Vol. 34 (Part II): *2009*, Sales No. E.10.IX.1]

Nuclear disarmament

Report of Secretary-General. In response to General Assembly resolutions 63/46 [YUN 2008, p. 574], 63/47 [ibid., p. 565] and 63/49 [ibid., p. 583], the Secretary-General in July submitted a report on nuclear disarmament [A/64/139] in which he recalled his warning about the risk of proliferation of nuclear and other weapons and his setting of non-proliferation and disarmament as one of his six priorities for action. He reported that a new momentum for nuclear disarmament had been spurred on by additional calls for a world free of nuclear weapons made by former statesmen in the United States, the United Kingdom, Italy, Germany and Norway. Global initiatives of civil society, such as the International Commission on Nuclear Non-Proliferation and Disarmament, the World Institute for Nuclear Security and Global Zero, had also been launched.

The United States and the Russian Federation had both stated their commitment to achieving a world free of nuclear weapons in accordance with their disarmament obligations under NPT. In a joint statement on 1 April, Presidents Obama and Medvedev announced that they had decided to move further along the path of reducing and limiting strategic offensive arms in accordance with obligations of United States and Russia under article VI of NPT; and that they had decided to begin bilateral negotiations to work out a new, comprehensive, legally binding agreement on reducing and limiting strategic offensive arms to replace START, which was due to expire in December. Negotiations had begun, with meetings held in Washington, D.C., and Geneva in May and June.

In his 2008 address to an event at UN Headquarters hosted by the East-West Institute [YUN 2008, p. 565], the Secretary-General had put forward a five-point proposal on nuclear disarmament. He had urged all NPT parties, in particular the nuclear-weapon States, to fulfil their Treaty obligations and undertake negotiations on effective measures leading to nuclear disarmament. He had encouraged States to make new efforts to bring the Comprehensive Nuclear-Test-Ban Treaty (CTBT) into force and called on the Conference on Disarmament to begin negotiations on a fissile material treaty immediately and without preconditions (see p. 509). He had expressed support for the entry into force of nuclear-weapon-free zone treaties and the establishment of such a zone in the Middle East. He had urged the nuclear-weapon States to assure non-nuclear-weapon States that they would not be the subject of the use or threat of use of nuclear weapons and underlined the need for further accountability and transparency with regard to nuclear disarmament measures.

Tangible progress had been made in several areas. The Treaty on a Central Asia Nuclear-Weapon-Free Zone had entered into force on 21 March. It was the first nuclear-weapon-free zone that required its parties to conclude with the International Atomic Energy Agency (IAEA) and bring into force an additional protocol to their safeguards agreements within 18 months after the entry into force of the Treaty; and to comply fully with the provisions of CTBT. The African Nuclear-Weapon-Free Zone Treaty was close to entry into force, with only one additional State required to ratify it so as to reach the required number of 28. However, progress on the creation of a nuclear-weapon-free zone in the Middle East remained difficult.

The parties to NPT had concluded the third session of its Preparatory Committee for the 2010 Review Conference in New York on 15 May with an agreement on the provisional agenda and draft rules of procedure. However, deep differences persisted among parties on the three pillars of the Treaty—disarmament, non-proliferation and peaceful uses of nuclear energy—and the Committee could not reach agreement on substantive recommendations for the Review Conference. Nevertheless, States parties had cleared the path for the immediate start of substantive discussions at the 2010 Review Conference.

The Secretary-General welcomed the Conference on Disarmament's agreement on its substantive programme of work for the 2009 session, after over a decade of stagnation and deadlock. That would allow the Conference to establish a working group to negotiate a treaty banning the production of fissile material for nuclear weapons or other nuclear explosive devices. The Conference would also establish a working group on practical steps for progressive and systematic efforts to reduce nuclear weapons, with the ultimate goal of their elimination; a working group on the prevention of an arms race in outer space; and a working group to discuss international arrangements to assure non-nuclear-weapon States against the use or threat of use of nuclear weapons.

The Disarmament Commission had launched a new three-year cycle of deliberations in April. It had adopted an agenda that allowed for two working groups to be formed during the first year and the beginning of substantive deliberations on recommendations for achieving the objective of nuclear disarmament and non-proliferation; and elements of a draft declaration of the 2010s as the fourth disarmament decade, as mandated by the General Assembly. Discussions on those items would continue in 2010.

Progress was still slow, however, in some areas. CTBT had not entered into force because it lacked ratification by nine States listed in Annex 2 of the Treaty. In October 2008, the Secretary-General, as depository of the Treaty, had sent letters to the nine countries urging them to ratify it.

Nuclear-weapon States had continued to emphasize the importance of nuclear deterrence in their security policies. Complete nuclear disarmament was a precondition to ensuring regional peace and stability, preventing the proliferation of nuclear weapons to non-State actors, making sure that all States possessing nuclear weapons—not just the five nuclear-weapon States—disarmed fully, and ensuring that the complete elimination of nuclear weapons from all arsenals was verifiable and irreversible. The Secretary-General noted that proposals for negotiating a universal nuclear-weapon convention were still referred to as premature.

On 25 May, the Democratic People's Republic of Korea (DPRK) had conducted a second underground nuclear test, in violation of Security Council resolution 1718(2006) [YUN 2006, p. 444]. The Council condemned the test and on 12 June, by **resolution 1874(2009)** (see p. 384), it strengthened financial and arms-related sanctions and called on States to inspect cargo to and from the DPRK for prohibited items referred to in resolution 1718(2006). States were also called on to exercise vigilance over the direct or indirect supply, sale or transfer to the DPRK of small arms or light weapons.

IAEA continued its efforts to verify the peaceful nature of the nuclear programme of Iran (see p. 530). The Agency had also investigated allegations concerning a destroyed building at the Dair Alzour site in the Syrian Arab Republic and sought to clarify the presence of uranium particles there [ibid.].

The Secretary-General and the High Representative for Disarmament Affairs continued to promote nuclear disarmament and non-proliferation globally through interaction with Governments and civil society.

Included in the report were replies from eight Member States—Cuba, El Salvador, Japan, Lebanon, Lithuania, Mexico, Nicaragua and Qatar—to the Secretary-General's invitation of February 2009 to inform him of measures they had taken with regard to the implementation of resolution 63/49 [YUN 2008, p. 583] concerning the follow-up to the International Court of Justice advisory opinion on the *Legality of the Threat or Use of Nuclear Weapons* (see p. 516).

Communication. On 8 May, Cuba, as Chair of the Coordinating Bureau of the Non-Aligned Movement (NAM), transmitted the Final Document of the NAM Coordinating Bureau at its Ministerial Meeting (Havana, Cuba, 27–30 April) [A/63/858], which addressed disarmament and international security.

GENERAL ASSEMBLY ACTION

On 2 December [meeting 55], the General Assembly, on the recommendation of the First Committee [A/64/391], adopted **resolution 64/37** by recorded vote (115-50-14) [agenda item 96 *(j)*].

Reducing nuclear danger

The General Assembly,

Bearing in mind that the use of nuclear weapons poses the most serious threat to mankind and to the survival of civilization,

Reaffirming that any use or threat of use of nuclear weapons would constitute a violation of the Charter of the United Nations,

Convinced that the proliferation of nuclear weapons in all its aspects would seriously enhance the danger of nuclear war,

Convinced also that nuclear disarmament and the complete elimination of nuclear weapons are essential to remove the danger of nuclear war,

Considering that, until nuclear weapons cease to exist, it is imperative on the part of the nuclear-weapon States

to adopt measures that assure non-nuclear-weapon States against the use or threat of use of nuclear weapons,

Considering also that the hair-trigger alert of nuclear weapons carries unacceptable risks of unintentional or accidental use of nuclear weapons, which would have catastrophic consequences for all mankind,

Emphasizing the need to adopt measures to avoid accidental, unauthorized or unexplained incidents arising from computer anomaly or other technical malfunctions,

Conscious that limited steps relating to de-alerting and de-targeting have been taken by the nuclear-weapon States and that further practical, realistic and mutually reinforcing steps are necessary to contribute to the improvement in the international climate for negotiations leading to the elimination of nuclear weapons,

Mindful that a diminishing role for nuclear weapons in the security policies of nuclear-weapon States would positively impact on international peace and security and improve the conditions for the further reduction and the elimination of nuclear weapons,

Reiterating the highest priority accorded to nuclear disarmament in the Final Document of the Tenth Special Session of the General Assembly and by the international community,

Recalling the advisory opinion of the International Court of Justice on the *Legality of the Threat or Use of Nuclear Weapons* that there exists an obligation for all States to pursue in good faith and bring to a conclusion negotiations leading to nuclear disarmament in all its aspects under strict and effective international control,

Recalling also the call in the United Nations Millennium Declaration to seek to eliminate the dangers posed by weapons of mass destruction and the resolve to strive for the elimination of weapons of mass destruction, particularly nuclear weapons, including the possibility of convening an international conference to identify ways of eliminating nuclear dangers,

1. *Calls for* a review of nuclear doctrines and, in this context, immediate and urgent steps to reduce the risks of unintentional and accidental use of nuclear weapons, including through the de-alerting and de-targeting of nuclear weapons;

2. *Requests* the five nuclear-weapon States to take measures towards the implementation of paragraph 1 above;

3. *Calls upon* Member States to take the necessary measures to prevent the proliferation of nuclear weapons in all its aspects and to promote nuclear disarmament, with the objective of eliminating nuclear weapons;

4. *Takes note* of the report of the Secretary-General submitted pursuant to paragraph 5 of resolution 63/47 of 2 December 2008;

5. *Requests* the Secretary-General to intensify efforts and support initiatives that would contribute towards the full implementation of the seven recommendations identified in the report of the Advisory Board on Disarmament Matters that would significantly reduce the risk of nuclear war, and also to continue to encourage Member States to consider the convening of an international conference, as proposed in the United Nations Millennium Declaration, to identify ways of eliminating nuclear dangers, and to report thereon to the General Assembly at its sixty-fifth session;

6.   *Decides* to include in the provisional agenda of its sixty-fifth session the item entitled "Reducing nuclear danger".

RECORDED VOTE ON RESOLUTION 64/37:

In favour: Afghanistan, Algeria, Angola, Antigua and Barbuda, Bahamas, Bahrain, Bangladesh, Barbados, Belize, Benin, Bhutan, Bolivia, Botswana, Brazil, Brunei Darussalam, Burkina Faso, Burundi, Cambodia, Cameroon, Cape Verde, Chile, Colombia, Comoros, Congo, Costa Rica, Côte d'Ivoire, Cuba, Democratic People's Republic of Korea, Democratic Republic of the Congo, Djibouti, Dominica, Dominican Republic, Ecuador, Egypt, El Salvador, Equatorial Guinea, Eritrea, Fiji, Gambia, Ghana, Grenada, Guatemala, Guinea, Guinea-Bissau, Guyana, Haiti, Honduras, India, Indonesia, Iran, Iraq, Jamaica, Jordan, Kenya, Kuwait, Lao People's Democratic Republic, Lebanon, Lesotho, Liberia, Libyan Arab Jamahiriya, Madagascar, Malawi, Malaysia, Maldives, Mali, Mauritania, Mauritius, Mexico, Mongolia, Morocco, Mozambique, Myanmar, Namibia, Nepal, Nicaragua, Niger, Nigeria, Oman, Pakistan, Panama, Papua New Guinea, Paraguay, Peru, Philippines, Qatar, Saint Kitts and Nevis, Saint Lucia, Saint Vincent and the Grenadines, Samoa, Saudi Arabia, Senegal, Singapore, Solomon Islands, Somalia, South Africa, Sri Lanka, Sudan, Suriname, Swaziland, Syrian Arab Republic, Thailand, Togo, Tonga, Trinidad and Tobago, Tunisia, Turkmenistan, Uganda, United Arab Emirates, United Republic of Tanzania, Uruguay, Venezuela, Viet Nam, Yemen, Zambia, Zimbabwe.

Against: Albania, Andorra, Australia, Austria, Belgium, Bosnia and Herzegovina, Bulgaria, Canada, Croatia, Cyprus, Czech Republic, Denmark, Estonia, Finland, France, Georgia, Germany, Greece, Hungary, Iceland, Ireland, Israel, Italy, Latvia, Liechtenstein, Lithuania, Luxembourg, Malta, Micronesia, Moldova, Monaco, Montenegro, Netherlands, New Zealand, Norway, Palau, Poland, Portugal, Romania, San Marino, Slovakia, Slovenia, Spain, Sweden, Switzerland, The former Yugoslav Republic of Macedonia, Turkey, Ukraine, United Kingdom, United States.

Abstaining: Argentina, Armenia, Azerbaijan, Belarus, China, Japan, Kazakhstan, Kyrgyzstan, Marshall Islands, Republic of Korea, Russian Federation, Serbia, Tajikistan, Uzbekistan.

Conference on Disarmament

The Conference on Disarmament held two rounds of informal meetings on "Cessation of the nuclear arms race and nuclear disarmament" and "Prevention of nuclear war, including all related matters" on 9 and 23 February [CD/1877, annex I]. Some nuclear-weapon States highlighted their unilateral actions in favour of reducing nuclear arsenals, while others underscored the shared responsibility in nuclear disarmament. In his report, the Chair said that some States viewed the conclusion of a legally binding agreement on fissile material as the first step towards nuclear disarmament. Other States referred to interim measures until complete disarmament was attained, such as the creation of additional nuclear-weapon-free zones, negative security and "no-first-use" assurances. Reference was made to the 13 practical steps adopted at the 2000 NPT Review Conference [YUN 2000, p. 487].

At both sessions, States insisted that nuclear disarmament was an objective of the highest importance. Nevertheless, diverging opinions persisted on timings, priorities, linkages, resources, interests, definitions and scope. In any case, real nuclear disarmament could be reached only through an incremental approach based on a comprehensive framework and on the principle of equitable security for all.

GENERAL ASSEMBLY ACTION

On 2 December [meeting 55], the General Assembly, on the recommendation of the First Committee [A/64/391], adopted **resolution 64/47** by recorded vote (171-2-8) [agenda item 96 *(y)*].

Renewed determination towards the total elimination of nuclear weapons

The General Assembly,

Recalling the need for all States to take further practical steps and effective measures towards the total elimination of nuclear weapons, with a view to achieving a peaceful and safe world, without nuclear weapons, and renewing the determination to do so,

Noting that the ultimate objective of the efforts of States in the disarmament process is general and complete disarmament under strict and effective international control,

Recalling its resolution 63/73 of 2 December 2008,

Convinced that every effort should be made to avoid nuclear war and nuclear terrorism,

Reaffirming the crucial importance of the Treaty on the Non-Proliferation of Nuclear Weapons as the cornerstone of the international nuclear non-proliferation regime and an essential foundation for the pursuit of nuclear disarmament and for the peaceful uses of nuclear energy, welcoming the results of the third session of the Preparatory Committee for the Review Conference of the Parties to the Treaty on the Non-Proliferation of Nuclear Weapons to be held in 2010, the year of the sixty-fifth anniversary of the atomic bombings in Hiroshima and Nagasaki, Japan, and noting the importance of achieving the success of the Review Conference,

Recalling the decisions and the resolution of the 1995 Review and Extension Conference of the Parties to the Treaty on the Non-Proliferation of Nuclear Weapons and the Final Document of the 2000 Review Conference of the Parties to the Treaty,

Recognizing that the enhancement of international peace and security and the promotion of nuclear disarmament are mutually reinforcing,

Reaffirming that further advancement in nuclear disarmament will contribute to consolidating the international regime for nuclear non-proliferation, which is, inter alia, essential to international peace and security,

Welcoming the recent global momentum of nuclear disarmament towards a world without nuclear weapons, which has been strengthened by concrete proposals and initiatives from political leaders of Member States, in particular by the Russian Federation and the United States of America, which currently together hold most of the nuclear weapons in the world,

Welcoming also the United Nations Security Council Summit on Nuclear Non-proliferation and Nuclear Disarmament, held on 24 September 2009, which confirmed the vision for a world without nuclear weapons,

Expressing deep concern regarding the growing dangers posed by the proliferation of weapons of mass destruction, inter alia, nuclear weapons, including that caused by proliferation networks,

Recognizing the importance of implementing Security Council resolution 1718(2006) of 14 October 2006 with regard to the nuclear test proclaimed by the Democratic People's Republic of Korea on 9 October 2006 and Council resolution 1874(2009) of 12 June 2009 with regard to the nuclear test conducted by the Democratic People's Republic of Korea on 25 May 2009, while calling upon the Democratic People's Republic of Korea to return immediately and without preconditions to the Six-Party Talks, and reiterating strong support for the early resumption of the Talks,

1. *Reaffirms* the importance of all States parties to the Treaty on the Non-Proliferation of Nuclear Weapons complying with their obligations under all the articles of the Treaty;

2. *Stresses* the importance of an effective Treaty review process, and calls upon all States parties to the Treaty to work together so that the 2010 Review Conference of the Parties to the Treaty on the Non-Proliferation of Nuclear Weapons can successfully strengthen the Treaty regime and can establish effective and practical measures in all the Treaty's three pillars;

3. *Reaffirms* the importance of the universality of the Treaty, and calls upon States not parties to the Treaty to accede to it as non-nuclear-weapon States without delay and without conditions and, pending their accession to the Treaty, to adhere to its terms as well as to take practical steps in support of the Treaty;

4. *Encourages* further steps leading to nuclear disarmament, in accordance with article VI of the Treaty, including deeper reductions in all types of nuclear weapons, and emphasizes the importance of applying the principles of irreversibility and verifiability, as well as increased transparency, in a way that promotes international stability and undiminished security for all, in the process of working towards the elimination of nuclear weapons;

5. *Calls upon* all nuclear-weapon States to undertake reductions of nuclear weapons in a transparent manner, and invites all nuclear-weapon States to agree on transparency and confidence-building measures, while noting in this regard the increased transparency demonstrated by nuclear-weapon States on their nuclear arsenals, including the current number of their nuclear warheads;

6. *Encourages* the Russian Federation and the United States of America to fully implement the obligations under the Treaty on Strategic Offensive Reductions and to undertake further steps in nuclear disarmament with greater transparency, including the conclusion of a legally binding successor to the Treaty on the Reduction and Limitation of Strategic Offensive Arms (START I), which is due to expire in December 2009, while welcoming the progress that has been made recently;

7. *Encourages* States to continue to pursue efforts, within the framework of international cooperation, contributing to the reduction of nuclear-weapons-related materials;

8. *Calls upon* the nuclear-weapon States to take measures to reduce the risk of an accidental or unauthorized launch of nuclear weapons and to also consider further reducing the operational status of nuclear weapons systems in ways that promote international stability and security;

9. *Stresses* the necessity of a diminishing role for nuclear weapons in security policies to minimize the risk that these weapons will ever be used and to facilitate the process of their total elimination, in a way that promotes international stability and based on the principle of undiminished security for all;

10. *Urges* all States that have not yet done so to sign and ratify the Comprehensive Nuclear-Test-Ban Treaty at the earliest opportunity with a view to its early entry into force and universalization, stresses the importance of maintaining existing moratoriums on nuclear-weapon test explosions or any other nuclear explosions pending the entry into force of the Treaty, and reaffirms the importance of the continued development of the Treaty verification regime, including the international monitoring system, which will be required to provide assurance of compliance with the Treaty;

11. *Welcomes* the adoption by the Conference on Disarmament of a programme of work for its 2009 session, and calls upon the Conference to start its substantive work when it convenes in January 2010, while taking into due consideration the increasing global momentum in favour of nuclear disarmament as well as progress and active engagement in deliberations at the Conference;

12. *Calls for* the immediate commencement of negotiations on a fissile material cut-off treaty at the 2010 session of the Conference on Disarmament and its early conclusion, and calls upon all nuclear-weapon States and States not parties to the Treaty on the Non-Proliferation of Nuclear Weapons to declare and maintain moratoriums on the production of fissile material for any nuclear weapons or other nuclear explosive devices pending the entry into force of the treaty;

13. *Calls upon* all States to redouble their efforts to prevent and curb the proliferation of nuclear and other weapons of mass destruction and their means of delivery;

14. *Stresses* the importance of preventing nuclear terrorism, and encourages every effort to secure all vulnerable nuclear and radiological material;

15. *Also stresses* the importance of further efforts for non-proliferation, including the universalization of the comprehensive safeguards agreements of the International Atomic Energy Agency to include States which have not yet adopted and implemented such an agreement, while also strongly encouraging further works for achieving the universalization of the Model Protocol Additional to the Agreement(s) between State(s) and the International Atomic Energy Agency for the Application of Safeguards approved by the Board of Governors of the Agency on 15 May 1997, and the full implementation of relevant Security Council resolutions, including resolution 1540(2004) of 28 April 2004;

16. *Encourages* all States to undertake concrete activities to implement, as appropriate, the recommendations contained in the report of the Secretary-General on the United Nations study on disarmament and non-proliferation education, submitted to the General Assembly

at its fifty-seventh session, and to voluntarily share information on efforts they have been undertaking to that end;

17. *Commends and further encourages* the constructive role played by civil society, including the International Commission on Nuclear Non-Proliferation and Disarmament, in promoting nuclear non-proliferation and nuclear disarmament;

18. *Decides* to include in the provisional agenda of its sixty-fifth session the item entitled "Renewed determination towards the total elimination of nuclear weapons".

RECORDED VOTE ON RESOLUTION 64/47:

In favour: Afghanistan, Albania, Algeria, Andorra, Angola, Antigua and Barbuda, Argentina, Armenia, Australia, Austria, Azerbaijan, Bahamas, Bahrain, Bangladesh, Barbados, Belarus, Belgium, Belize, Benin, Bolivia, Bosnia and Herzegovina, Botswana, Brazil, Brunei Darussalam, Bulgaria, Burkina Faso, Burundi, Cambodia, Cameroon, Canada, Cape Verde, Chile, Colombia, Comoros, Congo, Costa Rica, Croatia, Cyprus, Czech Republic, Democratic Republic of the Congo, Denmark, Djibouti, Dominica, Dominican Republic, Ecuador, Egypt, El Salvador, Equatorial Guinea, Eritrea, Estonia, Fiji, Finland, Gambia, Georgia, Germany, Ghana, Greece, Grenada, Guatemala, Guinea, Guinea-Bissau, Guyana, Haiti, Honduras, Hungary, Iceland, Indonesia, Iraq, Ireland, Italy, Jamaica, Japan, Jordan, Kazakhstan, Kenya, Kiribati, Kuwait, Kyrgyzstan, Lao People's Democratic Republic, Latvia, Lebanon, Lesotho, Liberia, Libyan Arab Jamahiriya, Liechtenstein, Lithuania, Luxembourg, Madagascar, Malawi, Malaysia, Maldives, Mali, Malta, Marshall Islands, Mauritania, Mauritius, Mexico, Micronesia, Moldova, Monaco, Mongolia, Montenegro, Morocco, Mozambique, Namibia, Nepal, Netherlands, New Zealand, Nicaragua, Niger, Nigeria, Norway, Oman, Palau, Panama, Papua New Guinea, Paraguay, Peru, Philippines, Poland, Portugal, Qatar, Republic of Korea, Romania, Russian Federation, Saint Kitts and Nevis, Saint Lucia, Saint Vincent and the Grenadines, Samoa, San Marino, Saudi Arabia, Senegal, Serbia, Seychelles, Sierra Leone, Singapore, Slovakia, Slovenia, Solomon Islands, Somalia, South Africa, Spain, Sri Lanka, Sudan, Suriname, Swaziland, Sweden, Switzerland, Syrian Arab Republic, Tajikistan, Thailand, The former Yugoslav Republic of Macedonia, Togo, Tonga, Trinidad and Tobago, Tunisia, Turkey, Turkmenistan, Uganda, Ukraine, United Arab Emirates, United Kingdom, United Republic of Tanzania, United States, Uruguay, Uzbekistan, Venezuela, Viet Nam, Yemen, Zambia, Zimbabwe.

Against: Democratic People's Republic of Korea, India.

Abstaining: Bhutan, China, Cuba, France, Iran, Israel, Myanmar, Pakistan.

Also on 2 December [meeting 55], the General Assembly, on the recommendation of the First Committee [A/64/391], adopted **resolution 64/53** by recorded vote (111-45-19) [agenda item 96 *(i)*].

Nuclear disarmament

The General Assembly,

Recalling its resolution 49/75 E of 15 December 1994 on a step-by-step reduction of the nuclear threat, and its resolutions 50/70 P of 12 December 1995, 51/45 O of 10 December 1996, 52/38 L of 9 December 1997, 53/77 X of 4 December 1998, 54/54 P of 1 December 1999, 55/33 T of

20 November 2000, 56/24 R of 29 November 2001, 57/79 of 22 November 2002, 58/56 of 8 December 2003, 59/77 of 3 December 2004, 60/70 of 8 December 2005, 61/78 of 6 December 2006, 62/42 of 5 December 2007 and 63/46 of 2 December 2008 on nuclear disarmament,

Reaffirming the commitment of the international community to the goal of the total elimination of nuclear weapons and the establishment of a nuclear-weapon-free world,

Bearing in mind that the Convention on the Prohibition of the Development, Production and Stockpiling of Bacteriological (Biological) and Toxin Weapons and on Their Destruction of 1972 and the Convention on the Prohibition of the Development, Production, Stockpiling and Use of Chemical Weapons and on Their Destruction of 1993 have already established legal regimes on the complete prohibition of biological and chemical weapons, respectively, and determined to achieve a nuclear weapons convention on the prohibition of the development, testing, production, stockpiling, loan, transfer, use and threat of use of nuclear weapons and on their destruction, and to conclude such an international convention at an early date,

Recognizing that there now exist conditions for the establishment of a world free of nuclear weapons, and stressing the need to take concrete practical steps towards achieving this goal,

Bearing in mind paragraph 50 of the Final Document of the Tenth Special Session of the General Assembly, the first special session devoted to disarmament, which called for the urgent negotiation of agreements for the cessation of the qualitative improvement and development of nuclear-weapon systems, and for a comprehensive and phased programme with agreed time frames, wherever feasible, for the progressive and balanced reduction of nuclear weapons and their means of delivery, leading to their ultimate and complete elimination at the earliest possible time,

Reaffirming the conviction of the States parties to the Treaty on the Non-Proliferation of Nuclear Weapons that the Treaty is a cornerstone of nuclear non-proliferation and nuclear disarmament, and the importance of the decision on strengthening the review process for the Treaty, the decision on principles and objectives for nuclear non-proliferation and disarmament, the decision on the extension of the Treaty and the resolution on the Middle East, adopted by the 1995 Review and Extension Conference of the Parties to the Treaty on the Non-Proliferation of Nuclear Weapons,

Stressing the importance of the thirteen steps for the systematic and progressive efforts to achieve the objective of nuclear disarmament leading to the total elimination of nuclear weapons, as agreed to by the States parties in the Final Document of the 2000 Review Conference of the Parties to the Treaty on the Non-Proliferation of Nuclear Weapons,

Reiterating the highest priority accorded to nuclear disarmament in the Final Document of the Tenth Special Session of the General Assembly and by the international community,

Reiterating its call for an early entry into force of the Comprehensive Nuclear-Test-Ban Treaty,

Taking note of the positive signals by the Russian Federation and the United States of America regarding their negotiations on the replacement for the Treaty on the

Reduction and Limitation of Strategic Offensive Arms (START I), which is due to expire by the end of 2009,

Urging the Russian Federation and the United States of America to conclude such negotiations urgently in order to achieve further deep cuts in their strategic and tactical nuclear weapons, and stressing that such cuts should be irreversible, verifiable and transparent,

Recalling the entry into force of the Treaty on Strategic Offensive Reductions ("the Moscow Treaty") between the United States of America and the Russian Federation as a significant step towards reducing their deployed strategic nuclear weapons, while calling for further irreversible deep cuts in their nuclear arsenals,

Noting the recent positive statements by nuclear-weapon States regarding their intention to pursue actions to achieve a world free of nuclear weapons, while reaffirming the need for urgent concrete actions by nuclear-weapon States to achieve this goal within a specified framework of time, and urging them to take further measures for progress on nuclear disarmament,

Recognizing the complementarity of bilateral, plurilateral and multilateral negotiations on nuclear disarmament, and that bilateral negotiations can never replace multilateral negotiations in this respect,

Noting the support expressed in the Conference on Disarmament and in the General Assembly for the elaboration of an international convention to assure non-nuclear-weapon States against the use or threat of use of nuclear weapons, and the multilateral efforts in the Conference on Disarmament to reach agreement on such an international convention at an early date,

Recalling the advisory opinion of the International Court of Justice on the *Legality of the Threat or Use of Nuclear Weapons*, issued on 8 July 1996, and welcoming the unanimous reaffirmation by all Judges of the Court that there exists an obligation for all States to pursue in good faith and bring to a conclusion negotiations leading to nuclear disarmament in all its aspects under strict and effective international control,

Mindful of paragraph 102 of the Final Document of the Coordinating Bureau of the Non-Aligned Movement at its Ministerial Meeting, held in Havana from 27 to 30 April 2009,

Recalling paragraph 112 and other relevant recommendations in the Final Document of the Fifteenth Summit Conference of Heads of State and Government of the Movement of Non-Aligned Countries, held in Sharm el-Sheikh, Egypt, on 15 and 16 July 2009, which called upon the Conference on Disarmament to establish, as soon as possible and as the highest priority, an ad hoc committee on nuclear disarmament and to commence negotiations on a phased programme for the complete elimination of nuclear weapons within a specified framework of time, including a nuclear weapons convention,

Noting the adoption of the programme of work for the 2009 session by the Conference on Disarmament on 29 May 2009, after years of stalemate, while reaffirming the importance of the Conference as the sole multilateral negotiating forum on disarmament,

Reaffirming the specific mandate conferred upon the Disarmament Commission by the General Assembly, in its decision 52/492 of 8 September 1998, to discuss the subject of nuclear disarmament as one of its main substantive agenda items,

Recalling the United Nations Millennium Declaration, in which Heads of State and Government resolved to strive for the elimination of weapons of mass destruction, in particular nuclear weapons, and to keep all options open for achieving this aim, including the possibility of convening an international conference to identify ways of eliminating nuclear dangers,

Reaffirming that, in accordance with the Charter of the United Nations, States should refrain from the use or threat of use of nuclear weapons in settling their disputes in international relations,

Seized of the danger of the use of weapons of mass destruction, particularly nuclear weapons, in terrorist acts and the urgent need for concerted international efforts to control and overcome it,

1. *Recognizes* that the time is now opportune for all the nuclear-weapon States to take effective disarmament measures to achieve the total elimination of these weapons at the earliest possible time;

2. *Reaffirms* that nuclear disarmament and nuclear non-proliferation are substantively interrelated and mutually reinforcing, that the two processes must go hand in hand and that there is a genuine need for a systematic and progressive process of nuclear disarmament;

3. *Welcomes and encourages* the efforts to establish new nuclear-weapon-free zones in different parts of the world on the basis of agreements or arrangements freely arrived at among the States of the regions concerned, which is an effective measure for limiting the further spread of nuclear weapons geographically and contributes to the cause of nuclear disarmament;

4. *Recognizes* that there is a genuine need to diminish the role of nuclear weapons in strategic doctrines and security policies to minimize the risk that these weapons will ever be used and to facilitate the process of their total elimination;

5. *Urges* the nuclear-weapon States to stop immediately the qualitative improvement, development, production and stockpiling of nuclear warheads and their delivery systems;

6. *Also urges* the nuclear-weapon States, as an interim measure, to de-alert and deactivate immediately their nuclear weapons and to take other concrete measures to reduce further the operational status of their nuclear-weapon systems, while stressing that reductions in deployments and in operational status cannot substitute for irreversible cuts in, and the total elimination of, nuclear weapons;

7. *Reiterates its call upon* the nuclear-weapon States to undertake the step-by-step reduction of the nuclear threat and to carry out effective nuclear disarmament measures with a view to achieving the total elimination of these weapons within a specified framework of time;

8. *Calls upon* the nuclear-weapon States, pending the achievement of the total elimination of nuclear weapons, to agree on an internationally and legally binding instrument on a joint undertaking not to be the first to use nuclear weapons, and calls upon all States to conclude an internationally and legally binding instrument on security assurances of non-use and non-threat of use of nuclear weapons against non-nuclear-weapon States;

9. *Urges* the nuclear-weapon States to commence pluri-lateral negotiations among themselves at an appropriate stage on further deep reductions of nuclear weapons as an effective measure of nuclear disarmament;

10. *Underlines* the importance of applying the princi-ples of transparency, irreversibility and verifiability to the process of nuclear disarmament and to nuclear and other related arms control and reduction measures;

11. *Underscores* the importance of the unequivocal un-dertaking by the nuclear-weapon States, in the Final Docu-ment of the 2000 Review Conference of the Parties to the Treaty on the Non-Proliferation of Nuclear Weapons, to accomplish the total elimination of their nuclear arsenals leading to nuclear disarmament, to which all States parties are committed under article VI of the Treaty, and the reaf-firmation by the States parties that the total elimination of nuclear weapons is the only absolute guarantee against the use or threat of use of nuclear weapons;

12. *Calls for* the full and effective implementation of the thirteen practical steps for nuclear disarmament contained in the Final Document of the 2000 Review Conference;

13. *Urges* the nuclear-weapon States to carry out fur-ther reductions of non-strategic nuclear weapons, based on unilateral initiatives and as an integral part of the nuclear arms reduction and disarmament process;

14. *Calls for* the immediate commencement of ne-gotiations in the Conference on Disarmament on a non-discriminatory, multilateral and internationally and effec-tively verifiable treaty banning the production of fissile ma-terial for nuclear weapons or other nuclear explosive devices on the basis of the report of the Special Coordinator and the mandate contained therein;

15. *Urges* the Conference on Disarmament to com-mence as early as possible its substantive work during its 2010 session, on the basis of a comprehensive and balanced programme of work that takes into consideration all the real and existing priorities in the field of disarmament and arms control, including the immediate commencement of negotiations on such a treaty with a view to their conclusion within five years;

16. *Calls for* the conclusion of an international legal instrument or instruments on adequate security assurances to non-nuclear-weapon States;

17. *Also calls for* the early entry into force and strict observance of the Comprehensive Nuclear-Test-Ban Treaty;

18. *Expresses its regret* that the 2005 Review Confer-ence of the Parties to the Treaty on the Non-Proliferation of Nuclear Weapons was unable to achieve any substantive result and that the 2005 World Summit Outcome adopted by the General Assembly failed to make any reference to nuclear disarmament and nuclear non-proliferation;

19. *Also expresses its regret* that the Conference on Disarmament was unable to establish an ad hoc committee to deal with nuclear disarmament early in 2009, as called for by the General Assembly in its resolution 63/46;

20. *Reiterates its call upon* the Conference on Disar-mament to establish, as soon as possible and as the high-est priority, an ad hoc committee on nuclear disarmament early in 2010, and to commence negotiations on a phased programme of nuclear disarmament leading to the total elimination of nuclear weapons within a specified frame-work of time;

21. *Calls for* the convening of an international confer-ence on nuclear disarmament in all its aspects at an early date to identify and deal with concrete measures of nuclear disarmament;

22. *Requests* the Secretary-General to submit to the General Assembly at its sixty-fifth session a report on the implementation of the present resolution;

23. *Decides* to include in the provisional agenda of its sixty-fifth session the item entitled "Nuclear disarmament".

RECORDED VOTE ON RESOLUTION 64/53:

In favour: Afghanistan, Algeria, Angola, Antigua and Bar-buda, Argentina, Bahamas, Bahrain, Bangladesh, Barbados, Belize, Benin, Bhutan, Botswana, Brazil, Brunei Darussalam, Burkina Faso, Burundi, Cambodia, Cameroon, Cape Verde, Chile, China, Colombia, Congo, Costa Rica, Cuba, Demo-cratic People's Republic of Korea, Democratic Republic of the Congo, Djibouti, Dominica, Dominican Republic, Ecuador, Egypt, El Salvador, Equatorial Guinea, Eritrea, Fiji, Gambia, Ghana, Grenada, Guatemala, Guinea, Guinea-Bissau, Guyana, Haiti, Honduras, Indonesia, Iran, Iraq, Jamaica, Jordan, Kenya, Kuwait, Lao People's Democratic Republic, Lebanon, Lesotho, Liberia, Libyan Arab Jamahiriya, Madagascar, Malawi, Malay-sia, Maldives, Mali, Mauritania, Mexico, Mongolia, Morocco, Mozambique, Myanmar, Namibia, Nepal, New Zealand, Nic-aragua, Niger, Nigeria, Oman, Panama, Papua New Guinea, Paraguay, Peru, Philippines, Qatar, Saint Kitts and Nevis, Saint Lucia, Saint Vincent and the Grenadines, Samoa, Saudi Arabia, Senegal, Singapore, Solomon Islands, Somalia, South Africa, Sri Lanka, Sudan, Suriname, Swaziland, Syrian Arab Repub-lic, Thailand, Togo, Tonga, Trinidad and Tobago, Tunisia, Uganda, United Arab Emirates, United Republic of Tanzania, Uruguay, Venezuela, Viet Nam, Yemen, Zambia, Zimbabwe.

Against: Albania, Andorra, Australia, Belgium, Bosnia and Herzegovina, Bulgaria, Canada, Croatia, Cyprus, Czech Re-public, Denmark, Estonia, Finland, France, Georgia, Germany, Greece, Hungary, Iceland, Israel, Italy, Latvia, Liechtenstein, Lithuania, Luxembourg, Micronesia, Moldova, Monaco, Montenegro, Netherlands, Norway, Palau, Poland, Portugal, Romania, San Marino, Slovakia, Slovenia, Spain, Switzerland, The former Yugoslav Republic of Macedonia, Turkey, Ukraine, United Kingdom, United States.

Abstaining: Armenia, Austria, Azerbaijan, Belarus, India, Ireland, Japan, Kazakhstan, Kyrgyzstan, Malta, Marshall Islands, Mauritius, Pakistan, Republic of Korea, Russian Fed-eration, Serbia, Sweden, Tajikistan, Uzbekistan.

Fissile material

The Conference on Disarmament held two infor-mal sessions on a fissile material cut-off treaty on 10 and 24 February [CD/1877, annex II]. The discussions focused on four topics: the definition of fissile materi-als, the scope of the treaty, stockpiles and plants, and verification.

Many delegations expressed preference for the defi-nition of fissile materials contained in article XX of the IAEA Statute: it had proved reliable and experts in the field had acquired sufficient familiarity with it, thus facilitating the drafting and implementation of a treaty on fissile materials. Certain delegations pointed out the close linkage between the issues of definitions and verification and observed that the adoption of excessively broad definitions might impair the conduct of verifications.

The scope of the treaty was no longer considered controversial. Several delegations stressed that the 1995 Shannon Report [CD/1299] remained the only one formally approved by consensus by the Conference on Disarmament that concerned the scope of a treaty. Some others stated that the wording on the scope of a treaty contained in document CD/1840 of 2008 [YUN 2008, p. 567] that called for negotiations without preconditions should also be taken into account. Other delegations stated that, in order to allow the Conference to proceed expeditiously towards the beginning of negotiations, discussions on the mandate should not be reopened.

The question of verification no longer appeared as contentious as in previous years, with most delegations in favour of an internationally verifiable treaty. The discussion on stockpiles was the most delicate and controversial, around the question whether the treaty should cover existing stocks of fissile materials or should only cover stocks manufactured after its entry into force. To a number of delegations, the question of stockpiles represented a priority national security concern. No delegation, however, considered reaching an understanding on stockpiles as a necessary precondition for starting negotiations on a treaty.

What clearly emerged from the sessions was that a treaty was ripe for negotiations. The only remaining contentious issue was that of fissile material stockpiles, which could be addressed within the framework of negotiations on the treaty.

GENERAL ASSEMBLY ACTION

On 2 December [meeting 55], the General Assembly, on the recommendation of the First Committee [A/64/391], adopted **resolution 64/29** without vote [agenda item 96].

Treaty banning the production of fissile material for nuclear weapons or other nuclear explosive devices

The General Assembly,

Recalling its resolutions 48/75 L of 16 December 1993, 53/77 I of 4 December 1998, 55/33 Y of 20 November 2000, 56/24 J of 29 November 2001, 57/80 of 22 November 2002, 58/57 of 8 December 2003 and 59/81 of 3 December 2004 on the subject of banning the production of fissile material for nuclear weapons or other nuclear explosive devices, and noting in this regard the support for the Conference on Disarmament expressed by the Security Council summit on nuclear disarmament and nuclear non-proliferation, held on 24 September 2009,

Convinced that a non-discriminatory, multilateral and internationally and effectively verifiable treaty banning the production of fissile material for nuclear weapons or other nuclear explosive devices would be a significant contribution to nuclear disarmament and non-proliferation,

Welcoming, after years of stalemate, the consensus adoption by the Conference on Disarmament of its decision (CD/1864) of 29 May 2009 on the establishment of a programme of work for its 2009 session, by which the Conference, inter alia, and without prejudice to any past, present or future position, established a Working Group to negotiate a treaty banning the production of fissile material for nuclear weapons or other nuclear explosive devices on the basis of document CD/1299 of 24 March 1995 and the mandate contained therein,

1. *Urges* the Conference on Disarmament to agree early in 2010 on a programme of work that includes the immediate commencement of negotiations on a treaty banning the production of fissile material for nuclear weapons or other nuclear explosive devices;

2. *Decides* to include in the provisional agenda of its sixty-fifth session an item entitled "Treaty banning the production of fissile material for nuclear weapons or other nuclear explosive devices".

Security assurances

The Conference on Disarmament held two informal meetings on 12 and 26 February on "Effective international arrangements to assure non-nuclear-weapon States against the use or threat of use of nuclear weapons" (or "negative security assurances") [CD/1877, annex IV], with many delegations in support of the legitimacy of the call by non-nuclear-weapon States for negative security assurances.

It was noted that statements by nuclear-weapon States that they would not use or threaten to use nuclear weapons against non-nuclear-weapon States were insufficient, given that the statements were unilateral, conditional and revocable. Some delegations maintained that the assurances given in nuclear-weapon-free zones were insufficient, conditional and geographically limited. Nevertheless, the creation of such zones in Africa, South-East Asia, Central Asia and South America, as well as Mongolia's nuclear-weapon-free status, constituted steps forward. In that spirit, some delegations called for the implementation of the relevant Council resolutions and the undertakings of the 1995 and 2000 NPT Review Conferences to make the Middle East a nuclear-weapon-free zone.

Furthermore, it was argued that granting negative security assurances would constitute a quid pro quo for States that renounced nuclear weapons and would help to combat proliferation. In that connection, granting legally binding assurances to non-nuclear-weapon States would be a confidence-building measure and a step towards the implementation by nuclear-weapon States of article VI of NPT concerning nuclear disarmament.

Several delegations stressed the need to start negotiations on a legally binding, non-discriminatory and universal international instrument that would provide assurances against the use or threat of use of nuclear weapons against non-nuclear-weapon States. It was proposed to establish an ad hoc committee within the Conference on Disarmament to prepare for and conduct such negotiations, in accordance with document CD/1693 of 2003, known as the five Ambassadors' proposal [YUN 2003, p. 532], which provided guidance on the matter. Some delegations considered that the basic details of a possible treaty could be dealt with in due course during the negotiations. One delegation put forward the idea that Security Council resolution 984(1995) [YUN 1995, p. 192] on security assurances could be reaffirmed to strengthen the current legal framework, if necessary by having more States align themselves with it.

The discussions once again revealed the complexity of negative security assurances, and there was no consensus on the framework in which negotiations over a possible treaty on such assurances might be conducted.

GENERAL ASSEMBLY ACTION

On 2 December [meeting 55], the General Assembly, on the recommendation of the First Committee [A/64/388], adopted **resolution 64/27** by recorded vote (118-0-58) [agenda item 93].

Conclusion of effective international arrangements to assure non-nuclear-weapon States against the use or threat of use of nuclear weapons

The General Assembly,

Bearing in mind the need to allay the legitimate concern of the States of the world with regard to ensuring lasting security for their peoples,

Convinced that nuclear weapons pose the greatest threat to mankind and to the survival of civilization,

Noting that the renewed interest in nuclear disarmament should be translated into concrete actions for the achievement of general and complete disarmament under effective international control,

Convinced that nuclear disarmament and the complete elimination of nuclear weapons are essential to remove the danger of nuclear war,

Determined to abide strictly by the relevant provisions of the Charter of the United Nations on the non-use of force or threat of force,

Recognizing that the independence, territorial integrity and sovereignty of non-nuclear-weapon States need to be safeguarded against the use or threat of use of force, including the use or threat of use of nuclear weapons,

Considering that, until nuclear disarmament is achieved on a universal basis, it is imperative for the international community to develop effective measures and arrangements to ensure the security of non-nuclear-weapon States against the use or threat of use of nuclear weapons from any quarter,

Recognizing that effective measures and arrangements to assure non-nuclear-weapon States against the use or threat of use of nuclear weapons can contribute positively to the prevention of the spread of nuclear weapons,

Bearing in mind paragraph 59 of the Final Document of the Tenth Special Session of the General Assembly, the first special session devoted to disarmament, in which it urged the nuclear-weapon States to pursue efforts to conclude, as appropriate, effective arrangements to assure non-nuclear-weapon States against the use or threat of use of nuclear weapons, and desirous of promoting the implementation of the relevant provisions of the Final Document,

Recalling the relevant parts of the special report of the Committee on Disarmament submitted to the General Assembly at its twelfth special session, the second special session devoted to disarmament, and of the special report of the Conference on Disarmament submitted to the Assembly at its fifteenth special session, the third special session devoted to disarmament, as well as the report of the Conference on its 1992 session,

Recalling also paragraph 12 of the Declaration of the 1980s as the Second Disarmament Decade, contained in the annex to its resolution 35/46 of 3 December 1980, which states, inter alia, that all efforts should be exerted by the Committee on Disarmament urgently to negotiate with a view to reaching agreement on effective international arrangements to assure non-nuclear-weapon States against the use or threat of use of nuclear weapons,

Noting the in-depth negotiations undertaken in the Conference on Disarmament and its Ad Hoc Committee on Effective International Arrangements to Assure Non-Nuclear-Weapon States against the Use or Threat of Use of Nuclear Weapons, with a view to reaching agreement on this question,

Taking note of the proposals submitted under the item in the Conference on Disarmament, including the drafts of an international convention,

Taking note also of the relevant decision of the Thirteenth Conference of Heads of State or Government of Non-Aligned Countries, held at Kuala Lumpur on 24 and 25 February 2003, which was reiterated at the Fourteenth and Fifteenth Conferences of Heads of State or Government of Non-Aligned Countries, held at Havana and Sharm el-Sheik, Egypt, on 15 and 16 September 2006, and 15 and 16 July 2009, respectively, as well as the relevant recommendations of the Organization of the Islamic Conference,

Taking note further of the unilateral declarations made by all the nuclear-weapon States on their policies of non-use or non-threat of use of nuclear weapons against the non-nuclear-weapon States,

Noting the support expressed in the Conference on Disarmament and in the General Assembly for the elaboration of an international convention to assure non-nuclear-weapon States against the use or threat of use of nuclear weapons, as well as the difficulties pointed out in evolving a common approach acceptable to all,

Taking note of Security Council resolution 984(1995) of 11 April 1995 and the views expressed on it,

Recalling its relevant resolutions adopted in previous years, in particular resolutions 45/54 of 4 December 1990, 46/32 of 6 December 1991, 47/50 of 9 December 1992, 48/73 of 16 December 1993, 49/73 of 15 December 1994, 50/68 of 12 December 1995, 51/43 of 10 December 1996, 52/36 of 9 December 1997, 53/75 of 4 December 1998, 54/52 of 1 December 1999, 55/31 of 20 November 2000, 56/22 of 29 November 2001, 57/56 of 22 November 2002, 58/35 of 8 December 2003, 59/64 of 3 December 2004, 60/53 of 8 December 2005, 61/57 of 6 December 2006, 62/19 of 5 December 2007 and 63/39 of 2 December 2008,

1. *Reaffirms* the urgent need to reach an early agreement on effective international arrangements to assure non-nuclear-weapon States against the use or threat of use of nuclear weapons;

2. *Notes with satisfaction* that in the Conference on Disarmament there is no objection, in principle, to the idea of an international convention to assure non-nuclear-weapon States against the use or threat of use of nuclear weapons, although the difficulties with regard to evolving a common approach acceptable to all have also been pointed out;

3. *Appeals* to all States, especially the nuclear-weapon States, to work actively towards an early agreement on a common approach and, in particular, on a common formula that could be included in an international instrument of a legally binding character;

4. *Recommends* that further intensive efforts be devoted to the search for such a common approach or common formula and that the various alternative approaches, including, in particular, those considered in the Conference on Disarmament, be explored further in order to overcome the difficulties;

5. *Also recommends* that the Conference on Disarmament actively continue intensive negotiations with a view to reaching early agreement and concluding effective international agreements to assure the non-nuclear-weapon States against the use or threat of use of nuclear weapons, taking into account the widespread support for the conclusion of an international convention and giving consideration to any other proposals designed to secure the same objective;

6. *Decides* to include in the provisional agenda of its sixty-fifth session the item entitled "Conclusion of effective international arrangements to assure non-nuclear-weapon States against the use or threat of use of nuclear weapons".

RECORDED VOTE ON RESOLUTION 64/27:

In favour: Afghanistan, Algeria, Angola, Antigua and Barbuda, Azerbaijan, Bahamas, Bahrain, Barbados, Belarus, Belize, Benin, Bhutan, Bolivia, Botswana, Brazil, Brunei Darussalam, Burundi, Cambodia, Cameroon, Cape Verde, Chile, China, Colombia, Comoros, Congo, Costa Rica, Côte d'Ivoire, Cuba, Democratic People's Republic of Korea, Djibouti, Dominica, Dominican Republic, Ecuador, Egypt, El Salvador, Equatorial Guinea, Eritrea, Fiji, Gambia, Ghana, Grenada, Guatemala, Guinea, Guinea-Bissau, Guyana, Haiti, Honduras, India, Indonesia, Iran, Iraq, Jamaica, Japan, Jordan, Kazakhstan, Kenya, Kuwait, Kyrgyzstan, Lao People's Democratic Republic, Lebanon, Lesotho, Liberia, Libyan Arab Jamahiriya, Madagascar, Malawi, Malaysia, Maldives, Mali, Mauritania, Mauritius, Mexico, Mongolia, Morocco, Mozambique, Myanmar, Namibia, Nepal, Nicaragua, Niger, Nigeria, Oman, Pakistan, Panama, Papua New Guinea, Paraguay, Peru, Philippines, Qa-

tar, Rwanda, Saint Kitts and Nevis, Saint Lucia, Saint Vincent and the Grenadines, Samoa, Saudi Arabia, Senegal, Singapore, Solomon Islands, Somalia, Sri Lanka, Sudan, Suriname, Syrian Arab Republic, Thailand, Togo, Tonga, Trinidad and Tobago, Tunisia, Turkmenistan, Uganda, United Arab Emirates, United Republic of Tanzania, Uruguay, Uzbekistan, Venezuela, Viet Nam, Yemen, Zambia, Zimbabwe.

Against: None.

Abstaining: Albania, Andorra, Argentina, Armenia, Australia, Austria, Belgium, Bosnia and Herzegovina, Bulgaria, Canada, Croatia, Cyprus, Czech Republic, Democratic Republic of the Congo, Denmark, Estonia, Finland, France, Georgia, Germany, Greece, Hungary, Iceland, Ireland, Israel, Italy, Latvia, Liechtenstein, Lithuania, Luxembourg, Malta, Marshall Islands, Micronesia, Moldova, Monaco, Montenegro, Netherlands, New Zealand, Norway, Palau, Poland, Portugal, Republic of Korea, Romania, Russian Federation, San Marino, Serbia, Slovakia, Slovenia, South Africa, Spain, Sweden, Switzerland, The former Yugoslav Republic of Macedonia, Turkey, Ukraine, United Kingdom, United States.

Comprehensive Nuclear-Test-Ban Treaty

Status

As at 31 December, 182 States had signed the 1996 Comprehensive Nuclear-Test-Ban Treaty (CTBT), adopted by General Assembly resolution 50/245 [YUN 1996, p. 454], and 151 had ratified it. During the year, instruments of ratification were deposited by Liberia, the Marshall Islands and Saint Vincent and the Grenadines. In accordance with article XIV, CTBT would enter into force 180 days after the 44 States possessing nuclear reactors, listed in annex 2 of the Treaty, had deposited their instruments of ratification. By year's end, 35 of those States had ratified the Treaty.

Report of Secretary-General. Pursuant to Assembly resolution 63/87 [YUN 2008, p. 579], the Secretary-General reported in July and September [A/64/137 & Add.1], in consultation with the Preparatory Commission for CTBT, on the efforts of States that had ratified the Treaty towards its universalization and possibilities for providing assistance on ratification procedures to States that so requested it.

Communication. On 12 May [A/64/81], Namibia, as President of the Inter-Parliamentary Union, transmitted to the Secretary-General the text of a resolution adopted by the 120th Assembly of the Inter-Parliamentary Union (Addis Ababa, Ethiopia, 10 April) on advancing nuclear non-proliferation and disarmament, and securing the entry into force of CTBT.

Preparatory Commission for the CTBT Organization

In advance of the entry into force of CTBT and the establishment of the Comprehensive Nuclear-Test-Ban Treaty Organization (CTBTO), a Preparatory

Commission was established by the States signatories in 1996 [YUN 1996, p. 452]. In 2009, the Preparatory Commission continued to develop the Treaty's verification regime. Further progress was made in setting up the International Monitoring System (IMS) [YUN 1999, p. 472], the global network of 337 facilities to be built in 90 countries and designed to detect nuclear explosions prohibited by CTBT. By the end of the year, 268 IMS stations, representing 83 per cent of the network, were installed and were transmitting information to the International Data Centre (IDC) in Vienna.

The operation and maintenance activities for the Global Communications Infrastructure (GCI) focused on consolidating the enhanced capabilities of the new GCI network, whose availability continued to improve. The volume of data traffic carried by GCI and by special links to IDC and in the other direction, from IDC to remote sites, increased during the year. Through new software applications, the detection capacity of IDC and the reliability of its operation were strengthened, and the means of access of authorized users in States signatories to IDC data and data products were developed further.

The Preparatory Commission held its thirty-second (8–9 June) [CTBT/PC-32/2] and thirty-third (16–17 November) [CTBT/PC-33/2] sessions, both in Vienna, to consider the reports of its working groups and to discuss organizational, budgetary and other matters.

Note by Secretary-General. In July [A/64/155], the Secretary-General submitted to the Assembly the report of the Commission's Executive Secretary for 2008, pursuant to article IV, paragraph 1, of the Agreement to Regulate the Relationship between the United Nations and the Preparatory Commission for CTBTO, annexed to Assembly resolution 54/280 [YUN 2000, p. 501].

Conference on facilitating entry into force

The sixth Conference on Facilitating the Entry into Force of CTBT (New York, 24–25 September) [CTBT-Art.XIV/2009/6], convened pursuant to article XIV of the Treaty, was opened by Sergio Duarte, United Nations High Representative for Disarmament Affairs, and attended by the Secretary-General. Bernard Kouchner, Minister for Foreign and European Affairs of France, and Taïb Fassi-Fihri, Minister for Foreign Affairs and Cooperation of Morocco, shared the Conference presidency. The conference was attended for the first time by the United States, represented by Secretary of State Hillary Clinton. Michael Douglas, United Nations Messenger of Peace, also attended the Conference.

At the event, attended by 103 States, an exchange of views was held by ratifiers and signatories on facilitating the entry into force of the Treaty. The President of the Carnegie Endowment for International Peace, Jessica Mathews, made a statement on behalf of the 19 NGOs attending the Conference.

In their final declaration, participants reaffirmed that the ultimate objective of States was general and complete disarmament under strict and effective international control. They reiterated that the cessation of all nuclear weapon test explosions and all other nuclear explosions, by constraining the development and improvement of nuclear weapons and ending the development of advanced new types of such weapons, constituted an effective measure of nuclear disarmament and non-proliferation. The end to all nuclear weapons testing was, thus, a meaningful step in the realization of a systematic process to achieve nuclear disarmament.

GENERAL ASSEMBLY ACTION

On 2 December [meeting 55], the General Assembly, on the recommendation of the First Committee [A/64/397], adopted **resolution 64/69** by recorded vote (175-1-3) [agenda item 102].

Comprehensive Nuclear-Test-Ban Treaty

The General Assembly,

Reiterating that the cessation of nuclear-weapon test explosions or any other nuclear explosions constitutes an effective nuclear disarmament and non-proliferation measure, and convinced that this is a meaningful step in the realization of a systematic process to achieve nuclear disarmament,

Recalling that the Comprehensive Nuclear-Test-Ban Treaty, adopted by its resolution 50/245 of 10 September 1996, was opened for signature on 24 September 1996,

Stressing that a universal and effectively verifiable Treaty constitutes a fundamental instrument in the field of nuclear disarmament and non-proliferation and that, after more than twelve years, its entry into force is more urgent than ever before,

Encouraged by the signing of the Treaty by one hundred and eighty-two States, including forty-one of the forty-four needed for its entry into force, and welcoming the ratification of one hundred and fifty States, including thirty-five of the forty-four needed for its entry into force, among which there are three nuclear-weapon States,

Recalling its resolution 63/87 of 2 December 2008,

Welcoming the Joint Ministerial Statement on the Comprehensive Nuclear-Test-Ban Treaty, adopted at the Ministerial Meeting held in New York on 24 September 2008,

Welcoming also the Final Declaration of the Sixth Conference on Facilitating the Entry into Force of the Comprehensive Nuclear-Test-Ban Treaty, held in New York on 24 and 25 September 2009, pursuant to article XIV of the Treaty, and noting the improved prospects for ratification in several Annex 2 countries,

1. *Stresses* the vital importance and urgency of signature and ratification, without delay and without conditions, to achieve the earliest entry into force of the Comprehensive Nuclear-Test-Ban Treaty;

2. *Welcomes* the contributions by the States signatories to the work of the Preparatory Commission for the Comprehensive Nuclear-Test-Ban Treaty Organization, in particular its efforts to ensure that the Treaty's verification regime will be capable of meeting the verification requirements of the Treaty upon its entry into force, in accordance with article IV of the Treaty;

3. *Underlines* the need to maintain momentum towards completion of all elements of the verification regime;

4. *Urges* all States not to carry out nuclear-weapon test explosions or any other nuclear explosions, to maintain their moratoriums in this regard and to refrain from acts that would defeat the object and purpose of the Treaty, while stressing that these measures do not have the same permanent and legally binding effect as the entry into force of the Treaty;

5. *Recalls* Security Council resolutions 1718(2006) of 14 October 2006 and 1874(2009) of 12 June 2009, calls for their early implementation, and calls for early resumption of the Six-Party Talks;

6. *Urges* all States that have not yet signed the Treaty to sign and ratify it as soon as possible;

7. *Urges* all States that have signed but not yet ratified the Treaty, in particular those whose ratification is needed for its entry into force, to accelerate their ratification processes with a view to ensuring their earliest successful conclusion;

8. *Welcomes*, since the last session of the General Assembly, the ratification of the Treaty by Lebanon, Liberia, Malawi, Mozambique and Saint Vincent and the Grenadines, as well as the signature by Trinidad and Tobago, as significant steps towards the early entry into force of the Treaty;

9. *Urges* all States to remain seized of the issue at the highest political level and, where in a position to do so, to promote adherence to the Treaty through bilateral and joint outreach, seminars and other means;

10. *Requests* the Secretary-General, in consultation with the Preparatory Commission for the Comprehensive Nuclear-Test-Ban Treaty Organization, to prepare a report on the efforts of States that have ratified the Treaty towards its universalization and possibilities for providing assistance on ratification procedures to States that so request it, and to submit such a report to the General Assembly at its sixty-fifth session;

11. *Decides* to include in the provisional agenda of its sixty-fifth session the item entitled "Comprehensive Nuclear-Test-Ban Treaty".

RECORDED VOTE ON RESOLUTION 64/69:

In favour: Afghanistan, Albania, Algeria, Andorra, Angola, Antigua and Barbuda, Argentina, Armenia, Australia, Austria, Azerbaijan, Bahamas, Bahrain, Bangladesh, Barbados, Belarus, Belgium, Belize, Benin, Bhutan, Bolivia, Bosnia and Herzegovina, Botswana, Brazil, Brunei Darussalam, Bulgaria, Burkina Faso, Burundi, Cambodia, Cameroon, Canada, Cape Verde, Chile, China, Colombia, Comoros, Congo, Costa Rica,

Côte d'Ivoire, Croatia, Cuba, Cyprus, Czech Republic, Democratic Republic of the Congo, Denmark, Djibouti, Dominica, Dominican Republic, Ecuador, Egypt, El Salvador, Equatorial Guinea, Eritrea, Estonia, Fiji, Finland, France, Gambia, Georgia, Germany, Ghana, Greece, Grenada, Guatemala, Guinea, Guinea-Bissau, Guyana, Haiti, Honduras, Hungary, Iceland, Indonesia, Iran, Iraq, Ireland, Israel, Italy, Jamaica, Japan, Jordan, Kazakhstan, Kenya, Kuwait, Kyrgyzstan, Lao People's Democratic Republic, Latvia, Lebanon, Lesotho, Liberia, Libyan Arab Jamahiriya, Liechtenstein, Lithuania, Luxembourg, Madagascar, Malawi, Malaysia, Maldives, Mali, Malta, Marshall Islands, Mauritania, Mexico, Micronesia, Moldova, Monaco, Mongolia, Montenegro, Morocco, Mozambique, Myanmar, Namibia, Nepal, Netherlands, New Zealand, Nicaragua, Niger, Nigeria, Norway, Oman, Pakistan, Palau, Panama, Papua New Guinea, Paraguay, Peru, Philippines, Poland, Portugal, Qatar, Republic of Korea, Romania, Russian Federation, Saint Kitts and Nevis, Saint Lucia, Saint Vincent and the Grenadines, Samoa, San Marino, Saudi Arabia, Senegal, Serbia, Sierra Leone, Singapore, Slovakia, Slovenia, Solomon Islands, Somalia, South Africa, Spain, Sri Lanka, Suriname, Swaziland, Sweden, Switzerland, Tajikistan, Thailand, The former Yugoslav Republic of Macedonia, Togo, Tonga, Trinidad and Tobago, Tunisia, Turkey, Turkmenistan, Uganda, Ukraine, United Arab Emirates, United Kingdom, United Republic of Tanzania, United States, Uruguay, Uzbekistan, Venezuela, Viet Nam, Yemen, Zambia, Zimbabwe.

Against: Democratic People's Republic of Korea.

Abstaining: India, Mauritius, Syrian Arab Republic.

Also on 2 December [meeting 55], the General Assembly, on the recommendation of the First Committee [A/64/391], adopted **resolution 64/57** by recorded vote (169-5-5) [agenda item 96 *(p)*].

Towards a nuclear-weapon-free world: accelerating the implementation of nuclear disarmament commitments

The General Assembly,

Recalling its resolution 63/58 of 2 December 2008,

Reiterating its grave concern at the danger to humanity posed by the possibility that nuclear weapons could be used,

Noting with satisfaction the renewed interest in nuclear disarmament on the part of international leaders expressed, inter alia, during the Security Council summit on nuclear non-proliferation and nuclear disarmament held on 24 September 2009, and underlining in this regard the urgent need for concrete, transparent, verifiable and irreversible steps to realize the goal of a world free of nuclear weapons,

Reaffirming that nuclear disarmament and nuclear non-proliferation are mutually reinforcing processes requiring urgent irreversible progress on both fronts,

Recognizing the continued vital importance of the early entry into force of the Comprehensive Nuclear-Test-Ban Treaty to the advancement of nuclear disarmament and nuclear non-proliferation objectives, and welcoming the recent ratifications of the Treaty by Lebanon, Liberia, Malawi, Mozambique and Saint Vincent and the Grenadines,

Recalling that the 2000 Review Conference of the Parties to the Treaty on the Non-Proliferation of Nuclear Weapons in its final document, inter alia, reaffirmed the conviction that the establishment of nuclear-weapon-free zones enhances global and regional peace and security, strengthens the nuclear non-proliferation regime and contributes towards realizing the objectives of nuclear disarmament,

Welcoming the entry into force, on 21 March 2009, of the Treaty on a Nuclear-Weapon-Free Zone in Central Asia and the entry into force, on 15 July 2009, of the Treaty of Pelindaba, which establishes a nuclear-weapon-free zone in Africa, and expressing the hope that these important steps will be followed by concerted international efforts to create nuclear-weapon-free zones in other areas in the world, especially in the Middle East,

Recalling the decisions entitled "Strengthening the review process for the Treaty", "Principles and objectives for nuclear non-proliferation and disarmament" and "Extension of the Treaty on the Non-Proliferation of Nuclear Weapons" and the resolution on the Middle East, all of which were adopted at the 1995 Review and Extension Conference of the Parties to the Treaty on the Non-Proliferation of Nuclear Weapons and the Final Document of the 2000 Review Conference of the Parties to the Treaty on the Non-Proliferation of Nuclear Weapons,

Recalling also the unequivocal undertaking by the nuclear-weapon States to accomplish the total elimination of their nuclear arsenals, leading to nuclear disarmament, in accordance with commitments made under article VI of the Treaty on the Non-Proliferation of Nuclear Weapons,

Welcoming the progress towards a follow-up agreement to the Strategic Arms Reduction Treaty, as reflected in recent statements made by the Presidents of the Russian Federation and of the United States of America,

Welcoming also the outcome of the third session of the Preparatory Committee for the 2010 Review Conference of the Parties to the Treaty on the Non-Proliferation of Nuclear Weapons, at which the Committee adopted the provisional agenda and decisions relating to the organization of the work of the Review Conference,

Welcoming further the recent positive developments in the Conference on Disarmament, which led to the adoption of a programme of work on 29 May 2009,

1. *Continues to emphasize* the central role of the Treaty on the Non-Proliferation of Nuclear Weapons and its universality in achieving nuclear disarmament and nuclear non-proliferation, and calls upon all States parties to respect their obligations;

2. *Calls upon* all States to comply fully with all commitments made regarding nuclear disarmament and nuclear non-proliferation and not to act in any way that may compromise either cause or that may lead to a new nuclear arms race;

3. *Reaffirms* that the outcome of the 2000 Review Conference of the Parties to the Treaty on the Non-Proliferation of Nuclear Weapons sets out the agreed process for systematic and progressive efforts towards nuclear disarmament, and in this regard renews its call upon the nuclear-weapon States to accelerate the implementation of the practical steps towards nuclear disarmament that were agreed upon at the 2000 Review Conference, thereby contributing to a safer world for all;

4. *Reiterates its call upon* all States parties to spare no effort to achieve the universality of the Treaty on the Non-Proliferation of Nuclear Weapons, and in this regard urges India, Israel and Pakistan to accede to the Treaty as non-nuclear-weapon States promptly and without conditions;

5. *Urges* the Democratic People's Republic of Korea to rescind its announced withdrawal from the Treaty on the Non-Proliferation of Nuclear Weapons, to re-establish cooperation with the International Atomic Energy Agency and to rejoin the Six-Party Talks, with a view to achieving the denuclearization of the Korean Peninsula in a peaceful manner;

6. *Calls upon* all Parties to the Treaty on the Non-Proliferation of Nuclear Weapons to spare no effort to ensure a successful and constructive outcome of the 2010 Review Conference;

7. *Stresses* that the outcome of the 2010 Review Conference should build upon the positive results reached at the 1995 and 2000 Conferences, contribute significantly to the concrete implementation of the outcomes of both Conferences, advance the objective of a nuclear-weapon-free world, strengthen the Treaty on the Non-Proliferation of Nuclear Weapons in all its aspects and contribute to achieving its full implementation and universality;

8. *Calls upon* all States parties to the Treaty on the Non-Proliferation of Nuclear Weapons to work towards the full implementation of the resolution on the Middle East adopted at the 1995 Review Conference;

9. *Calls upon* the States members of the Conference on Disarmament to pursue continued positive developments in that forum, in order to maintain the momentum that led to the adoption of a programme of work on 29 May 2009, and spare no efforts to ensure an early start to the substantive work of the Conference at the beginning of its 2010 session;

10. *Decides* to include in the provisional agenda of its sixty-fifth session the item entitled "Towards a nuclear-weapon-free world: accelerating the implementation of nuclear disarmament commitments" and to review the implementation of the present resolution at that session.

RECORDED VOTE ON RESOLUTION 64/57:

In favour: Afghanistan, Albania, Algeria, Andorra, Angola, Antigua and Barbuda, Argentina, Armenia, Australia, Austria, Azerbaijan, Bahamas, Bahrain, Bangladesh, Barbados, Belarus, Belgium, Belize, Benin, Bolivia, Bosnia and Herzegovina, Botswana, Brazil, Brunei Darussalam, Bulgaria, Burkina Faso, Burundi, Cambodia, Cameroon, Canada, Cape Verde, Chile, China, Colombia, Comoros, Congo, Costa Rica, Côte d'Ivoire, Croatia, Cuba, Cyprus, Czech Republic, Democratic Republic of the Congo, Denmark, Djibouti, Dominica, Dominican Republic, Ecuador, Egypt, El Salvador, Equatorial Guinea, Eritrea, Estonia, Fiji, Finland, Gambia, Georgia, Germany, Ghana, Greece, Grenada, Guatemala, Guinea, Guinea-Bissau, Guyana, Haiti, Honduras, Hungary, Iceland, Indonesia, Iran, Iraq, Ireland, Italy, Jamaica, Japan, Jordan, Kazakhstan, Kenya, Kuwait, Kyrgyzstan, Lao People's Democratic Republic, Latvia, Lebanon, Lesotho, Liberia, Libyan Arab Jamahiriya, Liechtenstein, Lithuania, Luxembourg, Madagascar, Malawi, Malaysia, Maldives, Mali, Malta, Marshall Islands, Mauritius, Mexico, Moldova, Mongolia, Montenegro, Morocco, Mozambique, Myanmar, Namibia, Nepal, Netherlands, New Zealand, Nicaragua, Niger, Nigeria, Norway, Oman, Panama,

Papua New Guinea, Paraguay, Peru, Philippines, Poland, Portugal, Qatar, Republic of Korea, Romania, Russian Federation, Saint Kitts and Nevis, Saint Lucia, Saint Vincent and the Grenadines, Samoa, San Marino, Saudi Arabia, Senegal, Serbia, Seychelles, Sierra Leone, Singapore, Slovakia, Slovenia, Solomon Islands, Somalia, South Africa, Spain, Sri Lanka, Sudan, Suriname, Swaziland, Sweden, Switzerland, Syrian Arab Republic, Tajikistan, Thailand, The former Yugoslav Republic of Macedonia, Togo, Tonga, Trinidad and Tobago, Tunisia, Turkey, Uganda, Ukraine, United Arab Emirates, United Republic of Tanzania, Uruguay, Uzbekistan, Venezuela, Viet Nam, Yemen, Zambia, Zimbabwe.

Against: Democratic People's Republic of Korea, France, India, Israel, United States.

Abstaining: Bhutan, Micronesia, Pakistan, Palau, United Kingdom.

Advisory opinion of the International Court of Justice

Pursuant to General Assembly resolutions 63/46 [YUN 2008, p. 574], 63/47 [ibid., p. 565] and 63/49 [ibid., p. 583], relating to the advisory opinion of the International Court of Justice that the threat or use of nuclear weapons was contrary to the UN Charter [YUN 1996, p. 461], the Secretary-General in July [A/64/139] presented information from eight States (Cuba, El Salvador, Japan, Lebanon, Lithuania, Mexico, Nicaragua, Qatar) on measures they had taken to implement resolution 63/49 and towards nuclear disarmament.

GENERAL ASSEMBLY ACTION

On 2 December [meeting 55], the General Assembly, on the recommendation of the First Committee [A/64/391], adopted **resolution 64/55** by recorded vote (124-31-21) [agenda item 96 *(l)*].

Follow-up to the advisory opinion of the International Court of Justice on the *Legality of the Threat or Use of Nuclear Weapons*

The General Assembly,

Recalling its resolutions 49/75 K of 15 December 1994, 51/45 M of 10 December 1996, 52/38 O of 9 December 1997, 53/77 W of 4 December 1998, 54/54 Q of 1 December 1999, 55/33 X of 20 November 2000, 56/24 S of 29 November 2001, 57/85 of 22 November 2002, 58/46 of 8 December 2003, 59/83 of 3 December 2004, 60/76 of 8 December 2005, 61/83 of 6 December 2006, 62/39 of 5 December 2007 and 63/49 of 2 December 2008,

Convinced that the continuing existence of nuclear weapons poses a threat to all humanity and that their use would have catastrophic consequences for all life on Earth, and recognizing that the only defence against a nuclear catastrophe is the total elimination of nuclear weapons and the certainty that they will never be produced again,

Reaffirming the commitment of the international community to the goal of the total elimination of nuclear weapons and the creation of a nuclear-weapon-free world,

Mindful of the solemn obligations of States parties, undertaken in article VI of the Treaty on the Non-Proliferation of Nuclear Weapons, particularly to pursue negotiations in good faith on effective measures relating to cessation of the nuclear arms race at an early date and to nuclear disarmament,

Recalling the principles and objectives for nuclear non-proliferation and disarmament adopted at the 1995 Review and Extension Conference of the Parties to the Treaty on the Non-Proliferation of Nuclear Weapons,

Emphasizing the unequivocal undertaking by the nuclear-weapon States to accomplish the total elimination of their nuclear arsenals leading to nuclear disarmament, adopted at the 2000 Review Conference of the Parties to the Treaty on the Non-Proliferation of Nuclear Weapons,

Recalling the adoption of the Comprehensive Nuclear-Test-Ban Treaty in its resolution 50/245 of 10 September 1996, and expressing its satisfaction at the increasing number of States that have signed and ratified the Treaty,

Recognizing with satisfaction that the Antarctic Treaty and the treaties of Tlatelolco, Rarotonga, Bangkok, Pelindaba and Central Asia, as well as Mongolia's nuclear-weapon-free status, are gradually freeing the entire southern hemisphere and adjacent areas covered by those treaties from nuclear weapons,

Stressing the importance of strengthening all existing nuclear-related disarmament and arms control and reduction measures,

Recognizing the need for a multilaterally negotiated and legally binding instrument to assure non-nuclear-weapon States against the threat or use of nuclear weapons,

Reaffirming the central role of the Conference on Disarmament as the sole multilateral disarmament negotiating forum,

Emphasizing the need for the Conference on Disarmament to commence negotiations on a phased programme for the complete elimination of nuclear weapons with a specified framework of time,

Expressing its regret over the failure of the 2005 Review Conference of the Parties to the Treaty on the Non-Proliferation of Nuclear Weapons to reach agreement on any substantive issues,

Expressing its deep concern at the lack of progress in the implementation of the thirteen steps to implement article VI of the Treaty on the Non-Proliferation of Nuclear Weapons agreed to at the 2000 Review Conference of the Parties to the Treaty,

Desiring to achieve the objective of a legally binding prohibition of the development, production, testing, deployment, stockpiling, threat or use of nuclear weapons and their destruction under effective international control,

Recalling the advisory opinion of the International Court of Justice on the *Legality of the Threat or Use of Nuclear Weapons*, issued on 8 July 1996,

Taking note of the relevant portions of the report of the Secretary-General relating to the implementation of resolution 63/49,

1. *Underlines once again* the unanimous conclusion of the International Court of Justice that there exists an obligation to pursue in good faith and bring to a conclusion negotiations leading to nuclear disarmament in all its aspects under strict and effective international control;

2. *Calls once again upon* all States immediately to fulfil that obligation by commencing multilateral negotiations leading to an early conclusion of a nuclear weapons convention prohibiting the development, production, testing, deployment, stockpiling, transfer, threat or use of nuclear weapons and providing for their elimination;

3. *Requests* all States to inform the Secretary-General of the efforts and measures they have taken on the implementation of the present resolution and nuclear disarmament, and requests the Secretary-General to apprise the General Assembly of that information at its sixty-fifth session;

4. *Decides* to include in the provisional agenda of its sixty-fifth session the item entitled "Follow-up to the advisory opinion of the International Court of Justice on the *Legality of the Threat or Use of Nuclear Weapons*".

RECORDED VOTE ON RESOLUTION 64/55:

In favour: Afghanistan, Algeria, Angola, Antigua and Barbuda, Argentina, Austria, Bahamas, Bahrain, Bangladesh, Barbados, Belize, Benin, Bhutan, Bolivia, Bosnia and Herzegovina, Botswana, Brazil, Brunei Darussalam, Burkina Faso, Burundi, Cambodia, Cameroon, Cape Verde, Chile, China, Colombia, Congo, Costa Rica, Côte d'Ivoire, Cuba, Democratic People's Republic of Korea, Democratic Republic of the Congo, Djibouti, Dominica, Dominican Republic, Ecuador, Egypt, El Salvador, Equatorial Guinea, Eritrea, Fiji, Gambia, Ghana, Grenada, Guatemala, Guinea, Guinea-Bissau, Guyana, Haiti, Honduras, India, Indonesia, Iran, Iraq, Ireland, Jamaica, Jordan, Kenya, Kuwait, Lao People's Democratic Republic, Lebanon, Lesotho, Liberia, Libyan Arab Jamahiriya, Madagascar, Malawi, Malaysia, Maldives, Mali, Malta, Mauritania, Mauritius, Mexico, Mongolia, Morocco, Mozambique, Myanmar, Namibia, Nepal, New Zealand, Nicaragua, Niger, Nigeria, Oman, Pakistan, Panama, Papua New Guinea, Paraguay, Peru, Philippines, Qatar, Saint Kitts and Nevis, Saint Lucia, Saint Vincent and the Grenadines, Samoa, San Marino, Saudi Arabia, Senegal, Serbia, Singapore, Solomon Islands, Somalia, South Africa, Sri Lanka, Sudan, Suriname, Swaziland, Sweden, Switzerland, Syrian Arab Republic, Thailand, Togo, Trinidad and Tobago, Tunisia, Turkmenistan, Uganda, United Arab Emirates, United Republic of Tanzania, Uruguay, Venezuela, Viet Nam, Yemen, Zambia, Zimbabwe.

Against: Albania, Belgium, Bulgaria, Czech Republic, Denmark, Estonia, France, Georgia, Germany, Greece, Hungary, Iceland, Israel, Italy, Latvia, Lithuania, Luxembourg, Montenegro, Netherlands, Norway, Palau, Poland, Portugal, Russian Federation, Slovakia, Slovenia, Spain, The former Yugoslav Republic of Macedonia, Turkey, United Kingdom, United States.

Abstaining: Andorra, Armenia, Australia, Azerbaijan, Belarus, Canada, Croatia, Cyprus, Finland, Japan, Kazakhstan, Kyrgyzstan, Liechtenstein, Marshall Islands, Micronesia, Moldova, Republic of Korea, Romania, Tajikistan, Ukraine, Uzbekistan.

Prohibition of the use of nuclear weapons

In 2009, no progress was made on a convention on the prohibition of the use of nuclear weapons, as the Conference on Disarmament was unable to undertake negotiations on the subject as called

for in Assembly resolution 63/75 [YUN 2008, p. 582]. As in previous years, the Assembly reiterated its request to the Conference to commence negotiations.

GENERAL ASSEMBLY ACTION

On 2 December [meeting 55], the General Assembly, on the recommendation of the First Committee [A/64/392], adopted **resolution 64/59** by recorded vote (116-50-12) [agenda item 97 *(b)*].

Convention on the Prohibition of the Use of Nuclear Weapons

The General Assembly,

Convinced that the use of nuclear weapons poses the most serious threat to the survival of mankind,

Bearing in mind the advisory opinion of the International Court of Justice of 8 July 1996 on the *Legality of the Threat or Use of Nuclear Weapons,*

Convinced that a multilateral, universal and binding agreement prohibiting the use or threat of use of nuclear weapons would contribute to the elimination of the nuclear threat and to the climate for negotiations leading to the ultimate elimination of nuclear weapons, thereby strengthening international peace and security,

Conscious that some steps taken by the Russian Federation and the United States of America towards a reduction of their nuclear weapons and the improvement in the international climate can contribute towards the goal of the complete elimination of nuclear weapons,

Recalling that paragraph 58 of the Final Document of the Tenth Special Session of the General Assembly states that all States should actively participate in efforts to bring about conditions in international relations among States in which a code of peaceful conduct of nations in international affairs could be agreed upon and that would preclude the use or threat of use of nuclear weapons,

Reaffirming that any use of nuclear weapons would be a violation of the Charter of the United Nations and a crime against humanity, as declared in its resolutions 1653(XVI) of 24 November 1961, 33/71 B of 14 December 1978, 34/83 G of 11 December 1979, 35/152 D of 12 December 1980 and 36/92 I of 9 December 1981,

Determined to achieve an international convention prohibiting the development, production, stockpiling and use of nuclear weapons, leading to their ultimate destruction,

Stressing that an international convention on the prohibition of the use of nuclear weapons would be an important step in a phased programme towards the complete elimination of nuclear weapons, with a specified framework of time,

Noting with regret that the Conference on Disarmament, during its 2009 session, was unable to undertake negotiations on this subject as called for in General Assembly resolution 63/75 of 2 December 2008,

1. *Reiterates its request* to the Conference on Disarmament to commence negotiations in order to reach agreement on an international convention prohibiting the use or threat of use of nuclear weapons under any circumstances;

2. *Requests* the Conference on Disarmament to report to the General Assembly on the results of those negotiations.

RECORDED VOTE ON RESOLUTION 64/59:

In favour: Afghanistan, Algeria, Angola, Antigua and Barbuda, Argentina, Bahamas, Bahrain, Bangladesh, Barbados, Belize, Benin, Bhutan, Bolivia, Botswana, Brazil, Brunei Darussalam, Burkina Faso, Burundi, Cambodia, Cameroon, Cape Verde, Chile, China, Colombia, Congo, Costa Rica, Côte d'Ivoire, Cuba, Democratic People's Republic of Korea, Democratic Republic of the Congo, Djibouti, Dominica, Dominican Republic, Ecuador, Egypt, El Salvador, Equatorial Guinea, Eritrea, Fiji, Gambia, Ghana, Grenada, Guatemala, Guinea, Guinea-Bissau, Guyana, Haiti, Honduras, India, Indonesia, Iran, Iraq, Jamaica, Jordan, Kenya, Kuwait, Lao People's Democratic Republic, Lebanon, Lesotho, Liberia, Libyan Arab Jamahiriya, Madagascar, Malawi, Malaysia, Maldives, Mali, Mauritania, Mauritius, Mexico, Mongolia, Morocco, Mozambique, Myanmar, Namibia, Nepal, Nicaragua, Niger, Nigeria, Oman, Pakistan, Panama, Papua New Guinea, Paraguay, Peru, Philippines, Qatar, Saint Kitts and Nevis, Saint Lucia, Saint Vincent and the Grenadines, Samoa, Saudi Arabia, Senegal, Singapore, Solomon Islands, South Africa, Sri Lanka, Sudan, Suriname, Swaziland, Syrian Arab Republic, Tajikistan, Thailand, Togo, Tonga, Trinidad and Tobago, Tunisia, Turkmenistan, Uganda, United Arab Emirates, United Republic of Tanzania, Uruguay, Venezuela, Viet Nam, Yemen, Zambia, Zimbabwe.

Against: Albania, Andorra, Australia, Austria, Belgium, Bosnia and Herzegovina, Bulgaria, Canada, Croatia, Cyprus, Czech Republic, Denmark, Estonia, Finland, France, Georgia, Germany, Greece, Hungary, Iceland, Ireland, Israel, Italy, Latvia, Liechtenstein, Lithuania, Luxembourg, Malta, Micronesia, Moldova, Monaco, Montenegro, Netherlands, New Zealand, Norway, Palau, Poland, Portugal, Romania, San Marino, Slovakia, Slovenia, Spain, Sweden, Switzerland, The former Yugoslav Republic of Macedonia, Turkey, Ukraine, United Kingdom, United States.

Abstaining: Armenia, Azerbaijan, Belarus, Comoros, Japan, Kazakhstan, Kyrgyzstan, Marshall Islands, Republic of Korea, Russian Federation, Serbia, Uzbekistan.

International Day against Nuclear Tests

The General Assembly declared 29 August the International Day against Nuclear Tests to increase awareness about the effects of nuclear weapon test explosions and the need for their cessation as a means of achieving a nuclear-weapon-free world. The resolution (see below) was initiated by Kazakhstan, together with a large number of cosponsors, to commemorate the closure of the Semipalatinsk nuclear test site on 29 August 1991.

GENERAL ASSEMBLY ACTION

On 2 December [meeting 55], the General Assembly, on the recommendation of the First Committee [A/64/391], adopted **resolution 64/35** without vote [agenda item 96].

International Day against Nuclear Tests

The General Assembly,

Recalling that the promotion of peace and security is among the main purposes and principles of the United Nations embodied in the Charter,

Convinced that every effort should be made to end nuclear tests in order to avert devastating and harmful effects on the lives and health of people and the environment,

Convinced also that the end of nuclear tests is one of the key means of achieving the goal of a nuclear-weapon-free world,

Welcoming the recent positive momentum in the international community to work towards this goal,

Emphasizing, in this context, the essential role of Governments, intergovernmental organizations, civil society, academia and mass media,

Acknowledging the related importance of education as a tool for peace, security, disarmament and non-proliferation,

1. *Declares* 29 August the International Day against Nuclear Tests, devoted to enhancing public awareness and education about the effects of nuclear weapon test explosions or any other nuclear explosions and the need for their cessation as one of the means of achieving the goal of a nuclear-weapon-free world;

2. *Invites* Member States, the United Nations system, civil society, academia, the mass media and individuals to commemorate the International Day against Nuclear Tests in an appropriate manner, including through all means of educational and public awareness-raising activities.

Non-proliferation issues

Non-proliferation treaty

Status

In 2009, the number of States parties to the Treaty on the Non-Proliferation of Nuclear Weapons (NPT) remained at 190. Regarded as the cornerstone of the global nuclear non-proliferation regime, the Treaty was adopted by the General Assembly in 1968, by resolution 2373(XXII) [YUN 1968, p. 17], and entered into force on 5 March 1970. It was extended indefinitely by Assembly resolution 50/70 in 1995 [YUN 1995, p. 189].

2010 review conference

Following the entry into force of NPT, quinquennial review conferences, as called for under article VIII, paragraph 3, of the Treaty, were held beginning in 1975 [YUN 1975, p. 27], and the most recent in 2005 [YUN 2005, p. 597].

The Preparatory Committee for the 2010 Review Conference held its third and last session in 2009 (New York, 4–15 May) [NPT/CONF.2010/1] prior to the Review Conference. Delegations of 135 States parties, Palestine (observer), IAEA, six intergovernmental organizations and 77 NGOs attended the session.

The Committee held 25 meetings, devoted to three main clusters and three blocks of issues. The clusters dealt with implementation of the provisions of the Treaty related to: non-proliferation of nuclear weapons, disarmament and international peace and security; non-proliferation of nuclear weapons, safeguards and nuclear-weapon-free zones; and the inalienable right of all NPT parties to develop research, production and use of nuclear energy for peaceful purposes. The blocks of issues addressed were: nuclear disarmament and security assurances; regional issues, including with respect to the Middle East and the implementation of the resolution on the Middle East adopted by the 1995 Review Conference [YUN 1995, p. 189]; and other Treaty provisions, including article X.

The Preparatory Committee was able to adopt procedural arrangements for the 2010 Review Conference. However, delegations were unable to achieve consensus on substantive recommendations to the Conference, as differences persisted among States parties towards achieving nuclear disarmament, strengthening non-proliferation and ensuring the peaceful use of nuclear energy in conformity with NPT.

The Committee decided that the 2010 Review Conference would be held from 3 to 28 May in New York. The Committee unanimously endorsed the candidacy of Libran N. Cabactulan (Philippines) for the presidency of the Conference.

GENERAL ASSEMBLY ACTION

On 2 December [meeting 55], the General Assembly, on the recommendation of the First Committee [A/64/391], adopted **resolution 64/31** by recorded vote (109-56-10) [agenda item 96 *(b)*].

Follow-up to nuclear disarmament obligations agreed to at the 1995 and 2000 Review Conferences of the Parties to the Treaty on the Non-Proliferation of Nuclear Weapons

The General Assembly,

Recalling its various resolutions in the field of nuclear disarmament, including its most recent, resolutions 62/24 of 5 December 2007, and 63/46, 63/49 and 63/75 of 2 December 2008,

Bearing in mind its resolution 2373(XXII) of 12 June 1968, the annex to which contains the Treaty on the Non-Proliferation of Nuclear Weapons,

Noting the provisions of article VIII, paragraph 3, of the Treaty regarding the convening of review conferences at five-year intervals,

Recalling its resolution 50/70 Q of 12 December 1995, in which the General Assembly noted that the States parties to the Treaty affirmed the need to continue to move with determination towards the full realization and effective implementation of the provisions of the Treaty, and accordingly adopted a set of principles and objectives,

Recalling also that, on 11 May 1995, the 1995 Review and Extension Conference of the Parties to the Treaty on the Non-Proliferation of Nuclear Weapons adopted three decisions on strengthening the review process for the Treaty, principles and objectives for nuclear non-proliferation and disarmament, and extension of the Treaty,

Reaffirming the resolution on the Middle East adopted on 11 May 1995 by the 1995 Review and Extension Conference of the Parties to the Treaty, in which the Conference reaffirmed the importance of the early realization of universal adherence to the Treaty and placement of nuclear facilities under full-scope International Atomic Energy Agency safeguards,

Reaffirming also its resolution 55/33 D of 20 November 2000, in which the General Assembly welcomed the adoption by consensus on 19 May 2000 of the Final Document of the 2000 Review Conference of the Parties to the Treaty on the Non-Proliferation of Nuclear Weapons, including, in particular, the documents entitled "Review of the operation of the Treaty, taking into account the decisions and the resolution adopted by the 1995 Review and Extension Conference" and "Improving the effectiveness of the strengthened review process for the Treaty",

Taking into consideration the unequivocal undertaking by the nuclear-weapon States, in the Final Document of the 2000 Review Conference of the Parties to the Treaty, to accomplish the total elimination of their nuclear arsenals leading to nuclear disarmament, to which all States parties to the Treaty are committed under article VI of the Treaty,

Gravely concerned over the failure of the 2005 Review Conference of the Parties to the Treaty to reach any substantive agreement on the follow-up to the nuclear disarmament obligations,

Noting with satisfaction that the Preparatory Committee for the 2010 Review Conference of the Parties to the Treaty finalized the procedural arrangements for the Review Conference,

1. *Determines* to pursue practical steps for systematic and progressive efforts to implement article VI of the Treaty on the Non-Proliferation of Nuclear Weapons and paragraphs 3 and 4 *(c)* of the decision on principles and objectives for nuclear non-proliferation and disarmament of the 1995 Review and Extension Conference of the Parties to the Treaty on the Non-Proliferation of Nuclear Weapons;

2. *Calls for* practical steps, as agreed to at the 2000 Review Conference of the Parties to the Treaty on the Non-Proliferation of Nuclear Weapons, to be taken by all nuclear-weapon States, which would lead to nuclear disarmament in a way that promotes international stability and, based on the principle of undiminished security for all:

(a) Further efforts to be made by the nuclear-weapon States to reduce their nuclear arsenals unilaterally;

(b) Increased transparency by the nuclear-weapon States with regard to nuclear weapons capabilities and the implementation of agreements pursuant to article VI of the Treaty and as a voluntary confidence-building measure to support further progress in nuclear disarmament;

(c) The further reduction of non-strategic nuclear weapons, based on unilateral initiatives and as an integral part of the nuclear arms reduction and disarmament process;

(d) Concrete agreed measures to reduce further the operational status of nuclear weapons systems;

(e) A diminishing role for nuclear weapons in security policies so as to minimize the risk that these weapons will ever be used and to facilitate the process of their total elimination;

(f) The engagement, as soon as appropriate, of all the nuclear-weapon States in the process leading to the total elimination of their nuclear weapons;

3. *Notes* that the 2000 Review Conference of the Parties to the Treaty agreed that legally binding security assurances by the five nuclear-weapon States to the non-nuclear-weapon States parties to the Treaty strengthen the nuclear non-proliferation regime;

4. *Urges* the States parties to the Treaty to follow up on the implementation of the nuclear disarmament obligations under the Treaty agreed to at the 1995 and 2000 Review Conferences of the Parties to the Treaty within the framework of Review Conferences of the Parties to the Treaty and their Preparatory Committees;

5. *Decides* to include in the provisional agenda of its sixty-sixth session the item entitled "Follow-up to nuclear disarmament obligations agreed to at the 1995 and 2000 Review Conferences of the Parties to the Treaty on the Non-Proliferation of Nuclear Weapons".

RECORDED VOTE ON RESOLUTION 64/31:

In favour: Algeria, Angola, Antigua and Barbuda, Argentina, Bahamas, Bahrain, Barbados, Belarus, Belize, Benin, Bhutan, Bolivia, Botswana, Brazil, Brunei Darussalam, Burundi, Cambodia, Cameroon, Cape Verde, Chile, Congo, Côte d'Ivoire, Cuba, Democratic People's Republic of Korea, Democratic Republic of the Congo, Djibouti, Dominica, Dominican Republic, Ecuador, Egypt, El Salvador, Equatorial Guinea, Eritrea, Fiji, Gambia, Ghana, Grenada, Guatemala, Guinea, Guinea-Bissau, Guyana, Haiti, Honduras, Indonesia, Iran, Iraq, Jamaica, Jordan, Kazakhstan, Kenya, Kuwait, Kyrgyzstan, Lao People's Democratic Republic, Lebanon, Lesotho, Liberia, Libyan Arab Jamahiriya, Madagascar, Malawi, Malaysia, Maldives, Mali, Mauritania, Mauritius, Mexico, Mongolia, Morocco, Mozambique, Myanmar, Namibia, Nepal, Nicaragua, Niger, Nigeria, Oman, Papua New Guinea, Paraguay, Philippines, Qatar, Rwanda, Saint Kitts and Nevis, Saint Lucia, Saint Vincent and the Grenadines, Saudi Arabia, Senegal, Singapore, Solomon Islands, Somalia, South Africa, Sri Lanka, Sudan, Suriname, Syrian Arab Republic, Tajikistan, Thailand, Togo, Trinidad and Tobago, Tunisia, Turkmenistan, Uganda, United Arab Emirates, United Republic of Tanzania, Uruguay, Uzbekistan, Venezuela, Viet Nam, Yemen, Zambia, Zimbabwe.

Against: Albania, Andorra, Australia, Austria, Belgium, Bosnia and Herzegovina, Bulgaria, Canada, Comoros, Croatia, Cyprus, Czech Republic, Denmark, Estonia, Finland, France, Georgia, Germany, Greece, Hungary, Iceland, Ireland, Israel, Italy, Japan, Latvia, Liechtenstein, Lithuania, Luxembourg, Malta, Marshall Islands, Micronesia, Moldova, Monaco, Montenegro, Netherlands, New Zealand, Norway, Palau, Panama, Poland, Portugal, Republic of Korea, Romania, Russian Federation, San Marino, Serbia, Slovakia, Slovenia, Spain, Sweden, Switzerland, The former Yugoslav Republic of Macedonia, Ukraine, United Kingdom, United States.

Abstaining: Armenia, Azerbaijan, China, Colombia, Costa Rica, India, Pakistan, Peru, Samoa, Tonga.

Hague Code of Conduct

At the Eighth Regular Meeting of the Hague Code of Conduct against Ballistic Missile Proliferation (Vienna, 28–29 May), the 130 subscribing States discussed the strengthening of confidence-building measures, such as pre-launch notifications and annual declarations of ballistic missiles, space-launch vehicles and the importance of outreach activities to foster the universalization of the Code and thereby increase the number of subscribing States.

Non-proliferation of weapons of mass destruction

Security Council Committee on WMDs

The Committee established pursuant to resolution 1540(2004) [YUN 2004, p. 544] was set up in 2004 by the Security Council for a period of no longer than two years, with a mandate to report to the Council on the implementation of that resolution, which dealt with the non-proliferation of weapons of mass destruction (WMDs). The Committee's mandate was extended for a further two years by resolution 1673(2006) [YUN 2006, p. 635]. By resolution 1810(2008) [YUN 2008, p. 585], the Council extended the mandate until 25 April 2011.

The Committee experts continued to update the matrices for Member States on the basis of new information about their efforts to implement resolution 1540(2004). Committee members and experts participated in seminars, workshops and conferences, explaining to participants the work of the Committee and the requirements of the resolution. The Committee also organized regional and subregional workshops on the implementation of the resolution.

On 2 March 2009 [S/2009/124], the Committee submitted to the Council its programme of work for the period from 1 February 2009 to 31 January 2010, featuring a new system of working groups dealing with monitoring and national implementation, assistance, cooperation with other Council committees, and transparency and media outreach.

The Committee established a working group to consider the modalities of a comprehensive review of the status of implementation of resolution 1540(2004), as requested by resolution 1810(2008), and on 27 March submitted proposals [S/2009/170] for such a review.

As part of the review, the Committee held an open meeting (New York, 30 September–2 October) with broad participation from Member States and international organizations. A final document on the 2009 comprehensive review [S/2010/52] stated that the adoption of resolution 1540(2004) had prompted significant steps across the globe to prevent non-State actors from manufacturing, acquiring, possessing, developing, transporting, transferring or using nuclear, chemical and biological weapons and their means of delivery. A large number of States had reported on the measures taken in accordance with the resolution. Member States had forged new working relationships across government bureaucracies, enhanced regulatory frameworks and expanded their efforts to address the nexus between non-State actors and WMDs. Since 2006, Member States had made demonstrable progress in addressing the threat of proliferation of WMDs. Nearly 160 Member States had reported on their capabilities and gaps in stopping the proliferation of WMDs, and the number of States reporting to have implemented legislative measures to penalize the involvement of non-State actors in prohibited WMD proliferation activities had grown considerably.

During the year, reports on implementation of the resolution were submitted by the Sudan [S/AC.44/2004/(02)/153], Bhutan [S/AC.44/2004/(02)/154], Bangladesh [S/AC.44/2004/(02)/133/Add.1] and the Dominican Republic [S/AC.44/2004/(02)/156].

At its summit on nuclear non-proliferation and nuclear disarmament of 24 September, the Council, by resolution 1887(2009) (see p. 525), reaffirmed the need for full implementation of resolution 1540(2004) by Member States.

New types of WMDs

Conference on Disarmament. The issue of radiological weapons had been on the agenda of the Conference on Disarmament since 1979. In accordance with the joint initiative by the 2008 Presidents, and under the guidance of the Coordinator (Bulgaria), the Conference [A/64/27], under its programme of work, held two informal meetings on 16 February and 2 March on "New types of WMDs and new systems of such weapons; radiological weapons".

During the discussions [CD/1877, annex V], one delegation raised the issue of "State terrorism", while others pointed out that the focus of the debate should be more on the nature of the weapon than on the user's characteristics. Emphasis was again placed on preventing the emergence of new WMDs since the prevention of an arms race was, after all, the major goal of disarmament. Delegations raised issues that fell within broader themes already established in 2008: radiological weapons; new types of WMDs and new systems of such weapons and the importance of prevention; and preventing terrorists from acquiring radiological materials and WMDs.

Terrorism and WMDs

During the year, the United Nations continued to promote international action against terrorism through collaborative efforts with Member States and regional and international organizations, and through the work of the Counter-Terrorism Committee (see

p. 70) and the Al-Qaida and Taliban Sanctions Committee (see p. 353).

Report of Secretary-General. Pursuant to General Assembly resolution 63/60 [YUN 2008, p. 589], the Secretary-General in July [A/64/140 & Add.1] presented the views of 13 Member States and 10 international organizations, including UN agencies, on measures they had taken to prevent terrorists from acquiring WMDs, their means of delivery, and related materials and technologies.

IAEA report. The Director General of IAEA, in a report [GOV/2009/53-GC(53)/16] issued in August in response to resolution GC(52)/RES/10 [YUN 2008, p. 589], presented activities undertaken by the Agency in the area of nuclear security and against nuclear terrorism between July 2008 and June 2009. In the framework of the Nuclear Security Plan 2006–2009, the Agency provided nuclear security assistance to States.

At an International Symposium on Nuclear Security (Vienna, 30 March–3 April), more than 500 participants from 76 countries and international organizations discussed the status of nuclear security and directions for the future. The Agency also organized the International Conference on Effective Nuclear Regulatory Systems: Further Enhancing the Global Nuclear Safety and Security Regime (Cape Town, South Africa, 14–18 December). The Nuclear Security Series documents were expanded to contain nuclear security guidance that States could use in establishing their national nuclear security systems.

The Agency's Illicit Trafficking Database programme continued to expand, with 107 participating States as at 30 June. Reports about incidents of illegal possession, movement and attempted sales of nuclear and other radioactive material showed a persistent picture of nuclear trafficking. The recovery rate of radioactive material reported lost or stolen remained low, the Director General said. During the period under discussion, only about 40 per cent of stolen or lost radioactive material was subsequently reported as recovered.

The Agency had established a process of developing integrated nuclear security support plans to consolidate the nuclear security needs of individual States into integrated plans for nuclear security improvements and assistance. As at 30 June, 49 such plans were developed by States and the Agency. The Agency offered services to evaluate and assess nuclear security arrangements in States through its nuclear security missions. Through the Nuclear Security Fund, 14 evaluation and advisory nuclear security missions were carried out between mid-2008 and mid-2009.

The Agency organized 57 nuclear security education and training events worldwide, which involved 1,400 participants in more than 105 countries. Participants were trained in physical protection, nuclear material accounting and control, registry of radioactive sources, regulatory systems, measures to combat illicit nuclear trafficking, response to nuclear security events and maintaining confidentiality of sensitive information. More than 300 training events had been conducted since 2003, in which about 8,000 participants from approximately 125 countries had been trained.

Between mid-2008 and mid-2009, the Agency provided technical assistance to 27 States to help establish effective border control, which included 985 radiation-monitoring instruments to detect any undeclared radioactive substance in cargo or in personal luggage. Moving radioactive material from a vulnerable to a secure location was an important IAEA contribution to nuclear risk reduction. The Agency conducted operations in seven States to improve the security of 575 radioactive sources; 31 of those sources were repatriated to the supplier State. Technical arrangements for increased security were applied to 539 radioactive sources in various countries.

The Agency assisted in the repatriation of high enriched uranium (HEU) research reactor fuel at the request of States. Between mid-2008 and mid-2009, the Agency was involved, in an auxiliary capacity, in the repatriation of four shipments of HEU fuel, totalling more than 40 kilograms (kg), to the United States; four shipments totalling 258 kg of spent fuel to the Russian Federation; and one shipment of 30 kg of fresh fuel to the Russian Federation. In June, the Agency assisted in repatriating HEU spent fuel from Romania to the Russian Federation by air—the first time that spent nuclear fuel had been transported in that manner.

IAEA action. On 18 September [GC(53)/RES/11], the IAEA General Conference, in a resolution on measures to protect against nuclear and radiological terrorism, called on Member States to support international efforts to enhance nuclear security through bilateral, regional and international arrangements.

Communication. In a letter of 24 July to the Secretary-General [A/63/965-S/2009/514], the Non-Aligned Movement communicated its long-held positions on disarmament and international security as affirmed in the Final Document of the Fifteenth Summit Conference of Heads of State and Government of the Movement of Non-Aligned Countries (Sharm el-Sheikh, Egypt, 11–16 July). The Movement stressed that reductions in deployments and in operational status could not substitute for irreversible cuts in, and the total elimination of, nuclear weapons; it called on the United States and the Russian Federation to apply the principles of transparency, irreversibility and verifiability to further reduce their nuclear arsenals, both warheads

and delivery systems, under the 2002 Strategic Offensive Reductions Treaty (Moscow Treaty) [YUN 2002, p. 493]. The Movement emphasized the importance of observing environmental norms in preparing and implementing disarmament and arms limitation agreements; expressed satisfaction with the consensus among States on measures to prevent terrorists from acquiring WMDs; underlined the need to ensure that any action by the Security Council did not undermine the UN Charter, multilateral treaties on WMDs and international organizations established in that regard, as well as the role of the General Assembly; and stressed the importance of the symbiotic relationship between disarmament and development and the role of security in that connection.

GENERAL ASSEMBLY ACTION

On 2 December [meeting 55], the General Assembly, on the recommendation of the First Committee [A/64/391], adopted **resolution 64/38** without vote [agenda item 96 *(q)*].

Measures to prevent terrorists from acquiring weapons of mass destruction

The General Assembly,

Recalling its resolution 63/60 of 2 December 2008,

Recognizing the determination of the international community to combat terrorism, as evidenced in relevant General Assembly and Security Council resolutions,

Deeply concerned by the growing risk of linkages between terrorism and weapons of mass destruction, and in particular by the fact that terrorists may seek to acquire weapons of mass destruction,

Cognizant of the steps taken by States to implement Security Council resolution 1540(2004) on the non-proliferation of weapons of mass destruction, adopted on 28 April 2004,

Welcoming the entry into force on 7 July 2007 of the International Convention for the Suppression of Acts of Nuclear Terrorism,

Welcoming also the adoption, by consensus, of amendments to strengthen the Convention on the Physical Protection of Nuclear Material by the International Atomic Energy Agency on 8 July 2005,

Noting the support expressed in the Final Document of the Fifteenth Summit Conference of Heads of State and Government of the Movement of Non-Aligned Countries, which was held in Sharm el-Sheikh, Egypt, from 11 to 16 July 2009, for measures to prevent terrorists from acquiring weapons of mass destruction,

Noting also that the Group of Eight, the European Union, the Regional Forum of the Association of Southeast Asian Nations and others have taken into account in their deliberations the dangers posed by the likely acquisition by terrorists of weapons of mass destruction, and the need for international cooperation in combating it,

Noting further the Global Initiative to Combat Nuclear Terrorism, launched jointly by the Russian Federation and the United States of America, and the proposed Global Summit on Nuclear Security to be hosted by the United States of America in 2010,

Acknowledging the consideration of issues relating to terrorism and weapons of mass destruction by the Advisory Board on Disarmament Matters,

Taking note of the relevant resolutions adopted by the General Conference of the International Atomic Energy Agency at its fifty-third regular session,

Taking note also of the 2005 World Summit Outcome adopted at the High-level Plenary Meeting of the General Assembly in September 2005 and the adoption of the United Nations Global Counter-Terrorism Strategy on 8 September 2006,

Taking note further of the report of the Secretary-General, submitted pursuant to paragraph 5 of resolution 63/60,

Mindful of the urgent need for addressing, within the United Nations framework and through international cooperation, this threat to humanity,

Emphasizing that progress is urgently needed in the area of disarmament and non-proliferation in order to maintain international peace and security and to contribute to global efforts against terrorism,

1. *Calls upon* all Member States to support international efforts to prevent terrorists from acquiring weapons of mass destruction and their means of delivery;

2. *Appeals* to all Member States to consider early accession to and ratification of the International Convention for the Suppression of Acts of Nuclear Terrorism;

3. *Urges* all Member States to take and strengthen national measures, as appropriate, to prevent terrorists from acquiring weapons of mass destruction, their means of delivery and materials and technologies related to their manufacture;

4. *Encourages* cooperation among and between Member States and relevant regional and international organizations for strengthening national capacities in this regard;

5. *Requests* the Secretary-General to compile a report on measures already taken by international organizations on issues relating to the linkage between the fight against terrorism and the proliferation of weapons of mass destruction and to seek the views of Member States on additional relevant measures, including national measures, for tackling the global threat posed by the acquisition by terrorists of weapons of mass destruction and to report to the General Assembly at its sixty-fifth session;

6. *Decides* to include in the provisional agenda of its sixty-fifth session the item entitled "Measures to prevent terrorists from acquiring weapons of mass destruction".

At the same meeting, the Assembly decided to include in the provisional agenda of its sixty-fifth (2010) session the item entitled "Preventing the acquisition by terrorists of radioactive materials and sources" **(decision 64/516).**

Multilateralism in disarmament and non-proliferation

Pursuant to General Assembly resolution 63/50 [YUN 2008, p. 591], the Secretary-General in July [A/64/117 & Add.1] presented the views of five Member States (Cuba, Lebanon, Qatar, Spain, United Arab Emirates) on the promotion of multilateralism in the area of disarmament and non-proliferation.

GENERAL ASSEMBLY ACTION

On 2 December [meeting 55], the General Assembly, on the recommendation of the First Committee [A/64/391], adopted **resolution 64/34** by recorded vote (122-5-49) [agenda item 96 *(m)*].

Promotion of multilateralism in the area of disarmament and non-proliferation

The General Assembly,

Determined to foster strict respect for the purposes and principles enshrined in the Charter of the United Nations,

Recalling its resolution 56/24 T of 29 November 2001 on multilateral cooperation in the area of disarmament and non-proliferation and global efforts against terrorism and other relevant resolutions, as well as its resolutions 57/63 of 22 November 2002, 58/44 of 8 December 2003, 59/69 of 3 December 2004, 60/59 of 8 December 2005, 61/62 of 6 December 2006, 62/27 of 5 December 2007 and 63/50 of 2 December 2008 on the promotion of multilateralism in the area of disarmament and non-proliferation,

Recalling also the purpose of the United Nations to maintain international peace and security and, to that end, to take effective collective measures for the prevention and removal of threats to the peace and for the suppression of acts of aggression or other breaches of the peace, and to bring about by peaceful means, and in conformity with the principles of justice and international law, adjustment or settlement of international disputes or situations which might lead to a breach of the peace, as enshrined in the Charter,

Recalling further the United Nations Millennium Declaration, which states, inter alia, that the responsibility for managing worldwide economic and social development, as well as threats to international peace and security, must be shared among the nations of the world and should be exercised multilaterally and that, as the most universal and most representative organization in the world, the United Nations must play the central role,

Convinced that, in the globalization era and with the information revolution, arms regulation, non-proliferation and disarmament problems are more than ever the concern of all countries in the world, which are affected in one way or another by these problems and, therefore, should have the possibility to participate in the negotiations that arise to tackle them,

Bearing in mind the existence of a broad structure of disarmament and arms regulation agreements resulting from non-discriminatory and transparent multilateral negotiations with the participation of a large number of countries, regardless of their size and power,

Aware of the need to advance further in the field of arms regulation, non-proliferation and disarmament on the basis of universal, multilateral, non-discriminatory and transparent negotiations with the goal of reaching general and complete disarmament under strict international control,

Recognizing the complementarity of bilateral, plurilateral and multilateral negotiations on disarmament,

Recognizing also that the proliferation and development of weapons of mass destruction, including nuclear weapons, are among the most immediate threats to international peace and security which need to be dealt with, with the highest priority,

Considering that the multilateral disarmament agreements provide the mechanism for States parties to consult one another and to cooperate in solving any problems which may arise in relation to the objective of, or in the application of, the provisions of the agreements and that such consultations and cooperation may also be undertaken through appropriate international procedures within the framework of the United Nations and in accordance with the Charter,

Stressing that international cooperation, the peaceful settlement of disputes, dialogue and confidence-building measures would contribute essentially to the creation of multilateral and bilateral friendly relations among peoples and nations,

Being concerned at the continuous erosion of multilateralism in the field of arms regulation, non-proliferation and disarmament, and recognizing that a resort to unilateral actions by Member States in resolving their security concerns would jeopardize international peace and security and undermine confidence in the international security system as well as the foundations of the United Nations itself,

Noting that the Fifteenth Summit Conference of Heads of State and Government of the Movement of Non-Aligned Countries, held in Sharm el-Sheikh, Egypt, from 11 to 16 July 2009, welcomed the adoption of resolution 63/50 on the promotion of multilateralism in the area of disarmament and non-proliferation, and underlined the fact that multilateralism and multilaterally agreed solutions, in accordance with the Charter, provide the only sustainable method of addressing disarmament and international security issues,

Reaffirming the absolute validity of multilateral diplomacy in the field of disarmament and non-proliferation, and determined to promote multilateralism as an essential way to develop arms regulation and disarmament negotiations,

1. *Reaffirms* multilateralism as the core principle in negotiations in the area of disarmament and non-proliferation with a view to maintaining and strengthening universal norms and enlarging their scope;

2. *Also reaffirms* multilateralism as the core principle in resolving disarmament and non-proliferation concerns;

3. *Urges* the participation of all interested States in multilateral negotiations on arms regulation, non-proliferation and disarmament in a non-discriminatory and transparent manner;

4. *Underlines* the importance of preserving the existing agreements on arms regulation and disarmament, which constitute an expression of the results of international cooperation and multilateral negotiations in response to the challenges facing mankind;

5. *Calls once again upon* all Member States to renew and fulfil their individual and collective commitments to multilateral cooperation as an important means of pursuing and achieving their common objectives in the area of disarmament and non-proliferation;

6. *Requests* the States parties to the relevant instruments on weapons of mass destruction to consult and cooperate among themselves in resolving their concerns with regard to cases of non-compliance as well as on implementation, in accordance with the procedures defined in those instruments, and to refrain from resorting or threatening to resort to unilateral actions or directing unverified non-compliance accusations against one another to resolve their concerns;

7. *Takes note* of the report of the Secretary-General containing the replies of Member States on the promotion of multilateralism in the area of disarmament and non-proliferation, submitted pursuant to resolution 63/50;

8. *Requests* the Secretary-General to seek the views of Member States on the issue of the promotion of multilateralism in the area of disarmament and non-proliferation and to submit a report thereon to the General Assembly at its sixty-fifth session;

9. *Decides* to include in the provisional agenda of its sixty-fifth session the item entitled "Promotion of multilateralism in the area of disarmament and non-proliferation".

RECORDED VOTE ON RESOLUTION 64/34:

In favour: Afghanistan, Algeria, Angola, Antigua and Barbuda, Argentina, Azerbaijan, Bahamas, Bahrain, Barbados, Belarus, Belize, Benin, Bhutan, Bolivia, Botswana, Brazil, Brunei Darussalam, Burundi, Cambodia, Cameroon, Cape Verde, Chile, China, Colombia, Comoros, Congo, Costa Rica, Côte d'Ivoire, Cuba, Democratic People's Republic of Korea, Democratic Republic of the Congo, Djibouti, Dominica, Dominican Republic, Ecuador, Egypt, El Salvador, Equatorial Guinea, Eritrea, Fiji, Gambia, Ghana, Grenada, Guatemala, Guinea, Guinea-Bissau, Guyana, Haiti, Honduras, India, Indonesia, Iran, Iraq, Jamaica, Jordan, Kazakhstan, Kenya, Kuwait, Kyrgyzstan, Lao People's Democratic Republic, Lebanon, Lesotho, Liberia, Libyan Arab Jamahiriya, Madagascar, Malawi, Malaysia, Maldives, Mali, Marshall Islands, Mauritania, Mauritius, Mexico, Mongolia, Morocco, Mozambique, Myanmar, Namibia, Nepal, Nicaragua, Niger, Nigeria, Oman, Pakistan, Panama, Papua New Guinea, Paraguay, Peru, Philippines, Qatar, Russian Federation, Saint Kitts and Nevis, Saint Lucia, Saint Vincent and the Grenadines, Saudi Arabia, Senegal, Serbia, Singapore, Solomon Islands, Somalia, South Africa, Sri Lanka, Sudan, Suriname, Syrian Arab Republic, Tajikistan, Thailand, Togo, Tonga, Trinidad and Tobago, Tunisia, Turkmenistan, Uganda, United Arab Emirates, United Republic of Tanzania, Uruguay, Uzbekistan, Venezuela, Viet Nam, Yemen, Zambia, Zimbabwe.

Against: Israel, Micronesia, Palau, United Kingdom, United States.

Abstaining: Albania, Andorra, Armenia, Australia, Austria, Belgium, Bosnia and Herzegovina, Bulgaria, Canada, Croatia, Cyprus, Czech Republic, Denmark, Estonia, Finland, France, Georgia, Germany, Greece, Hungary, Iceland, Ireland, Italy, Japan, Latvia, Liechtenstein, Lithuania, Luxembourg, Malta, Moldova, Monaco, Montenegro, Netherlands, New Zealand, Norway, Poland, Portugal, Republic of Korea, Romania, Samoa, San Marino, Slovakia, Slovenia, Spain, Sweden, Switzerland, The former Yugoslav Republic of Macedonia, Turkey, Ukraine.

Nuclear non-proliferation and nuclear disarmament

Security Council summit. On 24 September, the Security Council held a summit on nuclear non-proliferation and nuclear disarmament [meeting 6191] chaired by United States President Barack Obama and attended by 13 heads of State and Government, including the five nuclear-weapon States—China's President Hu Jintao, France's President Nicolas Sarkozy, Russia's President Dmitry Medvedev and United Kingdom's Prime Minister Gordon Brown. The Council adopted resolution 1887(2009) (see below), which called on States parties to NPT to comply fully with all their obligations under the Treaty and States that were not parties to accede to it so as to achieve its universality. The Council further called on States to sign and ratify the Comprehensive Nuclear-Test-Ban Treaty and to negotiate a treaty banning the production of fissile material.

A concept paper submitted by the United States [S/2009/463] provided the basis for the discussion. Documents were submitted by Egypt on behalf of NAM [S/2009/459, S/2009/631], the League of Arab States [S/2009/466], Australia [S/2009/476], Pakistan [S/2009/478], Iran [S/2009/480], the Philippines [S/2009/481], Kazakhstan [S/2009/482], India [S/2009/483], Brazil [S/2009/484], Italy [S/2009/485], Norway [S/2009/486], the Holy See [S/2009/492] and Canada [S/2009/505].

SECURITY COUNCIL ACTION

On 24 September [meeting 6191], the Security Council unanimously adopted **resolution 1887(2009)**. The draft [S/2009/473] was prepared in consultations among Council members.

The Security Council,

Resolving to seek a safer world for all and to create the conditions for a world without nuclear weapons, in accordance with the goals of the Treaty on the Non-Proliferation of Nuclear Weapons, in a way that promotes international stability, and based on the principle of undiminished security for all,

Reaffirming the statement by its President adopted at its meeting held at the level of Heads of State and Government on 31 January 1992, including the need for all Member States to fulfil their obligations in relation to arms control and disarmament and to prevent the proliferation in all its aspects of all weapons of mass destruction,

Recalling that the above statement underlined the need for all Member States to resolve peacefully in accordance with the Charter of the United Nations any problems in that context threatening or disrupting the maintenance of regional and global stability,

Reaffirming that the proliferation of weapons of mass destruction, and their means of delivery, constitutes a threat to international peace and security,

Bearing in mind the responsibilities of other organs of the United Nations and relevant international organizations in the field of disarmament, arms control and non-proliferation, as well as the Conference on Disarmament, and supporting them in continuing to play their due roles,

Underlining that the Treaty remains the cornerstone of the nuclear non-proliferation regime and the essential foundation for the pursuit of nuclear disarmament and for the peaceful uses of nuclear energy,

Reaffirming its firm commitment to the Treaty and its conviction that the international nuclear non-proliferation regime should be maintained and strengthened to ensure its effective implementation, and recalling in this regard the outcomes of past Review Conferences of the Parties to the Treaty, including the final documents of 1995 and 2000,

Calling for further progress on all aspects of disarmament to enhance global security,

Recalling the statement by its President adopted at its meeting held on 19 November 2008,

Welcoming the decisions of those non-nuclear-weapon States that have dismantled their nuclear weapons programmes or renounced the possession of nuclear weapons,

Welcoming also the nuclear arms reduction and disarmament efforts undertaken and accomplished by nuclear-weapon States, and underlining the need to pursue further efforts in the sphere of nuclear disarmament, in accordance with article VI of the Treaty,

Welcoming further, in this connection, the decision of the Russian Federation and the United States of America to conduct negotiations to conclude a new comprehensive legally binding agreement to replace the Treaty on the Reduction and Limitation of Strategic Offensive Arms (START I), which expires in December 2009,

Welcoming and supporting the steps taken to conclude nuclear-weapon-free zone treaties, and reaffirming the conviction that the establishment of internationally recognized nuclear-weapon-free zones on the basis of arrangements freely arrived at among the States of the region concerned, and in accordance with the Disarmament Commission guidelines of 1999, enhances global and regional peace and security, strengthens the nuclear non-proliferation regime and contributes towards realizing the objectives of nuclear disarmament,

Noting its support, in this context, for the convening of the second Conference of States Parties and Signatories to Treaties that Establish Nuclear-Weapon-Free Zones and Mongolia, to be held in New York on 30 April 2010,

Reaffirming its resolutions 825(1993) of 11 May 1993, 1695(2006) of 15 July 2006, 1718(2006) of 14 October 2006 and 1874(2009) of 12 June 2009,

Reaffirming also its resolutions 1696(2006) of 31 July 2006, 1737(2006) of 23 December 2006, 1747(2007) of 24 March 2007, 1803(2008) of 3 March 2008 and 1835(2008) of 27 September 2008,

Reaffirming further all other relevant non-proliferation resolutions adopted by the Security Council,

Gravely concerned about the threat of nuclear terrorism, and recognizing the need for all States to take effective measures to prevent nuclear material or technical assistance becoming available to terrorists,

Noting with interest the initiative to convene, in coordination with the International Atomic Energy Agency, an international conference on the peaceful uses of nuclear energy,

Expressing its support for the convening of the Global Summit on Nuclear Security in 2010,

Affirming its support for the Convention on the Physical Protection of Nuclear Material and its 2005 Amendment, and the International Convention for the Suppression of Acts of Nuclear Terrorism,

Recognizing the progress made by the Global Initiative to Combat Nuclear Terrorism and the Global Partnership of the Group of Eight,

Noting the contribution of civil society in promoting all the objectives of the Treaty on the Non-Proliferation of Nuclear Weapons,

Reaffirming its resolution 1540(2004) of 28 April 2004 and the necessity for all States to implement fully the measures contained therein, and calling upon all Member States and international and regional organizations to cooperate actively with the Security Council Committee established pursuant to that resolution, including in the course of the comprehensive review as called for in resolution 1810(2008) of 25 April 2008,

1. *Emphasizes* that a situation of non-compliance with non-proliferation obligations shall be brought to the attention of the Security Council, which shall determine if that situation constitutes a threat to international peace and security, and emphasizes the primary responsibility of the Council in addressing such threats;

2. *Calls upon* States parties to the Treaty on the Non-Proliferation of Nuclear Weapons to comply fully with all their obligations and fulfil their commitments under the Treaty;

3. *Notes* that enjoyment of the benefits of the Treaty by a State party can be assured only by its compliance with the obligations thereunder;

4. *Calls upon* all States that are not parties to the Treaty to accede to the Treaty as non-nuclear-weapon States so as to achieve its universality at an early date and, pending their accession to the Treaty, to adhere to its terms;

5. *Calls upon* the parties to the Treaty, pursuant to article VI of the Treaty, to undertake to pursue negotiations in good faith on effective measures relating to nuclear arms reduction and disarmament, and on a treaty on general and complete disarmament under strict and effective international control, and calls upon all other States to join in this endeavour;

6. *Calls upon* all States parties to the Treaty to cooperate so that the 2010 Review Conference of the Parties to the Treaty can successfully strengthen the Treaty and set realistic and achievable goals in all three pillars of the Treaty, namely, non-proliferation, the peaceful uses of nuclear energy, and disarmament;

7. *Calls upon* all States to refrain from conducting a nuclear test explosion and to sign and ratify the Comprehensive Nuclear-Test-Ban Treaty, thereby bringing the Treaty into force at an early date;

8. *Calls upon* the Conference on Disarmament to negotiate a treaty banning the production of fissile material for nuclear weapons or other nuclear explosive devices as soon as possible, welcomes the adoption by consensus by the Conference of its programme of work in 2009, and re-quests all Member States to cooperate in guiding the Conference to an early commencement of substantive work;

9. *Recalls* the statements made by each of the five nuclear-weapon States, noted in resolution 984(1995) of 11 April 1995, in which they give security assurances against the use of nuclear weapons to non-nuclear-weapon States parties to the Treaty on the Non-Proliferation of Nuclear Weapons, and affirms that such security assurances strengthen the nuclear non-proliferation regime;

10. *Expresses particular concern* at the current major challenges to the non-proliferation regime that the Council has acted upon, demands that the parties concerned comply fully with their obligations under the relevant Council resolutions, and reaffirms its call upon them to find an early negotiated solution to these issues;

11. *Encourages* efforts to ensure the development of peaceful uses of nuclear energy by countries seeking to maintain or develop their capacities in this field within a framework that reduces proliferation risk and adheres to the highest international standards for safeguards, security and safety;

12. *Underlines* that the Treaty recognizes in article IV the inalienable right of the parties to the Treaty to develop research, production and use of nuclear energy for peaceful purposes without discrimination and in conformity with articles I and II, and recalls in this context article III of the Treaty and article II of the statute of the International Atomic Energy Agency;

13. *Calls upon* States to adopt stricter national controls for the export of sensitive goods and technologies of the nuclear fuel cycle;

14. *Encourages* the work of the International Atomic Energy Agency on multilateral approaches to the nuclear fuel cycle, including assurances of nuclear fuel supply and related measures, as effective means of addressing the expanding need for nuclear fuel and nuclear fuel services and minimizing the risk of proliferation, and urges the Board of Governors of the Agency to agree upon measures to this end as soon as possible;

15. *Affirms* that effective Agency safeguards are essential to prevent nuclear proliferation and to facilitate cooperation in the field of peaceful uses of nuclear energy, and in that regard:

(a) Calls upon all non-nuclear-weapon States parties to the Treaty that have yet to bring into force a comprehensive safeguards agreement or a modified small quantities protocol to do so immediately;

(b) Calls upon all States to sign, ratify and implement an additional protocol, which, together with comprehensive safeguards agreements, constitute essential elements of the Agency safeguards system;

(c) Stresses the importance for all Member States to ensure that the Agency continues to have all the resources and authority necessary to verify the declared use of nuclear materials and facilities and the absence of undeclared activities, and for the Agency to report to the Council accordingly, as appropriate;

16. *Encourages* States to provide the Agency with the cooperation necessary for it to verify whether a State is in compliance with its safeguards obligations, and affirms the resolve of the Council to support the efforts of the Agency to that end, consistent with its authorities under the Charter of the United Nations;

17. *Undertakes* to address without delay any State's notice of withdrawal from the Treaty, including the events described in the statement provided by the State pursuant to article X of the Treaty, while noting ongoing discussions in the course of the review of the Treaty on identifying modalities under which States parties to the Treaty could collectively respond to notification of withdrawal, and affirms that a State remains responsible under international law for violations of the Treaty committed prior to its withdrawal;

18. *Encourages* States to require as a condition of nuclear exports that the recipient State agree that, in the event that it should terminate, withdraw from, or be found by the Board of Governors of the Agency to be in noncompliance with its safeguards agreement, the supplier State would have the right to require the return of nuclear material and equipment provided prior to such termination, non-compliance or withdrawal, as well as any special nuclear material produced through the use of such material or equipment;

19. *Also encourages* States to consider whether a recipient State has signed and ratified an additional protocol based on the Model Additional Protocol in making nuclear export decisions;

20. *Urges* States to require as a condition of nuclear exports that the recipient State agree that, in the event that it should terminate its safeguards agreement with the Agency, safeguards shall continue with respect to any nuclear material and equipment provided prior to such termination, as well as any special nuclear material produced through the use of such material or equipment;

21. *Calls for* universal adherence to the Convention on the Physical Protection of Nuclear Material and its 2005 Amendment, and the International Convention for the Suppression of Acts of Nuclear Terrorism;

22. *Welcomes* the March 2009 recommendations of the Security Council Committee established pursuant to resolution 1540(2004) to make more effective use of existing funding mechanisms, including the consideration of the establishment of a voluntary fund, and affirms its commitment to promote full implementation of resolution 1540(2004) by Member States by ensuring effective and sustainable support for the activities of the Committee;

23. *Reaffirms* the need for full implementation of resolution 1540(2004) by Member States and, with the aim of preventing access to, or assistance and financing for, weapons of mass destruction, related materials and their means of delivery by non-State actors, as defined in that resolution, calls upon Member States to cooperate actively with the Committee and the Agency, including rendering assistance, at their request, for their implementation of resolution 1540(2004) provisions, and in this context welcomes the forthcoming comprehensive review of the status of implementation of resolution 1540(2004) with a view to increasing its effectiveness, and calls upon all States to participate actively in this review;

24. *Calls upon* Member States to share best practices with a view to improved safety standards and nuclear security practices and raise standards of nuclear security to reduce the risk of nuclear terrorism, with the aim of securing all vulnerable nuclear material from such risks within four years;

25. *Calls upon* all States to manage responsibly and minimize to the greatest extent that is technically and economically feasible the use of highly enriched uranium for civilian purposes, including by working to convert research reactors and radioisotope production processes to the use of low enriched uranium fuels and targets;

26. *Also calls upon* all States to improve their national capabilities to detect, deter and disrupt illicit trafficking in nuclear materials throughout their territories, and calls upon those States in a position to do so to work to enhance international partnerships and capacity-building in this regard;

27. *Urges* all States to take all appropriate national measures in accordance with their national authorities and legislation, and consistent with international law, to prevent proliferation financing and shipments, to strengthen export controls, to secure sensitive materials and to control access to intangible transfers of technology;

28. *Declares its resolve* to monitor closely any situations involving the proliferation of nuclear weapons, their means of delivery or related material, including to or by non-State actors as they are defined in resolution 1540(2004) and, as appropriate, to take such measures as may be necessary to ensure the maintenance of international peace and security;

29. *Decides* to remain seized of the matter.

International Atomic Energy Agency

According to its annual report [GC(54)/4], the International Atomic Energy Agency (IAEA) continued to address global issues related to nuclear technology, providing advice in the application of nuclear technologies for development, promoting nuclear safety and security and carrying out nuclear verification activities.

The fifty-third session of the IAEA General Conference (Vienna, 14–18 September) adopted resolutions on measures to strengthen international cooperation in nuclear, radiation, transport and waste safety; nuclear security; strengthening the Agency's technical cooperation activities; strengthening the Agency's activities related to nuclear science, technology and applications; strengthening the effectiveness and improving the efficiency of the safeguards system and application of the Model Additional Protocol; implementing the NPT safeguards agreement between the Agency and the Democratic People's Republic of Korea (DPRK); and IAEA safeguards in the Middle East.

In August [A/64/257], the Secretary-General transmitted to the General Assembly the IAEA annual report for 2008 [YUN 2008, p. 593]. The Assembly took note of the report by **resolution 64/8** (see p. 995) of 2 November.

IAEA activities

During the year [GC(54)/4], IAEA assisted Member States in meeting their energy needs, responding to climate change concerns, helping to ensure food security and access to clean water, and improving health care through the use of nuclear techniques.

The financial crisis did not substantially change the factors driving rising expectations for nuclear power. Specifically, nuclear power's good performance and safety record and continuing concerns about climate change, security of energy supplies, high and volatile fossil fuel prices and energy demand growth remained key drivers. Both global energy demand and interest in nuclear power continued to grow during the year.

Construction started on 11 new nuclear power reactors, the largest number since 1987, and projections of future nuclear power growth were once again revised upwards. Growth targets were raised significantly in China, India and the Russian Federation. At year's end, there were 437 nuclear power reactors in operation, with a total capacity of 370 gigawatts. Fifty-five reactors were under construction, the largest number since 1992. Of the 11 construction starts, 10 were in Asia, as were 36 of the 55 reactors under construction and 30 of the last 41 new reactors to have been connected to the grid.

More than 60 countries—mostly in the developing world—had informed the Agency that they might be interested in launching nuclear power programmes. Fifty-eight Member States participated in technical cooperation projects related to the introduction of nuclear power, while 17 prepared national nuclear power programmes.

The growing interest in nuclear power had resulted in a comeback of uranium mining after a two-decade slump. It was expected to make a 12 per cent increase over the previous year. The establishment of low enriched uranium (LEU) reserves under the Agency's auspices, envisaged to assure States of LEU supply in case they experienced disruptions for non-technical or non-commercial reasons, had been the subject of discussions. In June, the Director General provided two reports on supply assurance to the IAEA Board of Governors: a proposal for the establishment of an IAEA LEU bank, and a Russian Federation initiative to establish a reserve of LEU for the supply of LEU to IAEA for its Member States. In addition, a report was issued on the German proposal to set up a multilateral enrichment sanctuary project, with Agency involvement. In November, the Board authorized the Director General to sign an agreement with the Russian Federation to establish a reserve of 120 tonnes of LEU in that country for the use of Member States, to be made available through the Agency at the prevailing market price to a country experiencing a non-commercial supply disruption.

A major development in the area of nuclear fusion was the completion in March of site preparations for the International Thermonuclear Experimental Reactor. The International Fusion Research Council (an advisory committee to IAEA) and the Fusion Power Coordinating Committee of the International Energy Agency held a joint meeting during the year. In addition, IAEA organized technical meetings on nuclear fusion topics that were attended by more than 450 experts.

Fifty per cent of all operating research reactors were over 40 years old. Progress was made, with Agency support, in developing cooperative networks in the Mediterranean, Eastern European, Caribbean and Central Asian regions. More than 20 Member States requested Agency advice on building new research reactors.

Early and rapid nuclear and nuclear-related molecular diagnostic technologies developed by the Agency were used to diagnose avian influenza, influenza A(H1N1) (swine flu) and Rift Valley fever, limiting the impact of those diseases on animal and public health. In South Africa, drought-resistant grain contributed to food security.

The incidence of cancer was growing rapidly in developing countries, with over 75 million people in low- and middle-income countries expected to suffer from it by 2020. The Programme of Action for Cancer Therapy (PACT) was leading the IAEA response to the cancer crisis. Following years of close collaboration, the Agency in February launched a Joint Programme for Cancer Control with the World Health Organization. The number of PACT Model Demonstration Sites grew to seven, with Ghana joining Albania, Nicaragua, Sri Lanka, the United Republic of Tanzania, Viet Nam and Yemen. PACT also provided opportunities for Member States to make contributions, as evidenced by India's donation through PACT of a "Bhabhatron" radiotherapy unit to Viet Nam.

The Agency's isotope studies and numerical models led to a better understanding of the impact of ocean acidification on marine resources. The results of those studies facilitated a scientific synthesis of the impacts of ocean acidification on marine biodiversity—the first of its kind—which was prepared for the United Nations Climate Change Conference in Copenhagen in December (see p. 1015).

A significant development during the year was the creation by the European Union (EU) of a common legal framework for nuclear safety, based on the Agency's main safety standards for nuclear installations and obligations under the Convention on Nuclear Safety. The EU was the first major regional body to adopt a binding legal framework on nuclear safety.

During the year, IAEA was informed of 211 events involving ionizing radiation. In most of those events no Agency action was required. In 22 events, however, the Agency took action, such as authenticating and verifying information with national authorities or offering its services.

The Agency continued its efforts to promote adherence to the various international legal instruments adopted under its auspices, in particular with respect to the Convention on Supplementary Compensation for Nuclear Damage, which remained the only such instrument to enter into force. In parallel, the International Expert Group on Nuclear Liability, an advisory body to the Director General, continued to serve as a central forum on questions related to nuclear liability.

The Agency conducted 14 nuclear security advisory missions, with more than half dealing with physical protection and with legal, regulatory and practical measures for controlling nuclear and other radioactive material.

In September, the Board of Governors approved the Agency's Nuclear Security Plan for 2010–2013. The plan recognized that the risk of malicious use of nuclear and other radioactive material continued to be a threat.

In Africa, the technical cooperation programme focused on building human and institutional capacity in the use of nuclear applications to achieve increased food security, better nutrition and health services. In Asia and the Pacific, the emphasis was on strengthening nuclear applications in health, agriculture and energy, with a focus on support for newcomers to nuclear power. In Europe, the focus was on safety and security standards in older nuclear plants and on mitigating the environmental degradation caused by uranium mining and milling. In Latin America, emphasis was placed on strengthening national regulatory frameworks and capacity-building for radiation safety. The programme was funded by contributions to the Technical Cooperation Fund, extrabudgetary contributions and government cost-sharing. Overall, new resources topped $112 million, with approximately $86 million for the Fund.

IAEA safeguards

IAEA's verification programme remained at the core of multilateral efforts to curb the proliferation of nuclear weapons. The Agency had an essential verification role under NPT as well as other treaties such as those establishing nuclear-weapon-free zones.

Comprehensive safeguards agreements, concluded pursuant to NPT, and the Model Additional Protocols to those agreements, which granted the Agency complementary verification authority, had been approved by the IAEA Board of Governors in 1997 [YUN 1997, p. 486]; they remained the principal legal instruments strengthening the Agency's safeguards regime. In 2009, comprehensive safeguards agreements entered into force for eight States and additional protocols for six States.

During the year, safeguards were applied for 170 States with safeguards agreements in force with the Agency. States for which both comprehensive safeguards agreements and additional protocols were in force numbered 89. For 52 of these States, the Agency concluded that all nuclear material remained in peaceful activities For the other 37 States, the Agency had not completed all the necessary evaluations under their additional protocol in order to conclude that the declared nuclear material remained in peaceful activities. For 73 States with a comprehensive safeguards agreement in force but without an additional protocol, the Agency was only able to draw the conclusion that declared nuclear material remained in peaceful nuclear activities. Integrated safeguards were implemented in 44 States. The Agency could not draw any safeguards conclusions for 22 NPT non-nuclear-weapon States without safeguards agreements in force.

Democratic People's Republic of Korea

Since December 2002, IAEA had not implemented safeguards in the DPRK and, therefore, could not draw any conclusion regarding nuclear material in that country. In the context of the ad hoc monitoring and verification arrangement agreed between the Agency and the DPRK, and foreseen in the Initial Actions agreed at the six-party talks (China, DPRK, Japan, Republic of Korea, Russian Federation, United States), the Agency continued to implement monitoring and verification measures related to the shutdown of three installations and construction of one installation at the Yongbyon nuclear facility, and the construction of one installation at Taechon.

On 5 April, the DPRK launched a long-range rocket with the stated aim of placing a satellite in orbit. On 13 April, by statement **S/PRST/2009/7** (see p. 384), the Security Council demanded that the DPRK conduct no further missile launches and adjusted the travel ban, assets freeze and arms embargo it had imposed by resolution 1718(2006). On 14 April, the DPRK informed the Agency that it had decided to cease all cooperation with IAEA immediately and requested Agency personnel to remove all their containment and surveillance equipment from the facilities, not allowing them to access the facilities thereafter. All Agency personnel were required to leave the country. The DPRK also informed the IAEA inspectors that it had decided to reactivate all facilities and to proceed with the reprocessing of spent fuel.

During 2009, until 14 April, IAEA neither observed any operation of the three shutdown installations at Yongbyon, nor any construction activities at the two installations under construction at Yongbyon and Taechon. On 15 April, following the DPRK's decision to cease all cooperation, the Agency inspectors at Yongbyon removed all seals, switched off the surveillance cameras and departed from the country the next day. Since that time, IAEA had not been able to implement the ad hoc monitoring and verification arrangement in the DPRK. Consequently, it was unable to make any statements in relation to nuclear material inventories in the DPRK.

Following the DPRK's announcement on 25 May that it had conducted an underground nuclear test, the Security Council adopted **resolution 1874(2009)** (see p. 384), which required the DPRK to abandon its nuclear weapons programme, return to NPT and Agency safeguards, and re-enter the six-party talks without preconditions.

In a resolution of 18 September [GC(53)/RES/15] on implementation of the NPT safeguards agreement between IAEA and the DPRK, the General Conference stressed its desire for a diplomatic resolution of the DPRK nuclear issue so as to achieve the complete, verifiable and irreversible denuclearization of the Korean peninsula; condemned the DPRK nuclear test of 25 May in violation of relevant Security Council resolutions; stressed the importance of Member States fully implementing their obligations pursuant to Council resolutions 1718(2006) [YUN 2006, p. 444] and 1874(2009) (see p. 384), including the DPRK's non-proliferation obligations; deplored the DPRK's actions to cease all cooperation with the Agency; recognized that the six-party talks were an effective mechanism for dealing with the DPRK nuclear issue; and called on the DPRK to return to the talks.

Iran

The IAEA Director General submitted four reports [GOV/2009/8, GOV/2009/35, GOV/2009/55, GOV/2009/74] to the Board of Governors on the implementation of Iran's NPT safeguards agreement and relevant Council resolutions—1737(2006) [YUN 2006, p. 436], 1747(2007) [YUN 2007, p. 374], 1803(2008) [YUN 2008, p. 409] and 1835(2008) [ibid., p. 414]. During the year, while the Agency continued to verify the non-diversion of declared nuclear material in Iran, Iran did not provide the necessary cooperation to permit the Agency to confirm that all nuclear material in the country was in peaceful activities. Since March 2007, Iran had not implemented the modified text of its Subsidiary Arrangements on the early provision of design information and had not been forthcoming in providing information about the design of facilities.

Contrary to the requests of the IAEA Board of Governors and of the Security Council, Iran had not implemented the Additional Protocol, without which the Agency remained unable to provide credible assurances about the absence of undeclared nuclear material and activities. Nor did Iran cooperate with the Agency to address a number of outstanding issues regarding possible military dimensions to its nuclear programme. Those issues related to the alleged studies on the green salt project; high explosives testing; the design of a missile re-entry vehicle; the circumstances of the acquisition of the "uranium metal" document; procurement and research and development activities of military-related institutes and companies that could be nuclear-related; and the production of nuclear equipment and components by companies belonging to defence industries. Contrary to the decisions of the Council, Iran did not suspend its enrichment-related activities, and continued with the operation of the pilot fuel enrichment plant and the construction and operation of the fuel enrichment plant in Natanz. Moreover, in October Iran announced that it was building an additional enrichment facility, the Fordow fuel enrichment plant. Subsequently, Iran announced its intention to build 10 new enrichment plants and continued its work on heavy-water-related projects, again contrary to the requirements of the Council, including the construction of the IR-40 heavy water moderated research reactor at Arak and the operation of a heavy water production plant.

Since August 2008, Iran had declined to discuss outstanding issues related to possible military dimensions of its nuclear programme, asserting that the allegations were baseless and that the Agency's information was based on forgeries. The Agency's information, however, was extensive, broadly consistent and credible. In order to confirm that all nuclear material was in peaceful activities, the Agency needed to have confidence in the absence of possible military dimensions to Iran's nuclear programme.

(See also p. 394.)

Syrian Arab Republic

The IAEA Director General submitted four reports [GOV/2009/9, GOV/2009/36, GOV/2009/56, GOV/2009/75] to the Board of Governors on the implementation of the NPT safeguards agreement in the Syrian Arab Republic. The Agency continued its verification activities in relation to the allegations that an installation destroyed by Israel at Dair Alzour in Syria in 2007 had been a nuclear reactor under construction. Syria had not cooperated with IAEA since 2008 in connection with the unresolved issues related to Dair Alzour and the three other locations to which it was allegedly functionally related. In 2009, the Agency found anthropogenic (i.e. produced as a result of chemical processing) natural uranium particles at the miniature neutron source reactor near Damascus. Syria had yet to provide a credible explanation for the origin and presence of those particles; although it had provided some information about the experiments carried out at the reactor and the origin of the material, it did not cooperate fully by providing design information related to the reactor, the required nuclear material accountancy reports and detailed explanations of experiments carried out with undeclared natural uranium.

Middle East

Report of Director General. In a report issued in August on the application of IAEA safeguards in the Middle East [GOV/2009/44-GC(53)/12], the IAEA Director General noted that all States in the region except Israel were parties to NPT and had undertaken to accept comprehensive Agency safeguards. There continued to be a fundamental difference between Israel and other States of the region with regard to the application of those safeguards to all nuclear activities in the region. Israel took the view that Agency safeguards, as well as all other regional security issues, should be addressed in the framework of a regional security and arms control dialogue in the context of a multilateral peace process; the other States emphasized that they were all parties to NPT and that there was no automatic sequence that linked the application of comprehensive safeguards to all nuclear activities in the Middle East, or the establishment of a nuclear-weapon-free zone, to the prior conclusion of a peace settlement. The Director General stated that he would continue his consultations regarding the early application of comprehensive safeguards on all nuclear activities in the region.

General Conference. In a resolution of 17 September [GC(53)/RES/16], the IAEA General Conference affirmed the need for all States in the region to accept the application of full-scope Agency safeguards to all their nuclear activities as a confidence-building measure, and to take steps to establish a mutually and effectively verifiable nuclear-weapon-free zone. It requested the Director General to continue consultations with the States of the region to facilitate the application of full-scope Agency safeguards to all nuclear activities. In a resolution of 18 September [GC(53)RES/17], the General Conference expressed concern about Israel's nuclear capabilities and called on the country to accede to NPT and place all its nuclear facilities under comprehensive Agency safeguards.

Report of Secretary-General. Pursuant to General Assembly resolution 63/84 [YUN 2008, p. 597], the Secretary-General in October reported [A/64/124 (Part II)] that apart from the 17 September IAEA resolution on the application of safeguards in the Middle East, he had not received any additional information since his 2008 report [YUN 2008, p. 597].

GENERAL ASSEMBLY ACTION

On 2 December [meeting 55], the General Assembly, on the recommendation of the First Committee [A/64/394], adopted **resolution 64/66** by recorded vote (167-6-6) [agenda item 99].

The risk of nuclear proliferation in the Middle East

The General Assembly,

Bearing in mind its relevant resolutions,

Taking note of the relevant resolutions adopted by the General Conference of the International Atomic Energy Agency, the latest of which are resolutions GC(53)/RES/16, adopted on 17 September 2009 and GC(53)/RES/17, adopted on 18 September 2009,

Cognizant that the proliferation of nuclear weapons in the region of the Middle East would pose a serious threat to international peace and security,

Mindful of the immediate need for placing all nuclear facilities in the region of the Middle East under full-scope safeguards of the Agency,

Recalling the decision on principles and objectives for nuclear non-proliferation and disarmament adopted by the 1995 Review and Extension Conference of the Parties to the Treaty on the Non-Proliferation of Nuclear Weapons on 11 May 1995, in which the Conference urged universal adherence to the Treaty as an urgent priority and called upon all States not yet parties to the Treaty to accede to it at the earliest date, particularly those States that operate unsafeguarded nuclear facilities,

Recognizing with satisfaction that, in the Final Document of the 2000 Review Conference of the Parties to the Treaty on the Non-Proliferation of Nuclear Weapons, the Conference undertook to make determined efforts towards the achievement of the goal of universality of the Treaty, called upon those remaining States not parties to the Treaty to accede to it, thereby accepting an international legally binding commitment not to acquire nuclear weapons or nuclear explosive devices and to accept Agency safeguards on all their nuclear activities, and underlined the necessity of universal adherence to the Treaty and of strict compliance by all parties with their obligations under the Treaty,

Recalling the resolution on the Middle East adopted by the 1995 Review and Extension Conference on 11 May 1995, in which the Conference noted with concern the continued existence in the Middle East of unsafeguarded nuclear facilities, reaffirmed the importance of the early realization of universal adherence to the Treaty and called upon all States in the Middle East that had not yet done so, without exception, to accede to the Treaty as soon as possible and to place all their nuclear facilities under full-scope Agency safeguards,

Noting that Israel remains the only State in the Middle East that has not yet become party to the Treaty,

Concerned about the threats posed by the proliferation of nuclear weapons to the security and stability of the Middle East region,

Stressing the importance of taking confidence-building measures, in particular the establishment of a nuclear-weapon-free zone in the Middle East, in order to enhance peace and security in the region and to consolidate the global non-proliferation regime,

Emphasizing the need for all parties directly concerned to seriously consider taking the practical and urgent steps required for the implementation of the proposal to establish a nuclear-weapon-free zone in the region of the Middle East in accordance with the relevant resolutions of the General Assembly and, as a means of promoting this objective, inviting the countries concerned to adhere to the Treaty and, pending the establishment of the zone, to agree to place all their nuclear activities under Agency safeguards,

Noting that one hundred and eighty-one States have signed the Comprehensive Nuclear-Test-Ban Treaty, including a number of States in the region,

1. *Welcomes* the conclusions on the Middle East of the 2000 Review Conference of the Parties to the Treaty on the Non-Proliferation of Nuclear Weapons;

2. *Reaffirms* the importance of Israel's accession to the Treaty on the Non-Proliferation of Nuclear Weapons and placement of all its nuclear facilities under comprehensive International Atomic Energy Agency safeguards in realizing the goal of universal adherence to the Treaty in the Middle East;

3. *Calls upon* that State to accede to the Treaty without further delay and not to develop, produce, test or otherwise acquire nuclear weapons, and to renounce possession of nuclear weapons, and to place all its unsafeguarded nuclear facilities under full-scope Agency safeguards as an important confidence-building measure among all States of the region and as a step towards enhancing peace and security;

4. *Requests* the Secretary-General to report to the General Assembly at its sixty-fifth session on the implementation of the present resolution;

5. *Decides* to include in the provisional agenda of its sixty-fifth session the item entitled "The risk of nuclear proliferation in the Middle East".

RECORDED VOTE ON RESOLUTION 64/66:

In favour: Afghanistan, Albania, Algeria, Andorra, Angola, Antigua and Barbuda, Argentina, Armenia, Austria, Azerbaijan, Bahamas, Bahrain, Bangladesh, Barbados, Belarus, Belgium, Belize, Benin, Bhutan, Bolivia, Bosnia and Herzegovina, Botswana, Brazil, Brunei Darussalam, Bulgaria, Burkina Faso, Burundi, Cambodia, Cape Verde, Chile, China, Colombia, Comoros, Congo, Costa Rica, Croatia, Cuba, Cyprus, Czech Republic, Democratic People's Republic of Korea, Democratic Republic of the Congo, Denmark, Djibouti, Dominica, Dominican Republic, Ecuador, Egypt, El Salvador, Equatorial Guinea, Eritrea, Estonia, Fiji, Finland, France, Gambia, Georgia, Germany, Ghana, Greece, Grenada, Guatemala, Guinea, Guinea-Bissau, Guyana, Haiti, Honduras, Hungary, Iceland, Indonesia, Iran, Iraq, Ireland, Italy, Jamaica, Japan, Jordan, Kazakhstan, Kenya, Kuwait, Kyrgyzstan, Lao People's Democratic Republic, Latvia, Lebanon, Lesotho, Liberia, Libyan Arab Jamahiriya, Liechtenstein, Lithuania, Luxembourg, Madagascar, Malawi, Malaysia, Maldives, Mali, Malta, Mauritania, Mauritius, Mexico, Moldova, Monaco, Mongolia, Montenegro, Morocco, Mozambique, Myanmar, Namibia, Nepal, Netherlands, New Zealand, Nicaragua, Niger, Nigeria, Norway, Oman, Pakistan, Papua New Guinea, Paraguay, Peru, Philippines, Poland, Portugal, Qatar, Republic of Korea, Romania, Russian Federation, Saint Kitts and Nevis, Saint Lucia, Saint Vincent and the Grenadines, Samoa, San Marino, Saudi Arabia, Senegal, Serbia, Sierra Leone, Singapore, Slovakia, Slovenia, Solomon Islands, South Africa, Spain, Sri Lanka, Sudan, Suriname, Swaziland, Sweden, Switzerland, Syrian Arab Republic, Tajikistan, Thailand, The former Yugoslav Republic of Macedonia, Togo, Trinidad and Tobago, Tunisia, Turkey, Turkmenistan, Uganda, Ukraine, United Arab Emirates, United Kingdom, United Republic of Tanzania, Uruguay, Uzbekistan, Venezuela, Viet Nam, Yemen, Zambia, Zimbabwe.

Against: Israel, Marshall Islands, Micronesia, Nauru, Palau, United States.

Abstaining: Australia, Cameroon, Canada, Côte d'Ivoire, India, Panama.

Radioactive waste

IAEA's safety standards provided the global reference for the high safety level required for the use of nuclear power and other applications. The third review meeting of the Contracting Parties to the Joint Convention on the Safety of Spent Fuel Management and on the Safety of Radioactive Waste Management (Vienna, 11–20 May) [JC/RM3/02/Rev.2] was attended by 45 Contracting Parties. The meeting emphasized policy and technical issues on the disposal of waste, decommissioning, disused sealed sources, knowledge management, stakeholder involvement and international cooperation. At the end of 2009, with the addition of Cyprus, Georgia, Portugal, the former Yugoslav Republic of Macedonia, the United Arab Emirates and Uzbekistan, the Joint Convention had 52 Contracting Parties.

Although Member States had made significant progress in managing their radioactive waste and spent fuel safely, efforts were still needed to develop national strategies and to strengthen national infrastructure. In 2009 IAEA launched an international low-level waste disposal network to facilitate the sharing of experience among operators and to coordinate support to Member States with less advanced programmes. Several international meetings discussed long-term management strategies for disused radioactive sources. IAEA convened an international workshop on "Demonstrating the Safety and Licensing of Radioactive Waste Disposal" (Cape Town, 14 December) and an international conference on "Effective Nuclear Regulatory Systems: Further Enhancing the Global Nuclear Safety and Security Regime" (Cape Town, 14–18 December). The Agency assisted seven Member States in managing 597 radioactive sources, of which 54 were classified as high activity sources. Most of the sources were conditioned and stored in the centralized storage facilities of the countries concerned. Of particular significance was the deployment of a mobile hot cell for operations in the Sudan and the United Republic of Tanzania. In response to requests for technical assistance from Kazakhstan, Kyrgyzstan, Tajikistan and Uzbekistan, and to address issues of legacy uranium production sites, IAEA organized workshops and scientific visits to learn from similar projects in other countries. Sampling and analytical equipment was upgraded, and management and laboratory staff were trained.

In a resolution of 18 September [GC(53)/RES/10], the IAEA General Conference invited Member States to become party to the Joint Convention, welcomed the efforts of the Convention's Contracting Parties to enhance the transparency, efficiency and effectiveness of the review process, and encouraged Member States to participate in the IAEA database on discharges of radionuclides to the atmosphere and the aquatic environment and in the Net-Enabled Waste Management Database on annual radioactive waste management data from Member States.

GENERAL ASSEMBLY ACTION

On 2 December [meeting 55], the General Assembly, on the recommendation of the First Committee [A/64/391], adopted **resolution 64/45** without vote [agenda item 96 *(d)*].

Prohibition of the dumping of radioactive wastes

The General Assembly,

Bearing in mind resolutions CM/Res.1153(XLVIII) of '1988 and CM/Res.1225(L) of 1989, adopted by the Council of Ministers of the Organization of African Unity, concerning the dumping of nuclear and industrial wastes in Africa,

Welcoming resolution GC(XXXIV)/RES/530 establishing a Code of Practice on the International Transboundary Movement of Radioactive Waste, adopted on 21 September 1990 by the General Conference of the International Atomic Energy Agency at its thirty-fourth regular session,

Taking note of the commitment by the participants in the Summit on Nuclear Safety and Security, held in Moscow on 19 and 20 April 1996, to ban the dumping at sea of radioactive wastes,

Considering its resolution 2602 C (XXIV) of 16 December 1969, in which it requested the Conference of the Committee on Disarmament, inter alia, to consider effective methods of control against the use of radiological methods of warfare,

Aware of the potential hazards underlying any use of radioactive wastes that would constitute radiological warfare and its implications for regional and international security, in particular for the security of developing countries,

Recalling all its resolutions on the matter since its forty-third session in 1988, including its resolution 51/45 J of 10 December 1996,

Recalling also resolution GC(45)/RES/10 adopted by consensus on 21 September 2001 by the General Conference of the International Atomic Energy Agency at its forty-fifth regular session, in which States shipping radioactive materials are invited to provide, as appropriate, assurances to concerned States, upon their request, that the national regulations of the shipping State take into account the Agency's transport regulations and to provide them with relevant information relating to the shipment of such materials; the information provided should in no case be contradictory to the measures of physical security and safety,

Welcoming the adoption at Vienna, on 5 September 1997, of the Joint Convention on the Safety of Spent Fuel Management and on the Safety of Radioactive Waste Management, as recommended by the participants in the Summit on Nuclear Safety and Security,

Noting with satisfaction that the Joint Convention entered into force on 18 June 2001,

Noting that the first Review Meeting of the Contracting Parties to the Joint Convention on the Safety of Spent Fuel Management and on the Safety of Radioactive Waste Management was convened in Vienna from 3 to 14 November 2003,

Desirous of promoting the implementation of paragraph 76 of the Final Document of the Tenth Special Session of the General Assembly, the first special session devoted to disarmament,

1. *Takes note* of the part of the report of the Conference on Disarmament relating to radiological weapons;

2. *Expresses grave concern* regarding any use of nuclear wastes that would constitute radiological warfare and have grave implications for the national security of all States;

3. *Calls upon* all States to take appropriate measures with a view to preventing any dumping of nuclear or radioactive wastes that would infringe upon the sovereignty of States;

4. *Requests* the Conference on Disarmament to take into account, in the negotiations for a convention on the prohibition of radiological weapons, radioactive wastes as part of the scope of such a convention;

5. *Also requests* the Conference on Disarmament to intensify efforts towards an early conclusion of such a convention and to include in its report to the General Assembly at its sixty-sixth session the progress recorded in the negotiations on this subject;

6. *Takes note* of resolution CM/Res.1356(LIV) of 1991, adopted by the Council of Ministers of the Organization of African Unity, on the Bamako Convention on the Ban on the Import of Hazardous Wastes into Africa and on the Control of Their Transboundary Movements within Africa;

7. *Expresses the hope* that the effective implementation of the International Atomic Energy Agency Code of Practice on the International Transboundary Movement of Radioactive Waste will enhance the protection of all States from the dumping of radioactive wastes on their territories;

8. *Appeals* to all Member States that have not yet taken the necessary steps to become party to the Joint Convention on the Safety of Spent Fuel Management and on the Safety of Radioactive Waste Management to do so as soon as possible;

9. *Decides* to include in the provisional agenda of its sixty-sixth session the item entitled "Prohibition of the dumping of radioactive wastes".

Nuclear-weapon-free zones

Africa

On 15 July, 13 years after being opened for signature in 1996 [YUN 1996, p. 486], the African Nuclear-Weapon-Free Zone Treaty (Treaty of Pelindaba) [YUN 1995, p. 203] entered into force when Burundi became the twenty-eighth State to ratify it. As at 31 December, the Treaty had been ratified by 29 countries; 24 of 56 signatory States had yet to ratify the Treaty. The African Nuclear-Weapon-Free Zone encompassed over 30 million square kilometres (km), making it the largest of the five nuclear-weapon-free zones in the world.

GENERAL ASSEMBLY ACTION

On 2 December [meeting 55], the General Assembly, on the recommendation of the First Committee [A/64/383], adopted **resolution 64/24** without vote [agenda item 88].

African Nuclear-Weapon-Free Zone Treaty

The General Assembly,

Recalling its resolutions 51/53 of 10 December 1996 and 56/17 of 29 November 2001 and all its other relevant resolutions, as well as those of the Organization of African Unity,

Recalling also the signing of the African Nuclear-Weapon-Free Zone Treaty (Treaty of Pelindaba) in Cairo on 11 April 1996,

Recalling further the Cairo Declaration adopted on that occasion, which emphasized that nuclear-weapon-free zones, especially in regions of tension, such as the Middle East, enhance global and regional peace and security,

Taking note of the statement made by the President of the Security Council on behalf of the members of the Council on 12 April 1996, affirming that the signature of the African Nuclear-Weapon-Free Zone Treaty constituted an important contribution by the African countries to the maintenance of international peace and security,

Considering that the establishment of nuclear-weapon-free zones, especially in the Middle East, would enhance the security of Africa and the viability of the African nuclear-weapon-free zone,

1. *Notes with satisfaction* the entry into force of the African Nuclear-Weapon-Free-Zone Treaty (Treaty of Pelindaba) on 15 July 2009;

2. *Calls upon* African States that have not yet done so to sign and ratify the Treaty as soon as possible;

3. *Expresses its appreciation* to the nuclear-weapon States that have signed the Protocols to the Treaty that concern them, and calls upon those that have not yet ratified the Protocols concerning them to do so as soon as possible;

4. *Calls upon* the States contemplated in Protocol III to the Treaty that have not yet done so to take all necessary measures to ensure the speedy application of the Treaty to territories for which they are, de jure or de facto, internationally responsible and that lie within the limits of the geographical zone established in the Treaty;

5. *Calls upon* the African States parties to the Treaty on the Non-Proliferation of Nuclear Weapons that have not yet done so to conclude comprehensive safeguards agreements with the International Atomic Energy Agency pursuant to the Treaty, thereby satisfying the requirements of article 9 *(b)* of and annex II to the Treaty of Pelindaba, and to conclude additional protocols to their safeguards agreements on the basis of the Model Protocol approved by the Board of Governors of the Agency on 15 May 1997;

6. *Expresses its gratitude* to the Secretary-General, the Chairperson of the African Union Commission and the Director General of the International Atomic Energy Agency

for the diligence with which they have rendered effective assistance to the signatories to the Treaty;

7. *Decides* to include in the provisional agenda of its sixty-fifth session the item entitled "African Nuclear-Weapon-Free Zone Treaty".

Asia

Central Asia

The Treaty on a Nuclear-Weapon-Free Zone in Central Asia entered into force on 21 March 2009 following ratification by Kazakhstan in December 2008, just over two years after the Treaty among the five Central Asian States was signed [YUN 2006, p. 644]. Kyrgyzstan, Tajikistan, Turkmenistan and Uzbekistan had already ratified the Treaty. Encompassing an area of roughly 4 million square km, the Treaty covered the smallest of the nuclear-weapon-free zones, but the only one where nuclear weapons previously existed. It was the first such treaty to oblige Central Asian countries to accept enhanced IAEA safeguards on their nuclear material and activities. The Treaty also required parties to meet international standards regarding security of nuclear facilities—a move that could reduce the risk of nuclear terrorism or smuggling of nuclear and radioactive materials in the region. Furthermore, all Treaty signatories must comply with the Comprehensive Nuclear-Test-Ban Treaty, which outlawed all nuclear test explosions. The Treaty encompassed an environmental component that addressed concerns unique to the Central Asian region. Each of the five States hosted former Soviet nuclear weapons infrastructure and confronted common problems of environmental remediation for damage resulting from the production and testing of nuclear weapons.

Mongolia

Efforts to define and institutionalize Mongolia's nuclear-weapon-free status, which it had been seeking since 2001, continued to be made through consultations for negotiating a draft trilateral treaty with the Russian Federation and China. In March and September, the three sides held preliminary meetings in Geneva to exchange views on a draft treaty. At the end of the second meeting, the Russia Federation and China presented a joint paper containing questions and comments on some provisions of the draft presented by Mongolia.

The General Assembly in resolution 64/52 (see below) decided to convene the second Conference of States Parties and Signatories to Treaties that Establish Nuclear-Weapon-Free Zones and Mongolia in April 2010 to strengthen the regime of nuclear disarmament and non-proliferation.

On 2 December [meeting 55], the General Assembly, on the recommendation of the First Committee [A/64/391], adopted **resolution 64/52** by recorded vote (166-3-6) [agenda item 96].

Second Conference of States Parties and Signatories to Treaties that Establish Nuclear-Weapon-Free Zones and Mongolia

The General Assembly,

Recognizing the right of any group of States to conclude regional treaties in order to ensure the total absence of nuclear weapons in their respective territories, under article VII of the Treaty on the Non-Proliferation of Nuclear Weapons,

Recognizing also the important contribution of the treaties of Tlatelolco, Rarotonga, Bangkok, Pelindaba and Central Asia, as well as the Antarctic Treaty, to the achievement of the objectives of nuclear non-proliferation and nuclear disarmament,

Recalling its resolution 63/56 of 2 December 2008 on Mongolia's international security and nuclear-weapon-free status,

Urging regions that have not yet established nuclear-weapon-free zone treaties to accelerate efforts in this direction, particularly in the Middle East, through agreements freely arrived at among the States of the region concerned, in accordance with the provisions of the Final Document of the First Special Session of the General Assembly devoted to disarmament and the principles adopted by the United Nations Disarmament Commission in 1999,

Taking note of paragraph 122 of the Final Document of the Fifteenth Summit Conference of Heads of State and Government of the Movement of Non-Aligned Countries, held in Sharm el-Sheikh, Egypt, from 11 to 16 July 2009, in which the Heads of State and Government stated their belief that those nuclear-weapon-free zones were positive steps and important measures towards strengthening global nuclear disarmament and nuclear non-proliferation,

Recognizing the progress made on increased collaboration within and between zones at the first Conference of States Parties and Signatories to Treaties that Establish Nuclear-Weapon-Free Zones, held in Tlatelolco, Mexico, from 26 to 28 April 2005, at which States reaffirmed their need to cooperate in order to achieve their common objectives,

Recalling the adoption of the Declaration of Santiago de Chile by the Governments of the States members of the Agency for the Prohibition of Nuclear Weapons in Latin America and the Caribbean and the States parties to the Treaty of Tlatelolco, during the nineteenth regular session of the General Conference of the Agency, held in Santiago on 7 and 8 November 2005,

Recalling also the support for nuclear-weapon-free zones expressed by the Security Council summit on nuclear non-proliferation and nuclear disarmament, held on 24 September 2009, and for the convening of the second Conference of States Parties and Signatories to Treaties that Establish Nuclear-Weapon-Free Zones and Mongolia, to be held in New York on 30 April 2010,

1. *Decides* to convene the second Conference of States Parties and Signatories to Treaties that Establish Nuclear-Weapon-Free Zones and Mongolia in New York on 30 April 2010;

2. *Notes* that the objective of the Conference will be to consider ways and means to enhance consultations and cooperation among States parties and signatories, the treaty agencies and other interested States, with the purpose of promoting coordination and convergence in the implementation of the provisions of the treaties and in strengthening the regime of nuclear disarmament and non-proliferation;

3. *Urges* the States parties and signatories to treaties that have established nuclear-weapon-free zones to develop activities of cooperation and coordination in order to promote their common objectives in the framework of the Conference;

4. *Requests* the Secretary-General to provide the necessary assistance and services as may be required for the second Conference of States Parties and Signatories to Treaties that Establish Nuclear-Weapon-Free Zones and Mongolia.

RECORDED VOTE ON RESOLUTION 64/52:

In favour: Afghanistan, Albania, Algeria, Andorra, Angola, Antigua and Barbuda, Argentina, Armenia, Australia, Austria, Azerbaijan, Bahamas, Bahrain, Bangladesh, Barbados, Belarus, Belgium, Belize, Benin, Bhutan, Bolivia, Bosnia and Herzegovina, Botswana, Brazil, Brunei Darussalam, Bulgaria, Burkina Faso, Burundi, Cambodia, Cameroon, Canada, Cape Verde, Chile, China, Colombia, Comoros, Congo, Costa Rica, Côte d'Ivoire, Croatia, Cuba, Cyprus, Czech Republic, Democratic Republic of the Congo, Denmark, Djibouti, Dominica, Dominican Republic, Ecuador, Egypt, El Salvador, Equatorial Guinea, Eritrea, Estonia, Fiji, Finland, Gambia, Georgia, Germany, Ghana, Greece, Grenada, Guatemala, Guinea, Guinea-Bissau, Guyana, Haiti, Honduras, Hungary, Iceland, India, Indonesia, Iran, Iraq, Ireland, Italy, Jamaica, Japan, Jordan, Kazakhstan, Kenya, Kuwait, Kyrgyzstan, Lao People's Democratic Republic, Latvia, Lebanon, Lesotho, Liberia, Libyan Arab Jamahiriya, Liechtenstein, Luxembourg, Madagascar, Malawi, Malaysia, Maldives, Mali, Malta, Mauritania, Mauritius, Mexico, Moldova, Monaco, Mongolia, Montenegro, Morocco, Mozambique, Myanmar, Namibia, Nepal, Netherlands, Nicaragua, Niger, Nigeria, Norway, Oman, Pakistan, Panama, Papua New Guinea, Paraguay, Peru, Philippines, Portugal, Qatar, Republic of Korea, Romania, Saint Kitts and Nevis, Saint Lucia, Saint Vincent and the Grenadines, Samoa, San Marino, Saudi Arabia, Senegal, Serbia, Singapore, Slovakia, Slovenia, Solomon Islands, Somalia, South Africa, Spain, Sri Lanka, Sudan, Suriname, Swaziland, Sweden, Switzerland, Syrian Arab Republic, Tajikistan, Thailand, The former Yugoslav Republic of Macedonia, Togo, Tonga, Trinidad and Tobago, Tunisia, Turkey, Uganda, Ukraine, United Arab Emirates, United Republic of Tanzania, Uruguay, Uzbekistan, Venezuela, Viet Nam, Yemen, Zambia, Zimbabwe.

Against: Lithuania, New Zealand, Poland.

Abstaining: France, Israel, Marshall Islands, Russian Federation, United Kingdom, United States.

South-East Asia

The 10 States parties to the Treaty on the South-East Asia Nuclear-Weapon-Free Zone (Bangkok

Treaty), which had opened for signature in 1995 [YUN 1995, p. 207] and entered into force in 1997 [YUN 1997, p. 495], continued to establish an institutional framework for implementing the Treaty. At the forty-second Foreign Ministers Meeting of the Association of Southeast Asian Nations (Phuket, Thailand, 19–20 July), the Ministers reviewed the implementation of the Treaty's plan of action and agreed to exert greater efforts to ensure that programmes and activities indicated in the plan were carried out.

GENERAL ASSEMBLY ACTION

On 2 December [meeting 55], the General Assembly, on the recommendation of the First Committee [A/64/391], adopted **resolution 64/39** by recorded vote (174-0-6) [agenda item 96 *(c)*].

Treaty on the South-East Asia Nuclear-Weapon-Free Zone (Bangkok Treaty)

The General Assembly,

Recalling its resolution 62/31 of 5 December 2007, entitled "Treaty on the South-East Asia Nuclear-Weapon-Free-Zone (Bangkok Treaty)",

Welcoming the desire of the South-East Asian States to maintain peace and stability in the region in the spirit of peaceful coexistence and mutual understanding and cooperation,

Noting the entry into force of the Charter of the Association of Southeast Asian Nations on 15 December 2008, which states, inter alia, that one of the purposes of the Association is to preserve South-East Asia as a nuclear-weapon-free zone, free of all other weapons of mass destruction,

Noting also the convening of the second Conference of States Parties and Signatories of Treaties that Establish Nuclear-Weapon-Free Zones and Mongolia,

Reaffirming its conviction of the important role of nuclear-weapon-free zones in strengthening the nuclear non-proliferation regime and in extending the areas of the world that are nuclear-weapon-free, and, with particular reference to the responsibilities of the nuclear-weapon States, calling upon all States to support the process of nuclear disarmament and to work for the total elimination of all nuclear weapons,

Convinced that the establishment of a South-East Asia Nuclear-Weapon-Free Zone, as an essential component of the Declaration on the Zone of Peace, Freedom and Neutrality, signed in Kuala Lumpur on 27 November 1971, will contribute towards strengthening the security of States within the Zone and towards enhancing international peace and security as a whole,

Noting the entry into force of the Treaty on the South-East Asia Nuclear-Weapon-Free Zone on 27 March 1997 and the tenth anniversary of its entry into force in 2007,

Welcoming the reaffirmation of South-East Asian States that the South-East Asia Nuclear-Weapon-Free Zone shall continue to play a pivotal role in the area of confidence-building measures, preventive diplomacy and the approaches to conflict resolution as enshrined in the Declaration of the Association of Southeast Asian Nations Concord II (Bali Concord II),

Reaffirming the inalienable right of all the parties to the Treaty on the South-East Asia Nuclear-Weapon-Free Zone to develop research, production and use of nuclear energy for peaceful purposes without discrimination and in conformity with the Treaty on the Non-Proliferation of Nuclear Weapons,

Recognizing that by signing and ratifying the relevant protocols to the treaties establishing nuclear-weapon-free zones, nuclear-weapon States undertake legally binding commitments to respect the status of such zones and not to use or threaten to use nuclear weapons against States parties to such treaties,

Recalling the applicable principles and rules of international law relating to the freedom of the high seas and the rights of innocent passage, archipelagic sea lanes passage or transit passage of ships and aircraft, particularly those of the United Nations Convention on the Law of the Sea,

1. *Welcomes* the commitment and efforts of the Commission for the Treaty on the South-East Asia Nuclear-Weapon-Free Zone to further enhance and strengthen the implementation of the Bangkok Treaty by implementing the Plan of Action for the period 2007–2012, adopted in Manila on 29 July 2007, and the recent decision of the Association of Southeast Asian Nations Political-Security Community Council, established under the Charter of the Association, to give priority to the implementation of the Plan of Action;

2. *Encourages* States parties to the Treaty to resume direct consultations with the five nuclear-weapon States to resolve comprehensively, in accordance with the objectives and principles of the Treaty, existing outstanding issues on a number of provisions of the Treaty and the Protocol thereto;

3. *Encourages* nuclear-weapon States and States parties to the Treaty to work constructively with a view to ensuring the early accession of the nuclear-weapon States to the Protocol to the Treaty;

4. *Underlines* the value of enhancing and implementing further ways and means of cooperation among nuclear-weapon-free zones;

5. *Decides* to include in the provisional agenda of its sixty-sixth session the item entitled "Treaty on the South-East Asia Nuclear-Weapon-Free Zone (Bangkok Treaty)".

RECORDED VOTE ON RESOLUTION 64/39:

In favour: Afghanistan, Albania, Algeria, Andorra, Angola, Antigua and Barbuda, Argentina, Armenia, Australia, Austria, Azerbaijan, Bahamas, Bahrain, Bangladesh, Barbados, Belarus, Belgium, Belize, Benin, Bhutan, Bolivia, Bosnia and Herzegovina, Botswana, Brazil, Brunei Darussalam, Bulgaria, Burkina Faso, Burundi, Cambodia, Cameroon, Canada, Cape Verde, Chile, China, Colombia, Comoros, Congo, Costa Rica, Côte d'Ivoire, Croatia, Cuba, Cyprus, Czech Republic, Democratic People's Republic of Korea, Democratic Republic of the Congo, Denmark, Djibouti, Dominica, Dominican Republic, Ecuador, Egypt, El Salvador, Equatorial Guinea, Eritrea, Estonia, Fiji, Finland, Gambia, Georgia, Germany, Ghana, Greece, Grenada, Guatemala, Guinea, Guinea-Bissau, Guyana, Haiti, Honduras, Hungary, Iceland, India, Indonesia, Iran, Iraq, Ireland, Italy, Jamaica, Japan, Jordan, Kazakhstan, Kenya, Kuwait, Kyrgyzstan, Lao People's Democratic Republic, Latvia, Lebanon, Lesotho, Liberia, Libyan Arab Jamahiriya, Liechtenstein, Lithuania, Luxembourg, Madagascar, Malawi, Malaysia, Maldives, Mali, Malta, Mauritania, Mauritius, Mexico, Moldova, Monaco, Mongolia, Montenegro, Morocco, Mozambique, Myanmar, Namibia, Nepal, Netherlands, New Zealand, Nicaragua, Niger, Nigeria, Norway, Oman, Pakistan, Panama, Papua New Guinea, Paraguay, Peru, Philippines, Poland, Portugal, Qatar, Republic of Korea, Romania, Russian Federation, Saint Kitts and Nevis, Saint Lucia, Saint Vincent and the Grenadines, Samoa, San Marino, Saudi Arabia, Senegal, Serbia, Seychelles, Singapore, Slovakia, Slovenia, Solomon Islands, Somalia, South Africa, Spain, Sri Lanka, Sudan, Suriname, Swaziland, Sweden, Switzerland, Syrian Arab Republic, Tajikistan, Thailand, The former Yugoslav Republic of Macedonia, Togo, Tonga, Trinidad and Tobago, Tunisia, Turkey, Turkmenistan, Uganda, Ukraine, United Arab Emirates, United Kingdom, United Republic of Tanzania, Uruguay, Uzbekistan, Venezuela, Viet Nam, Yemen, Zambia, Zimbabwe.

Against: None.

Abstaining: France, Israel, Marshall Islands, Micronesia, Palau, United States.

Latin America and the Caribbean

The 33 States parties to the Treaty for the Prohibition of Nuclear Weapons in Latin America and the Caribbean (Treaty of Tlatelolco) [YUN 1967, p. 13] continued to consolidate the Treaty regime. In a resolution [AG/RES. 2442(XXXIX-O/09)] adopted at its thirty-ninth session (San Pedro Sula, Honduras, 2 and 4 June), the General Assembly of the Organization of American States (OAS) reaffirmed that the consolidation of the nuclear-weapon-free zone set forth in the Treaty constituted a demonstration of the commitment of Latin America and the Caribbean to complete and verifiable disarmament and the non-proliferation of nuclear weapons. OAS recognized that the Treaty had become a model for other nuclear-weapon-free zones in various regions, and called on regional States that had not done so to sign or ratify the amendments to the Treaty. It reaffirmed the importance of strengthening the Agency for the Prohibition of Nuclear Weapons in Latin America and the Caribbean (OPANAL); recognized OPANAL's work in ensuring compliance with Treaty obligations; and expressed support to OPANAL's cooperation and coordination mechanisms with other nuclear-weapon-free zone treaties.

Middle East

In response to General Assembly resolution 63/38 [YUN 2008, p. 602], the Secretary-General in July reported [A/64/124 (Part I) & Add.1] on the establishment of a nuclear-weapon-free zone in the Middle East. He said that at the third session of the Preparatory Committee for the 2010 Review Conference of the Parties to NPT (see p. 503), States parties reiterated their support for establishing a nuclear-weapon-free zone in the Middle East; reaffirmed the importance of the implementation of the resolution on the Middle

East adopted by the 1995 NPT Review and Extension Conference [YUN 1995, p. 205]; and recognized that the resolution remained valid until its goals and objectives were achieved. Furthermore, the Arab Summit (Doha, Qatar, 30–31 March 2009), emphasized that the success of the 2010 NPT Review Conference required the implementation of the 1995 Middle East resolution and agreement on adopting practical and well-defined steps towards establishing the nuclear-weapon-free zone.

The Secretary-General said that he continued to carry out consultations with parties within and outside the region in order to explore ways and means to establish the zone. The major armed crisis in Gaza, the discontinuation of Israeli-Palestinian negotiations undertaken in the Annapolis framework [YUN 2007, p. 445] and limited progress towards Palestinian unity underscored the need for a renewed effort to resume direct talks on a two-State solution and comprehensive regional peace. He called upon all parties within and outside the region to resume dialogue with a view to creating stable security conditions and an eventual settlement that would facilitate the process of establishing a zone free of nuclear weapons in the Middle East.

The Secretary-General's report included the views of 10 Governments—Cuba, Egypt, Iran, Israel, Japan, Lebanon, Mali, Mexico, Nicaragua and Qatar.

GENERAL ASSEMBLY ACTION

On 2 December [meeting 55], the General Assembly, on the recommendation of the First Committee [A/64/387], adopted **resolution 64/26** without vote [agenda item 92].

Establishment of a nuclear-weapon-free zone in the region of the Middle East

The General Assembly,

Recalling its resolutions 3263(XXIX) of 9 December 1974, 3474(XXX) of 11 December 1975, 31/71 of 10 December 1976, 32/82 of 12 December 1977, 33/64 of 14 December 1978, 34/77 of 11 December 1979, 35/147 of 12 December 1980, 36/87 A and B of 9 December 1981, 37/75 of 9 December 1982, 38/64 of 15 December 1983, 39/54 of 12 December 1984, 40/82 of 12 December 1985, 41/48 of 3 December 1986, 42/28 of 30 November 1987, 43/65 of 7 December 1988, 44/108 of 15 December 1989, 45/52 of 4 December 1990, 46/30 of 6 December 1991, 47/48 of 9 December 1992, 48/71 of 16 December 1993, 49/71 of 15 December 1994, 50/66 of 12 December 1995, 51/41 of 10 December 1996, 52/34 of 9 December 1997, 53/74 of 4 December 1998, 54/51 of 1 December 1999, 55/30 of 20 November 2000, 56/21 of 29 November 2001, 57/55 of 22 November 2002, 58/34 of 8 December 2003, 59/63 of 3 December 2004, 60/52 of 8 December 2005, 61/56 of 6 December 2006, 62/18 of 5 December 2007 and 63/38 of 2 December 2008 on the establishment of a nuclear-weapon-free zone in the region of the Middle East,

Recalling also the recommendations for the establishment of a nuclear-weapon-free zone in the region of the Middle East consistent with paragraphs 60 to 63, and in particular paragraph 63 *(d)*, of the Final Document of the Tenth Special Session of the General Assembly,

Emphasizing the basic provisions of the above-mentioned resolutions, which call upon all parties directly concerned to consider taking the practical and urgent steps required for the implementation of the proposal to establish a nuclear-weapon-free zone in the region of the Middle East and, pending and during the establishment of such a zone, to declare solemnly that they will refrain, on a reciprocal basis, from producing, acquiring or in any other way possessing nuclear weapons and nuclear explosive devices and from permitting the stationing of nuclear weapons on their territory by any third party, to agree to place their nuclear facilities under International Atomic Energy Agency safeguards and to declare their support for the establishment of the zone and to deposit such declarations with the Security Council for consideration, as appropriate,

Reaffirming the inalienable right of all States to acquire and develop nuclear energy for peaceful purposes,

Emphasizing the need for appropriate measures on the question of the prohibition of military attacks on nuclear facilities,

Bearing in mind the consensus reached by the General Assembly since its thirty-fifth session that the establishment of a nuclear-weapon-free zone in the region of the Middle East would greatly enhance international peace and security,

Desirous of building on that consensus so that substantial progress can be made towards establishing a nuclear-weapon-free zone in the region of the Middle East,

Welcoming all initiatives leading to general and complete disarmament, including in the region of the Middle East, and in particular on the establishment therein of a zone free of weapons of mass destruction, including nuclear weapons,

Noting the peace negotiations in the Middle East, which should be of a comprehensive nature and represent an appropriate framework for the peaceful settlement of contentious issues in the region,

Recognizing the importance of credible regional security, including the establishment of a mutually verifiable nuclear-weapon-free zone,

Emphasizing the essential role of the United Nations in the establishment of a mutually verifiable nuclear-weapon-free zone,

Having examined the report of the Secretary-General on the implementation of resolution 63/38,

1. *Urges* all parties directly concerned seriously to consider taking the practical and urgent steps required for the implementation of the proposal to establish a nuclear-weapon-free zone in the region of the Middle East in accordance with the relevant resolutions of the General Assembly, and, as a means of promoting this objective, invites the countries concerned to adhere to the Treaty on the Non-Proliferation of Nuclear Weapons;

2. *Calls upon* all countries of the region that have not yet done so, pending the establishment of the zone, to agree to place all their nuclear activities under International Atomic Energy Agency safeguards;

3. *Takes note* of resolution GC(53)/RES/16, adopted on 17 September 2009 by the General Conference of the International Atomic Energy Agency at its fifty-third regular session, concerning the application of Agency safeguards in the Middle East;

4. *Notes* the importance of the ongoing bilateral Middle East peace negotiations and the activities of the multilateral Working Group on Arms Control and Regional Security in promoting mutual confidence and security in the Middle East, including the establishment of a nuclear-weapon-free zone;

5. *Invites* all countries of the region, pending the establishment of a nuclear-weapon-free zone in the region of the Middle East, to declare their support for establishing such a zone, consistent with paragraph 63 *(d)* of the Final Document of the Tenth Special Session of the General Assembly, and to deposit those declarations with the Security Council;

6. *Also invites* those countries, pending the establishment of the zone, not to develop, produce, test or otherwise acquire nuclear weapons or permit the stationing on their territories, or territories under their control, of nuclear weapons or nuclear explosive devices;

7. *Invites* the nuclear-weapon States and all other States to render their assistance in the establishment of the zone and at the same time to refrain from any action that runs counter to both the letter and the spirit of the present resolution;

8. *Takes note* of the report of the Secretary-General;

9. *Invites* all parties to consider the appropriate means that may contribute towards the goal of general and complete disarmament and the establishment of a zone free of weapons of mass destruction in the region of the Middle East;

10. *Requests* the Secretary-General to continue to pursue consultations with the States of the region and other concerned States, in accordance with paragraph 7 of resolution 46/30 and taking into account the evolving situation in the region, and to seek from those States their views on the measures outlined in chapters III and IV of the study annexed to the report of the Secretary-General of 10 October 1990 or other relevant measures, in order to move towards the establishment of a nuclear-weapon-free zone in the region of the Middle East;

11. *Also requests* the Secretary-General to submit to the General Assembly at its sixty-fifth session a report on the implementation of the present resolution;

12. *Decides* to include in the provisional agenda of its sixty-fifth session the item entitled "Establishment of a nuclear-weapon-free zone in the region of the Middle East".

South Pacific

As at 31 December, the number of States parties to the 1985 South Pacific Nuclear-Free Zone Treaty (Treaty of Rarotonga) [YUN 1985, p. 58] remained at 13. China and the Russian Federation had ratified Protocols 2 and 3, and France, the United Kingdom and the United States had ratified all three Protocols. Under Protocol 1, the States internationally responsible for territories situated within the zone would apply the relevant prohibitions of the Treaty to those territories; under Protocol 2, the five nuclear-weapon States would provide security assurances to parties or territories within the zone; and under Protocol 3, those five States would not carry out any nuclear tests in the zone.

Southern hemisphere and adjacent areas

On 2 December [meeting 55], the General Assembly, on the recommendation of the First Committee [A/64/391], adopted **resolution 64/44** by recorded vote (170-3-6) [agenda item 96 *(t)*].

Nuclear-weapon-free southern hemisphere and adjacent areas

The General Assembly,

Recalling its resolutions 51/45 B of 10 December 1996, 52/38 N of 9 December 1997, 53/77 Q of 4 December 1998, 54/54 L of 1 December 1999, 55/33 I of 20 November 2000, 56/24 G of 29 November 2001, 57/73 of 22 November 2002, 58/49 of 8 December 2003, 59/85 of 3 December 2004, 60/58 of 8 December 2005, 61/69 of 6 December 2006, 62/35 of 5 December 2007 and 63/65 of 2 December 2008,

Recalling also the adoption by the Disarmament Commission at its 1999 substantive session of a text entitled "Establishment of nuclear-weapon-free zones on the basis of arrangements freely arrived at among the States of the region concerned",

Determined to pursue the total elimination of nuclear weapons,

Determined also to continue to contribute to the prevention of the proliferation of nuclear weapons in all its aspects and to the process of general and complete disarmament under strict and effective international control, in particular in the field of nuclear weapons and other weapons of mass destruction, with a view to strengthening international peace and security, in accordance with the purposes and principles of the Charter of the United Nations,

Recalling the provisions on nuclear-weapon-free zones of the Final Document of the Tenth Special Session of the General Assembly, the first special session devoted to disarmament,

Stressing the importance of the treaties of Tlatelolco, Rarotonga, Bangkok and Pelindaba establishing nuclear-weapon-free zones, as well as the Antarctic Treaty, to, inter alia, achieve a world entirely free of nuclear weapons,

Noting the adoption of the Declaration of the first Conference of States Parties and Signatories to Treaties that Establish Nuclear-Weapon-Free Zones, held in Tlatelolco, Mexico, from 26 to 28 April 2005, where nuclear-weapon-free-zone States met for the purpose of strengthening the nuclear-weapon-free zone regime and contributing to the disarmament and the non-proliferation processes, and in particular to analyse ways of cooperating that could contribute to achieving the universal goal of a nuclear-weapon-free world,

Underlining the value of enhancing cooperation among the nuclear-weapon-free-zone treaty members by means of

mechanisms such as joint meetings of States parties, signatories and observers to those treaties, and in that regard, noting with satisfaction the meeting of focal points of nuclear-weapon-free zones and Mongolia, held in Ulaanbaatar on 27 and 28 April 2009,

Reaffirming the applicable principles and rules of international law relating to the freedom of the high seas and the rights of passage through maritime space, including those of the United Nations Convention on the Law of the Sea,

1. *Welcomes* the continued contribution that the Antarctic Treaty and the treaties of Tlatelolco, Rarotonga, Bangkok and Pelindaba are making towards freeing the southern hemisphere and adjacent areas covered by those treaties from nuclear weapons;

2. *Notes with satisfaction* that all nuclear-weapon-free zones in the southern hemisphere and adjacent areas are now in force;

3. *Welcomes* the ratification by all original parties of the Treaty of Rarotonga, and calls upon eligible States to adhere to the Treaty and the protocols thereto;

4. *Also welcomes* the entry into force, on 15 July 2009, of the Treaty of Pelindaba, which establishes a nuclear-weapon-free zone in Africa;

5. *Calls upon* all concerned States to continue to work together in order to facilitate adherence to the protocols to nuclear-weapon-free zone treaties by all relevant States that have not yet adhered to them;

6. *Urges* all relevant States to cooperate in resolving outstanding issues with a view to the full implementation of the Treaty on a Nuclear-Weapon-Free Zone in Central Asia, which entered into force on 21 March 2009;

7. *Welcomes* the steps taken to conclude further nuclear-weapon-free-zone treaties on the basis of arrangements freely arrived at among the States of the region concerned, and calls upon all States to consider all relevant proposals, including those reflected in its resolutions on the establishment of nuclear-weapon-free zones in the Middle East and South Asia;

8. *Affirms its conviction* of the important role of nuclear-weapon-free zones in strengthening the nuclear non-proliferation regime and in extending the areas of the world that are nuclear-weapon-free, and, with particular reference to the responsibilities of the nuclear-weapon States, calls upon all States to support the process of nuclear disarmament and to work for the total elimination of all nuclear weapons;

9. *Welcomes* the progress made on increased collaboration within and between zones at the first Conference of States Parties and Signatories to Treaties that Establish Nuclear-Weapon-Free Zones, held in Tlatelolco, Mexico, from 26 to 28 April 2005, at which States reaffirmed their need to cooperate in order to achieve their common objectives, and looks forward to the second Conference planned for 2010, which aims to further develop this collaboration;

10. *Congratulates* the States parties and signatories to the treaties of Tlatelolco, Rarotonga, Bangkok and Pelindaba, as well as Mongolia, for their efforts to pursue the common goals envisaged in those treaties and to promote the nuclear-weapon-free status of the southern hemisphere and adjacent areas, and calls upon them to explore and implement further ways and means of cooperation among themselves and their treaty agencies;

11.　*Encourages* the competent authorities of the nuclear-weapon-free-zone treaties to provide assistance to the States parties and signatories to those treaties so as to facilitate the accomplishment of the goals;

12.　*Decides* to include in the provisional agenda of its sixty-fifth session the item entitled "Nuclear-weapon-free southern hemisphere and adjacent areas".

RECORDED VOTE ON RESOLUTION 64/44:

In favour: Afghanistan, Albania, Algeria, Andorra, Angola, Antigua and Barbuda, Argentina, Armenia, Australia, Austria, Azerbaijan, Bahamas, Bahrain, Bangladesh, Barbados, Belarus, Belgium, Belize, Benin, Bhutan, Bolivia, Bosnia and Herzegovina, Botswana, Brazil, Brunei Darussalam, Bulgaria, Burkina Faso, Burundi, Cambodia, Cameroon, Canada, Cape Verde, Chile, China, Colombia, Comoros, Congo, Costa Rica, Côte d'Ivoire, Croatia, Cuba, Cyprus, Czech Republic, Democratic People's Republic of Korea, Democratic Republic of the Congo, Denmark, Djibouti, Dominica, Dominican Republic, Ecuador, Egypt, El Salvador, Equatorial Guinea, Eritrea, Estonia, Fiji, Finland, Gambia, Georgia, Germany, Ghana, Greece, Grenada, Guatemala, Guinea, Guinea-Bissau, Guyana, Haiti, Honduras, Hungary, Iceland, Indonesia, Iran, Iraq, Ireland, Italy, Jamaica, Japan, Jordan, Kazakhstan, Kenya, Kuwait, Kyrgyzstan, Lao People's Democratic Republic, Latvia, Lebanon, Lesotho, Liberia, Libyan Arab Jamahiriya, Liechtenstein, Lithuania, Luxembourg, Madagascar, Malawi, Malaysia, Maldives, Mali, Malta, Mauritania, Mauritius, Mexico, Moldova, Mongolia, Montenegro, Morocco, Mozambique, Myanmar, Namibia, Nepal, Netherlands, New Zealand, Nicaragua, Niger, Nigeria, Norway, Oman, Panama, Papua New Guinea, Paraguay, Peru, Philippines, Poland, Portugal, Qatar, Republic of Korea, Romania, Russian Federation, Saint Kitts and Nevis, Saint Lucia, Saint Vincent and the Grenadines, Samoa, San Marino, Saudi Arabia, Senegal, Serbia, Seychelles, Sierra Leone, Singapore, Slovakia, Slovenia, Solomon Islands, Somalia, South Africa, Spain, Sri Lanka, Sudan, Suriname, Swaziland, Sweden, Switzerland, Syrian Arab Republic, Tajikistan, Thailand, The former Yugoslav Republic of Macedonia, Togo, Tonga, Trinidad and Tobago, Tunisia, Turkmenistan, Uganda, Ukraine, United Arab Emirates, United Republic of Tanzania, Uruguay, Uzbekistan, Venezuela, Viet Nam, Yemen, Zambia, Zimbabwe.

Against: France, United Kingdom, United States.

Abstaining: India, Israel, Marshall Islands, Micronesia, Pakistan, Palau.

First Meeting of Focal Points
of Nuclear-Weapon-Free Zones and Mongolia

The focal points of the five nuclear-weapon-free zones and Mongolia met in Ulaanbaatar (27–28 April), along with representatives of Egypt and Turkey as observers, and others from CTBTO and civil society. The sessions addressed the implementation of the Tlatelolco Declaration and coordination and cooperation among nuclear-weapon-free zones; preparations for the follow-up conference of States parties and signatories to treaties that established nuclear-weapon-free zones and Mongolia; and preparations for the 2010 NPT Review Conference. Participants recalled that some nuclear-weapon States had yet to ratify protocols to the treaties and suggested that

zones could share experiences towards achieving such ratifications. Participants also stressed the importance of universalization of NPT and reinforced the need for entry into force of CTBT.

Bacteriological (biological) and chemical weapons

Bacteriological (biological) weapons

Annual meetings of the States parties to the 1972 Convention on the Prohibition of the Development, Production and Stockpiling of Bacteriological (Biological) and Toxin Weapons and on Their Destruction [YUN 1972, p. 5] (Biological Weapons Convention (BWC)) continued in 2009, covering international cooperation and capacity-building. Meetings of experts in August and of States parties in December sought to improve national implementation of agreed global norms and to promote universal adherence.

Meeting of States parties

As decided by the Sixth Review Conference of the States parties to BWC [YUN 2006, p. 650], a meeting of those States was convened in 2009 (Geneva, 7–11 December) [BWC/MSP/2009/5]. It was attended by 100 States parties, six signatory States, two observer States, UNODA, UNIDIR, the United Nations Interregional Crime and Justice Research Institute (UNICRI) and 14 NGOs and research institutes. The European Union (EU), the International Committee of the Red Cross, the Organization for the Prohibition of Chemical Weapons (OPCW) and the World Health Organization (WHO) participated as observers.

Sessions were devoted to enhancing international cooperation, assistance and exchange in biological sciences and technology for peaceful purposes; promoting capacity-building in disease surveillance, detection and diagnosis; and containment of infectious diseases. One working session was devoted to reports from the Chairman and States parties on universalization activities [BWC/MSP/2009/4], and the report of the UNODA Implementation Support Unit [BWC/MSP/2009/2 & Add.1]. Participants stressed that States parties had a legal obligation to facilitate the exchange of equipment, materials and scientific and technological information for the use of biological agents and toxins for peaceful purposes and not to hamper the economic and technological development of States parties. Participants agreed that although disease surveillance, mitigation and response were primarily national responsibilities, infectious diseases knew no boundaries and neither should efforts to combat them. They therefore noted that international organizations, such as the Food and Agriculture Organization of the United Nations (FAO), the International Plant Protection Convention secretariat, the World Organisation for Animal Health and WHO had a fundamental role to play in addressing disease and in supporting and financing national activities. It was recognized that infrastructure, equipment and technology were of little use without appropriately trained individuals, and that human resources should be developed for disease surveillance, detection, diagnosis and containment. Participants reviewed progress towards obtaining universality for the Convention and considered the Chairman's report on universalization activities, as well as States parties' reports on their activities to promote universalization.

Meeting of experts. A total of 103 States, including 96 States parties to the Convention, four signatory States and three observer States took part in the annual meeting of experts (Geneva, 24–28 August) [BWC/MSP/2009/MX/3 & Corr.1]. Among the nearly 500 participants were 16 NGOs and research institutes, UNODA, UNIDIR, UNICRI, FAO, WHO and other international scientific, professional, academic and industry bodies. Sessions were held on assistance and exchange in biological sciences and technology for peaceful purposes; promoting capacity-building in disease surveillance, detection and diagnosis; and containment of infectious diseases.

GENERAL ASSEMBLY ACTION

On 2 December [meeting 55], the General Assembly, on the recommendation of the First Committee [A/64/398], adopted **resolution 64/70** without vote [agenda item 103].

Convention on the Prohibition of the Development, Production and Stockpiling of Bacteriological (Biological) and Toxin Weapons and on Their Destruction

The General Assembly,

Recalling its previous resolutions relating to the complete and effective prohibition of bacteriological (biological) and toxin weapons and to their destruction,

Noting with satisfaction that there are one hundred and sixty-three States parties to the Convention on the Prohibition of the Development, Production and Stockpiling of Bacteriological (Biological) and Toxin Weapons and on Their Destruction, including all of the permanent members of the Security Council,

Bearing in mind its call upon all States parties to the Convention to participate in the implementation of the recommendations of the Review Conferences, including the exchange of information and data agreed to in the Final Declaration of the Third Review Conference of the Parties to the Convention, and to provide such information and data in conformity with standardized procedure to the Secretary-General on an annual basis and no later than 15 April,

Welcoming the reaffirmation made in the Final Declaration of the Fourth Review Conference that under all circumstances the use of bacteriological (biological) and toxin weapons and their development, production and stockpiling are effectively prohibited under article I of the Convention,

Recalling the decision reached at the Sixth Review Conference to hold four annual meetings of the States parties of one week's duration each year commencing in 2007, prior to the Seventh Review Conference, which is to be held no later than the end of 2011, and to hold a one-week meeting of experts to prepare for each meeting of the States parties,

1. *Notes* the increase in the number of States parties to the Convention on the Prohibition of the Development, Production and Stockpiling of Bacteriological (Biological) and Toxin Weapons and on Their Destruction, reaffirms the call upon all signatory States that have not yet ratified the Convention to do so without delay, and calls upon those States that have not signed the Convention to become parties thereto at an early date, thus contributing to the achievement of universal adherence to the Convention;

2. *Welcomes* the information and data provided to date, and reiterates its call upon all States parties to the Convention to participate in the exchange of information and data agreed to in the Final Declaration of the Third Review Conference of the Parties to the Convention;

3. *Also welcomes* the successful holding of meetings as part of the 2007–2010 intersessional process, and in this context also welcomes the discussion aimed at the promotion of common understanding and effective action on topics agreed at the Sixth Review Conference, and urges States parties to continue to participate actively in the remaining intersessional process;

4. *Notes with satisfaction* that the Sixth Review Conference agreed on several measures to update the mechanism for the transmission of information within the framework of the confidence-building measures;

5. *Recalls* the decisions reached at the Sixth Review Conference, and calls upon States parties to the Convention to participate in their implementation;

6. *Urges* States parties to continue to work closely with the Implementation Support Unit of the Office for Disarmament Affairs of the Secretariat in fulfilling its mandate, in accordance with the decision of the Sixth Review Conference;

7. *Requests* the Secretary-General to continue to render the necessary assistance to the depositary Governments and to provide such services as may be required for the implementation of the decisions and recommendations of the Review Conferences, including all assistance to the annual meetings of the States parties and the meetings of experts;

8. *Decides* to include in the provisional agenda of its sixty-fifth session the item entitled "Convention on the Prohibition of the Development, Production and Stockpiling of Bacteriological (Biological) and Toxin Weapons and on Their Destruction".

Chemical weapons
Chemical weapons convention

The Bahamas, the Dominican Republic and Iraq in 2009 acceded to the Convention on the Prohibition of the Development, Production, Stockpiling and Use of Chemical Weapons and on Their Destruction (cwc), bringing the number of States parties to 188. The number of signatories remained at 165. The Convention was adopted by the Conference on Disarmament in 1992 [YUN 1992, p. 65] and entered into force in 1997 [YUN 1997, p. 499].

Fourteenth session of Conference of States Parties

The fourteenth session of the Conference of States Parties to cwc (The Hague, Netherlands, 30 November–4 December) [C-14/5] was attended by 122 States parties, with two signatory States—Israel and Myanmar—attending as observers. The Conference noted that the final extended destruction deadline of 29 April 2012 for all categories of chemical weapons might not be fully met. It also noted that over 48 per cent of chemical weapons stockpiles remained to be destroyed as at 1 December 2009, and urged all possessor States parties to ensure their compliance with the final extended destruction deadline. The Conference extended the intermediate and final deadlines to 15 May 2011 for the destruction of category 1 chemical weapons by the Libyan Arab Jamahiriya. It approved the report of opcw on the implementation of the Convention in 2008. It requested the opcw Executive Council to intensify consultations so as to develop concrete measures and recommendations to ensure the implementation of article XI, dealing with international cooperation in the peaceful uses of chemistry. In that regard, the Conference requested the opcw Technical Secretariat to organize in 2010 a workshop for the exchange of ideas among States parties, chemical industry associations, NGOs and international institutions. The Conference appointed Ahmet Üzümcü (Turkey) as the next opcw Director-General for a four-year term beginning 25 July 2010.

GENERAL ASSEMBLY ACTION

On 2 December [meeting 55], the General Assembly, on the recommendation of the First Committee [A/64/391], adopted **resolution 64/46** without vote [agenda item 96 *(k)*].

Implementation of the Convention on the Prohibition of the Development, Production, Stockpiling and Use of Chemical Weapons and on Their Destruction

The General Assembly,

Recalling its previous resolutions on the subject of chemical weapons, in particular resolution 63/48 of 2 December 2008, adopted without a vote, in which it noted with appreciation the ongoing work to achieve the objective and purpose of the Convention on the Prohibition of the Development, Production, Stockpiling and Use of Chemical Weapons and on Their Destruction,

Determined to achieve the effective prohibition of the development, production, acquisition, transfer, stockpiling and use of chemical weapons and their destruction,

Noting with satisfaction that, since the adoption of resolution 63/48, four additional States have acceded to the Convention, bringing the total number of States parties to the Convention to one hundred and eighty-eight,

Reaffirming the importance of the outcome of the Second Special Session of the Conference of the States Parties to Review the Operation of the Chemical Weapons Convention (hereinafter "the Second Review Conference"), including the consensus final report, which addressed all aspects of the Convention and made important recommendations on its continued implementation,

Emphasizing that the Second Review Conference welcomed the fact that, eleven years after its entry into force, the Convention remains a unique multilateral agreement banning an entire category of weapons of mass destruction in a non-discriminatory and verifiable manner under strict and effective international control,

1. *Emphasizes* that the universality of the Convention on the Prohibition of the Development, Production, Stockpiling and Use of Chemical Weapons and on Their Destruction is fundamental to the achievement of its objective and purpose, acknowledges progress made in the implementation of the action plan for the universality of the Convention, and calls upon all States that have not yet done so to become parties to the Convention without delay;

2. *Underlines* the fact that implementation of the Convention makes a major contribution to international peace and security through the elimination of existing stockpiles of chemical weapons, the prohibition of the acquisition or use of chemical weapons, and provides for assistance and protection in the event of use, or threat of use, of chemical weapons and for international cooperation for peaceful purposes in the field of chemical activities;

3. *Stresses* the importance to the Convention that all possessors of chemical weapons, chemical weapons production facilities or chemical weapons development facilities, including previously declared possessor States, should be among the States parties to the Convention, and welcomes progress to that end;

4. *Reaffirms* the obligation of the States parties to the Convention to destroy chemical weapons and to destroy or convert chemical weapons production facilities within the time limits provided for by the Convention;

5. *Stresses* that the full and effective implementation of all provisions of the Convention, including those on national implementation (article VII) and assistance and protection (article X), constitutes an important contribution to the efforts of the United Nations in the global fight against terrorism in all its forms and manifestations;

6. *Notes* that the effective application of the verification system builds confidence in compliance with the Convention by States parties;

7. *Stresses* the importance of the Organization for the Prohibition of Chemical Weapons in verifying compliance with the provisions of the Convention as well as in promoting the timely and efficient accomplishment of all its objectives;

8. *Urges* all States parties to the Convention to meet in full and on time their obligations under the Convention and to support the Organization for the Prohibition of Chemical Weapons in its implementation activities;

9. *Welcomes* progress made in the national implementation of article VII obligations, commends the States parties and the Technical Secretariat for assisting other States parties, on request, with the implementation of the follow-up to the plan of action regarding article VII obligations, and urges States parties that have not fulfilled their obligations under article VII to do so without further delay, in accordance with their constitutional processes;

10. *Emphasizes* the continuing relevance and importance of the provisions of article X of the Convention, and welcomes the activities of the Organization for the Prohibition of Chemical Weapons in relation to assistance and protection against chemical weapons;

11. *Reaffirms* that the provisions of the Convention shall be implemented in a manner that avoids hampering the economic or technological development of States parties and international cooperation in the field of chemical activities for purposes not prohibited under the Convention, including the international exchange of scientific and technical information, and chemicals and equipment for the production, processing or use of chemicals for purposes not prohibited under the Convention;

12. *Emphasizes* the importance of article XI provisions relating to the economic and technological development of States parties, recalls that the full, effective and non-discriminatory implementation of those provisions contributes to universality, and also reaffirms the undertaking of the States parties to foster international cooperation for peaceful purposes in the field of chemical activities of the States parties and the importance of that cooperation and its contribution to the promotion of the Convention as a whole;

13. *Notes with appreciation* the ongoing work of the Organization for the Prohibition of Chemical Weapons to achieve the objective and purpose of the Convention, to ensure the full implementation of its provisions, including those for international verification of compliance with it, and to provide a forum for consultation and cooperation among States parties, and also notes with appreciation the substantial contribution of the Technical Secretariat and the outgoing Director-General, Rogelio Pfirter, whose mandate expires in July 2010, to the continued development and success of the Organization;

14. *Welcomes* the cooperation between the United Nations and the Organization for the Prohibition of Chemical Weapons within the framework of the Relationship Agreement between the United Nations and the Organization, in accordance with the provisions of the Convention;

15. *Decides* to include in the provisional agenda of its sixty-fifth session the item entitled "Implementation of the Convention on the Prohibition of the Development, Production, Stockpiling and Use of Chemical Weapons and on Their Destruction".

Organisation for the Prohibition of Chemical Weapons

OPCW, mandated to oversee CWC implementation and to provide a forum for consultations and cooperation among States parties, continued to make progress in the three areas of work under the Convention: chemical disarmament; non-proliferation, assistance and protection; and international cooperation, as detailed in a report on its activities during 2009 [C-15/4].

India became the third State party to complete the destruction of all chemical weapons declared to OPCW, after Albania in 2007, and an unnamed State party in 2008. OPCW verified the destruction of 9,697 tonnes of chemical weapons (5,560 tonnes more than in the previous year), with more than 40,000 tonnes of chemical weapons (10,000 tonnes more than in the previous year) having been verified as destroyed by 31 December.

As at 31 December, 70 chemical weapons production facilities had been declared to OPCW, including five newly declared Iraqi facilities. For 10 of the 13 States parties that had declared having such facilities, OPCW had certified that all of them had been either destroyed or converted. Four facilities remained to be certified as destroyed and four to be certified as converted. Under article VI of the Convention, the OPCW secretariat inspected 208 chemical industry facilities.

Under article X of the Convention, OPCW coordinated and delivered training on protection against chemical weapons to States parties. During the year, it conducted capacity-building courses, seminars, workshops and exercises for response specialists dealing with chemical weapons agents and toxic industrial chemicals in a number of States parties. OPCW also started preparations for a field exercise on the delivery of assistance and the investigation of alleged use of chemical weapons, which would be held in Tunisia in 2010.

OPCW's Associate Programme, designed to promote the peaceful uses of chemistry, expanded to accommodate more participants under the organization's programme for Africa. To promote stronger cooperation with the African Union, a task force composed of experts from across OPCW was established. In July, the EU decided to support OPCW activities in the framework of the EU Strategy against Proliferation of Weapons of Mass Destruction and agreed to provide €2,110,000 for OPCW activities.

The Secretary-General, in July [A/64/156], transmitted to the General Assembly the 2007 OPCW report on the implementation of the Convention and the 2008 draft report, in accordance with the Agreement concerning the Relationship between the United Nations and OPCW, signed in 2000 [YUN 2000, p. 516] and approved by Assembly resolution 55/283 [YUN 2001, p. 495], which entered into force in 2001.

Conventional weapons

Towards an arms trade treaty

In 2009, pursuant to General Assembly resolution 63/240 [YUN 2008, p. 612], the Open-ended Working Group towards an Arms Trade Treaty: establishing common international standards for the import, export and transfer of conventional arms, held an organizational session (23 January) and two substantive sessions (2–6 March, 13–17 July) [A/AC.277/2009/1] in New York. Through the Group, Member States expressed their points of view concerning the goals and objectives, scope, principles and draft parameters of a potential arms trade treaty and other aspects to be addressed by such a treaty. The Working Group recognized the need to address the problems relating to unregulated trade in conventional weapons and their diversion to the illicit market. Considering that such risks could fuel instability, international terrorism and transnational organized crime, the Group stated that international action should be taken to address the problem.

The Assembly decided to convene a United Nations Conference on the Arms Trade Treaty in 2012 (see below).

GENERAL ASSEMBLY ACTION

On 2 December [meeting 55], the General Assembly, on the recommendation of the First Committee [A/64/391], adopted **resolution 64/48** by recorded vote (151-1-20) [agenda item 96 *(z)*].

The arms trade treaty

The General Assembly,

Guided by the purposes and principles enshrined in the Charter of the United Nations, and reaffirming its respect for and commitment to international law,

Recalling its resolutions 46/36 L of 9 December 1991, 51/45 N of 10 December 1996, 51/47 B of 10 December 1996, 56/24 V of 24 December 2001, 60/69 and 60/82 of 8 December 2005, 61/89 of 6 December 2006 and 63/240 of 24 December 2008,

Recognizing that arms control, disarmament and non-proliferation are essential for the maintenance of international peace and security,

Reaffirming the inherent right of all States to individual or collective self-defence in accordance with Article 51 of the Charter,

Recalling its commitment to the principles of political independence, sovereign equality and territorial integrity of all States, and acknowledging that peace and security, development and human rights are the foundations for collective security,

Acknowledging the right of all States to manufacture, import, export, transfer and retain conventional arms for self-defence and security needs and in order to participate in peace support operations,

Acknowledging also the right of States to regulate internal transfers of arms and national ownership, including through national constitutional protections on private ownership, exclusively within their territory,

Recalling the obligations of all States to fully comply with arms embargoes decided by the Security Council in accordance with the Charter,

Reaffirming its respect for international law, including international human rights law and international humanitarian law, and the rights and responsibilities of every State under the Charter,

Noting and encouraging relevant initiatives undertaken at the international, regional and subregional levels between States, including those of the United Nations,

Taking note of the role played by non-governmental organizations and civil society to enhance cooperation, improve information exchange and transparency and assist States in implementing confidence-building measures in the field of responsible arms trade,

Recognizing that the absence of commonly agreed international standards for the transfer of conventional arms that address, inter alia, the problems relating to the unregulated trade of conventional arms and their diversion to the illicit market is a contributory factor to armed conflict, the displacement of people, organized crime and terrorism, thereby undermining peace, reconciliation, safety, security, stability and sustainable social and economic development,

Acknowledging the growing support across all regions for concluding a legally binding instrument, negotiated on a non-discriminatory, transparent and multilateral basis, to establish the highest possible common international standards for the import, export and transfer of conventional arms, including through several regional and subregional workshops and seminars held in order to discuss the initiative launched by the General Assembly in its resolution 61/89, as well as those sponsored by the European Union and organized through the United Nations Institute for Disarmament Research in different regions around the world,

Taking due note of the views expressed by Member States on the feasibility, scope and draft parameters for a comprehensive, legally binding instrument establishing common international standards for the import, export and transfer of conventional arms, submitted to the Secretary-General at his request,

Welcoming the report of the Group of Governmental Experts, which states that, in view of the complexity of the issues of conventional arms transfers, further consideration of efforts within the United Nations to address the international trade in conventional arms is required on a step-by-step basis in an open and transparent manner to achieve, on the basis of consensus, a balance that will provide benefit to all, with the principles of the Charter at the centre of such efforts,

Mindful of the need to prevent the diversion of conventional arms, including small arms and light weapons, from the legal to the illicit market,

1.　*Calls upon* all States to implement, on a national basis, the relevant recommendations contained in section VII of the report of the Group of Governmental Experts, recommends that all States carefully consider how to achieve such implementation in order to ensure that their national import and export control systems are of the highest possible standard, and urges those States in a position to do so to render assistance in this regard upon request;

2. *Endorses* the report of the Open-ended Working Group established by the General Assembly in its resolution 63/240 to further consider those elements in the report of the Group of Governmental Experts where consensus could be developed for their inclusion in an eventual legally binding treaty on the import, export and transfer of conventional arms, which provides a balance giving benefit to all, with the principles of the Charter of the United Nations and other existing international obligations at the centre of such considerations;

3. *Stresses* the need, as was underlined by consensus in the Open-ended Working Group, to address, inter alia, the problems relating to the unregulated trade in conventional weapons and their diversion to the illicit market, considering that such risks can fuel instability, transnational organized crime and terrorism, and that international action should be taken to address the problem;

4. *Decides*, therefore, to convene a United Nations Conference on the Arms Trade Treaty to meet for four consecutive weeks in 2012 to elaborate a legally binding instrument on the highest possible common international standards for the transfer of conventional arms;

5. *Also decides* that the United Nations Conference on the Arms Trade Treaty will be undertaken in an open and transparent manner, on the basis of consensus, to achieve a strong and robust treaty;

6. *Further decides* to consider the remaining sessions of the Open-ended Working Group in 2010 and 2011 as a preparatory committee for the United Nations Conference on the Arms Trade Treaty;

7. *Requests* the Preparatory Committee, at its four sessions in 2010 and 2011, to make recommendations to the United Nations Conference on the Arms Trade Treaty on the elements that would be needed to attain an effective and balanced legally binding instrument on the highest possible common international standards for the transfer of conventional arms, bearing in mind the views and recommendations expressed in the replies of Member States and those contained in the report of the Group of Governmental Experts and the report of the Open-ended Working Group, and to present a report containing those elements to the General Assembly at its sixty-sixth session;

8. *Decides* to establish a fifth session of the Preparatory Committee in 2012 of up to three days' duration to decide on all relevant procedural matters, including the composition of the Bureau, the draft agenda and the submission of documents, for the United Nations Conference on the Arms Trade Treaty;

9. *Requests* the Secretary-General to seek the views of Member States on proposed treaty elements and other relevant issues relating to the United Nations Conference on the Arms Trade Treaty, and to submit a report to the General Assembly at its sixty-sixth session;

10. *Decides* that intergovernmental organizations and specialized agencies, having received a standing invitation to participate as observers in the work of the General Assembly, may participate as observers in the sessions of the Preparatory Committee, and requests the Committee to take decisions on the modalities of attendance of non-governmental organizations at its sessions;

11. *Stresses* the need to ensure the widest possible and effective participation in the United Nations Conference on the Arms Trade Treaty in 2012;

12. *Requests* the Secretary-General to render the Preparatory Committee and the United Nations Conference on the Arms Trade Treaty all necessary assistance, including the provision of essential background information and relevant documents;

13. *Decides* to remain seized of the matter.

RECORDED VOTE ON RESOLUTION 64/48:

In favour: Afghanistan, Albania, Algeria, Andorra, Angola, Antigua and Barbuda, Argentina, Armenia, Australia, Austria, Azerbaijan, Bahamas, Bangladesh, Barbados, Belgium, Belize, Benin, Bhutan, Bosnia and Herzegovina, Botswana, Brazil, Brunei Darussalam, Bulgaria, Burkina Faso, Burundi, Cambodia, Cameroon, Canada, Cape Verde, Chile, Colombia, Comoros, Congo, Costa Rica, Côte d'Ivoire, Croatia, Cyprus, Czech Republic, Democratic Republic of the Congo, Denmark, Djibouti, Dominica, Dominican Republic, Ecuador, El Salvador, Equatorial Guinea, Eritrea, Estonia, Fiji, Finland, France, Gambia, Georgia, Germany, Ghana, Greece, Grenada, Guatemala, Guinea, Guinea-Bissau, Guyana, Haiti, Honduras, Hungary, Iceland, Indonesia, Iraq, Ireland, Israel, Italy, Jamaica, Japan, Jordan, Kazakhstan, Kenya, Latvia, Lebanon, Lesotho, Liberia, Liechtenstein, Lithuania, Luxembourg, Madagascar, Malawi, Malaysia, Maldives, Mali, Malta, Marshall Islands, Mauritania, Mauritius, Mexico, Micronesia, Moldova, Monaco, Mongolia, Montenegro, Morocco, Mozambique, Myanmar, Namibia, Nepal, Netherlands, New Zealand, Niger, Nigeria, Norway, Oman, Palau, Panama, Papua New Guinea, Paraguay, Peru, Philippines, Poland, Portugal, Republic of Korea, Romania, Saint Kitts and Nevis, Saint Lucia, Saint Vincent and the Grenadines, Samoa, San Marino, Senegal, Serbia, Sierra Leone, Singapore, Slovakia, Slovenia, Solomon Islands, Somalia, South Africa, Spain, Sri Lanka, Suriname, Swaziland, Sweden, Switzerland, Thailand, The former Yugoslav Republic of Macedonia, Togo, Tonga, Trinidad and Tobago, Tunisia, Turkey, Ukraine, United Kingdom, United Republic of Tanzania, United States, Uruguay, Zambia.

Against: Zimbabwe.

Abstaining: Bahrain, Belarus, Bolivia, China, Cuba, Egypt, India, Iran, Kuwait, Libyan Arab Jamahiriya, Nicaragua, Pakistan, Qatar, Russian Federation, Saudi Arabia, Sudan, Syrian Arab Republic, United Arab Emirates, Venezuela, Yemen.

Small arms

UN Programme of Action on illicit trade in small arms

The Third Biennial Meeting of States to Consider the Implementation of the Programme of Action to Prevent, Combat and Eradicate the Illicit Trade in Small Arms and Light Weapons in All Its Aspects [YUN 2008, p. 614] had stressed the importance of regional approaches to implement the 2001 Programme of Action [YUN 2001, p. 499] and the usefulness of convening regional meetings coordinated by the United Nations.

UNODA and regional sponsors organized a Pacific regional meeting (Sydney, Australia, 22–23 June) and a meeting for States in the Great Lakes region, the Horn of Africa and bordering States, and Southern Africa (Kigali, Rwanda, 8–9 July). The Sydney meeting issued draft regional implementation guidelines that covered national legislation for the control of small arms; illicit brokering; stockpile management; marking, record-keeping and tracing; and regional cooperation. The guidelines, tailored towards the region, aimed for achievement by the time of the Second Review Conference of the Programme of Action in 2012. The Kigali meeting emphasized the importance of the globally agreed sub-themes contained in the outcome document of the Third Biennial Meeting of States, namely to effectively respond to the problems of illicit arms brokering activities; to improve arms and ammunition stockpile management; and to implement the International Tracing Instrument. The meeting stressed that small arms control measures should be linked to wider peace and security and development efforts. Moreover, measures to curb small arms and light weapons supply would be more effective if demand factors were addressed simultaneously.

GENERAL ASSEMBLY ACTION

On 2 December [meeting 55], the General Assembly, on the recommendation of the First Committee [A/64/391], adopted **resolution 64/50** by recorded vote (180-0) [agenda item 96 *(x)*].

The illicit trade in small arms and light weapons in all its aspects

The General Assembly,

Recalling its resolution 63/72 of 2 December 2008 as well as all previous resolutions entitled "The illicit trade in small arms and light weapons in all its aspects", including resolution 56/24 V of 24 December 2001,

Emphasizing the importance of the continued and full implementation of the Programme of Action to Prevent, Combat and Eradicate the Illicit Trade in Small Arms and Light Weapons in All Its Aspects, adopted by the United Nations Conference on the Illicit Trade in Small Arms and Light Weapons in All Its Aspects,

Emphasizing also the importance of the continued and full implementation of the International Instrument to Enable States to Identify and Trace, in a Timely and Reliable Manner, Illicit Small Arms and Light Weapons (the International Tracing Instrument),

Recalling the commitment of States to the Programme of Action as the main framework for measures within the activities of the international community to prevent, combat and eradicate the illicit trade in small arms and light weapons in all its aspects,

Underlining the need for States to enhance their efforts to build national capacity for the effective implementation of the Programme of Action and the International Tracing Instrument,

Welcoming the early designation of Mexico as the Chair of the fourth biennial meeting of States to consider the implementation of the Programme of Action,

Welcoming also the efforts by Member States to submit, on a voluntary basis, national reports on their implementation of the Programme of Action,

Bearing in mind the importance of regular national reporting, which could greatly facilitate the rendering of international cooperation and assistance to affected States,

Noting the analysis of national reports prepared for the biennial meetings of States to consider the implementation of the Programme of Action by the United Nations Institute for Disarmament Research,

Taking into account the importance of regional approaches to the implementation of the Programme of Action,

Noting with satisfaction regional and subregional efforts being undertaken in support of the implementation of the Programme of Action, and commending the progress that has already been made in this regard, including tackling both supply and demand factors that are relevant to addressing the illicit trade in small arms and light weapons,

Welcoming the holding of such regional meetings in Australia, Nepal, Peru and Rwanda,

Recognizing that illicit brokering in small arms and light weapons is a serious problem that the international community should address urgently,

Recognizing also the efforts undertaken by nongovernmental organizations in the provision of assistance to States for the implementation of the Programme of Action,

Welcoming the coordinated efforts within the United Nations to implement the Programme of Action, including through developing the Programme of Action Implementation Support System, which forms an integrated clearing house for international cooperation and assistance for capacity-building in the area of small arms and light weapons,

Taking note of the report of the Secretary-General on the implementation of resolution 63/72,

1. *Underlines* the fact that the issue of the illicit trade in small arms and light weapons in all its aspects requires concerted efforts at the national, regional and international levels to prevent, combat and eradicate the illicit manufacture, transfer and circulation of small arms and light weapons and that their uncontrolled spread in many regions of the world has a wide range of humanitarian and socio-economic consequences and poses a serious threat to peace, reconciliation, safety, security, stability and sustainable development at the individual, local, national, regional and international levels;

2. *Encourages* all initiatives, including those of the United Nations, other international organizations, regional and subregional organizations, non-governmental organizations and civil society, for the successful implementation of the Programme of Action to Prevent, Combat and Eradicate the Illicit Trade in Small Arms and Light Weapons in All Its Aspects, and calls upon all Member States to

contribute towards the continued implementation of the Programme of Action at the national, regional and global levels;

3. *Encourages* States to implement the recommendations contained in the report of the Group of Governmental Experts established pursuant to resolution 60/81 to consider further steps to enhance international cooperation in preventing, combating and eradicating illicit brokering in small arms and light weapons;

4. *Recalls* its endorsement of the report adopted at the third biennial meeting of States to consider the implementation of the Programme of Action, and encourages all States to implement the measures highlighted in the section of the report entitled "The way forward";

5. *Encourages* all efforts to build national capacity for the effective implementation of the Programme of Action, including those highlighted in the report of the third biennial meeting of States;

6. *Decides* that, in conformity with the follow-up to the Programme of Action, the fourth biennial meeting of States to consider the national, regional and global implementation of the Programme of Action shall be held in New York from 14 to 18 June 2010;

7. *Recalls* that the meeting of States to consider the implementation of the International Instrument to Enable States to Identify and Trace, in a Timely and Reliable Manner, Illicit Small Arms and Light Weapons shall be held within the framework of the biennial meeting of States;

8. *Encourages* States at the fourth biennial meeting of States to promote substantive discussions on possible practical measures by sharing lessons learned in the implementation of practical measures highlighted in the report of the third biennial meeting of States;

9. *Encourages* States, as appropriate and where applicable, to develop common positions on issues relevant to the implementation of the Programme of Action and to present such common positions to the fourth biennial meeting of States;

10. *Encourages* States that have not yet done so to submit their national reports and, for those in a position to do so, to use the reporting template prepared by the United Nations Development Programme, and to include therein information on progress made in the implementation of the measures highlighted in the report of the third biennial meeting of States;

11. *Encourages* States to also submit, well in advance of the fourth biennial meeting of States, their national reports on the implementation of the International Tracing Instrument;

12. *Calls upon* all States to implement the International Tracing Instrument by, inter alia, including in their national reports the name and contact information of the national points of contact and information on national marking practices used to indicate country of manufacture and/or country of import, as applicable;

13. *Encourages* States, on a voluntary basis, to make increasing use of their national reports as another tool for communicating assistance needs and information on the resources and mechanisms available to address such needs, and encourages States in a position to render such assistance to make use of these national reports;

14. *Also encourages* States to identify, in cooperation with the Chair-designate, well in advance of the fourth biennial meeting of States, priority issues or topics of relevance in the illicit trade in small arms and light weapons in all its aspects, including their implementation challenges and opportunities, as well as any follow-up to the third biennial meeting of States;

15. *Recalls* its decision to convene an open-ended meeting of governmental experts for a period of one week, no later than in 2011, to address key implementation challenges and opportunities relating to particular issues and themes, including international cooperation and assistance;

16. *Also recalls* its decision to convene a conference to review progress made in the implementation of the Programme of Action, for a period of two weeks in New York, no later than in 2012;

17. *Encourages* interested States and international, regional and other relevant organizations in a position to do so, to convene regional meetings to consider and advance the implementation of the Programme of Action as well as the International Tracing Instrument in preparation for the fourth biennial meeting of States;

18. *Encourages* States to make use of the Programme of Action Implementation Support System and the United Nations Institute for Disarmament Research clearing house for matching assistance needs with potential donors as additional tools to facilitate global action on small arms and light weapons;

19. *Emphasizes* the need to facilitate the implementation at the national level of the Programme of Action through the strengthening of national coordination agencies or bodies and institutional infrastructure;

20. *Also emphasizes* the fact that initiatives by the international community with respect to international cooperation and assistance remain essential and complementary to national implementation efforts, as well as to those at the regional and global levels;

21. *Recognizes* the necessity for interested States to develop effective coordination mechanisms, where they do not exist, in order to match the needs of States with existing resources to enhance the implementation of the Programme of Action and to make international cooperation and assistance more effective;

22. *Encourages* States to consider, among other mechanisms, the coherent identification of needs, priorities, national plans and programmes that may require international cooperation and assistance from States and regional and international organizations in a position to do so;

23. *Encourages* civil society and relevant organizations to strengthen their cooperation and work with States at the respective national and regional levels to achieve the implementation of the Programme of Action;

24. *Requests* the Secretary-General to report to the General Assembly at its sixty-fifth session on the implementation of the present resolution;

25. *Decides* to include in the provisional agenda of its sixty-fifth session the item entitled "The illicit trade in small arms and light weapons in all its aspects".

RECORDED VOTE ON RESOLUTION 64/50:

In favour: Afghanistan, Albania, Algeria, Andorra, Angola, Antigua and Barbuda, Argentina, Armenia, Australia, Austria, Azerbaijan, Bahamas, Bahrain, Bangladesh, Barbados, Belarus, Belgium, Belize, Benin, Bhutan, Bolivia, Bosnia and Herzegovina, Botswana, Brazil, Brunei Darussalam, Bulgaria, Burkina Faso, Burundi, Cambodia, Cameroon, Canada, Cape Verde, Chile, China, Colombia, Comoros, Congo, Costa Rica, Côte d'Ivoire, Croatia, Cuba, Cyprus, Czech Republic, Democratic Republic of the Congo, Denmark, Djibouti, Dominica, Dominican Republic, Ecuador, Egypt, El Salvador, Equatorial Guinea, Eritrea, Estonia, Fiji, Finland, France, Gambia, Georgia, Germany, Ghana, Greece, Grenada, Guatemala, Guinea, Guinea-Bissau, Guyana, Haiti, Honduras, Hungary, Iceland, India, Indonesia, Iran, Iraq, Ireland, Israel, Italy, Jamaica, Japan, Jordan, Kazakhstan, Kenya, Kuwait, Kyrgyzstan, Lao People's Democratic Republic, Latvia, Lebanon, Lesotho, Liberia, Libyan Arab Jamahiriya, Liechtenstein, Lithuania, Luxembourg, Madagascar, Malawi, Malaysia, Maldives, Mali, Malta, Marshall Islands, Mauritania, Mauritius, Mexico, Micronesia, Moldova, Monaco, Mongolia, Montenegro, Morocco, Mozambique, Myanmar, Namibia, Nepal, Netherlands, New Zealand, Nicaragua, Niger, Nigeria, Norway, Oman, Pakistan, Palau, Panama, Papua New Guinea, Paraguay, Peru, Philippines, Poland, Portugal, Qatar, Republic of Korea, Romania, Russian Federation, Saint Kitts and Nevis, Saint Lucia, Saint Vincent and the Grenadines, Samoa, San Marino, Saudi Arabia, Senegal, Serbia, Seychelles, Sierra Leone, Singapore, Slovakia, Slovenia, Solomon Islands, Somalia, South Africa, Spain, Sri Lanka, Sudan, Suriname, Swaziland, Sweden, Switzerland, Syrian Arab Republic, Tajikistan, Thailand, The former Yugoslav Republic of Macedonia, Togo, Tonga, Trinidad and Tobago, Tunisia, Turkey, Turkmenistan, Uganda, Ukraine, United Arab Emirates, United Kingdom, United Republic of Tanzania, United States, Uruguay, Uzbekistan, Venezuela, Viet Nam, Yemen, Zambia, Zimbabwe.

Against: None.

Assistance to States for curbing illicit small arms traffic

Pursuant to General Assembly resolutions 63/66 [YUN 2008, p. 619] and 63/72 [ibid., p. 617], the Secretary-General in July reviewed [A/64/173] activities undertaken by the UN system, intergovernmental organizations and Member States to curb the illicit trade in small arms and light weapons, as well as implementation of the Programme of Action to Prevent, Combat and Eradicate the Illicit Trade in Small Arms and Light Weapons in All Its Aspects [YUN 2001, p. 499]. He noted that efforts to develop and implement small arms control measures had continued, with an increased emphasis not only on curbing the supply of illicit small arms and light weapons, but also on simultaneously stemming demand for those weapons. The reinvigoration of the Coordinating Action on Small Arms (CASA) mechanism, which brought together 22 UN system partners working to prevent violence and mitigate the impact of small arms and light weapons, was a reflection of the grow-

ing acknowledgement among UN entities of the importance of a coherent approach to small arms issues. CASA had been strengthening its coordination role, culminating in the endorsement of a strategic framework for 2009–2013 that included small arms demand and armed violence reduction issues. CASA had enhanced its capacity for information sharing since the launch in 2008 of the Programme of Action Implementation Support System [YUN 2008, p. 613], a web-based tool for stakeholders to contribute to the implementation of the Programme of Action. The UN system had been effective in setting technical standards in specific areas, such as mine action and disarmament, demobilization and reintegration. In the same vein, CASA had embarked on a project to develop international small arms control standards—a set of internationally accepted and validated technical standards that provided comprehensive guidance to practitioners and policymakers on legal, policy and operational issues surrounding small arms control. The project envisaged the completion of a set of standards by the Fourth Biennial Meeting of States to Consider the Implementation of the Programme of Action, scheduled for June 2010.

GENERAL ASSEMBLY ACTION

On 2 December [meeting 55], the General Assembly, on the recommendation of the First Committee [A/64/391], adopted **resolution 64/30** without vote [agenda item 96 *(u)*].

Assistance to States for curbing the illicit traffic in small arms and light weapons and collecting them

The General Assembly,

Recalling its resolution 63/66 of 2 December 2008 on assistance to States for curbing the illicit traffic in small arms and light weapons and collecting them,

Deeply concerned by the magnitude of human casualty and suffering, especially among children, caused by the illicit proliferation and use of small arms and light weapons,

Concerned by the negative impact that the illicit proliferation and use of those weapons continue to have on the efforts of States in the Sahelo-Saharan subregion in the areas of poverty eradication, sustainable development and the maintenance of peace, security and stability,

Bearing in mind the Bamako Declaration on an African Common Position on the Illicit Proliferation, Circulation and Trafficking of Small Arms and Light Weapons, adopted at Bamako on 1 December 2000,

Recalling the report of the Secretary-General entitled "In larger freedom: towards development, security and human rights for all", in which he emphasized that States must strive just as hard to eliminate the threat of illicit small arms and light weapons as they do to eliminate the threat of weapons of mass destruction,

Recalling also the International Instrument to Enable States to Identify and Trace, in a Timely and Reliable

Manner, Illicit Small Arms and Light Weapons, adopted on 8 December 2005,

Welcoming the expression of support in the 2005 World Summit Outcome for the implementation of the Programme of Action to Prevent, Combat and Eradicate the Illicit Trade in Small Arms and Light Weapons in All Its Aspects,

Welcoming also the adoption, at the thirtieth ordinary summit of the Economic Community of West African States, held in Abuja in June 2006, of the Convention on Small Arms and Light Weapons, Their Ammunition and Other Related Materials, in replacement of the moratorium on the importation, exportation and manufacture of small arms and light weapons in West Africa,

Welcoming further the decision taken by the Economic Community to establish a Small Arms Unit responsible for advocating appropriate policies and developing and implementing programmes, as well as the establishment of the Economic Community's Small Arms Control Programme, launched on 6 June 2006 in Bamako, in replacement of the Programme for Coordination and Assistance for Security and Development,

Taking note of the latest report of the Secretary-General on assistance to States for curbing the illicit traffic in small arms and light weapons and collecting them and the illicit trade in small arms and light weapons in all its aspects,

Welcoming, in that regard, the decision of the European Union to significantly support the Economic Community in its efforts to combat the illicit proliferation of small arms and light weapons,

Recognizing the important role that civil society organizations play, by raising public awareness, in efforts to curb the illicit traffic in small arms and light weapons,

Taking note of the report of the United Nations Conference to Review Progress Made in the Implementation of the Programme of Action to Prevent, Combat and Eradicate the Illicit Trade in Small Arms and Light Weapons in All Its Aspects, held in New York from 26 June to 7 July 2006,

1. *Commends* the United Nations and international, regional and other organizations for their assistance to States for curbing the illicit traffic in small arms and light weapons and collecting them;

2. *Encourages* the Secretary-General to pursue his efforts in the context of the implementation of General Assembly resolution 49/75 G of 15 December 1994 and the recommendations of the United Nations advisory missions aimed at curbing the illicit circulation of small arms and light weapons and collecting them in the affected States that so request, with the support of the United Nations Regional Centre for Peace and Disarmament in Africa and in close cooperation with the African Union;

3. *Encourages* the international community to support the implementation of the Economic Community of West African States Convention on Small Arms and Light Weapons, Their Ammunition and Other Related Materials;

4. *Encourages* the countries of the Sahelo-Saharan subregion to facilitate the effective functioning of national commissions to combat the illicit proliferation of small arms and light weapons, and, in that regard, invites the international community to lend its support wherever possible;

5. *Encourages* the collaboration of civil society organizations and associations in the efforts of the national commissions to combat the illicit traffic in small arms and light weapons and in the implementation of the Programme of Action to Prevent, Combat and Eradicate the Illicit Trade in Small Arms and Light Weapons in All Its Aspects;

6. *Also encourages* cooperation among State organs, international organizations and civil society in support of programmes and projects aimed at combating the illicit traffic in small arms and light weapons and collecting them;

7. *Calls upon* the international community to provide technical and financial support to strengthen the capacity of civil society organizations to take action to help to combat the illicit trade in small arms and light weapons;

8. *Invites* the Secretary-General and those States and organizations that are in a position to do so to continue to provide assistance to States for curbing the illicit traffic in small arms and light weapons and collecting them;

9. *Requests* the Secretary-General to continue to consider the matter and to report to the General Assembly at its sixty-fifth session on the implementation of the present resolution;

10. *Decides* to include in the provisional agenda of its sixty-fifth session the item entitled "Assistance to States for curbing the illicit traffic in small arms and light weapons and collecting them".

Stockpile management

In accordance with General Assembly resolution 61/72 [YUN 2006, p. 661], the Secretary-General in 2007 established a Group of Governmental Experts to consider further steps to enhance cooperation with regard to the issue of conventional ammunition stockpiles in surplus. The Group in 2008 issued recommendations [YUN 2008, p. 615] on measures to address the problem at the national, regional and global levels.

Acting on a recommendation of the Group, UNODA in 2009 embarked on a project for the development of technical guidelines for the management of stockpiles of conventional ammunition, which would be made available for States to use on a voluntary basis, in order to assist them in improving their national stockpile management capacity.

GENERAL ASSEMBLY ACTION

On 2 December [meeting 55], the General Assembly, on the recommendation of the First Committee [A/64/391], adopted **resolution 64/51** without vote [agenda item 96 *(r)*].

Problems arising from the accumulation of conventional ammunition stockpiles in surplus

The General Assembly,

Mindful of contributing to the process initiated within the framework of the United Nations reform to make the Organization more effective in maintaining peace and security by giving it the resources and tools it needs for conflict prevention, peaceful resolution of disputes, peacekeeping, post-conflict peacebuilding and reconstruction,

Underlining the importance of a comprehensive and integrated approach to disarmament through the development of practical measures,

Taking note of the report of the Group of Experts on the problem of ammunition and explosives,

Recalling the recommendation contained in paragraph 27 of the report submitted by the Chair of the Open-ended Working Group to Negotiate an International Instrument to Enable States to Identify and Trace, in a Timely and Reliable Manner, Illicit Small Arms and Light Weapons, namely, to address the issue of small arms and light weapons ammunition in a comprehensive manner as part of a separate process conducted within the framework of the United Nations,

Noting with satisfaction the work and measures pursued at the regional and subregional levels with regard to the issue of conventional ammunition,

Recalling its decision 59/515 of 3 December 2004 and its resolutions 60/74 of 8 December 2005 and 61/72 of 6 December 2006, as well as its resolution 63/61 of 2 December 2008, by which it welcomed the report of the Group of Governmental Experts established pursuant to resolution 61/72 to consider further steps to enhance cooperation with regard to the issue of conventional ammunition stockpiles in surplus and decided to include the issue of conventional ammunition stockpiles in surplus in the agenda of its sixty-fourth session,

1.   *Encourages* all interested States to assess, on a voluntary basis, whether, in conformity with their legitimate security needs, parts of their stockpiles of conventional ammunition should be considered to be in surplus, and recognizes that the security of such stockpiles must be taken into consideration and that appropriate controls with regard to the security and safety of stockpiles of conventional ammunition are indispensable at the national level in order to eliminate the risk of explosion, pollution or diversion;

2.   *Appeals* to all interested States to determine the size and nature of their surplus stockpiles of conventional ammunition, whether they represent a security risk, their means of destruction, if appropriate, and whether external assistance is needed to eliminate this risk;

3.   *Encourages* States in a position to do so to assist interested States within a bilateral framework or through international or regional organizations, on a voluntary and transparent basis, in elaborating and implementing programmes to eliminate surplus stockpiles or to improve their management;

4.   *Encourages* all Member States to examine the possibility of developing and implementing, within a national, regional or subregional framework, measures to address accordingly the illicit trafficking related to the accumulation of such stockpiles;

5.   *Takes note* of the replies submitted by Member States in response to the request of the Secretary-General for views regarding the risks arising from the accumulation of conventional ammunition stockpiles in surplus and regarding national ways of strengthening controls on conventional ammunition;

6.   *Strongly encourages* States to implement the recommendations of the report of the Group of Governmental Experts established pursuant to resolution 61/72 to consider further steps to enhance cooperation with regard to the issue of conventional ammunition stockpiles in surplus;

7.   *Continues to encourage* States in a position to do so to contribute, on a voluntary and transparent basis, to the development within the United Nations of technical guidelines for the stockpile management of conventional ammunition, which would be available for States to use on a voluntary basis, in order to assist States in improving their national stockpile management capacity, preventing the growth of conventional ammunition surpluses and addressing wider risk mitigation;

8.   *Reiterates its decision* to address the issue of conventional ammunition stockpiles in surplus in a comprehensive manner;

9.   *Decides* to include in the provisional agenda of its sixty-sixth session the item entitled "Problems arising from the accumulation of conventional ammunition stockpiles in surplus".

Convention on excessively injurious conventional weapons and Protocols

Status

As at 31 December, the accession of Kazakhstan, Qatar and the United Arab Emirates brought to 111 the number of States parties to the 1980 Convention on Prohibitions or Restrictions on the Use of Certain Conventional Weapons Which May Be Deemed to Be Excessively Injurious or to Have Indiscriminate Effects (ccw) and its annexed Protocols [YUN 1980, p. 76] on Non-Detectable Fragments (Protocol I); on Prohibitions or Restrictions on the Use of Mines, Booby Traps and Other Devices, as amended on 3 May 1996 (Protocol II) [YUN 1996, p. 484]; and on Prohibitions or Restrictions on the Use of Incendiary Weapons (Protocol III).

Amended Protocol II, which had entered into force on 3 December 1998 [YUN 1998, p. 844], had 93 parties. The 1995 Protocol on Blinding Laser Weapons (Protocol IV) [YUN 1995, p. 221], which took effect on 30 July 1998 [YUN 1998, p. 530], had 96 parties. The Protocol on Explosive Remnants of War (Protocol V), which was adopted in 2003 [YUN 2003, p. 566] and entered into force in 2006 [YUN 2006, p. 663], had 62 parties. The number of parties to the amendment to article I of the Convention, which entered into force on 18 May 2004 [YUN 2004, p. 563], stood at 73.

Group of Governmental Experts

The Group of Governmental Experts, established by the Second Review Conference of the States Parties to ccw [YUN 2001, p. 504], met in 2009 for two sessions (Geneva, 16–20 February, 14–17 April)

[CCW/GGE/2009-II/2]. States parties in 2008 [YUN 2008, p. 621] had mandated the Group to continue negotiations on a new protocol to the Convention that would address the humanitarian impact of cluster munitions while striking a balance between military and humanitarian considerations. The Group discussed the draft protocol's general provision and scope of application; definitions; protection of civilians, the civilian population and civilian objects during armed conflict; general prohibitions and restrictions; stockpile, storage, destruction, transfers, clearance and destruction of cluster munitions and their remnants; recording, retaining and transmission of information on the use or abandonment of cluster munitions; victim assistance; and other issues. The Chair's efforts, backed by the Friends of the Chair, resulted in incremental changes in the national positions of some key delegations. Despite their cooperation and flexibility, and despite some concessions by some key players, the text still remained unacceptable to many delegations. Based on the work of the two sessions and informal consultations held in August, the Chair, in his personal capacity, submitted a draft protocol [CCW/MSP/2009/WP.1] to the Meeting of the High Contracting Parties.

Meeting of High Contracting Parties

The Meeting of the High Contracting Parties to ccw (Geneva, 12–13 November) [CCW/MSP/2009/5] took note of the draft protocol submitted by the Chair of the Group of Governmental Experts. The Meeting decided that the Group would continue its negotiations, informed by the Chair's draft protocol and taking into account document CCW/GGE/2009-II/2, Annex I, on cluster munitions, along with other proposals by delegations; and that the Group would report to the next Meeting of the High Contracting Parties in 2010.

The Meeting emphasized the importance of compliance with the Convention and its annexed Protocols by all High Contracting Parties. It expressed satisfaction at the establishment and maintenance of a compliance database and a roster of experts, and decided to keep the issue of mines other than anti-personnel mines under consideration. The Meeting decided to establish an Implementation Support Unit within the UN Secretariat to assist States parties in their work.

Protocol V on explosive remnants of war

Meeting of Experts

The 2009 Protocol V Meeting of Experts (Geneva, 22–24 April) focused on five main topics identified by the First Conference of the High Contracting Parties to Protocol V [YUN 2007, p. 576]: clearance, removal or destruction of explosive remnants of war [CCW/P.V/CONF/2009/7]; victim assistance [CCW/P.V/CONF/2009/3]; cooperation and assistance and requests for assistance [CCW/P.V/CONF/2009/6]; national reporting [CCW/P.V/CONF/2009/4 & Add.1 & Add.1/Corr.1], including the article 4 generic electronic template for recording information [CCW/P.V/CONF/2009/5]; and generic preventive measures [CCW/P.V/CONF/2009/2 & Add.1]. Participants further developed the compliance and implementation tools.

Third Conference of High Contracting Parties to Protocol V

The Third Conference of the High Contracting Parties to Protocol V (Geneva, 9–10 November) welcomed 13 more countries that, since the Second Conference [YUN 2008, p. 622], had consented to be bound by Protocol V, bringing the total to 61 States parties. The Conference decided to continue the consideration of clearance, removal or destruction of explosive remnants of war and reiterated its invitation to all States in need of assistance to bring their case to the attention of the High Contracting Parties to Protocol V and make full use of the Protocol's implementation mechanism. The Conference decided to continue consideration of assistance to victims at future meetings. It also encouraged High Contracting Parties to identify themselves as requiring assistance or in the position to provide assistance for the purpose of matching needs and resources.

The Conference took note of the concept for a Web-based information system for Protocol V and decided to develop it. It decided that the Meeting of Experts should continue to consider the exchange of information on national procedures and experience in the implementation of Protocol V and the identification of the UN structure that could serve as the focal point for collecting and transmitting such information. It approved the draft "Guide to National Reporting under ccw Protocol V" and recommended that States parties use it in order to provide comprehensive information. It decided that the 2010 Meeting of Experts should complete the elaboration of the "Guide for the implementation of Part 3 of the Technical Annex", and continue to address one specific technical issue related to the implementation of article 9 and Part 3 of the Technical Annex, inviting States parties to share their technical approaches and experience in the matter.

The Conference adopted its report [CCW/P.V/CONF/2009/9], which contained the provisional agenda of the 2010 Conference and the mandate of the 2010 Meeting of Experts.

Amended Protocol II on Mines, Booby Traps and Other Devices

Group of Experts

The Group of Experts on Amended Protocol II on Mines, Booby Traps and Other Devices (Geneva, 20–21 April) reviewed the operation and status of the Protocol; considered matters arising from States parties' reports and the development of technologies to protect civilians against indiscriminate effects of mines; and addressed the issue of improvised explosive devices (IEDs). Two Friends of the President were appointed to assist him in his work. Abderrazzak Laassel (Morocco) helped review the operation and status of the Protocol, matters arising from reports by States parties, and the development of technologies to protect civilians against indiscriminate effects of mines [CCW/AP.II/CONF.11/3]; while Reto Wollenmann (Switzerland) helped review the issue of IEDs [CCW/AP.II/CONF.11/2]. Both reports were presented to the Eleventh Annual Conference (see below).

Annual Conference of States Parties

The Eleventh Annual Conference of the High Contracting Parties to Amended Protocol II to the CCW Convention (Geneva, 11 November) appealed to States that had not acceded to the Protocol to do so. It encouraged the States parties and the CCW secretariat to intensify their efforts to implement the Plan of Action to Promote the Universality of CCW [YUN 2006, p. 664], in particular by organizing national and regional seminars aimed at promoting and explaining CCW and its Protocols; and decided that the Group of Experts should analyse the implementation of the reporting obligations by States parties and the content of their national annual reports. The Conference also decided that the Group of Experts should consider the legal possibility and the feasibility of terminating the original CCW Protocol II and explore practical steps to address the challenges posed by IEDs. The Conference adopted its final document [CCW/AP.II/CONF.11/4 & Corr.1], which contained the mandate and dates of the 2010 Group of Experts.

GENERAL ASSEMBLY ACTION

On 2 December [meeting 55], the General Assembly, on the recommendation of the First Committee [A/64/395], adopted **resolution 64/67** without vote [agenda item 100].

Convention on Prohibitions or Restrictions on the Use of Certain Conventional Weapons Which May Be Deemed to Be Excessively Injurious or to Have Indiscriminate Effects

The General Assembly,

Recalling its resolution 63/85 of 2 December 2008,

Recalling with satisfaction the adoption and the entry into force of the Convention on Prohibitions or Restrictions on the Use of Certain Conventional Weapons Which May Be Deemed to Be Excessively Injurious or to Have Indiscriminate Effects, and its amended article 1, and the Protocol on Non-Detectable Fragments (Protocol I), the Protocol on Prohibitions or Restrictions on the Use of Mines, Booby Traps and Other Devices (Protocol II) and its amended version, the Protocol on Prohibitions or Restrictions on the Use of Incendiary Weapons (Protocol III), the Protocol on Blinding Laser Weapons (Protocol IV) and the Protocol on Explosive Remnants of War (Protocol V),

Welcoming the results of the Third Review Conference of the High Contracting Parties to the Convention on Prohibitions or Restrictions on the Use of Certain Conventional Weapons Which May Be Deemed to Be Excessively Injurious or to Have Indiscriminate Effects, held from 7 to 17 November 2006 in Geneva,

Welcoming also the results of the 2008 Meeting of the High Contracting Parties to the Convention, held on 13 and 14 November 2008 in Geneva,

Welcoming further the results of the Tenth Annual Conference of the High Contracting Parties to Amended Protocol II, held on 12 November 2008 in Geneva,

Welcoming the results of the Second Conference of the High Contracting Parties to Protocol V, held on 10 and 11 November 2008 in Geneva,

Recalling the role played by the International Committee of the Red Cross in the elaboration of the Convention and the Protocols thereto, and welcoming the particular efforts of various international, non-governmental and other organizations in raising awareness of the humanitarian consequences of explosive remnants of war,

1. *Calls upon* all States that have not yet done so to take all measures to become parties, as soon as possible, to the Convention on Prohibitions or Restrictions on the Use of Certain Conventional Weapons Which May Be Deemed to Be Excessively Injurious or to Have Indiscriminate Effects and the Protocols thereto, as amended, with a view to achieving the widest possible adherence to these instruments at an early date, and so as to ultimately achieve their universality;

2. *Calls upon* all States parties to the Convention that have not yet done so to express their consent to be bound by the Protocols to the Convention and the amendment extending the scope of the Convention and the Protocols thereto to include armed conflicts of a non-international character;

3. *Emphasizes* the importance of the universalization of the Protocol on Explosive Remnants of War (Protocol V);

4. *Welcomes* the additional ratifications and acceptances of or accessions to the Convention, as well as the consents to be bound by the Protocols thereto;

5. *Also welcomes* the adoption by the Third Review Conference of the High Contracting Parties to the Convention of a Plan of Action to promote universality of the Convention and its annexed Protocols, and expresses appreciation for the continued efforts of the Secretary-General, as depositary of the Convention and its annexed Protocols, the Chair of the Meeting of the High Contracting Parties to the Convention, the President of the Second Confer-

ence of the High Contracting Parties to Protocol V and the President of the Tenth Annual Conference of the High Contracting Parties to Amended Protocol II, on behalf of the High Contracting Parties, to achieve the goal of universality;

6. *Recalls* the decision by the Third Review Conference to establish a Sponsorship Programme within the framework of the Convention, and, with recognition of the value and importance of the programme, encourages States to contribute to the Sponsorship Programme;

7. *Welcomes* the commitment by States parties to continue to address the humanitarian problems caused by certain specific types of munitions in all their aspects, including cluster munitions, with a view to minimizing the humanitarian impact of these munitions;

8. *Expresses support* for the work conducted in 2009 by the Group of Governmental Experts of the High Contracting Parties to the Convention to continue its negotiations to address urgently the humanitarian impact of cluster munitions, while striking a balance between military and humanitarian considerations, in accordance with the mandate given to it by the Meeting of the High Contracting Parties, in November 2008;

9. *Welcomes* the commitment of States parties to the Protocol on Explosive Remnants of War (Protocol V) to the effective and efficient implementation of the Protocol and the implementation of the decisions of the First and Second Conferences of the High Contracting Parties to the Protocol establishing a comprehensive framework for the exchange of information and cooperation, and also welcomes the holding of the second Meeting of Experts of the High Contracting Parties to the Protocol, from 22 to 24 April 2009 in Geneva, as a mechanism for consultation and cooperation among the States parties;

10. *Notes* the decision of the Tenth Annual Conference of the High Contracting Parties to Amended Protocol II to establish an informal open-ended Group of Experts, and welcomes the holding of the first session of the Group of Experts of the High Contracting Parties to Amended Protocol II, on 20 and 21 April 2009 in Geneva, to exchange national practices and experiences and to assess the implementation of the Protocol;

11. *Also notes* that, in conformity with article 8 of the Convention, conferences may be convened to examine amendments to the Convention or to any of the Protocols thereto, to examine additional protocols concerning other categories of conventional weapons not covered by existing Protocols or to review the scope and application of the Convention and the Protocols thereto and to examine any proposed amendments or additional protocols;

12. *Requests* the Secretary-General to render the necessary assistance and to provide such services, including summary records, as may be required for the Third Conference of the High Contracting Parties to Protocol V, to be held on 9 and 10 November 2009, for the Eleventh Annual Conference of the High Contracting Parties to Amended Protocol II, to be held on 11 November 2009, and for the Meeting of the High Contracting Parties to the Convention, to be held on 12 and 13 November 2009, as well as for any continuation of work after the meetings;

13. *Also requests* the Secretary-General, in his capacity as depositary of the Convention and the Protocols thereto,

to continue to inform the General Assembly periodically, by electronic means, of ratifications and acceptances of and accessions to the Convention, its amended article 1 and the Protocols thereto;

14. *Decides* to include in the provisional agenda of its sixty-fifth session the item entitled "Convention on Prohibitions or Restrictions on the Use of Certain Conventional Weapons Which May Be Deemed to Be Excessively Injurious or to Have Indiscriminate Effects".

Cluster munitions

As at 31 December, the Convention on Cluster Munitions [YUN 2008, p. 623] had been signed by 104 States and ratified by 26. The Convention required four more ratifications for entry into force. The First Meeting of the States Parties was scheduled to be held in the Lao People's Democratic Republic in 2010. The Convention prohibited all use, stockpiling, production and transfer of cluster munitions causing unacceptable harm to civilians and provided for support to victims and affected communities.

GENERAL ASSEMBLY ACTION

On 2 December [meeting 55], the General Assembly, on the recommendation of the First Committee [A/64/391], adopted **resolution 64/36** without vote [agenda item 96].

Convention on Cluster Munitions

The General Assembly,

Recalling its resolution 63/71 of 2 December 2008,

Recalling also the conclusion of negotiations on the Convention on Cluster Munitions in Dublin on 30 May 2008 and the opening for signature of the Convention in Oslo on 3 December 2008, and thereafter at United Nations Headquarters pending its entry into force,

Noting the signature of the Convention on behalf of many States and the growing number of ratifications by signatories, which now approaches that required for entry into force of the Convention in accordance with its terms,

1. *Welcomes* the offer of the Government of the Lao People's Democratic Republic to host the First Meeting of States Parties to the Convention on Cluster Munitions following its entry into force;

2. *Requests* the Secretary-General, in accordance with article 11, paragraph 2, of the Convention, to undertake the preparations necessary to convene the First Meeting of States Parties to the Convention following its entry into force.

Anti-personnel mines
1997 Convention

The number of States parties to the Convention on the Prohibition of the Use, Stockpiling, Production and Transfer of Anti-personnel Mines and on Their Destruction (Mine-Ban Convention), which was adopted in 1997 [YUN 1997, p. 503], remained at 156 on the tenth anniversary of its entry into force in 1999 [YUN 1999, p. 498].

Second Review Conference

The Second Review Conference of the States Parties to the Mine-Ban Convention was held in Cartagena, Colombia, from 30 November to 4 December [APLC/CONF/2009/9], pursuant to a decision of the Ninth Meeting of the States Parties [YUN 2008, p. 624]. The Conference was attended by 108 States parties. Nineteen States non-parties, one signatory that had not ratified the Convention (Poland) and a number of international, regional and NGOs attended as observers. At its first six plenary meetings, the Conference reviewed the status and operation of the Convention and concluded that, while progress continued to be made, challenges remained.

The Conference agreed to extend deadlines for destruction of anti-personnel mines in mined areas under article 5 of the Convention by Argentina (until 1 January 2020), Cambodia (1 January 2020), Tajikistan (1 April 2020) and Uganda (1 August 2012). The Conference decided to hold annually, until a third review conference in 2014, a meeting of the States parties and intersessional meetings of the Standing Committees.

The Conference adopted three documents, included in its report: "Review of the operation and status of the Convention on the prohibition of the use, stockpiling, production and transfer of anti-personnel mines and on their destruction: 2005–2009", emphasizing that while great progress had been made in ending the suffering caused by anti-personnel mines, much more needed to be done; "Ending the suffering caused by anti-personnel mines: the Cartagena Action Plan 2010–2014", with the aim of supporting enhanced implementation and promotion of the Convention; and "A shared commitment for a mine-free world: the 2009 Cartagena Declaration". In the Declaration, States parties reaffirmed their adherence to the Convention's goals and appealed to those countries that had not ratified the Convention to do so.

GENERAL ASSEMBLY ACTION

On 2 December [meeting 55], the General Assembly, on the recommendation of the First Committee [A/64/391], adopted **resolution 64/56** by recorded vote (160-0-18) [agenda item 96].

Implementation of the Convention on the Prohibition of the Use, Stockpiling, Production and Transfer of Anti-personnel Mines and on Their Destruction

The General Assembly,

Recalling its resolutions 54/54 B of 1 December 1999, 55/33 V of 20 November 2000, 56/24 M of 29 November

2001, 57/74 of 22 November 2002, 58/53 of 8 December 2003, 59/84 of 3 December 2004, 60/80 of 8 December 2005, 61/84 of 6 December 2006, 62/41 of 5 December 2007 and 63/42 of 2 December 2008,

Reaffirming its determination to put an end to the suffering and casualties caused by anti-personnel mines, which kill or maim hundreds of people every week, mostly innocent and defenceless civilians, including children, obstruct economic development and reconstruction, inhibit the repatriation of refugees and internally displaced persons and have other severe consequences for years after emplacement,

Believing it necessary to do the utmost to contribute in an efficient and coordinated manner to facing the challenge of removing anti-personnel mines placed throughout the world and to assure their destruction,

Wishing to do the utmost in ensuring assistance for the care and rehabilitation, including the social and economic reintegration, of mine victims,

Recalling that 2009 marks the tenth anniversary of the entry into force of the Convention on the Prohibition of the Use, Stockpiling, Production and Transfer of Anti-personnel Mines and on Their Destruction,

Noting with satisfaction the work undertaken to implement the Convention and the substantial progress made towards addressing the global anti-personnel landmine problem,

Recalling the first to ninth meetings of the States parties to the Convention, held in Maputo (1999), Geneva (2000), Managua (2001), Geneva (2002), Bangkok (2003), Zagreb (2005), Geneva (2006), the Dead Sea (2007) and Geneva (2008) and the First Review Conference of the States Parties to the Convention, held in Nairobi (2004),

Recalling also the ninth meeting of the States parties to the Convention, held in Geneva from 24 to 28 November 2008, at which the international community monitored progress on implementation of the Convention, supported continued application of the Nairobi Action Plan 2005–2009, and established priorities to achieve further progress towards ending, for all people and for all time, the suffering caused by anti-personnel mines,

Recalling further the preparatory process for the Second Review Conference of the States Parties to the Convention on the Prohibition of the Use, Stockpiling, Production and Transfer of Anti-personnel Mines and on Their Destruction, entitled "The Cartagena Summit on a Mine-Free World", to be held in Cartagena, Colombia, from 29 November to 4 December 2009, and the two preparatory meetings held in 2009 pursuant to the decisions of the ninth meeting of the States parties,

Noting with satisfaction that one hundred and fifty-six States have ratified or acceded to the Convention and have formally accepted the obligations of the Convention,

Emphasizing the desirability of attracting the adherence of all States to the Convention, and determined to work strenuously towards the promotion of its universalization,

Noting with regret that anti-personnel mines continue to be used in conflicts around the world, causing human suffering and impeding post-conflict development,

1. *Invites* all States that have not signed the Convention on the Prohibition of the Use, Stockpiling, Production and Transfer of Anti-personnel Mines and on Their Destruction to accede to it without delay;

2. *Urges* all States that have signed but have not ratified the Convention to ratify it without delay;

3. *Stresses* the importance of the full and effective implementation of and compliance with the Convention, including through the continued implementation of the Nairobi Action Plan 2005–2009;

4. *Urges* all States parties to provide the Secretary-General with complete and timely information as required under article 7 of the Convention in order to promote transparency and compliance with the Convention;

5. *Invites* all States that have not ratified the Convention or acceded to it to provide, on a voluntary basis, information to make global mine action efforts more effective;

6. *Renews its call upon* all States and other relevant parties to work together to promote, support and advance the care, rehabilitation and social and economic reintegration of mine victims, mine risk education programmes and the removal and destruction of anti-personnel mines placed or stockpiled throughout the world;

7. *Urges* all States to remain seized of the issue at the highest political level and, where in a position to do so, to promote adherence to the Convention through bilateral, subregional, regional and multilateral contacts, outreach, seminars and other means;

8. *Reiterates its invitation and encouragement* to all interested States, the United Nations, other relevant international organizations or institutions, regional organizations, the International Committee of the Red Cross and relevant non-governmental organizations to attend the Second Review Conference of the States Parties to the Convention, entitled "The Cartagena Summit on a Mine-Free World", at the highest possible level and, pending a decision to be taken at the Second Review Conference, to participate in the future meetings programme;

9. *Requests* the Secretary-General, in accordance with article 11, paragraph 2, of the Convention, to undertake the preparations necessary to convene the next meeting of the States parties, pending a decision to be taken at the Second Review Conference, and on behalf of the States parties and in accordance with article 11, paragraph 4, of the Convention, to invite States not parties to the Convention, as well as the United Nations, other relevant international organizations or institutions, regional organizations, the International Committee of the Red Cross and relevant non-governmental organizations, to attend the Second Review Conference and future meetings as observers;

10. *Decides* to remain seized of the matter.

RECORDED VOTE ON RESOLUTION 64/56:

In favour: Afghanistan, Albania, Algeria, Andorra, Angola, Antigua and Barbuda, Argentina, Armenia, Australia, Austria, Azerbaijan, Bahamas, Bahrain, Bangladesh, Barbados, Belarus, Belgium, Belize, Benin, Bhutan, Bolivia, Bosnia and Herzegovina, Botswana, Brazil, Brunei Darussalam, Bulgaria, Burkina Faso, Burundi, Cambodia, Cameroon, Canada, Cape Verde, Chile, China, Colombia, Comoros, Congo, Costa Rica, Côte d'Ivoire, Croatia, Cyprus, Czech Republic, Democratic Republic of the Congo, Denmark, Djibouti, Dominica, Dominican Republic, Ecuador, El Salvador, Equatorial Guinea, Eritrea, Estonia, Fiji, Finland, France, Gambia, Georgia, Germany, Ghana, Greece, Grenada, Guatemala, Guinea, Guinea-Bissau, Guyana, Haiti, Honduras, Hungary, Iceland, Indonesia, Iraq, Ireland, Italy, Jamaica, Japan, Jordan, Kazakhstan, Kenya, Kuwait, Lao People's Democratic Republic, Latvia, Lesotho, Liberia, Liechtenstein, Lithuania, Luxembourg, Madagascar, Malawi, Malaysia, Maldives, Mali, Malta, Marshall Islands, Mauritania, Mauritius, Mexico, Micronesia, Moldova, Monaco, Mongolia, Montenegro, Morocco, Mozambique, Namibia, Netherlands, New Zealand, Niger, Nigeria, Norway, Oman, Palau, Panama, Papua New Guinea, Paraguay, Peru, Philippines, Poland, Portugal, Qatar, Romania, Saint Kitts and Nevis, Saint Lucia, Saint Vincent and the Grenadines, Samoa, San Marino, Senegal, Serbia, Sierra Leone, Singapore, Slovakia, Slovenia, Solomon Islands, Somalia, South Africa, Spain, Sri Lanka, Sudan, Suriname, Swaziland, Sweden, Switzerland, Tajikistan, Thailand, The former Yugoslav Republic of Macedonia, Togo, Tonga, Trinidad and Tobago, Tunisia, Turkey, Turkmenistan, Uganda, Ukraine, United Arab Emirates, United Kingdom, United Republic of Tanzania, Uruguay, Venezuela, Yemen, Zambia, Zimbabwe.

Against: None.

Abstaining: Cuba, Democratic People's Republic of Korea, Egypt, India, Iran, Israel, Kyrgyzstan, Lebanon, Libyan Arab Jamahiriya, Myanmar, Nepal, Pakistan, Republic of Korea, Russian Federation, Syrian Arab Republic, United States, Uzbekistan, Viet Nam.

Practical disarmament

The Disarmament Commission [A/64/42] included in its agenda the item "Practical confidence-building measures in the field of conventional weapons", but noted that the item would be taken up upon the conclusion of the elements of a draft declaration of the 2010s as the fourth disarmament decade, preferably by 2010 and in any case no later than 2011.

Transparency

While there was a decline in the number of States participating in the United Nations Register of Conventional Arms, there was an increase in the percentage of reports that referred to small arms. A Group of Governmental Experts was unable to reach a consensus on the inclusion of small arms as a new item in the Register. With respect to the Standardized Instrument for Reporting Military Expenditures, 2009 marked the lowest level of reporting since 2001.

Conference on Disarmament. During the general debate of the Conference [A/64/27], delegations reaffirmed or further elaborated their respective positions on "Transparency in armaments", an item also discussed at two informal meetings (17 February, 5 March) [CD/1877, Annex VII] where little real progress was achieved. Following the two meetings, the coordinator proposed that the issue of "increase in military expenditure and the necessity to make more effective the existing transparency measures", which arose during 2008 and was mentioned by several delegations in 2009, be highlighted for future discussions. Delegations said that the proposal was inspiring in its effort to shed light on common positions, and in principle they had no objection to it. Some delegations questioned the mandate of the informal discussion under the role of the Conference and commented on the work on military expenditure that was under way elsewhere, for instance in the framework of the General Assembly's First Committee. Delegations expressed support for continuing discussions, thus allowing Member States to share information on their policies and initiatives to increase transparency in armaments.

UN Register of Conventional Arms

In response to General Assembly resolution 63/69 [YUN 2008, p. 628], the Secretary-General in July submitted the seventeenth annual report on the United Nations Register of Conventional Arms [A/64/135 & Add.1–3], established in 1992 [YUN 1992, p. 75] to promote enhanced levels of transparency on arms transfers. The report presented information for the year 2008, provided by 80 countries, on imports and exports in the seven categories of conventional arms (battle tanks, armoured combat vehicles, large-calibre artillery systems, attack helicopters, combat aircraft, warships and missiles, and missile launchers). Governments also provided information on conventional arms transfers, military holdings, procurement through national production, and international transfers of small arms and light weapons. The report highlighted numerous activities undertaken by UNODA, in collaboration with Governments and regional organizations, to enhance awareness of the Register and encourage greater participation in it. Furthermore, UNODA produced background publications which could be accessed on its website.

In August [A/64/296], pursuant to resolution 63/69, the Secretary-General forwarded to the Assembly the report of the Group of Governmental Experts on the continuing operation of the Register and its further development. The report examined ways to improve the relevance of and promote universal participation in the Register; provided up-to-date data and analysis on information reported by States; assessed the operation of the Register, including regional priorities and relevance; and examined issues related to the further development of the Register, taking into account advanced armament technology, security and capacity concerns and emerging tactical methods. The Group considered expanding the reporting categories and adding new categories to the Register, representing both a new class of equipment that was just beginning to be widely used in combat operations and a category of small arms and light weapons. However, the Group was unable to reach consensus on expanding the Register's scope and adapting it to new political and military circumstances.

The Group encouraged increased and consistent participation by States in the Register in order to promote universality. In that regard, it recommended that the UN Secretariat continue to assist Member States to build capacity to submit meaningful reports, including capacity to report on small arms and light weapons, and encourage States to submit "nil" returns where appropriate. The Group recommended that the Secretary-General seek the views of Member States, including whether the continued absence of small arms and light weapons as a main category in the Register had limited its relevance and affected decisions on the participation of Member States in the instrument.

GENERAL ASSEMBLY ACTION

On 2 December [meeting 55], the General Assembly, on the recommendation of the First Committee [A/64/391], adopted **resolution 64/54** by recorded vote (153-0-23) [agenda item 96 *(w)*].

Transparency in armaments

The General Assembly,

Recalling its resolutions 46/36 L of 9 December 1991, 47/52 L of 15 December 1992, 48/75 E of 16 December 1993, 49/75 C of 15 December 1994, 50/70 D of 12 December 1995, 51/45 H of 10 December 1996, 52/38 R of 9 December 1997, 53/77 V of 4 December 1998, 54/54 O of 1 December 1999, 55/33 U of 20 November 2000, 56/24 Q of 29 November 2001, 57/75 of 22 November 2002, 58/54 of 8 December 2003, 60/226 of 23 December 2005, 61/77 of 6 December 2006 and 63/69 of 2 December 2008, entitled "Transparency in armaments",

Continuing to take the view that an enhanced level of transparency in armaments contributes greatly to confidence-building and security among States and that the establishment of the United Nations Register of Conventional Arms constitutes an important step forward in the promotion of transparency in military matters,

Welcoming the consolidated report of the Secretary-General on the Register, which includes the returns of Member States for 2008,

Welcoming also the response of Member States to the request contained in paragraphs 9 and 10 of resolution 46/36 L to provide data on their imports and exports of arms, as well as available background information regarding their military holdings, procurement through national production and relevant policies,

Welcoming further the inclusion by some Member States of their transfers of small arms and light weapons in their annual report to the Register as part of their additional background information,

Noting the focused discussions on transparency in armaments that took place in the Conference on Disarmament in 2009,

Noting with concern the reduction in reporting to the United Nations Register of Conventional Arms in the last two years,

Stressing that the continuing operation of the Register and its further development should be reviewed in order to secure a Register that is capable of attracting the widest possible participation,

1. *Reaffirms its determination* to ensure the effective operation of the United Nations Register of Conventional Arms, as provided for in paragraphs 7 to 10 of resolution 46/36 L;

2. *Endorses* the report of the Secretary-General on the continuing operation of the Register and its further development and the recommendations contained in the consensus report of the 2009 group of governmental experts;

3. *Calls upon* Member States, with a view to achieving universal participation, to provide the Secretary-General, by 31 May annually, with the requested data and information for the Register, including nil reports if appropriate, on the basis of resolutions 46/36 L and 47/52 L, the recommendations contained in paragraph 64 of the 1997 report of the Secretary-General on the continuing operation of the Register and its further development, the recommendations contained in paragraph 94 of the 2000 report of the Secretary-General and the appendices and annexes thereto, the recommendations contained in paragraphs 112 to 114 of the 2003 report of the Secretary-General, the recommendations contained in paragraphs 123 to 127 of the 2006 report of the Secretary-General and the recommendations contained in paragraphs 71 to 75 of the 2009 report of the Secretary-General;

4. *Invites* Member States in a position to do so, pending further development of the Register, to provide additional information on procurement through national production and military holdings and to make use of the "Remarks" column in the standardized reporting form to provide additional information such as types or models;

5. *Also invites* Member States in a position to do so to provide additional information on transfers of small arms and light weapons on the basis of the optional standardized reporting form, as adopted by the 2006 group of governmental experts, or by any other methods they deem appropriate;

6. *Reaffirms* its decision, with a view to further development of the Register, to keep the scope of and participation in the Register under review and, to that end:

(a) Recalls its request to Member States to provide the Secretary-General with their views on the continuing operation of the Register and its further development and on transparency measures related to weapons of mass destruction;

(b) Requests the Secretary-General to seek the views of Member States, including whether the absence of small arms and light weapons as a main category in the Register has limited its relevance and directly affected decisions on participation;

(c) Requests the Secretary-General to continue to assist Member States to build capacity to submit meaningful reports, including capacity to report on small arms and light weapons;

(d) Requests the Secretary-General, with a view to the three-year review cycle of the Register, to ensure that sufficient resources are made available for a group of governmental experts to be convened in 2012 to review the continuing operation of the Register and its further development, taking into account the work of the Conference on Disarmament, the views expressed by Member States and the reports of the Secretary-General on the continuing operation of the Register and its further development;

7. *Requests* the Secretary-General to implement the recommendations contained in his 2000, 2003, 2006 and 2009 reports on the continuing operation of the Register and its further development and to ensure that sufficient resources are made available for the Secretariat to operate and maintain the Register;

8. *Invites* the Conference on Disarmament to consider continuing its work undertaken in the field of transparency in armaments;

9. *Reiterates its call upon* all Member States to cooperate at the regional and subregional levels, taking fully into account the specific conditions prevailing in the region or subregion, with a view to enhancing and coordinating international efforts aimed at increased openness and transparency in armaments;

10. *Requests* the Secretary-General to report to the General Assembly at its sixty-fifth session on progress made in implementing the present resolution;

11. *Decides* to include in the provisional agenda of its sixty-sixth session the item entitled "Transparency in armaments".

RECORDED VOTE ON RESOLUTION 64/54:

In favour: Afghanistan, Albania, Andorra, Angola, Antigua and Barbuda, Argentina, Armenia, Australia, Austria, Azerbaijan, Bahamas, Bangladesh, Barbados, Belarus, Belgium, Belize, Benin, Bhutan, Bolivia, Bosnia and Herzegovina, Botswana, Brazil, Brunei Darussalam, Bulgaria, Burkina Faso, Burundi, Cambodia, Canada, Cape Verde, Chile, China, Colombia, Comoros, Congo, Costa Rica, Côte d'Ivoire, Croatia, Cyprus, Czech Republic, Democratic Republic of the Congo, Denmark, Dominica, Dominican Republic, Ecuador, El Salvador, Equatorial Guinea, Eritrea, Estonia, Fiji, Finland, France, Gambia, Georgia, Germany, Ghana, Greece, Grenada, Guatemala, Guinea, Guinea-Bissau, Guyana, Haiti, Honduras, Hungary, Iceland, India, Indonesia, Ireland, Israel, Italy, Jamaica, Japan, Kazakhstan, Kenya, Kyrgyzstan, Lao People's Democratic Republic, Latvia, Lesotho, Liberia, Liechtenstein, Lithuania, Luxembourg, Madagascar, Malawi, Malaysia, Maldives, Mali, Malta, Marshall Islands, Mauritius, Mexico, Micronesia, Moldova, Monaco, Mongolia, Montenegro, Mozambique, Namibia, Nepal, Netherlands, New Zealand, Nicaragua, Niger, Nigeria, Norway, Pakistan, Palau, Panama, Papua New Guinea, Paraguay, Peru, Philippines, Poland, Portugal, Republic of Korea, Romania, Russian Federation, Saint Kitts and Nevis, Saint Lucia, Saint Vincent and the Grenadines, Samoa, San Marino, Senegal, Serbia, Sierra Leone, Singapore, Slovakia, Slovenia, Solomon Islands, South Africa, Spain, Sri Lanka, Suriname, Swaziland, Sweden, Switzerland, Tajikistan, Thailand, The former Yugoslav Republic of Macedonia, Togo, Tonga, Trinidad and Tobago, Turkey, Turkmenistan, Ukraine, United Kingdom, United Republic of Tanzania, United States, Uruguay, Uzbekistan, Venezuela, Zambia, Zimbabwe.

Against: None.

Abstaining: Algeria, Bahrain, Cuba, Djibouti, Egypt, Iran, Iraq, Jordan, Kuwait, Lebanon, Libyan Arab Jamahiriya, Mauritania, Morocco, Myanmar, Oman, Qatar, Saudi Arabia, Somalia, Sudan, Syrian Arab Republic, Tunisia, United Arab Emirates, Yemen.

Also on 2 December [meeting 55], the General Assembly, on the recommendation of the First Committee [A/64/391], adopted **resolution 64/40** without vote [agenda item 96].

National legislation on transfer of arms, military equipment and dual-use goods and technology

The General Assembly,

Recognizing that disarmament, arms control and non-proliferation are essential for the maintenance of international peace and security,

Recalling that effective national control of the transfer of arms, military equipment and dual-use goods and technology, including those transfers that could contribute to proliferation activities, is an important tool for achieving those objectives,

Recalling also that the States parties to the international disarmament and non-proliferation treaties have undertaken to facilitate the fullest possible exchange of materials, equipment and technological information for peaceful purposes, in accordance with the provisions of those treaties,

Considering that the exchange of national legislation, regulations and procedures on the transfer of arms, military equipment and dual-use goods and technology contributes to mutual understanding and confidence among Member States,

Convinced that such an exchange would be beneficial to Member States that are in the process of developing such legislation,

Welcoming the electronic database established by the Office for Disarmament Affairs, in which all information exchanged pursuant to General Assembly resolutions 57/66 of 22 November 2002, 58/42 of 8 December 2003, 59/66 of 3 December 2004, 60/69 of 8 December 2005 and 62/26 of 5 December 2007, entitled "National legislation on transfer of arms, military equipment and dual-use goods and technology", can be consulted,

Reaffirming the inherent right of individual or collective self-defence in accordance with Article 51 of the Charter of the United Nations,

1. *Invites* Member States that are in a position to do so, without prejudice to the provisions contained in Security Council resolution 1540(2004) of 28 April 2004 and subsequent relevant Council resolutions, to enact or improve national legislation, regulations and procedures to exercise effective control over the transfer of arms, military equipment and dual-use goods and technology, while ensuring that such legislation, regulations and procedures are consistent with the obligations of States parties under international treaties;

2. *Encourages* Member States to provide, on a voluntary basis, information to the Secretary-General on their national legislation, regulations and procedures on the transfer of arms, military equipment and dual-use goods and technology, as well as the changes therein, and requests the Secretary-General to make that information accessible to Member States;

3. *Decides* to remain attentive to the matter.

Transparency of military expenditures

In response to General Assembly resolution 62/13 [YUN 2007, p. 579], the Secretary-General, in a report issued in June with later addenda [A/64/113 & Add.1,2], presented reports from 58 States on their military expenditures for the latest fiscal year for which data were available. As requested by the resolution, UNODA organized a workshop on transparency in armaments for West African States (Dakar, Senegal, 9–10 June), which devoted one session to the United Nations Standardized Instrument for Reporting Military Expenditures.

GENERAL ASSEMBLY ACTION

On 2 December [meeting 55], the General Assembly, on the recommendation of the First Committee [A/64/381], adopted **resolution 64/22** without vote [agenda item 86 *(b)*].

Objective information on military matters, including transparency of military expenditures

The General Assembly,

Recalling its resolutions 53/72 of 4 December 1998, 54/43 of 1 December 1999, 56/14 of 29 November 2001, 58/28 of 8 December 2003, 60/44 of 8 December 2005 and 62/13 of 5 December 2007 on objective information on military matters, including transparency of military expenditures,

Recalling also its resolution 35/142 B of 12 December 1980, which introduced the United Nations system for the standardized reporting of military expenditures, its resolutions 48/62 of 16 December 1993, 49/66 of 15 December 1994, 51/38 of 10 December 1996 and 52/32 of 9 December 1997, calling upon all Member States to participate in it, and its resolution 47/54 B of 9 December 1992, endorsing the guidelines and recommendations for objective information on military matters and inviting Member States to provide the Secretary-General with relevant information regarding their implementation,

Noting that, since then, national reports on military expenditures and on the guidelines and recommendations for objective information on military matters have been submitted by a number of Member States belonging to different geographical regions,

Convinced that the improvement of international relations forms a sound basis for promoting further openness and transparency in all military matters,

Convinced also that transparency in military matters is an essential element for building a climate of trust and confidence between States worldwide and that a better flow of objective information on military matters can help to relieve international tension and is therefore an important contribution to conflict prevention,

Noting the role of the standardized reporting system, as instituted through its resolution 35/142 B, as an important instrument to enhance transparency in military matters,

Conscious that the value of the standardized reporting system would be enhanced by a broader participation of Member States,

Noting that the continuing operation of the standardized reporting system should be reviewed with a view to improving its further development and to broadening participation in it,

Welcoming, therefore, the report of the Secretary-General on ways and means to implement the guidelines and recommendations for objective information on military matters, including, in particular, how to strengthen and broaden participation in the standardized reporting system,

Recalling that the guidelines and recommendations for objective information on military matters recommended certain areas for further consideration, such as the improvement of the standardized reporting system,

Noting the efforts of several regional organizations to promote transparency of military expenditures, including standardized annual exchanges of relevant information among their member States,

Recalling the establishment of a group of governmental experts, on the basis of equitable geographical representation, to review the operation and further development of the Standardized Instrument for Reporting Military Expenditures, commencing in 2010, taking into account the views expressed by Member States on the subject and the reports of the Secretary-General on objective information on military matters, including transparency of military expenditures,

Emphasizing the continuing importance of the Standardized Instrument under the current political and economic circumstances,

1. *Calls upon* Member States to report annually to the Secretary-General, by 30 April, their military expenditures for the latest fiscal year for which data are available, using, preferably and to the extent possible, the reporting instrument as recommended in its resolution 35/142 B or, as appropriate, any other format developed in conjunction with similar reporting on military expenditures to other international or regional organizations, and, in the same context, encourages Member States to submit nil returns, if appropriate;

2. *Recommends* the guidelines and recommendations for objective information on military matters to all Member States for implementation, fully taking into account specific political, military and other conditions prevailing in a region, on the basis of initiatives and with the agreement of the States of the region concerned;

3. *Encourages* relevant international bodies and regional organizations to promote transparency of military expenditures and to enhance complementarities among reporting systems, taking into account the particular characteristics of each region, and to consider the possibility of an exchange of information with the United Nations;

4. *Takes note* of the reports of the Secretary-General;

5. *Requests* the Secretary-General, within available resources:

(a) To continue the practice of sending an annual note verbale to Member States requesting the submission of data to the United Nations system for the standardized reporting of military expenditures, together with the reporting format and related instructions, and to publish in a timely fashion in appropriate United Nations media the due date for transmitting data on military expenditures;

(b) To circulate annually the reports on military expenditures as received from Member States, taking into account in his 2010 report the information received from Member States in accordance with paragraph 6 (b) below;

(c) To transmit the report of the group of governmental experts to the General Assembly for consideration at its sixty-sixth session;

(d) To continue consultations with relevant international bodies, with a view to ascertaining requirements for adjusting the present instrument, with a view to encouraging wider participation, and to make recommendations, based on the outcome of those consultations and taking into account the views of Member States, on necessary changes to the content and structure of the standardized reporting system;

(e) To encourage relevant international bodies and organizations to promote transparency of military expenditures and to consult with those bodies and organizations with emphasis on examining possibilities for enhancing complementarities among international and regional reporting systems and for exchanging related information between those bodies and the United Nations;

(f) To encourage the United Nations regional centres for peace and disarmament in Africa, in Asia and the Pacific, and in Latin America and the Caribbean to assist Member States in their regions in enhancing their knowledge of the standardized reporting system;

(g) To promote international and regional/subregional symposiums and training seminars to explain the purpose of the standardized reporting system and to give relevant technical instructions;

(h) To report on experiences gained during such symposiums and training seminars;

6. *Encourages* Member States:

(a) To inform the Secretary-General about possible problems with the standardized reporting system and their reasons for not submitting the requested data;

(b) To continue to provide the Secretary-General with their views and suggestions on ways and means to improve the future functioning of and broaden participation in the standardized reporting system, including necessary changes to its content and structure, which could be taken into account by the group of governmental experts during its mandated activity;

7. *Decides* to include in the provisional agenda of its sixty-sixth session the item entitled "Objective information on military matters, including transparency of military expenditures".

Verification

On 2 December, the General Assembly decided to include in the provisional agenda of its sixty-sixth (2011) session the item entitled "Verification in all its aspects, including the role of the United Nations in the field of verification" (**decision 64/512**).

Other disarmament issues

Prevention of an arms race in outer space

Conference on Disarmament. Delegations discussed the prevention of an arms race in outer space at two informal meetings on 10 and 24 February [CD/1877, Annex III], drawing on the discussions in 2008 on transparency and confidence-building measures and on legally binding instruments. Several delegations noted that the issue to be addressed was the placement or use of weapons in space and not the militarization of space, which had already occurred. On legally binding instruments, discussions focused on the Russian-Chinese draft "Treaty on the Prevention of the Placement of Weapons in Outer Space and of the Threat or Use of Force against Outer Space Objects", which had been submitted in 2008 [YUN 2008, p. 631]. In a letter of 18 August to the Conference, China and the Russian Federation transmitted their answers [CD/1872] to the principal questions and comments on their draft. Many delegations supported continued discussions on the draft treaty and welcomed the contributions made by the Russian Federation and China.

On transparency and confidence-building measures in outer space activities, most delegations supported the view that such measures could foster greater trust and serve as a complementary or even as a stand-alone measure. Some delegations, however, opposed the idea of those measures serving as a substitute for a legally binding instrument, as they did not believe that they could fill the gaps in the legal regime. Most delegations expressed interest in starting substantive discussions on outer space within the framework of an agreed programme of work in the Conference. Some delegations expressed optimism that a possible shift in the position of the new United States Administration could add a new element to the discussions.

Report of Secretary-General. Pursuant to General Assembly resolution 63/68 [YUN 2008, p. 633], the Secretary-General in July issued a report with a later addendum [A/64/138 & Add.1], containing proposals from 13 countries (Argentina, Canada, China, Colombia, Cuba, Czech Republic on behalf of the EU, Lebanon, Mexico, Nicaragua, Qatar, Russian Federation, Syria, Ukraine) on international outer space transparency and confidence-building measures in the interest of maintaining international peace and security and promoting international cooperation and the prevention of an arms race in outer space.

The EU drew attention to its draft code of conduct for outer space activities. The draft code covered civil as well as military outer space activities and was based on three principles: freedom of access to space for all

for peaceful purposes; preservation of the security and integrity of space objects in orbit; and due consideration for the legitimate defence interests of States. The voluntary code would be applicable to all outer space activities conducted by States and non-governmental entities under the jurisdiction of a subscribing State, including the activities carried out within the framework of international intergovernmental organizations.

GENERAL ASSEMBLY ACTION

On 2 December [meeting 55], the General Assembly, on the recommendation of the First Committee [A/64/389], adopted **resolution 64/28** by recorded vote (176-0-2) [agenda item 94].

Prevention of an arms race in outer space

The General Assembly,

Recognizing the common interest of all mankind in the exploration and use of outer space for peaceful purposes,

Reaffirming the will of all States that the exploration and use of outer space, including the Moon and other celestial bodies, shall be for peaceful purposes and shall be carried out for the benefit and in the interest of all countries, irrespective of their degree of economic or scientific development,

Reaffirming also the provisions of articles III and IV of the Treaty on Principles Governing the Activities of States in the Exploration and Use of Outer Space, including the Moon and Other Celestial Bodies,

Recalling the obligation of all States to observe the provisions of the Charter of the United Nations regarding the use or threat of use of force in their international relations, including in their space activities,

Reaffirming paragraph 80 of the Final Document of the Tenth Special Session of the General Assembly, in which it is stated that in order to prevent an arms race in outer space, further measures should be taken and appropriate international negotiations held in accordance with the spirit of the Treaty,

Recalling its previous resolutions on this issue, and taking note of the proposals submitted to the General Assembly at its tenth special session and at its regular sessions, and of the recommendations made to the competent organs of the United Nations and to the Conference on Disarmament,

Recognizing that prevention of an arms race in outer space would avert a grave danger for international peace and security,

Emphasizing the paramount importance of strict compliance with existing arms limitation and disarmament agreements relevant to outer space, including bilateral agreements, and with the existing legal regime concerning the use of outer space,

Considering that wide participation in the legal regime applicable to outer space could contribute to enhancing its effectiveness,

Noting that the Ad Hoc Committee on the Prevention of an Arms Race in Outer Space, taking into account its previous efforts since its establishment in 1985 and seeking to enhance its functioning in qualitative terms, continued the examination and identification of various issues, existing agreements and existing proposals, as well as future initiatives relevant to the prevention of an arms race in outer space, and that this contributed to a better understanding of a number of problems and to a clearer perception of the various positions,

Noting also that there were no objections in principle in the Conference on Disarmament to the re-establishment of the Ad Hoc Committee, subject to re-examination of the mandate contained in the decision of the Conference on Disarmament of 13 February 1992,

Emphasizing the mutually complementary nature of bilateral and multilateral efforts for the prevention of an arms race in outer space, and hoping that concrete results will emerge from those efforts as soon as possible,

Convinced that further measures should be examined in the search for effective and verifiable bilateral and multilateral agreements in order to prevent an arms race in outer space, including the weaponization of outer space,

Stressing that the growing use of outer space increases the need for greater transparency and better information on the part of the international community,

Recalling, in this context, its previous resolutions, in particular resolutions 45/55 B of 4 December 1990, 47/51 of 9 December 1992 and 48/74 A of 16 December 1993, in which, inter alia, it reaffirmed the importance of confidence-building measures as a means conducive to ensuring the attainment of the objective of the prevention of an arms race in outer space,

Conscious of the benefits of confidence- and security-building measures in the military field,

Recognizing that negotiations for the conclusion of an international agreement or agreements to prevent an arms race in outer space remain a priority task of the Conference on Disarmament and that the concrete proposals on confidence-building measures could form an integral part of such agreements,

Noting with satisfaction the constructive, structured and focused debate on the prevention of an arms race in outer space at the Conference on Disarmament in 2009,

Taking note of the introduction by China and the Russian Federation at the Conference on Disarmament of the draft treaty on the prevention of the placement of weapons in outer space and of the threat or use of force against outer space objects,

Taking note also of the decision of the Conference on Disarmament to establish for its 2009 session a working group to discuss, substantially, without limitation, all issues related to the prevention of an arms race in outer space,

1. *Reaffirms* the importance and urgency of preventing an arms race in outer space and the readiness of all States to contribute to that common objective, in conformity with the provisions of the Treaty on Principles Governing the Activities of States in the Exploration and Use of Outer Space, including the Moon and Other Celestial Bodies;

2. *Reaffirms its recognition*, as stated in the report of the Ad Hoc Committee on the Prevention of an Arms Race in Outer Space, that the legal regime applicable to outer space does not in and of itself guarantee the prevention of an arms race in outer space, that the regime plays a significant role in the prevention of an arms race in that environment, that there is a need to consolidate and reinforce that regime

and enhance its effectiveness and that it is important to comply strictly with existing agreements, both bilateral and multilateral;

3. *Emphasizes* the necessity of further measures with appropriate and effective provisions for verification to prevent an arms race in outer space;

4. *Calls upon* all States, in particular those with major space capabilities, to contribute actively to the objective of the peaceful use of outer space and of the prevention of an arms race in outer space and to refrain from actions contrary to that objective and to the relevant existing treaties in the interest of maintaining international peace and security and promoting international cooperation;

5. *Reiterates* that the Conference on Disarmament, as the sole multilateral disarmament negotiating forum, has the primary role in the negotiation of a multilateral agreement or agreements, as appropriate, on the prevention of an arms race in outer space in all its aspects;

6. *Invites* the Conference on Disarmament to establish a working group under its agenda item entitled "Prevention of an arms race in outer space" as early as possible during its 2010 session;

7. *Recognizes*, in this respect, the growing convergence of views on the elaboration of measures designed to strengthen transparency, confidence and security in the peaceful uses of outer space;

8. *Urges* States conducting activities in outer space, as well as States interested in conducting such activities, to keep the Conference on Disarmament informed of the progress of bilateral and multilateral negotiations on the matter, if any, so as to facilitate its work;

9. *Decides* to include in the provisional agenda of its sixty-fifth session the item entitled "Prevention of an arms race in outer space".

RECORDED VOTE ON RESOLUTION 64/28:

In favour: Afghanistan, Albania, Algeria, Andorra, Angola, Antigua and Barbuda, Argentina, Armenia, Australia, Austria, Azerbaijan, Bahamas, Bahrain, Barbados, Belarus, Belgium, Belize, Benin, Bhutan, Bolivia, Bosnia and Herzegovina, Botswana, Brazil, Brunei Darussalam, Bulgaria, Burundi, Cambodia, Cameroon, Canada, Cape Verde, Chile, China, Colombia, Comoros, Congo, Costa Rica, Côte d'Ivoire, Croatia, Cuba, Cyprus, Czech Republic, Democratic People's Republic of Korea, Democratic Republic of the Congo, Denmark, Djibouti, Dominica, Dominican Republic, Ecuador, Egypt, El Salvador, Equatorial Guinea, Eritrea, Estonia, Fiji, Finland, France, Gambia, Georgia, Germany, Ghana, Greece, Grenada, Guatemala, Guinea, Guinea-Bissau, Guyana, Haiti, Honduras, Hungary, Iceland, India, Indonesia, Iran, Iraq, Ireland, Italy, Jamaica, Japan, Jordan, Kazakhstan, Kenya, Kuwait, Kyrgyzstan, Lao People's Democratic Republic, Latvia, Lebanon, Lesotho, Liberia, Libyan Arab Jamahiriya, Liechtenstein, Lithuania, Luxembourg, Madagascar, Malawi, Malaysia, Maldives, Mali, Malta, Marshall Islands, Mauritania, Mauritius, Mexico, Micronesia, Moldova, Monaco, Mongolia, Montenegro, Morocco, Mozambique, Myanmar, Namibia, Nepal, Netherlands, New Zealand, Nicaragua, Niger, Nigeria, Norway, Oman, Pakistan, Palau, Panama, Papua New Guinea, Paraguay, Peru, Philippines, Poland, Portugal, Qatar, Republic of Korea, Romania, Russian Federation, Rwanda, Saint Kitts and Nevis, Saint Lucia, Saint Vincent and the Grenadines, Samoa,

San Marino, Saudi Arabia, Senegal, Serbia, Seychelles, Sierra Leone, Singapore, Slovakia, Slovenia, Solomon Islands, Somalia, South Africa, Spain, Sri Lanka, Sudan, Suriname, Sweden, Switzerland, Syrian Arab Republic, Thailand, The former Yugoslav Republic of Macedonia, Togo, Tonga, Trinidad and Tobago, Tunisia, Turkey, Turkmenistan, Uganda, Ukraine, United Arab Emirates, United Kingdom, United Republic of Tanzania, Uruguay, Uzbekistan, Venezuela, Viet Nam, Yemen, Zambia, Zimbabwe.

Against: None.

Abstaining: Israel, United States.

Also on 2 December [meeting 55], the Assembly, on the recommendation of the First Committee [A/64/391], adopted **resolution 64/49** without vote [agenda item 96 *(v)*].

Transparency and confidence-building measures in outer space activities

The General Assembly,

Recalling its resolutions 60/66 of 8 December 2005, 61/75 of 6 December 2006, 62/43 of 5 December 2007 and 63/68 of 2 December 2008,

Reaffirming that the prevention of an arms race in outer space would avert a grave danger to international peace and security,

Conscious that further measures should be examined in the search for agreements to prevent an arms race in outer space, including the weaponization of outer space,

Recalling, in this context, its previous resolutions, including resolutions 45/55 B of 4 December 1990 and 48/74 B of 16 December 1993, which, inter alia, emphasize the need for increased transparency and confirm the importance of confidence-building measures as a means conducive to ensuring the attainment of the objective of the prevention of an arms race in outer space,

Recalling also the report of the Secretary-General of 15 October 1993 to the General Assembly at its forty-eighth session, the annex to which contains the study by governmental experts on the application of confidence-building measures in outer space,

Noting the constructive debate which the Conference on Disarmament held on this subject in 2009, including the views expressed by Member States,

Noting also the introduction by China and the Russian Federation at the Conference on Disarmament of the draft treaty on the prevention of the placement of weapons in outer space and of the threat or use of force against outer space objects,

Noting further the presentation by the European Union of a draft code of conduct for outer space activities,

Noting the contribution of Member States which have submitted to the Secretary-General concrete proposals on international outer space transparency and confidence-building measures pursuant to paragraph 1 of resolution 61/75, paragraph 2 of resolution 62/43 and paragraph 2 of resolution 63/68,

1. *Takes note* of the reports of the Secretary-General containing concrete proposals from Member States on international outer space transparency and confidence-building measures;

2. *Invites* all Member States to continue to submit to the Secretary-General concrete proposals on international outer space transparency and confidence-building measures in the interest of maintaining international peace and security and promoting international cooperation and the prevention of an arms race in outer space;

3. *Requests* the Secretary-General to submit to the General Assembly at its sixty-fifth session a final report with an annex containing concrete proposals from Member States on international outer space transparency and confidence-building measures pursuant to resolutions 61/75, 62/43, 63/68 and the present resolution;

4. *Decides* to include in the provisional agenda of its sixty-fifth session the item entitled "Transparency and confidence-building measures in outer space activities".

Observance of environmental norms

Pursuant to General Assembly resolution 63/51 [YUN 2008, p. 636], the Secretary-General in July submitted a report with a later addendum [A/64/118 & Add.1] containing information from Cuba, the Czech Republic, El Salvador, Lebanon, Mexico, Spain and the United Arab Emirates on measures they had adopted to promote the observance of environmental norms in the drafting and implementation of agreements on disarmament and arms control.

GENERAL ASSEMBLY ACTION

On 2 December [meeting 55], the General Assembly, on the recommendation of the First Committee [A/64/391], adopted **resolution 64/33** without vote [agenda item 96 *(n)*].

Observance of environmental norms in the drafting and implementation of agreements on disarmament and arms control

The General Assembly,

Recalling its resolutions 50/70 M of 12 December 1995, 51/45 E of 10 December 1996, 52/38 E of 9 December 1997, 53/77 J of 4 December 1998, 54/54 S of 1 December 1999, 55/33 K of 20 November 2000, 56/24 F of 29 November 2001, 57/64 of 22 November 2002, 58/45 of 8 December 2003, 59/68 of 3 December 2004, 60/60 of 8 December 2005, 61/63 of 6 December 2006, 62/28 of 5 December 2007 and 63/51 of 2 December 2008,

Emphasizing the importance of the observance of environmental norms in the preparation and implementation of disarmament and arms limitation agreements,

Recognizing that it is necessary to take duly into account the agreements adopted at the United Nations Conference on Environment and Development, as well as prior relevant agreements, in the drafting and implementation of agreements on disarmament and arms limitation,

Taking note of the report of the Secretary-General submitted pursuant to resolution 63/51,

Noting that the Fifteenth Summit Conference of Heads of State and Government of the Movement of Non-Aligned

Countries, held in Sharm el-Sheikh, Egypt, from 11 to 16 July 2009, welcomed the adoption of resolution 63/51, the first resolution adopted without a vote by the General Assembly on the observance of environmental norms in the drafting and implementation of agreements on disarmament and arms control,

Mindful of the detrimental environmental effects of the use of nuclear weapons,

1. *Reaffirms* that international disarmament forums should take fully into account the relevant environmental norms in negotiating treaties and agreements on disarmament and arms limitation and that all States, through their actions, should contribute fully to ensuring compliance with the aforementioned norms in the implementation of treaties and conventions to which they are parties;

2. *Calls upon* States to adopt unilateral, bilateral, regional and multilateral measures so as to contribute to ensuring the application of scientific and technological progress within the framework of international security, disarmament and other related spheres, without detriment to the environment or to its effective contribution to attaining sustainable development;

3. *Welcomes* the information provided by Member States on the implementation of the measures they have adopted to promote the objectives envisaged in the present resolution;

4. *Invites* all Member States to communicate to the Secretary-General information on the measures they have adopted to promote the objectives envisaged in the present resolution, and requests the Secretary-General to submit a report containing that information to the General Assembly at its sixty-fifth session;

5. *Decides* to include in the provisional agenda of its sixty-fifth session the item entitled "Observance of environmental norms in the drafting and implementation of agreements on disarmament and arms control".

Science and technology and disarmament

By **decision 64/514** of 2 December, the General Assembly decided to include in the provisional agenda of its sixty-fifth (2010) session the item "Role of science and technology in the context of international security and disarmament".

The Assembly took related action on the same day in **resolution 64/25** (see p. 609) on developments in the field of information and telecommunications in the context of international security, calling on Member States to promote the consideration of existing and potential threats in the field of information security, as well as possible measures to limit the threats emerging in that field, consistent with the need to preserve the free flow of information. It requested the Secretary-General to study those threats as well as cooperative measures to address them, with the assistance of a group of governmental experts.

Studies, research and training

UN Institute for Disarmament Research

The Secretary-General presented to the General Assembly the report of the Director of the United Nations Institute for Disarmament Research (UNIDIR) [A/64/261] covering activities from August 2008 to July 2009, as well as the report of the UNIDIR Board of Trustees on the proposed 2009 and 2010 programme of work and estimated budget. During the reporting period, UNIDIR's work centred on three areas: global security and disarmament, regional security and disarmament, and human security and disarmament. The report outlined UNIDIR's activities regarding networking, dissemination and outreach to researchers, diplomats, government officials and NGOs; publications; and research activities for 2009–2011.

By means of the report, the Board of Trustees transmitted a recommendation for a subvention for the Institute from the UN regular budget for the biennium 2010–2011. The Director highlighted that such a subvention, which guaranteed the Institute's independence, currently covered only about 20 per cent of its core costs, or about 10 per cent of the overall budget. The Director also reported on the status of voluntary funds from Governments and philanthropic foundations, which comprised about 90 per cent of the Institute's budget and financed all operational costs.

The General Assembly, in section III of **resolution 64/245** of 24 December (see p. 1406), having considered the Secretary-General's request for a subvention to UNIDIR resulting from the recommendations of the Board of Trustees [A/64/270] and the related report of the Advisory Committee on Administrative and Budgetary Questions [A/64/7/Add.7], approved a subvention for the Institute in the amount of $558,200 from the UN regular budget for the 2010–2011 biennium.

Disarmament studies

The Group of Governmental Experts on the continuing operation and further development of the UN Register of Conventional Arms concluded its work and submitted a report [A/64/296] (see p. 556) on that topic. The report was mandated by General Assembly resolution 63/69 of 2 December 2008 [YUN 2008, p. 628] and endorsed by resolution 64/54 of 2 December 2009 [ibid.].

Disarmament fellowships

Twenty-four fellows participated in the 2009 UN disarmament fellowship, training and advisory services programme, which began in Geneva on 24 August and concluded in New York on 22 October.

The programme continued to be structured in three segments: a study session in Geneva; study visits to disarmament-related intergovernmental organizations and to Member States; and a study session at UN Headquarters in New York.

We Must Disarm campaign

On 13 June, the Secretary-General launched an advocacy campaign under the slogan "WMD-WeMustDisarm" to mark the 100-day countdown leading to the International Day of Peace on 21 September. He was joined in the campaign by United Nations Messenger of Peace Michael Douglas and actor Rainn Wilson. The campaign reached out to youth using a range of electronic media.

Annual DPI/NGO conference

Some 1,300 participants from more than 55 countries representing over 340 NGOs associated with the UN Department of Public Information (DPI) participated in the sixty-second annual DPI/NGO conference (Mexico City, 9–11 September), titled, "For Peace and Development: Disarm Now". DPI, the NGO/DPI Executive Committee, UNODA and the Government of Mexico jointly organized the event, which adopted a document titled "Disarming for Peace and Development". Participants urged Governments, the United Nations and civil society to work together and strengthen the regime of nuclear and conventional disarmament and non-proliferation. They urged the integration of security-related themes into the possible follow-up of the Millennium Development Goals; full implementation of Council resolution 1325(2000) [YUN 2000, p. 1113], in particular ensuring representation of women at all levels of decision-making on conflict prevention, management and resolution; and full implementation of Council resolution 1820(2008) [YUN 2008, p. 1265] to prevent sexual violence in armed conflict.

On 18 September [S/2009/477], Mexico transmitted to the Council the NGO Declaration: Disarming for Peace and Development, adopted at the conference.

Regional disarmament

Throughout 2009, regional organizations remained engaged with disarmament and non-proliferation issues. Regional and subregional initiatives aimed at preventing the spread of weapons of mass destruction, curbing the illicit trade in small arms and light weapons, promoting confidence- and security-building measures and advancing the prospects of additional nuclear-weapon-free zones. The year saw two major developments: the entry into force of the Treaty on

a Nuclear-Weapon-Free Zone in Central Asia (see p. 534) and of the African Nuclear-Weapon-Free Zone established under the Treaty of Pelindaba (see p. 533).

The General Assembly in resolution 64/41 (see below) noted that regional disarmament endeavours by countries, taking into account the specific characteristics of each region and in accordance with the principle of undiminished security at the lowest level of armaments, would enhance the security of all States and would thus contribute to international peace and security by reducing the risk of regional conflicts. The Assembly affirmed that global and regional approaches to disarmament complemented each other and should therefore be pursued simultaneously.

GENERAL ASSEMBLY ACTION

On 2 December [meeting 55], the General Assembly, on the recommendation of the First Committee [A/64/391], adopted **resolution 64/41** without vote [agenda item 96 *(f)*].

Regional disarmament

The General Assembly,

Recalling its resolutions 45/58 P of 4 December 1990, 46/36 I of 6 December 1991, 47/52 J of 9 December 1992, 48/75 I of 16 December 1993, 49/75 N of 15 December 1994, 50/70 K of 12 December 1995, 51/45 K of 10 December 1996, 52/38 P of 9 December 1997, 53/77 O of 4 December 1998, 54/54 N of 1 December 1999, 55/33 O of 20 November 2000, 56/24 H of 29 November 2001, 57/76 of 22 November 2002, 58/38 of 8 December 2003, 59/89 of 3 December 2004, 60/63 of 8 December 2005, 61/80 of 6 December 2006, 62/38 of 5 December 2007 and 63/43 of 2 December 2008 on regional disarmament,

Believing that the efforts of the international community to move towards the ideal of general and complete disarmament are guided by the inherent human desire for genuine peace and security, the elimination of the danger of war and the release of economic, intellectual and other resources for peaceful pursuits,

Affirming the abiding commitment of all States to the purposes and principles enshrined in the Charter of the United Nations in the conduct of their international relations,

Noting that essential guidelines for progress towards general and complete disarmament were adopted at the tenth special session of the General Assembly,

Taking note of the guidelines and recommendations for regional approaches to disarmament within the context of global security adopted by the Disarmament Commission at its 1993 substantive session,

Welcoming the prospects of genuine progress in the field of disarmament engendered in recent years as a result of negotiations between the two super-Powers,

Taking note of the recent proposals for disarmament at the regional and subregional levels,

Recognizing the importance of confidence-building measures for regional and international peace and security,

Convinced that endeavours by countries to promote regional disarmament, taking into account the specific characteristics of each region and in accordance with the principle of undiminished security at the lowest level of armaments, would enhance the security of all States and would thus contribute to international peace and security by reducing the risk of regional conflicts,

1. *Stresses* that sustained efforts are needed, within the framework of the Conference on Disarmament and under the umbrella of the United Nations, to make progress on the entire range of disarmament issues;

2. *Affirms* that global and regional approaches to disarmament complement each other and should therefore be pursued simultaneously to promote regional and international peace and security;

3. *Calls upon* States to conclude agreements, wherever possible, for nuclear non-proliferation, disarmament and confidence-building measures at the regional and subregional levels;

4. *Welcomes* the initiatives towards disarmament, nuclear non-proliferation and security undertaken by some countries at the regional and subregional levels;

5. *Supports and encourages* efforts aimed at promoting confidence-building measures at the regional and subregional levels to ease regional tensions and to further disarmament and nuclear non-proliferation measures at the regional and subregional levels;

6. *Decides* to include in the provisional agenda of its sixty-fifth session the item entitled "Regional disarmament".

Conventional arms control at regional and subregional levels

The Secretary-General, in response to General Assembly resolution 63/44 [YUN 2008, p. 644] on conventional arms control at the regional and subregional levels, in July submitted a report [A/64/126] containing the views of nine Member States (Bosnia and Herzegovina, Chile, Colombia, Greece, Lebanon, Mexico, Oman, Pakistan, Spain) on the issue.

GENERAL ASSEMBLY ACTION

On 2 December [meeting 55], the General Assembly, on the recommendation of the First Committee [A/64/391], adopted **resolution 64/42** by recorded vote (174-1-2) [agenda item 96 *(g)*].

Conventional arms control at the regional and subregional levels

The General Assembly,

Recalling its resolutions 48/75 J of 16 December 1993, 49/75 O of 15 December 1994, 50/70 L of 12 December 1995, 51/45 Q of 10 December 1996, 52/38 Q of 9 December 1997, 53/77 P of 4 December 1998, 54/54 M of 1 December 1999, 55/33 P of 20 November 2000, 56/24 I of 29 November 2001, 57/77 of 22 November 2002, 58/39 of 8 December 2003, 59/88 of 3 December 2004, 60/75 of 8 December 2005, 61/82 of 6 December 2006, 62/44 of 5 December 2007 and 63/44 of 2 December 2008,

Recognizing the crucial role of conventional arms control in promoting regional and international peace and security,

Convinced that conventional arms control needs to be pursued primarily in the regional and subregional contexts since most threats to peace and security in the post-cold-war era arise mainly among States located in the same region or subregion,

Aware that the preservation of a balance in the defence capabilities of States at the lowest level of armaments would contribute to peace and stability and should be a prime objective of conventional arms control,

Desirous of promoting agreements to strengthen regional peace and security at the lowest possible level of armaments and military forces,

Noting with particular interest the initiatives taken in this regard in different regions of the world, in particular the commencement of consultations among a number of Latin American countries and the proposals for conventional arms control made in the context of South Asia, and recognizing, in the context of this subject, the relevance and value of the Treaty on Conventional Armed Forces in Europe, which is a cornerstone of European security,

Believing that militarily significant States and States with larger military capabilities have a special responsibility in promoting such agreements for regional security,

Believing also that an important objective of conventional arms control in regions of tension should be to prevent the possibility of military attack launched by surprise and to avoid aggression,

1. *Decides* to give urgent consideration to the issues involved in conventional arms control at the regional and subregional levels;

2. *Requests* the Conference on Disarmament to consider the formulation of principles that can serve as a framework for regional agreements on conventional arms control, and looks forward to a report of the Conference on this subject;

3. *Requests* the Secretary-General, in the meantime, to seek the views of Member States on the subject and to submit a report to the General Assembly at its sixty-fifth session;

4. *Decides* to include in the provisional agenda of its sixty-fifth session the item entitled "Conventional arms control at the regional and subregional levels".

RECORDED VOTE ON RESOLUTION 64/42:

In favour: Afghanistan, Albania, Algeria, Andorra, Angola, Antigua and Barbuda, Argentina, Armenia, Australia, Austria, Azerbaijan, Bahamas, Bahrain, Bangladesh, Barbados, Belarus, Belgium, Belize, Benin, Bolivia, Bosnia and Herzegovina, Botswana, Brazil, Brunei Darussalam, Bulgaria, Burkina Faso, Burundi, Cambodia, Cameroon, Canada, Cape Verde, Chile, China, Colombia, Comoros, Congo, Costa Rica, Côte d'Ivoire, Croatia, Cyprus, Czech Republic, Democratic People's Republic of Korea, Democratic Republic of the Congo, Denmark, Djibouti, Dominica, Dominican Republic, Ecuador, Egypt, El Salvador, Equatorial Guinea, Eritrea, Estonia, Fiji, Finland, France, Gambia, Georgia, Germany, Ghana, Greece, Grenada, Guatemala, Guinea, Guinea-Bissau, Guyana, Haiti, Honduras, Hungary, Iceland, Indonesia, Iran, Iraq, Ireland, Israel, Italy, Jamaica, Japan, Jordan, Kazakhstan, Kenya, Kuwait, Kyrgyzstan, Latvia, Lebanon, Lesotho, Liberia, Libyan Arab Jamahiriya, Liechtenstein, Lithuania, Luxembourg, Madagascar, Malawi, Malaysia, Maldives, Mali, Malta, Marshall Islands, Mauritania,

Mauritius, Mexico, Micronesia, Moldova, Monaco, Mongolia, Montenegro, Morocco, Mozambique, Myanmar, Namibia, Nepal, Netherlands, New Zealand, Nicaragua, Niger, Nigeria, Norway, Oman, Pakistan, Palau, Panama, Papua New Guinea, Paraguay, Peru, Philippines, Poland, Portugal, Qatar, Republic of Korea, Romania, Saint Kitts and Nevis, Saint Lucia, Saint Vincent and the Grenadines, Samoa, San Marino, Saudi Arabia, Senegal, Serbia, Seychelles, Sierra Leone, Singapore, Slovakia, Slovenia, Solomon Islands, Somalia, South Africa, Spain, Sri Lanka, Sudan, Suriname, Swaziland, Sweden, Switzerland, Syrian Arab Republic, Tajikistan, Thailand, The former Yugoslav Republic of Macedonia, Togo, Tonga, Trinidad and Tobago, Tunisia, Turkey, Turkmenistan, Ukraine, United Arab Emirates, United Kingdom, United Republic of Tanzania, United States, Uruguay, Uzbekistan, Venezuela, Yemen, Zambia, Zimbabwe.

Against: India.

Abstaining: Bhutan, Russian Federation.

Confidence-building measures

In accordance with General Assembly resolution 63/45 [YUN 2008, p. 645] on confidence-building measures in the regional and subregional context, the Secretary-General in June presented a report with a later addendum [A/64/114 & Add.1] containing the views of 11 Member States (Bolivia, Bosnia and Herzegovina, Burundi, El Salvador, Greece, Lebanon, Mexico, Panama, Poland, Spain, Ukraine) on the issue.

On 2 December [meeting 55], the General Assembly, on the recommendation of the First Committee [A/64/391], adopted **resolution 64/43** without vote [agenda item 96 *(h)*].

Confidence-building measures in the regional and subregional context

The General Assembly,

Guided by the purposes and principles enshrined in the Charter of the United Nations,

Recalling its resolutions 58/43 of 8 December 2003, 59/87 of 3 December 2004, 60/64 of 8 December 2005, 61/81 of 6 December 2006, 62/45 of 5 December 2007 and 63/45 of 2 December 2008,

Recalling also its resolution 57/337 of 3 July 2003 entitled "Prevention of armed conflict", in which it calls upon Member States to settle their disputes by peaceful means, as set out in Chapter VI of the Charter, inter alia, by any procedures adopted by the parties,

Recalling further the resolutions and guidelines adopted by consensus by the General Assembly and the Disarmament Commission relating to confidence-building measures and their implementation at the global, regional and subregional levels,

Considering the importance and effectiveness of confidence-building measures taken at the initiative and with the agreement of all States concerned and taking into account the specific characteristics of each region, since such measures can contribute to regional stability,

Convinced that resources released by disarmament, including regional disarmament, can be devoted to economic and social development and to the protection of the environment for the benefit of all peoples, in particular those of the developing countries,

Recognizing the need for meaningful dialogue among States concerned to avert conflict,

Welcoming the peace processes already initiated by States concerned to resolve their disputes through peaceful means bilaterally or through mediation, inter alia, by third parties, regional organizations or the United Nations,

Recognizing that States in some regions have already taken steps towards confidence-building measures at the bilateral, subregional and regional levels in the political and military fields, including arms control and disarmament, and noting that such confidence-building measures have improved peace and security in those regions and contributed to progress in the socio-economic conditions of their people,

Concerned that the continuation of disputes among States, particularly in the absence of an effective mechanism to resolve them through peaceful means, may contribute to the arms race and endanger the maintenance of international peace and security and the efforts of the international community to promote arms control and disarmament,

1. *Calls upon* Member States to refrain from the use or threat of use of force in accordance with the purposes and principles of the Charter of the United Nations;

2. *Reaffirms its commitment* to the peaceful settlement of disputes under Chapter VI of the Charter, in particular Article 33, which provides for a solution by negotiation, enquiry, mediation, conciliation, arbitration, judicial settlement, resort to regional agencies or arrangements or other peaceful means chosen by the parties;

3. *Reaffirms* the ways and means regarding confidence- and security-building measures set out in the report of the Disarmament Commission on its 1993 session;

4. *Calls upon* Member States to pursue these ways and means through sustained consultations and dialogue, while at the same time avoiding actions that may hinder or impair such a dialogue;

5. *Urges* States to comply strictly with all bilateral, regional and international agreements, including arms control and disarmament agreements, to which they are party;

6. *Emphasizes* that the objective of confidence-building measures should be to help to strengthen international peace and security and to be consistent with the principle of undiminished security at the lowest level of armaments;

7. *Encourages* the promotion of bilateral and regional confidence-building measures, with the consent and participation of the parties concerned, to avoid conflict and prevent the unintended and accidental outbreak of hostilities;

8. *Requests* the Secretary-General to submit a report to the General Assembly at its sixty-fifth session containing the views of Member States on confidence-building measures in the regional and subregional context;

9. *Decides* to include in the provisional agenda of its sixty-fifth session the item entitled "Confidence-building measures in the regional and subregional context".

Central Africa Standing Advisory Committee

The United Nations Standing Advisory Committee on Security Questions in Central Africa met twice during 2009 at the ministerial level for its twenty-eighth (Libreville, Gabon, 4–8 May) [A/64/85-S/2009/288] and twenty-ninth (N'Djamena, Chad, 9–13 November) [A/64/638-S/2010/54] sessions. At both sessions, the Committee reviewed the geopolitical and security situation in Central Africa based on a report prepared by the Economic Community of Central African States.

At its twenty-eighth session, the Committee noted that since its meeting in 2008 [YUN 2008, p. 646], there had been sharply contrasting developments in the geopolitical and security situation among its members (Angola, Burundi, Cameroon, Central African Republic, Chad, Congo, Democratic Republic of the Congo (DRC), Equatorial Guinea, Gabon, Rwanda, Sao Tome and Principe). On the one hand, there had been notable progress in consolidation of democratic processes and the smooth functioning of institutions; on the other, the region had been confronted with a number of security situations. The Committee also focused on the status of bilateral relations between the DRC and Rwanda; developments in the situation among the members of the Economic Community of the Great Lakes Countries; implementation of the 2007 Sao Tome Initiative, which comprised a code of conduct for defence and security forces and a draft legal instrument on control of small arms and light weapons; cross-border crime; disarmament and arms limitation programmes; and the Committee's financial situation.

At its twenty-ninth session, the Committee additionally discussed the implementation of the Brazzaville Programme of priority activities on proliferation of small arms and light weapons and disarming civilians; implementation of the Yaoundé Agreement of 6 May 2009 on piracy in the Gulf of Guinea; report on the activities of the UN Subregional Centre for Human Rights and Democracy in Central Africa; and women, peace and security: implementation of Security Council resolutions 1325(2000) [YUN 2000, p. 1113], 1820(2008) [YUN 2008, p. 1265], 1888(2009) (see p. 1137) and 1889(2009) (see p. 1141). Congo and Gabon pledged to contribute $10,000 each to the Committee's trust fund.

Report of Secretary-General. In response to General Assembly resolution 63/78 [YUN 2008, p. 647], the Secretary-General in July [A/64/163] described the activities of the Committee between July 2008 and June 2009, which included the Committee's twenty-eighth ministerial meeting. The Secretary-General noted that Committee members adopted the Code of Conduct for the Defence and Security Forces in Central Africa, annexed to the Secretary-General's report, demonstrating their commitment to a set of principles guaranteeing the good governance of those forces. Moreover, in drafting a legal instrument on the control of small arms and light weapons in Central Africa, Committee members continued to pool their ideas on elements for inclusion in the future instrument and lessons to be drawn from the implementation of similar instruments.

GENERAL ASSEMBLY ACTION

On 2 December [meeting 55], the General Assembly, on the recommendation of the First Committee [A/64/392], adopted **resolution 64/61** without vote [agenda item 97 *(e)*].

Regional confidence-building measures: activities of the United Nations Standing Advisory Committee on Security Questions in Central Africa

The General Assembly,

Recalling its previous relevant resolutions, in particular resolution 63/78 of 2 December 2008,

Recalling also the guidelines for general and complete disarmament adopted at its tenth special session, the first special session devoted to disarmament,

Bearing in mind the establishment by the Secretary-General on 28 May 1992 of the United Nations Standing Advisory Committee on Security Questions in Central Africa, the purpose of which is to encourage arms limitation, disarmament, non-proliferation and development in the subregion,

Reaffirming that the purpose of the Standing Advisory Committee is to conduct reconstruction and confidence-building activities in Central Africa among its member States, including through confidence-building and arms limitation measures,

Convinced that the resources released by disarmament, including regional disarmament, can be devoted to economic and social development and to the protection of the environment for the benefit of all peoples, in particular those of the developing countries,

Considering the importance and effectiveness of confidence-building measures taken on the initiative and with the participation of all States concerned and taking into account the specific characteristics of each region, since such measures can contribute to regional stability and to international peace and security,

Convinced that development can be achieved only in a climate of peace, security and mutual confidence both within and among States,

Recalling the Brazzaville Declaration on Cooperation for Peace and Security in Central Africa, the Bata Declaration for the Promotion of Lasting Democracy, Peace and Development in Central Africa and the Yaoundé Declaration on Peace, Security and Stability in Central Africa,

Bearing in mind resolutions 1196(1998) and 1197(1998), adopted by the Security Council on 16 and 18 September 1998 respectively, following its consideration of the report of the Secretary-General on the causes of conflict and the promotion of durable peace and sustainable development in Africa,

Emphasizing the need to strengthen the capacity for conflict prevention and peacekeeping in Africa, and welcoming the close cooperation established between the United Nations and the Economic Community of Central African States for that purpose,

1. *Reaffirms its support* for efforts aimed at promoting confidence-building measures at the regional and subregional levels in order to ease tensions and conflicts in Central Africa and to further sustainable peace, stability and development in the subregion;

2. *Reaffirms* the importance of disarmament and arms limitation programmes in Central Africa carried out by the States of the subregion with the support of the United Nations, the African Union and other international partners;

3. *Welcomes* the adoption by the States members of the United Nations Standing Advisory Committee on Security Questions in Central Africa on 8 May 2009 of the Code of Conduct for the Defence and Security Forces in Central Africa and the major strides made by States in the drafting of a legal instrument on the control of small arms and light weapons in Central Africa, and encourages interested countries to provide their financial support to the implementation of the "Sao Tome Initiative";

4. *Encourages* the States members of the Standing Advisory Committee to carry out the programmes of activities adopted at their ministerial meetings;

5. *Also encourages* the States members of the Standing Advisory Committee to continue their efforts to render the early-warning mechanism for Central Africa fully operational as an instrument for analysing and monitoring the political situation in the subregion within the framework of the prevention of crises and armed conflicts, and requests the Secretary-General to provide the necessary assistance for its smooth functioning;

6. *Appeals* to the international community to support the efforts undertaken by the States concerned to implement disarmament, demobilization and reintegration programmes;

7. *Requests* the Secretary-General and the Office of the United Nations High Commissioner for Refugees to continue their assistance to the countries of Central Africa in tackling the problems of refugees and displaced persons in their territories;

8. *Requests* the Secretary-General and the United Nations High Commissioner for Human Rights to continue to provide their full assistance for the proper functioning of the Subregional Centre for Human Rights and Democracy in Central Africa;

9. *Welcomes* the adoption on 8 May 2009 of the Libreville Declaration calling upon States members of the Standing Advisory Committee to contribute to the Trust Fund for the United Nations Standing Advisory Committee on Security Questions in Central Africa;

10. *Urges* other Member States and intergovernmental and non-governmental organizations to support the activities of the Standing Advisory Committee effectively through voluntary contributions to the Trust Fund;

11. *Expresses its satisfaction* to the Secretary-General for his support for the revitalization of the activities of the Standing Advisory Committee, and requests him to continue to provide the assistance needed to ensure the success of its regular biannual meetings;

12. *Calls upon* the Secretary-General to submit to the General Assembly at its sixty-fifth session a report on the implementation of the present resolution;

13. *Decides* to include in the provisional agenda of its sixty-fifth session the item entitled "Regional confidence-building measures: activities of the United Nations Standing Advisory Committee on Security Questions in Central Africa".

Regional centres for peace and disarmament

On 2 December [meeting 55], the General Assembly, on the recommendation of the First Committee [A/64/392], adopted **resolution 64/58** without vote [agenda item 97 *(c)*].

United Nations regional centres for peace and disarmament

The General Assembly,

Recalling its resolutions 60/83 of 8 December 2005, 61/90 of 6 December 2006, 62/50 of 5 December 2007 and 63/76 of 2 December 2008 regarding the maintenance and revitalization of the three United Nations regional centres for peace and disarmament,

Recalling also the reports of the Secretary-General on the United Nations Regional Centre for Peace and Disarmament in Africa, the United Nations Regional Centre for Peace and Disarmament in Asia and the Pacific and the United Nations Regional Centre for Peace, Disarmament and Development in Latin America and the Caribbean,

Reaffirming its decision, taken in 1982 at its twelfth special session, to establish the United Nations Disarmament Information Programme, the purpose of which is to inform, educate and generate public understanding and support for the objectives of the United Nations in the field of arms control and disarmament,

Bearing in mind its resolutions 40/151 G of 16 December 1985, 41/60 J of 3 December 1986, 42/39 D of 30 November 1987 and 44/117 F of 15 December 1989 on the regional centres for peace and disarmament in Nepal, Peru and Togo,

Recognizing that the changes that have taken place in the world have created new opportunities as well as posed new challenges for the pursuit of disarmament, and, in this regard, bearing in mind that the regional centres for peace and disarmament can contribute substantially to understanding and cooperation among States in each particular region in the areas of peace, disarmament and development,

Noting that in paragraph 127 of the Final Document of the Fifteenth Summit Conference of Heads of State and Government of the Movement of Non-Aligned Countries, held in Sharm el-Sheikh, Egypt, from 11 to 16 July 2009, the Heads of State and Government emphasized the importance of the United Nations activities at the regional level to increase the stability and security of its Member States, which could be promoted in a substantive manner by the maintenance and revitalization of the three regional centres for peace and disarmament,

1. *Reiterates* the importance of the United Nations activities at the regional level to advancement in disarmament and to increase the stability and security of its Member States, which could be promoted in a substantive manner by the maintenance and revitalization of the three regional centres for peace and disarmament;

2. *Reaffirms* that, in order to achieve positive results, it is useful for the three regional centres to carry out dissemination and educational programmes that promote regional peace and security that are aimed at changing basic attitudes with respect to peace and security and disarmament so as to support the achievement of the purposes and principles of the United Nations;

3. *Appeals* to Member States in each region and those that are able to do so, as well as to international governmental and non-governmental organizations and foundations, to make voluntary contributions to the regional centres in their respective regions to strengthen their activities and initiatives;

4. *Emphasizes* the importance of the activities of the Regional Disarmament Branch of the Office for Disarmament Affairs of the Secretariat;

5. *Requests* the Secretary-General to provide all necessary support, within existing resources, to the regional centres in carrying out their programmes of activities;

6. *Decides* to include in the provisional agenda of its sixty-fifth session the item entitled "United Nations regional centres for peace and disarmament".

Africa

Pursuant to General Assembly resolution 63/80 [YUN 2008, p. 649], the Secretary-General in June reported [A/64/112] on the work of the United Nations Regional Centre for Peace and Disarmament in Africa between July 2008 and June 2009. The Centre was established in Lomé, Togo, in 1986 [YUN 1986, p. 85]. The Secretary-General noted that the revitalized Centre expanded its scope of action and achieved continental reach. It undertook and initiated activities covering an increased number of issues related to peace and disarmament, and did so in a majority of African subregions. The continental scope of the Centre's programmes went hand-in-hand with a strengthening of its partnerships with the African Union and subregional organizations. The numerous requests that the Centre had received, along with an upsurge of interest on the part of the States of the region, indicated that the Centre had achieved its goal of becoming recognized as the major expertise centre on peace and disarmament in Africa. The Secretary-General expressed his appreciation to the General Assembly for contributing to the Centre's financial revitalization. He also expressed gratitude to Austria, France, Germany, the Netherlands, Switzerland, Togo and the United Kingdom, as well as to the EU: their contributions in cash and in kind, in addition to funds from the UN regular budget, had provided the opportunity to develop and implement key peace and security programmes.

As at 31 December 2008, the balance of the trust fund for the Centre stood at $264,480.

GENERAL ASSEMBLY ACTION

On 2 December [meeting 55], the General Assembly, on the recommendation of the First Committee [A/64/392], adopted **resolution 64/62** without vote [agenda item 97 *(f)*].

United Nations Regional Centre for Peace and Disarmament in Africa

The General Assembly,

Mindful of the provisions of Article 11, paragraph 1, of the Charter of the United Nations stipulating that a function of the General Assembly is to consider the general principles of cooperation in the maintenance of international peace and security, including the principles governing disarmament and arms limitation,

Recalling its resolutions 40/151 G of 16 December 1985, 41/60 D of 3 December 1986, 42/39 J of 30 November 1987 and 43/76 D of 7 December 1988 on the United Nations Regional Centre for Peace and Disarmament in Africa and its resolutions 46/36 F of 6 December 1991 and 47/52 G of 9 December 1992 on regional disarmament, including confidence-building measures,

Recalling also its resolutions 48/76 E of 16 December 1993, 49/76 D of 15 December 1994, 50/71 C of 12 December 1995, 51/46 E of 10 December 1996, 52/220 of 22 December 1997, 53/78 C of 4 December 1998, 54/55 B of 1 December 1999, 55/34 D of 20 November 2000, 56/25 D of 29 November 2001, 57/91 of 22 November 2002, 58/61 of 8 December 2003, 59/101 of 3 December 2004, 60/86 of 8 December 2005, 61/93 of 6 December 2006, 62/216 of 22 December 2007 and 63/80 of 2 December 2008,

Reaffirming the role of the Regional Centre in promoting peace, security and disarmament at the regional level,

Taking into account the need to strengthen the existing cooperation between the Regional Centre and the African Union, in particular its institutions in the fields of peace, security and disarmament, as well as with relevant United Nations bodies and programmes in Africa for greater effectiveness, and considering the focus of its resolution 63/310 of 14 September 2009 on cooperation between the United Nations and the African Union, and in particular the need to address the problems related to peace and disarmament, and the communiqué adopted by the Peace and Security Council of the African Union at its two-hundredth meeting, held in Addis Ababa on 21 August 2009, in which the Council welcomes the increased collaboration between the Regional Centre and the African Union and regional organizations in the areas of peace, security and disarmament,

Recalling the report of the Secretary-General, in which he stated that an increase in the Regional Centre's human and operational capacity would enable it to discharge its mandate in full and to respond more effectively to requests for assistance from African States,

Taking note of the revitalization of the Regional Centre and the progress made in covering all of Africa and widening its scope of activities related to peace and disarmament in implementation of the recommendations made by the Consultative Mechanism for the Reorganization of the United Nations Regional Centre for Peace and Disarmament in Africa established by resolution 60/86 of 8 December 2005,

Noting the timely implementation by the Secretary-General of its resolution 62/216 of 22 December 2007 concerning the future work programme of the Regional Centre, as well as its staffing and funding,

Deeply concerned that, as noted in the report of the Secretary-General, despite the decision taken in Khartoum in January 2006 by the Executive Council of the African Union, in which the Council called upon member States to make voluntary contributions to the Regional Centre to maintain its operations, no such funds have been received to ensure its operations,

1. *Takes note* of the report of the Secretary-General;

2. *Notes* the successful conclusion of the process of revitalization of the United Nations Regional Centre for Peace and Disarmament in Africa through the strengthening of its financial and human capacities;

3. *Notes with appreciation* the efforts of the Regional Centre to align its actions with the priorities identified in the recommendations of the Consultative Mechanism for the Reorganization of the United Nations Regional Centre for Peace and Disarmament in Africa;

4. *Welcomes* the undertaking by the Regional Centre of new initiatives and projects in the fields of security sector reform and practical disarmament measures, as detailed in the report of the Secretary-General;

5. *Also welcomes* the efforts made by the Regional Centre to revitalize its activities and extend its operations to cover all of Africa, in order to respond to the evolving needs of the continent in the areas of peace, security and disarmament;

6. *Urges* all States, as well as international governmental and non-governmental organizations and foundations, to make voluntary contributions to support the programmes and activities of the Regional Centre and facilitate their implementation;

7. *Urges*, in particular, States members of the African Union to make voluntary contributions to the Regional Centre's trust fund in conformity with the decision taken by the Executive Council of the African Union in Khartoum in January 2006;

8. *Requests* the Secretary-General to facilitate closer cooperation between the Regional Centre and the African Union, in particular in the areas of peace, security and disarmament;

9. *Also requests* the Secretary-General to continue to provide the necessary support to the Regional Centre for greater achievements and results;

10. *Further requests* the Secretary-General to report to the General Assembly at its sixty-sixth session on the implementation of the present resolution;

11. *Decides* to include in the provisional agenda of its sixty-sixth session the item entitled "United Nations Regional Centre for Peace and Disarmament in Africa".

Asia and the Pacific

Pursuant to General Assembly resolution 63/77 [YUN 2008, p. 651], the Secretary-General in June reported [A/64/111] on the work of the United Nations Regional Centre for Peace and Disarmament in Asia and the Pacific between July 2008 and June 2009 on promoting global disarmament and non-proliferation norms; enhancing regional dialogue on disarmament, non-proliferation and security matters; and outreach and advocacy activities. The Centre, inaugurated in 1989 [YUN 1989, p. 88] and located in Kathmandu, Nepal, organized workshops, seminars and, in 2008, two conferences [YUN 2008, p. 650]. The Centre launched a new project aimed at enhancing international and regional cooperation to prevent, combat and eradicate illicit brokering in small arms and light weapons in the region. It was essential that Member States, in particular those from the region, took full ownership of the Centre and provided political and financial support to its operations and activities benefiting the region.

As at 31 December 2008, the Centre's trust fund balance stood at $537,792.

GENERAL ASSEMBLY ACTION

On 2 December [meeting 55], the General Assembly, on the recommendation of the First Committee [A/64/392], adopted **resolution 64/63** without vote [agenda item 97 *(d)*].

United Nations Regional Centre for Peace and Disarmament in Asia and the Pacific

The General Assembly,

Recalling its resolutions 42/39 D of 30 November 1987 and 44/117 F of 15 December 1989, by which it established the United Nations Regional Centre for Peace and Disarmament in Asia and renamed it the United Nations Regional Centre for Peace and Disarmament in Asia and the Pacific, with headquarters in Kathmandu and with the mandate of providing, on request, substantive support for the initiatives and other activities mutually agreed upon by the Member States of the Asia-Pacific region for the implementation of measures for peace and disarmament, through appropriate utilization of available resources,

Welcoming the physical operation of the Regional Centre from Kathmandu in accordance with General Assembly resolution 62/52 of 5 December 2007,

Recalling the Regional Centre's mandate of providing, on request, substantive support for the initiatives and other activities mutually agreed upon by the Member States of the Asia-Pacific region for the implementation of measures for peace and disarmament,

Expressing its appreciation to the Regional Centre for its important work in promoting confidence-building measures through the organization of meetings, conferences and workshops in the region, including conferences held on Jeju Island, Republic of Korea, from 24 to 26 November 2008 and in Niigata, Japan, from 26 to 28 August 2009,

Concerned by the report of the Secretary-General, in which he indicates that in order to be able to carry out its mandate fully and effectively, the Regional Centre needs to rely on a stable core team of skilled professional and support staff,

Appreciating the timely execution by Nepal of its financial commitments for the physical operation of the Regional Centre,

1. *Welcomes* the physical operation of the United Nations Regional Centre for Peace and Disarmament in Asia and the Pacific from Kathmandu in close cooperation with Member States;

2. *Expresses its gratitude* to the Government of Nepal for its cooperation and financial support, which has allowed the new office of the Regional Centre to operate from Kathmandu;

3. *Expresses its appreciation* to the Secretary-General and the Office for Disarmament Affairs of the Secretariat for providing necessary support with a view to ensuring the smooth operation of the Regional Centre from Kathmandu and to enabling the Centre to function effectively;

4. *Appeals* to Member States, in particular those within the Asia-Pacific region, as well as to international governmental and non-governmental organizations and foundations, to make voluntary contributions, the only resources of the Regional Centre, to strengthen the programme of activities of the Centre and the implementation thereof;

5. *Reaffirms its strong support* for the role of the Regional Centre in the promotion of United Nations activities at the regional level to strengthen peace, stability and security among its Member States;

6. *Underlines* the importance of the Kathmandu process for the development of the practice of region-wide security and disarmament dialogues;

7. *Requests* the Secretary-General to report to the General Assembly at its sixty-fifth session on the implementation of the present resolution;

8. *Decides* to include in the provisional agenda of its sixty-fifth session the item entitled "United Nations Regional Centre for Peace and Disarmament in Asia and the Pacific".

Latin America and the Caribbean

The United Nations Regional Centre for Peace, Disarmament and Development in Latin America and the Caribbean was inaugurated in Lima, Peru, in 1987 [YUN 1987, p. 88]. In a report issued in June [A/64/116], submitted pursuant to General Assembly resolution 63/74 [YUN 2008, p. 654], the Secretary-General described the work of the Centre from July 2008 to June 2009 in the areas of armed violence and public security; conventional and small arms instruments; and promotion of regional non-proliferation. The Centre focused on the issue of armed violence, which had been identified as a primary security con-

cern in the region, and contributed to the development of plans to reduce and prevent armed violence from an arms control perspective. In particular, the Centre assisted in building the capacity of States to combat illicit firearms trafficking. As a result of the Centre's efforts and joint initiatives, States were better equipped to confront armed violence and illicit firearms trafficking, which had a negative impact on sustainable development in the region. Similarly, States of the region gained greater access to standardized tools to assist in the development of firearms legislation and small arms policies. The Centre's dependency on extrabudgetary funds for both projects and operational costs continued to represent a challenge, and the Centre had therefore intensified its resource mobilization efforts to guarantee the sustainability of its operation.

As at 31 December 2008, the balance of the trust fund for the Centre stood at $1,236,976.

GENERAL ASSEMBLY ACTION

On 2 December [meeting 55], the General Assembly, on the recommendation of the First Committee [A/64/392], adopted **resolution 64/60** without vote [agenda item 97 *(a)*].

United Nations Regional Centre for Peace, Disarmament and Development in Latin America and the Caribbean

The General Assembly,

Recalling its resolutions 41/60 J of 3 December 1986, 42/39 K of 30 November 1987 and 43/76 H of 7 December 1988 on the United Nations Regional Centre for Peace, Disarmament and Development in Latin America and the Caribbean, with headquarters in Lima,

Recalling also its resolutions 46/37 F of 9 December 1991, 48/76 E of 16 December 1993, 49/76 D of 15 December 1994, 50/71 C of 12 December 1995, 52/220 of 22 December 1997, 53/78 F of 4 December 1998, 54/55 F of 1 December 1999, 55/34 E of 20 November 2000, 56/25 E of 29 November 2001, 57/89 of 22 November 2002, 58/60 of 8 December 2003, 59/99 of 3 December 2004, 60/84 of 8 December 2005, 61/92 of 6 December 2006, 62/49 of 5 December 2007 and 63/74 of 2 December 2008,

Recognizing that the Regional Centre has continued to provide substantive support for the implementation of regional and subregional initiatives and has intensified its contribution to the coordination of United Nations efforts towards peace and disarmament and for the promotion of economic and social development,

Reaffirming the mandate of the Regional Centre to provide, on request, substantive support for the initiatives and other activities of the Member States of the region for the implementation of measures for peace and disarmament and for the promotion of economic and social development,

Taking note of the report of the Secretary-General, and expressing its appreciation for the important assistance provided by the Regional Centre to many countries in the region for the development of plans to reduce and prevent armed violence from an arms control perspective and for promoting the implementation of relevant agreements and treaties,

Emphasizing the need for the Regional Centre to develop and strengthen its activities and programmes in a comprehensive and balanced manner, in accordance with its mandate,

Recalling the report of the Group of Governmental Experts on the relationship between disarmament and development, referred to in General Assembly resolution 59/78 of 3 December 2004, which is of utmost interest with regard to the role that the Regional Centre plays in promoting the issue in the region in pursuit of its mandate to promote economic and social development related to peace and disarmament,

Noting that security and disarmament issues have always been recognized as significant topics in Latin America and the Caribbean, the first inhabited region in the world to be declared a nuclear-weapon-free zone,

Welcoming the support provided by the Regional Centre to strengthening the nuclear-weapon-free zone established by the Treaty for the Prohibition of Nuclear Weapons in Latin America and the Caribbean (Treaty of Tlatelolco), as well as to promoting and assisting the ratification and implementation of existing multilateral agreements related to weapons of mass destruction and to promoting peace and disarmament education projects during the period under review,

Bearing in mind the important role of the Regional Centre in promoting confidence-building measures, arms control and limitation, disarmament and development at the regional level,

Bearing in mind also the importance of information, research, education and training for peace, disarmament and development in order to achieve understanding and cooperation among States,

1. *Reiterates its strong support* for the role of the United Nations Regional Centre for Peace, Disarmament and Development in Latin America and the Caribbean in the promotion of United Nations activities at the regional level to strengthen peace, disarmament, stability, security and development among its member States;

2. *Expresses its satisfaction* for the activities carried out in the past year by the Regional Centre, and requests the Centre to take into account the proposals to be submitted by the countries of the region in promoting confidence-building measures, arms control and limitation, transparency, disarmament and development at the regional level;

3. *Expresses its appreciation* for the political support and financial contributions to the Regional Centre, which are essential for its continued operation;

4. *Appeals* to Member States, in particular those within the Latin American and Caribbean region, and to international governmental and non-governmental organizations and foundations to make and to increase voluntary contributions to strengthen the Regional Centre, its programme of activities and the implementation thereof;

5. *Invites* all States of the region to continue to take part in the activities of the Regional Centre, proposing items for inclusion in its programme of activities and making greater and better use of the potential of the Centre to meet the current challenges facing the international community with a view to fulfilling the aims of the Charter of the United Nations in the areas of peace, disarmament and development;

6. *Recognizes* that the Regional Centre has an important role in the promotion and development of regional initiatives agreed upon by the countries of Latin America and the Caribbean in the field of weapons of mass destruction, in particular nuclear weapons, and conventional arms, including small arms and light weapons, as well as in the relationship between disarmament and development;

7. *Encourages* the Regional Centre to further develop activities in all countries of the region in the important areas of peace, disarmament and development;

8. *Requests* the Secretary-General to report to the General Assembly at its sixty-fifth session on the implementation of the present resolution;

9. *Decides* to include in the provisional agenda of its sixty-fifth session the item entitled "United Nations Regional Centre for Peace, Disarmament and Development in Latin America and the Caribbean".

Chapter VIII

Other political and security questions

In 2009, the United Nations continued to consider political and security questions related to its efforts in support of democratization worldwide, the promotion of decolonization, the peaceful uses of outer space and the Organization's public information activities.

Following a September report of the Secretary-General, the General Assembly encouraged Governments to strengthen programmes for the promotion and consolidation of democracy through increased cooperation and by highlighting the role of the International Day of Democracy.

The Special Committee on the Situation with regard to the Implementation of the Declaration on the Granting of Independence to Colonial Countries and Peoples reviewed progress in implementing the 1960 Declaration, particularly the exercise of self-determination by the remaining Non-Self-Governing Territories (NSGTs). During the year, the Special Committee organized a Caribbean regional seminar in Frigate Bay, Saint Kitts and Nevis, as part of its efforts to implement the plan of action for the Second International Decade for the Eradication of Colonialism (2001–2010). Highlighting the economic vulnerability brought about by climate change and the global economic and financial crisis, the seminar suggested that relevant stakeholders, particularly the territorial Governments and the administering Powers, increase their attention to community-based sustainable development and the empowerment of vulnerable groups in the NSGTs. The seminar suggested that the Special Committee consider proposing to the General Assembly the possibility of launching a Third International Decade for the Eradication of Colonialism.

The Committee on the Peaceful Uses of Outer Space considered the implementation of the recommendations of the Third (1999) United Nations Conference on the Exploration and Peaceful Uses of Outer Space (UNISPACE III) and welcomed the link between the work on UNISPACE III and the work of the Commission on Sustainable Development.

The United Nations Platform for Space-based Information for Disaster Management and Emergency Response (UN-SPIDER) inaugurated a new office in Bonn, Germany, and made progress towards formalizing a network of UN-SPIDER regional support offices, for which Algeria, Iran, Nigeria, Pakistan, Romania, South Africa and Ukraine had either signed a cooperation agreement or offered to host an office. The support provided by Member States, interna-

tional and regional organizations and UN-SPIDER in the provision of space-based information to support relief efforts was timely and useful.

The United Nations Scientific Committee on the Effects of Atomic Radiation could not hold its fifty-seventh session, originally scheduled for 25–29 May in Vienna, due to an unforeseen crisis and was rescheduled to the spring of the following year.

In a December resolution on developments in information and telecommunications in the context of international security, the Assembly called on Member States to promote consideration of existing and potential threats in the field of information security, as well as possible measures to limit threats emerging in the field, consistent with the need to preserve the free flow of information.

The Committee on Information continued to review UN information policies and activities and the management and operation of the UN Department of Public Information (DPI). At its May session, the Committee considered reports by the Secretary-General on several DPI activities in promoting the work of the United Nations to a global audience. Among other initiatives, DPI started a programme called Academic Impact to engage with centres of higher education, learning and research and facilitate a more direct input of the ideas generated by such institutions into UN policies and programmes. Also noteworthy was the launch of the Secretary-General's Creative Community Outreach Initiative, which would function as a one-stop-shop for writers, directors, producers and broadcasters interested in portraying the United Nations and its issues in their work.

General aspects of international security

Support for democracies

UN system activities

In a September report [A/64/372] submitted in response to General Assembly resolution 62/7 [YUN 2007, p. 605], the Secretary-General made observations and recommendations on UN cooperation with global democracy movements as well as with regional and other intergovernmental organizations working to promote democracy. The report recommended that the annual commemoration of the International Day of Democracy be sustained, broadened and deepened by including young people and by encompassing activities in all corners of the world. It was further suggested that the International Conference of New or Restored Democracies and the Community of Democracies seek to build synergies in their work, including through the establishment of mechanisms for enhanced coordination, cooperation and strategic partnership. There was also need for more effective follow-up between the conferences of the New or Restored Democracies Movement and strengthened democracy assistance of the United Nations, including by ensuring it was delivered coherently and consistently.

GENERAL ASSEMBLY ACTION

On 9 November [meeting 41], the General Assembly adopted **resolution 64/12** [draft: A/64/L.12 & Add.1] without vote [agenda item 11].

Support by the United Nations system of the efforts of Governments to promote and consolidate new or restored democracies

The General Assembly,

Recalling its resolutions 49/30 of 7 December 1994, 50/133 of 20 December 1995, 51/31 of 6 December 1996, 52/18 of 21 November 1997, 53/31 of 23 November 1998, 54/36 of 29 November 1999, 55/43 of 27 November 2000, 56/96 of 14 December 2001, 56/269 of 27 March 2002, 58/13 of 17 November 2003, 58/281 of 9 February 2004, 60/253 of 2 May 2006, 61/226 of 22 December 2006 and 62/7 of 8 November 2007,

Recalling also the United Nations Millennium Declaration adopted by Heads of State and Government on 8 September 2000, in particular paragraphs 6 and 24 thereof, and the 2005 World Summit Outcome,

Recalling further the declarations and plans of action of the six international conferences of new or restored democracies adopted in Manila in 1988, Managua in 1994, Bucharest in 1997, Cotonou in 2000, Ulaanbaatar in 2003 and Doha in 2006,

Reaffirming the Charter of the United Nations, including the principles and purposes contained therein, and recognizing that human rights, the rule of law and democracy are interlinked and mutually reinforcing and that they belong to the universal and indivisible core values and principles of the United Nations,

Stressing that democracy, development and respect for all human rights and fundamental freedoms are interdependent and mutually reinforcing,

Reaffirming that democracy is a universal value based on the freely expressed will of people to determine their own political, economic, social and cultural systems and their full participation in all aspects of their lives,

Reaffirming also that, while democracies share common features, there is no single model of democracy and that democracy does not belong to any country or region, and reaffirming further the necessity of due respect for sovereignty, the right to self-determination and territorial integrity,

Bearing in mind that the activities of the United Nations carried out in support of efforts of Governments to promote and consolidate democracy are undertaken in accordance with the Charter and only at the specific request of the Member States concerned,

Mindful of the central role of parliaments and the active involvement of civil society organizations and media and their interaction with Governments at all levels in promoting democracy, freedom, equality, participation, development, respect for human rights and fundamental freedoms and the rule of law, and welcoming in this regard the expanded tripartite participation in the Sixth International Conference of New or Restored Democracies, hosted by the Government of Qatar in Doha from 29 October to 1 November 2006, which focused on capacity-building, democracy and social progress,

Noting the role of the International Institute for Democracy and Electoral Assistance in support of the New or Restored Democracies Movement,

Noting also the achievement of the Sixth International Conference, under the chairmanship of Qatar, of the establishment of the International Day of Democracy on 15 September, as noted in General Assembly resolution 62/7, which was celebrated for the first time in 2008,

Convinced of the need to continue to encourage and promote democratization, development and respect for human rights and fundamental freedoms and of the importance of action-oriented follow-up to the Sixth International Conference,

1. *Takes note with appreciation* of the report of the Secretary-General;

2. *Welcomes* the work carried out as part of the follow-up mechanisms of the Sixth International Conference of New or Restored Democracies and the efforts of the Chair of the Conference to make the Conference and the follow-up thereto more effective and efficient, and in this regard takes note of the outcomes of the four meetings of the Advisory Board of the Conference, particularly the implementation of the programme of work of the Conference for 2007–2009 and the convening of the ministerial meeting of the New or Restored Democracies Movement, on the sidelines of the sixty-fourth session of the General Assembly, at which various initiatives on the future sustainability of the Movement were considered;

3. *Invites* Member States, the relevant organizations of the United Nations system, other intergovernmental organizations, national parliaments, including in collaboration with the Inter-Parliamentary Union and other parliamentary organizations, and non-governmental organizations to contribute actively to the follow-up to the Sixth International Conference and to make additional efforts to identify possible steps in support of the efforts of Governments to promote and consolidate new or restored democracies, including through those steps set out in the Doha Declaration, and to inform the Secretary-General of the actions taken;

4. *Encourages* Governments to strengthen national programmes devoted to the promotion and consolidation of democracy, including through increased bilateral, regional and international cooperation, taking into account innovative approaches and best practices;

5. *Invites* all Member States, organizations of the United Nations system, regional and intergovernmental

organizations, non-governmental organizations and individuals to continue to commemorate the International Day of Democracy in an appropriate manner that contributes to raising public awareness;

6. *Requests* the Secretary-General to continue to take necessary measures, within existing resources, for the observance by the United Nations of the International Day of Democracy;

7. *Urges* the Secretary-General to continue to improve the capacity of the Organization to respond effectively to the requests of Member States by providing sustainable assistance for building national capacity and adequate support for their efforts to achieve the goals of good governance and democratization, including through the activities of the United Nations Democracy Fund;

8. *Also urges* the Secretary-General to continue efforts to improve coherence and coordination among United Nations initiatives in the area of democracy assistance, including interactions with all stakeholders, in order to ensure that democracy assistance is more effectively integrated into the work of the Organization;

9. *Requests* the Secretary-General to examine options for strengthening the support provided by the United Nations system for the efforts of Member States to consolidate democracy and achieve good governance, including the provision of support to the Chair of the Sixth International Conference in his efforts to make the Conference and the follow-up thereto more effective and efficient;

10. *Welcomes* the decision of the Government of the Bolivarian Republic of Venezuela to host the Seventh International Conference of New or Restored Democracies in 2010;

11. *Invites* the Secretary-General, Member States, the relevant specialized agencies and bodies of the United Nations system and other intergovernmental organizations to collaborate in the holding of the Seventh International Conference;

12. *Requests* the Secretary-General to submit a report to the General Assembly at its sixty-sixth session on the implementation of the present resolution, including therein the information requested in paragraph 3 above;

13. *Decides* to include in the provisional agenda of its sixty-sixth session the item entitled "Support by the United Nations system of the efforts of Governments to promote and consolidate new or restored democracies".

Regional aspects of international peace and security

Indian Ocean

In 2009, the Ad Hoc Committee on the Indian Ocean continued its efforts to reach agreement on ways forward in implementing the 1971 Declaration of the Indian Ocean as a Zone of Peace, as adopted by the General Assembly in resolution 2832(XXVI) [YUN 1971, p. 34]. The Committee held its formal session in New York on 24 July [A/64/29], at which the Committee Chairman stated that while Member States shared the conviction that the objectives of the Declaration remained worthwhile, the changing security and geopolitical scenario in the Indian Ocean region continued to generate more issues and greater complexities. New challenges in arms trafficking and disarmament had emerged, while non-State players, including terrorist groups and transnational subversive elements, had become threats to peace and security within and between States. Such manifestations were working against the positive socio-economic developments and exponential growth in people-to-people contacts that had been seen in the Indian Ocean Zone. The Committee therefore had a continuing deliberating role to play, as it provided broad-based participation to all Member States within the region and beyond. The Chairman noted, however, that the Committee might wish to explore new approaches, including a revision of the Declaration in line with current regional challenges and realities. The Chairman was requested to continue consultations with Committee members and report to the Assembly's sixty-sixth (2011) session.

GENERAL ASSEMBLY ACTION

On 2 December [meeting 55], the General Assembly, on the recommendation of the First (Disarmament and International Security) Committee [A/64/382], adopted **resolution 64/23** by recorded vote (128-3-45) [agenda item 87].

Implementation of the Declaration of the Indian Ocean as a Zone of Peace

The General Assembly,

Recalling the Declaration of the Indian Ocean as a Zone of Peace, contained in its resolution 2832(XXVI) of 16 December 1971, and recalling also its resolutions 54/47 of 1 December 1999, 56/16 of 29 November 2001, 58/29 of 8 December 2003, 60/48 of 8 December 2005 and 62/14 of 5 December 2007 and other relevant resolutions,

Recalling also the report of the Meeting of the Littoral and Hinterland States of the Indian Ocean held in July 1979,

Recalling further paragraph 102 of the Final Document of the Thirteenth Conference of Heads of State or Government of Non-Aligned Countries, held in Kuala Lumpur on 24 and 25 February 2003, in which it was noted, inter alia, that the Chair of the Ad Hoc Committee on the Indian Ocean would continue his informal consultations on the future work of the Committee,

Emphasizing the need to foster consensual approaches that are conducive to the pursuit of such endeavours,

Noting the initiatives taken by countries of the region to promote cooperation, in particular economic cooperation, in the Indian Ocean area and the possible contribution of such initiatives to overall objectives of a zone of peace,

Convinced that the participation of all permanent members of the Security Council and the major maritime users of the Indian Ocean in the work of the Ad Hoc Committee is important and would assist the progress of a mutually beneficial dialogue to develop conditions of peace, security and stability in the Indian Ocean region,

Considering that greater efforts and more time are required to develop a focused discussion on practical measures to ensure conditions of peace, security and stability in the Indian Ocean region,

Having considered the report of the Ad Hoc Committee on the Indian Ocean,

1. *Takes note* of the report of the Ad Hoc Committee on the Indian Ocean;

2. *Reiterates its conviction* that the participation of all permanent members of the Security Council and the major maritime users of the Indian Ocean in the work of the Ad Hoc Committee is important and would greatly facilitate the development of a mutually beneficial dialogue to advance peace, security and stability in the Indian Ocean region;

3. *Requests* the Chair of the Ad Hoc Committee to continue his informal consultations with the members of the Committee and to report through the Committee to the General Assembly at its sixty-sixth session;

4. *Requests* the Secretary-General to continue to render, within existing resources, all necessary assistance to the Ad Hoc Committee, including the provision of summary records;

5. *Decides* to include in the provisional agenda of its sixty-sixth session the item entitled "Implementation of the Declaration of the Indian Ocean as a Zone of Peace".

RECORDED VOTE ON RESOLUTION 64/23:

In favour: Afghanistan, Algeria, Angola, Antigua and Barbuda, Argentina, Armenia, Australia, Azerbaijan, Bahamas, Bahrain, Barbados, Belarus, Belize, Benin, Bhutan, Bolivia, Bosnia and Herzegovina, Botswana, Brazil, Brunei Darussalam, Burundi, Cambodia, Cameroon, Cape Verde, Chile, China, Colombia, Comoros, Congo, Costa Rica, Côte d'Ivoire, Cuba, Democratic People's Republic of Korea, Democratic Republic of the Congo, Djibouti, Dominica, Dominican Republic, Ecuador, Egypt, El Salvador, Eritrea, Fiji, Gambia, Ghana, Grenada, Guatemala, Guinea, Guinea-Bissau, Guyana, Haiti, Honduras, India, Indonesia, Iran, Iraq, Jamaica, Japan, Jordan, Kazakhstan, Kenya, Kuwait, Kyrgyzstan, Lao People's Democratic Republic, Lebanon, Lesotho, Liberia, Libyan Arab Jamahiriya, Madagascar, Malawi, Malaysia, Maldives, Mali, Mauritania, Mauritius, Mexico, Mongolia, Morocco, Mozambique, Myanmar, Namibia, Nepal, New Zealand, Nicaragua, Niger, Nigeria, Oman, Pakistan, Panama, Papua New Guinea, Paraguay, Peru, Philippines, Qatar, Republic of Korea, Russian Federation, Rwanda, Saint Kitts and Nevis, Saint Lucia, Saint Vincent and the Grenadines, Samoa, Saudi Arabia, Senegal, Serbia, Sierra Leone, Singapore, Solomon Islands, Somalia, South Africa, Sri Lanka, Sudan, Suriname, Syrian Arab Republic, Thailand, Togo, Tonga, Trinidad and Tobago, Tunisia, Turkmenistan, Uganda, United Arab Emirates, United Republic of Tanzania, Uruguay, Uzbekistan, Venezuela, Viet Nam, Yemen, Zambia, Zimbabwe.

Against: France, United Kingdom, United States.

Abstaining: Albania, Andorra, Austria, Belgium, Bulgaria, Canada, Croatia, Cyprus, Czech Republic, Denmark, Estonia, Finland, Georgia, Germany, Greece, Hungary, Iceland, Ireland, Israel, Italy, Latvia, Liechtenstein, Lithuania, Luxembourg, Malta, Marshall Islands, Micronesia, Moldova, Monaco, Montenegro, Netherlands, Norway, Palau, Poland, Portugal, Romania, San Marino, Slovakia, Slovenia, Spain, Sweden, Switzerland, The former Yugoslav Republic of Macedonia, Turkey, Ukraine.

Decolonization

The General Assembly's Special Committee on the Situation with regard to the Implementation of the Declaration on the Granting of Independence to Colonial Countries and Peoples (Special Committee on decolonization) held its annual session in New York in two parts—27 February and 6 April (first part); and 8–9, 15–19 and 23 June (second part). Various aspects of the implementation of the 1960 Declaration, adopted by the Assembly in resolution 1514(XV) [YUN 1960, p. 49], were considered by the Special Committee, including general decolonization issues and the situation in the individual Non-Self-Governing Territories (NSGTs). The Special Committee adopted three draft resolutions and recommended eight draft resolutions for adoption by the General Assembly. In accordance with resolution 63/110 [YUN 2008, p. 659], the Special Committee reported to the Assembly on its 2009 activities [A/64/23].

Decade for the Eradication of Colonialism
Caribbean regional seminar

The Special Committee on decolonization organized a Caribbean regional seminar (Frigate Bay, Saint Kitts and Nevis, 12–14 May) [A/64/23] to review implementation of the plan of action for the Second International Decade for the Eradication of Colonialism (2001–2010) [YUN 2001, p. 530] and define priority action for the remaining years of the Decade, as declared by General Assembly resolution 55/146 [YUN 2000, p. 548]. The objective of the seminar was to enable the Special Committee to hear the views of representatives of NSGTs, experts, civil society and other stakeholders in the process of decolonization.

Seminar participants reaffirmed that all peoples have the right to self-determination, by virtue of which they freely determine their political status and pursue their economic, social and cultural development, and that the UN system had a valid ongoing role in the process of decolonization. The seminar recommended that the Special Committee develop a proactive and focused approach, in fulfilment of the goal of decolonization vis-à-vis the NSGTs on the UN list. In view of the economic vulnerability brought about by climate change and the global economic and financial crisis, the seminar suggested that relevant stakeholders, particularly the territorial Governments and the administering Powers, step up their attention to community-based sustainable development and the empowerment of vulnerable groups in the NSGTs. Participants advised that the Special Committee, in collaboration with the Department of Public Information, engage the peoples of the NSGTs in fostering an understanding of the various options for self-determination in accordance with relevant UN resolutions and decisions. The seminar further suggested that the Special Committee consider proposing to the Assembly the possibility of launching a Third International Decade for the Eradication of Colonialism, reaffirming that the process of decolonization was incomplete until all outstanding decolonization issues were resolved in a satisfactory manner.

GENERAL ASSEMBLY ACTION

On 10 December [meeting 62], the General Assembly, on the recommendation of the Fourth (Special Political and Decolonization) Committee [A/64/413], adopted **resolution 64/106** by recorded vote (172-3-2) [agenda item 39].

Implementation of the Declaration on the Granting of Independence to Colonial Countries and Peoples

The General Assembly,

Having examined the report of the Special Committee on the Situation with regard to the Implementation of the Declaration on the Granting of Independence to Colonial Countries and Peoples,

Recalling its resolution 1514(XV) of 14 December 1960, containing the Declaration on the Granting of Independence to Colonial Countries and Peoples, and all its subsequent resolutions concerning the implementation of the Declaration, the most recent of which was resolution 63/110 of 5 December 2008, as well as the relevant resolutions of the Security Council,

Bearing in mind its resolution 55/146 of 8 December 2000, by which it declared the period 2001–2010 the Second International Decade for the Eradication of Colonialism, and the need to examine ways to ascertain the wishes of the peoples of the Non-Self-Governing Territories on the basis of resolution 1514(XV) and other relevant resolutions on decolonization,

Recognizing that the eradication of colonialism has been one of the priorities of the United Nations and continues to be one of its priorities for the decade that began in 2001,

Reconfirming the need to take measures to eliminate colonialism by 2010, as called for in its resolution 55/146,

Reiterating its conviction of the need for the eradication of colonialism, as well as racial discrimination and violations of basic human rights,

Noting with satisfaction the achievements of the Special Committee in contributing to the effective and complete implementation of the Declaration and other relevant resolutions of the United Nations on decolonization,

Stressing the importance of the formal participation of the administering Powers in the work of the Special Committee,

Noting with satisfaction the cooperation and active participation of administering Powers in the work of the Special Committee, and encouraging the others also to do so,

Noting that the Caribbean regional seminar was held in Frigate Bay, Saint Kitts and Nevis, from 12 to 14 May 2009,

1. *Reaffirms* its resolution 1514(XV) and all other resolutions and decisions on decolonization, including its reso-

lution 55/146, by which it declared the period 2001–2010 the Second International Decade for the Eradication of Colonialism, and calls upon the administering Powers, in accordance with those resolutions, to take all steps necessary to enable the peoples of the Non-Self-Governing Territories concerned to exercise fully as soon as possible their right to self-determination, including independence;

2. *Reaffirms once again* that the existence of colonialism in any form or manifestation, including economic exploitation, is incompatible with the Charter of the United Nations, the Declaration on the Granting of Independence to Colonial Countries and Peoples and the Universal Declaration of Human Rights;

3. *Reaffirms its determination* to continue to take all steps necessary to bring about the complete and speedy eradication of colonialism and the faithful observance by all States of the relevant provisions of the Charter, the Declaration on the Granting of Independence to Colonial Countries and Peoples and the Universal Declaration of Human Rights;

4. *Affirms once again its support* for the aspirations of the peoples under colonial rule to exercise their right to self-determination, including independence, in accordance with the relevant resolutions of the United Nations on decolonization;

5. *Calls upon* the administering Powers to cooperate fully with the Special Committee on the Situation with regard to the Implementation of the Declaration on the Granting of Independence to Colonial Countries and Peoples to develop and finalize, before the end of the Second International Decade for the Eradication of Colonialism, a constructive programme of work on a case-by-case basis for the Non-Self-Governing Territories to facilitate the implementation of the mandate of the Special Committee and the relevant resolutions on decolonization, including resolutions on specific Territories;

6. *Recalls with satisfaction* the professional, open and transparent conduct of both the February 2006 and the October 2007 referendums to determine the future status of Tokelau, monitored by the United Nations;

7. *Requests* the Special Committee to continue to seek suitable means for the immediate and full implementation of the Declaration and to carry out the actions approved by the General Assembly regarding the International Decade for the Eradication of Colonialism and the Second International Decade for the Eradication of Colonialism in all Territories that have not yet exercised their right to self-determination, including independence, and in particular:

(a) To formulate specific proposals to bring about an end to colonialism and to report thereon to the General Assembly at its sixty-fifth session;

(b) To continue to examine the implementation by Member States of resolution 1514(XV) and other relevant resolutions on decolonization;

(c) To continue to examine the political, economic and social situation in the Non-Self-Governing Territories, and to recommend, as appropriate, to the General Assembly the most suitable steps to be taken to enable the populations of those Territories to exercise their right to self-determination, including independence, in accordance with the relevant resolutions on decolonization, including resolutions on specific Territories;

(d) To develop and finalize, before the end of the Second International Decade for the Eradication of Colonialism and in cooperation with the administering Power and the Territory in question, a constructive programme of work on a case-by-case basis for the Non-Self-Governing Territories to facilitate the implementation of the mandate of the Special Committee and the relevant resolutions on decolonization, including resolutions on specific Territories;

(e) To continue to dispatch visiting and special missions to the Non-Self-Governing Territories in accordance with the relevant resolutions on decolonization, including resolutions on specific Territories;

(f) To conduct seminars, as appropriate, for the purpose of receiving and disseminating information on the work of the Special Committee, and to facilitate participation by the peoples of the Non-Self-Governing Territories in those seminars;

(g) To take all steps necessary to enlist worldwide support among Governments, as well as national and international organizations, for the achievement of the objectives of the Declaration and the implementation of the relevant resolutions of the United Nations;

(h) To observe annually the Week of Solidarity with the Peoples of Non-Self-Governing Territories;

8. *Recognizes* that the plan of action for the Second International Decade for the Eradication of Colonialism represents an important legislative authority for the attainment of self-government by the Non-Self-Governing Territories, and that the case-by-case assessment of the attainment of self-government in each Territory can make an important contribution to this process;

9. *Calls upon* all States, in particular the administering Powers, as well as the specialized agencies and other organizations of the United Nations system, to give effect within their respective spheres of competence to the recommendations of the Special Committee for the implementation of the Declaration and other relevant resolutions of the United Nations;

10. *Calls upon* the administering Powers to ensure that economic and other activities in the Non-Self-Governing Territories under their administration do not adversely affect the interests of the peoples but instead promote development, and to assist them in the exercise of their right to self-determination;

11. *Urges* the administering Powers concerned to take effective measures to safeguard and guarantee the inalienable rights of the peoples of the Non-Self-Governing Territories to their natural resources, and to establish and maintain control over the future development of those resources, and requests the relevant administering Power to take all steps necessary to protect the property rights of the peoples of those Territories;

12. *Urges* all States, directly and through their action in the specialized agencies and other organizations of the United Nations system, to provide moral and material assistance, as needed, to the peoples of the Non-Self-Governing Territories, and requests the administering Powers to take steps to enlist and make effective use of all possible assistance, on both a bilateral and a multilateral basis, in the strengthening of the economies of those Territories;

13. *Requests* the Secretary-General, the specialized agencies and other organizations of the United Nations

system to provide economic, social and other assistance to the Non-Self-Governing Territories and to continue to do so, as appropriate, after they exercise their right to self-determination, including independence;

14. *Reaffirms* that the United Nations visiting missions to the Territories are an effective means of ascertaining the situation in the Territories, as well as the wishes and aspirations of their inhabitants, and calls upon the administering Powers to continue to cooperate with the Special Committee in the discharge of its mandate and to facilitate visiting missions to the Territories;

15. *Calls upon* all the administering Powers to cooperate fully in the work of the Special Committee and to participate formally in its future sessions;

16. *Approves* the report of the Special Committee on the Situation with regard to the Implementation of the Declaration on the Granting of Independence to Colonial Countries and Peoples covering its work during 2009, including the programme of work envisaged for 2010;

17. *Requests* the Secretary-General to provide the Special Committee with the facilities and services required for the implementation of the present resolution, as well as the other resolutions and decisions on decolonization adopted by the General Assembly and the Special Committee.

RECORDED VOTE ON RESOLUTION 64/106:

In favour: Afghanistan, Albania, Algeria, Andorra, Angola, Antigua and Barbuda, Argentina, Armenia, Australia, Austria, Azerbaijan, Bahamas, Bahrain, Bangladesh, Barbados, Belarus, Belize, Benin, Bhutan, Bolivia, Bosnia and Herzegovina, Botswana, Brazil, Brunei Darussalam, Bulgaria, Burkina Faso, Burundi, Cameroon, Canada, Cape Verde, Chile, China, Colombia, Comoros, Congo, Costa Rica, Côte d'Ivoire, Croatia, Cuba, Cyprus, Czech Republic, Democratic People's Republic of Korea, Denmark, Djibouti, Dominica, Dominican Republic, Ecuador, Egypt, El Salvador, Eritrea, Estonia, Ethiopia, Fiji, Finland, Gambia, Georgia, Germany, Ghana, Greece, Grenada, Guatemala, Guinea, Guinea-Bissau, Guyana, Honduras, Hungary, Iceland, India, Indonesia, Iran, Iraq, Ireland, Italy, Jamaica, Japan, Jordan, Kazakhstan, Kenya, Kuwait, Kyrgyzstan, Lao People's Democratic Republic, Latvia, Lebanon, Lesotho, Liberia, Libyan Arab Jamahiriya, Liechtenstein, Lithuania, Luxembourg, Madagascar, Malawi, Malaysia, Maldives, Mali, Malta, Marshall Islands, Mauritania, Mauritius, Mexico, Moldova, Monaco, Mongolia, Montenegro, Morocco, Mozambique, Myanmar, Namibia, Nepal, Netherlands, New Zealand, Nicaragua, Niger, Nigeria, Norway, Oman, Pakistan, Palau, Panama, Papua New Guinea, Paraguay, Peru, Philippines, Poland, Portugal, Qatar, Republic of Korea, Romania, Russian Federation, Saint Lucia, Saint Vincent and the Grenadines, Samoa, San Marino, Saudi Arabia, Senegal, Serbia, Sierra Leone, Singapore, Slovakia, Slovenia, Solomon Islands, Somalia, South Africa, Spain, Sri Lanka, Sudan, Suriname, Swaziland, Sweden, Switzerland, Syrian Arab Republic, Tajikistan, Thailand, The former Yugoslav Republic of Macedonia, Timor-Leste, Togo, Tonga, Trinidad and Tobago, Tunisia, Turkey, Turkmenistan, Uganda, Ukraine, United Arab Emirates, United Republic of Tanzania, Uruguay, Uzbekistan, Vanuatu, Venezuela, Viet Nam, Yemen, Zambia, Zimbabwe.

Against: Israel, United Kingdom, United States.

Abstaining: Belgium, France.

Implementation
by international organizations

In a February report [A/64/62], the Secretary-General stated that he had brought General Assembly resolution 63/103 [YUN 2008, p. 663] to the attention of the specialized agencies and other international institutions associated with the United Nations and invited them to submit information regarding their implementation activities in support of NSGTs. Replies received from eight agencies or institutions were summarized in a May report of the Economic and Social Council President on his consultations with the Special Committee on decolonization [E/2009/69]. According to the information provided, a number of organizations continued to provide support to NSGTs from their own budgetary resources, in addition to their respective contributions as executing agencies of projects funded by UNDP, the primary provider of support.

ECONOMIC AND SOCIAL COUNCIL ACTION

On 31 July [meeting 45], the Economic and Social Council adopted **resolution 2009/33** [draft: E/2009/L.26] by a roll-call vote (25-0-22) [agenda item 9].

Support to Non-Self-Governing Territories by the specialized agencies and international institutions associated with the United Nations

The Economic and Social Council,

Having examined the report of the Secretary-General and the report of the President of the Economic and Social Council containing the information submitted by the specialized agencies and other organizations of the United Nations system on their activities with regard to the implementation of the Declaration on the Granting of Independence to Colonial Countries and Peoples,

Having heard the statement by the representative of the Special Committee on the Situation with regard to the Implementation of the Declaration on the Granting of Independence to Colonial Countries and Peoples,

Recalling General Assembly resolutions 1514(XV) of 14 December 1960 and 1541(XV) of 15 December 1960, the resolutions of the Special Committee and other relevant resolutions and decisions, including, in particular, Economic and Social Council resolution 2008/15 of 24 July 2008,

Bearing in mind the relevant provisions of the final documents of the successive Conferences of Heads of State or Government of Non-Aligned Countries and of the resolutions adopted by the Assembly of Heads of State and Government of the African Union, the Pacific Islands Forum and the Caribbean Community,

Conscious of the need to facilitate the implementation of the Declaration on the Granting of Independence to Colonial Countries and Peoples,

Welcoming the current participation, in their capacity as observers, of those Non-Self-Governing Territories that are associate members of the regional commissions in the world conferences in the economic and social sphere, subject to the rules of procedure of the General Assembly and in accordance with relevant United Nations resolutions and decisions, including resolutions and decisions of the Assembly and the Special Committee on specific Non-Self-Governing Territories,

Noting that only some specialized agencies and organizations of the United Nations system have been involved in providing assistance to Non-Self-Governing Territories,

Welcoming the assistance extended to Non-Self-Governing Territories by certain specialized agencies and other organizations of the United Nations system, in particular the United Nations Development Programme,

Stressing that, because their development options are limited, the small island Non-Self-Governing Territories face special challenges in planning for and implementing sustainable development and will be constrained in meeting those challenges without the continuing cooperation and assistance of the specialized agencies and other organizations of the United Nations system,

Stressing also the importance of securing the resources necessary for funding expanded programmes of assistance for the peoples concerned and the need to enlist the support of all the major funding institutions within the United Nations system in that regard,

Reaffirming the mandates of the specialized agencies and other organizations of the United Nations system to take all appropriate measures, within their respective spheres of competence, to ensure the full implementation of resolution 1514(XV) and other relevant resolutions,

Expressing its appreciation to the African Union, the Pacific Islands Forum, the Caribbean Community and other regional organizations for the continued cooperation and assistance that they have extended to the specialized agencies and other organizations of the United Nations system in that regard,

Expressing its conviction that closer contacts and consultations between and among the specialized agencies and other organizations of the United Nations system and regional organizations help to facilitate the effective formulation of programmes of assistance for the peoples concerned,

Mindful of the imperative need to keep under continuous review the activities of the specialized agencies and other organizations of the United Nations system in the implementation of the various United Nations decisions relating to decolonization,

Bearing in mind the extremely fragile economies of the small island Non-Self-Governing Territories and their vulnerability to natural disasters, such as hurricanes, cyclones and sea-level rise, and recalling the relevant resolutions of the General Assembly,

Recalling General Assembly resolution 63/103 of 5 December 2008, entitled "Implementation of the Declaration on the Granting of Independence to Colonial Countries and Peoples by the specialized agencies and the international institutions associated with the United Nations",

1. *Takes note* of the report of the President of the Economic and Social Council, and endorses the observations and suggestions arising therefrom;

2. *Also takes note* of the report of the Secretary-General;

3. *Recommends* that all States intensify their efforts within the specialized agencies and other organizations of

the United Nations system of which they are members to ensure the full and effective implementation of the Declaration on the Granting of Independence to Colonial Countries and Peoples, contained in resolution 1514(XV), and other relevant resolutions of the United Nations;

4.   *Reaffirms* that the specialized agencies and other organizations and institutions of the United Nations system should continue to be guided by the relevant resolutions of the United Nations in their efforts to contribute to the implementation of the Declaration and all other relevant General Assembly resolutions;

5.   *Also reaffirms* that the recognition by the General Assembly, the Security Council and other United Nations organs of the legitimacy of the aspirations of the peoples of the Non-Self-Governing Territories to exercise their right to self-determination entails, as a corollary, the extension of all appropriate assistance to those peoples;

6.   *Expresses its appreciation* to those specialized agencies and other organizations of the United Nations system that have continued to cooperate with the United Nations and the regional and subregional organizations in the implementation of resolution 1514(XV) and other relevant resolutions of the United Nations, and requests all the specialized agencies and other organizations of the United Nations system to implement the relevant provisions of those resolutions;

7.   *Requests* the specialized agencies and other organizations of the United Nations system and international and regional organizations to examine and review conditions in each Non-Self-Governing Territory so that they may take appropriate measures to accelerate progress in the economic and social sectors of those Territories;

8.   *Urges* those specialized agencies and organizations of the United Nations system that have not yet provided assistance to Non-Self-Governing Territories to do so as soon as possible;

9.   *Requests* the specialized agencies and other organizations and bodies of the United Nations system and regional organizations to strengthen existing measures of support and to formulate appropriate programmes of assistance to the remaining Non-Self-Governing Territories, within the framework of their respective mandates, in order to accelerate progress in the economic and social sectors of those Territories;

10. *Recommends* that the executive heads of the specialized agencies and other organizations of the United Nations system formulate, with the active cooperation of the regional organizations concerned, concrete proposals for the full implementation of the relevant resolutions of the United Nations and submit those proposals to their governing and legislative organs;

11. *Also recommends* that the specialized agencies and other organizations of the United Nations system continue to review, at the regular meetings of their governing bodies, the implementation of resolution 1514(XV) and other relevant resolutions of the United Nations;

12. *Welcomes* the preparation by the Department of Public Information and the Department of Political Affairs of the Secretariat, in consultation with the United Nations Development Programme, the specialized agencies and the Special Committee on the Situation with regard to the Implementation of the Declaration on the Granting of Independence to Colonial Countries and Peoples, of an informational leaflet on assistance programmes available to the Non-Self-Governing Territories and its updated 2009 online version, and requests that they be disseminated as widely as possible;

13. *Also welcomes* the continuing efforts made by the United Nations Development Programme in maintaining a close liaison between the specialized agencies and other organizations of the United Nations system, including the Economic Commission for Latin America and the Caribbean and the Economic and Social Commission for Asia and the Pacific, and in providing assistance to the peoples of the Non-Self-Governing Territories;

14. *Encourages* the Non-Self-Governing Territories to take steps to establish and/or strengthen institutions and policies for disaster preparedness and management;

15. *Requests* the administering Powers concerned to facilitate, when appropriate, the participation of appointed and elected representatives of Non-Self-Governing Territories in the relevant meetings and conferences of the specialized agencies and other organizations of the United Nations system, in accordance with relevant United Nations resolutions and decisions, including the resolutions and decisions of the General Assembly and the Special Committee, on specific Territories, so that they may benefit from the related activities of those agencies and organizations;

16. *Recommends* that all Governments intensify their efforts within the specialized agencies and other organizations of the United Nations system of which they are members to accord priority to the question of providing assistance to the peoples of the Non-Self-Governing Territories;

17. *Draws the attention* of the Special Committee to the present resolution and to the discussion held on the subject at the substantive session of 2009 of the Economic and Social Council;

18. *Recalls* the adoption by the Economic Commission for Latin America and the Caribbean on 16 May 1998 of its resolution 574(XXVII), in which the Commission called for the necessary mechanisms to be devised to permit the associate members of regional commissions, including the Non-Self-Governing Territories, to participate, subject to the rules of procedure of the General Assembly, in the special sessions of the Assembly to review and appraise the implementation of the programmes of action of those United Nations world conferences in which the Territories had originally participated in their capacity as observers and to participate in the work of the Economic and Social Council and its subsidiary bodies;

19. *Requests* the President of the Economic and Social Council to continue to maintain close contact on these matters with the Chair of the Special Committee and to report thereon to the Council;

20. *Requests* the Secretary-General to follow up on the implementation of the present resolution, paying particular attention to cooperation and integration arrangements for maximizing the efficiency of the assistance activities undertaken by various organizations of the United Nations system, and to report thereon to the Economic and Social Council at its substantive session of 2010;

21. *Decides* to keep the above questions under continuous review.

ROLL-CALL VOTE ON RESOLUTION 2009/33:

In favour: Algeria, Barbados, Belarus, Bolivia, Brazil, China, El Salvador, Guatemala, India, Indonesia, Iraq, Malaysia, Mauritius, Mozambique, Namibia, New Zealand, Pakistan, Peru, Philippines, Saint Kitts and Nevis, Saint Lucia, Saudi Arabia, Sudan, Uruguay, Venezuela.

Against: None.

Abstaining: Canada, Côte d'Ivoire, Estonia, France, Germany, Greece, Japan, Liechtenstein, Luxembourg, Malawi, Moldova, Morocco, Netherlands, Norway, Poland, Portugal, Republic of Korea, Romania, Russian Federation, Sweden, United Kingdom, United States.

GENERAL ASSEMBLY ACTION

On 10 December [meeting 62], the General Assembly, on the recommendation of the Fourth Committee [A/64/411], adopted **resolution 64/99** by recorded vote (123-0-53) [agenda item 37].

Implementation of the Declaration on the Granting of Independence to Colonial Countries and Peoples by the specialized agencies and the international institutions associated with the United Nations

The General Assembly,

Having considered the item entitled "Implementation of the Declaration on the Granting of Independence to Colonial Countries and Peoples by the specialized agencies and the international institutions associated with the United Nations",

Having also considered the report of the Secretary-General and the report of the Economic and Social Council on the item,

Having examined the chapter of the report of the Special Committee on the Situation with regard to the Implementation of the Declaration on the Granting of Independence to Colonial Countries and Peoples relating to the item,

Recalling its resolutions 1514(XV) of 14 December 1960 and 1541(XV) of 15 December 1960 and the resolutions of the Special Committee, as well as other relevant resolutions and decisions, including in particular Economic and Social Council resolution 2008/15 of 24 July 2008,

Bearing in mind the relevant provisions of the final documents of the successive Conferences of Heads of State or Government of Non-Aligned Countries and of the resolutions adopted by the Assembly of Heads of State and Government of the African Union, the Pacific Islands Forum and the Caribbean Community,

Conscious of the need to facilitate the implementation of the Declaration on the Granting of Independence to Colonial Countries and Peoples, contained in resolution 1514(XV),

Noting that the large majority of the remaining Non-Self-Governing Territories are small island Territories,

Welcoming the assistance extended to Non-Self-Governing Territories by certain specialized agencies and other organizations of the United Nations system, in particular the United Nations Development Programme,

Also welcoming the participation in the capacity of observers of those Non-Self-Governing Territories that are associate members of regional commissions in the world conferences in the economic and social spheres, subject to the rules

of procedure of the General Assembly and in accordance with relevant resolutions and decisions of the United Nations, including resolutions and decisions of the Assembly and the Special Committee on specific Territories,

Noting that only some specialized agencies and other organizations of the United Nations system have been involved in providing assistance to Non-Self-Governing Territories,

Stressing that, because the development options of the small island Non-Self-Governing Territories are limited, there are special challenges to planning for and implementing sustainable development and that those Territories will be constrained in meeting the challenges without the continuing cooperation and assistance of the specialized agencies and other organizations of the United Nations system,

Stressing also the importance of securing the necessary resources for funding expanded programmes of assistance for the peoples concerned and the need to enlist the support of all major funding institutions within the United Nations system in that regard,

Reaffirming the mandates of the specialized agencies and other organizations of the United Nations system to take all appropriate measures, within their respective spheres of competence, to ensure the full implementation of General Assembly resolution 1514(XV) and other relevant resolutions,

Expressing its appreciation to the African Union, the Pacific Islands Forum, the Caribbean Community and other regional organizations for the continued cooperation and assistance they have extended to the specialized agencies and other organizations of the United Nations system in this regard,

Expressing its conviction that closer contacts and consultations between and among the specialized agencies and other organizations of the United Nations system and regional organizations help to facilitate the effective formulation of programmes of assistance to the peoples concerned,

Mindful of the imperative need to keep under continuous review the activities of the specialized agencies and other organizations of the United Nations system in the implementation of the various resolutions and decisions of the United Nations relating to decolonization,

Bearing in mind the extremely fragile economies of the small island Non-Self-Governing Territories and their vulnerability to natural disasters, such as hurricanes, cyclones and sea-level rise, and recalling the relevant resolutions of the General Assembly,

Recalling its resolution 63/103 of 5 December 2008 on the implementation of the Declaration by the specialized agencies and the international institutions associated with the United Nations,

1. *Takes note* of the report of the Secretary-General;

2. *Recommends* that all States intensify their efforts in the specialized agencies and other organizations of the United Nations system in which they are members to ensure the full and effective implementation of the Declaration on the Granting of Independence to Colonial Countries and Peoples, contained in General Assembly resolution 1514(XV), and other relevant resolutions of the United Nations;

3. *Reaffirms* that the specialized agencies and other organizations and institutions of the United Nations system should continue to be guided by the relevant resolutions of the United Nations in their efforts to contribute to the

implementation of the Declaration and all other relevant resolutions of the General Assembly;

4. *Reaffirms also* that the recognition by the General Assembly, the Security Council and other United Nations organs of the legitimacy of the aspirations of the peoples of the Non-Self-Governing Territories to exercise their right to self-determination entails, as a corollary, the extension of all appropriate assistance to those peoples;

5. *Expresses its appreciation* to those specialized agencies and other organizations of the United Nations system that have continued to cooperate with the United Nations and the regional and subregional organizations in the implementation of General Assembly resolution 1514(XV) and other relevant resolutions of the United Nations, and requests all the specialized agencies and other organizations of the United Nations system to implement the relevant provisions of those resolutions;

6. *Requests* the specialized agencies and other organizations of the United Nations system to intensify their engagement with the work of the Special Committee on the Situation with regard to the Implementation of the Declaration on the Granting of Independence to Colonial Countries and Peoples as an important element for the implementation of General Assembly resolution 1514(XV), including possible participation at the regional seminars on decolonization, upon the invitation of the Special Committee;

7. *Requests* the specialized agencies and other organizations of the United Nations system and international and regional organizations to examine and review conditions in each Territory so as to take appropriate measures to accelerate progress in the economic and social sectors of the Territories;

8. *Urges* those specialized agencies and other organizations of the United Nations system that have not yet provided assistance to Non-Self-Governing Territories to do so as soon as possible;

9. *Requests* the specialized agencies and other organizations and institutions of the United Nations system and regional organizations to strengthen existing measures of support and formulate appropriate programmes of assistance to the remaining Non-Self-Governing Territories, within the framework of their respective mandates, in order to accelerate progress in the economic and social sectors of those Territories;

10. *Requests* the specialized agencies and other organizations of the United Nations system concerned to provide information on:

(a) Environmental problems facing the Non-Self-Governing Territories;

(b) The impact of natural disasters, such as hurricanes and volcanic eruptions, and other environmental problems, such as beach and coastal erosion and droughts, on those Territories;

(c) Ways and means to assist the Territories to fight drug trafficking, money-laundering and other illegal and criminal activities;

(d) Illegal exploitation of the marine and other natural resources of the Territories and the need to utilize those resources for the benefit of the peoples of the Territories;

11. *Recommends* that the executive heads of the specialized agencies and other organizations of the United Nations system formulate, with the active cooperation of the

regional organizations concerned, concrete proposals for the full implementation of the relevant resolutions of the United Nations and submit the proposals to their governing and legislative organs;

12. *Also recommends* that the specialized agencies and other organizations of the United Nations system continue to review at the regular meetings of their governing bodies the implementation of General Assembly resolution 1514(XV) and other relevant resolutions of the United Nations;

13. *Recalls* the adoption by the Economic Commission for Latin America and the Caribbean of its resolution 574(XXVII) of 16 May 1998, calling for the necessary mechanisms for its associate members, including Non-Self-Governing Territories, to participate in the special sessions of the General Assembly, subject to the rules of procedure of the Assembly, to review and assess the implementation of the plans of action of those United Nations world conferences in which the Territories originally participated in the capacity of observer, and in the work of the Economic and Social Council and its subsidiary bodies;

14. *Requests* the Chair of the Special Committee on the Situation with regard to the Implementation of the Declaration on the Granting of Independence to Colonial Countries and Peoples to continue to maintain close contact on these matters with the President of the Economic and Social Council;

15. *Recalls* the publication by the Department of Public Information and the Department of Political Affairs of the Secretariat, in consultation with the United Nations Development Programme, the specialized agencies and the Special Committee, of an information leaflet on assistance programmes available to the Non-Self-Governing Territories, which was updated for the United Nations website on decolonization, and requests its continued updating and wide dissemination;

16. *Welcomes* the continuing efforts made by the United Nations Development Programme in maintaining close liaison among the specialized agencies and other organizations of the United Nations system, including the Economic Commission for Latin America and the Caribbean and the Economic and Social Commission for Asia and the Pacific, and in providing assistance to the peoples of the Non-Self-Governing Territories;

17. *Encourages* the Non-Self-Governing Territories to take steps to establish and/or strengthen disaster preparedness and management institutions and policies, inter alia, with the assistance of the relevant specialized agencies;

18. *Requests* the administering Powers concerned to facilitate, when appropriate, the participation of appointed and elected representatives of Non-Self-Governing Territories in the relevant meetings and conferences of the specialized agencies and other organizations of the United Nations system, in accordance with relevant resolutions and decisions of the United Nations, including resolutions and decisions of the General Assembly and the Special Committee on specific Territories, so that the Territories may benefit from the related activities of those agencies and organizations;

19. *Recommends* that all Governments intensify their efforts in the specialized agencies and other organizations of the United Nations system of which they are members

to accord priority to the question of providing assistance to the peoples of the Non-Self-Governing Territories;

20.   *Requests* the Secretary-General to continue to assist the specialized agencies and other organizations of the United Nations system in working out appropriate measures for implementing the relevant resolutions of the United Nations and to prepare for submission to the relevant bodies, with the assistance of those agencies and organizations, a report on the action taken in implementation of the relevant resolutions, including the present resolution, since the circulation of his previous report;

21.   *Commends* the Economic and Social Council for its debate and resolution on this question, and requests it to continue to consider, in consultation with the Special Committee, appropriate measures for the coordination of the policies and activities of the specialized agencies and other organizations of the United Nations system in implementing the relevant resolutions of the General Assembly;

22.   *Requests* the specialized agencies to report periodically to the Secretary-General on the implementation of the present resolution;

23.   *Requests* the Secretary-General to transmit the present resolution to the governing bodies of the appropriate specialized agencies and international institutions associated with the United Nations so that those bodies may take the measures necessary to implement the resolution, and also requests the Secretary-General to report to the General Assembly at its sixty-fifth session on the implementation of the present resolution;

24.   *Requests* the Special Committee to continue to examine the question and to report thereon to the General Assembly at its sixty-fifth session.

RECORDED VOTE ON RESOLUTION 64/99:

In favour: Afghanistan, Algeria, Angola, Antigua and Barbuda, Australia, Azerbaijan, Bahamas, Bahrain, Bangladesh, Barbados, Belarus, Belize, Benin, Bhutan, Bolivia, Botswana, Brazil, Brunei Darussalam, Burkina Faso, Burundi, Cameroon, Cape Verde, Chile, China, Colombia, Comoros, Congo, Costa Rica, Côte d'Ivoire, Cuba, Democratic People's Republic of Korea, Djibouti, Dominica, Dominican Republic, Ecuador, Egypt, El Salvador, Eritrea, Ethiopia, Fiji, Gambia, Ghana, Grenada, Guatemala, Guinea, Guinea-Bissau, Guyana, Honduras, India, Indonesia, Iran, Iraq, Jamaica, Jordan, Kazakhstan, Kenya, Kuwait, Kyrgyzstan, Lao People's Democratic Republic, Lebanon, Lesotho, Liberia, Libyan Arab Jamahiriya, Madagascar, Malawi, Malaysia, Maldives, Mali, Marshall Islands, Mauritania, Mauritius, Mexico, Mongolia, Morocco, Mozambique, Myanmar, Nepal, New Zealand, Nicaragua, Niger, Nigeria, Oman, Pakistan, Palau, Panama, Papua New Guinea, Paraguay, Peru, Philippines, Qatar, Saint Lucia, Saint Vincent and the Grenadines, Samoa, Saudi Arabia, Senegal, Sierra Leone, Singapore, Solomon Islands, Somalia, South Africa, Sri Lanka, Sudan, Suriname, Swaziland, Syrian Arab Republic, Tajikistan, Thailand, Timor-Leste, Togo, Tonga, Trinidad and Tobago, Tunisia, Uganda, United Arab Emirates, United Republic of Tanzania, Uruguay, Uzbekistan, Vanuatu, Venezuela, Viet Nam, Yemen, Zambia, Zimbabwe.

Against: None.

Abstaining: Albania, Andorra, Argentina, Armenia, Austria, Belgium, Bosnia and Herzegovina, Bulgaria, Canada, Croatia, Cyprus, Czech Republic, Denmark, Estonia, Finland, France, Georgia, Germany, Greece, Hungary, Iceland, Ireland, Israel,

Italy, Japan, Latvia, Liechtenstein, Lithuania, Luxembourg, Malta, Micronesia, Moldova, Monaco, Montenegro, Netherlands, Norway, Poland, Portugal, Republic of Korea, Romania, Russian Federation, San Marino, Serbia, Slovakia, Slovenia, Spain, Sweden, Switzerland, The former Yugoslav Republic of Macedonia, Turkey, Ukraine, United Kingdom, United States.

Military activities and arrangements in colonial countries

In accordance with General Assembly decision 57/525 [YUN 2002, p. 564], Secretariat working papers submitted to the Special Committee on decolonization on Bermuda [A/AC.109/2009/7], Guam [A/AC.109/2009/16] and the United States Virgin Islands [A/AC.109/2009/14] contained information on, among other things, military activities and arrangements by the administering Powers in those Territories.

Economic and other activities affecting the interests of NSGTs

The Special Committee on decolonization, in June [A/64/23], continued its consideration of economic and other activities affecting the interests of the peoples of NSGTs. It had before it Secretariat working papers containing information on, among other topics, economic conditions in American Samoa [A/AC.109/2009/4], Anguilla [A/AC.109/2009/11], Bermuda [A/AC.109/2009/7], the British Virgin Islands [A/AC.109/2009/1], the Cayman Islands [A/AC.109/2009/8], the Falkland Islands (Malvinas) [A/AC.109/2009/13], Gibraltar [A/AC.109/2009/15], Guam [A/AC.109/2009/16], Montserrat [A/AC.109/2009/6], New Caledonia [A/AC.109/2009/9], Pitcairn [A/AC.109/2009/3], St. Helena [A/AC.109/2009/5], Tokelau [A/AC.109/2009/2], the Turks and Caicos Islands [A/AC.109/2009/10] and the United States Virgin Islands [A/AC.109/2009/14].

GENERAL ASSEMBLY ACTION

On 10 December [meeting 62], the General Assembly, on the recommendation of the Fourth Committee [A/64/410], adopted **resolution 64/98** by recorded vote (173-2-2) [agenda item 36].

Economic and other activities which affect the interests of the peoples of the Non-Self-Governing Territories

The General Assembly,

Having considered the item entitled "Economic and other activities which affect the interests of the peoples of the Non-Self-Governing Territories",

Having examined the chapter of the report of the Special Committee on the Situation with regard to the Implementation of the Declaration on the Granting of Independence to Colonial Countries and Peoples relating to the item,

Recalling General Assembly resolution 1514(XV) of 14 December 1960, as well as all other relevant resolutions of the Assembly, including, in particular, resolutions 46/181 of 19 December 1991 and 55/146 of 8 December 2000,

Reaffirming the solemn obligation of the administering Powers under the Charter of the United Nations to promote the political, economic, social and educational advancement of the inhabitants of the Territories under their administration and to protect the human and natural resources of those Territories against abuses,

Reaffirming also that any economic or other activity that has a negative impact on the interests of the peoples of the Non-Self-Governing Territories and on the exercise of their right to self-determination in conformity with the Charter and General Assembly resolution 1514(XV) is contrary to the purposes and principles of the Charter,

Reaffirming further that the natural resources are the heritage of the peoples of the Non-Self-Governing Territories, including the indigenous populations,

Aware of the special circumstances of the geographical location, size and economic conditions of each Territory, and bearing in mind the need to promote the economic stability, diversification and strengthening of the economy of each Territory,

Conscious of the particular vulnerability of the small Territories to natural disasters and environmental degradation,

Conscious also that foreign economic investment, when undertaken in collaboration with the peoples of the Non-Self-Governing Territories and in accordance with their wishes, could make a valid contribution to the socio-economic development of the Territories and also to the exercise of their right to self-determination,

Concerned about any activities aimed at exploiting the natural and human resources of the Non-Self-Governing Territories to the detriment of the interests of the inhabitants of those Territories,

Bearing in mind the relevant provisions of the final documents of the successive Conferences of Heads of State or Government of Non-Aligned Countries and of the resolutions adopted by the Assembly of Heads of State and Government of the African Union, the Pacific Islands Forum and the Caribbean Community,

1. *Reaffirms* the right of the peoples of the Non-Self-Governing Territories to self-determination in conformity with the Charter of the United Nations and with General Assembly resolution 1514(XV), containing the Declaration on the Granting of Independence to Colonial Countries and Peoples, as well as their right to the enjoyment of their natural resources and their right to dispose of those resources in their best interest;

2. *Affirms* the value of foreign economic investment undertaken in collaboration with the peoples of the Non-Self-Governing Territories and in accordance with their wishes in order to make a valid contribution to the socio-economic development of the Territories, especially during times of economic and financial crisis;

3. *Reaffirms* the responsibility of the administering Powers under the Charter to promote the political, economic, social and educational advancement of the Non-Self-Governing Territories, and reaffirms the legitimate rights of their peoples over their natural resources;

4. *Reaffirms its concern* about any activities aimed at the exploitation of the natural resources that are the heritage of the peoples of the Non-Self-Governing Territories, including the indigenous populations, in the Caribbean, the Pacific and other regions, and of their human resources, to the detriment of their interests, and in such a way as to deprive them of their right to dispose of those resources;

5. *Reaffirms* the need to avoid any economic and other activities that adversely affect the interests of the peoples of the Non-Self-Governing Territories;

6. *Calls once again upon* all Governments that have not yet done so to take, in accordance with the relevant provisions of General Assembly resolution 2621(XXV) of 12 October 1970, legislative, administrative or other measures in respect of their nationals and the bodies corporate under their jurisdiction that own and operate enterprises in the Non-Self-Governing Territories that are detrimental to the interests of the inhabitants of those Territories, in order to put an end to such enterprises;

7. *Calls upon* the administering Powers to ensure that the exploitation of the marine and other natural resources in the Non-Self-Governing Territories under their administration is not in violation of the relevant resolutions of the United Nations, and does not adversely affect the interests of the peoples of those Territories;

8. *Invites* all Governments and organizations of the United Nations system to take all possible measures to ensure that the permanent sovereignty of the peoples of the Non-Self-Governing Territories over their natural resources is fully respected and safeguarded in accordance with the relevant resolutions of the United Nations on decolonization;

9. *Urges* the administering Powers concerned to take effective measures to safeguard and guarantee the inalienable right of the peoples of the Non-Self-Governing Territories to their natural resources and to establish and maintain control over the future development of those resources, and requests the administering Powers to take all necessary steps to protect the property rights of the peoples of those Territories in accordance with the relevant resolutions of the United Nations on decolonization;

10. *Calls upon* the administering Powers concerned to ensure that no discriminatory working conditions prevail in the Territories under their administration and to promote in each Territory a fair system of wages applicable to all the inhabitants without any discrimination;

11. *Requests* the Secretary-General to continue, through all means at his disposal, to inform world public opinion of any activity that affects the exercise of the right of the peoples of the Non-Self-Governing Territories to self-determination in conformity with the Charter and General Assembly resolution 1514(XV);

12. *Appeals* to trade unions and non-governmental organizations, as well as individuals, to continue their efforts to promote the economic well-being of the peoples of the Non-Self-Governing Territories, and also appeals to the media to disseminate information about the developments in this regard;

13. *Decides* to follow the situation in the Non-Self-Governing Territories so as to ensure that all economic activities in those Territories are aimed at strengthening and diversifying their economies in the interest of their peoples,

including the indigenous populations, and at promoting the economic and financial viability of those Territories;

14. *Requests* the Special Committee on the Situation with regard to the Implementation of the Declaration on the Granting of Independence to Colonial Countries and Peoples to continue to examine this question and to report thereon to the General Assembly at its sixty-fifth session.

RECORDED VOTE ON RESOLUTION 64/98:

In favour: Afghanistan, Albania, Algeria, Andorra, Angola, Antigua and Barbuda, Argentina, Armenia, Australia, Austria, Azerbaijan, Bahamas, Bahrain, Bangladesh, Barbados, Belarus, Belgium, Belize, Benin, Bhutan, Bolivia, Bosnia and Herzegovina, Botswana, Brazil, Brunei Darussalam, Bulgaria, Burkina Faso, Burundi, Cameroon, Canada, Cape Verde, Chile, China, Colombia, Comoros, Congo, Costa Rica, Côte d'Ivoire, Croatia, Cuba, Cyprus, Czech Republic, Democratic People's Republic of Korea, Denmark, Djibouti, Dominica, Dominican Republic, Ecuador, Egypt, El Salvador, Eritrea, Estonia, Ethiopia, Fiji, Finland, Gambia, Georgia, Germany, Ghana, Greece, Grenada, Guatemala, Guinea, Guinea-Bissau, Guyana, Honduras, Hungary, Iceland, India, Indonesia, Iran, Iraq, Ireland, Italy, Jamaica, Japan, Jordan, Kazakhstan, Kenya, Kuwait, Kyrgyzstan, Lao People's Democratic Republic, Latvia, Lebanon, Lesotho, Liberia, Libyan Arab Jamahiriya, Liechtenstein, Lithuania, Luxembourg, Madagascar, Malawi, Malaysia, Maldives, Mali, Malta, Marshall Islands, Mauritania, Mauritius, Mexico, Micronesia, Moldova, Mongolia, Montenegro, Morocco, Mozambique, Myanmar, Nepal, Netherlands, New Zealand, Nicaragua, Niger, Nigeria, Norway, Oman, Pakistan, Palau, Panama, Papua New Guinea, Paraguay, Peru, Philippines, Poland, Portugal, Qatar, Republic of Korea, Romania, Russian Federation, Saint Kitts and Nevis, Saint Lucia, Saint Vincent and the Grenadines, Samoa, San Marino, Saudi Arabia, Senegal, Serbia, Sierra Leone, Singapore, Slovakia, Slovenia, Solomon Islands, Somalia, South Africa, Spain, Sri Lanka, Sudan, Suriname, Swaziland, Sweden, Switzerland, Syrian Arab Republic, Tajikistan, Thailand, The former Yugoslav Republic of Macedonia, Timor-Leste, Togo, Tonga, Trinidad and Tobago, Tunisia, Turkey, Turkmenistan, Uganda, Ukraine, United Arab Emirates, United Republic of Tanzania, Uruguay, Uzbekistan, Vanuatu, Venezuela, Viet Nam, Yemen, Zambia, Zimbabwe.

Against: Israel, United States.

Abstaining: France, United Kingdom.

Dissemination of information

In June [A/64/23], the Special Committee on decolonization held consultations with representatives of the UN Departments of Political Affairs and Public Information on the dissemination of information on decolonization. It also considered a report of the Secretary-General on the subject, covering the period from April 2008 to March 2009 [A/AC.109/2009/18 & Corr.1].

GENERAL ASSEMBLY ACTION

On 10 December [meeting 62], the General Assembly, on the recommendation of the Fourth Committee [A/64/413], adopted **resolution 64/105** by recorded vote (173-3-1) [agenda item 39].

Dissemination of information on decolonization

The General Assembly,

Having examined the chapter of the report of the Special Committee on the Situation with regard to the Implementation of the Declaration on the Granting of Independence to Colonial Countries and Peoples relating to the dissemination of information on decolonization and publicity for the work of the United Nations in the field of decolonization,

Recalling General Assembly resolution 1514(XV) of 14 December 1960, containing the Declaration on the Granting of Independence to Colonial Countries and Peoples, and other resolutions and decisions of the United Nations concerning the dissemination of information on decolonization, in particular Assembly resolution 63/109 of 5 December 2008,

Recognizing the need for flexible, practical and innovative approaches towards reviewing the options of self-determination for the peoples of Non-Self-Governing Territories with a view to implementing the plan of action for the Second International Decade for the Eradication of Colonialism,

Reiterating the importance of dissemination of information as an instrument for furthering the aims of the Declaration, and mindful of the role of world public opinion in effectively assisting the peoples of Non-Self-Governing Territories to achieve self-determination,

Recognizing the role played by the administering Powers in transmitting information to the Secretary-General in accordance with the terms of Article 73 *e* of the Charter of the United Nations,

Recognizing also the role of the Department of Public Information of the Secretariat, through the United Nations information centres, in the dissemination of information at the regional level on the activities of the United Nations,

Recalling the issuance by the Department of Public Information, in consultation with the United Nations Development Programme, the specialized agencies and the Special Committee, of an information leaflet on assistance programmes available to the Non-Self-Governing Territories,

Aware of the role of non-governmental organizations in the dissemination of information on decolonization,

1. *Approves* the activities in the field of dissemination of information on decolonization undertaken by the Department of Public Information and the Department of Political Affairs of the Secretariat, in accordance with the relevant resolutions of the United Nations on decolonization, in particular the publication, in accordance with General Assembly resolution 61/129 of 14 December 2006, of the information leaflet entitled "What the UN Can Do to Assist Non-Self-Governing Territories", which was updated for the United Nations website on decolonization in May 2009, and encourages continued updating and wide dissemination of the information leaflet;

2. *Considers it important* to continue and expand its efforts to ensure the widest possible dissemination of information on decolonization, with particular emphasis on the options of self-determination available for the peoples of Non-Self-Governing Territories, and to this end, requests the Department of Public Information through the United Nations information centres in the relevant regions to

actively engage and seek new and innovative ways to disseminate material to the Non-Self-Governing Territories;

3. *Requests* the Secretary-General to further enhance the information provided on the United Nations decolonization website and to continue to include the full series of reports of the regional seminars on decolonization, the statements and scholarly papers presented at those seminars and links to the full series of reports of the Special Committee on the Situation with regard to the Implementation of the Declaration on the Granting of Independence to Colonial Countries and Peoples;

4. *Requests* the Department of Public Information to continue its efforts to update web-based information on the assistance programmes available to the Non-Self-Governing Territories;

5. *Requests* the Department of Political Affairs and the Department of Public Information to implement the recommendations of the Special Committee and to continue their efforts to take measures through all the media available, including publications, radio and television, as well as the Internet, to give publicity to the work of the United Nations in the field of decolonization and, inter alia:

(a) To develop procedures to collect, prepare and disseminate, particularly to the Non-Self-Governing Territories, basic material on the issue of self-determination of the peoples of the Territories;

(b) To seek the full cooperation of the administering Powers in the discharge of the tasks referred to above;

(c) To explore further the idea of a programme of collaboration with the decolonization focal points of territorial Governments, particularly in the Pacific and Caribbean regions, to help improve the exchange of information;

(d) To encourage the involvement of non-governmental organizations in the dissemination of information on decolonization;

(e) To encourage the involvement of the Non-Self-Governing Territories in the dissemination of information on decolonization;

(f) To report to the Special Committee on measures taken in the implementation of the present resolution;

6. *Requests* all States, including the administering Powers, to accelerate the dissemination of information referred to in paragraph 2 above;

7. *Requests* the Special Committee to continue to examine this question and to report to the General Assembly at its sixty-fifth session on the implementation of the present resolution.

RECORDED VOTE ON RESOLUTION 64/105:

In favour: Afghanistan, Albania, Algeria, Andorra, Angola, Antigua and Barbuda, Argentina, Armenia, Australia, Austria, Azerbaijan, Bahamas, Bahrain, Bangladesh, Barbados, Belarus, Belgium, Belize, Benin, Bhutan, Bolivia, Bosnia and Herzegovina, Botswana, Brazil, Brunei Darussalam, Bulgaria, Burkina Faso, Burundi, Cameroon, Canada, Cape Verde, Chile, China, Colombia, Comoros, Congo, Costa Rica, Côte d'Ivoire, Croatia, Cuba, Cyprus, Czech Republic, Democratic People's Republic of Korea, Denmark, Djibouti, Dominica, Dominican Republic, Ecuador, Egypt, El Salvador, Eritrea, Estonia, Ethiopia, Fiji, Finland, Gambia, Georgia, Germany, Ghana, Greece, Grenada, Guatemala, Guinea, Guinea-Bissau, Guyana, Honduras, Hungary, Iceland, India, Indonesia, Iran, Iraq, Ireland,

Italy, Jamaica, Japan, Jordan, Kazakhstan, Kenya, Kuwait, Kyrgyzstan, Lao People's Democratic Republic, Latvia, Lebanon, Lesotho, Liberia, Libyan Arab Jamahiriya, Liechtenstein, Lithuania, Luxembourg, Madagascar, Malawi, Malaysia, Maldives, Mali, Malta, Marshall Islands, Mauritania, Mauritius, Mexico, Moldova, Monaco, Mongolia, Montenegro, Morocco, Mozambique, Myanmar, Namibia, Nepal, Netherlands, New Zealand, Nicaragua, Niger, Nigeria, Norway, Oman, Pakistan, Palau, Panama, Papua New Guinea, Paraguay, Peru, Philippines, Poland, Portugal, Qatar, Republic of Korea, Romania, Russian Federation, Saint Lucia, Saint Vincent and the Grenadines, Samoa, San Marino, Saudi Arabia, Senegal, Serbia, Sierra Leone, Singapore, Slovakia, Slovenia, Solomon Islands, Somalia, South Africa, Spain, Sri Lanka, Sudan, Suriname, Swaziland, Sweden, Switzerland, Syrian Arab Republic, Tajikistan, Thailand, The former Yugoslav Republic of Macedonia, Timor-Leste, Togo, Tonga, Trinidad and Tobago, Tunisia, Turkey, Turkmenistan, Uganda, Ukraine, United Arab Emirates, United Republic of Tanzania, Uruguay, Uzbekistan, Vanuatu, Venezuela, Viet Nam, Yemen, Zambia, Zimbabwe.

Against: Israel, United Kingdom, United States.

Abstaining: France.

Information on Territories

In response to General Assembly resolution 63/101 [YUN 2008, p. 668], the Secretary-General submitted a March report [A/64/67] indicating the dates of transmittal of information from the administering Powers on economic, social and educational conditions in NSGTs for 2008, under Article 73 *e* of the Charter of the United Nations.

GENERAL ASSEMBLY ACTION

On 10 December [meeting 62], the General Assembly, on the recommendation of the Fourth Committee [A/64/409], adopted **resolution 64/97** by recorded vote (171-0-4) [agenda item 35].

Information from Non-Self-Governing Territories transmitted under Article 73 *e* of the Charter of the United Nations

The General Assembly,

Recalling its resolution 1970(XVIII) of 16 December 1963, in which it requested the Special Committee on the Situation with regard to the Implementation of the Declaration on the Granting of Independence to Colonial Countries and Peoples to study the information transmitted to the Secretary-General in accordance with Article 73 *e* of the Charter of the United Nations and to take such information fully into account in examining the situation with regard to the implementation of the Declaration, contained in General Assembly resolution 1514(XV) of 14 December 1960,

Recalling also its resolution 63/101 of 5 December 2008, in which it requested the Special Committee to continue to discharge the functions entrusted to it under resolution 1970(XVIII),

Stressing the importance of timely transmission by the administering Powers of adequate information under Article 73 *e* of the Charter, in particular in relation to the preparation by the Secretariat of the working papers on the Territories concerned,

Having examined the report of the Secretary-General,

1. *Reaffirms* that, in the absence of a decision by the General Assembly itself that a Non-Self-Governing Territory has attained a full measure of self-government in terms of Chapter XI of the Charter of the United Nations, the administering Power concerned should continue to transmit information under Article 73 *e* of the Charter with respect to that Territory;

2. *Requests* the administering Powers concerned, in accordance with their Charter obligations, to transmit or continue to transmit regularly to the Secretary-General for information purposes, subject to such limitation as security and constitutional considerations may require, statistical and other information of a technical nature relating to economic, social and educational conditions in the Territories for which they are respectively responsible, as well as the fullest possible information on political and constitutional developments in the Territories concerned, including the constitution, legislative act or executive order providing for the government of the Territory and the constitutional relationship of the Territory to the administering Power, within a maximum period of six months following the expiration of the administrative year in those Territories;

3. *Requests* the Secretary-General to continue to ensure that adequate information is drawn from all available published sources in connection with the preparation of the working papers relating to the Territories concerned;

4. *Requests* the Special Committee on the Situation with regard to the Implementation of the Declaration on the Granting of Independence to Colonial Countries and Peoples to continue to discharge the functions entrusted to it under General Assembly resolution 1970(XVIII), in accordance with established procedures.

RECORDED VOTE ON RESOLUTION 64/97:

In favour: Afghanistan, Albania, Algeria, Andorra, Angola, Antigua and Barbuda, Argentina, Armenia, Australia, Austria, Azerbaijan, Bahamas, Bahrain, Bangladesh, Barbados, Belarus, Belgium, Belize, Benin, Bhutan, Bolivia, Bosnia and Herzegovina, Botswana, Brazil, Brunei Darussalam, Bulgaria, Burkina Faso, Burundi, Cameroon, Canada, Cape Verde, Chile, China, Colombia, Congo, Costa Rica, Côte d'Ivoire, Croatia, Cuba, Cyprus, Czech Republic, Democratic People's Republic of Korea, Denmark, Djibouti, Dominica, Dominican Republic, Ecuador, Egypt, El Salvador, Eritrea, Estonia, Ethiopia, Fiji, Finland, Gambia, Georgia, Germany, Ghana, Greece, Grenada, Guatemala, Guinea, Guinea-Bissau, Guyana, Honduras, Hungary, Iceland, India, Indonesia, Iran, Iraq, Ireland, Italy, Jamaica, Japan, Jordan, Kazakhstan, Kenya, Kuwait, Kyrgyzstan, Lao People's Democratic Republic, Latvia, Lebanon, Lesotho, Libyan Arab Jamahiriya, Liechtenstein, Lithuania, Luxembourg, Madagascar, Malawi, Malaysia, Maldives, Mali, Malta, Marshall Islands, Mauritania, Mauritius, Mexico, Micronesia, Moldova, Mongolia, Montenegro, Morocco, Mozambique, Myanmar, Nepal, Netherlands, New Zealand, Nicaragua, Niger, Nigeria, Norway, Oman, Pakistan, Palau, Panama, Papua New Guinea, Paraguay, Peru, Philippines, Poland, Portugal, Qatar, Republic of Korea, Romania, Russian Federation, Saint Kitts and Nevis, Saint Lucia, Saint Vincent and the Grenadines, Samoa, San Marino, Saudi Arabia, Senegal, Serbia, Sierra Leone, Singapore, Slovakia, Slovenia,

Solomon Islands, Somalia, South Africa, Spain, Sri Lanka, Sudan, Suriname, Swaziland, Sweden, Switzerland, Syrian Arab Republic, Tajikistan, Thailand, The former Yugoslav Republic of Macedonia, Timor-Leste, Togo, Tonga, Trinidad and Tobago, Tunisia, Turkey, Turkmenistan, Uganda, Ukraine, United Arab Emirates, United Republic of Tanzania, Uruguay, Uzbekistan, Vanuatu, Venezuela, Viet Nam, Yemen, Zambia, Zimbabwe.

Against: None.

Abstaining: France, Israel, United Kingdom, United States.

Study and training

In response to General Assembly resolution 63/104 [YUN 2008, p. 669], the Secretary-General submitted a March report [A/64/69 & Corr.1,2] on offers of study scholarships and training facilities for inhabitants of NSGTs during the period from 20 March 2008 to 24 March 2009 by the following Member States: Algeria, Argentina, Austria, Cuba, Mexico, New Zealand and the United Kingdom. Over the years, a total of 59 Member States and one non-member State—the Holy See—had made such offers.

GENERAL ASSEMBLY ACTION

On 10 December [meeting 62], the General Assembly, on the recommendation of the Fourth Committee [A/64/412], adopted **resolution 64/100** without vote [agenda item 38].

Offers by Member States of study and training facilities for inhabitants of Non-Self-Governing Territories

The General Assembly,

Recalling its resolution 63/104 of 5 December 2008,

Having examined the report of the Secretary-General on offers by Member States of study and training facilities for inhabitants of Non-Self-Governing Territories, prepared pursuant to its resolution 845(IX) of 22 November 1954,

Conscious of the importance of promoting the educational advancement of the inhabitants of Non-Self-Governing Territories,

Strongly convinced that the continuation and expansion of offers of scholarships is essential in order to meet the increasing need of students from Non-Self-Governing Territories for educational and training assistance, and considering that students in those Territories should be encouraged to avail themselves of such offers,

1. *Takes note* of the report of the Secretary-General;

2. *Expresses its appreciation* to those Member States that have made scholarships available to the inhabitants of Non-Self-Governing Territories;

3. *Invites* all States to make or continue to make generous offers of study and training facilities to the inhabitants of those Territories that have not yet attained self-government or independence and, wherever possible, to provide travel funds to prospective students;

4. *Urges* the administering Powers to take effective measures to ensure the widespread and continuous dissemination in the Territories under their administration of information relating to offers of study and training facilities

made by States and to provide all the necessary facilities to enable students to avail themselves of such offers;

5. *Requests* the Secretary-General to report to the General Assembly at its sixty-fifth session on the implementation of the present resolution;

6. *Draws the attention* of the Special Committee on the Situation with regard to the Implementation of the Declaration on the Granting of Independence to Colonial Countries and Peoples to the present resolution.

Visiting Missions

In June [A/64/23], the Special Committee on decolonization considered the question of sending visiting missions to NSGTs. It adopted a resolution in which it stressed the need to dispatch periodic visiting missions to facilitate the full implementation of the 1960 Declaration on decolonization, and called upon administering Powers to receive those missions in the Territories under their administration. It also requested the administering Powers to cooperate with the Special Committee in exploring the possibility of undertaking visiting or special missions in furtherance of the decolonization mandate of the General Assembly. The Committee Chair was asked to consult with the administering Powers concerned and report on the results.

The Special Committee recommended to the Assembly for adoption draft resolutions on 11 small NSGTs (see p. 592), on New Caledonia (see p. 589) and on Tokelau (see p. 590), endorsing a number of conclusions and recommendations concerning the sending of visiting and special missions to those Territories.

Puerto Rico

In accordance with the Special Committee on decolonization's 2008 resolution concerning the self-determination and independence of Puerto Rico [YUN 2008, p. 670], the Committee's Rapporteur, in a March report [A/AC.109/2009/L.13], provided information on Puerto Rico, including recent political, military and economic developments and UN action.

Following its usual practice, the Committee [A/64/23] acceded to requests for hearings from representatives of a number of organizations, which presented their views on 15 June [A/AC.109/2009/SR.5,6]. The Committee adopted a resolution by which it reaffirmed the inalienable right of the people of Puerto Rico to self-determination and independence; urged the United States to return the occupied land and installations on Vieques Island and in Ceiba to the people of Puerto Rico and to respect fundamental human rights, such as the right to health and economic development; and requested the General Assembly to consider the question of Puerto Rico. The Rapporteur was requested to report in 2010 on the resolution's implementation.

Territories under review

Falkland Islands (Malvinas)

The Special Committee on decolonization considered the question of the Falkland Islands (Malvinas) at two meetings on 18 and 19 June [A/64/23]. The Committee had before it a Secretariat working paper on the Territory [A/AC.109/2009/13] which addressed constitutional and political developments, mine clearance, economic and social conditions, and participation in international organizations and arrangements. Statements were heard from two members of the Legislative Assembly of the Falkland Islands; two petitioners representing the Malvinas Islands; and the Minister for Foreign Affairs, International Trade and Worship of Argentina. Further remarks were made by the representatives of Bolivia, Brazil, Chile, China, Cuba, Ecuador, El Salvador, Grenada, Guatemala, Honduras, Indonesia, Mali, Paraguay (on behalf of MERCOSUR), Peru, the Russian Federation, Saint Lucia, Sierra Leone, the Syrian Arab Republic, Tunisia, Uruguay and Venezuela [A/AC.109/2009/SR.9,10]. The Committee adopted a resolution [A/AC.109/2009/L.8] requesting Argentina and the United Kingdom to consolidate the process of dialogue and cooperation by resuming negotiations towards finding a peaceful solution to the sovereignty dispute relating to the Territory as soon as possible.

The Secretary-General received a series of letters from Argentina and the United Kingdom on the dispute [A/63/719, A/63/745, A/63/759, A/63/765, A/63/833, A/63/859, A/63/890, A/63/923, A/64/90, A/64/165, A/64/479], which addressed topics such as the assignment of the Internet domains ".fk" and ".gs" to the islands in question by the Internet Corporation for Assigned Names and Numbers; the use of part of the islands by the United Kingdom as a practice missile range; the issuance of postage stamps in the Territories by the United Kingdom; the 11 May submission by the United Kingdom to the Commission on the Limits of the Continental Shelf; the statement of 18 June by Argentina to the Special Committee on decolonization; the citation, in a report of the Secretary-General [A/64/70], of a reply from the United Kingdom on the implementation of a new constitution in the islands; and the United Kingdom's response to remarks by the Minister of Foreign Affairs of Nicaragua at the general debate in September.

On 24 December, the General Assembly decided that the agenda item on the question of the Falkland Islands (Malvinas) would remain for consideration during its resumed sixty-fourth (2010) session (**decision 64/549**).

Gibraltar

The Special Committee on decolonization considered the question of Gibraltar on 9 June [A/64/23]. Before it was a Secretariat working paper describing political developments and economic and social conditions in the Territory, and presenting the positions of the United Kingdom (the administering Power), Gibraltar and Spain concerning Gibraltar's future status [A/AC.109/2009/15]. The representative of Spain and the leader of the opposition in Gibraltar made statements at the meeting [A/AC.109/2009/SR.4] .

On 10 December (**decision 64/521**), the General Assembly, recalling its decision 63/525 of 5 December 2008 [YUN 2008, p. 673], as well as the statement agreed upon by Spain and the United Kingdom in Brussels on 27 November 1984 [YUN 1984, p. 1075] and the establishment of the tripartite Forum for Dialogue on Gibraltar in December of 2004 [YUN 2004, p. 606], urged both Governments to reach a solution to the question of Gibraltar, in light of the relevant Assembly resolutions and applicable principles, and in the spirit of the UN Charter. The Assembly also welcomed the successful trilateral ministerial meeting of the Forum for Dialogue in Gibraltar on 21 July and the shared commitment to make progress in six new areas of cooperation.

New Caledonia

The Special Committee on decolonization considered the question of New Caledonia on 16 June [A/64/23]. Before it was a Secretariat working paper [A/AC.109/2009/9] describing the political and socioeconomic conditions and developments in the Territory. The representative of Fiji, also speaking on behalf of co-sponsor Papua New Guinea [A/AC.109/2009/SR.7], introduced a draft resolution [A/AC.109/2009/L.3] which the Committee adopted at the meeting.

GENERAL ASSEMBLY ACTION

On 10 December [meeting 62], the General Assembly, on the recommendation of the Fourth Committee [A/64/413], adopted **resolution 64/102** without vote [agenda item 39].

Question of New Caledonia

The General Assembly,

Having considered the question of New Caledonia,

Having examined the chapter of the report of the Special Committee on the Situation with regard to the Implementation of the Declaration on the Granting of Independence to Colonial Countries and Peoples relating to New Caledonia,

Reaffirming the right of peoples to self-determination as enshrined in the Charter of the United Nations,

Recalling General Assembly resolutions 1514(XV) of 14 December 1960 and 1541(XV) of 15 December 1960,

Noting the importance of the positive measures being pursued in New Caledonia by the French authorities, in cooperation with all sectors of the population, to promote political, economic and social development in the Territory, including measures in the area of environmental protection and action with respect to drug abuse and trafficking, in order to provide a framework for its peaceful progress to self-determination,

Noting also, in this context, the importance of equitable economic and social development, as well as continued dialogue among the parties involved in New Caledonia in the preparation of the act of self-determination of New Caledonia,

Noting with satisfaction the intensification of contacts between New Caledonia and neighbouring countries of the South Pacific region,

1. *Welcomes* the significant developments that have taken place in New Caledonia since the signing of the Nouméa Accord on 5 May 1998 by the representatives of New Caledonia and the Government of France;

2. *Urges* all the parties involved, in the interest of all the people of New Caledonia, to maintain, in the framework of the Nouméa Accord, their dialogue in a spirit of harmony, and in this context welcomes the unanimous agreement, reached in Paris on 8 December 2008, on the transfer of powers to New Caledonia in 2009 and the conduct of provincial elections in May 2009;

3. *Notes* the relevant provisions of the Nouméa Accord aimed at taking more broadly into account the Kanak identity in the political and social organization of New Caledonia, and welcomes, in this context, the adoption on 26 June 2008 by the Government of New Caledonia of a draft country law (*loi du pays*) on the identity symbols to be adopted by the country in implementation of the Nouméa Accord and the acceptance, on 21 October 2008, of the draft law on the anthem, motto and banknote design;

4. *Acknowledges* those provisions of the Nouméa Accord relating to control of immigration and protection of local employment, and notes that unemployment remains high among Kanaks and that recruitment of foreign mine workers continues;

5. *Notes* the concerns expressed by a group of indigenous people in New Caledonia regarding their underrepresentation in the Territory's governmental and social structures;

6. *Also notes* the concerns expressed by representatives of indigenous people regarding incessant migratory flows and the impact of mining on the environment;

7. *Takes note* of the relevant provisions of the Nouméa Accord to the effect that New Caledonia may become a member or associate member of certain international organizations, such as international organizations in the Pacific region, the United Nations, the United Nations Educational, Scientific and Cultural Organization and the International Labour Organization, according to their regulations;

8. *Notes* the agreement between the signatories to the Nouméa Accord that the progress made in the emancipation process shall be brought to the attention of the United Nations;

9. *Recalls* the fact that the administering Power invited to New Caledonia, at the time the new institutions were established, a mission of information which comprised representatives of countries of the Pacific region;

10. _Notes_ the continuing strengthening of ties between New Caledonia and both the European Union and the European Development Fund in such areas as economic and trade cooperation, the environment, climate change and financial services;

11. _Calls upon_ the administering Power to continue to transmit to the Secretary-General information as required under Article 73 _e_ of the Charter of the United Nations;

12. _Invites_ all the parties involved to continue promoting a framework for the peaceful progress of the Territory towards an act of self-determination in which all options are open and which would safeguard the rights of all sectors of the population, according to the letter and the spirit of the Nouméa Accord, which is based on the principle that it is for the populations of New Caledonia to choose how to control their destiny;

13. _Recalls with satisfaction_ the efforts of the French authorities to resolve the question of voter registration by adopting, in the French Congress of Parliament, on 19 February 2007, amendments to the French Constitution allowing New Caledonia to restrict eligibility to vote in local polls to those voters registered on the 1998 electoral rolls when the Nouméa Accord was signed, thus ensuring strong representation of the Kanak population;

14. _Welcomes_ all measures taken to strengthen and diversify the New Caledonian economy in all fields, and encourages further such measures in accordance with the spirit of the Matignon and Nouméa Accords;

15. _Also welcomes_ the importance attached by the parties to the Matignon and Nouméa Accords to greater progress in housing, employment, training, education and health care in New Caledonia;

16. _Notes_ the financial assistance rendered by the Government of France to the Territory in areas such as health, education, payment of public-service salaries and funding development schemes;

17. _Acknowledges_ the contribution of the Melanesian Cultural Centre to the protection of the indigenous Kanak culture of New Caledonia;

18. _Notes_ the positive initiatives aimed at protecting the natural environment of New Caledonia, including the "Zonéco" operation designed to map and evaluate marine resources within the economic zone of New Caledonia;

19. _Welcomes_ the cooperation among Australia, France and New Zealand in terms of surveillance of fishing zones, in accordance with the wishes expressed by France during the France-Oceania Summits in July 2003 and June 2006;

20. _Acknowledges_ the close links between New Caledonia and the peoples of the South Pacific and the positive actions being taken by the French and territorial authorities to facilitate the further development of those links, including the development of closer relations with the countries members of the Pacific Islands Forum;

21. _Welcomes_, in this regard, the participation of New Caledonia at the 39th Summit of the Pacific Islands Forum, held in Niue from 19 to 21 August 2008, following its accession to the Forum as an associate member in October 2006;

22. _Also welcomes_ the continuing high-level visits to New Caledonia by delegations from countries of the Pacific region and high-level visits by delegations from New Caledonia to countries members of the Pacific Islands Forum;

23. _Further welcomes_ the cooperative attitude of other States and Territories in the region towards New Caledonia, its economic and political aspirations and its increasing participation in regional and international affairs;

24. _Recalls_ the endorsement of the report of the Forum Ministerial Committee on New Caledonia by leaders of the Pacific Islands Forum at its 36th Summit, held in Papua New Guinea in October 2005, and the continuing role of the Forum Ministerial Committee in monitoring developments in the Territory and encouraging closer regional engagements;

25. _Decides_ to keep under continuous review the process unfolding in New Caledonia as a result of the signing of the Nouméa Accord;

26. _Requests_ the Special Committee on the Situation with regard to the Implementation of the Declaration on the Granting of Independence to Colonial Countries and Peoples to continue the examination of the question of the Non-Self-Governing Territory of New Caledonia and to report thereon to the General Assembly at its sixty-fifth session.

Tokelau

On 23 June, the Special Committee on decolonization considered the question of Tokelau (the three small atolls of Nukunonu, Fakaofo and Atafu in the South Pacific), administered by New Zealand [A/64/23]. Before it was a Secretariat working paper [A/AC.109/2009/2] [YUN 2008, p. 675] covering constitutional and political developments, external relations and economic and social conditions in the Territory, and presenting the positions of New Zealand and Tokelau on the Territory's future status. Statements were made by the Ulu-o-Tokelau (titular head of the Territory, a position rotated annually among the three Faipule), the representative of New Zealand, and the representatives of Papua New Guinea and Fiji [A/AC.109/2009/SR.11], who introduced a draft resolution [A/AC.109/2009/L.15] that the Committee adopted. The resolution noted the ongoing recognition by New Zealand of the right of the people of Tokelau to undertake the act of self-determination when they considered it to be appropriate. It also requested the Committee to examine the question of Tokelau and report to the Assembly at its sixty-fifth (2010) session.

GENERAL ASSEMBLY ACTION

On 10 December [meeting 62], the General Assembly, on the recommendation of the Fourth Committee [A/64/413], adopted **resolution 64/103** without vote [agenda item 39].

Question of Tokelau

The General Assembly,

Having considered the question of Tokelau,

Having examined the chapter of the report of the Special Committee on the Situation with regard to the Implementation of the Declaration on the Granting of Independence to Colonial Countries and Peoples relating to Tokelau,

Recalling its resolution 1514(XV) of 14 December 1960, containing the Declaration on the Granting of Independence to Colonial Countries and Peoples, and all resolutions and decisions of the United Nations relating to Non-Self-Governing Territories, in particular General Assembly resolution 63/107 of 5 December 2008,

Noting with appreciation the continuing exemplary cooperation of New Zealand as the administering Power with regard to the work of the Special Committee relating to Tokelau and its readiness to permit access by United Nations visiting missions to the Territory,

Also noting with appreciation the collaborative contribution to the development of Tokelau by New Zealand and the specialized agencies and other organizations of the United Nations system, in particular the United Nations Development Programme,

Recalling the inauguration in 1996 of a national legislative body, the General Fono, based on village elections by universal adult suffrage and the assumption by that body in June 2003 of full responsibility for the Tokelau budget,

Noting that, as a small island Territory, Tokelau exemplifies the situation of most remaining Non-Self-Governing Territories and that, as a case study pointing to successful cooperation for decolonization, Tokelau has wider significance for the United Nations as it seeks to complete its work in decolonization,

Recalling that New Zealand and Tokelau signed in November 2003 a document entitled "Joint statement of the principles of partnership", which sets out in writing, for the first time, the rights and obligations of the two partner countries,

Bearing in mind the decision of the General Fono at its meeting in November 2003, following extensive consultations undertaken in all three villages, to explore formally with New Zealand the option of self-government in free association and its decision in August 2005 to hold a referendum on self-government on the basis of a draft constitution for Tokelau and a treaty of free association with New Zealand, and its subsequent decision to hold a further referendum in October 2007,

1. *Notes* that Tokelau and New Zealand remain firmly committed to the ongoing development of Tokelau for the long-term benefit of the people of Tokelau, with particular emphasis on the further development of facilities on each atoll that meet their current requirements;

2. *Notes also* the ongoing recognition by New Zealand of the complete right of the people of Tokelau to undertake the act of self-determination when this is considered by the people of Tokelau to be appropriate;

3. *Welcomes* the progress made towards the devolution of power to the three taupulega (village councils), in particular the delegation of the Administrator's powers to the three taupulega with effect from 1 July 2004 and the assumption by each taupulega from that date of full responsibility for the management of all its public services;

4. *Recalls* the decision of the General Fono in November 2003, following extensive consultations in all three villages and a meeting of the Special Committee on the Constitution of Tokelau, to explore formally with New Zealand the option of self-government in free association, and the discussions subsequently held between Tokelau and New Zealand pursuant to the decision of the General Fono;

5. *Recalls also* the decision of the General Fono in August 2005 to hold a referendum on self-government on the basis of a draft constitution for Tokelau and a draft treaty of free association with New Zealand, and notes the enactment by the General Fono of rules for the referendum;

6. *Notes* that two referendums to determine the status of Tokelau, held in February 2006 and October 2007, did not produce the two-thirds majority of the valid votes cast required by the General Fono to change Tokelau's status from that of a Non-Self-Governing Territory under the administration of New Zealand;

7. *Commends* the professional and transparent conduct of both the February 2006 and the October 2007 referendums, monitored by the United Nations;

8. *Acknowledges* the decision of the General Fono that consideration of any future act of self-determination by Tokelau will be deferred and that New Zealand and Tokelau will devote renewed effort and attention to ensuring that essential services and infrastructure on the atolls of Tokelau are enhanced and strengthened, thereby ensuring an enhanced quality of life for the people of Tokelau;

9. *Also acknowledges* Tokelau's initiative in devising a strategic economic development plan for the period 2007–2010;

10. *Further acknowledges* the ongoing and consistent commitment of New Zealand to meeting the social and economic requirements of the people of Tokelau, as well as the support and cooperation of the United Nations Development Programme;

11. *Acknowledges* Tokelau's need for continued support from the international community;

12. *Recalls with satisfaction* the establishment and operation of the Tokelau International Trust Fund to support the ongoing needs of Tokelau, and calls upon Member States and international and regional agencies to contribute to the Fund and thereby lend practical support to Tokelau in overcoming the problems of smallness, isolation and lack of resources;

13. *Welcomes* the assurance of the Government of New Zealand that it will meet its obligations with respect to Tokelau;

14. *Also welcomes* the cooperative attitude of the other States and territories in the region towards Tokelau, and their support for its economic and political aspirations and its increasing participation in regional and international affairs;

15. *Calls upon* the administering Power and United Nations agencies to continue to provide assistance to Tokelau as it further develops;

16. *Welcomes* the actions taken by the administering Power to transmit information regarding the political, economic and social situation of Tokelau to the Secretary-General;

17. *Also welcomes* the commitment of both Tokelau and New Zealand to continue to work together in the interests of Tokelau and its people;

18. *Requests* the Special Committee on the Situation with regard to the Implementation of the Declaration on the Granting of Independence to Colonial Countries and Peoples to continue to examine the question of the Non-Self-Governing Territory of Tokelau and to report thereon to the General Assembly at its sixty-fifth session.

Western Sahara

The Special Committee on decolonization considered the question of Western Sahara on 16 June [A/64/23]. A Secretariat working paper [A/AC.109/2009/12] described the Secretary-General's good offices with the parties concerned and actions taken by the General Assembly and the Security Council (see p. 304). The Committee granted a request for hearing to Ahmed Boukhari of the Frente Popular para la Liberación de Saguía el-Hamra y de Río de Oro (Frente Polisario), who made a statement [A/AC.109/2009/SR.7]. At the same meeting, the representatives of the United Republic of Tanzania, Cuba, Venezuela and Côte d'Ivoire also made statements [ibid.].

The Special Committee transmitted the relevant documentation to the Assembly's sixty-fourth (2009) session to facilitate the Fourth Committee's consideration of the question. The Secretary-General submitted his report [A/64/185] to the Assembly in July.

By **resolution 64/101** of 10 December (see p. 307), the Assembly supported the process of negotiations initiated by the Security Council since 2007, with a view to achieving a political solution that would provide for the self-determination of the people of Western Sahara; commended the efforts by the Secretary-General and his Personal Envoy in that respect; and requested the Special Committee to continue to consider the situation in Western Sahara and report to the Assembly's sixty-fifth (2010) session.

Island Territories

On 19 June, the Special Committee on decolonization [A/64/23] considered working papers on American Samoa [A/AC.109/2009/4], Anguilla [A/AC.109/2009/11], Bermuda [A/AC.109/2009/7], the British Virgin Islands [A/AC.109/2009/1], the Cayman Islands [A/AC.109/2009/8], Guam [A/AC.109/2009/16], Montserrat [A/AC.109/2009/6], Pitcairn [A/AC.109/2009/3], Saint Helena [A/AC.109/2009/5], the Turks and Caicos Islands [A/AC.109/2009/10] and the United States Virgin Islands [A/AC.109/2009/14] describing political developments and economic and social conditions in each of those 11 island Territories. The delegations of the United Kingdom and the United States, as the administering Powers concerned, did not participate in the Special Committee's consideration of the Territories under their administration. The Committee adopted a consolidated draft resolution [A/AC.109/2009/L.9], which it subsequently recommended for adoption by the General Assembly (see below).

GENERAL ASSEMBLY ACTION

On 10 December [meeting 62], the General Assembly, on the recommendation of the Fourth Committee [A/64/413], adopted **resolution 64/104A** and **B** without vote [agenda item 39].

Questions of American Samoa, Anguilla, Bermuda, the British Virgin Islands, the Cayman Islands, Guam, Montserrat, Pitcairn, Saint Helena, the Turks and Caicos Islands and the United States Virgin Islands

A

General

The General Assembly,

Having considered the questions of the Non-Self-Governing Territories of American Samoa, Anguilla, Bermuda, the British Virgin Islands, the Cayman Islands, Guam, Montserrat, Pitcairn, Saint Helena, the Turks and Caicos Islands and the United States Virgin Islands, hereinafter referred to as "the Territories",

Having examined the relevant chapter of the report of the Special Committee on the Situation with regard to the Implementation of the Declaration on the Granting of Independence to Colonial Countries and Peoples,

Recalling all resolutions and decisions of the United Nations relating to those Territories, including, in particular, the resolutions adopted by the General Assembly at its sixty-third session on the individual Territories covered by the present resolutions,

Recognizing that all available options for self-determination of the Territories are valid as long as they are in accordance with the freely expressed wishes of the peoples concerned and in conformity with the clearly defined principles contained in General Assembly resolutions 1514(XV) of 14 December 1960, 1541(XV) of 15 December 1960 and other resolutions of the Assembly,

Recalling its resolution 1541(XV), containing the principles that should guide Member States in determining whether or not an obligation exists to transmit the information called for under Article 73 *e* of the Charter of the United Nations,

Expressing concern that more than forty-eight years after the adoption of the Declaration on the Granting of Independence to Colonial Countries and Peoples, there still remain a number of Non-Self-Governing Territories,

Conscious of the importance of continuing effective implementation of the Declaration, taking into account the target set by the United Nations to eradicate colonialism by 2010 and the plan of action for the Second International Decade for the Eradication of Colonialism,

Recognizing that the specific characteristics and the aspirations of the peoples of the Territories require flexible, practical and innovative approaches to the options for self-determination, without any prejudice to territorial size, geographical location, size of population or natural resources,

Noting the stated position of the Government of the United Kingdom of Great Britain and Northern Ireland and the stated position of the Government of the United States of America on the Non-Self-Governing Territories under their administration,

Noting also the constitutional developments in some Non-Self-Governing Territories affecting the internal structure of governance about which the Special Committee has received information,

Convinced that the wishes and aspirations of the peoples of the Territories should continue to guide the development of their future political status and that referendums, free and fair elections and other forms of popular consultation play an important role in ascertaining the wishes and aspirations of the people,

Convinced also that any negotiations to determine the status of a Territory must take place with the active involvement and participation of the people of that Territory, under the aegis of the United Nations, on a case-by-case basis, and that the views of the peoples of the Non-Self-Governing Territories in respect of their right to self-determination should be ascertained,

Noting that a number of Non-Self-Governing Territories have expressed concern at the procedure followed by some administering Powers, contrary to the wishes of the Territories themselves, of amending or enacting legislation for application to the Territories, either through orders in council, in order to apply to the Territories the international treaty obligations of the administering Power, or through the unilateral application of laws and regulations,

Aware of the importance of the international financial services and tourism sectors for the economies of some of the Non-Self-Governing Territories,

Noting the continued cooperation of the Non-Self-Governing Territories at the local and regional levels, including participation in the work of regional organizations,

Mindful that United Nations visiting and special missions provide an effective means of ascertaining the situation in the Territories, that some Territories have not received a United Nations visiting mission for a long time and that no visiting missions have been sent to some of the Territories, and considering the possibility of sending further visiting missions to the Territories at an appropriate time, in consultation with the relevant administering Powers and in accordance with the relevant resolutions and decisions of the United Nations on decolonization,

Mindful also that, in order for the Special Committee to enhance its understanding of the political status of the peoples of the Territories and to fulfil its mandate effectively, it is important for it to be apprised by the relevant administering Powers and to receive information from other appropriate sources, including the representatives of the Territories, concerning the wishes and aspirations of the peoples of the Territories,

Acknowledging the regular transmission by the administering Powers to the Secretary-General of information called for under Article 73 *e* of the Charter,

Aware of the importance both to the Territories and to the Special Committee of the participation of elected and appointed representatives of the Territories in the work of the Committee,

Recognizing the need for the Special Committee to ensure that the appropriate bodies of the United Nations actively pursue a public awareness campaign aimed at assisting the peoples of the Territories in gaining a better understanding of the options for self-determination,

Mindful, in this connection, that the holding of regional seminars in the Caribbean and Pacific regions and at Headquarters, with the active participation of representatives of the Non-Self-Governing Territories, provides a helpful means for the Special Committee to fulfil its mandate, and that the regional nature of the seminars, which alternate between the Caribbean and the Pacific, is a crucial element in the context of a United Nations programme for ascertaining the political status of the Territories,

Noting the stated positions of the representatives of the Non-Self-Governing Territories before the Special Committee and at its regional seminars,

Mindful that the 2009 Caribbean regional seminar was held in Frigate Bay, Saint Kitts and Nevis, from 12 to 14 May,

Conscious of the particular vulnerability of the Territories to natural disasters and environmental degradation, and, in this connection, bearing in mind the applicability to the Territories of the programmes of action or outcome documents of all United Nations world conferences and special sessions of the General Assembly in the economic and social spheres,

Noting with appreciation the contribution to the development of some Territories by the specialized agencies and other organizations of the United Nations system, in particular the United Nations Development Programme, the Economic Commission for Latin America and the Caribbean and the Economic and Social Commission for Asia and the Pacific, as well as regional institutions such as the Caribbean Development Bank, the Caribbean Community, the Organization of Eastern Caribbean States, the Pacific Islands Forum and the agencies of the Council of Regional Organizations in the Pacific,

Aware that the Human Rights Committee, as part of its mandate under the International Covenant on Civil and Political Rights, reviews the status of the self-determination process, including in small island Territories under examination by the Special Committee,

Recalling the ongoing efforts of the Special Committee in carrying out a critical review of its work with the aim of making appropriate and constructive recommendations and decisions to attain its objectives in accordance with its mandate,

Recognizing that the annual working papers prepared by the Secretariat on developments in each of the small Territories, as well as the substantive documentation and information furnished by experts, scholars, non-governmental organizations and other sources, have provided important inputs to update the present resolutions,

Taking note of the report of the Secretary-General on the implementation of decolonization resolutions adopted since the declaration of the First and Second International Decades for the Eradication of Colonialism,

1. *Reaffirms* the inalienable right of the peoples of the Non-Self-Governing Territories to self-determination, in conformity with the Charter of the United Nations and with General Assembly resolution 1514(XV), containing the Declaration on the Granting of Independence to Colonial Countries and Peoples;

2. *Also reaffirms* that, in the process of decolonization, there is no alternative to the principle of self-determination, which is also a fundamental human right, as recognized under the relevant human rights conventions;

3. *Further reaffirms* that it is ultimately for the peoples of the Territories themselves to determine freely their future political status in accordance with the relevant provisions of the Charter, the Declaration and the relevant resolutions of the General Assembly, and in that connection reiterates its long-standing call for the administering Powers, in cooperation with the territorial Governments and appropriate bodies of the United Nations system, to develop political

education programmes for the Territories in order to foster an awareness among the people of their right to self-determination in conformity with the legitimate political status options, based on the principles clearly defined in General Assembly resolution 1541(XV) and other relevant resolutions and decisions;

4. *Stresses* the importance of the Special Committee being apprised of the views and wishes of the peoples of the Territories and enhancing its understanding of their conditions, including the nature and scope of the existing political and constitutional arrangements between the Non-Self-Governing Territories and their respective administering Powers;

5. *Requests* the administering Powers to continue to transmit regularly to the Secretary-General information called for under Article 73 *e* of the Charter;

6. *Calls upon* the administering Powers to participate in and cooperate fully with the work of the Special Committee in order to implement the provisions of Article 73 *e* of the Charter and the Declaration and in order to advise the Special Committee on the implementation of the provisions under Article 73 *b* of the Charter on efforts to promote self-government in the Territories, and encourages the administering Powers to facilitate visiting and special missions to the Territories;

7. *Reaffirms* the responsibility of the administering Powers under the Charter to promote the economic and social development and to preserve the cultural identity of the Territories, and, as a priority, to mitigate the effects of the current global financial crisis where possible, in consultation with the territorial Governments concerned, towards the strengthening and diversification of their respective economies;

8. *Requests* the Territories and the administering Powers to take all measures necessary to protect and conserve the environment of the Territories against any degradation, and once again requests the specialized agencies concerned to continue to monitor environmental conditions in the Territories and to provide assistance to those Territories, consistent with their prevailing rules of procedure;

9. *Welcomes* the participation of the Non-Self-Governing Territories in regional activities, including the work of regional organizations;

10. *Stresses* the importance of implementing the plan of action for the Second International Decade for the Eradication of Colonialism, in particular by expediting the application of the work programme for the decolonization of each Non-Self-Governing Territory, on a case-by-case basis, as well as by ensuring that periodic analyses are undertaken of the progress and extent of the implementation of the Declaration in each Territory, and that the working papers prepared by the Secretariat on each Territory should fully reflect developments in those Territories;

11. *Urges* Member States to contribute to the efforts of the United Nations to usher in a world free of colonialism within the Second International Decade for the Eradication of Colonialism, and calls upon them to continue to give their full support to the Special Committee in its endeavours towards that noble goal;

12. *Stresses* the importance of the various constitutional exercises in the respective Territories administered by the United Kingdom of Great Britain and Northern Ireland

and the United States of America, and led by the territorial Governments, designed to address internal constitutional structures within the present territorial arrangements, and decides to follow closely the developments concerning the future political status of those Territories;

13. *Requests* the Secretary-General to continue to report to the General Assembly on a regular basis on the implementation of decolonization resolutions adopted since the declaration of the First and Second International Decades for the Eradication of Colonialism;

14. *Reiterates its request* that the Human Rights Committee collaborate with the Special Committee, within the framework of its mandate on the right to self-determination as contained in the International Covenant on Civil and Political Rights, with the aim of exchanging information, given that the Human Rights Committee is mandated to review the situation, including political and constitutional developments, in many of the Non-Self-Governing Territories that are within the purview of the Special Committee;

15. *Requests* the Special Committee to continue to collaborate with the Economic and Social Council and its relevant subsidiary intergovernmental bodies, within the framework of their respective mandates, with the aim of exchanging information on developments in those Non-Self-Governing Territories which are reviewed by those bodies;

16. *Also requests* the Special Committee to continue to examine the question of the Non-Self-Governing Territories and to report thereon to the General Assembly at its sixty-fifth session and on the implementation of the present resolution.

B
Individual Territories

The General Assembly,

Referring to resolution A above,

I
American Samoa

Taking note of the working paper prepared by the Secretariat on American Samoa and other relevant information,

Aware that under United States law the Secretary of the Interior has administrative jurisdiction over American Samoa,

Noting the position of the administering Power and the statements made by representatives of American Samoa in regional seminars expressing satisfaction with the Territory's present relationship with the United States of America,

Aware of the work of the Future Political Status Study Commission, completed in 2006, and the release of its report, with recommendations, in January 2007, and the Governor's announcement early in 2009 that the report and recommendations of the Commission would be laid before a constitutional convention sometime in 2009,

Noting, in that regard, the information contained in the paper provided by the Chair of the Future Political Status Study Commission and distributed at the 2008 Pacific regional seminar requesting the Special Committee to review the Territory's status as a Non-Self-Governing Territory, with a view to accepting the Territory's future political status once chosen by its people,

Acknowledging the indication by the territorial Government that certain cost-of-living issues, such as inflation, are serious cause for concern,

Aware that American Samoa continues to be the only United States Territory to receive financial assistance from the administering Power for the operations of the territorial Government, and calling upon the administering Power to assist the territorial Government in the diversification of its economy,

1. *Welcomes* the work of the territorial Government and legislature with regard to the recommendations made by the Future Political Status Study Commission, in preparation for a constitutional convention sometime in 2009, addressing issues related to the future status of American Samoa;

2. *Calls upon* the administering Power to assist the Territory by facilitating its work concerning the intention of holding a constitutional convention sometime in 2009, if requested;

3. *Stresses* the importance of the invitation previously extended to the Special Committee by the Governor of American Samoa to send a visiting mission to the Territory, calls upon the administering Power to facilitate such a mission if the territorial Government so desires, and requests the Chair of the Special Committee to take all the steps necessary to that end;

4. *Requests* the administering Power to assist the Territory by facilitating its work concerning a public awareness programme recommended by the Future Political Status Study Commission in its 2007 report, consistent with Article 73 *b* of the Charter of the United Nations and, in that regard, calls upon the relevant United Nations organizations to provide assistance to the Territory, if requested;

5. *Welcomes* the efforts made by the territorial Government to address employment and cost-of-living issues in various economic sectors;

II

Anguilla

Taking note of the working paper prepared by the Secretariat on Anguilla and other relevant information,

Recalling the holding of the 2003 Caribbean regional seminar in Anguilla, hosted by the territorial Government and made possible by the administering Power, the first time that the seminar had been held in a Non-Self-Governing Territory,

Taking note of the statement of the representative of Anguilla at the Caribbean regional seminar, held in Frigate Bay, Saint Kitts and Nevis, from 12 to 14 May 2009,

Taking note also of the internal constitutional review process resumed by the territorial Government in 2006, the work of the Constitutional and Electoral Reform Commission, which prepared its report in August 2006, and the holding of public and other consultative meetings in 2007 on proposed constitutional amendments to be presented to the administering Power, as well as the 2008 decision to set up a drafting team consisting of territorial Government officials, members of the House of Assembly and lawyers to draft a new constitution, to be based on internal self-government for public consultation and subsequent discussion with the administering Power, with the aim of seeking full internal self-government,

Aware that the Government intends to continue its commitment to high-end tourism and the implementation of various regulations in the financial services sector,

Noting the participation of the Territory as an associate member in the Caribbean Community, the Organization of Eastern Caribbean States and the Economic Commission for Latin America and the Caribbean,

1. *Welcomes* the work of the Constitutional and Electoral Reform Commission and its report of 2006, the holding of a public forum in April 2008 to address constitutional reform issues and the subsequent agreement to seek full internal self-government, short of political independence, and the setting up of a drafting group, with the aim of making recommendations to the administering Power on proposed changes to the Constitution of the Territory, using the concept of internal self-government;

2. *Requests* the administering Power to assist the Territory in its current efforts with regard to advancing the internal constitutional review exercise, if requested;

3. *Stresses* the importance of the previously expressed desire of the territorial Government for a visiting mission by the Special Committee, calls upon the administering Power to facilitate such a mission, if the territorial Government so desires, and requests the Chair of the Special Committee to take all the necessary steps to that end;

4. *Requests* the administering Power to assist the Territory by facilitating its work concerning public consultative outreach efforts, consistent with Article 73 *b* of the Charter of the United Nations, and, in this regard, calls upon the relevant United Nations organizations to provide assistance to the Territory, if requested;

III

Bermuda

Taking note of the working paper prepared by the Secretariat on Bermuda and other relevant information,

Taking note also of the statement of the representative of Bermuda at the Caribbean regional seminar, held in Frigate Bay, Saint Kitts and Nevis, from 12 to 14 May 2009,

Conscious of the different viewpoints of the political parties on the future status of the Territory, and noting a recent survey by local media on the matter,

Recalling the dispatch of the United Nations special mission to Bermuda in 2005 at the request of the territorial Government and with the concurrence of the administering Power, which provided information to the people of the Territory on the role of the United Nations in the process of self-determination, on the legitimate political status options as clearly defined in General Assembly resolution 1541(XV) and on the experiences of other small States that have achieved a full measure of self-government,

1. *Stresses* the importance of the 2005 report of the Bermuda Independence Commission, which provides a thorough examination of the facts surrounding independence, and regrets that the plans for public meetings and the presentation of a Green Paper to the House of Assembly followed by a White Paper outlining the policy proposals for an independent Bermuda have so far not materialized;

2. *Requests* the administering Power to assist the Territory by facilitating its work concerning public educational outreach efforts, consistent with Article 73 *b* of the Charter of the United Nations, and, in this regard, calls upon the relevant United Nations organizations to provide assistance to the Territory, if requested;

IV

British Virgin Islands

Taking note of the working paper prepared by the Secretariat on the British Virgin Islands and other relevant information,

Taking note also of the statement of the representative of the British Virgin Islands at the Caribbean regional seminar, held in Frigate Bay, Saint Kitts and Nevis, from 12 to 14 May 2009,

Recalling the 1993 report of the Constitutional Commissioners, the 1996 debate on the report in the Legislative Council of the Territory, the establishment of the Constitutional Review Commission in 2004, the completion in 2005 of its report providing recommendations on internal constitutional modernization and the debate held in 2005 on the report in the Legislative Council, as well as the negotiations between the administering Power and the territorial Government, which resulted in the adoption of the new Constitution of the Territory in 2007,

Noting that the 2007 Constitution of the British Virgin Islands provides for a Governor, who maintains reserved powers in the Territory, to be appointed by the administering Power,

Noting also the view expressed in the aforementioned statement made by the representative of the British Virgin Islands at the 2009 Caribbean regional seminar, that, building on the conclusion of the recent internal constitutional modernization exercise, the Territory's focus was on economic development prior to a search for independence,

Noting further the impact of the global financial crisis on the Territory's financial and tourism services sectors,

Cognizant of the potential usefulness of regional ties for the development of a small island Territory,

1.   *Welcomes* the new Constitution of the British Virgin Islands, which took effect in June 2007, and notes the continued need expressed by the territorial Government for minor constitutional amendments in the years to come;

2.   *Requests* the administering Power to assist the Territory by facilitating its work concerning public outreach efforts, consistent with Article 73 *b* of the Charter of the United Nations and, in that regard, calls upon the relevant United Nations organizations to provide assistance to the Territory, if requested;

3.   *Welcomes* the efforts made by the Territory to focus its economic base more on local ownership and on professional service industries other than financial services;

V

Cayman Islands

Taking note of the working paper prepared by the Secretariat on the Cayman Islands and other relevant information,

Aware of the 2002 report of the Constitutional Modernization Review Commission, which contained a draft constitution for the consideration of the people of the Territory, the 2003 draft constitution offered by the administering Power and the subsequent discussions between the Territory and the administering Power in 2003, and the reopening of discussions between the administering Power and the territorial Government on internal constitutional modernization, in 2006, which resulted in the finalization

of a new draft constitution in February 2009 and its subsequent acceptance by referendum in May 2009,

Noting with interest the establishment of the Cayman Islands Constitutional Review Secretariat, which began its work in March 2007 in support of the Territory's constitution modernization initiative, which comprises four phases with regard to constitutional reform, including research and publicity, consultation and public education, a referendum on reform proposals, and negotiations between the administering Power and the territorial Government,

Welcoming the participation of the Territory as a new associate member of the Economic Commission for Latin America and the Caribbean,

Acknowledging the indication by the territorial Government that certain cost-of-living issues, such as inflation, continue to be cause for concern,

1.   *Welcomes* the finalization of a new draft constitution in February 2009 and its subsequent acceptance by referendum in May 2009;

2.   *Requests* the administering Power to assist the Territory by facilitating its work concerning public awareness outreach efforts, consistent with Article 73 *b* of the Charter of the United Nations, and, in this regard, calls upon the relevant United Nations organizations to provide assistance to the Territory, if requested;

3.   *Welcomes* the efforts made by the territorial Government to address cost-of-living issues in various economic sectors;

VI

Guam

Taking note of the working paper prepared by the Secretariat on Guam and other relevant information,

Aware that under United States law the relations between the territorial Government and the federal Government in all matters that are not the programme responsibility of another federal department or agency are under the general administrative supervision of the Secretary of the Interior,

Recalling that, in a referendum held in 1987, the registered and eligible voters of Guam endorsed a draft Guam Commonwealth Act that would establish a new framework for relations between the Territory and the administering Power, providing for a greater measure of internal self-government for Guam and recognition of the right of the Chamorro people of Guam to self-determination for the Territory,

Recalling also the previously expressed requests by the elected representatives and non-governmental organizations of the Territory that Guam not be removed from the list of the Non-Self-Governing Territories with which the Special Committee is concerned, pending the self-determination of the Chamorro people and taking into account their legitimate rights and interests,

Aware that negotiations between the administering Power and the territorial Government on the draft Guam Commonwealth Act ended in 1997 and that Guam has subsequently established a non-binding plebiscite process for a self-determination vote by the eligible Chamorro voters,

Cognizant of the importance that the administering Power continues to implement its programme of transferring surplus federal land to the Government of Guam,

Noting that the people of the Territory have called for reform in the programme of the administering Power with respect to the thorough, unconditional and expeditious transfer of land property to the people of Guam,

Aware of deep concerns expressed by civil society and others, including at the meeting of the Special Political and Decolonization Committee of the General Assembly in October 2008, regarding the potential social and other impacts of the impending transfer of additional military personnel of the administering Power to the Territory,

Aware also of the austerity and fiscal measures undertaken by the territorial Government since 2007, when the Governor declared a financial "state of emergency", and of subsequent developments,

Conscious that immigration into Guam has resulted in the indigenous Chamorros becoming a minority in their homeland,

1. *Calls once again upon* the administering Power to take into consideration the expressed will of the Chamorro people as supported by Guam voters in the referendum of 1987 and as subsequently provided for in Guam law regarding Chamorro self-determination efforts, and encourages the administering Power and the territorial Government to enter into negotiations on the matter;

2. *Requests* the administering Power, in cooperation with the territorial Government, to continue to transfer land to the original landowners of the Territory, to continue to recognize and to respect the political rights and the cultural and ethnic identity of the Chamorro people of Guam and to take all measures necessary to address the concerns of the territorial Government with regard to the question of immigration;

3. *Also requests* the administering Power to cooperate in establishing programmes for the sustainable development of the economic activities and enterprises of the Territory, noting the special role of the Chamorro people in the development of Guam;

4. *Recalls* the request made previously by the elected Governor to the administering Power to lift restrictions to allow for foreign airlines to transport passengers between Guam and the United States of America to provide for a more competitive market and increased visitor arrivals;

5. *Requests* the administering Power to assist the Territory by facilitating public outreach efforts, consistent with Article 73 *b* of the Charter of the United Nations, and, in this regard, calls upon the relevant United Nations organizations to provide assistance to the Territory, if requested;

VII

Montserrat

Taking note of the working paper prepared by the Secretariat on Montserrat and other relevant information,

Taking note also of the statement of the representative of Montserrat at the Caribbean regional seminar, held in Frigate Bay, Saint Kitts and Nevis, from 12 to 14 May 2009,

Recalling the 2002 report of the Constitutional Review Commission, the convening of a committee of the House of Assembly in 2005 to review the report and the subsequent discussions between the administering Power and the territorial Government on internal constitutional advancement and devolution of power,

Noting that the negotiating process with the administering Power on a draft constitution giving greater autonomy to the territorial Government proceeded during 2008, and that, since March 2009, the administering Power has accorded stronger emphasis to the redevelopment of the Territory,

Aware that Montserrat continues to receive budgetary aid from the administering Power for the operation of the territorial Government,

Recalling the statements made by participants at the 2007 Caribbean regional seminar encouraging the administering Power to commit sufficient resources to meet the Territory's special needs,

Noting with concern the continued consequences of the volcanic eruption, which led to the evacuation of three quarters of the Territory's population to safe areas of the island and to areas outside the Territory, which continues to have enduring consequences for the economy of the island,

Acknowledging the continued assistance provided to the Territory by States members of the Caribbean Community, in particular Antigua and Barbuda, which has offered safe refuge and access to educational and health facilities, as well as employment for thousands who have left the Territory,

Noting the continuing efforts of the administering Power and the territorial Government to deal with the consequences of the volcanic eruption,

1. *Welcomes* the efforts of the territorial Government to continue to negotiate improvements to the Constitution of the Territory so as to preserve its ability to move towards full self-government, notes the efforts of the administering Power to support the redevelopment of the Territory, and encourages them to mutually reinforce their efforts;

2. *Requests* the administering Power to assist the Territory by facilitating its work concerning public outreach efforts, consistent with Article 73 *b* of the Charter of the United Nations, and, in this regard, calls upon the relevant United Nations organizations to provide assistance to the Territory, if requested;

3. *Calls upon* the administering Power, the specialized agencies and other organizations of the United Nations system, as well as regional and other organizations, to continue to provide assistance to the Territory in alleviating the consequences of the volcanic eruption;

VIII

Pitcairn

Taking note of the working paper prepared by the Secretariat on Pitcairn and other relevant information,

Taking into account the unique character of Pitcairn in terms of population and area,

Noting that the internal review of the Constitution of the Territory is still deferred,

Aware that the administering Power and the territorial Government are in the process of restructuring the relationship between the Governor's Office and the territorial Government, based on consultations with the people of the Territory, and that Pitcairn continues to receive budgetary aid from the administering Power for the operation of the territorial Government,

1. *Welcomes* all efforts by the administering Power that would devolve operational responsibilities to the territorial Government, with a view to expanding self-government;

2. *Requests* the administering Power to assist the Territory by facilitating its work concerning public outreach efforts, consistent with Article 73 *b* of the Charter of the United Nations, and, in this regard, calls upon the relevant United Nations organizations to provide assistance to the Territory, if requested;

3. *Also requests* the administering Power to continue its assistance for the improvement of the economic, social, educational and other conditions of the population of the Territory and to continue its discussions with the territorial Government on how best to support economic security in Pitcairn;

IX

Saint Helena

Taking note of the working paper prepared by the Secretariat on Saint Helena and other relevant information,

Taking note also of the statement of the representative of Saint Helena at the Caribbean regional seminar, held in Frigate Bay, Saint Kitts and Nevis, from 12 to 14 May 2009,

Taking into account the unique character of Saint Helena in terms of its population, geography and natural resources,

Noting the internal constitutional review process led by the territorial Government since 2001, the completion of a draft constitution following negotiations between the administering Power and the territorial Government in 2003 and 2004, the consultative poll with regard to a new Constitution, held in Saint Helena in May 2005, the subsequent preparation of a revised draft constitution and its publication in June 2008 for further public consultation, and the entry into force of the new Constitution for Saint Helena, Ascension and Tristan da Cunha on 1 September 2009,

Noting in that regard the importance of the right to nationality for Saint Helenians and their previously expressed request that the right, in principle, be included in a new constitution,

Aware that Saint Helena continues to receive budgetary aid from the administering Power for the operation of the territorial Government,

Aware also of the efforts of the administering Power and the territorial Government to improve the socio-economic conditions of the population of Saint Helena, in particular in the areas of employment and transport and communications infrastructure,

Noting the efforts of the Territory to address the problem of unemployment on the island and the joint action of the administering Power and the territorial Government in dealing with it,

Noting also the importance of improving the infrastructure and accessibility of Saint Helena,

Noting in this regard the administering Power's decision in December 2008 to pause the negotiations on the Saint Helena airport,

1. *Welcomes* the entry into force of the Territory's new Constitution on 1 September 2009;

2. *Requests* the administering Power to assist the Territory by facilitating its work concerning public outreach efforts, consistent with Article 73 *b* of the Charter of the

United Nations and, in that regard, calls upon the relevant United Nations organizations to provide assistance to the Territory, if requested;

3. *Requests* the administering Power and relevant international organizations to continue to support the efforts of the territorial Government to address the Territory's socio-economic development challenges, including unemployment, and limited transport and communications infrastructure;

4. *Notes* the decision by the administering Power to consult on whether an airport is the most appropriate option for access to Saint Helena in the current economic climate, and calls upon the administering Power to take into account the unique geographical character of Saint Helena in the process of consultation;

X

Turks and Caicos Islands

Taking note of the working paper prepared by the Secretariat on the Turks and Caicos Islands and other relevant information,

Taking note also of the statement of the representative of the Turks and Caicos Islands at the Caribbean regional seminar, held in Frigate Bay, Saint Kitts and Nevis, from 12 to 14 May 2009,

Recalling the dispatch of the United Nations special mission to the Turks and Caicos Islands in 2006, at the request of the territorial Government and with the concurrence of the administering Power,

Recalling also the 2002 report of the Constitutional Modernization Review Body, and acknowledging the Constitution agreed between the administering Power and the territorial Government, which entered into force in 2006,

Noting that the 2006 Constitution of the Turks and Caicos Islands provides for a Governor, who maintains reserved powers in the Territory, to be appointed by the administering Power,

Noting also the administering Power's decision to suspend parts of the 2006 Constitution of the Turks and Caicos Islands, covering the constitutional right to trial by jury, ministerial Government, and the House of Assembly, following the recommendations of an independent Commission of Inquiry and the ruling of the administering Power's Court of Appeal,

Acknowledging the impact that the global financial crisis has had on tourism and related real estate development, the mainstays of the Territory's economy,

1. *Recalls* the Constitution of the Territory, which took effect in 2006, and notes the view of the former territorial Government that there remains scope for a degree of delegation of the Governor's power to the Territory so as to secure greater autonomy;

2. *Requests* the administering Power to assist the Territory by facilitating its work concerning public outreach efforts, consistent with Article 73 *b* of the Charter of the United Nations and, in that regard, calls upon the relevant United Nations organizations to provide assistance to the Territory, if requested;

3. *Notes with concern* the ongoing situation in the Turks and Caicos Islands, and also notes the efforts of the administering Power to restore good governance and sound financial management in the Territory;

4. *Calls for* restoration of constitutional arrangements providing for representative democracy through elected territorial Government as soon as possible;

5. *Welcomes* the continuing efforts made by the Government addressing the need for attention to be paid to the enhancement of social cohesion across the Territory;

XI
United States Virgin Islands

Taking note of the working paper prepared by the Secretariat on the United States Virgin Islands and other relevant information,

Aware that under United States law the relations between the territorial Government and the federal Government in all matters not the programme responsibility of another federal department or agency are under the general administrative supervision of the Secretary of the Interior,

Aware also of the ongoing Constitutional Convention, the fifth attempt of the Territory to review the existing Revised Organic Act, which organizes its internal governance arrangements, as well as the various related efforts in implementing a public education programme on the constitution, as outlined in a statement by a participant from the Territory presented at the Caribbean regional seminar, held in Frigate Bay, St. Kitts and Nevis, from 12 to 14 May 2009,

Cognizant that the draft constitution is expected to be finalized by the territorial Government in 2009 and forwarded to the administering Power for review and action,

Cognizant also of the potential usefulness of regional ties for the development of a small island Territory,

1. *Welcomes* the establishment of the Constitutional Convention in 2007, and requests the administering Power to assist the territorial Government in achieving its political, economic and social goals, in particular the successful conclusion of the ongoing internal Constitutional Convention exercise;

2. *Requests* the administering Power to facilitate the process for approval of the territorial draft constitution in the United States Congress, once agreed upon by the territorial Government;

3. *Also requests* the administering Power to assist the Territory by facilitating its work concerning a public education programme, consistent with Article 73 *b* of the Charter of the United Nations, and, in this regard, calls upon the relevant United Nations organizations to provide assistance to the Territory, if requested;

4. *Reiterates its call* for the inclusion of the Territory in regional programmes of the United Nations Development Programme, consistent with the participation of other Non-Self-Governing Territories.

Peaceful uses of outer space

The Committee on the Peaceful Uses of Outer Space (Committee on Outer Space), at its fifty-second session (Vienna, 3–12 June) [A/64/20], discussed ways and means to maintain outer space for peaceful purposes; the spin-off benefits of space technology; space and society; space and water; space and climate change; the use of space technology in the UN system; and international cooperation in promoting the use of space-derived geospatial data for sustainable development. It also considered the implementation of the recommendations of the Third (1999) United Nations Conference on the Exploration and Peaceful Uses of Outer Space (UNISPACE III) [YUN 1999, p. 556] and reviewed the work of its two subcommittees, one dealing with scientific and technical issues (see p. 603) and the other with legal questions (see p. 606).

GENERAL ASSEMBLY ACTION

On 10 December [meeting 62], the General Assembly, on the recommendation of the Fourth Committee [A/64/404], adopted **resolution 64/86** without vote [agenda item 30].

International cooperation in the peaceful uses of outer space

The General Assembly,

Recalling its resolutions 51/122 of 13 December 1996, 54/68 of 6 December 1999, 59/2 of 20 October 2004, 61/110 and 61/111 of 14 December 2006, 62/101 of 17 December 2007, 62/217 of 22 December 2007 and 63/90 of 5 December 2008,

Deeply convinced of the common interest of mankind in promoting and expanding the exploration and use of outer space, as the province of all mankind, for peaceful purposes and in continuing efforts to extend to all States the benefits derived therefrom, and also of the importance of international cooperation in this field, for which the United Nations should continue to provide a focal point,

Reaffirming the importance of international cooperation in developing the rule of law, including the relevant norms of space law and their important role in international cooperation for the exploration and use of outer space for peaceful purposes, and of the widest possible adherence to international treaties that promote the peaceful uses of outer space in order to meet emerging new challenges, especially for developing countries,

Seriously concerned about the possibility of an arms race in outer space, and bearing in mind the importance of article IV of the Treaty on Principles Governing the Activities of States in the Exploration and Use of Outer Space, including the Moon and Other Celestial Bodies (Outer Space Treaty),

Recognizing that all States, in particular those with major space capabilities, should contribute actively to the goal of preventing an arms race in outer space as an essential condition for the promotion and strengthening of international cooperation in the exploration and use of outer space for peaceful purposes,

Recognizing also that space debris is an issue of concern to all nations,

Noting the progress achieved in the further development of peaceful space exploration and applications as well as in various national and cooperative space projects, which contributes to international cooperation, and the importance of further developing the legal framework to strengthen international cooperation in this field,

Convinced of the importance of the recommendations in the resolution entitled "The Space Millennium: Vienna Declaration on Space and Human Development", adopted by the Third United Nations Conference on the Exploration and Peaceful Uses of Outer Space (UNISPACE III), held at Vienna from 19 to 30 July 1999, and the need to promote the use of space technology towards implementing the United Nations Millennium Declaration,

Seriously concerned about the devastating impact of disasters,

Desirous of enhancing international coordination and cooperation at the global level in disaster management and emergency response through greater access to and use of space-based services for all countries and facilitating capacity-building and institutional strengthening for disaster management, in particular in developing countries,

Deeply convinced that the use of space science and technology and their applications in areas such as telemedicine, tele-education, disaster management, environmental protection and other Earth observation applications contribute to achieving the objectives of the global conferences of the United Nations that address various aspects of economic, social and cultural development, particularly poverty eradication,

Taking note, in that regard, of the fact that the 2005 World Summit recognized the important role that science and technology play in promoting sustainable development,

Having considered the report of the Committee on the Peaceful Uses of Outer Space on the work of its fifty-second session,

1. *Endorses* the report of the Committee on the Peaceful Uses of Outer Space on the work of its fifty-second session;

2. *Agrees* that the Committee on the Peaceful Uses of Outer Space, at its fifty-third session, should consider the items recommended by the Committee at its fifty-second session;

3. *Notes* that, at its forty-eighth session, the Legal Subcommittee of the Committee on the Peaceful Uses of Outer Space continued its work, as mandated by the General Assembly in its resolution 63/90;

4. *Agrees* that the Legal Subcommittee, at its forty-ninth session, should consider the items recommended by the Committee, taking into account the concerns of all countries, in particular those of developing countries;

5. *Also agrees* that the Legal Subcommittee, at its forty-ninth session, should reconvene its Working Group on the Status and Application of the Five United Nations Treaties on Outer Space, its Working Group on Matters Relating to the Definition and Delimitation of Outer Space and its Working Group on National Legislation Relevant to the Peaceful Exploration and Use of Outer Space;

6. *Urges* States that have not yet become parties to the international treaties governing the uses of outer space to give consideration to ratifying or acceding to those treaties in accordance with their domestic law, as well as incorporating them in their national legislation;

7. *Notes* that, at its forty-sixth session, the Scientific and Technical Subcommittee of the Committee on the Peaceful Uses of Outer Space continued its work, as mandated by the General Assembly in its resolution 63/90;

8. *Agrees* that the Scientific and Technical Subcommittee, at its forty-seventh session, should consider the items recommended by the Committee, taking into account the concerns of all countries, in particular those of developing countries;

9. *Also agrees* that the Scientific and Technical Subcommittee, at its forty-seventh session, should reconvene its Working Group of the Whole, its Working Group on the Use of Nuclear Power Sources in Outer Space and its Working Group on Near-Earth Objects;

10. *Welcomes* the fact that the Scientific and Technical Subcommittee, at its forty-seventh session, will begin consideration under a multi-year workplan of two new items, entitled "International Space Weather Initiative" and "Long-term sustainability of outer space activities", as agreed by the Committee;

11. *Welcomes with satisfaction* the Safety Framework for Nuclear Power Source Applications in Outer Space, adopted by the Scientific and Technical Subcommittee at its forty-sixth session and endorsed by the Committee at its fifty-second session;

12. *Notes* that the International Atomic Energy Agency Commission on Safety Standards agreed on the Safety Framework at its twenty-fifth meeting, which was held in Vienna from 22 to 24 April 2009, and welcomes the constructive and efficient cooperation between the Scientific and Technical Subcommittee and the International Atomic Energy Agency in the preparation of the Safety Framework, which is an example of successful inter-agency cooperation within the United Nations system;

13. *Notes with appreciation* that some States are already implementing space debris mitigation measures on a voluntary basis, through national mechanisms and consistent with the Space Debris Mitigation Guidelines of the Inter-Agency Space Debris Coordination Committee and with the Space Debris Mitigation Guidelines of the Committee on the Peaceful Uses of Outer Space, endorsed by the General Assembly in its resolution 62/217;

14. *Invites* other States to implement, through relevant national mechanisms, the Space Debris Mitigation Guidelines of the Committee on the Peaceful Uses of Outer Space;

15. *Considers* that it is essential that Member States pay more attention to the problem of collisions of space objects, including those with nuclear power sources, with space debris, and other aspects of space debris, calls for the continuation of national research on this question, for the development of improved technology for the monitoring of space debris and for the compilation and dissemination of data on space debris, also considers that, to the extent possible, information thereon should be provided to the Scientific and Technical Subcommittee, and agrees that international cooperation is needed to expand appropriate and affordable strategies to minimize the impact of space debris on future space missions;

16. *Urges* all States, in particular those with major space capabilities, to contribute actively to the goal of preventing an arms race in outer space as an essential condition for the promotion of international cooperation in the exploration and use of outer space for peaceful purposes;

17. *Notes with appreciation* that the activities planned by the United Nations Programme on Space Applications

for 2010 would address, inter alia, water resources management, socio-economic benefits of space activities, small satellite technology for sustainable development, space weather, global navigation satellite systems, search and rescue and space law;

18. *Welcomes* the progress made by the International Committee on Global Navigation Satellite Systems towards achieving compatibility and interoperability among global and regional space-based positioning, navigation and timing systems and in the promotion of the use of global navigation satellite systems and their integration into national infrastructure, particularly in developing countries, and notes with satisfaction that the International Committee held its third meeting in Pasadena, United States of America, from 8 to 12 December 2008 and its fourth meeting in St. Petersburg, Russian Federation, from 14 to 18 September 2009, and that its fifth meeting will be jointly organized by Italy and the European Commission in 2010;

19. *Endorses* the recommendation of the Committee on the Peaceful Uses of Outer Space that the Office for Outer Space Affairs of the Secretariat should continue to serve as the executive secretariat of the International Committee on Global Navigation Satellite Systems and its Providers' Forum;

20. *Notes with satisfaction* the progress made within the framework of the United Nations Platform for Space-based Information for Disaster Management and Emergency Response (UN-spider) in the implementation of the platform programme for the period 2007–2009;

21. *Endorses* the workplan of the UN-spider programme for the biennium 2010–2011, and encourages Member States to provide all support necessary, on a voluntary basis, to UN-spider, including financial support, to enable it to carry out the workplan;

22. *Welcomes* the fact that, in accordance with General Assembly resolution 61/110, regional support offices were established in the Islamic Republic of Iran, Nigeria and Romania, and that a cooperation agreement was reached with the Asian Disaster Reduction Centre, to support the implementation of the activities of the UN-spider programme;

23. *Notes with appreciation* that the African regional centres for space science and technology education in the French and English languages, located in Morocco and Nigeria, respectively, as well as the Centre for Space Science and Technology Education in Asia and the Pacific and the Regional Centre for Space Science and Technology Education for Latin America and the Caribbean, affiliated to the United Nations, have continued their education programmes in 2009;

24. *Welcomes* the fact that the regional centres would serve as International Committee on Global Navigation Satellite Systems information centres;

25. *Agrees* that the regional centres should continue to report to the Committee on their activities on an annual basis;

26. *Emphasizes* that regional and interregional cooperation in the field of space activities is essential to strengthen the peaceful uses of outer space, assist States in the development of their space capabilities and contribute to the achievement of the goals of the United Nations Millennium Declaration, and to that end fosters interregional dialogue on space matters between Member States;

27. *Recognizes*, in this regard, the important role played by conferences and other mechanisms in strengthening regional and international cooperation among States, such as the Third African Leadership Conference on Space Science and Technology for Sustainable Development, to be held in Algiers from 7 to 9 December 2009; the sixteenth session of the Asia-Pacific Regional Space Agency Forum, to be held in Bangkok from 26 to 29 January 2010 in cooperation with the Sentinel Asia project; the Asia-Pacific Space Cooperation Organization, with headquarters in Beijing, which started operating formally in December 2008; and the International Air and Space Fair, to be held in Santiago from 23 to 28 March 2010;

28. *Notes with appreciation* that since the adoption of the Declaration of San Francisco de Quito by the Fifth Space Conference of the Americas in July 2006, more States in the Latin America and Caribbean region have set up national space entities of a civilian nature, thus laying the foundation for enhanced regional cooperation in the peaceful uses of outer space, and recalls that in the Declaration, States in the Latin America and Caribbean region were invited to, inter alia, "set up national space entities to lay the foundation for a regional entity for cooperation";

29. *Welcomes*, in that regard, the fact that the Government of Mexico will host the Sixth Space Conference of the Americas from 22 to 27 November 2010 and that the preparatory meeting for the Conference will be held in Santiago in June 2010;

30. *Emphasizes* the need to increase the benefits of space technology and its applications and to contribute to an orderly growth of space activities favourable to sustained economic growth and sustainable development in all countries, including mitigation of the consequences of disasters, in particular in the developing countries;

31. *Notes* that space science and technology and their applications could make important contributions to economic, social and cultural development and welfare, as indicated in the resolution entitled "The Space Millennium: Vienna Declaration on Space and Human Development", its resolution 59/2 and the Plan of Action of the Committee on the Peaceful Uses of Outer Space on the implementation of the recommendations of unispace iii;

32. *Notes with appreciation* that a number of the recommendations set out in the Plan of Action have been implemented and that satisfactory progress is being made in implementing the outstanding recommendations;

33. *Urges* all Member States to continue to contribute to the Trust Fund for the United Nations Programme on Space Applications to enhance the capacity of the Office for Outer Space Affairs to provide technical and legal advisory services in accordance with the Plan of Action, while maintaining the priority thematic areas agreed by the Committee;

34. *Reiterates* that the benefits of space technology and its applications should continue to be brought to the attention, in particular, of the major United Nations conferences and summits for economic, social and cultural development and related fields and that the use of space technology should be promoted towards achieving the objectives of those conferences and summits and for implementing the United Nations Millennium Declaration;

35. *Notes with appreciation* that the initiative of the Chair of the Committee on the Peaceful Uses of Outer Space to seek a holistic approach for enhancing coordination between Member States and the United Nations system in applying space science and technology to meet the challenges to development of all countries and to further promote and strengthen the use of space technology and its applications in the United Nations system would be further developed for the consideration of the Committee at its fifty-third session;

36. *Welcomes* the increased efforts to strengthen further the Inter-Agency Meeting on Outer Space Activities as the central United Nations mechanism for building partnerships and coordinating space-related activities within the framework of the ongoing reforms in the United Nations system to work in unison and deliver as one, and encourages entities of the United Nations system to participate fully in the work of the Inter-Agency Meeting;

37. *Urges* entities of the United Nations system, particularly those participating in the Inter-Agency Meeting on Outer Space Activities, to continue to examine, in cooperation with the Committee, how space science and technology and their applications could contribute to implementing the United Nations Millennium Declaration on the development agenda, particularly in the areas relating to, inter alia, food security and increasing opportunities for education;

38. *Invites* the Inter-Agency Meeting on Outer Space Activities to continue to contribute to the work of the Committee and to report to the Committee on the work conducted at its annual sessions;

39. *Notes with satisfaction* that the open informal meetings, held in conjunction with the annual sessions of the Inter-Agency Meeting on Outer Space Activities and in which representatives of member States and observers in the Committee participate, provide a constructive mechanism for an active dialogue between the entities of the United Nations system and member States and observers in the Committee;

40. *Welcomes* the contribution of the Committee to the work of the Commission on Sustainable Development, and agrees that the Director of the Office for Outer Space Affairs of the Secretariat should continue to participate in the sessions of the Commission to raise awareness and promote the benefits of space science and technology for sustainable development, and that the Director of the Division for Sustainable Development of the Department of Economic and Social Affairs of the Secretariat should continue to be invited to participate in the sessions of the Committee to inform it of how it could further contribute to the work of the Commission;

41. *Requests* the United Nations University and other scientific institutions and the Economic Commission for Latin America and the Caribbean to explore the possibilities of providing training and policy research at the crossroads of international law, climate change and outer space;

42. *Requests* the Committee to continue to consider, as a matter of priority, ways and means of maintaining outer space for peaceful purposes and to report thereon to the General Assembly at its sixty-fifth session, and agrees that during its consideration of the matter the Committee could continue to consider ways to promote regional and interregional cooperation based on experiences stemming from the Space Conferences of the Americas, the African Leadership Conferences on Space Science and Technology for Sustainable Development and the role space technology could play in the implementation of recommendations of the World Summit on Sustainable Development;

43. *Endorses* the composition of the bureaux of the Committee and its subcommittees for the period 2010–2011, and agrees that the Committee and its subcommittees should elect their officers at their respective sessions in 2010 in accordance with that composition;

44. *Also endorses* the decision of the Committee to grant permanent observer status to the Asia-Pacific Space Cooperation Organization;

45. *Notes* that each of the regional groups has the responsibility for actively promoting the participation in the work of the Committee and its subsidiary bodies of the member States of the Committee that are also members of the respective regional groups, and agrees that the regional groups should consider this Committee-related matter among their members;

46. *Requests* entities of the United Nations system and other international organizations to continue and, where appropriate, to enhance their cooperation with the Committee and to provide it with reports on the issues dealt with in the work of the Committee and its subsidiary bodies, notes with satisfaction that a panel discussion on space applications and global health was held at United Nations Headquarters on 20 October 2009, and agrees that a panel discussion should be held at the sixty-fifth session of the General Assembly on a topic to be selected by the Committee, taking into account the panel discussions held on climate change, food security and global health.

Implementation of UNISPACE III recommendations

In response to General Assembly resolution 63/90 [YUN 2008, p. 684], the Committee on Outer Space considered the implementation of the recommendations of UNISPACE III [YUN 1999, p. 556]. It noted that they were being effectively implemented through regional preparatory conferences; the establishment of Member State-led action teams; and the contribution of Member States to regional and national activities and programmes, including by supporting and participating in work related to the 10-Year Implementation Plan of the Global Earth Observation System of Systems. The Committee expressed the view that while a significant amount of work had been done, the implementation of the UNISPACE III recommendations should not be considered complete until the vast majority of people, especially those in developing countries, benefited from space technology and its applications.

The Committee finalized its contribution to the work of the Commission on Sustainable Development for the thematic cluster 2010–2011 [A/AC.105/944].

The contribution addressed several topics related to overall sustainable resource management, consumption and production, and specific areas such as transport, chemicals, waste management and mining. The Committee agreed that the implementation and follow-up of UNISPACE III recommendations relating to the use of space-based systems in areas such as agriculture and land use, water resource management, disaster management and overall resource management would help Member States support their sustainable development needs and achieve the Millennium Development Goals (MDGs).

Scientific and Technical Subcommittee

The Scientific and Technical Subcommittee of the Committee on Outer Space, at its forty-sixth session (Vienna, 9–20 February) [A/AC.105/933], considered the United Nations Programme on Space Applications and the implementation of the UNISPACE III recommendations. It also dealt with matters relating to remote sensing of the Earth by satellite, including applications for developing countries and monitoring of the Earth's environment; space debris; space-system-based disaster management support; developments in global navigation satellite systems (GNSS); the use of nuclear power sources in outer space; near-Earth objects; the examination of the physical nature and technical attributes of the geostationary orbit and its utilization and applications; and the International Heliophysical Year 2007.

UN Programme on Space Applications

The United Nations Programme on Space Applications, as mandated by General Assembly resolution 37/90 [YUN 1982, p. 163], continued to promote greater cooperation in space science and technology between developed and developing countries, as well as among developing countries, by providing long-term fellowships, training programmes and seminars, and by supporting pilot projects and technical advisory services in capacity-building and regional cooperation. The Programme increased the awareness of knowledge-based themes in space science, law and exploration through multi-year workplans and projects, and by convening outreach events and workshops.

The United Nations Expert on Space Applications [A/AC.105/969] reported that the Programme continued to provide support for education and training for capacity-building in developing countries through regional centres for space science and technology education affiliated with the United Nations Office for Outer Space Affairs. The goal of the regional centres— located in Morocco and Nigeria for the African region, India for Asia and the Pacific, and Brazil and Mexico

for Latin America and the Caribbean—remained to develop an indigenous capability for research and applications in remote sensing and geographic information systems; satellite communications; satellite meteorology and global climate; and space and atmospheric science. Education curricula for those disciplines had been developed through expert meetings held under the Programme, and two further model curricula were being developed in the areas of GNSS and space law. At its fourth meeting (Saint Petersburg, Russian Federation, 14–18 September), the International Committee on Global Navigation Satellite Systems (ICG) further developed the concept according to which the regional centres would act as ICG information centres. Efforts would be made to revise, update and expand education curricula at the fourth UN expert meeting on the regional centres in 2010.

One symposium and seven workshops were conducted within the framework of the Programme. The United Nations/United States of America Training Course on Satellite-Aided Search and Rescue (Miami, United States, 19–23 January) was organized by the Programme and the National Oceanic and Atmospheric Administration of the United States. The training course was the second—the first took place in 2004—organized by the Programme and the United States for participants from Latin America and the Caribbean. The United Nations/Azerbaijan/United States of America/European Space Agency (ESA) Workshop on Applications of GNSS (Baku, Azerbaijan, 11–15 May) addressed the strengthening of regional information and data exchange networks; identification of the needs of individual plans and projects on GNSS at the regional and international levels for short-, medium- and long-term applications; and the development of a regional plan of action that would contribute to the wider use of GNSS technology and its applications.

Several other meetings were convened throughout the year. With regard to natural resources management and environmental monitoring, the United Nations/Peru/ESA Workshop on Integrated Space Technology Applications for Sustainable Development in the Mountain Regions of Andean Countries (Lima, Peru, 14–18 September) discussed ways in which remote sensing and other technologies could be used to promote sustainable development in mountain areas. The United Nations/International Astronautical Federation Workshop on Integrated Space Technologies and Space-based Information for Analysis and Prediction of Climate Change (Daejeon, Republic of Korea, 9–11 October) discussed space-related technologies, services and information resources available for analysing and predicting climate change.

As to tele-health and tele-education, the main objective of the Workshop on Applications of Telehealth to Service Delivery in Public Health and Environment for the benefit of States members of the South Asian Association for Regional Cooperation (Thimphu, Bhutan, 27–30 July), co-organized by the Governments of Bhutan and India and supported by the Programme, was to cost-effectively connect the hospitals of Bhutan and India via a broadband satellite communications channel.

At the sixth European Congress on Tropical Medicine and International Health (Verona, Italy, 6–10 September), the United Nations Office for Outer Space Affairs organized a workshop on space technology's contribution to infection surveillance and the health-related MDGs.

Meetings on space applications for sustainable development included the United Nations/Austria/ ESA Symposium on Small Satellite Programmes for Sustainable Development (Graz, Austria, 8–11 September) and the Tenth United Nations/International Academy of Astronautics Workshop on Small Satellites in the Service of Developing Countries (Daejeon, 13 October). The objectives of the Daejeon workshop were to introduce small satellite programmes; demonstrate the effectiveness, including the cost-effectiveness, of small satellites; and encourage educational and training activities at universities in developing countries.

On space law, the United Nations/Iran Workshop on Space Law (Tehran, Iran, 8–11 November) examined the role of international space law in the development and strengthening of international and regional cooperation in the peaceful exploration and use of outer space.

Further meetings included the United Nations/ ESA/National Aeronautics and Space Administration of the United States/Japan Aerospace Exploration Agency Workshop on Basic Space Science and the International Heliophysical Year 2007 (Daejeon, 21–25 September), where participants reviewed space science activities carried out in the framework of the International Heliophysical Year 2007 (see p. 606) and the projects that had emanated from previous editions of the workshop.

Following its consideration of the report of the United Nations Expert on Space Applications [A/AC.105/925] describing 2008 activities, those scheduled for 2009 and the activities of UN-affiliated regional centres for space science and technology education scheduled for 2008–2010, the Subcommittee expressed concern over the limited financial resources available for carrying out the Programme and appealed to Member States for support through voluntary contributions.

The General Assembly, in resolution 64/86 (see p. 599), endorsed the Programme on Space Applications, as proposed by the Expert.

Cooperation

The Inter-Agency Meeting on Outer Space Activities, at its twenty-ninth session (Vienna, 4–6 March) [A/AC.105/939], discussed the coordination of plans and programmes in the practical application of space technology and related areas; implementation of the UNISPACE III recommendations; contribution of the Committee on Outer Space to the work of the Commission on Sustainable Development for the thematic cluster 2010–2011 and beyond; use of spatial data and activities related to the United Nations Geographic Information Working Group and the United Nations Spatial Data Infrastructure; participation in the process of the Group on Earth Observations; operational framework and good practices in the use of space-based technologies for disaster risk reduction and emergency response; and public outreach and information exchange to promote inter-agency cooperation.

Representatives of participating UN entities reported on their activities and plans for 2009–2010, the details of which were included in the Secretary-General's draft report on the coordination of space-related activities within the UN system: directions and anticipated results for the 2009–2010 period [A/AC.105/940]. The report was reviewed and amended by the Meeting.

The Meeting endorsed a draft report on the use of space technology for sustainable development in Africa, prepared by the Office for Outer Space Affairs in cooperation with the Economic Commission for Africa and other UN entities. The finalized report was issued in August [A/AC.105/941].

The Meeting agreed on the importance of enhancing inter-agency cooperation and coordination and identified the following key issues: strengthening the Meeting as the UN central mechanism for building partnerships and coordination of space-related activities; and enhancing the use of space science and technology and their application to implementing the development agenda, particularly in the areas of food security and increasing opportunities for education.

The Office for Outer Space Affairs briefed the Meeting on progress achieved in implementing the UNISPACE III recommendations. The Meeting noted that UN system entities would be invited to report on activities contributing to the implementation of UNISPACE III recommendations which remained to be addressed, and that the Scientific and Technical Subcommittee would, at its forty-seventh (2010) session, take that information into account in considering the way forward. In acknowledging the work of the ICG, established as a result of UNISPACE III, the ICG Providers Forum and the Office for Outer Space Affairs, the

Meeting noted there were opportunities for building partnerships between UN entities and ICG, taking into account the increasing importance of GNSS applications for the benefit of humankind, in particular the use of GNSS receivers (land- or space-based) for meteorology and climate monitoring.

The Meeting took note of the outline prepared by the Office for Outer Space Affairs on the contribution of the Committee on Outer Space to the work of the Commission on Sustainable Development for the thematic cluster 2010–2011. It agreed that the Office should contact relevant UN entities with the aim of including in the report the activities carried out by such entities, in line with the themes to be addressed by the Commission.

The Office for Outer Space Affairs provided the Meeting with information on developments regarding the United Nations Platform for Space-based Information for Disaster Management and Emergency Response (UN-SPIDER) (see below). The Meeting took note of the work carried out in the framework of UN-SPIDER in 2008, including the development of a knowledge portal, the establishment of the UN-SPIDER office in Bonn, and progress towards formalizing the network of regional support offices, in which Algeria, Iran, Nigeria, Pakistan, Romania, South Africa and Ukraine were participating.

Scientific and technical issues

In 2009, the Scientific and Technical Subcommittee [A/AC.105/933] continued to emphasize the importance of Earth observation satellite data for sustainable development and noted that an increased number of developing countries were becoming engaged in developing and deploying their own remote-sensing satellite systems and in utilizing space-based data to improve socio-economic development. The Subcommittee encouraged further international cooperation in the use of remote sensing satellites, in particular by sharing experiences and technologies through bilateral, regional and international collaborative projects.

For its consideration of space debris, the Subcommittee had before it a Secretariat note [A/AC.105/931 & Add.1,2] containing replies from four Member States on national research on space debris, and the safety of space objects with nuclear power sources on board and problems relating to their collision with space debris. The Subcommittee agreed that the implementation of voluntary guidelines for the mitigation of space debris at the national level would increase mutual understanding on acceptable activities in space, thereby enhancing stability in space and decreasing the likelihood of friction and conflict. The Subcommittee also noted that some States were implementing space debris mitigation measures consistent with

the Space Debris Mitigation Guidelines of the Committee on the Peaceful Uses of Outer Space, adopted in 2007 [YUN 2007, p. 640], and/or the Space Debris Mitigation Guidelines of the Inter-Agency Space Debris Coordination Committee, or that they had developed their own mitigation standards based on those guidelines.

The Subcommittee continued its consideration of the use of nuclear power sources (NPS) in outer space under the multi-year workplan for 2007–2010, adopted at its 2007 session [ibid.]. It noted the progress of the Joint Expert Group of the Subcommittee and of the International Atomic Energy Agency in developing an international technically based framework of goals and recommendations for the safety of NPS applications in outer space. The Subcommittee reconvened its Working Group on the Use of Nuclear Power Sources in Outer Space and finalized and approved the Working Group's safety framework [A/AC.105/934].

The Subcommittee agreed that national and international efforts to detect and track near-Earth objects should be continued and expanded. Pursuant to Assembly resolution 63/90 [YUN 2008, p. 684], it reconvened its Working Group on near-Earth Objects and endorsed the Working Group's report, which was annexed to the report of the Subcommittee. The Secretariat submitted to the Subcommittee a note [A/AC.105/949] on research in the field of near-Earth objects carried out by Member States, international organizations and other entities, containing replies from seven States and three scientific organizations.

Also submitted to the Subcommittee were Secretariat notes on international cooperation in the peaceful uses of outer space [A/AC.105/923/Add.1,2 & A/AC.105/953], containing replies from 15 Member States on their space activities.

Space-based disaster management and emergency response

The Scientific and Technical Subcommittee, at its forty-sixth session in February [A/AC.105/933], had before it a report on the activities carried out in 2008 in the framework of UN-SPIDER [A/AC.105/929], established by Assembly resolution 61/110 [YUN 2006, p. 748], and a report of the Secretariat on outreach activities carried out in 2008 in the framework of UN-SPIDER [A/AC.105/927]. The Subcommittee heard a statement by the UN-SPIDER Programme Coordinator on the 2008 activities and on the proposed workplan for 2010–2011. It took note of the progress made in the implementation of the 2008 activities, including inaugurating the UN-SPIDER office in Bonn and steps towards establishing an office in Beijing in 2009. The Subcommittee reconvened its

Working Group of the Whole and endorsed its report, which was annexed to the Subcommittee's report. The Committee on Outer Space [A/64/20] also acknowledged the progress made within the UN-SPIDER framework and the significant extrabudgetary resources provided by various States to support UN-SPIDER activities in 2008 and 2009.

Three December reports, which were to be considered at the Subcommittee's forty-seventh (2010) session, dealt with the implementation of UN-SPIDER activities in 2009 [A/AC.105/955]; outreach activities carried out in 2009 within the UN-SPIDER framework [A/AC.105/952]; and the UN-SPIDER capacity-building strategy [A/AC.105/947]. The report on 2009 activities highlighted several accomplishments, including the provision of technical advisory support to 13 Member States; the formalization of cooperation agreements with regional support offices; the establishment of SpaceAid (a framework for, inter alia, facilitating efficient access to space-based information to support emergency response and early recovery); and the launch of the beta version of the UN-SPIDER knowledge portal. The report on outreach activities described two international workshops, one regional workshop and one expert meeting; a special event to launch the SPIDER Global Thematic Partnership; an exhibition marking the International Day for Natural Disaster Reduction (14 October); and the participation of UN-SPIDER experts in numerous conferences and meetings. Outreach targets in the workplan for the 2008–2009 biennium were met, and the UN-SPIDER outreach strategy was updated and finalized.

International Heliophysical Year 2007

The Scientific and Technical Subcommittee [A/AC.105/933] welcomed the final report [ST/SPACE/43 & Corr.1] on the International Heliophysical Year [YUN 2007, p. 641], published by the Office for Outer Space Affairs. The report reviewed activities conducted worldwide between 2005 and 2008 to implement the programme. The Subcommittee expressed its appreciation to the secretariat of the International Heliophysical Year and the Office for Outer Space Affairs for conducting the international campaign, from 2005 to 2009, aimed at exploring solar terrestrial interaction and deploying ground-based worldwide instrument arrays for space weather investigation, particularly in developing countries. As a result, more than 90 States, of which over 70 were developing countries, were collecting data to be used to understand how space weather, caused by solar variability, could affect space systems and human space flight; electric power transmission; high-frequency radio communications; GNSS signals; long-range radar; and the well-being of passengers in high altitude aircraft. The Subcommittee agreed to consider, beginning at its forty-seventh

(2010) session, a new agenda item entitled "International Space Weather Initiative" under a three-year workplan in order to build upon the success of the International Heliophysical Year 2007.

Legal Subcommittee

The Legal Subcommittee, at its forty-eighth session (Vienna, 23 March–3 April) [A/AC.105/935], considered: the status and application of the five UN treaties on outer space; information on the activities of international organizations relating to space law; matters related to the definition and delimitation of outer space and the character and utilization of the geostationary orbit; the review and possible revision of the Principles Relevant to the Use of Nuclear Power Sources in Outer Space; the examination and review of developments concerning the draft protocol on matters specific to space assets to the Convention on International Interests in Mobile Equipment; capacity-building in space law; the exchange of information on national mechanisms relating to space debris mitigation measures; and the exchange of information on national legislation relevant to the peaceful exploration and use of outer space.

The Subcommittee appreciated the distribution by the Secretariat of an updated document containing information, as at 1 January, on States parties and additional signatories to the UN treaties and other international agreements relating to activities in outer space [ST/SPACE/11/Rev.2/Add.2].

The Subcommittee reconvened its Working Group on the Status and Application of the Five United Nations Treaties on Outer Space [YUN 2001, p. 570], the discussions of which included the status of the UN treaties on outer space, a review of their implementation and the obstacles to their universal acceptance, and the promotion of space law, especially through the United Nations Programme on Space Applications.

The Working Group had before it two Secretariat notes: one on activities carried out on the Moon and other celestial bodies, international and national rules governing those activities, and information from States parties to the 1979 Agreement Governing the Activities of States on the Moon and Other Celestial Bodies [YUN 1979, p. 111] about the benefits of adherence to that Agreement [A/AC.105/C.2/L.271 & Corr.1 & Add.1]; the other on a joint statement on the benefits of adherence to the Agreement by its States parties [A/AC.105/C.2/L.272]. The Subcommittee endorsed the report of the Working Group and the recommendation that its mandate be extended for one additional year.

The Subcommittee considered a Secretariat note with information on activities relating to space law received from the European Centre for Space Law, the International Institute of Space Law, the International Law Association and the International Organization of Space Communications [A/AC.105/C.2/L.275 & Corr.1 & Add.1]; as well as a conference room paper with information on the space law activities of the International Mobile Satellite Organization [A/AC.105/C.2/2009/CRP.3]. The Subcommittee noted that the activities of international intergovernmental and non-governmental organizations relating to space law were important and had contributed significantly to the development of space law.

The Subcommittee welcomed the General Assembly's endorsement, in resolution 62/217 [YUN 2007, p. 634], of the Space Debris Mitigation Guidelines of the Committee on the Peaceful Uses of Outer Space.

The Subcommittee also reconvened its Working Group on the Definition and Delimitation of Outer Space, which considered three Secretariat notes on: replies from Member States to the questionnaire on possible legal issues with regard to aerospace objects [A/AC.105/635/Add.17]; national legislation and practice [A/AC.105/865/Add.4]; and replies from Member States to questions relating to the definition and delimitation of outer space [A/AC.105/889/Add.2,3]. It also had before it two conference room papers—one contained replies from Qatar and Saudi Arabia on questions on the definition and delimitation of outer space [A/AC.105/C.2/2009/CRP.11], and the other a reply from Mexico on national legislation and practice relating to the definition and delimitation of outer space [A/AC.105/C.2/2009/CRP.15]. The Subcommittee endorsed the report of the Working Group.

For its consideration of capacity-building in space law, the Subcommittee had before it conference room papers on: a directory of education opportunities in space law [A/AC.105/C.2/2009/CRP.4]; a draft education curriculum on space law [A/AC.105/C.2/2009/CRP.5]; and actions and initiatives to build capacity in space law by seven Member States and the Office for Outer Space Affairs [A/AC.105/C.2/2009/CRP.7 & Add.1].

The Subcommittee agreed that capacity-building, training and education in space law were of paramount importance to international, regional and national efforts to develop space activities and increase knowledge of their legal framework. It acknowledged the space law capacity-building efforts undertaken by governmental and non-governmental organizations and UN entities and highlighted the role of the Office for Outer Space Affairs in providing legal advisory services and strengthening cooperation with space law organizations.

For its discussion on the exchange of information on national legislation relevant to the peaceful exploration and use of outer space, the Subcommittee considered a Secretariat note [A/AC.105/932 & Add.1] and

three conference room papers [A/AC.105/C.2/2009/CRP.13,17,18] containing information received from 11 Member States on national legislation governing their space activities. The Subcommittee noted the increasing number of space-related international cooperation programmes and the strengthening of efforts by States to develop international space law, particularly in view of the increase in problems associated with the exploration and uses of outer space, such as the problem of space debris. The Subcommittee established the Working Group on National Legislation Relevant to the Peaceful Exploration and Use of Outer Space, which examined responses received from Member States to develop an understanding of the manner in which they regulated governmental and non-governmental space activities. On 3 April, the Subcommittee endorsed the report of the Working Group, annexed to the report of the Subcommittee.

Effects of atomic radiation

In a letter dated 10 July [A/64/223], the Chairman of the United Nations Scientific Committee on the Effects of Atomic Radiation informed the General Assembly that the Committee's fifty-seventh session, originally scheduled for 25–29 May 2009 in Vienna, had been rescheduled to 19–23 April 2010 due to an unforeseen personal crisis of the Secretary of the Committee. The officers of the Committee had taken steps to mitigate the consequences. The Chairman informed the Assembly of the status and future plans regarding matters raised in paragraphs of General Assembly resolution 63/89 [YUN 2008, p. 695] requiring action by the Committee, namely, the assessment and review of the effects of ionizing radiation; data collection and cooperation with other bodies; staffing and resources; and aspiring members of the Scientific Committee.

GENERAL ASSEMBLY ACTION

On 10 December [meeting 62], the General Assembly, on the recommendation of the Fourth Committee [A/64/403], adopted **resolution 64/85** without vote [agenda item 29].

Effects of atomic radiation

The General Assembly,

Recalling its resolution 913(X) of 3 December 1955, by which it established the United Nations Scientific Committee on the Effects of Atomic Radiation, and its subsequent resolutions on the subject, including resolution 63/89 of 5 December 2008, in which, inter alia, it requested the Scientific Committee to continue its work,

Taking note with appreciation of the work of the Scientific Committee, and noting the letter from its Chair to the President of the General Assembly,

Reaffirming the desirability of the Scientific Committee continuing its work,

Concerned about the potentially harmful effects on present and future generations resulting from the levels of radiation to which mankind and the environment are exposed,

Conscious of the continuing need to examine and compile information about atomic and ionizing radiation and to analyse its effects on mankind and the environment, and conscious also of the increased volume, complexity and diversity of that information,

Noting the views expressed by Member States at its sixty-fourth session with regard to the work of the Scientific Committee,

Emphasizing the vital need for sustainable, appropriate and predictable resourcing, as well as efficient management, of the work of the secretariat of the Scientific Committee to arrange the annual sessions and coordinate the development of documents based on scientific reviews from Member States of the sources of ionizing radiation and its effects on human health and the environment,

Recalling the deep concern of the Scientific Committee expressed in the reports on its fifty-fifth and fifty-sixth sessions that reliance on a single post at the Professional level in its secretariat had left the Committee seriously vulnerable and had hampered the efficient implementation of its approved programme of work,

Recalling also the comprehensive report of the Secretary-General on the financial and administrative implications of increased membership of the Scientific Committee, staffing of its professional secretariat and methods to ensure sufficient, assured and predictable funding,

Recalling its request to the Secretary-General, in formulating his proposed programme budget for the biennium 2010–2011, to consider all options, including the possibility of internal reallocation, to provide the Scientific Committee with the resources outlined in paragraphs 48 to 50 of his report,

1. *Commends* the United Nations Scientific Committee on the Effects of Atomic Radiation for the valuable contribution it has been making in the course of the past fifty-four years, since its inception, to wider knowledge and understanding of the levels, effects and risks of ionizing radiation, and for fulfilling its original mandate with scientific authority and independence of judgement;

2. *Reaffirms* the decision to maintain the present functions and independent role of the Scientific Committee;

3. *Requests* the Scientific Committee to continue its work, including its important activities to increase knowledge of the levels, effects and risks of ionizing radiation from all sources;

4. *Endorses* the intentions and plans of the Scientific Committee, including those outlined in the letter from its Chair to the President of the General Assembly, for conducting its present programme of work of scientific review and assessment on behalf of the General Assembly, encourages the Committee at its earliest convenience to submit the related reports, including assessments of levels of radiation from energy production and the effects on human health and the environment, and on the attribution of

health effects due to radiation exposure, and to initiate, as far as possible, work on the remaining previously endorsed topics, and requests the Committee to submit plans for its future programme of work to the Assembly at its sixty-fifth session;

5. *Requests* the Scientific Committee to continue at its next session the review of the important questions in the field of ionizing radiation and to report thereon to the General Assembly at its sixty-fifth session;

6. *Re-emphasizes* the need for the Scientific Committee to hold regular sessions on an annual basis so that its report can reflect the latest developments and findings in the field of ionizing radiation and thereby provide updated information for dissemination among all States;

7. *Expresses its appreciation* for the assistance rendered to the Scientific Committee by Member States, the specialized agencies, the International Atomic Energy Agency and non-governmental organizations, and invites them to increase their cooperation in this field;

8. *Invites* the Scientific Committee to continue its consultations with scientists and experts from interested Member States in the process of preparing its future scientific reports, and requests the Secretariat to facilitate such consultations;

9. *Welcomes*, in this context, the readiness of Member States to provide the Scientific Committee with relevant information on the effects of ionizing radiation in affected areas, and invites the Committee to analyse and give due consideration to such information, particularly in the light of its own findings;

10. *Invites* Member States, the organizations of the United Nations system and non-governmental organizations concerned to provide further relevant data about doses, effects and risks from various sources of radiation, which would greatly help in the preparation of future reports of the Scientific Committee to the General Assembly;

11. *Requests* the United Nations Environment Programme to continue providing support for the effective conduct of the work of the Scientific Committee and for the dissemination of its findings to the General Assembly, the scientific community and the public;

12. *Urges* the United Nations Environment Programme to continue to review and strengthen the funding of the Scientific Committee, pursuant to paragraph 13 of resolution 63/89, and to continue to seek out and consider temporary funding mechanisms to complement existing ones, and, in that context, encourages Member States to consider making voluntary contributions to the general trust fund established by the Executive Director of the United Nations Environment Programme to receive and manage voluntary contributions to support the work of the Committee;

13. *Reminds* the Scientific Committee, as directed in paragraph 17 of resolution 63/89, to continue its reflection on how its current, as well as its potentially revised, membership could best support its essential work, including by developing, with the participation of the observer countries, detailed, objective and transparent criteria and indicators to be applied equitably to present and future members alike, and to report its conclusions by the end of June 2010;

14. *Welcomes* the attendance of Belarus, Finland, Pakistan, the Republic of Korea, Spain and Ukraine as observers at the fifty-sixth session of the Scientific Committee, invites each of those States to designate one scientist to attend, as an observer, the fifty-seventh session of the Committee, and resolves to take a decision on the membership of the Committee, including the membership of those six States, once a decision on resource allocation has been made, and after the fifty-seventh session of the Scientific Committee, but no later than the end of the sixty-fourth session of the General Assembly.

On 24 December, the General Assembly decided that the agenda item on the effects of atomic radiation would remain for consideration during its resumed sixty-fourth (2010) session (**decision 64/549**).

Information and telecommunications in international security

In response to General Assembly resolution 63/37 [YUN 2008, p. 696], the Secretary-General issued a report [A/64/129 & Add.1] transmitting the views of 12 Member States on their general appreciation of issues of information security; national efforts to strengthen information security and promote international cooperation in that field; the content of international concepts aimed at strengthening the security of global information and telecommunications systems; and possible measures the international community could take to strengthen information security at the global level.

GENERAL ASSEMBLY ACTION

On 2 December [meeting 55], the General Assembly, on the recommendation of the First Committee [A/64/386], adopted **resolution 64/25** without vote [agenda item 91].

Developments in the field of information and telecommunications in the context of international security

The General Assembly,

Recalling its resolutions 53/70 of 4 December 1998, 54/49 of 1 December 1999, 55/28 of 20 November 2000, 56/19 of 29 November 2001, 57/53 of 22 November 2002, 58/32 of 8 December 2003, 59/61 of 3 December 2004, 60/45 of 8 December 2005, 61/54 of 6 December 2006, 62/17 of 5 December 2007 and 63/37 of 2 December 2008,

Recalling also its resolutions on the role of science and technology in the context of international security, in which, inter alia, it recognized that scientific and technological developments could have both civilian and military applications and that progress in science and technology

for civilian applications needed to be maintained and encouraged,

Noting that considerable progress has been achieved in developing and applying the latest information technologies and means of telecommunication,

Affirming that it sees in this process the broadest positive opportunities for the further development of civilization, the expansion of opportunities for cooperation for the common good of all States, the enhancement of the creative potential of humankind and additional improvements in the circulation of information in the global community,

Recalling, in this connection, the approaches and principles outlined at the Information Society and Development Conference, held in Midrand, South Africa, from 13 to 15 May 1996,

Bearing in mind the results of the Ministerial Conference on Terrorism, held in Paris on 30 July 1996, and the recommendations that it made,

Bearing in mind also the results of the World Summit on the Information Society, held in Geneva from 10 to 12 December 2003 (first phase) and in Tunis from 16 to 18 November 2005 (second phase),

Noting that the dissemination and use of information technologies and means affect the interests of the entire international community and that optimum effectiveness is enhanced by broad international cooperation,

Expressing its concern that these technologies and means can potentially be used for purposes that are inconsistent with the objectives of maintaining international stability and security and may adversely affect the integrity of the infrastructure of States to the detriment of their security in both civil and military fields,

Considering that it is necessary to prevent the use of information resources or technologies for criminal or terrorist purposes,

Noting the contribution of those Member States that have submitted their assessments on issues of information security to the Secretary-General pursuant to paragraphs 1 to 3 of resolutions 53/70, 54/49, 55/28, 56/19, 57/53, 58/32, 59/61, 60/45, 61/54, 62/17 and 63/37,

Taking note of the reports of the Secretary-General containing those assessments,

Welcoming the initiative taken by the Secretariat and the United Nations Institute for Disarmament Research in convening international meetings of experts in Geneva in August 1999 and April 2008 on developments in the field of information and telecommunications in the context of international security, as well as the results of those meetings,

Considering that the assessments of the Member States contained in the reports of the Secretary-General and the international meetings of experts have contributed to a better understanding of the substance of issues of international information security and related notions,

Bearing in mind that the Secretary-General, in fulfilment of resolution 58/32, established in 2004 a group of governmental experts, which, in accordance with its mandate, considered existing and potential threats in the sphere of information security and possible cooperative measures to address them and conducted a study on relevant international concepts aimed at strengthening the security of global information and telecommunications systems,

Taking note of the report of the Secretary-General on the Group of Governmental Experts on Developments in the Field of Information and Telecommunications in the Context of International Security, prepared on the basis of the results of the Group's work,

1. *Calls upon* Member States to promote further at multilateral levels the consideration of existing and potential threats in the field of information security, as well as possible measures to limit the threats emerging in this field, consistent with the need to preserve the free flow of information;

2. *Considers* that the purpose of such measures could be served through the examination of relevant international concepts aimed at strengthening the security of global information and telecommunications systems;

3. *Invites* all Member States to continue to inform the Secretary-General of their views and assessments on the following questions:

(a) General appreciation of the issues of information security;

(b) Efforts taken at the national level to strengthen information security and promote international cooperation in this field;

(c) The content of the concepts mentioned in paragraph 2 above;

(d) Possible measures that could be taken by the international community to strengthen information security at the global level;

4. *Requests* the Secretary-General, with the assistance of the group of governmental experts, established in 2009 on the basis of equitable geographical distribution pursuant to General Assembly resolution 63/37, to continue to study existing and potential threats in the sphere of information security and possible cooperative measures to address them, as well as the concepts referred to in paragraph 2 above, and to submit a report on the results of this study to the Assembly at its sixty-fifth session;

5. *Notes with satisfaction* the holding, in Geneva in November 2009, of the first session of the group of governmental experts established by the Secretary-General and the intention of the group to convene three more sessions in 2010 in order to fulfil its mandate as specified in resolution 63/37;

6. *Decides* to include in the provisional agenda of its sixty-fifth session the item entitled "Developments in the field of information and telecommunications in the context of international security".

By **resolution 64/211** of 21 December (see p. 825), the Assembly invited Member States to use, if and when they deemed appropriate, the "Voluntary self-assessment tool for national efforts to protect critical information infrastructures", which was annexed to the resolution. The tool would assist States in assessing their efforts to strengthen cybersecurity, so as to highlight areas for further action. The Assembly also encouraged Member States and regional and international organizations with strategies for dealing with cybersecurity and the protection of information infrastructures to share their best practices by providing such information to the Secretary-General for compilation and dissemination.

Information

UN public information

The General Assembly's Committee on Information, at its thirty-first session (New York, 4–15 May) [A/64/21], continued to consider UN information policies and activities, and to evaluate and follow up on efforts made and progress achieved in information and communications.

The Committee had before it three February reports of the Secretary-General on activities of the Department of Public Information (DPI) from July 2008 to February 2009, which addressed the following areas: strategic communications services [A/AC.198/2009/2], with a review of communication campaigns and UN information centre activities; news services [A/AC.198/2009/3], with a summary of news products and activities; and outreach services [A/AC.198/2009/4], with a presentation of DPI's work with civil society groups, Member States and the general public. The Secretary-General also submitted an updated July report on questions relating to information [A/64/262].

By **decision 64/520** of 10 December, the Assembly increased the Committee's membership from 112 to 113 by appointing Sierra Leone as a member.

GENERAL ASSEMBLY ACTION

On 10 December [meeting 62], the General Assembly, on the recommendation of the Fourth Committee [A/64/408], adopted **resolution 64/96 A** and **B** without vote [agenda item 34].

Questions relating to information
A
Information in the service of humanity

The General Assembly,

Taking note of the comprehensive and important report of the Committee on Information,

Also taking note of the report of the Secretary-General on questions relating to information,

Urges all countries, organizations of the United Nations system as a whole and all others concerned, reaffirming their commitment to the principles of the Charter of the United Nations and to the principles of freedom of the press and freedom of information, as well as to those of the independence, pluralism and diversity of the media, deeply concerned by the disparities existing between developed and developing countries and the consequences of every kind arising from those disparities that affect the capability of the public, private or other media and individuals in developing countries to disseminate information and communicate their views and their cultural and ethical values through endogenous cultural production, as well as to ensure the diversity of sources and their free access to information, and recognizing the call in this context for what in the United Nations and at various international forums has been termed "a new world information and communication order, seen as an evolving and continuous process":

(a) To cooperate and interact with a view to reducing existing disparities in information flows at all levels by increasing assistance for the development of communications infrastructures and capabilities in developing countries, with due regard for their needs and the priorities attached to such areas by those countries, and in order to enable them and the public, private or other media in developing countries to develop their own information and communications policies freely and independently and increase the participation of media and individuals in the communication process, and to ensure a free flow of information at all levels;

(b) To ensure for journalists the free and effective performance of their professional tasks and condemn resolutely all attacks against them;

(c) To provide support for the continuation and strengthening of practical training programmes for broadcasters and journalists from public, private and other media in developing countries;

(d) To enhance regional efforts and cooperation among developing countries, as well as cooperation between developed and developing countries, to strengthen communications capacities and to improve the media infrastructure and communications technology in the developing countries, especially in the areas of training and dissemination of information;

(e) To aim at, in addition to bilateral cooperation, providing all possible support and assistance to the developing countries and their media, public, private or other, with due regard to their interests and needs in the field of information and to action already adopted within the United Nations system, including:

(i) The development of the human and technical resources that are indispensable for the improvement of information and communications systems in developing countries and support for the continuation and strengthening of practical training programmes, such as those already operating under both public and private auspices throughout the developing world;

(ii) The creation of conditions that will enable developing countries and their media, public, private or other, to have, by using their national and regional resources, the communications technology suited to their national needs, as well as the necessary programme material, especially for radio and television broadcasting;

(iii) Assistance in establishing and promoting telecommunication links at the subregional, regional and interregional levels, especially among developing countries;

(iv) The facilitation, as appropriate, of access by the developing countries to advanced communications technology available on the open market;

(f) To provide full support for the International Programme for the Development of Communication of the United Nations Educational, Scientific and Cultural Organization, which should support both public and private media.

B

United Nations public information policies and activities

The General Assembly,

Emphasizing the role of the Committee on Information as its main subsidiary body mandated to make recommendations to it relating to the work of the Department of Public Information of the Secretariat,

Reaffirming its resolution 13(I) of 13 February 1946, establishing the Department of Public Information, which states in paragraph 2 of annex I that "the activities of the Department should be so organized and directed as to promote to the greatest possible extent an informed understanding of the work and purposes of the United Nations among the peoples of the world",

Emphasizing that the contents of public information and communications should be placed at the heart of the strategic management of the United Nations and that a culture of communications and transparency should permeate all levels of the Organization, as a means of fully informing the peoples of the world of the aims and activities of the United Nations, in accordance with the purposes and principles enshrined in the Charter of the United Nations, in order to create broad-based global support for the United Nations,

Stressing that the primary mission of the Department of Public Information is to provide, through its outreach activities, accurate, impartial, comprehensive, balanced, timely and relevant information to the public on the tasks and responsibilities of the United Nations in order to strengthen international support for the activities of the Organization with the greatest transparency,

Recalling the comprehensive review of the work of the Department of Public Information, requested by the General Assembly in its resolution 56/253 of 24 December 2001, as well as the report of the Secretary-General entitled "Strengthening of the United Nations: an agenda for further change" and Assembly resolutions 57/300 of 20 December 2002 and 60/109 B of 8 December 2005, which provided an opportunity to take due steps to enhance the efficiency and effectiveness of the Department and to maximize the use of its resources,

Expressing its concern that the gap in information and communications technology between the developed and the developing countries has continued to widen and that vast segments of the population in developing countries are not benefiting from the present information and communications technologies, and, in this regard, underlining the necessity of rectifying the imbalances in the present development of information and communications technologies in order to make it more just, equitable and effective,

Recognizing that developments in information and communications technologies open vast new opportunities for economic growth and social development and can play an important role in the eradication of poverty in developing countries, and, at the same time, emphasizing that the development of these technologies poses challenges and risks and could lead to the further widening of disparities between and within countries,

Recalling its resolution 61/266 of 16 May 2007 on multilingualism, and emphasizing the importance of making appropriate use of the official languages of the United Nations in the activities of the Department of Public Information, with the aim of eliminating the disparity between the use of English and the five other official languages,

Welcoming Sierra Leone to membership in the Committee on Information,

I

Introduction

1. *Reaffirms* its resolution 13(I), in which it established the Department of Public Information, and all other relevant resolutions of the General Assembly related to the activities of the Department, and requests the Secretary-General, in respect of the public information policies and activities of the United Nations, to continue to implement fully the recommendations contained in paragraph 2 of its resolution 48/44 B of 10 December 1993 and other mandates as established by the General Assembly;

2. *Also reaffirms* that the United Nations remains the indispensable foundation of a peaceful and just world and that its voice must be heard in a clear and effective manner, and emphasizes the essential role of the Department of Public Information in this context;

3. *Stresses* the importance of the provision of clear, timely, accurate and comprehensive information by the Secretariat to Member States, upon their request, within the framework of existing mandates and procedures;

4. *Reaffirms* the central role of the Committee on Information in United Nations public information policies and activities, including the prioritization of those activities, and decides that recommendations relating to the programme of the Department of Public Information shall originate, to the extent possible, in the Committee and shall be considered by the Committee;

5. *Requests* the Department of Public Information, following the priorities laid down by the General Assembly in its resolution 63/247 of 24 December 2008, and guided by the United Nations Millennium Declaration and reaffirming the 2005 World Summit Outcome, to pay particular attention to peace and security, development and human rights and to major issues such as the eradication of poverty, including the global food crisis, conflict prevention, sustainable development, the HIV/AIDS epidemic, combating terrorism in all its forms and manifestations and the needs of the African continent;

6. *Also requests* the Department of Public Information to pay particular attention to progress in implementing the internationally agreed development goals, including those contained in the Millennium Declaration, and the outcomes of the major related United Nations summits and conferences in carrying out its activities, and calls upon the Department to play an active role in raising public awareness of the world financial and economic crisis and its impact on development, including the achievement of the Millennium Development Goals;

7. *Further requests* the Department of Public Information and its network of United Nations information centres to play an active role in raising public awareness of the global challenge of climate change, and encourages the Department to pay particular attention to the actions taken in the framework of the United Nations Framework Convention on Climate Change, in accordance with the principles of common but differentiated responsibilities, especially in the context of the Conference of the Parties and of the Meetings of the Parties to the Kyoto Protocol held in Poznan, Poland, from 1 to 12 December 2008, and to be held in Copenhagen from 7 to 18 December 2009;

8. *Reaffirms* the need to enhance the technological infrastructure of the Department of Public Information on a continuous basis in order to widen its outreach and to continue to improve the United Nations website;

II

General activities of the Department of Public Information

9. *Takes note* of the reports of the Secretary-General on the activities of the Department of Public Information;

10. *Requests* the Department of Public Information to maintain its commitment to a culture of evaluation and to continue to evaluate its products and activities with the objective of enhancing their effectiveness, and to continue to cooperate and coordinate with Member States and the Office of Internal Oversight Services of the Secretariat;

11. *Reaffirms* the importance of more effective coordination between the Department of Public Information and the Office of the Spokesperson for the Secretary-General, and requests the Secretary-General to ensure consistency in the messages of the Organization;

12. *Notes* the efforts of the Department of Public Information to continue to publicize the work and decisions of the General Assembly, and requests the Department to continue to enhance its working relationship with the Office of the President of the General Assembly;

13. *Encourages* continued collaboration between the Department of Public Information and the United Nations Educational, Scientific and Cultural Organization in the promotion of culture and in the fields of education and communication, bridging the existing gap between the developed and the developing countries;

14. *Notes with appreciation* the efforts of the Department of Public Information to work at the local level with other organizations and bodies of the United Nations system to enhance the coordination of their communications activities, and requests the Secretary-General to report to the Committee on Information at its thirty-second session on progress achieved in this regard and on the activities of the United Nations Communications Group;

15. *Reaffirms* that the Department of Public Information must prioritize its work programme, while respecting existing mandates and in line with regulation 5.6 of the Regulations and Rules Governing Programme Planning, the Programme Aspects of the Budget, the Monitoring of Implementation and the Methods of Evaluation, to focus its message and better concentrate its efforts and to match its programmes with the needs of its target audiences, on the basis of improved feedback and evaluation mechanisms;

16. *Requests* the Secretary-General to continue to exert all efforts to ensure that publications and other information services of the Secretariat, including the United Nations website and the United Nations News Service, contain comprehensive, balanced, objective and equitable information in all official languages about the issues before the Organization and that they maintain editorial independence, impartiality, accuracy and full consistency with resolutions and decisions of the General Assembly;

17. *Requests* the Department of Public Information and content-providing offices of the Secretariat to ensure that United Nations publications are produced in a cost-effective and environmentally friendly manner and to continue to coordinate closely with all other entities, including all other departments of the Secretariat and funds and programmes of the United Nations system, in order to avoid duplication, within their respective mandates, in the issuance of United Nations publications;

18. *Emphasizes* that the Department of Public Information should maintain and improve its activities in the areas of special interest to developing countries and, where appropriate, other countries with special needs, and that the activities of the Department should contribute to bridging the existing gap between the developing and the developed countries in the crucial field of public information and communications;

19. *Notes* the issuance of daily press releases, and reiterates its request to the Department of Public Information to continue to improve their production process and streamline their format, structure and length, keeping in mind the views of Member States, including their views on expanding them to the other official languages;

Multilingualism and public information

20. *Emphasizes* the importance of making appropriate use and ensuring equitable treatment of all the official languages of the United Nations in all the activities of the Department of Public Information, including in presentations to the Committee on Information, with the aim of eliminating the disparity between the use of English and the five other official languages;

21. *Reiterates its request* to the Secretary-General to ensure that the Department of Public Information has appropriate staffing capacity in all the official languages of the United Nations to undertake all its activities and to include this aspect in future programme budget proposals for the Department, bearing in mind the principle of parity of all six official languages, while respecting the workload in each official language;

22. *Welcomes* the ongoing efforts of the Department of Public Information to enhance multilingualism in all its activities, and stresses the importance of fully implementing resolution 61/266 by ensuring that the texts of all new public documents in all six official languages and information materials of the United Nations are made available daily through the United Nations website and are accessible to Member States without delay;

23. *Requests* the Secretary-General to continue towards completion of the task of uploading all important older United Nations documents on the United Nations website in all six official languages on a priority basis, so that these archives are also available to Member States through that medium;

Bridging the digital divide

24. *Recalls with satisfaction* its resolution 60/252 of 27 March 2006, in which it endorsed the Tunis Commitment and the Tunis Agenda for the Information Society, as adopted at the second phase of the World Summit on the Information Society, held in Tunis from 16 to 18 November 2005, and proclaimed 17 May annual World Information Society Day, recalls the adoption of the Declaration of Principles and the Plan of Action at the first phase of the World Summit on the Information Society, held in Geneva from 10 to 12 December 2003, and in this regard requests the Department of Public Information to contribute to the celebration of this event and to play a role in raising awareness of the possibilities that the use of the Internet and other information and communications technologies can bring to societies and economies, as well as of ways to bridge the digital divide;

25. *Calls upon* the Department of Public Information to contribute to raising the awareness of the international community of the importance of the implementation of the outcome documents of the World Summit on the Information Society;

Network of United Nations information centres

26. *Emphasizes* the importance of the network of United Nations information centres in enhancing the public image of the United Nations and in disseminating messages on the United Nations to local populations, especially in developing countries;

27. *Welcomes* the work done by the network of United Nations information centres in favour of the publication of United Nations information materials and the translation of important documents into languages other than the official languages of the United Nations, encourages the network of United Nations information centres to continue to develop web pages in local languages, and the Department of Public Information to provide necessary resources and technical facilities, with a view to reaching the widest possible spectrum of audiences and extending the United Nations message to all the corners of the world in order to strengthen international support for the activities of the Organization, and encourages the continuation of efforts in this regard;

28. *Stresses* the importance of rationalizing the network of United Nations information centres, and, in this regard, requests the Secretary-General to continue to make proposals in this direction, including through the redeployment of resources where necessary, and to report to the Committee on Information at its successive sessions;

29. *Reaffirms* that the rationalization of United Nations information centres must be carried out on a case-by-case basis in consultation with all concerned Member States in which existing information centres are located, the countries served by those information centres and other interested countries in the region, taking into consideration the distinctive characteristics of each region;

30. *Recognizes* that the network of United Nations information centres, especially in developing countries, should continue to enhance its impact and activities, including through strategic communications support, and calls upon the Secretary-General to report on the implementation of this approach to the Committee on Information at its successive sessions;

31. *Encourages* the Department of Public Information, through the information centres, to strengthen its cooperation with all other United Nations entities at the country level, in order to enhance coherence in communications and to avoid duplication of work;

32. *Stresses* the importance of taking into account the special needs and requirements of developing countries in the field of information and communications technology for the effective flow of information in those countries;

33.   *Also stresses* that the Department of Public Information, through the network of United Nations information centres, should continue to promote public awareness of and mobilize support for the work of the United Nations at the local level, bearing in mind that information in local languages has the strongest impact on local populations;

34.   *Further stresses* the importance of efforts to strengthen the outreach activities of the United Nations to those Member States remaining outside the network of United Nations information centres, and encourages the Secretary-General, within the context of rationalization, to extend the services of the network of United Nations information centres to those Member States;

35.   *Stresses* that the Department of Public Information should continue to review the allocation of both staff and financial resources to the United Nations information centres in developing countries, emphasizing the needs of the least developed countries;

36.   *Takes note* of the proposal by the Secretary-General to work closely with the Governments concerned to explore the possibility of identifying rent-free premises, while taking into account the economic condition of the host countries and bearing in mind that such support should not be a substitute for the full allocation of financial resources for the information centres in the context of the programme budget of the United Nations, and encourages host countries to respond to the needs of the United Nations information centres;

37.   *Also takes note* of the strengthening of the information centres in Cairo, Mexico City and Pretoria, and encourages the Secretary-General to explore the strengthening of other centres, especially in Africa, in cooperation with the Member States concerned and within existing resources;

38.   *Recalls* the offer made by the Government of Angola to host a United Nations information centre in Luanda to address the special needs of Portuguese-speaking African countries, through the provision of rent-free premises, regrets the lack of progress in this regard, and reiterates its request to the Secretary-General to report to the Committee on Information at its thirty-second session, on the measures necessary, including the budgetary requirements, to accommodate those needs, as well as any proposal to move this process forward;

39.   *Encourages* the Secretary-General, when appointing directors to the United Nations information centres, to fully consider, inter alia, the experience of candidates in the field of information and communications technology, as one of the highly desirable appointment criteria;

III
Strategic communications services

40.   *Reaffirms* the role of the strategic communications services in devising and disseminating United Nations messages by developing communications strategies, in close collaboration with the substantive departments, United Nations funds and programmes and the specialized agencies, in full compliance with their legislative mandates;

Promotional campaigns

41.   *Appreciates* the work of the Department of Public Information in promoting, through its campaigns, issues of importance to the international community, such as the United Nations Millennium Declaration and the progress made in implementing the internationally agreed development goals, United Nations reform, the eradication of poverty, conflict prevention, peacekeeping, peacebuilding, sustainable development, disarmament, decolonization, human rights, including the rights of women and children and of persons with disabilities, strategic coordination in humanitarian relief, especially in natural disasters and other crises, HIV/AIDS, malaria, tuberculosis and other diseases, the needs of the African continent and combating terrorism in all its forms and manifestations, dialogue among civilizations, the culture of peace and tolerance and the consequences of the Chernobyl disaster, as well as prevention of genocide, and requests the Department to continue to carry out information activities on all these issues;

42.   *Commends* the role of the Department of Public Information in observing the annual International Day of Remembrance of the Victims of Slavery and the Transatlantic Slave Trade, and looks forward to its further work in promoting the establishment of the permanent memorial to the victims of slavery and the transatlantic slave trade;

43.   *Requests* the Department of Public Information, in this regard, in cooperation with the countries concerned and with the relevant organizations and bodies of the United Nations system, to continue to take appropriate measures to enhance world public awareness of these and other important global issues;

44.   *Stresses* the need to continue the renewed emphasis in support of Africa's development, in particular by the Department of Public Information, in order to promote awareness in the international community of the nature of the critical economic and social situation in Africa and of the priorities of the New Partnership for Africa's Development;

45.   *Recognizes* the role of the Department of Public Information and its network of United Nations information centres in commemorating the sixtieth anniversary of the Universal Declaration of Human Rights;

Role of the Department of Public Information in United Nations peacekeeping operations

46.   *Commends* the role of the Department of Public Information and its network of United Nations information centres in commemorating the sixtieth anniversary of United Nations peacekeeping;

47.   *Requests* the Secretariat to continue to ensure the involvement of the Department of Public Information from the planning stage of future peacekeeping operations through interdepartmental consultations and coordination with other departments of the Secretariat, in particular with the Department of Peacekeeping Operations and the Department of Field Support;

48.   *Requests* the Department of Public Information, the Department of Peacekeeping Operations and the Department of Field Support to continue their cooperation in raising awareness of the new realities, far-reaching successes and challenges faced by peacekeeping operations, especially multidimensional and complex ones, and the recent surge in United Nations peacekeeping activities, and welcomes efforts by the three Departments to develop and implement a comprehensive communications strategy on current challenges facing United Nations peacekeeping;

49.   *Stresses* the importance of enhancing the public information capacity of the Department of Public Information in the field of peacekeeping operations and its role,

in close cooperation with the Department of Peacekeeping Operations and the Department of Field Support, in the process of selecting public information staff for United Nations peacekeeping operations or missions, and, in this regard, invites the Department of Public Information to second public information staff who have the skills necessary to fulfil the tasks of the operations or missions, taking into account the principle of equitable geographical distribution in accordance with Chapter XV, Article 101, paragraph 3, of the Charter of the United Nations, and to consider views expressed, especially by host countries, when appropriate, in this regard;

50. *Emphasizes* the importance of the peacekeeping gateway on the United Nations website, and requests the Department of Public Information to continue its efforts in supporting the peacekeeping missions to further develop their websites;

51. *Requests* the Department of Public Information and the Department of Peacekeeping Operations to continue to cooperate in implementing an effective outreach programme to explain the zero-tolerance policy of the Organization regarding sexual exploitation and abuse and to inform the public of the outcome of all such cases involving peacekeeping personnel, including cases where allegations are ultimately found to be legally unproven, and also to inform the public of the adoption by the General Assembly of the United Nations Comprehensive Strategy on Assistance and Support to Victims of Sexual Exploitation and Abuse by United Nations Staff and Related Personnel;

Role of the Department of Public Information in strengthening dialogue among civilizations and the culture of peace as means of enhancing understanding among nations

52. *Recalls* its resolutions on dialogue among civilizations and the culture of peace, requests the Department of Public Information, while ensuring the pertinence and relevance of subjects for promotional campaigns under this issue, to continue to provide the support necessary for the dissemination of information pertaining to dialogue among civilizations and the culture of peace, as well as the initiative on the Alliance of Civilizations, and to take due steps in fostering the culture of dialogue among civilizations and promoting cultural understanding, tolerance, respect for and freedom of religion or belief and effective enjoyment by all of all human rights and civil, political, economic, social and cultural rights, including the right to development;

53. *Invites* the United Nations system, especially the Department of Public Information, to continue to encourage and facilitate dialogue among civilizations and to formulate ways and means to promote dialogue among civilizations in the activities of the United Nations in various fields, taking into account the Programme of Action of the Global Agenda for Dialogue among Civilizations, and in this regard, looks forward to the report of the Secretary-General requested by the General Assembly in its resolution 60/4 of 20 October 2005;

54. *Recognizes* the achievements of the Alliance of Civilizations and the efforts made by the High Representative of the Secretary-General for the Alliance of Civilizations, takes note of the broad range of initiatives and partnerships in the areas of youth, education, the media and migration

launched at the second Alliance of Civilizations Forum, held in Istanbul, Turkey, on 6 and 7 April 2009, and welcomes the continued support of the Department of Public Information for the work of the Alliance of Civilizations, including its ongoing projects;

IV
News services

55. *Stresses* that the central objective of the news services implemented by the Department of Public Information is the timely delivery of accurate, objective and balanced news and information emanating from the United Nations system in all four mass media, namely, print, radio, television and the Internet, to the media and other audiences worldwide, with the overall emphasis on multilingualism, and reiterates its request to the Department to ensure that all news-breaking stories and news alerts are accurate, impartial and free of bias;

56. *Emphasizes* the importance of the Department of Public Information continuing to draw the attention of world media to stories that do not obtain prominent coverage, through the initiative entitled "10 Stories the World Should Hear More About" and through video and audio coverage by United Nations Television and United Nations Radio;

Traditional means of communication

57. *Welcomes* the initiative of United Nations Radio, which remains one of the most effective and far-reaching traditional media available to the Department of Public Information and an important instrument in United Nations activities, to enhance its live radio broadcasting service by making more frequently updated reports in all six official languages and features available to broadcasters on a daily basis on all United Nations activities, and requests the Secretary-General to continue to make every effort to achieve parity in the six official languages in United Nations Radio productions;

58. *Notes* the efforts being made by the Department of Public Information to disseminate programmes directly to broadcasting stations all over the world in the six official languages, with the addition of Portuguese and Kiswahili, as well as in other languages where possible;

59. *Requests* the Department of Public Information to continue building partnerships with local, national and regional broadcasters to extend the United Nations message to all the corners of the world in an accurate and impartial way, and requests the Radio and Television Service of the Department to continue to take full advantage of the technological infrastructure made available in recent years;

United Nations website

60. *Reaffirms* that the United Nations website is an essential tool for the media, non-governmental organizations, educational institutions, Member States and the general public, and, in this regard, reiterates the continued need for efforts by the Department of Public Information to maintain and improve it;

61. *Recognizes* the efforts made by the Department of Public Information to implement the basic accessibility requirements for persons with disabilities to access the United Nations website, and calls upon the Department to continue to work towards compliance with accessibility

requirements on all new and updated pages of the website, with the aim of ensuring its accessibility for persons with different kinds of disabilities;

62. *Takes note* of the fact that the multilingual development and enrichment of the United Nations website has improved, and, in this regard, requests the Department of Public Information, in coordination with content-providing offices, to further improve the actions taken to achieve full parity among the six official languages on the United Nations website, and especially reiterates its request to ensure the adequate distribution of financial and human resources within the Department allocated to the United Nations website among all official languages, taking into consideration the specificity of each official language;

63. *Welcomes* the cooperative arrangements undertaken by the Department of Public Information with academic institutions to increase the number of web pages available in some official languages, and reiterates its request to the Secretary-General to extend those arrangements to all the official languages of the United Nations;

64. *Recalls* paragraph 74 of its resolution 60/109 B, and in this regard reiterates that all content-providing offices in the Secretariat should continue their efforts to translate into all official languages all English-language materials and databases posted on the United Nations website and to make them available on the respective language websites in the most practical, efficient and cost-effective manner;

65. *Requests* the Secretary-General to continue to take full advantage of new developments in information technology in order to improve, in a cost-effective manner, the expeditious dissemination of information on the United Nations, in accordance with the priorities established by the General Assembly in its resolutions and taking into account the linguistic diversity of the Organization, welcomes the continuing growth in the popularity of the e-mail news alerts service provided by the Department of Public Information on the United Nations News Centre portal in English and French, and encourages the Department to consult with the Information Technology Services Division of the Department of Management and to explore, as a matter of priority, ways of upgrading the technical capabilities of the service and providing it in all official languages;

66. *Recognizes* that some official languages use non-Latin and bidirectional scripts and that technological infrastructures and supportive applications in the United Nations are based on Latin script, which leads to difficulties in processing non-Latin and bidirectional scripts, and urges the Information Technology Services Division of the Department of Management to further collaborate with the Department of Public Information and to continue its efforts to ensure that technological infrastructures and supportive applications in the United Nations fully support Latin, non-Latin and bidirectional scripts in order to enhance the equality of all official languages on the United Nations website;

V
Library services

67. *Calls upon* the Department of Public Information to continue to lead the Steering Committee for the Modernization and Integrated Management of United Nations Libraries, and further commends the steps taken by the Dag Hammarskjöld Library and the other member libraries of the Steering Committee to align their activities, services and outputs more closely with the goals, objectives and operational priorities of the Organization;

68. *Reiterates* the need to maintain a multilingual collection of books, periodicals and other materials in hard copy, accessible to Member States, ensuring that the Library continues to be a broadly accessible resource for information about the United Nations and its activities;

69. *Calls upon* the Department of Public Information, recognizing the importance of audio-visual archives in preserving our common heritage, to continue to examine its policies and activities regarding the durable preservation of its radio, television and photographic archives and to take action, within existing resources, in ensuring that such archives are preserved and are accessible, and encourages the Department to work further with all interested partners in order to reach that objective;

70. *Takes note* of the initiative taken by the Dag Hammarskjöld Library, in its capacity as the focal point, to expand the scope of the regional training and knowledge-sharing workshops organized for the depository libraries in developing countries to include outreach in their activities;

71. *Acknowledges* the role of the Dag Hammarskjöld Library in enhancing knowledge-sharing and networking activities to ensure access to the vast store of United Nations knowledge for delegates, permanent missions of Member States, the Secretariat, researchers and depository libraries worldwide;

72. *Notes with appreciation* the Personal Knowledge Management initiative to assist representatives of Member States and Secretariat staff in the use of information products and tools as a complement to the traditional training programmes;

73. *Encourages* the Secretariat to develop and implement cost-neutral measures to provide Member States with secure access to the information currently accessible only on the Intranet of the Secretariat (iSeek), taking note that Member States have access to iSeek only through the facilities of the Dag Hammarskjöld Library;

VI
Outreach services

74. *Acknowledges* that the outreach services provided by the Department of Public Information continue to work towards promoting awareness of the role and work of the United Nations;

75. *Welcomes* the educational outreach activities of the Department of Public Information, through the United Nations Works programme and the Global Teaching and Learning Project, to reach educators and young people worldwide via a range of multimedia platforms, and encourages the United Nations Works programme to continue to develop further its partnerships with global media networks and celebrity advocates and the Global Teaching and Learning Project to further expand its activities to teachers and students in primary, intermediate and secondary schools;

76. *Notes* the importance of the continued implementation by the Department of Public Information of the ongoing programme for broadcasters and journalists from

developing countries and countries with economies in transition, as mandated by the General Assembly, and requests the Department to consider how best to maximize the benefits derived from the programme by extending, inter alia, its duration and the number of its participants;

77. *Welcomes* the movement towards educational outreach and the orientation of the *UN Chronicle*, both print and online editions, and, to this end, encourages the *UN Chronicle* to continue to develop co-publishing partnerships, collaborative educational activities and events, including the "Unlearning Intolerance" seminar series, with civil society organizations and institutions of higher learning;

78. *Takes note* of the report on "UN Affairs" contained in the annex to the report of the Secretary-General, and requests the Department of Public Information to continue the publication of the *UN Chronicle*, with a view to improving it further within existing resources, to report to the Committee on Information at its thirty-second session on progress in this matter and to submit options for publishing the *UN Chronicle* in all six official languages;

79. *Also takes note* of the efforts undertaken by the Department of Public Information in organizing exhibitions on important United Nations-related issues, within existing mandates, at United Nations Headquarters and at other United Nations offices as a useful tool for reaching out to the general public, reaffirms the important role that guided tours play as a means of reaching out to the general public, and requests the Secretary-General to continue his efforts to ensure that the guided tours provided at United Nations Headquarters and other United Nations duty stations are consistently available, in accordance with their income-generating nature, in particular in all the United Nations official languages;

80. *Requests* the Department of Public Information to strengthen its role as a focal point for two-way interaction with civil society relating to those priorities and concerns of the Organization identified by Member States;

81. *Commends*, in a spirit of cooperation, the United Nations Correspondents Association for its ongoing activities and for its Dag Hammarskjöld Memorial Scholarship Fund, which sponsors journalists from developing countries to come to the United Nations Headquarters and report on the activities during the General Assembly, and further encourages the international community to continue its financial support for the Fund;

82. *Expresses its appreciation* for the efforts and contribution of United Nations Messengers of Peace, Goodwill Ambassadors and other advocates to promote the work of the United Nations and to enhance international public awareness of its priorities and concerns, and calls upon the Department of Public Information to continue to involve them in its communications and media strategies and outreach activities;

VII
Final remarks

83. *Requests* the Secretary-General to report to the Committee on Information at its thirty-second session and to the General Assembly at its sixty-fifth session on the activities of the Department of Public Information and on the implementation of all recommendations and requests contained in the present resolution;

84. *Also requests* the Secretary-General to make every effort to ensure that the level of services provided by the Department of Public Information is maintained throughout the period of the implementation of the capital master plan;

85. *Takes note* of the initiative taken by the Department of Public Information, in cooperation with the Department of Safety and Security and the Protocol and Liaison Service, during the general debate of the sixty-third session of the General Assembly, to issue special identification stickers to press officers of Member States to enable them to escort media covering the visits of high-level officials to restricted areas, and strongly urges the Secretary-General to improve this practice by acceding to the request by Member States to provide the needed number of additional passes to press officers of Member States to allow their access to all areas that are deemed restricted, in order to effectively and comprehensively report on high-level meetings that include officials of delegations of Member States;

86. *Requests* the Committee on Information to report to the General Assembly at its sixty-fifth session;

87. *Decides* to include in the provisional agenda of its sixty-fifth session the item entitled "Questions relating to information".

DPI activities

In response to General Assembly resolution 63/100 B [YUN 2008, p. 699], the Secretary-General submitted a July report [A/64/262] on questions relating to information, covering DPI's activities since his February reports to the Committee on Information.

DPI's strategic communication services developed the "Seal the Deal" climate change campaign with the United Nations Environment Programme, while UN information centres (UNICs) in Brussels and Mexico City led regional campaigns, all of which promoted support for a successful outcome of the 2009 United Nations Climate Change Conference (Copenhagen, Denmark, 7–18 December). DPI also publicized the work of the Assembly by providing communications support for the UN Conference on the World Financial and Economic Crises and Its Impact on Development (New York, 24–26 June 2009). Activities in observance of International Women's Day, including those at Headquarters and at UNICs in Bucharest, Cairo and Harare, were carried out and publicized by the Department. DPI cooperated with the Department of Peacekeeping Operations and the Department of Field Support on activities to mark the International Day of United Nations Peacekeepers, dedicated in 2009 to women in peacekeeping. Also, on 13 June, 100 days before the International Day of Peace, DPI launched a campaign dedicated to nuclear disarmament and non-proliferation called "WMD-WeMustDisarm". Each day DPI issued a "reason to disarm" message over Twitter, Facebook and MySpace, with the Secretary-General issuing the first 10 messages. On the question of Palestine, DPI organized the annual International Media Seminar on Peace in the Middle East (Rio de Janeiro, Brazil, 27–28 July), attended by 150 participants from Latin America, the Middle East and other parts of the world. DPI contributed to the fifteenth commemoration of the Rwanda genocide, held at Headquarters on 7 April. The event included a solemn candle-lighting ceremony, and the Department oversaw the production and installation of the "Visions of Rwanda" exhibit.

DPI's quarterly magazines *Africa Renewal* and *Afrique renouveau* continued to play an important role in raising awareness of the New Partnership for Africa's Development and generating support for its goals and achievements. The Department paid particular attention to producing information on Africa's special needs in relation to the global financial and economic crises.

Through its outreach services and programmes, DPI continued to expand its association with journalists, schools, the general public, advocacy groups, UN entities, NGOs and cultural organizations. Effective January 2009, the Department would give priority of association to NGOs from the region where the DPI-NGO annual conference would be held. As the 2009 Conference took place in Mexico City, UNICs in the Latin America and the Caribbean region organized several workshops to inform NGOs about the process of affiliation with the Department. As a result of their work and the support of the Government of Mexico, DPI associated 57 NGOs in the first half of 2009, 49 of which came from Latin America and the Caribbean. Also noteworthy was the launch, in 2009, of the Secretary-General's Creative Community Outreach Initiative, which would function as a one-stop shop for writers, directors, producers and broadcasters interested in portraying the United Nations and its issues in their work.

Other priority areas, for which communications activities took place, included the International Day of Commemoration in memory of the victims of the Holocaust and the International Day of Remembrance of the Victims of Slavery and the Transatlantic Slave Trade. The Department started a new programme called Academic Impact to engage with centres of higher education, learning and research and facilitate a more direct input of the ideas generated by such entities into the policies, programmes and activities of the United Nations. By July, Academic Impact had more than 30 international scholastic networks of institutions endorsing it and more than 100 individual institutions affiliated with it. In addition to geographical diversity, the networks and institutions commanded a range of thematic disciplines—from medicine and technology to art and social science—representative of the broad scope of the UN mandate. To achieve greater efficiency in sales and marketing, the Department phased out the sales office in Geneva and centralized its New York operations.

UN website, multilingualism and accessibility

Through its news services, as part of continuing efforts to improve the structure, usability and visual attractiveness of the UN website, the Department carried out a refurbishment of the top layers of the site—from the splash page to over 200 underlying pages in all six official languages. In parallel with the revamp, work continued on a new companion site for mobile devices that was being tested for compatibility in all languages. The Department also explored new ways to deliver more content on demand in the form of podcasts and video podcasts (vodcasts) and to make it easier for consumers to share UN materials with others. Overall, during the first half of 2009, visits to the website exceeded 44,460,000—a 34 per cent increase over the corresponding period in 2008. Likewise, page views over the same time frame rose by 21 per cent, to 317,939,596.

While efforts towards parity among the official languages remained a high priority, given the fact that more content was produced in English and that the resources available for translation were limited, it was impractical to expect a closing of the gap with the other official languages with the current level of resources.

The Web accessibility guidelines finalized in 2008 had gone a long way towards assisting content-providing offices in developing web pages accessible by persons with disabilities. At the same time, efforts to ensure accessibility had increased the time required to develop and launch new sites.

Radio, television, video and photo services

In his July report on questions relating to information [A/64/262], the Secretary-General considered DPI's activities in providing radio, television and photo services. The Department continued to expand its network of broadcasting partners, now spanning 126 countries, while making every effort to harness the power of the Internet to bring audio directly to listeners around the world. UN Radio news stories were updated on UN Radio websites throughout the day. In one example of the success of that approach, continuous news updates by the Spanish Unit of UN Radio led to a sharp increase in downloads, from 3,168 in July 2008 to 58,511 in June 2009. Progress was made in exploring new distribution platforms, with analysis showing that UN Radio programmes were rapidly gaining new listeners on iTunes, a popular podcast site with audiences in different parts of the world. The increase was particularly noticeable for Chinese and English programmes. During April and May, iTunes accounted for over a quarter of the 70,000 registered downloads.

The Web-based UNifeed service, enabling media outlets to easily download broadcast-quality video, had gained a wide array of users despite having been launched only in 2008. Major world broadcasters such as CNN International, the Canadian Broadcasting Corporation and CBS News had utilized the service. The number of UNifeed clients grew more than tenfold, bringing the total to 1,122 in 27 countries on four continents. A similar trend was noticeable on the UN-branded channel on the online video-sharing site YouTube, with the Secretary-General's news conference on the influenza A(H1N1) pandemic registering nearly 150,000 views. Use of the United Nations Photo site remained high, with 29,501 downloads made from January to June 2009. In February, the Department began posting selected UN photographs on Flickr.com, a photo-sharing site that attracted a large number of young users and the Internet blogging community. By July, the UN Flickr site had recorded over 42,000 views.

Library and knowledge services

In 2009, the training and customized coaching programmes and direct research support services of the Dag Hammarskjöld Library and its branch libraries in the fields of map, legal and economic and social affairs had been revised to respond to the loss of the Library training room owing to the capital master plan. As a result, emphasis was placed on one-on-one and small group training rather than large group sessions. That format would continue until an alternative training room was secured. In April, the Library completed the digitization of major Security Council documents in English, French and Spanish from sessions held between 1946 and 1992, thereby expanding the coverage of the UN Official Document System (ODS). Programmes in 2009 under the depository library programme included a workshop in Pretoria, South Africa, for depository librarians representing 10 countries and UNIC staff from southern Africa, and a workshop in Incheon, Republic of Korea, for nine depository librarians and representatives of local public and university libraries.

UN information centres

The UNICs network, comprised of 63 information centres, services and information components around the world, served as DPI's field presence. It provided the United Nations with a global public information capacity; enhanced the Organization's public image; and disseminated UN messages to local populations, especially in developing countries. Country-level communications efforts led by UNICS included joint websites, newsletters and other information materials, launches of major UN flagship reports, the joint observance of international days, and major campaigns. UNIC Vienna, with as many as 10 UN entities located in that city, developed a workplan that included strengthening the visitors' service at the Vienna International Centre, expanding a roster of speakers and organizing a teachers' conference about the United Nations. UNIC Dar es Salaam, as chair of the local United Nations Communications Group, produced several issues of a newsletter that reflected on the consolidated operation of the UN system in the United Republic of Tanzania. The effort was particularly noteworthy, as Tanzania was a participant country of the "One UN" pilot initiative.

UN Communications Group

The United Nations Communications Group, which had evolved into a communication platform for the entire UN system since its establishment in 2002 [YUN 2002, p. 589], held its eighth annual meeting in Bangkok on 25 and 26 June. The meeting agreed to create a task force on the global financial and economic crisis; broaden the "Seal the Deal" campaign in support of a global climate change treaty; call upon the senior leadership of UN system organizations to be open and supportive of staff efforts to engage in new media, including online social networks and blogs; and endorse a set of revised draft guidelines on the appointment and activities of United Nations Goodwill Ambassadors and Messengers of Peace.

PART TWO

Human rights

Chapter I

Promotion of human rights

Efforts to promote human rights were boosted in 2009 by several developments. The Human Rights Council examined the human rights record of 48 Member States through the Universal Periodic Review mechanism, designed to assess the human rights record of all States every four years. A variety of recommendations were made during the reviews, ranging from calls for ratification of human rights treaties, enactment of national legislation and deepened cooperation with human rights mechanisms, to specific action and measures at the national level. The Human Rights Council Advisory Committee, which provided expertise to the Council, held its second and third sessions and submitted 13 recommendations, while the Council's complaint procedure, which consisted of the Working Group on Communications and the Working Group on Situations, addressed consistent patterns of gross and reliably attested human rights violations throughout the world.

During the year, the Council held three regular sessions (tenth, eleventh and twelfth) and four special sessions (ninth, tenth, eleventh and twelfth), focusing on the human rights situation in Gaza and Sri Lanka, as well as the impact of the global economic and financial crises. Human rights were also promoted through the work of the treaty bodies—committees of experts monitoring States parties' compliance with the legally binding human rights treaties.

The Office of the High Commissioner for Human Rights provided support to the work of the Council and its mechanisms, including the treaty bodies and the special procedures. The Office strengthened its country engagement and expanded its presence at the country and regional levels.

The year marked the twentieth anniversary of the adoption of the Convention on the Rights of the Child. In June, the Council established an open-ended working group to draft an optional protocol to the Convention providing for a communications procedure.

Concerning the World Programme for Human Rights Education, the Council, in October, decided that the second phase of the Programme (2010–2014) would focus on human rights education for higher education and on human rights training programmes for teachers, educators, civil servants and others.

The General Assembly, in December, proclaimed 2011 the International Year for People of African Descent and addressed the follow-up to the International Year of Human Rights Learning (2009).

UN machinery

Human Rights Council
Council sessions

During the year, the Human Rights Council held its tenth (2–27 March) [A/HRC/10/29], eleventh (2–18 June) [A/HRC/11/37] and twelfth (14 September–2 October) [A/HRC/12/50 & Corr.1] regular sessions. The Council also held four special sessions: its ninth (9 and 12 January) [A/HRC/S-9/2] on grave violations of human rights in the Occupied Palestinian Territory (see p. 780); tenth (20 and 23 February) [A/HRC/S-10/2] on the impact of the global economic and financial crises on the universal realization and enjoyment of human rights (see p. 702); eleventh (26–27 May) [A/HRC/S-11/2] on the human rights situation in Sri Lanka (see p. 777); and twelfth (15–16 October) [A/HRC/S-12/1] on the human rights situation in the Occupied Palestinian Territory, including East Jerusalem (see p. 787). All sessions were held in Geneva.

The Council adopted 77 resolutions, 53 decisions and 1 president's statement. It recommended for adoption by the General Assembly a draft resolution [A/64/53 (res. 11/7)] on Guidelines for the Alternative Care of Children (see p. 1161) and a draft decision [A/64/53 (dec. 11/117)] on issuing reports of the Working Group on the Universal Periodic Review in all UN official languages (see p. 1434). The resolutions, decisions and president's statement adopted at the Council's 2009 sessions were contained in its reports to the Assembly [A/64/53 & Add.1 & A/65/53 & Corr.1].

The General Assembly addressed revised estimates resulting from resolutions and decisions adopted by the Council in section V of **resolution 64/245** of 24 December (see p. 1407).

GENERAL ASSEMBLY ACTION

On 18 December [meeting 65], the General Assembly, on the recommendation of the Third (Social, Humanitarian and Cultural) Committee [A/64/434], adopted **resolution 64/143** without vote [agenda item 64].

Report of the Human Rights Council

The General Assembly,

Having considered the recommendations contained in the report of the Human Rights Council,

Takes note of the report of the Human Rights Council, and acknowledges the recommendations contained therein.

On 24 December, the General Assembly decided that the agenda item on the report of the Human Rights Council would remain for consideration during its resumed sixty-fourth (2010) session (**decision 64/549**).

Election of Council members

On 12 May, by **decision 63/420**, the General Assembly, in accordance with resolution 60/251 [YUN 2006, p. 757], elected the following 18 countries as members of the Human Rights Council for a three-year term of office beginning on 19 June: Bangladesh, Belgium, Cameroon, China, Cuba, Djibouti, Hungary, Jordan, Kyrgyzstan, Mauritius, Mexico, Nigeria, Norway, the Russian Federation, Saudi Arabia, Senegal, the United States and Uruguay. They would fill the vacancies occurring on the expiration of the terms of office of Azerbaijan, Bangladesh, Cameroon, Canada, China, Cuba, Djibouti, Germany, Jordan, Malaysia, Mauritius, Mexico, Nigeria, the Russian Federation, Saudi Arabia, Senegal, Switzerland and Uruguay. Belgium, Hungary, Kyrgyzstan, Norway and the United States were elected for the first time.

On 24 December, the Assembly decided that the item on the election of 14 members of the Council would remain for consideration during its resumed sixty-fourth (2010) session (**decision 64/549**).

Work of the Council

Human Rights Council action. On 1 October [A/65/53 (res. 12/1)], the Council established an open-ended intergovernmental working group to review the work and functioning of the Council. The working group was requested to report to the Council at its seventeenth (2011) session.

Office of the Council President. Pursuant to Human Rights Council decision 9/103 [YUN 2008, p. 712], which recommended that the General Assembly ensure the establishment of an Office of the President of the Human Rights Council, the Assembly, by resolution 64/144 (see below), requested the Council to address the question of establishing the office in the context of the review of the first five years of its work.

GENERAL ASSEMBLY ACTION

On 18 December [meeting 65], the General Assembly, on the recommendation of the Third Committee [A/64/434], adopted **resolution 64/144** without vote [agenda item 64].

Office of the President of the Human Rights Council

The General Assembly,

Recalling its resolution 60/251 of 15 March 2006 and Human Rights Council resolution 5/1 of 18 June 2007,

Recalling also Human Rights Council decision 9/103 of 24 September 2008, and underlining the crucial importance of appropriate resources to support the work of the Council and its numerous mechanisms,

Bearing in mind that the Human Rights Council meets regularly throughout the year in no fewer than three sessions per year for a total duration of no less than ten weeks,

Acknowledges the recommendation of the Human Rights Council to establish an Office of the President of the Human Rights Council, and requests the Council to address the question of the establishment and the modalities of an office in the context of the review of its work and functioning five years after its establishment, in accordance with resolution 60/251.

Universal Periodic Review

The Human Rights Council established the Universal Periodic Review (UPR) [YUN 2007, p. 663] as an instrument for assessing every four years the human rights records of all Member States. Each review, conducted by the Working Group on UPR, was facilitated by groups of three States, or "troikas", acting as rapporteurs.

Working Group sessions. The Working Group on UPR, made up of the 47 Council members, held its fourth (2–13 February), fifth (4–15 May) and sixth (30 November–11 December) sessions in Geneva. It reviewed 48 countries in the order of consideration determined by the Council in 2007 [ibid.]. As provided for in Council resolution 5/1 [ibid.], the review was based on a national report prepared by the State under review; a compilation by the Office of the High Commissioner for Human Rights (OHCHR) of information about the human rights situation in the State concerned, as reported by treaty bodies and special procedures; and a summary by OHCHR of credible information from other stakeholders, including non-governmental organizations (NGOs).

At its fourth session, the Working Group considered and adopted reports on Germany [A/HRC/11/15], Djibouti [A/HRC/11/16], Canada [A/HRC/11/17], Bangladesh [A/HRC/11/18], the Russian Federation [A/HRC/11/19], Azerbaijan [A/HRC/11/20], Cameroon [A/HRC/11/21], Cuba [A/HRC/11/22], Saudi Arabia [A/HRC/11/23], Senegal [A/HRC/11/24], China [A/HRC/11/25], Nigeria [A/HRC/11/26], Mexico [A/HRC/11/27], Mauritius [A/HRC/11/28], Jordan [A/HRC/11/29] and Malaysia [A/HRC/11/30]. The reports summarized the presentation by the State under review; the interactive dialogue in the Working Group between State and Council; the response by the State; and the conclusions on and/or recommendations to the State under review. The outcome of the review comprised the report of the Working Group, together with the views of the State under review about the recommendations and/or conclusions, as well as its voluntary commitments and its replies to questions or issues that were not sufficiently addressed during the interactive dialogue.

Replies to recommendations made during the review were submitted by Germany [A/HRC/11/15/Add.1], Canada [A/HRC/11/17/Add.1], Bangladesh [A/HRC/11/18/Add.1], Cameroon [A/HRC/11/21/Add.1], Saudi Arabia [A/HRC/11/23/Add.1 & Corr.1] and Mauritius [A/HRC/11/28/Add.1]. Responses to the recommendations made by delegations were submitted by the Russian Federation [A/HRC/11/19/Add.1/Rev.1]. Additional written information was submitted by Cuba and Mexico. Replies to the recommendations of the Working Group were submitted by Azerbaijan [A/HRC/11/20/Add.1], Senegal [A/HRC/11/24/Add.1] and Malaysia [A/HRC/11/30/Add.1].

At its fifth session, the Working Group considered and adopted reports on the Central African Republic [A/HRC/12/2], Monaco [A/HRC/12/3], Belize [A/HRC/12/4], Chad [A/HRC/12/5], the Congo [A/HRC/12/6], Malta [A/HRC/12/7], New Zealand [A/HRC/12/8], Afghanistan [A/HRC/12/9], Chile [A/HRC/12/10], Viet Nam [A/HRC/12/11], Uruguay [A/HRC/12/12], Yemen [A/HRC/12/13], Vanuatu [A/HRC/12/14], the former Yugoslav Republic of Macedonia [A/HRC/12/15], the Comoros [A/HRC/12/16] and Slovakia [A/HRC/12/17].

Responses to the outcomes of the review were submitted by Belize [A/HRC/12/4/Add.1]. Responses to recommendations made at the review were submitted by Viet Nam [A/HRC/12/11/Add.1], Yemen [A/HRC/12/13/Add.1 & Corr.1] and Vanuatu [A/HRC/12/14/Add.1]. Responses to the recommendations made by countries participating at the review were submitted by Afghanistan [A/HRC/12/9/Add.1]. Replies to the recommendations presented during the interactive dialogue were made by the former Yugoslav Republic of Macedonia [A/HRC/12/15/Add.1 & Corr.1]. Responses to the recommendations contained in the report of the Working Group were submitted by Malta [A/HRC/12/7/Add.1/Rev.2], New Zealand [A/HRC/12/8/Add.1 & Corr.1] and Slovakia [A/HRC/12/17/Add.1].

At its sixth session, the Working Group considered and adopted reports on Eritrea [A/HRC/13/2], the Dominican Republic [A/HRC/13/3], Cambodia [A/HRC/13/4 & Corr.1], Norway [A/HRC/13/5 & Corr.1], Albania [A/HRC/13/6], Cyprus [A/HRC/13/7], the Democratic Republic of the Congo [A/HRC/13/8], Côte d'Ivoire [A/HRC/13/9], Portugal [A/HRC/13/10], Bhutan [A/HRC/13/11], Dominica [A/HRC/13/12], the Democratic People's Republic of Korea [A/HRC/13/13], Brunei Darussalam [A/HRC/13/14], Costa Rica [A/HRC/13/15], Equatorial Guinea [A/HRC/13/16] and Ethiopia [A/HRC/13/17].

Responses to the recommendations made during the review were provided by Eritrea [A/HRC/13/2/Add.1], Portugal [A/HRC/13/10/Add.1], Costa Rica [A/HRC/13/15/Add.1] and Ethiopia [A/HRC/13/17/Add.1]. Views on conclusions and/or recommendations, voluntary commitments and replies were presented by Cyprus [A/HRC/13/7/Add.1] and Côte d'Ivoire [A/HRC/13/9/Add.1/Rev.1]. Responses to recommendations in the report of the Working Group were submitted by Norway [A/HRC/13/5/Add.1], Bhutan [A/HRC/13/11/Add.1 & Corr.1] and Brunei Darussalam [A/HRC/13/14/Add.1].

Human Rights Council action. At its tenth session [A/HRC/10/29], the Council considered the outcome of the reviews conducted during the third session of the Working Group [YUN 2008, p. 714]. The Council adopted the outcomes of the reviews through standardized decisions. On 18 March, the Council adopted the outcomes on Botswana [dec. 10/101], the Bahamas [dec. 10/102], Burundi [dec. 10/103], Luxembourg [dec. 10/104], Barbados [dec. 10/105] and Montenegro [dec. 10/106]. On 19 March, it adopted the outcomes on the United Arab Emirates [dec. 10/107], Liechtenstein [dec. 10/108], Serbia [dec. 10/109], Turkmenistan [dec. 10/110] and Burkina Faso [dec. 10/111]. On 20 March, it adopted the outcomes on Israel [dec. 10/112], Cape Verde [dec. 10/113], Colombia [dec. 10/114], Uzbekistan [dec. 10/115] and Tuvalu [dec. 10/116].

At its eleventh session [A/HRC/11/37], the Council considered the outcome of the reviews conducted during the fourth session of the Working Group. On 9 June, the Council adopted the outcomes of the reviews of Germany [dec. 11/101], Djibouti [dec. 11/102] and Canada [11/103]. On 10 June, it adopted the outcome of the reviews of Bangladesh [dec. 11/104], the Russian Federation [dec. 11/105], Cameroon [dec. 11/106], Cuba [dec. 11/107] and Saudi Arabia [dec. 11/108]. On 11 June, the Council adopted the outcomes of the reviews of Senegal [dec. 11/109], China [dec. 11/110], Azerbaijan [dec. 11/111], Nigeria [dec. 11/112], Mexico [dec. 11/113] and Mauritius [dec. 11/114]. On 12 June, it adopted the outcomes of the reviews of Jordan [dec. 11/115] and Malaysia [dec. 11/116].

At its twelfth session [A/HRC/12/50], the Council considered the outcome of the reviews conducted during the fifth session of the Working Group. On 23 September, it adopted the outcomes of the reviews of the Central African Republic [dec. 12/101], Monaco [dec. 12/102], Belize [12/103], the Congo [dec. 12/104] and Malta [dec. 12/105]. On 24 September, the Council adopted the outcomes of the reviews of New Zealand [dec. 12/106], Afghanistan [dec. 12/107], Chile [dec. 12/108], Chad [dec. 12/109], Viet Nam [dec. 12/110], Uruguay [dec. 12/111] and Yemen [dec. 12/112]. On 25 September, it adopted the outcomes of the reviews of Vanuatu [dec. 12/113], the former Yugoslav Republic of Macedonia [dec. 12/114], the Comoros [dec. 12/115] and Slovakia [dec. 12/116].

The Council, on 15 September, confirmed, for the seventh, eighth and ninth sessions of the UPR Working Group, the order of the review, which was established by drawing lots on 14 September.

Report of High Commissioner. In her annual report [A/HRC/13/26], the United Nations High Commissioner for Human Rights, Navanethem Pillay, noted that the review confirmed her own view that there was no country free from human rights violations. The UPR process testified to the credibility of the Council and positive results had been achieved. By the end of December, half of all Member States had been reviewed, and recommendations relating to all areas of human rights were made. Those ranged from calls for ratification of human rights treaties, enactment of legislation and deepened cooperation with human rights mechanisms to recommendations for national action. However, devising mechanisms to follow up and ensure implementation of such recommendations was a challenge. Ways and means should be found to involve States, UN entities and other stakeholders in a common effort to accelerate implementation of the recommendations.

Human Rights Council Advisory Committee

The Human Rights Council Advisory Committee, a think-tank for the Council composed of 18 experts serving in their personal capacity, held its second (26–30 January) [A/HRC/AC/2/2] and third (3–7 August) [A/HRC/AC/3/2] sessions in Geneva.

At its second session, the Committee adopted seven recommendations to be submitted to the Council on: human rights education and training; subsidiary bodies of the Council; elimination of discrimination against persons affected by leprosy and their family members; gender mainstreaming; protection of civilians in armed conflict; missing persons; and the right to food. Pursuant to a Council request [YUN 2007, p. 697], the Committee reported on progress in drafting a declaration on human rights education and training [A/HRC/A/AC/2/2 (rec. 2/1)]. The Committee also recommended that the Council authorize it to prepare draft guidelines on methods to enhance the implementation of gender mainstreaming [rec. 2/4].

At its third session, the Advisory Committee adopted six recommendations on: the elimination of discrimination against persons affected by leprosy and their family members, on which draft principles and guidelines were annexed to the Committee's recommendation 3/1; missing persons; the drafting group on human rights education and training; a study on discrimination in the context of the right to food;

promotion of the right of peoples to peace; and the human rights of elderly people.

Human Rights Council action. On 26 March [A/64/53 (res. 10/12)], the Council requested the Advisory Committee to undertake a study on discrimination in the context of the right to food, including good practices of anti-discriminatory policies and strategies, and to report to the Council's thirteenth (2010) session.

On 27 March [res. 10/28], the Council requested the Advisory Committee to submit its draft Declaration on Human Rights Education and Training to the Council's thirteenth session. Also on 27 March, the Council President read a statement [PRST/10/1] which took note of the reports on the first and second sessions of the Committee, the latter of which included five suggestions for the Committee's work.

On 1 October [A/65/53 (res. 12/7)], the Council requested the Committee to finalize the draft set of principles and guidelines for the elimination of discrimination against persons affected by leprosy and their family members for submission to the Council's fifteenth (2010) session. The Council also requested the Committee [dec. 12/117] to submit its study on best practices in the matter of missing persons to the Council's fourteenth (2010) session.

Complaint procedure

The complaint procedure of the Human Rights Council comprised the Working Group on Communications, which examined communications of alleged violations and assessed their merits, and the Working Group on Situations, which, on the recommendation of the Working Group on Communications, reported to the Council on consistent patterns of gross violations and recommended a course of action.

Working Group on Communications. The fourth (30 March–3 April) [A/HRC/WG.5/4/R.2] and fifth (3–9 September) [A/HRC/WG.5/5/R.2] sessions of the five-member Working Group on Communications were held in Geneva. At its fourth session, the Group considered 40 files of communications concerning 23 countries. That included 23 new files containing communications and Government replies thereto in relation to 14 countries. A total of 17 replies to 17 files were received from Governments in relation to the communications. The Working Group also examined 17 files related to communications which, at its third session [YUN 2008, p. 716], it had decided to keep under review. The countries to which the pending communications pertained were: Bulgaria, Colombia, India, Iraq, Japan, the Libyan Arab Jamahiriya, the Philippines, the Republic of Korea, Romania, the Sudan, Tajikistan, Thailand, Tunisia and the

United States. In relation to those communications, the Group received 36 replies from Governments.

The Group adopted 40 decisions, including a decision to postpone consideration of eight files of communications. Decisions were taken on 17 of the 23 new files registered under the complaint procedure between July and November 2008, as well as on 15 of the 17 files of communications that had been kept under review from the third session. The Group decided to transmit files relating to two countries (Philippines, Tajikistan) to the Group on Situations. It decided to keep under review until its next session 11 files relating to seven countries (Canada, India, Iraq, Malaysia, Nepal, Turkmenistan, United States) and requested further information about those communications from the Governments concerned. The Group postponed consideration of communications relating to six countries (Colombia, Egypt, Mexico, Republic of Korea, Sudan, United States). The consideration of 19 files in relation to Angola, Bulgaria, Colombia, India, Iran, Japan, Libya, the Philippines, the Republic of Korea, Romania, Thailand, Tunisia, the United States and Viet Nam was discontinued. The Group received Government replies to 33 of the 40 files before it.

At its fifth session, the Group considered 39 files of communications concerning 24 countries. That included 20 new files containing communications and Government replies thereto in relation to 15 countries. A total of 19 replies to 15 files were received from Governments in relation to the communications. The Group examined 11 files related to communications concerning seven countries which it had decided to keep under review. In relation to those communications, the Group had received 15 replies from Governments. The Group also had before it eight files related to communications on six countries, the consideration of which, at its previous session, the Group had postponed. To those communications, the Group had received 12 replies from concerned Governments.

The Group adopted 37 decisions. Decisions were taken on 18 of the 20 new files registered between December 2008 and April 2009, as well as on all 11 files of communications that had been kept under review and the eight files of postponed communications. The Group transmitted five files relating to two countries (Democratic Republic of the Congo, Iraq) to the Group on Situations. It kept under review until its next session 16 files relating to 11 countries (Colombia, Czech Republic, India, Lao People's Democratic Republic, Mexico, Nepal, Republic of Korea, Sudan, Turkmenistan, United States, Zimbabwe) and requested further information about those communications from the Governments concerned. The consideration of 17 files on Bangladesh, Cameroon, Canada, Egypt, India, Malaysia, Pakistan, the Russian Federation, Sri Lanka, Switzerland, the United States and Uzbekistan was discontinued. The Group received Government replies to 34 out of the 39 files before it.

Working Group on Situations. The third (19–22 January) [A/HRC/10/R.1] and fourth (22–24 June) [A/HRC/12/R.1] sessions of the five-member Working Group on Situations were held in Geneva. At its third session, the Group had before it dossiers relating to the human rights situation in Botswana, Cambodia, Cameroon, Colombia, the Democratic Republic of the Congo, the Gambia, Guinea, Nigeria and the Syrian Arab Republic. Having examined communications concerning the human rights situation in the Democratic Republic of the Congo, the Group decided to refer the matter to the Human Rights Council. It decided to keep under review cases on Cambodia, Cameroon, Colombia, the Gambia, Guinea and Nigeria, and dismissed cases concerning Botswana and Syria.

At its fourth session, the Group had before it dossiers relating to the human rights situation in Cambodia, Cameroon, Colombia, the Gambia, Guinea, Nigeria, the Philippines and Tajikistan, which consisted of communications, Government replies and observations thereon. The Group decided to refer the case concerning Guinea to the Human Rights Council. It also decided to keep under review cases concerning Cambodia, the Gambia, the Philippines, Nigeria and Tajikistan. It dismissed cases related to Cameroon and Colombia.

Human Rights Council action. In March, the Council held two closed meetings on the complaint procedure. It examined and decided to discontinue its consideration of the human rights situation in Turkmenistan. In June, the Council held two closed meetings and decided, by a recorded vote of 28 to 17, with 2 abstentions, to discontinue its consideration of the human rights situation in the Democratic Republic of the Congo. The Council held two more closed meetings on the complaint procedure in September, after which it decided to keep the human rights situation in Guinea under review and requested the Government of Guinea to provide further information to the Council's thirteenth (2010) session.

Office of the High Commissioner for Human Rights

Reports of High Commissioner. In her annual report to the General Assembly [A/64/36] covering activities since the previous report [YUN 2008, p. 718], the High Commissioner said that in the last 12 months the OHCHR Rapid Response Unit contributed to four missions providing technical advice in the aftermath of crises. It dispatched a human rights adviser

(August–September 2008) to support the UN country team in the context of the Georgia/South Ossetia crisis; a human rights officer (December 2008–March 2009) to its Regional Office for Southern Africa to deal with the situation in Zimbabwe; a rapid response officer (January 2009) to the OHCHR office in the Occupied Palestinian Territory in the wake of the Israeli military operations in Gaza; and a human rights adviser (July 2009) to the UN country team in Honduras responding to the political crisis. OHCHR provided advice to Member States on the establishment and responsibilities of national human rights institutions, and enhanced its cooperation with regional and intergovernmental organizations. The United Nations Human Rights Training and Documentation Centre for South-West Asia and the Arab Region was inaugurated in Doha, Qatar, on 27 May.

The Office had adopted new approaches and made full use of the UN human rights system, particularly its early warning mechanisms, to make a difference for the victims of human rights violations. Against that background, the High Commissioner defined six priorities during her tenure: ensuring the realization of human rights in the context of migration; eliminating discrimination, particularly on the basis of race, sex or religion, and against marginalized groups; protecting economic, social and cultural rights in an effort to combat inequalities and poverty, including in the context of the economic, food and climate crises; protecting human rights in situations of armed conflict, violence and insecurity; combating impunity and strengthening accountability, the rule of law, and democratic societies; and strengthening international human rights mechanisms and the development of international human rights law. Those six priorities would become the framework of the High Commissioner's 2010–2011 Strategic Management Plan.

The General Assembly took note of the report on 18 December (**decision 64/536**).

In her annual report to the Human Rights Council [A/HRC/13/26] on the 2009 activities of OHCHR, the High Commissioner noted the predominant challenges during the year, particularly the food, economic and financial crises, and the subsequent deterioration of the ability of vulnerable groups to enjoy their basic rights. Her Office addressed those challenges by reinforcing the work of the international human rights mechanisms and engaging in dialogue and cooperation with Member States and other stakeholders. The Office took action on combating discrimination and providing support to victims, selecting the theme of "Embrace diversity, stop discrimination" for the 2009 Human Rights Day activities which took place around the world. It also promoted the use of the United Nations Declaration on the Rights of Indigenous Peoples [YUN 2007, p. 690] by national human

rights institutions and other actors; and facilitated the integration of women's rights and a gender perspective into the work of the Human Rights Council, including through the recruitment of gender advisers to the OHCHR regional offices in Fiji, Lebanon, Panama and Senegal in response to Government requests for guidance on integrating a gender dimension into national policies and programmes.

As at December, OHCHR had 56 field presences: 12 regional presences, 11 country offices, 15 human rights components in UN peace missions and 18 human rights advisers in UN country teams. The United Nations Regional Office for Europe in Brussels, Belgium, was inaugurated in October, and an agreement was signed with Mauritania in September on the establishment of an OHCHR country office. Uganda and Nepal renewed agreements for existing offices. Through its rapid response capacity, OHCHR deployed two human rights officers to Madagascar in the context of the political crisis, and a team of four human rights officers to Gabon to monitor the human rights situation during the presidential electoral period. Following the violence of 28 September in Conakry, OHCHR supported the Commission of Inquiry on the events in Guinea established by the Secretary-General. The Office assisted in establishing or strengthening 43 national human rights institutions worldwide, in collaboration with UN partners and regional networks of such institutions.

In 2009, the Office produced a large number of reports to the Human Rights Council and the General Assembly, which placed significant demands on both the Office and UN conference services. Efforts were being made to rationalize required submissions and ensure that there was adequate support to the Secretariat for the effective functioning of the human rights machinery.

In a February report [A/HRC/10/31], the High Commissioner outlined the efforts of her Office to implement its mandate. She described the support given to the work of the Human Rights Council and its mechanisms, including UPR, and elaborated on the themes identified in the Strategic Management Plan for 2008–2009 and their implementation. She reviewed efforts in the field and activities related to the sixtieth anniversary of the Universal Declaration of Human Rights [YUN 2008, p. 726]. She focused on the Office's support for an inclusive and successful Durban Review Conference (see p. 657) and its leadership in enhancing a rights-based approach on issues such as migration, freedom of expression and incitement to racial and religious hatred. She also highlighted the support provided to human rights treaty bodies and the importance of ensuring follow-up to their recommendations.

Composition of staff

Report of High Commissioner. As requested by the Human Rights Council [ibid., p. 719], the High Commissioner reported in February [A/HRC/10/45] on the composition of OHCHR staff and efforts to achieve equitable geographical representation. In that regard, noticeable progress had been achieved, but OHCHR remained attentive to the need to attain the broadest possible geographic diversity and would continue implementing measures to redress the imbalance.

Human Rights Council action. On 26 March [A/64/53 (res. 10/5)], by a recorded vote of 33 to 12, with 2 abstentions, the Council noted the increase in the percentage of staff from regions requiring better representation, stressed that the imbalance was still prominent, and requested the High Commissioner to work on the broadest geographic diversity of her staff by enhancing the implementation of measures to achieve better representation of unrepresented or underrepresented countries and regions, particularly from the developing world, while considering the application of a zero-growth cap on representation from overrepresented countries and regions.

Auditing of OHCHR

OIOS reports. Pursuant to General Assembly resolution 62/236 [YUN 2007, p. 1446], the Office of Internal Oversight Services (OIOS) issued a July report [A/64/203 & Corr.1] reviewing the efficiency of the implementation of the OHCHR mandate, which concluded that the Office had contributed to raising the visibility of human rights issues in the international community, supporting human rights capacity-building in national legislation and institutions, and contributing to the implementation of the human rights-based approach across the UN system. However, in order to mitigate the risk of the Office's activities being spread too thinly, its strategic focus needed sharpening. As the only UN entity with a mandate exclusively dedicated to human rights, and one that worked within a crowded international human rights community, OIOS found it to be imperative that OHCHR be more strategic in identifying critical activities and establishing its organizational priorities.

OIOS concluded that the comparative advantage of OHCHR in fulfilling its mandate lay in its position as the central reference point and advocate for international human rights standards and mechanisms. In that regard, OHCHR had the potential for global impact as the authoritative source of advice and assistance to Governments, civil society and UN entities concerning compliance with those standards. It further concluded that while OHCHR monitoring and reporting activities made an important contribution to the pro-tection of international human rights, those activities were largely confined to countries and regions with a field presence. OHCHR could most efficiently utilize its finite resources by strategically focusing its activities in line with its comparative advantage.

OIOS also found that the rapid growth of OHCHR field operations had not been fully coherent. More explicit terms of engagement, including the development of entry and exit strategies, would increase their effectiveness. A more coordinated approach to the development and management of partnerships would enable OHCHR to extend the reach of its activities and increase the impact of its work. In addition, OHCHR follow-up to the work of human rights bodies needed strengthening. Finally, OIOS identified management challenges in the Office, including unclear leadership, inefficient coordination and undocumented processes for some critical tasks.

OIOS recommended that OHCHR sharpen its focus in finalizing and implementing the High Commissioner's Strategic Management Plan for 2010–2011; develop an overarching field strategy document; improve its work with the human rights bodies through more systematic follow-up of their recommendations; strengthen its partnerships; improve internal coordination and communication; and identify and document all critical work processes.

In September [A/64/203/Add.1], the Secretary-General submitted his comments on the OIOS report. He welcomed the overall conclusion and recommendations of the report, but also sought to provide greater context and clarity to its findings.

Also pursuant to General Assembly resolution 62/236, a July report from OIOS presented the findings of its audit of OHCHR human resources management [A/64/201]. The report concluded that OHCHR needed additional delegation of authority in human resources management to improve operational efficiency and, in that context, recommended that OHCHR pursue its case with the Office of Human Resources Management. OIOS also recommended that OHCHR develop a strategy to enhance staff recruitment from unrepresented and underrepresented countries; reduce the impact of delays in recruiting consultants by starting the recruitment process from the time the need for such services was identified; ensure the competitive selection of consultants by announcing opportunities for such employment on its website; and clarify with the Human Resources Management Service of the United Nations Office at Geneva the responsibility for consultants' reference checks.

Management review

JIU report. In June [A/64/94], the Secretary-General transmitted to the General Assembly the report of the Joint Inspection Unit (JIU) on the second follow-up to the management review of OHCHR [JIU/REP/2009/2-A/64/94]. The report assessed progress in the implementation of three recommendations on the issue of geographic distribution of staff, which had remained in question from the initial JIU report of 2003 [YUN 2004, p. 650], the first follow-up in 2006 [YUN 2006, p. 765] and the JIU progress report of 2007 [YUN 2008, p. 719]. JIU determined that the issue should be monitored by the Human Rights Council, with due care also given to issues of gender balance, staff mobility and career development. It also recommended that the Council monitor, on a biennial basis, OHCHR staffing to ensure compliance with General Assembly mandates, and that the Council encourage Member States to promote the selection and financing of candidates from developing countries in the OHCHR Associate Expert Programme.

In September [A/64/94/Add.1], the Secretary-General submitted his comments on the JIU report. As OHCHR had undertaken many efforts to diversify its staff, the Secretary-General welcomed the JIU report and the recognition it provided to the progress made in addressing the issue.

Joint workplan with the Division for the Advancement of Women

A report of the Secretary-General issued in December [A/HRC/13/70-E/CN.6/2010/7] reviewed the implementation of the 2009 joint workplan of the Division for the Advancement of Women and OHCHR and provided the joint workplan for 2010.

Human rights instruments

In 2009, eight UN human rights instruments were in force with expert bodies monitoring their implementation. Those instruments and their treaty bodies were: the 1965 International Convention on the Elimination of All Forms of Racial Discrimination [YUN 1965, p. 440, GA res. 2106 A (XX)] (Committee on the Elimination of Racial Discrimination); the 1966 International Covenant on Civil and Political Rights and the Optional Protocol thereto [YUN 1966, p. 423, GA res. 2200 A (XXI)] and the Second Optional Protocol aiming at the abolition of the death penalty [YUN 1989, p. 484, GA res. 44/128] (Human Rights Committee); the 1966 International Covenant on Economic, Social and Cultural Rights [YUN 1966, p. 419, GA res. 2200 A (XXI)] and the Optional Protocol thereto [YUN 2008, p. 729, GA res. 63/117] (Committee on Economic, Social and Cultural Rights); the 1979 Convention on the Elimination of All Forms of Discrimination against Women [YUN 1979, p. 895, GA res. 34/180] and the Optional Protocol thereto [YUN 1999, p. 1100, GA res. 54/4] (Committee on the Elimination of Discrimination against Women); the 1984 Convention against Torture and Other Cruel, Inhuman or Degrading Treatment or Punishment [YUN 1984, p. 813, GA res. 39/46] and the 2002 Optional Protocol thereto [YUN 2002, p. 631, GA res. 57/199] (Committee against Torture and Subcommittee on Prevention of Torture); the 1989 Convention on the Rights of the Child [YUN 1989, p. 560, GA res. 44/25] and the Optional Protocols on the involvement of children in armed conflict and on the sale of children, child prostitution and child pornography [YUN 2000, pp. 616 & 618, GA res. 54/263] (Committee on the Rights of the Child); the 1990 International Convention on the Protection of the Rights of All Migrant Workers and Members of Their Families [YUN 1990, p. 594, GA res. 45/158] (Committee on the Protection of the Rights of All Migrant Workers and Members of Their Families); and the 2006 Convention on the Rights of Persons with Disabilities and its Optional Protocol [YUN 2006, p. 785, GA res. 61/106] (Committee on the Rights of Persons with Disabilities).

The 2006 International Convention for the Protection of All Persons from Enforced Disappearance [ibid., p. 800] provided for the subsequent establishment of a Committee on Enforced Disappearances that would monitor the implementation of the Convention upon its entry into force. The 1948 Convention on the Prevention and Punishment of the Crime of Genocide [YUN 1948–49, p. 959] did not establish a treaty body, but the mandate of the Office of the Special Adviser on the Prevention of Genocide [YUN 2004, p. 730] included collecting information on situations where there might be a risk of genocide, war crimes, ethnic cleansing and crimes against humanity; alerting relevant actors where such a risk existed; and advocating and mobilizing for appropriate action.

Effective implementation of international human rights instruments

Pursuant to Human Rights Council resolution 9/8 [YUN 2008, p. 725], the Secretary-General submitted a report [A/HRC/13/69] which reviewed developments in the effective implementation of international human rights instruments, including recommendations for improving, harmonizing and reforming the treaty body system. During the year, human rights treaty bodies held 20 sessions amounting to 64 weeks in Geneva and New York, during which 103 State party reports were reviewed in plenary sessions and an equivalent number in working groups. The Committee on the Elimination of Discrimination against Women held one of its sessions in two chambers and the Committee on the Elimination of Racial Discrimination extended one of its sessions by one week to address the backlog of reports awaiting review. Treaty bodies received 150 State party reports during the year. The Committee on the Rights of Persons with Disabilities held its first two sessions and began work on its rules of procedure and working methods.

The treaty bodies continued their work on finalizing treaty-specific reporting guidelines to complement the guidelines for the common core document. The Committee on the Rights of Persons with Disabilities adopted its treaty-specific reporting guidelines in 2009, while the Human Rights Committee started its work in that regard. The treaty bodies continued to develop and implement new working methods, such as by establishing a list of issues for States to consider prior to reporting, and refining the follow-up procedures to concluding observations and views on petitions.

The Secretariat and the treaty bodies examined some 9,000 items of correspondence, and over 110 new individual complaints received by the treaty bodies were registered. The Human Rights Committee, the Committee against Torture, the Committee on the Elimination of Racial Discrimination and the Committee on the Elimination of Discrimination against Women examined and adopted final decisions on some 100 communications. They issued over 30 requests for interim measures of protection in cases where lack of such protection might lead to irreparable harm for the petitioners. They also followed up on over 50 decisions in which violations of the International Covenant on Civil and Political Rights, the Convention against Torture or the Convention on the Elimination of Discrimination against Women had been found.

Convention against racial discrimination

Accessions and ratifications

As at 31 December, the number of parties to the International Convention on the Elimination of All Forms of Racial Discrimination, adopted by the General Assembly in resolution 2106 A (XX) [YUN 1965, p. 440], stood at 173.

The amendment to article 8 of the Convention, regarding the financing of the Committee on the Elimination of Racial Discrimination [YUN 1992, p. 714], had been accepted by 43 States parties as at 31 December. The amendment would enter into force when accepted by a two-thirds majority of States parties, comprising 115 of the 173 States parties to the Convention.

A January note by the Secretariat [A/HRC/10/33], submitted in response to resolution 2005/64 of the Commission on Human Rights [YUN 2005, p. 728] and decision 2/102 of the Human Rights Council [YUN 2006, p. 760], described OHCHR efforts towards universal ratification of the Convention. It listed six States

that had signed but not ratified the instrument, and 16 others that had neither signed nor ratified it. OHCHR had written to those States, most of them small island developing nations or least developed countries, encouraging them to take the necessary action.

Implementation

Monitoring body. The Committee on the Elimination of Racial Discrimination (CERD), established under article 8 of the Convention, held its seventy-fourth (16 February–6 March) and seventy-fifth (3–28 August) sessions in Geneva [A/64/18]. It considered reports submitted by 20 countries—Azerbaijan, Bulgaria, Chad, Chile, China, Colombia, Congo, Croatia, Ethiopia, Finland, Greece, Montenegro, Pakistan, Peru, Philippines, Poland, Suriname, Tunisia, Turkey, United Arab Emirates—and adopted concluding observations on them.

With regard to the Convention's implementation by States parties whose reports were seriously overdue, the Committee noted that 18 of them were at least 10 years late in submitting their reports, and 34 were at least 5 years late. The review of the Convention's implementation by those States continued on the basis of the last reports submitted, in addition to information prepared by UN entities and other sources, including NGOs. The Committee reviewed the implementation of the Convention in the Gambia and adopted concluding observations in the absence of a delegation.

Under article 14 of the Convention, CERD considered communications from individuals or groups claiming violation by a State party of their rights as enumerated in the Convention. Fifty-three States parties had recognized CERD competence to do so.

Pursuant to article 15, which empowered the Committee to consider petitions, reports and other information relating to Trust and Non-Self-Governing Territories, CERD noted, as it had in the past, the difficulty in fulfilling its functions in that regard, owing to the scant information relating to the Convention's principles and objectives in the reports received.

The Committee considered a number of situations under its early warning and urgent action procedure, including situations in Australia, Brazil, El Salvador, Guatemala, India, Indonesia, the Lao People's Democratic Republic, Nepal, the Niger, Panama, Peru and the United Republic of Tanzania.

At the seventy-fifth session, the Committee adopted general recommendation No. 32 on the meaning and scope of special measures in the Convention, and general recommendation No. 33 on follow-up to the Durban Review Conference.

(For further information on the Organization's activities to combat racial discrimination, see p. 657.)

Complementary standards

Human Rights Council action. On 27 March [A/64/53 (res. 10/30)], by a recorded vote of 34 to 13, the Council endorsed as a framework for its future work the road map adopted by the Ad Hoc Committee on the Elaboration of Complementary Standards during the second part of its first session [YUN 2008, p. 734]. It also decided the Ad Hoc Committee's second session would be held in October (see below). The Ad Hoc Committee was established by the Council in 2006 [YUN 2006, p. 774] to elaborate complementary standards to the Convention in the form of a convention or additional protocol(s), fill gaps in the treaty, and provide new normative standards for combating racism.

Committee session. During its second session (Geneva, 19–30 October) [A/HRC/13/58], the Ad Hoc Committee considered submissions received from States and groups of States [A/HRC/AC.1/2/2] in response to a request for contributions. Among the topics examined were anti-discrimination legislation; discrimination based on religion or belief; incitement to racial, ethnic, national and religious hatred; national anti-discrimination mechanisms; hate crimes; impunity; human rights education; genocide; intercultural and interreligious dialogue; and implementation of existing norms and standards. The session revealed an absence of consensus, with some countries expressing support for drafting complementary standards, and others remaining unconvinced that such standards were necessary.

Covenant on Civil and Political Rights and Optional Protocols

Accessions and ratifications

As at 31 December, parties to the International Covenant on Civil and Political Rights and the Optional Protocol thereto, adopted by the General Assembly in resolution 2200A (XXI) [YUN 1966, p. 423], numbered 165 and 113, respectively. During the year, the Lao People's Democratic Republic became party to the Covenant, and Brazil and Kazakhstan became parties to the Optional Protocol.

The Second Optional Protocol, aimed at the abolition of the death penalty and adopted by the Assembly in resolution 44/128 [YUN 1989, p. 484], was acceded to by Brazil and ratified by Nicaragua, which brought the number of States parties to 72 as at 31 December.

Implementation

Monitoring body. The Human Rights Committee, established under article 28 of the Covenant, held three sessions in 2009: its ninety-fifth (New York, 16 March–3 April), ninety-sixth (Geneva, 13–31 July) [A/64/40, Vol. I] and ninety-seventh (Geneva, 12–30 October) [A/65/40, Vol. I]. It considered reports submitted under article 40 from 12 States—Australia, Azerbaijan, Chad, Croatia, Ecuador, Moldova, Netherlands, Switzerland, Russian Federation, Rwanda, Sweden, United Republic of Tanzania—and adopted concluding observations on them. It also adopted provisional concluding observations on Grenada in the absence of a report. The Committee adopted views on communications from individuals alleging violations of their rights under the Covenant, and decided that other such communications were inadmissible. Those views and decisions were annexed to the Committee's reports [A/64/40, Vol. II; A/65/40, Vol. II].

The Committee continued work on draft General Comment No. 34 on article 19 of the Covenant (freedoms of opinion and expression), which would replace General Comment No. 10 (1983). At the ninety-fifth session, the Committee adopted a decision on ways to strengthen the procedure for follow-up on concluding observations.

Pursuant to article 4 of the Covenant, Peru, on 15 May, 9 June and 23 November, notified the other States parties, through the intermediary of the Secretary-General, that it had extended or declared a state of emergency in different provinces and parts of the country, during which certain rights covered by the Covenant would be suspended. On 20 May, Guatemala notified the other States parties, through the intermediary of the Secretary-General, of a 6 May declaration of a national public health emergency, which had restricted certain rights contained in the Covenant; the decree was repealed on 12 May.

(For information on the Organization's efforts to protect civil and political rights, see p. 657.)

Covenant on Economic, Social and Cultural Rights and Optional Protocol

Accessions and ratifications

As at 31 December, there were 160 parties to the International Covenant on Economic, Social and Cultural Rights, adopted by the General Assembly in resolution 2200A (XXI) [YUN 1966, p. 419].

The Optional Protocol to the Covenant, adopted by the Assembly in resolution 63/117 [YUN 2008, p. 729], on a procedure of individual communications for alleged violations of economic, social and cultural rights, would enter into force when ratified by 10 parties.

Implementation

Monitoring body. The Committee on Economic, Social and Cultural Rights held its forty-second (4–22 May) and forty-third (2–20 November) sessions in Geneva [E/2010/22]. Its pre-sessional working group met in Geneva from 25 to 29 May and from 23 to 26 November to identify issues to be discussed with reporting States. The Committee examined reports submitted under articles 16 and 17 of the Covenant by Australia, Brazil, Cambodia, Chad, Cyprus, the Democratic Republic of the Congo, Madagascar, Poland, the Republic of Korea and the United Kingdom and adopted concluding observations on them. On 18 May, the Committee adopted General Comment No. 20 on non-discrimination in economic, social and cultural rights. On 13 November, it adopted General Comment No. 21 on the right of everyone to take part in cultural life.

The Economic and Social Council, on 30 July, took note of the Committee's report on its fortieth and forty-first sessions [YUN 2008, p. 729] (**decision 2009/256**).

(For information on the Organization's efforts to protect economic, social and cultural rights, see p. 702.)

GENERAL ASSEMBLY ACTION

On 18 December [meeting 65], the General Assembly, on the recommendation of the Third Committee [A/64/439/Add.1 & Corr.1, as orally amended], adopted **resolution 64/152** by recorded vote (185-0) [agenda item 69 *(a)*].

International Covenants on Human Rights

The General Assembly,

Recalling its resolution 62/147 of 18 December 2007 and Commission on Human Rights resolution 2004/69 of 21 April 2004,

Mindful that the International Covenants on Human Rights constitute the first all-embracing and legally binding international treaties in the field of human rights and, together with the Universal Declaration of Human Rights, form the core of the International Bill of Human Rights,

Recalling the International Covenant on Economic, Social and Cultural Rights and the International Covenant on Civil and Political Rights, and reaffirming that all human rights and fundamental freedoms are universal, indivisible, interdependent and interrelated, that they should be treated in a fair and equal manner, on the same footing and with the same emphasis, and that the promotion and protection of one category of rights should never exempt or excuse States from the promotion and protection of the other rights,

Recalling also the adoption of the Optional Protocol to the International Covenant on Economic, Social and Cultural Rights by the General Assembly on the occasion of the sixtieth anniversary of the Universal Declaration of Human Rights,

Recognizing the important role of the Human Rights Committee and the Committee on Economic, Social and Cultural Rights in examining the progress made by States parties in fulfilling the obligations undertaken in the International Covenants on Human Rights and the Optional Protocols thereto and in providing recommendations to States parties on their implementation,

Considering that the effective functioning of the Human Rights Committee and the Committee on Economic, Social and Cultural Rights is indispensable for the full and effective implementation of the International Covenants on Human Rights,

Recognizing the importance of regional human rights instruments and monitoring mechanisms in complementing the universal system of promotion and protection of human rights,

1. *Reaffirms* the importance of the International Covenants on Human Rights as major components of international efforts to promote universal respect for and observance of human rights and fundamental freedoms;

2. *Strongly appeals* to all States that have not yet done so to become parties to the International Covenant on Economic, Social and Cultural Rights and the International Covenant on Civil and Political Rights, and to consider acceding to the Optional Protocols thereto and making the declarations provided for in article 41 of the International Covenant on Civil and Political Rights and in articles 10 and 11 of the Optional Protocol to the International Covenant on Economic, Social and Cultural Rights, and, while acknowledging that additional States have recently become parties to these instruments, requests the Secretary-General to continue to support the annual treaty event to this end;

3. *Acknowledges* the ceremony of opening for signature of the Optional Protocol to the International Covenant on Economic, Social and Cultural Rights on 24 September 2009 during the 2009 treaty event and the signatures deposited at the event, with a view to its entry into force;

4. *Invites* the United Nations High Commissioner for Human Rights to intensify systematic efforts to encourage States to become parties to the International Covenants on Human Rights with a view to achieving universal adherence and, through the programme of advisory services in the field of human rights, to assist such States, at their request, in ratifying or acceding to the Covenants and to the Optional Protocols thereto;

5. *Calls for* the strictest compliance by States parties with their obligations under the International Covenant on Economic, Social and Cultural Rights and the International Covenant on Civil and Political Rights and, where applicable, the Optional Protocols thereto;

6. *Emphasizes* that States must ensure that any measure to combat terrorism complies with their obligations under relevant international law, including their obligations under the International Covenants on Human Rights;

7. *Stresses* the importance of avoiding the erosion of human rights by derogation, and recalls that certain rights are recognized as non-derogable in any circumstances, underlines the exceptional and temporary nature of any such derogations, and that they must be in accordance with the conditions and procedures stipulated under article 4 of the International Covenant on Civil and Political Rights, bearing in mind the need for States parties to provide the full-

est possible information during states of emergency so that the justification for the appropriateness of measures taken in those circumstances can be assessed, and in this regard takes note of General Comment No. 29 adopted by the Human Rights Committee;

8.   *Encourages* States parties to consider limiting the extent of any reservations that they lodge to the International Covenants on Human Rights and the Optional Protocols thereto, to formulate any reservations as precisely and narrowly as possible and to regularly review such reservations with a view to withdrawing them so as to ensure that no reservation is incompatible with the object and purpose of the relevant treaty;

9.   *Welcomes* the annual reports of the Human Rights Committee submitted to the General Assembly at its sixty-third and sixty-fourth sessions;

10.   *Also welcomes* the reports of the Committee on Economic, Social and Cultural Rights on its thirty-eighth and thirty-ninth sessions and on its fortieth and forty-first sessions, and takes note of General Comment No. 19 on the right to social security adopted by the Committee;

11.   *Expresses regret* at the number of States parties that have failed to fulfil their reporting obligations under the International Covenants on Human Rights, urges States parties to fulfil their reporting obligations on time, invites them to make use of the harmonized guidelines on reporting under the international human rights treaties, including guidelines on a common core document and treaty-specific documents, when submitting reports, and urges States to attend and participate in the consideration of the reports by the Human Rights Committee and the Committee on Economic, Social and Cultural Rights when so requested;

12.   *Urges* States parties to make use in their reports of sex-disaggregated data, and stresses the importance of integrating a gender perspective in the implementation of the International Covenants on Human Rights at the national level, including in the national reports of States parties and in the work of the Human Rights Committee and the Committee on Economic, Social and Cultural Rights;

13.   *Strongly encourages* States parties that have not yet submitted core documents to the Office of the United Nations High Commissioner for Human Rights to do so, invites them to make use of the harmonized guidelines on reporting, and also invites all States parties regularly to review and update their core documents while bearing in mind the current discussion on the elaboration of an expanded core document;

14.   *Urges* States parties to take duly into account, in implementing the provisions of the International Covenants on Human Rights, the recommendations and observations made during the consideration of their reports by the Human Rights Committee and the Committee on Economic, Social and Cultural Rights, and urges States parties to the respective Optional Protocols to take duly into account the views adopted by the Human Rights Committee under the first Optional Protocol to the International Covenant on Civil and Political Rights and the Committee on Economic, Social and Cultural Rights under the Optional Protocol to the International Covenant on Economic, Social and Cultural Rights following its entry into force;

15.   *Takes note with appreciation*, in this regard, of measures taken by both Committees to follow up on their concluding observations;

16.   *Urges* all States to publish the texts of the International Covenants on Human Rights and the Optional Protocols thereto in as many local languages as possible and to distribute them and make them known as widely as possible to all individuals within their territory and subject to their jurisdiction;

17.   *Urges* each State party to give particular attention to the dissemination at the national level of their reports submitted to the Human Rights Committee and the Committee on Economic, Social and Cultural Rights and, further, to translate, publish and make available as widely as possible to all individuals within its territory and subject to its jurisdiction by appropriate means the full text of the recommendations and observations made by the Committees after the examination of those reports;

18.   *Reiterates* that States parties should take into account, in their nomination of members to the Human Rights Committee and the Committee on Economic, Social and Cultural Rights, that the Committees shall be composed of persons of high moral character and recognized competence in the field of human rights, consideration being given to the usefulness of the participation of some persons having legal experience, and to equal representation of women and men, and that members shall serve in their personal capacity, and also reiterates that, in the elections to the Committees, consideration shall be given to equitable geographical distribution of membership and to the representation of the different forms of civilization and of the principal legal systems;

19.   *Invites* the Human Rights Committee and the Committee on Economic, Social and Cultural Rights, when considering the reports of States parties, to continue to identify specific needs that might be addressed by United Nations departments, funds and programmes and the specialized agencies, including through the programme of advisory services and technical cooperation of the Office of the United Nations High Commissioner for Human Rights;

20.   *Stresses* the need for improved coordination among relevant United Nations mechanisms and bodies in supporting States parties, upon their request, in implementing the International Covenants on Human Rights and the Optional Protocols thereto, and encourages continued efforts in this direction;

21.   *Expresses its appreciation* for the efforts made thus far by the Human Rights Committee and the Committee on Economic, Social and Cultural Rights to improve the efficiency of their working methods, encourages the Committees to pursue their efforts, welcomes in this regard the meetings held by the Committees and States parties to exchange ideas on how to render the working methods of the Committees more efficient, and encourages all States parties to continue to contribute to the dialogue with practical and concrete proposals and ideas on ways to improve the effective functioning of the Committees;

22.   *Encourages* the specialized agencies that have not yet done so to submit their reports on the progress made in achieving the observance of the provisions of the International Covenant on Economic, Social and Cultural

Rights, in accordance with article 18 of the Covenant, and expresses its appreciation to those that have done so;

23. *Encourages* the Secretary-General to continue to assist States parties to the International Covenants on Human Rights in the timely preparation of their reports, including by convening seminars or workshops at the national level for the training of government officials engaged in the preparation of such reports and by exploring other possibilities at the request of States, such as the programme of advisory services and technical cooperation in the field of human rights;

24. *Requests* the Secretary-General to ensure that the Office of the United Nations High Commissioner for Human Rights and relevant United Nations entities effectively assist the Human Rights Committee and the Committee on Economic, Social and Cultural Rights in the implementation of their respective mandates by providing, inter alia, adequate Secretariat staff resources and conference and other relevant support services, including translation;

25. *Also requests* the Secretary-General to keep the General Assembly informed of the status of the International Covenants on Human Rights and the Optional Protocols thereto, including all reservations and declarations, through the United Nations websites.

RECORDED VOTE ON RESOLUTION 64/152:

In favour: Afghanistan, Albania, Algeria, Andorra, Angola, Antigua and Barbuda, Argentina, Armenia, Australia, Austria, Azerbaijan, Bahamas, Bahrain, Bangladesh, Barbados, Belarus, Belgium, Belize, Benin, Bhutan, Bolivia, Bosnia and Herzegovina, Botswana, Brazil, Brunei Darussalam, Bulgaria, Burkina Faso, Burundi, Cambodia, Cameroon, Canada, Cape Verde, Chad, Chile, China, Colombia, Comoros, Congo, Costa Rica, Côte d'Ivoire, Croatia, Cuba, Cyprus, Czech Republic, Democratic People's Republic of Korea, Democratic Republic of the Congo, Denmark, Djibouti, Dominica, Dominican Republic, Ecuador, Egypt, El Salvador, Equatorial Guinea, Eritrea, Estonia, Ethiopia, Fiji, Finland, France, Gabon, Georgia, Germany, Ghana, Greece, Grenada, Guatemala, Guinea, Guinea-Bissau, Guyana, Haiti, Honduras, Hungary, Iceland, India, Indonesia, Iran, Iraq, Ireland, Israel, Italy, Jamaica, Japan, Jordan, Kazakhstan, Kenya, Kuwait, Kyrgyzstan, Lao People's Democratic Republic, Latvia, Lebanon, Lesotho, Liberia, Libyan Arab Jamahiriya, Liechtenstein, Lithuania, Luxembourg, Madagascar, Malawi, Malaysia, Maldives, Mali, Malta, Marshall Islands, Mauritania, Mauritius, Mexico, Micronesia, Moldova, Monaco, Mongolia, Montenegro, Morocco, Mozambique, Myanmar, Namibia, Nepal, Netherlands, New Zealand, Nicaragua, Niger, Nigeria, Norway, Oman, Pakistan, Palau, Panama, Papua New Guinea, Paraguay, Peru, Philippines, Poland, Portugal, Qatar, Republic of Korea, Romania, Russian Federation, Rwanda, Saint Kitts and Nevis, Saint Lucia, Saint Vincent and the Grenadines, Samoa, San Marino, Saudi Arabia, Senegal, Serbia, Sierra Leone, Singapore, Slovakia, Slovenia, Solomon Islands, Somalia, South Africa, Spain, Sri Lanka, Sudan, Suriname, Swaziland, Sweden, Switzerland, Syrian Arab Republic, Tajikistan, Thailand, The former Yugoslav Republic of Macedonia, Timor-Leste, Togo, Trinidad and Tobago, Tunisia, Turkey, Turkmenistan, Tuvalu, Uganda, Ukraine, United Arab Emirates, United Kingdom, United Republic of Tanzania, United States, Uruguay, Uzbekistan, Vanuatu, Venezuela, Viet Nam, Yemen, Zambia, Zimbabwe.

Against: None.

Convention on elimination of discrimination against women and Optional Protocol

(For the status of the Convention and Optional Protocol, see p. 1171. For details on activities to protect the rights of women and girls worldwide, in accordance with the provisions of the Convention, see the work of the Special Rapporteur on violence against women, its causes and consequences on p. 733.)

Convention against torture

Accessions and ratifications

As at 31 December, 146 States were parties to the 1984 Convention against Torture and Other Cruel, Inhuman or Degrading Treatment or Punishment, adopted by the General Assembly in resolution 39/46 [YUN 1984, p. 813].

States parties to the Optional Protocol to the Convention establishing an international inspection system for places of detention, which was adopted by the Assembly in resolution 57/199 [YUN 2002, p. 631] and entered into force in 2006 [YUN 2006, p. 776], rose to 50, with Azerbaijan, Cyprus, Montenegro, Nicaragua, Nigeria, Romania, Switzerland and the former Yugoslav Republic of Macedonia becoming parties during the year.

As at 15 May, 56 parties had made the required declarations under articles 21 and 22, which recognized the competence of the Committee against Torture to receive and consider communications by which a State party claimed that another party was not fulfilling its obligations under the Convention, and from or on behalf of individuals who claimed to be victims of a violation of the Convention's provisions by a State party. Four parties had made the declaration under article 21, concerning inter-State communications, bringing the number of declarations under that article to 60, while eight had done so under article 22, concerning individual communications, bringing the total under that article to 64. Amendments to articles 17 and 18, adopted in 1992 [YUN 1992, p. 735], had been accepted by 28 States parties as at year's end.

Implementation

Monitoring body. During the year, the Committee against Torture, established as a monitoring body under the Convention, held its forty-second (27 April–15 May) [A/64/44] and forty-third (2–20 November) [A/65/44] sessions in Geneva. Under article 19 of the Convention, it considered reports submitted by 14 countries—Azerbaijan, Chad, Chile, Colombia, El Salvador, Honduras, Israel, Moldova, New Zealand,

Nicaragua, Philippines, Slovakia, Spain, Yemen—and adopted concluding observations on them.

The Committee continued, in accordance with article 20, to study reliable information that appeared to contain well-founded indications that torture was systematically practised by a State party. The Rapporteur on article 20 encouraged States parties on which enquiries had been conducted to implement the Committee's related recommendations. Under article 22, the Committee considered communications submitted by individuals claiming that their rights under the Convention had been violated by a State party and who had exhausted all available domestic remedies.

On 18 December, the General Assembly took note of the report of the Committee against Torture on its forty-first [YUN 2008, p. 737] and forty-second (see above) sessions (**decision 64/536**).

Subcommittee on Prevention. The Subcommittee on Prevention of Torture and Other Cruel, Inhuman or Degrading Treatment or Punishment (Subcommittee on Prevention), established in 2006 [YUN 2006, p. 776] to carry out the functions laid down in the Optional Protocol adopted by resolution 57/199 [YUN 2002, p. 631], held its seventh (8–14 February) [CAT/C/42/2 & Corr.1], eighth (22–26 June) and ninth (16–20 November) [CAT/C/44/2] sessions in Geneva. The three pillars of the Subcommittee's mandate comprised visits to places of deprivation of liberty; direct contact with national mechanisms for the prevention of torture; and cooperation with UN bodies, international and regional organizations, and national bodies, including NGOs.

In 2009, the Subcommittee visited Paraguay [CAT/OP/PRY/1 & Add.1], Honduras [CAT/OP/HND/1] and Cambodia [CAT/C/44/2, annex III], respectively, focusing on the development of national preventive mechanisms and on the protection of people held in various types of places of deprivation of liberty. After the visits, the Subcommittee presented confidential preliminary observations to the State authorities, both orally and in writing. The authorities were requested to provide feedback and information on steps taken or planned in response to those observations, particularly on issues that could have been addressed in the weeks following the visit. That process was followed by the submission of a confidential visit report to the Governments in question, which included recommendations. The Subcommittee issued its second annual report [CAT/C/42/2 & Corr.1] on its activities from February 2008 to March 2009. Its third annual report [CAT/C/44/2] covered activities from April 2009 to March 2010.

(For the protection of the right not to be subjected to torture and other cruel, inhuman or degrading treatment or punishment, see the work of the Special Rapporteur on the question of torture on p. 692.)

Convention on the Rights of the Child

Accessions and ratifications

As at 31 December, the number of States parties to the 1989 Convention on the Rights of the Child, adopted by the General Assembly in resolution 44/25 [YUN 1989, p. 560], stood at 193. States parties to the Optional Protocol to the Convention on the involvement of children in armed conflict, adopted by Assembly resolution 54/263 [YUN 2000, p. 615], rose to 131, with Algeria, Bhutan, Mauritius, the Netherlands and South Africa becoming parties in 2009. The Optional Protocol on the sale of children, child prostitution and child pornography, also adopted by resolution 54/263, had 135 States parties, with Bhutan, the Congo, Germany, Malawi and the United Kingdom becoming parties in 2009.

The Secretary-General reported on the status of the Convention and its Optional Protocols as at 1 July [A/64/172].

Implementation

Monitoring body. The Committee on the Rights of the Child (CRC) held its fiftieth (12–30 January) [CRC/C/50/3], fifty-first (25 May–12 June) [CRC/C/51/3] and fifty-second (14 September–2 October) [CRC/C/52/3] sessions in Geneva. Each session was preceded by a working group meeting to review State party reports and identify the main questions to be discussed with representatives of the reporting States.

Under article 44 of the Convention, CRC considered initial or periodic reports submitted by Bangladesh, Bolivia, Chad, the Democratic People's Republic of Korea, the Democratic Republic of the Congo, France, Malawi, Mauritania, Moldova, Mozambique, the Netherlands, the Niger, Pakistan, the Philippines, Qatar, Romania and Sweden, and adopted concluding observations on them.

At its fiftieth session, the Committee adopted General Comment No. 11 (2009) on indigenous children and their rights under the Convention [CRC/C/GC/11]. At its fifty-first session, the Committee adopted General Comment No. 12 (2009) on the right of the child to be heard [CRC/C/GC/12].

In lieu of its annual day of general discussion, the Committee, on 8 and 9 October, commemorated the twentieth anniversary of the adoption of the Convention.

The Committee submitted to the General Assembly its biennial report [A/65/41] covering activities from its forty-eighth to its fifty-third sessions.

Human Rights Council action. On 26 March [A/64/53 (res. 10/14)], the Council celebrated the twentieth anniversary of the Convention and called for its implementation by all States parties. The Council requested States parties to ensure that their obligations arising from the Convention were given effect through policy and legislation. It called on States parties to assess any proposed law, administrative guidance, policy or budgetary allocation that was likely to affect children and their rights.

Optional protocol on communications. On 17 June [A/64/53 (res. 11/1)], the Council established an open-ended working group to explore the possibility of elaborating an optional protocol to the Convention to provide a communications procedure complementary to the reporting procedure under the Convention. It requested the working group to report to the Council's thirteenth (2010) session.

At its first session (16–18 December) [A/HRC/13/43], the working group discussed reasons and timing for elaborating a communications procedure; existing international mechanisms and their efficiency in child protection; the nature of the rights of the child and the specific rights emanating from the Convention; and the implications and feasibility of a communications procedure.

(For information on the Organization's efforts to protect the rights of the child, see p. 735.)

GENERAL ASSEMBLY ACTION

On 18 December [meeting 65], the General Assembly, on the recommendation of the Third Committee [A/64/435 & Corr.1], adopted **resolution 64/146** without vote [agenda item 65 *(a)*].

Rights of the child

The General Assembly,

Reaffirming all its previous resolutions on the rights of the child in their entirety, the most recent of which is resolution 63/241 of 24 December 2008,

Emphasizing that the Convention on the Rights of the Child must constitute the standard in the promotion and protection of the rights of the child, and bearing in mind the importance of the Optional Protocols to the Convention, as well as other human rights instruments,

Reaffirming that the general principles of, inter alia, the best interests of the child, non-discrimination, participation and survival and development provide the framework for all actions concerning children, including adolescents,

Reaffirming also the Vienna Declaration and Programme of Action, the United Nations Millennium Declaration and the outcome document of the twenty-seventh special session of the General Assembly on children, entitled "A world fit for children", and recalling the Copenhagen Declaration on Social Development and the Programme of Action, the Dakar Framework for Action adopted at the World Education Forum, the Declaration on Social Progress and Development, the Universal Declaration on the Eradication of Hunger and Malnutrition, the Declaration on the Right to Development and the Declaration of the commemorative high-level plenary meeting devoted to the follow-up to the

outcome of the special session on children, held in New York from 11 to 13 December 2007,

Taking note with appreciation of the reports of the Secretary-General on progress made towards achieving the commitments set out in the outcome document of the twenty-seventh special session of the General Assembly and on the status of the Convention on the Rights of the Child and the issues addressed in Assembly resolution 63/241, as well as the report of the Special Representative of the Secretary-General for Children and Armed Conflict, whose recommendations should be carefully studied, taking fully into account the views of Member States, and taking note of the report of the Secretary-General on children and armed conflict,

Acknowledging the important role played by national governmental structures for children, including, where they exist, ministries and institutions in charge of child, family and youth issues and independent ombudspersons for children or other national institutions for the promotion and protection of the rights of the child,

Taking note with appreciation of the work to promote and protect the rights of the child carried out by all relevant organs, bodies, entities and organizations of the United Nations system, within their respective mandates, and relevant mandate holders and special procedures of the United Nations, as well as relevant regional organizations, where appropriate, and intergovernmental organizations, and recognizing the valuable role of civil society, including non-governmental organizations,

Profoundly concerned that the situation of children in many parts of the world has been negatively impacted by the world financial and economic crisis, and reaffirming that eradicating poverty continues to be the greatest global challenge facing the world today, recognizing its impact beyond the socio-economic context,

Profoundly concerned also that the situation of children in many parts of the world remains critical, in an increasingly globalized environment, as a result of the persistence of poverty, social inequality, inadequate social and economic conditions, pandemics, in particular HIV/AIDS, malaria and tuberculosis, environmental damage, natural disasters, armed conflict, foreign occupation, displacement, violence, terrorism, abuse, trafficking in children and their organs, all forms of exploitation, commercial sexual exploitation of children, child prostitution, child pornography and child sex tourism, neglect, illiteracy, hunger, intolerance, discrimination, racism, xenophobia, gender inequality, disability and inadequate legal protection, and convinced that urgent and effective national and international action is called for,

I

Implementation of the Convention on the Rights of the Child and the Optional Protocols thereto

1. *Commemorates* the twentieth anniversary of the adoption of the Convention on the Rights of the Child and the fiftieth anniversary of the adoption of the Declaration of the Rights of the Child, which provided a foundation for the Convention, and takes this opportunity to call for the effective implementation of the Convention by all States parties to ensure that all children may fully enjoy all their human rights and fundamental freedoms;

2. *Reaffirms* paragraphs 1 to 8 of its resolution 63/241, and urges States that have not yet done so to become parties to the Convention and the Optional Protocols thereto as a matter of priority and to implement them fully;

3. *Calls upon* States parties to withdraw reservations that are incompatible with the object and purpose of the Convention or the Optional Protocols thereto and to consider reviewing regularly other reservations with a view to withdrawing them in accordance with the Vienna Declaration and Programme of Action;

4. *Encourages* States parties, in implementing the provisions of the Convention and the Optional Protocols thereto, to take duly into account the recommendations, observations and general comments of the Committee on the Rights of the Child, including, inter alia, general comment No. 12 (2009) entitled "The right of the child to be heard";

5. *Welcomes* actions of the Committee to monitor the implementation by State parties of the Convention, and notes with appreciation its actions to follow up on its concluding observations and recommendations, and in this regard underlines, in particular, the regional workshops and the participation of the Committee in national-level initiatives;

6. *Recalls* Human Rights Council resolution 10/14 of 26 March 2009 entitled "Implementation of the Convention on the Rights of the Child and the Optional Protocols thereto";

II

Promotion and protection of the rights of the child and non-discrimination against children

Non-discrimination

7. *Reaffirms* paragraphs 9 to 11 of its resolution 63/241, and calls upon States to ensure the enjoyment by children of all their civil, cultural, economic, political and social rights without discrimination of any kind;

Registration, family relations and adoption or other forms of alternative care

8. *Also reaffirms* paragraphs 12 to 16 of its resolution 63/241, and urges all States parties to intensify their efforts to comply with their obligations under the Convention on the Rights of the Child to protect children in matters relating to registration, family relations and adoption or other forms of alternative care, and, in cases of international parental or familial child abduction, encourages States to facilitate, inter alia, the return of the child to the country in which he or she resided immediately before the removal or retention;

9. *Welcomes* the accomplishment of the Guidelines for the Alternative Care of Children and the decision of the Human Rights Council, by its resolution 11/7 of 17 June 2009, to submit them to the General Assembly for action;

Economic and social well-being of children, eradication of poverty, right to education, right to enjoyment of the highest attainable standard of physical and mental health and right to food

10. *Reaffirms* paragraphs 17 to 26 of its resolution 63/241, paragraphs 42 to 52 of its resolution 61/146 of 19 December 2006, on the theme of children and poverty, and paragraphs 37 to 42 of its resolution 60/231 of 23 December 2005, on the theme of children infected with and affected by HIV/AIDS, and calls upon all States and the international community to create an environment in which the well-being of the child is ensured, including by strengthening international cooperation in this field and by implementing their previous commitments relating to poverty eradication, the right to education, the right to the enjoyment of the highest attainable standard of physical and mental health, including efforts to address the situation of children living with or affected by HIV/AIDS and to eliminate mother-to-child transmission of HIV, the right to food for all and the right to an adequate standard of living, including housing and clothing;

11. *Recognizes* the threat to the achievement of the internationally agreed development goals, including the Millennium Development Goals, posed by the global financial and economic crisis, which is connected to multiple, interrelated global crises and challenges, such as the food crisis and continuing food insecurity, volatile energy and commodity prices and climate change, and calls upon States to address, in their response to this crisis, any impact on the full enjoyment of the rights of children;

Elimination of violence against children

12. *Reaffirms* paragraphs 27 to 32 of its resolution 63/241 and paragraphs 47 to 62 of its resolution 62/141 of 18 December 2007, on the theme of elimination of violence against children, condemns all forms of violence against children, and urges all States to implement the measures set out in paragraph 27 of its resolution 63/241;

13. *Welcomes* the appointment of the Special Representative of the Secretary-General on violence against children, and encourages all States, requests United Nations entities and agencies and invites regional organizations and civil society, including non-governmental organizations, to cooperate with the Special Representative and provide support, including financial support, to her for the effective and independent performance of her mandate, as set out in resolution 62/141, and in promoting the further implementation of the recommendations of the United Nations study on violence against children, while promoting and ensuring country ownership and national plans and programmes in this regard, and calls upon States and institutions concerned, and invites the private sector, to provide voluntary contributions for that purpose;

Promoting and protecting the rights of children, including children in particularly difficult situations

14. *Reaffirms* paragraphs 34 to 42 of its resolution 63/241, and calls upon all States to promote and protect all human rights of all children in particularly difficult situations and to implement programmes and measures that provide them with special protection and assistance, including access to health care, education and social services, as well as, where appropriate and feasible, voluntary repatriation, reintegration, family tracing and family reunification, in particular for children who are unaccompanied, and to ensure that the best interests of the child are accorded a primary consideration;

Children alleged to have infringed or recognized as having infringed penal law and children of persons alleged to have infringed or recognized as having infringed penal law

15. *Also reaffirms* paragraphs 43 to 47 of its resolution 63/241, and calls upon all States to respect and protect the rights of children alleged to have infringed or recognized as having infringed penal law, as well as children of persons alleged to have infringed or recognized as having infringed penal law;

Prevention and eradication of the sale of children, child prostitution and child pornography

16. *Further reaffirms* paragraphs 48 to 50 of its resolution 63/241, and calls upon all States to prevent, criminalize, prosecute and punish all forms of sale of children, including for the purposes of transfer of organs of the child for profit, child slavery, commercial sexual exploitation of children, child prostitution and child pornography, with the aim of eradicating those practices and the use of the Internet and other information and communications technologies for these purposes, to combat the existence of a market that encourages such criminal practices and take measures to eliminate the demand that fosters them, as well as to address the needs of victims effectively and take effective measures against the criminalization of children who are victims of exploitation;

17. *Welcomes* the Third World Congress against Sexual Exploitation of Children and Adolescents, held in Rio de Janeiro, Brazil, from 25 to 28 November 2008, and the Rio de Janeiro Declaration and Call for Action to Prevent and Stop Sexual Exploitation of Children and Adolescents;

18. *Calls upon* all States to enact and enforce necessary legislative or other measures, in cooperation with relevant stakeholders, to prevent the distribution over the Internet of child pornography and including depictions of child sexual abuse, ensuring that adequate mechanisms are in place to enable reporting and removal of such material and that its creators, distributors and collectors are prosecuted as appropriate;

Children affected by armed conflict

19. *Reaffirms* paragraphs 51 to 63 of its resolution 63/241, condemns in the strongest terms all violations and abuses committed against children affected by armed conflict, and in this regard urges all States and other parties to armed conflict that are engaged, in contravention of applicable international law, including humanitarian law, in recruitment and use of children, in patterns of killing and maiming of children and/or rape and other sexual violence against children, as well as in all other violations and abuses against children, to take time-bound and effective measures to end them, and urges all States, United Nations agencies, funds and programmes, other relevant international and regional organizations and civil society to continue to give serious attention to, and to protect and assist child victims of, all violations and abuses committed against children in situations of armed conflict, in accordance with international humanitarian law, including the First to Fourth Geneva Conventions;

20. *Also reaffirms* the essential roles of the General Assembly, the Economic and Social Council and the Human Rights Council for the promotion and protection of the rights and welfare of children, including children affected by armed conflict, notes the increasing role played by the Security Council in ensuring protection for children affected by armed conflict, and notes also the activities undertaken by the Peacebuilding Commission, within its mandate, in areas that promote and contribute to the enjoyment of the rights and welfare of children;

21. *Notes with appreciation* the steps taken regarding Security Council resolutions 1539(2004) of 22 April 2004 and 1612(2005) of 26 July 2005, the adoption of Council resolution 1882(2009) on 4 August 2009 and the efforts of the Secretary-General to implement the monitoring and reporting mechanism on children and armed conflict in accordance with those resolutions, with the participation of and in cooperation with national Governments and relevant United Nations and civil society actors, including at the country level, requests the Secretary-General to ensure that information collected and communicated by the monitoring and reporting mechanism is accurate, objective, reliable and verifiable, and in this regard encourages the work and the deployment, as appropriate, of United Nations child protection advisers in peacekeeping operations and political and peacebuilding missions;

Child labour

22. *Reaffirms* paragraphs 64 to 80 of its resolution 63/241, on the theme of child labour, and calls upon all States to translate into concrete action their commitment to the progressive and effective elimination of child labour that is likely to be hazardous or to interfere with the child's education or to be harmful to the child's health or physical, mental, spiritual, moral or social development and to eliminate immediately the worst forms of child labour;

23. *Takes note with appreciation* of the report of the United Nations Educational, Scientific and Cultural Organization entitled "Education for All: Global Monitoring Report 2009", which emphasizes the need to increase the quality of education as a way to attract and keep children in school, as a tool in the prevention and elimination of child labour, and calls upon all States to take fully into account the report of the International Labour Organization entitled "The end of child labour: within reach" and the global action plan endorsed by the Governing Body of the International Labour Office in 2006 in their national efforts to tackle child labour and to monitor progress towards meeting the target of eliminating the worst forms of child labour by 2016;

III

The right of the child to express his or her views freely in all matters affecting him or her

24. *Recognizes* that the child who is capable of forming his or her own views should be assured the right to express those views freely in all matters affecting him or her, the views of the child being given due weight in accordance with his or her age and maturity, referred to in the present resolution as "the right to be heard";

25. *Reaffirms* that the general principle of participation forms part of the framework for the interpretation and implementation of all other rights incorporated in the Convention on the Rights of the Child;

26. *Recognizes* that, in the exercise by the child of his or her right to be heard, States shall respect the responsibilities, rights and duties of parents or, where applicable, the members of the extended family or community, as provided for by local custom, legal guardians or other persons legally responsible for the child to provide, in a manner consistent with the age, maturity and evolving capacities of the child, appropriate direction and guidance;

27. *Reaffirms* the international agreement on the 2015 target date for achieving universal primary education in all countries, emphasizes, recognizing the impact and interlinkage of poverty and education on the full enjoyment by children of the right to be heard and to participate, that literacy and universal access to free and compulsory primary education of good quality for all children are a key element in promoting the right of the child to be heard, and encourages international cooperation in this regard, including regional cooperation as well as South-South cooperation;

28. *Recognizes* that the free engagement of children in extracurricular activities, such as cultural, artistic, recreational, leisure, ecological and sports activities at the local and national levels, could develop the ability of children to express their views;

29. *Also recognizes* the key role that can be played by educational institutions and community-based organizations and projects, as well as by different local and national institutions, such as children's organizations and parliaments, in assuring the meaningful participation of children, and in this regard encourages States to ensure the institutionalization of children's participation and encourage the active consultation of children and the consideration of their views in all matters affecting them, in accordance with their age and maturity and their evolving capacities;

30. *Further recognizes* the role that can be played by the private sector, including the media, in promoting the participation and active consultation of children in issues affecting them, and stresses the importance of these actors taking into account the best interests of the child;

31. *Expresses deep concern* that, despite the recognition of children as rights holders entitled to be heard on all matters affecting them, children are seldom seriously consulted and involved in such matters owing to a variety of constraints and impediments and that the full implementation of this right in many parts of the world has yet to be fully realized;

32. *Recognizes* that the full enjoyment of the right of the child to be heard and to participate requires adults to adopt an appropriate child-centred attitude, listening to children and respecting their rights and individual points of view;

33. *Calls upon* all States:

(a) To assure that children are given the opportunity to be heard on all matters affecting them, without discrimination on any grounds, by adopting and/or continuing to implement regulations and arrangements that provide for and encourage, as appropriate, the participation of children in all settings, including within the family, in school and in their communities, and that are firmly anchored in laws and institutional codes and are regularly evaluated with regard to their effectiveness;

(b) To designate, establish or strengthen relevant governmental structures for children, including, where appropriate, ministers in charge of children's issues and independent ombudspersons for children, have mechanisms in place for allowing and promoting the involvement and participation of children in the formulation and implementation of public policies, in particular those designed to meet national goals and targets for children and adolescents, and ensure adequate and systematic training in the rights of the child for professional groups working with and for children;

(c) To involve children, as appropriate, in the planning, design, implementation and evaluation of the national plans of action set out in the document entitled "A world fit for children" that relate to the rights of the child, in recognition of the role of the child as a core stakeholder in the process;

(d) To develop policies and effective mechanisms at the local and national levels to enable children to be heard and to participate safely and meaningfully in the monitoring and reporting processes related to the implementation of the Convention;

(e) To provide support to children and adolescents to enable them to form and register their own associations and other child- and adolescent-led initiatives, in conformity with national and international law;

(f) To ensure that funding for the participation of children is considered in resource allocation and that policies and programmes to facilitate the participation of children are institutionalized and fully implemented;

(g) To ensure the equal participation of girls, including adolescents, on the basis of non-discrimination and in partnership with boys, including adolescents, in the development of strategies and the implementation of action aimed at achieving gender equality, development, non-violence and peace;

(h) To support the integration, in a systematic manner, of the participation and safe and meaningful involvement of children in United Nations activities and processes that are related to the promotion and protection of the rights of the child;

(i) To support the participation of children in initiatives to prevent and respond to violence against children, including in the work of the Special Representative of the Secretary-General on violence against children;

(j) To take measures to support the participation of children in the design and implementation of preventive and comprehensive anti-bullying policies;

(k) To address all the root causes preventing children from exercising their right to be heard and to be consulted on matters affecting them; inform children, parents, guardians, other caregivers and the general public about the rights of the child; and raise awareness of the importance and benefits of the participation of children in society, including through partnerships with civil society, the private sector and the media, while being attentive to their influence on children;

(l) To take appropriate measures to ensure the full realization of the right to education on the basis of equal opportunity for every child, including by providing accessible, free and compulsory primary education directed to the development of the personality, talents and abilities of the child to their fullest potential, in recognition of the importance of education to civic engagement by children and to their full enjoyment of the right to be heard and to participate in all matters affecting them;

(m) To develop and implement policies and programmes to promote the creation by public authorities, parents, guardians, other caregivers and other adults working with or for children of a safe and enabling environment based on trust, information-sharing, the capacity to listen and sound guidance that is conducive to the informed and voluntary participation of children, including in decision-making processes;

(n) To take all appropriate measures to promote the active involvement of parents, professionals and relevant authorities in the creation of opportunities for children to exercise their right to be heard within their everyday activities in all relevant settings, including by providing training in the necessary skills;

(o) To provide support to girls, including adolescents, if needed, to voice their views and for their views to be given due weight, and adopt measures to eliminate gender stereotypes that undermine and place severe limitations on girls in the enjoyment of their right to be heard;

(p) To ensure that child-sensitive procedures are made available to children and their representatives so that children have access to means of facilitating effective remedies for any breaches of any of their rights arising from the Convention through independent advice, advocacy and complaint procedures, including justice mechanisms, and that their views are heard when they are involved or their interests are concerned in judicial or administrative procedures in a manner consistent with the procedural rules of national law;

(q) To ensure that, when the necessary measures are taken to prevent and punish the wrongful removal of children who are subjected to enforced disappearance, of children whose father, mother or legal guardian is subjected to enforced disappearance or of children born during the captivity of a mother subjected to enforced disappearance, in accordance with legal procedures and applicable international agreements, the right of the child to be heard is respected, and that the best interests of the child are a primary consideration;

(r) To encourage and enable children affected by natural and man-made disasters and complex emergencies, in particular adolescents, to participate in analysing their situations and future prospects in crisis, post-crisis and transition processes, while ensuring that such participation is in accordance with their age, maturity and evolving capacities and is consistent with the best interests of the child and recognizing that appropriate care needs to be taken to protect children from exposure to situations that are likely to be traumatic or harmful;

(s) To take measures to ensure the enjoyment of the right to be heard by children belonging to minorities and/or vulnerable groups, including migrant children and indigenous children within their cultural values or ethnic identities;

(t) To adopt measures, including providing or promoting the use of accessible means, modes and formats of communication, to facilitate the enjoyment of the right to be heard by children with disabilities;

IV
Follow-up

34. *Decides:*

(a) To request the Secretary-General to submit to the General Assembly at its sixty-fifth session a comprehensive report on the rights of the child containing information on the status of the Convention on the Rights of the Child and the issues addressed in the present resolution, with a focus on implementing child rights in early childhood;

(b) To request the Special Representative of the Secretary-General for Children and Armed Conflict to continue to submit reports to the General Assembly and the Human Rights Council on the activities undertaken in the discharge of her mandate, including information on her field visits and on the progress achieved and the challenges remaining on the children and armed conflict agenda;

(c) To request the Special Representative of the Secretary-General on violence against children to submit annual reports to the General Assembly and the Human Rights Council on the activities undertaken in the discharge of her mandate;

(d) To request the Special Rapporteur on the sale of children, child prostitution and child pornography to submit reports to the General Assembly and the Human Rights Council on the activities undertaken in the discharge of her mandate;

(e) To invite the Chair of the Committee on the Rights of the Child to present an oral report on the work of the Committee to the General Assembly at its sixty-fifth session as a way to enhance communication between the Assembly and the Committee;

(f) To invite all Member States, organizations of the United Nations system, non-governmental organizations and individuals to observe the twentieth anniversary of the adoption of the Convention;

(g) To continue its consideration of the question at its sixty-fifth session under the item entitled "Promotion and protection of the rights of children", focusing section III of the resolution on the rights of the child on implementing child rights in early childhood.

Convention on migrant workers

Accessions and ratifications

As at 31 December, the number of States parties to the International Convention on the Protection of the Rights of All Migrant Workers and Members of Their Families, adopted by the General Assembly in resolution 45/158 [YUN 1990, p. 594] and which entered into force in 2003 [YUN 2003, p. 676], had risen to 42, with the Niger and Nigeria acceding in 2009.

Implementation

Monitoring body. The Committee on the Protection of the Rights of All Migrant Workers and Members of Their Families held its tenth (20 April–1 May) [A/64/48] and eleventh (12–16 October) [A/65/48] sessions in Geneva. Under article 74 of the Convention, the Committee considered the reports of Azerbaijan,

Bosnia and Herzegovina, Colombia, the Philippines and Sri Lanka, and adopted concluding observations on them. The Committee noted with concern that many initial reports from States parties under article 73 of the Convention, which required them to report on measures taken to give effect to the provisions of the Convention, had not been received. During its tenth session, the Committee met with representatives of States parties and encouraged them to present their reports without delay.

(Regarding efforts to protect the rights of migrants beyond national borders in accordance with the Convention, see p. 668.)

Convention on rights of persons with disabilities

Accessions and ratifications

As at 31 December, the number of States parties to the Convention on the Rights of Persons with Disabilities, adopted by the General Assembly in resolution 61/106 [YUN 2006, p. 785], stood at 76. During the year, the Convention was ratified or acceded to by Algeria, Azerbaijan, Belgium, Bolivia, Burkina Faso, the Cook Islands, the Czech Republic, Denmark, the Dominican Republic, Germany, Guatemala, Haiti, Iran, Italy, the Lao People's Democratic Republic, Malawi, Mongolia, Montenegro, Morocco, Oman, Portugal, Serbia, Seychelles, the Sudan, Syria, Turkey, the United Kingdom, the United Republic of Tanzania, Uruguay and Yemen. As at 31 December, the number of States parties to the Optional Protocol, which established an individual complaints mechanism, had increased to 48. During the year, the Protocol was ratified or acceded to by Australia, Azerbaijan, Belgium, Bolivia, Burkina Faso, the Cook Islands, the Dominican Republic, Germany, Guatemala, Haiti, Italy, Mongolia, Montenegro, Morocco, Portugal, Serbia, the Sudan, Syria, the United Kingdom, the United Republic of Tanzania and Yemen.

In July, the Secretary-General reported on the status of the Convention and the Optional Protocol [A/64/128 & Corr.1, 2].

Implementation

Monitoring body. The Committee on the Rights of Persons with Disabilities held its first (23–27 February) [CRPD/C/1/2] and second (19–23 October) [CRPD/C/2/2] sessions in Geneva. At its first session, the Committee established working groups to prepare draft rules of procedure, and to draft reporting guidelines and proposals to govern its working methods. At its second session, the Committee decided to adopt the draft reporting guidelines and send the text to States

parties and civil society. It also decided to study the comments and recommendations made during the day of general discussion, particularly the suggestion for formulating and adopting a general comment on article 12, dealing with equal recognition before the law.

Conference of States Parties. The Conference of States Parties to the Convention, at its second session (New York, 2–4 September) [CRPD/CSP/2008/42], discussed legislative measures to implement the Convention.

OHCHR studies. In January, OHCHR submitted a study [A/HRC/10/48] focusing on legal measures required for the ratification and effective implementation of the Convention. The study clarified the national and international steps that States needed to take for ratifying the Convention; identified measures required to give effect to the Convention in the national legal order; reviewed the national monitoring and implementation system envisaged by the Convention; and set out recommendations for ratification and effective implementation.

In December, OHCHR submitted a study [A/HRC/13/29] on the structure and role of national mechanisms for the implementation and monitoring of the Convention, including, to the same end, recommendations for the establishment of frameworks.

Human Rights Council action. On 26 March [A/64/53 (res. 10/7)], the Council invited all stakeholders to consider the OHCHR study on legal measures when establishing national frameworks to implement the Convention; encouraged States to review their legislation and other measures so as to modify or abolish laws, regulations, customs and practices that constituted discrimination against persons with disabilities; and called on States to prohibit and eliminate any form of discrimination on the basis of disability. OHCHR was requested to prepare a study to enhance awareness of the structure and role of national mechanisms for the implementation and monitoring of the Convention.

(For further information on the Organization's activities to promote and protect the rights of persons with disabilities, see p. 1067.)

On 18 December [meeting 65], the General Assembly, on the recommendation of the Third Committee [A/64/439/Add.1 & Corr.1], adopted **resolution 64/154** without vote [agenda item 69 *(a)*].

Convention on the Rights of Persons with Disabilities and the Optional Protocol thereto

The General Assembly,

Recalling its previous relevant resolutions, the most recent of which was resolution 63/192 of 18 December 2008, as well as relevant resolutions of the Human Rights Council, the Commission for Social Development and the Commission on Human Rights,

1. *Welcomes* the fact that, since the opening for signature of the Convention on the Rights of Persons with Disabilities and the Optional Protocol thereto on 30 March 2007, one hundred and forty-three States have signed and seventy-six States have ratified the Convention and eighty-seven States have signed and forty-eight States have ratified the Optional Protocol, and that one regional integration organization has signed the Convention;

2. *Calls upon* those States that have not yet done so to consider signing and ratifying the Convention and the Optional Protocol as a matter of priority;

3. *Welcomes* the holding of the second session of the Conference of States Parties to the Convention, from 2 to 4 September 2009, and the commencement of work of the Committee on the Rights of Persons with Disabilities;

4. *Also welcomes* the report of the Secretary-General and the activities undertaken in support of the Convention;

5. *Encourages* the Inter-Agency Support Group on the Convention to continue its work to mainstream the Convention on the Rights of Persons with Disabilities throughout the United Nations system, and calls upon the Department of Economic and Social Affairs and the Office of the United Nations High Commissioner for Human Rights to continue strengthening their cooperation in this regard;

6. *Invites* the Secretary-General to intensify efforts to assist States to become parties to the Convention and the Optional Protocol, including by providing assistance with a view to achieving universal adherence;

7. *Requests* the Secretary-General to continue the progressive implementation of standards and guidelines for the accessibility of facilities and services of the United Nations system, taking into account relevant provisions of the Convention, in particular when undertaking renovations, including interim arrangements;

8. *Also requests* the Secretary-General to take further actions to promote the rights of persons with disabilities in the United Nations system in accordance with the Convention, including the retention and recruitment of persons with disabilities;

9. *Requests* United Nations agencies and organizations, and invites intergovernmental and non-governmental organizations, to continue to strengthen efforts undertaken to disseminate accessible information on the Convention and the Optional Protocol, including to children and young people to promote their understanding, and to assist States parties in implementing their obligations under those instruments;

10. *Requests* the Secretary-General to submit to the General Assembly at its sixty-sixth session a report on the status of the Convention and the Optional Protocol and the implementation of the present resolution.

On the same day, the General Assembly adopted **resolution 64/131** (see p. 1068) on realizing the Millennium Development Goals for persons with disabilities.

International Convention for protection from enforced disappearance

Accessions and ratifications

As at 31 December, the International Convention for the Protection of All Persons from Enforced Disappearance, adopted by the General Assembly in resolution 61/177 [YUN 2006, p. 800], had 18 States parties. In 2009, Burkina Faso, Chile, Cuba, Ecuador, Germany, Japan, Kazakhstan, Mali, Nigeria, Spain and Uruguay became parties to the Convention, which would enter into force when ratified or acceded to by 20 States.

Pursuant to Assembly resolution 63/186 [YUN 2008, p. 751], the Secretary-General, in July, submitted a report [A/64/171] summarizing information on the implementation of the Convention received from 16 Governments (Argentina, Austria, Costa Rica, Greece, Guatemala, Iraq, Kazakhstan, Lebanon, Madagascar, Monaco, Netherlands, Paraguay, Qatar, Slovenia, Switzerland, Ukraine). The report also included information on the activities of OHCHR and the Working Group on Enforced or Involuntary Disappearances in disseminating information on the Convention and promoting its ratification (see p. 689).

GENERAL ASSEMBLY ACTION

On 18 December [meeting 65], the General Assembly, on the recommendation of the Third Committee [A/64/439/Add.2 (Part II)], adopted **resolution 64/167** without vote [agenda item 69 *(b)*].

International Convention for the Protection of All Persons from Enforced Disappearance

The General Assembly,

Reaffirming its resolution 61/177 of 20 December 2006, by which it adopted and opened for signature, ratification and accession the International Convention for the Protection of All Persons from Enforced Disappearance,

Recalling its resolution 47/133 of 18 December 1992, by which it adopted the Declaration on the Protection of All Persons from Enforced Disappearances as a body of principles for all States,

Recalling also its resolution 63/186 of 18 December 2008, as well as relevant resolutions adopted by the Human Rights Council, including resolution 10/10 of 26 March 2009, in which the Council took note of the report of the Working Group on Enforced or Involuntary Disappearances and the recommendations contained therein,

Deeply concerned, in particular, by the increase in enforced or involuntary disappearances in various regions of the world, including arrest, detention and abduction, when these are part of or amount to enforced disappearances, and by the growing number of reports concerning harassment, ill-treatment and intimidation of witnesses of disappearances or relatives of persons who have disappeared,

Recalling that the Convention sets out the right of victims to know the truth regarding the circumstances of the enforced disappearance, the progress and results of the investigation and the fate of the disappeared person, and sets forth State party obligations to take appropriate measures in this regard,

Acknowledging that acts of enforced disappearance are recognized in the Convention as crimes against humanity, in certain circumstances,

Acknowledging also the valuable work of the International Committee of the Red Cross in promoting compliance with international humanitarian law in this field,

Recognizing that the entry into force of the Convention, as soon as possible, through its ratification by twenty States, and its implementation, will be a significant contribution to ending impunity and to the promotion and protection of all human rights for all,

1. *Welcomes* the adoption of the International Convention for the Protection of All Persons from Enforced Disappearance;

2. *Also welcomes* the fact that eighty-one States have signed the Convention and eighteen have ratified or acceded to it, and calls upon States that have not yet done so to consider signing and ratifying or acceding to the Convention as a matter of priority, as well as to consider the option provided for in articles 31 and 32 of the Convention regarding the Committee on Enforced Disappearances, with a view to its entry into force by December 2009;

3. *Further welcomes* the report of the Secretary-General;

4. *Requests* the Secretary-General and the United Nations High Commissioner for Human Rights to continue with their intensive efforts to assist States to become parties to the Convention, with a view to achieving universal adherence;

5. *Requests* United Nations agencies and organizations, and invites intergovernmental and non-governmental organizations and the Working Group on Enforced or Involuntary Disappearances, to continue undertaking efforts to disseminate information on the Convention, to promote understanding of it, to prepare for its entry into force and to assist States parties in implementing their obligations under this instrument;

6. *Requests* the Secretary-General to submit to the General Assembly at its sixty-fifth session a report on the status of the Convention and the implementation of the present resolution.

Convention on genocide

As at 31 December, 141 States were parties to the 1948 Convention on the Prevention and Punishment of the Crime of Genocide, adopted by the General Assembly in resolution 260 A (III) [YUN 1948–49, p. 959]. Nigeria became a party in 2009.

Genocide prevention

Report of Secretary-General. The Secretary-General, in February, reported [A/HRC/10/30 & Corr.1] on the efforts of the UN system to prevent genocide

and on the activities of his Special Adviser on the Prevention of Genocide, Francis M. Deng. The Secretary-General described a new framework of analysis designed by the office of the Special Adviser to determine whether there was a genocide risk in a given situation. The framework sought to prompt information collection and analysis about the existence and vulnerability of national, ethnic, racial or religious groups; human rights violations committed against such groups; domestic capacity to prevent genocide; the existence of armed opposition; the existence of any political, economic or other motivation encouraging political leaders to stoke divisions between groups; whether elements of the crime of genocide were already occurring; whether there were moments of particular vulnerability approaching; and whether there was a discernible intent to commit to destroy a national, ethnic, racial or religious population group.

The report described the efforts of the office of the Special Adviser, in partnership with legal experts and NGOs, to identify ways in which human rights law provisions could be used as a guide in genocide prevention. It reviewed progress in operationalizing the "responsibility to protect" and described the contributions of UN operational departments and specialized agencies in preventing genocide, including through monitoring and early warning, building peace and restoring justice. It also provided an update on the activities of the Advisory Committee on the prevention of genocide.

The Special Adviser had prepared an inventory of the capacity of the Secretariat and specialized agencies assigned to monitoring, analysis and early warning, including several hundred staff that focused on almost all the criteria relevant to genocide prevention. On the basis of the inventory, the Special Adviser's office had designed an information management system to ensure that its staff could rapidly draw upon the vast information resources available within the United Nations for the specialized monitoring conducted by the office.

The Secretary-General described the response of the Special Adviser to situations of concern, including a recent visit to the Democratic Republic of the Congo, from which he concluded that there was cause for concern regarding the situation in North Kivu, including the risk of genocidal violence, with implications for the entire subregion. The Special Adviser followed up on his conclusions and recommendations from February 2008 on the situation in Kenya, particularly those regarding long-term prevention. He also responded to the situation in Darfur, insisting that any decision by the International Criminal Court regarding the request for indictment of Sudanese President Omar al-Bashir should under no circumstances lead to reprisals exposing civilians to even greater levels of violence, including the risk of genocide.

The Secretary-General concluded that it was only through the mutual efforts of Member States and UN operational departments that the international community could succeed in preventing genocide. He therefore urged a continued and strengthened collaboration to that end.

Report of High Commissioner. Pursuant to Human Rights Council resolution 7/25 [YUN 2008, p. 749], the High Commissioner submitted a March report [A/HRC/10/25] on the prevention of genocide that contained the views of five States (Armenia, Bosnia and Herzegovina, Finland, Russian Federation, Turkey) on two reports of the Secretary-General [YUN 2006, p. 784; YUN 2008, p. 749] on the implementation of the Five-Point Action Plan to Prevent Genocide [YUN 2004, p. 33]. The report also outlined the role of the human rights treaty bodies and the special procedures.

General aspects

Human rights treaty body system

Meeting of chairpersons. In August [A/64/276], the Secretary-General submitted the report on the twenty-first meeting of chairpersons of human rights treaty bodies (Geneva, 2–3 July), which considered follow-up to the recommendations of the twentieth meeting of chairpersons [YUN 2008, p. 723] and reviewed developments related to the work of the treaty bodies. Also discussed was the reform of the treaty body system, including harmonization of working methods and UPR, as well as the work of the Council. Participants met with representatives of States parties and the Council President. The meeting had before it reports on: the implementation of recommendations of the seventh and eighth inter-committee meetings and the twentieth meeting of chairpersons [HRI/MC/2009/2]; working methods of the human rights treaty bodies relating to the State party reporting process [HRI/MC/2009/4]; and reservations by States parties to human rights treaties [HRI/MC/2009/5]. The chairpersons also considered the reports on the eighth (1–3 December 2008) and ninth (29 June–1 July 2009) inter-committee meetings of human rights treaty bodies [A/64/276, Annexes].

The eleventh joint meeting of treaty body chairpersons, special rapporteurs/representatives, independent experts and chairpersons of working groups of the special procedures of the Council took place on 2 July. The chairpersons adopted recommendations on their relationship with special procedures mandate holders, the Human Rights Council, equitable geographical distribution in the membership of the human rights treaty bodies, the report of the independent expert on minorities [A/HRC/10/11/Add.1] and treaty body documentation.

The General Assembly took note of the report on the chairpersons' twenty-first meeting on 18 December (**decision 64/536**).

The tenth inter-committee meeting of human rights treaty bodies (30 November–1 December) [HRI/ICM/2010/CRP.1] focused on the strengthening and harmonization of follow-up procedures.

Meeting of special rapporteurs, independent experts and chairpersons. In July [A/HRC/12/47], the High Commissioner transmitted to the Human Rights Council the report on the sixteenth meeting of special rapporteurs/representatives, independent experts and chairpersons of working groups of the Council's special procedures (Geneva, 29 June–3 July). Mandate holders exchanged views with the High Commissioner, the Council President, the former Council President and members of the Bureau. They held a joint meeting with participants attending the twenty-first meeting of chairpersons of human rights treaty bodies (see above) and held exchanges of views with the Chair of the Committee on the Rights of Persons with Disabilities, the Special Representative of the Secretary-General on violence against children and the Special Adviser to the Secretary-General on the Prevention of Genocide. They met with representatives of NGOs and national human rights institutions. Participants focused on the independence and effectiveness of the special procedures and on harmonization of the working methods of mandate holders. They also discussed their linkages with UPR and thematic issues, such as protection of victims and witnesses and climate change.

Membership of human rights treaty bodies

Report of High Commissioner. As requested by the General Assembly in resolution 63/167 [YUN 2008, p. 724], the High Commissioner, in August, reported [A/64/212] on the equitable geographical distribution in the membership of human rights treaty bodies. She noted that under the terms of the eight human rights treaties with established treaty bodies, the modalities for nominating and electing treaty body members were a matter for the States parties. Regarding the Committee on Economic, Social and Cultural Rights, the nomination of candidates for election was a matter for States parties, whereas election was a matter for the Economic and Social Council, with geographical distribution being subject to Council resolution 1985/17 [YUN 1985, p. 878]. The High Commissioner also recommended that States parties, when nominating and electing members, apply the provisions on the nomination and election of treaty body members contained in the human rights treaties and Economic and Social Council resolution 1985/17.

The General Assembly took note of the report on 18 December (**decision 64/536**).

On 18 December [meeting 65], the General Assembly, on the recommendation of the Third Committee [A/64/439/Add.2 (Part II)], adopted **resolution 64/173** by recorded vote (131-53-2) [agenda item 69 *(b)*].

Promotion of equitable geographical distribution in the membership of the human rights treaty bodies

The General Assembly,

Recalling its previous resolutions on this question,

Reaffirming the importance of the goal of universal ratification of the United Nations human rights instruments,

Welcoming the significant increase in the number of ratifications of United Nations human rights instruments, which has especially contributed to their universality,

Reiterating the importance of the effective functioning of treaty bodies established pursuant to United Nations human rights instruments for the full and effective implementation of those instruments,

Recalling that, with regard to the election of the members of the human rights treaty bodies, the General Assembly as well as the former Commission on Human Rights recognized the importance of giving consideration in their membership to equitable geographical distribution, gender balance and representation of the principal legal systems and of bearing in mind that the members shall be elected and shall serve in their personal capacity, and shall be of high moral character, acknowledged impartiality and recognized competence in the field of human rights,

Reaffirming the significance of national and regional particularities and various historical, cultural and religious backgrounds, as well as of different political, economic and legal systems,

Recognizing that the United Nations pursues multilingualism as a means of promoting, protecting and preserving diversity of languages and cultures globally and that genuine multilingualism promotes unity in diversity and international understanding,

Recalling that the General Assembly as well as the former Commission on Human Rights encouraged States parties to United Nations human rights treaties, individually and through meetings of States parties, to consider how to give better effect, inter alia, to the principle of equitable geographical distribution in the membership of treaty bodies,

Expressing concern at the regional imbalance in the current composition of the membership of some of the human rights treaty bodies,

Noting in particular that the status quo tends to be detrimental to the election of experts from some regional groups, in particular the African, Asian, Latin American and Caribbean and Eastern European groups,

Convinced that the goal of equitable geographical distribution in the membership of human rights treaty bodies is perfectly compatible and can be fully realized and achieved in harmony with the need to ensure gender balance and the representation of the principal legal systems in those bodies and the high moral character, acknowledged impartiality and recognized competence in the field of human rights of their members,

1. *Reiterates* that the States parties to the United Nations human rights instruments should take into account, in their nomination of members to the human rights treaty bodies, that these committees shall be composed of persons of high moral character and recognized competence in the field of human rights, consideration being given to the usefulness of the participation of some persons having legal experience, and to equal representation of women and men, and that members shall serve in their personal capacity, and also reiterates that, in the elections to the human rights treaty bodies, consideration shall be given to equitable geographical distribution of membership and to the representation of the different forms of civilization and of the principal legal systems;

2. *Encourages* the States parties to the United Nations human rights instruments to consider and adopt concrete actions, inter alia, the possible establishment of quota distribution systems by geographical region for the election of the members of the treaty bodies, thereby ensuring the paramount objective of equitable geographical distribution in the membership of those human rights bodies;

3. *Urges* the States parties to the United Nations human rights instruments, including the bureau members, to include this matter in the agenda of each meeting and/or Conference of States Parties to those instruments in order to initiate a debate on ways and means to ensure equitable geographical distribution in the membership of the human rights treaty bodies, based on previous recommendations of the Commission on Human Rights and the Economic and Social Council and the provisions of the present resolution;

4. *Recommends*, when considering the possible establishment of a quota by region for the election of the membership of each treaty body, the introduction of flexible procedures that encompass the following criteria:

    (a) Each of the five regional groups established by the General Assembly must be assigned a quota of the membership of each treaty body in equivalent proportion to the number of States parties to the instrument that it represents;

    (b) There must be provision for periodic revisions that reflect the relative changes in the geographical distribution of States parties;

    (c) Automatic periodic revisions should be envisaged in order to avoid amending the text of the instrument when the quotas are revised;

5. *Stresses* that the process needed to achieve the goal of equitable geographical distribution in the membership of human rights treaty bodies can contribute to raising awareness of the importance of gender balance, the representation of the principal legal systems and the principle that the members of the treaty bodies shall be elected and shall serve in their personal capacity, and shall be of high moral character, acknowledged impartiality and recognized competence in the field of human rights;

6. *Requests* the chairs of the human rights treaty bodies to consider at their next meeting the content of the present resolution and to submit, through the United Nations High Commissioner for Human Rights, specific recommendations for the achievement of the goal of equitable geographical distribution in the membership of the human rights treaty bodies;

7. *Requests* the High Commissioner to submit concrete recommendations on the implementation of the present resolution to the General Assembly at its sixty-sixth session;

8. *Decides* to continue its consideration of the question at its sixty-sixth session under the item entitled "Promotion and protection of human rights".

RECORDED VOTE ON RESOLUTION 64/173:

In favour: Afghanistan, Algeria, Angola, Antigua and Barbuda, Argentina, Azerbaijan, Bahamas, Bahrain, Bangladesh, Barbados, Belarus, Belize, Benin, Bhutan, Bolivia, Botswana, Brazil, Brunei Darussalam, Burkina Faso, Burundi, Cambodia, Cameroon, Cape Verde, Central African Republic, Chad, China, Colombia, Comoros, Congo, Costa Rica, Côte d'Ivoire, Cuba, Democratic People's Republic of Korea, Democratic Republic of the Congo, Djibouti, Dominica, Dominican Republic, Ecuador, Egypt, El Salvador, Equatorial Guinea, Eritrea, Ethiopia, Fiji, Gabon, Ghana, Grenada, Guatemala, Guinea, Guinea-Bissau, Guyana, Haiti, Honduras, India, Indonesia, Iran, Iraq, Jamaica, Jordan, Kazakhstan, Kenya, Kuwait, Kyrgyzstan, Lao People's Democratic Republic, Lebanon, Lesotho, Liberia, Libyan Arab Jamahiriya, Madagascar, Malawi, Malaysia, Maldives, Mali, Marshall Islands, Mauritania, Mauritius, Mexico, Mongolia, Morocco, Mozambique, Myanmar, Namibia, Nepal, Nicaragua, Niger, Nigeria, Oman, Pakistan, Panama, Papua New Guinea, Paraguay, Peru, Philippines, Qatar, Russian Federation, Rwanda, Saint Kitts and Nevis, Saint Lucia, Saint Vincent and the Grenadines, Samoa, Saudi Arabia, Senegal, Sierra Leone, Singapore, Solomon Islands, Somalia, South Africa, Sri Lanka, Sudan, Suriname, Swaziland, Syrian Arab Republic, Tajikistan, Thailand, Togo, Tonga, Trinidad and Tobago, Tunisia, Turkmenistan, Tuvalu, Uganda, United Arab Emirates, United Republic of Tanzania, Uruguay, Uzbekistan, Vanuatu, Venezuela, Viet Nam, Yemen, Zambia, Zimbabwe.

Against: Albania, Andorra, Armenia, Australia, Austria, Belgium, Bosnia and Herzegovina, Bulgaria, Canada, Croatia, Cyprus, Czech Republic, Denmark, Estonia, Finland, France, Georgia, Germany, Greece, Hungary, Iceland, Ireland, Israel, Italy, Japan, Latvia, Liechtenstein, Lithuania, Luxembourg, Malta, Moldova, Monaco, Montenegro, Netherlands, New Zealand, Norway, Palau, Poland, Portugal, Republic of Korea, Romania, San Marino, Serbia, Slovakia, Slovenia, Spain, Sweden, Switzerland, The former Yugoslav Republic of Macedonia, Turkey, Ukraine, United Kingdom, United States.

Abstaining: Chile, Timor-Leste.

Other activities

Strengthening action to promote human rights

International cooperation in the field of human rights

Report of High Commissioner. Pursuant to a request of the Human Rights Council [YUN 2008, p. 759], the High Commissioner submitted a January report [A/HRC/10/26 & Add.1 & Add.1/Corr.1] on the enhancement of international cooperation in the field of human rights, which summarized replies received from Algeria, Greece, Lebanon, Mexico, Spain, Venezuela, the United Nations Population Fund, the National Human Rights Committee of Qatar, the Office of the Salvadorian human rights Ombudsman and an NGO: the Federation of Cuban Women.

Human Rights Council action. On 26 March [A/64/53 (res. 10/6)], the Council took note of the report of the High Commissioner; reaffirmed the importance of international cooperation for the promotion and protection of human rights; called on Member States, specialized agencies and intergovernmental organizations to continue carrying out a constructive dialogue for enhancing understanding and promoting and protecting human rights; and requested the High Commissioner to consult States, intergovernmental organizations and NGOs on ways and means of enhancing cooperation and dialogue within the UN human rights machinery and report to the Council in 2010.

Report of Secretary-General. In compliance with resolution 62/165 [YUN 2007, p. 700], the Secretary-General, in July, submitted a report [A/64/175] summarizing responses from six Member States (Algeria, Brazil, Qatar, Serbia, Syria, Ukraine) on practical proposals and ideas that would strengthen UN action in the field of human rights through the promotion of international cooperation based on the principles of non-selectivity, impartiality and objectivity.

The General Assembly took note of the report on 18 December (**decision 64/536**).

GENERAL ASSEMBLY ACTION

On 18 December [meeting 65], the General Assembly, on the recommendation of the Third Committee [A/64/439/Add.2 (Part II)], adopted **resolution 64/171** without vote [agenda item 69 *(b)*].

Enhancement of international cooperation in the field of human rights

The General Assembly,

Reaffirming its commitment to promoting international cooperation, as set forth in the Charter of the United Nations, in particular Article 1, paragraph 3, as well as relevant provisions of the Vienna Declaration and Programme of Action adopted by the World Conference on Human Rights on 25 June 1993 for enhancing genuine cooperation among Member States in the field of human rights,

Recalling its adoption of the United Nations Millennium Declaration on 8 September 2000 and of its resolution 63/180 of 18 December 2008, Human Rights Council resolution 10/6 of 26 March 2009 and the resolutions of the Commission on Human Rights on the enhancement of international cooperation in the field of human rights,

Recalling also the World Conference against Racism, Racial Discrimination, Xenophobia and Related Intolerance, held at Durban, South Africa, from 31 August to 8 September 2001, and the Durban Review Conference, held at Geneva from 20 to 24 April 2009, and their role in the enhancement of international cooperation in the field of human rights,

Recognizing that the enhancement of international cooperation in the field of human rights is essential for the full achievement of the purposes of the United Nations, including the effective promotion and protection of all human rights,

Recognizing also that the promotion and protection of human rights should be based on the principle of cooperation and genuine dialogue and aimed at strengthening the capacity of Member States to comply with their human rights obligations for the benefit of all human beings,

Reaffirming that dialogue among religions, cultures and civilizations in the field of human rights could contribute greatly to the enhancement of international cooperation in this field,

Emphasizing the need for further progress in the promotion and encouragement of respect for human rights and fundamental freedoms through, inter alia, international cooperation,

Underlining the fact that mutual understanding, dialogue, cooperation, transparency and confidence-building are important elements in all activities for the promotion and protection of human rights,

Recalling the adoption of resolution 2000/22 of 18 August 2000, on the promotion of dialogue on human rights issues, by the Subcommission on the Promotion and Protection of Human Rights at its fifty-second session,

1. *Reaffirms* that it is one of the purposes of the United Nations and the responsibility of all Member States to promote, protect and encourage respect for human rights and fundamental freedoms through, inter alia, international cooperation;

2. *Recognizes* that, in addition to their separate responsibilities to their individual societies, States have a collective responsibility to uphold the principles of human dignity, equality and equity at the global level;

3. *Reaffirms* that dialogue among cultures and civilizations facilitates the promotion of a culture of tolerance and respect for diversity, and welcomes in this regard the holding of conferences and meetings at the national, regional and international levels on dialogue among civilizations;

4. *Urges* all actors on the international scene to build an international order based on inclusion, justice, equality and equity, human dignity, mutual understanding and promotion of and respect for cultural diversity and universal human rights, and to reject all doctrines of exclusion based on racism, racial discrimination, xenophobia and related intolerance;

5. *Reaffirms* the importance of the enhancement of international cooperation for the promotion and protection of human rights and for the achievement of the objectives of the fight against racism, racial discrimination, xenophobia and related intolerance;

6. *Considers* that international cooperation in the field of human rights, in conformity with the purposes and principles set out in the Charter of the United Nations and international law, should make an effective and practical contribution to the urgent task of preventing violations of human rights and fundamental freedoms;

7. *Reaffirms* that the promotion, protection and full realization of all human rights and fundamental freedoms should be guided by the principles of universality, non-selectivity, objectivity and transparency, in a manner consistent with the purposes and principles set out in the Charter;

8. *Calls upon* Member States, the specialized agencies and intergovernmental organizations to continue to carry out a constructive dialogue and consultations for the enhancement of understanding and the promotion and protection of all human rights and fundamental freedoms, and encourages non-governmental organizations to contribute actively to this endeavour;

9. *Invites* States and relevant United Nations human rights mechanisms and procedures to continue to pay attention to the importance of mutual cooperation, understanding and dialogue in ensuring the promotion and protection of all human rights;

10. *Requests* the Secretary-General, in collaboration with the United Nations High Commissioner for Human Rights, to consult States and intergovernmental and non-governmental organizations on ways and means, as well as obstacles and challenges and possible proposals to overcome them, for the enhancement of international cooperation and dialogue in the United Nations human rights machinery, including the Human Rights Council;

11. *Decides* to continue its consideration of the question at its sixty-fifth session.

Also on 18 December [meeting 65], the General Assembly, on the recommendation of the Third Committee [A/64/439/Add.2 (Part II)], adopted **resolution 64/158** without vote [agenda item 69 *(b)*].

Strengthening United Nations action in the field of human rights through the promotion of international cooperation and the importance of non-selectivity, impartiality and objectivity

The General Assembly,

Bearing in mind that among the purposes of the United Nations are those of developing friendly relations among nations based on respect for the principle of equal rights and self-determination of peoples and taking other appropriate measures to strengthen universal peace, as well as achieving international cooperation in solving international problems of an economic, social, cultural or humanitarian character and in promoting and encouraging respect for human rights and fundamental freedoms for all without distinction as to race, sex, language or religion,

Desirous of achieving further progress in international cooperation in promoting and encouraging respect for human rights and fundamental freedoms,

Considering that such international cooperation should be based on the principles embodied in international law, especially the Charter of the United Nations, as well as the Universal Declaration of Human Rights, the International Covenants on Human Rights and other relevant instruments,

Deeply convinced that United Nations action in the field of human rights should be based not only on a profound understanding of the broad range of problems existing in all societies but also on full respect for the political, economic and social realities of each of them, in strict compliance with the purposes and principles of the Charter and for the basic purpose of promoting and encouraging respect for human rights and fundamental freedoms through international cooperation,

Recalling its previous resolutions in this regard,

Reaffirming the importance of ensuring the universality, objectivity and non-selectivity of the consideration of human rights issues, as affirmed in the Vienna Declaration and Programme of Action adopted by the World Conference on Human Rights on 25 June 1993, and the elimination of double standards,

Affirming the importance of the objectivity, independence, impartiality and discretion of the special rapporteurs and representatives on thematic issues and on countries, as well as of the members of the working groups, in carrying out their mandates,

Underlining the obligation that Governments have to promote and protect human rights and to carry out the responsibilities that they have undertaken under international law, especially the Charter, as well as various international instruments in the field of human rights,

1. *Reiterates* that, by virtue of the principle of equal rights and self-determination of peoples enshrined in the Charter of the United Nations, all peoples have the right freely to determine, without external interference, their political status and to pursue their economic, social and cultural development, and that every State has the duty to respect that right within the provisions of the Charter, including respect for territorial integrity;

2. *Reaffirms* that it is a purpose of the United Nations and the task of all Member States, in cooperation with the Organization, to promote and encourage respect for human rights and fundamental freedoms and to remain vigilant with regard to violations of human rights wherever they occur;

3. *Calls upon* all Member States to base their activities for the promotion and protection of human rights, including the development of further international cooperation in this field, on the Charter of the United Nations, the Universal Declaration of Human Rights, the International Covenant on Economic, Social and Cultural Rights, the International Covenant on Civil and Political Rights and other relevant international instruments, and to refrain from activities that are inconsistent with that international framework;

4. *Considers* that international cooperation in this field should make an effective and practical contribution to the urgent task of preventing mass and flagrant violations of human rights and fundamental freedoms for all and to the strengthening of international peace and security;

5. *Reaffirms* that the promotion, protection and full realization of all human rights and fundamental freedoms for all, as a legitimate concern of the world community, should be guided by the principles of non-selectivity, impartiality and objectivity and should not be used for political ends;

6. *Requests* all human rights bodies within the United Nations system, as well as the special rapporteurs and representatives, independent experts and working groups, to take duly into account the contents of the present resolution in carrying out their mandates;

7. *Expresses its conviction* that an unbiased and fair approach to human rights issues contributes to the promotion of international cooperation as well as to the effective promotion, protection and realization of human rights and fundamental freedoms;

8. *Stresses*, in this context, the continuing need for impartial and objective information on the political, economic and social situations and events of all countries;

9. *Invites* Member States to consider adopting, as appropriate, within the framework of their respective legal systems and in accordance with their obligations under international law, especially the Charter, and international human rights instruments, the measures that they may deem appropriate to achieve further progress in international cooperation in promoting and encouraging respect for human rights and fundamental freedoms;

10. *Requests* the Human Rights Council to continue taking duly into account the present resolution and to consider further proposals for the strengthening of United Nations action in the field of human rights through the promotion of international cooperation and the importance of the principles of non-selectivity, impartiality and objectivity, including in the context of the universal periodic review;

11. *Requests* the Secretary-General to invite Member States and intergovernmental and non-governmental organizations to present further practical proposals and ideas that would contribute to the strengthening of United Nations action in the field of human rights through the promotion of international cooperation based on the principles of non-selectivity, impartiality and objectivity, and to submit a comprehensive report on the question to the General Assembly at its sixty-sixth session;

12. *Decides* to consider the matter at its sixty-sixth session under the item entitled "Promotion and protection of human rights".

Advisory services and technical cooperation

Report of Secretary-General. A report of the Secretary-General [A/HRC/13/61] reviewed human rights advisory services and technical cooperation. Activities in Africa were carried out by the OHCHR country offices in Togo and Uganda; by the human rights components of UN peace missions in Côte d'Ivoire, Liberia, Sierra Leone and the Sudan; and by human rights advisers in Guinea, Kenya, the Niger, Rwanda and Somalia. Cooperation was carried out with regional mechanisms, in particular the African Union and the Economic Community of West African States.

In the Middle East and North Africa, OHCHR had a field presence in the Occupied Palestinian Territories; an OHCHR office was established in Mauritania; and in May, the United Nations Human Rights Training and Documentation Centre for South-West Asia and the Arab Region opened in Qatar. In Asia and the Pacific, OHCHR ran the human rights components of UN peace missions in Afghanistan and Timor-Leste and had human rights advisers in Indonesia, Papua New Guinea and Sri Lanka. The OHCHR Regional Office for South-East Asia (Bangkok) assisted the

Association of Southeast Asian Nations (ASEAN) in establishing a human rights body in accordance with the ASEAN Charter.

In Europe and Central Asia, the field presence in Kosovo was supplemented by human rights advisers in Georgia, Moldova and the Russian Federation. In the Russian Federation, OHCHR facilitated the establishment of a human rights master's programme at leading Russian universities and the OHCHR fellowship programme for indigenous people in the Russian language. A Regional Office for Europe opened in Brussels. Activities in the Americas were carried out by the human rights component in the UN peace mission in Haiti, the human rights advisers in Ecuador and Nicaragua, the country offices in Bolivia, Colombia, Guatemala and Mexico, and the regional offices in Chile and Panama.

Voluntary Fund

During the year, the Board of Trustees of the United Nations Voluntary Fund for Technical Cooperation in the Field of Human Rights held its thirtieth (20–23 April) and thirty-first (27–30 October) sessions in Geneva [ibid.]. The Board examined various components of the United Nations Human Rights Programme on Technical Cooperation funded by the Voluntary Fund. The Fund supported the activities of human rights advisers in 14 countries, human rights components in 7 peace missions, and 6 country offices. As at 30 September, the estimated balance of the Fund was $19,800,317; from 1 January 2008 to 30 September 2009, income was $32,882,934 and total expenditure $24,042,581.

Regional arrangements

Human Rights Council action. On 1 October [A/65/53 (res. 12/15)], the Council welcomed the progress made by Governments in establishing regional and subregional arrangements for human rights promotion and protection; welcomed the efforts made by member States of ASEAN, as manifested by the establishment of the ASEAN Intergovernmental Commission on Human Rights; and requested the High Commissioner to convene a workshop on regional arrangements in the first semester of 2010, and to report thereon to the Council's fifteenth (2010) session.

Africa

Report of Secretary-General. In accordance with General Assembly resolution 63/177 [YUN 2008, p. 758], the Secretary-General, in August, reviewed [A/64/333] the work carried out by the Subregional Centre for Human Rights and Democracy in

Central Africa, based in Yaoundé, Cameroon. The report detailed activities carried out from September 2008 to August 2009 in the areas of capacity-building for Governments, technical cooperation and advisory activities, democracy and peace support, public information and dissemination of documentation, as well as the creation of partnerships with Governments, subregional organizations, civil society organizations, UN agencies and diplomatic missions. The Centre had been solicited by many governmental and non-governmental human rights actors. It had given training to State and non-State actors; created networks of experts in the areas of media, transitional justice and indigenous peoples; worked on a joint programme for strengthening democracy with the UN Department of Political Affairs; provided technical expertise to Governments; and supported the capacity of non-governmental entities.

GENERAL ASSEMBLY ACTION

On 18 December [meeting 65], the General Assembly, on the recommendation of the Third Committee [A/64/439/Add.2 (Part II)], adopted **resolution 64/165** without vote [agenda item 69 *(b)*].

Subregional Centre for Human Rights and Democracy in Central Africa

The General Assembly,

Recalling its resolution 55/105 of 4 December 2000 concerning regional arrangements for the promotion and protection of human rights,

Recalling also its resolutions 55/34 B of 20 November 2000 and 55/233 of 23 December 2000, section III of its resolution 55/234 of 23 December 2000, its resolution 56/253 of 24 December 2001 and its resolutions 58/176 of 22 December 2003, 59/183 of 20 December 2004, 60/151 of 16 December 2005, 61/158 of 19 December 2006, 62/221 of 22 December 2007 and 63/177 of 18 December 2008 on the Subregional Centre for Human Rights and Democracy in Central Africa,

Recalling further that the World Conference on Human Rights recommended that more resources be made available for the strengthening of regional arrangements for the promotion and protection of human rights under the programme of technical cooperation in the field of human rights of the Office of the United Nations High Commissioner for Human Rights,

Recalling the report of the High Commissioner,

Taking note of the holding of the twenty-eighth ministerial meeting of the United Nations Standing Advisory Committee on Security Questions in Central Africa, in Libreville from 4 to 8 May 2009,

Taking note also of the report of the Secretary-General,

Welcoming the 2005 World Summit Outcome, in particular the decision confirmed therein to double the regular budget of the Office of the High Commissioner over the next five years,

1. *Welcomes* the activities of the Subregional Centre for Human Rights and Democracy in Central Africa at Yaoundé;

2. *Notes with satisfaction* the support provided for the establishment of the Centre by the host country;

3. *Takes note* of the implementation of the three-year strategy (2007–2009) for the Centre, which aims to reinforce its activities;

4. *Welcomes* the brainstorming session held in Yaoundé on 28 May 2009 between the Centre and the ambassadors of the subregion as well as the main Cameroonian ministries on possible orientations and activities of the Centre for the period 2009–2011, and encourages the Director of the Centre to institutionalize such exchanges in the future;

5. *Notes* the efforts of the Secretary-General and the United Nations High Commissioner for Human Rights to ensure the full implementation of the relevant resolutions of the General Assembly in order to provide sufficient funds and human resources for the missions of the Centre;

6. *Requests* the Secretary-General and the High Commissioner to continue to provide additional funds and human resources within the existing resources of the Office of the High Commissioner to enable the Centre to respond positively and effectively to the growing needs in the promotion and protection of human rights and in developing a culture of democracy and the rule of law in the Central African subregion;

7. *Requests* the Secretary-General to submit to the General Assembly at its sixty-sixth session a report on the implementation of the present resolution.

National institutions

Reports of Secretary-General. In a January report [A/HRC/10/54] on national institutions for the promotion and protection of human rights, the Secretary-General reviewed the 2008 activities of OHCHR in relation to those institutions; measures taken by Governments and other institutions; partnership initiatives of UN agencies and other international and regional organizations; and cooperation between national human rights institutions and international human rights mechanisms. The report highlighted the achievements, challenges and priorities for OHCHR, which ranged from encouraging the establishment of national human rights institutions to supporting their longevity and effectiveness.

The report summarized the role played by OHCHR in facilitating cooperation between national human rights institutions at the regional and international levels, such as by organizing and supporting the ninth International Conference of National Human Rights Institutions (Nairobi, 21–24 October 2008). It also provided information on the work of national human rights institutions in respect of specific issues, including conflict prevention and the prevention of torture, the sixtieth anniversary of the Universal Declaration of Human Rights, the rule of law and the administration of justice, and transitional justice.

A complementary report [A/64/320], issued in August and covering the period from September 2008 to September 2009, further reviewed the activities undertaken by OHCHR to establish and strengthen national human rights institutions; measures taken by Governments and such institutions in that regard; support provided for the international and regional activities of such institutions; technical assistance provided to such institutions, together with other UN agencies and programmes; and cooperation between such institutions and international human rights mechanisms.

A related report of the Secretary-General [A/HRC/10/55], issued in January, reviewed the progress and procedure of the Geneva-based International Coordinating Committee of National Institutions for the Promotion and Protection of Human Rights in accrediting national human rights institutions compliant with the principles relating to the status of national institutions (Paris Principles), as adopted by the General Assembly in 1993 [YUN 1993, p. 900]. An annex to the report listed 64 national institutions that were in compliance with the Paris Principles ("A status"); 3 institutions which were accredited that status with reserve; 13 institutions not fully in compliance or which had provided insufficient information ("B status"); 8 institutions that were non-compliant ("C status"); and 1 institution that had been suspended.

GENERAL ASSEMBLY ACTION

On 18 December [meeting 65], the General Assembly, on the recommendation of the Third Committee [A/64/439/Add.2 (Part II)], adopted **resolution 64/161** without vote [agenda item 69 *(b)*].

National institutions for the promotion and protection of human rights

The General Assembly,

Recalling its previous resolutions, the most recent of which is resolution 63/172 of 18 December 2008, and those of the Commission on Human Rights concerning national institutions and their role in the promotion and protection of human rights,

Welcoming the rapidly growing interest throughout the world in the creation and strengthening of independent, pluralistic national institutions for the promotion and protection of human rights,

Recalling the principles relating to the status of national institutions for the promotion and protection of human rights ("the Paris Principles"),

Reaffirming the important role that such national institutions play and will continue to play in promoting and protecting human rights and fundamental freedoms, in strengthening participation and the rule of law and in developing and enhancing public awareness of those rights and freedoms,

Recognizing the important role of the United Nations, in particular the Office of the United Nations High Commissioner for Human Rights, in assisting the development of independent and effective national human rights institutions, guided by the Paris Principles, and recognizing also in this regard the potential for strengthened and complementary cooperation among the United Nations, the International Coordinating Committee of National Institutions for the Promotion and Protection of Human Rights and those national institutions in the promotion and protection of human rights,

Recalling the Vienna Declaration and Programme of Action adopted by the World Conference on Human Rights on 25 June 1993, which reaffirmed the important and constructive role played by national human rights institutions, in particular in their advisory capacity to the competent authorities and their role in preventing and remedying human rights violations, in disseminating information on human rights and in education in human rights,

Reaffirming that all human rights are universal, indivisible, interrelated, interdependent and mutually reinforcing, and that all human rights must be treated in a fair and equal manner, on the same footing and with the same emphasis,

Bearing in mind the significance of national and regional particularities and various historical, cultural and religious backgrounds, and that all States, regardless of their political, economic and cultural systems, have the duty to promote and protect all human rights and fundamental freedoms,

Recalling the programme of action adopted by national institutions, at their meeting held in Vienna in June 1993 during the World Conference on Human Rights, for the promotion and protection of human rights, in which it was recommended that United Nations activities and programmes should be reinforced to meet the requests for assistance from States wishing to establish or strengthen their national institutions for the promotion and protection of human rights,

Taking note with appreciation of the reports of the Secretary-General to the Human Rights Council on national institutions for the promotion and protection of human rights and on the accreditation process of the International Coordinating Committee,

Welcoming the strengthening in all regions of regional cooperation among national human rights institutions, noting with appreciation the continuing work of the European Group of National Human Rights Institutions, the Network of National Institutions for the Promotion and Protection of Human Rights in the Americas, the Asia-Pacific Forum of National Human Rights Institutions and the Network of African National Human Rights Institutions, and encouraging them to participate in the workshop on regional arrangements for the promotion and protection of human rights to be organized by the Office of the High Commissioner in 2010,

1. *Takes note with appreciation* of the report of the Secretary-General and the conclusions contained therein;

2. *Reaffirms* the importance of the development of effective, independent and pluralistic national institutions for the promotion and protection of human rights, in accordance with the Paris Principles;

3. *Recognizes* the role of independent national institutions for the promotion and protection of human rights in working together with Governments to ensure full respect for human rights at the national level, including by contributing to follow-up actions, as appropriate, to the recommendations resulting from the international human rights mechanisms;

4. *Welcomes* the increasingly important role of national institutions for the promotion and protection of human rights in supporting cooperation between their Governments and the United Nations in the promotion and protection of human rights;

5. *Recognizes* that, in accordance with the Vienna Declaration and Programme of Action, it is the right of each State to choose the framework for national institutions that is best suited to its particular needs at the national level in order to promote human rights in accordance with international human rights standards;

6. *Encourages* Member States to establish effective, independent and pluralistic national institutions or, where they already exist, to strengthen them for the promotion and protection of all human rights and fundamental freedoms for all, as outlined in the Vienna Declaration and Programme of Action;

7. *Welcomes* the growing number of States establishing or considering the establishment of national institutions for the promotion and protection of human rights;

8. *Encourages* national institutions for the promotion and protection of human rights established by Member States to continue to play an active role in preventing and combating all violations of human rights as enumerated in the Vienna Declaration and Programme of Action and relevant international instruments;

9. *Recognizes* the role played by national institutions for the promotion and protection of human rights in the Human Rights Council, including its universal periodic review mechanism, in both preparation and follow-up, and the special procedures, as well as in the human rights treaty bodies, in accordance with Council resolutions 5/1 and 5/2 of 18 June 2007 and Commission on Human Rights resolution 2005/74 of 20 April 2005;

10. *Stresses* the importance of the financial and administrative independence and stability of national human rights institutions for the promotion and protection of human rights, and notes with satisfaction the efforts of those States that have provided their national institutions with more autonomy and independence, including by giving them an investigative role or enhancing such a role, and encourages other Governments to consider taking similar steps;

11. *Urges* the Secretary-General to continue to give high priority to requests from Member States for assistance in the establishment and strengthening of national human rights institutions;

12. *Underlines* the importance of the autonomy and independence of Ombudsman institutions, encourages increased cooperation between national human rights institutions and regional and international associations of Ombudsmen, also encourages Ombudsman institutions to actively draw on the standards enumerated in international instruments and the Paris Principles to strengthen their independence and increase their capacity to act as national human rights protection mechanisms, and in this

regard reaffirms General Assembly resolution 63/169 of 18 December 2008 on the role of Ombudsman institutions;

13. *Commends* the high priority given by the Office of the United Nations High Commissioner for Human Rights to work on national human rights institutions, encourages the High Commissioner, in view of the expanded activities relating to national institutions, to ensure that appropriate arrangements are made and budgetary resources provided to continue and further extend activities in support of national institutions, and invites Governments to contribute additional voluntary funds to that end;

14. *Requests* the Secretary-General to continue to provide the necessary assistance for holding international and regional meetings of national institutions, including meetings of the International Coordinating Committee of National Institutions for the Promotion and Protection of Human Rights, in cooperation with the Office of the High Commissioner;

15. *Encourages* national institutions, including Ombudsman institutions, to seek accreditation status through the International Coordinating Committee;

16. *Encourages* all Member States to take appropriate steps to promote the exchange of information and experience concerning the establishment and effective operation of national institutions;

17. *Encourages* all United Nations human rights mechanisms as well as agencies, funds and programmes to work within their respective mandates with Member States and national institutions in the promotion and protection of human rights with respect to, inter alia, projects in the area of good governance and the rule of law, and in this regard welcomes the efforts made by the High Commissioner to develop partnerships in support of national institutions;

18. *Requests* the Secretary-General to report to the General Assembly at its sixty-sixth session on the implementation of the present resolution.

Human rights education

Declaration on human rights education and training

At its second session (Geneva, 26–30 January), the Human Rights Council Advisory Committee submitted to the Council a progress report on its drafting group on human rights and training [A/HRC/AC/2/2 (rec. 2/1)]. The report was issued in response to the Council's request [YUN 2007, p. 697] that the Advisory Committee prepare a draft declaration on human rights education and training, including by seeking the views of relevant stakeholders.

Human Rights Council action. On 27 March [A/64/53 (res. 10/28)], the Council urged all stakeholders to respond to the questionnaire prepared by the Advisory Committee on the draft declaration; welcomed the initiative of the Platform for Human Rights Education and Training to organize a seminar to further the reflection on the draft declaration; and requested the Advisory Committee to submit the draft declaration to the Council's thirteenth (2010) session.

On 1 October [A/65/53 (dec. 12/118)], the Council welcomed the various initiatives aimed at furthering the discussions on the draft declaration, in particular the holding of a seminar in Marrakech, Morocco, on 16 and 17 July, and decided to hold a high-level discussion on the draft during its thirteenth session.

World Programme for Human Rights Education

Human Rights Council action. On 25 March [A/64/53 (res. 10/3)], the Council requested that the High Commissioner for Human Rights consult with States, national human rights institutions, intergovernmental organizations and NGOs on the possible focus of the second phase of the World Programme for Human Rights Education [YUN 2004, p. 678], to begin on 1 January 2010, and to report on those consultations to the Council's twelfth (2009) session. The Council also encouraged Member States to prepare national evaluation reports on the first phase (2005–2007) [YUN 2005, p. 745], to be provided to the United Nations Inter-Agency Coordinating Committee on Human Rights Education in the School System (UNIACC) early in 2010.

Report of High Commissioner. As requested by the Council, the High Commissioner, in August, reported [A/HRC/12/36] on the contributions received from 17 Governments, 15 national human rights institutions, 8 international organizations and 16 NGOs on the possible focus of the second phase of the World Programme. The responses contained a wide variety of approaches. Several respondents highlighted that the focus on human rights education in primary and secondary schools should continue, as the aims of the first phase had not been achieved. A considerable number of respondents expressed the need to focus on human rights training for teachers and educators where not enough had been achieved. A number of respondents cited tertiary or university education as the next proposed target area, while several pointed to the need for human rights training of civil servants, including law enforcement officials, government officials, parliamentarians, military officers and health workers. The thematic areas mentioned most frequently were the role of human rights education in tackling poverty and the importance of focusing on non-discrimination and equality. Most respondents proposed a period of five years for the second phase.

Human Rights Council action. On 1 October [A/65/53 (res. 12/4)], the Council decided to focus the second phase of the World Programme (2010–2014) on human rights education for higher education and on human rights training programmes for teachers and educators, civil servants, law enforcement officials and military personnel at all levels. It requested

OHCHR to submit to the Council's fifteenth (2010) session a plan of action for the second phase, and requested UNIACC to submit a final evaluation report on the implementation of the first phase, based on national evaluation reports and in cooperation with international, regional and non-governmental organizations, to the General Assembly's sixty-fifth (2010) session.

International Year of Human Rights Learning

Report of Secretary-General. In response to General Assembly resolutions 62/171 [YUN 2007, p. 697] and 63/173 [YUN 2008, p. 752], the Secretary-General submitted an August report [A/64/293] on the implementation of the International Year of Human Rights Learning, which commenced on 10 December 2008 with the goal of broadening and deepening human rights learning. The report reviewed a range of national and international efforts. Information from 18 Member States indicated that interest in human rights education and learning had grown among Government bodies, local authorities, teaching personnel, civil society and international entities. Synergies created by the complementarity between the International Year and the World Programme for Human Rights Education had resulted in new strategies for incorporating human rights into education and learning, greater regional cooperation, more extensive in-service training of civil servants, strengthened teacher training, and more programmes and projects involving schools, civil society and the general public.

GENERAL ASSEMBLY ACTION

On 10 December [meeting 61], the General Assembly, on the recommendation of the Third Committee [A/64/439/Add.2 (Part I)], adopted **resolution 64/82** without vote [agenda item 69 *(b)*].

Follow-up to the International Year of Human Rights Learning

The General Assembly,

Recalling that the purposes and principles contained in the Charter of the United Nations include promoting and encouraging respect for human rights and fundamental freedoms for all,

Recalling also its resolution 60/251 of 15 March 2006, in which it decided that the Human Rights Council should, inter alia, promote human rights education and learning as well as advisory services, technical assistance and capacity-building,

Recalling further the 2005 World Summit Outcome, in which Heads of State and Government expressed their support for the promotion of human rights education and learning at all levels, including through the implementation of the World Programme for Human Rights Education, as

appropriate, and encouraged all States to develop initiatives in that regard,

Recalling its resolutions 62/171 of 18 December 2007 and 63/173 of 18 December 2008 on the International Year of Human Rights Learning,

Welcoming resolution 12/4 adopted by the Human Rights Council on 1 October 2009, in which the Council decided on the focus of the second phase of the World Programme for Human Rights Education, and stressing the complementarity between human rights learning and human rights education,

Acknowledging that civil society, academia, the private sector, the media and, where appropriate, parliamentarians can play an important role at the national, regional and international levels in the development and facilitation of ways and means to promote and implement learning about human rights as a way of life at the community level,

Convinced that integrating human rights learning into all relevant development policies and programmes contributes to enabling people to participate as equals in the decisions that determine their lives,

Having considered the report of the Secretary-General,

1. *Reaffirms its conviction* that every woman, man, youth and child can realize his or her full human potential by learning about the comprehensive framework of human rights and fundamental freedoms, including the ability to act on that knowledge in order to ensure the effective realization of human rights and fundamental freedoms for all;

2. *Encourages* Member States to expand on efforts made during the International Year of Human Rights Learning and to consider devoting the financial and human resources necessary to design and implement international, regional, national and local long-term human rights learning programmes of action aimed at broad-based and sustained human rights learning at all levels, in coordination with civil society, the media, the private sector, academia, parliamentarians and regional organizations, including the appropriate specialized agencies, funds and programmes of the United Nations system, and, where possible, to designate human rights cities;

3. *Calls upon* the United Nations High Commissioner for Human Rights and the Human Rights Council to support, cooperate and collaborate closely with civil society, the private sector, academia, regional organizations, the media and other relevant stakeholders, as well as with organizations, programmes and funds of the United Nations system, in efforts to develop, in particular, the design of strategies and international, regional, national and local programmes of action aimed at broad-based and sustained human rights learning at all levels;

4. *Recommends* that the Human Rights Council integrate human rights learning into the preparation of the draft United Nations declaration on human rights education and training, bearing in mind the complementarity of this initiative with the World Programme for Human Rights Education and human rights learning;

5. *Encourages* civil society organizations worldwide, in particular those working at the community level, to integrate human rights learning into dialogue and consciousness-raising programmes with groups working on education, development, poverty eradication, participation, children, indigenous peoples, gender equality, persons with

disabilities, elder persons and migrants, as well as on other relevant political, civil, economic, social and cultural issues of concern;

6. *Encourages* relevant actors in civil society, including sociologists, anthropologists, members of academia and of the media and community leaders, to develop the concept of human rights learning as a way to promote the full realization of all human rights and fundamental freedoms for all;

7. *Invites* relevant treaty bodies to take human rights learning into account in their interaction with States parties;

8. *Requests* the Secretary-General to submit to the General Assembly at its sixty-sixth session a report on the implementation of the present resolution.

International Year for People of African Descent

The General Assembly, on 18 December, proclaimed 2011 the International Year for People of African Descent, in order to strengthen national actions and international cooperation for the benefit of people of African descent, to advance their participation in society, and to promote knowledge of and respect for their heritage and culture.

GENERAL ASSEMBLY ACTION

On 18 December [meeting 65], the General Assembly, on the recommendation of the Third Committee [A/64/439/Add.2 (Part II)], adopted **resolution 64/169** without vote [agenda item 69 *(b)*].

International Year for People of African Descent

The General Assembly,

Reaffirming the Universal Declaration of Human Rights, which proclaims that all human beings are born free and equal in dignity and rights and that everyone is entitled to all the rights and freedoms set forth therein, without distinction of any kind,

Recalling the International Covenant on Civil and Political Rights, the International Covenant on Economic, Social and Cultural Rights, the International Convention on the Elimination of All Forms of Racial Discrimination, the Convention on the Elimination of All Forms of Discrimination against Women, the Convention on the Rights of the Child, the International Convention on the Protection of the Rights of All Migrant Workers and Members of Their Families, the Convention on the Rights of Persons with Disabilities and other relevant international human rights instruments,

Recalling also the relevant provisions of the outcomes of all major United Nations conferences and summits, in particular the Vienna Declaration and Programme of Action and the Durban Declaration and Programme of Action,

Recalling further its resolutions 62/122 of 17 December 2007, 63/5 of 20 October 2008 and 64/15 of 16 November 2009 on the permanent memorial to and remembrance of the victims of slavery and the transatlantic slave trade,

1. *Proclaims* the year beginning on 1 January 2011 the International Year for People of African Descent, with a view to strengthening national actions and regional and international cooperation for the benefit of people of African descent in relation to their full enjoyment of economic, cultural, social, civil and political rights, their participation and integration in all political, economic, social and cultural aspects of society, and the promotion of a greater knowledge of and respect for their diverse heritage and culture;

2. *Encourages* Member States, the specialized agencies of the United Nations system, within their respective mandates and existing resources, and civil society to make preparations for and identify possible initiatives that can contribute to the success of the Year;

3. *Requests* the Secretary-General to submit to the General Assembly at its sixty-fifth session a report containing a draft programme of activities for the Year, taking into account the views and recommendations of Member States, the United Nations High Commissioner for Human Rights, the Committee on the Elimination of Racial Discrimination, the Working Group of Experts on People of African Descent of the Human Rights Council and other relevant United Nations agencies, funds and programmes, as appropriate.

Follow-up to 1993 World Conference

Report of Third Committee. The Third Committee of the General Assembly reported [A/64/439/Add.4] on the implementation of and follow-up to the Vienna Declaration and Programme of Action, adopted at the 1993 World Conference on Human Rights [YUN 1993, p. 908]. It noted that on 18 September, the Assembly, on the recommendation of the General Committee, decided to include in the agenda of its sixty-fourth session, under the item entitled "Promotion and protection of human rights", the sub-item entitled "Comprehensive implementation of and follow-up to the Vienna Declaration and Programme of Action" and to allocate it to the Third Committee. The Third Committee considered the sub-item on 20 October and 24 November [A/C.3/64/SR.21 & 47]. No proposals were submitted under that sub-item.

The General Assembly took note of the report of the Third Committee on 18 December (**decision 64/537**).

Chapter II

Protection of human rights

Human rights protection was advanced in 2009 by the adoption by 182 States of the outcome document of the anti-racism Durban Review Conference, held in Geneva from 20 to 24 April. Participating States emphasized the need to address with greater resolve all manifestations of racism and related intolerance; called on States to take effective measures to prevent, combat and eradicate all forms of racism; and urged them to create and implement national plans to combat racism and intolerance. The Review Conference assessed progress made since the World Conference against Racism, Racial Discrimination, Xenophobia and Related Intolerance held in Durban, South Africa, in 2001.

Central to human rights protection were the special procedures of the Human Rights Council—independent experts with mandates to investigate, report and advise on human rights from a thematic or country-specific perspective. At the end of 2009, there were 39 special procedures (31 thematic mandates and 8 mandates relating to countries or territories) with 55 mandate holders. Those special rapporteurs, independent experts, working groups and representatives of the Secretary-General served in their personal capacity, were not UN staff members and did not receive financial remuneration.

In 2009, special procedures sent 689 communications to 119 countries, covering 1,840 individuals. Governments replied to 32 per cent of communications sent between 1 January and 31 December. The number of fact-finding missions increased significantly, from 53 missions to 48 countries in 2008 to 73 missions to 51 countries and territories in 2009. Special procedures mandates submitted 136 reports to the Human Rights Council and 24 reports to the General Assembly. Reports included 47 annual reports of the mandate-holders and 51 mission reports. Special procedures also issued 223 press releases and public statements on situations of concern.

The Council in March established a new special procedure—the independent expert in the field of cultural rights. In May, the Secretary-General appointed a Special Representative on violence against children.

Human rights were also protected through the network of human rights defenders in individual countries, operating within the framework of the 1998 Declaration on Human Rights Defenders.

Economic, social and cultural rights continued to be a major focus of activity. The Council in February held its tenth special session, addressing the impact of the global economic and financial crises on the effective enjoyment of human rights. Highlighting the threat posed by the crises to human rights, the Council stressed the need to broaden the participation of developing countries in decisions regarding the global economy. The General Assembly in December welcomed the completion of the Guidelines for the Alternative Care of Children, designed to improve the protection of children deprived of parental care.

Special procedures

Report of High Commissioner. In her annual report to the Human Rights Council [A/HRC/13/26], the UN High Commissioner for Human Rights noted that the work undertaken by the special procedures—their dialogue with States, monitoring, public reporting, country visits, outreach, accessibility and direct interventions, including through the hundreds of communications they sent each year—was critical to the promotion and protection of human rights worldwide. A hallmark of special procedures mandate holders was their direct access to victims and witnesses, and their capacity to work closely with human rights defenders. During 2009, there had been several incidents, including killings of persons who had engaged with special procedures mandate holders. The comprehensive system of special rapporteurs, representatives, independent experts and working groups covered all sets of rights and several country situations. In all there were 39 mandates—31 thematic, including the new mandate in the field of cultural rights, and 8 country mandates—with 55 mandate holders. The special procedures provided early warning and drew international attention to emerging issues and global crises.

Report of Secretary-General. In response to a Human Rights Council request [YUN 2006, p. 760], the Secretary-General in March submitted a report [A/HRC/10/39] listing special procedures' conclusions and recommendations, contained in their reports to the Council's eighth, ninth and tenth sessions.

Human Rights Council action. On 18 June [A/64/53 (res. 11/11)], the Council reaffirmed that the code of conduct for special procedures mandate holders [YUN 2007, p. 666] was aimed at strengthening the capacity of mandate holders to exercise their functions while enhancing their moral authority and credibility, and that it required support by States. The Council recalled that it was incumbent on mandate holders to exercise their functions with strict observance of their mandates and to comply with the provisions of the code of conduct.

Civil and political rights

Racism and racial discrimination

Durban Review Conference

The Durban Review Conference (Geneva, 20–24 April) [A/CONF.211/8] evaluated progress towards the goals set by the 2001 World Conference against Racism, Racial Discrimination, Xenophobia and Related Intolerance [YUN 2001, p. 615]. The event was attended by 151 countries. Australia, Canada, Germany, Israel, Italy, the Netherlands, New Zealand, Poland and the United States did not attend, citing concerns that the Conference would be used to promote anti-Semitism as well as laws against defamation of religion perceived as contrary to freedom of expression.

The Secretary-General and United Nations High Commissioner for Human Rights Navanethem Pillay—the Secretary-General of the Conference—addressed the opening meeting on 20 April [A/CONF.211/SR.1]. They deplored the speech of Iranian President Mahmoud Ahmadinejad [A/CONF.211/SR.2] at the high-level segment and his use of the platform "to accuse, divide and even incite" [SG/SM/12193]. The Prime Minister of Namibia and several Ministers for Foreign Affairs and Justice also addressed the Conference.

The Conference unanimously adopted an outcome document which emphasized the need to address with greater resolve and political will all forms and manifestations of racism, racial discrimination, xenophobia and related intolerance. The document called on States to take effective, tangible and comprehensive measures to prevent, combat and eradicate all forms and manifestations of racism and related phenomena.

The five sections of the outcome document addressed: review of progress and assessment of implementation of the Durban Declaration and Programme of Action (DDPA), adopted at the 2001 World Conference; assessment of the effectiveness of the Durban follow-up mechanisms and other UN mechanisms; promotion of the universal ratification and implementation of the International Convention on the Elimination of All Forms of Racial Discrimination [YUN 1965, p. 440]; identification and sharing of best

practices; and identification of concrete measures and initiatives for combating and eliminating manifestations of racism and related phenomena.

The outcome document acknowledged the need to enhance the effectiveness of the mechanisms dealing with or addressing racism and related phenomena, with a view to achieving better synergy, coordination, coherence and complementarity in their work; renewed its call to States that had not done so to consider ratifying or acceding to the International Convention; urged States to punish violent, racist and xenophobic activities by groups that were based on neo-Nazi, neo-Fascist and other violent national ideologies; and urged States that had not developed or implemented national action plans to combat racism and related phenomena to elaborate such plans and monitor their implementation, in consultation with national human rights institutions and civil society.

Preparatory Committee. The Preparatory Committee for the Conference, at its third substantive session (Geneva, 15–17 April) [A/CONF.211/PC.4/10], decided to submit the revised text of the draft outcome document, annexed to the report, for consideration and adoption by the Review Conference; it agreed to accredit 81 non-governmental organizations (NGOs) to participate in the Conference.

Communication. On 27 April [A/HRC/11/G/2], Iran conveyed its official position with regard to the outcome document of the Durban Review Conference.

General Assembly action. Endorsing the outcome document of the Review Conference on 18 December (**decision 64/534**), the General Assembly decided to implement the outcome of the Conference as part of the wider implementation of DDPA.

Follow-up to 2001 World Conference

Intergovernmental Working Group. At its seventh session (Geneva, 5–16 October) [A/HRC/13/60], the Intergovernmental Working Group on the Effective Implementation of the Durban Declaration and Programme of Action, established in 2002 [YUN 2002, p. 661] to make recommendations for the effective implementation of DDPA and to prepare complementary standards, discussed issues pertaining to its effectiveness and to the implementation of its previous decisions. Presentations by experts on the issues of migration, protection of children and employment were followed by interactive discussions. The Working Group adopted conclusions and recommendations on those issues.

Human Rights Council action. On 18 June [A/64/53 (res. 11/12)], the Council extend the mandate of the Working Group for a three-year period.

Working Group on people of African descent.
At its seventh session (Geneva, 12–16 January)
[A/HRC/10/66], the Working Group of Experts on
People of African Descent, established in 2002 [YUN
2002, p. 661] to consider problems of racial discrimination affecting people of African descent, in accordance with DDPA, reviewed the themes it had discussed at previous sessions and identified new ones
with a view to developing its workplan for 2009–
2011. It examined its country visits and its continued
engagement with the Durban Review process, and
held a thematic discussion on the situation of children of African descent.

Following its mission to Ecuador (22–26 June)
[A/HRC/13/59], the Group issued recommendations
aimed at improving the situation of people of African
descent in that country. Those included the adoption
of legislation on non-discrimination; the development
of a national campaign to promote multiculturalism
and respect for the dignity of the Afro-Ecuadorian
people; the adoption of measures to reduce the educational gap between Afro-Ecuadorians and the
wider population; measures to eliminate racism and
discrimination in the media; efforts to encourage
participation of persons of African descent in public administration; the development of free legal aid
services; the creation within the office of the Ombudsman of a sub-unit dedicated to issues related to
Afro-Ecuadorians; and the creation of programmes to
promote the education of women of African descent.

Human Rights Council action. On 27 March
[A/64/53 (res. 10/31)], the Council welcomed the report
of the Intergovernmental Working Group on the
implementation of DDPA; took note of the report of
the Working Group of Experts on People of African
Descent and welcomed its workplan for 2009–2011.

Report of High Commissioner. In February
[A/CONF.211/PC.4/5], the High Commissioner addressed challenges to the fight against racism and assessed the strengths and shortcomings of the Office of
the High Commissioner for Human Rights (OHCHR)
anti-discrimination programme, as well as the Durban
follow-up intergovernmental and expert mechanisms.
She put forward proposals to help States overcome
differences in curtailing freedom of speech in order
to protect individuals and groups from hate speech,
and provided a vision to take forward the struggle
against racism, discrimination and intolerance. The
High Commissioner observed that while some progress had been made since the adoption of DDPA,
new challenges to the principles of equality and non-
discrimination had appeared. Those included the convergence of the global food crisis and the economic
and financial crisis and their disproportionate impact
on the most vulnerable; the intensification of hate
speech against racial, ethnic and religious minorities;

extreme xenophobic reactions against migrants; the
political exploitation of real and perceived differences;
and some counter-terrorism measures.

Report of Secretary-General. In response to
General Assembly resolution 63/242 [YUN 2008,
p. 764], the Secretary-General in August reported
[A/64/309] on global efforts for the total elimination of
racism, racial discrimination, xenophobia and related
intolerance and the comprehensive implementation of
and follow-up to DDPA. The report summarized contributions on the topic received from nine countries,
three UN bodies, two regional and intergovernmental
organizations, four national human rights institutions
and three NGOs. It reviewed activities undertaken by
UN bodies since the submission of the last report
[ibid., p. 762], and concluded that DDPA had provided
a platform for developing programmes, activities and
institutions to combat racism and related phenomena.
National efforts to realize constitutional guarantees of
equality and prohibition of discrimination had been
complemented by the harmonization of laws and
institutional developments at the regional level.

The General Assembly took note of that report on
18 December (**decision 64/535**).

Contemporary forms of racism

Reports of Special Rapporteur. Pursuant to a
Human Rights Council request [YUN 2008, p. 770], the
Special Rapporteur on contemporary forms of racism,
racial discrimination, xenophobia and related intolerance, Githu Muigai (Kenya), in a report issued in May
[A/HRC/11/36], addressed the issue of poverty and
racism—a fundamental challenge in the fight against
racism. A central dimension of the fight against racism was the overlap between two key social indicators: class and race or ethnicity. For many reasons,
including the lack of ethnically disaggregated data,
the links between race and poverty had yet to be fully
elucidated. There were no instruments for that type
of data collection worldwide, which would allow for
cross-regional comparison of the levels of poverty in
minorities. However, national data for many countries
showed that racial or ethnic minorities were disproportionately affected by poverty. The socio-economic
vulnerability of minorities was frequently the result of
historical legacies, such as slavery across the American
continent, systems of inherited status in other continents, and systems of formalized and State-sponsored
discrimination against minorities that were long in
place in many parts of the world. Because of the inaction of Governments, historically created imbalances
continued to profoundly affect minority groups long
after formal discrimination was dismantled. Concrete
measures were needed to address the disproportionate
levels of poverty affecting minorities.

An addendum [A/HRC/11/36/Add.1 & Corr.1] summarized communications sent to Governments in 2008, replies received from Governments until 15 May 2009, and observations of the Rapporteur.

As requested by the Human Rights Council (see below) the Rapporteur in July reported [A/HRC/12/38] on the manifestations of defamation of religions, and in particular on the serious implications of Islamophobia, on the enjoyment of all rights by their followers. The report took stock of the debate on the issue of "defamation of religions" and incitement to religious hatred. It distinguished between intolerant mentalities, incitement to religious hatred, religious discrimination and violence perpetrated against members of religious or belief communities. In his recommendations, the Rapporteur proposed a way forward in international efforts to combat incitement to racial or religious hatred, calling for a shift away from the sociological concept of defamation of religions towards the legal norm of non-incitement to national, racial or religious hatred. Policymakers should rely on the robust language of the outcome document of the Durban Review Conference and implement it domestically. Strong emphasis should be placed on the implementation of the core obligations of States relating to the protection of individuals and groups against violations of their rights incurred by hate speech, and members of religious or belief communities should be protected from violation of their rights.

Pursuant to General Assembly resolution 63/242 [YUN 2008, p. 764], the Secretary-General in August transmitted to the Assembly the interim report [A/64/271] by the Rapporteur, who described his activities, including country visits and press releases. In his recommendations, the Rapporteur said that while States needed to take measures to fight incitement to racial or religious hatred, they should refrain from adopting overly broad restrictions on freedom of expression, which often led to abuse by the authorities and to the silencing of dissenting voices. Freedom of expression made an essential contribution to the fight against racism: it empowered individuals and groups in vulnerable situations to fight for their rights and allowed them to respond to hate speech. The Rapporteur recalled that a national agenda against racism was the best way to prevent hate speech. Although legislative measures were necessary, States should also resort to non-legislative measures, such as education and intercultural dialogue.

Also in August the Secretary-General transmitted the Rapporteur's report [A/64/295] on the implementation of General Assembly resolution 63/162 [YUN 2008, p. 770] on the inadmissibility of practices that contributed to fuelling contemporary forms of racism and related phenomena, which summarized contributions from 18 States and put forward a number of recommendations.

Following his mission to Germany (22 June–1 July) [A/HRC/14/43/Add.2], the Rapporteur recommended that: an explicit reference to racism as an aggravating circumstance in crimes should be added under section 46 of the Criminal Code; the Government should develop training for police officers, prosecutors and judges on the identification of hate crimes; measures should be taken to ensure an adequate representation of persons with a migration background in State institutions, particularly in the areas of employment and education, in political institutions and the civil administration; the Federal Anti-Discrimination Agency should be provided with the resources necessary for it to be present in all 16 *Länder*, and the Agency should be allowed to investigate complaints brought to its attention and to bring proceedings before the courts; and the Agency should be empowered to initiate investigations in areas such as employment and housing discrimination.

Following his mission to the United Arab Emirates (4–8 October) [A/HRC/14/43/Add.3], the Rapporteur noted that in that unique country non-nationals were the vast majority of the population and nationals were a minority in their own country. The influx of foreign workers had created tremendous challenges in terms of national identity, social integration and capacity for absorption. The Rapporteur recommended that: a public debate be held on the definition of national identity; applications for citizenship by individuals who lawfully lived in the country for a certain period be reviewed and processed in a non-discriminatory manner; the Government address the risk of exploitation of unskilled foreign workers under the sponsorship system, the confiscation of their passports, the prohibition to constitute trade unions and their contracted debts with labour recruitment agencies; stateless individuals be provided with access to health, education, social services, employment, administrative procedures and the administration of justice; public schools be open to all children, including non-nationals; and the constitutional provisions restricting certain human rights to Emirati nationals be revised so as to extend human rights protection to all residents.

Human Rights Council action. On 26 March [A/64/53 (res. 10/22)], by a recorded vote of 23 to 11, with 13 abstentions, the Council urged States to provide adequate protection against acts of hatred, discrimination, intimidation and coercion resulting from defamation of religions and incitement to religious hatred, and called on States to ensure that religious places, sites, shrines and symbols were fully respected and protected. It requested the Special Rapporteur to report on all manifestations of defamation of religions, in particular on the implications of Islamophobia on the enjoyment of human rights, to the Council's twelfth (2009) session; and requested the High Commissioner to report at that session.

OHCHR note. In response to that request, OHCHR in July [A/HRC/12/39] informed the Council that on 10 June it had sent a note inviting Member States to provide contributions to the High Commissioner's report. In order for the report to include the broadest number of contributions, the High Commissioner requested that the submission of her report be delayed to the Council's thirteenth (2010) session.

GENERAL ASSEMBLY ACTION

On 18 December [meeting 65], the General Assembly, on the recommendation of the Third (Social, Humanitarian and Cultural) Committee [A/64/437], adopted **resolution 64/148** by recorded vote (128-13-43) [agenda item 67 *(b)*].

Global efforts for the total elimination of racism, racial discrimination, xenophobia and related intolerance and the comprehensive implementation of and follow-up to the Durban Declaration and Programme of Action

The General Assembly,

Recalling its resolution 52/111 of 12 December 1997, in which it decided to convene the World Conference against Racism, Racial Discrimination, Xenophobia and Related Intolerance, and its resolutions 56/266 of 27 March 2002, 57/195 of 18 December 2002, 58/160 of 22 December 2003, 59/177 of 20 December 2004 and 60/144 of 16 December 2005, which guided the comprehensive follow-up to and effective implementation of the World Conference, and in this regard underlining the importance of their full and effective implementation,

Welcoming the outcome of the Durban Review Conference convened in Geneva from 20 to 24 April 2009 within the framework of the General Assembly in accordance with its resolution 61/149 of 19 December 2006,

Noting the approaching commemoration of the tenth anniversary of the adoption of the Durban Declaration and Programme of Action,

Recalling all of the relevant resolutions and decisions of the Commission on Human Rights and of the Human Rights Council on this subject, and calling for their implementation to ensure the successful implementation of the Durban Declaration and Programme of Action,

Noting Human Rights Council decision 3/103 of 8 December 2006, by which, heeding the decision and instruction of the World Conference, the Council established the Ad Hoc Committee of the Human Rights Council on the Elaboration of Complementary Standards,

Bearing in mind the responsibility and obligations of the Human Rights Council emanating from the outcome of the Durban Review Conference,

Reiterating that all human beings are born free and equal in dignity and rights and have the potential to contribute constructively to the development and well-being of their societies, and that any doctrine of racial superiority is scientifically false, morally condemnable, socially unjust and dangerous and must be rejected, together with theories that attempt to determine the existence of separate human races,

Convinced that racism, racial discrimination, xenophobia and related intolerance manifest themselves in a differentiated manner for women and girls and may be among the factors leading to a deterioration in their living conditions, poverty, violence, multiple forms of discrimination and the limitation or denial of their human rights, and recognizing the need to integrate a gender perspective into relevant policies, strategies and programmes of action against racism, racial discrimination, xenophobia and related intolerance in order to address multiple forms of discrimination,

Underlining the primacy of political will, international cooperation and adequate funding at the national, regional and international levels needed to address all forms and manifestations of racism, racial discrimination, xenophobia and related intolerance,

Alarmed at the increase in racist violence and xenophobic ideas in many parts of the world, in political circles, in the sphere of public opinion and in society at large, inter alia, as a result of the resurgent activities of associations established on the basis of racist and xenophobic platforms and charters, and the persistent use of those platforms and charters to promote or incite racist ideologies,

Underlining the importance of urgently eliminating continuing and violent trends involving racism and racial discrimination, and conscious that any form of impunity for crimes motivated by racist and xenophobic attitudes plays a role in weakening the rule of law and democracy, tends to encourage the recurrence of such crimes and requires resolute action and cooperation for its eradication,

Welcoming the continued commitment of the United Nations High Commissioner for Human Rights to profile and increase the visibility of the struggle against racism, racial discrimination, xenophobia and related intolerance, and recognizing the need for the High Commissioner to make this a cross-cutting issue in the activities and programmes of her Office,

I

Outcomes of the 2001 World Conference against Racism, Racial Discrimination, Xenophobia and Related Intolerance and the 2009 Durban Review Conference

1. *Reaffirms* that the General Assembly is the highest intergovernmental mechanism for the formulation and appraisal of policy on matters relating to the economic, social and related fields, in accordance with Assembly resolution 50/227 of 24 May 1996, and that, together with the Human Rights Council, it shall constitute an intergovernmental process for the comprehensive implementation of and follow-up to the Durban Declaration and Programme of Action;

2. *Expresses its satisfaction* that the Durban Review Conference and Preparatory Committee for the Conference provided for the active participation of Member States and Observers of the United Nations, the specialized agencies, United Nations funds and programmes, various intergovernmental organizations as well as the major groups representing all regions of the world, at the highest level, and notes the contributions of non-governmental organizations in the preparation for the Durban Review Conference, which were broad-based, regionally balanced and consistent with the objectives of the Conference;

3. *Emphasizes* that the basic responsibility for effectively combating racism, racial discrimination, xenophobia and related intolerance lies with States, and to this end stresses that States have the primary responsibility to ensure full and effective implementation of all commitments and recommendations contained in the Durban Declaration and Programme of Action as well as the outcome of the Durban Review Conference and, in this regard, welcomes the steps taken by numerous Governments;

4. *Calls upon* all States that have not yet elaborated their national action plans on combating racism, racial discrimination, xenophobia and related intolerance to comply with their commitments undertaken at the World Conference;

5. *Calls upon* all States to formulate and implement without delay, at the national, regional and international levels, policies and plans of action to combat racism, racial discrimination, xenophobia and related intolerance, including their gender-based manifestations;

6. *Urges* States to support the activities of existing regional bodies or centres that combat racism, racial discrimination, xenophobia and related intolerance in their respective regions, and recommends the establishment of such bodies in all regions where they do not exist;

7. *Calls upon* those States that have not yet done so to consider signing and ratifying or acceding to the instruments enumerated in paragraph 78 of the Durban Programme of Action, including the International Convention on the Protection of the Rights of All Migrant Workers and Members of Their Families of 1990;

8. *Emphasizes* the fundamental and complementary role of national human rights institutions, regional bodies or centres and civil society, working jointly with States towards the elimination of all forms of racism and, in particular, towards the achievement of the objectives of the Durban Declaration and Programme of Action;

9. *Recognizes* the fundamental role of civil society in the fight against racism, racial discrimination, xenophobia and related intolerance, in particular in assisting States to develop regulations and strategies, in taking measures and action against such forms of discrimination and through follow-up implementation;

10. *Reaffirms its commitment* to eliminating all forms of racism, racial discrimination, xenophobia and other forms of related intolerance against indigenous peoples, and in this regard notes the attention paid to the objectives of combating prejudice and eliminating discrimination and promoting tolerance, understanding and good relations among indigenous peoples and all other segments of society in the United Nations Declaration on the Rights of Indigenous Peoples;

11. *Acknowledges* that the World Conference, which was the third world conference against racism, was significantly different from the previous two conferences, as evidenced by the inclusion in its title of two important components relating to contemporary forms of racism, namely, xenophobia and related intolerance;

12. *Also acknowledges* that the outcomes of the World Conference against Racism, Racial Discrimination, Xenophobia and Related Intolerance and the Durban Review Conference are on an equal footing with the outcomes of all the major United Nations conferences, summits and special sessions in the human rights and social fields;

13. *Recalls* that 2011 will mark the tenth anniversary of the World Conference, and decides to call for a one-day plenary event to commemorate the ten-year anniversary during the high-level segment of the General Assembly to be devoted to the elimination of racism, racial discrimination, xenophobia and related intolerance during its sixty-sixth session, in 2011, the modalities of which will be finalized during the sixty-fifth session;

14. *Welcomes* the adoption of the laudable initiative led by the States members of the Caribbean Community and other Member States for the establishment of a permanent memorial at the United Nations to the victims of slavery and the transatlantic slave trade as a contribution towards the fulfilment of paragraph 101 of the Durban Declaration, expresses its appreciation for contributions made to the voluntary fund established in this regard, and urges other countries to contribute to the fund;

15. *Expresses its appreciation* for the continuing work of the mechanisms mandated to follow up the World Conference;

16. *Decides* that the implementation of the outcome of the Durban Review Conference shall be undertaken in the same framework and by the same mechanisms as the outcome of the World Conference;

17. *Acknowledges* the centrality of resource mobilization, effective global partnership and international cooperation in the context of paragraphs 157 and 158 of the Durban Programme of Action for the successful realization of commitments undertaken at the World Conference, and to this end emphasizes the importance of the mandate of the group of independent eminent experts on the implementation of the Durban Declaration and Programme of Action, especially in mobilizing the political will necessary for the successful implementation of the Declaration and Programme of Action;

18. *Requests* the Secretary-General to provide the resources necessary for the effective fulfilment of the mandates of the Intergovernmental Working Group on the Effective Implementation of the Durban Declaration and Programme of Action, the Working Group of Experts on People of African Descent, the group of independent eminent experts on the implementation of the Durban Declaration and Programme of Action and the Ad Hoc Committee on the Elaboration of Complementary Standards;

19. *Expresses concern* at the increasing incidence of racism in various sporting events, while noting with appreciation the efforts made by some governing bodies of the various sporting codes to combat racism, and in this regard invites all international sporting bodies to promote, through their national, regional and international federations, a world of sport free from racism and racial discrimination;

20. *Welcomes*, in this context, the initiative of the Fédération internationale de football association to introduce a visible theme on non-racism in football, and invites the Fédération to continue with this initiative at the 2010 World Cup soccer tournament to be held in South Africa;

21. *Acknowledges* the guidance and leadership role of the Human Rights Council, and encourages it to continue overseeing the implementation of the Durban Declaration and Programme of Action and the outcome of the Durban Review Conference;

22.   *Requests* the Office of the United Nations High Commissioner for Human Rights to continue to provide the Human Rights Council with all the necessary support in order for it to achieve its objectives in this regard;

II
General principles

23.   *Acknowledges* that no derogation from the prohibition of racial discrimination, genocide, the crime of apartheid or slavery is permitted, as defined in the obligations under the relevant human rights instruments;

24.   *Expresses its profound concern about and its unequivocal condemnation* of all forms of racism and racial discrimination, including related acts of racially motivated violence, xenophobia and intolerance, as well as propaganda activities and organizations that attempt to justify or promote racism, racial discrimination, xenophobia and related intolerance in any form;

25.   *Expresses deep concern* at inadequate responses to emerging and resurgent forms of racism, racial discrimination, xenophobia and related intolerance, and urges States to adopt measures to address these scourges vigorously with a view to preventing their practice and protecting victims;

26.   *Stresses* that States and international organizations have a responsibility to ensure that measures taken in the struggle against terrorism do not discriminate in purpose or effect on grounds of race, colour, descent or national or ethnic origin, and urges all States to rescind or refrain from all forms of racial profiling;

27.   *Recognizes* that States should implement and enforce appropriate and effective legislative, judicial, regulatory and administrative measures to prevent and protect against acts of racism, racial discrimination, xenophobia and related intolerance, thereby contributing to the prevention of human rights violations;

28.   *Also recognizes* that racism, racial discrimination, xenophobia and related intolerance occur on the grounds of race, colour, descent or national or ethnic origin and that victims can suffer multiple or aggravated forms of discrimination based on other related grounds, such as sex, language, religion, political or other opinion, social origin, property, birth or other status;

29.   *Reaffirms* that any advocacy of national, racial or religious hatred that constitutes incitement to discrimination, hostility or violence shall be prohibited by law;

30.   *Emphasizes* that it is the responsibility of States to adopt effective measures to combat criminal acts motivated by racism, racial discrimination, xenophobia and related intolerance, including measures to ensure that such motivations are considered an aggravating factor for the purposes of sentencing, to prevent those crimes from going unpunished and to ensure the rule of law;

31.   *Urges* all States to review and, where necessary, revise their immigration laws, policies and practices so that they are free of racial discrimination and compatible with their obligations under international human rights instruments;

32.   *Calls upon* all States, in accordance with the commitments undertaken in paragraph 147 of the Durban Programme of Action, to take all measures necessary to combat incitement to violence motivated by racial hatred, including through the misuse of print, audio-visual and electronic media and new communication technologies, and, in collaboration with service providers, to promote the use of such technologies, including the Internet, to contribute to the fight against racism, in conformity with international standards of freedom of expression and taking all measures necessary to guarantee that right;

33.   *Encourages* all States to include in their educational curricula and social programmes at all levels, as appropriate, knowledge of and tolerance and respect for all cultures, civilizations, religions, peoples and countries, as well as information on the follow-up to and implementation of the Durban Declaration and Programme of Action;

34.   *Stresses* the responsibility of States to mainstream a gender perspective in the design and development of prevention, education and protection measures aimed at the eradication of racism, racial discrimination, xenophobia and related intolerance at all levels, to ensure that they effectively target the distinct situations of women and men;

III
International Convention on the Elimination of All Forms of Racial Discrimination

35.   *Reaffirms* that universal adherence to and full implementation of the International Convention on the Elimination of All Forms of Racial Discrimination are of paramount importance for the fight against racism, racial discrimination, xenophobia and related intolerance, and for the promotion of equality and non-discrimination in the world;

36.   *Expresses grave concern* that universal ratification of the Convention has not yet been reached, despite commitments under the Durban Declaration and Programme of Action, and calls upon those States that have not yet done so to accede to the Convention as a matter of urgency;

37.   *Urges*, in the above context, the Office of the United Nations High Commissioner for Human Rights to maintain on its website and issue regular updates on a list of countries that have not yet ratified the Convention and to encourage those countries to ratify it at the earliest;

38.   *Expresses concern* at the serious delays in the submission of overdue reports to the Committee on the Elimination of Racial Discrimination, which impede the effectiveness of the Committee, makes a strong appeal to all States parties to the Convention to comply with their treaty obligations, and reaffirms the importance of the provision of technical assistance to requesting countries in the preparation of their reports to the Committee;

39.   *Invites* States parties to the Convention to ratify the amendment to article 8 of the Convention on the financing of the Committee, and calls for adequate additional resources from the regular budget of the United Nations to enable the Committee to discharge its mandate fully;

40.   *Urges* all States parties to the Convention to intensify their efforts to implement the obligations that they have accepted under article 4 of the Convention, with due regard to the principles of the Universal Declaration of Human Rights and article 5 of the Convention;

41.   *Recalls* that the Committee holds that the prohibition of the dissemination of ideas based on racial superiority or racial hatred is compatible with the right to freedom of opinion and expression as outlined in article 19 of the

Universal Declaration of Human Rights and in article 5 of the Convention;

42. *Welcomes* the emphasis placed by the Committee on the importance of follow-up to the World Conference and the measures recommended to strengthen the implementation of the Convention as well as the functioning of the Committee;

IV

Special Rapporteur on contemporary forms of racism, racial discrimination, xenophobia and related intolerance, and follow-up to his visits

43. *Takes note* of the work done by the Special Rapporteur on contemporary forms of racism, racial discrimination, xenophobia and related intolerance, and welcomes Human Rights Council resolution 7/34 of 28 March 2008, by which the Council decided to extend the mandate of the Special Rapporteur for a period of three years;

44. *Also takes note* of the reports of the Special Rapporteur, and encourages Member States and other relevant stakeholders to consider implementing the recommendations contained in the reports;

45. *Reiterates its call* to all Member States, intergovernmental organizations, relevant organizations of the United Nations system and non-governmental organizations to cooperate fully with the Special Rapporteur, and calls upon States to consider responding favourably to his requests for visits so as to enable him to fulfil his mandate fully and effectively;

46. *Recognizes with deep concern* the increase in anti-Semitism, Christianophobia and Islamophobia in various parts of the world, as well as the emergence of racial and violent movements based on racism and discriminatory ideas directed against Arab, Christian, Jewish and Muslim communities, as well as all religious communities, communities of people of African descent, communities of people of Asian descent, communities of indigenous people and other communities;

47. *Encourages* closer collaboration between the Special Rapporteur and the Office of the United Nations High Commissioner for Human Rights, in particular the Anti-Discrimination Unit;

48. *Urges* the High Commissioner to provide States, at their request, with advisory services and technical assistance to enable them to implement fully the recommendations of the Special Rapporteur;

49. *Requests* the Secretary-General to provide the Special Rapporteur with all the human and financial assistance necessary to carry out his mandate efficiently, effectively and expeditiously and to enable him to submit a report to the General Assembly at its sixty-fifth session;

50. *Requests* the Special Rapporteur to continue giving particular attention to the negative impact of racism, racial discrimination, xenophobia and related intolerance on the full enjoyment of civil, cultural, economic, political and social rights by national or ethnic, religious and linguistic minorities, immigrant populations, asylum-seekers and refugees;

51. *Invites* Member States to demonstrate greater commitment to fighting racism in sport by conducting educational and awareness-raising activities and by strongly condemning the perpetrators of racist incidents, in cooperation with national and international sports organizations;

V
General

52. *Recommends* that the meetings of the Human Rights Council focusing on the follow-up to the World Conference and the implementation of the Durban Declaration and Programme of Action be scheduled in a manner that allows broad participation and that avoids overlap with the meetings devoted to the consideration of this item in the General Assembly;

53. *Requests* the Secretary-General to submit to the General Assembly at its sixty-fifth session a report on the implementation of the present resolution, with recommendations;

54. *Decides* to remain seized of this important matter at its sixty-fifth session under the item entitled "Elimination of racism, racial discrimination, xenophobia and related intolerance".

RECORDED VOTE ON RESOLUTION 64/148:

In favour: Afghanistan, Algeria, Angola, Antigua and Barbuda, Argentina, Armenia, Azerbaijan, Bahamas, Bahrain, Bangladesh, Barbados, Belarus, Belize, Benin, Bhutan, Bolivia, Botswana, Brazil, Brunei Darussalam, Burkina Faso, Burundi, Cambodia, Cameroon, Cape Verde, Central African Republic, Chad, Chile, China, Colombia, Comoros, Congo, Costa Rica, Côte d'Ivoire, Cuba, Democratic People's Republic of Korea, Democratic Republic of the Congo, Djibouti, Dominica, Dominican Republic, Ecuador, Egypt, El Salvador, Equatorial Guinea, Eritrea, Ethiopia, Fiji, Gabon, Ghana, Grenada, Guatemala, Guinea, Guinea-Bissau, Guyana, Haiti, Honduras, India, Indonesia, Iran, Iraq, Jamaica, Jordan, Kazakhstan, Kenya, Kuwait, Kyrgyzstan, Lao People's Democratic Republic, Lebanon, Lesotho, Liberia, Libyan Arab Jamahiriya, Madagascar, Malawi, Malaysia, Maldives, Mali, Mauritania, Mauritius, Mexico, Mongolia, Morocco, Mozambique, Namibia, Nepal, Nicaragua, Niger, Nigeria, Oman, Pakistan, Panama, Paraguay, Peru, Philippines, Qatar, Russian Federation, Rwanda, Saint Kitts and Nevis, Saint Lucia, Saint Vincent and the Grenadines, Saudi Arabia, Senegal, Sierra Leone, Singapore, Solomon Islands, South Africa, Sri Lanka, Sudan, Suriname, Swaziland, Syrian Arab Republic, Tajikistan, Thailand, Timor-Leste, Togo, Trinidad and Tobago, Tunisia, Turkey, Turkmenistan, Tuvalu, Uganda, United Arab Emirates, United Republic of Tanzania, Uruguay, Uzbekistan, Venezuela, Viet Nam, Yemen, Zambia, Zimbabwe.

Against: Australia, Canada, Czech Republic, Denmark, Germany, Israel, Italy, Marshall Islands, Netherlands, Palau, Poland, Romania, United States.

Abstaining: Albania, Andorra, Austria, Belgium, Bosnia and Herzegovina, Bulgaria, Croatia, Cyprus, Estonia, Finland, France, Georgia, Greece, Hungary, Iceland, Ireland, Japan, Latvia, Liechtenstein, Lithuania, Luxembourg, Malta, Moldova, Monaco, Montenegro, New Zealand, Norway, Papua New Guinea, Portugal, Republic of Korea, Samoa, San Marino, Serbia, Slovakia, Slovenia, Spain, Sweden, Switzerland, The former Yugoslav Republic of Macedonia, Tonga, Ukraine, United Kingdom, Vanuatu.

Also on 18 December, [meeting 65], the General Assembly, on the recommendation of the Third Committee [A/64/437], adopted **resolution 64/147** by recorded vote (127-1-54) [agenda item 67 *(a)*].

Inadmissibility of certain practices that contribute to fuelling contemporary forms of racism, racial discrimination, xenophobia and related intolerance

The General Assembly,

Guided by the Charter of the United Nations, the Universal Declaration of Human Rights, the International Covenant on Civil and Political Rights, the International Convention on the Elimination of All Forms of Racial Discrimination and other relevant human rights instruments,

Recalling the provisions of Commission on Human Rights resolutions 2004/16 of 16 April 2004 and 2005/5 of 14 April 2005 and relevant Human Rights Council resolutions, in particular resolution 7/34 of 28 March 2008, as well as General Assembly resolutions 60/143 of 16 December 2005, 61/147 of 19 December 2006, 62/142 of 18 December 2007 and 63/162 of 18 December 2008 on this issue and resolutions 61/149 of 19 December 2006, 62/220 of 22 December 2007 and 63/242 of 24 December 2008 entitled "Global efforts for the total elimination of racism, racial discrimination, xenophobia and related intolerance and the comprehensive implementation of and follow-up to the Durban Declaration and Programme of Action",

Recalling also the Charter of the Nuremberg Tribunal and the Judgement of the Tribunal, which recognized, inter alia, the SS organization and all its integral parts, including the Waffen SS, as criminal and declared it responsible for many war crimes and crimes against humanity,

Recalling further the relevant provisions of the Durban Declaration and Programme of Action adopted by the World Conference against Racism, Racial Discrimination, Xenophobia and Related Intolerance on 8 September 2001, in particular paragraph 2 of the Declaration and paragraph 86 of the Programme of Action, as well as the relevant provisions of the outcome document of the Durban Review Conference, of 24 April 2009, in particular paragraphs 11 and 54,

Alarmed, in this regard, at the spread in many parts of the world of various extremist political parties, movements and groups, including neo-Nazis and skinhead groups, as well as similar extremist ideological movements,

Recalling that the sixty-fourth session of the General Assembly coincides with the sixty-fifth anniversary of victory in the Second World War,

1. *Reaffirms* the relevant provisions of the Durban Declaration and of the outcome document of the Durban Review Conference, in which States condemned the persistence and resurgence of neo-Nazism, neo-Fascism and violent nationalist ideologies based on racial and national prejudice and stated that those phenomena could never be justified in any instance or in any circumstances;

2. *Takes note with appreciation* of the report of the Special Rapporteur on contemporary forms of racism, racial discrimination, xenophobia and related intolerance, prepared in accordance with the request contained in General Assembly resolution 63/162;

3. *Expresses its appreciation* to the United Nations High Commissioner for Human Rights for her commitment to maintain the fight against racism as one of the priority activities of her Office;

4. *Expresses deep concern* about the glorification of the Nazi movement and former members of the Waffen SS organization, including by erecting monuments and memorials and holding public demonstrations in the name of the glorification of the Nazi past, the Nazi movement and neo-Nazism, as well as by declaring or attempting to declare such members and those who fought against the anti-Hitler coalition and collaborated with the Nazi movement participants in national liberation movements;

5. *Expresses concern* at recurring attempts to desecrate or demolish monuments erected in remembrance of those who fought against Nazism during the Second World War, as well as to unlawfully exhume or remove the remains of such persons, and urges States in this regard to fully comply with their relevant obligations, inter alia, under article 34 of Additional Protocol I to the Geneva Conventions of 1949;

6. *Notes with concern* the increase in the number of racist incidents in several countries and the rise of skinhead groups, which have been responsible for many of these incidents, as well as the resurgence of racist and xenophobic violence targeting members of ethnic, religious or cultural communities and national minorities, as observed by the Special Rapporteur on contemporary forms of racism, racial discrimination, xenophobia and related intolerance in his latest report;

7. *Reaffirms* that such acts may be qualified to fall within the scope of activities described in article 4 of the International Convention on the Elimination of All Forms of Racial Discrimination and that they may represent a clear and manifest abuse of the rights to freedom of peaceful assembly and of association as well as the rights to freedom of opinion and expression within the meaning of those rights as guaranteed by the Universal Declaration of Human Rights, the International Covenant on Civil and Political Rights and the International Convention on the Elimination of All Forms of Racial Discrimination;

8. *Stresses* that the practices described above do injustice to the memory of the countless victims of crimes against humanity committed in the Second World War, in particular those committed by the SS organization and those who fought against the anti-Hitler coalition and collaborated with the Nazi movement, and poison the minds of young people, and that failure by States to effectively address such practices is incompatible with the obligations of States Members of the United Nations under its Charter and is incompatible with the goals and principles of the Organization;

9. *Also stresses* that such practices fuel contemporary forms of racism, racial discrimination, xenophobia and related intolerance and contribute to the spread and multiplication of various extremist political parties, movements and groups, including neo-Nazis and skinhead groups;

10. *Emphasizes* the need to take the measures necessary to put an end to the practices described above, and calls upon States to take more effective measures in accordance with international human rights law to combat those phenomena and the extremist movements, which pose a real threat to democratic values;

11. *Reaffirms*, in this regard, the particular importance of all forms of education, including human rights education, as a complement to legislative measures, as outlined by the Special Rapporteur in his report to the General Assembly;

12. *Emphasizes* the recommendation of the Special Rapporteur regarding the importance of history classes in teaching the dramatic events and human suffering that resulted from the ideologies of Nazism and Fascism, especially in view of the upcoming sixty-fifth anniversary of victory in the Second World War;

13. *Stresses* the importance of other positive measures and initiatives aimed at bringing communities together and providing them with space for genuine dialogue, such as round tables, working groups and seminars, including training seminars for State agents and media professionals, as well as awareness-raising activities, especially those initiated by civil society representatives which require continued State support;

14. *Underlines* the potentially positive role that relevant United Nations entities and programmes, in particular the United Nations Educational, Scientific and Cultural Organization, can play in the aforementioned areas;

15. *Reaffirms* that, according to article 4 of the International Convention on the Elimination of All Forms of Racial Discrimination, States parties to that instrument are, inter alia, under the obligation:

   (a) To condemn all propaganda and all organizations that are based on ideas of racial superiority or that attempt to justify or promote racial hatred and discrimination in any form;

   (b) To undertake to adopt immediate and positive measures designed to eradicate all incitement to, or acts of, such discrimination with due regard to the principles embodied in the Universal Declaration of Human Rights and the rights expressly set forth in article 5 of the Convention;

   (c) To declare as an offence punishable by law all dissemination of ideas based on racial superiority or hatred, and incitement to racial discrimination, as well as all acts of violence or incitement to such acts against any race or group of persons of another colour or ethnic origin, and also the provision of any assistance to racist activities, including the financing thereof;

   (d) To declare illegal and prohibit organizations and organized and all other propaganda activities that promote and incite racial discrimination and to recognize participation in such organizations or activities as an offence punishable by law;

   (e) To prohibit public authorities or public institutions, national or local, from promoting or inciting racial discrimination;

16. *Reaffirms also* that, as underlined in paragraph 13 of the outcome document of the Durban Review Conference, any advocacy of national, racial or religious hatred that constitutes incitement to discrimination, hostility or violence should be prohibited by law, that the dissemination of ideas based on racial superiority, hatred, acts of violence or incitement to such acts shall be declared offences punishable by law, and that these prohibitions are consistent with freedom of opinion and expression;

17. *Underlines*, at the same time, the positive role that the exercise of the right to freedom of opinion and expression, as well as the full respect for the freedom to seek, receive and impart information, can play in combating racism, racial discrimination, xenophobia and related intolerance;

18. *Encourages* those States that have made reservations to article 4 of the International Convention on the Elimination of All Forms of Racial Discrimination to give serious consideration to withdrawing such reservations as a matter of priority;

19. *Recalls* the request of the Commission on Human Rights in its resolution 2005/5 that the Special Rapporteur continue to reflect on this issue, make relevant recommendations in his future reports and seek and take into account in this regard the views of Governments and non-governmental organizations;

20. *Requests* the Special Rapporteur to prepare, for submission to the General Assembly at its sixty-fifth session and to the Human Rights Council, reports on the implementation of the present resolution based on the views collected in accordance with the request of the Commission on Human Rights, as recalled by the Assembly in paragraph 19 above;

21. *Expresses its appreciation* to those Governments that have provided information to the Special Rapporteur in the course of the preparation of his report to the General Assembly;

22. *Encourages* Governments and non-governmental organizations to cooperate fully with the Special Rapporteur in the exercise of the tasks outlined in paragraph 19 above;

23. *Decides* to remain seized of the issue.

RECORDED VOTE ON RESOLUTION 64/147:

In favour: Afghanistan, Algeria, Angola, Antigua and Barbuda, Argentina, Armenia, Azerbaijan, Bahamas, Bahrain, Bangladesh, Barbados, Belarus, Belize, Benin, Bhutan, Bolivia, Botswana, Brazil, Brunei Darussalam, Burkina Faso, Burundi, Cambodia, Cameroon, Cape Verde, Central African Republic, Chile, China, Colombia, Comoros, Congo, Costa Rica, Côte d'Ivoire, Cuba, Democratic People's Republic of Korea, Democratic Republic of the Congo, Djibouti, Dominica, Dominican Republic, Ecuador, Egypt, El Salvador, Equatorial Guinea, Eritrea, Ethiopia, Gabon, Ghana, Grenada, Guatemala, Guinea, Guinea-Bissau, Guyana, Haiti, Honduras, India, Indonesia, Iran, Iraq, Israel, Jamaica, Jordan, Kazakhstan, Kenya, Kuwait, Kyrgyzstan, Lao People's Democratic Republic, Lebanon, Lesotho, Liberia, Libyan Arab Jamahiriya, Madagascar, Malawi, Malaysia, Maldives, Mali, Mauritania, Mauritius, Mexico, Mongolia, Morocco, Mozambique, Namibia, Nepal, Nicaragua, Niger, Nigeria, Oman, Pakistan, Paraguay, Peru, Philippines, Qatar, Russian Federation, Rwanda, Saint Kitts and Nevis, Saint Lucia, Saint Vincent and the Grenadines, Saudi Arabia, Senegal, Serbia, Sierra Leone, Singapore, Solomon Islands, South Africa, Sri Lanka, Sudan, Suriname, Swaziland, Syrian Arab Republic, Tajikistan, Thailand, Timor-Leste, Togo, Trinidad and Tobago, Tunisia, Turkey, Turkmenistan, Tuvalu, Uganda, United Arab Emirates, United Republic of Tanzania, Uruguay, Uzbekistan, Venezuela, Viet Nam, Yemen, Zambia, Zimbabwe.

Against: United States.

Abstaining: Albania, Andorra, Australia, Austria, Belgium, Bosnia and Herzegovina, Bulgaria, Canada, Croatia, Cyprus, Czech Republic, Denmark, Estonia, Fiji, Finland, France, Georgia, Germany, Greece, Hungary, Iceland, Ireland, Italy, Japan, Latvia, Liechtenstein, Lithuania, Luxembourg, Malta, Moldova, Monaco, Montenegro, Netherlands, New Zealand, Norway, Palau, Panama, Papua New Guinea, Poland, Portugal, Republic of Korea, Romania, Samoa, San Marino, Slovakia, Slovenia, Spain, Sweden, Switzerland, The former Yugoslav Republic of Macedonia, Tonga, Ukraine, United Kingdom, Vanuatu.

Human rights defenders

Reports of Special Rapporteur. The new Special Rapporteur on the situation of human rights defenders, Margaret Sekaggya (Uganda), described her activities in her first report [A/HRC/10/12] to the Human Rights Council, submitted pursuant to a Council request [YUN 2008, p. 721]. She drew the attention of Member States to the 493 communications that were sent under the mandate during 2008. Focusing on the potential of the Universal Periodic Review in enhancing the protection of human rights defenders, the Rapporteur made recommendations to the United Nations, States, NGOs and defenders on utilizing the Review to improve the situation of defenders.

An addendum [A/HRC/10/12/Add.1] summarized communications sent to 80 Governments from 11 December 2007 to 10 December 2008 and replies received until 10 February 2009.

In August, in response to General Assembly resolution 62/152 [YUN 2007, p. 670], the Secretary-General transmitted to the Assembly a report [A/64/226] of the Rapporteur, which focused on the right to freedom of association, its content and its implementation. The report reviewed the legal framework for protecting that right at the international and regional levels, described the scope and content of the right and analysed permissible restrictions. Decisions of the Human Rights Committee, the African Commission of Human Rights, the Inter-American Court of Human Rights and the European Court of Human Rights demonstrated the scope and content of the right. The report highlighted the difficulties in forming and registering human rights associations; criminal sanctions for unregistered activities; the denial of registration and deregistration; and burdensome and lengthy registration procedures. It provided examples of restriction on the registration of international NGOs, of government supervision and monitoring, of administrative and judicial harassment, and of restrictions on the access to funding. The report's recommendations sought to address those problems.

Following her mission to the Democratic Republic of the Congo (21 May–3 June) [A/HRC/13/22/Add.2], the Rapporteur pointed out the stigmatization and related insecurity suffered by defenders, who were killed, "disappeared", tortured, threatened, arbitrarily arrested and detained, under surveillance, banned from travelling, displaced or forced into exile. The widespread impunity for violations against defenders by State authorities and members of armed groups was a cause of concern. The Rapporteur recommended that the Government: give legitimacy to the work of human rights defenders; recognize human rights work and criticism of the Government and its officials as a natural part of a democratic society; decriminalize

press offences; make the fight against impunity for violations against defenders a priority; and investigate abuses against defenders, hold fair trials of alleged perpetrators and sentence them if convicted.

Following her mission to Colombia (7–18 September) [A/HRC/13/22/Add.3], the Rapporteur pointed out the insecurity faced by several categories of defenders; their stigmatization by public officials and non-State actors; their illegal surveillance by State intelligence services; their arbitrary arrest and detention; their judicial harassment; and raids on NGO premises and theft of information. The Rapporteur recommended that: the agreements reached with defenders on guarantees for their work, in the framework of the National Guarantee Round Table, should be promptly implemented; a new presidential decree should give recognition to the legitimate work of defenders, in particular women defenders; the Attorney-General's Office should thoroughly investigate all threats and attacks against defenders and prosecute the perpetrators; and the Criminal Code should be amended in order to decriminalize slander and libel.

Communication. In March [A/HRC/10/G/3], Togo submitted its observations on the Special Rapporteur's report on her mission to the country [YUN 2008, p. 721].

GENERAL ASSEMBLY ACTION

On 18 December [meeting 65], the General Assembly, on the recommendation of the Third Committee [A/64/439/Add.2 (Part II)], adopted **resolution 64/163** without vote [agenda item 69 *(b)*].

Declaration on the Right and Responsibility of Individuals, Groups and Organs of Society to Promote and Protect Universally Recognized Human Rights and Fundamental Freedoms

The General Assembly,

Recalling its resolution 53/144 of 9 December 1998, by which it adopted by consensus the Declaration on the Right and Responsibility of Individuals, Groups and Organs of Society to Promote and Protect Universally Recognized Human Rights and Fundamental Freedoms annexed to that resolution, and reiterating the importance of the Declaration and its promotion and implementation,

Recalling also all previous resolutions on this subject, in particular its resolution 62/152 of 18 December 2007 and Human Rights Council resolution 7/8 of 27 March 2008,

Noting with deep concern that in many countries persons and organizations engaged in promoting and defending human rights and fundamental freedoms frequently face threats and harassment and suffer insecurity as a result of those activities, including through restrictions on freedom of association or expression or the right to peaceful assembly, or abuse of civil or criminal proceedings,

Gravely concerned that, in some instances, national security and counter-terrorism legislation and other measures have been misused to target human rights defenders or have hindered their work and safety in a manner contrary to international law,

Gravely concerned also by the continuing high level of human rights violations committed against persons engaged in promoting and defending human rights and fundamental freedoms around the world and by the fact that in many countries impunity for threats, attacks and acts of intimidation against human rights defenders persists and that this has a negative impact on their work and safety,

Gravely concerned further by the considerable number of communications received by the Special Rapporteur of the Human Rights Council on the situation of human rights defenders that, together with the reports submitted by some of the other special procedure mechanisms, indicates the serious nature of the risks faced by human rights defenders, in particular women human rights defenders,

Stressing the important role that individuals, civil society organizations, non-governmental organizations, groups, organs of society and independent national institutions play in the promotion and protection of all human rights and fundamental freedoms for all, including in addressing all forms of human rights violations, combating impunity, fighting poverty and discrimination, and promoting access to justice, democracy, tolerance, human dignity and the right to development, and recalling that all have rights as well as responsibilities and duties within and towards the community,

Recognizing the substantial role that human rights defenders can play in supporting efforts to strengthen peace and development, through dialogue, openness, participation and justice, including by monitoring, reporting on and contributing to the promotion and protection of human rights,

Recalling that, in accordance with article 4 of the International Covenant on Civil and Political Rights, certain rights are recognized as non-derogable in any circumstances and that any measures derogating from other provisions of the Covenant must be in accordance with that article in all cases, and underlining the exceptional and temporary nature of any such derogations, as stated in General Comment No. 29 on states of emergency adopted by the Human Rights Committee on 24 July 2001,

Welcoming the cooperation between the Special Rapporteur and other special procedures of the Human Rights Council, as well as other relevant United Nations bodies, offices, departments, specialized agencies and personnel, both at Headquarters and at the country level, within their mandates,

Welcoming also regional initiatives for the promotion and protection of human rights and the strengthened cooperation between international and regional mechanisms for the protection of human rights defenders, and encouraging further development in this regard,

Welcoming further the steps taken by some States towards adopting national policies or legislation for the protection of individuals, groups and organs of society engaged in promoting and defending human rights, including as follow-up to the universal periodic review mechanism of the Human Rights Council,

Recalling that the primary responsibility for promoting and protecting human rights rests with the State, reaffirm-

ing that national legislation consistent with the Charter of the United Nations and other international obligations of the State in the field of human rights and fundamental freedoms is the juridical framework within which human rights defenders conduct their activities, and noting with deep concern that the activities of some non-State actors pose a major threat to the security of human rights defenders,

Emphasizing the need for strong and effective measures for the protection of human rights defenders,

1. *Calls upon* all States to promote and give full effect to the Declaration on the Right and Responsibility of Individuals, Groups and Organs of Society to Promote and Protect Universally Recognized Human Rights and Fundamental Freedoms, including by taking, as appropriate, practical steps to that end;

2. *Welcomes* the reports of the Special Rapporteur of the Human Rights Council on the situation of human rights defenders and her contribution to the effective promotion of the Declaration and the improvement of the protection of human rights defenders worldwide;

3. *Condemns* all human rights violations committed against persons engaged in promoting and defending human rights and fundamental freedoms around the world, and urges States to take all appropriate action, consistent with the Declaration and all other relevant human rights instruments, to prevent and eliminate such human rights violations;

4. *Calls upon* all States to take all measures necessary to ensure the protection of human rights defenders, at both the local and the national levels, including in times of armed conflict and peacebuilding;

5. *Calls upon* States to respect, protect and ensure the rights to freedom of expression and association of human rights defenders and in this regard to ensure, where procedures governing registration of civil society organizations exist, that these are transparent, non-discriminatory, expeditious, inexpensive, allow for the possibility to appeal and avoid requiring re-registration, in accordance with national legislation, and are in conformity with international human rights law;

6. *Urges* States to ensure that any measures to combat terrorism and preserve national security are in compliance with their obligations under international law, in particular under international human rights law, and do not hinder the work and safety of individuals, groups and organs of society engaged in promoting and defending human rights;

7. *Also urges* States to take appropriate measures to address the question of impunity for attacks, threats and acts of intimidation, including cases of gender-based violence, against human rights defenders and their relatives, including by ensuring that complaints from human rights defenders are promptly investigated and addressed in a transparent, independent and accountable manner;

8. *Urges* all States to cooperate with and assist the Special Rapporteur in the performance of her mandate and to provide all information in a timely manner, as well as to respond without undue delay to communications transmitted to them by the Special Rapporteur;

9. *Calls upon* States to give serious consideration to responding favourably to the requests of the Special Rap-

porteur to visit their countries, and urges them to enter into a constructive dialogue with the Special Rapporteur with respect to the follow-up to and implementation of her recommendations, so as to enable the Special Rapporteur to fulfil her mandate even more effectively;

10. *Strongly encourages* States to translate the Declaration and to take measures to ensure its widest possible dissemination at the national and local levels;

11. *Encourages* States to promote awareness and training in regard to the Declaration in order to enable officials, agencies, authorities and members of the judiciary to observe the provisions of the Declaration and thus to promote better understanding and respect for individuals, groups and organs of society engaged in promoting and defending human rights, as well as for their work;

12. *Encourages* relevant United Nations bodies, including at the country level, within their respective mandates and working in cooperation with States, to give due consideration to the Declaration and to the reports of the Special Rapporteur, and in this context requests the Office of the United Nations High Commissioner for Human Rights to draw the attention of all relevant United Nations bodies, including at the country level, to the reports of the Special Rapporteur;

13. *Requests* the Office of the High Commissioner, as well as other relevant United Nations bodies, offices, departments and specialized agencies, within their respective mandates, to consider ways in which they can assist States in strengthening the role and security of human rights defenders, including in situations of armed conflict and peacebuilding;

14. *Requests* all concerned United Nations agencies and organizations, within their mandates, to provide all possible assistance and support to the Special Rapporteur for the effective fulfilment of her mandate, including through country visits;

15. *Requests* the Special Rapporteur to continue to report annually on her activities to the General Assembly and to the Human Rights Council in accordance with her mandate;

16. *Decides* to consider the question at its sixty-sixth session under the item entitled "Promotion and protection of human rights".

Reprisals for cooperation with human rights bodies

Report of Secretary-General. In February [A/HRC/10/36], the Secretary-General submitted a compilation and analysis of information on alleged reprisals against individuals or groups who had cooperated or sought to cooperate with representatives of UN human rights bodies. The report contained information brought to the attention of the mechanisms of the Human Rights Council and to OHCHR, including communications sent to Governments by representatives of the mechanisms and Government replies.

The report reviewed cases in Colombia, Iran, Mexico, Namibia and Thailand, adding that in many instances it had not been possible to record additional

cases due to security concerns or because the individuals exposed to reprisals had requested that their cases should not be raised publicly. Of particular concern was the continued seriousness of reprisals, as victims suffered violations of the rights to life, to liberty and to security of person. The gravity of reported acts of reprisal reinforced the need for all representatives of UN human rights bodies to help prevent the occurrence of such acts and ensure that they were not treated with impunity.

Human Rights Council action. On 1 October [A/65/53 (res. 12/2)], the Council urged Governments to prevent and refrain from all such acts of intimidation or reprisal. It invited the Secretary-General to submit a report to the Council's fourteenth (2010) session and annually thereafter, containing a compilation and analysis of any available information, from all appropriate sources, on alleged reprisals, as well as recommendations on how to address the issue.

Protection of migrants

Reports of Special Rapporteur. In response to a request by the Human Rights Council [YUN 2008, p. 773], the Special Rapporteur on the human rights of migrants, Jorge Bustamante (Mexico), in May reported [A/HRC/11/7] on his activities in 2008. He focused on the protection of children in the context of migration, recalling the obligation of the State to ensure the protection of children in all stages of the migration process. The Rapporteur reviewed the applicable international legal framework, proposed a conceptual framework and referred to three categories of children affected by the migration process: those left behind by migrating family members; migrant children moving across borders; and migrant children in host countries. The Rapporteur recommended, among other things, that protection of the human rights of the child be ensured in States of origin, transit and destination at every stage of the migration process; that States devote special attention to the protection of undocumented, unaccompanied and separated children, as well as to the protection of children seeking asylum and children victims of transnational organized crime; and that States address the specific vulnerability of the migrant girl child in policies and programmes, addressing gaps in protection.

An addendum [A/HRC/11/7/Add.1 & Corr.1] summarized 26 communications—urgent appeals and letters of allegations—addressed to 19 Governments between 1 January 2008 and 6 March 2009, as well as replies received until 6 May 2009.

In response to General Assembly resolution 63/184 [YUN 2008, p. 773] and Human Rights Council resolution 8/10 [ibid.], the Secretary-General in August transmitted to the Assembly the report of the Special

Rapporteur [A/64/213 & Corr.1], which summarized activities carried out between January 2008 and June 2009. The report highlighted issues related to the protection of the rights of migrants, including the protection of children in the context of migration, a number of illustrative good practices and the challenges encountered. The Rapporteur recommended that: the guiding principle of migration governance should ensure that all migrants, regardless of their immigration status, enjoyed their human rights; States should promote and protect the rights of all migrants, in particular those of women and children; and States should review their laws and policies to harmonize them with the international legal framework on the protection of the rights of migrants, with particular attention to the protection of the rights of the child.

The General Assembly took note of that report on 18 December (**decision 64/536**).

Following his mission to Romania (15–20 June) [A/HRC/14/30/Add.2], the Rapporteur analysed the situation of the Romanian diaspora, migrant workers, children left behind by migrating parents and victims of trafficking in persons. He recommended that the Government restrict the use of detention for immigration purposes, making it a measure of last resort; harmonize laws applicable to the detention of migrants with international human rights norms; and ratify the 1990 International Convention on the Protection of the Rights of All Migrant Workers and Members of Their Families.

Following his mission to the United Kingdom (22–26 June) [A/HRC/14/30/Add.3], the Rapporteur recommended that the Government restrict the use of detention for immigration purposes, making it a measure of last resort; establish channels allowing migrant workers, including irregular migrant workers, to lodge complaints of violations of their rights without fear of retaliation; and ratify the 1990 International Convention and the International Labour Organization Convention No. 143 concerning Migrations in Abusive Conditions and the Promotion of Equality of Opportunity and Treatment of Migrant Workers.

Following his mission to Senegal (17–24 August) [A/HRC/17/33/Add.2], the Rapporteur recommended that the Government elaborate a holistic and strategic migration policy; negotiate with the countries of migration provisions to facilitate the transfer—upon migrants' return to Senegal—of the social security contributions paid by Senegalese living abroad in the countries of migration; build the business capacity of young people and potential migrants; and conduct regular minimum-wage reviews.

Reports of Secretary-General. Pursuant to General Assembly resolution 62/132 [YUN 2007,

p. 1162], the Secretary-General in July submitted a report [A/64/152] reviewing measures taken by Member States and activities undertaken within the UN system to address violence against women migrant workers and ensure protection of their rights. The report recommended establishing legislation that protected the rights of women workers and addressed violence against them. Occupations dominated by women migrant workers, such as domestic work, should be regulated and include mechanisms for monitoring workplace conditions; women migrant workers should have access to legal remedies and redress for violence against them and should not be penalized for bringing complaints; recruiting and employment agencies should be regulated and monitored; perpetrators of violence should be prosecuted and punished; and victims should be able to apply for residency permits independently of an abusive employer or spouse.

In response to General Assembly resolution 63/184 [YUN 2008, p. 773], the Secretary-General submitted a July report [A/64/188] summarizing communications received from 21 Governments on the implementation of resolutions 63/184 and 62/156 [YUN 2007, p. 719] on protection of migrants. The report also provided information on the status of the 1990 International Convention and on the activities of the Committee on the Protection of the Rights of All Migrant Workers and Members of Their Families, the Special Rapporteur on the human rights of migrants, the Universal Periodic Review and OHCHR.

The General Assembly took note of that report on 18 December (**decision 64/536**).

Human Rights Council action. On 18 June [A/64/53 (res. 11/9)], the Council decided to hold at its twelfth session a panel discussion on the situation of migrants in detention centres and in administrative detention, which created conditions for the potential violation of their rights. The panel discussion was held on 17 September [A/HRC/12/50].

On 1 October [A/65/53 (res. 12/6)], the Council called on States: to promote and protect the human rights of migrants, especially those of children, regardless of their status; to establish or strengthen policies and programmes aimed at addressing the situation of children in the context of migration; to promote and protect the rights of children who were left behind in their country of origin by migrating family members; and to prevent the violation of the rights of migrant children while in transit. OHCHR was requested to prepare a study on challenges and best practices in the implementation of the international framework for the protection of the rights of the child in the context of migration, and make it available on its website prior to the Council's fifteenth (2010) session.

On 18 December [meeting 65], the General Assembly, on the recommendation of the Third Committee [A/64/439/Add.2 (Part II)], adopted **resolution 64/166** without vote [agenda item 69 *(b)*].

Protection of migrants

The General Assembly,

Recalling all its previous resolutions on the protection of migrants, the most recent of which is resolution 63/184 of 18 December 2008, and recalling also Human Rights Council resolution 12/6 of 1 October 2009,

Reaffirming the Universal Declaration of Human Rights, which proclaims that all human beings are born free and equal in dignity and rights and that everyone is entitled to all the rights and freedoms set out therein, without distinction of any kind, in particular as to race, colour or national origin,

Reaffirming also that everyone has the right to freedom of movement and residence within the borders of each State, and to leave any country, including his own, and return to his country,

Recalling the International Covenant on Civil and Political Rights and the International Covenant on Economic, Social and Cultural Rights, the Convention against Torture and Other Cruel, Inhuman or Degrading Treatment or Punishment, the Convention on the Elimination of All Forms of Discrimination against Women, the Convention on the Rights of the Child, the International Convention on the Elimination of All Forms of Racial Discrimination, the Convention on the Rights of Persons with Disabilities, the Vienna Convention on Consular Relations and the International Convention on the Protection of the Rights of All Migrant Workers and Members of Their Families,

Recalling also the provisions concerning migrants contained in the outcome documents of all major United Nations conferences and summits, including the Outcome of the Conference on the World Financial and Economic Crisis and Its Impact on Development, which recognizes that migrant workers are among the most vulnerable in the context of the current crisis,

Recalling further Commission on Population and Development resolutions 2006/2 of 10 May 2006 and 2009/1 of 3 April 2009,

Taking note with appreciation of the United Nations Development Programme *Human Development Report 2009: Overcoming Barriers—Human Mobility and Development*,

Taking note of advisory opinion OC-16/99 of 1 October 1999 on the Right to Information on Consular Assistance in the Framework of the Guarantees of the Due Process of Law and advisory opinion OC-18/03 of 17 September 2003 on the Juridical Condition and Rights of Undocumented Migrants, issued by the Inter-American Court of Human Rights,

Taking note also of the Judgment of the International Court of Justice of 31 March 2004 in the case concerning *Avena and Other Mexican Nationals*, and the Judgment of the Court of 19 January 2009 regarding the Request for interpretation of the *Avena* Judgment, and recalling the obligations of States reaffirmed in both decisions,

Underlining the importance of the Human Rights Council in promoting respect for the protection of the human rights and fundamental freedoms of all, including migrants,

Recognizing the increasing participation of women in international migration movements,

Recalling the High-level Dialogue on International Migration and Development, held in New York on 14 and 15 September 2006 for the purpose of discussing the multidimensional aspects of international migration and development, which recognized the relationship between international migration, development and human rights,

Noting the second and third meetings of the Global Forum on Migration and Development, held in Manila from 27 to 30 October 2008 and in Athens from 2 to 5 November 2009, respectively, recognizing the discussion on the theme "Inclusion, protection and acceptance of migrants in society: linking human rights and migrant empowerment for development" as a step to address the multidimensional nature of international migration, and taking note with appreciation of the generous offers of the Governments of Mexico and Spain to host the meetings of the Global Forum in 2010 and 2011, respectively,

Recognizing the cultural and economic contributions made by migrants to receiving societies and their communities of origin, as well as the need to identify appropriate means of maximizing development benefits and responding to the challenges which migration poses to countries of origin, transit and destination, especially in the light of the impact of the economic and financial crisis, and committing to ensuring dignified, humane treatment with applicable protections and to strengthening mechanisms for international cooperation,

Emphasizing the global character of the migratory phenomenon, the importance of international, regional and bilateral cooperation and dialogue in this regard, as appropriate, and the need to protect the human rights of migrants, particularly at a time in which migration flows have increased in the globalized economy and take place in a context of new security concerns,

Bearing in mind that policies and initiatives on the issue of migration, including those that refer to the orderly management of migration, should promote holistic approaches that take into account the causes and consequences of the phenomenon, as well as full respect for the human rights and fundamental freedoms of migrants,

Stressing the importance of regulations and laws regarding irregular migration being in accordance with the obligations of States under international law, including international human rights law,

Concerned about the large and growing number of migrants, especially women and children, who place themselves in a vulnerable situation by attempting to cross international borders without the required travel documents, and recognizing the obligation of States to respect the human rights of those migrants,

Stressing that penalties and the treatment given to irregular migrants should be commensurate with their infraction,

Recognizing the importance of having a comprehensive and balanced approach to international migration, and bearing in mind that migration enriches the economic, political, social and cultural fabric of States and the historical and cultural ties that exist among some regions,

Recognizing also the obligations of countries of origin, transit and destination under international human rights law,

Underlining the importance for States, in cooperation with non-governmental organizations, to undertake information campaigns aimed at clarifying opportunities, limitations and rights in the event of migration, so as to enable everyone to make informed decisions and to prevent anyone from utilizing dangerous means to cross international borders,

1. *Calls upon* States to promote and protect effectively the human rights and fundamental freedoms of all migrants, regardless of their migration status, especially those of women and children, and to address international migration through international, regional or bilateral cooperation and dialogue and through a comprehensive and balanced approach, recognizing the roles and responsibilities of countries of origin, transit and destination in promoting and protecting the human rights of all migrants, and avoiding approaches that might aggravate their vulnerability;

2. *Expresses its concern* over the impact of the current economic and financial crisis on international migration and migrants, and in that regard urges Governments to combat unfair and discriminatory treatment of migrants, particularly migrant workers and their families;

3. *Reaffirms* the rights set forth in the Universal Declaration of Human Rights and the obligations of States under the International Covenants on Human Rights, and in this regard:

 (a) Strongly condemns the manifestations and acts of racism, racial discrimination, xenophobia and related intolerance against migrants and the stereotypes often applied to them, including on the basis of religion or belief, and urges States to apply and, where needed, reinforce the existing laws when xenophobic or intolerant acts, manifestations or expressions against migrants occur, in order to eradicate impunity for those who commit xenophobic and racist acts;

 (b) Expresses concern at legislation and measures adopted by some States that may restrict the human rights and fundamental freedoms of migrants, and reaffirms that, when exercising their sovereign right to enact and implement migratory and border security measures, States have the duty to comply with their obligations under international law, including international human rights law, in order to ensure full respect for the human rights of migrants;

 (c) Calls upon States to ensure that their laws and policies, including in the areas of counter-terrorism and combating transnational organized crime, such as trafficking in persons and smuggling of migrants, fully respect the human rights of migrants;

 (d) Calls upon States that have not done so to consider signing and ratifying or acceding to the International Convention on the Protection of the Rights of All Migrant Workers and Members of Their Families as a matter of priority, and requests the Secretary-General to continue his efforts to promote and raise awareness of the Convention;

 (e) Takes note of the report of the Committee on the Protection of the Rights of All Migrant Workers and Members of Their Families on its ninth and tenth sessions;

4. *Also reaffirms* the duty of States to effectively promote and protect the human rights and fundamental freedoms of all migrants, especially those of women and children, regardless of their immigration status, in conformity with the Universal Declaration of Human Rights and the international instruments to which they are party, and therefore:

 (a) Calls upon all States to respect the human rights and the inherent dignity of migrants and to put an end to arbitrary arrest and detention and, where necessary, to review detention periods in order to avoid excessive detention of irregular migrants, and to adopt, where applicable, alternative measures to detention;

 (b) Urges all States to adopt effective measures to prevent and punish any form of illegal deprivation of liberty of migrants by individuals or groups;

 (c) Takes note with appreciation of the measures adopted by some States to reduce detention periods in cases of undocumented migration, in the application of domestic regulations and laws regarding irregular migration;

 (d) Also takes note with appreciation of the successful implementation by some States of alternative measures to detention in cases of undocumented migration as a practice that deserves consideration by all States;

 (e) Requests States to adopt concrete measures to prevent the violation of the human rights of migrants while in transit, including in ports and airports and at borders and migration checkpoints, to train public officials who work in those facilities and in border areas to treat migrants respectfully and in accordance with the law, and to prosecute, in conformity with applicable law, any act of violation of the human rights of migrants, inter alia, arbitrary detention, torture and violations of the right to life, including extrajudicial executions, during their transit from their country of origin to the country of destination and vice versa, including their transit through national borders;

 (f) Underlines the right of migrants to return to their country of citizenship, and recalls that States must ensure that their returning nationals are duly received;

 (g) Reaffirms emphatically the duty of States parties to ensure full respect for and observance of the Vienna Convention on Consular Relations, in particular with regard to the right of all foreign nationals, regardless of their immigration status, to communicate with a consular official of the sending State in case of arrest, imprisonment, custody or detention, and the obligation of the receiving State to inform the foreign national without delay of his or her rights under the Convention;

 (h) Requests all States, in conformity with national legislation and applicable international legal instruments to which they are party, to enforce labour law effectively, including by addressing violations of such law, with regard to migrant workers' labour relations and working conditions, inter alia, those related to their remuneration and conditions of health, safety at work and the right to freedom of association;

 (i) Encourages all States to remove unlawful obstacles that may prevent the safe, transparent, unrestricted and expeditious transfer of remittances, earnings, assets and pensions of migrants to their country of origin or to any other countries, in conformity with applicable legislation, and to consider, as appropriate, measures to solve other problems that may impede such transfers;

(j) Recalls that the Universal Declaration of Human Rights recognizes that everyone has the right to an effective remedy by the competent national tribunals for acts violating the fundamental rights granted to him or her;

5. *Emphasizes* the importance of protecting persons in vulnerable situations, and in this regard:

(a) Welcomes immigration programmes, adopted by some countries, that allow migrants to integrate fully into the host countries, facilitate family reunification and promote a harmonious, tolerant and respectful environment, and encourages States to consider the possibility of adopting these types of programmes;

(b) Encourages all States to develop international migration policies and programmes that include a gender perspective, in order to adopt the measures necessary to better protect women and girls against dangers and abuse during migration;

(c) Calls upon States to protect the human rights of migrant children, given their vulnerability, particularly unaccompanied migrant children, ensuring that the best interests of the child are a primary consideration in their policies of integration, return and family reunification;

(d) Encourages all States to prevent and eliminate discriminatory policies that deny migrant children access to education;

(e) Urges States to ensure that repatriation mechanisms allow for the identification and special protection of persons in vulnerable situations, including persons with disabilities, and take into account, in conformity with their international obligations and commitments, the principle of the best interests of the child and family reunification;

(f) Urges States parties to the United Nations Convention against Transnational Organized Crime and supplementing protocols thereto, namely, the Protocol against the Smuggling of Migrants by Land, Sea and Air and the Protocol to Prevent, Suppress and Punish Trafficking in Persons, Especially Women and Children, to implement them fully, and calls upon States that have not done so to consider ratifying or acceding to them as a matter of priority;

6. *Stresses* the importance of international, regional and bilateral cooperation in the protection of the human rights of migrants, and therefore:

(a) Requests all States, international organizations and relevant stakeholders to take into account in their policies and initiatives on migration issues the global character of the migratory phenomenon and to give due consideration to international, regional and bilateral cooperation in this field, including by undertaking dialogues on migration that include countries of origin, destination and transit, as well as civil society, including migrants, with a view to addressing, in a comprehensive manner, inter alia, its causes and consequences and the challenge of undocumented or irregular migration, granting priority to the protection of the human rights of migrants;

(b) Requests Member States, the United Nations system, international organizations, civil society and all relevant stakeholders, especially the United Nations High Commissioner for Human Rights and the Special Rapporteur of the Human Rights Council on the human rights of migrants, to ensure that the perspective of the human rights of migrants is included among the priority issues in the ongoing discussions on international migration and development within the United Nations system, and in this regard underlines the importance of adequately taking into account the human rights perspective as one of the priorities of the informal thematic debate on international migration and development, to be held in 2011, as well as in the High-level Dialogue on International Migration and Development, which will take place during the sixty-eighth session of the General Assembly, in 2013, as decided by the Assembly in its resolution 63/225 of 19 December 2008;

(c) Invites the Chair of the Committee to address the General Assembly at its sixty-fifth session under the item entitled "Promotion and protection of human rights";

(d) Invites the Special Rapporteur to submit his report to the General Assembly at its sixty-fifth session under the item entitled "Promotion and protection of human rights";

7. *Requests* the Secretary-General to provide the resources necessary, from within existing resources of the United Nations, for the Committee to meet for a maximum of three weeks in one session or in two separate sessions in 2010, as required by the number of reports submitted to the Committee, and requests the Committee to further consider ways of improving the effectiveness of its working sessions and to report to the General Assembly on the use of its meeting time;

8. *Also requests* the Secretary-General to submit a report on the implementation of the present resolution to the General Assembly at its sixty-fifth session and to include in that report an analysis of the ways and means to promote the human rights of migrants, in particular children, and decides to examine the question further under the item entitled "Promotion and protection of human rights".

Discrimination against minorities

Forum on minority issues. The Forum on Minority Issues, at its second session (Geneva, 12–13 November), focused on minorities and effective political participation. The more than 500 participants included representatives of Governments, treaty bodies, UN specialized agencies and civil society. The Forum had before it a note by the independent expert on minority issues concerning minorities and effective political participation [HRC/FMI/2009/2], a background document by the independent expert on the same topic [HRC/FMI/2009/3] and an OHCHR note providing draft recommendations on the topic [HRC/FMI/2009/4].

The Forum issued recommendations [A/HRC/13/25] aimed at increasing the inclusion and recognition of minorities within the State, while enabling them to maintain their own identity and characteristics. The recommendations were directed to Governments and Parliaments, political parties, national human rights institutions, civil society, UN human rights mechanisms, the international community, UN agencies and the media.

Reports of independent expert. In her annual report to the Human Rights Council [A/HRC/10/11], the independent expert on minority issues, Gay Mc-Dougall (United States), summarized activities undertaken since the submission of her previous annual report [YUN 2008, p. 777]. The report reviewed her collaboration with the United Nations Development Programme (UNDP) to strengthen UNDP engagement with minorities in development processes. It also provided details of the inaugural Forum on Minority Issues and its recommendations [ibid., p. 776].

Following her mission to Kazakhstan (6–15 July) [A/HRC/13/23/Add.1], the independent expert recommended the adoption of legislation addressing racial discrimination to enforce the rights of individuals from all communities to seek remedies for acts of discrimination. During the transition towards the use of Kazakh as the primary language of State administration, proficiency in Kazakh should in no way be used as a basis to deny rights and freedoms. The rights and freedoms accorded to traditional religious groups should be extended to all religious groups, and a wide-ranging dialogue should be held with "non-traditional" groups, such as Jehovah's Witnesses, Baptists, evangelicals, Scientologists and non-recognized forms of Islam.

Following her mission to Canada (13–23 October) [A/HRC/13/23/Add.2], the expert recommended taking robust action to achieve equality in employment; targeting poverty elimination policies to the special needs of ethnic, racial and religious minorities; addressing inequalities in educational outcomes; increasing political participation of minorities; taking steps against racial profiling; ensuring that counter-terrorism measures met human rights standards; and strengthening mechanisms of redress and access to justice.

Communications. On 6 March [A/HRC/10/G/5], Greece issued its comments on the report of the expert following her mission to the country [YUN 2008, p. 778].

On 11 and 12 March [A/HRC/10/G/7], Guyana issued its comments on the report of the expert following her mission there [YUN 2008, p. 777].

Reports of Secretary-General. A report of the Secretary-General [A/HRC/10/38 & Corr.1] covered the work in 2007 and 2008 of the treaty bodies, special procedures and OHCHR to promote the rights of minorities.

An addendum [A/HRC/10/38/Add.1] provided information on the expert meeting on integration with diversity in policing (Vienna, 15–16 January 2008), which brought together 10 professionals from the police services of Brazil, Cameroon, Canada, Hungary, India, Ireland, Nigeria, Pakistan, Samoa and South Africa.

Leprosy victims

OHCHR report. In response to a Human Rights Council request [YUN 2008, p. 780], OHCHR in February submitted a report [A/HRC/10/62] summarizing submissions received from Governments, NGOs and other stakeholders on measures they had taken to eliminate discrimination against persons affected by leprosy and their family members. The report presented the outcome of an open-ended consultation on the impact of health-related discrimination against persons affected by leprosy and their family members on the enjoyment of human rights (Geneva, 15 January), attended by Member States, international organizations, NGOs, experts and persons affected by leprosy.

Human Rights Council action. On 1 October [A/65/53 (res. 12/7)], the Council expressed its appreciation to the Human Rights Council Advisory Committee for submitting the draft set of principles and guidelines for the elimination of discrimination against persons affected by leprosy and their family members, annexed to its recommendation 3/1 [A/HRC/AC/3/2]. The Council requested OHCHR to collect the views of relevant actors on the draft and make those views available to the Advisory Committee; and requested the Advisory Committee to finalize the draft for submission to the Council's fifteenth (2010) session.

Religious intolerance

Reports of Special Rapporteur. Pursuant to a Human Rights Council request [YUN 2007, p. 726], the Special Rapporteur on freedom of religion or belief, Asma Jahangir (Pakistan), in January reported [A/HRC/10/8] on her activities. She highlighted the importance of initiatives in the fields of education, public awareness and interreligious dialogue, and examined discriminatory and harmful practices against women. She stressed the need to prevent discrimination with regard to the enjoyment of economic, social and cultural rights, since minorities and vulnerable groups were particularly affected when States did not abide by their obligations to respect those rights. The Rapporteur concluded that discrimination based on religion or belief often emanated from deliberate State policies to ostracize certain religious or belief communities and to restrict or deny their access, for example, to health services, public education or public-sector jobs.

An addendum [A/HRC/10/8/Add.1] summarized cases transmitted to 25 Governments between 1 December 2007 and 30 November 2008 and replies received by 30 January 2009.

In response to General Assembly resolution 63/181 [YUN 2008, p. 786], the Secretary-General in July transmitted to the Assembly the Rapporteur's interim report [A/64/159], which focused on persons deprived of their liberty, refugees, asylum-seekers, internally displaced persons, children, persons belonging to national or ethnic, religious and linguistic minorities and migrants as regards their ability to exercise their right to freedom of religion or belief. The Rapporteur reviewed her activities since her previous report [YUN 2008, p. 780] and recommended providing training to personnel of detention facilities about the duty to respect the right to freedom of religion or belief of detainees; and detecting signs of intolerance that might not be human rights violations themselves, but that might lead to religious discrimination. Parents should be supported in educating their children on tolerance and non-discrimination, teaching about religions and beliefs should be carried out in a fair and balanced manner, and political leaders should take a clear, human rights-based approach on the question of religious tolerance and communicate such position to the public.

Following her mission to the former Yugoslav Republic of Macedonia (26–29 April) [A/HRC/13/40/Add.2], the Rapporteur reminded those religious and political leaders who voiced their outrage at the judgement of the Constitutional Court of 15 April 2009 affirming the separation of church and State in religious instruction in public schools that an independent judiciary was crucial to safeguard freedom of religion. To foster a climate of religious tolerance, political and religious leaders should take a human rights-based approach and clearly affirm the importance of the right to freedom of religion or belief in all its dimensions.

Following her mission to Serbia, including Kosovo (30 April–8 May) [A/HRC/13/40/Add.3], the Rapporteur recommended reforming Serbia's 2006 Law on Churches and Religious Communities, which had been criticized for its discriminatory effects with regard to "non-traditional" religious communities. The Ministry of Religious Affairs should be more transparent and streamline the registration process to ensure equal access and treatment in the application procedure for all religious communities wishing to register. The authorities should remain neutral and impartial, avoiding any State measures favouring a particular leader or specific organs of a divided religious community. All places of worship needed to be fully respected and protected, and the State should take adequate measures to prevent all acts or threats of violence.

Regarding Kosovo, the Rapporteur recommended that the authorities take swift action and devise creative measures to counter coercion and violence in the name of religion. She reminded religious leaders of their responsibility to play a constructive role, so as to enhance freedom of religion. The international community

should send a clear message that violence and incitement to racial or religious hatred would not be tolerated.

Following her mission to the Lao People's Democratic Republic (23–30 November) [A/HRC/13/40/Add.4], the Rapporteur recommended: bringing in line with international human rights standards the Decree No. 92/PM for the Management and Protection of Religious Activities; passing on the Decree's explanatory policy directions to the provincial and district levels to avoid any discriminatory interpretation; extending the affirmative action schemes, which already existed for members of ethnic minorities, to religious minorities to increase their access to higher education; discontinuing bureaucratic controls over and impediments to liberty of movement in the context of religious activities; and providing the personnel of detention facilities with adequate training to raise awareness of their duty to promote and respect freedom of religion or belief.

Report of Secretary-General. In response to General Assembly resolution 63/171 [YUN 2008, p. 783], the Secretary-General in July submitted a report [A/64/209] on combating defamation of religions, examining the possible correlation between defamation of religions and the upsurge in incitement, intolerance and hatred in many parts of the world. The report examined the activities of OHCHR, UN human rights treaty bodies and special procedures, and concluded that hate speech was but a symptom of something much more profound—intolerance and bigotry. Legal responses, such as restrictions on freedom of expression alone, were far from being sufficient to bring about real changes in mindsets, perceptions and discourse. Tackling the root causes of intolerance required a much broader set of policy measures, covering the areas of intercultural dialogue as well as education for tolerance and diversity.

Human Rights Council action. On 27 March [A/64/53 (res. 10/25)], by a recorded vote of 22 to 1, with 24 abstentions, the Council urged States to ensure that everyone had the right to education, work, an adequate standard of living, the enjoyment of the highest attainable standard of physical and mental health and to take part in cultural life, without any discrimination on the basis of religion or belief; and to ensure that no one was discriminated against on the basis of religion or belief in regard to access to humanitarian assistance, social benefits or public services. The Special Rapporteur was requested to report to the Council's thirteenth (2010) session.

GENERAL ASSEMBLY ACTION

On 18 December [meeting 65], the General Assembly, on the recommendation of the Third Committee [A/64/439/Add.2 (Part II)], adopted **resolution 64/156** by recorded vote (80-61-42) [agenda item 69 *(b)*].

Combating defamation of religions

The General Assembly,

Reaffirming the pledge made by all States, under the Charter of the United Nations, to promote and encourage universal respect for and observance of all human rights and fundamental freedoms without distinction as to race, sex, language or religion,

Recalling the relevant international instruments on the elimination of discrimination, in particular the International Convention on the Elimination of All Forms of Racial Discrimination, the International Covenant on Civil and Political Rights, the Declaration on the Elimination of All Forms of Intolerance and of Discrimination Based on Religion or Belief, the Declaration on the Human Rights of Individuals Who are not Nationals of the Country in which They Live and the Declaration on the Rights of Persons Belonging to National or Ethnic, Religious and Linguistic Minorities,

Reaffirming that all human rights are universal, indivisible, interdependent and interrelated,

Recalling the relevant resolutions of the Commission on Human Rights and the Human Rights Council in this regard,

Welcoming the resolve expressed in the United Nations Millennium Declaration adopted by the General Assembly on 8 September 2000 to take measures to eliminate the increasing acts of racism and xenophobia in many societies and to promote greater harmony and tolerance in all societies, and looking forward to its effective implementation at all levels,

Underlining, in this regard, the importance of the Durban Declaration and Programme of Action adopted by the World Conference against Racism, Racial Discrimination, Xenophobia and Related Intolerance, held in Durban, South Africa, from 31 August to 8 September 2001 and the outcome document of the Durban Review Conference, held in Geneva from 20 to 24 April 2009, welcoming the progress achieved in implementing them, and emphasizing that they constitute a solid foundation for the elimination of the scourges and all manifestations of racism, racial discrimination, xenophobia and related intolerance,

Expressing serious concern at the increase in racist violence and xenophobic ideas in many parts of the world, in political circles, in the sphere of public opinion and in society at large, as a result, inter alia, of the resurgence of activities of political parties and associations established on the basis of racist, xenophobic and ideological superiority platforms and charters, and the persistent use of those platforms and charters to promote or incite racist ideologies,

Deeply alarmed at the rising trends towards discrimination based on religion or belief, including in some national policies, laws and administrative measures that stigmatize groups of people belonging to certain religions and beliefs under a variety of pretexts relating to security and irregular immigration, thereby legitimizing discrimination against them and consequently impairing their enjoyment of the right to freedom of thought, conscience and religion and impeding their ability to observe, practise and manifest their religion freely and without fear of coercion, violence or reprisal,

Noting with deep concern the serious instances of intolerance, discrimination and acts of violence based on religion or belief, intimidation and coercion motivated by extremism, religious or otherwise, occurring in many parts of the world, in addition to the negative projection of certain religions in the media and the introduction and enforcement of laws and administrative measures that specifically discriminate against and target persons with certain ethnic and religious backgrounds, particularly Muslim minorities following the events of 11 September 2001, and that threaten to impede their full enjoyment of human rights and fundamental freedoms,

Stressing that defamation of religions is a serious affront to human dignity leading to the illicit restriction of the freedom of religion of their adherents and incitement to religious hatred and violence,

Stressing also the need to effectively combat defamation of all religions, and incitement to religious hatred in general,

Reaffirming that discrimination on the grounds of religion or belief constitutes a violation of human rights and a disavowal of the principles of the Charter,

Noting with concern that defamation of religions, and incitement to religious hatred in general, could lead to social disharmony and violations of human rights, and alarmed at the inaction of some States to combat this burgeoning trend and the resulting discriminatory practices against adherents of certain religions,

Taking note of the reports of the Special Rapporteur on contemporary forms of racism, racial discrimination, xenophobia and related intolerance submitted to the Human Rights Council at its fourth, sixth, ninth and twelfth sessions, in which the Special Rapporteur highlighted the serious nature of the defamation of all religions and the need to complement legal strategies, and reiterating the call of the Special Rapporteur to all States to wage a systematic campaign against incitement to racial and religious hatred by maintaining a careful balance between the defence of secularism and respect for freedom of religion and by acknowledging and respecting the complementarity of all the freedoms embodied in internationally agreed human rights instruments, including the International Covenant on Civil and Political Rights,

Recalling the proclamation of the Global Agenda for Dialogue among Civilizations, and inviting States, the organizations and bodies of the United Nations system, within existing resources, other international and regional organizations and civil society to contribute to the implementation of the Programme of Action contained in the Global Agenda,

Welcoming the efforts of the Alliance of Civilizations initiative in promoting mutual respect and understanding among different cultures and societies, including its first forum, held in Spain in 2008, its second forum, held in Turkey in 2009, its third forum, to be held in Brazil in 2010, and its fourth forum, to be held in Qatar in 2011,

Recognizing the valuable contributions of all religions and beliefs to modern civilization and the contribution that dialogue among civilizations can make to an improved awareness and understanding of common values,

Convinced that respect for cultural, ethnic, religious and linguistic diversity, as well as dialogue among and within civilizations, is essential for peace, understanding and friendship among individuals and people of the different cultures and nations of the world, while manifestations of cultural prejudice, intolerance and xenophobia towards people belonging to different cultures, religions and beliefs give rise to polarization and disturb social cohesion, generating hatred and violence among peoples and nations throughout the world,

Underlining the important role of education in the promotion of tolerance, which involves acceptance by the public of, and its respect for, diversity, including with regard to religious expression, and underlining also the fact that education should contribute in a meaningful way to promoting tolerance and the elimination of discrimination based on religion or belief,

Reaffirming the need for all States to continue their national and international efforts to enhance dialogue and broaden understanding among civilizations, cultures, religions and beliefs, and emphasizing that States, regional organizations, non-governmental organizations, religious bodies and the media have an important role to play in promoting tolerance, and respect for and freedom of religion and belief,

Welcoming all international and regional initiatives aimed at promoting cross-cultural and interfaith harmony, including the international dialogue on interfaith cooperation, the World Conference on Dialogue, held in Madrid from 16 to 18 July 2008, and the high-level meeting of the General Assembly on the culture of peace, held on 12 and 13 November 2008, and their valuable efforts towards the promotion of a culture of peace and dialogue at all levels, and taking note with appreciation of the programmes led by the United Nations Educational, Scientific and Cultural Organization in this regard,

Underlining the importance of increasing contacts at all levels in order to deepen dialogue and reinforce understanding among different cultures, religions, beliefs and civilizations, and in this regard taking note with appreciation of the Declaration and Programme of Action adopted by the Ministerial Meeting on Human Rights and Cultural Diversity of the Movement of Non-Aligned Countries, held in Tehran on 3 and 4 September 2007,

Recognizing the importance of the intersection of religion and race and that instances can arise of multiple or aggravated forms of discrimination on the basis of religion and other grounds, such as race, colour, descent or national or ethnic origin,

Recalling its resolution 63/171 of 18 December 2008,

1.   *Takes note* of the report of the Secretary-General;

2.   *Expresses deep concern* at the negative stereotyping of religions and manifestations of intolerance and discrimination in matters of religion or belief still evident in the world;

3.   *Strongly deplores* all acts of psychological and physical violence and assaults, and incitement thereto, against persons on the basis of their religion or belief, and such acts directed against their businesses, properties, cultural centres and places of worship, as well as targeting of holy sites and religious symbols of all religions;

4.   *Expresses deep concern* at the programmes and agendas pursued by extremist organizations and groups aimed at creating and perpetuating stereotypes about certain religions, in particular when condoned by Governments;

5.   *Notes with deep concern* the intensification of the overall campaign of defamation of religions, and incitement

to religious hatred in general, including the ethnic and religious profiling of Muslim minorities in the aftermath of the tragic events of 11 September 2001;

6.   *Recognizes* that, in the context of the fight against terrorism, defamation of religions, and incitement to religious hatred in general, become aggravating factors that contribute to the denial of fundamental rights and freedoms of members of target groups, as well as to their economic and social exclusion;

7.   *Expresses deep concern*, in this respect, that Islam is frequently and wrongly associated with human rights violations and terrorism;

8.   *Reiterates* the commitment of all States to the implementation, in an integrated manner, of the United Nations Global Counter-Terrorism Strategy, which was adopted without a vote by the General Assembly on 8 September 2006 and reaffirmed by the Assembly in its resolution 62/272 of 5 September 2008, and which clearly confirms, inter alia, that terrorism cannot and should not be associated with any religion, nationality, civilization or ethnic group, stressing the need to reinforce the commitment of the international community to promote a culture of peace, justice and human development, ethnic, national and religious tolerance, and respect for all religions, religious values, beliefs or cultures and prevent the defamation of religions;

9.   *Deplores* the use of the print, audio-visual and electronic media, including the Internet, and any other means to incite acts of violence, xenophobia or related intolerance and discrimination against any religion, as well as targeting of religious symbols;

10.   *Emphasizes* that, as stipulated in international human rights law, everyone has the right to hold opinions without interference and has the right to freedom of expression, the exercise of which carries with it special duties and responsibilities and may therefore be subject to limitations as are provided for by law and are necessary for respect of the rights or reputations of others, protection of national security or of public order, public health or morals;

11.   *Reaffirms* that general recommendation XV(42) of the Committee on the Elimination of Racial Discrimination, in which the Committee stipulated that the prohibition of the dissemination of all ideas based upon racial superiority or hatred is compatible with freedom of opinion and expression, is equally applicable to the question of incitement to religious hatred;

12.   *Takes note* of the work undertaken by the Special Rapporteur on contemporary forms of racism, racial discrimination, xenophobia and related intolerance and the Special Rapporteur on the promotion and protection of the right to freedom of opinion and expression in accordance with their mandates defined by the Human Rights Council in its resolutions 7/34 and 7/36 of 28 March 2008;

13.   *Strongly condemns* all manifestations and acts of racism, racial discrimination, xenophobia and related intolerance against national or ethnic, religious and linguistic minorities and migrants and the stereotypes often applied to them, including on the basis of religion or belief, and urges all States to apply and, where applicable, reinforce existing laws when such xenophobic or intolerant acts, manifestations or expressions occur in order to eradicate impunity for those who commit xenophobic and racist acts;

14. *Reaffirms* the obligation of all States to enact the legislation necessary to prohibit the advocacy of national, racial or religious hatred that constitutes incitement to discrimination, hostility or violence, and encourages States, in their follow-up to the World Conference against Racism, Racial Discrimination, Xenophobia and Related Intolerance, to include aspects relating to national or ethnic, religious and linguistic minorities in their national plans of action and in this context to take forms of multiple discrimination against minorities fully into account;

15. *Invites* all States to put into practice the provisions of the Declaration on the Elimination of All Forms of Intolerance and of Discrimination Based on Religion or Belief;

16. *Urges* all States to provide, within their respective legal and constitutional systems, adequate protection against acts of hatred, discrimination, intimidation and coercion resulting from defamation of religions, and incitement to religious hatred in general;

17. *Also urges* all States to take all possible measures to promote tolerance and respect for all religions and beliefs and the understanding of their value systems and to complement legal systems with intellectual and moral strategies to combat religious hatred and intolerance;

18. *Recognizes* that the open, constructive and respectful debate of ideas, as well as interfaith and intercultural dialogue at the local, national and international levels, can play a positive role in combating religious hatred, incitement and violence;

19. *Welcomes* the recent steps taken by Member States to protect freedom of religion through the enactment or strengthening of domestic frameworks and legislation to prevent the defamation of religions and the negative stereotyping of religious groups;

20. *Urges* all States to ensure that all public officials, including members of law enforcement bodies, the military, civil servants and educators, in the course of their official duties, respect people regardless of their different religions and beliefs and do not discriminate against persons on the grounds of their religion or belief, and that any necessary and appropriate education or training is provided;

21. *Underscores* the need to combat defamation of religions, and incitement to religious hatred in general, by strategizing and harmonizing actions at the local, national, regional and international levels through education and awareness-raising, and urges all States to ensure equal access to education for all, in law and in practice, including access to free primary education for all children, both girls and boys, and access for adults to lifelong learning and education based on respect for human rights, diversity and tolerance, without discrimination of any kind, and to refrain from any legal or other measures leading to racial segregation in access to schooling;

22. *Calls upon* all States to exert the utmost efforts, in accordance with their national legislation and in conformity with international human rights and humanitarian law, to ensure that religious places, sites, shrines and symbols are fully respected and protected, and to take additional measures in cases where they are vulnerable to desecration or destruction;

23. *Calls upon* the international community to foster a global dialogue to promote a culture of tolerance and peace at all levels, based on respect for human rights and diversity of religion and belief, and urges States, non-governmental organizations, religious leaders and bodies and the print and electronic media to support and foster such a dialogue;

24. *Affirms* that the Human Rights Council shall promote universal respect for all religious and cultural values and address instances of intolerance, discrimination and incitement of hatred against members of any community or adherents of any religion, as well as the means to consolidate international efforts in order to combat impunity for such deplorable acts;

25. *Welcomes* the initiative of the United Nations High Commissioner for Human Rights on the expert seminar on freedom of expression and advocacy of religious hatred that constitutes incitement to discrimination, hostility or violence, held on 2 and 3 October 2008, and requests the High Commissioner to continue to build on this initiative, with a view to concretely contributing to the prevention and elimination of all such forms of incitement and the consequences of negative stereotyping of religions or beliefs, and their adherents, on the human rights of those individuals and their communities;

26. *Takes note* of the efforts of the High Commissioner to promote and include human rights aspects in educational programmes, particularly the World Programme for Human Rights Education proclaimed by the General Assembly on 10 December 2004, and calls upon the High Commissioner to continue those efforts, with particular focus on:

(a) The contributions of cultures, as well as religious and cultural diversity;

(b) Collaboration with other relevant bodies of the United Nations system and regional and international organizations in holding joint conferences designed to encourage dialogue among civilizations and promote understanding of the universality of human rights and their implementation at various levels, in particular the Office of the United Nations High Representative for the Alliance of Civilizations, the United Nations Educational, Scientific and Cultural Organization and the unit within the Secretariat mandated to interact with various entities within the United Nations system and coordinate their contribution to the intergovernmental process;

27. *Requests* the Secretary-General to submit a report on the implementation of the present resolution, including the correlation between defamation of religions and the intersection of religion and race, the upsurge in incitement, intolerance and hatred in many parts of the world and steps taken by States to combat this phenomenon, to the General Assembly at its sixty-fifth session.

RECORDED VOTE ON RESOLUTION 64/156:

In favour: Afghanistan, Algeria, Angola, Azerbaijan, Bahrain, Bangladesh, Barbados, Belarus, Bhutan, Bolivia, Brunei Darussalam, Cambodia, Chad, China, Comoros, Congo, Côte d'Ivoire, Cuba, Democratic People's Republic of Korea, Democratic Republic of the Congo, Djibouti, Dominica, Dominican Republic, Egypt, El Salvador, Eritrea, Ethiopia, Gabon, Guinea, Guinea-Bissau, Guyana, Indonesia, Iran, Iraq, Jordan, Kazakhstan, Kuwait, Kyrgyzstan, Lao People's Democratic Republic, Lebanon, Libyan Arab Jamahiriya, Malaysia, Maldives, Mali, Mauritania, Morocco, Mozambique, Myanmar, Namibia, Nicaragua, Niger, Nigeria, Oman, Pakistan, Philippines,

Qatar, Russian Federation, Saint Vincent and the Grenadines, Saudi Arabia, Senegal, Singapore, Somalia, South Africa, Sri Lanka, Sudan, Suriname, Swaziland, Syrian Arab Republic, Tajikistan, Thailand, Togo, Tunisia, Turkey, Turkmenistan, Uganda, United Arab Emirates, Uzbekistan, Venezuela, Viet Nam, Yemen.

Against: Andorra, Australia, Austria, Belgium, Bulgaria, Canada, Chile, Croatia, Cyprus, Czech Republic, Denmark, Estonia, Finland, France, Georgia, Germany, Greece, Hungary, Iceland, Ireland, Israel, Italy, Latvia, Liechtenstein, Lithuania, Luxembourg, Malta, Marshall Islands, Mexico, Micronesia, Moldova, Monaco, Montenegro, Nauru, Netherlands, New Zealand, Norway, Palau, Panama, Papua New Guinea, Poland, Portugal, Republic of Korea, Romania, Saint Lucia, Samoa, San Marino, Serbia, Slovakia, Slovenia, Spain, Sweden, Switzerland, The former Yugoslav Republic of Macedonia, Timor-Leste, Tonga, Ukraine, United Kingdom, United States, Uruguay, Vanuatu.

Abstaining: Albania, Antigua and Barbuda, Argentina, Armenia, Bahamas, Belize, Benin, Bosnia and Herzegovina, Botswana, Brazil, Burkina Faso, Burundi, Cameroon, Cape Verde, Colombia, Costa Rica, Ecuador, Equatorial Guinea, Fiji, Ghana, Grenada, Guatemala, Haiti, Honduras, India, Jamaica, Japan, Kenya, Lesotho, Liberia, Malawi, Mauritius, Mongolia, Nepal, Paraguay, Peru, Rwanda, Saint Kitts and Nevis, Trinidad and Tobago, Tuvalu, United Republic of Tanzania, Zambia.

Also on 18 December [meeting 65], the General Assembly, on the recommendation of the Third Committee [A/64/439/Add.2 (Part II)], adopted **resolution 64/164** without vote [agenda item 69 *(b)*].

Elimination of all forms of intolerance and of discrimination based on religion or belief

The General Assembly,

Recalling its resolution 36/55 of 25 November 1981, by which it proclaimed the Declaration on the Elimination of All Forms of Intolerance and of Discrimination Based on Religion or Belief,

Recalling also article 18 of the International Covenant on Civil and Political Rights, article 18 of the Universal Declaration of Human Rights and other relevant human rights provisions,

Recalling further its previous resolutions on the elimination of all forms of intolerance and of discrimination based on religion or belief, including resolution 63/181 of 18 December 2008, as well as Human Rights Council resolution 10/25 of 27 March 2009,

Recognizing the important work carried out by the Human Rights Committee in providing guidance with respect to the scope of the freedom of religion or belief,

Considering that religion or belief, for those who profess either, is one of the fundamental elements in their conception of life and that freedom of religion or belief should be fully respected and guaranteed,

Reaffirming that everyone has the right to freedom of thought, conscience and religion or belief, which includes the freedom to have or to adopt a religion or belief of one's choice and the freedom, either alone or in community with others and in public or private, to manifest one's religion or belief in teaching, practice, worship and observance,

Deeply concerned at the limited progress that has been made in the elimination of all forms of intolerance and of discrimination based on religion or belief, and believing that further intensified efforts are therefore required to promote and protect the right to freedom of thought, conscience and religion or belief and to eliminate all forms of hatred, intolerance and discrimination based on religion or belief, as also noted at the World Conference against Racism, Racial Discrimination, Xenophobia and Related Intolerance, as well as at the Durban Review Conference,

Concerned that acts of violence, or credible threats of violence, against persons belonging to religious minorities are sometimes tolerated or encouraged by official authorities,

Expressing deep concern at all forms of discrimination and intolerance, including prejudices against persons and derogatory stereotyping of persons, based on religion or belief,

Concerned about the rise in the number of laws or regulations that limit the freedom of religion or belief and the implementation of existing laws in a discriminatory manner,

Convinced of the need to address the rise in various parts of the world of religious extremism that affects the rights of individuals, the situations of violence and discrimination that affect many women as well as other individuals on the grounds or in the name of religion or belief or in accordance with cultural and traditional practices, and the misuse of religion or belief for ends inconsistent with the Charter of the United Nations, as well as other relevant instruments of the United Nations,

Seriously concerned at all attacks on religious places, sites and shrines in violation of international law, in particular human rights and humanitarian law, including any deliberate destruction of relics and monuments,

Emphasizing that States, regional organizations, nongovernmental organizations, religious bodies and the media have an important role to play in promoting tolerance and respect for religious and cultural diversity and in the universal promotion and protection of human rights, including freedom of religion or belief,

Underlining the importance of education in the promotion of tolerance, which involves the acceptance by the public of, and its respect for, diversity, including with regard to religious expression, and underlining also the fact that education, in particular at school, should contribute in a meaningful way to promoting tolerance and the elimination of discrimination based on religion or belief,

1. *Condemns* all forms of intolerance and of discrimination based on religion or belief, as well as violations of freedom of thought, conscience and religion or belief;

2. *Stresses* that the right to freedom of thought, conscience and religion applies equally to all persons, regardless of their religions or beliefs, and without any discrimination as to their equal protection by the law;

3. *Emphasizes* that, as underlined by the Human Rights Committee, restrictions on the freedom to manifest one's religion or belief are permitted only if limitations are prescribed by law, are necessary to protect public safety, order, health or morals, or the fundamental rights and freedoms of others, are non-discriminatory and are applied in a manner that does not vitiate the right to freedom of thought, conscience and religion;

4. *Also emphasizes* that freedom of religion or belief and freedom of expression are interdependent, interrelated and mutually reinforcing;

5. *Recognizes with deep concern* the overall rise in instances of intolerance and violence directed against members of many religious and other communities in various parts of the world, including cases motivated by Islamophobia, anti-Semitism and Christianophobia;

6. *Condemns* any advocacy of religious hatred that constitutes incitement to discrimination, hostility or violence, whether it involves the use of print, audio-visual or electronic media or any other means;

7. *Expresses concern* over the persistence of institutionalized social intolerance and discrimination practiced against many on the grounds of religion or belief, and emphasizes that legal procedures pertaining to religious or belief-based groups and places of worship are not a prerequisite for the exercise of the right to manifest one's religion or belief, and that such procedures, when legally required at the national or local level, should be non-discriminatory in order to contribute to the effective protection of the right of all persons to practise their religion or belief, either individually or in community with others and in public or private;

8. *Recognizes with concern* the situation of persons in vulnerable situations, including persons deprived of their liberty, refugees, asylum-seekers and internally displaced persons, children, persons belonging to national or ethnic, religious and linguistic minorities and migrants, as regards their ability to freely exercise their right to freedom of religion or belief;

9. *Emphasizes* that States have an obligation to exercise due diligence to prevent, investigate and punish acts of violence against persons belonging to religious minorities, regardless of the perpetrator, and that failure to do so may constitute a human rights violation;

10. *Also emphasizes* that no religion should be equated with terrorism, as this may have adverse consequences on the enjoyment of the right to freedom of religion or belief of all members of the religious communities concerned;

11. *Urges* States to step up their efforts to protect and promote freedom of thought, conscience and religion or belief, and to this end:

(a) To ensure that their constitutional and legislative systems provide adequate and effective guarantees of freedom of thought, conscience, religion and belief to all without distinction, inter alia, by the provision of effective remedies in cases where the right to freedom of thought, conscience, religion or belief, or the right to practise freely one's religion, including the right to change one's religion or belief, is violated;

(b) To ensure that no one within their jurisdiction is deprived of the right to life, liberty or security of person because of religion or belief and that no one is subjected to torture or other cruel, inhuman or degrading treatment or punishment, or arbitrary arrest or detention on that account and to bring to justice all perpetrators of violations of these rights;

(c) To end violations of the human rights of women and to devote particular attention to abolishing practices that discriminate against women, including in the exercise of their right to freedom of thought, conscience and religion or belief;

(d) To ensure that no one is discriminated against on the basis of his or her religion or belief when accessing, inter alia, education, medical care, employment, humanitarian assistance or social benefits, and to ensure that everyone has the right and the opportunity to have access, on general terms of equality, to public services in one's country, without any discrimination on the basis of religion or belief;

(e) To review, whenever relevant, existing registration practices in order to ensure that such practices do not limit the right of all persons to manifest their religion or belief, either alone or in community with others and in public or private;

(f) To ensure that no official documents are withheld from the individual on the grounds of religion or belief and that everyone has the right to refrain from disclosing information concerning one's religious affiliation on such documents against one's will;

(g) To ensure, in particular, the right of all persons to worship, assemble or teach in connection with a religion or belief and their right to establish and maintain places for these purposes and the right of all persons to write, issue and disseminate relevant publications in these areas;

(h) To exert the utmost efforts, in accordance with their national legislation and in conformity with international human rights law, to ensure that religious places, sites, shrines and symbols are fully respected and protected and to take additional measures in cases where they are vulnerable to desecration and destruction;

(i) To ensure that, in accordance with appropriate national legislation and in conformity with international human rights law, the freedom of all persons and members of groups to establish and maintain religious, charitable or humanitarian institutions is fully respected and protected;

(j) To ensure that all public officials and civil servants, including members of law enforcement bodies and personnel of detention facilities, the military and educators, in the course of fulfilling their official duties, respect freedom of religion or belief and do not discriminate for reasons based on religion or belief, and that all necessary and appropriate awareness-raising, education or training is provided;

(k) To take all necessary and appropriate action, in conformity with international standards of human rights, to combat hatred, discrimination, intolerance and acts of violence, intimidation and coercion motivated by intolerance based on religion or belief, as well as incitement to hostility and violence, with particular regard to members of religious minorities in all parts of the world;

(l) To promote, through education and other means, understanding, tolerance, non-discrimination and respect in all matters relating to freedom of religion or belief by encouraging a wider knowledge in the society at large of the history, traditions, languages and culture of the various religious minorities existing within their jurisdiction;

(m) To prevent any distinction, exclusion, restriction or preference based on religion or belief which impairs the recognition, enjoyment or exercise of human rights and fundamental freedoms on an equal basis, and to detect signs of intolerance that may lead to discrimination based on religion or belief;

12. *Stresses* the importance of a continued and strengthened dialogue in all its forms, including among

and within religions or beliefs, and with broader participation, including of women, to promote greater tolerance,
respect and mutual understanding, and welcomes different
initiatives in this regard, including the Alliance of Civilizations and the programmes led by the United Nations
Educational, Scientific and Cultural Organization;

13. *Welcomes and encourages* the continuing efforts of
all actors in society, including non-governmental organizations and bodies and groups based on religion or belief,
to promote the implementation of the Declaration on the
Elimination of All Forms of Intolerance and of Discrimination Based on Religion or Belief, and further encourages
their work in promoting freedom of religion or belief and in
highlighting cases of religious intolerance, discrimination
and persecution;

14. *Recommends* that States, the United Nations and
other actors, including non-governmental organizations
and bodies and groups based on religion or belief, in their
efforts to promote freedom of religion or belief, ensure the
widest possible dissemination of the text of the Declaration,
in as many different languages as possible, and promote its
implementation;

15. *Welcomes* the work and the interim report of the
Special Rapporteur of the Human Rights Council on freedom of religion or belief;

16. *Urges* all Governments to cooperate fully with the
Special Rapporteur, to respond favourably to her requests
to visit their countries and to provide all necessary information for the effective fulfilment of her mandate;

17. *Requests* the Secretary-General to ensure that the
Special Rapporteur receives the resources necessary to fully
discharge her mandate;

18. *Requests* the Special Rapporteur to submit an
interim report to the General Assembly at its sixty-fifth
session;

19. *Decides* to consider the question of the elimination
of all forms of religious intolerance at its sixty-fifth session
under the item entitled "Promotion and protection of
human rights".

Right to self-determination

Report of Secretary-General. In response to
General Assembly resolution 63/163 [YUN 2008,
p. 789], the Secretary-General submitted a report
[A/64/360] on the question of the universal realization
of the right of peoples to self-determination. The report summarized developments relating to the consideration of that subject by the Human Rights Council
and outlined the jurisprudence of the Human Rights
Committee and the Committee on Economic, Social
and Cultural Rights on the treaty-based human rights
norms relating to the realization of that right.

GENERAL ASSEMBLY ACTION

On 18 December [meeting 65], the General Assembly,
on the recommendation of the Third Committee
[A/64/438], adopted **resolution 64/149** without vote
[agenda item 68].

Universal realization of the right of peoples to self-determination

The General Assembly,

Reaffirming the importance, for the effective guarantee
and observance of human rights, of the universal realization of the right of peoples to self-determination enshrined
in the Charter of the United Nations and embodied in the
International Covenants on Human Rights, as well as in
the Declaration on the Granting of Independence to Colonial Countries and Peoples contained in General Assembly
resolution 1514(XV) of 14 December 1960,

Welcoming the progressive exercise of the right to self-
determination by peoples under colonial, foreign or alien
occupation and their emergence into sovereign statehood
and independence,

Deeply concerned at the continuation of acts or threats
of foreign military intervention and occupation that are
threatening to suppress, or have already suppressed, the
right to self-determination of peoples and nations,

Expressing grave concern that, as a consequence of the
persistence of such actions, millions of people have been
and are being uprooted from their homes as refugees and
displaced persons, and emphasizing the urgent need for
concerted international action to alleviate their condition,

Recalling the relevant resolutions regarding the violation
of the right of peoples to self-determination and other
human rights as a result of foreign military intervention,
aggression and occupation, adopted by the Commission
on Human Rights at its sixty-first and previous sessions,

Reaffirming its previous resolutions on the universal
realization of the right of peoples to self-determination,
including resolution 63/163 of 18 December 2008,

Reaffirming also its resolution 55/2 of 8 September 2000,
containing the United Nations Millennium Declaration,
and recalling its resolution 60/1 of 16 September 2005,
containing the 2005 World Summit Outcome, which, inter
alia, upheld the right to self-determination of peoples under
colonial domination and foreign occupation,

Taking note of the report of the Secretary-General on
the right of peoples to self-determination,

1. *Reaffirms* that the universal realization of the right
of all peoples, including those under colonial, foreign and
alien domination, to self-determination is a fundamental
condition for the effective guarantee and observance of
human rights and for the preservation and promotion of
such rights;

2. *Declares its firm opposition* to acts of foreign military
intervention, aggression and occupation, since these have
resulted in the suppression of the right of peoples to self-
determination and other human rights in certain parts of
the world;

3. *Calls upon* those States responsible to cease immediately their military intervention in and occupation of foreign countries and territories and all acts of repression, discrimination, exploitation and maltreatment, in particular
the brutal and inhuman methods reportedly employed for
the execution of those acts against the peoples concerned;

4. *Deplores* the plight of millions of refugees and
displaced persons who have been uprooted as a result of the
aforementioned acts, and reaffirms their right to return to
their homes voluntarily in safety and honour;

5. *Requests* the Human Rights Council to continue to give special attention to the violation of human rights, especially the right to self-determination, resulting from foreign military intervention, aggression or occupation;

6. *Requests* the Secretary-General to report on the question to the General Assembly at its sixty-fifth session under the item entitled "Right of peoples to self-determination".

Rights of Palestinians to self-determination

During the year, the General Assembly reaffirmed the right of the Palestinian people to self-determination, including the right to their independent State of Palestine, as well as the right of all States in the region to live in peace within secure and internationally recognized borders. States and UN system bodies were urged to assist Palestinians in the early realization of the right.

Human Rights Council action. On 26 March [A/64/53 (res. 10/20)], the Council urged Member States and UN system bodies to support and assist the Palestinian people in the early realization of their right to self-determination.

GENERAL ASSEMBLY ACTION

On 18 December [meeting 65], the General Assembly, on the recommendation of the Third Committee [A/64/438], adopted **resolution 64/150** by recorded vote (176-6-3) [agenda item 68].

The right of the Palestinian people to self-determination

The General Assembly,

Aware that the development of friendly relations among nations, based on respect for the principle of equal rights and self-determination of peoples, is among the purposes and principles of the United Nations, as defined in the Charter,

Recalling, in this regard, its resolution 2625(XXV) of 24 October 1970 entitled "Declaration on Principles of International Law concerning Friendly Relations and Cooperation among States in accordance with the Charter of the United Nations",

Bearing in mind the International Covenants on Human Rights, the Universal Declaration of Human Rights, the Declaration on the Granting of Independence to Colonial Countries and Peoples and the Vienna Declaration and Programme of Action adopted at the World Conference on Human Rights on 25 June 1993,

Recalling the Declaration on the Occasion of the Fiftieth Anniversary of the United Nations,

Recalling also the United Nations Millennium Declaration,

Recalling further the advisory opinion rendered on 9 July 2004 by the International Court of Justice on the *Legal Consequences of the Construction of a Wall in the Occupied Palestinian Territory*, and noting in particular the reply of the Court, including on the right of peoples to self-determination, which is a right *erga omnes*,

Recalling the conclusion of the Court, in its advisory opinion of 9 July 2004, that the construction of the wall

by Israel, the occupying Power, in the Occupied Palestinian Territory, including East Jerusalem, along with measures previously taken, severely impedes the right of the Palestinian people to self-determination,

Expressing the urgent need for the resumption of negotiations within the Middle East peace process, based on the relevant United Nations resolutions, the Madrid terms of reference, including the principle of land for peace, the Arab Peace Initiative and the Quartet road map to a permanent two-State solution to the Israeli-Palestinian conflict, and for the speedy achievement of a just, lasting and comprehensive peace settlement between the Palestinian and Israeli sides,

Stressing the need for respect for and preservation of the territorial unity, contiguity and integrity of all of the Occupied Palestinian Territory, including East Jerusalem,

Recalling its resolution 63/165 of 18 December 2008,

Affirming the right of all States in the region to live in peace within secure and internationally recognized borders,

1. *Reaffirms* the right of the Palestinian people to self-determination, including the right to their independent State of Palestine;

2. *Urges* all States and the specialized agencies and organizations of the United Nations system to continue to support and assist the Palestinian people in the early realization of their right to self-determination.

RECORDED VOTE ON RESOLUTION 64/150:

In favour: Afghanistan, Albania, Algeria, Andorra, Angola, Antigua and Barbuda, Argentina, Armenia, Australia, Austria, Azerbaijan, Bahamas, Bahrain, Bangladesh, Barbados, Belarus, Belgium, Belize, Benin, Bhutan, Bolivia, Bosnia and Herzegovina, Botswana, Brazil, Brunei Darussalam, Bulgaria, Burkina Faso, Burundi, Cambodia, Cape Verde, Central African Republic, Chad, Chile, China, Colombia, Comoros, Congo, Costa Rica, Côte d'Ivoire, Croatia, Cuba, Cyprus, Czech Republic, Democratic People's Republic of Korea, Democratic Republic of the Congo, Denmark, Djibouti, Dominica, Dominican Republic, Ecuador, Egypt, El Salvador, Equatorial Guinea, Eritrea, Estonia, Ethiopia, Fiji, Finland, France, Gabon, Georgia, Germany, Ghana, Greece, Grenada, Guatemala, Guinea, Guinea-Bissau, Guyana, Haiti, Honduras, Hungary, Iceland, India, Indonesia, Iran, Iraq, Ireland, Italy, Jamaica, Japan, Jordan, Kazakhstan, Kenya, Kuwait, Kyrgyzstan, Lao People's Democratic Republic, Latvia, Lebanon, Lesotho, Liberia, Libyan Arab Jamahiriya, Liechtenstein, Lithuania, Luxembourg, Madagascar, Malawi, Malaysia, Maldives, Mali, Malta, Mauritania, Mauritius, Mexico, Moldova, Monaco, Mongolia, Montenegro, Morocco, Mozambique, Namibia, Nepal, Netherlands, New Zealand, Nicaragua, Niger, Nigeria, Norway, Oman, Pakistan, Panama, Papua New Guinea, Paraguay, Peru, Philippines, Poland, Portugal, Qatar, Republic of Korea, Romania, Russian Federation, Rwanda, Saint Kitts and Nevis, Saint Lucia, Saint Vincent and the Grenadines, Samoa, San Marino, Saudi Arabia, Senegal, Serbia, Sierra Leone, Singapore, Slovakia, Slovenia, Solomon Islands, South Africa, Spain, Sri Lanka, Sudan, Suriname, Swaziland, Sweden, Switzerland, Syrian Arab Republic, Tajikistan, Thailand, The former Yugoslav Republic of Macedonia, Timor-Leste, Togo, Trinidad and Tobago, Tunisia, Turkey, Turkmenistan, Tuvalu, Uganda, Ukraine, United Arab Emirates, United Kingdom, United Republic of Tanzania, Uruguay, Uzbekistan, Venezuela, Viet Nam, Yemen, Zambia, Zimbabwe.

Against: Israel, Marshall Islands, Micronesia, Nauru, Palau, United States.

Abstaining: Cameroon, Canada, Tonga.

Mercenaries

Reports of Working Group. In its annual report [A/HRC/10/14], issued in January, the five-member Working Group on the use of mercenaries as a means of violating human rights and impeding the exercise of the right of peoples to self-determination reviewed its activities and described envisioned future activities, notably a process of regional consultations with States to discuss the fundamental question of the role of the State as a holder of the monopoly of the use of force. The Group devoted a section of the report to standards, principles and guidelines for a new international convention on regulating private military and security companies and other legal regulatory instruments. The Group recommended the elaboration and adoption of such a convention, as well as an accompanying model law to assist Governments in adopting national legislation. The Group also proposed basic principles for regulating private military and security companies and recommended, when those principles were converted by it into draft legal instruments, the establishment of an intersessional, intergovernmental open-ended working group to prepare such a convention.

An addendum [A/HRC/10/14/Add.1] summarized allegations transmitted to seven Governments between 1 October 2007 and 15 December 2008 and Government replies received until 31 January 2009.

In response to General Assembly resolution 63/164 [YUN 2008, p. 792], the Secretary-General in August transmitted the report [A/64/311] of the Working Group, which outlined its activities, including work on a possible new draft international convention. The Group recommended that the approach to private military and security companies should imply greater State responsibility for the activities of those companies worldwide, including responsibility for where and how they operated and their impact on human rights. Governments should devise national and international mechanisms to monitor human rights violations and ensure that victims had access to remedies. A complaint mechanism open to individuals, State agencies, foreign Governments and other companies and entities should be established to provide an avenue for victims to be heard and a means to request information from the concerned Government. The Group reported on the status of the International Convention against the Recruitment, Use, Financing and Training of Mercenaries, adopted by the General Assembly in 1989 [YUN 1989, p. 825], which by year's end had 32 States parties.

After its mission to Afghanistan (4–9 April) [A/HRC/15/25/Add.2], the Working Group recommended that the Government investigate all private military and security companies operating without licences and take action to disarm them; investigate incidents involving casualties caused by private security contractors, prosecute the perpetrators and provide remedies for victims; establish a regulation mechanism with oversight of the companies that had been licensed; and establish a complaints mechanism through which the local population and civilian international actors could submit complaints.

After its mission to the United States (20 July– 3 August) [A/HRC/15/25/Add.3], the Working Group recommended that the Government: support the Stop Outsourcing Security (sos) Act, which defined the functions that were inherently governmental and could not be outsourced to the private sector; rescind immunity to contractors carrying out activities in other countries under bilateral agreements; investigate human rights violations committed by private military and security companies and prosecute alleged perpetrators; ensure that the oversight of private military and security contractors was not outsourced to the private sector; establish a system of federal licensing of those companies for their activities abroad; set up a vetting procedure for awarding contracts to those companies; ensure that United States criminal jurisdiction apply to private military and security companies contracted by the Government to carry out activities abroad; and respond to pending communications from the Group, including its long-standing case related to Luis Posada Carriles, allegedly involved in mercenary activities in the Americas in the 1980s and residing in the United States.

The Group reported [A/HRC/15/25/Add.4] on the regional consultation for Asia and the Pacific (Bangkok, 26–27 October). Through the consultation, the Group sought to gain a regional perspective on practices related to mercenaries and private military and security companies registered, operating or recruiting personnel in the Asia, Pacific and Middle East regions.

Human Rights Council action. On 26 March [A/64/53 (res. 10/11)], the Council, by a recorded vote of 32 to 12, with 3 abstentions, urged States to take the necessary steps against the menace posed by the activities of mercenaries, and to take legislative measures to ensure that their territories, as well as their nationals, were not used for the recruitment, assembly, financing, training and transit of mercenaries for activities designed to impede the right to self-determination. The Working Group was requested to report to the Council's fifteenth (2010) session, including on progress achieved in elaborating a possible draft convention on private companies offering military assistance, consultancy and other military security-related services on the international market.

On 18 December [meeting 65], the General Assembly, on the recommendation of the Third Committee [A/64/438], adopted **resolution 64/151** by recorded vote (126-53-4) [agenda item 68].

Use of mercenaries as a means of violating human rights and impeding the exercise of the right of peoples to self-determination

The General Assembly,

Recalling all of its previous resolutions on the subject, including resolution 63/164 of 18 December 2008, and Human Rights Council resolution 10/11 of 26 March 2009, as well as all resolutions adopted by the Commission on Human Rights in this regard,

Recalling also all of its relevant resolutions in which, inter alia, it condemned any State that permitted or tolerated the recruitment, financing, training, assembly, transit and use of mercenaries with the objective of overthrowing the Governments of States Members of the United Nations, especially those of developing countries, or of fighting against national liberation movements, and recalling further the relevant resolutions and international instruments adopted by the General Assembly, the Security Council, the Economic and Social Council and the Organization of African Unity, inter alia, the Organization of African Unity Convention for the elimination of mercenarism in Africa, as well as by the African Union,

Reaffirming the purposes and principles enshrined in the Charter of the United Nations concerning the strict observance of the principles of sovereign equality, political independence, the territorial integrity of States, the self-determination of peoples, the non-use of force or of the threat of use of force in international relations and non-interference in affairs within the domestic jurisdiction of States,

Reaffirming also that, by virtue of the principle of self-determination, all peoples have the right freely to determine their political status and to pursue their economic, social and cultural development, and that every State has the duty to respect this right in accordance with the provisions of the Charter,

Reaffirming further the Declaration on Principles of International Law concerning Friendly Relations and Cooperation among States in accordance with the Charter of the United Nations,

Alarmed and concerned at the danger that the activities of mercenaries constitute to peace and security in developing countries, in particular in Africa and in small States,

Deeply concerned at the loss of life, the substantial damage to property and the negative effects on the policy and economies of affected countries resulting from criminal mercenary activities,

Extremely alarmed and concerned about recent mercenary activities in some developing countries in various parts of the world, including in areas of armed conflict, and the threat they pose to the integrity of and respect for the constitutional order of the affected countries,

Convinced that, notwithstanding the way in which they are used or the form that they take to acquire some semblance of legitimacy, mercenaries or mercenary-related activities are a threat to peace, security and the self-determination of peoples and an obstacle to the enjoyment of all human rights by peoples,

1. *Takes note with appreciation* of the report of the Working Group on the use of mercenaries as a means of violating human rights and impeding the exercise of the right of peoples to self-determination, and expresses its appreciation for the work of the experts of the Working Group;

2. *Reaffirms* that the use of mercenaries and their recruitment, financing and training are causes for grave concern to all States and violate the purposes and principles enshrined in the Charter of the United Nations;

3. *Recognizes* that armed conflict, terrorism, arms trafficking and covert operations by third Powers, inter alia, encourage the demand for mercenaries on the global market;

4. *Urges once again* all States to take the steps necessary and to exercise the utmost vigilance against the menace posed by the activities of mercenaries and to take legislative measures to ensure that their territories and other territories under their control, as well as their nationals, are not used for the recruitment, assembly, financing, training and transit of mercenaries for the planning of activities designed to impede the right of peoples to self-determination, to destabilize or overthrow the Government of any State or to dismember or impair, totally or in part, the territorial integrity or political unity of sovereign and independent States conducting themselves in compliance with the right of peoples to self-determination;

5. *Requests* all States to exercise the utmost vigilance against any kind of recruitment, training, hiring or financing of mercenaries by private companies offering international military consultancy and security services, as well as to impose a specific ban on such companies intervening in armed conflicts or actions to destabilize constitutional regimes;

6. *Encourages* States that import the military assistance, consultancy and security services provided by private companies to establish regulatory national mechanisms for the registering and licensing of those companies in order to ensure that imported services provided by those private companies neither impede the enjoyment of human rights nor violate human rights in the recipient country;

7. *Calls upon* all States that have not yet done so to consider taking the action necessary to accede to or ratify the International Convention against the Recruitment, Use, Financing and Training of Mercenaries;

8. *Welcomes* the cooperation extended by those countries that received a visit by the Working Group and the adoption by some States of national legislation that restricts the recruitment, assembly, financing, training and transit of mercenaries;

9. *Condemns* recent mercenary activities in developing countries in various parts of the world, in particular in areas of conflict, and the threat they pose to the integrity of and respect for the constitutional order of those countries and the exercise of the right of their peoples to self-determination, and stresses the importance for the Working Group of looking into sources and root causes, as well as the political motivations of mercenaries and for mercenary-related activities;

10. *Calls upon* States to investigate the possibility of mercenary involvement whenever and wherever criminal acts of a terrorist nature occur and to bring to trial those found responsible or to consider their extradition, if so re-

quested, in accordance with domestic law and applicable bilateral or international treaties;

11.	*Condemns* any form of impunity granted to perpetrators of mercenary activities and to those responsible for the use, recruitment, financing and training of mercenaries, and urges all States, in accordance with their obligations under international law, to bring them, without distinction, to justice;

12.	*Calls upon* Member States, in accordance with their obligations under international law, to cooperate with and assist the judicial prosecution of those accused of mercenary activities in transparent, open and fair trials;

13.	*Requests* the Working Group to continue the work already done by the previous Special Rapporteurs on the strengthening of the international legal framework for the prevention and sanction of the recruitment, use, financing and training of mercenaries, taking into account the proposal for a new legal definition of a mercenary drafted by the Special Rapporteur in his report to the Commission on Human Rights at its sixtieth session, including the elaboration and presentation of concrete proposals on possible complementary and new standards aimed at filling existing gaps, as well as general guidelines or basic principles encouraging the further protection of human rights, in particular the right of peoples to self-determination, while facing current and emergent threats posed by mercenaries or mercenary-related activities;

14.	*Requests* the Office of the United Nations High Commissioner for Human Rights, as a matter of priority, to publicize the adverse effects of the activities of mercenaries on the right of peoples to self-determination and, when requested and where necessary, to render advisory services to States that are affected by those activities;

15.	*Expresses its appreciation* to the Office of the High Commissioner for its support for convening the regional governmental consultations in the Russian Federation for States in the Eastern European Group and Central Asia region and in Thailand for States in the Asian region on traditional and new forms of mercenary activities as a means of violating human rights and impeding the exercise of the right of peoples to self-determination, in particular regarding the effects of the activities of private military and security companies on the enjoyment of human rights;

16.	*Requests* the Office of the High Commissioner to continue to support the Working Group in the convening of regional governmental consultations on this matter, with the remaining two to be held before the end of 2010, bearing in mind that this process may lead to the holding of a high-level round table of States, under the auspices of the United Nations, to discuss the fundamental question of the role of the State as holder of the monopoly of the use of force, with the objective of facilitating a critical understanding of the responsibilities of the different actors, including private military and security companies, in the current context, and their respective obligations for the promotion and protection of human rights and in reaching a common understanding as to which additional regulations and controls are needed at the international level;

17.	*Notes with appreciation* the work of the Working Group on its elaboration of concrete principles on the regulation of private companies offering military assistance, consultancy and other military security-related services on the international market, which it carried out after country visits and through the process of regional consultations, and in consultation with academics and intergovernmental and non-governmental organizations;

18.	*Urges* all States to cooperate fully with the Working Group in the fulfilment of its mandate;

19.	*Requests* the Secretary-General and the United Nations High Commissioner for Human Rights to provide the Working Group with all the assistance and support necessary for the fulfilment of its mandate, both professional and financial, including through the promotion of cooperation between the Working Group and other components of the United Nations system that deal with countering mercenary-related activities, in order to meet the demands of its current and future activities;

20.	*Requests* the Working Group to consult States and intergovernmental and non-governmental organizations in the implementation of the present resolution and to report, with specific recommendations, to the General Assembly at its sixty-fifth session its findings on the use of mercenaries to undermine the enjoyment of all human rights and to impede the exercise of the right of peoples to self-determination;

21.	*Decides* to consider at its sixty-fifth session the question of the use of mercenaries as a means of violating human rights and impeding the exercise of the right of peoples to self-determination under the item entitled "Right of peoples to self-determination".

RECORDED VOTE ON RESOLUTION 64/151:

In favour: Afghanistan, Algeria, Angola, Antigua and Barbuda, Argentina, Armenia, Azerbaijan, Bahamas, Bahrain, Bangladesh, Barbados, Belarus, Belize, Benin, Bhutan, Bolivia, Botswana, Brazil, Brunei Darussalam, Burkina Faso, Burundi, Cambodia, Cameroon, Cape Verde, Central African Republic, Chad, Chile, China, Colombia, Comoros, Congo, Costa Rica, Côte d'Ivoire, Cuba, Democratic People's Republic of Korea, Democratic Republic of the Congo, Djibouti, Dominica, Dominican Republic, Ecuador, Egypt, El Salvador, Equatorial Guinea, Eritrea, Ethiopia, Gabon, Ghana, Grenada, Guatemala, Guinea, Guinea-Bissau, Guyana, Haiti, Honduras, India, Indonesia, Iran, Iraq, Jamaica, Jordan, Kazakhstan, Kenya, Kuwait, Kyrgyzstan, Lao People's Democratic Republic, Lebanon, Lesotho, Liberia, Libyan Arab Jamahiriya, Madagascar, Malawi, Malaysia, Maldives, Mali, Mauritania, Mauritius, Mexico, Mongolia, Morocco, Mozambique, Namibia, Nepal, Nicaragua, Niger, Nigeria, Oman, Pakistan, Panama, Papua New Guinea, Paraguay, Peru, Philippines, Qatar, Russian Federation, Rwanda, Saint Kitts and Nevis, Saint Lucia, Saint Vincent and the Grenadines, Samoa, Saudi Arabia, Senegal, Sierra Leone, Singapore, Solomon Islands, South Africa, Sri Lanka, Sudan, Suriname, Swaziland, Syrian Arab Republic, Tajikistan, Thailand, Togo, Trinidad and Tobago, Tunisia, Tuvalu, Uganda, United Arab Emirates, United Republic of Tanzania, Uruguay, Uzbekistan, Venezuela, Viet Nam, Yemen, Zambia, Zimbabwe.

Against: Albania, Andorra, Australia, Austria, Belgium, Bosnia and Herzegovina, Bulgaria, Canada, Croatia, Cyprus, Czech Republic, Denmark, Estonia, Finland, France, Georgia, Germany, Greece, Hungary, Iceland, Ireland, Israel, Italy, Japan, Latvia, Liechtenstein, Lithuania, Luxembourg, Malta, Marshall Islands, Micronesia, Moldova, Monaco, Montenegro, Netherlands, New Zealand, Norway, Palau, Poland, Portugal, Republic of Korea, Romania, San Marino, Serbia, Slovakia, Slovenia, Spain, Sweden, The former Yugoslav Republic of Macedonia, Turkey, Ukraine, United Kingdom, United States.

Abstaining: Fiji, Switzerland, Timor-Leste, Tonga.

Rule of law, democracy and human rights

Administration of justice

Human Rights Council action. On 25 March [A/64/53 (res. 10/2)], the Council called on Member States to provide for effective legislative, judicial, social and educative mechanisms and procedures to ensure the full implementation of UN human rights standards in the administration of justice. The Council encouraged States to integrate children's issues in their rule of law efforts, develop and implement a comprehensive juvenile justice policy to prevent and address juvenile delinquency, promote alternative measures, such as diversion and restorative justice, ensure that deprivation of children's liberty be used as a last resort and avoid pretrial detention for children. The Secretary-General was requested to report to the Council's thirteenth (2010) session on the latest developments, challenges and good practices in human rights in the administration of justice, including juvenile justice and conditions for women and children in detention, as well as in activities undertaken by the UN system.

Transitional justice

OHCHR study. Pursuant to a Human Rights Council request [YUN 2008, p. 794], OHCHR in August submitted a study [A/HRC/12/18] on human rights and transitional justice, which reviewed OHCHR field presences and human rights components of UN peacekeeping and political missions. OHCHR had supported transitional justice programmes in more than 20 countries, offering expertise during peace negotiations, and assisting in the design and implementation of truth commissions, prosecution initiatives, reparations programmes and institutional reform. The study discussed the relationship between justice and peace, including human rights and transitional justice aspects of peace agreements; explored the potential for greater inclusion of economic, social and cultural rights in transitional justice mechanisms and processes; and considered the linkages between disarmament, demobilization and reintegration, and transitional justice processes. There was a need for further understanding of the human rights aspects of vetting processes, witness and victim protection, and the relationship between traditional justice and transitional justice mechanisms.

An addendum [A/HRC/12/18/Add.1] provided an inventory of human rights and transitional justice aspects of recent peace agreements.

Human Rights Council action. On 1 October [A/65/53 (res. 12/11)], the Council emphasized the importance of a comprehensive approach to transitional justice, incorporating the full range of judicial and non-judicial measures, including individual prosecutions, reparations, truth-seeking, institutional reform, and vetting of public employees and officials, in order to ensure accountability, serve justice, provide remedies to victims, promote healing and reconciliation, establish independent oversight of the security system, restore confidence in State institutions and promote the rule of law. OHCHR was requested to submit to the Council's eighteenth (2011) session a report containing an update of the activities undertaken by the Office in the context of transitional justice.

Right to the truth

OHCHR study. Pursuant to a Human Rights Council request [YUN 2008, p. 799], OHCHR in August submitted a study [A/HRC/12/19] on best practices for the effective implementation of the right to the truth, in particular practices relating to archives and records concerning gross violations of human rights, and the protection of witnesses and other persons involved in trials connected with such violations.

Human Rights Council action. On 1 October [A/65/53 (res. 12/12)], the Council encouraged the States concerned to implement the recommendations of non-judicial mechanisms such as truth and reconciliation commissions, and encouraged other States to establish judicial mechanisms and truth and reconciliation commissions to complement the justice system, in order to investigate and address gross human rights violations. It requested OHCHR to report to the Council's fifteenth (2010) session on programmes for the protection of witnesses of gross human rights violations for the possible development of guidelines. OHCHR was invited to convene a seminar on creating, organizing and managing public systems of archives as a means to guarantee the right to the truth, and to report to the Council at its seventeenth (2011) session.

Independence of the judicial system

Reports of Special Rapporteur. In a report issued in March [A/HRC/11/41], the Special Rapporteur on the independence of judges and lawyers, Leandro Despouy (Argentina), described his activities between May 2008 and March 2009. The Rapporteur devoted this last thematic report to an analysis of parameters necessary to guarantee the independence of judges: those included both individual and institutional elements, which could either reinforce or hamper the independent administration of justice. He addressed developments in the cases before the International Criminal Court, discussed recent judgments of the International Tribunal for the Former

Yugoslavia and the International Criminal Tribunal for Rwanda and examined progress made by the Extraordinary Chambers in the Courts of Cambodia. He also referred to the Special Tribunal for Lebanon and the institution of proceedings by Belgium before the International Court of Justice concerning the case of the former President of Chad, Hissène Habré. The Rapporteur recommended measures to be taken by Member States to strengthen the independence of judges in both its individual and institutional dimensions.

An addendum [A/HRC/11/41/Add.1] summarized communications sent to 52 Governments between 16 March 2008 and 15 March 2009 and replies received between 1 May 2008 and 10 May 2009.

In response to a Human Rights Council request [YUN 2008, p. 801], the Secretary-General in July transmitted to the General Assembly the report of the Rapporteur [A/64/181], which analysed safeguards established by international law to ensure the independence of lawyers and the legal profession. In his concluding report, the Rapporteur said that throughout his tenure he had witnessed that the independence of the judiciary was at risk in all parts of the world, and that key actors in the field were the targets of attacks affecting their professional and personal integrity. Lawyers, in particular, were often the targets of attacks affecting them in the discharge of their duty as well as on their physical and moral integrity. The Rapporteur recommended that the right to legal counsel of choice be enshrined at the constitutional level or be considered as a fundamental principle of law and be translated into domestic legislation. Among other things, the authorities should refrain from directly or indirectly interfering in the work and functioning of lawyers; acts of harassment, threats or physical assaults should be promptly investigated; where the security of lawyers was threatened the authorities should be required to adopt effective security measures; and when a lawyer was arrested or detained, the legal profession should be informed immediately of the reason and be granted access to the lawyer in question.

The General Assembly took note of that report on 18 December (**decision 64/536**).

Following his mission to Guatemala (26–30 January) [A/HRC/11/41/Add.3], the Rapporteur observed that one main cause of the prevalence of impunity was the violence to which justice professionals were subjected. Urgent reforms were needed. A unified justice policy should be established, addressing the problem of many different institutions acting in a fragmentary and disjointed manner. It was necessary to define a State criminal and criminological policy, and the establishment of a Ministry of Justice could help to solve those problems. At the same time, it was

necessary to regulate the way in which justice officials were elected. The current system was open to external interference and was highly politicized, affecting the independence of the judiciary. The criminal investigative bodies should coordinate and harmonize their actions so as to guarantee their effectiveness, and the International Commission against Impunity in Guatemala played a vital role in that regard. Finally, it was necessary to adopt a set of legislative reforms, including in respect of access to justice. The legislature had a basic responsibility to step up the effort to combat impunity.

Appointment of Special Rapporteur. On 18 June, the Human Rights Council appointed Gabriela Carina Knaul de Albuquerque e Silva (Brazil) as Special Rapporteur. She assumed the post on 1 August.

Report of Special Rapporteur. Following her mission to Colombia (7–16 December) [A/HRC/14/26/Add.2], the Rapporteur recommended revising the system of appointment of the members of the Disciplinary Chamber of the Supreme Judicial Council, securing a majority of career staff and a substantive participation of magistrates, judges, lawyers and academics; developing mechanisms to resolve the conflicts of jurisdiction between military and ordinary courts, sending cases to ordinary courts in case of doubt; establishing a single legal career in the judiciary and a career in the Attorney General's Office through objective and impartial competitive examinations; and investigating all murders, attacks, threats and intimidations against magistrates and judges. Progress was needed in demarcating, titling and registering land ownership, as uncertainty in those matters was an underlying cause of many crimes and human rights violations.

Human Rights Council action. On 1 October [A/65/53 (res. 12/3)], the Council called on Governments to respect and uphold the independence of judges and lawyers and to take legislative, law enforcement and other measures enabling them to carry out their duties without harassment or intimidation. The Council encouraged States to promote diversity in the composition of the members of the judiciary and to ensure that the requirements for joining the judiciary and the selection process thereof were non-discriminatory.

Electoral processes

Report of Secretary-General. In conformity with General Assembly resolution 62/150 [YUN 2007, p. 740], the Secretary-General in August submitted a report [A/64/304] describing the activities of the UN system in providing electoral assistance to Member States over the previous two years. Assistance was provided to 52 Member States, 8 of them on the basis of a Security Council mandate. As the focal point for electoral assistance activities, the Under-Secretary-General for Political Affairs was responsible for ensuring organizational coherence as well as political and technical consistency, supported by the Electoral Assistance Division, which assisted with the design and staffing of UN electoral activities, provided technical guidance and maintained both the roster of electoral experts and the Organization's electoral institutional memory. In peacekeeping or post-conflict environments, electoral assistance was generally provided through field components of the Departments of Peacekeeping Operations or of Political Affairs. Also involved were the United Nations Development Programme, OHCHR, the United Nations Volunteers programme and other UN entities.

The report indicated that the demand from Member States for such assistance remained high, and highlighted positive trends, including the increasing number of States that were using elections as a peaceful means of discerning the will of the people, the growing capacity among new democracies to administer credible elections, and increasing South-South cooperation among electoral administrators. Challenges included the potential for elections to be overshadowed by political discord or violence, especially after results were announced; concerns regarding the cost of elections and sustainability; and, following the increase of actors involved in electoral assistance both inside and outside the United Nations, the need to ensure coordination and cohesion and safeguard UN impartiality. The report observed the need to: make sustainability and cost-effectiveness more central in the design and provision of electoral assistance; ensure that elections contributed to peace and good governance, rather than violence or instability; and increase the use of special or more flexible administrative procedures for electoral projects in a crisis situation or under a Security Council mandate. The report concluded by recalling that while elections were technical processes, they were fundamentally political events. The true measure of an election was whether it engendered broad public confidence in the process and trust in the outcome. An election run honestly and transparently, respecting basic rights, with the support of State institutions and responsible conduct of participants—leaders, candidates and voters—was most likely to achieve an accepted and peaceful outcome.

GENERAL ASSEMBLY ACTION

On 18 December [meeting 65], the General Assembly, on the recommendation of the Third Committee [A/64/439/Add.2 (Part II)], adopted **resolution 64/155** without vote [agenda item 69 *(b)*].

Strengthening the role of the United Nations in enhancing periodic and genuine elections and the promotion of democratization

The General Assembly,

Reaffirming that democracy is a universal value based on the freely expressed will of the people to determine their own political, economic, social and cultural systems and their full participation in all aspects of their lives,

Reaffirming also that, while democracies share common features, there is no single model of democracy and that democracy does not belong to any country or region, and reaffirming further the necessity of due respect for sovereignty and the right to self-determination,

Stressing that democracy, development and respect for all human rights and fundamental freedoms are interdependent and mutually reinforcing,

Reaffirming that Member States are responsible for organizing, conducting and ensuring free and fair electoral processes and that Member States, in the exercise of their sovereignty, may request that international organizations provide advisory services or assistance for strengthening and developing their electoral institutions and processes, including sending preliminary missions for that purpose,

Recalling its previous resolutions on the subject, in particular resolution 62/150 of 18 December 2007,

Reaffirming that United Nations electoral assistance and support for the promotion of democratization are provided only at the specific request of the Member State concerned,

Noting with satisfaction that increasing numbers of Member States are using elections as a peaceful means of discerning the will of the people, which builds confidence in representative governance and contributes to greater national peace and stability,

Recalling the Universal Declaration of Human Rights, adopted on 10 December 1948, in particular the principle that the will of the people, as expressed through periodic and genuine elections, shall be the basis of government authority, as well as the right freely to choose representatives through periodic and genuine elections, which shall be by universal and equal suffrage and shall be held by secret vote or by equivalent free voting procedures,

Reaffirming the International Covenant on Civil and Political Rights, the Convention on the Elimination of All Forms of Discrimination against Women and the International Convention on the Elimination of All Forms of Racial Discrimination, in particular that citizens, without distinction of any kind, have the right and the opportunity to take part in the conduct of public affairs, directly or through freely chosen representatives, and to vote and to be elected in genuine periodic elections which shall be by universal and equal suffrage and shall be held by secret ballot, guaranteeing the free expression of the will of the electors,

Stressing the importance, generally and in the context of promoting fair and free elections, of respect for the freedom to seek, receive and impart information, in accordance with the International Covenant on Civil and Political Rights, and noting in particular the fundamental importance of access to information and media freedom,

Recognizing the need for strengthening democratic processes, electoral institutions and national capacity-building in requesting countries, including the capacity to administer fair elections, promote the participation of women on equal terms with men, increase citizen participation and provide civic education in requesting countries in order to consolidate and regularize the achievements of previous elections and support subsequent elections,

Noting the importance of ensuring orderly, open, fair and transparent democratic processes that preserve the right of peaceful assembly,

Noting also that the international community can contribute to creating conditions which could foster stability and security throughout the pre-election, election and post-election periods in transitional and post-conflict situations,

Reiterating that transparency is a fundamental basis for free and fair elections, which contribute to the accountability of leaders to their citizens, which, in turn, is an underpinning of democratic societies,

Acknowledging, in this regard, the importance of international election observation for the promotion of free and fair elections and its contribution to enhancing the integrity of election processes in requesting countries, to promoting public confidence and electoral participation and to mitigating the potential for election-related disturbances,

Acknowledging also that extending invitations regarding international electoral assistance and/or observation is the sovereign right of Member States, and welcoming the decisions of those States that have requested such assistance and/or observation,

Welcoming the support provided by Member States to the electoral assistance activities of the United Nations, inter alia, through the provision of electoral experts, including electoral commission staff, and observers, as well as through contributions to the United Nations Trust Fund for Electoral Assistance, the Democratic Governance Thematic Trust Fund and the United Nations Democracy Fund,

Recognizing that electoral assistance, particularly through appropriate, sustainable and cost-effective electoral technology, supports the electoral processes of developing countries,

Recognizing also the coordination challenges posed by the multiplicity of actors involved in electoral assistance both within and outside the United Nations,

Welcoming the contributions made by international and regional organizations and also by non-governmental organizations to enhancing the effectiveness of the principle of periodic and genuine elections and the promotion of democratization,

1. *Welcomes* the report of the Secretary-General;

2. *Commends* the electoral assistance provided upon request to Member States by the United Nations, and requests that such assistance continue on a case-by-case basis in accordance with the evolving needs and legislation of requesting countries to develop, improve and refine their electoral institutions and processes, recognizing that the responsibility for organizing free and fair elections lies with Governments;

3. *Reaffirms* that the electoral assistance provided by the United Nations should continue to be carried out in an objective, impartial, neutral and independent manner;

4. *Requests* the Under-Secretary-General for Political Affairs, in his role as United Nations focal point for electoral assistance matters, to continue to inform Member States regularly about the requests received and the nature of any assistance provided;

5. *Requests* that the United Nations continue its efforts to ensure, before undertaking to provide electoral assistance to a requesting State, that there is adequate time to organize and carry out an effective mission for providing such assistance, including the provision of long-term technical cooperation, that conditions exist to allow a free and fair election and that the results of the mission will be reported comprehensively and consistently;

6. *Recommends* that, throughout the time span of the entire electoral cycle, including before and after elections, as appropriate, based on a needs assessment and in accordance with the evolving needs of requesting Member States, bearing in mind sustainability and cost-effectiveness, the United Nations continue to provide technical advice and other assistance to requesting States and electoral institutions in order to help to strengthen their democratic processes;

7. *Notes with appreciation* the additional efforts being made to enhance cooperation with other international, governmental and non-governmental organizations in order to facilitate more comprehensive and needs-specific responses to requests for electoral assistance, encourages those organizations to share knowledge and experience in order to promote best practices in the assistance they provide and in their reporting on electoral processes, and expresses its appreciation to those Member States, regional organizations and non-governmental organizations that have provided observers or technical experts in support of United Nations electoral assistance efforts;

8. *Acknowledges* the aim of harmonizing the methods and standards of the many intergovernmental and non-governmental organizations engaged in observing elections, and in this regard expresses appreciation for the Declaration of Principles for International Election Observation and the Code of Conduct for International Election Observers, which elaborate guidelines for international electoral observation;

9. *Recalls* the establishment by the Secretary-General of the United Nations Trust Fund for Electoral Assistance, and, bearing in mind that the Fund is currently close to depletion, calls upon Member States to consider contributing to the Fund;

10. *Encourages* the Secretary-General, through the United Nations focal point for electoral assistance matters and with the support of the Electoral Assistance Division of the Department of Political Affairs of the Secretariat, to continue responding to the evolving nature of requests for assistance and the growing need for specific types of medium-term expert assistance aimed at supporting and strengthening the existing capacity of the requesting Government, in particular by enhancing the capacity of national electoral institutions;

11. *Requests* the Secretary-General to provide the Electoral Assistance Division with adequate human and financial resources to allow it to carry out its mandate, including to enhance the accessibility and diversity of the roster of electoral experts and the Organization's electoral institutional memory, and to continue to ensure that the Office of

the United Nations High Commissioner for Human Rights is able to respond, within its mandate and in close coordination with the Division, to the numerous and increasingly complex and comprehensive requests from Member States for advisory services;

12. *Reiterates* the need for ongoing comprehensive coordination, under the auspices of the United Nations focal point for electoral assistance matters, between the Electoral Assistance Division and the United Nations Development Programme and the Department of Peacekeeping Operations and the Department of Field Support of the Secretariat to ensure coordination and coherence and avoid duplication of United Nations electoral assistance, and encourages further engagement of the Office of the United Nations High Commissioner for Human Rights in this context;

13. *Requests* the United Nations Development Programme to continue its democratic governance assistance programmes in cooperation with other relevant organizations, in particular those that promote the strengthening of democratic institutions and linkages between civil society and Governments;

14. *Reiterates* the importance of reinforced coordination within and outside the United Nations system, and reaffirms the role of the United Nations focal point for electoral assistance matters in ensuring system-wide coherence and consistency and in strengthening the institutional memory and the development and dissemination of electoral policies;

15. *Requests* the Secretary-General to report to the General Assembly at its sixty-sixth session on the implementation of the present resolution, in particular on the status of requests from Member States for electoral assistance, and on his efforts to enhance support by the Organization for the democratization process in Member States.

Right to a nationality

Report of Secretary-General. As requested by the Human Rights Council [YUN 2008, p. 772], the Secretary-General in January submitted a report [A/HRC/10/34] on arbitrary deprivation of nationality, summarizing replies received from 28 Governments (Algeria, Angola, Azerbaijan, Belarus, Bosnia and Herzegovina, Bulgaria, Burkina Faso, Colombia, Congo, Costa Rica, Ecuador, Finland, Georgia, Greece, Guatemala, Iran, Iraq, Jamaica, Kuwait, Mauritius, Monaco, Montenegro, Qatar, Russian Federation, Spain, Syrian Arab Republic, Ukraine, Venezuela). The Office of the United Nations High Commissioner for Refugees and Refugees International also provided information, noting that it was a general principle of international law that State discretion on nationality matters was limited by international law and in particular obligations under international human rights law.

Human Rights Council action. On 26 March [A/64/53 (res. 10/13)], the Council called on States to refrain from taking discriminatory measures and from enacting or maintaining legislation that would

arbitrarily deprive persons of their nationality; urged States to adopt and implement nationality legislation with a view to avoiding statelessness, in particular by preventing arbitrary deprivation of nationality and statelessness as a result of State succession; and requested the Secretary-General to report on the issue to the Council's thirteenth (2010) session.

Civilians in armed conflict

OHCHR consultation. An OHCHR report issued in June [A/HRC/11/31] summarized the outcome of the expert consultation on protecting the human rights of civilians in armed conflict (Geneva, 15 April) organized in response to a Human Rights Council request [YUN 2008, p. 796].

Human Rights Council action. On 1 October [A/65/53 (res. 12/5)], the Council invited OHCHR to convene a second expert consultation on the issue, with a view to enabling the completion of the consultations, and requested OHCHR to prepare a report on the outcome of the consultation prior to its fourteenth (2010) session.

(For information on the protection of civilians in armed conflict, see p. 50.)

Other issues

Disappearance of persons

Working Group activities. The five-member Working Group on Enforced or Involuntary Disappearances in 2009 held three sessions: its eighty-seventh (Geneva, 9–13 March), eighty-eighth (Rabat, Morocco, 26–28 June) and eighty-ninth (Geneva, 4–13 November) [A/HRC/13/31 & Corr.1]. In addition to its core mandate to assist families in determining the fate or whereabouts of their family members who were reportedly "disappeared" and to act as a communication channel between families and the Government concerned, the Group monitored compliance with the 1992 Declaration on the Protection of All Persons from Enforced Disappearance [YUN 1992, p. 744]. Cases under consideration by the Group totalled 42,600, concerning 82 countries. The Group had clarified 1,776 cases over the previous five years. Between 5 December 2008 and 13 November 2009, the Group transmitted 456 new cases of enforced disappearance to 25 Governments, 54 of which allegedly occurred during the same period. Of those, 60 were urgent action appeals sent to 13 countries. The Group also clarified 37 cases in 15 countries. The Group's report summarized information on disappearances relating to 98 countries and the Palestinian Authority.

The Working Group remained concerned that of the 82 States with outstanding cases, some Governments had never replied to the Group's communications while some provided responses that did not contain relevant information. The Group urged those Governments to fulfil their obligations under international law. The Group continued to be concerned about measures taken by States while addressing terrorism and its implications for enforced disappearances, which included extraordinary renditions. The Group also noted that 81 countries had signed and 16 had ratified the International Convention for the Protection of All Persons from Enforced Disappearance, adopted in 2006 [YUN 2006, p. 800], reiterating that the Convention's entry into force would help strengthen the capacities of States to reduce the number of disappearances.

The Group finalized and adopted a general comment on enforced disappearance as a crime against humanity, whose text was included in its report.

Following its mission to Morocco (22–25 June) [A/HRC/13/31/Add.1], the Group recommended the adoption of legislative measures, such as the introduction in the Criminal Code of a separate offence of enforced disappearance; the ratification of several international instruments, in particular the International Convention; and the adoption of measures to put an end to impunity. It also recommended strengthening the independence of the judicial system, reforming the oversight of the security services and strengthening the independence and authority of the Consultative Council on Human Rights.

Human Rights Council action. On 26 March [A/64/53 (res. 10/10)], the Council called on the Governments that had not provided for a long period substantive replies concerning claims of enforced disappearances in their countries to do so. It urged States to prevent the occurrence of disappearances, including by guaranteeing that any person deprived of liberty was held solely in officially recognized and supervised places of detention; guaranteeing access to all places of detention by competent authorities and institutions; maintaining accessible; up-to-date registers and records of detainees; and ensuring that detainees were promptly brought before a judicial authority.

Missing persons

OHCHR note. In January, OHCHR submitted a summary [A/HRC/10/10] of a panel discussion on the question of missing persons (Geneva, 22 September 2008) organized at the request of the Human Rights Council [YUN 2008, p. 796]. The Council had requested OHCHR to summarize the panel's deliberations with a view to charging the Human Rights Council Advisory Committee with the preparation of a study on best practices.

Report of Secretary-General. As requested by the Human Rights Council [ibid.], the Secretary-General in February submitted a report on missing persons [A/HRC/10/28], reviewing action by the General Assembly; the 2008 panel discussion on the question (see above); the rights of families to know the fate of their relatives reported missing during armed conflicts; and the assistance provided to States and measures taken to address the issue by the International Committee of the Red Cross, the International Commission on Missing Persons and the Council of Europe. The Secretary-General called on States, intergovernmental organizations and NGOs to take additional measures to prevent persons from going missing; to establish the right to know; to collect, protect and manage credible and reliable data on missing persons; to develop their forensic science capacities; and to address impunity. As the issue was particularly severe in the context of armed conflict, measures should be taken to minimize the phenomenon, including through the judiciary, parliamentary commissions and truth-seeking mechanisms.

Advisory Committee action. The Human Rights Council Advisory Committee, at its third session in August, requested its drafting group to continue its work on the study on best practices in the matter of missing persons and to submit the results of its work to the Advisory Committee's fourth session, with a view to submitting them to the Council's fourteenth (2010) session [A/HRC/AC/3/2 (rec. 3/2)].

Human Rights Council action. On 1 October [A65/53 (dec. 12/117)], the Council took note of the Advisory Committee's action and requested the Committee to submit the study to the Council's fourteenth session.

Capital punishment

Communication. By a note of 10 February [A/63/716], 53 States referred to General Assembly resolution 63/168 [YUN 2008, p. 802] on a moratorium on the use of the death penalty, and placed on record their objection to any attempt to impose such a moratorium, in contravention to international law, for several reasons. There was no international consensus that the death penalty should be abolished; while capital punishment had been characterized as a human rights issue in the context of the right of the convicted prisoner to life, it was first and foremost an issue of the criminal justice system and a deterrent element vis-à-vis the most serious crimes, and should therefore be weighed against the rights of the victims and the right of the community to live in peace and security; and every State had an inalienable right to choose its political, economic, social, cultural and legal justice systems, without interference in any form by another

State. Some Member States had voluntarily decided to abolish the death penalty, whereas others had chosen to apply a moratorium on executions. Meanwhile, many Member States had retained the death penalty in their legislations. All sides were acting in compliance with their international obligations. Each Member State had decided freely, in accordance with its own sovereign right, to determine the path that corresponded to its own social, cultural and legal needs in order to maintain social security, order and peace. No side had the right to impose its standpoint on the other.

Report of Secretary-General. Pursuant to a Human Rights Council request [YUN 2006, p. 760], the Secretary-General in August reported [A/HRC/12/45] on the question of the death penalty, covering the period from June 2008 to July 2009. Burundi and Togo had abolished the death penalty for all crimes, Kazakhstan, the United States and Viet Nam had restricted its scope or were limiting its use, while Saint Kitts and Nevis had carried out its first execution in 10 years. Papua New Guinea, although maintaining the death penalty, had not carried out an execution since the country's independence in 1975. While the trend towards abolition continued, some States were maintaining the punishment while gradually restricting its use. A number of States were engaging in a national debate on whether to lift moratoriums or to abolish the death penalty. However, any analysis of the application of the death penalty remained difficult due to a lack of transparency by States in providing information.

Extralegal executions

Reports of Special Rapporteur. Pursuant to a Human Rights Council request [YUN 2008, p. 803], the Special Rapporteur on extrajudicial, summary or arbitrary executions, Philip Alston (Australia), in May reported [A/HRC/11/2] on his activities in 2008 and the first three months of 2009. He also examined four issues: responding to reprisals against individuals assisting him in his work; upholding the prohibition against the execution of juvenile offenders; the killing of witches; and the use of lethal force in policing public assemblies. The Rapporteur recommended that civil society organizations and States through their diplomatic missions provide financial and other assistance to individuals who were at risk for having cooperated with UN special procedures, including assisting them in relocation to a secure place. The Council President should designate a member of the Council Bureau to seek to visit Iran with a view to identifying measures to halt the sentencing and execution of juvenile offenders. The Council should call on Governments to treat extrajudicial killings of individuals accused of witchcraft as murder, investigating, prosecuting and punishing such killings accordingly.

An addendum [A/HRC/11/2/Add.1] covered 130 communications sent to 42 Governments from 16 March 2008 to 15 March 2009 and replies received from 1 May 2008 to 30 April 2009. Those included 64 urgent appeals and 66 allegation letters. The main issues covered in the communications were the death penalty (54); deaths in custody (21); the death penalty for minors (20); excessive use of force (18); impunity (11); attacks or killings (23); armed conflict (3); and death threats (7).

Other addenda tracked the implementation of the Rapporteur's recommendations following his missions to Guatemala [YUN 2006, p. 870] and the Philippines [YUN 2007, p. 746]. Regarding Guatemala [A/HRC/11/2/Add.7], the Rapporteur said that while improvements had been achieved with the establishment of the International Commission against Impunity in Guatemala, much-needed improvements to the criminal justice institutions, witness protection, budget allocations and fiscal policy had not been implemented. Regarding the Philippines [A/HRC/11/2/Add.8], he noted that the Supreme Court had promulgated and improved the operation of two important writs, and the Commission on Human Rights was taking steps to investigate unlawful killings. However, the Davao death squad continued to operate and increased numbers of death squad killings had been recorded. Reforms directed at institutionalizing the reduction of killings of leftist activists and others and ensuring command responsibility for abuses had not been implemented. Witness protection remained inadequate, and impunity for unlawful killings was widespread. Likewise, no improvement had been made by the Communist Party of the Philippines and the New People's Army to reduce the extrajudicial executions for which they bore responsibility.

The Secretary-General in July transmitted to the General Assembly the report of the Rapporteur [A/64/187], submitted in response to Assembly resolution 63/182 [YUN 2008, p. 805]. The report focused on vigilante killings and mob justice, an issue that had received far too little attention; it explored the phenomenon and analysed the victims and perpetrators, the human rights and security implications, and the context and motives. A survey carried out by the Rapporteur showed that such killings were reported from around the world, indicating that the problem concerned all States. The Rapporteur called on States to ensure that they were not supporting or encouraging vigilante killings in any way, and to take targeted action to prevent their occurrence and to punish perpetrators.

The General Assembly took note of that report on 18 December (**decision 64/536**).

Following his mission to Kenya (16–25 February) [A/HRC/11/2/Add.6], the Rapporteur concluded that the causes of many unlawful killings were well defined, and relatively straightforward steps could improve the situation. The Government could choose to deny the existence of problems or insist that they were under control, while the killings and impunity continued; or it could choose to acknowledge the scale of the problem and implement a reform programme to end extrajudicial executions, thus sending the message that impunity would not be tolerated. The President of Kenya should publicly acknowledge his commitment to ending unlawful killings by the police; police death squad killings should be prevented, investigated and punished; and the "Mungiki" should immediately cease their harassment, abuse and murder of Kenyans. Political control over prosecutions should be eliminated, and there should be accountability for the violence that followed the 2007 general election [YUN 2008, p. 326].

Following his mission to Colombia (8–18 June) [A/HRC/14/24/Add.2], the Rapporteur recommended that the Government: scrutinize and reform its security policies, including the armed forces, by increasing transparency, respect for the rule of law and accountability; bolster the ability of State institutions to provide accountability for human rights and humanitarian law violations committed by all actors—State forces, guerrillas and illegal armed groups; establish a truth commission to investigate the history of, and responsibility for, killings and other crimes committed by the paramilitaries, guerrillas and State forces during the conflict; and ensure that its policies did not directly or indirectly contribute to the further victimization of groups that had been disproportionately targeted by all sides throughout the years of the conflict: human rights defenders, Afro-Colombian and indigenous communities and persons with disabilities.

Communication. On 16 June [A/HRC/11/G/3], Guatemala transmitted its observations on the Rapporteur's follow-up report (see above).

Torture and cruel treatment

Reports of Special Rapporteur. In a report issued in January [A/HRC/10/44 & Corr.1], the Special Rapporteur on the question of torture, Manfred Nowak (Austria), summarized his activities between August and December 2008 and focused on the compatibility of the death penalty with the prohibition of cruel, inhuman and degrading punishment. He concluded that the historic interpretation of the right to personal integrity and human dignity in relation to the death penalty was increasingly challenged by the dynamic interpretation of that right in relation to corporal punishment and the inconsistencies deriv-

ing from the distinction between corporal and capital punishment, as well as by the universal trend towards abolishing capital punishment. The Rapporteur discussed a human rights-based approach to drug policies, concluding that drug users were often subjected to discriminatory treatment and that States had an obligation to ensure the same access to prevention and treatment in places of detention as outside them.

An addendum [A/HRC/10/44/Add.4 & Corr.1] summarized 77 letters of allegations of torture to 48 Governments and 155 urgent appeals to 49 Governments on behalf of persons who might be at risk of torture or ill-treatment sent between 16 December 2007 and 14 December 2008, as well as Government responses received up to 31 December 2008.

Another addendum [A/HRC/10/44/Add.5] summarized information provided by Governments, national human rights institutions and NGOs on the implementation of the Rapporteur's recommendations following country visits to China [YUN 2006, p. 875], Georgia [YUN 2005, p. 813], Jordan [YUN 2006, p. 875], Nepal [YUN 2005, p. 814], Nigeria [YUN 2007, p. 749] and Togo [ibid.].

The Secretary-General in August transmitted to the General Assembly the interim report [A/64/215 & Corr.1] of the Rapporteur, submitted in response to Assembly resolution 63/166 [YUN 2008, p. 810]. The Rapporteur drew the attention of the Assembly to his assessment that conditions of detention in most parts of the world did not respect the dignity of detainees and therefore failed to live up to international standards. He distinguished among three categories of human rights of detainees: certain rights, which detainees had forfeited as a result of their lawful deprivation of liberty; relative rights, which might be restricted for justified reasons; and absolute rights, which detainees enjoyed in full equality with other human beings. The Rapporteur also addressed the question of children in detention, and expressed his concern that too many children were still deprived of their liberty, in spite of the existence of clear international norms. If the detention of children was indispensable, conditions must adequately address their particular needs, including education, recreation and vocational training.

Following his mission to Uruguay (21–27 March) [A/HRC/13/39/Add.2], the Rapporteur recommended that the Government criminalize torture in line with the Convention against Torture, prevent the use of excessive force by the police, expedite judicial proceedings, ensure that the perpetrators of human rights violations committed during the dictatorship were brought to justice and fully implement the National Action Plan on Fighting Domestic Violence. The Government should undertake a reform of the criminal justice and penitentiary systems aimed at the rehabilitation and better reintegration of offenders into society, introducing and strengthening non-custodial measures of punishment; improve the conditions of detention; and close prisons with inhuman conditions of detention. The international community should assist the Government by providing financial and technical support.

Following his mission to Kazakhstan (5–13 May) [A/HRC/13/39/Add.3], the Rapporteur recommended that the Government create an independent national preventive mechanism mandated to undertake unannounced visits to places of detention at any time. The penitentiary system should be conceived in a way that truly aimed at the rehabilitation and reintegration of offenders. Complaints mechanisms needed to be made accessible and credible; a mechanism to investigate allegations of torture and ill-treatment should be put in place and be independent of the alleged perpetrators; the time of apprehension should be recorded and terms of police custody reduced to international standards; temporary detention units should be transferred from the Ministry of the Interior to the Ministry of Justice; and the burden of proof to show that a confession had not been extracted by torture should be transferred to the prosecutor.

Human Rights Council action. On 27 March [A/64/53 (res. 10/24)], the Council, by a recorded vote of 34 to none, with 13 abstentions, urged States to respect the professional and moral independence, duties and responsibilities of medical and other health personnel; to ensure that such personnel might fulfil their duty to report or denounce acts of torture or cruel, inhuman or degrading treatment to relevant authorities without fear of retribution or harassment; and to provide all persons deprived of their liberty with a medical examination at their admission to and transfer between detention facilities and thereafter on a regular basis as a means to help prevent torture or other cruel, inhuman or degrading treatment or punishment.

Voluntary Fund for torture victims

Reports of Secretary-General. In his annual report [A/64/264] to the General Assembly on the status of the United Nations Voluntary Fund for Victims of Torture, the Secretary-General provided information on the recommendations of the Fund's Board of Trustees at its twenty-ninth [YUN 2008, p. 810] and thirtieth (Geneva, 4–6 February) sessions. At those sessions, the Board made recommendations for grants for 2009 for more than 205 projects carried out by NGOs in over 65 countries, for an amount of $10,615,250. The High Commissioner for Human Rights approved those recommendations on behalf of the Secretary-General. Contributions from 29 countries and two individuals from 17 October 2008 to 31 July 2009

amounted to $3,602,026, while pledges from four countries totalled $1,390,071.

The General Assembly took note of that report on 18 December **(decision 64/536)**.

The Secretary-General further reported [A/HRC/13/75] on the Board's thirty-first session (Geneva, 19–23 October), at which the Board made recommendations for allocating in 2010 $11,809,050 in grants for over 200 projects in more than 70 countries. The High Commissioner approved the recommendations on 3 November on behalf of the Secretary-General. Between 1 January and 24 November, the Fund received $2,535,126 in contributions from 26 countries, as well as pledges for $8,347,887 from four countries. The Board maintained its practice of financing requests for training and seminars, and recommended allocating in 2010 $276,100 to 15 organizations in 13 countries for that purpose.

GENERAL ASSEMBLY ACTION

On 18 December [meeting 65], the General Assembly, on the recommendation of the Third Committee [A/64/439/Add.1 & Corr.1], adopted **resolution 64/153** without vote [agenda item 69 *(a)*].

Torture and other cruel, inhuman or degrading treatment or punishment

The General Assembly,

Reaffirming that no one shall be subjected to torture or to other cruel, inhuman or degrading treatment or punishment,

Recalling that freedom from torture and other cruel, inhuman or degrading treatment or punishment is a nonderogable right that must be protected under all circumstances, including in times of international or internal armed conflict or disturbance, and that the absolute prohibition of torture and other cruel, inhuman or degrading treatment or punishment is affirmed in relevant international instruments,

Recalling also that the prohibition of torture is a peremptory norm of international law and that international, regional and domestic courts have held the prohibition of cruel, inhuman or degrading treatment or punishment to be customary international law,

Recalling further the definition of torture contained in article 1 of the Convention against Torture and Other Cruel, Inhuman or Degrading Treatment or Punishment, without prejudice to any international instrument or national legislation which contains or may contain provisions of wider application,

Emphasizing the importance of properly interpreting and implementing the obligations of States with respect to torture and other cruel, inhuman or degrading treatment or punishment, and of abiding strictly by the definition of torture contained in article 1 of the Convention,

Noting that under the Geneva Conventions of 1949, torture and inhuman treatment are a grave breach and that under the statute of the International Tribunal for the Prosecution of Persons Responsible for Serious Violations of International Humanitarian Law Committed in the Territory of the Former Yugoslavia since 1991, the statute of the International Criminal Tribunal for the Prosecution of Persons Responsible for Genocide and Other Serious Violations of International Humanitarian Law Committed in the Territory of Rwanda and Rwandan Citizens Responsible for Genocide and Other Such Violations Committed in the Territory of Neighbouring States between 1 January and 31 December 1994 and the Rome Statute of the International Criminal Court, acts of torture can constitute crimes against humanity and, when committed in a situation of armed conflict, constitute war crimes,

Emphasizing that the entry into force as soon as possible of the International Convention for the Protection of All Persons from Enforced Disappearance and its implementation will make a significant contribution to the prevention and prohibition of torture, including by prohibiting secret places of detention, and encouraging all States that have not done so to consider signing, ratifying or acceding to the Convention,

Commending the persistent efforts of civil society organizations, including non-governmental organizations, national human rights institutions and the considerable network of centres for the rehabilitation of victims of torture, to combat torture and to alleviate the suffering of victims of torture,

1.   *Condemns* all forms of torture and other cruel, inhuman or degrading treatment or punishment, including through intimidation, which are and shall remain prohibited at any time and in any place whatsoever and can thus never be justified, and calls upon all States to implement fully the absolute prohibition of torture and other cruel, inhuman or degrading treatment or punishment;

2.   *Emphasizes* that States must take persistent, determined and effective measures to prevent and combat all acts of torture and other cruel, inhuman or degrading treatment or punishment, stresses that all acts of torture must be made offences under domestic criminal law, and encourages States to prohibit under domestic law acts constituting cruel, inhuman or degrading treatment or punishment;

3.   *Welcomes* the establishment of national preventive mechanisms to prevent torture, encourages all States that have not yet done so to establish such mechanisms, and calls upon States parties to the Optional Protocol to the Convention against Torture and Other Cruel, Inhuman or Degrading Treatment or Punishment to fulfil their obligation to designate or establish truly independent and effective national preventive mechanisms for the prevention of torture;

4.   *Emphasizes* the importance of States' ensuring proper follow-up to the recommendations and conclusions of the relevant treaty bodies and mechanisms, including the Committee against Torture, the Subcommittee on Prevention of Torture and Other Cruel, Inhuman or Degrading Treatment or Punishment and the Special Rapporteur of the Human Rights Council on torture and other cruel, inhuman or degrading treatment or punishment;

5.   *Condemns* any action or attempt by States or public officials to legalize, authorize or acquiesce in torture and other cruel, inhuman or degrading treatment or punishment under any circumstances, including on grounds of national security or through judicial decisions;

6.   *Stresses* that an independent, competent domestic authority must promptly, effectively and impartially examine all allegations of torture or other cruel, inhuman or degrading treatment or punishment and wherever there is reasonable ground to believe that such an act has been committed, and that those who encourage, order, tolerate or perpetrate such acts must be held responsible, brought to justice and punished in a manner commensurate with the severity of the offence, including the officials in charge of the place of detention where the prohibited act is found to have been committed;

7.   *Takes note* in this respect of the Principles on the Effective Investigation and Documentation of Torture and Other Cruel, Inhuman or Degrading Treatment or Punishment (the Istanbul Principles) as a useful tool in efforts to prevent and combat torture and of the updated set of principles for the protection of human rights through action to combat impunity;

8.   *Calls upon* all States to implement effective measures to prevent torture and other cruel, inhuman or degrading treatment or punishment, particularly in places of detention and other places where persons are deprived of their liberty, including education and training of personnel who may be involved in the custody, interrogation or treatment of any individual subjected to any form of arrest, detention or imprisonment;

9.   *Also calls upon* all States to adopt a gender-sensitive approach in the fight against torture and other cruel, inhuman or degrading treatment or punishment, paying special attention to gender-based violence;

10.   *Calls upon* States to ensure that the rights of persons with disabilities, bearing in mind the Convention on the Rights of Persons with Disabilities, are fully integrated into torture prevention and protection, and welcomes the efforts of the Special Rapporteur in this regard;

11.   *Encourages* all States to ensure that persons convicted of torture or other cruel, inhuman or degrading treatment or punishment have no subsequent involvement in the custody, interrogation or treatment of any person under arrest, detention, imprisonment or other deprivation of liberty;

12.   *Emphasizes* that acts of torture in armed conflict are serious violations of international humanitarian law and in this regard constitute war crimes, that acts of torture can constitute crimes against humanity and that the perpetrators of all acts of torture must be prosecuted and punished;

13.   *Strongly urges* States to ensure that no statement that is established to have been made as a result of torture is invoked as evidence in any proceedings, except against a person accused of torture as evidence that the statement was made, and calls upon States to consider extending that prohibition to statements made as a result of cruel, inhuman or degrading treatment or punishment;

14.   *Stresses* that States must not punish personnel for not obeying orders to commit or conceal acts amounting to torture or other cruel, inhuman or degrading treatment or punishment;

15.   *Urges* States not to expel, return ("refouler"), extradite or in any other way transfer a person to another State where there are substantial grounds for believing that the person would be in danger of being subjected to torture, and recognizes that diplomatic assurances, where used, do

not release States from their obligations under international human rights, humanitarian and refugee law, in particular the principle of non-refoulement;

16. *Recalls* that, for the purpose of determining whether there are such grounds, the competent authorities shall take into account all relevant considerations, including, where applicable, the existence in the State concerned of a consistent pattern of gross, flagrant or mass violations of human rights;

17. *Calls upon* States parties to the Convention against Torture and Other Cruel, Inhuman or Degrading Treatment or Punishment to fulfil their obligation to submit for prosecution or extradite those alleged to have committed acts of torture, and encourages other States to do likewise, bearing in mind the need to fight impunity;

18. *Stresses* that national legal systems must ensure that victims of torture and other cruel, inhuman or degrading treatment or punishment obtain redress, are awarded fair and adequate compensation and receive appropriate social and medical rehabilitation, urges States to take effective measures to this end, and in this regard encourages the development of rehabilitation centres;

19. *Recalls* its resolution 43/173 of 9 December 1988 on the Body of Principles for the Protection of All Persons under Any Form of Detention or Imprisonment, and in this context stresses that ensuring that any individual arrested or detained is promptly brought before a judge or other independent judicial officer in person and permitting prompt and regular medical care and legal counsel as well as visits by family members and independent monitoring mechanisms are effective measures for the prevention of torture and other cruel, inhuman or degrading treatment or punishment;

20. *Reminds* all States that prolonged incommunicado detention or detention in secret places can facilitate the perpetration of torture and other cruel, inhuman or degrading treatment or punishment and can in itself constitute a form of such treatment, and urges all States to respect the safeguards concerning the liberty, security and dignity of the person and to ensure that secret places of detention and interrogation are abolished;

21. *Emphasizes* that conditions of detention must respect the dignity and human rights of detainees, highlights the importance of reflecting on this in efforts to promote respect for and protection of the rights of detainees, and notes in this regard concerns about solitary confinement;

22. *Calls upon* all States to take appropriate effective legislative, administrative, judicial and other measures to prevent and prohibit the production, trade, export and use of equipment that is specifically designed to inflict torture or other cruel, inhuman or degrading treatment or punishment;

23. *Urges* all States that have not yet done so to become parties to the Convention as a matter of priority, and calls upon States parties to give early consideration to signing and ratifying the Optional Protocol to the Convention;

24. *Urges* all States parties to the Convention that have not yet done so to make the declarations provided for in articles 21 and 22 concerning inter-State and individual communications, to consider the possibility of withdrawing their reservations to article 20, and to notify the Secretary-General of their acceptance of the amendments to articles

17 and 18 with a view to enhancing the effectiveness of the Committee against Torture as soon as possible;

25. *Urges* States parties to comply strictly with their obligations under the Convention, including, in view of the high number of reports not submitted in time, their obligation to submit reports in accordance with article 19 of the Convention, and invites States parties to incorporate a gender perspective and information concerning children and juveniles and persons with disabilities when submitting reports to the Committee;

26. *Welcomes* the work of the Committee and its report submitted in accordance with article 24 of the Convention, recommends that the Committee continue to include information on the follow-up by States to its recommendations, and supports the Committee in its intention to further improve the effectiveness of its working methods;

27. *Invites* the Chairs of the Committee and the Subcommittee to present oral reports on the work of the committees and to engage in an interactive dialogue with the General Assembly at its sixty-fifth session under the sub-item entitled "Implementation of human rights instruments";

28. *Calls upon* the United Nations High Commissioner for Human Rights, in conformity with her mandate established by the General Assembly in its resolution 48/141 of 20 December 1993, to continue to provide, at the request of States, advisory services for the prevention of torture and other cruel, inhuman or degrading treatment or punishment, including for the preparation of national reports to the Committee and for the establishment and operation of national preventive mechanisms, as well as technical assistance for the development, production and distribution of teaching material for this purpose;

29. *Takes note with appreciation* of the interim report of the Special Rapporteur, and encourages the Special Rapporteur to continue to include in his recommendations proposals on the prevention and investigation of torture and other cruel, inhuman or degrading treatment or punishment, including its gender-based manifestations;

30. *Requests* the Special Rapporteur to continue to consider including in his report information on the follow-up by States to his recommendations, visits and communications, including progress made and problems encountered, and on other official contacts;

31. *Calls upon* all States to cooperate with and assist the Special Rapporteur in the performance of his task, to supply all necessary information requested by the Special Rapporteur, to fully and expeditiously respond to and follow up on his urgent appeals, to give serious consideration to responding favourably to requests by the Special Rapporteur to visit their countries and to enter into a constructive dialogue with the Special Rapporteur on requested visits to their countries as well as with respect to the follow-up to his recommendations;

32. *Stresses* the need for the continued regular exchange of views among the Committee, the Subcommittee, the Special Rapporteur and other relevant United Nations mechanisms and bodies, as well as for the pursuance of cooperation with relevant United Nations programmes, notably the United Nations Crime Prevention and Criminal Justice Programme, with regional organizations and mechanisms, as appropriate, and civil society organizations,

including non-governmental organizations, with a view to enhancing further their effectiveness and cooperation on issues relating to the prevention and eradication of torture, inter alia, by improving their coordination;

33. *Recognizes* the global need for international assistance to victims of torture, stresses the importance of the work of the Board of Trustees of the United Nations Voluntary Fund for Victims of Torture, appeals to all States and organizations to contribute annually to the Fund, preferably with a substantial increase in the level of contributions, and encourages contributions to the Special Fund established by the Optional Protocol to help finance the implementation of the recommendations made by the Subcommittee as well as education programmes of the national preventive mechanisms;

34. *Requests* the Secretary-General to continue to transmit to all States the appeals of the General Assembly for contributions to the Funds and to include the Funds on an annual basis among the programmes for which funds are pledged at the United Nations Pledging Conference for Development Activities;

35. *Also requests* the Secretary-General to submit to the Human Rights Council and to the General Assembly at its sixty-fifth session a report on the operations of the Funds;

36. *Further requests* the Secretary-General to ensure, within the overall budgetary framework of the United Nations, the provision of adequate staff and facilities for the bodies and mechanisms involved in preventing and combating torture and assisting victims of torture or other cruel, inhuman or degrading treatment or punishment, including in particular the Subcommittee on Prevention of Torture, commensurate with the strong support expressed by Member States for preventing and combating torture and assisting victims of torture;

37. *Calls upon* all States, the Office of the United Nations High Commissioner for Human Rights and other United Nations bodies and agencies, as well as relevant intergovernmental and civil society organizations, including non-governmental organizations, to commemorate, on 26 June, the United Nations International Day in Support of Victims of Torture;

38. *Decides* to consider at its sixty-fifth session the reports of the Secretary-General, including the report on the United Nations Voluntary Fund for Victims of Torture and the Special Fund established by the Optional Protocol, the report of the Committee against Torture and the interim report of the Special Rapporteur on torture and other cruel, inhuman or degrading treatment or punishment.

Arbitrary detention

Working Group activities. The five-member Working Group on Arbitrary Detention held its fifty-fourth (4–8 May), fifty-fifth (31 August–4 September) and fifty-sixth (18–26 November) sessions in Geneva [A/HRC/13/30]. During the year, the Group adopted 29 opinions concerning 71 persons in 23 States; the texts of those opinions were contained in an addendum [A/HRC/13/30/Add.1]. The Group transmitted 138 urgent appeals to 58 States concerning 844 individuals, including 50 women and 29 boys.

The States informed the Group that they had taken measures to remedy the situation of the detainees: in some cases, the detainees were released; in other cases, the Working Group was assured that the detainees concerned would be guaranteed a fair trial.

The Working Group engaged in a continuous dialogue with the countries it visited, in respect of which it recommended changes to domestic legislation governing detention or the adoption of other measures. Information about the implementation of the recommendations made by the Group to the countries visited in 2007 [YUN 2007, pp. 738–739] was received from Norway and Equatorial Guinea; Angola requested an extension of the deadline for submitting its comments.

The Working Group's report [A/HRC/13/30] addressed issues that had given rise to concern during 2009. The rights of detained migrants in an irregular situation and those of asylum-seekers and refugees were not fully guaranteed, and the Group emphasized that where the obstacles to the removal of detained migrants did not lie within their sphere of responsibility, the principle of proportionality required that they should be released. On the question of detention in connection with military tribunals and states of emergency, the Group observed that a weak or nonexistent institution of habeas corpus still prevailed in some States, particularly in the context of administrative detention, despite recommendations addressed to States by the Group aimed at strengthening that common-law prerogative writ.

On the basis of an analysis of its jurisprudence and recommendations on compliance with international human rights norms, the Group concluded that the typical remedy for arbitrarily detained individuals was their immediate release. That included the release of foreign detainees arbitrarily deprived of their liberty into the territory of the detaining State. The Group also raised concerns over an increase in alleged reprisals suffered by individuals who were the subject of an urgent appeal or opinion. The Group had decided to focus in 2010 on the issues of video and audio surveillance in interrogation rooms, alternatives to detention and the detention of drug users. To enable the Group to report more systematically and comprehensively, it reiterated its proposal to the Human Rights Council to expand its mandate, if renewed in 2010, so as to include the examination of conditions of detention around the world and the monitoring of State compliance with obligations concerning all human rights of detained and imprisoned persons.

After its mission to Malta [A/HRC/13/30/Add.2], the Working Group recommended that the Government: change its laws and policies on administrative detention of migrants in an irregular situation and asylum-seekers, so that detention was decided upon by a court of law on a case-by-case basis and pursuant to clearly and exhaustively defined criteria; rule out immigration detention of vulnerable groups of migrants; and provide for automatic periodic review by a court of law on the necessity and legality of detention in all cases, as well as for an effective remedy for detainees. In relation to criminal justice, the Group recommended that persons arrested on suspicion of having committed a criminal offence be allowed access to lawyers during the first period of up to 48 hours while in police custody. Concerning juvenile justice, the Group recommended that the minimum age of criminal responsibility for juveniles be increased to 12 years; the assumption that a juvenile aged between 9 and 14 years could act with "mischievous discretion" be eliminated; and provision be made for the juvenile justice system to extend to minors between the age of 16 and 18 years.

After its mission to Senegal (5–15 September) [A/HRC/13/30/Add.3], the Working Group recommended improving and guaranteeing the right to a fair trial, reducing the duration of pretrial detention and eliminating unsafe conditions of detention. The Government should establish habeas corpus as a means of combating arbitrary detentions, make legal assistance mandatory in misdemeanour cases and authorize the presence of a lawyer during the first 24 hours of police custody. The Group called on the international community, and the Human Rights Council in particular, to provide the technical and financial support necessary to reinforce Senegal's capacities in human rights protection and to support the reform process begun by the Government.

Human Rights Council action. On 26 March [A/64/53 (res. 10/9)], the Council encouraged States to give due consideration to the recommendations of the Group and to ensure that their legislation, regulations and practices remained in conformity with international standards and international legal instruments. States were encouraged to ensure that immigrants in an irregular situation and asylum-seekers were protected from arbitrary arrest and detention and were not subjected to arbitrary deprivation of liberty.

Terrorism

Reports of Special Rapporteur. The Special Rapporteur on the promotion and protection of human rights and fundamental freedoms while countering terrorism, Martin Scheinin (Finland), in February reported [A/HRC/10/3] on his activities from 17 December 2007 to 31 December 2008. He highlighted concerns regarding the role of intelligence agencies in the fight against terrorism, stressing the need for a legislative framework to regulate the broader powers that had been given to those agencies in the aftermath of the terrorist attacks of 11 September 2001. The

collection and sharing of "signal intelligence"—the gathering of intelligence by interception of signals— had led to violations of the right to privacy and the principle of non-discrimination, while "human intelligence"—the gathering of intelligence by means of interpersonal contact—had led to violations of universal norms such as the prohibition of torture and other inhuman treatment. The lack of oversight and political and legal accountability appeared to have facilitated illegal activities by intelligence agencies. The increased cooperation between those agencies posed challenges, and States had human rights obligations when their agencies performed joint operations, participated in interrogations and exchanged intelligence for operational use. When unlawful conduct by those agencies occurred, it might have been condoned or even secretly directed by government officials. In that context, the Rapporteur reviewed best practices by oversight bodies. State secrecy or public interest immunity clauses did not negate the obligations of States to investigate violations and provide victims with an effective remedy. The Rapporteur made recommendations to key actors—intelligence agencies, Governments, parliaments and the United Nations— to improve the accountability of intelligence agencies in the fight against terrorism.

An addendum [A/HRC/10/3/Add.1] summarized 30 communications transmitted to 26 Governments between 15 September 2007 and 31 December 2008, as well as replies received up to 31 January 2009.

In response to General Assembly resolution 62/159 [YUN 2007, p. 757], the Secretary-General in August transmitted to the Assembly the report of the Rapporteur [A/64/211 & Corr.1], which summarized his activities from 1 January to 31 July and analysed counter-terrorism measures from a gender perspective. The report reviewed the frequency and nature of gender-based human rights abuses in counter-terrorism measures and explored the relationship between gender equality and countering terrorism. While many of the measures discussed related to the human rights of women, gender also encompassed the social constructions that underlay how women's and men's roles, functions and responsibilities were understood. The report therefore also discussed the impact of counter-terrorism measures on men and persons of diverse sexual orientations and gender identities. Those subject to gender-based abuse were often caught between targeting by terrorist groups and State counter-terrorism measures that might lead to new violations. Those violations were amplified through war rhetoric and increased militarization in countering terrorism, both of which marginalized those who challenged or fell outside the boundaries of gender roles. Women were often victims of terrorism and counter-terrorism measures. Counter-terrorism measures had significant adverse impacts on female family members of victims of dis-appearances and extraordinary rendition. Collective sanctions had been used against female relatives of suspected terrorists, and women not suspected of ter-rorism offences had been unlawfully detained and ill-treated to gain information about male family mem-bers or to compel male terrorism suspects to provide information or confessions. Gender-specific forms of interrogation techniques in the name of countering terrorism included sexual violence and other tech-niques aimed at emasculating male detainees. At the same time, a gender perspective was integral to combating the conditions conducive to the spread of terrorism, and women should be considered as key stakeholders in counter-terrorism measures. The Rap-porteur addressed recommendations to States and UN organs and bodies.

The General Assembly took note of that report on 18 December **(decision 64/536)**.

Following his mission to Egypt (17–21 April) [A/HRC/13/37/Add.2], the Rapporteur urged the Gov-ernment to lift the state of emergency and repeal the Emergency Law, including all decrees issued under it; to ensure that all provisions establishing terror-ist crimes adhered strictly to the principle of legal-ity; to proscribe terrorist organizations on the basis of factual evidence of genuine terrorist activities as well as of the actual involvement of the individuals concerned; to abolish any legal provisions allowing for administrative detention and to release or bring to trial all detainees subjected to that regime; to prohibit any detention without charge or trial; and to adopt a mechanism providing for the mandatory conduct of independent, unrestricted and unannounced inspec-tions at all places of detention.

Communication. On 10 February [A/HRC/10/G/2], Spain submitted its response and observations con-cerning the Rapporteur's visit to the country [YUN 2008, p. 814].

Report of Secretary-General. Pursuant to General Assembly resolution 63/185 [ibid., p. 815], the Secretary-General in July reported [A/64/186] on developments within the UN system in relation to human rights and counter-terrorism, including through the activi-ties of the High Commissioner for Human Rights, the Human Rights Council and its special proce-dures mandates, the human rights treaty bodies, the Counter-Terrorism Implementation Task Force and its Working Group on Protecting Human Rights while Countering Terrorism, the Counter-Terrorism Committee and the Counter-Terrorism Committee Executive Directorate. He reported on the considera-tion by the UN human rights system of issues relating to human rights and counter-terrorism, including the absolute prohibition of torture, detention in the con-text of countering terrorism, access to justice and the

fundamental right to a fair trial. He recommended that States ensure respect for non-derogable rights, such as the right to life and the prohibition of torture; prosecute those responsible for inflicting torture and ill-treatment; ensure access by monitoring bodies to all prisoners in all places of detention; and abolish places of secret detention.

Report of High Commissioner. Pursuant to a Human Rights Council request [YUN 2008, p. 814], the High Commissioner in September submitted a report [A/HRC/12/22] analysing the links between counter-terrorism measures and economic, social and cultural rights. The report examined how international treaty obligations to promote and protect those rights should form part of the counter-terrorism strategy of a State. It highlighted the need to protect all rights and in particular economic, social and cultural rights, while at the same time taking effective counter-terrorism measures. Protecting and promoting all rights while countering terrorism were mutually reinforcing objec-tives. Through specific examples, the report focused on key aspects of economic, social and cultural rights, the legal framework in the context of countering ter-rorism, as well as the impact of terrorism and counter-terrorism measures and policies on the enjoyment of those rights.

Human Rights Council action. On 26 March [A/64/53 (res. 10/15)], the Council called on States, while countering terrorism, to ensure that any per-son whose human rights had been violated had ac-cess to an effective remedy and reparations, includ-ing by bringing to justice the perpetrators. It urged States, while countering terrorism, to respect the right to equality before the courts and tribunals and to a fair trial. The High Commissioner and the Special Rapporteur were requested to report to the Council's thirteenth (2010) session.

GENERAL ASSEMBLY ACTION

On 18 December [meeting 65], the General Assembly, on the recommendation of the Third Committee [A/64/439/Add.2 (Part II)], adopted **resolution 64/168** without vote [agenda item 69 *(b)*].

Protection of human rights and fundamental freedoms while countering terrorism

The General Assembly,

Reaffirming the purposes and principles of the Charter of the United Nations,

Reaffirming also the Universal Declaration of Human Rights,

Recalling the Vienna Declaration and Programme of Action,

Reaffirming the fundamental importance, including in response to terrorism and the fear of terrorism, of respect-ing all human rights and fundamental freedoms and the rule of law,

Reaffirming also that States are under the obligation to protect all human rights and fundamental freedoms of all persons,

Reiterating the important contribution of measures taken at all levels against terrorism, consistent with international law, in particular international human rights, refugee and humanitarian law, to the functioning of democratic institutions and the maintenance of peace and security and thereby to the full enjoyment of human rights, as well as the need to continue this fight, including through international cooperation and the strengthening of the role of the United Nations in this respect,

Deeply deploring the occurrence of violations of human rights and fundamental freedoms in the context of the fight against terrorism, as well as violations of international refugee and humanitarian law,

Noting with concern measures that can undermine human rights and the rule of law, such as the detention of persons suspected of acts of terrorism in the absence of a legal basis for detention and due process guarantees, the deprivation of liberty that amounts to placing a detained person outside the protection of the law, the trial of suspects without fundamental judicial guarantees, the illegal deprivation of liberty and transfer of individuals suspected of terrorist activities, and the return of suspects to countries without individual assessment of the risk of there being substantial grounds for believing that they would be in danger of subjection to torture, and limitations to effective scrutiny of counter-terrorism measures,

Stressing that all measures used in the fight against terrorism, including the profiling of individuals and the use of diplomatic assurances, memorandums of understanding and other transfer agreements or arrangements, must be in compliance with the obligations of States under international law, including international human rights, refugee and humanitarian law,

Recalling article 30 of the Universal Declaration of Human Rights, and reaffirming that acts, methods and practices of terrorism in all its forms and manifestations are activities aimed at the destruction of human rights, fundamental freedoms and democracy, threatening the territorial integrity and security of States and destabilizing legitimately constituted Governments, and that the international community should take the necessary steps to enhance cooperation to prevent and combat terrorism,

Reaffirming its unequivocal condemnation of all acts, methods and practices of terrorism in all its forms and manifestations, wherever and by whomsoever committed, regardless of their motivation, as criminal and unjustifiable, and renewing its commitment to strengthen international cooperation to prevent and combat terrorism,

Recognizing that respect for all human rights, respect for democracy and respect for the rule of law are interrelated and mutually reinforcing,

Reaffirming that terrorism cannot and should not be associated with any religion, nationality, civilization or ethnic group,

Emphasizing the importance of properly interpreting and implementing the obligations of States with respect to torture and other cruel, inhuman or degrading treatment or punishment, and of abiding strictly by the definition of torture contained in article 1 of the Convention against Torture and Other Cruel, Inhuman or Degrading Treatment or Punishment, in the fight against terrorism,

Recalling its resolutions 57/219 of 18 December 2002, 58/187 of 22 December 2003, 59/191 of 20 December 2004, 60/158 of 16 December 2005, 61/171 of 19 December 2006, 62/159 of 18 December 2007 and 63/185 of 18 December 2008, Commission on Human Rights resolutions 2003/68 of 25 April 2003, 2004/87 of 21 April 2004 and 2005/80 of 21 April 2005, and other relevant resolutions and decisions of the General Assembly, the Commission on Human Rights and the Human Rights Council, including Council decision 2/112 of 27 November 2006 and Council resolutions 7/7 of 27 March 2008 and 10/15 of 26 March 2009,

Recognizing the importance of the United Nations Global Counter-Terrorism Strategy, adopted on 8 September 2006, reaffirming that the promotion and protection of human rights for all and the rule of law are essential to the fight against terrorism, recognizing that effective counter-terrorism measures and the protection of human rights are not conflicting goals but complementary and mutually reinforcing, and stressing the need to promote and protect the rights of victims of terrorism,

Recalling Human Rights Council resolution 6/28 of 14 December 2007, by which the Council decided to extend the mandate of the Special Rapporteur on the promotion and protection of human rights and fundamental freedoms while countering terrorism,

1. *Reaffirms* that States must ensure that any measure taken to combat terrorism complies with their obligations under international law, in particular international human rights, refugee and humanitarian law;

2. *Deeply deplores* the suffering caused by terrorism to the victims and their families, expresses its profound solidarity with them, and stresses the importance of providing them with assistance;

3. *Expresses serious concern* at the occurrence of violations of human rights and fundamental freedoms, as well as international refugee and humanitarian law, committed in the context of countering terrorism;

4. *Reaffirms* that counter-terrorism measures should be implemented in accordance with international law, including international human rights, refugee and humanitarian law, thereby taking into full consideration the human rights of all, including persons belonging to national or ethnic, religious and linguistic minorities, and in this regard must not be discriminatory on grounds such as race, colour, sex, language, religion or social origin;

5. *Also reaffirms* the obligation of States, in accordance with article 4 of the International Covenant on Civil and Political Rights, to respect certain rights as non-derogable in any circumstances, recalls, in regard to all other Covenant rights, that any measures derogating from the provisions of the Covenant must be in accordance with that article in all cases, and underlines the exceptional and temporary nature of any such derogations, and in this regard calls upon States to raise awareness about the importance of these obligations among national authorities involved in combating terrorism;

6. *Urges* States, while countering terrorism:

(a) To fully comply with their obligations under international law, in particular international human rights, refugee and humanitarian law, with regard to the absolute prohibition of torture and other cruel, inhuman or degrading treatment or punishment;

(b) To take all necessary steps to ensure that persons deprived of liberty, regardless of the place of arrest or detention, benefit from the guarantees to which they are entitled under international law, including the review of the detention and other fundamental judicial guarantees;

(c) To ensure that no form of deprivation of liberty places a detained person outside the protection of the law, and to respect the safeguards concerning the liberty, security and dignity of the person, in accordance with international law, including international human rights and humanitarian law;

(d) To treat all prisoners in all places of detention in accordance with international law, including international human rights and humanitarian law;

(e) To respect the right of persons to equality before the law, courts and tribunals and to a fair trial as provided for in international law, including international human rights law, such as the International Covenant on Civil and Political Rights, and international humanitarian and refugee law;

(f) To protect all human rights, including economic, social and cultural rights, bearing in mind that certain counter-terrorism measures may have an impact on the enjoyment of these rights;

(g) To ensure that guidelines and practices in all border control operations and other pre-entry mechanisms are clear and fully respect their obligations under international law, particularly international refugee and human rights law, towards persons seeking international protection;

(h) To fully respect non-refoulement obligations under international refugee and human rights law and, at the same time, to review, with full respect for these obligations and other legal safeguards, the validity of a refugee status decision in an individual case if credible and relevant evidence comes to light that indicates that the person in question has committed any criminal acts, including terrorist acts, falling under the exclusion clauses under international refugee law;

(i) To refrain from returning persons, including in cases related to terrorism, to their countries of origin or to a third State whenever such transfer would be contrary to their obligations under international law, in particular international human rights, humanitarian and refugee law, including in cases where there are substantial grounds for believing that they would be in danger of subjection to torture, or where their life or freedom would be threatened in violation of international refugee law on account of their race, religion, nationality, membership of a particular social group or political opinion, bearing in mind obligations that States may have to prosecute individuals not returned;

(j) Insofar as such an act runs contrary to their obligations under international law, not to expose individuals to cruel, inhuman or degrading treatment or punishment by way of return to another country;

(k) To ensure that their laws criminalizing acts of terrorism are accessible, formulated with precision, non-discriminatory, non-retroactive and in accordance with international law, including human rights law;

(l) Not to resort to profiling based on stereotypes founded on grounds of discrimination prohibited by in-

ternational law, including on racial, ethnic and/or religious grounds;

(m) To ensure that the interrogation methods used against terrorism suspects are consistent with their international obligations and are reviewed to prevent the risk of violations of their obligations under international law, including international human rights, refugee and humanitarian law;

(n) To ensure that any person whose human rights or fundamental freedoms have been violated has access to an effective remedy and that victims receive adequate, effective and prompt reparations, where appropriate, including by bringing to justice those responsible for such violations;

(o) To ensure due process guarantees, consistent with all relevant provisions of the Universal Declaration of Human Rights, and their obligations under the International Covenant on Civil and Political Rights, the Geneva Conventions of 1949 and the Additional Protocols thereto, of 1977, and the 1951 Convention relating to the Status of Refugees and the 1967 Protocol thereto in their respective fields of applicability;

(p) To shape and implement all counter-terrorism measures in accordance with the principles of gender equality and non-discrimination;

7. *Encourages* States, while countering terrorism, to take into account relevant United Nations resolutions and decisions on human rights, and encourages them to give due consideration to the recommendations of the special procedures and mechanisms of the Human Rights Council and to the relevant comments and views of United Nations human rights treaty bodies;

8. *Acknowledges* the adoption of the International Convention for the Protection of All Persons from Enforced Disappearance in its resolution 61/177 of 20 December 2006, and recognizes that the entry into force of the Convention and its implementation will be an important step in support of the rule of law in countering terrorism;

9. *Recognizes* the need to continue ensuring that fair and clear procedures under the United Nations terrorism-related sanctions regime are strengthened in order to enhance their efficiency and transparency, and welcomes and encourages the ongoing efforts of the Security Council in support of these objectives, including by continuing to review all the names of individuals and entities in the regime, while emphasizing the importance of these sanctions in countering terrorism;

10. *Urges* States, while ensuring full compliance with their international obligations, to ensure the rule of law and to include adequate human rights guarantees in their national procedures for the listing of individuals and entities with a view to combating terrorism;

11. *Requests* the Office of the United Nations High Commissioner for Human Rights and the Special Rapporteur of the Human Rights Council on the promotion and protection of human rights and fundamental freedoms while countering terrorism to continue to contribute to the work of the Counter-Terrorism Implementation Task Force, including by raising awareness about the need to respect human rights and the rule of law while countering terrorism;

12. *Takes note* of the report of the Secretary-General on protecting human rights and fundamental freedoms while countering terrorism and the previous work of the

Special Rapporteur on the promotion and protection of human rights and fundamental freedoms while countering terrorism undertaken in accordance with his mandate, based on Commission on Human Rights resolution 2005/80 of 21 April 2005, and Human Rights Council resolutions 5/1 and 5/2 of 18 June 2007 and 6/28 of 14 December 2007;

13.   *Welcomes* the ongoing dialogue established in the context of the fight against terrorism between the Security Council and its Counter-Terrorism Committee and the relevant bodies for the promotion and protection of human rights, and encourages the Security Council and its Counter-Terrorism Committee to strengthen the links, cooperation and dialogue with relevant human rights bodies, in particular with the Office of the United Nations High Commissioner for Human Rights, the Special Rapporteur on the promotion and protection of human rights and fundamental freedoms while countering terrorism, other relevant special procedures and mechanisms of the Human Rights Council, and relevant treaty bodies, giving due regard to the promotion and protection of human rights and the rule of law in the ongoing work pursuant to relevant Security Council resolutions relating to terrorism;

14.   *Calls upon* States and other relevant actors, as appropriate, to continue to implement the United Nations Global Counter-Terrorism Strategy, which, inter alia, reaffirms respect for human rights for all and the rule of law as the fundamental basis of the fight against terrorism;

15.   *Requests* the Counter-Terrorism Implementation Task Force to continue its efforts to ensure that the United Nations can better coordinate and enhance its support to Member States in their efforts to comply with their obligations under international law, including international human rights, refugee and humanitarian law, while countering terrorism;

16.   *Encourages* relevant United Nations bodies and entities and international, regional and subregional organizations, in particular those participating in the Counter-Terrorism Implementation Task Force, which provide technical assistance, upon request, consistent with their mandates and as appropriate, related to the prevention and suppression of terrorism to step up their efforts to ensure, as an element of technical assistance, respect for international human rights, refugee and humanitarian law, as well as the rule of law;

17.   *Urges* relevant United Nations bodies and entities and international, regional and subregional organizations, including the United Nations Office on Drugs and Crime, within its mandate related to the prevention and suppression of terrorism, to step up their efforts to provide, upon request, technical assistance for building the capacity of Member States in the development and implementation of programmes of assistance and support for victims of terrorism in accordance with relevant national legislation;

18.   *Calls upon* international, regional and subregional organizations to strengthen information-sharing, coordination and cooperation in promoting the protection of human rights, fundamental freedoms and the rule of law while countering terrorism;

19.   *Requests* the Special Rapporteur on the promotion and protection of human rights and fundamental freedoms while countering terrorism to make recommendations in the context of his mandate, with regard to preventing, combating and redressing violations of human rights and fundamental freedoms in the context of countering terrorism;

20.   *Requests* all Governments to cooperate fully with the Special Rapporteur on the promotion and protection of human rights and fundamental freedoms while countering terrorism in the performance of the tasks and duties mandated, including by reacting promptly to the urgent appeals of the Special Rapporteur and providing the information requested, and to give serious consideration to responding favourably to his requests to visit their countries, as well as to cooperate with other relevant procedures and mechanisms of the Human Rights Council regarding the promotion and protection of human rights and fundamental freedoms while countering terrorism;

21.   *Welcomes* the work of the United Nations High Commissioner for Human Rights to implement the mandate given to her in 2005, in resolution 60/158, and requests the High Commissioner to continue her efforts in this regard;

22.   *Requests* the Secretary-General to submit a report on the implementation of the present resolution to the Human Rights Council and to the General Assembly at its sixty-fifth session;

23.   *Decides* to consider at its sixty-fifth session the report of the Special Rapporteur on the promotion and protection of human rights and fundamental freedoms while countering terrorism.

Freedom of expression

Reports of Special Rapporteur. Pursuant to a Human Rights Council request [YUN 2008, p. 814], the Special Rapporteur on the promotion and protection of the right to freedom of opinion and expression, Frank La Rue (Guatemala), in April submitted his first report [A/HRC/11/4] focusing on his vision and priorities. He made preliminary reflections on the issue of limitations to the right to freedom of opinion and expression, also addressing the right of access to information in situations of extreme poverty, and the safety and protection of media professionals, including those working in conflict zones. The Rapporteur summarized his activities since the beginning of his tenure in August 2008, including an analysis of communication trends in that period.

An addendum [A/HRC/11/4/Add.1] summarized 420 communications sent in 2008 to 80 Governments on behalf of 1,116 persons, and replies received until 15 May 2009.

Following his mission to Maldives (1–5 March) [A/HRC/11/4/Add.3], the Rapporteur recommended that the Government establish a mechanism of public communication and consultation about the measures being taken under the process of constitutional and legislative reform launched in 2005; continue the decentralization process by empowering people living on islands and atolls to make certain decisions for themselves; implement the media reform package initiated in 2004; establish a Broadcasting Corporation and a Telecommunications Authority as fully independent public bodies; ensure that cases of defamation be established by law as a civil and not a criminal offence; and guarantee freedom of religion or belief.

Human Rights Council action. On 2 October [A/65/53 (res. 12/16)], the Council called on States to respect and ensure the respect for the rights to freedom of opinion and expression; to put an end to violations of those rights; to ensure that victims of violations had an effective remedy; to investigate threats and acts of violence against journalists; and to ensure that persons exercising those rights were not discriminated against. The Council requested the Rapporteur to submit an annual report to it and to the General Assembly.

Communication. On 12 May [A/64/81], Namibia, as President of the Inter-Parliamentary Union, transmitted to the Secretary-General the text of a resolution adopted by the one hundred twentieth Assembly of the Inter-Parliamentary Union (Addis Ababa, Ethiopia, 10 April) on freedom of expression and the right to information.

Peace and security

Human Rights Council action. On 17 June [A/64/53 (res. 11/4)], the Council, by a recorded vote of 32 to 13, with 1 abstention, reaffirmed that the peoples of our planet had a sacred right to peace; stressed that the deep fault line that divided human society between the rich and the poor and the ever-increasing gap between the developed and the developing world posed a major threat to global prosperity, peace, human rights, security and stability; emphasized that the right of peoples to peace and its promotion demanded that the policies of States be directed towards the elimination of the threat of war, particularly nuclear war; underlined the vital importance of education for peace as a tool to foster the realization of the right of peoples to peace; reiterated its request to the High Commissioner to convene, before February 2010, a workshop on the right of peoples to peace; and requested the High Commissioner to report on the workshop to the Council's fourteenth (2010) session.

Traditional values

Human Rights Council action. On 2 October [A/65/53 (res. 12/21)], by a recorded vote of 26 to 15, with 6 abstentions, the Council requested the High Commissioner to convene, in 2010, a workshop discussing how a better understanding of traditional values of humankind underpinning international human rights norms and standards could contribute to human rights promotion and protection. OHCHR was requested to present to the Council a summary of the discussion.

Economic, social and cultural rights

Realizing economic, social and cultural rights

Report of Secretary-General. In response to a Human Rights Council request [YUN 2007, p. 761], the Secretary-General in January submitted a report [A/HRC/10/46] on the question of the realization in all countries of economic, social and cultural rights. The report outlined the activities of OHCHR, treaty bodies and special procedures in relation to those rights. Activities included those of the Committees on Economic, Social and Cultural Rights, on the Rights of the Child, and on Migrant Workers; of several special procedures; and of the Open-ended Working Group on an optional protocol to the International Covenant on Economic, Social and Cultural Rights. The report reflected a continued focus in the work on those rights, highlighting major areas of enhanced capacity and engagement.

Report of High Commissioner. Pursuant to General Assembly resolution 48/141 [YUN 1993, p. 906], the High Commissioner, in a June report [E/2009/90], addressed ways and means to measure progress in implementing economic, social and cultural rights through monitoring mechanisms, including budget and policy processes. She outlined ways of monitoring legislation and other measures, such as regulations, policies, plans and programmes; elaborated on monitoring the realization of those rights through human rights impact assessments, the use of indicators and benchmarks, and budget analysis; and addressed the issue of monitoring violations.

The Economic and Social Council took note of the report on 30 July **(decision 2009/256)**.

Human Rights Council action. On 25 March [A/64/53 (res. 10/1)], the Council called on States to take measures to implement Council resolution 4/1 [YUN 2007, p. 761], on the question of the realization in all countries of economic, social and cultural rights, with a view to improving the realization of those rights. It requested the High Commissioner to continue to submit an annual report on the question.

Human Rights Council special session

At the request of Egypt, on behalf of the African Group, and Brazil [A/HRC/S-10/1], backed by 25 other Human Rights Council members, the Council held its tenth special session (Geneva, 20 and 23 February) [A/HRC/S-10/2] to consider and take action on the impact of the global economic and financial crises on the universal realization and effective enjoyment of human rights. During its consideration of the issue, the

Council heard statements from its members, observer States, UN entities, intergovernmental organizations and NGOs.

On 23 February, by a recorded vote of 31 to none, with 14 abstentions, the Council adopted a resolution [A/HRC/S-10/2 (res. S-10/1)] by which it called on States to note that the global economic and financial crises did not diminish the responsibility of national authorities and the international community in the realization of human rights; called on them to assist the most vulnerable; and urged the international community to support national efforts to establish and preserve social safety nets for the protection of the most vulnerable. The Council called on States to ensure that those at risk of being most affected by the global economic and financial crises were protected in a non-discriminatory way; and reaffirmed that an open, equitable, predictable and non-discriminatory multilateral trading system could substantially stimulate development worldwide, benefiting all countries, particularly developing countries, and thereby contribute to the universal realization and effective enjoyment of all human rights. The special procedures were invited to consider any of the impacts of the global economic and financial crises on the realization and effective enjoyment of all human rights, particularly economic, social and cultural rights, and to integrate their findings in that regard in their reports to the Council.

Follow-up to special session. On 2 October [A/65/53 (res. 12/28)], the Human Rights Council recognized the fact that multiple and interrelated global economic and financial crises posed additional challenges to the universal realization and effective enjoyment of all human rights, and stressed the central importance of recognizing human dignity for all people when they were faced with economic circumstances beyond their control that deprived them of their capacity to realize their rights fully. The Council decided to hold a panel discussion during its thirteenth (2010) session to discuss and evaluate the impact of the financial and economic crises on the realization of all human rights worldwide.

Right to development

Task force activities. The high-level task force of the Working Group on the Right to Development was established in 2004 [YUN 2004, p. 746] to assist the Group in making recommendations to various actors on issues related to the implementation of the right to development. The task force examined Millennium Development Goal (MDG) 8, on a global partnership for development, and elaborated criteria for evaluating global partnerships with the aim of improving their effectiveness in support of the realization of the right to development.

At its fifth session (Geneva, 1–9 April) [A/HRC/12/WG.2/TF/2], the task force substantively reviewed and refined the right-to-development criteria, conceptualized around the key attributes of comprehensive human development, an enabling environment, and social justice and equity. The task force reviewed partnerships such as the Cotonou Agreement, the Common Market of the South (MERCOSUR), the Global Fund to Fight AIDS, Tuberculosis and Malaria, and the Special Programme for Research and Training in Tropical Diseases.

Working Group activities. The Working Group on the Right to Development, at its tenth session (Geneva, 22–26 June) [A/HRC/12/28], considered the report of the task force on its fifth session, which contained the assessments of the selected global development partnerships in the context of further elaboration of the right-to-development criteria, and the revised list of those criteria. The Group recommended that the task force should focus on the refinement of the criteria and the elaboration of corresponding operational subcriteria, to be submitted to the Group's eleventh (2010) session, and continue to study development partnerships on selected thematic areas with a view towards further refinement of the criteria.

Reports of Secretary-General and High Commissioner. In response to General Assembly resolution 63/178 [YUN 2008, p. 819], the Secretary-General and the High Commissioner in July reported [A/HRC/12/29] on the activities undertaken by OHCHR with regard to the implementation of the right to development, particularly the activities of the Group and its high-level task force.

In August [A/64/256], the Secretary-General reported to the General Assembly on the tenth session of the Group.

Human Rights Council action. On 2 October [A/65/53 (res. 12/23)], by a recorded vote of 33 to none, with 14 abstentions, the Council welcomed the report of the Working Group on the Right to Development; decided to continue to ensure that its agenda promoted sustainable development and the achievement of the MDGs and led to raising the right to development to the same level and on a par with all other human rights; and endorsed the recommendations of the Group, which would ensure that the right-to-development criteria and corresponding operational subcriteria, to be submitted by the task force to the Group's eleventh session, addressed the essential features of the right to development. The Council decided that, once considered, revised and endorsed by the Group, the criteria and subcriteria should be used to elaborate a comprehensive and coherent set of standards for the implementation of the right to development. Upon completion of the three phases of the 2008–2010 workplan of the high-level task force, the Group would take steps to ensure respect for and practical application of those standards, which could take various forms, including guidelines on the implementation of the right to development, and evolve into a basis for consideration of an international binding legal standard.

GENERAL ASSEMBLY ACTION

On 18 December [meeting 65], the General Assembly, on the recommendation of the Third Committee [A/64/439/Add.2 (Part II)], adopted **resolution 64/172** by recorded vote (133-23-30) [agenda item 69 *(b)*].

The right to development

The General Assembly,

Guided by the Charter of the United Nations, which expresses, in particular, the determination to promote social progress and better standards of life in larger freedom and, to that end, to employ international mechanisms for the promotion of the economic and social advancement of all peoples,

Recalling the Universal Declaration of Human Rights, as well as the International Covenant on Civil and Political Rights and the International Covenant on Economic, Social and Cultural Rights,

Recalling also the outcomes of all the major United Nations conferences and summits in the economic and social fields,

Recalling further that the Declaration on the Right to Development, adopted by the General Assembly in its resolution 41/128 of 4 December 1986, confirmed that the right to development is an inalienable human right and that equality of opportunity for development is a prerogative both of nations and of individuals who make up nations, and that the individual is the central subject and beneficiary of development,

Stressing that the Vienna Declaration and Programme of Action reaffirmed the right to development as a universal and inalienable right and an integral part of fundamental human rights, and the individual as the central subject and beneficiary of development,

Reaffirming the objective of making the right to development a reality for everyone, as set out in the United Nations Millennium Declaration, adopted by the General Assembly on 8 September 2000,

Deeply concerned that the majority of indigenous peoples in the world live in conditions of poverty, and recognizing the critical need to address the negative impact of poverty and inequity on indigenous peoples by ensuring their full and effective inclusion in development and poverty eradication programmes,

Reaffirming the universality, indivisibility, interrelatedness, interdependence and mutually reinforcing nature of all civil, cultural, economic, political and social rights, including the right to development,

Expressing deep concern over the lack of progress in the trade negotiations of the World Trade Organization, and reaffirming the need for a successful outcome of the Doha Development Round in key areas such as agriculture, market access for non-agricultural products, trade facilitation, development and services,

Recalling the outcome of the twelfth session of the United Nations Conference on Trade and Development, held in Accra from 20 to 25 April 2008, on the theme "Addressing the opportunities and challenges of globalization for development",

Recalling also all its previous resolutions, Human Rights Council resolution 12/23 of 2 October 2009, previous resolutions of the Council and those of the Commission on Human Rights on the right to development, in particular Commission resolution 1998/72 of 22 April 1998 on the urgent need to make further progress towards the realization of the right to development as set out in the Declaration on the Right to Development,

Welcoming the outcome of the tenth session of the Working Group on the Right to Development of the Human Rights Council, held in Geneva from 22 to 26 June 2009, as contained in the report of the Working Group and as referred to in the report of the Secretary-General,

Recalling the Fifteenth Summit Conference of Heads of State and Government of the Movement of Non-Aligned Countries, held in Sharm el-Sheikh, Egypt, from 11 to 16 July 2009, and the previous summits and conferences at which the States members of the Movement stressed the need to operationalize the right to development as a priority,

Reiterating its continuing support for the New Partnership for Africa's Development as a development framework for Africa,

Deeply concerned by the negative impacts of the global economic and financial crises on the realization of the right to development,

Recognizing that poverty is an affront to human dignity,

Recognizing also that extreme poverty and hunger are the greatest global threat that requires the collective commitment of the international community for its eradication, pursuant to Millennium Development Goal 1, and therefore calling upon the international community, including the Human Rights Council, to contribute towards achieving that goal,

Recognizing further that historical injustices have undeniably contributed to the poverty, underdevelopment, marginalization, social exclusion, economic disparity, instability and insecurity that affect many people in different parts of the world, in particular in developing countries,

Stressing that poverty eradication is one of the critical elements in the promotion and realization of the right to development and that poverty is a multifaceted problem that requires a multifaceted and integrated approach in addressing economic, political, social, environmental and institutional dimensions at all levels, especially in the context of the Millennium Development Goal of halving, by 2015, the proportion of the world's people whose income is less than one dollar a day and the proportion of people who suffer from hunger,

1.　*Endorses* the conclusions and recommendations adopted by consensus by the Working Group on the Right to Development of the Human Rights Council at its tenth session, and calls for their immediate, full and effective implementation by the Office of the United Nations High Commissioner for Human Rights and other relevant actors;

2. *Supports* the realization of the mandate of the Working Group, as renewed by the Human Rights Council in its resolution 9/3 of 24 September 2008, with the recognition that the Working Group will convene annual sessions of five working days and submit its reports to the Council;

3. *Also supports* the realization of the mandate of the high-level task force on the implementation of the right to development established within the framework of the Working Group, as renewed by the Human Rights Council in its resolution 9/3, with the further recognition that the task force will convene annual sessions of seven working days and submit its reports to the Working Group;

4. *Emphasizes* the relevant provisions of General Assembly resolution 60/251 of 15 March 2006 establishing the Human Rights Council, and in this regard calls upon the Council to implement the agreement to continue to act to ensure that its agenda promotes and advances sustainable development and the achievement of the Millennium Development Goals, and also in this regard to lead to raising the right to development, as set out in paragraphs 5 and 10 of the Vienna Declaration and Programme of Action, to the same level as and on a par with all other human rights and fundamental freedoms;

5. *Notes with appreciation* that the high-level task force, at its second meeting, examined Millennium Development Goal 8, on developing a global partnership for development, and suggested criteria for a periodic evaluation with the aim of improving the effectiveness of global partnership with regard to the realization of the right to development;

6. *Endorses* the recommendations of the Working Group, as outlined in paragraphs 44 to 46 of its report, which would ensure that the right to development criteria and corresponding operational sub-criteria, to be submitted by the high-level task force to the Working Group at its eleventh session in 2010, together with suggestions for further work, address, in a comprehensive and coherent manner, the essential features of the right to development, as defined in the Declaration on the Right to Development, including the priority concerns of the international community beyond those enumerated in Millennium Development Goal 8;

7. *Stresses* that the above-mentioned criteria and corresponding operational sub-criteria, once considered, revised and endorsed by the Working Group, should be used, as appropriate, in the elaboration of a comprehensive and coherent set of standards for the implementation of the right to development;

8. *Emphasizes* the importance, upon completion of the workplan of the high-level task force for the period 2008–2010, endorsed by the Human Rights Council in its resolution 9/3, of the Working Group taking appropriate steps to ensure respect for and practical application of the above-mentioned standards, which could take various forms, including the elaboration of guidelines on the implementation of the right to development, and which could evolve into a basis for consideration of an international legal standard of a binding nature, through a collaborative process of engagement;

9. *Stresses* the importance of the core principles contained in the conclusions of the Working Group at its third session, congruent with the purpose of international human rights instruments, such as equality, non-discrimination, accountability, participation and international cooperation, as critical to mainstreaming the right to development at the national and international levels, and underlines the importance of the principles of equity and transparency;

10. *Also stresses* that it is important that the high-level task force and the Working Group, in the discharge of their mandates, take into account the need:

(a) To promote the democratization of the system of international governance in order to increase the effective participation of developing countries in international decision-making;

(b) To also promote effective partnerships such as the New Partnership for Africa's Development and other similar initiatives with the developing countries, particularly the least developed countries, for the purpose of the realization of their right to development, including the achievement of the Millennium Development Goals;

(c) To strive for greater acceptance, operationalization and realization of the right to development at the international level, while urging all States to undertake at the national level the necessary policy formulation and to institute the measures required for the implementation of the right to development as an integral part of fundamental human rights, and also urging all States to expand and deepen mutually beneficial cooperation in ensuring development and eliminating obstacles to development in the context of promoting effective international cooperation for the realization of the right to development, bearing in mind that lasting progress towards the implementation of the right to development requires effective development policies at the national level and a favourable economic environment at the international level;

(d) To consider ways and means to continue to ensure the operationalization of the right to development as a priority;

(e) To mainstream the right to development in the policies and operational activities of the United Nations and the specialized agencies, funds and programmes, as well as in the policies and strategies of the international financial and multilateral trading systems, bearing in mind in this regard that the core principles of the international economic, commercial and financial spheres, such as equity, non-discrimination, transparency, accountability, participation and international cooperation, including effective partnerships for development, are indispensable in achieving the right to development and preventing discriminatory treatment arising from political or other non-economic considerations in addressing the issues of concern to the developing countries;

11. *Encourages* the Human Rights Council to consider how to ensure follow-up to the work of the former Subcommission on the Promotion and Protection of Human Rights on the right to development, in accordance with the relevant provisions of the resolutions adopted by the General Assembly and the Commission on Human Rights and in compliance with decisions to be taken by the Council;

12. *Invites* Member States and all other stakeholders to participate actively in future sessions of the Social Forum, while recognizing the strong support extended to the Forum at its first four sessions by the Subcommission on the Promotion and Protection of Human Rights;

13. *Reaffirms* the commitment to implement the goals and targets set out in all the outcome documents of the major United Nations conferences and summits and their review processes, in particular those relating to the realization of the right to development, recognizing that the realization of the right to development is critical to achieving the objectives, goals and targets set in those outcome documents;

14. *Also reaffirms* that the realization of the right to development is essential to the implementation of the Vienna Declaration and Programme of Action, which regards all human rights as universal, indivisible, interdependent and interrelated, places the human person at the centre of development and recognizes that, while development facilitates the enjoyment of all human rights, the lack of development may not be invoked to justify the abridgement of internationally recognized human rights;

15. *Stresses* that the primary responsibility for the promotion and protection of all human rights lies with the State, and reaffirms that States have the primary responsibility for their own economic and social development and that the role of national policies and development strategies cannot be overemphasized;

16. *Reaffirms* the primary responsibility of States to create national and international conditions favourable to the realization of the right to development, as well as their commitment to cooperate with each other to that end;

17. *Also reaffirms* the need for an international environment that is conducive to the realization of the right to development;

18. *Stresses* the need to strive for greater acceptance, operationalization and realization of the right to development at the international and national levels, and calls upon States to institute the measures required for the implementation of the right to development as an integral part of fundamental human rights;

19. *Emphasizes* the critical importance of identifying and analysing obstacles impeding the full realization of the right to development at both the national and the international levels;

20. *Affirms* that, while globalization offers both opportunities and challenges, the process of globalization remains deficient in achieving the objectives of integrating all countries into a globalized world, and stresses the need for policies and measures at the national and global levels to respond to the challenges and opportunities of globalization if this process is to be made fully inclusive and equitable;

21. *Recognizes* that, despite continuous efforts on the part of the international community, the gap between developed and developing countries remains unacceptably wide, that most of the developing countries continue to face difficulties in participating in the globalization process and that many risk being marginalized and effectively excluded from its benefits;

22. *Expresses its deep concern*, in this regard, at the negative impact on the realization of the right to development owing to the further aggravation of the economic and social situation, in particular of developing countries, as a result of the ongoing international energy, food and financial crises as well as global climate change;

23. *Underlines* the fact that the international community is far from meeting the target set in the United Nations Millennium Declaration of halving the number of people living in poverty by 2015, reaffirms the commitment made to meet that target, and emphasizes the principle of international cooperation, including partnership and commitment, between developed and developing countries towards achieving the goal;

24. *Urges* developed countries that have not yet done so to make concrete efforts towards meeting the targets of 0.7 per cent of their gross national product for official development assistance to developing countries and 0.15 to 0.2 per cent of their gross national product to least developed countries, and encourages developing countries to build on the progress achieved in ensuring that official development assistance is used effectively to help to meet development goals and targets;

25. *Recognizes* the need to address market access for developing countries, including in agriculture, services and non-agricultural products, in particular those of interest to developing countries;

26. *Calls for* the implementation of a desirable pace of meaningful trade liberalization, including in areas under negotiation in the World Trade Organization; the implementation of commitments on implementation-related issues and concerns; a review of special and differential treatment provisions, with a view to strengthening them and making them more precise, effective and operational; the avoidance of new forms of protectionism; and capacity-building and technical assistance for developing countries as important issues in making progress towards the effective implementation of the right to development;

27. *Recognizes* the important link between the international economic, commercial and financial spheres and the realization of the right to development; stresses in this regard the need for good governance and for broadening the base of decision-making at the international level on issues of development concern and the need to fill organizational gaps, as well as to strengthen the United Nations system and other multilateral institutions; and also stresses the need to broaden and strengthen the participation of developing countries and countries with economies in transition in international economic decision-making and norm-setting;

28. *Also recognizes* that good governance and the rule of law at the national level assist all States in the promotion and protection of human rights, including the right to development, and agrees on the value of the ongoing efforts being made by States to identify and strengthen good governance practices, including transparent, responsible, accountable and participatory government, that are responsive and appropriate to their needs and aspirations, including in the context of agreed partnership approaches to development, capacity-building and technical assistance;

29. *Further recognizes* the important role and the rights of women and the application of a gender perspective as a cross-cutting issue in the process of realizing the right to development, and notes in particular the positive relationship between women's education and their equal participation in the civil, cultural, economic, political and social activities of the community and the promotion of the right to development;

30. *Stresses* the need for the integration of the rights of children, girls and boys alike, in all policies and programmes and for ensuring the promotion and protection of those rights, especially in areas relating to health, education and the full development of their capacities;

31. *Welcomes* the Political Declaration on HIV/AIDS adopted at the High-level Meeting on HIV/AIDS of the General Assembly on 2 June 2006, stresses that further and additional measures must be taken at the national and international levels to fight HIV/AIDS and other communicable diseases, taking into account ongoing efforts and programmes, and reiterates the need for international assistance in this regard;

32. *Recalls* the Convention on the Rights of Persons with Disabilities, which entered into force on 3 May 2008, and stresses the need to take into consideration the rights of persons with disabilities and the importance of international cooperation in the realization of the right to development;

33. *Stresses its commitment* to indigenous peoples in the process of the realization of the right to development, and reaffirms the commitment to promote their rights in the areas of education, employment, vocational training and retraining, housing, sanitation, health and social security, in accordance with recognized international human rights obligations and taking into account, as appropriate, the United Nations Declaration on the Rights of Indigenous Peoples, adopted by the General Assembly in its resolution 61/295 of 13 September 2007;

34. *Recognizes* the need for strong partnerships with civil society organizations and the private sector in pursuit of poverty eradication and development, as well as for corporate social responsibility;

35. *Emphasizes* the urgent need for taking concrete and effective measures to prevent, combat and criminalize all forms of corruption at all levels, to prevent, detect and deter in a more effective manner international transfers of illicitly acquired assets and to strengthen international cooperation in asset recovery, consistent with the principles of the United Nations Convention against Corruption, particularly chapter V thereof, stresses the importance of a genuine political commitment on the part of all Governments through a firm legal framework, and in this context urges States to sign and ratify the Convention as soon as possible and States parties to implement it effectively;

36. *Also emphasizes* the need to strengthen further the activities of the Office of the United Nations High Commissioner for Human Rights in the promotion and realization of the right to development, including by ensuring effective use of the financial and human resources necessary to fulfil its mandate, and calls upon the Secretary-General to provide the Office of the High Commissioner with the necessary resources;

37. *Reaffirms* the request to the United Nations High Commissioner for Human Rights, in mainstreaming the right to development, to undertake effectively activities aimed at strengthening the global partnership for development between Member States, development agencies and the international development, financial and trade institutions, and to reflect those activities in detail in her next report to the Human Rights Council;

38. *Calls upon* the United Nations funds and programmes, as well as the specialized agencies, to mainstream the right to development in their operational programmes and objectives, and stresses the need for the international financial and multilateral trading systems to mainstream the right to development in their policies and objectives;

39. *Requests* the Secretary-General to bring the present resolution to the attention of Member States, United Nations organs and bodies, specialized agencies, funds and programmes, international development and financial institutions, in particular the Bretton Woods institutions, and non-governmental organizations;

40. *Also requests* the Secretary-General to submit a report to the General Assembly at its sixty-fifth session and an interim report to the Human Rights Council on the implementation of the present resolution, including efforts undertaken at the national, regional and international levels in the promotion and realization of the right to development, and invites the Chair of the Working Group on the Right to Development to present a verbal update to the Assembly at its sixty-fifth session.

RECORDED VOTE ON RESOLUTION 64/172:

In favour: Afghanistan, Algeria, Angola, Antigua and Barbuda, Argentina, Armenia, Azerbaijan, Bahamas, Bahrain, Bangladesh, Barbados, Belarus, Belize, Benin, Bhutan, Bolivia, Bosnia and Herzegovina, Botswana, Brazil, Brunei Darussalam, Burkina Faso, Burundi, Cambodia, Cameroon, Cape Verde, Central African Republic, Chad, Chile, China, Colombia, Comoros, Congo, Costa Rica, Côte d'Ivoire, Cuba, Democratic People's Republic of Korea, Democratic Republic of the Congo, Djibouti, Dominica, Dominican Republic, Ecuador, Egypt, El Salvador, Equatorial Guinea, Eritrea, Ethiopia, Fiji, Gabon, Ghana, Grenada, Guatemala, Guinea, Guinea-Bissau, Guyana, Haiti, Honduras, India, Indonesia, Iran, Iraq, Jamaica, Jordan, Kazakhstan, Kenya, Kuwait, Kyrgyzstan, Lao People's Democratic Republic, Lebanon, Lesotho, Liberia, Libyan Arab Jamahiriya, Madagascar, Malawi, Malaysia, Maldives, Mali, Mauritania, Mauritius, Mexico, Mongolia, Morocco, Mozambique, Myanmar, Namibia, Nepal, Nicaragua, Niger, Nigeria, Oman, Pakistan, Panama, Papua New Guinea, Paraguay, Peru, Philippines, Qatar, Russian Federation, Rwanda, Saint Kitts and Nevis, Saint Lucia, Saint Vincent and the Grenadines, Saudi Arabia, Senegal, Serbia, Sierra Leone, Singapore, Solomon Islands, Somalia, South Africa, Sri Lanka, Sudan, Suriname, Swaziland, Syrian Arab Republic, Tajikistan, Thailand, Timor-Leste, Togo, Tonga, Trinidad and Tobago, Tunisia, Turkmenistan, Tuvalu, Uganda, United Arab Emirates, United Republic of Tanzania, Uruguay, Uzbekistan, Venezuela, Viet Nam, Yemen, Zambia, Zimbabwe.

Against: Australia, Belgium, Bulgaria, Canada, Czech Republic, Denmark, Estonia, Georgia, Germany, Hungary, Israel, Lithuania, Marshall Islands, Netherlands, New Zealand, Palau, Poland, Slovakia, Sweden, Switzerland, The former Yugoslav Republic of Macedonia, United Kingdom, United States.

Abstaining: Albania, Andorra, Austria, Croatia, Cyprus, Finland, France, Greece, Iceland, Ireland, Italy, Japan, Latvia, Liechtenstein, Luxembourg, Malta, Moldova, Monaco, Montenegro, Norway, Portugal, Republic of Korea, Romania, Samoa, San Marino, Slovenia, Spain, Turkey, Ukraine, Vanuatu.

Human rights and international solidarity

Report by independent expert. The independent expert on human rights and international solidarity, Rudi Muhammad Rizki (Indonesia), in July reported to the Human Rights Council [A/HRC/12/27 & Corr.1], in accordance with a Council request [YUN 2008, p. 823], on his work on a draft declaration on the right of peoples and individuals to international solidarity. The expert considered international solidarity as a principle of international human rights law; dealt with international solidarity in relation to the eradication of poverty; and reviewed international solidarity and cooperation in natural disasters and combating diseases. He highlighted elements of the scope, content and nature of obligations in the promotion and protection of the right to international solidarity. He concluded that there was adequate evidence of the existence of a principle of international solidarity and of numerous global public values, policies and both hard and soft laws, followed in practice, which could support the construction of a normative framework for human rights and international solidarity, as well as the emergence of a right of peoples and individuals to international solidarity.

Human Rights Council action. On 1 October [A/65/53 (res. 12/9)], by a recorded vote of 33 to 14, the Council called on the international community to promote international solidarity and cooperation to overcome the negative effects of the economic, financial and climate crisis, particularly in developing countries. It requested the expert to continue his work in preparing a draft declaration on the right of peoples and individuals to international solidarity and in developing guidelines, standards, norms and principles promoting that right, and to report to the Council's fifteenth (2010) session. The Council's Advisory Committee was requested to contribute to those tasks.

Democratic and equitable international order

On 18 December [meeting 65], the General Assembly, on the recommendation of the Third Committee [A/64/439/Add.2 (Part II)], adopted **resolution 64/157** by recorded vote (127-54-5) [agenda item 69 *(b)*].

Promotion of a democratic and equitable international order

The General Assembly,

Recalling its previous resolutions on the promotion of a democratic and equitable international order, including resolution 63/189 of 18 December 2008, and taking note of Human Rights Council resolution 8/5 of 18 June 2008,

Reaffirming the commitment of all States to fulfil their obligations to promote universal respect for, and observance and protection of, all human rights and fundamental freedoms for all, in accordance with the Charter of the United Nations, other instruments relating to human rights and international law,

Affirming that the enhancement of international cooperation for the promotion and protection of all human rights should continue to be carried out in full conformity with the purposes and principles of the Charter and international law as set forth in Articles 1 and 2 of the Charter and, inter alia, with full respect for sovereignty, territorial integrity, political independence, the non-use of force or the threat of force in international relations and non-intervention in matters that are essentially within the domestic jurisdiction of any State,

Recalling the Preamble to the Charter, in particular the determination to reaffirm faith in fundamental human rights, in the dignity and worth of the human person and in the equal rights of men and women and of nations large and small,

Reaffirming that everyone is entitled to a social and international order in which the rights and freedoms set forth in the Universal Declaration of Human Rights can be fully realized,

Reaffirming also the determination expressed in the Preamble to the Charter to save succeeding generations from the scourge of war, to establish conditions under which justice and respect for the obligations arising from treaties and other sources of international law can be maintained, to promote social progress and better standards of life in larger freedom, to practise tolerance and good-neighbourliness, and to employ international machinery for the promotion of the economic and social advancement of all peoples,

Stressing that the responsibility for managing worldwide economic and social issues, as well as threats to international peace and security, must be shared among the nations of the world and should be exercised multilaterally, and that in this regard the central role must be played by the United Nations, as the most universal and representative organization in the world,

Considering the major changes taking place on the international scene and the aspirations of all peoples for an international order based on the principles enshrined in the Charter, including promoting and encouraging respect for human rights and fundamental freedoms for all and respect for the principle of equal rights and self-determination of peoples, peace, democracy, justice, equality, the rule of law, pluralism, development, better standards of living and solidarity,

Recognizing that the enhancement of international cooperation in the field of human rights is essential for the full achievement of the purposes of the United Nations, including the effective promotion and protection of all human rights,

Considering that the Universal Declaration of Human Rights proclaims that all human beings are born free and equal in dignity and rights and that everyone is entitled to all the rights and freedoms set out therein, without distinction of any kind, such as race, colour, sex, language, religion, political or other opinion, national or social origin, property, birth or other status,

Reaffirming that democracy, development and respect for human rights and fundamental freedoms are interdependent and mutually reinforcing, and that democracy is based on the freely expressed will of the people to determine their own political, economic, social and cultural systems and their full participation in all aspects of their lives,

Recognizing that the promotion and protection of human rights should be based on the principle of cooperation and genuine dialogue and aimed at strengthening the capacity of Member States to comply with their human rights obligations for the benefit of all human beings,

Emphasizing that democracy is not only a political concept, but that it also has economic and social dimensions,

Recognizing that democracy, respect for all human rights, including the right to development, transparent and accountable governance and administration in all sectors of society, and effective participation by civil society are an essential part of the necessary foundations for the realization of social and people-centred sustainable development,

Noting with concern that racism, racial discrimination, xenophobia and related intolerance may be aggravated by, inter alia, inequitable distribution of wealth, marginalization and social exclusion,

Underlining the fact that it is imperative for the international community to ensure that globalization becomes a positive force for all the world's people, and that only through broad and sustained efforts, based on common humanity in all its diversity, can globalization be made fully inclusive and equitable,

Concerned that the current global economic, financial, energy and food crises, resulting from a combination of several major factors, including macroeconomic and other factors, such as environmental degradation, desertification and global climate change, natural disasters and the lack of financial resources and the technology necessary to confront their negative impact in developing countries, particularly in the least developed countries and small island developing States, represent a global scenario that is threatening the adequate enjoyment of all human rights and widening the gap between developed and developing countries,

Stressing that efforts to make globalization fully inclusive and equitable must include policies and measures, at the global level, that correspond to the needs of developing countries and countries with economies in transition and are formulated and implemented with their effective participation,

Stressing also the need for adequate financing of and technology transfer to developing countries, in particular the landlocked developing countries and small island developing States, including to support their efforts to adapt to climate change,

Having listened to the peoples of the world, and recognizing their aspirations to justice, to equality of opportunity for all, to the enjoyment of their human rights, including the right to development, to live in peace and freedom and to equal participation without discrimination in economic, social, cultural, civil and political life,

Resolved to take all measures within its power to secure a democratic and equitable international order,

1. *Affirms* that everyone is entitled to a democratic and equitable international order;

2. *Also affirms* that a democratic and equitable international order fosters the full realization of all human rights for all;

3. *Calls upon* all Member States to fulfil their commitment expressed in Durban, South Africa, during the World Conference against Racism, Racial Discrimination, Xenophobia and Related Intolerance to maximize the benefits of globalization through, inter alia, the strengthening and enhancement of international cooperation to increase equality of opportunities for trade, economic growth and sustainable development, global communications through the use of new technologies and increased intercultural exchange through the preservation and promotion of cultural diversity, and reiterates that only through broad and sustained efforts to create a shared future based upon our common humanity and all its diversity can globalization be made fully inclusive and equitable;

4. *Affirms* that a democratic and equitable international order requires, inter alia, the realization of the following:

(a) The right of all peoples to self-determination, by virtue of which they can freely determine their political status and freely pursue their economic, social and cultural development;

(b) The right of peoples and nations to permanent sovereignty over their natural wealth and resources;

(c) The right of every human person and all peoples to development;

(d) The right of all peoples to peace;

(e) The right to an international economic order based on equal participation in the decision-making process, interdependence, mutual interest, solidarity and cooperation among all States;

(f) International solidarity, as a right of peoples and individuals;

(g) The promotion and consolidation of transparent, democratic, just and accountable international institutions in all areas of cooperation, in particular through the implementation of the principle of full and equal participation in their respective decision-making mechanisms;

(h) The right to equitable participation of all, without any discrimination, in domestic and global decision-making;

(i) The principle of equitable regional and gender-balanced representation in the composition of the staff of the United Nations system;

(j) The promotion of a free, just, effective and balanced international information and communications order, based on international cooperation for the establishment of a new equilibrium and greater reciprocity in the international flow of information, in particular correcting the inequalities in the flow of information to and from developing countries;

(k) Respect for cultural diversity and the cultural rights of all, since this enhances cultural pluralism, contributes to a wider exchange of knowledge and understanding of cultural backgrounds, advances the application and enjoyment of universally accepted human rights across the world and fosters stable, friendly relations among peoples and nations worldwide;

(l) The right of every person and all peoples to a healthy environment and to enhanced international cooperation that responds effectively to the needs for assistance of national efforts to adapt to climate change, particularly in developing countries, and that promotes the fulfilment of international agreements in the field of mitigation;

(m) The promotion of equitable access to benefits from the international distribution of wealth through enhanced international cooperation, in particular in economic, commercial and financial international relations;

(n) The enjoyment by everyone of ownership of the common heritage of mankind in connection to the public right of access to culture;

(o) The shared responsibility of the nations of the world for managing worldwide economic and social development as well as threats to international peace and security that should be exercised multilaterally;

5. *Stresses* the importance of preserving the rich and diverse nature of the international community of nations and peoples, as well as respect for national and regional particularities and various historical, cultural and religious backgrounds in the enhancement of international cooperation in the field of human rights;

6. *Also stresses* that all human rights are universal, indivisible, interdependent and interrelated and that the international community must treat human rights globally in a fair and equal manner, on the same footing and with the same emphasis, and reaffirms that, while the significance of national and regional particularities and various historical, cultural and religious backgrounds must be borne in mind, it is the duty of States, regardless of their political, economic and cultural systems, to promote and protect all human rights and fundamental freedoms;

7. *Urges* all actors on the international scene to build an international order based on inclusion, justice, equality and equity, human dignity, mutual understanding and promotion of and respect for cultural diversity and universal human rights, and to reject all doctrines of exclusion based on racism, racial discrimination, xenophobia and related intolerance;

8. *Reaffirms* that all States should promote the establishment, maintenance and strengthening of international peace and security and, to that end, should do their utmost to achieve general and complete disarmament under effective international control, as well as to ensure that the resources released by effective disarmament measures are used for comprehensive development, in particular that of the developing countries;

9. *Also reaffirms* the need to continue working urgently for the establishment of an international economic order based on equity, sovereign equality, interdependence, common interest and cooperation among all States, irrespective of their economic and social systems, which shall correct inequalities and redress existing injustices, make it possible to eliminate the widening gap between the developed and the developing countries and ensure steadily accelerating economic and social development and peace and justice for present and future generations;

10. *Further reaffirms* that the international community should devise ways and means to remove the current obstacles and meet the challenges to the full realization of all human rights and to prevent the continuation of human rights violations resulting therefrom throughout the world;

11. *Urges* States to continue their efforts, through enhanced international cooperation, towards the promotion of a democratic and equitable international order;

12. *Requests* the Human Rights Council, the human rights treaty bodies, the Office of the United Nations High Commissioner for Human Rights, the special mechanisms extended by the Council and the Human Rights Council Advisory Committee to pay due attention, within their respective mandates, to the present resolution and to make contributions towards its implementation;

13. *Calls upon* the Office of the High Commissioner to build upon the issue of the promotion of a democratic and equitable international order;

14. *Requests* the Secretary-General to bring the present resolution to the attention of Member States, United Nations organs, bodies and components, intergovernmental organizations, in particular the Bretton Woods institutions, and non-governmental organizations, and to disseminate it on the widest possible basis;

15. *Decides* to continue consideration of the matter at its sixty-fifth session under the item entitled "Promotion and protection of human rights".

RECORDED VOTE ON RESOLUTION 64/157:

In favour: Afghanistan, Algeria, Angola, Antigua and Barbuda, Azerbaijan, Bahamas, Bahrain, Bangladesh, Barbados, Belarus, Belize, Benin, Bhutan, Bolivia, Botswana, Brazil, Brunei Darussalam, Burkina Faso, Burundi, Cambodia, Cameroon, Cape Verde, Central African Republic, Chad, China, Colombia, Comoros, Congo, Costa Rica, Côte d'Ivoire, Cuba, Democratic People's Republic of Korea, Democratic Republic of the Congo, Djibouti, Dominica, Dominican Republic, Ecuador, Egypt, El Salvador, Equatorial Guinea, Eritrea, Ethiopia, Fiji, Gabon, Ghana, Grenada, Guatemala, Guinea, Guinea-Bissau, Guyana, Haiti, Honduras, India, Indonesia, Iran, Iraq, Jamaica, Jordan, Kazakhstan, Kenya, Kuwait, Kyrgyzstan, Lao People's Democratic Republic, Lebanon, Lesotho, Liberia, Libyan Arab Jamahiriya, Madagascar, Malawi, Malaysia, Maldives, Mali, Mauritania, Mauritius, Mongolia, Morocco, Mozambique, Myanmar, Namibia, Nepal, Nicaragua, Niger, Nigeria, Oman, Pakistan, Panama, Papua New Guinea, Paraguay, Philippines, Qatar, Russian Federation, Rwanda, Saint Kitts and Nevis, Saint Lucia, Saint Vincent and the Grenadines, Saudi Arabia, Senegal, Sierra Leone, Singapore, Solomon Islands, Somalia, South Africa, Sri Lanka, Sudan, Suriname, Swaziland, Syrian Arab Republic, Tajikistan, Thailand, Timor-Leste, Togo, Tonga, Trinidad and Tobago, Tunisia, Turkmenistan, Tuvalu, Uganda, United Arab Emirates, United Republic of Tanzania, Uruguay, Uzbekistan, Vanuatu, Venezuela, Viet Nam, Yemen, Zambia, Zimbabwe.

Against: Albania, Andorra, Australia, Austria, Belgium, Bosnia and Herzegovina, Bulgaria, Canada, Croatia, Cyprus, Czech Republic, Denmark, Estonia, Finland, France, Georgia, Germany, Greece, Hungary, Iceland, Ireland, Israel, Italy, Japan, Latvia, Liechtenstein, Lithuania, Luxembourg, Malta, Marshall Islands, Moldova, Monaco, Montenegro, Netherlands, New Zealand, Norway, Palau, Poland, Portugal, Republic of Korea, Romania, Samoa, San Marino, Serbia, Slovakia, Slovenia, Spain, Sweden, Switzerland, The former Yugoslav Republic of Macedonia, Turkey, Ukraine, United Kingdom, United States.

Abstaining: Argentina, Armenia, Chile, Mexico, Peru.

Globalization

Report of Secretary-General. In response to General Assembly resolution 63/176 [YUN 2008, p. 826], the Secretary-General in August submitted a report [A/64/265] that summarized the views on globalization and its impact on the full enjoyment of all human rights received from Oman and the Holy See, as well as from the UN Department of Economic and Social Affairs, the International Labour Organization, the International Monetary Fund, the United Nations Conference on Trade and Development, the United Nations Development Programme and the World Trade Organization.

GENERAL ASSEMBLY ACTION

On 18 December [meeting 65], the General Assembly, on the recommendation of the Third Committee [A/64/439/Add.2 (Part II)], adopted **resolution 64/160** by recorded vote (129-54-3) [agenda item 69 *(b)*].

Globalization and its impact on the full enjoyment of all human rights

The General Assembly,

Guided by the purposes and principles of the Charter of the United Nations, and expressing, in particular, the need to achieve international cooperation in promoting and encouraging respect for human rights and fundamental freedoms for all without distinction,

Recalling the Universal Declaration of Human Rights, as well as the Vienna Declaration and Programme of Action adopted by the World Conference on Human Rights on 25 June 1993,

Recalling also the International Covenant on Civil and Political Rights and the International Covenant on Economic, Social and Cultural Rights,

Recalling further the Declaration on the Right to Development adopted by the General Assembly in its resolution 41/128 of 4 December 1986,

Recalling the United Nations Millennium Declaration and the outcome documents of the twenty-third and twenty-fourth special sessions of the General Assembly, held in New York from 5 to 10 June 2000 and in Geneva from 26 June to 1 July 2000, respectively,

Recalling also its resolution 63/176 of 18 December 2008,

Recalling further Commission on Human Rights resolution 2005/17 of 14 April 2005 on globalization and its impact on the full enjoyment of all human rights,

Recognizing that all human rights are universal, indivisible, interdependent and interrelated and that the international community must treat human rights globally in a fair and equal manner, on the same footing and with the same emphasis,

Realizing that globalization affects all countries differently and makes them more exposed to external developments, positive as well as negative, inter alia, in the field of human rights,

Realizing also that globalization is not merely an economic process, but that it also has social, political, environmental, cultural and legal dimensions, which have an impact on the full enjoyment of all human rights,

Emphasizing the need to fully implement the global partnership for development and enhance the momentum generated by the 2005 World Summit in order to operationalize and implement the commitments made in the outcomes of the major United Nations conferences and summits, including the 2005 World Summit, in the economic, social and related fields, and reaffirming in particular the commitment contained in paragraphs 19 and 47 of the 2005 World Summit Outcome to promote fair globalization and the development of the productive sectors in developing countries to enable them to participate more effectively in and benefit from the process of globalization,

Realizing the need to undertake a thorough, independent and comprehensive assessment of the social, environmental and cultural impact of globalization on societies,

Recognizing in each culture a dignity and value that deserve recognition, respect and preservation, convinced that, in their rich variety and diversity and in the reciprocal influences that they exert on one another, all cultures form part of the common heritage belonging to all humankind, and aware of the risk that globalization poses more of a threat to cultural diversity if the developing world remains poor and marginalized,

Recognizing also that multilateral mechanisms have a unique role to play in meeting the challenges and opportunities presented by globalization,

Emphasizing the global character of the migratory phenomenon, the importance of international, regional and bilateral cooperation and the need to protect the human rights of migrants, particularly at a time in which migration flows have increased in the globalized economy,

Expressing concern at the negative impact of international financial turbulence on social and economic development and on the full enjoyment of all human rights, particularly in the light of the current global financial and economic crisis, which has an adverse impact on the realization of the internationally agreed development goals, particularly the health-related Millennium Development Goals,

Expressing deep concern at the negative impact of the rising global food and energy challenges and climate change on social and economic development and on the full enjoyment of all human rights for all,

Recognizing that globalization should be guided by the fundamental principles that underpin the corpus of human rights, such as equity, participation, accountability, non-discrimination at both the national and the international levels, respect for diversity, tolerance and international cooperation and solidarity,

Emphasizing that the existence of widespread extreme poverty inhibits the full realization and effective enjoyment of human rights, and that its immediate alleviation and eventual elimination must remain a high priority for the international community,

Strongly reiterating the determination to ensure the timely and full realization of the development goals and objectives agreed at the major United Nations conferences and summits, including those agreed at the Millennium Summit, that are described as the Millennium Development Goals, which have helped to galvanize efforts towards poverty eradication,

Deeply concerned at the inadequacy of measures to narrow the widening gap between the developed and the developing countries, and within countries, which has contributed to, inter alia, deepening poverty and has adversely affected the full enjoyment of all human rights, in particular in developing countries,

Underlining that human beings strive for a world that is respectful of human rights and cultural diversity and that, in this regard, they work to ensure that all activities, including those affected by globalization, are consistent with those aims,

1. *Recognizes* that, while globalization, by its impact on, inter alia, the role of the State, may affect human rights, the promotion and protection of all human rights is first and foremost the responsibility of the State;

2. *Emphasizes* that development should be at the centre of the international economic agenda and that coherence between national development strategies and international obligations and commitments is imperative for an enabling environment for development and an inclusive and equitable globalization;

3. *Reaffirms* that narrowing the gap between rich and poor, both within and between countries, is an explicit goal at the national and international levels, as part of the effort to create an enabling environment for the full enjoyment of all human rights;

4. *Also reaffirms* the commitment to create an environment at both the national and the global levels that is conducive to development and to the elimination of poverty by, inter alia, promoting good governance within each country and at the international level, avoiding protectionism, enhancing transparency in the financial, monetary and trading systems, and committing to an open, equitable, rule-based, predictable and non-discriminatory multilateral trading and financial system;

5. *Recognizes* that, while globalization offers great opportunities, the fact that its benefits are very unevenly shared and its costs unevenly distributed represents an aspect of the process that affects the full enjoyment of all human rights, in particular in developing countries;

6. *Welcomes* the report of the United Nations High Commissioner for Human Rights on globalization and its impact on the full enjoyment of human rights, which focuses on the liberalization of agricultural trade and its impact on the realization of the right to development, including the right to food, and takes note of the conclusions and recommendations contained therein;

7. *Reaffirms* the international commitment to eliminating hunger and to securing food for all, today and tomorrow, and reiterates that the relevant United Nations organizations should be assured the resources needed to expand and enhance their food assistance, and support safety net programmes designed to address hunger and malnutrition, when appropriate, through the use of local or regional purchase;

8. *Calls upon* Member States, relevant agencies of the United Nations system, intergovernmental organizations and civil society to promote equitable and environmentally sustainable economic growth for managing globalization so that poverty is systematically reduced and the international development targets are achieved;

9. *Recognizes* that only through broad and sustained efforts, including policies and measures at the global level to create a shared future based upon our common humanity in all its diversity, can globalization be made fully inclusive and equitable and have a human face, thus contributing to the full enjoyment of all human rights;

10. *Underlines* the urgent need to establish an equitable, transparent and democratic international system to strengthen and broaden the participation of developing countries in international economic decision-making and norm-setting;

11. *Affirms* that globalization is a complex process of structural transformation, with numerous interdisciplinary aspects, which has an impact on the enjoyment of civil, political, economic, social and cultural rights, including the right to development;

12. *Also affirms* that the international community should strive to respond to the challenges and opportunities posed by globalization in a manner that promotes and protects human rights while ensuring respect for the cultural diversity of all;

13. *Underlines*, therefore, the need to continue to analyse the consequences of globalization for the full enjoyment of all human rights;

14. *Takes note* of the report of the Secretary-General, and requests him to seek further the views of Member States and relevant agencies of the United Nations system and to submit to the General Assembly at its sixty-fifth session a substantive report on the subject based on these views, including recommendations on ways to address the impact of globalization on the full enjoyment of all human rights.

RECORDED VOTE ON RESOLUTION 64/160:

In favour: Afghanistan, Algeria, Angola, Antigua and Barbuda, Armenia, Azerbaijan, Bahamas, Bahrain, Bangladesh, Barbados, Belarus, Belize, Benin, Bhutan, Bolivia, Botswana, Brunei Darussalam, Burkina Faso, Burundi, Cambodia, Cameroon, Cape Verde, Central African Republic, Chad, China, Colombia, Comoros, Congo, Costa Rica, Côte d'Ivoire, Cuba, Democratic People's Republic of Korea, Democratic Republic of the Congo, Djibouti, Dominica, Dominican Republic, Ecuador, Egypt, El Salvador, Equatorial Guinea, Eritrea, Ethiopia, Fiji, Gabon, Ghana, Grenada, Guatemala, Guinea, Guinea-Bissau, Guyana, Haiti, Honduras, India, Indonesia, Iran, Iraq, Jamaica, Jordan, Kazakhstan, Kenya, Kuwait, Kyrgyzstan, Lao People's Democratic Republic, Lebanon, Lesotho, Liberia, Libyan Arab Jamahiriya, Madagascar, Malawi, Malaysia, Maldives, Mali, Mauritania, Mauritius, Mexico, Mongolia, Morocco, Mozambique, Myanmar, Namibia, Nepal, Nicaragua, Niger, Nigeria, Oman, Pakistan, Panama, Papua New Guinea, Paraguay, Peru, Philippines, Qatar, Russian Federation, Rwanda, Saint Kitts and Nevis, Saint Lucia, Saint Vincent and the Grenadines, Samoa, Saudi Arabia, Senegal, Sierra Leone, Solomon Islands, Somalia, South Africa, Sri Lanka, Sudan, Suriname, Swaziland, Syrian Arab Republic, Tajikistan, Thailand, Timor-Leste, Togo, Tonga, Trinidad and Tobago, Tunisia, Turkmenistan, Tuvalu, Uganda, United Arab Emirates, United Republic of Tanzania, Uruguay, Uzbekistan, Vanuatu, Venezuela, Viet Nam, Yemen, Zambia, Zimbabwe.

Against: Albania, Andorra, Australia, Austria, Belgium, Bosnia and Herzegovina, Bulgaria, Canada, Croatia, Cyprus, Czech Republic, Denmark, Estonia, Finland, France, Georgia, Germany, Greece, Hungary, Iceland, Ireland, Israel, Italy, Japan, Latvia, Liechtenstein, Lithuania, Luxembourg, Malta, Marshall Islands, Micronesia, Moldova, Monaco, Montenegro, Netherlands, New Zealand, Norway, Palau, Poland, Portugal, Republic of Korea, Romania, San Marino, Serbia, Slovakia, Slovenia, Spain, Sweden, Switzerland, The former Yugoslav Republic of Macedonia, Turkey, Ukraine, United Kingdom, United States.

Abstaining: Brazil, Chile, Singapore.

Foreign debt

Reports of independent expert. In response to a Human Rights Council request [YUN 2008, p. 828], the independent expert on the effects of foreign debt and other related international financial obligations of States on the full enjoyment of all human rights, particularly economic, social and cultural rights, Cephas Lumina (Zambia), in April reported [A/HRC/11/10] on his activities since assuming his mandate in May 2008. He proposed a preliminary conceptual framework for understanding the connection between foreign debt and human rights, based on international legal standards. The framework included a definition of foreign debt, a brief discussion of the relationship between foreign debt and human rights, the value of a human rights-based approach to foreign debt, a review of international standards, States' obligations in the framework of international cooperation, the obligations of international financial institutions, and the principle of shared responsibility. The expert argued that a human rights-based approach to foreign debt offered specific value through its emphasis on participation, non-discrimination, transparency, accountability and the universality, interdependence and indivisibility of all human rights, to ensure that the goals of debt relief measures were consistent with international human rights standards. In 2009 and 2010, the expert would review and develop the draft general guidelines on foreign debt and human rights, explore the linkages between trade and debt and examine the issue of "illegitimate debt". In that regard, the expert observed that although the debate concerning the responsibility for sovereign debt incurred in questionable circumstances had a long history, it had, since the Monterrey Consensus [YUN 2002, p. 953], assumed a prominent place in discussions regarding the just, equitable and sustainable resolution of the debt problem of developing countries. In particular, the recognition in the Monterrey Consensus that creditor and debtor countries were both equally responsible for preventing and resolving unsustainable debt situations had opened up the debate on the issue of creditor co-responsibility for illegitimate debt.

The Secretary-General in August submitted to the General Assembly the expert's report [A/64/289 & Corr.1], which highlighted the relevance of the concept of illegitimate debt to global efforts to find a fair and durable solution to the debt crisis. The report argued that human rights considerations must form part of the efforts towards a precise formulation of that concept. The report reviewed the various definitions of illegitimate debt set forth by debt relief campaigners and others, and proposed that the human rights principles of participation, inclusion, transparency, accountability, the rule of law, equality and non-discrimination might provide guidance in formulating an internationally accepted definition. National audits of debt/lending portfolios and international debt arbitration were potentially useful tools in addressing the problem of illegitimate debt. Debt relief initiatives had limitations, and concerted efforts should be made towards reform of the global financial system. The report called on States to support efforts to find a precise and meaningful definition of illegitimate debt, to establish an international independent arbitration mechanism on debt and to reform the international financial system.

The General Assembly took note of that report on 18 December **(decision 64/536)**.

The expert visited Norway (28–30 April) and Ecuador (2–8 May) [A/HRC/14/21/Add.1], following Norway's cancellation of Ecuador's debt in 2006 as a one-off unilateral act and the work of an audit commission in Ecuador, which concluded that due to numerous irregularities in the contraction of loans by successive Governments of Ecuador during the period 1976–2006, many of the loans and their impact breached numerous principles of international and domestic law and were therefore "illegitimate". The expert concluded that the decisions by Norway and Ecuador were significant steps in the global campaign against unsustainable debt and for the creation of an equitable global financial system. They also represented a reaffirmation by both countries of the principle of shared responsibility as underscored in the Monterrey Consensus. The principle of shared responsibility for preventing and resolving unsustainable debt situations was a critical element of global efforts to create an equitable global financial system, and the expert encouraged all States—creditors and debtors alike—to fulfil their pledges in that regard.

Human Rights Council action. On 17 June [A/64/53 (res. 11/5)], by a recorded vote of 31 to 13, with 2 abstentions, the Council, noting that the total external debt of low- and middle-income countries had risen to $2,983 billion by 2006, and that by 2007 the total debt service payments of developing countries had risen to $523 billion, urged the international community to implement the pledges, commitments, agreements and decisions of the major UN conferences and summits relating to the external debt problem of developing countries. The Council called on creditors, particularly international financial institutions, and debtors alike to prepare human rights impact assessments with regard to development projects, loan agreements or Poverty Reduction Strategy Papers.

Transnational corporations

Reports of Special Representative. In a report issued in April [A/HRC/11/13], the Special Representative of the Secretary-General on the issue of human rights and transnational corporations and other business enterprises, John Ruggie (United States), recapitulated the key features of the "protect, respect and remedy" framework welcomed by the Human Rights Council in 2008 [YUN 2008, p. 830] and outlined the directions of his work in operationalizing the framework. The framework rested on three pillars: the State duty to protect against human rights abuses by third parties, including business, through policies, regulation and adjudication; the corporate responsibility to respect human rights, which in essence meant to act with due diligence to avoid infringing on the rights of others; and greater access by victims to remedy. Answering those who questioned whether, in the face of a major worldwide economic downturn, it was an appropriate time to be addressing business and human rights, the Representative pointed out that human rights were most at risk in times of crisis, and economic crises posed a particular risk to economic and social rights. The business and human rights agenda mattered, therefore, more than ever. The same types of governance gaps and failures that had produced the economic crisis also constituted what the Representative had called the permissive environment for corporate wrongdoing in relation to human rights. The necessary solutions pointed in the same direction: Governments adopting policies that induced greater corporate responsibility, and companies adopting strategies reflecting the fact that their own long-term prospects were tightly coupled with the well-being of society. The "protect, respect and remedy" framework identified specific ways to achieve the desired objectives. For Governments, the key was to drive the business and human rights agenda more deeply into the policy domains that shaped business practices. For companies, the key was to become fully aware of their infringements on the rights of others.

An addendum [A/HRC/11/13/Add.1] reviewed international and regional provisions, commentary and decisions on State obligations to provide access to remedy for human rights abuses by third parties, including business.

In August, the Secretary-General submitted to the General Assembly a report of the Representative [A/64/216] reviewing his work since the presentation of the above report. The report noted that the bifurcation of voluntary and mandatory approaches to business and human rights was an impediment to innovative thinking and action.

The General Assembly took note of that report on 18 December (**decision 64/536**).

Report of High Commissioner. A report of the High Commissioner [A/HRC/14/29] summarized the proceedings of the consultation on the issue of human rights and transnational corporations and other busi-

ness enterprises (Geneva, 5–6 October), convened in response to a Human Rights Council request [YUN 2008, p. 830]. The consultation, attended by representatives of States, the private sector and civil society, sought to operationalize the "protect, respect and remedy" framework put forward by the Representative.

An addendum [A/HRC/14/29/Add.1] summarized the proceedings of side events to the consultation.

Coercive economic measures

Reports of Secretary-General. A report of the Secretary-General [A/HRC/12/30] issued in July and submitted in response to a Human Rights Council request [YUN 2008, p. 830] summarized the responses from five Governments (Belarus, Costa Rica, Iraq, Spain, Ukraine) on the implications and negative effects of unilateral coercive measures on their populations. A report [A/64/219] issued in August in response to General Assembly resolution 63/179 [YUN 2008, p. 831] summarized information received from seven Governments (Algeria, Angola, Belarus, Costa Rica, Jamaica, Paraguay, Syrian Arab Republic) on the same topic.

Human Rights Council action. On 2 October [A/65/53 (res. 12/22)], by a recorded vote of 32 to 14, the Council called upon States to stop adopting or implementing unilateral coercive measures not in accordance with international law, in particular those of a coercive nature with extraterritorial effects, which hampered trade relations among States, thus impeding the full realization of the right of individuals and peoples to development. The Secretary-General was requested to submit an analytical report to the Council's fifteenth (2010) session.

GENERAL ASSEMBLY ACTION

On 18 December [meeting 65], the General Assembly, on the recommendation of the Third Committee [A/64/439/Add.2 (Part II)], adopted **resolution 64/170** by recorded vote (134-54) [agenda item 69 *(b)*].

Human rights and unilateral coercive measures

The General Assembly,

Recalling all its previous resolutions on this subject, the most recent of which was resolution 63/179 of 18 December 2008, Human Rights Council resolution 12/22 of 2 October 2009 and previous resolutions of the Council and the Commission on Human Rights,

Reaffirming the pertinent principles and provisions contained in the Charter of Economic Rights and Duties of States proclaimed by the General Assembly in its resolution 3281(XXIX) of 12 December 1974, in particular article 32 thereof, in which it declared that no State may use or encourage the use of economic, political or any other type of measures to coerce another State in order to obtain from it the subordination of the exercise of its sovereign rights,

Taking note of the report of the Secretary-General submitted pursuant to General Assembly resolution 63/179 and the reports of the Secretary-General on the implementation of Assembly resolutions 52/120 of 12 December 1997 and 55/110 of 4 December 2000,

Stressing that unilateral coercive measures and legislation are contrary to international law, international humanitarian law, the Charter of the United Nations and the norms and principles governing peaceful relations among States,

Recognizing the universal, indivisible, interdependent and interrelated character of all human rights, and in this regard reaffirming the right to development as an integral part of all human rights,

Recalling the Final Document of the Fifteenth Summit Conference of Heads of State and Government of the Movement of Non-Aligned Countries, held in Sharm el-Sheikh, Egypt, from 11 to 16 July 2009 and those adopted at previous summits and conferences, in which States members of the Movement agreed to oppose and condemn those measures or laws and their continued application, persevere with efforts to effectively reverse them and urge other States to do likewise, as called for by the General Assembly and other United Nations organs, and request States applying those measures or laws to revoke them fully and immediately,

Recalling also that at the World Conference on Human Rights, held in Vienna from 14 to 25 June 1993, States were called upon to refrain from any unilateral measure not in accordance with international law and the Charter that creates obstacles to trade relations among States and impedes the full realization of all human rights, and also severely threatens the freedom of trade,

Bearing in mind all the references to this question in the Copenhagen Declaration on Social Development adopted by the World Summit for Social Development on 12 March 1995, the Beijing Declaration and Platform for Action adopted by the Fourth World Conference on Women on 15 September 1995, the Istanbul Declaration on Human Settlements and the Habitat Agenda adopted by the second United Nations Conference on Human Settlements (Habitat II) on 14 June 1996, and their five-year reviews,

Expressing concern about the negative impact of unilateral coercive measures on international relations, trade, investment and cooperation,

Expressing grave concern that, in some countries, the situation of children is adversely affected by unilateral coercive measures not in accordance with international law and the Charter that create obstacles to trade relations among States, impede the full realization of social and economic development and hinder the well-being of the population in the affected countries, with particular consequences for women and children, including adolescents,

Deeply concerned that, despite the recommendations adopted on this question by the General Assembly, the Human Rights Council, the Commission on Human Rights and recent major United Nations conferences, and contrary to general international law and the Charter, unilateral coercive measures continue to be promulgated and implemented with all their negative implications for the social humanitarian activities and economic and social development of developing countries, including their extraterritorial effects, thereby creating additional obstacles to the full enjoyment of all human rights by peoples and individuals under the jurisdiction of other States,

Bearing in mind all the extraterritorial effects of any unilateral legislative, administrative and economic measures, policies and practices of a coercive nature against the development process and the enhancement of human rights in developing countries, which create obstacles to the full realization of all human rights,

Reaffirming that unilateral coercive measures are a major obstacle to the implementation of the Declaration on the Right to Development,

Recalling article 1, paragraph 2, common to the International Covenant on Civil and Political Rights and the International Covenant on Economic, Social and Cultural Rights, which provides, inter alia, that in no case may a people be deprived of its own means of subsistence,

Noting the continuing efforts of the open-ended Working Group on the Right to Development of the Human Rights Council, and reaffirming in particular its criteria, according to which unilateral coercive measures are one of the obstacles to the implementation of the Declaration on the Right to Development,

1. *Urges* all States to cease adopting or implementing any unilateral measures not in accordance with international law, the Charter of the United Nations and the norms and principles governing peaceful relations among States, in particular those of a coercive nature with all their extraterritorial effects, which create obstacles to trade relations among States, thus impeding the full realization of the rights set forth in the Universal Declaration of Human Rights and other international human rights instruments, in particular the right of individuals and peoples to development;

2. *Also urges* all States not to adopt any unilateral measures not in accordance with international law and the Charter that impede the full achievement of economic and social development by the population of the affected countries, in particular children and women, that hinder their well-being and that create obstacles to the full enjoyment of their human rights, including the right of everyone to a standard of living adequate for his or her health and well-being and his or her right to food, medical care and the necessary social services, as well as to ensure that food and medicine are not used as tools for political pressure;

3. *Strongly objects* to the extraterritorial nature of those measures which, in addition, threaten the sovereignty of States, and in this context calls upon all Member States neither to recognize those measures nor to apply them, as well as to take administrative or legislative measures, as appropriate, to counteract the extraterritorial applications or effects of unilateral coercive measures;

4. *Condemns* the continuing unilateral application and enforcement by certain Powers of unilateral coercive measures, and rejects those measures with all their extraterritorial effects as being tools for political or economic pressure against any country, in particular against developing countries, adopted with a view to preventing those countries from exercising their right to decide, of their own free will, their own political, economic and social systems,

and because of the negative effects of those measures on the realization of all the human rights of vast sectors of their populations, in particular children, women and the elderly;

5. *Reaffirms* that essential goods such as food and medicines should not be used as tools for political coercion and that under no circumstances should people be deprived of their own means of subsistence and development;

6. *Calls upon* Member States that have initiated such measures to abide by the principles of international law, the Charter, the declarations of the United Nations and world conferences and relevant resolutions and to commit themselves to their obligations and responsibilities arising from the international human rights instruments to which they are parties by revoking such measures at the earliest possible time;

7. *Reaffirms*, in this context, the right of all peoples to self-determination, by virtue of which they freely determine their political status and freely pursue their economic, social and cultural development;

8. *Recalls* that, according to the Declaration on Principles of International Law concerning Friendly Relations and Cooperation among States in accordance with the Charter of the United Nations, contained in the annex to General Assembly resolution 2625(XXV) of 24 October 1970, and the relevant principles and provisions contained in the Charter of Economic Rights and Duties of States proclaimed by the Assembly in its resolution 3281(XXIX), in particular article 32 thereof, no State may use or encourage the use of economic, political or any other type of measures to coerce another State in order to obtain from it the subordination of the exercise of its sovereign rights and to secure from it advantages of any kind;

9. *Rejects* all attempts to introduce unilateral coercive measures, and urges the Human Rights Council to take fully into account the negative impact of those measures, including through the enactment of national laws and their extraterritorial application which are not in conformity with international law, in its task concerning the implementation of the right to development;

10. *Requests* the United Nations High Commissioner for Human Rights, in discharging her functions relating to the promotion, realization and protection of the right to development and bearing in mind the continuing impact of unilateral coercive measures on the population of developing countries, to give priority to the present resolution in her annual report to the General Assembly;

11. *Underlines* the fact that unilateral coercive measures are one of the major obstacles to the implementation of the Declaration on the Right to Development, and in this regard calls upon all States to avoid the unilateral imposition of economic coercive measures and the extraterritorial application of domestic laws that run counter to the principles of free trade and hamper the development of developing countries, as recognized by the Working Group on the Right to Development of the Human Rights Council;

12. *Recognizes* that, in the Declaration of Principles adopted at the first phase of the World Summit on the Information Society, held in Geneva from 10 to 12 December 2003, States were strongly urged to avoid and refrain from any unilateral measure not in accordance with international law and the Charter of the United Nations in building the information society;

13. *Supports* the invitation of the Human Rights Council to all special rapporteurs and existing thematic mechanisms of the Council in the field of economic, social and cultural rights to pay due attention, within the scope of their respective mandates, to the negative impact and consequences of unilateral coercive measures;

14. *Requests* the Secretary-General to bring the present resolution to the attention of all Member States, to continue to collect their views and information on the implications and negative effects of unilateral coercive measures on their populations and to submit an analytical report thereon to the General Assembly at its sixty-fifth session, while reiterating once again the need to highlight the practical and preventive measures in this respect;

15. *Decides* to examine the question on a priority basis at its sixty-fifth session under the sub-item entitled "Human rights questions, including alternative approaches for improving the effective enjoyment of human rights and fundamental freedoms".

RECORDED VOTE ON RESOLUTION 64/170:

In favour: Afghanistan, Algeria, Angola, Antigua and Barbuda, Argentina, Armenia, Azerbaijan, Bahamas, Bahrain, Bangladesh, Barbados, Belarus, Belize, Benin, Bhutan, Bolivia, Botswana, Brazil, Brunei Darussalam, Burkina Faso, Burundi, Cambodia, Cameroon, Cape Verde, Central African Republic, Chad, Chile, China, Colombia, Comoros, Congo, Costa Rica, Côte d'Ivoire, Cuba, Democratic People's Republic of Korea, Democratic Republic of the Congo, Djibouti, Dominica, Dominican Republic, Ecuador, Egypt, El Salvador, Equatorial Guinea, Eritrea, Ethiopia, Gabon, Ghana, Grenada, Guatemala, Guinea, Guinea-Bissau, Guyana, Haiti, Honduras, India, Indonesia, Iran, Iraq, Jamaica, Jordan, Kazakhstan, Kenya, Kuwait, Kyrgyzstan, Lao People's Democratic Republic, Lebanon, Lesotho, Liberia, Libyan Arab Jamahiriya, Madagascar, Malawi, Malaysia, Maldives, Mali, Mauritania, Mauritius, Mexico, Mongolia, Morocco, Mozambique, Myanmar, Namibia, Nepal, Nicaragua, Niger, Nigeria, Oman, Pakistan, Panama, Papua New Guinea, Paraguay, Peru, Philippines, Qatar, Russian Federation, Rwanda, Saint Kitts and Nevis, Saint Lucia, Saint Vincent and the Grenadines, Samoa, Saudi Arabia, Senegal, Sierra Leone, Singapore, Solomon Islands, Somalia, South Africa, Sri Lanka, Sudan, Suriname, Swaziland, Syrian Arab Republic, Tajikistan, Thailand, Timor-Leste, Togo, Tonga, Trinidad and Tobago, Tunisia, Turkmenistan, Tuvalu, Uganda, United Arab Emirates, United Republic of Tanzania, Uruguay, Uzbekistan, Vanuatu, Venezuela, Viet Nam, Yemen, Zambia, Zimbabwe.

Against: Albania, Andorra, Australia, Austria, Belgium, Bosnia and Herzegovina, Bulgaria, Canada, Croatia, Cyprus, Czech Republic, Denmark, Estonia, Finland, France, Georgia, Germany, Greece, Hungary, Iceland, Ireland, Israel, Italy, Japan, Latvia, Liechtenstein, Lithuania, Luxembourg, Malta, Marshall Islands, Micronesia, Moldova, Monaco, Montenegro, Netherlands, New Zealand, Norway, Palau, Poland, Portugal, Republic of Korea, Romania, San Marino, Serbia, Slovakia, Slovenia, Spain, Sweden, Switzerland, The former Yugoslav Republic of Macedonia, Turkey, Ukraine, United Kingdom, United States.

Social Forum

Human Rights Council action. On 27 March [A/64/53 (res. 10/29)], the Council reaffirmed the Social Forum as a unique space for interactive dialogue between representatives of Member States, civil society, including grass-roots organizations and intergovernmental organizations, and the UN human rights machinery. It requested that the next Forum meeting be held during 2009 in Geneva, focusing on the negative impact of economic and financial crises on efforts to combat poverty; national anti-poverty programmes: best practices of States in implementing social security programmes from a human rights perspective; and international assistance and cooperation in combating poverty. The Council invited the 2009 Forum to submit a report.

Social Forum session. In accordance with that request, the 2009 Social Forum (Geneva, 31 August–2 September) [A/HRC/13/51] brought together representatives of Member States, intergovernmental organizations, UN system entities, NGOs and academia. Participants exchanged views and made proposals on the social protection gap; protecting the human rights of vulnerable groups during economic and financial crises; and strengthening the effectiveness of international assistance in combating poverty. Participants stressed that social security was not optional, but an obligation enshrined in international human rights law; social security systems were important in times of crisis to protect those who suffered from the crisis and to contribute to job creation and economic recovery. Since poverty prevented the realization and enjoyment of human rights, poverty eradication should remain an international priority, and the poor must be at the centre of public policies.

Extreme poverty

Reports of independent expert. Pursuant to a Human Rights Council request [YUN 2008, p. 833], the independent expert on the question of human rights and extreme poverty, Magdalena Sepúlveda Carmona (Chile), submitted a report [A/HRC/11/9] focusing on cash transfer programmes (CTPs), non-contributory programmes providing cash payments to individuals or households. Their primary objective was to increase the real income of beneficiaries in order to enable a minimum level of consumption within the household. CTPs had been identified as effective tools for poverty eradication due to their capacity to reduce economic inequalities and break the transmission of poverty between generations. Yet they had seldom been analysed from a human rights perspective. The expert recognized that CTPs could assist States in fulfilling their obligations under human rights law. The transfers might have an impact on the exercise of economic, social, cultural, civil and political rights: in particular, they had the potential to assist in realizing the right to an adequate standard of living, including adequate food, clothing and housing. Nonetheless, CTPs were not the most effec-

tive means of tackling extreme poverty and protecting human rights in all contexts, and should be seen as only one component of social assistance policies. As such, they must be integrated within social protection systems and grounded by solid legal and institutional frameworks framed by human rights standards and principles.

Also in response to a request of the Council [YUN 2008, p. 833], the Secretary-General in August transmitted to the General Assembly a report [A/64/279] of the expert addressing the impact of the global financial crisis on people living in extreme poverty and the enjoyment of their human rights. The report stressed that the crisis offered an opportunity to move beyond the restructuring of the global financial and monetary systems and to place people at the centre of policy measures by enhancing social protection systems from a human rights-based approach. Human rights standards provided a normative framework for the adoption of social protection measures and provided guidance for their design, implementation and evaluation. Beyond reaffirming political will to rescue economies, the report urged the international community to take action and mobilize support in order to ensure that those who suffered the most acute consequences of economic crises were protected and supported through the strengthening of social protection systems.

The General Assembly took note of that report on 18 December (**decision 64/536**).

Following her mission to Zambia (20–28 August) [A/HRC/14/31/Add.1], the expert underlined the importance of enhancing support to social protection measures through increased public financial resources and better coordination of social protection initiatives. Focusing on a set of pilot social cash transfers schemes, the expert called on the Government to increase support for the schemes and convert those limited pilots into well-funded and stable public policies that could be the basis of a national social protection system. The expert reiterated the importance of investing in social protection to avoid expanding and deepening poverty; called for the enhancement of accountability mechanisms, in particular to fight corruption; urged the Government to ensure participation of civil society organizations and local communities in public policies; and called on the international community to support Zambia.

The independent expert undertook a mission to Bangladesh (3–10 December) together with the independent expert on the issue of human rights obligations related to access to safe drinking water and sanitation. In their joint report [A/HRC/15/55 & Corr.1], the experts recommended that the Government: ensure equal protection of all human rights—civil, cultural, economic, political and social—in the law, in their independent monitoring and in their enforcement; provide greater political and financial support to the National Human Rights Commission, the Ombudsman and the Anti-Corruption Commission while assuring their continued independence; and collect disaggregated data on the most vulnerable groups to have a clear picture of who was living in urban slums. On the basis of that information, the Government should draw up a comprehensive plan for people living in poverty in urban areas, including measures to ensure their access to sanitation and safe drinking water. The Government should address the situation of those who lacked secure land tenure and put an end to forced evictions, which were contrary to its human rights obligations.

Draft guiding principles. In 2001, the Commission on Human Rights had requested its Sub-commission on the Promotion and Protection of Human Rights to develop guiding principles on the implementation of human rights norms and standards in the context of the fight against extreme poverty [YUN 2001, p. 668]. The Subcommission entrusted an ad hoc group of experts with the task of preparing draft principles [ibid., p. 669], which were annexed to a report submitted to the Subcommission and the Human Rights Council [YUN 2006, p. 900]. The Council took note of the draft guiding principles and requested the High Commissioner to obtain the views of all stakeholders [ibid.]. The High Commissioner in 2008 reported on the consultations [YUN 2008, p. 833], and the Council requested her to continue the consultations and organize a seminar on the guiding principles [ibid.].

Following that request, the High Commissioner in April submitted a report [A/HRC/11/32] summarizing all submissions collected during the two rounds of consultation (2007–2008), which concluded with a seminar (Geneva, 27–28 January 2009) attended by States, civil society organizations, international experts, including the independent expert, and other stakeholders. The consultations disclosed a broad consensus on the importance of preparing guiding principles on extreme poverty and human rights. Such principles had the potential to strengthen the implementation of international human rights law, rendering international human rights law and policy directly relevant to people living in extreme poverty. However, the draft guiding principles required work. Their language and terms needed to conform more systematically with those of international human rights law. Topics requiring further discussion included how to strike a balance between normative clarification and operational guidance, and whether or how to deal with global and structural causes of poverty. At the end of the seminar, France made a proposal on the way forward, recommending that the Human Rights Council mandate the independent expert to revise the

draft guiding principles. The proposal received unanimous support.

Human Rights Council action. On 2 October [A/65/53 (res. 12/19)], the Council invited the expert to pursue further work on the draft guiding principles; to consult Member States further; and to submit a progress report presenting her recommendations on how to improve the principles to the Council no later than its fifteenth (2010) session, to allow the Council to take a decision on the way forward with a view to a possible adoption of guiding principles by 2012.

Right to food

Reports of Special Rapporteur. The Special Rapporteur on the right to food, Olivier De Schutter (Belgium), in February submitted to the Human Rights Council a report [A/HRC/10/5] examining the contribution of development cooperation and food aid to the realization of the right to food, which ranged from long-term support for food security to short-term answers to emergency situations. Both policies had been under increased scrutiny, and both were in need of reform. The report made suggestions to reorient them by better integrating three perspectives grounded in the human right to adequate food: the definition of the obligations of donor States, the identification of the tools on which those policies relied, and the evaluation of such policies. At its core, a human rights approach turned what had been a bilateral relationship between donor and partner into a triangular relationship in which policy beneficiaries played an active role. Seeing the provision of foreign aid as a means to fulfil the right to adequate food had concrete implications, which assumed that donor and partner Governments were duty-bearers and beneficiaries were rights-holders.

An addendum [A/HRC/10/5/Add.1] summarized 21 communications sent between 5 December 2007 and 5 December 2008 to 17 Member States and two transnational corporations (Syngenta Limited and ITM-Mining Angola), as well as responses received by 6 February 2009.

In a report to the Council submitted in July [A/HRC/12/31], the Rapporteur said that since the global food crisis had put hunger at the top of the political agenda, important efforts had been put into increasing the supply of food. Producing more food would not, however, reduce hunger without rethinking the political economy of the food systems and without producing and consuming in ways that were more equitable and sustainable. Nor would increased production suffice if policies were not grounded on the right to food as a means to ensure adequate targeting, monitoring, accountability and participation, all of which could improve the effectiveness of the strategies put in place. The Rapporteur called on States to: assess the contribution of different modes of agricultural development to the realization of the right to food; accelerate progress towards an international consensus on the production and use of agrofuels and on large-scale land acquisitions or leases; guarantee the right to social security and strengthen social protection; combat the sources of price volatility on the international markets through international cooperation; improve the global governance of food security; and effectively realize the right to food by strengthening multilateralism.

In response to General Assembly resolution 63/187 [YUN 2008, p. 837], the Secretary-General transmitted to the Assembly the interim report [A/64/170] of the Rapporteur, which focused on seed policies and the right to food. The Rapporteur argued that the professionalization of breeding and its separation from farming had led to the emergence of a commercial seed system, alongside the farmers' seed systems through which farmers traditionally saved, exchanged and sold seeds, often informally. That shift had led to the granting of temporary monopoly privileges to plant breeders and patent-holders through the tools of intellectual property as a means to encourage research and innovation in plant breeding. In that process, however, the poorest farmers might become dependent on expensive inputs, creating the risk of indebtedness in the face of unstable incomes. Private-led research might seek to satisfy the needs of farmers in industrialized countries while neglecting those of poor farmers in developing countries. The farmers' seed systems might be put in jeopardy, although most farmers in developing countries relied on such systems, which, for them, were a source of economic independence and resilience in the face of threats such as pests, diseases or climate change. Agrobiodiversity might be threatened by the uniformization encouraged by the spread of commercial varieties. The report explored how States could implement seed policies that contributed to the full realization of human rights; identified how research and development could best serve the poorest farmers in developing countries, and how commercial seed systems could be regulated to serve the right to food and the right of all to the benefits of scientific progress; and examined how farmers' seed systems could be supported to preserve agrobiodiversity.

Following his mission to Benin (12–20 March) [A/HRC/13/33/Add.3], the Rapporteur recommended more ambitious support to the dissemination of sustainable agriculture best practices, continued reinvestment in agricultural extension systems, and a special focus on the impact of international trade on small producers and on the integration of such producers in export channels. Those efforts should be coordinated as part of a national strategy for realizing the right to food.

Following his mission to Guatemala (3–5 September) [A/HRC/13/33/Add.4], the Rapporteur recommended addressing unequal access to land, including full implementation and codification into law of the Policy for Integral Rural Development; integrating human rights principles into social programmes, in particular the Mi Familia Progresa (My Family Progresses) cash transfer programme; raising the minimum salary; reinforcing the capacity of the Labour Inspectorate; strengthening the System of Information and Communication on Food and Nutrition Security; and reforming the taxation system, including by amending the Solidarity Tax and increasing the income tax on the highest revenues.

Following his mission to Nicaragua (6–12 September) [A/HRC/13/33/Add.5], the Rapporteur recommended improved protection against forced evictions; impact assessments of trade agreements; an increase in the minimum wage; improved capacity of the labour inspectorates and regulation of subcontracting; full implementation of the Law on Food and Nutrition Security and Sovereignty; strengthened capacity of the Nicaraguan State Enterprise for Staple Foods; integration of human rights principles into the programmes placed under the Hambre Cero (Zero Hunger) strategy; acceleration of the land titling programme and efforts to improve the productive capacities of smallholders and women's access to land; adequate resources for the Office of the Ombudsman and for the special ombudsman for indigenous peoples; adoption of the act relating to the indigenous peoples of the Pacific, central and northern regions and ratification of ILO Convention No. 169 (1989) concerning Indigenous and Tribal Peoples in Independent Countries; and resumption of the global round table with the donor community.

Following his mission to Brazil (12–18 October) [A/HRC/13/33/Add.6], the Rapporteur recommended the establishment of an independent national institution for human rights promotion and protection; the strengthening of the National Food and Nutritional Security System; further capacity-building within the Federal Public Ministry; the improvement of the rights of indigenous peoples; ex ante impact assessments on the right to food in large-scale infrastructural projects; respect for freedom of expression and assembly exercised through legitimate forms of social protest; further consolidation of social policies of the "Zero Hunger" strategy; maximum use of public resources for the progressive realization of the right to food; acceleration of land distribution; participatory assessment of the different forms of agriculture—large-scale and small-scale family farming—and the support the State provided to them; participatory right-to-food impact assessment of trade policies; and compliance with social and environmental requirements in sugar-cane plantations.

Human Rights Council action. On 26 March [A/64/53 (res. 10/12)], the Council encouraged States to achieve progressively the full realization of the right to food and adopt national strategies for realizing that right; and requested States, private actors and international organizations to take fully into account the need to promote the effective realization of that right for all. The Council requested its Advisory Committee to undertake a study on discrimination in the context of the right to food and to report to the its thirteenth (2010) session; and requested the Rapporteur to report to that session.

Following up on its seventh special session on the negative impact of the worsening of the world food crisis on the realization of the right to food for all [YUN 2008, p. 835], the Council on 1 October [A/65/53 (res. 12/10)] encouraged States to incorporate a human rights perspective in building and reviewing their national strategies for the realization of the right to adequate food for all; encouraged States to invest or promote investment in agriculture and rural infrastructure to benefit the most vulnerable and affected by the crisis; and called on States, multilateral institutions and other stakeholders to take all necessary measures to ensure the realization of the right to food and to review any policy or measure that could have a negative impact on the realization of that right before instituting such a policy or measure.

GENERAL ASSEMBLY ACTION

On 18 December [meeting 65], the General Assembly, on the recommendation of the Third Committee [A/64/439/Add.2 (Part II)], adopted **resolution 64/159** without vote [agenda item 69 *(b)*].

The right to food

The General Assembly,

Reaffirming all previous resolutions and decisions on the right to food adopted within the framework of the United Nations,

Recalling the Universal Declaration of Human Rights, which provides that everyone has the right to a standard of living adequate for her or his health and well-being, including food, the Universal Declaration on the Eradication of Hunger and Malnutrition and the United Nations Millennium Declaration, in particular Millennium Development Goal 1 on eradicating extreme poverty and hunger by 2015,

Recalling also the provisions of the International Covenant on Economic, Social and Cultural Rights, in which the fundamental right of every person to be free from hunger is recognized,

Bearing in mind the Rome Declaration on World Food Security and the World Food Summit Plan of Action and

the Declaration of the World Food Summit: five years later, adopted in Rome on 13 June 2002,

Reaffirming the concrete recommendations contained in the Voluntary Guidelines to Support the Progressive Realization of the Right to Adequate Food in the Context of National Food Security, adopted by the Council of the Food and Agriculture Organization of the United Nations in November 2004,

Reaffirming also that all human rights are universal, indivisible, interdependent and interrelated, and that they must be treated globally, in a fair and equal manner, on the same footing and with the same emphasis,

Reaffirming further that a peaceful, stable and enabling political, social and economic environment, at both the national and the international levels, is the essential foundation that will enable States to give adequate priority to food security and poverty eradication,

Reiterating, as in the Rome Declaration on World Food Security and the Declaration of the World Food Summit: five years later, that food should not be used as an instrument of political or economic pressure, and reaffirming in this regard the importance of international cooperation and solidarity, as well as the necessity of refraining from unilateral measures that are not in accordance with international law and the Charter of the United Nations and that endanger food security,

Convinced that each State must adopt a strategy consistent with its resources and capacities to achieve its individual goals in implementing the recommendations contained in the Rome Declaration on World Food Security and the World Food Summit Plan of Action and, at the same time, cooperate regionally and internationally in order to organize collective solutions to global issues of food security in a world of increasingly interlinked institutions, societies and economies where coordinated efforts and shared responsibilities are essential,

Recognizing that the complex character of the global food crisis, in which the right to adequate food is threatened to be violated on a massive scale, is a combination of several major factors, such as the global financial and economic crisis, environmental degradation, desertification and the impacts of global climate change, as well as natural disasters and the lack in many countries of the appropriate technology, investment and capacity-building necessary to confront its impact, particularly in developing countries, least developed countries and small island developing States,

Resolved to act to ensure that the human rights perspective is taken into account at the national, regional and international levels in measures to address the current global food crisis,

Expressing its deep concern at the number and scale of natural disasters, diseases and pests and their increasing impact in recent years, which have resulted in massive loss of life and livelihood and threatened agricultural production and food security, in particular in developing countries,

Stressing the importance of reversing the continuing decline of official development assistance devoted to agriculture, both in real terms and as a share of total official development assistance,

Recognizing the importance of the protection and preservation of agrobiodiversity in guaranteeing food security and the right to food for all,

Recognizing also the role of the Food and Agriculture Organization of the United Nations as the key United Nations agency for rural and agricultural development and its work in supporting the efforts of Member States to achieve the full realization of the right to food, including through its provision of technical assistance to developing countries in support of the implementation of national priority frameworks,

Taking note of the final Declaration adopted at the International Conference on Agrarian Reform and Rural Development of the Food and Agriculture Organization of the United Nations in Porto Alegre, Brazil, on 10 March 2006,

Acknowledging the High-level Task Force on the Global Food Security Crisis established by the Secretary-General, and supporting the Secretary-General in his continuing efforts in this regard, including continued engagement with Member States and the Special Rapporteur of the Human Rights Council on the right to food,

1. *Reaffirms* that hunger constitutes an outrage and a violation of human dignity and therefore requires the adoption of urgent measures at the national, regional and international levels for its elimination;

2. *Also reaffirms* the right of everyone to have access to safe, sufficient and nutritious food, consistent with the right to adequate food and the fundamental right of everyone to be free from hunger, so as to be able to fully develop and maintain his or her physical and mental capacities;

3. *Considers it intolerable* that, as estimated by the United Nations Children's Fund, more than one third of the children who die every year before the age of 5 do so from hunger-related illness, and that, as estimated by the Food and Agriculture Organization of the United Nations, the number of people who are undernourished has grown to about 1.02 billion worldwide, including as a result of the global food crisis, while, according to the latter organization, the planet could produce enough food to feed everyone around the world;

4. *Expresses its concern* that women and girls are disproportionately affected by hunger, food insecurity and poverty, in part as a result of gender inequality and discrimination, that in many countries, girls are twice as likely as boys to die from malnutrition and preventable childhood diseases and that it is estimated that almost twice as many women as men suffer from malnutrition;

5. *Encourages* all States to take action to address gender inequality and discrimination against women, in particular where it contributes to the malnutrition of women and girls, including measures to ensure the full and equal realization of the right to food and ensuring that women have equal access to resources, including income, land and water and their ownership, as well as full and equal access to education, science and technology, to enable them to feed themselves and their families;

6. *Encourages* the Special Rapporteur of the Human Rights Council on the right to food to continue mainstreaming a gender perspective in the fulfilment of his mandate, and encourages the Food and Agriculture Organization of the United Nations and all other United Nations bodies and mechanisms addressing the right to food and food insecurity to integrate a gender perspective into their relevant policies, programmes and activities;

7. *Reaffirms* the need to ensure that programmes delivering safe and nutritious food are inclusive of and accessible to persons with disabilities;

8. *Encourages* all States to take steps with a view to achieving progressively the full realization of the right to food, including steps to promote the conditions for everyone to be free from hunger and, as soon as possible, to enjoy fully the right to food, and to create and adopt national plans to combat hunger;

9. *Recognizes* the advances reached through South-South cooperation in developing countries and regions in connection with food security and the development of agricultural production for the full realization of the right to food;

10. *Stresses* that improving access to productive resources and public investment in rural development are essential for eradicating hunger and poverty, in particular in developing countries, including through the promotion of investments in appropriate small-scale irrigation and water management technologies in order to reduce vulnerability to droughts;

11. *Recognizes* that 80 per cent of hungry people live in rural areas and 50 per cent are small-scale farm-holders, and that these people are especially vulnerable to food insecurity, given the increasing cost of inputs and the fall in farm incomes; that access to land, water, seeds and other natural resources is an increasing challenge for poor producers; that sustainable and gender-sensitive agricultural policies are important tools for promoting land and agrarian reform, rural credit and insurance, technical assistance and other associated measures to achieve food security and rural development; and that support by States for small farmers, fishing communities and local enterprises is a key element for food security and the provision of the right to food;

12. *Stresses* the importance of fighting hunger in rural areas, including through national efforts supported by international partnerships to stop desertification and land degradation and through investments and public policies that are specifically appropriate to the risk of drylands, and in this regard calls for the full implementation of the United Nations Convention to Combat Desertification in Those Countries Experiencing Serious Drought and/or Desertification, Particularly in Africa;

13. *Urges* States that have not yet done so to favourably consider becoming parties to the Convention on Biological Diversity and to consider becoming parties to the International Treaty on Plant Genetic Resources for Food and Agriculture as a matter of priority;

14. *Recalls* the United Nations Declaration on the Rights of Indigenous Peoples and acknowledges that many indigenous organizations and representatives of indigenous peoples have expressed in different forums their deep concerns over the obstacles and challenges they face for the full enjoyment of the right to food, and calls upon States to take special actions to combat the root causes of the disproportionately high level of hunger and malnutrition among indigenous peoples and the continuous discrimination against them;

15. *Notes* the need to further examine various concepts such as, inter alia, "food sovereignty" and their relation with food security and the right to food, bearing in mind

the need to avoid any negative impact on the enjoyment of the right to food for all people at all times;

16.   *Requests* all States and private actors, as well as international organizations within their respective mandates, to take fully into account the need to promote the effective realization of the right to food for all, including in the ongoing negotiations in different fields;

17.   *Recognizes* the need to strengthen national commitment as well as international assistance, upon the request of and in cooperation with the affected countries, towards the full realization and protection of the right to food, and in particular to develop national protection mechanisms for people forced to leave their homes and land because of hunger or humanitarian emergencies affecting the enjoyment of the right to food;

18.   *Stresses* the need to make efforts to mobilize and optimize the allocation and utilization of technical and financial resources from all sources, including external debt relief for developing countries, and to reinforce national actions to implement sustainable food security policies;

19.   *Calls for* the early conclusion and a successful, development-oriented outcome of the Doha Round of trade negotiations of the World Trade Organization as a contribution to creating international conditions that permit the full realization of the right to food;

20.   *Stresses* that all States should make all efforts to ensure that their international policies of a political and economic nature, including international trade agreements, do not have a negative impact on the right to food in other countries;

21.   *Recalls* the importance of the New York Declaration on Action against Hunger and Poverty, and recommends the continuation of efforts aimed at identifying additional sources of financing for the fight against hunger and poverty;

22.   *Recognizes* that the promises made at the World Food Summit in 1996 to halve the number of persons who are undernourished are not being fulfilled, while recognizing the efforts of Member States in this regard, and invites once again all international financial and development institutions, as well as the relevant United Nations agencies and funds, to give priority to and provide the necessary funding to realize the aim of halving by 2015 the proportion of people who suffer from hunger, as well as the right to food as set out in the Rome Declaration on World Food Security and the United Nations Millennium Declaration;

23.   *Reaffirms* that integrating food and nutritional support, with the goal that all people at all times will have access to sufficient, safe and nutritious food to meet their dietary needs and food preferences for an active and healthy life, is part of a comprehensive effort to improve public health, including the response to the spread of HIV/AIDS, tuberculosis, malaria and other communicable diseases;

24.   *Urges* States to give adequate priority in their development strategies and expenditures to the realization of the right to food;

25.   *Stresses* the importance of international cooperation and development assistance as an effective contribution both to the expansion and improvement of agriculture and its environmental sustainability, food production, breeding projects on diversity of crops and livestock, and institutional innovations such as community seed banks,

farmer field schools and seed fairs, and to the provision of humanitarian food assistance in activities related to emergency situations, for the realization of the right to food and the achievement of sustainable food security, while recognizing that each country has the primary responsibility for ensuring the implementation of national programmes and strategies in this regard;

26.   *Also stresses* that States parties to the World Trade Organization Agreement on Trade-Related Aspects of Intellectual Property Rights should consider implementing that agreement in a manner supportive of food security, while mindful of the obligation of Member States to promote and protect the right to food;

27.   *Calls upon* Member States, the United Nations system and other relevant stakeholders to support national efforts aimed at responding rapidly to the food crises currently occurring across Africa, and expresses its deep concern that funding shortfalls are forcing the World Food Programme to cut operations across different regions, including Southern Africa;

28.   *Invites* all relevant international organizations, including the World Bank and the International Monetary Fund, to continue to promote policies and projects that have a positive impact on the right to food, to ensure that partners respect the right to food in the implementation of common projects, to support strategies of Member States aimed at the fulfilment of the right to food and to avoid any actions that could have a negative impact on the realization of the right to food;

29.   *Takes note with appreciation* of the interim report of the Special Rapporteur;

30.   *Supports* the realization of the mandate of the Special Rapporteur, as extended by the Human Rights Council in its resolution 6/2 of 27 September 2007;

31.   *Requests* the Secretary-General and the United Nations High Commissioner for Human Rights to provide all the human and financial resources necessary for the effective fulfilment of the mandate of the Special Rapporteur;

32.   *Welcomes* the work already done by the Committee on Economic, Social and Cultural Rights in promoting the right to adequate food, in particular its General Comment No. 12 (1999) on the right to adequate food (article 11 of the International Covenant on Economic, Social and Cultural Rights), in which the Committee affirmed, inter alia, that the right to adequate food is indivisibly linked to the inherent dignity of the human person and is indispensable for the fulfilment of other human rights enshrined in the International Bill of Human Rights, and is also inseparable from social justice, requiring the adoption of appropriate economic, environmental and social policies, at both the national and the international levels, oriented to the eradication of poverty and the fulfilment of all human rights for all;

33.   *Recalls* General Comment No. 15 (2002) of the Committee on Economic, Social and Cultural Rights on the right to water (articles 11 and 12 of the Covenant), in which the Committee noted, inter alia, the importance of ensuring sustainable water resources for human consumption and agriculture in realization of the right to adequate food;

34.   *Reaffirms* that the Voluntary Guidelines to Support the Progressive Realization of the Right to Adequate

Food in the Context of National Food Security, adopted by the Council of the Food and Agriculture Organization of the United Nations in November 2004, represent a practical tool to promote the realization of the right to food for all, contribute to the achievement of food security and thus provide an additional instrument in the attainment of internationally agreed development goals, including those contained in the Millennium Declaration;

35. *Welcomes* the continued cooperation of the High Commissioner, the Committee and the Special Rapporteur, and encourages them to continue their cooperation in this regard;

36. *Calls upon* all Governments to cooperate with and assist the Special Rapporteur in his task, to supply all necessary information requested by him and to give serious consideration to responding favourably to the requests of the Special Rapporteur to visit their countries to enable him to fulfil his mandate more effectively;

37. *Requests* the Special Rapporteur to submit an interim report to the General Assembly at its sixty-fifth session on the implementation of the present resolution and to continue his work, including by examining the emerging issues with regard to the realization of the right to food within his existing mandate;

38. *Invites* Governments, relevant United Nations agencies, funds and programmes, treaty bodies, civil society actors and non-governmental organizations, as well as the private sector, to cooperate fully with the Special Rapporteur in the fulfilment of his mandate, inter alia, through the submission of comments and suggestions on ways and means of realizing the right to food;

39. *Decides* to continue the consideration of the question at its sixty-fifth session under the item entitled "Promotion and protection of human rights".

Right to adequate housing

Reports of Special Rapporteur. In response to a Human Rights Council request [YUN 2007, p. 780], the Special Rapporteur on adequate housing as a component of the right to an adequate standard of living, and on the right to non-discrimination in that context, Raquel Rolnik (Brazil), submitted a report [A/HRC/10/7] focusing on the consequences of economic, financial and housing policies and approaches that had affected the right to adequate housing and had contributed to the crisis in the housing, mortgage and financial sectors. Within the context of the globalization of the housing and real estate finance markets and economic adjustment policies, cities had become unaffordable for lower-income—and increasingly middle-income—people. In most countries, the market had become the regulating institution, setting benchmarks for the price, location and availability of housing and land, while the role of the State in managing public housing had generally decreased. As a result, housing was seen as a mere commodity and a financial asset, neglecting other dimensions of the right to adequate housing and negatively affecting the enjoyment of human rights. The crisis provided an opportunity to introduce changes to make the system sustainable and allow the provision of adequate housing for all. Markets alone could not provide adequate housing for all, and in some circumstances public intervention was needed. The Rapporteur advocated the adoption of human rights-based public housing policies supporting access to adequate housing by different means, including through alternatives to private mortgage and ownership-based housing systems, and through new financial mechanisms and tenure arrangements. She called for an increase in public funding for housing and the construction of public housing to address the crisis.

An addendum [A/HRC/10/7/Add.1] summarized 34 communications sent to 25 States between 5 December 2007 and 5 December 2008 and 17 replies received between 24 January 2008 and 6 February 2009.

Another addendum [A/HRC/10/7/Add.2] assessed implementation of recommendations following visits to Mexico [YUN 2002, p. 739], Romania [ibid.], Afghanistan [YUN 2003, p. 769] and Peru [ibid.]. The Rapporteur noted that actors dealing with issues related to the right to adequate housing, including public officials and institutions, UN agencies, international organizations and donors, continued to work without applying a rights-based approach and ignoring the right to adequate housing in their activities, planning and programmes. Ignoring human rights entitlements was one factor that might partly explain the mixed results of many programmes and initiatives. The Rapporteur encouraged all those involved in housing to seek appropriate training on human rights and the right to adequate housing.

In response to a Human Rights Council request [YUN 2007, p. 780], the Secretary-General in August transmitted to the General Assembly the report of the Rapporteur [A/64/255], which discussed how the impacts of climate change had consequences for the fulfilment of the right to adequate housing. The report reviewed the scope and severity of climate change, its implications for extreme weather events and its impact on urban and rural areas, including unplanned and unserviced settlements, on human mobility and on small islands and low-lying coastal zones. It outlined the relevant international human rights frameworks and obligations in connection to the right to housing; discussed the role of international cooperation to address the inevitable impacts of climate change; and considered policies on mitigation and adaptation as they related to the right to adequate housing. The Rapporteur urged States to uphold their human rights obligations when mitigating climate change and adapting to its impacts.

The General Assembly took note of that report on 18 December **(decision 64/536)**.

Following her mission to Maldives (18–25 February) [A/HRC/13/20/Add.3], the Rapporteur recommended establishing a land and housing policy council, with the participation of community representatives from the different atolls and members of governmental agencies and the private sector, to participate in the formulation of land and housing policies and monitor reform implementation. Programmes of adaptation to climate change should give priority to eco-friendly solutions and carefully evaluate the impact of hard engineering solutions. While various factors, including population growth and land scarcity, made a new approach to land distribution and territorial planning unavoidable, such an approach should keep the positive aspects of traditional land allocation, which provided for access to land for housing purposes to all, regardless of social class and wealth.

Following her mission to the United States (22 October–8 November) [A/HRC/13/20/Add.4], the Rapporteur recommended increased funding of the federal housing assistance programmes, which played a major role in providing affordable housing to low-income residents. Additional funding was needed to maintain and restore the public housing stock. The Government should strengthen legislation on health standards for subsidized buildings and ensure proper maintenance and pest control. Tenant protection legislation should be strengthened for renters of foreclosed properties. Empty foreclosed properties should be made available using incentives for the sale of the property to non-profit organizations or community land trusts, in order to increase the stock of affordable housing. Homelessness prevention strategies should increase the stock of affordable housing available to low-income workers and those at risk of becoming homeless.

Cultural rights

Report of High Commissioner. Pursuant to a Human Rights Council request [YUN 2007, p. 721] the High Commissioner in January submitted a report [A/HRC/10/60] summarizing the views of 15 Governments, the United Nations Educational, Scientific and Cultural Organization (unesco) and one ngo on the content and scope of a possible future mandate of an independent expert in the field of cultural rights. Fifteen of the 17 responses supported such action.

Human Rights Council action. On 26 March [A/64/53 (res. 10/23)], the Council established for a three-year period a new special procedure entitled "independent expert in the field of cultural rights".

The expert was requested to report to the Council in March 2010.

On 2 October, the Council appointed Farida Shaheed (Pakistan) as independent expert.

Report of Secretary-General. Pursuant to General Assembly resolution 62/155 [YUN 2007, p. 721], the Secretary-General in July submitted a report [A/64/160] summarizing measures taken by 10 Governments to promote cultural diversity and tolerance.

GENERAL ASSEMBLY ACTION

On 18 December [meeting 65], the General Assembly, on the recommendation of the Third Committee [A/64/439/Add.2 (Part II)], adopted **resolution 64/174** by recorded vote (126-52-5) [agenda item 69 *(b)*].

Human rights and cultural diversity

The General Assembly,

Recalling the Universal Declaration of Human Rights, the International Covenant on Economic, Social and Cultural Rights and the International Covenant on Civil and Political Rights, as well as other pertinent human rights instruments,

Recalling also its resolutions 54/160 of 17 December 1999, 55/91 of 4 December 2000, 57/204 of 18 December 2002, 58/167 of 22 December 2003, 60/167 of 16 December 2005 and 62/155 of 18 December 2007, and recalling further its resolutions 54/113 of 10 December 1999, 55/23 of 13 November 2000 and 60/4 of 20 October 2005 concerning the United Nations Year of Dialogue among Civilizations,

Noting that numerous instruments within the United Nations system promote cultural diversity, as well as the conservation and development of culture, in particular the Declaration of the Principles of International Culture Cooperation proclaimed on 4 November 1966 by the General Conference of the United Nations Educational, Scientific and Cultural Organization at its fourteenth session,

Taking note of the report of the Secretary-General,

Recalling that, as stated in the Declaration on Principles of International Law concerning Friendly Relations and Cooperation among States in accordance with the Charter of the United Nations, contained in the annex to its resolution 2625(XXV) of 24 October 1970, States have the duty to cooperate with one another, irrespective of the differences in their political, economic and social systems, in the various spheres of international relations, in the promotion of universal respect for and observance of human rights and fundamental freedoms for all, and in the elimination of all forms of racial discrimination and all forms of religious intolerance,

Welcoming the adoption of the Global Agenda for Dialogue among Civilizations by its resolution 56/6 of 9 November 2001,

Welcoming also the contribution of the World Conference against Racism, Racial Discrimination, Xenophobia and Related Intolerance, held in Durban, South Africa, from 31 August to 8 September 2001, to the promotion of respect for cultural diversity,

Welcoming further the Universal Declaration on Cultural Diversity of the United Nations Educational, Scientific and Cultural Organization, together with its Action Plan, adopted on 2 November 2001 by the General Conference of the United Nations Educational, Scientific and Cultural Organization at its thirty-first session, in which member States invited the United Nations system and other inter-governmental and non-governmental organizations concerned to cooperate with the United Nations Educational, Scientific and Cultural Organization in the promotion of the principles set forth in the Declaration and its Action Plan with a view to enhancing the synergy of actions in favour of cultural diversity,

Taking note of the Ministerial Meeting on Human Rights and Cultural Diversity of the Movement of Non-Aligned Countries, held in Tehran on 3 and 4 September 2007,

Reaffirming that all human rights are universal, indivisible, interdependent and interrelated and that the international community must treat human rights globally in a fair and equal manner, on the same footing and with the same emphasis, and that, while the significance of national and regional particularities and various historical, cultural and religious backgrounds must be borne in mind, it is the duty of States, regardless of their political, economic and cultural systems, to promote and protect all human rights and fundamental freedoms,

Recognizing that cultural diversity and the pursuit of cultural development by all peoples and nations are a source of mutual enrichment for the cultural life of humankind,

Taking into account that a culture of peace actively fosters non-violence and respect for human rights and strengthens solidarity among peoples and nations and dialogue between cultures,

Recognizing that all cultures and civilizations share a common set of universal values,

Recognizing also that the promotion of the rights of indigenous people and their cultures and traditions will contribute to the respect for and observance of cultural diversity among all peoples and nations,

Considering that tolerance of cultural, ethnic, religious and linguistic diversities, as well as dialogue among and within civilizations, is essential for peace, understanding and friendship among individuals and people of different cultures and nations of the world, while manifestations of cultural prejudice, intolerance and xenophobia towards different cultures and religions generate hatred and violence among peoples and nations throughout the world,

Recognizing in each culture a dignity and value that deserve recognition, respect and preservation, and convinced that, in their rich variety and diversity, and in the reciprocal influences that they exert on one another, all cultures form part of the common heritage belonging to all humankind,

Convinced that the promotion of cultural pluralism and tolerance towards and dialogue among various cultures and civilizations would contribute to the efforts of all peoples and nations to enrich their cultures and traditions by engaging in a mutually beneficial exchange of knowledge and intellectual, moral and material achievements,

Acknowledging the diversity of the world, recognizing that all cultures and civilizations contribute to the enrichment of humankind, acknowledging the importance of respect and understanding for religious and cultural diversity

throughout the world, and, in order to promote international peace and security, committing itself to advancing human welfare, freedom and progress everywhere, as well as to encouraging tolerance, respect, dialogue and cooperation among different cultures, civilizations and peoples,

1. *Affirms* the importance for all peoples and nations to hold, develop and preserve their cultural heritage and traditions in a national and international atmosphere of peace, tolerance and mutual respect;

2. *Welcomes* the adoption on 8 September 2000 of the United Nations Millennium Declaration, in which Member States consider, inter alia, that tolerance is one of the fundamental values essential to international relations in the twenty-first century and that it should include the active promotion of a culture of peace and dialogue among civilizations, with human beings respecting one another in all their diversity of belief, culture and language, neither fearing nor repressing differences within and between societies but cherishing them as a precious asset of humanity;

3. *Recognizes* the right of everyone to take part in cultural life and to enjoy the benefits of scientific progress and its applications;

4. *Affirms* that the international community should strive to respond to the challenges and opportunities posed by globalization in a manner that ensures respect for the cultural diversity of all;

5. *Expresses its determination* to prevent and mitigate cultural homogenization in the context of globalization, through increased intercultural exchange guided by the promotion and protection of cultural diversity;

6. *Affirms* that intercultural dialogue essentially enriches the common understanding of human rights and that the benefits to be derived from the encouragement and development of international contacts and cooperation in the cultural fields are important;

7. *Welcomes* the recognition at the World Conference against Racism, Racial Discrimination, Xenophobia and Related Intolerance of the necessity of respecting and maximizing the benefits of diversity within and among all nations in working together to build a harmonious and productive future by putting into practice and promoting values and principles such as justice, equality and non-discrimination, democracy, fairness and friendship, tolerance and respect within and among communities and nations, in particular through public information and educational programmes to raise awareness and understanding of the benefits of cultural diversity, including programmes in which the public authorities work in partnership with international and non-governmental organizations and other sectors of civil society;

8. *Recognizes* that respect for cultural diversity and the cultural rights of all enhances cultural pluralism, contributing to a wider exchange of knowledge and understanding of cultural background, advancing the application and enjoyment of universally accepted human rights throughout the world and fostering stable, friendly relations among peoples and nations worldwide;

9. *Emphasizes* that the promotion of cultural pluralism and tolerance at the national, regional and international levels is important for enhancing respect for cultural rights and cultural diversity;

10. *Also emphasizes* that tolerance and respect for diversity facilitate the universal promotion and protection of human rights, including gender equality and the enjoyment of all human rights by all, and underlines the fact that tolerance and respect for cultural diversity and the universal promotion and protection of human rights are mutually supportive;

11. *Urges* all actors on the international scene to build an international order based on inclusion, justice, equality and equity, human dignity, mutual understanding and promotion of and respect for cultural diversity and universal human rights, and to reject all doctrines of exclusion based on racism, racial discrimination, xenophobia and related intolerance;

12. *Urges* States to ensure that their political and legal systems reflect the multicultural diversity within their societies and, where necessary, to improve democratic institutions so that they are more fully participatory and avoid marginalization and exclusion of, and discrimination against, specific sectors of society;

13. *Calls upon* States, international organizations and United Nations agencies and invites civil society, including non-governmental organizations, to recognize and promote respect for cultural diversity for the purpose of advancing the objectives of peace, development and universally accepted human rights;

14. *Stresses* the necessity of freely using the media and new information and communications technologies to create the conditions for a renewed dialogue among cultures and civilizations;

15. *Requests* the Office of the United Nations High Commissioner for Human Rights to continue to bear in mind fully the issues raised in the present resolution in the course of its activities for the promotion and protection of human rights;

16. *Also requests* the Office of the High Commissioner and invites the United Nations Educational, Scientific and Cultural Organization to support initiatives aimed at promoting intercultural dialogue on human rights;

17. *Urges* relevant international organizations to conduct studies on how respect for cultural diversity contributes to fostering international solidarity and cooperation among all nations;

18. *Requests* the Secretary-General, in the light of the present resolution, to prepare a report on human rights and cultural diversity, taking into account the views of Member States, relevant United Nations agencies and non-governmental organizations, as well as the considerations in the present resolution regarding the recognition and importance of cultural diversity among all peoples and nations in the world, and to submit the report to the General Assembly at its sixty-sixth session;

19. *Decides* to continue consideration of the question at its sixty-sixth session under the sub-item entitled "Human rights questions, including alternative approaches for improving the effective enjoyment of human rights and fundamental freedoms".

RECORDED VOTE ON RESOLUTION 64/174:

In favour: Afghanistan, Algeria, Angola, Antigua and Barbuda, Argentina, Azerbaijan, Bahamas, Bahrain, Bangladesh, Barbados, Belarus, Belize, Benin, Bhutan, Bolivia, Botswana, Brazil, Brunei Darussalam, Burkina Faso, Burundi, Cambodia, Cameroon, Cape Verde, Central African Republic, Chad, Chile, China, Colombia, Comoros, Congo, Costa Rica, Côte d'Ivoire, Cuba, Democratic People's Republic of Korea, Democratic Republic of the Congo, Djibouti, Dominica, Dominican Republic, Ecuador, Egypt, El Salvador, Equatorial Guinea, Eritrea, Ethiopia, Gabon, Ghana, Grenada, Guatemala, Guinea, Guinea-Bissau, Guyana, Haiti, Honduras, India, Indonesia, Iran, Iraq, Jamaica, Jordan, Kazakhstan, Kenya, Kuwait, Kyrgyzstan, Lao People's Democratic Republic, Lebanon, Lesotho, Liberia, Libyan Arab Jamahiriya, Madagascar, Malawi, Malaysia, Mali, Mauritania, Mauritius, Mexico, Mongolia, Morocco, Mozambique, Namibia, Nepal, Nicaragua, Niger, Nigeria, Oman, Pakistan, Panama, Papua New Guinea, Paraguay, Peru, Philippines, Qatar, Russian Federation, Saint Kitts and Nevis, Saint Lucia, Saint Vincent and the Grenadines, Saudi Arabia, Senegal, Serbia, Sierra Leone, Singapore, Solomon Islands, Somalia, South Africa, Sri Lanka, Sudan, Suriname, Swaziland, Syrian Arab Republic, Tajikistan, Thailand, Togo, Trinidad and Tobago, Tunisia, Turkmenistan, Tuvalu, Uganda, United Arab Emirates, United Republic of Tanzania, Uruguay, Uzbekistan, Vanuatu, Venezuela, Viet Nam, Yemen, Zambia, Zimbabwe.

Against: Albania, Andorra, Australia, Austria, Belgium, Bosnia and Herzegovina, Bulgaria, Canada, Croatia, Cyprus, Czech Republic, Denmark, Estonia, Finland, France, Georgia, Germany, Greece, Hungary, Iceland, Ireland, Israel, Italy, Latvia, Liechtenstein, Lithuania, Luxembourg, Malta, Marshall Islands, Micronesia, Moldova, Monaco, Montenegro, Netherlands, New Zealand, Norway, Palau, Poland, Portugal, Republic of Korea, Romania, San Marino, Slovakia, Slovenia, Spain, Sweden, Switzerland, The former Yugoslav Republic of Macedonia, Turkey, Ukraine, United Kingdom, United States.

Abstaining: Armenia, Fiji, Japan, Maldives, Timor-Leste.

Right to education

Reports of Special Rapporteur. In response to a Human Rights Council request [YUN 2008, p. 842], the Special Rapporteur on the right to education, Vernor Muñoz (Costa Rica), in April submitted a report [A/HRC/11/8] devoted to the right to education of persons in detention, a group subject to discrimination generally and to discrimination in the provision of education specifically. Learning in prison through educational programmes was considered to have an impact on recidivism, reintegration and employment upon release. Education, however, was much more than a tool for change; it was an imperative in its own right. Nevertheless, prisoners faced significant educational challenges owing to environmental, social, organizational and individual factors. The Rapporteur aimed to assist Governments and interested parties to develop best practices so as to ensure the unfulfilled right to education for persons in detention. Among his recommendations to States were: education for people in detention should be guaranteed and entrenched in Constitutional and other legislative instruments; the provision of education for persons in detention should be adequately resourced from public funds; and compliance with the standards set forth in international law and guidance pertaining to education in detention should be ensured. Authorities in charge of public education should make available to all detainees education programmes covering at least the curriculum of compulsory education, and arrange comprehensive education programmes aimed at the development of the full potential of each detainee; curricula and educational practices in places of detention must be gender sensitive; and attention should be given to minority and indigenous groups, those of foreign origin and persons with physical, learning and psychosocial disabilities.

An addendum [A/HRC/11/8/Add.1] summarized 16 letters of allegations and urgent appeals transmitted to 15 Governments between 1 March 2008 and 15 March 2009, as well as replies received between 15 April 2008 and 30 April 2009.

In response to a Human Rights Council request [YUN 2008, p. 842], the Secretary-General in August transmitted to the General Assembly the interim report of the Rapporteur [A/64/273], which summarized his activities since the previous report [YUN 2008, p. 842]. The report also raised the issue of lifelong learning and human rights. Lifelong learning encompassed formal, informal and non-formal education, and the report reviewed national and international initiatives to promote that learning by Governments and the non-governmental sector. The report argued that lifelong learning needed to move closer to the context of human rights, as that was essential for progressing to a society free from prejudice, exclusion and discrimination and for realizing a global human rights culture.

The General Assembly took note of that report on 18 December **(decision 64/536)**.

Following his mission to Paraguay (14–22 April) [A/HRC/14/25/Add.2], the Rapporteur recommended that Congress progressively increase the budget allocated to education, in line with the State's domestic and international obligation to gradually invest in education to the maximum of its available resources. He recommended that the education budget grow by 0.5 per cent of gross domestic product per year until it reached at least the level of 6 per cent established by international standards. It was also necessary to build a national consensus on education. Debate should be encouraged, and education should be made a national priority. The education system needed resources to solve infrastructure problems and to ensure drinking water, school meals, culturally diverse teaching materials, teacher training and affirmative measures, making sure that the poorest members of the community could get to school, stay there and do well.

Human Rights Council action. On 17 June [A/64/53 (res. 11/6)], the Council urged all stakeholders to increase their efforts so that the goals of the Education for All initiative [YUN 2000, p. 1080] could be achieved by 2015, including by tackling persistent inequalities; stressed the need for developing cultural

and educational programmes with a view to raising awareness on human rights; and urged States to ensure the right to education of persons in detention, and to provide appropriate education to foster their reintegration into society.

Environmental and scientific concerns

Climate change

OHCHR study. Pursuant to a Human Rights Council request [YUN 2008, p. 842], OHCHR in January submitted a study [A/HRC/10/61] on the relationship between climate change and human rights. The study outlined the relationship between the environment and human rights; implications of climate change for the enjoyment of specific rights; vulnerabilities of specific groups; human rights implications of climate change-induced displacement and conflict; and human rights implications of measures to address climate change. The effects on human rights could be direct, such as the threat extreme weather events might pose to the right to life, but would often have an indirect and gradual effect, such as increasing stress on health systems and vulnerabilities related to climate change-induced migration. The application of a human rights approach in preventing and responding to climate change served to empower vulnerable individuals and groups, who should be perceived as agents of change and not as passive victims. The impacts of global warming could not easily be classified as human rights violations, not least because climate change-related harm often could not clearly be attributed to acts or omissions of specific States. Yet addressing that harm remained a critical human rights concern and obligation under international law. International human rights law complemented the United Nations Framework Convention on Climate Change by underlining that international cooperation was not only expedient but also a human rights obligation, and that its central objective was the realization of human rights.

Human Rights Council action. On 25 March [A/64/53 (res. 10/4)], the Council decided to hold a panel discussion on the relationship between climate change and human rights at its eleventh session, and requested OHCHR to prepare a summary of the panel discussion and to make it available to the Conference of the Parties to the United Nations Framework Convention on Climate Change.

At the panel discussion (Geneva, 15 June), delegates noted that climate change-related events would directly affect the enjoyment of a range of human rights and would negatively affect the capacity of States to protect those rights. Adopting a human rights perspective focused the debate on the effects on the lives of individuals and communities; directed attention to the situation of the most vulnerable and to the need to protect their rights; empowered individuals and communities and gave them a voice in decision-making; introduced an accountability framework, holding Governments accountable for reducing the vulnerability of their populations to global warming; and strengthened policymaking, drawing attention to the interactions between climate and human rights policies and promoting a more coherent and effective global response.

Forensic genetics

Human Rights Council action. On 27 March [A/64/53 (res. 10/26)], the Council encouraged States to use forensic genetics to contribute to the identification of the remains of victims of violations of human rights and international humanitarian law, and address the issue of impunity; and to contribute to the restoration of identity to persons who were separated from their families, including those taken away from their relatives when they were children, in situations of violations of human rights, and in the context of violations of international humanitarian law during armed conflicts. OHCHR was requested to solicit information on best practices in the use of forensic genetics for identifying victims of violations, and to report on the use of forensic experts to the Council's fifteenth (2010) session.

Toxic wastes

Reports of Special Rapporteur. In response to a Human Rights Council request [YUN 2008, p. 843], the Special Rapporteur on the adverse effects of the movement and dumping of toxic and dangerous products and wastes on the enjoyment of human rights, Okechukwu Ibeanu (Nigeria), submitted a report [A/HRC/12/26] focusing on shipbreaking—an important industry for developing countries, especially in South Asia. Shipbreaking represented an important source of raw material supply and provided jobs to tens of thousands of persons. The practice was inherently sustainable, given that over 95 per cent of a ship could be recycled. However, the extremely poor working practices and environmental conditions prevailing in most shipbreaking yards were a source of concern. Every year, about 600 end-of-life ships containing large amounts of toxic and hazardous substances and materials were sent to the beaches of South Asia, where they were dismantled without concrete covering or any containment other than the hull of the ship itself. That method of ship dismantling, commonly referred to as "beaching", generated high levels of pollution of coastal soil, air, sea and groundwater resources, and adversely affected local communities, which often relied on agriculture and fishing for

their subsistence. Working in shipbreaking yards was a dirty and dangerous job. Every year, many workers died or were seriously injured because of work-related accidents or occupational diseases related to long-term exposure to hazardous materials. Workers did not usually receive any information or safety training. They lived in makeshift facilities that often lacked basic minimum requirements such as sanitation, electricity and even drinking water. There was a general lack of medical facilities and social protection, and injured workers or their relatives hardly received any compensation for work-related accidents resulting in fatal injuries or permanent disabilities. Efforts by several organizations and mechanisms to develop an international regulatory framework had culminated in the Hong Kong International Convention for the Safe and Environmentally Sound Recycling of Ships, adopted on 15 May under the auspices of the International Maritime Organization (IMO). That Convention represented a positive step towards creating an enforceable regulatory regime aimed at ensuring that end-of-life ships did not pose unnecessary risks to human health or the environment. Nevertheless, the Convention alone was not sufficient to bring about significant improvements in working practices or in the elimination of pollution. The Rapporteur called on shipbreaking States, flag States, the shipbreaking industry and international organizations to adopt and implement additional measures to address negative impacts that were not covered by the Convention.

An addendum [A/HRC/12/26/Add.1] summarized communications sent by the Rapporteur between 5 December 2007 and 30 June 2009, as well as responses from Governments received between 22 January 2008 and 18 August 2009.

Following his mission to Kyrgyzstan (30 September–9 October) [A/HRC/15/22/Add.2], the Rapporteur recommended: relocation of the most dangerous uranium tailings and pesticides to more secure locations; rehabilitation of abandoned mines, uranium tailings and waste storage facilities to prevent environmental contamination and unauthorized access; comprehensive assessment of the harmful impact of radioactive and hazardous substances on the health of individuals and communities living close to tailings sites and storage facilities for hazardous chemicals; improvement of the regulatory framework on radioactive waste and chemicals management to ensure its consistency with international standards; clarification of the roles and functions of the different ministries and State agencies responsible for radioactive waste and chemicals management; and creation of mechanisms to ensure better coordination.

Human Rights Council action. On 2 October [A/65/53 (res. 12/18)], the Council condemned the movement and dumping of toxic and dangerous products and wastes, which had a negative impact on the enjoyment of human rights. It decided to hold a panel discussion on the matter at its thirteenth (2010) session, with a view to informing the future work of the Rapporteur.

Right to health

Reports of Special Rapporteur. In response to a Human Rights Council request [YUN 2007, p. 783], the Special Rapporteur on the right of everyone to the enjoyment of the highest attainable standard of physical and mental health (right to health), Anand Grover (India), in March submitted a report [A/HRC/11/12] analysing access to medicines and intellectual property rights. The Rapporteur said that the framework of the right to health made it clear that medicines must be available, accessible, acceptable and of good quality to reach ailing populations without discrimination. The Agreement on Trade-Related Aspects of Intellectual Property Rights (TRIPS) and free trade agreements had an adverse impact on prices and availability of medicines, making it difficult for countries to comply with their obligations to respect, protect and fulfil the right to health. Flexibilities had been included in TRIPS to allow States to meet their economic and development needs, but States had varied in the extent to which they had implemented the TRIPS flexibilities, with some lacking sufficient awareness, some having limited technical capacity and others not having sufficiently streamlined their patent laws to facilitate the use of those flexibilities. External pressures from developed countries had also made it difficult for developing countries to use flexibilities to promote access to medicines. Developing countries should review their laws and policies and, if necessary, amend them to make full use of the flexibilities.

An addendum [A/HRC/11/12/Add.1] summarized 37 communications sent to 23 States and to the Global Fund to Fight AIDS, Tuberculosis and Malaria between 2 December 2007 and 15 March 2009, and replies received between 1 February 2008 and 1 May 2009.

In response to a Human Rights Council request [YUN 2007, p. 783], the Secretary-General in August transmitted to the General Assembly the report of the Rapporteur [A/64/272], which discussed the role of informed consent in realizing the right to health and the duties and obligations of States and health-care providers in guaranteeing informed consent in clinical practice, public health and medical research. Guaranteeing informed consent involved practices, policies and research that were respectful of autonomy, self-determination and human dignity. That required States to ensure that information was available, acceptable, accessible and of good quality, and imparted

through measures such as counselling and involvement of community networks. Informed consent should be a critical element of a voluntary counselling, testing and treatment continuum in the development of guidance for clinical practice, public health evidence and medical research protocols, with special attention to the needs of vulnerable groups.

The General Assembly took note of that report on 18 December (**decision 64/536**).

Following his mission to Poland (5–11 May) [A/HRC/14/20/Add.3], the Rapporteur noted that the 1993 Act on Family Planning had restricted access to legal terminations of pregnancies by revoking the ground for abortion for economic and social reasons, resulting in an increase in unsafe, clandestine abortions. The Law on Counteracting Drug Addiction penalized possession of very small amounts of drugs, making it difficult for people to receive necessary substitution treatment. There had been a gap in funding and work on HIV prevention, which in turn affected the availability of prevention services, including harm reduction measures. The Rapporteur recommended that Poland: adopt a comprehensive strategy for the promotion of rights to sexual and reproductive health; promote dialogue on rights to sexual and reproductive health in public health policies; amend the Law on Counteracting Drug Addiction to avoid penalization of the possession of minute quantities of drugs, in order to foster access to substitution therapy for people using drugs; and include the participation of people living with HIV and those groups most at risk of contracting HIV in HIV/AIDS-related educational projects and campaigns.

Following his mission to Australia (23 November–4 December) [A/HRC/14/20/Add.4], the Rapporteur expressed concern about health service delivery to Aboriginal people and to those in detention. He recommended that the Government develop a national health policy that included a detailed plan for the full realization of the right to health; implement legislative or other guarantees to ensure that the opinions of national representative indigenous bodies, such as the National Congress of Australia's First Peoples, were taken into account; and improve health information exchange within the prison system and between prisons and health providers.

Human Rights Council action. On 17 June [A/64/53 (res. 11/8)], the Council expressed concern at the unacceptably high global rate of preventable maternal mortality and morbidity, noting that the World Health Organization had assessed that over 1,500 women and girls died every day as a result of preventable complications occurring before, during and after pregnancy and childbirth, and that, globally, maternal mortality was the leading cause of death among women and girls of reproductive age. It requested States to renew their political commitment to eliminating preventable maternal mortality and morbidity and to redouble their efforts to ensure the full and effective implementation of their human rights obligations, including through the allocation of necessary resources to health systems. The Council requested OHCHR to prepare a study on preventable maternal mortality and morbidity and human rights, to be addressed at the Council's fourteenth (2010) session.

On 2 October [A/65/53 (res. 12/24)], the Council stressed the responsibility of States to ensure access to all, without discrimination, of medicines, in particular essential medicines, that were affordable, safe, effective and of good quality. The Council invited OHCHR to convene an expert consultation on human rights considerations relating to the realization of access to medicines, and invited the Rapporteur to present a summary of the consultation to the Council.

Human rights and HIV/AIDS

Report of Secretary-General. Further to a Human Rights Council request [YUN 2006, p. 760], the Secretary-General in February submitted a progress report [A/HRC/10/47] summarizing replies received from 21 Governments, 9 international organizations and 8 NGOs on action taken for the protection of human rights in the context of human immunodeficiency virus (HIV) and acquired immunodeficiency syndrome (AIDS). The report concluded that, while some progress had been made in the global response to the epidemic, human rights challenges remained, which posed barriers to achieving universal access to HIV prevention, treatment, care and support.

Human Rights Council action. On 2 October [A/65/53 (res. 12/27)], the Council called on States, UN bodies, international organizations and NGOs to ensure the respect, protection and fulfilment of human rights in the context of HIV/AIDS. The Council requested the Secretary-General to prepare an analytical study on the steps taken to promote and implement programmes to address HIV/AIDS-related human rights, and to report to the Council's sixteenth (2011) session.

Water and sanitation

Reports of independent expert. In response to a Human Rights Council request [YUN 2008, p. 844], the independent expert on the issue of human rights obligations related to access to safe drinking water and sanitation, Catarina de Albuquerque (Portugal), in February submitted her first report to the Council [A/HRC/10/6]. She explained that she would take a thematic approach to her mandate, focusing on different themes each year, with the first year concentrated on sanitation.

In her first annual report [A/HRC/12/24], submitted in July, the expert focused on the human rights obligations related to sanitation. After reviewing the inextricable links between sanitation and a range of human rights, the expert concluded that an analysis of sanitation in a human rights context must go beyond linking it to other human rights, because that would fail to capture all of the dimensions of sanitation. Although a discussion was ongoing on whether sanitation should be recognized as a distinct right, recent developments demonstrated a trend towards recognition, specifically, considering the right to sanitation as a component of the right to an adequate standard of living. While opinions might differ on whether to recognize sanitation as a distinct right, there were clear human rights obligations related to sanitation because it was inextricably linked to, and indispensable for, the realization of many other rights. The expert recommended that States support legal and political developments towards broader recognition of sanitation as a distinct human right; abide by their human rights obligations related to sanitation; adopt a national action plan on sanitation; and adopt policies to expand access to unserved and underserved areas.

Following her mission to Costa Rica (19–27 March) [A/HRC/12/24/Add.1 & Corr.1], the expert recommended that the country move expeditiously towards the adoption of a new water law, which should rationalize the legal framework for the management and use of water resources and adapt it to the economic and social situation. Costa Rica should review its normative framework on sanitation, with a view to establishing a coherent and comprehensive system for the collection, management, treatment and disposal of human excreta and wastewater. Costa Rica should develop and implement appropriate policies to ensure the sustainable development of tourist and real estate activities, avoiding the depletion of water sources used by local communities.

Following her mission to Egypt (21–28 June) [A/HRC/15/31/Add.3], the expert said that the Government must place priority attention on the areas where people were unserved or underserved, particularly in rural areas and in informal settlements. She encouraged the Government to embrace and foster a human rights culture, including greater transparency, access to information and participation. The Government should adopt the draft water act, which should: recognize water and sanitation as human rights; provide for clear responsibilities of different agencies for testing water quality, controlling pollution and ensuring the safety of sanitation facilities; and include measures for ensuring affordable access to water and sanitation for the poorest people.

The independent expert, in December, undertook a joint mission to Bangladesh with the independent expert on the question of human rights and extreme poverty [A/HRC/15/55 & Corr.1] (see p. 717).

Communication. On 10 August [A/HRC/12/G/3], Costa Rica transmitted its response to the report of the independent expert.

Human Rights Council action. On 1 October [A/65/53 (res. 12/8)], the Council called on States to create an enabling environment to address the issue of lack of sanitation, including by budgeting; legislation; the establishment of regulatory, monitoring and accountability frameworks and mechanisms; the assignment of clear institutional responsibilities; and the inclusion of sanitation in national poverty reduction strategies and development plans. The Council requested the expert to submit annual reports to the Council and to the General Assembly.

Slavery and related issues

Reports of Special Rapporteur. Pursuant to a Human Rights Council request [YUN 2007, p. 784], the Special Rapporteur on contemporary forms of slavery, including its causes and consequences, Gulnara Shahinian (Armenia), in July submitted a report [A/HRC/12/21] exploring the issue of forced labour, which, as a form of slavery, was a global issue. Neither its traditional form nor its subtle and new forms had been sufficiently addressed, irrespective of the fact that many countries had ratified the slavery conventions and the relevant conventions of the International Labour Organization. Where laws on forced labour existed, their enforcement was limited, and there were few policies and programmes that addressed bonded labour (debt bondage). Comprehensive action to eliminate the phenomenon required strong political will and the coordinated actions of Governments to enforce international law. The Rapporteur recommended that Governments, NGOs, UN agencies and private actors take prevention, prosecution and protection measures to combat forced and bonded labour.

During her mission to Haiti (1–10 June) [A/HRC/12/21/Add.1], the Rapporteur discussed with Government representatives, civil society organizations, and UN and other international organizations the situation of *restavèk* children—children who were given by their families to more affluent families in the hope that they would be provided with food, clothing, shelter, schooling and health care in return for domestic labour. Their estimated number was between 150,000 and 500,000. The Rapporteur was concerned that *restavèk* children were economically exploited, as they were not being compensated for their work and were performing tasks interfering with their education and harmful to their health and development. Many were malnourished and given food only at school, with little or no access to health care. Some were subjected

to violence, injury, abuse, neglect, maltreatment or exploitation, including sexual abuse. The Rapporteur urged the Government to establish a national commission on children to ensure protection of their rights. The Government should develop prevention programmes to eliminate the practice; bring legislation into conformity with international legal instruments ratified by Haiti; and adopt measures to address shortcomings in the administration of justice.

Following her mission to Mauritania (24 October–4 November) [A/HRC/15/20/Add.2], the Rapporteur recommended that the 2007 Slavery Act be amended to contain a clearer definition of slavery to aid judicial enforcement, and provide for victim assistance and encourage socio-economic programmes to aid victims' reintegration into society. The Government should develop a comprehensive national strategy to combat slavery. To be effective, the amended law should be supported by programmes providing access to basic education, vocational training, microcredit and equal access to employment opportunities.

Fund on slavery

Report of Secretary-General. The Secretary-General reported [A/65/94] on the financial status of the United Nations Voluntary Trust Fund on Contemporary Forms of Slavery. At its fourteenth session (Geneva, 14–18 September), the Fund's Board of Trustees recommended 63 new project grants amounting to $726,090 to assist 63 NGO projects in 44 countries in Africa, the Americas, Asia and Europe. Thirteen countries and two individuals had contributed $936,536 since the Board's thirteenth session [YUN 2008, p. 846]. The Board estimated that the Fund would need an additional $4 million before its fifteenth session, scheduled for December 2010. The High Commissioner, on behalf of the Secretary-General, approved the Board's recommendations.

Transatlantic slave trade and slavery

Report of Secretary-General. The Secretary-General in August reported [A/64/299] on the programme of educational outreach on the transatlantic slave trade and slavery, as requested by General Assembly resolution 63/5 [YUN 2008, p. 845]. The Department of Public Information (DPI) carried out activities aimed at educating people about the causes, consequences, lessons and legacy of the 400-year transatlantic slave trade and communicating the dangers of racism and prejudice. For the observance of the International Day of Remembrance of the Victims of Slavery and the Transatlantic Slave Trade on 25 March, DPI organized a cultural evening and concert in the General Assembly Hall. Other events at UN Headquarters included an exhibit, a student videoconference, the screening of documentary films, a briefing for NGOs and a "meet the author" book programme. The outreach strategy included follow-up activities throughout the year, targeting and responding to communities and civil society organizations.

GENERAL ASSEMBLY ACTION

On 16 November [meeting 47], the General Assembly adopted **resolution 64/15** [draft: A/64/L.10 & Add.1, as orally revised] without vote [agenda item 116].

Permanent memorial to and remembrance of the victims of slavery and the transatlantic slave trade

The General Assembly,

Recalling its resolution 61/19 of 28 November 2006, entitled "Commemoration of the two-hundredth anniversary of the abolition of the transatlantic slave trade" and resolutions 62/122 of 17 December 2007 and 63/5 of 20 October 2008, entitled "Permanent memorial to and remembrance of the victims of slavery and the transatlantic slave trade",

Recalling also its resolution 63/100 B of 5 December 2008, entitled "United Nations public information policies and activities",

Recalling further the designation of 25 March as the annual International Day of Remembrance of the Victims of Slavery and the Transatlantic Slave Trade, beginning in 2008, as a complement to the existing International Day for the Remembrance of the Slave Trade and its Abolition of the United Nations Educational, Scientific and Cultural Organization,

Noting the initiatives undertaken by States in reaffirming their commitment to implement paragraphs 101 and 102 of the Durban Declaration of the World Conference against Racism, Racial Discrimination, Xenophobia and Related Intolerance, aimed at countering the legacy of slavery and contributing to the restoration of the dignity of the victims of slavery and the slave trade,

Recalling, in particular, paragraph 101 of the Durban Declaration, which, inter alia, invited the international community and its members to honour the memory of the victims,

Stressing the importance of educating and informing current and future generations about the causes, consequences and lessons of slavery and the transatlantic slave trade,

Recognizing how little is known about the four-hundred-year-long transatlantic slave trade and its lasting consequences, felt throughout the world, and welcoming the increased attention that the General Assembly commemoration brought to the issue, including the raising of its profile in many States,

Recalling that the permanent memorial initiative within the General Assembly complements the work being done at the United Nations Educational, Scientific and Cultural Organization on the Slave Route Project, including its commemorative activities,

1. *Welcomes* the initiative of the States members of the Caribbean Community to erect, at a place of prominence at United Nations Headquarters that is easily accessible to delegates, United Nations staff and visitors, a permanent memorial in acknowledgement of the tragedy and in consideration of the legacy of slavery and the transatlantic slave trade;

2. *Also welcomes* the establishment of a committee of interested States to oversee the permanent memorial project, drawn from all geographical regions of the world, with Member States from the Caribbean Community and the African Union playing a primary role, in collaboration with the United Nations Educational, Scientific and Cultural Organization, representatives of the Secretariat, the Schomburg Center for Research in Black Culture of the New York Public Library and civil society;

3. *Endorses* the establishment of a trust fund for the permanent memorial, to be referred to as the United Nations Trust Fund for Partnerships–Permanent Memorial, which will be administered by the United Nations Office for Partnerships, and notes the status of voluntary contributions currently held in the Trust Fund, which currently amount to 346,118 United States dollars;

4. *Welcomes* the appointment of a Goodwill Ambassador to assist with re-engaging international attention on the horrific nature of slavery, the transatlantic slave trade and their legacy of discrimination, while promoting and supporting the media outreach and resource mobilization efforts of the initiative;

5. *Recognizes* the importance and necessity of sustained voluntary contributions in order to achieve in a timely manner the goal of erecting a permanent memorial in honour of the victims of slavery and the transatlantic slave trade;

6. *Expresses sincere appreciation* to those Member States that have already made contributions to the Trust Fund, and invites Member States and other interested parties that have not done so to do likewise;

7. *Expresses its appreciation* to the Secretary-General, the Secretariat and, in particular, the United Nations Office for Partnerships and members of the committee for their invaluable support, technical advice and assistance towards implementation of the project;

8. *Reiterates its request* contained in resolutions 61/19 and 63/5 for Member States that have not already done so to develop educational programmes, including through school curricula, designed to educate and inculcate in future generations an understanding of the lessons, history and consequences of slavery and the slave trade;

9. *Encourages* the United Nations Educational, Scientific and Cultural Organization to launch an international design competition for the permanent memorial, which is to be funded from the Trust Fund, in view of the considerable experience of that Organization with the Slave Route Project, international competitions and its worldwide presence through its network of field offices and National Commissions;

10. *Invites* the United Nations Educational, Scientific and Cultural Organization to assist the committee in defining guidelines for the selection process and in identifying qualified candidates from its pool of international specialists to serve on the international jury;

11. *Requests* the Department of Public Information, in cooperation with the countries concerned and with relevant organizations and bodies of the United Nations system, to continue to take appropriate steps to enhance world public awareness of the commemorative activities and the permanent memorial initiative, and to continue to facilitate efforts to erect the permanent memorial at United Nations Headquarters, within existing resources;

12. *Takes note* of the report of the Secretary-General on the programme of educational outreach on the transatlantic slave trade and slavery, which highlights developments relating to the diverse educational outreach strategy to increase awareness of and to educate future generations about the causes, consequences, lessons and legacy of the four-hundred-year-long slave trade and to communicate the dangers of racism and prejudice, and encourages continued action in this regard;

13. *Requests* the Secretary-General to report to the General Assembly at its sixty-fifth session on continued action to implement the programme of educational outreach, including action by Member States, as well as steps to enhance world public awareness of the commemorative activities and the permanent memorial initiative;

14. *Requests* the United Nations Office for Partnerships, through the Secretary-General, to submit a comprehensive report to the General Assembly at its sixty-fifth session on the status of the Trust Fund, and in particular on contributions received and their utilization;

15. *Decides* to include in the provisional agenda of its sixty-fifth session the item entitled "Follow-up to the commemoration of the two-hundredth anniversary of the abolition of the transatlantic slave trade".

Vulnerable groups

Women

Human Rights Council action. On 2 October [A/65/53 (res. 12/17)], the Council reaffirmed the obligation of States to take all appropriate measures to eliminate discrimination against women by any person, organization or enterprise; called on States to fulfil their international obligations and commitments to revoke any remaining laws discriminating on the basis of sex and to remove gender bias in the administration of justice; requested the High Commissioner to prepare a study on discrimination against women in law and practice, and on how the issue was addressed throughout the UN human rights system; and decided to address the study at its fifteenth (2010) session.

Violence against women

Reports of Special Rapporteur. Pursuant to a Human Rights Council request [YUN 2008, p. 848], the Special Rapporteur on violence against women, its causes and consequences, Yakin Ertürk (Turkey), in May submitted a report [A/HRC/11/6] highlighting her activities in 2008 and early 2009 and addressing the political economy of women's human

rights. The political economic order—too often neglected in the analyses of women's rights—profoundly affected both the prevalence of violence against women and efforts to eliminate it. Women's security and freedom from violence were inextricably linked to the material basis of relationships governing the distribution and use of resources and entitlements, as well as authority within the home, the community and the nation. Cultural rationales for limiting women's rights were grounded in economic interests and power dynamics. Preventing violence against women and ensuring gender equality required a holistic approach to women's rights beyond the dichotomized treatment of rights into civil and political on the one hand, and economic and social on the other. Unless women's agency was recognized and their capabilities supported through social, economic and political empowerment, the rights they were promised would remain abstract concepts. Economic and social rights were directly linked to women's socio-economic security and their capacity to assert their will and resist violence. Nowhere in the world did women share equal social and economic rights or equal access to productive resources. The neoliberal policy environment and the proliferation of armed conflicts had set back women's access to productive resources and increased their exposure to violence. Conflicts and humanitarian crises often built upon gender, class and ethnic inequalities—deepening some and creating new ones, thus reconfiguring entitlement structures and rarely benefiting women. Yet, although globalization, conflicts and the economic recession held new risks for women and their rights, they also offered new opportunities for taming globalization and patriarchy. The unprecedented entry of women into paid employment had created new contradictions with the potential to rupture the inequality structures that perpetuated women's subordination. The Rapporteur called for gender-aware, competent governance and joint international responsibility for integrating initiatives to end violence against women in the context of the struggle for social and economic equality within the human rights movement.

Political economy and violence against women was the subject of an addendum [A/HRC/11/6/Add.6] that identified how lack of access to economic and social rights, such as the right to land, housing and food, was directly linked to the increased risk of violence against women. Economic and social security was crucial for protecting and preventing such violence. Current approaches to responding to violence against women should be broadened to take account of causes and consequences of violence evident in women's poverty and labour exploitation, their socio-economic inequality with men and their exclusion from political decision-making. To attend to prevention as well as protection and prosecution of violence against women, the Rapporteur called for integrating assessments of violence against women into public policies and for including initiatives to end such violence within the larger struggle for social and economic equality of the human rights movement.

Another addendum [A/HRC/11/6/Add.1] summarized 93 communications—51 allegation letters and 42 urgent appeals—sent to 34 Member States from 5 December 2007 to 2 April 2009; 37 of them, or 40 per cent, were sent to five States alone: India, Iran, Mexico, Pakistan and the Sudan; 80 were sent jointly with other Human Rights Council mandate holders. The Rapporteur remained concerned that only 19 Governments had replied.

A further addendum [A/HRC/11/6/Add.5] provided a critical review of the 15 years of the Special Rapporteur's mandate (1994–2009), and concluded that the role of the mandate was invaluable as the forum that could make visible hidden violations, lent support to the voices of the most vulnerable women and acted as a channel to access justice and accountability where national systems of justice failed to respond.

Appointment of new Rapporteur. On 18 June, the Human Rights Council appointed Rashida Manjoo (South Africa) as Special Rapporteur.

Following her mission to Kyrgyzstan (9–16 November) [A/HRC/14/22/Add.2], the new Rapporteur recommended that the Government establish an independent body responsible for women's rights and gender equality; treat violence against women as a criminal offence and investigate and prosecute cases within the formal justice system; develop mechanisms to combat internal trafficking and sexual exploitation of women and girls; support awareness-raising campaigns on domestic violence and women's rights; and amend legislation to set a uniform minimum legal age for marriage at 18 for both women and men, in line with international standards.

Human Rights Council action. On 17 June [A/64/53 (res. 11/2)], the Council called on States to enact, reinforce or amend domestic legislation to investigate, prosecute, punish and redress the wrongs done to women and girls subjected to any form of violence; called on States to support initiatives undertaken by women's organizations and NGOs to eliminate violence against women and girls; and requested OHCHR to convene in 2010 an expert workshop to discuss measures for overcoming obstacles and challenges that States might face in preventing, investigating, prosecuting and punishing the perpetrators of violence against women and girls, as well as measures for providing protection, assistance and redress for victims. The Office was requested to submit a summary report of the workshop to the Council.

Integrating women's rights in the UN system

OHCHR report. Pursuant to a Human Rights Council request [YUN 2007, p. 787], OHCHR in August submitted a report [A/HRC/12/46] on integrating the human rights of women throughout the UN system that identified obstacles and challenges in that regard. The report recommended increasing cooperation among UN agencies, making women's rights a main element of the Universal Periodic Review and integrating a gender perspective into the work of the special procedures and the Human Rights Council Advisory Committee.

Trafficking in women and girls

Reports of Special Rapporteur. In response to a Human Rights Council request [YUN 2008, p. 848], the Special Rapporteur on trafficking in persons, especially women and children, Joy Ngozi Ezeilo (Nigeria), submitted a report [A/HRC/10/16 & Corr.1] providing a global perspective of the trafficking phenomenon and its trends, forms and manifestations, including the challenges relating to the lack of coherent and reliable statistical information capturing different dimensions of trafficking in human beings. The Rapporteur outlined her vision and agenda for the mandate and the working methods she intended to use. She recommended that States establish dedicated national anti-trafficking machinery; work towards a global plan of action to combat trafficking; put in place harmonized data collection mechanisms to improve data collection and reporting; and improve cooperation through bilateral and multilateral agreements for joint actions against human trafficking among countries of origin, transit and destination.

Pursuant to a Council request [YUN 2008, p. 848], the Secretary-General in August transmitted to the General Assembly the report of the Rapporteur [A/64/290], which summarized her activities and focused on the identification and protection of and assistance to victims of trafficking. The report presented cases of trafficked victims, examined the responsibilities of States and non-State actors, outlined a child-centred approach to children who were victims of trafficking and examined issues of protection of and assistance to refugees, asylum-seekers, returnees and stateless and internally displaced persons. The Rapporteur recommended developing operational guidelines, procedures and tools for identifying victims of trafficking, based on models developed by UN agencies and programmes.

Following her mission to Belarus (18–24 May) [A/HRC/14/32/Add.2], the Rapporteur recommended adopting and implementing a law on domestic violence; establishing a national special rapporteur on trafficking in persons, under the aegis of the Presidential Administration, to enhance coordination of counter-trafficking activities; and address the root causes of trafficking, including gender inequality and demand for exploitative labour.

In Poland (24–29 May) [A/HRC/14/32/Add.3], the Rapporteur observed that joining the European Union and acceding to the Schengen area had contributed to transforming Poland, once primarily a source country, into a transit and destination country as well. She recommended adopting a definition of trafficking in relevant legislation; including in the Criminal Code a specific provision for child victims of trafficking; increasing prevention efforts, including awareness-raising for the general public; strengthening training of law enforcement authorities and NGOs on identification of victims; expanding Government programmes of assistance to victims; and developing a comprehensive data collection system.

Following her mission to Japan (12–17 July) [A/HRC/14/32/Add.4], a destination country for many victims of human trafficking, the Rapporteur urged the country to adopt a clearer definition of trafficking and spell out clear criteria and guidelines for the identification of victims. A comprehensive legal and policy framework on the protection of victims should be adopted, and better assistance, including possibilities for rehabilitation, recovering, reintegration and redress, should be provided to victims. Training of law enforcement officials on the identification of victims should be urgently pursued. A permanent coordination agency should be established, solely dedicated to promoting, coordinating and monitoring policies and actions related to the fight against human trafficking, in cooperation with international organizations, civil society and other stakeholders.

OHCHR report. In response to a Human Rights Council request [YUN 2008, p. 848], OHCHR in February reported [A/HRC/10/64] on policy developments and activities within the UN system to combat trafficking in persons, including the activities of UN entities, OHCHR and the UN human rights mechanisms.

Human Rights Council action. On 17 June [A/64/53 (res. 11/3)], the Council urged Governments to take measures to address the root factors that encouraged trafficking in persons for prostitution and other forms of commercialized sex, forced marriages and forced labour, slavery or practices similar to slavery, servitude or the removal of organs; to criminalize trafficking in persons in all its forms and to condemn and penalize traffickers, facilitators and intermediaries; and to ensure protection and assistance to the victims. The Council requested OHCHR to organize a two-day seminar aimed at identifying opportunities and challenges in the development of rights-based responses to trafficking in persons, and to submit a report on the seminar to the Council.

Children

Guidelines for alternative care

Human Rights Council action. On 26 March [A/64/53 (res. 10/8)], the Council welcomed the progress made during consultations on the draft United Nations guidelines for the appropriate use and conditions of alternative care for children [YUN 2008, p. 738] and decided to continue efforts to take action on them at its eleventh session.

At that session [res. 11/7], the Council on 17 June considered that the Guidelines for the Alternative Care of Children, the text of which was annexed to the resolution, set out desirable orientations for policy and practice that would enhance the implementation of the Convention on the Rights of the Child and other international instruments regarding the protection and well-being of children deprived of parental care. Welcoming the accomplishment of the Guidelines, the Council submitted them to the General Assembly for consideration, with a view to their adoption in 2009, the twentieth anniversary of the Convention.

The General Assembly welcomed the Guidelines by **resolution 64/142** of 18 December (see p. 1161).

Violence against children

Appointment of Special Representative. Pursuant to General Assembly resolution 62/141 [YUN 2007, p. 681], in which the Assembly requested the Secretary-General to appoint a Special Representative on violence against children, the Secretary-General announced [A/64/182-E/2009/110] on 1 May the appointment of Marta Santos Pais (Portugal) as his Special Representative for a three-year period. She would act as a high-profile and independent global advocate to promote the prevention and elimination of all forms of violence against children in all regions, and would chair the Inter-Agency Working Group on Violence against Children. Her Office would be provided with administrative support by the United Nations Children's Fund (UNICEF). Her position, as well as the Office to support her, would be funded from voluntary contributions.

The General Assembly took note of the appointment on 18 December (**decision 64/532**).

Sale of children, child prostitution and child pornography

Reports of Special Rapporteur. In response to a Human Rights Council request [YUN 2008, p. 849], the Special Rapporteur on the sale of children, child prostitution and child pornography, Najat M'jid Maalla (Morocco), in July submitted a report [A/HRC/12/23] on child pornography on the Internet, which constituted a worldwide problem: the development of new technologies which greatly increased ways of accessing, disseminating and selling that criminal material had contributed to the growth of the phenomenon. Despite many and varied initiatives to combat it, there was more and more child pornography on the Internet, constituting a profitable business with a global market value estimated at billions of dollars. Given the seriousness of the crime, relevant legislation should be clear and comprehensive and treat child pornography on the Internet as a grave violation of the rights of the child and as a criminal act. All forms of child pornography should be criminalized and penalized. The victim's privacy must be protected and protection measures and care adapted to the needs and characteristics of children must be available. Actions should be specific and targeted and comprise specialized resources for the identification of victims, protection for child victims and child Internet users, a committed and responsible private sector, and coordinated and structured international cooperation. The Rapporteur recommended that States that had not done so ratify the Optional Protocol to the Convention on the Rights of the Child on the sale of children, child prostitution and child pornography.

An addendum [A/HRC/12/23/Add.3] summarized six general and individual allegations and urgent appeals sent to six Governments between 1 December 2007 and 15 April 2009, as well as two replies received by 15 June 2009.

Following her mission to the United Arab Emirates (12–18 October) [A/HRC/16/57/Add.2], the Rapporteur recommended that the Government: define and criminalize the sale of children; ensure that children under 18 years of age who were sexually exploited were not treated as criminals but as victims; include in the Federal Law on Combating Human Trafficking Crimes provisions regarding trafficking in children and protection of victims (care, rehabilitation, reintegration, repatriation); strengthen training given to relevant authorities on combating sexual exploitation of children online; pursue partnerships with tourism agencies, Internet service providers, telecommunication companies and banks in efforts to combat child sex tourism and the exploitation of children online; and guarantee birth registration of all children born in the country as well as access to social services and health care to all children, whether citizen or not.

Following her mission to Senegal (21–30 October) [A/HRC/16/57/Add.3], the Rapporteur recommended that the Government: conclude the drafting of a national strategy for the protection of children's rights; use the Criminal Code reform as an opportunity to incorporate a clear definition of "sale of children" and specify the penalties for offenders; equip the police

and the judiciary with sufficient material and human resources and secure reception centres for children; provide officers and officials with training in child counselling and interviewing techniques, as well as in cybercrime; and ensure strict compliance with adoption controls and procedures.

Children and armed conflict

Report of Secretary-General. The Secretary-General in March submitted a report on children and armed conflict [A/63/785-S/2009/158 & Corr.1], covering the period from September 2007 to December 2008. The report reviewed compliance and progress in ending six grave violations against children caught up in armed conflict: the recruitment and use of children; killing and maiming of children; rape and other grave sexual violence; abductions; attacks on schools and hospitals; and denial of humanitarian access to children.

Submitted pursuant to presidential statement S/PRST/2008/6 [YUN 2008, p. 850], the report reviewed progress made in the implementation of monitoring and reporting mechanisms and action plans to halt the recruitment and use of children. It assessed progress made in mainstreaming children and armed conflict issues in UN peacekeeping and political missions and summarized the progress and conclusions of the Security Council Working Group on Children and Armed Conflict. Annexes to the report listed 56 parties, both State and non-State, which recruited or used children in situations of armed conflict in Afghanistan, Burundi, the Central African Republic, Chad, Colombia, the Democratic Republic of the Congo, Iraq, Myanmar, Nepal, the Philippines, Somalia, Sri Lanka, southern Sudan, Darfur and Uganda.

The Secretary-General underlined the particular vulnerability of children to rape and sexual violence in armed conflict situations, as well as the culture of impunity that prevailed for such crimes, and recommended strengthening mechanisms and arrangements for monitoring and reporting violations. He encouraged the Security Council to insist that parties listed in the report's annexes prepare and implement concrete, time-bound action plans to halt the recruitment and use of children, and to take measures against any parties that failed to comply. Concerned Member States should allow contact between the United Nations and non-State parties to ensure the broad and effective protection of children. Systematic communication should be established between the Security Council Working Group on Children and Armed Conflict and the relevant sanctions committees and their expert groups in country situations of common concern. Where no sanctions committees existed, the Security Council should consider means by which targeted measures might be applied against persistent perpetrators of grave violations against children. All relevant UN peacekeeping operations and political missions should include provisions for the protection of children. Given the regional dimension of some conflicts, appropriate strategies and coordination mechanisms for information exchange and cooperation on cross-border child protection, such as recruitment, release and reintegration of children, should be established. Member States should take strong action to bring to justice individuals responsible for the recruitment and use of children through national justice systems. The Security Council should refer to the International Criminal Court, for investigation and prosecution, violations against children in armed conflict that fell within its jurisdiction. Other international justice mechanisms should also prioritize accountability for crimes against children. Since effective disarmament, demobilization and reintegration programmes for children were crucial, Governments and donors should ensure that such programmes received timely and adequate resources and were community-based.

Security Council consideration (April). On 29 April [meeting 6114], the Security Council considered the Secretary-General's report (see above). Speaking at the meeting, the Secretary-General called on the Security Council to strike a blow against impunity and to stop violators from continuing to victimize children. All countries and all groups must put the protection of children in situations of armed conflict above politics.

The Special Representative of the Secretary-General for Children and Armed Conflict (see p. 739) said that the Council's decision to demand that annexes of the report of the Secretary-General contain lists of parties to conflict that recruited and used children, and to consider possible targeted measures against them had led to thousands of children being identified and released. She called for the Council to extend its focus beyond child soldiers to deal with other violations, such as rape and other grave sexual violence against children and the intentional killing and maiming of children.

Representatives of 56 countries spoke in the ensuing debate.

SECURITY COUNCIL ACTION

At the same meeting, following consultations among Security Council members, the President made statement **S/PRST/2009/9** on behalf of the Council:

The Security Council takes note with appreciation of the eighth report of the Secretary-General on children and armed conflict and of the positive developments referred to in the report, and notes the continuing challenges in the implementation of its resolution 1612(2005) reflected therein.

The Council reaffirms its commitment to address the widespread impact of armed conflict on children and its determination to ensure respect for and the implementation of resolution 1612(2005) and all its previous resolutions on children and armed conflict, as well as respect for other applicable international law related to the protection of children affected by armed conflict.

The Council stresses in this regard the importance of adopting a broad strategy of conflict prevention which addresses the root causes of armed conflict in a comprehensive manner in order to enhance the protection of children on a long-term basis, including by promoting sustainable development, poverty eradication, national reconciliation, good governance, democracy, the rule of law and respect for and protection of human rights.

The Council acknowledges that the implementation of resolution 1612(2005) in situations listed in the annexes to the report of the Secretary-General has generated progress and invites the Secretary-General, where applicable, to strengthen the efforts to bring the monitoring and reporting mechanism to its full capacity in order to allow for prompt advocacy and effective response to all violations and abuses committed against children. In this regard, the Council reiterates its request to the Secretary-General to provide additional administrative support to its Working Group on Children and Armed Conflict.

The Council reiterates its equally strong condemnation of the continuing recruitment and use of children in armed conflict in violation of applicable international law, the killing and maiming of children, rape and other sexual violence, abductions, the denial of humanitarian access to children and attacks against schools and hospitals by parties to armed conflict. The Council condemns all other violations of international law, including international humanitarian law, human rights law and refugee law, committed against children in situations of armed conflict. The Council demands that all relevant parties immediately put an end to such practices and take special measures to protect children.

The Council expresses deep concern that civilians, in particular children, continue to account for a considerable number of casualties resulting from killing and maiming in armed conflicts, including as a result of deliberate targeting, indiscriminate and excessive use of force, indiscriminate use of landmines and cluster munitions and use of children as human shields.

The Council further expresses deep concern about the high incidence and appalling levels of brutality of rape and other forms of sexual violence against children, girls and boys, committed in the context of and associated with armed conflict, including the use or commission of rape and other forms of sexual violence in some situations as a tactic of war.

The Council recognizes the importance of including in the annexes to the reports of the Secretary-General on children and armed conflict those parties to armed conflict that commit acts of killing and maiming of children that are prohibited under applicable international law or acts of rape and other sexual violence against children that are prohibited under applicable international law in situations of armed conflict, and expresses its intention to continue its consideration of this issue in order to take action within three months of this date.

The Council reiterates its call upon the parties to armed conflict listed in the annexes to the report of the Secretary-General that have not already done so to prepare and implement, without further delay, concrete time-bound action plans to halt the recruitment and use of children in violation of applicable international law, and to address all other violations and abuses committed against children and undertake specific commitments and measures in this regard, in close cooperation with the Special Representative of the Secretary-General for Children and Armed Conflict and the United Nations country-level task forces on monitoring and reporting.

The Council expresses its concern about situations where insufficient or no progress has been made by parties listed in the annexes to the reports of the Secretary-General in halting the recruitment and use of children in violation of applicable international law, including through the preparation and implementation of concrete time-bound action plans, and reiterates its determination to ensure respect for its resolutions on children and armed conflict, making use of all the tools provided in resolution 1612(2005), including action, as appropriate, in accordance with paragraph 9 of resolution 1612(2005).

The Council strongly emphasizes the need for the Member States concerned to take decisive and immediate action against persistent perpetrators of violations against children and to bring to justice those responsible for the recruitment and use of children in violation of applicable international law and other violations against children through national justice systems and, where applicable, international justice mechanisms and mixed criminal courts and tribunals, with a view to ending impunity for those committing crimes against children.

The Council reiterates the primary responsibility of States in providing effective protection and relief to all children affected by armed conflict and calls upon them to comply with their obligations under applicable international law, including the Convention on the Rights of the Child and the Optional Protocols thereto, encourages States to strengthen national measures for the prevention of violations against children in armed conflict, including the recruitment and use of children and their use in hostilities in violation of applicable international law, inter alia, by enacting legislation that explicitly prohibits such recruitment and use as well as other violations, and urges States that have not yet done so to consider ratifying or acceding to the Convention and the Optional Protocols thereto.

The Council reiterates the importance of the full, safe and unhindered access of humanitarian personnel and goods and the delivery of humanitarian assistance to all children affected by armed conflict, and stresses the importance for all, within the framework of humanitarian assistance, of upholding and respecting the humanitarian principles of humanity, neutrality, impartiality and independence.

The Council remains concerned about the illicit trafficking in small arms and light weapons and its effect on and their use by children in armed conflict.

The Council welcomes the sustained engagement of its Working Group on Children and Armed Conflict and requests it to adopt, with the administrative support of the Secretariat, timely conclusions and recommendations

in line with resolution 1612(2005). The Council encourages the Working Group to continue its review process, to enhance its ability to follow up the implementation of its recommendations and the development and implementation of action plans to halt the recruitment and use of children, and to consider and react in a timely manner to information on situations of children and armed conflict, in collaboration with the Office of the Special Representative and the United Nations Children's Fund. It also invites the Working Group to enhance its communication with relevant sanctions committees of the Council, including by forwarding pertinent information.

The Council commends the work carried out by the Special Representative, Ms. Radhika Coomaraswamy, and emphasizes the importance of her country visits in promoting collaboration between the United Nations and Governments and enhancing dialogue with parties to armed conflict.

The Council also commends the work carried out by the United Nations Children's Fund as well as other relevant United Nations agencies, funds and programmes within their respective mandates, the child protection advisers of United Nations peacekeeping, peacebuilding and political missions in cooperation with national Governments and relevant civil society actors.

The Council encourages the efforts of the Department of Peacekeeping Operations of the Secretariat in mainstreaming child protection into all peacekeeping missions, in close collaboration with the Office of the Special Representative and the United Nations Children's Fund, and encourages the deployment of child protection advisers to peacekeeping operations, as well as to relevant peacebuilding and political missions.

The Council invites the Peacebuilding Commission to continue to promote child protection in post-conflict situations under its consideration.

Given the regional dimension of some conflicts, the Council encourages Member States, United Nations peacekeeping, peacebuilding and political missions and United Nations country teams to establish appropriate strategies and coordination mechanisms for information exchange and cooperation on cross-border child protection concerns, such as the recruitment, release and reintegration of children.

The Council recognizes the important role of education in armed conflict areas, including as a means to achieve the goal of halting and preventing the recruitment and re-recruitment of children in violation of applicable international law, and calls upon all parties concerned to continue to ensure that all children associated with armed forces and groups systematically have access to disarmament, demobilization and reintegration processes through which they can benefit, inter alia, from education.

The Council also urges parties to armed conflict to refrain from actions that impede children's access to education, in particular attacks or threats of attack on school children or teachers as such, the use of schools for military operations, and attacks on schools that are prohibited by applicable international law.

The Council requests the Secretary-General to submit his next report on the implementation of its resolutions on children and armed conflict by May 2010.

Reports of Special Representative. Pursuant to General Assembly resolution 63/241 [YUN 2008, p. 739], the Secretary-General's Special Representative for Children and Armed Conflict, Radhika Coomaraswamy (Sri Lanka), in a report [A/HRC/12/49] submitted in July, outlined emerging concerns, including rampant sexual violence against girls and boys in situations of armed conflict, the special vulnerabilities of children internally displaced, the effects of terrorism and counter-terrorism measures on children, attacks on schools and accountability for acts committed by children during armed conflict. She recommended that States comply with international norms and standards on child protection and take strong action to bring to justice individuals responsible for recruiting and using children in the armed forces or armed groups. Children accused of crimes allegedly committed while they were associated with armed forces or groups should be considered primarily as victims, and should be treated in accordance with international law and other standards on juvenile justice, and within a framework of restorative justice and social rehabilitation. Neither capital punishment nor life imprisonment without the possibility of release should be imposed for offences committed by persons below 18 years of age. Detention of children should be used as a last resort and for the shortest period of time. The report listed 50 State and non-State parties that recruited children in situations of armed conflict in Afganistan, Burundi, the Central African Republic, Chad, Colombia, the Democratic Republic of the Congo, Iraq, Myanmar, Nepal, the Philippines, southern Sudan and Darfur, Sri Lanka, and Uganda.

Pursuant to General Assembly resolution 62/141 [YUN 2007, p. 681], the Representative in August submitted a report [A/64/254] highlighting issues of concern, such as the need for education for children in emergency situations and the need to ensure avenues for the contribution of children and youth to national processes. The report also focused on integrating the issue of children and armed conflict in UN system-wide activities and within UN entities as a strategy to ensure the practical application of standards and norms for child protection. Significant progress had been made in integrating the issue in the UN system, particularly in the peace and security sector. Yet progress made remained fragile and should be consolidated.

Working Group activities. In July [S/2009/378], the Chairman of the Security Council Working Group on Children and Armed Conflict reported on the Group's activities since the submission of its last report [YUN 2008, p. 852]. The Group held four meetings in 2009 (24 February, 1 July, 12 October, 18 December), during which it adopted conclusions on children and armed conflict in Afghanistan

[S/AC.51/2009/1], Burundi [S/AC.51/2009/6], the Central African Republic [S/AC.51/2009/2], the Democratic Republic of the Congo (DRC) [S/AC.51/2009/3], Myanmar [S/AC.51/2009/4] and the Sudan [S/AC.51/2009/5].

On 27 August, the Security Council President sent letters to the Secretary-General based on the Working Group's conclusions on Afghanistan [S/2009/435], the Central African Republic [S/2009/436] and the DRC [S/2009/437]. On 27 October, he sent a letter [S/2009/564] to the Secretary-General based on the Group's conclusions on Myanmar.

Security Council consideration (August). On 4 August [meeting 6176], the Council adopted resolution 1882(2009) (see below), by which it decided that parties to armed conflict engaging in patterns of killing and maiming of children and rape and other sexual violence against children should be listed in the Secretary-General's reports on children in armed conflict. Previously only State and non-State parties who had recruited child soldiers or used children in situations of armed conflict were explicitly named—the so-called list of shame—in annexes to the Secretary-General's annual report.

The Chairman of the Working Group on Children and Armed Conflict told the Council that the resolution represented a fundamental step forward in the child-protection agenda as it expanded the criteria by which parties could be included in the Secretary-General's annual report. Parties engaging in other forms of violence against children could now fall under the Council's scrutiny. The resolution dealt with major aspects, especially the preparation of plans of action directed towards putting an end to those practices. Likewise, in order to fight impunity, the text requested Member States to bring to justice—both national and international—the perpetrators of those crimes. For those reasons, the resolution was a formidable tool to be used by the Office of the Special Representative, UNICEF, the Department of Peacekeeping Operations, UN monitoring teams and NGOs.

SECURITY COUNCIL ACTION

On the same day [meeting 6176], the Security Council unanimously adopted **resolution 1882(2009)**. The draft [S/2009/399] was submitted by Argentina, Australia, Austria, Belgium, Benin, Burkina Faso, Canada, Chile, the Comoros, Costa Rica, Côte d'Ivoire, Croatia, the Czech Republic, Denmark, Finland, France, Germany, Greece, Guatemala, Iceland, Ireland, Italy, Japan, Kazakhstan, Latvia, Liechtenstein, Luxembourg, Mexico, Monaco, the Netherlands, New Zealand, Norway, Peru, Portugal, the Republic of Korea, Rwanda, Slovenia, South Africa, Spain, Sweden, Switzerland, Turkey, the United Kingdom, the United Republic of Tanzania, the United States and Uruguay.

The Security Council,

Reaffirming its resolutions 1261(1999) of 25 August 1999, 1314(2000) of 11 August 2000, 1379(2001) of 20 November 2001, 1460(2003) of 30 January 2003, 1539(2004) of 22 April 2004 and 1612(2005) of 26 July 2005, and the statements by its President of 24 July 2006, 28 November 2006, 12 February 2008, 17 July 2008 and 29 April 2009, which contribute to a comprehensive framework for addressing the protection of children affected by armed conflict,

Acknowledging that the implementation of resolution 1612(2005) has generated progress, resulting in the release and reintegration of children into their families and communities and in a more systematic dialogue between the United Nations country-level task forces and parties to armed conflict on the implementation of time-bound action plans, while remaining deeply concerned over the lack of progress on the ground in some situations of concern, where parties to conflict continue to violate with impunity the relevant provisions of applicable international law relating to the rights and protection of children in armed conflict,

Stressing the primary role of national Governments in providing protection and relief to all children affected by armed conflict,

Reiterating that all actions undertaken by United Nations entities within the framework of the monitoring and reporting mechanism must be designed to support and supplement, as appropriate, the protection and rehabilitation roles of national Governments,

Recalling the responsibilities of States to end impunity and to prosecute those responsible for genocide, crimes against humanity, war crimes and other egregious crimes perpetrated against children,

Welcoming the fact that several individuals who are alleged to have committed crimes against children in situations of armed conflict have been brought to justice by national justice systems, international justice mechanisms and mixed criminal courts and tribunals,

Convinced that the protection of children in armed conflict should be an important aspect of any comprehensive strategy to resolve conflict,

Calling upon all parties to armed conflicts to comply strictly with the obligations applicable to them under international law for the protection of children in armed conflict, including those contained in the Convention on the Rights of the Child and the Optional Protocol thereto on the involvement of children in armed conflict, as well as the Geneva Conventions of 12 August 1949 and the Additional Protocols thereto, of 1977,

Reiterating its primary responsibility for the maintenance of international peace and security and, in this connection, its commitment to address the widespread impact of armed conflict on children,

Stressing its determination to ensure respect for its resolutions and other international obligations and applicable norms on the protection of children affected by armed conflict,

Having considered the report of the Secretary-General of 26 March 2009, and stressing that the present resolution does not seek to make any legal determination as to whether situations which are referred to in the report of the Secretary-General are or are not armed conflicts in the context of the Geneva Conventions and the Additional Protocols thereto, nor does it prejudge the legal status of the non-State parties involved in those situations,

Deeply concerned that children continue to account for a considerable number of casualties resulting from killing and maiming in armed conflicts, including as a result of deliberate targeting, indiscriminate and excessive use of force, indiscriminate use of landmines, cluster munitions and other weapons and use of children as human shields, and equally deeply concerned about the high incidence and appalling levels of brutality of rape and other forms of sexual violence committed against children, in the context of and associated with armed conflict, including the use or commissioning of rape and other forms of sexual violence in some situations as a tactic of war,

1.   *Strongly condemns* all violations of applicable international law involving the recruitment and use of children by parties to armed conflict, as well as their re-recruitment, killing and maiming, rape and other sexual violence, abductions, attacks against schools or hospitals and denial of humanitarian access by parties to armed conflict and all other violations of international law committed against children in situations of armed conflict;

2.   *Reaffirms* that the monitoring and reporting mechanism will continue to be implemented in situations listed in the annexes to the reports of the Secretary-General on children and armed conflict in line with the principles set out in paragraph 2 of resolution 1612(2005) and that its establishment and implementation shall not prejudge or imply a decision by the Security Council as to whether or not to include a situation on its agenda;

3.   *Recalls* paragraph 16 of resolution 1379(2001), and requests the Secretary-General also to include in the annexes to his reports on children and armed conflict those parties to armed conflict that engage, in contravention of applicable international law, in patterns of killing and maiming of children and/or rape and other sexual violence against children, in situations of armed conflict, bearing in mind all other violations and abuses against children, and notes that the present paragraph will apply to situations in accordance with the conditions set out in paragraph 16 of resolution 1379(2001);

4.   *Invites* the Secretary-General, through his Special Representative for Children and Armed Conflict, to exchange appropriate information and maintain interaction from the earliest opportunity with the Governments concerned regarding violations and abuses committed against children by parties which may be included in the annexes to his periodic reports;

5.   While noting that some parties to armed conflict have responded to its call upon them to prepare and implement concrete time-bound action plans to halt the recruitment and use of children in violation of applicable international law:

(a)   *Reiterates its call upon* those parties to armed conflict listed in the annexes to the report of the Secretary-General on children and armed conflict that have not already done so to prepare and implement, without further delay, action plans to halt the recruitment and use of children in violation of applicable international law;

(b) *Calls upon* those parties listed in the annexes to the report of the Secretary-General on children and armed conflict that commit, in contravention of applicable international law, killing and maiming of children and/or rape and other sexual violence against children in situations of armed conflict to prepare concrete time-bound action plans to halt those violations and abuses;

(c) *Further calls upon* all parties listed in the annexes to the report of the Secretary-General on children and armed conflict to address all other violations and abuses committed against children and undertake specific commitments and measures in this regard;

(d) *Urges* those parties listed in the annexes to the report of the Secretary-General on children and armed conflict to implement the provisions contained in the present paragraph, in close cooperation with the Special Representative of the Secretary-General for Children and Armed Conflict and the United Nations country-level task forces on monitoring and reporting;

6. In this context, *encourages* Member States to devise ways, in close consultation with the United Nations country-level task forces on monitoring and reporting and United Nations country teams, to facilitate the development and implementation of time-bound action plans, and the review and monitoring by the United Nations country-level task forces of obligations and commitments relating to the protection of children in armed conflict;

7. *Reiterates its determination* to ensure respect for its resolutions on children and armed conflict, and in this regard:

(a) Welcomes the sustained activity and recommendations of the Security Council Working Group on Children and Armed Conflict, as called for in paragraph 8 of resolution 1612(2005), and invites the Working Group to continue reporting regularly to the Council;

(b) Requests enhanced communication between the Working Group and relevant Security Council sanctions committees, including through the exchange of pertinent information on violations and abuses committed against children in armed conflict;

(c) Reaffirms its intention to take action against persistent perpetrators in line with paragraph 9 of resolution 1612(2005);

8. *Stresses* the responsibility of the United Nations country-level task forces on monitoring and reporting and United Nations country teams, consistent with their respective mandates, to ensure effective follow-up to Council resolutions on children and armed conflict, to monitor and report progress to the Secretary-General in close cooperation with his Special Representative for Children and Armed Conflict and to ensure a coordinated response to issues related to children and armed conflict;

9. *Requests* the Secretary-General to include more systematically in his reports on children and armed conflict specific information regarding the implementation of the recommendations of the Working Group;

10. *Reiterates its request* to the Secretary-General to ensure that, in all his reports on country-specific situations, the matter of children and armed conflict is included as a specific aspect of the report, and expresses its intention to give its full attention to the information provided therein, including the implementation of relevant Council resolu-

tions and of the recommendations of the Working Group, when dealing with those situations on its agenda;

11. *Welcomes* the efforts of the Department of Peacekeeping Operations of the Secretariat in mainstreaming child protection into peacekeeping missions, in line with the child protection policy directive recently adopted by the Department, encourages the deployment of child protection advisers to peacekeeping operations, as well as to relevant peacebuilding and political missions, and decides to continue the inclusion of specific provisions for the protection of children in such mandates;

12. *Requests* Member States, United Nations peacekeeping, peacebuilding and political missions and United Nations country teams, within their respective mandates and in close cooperation with the Governments of the countries concerned, to establish appropriate strategies and coordination mechanisms for information exchange and cooperation on child protection concerns, in particular cross-border issues, bearing in mind relevant conclusions of the Working Group and paragraph 2 *(d)* of resolution 1612(2005);

13. *Stresses* that effective disarmament, demobilization and reintegration programmes for children, building on best practices identified by the United Nations Children's Fund and other relevant child protection actors, are crucial for the well-being of all children who, in contravention of applicable international law, have been recruited or used by armed forces and groups, and are a critical factor for durable peace and security, and urges national Governments and donors to ensure that these community-based programmes receive timely, sustained and adequate resources and funding;

14. *Also stresses* the importance of timely, sustained and adequate resources and funding for effective welfare programmes for all children affected by armed conflict;

15. *Calls upon* Member States, United Nations entities, including the Peacebuilding Commission, and other parties concerned to ensure that the protection, rights, well-being and empowerment of children affected by armed conflict are integrated into all peace processes and that post-conflict recovery and reconstruction planning, programmes and strategies prioritize issues concerning children affected by armed conflict;

16. *Calls upon* concerned Member States to take decisive and immediate action against persistent perpetrators of violations and abuses against children in situations of armed conflict, and further calls upon them to bring to justice those responsible for such violations that are prohibited under applicable international law, including with regard to the recruitment and use of children, killing and maiming and rape and other sexual violence, through national justice systems, and where applicable, international justice mechanisms and mixed criminal courts and tribunals, with a view to ending impunity for those committing crimes against children;

17. *Requests* the Secretary-General to continue to take the necessary measures, including, where applicable, to bring the monitoring and reporting mechanism to its full capacity, to allow for prompt advocacy and effective response to all violations and abuses committed against children and to ensure that information collected and com-

municated by the mechanism is accurate, objective, reliable and verifiable;

18. *Also requests* the Secretary-General to provide administrative and substantive support for the Working Group, taking into consideration its current workload and the need to strengthen its capacities and institutional memory;

19. *Further requests* the Secretary-General to submit a report by May 2010 on the implementation of its resolutions and the statements by its President on children and armed conflict, including the present resolution, which would include, inter alia:

(a) Annexed lists of parties in situations of armed conflict on the agenda of the Council or in other situations of concern, in accordance with paragraph 3 of the present resolution;

(b) Information on measures undertaken by parties listed in the annexes to end all violations and abuses committed against children in armed conflict;

(c) Information on progress made in the implementation of the monitoring and reporting mechanism established in resolution 1612(2005);

(d) Information on the criteria and procedures used for listing and de-listing parties to armed conflict in the annexes to his periodic reports, bearing in mind the views expressed by all the members of the Working Group during informal briefings to be held before the end of 2009;

20. *Decides* to remain actively seized of the matter.

Internally displaced persons

Reports of Secretary-General's Representative. As requested by the Human Rights Council [YUN 2007, p. 793], the Secretary-General's Representative on the human rights of internally displaced persons (IDPs), Walter Kälin (Switzerland), in February submitted a report [A/HRC/10/13] that addressed three issues: the status of the Guiding Principles on Internal Displacement [YUN 1998, p. 675] 10 years after their submission to the Commission on Human Rights; the protection of persons displaced by natural disaster; and the inclusion of the issue of internal displacement and the people it affected in peace processes. The report also reviewed the Representative's country mission, his working visits and other activities supporting dialogue with Governments, intergovernmental organizations and NGOs involved in the response to internal displacement. The Representative called on Member States to: draft national legislation and policies or revisit existing norms to ensure that the needs of displaced persons received an appropriate response; refrain from any acts against IDPs amounting to violations of their obligations under international human rights law, international humanitarian law and international criminal law; and investigate, prosecute and punish crimes against humanity and war crimes causing internal displacement or committed against those who had been displaced. He called on de facto authorities and armed groups to scrupulously respect

their obligation under international humanitarian and criminal law, to refrain from all acts causing displacement or violating the rights of the displaced and to grant safe humanitarian access to agencies and organizations.

An addendum [A/HRC/10/13/Add.1] on the protection of IDPs in situations of natural disasters set out the relevant legal framework and reviewed typical human rights protection challenges which seemed to be symptomatic of disaster-induced displacement, particularly in the context of sudden-onset disasters such as flooding, earthquakes or cyclones, which provoked a sudden displacement. The report examined how protection could be strengthened and offered recommendations.

A further addendum [A/HRC/10/13/Add.3] summarized the conclusions of the high-level conference on "Ten years of the Guiding Principles on Internal Displacement: achievements and future challenges" (Oslo, Norway, 16–17 October 2008).

In response to General Assembly resolution 62/153 [YUN 2007, p. 793], the Secretary-General transmitted the report of the Representative [A/64/214], which outlined his activities from August 2008 to July 2009, reviewed the situation of internal displacement and discussed the nexus between climate change and internal displacement. At the beginning of 2009, the number of persons internally displaced as a result of armed conflict, generalized violence or human rights violations stood at approximately 26 million. Reported returns of about 2.6 million people in 2008, particularly in the Central African Republic, Côte d'Ivoire, the DRC, Georgia, Iraq, Kenya, the Philippines, Sri Lanka, the Sudan, Timor-Leste, Uganda and Yemen, were outweighed by the displacement of about 4.6 million people during the same period. New internal displacement was reported mainly from the Philippines (600,000 persons), the Sudan (550,000), Kenya (500,000), the DRC (at least 400,000), Iraq (360,000), Pakistan (over 310,000), Somalia (300,000), Colombia (270,000), Sri Lanka (230,000), India (over 220,000) and Georgia (128,000). The first half of 2009 had seen more displacement, particularly in Sri Lanka, with almost 300,000 persons displaced during the course of the army's operation against the Liberation Tigers of Tamil Eelam, and in Pakistan, with up to 2 million persons displaced in the context of armed operations against Taliban militants in the north-west of the country. The Representative recommended that States: criminalize arbitrary displacement and bring perpetrators to justice; enhance the protection of displaced persons by adopting laws and policies outlining the duties of national actors, assigning responsibilities among State institutions and establishing adequate funding mechanisms; and establish processes and conditions to ensure that IDPs could find a durable solution of their choice.

Following his mission to Chad (3–9 February) [A/HRC/13/21/Add.5], the Representative highlighted the crisis in the country with regard to protection, characterized by the precarious situation in which displaced persons lived and the general insecurity that prevailed in the east. He called on the Government to restore and reinforce a State presence, in particular the judicial system, a police presence and basic services. Mechanisms for conflict resolution and reconciliation among local communities should be strengthened. The Government should implement child demobilization programmes in all units of the armed forces, respect the civilian character of displacement camps and incorporate its international obligations relating to child protection into domestic legislation, with a view to criminalizing any actions violating those obligations. All parties to the conflict should comply with international child protection standards and refrain from recruiting children into armed forces and armed groups. The Government, with significant international support, should devote its efforts to reconciliation among the various communities; the fight against impunity and the implementation of transitional justice measures; the resolution of disputes over property rights and resources; and the provision of basic services.

Following his mission to Serbia, including Kosovo (28 June–4 July) [A/HRC/13/21/Add.1], the Representative called on Serbia to find ways to engage with the Kosovo authorities at a technical level to resolve displacement-related challenges. The Kosovo authorities should ensure that municipal authorities facilitate the reintegration of returnees. Efforts to facilitate return should include the large number of persons displaced within Kosovo. The European Union Rule of Law Mission in Kosovo should pay particular attention to how housing, land and property cases involving displaced parties were handled by the courts, police and other authorities to prevent further miscarriages of justice and protect the human rights of IDPs.

In Somalia (14–21 October) [A/HRC/13/21/Add.2], the Representative visited Puntland and Somaliland. He was unable to travel to south and central Somalia due to the security situation, but managed to interview IDPs who had recently arrived from there. He urged all actors, including de facto authorities and armed groups with territorial control, to grant full humanitarian access to ensure delivery of goods to all those displaced. Enhancing the protection of civilians and tackling impunity for atrocities were imperative, and it was essential to put in place mechanisms to address impunity, justice and reconciliation with regard to past atrocities, including by considering at an appropriate stage the establishment of an independent commission of inquiry or referral of the situation to the International Criminal Court. The Representative urged donors to provide support to programmes aimed at improving assistance to and protection of the internally displaced, and to embark on bringing robust recovery and development activities to areas that were sufficiently stable, in order to prevent further deterioration of the humanitarian and security situation.

Following his mission to the Tskhinvali region/South Ossetia (5–6 November) [A/HRC/13/21/Add.3 & Corr.1,2] as a follow-up to his mission to Georgia in October 2008 [YUN 2008, p. 855], the Representative urged the parties to ensure that all persons displaced by recent and past conflicts be able to return to their former homes in safety and dignity, recover their property or obtain compensation. He urged the South Ossetian de facto authorities not to link political demands with the right to return. In the light of the complex housing, land and property situation, caused by several waves of violence and displacement, the Representative recommended establishing a property resolution mechanism involving international expertise. Until a comprehensive solution to the conflict was found, the parties should come to pragmatic agreements to improve the situation of idps and other conflict-affected populations.

GENERAL ASSEMBLY ACTION

On 18 December [meeting 65], the General Assembly, on the recommendation of the Third Committee [A/64/439/Add.2 (Part II)], adopted **resolution 64/162** without vote [agenda item 69 *(b)*].

Protection of and assistance to internally displaced persons

The General Assembly,

Recalling that internally displaced persons are persons or groups of persons who have been forced or obliged to flee or to leave their homes or places of habitual residence, in particular as a result of or in order to avoid the effects of armed conflict, situations of generalized violence, violations of human rights or natural or human-made disasters, and who have not crossed an internationally recognized State border,

Recognizing that internally displaced persons are to enjoy, in full equality, the same rights and freedoms under international and domestic law as do other persons in their country,

Deeply disturbed by the alarmingly high numbers of internally displaced persons throughout the world, for reasons including armed conflict, violations of human rights and natural or human-made disasters, who receive inadequate protection and assistance, and conscious of the serious challenges that this is creating for the international community,

Recognizing that natural disasters are a cause of internal displacement, and concerned about factors, such as climate change, that are expected to exacerbate the impact of natural hazards, and climate-related slow-onset events,

Recognizing also that the consequences of hazards can be prevented or substantially mitigated by integrating disaster risk reduction strategies into national development policies and programmes,

Conscious of the human rights and humanitarian dimensions of the problem of internally displaced persons, including in long-term displacement situations, and the responsibilities of States and the international community to strengthen further their protection and assistance,

Emphasizing that States have the primary responsibility to provide protection and assistance to internally displaced persons within their jurisdiction, as well as to address the root causes of the displacement problem in appropriate cooperation with the international community,

Reaffirming that all persons, including those internally displaced, have the right to freedom of movement and residence and should be protected against being arbitrarily displaced,

Noting the international community's growing awareness of the issue of internally displaced persons worldwide and the urgency of addressing the root causes of their displacement and finding durable solutions, including voluntary return in safety and with dignity, as well as voluntary local integration in the areas to which persons have been displaced or voluntary settlement in another part of the country,

Recalling the relevant norms of international law, including international human rights law, international humanitarian law and international refugee law, and recognizing that the protection of internally displaced persons has been strengthened by identifying, reaffirming and consolidating specific standards for their protection, in particular through the Guiding Principles on Internal Displacement,

Noting, in this regard, that 2009 marks the sixtieth anniversary of the Geneva Conventions of 1949, which constitute one vital legal framework for the protection of and assistance to civilians in armed conflict and under foreign occupation, including internally displaced persons,

Welcoming the adoption on 22 October 2009 of the African Union Convention for the Protection and Assistance of Internally Displaced Persons in Africa, which marks a significant step towards strengthening the national and regional normative framework for the protection of and assistance to internally displaced persons,

Welcoming also the increasing dissemination, promotion and application of the Guiding Principles when dealing with situations of internal displacement,

Deploring practices of forced displacement and their negative consequences for the enjoyment of human rights and fundamental freedoms by large groups of populations, and recalling the relevant provisions of the Rome Statute of the International Criminal Court that define the deportation or forcible transfer of population as a crime against humanity, and the unlawful deportation, transfer, or ordering the displacement of the civilian population as war crimes,

Welcoming the cooperation established between the Representative of the Secretary-General on the human rights of internally displaced persons and national Governments, the relevant offices and agencies of the United Nations as well as with other international and regional organizations, and encouraging further strengthening of this collaboration in order to promote better strategies for, protection of,

assistance to and durable solutions for internally displaced persons,

Acknowledging with appreciation the important and independent contribution of the International Red Cross and Red Crescent Movement and other humanitarian agencies in protecting and assisting internally displaced persons, in cooperation with relevant international bodies,

Recalling the Vienna Declaration and Programme of Action adopted by the World Conference on Human Rights on 25 June 1993, regarding the need to develop global strategies to address the problem of internal displacement,

Recalling also its resolution 62/153 of 18 December 2007 and Human Rights Council resolution 6/32 of 14 December 2007,

1. *Welcomes* the report of the Representative of the Secretary-General on the human rights of internally displaced persons and the conclusions and recommendations contained therein;

2. *Commends* the Representative of the Secretary-General for the activities undertaken so far, for the catalytic role that he plays in raising the level of awareness about the plight of internally displaced persons and for his ongoing efforts to address their development and other specific needs, including through the mainstreaming of the human rights of internally displaced persons into all relevant parts of the United Nations system;

3. *Encourages* the Representative of the Secretary-General, through continuous dialogue with Governments and all intergovernmental and non-governmental organizations concerned, to continue his analysis of the root causes of internal displacement and of the needs and human rights of those displaced, to continue the development of benchmarks for achieving durable solutions and measures of prevention, including early warning, as well as ways to strengthen protection, assistance and durable solutions for internally displaced persons, and to continue to promote comprehensive strategies, taking into account the primary responsibility of States for the protection of and assistance to internally displaced persons within their jurisdiction;

4. *Expresses its appreciation* to those Governments and intergovernmental and non-governmental organizations that have provided protection and assistance to internally displaced persons and have supported the work of the Representative of the Secretary-General;

5. *Calls upon* States to provide durable solutions, and encourages strengthened international cooperation, including through the provision of resources and expertise to assist affected countries, and in particular developing countries, in their national efforts and policies related to assistance, protection and rehabilitation for internally displaced persons;

6. *Expresses particular concern* at the grave problems faced by many internally displaced women and children, including violence and abuse, sexual exploitation, trafficking in persons, forced recruitment and abduction, and encourages the continued commitment of the Representative of the Secretary-General to promote action to address their particular assistance, protection and development needs, as well as those of other groups with special needs, such as severely traumatized individuals, older persons and persons with disabilities, taking into account the relevant resolutions of the General Assembly and of the Security Council

and giving appropriate consideration to annex I to the report of the Special Representative of the Secretary-General for Children and Armed Conflict, entitled "Rights and guarantees for internally displaced children";

7. *Emphasizes* the importance of consultation with internally displaced persons and host communities by Governments and other relevant actors, in accordance with their specific mandates, during all phases of displacement, as well as the participation of internally displaced persons, where appropriate, in programmes and activities pertaining to them, taking into account the primary responsibility of States for the protection of and assistance to internally displaced persons within their jurisdiction;

8. *Notes* the importance of taking the human rights and the specific protection and assistance needs of internally displaced persons into consideration, when appropriate, in peace processes, and emphasizes that durable solutions for internally displaced persons, including through voluntary return, sustainable reintegration and rehabilitation processes and their active participation, as appropriate, in the peace process, are necessary elements of effective peacebuilding;

9. *Welcomes* the role of the Peacebuilding Commission in this regard, and continues to urge the Commission to intensify its efforts, within its mandate, in cooperation with national and transitional Governments and in consultation with the relevant United Nations entities, to incorporate the rights and the specific needs of internally displaced persons, including their voluntary return in safety and with dignity, reintegration and rehabilitation, as well as related land and property issues, when advising on or proposing country-specific peacebuilding strategies for post-conflict situations in cases under consideration;

10. *Recognizes* the Guiding Principles on Internal Displacement as an important international framework for the protection of internally displaced persons, welcomes the fact that an increasing number of States, United Nations organizations and regional and non-governmental organizations are applying them as a standard, and encourages all relevant actors to make use of the Guiding Principles when dealing with situations of internal displacement;

11. *Welcomes* the ongoing use of the Guiding Principles by the Representative of the Secretary-General in his dialogue with Governments, intergovernmental and non-governmental organizations and other relevant actors, and requests him to continue his efforts to further the dissemination, promotion and application of the Guiding Principles and to provide support for efforts to promote capacity-building and the use of the Guiding Principles, as well as the development of domestic legislation and policies;

12. *Encourages* States to continue to develop and implement domestic legislation and policies dealing with all stages of displacement, in an inclusive and non-discriminatory way, including through the identification of a national focal point within the Government for issues of internal displacement, and through the allocation of budget resources, and encourages the international community and national actors to provide financial support and cooperation to Governments, upon request, in this regard;

13. *Expresses its appreciation* that an increasing number of States have adopted domestic legislation and policies dealing with all stages of displacement;

14. *Urges* all Governments to continue to facilitate the activities of the Representative of the Secretary-General, in particular Governments with situations of internal displacement, and to respond favourably to requests from the Representative for visits so as to enable him to continue and enhance dialogue with Governments in addressing situations of internal displacement, and thanks those Governments that have already done so;

15. *Invites* Governments to give serious consideration, in dialogue with the Representative of the Secretary-General, to the recommendations and suggestions addressed to them, in accordance with his mandate, and to inform him of measures taken thereon;

16. *Calls upon* Governments to provide protection and assistance, including reintegration and development assistance, to internally displaced persons, and to facilitate the efforts of the relevant United Nations agencies and humanitarian organizations in these respects, including by further improving access to internally displaced persons and by maintaining the civilian and humanitarian character of camps and settlements for internally displaced persons where they exist;

17. *Emphasizes* the central role of the Emergency Relief Coordinator for the inter-agency coordination of protection of and assistance to internally displaced persons, welcomes continued initiatives taken in order to ensure better protection, assistance and development strategies for internally displaced persons, as well as better coordination of activities regarding them, and emphasizes the need to strengthen the capacities of the United Nations organizations and other relevant actors to meet the immense humanitarian challenges of internal displacement;

18. *Encourages* all relevant United Nations organizations and humanitarian assistance, human rights and development organizations to enhance their collaboration and coordination, through the Inter-Agency Standing Committee and United Nations country teams in countries with situations of internal displacement, and to provide all possible assistance and support to the Representative of the Secretary-General, and requests the continued participation of the Representative in the work of the Inter-Agency Standing Committee and its subsidiary bodies;

19. *Notes with appreciation* the increased attention paid to the issue of internally displaced persons in the consolidated appeals process, and encourages further efforts in this regard;

20. *Also notes with appreciation* the increasing role of national human rights institutions in assisting internally displaced persons and in promoting and protecting their human rights;

21. *Recognizes* the relevance of the global database on internally displaced persons advocated by the Representative of the Secretary-General, and encourages the members of the Inter-Agency Standing Committee and Governments to continue to collaborate on and support this effort, including by providing financial resources and relevant data on situations of internal displacement;

22. *Welcomes* the initiatives undertaken by regional organizations, such as the African Union, the International

Conference on the Great Lakes Region, the Organization of American States and the Council of Europe, to address the protection, assistance and development needs of internally displaced persons and to find durable solutions for them, and encourages regional organizations to strengthen their activities and their cooperation with the Representative of the Secretary-General;

23. *Requests* the Secretary-General to provide his Representative, from within existing resources, with all assistance necessary to carry out his mandate effectively, and encourages the Office of the United Nations High Commissioner for Human Rights, in close cooperation with the Emergency Relief Coordinator, the Office for the Coordination of Humanitarian Affairs of the Secretariat and the Office of the United Nations High Commissioner for Refugees and all other relevant United Nations offices and agencies, to continue to support the Representative;

24. *Encourages* the Representative of the Secretary-General to continue to seek the contributions of States, relevant organizations and institutions in order to create a more stable basis for his work;

25. *Requests* the Representative of the Secretary-General to prepare, for the General Assembly at its sixty-fifth and sixty-sixth sessions, a report on the implementation of the present resolution;

26. *Decides* to continue its consideration of the question of protection of and assistance to internally displaced persons at its sixty-sixth session.

Indigenous peoples

Reports of Special Rapporteur. In accordance with a Human Rights Council request [YUN 2007, p. 798], the Special Rapporteur on the situation of human rights and fundamental freedoms of indigenous people, S. James Anaya (United States), in July submitted his second report to the Council [A/HRC/12/34], which summarized his activities as they related to four principal areas: promoting good practices, thematic studies, country reports and cases of alleged human rights violations. The Rapporteur examined his mandate in relation to those of the Permanent Forum on Indigenous Issues and the Expert Mechanism on the Rights of Indigenous Peoples. He recommended strengthening and consolidating coordination among those mechanisms, which were created at different times and in response to different moments in the international movement to protect indigenous rights. The Rapporteur analysed the duty of States to consult with indigenous peoples on matters affecting them, and recommended that States develop mechanisms for determining whether proposed legislative or administrative measures—including those for natural resource extraction or other development activities—affected indigenous interests, to determine the need for special consultation procedures well before the measures were taken.

An addendum [A/HRC/12/34/Add.1] summarized communications sent to 29 Governments and to the

African Commission on Human and Peoples' Rights between 10 June 2008 and 26 August 2009, and responses received.

The Rapporteur addressed [A/HRC/12/34/Add.2] the situation of indigenous peoples of Brazil in relation to the realization of their right to self-determination and related rights, following a mission to Brazil (18–25 August 2008) and subsequent research and exchanges of information. He noted that the Government was committed to advancing indigenous rights in accordance with international standards, having ratified International Labour Organization (ILO) Convention (No. 169) concerning Indigenous and Tribal Peoples in Independent Countries and supported adoption of the United Nations Declaration on the Rights of Indigenous Peoples [YUN 2007, p. 691]. Additionally, Brazil had constitutional and other legal protections for indigenous peoples, and the Government had developed significant programmes in the areas of indigenous land rights, development, health and education. Nonetheless, further efforts were needed to ensure that they fully exercised the right to self-determination; the Rapporteur offered recommendations in the areas of awareness-raising, demarcation and protection of lands, health, education, security enforcement, and law and policy reform.

The Rapporteur focused [A/HRC/12/34/Add.3] on the indigenous peoples of Nepal, comprehensively referred to as Adivasi Janajati, following a visit (24 November–2 December 2008) and subsequent exchange of information and research. He was encouraged by the Government's commitment to advance indigenous rights, which was manifested by the ratification of the ILO Convention No. 169 and the Government's support for the United Nations Declaration. At the same time, he noted a number of human rights concerns and offered recommendations concerning legal and institutional reform; federalism, local government and autonomy; land, territory and resource rights; cultural heritage; social and economic development; and the rights of indigenous women and children.

After visiting Panama (27–30 January), the Rapporteur provided his observations [A/HRC/12/34/Add.5] on the situation of the Charco la Pava community and other communities affected by the Chan 75 hydroelectric project. He pointed out that the project had a significant impact on indigenous communities, without the consultation process required by international standards on free, prior and informed consultation with indigenous peoples. Insecurity as regards land tenure and natural resources contributed to the vulnerability of the communities affected by the project. The Rapporteur recommended that steps be taken to remedy the lack of adequate consultation with the communities and to address their territorial claims, especially in view of the level of discontent among the communities and the inadequate negotiations that were held in order to relocate them.

The Rapporteur submitted [A/HRC/12/34/Add.7] the conclusions and recommendations of the international expert seminar on the role of UN mechanisms with a specific mandate regarding the rights of indigenous peoples (Madrid, 4–6 February), organized by the Almáciga Intercultural Working Group and the International Work Group for Indigenous Affairs and hosted by the Spanish Agency for International Development Cooperation. Participants discussed methods for streamlining the work of the three UN mechanisms—the Expert Mechanism, on the Permanent Forum and the Special Rapporteur—by examining the priority work areas of the respective mandates and identifying ways in which those aspects might be maximized.

The Rapporteur presented his observations [A/HRC/12/34/Add.8] on the situation of the indigenous peoples of the Amazon region, particularly in relation to the clashes that occurred on 5 June and the events of the following days in the Peruvian provinces of Bagua and Utcubamba, Amazonas department, which resulted in deaths and injuries. He recommended establishing an independent commission to shed light on those incidents, conducting consultations and reviewing the criminal charges against indigenous leaders. The absence of an adequate mechanism to address the right of indigenous peoples to be consulted and to protect their rights over their lands had been a factor in the feeling among indigenous peoples that they lacked adequate options to defend their rights.

In accordance with General Assembly resolution 63/161 [YUN 2008, p. 858], the Secretary-General in September transmitted the report of the Rapporteur [A/64/338], which reviewed his activities and provided an analysis of the United Nations Declaration on the Rights of Indigenous Peoples. The Rapporteur observed that the standards affirmed in the Declaration shared an essentially remedial character, seeking to redress the obstacles and discrimination that indigenous peoples had faced. The Rapporteur encouraged States to raise awareness of the Declaration and provide technical training to Government officials, members of legislative bodies, judicial authorities, civil society and indigenous peoples themselves.

The General Assembly took note of that report on 18 December (**decision 64/533**).

Following his mission to Botswana (19–27 March) [A/HRC/15/37/Add.2], the Rapporteur noted that the Government had developed programmes aimed at preserving and celebrating the unique cultural attributes of the country's many indigenous tribes. However, such programmes should not be limited to the recognition of ceremonial and artistic expression, but should be expanded to include a real respect for and promotion of cultural diversity as it was manifested in political and social structures, land-use patterns and approaches to development. Too often, the practices of the dominant Tswana tribes had been incorporated in the design and implementation of Government initiatives to the exclusion of the practices of minority tribes. The Government should adopt measures to protect the rights of non-dominant indigenous groups to develop their cultural identities, particularly those related to land rights, approaches to development, and political and decision-making structures. Laws and Government programmes should be reviewed and reformed to ensure that they did not discriminate against particular groups, but accommodated and strengthened cultural diversity. The Government should modify, in consultation with the affected indigenous peoples, its educational curriculum to better reflect the cultural diversity of Botswana, including the history, culture, identity and current situation of non-dominant tribes throughout the country.

Following his mission to Chile (5–9 April) [A/HRC/12/34/Add.6], the Rapporteur observed that the State must still address major challenges, particularly regarding consultation and cooperation, rights to land and territory, development of natural resources, and policies on conflicts connected with claims to Mapuche lands. He called for stronger and more effective consultation mechanisms between the State and indigenous people, and recommended that the State establish a mechanism to recognize indigenous rights over lands and natural resources and consult with indigenous peoples on any project affecting indigenous lands and resources.

Following his mission to Australia (17–28 August) [A/HRC/15/37/Add.4], the Rapporteur stressed the need to incorporate into government programmes a more integrated approach to addressing indigenous disadvantage, one not just promoting social and economic well-being of indigenous peoples, but also advancing their self-determination and strengthening their cultural bonds. The Government should advance self-determination by encouraging indigenous self-governance at the local level, ensuring indigenous participation in the design, delivery and monitoring of programmes and promoting culturally appropriate programmes incorporating or building on indigenous peoples' own initiatives. Further efforts were needed to secure indigenous rights over lands, resources and heritage sites and to ensure that indigenous peoples living in remote areas could enjoy the same social and economic rights as other segments of the Australian population, without having to sacrifice important aspects of their cultures and ways of life.

Report of High Commissioner. In a report to the Council issued in January [A/HRC/10/51], the High Commissioner reviewed developments in indigenous rights arising out of the work of the treaty bodies, special procedures and OHCHR field presences from 2007 to 2008. She reviewed the work of treaty bodies and special procedures, and presented good practices by OHCHR field presences to advance indigenous rights at the national and regional levels. The High Commissioner recommended that she submit a single consolidated report on indigenous rights annually, covering the activities of human rights bodies and mechanisms as well as of OHCHR. She also recommended that all reports on indigenous peoples be submitted at one Council session in the year.

Human Rights Council action. On 1 October [A/65/53 (res. 12/13)], the Council requested the High Commissioner to submit an annual report on the rights of indigenous peoples, covering developments of human rights bodies and OHCHR activities. It decided that the reports of the Special Rapporteur, the Expert Mechanism and the High Commissioner would be considered by the Council at its annual September session and that the Expert Mechanism should hold its future annual sessions well in advance of that session, if possible in June. It requested the Special Rapporteur to report to the General Assembly's sixty-fifth (2010) session.

Expert Mechanism on rights of indigenous peoples

Expert Mechanism study. In response to a Human Rights Council request [YUN 2008, p. 857], the five-member Expert Mechanism on the Rights of Indigenous Peoples in August submitted a study [A/HRC/12/33] on lessons learned and challenges to achieve the implementation of the right of indigenous peoples to education. The study analysed the scope and content of the right to education; indigenous education systems and institutions; lessons learned; and challenges and measures to achieve the implementation of the right of indigenous peoples to education. An annex contained Expert Mechanism advice No. 1 (2009) on the right of indigenous peoples to education.

Meeting of Expert Mechanism. The Expert Mechanism, at its second session (Geneva, 10–14 August) [A/HRC/12/32], held a discussion on the draft study on lessons learned and challenges (see above) in order to finalize the study. It also held a discussion on the United Nations Declaration on the Rights of Indigenous Peoples, addressing the implementation of the Declaration and provisions in the Declaration identifying remedies for infringements of rights—such as rights to adjudication, remedies, repatriation, redress and compensation.

The Expert Mechanism adopted the study and adopted six proposals. Five were addressed to the Human Rights Council and related to: a suggested thematic study on indigenous peoples' right to par-

ticipate in decision-making; human rights institutions and mechanisms; consideration of indigenous rights during the Human Rights Council sessions; the UN Voluntary Fund for Indigenous Populations; and follow-up to the Durban Review Conference. The sixth proposal related to the United Nations Declaration and was addressed to UN specialized agencies.

The session was attended by representatives of States, UN bodies, NGOs, academics and a large number of indigenous peoples. The participation of some of the indigenous peoples was funded through the Voluntary Fund.

Human Rights Council action. On 1 October [res. 12/13], the Council requested the Expert Mechanism to carry out a study on indigenous peoples and the right to participate in decision-making, submitting a progress report to the Council's fifteenth (2010) session and a final study to the eighteenth (2011) session.

Voluntary Fund for Indigenous Populations

The Board of Trustees of the United Nations Voluntary Fund for Indigenous Populations, at its twenty-second session (Geneva, 16–20 March) [A/65/163], recommended 75 travel grants totalling $307,437 to enable indigenous representatives to attend the eighth session of the Permanent Forum on Indigenous Issues (see p. 749) and another 36 grants totalling $104,585 to enable representatives to attend the second session of the Expert Mechanism (see above). On 26 March, the High Commissioner approved the Board's recommendations on behalf of the Secretary-General.

Human Rights Council action. On 1 October [res. 12/13], the Council requested OHCHR to prepare a document outlining the practical implications of a change in mandate of the Voluntary Fund, in particular if it was expanded, the working methods and resources of the Fund, for submission to the Council's fifteenth (2010) session.

Voluntary Fund for International Decade

The Voluntary Fund for the Second International Decade of the World's Indigenous People, 2005–2014, established in General Assembly resolution 59/174 [YUN 2004, p. 799], continued to promote, support and implement the goals of the Second Decade in terms of promoting indigenous peoples' culture, education, health, human rights, environment and economic development. In May, the Bureau of the United Nations Permanent Forum on Indigenous Issues (see p. 749), serving as the Advisory Group for the Fund, considered project proposals for funding received by the Secretariat, in accordance with resolution 59/174. It proposed to award grants to 19 projects being implemented by indigenous organizations and related NGOs in Africa; Asia; Central and South America and the Caribbean; Eastern Europe, the Russian Federation, Central Asia and Transcaucasia; North America; and the Pacific.

Permanent Forum on Indigenous Issues

Report of Permanent Forum. The 16-member Permanent Forum on Indigenous Issues, established by Economic and Social Council resolution 2000/22 [YUN 2000, p. 731] to address indigenous issues relating to economic and social development, the environment, health, education and culture, and human rights, at its eighth session (New York, 18–29 May) [E/2009/43], considered as its theme "Indigenous peoples: development with culture and identity: articles 3 and 32 of the United Nations Declaration on the Rights of Indigenous Peoples". It had before it background reports relating to its work submitted by its secretariat and subsidiary mechanisms, Governments, UN system bodies, intergovernmental organizations, regional organizations and NGOs [E/C.19/2009/1–11]. The Forum recommended three draft decisions for adoption by the Economic and Social Council on: an international expert group meeting on the Forum's theme (see above); the dates of the Forum's ninth session; and the provisional agenda for that session. Matters brought to the Council's attention related to the recommendations of the Forum on; follow-up to the Forum's recommendations on economic and social development, indigenous women and the Second International Decade of the World's Indigenous People; economic and social development; the Arctic; future work of the Forum: and follow-up to its recommendations on implementation of the Declaration on the Rights of Indigenous Peoples and on dialogue with the Special Rapporteur on the situation of human

rights and fundamental freedoms of indigenous peoples and other special rapporteurs. The Forum held a half-day discussion on the Arctic and a comprehensive dialogue with six UN agencies and funds.

On 30 July [E/2009/99], the Economic and Social Council took note of the report of the Permanent Forum on its eighth session **(decision 2009/256)**. It authorized a three-day international expert group meeting on the theme "Indigenous peoples: development with culture and identity—articles 3 and 32 of the United Nations Declaration on the Rights of Indigenous Peoples" and requested that the results of the meeting be reported to the Permanent Forum at its ninth session **(decision 2009/253)**, which would be held from 19 to 30 April 2010 **(decision 2009/254)**. The Council also approved the provisional agenda for that session **(decision 2009/255)**.

Expert meetings and conferences

An international expert group meeting (New York, 14–16 January) [E/C.19/2009/2] discussed the role of the Permanent Forum in the implementation of article 42 of the United Nations Declaration on the Rights of Indigenous Peoples, which called on the UN system and States to promote respect for and full application of the provisions of the Declaration.

The 2009 meeting of the Inter-Agency Support Group on Indigenous Issues (Nairobi, 28–30 September) [E/C.19/2010/8], hosted by the United Nations Environment Programme and the United Nations Human Settlements Programme, examined indigenous rights and challenges in Africa, such as the effects of climate change, and preparations for the 2010 session of the Permanent Forum, including the development of a Support Group reflection paper on development with culture and identity.

Chapter III

Human rights country situations

In 2009, human rights situations of concern in Member States, particularly regarding alleged violations and how best to assist and guide Governments and national institutions in combating them, were addressed by the General Assembly and the Human Rights Council, and by special rapporteurs, special representatives of the Secretary-General and independent experts appointed to examine those situations.

Political developments in some African countries led to new opportunities for improving the human rights situation, while in others the conditions deteriorated. In Somalia, the election of a new President, the formation of a new Government of national unity, the expansion of Parliament, and the withdrawal of Ethiopian troops created momentum for further implementation of the 2008 Djibouti Agreement. Despite that progress, the human rights situation remained precarious. The need for strengthening security remained urgent, as the parties to the conflict continued to violate international humanitarian and human rights laws within a culture of impunity. In Sierra Leone, elections for local representatives were held with credible results. The Government launched justice sector reform, and projects were aimed at building capacity within that sector. In both the Democratic Republic of the Congo and the Sudan, the human rights situation remained grave and, according to reports by experts, deteriorated during the year. In the Sudan, despite some positive legislative developments, the situation remained critical, in particular with regard to the rights to life and security of the person, and the country appeared to lack the political will to ensure justice and accountability.

The human rights situation deteriorated markedly in Iran following the presidential election on 12 June. Following the announcement of results, tens of thousands took to the streets over several days in protest, and there were reports of at least seven protesters killed, many arrests and the excessive use of force by security forces. In general, there had been impediments to the fundamental rights enshrined in the 1979 Constitution; in particular, civil and political rights had seen negative developments.

In Myanmar, the human rights situation remained serious, despite the approval by referendum in 2008 of a new Constitution and the Government's affirmation that it would proceed towards national parliamentary elections in 2010 and would review existing laws for conformity to international standards. The Secretary-General visited the country on 3 and 4 July for discussions that focused on the release of all political prisoners, conditions for a political transition to a civilian and democratic government, improvement of socio-economic conditions, and regularization of the good offices process between Myanmar and the United Nations. According to the Special Rapporteur, the Government's seven-step road to democracy suffered a setback when Daw Aung San Suu Kyi, General Secretary of the National League for Democracy, was sentenced on 11 August 2009 to an additional 18-month house arrest, barring her from participating in the 2010 elections.

On 3 January, following rocket and mortar attacks on Southern Israel by Palestinian groups in Gaza, Israel launched a ground attack against the Gaza Strip. That led to the Human Rights Council convening a special session to consider the resulting violations of human rights. The Israeli military operation ended after 22 days. Estimates of the number of Palestinians killed ranged from 1,200 to 1,400 civilians, and 4 Israeli civilians were killed. Civilians were reported to be the target of Israeli attacks, as were Palestinian administrative buildings. The Council established a fact-finding mission on the operation which reported in September on its findings, particularly violations of humanitarian and human rights laws.

The Human Rights Council held three special sessions in 2009 on particular situations—its ninth special session (9 and 12 January) on human rights violations in the Occupied Palestinian Territory, particularly those emanating from the Israeli military attacks against the occupied Gaza Strip; its eleventh special session (26–27 May) on assistance to Sri Lanka for promoting and protecting human rights; and its twelfth special session (15–16 October) on the human rights situation in the Occupied Palestinian Territory, including East Jerusalem.

General aspects

In the 2009 annual report on the activities undertaken by the Office of the United Nations High Commissioner for Human Rights (OHCHR) [A/HRC/13/26], the High Commissioner provided an overview of its work at the country and regional levels, including its field presences and their efforts to respond to deteriorating human rights situations. The approach of OHCHR to addressing human rights concerns was through constructive dialogue with national counterparts, and through partnerships within the UN system and with regional organizations. At the country level, its work was conducted through human rights field presences, support for human rights mechanisms and dialogue between the High Commissioner and Member States—including through bilateral meetings, open or confidential communication, country visits by the High Commissioner, technical cooperation programmes and rapid-response operations.

In 2009, OHCHR had 56 field presences: 12 regional presences, 11 country offices, 15 human rights components in UN peace missions, and 18 human rights advisers in UN country teams. Regional presences included Regional Offices for Southern Africa (Pretoria, South Africa); East Africa (Addis Ababa, Ethiopia); West Africa (Dakar, Senegal); the Pacific (Suva, Fiji); the Middle East (Beirut, Lebanon); Central Asia (Bishkek, Kyrgyzstan); Southeast Asia (Bangkok, Thailand); Central America (Panama City); and South America (Santiago, Chile); in addition to the Subregional Centre for Human Rights and Democracy in Central Africa (Yaoundé, Cameroon). New offices established in 2009 were the United Nations Human Rights Training and Documentation Centre for South-West Asia and the Arab Region in Doha, Qatar, inaugurated in May, and the Regional Office for Europe in Brussels, Belgium, opened in October. Country offices were located in Bolivia, Cambodia, Colombia, Guatemala, Mexico, Nepal, Togo and Uganda. In addition, OHCHR had a presence in the Occupied Palestinian Territory and in Kosovo. In September an agreement was signed with Mauritania on the establishment of an OHCHR country office. The establishment of an OHCHR Regional Office for North Africa remained under discussion. Within peace missions, OHCHR supported human rights components in Afghanistan, Burundi, the Central African Republic, Chad, Côte d'Ivoire, the Democratic Republic of the Congo, Guinea-Bissau, Haiti, Iraq, Liberia, Sierra Leone, Somalia, the Sudan and Timor-Leste. Human rights advisers were posted in Albania, Burundi (covering the Great Lakes region), Ecuador, Georgia (covering the South Caucasus), Guinea, Indonesia, Kenya, Moldova, Nicaragua, Niger, Papua New Guinea, the Russian Federation, Rwanda, Serbia, Sri Lanka, Tajikistan and the former Yugoslav Republic of Macedonia. That number included a human rights adviser within the United Nations Office in West Africa.

Since the establishment of a rapid-response unit in 2006 [YUN 2006, p. 763], OHCHR had strengthened its capacity to act promptly on the ground to confront deteriorating human rights situations. It supported short-term missions and commissions of inquiry aimed at providing technical advice following crises, as well as for implementation of Human Rights Council resolutions. Through its rapid-response capacity, OHCHR provided a human rights officer to Honduras to respond to the political crisis, two such officers to Madagascar in the context of the political crisis, and four to Gabon to monitor the human rights situation during the presidential electoral period. Following the violence of 28 September in Conakry, Guinea, OHCHR provided support to the Secretary-General's commission of inquiry on those events (see p. 230). It provided operational and technical support to the United Nations Fact-Finding Mission on the Gaza Conflict established by the President of the Human Rights Council on 3 April (see p. 783). OHCHR continued to reinforce national human rights institutions in Member States.

Africa

Burundi

Report of High Commissioner. The High Commissioner for Human Rights on 31 August reported [A/HRC/12/43] to the Human Rights Council on the human rights situation and OHCHR activities in Burundi. The report noted that the highly politicized environment had manifested itself in restrictions on civil and political rights and in targeted violence. The legal framework for the protection of human rights, while significantly improved through a revised Criminal Code, had stagnated with respect to other laws. By those revisions, the Code abolished the death penalty, prohibited torture, strengthened the punishment of violence against women and children, and criminalized genocide, war crimes and crimes against humanity.

The consolidation of peace remained the main challenge facing Burundi in protecting human rights. In April, the only remaining armed group reached agreement on its combatants' integration into the national security forces. However, worrisome trends in the human rights situation included violations of freedom of expression, association and assembly, politically motivated assassinations, and the emergence of violent militant youth groups affiliated with political parties, particularly in view of scheduled national elections in 2010. Reports of restrictions on political rights increased between August 2008 and June 2009, including interference with meetings of opposition political parties and detention of opposition party members. Impunity remained prevalent. Justice, not granted in courts, tended to be claimed in the streets, and the judiciary lacked the means and capability to perform its functions. Arbitrary detention remained widespread, and torture, ill-treatment and abductions were reported. One of the most endemic human rights violations was sexual and gender-based violence, and most of the victims were children. The report made recommendations to the Government, including that it: undertake consultations on revising the Criminal Procedure Code; begin voter registration to ensure the right to vote to all those eligible; end violence for political purposes; ensure independence of the judiciary and accountability; prevent arbitrary detentions; strengthen mechanisms within security and defence forces for investigating human rights violations by their personnel; address sexual and gender-based violence; and establish a national human rights commission.

Report of independent expert. The independent expert on the human rights situation in Burundi, Akich Okola (Kenya), pursuant to a 2008 request of the Human Rights Council [YUN 2008, p. 862], in May issued a note [A/HRC/11/40] on the expected delay of his report.

Democratic Republic of the Congo

Report of thematic special procedures. In response to requests of the Human Rights Council [YUN 2008, p. 863], seven special procedures mandate-holders in March issued a combined report [A/HRC/10/59] on how best to assist technically the Democratic Republic of the Congo (DRC) in addressing the human rights situation. The authors were the Special Rapporteur on violence against women, its causes and consequences, the Representative of the Secretary-General on the human rights of internally displaced persons, the Special Rapporteur on the independence of judges and lawyers, the Special Rapporteur on the right of everyone to the enjoyment of the highest attainable standard of physical and mental health, the Special Rapporteur on the situation of human rights defenders, the Special Representative of the Secretary-General on the issue of human rights and transnational corporations and other business enterprises, and the Special Representative of the Secretary-General for children and armed conflict. They found that the human rights situation in the DRC had deteriorated since March 2008. In particular, systematic and gross human rights violations and grave breaches of humanitarian law were taking place in the east. The report highlighted forced and arbitrary displacement, the effect of the humanitarian crisis on economic, social and cultural rights, violence against women and girls, the situation of human rights defenders and the impact of armed conflict on children in the east. Impunity, the existence of non-State armed actors, the state of the security and justice sectors, illegal exploitation of natural resources, the political use of ethnic cleavages and the lack of equality for women were identified as root causes of human rights concerns.

Members of the armed forces and police continued to be responsible for serious violations, including summary executions, rape, torture and cruel, inhuman or degrading treatment. National security forces and armed groups, as well as political, judicial and administrative officials, targeted journalists and human rights defenders, subjecting them to threats, arbitrary arrest, detention and other forms of ill-treatment. Little progress had been made to ensure economic and social rights, such as health and education. There remained high rates of severe malnutrition among vulnerable groups, especially the poor, women and children. The Batwa, often referred to as "pygmies", were also marginalized.

The situation in eastern DRC had deteriorated in the past year, with evidence of systematic and gross violations of civilians' human rights. By the end of 2008, the Office for the Coordination of Humanitarian Affairs (OCHA) estimated that 1,373,169 Congolese had been displaced in the east, mostly due to clashes between armed groups. The strength of the United Nations Organization Mission in the Democratic Republic of the Congo (MONUC) had proved to be inadequate for protecting civilians in the east. The displaced population often lacked basic food, potable water, shelter, health care or basic education, and a large percentage of the displaced had been cut off from humanitarian aid. The prevalence of sexual violence could be explained by the climate of impunity, absence of the rule of law and the normalization of violence as an aspect of women's oppression.

The authors outlined priority objectives for Government action along with technical assistance needs, focusing on fighting impunity and strengthening the law enforcement and justice sectors, reforming the security sector, preventing recruitment of children by armed actors, socially reintegrating children already recruited, protecting women's rights, ensuring gender equality, addressing the economic root causes of human rights violations, such as the illegal exploitation of natural resources, protecting the rights of the displaced and minorities, providing access to health care, especially for marginalized groups, and strengthening State and civil society structures to promote and protect human rights. The authors recommended compensation for victims and transitional justice for violations that occurred between 1993 and 2003. They called for benchmarks as an accountability measure that would help steer donor priorities. They urged the Human Rights Council to include the human rights dimension in peacebuilding through a follow-up and monitoring mechanism. The Council was also urged to create a special procedures mandate on the human rights situation in the DRC, in particular for areas threatened by conflict.

Report of High Commissioner (April). In a report [A/HRC/10/58 & Corr.1] issued on 2 April on the situation of human rights and the activities of OHCHR in the DRC, the High Commissioner said that acute conflicts and long-standing structural challenges had worsened the already precarious living conditions of the Congolese. In eastern DRC, Government control was often challenged or replaced by various armed groups, resulting in or perpetuating conflicts that engendered serious violations of human rights, such as arbitrary executions, sexual violence, torture, abductions and pillaging. At the same time, the authorities often repressed those critical of their policies, and a climate of intimidation hampered any critical dialogue, political tolerance or free expression. Police and army officers commonly used their position to extract payment from civilians, often through the use of arbitrary arrests and physical force. The judiciary lacked adequate resources and faced widespread corruption and political and military interference. During the reporting period, the United Nations Joint Human Rights Office in the Democratic Republic of the Congo (UNJHRO) stepped up its monitoring and advocacy activities. In areas of armed conflict, it took part in joint protection teams established by MONUC to enhance its capacity to protect civilians under imminent threat of physical violence. A comprehensive strategy to combat sexual violence was finalized in late 2008. OHCHR was undertaking a mapping exercise to create an inventory of the most serious violations of human rights and international humanitarian law committed between 1993 and 2003, as a means to address justice and accountability issues and to make recommendations for transitional justice. Despite the peace agreements signed in early 2008 [YUN 2008, p. 120], large-scale human rights violations increased, particularly in eastern DRC. Impunity and the passivity of the judiciary remained obstacles to improving the human rights situation.

The High Commissioner recommended that the DRC: prioritize resources for the realization of human rights; increase training and awareness-raising for army and police officers; set up follow-up committees for human rights violations committed by the main armed groups; establish an independent national human rights commission; enable the judiciary to fulfil its constitutional role in full independence; ensure that UNJHRO had access to all prisons and detention centres in accordance with the mandate of MONUC; execute arrest warrants of the International Criminal Court and combat impunity domestically; allocate adequate resources to the penitentiary system; clarify charges against persons held in pre-trial detention; release those detained solely for their opinions or for belonging to the opposition; and combat sexual violence through such means as the Comprehensive Strategy to Combat Sexual Violence adopted in March 2009.

The High Commissioner recommended that the international community: assist the DRC in reforming the justice and security sectors, including by implementing a transitional justice strategy based on the recommendations of the OHCHR-led mapping exercise of human rights violations; assist the authorities in controlling resources from the extractive industry and other business activities, including by refraining from participation in the illegal exploitation of natural resources and by holding accountable those involved in such illegal activities; encourage reorientation of peacekeeping activities towards protection of civilians; engage with the authorities and armed groups in reaching a peace agreement that included mechanisms to deal with human rights violations; and ensure that adequate resources were allocated for implementing the Comprehensive Strategy to Combat Sexual Violence.

Human Rights Council action. On 27 March [A/64/53 (res. 10/33)], by a recorded vote of 33 to none, with 14 abstentions, the Human Rights Council welcomed the DRC's commitment to pursue technical cooperation with the thematic representatives and special rapporteurs. It welcomed the Government's cooperation with the thematic special procedures mandate-holders and its invitation to a number of them to make recommendations on technical assistance on human rights issues. The Council encouraged the DRC to finalize the establishment of a national commission for human rights, and invited the Government to promote human rights education at school and in academia, the armed forces, the police and the security services. Noting the report of the seven special procedures, the Council invited them to report again on the situation in 2010. Also noting the High Commissioner's report, it invited her Office to report again in 2010. The international community was urged to support the establishment of a local cooperation mechanism by the DRC, the High Commissioner and the Human Rights Section of MONUC.

Further report of High Commissioner. In a report [A/HRC/13/64 & Corr.1] submitted pursuant to the Council's resolution, the High Commissioner acknowledged the tentative efforts of the Government to align its policy and practice with its international human rights obligations. However, improvement in the human rights situation, critical to achieving a well-functioning democracy, had been limited and the human rights situation remained problematic. Numerous recommendations had been made to the Government, yet very limited progress had been made in their implementation. Consequently, the Congolese people remained insecure in enjoying even their most fundamental rights. As an emerging "recommendation fatigue" could be observed, the report did not make new recommendations; rather it recalled conclusions and recommendations made in previous reports to the Council. The report assessed the Government's response to those recommendations from March to November to determine the causes for their insufficient implementation and to identify setbacks. Obstacles to implementing the recommendations included poor governance, absence of the rule of law and lack of political will. All public sectors were under-resourced, and the Government failed to ensure basic economic and social rights, such as health care and education. A dysfunctional and understaffed justice system contributed to a climate of impunity for human rights violations and undermined the security of citizens. The insufficient allocation of funding to civil servants, the penitentiary system and State security forces fed systemic corruption and fostered the "privatization" of State functions. The Government must take coherent, systematic and human rights-focused measures, with the assistance of local, national and international stakeholders, to implement the recommendations that had already been made in order to respect, protect and fulfil the human rights of its citizens.

During the period under review, UNJHRO took steps against arbitrary and illegal arrests and detentions to prompt the Government to provide the protection that detainees were entitled to under Congolese law and international human rights law. It visited numerous holding cells and prisons throughout the country, in several cases with national prosecutors, to verify the legality of detentions, and obtained the release of scores of people who had been illegally detained. UNJHRO made frequent visits to prisons throughout the country, including joint visits with the Minister for Human Rights in some provinces, and documented crumbling cells, lack of food and medical care, corruption and unqualified prison staff. To counter sexual violence and impunity, the Office monitored and reported on cases of sexual violence to ensure that those responsible, particularly those in the security forces, were prosecuted. The Office provided information to military justice officials, the Defence Ministry, and the hierarchy of the national armed force and national police on the human rights violations perpetrated by members of the armed forces and the police. It provided logistical and substantive support for joint investigation missions to Congolese civilian and military justice officials. The Office paid special attention to allegations of human rights violations against human rights activists, journalists, victims and witnesses, as they were often the target of repression by the authorities for speaking out against government policy or the problematic realities in the country. Besides intervening in such cases, UNJHRO also took measures to prevent them. To increase the judicial response to human rights violations, UNJHRO provided technical assistance in drafting laws, as well

as in completing judicial reform through the establishment of high courts.

Liberia

In September 2008, the independent expert on technical cooperation and advisory services in Liberia, Charlotte Abaka (Ghana), presented her report on the situation of human rights in Liberia to the Human Rights Council [YUN 2008, p. 864]. The mandate of the independent expert was not renewed; instead, in resolution 9/16 [ibid., p. 865], the Council invited OHCHR to report to the Council at its twelfth session on the progress made in the human rights situation in Liberia and the activities undertaken there.

Report of OHCHR. In a report issued in August [A/HRC/12/42] covering the period from September 2008 to June 2009, OHCHR reviewed the human rights situation in the country. The Government had made some advances towards improving institutional human rights protection, including drafting strategic plans for reform of the judiciary and corrections sectors, and finalizing a strategic plan for the police. The legislature passed amendments to the act establishing the Independent National Commission on Human Rights (INCHR). The Truth and Reconciliation Commission concluded its public hearings and produced a final report (see p. 194). Nevertheless, serious human rights concerns persisted. Institutions in the criminal justice sector remained weak due to shortages of qualified personnel, insufficient funding, lack of infrastructure, poor administration and corruption. Despite efforts to combat sexual and gender-based violence, cases of rape and other sexual crimes were prevalent. Harmful traditional practices, including trials by ordeal, ritual killings and female genital mutilation, were common. Protection of children's rights was inadequate and children suffered violence, both physical and sexual. Although the humanitarian situation had improved, much of the population had limited or no access to education, health care or social welfare.

OHCHR recommended that the Government: appoint commissioners to INCHR and ensure that it was functional; establish a commission to facilitate land reform and settle disputes; provide resources to criminal justice institutions and training for legal system personnel; clarify the status of Justices of the Peace, as their continued illegal operation violated international standards on fair trial; provide training on juvenile justice for magistrates and establish a juvenile justice system; close unauthorized detention facilities and open prisons, where needed; raise awareness on child development so as to prevent child neglect; and prohibit violence against children. The international community was called on to work with the Government to raise awareness of the harmful effects of traditional practices such as female genital mutilation, trials by ordeal, ritual killings and witchcraft, and to provide assistance to improve the human rights situation and consolidate peace and security.

Sierra Leone

Reports of High Commissioner. The High Commissioner, in a report of 4 March [A/HRC/10/52] on human rights assistance to Sierra Leone, described developments in 2008. Sierra Leone registered a positive trend towards respect for civil and political rights, although concerns remained in the areas of sexual violence, legal and constitutional reform, and capacity-building of justice sector institutions. Elections for local representatives were held on 5 July 2008, resulting in a generally credible outcome. Political, legal and security institutions made progress towards securing respect for the right to life and security of the person. The moratorium on the execution of the death penalty remained in force. Some progress was made in protecting the rights of women and children. A change of attitude by some traditional leaders regarding female genital mutilation was noted—they committed not to subject girls younger than 18 years to the practice. Acts were drafted on women's rights and protection in cases of domestic violence. The Government launched a Justice Sector Reform Strategy and Investment Plan for 2008–2010. Projects under the United Nations Peacebuilding Fund aimed at building capacity within the justice sector, operationalizing the national Human Rights Commission and establishing a reparations programme. The Anti-Corruption Commission was strengthened by legislation passed in August 2008, giving it prosecutorial powers and enabling it to initiate proceedings. The United Nations Integrated Peacebuilding Office in Sierra Leone (UNIPSIL) (see p. 213) assisted national institutions in promoting and monitoring good governance, human rights, democratic institutions and the rule of law, and provided policy advice, joint programming, training and material support. Still, serious human rights concerns persisted. Police were not held accountable in many cases of arbitrary arrest and detention. The recommendations of the Truth and Reconciliation Commission were not fully implemented. The High Commissioner urged the Government to complete the constitutional reform process, implement the outstanding Truth and Reconciliation Commission recommendations [YUN 2004, p. 219], establish a fund for reparations to victims of the conflict, provide financial support for the Human Rights Commission, enhance press freedom, protect women's rights by enacting laws on sexual offences and on matrimony, develop a land reform policy and include mechanisms for resolution of land disputes.

In a further report covering developments in 2009 [A/HRC/13/28], the High Commissioner said that Sierra Leone continued to progress in building its capacity for human rights promotion and protection. The passage of the Chieftaincy Act, the ratification of the Convention on the Rights of Persons with Disabilities, and various sensitization programmes organized on the Child Rights Act, the Domestic Violence Act, and the Registration of Customary Marriage and the Divorce Act were notable in that regard. The capacity of civil society organizations, government officials and the Human Rights Commission was developed through training and other activities.

Progress was made in strengthening the rule of law. The Anti-Corruption Commission took action against corrupt practices. Significant activities were carried out to strengthen the justice sector institutions, including the judiciary, prisons and the police. Progress was also made in improving prison conditions through the supply of necessary logistics and the provision of water and regular food supplies. However, challenges remained, as detention by police for periods beyond the lawful detention period, the poor condition of police detention cells, inadequate supplies of medicine in prisons and overcrowding in some prisons continued to pose a threat to the protection of the rights of accused persons. The Government adopted the second poverty reduction strategy, which aimed at improving the socio-economic conditions of people. It also adopted a strategy to address the challenges in the health sector. However, effective implementation of those strategies depended on the mobilization of resources by the Government, as well as on the support of international partners. The law reform process, including constitutional review, was making little progress. The issues of the separation of Attorney General from the Ministry of Justice, the removal of the death penalty from the Constitution, the amendment of discriminatory provisions of the Constitution and the review of the seditious libel provision of the Public Order Act had yet to be addressed. In the area of women's and children's rights, customs and traditions continued to bar full implementation of certain laws, such as the Child Rights Act and the Domestic Violence Act. Capacity constraints on investigating authorities, the low rate of prosecution, out of court settlements and interference by traditional leaders in judicial matters undermined the judicial process, thus creating room for impunity, particularly regarding sexual and gender-based violence.

In the light of those challenges, the High Commissioner urged the Government: to speed up the implementation of the recommendations of the Truth and Reconciliation Commission, including through the allocation of adequate resources, and to mobilize resources to implement the reparations programme; to fast-track the law reform process; to prosecute security officials involved in violating human rights; to improve the conditions of service of judges and magistrates to strengthen the independence of the judiciary and prosecutors, and to fill vacant positions of magistrates and prosecutors; to provide adequate budget resources to the Human Rights Commission, and to implement the recommendations made by the Commission in its state of human rights reports for 2007 and 2008; to adopt a clear land policy, including with regard to the demarcation and registration of land; to repeal the criminal libel provision of the Public Order Act of 1965; and to adopt a national strategy for eliminating violence against women. The High Commissioner urged international partners to continue supporting the Government in addressing the human rights challenges and, in particular, to assist in funding the reparations programme.

Somalia

Report of independent expert (February). On 24 February [A/HRC/10/85], the independent expert on the situation of human rights in Somalia, Shamsul Bari (Bangladesh), reported to the Human Rights Council after two visits to the Horn of Africa in 2008. The election of a new President, Sheikh Sharif Ahmed, the formation of a new Government of national unity, the expansion of Parliament and the withdrawal of Ethiopian troops in January 2009 created momentum for implementing the 2008 Djibouti Agreement [YUN 2008, p. 281]. Elsewhere in Somalia, elections in "Puntland" in January resulted in the election of a new President and a government which expressed commitment to democratization. Nevertheless, the situation remained unpredictable. The need for strengthening security, including through the development of Somali transitional forces and a new civilian police force, remained urgent. The African Union (AU) urged reinforcement of its Mission in Somalia (AMISOM) (see p. 293) and asked the United Nations to provide financial and political support. The parties to the conflict continued to commit serious violations of international humanitarian and human rights law, within a culture of impunity and a lack of accountability. Indiscriminate violence and attacks against civilians continued, including the use of heavy artillery, mortars and roadside bombs; targeted attacks, abduction and killings of aid workers and human rights defenders; smuggling and human trafficking; looting and property destruction; and sexual and gender-based violence. The widespread violence led to an increase in displaced persons, estimated at 1.1 million as at September 2008. The right to food was severely affected by drought, and the rights to education, health, shelter, water and sanitation were seriously challenged.

According to the independent expert, the regime for the protection of human rights and humanitarian law in Somalia was one of the most challenged in the world, after almost two decades of armed conflicts and the consequent absence of law and order. He recommended that the new Government: make human rights the foundation of the transition with a focus on protecting lives; provide security to allow humanitarian access; reopen schools and develop health care; and ensure appropriate training and structures for security forces. He encouraged the Security Council to establish an international commission of inquiry to investigate violations of human rights and humanitarian law, commended the United Nations Political Office for Somalia (UNPOS) (see p. 292) for its commitment to contribute towards ending impunity, and called on international organizations to assist Somali refugees. OHCHR was called upon to collaborate with other organizations to monitor human rights abuses in refugee camps in Djibouti, Kenya and Yemen and identify solutions.

Human Rights Council action. On 27 March 2009 [A/64/53 (res. 10/32)], the Human Rights Council, while welcoming the positive developments made in the Djibouti peace process in Somalia, expressed concern at the human rights and humanitarian situation and called for an immediate end to all violations. The Council invited the independent expert to continue his work through September 2009. It encouraged OHCHR to reach an agreement with the Somali authorities on technical cooperation and human and institutional capacity-building in human rights. The international community was called upon to provide support to the Somali institutions to enhance their capacity.

Report of independent expert (September). As requested by the Council, the independent expert in September reported [A/HRC/12/44] on the situation in Somalia from March to August, stating that condiions had worsened in recent months, with renewed violence and bloodshed. The Somalis with whom the independent expert met almost universally expressed their dismay at the fact that the international community's attention to Somalia remained woefully limited. However, during his third mission to Somalia and neighbouring countries (1–13 June), the expert observed new hope among Somalis and others in the region. Contrary to the situation in November–December 2008 when he was unable to visit Somalia, as the entire country was under the highest UN security alert, in June 2009 he was able to visit the north-western and north-eastern regions, namely Somaliland and Puntland.

The independent expert recommended that the Government demonstrate that it was taking all measures possible to protect basic rights, such as the right to life and safety, including ensuring that its own security forces were not the source of violations. An excellent beginning would be to dismiss officials and commanders who were known for their corruption, inefficiency and human rights violations. Measures to end the deep-rooted culture of impunity and to ensure accountability for all Government officials must be a priority. Capacity-building and the training of Government forces and officials on human rights and humanitarian law principles should continue. The AU should consider providing AMISOM with a mandate to protect civilians, including, if necessary, through the use of force.

Human Rights Council action. On 2 October [A/65/53 (res. 12/26)], the Council, expressing concern at the deteriorating human rights and humanitarian conditions in Somalia, in particular indiscriminate attacks against civilians by armed groups, called on all parties to allow unhindered access of civilians and non-combatants to humanitarian assistance. Noting the plight of internally displaced people and refugees, it urged all parties to refrain from violence against civilians and to prevent human rights abuses. The Council stressed the need to implement technical assistance and institutional capacity-building programmes to support Somali-led efforts to identify the best means for prevention of and accountability for abuses. The Council renewed the mandate of the independent expert for one year and requested him to report in 2010.

Sudan

Report of Special Rapporteur. In a report issued in June [A/HRC/11/14], the Special Rapporteur on the situation of human rights in the Sudan, Sima Samar (Afghanistan), covered events from August 2008 to May 2009 in four regions—northern Sudan, Darfur, southern Sudan and the transitional areas. Despite some positive legislative developments, the human rights situation remained critical, in particular with regard to the rights to life and security of the person, and the whole country was marked by a lack of political will and capacity to ensure justice and accountability. Arbitrary arrest and detention by the intelligence service, military and police was widespread. The administration of justice was restricted by an inadequate number of qualified police, prosecutors and judges; lack of basic communication and transportation equipment for such officials; prosecutors and judges unfamiliar with international human rights standards; and challenging distances and terrain preventing access to justice for rural populations. In northern Sudan, there was an increase in arrests, harassment, intimidation, ill-treatment and alleged torture of human rights defenders and humanitarian workers. The human rights consequences of the 10 May 2008 attack on Omdurman, Khartoum [YUN

2008, p. 236], by the Darfur-based Justice and Equality Movement (JEM) continued to be felt. The announcement of death sentences following unfair trials for a further 41 alleged JEM combatants brought the total number of such sentences to 91 as at May 2009. As the conflict in Darfur continued, violations of human rights and international humanitarian law continued unabated. Civilians were attacked by Government security forces, Government-supported militia groups and armed movements. As in other parts of the Sudan, sexual and gender-based violence continued to be reported, in particular in internally displaced persons camps. In northern Sudan, a crackdown on human rights defenders had resulted in reduced capacity for human rights monitoring and reporting from national partners. In southern Sudan, hundreds of civilians had died during armed clashes and inter-tribal cattle raiding. Inter-tribal fighting had resulted in several hundred civilian deaths, and more than 5,000 persons were displaced.

Although the Government of National Unity and the Government of Southern Sudan had taken some positive steps in law reform, there was little if any improvement of the human rights situation on the ground. Interlocutors in Khartoum and Darfur reported a climate of fear and an inability to exercise freedom of speech or association for fear of reprisal. Land and air attacks by Government forces on civilians in Darfur took place during the reporting period. An increased number of arbitrary arrests and detention, incommunicado detention and torture of human rights defenders and humanitarian workers were documented in northern Sudan. In southern Sudan, the deaths of hundreds of civilians in tribal conflict and attacks by the Lord's Resistance Army were of particular concern.

The Special Rapporteur recommended that the Government of National Unity: ensure that human rights defenders and humanitarian workers were not subjected to maltreatment; review national laws in order to guarantee their compatibility with human rights obligations; establish the National Human Rights Commission through a transparent procedure; ensure that all allegations of violations of human rights and humanitarian law were investigated; provide access to detention places to UN human rights officials; ensure deployment of remaining components for the African Union-United Nations Hybrid Operation in Darfur (UNAMID) so that it could fulfil its mandate to protect civilians; establish an inquiry into allegations of deliberate killings of civilians by security forces in Abyei; and address the absence of justice institutions in the transitional areas. The Government of Southern Sudan was called upon to: address the increasing levels of conflict which resulted in massive loss of life and livelihoods through deployment of army and police forces; address impunity and investigate all allegations of human rights violations, including from the Abyei clashes, and of abuse of power; and ensure adequate means for the administration of justice and rule of law. Other recommendations were made to armed groups and non-State actors, as well as to the international community. The Special Rapporteur recommended that the United Nations, through UN-AMID and the United Nations Mission in the Sudan (UNMIS), protect civilians and provide support to the Government of National Unity.

An addendum [A/HRC/11/14/Add.1] assessed the implementation of the recommendations made by the group of experts on the Sudan [YUN 2007, pp. 806–807]. The Special Rapporteur concluded that little progress had been made. While a few recommendations had been followed, others in the area of humanitarian access had taken a step back with the expulsion of international non-governmental organizations (NGOs) and attacks on human rights defenders.

Human Rights Council action. On 18 June [A/64/53 (res. 11/10)], by a recorded vote of 20 to 18, with 9 abstentions, the Council acknowledged the steps by the Government of National Unity to strengthen the human rights legal and institutional framework, principally in law reform, and to hold general elections in February 2010. It welcomed the Government's measures to implement the recommendations of the group of experts, including deployment of police in Darfur and the sentencing of several perpetrators of human rights abuses, but noted that some had not been implemented. The Council called on the signatories of the Darfur Peace Agreement to comply with their obligations, and on non-signatory parties to commit to the peace process. It welcomed the Government's invitation to the High Commissioner to visit the country and its deployment of more than 75 human rights monitors throughout the Sudan. The Council created the mandate of an independent expert on the situation of human rights in the Sudan for one year, to assume the mandate of the Special Rapporteur, who should engage with the new human rights forums in the Sudan and with the AU, UNMIS and UNAMID.

On 2 October, the Council appointed Mohamed Chande Othman (United Republic of Tanzania) as independent expert.

Americas

Bolivia

Reports of High Commissioner. As per the agreement signed in 2007 between OHCHR and the Government, the High Commissioner in March reported [A/HRC/10/31/Add.2] on the human rights situation and the activities of her office in Bolivia in 2008. OHCHR-Bolivia carried out 41 field missions to

monitor human rights developments, and also provided advisory services and training to Government institutions and civil society. In particular, OHCHR-Bolivia provided technical comments on the new draft constitution and various legislative proposals and provided technical assistance to the Ministry of Justice in elaborating the recently adopted National Human Rights Action Plan. OHCHR-Bolivia welcomed positive steps taken by the Government in the field of economic, social and cultural rights, including the "dignity pension"—a new non-contributory benefit for persons over the age of 60—and Bono Juancito Pinto social programmes, as well as the "Yo, sí puedo" ("Yes I can") literacy initiative. The United Nations Declaration on the Rights of Indigenous Peoples was enacted as law and those rights were being incorporated into public policies and programmes. However, despite progress, challenges remained. A controversial Constituent Assembly process that took place in 2007 created political tensions in 2008. The quest for autonomy by the departments in the south and the east exacerbated antagonisms. At the height of tensions was the Pando massacre on 11 September, where at least 11 persons, mostly indigenous people, were killed and which led the Government to declare a state of emergency in the department. In October 2008, the Government and the opposition reached an agreement on changes to the new Constitution, including on issues of departmental autonomy. There was an increase of reported acts and practices of racism and discrimination against indigenous persons; attacks against human rights defenders; undermining of freedom of expression and the press; and instances of excessive use of force by security forces, the weakening of the administration of justice and interference in due process.

The High Commissioner called on the Government, the prefectures, Congress and other political actors to promote tolerant attitudes and to address political, social and regional demands in a constructive manner in order to prevent political violence. The authorities should prosecute all cases of human rights violations, combat impunity and comply with judicial decisions. Other recommendations concerned security, indigenous rights, racism and discrimination, human rights defenders, and freedom of expression.

Reporting on the human rights situation in 2009 [A/HRC/13/26/Add.2], the High Commissioner said that a new Constitution had been adopted on 25 January, providing for numerous human rights and incorporating the collective rights of indigenous peoples. General elections were held on 6 December, with high voter participation leading to the re-election of President Evo Morales. Economic, social and cultural rights were reflected in the new Constitution and, compared with 2008, there was an overall improvement in the human rights situation. There was less political violence, although political division between the Government and the opposition continued throughout the year, with consequences for the human rights situation. Problems affecting the rule of law and the judicial system became more acute in 2009. Despite Government efforts, indigenous peoples continued to register adverse social and economic living conditions and some were subjected to servitude and forced labour. In the fight against impunity, the search for the remains of those who disappeared during the military dictatorships, the start of the trial against former President Gonzalo Sánchez de Lozada and others, and the beginning of reparation payments to victims in that case represented significant advances. Progress was still needed in reparation to victims of other violations. Investigations were ongoing into the Pando massacre of September 2008 and into racist incidents in Sucre in May 2008. The judicial system was experiencing an institutional crisis amid political division between the Government and the opposition, while the failure to fill senior judicial posts continued to paralyse the Constitutional Court. OHCHR monitored human rights developments and gave attention to judicial developments in human rights cases, attacks on freedom of expression and human rights defenders, and human rights issues during the national referendum and the general elections. Some progress was noted in implementing the National Human Rights Action Plan, adopted in 2008, including the installation of the National Human Rights Council and efforts to combat racism and discrimination.

Among her recommendations, the High Commissioner called on judicial authorities to investigate and prosecute all cases of human rights violations reported in 2008, ensuring that victims had access to justice and were guaranteed reparation, in particular with regard to the incidents in Sucre and the massacre in Pando; and to investigate whether the actions taken by the police on 11 September 2008 in Pando were appropriate to avoid the escalation of violence, prevent human rights violations and protect victims. She urged the development of legislation to strengthen human rights, in particular of indigenous peoples, and called for consultations and environmental impact analyses of extraction and development projects in indigenous areas. The Government was encouraged to reinforce measures on eradicating contemporary forms of slavery, in particular conditions to which Guaraní families and communities were subjected, and to overcome manifestations of racism and discrimination. The High Commissioner called for measures to combat impunity and ensure the rule of law through such means as establishing transparent procedures for appointing judicial authorities, guaranteeing reparation for victims of human rights violations, and bringing to justice those responsible for such violations, in-

cluding incidents that occurred during the electoral campaigns. Impartial investigations should be held on the alleged terrorist group in Santa Cruz and on allegations of excessive use of force by security officials. The Government was urged to adopt a plan to prevent and sanction lynching, and to investigate promptly cases of lynching. The High Commissioner called on law enforcement authorities to ensure that human rights defenders enjoyed full protection, and urged authorities to investigate attacks on journalists and to guarantee freedom of expression. She recommended that the Legislative Assembly eliminate the crime of contempt for legally constituted authorities from Bolivia's criminal legislation. The Government was urged to promote improvement of access to health and education, particularly in rural areas, and to end forced labour of children.

Colombia

Report of High Commissioner. In a report on the situation of human rights in Colombia in 2009 [A/HRC/13/72], the High Commissioner described the main developments in the country within the framework of the 1996 agreement between the Government and OHCHR. She noted that significant progress had been made in the reduction of complaints of extrajudicial executions and the prosecution of members of Congress and public officials for alleged links with paramilitary organizations. The full realization of human rights, however, continued to be affected by an internal armed conflict exacerbated by organized violence related to drug trafficking. That situation had negatively affected the functioning of democratic institutions and the socio-economic development of the country. An increase in killing rates was reported in some cities as well as a rise in violence against civilians from armed groups. Other developments that affected human rights were serious irregularities involving the Department of National Security; ongoing tension between the Government and the Supreme Court; difficulties in achieving more releases of kidnapped policemen and politicians held by the Revolutionary Armed Forces of Colombia-People's Army (FARC-EP); disregard for international humanitarian law by guerrilla groups and their attacks on the civilian population; and the political polarization fuelled by a possible referendum that could allow President Alvaro Uribe to run for a third term. Problems remained in the administration of justice, illegal activities of the intelligence services, violations and abuse of human rights defenders and journalists, alleged links of members of Congress and public officials with paramilitary organizations, extrajudicial executions, an increase in sexual violence, torture and other cruel treatment, enforced disappearances, expansion of illegal armed groups after the demobilization of paramilitary organizations, and increased forced displacement. Other areas of concern were the need for full realization of economic, social and cultural rights and the discrimination and marginalization of Afro-Colombian and indigenous populations. OHCHR-Colombia received 1,387 complaints during the year and followed up on 1,279. The High Commissioner called on the parties to the conflict to abide by international humanitarian law and insisted that illegal armed groups release all kidnapped persons, stop child recruitment and release all recruited children. She called on the Government to protect victims, witnesses and judicial officials involved in the prosecution of extrajudicial executions, and requested adherence to the limitations of military jurisdiction. The Government was urged to protect civilians from violence perpetuated by illegal armed groups and to sanction public officials whose statements put at risk the work of human rights defenders.

Communication. On 2 February [A/HRC/10/G/4], Colombia transmitted to the Human Rights Council its observations on the 2008 report of the High Commissioner [YUN 2008, p. 870]. Colombia described the report as a full and comprehensive picture of the workings of human rights and international humanitarian law in the country.

Guatemala

Report of High Commissioner. Reporting on the work of OHCHR in Guatemala in 2009 [A/HRC/13/26/Add.1], the High Commissioner said that the Office monitored the human rights situation and provided assistance to State institutions and civil society. During 2009, Guatemala experienced political instability, social unrest and persistent and increasing violence and insecurity. OHCHR-Guatemala followed the impact of the security situation on human rights, as well as the challenges met in fighting against impunity, in strengthening the rule of law, and in combating discrimination and poverty. The report addressed the issues of insecurity and the right to life, rule of law, violence against women, attacks against human rights defenders, impunity, racism and discrimination, transitional justice, and economic, social and cultural rights. The heads of three branches of the State signed in April the National Agreement for the Advancement of Security and Justice, containing 101 commitments that could serve as a strategy to overcome human rights challenges. State institutions remained fragile and were unable to assume their role in preventing violence. Security was provided in great part by private companies over which there was minimal control, and illegal armed groups committed abuses. The police reported 6,498 violent deaths in 2009, compared with 6,244 in 2008, and 119 cases of lynching, an increase from 56. The number of violent deaths of women amounted to 720 in 2009, and do-

mestic violence complaints increased to 48,437, from 37,358 in 2008. In February, Congress passed a law on sexual violence and trafficking in persons. In the justice sector, legislation was passed concerning the system for the selection and promotion of judges and others. Despite the opening of new courts in 2009, access to justice remained limited due to insufficient geographic coverage of the justice system. The High Commissioner called for strengthening the legislative framework for protecting human rights, protecting the right to life, consolidating the rule of law, combating impunity, protecting the rights of women and indigenous peoples, and improving the enjoyment of economic, social and cultural rights. She called on the Government: to ratify international conventions on human rights; to ensure that the police assumed its public security role and that no private citizen or company assumed that role; to ensure access to justice based on non-discrimination, transparency, celerity, independence and impartiality, as well as on multicultural and linguistic sensitivity; to realize the rights to food and free education; and to improve human rights statistical information systems.

Report of Secretary-General. The Secretary-General, in response to General Assembly resolution 63/19 [YUN 2008, p. 333], reported on 23 September [A/64/370] on the activities of the International Commission against Impunity in Guatemala (see p. 312), a non-UN body established in 2006 and funded through voluntary contributions. The key goal of the Commission was to support and strengthen Guatemalan State institutions in investigating and prosecuting crimes by illegal security forces and clandestine security organizations. During the reporting period, the Commission made progress in criminal prosecutions and investigations, as well as in obtaining the approval of important legal reforms. A Special Prosecutor's Office was created in September 2008 to investigate cases within the scope of the Commission's mandate. The Commission had been accepted as a complementary prosecutor in nine cases, including a case in which a Nicaraguan bus was burned and 16 people died, and a case against former President Alfonso Portillo. At the same time, the Commission faced challenges to its authority, resulting in delays and appeals. The Commission recommended policies and legal reforms to help eradicate clandestine security organizations, prevent trafficking in persons, fight corruption and establish disciplinary measures in the criminal justice sector. It advocated for the selection of suitable magistrates to the Supreme Court, whose members were selected by Congress on 30 September 2009. As the profile of the Commission had increased, so had the security risks facing it, and ensuring the safety of its staff was one of its greatest challenges. At the request of Guatemala, the Secretary-General agreed in April to extend the Commission's mandate until 4 September 2011. He renewed the appointment of Carlos Castresana (Spain) as Commissioner.

Haiti

Report of independent expert. In a report of 26 March [A/HRC/11/5], the independent expert on the situation of human rights in Haiti, Michel Forst (France), reviewed developments from January 2008 to February 2009. He stated that the appointment of the Prime Minister, the installation of the Government and the adoption of a policy statement by Parliament were generally viewed as signs of the re-establishment of constitutional legality. In February 2009, President René Préval set up a commission for drafting proposals to reform the Constitution. Progress was made with the passing of framework laws on the reform of the judicial profession, the Supreme Council of the Judiciary and the independence of the Judicial Training College, but the reforms were stagnating and much remained to be done to establish the rule of law. The keystone of the reform of the judicial system was the appointment of the President of the Court of Cassation, but that decision had not been made. The security situation had improved, the number of kidnappings had fallen and the main gang bosses had been arrested; nevertheless, the situation remained precarious. The reform of the national police and the vetting process begun by it with the support of the United Nations Stabilization Mission in Haiti (MINUSTAH) (see p. 326) were a major test of the rule of law. The aim was doubling police strength by 2011 to provide 14,000 well-trained officers. The relationship between the population and the police was characterized by suspicion, accusations of brutality, human rights violations and complicity with criminal elements. Other human rights issues included: overcrowding and mismanagement in places of detention; violence against women and girls; lynching and extrajudicial arrests; mass expulsions of migrants and labour exploitation; detention of Haitian nationals expelled from other countries after committing a crime; and economic, social and cultural rights.

The independent expert made recommendations on the judicial system, calling for a judicial inspectorate composed of judges to ensure proper court functioning, and for two specialized chambers to deal with serious political offences and economic and financial crimes. Other recommendations called for improvements in youth imprisonment and children's rights, better youth crime prevention strategies, new prisons to relieve overcrowding, adoption of the law on violence against women including domestic violence, greater attention to certification of police officers and monitoring of police procedures.

Honduras

Human Rights Council action. On 1 October [A/65/53 (res. 12/14)], the Human Rights Council condemned the human rights violations in Honduras since the coup d'état on 28 June (see p. 314), and in particular following the return of President José Manuel Zelaya Rosales on 21 September. Such violations had been reported by several special procedures of the Council and by regional organizations. The Council called for the immediate end to all human rights violations and for the unconditional respect for human rights and fundamental freedoms, as well as restoration of democracy and the rule of law. It called on all actors and institutions to refrain from violence and to respect human rights and fundamental freedoms, and expressed support for regional and subregional efforts to restore democratic order and the rule of law. The Council requested the High Commissioner to report on the human rights situation since the coup d'état, and to submit a preliminary report to the General Assembly in 2009 and to the Council in early 2010.

OHCHR mission. Following the Council's resolution, OHCHR sent a mission to Honduras from 18 October to 7 November. In its report [A/HRC/13/66], the mission analysed the provisions and measures taken during the state of emergency, raising concerns about the procedures used to impose them, their legality and proportionality, and their impact on the human rights situation. It also examined the impact of the coup d'état on the human rights of particular groups, and assessed specific human rights situations with a particular focus on economic and social rights. The mission concluded that the main human rights violations related to the excessive use of force by the security forces and massive numbers of arrests, disrespect for the principles of legality, necessity and proportionality through the imposition of restrictions on fundamental rights, and selective and discriminatory application of legislation. Some violations were based on pre-existing legal provisions that OHCHR considered to be incompatible with international human rights instruments or not implemented in accordance with international human rights law.

Based on that analysis, the High Commissioner recommended that the authorities: conduct independent investigations on the violations committed after the coup, particularly regarding cases of violations of the right to life, torture, ill-treatment, arbitrary detentions and rape, and initiate legal proceedings against those found responsible; ensure respect for the due process of law and judicial guarantees in all investigations against people who participated in demonstrations against the coup; review decisions taken regarding judges and public defenders under investigation; and ensure reparation, support and assistance to the victims of violations. To deal with structural problems, the High Commissioner recommended: revising or abrogating legislation incompatible with international standards; developing a national human rights plan of action to address structural problems; avoiding the use of the military in law enforcement functions, unless in extreme and exceptional cases, and always subject to independent judicial control; and establishing an independent national mechanism to prevent torture and other cruel, inhuman or degrading treatment or punishment.

Asia

Afghanistan

Reports of High Commissioner. In a report of 16 January [A/HRC/10/23] on the situation of human rights in Afghanistan and on the achievements of technical assistance in the field of human rights, submitted pursuant to a Human Rights Council decision [YUN 2006, p. 948], the High Commissioner stated that throughout 2008, efforts to transform Afghan society were undermined by the intensification of the armed conflict, growing lawlessness, widespread abuse of power, violence against women and their marginalization, and a clampdown on freedom of expression. Compounded by a surge in criminal violence and a decline of law enforcement's control over parts of the country, a culture of impunity prevailed. Abusive structures of society and the leeway given to traditional power brokers had limited prospects for the realization of human rights, in particular for vulnerable groups. Discrimination against women and minority groups was manifested in their lack of access to justice and other basic services. Recent gains made by women in the public sphere were in danger of receding. Attacks on the freedom to express views that challenged power structures as well as social and religious norms cast doubts on the Government's ability to ensure a free and democratic space where human rights were respected. While initiatives to reform the justice sector and improve the administration of justice were launched in 2008, the judicial system remained weak, corrupt and dysfunctional. The High Commissioner recommended that further efforts be made to integrate a human rights perspective into development strategies. The implementation of the 2008 Afghanistan National Development Strategy needed to be consistent with Afghanistan's national and international human rights obligations, and those obligations should be monitored and evaluated. Pro-Government forces and anti-Government elements should ensure greater respect for the protection of civilians. National and international security forces should establish systems of accountability. The Gov-

ernment and its international partners should address impunity as a matter of priority. The independence and impartiality of law enforcement and judicial authorities must be guaranteed, and resources put at their disposal so that they could deliver justice efficiently. The Government and the international community should ensure the integrity and independence of the upcoming electoral process. The Afghan Independent Human Rights Commission should continue to carry out its vigilant role in monitoring, promoting and protecting human rights with international support.

In a report covering developments in 2009 [A/HRC/13/62], the High Commissioner said that the year was a difficult one for Afghanistan as hard-won gains had been put in jeopardy. Confidence in the State-building project diminished as many Afghans questioned the commitment of elected authorities and their international partners to safeguarding their core rights and freedoms. The escalation of the armed conflict resulted in the highest number of civilian casualties recorded since the fall of the Taliban regime in 2001 and in the further erosion of humanitarian space. While the armed opposition was responsible for the majority of civilian casualties, deaths as a result of air strikes by international forces was a high-profile and contentious issue. However, new tactical directives adopted by the international forces to reduce civilian casualties appeared to have had a positive impact. Attacks by anti-Government elements produced high levels of violence including, in particular, around the presidential and provincial council elections held in August. The presidential election, widely regarded as deeply flawed, further weakened support for the Government and its international partners. While greater numbers of women stood for election to public office, threats against women in public life and crimes of sexual violence remained serious concerns. The adoption of the Shia Personal Status Law, which legitimized discriminatory practices against women, represented a setback for women's rights. Widespread impunity undermined effective governance and little progress was achieved in terms of accountability for crimes associated with a long history of abuse of power. Journalists and media workers continued to be harassed for exercising their profession. Conditions of extreme poverty, which affected one third of the population, were exacerbated by the intensifying conflict, abusive power structures and corrosive impunity.

OHCHR supported the Ministry of Foreign Affairs with respect to its submission under the Universal Periodic Review of the Human Rights Council. The high-quality report was praised by other States as a frank account of the human rights situation that gave a balanced view of progress as well as persistent challenges. OHCHR was engaged in other technical assistance initiatives, including with the Ministry of Justice and the Afghan Independent Human Rights

Commission. The High Commissioner recommended that: the Government assume with serious commitment its responsibilities to meet its human rights obligations; parties to the conflict secure respect for the protection of civilians; pro-Government forces strengthen procedures to mitigate the impact of the conflict on the civilian population; the Government take all necessary steps to end discrimination against women; and the Government and its international partners address impunity and ensure the rights of all Afghans to reparation for egregious human rights violations.

Cambodia

Report of Secretary-General. In a report of 5 August [A/HRC/12/41] on the role and achievements of OHCHR in assisting the Government and people of Cambodia to promote and protect human rights, submitted pursuant to a Human Rights Council request [YUN 2008, p. 874], the Secretary-General stated that over the previous 18 months, OHCHR in Cambodia had stepped up efforts to engage in dialogue and cooperation with the Government. It developed initiatives with government institutions concerned with human rights and offered technical and other assistance for their implementation. That approach, through dialogue with government interlocutors, aimed at building working relationships based on mutual confidence. At the same time, OHCHR drew public attention to certain issues of concern when avenues for dialogue were insufficient to address them. OHCHR developed cooperation with community-based organizations, NGOs and other civil society actors, and development cooperation agencies. Under its rule of law programme, OHCHR advised Cambodia on the establishment of a national human rights institution and a national mechanism to prevent torture, provided technical advice on conducting prison inspections, and promoted international trial standards in domestic courts. Among activities to strengthen the capacity of individuals and civil society organizations to exercise freedoms of association, expression and assembly, OHCHR assisted the Government in developing legislation and policies that would enable groups and individuals to organize and participate in public affairs. Prior to the general elections on 27 July 2008, OHCHR reported the ruling party's efforts to pressure opposition members to switch allegiance, mobilization of civil servants to campaign for the ruling party, and the use of threats and intimidation. OHCHR advocated the removal of defamation and disinformation charges from penal law, tolerance by public officials for criticism, and the right to peaceful assembly. Through its land and livelihoods programme, OHCHR worked to ensure that government policy complied with national law and international

standards pertaining to land and housing, to improve the protection of land and housing rights, and to find fair solutions to land disputes. In recent years, over 150,000 people had been evicted and as many were estimated to be facing eviction. Land conflicts were rooted in insecurity of land tenure and the lack of implementation of laws protecting land and property rights, in particular the Land Law of 2001. OHCHR assisted the Government in reporting on human rights under treaty obligations. By mid-2009, Cambodia had cleared its backlog from 15 reports overdue to 7.

Report of Special Rapporteur. In a report of 31 August [A/HRC/12/40 & Corr.1], the Special Rapporteur on the situation of human rights in Cambodia, Surya Subedi (Nepal), who was appointed with effect from 1 May 2009 and undertook his first mission to the country from 16 to 26 June, said that his focus at that time was on familiarizing himself with the complex realities on the ground, re-establishing conditions for a fruitful dialogue with the Government, and strengthening cooperation between the Government, civil society and the international community. A number of issues arose during his talks, namely, freedom of expression, independence of the judiciary, land and housing rights in urban and rural areas, and prison reform. The Rapporteur was of the preliminary view that while Cambodia had made remarkable progress in a number of areas given its legacy, there were still serious human rights challenges. What was needed was not only a formal commitment to human rights by the Government, but implementation through action in key areas—strengthening the rule of law, creating a clearer separation of power between the three main branches of the Government, protecting the independence of the judiciary, including that of the Extraordinary Chambers in the Courts of Cambodia (ECCC), and addressing issues such as conflicts over land, impunity and corruption. Among the Government's recent achievements, the Rapporteur pointed to improving land tenure, a project of land titling in rural areas, combating trafficking in human beings for sexual exploitation, closing down a number of gambling places, and combating HIV/AIDS. Among the challenges facing the Government were the issues of property safeguards, intimidation or imprisonment of opposition leaders, and fulfilment of obligations under international human rights treaties.

Communications. Cambodia, in three communications addressed to OHCHR or the Human Rights Council, commented on the Special Rapporteur's remarks. In a note of 29 September [A/HRC/12/G/5], Cambodia listed actions it had taken or planned to take on land issues and freedom of expression. In another note of the same date [A/HRC/12/G/6], Cambodia commented on a number of claims made by the

Rapporteur in his report. In a letter of 12 October [A/HRC/12/G/11], Cambodia rejected some of the claims made by the Rapporteur regarding the rule of law and freedom of expression.

Human Rights Council action. On 2 October [A/65/53 (res. 12/25)], the Human Rights Council, taking note of recent progress by Cambodia to promote and protect human rights, reaffirmed the importance of ECCC as an independent body which would contribute to eradicating impunity and establishing the rule of law. The Council welcomed the progress made by ECCC, including the hearing concerning former Khmer Rouge leader Kaing Guek Eav, and supported Cambodia's position to proceed with the tribunal, given the age and health of the persons charged and the long overdue justice for the Cambodian people. It also welcomed the Government's efforts in: promoting legal and judicial reform; combating corruption, including the drafting of an anti-corruption law and bringing corrupt officials to justice; stopping political appointments based on party allocations; combating trafficking in persons, including the enforcement of laws on suppression of human trafficking and commercial sexual exploitation; resolving land issues; fulfilling obligations under international human rights conventions; improving the conditions in prisons; promoting decentralization reform, including the local elections at provincial/municipal and district/ *sangkat* levels held in May; and approving a national disability law and a policy on development for indigenous minorities. The Council expressed concern about some areas of human rights practices, and urged the Government to take steps to promote the rule of law, address impunity, investigate and prosecute those who perpetrated serious crimes, resolve land ownership issues in accordance with national law and cadastral committees, promote an environment conducive to the conduct of legitimate political activity, improve the rights of women and children, address problems such as human trafficking, issues related to poverty, sexual violence, domestic violence and sexual exploitation, and promote civil and political rights. The Council extended by one year the mandate of the Special Rapporteur, and requested him and the Secretary-General to report to the Council in 2010.

Democratic People's Republic of Korea

Report of Special Rapporteur. In a report of 24 February [A/HRC/10/18], the Special Rapporteur on the situation of human rights in the Democratic People's Republic of Korea (DPRK), Vitit Muntarbhorn (Thailand), said that the predicament ensuing from the systematic and widespread human rights violations in the country required urgent attention. Of particular concern were problems related to food and other basic necessities, personal security and freedoms, asylum and migration, and vulnerable groups. The tragedy of the country was that the powerful sought to survive at the expense of the majority of the population, leading to the environment of human rights abuses. Among recommendations in the short term, the Special Rapporteur called for: providing food and other basic necessities, and enabling people to undertake economic activities to satisfy their basic needs and supplement their livelihood without State interference; ending the punishment of those who sought asylum abroad and who were sent back to the DPRK; terminating public executions and abuses against security of the person, and other violations of fundamental rights; cooperating to resolve the issue of foreigners abducted by the DPRK; and responding constructively to the Rapporteur's recommendations. In the longer term, the DPRK should: seek to modernize its national system by instituting reforms to ensure greater participation of the people in the process and compliance with human rights standards; institute equitable development measures based on a "people first" policy and reallocate national budgets to the social sector; take more food security-related measures; guarantee personal security and freedoms by dismantling the pervasive surveillance and intelligence system, reforming the justice system, and abiding by the rule of law; become a party to human rights treaties and implement them; address the vulnerability of specific groups; address the root causes of refugee outflows; and act against the impunity of those responsible for human rights violations. The international community was invited to take more proactive measures in relation to those issues and to adopt an integrated approach to impel more protection for citizens, with due regard for the responsibility of State authorities and their accountability for the violence and violations that had led to the sufferings of millions of people.

In recent years, the Rapporteur said, the authorities had opened the door slightly to engage with the international community, in particular by becoming more accessible to international aid organizations, including UN agencies. Nevertheless, the overall human rights picture was grim and the lack of sufficient food and basic necessities for the general population remained serious. Under one-party rule premised on an ideology described as ruler-based nationalism, the people lived in fear and were pressed to inform on each other. The regime placed the military above other concerns and had armed itself with nuclear weapons. In 2008, a new agreement was reached between the DPRK and the World Food Programme (WFP) on food assistance. WFP estimated that 8.7 million people were food insecure and needed help, and it targeted extensive emergency operations for 2009, particularly for vulnerable groups such as lactating women, young children, the elderly and persons with disabilities. It estimated that at the beginning of 2009, only 1.8 million people were receiving food assistance. Regarding personal security, the Rapporteur described some law reforms aimed at bringing national security standards more in line with international ones, but in reality there were gaps in implementation, resulting in grave human rights violations. Collective punishment was used against people; for example, whole families were persecuted and sent into detention when a member fell afoul of the authorities. Torture, although prohibited by law, was practised extensively. Conditions in prisons included insufficient food, poor hygiene, forced labour and corporal punishment. Basic freedoms associated with human rights, including freedom of association, freedom of expression, freedom of information, privacy and freedom of religion were infringed on a daily basis. Political dissent was heavily punished. The media were rigidly controlled and censored, and formed the backbone of the State's propaganda machine.

The Special Rapporteur, together with three other Special Rapporteurs (on executions, on the right to food, and on torture and other punishment), had addressed on 20 March 2008 a joint communication to the DPRK Government concerning the alleged public executions of 15 nationals who were accused of planning to cross into a neighbouring country to receive economic assistance. The Government had not replied. The Government had also failed to reply to a communication, sent by the Special Rapporteur on 7 April 2008, requesting clarification on reports of 22 nationals who had been returned to the DPRK after accidently drifting in a boat outside DPRK waters.

Communication. The DPRK, in a letter of 29 January 2009 [A/HRC/10/G/6] to the Human Rights Council, reiterated its position that the "special rapporteur" was a product of political confrontation and plot, particularly by the United States, Japan and European Union countries, and that the human rights issue was being abused along with the nuclear issue for those purposes. Furthermore, the "special rapporteur" remained a fundamental impediment to the work of the Council.

Human Rights Council action. On 26 March [A/64/53 (res. 10/16)], the Human Rights Council, by a recorded vote of 26 to 6, with 15 abstentions, expressed concern at the ongoing systematic human rights violations in the DPRK and extended the Special Rapporteur's mandate for one year. It urged the DPRK to cooperate with the Rapporteur and to permit him unrestricted access to visit the country and to provide him with all necessary information. It urged the Government to engage fully with the Universal Periodic Review process in December, and to ensure unimpeded access of humanitarian assistance.

Further report of Special Rapporteur. The Special Rapporteur, in an August report to the General Assembly [A/64/224], covered the human rights situation from mid-2008 to mid-2009. That analysis reviewed human rights and freedoms, in particular freedom from want, fear, discrimination, persecution and exploitation. Those rights were violated with impunity by the authorities on a daily basis. The violations were widespread, systematic and abhorrent in their impact and implications. The array of violations cut across civil, political, economic, social and cultural rights. During the reporting period, WFP had more access to the field than it had had since 2005, accessing 6,237,000 beneficiaries, mainly vulnerable groups. However, by mid-2009, the authorities had limited WFP operations. The pervasive repression imposed by the authorities ensured that people lived in fear. The State practised surveillance over its inhabitants. Public executions continued to take place, particularly for human traffickers. The Rapporteur reiterated his recommendations for action by the DPRK authorities and the international community.

Report of Secretary-General. The Secretary-General, in a report of 24 August [A/64/319 & Corr.1] submitted pursuant to General Assembly resolution 63/190 [YUN 2008, p. 877], described the human rights situation in the DPRK, noting that the Government had not taken significant steps to address reports of systematic and widespread human rights violations, nor had it accepted technical assistance from OHCHR or granted access to the Special Rapporteur. The DPRK faced complex humanitarian problems and it continued to decline food assistance offered by the international community, despite the worsening shortage of food. The report covered the DPRK's cooperation with international human rights mechanisms such as treaty bodies, special procedures, the Special Rapporteur, the Working Group on Enforced or Involuntary Disappearances, and the Universal Periodic Review carried out by the Human Rights Council. It described the role of OHCHR in assisting the Government in promoting and protecting human rights. The Secretary-General urged the Government to provide safeguards for human rights and ensure domestic legal reforms, in accordance with its international treaty obligations. He called on the DPRK to engage with OHCHR in technical cooperation, to cooperate with the Special Rapporteur, to prioritize its resources in order to address the humanitarian needs of its population, and to allow UN agencies and their humanitarian partners on the ground to increase their operations. The Secretary-General urged the international community to help address the critical humanitarian needs of the DPRK citizens.

On 18 December [meeting 65], the General Assembly, on the recommendation of the Third (Social, Humanitarian and Cultural) Committee [A/64/439/Add.3], adopted **resolution 64/175** by recorded vote (99-20-63) [agenda item 69 *(c)*].

Situation of human rights in the Democratic People's Republic of Korea

The General Assembly,

Reaffirming that States Members of the United Nations have an obligation to promote and protect human rights and fundamental freedoms and to fulfil the obligations that they have undertaken under the various international instruments,

Mindful that the Democratic People's Republic of Korea is a party to the International Covenant on Civil and Political Rights, the International Covenant on Economic, Social and Cultural Rights, the Convention on the Rights of the Child and the Convention on the Elimination of All Forms of Discrimination against Women,

Noting the constructive dialogue with the Committee on the Rights of the Child during the consideration of the Democratic People's Republic of Korea's combined third and fourth periodic reports on the implementation of the Convention on the Rights of the Child as a sign of engagement in international cooperative efforts in the field of human rights, and hoping that the enhanced dialogue will contribute to improving the situation of children in the country,

Taking note of the concluding observations of the treaty-monitoring bodies under the four treaties to which the Democratic People's Republic of Korea is a party, the most recent of which were given by the Committee on the Rights of the Child in January 2009,

Noting with appreciation the collaboration established between the Government of the Democratic People's Republic of Korea and the United Nations Children's Fund and the World Health Organization in order to improve the health situation in the country, and the collaboration established with the United Nations Children's Fund in order to improve the quality of education for children,

Noting the decision on the resumption, on a modest scale, of the activities of the United Nations Development Programme in the Democratic People's Republic of Korea, and encouraging the engagement of the Government with the international community to ensure that the programmes benefit the persons in need of assistance,

Recalling its resolutions 60/173 of 16 December 2005, 61/174 of 19 December 2006, 62/167 of 18 December 2007 and 63/190 of 18 December 2008, Commission on Human Rights resolutions 2003/10 of 16 April 2003, 2004/13 of 15 April 2004 and 2005/11 of 14 April 2005, Human Rights Council decision 1/102 of 30 June 2006 and Council resolutions 7/15 of 27 March 2008 and 10/16 of 26 March 2009, and mindful of the need for the international community to strengthen its coordinated efforts aimed at achieving the implementation of those resolutions,

Taking note of the report of the Special Rapporteur on the situation of human rights in the Democratic People's Republic of Korea, regretting that he still has not been al-

lowed to visit the country and that he received no cooperation from the authorities of the Democratic People's Republic of Korea, and taking note also of the comprehensive report of the Secretary-General on the situation of human rights in the Democratic People's Republic of Korea submitted in accordance with resolution 63/190,

Noting the importance of the inter-Korean dialogue, which could contribute to the improvement of the human rights and humanitarian situation in the country,

Welcoming the recent resumption of the reunion of separated families across the border, which is an urgent humanitarian concern of the entire Korean people,

1. *Expresses its very serious concern* at:

(a) The persistence of continuing reports of systematic, widespread and grave violations of civil, political, economic, social and cultural rights in the Democratic People's Republic of Korea, including:

(i) Torture and other cruel, inhuman or degrading treatment or punishment, including inhuman conditions of detention, public executions, extrajudicial and arbitrary detention; the absence of due process and the rule of law, including fair trial guarantees and an independent judiciary; the imposition of the death penalty for political and religious reasons; collective punishments; and the existence of a large number of prison camps and the extensive use of forced labour;

(ii) Limitations imposed on every person who wishes to move freely within the country and travel abroad, including the punishment of those who leave or try to leave the country without permission, or their families, as well as punishment of persons who are returned;

(iii) The situation of refugees and asylum-seekers expelled or returned to the Democratic People's Republic of Korea and sanctions imposed on citizens of the Democratic People's Republic of Korea who have been repatriated from abroad, leading to punishments of internment, torture, cruel, inhuman or degrading treatment or the death penalty, and, in this regard, urges all States to respect the fundamental principle of non-refoulement, to treat those who seek refuge humanely and to ensure unhindered access to the United Nations High Commissioner for Refugees and his Office, with a view to improving the situation of those who seek refuge, and once again urges States parties to comply with their obligations under the 1951 Convention relating to the Status of Refugees and the 1967 Protocol thereto in relation to refugees from the Democratic People's Republic of Korea who are covered by those instruments;

(iv) All-pervasive and severe restrictions on the freedoms of thought, conscience, religion, opinion and expression, peaceful assembly and association, the right to privacy and equal access to information, by such means as the persecution of individuals exercising their freedom of opinion and expression, and their families, and on the right of everyone to take part in the conduct of public affairs, directly or through freely chosen representatives, of his or her country;

(v) The violations of economic, social and cultural rights, which have led to severe malnutrition, widespread health problems and other hardship for the population in the Democratic People's Republic of Korea, in particular for persons belonging to particularly exposed groups, inter alia, women, children and the elderly;

(vi) Continuing violations of the human rights and fundamental freedoms of women, in particular the trafficking of women for the purpose of prostitution or forced marriage and the subjection of women to human smuggling, forced abortions, gender-based discrimination, including in the economic sphere, and gender-based violence;

(vii) Continuing reports of violations of the human rights and fundamental freedoms of children, in particular the continued lack of access to basic economic, social and cultural rights for many children, and in this regard notes the particularly vulnerable situation faced by, inter alia, returned or repatriated children, street children, children with disabilities, children whose parents are detained, children living in detention or in institutions and children in conflict with the law;

(viii) Continuing reports of violations of the human rights and fundamental freedoms of persons with disabilities, especially on the use of collective camps and of coercive measures that target the rights of persons with disabilities to decide freely and responsibly on the number and spacing of their children;

(ix) Violations of workers' rights, including the right to freedom of association and collective bargaining, the right to strike as defined by the obligations of the Democratic People's Republic of Korea under the International Covenant on Economic, Social and Cultural Rights, and the prohibition of the economic exploitation of children and of any harmful or hazardous work of children as defined by the obligations of the Democratic People's Republic of Korea under the Convention on the Rights of the Child;

(b) The continued refusal of the Government of the Democratic People's Republic of Korea to recognize the mandate of the Special Rapporteur on the situation of human rights in the Democratic People's Republic of Korea or to extend cooperation to him, despite the renewal of the mandate by the Human Rights Council in its resolutions 7/15 and 10/16;

2. *Reiterates its very serious concern* at unresolved questions of international concern relating to abductions in the form of enforced disappearance, which violates the human rights of nationals of other sovereign countries, and in this regard strongly calls upon the Government of the Democratic People's Republic of Korea urgently to resolve these questions, including through existing channels, in a transparent manner, including by ensuring the immediate return of abductees;

3. *Expresses its very deep concern* at the precarious humanitarian situation in the country, partly as a result of frequent natural disasters, compounded by the misallocation of resources away from the satisfaction of basic needs, and the increasing State restrictions on the cultivation and trade in foodstuffs, as well as the prevalence of maternal malnutrition and of infant malnutrition, which, despite some progress, continues to affect the physical and mental development of a significant proportion of children, and urges the Government of the Democratic People's Republic of Korea, in this regard, to take preventive and remedial action;

4. *Commends* the Special Rapporteur for the activities undertaken so far and for his continued efforts in the conduct of his mandate despite the limited access to information;

5. *Strongly urges* the Government of the Democratic People's Republic of Korea to respect fully all human rights and fundamental freedoms and, in this regard:

(a) To immediately put an end to the systematic, widespread and grave violations of human rights mentioned above, inter alia, by implementing fully the measures set out in the above-mentioned resolutions of the General Assembly, the Commission on Human Rights and the Human Rights Council, and the recommendations addressed to the Democratic People's Republic of Korea by the United Nations special procedures and treaty bodies;

(b) To protect its inhabitants, address the issue of impunity and ensure that those responsible for violations of human rights are brought to justice before an independent judiciary;

(c) To tackle the root causes leading to refugee outflows and prosecute those who exploit refugees by human smuggling, trafficking and extortion, while not criminalizing the victims, and to ensure that citizens of the Democratic People's Republic of Korea expelled or returned to the Democratic People's Republic of Korea are able to return in safety and dignity, are humanely treated and are not subjected to any kind of punishment;

(d) To extend its full cooperation to the Special Rapporteur, including by granting him full, free and unimpeded access to the Democratic People's Republic of Korea, and to other United Nations human rights mechanisms;

(e) To engage in technical cooperation activities in the field of human rights with the United Nations High Commissioner for Human Rights and her Office, as pursued by the High Commissioner in recent years, with a view to improving the situation of human rights in the country, and in the universal periodic review by the Human Rights Council;

(f) To engage in cooperation with the International Labour Organization with a view to significantly improving workers' rights;

(g) To continue and reinforce its cooperation with United Nations humanitarian agencies;

(h) To ensure full, safe and unhindered access to humanitarian aid and take measures to allow humanitarian agencies to secure its impartial delivery to all parts of the country on the basis of need in accordance with humanitarian principles, as it pledged to do, and to ensure access to adequate food and implement food security policies, including through sustainable agriculture;

6. *Decides* to continue its examination of the situation of human rights in the Democratic People's Republic of Korea at its sixty-fifth session, and to this end requests the Secretary-General to submit a comprehensive report on the situation in the Democratic People's Republic of Korea and the Special Rapporteur to continue to report his findings and recommendations.

RECORDED VOTE ON RESOLUTION 64/175:

In favour: Afghanistan, Albania, Andorra, Argentina, Australia, Austria, Bahrain, Belgium, Belize, Bhutan, Bosnia and Herzegovina, Botswana, Bulgaria, Burundi, Canada, Chile, Costa Rica, Croatia, Cyprus, Czech Republic, Denmark, El Salvador, Eritrea, Estonia, Fiji, Finland, France, Georgia, Germany, Ghana, Greece, Guinea-Bissau, Honduras, Hungary, Iceland, Iraq, Ireland, Israel, Italy, Jamaica, Japan, Jordan, Kazakhstan, Kiribati, Latvia, Lebanon, Liberia, Liechtenstein, Lithuania, Luxembourg, Madagascar, Malawi, Maldives, Malta, Marshall Islands, Mexico, Micronesia, Moldova, Monaco, Montenegro, Morocco, Nauru, Netherlands, New Zealand, Norway, Palau, Panama, Papua New Guinea, Paraguay, Peru, Poland, Portugal, Republic of Korea, Romania, Saint Lucia, Samoa, San Marino, Saudi Arabia, Sierra Leone, Slovakia, Slovenia, Solomon Islands, Somalia, Spain, Sweden, Switzerland, The former Yugoslav Republic of Macedonia, Timor-Leste, Togo, Tonga, Turkey, Tuvalu, Ukraine, United Arab Emirates, United Kingdom, United Republic of Tanzania, United States, Uruguay, Vanuatu.

Against: Algeria, Belarus, China, Cuba, Democratic People's Republic of Korea, Egypt, Equatorial Guinea, Indonesia, Iran, Libyan Arab Jamahiriya, Malaysia, Myanmar, Namibia, Oman, Russian Federation, Sudan, Syrian Arab Republic, Venezuela, Viet Nam, Zimbabwe.

Abstaining: Angola, Antigua and Barbuda, Azerbaijan, Bahamas, Bangladesh, Barbados, Benin, Bolivia, Brazil, Brunei Darussalam, Burkina Faso, Cambodia, Cameroon, Cape Verde, Central African Republic, Chad, Colombia, Comoros, Congo, Côte d'Ivoire, Democratic Republic of the Congo, Dominica, Dominican Republic, Ecuador, Ethiopia, Gabon, Grenada, Guatemala, Guinea, Guyana, Haiti, India, Kenya, Kuwait, Kyrgyzstan, Lesotho, Mali, Mauritania, Mauritius, Mozambique, Nepal, Nicaragua, Niger, Nigeria, Pakistan, Philippines, Qatar, Rwanda, Saint Kitts and Nevis, Saint Vincent and the Grenadines, Senegal, Singapore, South Africa, Sri Lanka, Suriname, Swaziland, Tajikistan, Thailand, Trinidad and Tobago, Turkmenistan, Uganda, Yemen, Zambia.

Iran

Report of Secretary-General. The Secretary-General, in a report of 23 September [A/64/357] on the human rights situation in Iran, submitted in accordance with General Assembly resolution 63/191 [YUN 2008, p. 880], covered developments since June 2008, including events following the 12 June 2009 presidential election, Iran's cooperation with international human rights mechanisms and OHCHR, and communications by Special Rapporteurs on allegations of human rights violations by the Government. While the 1979 Constitution guaranteed a wide range of human rights and fundamental freedoms, in practice there were impediments to the full protection of human rights and the functioning of State institutions. A revised penal code under consideration included provisions incompat-

ible with international human rights standards, such as capital punishment, flogging and amputation. Iran had made gains during the past decade in the area of economic, social and cultural rights, and poverty levels had declined significantly. In recent years, however, those trends had slowed owing to high inflation, offset somewhat by State support and an extensive social protection system that provided health and unemployment insurance, and disability and old-age pensions.

Negative developments were noted in civil and political rights, with an increase in human rights violations targeting women, minorities, university students, teachers, workers and other activist groups, particularly in the aftermath of the elections. Following the announcement of the election result, tens of thousands of people protested in the streets and seven people were reported killed. On 19 June, five independent UN experts voiced concern about the use of excessive police force, arbitrary arrests and killings, despite the mainly peaceful demonstrations. On the same day, the High Commissioner issued a press statement expressing concern about reports of increasing arrests that were not in conformity with the law, and the use of excessive force. She expressed concern about reported violence by the Basij militia, adding that it was the Government's responsibility to ensure that militia members and regular law enforcement agencies did not resort to illegal acts of violence. The Government responded by stating that more than 85 per cent of those eligible had cast votes in a peaceful atmosphere and that all four candidates had been given opportunities to express their policies; complaints had been reviewed and the results confirmed. Rallies continued in Tehran over several days. On 20 June, Neda Agha Soltan, a young woman, was killed by a shot during a demonstration, an incident that received much international attention. The authorities said that the case was being investigated. On 22 June, the Secretary-General expressed dismay at the violence, particularly the use of force against civilians, which had led to the loss of life and injuries.

Various special procedures mandate-holders signed urgent action appeals regarding the alleged arrest and arbitrary detention of several hundred opposition activists carried out by the police, security forces, the Basij militia and plain-clothes officers of the intelligence services during demonstrations or at private residences. In a joint statement of 7 July expressing concern about mass arrests, six mandate holders stated that at least 20 people had been killed and hundreds injured. On 1 August, the trial of about 100 defendants began on a variety of charges, ranging from participation in the unrest to leading riots, acting against national security, disturbing public order, damaging public property, and maintaining relations with anti-revolutionary groups.

The Special Rapporteur on torture and other cruel, inhuman or degrading treatment or punishment sent numerous communications to the Government regarding allegations of torture, including in the cases of Mahdi Hanafi, a student who reportedly died from injuries inflicted during detention, and Ya'qub Mehrnehad, a journalist who was executed in August 2008. Although the head of the judiciary in January 2008 had banned public executions, there were reports that on 11 July 2008 another public execution had been held. There were also executions by stoning of two men, as confirmed on 13 January 2009 by the judiciary. According to Amnesty International, eight juvenile offenders were executed in 2008 and three in 2009. OHCHR continued to receive reports of human rights abuses against minorities, particularly members of the Baha'i community. Serious impediments were placed on the right to freedom of opinion and expression. The home of Nobel Peace Prize laureate Shirin Ebadi, a lawyer and human rights activist, was reportedly attacked and materials were removed from her office. On 3 January, the Secretary-General called on the authorities to prevent any further harassment and to ensure the safety and security of Ms. Ebadi. Iran replied on 5 January that the Defenders of Human Rights Centre, led by Ms. Ebadi, had been closed because it did not comply with the law. The Chairperson of the Working Group on Arbitrary Detention and some Special Rapporteurs issued several communications to the Government on cases that suggested a widespread lack of due process rights and the failure to respect the rights of detainees.

The Secretary-General encouraged the Government to continue to revise national laws to ensure compliance with international human rights standards; to prevent discriminatory practices against women, ethnic and religious minorities and other minority groups; to address regional disparities in the enjoyment of economic, social and cultural rights; to ratify major international human rights treaties; to submit its long-outstanding periodic reports under human rights treaties; and to allow special procedures mandate holders to visit the country.

GENERAL ASSEMBLY ACTION

On 18 December [meeting 65], the General Assembly, on the recommendation of the Third Committee [A/64/439/Add.3], adopted **resolution 64/176** by recorded vote (74-49-59) [agenda item 69 *(c)*].

Situation of human rights in the Islamic Republic of Iran

The General Assembly,

Guided by the Charter of the United Nations, as well as the Universal Declaration of Human Rights, the Inter-

national Covenants on Human Rights and other international human rights instruments,

Recalling its previous resolutions on the situation of human rights in the Islamic Republic of Iran, the most recent of which is resolution 63/191 of 18 December 2008,

1. *Takes note* of the report of the Secretary-General submitted pursuant to resolution 63/191, which highlights many areas of continuing concern with respect to the promotion and protection of human rights in the Islamic Republic of Iran and notes with particular concern negative developments in the area of civil and political rights since June 2008, and which discusses some positive achievements with respect to economic and social indicators;

2. *Expresses deep concern* at serious ongoing and recurring human rights violations in the Islamic Republic of Iran relating to, inter alia:

(a) Torture and cruel, inhuman or degrading treatment or punishment, including flogging and amputations;

(b) The continuing high incidence and increase in the rate of executions carried out in the absence of internationally recognized safeguards, including public executions and executions of juveniles;

(c) Stoning as a method of execution and persons in prison who continue to face sentences of execution by stoning, notwithstanding a circular from the head of the judiciary prohibiting stoning;

(d) Arrests, violent repression and sentencing of women exercising their right to peaceful assembly, a campaign of intimidation against women's human rights defenders, and continuing discrimination against women and girls in law and in practice;

(e) Increasing discrimination and other human rights violations against persons belonging to religious, ethnic, linguistic or other minorities, recognized or otherwise, including, inter alia, Arabs, Azeris, Baluchis, Kurds, Christians, Jews, Sufis and Sunni Muslims and their defenders, and, in particular, attacks on Baha'is and their faith in State-sponsored media, increasing evidence of efforts by the State to identify, monitor and arbitrarily detain Baha'is, preventing members of the Baha'i faith from attending university and from sustaining themselves economically, and the continuing detention of seven Baha'i leaders who were arrested in March and May 2008 and faced with serious charges without adequate or timely access to legal representation;

(f) Ongoing, systemic and serious restrictions of freedom of peaceful assembly and association and freedom of opinion and expression, including those imposed on the media, Internet users and trade unions, and increasing harassment, intimidation and persecution of political opponents and human rights defenders from all sectors of Iranian society, including arrests and violent repression of labour leaders, labour members peacefully assembling and students, noting in particular the forced closure of the Defenders of Human Rights Centre and the subsequent arrest and harassment of a number of its staff;

(g) Severe limitations and restrictions on freedom of religion and belief, including arbitrary arrest, indefinite detention and lengthy jail sentences for those exercising their right to freedom of religion or belief;

(h) Persistent failure to uphold due process of law rights, and violation of the rights of detainees, including

defendants held without charge or held incommunicado, the systematic and arbitrary use of prolonged solitary confinement, and lack of timely access to legal representation;

3. *Also expresses particular concern* at the response of the Government of the Islamic Republic of Iran following the presidential election of 12 June 2009 and the concurrent rise in human rights violations including, inter alia:

(a) Harassment, intimidation and persecution, including by arbitrary arrest, detention or disappearance, of opposition members, journalists and other media representatives, bloggers, lawyers, clerics, human rights defenders, academics, students and others exercising their rights to peaceful assembly and association and freedom of opinion and expression, resulting in numerous deaths and injuries;

(b) Use of violence and intimidation by Government-directed militias to forcibly disperse Iranian citizens engaged in the peaceful exercise of freedom of association, also resulting in numerous deaths and injuries;

(c) Interfering in the right to a fair trial by, inter alia, holding mass trials and denying defendants access to adequate legal representation, resulting in death sentences and lengthy jail sentences for some individuals;

(d) Reported use of forced confessions and abuse of prisoners including, inter alia, rape and torture;

(e) Escalation in the rate of executions in the months following the election;

(f) Further restrictions on freedom of expression, including severe restrictions on media coverage of public demonstrations and the disruption of telecommunications and Internet technology and the forcible closure of the offices of several organizations involved in the investigation of the situation of persons imprisoned following the election;

(g) Arbitrary arrest and detention of employees of foreign embassies in Tehran, thereby unduly interfering with the performance of the functions of those missions in a manner inconsistent with the Vienna Convention on Diplomatic Relations and the Vienna Convention on Consular Relations;

4. *Calls upon* the Government of the Islamic Republic of Iran to address the substantive concerns highlighted in the report of the Secretary-General and the specific calls to action found in previous resolutions of the General Assembly, and to respect fully its human rights obligations, in law and in practice, in particular:

(a) To eliminate, in law and in practice, amputations, flogging and other forms of torture and other cruel, inhuman or degrading treatment or punishment;

(b) To abolish, in law and in practice, public executions and other executions carried out in the absence of respect for internationally recognized safeguards;

(c) To abolish, pursuant to its obligations under article 37 of the Convention on the Rights of the Child and article 6 of the International Covenant on Civil and Political Rights, executions of persons who at the time of their offence were under the age of 18;

(d) To abolish the use of stoning as a method of execution;

(e) To eliminate, in law and in practice, all forms of discrimination and other human rights violations against women and girls;

(f) To eliminate, in law and in practice, all forms of discrimination and other human rights violations against persons belonging to religious, ethnic, linguistic or other minorities, recognized or otherwise, to refrain from monitoring individuals on the basis of their religious beliefs, and to ensure that access of minorities to education and employment is on par with that of all Iranians;

(g) To implement, inter alia, the 1996 report of the Special Rapporteur on religious intolerance, which recommended ways in which the Islamic Republic of Iran could emancipate the Baha'i community, and also to accord the seven Baha'i leaders held since 2008 the due process of law rights they are constitutionally guaranteed, including the right to adequate legal representation and the right to a fair trial;

(h) To end the harassment, intimidation and persecution of political opponents and human rights defenders, students, academics, journalists, other media representatives, bloggers, clerics and lawyers, including by releasing persons imprisoned arbitrarily or on the basis of their political views, including those detained following the presidential election of 12 June 2009;

(i) To uphold due process of law rights, to end impunity for human rights violations, and to launch a credible, impartial and independent investigation into the allegations of post-presidential election human rights violations;

5. *Further calls upon* the Government of the Islamic Republic of Iran to redress its inadequate record of cooperation with international human rights mechanisms by, inter alia, reporting pursuant to its obligations to the treaty bodies of the instruments to which it is a party and cooperating fully with all international human rights mechanisms, and encourages the Government of the Islamic Republic of Iran to continue exploring cooperation on human rights and justice reform with the United Nations, including the Office of the United Nations High Commissioner for Human Rights;

6. *Expresses deep concern* that, despite the Islamic Republic of Iran's standing invitation to all thematic special procedures mandate holders, it has not fulfilled any requests from those special mechanisms to visit the country in four years and has not answered numerous communications from those special mechanisms, and strongly urges the Government of the Islamic Republic of Iran to fully cooperate with the special mechanisms, including facilitating their visits to its territory, so that credible and independent investigations of all allegations of human rights violations, particularly those arising since 12 June 2009, can be conducted;

7. *Invites* the thematic special procedures mandate holders to pay particular attention to the human rights situation in the Islamic Republic of Iran, in particular the Special Rapporteur on extrajudicial, summary or arbitrary executions, the Special Rapporteur on torture and other cruel, inhuman or degrading treatment or punishment, the Special Rapporteur on the promotion and protection of the right to freedom of opinion and expression, the Special Rapporteur on the situation of human rights defenders, the Working Group on Arbitrary Detention and the Working Group on Enforced or Involuntary Disappearances, with a view to investigating and reporting on the various human rights violations that have arisen since 12 June 2009;

8. *Requests* the Secretary-General to report to it at its sixty-fifth session on the progress made in the implementation of the present resolution;

9. *Decides* to continue its examination of the situation of human rights in the Islamic Republic of Iran at its sixty-fifth session under the item entitled "Promotion and protection of human rights".

RECORDED VOTE ON RESOLUTION 64/176:

In favour: Albania, Andorra, Argentina, Australia, Austria, Belgium, Belize, Bosnia and Herzegovina, Botswana, Bulgaria, Canada, Chile, Costa Rica, Croatia, Cyprus, Czech Republic, Denmark, Dominican Republic, El Salvador, Estonia, Fiji, Finland, France, Germany, Greece, Honduras, Hungary, Iceland, Ireland, Israel, Italy, Japan, Kiribati, Latvia, Liberia, Liechtenstein, Lithuania, Luxembourg, Madagascar, Malta, Marshall Islands, Mexico, Micronesia, Moldova, Monaco, Montenegro, Nauru, Netherlands, New Zealand, Norway, Palau, Panama, Papua New Guinea, Peru, Poland, Portugal, Romania, Saint Lucia, Samoa, San Marino, Saudi Arabia, Slovakia, Slovenia, Solomon Islands, Spain, Sweden, Switzerland, The former Yugoslav Republic of Macedonia, Timor-Leste, Tonga, Ukraine, United Kingdom, United States, Vanuatu.

Against: Afghanistan, Algeria, Armenia, Azerbaijan, Bangladesh, Belarus, Bolivia, Brunei Darussalam, China, Comoros, Cuba, Democratic People's Republic of Korea, Ecuador, Egypt, Equatorial Guinea, Eritrea, Guinea, India, Indonesia, Iran, Iraq, Kazakhstan, Kuwait, Kyrgyzstan, Lebanon, Libyan Arab Jamahiriya, Malaysia, Mauritania, Myanmar, Namibia, Nicaragua, Niger, Nigeria, Oman, Pakistan, Qatar, Russian Federation, Senegal, Somalia, Sri Lanka, Sudan, Syrian Arab Republic, Tajikistan, Tunisia, Turkmenistan, United Arab Emirates, Venezuela, Viet Nam, Zimbabwe.

Abstaining: Angola, Antigua and Barbuda, Bahamas, Barbados, Benin, Bhutan, Brazil, Burkina Faso, Burundi, Cambodia, Cameroon, Cape Verde, Central African Republic, Chad, Colombia, Congo, Côte d'Ivoire, Democratic Republic of the Congo, Dominica, Ethiopia, Gabon, Georgia, Ghana, Grenada, Guatemala, Guinea-Bissau, Guyana, Haiti, Jamaica, Jordan, Kenya, Lao People's Democratic Republic, Lesotho, Malawi, Mali, Mauritius, Mongolia, Morocco, Mozambique, Nepal, Paraguay, Philippines, Republic of Korea, Rwanda, Saint Kitts and Nevis, Saint Vincent and the Grenadines, Sierra Leone, Singapore, South Africa, Suriname, Swaziland, Thailand, Togo, Trinidad and Tobago, Tuvalu, Uganda, United Republic of Tanzania, Uruguay, Zambia.

Myanmar

Report of Special Rapporteur. The Special Rapporteur on the situation of human rights in Myanmar, Tomás Ojea Quintana (Argentina), in a report of 11 March [A/HRC/10/19] covering the previous year, stated that he had visited the country twice since his appointment in 2008 and established good working relations with the Government. The report focused on the situation of prisoners of conscience, their right to a fair trial and due process of law and their conditions of detention, as well as freedom of expression, assembly and association in the context of forthcoming elections in 2010. The Rapporteur reviewed internal conflicts with regard to international humanitarian law and protection of civilians, issues of discrimination and the need for humanitarian assistance. He

reiterated his 2008 recommendation of four core human rights elements to set a path towards democracy: a review of national legislation in accordance with the new Constitution and international obligations; the progressive release of prisoners of conscience; training within the armed forces to ensure respect for international human rights and humanitarian law; and an independent and impartial judiciary [YUN 2008, p. 885]. The human rights situation remained challenging and poverty remained the main reason for many problems and a hindrance to the realization of human rights. At the time of the report, there were more than 2,100 prisoners of conscience in Myanmar. From October to December 2008, some 400 prisoners of conscience were brought before prison courts and given harsh sentences. The process leading to the sentences illustrated the flaws in the administration of justice system. Defence lawyers had reportedly been convicted of contempt of court and imprisoned. The right to legal counsel was not fully respected and the Government was not obliged to provide a lawyer to those unable to afford one. Prisoners of conscience were often subjected to ill-treatment.

During his visit to Myanmar from 14 to 19 February 2009, the Rapporteur was allowed to meet with five prisoners of his choice. He received reports about the dire health conditions of many prisoners of conscience and the deaths of some due to lack of medical care. Most prisoners of conscience relied on their families for medication and food supplies. The Rapporteur reiterated his call for ending the detention under house arrest of Daw Aung San Suu Kyi, the leader of the National League for Democracy (NLD) party. Despite his request, the Rapporteur could not meet with leaders of political parties—including Ms. Suu Kyi, Min Ko Naing, leader of the 88 Generation Students Group, Khun Htun Oo, leader of the Shan Nationalities League for Democracy, and U Myint Aye, leader of Human Rights Defenders and Promoters Group—because they were all either under house arrest or in remote prisons. In September 2008, the Government released 9,000 prisoners, although only 7 were prisoners of conscience. On 21 February 2009, it released 6,313 prisoners, of whom 29 were prisoners of conscience. The release, although welcomed, lacked proportionality when compared with the total number of prisoners of conscience. Freedom of opinion and expression, as well as of assembly and association, were enshrined in the new Constitution and were essential elements for achieving the Government's seven-step road map to democracy through elections in 2010. Restrictions reportedly continued to be imposed on the right to form trade unions. Several individuals who were associated with trade unions, including the banned Federation of Trade Unions of Burma, were detained and sentenced to long prison terms. The Rapporteur also received information that several journalists had been convicted, and that the media had been restricted and censored.

The Rapporteur was concerned about the unfolding armed conflict in Kayin State between the Myanmar army and the Karen National Union (KNU), which severely affected the civilian population. Both parties were responsible for extrajudicial killings, torture, enforced disappearances and arbitrary arrests, forcible displacement and the destruction of villages. Other conflicts and human rights abuses were reported in Southern Shan, Kaya and Mon States. In November 2008, the Committee on the Elimination of Discrimination against Women expressed concern at the high prevalence of sexual and other forms of violence perpetrated against rural women from the Shan, Mon, Karen, Palaung and Chin ethnic groups by members of the armed forces, and the apparent impunity of the perpetrators. The Rapporteur urged the Government and all armed groups to ensure the protection of civilians, in particular children and women, during armed conflict. He also expressed concern over the use of anti-personnel mines along the border areas, the practice of forced labour without compensation, and the continued discrimination against the Muslim population of Rakhine State.

The Rapporteur recommended that the Government: sign and ratify the remaining core international human rights instruments; expand the mandate of the Tripartite Core Group (Myanmar, the Association of Southeast Asian Nations and the United Nations) to include all other regions in Myanmar in need of humanitarian aid; establish accountability for the widespread human rights violations and combat impunity enjoyed by the perpetrators; and review national legislation in accordance with the new Constitution and international obligations. He called on the armed forces to repeal discriminatory legislation and avoid discriminatory practices, particularly in Northern Rakhine State, refrain from recruiting child soldiers, forbid the use of anti-personnel landmines, respect international human rights and humanitarian law in areas affected by armed conflict, particularly in Kayin State, refrain from the use of forced labour of civilians, particularly in Kayin State, and establish a training programme on human rights for the armed forces and police and prison personnel. The Rapporteur called on the judiciary to exercise independence and impartiality, particularly for prisoners of conscience, guarantee due process of law, and establish mechanisms to investigate human rights abuses.

Human Rights Council action (March). On 27 March [A/64/53 (res. 10/27)], the Council condemned the ongoing systematic violations of human rights and fundamental freedoms of the people of Myanmar. It urged the Government to desist from further politi-

cally motivated arrests, to release all political prisoners, including Ms. Suu Kyi, Khun Htun Oo and Min Ko Naing. It called for public hearings by independent tribunals and for rectification of trial deficiencies that had led to harsh sentences in Yangon and Mandalay since October 2008. The Council called for a full and transparent investigation into all reports of human rights violations, and for bringing those responsible to justice. It welcomed the prolongation in February 2009 of the understanding between the Government and the International Labour Organization, and urged the Government to end its practice of forced labour. The Government was urged to end the recruitment and use of child soldiers and to ensure the protection of children from armed conflict. The Council expressed appreciation for the Government's cooperation with the international community in delivering humanitarian assistance and called on it to allow unimpeded humanitarian access to all persons in need in all areas, with special attention to internally displaced persons. The Council expressed concern over the situation of the Rohingya ethnic minority in Northern Rakhine State, and urged the Government to recognize their right to nationality. It urged the Government: to ensure a comprehensive review of compliance of all its legislation with international human rights law; to ensure the independence of the judiciary; to guarantee due process of law; to provide human rights and international humanitarian law training for its armed forces, police and prison personnel; to ensure a free and fair electoral process; and to guarantee the rights to freedom of assembly, association and expression. The Council extended for one year the mandate of the Special Rapporteur and requested him to report to the General Assembly and to the Council.

Further report of Special Rapporteur. In a report of 24 August [A/64/318], submitted pursuant to General Assembly resolution 63/245 [YUN 2008, p. 886], the Rapporteur focused on human rights developments since his March report. The trial of Ms. Suu Kyi, with sentencing on 11 August to an additional 18-month house arrest, was the most significant event as it barred her from participating in the 2010 elections. The Rapporteur considered that the new sentence, in connection with the intrusion of a United States national into her house, was a blow to the Government's seven-step road map to democracy, and regretted that the Government had missed another opportunity to prove its commitment to hold inclusive, free and fair elections. The report highlighted the situation of prisoners of conscience and called for their progressive release, beginning with those with health problems, and noted that their prison conditions were reportedly harsh, including solitary confinement, forced labour and shackling. The Rapporteur was informed of new arrests and sentences by special courts and of the arrest of a number of lawyers for contempt of court. He was able to meet in private with imprisoned lawyers who had defended prisoners of conscience. He regretted that the independence of lawyers had been hindered for political motivations.

In February, the authorities informed the Rapporteur that 380 domestic laws had been sent to the concerned Ministries for compliance checks with the provisions of the new Constitution and Myanmar's international obligations. Welcoming the move, the Rapporteur recommended that priority be given to laws affecting the exercise of the freedom of expression and association in view of the upcoming elections. He pointed out that some legislation contained provisions allowing misuse and arbitrary application, and he named certain laws dealing with emergency powers, the media, computers, the Internet and publications, which he hoped would be revised. The electoral law governing the 2010 elections had not been made public. It was urgent to ensure proper registration of political parties and to allow for adequate campaigning and civic education. The Rapporteur saw problems in the Constitution in that it provided for an overly dominant role for the military without effective counter-balancing and control mechanisms; in addition, human rights could be compromised by exception clauses, which were formulated in broad terms and could allow justifications for the security of the Union, prevalence of law and order, community peace or public morality.

Another concern was the treatment of ethnic minorities, and Myanmar had seen a large scale of population displacements, especially along border areas. Owing to the ongoing fighting between the Government and KNU, some 500,000 people were forced to leave their villages in the east, while others had fled the country. The conflict led to problems of law and order violations, the use of anti-personnel mines, recruitment of children, rape and sexual assault by military personnel, and forced labour. Another concern raised by the Rapporteur was the situation of the Muslim population in Northern Rakhine State, who, because they were not recognized as one of the 135 national races in Myanmar, were not granted citizenship despite having lived there for generations. However, the population, having been given temporary registration cards for participating in the referendum on the new Constitution, would be allowed to vote. The Rapporteur recommended that the Government repeal discriminatory legislation, particularly in Northern Rakhine State. He reiterated recommendations made in his previous report, while regretting that the Government had not accepted his request to visit Myanmar again.

Report of Secretary-General. The Secretary-General, having visited Myanmar on 3 and 4 July, submitted a report [A/64/334] on the human rights situation in the country, pursuant to General Assembly resolution 63/245, covering the period from 25 August 2008 to 25 August 2009. His Special Adviser, Ibrahim Gambari, visited Myanmar at the Government's invitation, from 31 January to 3 February and on 26 and 27 June, and accompanied the Secretary-General in July.

Discussions with senior leaders focused on the release of all political prisoners, including Ms. Suu Kyi; the need for an inclusive, substantive and time-bound dialogue; the conditions for a credible process of political transition to civilian and democratic government; improvement of socio-economic conditions; and regularization of the good offices process between Myanmar and the United Nations. The Government enacted two prisoner amnesties, announcing that it had released 9,002 prisoners in September 2008 and 6,313 prisoners in February 2009. However, during that time, the Government imposed lengthy prison terms on some 400 individuals connected to protests in 2007. The Government expressed its determination to proceed with multiparty elections. Several key stakeholders, including NLD and some ethnic groups, objected to the new Constitution and the process by which it had been adopted, and reserved their position on participating in the 2010 election. The Secretary-General emphasized that only a credible and inclusive political process, based on mutual understanding and constructive compromise by all stakeholders, could advance the prospects of durable peace, democracy and respect for human rights. On 9 June, the Office of the United Nations High Commissioner for Refugees (UNHCR) reported an influx of some 3,000 refugees from Myanmar into Thailand, coinciding with reports of renewed fighting in eastern border areas.

The Special Adviser suggested a review of the recent sentencing of individuals connected to the 2007 demonstrations, but the Government explained that that could be done only through the legal appeal channels. The Special Adviser raised the cases of individuals who could contribute to the political process and whose release on compassionate grounds should be considered. He encouraged Government officials and Ms. Suu Kyi to meet for discussions with a view to creating conditions conducive to lifting sanctions against Myanmar. He stressed the need for the Government to create conditions conducive to a process leading to elections and made suggestions to that end, including a constitutional review. The Government ruled out a constitutional review while reiterating its determination to proceed with elections. The Prime Minister affirmed that once election laws were adopted, all political parties would be able to participate. The Special Adviser stressed the positive implications of establishing a broad-based national forum on socio-economic issues, while the Government reiterated its demand that sanctions be lifted.

During his visit, the Secretary-General met with the Chairman of the State Peace and Development Council (spDC), Senior General Than Shwe, other spDC members, the Prime Minister and other ministers, and representatives of the political parties, including those representing ethnic constituencies. He emphasized the need to address development issues, as peace and security could be affected by underlying socio-economic conditions, and offered to work on the question of sanctions and restrictions on the work of international aid organizations. He recommended the early announcement of a date for the elections, publication of sound election laws, establishment of an independent electoral commission, the reopening of all NLD offices, and re-registration of deregistered political parties. He encouraged the leadership to consider establishing a UN presence in Yangon for liaison and facilitation of communication in the run-up to elections. The Senior General replied that elections would be arranged to allow for the participation of all and would be free and fair. He highlighted the fact that while some insurgent groups remained, 17 armed groups had made peace with the Government and were concentrating on regional development. According to him, efforts had been made to engage directly with Ms. Suu Kyi with a view to including her in the national reconciliation process.

As the Government prepared for the first elections in 20 years, the Secretary-General expected it to take the necessary steps to ensure that the elections were inclusive, participatory and transparent, and conducted in accordance with international standards. In addition, Myanmar needed to give attention to longer-term issues such as the future status of armed groups, development needs in border areas, and cessation of hostilities, particularly in Kayin and Kayah States, where there were reports of armed conflict and associated human rights abuses.

Human Rights Council action (October). On 2 October [A/65/53 (res. 12/20)], the Council expressed concern at the conviction and sentencing of Ms. Suu Kyi and called for her release. It called on Myanmar: to release all political prisoners, enabling them to participate fully in the 2010 elections; to engage in a process of dialogue and national reconciliation with the participation of representatives of all political parties and ethnic groups; and to create the conditions for inclusive, transparent and credible democratic elections.

Communication. Myanmar, in a letter of 23 October [A/C.3/64/2] to the Secretary-General, referred to General Assembly resolution 63/245 [YUN 2008, p. 886] on its human rights situation, which it found to be procedurally and factually flawed. Human rights could best be promoted through understanding rather than through country-specific resolutions. Myanmar outlined its actions on illicit narcotic drugs, steps to

enforce the law prohibiting production and trafficking of illegal arms and ammunition, efforts to halt the recruitment of child soldiers and trafficking in persons, and measures for protecting women and girls from sexual and gender-based violence. Myanmar affirmed that a democratic State would emerge after the 2010 general elections, which would be free and fair.

GENERAL ASSEMBLY ACTION

On 24 December [meeting 68], the General Assembly, on the recommendation of the Third Committee [A/64/439/Add.3], adopted **resolution 64/238** by recorded vote (86-23-39) [agenda item 69 *(c)*].

Situation of human rights in Myanmar

The General Assembly,

Guided by the Charter of the United Nations and the Universal Declaration of Human Rights, and recalling the International Covenants on Human Rights and other relevant human rights instruments,

Reaffirming that all Member States have an obligation to promote and protect human rights and fundamental freedoms and the duty to fulfil the obligations they have undertaken under the various international instruments in this field,

Reaffirming also its previous resolutions on the situation of human rights in Myanmar, the most recent of which is resolution 63/245 of 24 December 2008, those of the Commission on Human Rights, and the resolutions of the Human Rights Council, the most recent of which are 10/27 of 27 March 2009 and 12/20 of 2 October 2009,

Welcoming the statements made by the President of the Security Council on 11 October 2007 and 2 May 2008, and the Security Council statements to the press of 22 May 2009 and 13 August 2009,

Welcoming also the report of the Secretary-General on the situation of human rights in Myanmar, as well as his visit to the country on 3 and 4 July 2009, and the visits of his Special Adviser on Myanmar from 31 January to 3 February and on 26 and 27 June 2009 respectively, while regretting that the Government of Myanmar did not seize the opportunity of those visits to work towards the fulfilment of the good offices mission,

Welcoming further the reports of the Special Rapporteur on the situation of human rights in Myanmar and his oral presentations, and the fact that a date has now been established for a follow-up visit by the Special Rapporteur,

Deeply concerned that the urgent calls contained in the above-mentioned resolutions, as well as the statements of other United Nations bodies concerning the situation of human rights in Myanmar, have not been met, and emphasizing that, without significant progress towards meeting these calls of the international community, the situation of human rights in Myanmar will continue to deteriorate,

Deeply concerned also at restrictions to effective and genuine participation of the representatives of the National League for Democracy and other political parties and other relevant stakeholders, including some ethnic groups, in a genuine process of dialogue, national reconciliation and transition to democracy,

Calling upon the Government of Myanmar to cooperate with the international community in order to achieve concrete progress with regard to human rights and fundamental freedoms, and political processes, and to take immediate steps to ensure a free and fair electoral process which is transparent and inclusive, leading to a genuine democratic transition through concrete measures,

1. *Strongly condemns* the ongoing systematic violations of human rights and fundamental freedoms of the people of Myanmar;

2. *Expresses grave concern* at the recent trial, conviction and sentencing of Daw Aung San Suu Kyi, resulting in her return to house arrest, and calls for her immediate and unconditional release;

3. *Urges* the Government of Myanmar to release all prisoners of conscience, currently estimated at more than 2,000, without delay, without conditions and with full restoration of their political rights, while noting the recent release of more than 100 prisoners of conscience, and strongly calls upon the Government of Myanmar to reveal the whereabouts of persons who are detained or have been subjected to enforced disappearance, and to desist from further politically motivated arrests;

4. *Reaffirms* the essential importance of a genuine process of dialogue and national reconciliation for a transition to democracy, notes with appreciation recent contact between the Government of Myanmar and Daw Aung San Suu Kyi, and calls upon the Government of Myanmar to take immediate measures to undertake a genuine dialogue with Daw Aung San Suu Kyi and all other concerned parties and ethnic groups, and to permit Daw Aung San Suu Kyi contact with the National League for Democracy and other domestic stakeholders;

5. *Strongly urges* the Government of Myanmar to ensure the necessary steps to be taken towards a free, fair, transparent and inclusive electoral process and calls upon the Government to take such steps without delay, including by enacting the required electoral laws and allowing the participation of all voters, all political parties and all other relevant stakeholders in the electoral process;

6. *Strongly calls upon* the Government of Myanmar to lift restrictions on the freedom of assembly, association, movement and freedom of expression, including for free and independent media, including through the openly available and accessible use of Internet and mobile telephone services, and ending the use of censorship;

7. *Expresses grave concern* at the continuing practice of arbitrary detentions, enforced disappearances, rape and other forms of sexual violence, torture and cruel, inhuman and degrading treatment, and strongly calls upon the Government of Myanmar to allow a full, transparent, effective, impartial and independent investigation into all reports of human rights violations, and to bring to justice those responsible in order to end impunity for such crimes;

8. *Calls upon* the Government of Myanmar to undertake a transparent, inclusive and comprehensive review of compliance of the Constitution and all national legislation with international human rights law, while fully engaging with democratic opposition and ethnic groups, while recalling that the procedures established for the drafting of the Constitution resulted in a de facto exclusion of the opposition from the process;

9. *Urges* the Government of Myanmar to ensure the independence and impartiality of the judiciary and to guarantee due process of law, and to fulfil earlier assurances made to the Special Rapporteur on the situation of human rights in Myanmar to begin a dialogue on judicial reform;

10. *Expresses concern* about the conditions in prisons and other detention facilities, and consistent reports of ill-treatment of prisoners of conscience, including torture, and about the moving of prisoners of conscience to isolated prisons far from their families where they cannot receive food and medicine;

11. *Expresses deep concern* about the resumption of armed conflict in some areas, and calls upon the Government of Myanmar to protect the civilian population in all parts of the country and for all concerned to respect existing ceasefire agreements;

12. *Strongly calls upon* the Government of Myanmar to take urgent measures to put an end to violations of international human rights and humanitarian law, including the targeting of persons belonging to particular ethnic groups, the targeting of civilians by military operations, and rape and other forms of sexual violence, and to end impunity for such acts;

13. *Also strongly calls upon* the Government of Myanmar to end the practice of systematic forced displacement of large numbers of persons within their country and other causes of refugee flows into neighbouring countries;

14. *Expresses its concern* about the continuing discrimination, human rights violations, violence, displacement and economic deprivation affecting numerous ethnic minorities, including, but not limited to, the Rohingya ethnic minority in Northern Rakhine State, and calls upon the Government of Myanmar to take immediate action to bring about an improvement in their respective situations, and to grant citizenship to the Rohingya ethnic minority;

15. *Urges* the Government of Myanmar to provide, in cooperation with the Office of the United Nations High Commissioner for Human Rights, adequate human rights and international humanitarian law training for its armed forces, police and prison personnel, to ensure their strict compliance with international human rights law and international humanitarian law and to hold them accountable for any violations thereof;

16. *Welcomes* the dialogue between the Government of Myanmar and the Committee on the Elimination of Discrimination against Women on the occasion of the consideration of the Government's report in November 2008, as a sign of engagement in international cooperative efforts in the field of human rights, and encourages the Government to work to fulfil the recommendations of the Committee;

17. *Calls upon* the Government of Myanmar to consider acceding to remaining international human rights treaties, which would enable a dialogue with the other human rights treaty bodies;

18. *Also calls upon* the Government of Myanmar to allow human rights defenders to pursue their activities unhindered and to ensure their safety, security and freedom of movement in that pursuit;

19. *Strongly calls upon* the Government of Myanmar to put an immediate end to the continuing recruitment and use of child soldiers in violation of international law by all parties, to intensify measures to ensure the protection of

children from armed conflict and to pursue its collaboration with the Special Representative of the Secretary-General for Children and Armed Conflict, including by granting access to areas where children are recruited, for the purpose of implementing an action plan to halt this practice;

20. *Notes with appreciation* that some further steps have been taken with regard to the supplementary understanding between the International Labour Organization and the Government of Myanmar to eliminate the use of forced labour, but expresses grave concern at the continuing practice of forced labour, and urges the Government to continue to work with the International Labour Organization on the basis of the understanding, including through awareness-raising activities, with a view to extending action against forced labour as widely as possible throughout the country and to fully implementing the recommendations of the Commission of Inquiry of the International Labour Organization;

21. *Notes* the continued cooperation of the Government of Myanmar with the international community, including the United Nations, in delivering humanitarian assistance to the people affected by Cyclone Nargis, and in the light of ongoing humanitarian need encourages the Government of Myanmar to ensure that cooperation is maintained, and the continuation of the Tripartite Core Group mechanism;

22. *Calls upon* the Government of Myanmar to ensure timely, safe, full and unhindered access to all parts of Myanmar, including conflict and border areas, for the United Nations, international humanitarian organizations and their partners and to cooperate fully with those actors to ensure that humanitarian assistance is delivered to all persons in need throughout the country, including displaced persons;

23. *Also calls upon* the Government of Myanmar to resume its humanitarian dialogue with the International Committee of the Red Cross and to allow it to carry out its activities according to its mandate, in particular by granting access to persons detained and to areas of internal armed conflict;

24. *Welcomes* the progress reported on the work conducted by the Government of Myanmar and international humanitarian entities on HIV/AIDS;

25. *Reaffirms its full support* for the good offices of the Secretary-General pursued through his Special Adviser on Myanmar, consistent with the report of the Secretary-General on the situation of human rights in Myanmar, and urges the Government of Myanmar to cooperate fully with the good offices mission in the fulfilment of its responsibilities as mandated by the General Assembly, including by facilitating the visits of the Special Adviser to the country and granting him unrestricted access to all relevant parties, including the highest level of leadership within the regime, human rights defenders, representatives of ethnic minorities, student leaders and other opposition groups, and to respond substantively and without delay to the five-point plan of the Secretary-General, including the establishment of a United Nations office in support of the mandate of the good offices;

26. *Welcomes* the role played by countries neighbouring Myanmar and members of the Association of Southeast Asian Nations in support of the good offices mission of the Secretary-General, and in relief efforts following Cyclone Nargis, and encourages the continuation and intensification of efforts in this regard;

27. *Welcomes also* the continued contribution of the Group of Friends of the Secretary-General on Myanmar to facilitate the work of the good offices mission;

28. *Welcomes further* the favourable response to granting the Special Rapporteur's requests to visit the country, and urges the Government to cooperate fully with him in the exercise of his work as mandated by the Human Rights Council, and to implement the four core human rights elements recommended by the Special Rapporteur;

29. *Calls upon* the Government of Myanmar to engage in a dialogue with the Office of the United Nations High Commissioner for Human Rights with a view to ensuring full respect for all human rights and fundamental freedoms;

30. *Requests* the Secretary-General:

(a) To continue to provide his good offices and to pursue his discussions on the situation of human rights, the transition to democracy and the national reconciliation process with the Government and the people of Myanmar, including democracy and human rights groups and all relevant parties, and to offer technical assistance to the Government in this regard;

(b) To give all necessary assistance to enable the Special Adviser and the Special Rapporteur to discharge their mandates fully and effectively and in a coordinated manner;

(c) To report to the General Assembly at its sixty-fifth session, as well as to the Human Rights Council, on the progress made in the implementation of the present resolution;

31. *Decides* to continue the consideration of the question at its sixty-fifth session, on the basis of the report of the Secretary-General and the interim report of the Special Rapporteur.

RECORDED VOTE ON RESOLUTION 64/238:

In favour: Afghanistan, Albania, Andorra, Antigua and Barbuda, Argentina, Armenia, Australia, Austria, Belgium, Bosnia and Herzegovina, Botswana, Bulgaria, Burundi, Canada, Chile, Costa Rica, Croatia, Cyprus, Czech Republic, Denmark, Estonia, Finland, France, Georgia, Germany, Ghana, Greece, Guatemala, Guyana, Haiti, Hungary, Iceland, Iraq, Ireland, Israel, Italy, Jamaica, Japan, Kazakhstan, Latvia, Lebanon, Liberia, Liechtenstein, Lithuania, Luxembourg, Malawi, Maldives, Malta, Marshall Islands, Mauritius, Mexico, Micronesia, Moldova, Monaco, Mongolia, Montenegro, Morocco, Namibia, Nauru, Netherlands, New Zealand, Nigeria, Palau, Panama, Peru, Poland, Portugal, Republic of Korea, Romania, Slovakia, Slovenia, Solomon Islands, South Africa, Spain, Sweden, Switzerland, The former Yugoslav Republic of Macedonia, Timor-Leste, Togo, Tonga, Turkey, Ukraine, United Kingdom, United Republic of Tanzania, United States, Uruguay.

Against: Algeria, Azerbaijan, Bangladesh, Belarus, Brunei Darussalam, China, Cuba, Democratic People's Republic of Korea, Egypt, India, Lao People's Democratic Republic, Libyan Arab Jamahiriya, Malaysia, Myanmar, Nicaragua, Oman, Russian Federation, Sri Lanka, Sudan, Syrian Arab Republic, Venezuela, Viet Nam, Zimbabwe.

Abstaining: Bahamas, Bahrain, Benin, Bolivia, Brazil, Burkina Faso, Cambodia, Cameroon, Colombia, Congo, Côte d'Ivoire, Dominica, Dominican Republic, Ecuador, Ethiopia, Gabon, Indonesia, Jordan, Kenya, Kuwait, Kyrgyzstan, Madagascar, Mali, Mauritania, Nepal, Niger, Norway, Pakistan, Qatar, Saint Lucia, Saudi Arabia, Senegal, Singapore, Swaziland, Tajikistan, Thailand, Trinidad and Tobago, United Arab Emirates, Yemen.

Nepal

Report of High Commissioner. In a report [A/HRC/13/73 & Corr.1] on the human rights situation and OHCHR activities in Nepal, including technical cooperation, covering events in 2009, the High Commissioner described some positive developments since the previous report [YUN 2008, p. 889], including in relation to policies on violence against women and reducing discrimination. Although the peace process had delivered improvements in the human rights situation since 2006, it had lost considerable momentum during the year, giving rise to concerns about longer-term peace and stability. Political instability, the impasse in the implementation of several key provisions in the 2006 Comprehensive Peace Agreement [YUN 2006, p. 449], de facto impunity for serious human rights violations, and deficiencies in the rule of law framework aggravated an already weakened security situation and had a negative impact on the overall human rights situation. The widespread inequality and discrimination that gave rise to the conflict persisted, and expectations that the new political order signalled by the 2006 people's movement would foster greater respect for human rights and democracy had been severely tested. Despite those challenges, the peace process continued to hold promise, provided all parties recommitted themselves to the human rights principles at the centre of the Peace Agreement.

The High Commissioner recommended that the Government fulfil its commitments to end impunity, including by implementing transitional justice mechanisms, investigating the disappearances at Maharajgunj barracks and Bardiya documented by OHCHR, and prosecuting cases committed both by members of the Unified Communist Party of Nepal (Maoist) (UCPN-M) and the State security forces. The army and UCPN-M were urged to comply with court orders regarding alleged crimes committed by their members. Comprehensive reforms in the security sector institutions would enhance human rights protection. The establishment of an independent special unit to investigate serious allegations against the police and the armed police force, including allegations of extrajudicial killings, would be an important first step. The Government's efforts to address long-standing discrimination were welcomed, and further legislative and practical measures were encouraged, including implementation of the national plan of action for the elimination of violence against women.

Sri Lanka

Human Rights Council special session

At the request of Germany [A/HRC/S-11/1], supported by 16 other Council members, the Council held its eleventh special session (Geneva, 26–27 May) [A/HRC/S-11/2] to consider the human rights situation in Sri Lanka. During its consideration, the Council heard statements from its members, Sri Lanka, other countries, the High Commissioner, the independent expert on the question of human rights and extreme poverty on behalf of special procedures mandate-holders, UN entities and NGOs.

On 27 May [ibid. (res. S-11/1)], by a recorded vote of 29 to 12, with 6 abstentions, the Council, welcoming the conclusion of hostilities and the liberation by the Sri Lankan Government of tens of thousands of its citizens who were held by the Liberation Tigers of Tamil Eelam as hostages, commended the Government's efforts to bring peace to the country and to address the needs of internally displaced persons (IDPs). Emphasizing that the human rights priorities remained assistance for the relief and rehabilitation of persons affected by the conflict and reconstruction of the economy and infrastructure, the Council welcomed Sri Lanka's commitment to the promotion and protection of all human rights and encouraged it to continue to uphold its obligations under international human rights law. The Council encouraged the Government to cooperate with UN organizations in providing basic humanitarian assistance to IDPs. It welcomed the Government's proposal to resettle most IDPs within six months, and acknowledged its commitment to provide access to international agencies in order to ensure assistance to those affected by the conflict. The Government was encouraged to persevere in disarmament, demobilization and rehabilitation of former child soldiers, their physical and psychological recovery and reintegration into society, in cooperation with UN organizations. The Council urged Sri Lanka to ensure that there was no discrimination against ethnic minorities in the enjoyment of human rights. It welcomed the cooperation between the Government, UN agencies and other organizations in providing humanitarian assistance and urged them to continue to cooperate. It welcomed the visits to Sri Lanka by the Under-Secretary-General for Humanitarian Affairs and the Representative of the Secretary-General on the human rights of IDPs, and encouraged them to continue to cooperate. The Council further welcomed the visit of the Secretary-General and endorsed the joint communiqué issued at the conclusion of that visit (see p. 398). It welcomed the resolve of the authorities to begin a broader dialogue with all parties in order to enhance the political settlement process and to bring about lasting peace and development based on consensus among and respect for all ethnic and religious groups, and invited all stakeholders to participate in it. The Council urged the international community to cooperate with the Government in reconstruction, including by increasing financial assistance to help the country fight poverty and underdevelopment and to ensure the promotion and protection of human rights.

Europe and the Mediterranean

Cyprus

In accordance with a request of the Human Rights Council [YUN 2006, p. 760], the Secretary-General transmitted to the Council an OHCHR report on the question of human rights in Cyprus [A/HRC/13/24] covering the period up to 31 December 2009. Without an OHCHR field presence in Cyprus, the report relied on a variety of sources. The persisting division of Cyprus continued to have consequences in relation to a number of human rights issues, including freedom of movement, missing persons, property rights, discrimination, freedom of religion, the right to education and economic rights. With regard to freedom of movement, the United Nations Peacekeeping Force in Cyprus (UNFICYP) recorded approximately 873,700 crossings through the buffer zone during the period from November 2008 to May 2009 and approximately 928,200 in the period from May to November 2009. The Committee on Missing Persons continued the exhumation, identification and return of the remains of missing persons. By December, the remains of 585 individuals had been exhumed on both sides of the buffer zone, the remains of 352 missing persons had undergone examination, and the remains of 196 individuals had been returned to their families. Property rights remained the main issue of concern, and the Council of Europe Committee of Ministers' Deputies continued to supervise the execution of judgements of the European Court on Human Rights on landmark property cases from previous years. UNFICYP assisted Turkish Cypriots living in the south to obtain identity documents, housing, welfare services, medical care, employment and education. With regard to freedom of religion, UNFICYP facilitated access to sites and icons of religious and cultural significance. From November 2008 to May 2009, the mission facilitated five religious and commemorative events, which took place without incident. The report concluded that the persisting de facto partition of the island continued to constitute an obstacle to the full enjoyment of human rights. It was hoped that the new momentum to achieve a comprehensive settlement of the Cyprus problem would provide avenues to improve the human rights situation and that relevant stakeholders would contribute to achieving enhanced human rights protection and promotion.

Communications. In a note of 26 March [A/HRC/10/G/12], Turkey transmitted a letter reflecting the Turkish Cypriot views on the Secretary-General's 2008 report on the question of human rights in Cyprus [YUN 2008, p. 890]. Cyprus replied to that note by a letter of 28 April [A/HRC/10/G/13].

Georgia

Report of Secretary-General. The Secretary-General, pursuant to General Assembly resolution 62/249 [YUN 2008, p. 891], reported on 24 August [A/63/950] on the status of IDPs and refugees from Abkhazia, Georgia, covering the period from 16 May 2008 to 15 July 2009. Referring to his report of 3 October 2008 on Georgia to the Security Council [YUN 2008, p. 457], the Secretary-General stated that the outbreak of hostilities in South Ossetia on 7 and 8 August 2008 had had a profound impact on the situation in the Georgian-Abkhaz conflict zone and the overall conflict settlement process begun in 1994 with the signing of the Quadripartite Agreement on Voluntary Return of Refugees and Displaced Persons [YUN 1994, p. 581] and the Agreement on a Ceasefire and Separation of Forces [ibid., p. 583]. Since the events of August 2008, the United Nations, the European Union and the Organization for Security and Cooperation in Europe had held, as co-chairs, six rounds of discussions in Geneva pursuant to the six-point agreement of 12 August 2008 and the subsequent implementing measures of 8 September 2008. Issues relating to security and stability, as well as humanitarian issues, including refugees and IDPs, were reviewed. The Co-Chairpersons undertook frequent missions to the conflict area and submitted various proposals to the sides; however, they were unable to reach a comprehensive settlement of the conflict addressing the needs of all refugees and IDPs, regardless of where they were displaced. Thus, the conditions required to allow for the organized return of displaced persons had not been met. Provided that adequate security conditions could be put in place, the competent UN entities would continue to support the humanitarian needs of the refugees, IDPs and returnees and concentrate their efforts on providing assistance to the war-affected population, including spontaneous returnees. (See also p. 418.)

Georgian authorities reported that more than 293,048 IDPs resided in Georgia, of whom 245,363 (83.7 per cent) were displaced following the Georgian-Abkhaz conflict in the 1990s. Of the latter number, it was estimated that approximately 45,000 people had spontaneously returned or were in the process of returning to their homes in the Gali, Ochamchira and Tkvarcheli districts, although they were still considered IDPs and were eligible for Government assistance. For several years, the United Nations High Commissioner for Refugees had called upon the parties to conduct a verification and profiling exercise to better assess the needs of spontaneous returnees and their host communities; the exercise had not taken place owing to lack of agreement between the parties. The exercise was considered critical to obtaining a clearer picture of the legal, social, economic and security conditions in areas of return as well as the number, profile and needs of returnees and receiving communities. Humanitarian assistance was provided in both returnee and non-returnee areas, including measures to increase the capacity of civil society actors to assist the beneficiary population. Many returnees seasonally migrated or had families living in different places. Returnees were concerned in particular with their security and access to livelihood programmes. Other issues included personal identity documentation, freedom of movement and access to social and health-care services. Ideally, a peace agreement should be secured prior to a return process; in the absence of a political settlement, verifiable security guarantees were needed. It was essential to recognize return both as a human right and as a humanitarian issue. International law as well as commitments made by the parties, expressed in the Quadripartite Agreement, underscored that responsibility for IDPs and refugees rested with the parties to the conflict. To preserve and protect the property rights of refugees, IDPs and their descendants, the parties must resolve the legal and political issues impeding their implementation. In doing so, the principles on housing and property restitution for refugees and displaced persons (the "Pinheiro principles") and international law had to be respected. UN agencies were ready to assist the parties in addressing establishment, registration and documentation of property rights; preservation of property rights; permitting safeguarded property transactions; and establishment of property restitution procedures. In addition, they were ready to proceed with developing a timetable for the voluntary return of all refugees and IDPs.

GENERAL ASSEMBLY ACTION

On 9 September [meeting 104], the General Assembly adopted **resolution 63/307** [draft: A/63/L.79] by recorded vote (48-19-78) [agenda item 13].

Status of internally displaced persons and refugees from Abkhazia, Georgia, and the Tskhinvali region/South Ossetia, Georgia

The General Assembly,

Recalling all its relevant resolutions on the protection of and assistance to internally displaced persons, including its resolutions 62/153 of 18 December 2007 and 62/249 of 15 May 2008,

Recalling also all relevant Security Council resolutions on Georgia relating to the need for all parties to work towards a comprehensive peace and the return of internally displaced persons and refugees to their places of origin, and stressing the importance of their full and timely implementation,

Recognizing the Guiding Principles on Internal Displacement as the key international framework for the protection of internally displaced persons,

Concerned by forced demographic changes resulting from the conflicts in Georgia,

Concerned also by the humanitarian situation caused by armed conflict in August 2008, which resulted in the further forced displacement of civilians,

Mindful of the urgent need to find a solution to the problems related to forced displacement in Georgia,

Underlining the importance of the discussions that commenced in Geneva on 15 October 2008 and of continuing to address the issue of the voluntary, safe, dignified and unhindered return of internally displaced persons and refugees on the basis of internationally recognized principles and conflict-settlement practices,

Taking note of the report of the Secretary-General concerning the implementation of General Assembly resolution 62/249,

1. *Recognizes* the right of return of all internally displaced persons and refugees and their descendants, regardless of ethnicity, to their homes throughout Georgia, including in Abkhazia and South Ossetia;

2. *Stresses* the need to respect the property rights of all internally displaced persons and refugees affected by the conflicts in Georgia and to refrain from obtaining property in violation of those rights;

3. *Reaffirms* the unacceptability of forced demographic changes;

4. *Underlines* the urgent need for unimpeded access for humanitarian activities to all internally displaced persons, refugees and other persons residing in all conflict-affected areas throughout Georgia;

5. *Calls upon* all participants in the Geneva discussions to intensify their efforts to establish a durable peace, to commit to enhanced confidence-building measures and to take immediate steps to ensure respect for human rights and create favourable security conditions conducive to the voluntary, safe, dignified and unhindered return of all internally displaced persons and refugees to their places of origin;

6. *Underlines* the need for the development of a timetable to ensure the voluntary, safe, dignified and unhindered return of all internally displaced persons and refugees affected by the conflicts in Georgia to their homes;

7. *Requests* the Secretary-General to submit to the General Assembly at its sixty-fourth session a comprehensive report on the implementation of the present resolution;

8. *Decides* to include in the provisional agenda of its sixty-fourth session the item entitled "Protracted conflicts in the GUAM area and their implications for international peace, security and development".

RECORDED VOTE ON RESOLUTION 63/307:

In favour: Albania, Andorra, Australia, Austria, Azerbaijan, Belgium, Bosnia and Herzegovina, Bulgaria, Canada, Croatia, Czech Republic, Denmark, Estonia, Finland, France, Georgia, Germany, Greece, Hungary, Iceland, Ireland, Italy, Japan, Latvia, Liechtenstein, Lithuania, Luxembourg, Malta, Monaco, Montenegro, Netherlands, New Zealand, Norway, Poland, Portugal, Romania, Saint Lucia, San Marino, Slovakia, Slovenia, Spain, Sweden, The former Yugoslav Republic of Macedonia, Uganda, Ukraine, United Kingdom, United States, Vanuatu.

Against: Algeria, Armenia, Belarus, Bolivia, Cuba, Democratic People's Republic of Korea, Ecuador, Ethiopia, India,

Iran, Lao People's Democratic Republic, Myanmar, Nicaragua, Russian Federation, Sri Lanka, Syrian Arab Republic, Venezuela, Viet Nam, Zimbabwe.

Abstaining: Antigua and Barbuda, Argentina, Bahamas, Bahrain, Bangladesh, Barbados, Benin, Botswana, Brazil, Brunei Darussalam, Burkina Faso, Cameroon, Chile, China, Colombia, Congo, Costa Rica, Cyprus, Djibouti, Dominica, Dominican Republic, Egypt, El Salvador, Fiji, Gabon, Ghana, Guatemala, Guyana, Indonesia, Israel, Jamaica, Jordan, Kazakhstan, Kenya, Kuwait, Kyrgyzstan, Lebanon, Libyan Arab Jamahiriya, Malaysia, Mauritius, Mexico, Moldova, Mongolia, Morocco, Namibia, Nepal, Nigeria, Oman, Pakistan, Panama, Papua New Guinea, Paraguay, Peru, Philippines, Qatar, Republic of Korea, Rwanda, Samoa, Saudi Arabia, Senegal, Serbia, Singapore, South Africa, Suriname, Swaziland, Switzerland, Thailand, Timor-Leste, Togo, Trinidad and Tobago, Tunisia, Turkey, United Arab Emirates, United Republic of Tanzania, Uruguay, Uzbekistan, Yemen, Zambia.

Middle East

Territories occupied by Israel

In 2009, human rights questions, including cases of violations in the territories occupied by Israel following the 1967 hostilities in the Middle East, were addressed by the Human Rights Council. Political and other aspects were considered by the Security Council, the General Assembly, its Special Committee to Investigate Israeli Practices Affecting the Human Rights of the Palestinian People and Other Arabs of the Occupied Territories (Committee on Israeli Practices) and other bodies (see PART ONE, Chapter VI).

Israeli military operation in Gaza Strip

Human Rights Council special session. At the request of Egypt, on behalf of the Arab Group and the African Group; Pakistan, on behalf of the Organization of the Islamic Conference; Cuba, on behalf of the Non-Aligned Movement; and supported by 30 other States [A/HRC/S-9/1], the Human Rights Council held its ninth special session (Geneva, 9 and 12 January) [A/HRC/S-9/2] on the grave violations of human rights in the Occupied Palestinian Territory including recent aggression in the occupied Gaza Strip. During its consideration of the issue, the Council heard statements from its members and non-members, Israel and Palestine, the High Commissioner for Human Rights, intergovernmental organizations and NGOs. Other UN bodies, including the Security Council and the General Assembly, took action regarding the attacks (see PART ONE, Chapter VI).

On 12 January [ibid. (res. S-9/1)], by a recorded vote of 33 to 1, with 13 abstentions, the Council condemned the ongoing Israeli military operation carried out in the Occupied Palestinian Territory, particularly in the Gaza Strip, which had resulted in massive vio-

lations of the human rights of the Palestinian people and systematic destruction of infrastructure. It called for the immediate cessation of Israeli attacks, which had resulted in more than 900 deaths, and the end to rocket launchings against Israeli civilians, which had resulted in the loss of four civilians. The Council demanded that the occupying Power, Israel: withdraw its military forces from the Gaza Strip; stop the targeting of civilians and medical facilities and staff and the systematic destruction of the cultural heritage of the Palestinian people, in addition to property destruction; lift its siege and open all borders to allow access of humanitarian aid to the Gaza Strip, including through humanitarian corridors; and ensure access of the media to conflict areas through media corridors. Israel was called on to end its occupation of all Palestinian lands occupied since 1967 and to respect its commitment within the peace process towards the establishment of the independent sovereign Palestinian State, with East Jerusalem as its capital. The Council called for international action to end the violations by Israel in the Occupied Palestinian Territory, particularly in Gaza, and for international protection of the Palestinian people in the Territory, in compliance with international law. It urged all parties to respect international human rights law and international humanitarian law and to refrain from violence against the civilian population. The Council requested the High Commissioner to report on human rights violations of the Palestinian people by Israel by: strengthening the OHCHR field presence in the Occupied Palestinian Territory, particularly in Gaza; monitoring Israeli violations of the human rights of Palestinians and the destruction of their properties; and submitting periodic reports. The Council requested relevant special procedures mandate-holders to report to the Council on violations of the human rights of Palestinians. The Council decided to dispatch an independent international fact-finding mission, to be appointed by its President, to investigate violations of international human rights law and international humanitarian law by Israel against the Palestinian people in the Occupied Palestinian Territory, particularly in Gaza, due to the current aggression, and called on Israel not to obstruct the investigation and to cooperate with the mission. The Secretary-General was requested to investigate the targeting of facilities of the United Nations Relief and Works Agency for Palestine Refugees in the Near East (UNRWA) in Gaza, which resulted in the killing of tens of Palestinian civilians, and to report to the General Assembly thereon.

Communication. Cuba, in a note dated 6 January to the Human Rights Council [A/HRC/S-9/G/1], transmitted two statements by the Coordinating Bureau of the Non-Aligned Movement on the situation in the Occupied Palestinian Territory, in the light of the latest assaults by Israel against the Gaza Strip. The

Movement expressed regret at the loss of innocent life and injury as a result of the attacks, as well as the destruction of property and infrastructure.

Report of High Commissioner. As mandated by the Council, the High Commissioner reported on 19 August [A/HRC/12/37] on the implementation of resolution S-9/1 (see p. 780), focusing on key concerns of OHCHR in the Occupied Palestinian Territory during the period of the Israeli military operations in Gaza codenamed "Cast Lead". The report reviewed Israel's obligations as a State party to many international human rights conventions, noting that a situation of armed conflict or occupation did not release a State from its obligations. The Palestinian Authority (PA), the Palestine Liberation Organization and the Palestinian Legislative Council had declared themselves bound by international human rights obligations, as had Hamas. With respect to Hamas, it was recalled that non-State actors that exercised government-like functions were obliged to respect human rights norms when their conduct affected the human rights of individuals under their control. The report also stated that the principles of customary international humanitarian law concerning the protection of civilians in the conduct of hostilities—including the principles of distinction between civilians and combatants and between civilian objects and military objectives, proportionality and precautions in attack, and humane treatment of those not taking part in hostilities—were applicable to all parties of the conflict. In addition, Israel, as the occupying Power, should apply rules of international humanitarian law regarding military occupation in the West Bank and the Gaza Strip.

The report described the military operations in the Gaza Strip which began on 27 December 2008 with Israel's launch of a large-scale aerial and naval offensive, followed by the launch of a ground offensive on 3 January 2009. The hostilities lasted 22 days, until Israel announced a unilateral ceasefire effective 18 January. Hamas and other Palestinian groups, which had fired rockets and mortars into Israel prior to and during Operation Cast Lead, also declared unilateral ceasefires on the same day. Israeli troops subsequently withdrew from the Gaza Strip.

Estimates of the number of Palestinian civilians killed ranged from 1,200 to 1,400, and around 5,300 people were wounded. Israel reported that 10 Israeli soldiers were killed during the operation, while in southern Israel 4 Israeli civilians were killed and 182 were injured by rockets and mortar shells fired from Gaza. Referring to reports of civilians being attacked by Israeli forces, the report highlighted a few cases in which civilians were targeted; in one of the gravest incidents, Israeli soldiers on 4 January ordered over 100 Palestinians into a house in Gaza City, and a day later Israeli forces shelled the house repeatedly, killing

about 23 people. With regard to allegations of attacks by Palestinian militants, 571 rockets and 205 mortars landed in Israel from Gaza during the offensive. Israel reported that up to 40 per cent of the inhabitants of Ashkelon had felt forced to flee their homes. The Israeli military targeted and damaged numerous civilian administrative facilities, including buildings of the Palestinian Legislative Council, the Ministry of Foreign Affairs, the Ministry of Justice, prisons and police stations, and a medical centre. Even facilities clearly marked as being operated by the United Nations were damaged, including schools, health centres and warehouses run by UNRWA. OHCHR was not currently in a position to assess each incident but found sufficient evidence of serious violations of international humanitarian law having been committed by both sides. On 11 February, the Secretary-General appointed a Board of Inquiry to investigate nine incidents that had occurred between 27 December 2008 and 18 January 2009 at UN premises in Gaza causing death, injury or damage. Of those nine incidents, the Board of Inquiry [A/63/855-S/2009/250] found Israeli forces responsible for casualties and damages in seven. In one incident, it found that the worst damage had been caused by a Palestinian rocket probably fired by Hamas, and in the final incident it was unable to reach a conclusion. Israel asserted that it took measures to warn the civilian population of Gaza of imminent attacks, including through dropping leaflets, recorded telephone calls and text messages. In any event, the use of such warnings did not discharge Israel of the duty to consider the proportionality of any attack on a target which might include civilians.

There were reports of failures on the part of the Israeli military to meet its obligation under international humanitarian law to protect medical personnel and to care for the wounded. Following shelling in Gaza City, the Israeli military hindered medical personnel from assisting the wounded for several days. Apart from limited openings, including to facilitate medical evacuation of some seriously injured persons, all borders of Gaza remained closed during the military operation, preventing persons from fleeing the area for safety, contrary to the principles of international human rights law. The blockade itself was a violation of international humanitarian law and had wide effects on the economic, social and cultural rights, as well as the civil and political rights of the Gaza population. Reports indicated that the Hamas security forces had conducted a large number of extrajudicial executions, torture and ill-treatment against alleged collaborators with Israeli forces, former PA security personnel and Fatah supporters during and after the Israeli operation. Most of the victims were reportedly abducted from their homes and subsequently found dead or injured. At least 32 Palestinians had allegedly been extrajudicially executed.

Reports of Special Rapporteur. The Special Rapporteur on the situation of human rights in the Palestinian territories occupied since 1967, Richard Falk (United States), issued a report dated 11 February [A/HRC/10/20] in the light of Human Rights Council resolution S-9/1 (see p. 780), focusing on the international law and human rights issues raised by the attacks by Israel on Gaza. He considered whether Israeli force was legally justified, and concluded that such recourse to force was not, given the circumstances and diplomatic alternatives available, and was potentially a crime against peace. The Rapporteur reviewed the pre-existing blockade of Gaza, which was in violation of the Fourth Geneva Convention, suggesting the presence of war crimes and possibly crimes against humanity. He considered the tactics pursued during the attacks by both sides, condemned the firing of rockets at Israeli civilian targets, and noted the unlawfulness of disallowing civilians in Gaza to have an option to leave the war zone to become refugees. He recommended that an inquiry be conducted to confirm the status under international law of war crimes allegations, and to consider alternative approaches to accountability. The Rapporteur maintained that Israeli security and the realization of the Palestinian right of self-determination were fundamentally connected, and that the recognition of that aspect of the situation highlighted the importance of an intensified diplomatic effort, respect by all parties of international law and implementation of Israeli withdrawal from occupied Palestine as initially prescribed by the Security Council in 1967. Until such steps were taken, the Palestinian right of resistance within the limits of international humanitarian law and Israeli security policy would inevitably clash, giving rise to new cycles of violence.

The Rapporteur recommended that: an advisory opinion be requested from the International Court of Justice (ICJ) on the obligations of a Member State to cooperate with special procedures; a procedure for conducting an expert inquiry into allegations of war crimes associated with the Israeli military operation be established; and it be recognized that the Palestinian right of resistance under international law within the limits of international humanitarian law collided with Israeli security concerns, requiring adjustments in the relationship of the parties premised on respect for the legal rights of the Palestinian people, and that sustainable peace in Gaza required the lifting of the blockade and a diplomatic process seeking peace.

In a report of 25 August [A/64/328], the Special Rapporteur examined the observance of international humanitarian and international human rights standards in the occupied territories from December 2008 to July 2009. He noted the continuing unlawful non-cooperation of Israel with the mandate-holder and the continuation of the blockade, which jeopardized fundamental rights and hindered reconstruction and repair of infrastructure. The report reviewed alleged war crimes committed during Operation Cast Lead and the issue of accountability. It considered information regarding attacks on UN facilities and civilians and analysed their legal merit. It reviewed testimony of combat soldiers involved in the operation, which provided evidence of loose rules of engagement and widespread destruction of targets that could not be justified from a military or security perspective. The issue of Israeli settlements was discussed, and it was noted that the possibility of a freeze on settlements had been raised as a political move and not with reference to Palestinian rights under international humanitarian law. The report also discussed the construction of a wall in the occupied Palestinian territories and Israeli non-compliance with the 2004 advisory opinion of ICJ on that issue [YUN 2004, p. 452]. The Rapporteur recommended that: the General Assembly request an ICJ advisory opinion on Member States' obligations to cooperate with the United Nations and its representatives; Member States be encouraged to use national means, including courts, to implement international criminal law as it pertained to the Occupied Palestinian Territory; Israeli respect for international law and Palestinian rights be an integral element in future peace negotiations; and consideration be given to limiting the supply of arms to the parties to the Israeli-Palestinian conflict.

In a further report [A/HRC/13/53/Rev.1], the Special Rapporteur examined developments from July through December, focusing on the main findings of the United Nations Fact-Finding Mission on the Gaza Conflict (see p. 783). The Rapporteur considered the question of Israeli settlements and their impact on the enjoyment of human rights, also discussing the initiatives of the Israeli Government in relation to the settlements and recent efforts to demonstrate against the construction of a wall in the West Bank. Addressing the ongoing blockade of Gaza, the Rapporteur highlighted its implications for efforts to rebuild following Operation Cast Lead, as well as persistent calls from the international community for Israel to lift the blockade. The Rapporteur recalled the situation of Palestinian refugees, and emphasized the need to keep their plight on the agenda of any effort to establish peace. The report welcomed the civil society-led campaign to boycott, divest from and sanction Israel for its occupation of Palestinian territories.

Report of special procedures. As requested by the Council in resolution S-9/1 (see p. 780), the relevant special procedures mandate-holders issued on 29 May a combined report [A/HRC/10/22] on the human rights situation in Palestine and other occupied Arab territories, focusing on the effects of the Israeli operation in the Gaza Strip. Contributions were submitted by the

Special Rapporteur on the right of everyone to the enjoyment of the highest attainable standard of physical and mental health, the Special Representative of the Secretary-General for Children and Armed Conflict, the Special Rapporteur on violence against women, its causes and consequences, the Representative of the Secretary-General on the human rights of internally displaced persons, the Special Rapporteur on adequate housing, the Special Rapporteur on the right to food, the Special Rapporteur on extrajudicial, summary or arbitrary executions, the Special Rapporteur on the right to education and the independent expert on the question of human rights and extreme poverty.

Human Rights Council action. On 26 March [A/64/53 (res. 10/19)], the Council, by a recorded vote of 35 to 4, with 8 abstentions, demanded that the occupying Power, Israel: end its occupation of the Palestinian land, and respect its commitments within the peace process towards the establishment of the independent sovereign Palestinian State, with East Jerusalem as its capital; stop the targeting of civilians and UN facilities, the destruction of the cultural heritage of the Palestinian people, and destruction of property; cease excavations around the Al-Aqsa Mosque and refrain from endangering Islamic and Christian holy sites in the Occupied Palestinian Territory; stop its illegal decision to demolish many Palestinian houses in East Jerusalem near the Al-Aqsa Mosque, which would result in the displacement of some 1,500 Palestinian residents; and release Palestinian prisoners and detainees. The Council condemned the Israeli military attacks in the Territory, particularly the recent ones in Gaza, which resulted in the killing and injury of thousands of Palestinian civilians, and also condemned the firing of crude rockets on Israeli civilians. It called for protection of all civilians, including international protection for the Palestinians in the Territory, and for the cessation of Israeli military attacks in the Territory and the firing of crude rockets by Palestinian combatants against southern Israel. Israel was called on to lift checkpoints and to open all crossing points and borders.

On the same day [res. 10/21], the Council, by a recorded vote of 33 to 1, with 13 abstentions, expressing regret that resolution S-9/1 (see p. 780) had not been fully implemented, requested its President to continue his efforts to appoint the independent international fact-finding mission to investigate the Israeli aggression in Gaza. It called on Israel to abide by international law, and demanded that it provide access to the fact-finding mission.

UN Fact-Finding Mission on the Gaza Conflict. On 3 April, the Council President established the United Nations Fact-Finding Mission on the Gaza Conflict, with the mandate "to investigate all violations of international human rights law and inter-national humanitarian law that might have been committed at any time in the context of the military operations that were conducted in Gaza during the period from 27 December 2008 to 18 January 2009, whether before, during or after". The President appointed Justice Richard Goldstone, former judge of the Constitutional Court of South Africa and former Prosecutor of the International Criminal Tribunals for the former Yugoslavia and Rwanda, to head the Mission, which convened in Geneva (4–8 May, 20 May, 4–5 July and 1–4 August). Having repeatedly sought but failed to obtain the cooperation of Israel, the Mission obtained the assistance of Egypt to enter Gaza through the Rafah crossing. The Mission conducted three field visits: two to the Gaza Strip (30 May–6 June and 25 June–1 July) and one to Amman, Jordan (2–3 July). In Gaza, the Mission investigated 36 incidents, interviewed 188 persons and reviewed more than 300 reports and other documentation. It was unable to meet Israeli Government officials or to travel to Israel to speak to Israeli victims. The Mission submitted its report [A/HRC/12/48], also referred to as the "Goldstone Report", on 25 September. The Secretary-General transmitted the report to the Security Council on 10 November [S/2009/586].

Report of Fact-Finding Mission ("Goldstone Report"). The Mission was of the view that Israel's military operation in Gaza and its impact could not be fully understood or assessed in isolation from developments prior and subsequent to it; the operation fit into a continuum of policies aimed at pursuing Israel's political objectives with regard to Gaza and the Occupied Palestinian Territory as a whole. Military objectives as stated by Israel did not explain the facts ascertained by the Mission, nor were they congruous with patterns identified by the Mission.

The Gaza military operations were, according to the Israeli Government, extensively planned. While the Israeli Government maintained that its operations were a response to rocket attacks and an exercise of the right to self-defence, the Mission considered the plan to have been directed, at least in part, at the people of Gaza as a whole. Both Palestinians and Israelis who met with the Mission stressed that the Israeli military operations in Gaza were qualitatively different from any previous military action by Israel in the Occupied Palestinian Territory. Victims and long-time observers stated that the operations were unprecedented in their severity and that their consequences would be long-lasting.

The Mission considered whether the series of acts that deprived Palestinians in the Gaza Strip of their means of sustenance, employment, housing and water, freedom of movement and their right to leave and enter their own country and limited access to courts of law and effective remedies could amount to persecution, a crime against humanity. It concluded that some of the actions of the Israeli Government might justify a competent court finding that crimes against humanity had been committed. The Mission said that the Israeli blockade restricted the import of goods and closed border crossings for people, goods and services, sometimes for days, including cuts in fuel and electricity. Israel was duty-bound under the Fourth Geneva Convention to ensure the supply of food and medical and hospital items, and to meet the humanitarian needs of the population. The overall number of Palestinians killed was between 1,387 and 1,417, and Israel reported four fatalities in southern Israel.

The Israeli armed forces had launched numerous attacks against buildings and persons of the Gaza authorities. Attacks on the buildings constituted deliberate attacks on civilian objects in violation of the rule of customary international humanitarian law whereby attacks must be limited to military objectives. The Mission examined the attacks against six police facilities that resulted in the death of 99 policemen and 9 civilians, and determined that the policemen had been deliberately targeted on the grounds that they were, in Israel's view, part of the Palestinian military forces in Gaza. The Mission found that the attacks failed to strike an acceptable balance between the military advantage anticipated and the loss of civilian life, and therefore violated international humanitarian law. The Mission examined attacks by Israeli forces resulting in the loss of life and injury to civilians and determined that the shelling of al-Fakhura junction near an UNRWA school was indiscriminate, in violation of international law, and violated the right to life of the Palestinian civilians killed.

The Mission investigated 11 incidents in which the Israeli armed forces launched direct attacks against civilians with lethal outcomes, and in 10 of those cases, there were no indications of justifiable military objective. It found that the conduct of the Israeli forces constituted breaches of the Fourth Geneva Convention in respect of wilful killings and wilfully causing suffering to protected persons and gave rise to individual criminal responsibility. In its investigation of several incidents involving the destruction of industrial infrastructure, food production, water installations, sewage treatment plants and housing, the Mission found a deliberate and systematic policy on the part of the Israeli armed forces to target such facilities. The Mission investigated four incidents in which the Israeli armed forces coerced Palestinian civilian men at gunpoint to take part in house searches during the military operations, and it concluded that the practice amounted to the use of Palestinian civilians as human shields, was therefore prohibited by international humanitarian law and was a war crime.

The Mission noted the continued detention of Gilad Shalit, an Israeli soldier captured in 2006 by a Palestinian armed group, and said that he met the requirements for prisoner-of-war status under the Third Geneva Convention. As such, he should be protected, treated humanely and allowed communication. The Mission was concerned by Israeli officials' declarations of intention to maintain the blockade until his release, which it believed would constitute collective punishment of the civilian population of Gaza. The Mission obtained information about violence against political opponents by the security services that reported to the Gaza authorities, and it found that such actions constituted violations of human rights.

The Mission found that, in a number of cases, Israel failed to take feasible precautions required by customary law to avoid or minimize incidental loss of civilian life, injury to civilians or damage to civilian objects. The Mission also found that the warnings to civilians issued by Israel in Gaza preceding their military action could not be considered sufficiently effective in the circumstances as to comply with customary law. There were numerous instances of deliberate attacks on civilians and civilian objects (individuals, families, houses, mosques) in violation of the fundamental international humanitarian law principle of distinction, resulting in deaths and serious injuries, in addition to unlawful attacks on food production and processing facilities, drinking water installations, farms and animals.

From the facts gathered, the Mission found that the following breaches of the Fourth Geneva Convention were committed by the Israeli armed forces in Gaza: wilful killing; torture or inhuman treatment; wilfully causing great suffering or serious injury to body or health; and extensive destruction of property, not justified by military necessity and carried out unlawfully.

In relation to the firing of rockets and mortars into southern Israel by Palestinian armed groups operating in the Gaza Strip, the Mission found that those groups failed to distinguish between military targets and the civilian population. The launching of rockets and mortars that could not be aimed with sufficient precision at military targets breached the fundamental principle of distinction; those actions would constitute war crimes and might amount to crimes against humanity.

In the light of the information it reviewed, the Mission concluded that there were doubts about the willingness of Israel to carry out investigations in an impartial, independent, prompt and effective way, as required by international law. With regard to allegations of violations of international humanitarian law falling within the jurisdiction of Palestinian authorities in Gaza, the Mission found that those allegations had not been investigated. There was little potential for accountability for serious violations of international humanitarian and human rights laws through domestic institutions in Israel, and even less in Gaza. The Mission considered the violations recounted in the report to fall within the jurisdiction of the International Criminal Court.

The Mission made recommendations to the Human Rights Council, the Security Council, the General Assembly, Israel, Palestinian armed groups, the Palestinian authorities and the international community on: violations of international humanitarian law and human rights law; accountability and reparations; the blockade and reconstruction; the use of weapons and military procedures; the protection of human rights organizations and defenders; and follow-up to the Mission's recommendations.

Communications. By a communication transmitted to the Council on 4 September [A/HRC/12/NI/5], the Palestinian Independent Commission for Human Rights outlined its position on the report of the Fact-Finding Mission.

By a letter of 25 September [A/HRC/12/G/4], Israel transmitted a report on the factual and legal aspects of the operation in Gaza.

Human Rights Council action. The Council, on 16 October, at its twelfth special session (see p. 787), by a recorded vote of 25 to 6, with 11 abstentions [A/64/53/Add.1 (res. S-12/1 B)], condemned the non-cooperation by Israel with the independent international Fact-Finding Mission. It welcomed the Mission's report, endorsed its recommendations, and recommended that the General Assembly consider it at its current session. On the same day [res. S-12/1 C], the Council welcomed the first periodic report of the High Commissioner on the implementation of Council resolution S-9/1 (see p. 780), and called on all concerned parties to ensure the implementation of the report's recommendations.

GENERAL ASSEMBLY ACTION

On 5 November [meeting 39], the General Assembly adopted **resolution 64/10** [draft A/64/L.11 & Add.1] by recorded vote (114-18-44) [agenda item 64].

Follow-up to the report of the United Nations Fact-Finding Mission on the Gaza Conflict

The General Assembly,

Guided by the purposes and principles of the Charter of the United Nations,

Recalling the relevant rules and principles of international law, including international humanitarian and human rights law, in particular the Geneva Convention relative to the Protection of Civilian Persons in Time of War, of 12 August 1949, which is applicable to the Occupied Palestinian Territory, including East Jerusalem,

Recalling also the Universal Declaration of Human Rights and the other human rights covenants, including the International Covenant on Civil and Political Rights, the International Covenant on Economic, Social and Cultural Rights and the Convention on the Rights of the Child,

Recalling further its relevant resolutions, including resolution ES-10/18 of 16 January 2009 of its tenth emergency special session,

Recalling the relevant Security Council resolutions, including resolution 1860(2009) of 8 January 2009,

Recalling also the relevant resolutions of the Human Rights Council, including resolution S-12/1 of 16 October 2009,

Expressing its appreciation to the United Nations Fact-Finding Mission on the Gaza Conflict, led by Justice Richard Goldstone, for its comprehensive report,

Affirming the obligation of all parties to respect international humanitarian law and international human rights law,

Emphasizing the importance of the safety and well-being of all civilians, and reaffirming the obligation to ensure the protection of civilians in armed conflict,

Gravely concerned by reports regarding serious human rights violations and grave breaches of international humanitarian law committed during the Israeli military operations in the Gaza Strip that were launched on 27 December 2008, including the findings of the Fact-Finding Mission and of the Board of Inquiry convened by the Secretary-General,

Condemning all targeting of civilians and civilian infrastructure and institutions, including United Nations facilities,

Stressing the need to ensure accountability for all violations of international humanitarian law and international human rights law in order to prevent impunity, ensure justice, deter further violations and promote peace,

Convinced that achieving a just, lasting and comprehensive settlement of the question of Palestine, the core of the Arab-Israeli conflict, is imperative for the attainment of a comprehensive, just and lasting peace and stability in the Middle East,

1. *Endorses* the report of the Human Rights Council on its twelfth special session, held on 15 and 16 October 2009;

2. *Requests* the Secretary-General to transmit the report of the United Nations Fact-Finding Mission on the Gaza Conflict to the Security Council;

3. *Calls upon* the Government of Israel to take all appropriate steps, within a period of three months, to undertake investigations that are independent, credible and in conformity with international standards into the serious violations of international humanitarian and international human rights law reported by the Fact-Finding Mission, towards ensuring accountability and justice;

4. *Urges*, in line with the recommendation of the Fact-Finding Mission, the undertaking by the Palestinian side, within a period of three months, of investigations that are independent, credible and in conformity with international standards into the serious violations of international humanitarian and international human rights law reported

by the Fact-Finding Mission, towards ensuring accountability and justice;

5. *Recommends* that the Government of Switzerland, in its capacity as depositary of the Geneva Convention relative to the Protection of Civilian Persons in Time of War, undertake as soon as possible the steps necessary to reconvene a Conference of High Contracting Parties to the Fourth Geneva Convention on measures to enforce the Convention in the Occupied Palestinian Territory, including East Jerusalem, and to ensure its respect in accordance with article 1;

6. *Requests* the Secretary-General to report to the General Assembly, within a period of three months, on the implementation of the present resolution, with a view to the consideration of further action, if necessary, by the relevant United Nations organs and bodies, including the Security Council;

7. *Decides* to remain seized of the matter.

RECORDED VOTE ON RESOLUTION 64/10:

In favour: Afghanistan, Albania, Algeria, Angola, Antigua and Barbuda, Argentina, Armenia, Azerbaijan, Bahamas, Bahrain, Bangladesh, Barbados, Belarus, Belize, Benin, Bolivia, Bosnia and Herzegovina, Botswana, Brazil, Brunei Darussalam, Cambodia, Central African Republic, Chad, Chile, China, Comoros, Congo, Cuba, Cyprus, Democratic People's Republic of Korea, Democratic Republic of the Congo, Djibouti, Dominica, Dominican Republic, Ecuador, Egypt, El Salvador, Eritrea, Gabon, Gambia, Ghana, Grenada, Guatemala, Guinea, Guinea-Bissau, Guyana, Haiti, India, Indonesia, Iran, Iraq, Ireland, Jamaica, Jordan, Kazakhstan, Kuwait, Lao People's Democratic Republic, Lebanon, Lesotho, Libyan Arab Jamahiriya, Malawi, Malaysia, Maldives, Mali, Malta, Mauritania, Mauritius, Mexico, Mongolia, Morocco, Mozambique, Myanmar, Namibia, Nepal, Nicaragua, Niger, Nigeria, Oman, Pakistan, Paraguay, Peru, Philippines, Portugal, Qatar, Saint Lucia, Saint Vincent and the Grenadines, Saudi Arabia, Senegal, Serbia, Sierra Leone, Singapore, Slovenia, Solomon Islands, Somalia, South Africa, Sri Lanka, Sudan, Suriname, Switzerland, Syrian Arab Republic, Tajikistan, Thailand, Timor-Leste, Trinidad and Tobago, Tunisia, Turkey, United Arab Emirates, United Republic of Tanzania, Uzbekistan, Venezuela, Viet Nam, Yemen, Zambia, Zimbabwe.

Against: Australia, Canada, Czech Republic, Germany, Hungary, Israel, Italy, Marshall Islands, Micronesia, Nauru, Netherlands, Palau, Panama, Poland, Slovakia, The former Yugoslav Republic of Macedonia, Ukraine, United States.

Abstaining: Andorra, Austria, Belgium, Bulgaria, Burkina Faso, Burundi, Cameroon, Colombia, Costa Rica, Croatia, Denmark, Estonia, Ethiopia, Fiji, Finland, France, Georgia, Greece, Iceland, Japan, Kenya, Latvia, Liberia, Liechtenstein, Lithuania, Luxembourg, Moldova, Monaco, Montenegro, New Zealand, Norway, Papua New Guinea, Republic of Korea, Romania, Russian Federation, Samoa, San Marino, Spain, Swaziland, Sweden, Tonga, Uganda, United Kingdom, Uruguay.

Other developments

Report of Secretary-General. The Secretary-General, pursuant to a Human Rights Council resolution on human rights in the occupied Syrian Golan [YUN 2008, p. 895], submitted in February/March [A/HRC/10/15 & Add.1] information from three Governments on their position on the Golan.

On 6 March, pursuant to a Council request [YUN 2008, p. 898], the Secretary-General reported [A/HRC/10/27] on the implementation of the recommendations contained in the report of the high-level fact-finding mission to Beit Hanoun [YUN 2008, p. 897].

Report of High Commissioner. The High Commissioner, pursuant to a request of the Commission on Human Rights [YUN 2005, p. 904], reported on 26 February [A/HRC/10/35] on the issue of Palestinian pregnant women giving birth at Israeli checkpoints owing to denial of access by Israel to hospitals. The United Nations did not maintain a systematic monitoring mechanism on the issue, but the report mentioned a few incidents and described difficulties encountered at border checkpoints.

Human Rights Council action. On 26 March [A/64/53 (res. 10/18)], the Council, by a recorded vote of 46 to 1, deplored the Israeli announcements of construction of new housing units in the Occupied Palestinian Territory as it undermined the peace process. It expressed concern at the continuing Israeli settlement activities; the destruction of property; the expulsion of Palestinians; the announcement by Israel that it would retain major settlement blocks in the Occupied Palestinian Territory, including settlements in the Jordan Valley; the restriction of the freedom of movement of people and goods, including closures of crossing points of the Gaza Strip; and the continued construction of the wall inside the Territory, including in and around East Jerusalem. The Council urged Israel to reverse the settlement policy in the occupied territories, including in East Jerusalem and the Syrian Golan, and to prevent any new installation of settlers there. It called for the reopening of the Rafah and Karni crossings, which were crucial to the passage of food and essential supplies, and demanded that Israel comply with its obligations as mentioned in the 2004 ICJ advisory opinion [YUN 2004, p. 1273].

On the same day [res. 10/17], the Council, by a recorded vote of 33 to 1, with 13 abstentions, called upon Israel: to comply with UN resolutions on the occupied Syrian Golan which determined that the occupation was null and void; to desist from changing the physical character, demographic composition, institutional structure and legal status of the Syrian Golan; to desist from imposing Israeli citizenship and identity cards on the Syrian citizens in the Golan and to desist from its repressive measures against them; to allow the Syrian population of the Golan to visit Syria through the Quneitra checkpoint; to release the Syrian detainees in Israeli prisons and treat them in conformity with international humanitarian law; and to allow delegates of the International Committee of the Red Cross to visit Syrian detainees in Israeli prisons.

Also on 26 March [res. 10/20], the Council reaffirmed the inalienable right of the Palestinian people to self-determination, including their right to live in freedom and to establish their sovereign, independent, democratic and viable contiguous State. It reaffirmed support for the solution of two States, Palestine and Israel, living in peace and security. The Council stressed the need for respect for the territorial unity, contiguity and integrity of all of the Occupied Palestinian Territory, including East Jerusalem.

Report of High Commissioner. The High Commissioner, in the first periodic report mandated by the Human Rights Council in resolution S-9/1 (see p. 780), reported on 19 August [A/HRC/12/37] on violations of international humanitarian and human rights laws resulting from the Israeli military attacks on Gaza, as well as on violations in other areas of the Occupied Palestinian Territory, in particular the West Bank, including East Jerusalem. Reported violations in the Territory included arbitrary detentions, torture and ill-treatment, extrajudicial executions, forced evictions and home demolitions, settlement expansion and related violence, and restrictions on freedom of movement and freedom of expression. The nearly total impunity that persisted was also a concern.

The human rights situation in the West Bank continued to be critical, primarily as a result of reported violations committed by Israel, but also due to a rise in alleged violations of rights of political opponents, committed in a context of continued political separation between the PA and Hamas. Israeli forces conducted military operations in the West Bank, with the purpose of detaining persons suspected of involvement in activities against Israeli security. In March alone, more than 120 operations of that nature took place, resulting in the arrest of more than 300 Palestinians, who were generally held under administrative detention orders issued by a military commander, as opposed to a judicial decision, without indictment or trial and with restrictions on access to counsel. The PA security forces in the West Bank reportedly carried out arbitrary detention of persons accused of supporting Hamas or of collaborating with Israel, and there were complaints from Palestinians of having been subjected to torture. During the military offensive in Gaza, mass demonstrations took place in the West Bank, resulting in clashes with Israeli forces who used rubber-coated metal bullets, sound bombs and tear gas. Five Palestinian demonstrators were killed as a result. Forced evictions and home demolitions continued in the West Bank, including East Jerusalem, resulting in the displacement of 296 persons. Meanwhile, Israel expanded settlements by building new structures in the West Bank, in violation of humanitarian law. By the beginning of 2009, approximately 485,000 settlers were residing in 121 settlements in the West Bank, including 195,000 in 12 settlements in East Jerusalem.

The wall enclosing, and in many areas encroaching into, the West Bank, caused a wide scope of human rights violations. As of August 2008, approximately 57 per cent of the wall's planned route of 723 kilometres had been completed. Approximately 86 per cent of the wall was actually in the West Bank, and not along the Green Line (the armistice line between Israel and the West Bank), and would effectively annex large parts of the West Bank to Israel. Almost 12 per cent of the land of the West Bank (including East Jerusalem) would remain either west of the wall or in enclaves created by the route. Over 80 per cent of the Israeli settlers in the West Bank would be connected to Israel, whereas Palestinians would be separated from land, livelihoods and services, with access limited by a restrictive permit regime. ICJ had found the wall to be in contravention of Israel's obligations under international law, insofar as it departed from the Green Line. Access through the 66 gates was limited, with only half of them open to Palestinians. Travel on many of the roads in the West Bank was restricted or prohibited for Palestinians. The High Commissioner remained concerned that Israel had not complied with the ICJ advisory opinion on the wall, and that severe restrictions on movement of Palestinians in the West Bank continued.

Human Rights Council twelfth special session. Acting on a request supported by 19 Council members, the Council held its twelfth special session (Geneva, 15–16 October) [A/64/53/Add.1] on the human rights situation in the Occupied Palestinian Territory, including East Jerusalem. During the session, the Council heard statements from its members, other States, Israel and Palestine, the High Commissioner, intergovernmental organizations and NGOs.

On 16 October [ibid. (res. S-12/1 A)], by a recorded vote of 25 to 6, with 11 abstentions, the Council condemned policies and measures taken by Israel, including those limiting access of Palestinians to their properties and holy sites, particularly in Occupied East Jerusalem, on the basis of national origin, religion, sex, age or any other discriminatory ground, which were in violation of the Palestinian people's civil, political, economic, social and cultural rights. It condemned the recent violations of human rights by Israel in Occupied East Jerusalem, particularly the confiscation of lands and properties, the demolition of houses and private properties, the construction and expansion of settlements, the continuous construction of the separation wall, the restrictions on freedom of movement of the Palestinian citizens of East Jerusalem, and excavation around the Al-Aqsa Mosque. It demanded that Israel respect the religious and cultural rights in the Territory as provided for in international human rights instruments and the Geneva Conventions, allow Palestinian citizens access to their properties and religious sites, cease excavation around Al-Aqsa, and refrain from acts endangering holy sites in the Occupied Palestinian Territory, including East Jerusalem. In other parts of the resolution (see p. 780), the Council took action on the Israeli military operation in Gaza.

The General Assembly, by **decision 64/507** of 28 October, decided to consider directly in plenary meeting the Council's report on its twelfth special session.

Communication. In a letter dated 27 October [A/HRC/13/G/1], Syria stated that seven Syrian students from the Occupied Syrian Golan had been prevented by Israeli authorities from returning there.

PART THREE

Economic and social questions

Chapter I

Development policy and international economic cooperation

In 2009, with the world economy mired in the worst financial and economic crisis since the Second World War, most advanced economies were already in recession, and the outlook for emerging and other developing economies was deteriorating rapidly, including those with a recent history of strong economic performance. Key issues in development policy and international economic cooperation for the United Nations included the global recession, including its relation to the food crisis; policy responses, including reform of the international monetary and financial system; and climate change mitigation and development, along with human mobility. The General Assembly reaffirmed the need for the United Nations to play a fundamental role in promoting international cooperation for development, and to continue working towards a new international economic order based on the principles of equity, sovereign equality, interdependence, common interest, cooperation and solidarity among States.

Sustainable development remained a major focus of UN system work in the context of international economic relations. The Commission on Sustainable Development reviewed progress in the follow-up to the 2002 World Summit on Sustainable Development and implementation of Agenda 21, the action plan on sustainable development adopted by the 1992 United Nations Conference on Environment and Development. Jointly with Namibia, the Commission organized a high-level meeting (Windhoek, Namibia, 9–10 February) whose resultant Ministerial Declaration called for an integrated response by African countries and the international community in support of sustainable agriculture and rural development approaches, and stressed the importance of food security and strengthening the agriculture sector in Africa. The Commission's high-level segment (13–15 May) addressed the thematic cluster for its 2008–2009 implementation cycle: agriculture, rural development, land, drought, desertification and Africa.

The Economic and Social Council, at its high-level segment (6–9 July), held a special event on Africa and the least developed countries, along with a high-level policy dialogue with the international financial and trade institutions on current developments in the world economy. The Council also reviewed implementation of its 2008 Ministerial Declaration on

implementing the internationally agreed sustainable development goals and commitments.

With regard to the implementation of Agenda 21, the Programme for the Further Implementation of Agenda 21 and the outcomes of the World Summit on Sustainable Development, the Secretary-General provided an update to the General Assembly on actions taken by Governments, UN system organizations and major groups in advancing the implementation of sustainable development goals and targets, including through partnerships. In December, the General Assembly decided to organize, in 2012, the United Nations Conference on Sustainable Development and accepted the offer of Brazil to host the event.

The eradication of poverty and the achievement of the Millennium Development Goals (MDGs) remained a major focus of UN system attention. The General Assembly reviewed progress made in the implementation of the Second United Nations Decade for the Eradication of Poverty (2008–2017), and decided that the high-level plenary meeting of its sixty-fifth (2010) session would focus on accelerating progress towards the achievement of all the MDGs by 2015.

At its twelfth session (Geneva, 25–29 May), the Commission on Science and Technology for Development considered regional and international progress made in the implementation of and follow-up to the outcomes of the World Summit on the Information Society. In a March report to the Economic and Social Council, the Secretary-General presented responses provided by 20 international and regional organizations on trends, achievements and obstacles to implementation of those outcomes. To strengthen cybersecurity, the General Assembly in December endorsed a voluntary self-assessment tool for national efforts to protect critical information infrastructures.

As for development policy and public administration, the Committee for Development Policy (CDP), at its eleventh session (New York, 9–13 March) addressed international cooperation on global public health, particularly the importance of tackling inequalities; the global financial turmoil and its impact on developing countries; and climate change and development. The Committee of Experts on Public Administration, at its eighth session (New York, 30 March–3 April), considered as its main theme the human factor in capacity-building for development, along with a review of the United Nations Programme in Public Administration and Finance and mainstreaming of health issues and human-capacity building in public administration.

Finally, the UN system continued to address the development problems of groups of countries in special situation. CDP conducted its triennial review of the list of the least developed countries (LDCs), and found two countries—Papua New Guinea and Zimbabwe—eligible for inclusion in the list of LDCs; however, both declined to join the category. The number of countries officially designated as LDCs remained at 49. The General Assembly in December decided to convene the Fourth United Nations Conference on the Least Developed Countries in Turkey in the first half of 2011. The Assembly also decided on the structure of the high-level review, planned for 2010, of progress made in addressing the vulnerabilities of small island developing States. In addition, the Assembly reviewed progress in the implementation of the 1994 Programme of Action for the Sustainable Development of Small Island Developing States and the related 2005 Mauritius Strategy, as well as of the 2003 Almaty Programme of Action for assisting landlocked developing countries.

International economic relations

Development and international economic cooperation

International economic cooperation issues were considered in 2009 by various UN bodies, including the General Assembly and the Economic and Social Council.

On 27 April, the Economic and Social Council held in New York its twelfth special high-level meeting with the Bretton Woods institutions (the World Bank Group and the International Monetary Fund), the World Trade Organization and the United Nations Conference on Trade and Development (see p. 940).

On 21 December, the Assembly took note of the report of the Second (Economic and Financial) Committee [A/64/418] on its discussion of macroeconomic policy questions (**decision 64/540**).

High-level segment of Economic and Social Council

In accordance with its decision 2008/257 [YUN 2008, p. 1339], the Economic and Social Council, at the high-level segment of its 2009 substantive session (Geneva, 6–9 July) [A/64/3/Rev.1], discussed the theme of "Current global and national trends and their impact on social development, including public health"

(see p. 1226). Following its annual ministerial review, on 9 July, the Council adopted the ministerial declaration of the high-level segment, entitled "Implementing the internationally agreed goals and commitments in regard to global public health" (see p. 1227). It also held a special event on Africa and the least developed countries (LDCs) and a high-level policy dialogue with the international financial and trade institutions on developments in the world economy.

The Council had before it a May report of the Secretary-General on regional cooperation in the economic, social and related fields [E/2009/15 & Add.1], submitted in response to General Assembly resolution 1823(XVII) [YUN 1962, p. 266] and Economic and Social Council resolution 1817(LV) [YUN 1973, p. 449]. The report examined how the different regions were being affected by and were responding to the economic and financial crisis, how their efforts could be enhanced, and how the United Nations regional commissions were supporting Member States. It also covered developments in selected areas of regional and interregional cooperation, efforts to promote coherence at the regional level, and cooperation among the commissions.

Policy dialogue. On 6 July, the Council held a high-level policy dialogue on developments in the world economy with the international financial and trade institutions of the UN system.

Communications. On 12 May [A/64/81], Namibia, as President of the Inter-Parliamentary Union (IPU), transmitted to the Secretary-General the text of a resolution adopted by the 120th Assembly of the IPU (Addis Ababa, Ethiopia, 10 April) on the role of parliaments in mitigating the social and political impact of the international economic and financial crisis on the most vulnerable sectors of the global community, especially in Africa.

In a letter to the Secretary-General dated 4 June [A/63/893], the Syrian Arab Republic transmitted the Damascus Declaration on responding to the International Financial Crisis in the ESCWA Region, adopted at the Regional High-Level Consultative Forum on the Impacts of the International Financial Crisis on ESCWA Member Countries (Damascus, Syria, 5–7 May).

On 30 September [A/64/489], the Sudan, as Chairman of the Group of 77, transmitted to the Secretary-General the Ministerial Declaration adopted at the thirty-third annual meeting of the Ministers for Foreign Affairs of the Group of 77 and China (New York, 25 September), which reviewed the world economic situation and addressed development challenges facing developing countries, particularly in the context of the world financial and economic as well as food crisis, volatile energy prices and climate change, insofar as those could undermine the achievement of the internationally agreed development goals, including the Millennium Development Goals (MDGs).

Globalization and interdependence

In response to General Assembly resolution 63/222 [YUN 2008, p. 904], the Secretary-General in August submitted a report [A/64/310] on the role of the United Nations in promoting development in the context of globalization and interdependence. In response to General Assembly resolution 63/224 [YUN 2008, p. 909], the Secretary-General also provided an overview of the international economic and policy challenges for achieving equitable and inclusive sustained economic growth and sustainable development, and the corresponding role of the United Nations. The report examined strains placed on the global trade and investment system by the economic crisis; its effects on poverty reduction, including food insecurity; and its consequences for sustainable development. Commodity prices and trade and investment flows had declined as a result of the crisis, the brunt of which was being borne by the poorest and most vulnerable populations of developing countries. If aid flows continued to decline, the impact would be even more devastating for low-income countries and the poor. The Secretary-General outlined a Global Sustainable New Deal to establish a new public policy agenda placing countries on a different development pathway, protecting the natural resource base in an equitable manner without compromising job creation and catch-up growth. He called for the developed world to consider the impact of its responses to the crisis on developing countries, and for the latter to implement policies enabling them to make their economies more robust. The United Nations could ensure dialogue and enable a coordinated response based on inclusive decision-making, and could provide impartial analysis and pragmatic policy recommendations.

On 21 December (**decision 64/541**), the Assembly took note of the report of the Second Committee [A/64/422 & Add.1] on its discussion of globalization and interdependence.

GENERAL ASSEMBLY ACTION

On 21 December [meeting 66], the General Assembly, on the recommendation of the Second Committee [A/64/422/Add.1], adopted **resolution 64/210** without vote [agenda item 55 *(a)*].

Role of the United Nations in promoting development in the context of globalization and interdependence

The General Assembly,

Recalling its resolutions 62/199 of 19 December 2007 and 63/222 of 19 December 2008 on the role of the United Nations in promoting development in the context of globalization and interdependence,

Recalling also the Monterrey Consensus of the International Conference on Financing for Development and the Doha Declaration on Financing for Development,

Recalling further its resolution 63/303 of 9 July 2009 on the Outcome of the Conference on the World Financial and Economic Crisis and Its Impact on Development,

Recalling General Assembly resolution 63/199 of 19 December 2008 on social justice for a fair globalization, in which the Assembly took note with interest of the adoption of the Declaration on Social Justice for a Fair Globalization,

Recalling also the 2005 World Summit Outcome and all relevant General Assembly resolutions, in particular those that have built upon the 2005 World Summit Outcome, in the economic, social and related fields, including Assembly resolution 60/265 of 30 June 2006 entitled "Follow-up to the development outcome of the 2005 World Summit, including the Millennium Development Goals and the other internationally agreed development goals",

Reaffirming that the United Nations has a central role in promoting international cooperation for development and in promoting policy coherence on global development issues, including in the context of globalization and interdependence,

Reaffirming also the resolve expressed in the United Nations Millennium Declaration to ensure that globalization becomes a positive force for all,

Recognizing that globalization, driven largely by economic liberalization and technology, implies that the economic performance of a country is increasingly affected by factors outside its geographical borders and that maximizing in an equitable manner the benefits of globalization requires developing responses to globalization through a strengthened global partnership for development to achieve the internationally agreed development goals, including the Millennium Development Goals,

Reaffirming its strong support for fair and inclusive globalization and the need to translate growth into poverty reduction and in this regard its resolve to make the goals of full and productive employment and decent work for all, including for women and young people, a central objective of relevant national and international policies as well as national development strategies, including poverty reduction strategies, as part of efforts to achieve the Millennium Development Goals,

1. *Takes note* of the report of the Secretary-General;

2. *Recognizes* that some countries have successfully adapted to the changes and have benefited from globalization but that many others, especially the least developed countries, have remained marginalized in the globalizing world economy, and recognizes also that, as stated in the United Nations Millennium Declaration, the benefits are very unevenly shared, while the costs are unevenly distributed;

3. *Reaffirms* the need for the United Nations to play a fundamental role in the promotion of international cooperation for development and the coherence, coordination and implementation of development goals and actions agreed upon by the international community, and resolves to strengthen coordination within the United Nations system in close cooperation with all other multilateral financial, trade and development institutions in order to sup-

port sustained economic growth, poverty eradication and sustainable development;

4. *Welcomes* the joint crisis initiative launched by the United Nations System Chief Executives Board for Coordination in 2009 to provide coordination on social protection floors, which aims at advocating for and advising on the provision of social protection floors and public spending in ways that will both kick-start growth and support more inclusive and sustainable social and economic development;

5. *Recognizes* that policies which link economic and social development can contribute to reducing inequalities within and among countries with a view to guaranteeing that the poor and vulnerable groups maximize their benefits from economic growth and development;

6. *Notes with concern* the unprecedented rise in unemployment as a consequence of the current global financial and economic crisis, recognizes that decent work remains one of the best routes out of poverty, and in this regard invites donor countries, multilateral organizations and other development partners to consider assisting developing countries to implement the resolution entitled "Recovering from the crisis: a Global Jobs Pact" adopted by the International Labour Conference at its ninety-eighth session, in consultation and cooperation with the International Labour Organization;

7. *Stresses* the need for all countries to harness knowledge and technology and stimulate innovation if they are to improve their competitiveness and benefit from trade and investment, and in this regard underlines the importance of concrete actions to facilitate the transfer of technology under fair, transparent and mutually agreed terms to developing countries in support of the implementation of their sustainable development strategies;

8. *Decides* to include in the provisional agenda of its sixty-fifth session, under the item entitled "Globalization and interdependence" the sub-item entitled "Role of the United Nations in promoting development in the context of globalization and interdependence".

New international economic order

In 2009, the year marking the thirty-fifth anniversary of the adoption of the Declaration on the Establishment of a New International Economic Order and the Programme of Action on the Establishment of a New International Economic Order [YUN 1974, p. 306], the General Assembly took action on the issue.

GENERAL ASSEMBLY ACTION

On 21 December [meeting 66], the General Assembly, on the recommendation of the Second Committee [A/64/422/Add.1], adopted **resolution 64/209** by recorded vote (124-0-50) [agenda item 55 *(a)*].

Towards a New International Economic Order

The General Assembly,

Bearing in mind the purposes and principles of the Charter of the United Nations to promote the economic advancement and social progress of all peoples,

Recalling the principles of the Declaration on the Establishment of a New International Economic Order and the Programme of Action on the Establishment of a New International Economic Order, as set out in resolutions 3201(S-VI) and 3202(S-VI), respectively, adopted by the General Assembly at its sixth special session, on 1 May 1974,

Taking into account the fact that the year 2009 marks the thirty-fifth anniversary of the adoption of the Declaration and the Programme of Action,

Recalling its resolution 63/224 of 19 December 2008,

Reaffirming the United Nations Millennium Declaration,

Recalling the outcomes of the major United Nations conferences and summits in the economic, social and related fields, including the development goals and objectives contained therein, and recognizing the vital role played by those conferences and summits in shaping a broad development vision and in identifying commonly agreed objectives,

Concerned that the current international economic, financial, energy and food crises, as well as the challenges posed by climate change, aggravate the existing international situation and have a negative impact on the development prospects of developing countries, while threatening to further widen the gap between developed and developing countries, including the technological and income gap,

1. *Reaffirms* the need to continue working towards a new international economic order based on the principles of equity, sovereign equality, interdependence, common interest, cooperation and solidarity among all States;

2. *Decides* to continue considering the international economic situation and its impact on development during the sixty-fifth session of the General Assembly, and in that regard requests the Secretary-General to include in his next report, under the item entitled "Globalization and interdependence", an overview of the major international economic and policy challenges for equitable and inclusive sustained economic growth and sustainable development, and of the role of the United Nations in addressing these issues, in the light of the relevant principles contained in the Declaration on the Establishment of a New International Economic Order and the Programme of Action on the Establishment of a New International Economic Order.

RECORDED VOTE ON RESOLUTION 64/209:

In favour: Afghanistan, Algeria, Angola, Antigua and Barbuda, Argentina, Armenia, Bahamas, Bahrain, Bangladesh, Belarus, Belize, Benin, Bhutan, Bolivia, Botswana, Brazil, Brunei Darussalam, Burkina Faso, Burundi, Cambodia, Cameroon, Cape Verde, Central African Republic, Chad, Chile, China, Comoros, Congo, Costa Rica, Côte d'Ivoire, Cuba, Democratic People's Republic of Korea, Djibouti, Dominica, Dominican Republic, Ecuador, Egypt, El Salvador, Eritrea, Ethiopia, Fiji, Gabon, Ghana, Grenada, Guatemala, Guinea, Guinea-Bissau, Guyana, Haiti, India, Indonesia, Iran, Iraq, Jamaica, Jordan, Kazakhstan, Kuwait, Kyrgyzstan, Lao People's Democratic Republic, Lebanon, Lesotho, Liberia, Libyan Arab Jamahiriya, Madagascar, Malawi, Malaysia, Maldives, Mali, Marshall Islands, Mauritania, Mauritius, Mexico, Mongolia, Morocco, Mozambique, Myanmar, Namibia, Nepal, Nicaragua, Niger, Nigeria, Oman, Pakistan, Panama, Papua New Guinea, Paraguay, Peru, Philippines, Qatar, Russian Federation, Rwanda, Saint Kitts and Nevis, Saint Lucia, Saint Vincent and the Grenadines, Samoa, Saudi Arabia, Sierra Leone, Singapore, Solomon

Islands, Somalia, South Africa, Sri Lanka, Sudan, Suriname, Swaziland, Syrian Arab Republic, Tajikistan, Thailand, Timor-Leste, Togo, Tonga, Trinidad and Tobago, Tunisia, Tuvalu, Uganda, United Arab Emirates, United Republic of Tanzania, Uruguay, Uzbekistan, Venezuela, Viet Nam, Yemen, Zambia, Zimbabwe.

Against: None.

Abstaining: Andorra, Australia, Austria, Belgium, Bosnia and Herzegovina, Bulgaria, Canada, Croatia, Cyprus, Czech Republic, Denmark, Estonia, Finland, France, Georgia, Germany, Greece, Hungary, Iceland, Ireland, Israel, Italy, Japan, Latvia, Liechtenstein, Lithuania, Luxembourg, Malta, Moldova, Monaco, Montenegro, Netherlands, New Zealand, Norway, Palau, Poland, Portugal, Republic of Korea, Romania, San Marino, Serbia, Slovakia, Slovenia, Spain, Sweden, Switzerland, Turkey, Ukraine, United Kingdom, United States.

Development cooperation with middle-income countries

In response to resolution 663/223 [YUN 2008, p. 906], the Secretary-General in August submitted a report [A/64/253] on development cooperation with middle-income countries. The report focused on strategies and actions of the UN system with regard to development cooperation with middle-income countries, taking into account the work of other international organizations, including international financial institutions. As home to almost two thirds of the world's poor, middle-income countries were of considerable importance for promoting the UN agenda of development for all, including the achievement of the MDGs. Accounting for two thirds of the world population and almost 40 per cent of world gross product, they also played an increasing role in advancing equitable and sustainable growth of the world economy. The report examined progress in the development of, as well as challenging international economic conditions for, middle-income countries. It described major achievements in UN development cooperation with middle-income countries, along with the engagement of international financial institutions. According to the Secretary-General, the UN system needed a better-defined agenda to address both the common and the idiosyncratic challenges that middle-income countries faced. Priorities should be given to perennial development challenges such as poverty eradication and financial stability, and to emerging issues, especially climate change. The UN system should also enhance its support of South-South cooperation.

GENERAL ASSEMBLY ACTION

On 21 December [meeting 66], the General Assembly, on the recommendation of the Second Committee [A/64/422/Add.1], adopted **resolution 64/208** without vote [agenda item 55 *(a)*].

Development cooperation with middle-income countries

The General Assembly,

Recalling the outcomes of the United Nations major international conferences and summits, including the United Nations Millennium Declaration and the 2005 World Summit Outcome, as well as the relevant provisions of General Assembly resolutions,

Reaffirming its resolution 62/208 of 19 December 2007, entitled "Triennial comprehensive policy review of operational activities for development of the United Nations system", in which it recognized that middle-income developing countries still face significant challenges in the area of poverty eradication and that efforts to address those challenges should be supported in order to ensure that achievements made to date are sustained, including through support to the effective development of comprehensive cooperation policies,

Recalling its resolution 63/223 of 19 December 2008,

Emphasizing that middle-income countries must take primary responsibility for their own development, and that their national efforts should be complemented by supportive global programmes, measures and policies aimed at expanding the development opportunities of middle-income countries, while taking into account their specific national conditions,

Noting that national averages based on criteria such as per capita income do not always reflect the actual particularities and development needs of middle-income countries, and recognizing the significant diversity of middle income countries,

Recognizing that, despite the achievements and efforts of middle-income countries, a significant number of people are still living in poverty and inequalities remain, and that further investment in social services and economic opportunities are needed in order to reduce those inequalities,

Recognizing also the actions that middle-income countries have taken to address their particular challenges and the needs of their people, and recognizing the need for further international efforts to support middle-income countries in this regard,

Acknowledging the negative effects of the current global financial and economic crisis on the development efforts of middle-income countries, which are vulnerable to external shocks,

Expressing concern that some middle-income countries are highly indebted and face increased challenges to their long-term debt sustainability,

Recognizing that climate change is one of the challenges to the sustainable development of middle-income countries,

Taking note of the outcomes of the international conferences on development cooperation with middle-income countries held in Madrid, El Salvador and Windhoek, and the regional conference on the theme "Increasing the competitiveness of African middle-income countries", held in Cairo,

1. *Takes note* of the report of the Secretary-General;

2. *Recognizes* that middle-income countries still face significant challenges in their efforts to achieve the internationally agreed development goals, including the Millennium Development Goals, and in that regard underlines

the importance of international support, through various forms, that is well aligned with national priorities to address the development needs of middle-income countries;

3. *Acknowledges* the efforts made and successes achieved by many middle-income countries to eradicate poverty and achieve the internationally agreed development goals, including the Millennium Development Goals, as well as their significant contribution to global and regional development and economic stability;

4. *Also acknowledges* that good governance and the rule of law at the national and international levels are essential for sustained economic growth, sustainable development and the eradication of poverty and hunger;

5. *Recognizes* the solidarity of middle-income countries with other developing countries with a view to supporting their development efforts, including in the context of South-South and triangular cooperation;

6. *Invites* the United Nations development system, in particular the funds and programmes, and at the regional level, in accordance with their respective mandates, to improve support, as appropriate, to middle-income countries and to improve coordination and exchange of experiences with other international organizations, international financial institutions and regional organizations in this field as well as to align the programming of its activities more closely with national development strategies while targeting specific existing and emerging needs of middle-income countries;

7. *Invites* the international community, including international financial institutions, to further strengthen their support to the development efforts of middle-income countries through targeted technical assistance, provision of resources, technology transfer and capacity-building, as appropriate, while taking into account their national priorities and development policies;

8. *Acknowledges* that official development assistance is still essential for a number of middle-income countries and that it has a role to play in targeted areas, taking into account the needs and domestic resources of these countries;

9. *Calls upon* the international community to continue to further undertake timely, appropriate and targeted measures to address the new and additional challenges that the current economic and financial crisis has imposed on middle income countries, on a case-by-case basis, based on the specific needs and national priorities of each of those countries;

10. *Underlines* the need for sustained efforts towards achieving debt sustainability in middle-income countries in order to avoid a debt crisis, and to that end notes and encourages further efforts by international financial institutions to enhance facilities for them;

11. *Requests* the Secretary-General to submit to the General Assembly at its sixty-sixth session a report on the implementation of the present resolution, and decides to include in its provisional agenda, under the item entitled "Globalization and interdependence", a sub-item entitled "Development cooperation with middle-income countries".

Development through partnership

In compliance with resolution 62/211 [YUN 2007, p. 837], the Secretary-General in September submit-ted a report [A/64/337] on the implementation of the proposed modalities for enhanced cooperation between the United Nations and all relevant partners, in particular the private sector. The report reviewed partnership types; the impact of the global economic downturn on the partnership agenda; the role of Governments; partnering at the system level; partnership developments at the level of agencies, funds and programmes; and actions to overcome operational challenges. According to the Secretary-General, efforts were needed to develop a more strategic and coherent approach to select and engage partners; integrate small companies and those from low-income countries; align global partnerships with country development agendas; build an enabling framework for partnerships; build staff capacity; enhance mechanisms to share best practices; and improve evaluation and impact assessment. Caretaking of the United Nations-business relationship was required to undertake a new process to continuously assess and improve the value proposition of partnerships, and to ensure maximum alignment with the priorities set by Member States. Continued and increased engagement by Governments would enable the Organization to better define its strategic goals with the private sector. The revised Guidelines on Cooperation between the United Nations and the Business Community, now called the Guidelines on Cooperation between the United Nations and the Private Sector, and the new UN and Business website, were milestones in that collaboration.

GENERAL ASSEMBLY ACTION

On 21 December [meeting 66], the General Assembly, on the recommendation of the Second Committee [A/64/426], adopted **resolution 64/223** without vote [agenda item 59].

Towards global partnerships

The General Assembly,

Recalling its resolutions 55/215 of 21 December 2000, 56/76 of 11 December 2001, 58/129 of 19 December 2003, 60/215 of 22 December 2005 and 62/211 of 19 December 2007,

Reaffirming the vital role of the United Nations, including the General Assembly and the Economic and Social Council, in the promotion of partnerships in the context of globalization,

Underlining the intergovernmental nature of the United Nations, and the central role and responsibility of Governments in national and international policymaking,

Reaffirming its resolve to create an environment, at the national and global levels alike, that is conducive to sustainable economic development, poverty alleviation and environmental sustainability,

Taking note of the continuing increase in the number of public-private partnerships worldwide,

Recalling the objectives formulated in the United Nations Millennium Declaration, notably the Millennium Development Goals, and the reaffirmation they received in the 2005 World Summit Outcome, particularly in regard to developing partnerships through the provision of greater opportunities to the private sector, non-governmental organizations and civil society in general so as to enable them to contribute to the realization of the goals and programmes of the Organization, in particular in the pursuit of development and the eradication of poverty,

Recalling also the 2005 World Summit encouragement to pursue responsible business practices,

Underlining the fact that cooperation between the United Nations and all relevant partners, including the private sector, shall serve the purposes and principles embodied in the Charter of the United Nations, can make concrete contributions to the realization of the internationally agreed development goals, including the Millennium Development Goals, as well as the outcomes of major United Nations conferences and summits and their reviews, in particular in the area of development and the eradication of poverty, and shall be undertaken in a manner that maintains the integrity, impartiality and independence of the Organization,

Underlining also the importance of the contribution of the private sector, non-governmental organizations and civil society to the implementation of the outcomes of United Nations conferences in the economic, social and related fields,

Reiterating that maintaining a comprehensive and diverse multi-stakeholder follow-up process to the 2002 International Conference on Financing for Development and the 2008 Follow-up International Conference on Financing for Development, including with civil society and the private sector, is critical, bearing in mind the core responsibility of all participants in the financing for development process to exercise ownership of it and to implement their respective commitments in an integrated fashion, and welcoming in this regard the active participation of civil society and private-sector entities,

Recognizing the need, where appropriate, for enhancing the capacity of Member States for their effective participation in partnerships, at all levels, in accordance with national priorities and national legislation, and encouraging international support for such efforts in developing countries,

Emphasizing that all relevant partners, including the private sector, can contribute in several ways to addressing the obstacles confronted by developing countries in mobilizing the resources needed to finance their sustainable development and to the realization of the development goals of the United Nations through, inter alia, financial resources, access to technology, management expertise and support for programmes, including through the reduced pricing of drugs, where appropriate, for the prevention, care and treatment of HIV/AIDS, malaria and tuberculosis and other diseases,

Welcoming the efforts and encouraging further efforts by all relevant partners, including the private sector, to engage as reliable and consistent partners in the development process and to take into account not only the economic and financial, but also the developmental, social, human rights,

gender and environmental implications of their undertakings and, in general, towards accepting and implementing corporate social and environmental responsibility, that is, bringing such values and responsibilities to bear on their conduct and policy premised on profit incentives, in conformity with national laws and regulations,

Underlining the fact that, in the face of the current multiple, interrelated global crises and challenges, such as the financial and economic crisis, the food crisis, volatile energy and commodity prices, and climate change, cooperation and increased commitment by all relevant partners, including the public sector, the private sector and civil society, are needed more than ever, and recognizing, in this context, the potential that partnerships have in contributing to the achievement of the internationally agreed development goals, including the Millennium Development Goals,

Reaffirming the principles of sustainable development, and underlining the need for a global consensus on the key values and principles that will promote sustainable, fair and equitable economic development, and that corporate social and environmental responsibility are important elements of such a consensus,

Noting that the financial and economic crisis has demonstrated the need for values and principles in business, including for sustainable business practices, which in turn has led to broader private sector engagement in support of United Nations goals,

Recognizing the importance of promoting a gender perspective in global partnerships,

Taking note of the Principles for Responsible Investment initiative, created to help investors to integrate environmental, social and corporate governance issues into investment decisions, and the Principles for Responsible Management Education initiative, which seeks to embed corporate responsibility principles in business school curricula and research,

Welcoming the continuous efforts by the Commission on Sustainable Development, through its secretariat, to promote partnerships for sustainable development, inter alia, by the implementation and expansion of an interactive online database as a platform to provide access to information on partnerships and to facilitate the exchange of experiences and best practices and by the regular holding of partnership fairs at the sessions of the Commission,

Taking note with appreciation of the progress achieved in the work of the United Nations on partnerships, notably in the framework of various United Nations organizations, agencies, funds, programmes, task forces, commissions and initiatives, such as the Global Compact, launched by the Secretary-General, the Global Alliance for Information and Communication Technologies and Development and the United Nations Fund for International Partnerships, and welcoming the establishment of a multitude of partnerships at the field level, entered into by various United Nations agencies, non-public partners and Member States, such as the United Nations Public-Private Alliance for Rural Development,

Recognizing the vital role the Global Compact Office continues to play with regard to strengthening the capacity of the United Nations to partner strategically with the private sector in accordance with its General Assembly mandate,

1.   *Takes note* of the report of the Secretary-General on enhanced cooperation between the United Nations and all relevant partners, in particular the private sector;

2.   *Stresses* that partnerships are voluntary and collaborative relationships between various parties, both public and non-public, in which all participants agree to work together to achieve a common purpose or undertake a specific task and, as mutually agreed, to share risks and responsibilities, resources and benefits;

3.   *Also stresses* the importance of the contribution of voluntary partnerships to the achievement of the internationally agreed development goals, including the Millennium Development Goals, while reiterating that they are a complement to, but not intended to substitute for, the commitment made by Governments with a view to achieving these goals;

4.   *Further stresses* that partnerships should be consistent with national laws and national development strategies and plans, as well as the priorities of countries where their implementation takes place, bearing in mind the relevant guidance provided by Governments;

5.   *Emphasizes* the vital role played by Governments in promoting responsible business practices, including providing the necessary legal and regulatory frameworks, where appropriate;

6.   *Recalls* that the 2005 World Summit welcomed the positive contributions of the private sector and civil society, including non-governmental organizations, in the promotion and implementation of development and human rights programmes, and also recalls that the 2005 World Summit resolved to enhance the contribution of non-governmental organizations, civil society, the private sector and other stakeholders in national development efforts, as well as in the promotion of the global partnership for development, and encouraged public-private partnerships in the following areas: the generation of new investments and employment, financing for development, health, agriculture, conservation, sustainable use of natural resources and environmental management, energy, forestry and the impact of climate change;

7.   *Recognizes* the role that public-private partnerships can play in efforts to eradicate poverty and hunger, and in improving health as well as contributing to the implementation of national strategies and action plans, inter alia, on social services delivery and in making progress towards more equitable health outcomes, bearing in mind the need to ensure that their activities conform fully with the principle of national ownership of development strategies, and also recognizes the need for effective accountability and transparency in their implementation;

8.   *Calls upon* the international community to continue to promote multi-stakeholder approaches in addressing the challenges of development in the context of globalization;

9.   *Encourages* the United Nations system to continue to develop, for those partnerships in which it participates, a common and systemic approach, which places greater emphasis on impact, transparency, accountability and sustainability, without imposing undue rigidity in partnership agreements, and with due consideration being given to the following partnership principles: common purpose, transparency, bestowing no unfair advantages upon any partner of the United Nations, mutual benefit and mutual respect,

accountability, respect for the modalities of the United Nations, striving for balanced representation of relevant partners from developed and developing countries and countries with economies in transition, sectoral and geographic balance, and not compromising the independence and neutrality of the United Nations;

10.   *Takes note with appreciation* of the efforts of the Secretary-General to streamline and update the United Nations guidelines for partnerships between the United Nations and the private sector, including through the approval of the revised Guidelines on Cooperation between the United Nations and the Business Sector;

11.   *Invites* the United Nations, when considering partnerships, to seek to engage in a more coherent manner with private sector entities that support the core values of the United Nations as reflected in the Charter and other relevant conventions and treaties and that commit to the principles of the Global Compact by translating them into operational corporate policies, codes of conduct and management, monitoring and reporting systems;

12.   *Calls upon* United Nations entities to ensure that information on the nature and scope of partnership arrangements with the private sector is available within the United Nations system, as well as to Member States and the public at large, so as to enhance transparency;

13.   *Encourages* the Global Compact to continue its activities as an innovative public-private partnership to advance United Nations values and responsible business practices within the United Nations system and among the global business community, including through an increased number of local networks;

14.   *Acknowledges* the positive contribution of the Global Compact and its ten principles in the promotion of responsible business practices;

15.   *Takes note with interest* of the decision of the Secretary-General to hold an annual Private Sector Forum, beginning with the United Nations Private Sector Forum in September 2008, focusing on food sustainability and achieving the Millennium Development Goals, and followed by the United Nations Leadership Forum on Climate Change in September 2009;

16.   *Welcomes* the collaboration between the African Private Sector Forum and the Global Compact, and encourages the strengthening of this partnership in conjunction with the Commission of the African Union to support the development of the African private sector, the promotion of public-private partnership projects and the achievement of the Millennium Development Goals in line with the relevant executive decisions of the African Union;

17.   *Welcomes* the establishment of the Global Compact Regional Centre for Latin America and the Caribbean in Bogotá, aiming at providing support to the Global Compact Local Networks and at promoting social and environmental responsibility and public-private partnerships for development in the region;

18.   *Acknowledges* the ongoing work of the United Nations on partnerships, notably in the framework of various United Nations organizations, agencies, funds, programmes, task forces and commissions, within their respective mandates, and in this regard encourages the provision of adequate training, as appropriate;

19. *Encourages* the relevant United Nations organizations and agencies to share relevant lessons learned and positive experiences from partnerships, including with the business community, as a contribution to the development of more effective United Nations partnerships;

20. *Takes note with appreciation* of the efforts of the Secretary-General to enhance partnership management through the promotion of adequate training at all levels concerned, institutional capacity in country offices, strategic focus and local ownership, the sharing of best practices and the improvement of partner selection processes, calls upon United Nations entities that engage the private sector as partners in their work to develop the policy frameworks and institutional capacities needed for engagement in a mutually beneficial way, and encourages the further development of United Nations private sector focal points for the purposes of learning and sharing best practices and information;

21. *Requests* the Secretary-General, in consultation with Member States, to promote, within existing resources, impact-assessment mechanisms of partnerships, taking into account best tools available, in order to enable effective management, ensure accountability and facilitate effective learning from both successes and failures;

22. *Welcomes* innovative approaches to using partnerships as a means to better implement goals and programmes, in particular in support of the pursuit of development and the eradication of poverty, encourages relevant United Nations bodies and agencies, and invites the Bretton Woods institutions and the World Trade Organization to further explore such possibilities, bearing in mind their different mandates, modes of operation and objectives, as well as the particular roles of the non-public partners involved;

23. *Recommends*, in this context, that partnerships should also foster the elimination of all forms of discrimination, including on gender grounds, in respect of employment and occupation;

24. *Reiterates its call upon:*

(a) All bodies within the United Nations system that engage in partnerships to ensure the integrity and independence of the Organization and to include information on partnerships in their regular reporting, as appropriate, on their websites and through other means;

(b) Partners to provide to and exchange relevant information with Governments, other stakeholders and the relevant United Nations agencies and bodies and other international organizations with which they engage, in an appropriate way, including through reports, with particular attention to the importance of sharing among partnerships information on their practical experience;

25. *Requests* the Secretary-General to report to the General Assembly at its sixty-sixth session on the implementation of the present resolution.

Sustainable development

In 2009, several UN bodies, including the General Assembly, the Economic and Social Council and the Commission on Sustainable Development, considered the implementation of outcomes of the 2002

World Summit on Sustainable Development [YUN 2002, p. 821], particularly the Johannesburg Declaration and Plan of Implementation, which outlined actions and targets for stepping up implementation of Agenda 21—a programme of action for sustainable development worldwide, adopted at the 1992 United Nations Conference on Environment and Development [YUN 1992, p. 670]—and of the Programme for the Further Implementation of Agenda 21, adopted by the Assembly at its nineteenth special session in 1997 [YUN 1997, p. 792].

By **resolution 64/196** of 21 December (see p. 1038), the General Assembly decided to include in the provisional agenda of its sixty-fifth (2011) session a sub-item entitled "Harmony with Nature" under the item entitled "Sustainable development".

Commission on Sustainable Development

As the main body responsible for coordinating and monitoring implementation of the 2002 World Summit on Sustainable Development outcomes, the Commission on Sustainable Development held its seventeenth (policy) session in New York on 16 May 2008 and from 4 to 15 May 2009 [E/2009/29], electing members of the Bureau at its second meeting on 4 May.

Intersessional events. A summary of the recommendations [E/CN.17/2009/13] emanating from the Capacity Development Workshop for Improving Agricultural Productivity, Water-use Efficiency and Rural Livelihood (Bangkok, 28–30 January) [E/CN.17/2009/16] emphasized that improving agricultural productivity, promoting integrated management of land and water resources, providing access to social capital, securing access to tenure and adapting to climate change were prerequisites for sustainable agriculture and food security. A high-level regional meeting (Windhoek, Namibia, 9–10 February) [E/CN.17/2009/15] organized by the Commission jointly with Namibia on the theme "African Agriculture in the Twenty-first Century: Meeting the Challenges, Making a Sustainable Green Revolution" focused on operationalizing a green revolution in Africa, integrating African agriculture into global markets and managing Africa's agricultural transition. In a letter dated 20 February [A/63/740], Namibia transmitted to the Secretary-General the resultant Windhoek High-level Ministerial Declaration, which called for an integrated response by African countries and the international community in support of sustainable agriculture and rural development approaches, and stressed the importance of food security and strengthening the agriculture sector in Africa.

Preparatory meeting. The Intergovernmental Preparatory Meeting (New York, 23–27 February) for the seventeenth session of the Commission [E/CN.17/2009/2], held in accordance with Economic and Social Council resolution 2007/234 [YUN 2007, p. 847], had before it the Secretary-General's reports on policy options and actions for expediting progress in implementation in: agriculture [E/CN.17/2009/3]; rural development [E/CN.17/2009/4]; land [E/CN.17/2009/5]; drought [E/CN.17/2009/6]; desertification [E/CN.17/2009/7]; Africa [E/CN.17/2009/8]; and interlinkages and cross-cutting issues [E/CN.17/2009/9].

Agriculture required renewed commitment and a new vision for global cooperation to implement policies that simultaneously aimed at increasing agricultural productivity, creating fair trade regimes, conserving natural resources and promoting investment in agricultural-related infrastructure, along with investments to bridge gaps in agricultural research and technology, and improved land and water management programmes and sustainable farming practices.

Important for rural development was enhancing the capacities of the rural population through access to education, skills development and the use of information and communication technologies for sustaining the impact of rural development programmes. Equally needed were the development of infrastructure, the integrated and holistic management of natural resources, and the promotion of alternative livelihoods options that did not depend on agriculture, yet provided sustainable income opportunities.

Central to achieving sustainable development and eradicating poverty was ensuring equitable access to land and other natural resources and land tenure security, including the recognition of customary tenure arrangements. There was a need to empower and provide access to land to marginalized people in order to eradicate poverty and ensure food security.

Improved drought-management planning, monitoring and implementation required support by capable national institutions and technical backstopping from international institutions. In addition to natural resources conservation and structural adaptation to climatic variability, policies that focused on exploiting alternative sources of water were crucial. Better access by developing countries to drought-tolerant crop varieties was essential.

National policies aimed at combating desertification needed to take into account the linkages among land degradation, desertification and poverty, in addition to addressing the root cause of land degradation itself. Local community policy ownership, regional cooperation and improved land tenure security were also important for attaining sustainable development goals.

As for Africa, priorities involved economic growth and diversification, including increasing investment in infrastructure; expanding agricultural productivity and promoting sustainable agriculture; making long-term investments in social and human capital; and preserving the environment and the natural resource base, including coping with drought, desertification, and climate change.

Interlinkages among the six issues required building institutional capacity and including agriculture, rural development, land, drought and desertification in national sustainable development strategies and other development plans, especially in Africa. Key cross-cutting issues involved gender equality, sustainable patterns of consumption and production, integrating trade of developing countries into the world trade arena, sustainable management of natural resources in small island developing States, primary health care, and public investment in rural education.

The meeting also considered a note by the Secretariat on major groups priorities for action in agriculture, rural development, land, drought, desertification and Africa [E/CN.17/2009/10]; and a letter dated 15 July 2008 from Zimbabwe to the Secretary-General transmitting the statement of African Ministers emanating from the African ministerial retreat held at Glen Cove, New York on 10 and 11 May 2008 [E/CN.17/2009/12]. The Commission took note of the Chairman's draft negotiating document for transmittal to the Commission at its seventeenth session. It also approved the request of the Nordic Council of Ministers, transmitted in a note by the Secretariat [E/CN.17/2009/L.1], to participate as an observer in the work of the Commission at its seventeenth session.

Communications. Contributions to the preparations for the seventeenth session of the Commission were received from Belarus [E/CN.17/2009/18] and Israel [E/CN.17/2009/17].

Policy session. At its seventeenth session—the policy session of the 2008–2009 implementation cycle—the Commission discussed, in line with the multi-year programme adopted by the Economic and Social Council in resolution 2003/61 [YUN 2003, p. 842], the thematic cluster for the cycle: agriculture, rural development, land, drought, desertification and Africa. The Commission focused its deliberations on those policy options and practical measures which could advance implementation in those areas, with a particular focus on how implementation could be advanced through a concerted global effort. Delegations noted that the world faced multiple crises that affected the topics under discussion, and that renewed commitment and a new vision were needed to make progress in those areas while responding to those crises.

The Commission recommended to the Economic and Social Council for adoption one draft decision on the dates of its meetings during its 2010/2011 cycle and another on the adoption of its report on its seventeenth session and the provisional agenda for its eighteenth session. It also took note of the draft programme of work for the biennium 2010–2011 for the Division for Sustainable Development of the Department of Economic and Social Affairs [E/2009/29 (dec. 17/1)]. Further, the Commission brought to the attention of the Council a resolution on "Policy options and practical measures to expedite implementation in agriculture, rural development, land, drought, desertification and Africa" [res. 17/1] and another on "Preparations for the high-level meeting to review progress made in addressing the vulnerabilities of small island developing States through the implementation of the Mauritius Strategy for Implementation" [res. 17/2], as well as the Chairperson's summary "Shared vision" on the way to meet both the near- and long-term challenges facing agriculture and to realize a green revolution based on the three pillars of sustainable development.

High-level segment. The Commission's high-level segment (13–15 May) addressed the six thematic areas under consideration. Pairs of parallel interactive round tables concerned "Responding to the food crisis through sustainable development", "Realizing a sustainable green revolution in Africa", and "Integrated management of land and water resources for sustainable agriculture and rural development".

Speaking at the opening of the segment, the Secretary-General stressed that the idea of an integrated and comprehensive approach to development—the essence of sustainable development—remained as valid then as ever for addressing the climate, food and energy crises. He underlined a strong link between climate change mitigation and sustainable agriculture. Left unchecked, climate change would have a devastating effect on the poor. Farmers, especially in Africa, must have access to land, security of tenure, access to markets, technology and improved infrastructure, in particular to empower women to become full partners in development.

Activities in the partnerships fair (4–8 May) focused on policy options and practical measures to expedite implementing sustainable development goals and commitments through partnerships. The Learning Centre offered 12 courses on topics related to the Commission's themes and cross-cutting issues.

The Economic and Social Council, on 29 July (**decision 2009/236**), took note of the Commission's report on its seventeenth session [E/2009/29] and approved the provisional agenda for its eighteenth (2010) session. Also on 29 July (**decision 2009/235**), the Council decided on the dates of the Commission's meetings during its 2010/2011 cycle.

Implementation of Agenda 21, Programme for Further Implementation of Agenda 21 and Johannesburg Plan of Implementation

In response to General Assembly resolution 63/212 [YUN 2008, p. 912], the Secretary-General in August submitted a report [A/64/275] on the implementation of Agenda 21, the Programme for the Further Implementation of Agenda 21 and the outcomes of the World Summit on Sustainable Development that provided an update on actions taken by Governments, UN system organizations and major groups in advancing the implementation of sustainable development goals and targets, including through partnerships. The report gave an overview of outcomes in sustainable human development, conservation and management of resources for development, and environmentally sound management of toxic chemicals and wastes; reviewed progress on the elements of Agenda 21 pertaining to governance and institutions, covering structures developed at international levels to oversee the implementation of Agenda 21, including the role and contributions of major groups; and summarized capacity-building actions in support of Agenda 21 with regard to international cooperation and means of implementation. The report, which recorded positive and negative trends in each of those areas, also featured views of Member States regarding the possibility of convening a high-level event on sustainable development.

The Secretary-General recommended that the General Assembly call on Governments, UN system organizations and major groups to deepen their commitments to sustainable development by redoubling their efforts to implement Agenda 21, the Programme for the Further Implementation of Agenda 21 and the Johannesburg Plan of Implementation; call on Governments to continue providing their support to the Commission on Sustainable Development and to organize intersessional activities, taking into account the thematic cluster of issues considered by the Commission in 2010–2011; call on Governments to continue providing their support to the Commission and to contribute to the Commission's trust fund in support of enhanced participation of representatives of developing countries and representatives of major groups in the work of the Commission; invite the United Nations System Chief Executives Board for Coordination (CEB) to continue monitoring, through its High-Level Committee on Programmes, the operational efficiency and effectiveness of inter-agency collaborative mechanisms, including UN-Energy, UN-Water, UN-Oceans and other collaborative arrangements, in the follow-up to the World Summit on Sustainable Development; invite Governments to continue discussing the possibility of convening a high-level event on sustainable development in order to reach a consensus; call on donor Governments and international financial institutions to support developing countries in the areas of transport, chemicals, waste management, mining and a Ten-Year Framework of Programmes on Sustainable Consumption and Production Patterns; and encourage Governments, in collaboration with UN system organizations and major groups, including business and industry, to consider enhancing the implementation and increasing the effectiveness of national sustainable development strategies, including through development cooperation frameworks, shared learning and exchange of experiences and best practices.

GENERAL ASSEMBLY ACTION

On 24 December [meeting 68], the General Assembly, on the recommendation of the Second Committee [A/64/420/Add.1], adopted **resolution 64/236** without vote [agenda item 53 *(a)*].

**Implementation of Agenda 21,
the Programme for the Further Implementation
of Agenda 21 and the outcomes of the World Summit
on Sustainable Development**

The General Assembly,

Recalling its resolutions 55/199 of 20 December 2000, 56/226 of 24 December 2001, 57/253 of 20 December 2002, 57/270 A and B of 20 December 2002 and 23 June 2003, respectively, 62/189 of 19 December 2007 and 63/212 of 19 December 2008, and all other previous resolutions on the implementation of Agenda 21, the Programme for the Further Implementation of Agenda 21 and the outcomes of the World Summit on Sustainable Development,

Recalling also the Rio Declaration on Environment and Development, Agenda 21, the Programme for the Further Implementation of Agenda 21, the Johannesburg Declaration on Sustainable Development and the Plan of Implementation of the World Summit on Sustainable Development ("Johannesburg Plan of Implementation"), as well as the Monterrey Consensus of the International Conference on Financing for Development and the Doha Declaration on Financing for Development: outcome document of the Follow-up International Conference on Financing for Development to Review the Implementation of the Monterrey Consensus,

Recalling further the Programme of Action for the Sustainable Development of Small Island Developing States, the Declaration and state of progress and initiatives for the future implementation of the Programme of Action for the Sustainable Development of Small Island Developing States, and the Mauritius Strategy for the Further Implementation of the Programme of Action for the Sustainable Development of Small Island Developing States,

Reaffirming the commitment to implement Agenda 21, the Programme for the Further Implementation of Agenda 21, the Johannesburg Plan of Implementation, including the time-bound goals and targets, and the other internationally agreed development goals, including the Millennium Development Goals,

Recalling the 2005 World Summit Outcome,

Reaffirming the decisions taken at the eleventh session of the Commission on Sustainable Development,

Recalling the adoption by the Commission of a multi-year programme of work designed to contribute to advancing the implementation of Agenda 21, the Programme for the Further Implementation of Agenda 21 and the Johannesburg Plan of Implementation at all levels,

Recalling also the decision taken by the Commission at its eleventh session that in review years it should discuss the contribution of partnerships towards supporting the implementation of Agenda 21, the Programme for the Further Implementation of Agenda 21 and the Johannesburg Plan of Implementation with a view to sharing lessons learned and best practices, identifying and addressing problems, gaps and constraints and providing further guidance, including on reporting, during policy years, as necessary,

Reiterating that sustainable development in its economic, social and environmental aspects is a key element of the overarching framework for United Nations activities, and reaffirming the continuing need to ensure a balance among economic development, social development and environmental protection as interdependent and mutually reinforcing pillars of sustainable development,

Noting that challenges remain in achieving the goals of the three pillars of sustainable development, particularly in the context of the current global crises,

Taking note with appreciation of the offer of the Government of Brazil to host a United Nations conference on sustainable development in 2012,

Reaffirming that eradicating poverty, changing unsustainable patterns of production and consumption and protecting and managing the natural resource base of economic and social development are overarching objectives of and essential requirements for sustainable development,

Recognizing that good governance within each country and at the international level is essential for sustainable development,

Recalling that the Johannesburg Plan of Implementation designated the Commission to serve as the focal point for discussion on partnerships that promote sustainable development and contribute to the implementation of intergovernmental commitments in Agenda 21, the Programme for the Further Implementation of Agenda 21 and the Johannesburg Plan of Implementation,

Recognizing that eradicating poverty is the greatest global challenge facing the world today and an indispensable requirement for sustainable development, in particular for developing countries, and that although each country has the primary responsibility for its own sustainable development and poverty eradication and the role of national policies and development strategies cannot be overemphasized, concerted and concrete measures are required at all levels to enable developing countries to achieve their sustainable development goals as related to the internationally agreed poverty-related targets and goals, including those contained in Agenda 21, the relevant outcomes of other United Nations conferences and the United Nations Millennium Declaration,

Recalling that the Economic and Social Council should increase its role in overseeing system-wide coordination and the balanced integration of economic, social and environmental aspects of United Nations policies and programmes aimed at promoting sustainable development, and reaffirming that the Commission should continue to be the high-level commission on sustainable development within the United Nations system and serve as a forum for consideration of issues related to the integration of the three dimensions of sustainable development,

Welcoming the outcome of the seventeenth session of the Commission on the thematic issues of agriculture, rural development, land, drought, desertification and Africa,

Recalling that the themes of the eighteenth and nineteenth sessions of the Commission, namely, transport, chemicals, waste management, mining and a ten-year framework of programmes on sustainable consumption and production patterns are interlinked and should be addressed in an integrated manner, taking into account the economic, social and environmental dimensions of sustainable development, related sectoral policies and cross-cutting issues, including means of implementation, as identified at the eleventh session of the Commission,

Reiterating that fundamental changes in the way societies produce and consume are indispensable for achieving global sustainable development and that all countries should promote sustainable consumption and production patterns, with the developed countries taking the lead and with all countries benefiting from the process, taking into account the Rio principles, including the principle of common but differentiated responsibilities as set out in paragraph 7 of the Rio Declaration on Environment and Development, and also reiterating that Governments, relevant international organizations, the private sector and all major groups should play an active role in changing unsustainable consumption and production patterns,

1. *Takes note* of the report of the Secretary-General;

2. *Reiterates* that sustainable development is a key element of the overarching framework for United Nations activities, in particular for achieving the internationally agreed development goals, including the Millennium Development Goals, and those contained in the Johannesburg Plan of Implementation;

3. *Calls upon* Governments, all relevant international and regional organizations, the Economic and Social Council, the United Nations funds and programmes, the regional commissions and specialized agencies, the international financial institutions, the Global Environment Facility and other intergovernmental organizations, in accordance with their respective mandates, as well as major groups, to take action to ensure the effective implementation of and follow-up to the commitments, programmes and time-bound targets adopted at the World Summit on Sustainable Development, and encourages them to report on concrete progress in that regard;

4. *Calls for* the effective implementation of the commitments, programmes and time-bound targets adopted at the World Summit on Sustainable Development and for the fulfilment of the provisions relating to the means of implementation, as contained in the Johannesburg Plan of Implementation;

5. *Reiterates* that the Commission on Sustainable Development is the high-level body responsible for sustainable development within the United Nations system and serves as a forum for the consideration of issues related to the integration of the three dimensions of sustainable development, and underlines the need to further support the work of the Commission, taking into account its existing mandate and the decisions taken at its eleventh session;

6. *Encourages* countries to present, on a voluntary basis, in particular at the Commission's review sessions, national reports focusing on concrete progress in implementation, including achievements, constraints, challenges and opportunities;

7. *Emphasizes* the importance of a consensus outcome and action-oriented policy sessions;

8. *Encourages* Governments to participate, at the appropriate level, in the eighteenth session of the Commission, with representatives, including ministers, from the relevant departments and organizations working in the areas of transport, chemicals, waste management, mining and sustainable consumption and production, as well as finance;

9. *Recalls* the decision of the Commission at its eleventh session that activities during Commission meetings should provide for the balanced involvement of participants from all regions, as well as for gender balance;

10. *Invites* donor countries to consider supporting the participation of representatives from the developing countries in the eighteenth session of the Commission, inter alia, through contributions to the Commission's trust fund;

11. *Reaffirms* the objective of strengthening the implementation of Agenda 21, including through the mobilization of financial and technological resources, as well as capacity-building programmes, in particular for developing countries;

12. *Also reaffirms* the objective of enhancing the participation and effective involvement of civil society and other relevant stakeholders, as well as promoting transparency and broad public participation, in the implementation of Agenda 21;

13. *Requests* the secretariat of the Commission to coordinate the participation of the relevant major groups in the thematic discussions at the eighteenth session of the Commission and the reporting on the fulfilment of corporate responsibility and accountability with respect to the thematic cluster of issues, in accordance with the provisions of the Johannesburg Plan of Implementation;

14. *Reaffirms* the need to promote corporate social responsibility and accountability as envisaged by the Johannesburg Plan of Implementation;

15. *Requests* the secretariat of the Commission to make arrangements to facilitate the balanced representation of major groups from developed and developing countries in the sessions of the Commission, and in this regard invites donor countries to consider supporting the participation of major groups from developing countries, inter alia, through contributions to the Commission's trust fund;

16. *Encourages* contributions by the regional implementation meetings and other regional events to the Commission at its eighteenth session;

17. *Reiterates its invitation* to the relevant United Nations funds and programmes, the regional commissions

and specialized agencies, the international and regional financial and trade institutions and the Global Environment Facility, as well as the secretariats of the multilateral environmental agreements and other relevant bodies, to actively participate, within their mandates, in the work of the Commission at its eighteenth session;

18. *Encourages* Governments and organizations at all levels, as well as major groups, to undertake results-oriented initiatives and activities to support the work of the Commission and to promote and facilitate the implementation of Agenda 21, the Programme for the Further Implementation of Agenda 21 and the Johannesburg Plan of Implementation, including through voluntary multi-stakeholder partnership initiatives;

19. *Requests* the Secretary-General, in reporting to the Commission at its eighteenth session, on the basis of appropriate inputs from all levels, to submit a thematic report on each of the five issues contained in the thematic cluster to be considered at the session, namely, transport, chemicals, waste management, mining and a ten-year framework of programmes on sustainable consumption and production patterns, taking into account their interlinkages as well as cross-cutting issues, including means of implementation identified by the Commission at its eleventh session, and takes into account the relevant provisions of paragraphs 10, 14 and 15 of draft resolution I adopted by the Commission at its eleventh session;

20. *Decides* to organize, in 2012, the United Nations Conference on Sustainable Development at the highest possible level, including Heads of State and Government or other representatives, in this regard accepts with gratitude the generous offer of the Government of Brazil to host the Conference, and decides that:

(a) The objective of the Conference will be to secure renewed political commitment for sustainable development, assessing the progress to date and the remaining gaps in the implementation of the outcomes of the major summits on sustainable development and addressing new and emerging challenges. The focus of the Conference will include the following themes to be discussed and refined during the preparatory process: a green economy in the context of sustainable development and poverty eradication and the institutional framework for sustainable development;

(b) The Conference will result in a focused political document;

(c) The Conference and its preparatory process should take into account the decision taken at the eleventh session of the Commission to carry out, at the conclusion of the multi-year programme of work, an overall appraisal of the implementation of Agenda 21, the Programme for the Further Implementation of Agenda 21 and the Johannesburg Plan of Implementation;

(d) The Conference, including its preparatory process, should ensure the balanced integration of economic development, social development and environmental protection, as these are interdependent and mutually reinforcing components of sustainable development;

(e) It is important that there be efficient and effective preparations at the local, national, regional and international levels by Governments and the United Nations system so as to ensure high-quality inputs without placing undue strain on Member States;

(f) It must be ensured that the Conference and related preparations do not adversely affect other ongoing activities;

21. *Encourages* the active participation of all major groups, as identified in Agenda 21 and further elaborated in the Johannesburg Plan of Implementation and decisions taken at the eleventh session of the Commission, at all stages of the preparatory process, in accordance with the rules and procedures of the Commission as well as its established practices related to the participation and engagement of major groups;

22. *Invites* relevant stakeholders, including organizations and bodies of the United Nations, international financial institutions and major groups involved in the area of sustainable development, to provide ideas and proposals reflecting their experiences and lessons learned as a contribution to the preparatory process;

23. *Decides* that a preparatory committee will be established within the framework of the Commission to carry out the preparations for the United Nations Conference on Sustainable Development, which will provide for the full and effective participation of all States Members of the United Nations and members of the specialized agencies, as well as other participants in the Commission, in accordance with the rules of procedure of the functional commissions of the Economic and Social Council and the supplementary arrangements established for the Commission by the Council in its decisions 1993/215 of 12 February 1993 and 1995/201 of 8 February 1995;

24. *Invites* regional groups to nominate their candidates for the ten-member Bureau of the Preparatory Committee no later than 28 February 2010 so that they can be involved in its preparations in advance of the first session of the Preparatory Committee;

25. *Decides* that:

(a) The first meeting of the Preparatory Committee will be held in 2010 for three days, immediately after the conclusion of the eighteenth session and the first meeting of the nineteenth session of the Commission to discuss the substantive themes of the Conference, as decided in accordance with the present resolution, and pending procedural matters, as well as to elect the Bureau;

(b) The second meeting of the Preparatory Committee will be held in 2011 for two days immediately after the conclusion of the Intergovernmental Preparatory Meeting for the nineteenth session of the Commission to discuss further the substantive themes of the Conference;

(c) The third and final meeting of the Preparatory Committee will be held in Brazil in 2012 for three days to discuss the outcome of the Conference, immediately preceding the United Nations Conference on Sustainable Development, which will also be held for three days. In this regard, the Commission will postpone its multi-year programme of work for one year;

(d) Regional implementation meetings will become regional preparatory meetings for the Conference in 2011;

26. *Requests* the Secretary-General to submit a report on progress to date and remaining gaps in the implementation of the outcomes of the major summits in the area of sustainable development, as well as an analysis of the themes identified above, to the Preparatory Committee at its first meeting;

27. *Also requests* the Secretary-General to provide all appropriate support to the work of the preparatory process and the Conference, ensuring inter-agency participation and coherence as well as the efficient use of resources;

28. *Encourages* international and bilateral donors and other countries in a position to do so to support the preparations for the Conference through voluntary contributions to the Commission's trust fund and to support the participation of representatives of developing countries, and invites voluntary contributions to support the participation of major groups of developing countries in the regional and international preparatory processes and the Conference itself;

29. *Decides* to include in the provisional agenda of its sixty-fifth session the sub-item entitled "Implementation of Agenda 21, the Programme for the Further Implementation of Agenda 21 and the outcomes of the World Summit on Sustainable Development", and requests the Secretary-General, at that session, to submit a report on the implementation of the present resolution, including on the progress of the preparations for the United Nations Conference on Sustainable Development.

On 24 December (**decision 64/549**), the General Assembly decided that the agenda items on the follow-up to and implementation of the outcome of the 2002 International Conference on Financing for Development and the 2008 Review Conference, and sustainable development: protection of global climate for present and future generations would remain for consideration during its resumed sixty-fourth (2010) session.

Communications. In a letter dated 4 May [A/63/843], Turkmenistan transmitted the statement of the Chairmanship of the High-level Ashgabat Conference on "Reliable and stable transit of energy and its role in ensuring sustainable development and international cooperation" (Ashgabat, Turkmenistan, 23–24 April). In respective letters dated 17 February [A/63/723] and 7 May [A/63/847], Uzbekistan and Belarus submitted information on their respective declarations of 2009 as the Year of Development and Improvement of the Countryside in Uzbekistan and as the Year of Our Native Land in Belarus.

Implementation of Ministerial Declaration on internationally agreed sustainable development goals

Coordination segment of Economic and Social Council. At its 2009 coordination segment (10, 13–14 and 31 July) [A/64/3/Rev.1], the Economic and Social Council considered the role of the UN system in implementing the Ministerial Declaration on implementing the internationally agreed goals and commitments in regard to sustainable development, adopted at its 2008 high-level segment [YUN 2008, p. 903]. The Council had before it a report of the Secretary-General [E/2009/56] that reviewed UN sys-

tem efforts to further the sustainable development agenda against the backdrop of current challenges. The report assessed progress and challenges in priority areas identified in the 2008 Ministerial Declaration; identified lessons learned from country-level experience to strengthen support for national sustainable development strategies; and assessed the impact of current challenges on those efforts. The report made recommendations in the areas of energy, climate change, water, agricultural and rural development, sustainable urbanization, social equality, and institutions for sustainable development, and concluded that the UN system had made important strides in strengthening its role in support of sustainable development, as evidenced in several initiatives; it had addressed specific challenges, including climate change, water resource management, energy supply and agricultural and rural development, and those efforts could be scaled up to involve all relevant partners.

The Economic and Social Council took note of the Secretary-General's report on 31 July (**decision 2009/257**).

ECONOMIC AND SOCIAL COUNCIL ACTION

On 31 July [meeting 45], the Economic and Social Council adopted **resolution 2009/28** [draft: E/2009/L.44] without vote [agenda item 4].

The role of the United Nations system in implementing the ministerial declaration of the high-level segment of the substantive session of 2008 of the Economic and Social Council, on the theme "Implementing internationally agreed goals and commitments in regard to sustainable development"

The Economic and Social Council,

Recalling the United Nations Millennium Declaration and the 2005 World Summit Outcome,

Recalling also the ministerial declaration of the high-level segment of its substantive session of 2008,

Recalling further its resolutions 2008/28 and 2008/29 of 24 July 2008, adopted at the coordination segment of its substantive session of 2008, as well as other relevant resolutions,

Reaffirming that effective sustainable development strategies need to pursue an integrated approach to economic, social and environmental dimensions of sustainable development, in line with the Rio Declaration on Environment and Development, the Johannesburg Declaration on Sustainable Development, the Plan of Implementation of the World Summit on Sustainable Development ("Johannesburg Plan of Implementation") and other relevant outcomes of United Nations conferences and summits,

Expressing concern regarding the number of people living in poverty and the fact that the current economic and food insecurity crises and unpredictable energy prices may pose significant challenges for the achievement of the internationally agreed development goals, including the Millennium Development Goals, and in this context highlighting the importance of improved coordination of United Nations system activities in support of achieving sustainable development,

Recalling that the Economic and Social Council should further increase its role in overseeing system-wide coordination and the balanced integration of economic, social and environmental aspects of United Nations policies and programmes aimed at achieving sustainable development, and reaffirming that the Commission on Sustainable Development should continue to act as the high-level body on sustainable development within the United Nations system and to serve as a forum for the consideration of issues related to the integration of the three dimensions of sustainable development,

1. *Reiterates* that sustainable development in its economic, social and environmental aspects is a key element of the overarching framework for United Nations activities, and reaffirms the continuing need to ensure a balance among economic development, social development and environmental protection as interdependent and mutually reinforcing pillars of sustainable development;

2. *Requests* all member organizations of the United Nations System Chief Executives Board for Coordination to further mainstream, at all levels, the sustainable development agenda, including recommendations of the Commission on Sustainable Development, and to align and coordinate, as well as promote coherence among, their policies, programmes, initiatives and activities, as appropriate;

3. *Requests* the funds, programmes and agencies of the United Nations system, as appropriate within their mandates, to continue to lend and further strengthen their support to developing countries in:

(a) Building their capacity to formulate effective sustainable development strategies;

(b) Mobilizing adequate and sustained levels of financial resources for meeting the priority objectives of sustainable development;

(c) Enhancing access to external resources as well as to key technologies for sustainable development;

4. *Notes* the progress made by UN-Energy in enhancing United Nations system cooperation and coordination with respect to following up the energy agenda of the World Summit on Sustainable Development, and calls upon UN-Energy to further promote system-wide policy coherence in relation to, inter alia, energy efficiency and renewable energy technologies;

5. *Invites* the United Nations system to further strengthen a coordinated and coherent system-wide approach to addressing the adverse impacts of climate change, particularly in developing countries;

6. *Encourages* the United Nations system to support and participate in, as appropriate, the activities being envisaged for the observance of 2010 as the International Year of Biodiversity, including those organized under the auspices of the secretariat of the Convention on Biological Diversity;

7. *Invites* the funds, programmes and agencies of the United Nations system, as appropriate within their mandates, to support, in a coordinated manner, initiatives directed towards implementing green initiatives in developing countries, encompassing, inter alia, the preparation of strategies for achieving a green economy in the context of sustainable development, including through capacity-building and the transfer and diffusion of environmentally sound technologies and corresponding know-how, in particular to developing countries and countries with economies in transition, on favourable terms, including on concessional and preferential terms, as mutually agreed, while taking note of the coordination work of UN-Energy in this regard;

8. *Also invites* the funds, programmes and agencies of the United Nations system, as appropriate within their mandates, to integrate their work on water issues at the regional and local levels into United Nations efforts at the country level to support national sustainable development strategies and to promote the implementation of the priorities agreed within the framework of the Commission on Sustainable Development, while taking note, inter alia, of the coordination work of UN-Water in this regard;

9. *Calls upon* the United Nations system to support efforts to promote sustainable consumption and production patterns, including through the Marrakech Process, with developed countries taking the lead and with all countries benefiting from the process, while taking into account the principles contained in the Rio Declaration on Environment and Development, including the principle of common but differentiated responsibilities;

10. *Requests* the funds, programmes and agencies of the United Nations system, as appropriate within their mandates, to mainstream, in a coordinated manner, sustainable urbanization, urban poverty reduction and slum upgrading in their efforts to assist developing countries, in accordance with national strategies and programmes, in achieving the Millennium Development Goals, and notes the efforts of the United Nations Development Group in facilitating the inclusion of these concerns in the United Nations Development Assistance Framework guidelines;

11. *Encourages* the funds, programmes and agencies of the United Nations system, as appropriate within their mandates, to continue integrating social justice and equity concerns into their programmes and activities to support national sustainable development strategies and to promote a greater understanding of the social impact of current crises;

12. *Requests* the funds, programmes and agencies of the United Nations system, as appropriate within their mandates, to continue to promote gender equality and the empowerment of women, as well as multi-stakeholder approaches involving local authorities, civil society and the private sector, in their efforts to ensure the achievement of sustainable development.

Agricultural technology for development

In response to General Assembly resolution 62/190 [YUN 2007, p. 844], the Secretary-General in August submitted a report [A/64/258] on agricultural technology for development. The report assessed the contribution of agricultural technologies to boosting productivity and promoting growth and food security, especially in low-productivity agricultural systems, and ensuring resilience and long-run stability of production. The report reviewed areas such as, agricultural productivity and sustainability challenges; supporting technology development with regard to factors affecting the productivity, resilience and sustainability of agricultural systems; and boosting agriculture sustainability through programmes for technology development and adaptation, as well as support institutions and infrastructure.

The Secretary-General recommended incorporating agricultural technology and broader development into national sustainable development strategies; and supporting a new, sustainable green revolution that would revitalize agricultural sectors in developing countries by enhancing agricultural production, productivity and sustainability by using science-based approaches and local indigenous knowledge in a manner that protected and conserved natural resources, limited the use of scarce inputs and pollutants, and enhanced the quality of natural resources. He also recommended implementing a social strategy for sustainable rural development, including enhanced support for small farmers; ensuring land tenure protection as well as secure access to water, especially for poor and vulnerable groups; promoting the empowerment of rural women; and scaling up of best practices. International cooperation would be essential to implement those national actions.

GENERAL ASSEMBLY ACTION

On 21 December [meeting 66], the General Assembly, on the recommendation of the Second Committee [A/64/420/Add.1], adopted **resolution 64/197** by recorded vote (146-1-32) [agenda item 53 (a)].

Agricultural technology for development

The General Assembly,

Recalling its resolution 62/190 of 19 December 2007 on agricultural technology for development,

Recalling also the Rio Declaration on Environment and Development, Agenda 21, the Programme for the Further Implementation of Agenda 21, the Johannesburg Declaration on Sustainable Development and the Plan of Implementation of the World Summit on Sustainable Development ("Johannesburg Plan of Implementation"),

Recalling further the 2005 World Summit Outcome,

Recalling its resolution 63/235 of 22 December 2008 on agriculture development and food security,

Recognizing the work done by the Commission on Sustainable Development, in particular at its sixteenth and seventeenth sessions, highlighting the thematic focus on agriculture-related issues, and applauding its call to increase investment in training research and development, in particular on sustainable practices and technologies, including agricultural technologies, and to accelerate the transfer and diffusion of such technologies, information, methods and practices in order to reach all users, including farmers, women, youth and indigenous people as well as those in remote rural areas,

Acknowledging the work performed by the High-level Task Force on the Global Food Security Crisis, established by the Secretary-General in 2008, and the Comprehensive

Framework for Action that it produced, specifically its call for increased investments in the development of agricultural technology as well as the transfer and use of existing technologies, as appropriate, especially for smallholder farmers as a means to achieve global food security and poverty reduction,

Recalling the World Summit on Food Security convened by the Food and Agriculture Organization of the United Nations in Rome from 16 to 18 November 2009, and stressing the vital role of international cooperation in advancing and implementing agricultural technologies,

Welcoming the commitment by the Group of Eight and more than twenty-five countries and organizations in the Joint Statement on Global Food Security, adopted in L'Aquila, Italy, on 10 July 2009, towards the goal of mobilizing 20 billion United States dollars over three years focused on sustainable agriculture development,

Reaffirming its commitment to achieve the Millennium Development Goals, and recognizing the beneficial impact that the adoption of agricultural technologies can have for the achievement of those goals, including for eradicating extreme poverty and hunger, empowering women and ensuring environmental sustainability,

Concerned by the slow progress so far in achieving the above-mentioned goals, in particular by the fact that Africa remains the only continent currently not on track to achieve any of the goals of the United Nations Millennium Declaration by 2015, and recognizing the need to intensify the efforts of the international community in its attempt to reach the internationally agreed development goals, including the Millennium Development Goals,

Acknowledging the importance and the potential of smallholder farmers in increasing agricultural production, achieving economic growth and reducing poverty,

Stressing the critical role of women in the agricultural sector and their contribution to enhancing agricultural and rural development, improving food security and eradicating rural poverty, and underlining further the fact that meaningful progress in agricultural development necessitates a focus on supporting and empowering women,

Acknowledging the role and work of civil society in furthering progress in developing countries, in promoting the use of sustainable agricultural technology and the training of smallholder farmers, in raising awareness and in the provision and dissemination of information,

Aware that the world financial and economic crisis, in addition to other global challenges, has a negative impact on food security and development, specifically in the agricultural sector, thereby negatively impacting the most vulnerable groups and potentially setting back progress made in achieving the Millennium Development Goals,

Considering the increasing need to innovate in agriculture and food production in order to respond to the challenges posed by, inter alia, climate change, depletion and scarcity of natural resources, urbanization and globalization, and recognizing that sustainable agricultural technologies can greatly contribute to the adaptation of agriculture to, and help to mitigate the negative impact of, climate change, land degradation and desertification,

Underlining the importance of collaboration, sharing of information and dissemination of agricultural technology research results as well as wide consultation when defining the global, regional and national research agendas, and in this regard noting the valuable role of, inter alia, the Global Forum on Agricultural Research and its affiliated or associated organizations,

1. *Welcomes* the report of the Secretary-General on agricultural technology for development;

2. *Calls upon* Member States and relevant United Nations organizations to make greater efforts to develop and disseminate appropriate sustainable agricultural technologies, particularly in and with developing countries, under fair, transparent and mutually agreed terms, and to support national efforts to foster utilization of local know-how and agricultural technologies, promote agricultural technology research and enable poor rural women, men and youth to increase sustainable agricultural productivity and enhance food security;

3. *Calls attention* to the crucial role of women in the agricultural sector, and therefore calls upon Member States to promote and support better access of women to agricultural technology information and know-how, equipment and decision-making forums;

4. *Underlines* the importance of supporting and advancing research in improving and diversifying crop varieties, as well as supporting the establishment of agricultural systems and sustainable management practices, in order to make agriculture more resilient and, in particular, to make crops more tolerant to environmental stress, including drought and climate change, in a manner consistent with national regulations and relevant international agreements;

5. *Also underlines* the importance of the sustainable use and management of water resources to increase and ensure agricultural productivity, and calls for further efforts to strengthen the provision and proper maintenance of irrigation facilities as well as to introduce water-saving technology, considering the possible impact of climate change on water resources;

6. *Encourages* Member States, civil society and public and private institutions to develop partnerships to support financial and market services, including training, capacity-building, infrastructure and extension services to farmers, in particular smallholder farmers, and calls for further efforts by all stakeholders to make appropriate sustainable agricultural technologies available and affordable to smallholder farmers;

7. *Calls upon* Member States to include sustainable agricultural development as an integral part of their national policies and strategies, notes the positive impact that North-South, South-South and triangular cooperation can have in this regard, and urges the relevant bodies of the United Nations system to include elements of agricultural technology, research and development in efforts to achieve the Millennium Development Goals;

8. *Requests* relevant United Nations organizations, including the Food and Agriculture Organization of the United Nations and the International Fund for Agricultural Development, to promote, support and facilitate the exchange of experience among Member States on ways to sustainably expand areas for agriculture and increase opportunities for agricultural development through technologies that allow soil recovery, improve soil fertility and increase agricultural production in pressing environmental circumstances;

9. *Underlines* the instrumental role of agricultural technology in furthering sustainable development and in achieving the Millennium Development Goals, calls therefore upon Member States and encourages relevant international bodies to support sustainable agricultural research and development, and in this regard calls for continued support to the international agricultural research system, including the Consultative Group on International Agricultural Research and other relevant international organizations;

10. *Requests* the Secretary-General to submit to the General Assembly at its sixty-sixth session a report on the implementation of the present resolution.

RECORDED VOTE ON RESOLUTION 64/197:

In favour: Albania, Algeria, Andorra, Angola, Antigua and Barbuda, Argentina, Armenia, Australia, Austria, Azerbaijan, Bahamas, Barbados, Belarus, Belgium, Belize, Benin, Bhutan, Bolivia, Bosnia and Herzegovina, Botswana, Brazil, Bulgaria, Burkina Faso, Burundi, Cambodia, Cameroon, Canada, Cape Verde, Central African Republic, Chad, Chile, China, Colombia, Congo, Costa Rica, Côte d'Ivoire, Croatia, Cyprus, Czech Republic, Denmark, Dominica, Dominican Republic, El Salvador, Eritrea, Estonia, Ethiopia, Fiji, Finland, France, Gabon, Georgia, Germany, Ghana, Greece, Grenada, Guatemala, Guinea, Guinea-Bissau, Guyana, Haiti, Hungary, Iceland, India, Ireland, Israel, Italy, Jamaica, Japan, Jordan, Kazakhstan, Kenya, Kyrgyzstan, Latvia, Lesotho, Liberia, Liechtenstein, Lithuania, Luxembourg, Madagascar, Malawi, Maldives, Malta, Marshall Islands, Mauritius, Mexico, Micronesia, Moldova, Monaco, Mongolia, Montenegro, Mozambique, Myanmar, Nauru, Nepal, Netherlands, New Zealand, Niger, Nigeria, Norway, Palau, Panama, Papua New Guinea, Paraguay, Peru, Philippines, Poland, Portugal, Republic of Korea, Romania, Russian Federation, Rwanda, Saint Kitts and Nevis, Saint Lucia, Saint Vincent and the Grenadines, Samoa, San Marino, Senegal, Serbia, Sierra Leone, Singapore, Slovakia, Slovenia, Solomon Islands, Spain, Sri Lanka, Suriname, Sweden, Switzerland, Tajikistan, Thailand, The former Yugoslav Republic of Macedonia, Timor-Leste, Togo, Tonga, Trinidad and Tobago, Turkey, Tuvalu, Uganda, Ukraine, United Kingdom, United States, Uruguay, Uzbekistan, Viet Nam, Zambia, Zimbabwe.

Against: Somalia.

Abstaining: Afghanistan, Bahrain, Bangladesh, Brunei Darussalam, Comoros, Cuba, Democratic People's Republic of Korea, Djibouti, Ecuador, Indonesia, Iraq, Kuwait, Lebanon, Libyan Arab Jamahiriya, Malaysia, Mali, Mauritania, Morocco, Namibia, Nicaragua, Oman, Pakistan, Qatar, Saudi Arabia, South Africa, Sudan, Swaziland, Syrian Arab Republic, Tunisia, United Arab Emirates, Venezuela, Yemen.

Communication. By a 7 August letter [A/64/301], Israel submitted a report on its implementation of General Assembly resolution 62/190 [YUN 2007, p. 844].

Eradication of poverty

Second UN Decade for the Eradication of Poverty

In response to General Assembly resolution 63/230 [YUN 2008, p. 917], the Acting Director of the Division for Social Policy and Development in the

Department of Economic and Social Affairs (DESA) on 22 October briefed the Second Committee [A/C.2/64/SR.18] on progress made in implementing the Second United Nations Decade for the Eradication of Poverty (2008–2017), proclaimed by the Assembly in 2007 [YUN 2007, p. 847]. The CEB High-level Committee on Programmes (HLCP) had reviewed and endorsed the framework of a system-wide plan of action for poverty eradication, with a focus on employment and decent work, prepared by a cluster group of HLCP members, co-led by DESA and the International Labour Organization. The plan covered four types of joint activity: raising awareness about employment and decent work as an effective development strategy for poverty eradication; strengthening capacity-building; sharing good practices in promoting employment and decent work nationally and internationally; and supporting the integration of decent work towards poverty eradication into national and international policies and programmes. The plan focused on youth employment, the working poor, social protection, support for sustainable enterprises, gender equality, standards and rights at work, and social dialogue. The UN system would work closely with social partners, civil society organizations and other actors with a view to supporting Governments in implementing internationally agreed development goals, including the MDGs, related to poverty eradication. The Secretary-General had decided to appoint the Under-Secretary-General for Economic and Social Affairs as UN focal point for the implementation of the Second United Nations Decade for the Eradication of Poverty.

GENERAL ASSEMBLY ACTION

On 21 December [meeting 66], the General Assembly, on the recommendation of the Second Committee [A/64/424/Add.1], adopted **resolution 64/216** without vote [agenda item 57 (a)].

Second United Nations Decade for the Eradication of Poverty (2008–2017)

The General Assembly,

Recalling its resolutions 47/196 of 22 December 1992, 48/183 of 21 December 1993, 50/107 of 20 December 1995, 56/207 of 21 December 2001, 57/265 and 57/266 of 20 December 2002, 58/222 of 23 December 2003, 59/247 of 22 December 2004, 60/209 of 22 December 2005, 61/213 of 20 December 2006, 62/205 of 19 December 2007 and 63/230 of 19 December 2008,

Recalling also the United Nations Millennium Declaration, adopted by Heads of State and Government on the occasion of the Millennium Summit, as well as the international commitment to eradicate extreme poverty and to halve, by 2015, the proportion of the world's people whose income is less than one dollar a day and the proportion of people who suffer from hunger,

Recalling further the 2005 World Summit Outcome,

Recalling its resolution 60/265 of 30 June 2006 on the follow-up to the development outcome of the 2005 World Summit, including the Millennium Development Goals and the other internationally agreed development goals,

Recalling also its resolution 61/16 of 20 November 2006 on the strengthening of the Economic and Social Council,

Welcoming the poverty-related discussions in the annual ministerial reviews held by the Economic and Social Council, which play an important supporting role in the implementation of the Second United Nations Decade for the Eradication of Poverty (2008–2017),

Noting with appreciation the ministerial declaration adopted at the high-level segment of the substantive session of 2006 of the Economic and Social Council on creating an environment at the national and international levels conducive to generating full and productive employment and decent work for all, and its impact on sustainable development, and also Economic and Social Council resolution 2009/5 of 24 July 2009 entitled "Recovering from the crisis: a Global Jobs Pact",

Recalling its resolution 63/303 of 9 July 2009 on the outcome of the Conference on the World Financial and Economic Crisis and Its Impact on Development,

Recalling also the Doha Declaration on Financing for Development: outcome document of the Follow-up International Conference on Financing for Development to Review the Implementation of the Monterrey Consensus,

Recalling further the outcomes of the World Summit for Social Development and the twenty-fourth special session of the General Assembly,

Underlining the fact that, in the face of the current multiple, interrelated global crises and challenges, such as the financial and economic crisis, the food crisis, volatile energy and commodity prices and climate change, cooperation and increased commitment by all relevant partners, including the public sector, the private sector and civil society, are needed more than ever, and recognizing in this context the urgent need to achieve the internationally agreed development goals, including the Millennium Development Goals,

Expressing concern that, after the First United Nations Decade for the Eradication of Poverty (1997–2006) and six years from the 2015 target date of the Millennium Development Goals, while there has been progress in reducing poverty in some regions, this progress has been uneven and the number of people living in poverty in some countries continues to increase, with women and children constituting the majority of the most affected groups, especially in the least developed countries and particularly in sub-Saharan Africa,

Recognizing that rates of economic growth vary among countries and that these differences must be addressed by, among other actions, promoting pro-poor growth and social protection,

Concerned at the global nature of poverty and inequality, and underlining the fact that the eradication of poverty and hunger is an ethical, social, political and economic imperative of humankind,

Reaffirming that eradicating poverty is one of the greatest global challenges facing the world today, particularly in Africa and in least developed countries, and underlining the fact that the importance of accelerating sustainable broad-based and inclusive economic growth, including full, productive employment generation and decent work,

Recognizing that mobilizing financial resources for development at the national and international levels and the effective use of those resources are central to a global partnership for development in support of the achievement of the internationally agreed development goals, including the Millennium Development Goals,

Recognizing also the contributions of South-South and triangular cooperation to the efforts of developing countries to eradicate poverty and to pursue sustainable development,

Acknowledging that good governance at the national and international levels and sustained and inclusive economic growth, supported by full employment and decent work, rising productivity and a favourable environment, including public and private investment and entrepreneurship, are necessary to eradicate poverty, achieve the internationally agreed development goals, including the Millennium Development Goals, and realize a rise in living standards, and that corporate social responsibility initiatives play an important role in maximizing the impact of public and private investment,

Underlining the priority and urgency given by the Heads of State and Government to the eradication of poverty, as expressed in the outcomes of the major United Nations conferences and summits in the economic and social fields,

1. *Reaffirms* that the objective of the Second United Nations Decade for the Eradication of Poverty (2008–2017) is to support, in an efficient and coordinated manner, the follow-up to the implementation of the internationally agreed development goals, including the Millennium Development Goals, related to the eradication of poverty and to coordinate international support to that end;

2. *Also reaffirms* that each country must take primary responsibility for its own development and that the role of national policies and strategies cannot be overemphasized in the achievement of sustainable development and poverty eradication, and recognizes that increased effective national efforts should be complemented by concrete, effective and supportive international programmes, measures and policies aimed at expanding the development opportunities of developing countries, while taking into account national conditions and ensuring respect for national ownership, strategies and sovereignty;

3. *Emphasizes* the need to accord the highest priority to poverty eradication within the United Nations development agenda, while stressing the importance of addressing the causes and challenges of poverty through integrated, coordinated and coherent strategies at the national, inter-governmental and inter-agency levels;

4. *Reiterates* the need to strengthen the leadership role of the United Nations in promoting international cooperation for development, which is critical for the eradication of poverty;

5. *Stresses* the importance of ensuring, at the national, intergovernmental and inter-agency levels, coherent, comprehensive and integrated activities for the eradication of poverty in accordance with the outcomes of the major United Nations conferences and summits in the economic, social and related fields;

6. *Reaffirms* the commitment to promote opportunities for full, freely chosen and productive employment, including for the disadvantaged, as well as decent work for all, with full respect for fundamental principles and rights at work under conditions of equity, equality, security and dignity, and also reaffirms that macroeconomic policies should, inter alia, support employment creation, taking fully into account the social and environmental impact and dimensions of globalization, and that these concepts are key elements of sustainable development for all countries and are therefore a priority objective of international cooperation;

7. *Emphasizes* that education and training are among the critical factors in empowering those living in poverty, while recognizing the complexity of the challenge of poverty eradication;

8. *Calls upon* the international community to continue to give priority to the eradication of poverty and upon donor countries in a position to do so to support the effective national efforts of developing countries in this regard, through adequate predictable financial resources on either a bilateral or a multilateral basis;

9. *Reaffirms* the need to fulfil all official development assistance commitments, including the commitments made by many developed countries to achieve the target of 0.7 per cent of gross national product for official development assistance to developing countries by 2015, and to reach the level of at least 0.5 per cent of gross national product for development assistance by 2010, as well as a target of 0.15 to 0.20 per cent of gross national product for official development assistance to least developed countries;

10. *Welcomes* the increased efforts to improve the quality of official development assistance and to increase its impact on development, including through the Development Cooperation Forum of the Economic and Social Council, the 2005 Paris Declaration on Aid Effectiveness and the 2008 Accra Agenda for Action, which make important contributions to the efforts of those countries which have committed to them, and through the adoption of the fundamental principles of national ownership, alignment, harmonization and management of results and through the further alignment of assistance with countries' strategies, the building of institutional capacities, the reduction of transaction costs, the elimination of bureaucratic procedures, the achievement of progress on untying aid, the enhancement of the absorptive capacity and financial management of recipient countries and the strengthening of the focus on development results, and bears in mind that there is no one-size-fits-all formula that will guarantee effective assistance and that the specific situation of each country needs to be fully considered;

11. *Recognizes* that sustained and inclusive economic growth is essential for eradicating poverty and hunger, in particular in developing countries, and stresses that national efforts in this regard should be complemented by an enabling international environment;

12. *Calls upon* Member States to continue their ambitious efforts to strive for more inclusive, equitable, balanced, stable and development-oriented sustainable socioeconomic approaches to overcoming poverty and inequality;

13. *Takes note* of the decision of the Secretary-General to appoint the Under-Secretary-General for Economic and

Social Affairs as the coordinator for the Second United Nations Decade for the Eradication of Poverty (2008–2017);

14. *Calls upon* the relevant organizations of the United Nations system to consider activities to implement the Second Decade, in consultation with Member States and other relevant stakeholders;

15. *Takes note* of the inter-agency system-wide plan of action for poverty eradication involving more than twenty-one agencies, funds, programmes and regional commissions, and requests the Secretary-General to provide further details of this plan of action to the Member States;

16. *Reaffirms* the need to give the highest priority to its consideration of the item on poverty eradication in its agenda, and in that regard recalls its decision, in resolution 63/230, as a contribution to the Second Decade, to convene, during its sixty-eighth session, a meeting of the General Assembly at the highest appropriate political level centred on the review process devoted to the theme relating to the issue of poverty eradication, and stresses that the meeting and the preparatory activities should be carried out within the budget level proposed by the Secretary-General for the biennium 2012–2013 and should be organized in the most effective and efficient manner;

17. *Decides* to include in the provisional agenda of its sixty-fifth session the item entitled "Implementation of the Second United Nations Decade for the Eradication of Poverty (2008–2017)", and requests the Secretary-General to submit a report that details the current response of the United Nations system related to the theme of the Second Decade.

Rural development

United Nations Alliance

In response to Economic and Social Council resolution 2007/36 [YUN 2007, p. 849], the Secretary-General in May submitted a report [E/2009/72] on the United Nations Public-Private Alliance for Rural Development [YUN 2004, p. 841]. The report provided updated information on activities undertaken by Governments, UN bodies and civil society organizations in the first two pilot countries (Dominican Republic and Madagascar) and gave examples of similar initiatives in support of rural development in the two new pilot countries (Angola and Ethiopia). In addition to presenting UN Headquarters activities in support of the four pilot countries, the report also examined the impact of the financial and economic crisis on efforts to achieve rural development in those countries. The report recommended that in order to strengthen public-private partnerships in support of rural development in the four pilot countries, there had to be a major scaling up of engagement by UN system organizations with civil society and private sector partners, in close collaboration with the Governments of those countries. As the global crisis was threatening both recent gains made towards achieving the MDGs and the achievement of their targets by 2015, it was important for the international community to pro-

vide sufficient additional resources for rural and agricultural development programmes and to address the challenge of food insecurity. The integral role that rural women played should be highlighted during the consideration by the Commission on the Status of Women of the priority theme of its fifty-fourth (2010) session, review and appraisal of the implementation of the Beijing Platform for Action.

The Economic and Social Council took note of the Secretary-General's report on 31 July (**decision 2009/264**).

Legal empowerment of the poor and eradication of poverty

Pursuant to General Assembly resolution 63/142 [YUN 2008, p. 925], which took note of the final report of the Commission on Legal Empowerment of the Poor [ibid.], the Secretary-General in July submitted a report [A/64/133] on the legal empowerment of the poor and eradication of poverty. The report set forth the emerging approach to the matter in terms of the international human rights framework; its operational scope and focus, including access to justice as well as property, labour and entrepreneurship rights; national and regional experiences and the role of various UN system organizations in fostering legal empowerment of the poor; and relevant challenges and lessons learned in consideration of the matter as both a development strategy and a development objective.

GENERAL ASSEMBLY ACTION

On 21 December [meeting 66], the General Assembly, on the recommendation of the Second Committee [A/64/424], adopted **resolution 64/215** without vote [agenda item 57].

Legal empowerment of the poor and eradication of poverty

The General Assembly,

Recalling the 2005 World Summit Outcome,

Recalling also its resolution 63/142 of 11 December 2008,

Recalling further the United Nations Millennium Declaration, the Monterrey Consensus of the International Conference on Financing for Development, the Plan of Implementation of the World Summit on Sustainable Development ("Johannesburg Plan of Implementation"), the Doha Declaration on Financing for Development and the Outcome of the Conference on the World Financial and Economic Crisis and Its Impact on Development,

Reaffirming the importance of the timely and full realization of the development goals and objectives agreed upon at the major United Nations conferences and summits, including the Millennium Development Goals,

Reiterating that all human rights are universal, indivisible, interdependent and interrelated,

Remaining committed to the objective of making the right to development a reality for everyone, as set out in the Millennium Declaration,

Concerned by the global nature of poverty and inequality, reaffirming that eradicating poverty is one of the greatest global challenges facing the world today, particularly in Africa and in the least developed countries, and underlining the importance of accelerating sustainable broad-based and inclusive economic growth, including full, productive employment generation and decent work,

Stressing that poverty is a multifaceted problem that requires a multifaceted and integrated approach in addressing the economic, political, social, environmental and institutional dimensions at all levels,

Recognizing that empowerment of the poor is essential for the effective eradication of poverty and hunger,

Recognizing also, in this regard, that access to justice and the realization of rights related, inter alia, to property, labour and business are mutually reinforcing and essential determinants of the effective eradication of poverty,

Taking note of the report of the Commission on Legal Empowerment of the Poor, entitled "Making the Law Work for Everyone", as a useful reference in the area of poverty eradication,

Reaffirming that the rule of law at the national and international levels is essential for sustained economic growth, sustainable development and the eradication of poverty and hunger,

Stressing that gender equality and the empowerment of women are essential to achieving equitable and effective development and to fostering a vibrant economy, and reaffirming its commitment to eliminating gender-based discrimination in all its forms, including in the labour and financial markets, as well as, inter alia, in respect of the ownership of assets and property rights, to promoting women's rights, including their economic empowerment, and effectively mainstreaming gender in law reforms, business support services and economic programmes, and to giving women full and equal access to economic resources,

Reaffirming that each country must take primary responsibility for its own development and that the role of national policies and development strategies cannot be overemphasized in the achievement of sustainable development, and recognizing that national efforts should be complemented by supportive global programmes, measures and policies aimed at expanding the development opportunities of developing countries, while taking into account national conditions and ensuring respect for national ownership, strategies and sovereignty,

Deeply concerned by the significant challenges that the financial and economic crisis poses for the eradication of poverty, and in this regard reiterating that national efforts should be complemented by an enabling international environment, to ensure the achievement of a more inclusive, equitable, balanced, development-oriented and sustainable economic development that would help to overcome poverty and inequality,

1. *Takes note* of the report of the Secretary-General;

2. *Also takes note* of the broad diversity of national experiences in the area of legal empowerment of the poor, recognizes the initiatives undertaken and progress made by some countries in advancing legal empowerment of the poor as an integral part of their national strategies and objectives, and stresses the importance of promoting the sharing of national best practices;

3. *Welcomes*, in this regard, the ongoing work of the United Nations funds and programmes as well as of the specialized agencies;

4. *Emphasizes* the need to accord the highest priority to poverty eradication within the United Nations development agenda, while stressing the importance of addressing the causes and challenges of poverty through integrated, coordinated and coherent strategies at the national, inter-governmental and inter-agency levels;

5. *Also emphasizes* the importance of access to justice for all, and in this regard encourages the strengthening and improvement of the administration of justice and identity and birth registration systems, as well as awareness-raising concerning existing legal rights;

6. *Recognizes* that respect for the rule of law and property rights, and the pursuit of appropriate policy and regulatory frameworks, inter alia, encourage business formation, including entrepreneurship, and contribute to poverty eradication;

7. *Reiterates* the importance of pursuing appropriate policy and regulatory frameworks at national levels to promote employment and decent work for all and to protect labour rights, including through respect for the fundamental principles and rights at work proclaimed by the International Labour Organization;

8. *Recognizes* the importance of pursuing appropriate policy and regulatory frameworks at national levels to promote a dynamic, inclusive, well-functioning and socially responsible private sector as a valuable instrument for generating economic growth and reducing poverty, and encourages the promotion of an enabling environment that facilitates entrepreneurship and doing business by all, including women, the poor and the vulnerable;

9. *Encourages* countries to continue their efforts in the area of legal empowerment of the poor, including access to justice and the realization of rights related to property, labour and business, addressing both formal and informal settings by taking into account those dimensions in their national policies and strategies, while bearing in mind the importance of national circumstances, ownership and leadership;

10. *Emphasizes* that education and training are among the critical factors in empowering those living in poverty, and in this regard calls for action at all levels to give high priority to improving and expanding literacy, while recognizing the complexity of the challenge of poverty eradication;

11. *Calls upon* the international community to continue to give priority to the eradication of poverty, and calls upon countries in a position to do so to support the national efforts of developing countries in promoting legal empowerment of the poor through the provision of adequate, predictable financial resources or technical assistance;

12. *Requests* the Secretary-General to submit a report to the General Assembly at its sixty-sixth session on the implementation of the present resolution, under the item entitled "Follow-up to the outcome of the Millennium Summit" and to continue the consideration of legal empowerment of the poor, taking into account national experiences and the views of Member States.

Millennium Development Goals

The Millennium Development Goals Report 2009, published by DESA [Sales No. E.09.I.12] and based on data available as of June, summarized regional progress on official MDG indicators. Although data were not available to reveal the full impact of the recent economic downturn, they pointed to areas where progress was threatened or had been reversed by sluggish—or even negative—economic growth, diminished resources, fewer trade opportunities for developing countries, and possible reductions in aid flows from donor nations. Living in extreme poverty were an estimated 55 million to 90 million more people than anticipated before the crisis. The encouraging trend in the eradication of hunger since the early 1990s was reversed in 2008, largely due to higher food prices. The prevalence of hunger in the developing regions was on the rise, from 16 per cent in 2006 to 17 per cent in 2008.

The report portrayed advances that many countries and regions had made before the economic landscape changed in 2008, especially in advancing education and reducing child mortality. Those were most evident where targeted interventions had an immediate effect, and where increased funding translated into expanded delivery of services and tools directly to those in need, for example, in the fight against malaria, the dramatic reduction in measles deaths, and the coverage of antiretroviral treatment for HIV and AIDS. Progress had been more modest when it required structural changes and strong political commitment to guarantee sufficient and sustained funding. That was likely the reason behind the poor performance of most countries in reducing maternal mortality and increasing access of the rural poor to improved sanitation. Achieving the MDGs would require that the development agenda be fully integrated into efforts to jumpstart and rebuild the global economy.

2010 General Assembly
high-level plenary meeting on MDGs

In response to General Assembly **resolution 63/302** (see p. 1375), the Secretary-General in August submitted a report [A/64/263] to serve as a basis for further consultations on the scope, modalities, format and organization of the high-level plenary meeting of the sixty-fifth session of the Assembly with the participation of heads of State and Government.

By **resolution 64/184** of 21 December (see p. 1375), the General Assembly decided that the high-level plenary meeting, to be held from 20 to 22 September 2010, would focus on accelerating progress towards the achievement of all the MDGs by 2015, taking into account the progress made with regard to the internationally agreed development goals.

Science and technology for development

Commission on Science and Technology for Development

At its twelfth session (Geneva, 25–29 May) [E/2009/31], the Commission on Science and Technology for Development (CSTD) considered regional and international progress made in the implementation of and follow-up to the outcomes of the World Summit on the Information Society (WSIS) [YUN 2003, p. 857 & YUN 2005, p. 933] at the regional and international levels. It also addressed its priority themes "Development-oriented policies for a socio-economic inclusive information society, including access, infrastructure and an enabling environment" and "Science, technology and engineering for innovation and capacity-building in education and research". The Commission had before it respective reports of the Secretary-General on the priority themes [E/CN.16/2009/2 & E/CN.16/2009/3] and a summary report by the UNCTAD secretariat on the Commission's intersessional panel meeting (Santiago, Chile, 12–14 November 2008) [E/CN.16/2009/CRP.1]. It also had before it a report [E/CN.16/2009/CRP.2] on the Conference on Global Food Security: The Role of Science and Technology (Kota Kinabalu, Sabah, Malaysia, 17–18 February), attended by representatives of CSTD member States, government agencies, private companies, researchers and non-governmental organizations (NGOs), and centred on action plans to be implemented in the short to medium term; regional development; and the way forward in addressing the food crisis through science and technology.

The Secretary-General stated [E/CN.16/2009/2] that international organizations, corporations and public-private partnerships were critical players in the promotion of access to information and communication technologies (ICT) and improved facilities; and that indigenous science, technology and innovation capabilities were essential for the achievement of both short- and long-term development goals. He recommended that efforts be stepped up to share policy-related experiences through North-South and South-South cooperation, and through existing and new regional and international agreements [E/CN.16/2009/3].

The Commission recommended two draft resolutions and one draft decision for adoption by the Economic and Social Council.

On 24 July (**decision 2009/219**), the Economic and Social Council took note of the Commission's report on its twelfth session and approved the provisional agenda and documentation for its thirteenth (2010) session.

ECONOMIC AND SOCIAL COUNCIL ACTION

On 24 July [meeting 36], the Economic and Social Council, on the recommendation of the Commission on Science and Technology for Development [E/2009/31], adopted **resolution 2009/8** without vote [agenda item 13 *(b)*].

Science and technology for development

The Economic and Social Council,

Recalling its decision 2008/219 of 18 July 2008, in which it requested the Secretary-General to report to the Commission on Science and Technology for Development at its twelfth session on the science, technology and innovation priority themes addressed during the current biennium,

Recalling also the 2005 World Summit Outcome, which recognizes that science and technology, including information and communications technologies, are vital for the achievement of the internationally agreed development goals, and reaffirming the commitments contained therein, especially the commitment to support the efforts of developing countries, individually and collectively, to harness new agricultural technologies in order to increase agricultural productivity through environmentally sustainable means,

Recalling further that the United Nations Conference on Trade and Development is the secretariat of the Commission,

Welcoming the work of the Commission on its two priority themes, "Development-oriented policies for a socioeconomically inclusive information society, including access, infrastructure and an enabling environment" and "Science, technology and engineering for innovation and capacity-building in education and research",

Recognizing the critical role of innovation in maintaining national competitiveness in the global economy,

Noting the outcomes of the intersessional panel meeting of the Commission, held in Santiago from 12 to 14 November 2008, and the summary report prepared by the secretariat of the United Nations Conference on Trade and Development,

Taking note of the reports submitted by the Secretary-General to the Commission at its twelfth session,

Welcoming the revision of the terms of reference of the United Nations Group on the Information Society to expand its mandate to include science and technology pursuant to General Assembly resolution 62/208 of 19 December 2007 and the decision adopted by the High-level Committee on Programmes at its seventeenth session, held in Geneva on 26 and 27 February 2009,

Extending its appreciation to the Secretary-General for his role in helping to ensure that the aforementioned reports were completed in a timely manner,

Noting that, while there is broad consensus that technological innovation is a driver and critical source of sustainable economic growth in the new millennium, many developing countries have yet to benefit from the promises of science, technology and innovation,

Stressing the role of education for all as a precondition for the development of science, technology and innovation,

Reaffirming that the training and retention of scientific, technological and engineering talent, mechanisms for the funding of research, the commercialization of scientific knowledge, the building of strategic partnerships for the transfer of technology, innovative financing strategies and an innovation-friendly culture can all play critical roles in harnessing scientific and technological knowledge for development,

Recognizing the role that science, technology and engineering can play in developing solutions for the problems facing the world today, including climate change and the food and energy crises, and that most of the knowledge that countries need in order to address their most urgent social and economic problems already exists,

Extending its appreciation to the United Nations Conference on Trade and Development for the particular attention given to the needs of African countries in the areas of science and technology in order to stimulate economic growth and to reduce poverty, by undertaking science, technology and innovation policy reviews for Angola, Ghana, Lesotho and Mauritania and by organizing training sessions,

1. *Invites* the Secretary-General to initiate a process aimed at developing and making available a guide to help United Nations personnel to prepare United Nations Development Assistance Frameworks and common country assessments and to help relevant stakeholders to prepare poverty reduction strategy papers, identifying opportunities that science, technology and innovation can provide at the country level towards the eradication of poverty and the achievement of the Millennium Development Goals;

2. *Decides* to make the following recommendations for consideration by national Governments, the Commission on Science and Technology for Development and the United Nations Conference on Trade and Development:

(*a*) Governments are encouraged to take into account the findings of the Commission and to undertake the following actions:

   (i) Mainstream science and technology promotion and investment into their national development plans;

   (ii) Formulate and implement policies and programmes to:

     a. Strengthen science and mathematics education and mentorship for students in primary and secondary schools;

     b. Expand opportunities for science, technology and engineering education and research for their population, especially women and particularly in the emerging technologies such as biotechnology and nanotechnology, as appropriate;

     c. Provide, where possible, suitable working conditions for their scientific, technological and engineering talent, especially young graduates and women, in order to prevent brain drain;

     d. Develop mechanisms, including innovative solutions for expanding rural power supply and the provision of broadband access to poor communities in rural areas not covered by market-driven investment, to ensure access to science, technology and engineering for women, youth, the rural poor and other marginalized groups in all countries;

e.	Promote research and development in scientific, technological and engineering-related fields, to support, inter alia, grass-roots food production and entrepreneurial activities by the rural population;

f.	Strengthen, as appropriate, linkages between the private sector, academia and financial institutions and incentives for the commercialization of research and development, by promoting entrepreneurship, increased venture capital funding, the establishment of technology parks and incubators, and greater international collaboration;

g.	Increase the number of full-time researchers in science, technology and engineering;

(iii)	Create innovative funding strategies and compensation and reward structures in academic and research institutions to provide incentives for scientific and technological talent to remain within their countries and promote research directed at addressing national and regional development challenges;

(iv)	Establish international needs-based partnerships, where countries and their private sectors can collaborate on research and development, including the commercialization of research results, to address similar development challenges, especially those related to health, agriculture, conservation, sustainable use of natural resources and environmental management, energy, forestry and the impact of climate change;

(v)	Develop a culture of innovation and entrepreneurship, support the development of technological capabilities in small and medium-sized enterprises and promote incubators for promising technologies;

(vi)	Launch campaigns to raise awareness of the importance of innovation for wealth creation and national welfare through the mass media and high-profile awards;

(vii)	Reaffirm the essential role that official development assistance plays as a complement to other sources of financing for development and fulfil the internationally agreed commitments regarding official development assistance in order to contribute to the efforts of developing countries in building their indigenous capabilities in science and technology;

(viii)	Make considered decisions to balance short- and long-term science, technology and innovation goals and policies, evaluating the advantages and disadvantages of procuring or licensing technologies, as compared with producing them indigenously;

(ix)	Focus national efforts, when facing a generally low level of science, technology and innovation capacity, on building and strengthening indigenous scientific, technical, vocational and engineering capacities to select and use existing knowledge resources, in order to create jobs, to generate wealth and to achieve the Millennium Development Goals;

(b)	The Commission on Science and Technology for Development is encouraged to:

(i)	Play the role of torch-bearer for innovation and innovation-oriented planning and support efforts by national Governments to integrate science, technology and innovation into national development strategies by providing a forum for developing countries, the international community, the science, technology and innovation policy research community and other interested parties to:

a.	Share and analyse available empirical evidence on technological earning and science, technology and innovation policy impacts;

b.	Identify critical gaps in "innovation system" understanding that the policy research community might usefully address;

c.	Share best practices and information on new technologies, financing mechanisms and regulatory measures related to the provision of broadband connectivity in their respective communities, as well as on a range of access strategies and technologies aimed at supplementing broadband Internet access and supporting all levels of socio-economic activity in a country, with a focus on reaching women and the population in rural areas;

(ii)	Explore the possibility of organizing an Internet-based science, technology and innovation collaborative network, in conjunction with the United Nations Conference on Trade and Development, the regional commissions and other appropriate stakeholders, which could promote regional and global cooperation by collecting information related to science, technology and engineering capacity-building in education, research and innovation, technology development and transfer, prospects for commercialization of knowledge-based products, opportunities for collaboration and joint ventures and related issues and which could also serve as a repository of regional and subregional initiatives that could encourage further use of the Internet by all interested stakeholders;

(c)	The United Nations Conference on Trade and Development is encouraged to:

(i)	Reaffirm its mandate in respect of science and technology for development and place greater emphasis on the role of innovation within its mandate;

(ii)	Improve the collaboration on science and technology for development existing within the United Nations system, particularly with the United Nations Educational, Scientific and Cultural Organization, the Commission on Science and Technology for Development and the regional commissions and with other appropriate stakeholders, including the World Bank;

(iii)	Continue providing its expertise and analytical skills for science, technology and innovation policy reviews and organizing training sessions, particularly for African countries, aimed at providing information-based policy recommendations and proposed action plans to assist developing countries with their specific needs and circumstances;

(iv) Develop a clearing house for common development challenges that can be addressed through scientific, technological and innovation-related issues, including financing and regulation, and convene meetings of representatives of developing countries with similar concerns to explore concrete ways of engaging and partnering in solutions;

(v) Collaborate with less developed countries to create conditions that make them attractive to foreign direct investment in science and technology, including information and communications technologies;

(vi) Develop a training programme for sharing best practices on science, technology and innovation capacity-building in developing countries, using extrabudgetary resources;

(vii) Continue to assist African countries in their efforts to build science, technology and innovation capacities through training and workshops, particularly in the areas of biotechnology and cyber-security, and invite donors to support the network of centres of excellence, currently sponsored by the Government of Italy, and to expand it to include other regions.

Report of Secretary-General. In response to General Assembly resolution 62/201 [YUN 2007, p. 851], the Secretary-General in July submitted a report [A/64/168] on science and technology for development, in particular on the work carried out by CSTD in agriculture, rural development, ICT and environmental management. It also provided information on activities carried out by UNCTAD and other organizations to assist developing countries in their efforts to integrate science, technology and innovation policies in their national development plans and strategies.

In November 2008, the Government of Tunisia, in collaboration with UNCTAD and the International Telecommunication Union, and in partnership with the Global Alliance for Information and Communications Technologies and Development and the African Development Bank, organized the third Information and Communications Technology for All Forum, "Tunis+3: broadband, industry of content for development" (Hammamet, Tunisia, 27–28 November). The Forum addressed strategies and options to expand access among low-income countries to low-cost fixed or wireless broadband technology. CSTD continued to collaborate with UNCTAD on the Network of Centres of Excellence project, which organized training courses and workshops for scientists and engineers from developing countries at scientific and technological institutions in developing countries selected for their competence and state-of-the-art facilities. The Network organized three training sessions in 2008, one in

Tunisia and two in Egypt, with the first francophone session of the Network having been held in Tunisia, in collaboration with the National Agency for Computer Security. UNCTAD science, technology and innovation policy reviews were completed for 5 countries.

In 2009, the first session of the UNCTAD multi-year expert meeting on enterprise development policies and capacity-building in science, technology and innovation (Geneva, 20–22 January) discussed how innovation and entrepreneurship could help developing countries overcome global challenges, such as climate change, energy and food security. Experts shared ideas on how to fight poverty through improving productivity and competitiveness of enterprises in developing countries. UNCTAD and the Malaysian Ministry of Science, Technology and Innovation organized a conference on the theme "Global food security: the role of science and technology" (Kota Kinabalu, Malaysia, 17–18 February) that examined whether the food crisis could be resolved by way of science and technology policies, and called for continued investment and research efforts in developing and sharing new technologies and technological solutions in the agriculture sector.

Intersessional panel meeting. The CSTD intersessional panel meeting (Geneva, 9–11 November) [E/CN.16/2010/CRP.1] addressed improvements and innovations in financial mechanisms for ICT; new and emerging technologies; and the follow-up to the World Summit on the Information Society.

GENERAL ASSEMBLY ACTION

On 21 December [meeting 66], the General Assembly, on the recommendation of the Second Committee [A/64/422/Add.3], adopted **resolution 64/212** without vote [agenda item 55 *(c)*].

Science and technology for development

The General Assembly,

Recalling its resolutions 58/200 of 23 December 2003, 59/220 of 22 December 2004, 60/205 of 22 December 2005 and 62/201 of 19 December 2007,

Recalling also its resolution 61/207 of 20 December 2006 and its reference to science and technology,

Taking note of Economic and Social Council resolutions 2006/46 of 28 July 2006 and 2009/8 of 24 July 2009,

Recognizing the vital role that science and technology, including environmentally sound technologies, can play in development and in facilitating efforts to eradicate poverty, achieve food security, fight diseases, improve education, protect the environment, accelerate the pace of economic diversification and transformation and improve productivity and competitiveness,

Recalling the 2005 World Summit Outcome,

Recalling also the outcomes of the World Summit on the Information Society,

Recognizing that international support can help developing countries to benefit from technological advances and can enhance their productive capacity,

Underscoring the role that traditional knowledge can play in technological development, and in the sustainable management and use of natural resources,

Acknowledging the urgent need to bridge the digital divide and to assist developing countries in accessing the potential benefits of information and communications technologies,

Encouraging continued efforts towards the implementation of the Bali Strategic Plan for Technology Support and Capacity-building of the United Nations Environment Programme,

Reaffirming the need to enhance the science and technology programmes of the relevant entities of the United Nations system,

Noting with appreciation the collaboration between the Commission on Science and Technology for Development and the United Nations Conference on Trade and Development in establishing a network of centres of excellence in science and technology for developing countries and in designing and carrying out science, technology and innovation policy reviews,

Taking note with interest of the establishment of the inter-agency cooperation network on biotechnology, UN-Biotech, as described in the report of the Secretary-General,

Taking note of the report of the Secretary-General,

Encouraging the development of initiatives to promote private sector engagement in technology transfer and technological and scientific cooperation,

1. *Reaffirms its commitment*:

(a) To strengthen and enhance existing mechanisms and to support initiatives for research and development, including through voluntary partnerships between the public and private sectors, to address the special needs of developing countries in the areas of health, agriculture, conservation, sustainable use of natural resources and environmental management, energy, forestry and the impact of climate change;

(b) To promote and facilitate, as appropriate, access to, and development, transfer and diffusion of, technologies, including environmentally sound technologies and the corresponding know-how, to developing countries;

(c) To assist developing countries in their efforts to promote and develop national strategies for human resources and science and technology, which are primary drivers of national capacity-building for development;

(d) To promote and support greater efforts to develop renewable sources of energy, including appropriate technology;

(e) To implement policies at the national and international levels to attract both public and private investment, domestic and foreign, that enhances knowledge, transfers technology on mutually agreed terms and raises productivity;

(f) To support the efforts of developing countries, individually and collectively, to harness new agricultural technologies in order to increase agricultural productivity through environmentally sustainable means;

2. *Recognizes* that science and technology, including information and communications technologies, are vital for the achievement of the internationally agreed development goals, including the Millennium Development Goals, and for the full participation of developing countries in the global economy;

3. *Requests* the Commission on Science and Technology for Development to provide a forum within which to continue to assist the Economic and Social Council as the focal point in the system-wide follow-up to the outcomes of the World Summit on the Information Society and to address within its mandate, in accordance with Council resolution 2006/46, the special needs of developing countries in areas such as agriculture, rural development, information and communications technologies and environmental management;

4. *Encourages* the United Nations Conference on Trade and Development, in collaboration with relevant partners, to continue to undertake science, technology and innovation policy reviews, with a view to assisting developing countries and countries with economies in transition in identifying the measures that are needed to integrate science, technology and innovation policies into their national development strategies;

5. *Encourages* the United Nations Conference on Trade and Development and other relevant organizations to assist developing countries in their efforts to integrate science, technology and innovation policies into national development strategies;

6. *Encourages* Governments to strengthen and foster investment in research and development for environmentally sound technologies and to promote the involvement of the business and financial sectors in the development of those technologies, and invites the international community to support those efforts;

7. *Encourages* existing arrangements and the further promotion of regional, subregional and interregional joint research and development projects, where feasible, by mobilizing existing scientific and research and development resources and by networking sophisticated scientific facilities and research equipment;

8. *Encourages* the international community to continue to facilitate, in view of the difference in level of development between countries, an adequate diffusion of scientific and technical knowledge and transfer of, access to and acquisition of technology for developing countries, under fair, transparent and mutually agreed terms, in a manner conducive to social and economic welfare for the benefit of society;

9. *Calls for* continued collaboration between United Nations entities and other international organizations, civil society and the private sector in implementing the outcomes of the World Summit on the Information Society, with a view to putting the potential of information and communications technologies at the service of development through policy research on the digital divide and on new challenges of the information society, as well as technical assistance activities, involving multi-stakeholder partnerships;

10. *Requests* the Secretary-General to submit to the General Assembly at its sixty-sixth session a report on the implementation of the present resolution and recommendations for future follow-up, including lessons learned in integrating science, technology and innovation policies into national development strategies.

Information and communication technologies

During 2009, the United Nations continued to consider how the benefits of new technologies, especially ICT, could be made available to all, in keeping with recommendations contained in the ministerial declaration adopted by the Economic and Social Council at its 2000 high-level segment [YUN 2000, p. 799], the Millennium Declaration [ibid., p. 49] and the Geneva Declaration of Principles and Plan of Action [YUN 2003, p. 857] adopted at the first phase of WSIS [ibid.], and the Tunis Commitment and the Tunis Agenda adopted at its second phase [YUN 2005, p. 933].

GENERAL ASSEMBLY ACTION

On 21 December [meeting 66], the General Assembly, on the recommendation of the Second Committee [A/64/417], adopted **resolution 64/186** without vote [agenda item 50].

Building connectivity through the Trans-Eurasian Information Super Highway

The General Assembly,

Recalling the Declaration of Principles and the Plan of Action adopted by the World Summit on the Information Society at its first phase, held in Geneva from 10 to 12 December 2003, and endorsed by the General Assembly, and the Tunis Commitment and the Tunis Agenda for the Information Society adopted by the Summit at its second phase, held in Tunis from 16 to 18 November 2005, and endorsed by the General Assembly,

Recalling also the 2005 World Summit Outcome,

Stressing the need to reduce the digital divide and to ensure that the benefits of new technologies, especially information and communication technologies, are available to all,

Noting that Governments, as well as the private sector, civil society and the United Nations, and other international organizations, have an important role in bridging the digital divide for the benefit of all and in building an inclusive and people-centred information society,

Recognizing that well-developed information and communication network infrastructures, such as information superhighways, act as one of the main technological enablers of the digital opportunities, and noting, in this regard, the Regional Ministerial Meeting on the Trans-Eurasian Information Super Highway convened by the Government of Azerbaijan in cooperation with the Department of Economic and Social Affairs of the Secretariat, held in Baku on 11 November 2008,

1. *Recognizes* that information and communication technologies have the potential to provide new solutions to development challenges, particularly in the context of globalization, and can foster economic growth, competitiveness, access to information and knowledge, poverty eradication and social inclusion that will help to expedite the integration of all countries, particularly developing countries, into the global economy;

2. *Also recognizes* the immense potential that building connectivity can have in contributing to social progress, including in advancing the status of women and promoting social integration and tolerance;

3. *Stresses* the importance of strengthened and continued cooperation among all stakeholders to build and run information infrastructures to bridge the digital divide in the region, and encourages interested Member States to participate in the development of regional connectivity solutions;

4. *Recognizes* the need to build connectivity in the region to help to bridge the digital divide, and in this regard welcomes the Trans-Eurasian Information Super Highway initiative and the readiness of the Republic of Azerbaijan to coordinate regional efforts aimed at realizing this initiative.

Also on 21 December [meeting 66], the General Assembly, on the recommendation of the Second Committee [A/64/417], adopted **resolution 64/187** without vote [agenda item 50].

Information and communication technologies for development

The General Assembly,

Recalling its resolutions 56/183 of 21 December 2001, 57/238 of 20 December 2002, 57/270 B of 23 June 2003, 59/220 of 22 December 2004, 60/252 of 27 March 2006 and 62/182 of 19 December 2007, Economic and Social Council resolution 2008/3 of 18 July 2008, its resolution 63/202 of 19 December 2008 and other relevant resolutions,

Noting that cultural diversity is the common heritage of humankind and that the information society should be founded on and stimulate respect for cultural identity, cultural and linguistic diversity, traditions and religions, and foster dialogue among cultures and civilizations, and noting also that the promotion, affirmation and preservation of diverse cultural identities and languages as reflected in relevant agreed United Nations documents, including the Universal Declaration on Cultural Diversity of the United Nations Educational, Scientific and Cultural Organization, will further enrich the information society,

Recalling the Declaration of Principles and the Plan of Action adopted by the World Summit on the Information Society at its first phase, held in Geneva from 10 to 12 December 2003, as endorsed by the General Assembly, and the Tunis Commitment and the Tunis Agenda for the Information Society adopted by the Summit at its second phase, held in Tunis from 16 to 18 November 2005, and endorsed by the General Assembly,

Recalling also the 2005 World Summit Outcome,

Taking note of the report of the Secretary-General on progress made in the implementation of and follow-up to the World Summit on the Information Society outcomes at the regional and international levels,

Stressing the need to reduce the digital divide and to ensure that the benefits of new technologies, especially information and communication technologies, are available to all,

Recognizing the importance of the mandate of the Internet Governance Forum, as a multi-stakeholder dialogue to discuss various matters, including public policy issues related to key elements of Internet governance, in order to foster the sustainability, robustness, security, stability and development of the Internet, and reiterating that all Governments, on an equal footing, should carry out their roles and responsibilities for international Internet governance and for ensuring the stability, security and continuity of the Internet, but not with regard to the day-to-day technical and operational matters that do not impact on international public policy issues,

Taking note of the discussions at the fourth meeting of the Internet Governance Forum, held in Sharm el-Sheikh, Egypt, from 15 to 18 November 2009, on the future of the Forum, which generally welcomed the renewal of its mandate and recognized the need for further discussion on the improvement of its working methods,

Recalling the first, second, third and fourth meetings of the Internet Governance Forum, held in Athens from 30 October to 2 November 2006, in Rio de Janeiro, Brazil, from 12 to 15 November 2007, in Hyderabad, India, from 3 to 6 December 2008, and in Sharm el-Sheikh, Egypt, from 15 to 18 November 2009, respectively, and welcoming the convening of the fifth meeting of the Forum, to be held in Vilnius from 14 to 17 September 2010,

Welcoming, in view of the existing gaps in information and communication technologies infrastructure, the Connect Africa summits held in Kigali on 29 and 30 October 2007 and in Cairo from 12 to 15 May 2008 and the Connect the Commonwealth of Independent States summit held in Minsk on 26 and 27 November 2009, which are regional initiatives aimed at mobilizing human, financial and technical resources to accelerate the implementation of the connectivity goals of the World Summit on the Information Society,

Recognizing the role of the Commission on Science and Technology for Development in assisting the Economic and Social Council as the focal point in the system-wide follow-up, in particular the review and assessment, of the progress made in implementing the outcomes of the World Summit on the Information Society, while at the same time maintaining its original mandate on science and technology for development,

Noting the contribution of the Global Alliance for Information and Communication Technologies and Development to the Commission on Science and Technology for Development,

Noting also the twelfth session of the Commission, held in Geneva from 25 to 29 May 2009, and the intersessional meeting of the Commission held in Geneva from 9 to 11 November 2009,

Taking note of Economic and Social Council resolution 2009/7 of 24 July 2009, on the assessment of the progress made in the implementation of and follow-up to the outcomes of the World Summit on the Information Society,

Stressing that, for the majority of the poor, the developmental promise of science and technology, including information and communication technologies, remains unfulfilled, and emphasizing the need to effectively harness technology, including information and communication technologies, to bridge the digital divide,

Recognizing the pivotal role of the United Nations system in promoting development, including with respect to enhancing access to information and communication technologies, inter alia, through partnerships with all relevant stakeholders,

1. *Recognizes* that information and communication technologies have the potential to provide new solutions to development challenges, particularly in the context of globalization, and can foster economic growth, competitiveness, access to information and knowledge, poverty eradication and social inclusion that will help to expedite the integration of all countries, particularly developing countries, into the global economy;

2. *Stresses* the important role of Governments in the design of public policies and in the provision of public services responsive to national needs and priorities through, inter alia, the effective use of information and communication technologies, on the basis of a multi-stakeholder approach, to support national development efforts;

3. *Recognizes* that, in addition to financing by the public sector, financing of information and communication technologies infrastructure by the private sector has come to play an important role in many countries and that domestic financing is being augmented by North-South flows and South-South cooperation;

4. *Also recognizes* that information and communication technologies present new opportunities and challenges, and that there is a pressing need to address the major impediments that developing countries face in accessing the new technologies, such as insufficient resources, infrastructure, education, capacity, investment and connectivity and issues related to technology ownership, standards and flows, and in this regard calls upon all stakeholders to provide adequate resources, enhanced capacity-building and technology transfer, on mutually agreed terms, to developing countries, particularly the least developed countries;

5. *Further recognizes* the immense potential that information and communication technologies have in promoting the transfer of technologies in a wide spectrum of socio-economic activity;

6. *Acknowledges* that a gender divide exists as part of the digital divide, and encourages all stakeholders to ensure the full participation of women in the information society and women's access to the new technologies, especially information and communication technologies for development;

7. *Recalls* the improvements and innovations in financing mechanisms, including the creation of a voluntary Digital Solidarity Fund, as mentioned in the Geneva Declaration of Principles, and in this regard invites voluntary contributions to its financing;

8. *Recognizes* that South-South cooperation, particularly through triangular cooperation, can be a useful tool to promote the development of information and communication technologies;

9. *Encourages* strengthened and continuing cooperation between and among stakeholders to ensure effective implementation of the outcomes of the Geneva and Tunis phases of the World Summit on the Information Society, through, inter alia, the promotion of national, regional and international multi-stakeholder partnerships, including public-private partnerships, and the promotion of national and regional multi-stakeholder thematic platforms, in a joint effort and dialogue with developing and least

developed countries, development partners and actors in the information and communication technologies sector;

10. *Welcomes* the efforts undertaken by Tunisia, host of the second phase of the World Summit on the Information Society in collaboration with the United Nations Conference on Trade and Development, the International Telecommunication Union and other relevant international and regional organizations, for organizing annually the ICT 4 All Forum and technological exhibition as a platform within the framework of the follow-up to the Summit to promote a dynamic business environment for the information and communication technologies sector worldwide;

11. *Encourages* the United Nations funds and programmes and the specialized agencies, within their respective mandates, to contribute to the implementation of the outcomes of the World Summit on the Information Society, and emphasizes the need for resources in this regard;

12. *Notes* the organization of the World Summit on the Information Society Forum 2009 by the International Telecommunication Union, the United Nations Conference on Trade and Development, the United Nations Development Programme and the United Nations Educational, Scientific and Cultural Organization to facilitate interaction among actors implementing the Summit's action lines, and invites the organizers to fully engage Governments, international organizations, civil society and the private sector in the preparations for the World Summit on the Information Society Forum 2010, to be held from 10 to 14 May 2010 in Geneva;

13. *Recognizes* the urgent need to harness the potential of knowledge and technology, and in that regard encourages the United Nations development system to continue its effort to promote the use of information and communication technologies as a critical enabler of development and a catalyst for the achievement of the internationally agreed development goals, including the Millennium Development Goals;

14. *Also recognizes* the role of the United Nations Group on the Information Society as an inter-agency mechanism of the United Nations System Chief Executives Board for Coordination designed to coordinate United Nations implementation of the World Summit on the Information Society outcomes;

15. *Invites* the Economic and Social Council to consider the report of the Secretary-General on enhanced cooperation on public policy issues pertaining to the Internet;

16. *Invites* Member States to support the meaningful participation of stakeholders from developing countries in the preparatory meetings of the Internet Governance Forum and in the Forum itself in 2010;

17. *Encourages* Member States, the private sector and all other relevant stakeholders to consider strengthening the secretariat of the Internet Governance Forum in order to support its activities and operations, in accordance with its mandate, including by providing additional funds, where possible, to the Trust Fund in support of the secretariat;

18. *Requests* the Commission on Science and Technology for Development, during its thirteenth session, which will be held at the halfway point to the 2015 overall review, to organize a substantive discussion on the progress made over five years in the implementation of the Summit outcomes, including consideration of the modalities of im-

plementation and follow-up to the Summit, and invites all facilitators and stakeholders to take this into account with regard to their contribution to that session;

19. *Requests* the Secretary-General to submit to the General Assembly at its sixty-fifth session, through the Economic and Social Council, a report on the status of the implementation of and follow-up to the present resolution.

Inter-Agency Round Table on Communication for Development

The Secretary-General transmitted the report [A/65/276] of the Director-General of the United Nations Educational, Scientific and Cultural Organization on the implementation of General Assembly resolution 50/130 [YUN 1995, p. 1438], including the recommendations of the eleventh United Nations Inter-Agency Round Table on Communication for Development (Washington, D.C., 11–13 March 2009).

The Round Table reviewed communication for development coordination arrangements around the theme "Moving communication for development up the international development agenda: demonstrating impact and positioning institutionally". Participants included 14 UN agencies, funds and programmes, along with representatives of the UN Secretariat, the Organization for Economic Cooperation and Development/Development Assistance Committee, academia, civil society and donors.

Participants agreed to articulate and promote communication for development at country and regional levels and to coordinate more closely with other agency mechanisms, including the United Nations Development Group. It was considered necessary to plan advocacy measures that would promote communication for development in policy guidelines within UN agencies; and important to produce practical tools that could demonstrate how communication for development contributed to programme priorities, and to strengthen UN capacity through learning frameworks. Participants decided to develop communication for development indicators and compile tools and resource material available with different agencies, and to pursue the institutionalization of communication for development, including integration in the United Nations Development Assistance Framework "90" rollout. Participating UN system organizations agreed to design and implement advocacy actions to integrate communication for development practice in national development plans; develop communication monitoring and evaluation indicators that were valid for the UN system and its Member States; introduce learning and capacity enhancement measures; and consolidate case studies demonstrating the diverse approaches of communication for development practice in the UN system.

Cooperation on public policy issues pertaining to the Internet

In a June report [E/2009/92], submitted in response to General Assembly resolution 63/202 [YUN 2008, p. 928], the Secretary-General reviewed steps taken to enhance cooperation on public policy issues pertaining to the Internet, and summarized recommendations proposed by relevant organizations on the way forward. All organizations reported that they had made efforts to reach out to other stakeholders; almost all had participated in the Internet Governance Forum (see below), and most were represented in the Multi-stakeholder Advisory Group of the Forum. While most organizations interpreted enhanced cooperation as a process to facilitate and contribute to multi-stakeholder dialogue through formal or informal cooperative arrangements, one challenge to the effective monitoring of progress towards implementation of the Tunis Agenda was the absence of practical guidance on what constituted an enhanced level of cooperation. The report summarized recommendations made by the Internet Corporation for Assigned Names and Numbers (icann), the International Telecommunication Union, the World Wide Web Consortium, the Council of Europe, the Internet Society and the Organization for Economic Cooperation and Development.

The Economic and Social Council on 24 July deferred consideration of the Secretary-General's report until its substantive 2010 session (**decision 2009/220**).

Global Alliance for ICT and Development. The Global Alliance for Information and Communications Technologies and Development, established in 2006 [YUN 2006, p. 1004], continued to focus its attention on helping to mainstream ICT into the UN development agenda and on helping developing countries to integrate ICT into their national development strategies and programmes. The annual meeting of the Global Alliance and its forum (Monterrey, Mexico, 31 August–4 September) discussed how best to use ICT to strengthen education.

Internet Governance Forum. Established in 2006 [YUN 2006, p. 1001] to support the Secretary-General in carrying out the wsis mandate to convene a multi-stakeholder policy dialogue on Internet governance issues, the Internet Governance Forum held its fourth meeting (Sharm el-Sheikh, Egypt, 15–18 November) on the theme "Internet Governance–Creating Opportunities for All". Its sessions addressed managing critical Internet resources; security, openness and privacy; diversity; access; Internet governance in the light of wsis principles; and the impact of social networks. More than 1,800 participants from 112 countries attended the event.

Follow-up to World Summit on the Information Society

In response to Economic and Social Council resolutions 2006/46 [YUN 2006, p. 1001] and 2007/8 [YUN 2007, p. 853], the Secretary-General in March reported [A/64/64-E/2009/10] on progress made in the implementation of and follow-up to the wsis outcomes at the regional and international levels. The report incorporated analyses of responses provided by 20 international and regional organizations on trends, achievements and obstacles to wsis implementation. It also highlighted major initiatives undertaken since February 2008, as reported by the relevant organizations.

At the regional level, the UN regional commissions continued to support wsis implementation through their respective action plans. Activities reported included the facilitation of the sharing of best-practice experiences at the regional level, support for national Governments in policy development, e-services deployment and capacity-building efforts.

At the international level, the United Nations Group on the Information Society (ungis) [YUN 2006, p. 1000] held its third meeting on 18 September 2008, attended by representatives from 12 UN bodies. Among other issues, the Group discussed the relationship between ungis and the United Nations Development Group and how to achieve a better integration of strategies and actions harnessing ict for development into the United Nations Development Assistance Frameworks and the Common Country Assessments. UN system entities working closely with Governments, regional commissions and other stakeholders, including ngos and the private sector, reported on programme activities in wsis implementation.

The Secretary-General concluded that there was a need for greater coordination among the leading facilitator agencies and the Commission on Science and Technology for Development secretariat, with a view to streamlining and clustering wsis-related events into a one-week event, to take place back-to-back with the Commission's annual regular session. There was also a need to benchmark progress towards the attainment of the targets and goals set out in the Geneva Plan of Action and the Tunis Agenda for the Information Society. The Secretary-General also recommended that the Commission focus not only on the positive sides of the emerging information society, but also on the various risks, including cybercrime. Empowerment and the strengthening of democratic processes and ict in education should be priority themes for the Commission. Greater attention should also be given by all stakeholders to the potential contributions of ict towards the mdgs and the reduction of poverty.

The Economic and Social Council took note of the Secretary-General's report on 31 July (**decision 2009/257**).

ECONOMIC AND SOCIAL COUNCIL ACTION

On 24 July [meeting 36], the Economic and Social Council, on the recommendation of the Commission on Science and Technology for Development [E/2009/31], adopted **resolution 2009/7** without vote [agenda item 13 *(b)*].

Assessment of the progress made in the implementation of and follow-up to the outcomes of the World Summit on the Information Society

The Economic and Social Council,

Recalling the outcomes of the World Summit on the Information Society,

Recognizing the efforts by all stakeholders to implement the outcomes of the two phases of the World Summit, while recognizing also the efforts of United Nations entities and other intergovernmental organizations in facilitating activities among different stakeholders,

Recalling the agreements by which the United Nations recognized various organizations as specialized agencies within the United Nations system,

Recalling also the relevant resolutions founding the United Nations programmes,

Recalling further its resolution 2006/46 of 28 July 2006 entitled "Follow-up to the World Summit on the Information Society and review of the Commission on Science and Technology for Development" and the mandate that it gave to the Commission,

Recalling General Assembly resolution 61/16 of 20 November 2006 on the strengthening of the Economic and Social Council,

Recalling also its resolutions 2007/8 of 25 July 2007 on the flow of information for the follow-up to the World Summit and 2008/3 of 18 July 2008 on the assessment of the progress made in the implementation of and follow-up to the outcomes of the World Summit,

Recalling further General Assembly resolution 63/202 of 19 December 2008 on information and communication technologies for development,

Noting the outcomes of the intersessional panel meeting of the Commission on Science and Technology for Development, held in Santiago from 12 to 14 November 2008, and the summary report prepared by the secretariat of the United Nations Conference on Trade and Development,

Taking note with satisfaction of the report of the Secretary-General on the progress made in the implementation of and follow-up to the outcomes of the World Summit at the regional and international levels,

Taking note of the respective reports of the Council of Europe, the Department of Economic and Social Affairs of the Secretariat, the Economic Commission for Africa, the Economic Commission for Europe, the Economic Commission for Latin America and the Caribbean, the Economic and Social Commission for Asia and the Pacific, the Economic and Social Commission for Western Asia, the Food and Agriculture Organization of the United Nations, the Global Alliance for Information and Communication Technologies and Development, the Internet Governance Forum, the International Trade Centre UNCTAD/WTO, the International Telecommunication Union, the United Nations Educational, Scientific and Cultural Organization, the United Nations Industrial Development Organization, the Universal Postal Union, the World Health Organization, the World Intellectual Property Organization and the World Meteorological Organization, all of which were used as inputs to the report of the Secretary-General,

Taking stock: reviewing the implementation of the outcomes of the World Summit on the Information Society

1. *Reaffirms* that information and communications technologies have the potential to provide new solutions to development challenges;

2. *Recognizes* that the economic downturn has led to a slowdown in investment, but at the same time notes the resilience of the information and communications technology sectors and their potential contribution to speeding up global economic recovery;

3. *Notes* that, while the digital divide may be shrinking in some areas, many challenges remain, with large disparities still existing in terms of access to information and communications technologies and knowledge, penetration and affordability, both between developed and developing countries and within countries and regions, and, moreover, new forms of digital divide emerging with regard to broadband access and local digital content;

4. *Stresses* the need to bridge the digital divide and to ensure that the benefits of new technologies, especially information and communications technologies, are available to all, a need that poses a challenge for many countries, which are forced to choose between many competing objectives in their development planning and in demands for development funds, while having limited resources;

5. *Notes with dissatisfaction* that, for the majority of the poor, the developmental promise of science and technology, including information and communications technologies, remains unfulfilled, and emphasizes the need to effectively harness technology, including information and communications technologies, to bridge the digital divide;

6. *Recognizes* that information and communications technologies present new opportunities and challenges and that there is a pressing need to address the major impediments that developing countries face in accessing new technologies, such as insufficient resources, infrastructure, education, capacity, investment and connectivity and issues related to technology ownership, standards and flows, and in this regard calls upon all stakeholders to provide adequate resources, enhanced capacity-building and transfer of technology to developing countries, particularly the least developed countries;

7. *Notes* that considerable efforts were undertaken and progress was made in 2008 towards the implementation of the outcomes of the World Summit on the Information Society and that numerous activities have been reported by the different entities of the United Nations system, although various relevant activities by non-governmental actors were not reflected by the reporting mechanism in place;

8. *Takes note* of the respective reports of many United Nations entities, with their own executive summaries, submitted as inputs for the preparation of the annual report of the Secretary-General to the Commission on Science and Technology for Development and published on the website of the Commission, as mandated by the Economic and Social Council in its resolution 2007/8;

9. *Notes* the holding of the cluster of events related to the World Summit in an improved format, renamed the World Summit on the Information Society Forum 2009, organized by the International Telecommunication Union, the United Nations Educational, Scientific and Cultural Organization, the United Nations Conference on Trade and Development and the United Nations Development Programme to facilitate the implementation of the World Summit action lines, and notes that the inclusiveness, interactivity and depth of the discussions of the Forum on the implementation of those action lines in a multi-stakeholder framework can be further enhanced;

10. *Recalls* the importance of close coordination among the leading action line facilitators and with the secretariat of the Commission;

11. *Notes* the results of the fourth meeting of the United Nations Group on the Information Society, held in Geneva on 22 May 2009, which included an agreement to organize open consultations on financial mechanisms, as requested by the Economic and Social Council in its resolution 2008/3, and highlights the role of the Group in facilitating the implementation of the outcomes of the World Summit under the United Nations System Chief Executives Board for Coordination, pursuant to paragraph 103 of the Tunis Agenda for the Information Society;

12. *Calls upon* international and regional organizations to assess and report on a regular basis on the universal accessibility of nations to information and communications technologies, with the aim of creating equitable opportunities for the growth of the information and communications technology sectors of developing countries;

13. *Notes with regret* that, more than three years after the second phase of the World Summit, held in Tunis from 16 to 18 November 2005, the updated guidelines for United Nations country teams on preparing common country assessments and United Nations Development Assistance Frameworks still do not reflect the recommendations contained in the outcomes of the World Summit and do not contain a component on information and communications technology for development, and urges that the coordinated action necessary for the implementation of the recommendations contained in paragraph 100 of the Tunis Agenda be taken;

14. *Reaffirms* the principles enunciated in the first phase of the World Summit, held in Geneva from 10 to 12 December 2003, that the Internet has evolved into a global facility available to the public, that its governance should constitute a core issue of the information society agenda and that the international management of the Internet should be multilateral, transparent and democratic, with the full involvement of Governments, the private sector, civil society and international organizations, and should ensure an equitable distribution of resources, facilitate access for all and ensure a stable and secure functioning of the Internet, taking into account multilingualism;

15. *Notes* the discussions in the Internet Governance Forum, in its capacity as a multi-stakeholder platform for discussing public policy issues related to Internet governance, which were reflected by the Secretary-General in his report, expresses appreciation for the work done by the Chair, the secretariat and the host Governments of the Forum, and looks forward to the convening of the fourth meeting of the Forum, to be held in Sharm el-Sheikh, Egypt, from 15 to 18 November 2009;

16. *Encourages* all stakeholders to contribute to the online consultations regarding the "desirability of the continuation" of the Internet Governance Forum, as envisaged in paragraph 76 of the Tunis Agenda, taking into consideration the stakeholders in developing areas that have been unable to get connected online, and urges the Secretary-General to take all appropriate measures to have broad-based consultations;

17. *Notes* that paragraph 80 of the Tunis Agenda refers to the development of multi-stakeholder processes at the national, regional and international levels;

18. *Recognizes* the contribution of the World Telecommunication Standardization Assembly 2008 towards enhanced cooperation;

19. *Notes* the conclusion reached by the Secretary-General on the basis of performance reports received from ten organizations relevant to Internet governance that, while the efforts made varied in nature among the organizations, the call in the Tunis Agenda for enhanced cooperation has been taken seriously by these organizations, and requests the Secretary-General to report to the Economic and Social Council through the Commission on progress made towards enhanced cooperation;

20. *Also notes* that topics that were not central at the first and second phases of the World Summit continue to emerge, such as the potential of information and communications technologies to combat climate change, the protection of online privacy and the empowerment and protection, particularly against cyberexploitation and abuse, of vulnerable groups of society, in particular children and young people;

21. *Further notes* that a rising level of Internet penetration alone does not necessarily guarantee an information society for all and that the information society requires complementary efforts and funds to make access affordable and to facilitate the development of the skills needed to make use of services and equipment and to develop local content;

22. *Notes* the contribution of the Global Alliance for Information and Communication Technologies and Development to the twelfth session of the Commission, held in Geneva from 25 to 29 May 2009;

23. *Welcomes* the efforts undertaken by Tunisia, host of the second phase of the World Summit, to organize annually the ICT 4 All Forum and technological exhibition as a platform for promoting a dynamic business environment for the information and communications technology sector worldwide;

24. *Calls upon* all States, in building the information society, to take steps to avoid and to refrain from taking any unilateral measure not in accordance with international law and the Charter of the United Nations that impedes the full achievement of economic and social development by the population of affected countries and hinders their well-being;

The road ahead

25. *Encourages* all stakeholders to continue their efforts to implement the World Summit vision of a people-centred, inclusive and development-oriented information society, so as to enhance digital opportunities for all people and thereby help to bridge the digital divide;

26. *Calls upon* all stakeholders to assist developing countries in their efforts towards narrowing the digital divide, particularly with regard to access, affordability, broadband speed, local content and data privacy;

27. *Encourages* all stakeholders to continue to cooperate on and to develop information and communications technology partnerships towards capacity-building, transfer of technology and knowledge, and research and development;

28. *Recognizes* the work of the Partnership on Measuring Information and Communications Technologies for Development, its institutional strengthening and the creation of a working group to measure the economic and social impact of information and communications technologies, recalls Economic and Social Council resolution 2008/3, in which the Council acknowledged the work of the Partnership on developing indicators, and recommends that the Partnership consider the development of benchmarks and impact indicators for further consideration by the Statistical Commission;

29. *Notes* the efforts made in developing tools to assess the global digital divide, including the International Telecommunication Union Information and Communications Technology Development Index;

30. *Encourages* all stakeholders to continue to focus on pro-poor information and communications technology policies and applications, including the need for broadband access at the grass-roots level, with a view to narrowing the digital divide between and within countries;

31. *Also encourages* all stakeholders to increase efforts to implement the information and communications technology accessibility concept as contained in article 9 of the Convention on the Rights of Persons with Disabilities;

32. *Calls upon* all stakeholders, in the interest of future generations, to give due attention to digital preservation, and commends the United Nations Educational, Scientific and Cultural Organization and its partners for their work on the World Digital Library, which was inaugurated on 21 April 2009;

33. *Takes note* of the importance of efforts to reduce the environmental effects of the information and communications technology sector and at the same time of the potential of information and communications technologies to reduce environmental impacts in other sectors;

34. *Recognizes* the importance of continuing efforts at the national and international levels to address privacy and security concerns in the use of information and communications technology, and encourages Governments, in cooperation with other stakeholders, to develop effective approaches in this regard;

35. *Urges* those United Nations entities still not actively cooperating in the implementation of and follow-up to the outcomes of the World Summit, through the United Nations system, to take the necessary steps for and commit to a people-centred, inclusive and development-oriented information society and to catalyse the attainment of the internationally agreed development goals, including those contained in the United Nations Millennium Declaration;

36. *Encourages* the World Summit action line facilitators to increase their efforts to include all stakeholders in the process designed to facilitate the implementation of the World Summit action lines and to further enhance the interactivity of this process;

37. *Encourages* the regional commissions to continue to share best practices among themselves in order to improve the overall implementation of the outcomes of the World Summit;

38. *Encourages* all relevant United Nations entities, including the regional commissions, to support the development and implementation of national e-strategies in developing and least developed countries, while encouraging international collaboration, especially South-South cooperation and North-South partnerships, with a view to determining best practices and sharing experiences and resources;

39. *Takes note* of World Summit action line C7 (e-health) and the Millennium Development Goals related to health, as well as the theme for the 2009 annual ministerial review of the Economic and Social Council, "Implementing the internationally agreed goals and commitments in regard to global public health";

40. *Encourages* Governments to strive to use information and communications technology to achieve the health-related internationally agreed development goals by increasing multi-stakeholder coordinated efforts at the national and international levels;

41. *Encourages* the development of identified national health priorities and of a national e-health policy and strategy that brings together the health and information and communications technology sectors to articulate information and communications technology implementation policies and plans for public health;

42. *Encourages* the World Health Organization, the International Telecommunication Union and other United Nations agencies and bodies to coordinate their activities and to work closely with relevant stakeholders to develop guidelines for data exchange, which is essential to the successful implementation of health-related information and communications technology applications and the infrastructure that supports them;

43. *Invites* the international community to make voluntary contributions to the special trust fund established by the United Nations Conference on Trade and Development to support the review and assessment work of the Commission on Science and Technology for Development regarding follow-up to the World Summit;

44. *Recommends* mainstreaming information and communications technologies in the economy as a driver of growth and sustainable development, and encourages all stakeholders to continue engaging in people-centred partnerships as an effective way forward;

45. *Encourages* the World Summit action line facilitators and moderators for action lines C3 (access to information and knowledge) and C7 (e-science and e-health) to collaborate with the Commission in the context of its traditional mandate;

46. *Requests* the Commission, during its thirteenth session, to be held at the halfway point to the overall review of the implementation of the outcomes of the World Sum-

mit in 2015, to organize a substantive discussion on the progress made in the implementation of those outcomes during the first five years, to include consideration of modalities for the implementation of and follow-up to those outcomes, and invites all facilitators and stakeholders to take this into account in the context of their contribution to that session;

47.   *Requests* the Secretary-General to submit to the Economic and Social Council, through the Commission, an executive summary on the implementation of the outcomes of the World Summit by each United Nations agency and programme;

48.   *Urges* all United Nations bodies to contribute to the executive summary mentioned in paragraph 47 above, by listing the decisions and resolutions of their relevant organs as well as their relevant plans and activities;

49.   *Requests* the Secretary-General to submit to the Commission, on a yearly basis, a report on the implementation of the recommendations contained in the Economic and Social Council resolutions on the assessment of the progress made in the implementation of and follow-up to the outcomes of the World Summit.

Cybersecurity

The General Assembly in 2009 considered the issue of cybersecurity, and offered Member States a voluntary self-assessment tool to aid them in reviewing national efforts on cybersecurity and the protection of critical information infrastructures.

GENERAL ASSEMBLY ACTION

On 21 December [meeting 66], the General Assembly, on the recommendation of the Second Committee [A/64/422/Add.3], adopted **resolution 64/211** without vote [agenda item 55 *(c)*].

Creation of a global culture of cybersecurity and taking stock of national efforts to protect critical information infrastructures

The General Assembly,

Recalling its resolutions 55/63 of 4 December 2000 and 56/121 of 19 December 2001 on combating the criminal misuse of information technologies, 57/239 of 20 December 2002 on the creation of a global culture of cybersecurity and 58/199 of 23 December 2003 on the creation of a global culture of cybersecurity and the protection of critical information infrastructures,

Recalling also its resolutions 53/70 of 4 December 1998, 54/49 of 1 December 1999, 55/28 of 20 November 2000, 56/19 of 29 November 2001, 57/53 of 22 November 2002, 58/32 of 8 December 2003, 59/61 of 3 December 2004, 60/45 of 8 December 2005, 61/54 of 6 December 2006, 62/17 of 5 December 2007 and 63/37 of 2 December 2008 on developments with respect to information technologies in the context of international security,

Recalling further the outcomes of the World Summit on the Information Society, held in Geneva from 10 to 12 December 2003 (first phase) and in Tunis from 16 to 18 November 2005 (second phase),

Recognizing that confidence and security in the use of information and communications technologies are among the main pillars of the information society and that a robust global culture of cybersecurity needs to be encouraged, promoted, developed and vigorously implemented,

Recognizing also the increasing contribution made by networked information technologies to many of the essential functions of daily life, commerce and the provision of goods and services, research, innovation and entrepreneurship, and to the free flow of information among individuals and organizations, Governments, business and civil society,

Recognizing further that, in a manner appropriate to their roles, Governments, business, organizations and individual owners and users of information technologies must assume responsibility for and take steps to enhance the security of these information technologies,

Recognizing the importance of the mandate of the Internet Governance Forum as a multi-stakeholder dialogue to discuss various matters, including public policy issues related to key elements of Internet governance in order to foster sustainability, robustness, security, stability and development of the Internet, and reiterating that all Governments should have an equal role and responsibility for international Internet governance and for ensuring the stability, security and continuity of the Internet,

Reaffirming the continuing need to enhance cooperation, to enable Governments, on an equal footing, to carry out their roles and responsibilities in international public policy issues pertaining to the Internet, but not the day-to-day technical and operational matters that do not impact on international public policy issues,

Recognizing that each country will determine its own critical information infrastructures,

Reaffirming the need to harness the potential of information and communications technologies to promote the achievement of the internationally agreed development goals, including the Millennium Development Goals, recognizing that gaps in access to and use of information technologies by States can diminish their economic prosperity, and reaffirming also the effectiveness of cooperation in combating the criminal misuse of information technology and in creating a global culture of cybersecurity,

Stressing the need for enhanced efforts to close the digital divide in order to achieve universal access to information and communications technologies and to protect critical information infrastructures by facilitating the transfer of information technology and capacity-building to developing countries, especially the least developed countries, in the areas of cybersecurity best practices and training,

Expressing concern that threats to the reliable functioning of critical information infrastructures and to the integrity of the information carried over those networks are growing in both sophistication and gravity, affecting domestic, national and international welfare,

Affirming that the security of critical information infrastructures is a responsibility Governments must address systematically and an area in which they must lead nationally, in coordination with relevant stakeholders, who in turn must be aware of relevant risks, preventive measures and effective responses in a manner appropriate to their respective roles,

Recognizing that national efforts should be supported by international information-sharing and collaboration, so as to effectively confront the increasingly transnational nature of such threats,

Noting the work of relevant regional and international organizations on enhancing cybersecurity, and reiterating their role in encouraging national efforts and fostering international cooperation,

Noting also the 2009 report of the International Telecommunication Union on securing information and communication networks and best practices for developing a culture of cybersecurity, which focused on a comprehensive national approach to cybersecurity consistent with free speech, the free flow of information and due process of law,

Recognizing that national efforts to protect critical information infrastructures benefit from a periodic assessment of their progress,

1. *Invites* Member States to use, if and when they deem appropriate, the annexed voluntary self-assessment tool for national efforts to protect critical information infrastructures in order to assist in assessing their efforts in this regard to strengthen their cybersecurity, so as to highlight areas for further action, with the goal of increasing the global culture of cybersecurity;

2. *Encourages* Member States and relevant regional and international organizations that have developed strategies to deal with cybersecurity and the protection of critical information infrastructures to share their best practices and measures that could assist other Member States in their efforts to facilitate the achievement of cybersecurity by providing such information to the Secretary-General for compilation and dissemination to Member States.

ANNEX

Voluntary self-assessment tool for national efforts to protect critical information infrastructures

Taking stock of cybersecurity needs and strategies

1. Assess the role of information and communications technologies in your national economy, national security, critical infrastructures (such as transportation, water and food supplies, public health, energy, finance, emergency services) and civil society.

2. Determine the cybersecurity and critical information infrastructure protection risks to your economy, national security, critical infrastructures and civil society that must be managed.

3. Understand the vulnerabilities of the networks in use, the relative levels of threat faced by each sector at present and the current management plan; note how changes in the economic environment, national security priorities and civil society needs affect these calculations.

4. Determine the goals of the national cybersecurity and critical information infrastructure protection strategy; describe its goals, the current level of implementation, measures that exist to gauge its progress, its relation to other national policy objectives and how such a strategy fits within regional and international initiatives.

Stakeholder roles and responsibilities

5. Determine key stakeholders with a role in cybersecurity and critical information infrastructure protection

and describe the role of each in the development of relevant policies and operations, including:

- National Government ministries or agencies, noting primary points of contact and responsibilities of each;
- Other government (local and regional) participants;
- Non-governmental actors, including industry, civil society and academia;
- Individual citizens, noting whether average users of the Internet have access to basic training in avoiding threats online and whether there is a national awareness-raising campaign regarding cybersecurity.

Policy processes and participation

6. Identify formal and informal venues that currently exist for Government-industry collaboration in the development of cybersecurity and critical information infrastructure protection policy and operations; determine participants, role(s) and objectives, methods for obtaining and addressing input, and adequacy in achieving relevant cybersecurity and critical information infrastructure protection goals.

7. Identify other forums or structures that may be needed to integrate the government and non-government perspectives and knowledge necessary to realize national cybersecurity and critical information infrastructure protection goals.

Public-private cooperation

8. Collect all actions taken and plans to develop collaboration between government and the private sector, including any arrangements for information-sharing and incident management.

9. Collect all current and planned initiatives to promote shared interests and address common challenges among both critical infrastructure participants and private-sector actors mutually dependent on the same interconnected critical infrastructure.

Incident management and recovery

10. Identify the Government agency that serves as the coordinator for incident management, including capability for watch, warning, response and recovery functions; the cooperating Government agencies; non-governmental cooperating participants, including industry and other partners; and any arrangements in place for cooperation and trusted information-sharing.

11. Separately, identify national-level computer incident response capacity, including any computer incident response team with national responsibilities and its roles and responsibilities, including existing tools and procedures for the protection of Government computer networks, and existing tools and procedures for the dissemination of incident-management information.

12. Identify networks and processes of international cooperation that may enhance incident response and contingency planning, identifying partners and arrangements for bilateral and multilateral cooperation, where appropriate.

Legal frameworks

13. Review and update legal authorities (including those related to cybercrime, privacy, data protection, commercial law, digital signatures and encryption) that may

be outdated or obsolete as a result of the rapid uptake of and dependence upon new information and communications technologies, and use regional and international conventions, arrangements and precedents in these reviews. Ascertain whether your country has developed necessary legislation for the investigation and prosecution of cybercrime, noting existing frameworks, for example, General Assembly resolutions 55/63 and 56/121 on combating the criminal misuse of information technologies, and regional initiatives, including the Council of Europe Convention on Cybercrime.

14. Determine the current status of national cybercrime authorities and procedures, including legal authorities and national cybercrime units, and the level of understanding among prosecutors, judges and legislators of cybercrime issues.

15. Assess the adequacy of current legal codes and authorities in addressing the current and future challenges of cybercrime, and of cyberspace more generally.

16. Examine national participation in international efforts to combat cybercrime, such as the round-the-clock Cybercrime Point of Contact Network.

17. Determine the requirements for national law enforcement agencies to cooperate with international counterparts to investigate transnational cybercrime in those instances in which infrastructure is situated or perpetrators reside in national territory, but victims reside elsewhere.

Developing a global culture of cybersecurity

18. Summarize actions taken and plans to develop a national culture of cybersecurity referred to in General Assembly resolutions 57/239 and 58/199, including implementation of a cybersecurity plan for Government-operated systems, national awareness-raising programmes, outreach programmes to, among others, children and individual users, and national cybersecurity and critical information infrastructure protection training requirements.

Economic and social trends

The *World Economic and Social Survey 2009* [Sales No. E.09.II.C.1; overview E/2009/50], published by DESA, focused on the relation between promoting development and saving the planet. The survey examined climate change and the development challenge; climate mitigation and the energy challenge; adaptation; development policy and the climate challenge; technology transfer and the climate challenge; and financing the development response to climate change. According to the report, the climate challenge required much stronger efforts by advanced countries to cut their emissions. Active participation of developing countries was also required, but such participation could occur only if it allowed economic growth and development to proceed in a rapid and sustainable manner. Switching to low-emissions, high-growth pathways in order to meet the development and climate challenge was both necessary—combating global warm-

ing could not be achieved without eventual emissions reductions from developing countries—and feasible—as technological solutions that could enable a shift towards such pathways did in fact exist. Such a switch would entail unprecedented and potentially very costly socio-economic adjustments in developing countries—adjustments that would require international support and solidarity. Achieving such a transformation hinged on the creation of a global new deal capable of raising investment levels and channelling resources towards lowering the carbon content of economic activity and building resilience with respect to unavoidable climate changes. Most developing countries did not have the financial resources, technological know-how and institutional capacity to deploy such strategies at a speed commensurate with the urgency of the climate challenge. Failure to honour long-standing commitments of international support in those three areas remained the single biggest obstacle to meeting the challenge. In line with common but differentiated responsibilities, the switch would demand an approach to climate policy in developing countries different from that in developed ones. It would, in particular, require a new public policy agenda—one focused on a broad mix of market and non-market measures while placing greater emphasis on public investment and effective industrial policies, to be managed by a developmental State. The mix in developed countries would likely entail a larger role for carbon markets, taxes and regulations. Finally, issues of trust and justice would need to be taken much more seriously so as to ensure fair and inclusive responses to the climate challenge. One determinant of success would be the capacity of developed and developing countries to create a more integrated framework and joint programmes with shared goals on climate adaptation, forestry, energy and poverty eradication.

The *World Economic Situation and Prospects 2009* [Sales No. E.09.II.C.2; update E/2009/73], jointly produced by DESA, the United Nations Conference on Trade and Development (UNCTAD) and the five United Nations regional commissions, examined the global outlook for the world economy, international trade, financing for development, and regional developments and outlook. With the world economy mired in the worst financial and economic crisis since the Second World War, most advanced economies were already in recession, and the outlook for emerging and other developing economies was deteriorating rapidly, including those with a recent history of strong economic performance. The report recommended the implementation of massive, internationally coordinated fiscal stimulus packages that were coherent and mutually reinforcing and aligned with sustainable development goals. That should be effected in addition to the liquidity and recapitalization measures already undertaken by countries in response to the economic crisis.

As immediate solutions were being worked out, it was important to address the systemic causes that led to the crisis through the establishment of a credible and effective mechanism for international policy coordination; fundamental reforms of existing systems of financial regulation and supervision; reform of the international reserve system away from the almost exclusive reliance on the United States dollar and towards a multilaterally backed multi-currency system; and reforms of liquidity provisioning and compensatory financing mechanisms backed through better multilateral and regional pooling of national foreign-exchange reserves that would avoid the onerous policy conditionality attached to existing mechanisms.

The *Trade and Development Report, 2009* [Sales No. E.09.II.D.16], published by UNCTAD, discussed the impact of the global recession, including its relation to the food crisis, and the short-term policy response; the financialization of commodity markets; policies for safer and sounder financial systems; reform of the international monetary and financial system; and climate change mitigation and development. According to the report, an internationally agreed exchange-rate system based on the principle of constant and sustainable real exchange rates of all countries would go a long way towards reducing the scope for speculative capital flows that generated volatility in the international financial system and distorted the pattern of exchange rates. Such a multilateral system would tackle the problem of destabilizing capital flows at its source. It would remove a major incentive for speculation, ensure that monetary factors did not stand in the way of achieving a level playing field for international trade, and avoid debt traps for developing countries. The large fiscal stimulus packages launched in response to the financial and economic crisis offered an ideal opportunity to accelerate structural change towards a low-carbon economy through additional public investment in activities and infrastructure in support of climate change mitigation, and through the provision of subsidies for acquisition of climate-friendly capital goods and durable consumer goods.

Human development

Prepared by the United Nations Development Programme, the *Human Development Report 2009* (HDR 2009) [Sales No. 09.III.B.1] explored how better policies towards human mobility could enhance human development. Topics addressed included freedom and movement: how mobility could foster human development; people in motion: who moved where, when and why; how movers fared; impacts at origin and destination; and policies to enhance human development outcomes. According to the report, large gains to human development could be achieved by lowering barriers to movement and improving the treatment of

movers. The two most important dimensions of the mobility agenda that offered scope for better policies were admissions and treatment. Principal proposed reforms centred around opening up entry channels so that more workers could emigrate; ensuring basic rights for migrants; lowering the transaction costs of migration; finding solutions that benefited both destination communities and the migrants they received; making it easier for people to move within their own countries; and integrating migration into national development strategies.

UNDP consideration. The Executive Board of the United Nations Development Programme/United Nations Population Fund, at its 2009 annual session (New York, 26 May–3 June) [E/2009/35], took note of a March update [DP/2009/17] on HDR 2009 network consultations underpinning the selection of its theme and the informal Executive Board consultations held during its preparation, as well as participatory consultations with experts worldwide.

Development policy and public administration

Committee for Development Policy

The Committee for Development Policy (CDP), at its eleventh session (New York, 9–13 March) [E/2009/33], addressed three themes: international cooperation on global public health, particularly the importance of tackling inequalities; the global financial turmoil and its impact on developing countries; and climate change and development. It also conducted its triennial review of the list of the least developed countries (LDCs) (see p. 832).

With regard to international cooperation for health, CDP concluded that much greater consideration should be given to the persistently high inequalities in access to health services and in health outcomes. Such inequalities existed by income groups, gender, race, ethnicity and geography, and were manifest especially in disadvantageous health outcomes for the poorest. Poor health conditions, in turn, affected other dimensions of well-being and were a cause of poorer education performance and lower incomes. Addressing health inequalities required redressing international cooperation in health. It also required that both recipient and donor Governments take an integrated view of the health system, giving priority to primary care and the strengthening of the institutional and technical capacities of health delivery systems.

As for the implications of the global financial crisis for developing countries, the Committee concluded that there was a need to raise the revenue capacity of

Governments through measures that would improve tax collection. International cooperation to combat tax evasion taking place through international tax havens should be a crucial ingredient of those efforts. Enhanced compensatory finance was urgently needed and should be made accessible without the restrictive policy conditions attached to existing mechanisms. A significant part of financing should come from counter-cyclical issuance of special drawing rights (SDRs) by the International Monetary Fund, and the role of SDRs as a global reserve currency should be gradually increased. A global regulatory mechanism of the international financial system needed to be established in order to prevent new crises.

With regard to climate change, every country needed to adopt carbon-saving technologies. Improved governance and a review of the financial architecture for addressing climate change were required in order to ensure policy coherence and a focus on sustainable development. A climate impact vulnerability indicator at the national level to guide adaptation strategies should be developed.

For its forthcoming twelfth session, the Committee would undertake work on the theme of the 2010 annual ministerial review of the Economic and Social Council, "Implementing the internationally agreed goals and commitments in regard to gender equality and the empowerment of women".

ECONOMIC AND SOCIAL COUNCIL ACTION

On 31 July [meeting 45], the Economic and Social Council adopted **resolution 2009/35** [draft: E/2009/L.43] without vote [agenda item 13 (a)].

Report of the Committee for Development Policy on its eleventh session

The Economic and Social Council,

Recalling General Assembly resolution 59/209 of 20 December 2004 on a smooth transition strategy for countries graduating from the list of least developed countries,

Recalling also its resolutions 2007/34 and 2007/35 of 27 July 2007,

Expressing its conviction that countries graduating from the least developed country category should not have their positive development disrupted or reversed, but rather should be able to continue and sustain their progress and development,

1. *Takes note* of the report of the Committee for Development Policy on its eleventh session;

2. *Requests* the Committee, at its twelfth session, to examine and make recommendations on the themes chosen by the Economic and Social Council for the high-level segment of its substantive session of 2010;

3. *Takes note* of the proposals made by the Committee regarding its future work programme;

4. *Endorses* the recommendation of the Committee that Equatorial Guinea be graduated from the list of least developed countries;

5. *Recommends* that the General Assembly take note of the recommendation of the Committee that Equatorial Guinea be graduated from the list of least developed countries;

6. *Reiterates* the importance for development partners to implement concrete measures in support of the transition strategy of ensuring durable graduation;

7. *Requests* the Committee to monitor the development progress of countries graduating from the list of least developed countries and to include its findings in its annual report to the Economic and Social Council;

8. *Invites* the Chair and, as necessary, other members of the Committee to continue the practice of reporting orally on the work of the Committee.

Public administration

Committee of Experts. The Committee of Experts on Public Administration, at its eighth session (New York, 30 March–3 April) [E/2009/44], had before it notes by the Secretariat on the human factor in capacity-building for development [E/C.16/2009/2], review of the United Nations Programme in Public Administration and Finance [E/C.16/2009/3] and mainstreaming of health issues and human capacity-building in public administration [E/C.16/2009/4].

The Committee considered as its main theme the human factor in capacity-building and development. Its principal conclusions were that: there had to be much stronger emphasis on this topic on the part of both the United Nations and Member States; human resources management should be fully integrated into development by repositioning it as a strategic function in public administration and by investing in the development of competent and professional human resources managers in the public service; an efficient, professional and high-performing civil service went hand in hand with legitimate institutions that both implemented public policies efficiently and was accountable, transparent and inclusive; concerted efforts should be made to improve the information technology skill sets of both public employees and citizens, and the enabling power of e-tools harnessed to improve governance and help achieve development goals; and the versatility of the notion of leadership must be recognized in order to link it effectively with the human factor in capacity-building and development.

Regarding the mainstreaming of health issues and human capacity-building in public administration, the Committee recommended that Member States: raise awareness in all sectors and at all levels of government about their respective responsibilities and opportunities to promote, restore and maintain public health and to provide health delivery services;

develop an integrated health policy coordinated with all other policies that had an impact on public health and health services; adopt participatory and citizen-centred approaches to developing national health policies, including via the adequate use of ICT tools; promote reforms of health institutions and establish a strategy based on primary care, universal access and equity in health care; cooperate with each other and with global institutions on a regular basis in order to avoid possible risks posed by a global threat as a result of a new global pandemic and illnesses; promote long-term funding, including public-private partnerships where appropriate, for research and development, and ensure that the health sector did not suffer from budgetary retrenchments during economic crisis; and involve civil society organizations to enhance awareness on health issues among different stakeholders, including public service providers.

As for the United Nations Programme in Public Administration and Finance, the Committee requested the Secretariat to continue giving due recognition to innovative public sector initiatives by Member States in support of the implementation of the internationally agreed development goals, including the MDGs; enhance its work on the development of public sector institutions and resources for the achievement of those goals; support and facilitate the work of the Global Alliance for Information and Communication Technologies and Development, the Internet Governance Forum, and the Global Centre for Information and Communication Technologies in Parliament, and the implementation of the WSIS Action Plan on e-government related issues; and work with relevant partners and further develop a global knowledge base of administrative strategies, public policies, expert networks, best practices and lessons learned at the national and subnational levels, within the United Nations Public Administration Network, in order to promote efficiency, effectiveness, transparency, accountability and participation in the public sector, and to support the achievement of the internationally agreed development goals, including the MDGS.

Appointments. In notes of 17 February [E/2009/9/Add.11] and 23 April [E/2009/9/Add.16], the Secretary-General nominated 24 experts to the Committee for a four-year term beginning on 1 January 2010. At its seventh meeting on 18 May, the Council approved the nominations [E/2009/SR.7].

ECONOMIC AND SOCIAL COUNCIL ACTION

On 29 July [meeting 42], the Economic and Social Council, on the recommendation of the Committee of Experts on Public Administration [E/2009/44], adopted **resolution 2009/18** without vote [agenda item 13 *(g)*].

Report of the Committee of Experts on Public Administration on its eighth session

The Economic and Social Council,

Recalling its resolutions 2002/40 of 19 December 2002, 2003/60 of 25 July 2003, 2005/3 of 31 March 2005, 2005/55 of 21 October 2005, 2006/47 of 28 July 2006, 2007/38 of 4 October 2007 and 2008/32 of 25 July 2008, as well as General Assembly resolutions 50/225 of 19 April 1996, 56/213 of 21 December 2001, 57/277 of 20 December 2002, 58/231 of 23 December 2003, 59/55 of 2 December 2004, 60/34 of 30 November 2005 and 63/202 of 19 December 2008,

Taking note with appreciation of the pioneering work of the United Nations Programme on Public Administration, Finance and Development in supporting Member States with analytical research, advocacy and advisory and training services for public administrations in the areas of human capacity development, e-government development and citizen engagement since its inception in 1948,

Taking note with appreciation also of the work done by the Committee of Experts on Public Administration at its eighth session, including on the human factor in capacity-building and development, the mainstreaming of health issues and human capacity-building in public administration and the United Nations online glossary on governance and public administration, and taking note with appreciation also of its continual support for the work of the Economic and Social Council concerning the promotion and development of public administration and governance among Member States,

Recognizing that, especially because the conditions and context of development, growth and governance have changed, public administration priorities, including capacity-building for growth and development and ownership of national development, still remain critical cross-cutting issues in addressing the current global financial crisis, climate change and gender equality challenges, as well as for the achievement of the internationally agreed development goals, including the Millennium Development Goals,

Recognizing with appreciation the substantive contributions made by the current members of the Committee in strengthening public administration capacity at the regional, national and local levels,

1. *Takes note* of the conclusions contained in the report of the Committee of Experts on Public Administration on its eighth session that relate to the need for continual capacity-building for development at the national and subnational levels and the need for the Secretariat to continue to enhance its support for capacity-building in the public sector;

2. *Takes note with appreciation* of the input by the Committee to the 2009 annual ministerial review of the Economic and Social Council on the theme "Implementing the internationally agreed goals and commitments in regard to global public health";

3. *Requests* the Secretariat to continue to give due recognition to innovative public sector initiatives by Member States through the flagship work of the United Nations Public Service Day and the Public Service Awards in support of the implementation of the internationally agreed

development goals, including the Millennium Development Goals;

4. *Also requests* the Secretariat to further enhance its support for capacity-building through analytical research, advisory services and online and offline training, emphasizing trust building, citizen engagement, human resources and institutional development;

5. *Further requests* the Secretariat, in the light of the fact that the current economic and financial crisis is a daunting challenge to public administration, to enhance its important work on the development of public sector institutions and resources for the achievement of the internationally agreed development goals, including the Millennium Development Goals, by further developing its analytical and advisory capacity and further integrating research and analysis into its normative and operational work and by continuing to work with other partners in developing joint products;

6. *Requests* the Secretariat, in order to facilitate advocacy for and the implementation of the Plan of Action adopted by the World Summit on the Information Society at its first phase, held in Geneva from 10 to 12 December 2003, to continue to support and facilitate the work of the Global Alliance for Information and Communication Technologies and Development, the Internet Governance Forum and the Global Centre for Information and Communication Technologies in Parliament, as well as the implementation of the provisions of the Plan of Action that relate to e-government;

7. *Also requests* the Secretariat to work with relevant partners, especially public administration schools and research institutes worldwide, and to further develop and maintain a global knowledge base at the national and subnational levels, within the United Nations Public Administration Network, of administrative strategies, public policies, expert networks, best practices and lessons learned in the areas mentioned above, with the overarching objective of promoting efficiency, effectiveness, transparency, accountability and participation in the public sector and supporting the achievement of the internationally agreed development goals, including the Millennium Development Goals;

8. *Approves* the convening of the ninth session of the Committee.

Groups of countries in special situations

On 18 September [A/64/423], the General Assembly, on the recommendation of the General Committee, included in the agenda of its sixty-fourth session the item entitled "Groups of countries in special situations", covering least developed countries and landlocked and transit developing countries, and allocated it to the Second Committee.

On 21 December (**decision 64/542**), the General Assembly took note of the report of the Second Committee on the subject [A/64/423 & Add.1 & Add.2].

OIOS report. In April, the Office of Internal Oversight Services (OIOS) issued a report [E/AC.51/2009/2] on the relevance, efficiency and effectiveness of the Office of the High Representative for Least Developed Countries, Landlocked Developing Countries and Small Island Developing States (OHRLLS) and UN support for the New Partnership for Africa's Development (NEPAD). OIOS found that the results frameworks mandated for and embedded in the budgets of both OHRLLS and UN support for NEPAD involved the expectation of contributions to change far beyond the realm of the respective programme managers' influence. Resource and capacity constraints made it unrealistic to exert any detectable influence on, for example, the coordination of UN affairs in Africa. A lack of programmatic focus and insufficient communication with stakeholders worsened the situation.

The main achievement of the two programmes was their contribution to heightened policy attention to the special development needs of the least developed countries, landlocked developing countries, small island developing States and Africa at UN-convened global forums. There was an unclear division of labour between the programmes and other UN actors. As perceived by Member States and UN partners, and within the entities themselves, there were multiple interpretations of what their operational priorities should be.

According to the report, considerable overlaps existed between the countries that OHRLLS and UN support for NEPAD covered. The potential for synergy between OHRLLS and the Office of the Special Adviser on Africa (OSAA), as small offices with overlapping mandates, had not been exploited.

Misalignment between budget and organizational structure had led to little coordination within the three subprogrammes under UN support for NEPAD. At the same time, the parallel arrangements of OHRLLS and DESA amid a fragmented structure in support of small island developing States needed better coordination.

OIOS recommended that a review be undertaken to translate the respective mandates into a narrower and more clearly defined programmatic focus, and that revised strategic frameworks be submitted for consideration by the General Assembly. OIOS also recommended that reviews be undertaken to combine administrative and advocacy functions of OSAA and OHRLLS, and that the three subprogrammes under UN support for NEPAD be brought under the responsibility and oversight of one senior officer. Likewise, the programme of UN system support for NEPAD should formulate a proposal for strengthening support for the regional consultative mechanism for Africa. Lastly, OHRLLS and DESA should clarify their respective roles and develop a joint action plan to bring coherence and provide guidance to UN system efforts in support of small island developing States.

Least developed countries

The special problems of the officially designated least developed countries (LDCs) were considered in several UN forums in 2009, particularly in connection with the implementation of the Brussels Declaration and Programme of Action for the Least Developed Countries for the Decade 2001–2010, adopted at the Third United Nations Conference on LDCs in 2001 [YUN 2001, p. 770] and endorsed by the General Assembly in resolution 55/279 in July of that year [ibid., p. 771]. The Committee for Development Policy (CDP) and the United Nations Conference on Trade and Development (UNCTAD) also considered LDC-related issues.

LDC list

In its triennial review of the list of the least developed countries (LDCs) [E/2009/33], defined as low-income countries suffering from severe structural handicaps to growth, CDP found two countries—Papua New Guinea and Zimbabwe—eligible for inclusion in the list of LDCs. Both declined, however, to join the category. The Committee found Equatorial Guinea eligible for graduation from the list, and recommended the country's graduation. Tuvalu and Vanuatu were also considered eligible, but were not recommended for graduation. CDP reiterated the importance for graduating countries of developing a smooth transition strategy with the support of their respective development partners. Consequently, in 2009, the number of countries officially designated as LDCs remained at 49 [YUN 2008, p. 938].

The list of LDCs comprised: Afghanistan, Angola, Bangladesh, Benin, Bhutan, Burkina Faso, Burundi, Cambodia, the Central African Republic, Chad, Comoros, Democratic Republic of the Congo, Djibouti, Equatorial Guinea, Eritrea, Ethiopia, the Gambia, Guinea, Guinea-Bissau, Haiti, Kiribati, the Lao People's Democratic Republic, Lesotho, Liberia, Madagascar, Malawi, Maldives, Mali, Mauritania, Mozambique, Myanmar, Nepal, the Niger, Rwanda, Samoa, Sao Tome and Principe, Senegal, Sierra Leone, Solomon Islands, Somalia, the Sudan, Timor-Leste, Togo, Tuvalu, Uganda, United Republic of Tanzania, Vanuatu, Yemen and Zambia.

Programme of Action (2001–2010)

Report of Secretary-General. In accordance with General Assembly resolution 63/227 [YUN 2008, p. 944] and Economic and Social Council resolution 2007/31 [YUN 2007, p. 863], the Secretary-General in May submitted a report [A/64/80-E/2009/79] on the implementation of the Programme of Action for the Least Developed Countries for the Decade 2001–2010. The report examined the impact of the financial and economic crises on LDCs; reviewed the progress made towards the international goals and targets contained in the Programme of Action; and described preparations for the Fourth United Nations Conference on the Least Developed Countries, to be held in 2011.

The Secretary-General concluded that the first and immediate concern was to mitigate the effects of the global recession on LDCs. Efforts were required to make the LDCs more resilient to the development shocks caused by their increased integration into the global economy. LDCs, supported by their development partners, needed to integrate actions that would mitigate the anticipated effects of climate change into their national development strategies.

The Secretary-General recommended that the international community ensure that sufficient resources were available to provide food to the most vulnerable people in LDCs and other countries with food deficits. Because LDCs faced not only short-term but also potential long-term food shortage, they and their development partners needed to implement corresponding measures to address that challenge. Since LDCs had very little scope for mitigating the effects of the global recession on their economies and peoples without substantial additional external financial support, all development partners should honour their commitments to increase their official development assistance (ODA), ensuring that those did not fall victim to domestic budgetary pressures. Developing countries in a position to do so, such as oil-producing countries, should consider providing or expanding their support to LDCs. Because LDCs required additional funding to avoid immediate economic hardship and massive human suffering, development partners should respond by fully and promptly implementing the commitments they made at the most recent meetings of the Group of Twenty, the Development Committee and the International Monetary and Financial Committee.

Towards reducing vulnerability through diversification of their economies, Governments of LDCs and their development partners should endeavour to sustain their long-term investment in infrastructure, but should continue to rely mainly on the private sector to identify and organize new investments in production facilities. To encourage such diversification, all other countries, including other developing countries, should reduce trade barriers to exports from LDCs, including subsidies granted to their own exports and domestic production. LDCs needed to reduce their exposure to the volatility of primary commodity markets by enhancing arrangements to absorb the impact of short-term fluctuations in the domestic commodity sector itself, export earnings, Government revenue and in the economy as a whole. LDCs should lay the foundations for systems that would reduce the impact of future shocks on vulnerable groups. Because the high rate of population growth in LDCs continued to intensify their development challenge, dilute achievements and increase vulnerability to shocks, particularly those such as the food crisis and climate change, LDCs should give increased attention to their commitment to making reproductive health accessible to all individuals of appropriate ages no later than 2015.

The ongoing negotiations for a new international agreement on climate change should fully embrace and apply the principle of common but differentiated responsibility to LDCs. LDCs should continue to prepare and implement national adaptation programmes of action for climate change, focusing on the needs of the most vulnerable groups and ecosystems. Development partners, including other developing countries, should give urgent attention to increasing the funding for projects that would enable LDCs to adapt to climate change. Those issues should be among those addressed in the context of the upcoming Fourth United Nations Conference on the Least Developed Countries.

Communications. In a letter of 10 April [A/63/819-S/2009/204], Mexico transmitted the statement by the States members of the Rio Group and of the Caribbean Community entitled "Towards a new paradigm of cooperation", issued on 8 April in preparation for the Conference on the Economic and Social Development of Haiti convened by the Government of Haiti (Washington, D.C., 14 April) under the auspices of the Inter-American Development Bank. In a letter of 8 October [A/C.2/64/3], Nepal transmitted the Ministerial Declaration of the Least Developed Countries, adopted during the general debate of the sixty-fourth session of the General Assembly (New York, 29 September).

ECONOMIC AND SOCIAL COUNCIL ACTION

On 31 July [meeting 45], the Economic and Social Council adopted **resolution 2009/31** [draft: E/2009/L.39 & E/2009/SR.45] without vote [agenda item 6 *(b)*].

Implementation of the Programme of Action for the Least Developed Countries for the Decade 2001–2010

The Economic and Social Council,

Recalling the Brussels Declaration and the Programme of Action for the Least Developed Countries for the Decade 2001–2010,

Recalling also its decision 2001/320 of 24 October 2001, in which it decided to establish, under the regular agenda item entitled "Integrated and coordinated implementation of and follow-up to the major United Nations conferences and summits", a regular sub-item entitled "Review and coordination of the implementation of the Programme of Action for the Least Developed Countries for the Decade 2001–2010",

Reaffirming the ministerial declaration of the high-level segment of its substantive session of 2009, on the theme "Implementing the internationally agreed goals and commitments in regard to global public health",

Recalling the ministerial declaration of the high-level segment of its substantive session of 2004 on the theme "Resources mobilization and enabling environment for poverty eradication in the context of the implementation of the Programme of Action for the Least Developed Countries for the Decade 2001–2010",

Recognizing the outcome document of the Conference on the World Financial and Economic Crisis and Its Impact on Development,

Taking note of the Doha Declaration on Financing for Development of 2008,

Recalling its resolution 2008/37 of 25 July 2008 on the implementation of the Programme of Action for the Least Developed Countries for the Decade 2001–2010,

Recalling also General Assembly resolution 63/227 of 19 December 2008, in which the Assembly decided to convene the Fourth United Nations Conference on the Least Developed Countries at a high level in 2011,

Recalling further the declaration of the high-level meeting of the sixty-first session of the General Assembly on the midterm comprehensive global review of the implementation of the Programme of Action, in which participating Heads of State and Government and heads of delegations recommitted themselves to meeting the special needs of the least developed countries by making progress towards the goals of poverty eradication, peace and development,

Emphasizing that the Fourth United Nations Conference on the Least Developed Countries should strengthen concerted global actions in support of the least developed countries,

1. *Takes note* of the annual progress report of the Secretary-General;

2. *Notes* the economic and social progress made by many least developed countries in recent years, as a result of which a number are moving towards graduation from the list of least developed countries and some are on track to achieve the growth and investment targets of the Programme of Action for the Least Developed Countries for the Decade 2001–2010 by 2010;

3. *Remains concerned*, however, about the uneven and insufficient progress made in the implementation of the Programme of Action at a time when the international community has embarked on preparations for the Fourth United Nations Conference on the Least Developed Countries, which will undertake a comprehensive appraisal of such implementation, and stresses the urgent need to address areas of weakness in the implementation of the Programme of Action and the continued precarious socio-economic situation in many least developed countries

through a strong commitment to the objectives, goals and targets of the Programme of Action;

4. *Expresses deep concern* that the number of people living in extreme poverty remains very high in the least developed countries while an increasing number of people, in particular children and women, are at risk of malnutrition, and recognizes that there are important linkages between development, poverty eradication and gender equality;

5. *Expresses concern* about the severe impact of the global financial and economic crisis on developing countries and recognizes that the social and economic progress made in recent years, particularly on the internationally agreed development goals, including the Millennium Development Goals, is now threatened in developing countries, particularly the least developed countries, and resolves to strive to combine short-term responses designed to meet the immediate impact of the financial and economic crisis, particularly on the most vulnerable countries, with medium- and long-term responses;

6. *Encourages* the United Nations system organizations, the Bretton Woods institutions, bilateral and multilateral donors and other development partners, in view of the global crises, to assist the least developed countries in translating the goals and targets of the Programme of Action into concrete actions, taking into account their national development priorities, and to collaborate with and provide support to the relevant national development forums and follow-up mechanisms, as appropriate;

7. *Reaffirms* that progress in the implementation of the Programme of Action will require effective implementation of national policies and priorities for the sustained economic growth and sustainable development of the least developed countries, as well as strong and committed partnership between those countries and their development partners;

8. *Underlines* the fact that, for the further implementation of the Programme of Action, the least developed countries and their development partners must be guided by an integral approach, a broader genuine partnership, country ownership, market considerations and results-oriented actions aimed, inter alia, at:

(a) Fostering a people-centred policy framework;

(b) Ensuring good governance at both the national and the international levels as essential for the implementation of the commitments embodied in the Programme of Action;

(c) Building human and institutional capacities;

(d) Building productive capacities to make globalization work for the least developed countries;

(e) Enhancing the role of trade in development;

(f) Reducing vulnerability and protecting the environment;

(g) Mobilizing financial resources;

9. *Urges* the least developed countries to strengthen country ownership in the implementation of the Programme of Action, inter alia, by translating its goals and targets into specific measures within their national development frameworks and poverty eradication strategies, including, where they exist, poverty reduction strategy papers, by promoting broad-based and inclusive dialogue on development with relevant stakeholders, including civil society and the private sector, and by enhancing domestic resource mobilization and aid management;

10. *Urges* development partners to fully implement, in a timely manner, commitments in the Programme of Action and to make every effort to continue to increase their financial and technical support for its implementation;

11. *Reiterates its invitation* to all development and trading partners to support the implementation of the transition strategy of countries graduating from the list of least developed countries, to avoid any abrupt reductions in either official development assistance or technical assistance provided to the graduated country and to consider either extending to the graduated country trade preferences previously made available as a result of least developed country status or reducing such trade preferences in a phased manner;

12. *Welcomes with appreciation* the generous offers of the Governments of Austria and Turkey to host the Fourth United Nations Conference on the Least Developed Countries, to be held in 2011;

13. *Reiterates* the decision of the General Assembly in its resolution 63/227 that the Office of the High Representative for the Least Developed Countries, Landlocked Developing Countries and Small Island Developing States would be the focal point for the preparations for the Fourth United Nations Conference on the Least Developed Countries, in accordance with mandates given in Assembly resolution 56/227 of 24 December 2001, to ensure that those preparations are carried out effectively and to mobilize and coordinate the active involvement of the organizations of the United Nations system;

14. *Reiterates its invitation* to the organs, organizations and bodies of the United Nations system and other relevant multilateral organizations to provide full support to and cooperation with the Office of the High Representative for the Least Developed Countries, Landlocked Developing Countries and Small Island Developing States;

15. *Requests* the Secretary-General to continue to take appropriate measures to prepare for the Fourth United Nations Conference on the Least Developed Countries as well as to implement the advocacy strategy on the effective and timely implementation of the Programme of Action, in coordination with all relevant stakeholders;

16. *Also requests* the Secretary-General to ensure the active involvement of the organizations of the United Nations system in the preparatory process for the Fourth United Nations Conference on the Least Developed Countries in a coordinated and coherent manner, inter alia, by making use of the existing coordination mechanisms of the United Nations system;

17. *Reiterates* the request of the General Assembly to the organizations of the United Nations system and the invitation of the General Assembly to the Bretton Woods institutions, the World Trade Organization and other relevant international and regional organizations, within their respective mandates, to provide necessary support and actively contribute to the preparatory process for the Fourth United Nations Conference on the Least Developed Countries and to the Conference itself;

18. *Expresses concern* about the insufficient resources in the trust fund established for the participation of the least developed countries in the annual review of the implementation of the Programme of Action by the Economic and Social Council, and expresses appreciation to those countries that have made voluntary contributions;

19. *Reiterates* the critical importance of the participation of Government representatives from the least developed countries in the annual review of the Programme of Action by the Economic and Social Council, invites donor countries to continue to support the participation of two representatives from each least developed country in the annual review, including by contributing in an adequate and timely manner to the special trust fund established for that purpose, and requests the Secretary-General to intensify his efforts to mobilize the necessary resources in order to ensure that the trust fund is adequately resourced and to provide information on the status of the trust fund;

20. *Reiterates its request* to the Secretary-General to include least developed country issues in all relevant reports in the economic, social and related fields in order to ensure follow-up to the development of such countries in the broader context of the world economy and to contribute to preventing their marginalization while promoting their further integration into the world economy;

21. *Requests* the Secretary-General to submit an analytical and results-oriented annual progress report on the further implementation of the Programme of Action and to make available adequate resources, within existing resources, for the preparation of such a report.

Trade and Development Board action. The UNCTAD Trade and Development Board, at its fifty-sixth session (Geneva, 14–25 September and 12 October) [A/64/15 (Part IV)], considered the eighth progress report [TD/B/56/2 & Corr.1] on UNCTAD-wide activities in the implementation of the Programme of Action for the Least Developed Countries for the Decade 2001–2010, and adopted agreed conclusions [496 (LVI)] on the review of progress in the implementation of the Programme of Action. The Board took note of *The Least Developed Countries Report 2009: The State and Development Governance* [Sales No. E.09.II.D.9], prepared by the UNCTAD secretariat, and stressed the importance of government policies to promote development and poverty reduction in LDCs, including agricultural and industrial policies which contributed to developing productive capacities, while stressing the importance of a conducive environment for business and private sector initiative. According to the report, whose topics included the global economic crisis, the role of the State, macroeconomic challenges, agricultural policy, and industrial policy, LDC Governments should view the global economic crisis as a potential turning point in their development. They needed to shift towards a catch-up growth strategy based on the development of productive capacities and expansion of productive employment opportunities.

Preparatory process for Fourth UN Conference on LDCs

In May [A/64/80-E/2009/79], the Secretary-General reported on the substantive, organizational and logistical preparations for the Fourth United Nations Con-

ference on the Least Developed Countries, which the General Assembly, in its resolution 63/227, decided to convene in 2011 [YUN 2008, p. 944]. OHRLLS—the focal point for the preparations for the Conference—had prepared a concept note to facilitate intergovernmental, regional and national preparations and to ensure the involvement of all stakeholders. The concept note was presented to the first meeting of the inter-agency consultative group convened by OHRLLS (New York, March 2008), attended by senior officials from more than 30 UN system and international organizations, which served to launch the system-wide preparations for the Conference. Guidelines were being prepared to assist LDCs in the organization of national reviews and the preparation of national reports. OHRLLS had been consulting with two potential host countries, Austria and Turkey, on the venue for the event.

The Conference, the Secretary-General said, would be critical to restoring the momentum of development to the world's most vulnerable countries and to providing hope for many of the world's poorest people. To facilitate the preparatory process, the General Assembly should decide on the pending organizational aspects of the Conference, including the schedule of meetings for the Intergovernmental Preparatory Committee and the venue of the Conference itself.

GENERAL ASSEMBLY ACTION

On 21 December [meeting 66], the General Assembly, on the recommendation of the Second Committee [A/64/423/Add.1], adopted **resolution 64/213** without vote [agenda item 56 (a)].

Fourth United Nations Conference on the Least Developed Countries

The General Assembly,

Recalling the Brussels Declaration and the Programme of Action for the Least Developed Countries for the Decade 2001–2010, adopted at the Third United Nations Conference on the Least Developed Countries,

Recalling also the United Nations Millennium Declaration,

Recalling further the 2005 World Summit Outcome,

Recalling its resolution 61/1 of 19 September 2006, entitled "Declaration of the high-level meeting of the sixty-first session of the General Assembly on the midterm comprehensive global review of the implementation of the Programme of Action for the Least Developed Countries for the Decade 2001–2010",

Recalling also its resolution 63/227 of 19 December 2008, in which it decided to convene the Fourth United Nations Conference on the Least Developed Countries in 2011 at a high level,

Taking note of the Ministerial Declaration adopted at the Ministerial Meeting of the Least Developed Countries held in New York on 29 September 2009,

Recalling Economic and Social Council resolution 2009/31 of 31 July 2009 on the implementation of the Programme of Action for the Least Developed Countries for the Decade 2001–2010,

Recalling also the Cotonou Strategy for the Further Implementation of the Programme of Action for the Least Developed Countries for the Decade 2001–2010, as an initiative owned and led by the least developed countries,

Recalling further the Outcome of the Conference on the World Financial and Economic Crisis and Its Impact on Development, where it was recognized that the economic and social progress achieved by the least developed countries in recent years is being threatened by the global economic and financial crisis and that, in order to adequately respond to the crisis, developing countries, especially the least developed countries, will need a larger share of any additional resources, both short-term liquidity and long-term development financing,

Reaffirming that the Programme of Action constitutes a fundamental framework for a strong global partnership, whose goal is to accelerate sustained economic growth, sustainable development and poverty eradication in the least developed countries,

Urging the least developed countries to strengthen country ownership in the implementation of the Programme of Action by, inter alia, translating its goals and targets into specific measures within their national development frameworks and poverty eradication strategies, including, where they exist, poverty reduction strategy papers, promoting broad-based and inclusive dialogue on development with relevant stakeholders, including civil society and the private sector, and enhancing domestic resource mobilization and aid management,

Urging development partners to fully implement, in a timely manner, commitments in the Programme of Action, and to exercise individual best efforts to continue to increase their financial and technical support for its implementation,

1. *Takes note* of the report of the Secretary-General on the implementation of the Programme of Action for the Least Developed Countries for the Decade 2001–2010;

2. *Also takes note* of the progress being made in the preparatory process for the Fourth United Nations Conference on the Least Developed Countries;

3. *Welcomes and accepts with appreciation* the offer of the Government of Turkey to host the Conference;

4. *Decides* to convene the Conference in the first half of 2011 for a duration of five days, from within existing resources, at a venue and time to be determined in consultation with the host Government;

5. *Also decides* that the meeting of the intergovernmental preparatory committee envisaged in paragraph 5 of resolution 63/227 will be organized in New York in two parts, from 10 to 14 January 2011 and from 18 to 25 April 2011, each of five working days;

6. *Requests* the Office of the High Representative for the Least Developed Countries, Landlocked Developing Countries and Small Island Developing States, as the focal point for the preparations for the Conference, as requested in resolution 63/227, to ensure effective, efficient and timely preparations for the Conference and to further mobilize and coordinate the active involvement of the organizations of the United Nations system;

7. *Requests* the organizations of the United Nations system, including the United Nations Development Programme, the United Nations Conference on Trade and Development, the regional commissions, the specialized agencies, and funds and programmes, and invites the Bretton Woods institutions, the World Trade Organization and other relevant international and regional organizations, within their respective mandates, to provide necessary support and actively contribute to the preparatory process and to the Conference itself;

8. *Requests* the Secretary-General to ensure, as appropriate, the full involvement of resident coordinators and country teams in preparations for the Conference, in particular in country- and regional-level preparations;

9. *Invites* Governments, intergovernmental and non-governmental organizations, major groups and other donors to contribute to the Trust Fund for the participation of representatives of the least developed countries in both the preparatory process and the Conference itself;

10. *Recognizes* the importance of the contributions of all relevant stakeholders, including parliaments, civil society, non-governmental organizations and the private sector, to the Conference and its preparatory process, stresses, in this regard, the need for active participation, including from the least developed countries, and invites donors to make appropriate contributions for that purpose;

11. *Requests* the Secretary-General, with the assistance of concerned organizations and bodies of the United Nations system, including the Department of Public Information of the Secretariat, in collaboration with the Office of the High Representative for the Least Developed Countries, Landlocked Developing Countries and Small Island Developing States, to take the necessary measures to intensify their public information efforts and other appropriate initiatives to enhance public awareness in favour of the Conference, including by highlighting its objectives and its significance;

12. *Emphasizes* the importance of country-level preparations as a critical input to the preparatory process for the Conference and the implementation of and follow-up to its outcome, and calls upon the Governments of the least developed countries to submit their reports in a timely manner;

13. *Requests* the executive secretaries of the Economic Commission for Africa and the Economic and Social Commission for Asia and the Pacific, in close coordination and cooperation with the Office of the High Representative for the Least Developed Countries, Landlocked Developing Countries and Small Island Developing States, to provide the necessary substantive and organizational arrangements and to organize the regional-level preparatory review meetings in the context of the annual sessions of 2010 of their respective commissions, as called for by the General Assembly in its resolution 63/227;

14. *Requests* the Secretary-General to submit to the General Assembly at its sixty-fifth session a report on the further implementation of the Programme of Action for the Least Developed Countries for the Decade 2001–2010 as well as on the implementation of the present resolution, including the state of the substantive, organizational and logistic preparations for the Conference.

Small island developing States

During 2009, UN bodies continued to review progress in the implementation of the Programme of Action for the Sustainable Development of Small Island Developing States (Barbados Programme of Action), adopted in 1994 [YUN 1994, p. 783]. Member States also reviewed the Mauritius Strategy for the Further Implementation of the Programme of Action for the Sustainable Development of Small Island Developing States, adopted by the 2005 International Meeting to Review the Implementation of the 1994 Programme of Action [YUN 2005, p. 946].

Commission on Sustainable Development consideration. Recalling General Assembly resolution 63/213 [YUN 2008, p. 946], the Commission on Sustainable Development, on 15 May [E/2009/29 (res. 17/2)], resolved to use the Small Island Developing States Day (10 May) in 2010 as a preparatory committee meeting for the high-level review, in September 2010, of progress made in addressing the vulnerabilities of small island developing States through the implementation of the Mauritius Strategy. The meeting would consider a synthesis report to be prepared by the Secretary-General.

ECONOMIC AND SOCIAL COUNCIL ACTION

On 29 July [meeting 42], the Economic and Social Council adopted **resolution 2009/17** [draft: E/2009/L.35 & E/2009/SR.42] without vote [agenda item 13 *(a)*].

Review of United Nations support for small island developing States

The Economic and Social Council,

Guided by the Charter of the United Nations,

Recalling the Rio Declaration on Environment and Development, Agenda 21, the Programme for the Further Implementation of Agenda 21, the Johannesburg Declaration on Sustainable Development and the Plan of Implementation of the World Summit on Sustainable Development ("Johannesburg Plan of Implementation"), as well as the outcomes of other relevant major United Nations conferences and summits,

Recalling also the Declaration of Barbados, the Programme of Action for the Sustainable Development of Small Island Developing States and the Mauritius Strategy for the Further Implementation of the Programme of Action for the Sustainable Development of Small Island Developing States,

Recalling further General Assembly resolution 63/213 of 19 December 2008 and reaffirming the importance of follow-up to and implementation of the Mauritius Strategy for the Further Implementation of the Programme of Action for the Sustainable Development of Small Island Developing States, and reaffirming also the importance of the two-day high-level review, to be conducted at the sixty-fifth session of the Assembly, of the progress made in addressing the vulnerabilities of small island developing States,

Recognizing that, although they are afflicted by economic difficulties and confronted by development imperatives similar to those of developing countries generally, small island developing States also have their own peculiar vulnerabilities and characteristics, which render the difficulties that they face in the pursuit of sustainable development particularly severe and complex,

Noting that the United Nations designation "small island developing States" is a useful and important tool for recognizing and responding to the particular vulnerabilities and characteristics of small island developing States and for assisting them in their pursuit of sustainable development,

1. *Requests* all relevant subsidiary bodies of the Economic and Social Council, as appropriate and in accordance with their relevant mandates, to contribute to the report requested by the General Assembly in paragraph 21 of its resolution 63/213;

2. *Invites* the Committee for Development Policy to consider the findings of the report requested by the General Assembly in paragraph 21 of its resolution 63/213, as well as supporting documentation, and to submit its independent views and perspectives on United Nations support for small island developing States to the Economic and Social Council, prior to its substantive session of 2010, and notes, in this regard, that the Secretary-General may wish to provide the Committee with supplemental information on United Nations institutional, administrative and technical support for small island developing States;

3. *Decides* to consider the issue at its substantive session of 2010 and to make available a summary of the debate held during that session, together with the independent views and perspectives of the Committee for Development Policy, as a contribution to the two-day high-level review, to be conducted at the sixty-fifth session of the General Assembly, of the progress made in addressing the vulnerabilities of small island developing States.

Report of Secretary-General. In an August report [A/64/278], submitted in accordance with General Assembly resolution 63/213 [YUN 2008, p. 946], the Secretary-General presented an overview of arrangements being made for the high-level review (see above). The report also provided an account of the continuing efforts of small island developing States, with the support of the UN system and the international community, for follow-up to and implementation of the Mauritius Strategy.

The Secretary-General concluded that concerted efforts were being made by small island developing States to implement meaningful policies and adaptation strategies to address their vulnerabilities and build resilience at the national level. It was expected that the forthcoming review process would promote a thorough examination and assessment of the ongoing and emerging economic, social and environmental vulnerabilities of small island developing States and provide an opportunity for them to showcase their successes and demonstrate the continuing shortfalls in capacity which undermined their efforts to pursue a sustainable development path or to respond to exogenous shocks. The scaling-up of support from the international community, especially through concessionary financing, the transfer of technology and support for capacity-building would enhance the efforts of small island developing States to achieve sustainable development. Work in preparation for the five-year review of the Mauritius Strategy was progressing steadily, with strong involvement and commitment on the part of UN system partners and regional organizations, and with the support of the international community. The fullest participation of all Member States, the UN system, international organizations and civil society was strongly encouraged to ensure the success of the high-level meeting in reviewing progress made by small island developing States in strengthening indigenous capacity to address their vulnerabilities, and in assessing how those Member States might best be served through the continued support of the international community. It was also anticipated that the confluence of important, mutually reinforcing review processes during 2010, notably those relating to implementation of the MDGs, biodiversity and the least developed countries, would result in a richer debate and a more meaningful outcome to the review of the Mauritius Strategy.

GENERAL ASSEMBLY ACTION

On 21 December [meeting 66], the General Assembly, on the recommendation of the Second Committee [A/64/420/Add.2], adopted **resolution 64/199** without vote [agenda item 53 *(b)*].

Follow-up to and implementation of the Mauritius Strategy for the Further Implementation of the Programme of Action for the Sustainable Development of Small Island Developing States

The General Assembly,

Reaffirming the Declaration of Barbados and the Programme of Action for the Sustainable Development of Small Island Developing States, adopted by the Global Conference on the Sustainable Development of Small Island Developing States, and recalling its resolution 49/122 of 19 December 1994 on the Global Conference,

Reaffirming also the Mauritius Declaration and the Mauritius Strategy for the Further Implementation of the Programme of Action for the Sustainable Development of Small Island Developing States ("Mauritius Strategy for Implementation"), adopted by the International Meeting to Review the Implementation of the Programme of Action for the Sustainable Development of Small Island Developing States on 14 January 2005,

Recalling its resolutions 59/311 of 14 July 2005, 60/194 of 22 December 2005, 61/196 of 20 December 2006, 62/191 of 19 December 2007 and 63/213 of 19 December 2008,

Recalling also the 2005 World Summit Outcome,

Reaffirming that the Commission on Sustainable Development is the primary intergovernmental forum for monitoring the implementation of the Barbados Programme of Action and the Mauritius Strategy for Implementation,

Reaffirming also that the adverse effects of climate change and sea-level rise present significant and specific risks to the sustainable development of small island developing States, that the effects of climate change may threaten the very existence of some of them and that, given their vulnerability, adaptation to the adverse effects of climate change and sea-level rise therefore remains a major priority for small island developing States,

Recognizing the urgent need to increase the level of resources provided to small island developing States for the effective implementation of the Mauritius Strategy for Implementation,

Underlining the importance of developing and strengthening national sustainable development strategies in small island developing States,

Recalling the decision to review progress made in addressing the vulnerabilities of small island developing States through the implementation of the Mauritius Strategy for Implementation at the sixty-fifth session of the General Assembly,

1. *Takes note* of the report of the Secretary-General on the follow-up to and implementation of the Mauritius Strategy for Implementation;

2. *Reaffirms* its decision to convene a two-day high-level review in September 2010 as part of its sixty-fifth session, to assess progress made in addressing the vulnerabilities of small island developing States through the implementation of the Mauritius Strategy for Implementation;

3. *Decides* that the high-level review will be structured around an opening plenary meeting, followed by two multi-stakeholder round-table sessions, an interactive dialogue on cross-regional perspectives and a closing plenary meeting;

4. *Also decides* that the review will be chaired by the President of the General Assembly, and requests the President of the General Assembly to present a concise draft political declaration based on, inter alia, inputs from the preparatory meetings, at an appropriate date to enable sufficient consideration and agreement by Member States;

5. *Reaffirms* that the review should provide the international community with an opportunity to conduct a thorough assessment of the progress made, lessons learned and constraints encountered in the implementation of the Mauritius Strategy for Implementation and to agree on what needs to be done to further address the vulnerabilities of small island developing States;

6. *Decides* to convene regional preparatory meetings of small island developing States in their respective regions, as well as an interregional meeting for all small island developing States, to undertake the review of the Mauritius Strategy for Implementation at the national and regional levels, and also decides that, for this purpose, the Department of Economic and Social Affairs of the Secretariat, through its Small Island Developing States Unit, the Office of the High Representative for the Least Developed Countries, Landlocked Developing Countries and Small Island Developing States and the relevant agencies of the United Nations system, including regional commissions, within their respective mandates and existing resources, should organize, facilitate and provide necessary support to the review process at the national, regional and international levels;

7. *Requests* the Secretary-General, in this context, to provide a comprehensive report on progress made and on the continuing challenges faced in the implementation of the Mauritius Strategy for Implementation, noting the importance of paragraphs 87, 88 and 101 of the Mauritius Strategy and of taking into account cross-cutting implementation issues;

8. *Decides* that the meeting of the preparatory committee for the high-level review will be convened during the eighteenth session of the Commission on Sustainable Development, in accordance with Commission resolution 17/2 of 15 May 2009;

9. *Invites* the participation of associate members of regional commissions in the high-level review, subject to the rules of procedure of the General Assembly, and in the preparatory process thereof, as observers, in the same capacity specified for their participation at the International Meeting to Review the Implementation of the Programme of Action for the Sustainable Development of Small Island Developing States, held in Mauritius from 10 to 14 January 2005;

10. *Invites* all Member States and States members of the specialized agencies, relevant regional and international agencies and organizations, in accordance with the rules of procedure of the Commission on Sustainable Development and the General Assembly, to participate fully in the preparatory activities and the high-level review;

11. *Urges* that representation and participation at the high-level review be at the highest possible level, including with the participation of Heads of State or Government;

12. *Invites* heads of the United Nations funds and programmes, the specialized agencies and regional commissions, as well as heads of intergovernmental organizations and entities having observer status in the General Assembly, to participate, as appropriate, in the review, in accordance with the rules and procedures as established by the General Assembly;

13. *Stresses* the need for the effective participation of civil society, in particular non-governmental organizations and other major groups, in preparing for the high-level review, as well as the need to ensure appropriate arrangements, taking into account the practice and experience gained at the International Meeting held in Mauritius, for their substantive contributions to and active involvement in the preparatory meetings and the high-level review, and in this context invites the President of the General Assembly, in consultation with Member States, to propose to Member States appropriate modalities for their effective involvement in the high-level review;

14. *Encourages* relevant major groups organizations that are not currently accredited by the Economic and Social Council to submit applications to participate as observers in the high-level review, as well as its preparatory meeting, in accordance with the rules of procedure of the General Assembly, following the accreditation procedures established during the International Meeting held in Mauritius;

15. *Acknowledges with appreciation* the contribution of Member States and other international donors to support activities related to small island developing States, including through the voluntary trust fund;

16. *Invites* Governments, intergovernmental and non-governmental organizations, other major groups and other donors to contribute to the voluntary trust fund for the purpose of assisting small island developing States in participating fully and effectively in the high-level review and the various preparatory processes;

17. *Urges* Governments and all relevant international and regional organizations, United Nations funds and programmes, the specialized agencies and regional commissions, international financial institutions and the Global Environment Facility, as well as other intergovernmental organizations and major groups, to take timely action for the effective implementation of and follow-up to the Mauritius Declaration and the Mauritius Strategy for Implementation, including the further development and operationalization of concrete projects and programmes;

18. *Calls for* the full and effective implementation of the commitments, programmes and targets adopted at the International Meeting to Review the Implementation of the Programme of Action for the Sustainable Development of Small Island Developing States and, to this end, for the fulfilment of the provisions for the means of implementation, as contained in the Mauritius Strategy for Implementation, and encourages small island developing States and their development partners to continue to consult widely in order to develop further concrete projects and programmes for the implementation of the Mauritius Strategy for Implementation;

19. *Encourages* enhanced, closer and early consultation with small island developing States in the planning and coordination, as appropriate, of the activities related to the high-level review of the Mauritius Strategy for Implementation, and emphasizes the importance of enhanced interaction between small island developing States and the relevant agencies of the United Nations system addressing issues concerning small island developing States;

20. *Reiterates* the importance of providing the Small Island Developing States Unit with adequate, stable and predictable funding to facilitate the full and effective implementation of its mandates in accordance with the priority accorded to the Unit and in view of the demand for its services, in particular with respect to the provision of assistance, technical cooperation services and support to small island developing States;

21. *Also reiterates* the importance of ensuring sufficient and sustainable staffing of the Small Island Developing States Unit so that it may undertake its broad range of mandated functions with a view to facilitating the full and effective implementation of the Mauritius Strategy for Implementation;

22. *Calls for* the provision of new and additional voluntary resources to ensure the revitalization and sustainability of the Small Island Developing States Information Network, and in this regard welcomes the contribution of the Government of Spain to support the revitalization of the Network;

23. *Calls upon* the international community to enhance support for the efforts of small island developing States to adapt to the adverse impacts of climate change, including through the provision of dedicated sources of financing, capacity-building and the transfer of appropriate technologies to address climate change;

24. *Reiterates its request* to the relevant agencies of the United Nations system, within their respective mandates, to intensify efforts aimed at mainstreaming the Mauritius Strategy for Implementation in their work programmes and to establish a focal point for matters related to small island developing States within their respective secretariats to support coordinated implementation of the Programme of Action at the national, subregional, regional and global levels;

25. *Calls upon* the international community to enhance its support for the implementation of the programme of work on island biodiversity as a set of actions to address characteristics and problems that are specific to islands, adopted by the Conference of the Parties to the Convention on Biological Diversity at its eighth meeting, in 2006;

26. *Calls for* continued support for the design and implementation of national sustainable development strategies in all small island developing States;

27. *Encourages* the implementation of partnership initiatives, within the framework of the Mauritius Strategy for Implementation, in support of the sustainable development of small island developing States;

28. *Invites* the small island developing States to consider, at their relevant intergovernmental meetings, assessments of and relevant contributions to the review process;

29. *Calls upon* the international community to support the efforts to review progress made in addressing the vulnerabilities of small island developing States through the implementation of the Mauritius Strategy for Implementation, including by facilitating the participation of small island developing States in review activities;

30. *Decides* to include in the provisional agenda of its sixty-fifth session, under the item entitled "Sustainable development", the sub-item entitled "Follow-up to and implementation of the Mauritius Strategy for the Further Implementation of the Programme of Action for the Sustainable Development of Small Island Developing States".

Communication. In a letter to the Secretary-General dated 20 October [A/C.2/64/11], Grenada transmitted the Alliance of Small Island States (AOSIS) Declaration on Climate Change 2009, adopted at the AOSIS Summit on Climate Change (New York, 21 September).

Landlocked developing countries

Report of Secretary-General. In response to General Assembly resolution 63/228 [YUN 2008, p. 954], the Secretary-General in August reported [A/64/268] on the implementation of the Almaty Programme of Action: Addressing the Special Needs of Landlocked Developing Countries within a New Global Framework for Transit Transport Cooperation for Landlocked and Transit Developing Countries, adopted in 2003 by the International Ministerial Conference of Landlocked and Transit Developing Countries and Donor Countries and International Financial and Development Institutions on Transit Transport Cooperation [YUN 2003, p. 875]. The report described the overall socio-economic situation in landlocked developing countries and the four priority areas of the Pro-

gramme of Action: fundamental transit policy issues; infrastructure development and maintenance; international trade and trade facilitation; and international support measures. It also outlined the implementation and review of the Programme of Action.

The Secretary-General stated that in response to the declaration on the midterm review of the Programme of Action adopted by the Assembly in its resolution 63/2 [YUN 2008, p. 949], OHRLLS convened the Fifth Inter-agency Consultative Meeting on the Almaty Programme Implementation (Geneva, 2 March). The Meeting endorsed a matrix containing activities and programmes to be implemented by UN system and other international organizations in order to ensure better coordination of and synergy in their efforts regarding intergovernmental processes; transit policy issues; transit transport infrastructure; international trade and trade facilitation; and resources mobilization. The matrix would be reviewed regularly to monitor progress.

UN system organizations continued their efforts to develop internationally acceptable indicators to measure progress in implementing the Almaty Programme of Action. OHRLLS compiled revised statistics with the latest available data on macroeconomic variables, ODA, debt sustainability and participation in international trade, as well as selected transport infrastructure indicators. The Economic and Social Commission for Asia and the Pacific expanded its training and advisory services on the practical applications of the time/cost-distance methodology as a tool for identifying, isolating and addressing the major bottlenecks impeding smooth and efficient cross-border transport.

The Secretary-General concluded that inherent geographical difficulties and poorly developed transport, communications and border management and logistics systems in both landlocked and transit developing countries hampered their productivity, growth, and poverty reduction. High trade transaction costs lay at the core of the continued marginalization of the landlocked developing countries within the world economy. Lack of export diversification, and concentration on few export commodities, associated with low foreign-exchange reserves and dependence on external financial flows, exposed them to severe external shocks. The Almaty Programme of Action remained a sound global framework for establishing genuine partnerships at the bilateral, regional and international levels aimed at addressing the special needs of landlocked developing countries by establishing efficient transit transport systems. Its implementation and that of the declaration on the midterm review of the Programme of Action should be accelerated.

The Secretary-General recommended pursuing policies to enhance domestic competitiveness of landlocked developing countries through investment in building productive capacities, reducing commodity dependence, improving transit transport infrastructure, reforming transit policies, liberalizing transport services and implementing trade facilitation measures at national and regional levels. Broader and more effective cooperation between landlocked and transit developing countries was necessary to ensure a harmonized approach to the design, implementation and monitoring of trade and transport facilitation policy reforms across borders. The role of regional and subregional organizations should be strengthened, as they were crucial to the development of regional integrated infrastructure networks, completion of missing links, implementation of trade facilitation measures and broader application of information technology.

The United Nations and other international organizations should provide greater support to landlocked and transit developing countries through technical assistance programmes in transit transport and trade facilitation. Landlocked and transit developing countries should also continue to make efforts to accede to multilateral conventions in the area of transit transport and trade. There was a need for additional international development assistance in the form of flexible, concessional and fast-disbursing financial resources to assist landlocked developing countries facing financing gaps. Bilateral and multilateral donors should increase their financial support to fill infrastructure gaps in landlocked and transit developing countries through grants and concessional loans so as to improve the level of intraregional connectivity, with a view to ensuring completion, upgrading and maintenance of strategic sea corridors extended into landlocked countries.

Special attention should be given to landlocked developing countries in the context of the Aid for Trade initiative [YUN 2005, p. 1043]. A development-supportive accession of landlocked developing countries to the World Trade Organization should be ensured through targeted technical assistance. The United Nations and other international organizations should provide greater support for the strengthening of the negotiating capacities of landlocked developing countries and their ability to implement trade facilitation measures. Strong political commitment was needed to promote combined climate and development goals and ensure increasing adaptive resilience with respect to the unavoidable consequences of climate change.

Communications. In separate letters of 5 October, Mali transmitted the communiqué adopted by the Ministers for Foreign Affairs of the States members of the Group of Landlocked Developing Countries at their eighth annual meeting (New York, 25 September) [A/C.2/64/4] and the rules of procedure adopted by them at the same meeting [A/C.2/64/5].

GENERAL ASSEMBLY ACTION

On 21 December [meeting 66], the General Assembly, on the recommendation of the Second Committee [A/64/423/Add.2], adopted **resolution 64/214** without vote [agenda item 56 *(b)*].

Groups of countries in special situations: specific actions related to the particular needs and problems of landlocked developing countries: outcome of the International Ministerial Conference of Landlocked and Transit Developing Countries and Donor Countries and International Financial and Development Institutions on Transit Transport Cooperation

The General Assembly,

Recalling its resolutions 58/201 of 23 December 2003, 60/208 of 22 December 2005, 61/212 of 20 December 2006, 62/204 of 19 December 2007 and 63/228 of 19 December 2008,

Recalling also the United Nations Millennium Declaration and the 2005 World Summit Outcome,

Recalling further the Almaty Declaration and the Almaty Programme of Action: Addressing the Special Needs of Landlocked Developing Countries within a New Global Framework for Transit Transport Cooperation for Landlocked and Transit Developing Countries,

Recalling its resolution 63/2 of 3 October 2008, by which it adopted the Declaration of the high-level meeting of the sixty-third session of the General Assembly on the midterm review of the Almaty Programme of Action,

Taking note of the Communiqué of the Eighth Annual Ministerial Meeting of Landlocked Developing Countries, held at United Nations Headquarters on 25 September 2009,

Recalling the New Partnership for Africa's Development, an initiative for accelerating regional economic cooperation and development, as many landlocked and transit developing countries are located in Africa,

Recognizing that the lack of territorial access to the sea, aggravated by remoteness from world markets, and prohibitive transit costs and risks continue to impose serious constraints on export earnings, private capital inflow and domestic resource mobilization of landlocked developing countries and therefore adversely affect their overall growth and socio-economic development,

Expressing support to those landlocked developing countries that are emerging from conflict, with a view to enabling them to rehabilitate and reconstruct, as appropriate, political, social and economic infrastructure and to assisting them in achieving their development priorities in accordance with the goals and targets of the Almaty Programme of Action,

Recognizing that the primary responsibility for establishing effective transit systems rests with the landlocked and transit developing countries,

Reaffirming that the Almaty Programme of Action constitutes a fundamental framework for genuine partnerships between landlocked and transit developing countries and their development partners at the national, bilateral, subregional, regional and global levels,

1. *Takes note* of the report of the Secretary-General on the implementation of the Almaty Programme of Action;

2. *Reaffirms* the right of access of landlocked countries to and from the sea and freedom of transit through the territory of transit countries by all means of transport, in accordance with the applicable rules of international law;

3. *Also reaffirms* that transit countries, in the exercise of their full sovereignty over their territory, have the right to take all measures necessary to ensure that the rights and facilities provided for landlocked countries in no way infringe upon their legitimate interests;

4. *Calls upon* landlocked and transit developing countries to take all appropriate measures, as set out in the Declaration of the high-level meeting of the sixty-third session of the General Assembly on the midterm review of the Almaty Programme of Action, to speed up the implementation of the Almaty Programme of Action;

5. *Reaffirms its full commitment* to address urgently the special development needs of and challenges faced by the landlocked developing countries through the full, timely and effective implementation of the Almaty Programme of Action, as contained in the Declaration on the midterm review;

6. *Invites* Member States, organizations of the United Nations system and other relevant international, regional and subregional organizations and multilateral financial and development institutions to accelerate the implementation of the specific actions in the five priorities agreed upon in the Almaty Programme of Action and those contained in the Declaration on the midterm review;

7. *Acknowledges* that landlocked and transit developing countries in Africa, Asia, Europe and Latin America have strengthened their policy and governance reform efforts and that donor countries, financial and development institutions and international and regional organizations have paid greater attention to the establishment of efficient transit systems;

8. *Notes with concern* that, despite the progress made, landlocked developing countries continue to be marginalized in international trade, which prevents them from fully harnessing the potential of trade as an engine of sustained economic growth and development, and face challenges in their efforts to establish efficient transit transport systems and achieve their development goals, including the internationally agreed development goals and the Millennium Development Goals;

9. *Expresses concern* that the economic growth and social well-being of landlocked developing countries remain very vulnerable to external shocks and to the multiple challenges the international community faces, and stresses the need for the international community to enhance development assistance to landlocked developing countries;

10. *Calls upon* donors and multilateral and regional financial and development institutions to provide landlocked and transit developing countries with appropriate, substantial and better-coordinated technical and financial assistance, particularly in the form of grants or concessionary loans, for the implementation of the Almaty Programme of Action, in particular for the construction, maintenance and improvement of their transport, storage and other transit-related facilities, including alternative routes, completion of missing links and improved communications, so as to promote subregional, regional and interregional projects and programmes;

11. *Stresses* the need to attract private investment, including foreign direct investment, and that private sector participation through co-financing can play a catalytic role in this regard, and recalls that, notwithstanding the increase of flows in foreign direct investment, private sector involvement in infrastructure development still has considerable potential;

12. *Underscores* the importance of international trade and trade facilitation as one of the priorities of the Almaty Programme of Action, and notes that the ongoing World Trade Organization Doha Round negotiations on trade facilitation, particularly on the relevant articles of the General Agreement on Tariffs and Trade, such as those referred to in the Declaration on the midterm review, are important for landlocked developing countries to gain a more efficient flow of goods and services as well as improved international competitiveness resulting from lower transaction costs;

13. *Calls upon* the development partners to effectively operationalize the Aid for Trade Initiative so as to support trade facilitation measures and trade-related technical assistance, as well as the diversification of export products through the development of small and medium-sized enterprises and private-sector involvement in landlocked developing countries;

14. *Encourages* the international community to enhance efforts to facilitate access to and encourage the transfer of technologies related to transit transport systems, including information and communications technology;

15. *Encourages* the further strengthening of South-South cooperation and triangular cooperation with the involvement of donors, as well as cooperation among subregional and regional organizations, in support of the efforts of landlocked and transit developing countries towards achieving the full and effective implementation of the Almaty Programme of Action;

16. *Encourages* landlocked and transit developing countries to pursue the harmonization of trade and transit transport facilitation procedures and to continue to make efforts to accede to relevant multilateral conventions in the area of transit transport and trade;

17. *Calls upon* the relevant organizations of the United Nations system, the regional commissions, the United Nations Development Programme and the United Nations Conference on Trade and Development, and invites other international organizations, including the World Bank, the regional development banks, the World Customs Organization, the World Trade Organization, regional economic integration organizations, and other relevant regional and subregional organizations, to further integrate the Almaty Programme of Action into their relevant programmes of work, taking full account of the Declaration on the midterm review, and encourages them to continue, as appropriate, within their respective mandates, their support to the landlocked and transit developing countries, inter alia, through well-coordinated and coherent technical assistance programmes in transit transport and trade facilitation;

18. *Encourages* the Office of the High Representative for the Least Developed Countries, Landlocked Developing Countries and Small Island Developing States to continue to ensure coordinated follow-up to and effective

monitoring and reporting on the implementation of the Almaty Programme of Action, in line with General Assembly resolution 57/270 B of 23 June 2003, and to step up its advocacy efforts directed towards raising international awareness and mobilizing resources, as well as to further develop cooperation and coordination with organizations within the United Nations system in order to ensure the timely and effective implementation of the Almaty Programme of Action and the Declaration on the midterm review;

19. *Welcomes* the establishment of the international think tank for the landlocked developing countries in Ulaanbaatar to enhance analytical capability within landlocked developing countries and to promote the exchange of experiences and best practices needed to maximize their coordinated efforts for the full and effective implementation of the Almaty Programme of Action and the Millennium Development Goals, and invites the Office of the High Representative for the Least Developed Countries, Landlocked Developing Countries and Small Island Developing States, other relevant organizations of the United Nations system, Member States, as well as relevant international and regional organizations, to assist the landlocked developing countries in implementing the activities of the international think tank;

20. *Encourages* donors and the international financial and development institutions, as well as private entities, to make voluntary contributions to the trust fund established by the Secretary-General to support the activities related to the follow-up to the implementation of the outcome of the Almaty International Ministerial Conference;

21. *Requests* the Secretary-General to submit to the General Assembly at its sixty-fifth session an analytical report on the implementation of the Almaty Programme of Action and the Declaration on the midterm review;

22. *Decides* to include in the provisional agenda of its sixty-fifth session the sub-item entitled "Specific actions related to the particular needs and problems of landlocked developing countries: outcome of the International Ministerial Conference of Landlocked and Transit Developing Countries and Donor Countries and International Financial and Development Institutions on Transit Transport Cooperation".

Chapter II

Operational activities for development

In 2009, the UN system continued to provide development assistance to developing countries and countries with economies in transition through the United Nations Development Programme (UNDP)— the central UN body for technical assistance. During the year, UNDP income fell to $5.79 billion, while overall expenditure increased to $5.53 billion. Total income for the United Nations Capital Development Fund (UNCDF) amounted to $36.2 million. At year's end, cumulative allocations to projects of the United Nations Fund for International Partnerships reached approximately $1.09 billion.

In May, the Secretary-General reported on progress in the implementation of General Assembly resolution 62/208 on the 2007 triennial comprehensive policy review of operational activities for development of the UN system. In June, the UNDP/United Nations Population Fund Executive Board extended the UNDP strategic plan, 2008–2011, until 2013.

In 2009, the United Nations Office for Project Services (UNOPS) delivered $1.1 billion through project implementation and spent $62.1 million administering it. The contribution to the operational reserve was $12 million, bringing the reserve to $42.1 million. In January, the Executive Board approved the revised UNOPS financial regulations and rules. In September, the Board endorsed the UNOPS strategic plan, 2010–2013, proposed by the UNOPS Executive Director in July.

The High-level United Nations Conference on South-South Cooperation was held at the United Nations Office at Nairobi from 1 to 3 December on the occasion of the thirtieth anniversary of the 1978 United Nations Conference on Technical Cooperation among Developing Countries. The Conference adopted the Nairobi outcome document, which reaffirmed the key role of the United Nations in supporting and promoting cooperation among developing countries, and reiterated that every country had the primary responsibility for its own development. The Assembly endorsed the Nairobi outcome document in December.

In 2009, 7,545 volunteers working for the UNDP-administered United Nations Volunteers (UNV) programme carried out 7,716 assignments in 128 countries. UNCDF conducted operations in 40 of the 49 least developed countries, with a particular focus on post-crisis countries.

In March, the Assembly confirmed the appointment of Helen Clark (New Zealand) as UNDP Administrator for a four-year term of office ending in April 2013.

System-wide activities

Operational activities segment of the Economic and Social Council

On 10 February (**decision 2009/206**), the Economic and Social Council decided to devote the work of the operational activities segment to progress on and implementation of General Assembly resolutions 62/208 [YUN 2007, p. 877] on the triennial comprehensive policy review of operational activities for development of the UN system and 63/232 [YUN 2008, p. 962] on operational activities for development. During its 2009 substantive session [A/64/3/Rev.1], the Council considered the question of operational activities of the United Nations for international development cooperation at meetings held from 15 to 17 July and on 22 July. The Council considered follow-up to policy recommendations of the Assembly and the Council; the reports of the Executive Boards of the United Nations Development Programme (UNDP)/United Nations Population Fund (UNFPA), the United Nations Children's Fund and the World Food Programme; and South-South cooperation for development.

Among the documents before the Council were the Secretary-General's reports on the comprehensive statistical analysis of the financing of operational activities for development of the UN system [A/64/75-E/2009/59]; actions taken by the executive boards and governing bodies of the UN funds, programmes and specialized agencies in the area of simplification and harmonization of the UN development system [E/2009/61]; results achieved and measures and processes implemented in follow-up to Assembly resolution 62/208 [E/2009/68]; the human resources challenges within the UN development system at the country level [E/2009/75]; and the functioning of the resident coordinator system, including costs and benefits [E/2009/76]. The Council also had before it a May note by the Secretary-General [E/2009/85] on the review of trends and perspectives in funding for development cooperation; and the report of the Joint Inspection Unit (JIU) on the national execution of technical cooperation projects [JIU/REP/2008/4], as contained in a June note by the Secretary-General [A/64/375-E/2009/103 & Corr.1].

On 15 July, the Council held a panel discussion on the economic, food and climate change crises and their effects on the achievement of the Millennium Development Goals (MDGs) [YUN 2000, p. 51]: the role of UN system support to national efforts; and a dialogue on UN system funding. On 16 July, it held a panel discussion with the heads of UN funds and programmes. On 17 July, the Council held a dialogue with UN country teams on strengthening the teams' support to public health.

Implementation of resolution 62/208

In April [A/64/75-E/2009/59], the Secretary-General issued a report on the comprehensive statistical analysis of the financing of operational activities for development of the UN system for 2007, which was to be read in conjunction with his report (see below) on the implementation of General Assembly resolution 62/208 [YUN 2007, p. 877] on the 2007 triennial comprehensive policy review of operational activities for development of the UN system [ibid., p. 874]. It contained information on the 37 UN system entities that reported funding for operational activities for development and examined the extent to which such entities relied on a limited set of donors to fund their operational activities. The report also outlined plans for strengthening future reports towards a comprehensive and sustainable UN system-wide financial data and reporting system.

On 7 May [E/2009/68] the Secretary-General issued the first progress report on the implementation of Assembly resolution 62/208. It was based on the Secretary-General's 2008 report on the management process for the implementation of resolution 62/208 [YUN 2008, p. 958]. The report provided an overview of progress achieved, and information on funding for UN system operational activities for development and the contribution of UN operational activities to national capacity development in the areas of capacity-building and development, South-South cooperation, gender equality and women's empowerment, and the transition from relief to development. It also discussed improved functioning of the UN development system in coherence, effectiveness and relevance; regional coordination; transaction costs and efficiency; country-level capacity; and evaluation of operational activities for development. An annex to the report contained a matrix setting out actions taken by the UN system to implement resolution 62/208. Overall, significant advances had been made in implementing the policy review since 2008. System-wide coordination and the mobilization of UN system capacities at all levels was improved through the streamlining of inter-agency governance and management structures and the development of mutual accountability frameworks,

tools and joint programming operational documents, as well as the mobilization of common resources and funding instruments. The policy review's emphasis on national ownership and alignment of the UN country-level programming process with national systems was reflected in the programming guidance issued by the United Nations Development Group (UNDG), and there were indications of greater alignment of United Nations Development Assistance Frameworks (UNDAFs) with national processes.

Among the remaining challenges was the imbalance between core and non-core resources received by the UN system, which persisted against the backdrop of growing concerns about the possible negative impact of the global economic crisis on UN system aid and funding. Further progress needed to be made in supporting UN country teams in such areas as capacity development, the use of South-South cooperation as a modality for programme delivery and improving coordination, and strengthening of support structures in situations of transition from relief to development. A growing number of normative mandates needed to be implemented at the country level, which would require greater substantive capacities and coherence in approaches. Consistency in the quality of UNDAFs needed to be ensured. Responses from Headquarters to innovations at the country level on simplification and harmonization in terms of procedural and regulatory policy changes needed to keep pace with those developments. The combined economic, food security and climate change crises threatened development and challenged the UN system to provide strategic and cohesive support to Governments.

On 15 May [E/2009/76], the Secretary-General submitted a report on the functioning of the resident coordinator system, including costs and benefits. The report assessed progress since the 2008 report [YUN 2008, p. 958] and reviewed participation and support to the functioning of the system by UN system organizations, with a special focus on coordination in countries in crisis and post-crisis situations. It discussed the enhanced management of the resident coordinator system; examined the support provided by the UN system to the resident/humanitarian coordinator system in situations of early recovery and transition from relief to recovery; outlined the work of the resident coordinator system in contributing to national development priorities and increased efficiency in business processes; and provided information on the costs and funding of country-level coordination. Total expenditure on UN operational activities in 2007, the latest year for which full system-wide data were available, totalled $17.4 billion. Actual support for the UN resident coordinator system from or through UNDP in 2007 totalled $92 million, $76 million of which was provided by UNDP and $16 million of which was raised from donors by the United Nations Development Operations Coordination Office. Coordination costs in 2007 stood at 0.53 per cent of the total expenditures for UN system operational activities. Expenditures for the UN resident coordinator system from or through UNDP amounted to $111.3 million in 2008.

The report concluded that, over the previous two years, progress had been made in enhancing the functioning of the resident coordinator system, including support, in the areas of: management and accountability; resident coordinator recruitment, selection and training; system-wide participation; and coherence in country programming and harmonization in country business processes. Innovations from "Delivering as one" pilot countries [YUN 2007, p. 1418] were producing better tools and business practices. UNDG would further refine and develop additional operational frameworks, guidance and tools in the 2009–2010 period.

The report identified a number of remaining challenges. In general, there was a need to review the appropriate level and type of support that a resident coordinator office required in order to perform effectively in different country contexts, especially in complex situations. Although resident coordinators were expected to function on behalf of the the UN system as a whole, and were subject to performance review by various agencies, there was a need to build on the resident coordinator management and accountability system in order to identify resources and contributions by UN system members in support of the resident coordinator system and to balance mutual accountability between the resident coordinator and UN country team. There was a need for more systematic and consistent reporting among agencies of their participation and support to the resident coordinator system as part of their strategic plans, programme budgets and reports to their governing bodies. Headquarters units/mechanisms needed to coordinate effectively in order to provide relevant and efficient support and guidance to the resident coordinators in managing the UN system country strategy in response to national priorities, especially in crisis and post-crisis transition countries.

The report recommended, among other measures, that the Economic and Social Council might wish to request UNDG to undertake a review of the scope of country coordination functions and requirements in a range of country settings, including in post-crisis transition countries, and establish standards for the type, level of staff and operational support capacities that would be needed to effectively fulfil those functions. Based on such an assessment, the Council might wish to ask UNDG to develop a strategy for mobilizing resources to support functioning resident coordinator offices.

A 15 May report [E/2009/75] on human resources challenges within the UN development system, prepared in collaboration with UN system organizations and the International Civil Service Commission (ICSC), focused on how the UN system could best meet the demands of programme countries while recognizing the differences and unique country requirements. UN country capacities needed to be adjusted regularly so that the system's operational support remained fully aligned with development priorities and policies in various countries. To that end, the UN system needed to implement policies related to workforce planning, development and reprofiling, and to facilitate mobility and redeployment of staff at the global, regional and country levels.

The report provided information on the diverse and increasingly field-based UN development system workforce. Between 2004 and 2007, the number of international staff members serving with organizations of the UN common system increased by 33 per cent; most of the increase was in the field. The number of staff in offices other than those established at headquarters expanded by 31 per cent for the Professional and above category and by 96 per cent for the General Service category. At the end of 2007, the majority of UN development system staff was located in the field. UN system organizations were increasing the number of field offices and staff as a way to respond to the needs of recipient countries in a timely and efficient manner. Policies aimed at deploying staff to the field were in some cases part of broader reforms of the organizations.

The report identified six human resources challenges faced by the UN system that should be taken into account in designing comprehensive human resources policies and strategies: aligning UN response capacities to national priorities; optimizing the recruitment and career management of UN system staff; dealing with the multiple human resources policies and procedures across the UN system; planning for the succession of retiring staff members; ensuring staff security; and securing the equal representation of women.

The report recommended, among other measures, that the Economic and Social Council might wish to request UN system organizations to: mobilize adequate human resources to support the development of new UNDAFs and invite donors to provide support in that regard; adjust recruitment processes and intensify efforts to identify qualified national and international staff to be placed on a roster of candidates for rapid deployment to situations of transition from relief to development; support UNDG efforts to strengthen the capability of the UN system to attract, develop and retain suitable candidates for the post of resident coordinator; and make greater use of the United Nations System Staff College to train their staff, notably members of UN country teams. The Council might also wish to call upon UNDG and the Staff College to further develop training on capacity development, and encourage the UN system to conduct, when appropriate, assessments of human resources capacities in UN country teams to respond to UNDAF or country programme priorities. The Council might wish to encourage efforts by: UN system organizations, through UNDG, to make use of each other's training facilities, so as to maximize opportunities and substantive coverage of training offered to UN system staff; the United Nations System Chief Executives Board for Coordination (CEB), in collaboration with ICSC, to pursue its work on harmonizing the conditions of service for National Professional Officers; the UN system to intensify its efforts to achieve gender balance in appointments for positions that affect operational activities for development, including high-level (D-1 and D-2) and resident coordinator posts; and ICSC, CEB and the UN system to promote further research to inform policy decisions on key human resources management issues and develop indicators to monitor human resources effectiveness management in the UN common system. The Council might also wish to encourage the UN system to continue efforts to make human resources procedures coherent across the UN system through the CEB High-level Committee on Management (HLCM) Plan of Action for the Harmonization of Business Practices in the United Nations System [CEB/2008/HLCM/10], excerpts of which were contained in a June CEB report [CEB/2009/HLCM/HR/45/Rev.1].

In response to General Assembly resolution 59/250 [YUN 2004, p. 868] on the triennial comprehensive policy review of operational activities for development of the UN system, the Secretary-General, on 27 May [E/2009/85], submitted a note on the review of trends and perspectives in funding for development cooperation in six major areas: UN operational activities for development; multilateral and regional development banks; global funds; innovative sources of financing for development; South-South and triangular development cooperation; and private philanthropy. According to Organisation for Economic Cooperation and Development (OECD) Development Assistance Committee (DAC) figures released on 30 March, official development assistance (ODA) by DAC countries in 2008 reached $119.8 billion—the highest dollar figure ever recorded and an increase in real terms of 10.2 per cent over the previous year. However, since 2005, the ODA/gross national income (GNI) ratio had declined from 0.33 per cent to 0.30 per cent. A key factor explaining the volatility of ODA flows was debt relief, which reached $25 billion in 2005, declined to $9.6 billion in 2007 and in-

creased again to $11.3 billion in 2008. The 2008 ODA level of nearly $120 billion for DAC countries remained short of the $150 billion deemed necessary to attain the MDGs. The current outlook suggested that at least $10 billion to $15 billion had to be added to forward spending plans if donors were to meet the 2010 commitment of $130 billion in ODA (at constant 2004 prices). Net bilateral ODA from DAC donors to Africa in 2008 totalled $26 billion, of which $22 billion went to sub-Saharan Africa. Excluding volatile debt relief grants, bilateral aid to Africa and sub-Saharan Africa in 2008 rose in real terms by 10.6 per cent and 10 per cent, respectively.

The annual growth in contributions to UN operational activities for development slowed to 5.6 per cent in the 2002–2007 period, while non-UN multilateral ODA grew at 6.6 per cent and bilateral ODA at 6.1 per cent (in constant 2006 dollars). In 2007, total private grants from donor countries amounted to $18.5 billion, equivalent to almost 18 per cent of overall ODA flows. The volume of private grants as a share of overall ODA from OECD/DAC countries averaged an estimated 15 per cent, representing faster growth than overall ODA. There were early indications, however, that the global financial and economic crisis that began in 2008 was beginning to affect funding to international development cooperation, including the UN development system.

A notable long-term trend in the funding of UN operational activities for development was the decline in core resources as a share of overall contributions, from 37.1 per cent in 2002 to 28.8 per cent in 2007. The reliance on non-core resources, with the corresponding unpredictability of funding and timing of payments and the restricted use for which voluntary contributions might be earmarked, made the management and implementation of UN operational activities for development more challenging. The growth in non-core funding in the previous decade was also an important factor in increasing transaction costs for UN entities.

On 22 July (**decision 2009/214**), the Economic and Social Council recommended that the General Assembly, at its sixty-fourth (2009) session, request the Secretary-General to postpone to its sixty-seventh (2012) session the submission, through the Council, of the comprehensive analysis of the implementation of Assembly resolution 62/208, to be prepared in accordance with that resolution.

ECONOMIC AND SOCIAL COUNCIL ACTION

On 22 July [meeting 32], the Economic and Social Council adopted **resolution 2009/1** [draft: E/2009/L.18] without vote [agenda item 3 *(a)*].

Progress in the implementation of General Assembly resolution 62/208 on the triennial comprehensive policy review of operational activities for development of the United Nations system

The Economic and Social Council,

Recalling General Assembly resolutions 62/208 of 19 December 2007 on the triennial comprehensive policy review of operational activities for development of the United Nations system and 63/232 of 19 December 2008 on operational activities for development and Economic and Social Council resolution 2008/2 of 18 July 2008 on progress in the implementation of resolution 62/208,

Reaffirming the importance of the comprehensive policy review of operational activities for development, through which the General Assembly establishes key system-wide policy orientations for the development cooperation and country-level modalities of the United Nations system,

Underscoring the fact that there is no "one size fits all" approach to development and that development assistance by the United Nations development system should be able to respond to the varying development needs of programme countries and should be in alignment with their national development plans and strategies, in accordance with its mandates,

Reaffirming the need to strengthen the United Nations with a view to enhancing its authority and efficiency, as well as its capacity to address effectively, and in accordance with the purposes and principles of the Charter of the United Nations, the full range of development challenges of our time, and emphasizing that operational activities for development of the United Nations system should be valued and assessed on the basis of their impact on the programme countries as contributions to enhancing their capacity to pursue poverty eradication, sustained economic growth and sustainable development,

Acknowledging the importance of delivering assistance in order to overcome the challenges to improving human life through the implementation of resolution 62/208,

Recalling the role of the Economic and Social Council in providing coordination and guidance to the United Nations system so as to ensure that policy orientations established by the General Assembly are implemented on a system-wide basis in accordance with Assembly resolutions 57/270 B of 23 June 2003, 61/16 of 20 November 2006 and 62/208 and other relevant resolutions,

Results achieved and measures and processes implemented in follow-up to General Assembly resolution 62/208

1. *Takes note* of the report of the Secretary-General on results achieved and measures and processes implemented in follow-up to General Assembly resolution 62/208 and of the efforts of the Secretary-General to identify results and fine-tune targets, benchmarks and time frames, in line with paragraph 7 of Economic and Social Council resolution 2008/2;

2. *Notes* the advances made in some areas by the United Nations system in implementing resolution 62/208, including through the development of guidance by the United Nations Development Group reflecting the principles and guidance contained in resolution 62/208;

3. *Reiterates* the call of the General Assembly for the governing bodies of the funds, programmes and specialized agencies of the United Nations development system to take appropriate actions for the full implementation of resolution 62/208;

4. *Also reiterates* the request of the General Assembly to the executive heads of those organizations to continue to report annually to their governing bodies on measures taken and envisaged for the implementation of resolution 62/208;

5. *Reaffirms* that the fundamental characteristics of operational activities for development of the United Nations system should be, inter alia, their universal, voluntary and grant nature, their neutrality and their multilateralism, as well as their ability to respond to the development needs of programme countries in a flexible manner, and that operational activities are carried out for the benefit of programme countries, at the request of those countries and in accordance with their own policies and priorities for development;

6. *Notes* the improvements in respect of the participation of United Nations system organizations in the functioning of the resident coordinator system, including through the streamlining of inter-agency governance and management structures;

7. *Acknowledges* the interim assessments of the progress made and the challenges remaining in efforts to increase coherence in country-level programming, including in the pilot programme countries;

8. *Notes* the voluntary efforts made to improve coherence, coordination and harmonization in the United Nations development system, including at the request of some pilot programme countries, encourages the Secretary-General to support pilot programme countries in evaluating and exchanging their experiences, with the support of the United Nations Evaluation Group, and emphasizes, in addition, the need for an independent evaluation of lessons learned from such efforts, according to the principles contained in resolution 62/208, with regard to national ownership and leadership and in the context of system-wide norms and standards, for consideration by Member States, without prejudice to a future intergovernmental decision;

9. *Encourages* United Nations system organizations to take the necessary steps to further enhance their participation in United Nations country-level coordination mechanisms, including through decentralization, delegation of authority and multi-year programming, encourages the participation of the United Nations development system, by invitation and ex officio, in current and new aid modalities and coordination mechanisms, at the request of the programme country, and invites the United Nations development system to enhance its participation in this regard;

10. *Recalls* the underscoring by the General Assembly, in paragraph 96 of its resolution 62/208, that resident coordinators, supported by United Nations country teams, should report to national authorities on progress made against results agreed in the United Nations Development Assistance Framework, and requests the Secretary-General, through the United Nations Development Group and its member organizations, to develop a standard operational format on reporting for this purpose, bearing in mind the need to reduce the administrative burden and transaction costs;

11. *Encourages* the United Nations Evaluation Group to continue its work to harmonize evaluation practices across the system, to bring evaluation practices up to standard and to professionalize evaluation capacities;

12. *Reiterates its encouragement* to all United Nations organizations involved in operational activities for development that have not already done so to adopt, as appropriate, monitoring and evaluation policies that are in line with system-wide norms and standards and to make the necessary financial and institutional arrangements for the creation and/or strengthening of independent, credible and useful evaluation functions within each organization;

13. *Encourages* the United Nations Development Group to develop indicators to assess the sustainability of the capacity-building activities of the United Nations system, and reiterates that the United Nations development system should use national execution, available national expertise and technologies, and national procurement systems in the implementation of operational activities, in line with paragraph 39 of resolution 62/208;

14. *Recalls* paragraphs 48, 49, 51 and 52 of resolution 62/208, and calls upon the organizations of the United Nations development system to continue to mainstream support to South-South and triangular cooperation into their strategic plans and operational activities for development, including through United Nations Development Assistance Frameworks, at the request of recipient countries;

15. *Encourages* regional, subregional and international organizations to strengthen their support for South-South cooperation, including triangular cooperation;

16. *Calls upon* the organizations of the United Nations development system, within their organizational mandates, to further improve their institutional accountability mechanisms, welcoming in this regard the development of performance indicators for gender equality and women's empowerment (the scorecard) by the United Nations Development Group and encouraging their systematic use by United Nations country teams, and to include, in particular, intergovernmentally agreed gender equality results and gender-sensitive indicators in their strategic frameworks, and takes note of their progress in this regard;

17. *Reiterates* paragraph 20 of General Assembly resolution 63/232, in which the Assembly urged the funds and programmes and encouraged the specialized agencies to carry out any changes required to align their planning cycles with the quadrennial comprehensive policy review, including the implementation of midterm reviews as necessary, and to report to the Economic and Social Council on adjustments made to fit the new comprehensive review cycle;

18. *Recalls* the decision of the General Assembly in its resolution 63/232 to hold its next comprehensive policy review in 2012 and subsequent reviews on a quadrennial basis, and in this regard requests the Secretary-General to continue to submit to the Economic and Social Council detailed reports on results achieved and measures and processes implemented, in accordance with paragraph 142 of resolution 62/208, including at its substantive sessions of 2011 and 2012;

Functioning of the resident coordinator system, including costs and benefits

19. *Takes note* of the report of the Secretary-General on the functioning of the resident coordinator system, including costs and benefits;

20. *Requests* the United Nations Development Group, in close cooperation with the United Nations Development Programme, to further develop approaches and tools for measuring and reporting on the costs and benefits of coordination, including input on best practices and lessons learned from the field on the functioning of the resident coordinator system, and requests the Secretary-General to include in his report to be submitted to the Economic and Social Council at its substantive session of 2010 information on challenges and achievements;

21. *Urges* the accelerated coordination of efforts by headquarters units and mechanisms within the United Nations development system in order to provide relevant, efficient and timely support and guidance to resident coordinators, bearing in mind their various coordination functions;

22. *Encourages* the United Nations Development Group, in close cooperation with the United Nations Development Programme, as manager of the resident coordinator system, to develop standards for the type and level of staff and options for operational support that need to be provided to ensure effective United Nations system coordination in addressing the many interlinked development needs, including for those countries in transition from relief to development, taking into account countries in complex situations and their challenges as well as the country-specific character of those challenges;

23. *Reiterates* the request of the General Assembly to the United Nations development system to provide further financial, technical and organizational support for the resident coordinator system, and requests the organizations of the United Nations development system to include the provision of resources and support to the resident coordinator system in their respective strategic plans and budgets and to continue to include information on their support to the resident coordinator system in their reports to their respective governing bodies;

24. *Encourages* the United Nations development system to continue broadening the system-wide support provided to the resident coordinator system and to improve the response to requests for support from United Nations country teams, bearing in mind the national ownership and leadership of programme countries, and to ensure that the cost of funding the resident coordinator system does not entail a reduction of the resources that are destined for development programmes in programme countries;

25. *Stresses* that the contribution of non-resident agencies in country programming processes, in response to the priorities of national Governments, should be appropriately facilitated, as necessary, by working through the resident coordinator system and by strengthening the accountability of the resident coordinator, and underlines the need for participating non-resident agencies, where they have commitments in relation to programme planning and implementation, to provide the resources necessary to fulfil those commitments;

26.   *Requests* United Nations system organizations to support efforts by the United Nations Development Group to strengthen the capability of the United Nations system for improving the process through which resident coordinators are selected and trained, as well as for attracting and retaining suitable and high-performing resident coordinators, without infringing upon or prejudging the decisions of the General Assembly;

27.   *Requests* the Secretary-General to include in his annual report to the Economic and Social Council on the functioning of the resident coordinator system information on the operational modalities and the implementation of the management and accountability system of the United Nations development and resident coordinator systems, including the functional firewall of the resident coordinator system, and to report on the independent comprehensive assessment thereof to the Council at its substantive session of 2012, within the framework of the comprehensive analysis of the implementation of resolution 62/208;

28.   *Requests* the United Nations funds and programmes to reflect in their respective annual reports to the Economic and Social Council and to their governing bodies their specific contributions to and the challenges faced in the implementation of the management and accountability framework of the United Nations development and resident coordinator systems, including the functional firewall of the resident coordinator system, bearing in mind the authorities established for the Council and the executive boards, including by the General Assembly in its resolutions 48/162 of 20 December 1993, 50/227 of 24 May 1996, 57/270 B, 60/265 of 30 June 2006 and 61/16;

Country-level capacity of the United Nations development system

29.   *Takes note* of the report of the Secretary-General on human resources challenges within the United Nations development system at the country level;

30.   *Encourages* the United Nations development system to assess, when appropriate, the adequacy of human resource capacities in United Nations country teams with a view to improving their capacity to deliver results in response to the priorities set out in the United Nations Development Assistance Framework, in line with national development priorities and plans;

31.   *Calls upon* the organizations of the United Nations development system to continue their efforts to achieve gender balance within the United Nations system at all levels, both in headquarters and at field duty stations;

32.   *Recalls* paragraphs 125 and 126 of resolution 62/208 and the need to adopt comprehensive policies and strategies for human resources and workforce planning and development, and in this regard stresses the need to address obstacles to inter-agency mobility, the rapid deployment of qualified national and international staff to situations of crisis and the transparency and competitiveness of recruitment processes for senior high-level posts, while not infringing upon or prejudging the decisions of the Assembly, and to integrate these issues into the annual reports on results achieved and measures and processes implemented in follow-up to resolution 62/208;

Funding of operational activities for development of the United Nations system

33.   *Takes note* of the report of the Secretary-General on the comprehensive statistical analysis of the financing of operational activities for development of the United Nations system for 2007 and notes the progress made on broadening and improving the reporting, in line with paragraph 28 of resolution 62/208, and in this regard requests that future reports include further analysis of the current situation and perspectives in respect of core and non-core funding for the United Nations development system;

34.   *Also takes note* of the note by the Secretary-General on the review of trends and perspectives in funding for development cooperation;

35.   *Stresses* that core resources, because of their untied nature, continue to be the bedrock of operational activities for development of the United Nations system;

36.   *Notes* that non-core resources represent an important supplement to the regular resource base of the United Nations development system for supporting operational activities for development, thus contributing to an increase in total resources, while recognizing that non-core resources are not a substitute for core resources and that non-earmarked contributions are vital for the coherence and harmonization of operational activities for development;

37.   *Notes with concern* the continuing imbalance between the core and non-core resources received for operational activities for development of the United Nations system and the potential negative impact of non-core funding on the coordination and effectiveness of United Nations operational activities for development at the country level, while recognizing that thematic trust funds, multi-donor trust funds and other voluntary non-earmarked funding mechanisms linked to organization-specific funding frameworks and strategies, as established by the respective governing bodies, constitute some of the funding modalities that are complementary to regular budgets;

38.   *Also notes with concern* the negative impact of the financial crisis, and urges countries in a position to do so to increase their voluntary contributions to the United Nations development system, on a predictable basis, to support development activities at the country level;

39.   *Calls upon* the United Nations development system to strengthen its ability to support efforts at the country level to mitigate the impact of the crisis;

40.   *Recalls* the request by the General Assembly, in paragraph 23 of its resolution 59/250 of 22 December 2004, that the Economic and Social Council undertake triennially a comprehensive review of trends and perspectives in funding for development cooperation, and requests the Secretary-General to integrate all the elements of that review into his biennial report to the Development Cooperation Forum as of 2012;

41.   *Emphasizes* that increasing financial contributions to the United Nations development system is key to achieving the internationally agreed development goals, including the Millennium Development Goals, and in this regard recognizes the mutually reinforcing links among increased effectiveness, efficiency and coherence

of the United Nations development system, the achievement of concrete results in assisting developing countries in eradicating poverty and achieving sustained economic growth and sustainable development through operational activities for development, and the overall resourcing of the United Nations development system;

Simplification and harmonization of the United Nations development system

42. *Takes note* of the actions taken by the executive boards and governing bodies of the United Nations funds and programmes and the specialized agencies in the area of simplification and harmonization of the United Nations development system to reduce transaction costs, to enhance efficiency and to achieve financial savings, to be invested back in country programmes;

43. *Encourages* United Nations system organizations to continue to work towards simplification and harmonization under the guidance of their executive boards and governing bodies;

44. *Notes* that, while progress is being made towards the simplification and harmonization of business practices within the United Nations development system, many procedures require further harmonization, as identified in the Plan of Action for the Harmonization of Business Practices in the United Nations System, developed by the High-level Committee on Management of the United Nations System Chief Executives Board for Coordination and its functional networks, and requests the United Nations funds and programmes and the specialized agencies to explore sources of financing to support the implementation of this Plan, including through discussions with their respective governing bodies on the allocation of funds through their respective support budgets;

45. *Urges* the Secretary-General, through the High-level Committee, to step up efforts to standardize and harmonize the concepts, practices and cost classifications related to transaction costs and cost recovery, while maintaining the principle of full cost recovery in the administration of all non-core/supplementary/extrabudgetary contributions, including in joint programmes;

46. *Recalls* the importance of continuing to strengthen national execution, bearing in mind the importance of building national capacity, simplifying procedures and aligning those procedures with national procedures;

47. *Requests* the United Nations funds and programmes and the specialized agencies that practise cash transfer to accelerate the roll-out of the harmonized approach to cash transfers;

48. *Urges* the United Nations funds and programmes and encourages the specialized agencies to ensure that adequate information is included in the existing reporting on simplification and harmonization to their respective executive boards and governing bodies so as to enable intergovernmental bodies to make informed decisions on policy changes in a timely manner, and requests the Secretary-General, in his capacity as Chair of the United Nations System Chief Executives Board for Coordination, to ensure that information on the Plan of Action for the Harmonization of Business Practices, as well as periodically updated information on its implementation, including related costs and possible savings, is made available.

Operational activities

National execution of technical cooperation projects

A June note by the Secretary-General [A/64/375-E/2009/103 & Corr.1] contained the report of the Joint Inspection Unit (JIU) on the national execution of technical cooperation projects [JIU/REP/2008/4]. The report identified and disseminated lessons learned and best practices in the implementation of national execution (NEX) projects and programmes, including the related issues of auditing, monitoring and evaluation. NEX programmes aimed to achieve greater national self-reliance, enhanced sustainability of development programmes and projects, a reduction of workload and integration with national programmes.

Constraints were identified in the implementation of training programmes, including the lack of clear purpose of such programmes to serve project outcomes. The JIU inspectors were of the opinion that additional efforts should be made to strengthen the capacity of the recipient Government institutions and improve the public professional sector. A fundamental challenge identified in the execution/implementation of NEX projects and programmes was to regard civil society—including non-governmental organizations (NGOs)—as executing entities/implementing partners in development. The inspectors noted that in certain cases, the NEX project manager was substituting the recipient Governments in monitoring and evaluation despite General Assembly resolution 56/201 [YUN 2001, p. 783] on the triennial policy review, which stipulated that such activities should be Government-led. In order to address internal and external challenges related to NEX, more coherence among UN system organizations was required, including further simplification and harmonization of their rules and procedures at the headquarters level. The knowledge possessed by UN regional commissions should be used for the preparation of country programmes, particularly in the planning, implementation and follow-up of NEX projects. The report concluded that the existence of reliable Government institutions was a prerequisite for viable NEX projects. Government-led execution required implementing partners to assume greater risk. Such partners should mitigate risk by promoting sound national policies that advanced accountability and built capacity.

JIU recommended that the Assembly, in the context of the triennial comprehensive policy review, should invite CEB to coordinate compliance with the provisions of Assembly resolutions, including resolution 62/208 [YUN 2007, p. 877], by which it adopted NEX as the norm in the implementation of operational activities. The Assembly and legislative bodies of corresponding organizations should reiterate that donors should provide less conditioned extrabudgetary contributions, including those financing NEX, with a view to realizing the priorities of the recipient countries and ensuring more flexibility, predictability and geographic balance in NEX expenditures. They should assist recipient Governments in strengthening their capacity in the accounting and audit field, through focused training, as required, to enable them to match international standards. The Assembly and the Economic and Social Council should request UN system organizations to strengthen coordination with the resident coordinator system and the Regional Coordination Mechanism to include the regional perspective and to establish synergies between regional, subregional and national programmes.

The Economic and Social Council, by **decision 2009/215** of 22 July, took note of the JIU report.

In an October note [A/64/375/Add.1-E/2009/103/Add.1], the Secretary-General transmitted to the Assembly his comments and those of CEB concerning the JIU report. CEB welcomed the report and expressed overall agreement with the recommendations contained therein.

GENERAL ASSEMBLY ACTION

On 21 December [meeting 66], the General Assembly, on the recommendation of the Second (Economic and Financial) Committee [A/64/425/Add.1], adopted **resolution 64/220** without vote [agenda item 58 *(a)*].

Operational activities for development of the United Nations system

The General Assembly,

Recalling its resolution 62/208 of 19 December 2007 on the triennial comprehensive policy review of operational activities for development of the United Nations system,

Reaffirming the importance of the triennial comprehensive policy review of operational activities for development, through which the General Assembly establishes key system-wide policy orientations for development cooperation and country-level modalities of the United Nations system,

Recalling the role of the Economic and Social Council in providing coordination and guidance to the United Nations system to ensure that those policy orientations are implemented on a system-wide basis in accordance with General Assembly resolution 62/208,

1. *Takes note* of the report of the Secretary-General on the comprehensive statistical analysis of the financing of operational activities for development of the United Nations system for 2007, and notes the progress made in broadening and improving the reporting, in line with paragraph 28 of its resolution 62/208;

2. *Also takes note* of the report on the activities of the United Nations Development Fund for Women;

3. *Further takes note* of the report of the Joint Inspection Unit on the national execution of technical cooperation projects, and of the comments of the Secretary-

General and the member organizations of the United Nations system thereon;

4. *Takes note* of Economic and Social Council decision 2009/214 of 22 July 2009 on operational activities for development and its resolution 2009/1 of 22 July 2009 on progress in the implementation of General Assembly resolution 62/208, and expresses appreciation for the guidance provided by the Council on the further implementation of resolution 62/208 as contained therein;

5. *Recalls* General Assembly resolution 63/232 of 19 December 2008, in which it decided to hold its next comprehensive policy review of operational activities for development of the United Nations system in 2012 and subsequent reviews on a quadrennial basis, and requests the Secretary-General to postpone to its sixty-seventh session the submission, through the Economic and Social Council, of the comprehensive analysis of the implementation of Assembly resolution 62/208 to be prepared in accordance with the guidance contained in paragraph 143 thereof.

Simplification and harmonization of UN development system

On 5 May [E/2009/61], the Secretary-General reported on actions taken by the executive boards and governing bodies of the UN funds, programmes and specialized agencies to simplify and harmonize the UN development system. The report provided an overview of progress achieved system-wide and by individual agencies. It focused on the simplification of cost recovery rates, practices and policies, and of rules, procedures and business practices; and the rationalization of the UN country presence through the use of common premises, co-location and common services.

The Secretary-General concluded that, in the context of the changing aid environment, both programme and donor countries placed growing demand on the UN development system to translate accountability and render processes into more simple and harmonized working modalities that were results-oriented and transparent. The UN development system started to identify and operationalize solutions for streamlining, rationalizing and optimizing key business processes and practices at headquarters and in the field. The endorsement by CEB of the High-level Committee on Management (HLCM) Plan of Action for the Harmonization of Business Practices in the United Nations System [CEB/2008/HLCM/10], excerpts of which were contained in a June report [CEB/2009/HLCM/HR/45/Rev.1], set out a road map for the collective effort. The "Delivering as one" country pilots [YUN 2007, p. 1418] provided a platform to test innovative solutions for application on a wider scale. Management reform had to go hand in hand with progress in reinforcing policy coherence among the various intergovernmental processes. In addition, UN commitment to coherence and effectiveness should be matched with sustained financing. In that regard, the availability of extrabudgetary resources requested in the funding proposal for the CEB/HLCM Plan of Action remained critical to sustaining the growing momentum towards simplification and harmonization. Fast-paced reform in the field required corresponding policy changes at headquarters, and it was important to ensure adequate sharing of information with the executive boards and governing bodies about the progress of reform system-wide.

The Economic and Social Council took note of the Secretary-General's report on 22 July (**decision 2009/215**).

System-wide coherence

General Assembly action. The General Assembly, during its resumed sixty-third (2009) session, considered discussion notes on "Strengthening the governance of operational activities for development of the United Nations system for enhanced system-wide coherence" and "Strengthening the system-wide funding architecture of operational activities of the United Nations for development", of 15 April and 3 May, respectively. Both notes contained recommendations related to UN operational activities for development, including, in the 15 April note, a recommendation on the creation of a central repository of information on such activities.

In **resolution 63/311** of 14 September (see p. 1368) on system-wide coherence, the General Assembly adopted measures aimed at strengthening the governance of UN system operational activities for development and improving the funding system of such activities for enhanced system-wide coherence. It requested the Secretary-General, in consultation with CEB, to propose to the Assembly, at its sixty-fourth (2009) session, measures for the further improvement of the governance of the operational activities for development, as well as modalities for the submission and approval of common country programmes; and for the establishment of an independent evaluation mechanism to assess system-wide efficiency, effectiveness and performance. The Assembly noted with concern the continuing imbalance between core and non-core resources received by UN system operational activities for development and the potential negative impact of non-core funding on the coordination and effectiveness of operational activities at the country level. It urged countries in a position to do so to increase substantially their voluntary contributions to the core/regular budgets of the UN development system; contribute on a multi-year basis, in a sustained and predictable manner; and undertake voluntary commitments to provide a greater share of system-wide contributions to operational activities for development as core/regular resources. The Secretary-General was requested to create a cen-

tral repository of information on operational activities for development, including disaggregated statistics on all funding sources and expenditures, building on his comprehensive statistical analysis of the financing of operational activities for development.

Report of Secretary-General. In December [A/64/589], the Secretary-General issued a report on follow-up to Assembly resolution 63/311 on system-wide coherence related to operational activities for development. The report put forward proposals for improving the functioning of the governing bodies. The proposals were intended to help ensure that the tiers of governance—including the Assembly, the Economic and Social Council, the executive boards of the funds and programmes and the governing bodies of the specialized agencies—engaged in operational activities for development functioned as an integrated system with clear roles and well-defined lines of responsibility and accountability. It identified four priority areas for enhancing the functioning of intergovernmental bodies governing UN operational activities for development, including key challenges and a possible way forward. The priorities were to: strengthen functional coherence between the Assembly, the Economic and Social Council and the executive boards of funds and programmes, as well as the governing bodies of specialized agencies; ensure that countries participated in governing bodies on an equal basis; improve substantive preparations for meetings of governing bodies; and enhance the impact of intergovernmental decisions. The report concluded that improving the functioning of intergovernmental bodies was critical for more effective UN operational activities for development at the country level. Such improvement would require Member States to take action in several areas, including committing to greater coherence in policymaking; establishing enhanced clarity on the roles and functions of different tiers of the governance system; significantly strengthening the capacity of programme countries to participate in intergovernmental policymaking on UN operational activities for development; making decision-making processes at all levels more action-oriented; and stepping up secretariat support to governing bodies based on a functional needs analysis.

The report outlined possible modalities for submission and approval of common country programmes on a voluntary basis. Options included a common country programme presented to governing bodies of participating UN agencies; a programme consistent with the United Nations Development Assistance Framework (UNDAF) presented to each governing body and internal agency mechanism a programme presented to the Economic and Social Council; and a programme presented to the joint meeting of executive boards. The report also set out key principles for establishing an independent, system-wide evaluation mechanism and discussed efforts to strengthen financial reporting on operational activities for development.

The Secretary-General reported that a central repository of information on operational activities for development would be created as part of a system-wide financial statistics database and reporting system, building on the CEB mandate to collect and publish financial information on the entire UN system. The database was expected to enhance the scope and detail of financial reporting to Member States, including on operational activities. The first phase of the project included the launch, expected in 2010, of a dedicated section of the CEB website, with analysis based on the 2008 report on the budgetary and financial situation of the UN system organizations [YUN 2008, p. 1562]. The second and final phase of the project—the launch of a central repository—was expected to be completed within two years. The report also addressed the purpose, timing and scope of the independent evaluation, requested by the Assembly in resolution 63/311, of lessons learned from the "Delivering as one" pilot countries [YUN 2007, p. 1418] and proposed options for the management of the evaluation.

CEB was leading efforts to simplify and harmonize business practices within the UN development system through the Plan of Action for the Harmonization of Business Practices in the UN system, excerpts of which were contained in a June report. A funding proposal outlining the scope and objective of the Plan was transmitted to potential donors in October 2008. CEB reviewed projects included in the Plan of Action to ensure their relevance in the context of financial constraints, and it selected priorities among the activities included in the original funding proposals. Further action was taken on the simplification and harmonization of business practices called for in Economic and Social Council resolution 2009/1 of 22 July 2009 (see p. 847).

Financing of operational activities

The UNDP/UNFPA Executive Board, at its September session [E/2009/35 (dec. 2009/21)], took note of the report of the UNDP Administrator on UN system technical cooperation expenditures in 2008 and its addendum [YUN 2008, p. 964]. The Board supported the integration of information from that report into the report on the comprehensive statistical analysis of the financing of operational activities for development of the UN system, in accordance with General Assembly resolution 63/232 [ibid., p. 962], and noted that the UN Department of Economic and Social Affairs (DESA) would prepare such an analysis effective 2010.

UN system expenditures on operational activities amounted to $18.6 billion in 2008 [A/65/79-

E/2010/76], the most recent year for which figures were available, compared with $17.3 billion in 2007, representing a 7 per cent increase over the previous year. Of the total expenditures, $4,270 million was distributed by UNDP; $3,536 million by the World Food Programme; $2,808 million by the United Nations Children's Fund (UNICEF); $1,691 million by the World Health Organization; $1,597 million by the Office of the United Nations High Commissioner for Refugees; $807 million by the United Nations Relief and Works Agency for Palestine Refugees in the Near East; $691 million by the Food and Agriculture Organization of the United Nations (FAO); $436 million by UNFPA; $424 million by the International Labour Organization; $347 million by the United Nations Educational, Scientific and Cultural Organization; $231 million by the United Nations Office on Drugs and Crime/United Nations International Drug Control Programme; $231 million by the United Nations Industrial Development Organization (UNIDO); $142 million by the Joint United Nations Programme on HIV/AIDS (UNAIDS); $131 million by the United Nations Environment Programme (UNEP); $125 million by the United Nations Human Settlements Programme; $121 million by the Office for the Coordination of Humanitarian Affairs; $69 million by DESA; $59 million by the UN regional commissions; $35 million by the United Nations Conference on Trade and Development (UNCTAD) and an additional $49 million by the International Trade Centre of UNCTAD; and $379 million by other specialized agencies. The International Fund for Agricultural Development disbursed $450 million in loans.

The 2009 United Nations Pledging Conference for Development Activities was held in New York on 9 November [A/CONF.208/2009/3]. In August [A/CONF.208/2009/2], the Secretary-General provided a statement of contributions pledged or paid at the 2008 Pledging Conference to 25 funds and programmes, amounting to some $1.4 billion as at 30 June 2009.

Technical cooperation through UNDP

UNDP/UNFPA Executive Board

In 2009, the UNDP/UNFPA Executive Board held its first (19–22 January) and second (8–11 September) sessions, its annual session (26 May–3 June) and a special session (17 November), all in New York [E/2009/35].

The Board adopted 30 decisions in 2009, including those providing an overview of actions taken at its January [E/2009/35 (dec. 2009/8)], June [dec. 2009/19] and September [dec. 2009/28] sessions. Other decisions dealt with the work of UNDP, the United Nations

Office for Project Services (UNOPS) and the United Nations Capital Development Fund (UNCDF) (see p. 880), as well as that of UNFPA (see PART THREE, Chapter VIII) and the United Nations Development Fund for Women (see PART THREE, Chapter X).

The Economic and Social Council, by **decision 2009/215** of 22 July, took note of the Board's report on its work in 2008 [YUN 2008, p. 966].

Appointment of Administrator

On 21 January [dec. 2009/7], the Executive Board noted with regret that Kemal Derviş would leave his position as UNDP Administrator effective 1 March. The Board commended him on his effective guidance and management of UNDP from 2005 to 2009.

In a 26 March note [A/63/109], the Secretary-General requested the General Assembly to confirm the appointment of Helen Clark (New Zealand) as UNDP Administrator for a four-year term of office beginning on 20 April and ending on 19 April 2013. The Assembly confirmed the appointment on 31 March 2009 (**decision 63/419**).

UNDP/UNFPA reports

On 22 January [dec. 2009/3], the UNDP/UNFPA Executive Board took note of the 2008 report of the UNDP Administrator and the UNFPA Executive Director on the implementation of the Secretary-General's reform programme and the triennial comprehensive policy review of operational activities for development [YUN 2008, p. 966] and transmitted it to the Economic and Social Council, along with a summary of the comments and guidance provided by delegations at the Board's January session. The Board underscored the importance of the full implementation of General Assembly resolution 62/208 on the policy review [YUN 2007, p. 877] and requested that future reports adhere to the structure established in the resolution and include recommendations to improve its implementation further. The Administrator and Executive Director were asked to consider ways to improve the reports, taking into account the need to achieve efficiency and effectiveness in their reporting practices, and to consult with the Board in order to prepare a proposal on the matter at its September session.

The Council took note of the 2008 report on 22 July (**decision 2009/215**).

In response to Assembly resolutions 56/201 [YUN 2001, p. 783], 59/250 [YUN 2004, p. 868] and 62/208, the UNDP Administrator and the UNFPA Executive Director issued, in November [E/2010/5], a joint report containing information on funding for operational activities of the UN development system; the contribution of UN operational activities to national capac-

ity development and development effectiveness; improved functioning of the UN development system; and follow-up to the triennial comprehensive policy review. UNDP and UNFPA were establishing partnerships with regional and national institutions and using knowledge-sharing platforms and communities of practice—networks of development experts who share an interest in a particular area—to carry out capacity assessments and provide policy advice and programme support. In 2008 and 2009, UNDP and UNFPA forged or strengthened partnerships with the World Bank, the African Development Bank, the United Nations University, the New Partnership for Africa's Development, the Asian Institute of Technology, the Council of Europe and the League of Arab States, among other institutions. The partnerships were essential to enhancing capacity-development initiatives. In the Asia and the Pacific region, UNFPA, UNDP and UNICEF established a regional working group on capacity development, which provided support to UN country teams. Similar initiatives were undertaken in Latin America and in Southern Africa.

UNDP and UNFPA launched initiatives to strengthen national capacity to integrate gender equality into national development planning and budget frameworks. Both organizations sought to improve accountability and build capacity to advance gender equality and support women's political empowerment. UNDP worked with electoral management bodies and political parties to enhance women's civic and political participation. It focused its efforts on the implementation of an eight-point agenda for women's empowerment and gender equality in crisis prevention and recovery. In mid-2009, UNDP deployed senior gender advisers to work in seven conflict or post-conflict countries. It launched initiatives to examine financing for gender equality in early recovery programmes and ensure women's political and civic participation in post-conflict elections. UNDP and UNEP were integrating gender issues into their poverty and environment initiative, and developed partnerships with civil society networks that integrated gender issues into national development planning processes.

As a result of their field presence and their ability to liaise with local partners, UNDP and UNFPA were able to support efforts to reduce the vulnerability of countries to crises and conflicts, promote human development principles in humanitarian settings, and establish the foundations for a transition from relief to development. They had to build stronger national and regional capacities and pool regional resources to enable countries to respond jointly to common concerns. UNDP was providing technical support to more than 40 disaster-prone countries by integrating disaster risk management into development planning and programming, and by strengthening institutional structures for disaster preparedness. It was strengthening national technical expertise to analyse the risks related to climate variability and develop risk-management solutions. In collaboration with the World Bank and UN system partners, UNDP supported post-disaster needs assessments and the design of recovery frameworks in Western Africa and South-East Asia. The UNDP Bureau for Crisis Prevention and Recovery was implementing plans of action for early recovery in five countries. The plans included strengthening early recovery coordination and programming capacity and early recovery projects at the local level. As part of the Inter-Agency Standing Committee—the primary mechanism for the inter-agency coordination of humanitarian assistance—UNDP helped establish early recovery coordination mechanisms in 32 countries and supported needs assessments and strategic frameworks in 10 countries. UNDP provided technical support to 24 national disarmament, demobilization and reintegration programmes that contributed to the disarmament and demobilization of more than 350,000 former combatants and provided reintegration assistance to 60 per cent of them.

Human Development Report

The UNDP/UNFPA Executive Board, at its annual session, considered a March update [DP/2009/17] on the *Human Development Report* consultations, submitted in response to General Assembly resolution 57/264 [YUN 2002, p. 841]. In 2009, the Human Development Report Office, charged with preparing the *Report* (see p. 828), held two informal consultations with the UNDP/UNFPA Executive Board, focusing on the key findings of the research and writing process, and the statistical data and main messages contained in the *Report*. The Board took note of the update on 3 June [dec. 2009/19].

UNDP operational activities

Country and regional programmes

The UNDP/UNFPA Executive Board, at its January session, considered a report containing proposed measures for the resumption of programme operations in the Democratic People's Republic of Korea (DPRK) [DP/2009/8]. The report requested the Board to authorize the Administrator to approve assistance to the DPRK, and outlined the programme interventions to be supported by UNDP and the operational modalities to be used. On 22 January [dec. 2009/1], the Board took note of the proposed measures and authorized the resumption of programme activities in the DPRK based on those measures, which were further clarified in statements made by UNDP to the Board during the session. The Administrator was authorized to approve

additional projects in the DPRK on a project-by-project basis for the 2009–2010 period.

Also at its January session [dec. 2009/8], the Board approved country programme documents for eight countries.

At its annual session in June [dec. 2009/19], the Executive Board took note of the first one-year extensions of the country programmes for Azerbaijan, Chile, Iran, Serbia, Somalia and Zimbabwe; and approved the second one-year extension of the country programme for the Turks and Caicos Islands and the first two-year extensions of the country programmes for Barbados and the Organization of Eastern Caribbean States, Mozambique and the Philippines [DP/2009/18]. The Board also took note of the draft country programme documents and the comments made thereon for 12 countries.

At its September session [dec. 2009/28], the Executive Board approved the final country programme documents for 12 countries on a no-objection basis, without presentation or discussion, in accordance with a 2006 Board decision [YUN 2006, p. 1038]. It took note of the one-year extension of the country programme for the Libyan Arab Jamahiriya [DP/2009/35], the draft regional programme documents for the Arab States, and the draft country programme documents and the comments made thereon for four countries.

Also at the September session [dec. 2009/24], the Board took note of the UNDP Administrator's July note on assistance to Myanmar [DP/2009/34]; requested that the Administrator take account of and implement the findings of the independent assessment mission under the Human Development Initiative; and endorsed the proposed one-year extension of phase IV of the Initiative until 2011. The Administrator was authorized to allocate for the revised period (2008–2011) an estimated $38.9 million from regular (core) resources and mobilize other (non-core) resources up to $65 million; both amounts were inclusive of the $24.1 million core and $24.9 million non-core resources authorized by the 2007 Board decision [YUN 2007, p. 889].

Evaluation of regional cooperation framework for Arab States

In March [DP/2009/14], the UNDP Evaluation Office submitted to the Executive Board a report summarizing the findings of the evaluation of the third regional cooperation framework (RCF) for the Arab States. The evaluation, conducted between August 2008 and January 2009, was designed to assess the overall programme performance and outcomes of the RCF and evaluate the contributions of UNDP through the RCF to regional development. RCF activities were organized under three pillars: MDG achievement, democratic governance and building a knowledge society, with youth as a cross-cutting issue. The total budget for the first three years of the 2006–2008 RCF amounted to some $30.2 million, with core and other resources totalling $9.5 million and $20.7 million, respectively.

The evaluation found that the 2006–2009 RCF had been relevant to the priorities and needs of the Arab region. In most cases, the RCF was positioned to deal with issues that could not have been adequately addressed within the country programmes. The programme on HIV/AIDS was particularly relevant to the region, where the epidemic was not openly discussed. Projects related to education under the knowledge society pillar provided assistance to Arab universities to promote a culture of evaluation, educational quality and reform. Programmes under the democratic governance pillar addressed good governance and judicial reform through advocacy, policy dialogue and training.

RCF programmes were most effective in advocacy and policy dialogue on common priority issues in the region. The programmes developed the capacities of NGOs, governmental organizations and religious leaders, and created partnerships with Governments, civil society and NGOs, and academic and policy institutions.

The RCF faced several shortcomings, most of which stemmed from its design. The regional programme document did not define the expected outcomes or the corresponding indicators that would allow for measuring results in a meaningful manner. Coordination between the RCF and the country programmes in the region was weak at best, and in many cases non-existent. There was a marked absence of concrete projects with sustainable results at the operational level, and funding for the RCF from UNDP core resources was limited. The evaluation report outlined a number of broad conclusions related to the need for an RCF results framework and focused programmes, coordination with country programmes, and greater participation by net contributor countries and least developed countries.

The evaluation recommended that the overall objectives of the RCF be reviewed, with a view to concentrating on fewer areas with clearly defined outcomes and strategic trust. The RCF should be aligned with the 2008–2011 UNDP strategic plan [YUN 2007, p. 898], recognizing country-specific circumstances. Country office management should be involved at all stages of the RCF planning and implementation to ensure alignment with country programmes. Activities under environment and sustainable development—a new RCF component—should be closely aligned with the governance and poverty reduction focus areas. The *Arab Human Development Report* should become independent from the regional programme but remain under the purview of UNDP in

order to maintain its neutrality and quality. The evaluation suggested that a separate fund be set up with, inter alia, private sector contributions from the region. Resource mobilization efforts should tap into the financial resources of the region, and individual programmes should be encouraged to mobilize additional resources and facilitate the application procedures of the funds.

UNDP responded to the evaluation in a March report [DP/2009/15], in which it took note of the issues raised and the recommendations made by the evaluation and proposed follow-up action.

In June [dec. 2009/19], the UNDP/UNFPA Executive Board took note of the evaluation of the third (2006–2009) RCF for the Arab States and the management response thereto.

UNDP programme results

UNDP activities under the 2008–2011 strategic plan, endorsed by the UNDP/UNFPA Executive Board in 2007 [YUN 2007, p. 898] and updated in 2008 [YUN 2008, p. 975], were conducted in four focus areas: poverty reduction and MDG achievement, democratic governance, crisis prevention and recovery, and environment and sustainable development. The annual report of the UNDP Administrator on the strategic plan: performance and results for 2009 [DP/2010/17] provided an in-depth analysis of six outcomes in the poverty and MDG achievement, environment and sustainable development and crisis prevention and recovery focus areas. Other areas of UNDP work discussed in the report included gender equality and South-South cooperation.

(For information on South-South cooperation see p. 873; for other areas of UNDP work, see sections below.)

Poverty reduction and MDG achievement

The UNDP approach to responding to country demand for support in MDG achievement was focused primarily in four interconnected areas: advocacy, assessment and planning, implementation for inclusive development and building resilience. The economic crisis necessitated urgent responses to help countries identify and protect the vulnerable. In addition, the imminent impacts of climate change threatened developing countries, especially the poorest and most vulnerable. UNDP work on poverty reduction and acceleration of the achievement of the MDGs in 2009 was driven by the confluence of those factors. It focused its investments on country capacities and partnerships to deliver sustainable development results and build resilience. UNDP also maintained its focus on the longer-term objective of supporting national efforts to accelerate and sustain progress on the MDGs at the national and local levels. During the year, UNDP initiated steps towards the 2010 MDG summit and took the lead to work with stakeholders at the global, regional, country and subnational levels to ensure a comprehensive and coherent set of inputs that would inform plans for MDG acceleration until 2015. As part of the UN system-wide effort to support partner nations in accelerating progress on the MDGs, UNDP was developing an MDG breakthrough strategy to ensure the best possible impact of UNDP support. It focused on scaling up local development and innovative approaches; sustaining MDG progress through addressing structural constraints; and developing partnerships and mobilizing resources. UNDP, through the provision of guidelines updated in 2009, helped countries prepare national MDG reports that would inform a strategic update of progress, constraints and emerging challenges.

UNDP, as a co-sponsor of UNAIDS, addressed dimensions of HIV related to development planning, governance, human rights, gender and sexual diversity. It also supported countries in implementing HIV and health programmes financed by the Global Fund to Fight AIDS, Tuberculosis and Malaria. As a principal recipient for Global Fund programmes in 34 countries, UNDP contributed to providing community outreach for HIV, tuberculosis and malaria prevention to more than 20 million people. HIV counselling and testing was provided to nearly 3.5 million people, and antiretroviral treatment to more than 100,000 people living with the virus. In more than 30 countries, UNDP contributed to implementation efforts, including audits of national legal frameworks to ensure sensitivity and responsiveness to HIV and gender equality; enactment of protective laws for women and people living with HIV; and improved access to justice for women and men affected by HIV. Those efforts created enabling legal environments for scaling up and sustaining effective responses to the HIV epidemic. UNDP worked with networks of people living with HIV in Kenya to enhance legal and human rights awareness, especially among women. In Ukraine, it sought to extend the network on monitoring and response to human rights violations and conducted information campaigns on tolerance for youth. It supported capacity development of districts, municipalities, civil society and community-based organizations in more than 40 countries to plan and implement inclusive HIV programmes and effectively deliver services at the local level.

Democratic governance

UNDP work in the area of democratic governance focused on support for the expansion of opportunities to participate in political decision-making; on accountable and responsive democratic institutions; and on promotion of the principles of democratic govern-

ance, particularly anti-corruption efforts, gender equality and human rights. In 2009, UNDP supported special measures in 59 countries to increase the representation of women at all levels of government, including training for women candidates on leadership and campaign management. It continued to work on a national level worldwide to strengthen women's property, inheritance and land rights; examine how informal law could be brought closer to international norms and standards; and improve women's legal rights and access to justice. In 2009, 112 countries benefited from UNDP technical support for action aimed at forming anti-corruption policies and organizations, as well as improving the participation of civil society and the media. UNDP organized anti-corruption training activities initiated from a South-South perspective—a development approach that called for the exchange of knowledge and experience between developing countries. UNDP and the Media Institute of Southern Africa organized a training workshop for regional journalists on the investigation and reporting of corruption (Johannesburg, South Africa, 3–5 December), which brought together 20 senior journalists from 11 African countries in addition to trainers from the Philippine Centre for Investigative Journalism. UNDP also provided 16 countries with technical and financial support to strengthen country-led assessments of governance reforms.

Crisis prevention and recovery

UNDP contributed to greater harmonization and coherence in the area of crisis prevention and recovery through stronger partnerships established with UN entities, including the Departments of Peacekeeping Operations and Political Affairs, the Peacebuilding Support Office and international financial institutions. UNDP support to national recovery efforts in 2009 reflected the complexity of recovery. The Programme provided assistance that combined swift support at the outset of a crisis with longer-term approaches dealing with a range of interlinked technical issues. The aim was to support Government capacities to deliver services and drive the coordination of recovery efforts. Rapid assistance in early recovery efforts in 29 countries represented an almost 50 per cent increase compared to 2008. Forging a closer link between jobs and recovery was an increasingly important area for UNDP, along with the overriding priority to focus on women and other vulnerable groups, including refugees and internally displaced persons.

UNDP continued to face a number of challenges, including the need to adapt continuously to a changing global agenda, uncertain funding scenarios and increasingly complex field operations. It needed to hone its capacities and expertise to maximize its comparative advantages, particularly in supporting the coherence of the United Nations on the ground in both prevention and recovery. UNDP was spearheading an initiative to embed disaster risk management and prevention in the MDGs and securing the resources required to formulate and implement multi-year programmes.

Environment and sustainable development

UNDP provided a cross-practice and cross-sector approach to inclusive development that assisted countries in managing the nexus of climate change, poverty reduction and capacity development. It led the UN system in integrating gender equality in global and national climate change policies and finance mechanisms. UNDP provided planning support to countries in Africa that were vulnerable to the impacts associated with climate change through the African Adaptation Programme and in the preparation of National Adaptation Programmes of Action, which identified needs and priorities for adaptation and access to international funding. UNDP was helping countries harness the economic potential of 453 protected areas covering 85.2 million hectares by promoting sustainable tourism and the sustainable harvest of natural resources, and by developing markets for ecosystem services. As part of the United Nations Collaborative Programme on Reducing Emissions from Deforestation and Forest Degradation in Developing Countries, a partnership between UNDP, UNEP and FAO started in 2008, Panama produced the region's first joint programme to participate in the forest carbon market.

UNDP supported inclusive development to enable policy frameworks and financial mechanisms that promoted energy efficiency and made renewable energy more affordable. Through those efforts, 44 countries were able to avoid approximately 26 million tons of carbon dioxide in 2009. UNDP assisted 32 of China's provinces and regions in responding to climate change; by the end of the year, 17 provincial/regional governments in China had endorsed provincial climate change programmes, 13 had established climate change divisions and 22 leading groups on climate change. It supported capacity development programmes that focused on designing, planning and managing low-carbon growth strategies. Under the 1987 Montreal Protocol [YUN 1987, p. 686], UNDP implementation support contributed to the reduction of the use of ozone-depleting substances in over 100 countries. It supported Governments in expanding access to sustainable energy services to the energy poor, including the 3 billion people who relied on traditional biomass and coal for cooking and heating and the 1.5 billion who lived without access to electricity. It was also helping countries identify, finance and implement cost-effective energy efficiency

and renewable energy projects, while at the same time enhancing the quality, reliability and affordability of energy services.

Gender equality

At the January session of the UNDP/UNFPA Executive Board [E/2009/35], the Assistant Administrator and Director of the Bureau for Development Policy and the Bureau's Gender Unit Director provided a comprehensive overview of UNDP's gender equality strategy. The Gender Unit Director also updated the Board with detailed information on enhancing capacity for gender mainstreaming and corporate accountability for gender equality results through improved monitoring and reporting; strengthened knowledge management for gender equality; and increased inter-agency joint programming through UN country team gender thematic groups and inter-agency task forces. The Director discussed the finances for gender equality, including the total regular resources contribution of $12,800,000 for implementing the gender equality strategy; and human resources for gender mainstreaming, including staffing for regional programmes intended to stimulate and complement country-level gender action.

In January [dec. 2009/6], the Executive Board took note of the oral report on the implementation of the UNDP gender strategy and action plan and requested the Administrator to provide such a report annually, for the remainder of UNDP's strategic plan 2008–2011 [YUN 2007, p. 898], at its first regular session each year.

Programming arrangements

Monitoring and evaluation

The UNDP/UNFPA Executive Board, at its May/June session, considered the annual report on evaluation in UNDP, issued in March [DP/2009/13]. The report, which covered the period from March 2008 to February 2009, provided information on evaluation coverage, compliance, quality, resources and capacity; initiatives undertaken by the United Nations Evaluation Group (UNEG); and evaluation use. It also presented key findings and the Evaluation Office programme of work for the 2009–2010 period.

The methodology of the country-level programme evaluations, known as the assessment of development results, was enhanced and harmonized across all evaluations, which positioned the Evaluation Office to expand coverage of the assessments. The Office codified good practices; identified measures for improving the technical quality of thematic evaluations; and institutionalized an external quality-assurance system. Coverage of assessments of development results increased by more than 100 per cent. Nine such assessments, compared with four in the previous year, were completed in Afghanistan, Argentina, Barbados and the Organization of Eastern Caribbean States, Bosnia and Herzegovina, Botswana, Guatemala, the Philippines, Tajikistan and Uzbekistan. UNDP developed a directive to reinforce the roles and oversight responsibilities of the regional bureaux with respect to country offices, and UNEG developed ethical guidelines that expanded on its code of conduct for evaluation.

During the reporting period, 50 per cent of country offices carried out 158 evaluations, including 121 project evaluations and 24 outcome evaluations. Audits conducted by the Office of Audit and Investigation highlighted weak compliance in planning and undertaking outcome evaluations. Of the 701 audit recommendations made in 2008, 13 were made in response to the absence of planned outcome evaluations or their delayed execution.

The independent evaluations found that UNDP had made a concerted effort to provide expert policy advice, but more needed to be done in that regard. UNDP was often seen as an effective administrator of donor funds rather than a substantive development partner. In countries where a high proportion of the budget came from the programme country, evaluations pointed to the tendency of UNDP to become a service provider to the Government, and found that UNDP should focus on building the substantive capacities of its staff. Where Government capacity was not sufficiently strong, UNDP might have to engage in the administration of public funds in the short term. UNDP did not, however, always integrate the development of the capacity of national partners and institutions in those programmes. UNDP business services, including procurement and recruitment, risked substituting the implementation capacity of national institutions instead of strengthening them. Nearly every assessment of development results mentioned the lack of an exit strategy. While most programmes were in line with the UNDP mandate and national priorities, they often lacked focus. UNDP programmes were largely relevant to national challenges, but there was often a missing link between the broad strategic goals and outcomes, and associated projects and outputs.

UNDP was seen as an impartial development partner with a nearly universal global presence, which provided the Programme with strategic advantages in facilitating policy dialogue, knowledge-sharing and coordination for development results. Women were increasingly serving as administrators and experts in planning and executing UNDP projects, but seven evaluations highlighted the fact that gender had not been adequately mainstreamed into programme work. Regarding UN coordination, UNDP was generally seen as an effective convener of disparate partners on the ground, and was facilitating joint planning through the United Nations Development Assistance

Framework (UNDAF), but the assessments of development results showed few examples of implementation collaboration through joint programmes. The uneven application of results-based management principles in programming, monitoring and evaluation was a common theme in many evaluations. Although most projects in the country programmes achieved the stated outputs, it was less clear that UNDP contributed to outcomes.

An April report [DP/2009/16], submitted in response to a 2008 Executive Board decision [YUN 2008, p. 973], provided a statistical overview of the status of implementation of key actions in management responses to independent evaluations since the Board had approved the evaluation policy in 2006 [YUN 2006, p. 1040], and a statistical overview of the status of implementation of key actions in management responses to mandatory outcome evaluations at the decentralized level in 2008. It also described internal systems for follow-up to management responses. While those systems had led to progress in the submission and tracking of responses, further efforts were needed to ensure stricter compliance with the management response system as a key element of the UNDP commitment to a culture of monitoring, evaluation and learning across the Programme. Follow-up actions were described in an annex to the report.

On 2 June [dec. 2009/11], the Executive Board took note of the report on evaluation in UNDP and requested UNDP to address the issues raised therein. It noted the decline in the number of decentralized evaluations and asked UNDP to strengthen decentralized evaluation capacity to monitor and evaluate programmes at the country level, and to increase the use of those evaluations as the basis for decision-making for improvements. The Board also requested UNDP to improve compliance with conducting outcome evaluations through the establishment and resourcing of achievable country programme evaluation plans. It emphasized the need for UNDP to improve programme planning and results-based management in order to improve the design and methodology of decentralized evaluations. The Board acknowledged the increase in dedicated monitoring and evaluation specialists in 2008, and encouraged UNDP to continue professionalizing the function through improvements in dedicated personnel and their sustainability to address the fact that some programming units were without such expertise. It encouraged UNDP to further improve the submission and tracking of management responses to evaluations to improve accountability and transparency on evaluation follow-up, and requested UNDP to support national evaluation capacity development. UNDP was encouraged to continue to conduct joint evaluations with other UN organizations while retaining a focus on its accountability.

The Board approved the 2009–2010 programme of work proposed by the Evaluation Office.

On 3 June [dec. 2009/19], the Executive Board took note of the April report on follow-up to management responses to independent and decentralized evaluations.

Evaluation of cooperation agreement between UNIDO and UNDP

The UNDP/UNFPA Executive Board, at its September session, considered a July report [DP/2009/32] containing the Executive Summary of the joint terminal evaluation of the cooperation agreement between UNIDO and UNDP, which was signed on 23 September 2004 for a period of five years. The purpose of the evaluation was to present evidence and findings on past performance, as well as recommendations for both organizations. The evaluation focused on the 2006–2009 period and was conducted jointly from March to July 2009 by the UNDP Evaluation Office and the UNIDO Evaluation Group. It covered the two components of the cooperation agreement: the "UNIDO desks" component and the "joint private sector development" component.

The evaluation concluded, among other things, that the cooperation agreement addressed, at an early stage, issues of enhanced system-wide coherence but did not fully take into account the country-level conditions or the existing modalities for inter-agency collaboration. The UNIDO/UNDP partnership failed to avail itself of the opportunity to involve other UN organizations working in the area of private sector development. The systemic asymmetries in programming arrangements posed a considerable challenge to the successful implementation of the agreement, which was of limited relevance and effectiveness as an incentive for joint programming. Several UNIDO desks demonstrated that the concept worked, but not every UNIDO desk added value to the programme country, and it was a shortcoming that UNIDO had not established a functioning review mechanism for the component. As a result of the agreement, UNIDO expanded its country presence by over 50 per cent, with field representation in 46 countries by the end of 2009. Nevertheless, the goal of UNIDO to expand its presence to 80 countries appeared unrealistic unless the technical cooperation implementation capacity of UNIDO headquarters was increased.

The private sector development component of the agreement did not achieve any results. Only two projects—in the Lao People's Democratic Republic and Rwanda—from the original joint programming exercise passed the formulation stage and were implemented; in both cases, only a small fraction of the original budget could be mobilized. The lack of established procedures and clear operational guidance for the implementation of the agreement at the country level led each organization to proceed according to its respective modus operandi, slowing progress in joint programming and fundraising for private sector development.

The evaluation recommended that, in line with UN reform efforts, bilateral agreements among UN organizations working on private sector development should be replaced with a system-wide cluster approach involving all relevant units in order to further coordination, coherence and synergies. Until a system-wide approach was developed, the existing partnership agreement between UNIDO and UNDP should be replaced with a memorandum of understanding that defined operational and administrative arrangements at the country level, including provisions for UNIDO desks. The memorandum of understanding should provide an institutional framework of cooperation and facilitate collaboration between the parties. Further recommendations dealt with issues related to UNIDO desks and joint private sector development programmes.

On 11 September [dec. 2009/23], the Executive Board took note of the evaluation and requested UNDP to implement its recommendations, taking into consideration the deliberations of the upcoming UNIDO General Conference (Vienna, 7–11 December). UNDP was encouraged to replace the existing partnership agreement with a memorandum of understanding that described the thematic areas of interest and simplified and standardized cooperation, including administrative arrangements, to ensure flexible and relevant support to national priorities.

Strategic plan, 2008–2011

At its May/June session, the Executive Board considered an April report on the operationalization of the UNDP strategic plan, 2008–2011 [DP/2009/11]. The report outlined proposals for providing the Board with a comprehensive report on performance and results and a midterm review in 2010. It provided information on the status of strategic plan commitments, including baselines for the first of three indicators in the plan's development results framework: the number of programme countries requesting UNDP support for each outcome; adjustments of priorities and operations in response to events or lessons learned; and priority actions needed to meet those commitments. The report also discussed global development challenges; as well as achievements, challenges and priority actions related to operationalizing the strategic plan, and to coordination and management results. Also before the Board were a March report [DP/2009/11/Add.1] summarizing UNDP management responses to recommendations contained in the reports issued by

JIU in 2008; and a statistical annex issued in May [DP/2009/11/Add.2 & Corr.1].

On 2 June [dec. 2009/9], the Executive Board took note of the annual report on the operationalization of the strategic plan, 2008–2011. It urged UNDP to continue to strengthen the report, starting in 2010, to integrate information on its contributions to the development outcomes of the strategic plan; and supported the UNDP plan to provide more in-depth analysis, starting in programme areas with higher demand. The Board noted with concern that earmarked resources continued to far exceed UNDP regular resources, and that core resources, because of their untied nature, formed the bedrock of UNDP finances. It extended the UNDP strategic plan, 2008–2011, including the integrated financial resources framework and relevant UNDP global and regional programmes, to 2013. The Board requested the Administrator to submit to the Executive Board in 2011 a midterm review of the extended strategic plan, 2008–2013, including the integrated financial resources framework and the relevant UNDP global and regional programmes. The Administrator was also asked to submit to the Executive Board, at its first regular session in 2013, a cumulative review of the extended strategic plan prior to the submission of a draft of the UNDP strategic plan, 2014–2017, at the annual session, and ahead of its formal submission at the second regular session.

On 3 June [dec. 2009/19], the Executive Board took note of the report on the 2008 JIU recommendations and the statistical annex.

Financial and administrative matters

The UNDP Administrator, in the annual review of the financial situation [DP/2010/35 & Add.1], reported that total income—comprised of contributions, interest and other income—decreased by 4 per cent, from $6.03 billion in 2008 to $5.79 billion in 2009. Contributions decreased from $5.50 billion in 2008 to $5.34 billion in 2009; interest income from $0.18 billion to $0.10 billion; and other income from $0.36 billion to $0.35 billion. Total regular resources income, including interest and other income, decreased by 13 per cent, from $1.21 billion to $1.05 billion. Contributions to core resources decreased by 8 per cent in 2009, to $1.01 billion, compared with $1.10 billion contributed in 2008. In 2009, core resources fell short of the projected target of $1.25 billion of the integrated financial resources framework of the 2008–2011 strategic plan [YUN 2007, p. 897] by 19 per cent. Contributions from the top 10 donors to regular resources decreased by 4 per cent in dollar terms, to $828 million from $859 million in 2008.

Non-core contributions reached $4.13 billion in 2009, just below the $4.16 billion contributed in 2008. Bilateral contributions amounted to $1.56 billion in 2009, representing an increase of 8 per cent compared with 2008 and exceeding the annual average of $1.25 billion estimated in the strategic plan. Non-core resources entrusted to UNDP by non-bilateral partners and multilateral funds reached $1.55 billion, representing an increase of 15 per cent over 2008 and exceeding the estimated annual average of $1.37 billion. Local resources amounted to $0.72 billion, a decrease of 25 per cent compared with 2008. Multi-donor trust fund income, including joint programmes and management and operational services provided by UNDP, increased to $1.78 billion compared with $1.5 billion in 2008. Overall income for other resources decreased by $0.03 billion (1 per cent), from $4.55 billion in 2008 to $4.52 billion in 2009.

Overall UNDP expenditures increased by 3 per cent, from $5.39 billion in 2008 to $5.53 billion in 2009. Total regular resources expenditure increased by 11 per cent, from $1.05 billion to $1.17 billion in 2009. Programme expenditure from regular resources, including programme support to the resident coordinator system, development support services and the UNDP economist programme, increased by 3 per cent, from $617 million to $635 million in 2009. By category, 74 per cent of the expenditure was spent on biennial support budget functions, 19 per cent on the UNDP-specific function of country-office support to UN activities, 1 per cent on the United Nations Development Operations Coordination Office, 5 per cent on the United Nations Volunteers (UNV) programme and 1 per cent on UNCDF. In total, 60 per cent of the expenditure related to country offices, with the remaining 40 per cent attributed to headquarters locations, including UNV.

By region, Africa recorded the highest expenditure of regular resources, with $270 million, followed by Asia and the Pacific with $161 million, Europe and the Commonwealth of Independent States with $45 million, and Arab States and Latin America, each with $41 million. The expenditure for global and other programmes was $72 million.

At the end of 2009, the overall balance of unexpended resources amounted to $5.19 billion, compared with $5.05 billion in 2008. The balance of unexpended regular resources, excluding the operational reserve, was $354 million, compared with $499 million in 2008, representing 7 per cent of the overall balance. The balance of unexpended other resources at the end of 2009 increased by 6 per cent with $4.55 billion, compared to $4.30 billion at the end of 2008.

In September [dec. 2009/20], the Executive Board took note of the annual review of the financial situation for 2008 [YUN 2008, p. 975] and requested that UNDP include information on cost recovery income and expenditure in its future financial reviews.

Regular funding commitments to UNDP

In May [DP/2009/12], UNDP submitted a report on the status of regular funding commitments to the Programme and its associated funds and programmes for 2009 and onward. Provisional data showed that contributions to regular resources for 2008 amounted to $1.10 billion, slightly below the $1.12 billion achieved in 2007 but meeting the first annual target for regular resources as set out in the UNDP strategic plan, 2008–2011 [YUN 2007, p. 897]. Although not all donor countries were in a position to maintain their contributions, the 2007 level was reached due to volume increases in regular contributions in nominal local currency terms in some countries; exchange rate gains; and full payment of pledges made by Member States. Based on UN exchange rates as at 1 May, contributions were expected to decrease to approximately $985 million in 2009, falling considerably short of the second annual target set out in the strategic plan. Most donors pledged to maintain their contributions in 2009, but for the first time in many years, some countries would decrease their contributions. Eight members of the Organisation for Economic Cooperation and Development/ Development Assistance Committee (OECD/DAC) increased their contributions to regular resources in 2008; one increased its contribution by 71 per cent and two increased their contributions by 40 per cent or more. Twenty-five Member States, including 21 of the 22 OECD/DAC members, contributed $1 million or more to regular resources. Although a number of donors delayed payment of significant proportions of their pledges, UNDP did not have to draw upon its operational reserves.

In June [dec. 2009/10], the Executive Board took note of the report. It noted that UNDP was able to meet the first annual (2008) funding target for regular ("core") resources set out in the 2008–2011 strategic plan, and requested all countries that had not done so to make contributions to regular resources for 2009. The Board also noted with concern that UNDP regular resources were expected to fall to $965 million and therefore not reach the targeted $1.25 billion in 2009, in addition to being highly unpredictable for 2010. In that regard, it called on UNDP to hold an informal consultation with the Board on a strategy to address the projected funding gap. The Board recognized that strengthening the role and capacity of UNDP to assist countries in achieving their development goals required an increase in resources in line with the projections calculated in the UNDP 2008–2011 strategic plan and an expansion of its resource base on a continuous, predictable and assured basis. Member States were encouraged to announce and adhere to multi-year pledges and payment schedules.

Biennial support budget, 2010–2011

The UNDP/UNFPA Executive Board, at its September session, considered an August report [DP/2009/30] on the methodology and approach to the UNDP biennial support budget, 2010–2011. The report contained an overview of major areas and proposals that would be included in the biennial support budget. The proposals sought to ensure that UNDP was able to provide high-quality policy advice and capacity development support in providing demand-driven development, coordination and management services funded from regular and other resources, in response to the needs of programme countries. Within the overall framework of the strategic plan, 2008–2011, the Administrator determined that priority should be given to working effectively with programme countries to reduce poverty and achieve the MDGs [YUN 2000, p. 51]. The report described the financial context for the 2010–2011 budget, including cost efficiency, investing in the organization and improving transparency. It contained a proposed outline of the integrated resources plan, which sought to provide a coherent, transparent presentation of UNDP activities, costs and budgetary allocations, and their linkages to organizational goals and plans, primarily through improved alignment, integration and harmonization. In order to implement a strategic alignment in which all activities funded from regular and other resources were classified transparently, UNDP was seeking guidance from the Executive Board on three broad cost classifications defined in the report: development, management and special-purpose costs. The report also described a series of harmonization review initiatives launched in 2009 that supported the overall objective of the integrated resources plan and the classification of activities and costs. The reviews included an internal UNDP country office cost classification review; an internal central programme unit cost classification review; an external cost classification benchmarking exercise with bilateral agencies; and a harmonization review with UNFPA and UNICEF. The methodology and approach for results-based budgeting in the biennial support budget, 2010–2011, would continue to be based on the 16 harmonized and 3 UNDP-specific management functions introduced in the biennial support budget, 2008–2009 [YUN 2008, p. 976]. UNDP recommended that the biennial support budget, 2010–2011, be considered in the context of a comprehensive discussion of the resources framework, encompassing the UNDP integrated resources plan, with an emphasis on the biennial support budget and the programming arrangements framework, and the link between them.

In an 11 September decision [dec. 2009/22], the Executive Board took note of the report on the methodology and approach to the UNDP biennial support budget, 2010–2011. It endorsed the approach proposed in the report, with the provisions outlined in the decision. In the context of improving transparency, the Board recommended four broad classifications of activities and costs: development, management, UN development coordination and special purpose. In that regard, it requested UNDP to propose how to treat costs relating to UN development coordination as a separate cost category within its budget instruments. As to improving transparency, accountability and harmonization, it endorsed the UNDP decision to base post cost classification on the "whole post" approach—whereby each individual post was paid from a single cost category—for all posts charged against budget categories and functions within the budget instrument(s) of the organization, with the exception of the posts relating to UN development coordination. Regarding development activities and costs, the Board endorsed two subclassifications of activities and costs: programmes and development effectiveness. It endorsed those categories of activities and costs that were more appropriately considered "programmes", and those that were more appropriately considered "development effectiveness". The Board also endorsed two categories of activities and costs: programme development and implementation, and programme policy advisory services. Under special-purpose costs and activities, it endorsed three sub-classifications of activities and costs: General Assembly—mandated activities, capital investments and non-UNDP operations administered by UNDP.

The Board requested UNDP, in applying the decision, to strengthen harmonization in cooperation with UNFPA and UNICEF; underlined that the changes would not cause a reduction in the allocation for programme activities; and stressed the need to outline clearly the costs relating to the sub-classifications shifted between budget instruments. UNDP was also asked to engage in an informal consultation process with the Board, with a view to taking action on the biennial support budget, 2010–2011, in 2010. The Board requested the UNDP Administrator to continue to improve the method of budgeting in collaboration with UNFPA and UNICEF, with a view to presentation by each organization of a single, integrated budget that included all budgetary categories to complement the next strategic plan, and, in that regard, requested a joint preliminary briefing note on steps taken and progress achieved in 2011 and a joint report in 2012. The Administrator was also asked to collaborate with UNFPA and UNICEF towards greater harmonization in the UNDP biennial support budget, 2012–2013, and to submit a joint report in 2010 on: improved results focus and enhanced linkages with the institutional results of the strategic plan; and further harmonized budget methodologies, including the attribution of costs between programme and support budgets, and the determination of a common method for the treat-

ment of similar cost items across and within respective budgets and funding frameworks. The Administrator was further asked, as a step towards the single, integrated budget for UNDP, to improve the UNDP biennial support budget, 2012–2013, by: improving the linkages between biennial support budget resources and results; providing summary explanations of any proposed budgetary changes and their attribution to volume and to nominal and statutory changes; and providing information on cost recovery by describing how projected recoveries from extrabudgetary resources were calculated, including updated information on UNDP variable indirect costs. The Board emphasized the need for consultation with its members in making improvements to the UNDP biennial support budget, 2012–2013, and to the single, integrated budget for each organization, beginning in 2014. In that regard, it requested UNDP, in collaboration with UNFPA and UNICEF, to present, in 2010, a note outlining a road map for achieving the objectives identified in the decision.

At its special session held on 17 November [dec. 2009/29], the Board approved an interim budget allocation for January 2010 in the amount of $38.1 million, pending final approval of the UNDP biennial support budget for 2010–2011. It agreed that the interim budget allocation would be part of, and not incremental to, the 2010–2011 budget.

Audit reports

The UNDP/UNFPA Executive Board, at its January session [DP/2009/5], considered the Administrator's report on the implementation of the recommendations of the United Nations Board of Auditors for the 2006–2007 biennium [YUN 2008, p. 1559]. The Board of Auditors issued an unqualified audit opinion on the UNDP financial statements for that period; UNDP was one of 7 UN organizations of the 16 audited to receive such an opinion. The significance of the unqualified opinion was that for the 2004–2005 biennium, the Board had issued a modified opinion, which signified audit concerns. The Administrator stated that the positive result reaffirmed the strategic thrust of management initiatives implemented over several years aimed at addressing key audit findings, as well as systemic issues underlying those findings.

Of the 82 audit recommendations made by the Board of Auditors for the 2006–2007 biennium, 5 were fully implemented as at 31 October and another 70 were partially implemented. Together, those numbers represented 91 per cent of the recommendations. UNDP targeted full implementation of at least 80 per cent of the recommendations by the fourth quarter of 2009 and the remaining recommendations by the second quarter of 2010.

The report also reviewed progress made since the Administrator's previous update in 2008 [ibid., p. 979] in addressing the top 15 audit priorities in UNDP in the 2006–2007 biennium, as set out in the Administrator's 2007 report [YUN 2007, p. 900]. Significant progress included improved management of fiduciary risks associated with nationally executed projects and audit results; reconciliation of all headquarters and country office bank accounts; mitigation of key risks with enhanced internal controls in the Atlas enterprise resource planning system and exception transaction monitoring; and, with the migration of UNDP Brazil human and financial resources management to Atlas in 2008, the achievement of a truly global financial and human resources management system covering all UNDP offices. UNDP was revising its top 15 audit priorities to better reflect remaining risk and new or emerging risks highlighted by the Board of Auditors. Progress in addressing the priorities reflected the significant investment made in implementing specific management strategies. It was envisaged that UNDP would move towards 10 top priorities for the 2008–2009 period.

In January [dec. 2009/2], the Executive Board, having reviewed the reports of UNDP, UNFPA and the United Nations Office for Project Services (UNOPS) on the implementation of the recommendations of the Board of Auditors, 2006–2007, requested the three bodies to provide a joint briefing at the annual Executive Board session in May and June, including a conference room paper, on the preparations, implementation and implications of the International Public Sector Accounting Standards on those bodies. It noted that the Board of Auditors had issued an unqualified audit opinion for UNDP with respect to the biennium ended 31 December 2007; recognized the progress made by UNDP in addressing the top 15 audit priorities in the 2006–2007 biennium; expressed its support for the specific efforts made by UNDP to address key audit priorities in the 2008–2009 biennium; and stressed the importance of timely and full implementation of the recommendations of the Board of Auditors. UNDP was requested to provide, with future reports to the Executive Board, an accompanying matrix illustrating the status of implementation of the recommendations of the Board of Auditors, including proposed actions.

In March [DP/2009/23], the UNDP Office of Audit and Investigations (OAI) submitted to the Executive Board its report on internal audit and investigation activities for the year ended 31 December 2008. As requested by the Board in a 2008 decision [YUN 2008, p. 980], the report contained a list of the key findings and audit ratings; a table containing the unresolved recommendations by year and category; an explanation of findings that had remained unresolved for 18 months or more; the outcome of investigations

on the misconduct of staff members; an update on progress made regarding audits rated unsatisfactory; the outcome of risk-based audit planning; and the status of the OAI staffing situation. The annual report of the Audit Advisory Committee was appended to the report.

OAI issued 57 reports in 2008, pertaining to 3 headquarters audits and 54 country office audits, which included 3 special audits and 2 audits of projects directly executed by country offices. The 54 country office audits accounted for about $0.95 billion, or 25 per cent of the $3.9 billion in expenditures incurred by UNDP at the country-office level in 2007. The country office audit risk assessment conducted in 2008 for the planning of 2009 audits resulted in 4 (3 per cent) of the 141 offices assessed being ranked high audit risk, 84 (60 per cent) ranked medium risk, and the remainder ranked low risk. Six of the internal audit reports pertaining to country offices had no overall rating, since they were either special reviews or follow-up audits. Based on the results of the remaining 48 audits, with 40 having either satisfactory or partially satisfactory ratings, OAI found that the internal controls and risk-management practices were generally established and functioning, but needed improvement. Eight audits resulted in an unsatisfactory rating. The majority of the issues identified in the audits were rated high-risk, and originated mostly in the areas of strategic management and procurement, thus jeopardizing country office objectives. Periodic desk reviews showed that two of the eight country offices rated unsatisfactory had already made substantial progress in implementing recommendations as at 31 December 2008. The 54 reports issued in 2008 contained 701 recommendations.

OAI introduced a risk-assessment methodology in selecting projects to be audited, resulting in a sharper focus on high-risk projects and a reduction of about 200 audit reports compared with the previous year. A total of 1,765 audit reports from 122 countries were expected, covering $2 billion, or 85 per cent, of the total expenditure of $2.4 billion related to projects executed by NGOs or Governments for fiscal year 2007. As at 31 December 2008, OAI had received 1,733 (98 per cent) of the audit reports required, encompassing project expenditures amounting to $1.96 billion (98 per cent). The audit reports covered audit opinion and net financial impact, outcome, scope, and administration.

Regarding investigation activities, OAI received 135 complaints in 2008, which constituted a 19 per cent increase in caseload compared with the 113 complaints received in 2007. In addition, 85 complaints were carried forward from 2007. The majority of complaints related to fraud or other financial misconduct (31 per cent) and abuse of authority or workplace harassment (26 per cent), followed by staff misconduct, such as insubordination, inappropriate acts, or violation of local laws (21 per cent), and personal disputes (18 per cent). A total of 142 complaints were closed in 2008, reducing the caseload by 9 per cent. As a result of the preliminary assessment, 69 per cent of the 142 complaints processed were found to be unsubstantiated and did not require further investigation. The rest (31 per cent) were formally investigated by OAI and were found to be substantiated, leading to submission of an investigation report to the Legal Support Office. Twenty cases were closed, and 20 investigation reports were submitted to the Office recommending disciplinary proceedings against 19 staff members. From February to December 2008, the Legal Support Office concluded such proceedings in 10 cases, of which 8 resulted in the imposition of disciplinary measures. During the period, an additional 8 staff members were formally charged with misconduct.

At the beginning of 2009, OAI subjected itself to an external quality-assurance review of its investigation function. The review would assess the conformity of OAI with generally accepted standards for investigators in international organizations and identify potential areas for further improvement.

In June [dec. 2009/15], the Executive Board took note of the report on internal audit and investigations and the annual report of the Audit Advisory Committee for 2008; the report on UNFPA internal audit and oversight activities in 2008 (see p. 1053); and the report of UNOPS on internal audit services to the organization in 2008. It requested UNDP and UNFPA to address all operational issues identified in the reports, with particular attention given to capacity-building. It also requested UNDP, UNFPA and UNOPS to provide the concerned Governments with adequate time to review and comment on the internal audit reports, prior to disclosure. The Board endorsed the decision of UNDP, UNFPA and UNOPS to defer implementation of the International Public Sector Accounting Standards (IPSAS) by 2012, and requested the UNDP Administrator and the UNFPA and UNOPS Executive Directors to commit, as a matter of priority, to adopting IPSAS no later than 2012 and submitting to the Board their IPSAS-compliant financial statements for the year 2012 in 2013. UNDP, UNFPA and UNOPS were asked to make their IPSAS implementation plans available on their respective websites, and to update the Executive Board on a regular basis until the financial statements were submitted in 2013. The Board shared the concern of UNDP and UNFPA management on the recurrent findings outlined in their respective internal audit reports relating to project and programme management and monitoring and evaluation, and looked forward to significant improvements in audit findings relating to those areas by 2010, to be reported to the Board in 2011. UNDP and UNFPA management were asked to

inform the Board on strategies and activities they had implemented to address the recurrent audit findings identified. The Board encouraged UNDP to expand its audit coverage of headquarters units, and noted with concern the number of country office audits, which gave rise to an unsatisfactory audit rating. It noted the decreasing number of audit recommendations that remained outstanding after more than 18 months, and requested UNDP to maintain its follow-up efforts for implementing those recommendations. The Board noted with appreciation the significant progress made in the timely submission of audit reports covering projects executed by NGOs and/or Governments. UNDP was requested to address the recurrent findings on audit issues identified in its report on internal audit and investigation, including weaknesses in procurement, asset management and financial resources, as a matter of priority and in future planning efforts in country offices and at headquarters.

Regarding UNOPS, the Board took note of the annual report of the Strategic and Advisory Committee for 2008 and endorsed the revised terms of reference included therein, subject to modifications set out in the decision.

UNDP Ethics Office

In response to a 2008 Executive Board decision [YUN 2008, p. 980], the UNDP Ethics Office in March submitted to the Administrator, the first report on its activities from 1 December 2007 to 31 December 2008 [DP/2009/25]. The Administrator established the Office on 1 December 2007 pursuant to the Secretary-General's bulletin ST/SGB/2007/11 on UN system-wide application of ethics: separately administered organs and programmes. The Office's main areas of responsibility included developing standards, training and education on ethics issues; providing guidance to ensure that UNDP rules, policies, procedures and practices reinforced and promoted the standards of integrity called for under the Charter of the United Nations; providing confidential advice and guidance to staff on ethical issues; serving as a focal point for raising staff awareness on ethical standards and expected behavior; protecting staff against retaliation for having reported misconduct and having cooperated with authorized audits or investigations; administering the financial disclosure policy; and reporting annually to the executive head on its activities.

During the reporting period, the Ethics Office received 186 requests, including 89 related to ethics advice; 29 to training; 17 to protection against retaliation for reports of wrongdoing; 45 to general information; and 6 to standard-setting. Of the 17 complaints of retaliation received, 1 was dropped and 7 were found to be outside the scope of the Ethics

Office mandate. Advice was provided in three cases, and referrals to other offices were made in four cases. Of the remaining nine complaints that warranted preliminary review, three were determined to meet the test of a prima facie case, and were referred to OAI for investigation. At the conclusion of the investigation, evidence of retaliation was found in one case.

The 2007 financial disclosure exercise filing period began in October 2008. Of the 1,718 staff members who were required to comply, 1,716 fulfilled the filing requirement, representing a 99.9 per cent compliance rate. The Office was following up on those staff members who had not complied with the mandatory disclosure exercises in 2006 and 2007, and was reviewing 3,309 statements submitted during those exercises by staff, who reported 14,227 transactions.

The report also contained information on the United Nations Ethics Committee, which was established in 2008. The Committee's mandate was to create a unified set of ethical standards and policies across UN funds and programmes, and to consult on issues raised by the Committee Chairperson or members that had implications for the UN system. The Ethics Office participated regularly in the Committee meetings in 2008. The Committee's 2008 work programme focused on drafting the UN system-wide code of ethics, comparing the protection against retaliation policies of its members, with a view to harmonization, and reviewing existing ethics training programmes.

The report concluded that there was a need to clarify UN staff regulations and rules, as well as UNDP human resources practices, in regulating outside gifts, hospitality and honours. Although the Office's work should be characterized by independence, it needed to be seen within the larger context of the UNDP goals. In particular, the Office needed to support initiatives for strengthening human resources management and organizational accountability. The Ethics Office would support UNDP efforts to operationalize the accountability framework approved by the Executive Board in 2008 [YUN 2008, p. 980].

The Board took note of the report in June [dec. 2009/15] (see p. 854).

Other technical cooperation

Development Account

In response to General Assembly resolution 56/237 [YUN 2001, p. 810], the Secretary-General submitted, in June [A/64/89], the sixth progress report on the implementation of projects financed from the

Development Account. The report provided an update on the management and coordination of the Account and contained proposals for the way forward. Since the establishment of the Account by the Assembly in 1997 [YUN 1997, p. 1394], 138 projects had been or were being implemented under six consecutive tranches, for an overall budget of $92.5 million. A four-year implementation cycle and the corresponding submission of mandatory detailed project documents and final evaluation reports were instituted. Although all 23 projects of the fourth tranche were closed as at 31 December 2008, 7 projects remained open for evaluation. The fifth tranche—the largest to date—comprised 24 projects, and its resource level totalled $21,551,900. The sixth tranche comprised 32 projects. Seventy-two projects—nearly half of all projects programmed since the inception of the Account—were being implemented through the fifth and sixth tranches for a total budget of approximately $40 million. The rate of implementation of the initial 24 projects of the fifth tranche was 59.6 per cent. Implementation of the six projects added through the recosting of the Account implemented following the adoption of resolution 60/246 [YUN 2005, p. 1489] and the additional appropriation of $2.5 million provided by the Assembly in section IV of resolution 61/252 [YUN 2006, p. 1615] was 53.2 per cent. The implementation rate for the initial 27 projects of the sixth tranche was 13 per cent. Activities under the 10 additional projects of the fifth tranche included through the additional funding of $5 million provided in resolution 62/235 A [YUN 2007, p. 1436], as well as the five additional projects of the sixth tranche funded from the $2.5 million appropriated by the Assembly in resolution 62/238 [ibid., 1436], were expected to be completed by 2011.

Preparations for the launch of the seventh tranche were made in the context of the proposed programme budget for 2010–2011 concerning the Development Account, as set out in a March report [A/64/6 (Sect. 35)]. The report provided information on 28 projects proposed for funding under the seventh tranche, which required $18,651,300 in resources. That amount was the same level as the revised appropriation for the 2008–2009 biennium, but represented an increase of $5,586,300 over the level of $13,065,000 approved by the Assembly in resolution 52/221 A [YUN 1997, p. 1434] at the inception of the Account for the 1998–1999 biennium. With the Assembly's approval of the proposed projects (see below), the Development Account would comprise 166 projects.

Although the volume, scope and complexity of managing the Account had increased considerably since its inception, the Account was well positioned to support the response of the United Nations to key global development challenges. Management of the Account was strengthened through the formation, by the Under-Secretary-General for Economic and Social Affairs, of the Steering Committee of the Development Account, an inter-entity coordination framework of the Executive Committee on Economic and Social Affairs; the Steering Committee would provide advice and assistance to the Under-Secretary-General concerning the Account. The provision of support to the Under-Secretary-General in the exercise of his responsibility as programme manager was assigned to the newly established Capacity Development Office in DESA.

The Advisory Committee on Administrative and Budgetary Questions (ACABQ), in its first report on the proposed programme budget for 2010–2011 [A/64/7], recommended that the Assembly approve the Secretary-General's proposal concerning the Development Account. In **resolution 64/243** of 24 December (see p. 1395), the Assembly appropriated an additional $5 million for the Development Account.

UN activities

Department of Economic and Social Affairs

During 2009, the Department of Economic and Social Affairs (DESA) had approximately 442 technical cooperation projects under execution in a dozen substantive sectors, with a total project expenditure of $69.8 million. Projects financed by UNDP represented $2.5 million, and those by trust funds, $67.3 million. On a geographical basis, the DESA technical cooperation programme included expenditures of $40.5 million for interregional and global programmes; $22.9 million in Asia and the Pacific; $3.5 million in Africa; $2.5 million in the Middle East; and $0.4 million in the Americas.

Distribution of expenditures by substantive sectors was as follows: associate expert programme, $30.3 million; programme support, $24 million; regional development, $3.7 million; governance and public administration, $3.1 million; knowledge management, $1.9 million; statistics, $1.8 million; socio economic governance management, $1.8 million; communication and outreach, $1.4 million; water and energy, $1.1 million; small islands developing States, $0.2 million; advancement of women, $0.2 million; social development, $0.1 million; policy analysis and networks, $0.1 million; and the United Nations Forum on Forests, $0.1 million. Of the total delivery of $69.8 million, the associate expert programme comprised 43 per cent; programme support, 34 per cent; regional development, 5 per cent, and governance and public administration, 4 per cent.

On a component basis, the Department's delivery in 2009 included $61.6 million for project personnel; $3.2 million for training; $2.9 million for sub-contracts; $1.3 million for equipment; and $0.8 million for miscellaneous expenses.

The total expenditure for DESA against the UN regular programme of technical cooperation was $7.8 million. The total expenditure against the United Nations Development Account was $1.5 million.

UN Office for Partnerships

The United Nations Office for Partnerships, formed in 2006 [YUN 2006, p. 1046], served as the gateway for public-private partnerships with the UN system in furtherance of the MDGs. It oversaw the United Nations Fund for International Partnerships, the United Nations Democracy Fund, and Partnership Advisory Services and Outreach.

The Secretary-General, in his report on the activities of the Office in 2009 [A/65/347], said that it continued to facilitate innovative and rewarding partnerships and engage in valuable initiatives supporting the international development agenda. In addition to its work within the UN system, the Office's collaboration with the private sector and non-State actors continued to be essential in achieving the MDGs. The Office would focus on the regions most in need of support to achieve the final MDG targets: the Middle East, South-East Asia and sub-Saharan Africa.

The General Assembly, by **decision 64/547** of 24 December, took note of the Secretary-General's report on the 2008 activities of the Office for Partnerships [YUN 2008, p. 982].

UN Fund for International Partnerships

The United Nations Fund for International Partnerships (UNFIP) was established in 1998 [YUN 1998, p. 1297] to serve as an interface between the UN system and the United Nations Foundation, the public charity responsible for administering Robert E. Turner's $1 billion contribution in support of UN causes. As at 31 December, the cumulative allocations to UNFIP projects reached approximately $1.09 billion, of which $438.5 million represented core Turner funds and $651.2 million (59 per cent) was generated from other partners. More than 479 projects had been implemented by 43 UN entities in 124 countries.

In 2009, the projects of the children's health programme area were valued at $663.1 million for 103 projects; the population and women programme area, $137.9 million for 108 projects; the environment programme area, $165.9 million for 144 projects; and the peace, security and human rights programme area, $53.9 million for 61 projects. Sixty-three other projects were valued at $66.1 million.

United Nations Democracy Fund

The United Nations Democracy Fund (UNDEF) was established in 2005 [YUN 2005, p. 655] to support democratization throughout the world. It focused on supporting democratic institutions, promoting human rights and ensuring the participation of all groups in democratic processes. Through UNDEF, the United Nations Office for Partnerships had channelled approximately $75 million to 271 projects in 99 countries; 47 regional projects covering a further 28 countries; and 17 global projects. The projects ranged from strengthening civil society leadership skills and promoting the participation of women and youth, to media programmes allowing civil society to project its voice.

In 2009, UNDEF began funding its third round of projects. The Fund's Advisory Board recommended a portfolio of projects, which was approved by the Secretary-General. Following negotiations with the short-listed applicants, 67 projects were funded at a total cost of $18.9 million. UNDEF collected the required reports on projects funded under the first, second and third rounds; closed completed projects from the first round; reported on its achievements to the Advisory Board; and undertook initiatives to strengthen its donor base. As at 31 December, total contributions received exceeded $106 million.

UNDEF launched its fourth round of project proposals in November. By year's end, 1,966 applications from organizations in 137 countries had been received. The majority of applications came from local or regional organizations in Africa, Asia, the Americas and Europe.

Partnership Advisory Services and Outreach

Through Partnership Advisory Services and Outreach, the United Nations Office for Partnerships provided advice to academic institutions, companies, foundations, Government agencies, media groups, civil society organizations and other entities on how best to develop and implement public-private partnerships. Investment in high-impact initiatives was encouraged by providing advice to potential partners regarding procedures and best practices; assisting in the design of programmes and projects; advising companies on the conversion of the principles of the Global Compact, a multi-stakeholder corporate social responsibility initiative launched in 2000 [YUN 2000, p. 989], into practice; helping to establish and manage global and regional networks; and promoting the MDGs as a framework for action.

In 2009, the Office for Partnerships served on 17 task forces, including regionally focused groups, issue-based groups and coordination mechanisms. It received more than 1,400 external requests for advisory services, representing a 40 per cent increase compared with 2008. The majority of requests from non-State actors offered assistance in programmes focused on poverty reduction, education, health and disaster relief, and humanitarian assistance in the least developed countries. During the year, agreements and memorandums of understanding were established with external actors to formalize some of the partnerships in support of the MDGs. The Office provided advisory services concerning operational partnerships; policy and advocacy partnerships; resource- and expertise-sharing; and networks and alliances.

UN Office for Project Services

The United Nations Office for Project Services (UNOPS) was established in 1995 [YUN 1995, p. 900], in accordance with General Assembly decision 48/501 [YUN 1994, p. 806], as a separate, self-financing entity of the UN system to act as a service provider to UN organizations. It offered a broad range of services, from overall project management to the provision of single inputs.

2009 activities

The UNOPS Executive Director, in his annual report on UNOPS activities [DP/2010/30 & Corr.1], informed the Executive Board of progress made in 2009 towards the implementation of the 2007–2009 business strategy [YUN 2007, p. 905], which focused on financial viability, partner satisfaction, world-class business practices and performance, and workforce competence and motivation. In 2009, UNOPS delivered $1.1 billion through project implementation and spent $62.1 million administering it. The contribution to the operational reserve was $12 million, bringing the reserve to $42.1 million—a 40 per cent increase compared with 2008. Business acquisition in 2009 exceeded targets at $1.44 billion.

The UNOPS strategic plan, 2010–2013, endorsed by the UNDP/UNFPA Executive Board in September 2009 (see p. 854), articulated focus areas, known as implementation support practices (ISPs), which were demand-driven and would be reviewed annually. While the strategic plan did not come into effect until January 2010, the report reflected its structure and provided information on operational results in line with the goals outlined in the plan. The focus was to provide implementation support services to partners in the areas of physical infrastructure, public order and security, census and elections, environment, and health. In 2009, health was the largest ISP (30 per cent of total delivery), followed by public order and security (21 per cent); infrastructure (16 per cent); environment (10 per cent); and census and elections (2 per cent). UNDP continued to be the most important

UNOPS partner, accounting for 44 per cent of total implementation expenditures, with 6 per cent from core funds, about 10 per cent from trust funds (excluding United Nations Development Group multi-donor trust funds) and 28 per cent from management services agreements.

UNOPS issued or revised 12 of its 26 corporate policies, including the Legislative Framework, the Financial Regulations and Rules, the Engagement Acceptance Policy and the Client Pricing Policy. The UNOPS global structure was revised to institutionalize the "practice approach", which aligned policy, business processes, tools and people across functions, areas of service and support, and geography. It also enabled coordinated decision-making across the four management practices of project management, finance, procurement and human resources.

UNOPS was preparing to implement the International Public Sector Accounting Standards (IPSAS) by January 2012, in harmony with UNDP and UNFPA, which shared the same enterprise resource planning system. UNOPS was managing the transition from United Nations System Accounting Standards to IPSAS on the Prince2 project management methodology. The UNOPS Ethics Office was established as an independent office in February, and UNOPS adopted the draft United Nations Code of Ethics in April. In 2009, there were 96 referrals to the Ethics Officer, of which 92 were completed as a result of advice, the resolution of issues raised, or referrals to other officers. UNOPS implemented around 900 projects on behalf of its partners. It contributed to programme outcomes, which were split between the four goals described in the strategic plan (see below).

In May [dec. 2009/14], the Executive Board took note of the annual report of the UNOPS Executive Director on 2008 activities [YUN 2008, p. 983] and encouraged UNOPS to integrate additional information on analysis of its client satisfaction surveys into future reports.

Financial, administrative and operational matters

UNOPS strategic plan, 2010–2013

A July report [DP/2009/36] outlined the UNOPS strategic plan, 2010–2013, which focused and articulated the role of the Office as a provider of management services that contributed significantly to UN peacebuilding, humanitarian and development operations. In the spirit of UN coherence, the plan assumed a UNOPS without political, policy or substantive mandate. It recognized the UNOPS commitment to operating in a transparent, accountable manner, and emphasized the need to communicate openly and clearly with stakeholders. The report stated that the UNOPS mission was to expand the capacity of the UN system and its partners to implement peacebuilding, humanitarian and development operations that mattered for people in need. Its vision was to always satisfy partners with management services that met world-class standards of quality, speed and cost-effectiveness. UNOPS committed to the following core values and principles as the foundation for its organizational culture and operations: accountability for results and the efficient use of resources; respect of national ownership and capacity; harmonization within and beyond the UN system; and service to others. Through the strategic plan, the role and niches of UNOPS within the UN family should be well established and widely accepted. Essential elements of that objective included transparent, accountable management services meeting the highest international standards; external recognition through certification of core management functions, business processes and staff performing those functions; a proven track record of contributions to the operational results of the United Nations in peacebuilding, humanitarian and development operations; and systematically collected and shared knowledge in UNOPS focus areas. The four UNOPS management practices were project management, procurement, human resources and financial management. The strategic plan would commence with five ISPs: physical infrastructure; public order and security; census and elections; the environment; and health.

During the 2010–2013 period, four high-level "contribution goals" would define the work of UNOPS and contribute to the work and results of its partners. The goals included rebuilding peace and stability after conflict (contribution goal 1); promoting early recovery of communities affected by natural disasters (contribution goal 2); contributing to the ability of people to develop local economies and obtain social services (contribution goal 3); and contributing to environmental sustainability and adaptation to climate change (contribution goal 4). Cross-cutting concerns included gender equality and the empowerment of women; national capacity development; and environmental sustainability.

The report outlined a management results framework, which mapped goals and strategic performance objectives related to the partner, business, personnel and financial perspectives. Implementation of the strategic plan was supported by management tools based on the public sector version of the "balanced scorecard" and reinforced by target agreements with managers. Implementation of the plan would be reviewed in annual reports. The United Nations Board of Auditors would present audit reports to the Executive Board for the 2010–2011 biennium and annually thereafter.

In September [dec. 2009/25], the UNDP/UNFPA Executive Board endorsed the strategic plan proposed by the UNOPS Executive Director in July. It reaffirmed the UNOPS mandate to act as a service provider to the UN system agencies, funds and programmes; international and regional financial institutions; intergovernmental organizations; donor and recipient Governments; and NGOs. The Board reconfirmed the role of UNOPS as a central resource for the UN system in procurement and contracts management, as well as in civil works and physical infrastructure development, including the relevant capacity development activities. It authorized the Executive Director to: sign, in consultation with the resident coordinator or the humanitarian coordinator, as appropriate, direct service agreements with Governments; appoint UNOPS representatives; and, where it was not covered by a framework agreement of another UN entity, to sign host-country agreements on behalf of the United Nations with Governments regarding the activities of UNOPS in the host country, having previously informed the resident coordinator or the humanitarian coordinator, as appropriate. The Executive Director was requested to inform the Board, in his annual report, on the use of the authority given to sign host country agreements.

Financial regulations and rules

The UNDP/UNFPA Executive Board, at its January session, considered the UNOPS financial rules and regulations [DP/2009/4] proposed by the Office in response to a 2008 Board decision [YUN 2008, p. 984]. The regulations and rules codified and reinforced a number of institutional imperatives, including risk management; the internal financial controls mechanism; separation of duties; and internal and audit functions. They would enable UNOPS to operate on the basis of full cost recovery and generate sufficient net surplus to maintain operational reserves. Significant changes to the previous regulations and rules would permit the Executive Director to: accept contributions to the UNOPS biennial administrative budget or projects; enter into commitments and/or make project payments in advance of receipt of project funds; and redeploy funds within an approved biennial administrative budget. They also allowed the Executive Director to make such ex gratia payments as might be necessary in the best interests of UNOPS, provided the combined total of all such payments made in a biennium did not exceed 0.25 per cent of the biennial administrative budget approved by the Board. The proposed financial regulations and rules required that UNOPS make full accrual for the value of future personnel benefits, including post-employment, termination and other long-term personnel benefits.

The Executive Board also had before it the ACABQ report on the proposed revised UNOPS financial regulations and rules, and on the proposed comprehensive post classification contained in a 19 December 2008

letter from the Committee Chairman to the UNOPS Executive Director [AC/1673].

In a January decision [dec. 2009/4], the Executive Board took note of the proposed financial regulations and rules and the related ACABQ report. It approved the proposed financial regulations and rules, to take effect on 1 February 2009, with exceptions and modifications set out in the decision. The Board welcomed the engagement of UNOPS in inter-agency efforts to achieve harmonized financial regulations and rules, and recommended that the Executive Director review the financial regulations and rules, following completion of the inter-agency exercise, with a view to achieving harmonization to the extent possible, and that the Executive Director consult accordingly with the Board. It requested UNOPS to ensure that, when implementing rule 103.05 concerning the establishment of policies and procedures related to performance management, compensation schemes and increased competitiveness, its human resource practices did not contradict the United Nations Staff Regulations and Rules. The Strategy and Audit Advisory Committee was asked to inform the Board periodically on the implementation of the revised financial regulations and rules with a view to their further improvement. UNOPS and its UN partners were urged to continue to consult on the issue of trust funds and multi-donor trust funds, and their potential impact on the activities of UNOPS, and to present the recommended conclusions to the Executive Board at its May/June session.

Post classification

In January, the Executive Board considered a report [DP/2009/7] on comprehensive post classification at UNOPS and proposals concerning the implementation of the recommendations made by the team of consultants that conducted a comprehensive review of all 193 international posts approved by the Board. The Executive Director proposed a comprehensive package of post reclassifications to conform to UN job standards and reflect the operational realities of UNOPS. Existing gaps hampered optimal performance and the ability of the organization to contribute to UN development, peacebuilding and humanitarian operations. Based on the consultant's report, a number of posts were proposed for upgrade or downgrade. The most important upgrades included an Assistant Secretary-General position for the Deputy Executive Director and D-2 level positions for five regional directors and the directors of finance, human resources and procurement. Five deputy regional directors would be placed at the D-1 level. Operations Centre directors with large and complex portfolios were consistently placed at the D-1 level, whereas operations centre managers in other locations would serve at the

P-5 level. The oversight and policy functions were enhanced to appropriate levels, including an upgrade of the head of internal audit to D-1. The estimated costs of the proposed changes, if all were implemented as at 1 March 2009, was $1.045 million, or an increase of some 1.7 per cent over the total approved biennial administrative budget for the 2008–2009 biennium. The additional expenditure should contribute to the ability of UNOPS to meet its net revenue targets. Due to its fully self-financing status, UNOPS sought no external funding to meet those costs.

On 22 January [dec. 2009/5], the Executive Board took note of the report and of the UNOPS management objective to achieve, through the reclassification exercise, a reduction in the current attrition rates, as well as increased cost savings from greater productivity and reduced selection and training expenditures for new staff. The Board approved all the proposed post reclassifications set out in the report and the associated increase in the 2008–2009 biennial administrative budget of up to $1.045 million, and encouraged the Executive Director to prioritize the post upgrades for those positions with the greatest transformational impact for the Office. UNOPS was requested to report to the Board, in the Executive Director's annual report, on the implementation of the post upgrades, as well as on the productivity of the organization, including the impact on staff attrition rates and the ratio of administrative budget to programme expenditure.

Audit reports

In January [dec. 2009/2], the Executive Board, having reviewed the 2008 UNOPS report on the implementation of the recommendations of the Board of Auditors for the 2006–2007 biennium [YUN 2008, p. 985] noted that the Board of Auditors had issued an unqualified audit opinion for UNOPS with respect to that biennium, and stressed the importance of timely and full implementation of the recommendations. It acknowledged the progress made by UNOPS in strengthening internal controls and improving its financial viability since the release, in 2007, of the audit report for the biennium ending 31 December 2005 [YUN 2007, p. 906].

In April [DP/2009/24], the head of the UNOPS Internal Audit Office submitted the activity report on internal audit and related services for the year ended 31 December 2008, the first full year of operation for the Office. The report contained, among other details, a list of the key findings and the ratings of audit reports; information on unresolved audit recommendations; and an explanation of findings that had remained unresolved for 18 months or more. The audit strategy of the Office during the 2008–2009 period was to extend audit coverage to those UNOPS locations deemed as high and medium risk and to conduct func-

tional audits of key operational areas. The 2008 workplan was based on the overall objective of assisting the Executive Director in ensuring that internal controls and procedures function as envisaged. In preparing the workplan, the Office refined its risk assessment model to ensure consistency between internal audit priorities and UNOPS management goals. By early 2008, the Office was fully staffed and had significantly increased internal audit coverage, enhancing the overall UNOPS internal control environment.

During 2008, 40 audits were completed by the Office and submitted to the UNOPS Executive Director, a 67 per cent increase over the 24 audit reports issued in 2007. The reports generated 581 audit recommendations that could be analysed, a significant increase (505 per cent) from the 115 recommendations made in 2007. The results of the internal audit reports indicated that UNOPS did not have significant gaps in its internal controls, but rather that such controls were not being fully complied with and/or understood.

As at 31 December 2008, the implementation rate for 2007 audit recommendations was 72 per cent; for 2006, 77 per cent; and for 2005, 96 per cent. The percentage of outstanding audit recommendations unresolved for 18 months or more, when compared to the total unresolved recommendations at that date, was 4.6 per cent and 18.8 per cent as at 31 December 2007 and 31 December 2008, respectively, reflecting the increase in total recommendations issued in 2008.

Annexes to the Internal Audit Office report containing the 2008 annual report and the terms of reference of the UNOPS Strategy and Audit Advisory Committee, as well as the UNOPS management response to the Office's report, were provided on the UNDP/UNFPA Executive Board web page.

In a 3 June decision [dec. 2009/15], the Executive Board welcomed the progress made to increase the internal audit capacity and coverage of UNOPS in 2008. It took note of the 2008 annual report of the Strategic and Advisory Committee and endorsed the Committee's revised terms of reference, subject to modifications set out in the decision.

In October [DP/2010/14], UNOPS submitted a progress report on the implementation of the recommendations of the Board of Auditors for the 2006–2007 biennium. The report provided a response to each of the 48 recommendations, including three "matters of emphasis": unreconciled interfund amounts, the bulk of which concerned UNDP; deferred revenue; and non-expendable assets. The interfund balance with UNDP—about $43 million at the end of 2007—was fully reconciled as at 31 December 2008, and work aimed at eliminating discrepancies was nearing completion. Both UNDP and UNOPS reconciled interfund balances frequently, greatly reducing the likelihood of recurring interfund problems. The UNOPS–UNFPA interfund account was also fully reconciled and settled as at 31 December 2008. As to the problem of deferred revenue, work was well under way to complete the reconciliation exercise by the time the 2008–2009 accounts were closed. Unops made tangible improvements to its asset management systems during the 2008–2009 period. As at October 2009, unops began to manage property, plant and equipment using the Atlas assets module, and was on track to train personnel and strengthen procedures for proper "tagging" of assets. Implementation of ipsas represented a major hurdle for unops, and the Office embarked on a change management programme, including ipsas as one of its five pillars.

Procurement

In response to a 2007 Executive Board decision [YUN 2007, p. 905], the unops Executive Director submitted, in July, the executive summary of the annual statistical report on the procurement activities of the UN system in 2008 [DP/2009/37]. The report provided details on UN system procurement by country of supply. The report stated that the overall procurement volume of goods and services of UN organizations had increased to $13.6 billion in 2008, from $10.1 billion in 2007—a 34.4 per cent gain. Total procurement of goods increased by $1.5 billion (28.1 per cent), while procurement of services grew by $2 billion (41.3 per cent). Between 2004 and 2008, UN procurement more than doubled in volume, from $6.5 billion to $13.6 billion, primarily attributable to a $4.1 billion growth in the procurement of services. In 2008, the share of services exceeded that of goods by 0.6 per cent, reversing the 2007 data in which the procurement of goods exceeded that of services by 4.6 per cent.

In 2008, procurement from developing countries and countries with economies in transition increased by $1.5 billion over 2007, but their share of overall procurement volume decreased by 2.9 per cent. Procurement from such countries exceeded 50 per cent of total UN procurement volume in 2007 (53.6 per cent) and 2008 (50.7 per cent), while procurement from industrialized countries remained steady at 37.7 per cent in 2007 and 37.8 per cent in 2008.

In September [dec. 2009/25], the Executive Board took note of the annual statistical report on the procurement activities of the UN system organizations.

UN Volunteers

In 2009, 7,545 volunteers worked for the undp-administered United Nations Volunteers (unv) programme, compared with 7,753 in 2008. The volunteers, representing 158 nationalities, carried out 7,716 assignments in 128 countries. Volunteers from developing countries represented 80 per cent of the total number; women accounted for 37 per cent. By region, 48 per cent of assignments were carried out in sub-Saharan Africa, 19 per cent in the Arab States, 17 per cent in Asia and the Pacific, 13 per cent in Latin America and the Caribbean, and 4 per cent in Europe and the cis. Total contributions to unv in 2009 amounted to $214.7 million; other income totalled $9.98 million. The total expenditure for the year was $218.9 million.

Economic and technical cooperation among developing countries

South-South cooperation

In response to General Assembly resolution 62/209 [YUN 2007, p. 908], the Secretary-General submitted an August report [A/64/321] on the state of South-South cooperation. The report reviewed the progress, main trends and challenges in South-South cooperation for development from 2007 to mid-2009, especially in the areas of regional integration, trade, investment, and monetary and financial co-operation. Developing and developed countries alike continued to prioritize the strengthening of regional, interregional and global institutional mechanisms aimed at mitigating the impact of the financial crisis through mutual partnerships and cooperation mechanisms. Key issues that emerged as significant areas of South-South and triangular cooperation included climate change, energy and the environment. Developing countries consolidated interregional, regional and subregional cooperation to address larger global trends, including the increasing vulnerability of countries to financially volatile markets, rapid rates of urbanization, epidemics and food security problems.

The rapid deterioration of the global economy over the previous several years created new opportunities for South-South cooperation, as many countries looked to one another and to their cooperation mechanisms to facilitate market recovery and ensure greater stability. It was clear that South-South cooperation benefited countries regardless of their level of development, and was necessary for countries that wished to address transnational challenges successfully. The international community was increasingly using South-South cooperation as a practical framework and a flexible modality for partnership-building and collaboration towards achieving internationally agreed development goals, including the mdgs. Under the guidance of the High-level Committee on South-South Cooperation of the Assembly, the UN system prioritized South-South cooperation as a key modality for promoting collaborative initiatives at the national, regional and interregional levels. With the Special Unit for South-South Cooperation acting as system-wide coordinator and focal point, UN bodies and agencies, including regional commissions, supported innovative, demand-driven South-South cooperation initiatives. The UN system and other multilateral organizations increasingly sought to devise demand-based, South-South support facilities and innovative financing mechanisms to enable developing countries and their development partners to more systematically share knowledge, exchange experiences, transfer expertise and technologies and pool resources to deal effectively with development challenges. In December 2008, the Special Unit launched the first Global South-South Development Expo in New York, in conjunction with the fifth United Nations Day for South-South Cooperation.

The report stated that there was a need to translate the renewed commitments made by the international community in support of South-South and triangular cooperation into action in order to preserve the development achievements made over the previous decade. As global commitments increased, multilateral support for South-South development also needed to increase, which would require closer inter-agency collaboration. The report recommended that the United Nations Inter-agency Focal Points Network for South-South Cooperation, facilitated by the Special Unit for South-South Cooperation, be strengthened in order to achieve that objective.

Communications. In an 8 October letter to the Secretary-General [A/C.2/64/6], Venezuela transmitted the Declaration of Nueva Esparta II, issued by the Second Africa–South America Summit (Isla de Margarita, Nueva Esparta, Venezuela, 26–27 September).

On 21 October [A/C.2/64/8], Venezuela transmitted to the Secretary-General the Declaration of the Seventh Summit of the Bolivarian Alliance for the Peoples of Our America-Peoples' Trade Agreement (Cochabamba, Bolivia, 17 October).

In a 16 November letter [A/C.2/64/13], Qatar transmitted the summary report of the Second High-Level Meeting on Oil and Gas Management (Nairobi, 12–15 October). The Nairobi meeting was aimed at continuing the collaboration among southern oil and gas producers begun at the first South-South High-Level Meeting in 2007 [YUN 2007, p. 907].

GENERAL ASSEMBLY ACTION

On 21 December [meeting 66], the General Assembly, on the recommendation of the Second Committee [A/64/425/Add.2], adopted **resolution 64/221** without vote [agenda item 58 *(b)*].

South-South cooperation

The General Assembly,

Reaffirming its resolution 33/134 of 19 December 1978, in which it endorsed the Buenos Aires Plan of Action for

Promoting and Implementing Technical Cooperation among Developing Countries,

Recalling its resolutions 57/270 B of 23 June 2003, 60/212 of 22 December 2005, 62/209 of 19 December 2007, 63/233 of 19 December 2008, 64/1 of 6 October 2009 and other resolutions relevant to South-South cooperation,

Recalling also the 2005 World Summit Outcome,

Welcoming with appreciation the generous offer of the Government of Kenya to host the High-level United Nations Conference on South-South Cooperation,

1. *Takes note* of the report of the Secretary-General on the state of South-South cooperation;

2. *Decides* to hold the sixteenth session of the High-level Committee on South-South Cooperation on 4 February 2010, preceded by an organizational meeting on 21 January 2010 to elect the President and Bureau of the sixteenth session of the High-level Committee;

3. *Also decides* to include in the provisional agenda of its sixty-sixth session the sub-item entitled "South-South Cooperation for development", and requests the Secretary-General to submit at that session a comprehensive report of the state of South-South cooperation for development.

High-level Conference on South-South Cooperation

Preparations for High-level Conference

In response to General Assembly resolution 63/233 [YUN 2008, p. 989], the President of the High-level Committee on South-South Cooperation held consultations with Member States in preparation for the proposed High-level United Nations Conference on South-South Cooperation, which, in accordance with resolution 62/209 [YUN 2007, p. 908], was to be convened no later than the first half of 2009, on the occasion of the thirtieth anniversary of the adoption of the 1978 Buenos Aires Plan of Action for Promoting and Implementing Technical Cooperation among Developing Countries [YUN 1978, p. 467]. In a 30 January letter [A/63/741], Qatar, in its capacity as President of the High-level Committee on South-South Cooperation, submitted to the Assembly a report summarizing the outcomes and recommendations of the consultations, including the proposed nature of the Conference and its objectives, themes, venue, date, modalities and preparations. The Committee President recommended that the Assembly accept Kenya's offer to host the Conference in Nairobi. It was proposed that a comprehensive report be prepared, in the form of a report of the Secretary-General, highlighting the new dynamism and trends in South-South cooperation and the progress made in advancing such cooperation since the adoption of the Buenos Aires Plan of Action. The Conference should result in an intergovernmentally agreed outcome, including a declaration and plan of action.

On 6 October [meeting 15], the General Assembly adopted **resolution 64/1** [draft: A/64/L.1 & Add.1] without vote [agenda item 114].

High-level United Nations Conference on South-South Cooperation

The General Assembly,

Reaffirming its resolution 33/134 of 19 December 1978, in which it endorsed the Buenos Aires Plan of Action for Promoting and Implementing Technical Cooperation among Developing Countries,

Recalling its resolution 62/209 of 19 December 2007, in which it decided to convene a High-level United Nations Conference on South-South Cooperation on the occasion of the thirtieth anniversary of the adoption of the Buenos Aires Plan of Action, no later than the first half of 2009, and its resolution 63/233 of 19 December 2008,

Taking note with appreciation of the report of the President of the High-level Committee on South-South Cooperation submitted pursuant to resolution 63/233,

Reaffirming its previous resolutions relevant to South-South cooperation,

Taking note of the growing importance of South-South cooperation, and recognizing the increased role undertaken by the United Nations to support economic cooperation activities among developing countries,

Stressing that South-South cooperation, as an important element of international cooperation for development, offers viable opportunities for developing countries in their individual and collective pursuit of sustained economic growth and sustainable development,

Stressing also that South-South cooperation is not a substitute for, but rather a complement to, North-South cooperation,

Recalling the United Nations resolutions relevant to South-South cooperation and the outcomes of the major United Nations conferences and summits in the economic, social and related fields, including the Doha Declaration on Financing for Development, and acknowledging the Havana Programme of Action adopted at the first South Summit, the Marrakesh Framework for the Implementation of South-South Cooperation and the Doha Plan of Action adopted at the Second South Summit,

Welcoming with appreciation the generous offer of the Government of Kenya to host the High-level United Nations Conference on South-South Cooperation,

1. *Decides* that the High-level United Nations Conference on South-South Cooperation:

(a) Will be held in Nairobi from 1 to 3 December 2009;

(b) Will be held at the highest possible level;

(c) Will have as its overarching theme "Promotion of South-South cooperation for development";

(d) Will consist of plenary meetings and interactive multi-stakeholder round tables on the following sub-themes:

(i) Strengthening the role of the United Nations system in supporting South-South and triangular cooperation;

(ii) South-South and triangular cooperation for development: complementarities, specificities, challenges and opportunities;

(e) Will result in an intergovernmentally agreed outcome;

(f) Will also result in summaries by the Chair;

2. *Requests* the Secretary-General to prepare a comprehensive report, consistent with the overarching theme of the Conference, reviewing the trends in South-South cooperation, including triangular cooperation, reviewing also the progress made by the international community, in particular the United Nations, in supporting and promoting such cooperation and identifying new opportunities, as well as challenges and constraints and measures to overcome them;

3. *Reaffirms* the role of the Special Unit for South-South Cooperation within the United Nations Development Programme as a separate entity and a focal point for South-South cooperation within the United Nations system, and requests the Unit to continue to provide the necessary substantive and technical support to the preparatory process for the Conference;

4. *Encourages* Member States and their partners, including non-governmental organizations, to consider preparing reports on South-South and triangular cooperation for the purpose of the Conference, on a voluntary basis, taking into account the themes of the Conference and the outcomes of regional, subregional or sectoral United Nations meetings prior to the Conference;

5. *Requests* the President of the General Assembly to initiate informal consultations with all Member States, in an open, inclusive and transparent manner, commencing at an appropriate date to enable sufficient discussion, with a view to producing a draft outcome prior to the Conference, by the end of November 2009;

6. *Invites* United Nations organizations, including the specialized agencies, regional commissions and funds and programmes, to provide input to the preparations for the Conference;

7. *Invites* international and regional organizations, international financial institutions, non-governmental organizations and business sector entities to participate in the Conference, in accordance with the rules and procedures of the General Assembly;

8. *Invites* intergovernmental organizations and entities that have observer status with the General Assembly to participate in the Conference;

9. *Requests* the Secretary-General to provide all necessary assistance to the preparatory process and the Conference;

10. *Also requests* the Secretary-General to proceed with the organizational arrangements for the Conference in cooperation with the Government of Kenya, and further requests the Secretary-General to provide a note on the organizational aspects of the Conference;

11. *Encourages* all Member States and other relevant stakeholders that are in a position to do so to consider supporting the participation of developing countries, in particular the least developed countries, including by making voluntary contributions through the United Nations Fund for South-South Cooperation, in order to ensure the broadest possible participation;

12.   *Decides* to postpone the sixteenth session of the High-level Committee on South-South Cooperation, which was to be held from 2 to 5 June 2009, to one convenient day in January 2010.

On 6 July [A/63/919], Qatar informed the Assembly that the negotiations on the draft resolution on the High-level United Nations Conference on South-South Cooperation [A/63/L.68] had resulted in an agreement between Member States on the terms and modalities of the Conference. Nevertheless, a pending issue was delaying Conference preparations, and Member States were encouraged to demonstrate flexibility to reach a consensus.

In **decision 2009/216** of 22 July, the Economic and Social Council decided to defer consideration of the report of the High-level Committee on South-South Cooperation on its sixteenth session to the substantive session of the Council in 2010.

Report of Secretary-General. In October [A/64/504], the Secretary-General issued a report on the promotion of South-South cooperation for development: a thirty-year perspective. The report was submitted in response to General Assembly resolutions 62/209 [YUN 2007, p. 908] and 63/233 [YUN 2008, p. 989], by which the Assembly decided to convene the High-level United Nations Conference on South-South Cooperation. It reviewed the implementation of the Buenos Aires Plan of Action [YUN 1978, p. 467] by Member States and organizations of the UN system, including action at the national, interregional and global levels, and highlighted key priorities for South-South cooperation. The report found that developing countries as a group possessed the entire range of modern technical competencies, with centres of excellence in key areas that increased their national and collective self-reliance. Many developing countries, however, also continued to suffer from serious socio-economic deficits, and some were not on track to achieve the minimum goals set by the 2000 Millennium Summit [YUN 2000, p. 51]. A growing number of developing countries were becoming middle-income economies, and the largest of them were gaining a voice in global governance. Regional integration had fuelled economic progress, leading to further expansion of South-South flows of finance, technology and trade. The industrial growth of the South posed growing environmental problems. UN agencies and programmes had a key role in promoting cooperation among developing countries, but stronger mechanisms for coordination, monitoring, funding and reporting were needed to improve their performance further. Clear but uneven progress had been made in the 30 years since the Buenos Aires Conference. The first decade laid the foundations for action with the appointment of national focal points and clarification of concepts and procedures. Projects

and programmes proliferated in the second decade as conceptual barriers fell and South-South cooperation was redirected to deal with globalization. The third decade saw a large expansion of South-South trade, investment and tourism, mainly guided by policy reforms and driven by the private sector.

The Secretary-General observed that despite significant advances, developing countries needed stronger mechanisms for effective policy coordination and related institutions to spur greater collective action in a coherent manner. South-South flows of finance, trade and development assistance continued to be important for the growth of developing countries. Such assistance included knowledge- and experience-sharing, training, technology transfers, in-kind contributions, cost-sharing arrangements, soft loans, credit lines and other innovations. More advanced developing countries played a pivotal role as drivers of multi-country programmes, hubs for knowledge- and experience-sharing, and as sources of expertise, technology and funding. Nevertheless, there were areas in which those countries required assistance to build capacity and ensure that the benefits of growth were equitably distributed within their borders. Developing countries should ensure that the necessary policy and institutional infrastructure was in place for them to avail themselves of assistance. The United Nations should focus on national capacity development in priority areas through facilitating intra- and interregional knowledge-sharing. The UN system should support South-South and triangular cooperation primarily from the regional perspective by linking national centres of excellence; bringing in global normative expertise corresponding to the respective mandates of the UN funds, programmes and agencies; and exercising political neutrality in responding to local sensitivities.

High-level Conference

In accordance with Assembly resolution 64/1 (see p. 875), the High-level Conference on South-South Cooperation was held at the United Nations Office at Nairobi from 1 to 3 December [A/CONF.215/2]. The Conference held a general debate on the theme "Promotion of South-South cooperation for development", which offered a multifaceted view of the evolution of South-South cooperation over the previous three decades. There was general appreciation of the importance of such cooperation in the individual and collective pursuit of sustained and sustainable economic growth by developing countries, and of the need to strengthen and invigorate its processes, including through its support by developed countries and the UN system. South-South cooperation was seen as vital in reshaping global institutions that did not reflect the important role and new weight of developing countries in world affairs. The solidarity of the economically dynamic developing countries with those facing acute developmental challenges energized South-South cooperation and increased political, economic and institutional linkages between Southern countries. Representatives of developed countries said that there was inadequate documentation on what actually worked in South-South cooperation, which was "one of many instruments" for development; its "methodological framework" needed to be elaborated, and there was a need for a better understanding of its particularities, potential and impact. The value of increased support for South-South cooperation from developed countries was recognized, as was the key role of UN specialized agencies, funds and programmes in building the technical and technological capacities of developing countries. In calling on the UN system to mainstream support for South-South cooperation, representatives appealed for greater support for building institutional capacity in developing countries. UN specialized agencies, funds and programmes were requested to help developing countries establish centres of excellence and networks to improve information flows. Representatives also called for increased commitment of resources for South-South cooperation, appealing for more direct support from developed countries, cost-sharing arrangements, funding of joint research and development projects, third-country training programmes, arrangements to exchange experience and knowledge, and the establishment of institutional hubs for outreach and enhanced cooperation. Interactive round tables on the Conference theme focused on strengthening the role of the UN system in supporting South-South and triangular cooperation, and South-South and triangular cooperation for development: complementarities, specificities, challenges and opportunities.

The Conference adopted the draft Nairobi outcome document of the High-level United Nations Conference on South-South Cooperation, as contained in the Conference report, and recommended that the General Assembly endorse the document during its sixty-fourth (2009) session (see below).

GENERAL ASSEMBLY ACTION

On 21 December [meeting 66], the General Assembly adopted **resolution 64/222** [A/64/L.37] without vote [agenda item 58 *(b)*]

Nairobi outcome document of the High-level United Nations Conference on South-South Cooperation

The General Assembly,

Taking note of the holding of the High-level United Nations Conference on South-South Cooperation in Nairobi,

from 1 to 3 December 2009, and the adoption by the Conference of the Nairobi outcome document,

1. *Expresses its deep appreciation* to Kenya for hosting the High-level United Nations Conference on South-South Cooperation;

2. *Decides* to endorse the Nairobi outcome document of the High-level United Nations Conference on South-South Cooperation, which is annexed to the present resolution.

ANNEX

Nairobi outcome document of the High-level United Nations Conference on South-South Cooperation

1. We, heads of delegations and high representatives of Governments, gathered in Nairobi, from 1 to 3 December 2009 at the High-level United Nations Conference on South-South Cooperation, on the occasion of the thirtieth anniversary of the 1978 United Nations Conference on Technical Cooperation among Developing Countries, held in Buenos Aires, which produced the Buenos Aires Plan of Action for Promoting and Implementing Technical Cooperation among Developing Countries.

2. We recognize and contribute to the goal of the Conference to strengthen and further invigorate South-South cooperation.

3. We recall and renew our commitment to the full implementation of the outcomes of all major United Nations conferences and summits in the economic, social and related fields, and all General Assembly resolutions relevant to South-South and triangular cooperation.

4. We note the outcomes of the South Summits of the Group of 77 and other relevant South meetings.

5. We recognize the role of the Non-Aligned Movement in promoting South-South cooperation.

6. We take note of relevant processes and dialogues related to enhancing South-South cooperation.

7. Since the Buenos Aires meeting, the increasing economic dynamism of some developing countries in recent years has imparted greater energy to South-South cooperation, including through regional integration initiatives across the developing world, seen in, among other things, the creation of regional common markets, customs unions, cooperation in political fields, institutional and regulatory frameworks, and inter-State transport and communications networks. In this regard, we recognize the solidarity of middle-income countries with other developing countries with a view to supporting their development efforts, including in the context of South-South and triangular cooperation.

8. At the same time, we duly note that many developing countries continue to face serious development challenges and that many of them are not on track to achieve the internationally agreed development goals, including the Millennium Development Goals.

9. We stress that South-South cooperation, as an important element of international cooperation for development, offers viable opportunities for developing countries in their individual and collective pursuit of sustained economic growth and sustainable development.

10. We reaffirm the key role of the United Nations, including its funds, programmes, specialized agencies and

regional commissions, in supporting and promoting co-operation among developing countries, while reiterating that every country has the primary responsibility for its own development. We reaffirm resolution 33/134 of 19 December 1978, endorsing the Buenos Aires Plan of Action, which constitutes a major milestone in the evolution of South-South and triangular cooperation.

11. We recognize the importance and different history and particularities of South-South cooperation, and we reaffirm our view of South-South cooperation as a manifestation of solidarity among peoples and countries of the South that contributes to their national well-being, their national and collective self-reliance and the attainment of internationally agreed development goals, including the Millennium Development Goals. South-South cooperation and its agenda have to be set by countries of the South and should continue to be guided by the principles of respect for national sovereignty, national ownership and independence, equality, non-conditionality, non-interference in domestic affairs and mutual benefit.

12. We recognize that South-South cooperation takes different and evolving forms, including the sharing of knowledge and experience, training, technology transfer, financial and monetary cooperation and in-kind contributions.

13. We recognize the need to enhance local capacity in developing countries by supporting local capabilities, institutions, expertise and human resources and national systems, where appropriate, in contribution to national development priorities, at the request of developing countries.

14. We stress that South-South cooperation is not a substitute for, but rather a complement to, North-South cooperation.

15. We recognize the value of the increasing support provided by developed countries, international organizations and civil society to developing countries, upon their request, in improving their expertise and national capacities through triangular cooperation mechanisms, including direct support or cost-sharing arrangements, joint research and development projects, third-country training programmes and support for South-South centres, as well as by providing the necessary knowledge, experience and resources, so as to assist other developing countries, in accordance with their national development priorities and strategies.

16. We welcome efforts by multilateral, regional and bilateral financial and development institutions to increase financial resources to promote South-South cooperation, where appropriate, including for the least developed countries and countries with economies in transition.

17. We recognize that developing countries tend to share common views on national development strategies and priorities when faced with similar development challenges. The proximity of experience is therefore a key catalyst in promoting capacity development in developing countries and, in this regard, accentuates the principles of South-South cooperation. It is important to enhance South-South cooperation in order to fulfil its full development potential.

18. We reaffirm that South-South cooperation is a common endeavour of peoples and countries of the South, born out of shared experiences and sympathies, based on their common objectives and solidarity, and guided by, inter alia, the principles of respect for national sovereignty and ownership, free from any conditionalities. South-South cooperation should not be seen as official development assistance. It is a partnership among equals based on solidarity. In that regard, we acknowledge the need to enhance the development effectiveness of South-South cooperation by continuing to increase its mutual accountability and transparency, as well as coordinating its initiatives with other development projects and programmes on the ground, in accordance with national development plans and priorities. We also recognize that the impact of South-South cooperation should be assessed with a view to improving, as appropriate, its quality in a results-oriented manner.

19. South-South cooperation embraces a multistakeholder approach, including non-governmental organizations, the private sector, civil society, academia and other actors that contribute to meeting development challenges and objectives in line with national development strategies and plans.

20. In order to realize the potential of South-South cooperation in accordance with its principles and to attain the objectives of supporting national and regional development efforts, strengthening institutional and technical capacities, improving the exchange of experience and know-how among developing countries, responding to their specific development challenges and increasing the impact of international cooperation, we:

(a) Welcome the achievements made by developing countries towards promoting South-South cooperation initiatives and invite them to continue to intensify their efforts in this regard;

(b) Invite developed countries to support South-South cooperation through triangular cooperation, including for capacity development;

(c) Encourage developing countries to develop country-led systems to evaluate and assess the quality and impact of South-South and triangular cooperation programmes and improve data collection at the national level to promote cooperation in the development of methodologies and statistics to this end, as appropriate, while bearing in mind the specific principles and unique characteristics of South-South cooperation, and encourage all actors to support initiatives for information and data collection, coordination, dissemination and evaluation of South-South cooperation, upon the request of developing countries;

(d) Also encourage developing countries to enhance their national coordination mechanisms, as appropriate, in order to improve South-South and triangular cooperation through the dissemination of results, the sharing of lessons and good practices, and replication, including through the voluntary exchange of experience for the benefit of developing countries, and according to their policies and priorities for development;

(e) Recognize that interrelated global crises, in particular the financial and economic crisis, volatile energy prices, the food crisis, poverty and the challenges posed by climate change, as well as other challenges, including communicable and non-communicable diseases, are already reversing the gains achieved in developing countries and hence require action at all levels. In this regard, we invite developed

countries and multilateral institutions to enhance their support for South-South cooperation to contribute to addressing these challenges;

(f) Emphasize the need to promote, including through South-South cooperation, access to and the transfer of technology. In this regard, we welcome efforts made by developing countries in improving technology cooperation arrangements, such as the Consortium on Science, Technology and Innovation for the South. We also emphasize the need to promote, through South-South cooperation, broader technological developments such as technological management capabilities and information networks that are demand-oriented and involve participation by users of technology or by those involved in the process of technological development and infrastructure and human resources development;

(g) Call for the strengthening of various interregional dialogues and the exchange of experience among subregional and regional economic groupings for the purpose of expanding South-South cooperation by integrating the various approaches to economic and technical cooperation among developing countries;

(h) Acknowledge the various national, regional and subregional initiatives to enhance South-South cooperation in the social (particularly health and education), economic, environmental, technical and political fields;

(i) Recognize regional mechanisms and initiatives for infrastructure cooperation and integration, including in the energy field, based on solidarity and complementarity, to overcome asymmetries with regard to access to energy resources;

(j) Recognize that international support for South-South cooperation in trade, investment and other areas can be catalytic in strengthening and consolidating regional and subregional economic integration and take note of the São Paulo round of negotiations relating to the Global System of Trade Preferences among Developing Countries in order to reinvigorate and strengthen the agreement in general, promote greater interregional trade, diversify export markets and enhance investment flows among them.

21. We acknowledge the need to reinvigorate the United Nations development system in supporting and promoting South-South cooperation. To this effect, we:

(a) Urge the United Nations funds, programmes and specialized agencies to take concrete measures to mainstream support for South-South and triangular cooperation to help developing countries, at their request and with their ownership and leadership, to develop capacities to maximize the benefits and impact of South-South and triangular cooperation in order to achieve their national development goals and internationally agreed development goals, including the Millennium Development Goals;

(b) Call upon the United Nations funds and programmes and invite the specialized agencies to continue to enhance the capacities of developing countries to develop and formulate development cooperation programmes, strengthen the capacities of regional and subregional organizations and conduct research to identify areas where support for South-South cooperation will have the greatest impact;

(c) Call upon the United Nations funds, programmes and specialized agencies to continue to focus and coordinate their operational activities in support of South-South cooperation, in accordance with national development plans and their respective mandates, and to produce practical results, taking into account South-South characteristics and approaches;

(d) Call furthermore upon United Nations regional commissions to play a catalytic role in promoting South-South and triangular cooperation and in strengthening their technical, policy and research support for countries of their regions;

(e) Welcome the recent initiatives by the United Nations Conference on Trade and Development, the United Nations Industrial Development Organization, the Food and Agriculture Organization of the United Nations and other United Nations specialized agencies to establish, within their respective mandates, new units and work programmes to support and promote South-South cooperation, and request United Nations funds, programmes and specialized agencies, as well as regional commissions, to help developing countries to establish or strengthen existing South-South centres of excellence, within their respective areas of competence, and to enhance closer cooperation among such centres of excellence, especially at the regional and interregional levels, with a view to improving South-South knowledge-sharing, networking, mutual capacity-building, information and best practices exchanges, policy analysis and coordinated action among developing countries on major issues of common concern;

(f) Encourage such institutions and centres of excellence, as well as regional and subregional economic groupings, to establish closer links among themselves, with the support of the Special Unit for South-South Cooperation, including through its Global South-South Development Academy, Global South-South Development Expo and South-South Global Assets and Technology Exchange;

(g) Reaffirm the mandate of the Special Unit for South-South Cooperation, hosted by the United Nations Development Programme, as a separate entity and coordinator for promoting and facilitating South-South and triangular cooperation for development on a global and United Nations system-wide basis;

(h) Call for the effective implementation of the United Nations Development Programme fourth cooperation framework for South-South cooperation and, in this regard, encourage Member States in a position to do so to support the United Nations Development Programme and the Special Unit for South-South Cooperation in fully implementing this framework;

(i) Invite the Secretary-General, in consultation with States Members of the United Nations, to take measures to further strengthen the Special Unit for South-South Cooperation, as reaffirmed by the General Assembly in its resolutions 58/220 of 23 December 2003, 60/212 of 22 December 2005 and 62/209 of 19 December 2007, so as to enable it to carry out its full responsibilities, in particular through the mobilization of resources for the advancement of South-South cooperation, including triangular cooperation;

(j) Reaffirm the relevance of the previously established Guidelines for the Review of Policies and Procedures con-

cerning Technical Cooperation among Developing Countries in conducting and managing South-South cooperation. We therefore call for their full implementation and recognize the need for their continued improvement, in particular in strengthening the capacity of the United Nations Development Programme and United Nations funds, programmes and specialized agencies to promote and support South-South cooperation, as well as to further develop the specific framework of operational guidelines to facilitate the use of technical cooperation among developing countries in their programmes and projects;

(k) Emphasize that South-South cooperation needs adequate support from the United Nations funds, programmes and specialized agencies, including through triangular cooperation, and call upon all relevant United Nations organizations to consider increasing allocations of human, technical and financial resources for South-South cooperation, as appropriate;

(l) Recognize the need to mobilize adequate resources for enhancing South-South cooperation and, in this context, invite all countries in a position to do so to contribute in support of such cooperation through, inter alia, the Pérez-Guerrero Trust Fund for Economic and Technical Cooperation among Developing Countries and the United Nations Fund for South-South Cooperation. In this context, we encourage the Special Unit for South-South Cooperation to undertake additional resource mobilization initiatives to attract more financial and in-kind resources, while avoiding the proliferation and fragmentation of financing arrangements. In this regard, we reaffirm that regular resources will continue to fund the activities of the Special Unit, and invite the Executive Board of the United Nations Development Programme to consider measures to allocate adequate resources for the Special Unit.

22. We convey our appreciation and gratitude to the Republic of Kenya and its people for the excellent organization and hosting of the High-level United Nations Conference on South-South Cooperation and the warm hospitality extended to us in the city of Nairobi.

UN Capital Development Fund

The United Nations Capital Development Fund (UNCDF) worked to reduce poverty in the least developed countries by strengthening local services and increasing access to microfinance. In 2009, UNCDF operated in 40 of the 49 least developed countries, with a particular focus on post-crisis countries. Local development programmes accounted for 61 per cent of the 2009 programme expenditure; microfinance accounted for 39 per cent. The 2009 programme targets in both local development and microfinance were achieved and in some cases exceeded. While management targets were largely met, strengthening UNCDF operational effectiveness remained a priority.

Total contributions in 2009 amounted to $36.2 million, consisting of $19.7 million in regular resources, including a $1 million contribution from UNDP, and $16.5 million in other resources. The volume of regular resources grew by $1 million in 2009.

The decrease in other resources, from $26.6 million in 2008 to 16.5 million in 2009, was anticipated, as a large contribution from the Bill and Melinda Gates Foundation made in 2008 had been intended for both 2008 and 2009. UNCDF continued to be overly dependent on too few donors to regular resources: its six largest donors contributed 95 per cent of regular resources. Total expenditures in 2009 amounted to $49.1 million. Programme expenditures increased by 12.2 per cent to $41.5 million, from $37 million in 2008. Other resources expenditures increased by 35 per cent. Fund balances at the end of 2009 were approximately 53 million. Operational reserves amounted to approximately $26 million.

In response to a 2008 decision of the UNPD/UNFPA Executive Board [YUN 2008, p. 989], UNDP and UNCDF reported in April [DP/2009/20] on progress made in implementing their strategic partnership, proposed in 2007 [YUN 2007, p. 909]. The integration of the UNDP and UNCDF strategic planning and results agendas within the framework of the UNDP strategic plan helped to maximize synergies between the two organizations and reflected the complementary nature and added value of the organizations in local development and microfinance. UNDP and UNCDF formulated joint development outcomes and outcome indicators. The contributions of UNCDF in its two practice areas—local development and microfinance—were being integrated more effectively into UN common country programming, assessments, documents, action plans and United Nations Development Assistance Frameworks (UNDAF). While more progress was required, ongoing discussions with UNDP regional bureaux had led to more UNCDF engagement in UNDAF formulation processes.

UNDP and UNCDF began implementing programmes jointly. Over the previous two years, nearly 100 per cent of new UNCDF programmes were joint with UNDP and other UN system partners. Fourteen joint programmes were signed by UNDP and UNCDF as at 31 December 2008, generating $34 million in cost-sharing from seven donors. UNCDF and UNDP formalized their strategic partnership through regular headquarters, regional and country engagements. At the corporate level, the frequency of interaction between UNCDF, regional bureaux and the relevant practices in the UNDP Bureau for Development Policy increased. In early 2010, UNCDF and UNDP would co-host the Global Forum on Local Development in Addis Ababa, Ethiopia, and the two organizations were working together on a joint global initiative on scaling up local level support for the MDGs. Regionally, UNCDF technical advisers were co-located and worked closely with the staff of the UNDP regional service centres and participated in the thematic clusters of the UN regional teams. Joint programme formulation and implementation was becoming the norm at the country level.

The strategic partnership aimed at greater simplicity, coherence, effectiveness and increased resource flows. In that respect, the two organizations promoted the application of the 2005 Paris Declaration on Aid Effectiveness [YUN 2005, p. 957] through joint programmes that supported national decentralization efforts and local development, as well as national strategies for inclusive financial sectors. Financial alignment between the two organizations was evidenced by the integration of the UNCDF administrative budget in the UNDP biennial support budget. Knowledge-sharing and strong synergies in the local development and microfinance portfolios of both organizations resulted in increased joint programming and joint resource mobilization, especially at country level.

The annual report on results achieved by UNCDF, submitted in April [DP/2009/19], analysed performance against established programme, management and financial results targets in 2008. Total regular and other resources increased by 76 per cent, reaching $50.1 million, the highest level of income to UNCDF in at least 15 years. Regular resources totalled $23.5 million in 2008, short of the $25 million per year minimum called for in the 2008–2011 UNCDF investment plan. Total programme expenditure amounted to $37 million. Other resources expenditures reached $14.4 million and accounted for 39 per cent of total programme resources. The UNCDF support expenditure amounted to $6.8 million, compared with $5.4 million in 2007. The increase of $1.3 million could be attributed to 2007 outstanding service-level agreements and non-recurrent staff costs.

In June [dec. 2009/12], The Executive Board took note of the annual report on results for 2008. It encouraged Member States in a position to do so to contribute to UNCDF regular resources or to make multi-year thematic contributions at the level necessary to implement the UNCDF investment plan, 2008–2011, which would allow UNCDF to expand its services and investment support from 38 to 45 least developed countries. The Board recommended that UNDP and UNCDF further strengthen their strategic partnership as outlined in the April report, and requested that the two organizations report to the Board regularly on the challenges and lessons learned in that regard.

Chapter III

Humanitarian and special economic assistance

In 2009, the United Nations, through the Office for the Coordination of Humanitarian Affairs (OCHA), continued to mobilize and coordinate humanitarian assistance. During the year, consolidated inter-agency and flash appeals were launched for Afghanistan, Burkina Faso, the Central African Republic, Chad, Côte d'Ivoire, the Democratic Republic of the Congo, El Salvador, Indonesia, Iraq, Kenya, the Lao People's Democratic Republic, Madagascar, Namibia, the Occupied Palestinian Territory, Pakistan, the Philippines, Somalia, Sri Lanka, the Sudan, Uganda, West Africa, Yemen and Zimbabwe. OCHA received contributions for natural disaster assistance worth $311 million.

The Ad Hoc Advisory Group on Haiti continued to develop long-term programmes of support for the country, and former United States President William Clinton was named as the United Nations Special Envoy for Haiti. In other development activities, the General Assembly adopted resolutions in support of the New Partnership for Africa's Development and the rehabilitation and economic development of the Semipalatinsk region of Kazakhstan.

Efforts continued to implement the Hyogo Declaration and the Hyogo Framework for Action 2005–2015, the 10-year plan for reducing disaster risks adopted at the World Conference on Disaster Reduction in 2005. The second session of the Global Platform for Disaster Risk Reduction was convened in June. The General Assembly designated 13 October the International Day for Disaster Reduction.

During the year, the Economic and Social Council considered ways to strengthen UN humanitarian assistance coordination by implementing improved humanitarian response at all levels. Implementation of the humanitarian reform agenda advanced with the launch of the cluster approach in 13 additional countries. The Central Emergency Response Fund continued to allow for the rapid provision of assistance to populations affected by sudden-onset disasters and underfunded emergencies.

Humanitarian assistance

Coordination
Humanitarian affairs segment
of the Economic and Social Council

The humanitarian affairs segment of the Economic and Social Council (20–22 July) [A/64/3/Rev.1] consid-

ered, in accordance with Council **decision 2009/207**, the theme "Strengthening of the coordination of humanitarian assistance: present challenges and their impact on the future". It also convened panels on respecting and implementing guiding principles of humanitarian assistance at the operational level: assisting the affected populations; and on addressing the impact of current global challenges and trends on the effective delivery of humanitarian assistance. On 26 March, the Council decided to hold an informal event on 17 July to discuss transition from relief to development (**decision 2009/209**).

The Council considered the Secretary-General's May report [A/64/84-E/2009/87] on strengthening the coordination of UN emergency humanitarian assistance, submitted in response to General Assembly resolutions 46/182 [YUN 1991, p. 421] and 63/139 [YUN 2008, p. 996] and Council resolution 2008/36 [ibid., p. 993]. The report summarized humanitarian trends and challenges of disasters associated with natural hazards and complex emergencies; examined progress in coordinating humanitarian assistance; and analysed the themes of the Council's humanitarian affairs segment (see above). The analysis discussed challenges to humanitarian action, such as safety and security of humanitarian personnel; the increasing number of actors involved in humanitarian assistance; distinguishing between humanitarian and military or political actors; balancing coherence in UN operations and principled humanitarian action; and gaining access to people in need. It also explored how climate change, extreme poverty, the food and financial crises, water and energy scarcity, migration, population growth, urbanization, terrorism and health pandemics impacted humanitarian needs, as well as how those challenges would shape the environment in which humanitarian actors would have to operate.

In 2008, the Centre for the Research on the Epidemiology of Disasters reported 321 disasters associated with natural hazards. While the number of disasters decreased on average, their severity increased. During the reporting period, natural disasters, such as floods, cyclones, earthquakes and droughts, continued to trigger humanitarian emergencies, causing over 235,000 deaths and affecting more than 211 million people. The number of deaths was three times the average for 2000–2007 due to Cyclone Nargis [YUN 2008, p. 421] and the Sichuan earthquake [ibid., p. 1149]. As at the time of the report, the humanitarian consolidated appeal process had requested $8.6 billion to provide 30 million people with life-saving assistance for 2009, an increase of almost 23 per cent from 2008 requirements. Complex emergencies such as the humanitarian operation in Darfur, ongoing drought and food insecurity in Afghanistan and Somalia, fighting in Sri Lanka, the sustained closure of Gaza, and limited or no access to safe water and sanitation in Zimbabwe, affected tens of millions of people. In addition, internal and cross-border movements of people constituted major concerns. Although the Office of the United Nations High Commissioner for Refugees (UNHCR) reported a decrease in the global number of refugees from 11.4 million in 2007 to 10.5 million by the end of 2008—attributed to repatriation operations in Afghanistan, Burundi and the Sudan—some 26 million people were internally displaced due to conflict, insecurity and persecution, while millions were displaced owing to natural hazards.

On progress in the coordination of humanitarian assistance, the cluster approach [YUN 2006, p. 1057] was implemented in 13 additional countries, bringing the number of countries where the approach was implemented to 24. Other topics addressed included, enhanced humanitarian coordination: the resident and humanitarian coordinator system; predictability of response and humanitarian financing; equity and accountability of response and enhancing needs assessments; strengthening and expanding partnerships; the White Helmets (see p. 890); and strengthening capacities to support survivors of gender-based violence. In that regard, the Inter-Agency Standing Committee (IASC) Gender Standby Capacity project deployed 29 advisers to 18 humanitarian crises. The Secretary-General concluded with a series of recommendations for consideration by States, non-State actors, humanitarian organizations and the UN system.

ECONOMIC AND SOCIAL COUNCIL ACTION

On 22 July [meeting 32], the Economic and Social Council adopted resolution **2009/3** [E/2009/SR.32], without vote [agenda item 5].

Strengthening of the coordination of emergency humanitarian assistance of the United Nations

The Economic and Social Council,

Reaffirming General Assembly resolution 46/182 of 19 December 1991 and the guiding principles contained in the annex thereto, and recalling other relevant resolutions of the Assembly and relevant resolutions and agreed conclusions of the Economic and Social Council,

Recalling its decision to consider the theme "Strengthening of the coordination of humanitarian assistance: present challenges and their impact on the future" at the humanitarian affairs segment of its substantive session of 2009,

Recalling also its decision to convene two panels, on "Respecting and implementing guiding principles of

humanitarian assistance at the operational level: assisting the affected populations" and "Addressing the impact of current global challenges and trends on the effective delivery of humanitarian assistance", and its decision to hold an informal event entitled "Economic and Social Council event to discuss transition from relief to development",

Expressing grave concern at the increase in the number of people affected by humanitarian emergencies, including those associated with natural hazards and complex emergencies, at the increased impact of natural disasters and at the displacement resulting from humanitarian emergencies,

Reaffirming the need for all actors engaged in the provision of humanitarian assistance in situations of complex emergencies and natural disasters to promote and fully respect the principles of humanity, neutrality, impartiality and independence,

Reiterating the need to mainstream a gender perspective into humanitarian assistance in a comprehensive and consistent manner,

Expressing deep concern at the increasing challenges posed to Member States and the United Nations humanitarian response capacity by the consequences of natural disasters, including the impact of climate change, and by the humanitarian implications of the current global food crisis,

Acknowledging that the current financial and economic crisis has the potential to increase the need for resources for humanitarian assistance in developing countries,

Condemning the increasing number of attacks and other acts of violence against humanitarian personnel, facilities, assets and supplies, and expressing deep concern about the negative implications of such acts for the provision of humanitarian assistance to affected populations,

Noting with grave concern that violence, including gender-based violence, particularly sexual violence, and violence against children, continues to be deliberately directed against civilian populations in many emergency situations,

Recognizing that building and strengthening national and local preparedness and response capacity is critical to a more predictable and effective response,

Recognizing also the clear relationship between emergency relief, rehabilitation and development, and reaffirming that, in order to ensure a smooth transition from relief to rehabilitation and development, emergency assistance must be provided in ways that will be supportive of recovery and long-term development and that emergency measures should be seen as a step towards sustainable development,

Noting the contribution, as appropriate, of relevant regional and subregional organizations in the provision of humanitarian assistance within their region at the request of the affected State,

1. *Takes note* of the report of the Secretary-General;

2. *Encourages* Member States to create and strengthen an enabling environment for the capacity-building of national and local authorities, national societies of the International Red Cross and Red Crescent Movement, and national and local non-governmental and community-based organizations in providing timely humanitarian assistance, and encourages the international community, the relevant entities of the United Nations system and other relevant institutions and organizations to support national authorities in their capacity-building programmes, including through technical cooperation and long-term partnerships based on

recognition of their important role in providing humanitarian assistance;

3. *Stresses* that the United Nations system should make efforts to enhance existing humanitarian capacities, knowledge and institutions, including, as appropriate, through the transfer of technology and expertise to developing countries, and encourages the international community to support efforts of Member States aimed at strengthening their capacity to prepare for and respond to disasters;

4. *Notes with appreciation* the second session of the Global Platform for Disaster Risk Reduction, held in Geneva from 16 to 19 June 2009, urges Member States to develop, update and strengthen disaster preparedness and risk reduction measures at all levels, in accordance with the Hyogo Framework for Action, in particular priority 5 thereof, taking into account their own circumstances and capacities and in coordination with relevant actors, as appropriate, and encourages the international community and relevant United Nations entities to give increased priority to supporting national and local efforts in this regard;

5. *Encourages* Member States and, where applicable, relevant regional organizations to strengthen operational and legal frameworks for international disaster relief, taking into account, as appropriate, the Guidelines for the Domestic Facilitation and Regulation of International Disaster Relief and Initial Recovery Assistance, adopted at the thirtieth International Conference of the Red Cross and Red Crescent, held in Geneva from 26 to 30 November 2007;

6. *Encourages* efforts to enhance cooperation and coordination between United Nations humanitarian entities, other relevant humanitarian organizations and donor countries and the affected State, with a view to planning and delivering emergency humanitarian assistance in ways that are supportive of early recovery as well as sustainable rehabilitation and reconstruction efforts;

7. *Also encourages* efforts to provide education in emergencies, including in order to contribute to a smooth transition from relief to development;

8. *Requests* the Emergency Relief Coordinator to continue his efforts to strengthen the coordination of humanitarian assistance, and encourages relevant United Nations organizations and other relevant intergovernmental organizations, as well as other humanitarian and development actors, to continue to work with the Office for the Coordination of Humanitarian Affairs of the Secretariat to enhance the coordination, effectiveness and efficiency of humanitarian assistance;

9. *Encourages* United Nations humanitarian organizations, while strengthening the coordination of humanitarian assistance in the field, to continue to work in close coordination with national Governments, taking into account the primary role of the affected State in the initiation, organization, coordination and implementation of such assistance within its territory;

10. *Welcomes* the continued efforts to strengthen the humanitarian response capacity in order to provide a timely, predictable, coordinated and accountable response to humanitarian needs, and requests the Secretary-General to continue efforts in this regard, in consultation with Member States, including by strengthening the support provided to and improving the identification, selection and training of United Nations resident/humanitarian co-ordinators and by improving coordination mechanisms for the provision of humanitarian assistance at the field level;

11. *Urges* all actors engaged in the provision of humanitarian assistance to fully commit to and duly respect the guiding principles contained in the annex to General Assembly resolution 46/182, including the principles of humanity, neutrality and impartiality, as well as the guiding principle of independence, as recognized by the Assembly in its resolution 58/114 of 17 December 2003;

12. *Calls upon* all States and parties in complex humanitarian emergencies, in particular in armed conflict and in post-conflict situations, in countries in which humanitarian personnel are operating, in conformity with the relevant provisions of international law and national laws, to cooperate fully with the United Nations and other humanitarian agencies and organizations and to ensure the safe and unhindered access of humanitarian personnel, as well as delivery of supplies and equipment, in order to allow such personnel to efficiently perform their task of assisting affected civilian populations, including refugees and internally displaced persons;

13. *Calls upon* all parties to armed conflict to comply with their obligations under international humanitarian law, human rights law and refugee law;

14. *Calls upon* all States and parties to comply fully with the provisions of international humanitarian law, including all the Geneva Conventions of 12 August 1949, in particular the Geneva Convention relative to the Protection of Civilian Persons in Time of War, in order to protect and assist civilians in occupied territories, and in this regard urges the international community and the relevant organizations of the United Nations system to strengthen humanitarian assistance to civilians in such situations;

15. *Recognizes* the benefits of engagement and coordination with relevant humanitarian actors to the effectiveness of humanitarian response, and encourages the United Nations to continue to pursue efforts to strengthen partnerships at the global level with the International Red Cross and Red Crescent Movement, relevant humanitarian nongovernmental organizations and other participants in the Inter-Agency Standing Committee;

16. *Urges* Member States to continue to take the steps necessary to ensure the safety and security of humanitarian personnel, premises, facilities, equipment, vehicles and supplies located within their borders and in other territories under their effective control, recognizes the need for appropriate collaboration between humanitarian actors and the relevant authorities of the affected State in matters related to the safety and security of humanitarian personnel, requests the Secretary-General to expedite his efforts to enhance the safety and security of personnel involved in United Nations humanitarian operations, and urges Member States to ensure that perpetrators of crimes committed against humanitarian personnel on their territory or on other territories under their effective control do not operate with impunity and are brought to justice, as provided for by national laws and by obligations under international law;

17. *Encourages* Member States, as well as relevant regional and international organizations, in accordance with their specific mandates, to support adaptation to the effects of climate change and to strengthen disaster risk reduction and early warning systems in order to minimize the

humanitarian consequences of natural disasters, including the impact of climate change, takes note of the *2009 Global Assessment Report on Disaster Risk Reduction: Risk and poverty in a changing climate—Invest today for a safer tomorrow*, and encourages relevant entities to continue their research on the humanitarian implications of natural disasters;

18. *Emphasizes* the fundamentally civilian character of humanitarian assistance, and, in situations where military capacity and assets are used to support the implementation of humanitarian assistance, reaffirms the need for their use to be undertaken with the consent of the affected State and in conformity with international law, including international humanitarian law, as well as principles for the provision of humanitarian assistance;

19. *Requests* Member States, relevant United Nations organizations and other relevant actors to ensure that all aspects of humanitarian response address the specific needs of women, girls, men and boys, including through improved collection, analysis and reporting of sex- and age-disaggregated data, taking into account, inter alia, information provided by States;

20. *Urges* Member States to continue to prevent, investigate and prosecute acts of gender-based violence, including sexual violence, in humanitarian emergencies, calls upon Member States and relevant organizations to strengthen support services to victims of such violence, and calls for a more effective response in this regard;

21. *Encourages* Member States, the private sector and other relevant entities to make contributions and to consider increasing and diversifying their contributions to humanitarian funding mechanisms, including consolidated and flash appeals, the Central Emergency Response Fund and other funds, on the basis of and in proportion to assessed needs, as a means of ensuring flexible, predictable, timely, needs-based and, where possible, multi-year, non-earmarked and additional resources to meet global humanitarian challenges, encourages donors to adhere to the Principles and Good Practice of Humanitarian Donorship, and reiterates that contributions for humanitarian assistance should not be to the detriment of resources made available for international cooperation for development;

22. *Notes* that the current global financial and economic crisis has the potential to affect the ability of developing countries to respond to humanitarian emergencies, and stresses the need to take measures to ensure adequate resources for international cooperation in the provision of humanitarian assistance;

23. *Calls upon* United Nations humanitarian organizations, in consultation with Member States, as appropriate, to strengthen the evidence base for humanitarian assistance by further developing common mechanisms to improve the quality, transparency and reliability of humanitarian needs assessments, to assess their performance in providing assistance and to ensure the most effective use of humanitarian resources by these organizations;

24. *Requests* the Secretary-General to reflect the progress made in the implementation of and follow-up to the present resolution in his next report to the Economic and Social Council and to the General Assembly on the strengthening of the coordination of emergency humanitarian assistance of the United Nations.

Humanitarian reform agenda

In 2009, OCHA continued to build on the humanitarian reform process initiated in 2005 [YUN 2005, p. 991] and remained at the forefront of strengthening the predictability and accountability of the international humanitarian system, both at the policy and operational level. The OCHA 2007–2009 strategic framework focused on striving to ensure a better coordinated, more equitably supported international humanitarian response system. The cluster approach, a key element in humanitarian reform, had been applied in 36 countries and continued to be adapted and improved, based on continuous learning within the humanitarian system. During the year, OCHA rolled out the approach in six countries, as well as the Occupied Palestinian Territory, and managed the inter-agency evaluation of Phase II of the Cluster Approach (see below). OCHA also established a new system to ensure that the results and recommendations of evaluations, reviews and audits were addressed, as formalized in the 2009 evaluation policy.

In other developments, the Roster Management Programme, the primary mechanism for regular field recruitment, was introduced; two new surge mechanisms to help fill the gap between short-term deployments and longer-term staffing solutions through regular recruitment were developed; and the first phase of consolidating OCHA's web presence into a new OCHA portal was completed. OCHA also initiated an inter-agency review of protection from sexual exploitation and abuse, released the "Occasional Policy Paper: Global Challenges and their Impact on International Humanitarian Action"—a detailed analysis providing background for developing OCHA's strategic framework for 2010–2013, and, in order to advocate international humanitarian law and principles, played a major role in launching the first World Humanitarian Day in August. Efforts by OCHA also resulted in the establishment of an informal Security Council Expert Group on the Protection of Civilians in Armed Conflict. By year's end, owing to OCHA briefings to the Expert Group, Council members were receiving more detailed analysis and information on protection-related issues. Meanwhile, the OCHA strategic framework for 2010–2013 was developed over the course of the year and encompassed multi-year strategies detailing risks, milestones and a path to achieving the ends stated by 2013.

Global Cluster Approach Evaluation. Following the 2005 Humanitarian Response Review [YUN 2005, p. 991], IASC established the "cluster leadership approach" as a mechanism to improve humanitarian response effectiveness and to strengthen partnerships among all humanitarian actors [YUN 2006, p. 1057]. The first of a two-phase evaluation of the approach took place in 2007 [YUN 2007, p. 915] and phase II, based on a 2008 framework [YUN 2008, p. 996], was under way in 2009. In other activities, IASC clarified key terminology and reinforced the dual responsibility of cluster lead agencies to represent both their own agency and the clusters they lead in meetings at the country and global level.

GENERAL ASSEMBLY ACTION

On 7 December [meeting 60], the General Assembly adopted **resolution 64/76** [draft: A/64/L.32 & Add.1] without vote [agenda item 70 *(a)*].

Strengthening of the coordination of emergency humanitarian assistance of the United Nations

The General Assembly,

Reaffirming its resolution 46/182 of 19 December 1991 and the guiding principles contained in the annex thereto, other relevant General Assembly and Economic and Social Council resolutions and agreed conclusions of the Council,

Noting the reports of the Secretary-General on the strengthening of the coordination of emergency humanitarian assistance of the United Nations and on the Central Emergency Response Fund,

Reaffirming the principles of neutrality, humanity, impartiality and independence for the provision of humanitarian assistance,

Deeply concerned about the humanitarian impact of such global challenges as the global financial and economic crisis and the ongoing food crisis, including their effect on the increasing vulnerability of populations and their negative impact on the effective delivery of humanitarian assistance,

Emphasizing the need to mobilize adequate, predictable, timely and flexible resources for humanitarian assistance based on and in proportion to assessed needs, with a view to ensuring fuller coverage of the needs in all sectors and across humanitarian emergencies, and recognizing, in this regard, the achievements of the Central Emergency Response Fund,

Reiterating the need for Member States, relevant United Nations organizations and other relevant actors to mainstream a gender perspective into humanitarian assistance, including by addressing the specific needs of women, girls, boys and men in a comprehensive and consistent manner,

Expressing its deep concern at the increasing challenges faced by Member States and the United Nations humanitarian response capacity as a result of the consequences of natural disasters, including the impact of climate change, and reaffirming the importance of implementing the Hyogo Framework for Action 2005–2015: Building the Resilience of Nations and Communities to Disasters, inter alia, by providing adequate resources for disaster risk reduction, including disaster preparedness,

Recognizing that building national and local preparedness and response capacity is critical to a more predictable and effective response,

Emphasizing that enhancing international cooperation on emergency humanitarian assistance is essential, and reaffirming its resolution 63/141 of 11 December 2008 on international cooperation on humanitarian assistance in the field of natural disasters,

Condemning the increasing number of deliberate violent attacks against humanitarian personnel and facilities and the negative implications for the provision of humanitarian assistance to populations in need,

Recognizing the high numbers of persons affected by humanitarian emergencies, including internally displaced persons, and welcoming, in this regard, the adoption on 22 October 2009 of the African Union Convention for the Protection and Assistance of Internally Displaced Persons in Africa, which marks a significant step towards strengthening the national and regional normative framework for the protection of and assistance to internally displaced persons in Africa,

Recognizing also that 2009 marks the sixtieth anniversary of the Geneva Conventions of 1949, which include a vital legal framework for the Protection of Civilian Persons in Time of War, including the provision of humanitarian assistance,

Noting with grave concern that violence, including gender-based violence, particularly sexual violence, and violence against children, continues to be deliberately directed against civilian populations in many emergency situations,

Noting with appreciation the efforts made by the United Nations to improve humanitarian response, including by strengthening humanitarian response capacities, improving humanitarian coordination, enhancing predictable and adequate funding and strengthening the accountability of all stakeholders, and recognizing the importance of strengthening emergency administrative procedures and funding to allow for an effective response to emergencies,

Recognizing that in strengthening the coordination of humanitarian assistance in the field, United Nations organizations should continue to work in close coordination with national Governments,

1. *Welcomes* the outcome of the twelfth humanitarian affairs segment of the Economic and Social Council at its substantive session of 2009;

2. *Requests* the Emergency Relief Coordinator to continue his efforts to strengthen the coordination of humanitarian assistance, and calls upon relevant United Nations organizations and other relevant intergovernmental organizations, as well as other humanitarian and development actors, to continue to work with the Office for the Coordination of Humanitarian Affairs of the Secretariat to enhance the coordination, effectiveness and efficiency of humanitarian assistance;

3. *Calls upon* the relevant organizations of the United Nations system and, as appropriate, other relevant humanitarian actors to continue efforts to improve the humanitarian response to natural and man-made disasters and complex emergencies by further strengthening humanitarian response capacities at all levels, by continuing to strengthen the coordination of humanitarian assistance at the field level, including with national authorities of the affected State, as appropriate, and by further enhancing transparency, performance and accountability;

4. *Recognizes* the benefits of engagement and coordination with relevant humanitarian actors to the effectiveness of humanitarian response, and encourages the United Nations to continue to pursue efforts to strengthen partnerships at the global level with the International Red Cross and Red Crescent Movement, relevant humanitarian non-

governmental organizations and other participants in the Inter-Agency Standing Committee;

5. *Requests* the Secretary-General to strengthen the support provided to United Nations resident/humanitarian coordinators and to United Nations country teams, including by providing necessary training, identifying resources and improving the identification of and the selection process for United Nations resident/humanitarian coordinators;

6. *Reaffirms* the importance of implementing the Hyogo Framework for Action 2005–2015: Building the Resilience of Nations and Communities to Disasters, takes note with appreciation of the "2009 Global Assessment Report on Disaster Risk Reduction" and the outcome of the second session of the Global Platform for Disaster Risk Reduction, held in Geneva from 16 to 19 June 2009, and looks forward to the midterm review of the Hyogo Framework for Action in 2010;

7. *Calls upon* Member States and the international community to increase resources for disaster risk reduction measures, including in the areas of preparedness for effective response and contingency planning;

8. *Urges* Member States, the United Nations and other relevant organizations to take further steps to provide a coordinated emergency response to the food and nutrition needs of affected populations, while aiming to ensure that such steps are supportive of national strategies and programmes aimed at improving food security;

9. *Encourages* the international community, including relevant United Nations organizations and the International Federation of Red Cross and Red Crescent Societies, to support efforts of Member States aimed at strengthening their capacity to prepare for and respond to disasters and to support efforts, as appropriate, to strengthen systems for identifying and monitoring disaster risk, including vulnerability and natural hazards;

10. *Recognizes* the importance of the work of international and, as appropriate, regional organizations in supporting State efforts to improve international cooperation in disaster response, and encourages Member States and, where applicable, regional organizations to strengthen operational and legal frameworks for international disaster relief, taking into account, as appropriate, the Guidelines for the Domestic Facilitation and Regulation of International Disaster Relief and Initial Recovery Assistance, adopted at the Thirtieth International Conference of the Red Cross and Red Crescent, held in Geneva from 26 to 30 November 2007;

11. *Encourages* States to create an enabling environment for the capacity-building of local authorities and of national and local non-governmental and community-based organizations in order to ensure better preparedness in providing timely, effective and predictable humanitarian assistance, and encourages the United Nations and humanitarian organizations to provide support to such efforts, including, as appropriate, through the transfer of technology and expertise to developing countries and through support to programmes aimed at enhancing the coordination capacities of affected States;

12. *Encourages* efforts to enhance cooperation and coordination between United Nations humanitarian entities, other relevant humanitarian organizations and donor countries and the affected State, with a view to planning and delivering emergency humanitarian assistance in ways that are supportive of early recovery as well as of sustainable rehabilitation and reconstruction efforts;

13. *Requests* the Secretary-General, in consultation with the affected countries and relevant humanitarian and development actors, to carry out an assessment of steps taken by the United Nations and relevant partners to support efforts to strengthen local, national and regional humanitarian response capacity and to include his findings as well as recommendations for enhancing United Nations support in this regard in his report to the General Assembly at its sixty-fifth session;

14. *Encourages* efforts to provide education in emergencies, including in order to contribute to a smooth transition from relief to development;

15. *Calls upon* relevant United Nations organizations to support the improvement of the consolidated appeals process, inter alia by engaging in the preparation of needs analyses and common humanitarian action plans, including through a better analysis of gender-related allocations, in order to further the development of the process as an instrument for United Nations strategic planning and prioritization, and by involving other relevant humanitarian organizations in the process, while reiterating that consolidated appeals are prepared in consultation with affected States;

16. *Requests* Member States, relevant humanitarian organizations of the United Nations system and other relevant humanitarian actors to ensure that all aspects of humanitarian response, including disaster preparedness and needs assessment, take into account the specific needs of the affected population, recognizing that giving appropriate consideration to, inter alia, gender, age and disability is part of a comprehensive and effective humanitarian response;

17. *Calls upon* United Nations humanitarian organizations, in consultation with Member States, as appropriate, to strengthen the evidence base for humanitarian assistance by further developing common mechanisms to improve the quality, transparency and reliability of, and make further progress towards, common humanitarian needs assessments, to assess their performance in assistance and to ensure the most effective use of humanitarian resources by these organizations;

18. *Calls upon* donors to provide adequate, timely, predictable and flexible resources based on and in proportion to assessed needs, including for underfunded emergencies, and to continue to support diverse humanitarian funding channels, and encourages efforts to adhere to the Principles and Good Practice of Humanitarian Donorship;

19. *Welcomes* the important achievements of the Central Emergency Response Fund in ensuring a more timely and predictable response to humanitarian emergencies, and stresses the importance of continuing to improve the functioning of the Fund in order to ensure that resources are used in the most efficient, effective and transparent manner possible;

20. *Calls upon* all Member States and invites the private sector and all concerned individuals and institutions to consider increasing their voluntary contributions to the Central Emergency Response Fund, and emphasizes that

contributions should be additional to current commitments to humanitarian programming and should not be to the detriment of resources made available for international cooperation for development;

21. *Reiterates* that the Office for the Coordination of Humanitarian Affairs should benefit from adequate and more predictable funding;

22. *Reaffirms* the obligation of all States and parties to an armed conflict to protect civilians in armed conflicts in accordance with international humanitarian law, and invites States to promote a culture of protection, taking into account the particular needs of women, children, older persons and persons with disabilities;

23. *Calls upon* States to adopt preventive measures and effective responses to acts of violence committed against civilian populations in armed conflicts and to ensure that those responsible are promptly brought to justice, in accordance with national law and their obligations under international law;

24. *Urges* all Member States to address gender-based violence in humanitarian emergencies and to ensure that their laws and institutions are adequate to prevent, promptly investigate and prosecute acts of gender-based violence, and calls upon States, the United Nations and all relevant humanitarian organizations to improve coordination, harmonize response and strengthen capacity, with a view to reducing such violence, and in support services to victims of such violence;

25. *Recognizes* the Guiding Principles on Internal Displacement as an important international framework for the protection of internally displaced persons, encourages Member States and humanitarian agencies to continue to work together, in collaboration with host communities, in endeavours to provide a more predictable response to the needs of internally displaced persons, and in this regard calls for continued and enhanced international support, upon request, for capacity-building efforts of States;

26. *Calls upon* all States and parties in complex humanitarian emergencies, in particular in armed conflict and in post-conflict situations, in countries in which humanitarian personnel are operating, in conformity with the relevant provisions of international law and national laws, to cooperate fully with the United Nations and other humanitarian agencies and organizations and to ensure the safe and unhindered access of humanitarian personnel, as well as delivery of supplies and equipment, in order to allow such personnel to efficiently perform their task of assisting affected civilian populations, including refugees and internally displaced persons;

27. *Requests* the Secretary-General to report on action taken by the Secretariat to develop and apply special emergency rules and procedures to ensure the quick disbursement of emergency funds, the expeditious procurement of emergency supplies and equipment and the rapid recruitment of staff in order to improve the overall response to humanitarian emergencies;

28. *Also requests* the Secretary-General to report to the General Assembly at its sixty-fifth session, through the Economic and Social Council at its substantive session of 2010, on progress made in strengthening the coordination of emergency humanitarian assistance of the United Nations and to submit a report to the Assembly on the detailed use of the Central Emergency Response Fund.

UN and other humanitarian personnel

In response to Assembly resolution 63/138 [YUN 2008, p. 1611], the Secretary-General, in an August report [A/64/336], provided updates on the safety and security of humanitarian and UN personnel over the preceding year and on the efforts by the UN Department of Safety and Security to implement that resolution. He expressed concern over the increased number of security incidents against humanitarian and UN personnel and was disturbed by the trend of politically or criminally motivated targeting of humanitarian workers, which was most evident in Haiti, Somalia and the Sudan. He noted that the humanitarian community had embraced the Saving Lives Together framework for the United Nations and NGO/international organization/intergovernmental organization security collaboration and called on States to support that security initiative.

The Assembly, in **resolution 64/77** of 7 December, called on Governments and parties in complex humanitarian emergencies to cooperate fully with the United Nations and other humanitarian agencies and organizations and to ensure the safe and unhindered access of humanitarian personnel (see p. 1459).

Resource mobilization
Central Emergency Response Fund

In 2009, the Central Emergency Response Fund (CERF), formerly known as the Central Emergency Revolving Fund [YUN 2006, p. 1061], a cash-flow mechanism for the initial phase of humanitarian emergencies established in 1992 [YUN 1992, p. 584], continued to allow for the rapid provision of assistance to populations affected by sudden-onset disasters and underfunded emergencies. The Fund was upgraded by General Assembly resolution 60/124 [YUN 2005, p. 991] to include a grant element, targeted at $450 million, to ensure the availability of immediate resources to address humanitarian crises. The loan element of the Fund continued to operate as a distinct and separately managed revolving fund with a target of $50 million. The 16-member CERF Advisory Group, established to provide the Secretary-General with policy guidance and advice on the use and impact of the Fund, met in April and November. In 2009, donors contributed $401.7 million to the Fund, and as of 31 December, $397.4 million in CERF funds had been allocated to support relief operations in 50 countries and the Occupied Palestinian Territory.

Report of Secretary-General. In his August report on CERF [A/64/327] covering the period from 1 July 2008 to 30 June 2009, the Secretary-General indicated that $374.3 million was allocated from the Fund to implement 475 humanitarian projects in 50 countries/territories. That amount was comprised of $274.5 million through the rapid response window and $99.8 million through the underfunded window. Fourteen humanitarian agencies received funds directly from the Fund to address emergency needs and many projects were carried out in partnership with non-governmental organizations (NGOs). A breakdown of the rapid response grants indicated that projects in response to protracted conflict-related emergencies (including services for refugees and internally displaced persons (IDPs) received the highest allocations at $113.9 million, followed by natural disaster-related allocations of $84.2 million and global-food-crisis allocations of $72.4 million. Sub-Saharan Africa received the highest percentage of funding (57.4 per cent), while Asia and the Caucasus, Latin America and the Caribbean, and the Middle East received respectively, 26.1 per cent, 9.0 per cent and 7.5 per cent. The Fund's loan mechanism remained available as a cash flow instrument when funds expected from donors had not been received, yet no formal requests for loans were submitted during the reporting period. Disbursements were made for two loans approved prior to the reporting period totalling $30 million for World Food Programme (WFP) projects in Ethiopia and the Democratic Republic of the Congo. On the grant component of the Fund, $428.8 million was committed to humanitarian projects in 2008, while $194.6 million was committed in the first half of 2009.

As recommended in the two-year evaluation of CERF [YUN 2008, p. 998], the Fund secretariat, together with humanitarian agency partners, was carrying out a review of the underfunded window processes, which would result in updated guidelines for allocating funds and improvements in the management of the allocation process. A management response matrix—prepared in November 2008 in response to the 37 strategic and operational recommendations from the evaluation to serve as a road map for work that needed to be completed before the next evaluation of the Fund in 2011—was updated and circulated in April 2009. The matrix detailed the response and action to be taken for each of the evaluation's recommendations. Of the recommendations made, 22 had been accepted, 8 partially accepted, 1 rejected, and 6 were pending. The Fund secretariat was also leading an inter-agency process to revise the Secretary-General's Bulletin on the establishment and operation of CERF, which would refine the operational guidance on the use, management and administration of the Fund. The Secretary-General concluded that the Fund continued to be an essential part of the multilateral humanitarian financial architecture and that the Fund secretariat had continued to improve its operations, financial management and reporting. He also reminded States of the $450 million annual

funding goal set by the General Assembly and the need to maintain support for a diversity of humanitarian funding tools.

Advisory Group meetings. At its April meeting [A/63/910], the CERF Advisory Group noted that the Fund governing document [ST/SGB/2006/10] needed to be revised in order to implement some of the recommendations of the two-year evaluation (see above) and that the revision of the Fund's Life-Saving Criteria would be finalized by year's end. It discussed steps taken by the secretariat to develop the CERF Performance and Accountability Framework and asked the Under-Secretary-General for Humanitarian Affairs and the Emergency Relief Coordinator to devise and implement a complete Framework before the end of the year. Noting that NGOs continued to have concerns related to the slow disbursement of sub-grants from agencies receiving CERF funds, the Advisory Group stressed that an essential element of effective response was ensuring predictable, timely and cost-efficient funding arrangements between the United Nations and NGO implementing partners. The meeting also marked the Advisory Group's first opportunity to discuss directly with the Controller issues related to the administration of the Fund, including ways to use the 3 per cent programme support cost towards the direct administration of the Fund, as well as assurances of the Controller's imminent approval of the draft interim umbrella letter of understanding, which would constitute a standard agreement between the Emergency Relief Coordinator and each humanitarian agency.

In November [A/64/558], the Group continued discussions on: use and management of the Fund in 2009; development of a performance and accountability framework; definition of the Fund's "life-saving criteria"; review of the Fund's underfunded window; partnerships with NGOs; and administrative issues. Progress had been made to finalize the revised Secretary-General's Bulletin on CERF and on the umbrella letter of understanding. In that regard, the Advisory Group requested that steps be taken to ensure that the bulletin would enter into force by 1 January 2010 and that the umbrella letter of understanding would be finalized as soon as possible thereafter. The Group also agreed to revisions to its terms of reference, including an expansion to 18 full members each serving a single three-year term.

Consolidated appeals

The consolidated appeals process, an inclusive and coordinated programme cycle for analysing context, assessing needs and planning prioritized humanitarian response, was the humanitarian sector's main strategic planning and programming tool. In 2009, the United Nations and its humanitarian partners issued consolidated and flash appeals seeking $9.8 billion in assistance to Afghanistan, Burkina Faso, the Central African Republic, Chad, Côte d'Ivoire, the Democratic Republic of the Congo, El Salvador, Indonesia, Iraq, Kenya, the Lao People's Democratic Republic, Madagascar, Namibia, the Occupied Palestinian Territory, Pakistan, the Philippines, Somalia, Sri Lanka, the Sudan, Uganda, the West Africa subregion (Benin, Burkina Faso, Côte d'Ivoire, Ghana, Guinea, Guinea-Bissau, Liberia, Mali, Mauritania, Niger, Senegal, Sierra Leone, Togo), Yemen and Zimbabwe.

The latest available data indicated that 71 per cent ($7.0 billion) of requirements had been met.

White Helmets

In response to General Assembly resolution 61/220 [YUN 2006, p. 1062], the Secretary-General provided, in a May report [A/64/84-E/2009/87] on the coordination of UN humanitarian assistance, an update on the "White Helmets" initiative, as well as suggested measures to enhance its integration into the work of the UN system. The White Helmets initiative was established by Argentina in 1993 and adopted by the Assembly in 1994 [YUN 1994, p. 827] to promote pre-identified standby and trained teams of volunteers from various national volunteer corps to support relief, rehabilitation, reconstruction and development activities. Measures to strengthen its support to UN response efforts included, among others, the conduct of a joint assessment mission by the White Helmets Commission and WFP following floods in Beni, Bolivia in 2007 [YUN 2007, p. 957], and a WFP-hosted two-day seminar with the White Helmets on WFP operational modalities in 2008. It was agreed during the 2008 meeting that the White Helmets would initiate a proposal for community-level cooperation in the areas of common interest such as supply chain and storage management, distribution and needs assessment. The Secretary-General observed that with enhanced coordination with the international humanitarian system, the White Helmets could provide an interesting model for regional and local volunteer organizations responding to disasters. In that connection, he encouraged the White Helmets initiative to enhance coordination and explore mechanisms to share best practices on disaster response and preparedness with other regional organizations in disaster-prone areas.

GENERAL ASSEMBLY ACTION

On 7 December [meeting 60], the General Assembly adopted **resolution 64/75** [draft: A/64/L.31 & Add.1] without vote [agenda item 70 *(a)*].

Participation of volunteers, "White Helmets", in the activities of the United Nations in the field of humanitarian relief, rehabilitation and technical cooperation for development

The General Assembly,

Reaffirming its resolutions 50/19 of 28 November 1995, 52/171 of 16 December 1997, 54/98 of 8 December 1999, 56/102 of 14 December 2001, 58/118 of 17 December 2003 and 61/220 of 20 December 2006,

Reaffirming also its resolutions 46/182 of 19 December 1991, 47/168 of 22 December 1992, 48/57 of 14 December 1993, 49/139 A and B of 20 December 1994, 50/57 of 12 December 1995 and 51/194 of 17 December 1996 and Economic and Social Council resolutions 1995/56 of 28 July 1995 and 1996/33 of 25 July 1996,

Emphasizing the need for coordination between relief and development activities in the context of humanitarian emergencies, taking into account the internationally agreed development goals, including those contained in the United Nations Millennium Declaration,

Recognizing the importance of mobilizing the scientific and technical know-how of the international community as a way of mitigating the effects of disasters, bearing in mind the positive impact of technology transfer to developing countries in this field,

Recognizing also the responsibility of the United Nations system in the promotion of international cooperation to prevent and mitigate disasters, to provide assistance and to coordinate relief and prevention measures, highlighting the leading role of the Secretary-General in this regard,

Recognizing further that the international community, in addressing the growing magnitude and complexity of man-made and natural disasters and chronic situations characterized by hunger, malnutrition and poverty, must rely not only on the formulation of a well-coordinated global response within the framework of the United Nations but also on the promotion of a smooth transition from relief to rehabilitation, reconstruction and development,

Recognizing the effort made by the White Helmets model in helping to involve stricken populations or those at risk in the tasks of planning, training, mobilizing and providing an immediate response in disaster situations,

Recognizing also the need to integrate a gender perspective in the design and implementation of all phases of disaster management,

1. *Takes note* of the report of the Secretary-General, in particular section IV.C, on the strengthening of the coordination of emergency humanitarian assistance of the United Nations, prepared pursuant to its resolution 46/182 and submitted in response to resolutions 63/139 of 11 December 2008 and 61/220;

2. *Recognizes* the effort being made by the White Helmets initiative to strengthen national and regional agreements aimed at facilitating coordination between the United Nations system and trained standby national volunteer corps, in accordance with accepted United Nations procedures, through the United Nations Volunteers and other agencies of the system;

3. *Notes* the emphasis placed on the development of mechanisms to facilitate the local management of humanitarian emergencies, through the organization and

participatory involvement and empowerment of affected communities and the training of the members of local volunteer corps;

4. *Also notes* the importance of the international efforts being made by the White Helmets initiative to strengthen the comprehensive regional mechanisms for managing prevention and response activities in emergency and disaster situations, in particular its model for setting up regional networks of focal points, with a view to linkage with other international structures;

5. *Recognizes* that the White Helmets initiative can play an important role in the promotion, diffusion and implementation of the decisions contained in the United Nations Millennium Declaration, and invites Member States in a position to do so to consider means to ensure the integration of the White Helmets initiative into their programme activities and to make financial resources available to the Special Voluntary Fund of the United Nations Volunteers;

6. *Takes note* of the efforts made by the World Food Programme and the White Helmets to coordinate integration mechanisms that allow for joint action within the framework of food security, on the basis of their general agreements of 1998;

7. *Encourages* operational partners of the United Nations system, in particular the United Nations Volunteers and the World Health Organization, in providing psychosocial support to the disaster-affected population in emergency and disaster situations, to draw, as appropriate, on the voluntary expertise of the White Helmets, which has been successfully tested;

8. *Encourages* the White Helmets to continue enhancing coordination with the international humanitarian system and to explore mechanisms for sharing best practices on disaster response and preparedness with other regional organizations in disaster-prone areas, in an effort to improve the coordination of humanitarian assistance provided by the United Nations in emergency situations;

9. *Invites* the Secretary-General, on the basis of the experience acquired, to continue considering the use of the White Helmets initiative as a resource suitable for preventing and mitigating the effects of humanitarian disaster situations;

10. *Also invites* the Secretary-General, on the basis of the extensive international work experience acquired by the White Helmets, as recognized by the General Assembly since the adoption of its resolution 49/139 B, the first resolution on the White Helmets initiative, and in view of the success of coordinated actions carried out with, inter alia, the United Nations Children's Fund, the World Food Programme, the Food and Agriculture Organization of the United Nations, the Office for the Coordination of Humanitarian Affairs of the Secretariat, the United Nations Development Programme and the United Nations Volunteers, to suggest measures to enhance the integration of the White Helmets initiative into the work of the United Nations system and to report thereon to the Assembly at its sixty-seventh session in a separate section of the annual report on the strengthening of the coordination of emergency humanitarian assistance of the United Nations.

Mine clearance

In response to General Assembly resolution 62/99 [YUN 2007, p. 919], the Secretary-General, in an August report [A/64/287], described the achievements of the United Nations Mine Action Team (UNMAT) since his previous report in 2007 [YUN 2007, p. 919]. The Team's activities were guided by the four strategic objectives identified in the UNMAT Strategy for 2006–2010: reduce death and injury by at least 50 per cent; mitigate the risk to community livelihoods and expand freedom of movement for at least 80 per cent of the most seriously affected communities; integrate mine-action needs into national development and reconstruction plans and budgets in at least 15 countries; and assist the development of national institutions to manage the landmine/explosive remnants of war threat and at the same time prepare for residual capacity in at least 15 countries. On progress achieved, the report indicated that while the number of casualties globally had decreased significantly since 2007, the residual threat of mines, the threat of new mines and the increased use of improvised explosive devices in a few areas remained a concern. Surveys of suspected areas conducted in 13 countries and territories revealed that the number of cleared communities, the kilometres of roads cleared and area of land released for productive use had substantially increased. In addition, the United Nations had assisted 26 countries and territories in integrating mine action into their national development plans and budgets and 15 countries in developing national institutions and strategies for successful transition to national management responsibility. The report also noted the opening for signature in December 2008 of the Convention on Cluster Munitions [YUN 2008, p. 623] and indicated that on the occasion of the tenth anniversary of the entry into force of the Anti-Personnel Mine Ban Convention (March 2009) (see p. 553), over 41 million landmines had been destroyed.

The Secretary-General observed that as UNMAT neared the completion of its five-year strategy and considered priorities and benchmarks for its 2011–2015 Strategy, significant challenges remained, including emerging ones, such as the risks posed to UN peace operations by landmines and by improvised explosive devices that had been abandoned, stockpiled or failed to function. He urged UNMAT, Member States, and the mine-action community to remain committed to the remaining work and made recommendations for their consideration.

GENERAL ASSEMBLY ACTION

On 10 December [meeting 62], the General Assembly, on the recommendation of the Fourth (Special Political and Decolonization) Committee [A/64/402], adopted **resolution 64/84** without vote [agenda item 28].

Assistance in mine action

The General Assembly,

Recalling its resolution 62/99 of 17 December 2007 and all its previous resolutions on assistance in mine clearance and on assistance in mine action, all adopted without a vote,

Recalling also all relevant treaties and conventions and their review processes,

Noting with appreciation the extent to which the International Day for Mine Awareness and Assistance in Mine Action has been commemorated worldwide,

Reaffirming its deep concern at the tremendous humanitarian and development problems caused by the presence of mines and explosive remnants of war, which have serious and lasting social and economic consequences for the populations of countries affected by them,

Bearing in mind the serious threat that mines and explosive remnants of war pose to the safety, health and lives of local civilian populations, as well as of personnel participating in humanitarian, peacekeeping, rehabilitation and mine-clearance programmes and operations,

Deeply alarmed by the number of mines that continue to be laid each year as well as the presence of a decreasing but still very large number of, and area of square kilometres infested by, mines and explosive remnants of war as a result of armed conflicts, and therefore remaining convinced of the necessity and urgency of strengthening mine-action efforts by the international community with a view to eliminating the threat of landmines and explosive remnants of war to civilians as soon as possible,

Recognizing that, in addition to the primary role of States, the United Nations has a significant role to play in the field of assistance in mine action through the United Nations Mine Action Team, including the United Nations Mine Action Service, and considering mine action to be an important and integrated component of United Nations humanitarian and development activities, as well as noting the integration of mine action in numerous United Nations peacekeeping operations,

Recognizing also the valuable mine-action efforts of national and international mine-action practitioners, including United Nations personnel and peacekeepers, enabling local communities to resume normal lives and reclaim their livelihoods by regaining access to previously contaminated lands,

Stressing the pressing need to urge non-State actors to halt immediately and unconditionally new deployments of mines and other associated explosive devices,

1. *Takes note* of the report of the Secretary-General;

2. *Calls for*, in particular, the continuation of the efforts of States, with the assistance of the United Nations and relevant organizations involved in mine action, as appropriate, to foster the establishment and development of national mine-action capacities in countries in which mines and explosive remnants of war constitute a serious threat to the safety, health and lives of the local civilian population or an impediment to social and economic development efforts at the national and local levels;

3. *Urges* all States, in particular those that have the capacity to do so, as well as the United Nations system and other relevant organizations and institutions involved in mine action, to support mine-affected States and territories, as appropriate, by providing:

(a) Assistance to countries affected by mines and explosive remnants of war for the establishment and development of national mine-action capacities, including, where appropriate, in the fulfilment of the relevant international obligations of those countries;

(b) Support for national programmes, where appropriate, in cooperation with the relevant bodies of the United Nations system and relevant regional, governmental and non-governmental organizations, to reduce the risks posed by landmines and explosive remnants of war, taking into consideration the different needs of women, girls, boys and men;

(c) Reliable, predictable and timely contributions for mine-action activities, including through national mine-action efforts and mine-action programmes of non-governmental organizations, including those relating to victim assistance and mine-risk education, especially at the local level, as well as through relevant national, regional and global trust funds, including the Voluntary Trust Fund for Assistance in Mine Action;

(d) Necessary information and technical, financial and material assistance to locate, remove, destroy and otherwise render ineffective minefields, mines, booby traps, other devices and explosive remnants of war, in accordance with international law, as soon as possible;

(e) Technological assistance (i) to countries affected by mines and explosive remnants of war; and (ii) to promote user-oriented scientific research on and development of mine-action techniques and technology that are effective, sustainable, appropriate and environmentally sound;

4. *Encourages* efforts to conduct all mine-action activities in accordance with the International Mine Action Standards (IMAS) or IMAS-compliant national standards, and emphasizes the importance of using an information management system, such as the Information Management System for Mine Action, to help facilitate mine-action activities;

5. *Urges* all mine-affected States, pursuant to applicable international law, to identify all areas, as appropriate, under their jurisdiction or control containing mines and other explosive remnants of war in the most efficient manner possible and to employ land release techniques, including non-technical survey, technical survey and clearance when appropriate;

6. *Encourages* mine-affected States, with support from relevant development partners as appropriate, to proactively mainstream mine action and victim assistance requirements into development plans and processes to ensure that development priorities include mine action and that mine action is predictably funded;

7. *Encourages* all relevant multilateral, regional and national programmes and bodies to include activities related to mine action, including clearance, in their humanitarian, rehabilitation, reconstruction and development assistance activities, where appropriate, bearing in mind the need to ensure national and local ownership, sustainability and capacity-building, as well as to include a gender and age-appropriate perspective in all aspects of such activities;

8. *Encourages* Member States, as appropriate, and relevant organizations involved in mine action to continue efforts to ensure that mine-action programmes are gender-

and age-sensitive, so that women, girls, boys and men can benefit equally from them, and encourages the participation of all stakeholders in the programming of mine action;

9. *Stresses* the importance of cooperation and coordination in mine action, and emphasizes the primary responsibility of national authorities in that regard, also stresses the supporting role of the United Nations and other relevant organizations in that regard, and underlines the need for a comprehensive and independent evaluation of the scope, organization, effectiveness and approach of the work of the United Nations in mine action;

10. *Recognizes* the importance of explicitly incorporating references to mine action, when appropriate, in ceasefire and peace agreements in light of the potential that mine action can have as a peace and confidence-building measure in post-conflict situations among parties concerned;

11. *Requests* the Secretary-General to submit to the General Assembly at its sixty-sixth session a report on the implementation of the present resolution and on follow-up to previous resolutions on assistance in mine clearance and on assistance in mine action, including on relevant United Nations policies and activities;

12. *Decides* to include in the provisional agenda of its sixty-sixth session the item entitled "Assistance in mine action".

Humanitarian activities

Africa

Angola

In October, following a large-scale expulsion of irregular Congolese migrants from Angola's diamond mining areas in the northeast by the Angolan Government, an estimated 54,000 Angolans were expelled from the Democratic Republic of the Congo. The majority of the expelled resided in the border province of Bas-Congo. In the space of a few days, some 38,647 people arrived in the Angolan province of Zaire, 10,223 in Uige, and 2,638 in Cabinda. Many people were forced to leave without any notice, leaving behind their possessions and identity documents, and in a number of cases, were separated from their families. The Angolan Government provided assistance, including temporary shelter, food and medical services. It also carried out a basic registration of the expelled, gathering information on their identity, places of origin and family background. At the request of the Government, the UN and humanitarian organizations provided relief items to affected populations in Zaire province: non-food items, water and sanitation supplies and equipment, emergency medical kits, education materials and supplies, construction kits, tarpaulins and a truck. UNHCR also dispatched tents and blankets to Uige province.

The six-month response plan for the period 1 October 2009 to 31 March 2010 required $5.2 million and would focus on the provision of technical assistance to the Government and targeted provision of humanita-

rian assistance in gap sectors, jointly identified with the Government, in reception and transit centres.

Central African Republic

The UN Consolidated Inter-Agency Appeal for the Central African Republic in 2009 sought $100.4 million, of which 73 per cent ($73.3 million) was received.

While progress had been made over the previous year, the peace process in the Central African Republic remained fragile and limited. Nearly half of the IDPs, some 85,000 people, had returned to their villages only to find their houses destroyed and their fields overgrown. Another 209,000 Central Africans displaced in the country and in neighbouring Cameroon, Chad and Darfur, were afraid to return home. Displacement continued as renewed fighting between a militant group and Government forces in the northwest, as well as attacks by armed bandits across the north and incursions by the Ugandan Lord's Resistance Army rebel group in the southeast, forced more people away from their villages. Political conflict, banditry, the destruction of schools, health centres and houses, and forced displacement further exacerbated an already dire humanitarian situation. Meanwhile, basic health indicators in the Central African Republic were among the worst on the continent. The humanitarian aid strategy was limited to areas directly affected by conflict and violence: the seven northern prefectures and the far southeast. The four sectors identified as priorities were health; water, sanitation and hygiene; protection; and early recovery. An initial appeal sought $116.2 million for 105 projects. In July, humanitarian partners issued a revised strategy to continue assisting and protecting hundreds of thousands of people who had been affected by violence.

Chad

The UN Consolidated Inter-Agency Appeal for Chad in 2009 sought $400.6 million, of which 91 per cent ($365.9 million) was received.

Thanks to the funding, the humanitarian aid community in Chad was able to continue providing vital assistance to Sudanese and Central African refugees, to Chadian IDPs, and to members of the host population most affected by the presence of refugees and IDPs in the east and south-east of the country. That assistance contributed to the survival of more than half a million people. It was achieved in restricted humanitarian space, and in a complex and difficult security environment in which attacks and banditry had increased. Although the security situation remained fragile, in the absence of any large-scale fighting in Chad in 2009, the aid community agreed that the situation in Chad was predominately one of assistance to the various populations and that the acute emergency phase (in the sense of rapid worsening) was over. Humanitarian action would continue to focus on emergency relief needs, while emphasizing self-sufficiency and developing local capacities of people in Chad affected by the internal crisis and instability in the subregion. No new internal displacements had been reported since the beginning of the year. Between 20,000 and 25,000 people had returned home from 2008 to the end of 2009.

Côte d'Ivoire

The UN Consolidated Inter-Agency Appeal for Côte d'Ivoire, which sought $36.7 million in 2009, received 37 per cent ($13.7 million) of the requirement.

Following the signature of the Ouagadougou Agreement in March 2007 [YUN 2007, p. 174], Côte d'Ivoire entered a post-conflict phase, which led to positive changes in the socio-economic sector during the political transition period, including new commitments towards the country made by financial institutions. Nonetheless, those developments had not completely halted the degradation of social conditions resulting from five years of crisis. Although an estimated 78,000 out of 120,000 IDPs had voluntarily returned to their origins in the western part of the country as at 31 May 2009, land disputes and an overall weak social fabric posed a threat to the sustained pace of return of the remaining IDPs. Response to the high malnutrition rate continued to be a critical need in the north of the country. Assistance had reached 10,000 malnourished children under five years of age and mothers. Collecting data on malnutrition was identified as a priority in order to allow for better-targeted actions in the second half of the year. Humanitarian partners in Côte d'Ivoire agreed that the transitional context required responses that were more anchored in recovery and development objectives and coordination frameworks had been adapted to meet that new reality.

Democratic Republic of the Congo

The Democratic Republic of the Congo (DRC) was the scene of one of the worst humanitarian crises in the world. In 2009, despite positive signs of political progress and the improvement of relations between the DRC and neighbouring countries, the continued fighting in the east between the Armed Forces of the Democratic Republic of the Congo and rebel groups had serious impact on humanitarian activities. The year was also marked by aggravated attacks by the Lord's Resistance Army (LRA), which resulted in frequent looting and serious abuses against civilians.

In addition, harassment and attacks against humanitarian workers were on the rise, particularly in North Kivu.

However, thanks to the efforts of humanitarian actors, many positive results were achieved, including: more than 1 million people gained access to drinking water; some 55,000 schoolchildren were back in school; about 1.3 million people became reachable due to the rebuilding of bridges and roads and the introduction of flights; support was sent to more than 600 nutritional centres; the social and economic reintegration of over 12,000 people was accomplished; food rations to 2.8 million people and non-food item kits to 280,000 people were distributed; support was provided to more than 6,700 victims of sexual violence; and 80 per cent vaccine coverage of measles and diphtheria/pertusis/tetanus (DPT) in accessible areas were distributed.

The revised Humanitarian Action Plan for the Democratic Republic of the Congo sought $946.3 million, of which 65 per cent ($617.9 million) was received.

Kenya

In 2009, a number of factors—including poor short rains, rising food and commodity prices, reduced cereal production and livestock diseases—converged to increase food insecurity among vulnerable populations in Kenya, leading the President to declare an emergency on 16 January and launch an appeal for assistance. The short rains assessment revealed that 3.5 million people required emergency food assistance. Meanwhile, ongoing violence and insecurity in Somalia had prompted an increase in refugees entering Kenya, with more than 50,000 refugees entering the country in 2009. In March, the 2009 Emergency Humanitarian Response Plan for Kenya was revised to respond to existing and emerging needs, which represented a 48 per cent increase.

Thanks to the funding, 2.2 million people in the arid and semi-arid lands received food assistance. More than 420,000 schoolchildren in coastal districts received emergency school feeding. More than 100,000 people in the 2008 post-election violence affected areas received basic needs assistance, including improved access to safe water and food assistance. In addition, 20,000 IDP shelters had been constructed. Health sector partners responded to cholera outbreaks in 38 districts in five provinces and kala azar outbreaks in three districts of the Rift Valley and northeastern provinces. As of July 2009, approximately 51,300 children under five had been admitted into supplementary feeding programmes and 8,400 into therapeutic feeding programmes. That represented a significant increase from the previous year, during which 7,400 children were admitted in therapeutic feeding programmes for the whole of 2008.

The Plan, which sought $581.1 million for 2009, received 84 per cent ($490.3 million) of the requirements. In June, further revisions to the Plan reduced the requirements to $576 million.

Somalia

The UN Consolidated Inter-Agency Appeal for Somalia for 2009, which sought $851.8 million, received 66 per cent ($559.1 million) of the requirements.

Protracted conflict, economic collapse, and drought conditions continued to drive the humanitarian crisis in Somalia in 2009, resulting in increased population displacement, greater urban vulnerability and widespread acute malnutrition. The overall food security situation continued to deteriorate, with 43 per cent of the population (3.2 million people) remaining in need of humanitarian and livelihood assistance. While the *Gu* rains, which normally ran from March to June, had started in many parts of the country, they were insufficient to alleviate the water shortages in some areas. The global economic downturn also affected the country; remittances estimated at one billion dollars per year declined by 25 per cent owing to the global recession and increased unemployment among the Somali diaspora. Due to operational constraints, such as growing insecurity, targeting of humanitarian workers, and limited funding, the humanitarian community had prioritized emergency relief activities over medium- and long-term humanitarian programming. The four response objectives remained valid: provide humanitarian assistance to 3.2 million people in crisis, including 820,000 people in humanitarian emergency who would be targeted for life-saving assistance; increase community and local capacity to protect social and economic assets in emergencies; deliver an integrated minimum package of basic social services based on geographic specific priorities and target groups; and strengthen the protective environment of civilians. The initial appeal requirements were decreased by $70 million owing mainly to the withdrawal of a key food aid organization.

Sudan

The UN Consolidated Inter-Agency Appeal for the Sudan sought $2.1 billion, of which 70 per cent ($1.5 billion) was received, making Sudan the largest humanitarian operation in the world.

Events in early 2009 changed the operational environment for humanitarian actors in the Sudan. Key aspects of the Comprehensive Peace Agreement—the census, disarmament, demobilization and rehabilitation, and the Interim Abyei Administration—

advanced the movement towards recovery. However, each of those benchmarks had been offset by continued challenges. Insecurity and conflict caused displacement as well as protection and human rights concerns in Darfur, southern Sudan and the "Three Areas" (Abyei, Blue Nile, South Kordofan). In addition, the loss of Sudanese and international NGOs in March altered the humanitarian community's ability to implement programmes. During the first half of the year, the United Nations and NGOs provided 104,500 metric tonnes of food assistance; supplied chlorinated water to more than 1 million people; and maintained health facilities and serviced nearly 1.3 million outpatients. Despite those efforts, chronic gaps and concerns for strategic and sustainable solutions became more pressing. By August, 4 million people had received critical food assistance—including basic cereals, pulses, oil, sugar and salt while 800,000 households had received seed and tool kits and technical training on increasing yields. More than 21,000 severely malnourished children had been admitted to feeding programmes in northern Sudan and 18,600 in southern Sudan by October; and the mass distribution of vitamin A supplements to over 7 million children and mass de-worming campaigns were carried out in northern Sudan, reaching 5.1 million children. Gross enrolment in basic education rose to 73.2 per cent, a 3.3 per cent increase over 2008, although large numbers of children remained out of school.

Communication. On 19 June [S/2009/318], the Sudan transmitted to the Security Council a joint press advisory on the second meeting of the strengthened High-level Committee on humanitarian affairs (Khartoum, 17 June). The meeting built on the dialogue established at the first meeting on 7 May between the Government and the humanitarian community. The Committee approved terms of reference towards a predictable, less bureaucratic and more accountable and efficient aid system in Darfur.

Uganda

The UN Consolidated Inter-Agency Appeal for Uganda sought $247 million in 2009, of which 76 per cent ($188.2 million) was received.

In 2009, recovery was emerging as the main requirement in Uganda, yet humanitarian needs remained in danger of not being met due to poor funding. With some 1.6 million people across the Acholi, Karamoja and Teso sub-regions requiring humanitarian assistance, some aid organizations, particularly in Teso, were considering closing operations as funding was not forthcoming. Continuing stability in the country prompted the majority of IDPs to leave the camps in Acholi. Population movements out of IDP camps, where access to water and sanitation facilities had been good, had not been matched by increased provision of services in return sites. Latrine coverage in return areas in northern Uganda was less than 30 per cent, while access to improved water sources averaged only 30 per cent. The outbreak of hepatitis E that had killed 160 people and infected more than 10,000 since 2007 continued to spread and the threat of epidemic outbreaks of other diseases remained high. In Karamoja, humanitarian response provided food assistance to over 80 per cent of food-insecure individuals. Animal diseases imperilled the region's main source of livelihood; sustained funding for vaccinations was required to bring outbreaks under control. Over half of the food security sector funding had gone toward food assistance, even though agricultural interventions to expand land access and use were critical to ensuring food security in the Acholi and Teso sub-regions. In June, priorities identified for the remainder of the Appeal included boosting food and livelihood security; enhancing access to water and sanitation in areas of return; increasing immunization coverage and disease surveillance and response; and facilitating return and functional capacity of displaced schools.

West Africa

The UN Consolidated Inter-Agency Appeal for the West Africa subregion, which sought $404.2 million in 2009 to assist beneficiaries in Benin, Burkina Faso, Côte d'Ivoire, Ghana, Guinea, Guinea-Bissau, Liberia, Mali, Mauritania, the Niger, Senegal, Sierra Leone and Togo, received 64 per cent ($259.7 million) of requirements.

During the year, West Africa experienced humanitarian emergencies arising from a range of vulnerabilities. By mid-May, the region had suffered a meningitis epidemic that affected some 67,000 persons, killing 3,000, and a measles outbreak with 35,000 reported cases that killed 250 people. The epidemics showed the vulnerability of the population, as well as the lack of preparedness and capacity to respond to rapid onset, or to medium- to large-scale emergencies. At the same time, high food commodity prices affected the region and impacted already high rates of malnutrition. On the political front, a number of countries had achieved a measure of peace and stability, yet still struggled with the longer-term effects of past conflicts and instability. Military coups d'état (Guinea, Guinea-Bissau, Mauritania), constitutional changes to extend presidential mandates (Niger), and social unrest or uncertainty surrounding political elections were worrying indications of the potential for a deterioration in regional stability. The four priority areas agreed by the humanitarian community—food security and nutrition; health; protection and population movements; and water, sanita-

tion and hygiene—would continue to be the core of humanitarian action in the region. A fifth priority area, comprising coordination, information management and support services, would continue to ensure a principled humanitarian response and the provision of support and services to all humanitarian actors. The mid-year review of the Appeal included 14 new projects, as well as revisions of existing projects, and resulted in an 8.5 per cent increase in requirements, mainly due to increased food and nutrition needs.

Zimbabwe

The UN Consolidated Inter-Agency Appeal for Zimbabwe sought $722.2 million in 2009, of which 63 per cent ($456.4 million) was received.

During the year, the humanitarian situation in Zimbabwe deteriorated sharply. A country-wide cholera outbreak and increase in food insecurity exacerbated the socio-economic environment of hyper-inflation and led to the collapse of basic social services. The humanitarian response contained the cholera outbreak, provided food and agricultural assistance to vulnerable populations, and supported vital social services including health, water and education, in the face of operational difficulties. Despite those efforts, as of May, 6 million people had limited or no access to safe water and sanitation; 600,000 families needed key agricultural inputs for the 2009–2010 planting season; and 1.3 million people were living with HIV/AIDS. The decline of the water and sanitation, health, education, and protection sectors was one of the main reasons the cholera outbreak had spread uncontrollably and claimed over 4,200 lives. There was concern that, unless conditions changed, outbreaks of water-borne diseases at the onset of the next rainy season could lead to new cholera cases and increased humanitarian needs. A revision of the appeal resulted in the inclusion of projects that supported population stabilization and emergency recovery and risk reduction, such as the repair to basic infrastructure and payment of incentives to health workers and teachers. Other appeal objectives included saving and preventing loss of lives; supporting the restoration of livelihoods; preventing the depletion of productive household assets; and strengthening the institutional capacity at the local level of coordinating and implementing essential recovery activities.

Asia

Afghanistan

The humanitarian crisis in Afghanistan was characterized by some 235,000 IDPs, 7.4 million food-insecure people (31 per cent of the population), 400,000 persons seriously affected by natural disasters annually and 2.6 million registered Afghan refugees in the region. Many parts of the country were inaccessible for humanitarian actors, who continued to be affected by intimidation and kidnappings of national staff, which surged in April 2009. Since 2007, security had deteriorated, particularly in the southern and eastern regions. Insecurity was linked to the movement of insurgents into those provinces, the ongoing lack of development and weak government institutions. The conflict-based humanitarian needs were compounded by the chronic vulnerability of much of Afghanistan's population. Flooding in the north of the country had affected more than 22,000 households, and drought from the previous two years had affected the lives of 70 per cent of the population in remote rural areas. The objectives of the 2009 Humanitarian Action Plan remained valid: provide relief to those affected by conflict and disasters; mitigate food insecurity and treat malnutrition; monitor and advocate for the protection of civilians and respect for the law; improve preparedness for disasters and disease outbreaks; and improve humanitarian access and response. The Plan, which was revised at the mid-year review to include new and re-prioritized projects, sought $664.9 million, of which 76 per cent ($507.7 million) was received.

Iraq

The UN Consolidated Inter-Agency Appeal for Iraq and the Region sought $650.2 million in 2009, of which 67 per cent ($433 million) of the requirement was received.

Although Iraq was moving toward transition, with rates of violence down by 75 per cent since mid-2007, food insecurity at 25 per cent of the 2005 figures, and 21,000 IDP families returning home between June and September 2008, the situation in 2009 remained fragile. That included continued attacks against civilians; many underlying conflicts and grievances unresolved; and hundreds of thousands of Iraqi families inside and outside the country struggling with acute poverty, displacement and the continuing effects of conflict. In some areas, availability of water, sanitation, and health care was far below national averages. The 2009 Appeal for Iraq and the Region supplemented the Government response, addressing immediate humanitarian needs, contributing to stabilization and promoting recovery, not only within Iraq, but for 1.7 million Iraqi refugees in seven countries across the Middle East. It was presented in two pillars: one coordinated by Iraq's Humanitarian Coordinator, reflecting needs inside the country; and the other coordinated by UNHCR, addressing the needs of Iraqi refugees in the region. Countries hosting the largest number of Iraqi refugees (Syria, Jordan, Lebanon) assisted nearly 300,000 registered refugees. In Iraq, UN operations shifted towards addressing the needs of vulnerable groups including not only IDPs and re-

turnees but also female-headed households, particularly Iraq's widows, children and adolescents. New projects on returnees' protection and shelter requirements added at the mid-year review increased first pillar requirements by 61 per cent ($308.8 million).

Nepal

In 2009, significant humanitarian needs remained in Nepal due to a combination of national and global factors: a particularly severe winter drought, ongoing civil and political tensions, chronic underlying vulnerabilities, and susceptibility to sudden-onset natural disasters, compounded by the global financial, fuel, and food crises. Food insecurity was widespread, with more than 40 per cent of the population undernourished. In December 2008, 2.7 million people were identified as requiring urgent food assistance and a joint Government of Nepal and UN assessment undertaken in May 2009 identified an additional 707,000 individuals requiring food assistance due to drought-induced failure of winter crops and high food prices. Meanwhile, political issues remained unresolved—a crisis resulted in the resignation of Prime Minister Pushpa Kamal Dahal on 4 May, terminating the nine-month-old Government. A coalition government was being established. Nepal was also faced with prolonged disruptions in the movement of goods due to intermittent unrest in Terai-Madhes, daily electricity cuts lasting up to 16 hours, and deteriorating labour relations. At the mid-year review, the Humanitarian Country Team agreed that the three priorities set at the beginning of the year were still valid: response, preparedness and partnership. Priority was given to projects for food assistance and disaster preparedness activities. Consequently, the 2009 Nepal Humanitarian Transition Appeal was revised upwards to $145 million from the original $115 million, which represented increases attributed to the addition of 12 new and revised projects, mainly to cover additional food security needs.

Pakistan

In April, insecurity in Pakistan's North West Frontier Province (NWFP) and Federally Administered Tribal Areas (FATA) intensified, leading to mass forced displacement of the civilian population. Since mid-2008, some 577,167 people had fled their homes in NWFP, including FATA, and by the end of April 2009, the insecurity in the southern Malakand Division had led to further displacement of 1.2 million people and an estimated total of 1.8 million displaced people. Prior to the deterioration of the situation, the humanitarian community had been providing protection and assistance to 577,000 IDPs, the majority of whom were accommodated with host families, while the rest received shelter, food, water, sanitation and hygiene and other services, including non-food items, in the 11 IDP camps established across NWFP. The scale of the new displacement demanded an increased humanitarian response from the Government and necessitated a further revision of the Pakistan Humanitarian Response Plan (PHRP) [YUN 2008, p. 1005]. Reports indicated that the insecurity had resulted in significant civilian casualties, restricted freedom of movement and devastated civilian infrastructure. Rapid needs assessment and immediate response would be implemented as soon as access permitted.

The UN appeal for the revised PHRP sought $680.1 million in 2009, of which 77 per cent ($525.8 million) was received.

Occupied Palestinian Territory

The UN Consolidated Inter-Agency Appeal for the Occupied Palestinian Territory, which sought $804.5 million in 2009, received 79 per cent ($636.6 million) of the requirements.

The year 2009 witnessed one of the most violent periods experienced by Palestinian civilians since the beginning of Israel's occupation in 1967 [YUN 1967, p. 174]. Following an escalation of violence since November 2008—including incursions and air strikes by Israeli forces and rockets fired into Israel by Palestinian armed factions—Israeli forces, on 27 December, conducted a 23-day military operation in the Gaza Strip (see p. 434). Some 1,326 Palestinians were killed and 5,450 injured. The conflict resulted in the destruction of homes, livelihoods and infrastructure, and debilitated basic services throughout the Gaza strip, compounding the humanitarian situation arising from the 18-month closure of Gaza to all but the most essential commodities. Some 14,800 homes were destroyed or damaged and nearly 51,000 people were displaced in shelters. Five months after the military operation, access to essential goods remained severely restricted, hindering humanitarian response. Some 32,000 Gazans still had no or limited access to clean water. Early recovery had not begun on the damaged infrastructure due to Israel's ban on imports of building materials and supplies. In July, humanitarian needs in all sectors were reassessed. The Humanitarian Country Team developed a normative framework for the provision of humanitarian assistance to Gaza providing guidelines for all actors to follow to allow the unhindered and impartial delivery of humanitarian assistance.

Sri Lanka

In 2009, the humanitarian situation in Sri Lanka changed significantly. The Government advance into remaining rebel-held territory in the northern Vanni region continued until 18 May, when the Government announced the end of combat operations, concluding the 26-year long conflict with the separatist movement of the Liberation Tigers of Tamil Eelam. Over 230,000 people fled during the final month of the conflict, joining another 65,000 IDPs who had fled from the conflict area between the end of 2008 and mid-April 2009. The capacities of the Government and humanitarian aid agencies were strained, particularly in the Vavuniya District, where nearly 262,000 IDPs were being accommodated. The Government provided resources such as land clearing, drainage, electricity, and water supply to assist the displaced populations accommodated in IDP camps in Jaffna, Trincomalee and Vavuniya. UN agencies and NGOs provided basic assistance and monitored needs and gaps in IDP sites. The Humanitarian Country Team compiled a summary of emergency priorities to address IDP needs from May to July, which sought to clarify the nature and scale of the response within the framework of Sri Lanka's 2009 Common Humanitarian Action Plan and identified projects totalling $52 million. That exercise fed into the mid-year review process and enabled humanitarian partners to review needs and update response plans. The updated Plan included projects to assist up to 100,000 IDPs to return to their places of origin before year's end and to support economic recovery, infrastructure and agriculture, and mine action activities. Consequently, the revised Plan sought $270.1 million for 185 projects, of which 74 per cent ($200.7 million) was received.

Syrian Arab Republic

In 2009, drought continued to affect a population in Syria that was already suffering from the impact of previous drought spells. Syrian Government and UN assessment missions indicated that some 1.3 million inhabitants of eastern Syria had been affected by the disaster, out of which 803,000 had lost almost all their livelihoods and faced extreme hardship. Up to 80 per cent of those severely affected lived on a diet consisting of bread and sugared tea, covering only 50 per cent of both caloric and protein requirements. Communities inhabiting the drought-affected areas suffered from acute water shortage as many wells and rivers had dried up. Meanwhile, poor nutrition, heat, and dust storms had a detrimental effect on the health of those populations. One of the most visible effects of the drought had been an increase in the already substantial migration out of the affected areas since the previous year. A combination of actions—food and agriculture assistance, supplemented by water and health interventions, and measures aimed at increasing drought resilience—was required to allow affected populations to remain in their villages and restart agriculture production in October 2009. Assistance would need to continue until mid-2010, when new crops were expected to improve food security. The Syria Drought Response Plan was developed to supplement and enhance Government assistance. Through the Plan, seven agencies sought $52.9 million to work with Governmental partners and targeted communities in addressing emergency humanitarian needs and mitigating further impact on some 38,000 families (300,000 people) considered the most vulnerable for a period of 12 months.

Special economic assistance

African economic recovery and development
New Partnership for Africa's Development

The General Assembly, by resolution 57/7 [YUN 2002, p. 910], endorsed the Secretary-General's recommendation [ibid., p. 909] that the New Partnership for Africa's Development (NEPAD), adopted in 2001 by the Assembly of Heads of State and Government of the Organization of African Unity [YUN 2001, p. 900], should be the framework within which the international community should concentrate its efforts for Africa's development. During 2009, efforts continued to focus on UN and international support for NEPAD and its implementation.

Implementation and support for NEPAD

Report of Secretary-General (March). In response to a request of the Committee for Programme and Coordination (CPC) [YUN 2005, p. 1004], the Secretary-General in March submitted a report [E/AC.51/2009/7] on UN system support for NEPAD since May 2008. The report was organized around nine thematic clusters corresponding to the Partnership's priorities and strategies: infrastructure development; governance; peace and security; agriculture, food security and rural development; industry, trade and market access; environment, population and urbanization; social and human development; science and technology; and communications, advocacy and outreach. In addition, three selected policy issues in the implementation of NEPAD were examined: strengthening of the cluster system and impact of UN system support; support for the mobilization of financial resources for NEPAD implementation; and cross-cutting issues, such as the global economic and financial crisis, food and nutrition, governance, HIV/AIDS and public health, environmental sustainability and higher education. The report also identified challenges and constraints faced by the UN system

in supporting the African Union (AU) and the NEPAD programme.

The Secretary-General observed that the report coincided with the eighth anniversary of the adoption of NEPAD and that it was timely for UN system entities to develop an outcome-oriented monitoring approach whereby they could assess the impact of their support in the implementation of the NEPAD programme. He made recommendations for, among others, a specific monitoring and evaluation framework to be operationalized within the framework of the regional coordination mechanism; clusters to prepare and submit their business plans to be consolidated into one regional coordination plan; and UN system organizations to continue to collaborate closely with the AU Commission in support of AU priorities.

On 31 March [meeting 78], the General Assembly adopted **resolution 63/267** [draft: A/63/L.60/Rev.1 & Add.1] without vote [agenda item 57 (a)].

New Partnership for Africa's Development: progress in implementation and international support

The General Assembly,

Recalling its resolution 57/2 of 16 September 2002 on the United Nations Declaration on the New Partnership for Africa's Development,

Recalling also its resolution 57/7 of 4 November 2002 on the final review and appraisal of the United Nations New Agenda for the Development of Africa in the 1990s and support for the New Partnership for Africa's Development and resolutions 58/233 of 23 December 2003, 59/254 of 23 December 2004, 60/222 of 23 December 2005, 61/229 of 22 December 2006 and 62/179 of 19 December 2007 entitled "New Partnership for Africa's Development: progress in implementation and international support",

Recalling further the 2005 World Summit Outcome, including the recognition of the need to address the special needs of Africa, and recalling its resolution 60/265 of 30 June 2006,

Recalling the political declaration on Africa's development needs, adopted at the high-level meeting on Africa's development needs on 22 September 2008,

1. *Takes note* of the sixth consolidated report of the Secretary-General;

2. *Reaffirms its commitment* to the full implementation of the political declaration on Africa's development needs, as reaffirmed also in the Doha Declaration on Financing for Development, adopted as the outcome document of the Follow-up International Conference on Financing for Development to Review the Implementation of the Monterrey Consensus, held in Doha from 29 November to 2 December 2008;

3. *Reaffirms its full support* for the implementation of the New Partnership for Africa's Development;

4. *Requests* the Secretary-General to submit a comprehensive report on the implementation of the present resolution to the General Assembly at its sixty-fourth session on

the basis of inputs from Governments, organizations of the United Nations system and other stakeholders in the New Partnership.

CPC action. CPC, at its forty-ninth session (8 June–2 July) [A/64/16], welcomed the Secretary-General's report on NEPAD (see above) and the political declaration on Africa's development needs adopted during the 2008 high-level meeting of the Assembly by resolution 63/1 [YUN 2008, p. 1009]. The Committee recommended the urgent filling of the post of the Special Adviser on Africa and that the Special Adviser closely monitor the development and social effects of the financial crisis and its impact on the achievement of the Millennium Development Goals (MDGs) in Africa. CPC also requested the Secretary-General to emphasize mitigation of the impacts of the crisis on African countries when ensuring better coordination among UN system organizations.

Report of Secretary-General (July). In response to Assembly resolution 63/267 (see above), the Secretary-General submitted, in July, the seventh consolidated report [A/64/204] on progress achieved to implement and support NEPAD, which highlighted action taken by African countries and organizations in the implementation in NEPAD; the response of the international community in building on the momentum of international support for Africa's development; and support provided by the UN system in NEPAD implementation, ranging from advocacy and institutional support to technical assistance and capacity-building. Given the need for a comprehensive long-term infrastructural development plan for the continent, the AU Commission, NEPAD and the African Development Bank (AfDB) initiated the Programme for Infrastructure Development in Africa, a framework that would focus on translating sectoral policies into development action plans for the energy, transport, water and sanitation, and information and communications technology (ICT) sectors. Efforts were under way to determine the successful bidder to undertake the Programme study, which was expected to be completed by the end of 2010. The AU Commission, in collaboration with the NEPAD secretariat and AfDB, had also launched a number of quick-win infrastructure projects, such as the development of regional hydropower projects in response to the energy crisis, and projects concerning transcontinental transport infrastructure, including the missing links in the Trans-African Highway corridors. In other developments, the NEPAD e-Africa Commission was coordinating the development of the NEPAD ICT broadband infrastructure network in two segments: the Uhurunet submarine cable and the Umojanet terrestrial network. Uhurunet, which would provide for the connection of all coastal and island countries in Africa, was expected to become opera-

tional in 2010. A detailed feasibility study of part of Umojanet which would cover terrestrial networks in Eastern and Southern Africa was completed in April 2009.

The report also discussed the activities of the Regional Consultation Mechanism of UN entities and organizations working in Africa in support of AU and NEPAD, as well as progress achieved with the Millennium Villages Project and the peer review process. In that regard, some 30 countries had acceded to the African Peer Review Mechanism (APRM) as of July 2009. The Secretary-General concluded that progress had been achieved in implementing the NEPAD projects, moving the APRM process forward, and achieving the 10.2 per cent rise in net global official development assistance (ODA) from members of the Development Assistance Committee, which totalled $119.8 billion in 2008. However, the main challenge was for African countries to ensure that the financial crisis, combined with the latent food and energy crisis, did not reverse the progress achieved. He called on international development partners to take action to mitigate the socio-economic impact of the crisis and help African countries recover ground in their progress towards the implementation of NEPAD and the MDGs. He further urged those partners to take steps to successfully conclude the Doha Round of trade negotiations.

Follow-up to high-level meeting on Africa's development needs

In follow-up to the high-level meeting convened by the Assembly on Africa's development needs in 2008 [YUN 2008, p. 1009] and pursuant to Assembly resolution 63/1 [ibid.], the Secretary-General submitted a July report [A/64/208] on Africa's development needs: state of implementation of various commitments, challenges and the way forward. The report assessed the impact on development of three crises that were engulfing Africa: the financial and economic, the food, and the climate change and energy crises. It also identified other development challenges, such as the increased number of armed conflicts; the brain drain; the health, human and economic impact of HIV/AIDS; the growth of urban areas; and governance, which in some States was marked by personalized rule and corruption.

On commitments and the state of implementation, the Secretary-General reported that the turn of the millennium had heralded a new phase in Africa's development, characterized by bolder commitments, more rigorous monitoring, and the willingness of African States and institutions to take full responsibility over the helm. Africa's economy was estimated to have expanded 5.7 per cent in 2008—the first time in 45 years that growth had exceeded

5 per cent for five successive years. Political and economic reforms had led to better economic management and an improved business environment. However, due to the financial and economic crisis, the pace of growth had slowed and was projected to reach only 2.8 per cent in 2009, lower than the 7 per cent average rate estimated for achieving the MDGs. The World Bank's *Global Monitoring Report 2009* indicated that 386 million people in sub-Saharan Africa were living below the poverty line of $1.25 per day, a slight increase from 382.7 million in 2008. Progress in trade liberalization and economic diversification had led exports to increase from $159 billion in 2000 to $424 billion in 2007. On education, many African Governments had increased the priority of basic education, and primary enrolment in sub-Saharan Africa had grown from 60 per cent in 2000 to 71 per cent in 2007. Nonetheless, it was projected that the target of achieving universal primary enrolment by 2015 would be missed. On health-related issues, limited progress was made with regard to the 2001 Abuja Declaration [YUN 2001, p. 1133] on HIV/AIDS, tuberculosis and other related infectious diseases; only 6 countries had met the commitment of allocating 15 per cent of their national budgets to health. Despite some improvement, deaths of under-five children remained high in 2007, totalling 145 deaths per 1,000 children in sub-Saharan Africa and 35 per 1,000 in northern Africa. On gender, African leaders made notable progress with the adoption of the African Union Gender Policy and its 10-year implementation plan.

The Secretary-General observed that the three crises affecting the continent occurred at an inopportune time—when African economies were growing steadily—and should be assessed jointly rather than individually. In 2008, Africa took a step back in important key areas such as economic growth, agricultural development and poverty eradication, as well as many other human development indicators. He made recommendations on addressing the world financial and economic crisis, the food crisis, climate change, as well as official development assistance, governance, poverty and cooperation in the areas of aid, trade, development finance and debt sustainability.

On 24 December, the General Assembly decided that the agenda item on "NEPAD: progress in implementation and international support" would remain for consideration during its resumed sixty-fourth (2010) session (**decision 64/549**).

Social dimensions of NEPAD

The Commission for Social Development, at its forty-seventh session (New York, 22 February 2008 and 4–13 February 2009) [E/2009/26], recommended to the Economic and Social Council for adoption a resolution on the social dimensions of NEPAD. In resolution 2009/20 (see below), the Council requested the Commission to continue to give prominence to and raise awareness of the social dimensions of NEPAD. It also requested the Secretary-General to submit a report on the subject to the Commission's forty-eighth (2010) session.

ECONOMIC AND SOCIAL COUNCIL ACTION

On 30 July [meeting 44], the Economic and Social Council, on the recommendation of the Commission for Social Development [E/2009/26], adopted **resolution 2009/20** without vote [agenda item 14 *(c)*].

Social dimensions of the New Partnership for Africa's Development

The Economic and Social Council,

Recalling the outcomes of the World Summit for Social Development, held in Copenhagen from 6 to 12 March 1995, and the twenty-fourth special session of the General Assembly, entitled "World Summit for Social Development and beyond: achieving social development for all in a globalizing world", held in Geneva from 26 June to 1 July 2000,

Reaffirming the United Nations Millennium Declaration of 8 September 2000, the United Nations Declaration on the New Partnership for Africa's Development of 16 September 2002 and General Assembly resolution 57/7 of 4 November 2002 entitled "Final review and appraisal of the United Nations New Agenda for the Development of Africa in the 1990s and support for the New Partnership for Africa's Development",

Noting the conclusions of the African Union Extraordinary Summit on Employment and Poverty Alleviation in Africa, held in Ouagadougou on 8 and 9 September 2004,

Recognizing the commitments to address the special needs of Africa made at the 2005 World Summit and reaffirmed in the political declaration adopted at the high-level meeting on Africa's development needs, held at United Nations Headquarters on 22 September 2008,

Remaining concerned that Africa is the only continent currently not on track to achieve any of the goals set out in the United Nations Millennium Declaration by 2015, and in this regard emphasizing that concerted efforts and continued support are required to fulfil the commitments to address the special needs of Africa,

Expressing deep concern that attainment of the social development objectives may be hindered by the financial crisis, as well as by challenges brought about by the ongoing food and energy crisis,

Recognizing that capacity-building, knowledge-sharing and best practices are essential for the successful implementation of the New Partnership for Africa's Development, and recognizing also the need for continued support from the international community,

Bearing in mind that African countries have primary responsibility for their own economic and social development, that the role of national policies and development strategies cannot be overemphasized and that the development efforts of such countries need to be supported by an enabling international economic environment, and in this regard recalling the support given by the International Conference on Financing for Development to the New Partnership,

1.	*Takes note* of the report of the Secretary-General;

2.	*Welcomes* the progress made by African countries in fulfilling their commitments in the implementation of the New Partnership for Africa's Development to deepen democracy, human rights, good governance and sound economic management, and encourages African countries, with the participation of stakeholders, including civil society and the private sector, to intensify their efforts in this regard by developing and strengthening institutions for governance and by creating an environment conducive to attracting foreign direct investment for the development of the region;

3.	*Also welcomes* the good progress that has been made in implementing the African Peer Review Mechanism, as reflected, in particular, by the number of countries that have signed up to participate in the Mechanism, the completion of the peer review process and the progress in implementing the recommendations of those reviews in some countries and the completion of the self-assessment process, the hosting of country support missions and the launching of the national preparatory process for the peer review in others, and urges African States that have not yet done so to join the Mechanism, as a matter of priority, and to strengthen the peer review process so as to ensure its efficient performance;

4.	*Welcomes in particular* the organization of the first session of the African Union Conference of Ministers in charge of Social Development, held in Windhoek from 27 to 31 October 2008, and recalls in this regard the African Common Position on Social Integration and the Social Policy Framework for Africa, both of which have been endorsed by Africa's Heads of State;

5.	*Welcomes* the efforts made by African countries and regional and subregional organizations, including the African Union, to mainstream a gender perspective and the empowerment of women in the implementation of the New Partnership, including through the implementation of the Protocol to the African Charter on Human and Peoples' Rights on the Rights of Women in Africa;

6.	*Emphasizes* that the African Union and the regional economic communities have a critical role to play in the implementation of the New Partnership, and in this regard encourages African countries, with the assistance of their development partners, to increase and coordinate effectively their support for enhancing the capacities of those institutions and to promote regional cooperation and social and economic integration in Africa;

7.	*Also emphasizes* that progress in the implementation of the New Partnership depends also on a favourable national and international environment for Africa's growth and development, including measures to promote a policy environment conducive to private sector development and entrepreneurship;

8.	*Further emphasizes* that democracy, respect for all human rights and fundamental freedoms, including the right to development, transparent and accountable governance and administration in all sectors of society

and effective participation by civil society, including nongovernmental organizations, in particular communitybased organizations, and the private sector are among the indispensable foundations for the realization of social and people-centred sustainable development;

9.	*Emphasizes* that the increasingly unacceptable levels of poverty and social exclusion faced by most African countries require a comprehensive approach to the development and implementation of social and economic policies, inter alia, to reduce poverty, to promote economic activity, growth and sustainable development, to ensure employment creation and decent work for all, to promote education and health and to enhance social inclusion, political stability, democracy and good governance and the promotion and protection of human rights and fundamental freedoms, so as to ensure the achievement of Africa's social and economic objectives;

10.	*Recognizes* that, while social development is primarily the responsibility of Governments, international cooperation and assistance are essential for the full achievement of that goal;

11.	*Also recognizes* the contribution made by Member States to the implementation of the New Partnership in the context of South-South cooperation, and encourages the international community, including the international financial institutions, to support the efforts of African countries, including through trilateral cooperation;

12.	*Welcomes* the various important initiatives undertaken by Africa's development partners in recent years, and in this regard emphasizes the importance of coordinating such initiatives on Africa by ensuring effective implementation of existing commitments in the context of such initiatives;

13.	*Urges* continuous support for measures to address the challenges of poverty eradication and sustainable development in Africa, with a special emphasis on the Millennium Development Goals related to health, education, poverty and hunger, including, as appropriate, debt relief, improved market access, support for the private sector and entrepreneurship, enhanced official development assistance, increased foreign direct investment and technology transfer on mutually agreed terms, enhanced economic empowerment of women, the promotion of social protection systems and the conclusion of the current round of negotiations of the World Trade Organization;

14.	*Recognizes* that the implementation of the commitments made by Governments during the First United Nations Decade for the Eradication of Poverty (1997–2006) has fallen short of expectations, and welcomes the proclamation of the Second Decade (2008–2017) by the General Assembly in its resolution 62/205 of 19 December 2007 in order to support, in an efficient and coordinated manner, the internationally agreed development goals related to poverty eradication, including the Millennium Development Goals;

15.	*Encourages* all development partners to implement the principles of aid effectiveness recalled in the Doha Declaration on Financing for Development, adopted by the Follow-up International Conference on Financing for Development to Review the Implementation of the Monterrey Consensus on 2 December 2008;

16.	*Recognizes* the need for national Governments and the international community to make continued efforts to increase the flow of new and additional resources for financing for development from all sources, public and private, domestic and foreign, to support the development of African countries;

17. *Welcomes* the efforts by development partners to align their financial and technical support to Africa more closely with the priorities of the New Partnership, as reflected in national poverty reduction strategies or in similar strategies, and encourages development partners to increase their efforts in this regard;

18. *Acknowledges* the activities of the Bretton Woods institutions and the African Development Bank in African countries, and invites those institutions to continue to support the implementation of the priorities and objectives of the New Partnership;

19. *Notes* the growing collaboration among the entities of the United Nations system in support of the New Partnership, and requests the Secretary-General to promote greater coherence in the work of the United Nations system in support of the New Partnership, on the basis of the agreed clusters;

20. *Emphasizes* the importance for the communication, advocacy and outreach cluster to continue to muster international support for the New Partnership and to urge the United Nations system to demonstrate more evidence of cross-sectoral synergies in order to promote a comprehensive approach regarding successive phases of planning and implementation of social development programmes in Africa;

21. *Requests* the United Nations system to continue to provide assistance to the African Union, the secretariat of the New Partnership and African countries in developing projects and programmes within the scope of the priorities of the New Partnership;

22. *Invites* the Secretary-General, as a follow-up to the 2005 World Summit, to urge the organizations and bodies of the United Nations system to assist African countries in implementing quick-impact initiatives based on their national development priorities and strategies to enable them to achieve the Millennium Development Goals, and in this respect acknowledges recent commitments by some donor countries;

23. *Requests* the Secretary-General to continue to take measures to strengthen the Office of the Special Adviser on Africa, and requests the Office to collaborate with the Department of Economic and Social Affairs of the Secretariat and to include the social dimensions of the New Partnership in its comprehensive reports to the General Assembly at its sixty-fourth session;

24. *Requests* the Commission for Social Development to discuss in its annual programme of work those regional programmes that promote social development so as to enable all regions to share experiences and best practices, with the agreement of the countries concerned, and in this regard requests that the programmes of work of the Commission include priority areas of the New Partnership, as appropriate;

25. *Decides* that the Commission for Social Development should continue to give prominence to and raise awareness of the social dimensions of the New Partnership at its forty-eighth session;

26. *Requests* the Secretary-General, in collaboration with the Office of the Special Adviser on Africa, while also taking into consideration General Assembly resolution 62/179 of 19 December 2007 entitled "New Partnership for Africa's Development: progress in implementation and international support", to submit to the Commission for Social Development at its forty-eighth session a report on the social dimensions of the New Partnership.

Report of Secretary-General. In response to Council resolution 2009/20 (see above), the Secretary-General submitted a December report [E/CN.5/2010/3] on the social dimensions of NEPAD, which assessed the impact on social development of the converging global crises that had affected both developed and developing countries: the food and energy crises of 2007–2008, the existing global financial and economic crisis, and ongoing climate change. The Secretary-General observed that the gains achieved as a result of improved economic performance were likely to be lost, undoing advances made over the past decade. In addition, the lack of public social safety nets in Africa to offset the negative impact of a global recession would compound the situation, with the working poor and other vulnerable groups bearing the brunt of the global crises. Consequently, it was likely that African economies would experience decelerated growth, high unemployment and poverty rates, and diminished prospects for achieving NEPAD goals and other internationally agreed development goals, including the MDGs. The report concluded with recommendations for consideration by African countries and their development partners, including that proven initiatives in health, gender, sustainable agriculture, energy and infrastructure, and education, such as the Education for All-Fast Track Initiative, be scaled up and fully funded.

African countries emerging from conflict

On 23 July [E/2009/SR.34], the Chairman of the Organizational Committee of the Peacebuilding Commission addressed the Economic and Social Council on the question of ad hoc advisory groups on African countries emerging from conflict. He stressed the importance of cooperation between the Commission and the Council and the need to find ways to improve coordination of assistance to countries emerging from a conflict from the start. In the four countries on its agenda, namely Burundi (see p. 142), Guinea-Bissau (see p. 224), the Central African Republic (see p. 151) and Sierra Leone (see p. 211), the Commission continued to promote better coordination in order to maximize the impact of peacebuilding measures and to facilitate the channelling of resources. He briefed the Council on post-conflict recovery in those countries and said that five other African countries (Comoros, Côte d'Ivoire, Guinea, Liberia, the Democratic Republic of the Congo) had been declared eligible to benefit from the Peacebuilding Fund (see p. 47).

On 31 July [meeting 45], the Economic and Social Council adopted **resolution 2009/32** [draft: E/2009/L.33/Rev.1] without vote [agenda item 7 *(f)*].

African countries emerging from conflict

The Economic and Social Council,

Recalling its resolution 2008/30 of 25 July 2008,

1. *Expresses its appreciation* to the Chair of the Organizational Committee of the Peacebuilding Commission for providing insights and information on post-conflict recovery, on the basis of the engagement of the Commission with the countries on its agenda, and urges the Commission to continue to strengthen its support for peacebuilding processes in the African countries placed on its agenda;

2. *Invites* the Chair of the Organizational Committee of the Peacebuilding Commission to continue to inform the Economic and Social Council about best practices, particularly lessons learned from its experiences, that are relevant for addressing the economic and social challenges of peacebuilding in other African countries emerging from conflict;

3. *Invites* the Peacebuilding Commission to strengthen its cooperation with the Council, including through enhanced dialogue between the Council and the Chairs of the Commission's country-specific configurations;

4. *Decides* to consider the matter at its substantive session of 2010 under the agenda item entitled "African countries emerging from conflict".

Other economic assistance

Haiti

In response to Economic and Social Council resolution 2008/10 [YUN 2008, p. 1021], the Ad Hoc Advisory Group on Haiti reported in June [E/2009/105] on the Group's visit to Haiti from 4 to 7 May, the third conference on Haiti's economic and social development (Washington, D.C., 14 April), national ownership of development strategies, the strengthening of State institutions, the risks of donor impatience and fatigue and the challenges facing the country. The Group indicated that the appointment of Prime Minister Michèle Duvivier Pierre-Louis in September 2008 [YUN 2008, p. 337] and the return to stability allowed the Group to resume its practice of visiting the country and meeting with Haitian authorities, key civil society representatives and international development partners. The Group witnessed progress in various areas, particularly in the security and rule of law sectors. In addition, since the beginning of 2009, Haiti had received a high level of international attention and commitments of support: a joint visit by the UN Secretary-General and former United States President William Clinton; visits from high-level officials from partner countries; and the visit of the Security Council in March (see p. 319). Subsequently, President Clinton was named as the United Nations Special Envoy for Haiti. At the Washington, D.C.

donor conference in April, more than $378 million was pledged for the Government's plan for economic recovery and rehabilitation.

The Group also observed that the weakness of State institutions constituted a major obstacle to development. In the field of education, in 2002–2003, some 2.8 million persons (39 per cent of the population) had never attended school and only 18 per cent of children were educated in the public sector. The maternal mortality rate remained high (630 per 100,000 live births) due to the State's inability to provide access to basic health-care services. On security and stability, lack of equipment jeopardized progress made in the recruitment and training of the Haitian National Police. As a result of those institutional weaknesses, the share of development assistance that was spent through State institutions remained very low as donors did not have sufficient indications of improvement in the area of governance. Regarding the main areas for international assistance, the Group stressed the double challenges of providing immediate support to the population, including through rapid job creation and foreign investments, and the need to continue in-depth support to communities, including in rural areas, and called for simultaneous action in those directions. The report concluded with nine recommendations addressed to the Haitian authorities and their international partners to enhance the impact of development assistance.

Communications. On 10 April [E/2009/52], Mexico transmitted to the Secretary-General the statement by the States members of the Rio Group and of the Caribbean Community entitled "Towards a new paradigm of cooperation", issued on 8 April in preparation for the Conference on the Economic and Social Development of Haiti (Washington, D.C., 14 April).

In letters to the Economic and Social Council dated 20 March [E/2009/49] and 1 October [E/2009/117], Peru and El Salvador, respectively, expressed the wish to join the Ad Hoc Advisory Group on Haiti and requested a positive decision by the Council. By **decision 2009/211** of 20 April and **decision 2009/267** of 15 December, the Council decided to appoint, respectively, Peru and El Salvador as additional members.

(For more information on Haiti see p. 318.)

On 23 July [meeting 34], the Economic and Social Council adopted **resolution 2009/4** [draft: E/2009/L.13] without vote [agenda item 7 *(d)*].

Ad Hoc Advisory Group on Haiti

The Economic and Social Council,

Recalling its resolutions 2004/52 of 23 July 2004, 2005/46 of 27 July 2005, 2006/10 of 26 July 2006,

2007/13 of 25 July 2007 and 2008/10 of 23 July 2008 and its decisions 2004/322 of 11 November 2004 and 2009/211 of 20 April 2009,

1. *Takes note with appreciation* of the report of the Ad Hoc Advisory Group on Haiti and the recommendations contained therein;

2. *Notes* the political and economic evolution of the situation, and welcomes the support provided by the international community to this process;

3. *Also notes* the progress made towards the reform of rule-of-law institutions;

4. *Commends* the ongoing implementation of the growth and poverty reduction strategy paper by the authorities of Haiti, and looks forward to continued support from donors and other partners, including the United Nations system and the Bretton Woods institutions, in connection with the implementation of that strategy;

5. *Notes* the progress made by the Government of Haiti in terms of gender equality, and also notes the importance of gender equality as a necessary dimension of any strategy for development;

6. *Expresses its deep concern* over the particularly adverse effects of the 2008 hurricanes on Haiti, and encourages the international community to continue providing support for the short and long-term needs of Haiti for recovery;

7. *Welcomes* the nomination of a United Nations Special Envoy for Haiti, as well as the third conference on Haiti's economic and social development, held in Washington, D.C., on 14 April 2009 under the auspices of the Inter-American Development Bank, and looks forward to the timely and effective implementation of pledges made at that conference;

8. *Recognizes* the need for effective and continued coordination between the Government of Haiti and donors, as well as a standing mechanism for consultation with the main non-governmental organizations active in Haiti;

9. *Decides* to extend the mandate of the Advisory Group until the substantive session of 2010 of the Economic and Social Council, with the purpose of following closely and providing advice on Haiti's long-term development strategy to promote socio-economic recovery and stability, with particular attention to the need to ensure coherence and sustainability in international support for Haiti, on the basis of long-term national development priorities and building upon the Interim Cooperation Framework and the growth and poverty reduction strategy paper, and stressing the need to avoid overlap and duplication with respect to existing mechanisms;

10. *Expresses its satisfaction* to the Secretary-General for the support provided to the Advisory Group, and requests him to continue to support the activities of the Group adequately and from within existing resources;

11. *Requests* the Advisory Group, in accomplishing its mandate, to continue to cooperate with the Secretary-General and his Special Representative and Head of the United Nations Stabilization Mission in Haiti, the United Nations Special Envoy for Haiti, the United Nations Development Group, relevant United Nations funds and programmes, the specialized agencies, the Bretton Woods institutions, regional organizations and institutions, including the Economic Commission for Latin America and the Caribbean, the Organization of American States and the Caribbean Community, the Inter-American Development Bank and other major stakeholders;

12. *Also requests* the Advisory Group to submit a report on its work, with recommendations, as appropriate, to the Economic and Social Council for its consideration at its substantive session of 2010.

Kazakhstan

In 2009, the General Assembly continued its consideration of special economic assistance to individual countries or regions, including the Secretary-General's 2008 report [YUN 2008, p. 1021] on international cooperation and coordination for the human and ecological rehabilitation and economic development of the Semipalatinsk region of Kazakhstan, a former nuclear test site also referred to as the Semipalatinsk Polygon. The report indicated that despite actions undertaken by the Government of Kazakhstan, the UN system and the international community since the adoption of resolution 60/216 in 2005 [YUN 2005, p. 1013], those efforts had not been sufficient to mitigate the suffering caused by years of nuclear testing. The Secretary-General recommended the organization of a conference with the participation of international and national partners to review the work that had been accomplished and set future priorities. During the year, the International Atomic Energy Agency (IAEA) convened the International Conference on Remediation of Land Contaminated by Radioactive Material Residues (Kazakhstan, 18–22 May 2009), which provided a forum for all parties involved in the remediation of radioactive contaminated sites to exchange ideas, review progress and developments since the 1999 IAEA international symposium on the topic, compare technologies and methods, and disseminate information and experience.

In resolution 63/279 (see below), the General Assembly took note of the Secretary-General's report, welcomed the IAEA conference and requested the Secretary-General to pursue a consultative process on modalities for mobilizing and coordinating the support to seek solutions to the problems and needs of the Semipalatinsk region.

GENERAL ASSEMBLY ACTION

On 24 April [meeting 81], the General Assembly adopted **resolution 63/279** [draft: A/63/L.67 & Add.1] without vote [agenda item 65 *(b)*].

International cooperation and coordination for the human and ecological rehabilitation and economic development of the Semipalatinsk region of Kazakhstan

The General Assembly,

Recalling its resolutions 52/169 M of 16 December 1997, 53/1 H of 16 November 1998, 55/44 of 27 November 2000,

57/101 of 25 November 2002 and 60/216 of 22 December 2005,

Taking note of the report of the Secretary-General, and the information contained therein on measures taken to address health, environmental, economic and humanitarian development problems and satisfy the needs of the Semipalatinsk region,

Recognizing that the Semipalatinsk nuclear testing ground, inherited by Kazakhstan and closed in 1991, remains a matter of serious concern for the people and Government of Kazakhstan with regard to the long-term nature of its consequences for the lives and health of the people, especially children and other vulnerable groups, as well as for the environment of the region,

Taking into consideration the results of the international conference on the problems of the Semipalatinsk region, held in Tokyo in 1999, which have promoted the effectiveness of the assistance provided to the population of the region,

Recognizing the important role of national development policies and strategies in the rehabilitation of the Semipalatinsk region, and taking note with satisfaction of the successful implementation of the Kazakhstan national programme entitled "Complex solution of the former Semipalatinsk nuclear test site problems for 2005–2007" and the elaboration of the new cycle of the programme for 2009–2011,

Recognizing also the challenges Kazakhstan faces in the rehabilitation of the Semipalatinsk region, in particular in the context of the efforts by the Government of Kazakhstan to ensure the effective and timely achievement of the internationally agreed development goals, including the Millennium Development Goals, in particular with regard to health care and environmental sustainability,

Recognizing further that the Government of Kazakhstan may call upon the United Nations Resident Coordinator in Kazakhstan to render assistance conducting consultations for establishing a multi-stakeholders' mechanism, with the participation of various government bodies, local governments, civil society, the donor community and international organizations, to improve governance and enable the more efficient use of resources allocated for the rehabilitation of the Semipalatinsk region, in particular regarding the areas of radiation safety, socio-economic development, health and environmental protection, and for the provision of information on risks to the population,

Expressing profound concern regarding the negative effects of nuclear testing on the sustainability of the ecosystem in the region and about the accumulation of radioactive substances in the soil, which result in wide-ranging and complex consequences that create humanitarian, environmental, social, economic and health problems,

Taking note of the need for the utilization of modern technologies in minimizing and mitigating radiological, health, socio-economic, psychological and environmental challenges in the Semipalatinsk region,

Taking into account the fact that a number of international programmes in the Semipalatinsk region have been completed since the closure of the nuclear testing ground, but serious social, economic and ecological problems continue to exist,

Expressing deep concern that the current efforts are not sufficient to alleviate the consequences of nuclear testing, and regarding the fact that only five of the thirty-eight projects identified by the international conference held in Tokyo in 1999 were implemented,

Emphasizing the importance of support by donor States and international development organizations for the efforts by Kazakhstan to improve the social, economic and environmental situation in the Semipalatinsk region, and in this regard stressing the need for the international community to continue to pay due attention to the rehabilitation of the Semipalatinsk region,

Emphasizing also the importance of the new development-oriented approach in tackling problems in the Semipalatinsk region in the medium and long term,

Stressing the importance of the commemoration, in 2011, of the twentieth anniversary of the closure of the Semipalatinsk nuclear test site,

Expressing appreciation to donor countries, especially Japan, United Nations agencies, in particular the United Nations Development Programme, the United Nations Children's Fund, the United Nations Population Fund, the International Atomic Energy Agency and the World Bank, and the Organization for Security and Cooperation in Europe and the Global Environment Facility for their contribution to the rehabilitation of the Semipalatinsk region,

1. *Welcomes and recognizes* the important role of the Government of Kazakhstan in providing domestic resources to help to meet the needs of the Semipalatinsk region, including for the implementation of the Kazakhstan national multi-year programme entitled "Complex solution of the former Semipalatinsk nuclear test site problems for 2005–2007";

2. *Calls upon* the international community, including all Member States, in particular donor States, and United Nations institutions to continue to support Kazakhstan in addressing the challenges of the rehabilitation of the Semipalatinsk region and its population, taking additional actions, including by facilitating the implementation of the Kazakhstan national programme on addressing the problems of the former Semipalatinsk nuclear testing ground in a comprehensive manner, and stresses the importance of regional cooperation in this regard;

3. *Urges* the international community to provide assistance to Kazakhstan in the formulation and implementation of special programmes and projects for the treatment and care of the affected population as well as in efforts to ensure economic growth and sustainable development in the Semipalatinsk region;

4. *Calls upon* Member States, relevant multilateral financial organizations and other entities of the international community, including academia and non-governmental organizations, to share their knowledge and experience in order to contribute to the human and ecological rehabilitation and economic development of the Semipalatinsk region;

5. *Welcomes* initiatives commemorating the closure of the former Semipalatinsk test site and the twentieth anniversary of the international anti-nuclear movement "Nevada-Semei", and the international conference of the International Atomic Energy Agency on the remediation of land contaminated by radioactive material residues, to be

held in 2009 in Kazakhstan, and invites the international community to participate in these events;

6. *Invites* Member States to observe, in 2011, the twentieth anniversary of the closure of the Semipalatinsk nuclear test site by conducting events and functions to provide to the international community information on the deteriorating consequences of nuclear testing on human health and the environment;

7. *Requests* the Secretary-General to continue his efforts in implementing relevant resolutions of the General Assembly and to encourage the donor community and international and regional organizations to fulfil their commitments declared at the Tokyo international conference;

8. *Also requests* the Secretary-General to pursue a consultative process, with the participation of interested States and relevant United Nations agencies, on modalities for mobilizing and coordinating the necessary support to seek appropriate solutions to the problems and needs of the Semipalatinsk region, including those prioritized in his report;

9. *Calls upon* the Secretary-General to continue his efforts to enhance world public awareness of the problems and needs of the Semipalatinsk region;

10. *Requests* the Secretary-General to report to the General Assembly at its sixty-sixth session, under the item entitled "Sustainable development", on progress made in the implementation of the present resolution.

Third States affected by sanctions

In response to General Assembly resolution 63/127 [YUN 2008, p. 1476], the Secretary-General submitted an August report [A/64/225] that highlighted developments concerning Assembly and Economic and Social Council activities in the area of assistance to third States affected by the application of sanctions; arrangements in the Secretariat related to assistance to those States; and operational changes as a result of the shift in focus towards targeted sanctions in the procedures and working methods of the Security Council and its sanctions committees.

The Assembly took action with regard to the Secretary-General's report in **resolution 64/115** (see p. 1322).

Disaster response

In 2009, a reduced number of disasters associated with natural hazards, such as earthquakes, floods, cyclones and droughts, was recorded with some 328 disasters, spread across 111 countries, affecting 113 million people and causing more than 10,000 deaths. That number marked a significant divergence from the annual average of 392 disasters per year for the period 2000–2008. Experts attributed the reduced incidence of disasters to climate change variations, particularly the El Niño effect, leading to an unusually quiet

North Atlantic hurricane season in the Caribbean and drought in South Asia. Global temperatures were still predicted to continue to rise—globally, 2009 was warmer than the previous three years—increasing the likelihood of more frequent extreme weather events in the future. Globally, hydrometeorological hazards (hazards of an atmospheric, hydrological or oceanographic nature) caused 92 per cent of the disasters during the year. Floods were the most common type of disaster recorded with 147 events, followed by 84 storms and 30 landslides. Estimates of the economic costs of disasters in 2009 averaged between $35 and $50 billion. Despite high absolute financial losses in China, Europe and the United States, the relative economic impact of disasters was greatest in low- and middle-income countries.

The Horn of Africa continued to be in the grip of a severe and prolonged drought contributing to an acute need for humanitarian assistance and affecting food security. Devastating floods in several West African countries from June to October affected more than 770,000 people and killed 193. In Asia, two consecutive earthquakes in Indonesia affected 2.5 million people, causing 1,100 casualties, displacing 469,000 people and damaging 114,000 houses. Three consecutive typhoons struck the Philippines in September and October affecting over 10 million people, of whom an estimated 700,000 were displaced. In the Middle East, the north-eastern region of the Syrian Arab Republic experienced its third consecutive year of drought affecting 1.3 million people. In Latin America and the Caribbean, the combined effects of Hurricane Ida and a low pressure system off the Pacific coast led in November to unprecedented heavy rainfall in El Salvador, triggering severe flooding that affected more than 75,000 people and killed 198. Guatemala suffered from drought and food insecurity affecting some 136,000 families.

Human influenza. The United Nations continued to consider the issue of business continuity management [YUN 2008, p. 1551], including preparedness for a potential pandemic. By **resolution 63/268** of 7 April (see p. 1391) the General Assembly requested the Secretary-General to ensure that lessons learned within the Secretariat for human influenza pandemic preparedness were taken into account as the work of business continuity management was implemented.

International cooperation

Report of Secretary-General. In response to General Assembly resolution 63/141 [YUN 2008, p. 1023], the Secretary-General, in an August report on international cooperation on humanitarian assistance in the field of natural disasters [A/64/331], provided an overview of disasters associated with natural hazards and highlighted emerging trends, their humanitarian implications, key challenges and activities undertaken to strengthen disasters preparedness.

The report stated that global disaster risk was increasing and was highly concentrated in poorer countries with weaker governance. Rapid urbanization was exacerbating the vulnerability of urban dwellers to the impacts of disaster and climate change. More than 50 per cent of the world's population lived in urban areas and that figure was expected to rise to 60 per cent by 2030. The effects of disasters also magnified gender inequalities. Women represented the majority of deaths from natural disasters as they had less access to essential resources for disaster preparedness, mitigation and rehabilitation. Globally, natural disasters were also the greatest cause of internal displacement.

Key challenges in addressing disaster risk included global issues, such as extreme poverty, the food crisis, water and energy scarcity, forced displacement and migration, population growth, urbanization and pandemics, which were increasing the underlying vulnerability of communities, as well as climate change, which was increasing hazard intensity and frequency. Specific challenges facing humanitarian actors included adjusting their systems towards a greater focus on the multi-hazard environment, particularly climate change; on disaster preparedness; and on efforts to ensure an effective transition from relief to recovery. The Secretary-General concluded that within the changing humanitarian landscape, developing national and local capacities for humanitarian action, in terms of emergency preparedness, response and recovery, was fundamental to improving the overall delivery of humanitarian assistance. Enhancing capacity at local and national levels must be a priority in order to mitigate risks to population and to ensure the effectiveness of disaster preparedness, risk reduction and initial response operations. He encouraged Member States to underline the importance of early and multiyear commitments to the Central Emergency Response Fund (see p. 888) and other humanitarian financing mechanisms; strengthen support for humanitarian actors to enable them to cope with the increasing humanitarian burden associated with climate change; review and revise pandemic response plans, as well as take necessary preparedness measures to respond to pandemic influenza. The United Nations system and other humanitarian actors were encouraged to strengthen the ability to quickly and flexibly deploy humanitarian professionals to support Governments and country teams in the immediate aftermath of a disaster, as well as increase the level of human and financial resources provided to humanitarian and resident coordinators for leading and coordinating disaster preparedness and early recovery activities. Member States, the UN system and other humanitarian actors were also called upon to accelerate the implementa-

tion of the Hyogo Framework for Action [YUN 2005, p. 1016] and to place a strong emphasis on the promotion and strengthening of disaster preparedness activities at all levels.

UN-SPIDER programme. The Committee on the Peaceful Uses of Outer Space (see p. 599) submitted a report [A/AC.105/955] on the 2009 activities of the United Nations Platform for Space-based Information for Disaster Management and Emergency Response (UN-SPIDER). On 10 December, in **resolution 64/86**, the Assembly endorsed the workplan for the 2010–2011 UN-SPIDER programme (see p. 599). It also welcomed the establishment of regional support offices in Iran, Nigeria and Romania and the cooperation agreement reached with the Asian Disaster Reduction Centre to support the implementation of the programme's activities.

On 24 December, the Assembly decided that the agenda item on strengthening the coordination of UN emergency humanitarian assistance would remain for consideration during its resumed sixty-fourth (2010) session (**decision 64/549**).

Disaster reduction
International Strategy for Disaster Reduction

In response to General Assembly resolution 63/216 [YUN 2008, p. 1027], the Secretary-General, in an August report [A/64/280], reviewed the implementation of the International Strategy for Disaster Reduction (ISDR), which was adopted by the programme forum of the International Decade for Natural Disaster Reduction (1990–2000) in 1999 [YUN 1999, p. 859] and endorsed by the Assembly in resolution 54/219 [ibid., p. 861]. It detailed efforts to implement the Hyogo Framework for Action, the 10-year plan for reducing disaster risks adopted at the World Conference on Disaster Reduction in 2005 [YUN 2005, p. 1015] and endorsed by the Assembly in resolution 60/195 [ibid., p. 1018]. The report indicated that globally, disaster risk was increasing substantially with regard to most hazards, with the risk of economic loss increasing much faster than the risk of mortality. The main driver of the trend was rapidly increasing exposure to risk. As countries developed, vulnerability decreased, but not fast enough to compensate for the increased exposure. The report called for urgent action to invest more in systematic implementation of the strategy and to address the driving factors of disaster: rural poverty and vulnerability, unplanned urban growth and declining ecosystems.

Although progress was made in implementing some aspects of the Hyogo Framework for Action, acceleration in implementation was required towards all Framework goals. At the national level, 88 countries had issued systematic reports on Framework implementation and 120 Governments had designated focal points for implementation, follow-up and monitoring. At the regional level, progress was achieved through cooperation mechanisms, such as platforms networks and partnerships that catalysed increased action. At the international level, the United Nations Development Group finalized and disseminated guidelines on disaster risk reduction to UN country teams, while UNDP worked in 50 high-risk countries on enhancing disaster-risk reduction capacity. The international community also strove to invest systematically in disaster risk-reduction. Resource mobilization efforts of the Strategy contributed to increasing levels of voluntary contributions to the United Nations Trust Fund for Disaster Risk Reduction, which received income of $28.9 million in 2008. Pledges to the Global Facility for Disaster Reduction and Recovery [YUN 2006, p. 1093] during 2007–2008 exceeded $90 million. Annexed to the report was information on gains achieved in the five priority areas of the Hyogo Framework. The report also contained recommendations on accelerating implementation of the Framework at the national and international levels; ensuring climate change adaptation through disaster risk reduction; investing in disaster risk reduction, particularly by States in national budgets; securing the safety of schools and hospitals; commemorating the International Day for Disaster Risk Reduction (13 October) starting in 2010; and strengthening funding for the Strategy.

Global Platform for Disaster Risk Reduction. The Global Platform for Disaster Risk Reduction, established as the successor to the Inter-Agency Task Force on Disaster Reduction to provide a regular global forum for advocacy, information-sharing and the coordination of action [YUN 2007, p. 949], held its second session (Geneva, 16–19 June), which was attended by some 1,688 participants, including 152 Governments, 137 UN system entities, international financial institutions, regional bodies, and scientific and academic communities. The Global Platform placed an emphasis on lessons learned and the development of guidance to implement risk reduction measures; recognized the need to set targets in specific areas such as safe schools and hospitals, water risks and municipal disaster recovery plans; and identified a drastic mismatch between resources required to address disaster risk and those available. It urged the massive scaling up of funding from national budgets and international sources. The Global Platform also called for action to integrate disaster risk reduction and climate change adaptation efforts and to strengthen community-level action. The Global Platform proceedings [ISDR/2009/24] and outcomes, as well as other documents, including the Chair's summary, were available on the PreventionWeb site.

GENERAL ASSEMBLY ACTION

On 21 December [meeting 66], the General Assembly, on the recommendation of the Second (Economic and Financial) Committee [A/64/420/Add.3], adopted **resolution 64/200** without vote [agenda item 53 *(c)*].

International Strategy for Disaster Reduction

The General Assembly,

Recalling its resolutions 44/236 of 22 December 1989, 49/22 A of 2 December 1994, 49/22 B of 20 December 1994, 53/185 of 15 December 1998, 54/219 of 22 December 1999, 56/195 of 21 December 2001, 57/256 of 20 December 2002, 58/214 of 23 December 2003, 59/231 of 22 December 2004, 60/195 of 22 December 2005, 61/198 of 20 December 2006, 62/192 of 19 December 2007 and 63/216 of 19 December 2008 and Economic and Social Council resolutions 1999/63 of 30 July 1999 and 2001/35 of 26 July 2001, and taking into consideration its resolution 57/270 B of 23 June 2003 on the integrated and coordinated implementation of and follow-up to the outcomes of the major United Nations conferences and summits in the economic and social fields,

Recalling also the 2005 World Summit Outcome,

Reaffirming the Hyogo Declaration, the Hyogo Framework for Action 2005–2015: Building the Resilience of Nations and Communities to Disasters and the common statement of the special session on the Indian Ocean disaster: risk reduction for a safer future, as adopted by the World Conference on Disaster Reduction,

Reaffirming also its role in providing policy guidance on the implementation of the outcomes of the major United Nations conferences and summits,

Expressing its deep concern at the number and scale of natural disasters and their increasing impact in recent years, which have resulted in massive loss of life and long-term negative social, economic and environmental consequences for vulnerable societies throughout the world and hamper the achievement of their sustainable development, in particular in developing countries,

Expressing its deep concern also at the increasing challenges facing the disaster response and preparedness capacity of Member States and the United Nations system as a result of the combined impacts of current global challenges, including the global economic and financial crisis, climate change and the food crisis,

Emphasizing that disaster risk reduction, including the reduction of vulnerability to natural disasters, is an important cross-cutting element that contributes to the achievement of sustainable development,

Recognizing the clear relationship between sustainable development, poverty eradication, disaster risk reduction, disaster response and disaster recovery and the need to continue to deploy efforts in all these areas,

Recognizing also the urgent need to further develop and make use of the existing scientific and technical knowledge to build resilience to natural disasters, and emphasizing the need for developing countries to have access to appropriate, advanced, environmentally sound, cost-effective and easy-to-use technologies so as to seek more comprehensive solutions to disaster risk reduction and to effectively and efficiently strengthen their capabilities to cope with disaster risks,

Recognizing further that certain measures for disaster risk reduction in the context of the Hyogo Framework for Action can also support adaptation to climate change, and emphasizing the importance of strengthening the resilience of nations and communities to natural disasters through disaster risk reduction programmes,

Stressing the importance of advancing the implementation of the Plan of Implementation of the World Summit on Sustainable Development ("Johannesburg Plan of Implementation") and its relevant provisions on vulnerability, risk assessment and disaster management,

Recognizing the need to continue to develop an understanding of, and to address, socio-economic activities that exacerbate the vulnerability of societies to natural disasters and to build and further strengthen local authorities and community capabilities to reduce vulnerability to disasters,

Having considered the recommendation of the Secretary-General regarding General Assembly resolution 54/219,

Taking note with appreciation of the "Global Assessment Report on Disaster Risk Reduction" launched in Manama in May 2009,

Noting the *World Disasters Report 2009: Focus on early warning, early action,*

1. *Takes note* of the report of the Secretary-General on the implementation of the International Strategy for Disaster Reduction;

2. *Recalls* that the commitments of the Hyogo Declaration and the Hyogo Framework for Action 2005–2015: Building the Resilience of Nations and Communities to Disasters include the provision of assistance for developing countries that are prone to natural disasters and disaster-stricken States in the transition phase towards sustainable physical, social and economic recovery, for risk reduction activities in post-disaster recovery and for rehabilitation processes;

3. *Welcomes* the progress made in the implementation of the Hyogo Framework for Action, and stresses the need for a more effective integration of disaster risk reduction into sustainable development policies, planning and programming, for the development and strengthening of institutions, mechanisms and capacities at the regional, national and local levels to build resilience to hazards, and for a systematic incorporation of risk reduction approaches into the implementation of emergency preparedness, response and recovery programmes and long-term development plans, as a means to achieve the internationally agreed development goals, including the Millennium Development Goals;

4. *Calls upon* the international community to increase its efforts to fully implement the commitments of the Hyogo Declaration and the Hyogo Framework for Action;

5. *Invites* Member States, the United Nations system, international financial institutions, regional bodies and other international organizations, including the International Federation of Red Cross and Red Crescent Societies, as well as civil society, including non-governmental organizations and volunteers, the private sector and the scientific community, to increase efforts to support, implement and follow up the Hyogo Framework for Action, and stresses the importance in this regard of the continued cooperation and coordination of stakeholders at all levels with respect to addressing effectively the impact of natural disasters;

6. *Calls upon* the United Nations system, and invites international financial institutions and regional and international organizations, to integrate the goals of, and take into full account, the Hyogo Framework for Action in their strategies and programmes, making use of existing coordination mechanisms, and to assist developing countries with those mechanisms to design and implement, as appropriate, disaster risk reduction measures with a sense of urgency;

7. *Also calls upon* the United Nations system, and invites the international financial institutions and regional banks and other regional and international organizations, to support, in a timely and sustained manner, the efforts led by disaster-stricken countries for disaster risk reduction in post-disaster recovery and rehabilitation processes;

8. *Recognizes* that each State has the primary responsibility for its own sustainable development and for taking effective measures to reduce disaster risk, including for the protection of people on its territory, infrastructure and other national assets from the impact of disasters, including the implementation of and follow-up to the Hyogo Framework for Action, and stresses the importance of international cooperation and partnerships to support those national efforts;

9. *Also recognizes* the efforts made by Member States to develop national and local capacities to implement the Hyogo Framework for Action, including through the establishment of national platforms for disaster reduction, and encourages Member States that have not done so to develop such capacities;

10. *Further recognizes* the importance of coordinating adaptation to climate change with relevant disaster risk reduction measures, invites Governments and relevant international organizations to integrate these considerations in a comprehensive manner into, inter alia, development plans and poverty eradication programmes and, in least developed countries, national adaptation programmes of action, and invites the international community to support the ongoing efforts of developing countries in this regard;

11. *Urges* Member States to continue to develop, update and strengthen disaster risk reduction, including preparedness measures, at all levels, in accordance with the Hyogo Framework for Action, taking into account their own circumstances and capacities and in coordination with relevant actors, as appropriate, and encourages the international community and relevant United Nations entities to give increased priority to supporting national and local efforts in this regard;

12. *Welcomes* the regional and subregional initiatives developed in order to achieve disaster risk reduction, and reiterates the need to further develop regional initiatives and risk reduction capacities of regional mechanisms where they exist and to strengthen them and encourage the use and sharing of all existing tools, and requests United Nations regional commissions, within their mandates, to support the efforts of Member States in this regard, in close coordination with implementing entities of the United Nations system;

13. *Encourages* the Global Facility for Disaster Reduction and Recovery, a partnership of the Strategy system managed by the World Bank, to continue to support the implementation of the Hyogo Framework for Action;

14. *Encourages* the secretariat of the International Strategy for Disaster Reduction to continue to develop, promote and improve methods for predictive multirisk assessments, including on the economics of disaster risk reduction and socioeconomic cost-benefit analysis of risk reduction actions at all levels;

15. *Calls upon* the international community to support the development and strengthening of institutions, mechanisms and capacities at all levels, in particular at the community level, that can systematically contribute to building resilience to hazards;

16. *Encourages* Member States to increase their commitment to the effective implementation of the Hyogo Framework for Action, by strengthening their participation in the Strategy system, including national and regional platforms, thematic technical platforms and the midterm review process, as well as the Global Platform for Disaster Risk Reduction;

17. *Notes with appreciation* the second session of the Global Platform for Disaster Risk Reduction, on the theme "Disasters, poverty and vulnerability", held in Geneva from 16 to 19 June 2009, as an important forum for Member States and other stakeholders to assess progress made in the implementation of the Hyogo Framework for Action, enhance awareness of disaster risk reduction, share experiences and learn from good practices;

18. *Recognizes* the importance of integrating a gender perspective and empowering and engaging women in the design and implementation of all phases of disaster management, as well as in risk reduction strategies and programmes, and encourages the secretariat of the Strategy to continue to increase the promotion of gender mainstreaming and empowerment of women;

19. *Expresses its appreciation* to those countries that have provided financial support for the activities of the Strategy by making voluntary contributions to the United Nations Trust Fund for Disaster Reduction;

20. *Encourages* the international community to continue providing adequate voluntary financial contributions to the Trust Fund in the effort to ensure adequate support for the follow-up activities to the Hyogo Framework for Action, and encourages Member States to make multiannual, unmarked contributions as early in the year as possible;

21. *Encourages* Governments, multilateral organizations, international and regional organizations, international and regional financial institutions, the private sector and civil society to systematically invest in disaster risk reduction with a view to implementing the objectives of the Strategy;

22. *Stresses* the importance of disaster risk reduction and subsequent increased responsibilities of the secretariat of the Strategy, and reiterates the request to the Secretary-General to explore all means of securing additional funding to ensure predictable and stable financial resources for the operation of the secretariat;

23. *Acknowledges* the importance of early warning systems, encourages Member States to integrate such systems into their national disaster risk reduction strategies and plans, and encourages all stakeholders to share good practices on early warning, using existing information-sharing mechanisms within the Strategy system;

24. *Stresses* the need to foster better understanding and knowledge of the causes of disasters, as well as to build and strengthen coping capacities through, inter alia, the transfer and exchange of experiences and technical knowledge, educational and training programmes for disaster risk reduction, access to relevant data and information, the strengthening of institutional arrangements and the promotion of community participation and ownership through community-based disaster risk management approaches;

25. *Emphasizes* the need for the international community to maintain its focus beyond emergency relief and to support medium- and long-term rehabilitation, reconstruction and risk reduction, and stresses the importance of implementing and adapting long-term programmes related to the eradication of poverty, sustainable development and disaster risk reduction management in the most vulnerable regions, particularly in developing countries prone to natural disasters;

26. *Stresses* the need to address risk reduction of and vulnerabilities to all natural hazards, including geological and hydrometeorological hazards, in a comprehensive manner;

27. *Takes note* of the global initiative of the Strategy to secure the safety of schools and hospitals, in particular by investing in actions to undertake national assessments of the safety of existing education and health facilities by 2011 and to develop and implement, as appropriate, concrete action plans for safer schools and hospitals by 2015, and encourages Member States to report on this on a voluntary basis;

28. *Decides* to designate 13 October as the date to commemorate the International Day for Disaster Reduction;

29. *Requests* the Secretary-General to submit to the General Assembly at its sixty-fifth session a report on the implementation of the present resolution, under the item entitled "Sustainable development".

Natural disasters and vulnerability

In response to General Assembly resolution 63/216 [YUN 2008, p. 1027], the Secretary-General submitted an August report [A/64/280] on ISDR implementation, which included information on measures taken to reduce vulnerability to climate-related hazards. The ISDR secretariat continued to promote disaster risk reduction as an adaptation policy and to build close working relationships on the topic with the parties and the UN Framework Convention on Climate Change secretariat. Cooperation was also enhanced with the Inter-Agency Standing Committee on humanitarian aspects of climate change. In April, the Intergovernmental Panel on Climate Change decided to produce a special report on managing the risk of extreme events to advance climate change adaptation, which would provide an authoritative basis of factual information on climate-related disaster risk and methodologies for reducing and managing risks. The second session of the Global Platform for Disaster Risk Reduction also addressed climate change and reducing risks for all.

Regional meetings on partnerships. In a 24 February letter [A/63/747] to the Secretary-General, Canada and Mexico transmitted the report of the First Regional Meeting on Enhancing International Humanitarian Partnerships, held in September 2008 in Mexico on the initiative of the two countries and OCHA. The meeting was convened in light of the fact that the number of devastating natural disasters was on the increase and the region of Latin America and the Caribbean was the second most affected region. At the second regional meeting (Brazil, 2–4 September 2009), participating countries adopted the "Declaration of Florianopolis", which established a regional virtual tool to make information available in an updated, effective and transparent manner, on requirements of countries affected by disasters and on international humanitarian assistance offered.

Disaster assistance

Burkina Faso

During 2009, several West African countries were affected by unrelenting rains causing the loss of human lives, and massive destruction of infrastructure including dwellings and harvests. In Burkina Faso, the rain on 1 September around the capital, Ouagadougou, was unprecedented. Some 263 millimetres fell in 12 hours—more than one-third of the annual total precipitation—causing severe flooding and widespread displacement. The Government reported that all five districts of Ouagadougou, with an estimated population of 1.3 million, had been severely affected. Eight people had died and it was estimated that 90,000 people were sheltering in temporary accommodation. The fire department reported that 50 per cent of the city's territory had been affected. The Central University Hospital, as well as primary infrastructure such as bridges, roads, schools and agricultural land, suffered damage. Humanitarian organizations and the Government initiated a swift response in all accessible areas using in-country stocks. The overall humanitarian response was organized through the Humanitarian Country Team. On 2 September, the Government established a National Crisis Committee to improve the coordination of assistance. Priority humanitarian needs included support for food security and health; improvement of access to safe water, sanitation and hygiene; rehabilitation of basic shelter; rehabilitation of schools; and provision of non-food items.

The UN Flash Appeal for Burkina Faso, which sought $18.4 million to address the needs of 150,000 people affected by flooding for six months, received 46 per cent ($8.5 million) of requirements.

El Salvador

On 7 and 8 November, the combined effect of Hurricane Ida and a low-pressure system off the Pacific Coast led to heavy rainfall in El Salvador causing severe flooding and landslides in seven of the country's 14 departments. In just a few hours, a total of 355 millimetres of rainfall was registered in the most adversely affected areas. On 8 November, the President of El Salvador decreed a national emergency and on 10 November the Government officially requested international assistance. As of 18 November, some 192 people had been reported dead, 80 people were missing, and around 15,000 people were being supported in emergency collective centres. Approximately 15,000 families (75,000 people) were in need of humanitarian assistance. The Government requested the deployment of a UN disaster assessment and coordination team to support national efforts in damage and needs assessment, and the coordination of international assistance. Initial international efforts focused on the provision of emergency aid to the affected population, especially those in collective centres. Urgent action was needed to locate, quantify and deliver humanitarian aid to the affected population outside the collective centres, mainly in areas of limited access. Immediate support was also needed to improve the management of the established collective centres and aid quality. The initial UN Flash Appeal sought $13.1 million for a period of six months.

GENERAL ASSEMBLY ACTION

On 7 December [meeting 60], the General Assembly adopted **resolution 64/74** [draft: A/64/L.19 & Add.1] without vote [agenda item 70 (a)].

Humanitarian assistance, emergency relief and rehabilitation for El Salvador as a result of the devastating effects of Hurricane Ida

The General Assembly,

Recalling its resolutions 53/1 B of 5 October 1998, 53/1 C of 2 November 1998, 54/96 E of 15 December 1999, 58/117 of 17 December 2003, 59/212 of 20 December 2004, 59/231 and 59/233 of 22 December 2004 and 60/220 of 22 December 2005,

Reiterating the need for the United Nations system to respond to requests for assistance by Member States and for humanitarian assistance to be provided in accordance with the principles of humanity, neutrality, impartiality and independence,

Deeply regretting the loss of human life and the scores of victims caused by Hurricane Ida in El Salvador on 7 and 8 November 2009,

Conscious of the huge material losses sustained to crops, homes, basic infrastructure and tourist and other areas,

Acknowledging the efforts of the Government of El Salvador to protect the lives of its nationals and rapidly to assist the affected population,

Conscious that the Central American countries are vulnerable to cyclical weather patterns and prone to natural hazards owing to their geographical location and features, which impose additional challenges on their ability to achieve the Millennium Development Goals,

Noting the enormous effort, as well as the fullest coordinated support and solidarity of the international community, that will be required to rebuild the affected areas and to alleviate the grave situation wreaked by these natural hazards,

1. *Expresses its solidarity and support* to the Government and the people of El Salvador;

2. *Expresses its appreciation* to the members of the international community that have offered their support to the rescue and emergency assistance effort for the affected population;

3. *Appeals* to all Member States and all organs and bodies of the United Nations system, as well as international financial institutions and development agencies, to provide speedy support to the relief, rehabilitation and assistance effort for El Salvador;

4. *Calls upon* the international community to provide assistance in response to the United Nations flash appeal for El Salvador;

5. *Acknowledges* the efforts and progress made by El Salvador in strengthening its disaster-preparedness capacity, emphasizes the importance of investing in disaster risk reduction, and encourages the international community to continue to cooperate with the Government of El Salvador towards this end;

6. *Requests* the Secretary-General and all organs and bodies of the United Nations system, as well as international financial institutions and development agencies, to assist El Salvador, whenever possible, through continued effective humanitarian, technical and financial assistance that contributes to overcoming the emergency and achieving the rehabilitation and recovery of the economy and the affected population, in conformity with the priorities identified at the national level;

7. *Requests* the relevant organs and organizations of the United Nations system and other multilateral organizations to increase their support and assistance for strengthening the disaster-preparedness capacity of El Salvador;

8. *Requests* the Secretary-General to report to the General Assembly at its sixty-fifth session on the implementation of the present resolution and on the progress made in the relief, rehabilitation and reconstruction effort for El Salvador under the sub-item entitled "Strengthening of the coordination of emergency humanitarian assistance of the United Nations".

Following a later assessment by the national authorities, the UN system and other humanitarian partners, the revised UN Flash Appeal for El Salvador sought $14.5 million, of which 48 per cent ($6.9 million) was received.

Indonesia

On 30 September, an earthquake measuring 7.6 degrees on the Richter Scale struck off the western Sumatra coast in Indonesia. The epicentre was 45 kilometres west-northwest of the port city of Padang, Sumatra (population of approximately 900,000 people). A second quake measuring 6.2 degrees occurred 22 minutes later, while a third 6.8 quake struck an inland area southeast of Padang the following morning. The cumulative impact of the earthquakes resulted in significant destruction. Three villages in the Padang Pariaman District were completely leveled and there was concern that most of their inhabitants had been buried under a subsequent landslide. As at 8 October, according to provincial authorities, the official death toll was placed at 739 people, with another 296 people missing and presumed dead, primarily in Padang Pariaman District. Some 2,219 people had been injured and damage to houses was widespread with 231,395 homes damaged, rendering an estimated 250,000 families homeless, and many too frightened to return home. A state of emergency was proclaimed for one month and coordinated international assistance was welcomed. The Government led the response to the emergency in the affected areas. At least 21 search and rescue teams from 14 countries completed assessments of 31 collapsed buildings in Padang in the first days after the disaster, as the Indonesian military's emergency response teams deployed heavy equipment and recovered trapped victims.

In close coordination with the Indonesian Government, and based on reports and assessments from official sources, the UN system and humanitarian partners prepared the humanitarian response plan. The Plan, which sought $38 million for 90 days, received 42 per cent ($15.9 million) of requirements.

Communication. On 5 October [A/64/485], Egypt, on behalf of the Coordinating Bureau of the Non-Aligned Movement, transmitted a statement to the Secretary-General by its Chair urging States, UN humanitarian entities and the international community to provide support to the Government of Indonesia, which was open to receiving international assistance in support of its efforts to address the humanitarian situation in the country.

Lao People's Democratic Republic

On 29 September, Typhoon Ketsana crossed into the southern provinces of the Lao People's Democratic Republic, causing devastation in Attapeu, Sekong, Saravan, Savannakhet, and Champassack Provinces, which included some of the poorest districts in the country, with high levels of food insecurity. Some 178,000 people were affected by the subsequent floods and landslides with an estimated 9,602 households displaced and 15 storm-related deaths reported. There was limited access to the majority of the flood-affected population living in mountainous and remote areas. The typhoon also destroyed food stocks and damaged crops, significantly reducing the upcoming harvest. Reported infrastructure damage included 1,848 houses destroyed or damaged. Health risks increased significantly owing to damaged water supply systems, contaminated water supplies and disrupted access to health care services. The threat of displaced unexploded ordnance exposed by the flood waters exacerbated the protection concerns of the flood-affected population. Supported by humanitarian agencies on the ground, government agencies responded swiftly, launching search and rescue operations and releasing emergency relief stocks. To support the Government's relief actions, the international humanitarian community launched a flash appeal for $10.2 million. In November, the results of a joint assessment conducted by the Government, NGOs and UN partners indicated that further support was needed.

The revised UN Flash Appeal for the Lao People's Democratic Republic sought $12.8 million to address the immediate needs of 180,674 people affected by Typhoon Ketsana for six months, of which 75 per cent ($9.6 million) was received.

Madagascar

In April, the humanitarian situation in Madagascar was characterized by three concurrent crises: a period of political instability and violence since the beginning of the year that led to the ousting of President Marc Ravalomanana in March and the subsequent installation of a Transitional Authority; the drought that resulted in generalized food insecurity and severe child malnutrition in three regions in the south of the country; and the effects of cyclones and flooding along the eastern and south-western coasts, affecting over 114,000 people. UN-led assessments, which were conducted after an initial appeal was launched on 7 April, revealed that the most urgent humanitarian needs were in the drought-affected south. On the cyclones and flooding, the humanitarian response was largely covered through pre-positioned stocks and reallocation of funds from other programmes to meet the most urgent needs in the areas of water, sanitation and education. On food insecurity, the counter-season harvest in June had stabilized prices in local markets and enabled previously food-insecure areas to achieve self-sufficiency in the short term, although the respite was insufficient to enable families to meet basic needs during the traditional lean season from September through December. In addition, an estimated 7,000 children required nutritional support. Nonetheless, the country as a whole was benefiting from the year's good rice harvest.

The revised UN Flash Appeal for Madagascar, which was revised downwards by 37 per cent, sought $22.3 million, of which 82 per cent ($18.4 million) had been received. Activities under the appeal aimed to assist some 516,000 people, of which

276,000 had been affected by the drought; 140,000 beneficiaries in urban areas affected by the socio-political crisis; and 100,000 people affected by cyclone-related activities.

Namibia

In early 2009, the north-central and north-eastern regions of Namibia experienced torrential rains causing flooding along the country's northern borders. The water levels of the Cunene, Chobe, Zambezi and Kavango rivers increased significantly due to the combined effects of rain and water from tributaries in Angola and Zambia, affecting 350,000 people, causing 102 deaths and displacing over 13,500 persons. Six regions (Caprivi, Kavango, Oshana, Oshikoto, Ohangwena and Omusati), home to the majority of the rural poor, were worst affected. On 17 March, the President declared an emergency for the North-Central and North-Eastern part of Namibia and appealed for international assistance. The Government established relocation camps to host the displaced and distributed non-food items in the affected regions. Meanwhile, the number of affected and displaced populations continued to rise due to continued heavy rainfall upstream in Angola and Zambia and increasing river levels. April assessment reports from the Government and the international community indicated that an estimated 750,000 people were affected, including 54,000 people displaced. Further assessments were conducted in May, and by the end of June, the Government reported that 28,103 people were displaced in the Caprivi and Kavango regions, and residual humanitarian needs remained in the relocation camps.

The revised UN Flash Appeal for Namibia, which sought $7.1 million to address residual humanitarian needs as identified by further assessments, received 32 per cent ($2.3 million) of its target.

Philippines

On 26 September, Tropical Storm Ketsana swept across Manila and parts of Central Luzon, bringing months worth of rain in just 12 hours. On 3 October, Typhoon Parma made landfall in Northern Luzon with heavy rains over an area much larger than initially anticipated, only to be followed by Typhoon Mirinae on 31 October—the third typhoon within a period of just over a month. The Government requested the assistance of the international community in responding to the effects of Ketsana on 28 September, and on 19 October requested that the areas affected by Typhoon Parma be included in the revised flash appeal. In November, Government data and assessments by UN agencies and NGOs indicated that out of the 10 million people affected, some

4.2 million were in need. Of particular concern for humanitarian agencies were the estimated 1.7 million people still displaced or living in areas that remained flooded. Those areas were likely to remain flooded for another three or four months, resulting in serious health concerns. In addition, preliminary assessments by the country's Department of Agriculture and the Food and Agriculture Organization of the United Nations indicated that some 100,000 to 120,000 farming households (500,000 people) in Regions I, II, and III lost 100 per cent of their production and assets.

The UN revised Flash Appeal for the Philippines, which sought $143.8 million to address the need of some 4.2 million people, received 44 per cent ($62.9 million) of the requirements.

Communication. On 29 September [A/64/471], Egypt, on behalf of the Coordinating Bureau of the Non-Aligned Movement, transmitted a statement to the Secretary-General by its Chair urging UN humanitarian entities and the international community to provide support to the Government and people of the Philippines to address the urgent situation due to tropical storm Ketsana.

Tajikistan

In 2009, the organizations participating in the review of the Humanitarian Food Security Appeal for Tajikistan [YUN 2008, p. 1038] agreed that the situation in the country remained severe. Negative effects of the global economic and financial crises, combined with significant damage caused by natural disasters over the previous year, had undermined ongoing efforts to improve the humanitarian situation. In May, statistics indicated that in rural areas, severe food insecurity had decreased from 600,000 people in 2008 to 480,000 people in 2009, while moderate food insecurity had increased from 1.1 million people to 1.4 million. The main cause of the worsening situation of people suffering from moderate food insecurity was an increase in unemployment, which was affecting migrants abroad and local entrepreneurs. Meanwhile, the spring brought new losses from floods and mudflows that damaged 40,000 hectares of land in 40 out 58 districts in the country, including 22,000 hectares of cotton and over 12,000 hectares of cereals, fruit

and vegetable gardens, and potato fields. The aim of the revised appeal, which sought $39.9 million, was to provide a temporary safety net to the most vulnerable poor people in urban and rural areas through the provision of food and cash. In other efforts, the Tajikistan Humanitarian Partnership launched a $1.5 million appeal to address the humanitarian needs of some 12,000 individuals that had been severely affected by floods and mud flows during the spring.

Yemen

In Yemen, following sporadic clashes between Al Houthis groups and the Yemeni Government in July, the situation in Sa'ada Governorate escalated into open hostilities on 12 August, forcing tens of thousands of people to flee for their safety and generating new displacement in northern Yemen. Until July, humanitarian agencies had been assisting some 95,000 people in Sa'ada Governorate affected by previous rounds of fighting. The renewed fighting led tens of thousands of people from Sa'ada and Amran Governorates to flee for the first time and forced many previously displaced people into a second displacement; an estimated 150,000 people were displaced. Humanitarian partners were also concerned with the threats to, and needs of, civilian populations remaining in areas of intensified fighting to which the humanitarian community had little or no access due to insecurity. Additionally, the crisis was unfolding in the context of significant vulnerability due to poverty, lack of investment in basic services, and the impact of repeated confrontations on people's coping mechanisms. In areas where access was possible, humanitarian agencies had responded swiftly. Using in-country stocks, partners had delivered relief items to displaced populations in Haradh (Hajjah Governorate) and Amran Governorate, and in Sa'ada town, when security conditions allowed.

The revised UN Flash Appeal for Yemen sought $22.7 million to address the needs of a projected caseload of 175,000 IDPs, and up to 800,000 people indirectly affected by the conflict, including communities hosting IDPs and residents who had lost access to basic services such as food, water and health care. Of that amount, 88 per cent of the requirements ($19.9 million) had been received.

Chapter IV

International trade, finance and transport

In 2009, the work of the United Nations Conference on Trade and Development (UNCTAD) and the UN system on international trade, finance and transport dealt mainly with the global economic and financial crisis that began the previous year. During the crisis, world trade volume contracted by almost 13 per cent. The severe decline was attributed mainly to the financial crisis, which caused a free fall of 30 to 50 per cent in world trade volumes from the end of 2008 up to the second quarter of 2009, with Asian exporters being hit hardest. World trade rebounded somewhat thereafter, but recovery was fragile.

In response to the crisis, which the Secretary-General called the worst of its kind since the founding of the United Nations, the General Assembly convened, at the highest level, the Conference on the World Financial and Economic Crisis and Its Impact on Development in New York in June. The Conference considered measures to mitigate the impact of the crisis on development and the role of the United Nations in reforming the international financial and economic system. The Conference adopted an outcome document in which heads of State and Government committed to work in solidarity on a coordinated and comprehensive global response to the crisis through a number of actions outlined in the document. In July, the Assembly endorsed the outcome document and established an ad hoc open-ended working group to follow up on the issues contained therein.

In April, the high-level meeting between the Economic and Social Council and the Bretton Woods institutions (the World Bank Group and the International Monetary Fund), the World Trade Organization (WTO) and UNCTAD discussed coherence, coordination and cooperation in the context of the implementation of the Monterrey Consensus and the Doha Declaration on Financing for Development, focusing on addressing the impact of the global financial and economic crisis on development and strengthening the intergovernmental inclusive process to carry out the financing for development follow-up.

The Trade and Development Board, the governing body of UNCTAD, in September, adopted agreed conclusions on the implementation of the Programme of Action for the Least Developed Countries for the Decade 2001–2010 and on economic development in Africa. It also adopted a decision on UNCTAD technical cooperation activities.

International trade

On 21 December (**decision 64/540**), the Assembly took note of the report of the Second Committee [A/64/418] on its discussion of macroeconomic policy questions, including those related to international trade and development, and commodities.

Global trade activity

The *World Economic Situation and Prospects 2010* [Sales No. E.10.II.C.2], jointly issued by the UN Department of Economic and Social Affairs (DESA) and UNCTAD, stated that world trade volume contracted by almost 13 per cent in 2009, more than 20 per cent below its annualized 8.6 per cent trend growth during the 2004–2007 period. Developed country gross domestic product (GDP) contracted by 3.5 per cent and the volume of imports reduced by about 12 per cent. GDP growth for developing countries (excluding East Asia) dropped by 6 per cent while import demand fell by 17 per cent. In developing East Asia, the decline in import volume was 8 per cent and GDP growth dropped by 2 per cent. Trade in manufactures showed the greatest swings during the global crisis, characterized by a higher income elasticity than trade in other commodities. The deep recession in developed countries spread quickly, first to countries specializing in manufactures, especially in East Asia, and subsequently to countries providing industrial inputs and raw materials. The decline in export volumes, however, was greater in regions with higher specialization in manufactures. Many Asian exporters were among the hardest hit and saw their merchandise export revenues decline by 30 per cent or more during the first quarter of 2009. Decreases in exports, and thus in industrial production in developing countries, were transmitted into drops in energy imports from economies in transition. The least developed countries (LDCs) were least affected by a decline in the demand for their exports, possibly owing to the relatively low income elasticity of demand for primary export products. Nevertheless, the contraction in demand for LDC exports averaged about 1.6 per cent of GDP in 2009 and contributed to the substantial run-up of trade deficits amounting to 10 per cent of the combined GDP of the poorest countries.

A June report [E/2009/73] gave an update, as at mid-2009, of the *World Economic Situation and Prospects 2009* report [YUN 2008, p. 1047].

The *Trade and Development Report, 2009* [Sales No. E.09.II.D.16], published by UNCTAD, stated that world trade slowed down in 2007 and 2008 and had been shrinking in both volume and value at a faster rate since November 2008. Trade volume growth decelerated first in the United States and other developed countries. Import volume growth actually turned negative in the United States and Japan in 2008. Trade expansion was more resilient in developing and transition economies. In particular, countries that had benefited from terms-of-trade gains until mid-2008 were able to increase their imports significantly, although in some cases the volume of their exports slowed or even declined. In the final months of 2008, the contraction in investment and consumption of durable goods in many countries was reflected in lower private domestic and foreign demand, leading to a sharp reduction of trade in manufactures. All major developed economies were in recession.

A later report—*Trade and Development Report, 2010* [Sales No. E.10.II.D.3]—stated that world trade, which had plunged by more than 13 per cent in volume and by as much as 23 per cent in value in the first half of 2009, started to recover in mid-2009, and that the recovery was much faster in developing than in developed countries. Although the crisis-induced squeeze on trade credit played a role in reducing trade worldwide, the decline in domestic demand, amplified by the globally synchronized nature of the downturn since 2008, was the main cause of the slowdown in world trade in 2009. The sharp falls in wealth and expectations prompted households and firms to reduce or postpone spending. Expanded global supply chains— a dominant feature of transnational corporations in world trade—also played an important, though unquantifiable, role in the 2009 slump in world trade. In addition, lower production of manufactures translated into lower demand for energy and industrial raw materials. As a result, all countries and regions registered significant declines in their exports of goods, with larger declines in volume in developed and transition countries than in developing countries. In terms of the value of exports, the worst hit countries were exporters of oil and mining products. Recovery of trade volume started from the second half of the year and was led by strong demand from developing countries and relatively weaker demand from developed countries. External trade in developed countries had also grown since mid-2009, although at a slower pace.

Multilateral trading system

Report of Secretary-General. In response to General Assembly resolution 63/203 [YUN 2008, p. 1052], the Secretary-General submitted a July report [A/64/177] on international trade and development, prepared in collaboration with UNCTAD. The report discussed the global development crisis and governance; the ongoing financial and economic crisis; the effects of the crisis on international trade; trade-related policy developments; developments in the multilateral trading system; and regional trade arrangements.

The Secretary-General concluded that the global economy required a course correction towards more sustainable and inclusive development, which, in turn, necessitated addressing the root causes of the financial and economic crisis. The crisis underscored the need for a careful reassessment of development models and strategies and a redefinition of Governments' role in the markets as "enabling and development States". The global governance system needed to provide a coherent paradigm to comprehensively address global crises and promote development, and the United Nations played a key role in that effort. Governments needed to better adjust their economies to post-crisis realities and make them more resistant to external shocks through diversification into new products, services and markets, including South-South trade, and through bolstering domestic demand. Sustainable production and consumption could be supported by proactive policies and sound regulatory and institutional frameworks, including the provision of social safety nets and scaled-up international development support. Innovative approaches were required in the design of policy responses to ensure that post-crisis development was resilient and inclusive. International trade continued to be a driver of growth and the multilateral trading system could provide unique public good, including by addressing economic nationalism that could alter competitive conditions and production location, and by delivering the development agenda of the Doha Round.

UNCTAD consideration. At its fifty-sixth annual session (Geneva, 14–25 September and 12 October) [A/64/15 (Part IV)], the Trade and Development Board (TDB) discussed an UNCTAD secretariat note on the evolution of the international trading system and of international trade from a development perspective: impact of the crisis [TD/B/56/7]. Participants agreed that the global financial and economic crisis, which had originated in developed countries, affected all countries and had severe social, economic and developmental implications, particularly for developing countries. Combined with a series of crises affecting energy, food, commodities and climate change, and the limited ability of countries to put in place social safety nets, the crisis had aggravated poverty and social misery, and rendered the achievement of the Millennium Development Goals (MDGs) and poverty reduction by 2015 practically impossible. Many participants underlined the importance of a coordinated approach to the crisis, including through a stronger partnership among international organizations. There was a need for innovative and viable solutions to improve the availability and affordability of trade finance, including by activities of the network of export-import banks and by initiatives aimed at increasing global trade liquidity. The rapid spread of the crisis highlighted the extent of vulnerability facing developing countries from their excessive reliance on external demand, especially on a narrow range of commodities and markets. Many participants stressed that markets could not self-regulate and that Governments should play a central role in guiding investments and economic activities, regulating markets and facilitating trade in key sectors. Participants concurred that economic nationalism and protectionist sentiments were a matter of concern, as they affected developing countries in particular, and stressed the importance of concluding the Doha Round of trade negotiations with substantial development content by 2010. Participants also concurred on the value of the multilateral trading system in maintaining trade flows. There was a need to strengthen a multilateral trading that was universal, rules-based, open, non-discriminatory and equitable. Participants reaffirmed that UNCTAD played an important role as catalyst for monitoring the evolution of the crisis and building a consensus on measures needed to address its trade and development implications. UNCTAD should continue to help developing countries engage in the international trading system and build trade and productive capacities, including through Aid for Trade [YUN 2005, p. 1043].

Ministerial meetings. The seventh session of the WTO Ministerial Conference (Geneva, 30 November–2 December), held on the theme "The WTO, the Multilateral Trading System and the Current Global Economic Environment", reviewed the operation and functioning of the multilateral trading system. Proposals included revitalizing regular committees to improve monitoring of measures; improving oversight of regional trade agreements; and adopting an omnibus legal instrument to cover least developed countries' preferences.

Negotiating frameworks

Development of Doha Round negotiations

The Secretary-General, in his July report on international trade and development [A/64/177], said that in 2009 there were signs of re-engagement in the Doha Round of trade negotiations. Changes in the leadership in countries could lead to a redefinition of

the national trade policy agenda, and the renewal of the United States Trade Promotion Authority would facilitate the process. A possible two-track approach to the negotiations was suggested, whereby negotiations on modalities would continue in parallel with a scheduling exercise for outcome testing for greater clarity on the use of flexibilities. However, a significant challenge facing the WTO members was the effective management of the Doha Round in the context of the global crisis and related policy developments. Although the successful conclusion of the Round would be considered important in boosting the world economy and sending a strong signal of enhanced international cooperation as well as in containing rising protectionist tendencies, the recession and emerging social and developmental hardships, particularly unemployment, could discourage many countries from undertaking ambitious policy reform. He further stated that the protracted negotiations and recurrent setbacks implied that the modus operandi of the trading system needed to be assessed, bearing in mind the MDGs and the need for strengthened and operational special and differential treatment.

The report also discussed issues related to agriculture, non-agricultural market access, duty-free quota-free market access for least developed countries, services sectors and development.

Ministerial meetings. WTO held an informal ministerial meeting (New Delhi, India, 3–4 September) on the theme "Re-energising Doha—A Commitment to Development". The meeting affirmed the need to conclude the Doha Round in 2010.

The seventh session of the WTO Ministerial Conference, overdue since 2007, was held in Geneva from 30 November to 2 December 2009 on the theme "The WTO, the Multilateral Trading System and the Current Global Economic Environment". Participants took stock of the implementation of WTO agreements and reviewed issues facing WTO in the global economic environment.

GENERAL ASSEMBLY ACTION

On 21 December [meeting 66], the General Assembly, on the recommendation of the Second (Economic and Financial) Committee [A/64/418/Add.1], adopted **resolution 64/188** by recorded vote (122-47-8) [agenda item 51 *(a)*].

International trade and development

The General Assembly,

Recalling its resolutions 56/178 of 21 December 2001, 57/235 of 20 December 2002, 58/197 of 23 December 2003, 59/221 of 22 December 2004, 60/184 of 22 December 2005, 61/186 of 20 December 2006, 62/184 of 19 December 2007 and 63/203 of 19 December 2008 on international trade and development,

Recalling also the United Nations Millennium Declaration, as well as the outcomes of the International Conference on Financing for Development, the World Summit on Sustainable Development, the 2005 World Summit Outcome and the Doha Declaration on Financing for Development,

Recalling further the Outcome of the Conference on the World Financial and Economic Crisis and Its Impact on Development,

Reaffirming the value of multilateralism to the global trading system and the commitment to achieving a universal, rule-based, open, non-discriminatory and equitable multilateral trading system that contributes to growth, sustainable development and employment generation in all sectors, and emphasizing that bilateral and regional trading arrangements should contribute to the goals of the multilateral trading system,

Stressing the importance of open, transparent, inclusive, democratic and more orderly processes and procedures for the effective functioning of the multilateral trading system, including in the decision-making process, so as to enable developing countries to have their vital interests duly reflected in the outcome of trade negotiations,

Reiterating that development concerns form an integral part of the Doha Development Agenda, which places the needs and interests of developing and least developed countries at the heart of the Doha Work Programme,

Noting that agriculture lags behind the manufacturing sector in the process of the establishment of multilateral disciplines and in the reduction of tariff and non-tariff barriers and that, since most of the world's poor make their living from agriculture, the livelihood and standards of living of many of them are seriously jeopardized by the serious distortions in production and trade in agricultural products caused by the high levels of export subsidies, trade-distorting domestic support and protectionism by many developed countries,

1.   *Takes note* of the report of the Trade and Development Board and the report of the Secretary-General;

2.   *Reaffirms* that international trade can be an engine for development and sustained economic growth, underlines the need to fully harness its potential in that regard, and stresses the importance of upholding a universal, rule-based, open, non-discriminatory and equitable multilateral trading system that contributes to growth, sustainable development and employment, particularly in developing countries;

3.   *Notes with deep concern* that the world financial and economic crisis has severely impacted international trade, particularly affecting developing countries, including through the fall in exports and loss of export revenues, restricted access to trade finance and reduced export-oriented investment, which have resulted, in many cases, in lower fiscal revenues and balance-of-payment problems;

4.   *Notes* that the shortage and the high cost of trade finance for developing countries contributed significantly to the reduction in trade flows during the crisis, also notes the efforts of the international community, including through the World Bank Global Trade Liquidity Programme, to ensure additional resources at affordable rates, and calls upon bilateral and multilateral donors to redouble their efforts to increase the availability and affordability of trade finance for developing countries;

5.   *Underlines*, in this regard, the need for greater coherence in the trade, financial and monetary systems, with a view to promoting growth, sustainable development and employment;

6.   *Stresses* the need to resist all protectionist measures and tendencies, especially those affecting developing countries, particularly tariff, non-tariff and para-tariff barriers to trade, and to rectify any such measures already taken, recognizes the right of countries to fully utilize their policy space, consistent with World Trade Organization commitments, and calls upon the World Trade Organization and other relevant bodies, including the United Nations Conference on Trade and Development, to continue monitoring protectionist measures and assess their impact on developing countries;

7.   *Encourages* Member States to refrain from adopting any measures or restrictions related to trade and transit that affect the access by developing countries to medicines, especially generic medicines, and medical equipment;

8.   *Expresses serious concern* at the lack of progress in the negotiations of the World Trade Organization Doha Development Round, reiterates the call on developed countries to demonstrate the flexibility and political will necessary to make meaningful progress in the negotiations, with a view to concluding the Round by 2010, and calls upon all members of the World Trade Organization to adhere to the development mandate of the Doha Ministerial Declaration, the decision of 1 August 2004 of the General Council of the World Trade Organization and the Hong Kong Ministerial Declaration, which places development at the heart of the multilateral trading system;

9.   *Takes note* of the New Delhi informal ministerial meeting on re-energizing Doha, held on 3 and 4 September 2009, which led to the resumption of the negotiations of the Doha Round with the objective of concluding the Round by 2010;

10.   *Stresses* the importance of accelerating the negotiations, with a strong reaffirmation that development remains at the heart of the Doha Round, building upon the progress already made, particularly with regard to modalities, and based on the World Trade Organization agreed workplan on agriculture, non-agricultural market access, services, rules, trade facilitation and other remaining issues, with a view to concluding the Round by 2010;

11.   *Also stresses* that, in order for the Doha Round to be concluded satisfactorily, the negotiations should strengthen the rules and disciplines in the area of agriculture, eliminate agricultural export subsidies, substantially reduce the domestic measures of support by developed countries and promote enhanced market access to developed country markets, in a balanced and development-oriented outcome, while adhering to the development mandate of the Doha Ministerial Declaration, the decision of 1 August 2004 of the General Council of the World Trade Organization and the Hong Kong Ministerial Declaration;

12.   *Further stresses* the need for negotiations of the World Trade Organization in non-agricultural market access to fulfil the development mandate of the Doha Ministerial Declaration, the decision of 1 August 2004 of the General Council of the World Trade Organization and the Hong Kong Ministerial Declaration;

13. *Stresses* the need for negotiations of the World Trade Organization to make substantial progress in all areas under the single undertaking, such as services, rules and trade facilitation, so as to ensure that the development concerns of developing countries are fully reflected in any outcome, consistent with the development mandate of the Doha Ministerial Declaration, the decision of 1 August 2004 of the General Council of the World Trade Organization and the Hong Kong Ministerial Declaration;

14. *Reiterates its call for* accelerating work on the trade-related aspects of the World Intellectual Property Organization development agenda, as well as the development-related mandate concerning the Agreement on Trade-related Aspects of Intellectual Property Rights (TRIPS Agreement) in the Doha Ministerial Declaration, especially the examination of the relationship between the TRIPS Agreement and the Convention on Biological Diversity, the protection of traditional knowledge and folklore and the issues related to the full implementation of the Doha Declaration on the TRIPS Agreement and Public Health, affecting developing countries, including the least developed countries, especially those issues arising from HIV/AIDS, tuberculosis, malaria and other diseases;

15. *Reaffirms* the commitments made at the Fourth Ministerial Conference of the World Trade Organization and at the Third United Nations Conference on the Least Developed Countries, in this regard calls upon developed countries that have not already done so to provide immediate predictable, duty-free and quota-free market access on a lasting basis to all products originating from all least developed countries, calls upon developing countries that are in a position to do so to extend duty-free and quota-free market access to exports of these countries, in this context reaffirms also the need to consider additional measures for progressive improvement in market access for least developed countries, and reaffirms further the need for members of the World Trade Organization to take additional measures to provide effective market access, both at the border and otherwise, including simplified and transparent rules of origin so as to facilitate exports from least developed countries;

16. *Also reaffirms* the commitment to actively pursue the work programme of the World Trade Organization with respect to addressing the trade-related issues and concerns affecting the fuller integration of small, vulnerable economies into the multilateral trading system in a manner commensurate with their special circumstances and in support of their efforts towards sustainable development, in accordance with paragraph 35 of the Doha Ministerial Declaration and paragraph 41 of the Hong Kong Ministerial Declaration;

17. *Expresses its deep concern* at the imposition of laws and other forms of coercive economic measures, including unilateral sanctions, against developing countries, which undermine international law and the rules of the World Trade Organization and also severely threaten freedom of trade and investment;

18. *Recognizes* the special problems and needs of the landlocked developing countries within a new global framework for transit transport cooperation for landlocked and transit developing countries, calls, in this regard, for the full and effective implementation of the Almaty Programme of Action, and stresses the need for the implemen-

tation of the São Paulo Consensus and of the Accra Accord by the relevant international organizations and donors in a multi-stakeholder approach;

19. *Reaffirms* that developing countries should play an increasing role in the formulation of, inter alia, safety, environmental and health standards, calls for the full and fair representation of developing countries in the relevant international standard-setting organizations, and in this regard also calls for additional financial resources and technical capacity-building to ensure the adequate participation of developing countries;

20. *Recognizes* that South-South trade should be strengthened, notes that enhanced market access between developing countries can play a positive role in stimulating South-South trade, and calls for acceleration of the work of the ongoing third round of negotiations (the São Paulo Round) on the Global System of Trade Preferences among Developing Countries;

21. *Calls for* facilitating the accession of all developing countries that apply for membership in the World Trade Organization, in particular the least developed countries, including countries emerging from conflict that are least developed countries, bearing in mind paragraph 21 of resolution 55/182 of 20 December 2000 and subsequent developments, and also calls for the effective and faithful application of the World Trade Organization guidelines on accession by the least developed countries;

22. *Emphasizes* the need for further work to foster greater coherence between the multilateral trading system and the international financial system, and invites the United Nations Conference on Trade and Development, in fulfilment of its mandate, to undertake the relevant policy analysis in those areas and to operationalize such work, including through its technical assistance activities;

23. *Takes note* of the holding of the second Global Review on Aid for Trade, on 6 and 7 July 2009, aimed at reviewing progress achieved and identifying additional measures needed to support developing and least developed countries in building their supply and export capacities, and stresses the urgent need to implement the aid-for-trade commitments, especially with regard to the mobilization of additional, non-conditional and predictable funding;

24. *Welcomes* the efforts made to operationalize the Enhanced Integrated Framework for Trade-related Technical Assistance to Least Developed Countries, aimed at promoting the export and supply capacities of the least developed countries, as well as the establishment of the Enhanced Integrated Framework Trust Fund, and urges development partners to increase their contributions, with a view to ensuring increased additional, non-conditional and predictable financial resources on a multi-year basis;

25. *Reiterates* the important role of the United Nations Conference on Trade and Development as the focal point within the United Nations system for the integrated treatment of trade and development and interrelated issues in the areas of finance, technology, investment and sustainable development, and calls upon the international community to work towards the strengthening of the Conference in order to enable it to enhance its contribution in its three major pillars, namely, consensus-building, research and policy analysis and technical assistance, especially through increased core resources;

26. *Invites* the United Nations Conference on Trade and Development, in accordance with its mandate, to monitor and assess the evolution of the international trading system and of trends in international trade from a development perspective, and, in particular, to analyse issues of concern to developing countries, supporting them in building capacities to establish their own negotiating priorities and negotiate trade agreements, including under the Doha Work Programme;

27. *Urges* donors to provide the United Nations Conference on Trade and Development with the increased resources necessary to deliver effective and demand-driven assistance to developing countries, as well as to enhance their contributions to the trust funds of the Integrated Framework for Trade-related Technical Assistance to Least Developed Countries and the Joint Integrated Technical Assistance Programme;

28. *Requests* the Secretary-General, in collaboration with the secretariat of the United Nations Conference on Trade and Development, to submit to the General Assembly at its sixty-fifth session a report on the implementation of the present resolution and on developments in the multilateral trading system, including with regard to the implementation of the World Intellectual Property Organization development agenda, under the sub-item entitled "International trade and development" of the item entitled "Macroeconomic policy questions";

29. *Also requests* the Secretary-General to transmit the present resolution to the Director-General of the World Trade Organization for circulation as a document of the World Trade Organization.

RECORDED VOTE ON RESOLUTION 64/188:

In favour: Algeria, Angola, Antigua and Barbuda, Argentina, Armenia, Bahamas, Bahrain, Bangladesh, Barbados, Belarus, Belize, Benin, Bhutan, Bolivia, Botswana, Brazil, Brunei Darussalam, Burkina Faso, Burundi, Cambodia, Cameroon, Cape Verde, Central African Republic, Chad, Chile, China, Colombia, Comoros, Congo, Côte d'Ivoire, Cuba, Democratic People's Republic of Korea, Djibouti, Dominica, Dominican Republic, Ecuador, Egypt, El Salvador, Eritrea, Ethiopia, Fiji, Gabon, Ghana, Grenada, Guatemala, Guinea, Guinea-Bissau, Guyana, Haiti, India, Indonesia, Iran, Iraq, Jamaica, Jordan, Kazakhstan, Kenya, Kuwait, Kyrgyzstan, Lao People's Democratic Republic, Lebanon, Lesotho, Libyan Arab Jamahiriya, Madagascar, Malawi, Malaysia, Maldives, Mali, Mauritania, Mauritius, Micronesia, Mongolia, Morocco, Mozambique, Myanmar, Namibia, Nepal, Nicaragua, Niger, Nigeria, Oman, Pakistan, Panama, Papua New Guinea, Paraguay, Peru, Philippines, Qatar, Rwanda, Saint Kitts and Nevis, Saint Lucia, Saint Vincent and the Grenadines, Samoa, Saudi Arabia, Senegal, Singapore, Solomon Islands, Somalia, South Africa, Sri Lanka, Sudan, Suriname, Swaziland, Syrian Arab Republic, Tajikistan, Thailand, Timor-Leste, Togo, Tonga, Trinidad and Tobago, Tunisia, Turkmenistan, Tuvalu, Uganda, United Arab Emirates, Uruguay, Uzbekistan, Venezuela, Viet Nam, Yemen, Zambia, Zimbabwe.

Against: Albania, Andorra, Australia, Austria, Belgium, Bosnia and Herzegovina, Bulgaria, Canada, Croatia, Cyprus, Czech Republic, Denmark, Estonia, Finland, France, Georgia, Germany, Greece, Hungary, Iceland, Ireland, Israel, Italy, Japan, Latvia, Liechtenstein, Lithuania, Luxembourg, Malta, Moldova, Monaco, Montenegro, Netherlands, New Zealand,

Poland, Portugal, Romania, San Marino, Slovakia, Slovenia, Spain, Sweden, Switzerland, The former Yugoslav Republic of Macedonia, Ukraine, United Kingdom, United States.

Abstaining: Marshall Islands, Mexico, Norway, Palau, Republic of Korea, Russian Federation, Serbia, Turkey.

Coercive economic measures

Pursuant to General Assembly resolution 62/183 [YUN 2007, p. 840], the Secretary-General submitted a July report [A/64/179] on unilateral economic measures as a means of political and economic coercion against developing countries. The report summarized replies received from four Member States (Belarus, Burkina Faso, Iran, Jamaica), expressing disagreement with the imposition of such measures, and from three UN regional commissions reporting the continued application of such measures against five Member States: Cuba, the Democratic People's Republic of Korea, Myanmar, the Sudan and the Syrian Arab Republic, as well as against the Occupied Palestinian Territory.

GENERAL ASSEMBLY ACTION

On 21 December [meeting 66], the General Assembly, on the recommendation of the Second Committee [A/64/418/Add.1], adopted **resolution 64/189** by recorded vote (124-3-51) [agenda item 51 *(a)*].

Unilateral economic measures as a means of political and economic coercion against developing countries

The General Assembly,

Recalling the relevant principles set forth in the Charter of the United Nations,

Reaffirming the Declaration on Principles of International Law concerning Friendly Relations and Cooperation among States in accordance with the Charter of the United Nations, which states, inter alia, that no State may use or encourage the use of unilateral economic, political or any other type of measures to coerce another State in order to obtain from it the subordination of the exercise of its sovereign rights,

Bearing in mind the general principles governing the international trading system and trade policies for development contained in relevant resolutions, rules and provisions of the United Nations and the World Trade Organization,

Recalling its resolutions 44/215 of 22 December 1989, 46/210 of 20 December 1991, 48/168 of 21 December 1993, 50/96 of 20 December 1995, 52/181 of 18 December 1997, 54/200 of 22 December 1999, 56/179 of 21 December 2001, 58/198 of 23 December 2003, 60/185 of 22 December 2005 and 62/183 of 19 December 2007,

Gravely concerned that the use of unilateral coercive economic measures adversely affects the economy and development efforts of developing countries in particular and has a general negative impact on international economic cooperation and on worldwide efforts to move towards a non-discriminatory and open multilateral trading system,

Recognizing that such measures constitute a flagrant violation of the principles of international law as set forth in the Charter, as well as the basic principles of the multilateral trading system,

1. *Takes note* of the report of the Secretary-General;

2. *Urges* the international community to adopt urgent and effective measures to eliminate the use of unilateral coercive economic measures against developing countries that are not authorized by relevant organs of the United Nations or are inconsistent with the principles of international law as set forth in the Charter of the United Nations and that contravene the basic principles of the multilateral trading system;

3. *Calls upon* the international community to condemn and reject the imposition of the use of such measures as a means of political and economic coercion against developing countries;

4. *Requests* the Secretary-General to continue to monitor the imposition of measures of this nature and to study the impact of such measures on the affected countries, including the impact on trade and development;

5. *Also requests* the Secretary-General to submit to the General Assembly at its sixty-sixth session a report on the implementation of the present resolution.

RECORDED VOTE ON RESOLUTION 64/189:

In favour: Afghanistan, Algeria, Angola, Antigua and Barbuda, Argentina, Armenia, Bahamas, Bahrain, Bangladesh, Barbados, Belarus, Belize, Benin, Bhutan, Bolivia, Botswana, Brazil, Brunei Darussalam, Burkina Faso, Burundi, Cambodia, Cameroon, Cape Verde, Central African Republic, Chad, Chile, China, Colombia, Comoros, Congo, Costa Rica, Côte d'Ivoire, Cuba, Democratic People's Republic of Korea, Djibouti, Dominica, Dominican Republic, Ecuador, Egypt, El Salvador, Eritrea, Ethiopia, Fiji, Gabon, Ghana, Grenada, Guatemala, Guinea, Guinea-Bissau, Guyana, Haiti, India, Indonesia, Iran, Iraq, Jamaica, Jordan, Kazakhstan, Kenya, Kuwait, Kyrgyzstan, Lao People's Democratic Republic, Lebanon, Lesotho, Libyan Arab Jamahiriya, Madagascar, Malawi, Malaysia, Maldives, Mali, Mauritania, Mauritius, Mexico, Mongolia, Morocco, Mozambique, Myanmar, Namibia, Nepal, Nicaragua, Niger, Nigeria, Oman, Pakistan, Panama, Papua New Guinea, Paraguay, Peru, Philippines, Qatar, Russian Federation, Rwanda, Saint Kitts and Nevis, Saint Lucia, Saint Vincent and the Grenadines, Samoa, Saudi Arabia, Senegal, Singapore, Solomon Islands, Somalia, South Africa, Sri Lanka, Sudan, Suriname, Swaziland, Syrian Arab Republic, Tajikistan, Thailand, Togo, Tonga, Trinidad and Tobago, Tunisia, Turkmenistan, Tuvalu, United Arab Emirates, United Republic of Tanzania, Uruguay, Uzbekistan, Venezuela, Viet Nam, Yemen, Zambia, Zimbabwe.

Against: Israel, Uganda, United States.

Abstaining: Albania, Andorra, Australia, Austria, Belgium, Bosnia and Herzegovina, Bulgaria, Canada, Croatia, Cyprus, Czech Republic, Denmark, Estonia, Finland, France, Georgia, Germany, Greece, Hungary, Iceland, Ireland, Italy, Japan, Latvia, Liechtenstein, Lithuania, Luxembourg, Malta, Marshall Islands, Moldova, Monaco, Montenegro, Netherlands, New Zealand, Norway, Palau, Poland, Portugal, Republic of Korea, Romania, San Marino, Serbia, Slovakia, Slovenia, Spain, Sweden, Switzerland, The former Yugoslav Republic of Macedonia, Turkey, Ukraine, United Kingdom.

Trade policy

Trade and development

The Trade and Development Commission, established by the twelfth UNCTAD session (UNCTAD XII) [YUN 2008, p. 1044], at its first session (Geneva, 11–15 May) [TD/B/C.I/5], had before it reports on energy-related issues from the trade and development perspective [TD/B/C.I/2]; progress reports on the implementation of the provisions of the 2008 Accra Accord [YUN 2008, p. 1042], adopted by UNCTAD XII [ibid., p. 1041], related to key trade and development issues [TD/B/C.I/3] and commodities [TD/B/C.I/4]; and the global economic crisis: implications for trade and development [TD/B/C.I/CRP.1]. It also considered reports of the multi-year expert meetings on transport and trade facilitation [TD/B/C.I/MEM.1/3]; commodities and development [TD/B/C.I/MEM.2/5]; services, development and trade: the regulatory and institutional dimension [TD/B/C.I/MEM.3/3 & Corr.1]; and international cooperation: South-South cooperation and regional integration [TD/B/C.II/MEM.2/3]. Other documents before the Commission included the report of the Intergovernmental Group of Experts on Competition Law and Policy [TD/B/C.I/CLP/6], and reports of the single-year expert meetings on mainstreaming gender in trade policy [TD/B/C.I/EM.2/4] and on trade and climate change: trade and investment opportunities and challenges under the Clean Development Mechanism [TD/B/C.I/EM.1/3].

The UNCTAD Secretary-General, addressing the session, stated that the economic and financial crisis was being transmitted to developing countries through mutually reinforcing declines in exports of goods, services and commodities, and declines in commodity prices, remittances, investments and the availability of finance. That necessitated serious reflection on the process of globalization, the extent of developing countries' dependence on external sources of growth, the potential of domestic demand, resistance against protectionist trends, enhanced trade financing, reinforced South-South trade and cooperation, and more comprehensive development partnerships. Regarding the trade and development aspects of energy, the challenge was to make energy affordable and sustainable in a context of dramatic price fluctuations exacerbated by speculation, inadequate access to energy by many people in developing countries, investment needs, declining fossil fuel reserves, climate change challenges, and the financial and economic crisis. Economic stimulus should prioritize energy-related investment and trade, as well as the greater use of renewable energy. Delegates requested UNCTAD to further analyse the global crisis and help countries to take measures to mitigate its impact and increase development, provide assistance to UNCTAD member States on development issues in trade negotiations, and continue to provide a platform for dialogue and exchange of experiences and best practices.

In agreed conclusions, the Commission took note of the UNCTAD report on the global economic crisis:

implications for trade and development [TD/B/C.I/ CRP.1]. It requested UNCTAD to continue its analytical work on the impact of the global economic crisis on trade and development, especially on developing countries, and to periodically report its findings to member States. UNCTAD was asked to help countries to assess the trade and development impact of the global crisis on their economies, consider policy options and strategies for mitigation measures, build resilience, and engender sustainable development processes that promoted the achievement of internationally agreed development goals, including the MDGs.

TDB, at its forty-seventh executive session [A/64/15 (Part III)], took note of the Commission's report and endorsed the agreed conclusions contained therein.

Development strategies in a globalized world

In September [A/64/15 (Part IV)], TDB discussed development strategies in a globalized world: meeting the development challenges of climate change. Delegations based their discussion on the chapter of the *Trade and Development Report, 2009* on the compatibility of development and poverty reduction strategies with the imperative of climate change mitigation. They noted that many countries that had contributed least to climate change, especially many LDCs and small island developing States, were among those hardest hit by its effects. Climate change mitigation was considered to be one of several major challenges for developing countries, and it was felt that mitigation measures could not come at the expense of economic growth and poverty reduction. Delegations welcomed the balanced assessment of the microeconomic and macroeconomic costs of climate change mitigation put forward by UNCTAD and its emphasis on mitigation as a process of structural change. It was widely recognized that in order for development and poverty reduction strategies to be sustainable, they would need to include climate change mitigation and adaptation efforts. Delegations stressed that all countries would need to intensify their efforts to reduce greenhouse gas emissions. Developed countries had the ethical responsibilities, as well as the technological and financial capabilities, to lead mitigation efforts. There was wide consensus that technology and knowledge transfers to developing countries were necessary to facilitate a shift towards renewable sources of energy, the introduction of greener methods of production, and the development of green technologies and goods. Delegations requested UNCTAD to consider the issue of climate change in its work on productive capacities, trade, investment and technology, as well as its work on South-South cooperation and development strategies.

Trade promotion and facilitation

In 2009, UN bodies continued to assist developing countries and transition economies in promoting their exports and facilitating their integration into the multilateral trading system. The main originator of technical cooperation projects in that area was the International Trade Centre, under the joint sponsorship of UNCTAD and WTO.

International Trade Centre

According to its Annual Report 2009 [ITC/ AG(XLIV)/233 & Add.1], the UNCTAD/WTO International Trade Centre (ITC), increased its delivery of technical assistance by nearly 7 per cent to $31.5 million, from $29.4 million in 2008. The largest portion of programme funds was spent in Africa (47 per cent), followed by Asia and the Pacific (14 per cent), Latin America and the Caribbean (8 per cent), the Arab States (5 per cent), and Europe and the Commonwealth of Independent States (5 per cent). The remainder (21 per cent) was spent on global projects. The share of the technical cooperation expenditure for LDCs rose to 48 per cent.

During the year, ITC conducted the 2009 Client Survey which allowed it to gain better understanding of the impact of its products and services. It set up a dedicated unit to manage the process of scaling up for large programmes including the Netherlands Trust Fund. It also implemented the recommendations related to project-cycle management, ensuring synergies in project design across ITC and an increased ability for robust reporting. In addition, it held the first ever conference for women in the coffee sector in Africa, bringing together international and regional trade support institutions to increase opportunities for African women in coffee production. It continued to provide clients with monthly trade data to improve their knowledge of international markets. ITC also held 297 workshops and training sessions, with a combined total of 9,991 participants, of whom 3,149 were women, and conducted 172 operational projects. On programme delivery response, ITC updated its 2009–2012 Strategic Plan [YUN 2008, p. 1055]. Delivery of multi-year projects progressed unevenly, as ITC sought to improve product design. Work was due to start in 11 countries and three regions in the Programme for Building African Capacity for Trade, the Enhancing Arab Capacity for Trade and the Netherlands Trust Fund II programmes. Some of the new programmes, however, did not make as much progress in 2009 as planned, and some activities and expenditures had to be rescheduled for 2010. Particular attention was paid to clarifying and defining ITC partnerships with UNCTAD and WTO.

Joint Advisory Group

UNCTAD consideration. At its fifty-sixth session (Geneva, 14–25 September and 12 October) [A/64/15 (Part IV)], TDB took note of the ITC Joint Advisory Group (JAG) report on its forty-second session [YUN 2008, p. 1056].

JAG session. JAG, at its forty-third session (14–15 December) [ITC/AG(XLIII)/232], considered the annual report on ITC activities in 2008 [YUN 2008, p. 1055] and the preliminary report [ITC/AG(XLIII)/230] on 2009 activities; the consolidated programme document for 2010 [ITC/AG(XLIII)/229]; and the ITC strategic plan 2010–2013 [ITC/AG(XLIII)/228]. Statements were made by the WTO Director-General, the UNCTAD Deputy Secretary-General and the ITC Executive Director. Delegates emphasized the need for ITC to focus on its areas of comparative advantage, in particular working to build the capacity of small and medium-sized enterprises to integrate into the world trading system, and to enhance the performance of the trade support institutions that existed to support them. Regarding efforts to achieve the MDGs [YUN 2000, p. 51], delegates noted the importance of incorporating climate change, which would likely affect the poorest countries disproportionately, into ITC programmes, along with other environmental issues. Concern was expressed by some delegations that certain regions appeared to be receiving less support from ITC than was needed, and ITC was urged to develop larger programmes in those countries and regions.

The Consolidated Programme Document 2010 focused on providing clear description of ITC plans by region and area of work; described the links between ITC work and the MDGs; and provided greater detail on planned achievements and outcomes, sources of funding, and the intended uses of extrabudgetary funds. Delegates noted that poverty reduction was the overarching objective underpinning all ITC export and trade support work, and called for ITC to develop clearer indicators to measure the impact of trade and export programmes on poverty. Concern was expressed that a large part of extrabudgetary funding, which was projected to cover 55 per cent of ITC delivery in 2010, was hard earmarked. Delegates questioned how ITC would maintain its focus on strategic objectives given the level of reliance on extrabudgetary funds and donor earmarking, and expressed concern that increasing demands on the organization could make it less effective.

The Acting Deputy Executive Director stated that key elements of the Strategic Plan 2010–2013 included greater prominence given to the Aid for Trade programme [YUN 2005, p. 1043], including support to countries seeking WTO accession; taking into account the current global challenges; intensified collaboration with partner agencies; the improvement of quality assurance processes; and the shift in the ITC portfolio to domination by a number of multi-year programmes. Several delegations felt that while progress had been made, more needed to be done to align the Plan with results-based management approaches, and there were several requests for the establishment of clear baselines to facilitate performance measurements. There was also a need for greater clarity in articulating and defining objectives at various levels and the links between them. There were calls to strengthen analytical work to demonstrate the links between ITC projects and programmes and the MDGs, particularly between trade and poverty reduction. Delegates urged ITC to engage in comprehensive feasibility studies involving local expertise before engaging in projects and programmes. The ITC Executive Director, in her response to the issues raised during the meeting, said that prioritization between programmes and projects in the event of limited financial resources would be done in line with the priorities set out in the Strategic Plan, and that it was vital to maintain a balance between achieving impact and spreading services too thinly.

Pledges of trust fund contributions to ITC were announced by Canada, China, Finland, Germany, the Netherlands, New Zealand, Norway, Romania, Sweden, Switzerland and the United Kingdom.

ITC administrative and budgetary arrangements

In accordance with arrangements approved by the General Assembly in resolution 59/276 [YUN 2004, p. 1383], the Secretary General, in March [A/64/6 (Sect. 13)], submitted preliminary budget estimates for ITC for the 2010–2011 biennium. Requirements, expressed in Swiss francs (SwF) at 2008–2009 rates, were estimated at SwF 74,473,700. Since SwF 700,000 from various sources would be available to ITC during the biennium, the contribution of each organization (United Nations and WTO) was estimated at SwF 36,886,850 at 2008–2009 rates for the 2010–2011 biennium.

In October [A/64/6 (Sect. 13)/Add.1], the Secretary-General submitted revised budget estimates. The contribution of each organization was estimated at Swf 37,557,600, or $31,298,000.

In November [A/64/7/Add.10], ACABQ recommended that the Assembly approve the revised proposals, subject to the recommendations outlined by the Committee.

The Assembly, in section I of **resolution 64/245** of 24 December (see p. 1406), approved an amount of $29,459,792 for the 2010–2011 biennium.

Investment, enterprise and development

The Investment, Enterprise and Development Commission, established by UNCTAD XII [YUN 2008, p. 1044], at its first session (Geneva, 4–8 May) [TD/B/C.II/5], considered the report on releasing the productive capacities and boosting enterprise development through improved transparency, simplification and automation of administrative procedures [TD/B/C.II/2]; UNCTAD secretariat note on exchange of experiences: investment policy reviews, lessons learned and best practices [TD/B/C.II/3]; and the progress report on the implementation of the provisions of the 2008 Accra Accord [YUN 2008, p. 1042] related to the areas of work covered by the Commission [TD/B/C.II/4]. Also before the Commission were reports of the multi-year expert meetings on enterprise development policies and capacity-building in science, technology and innovation [TD/B/C.II/MEM.1/4 & Corr.1]; international cooperation: South-South Cooperation and Regional Integration [TD/B/C.II/MEM.2/3]; and investment for development [TD/B/C.II/MEM.3/3], as well as the report of the Intergovernmental Working Group of Experts on of the International Standards of Accounting and Reporting [TD/B/C.II/ISAR/51, Corr.1 & Corr.2] [YUN 2008, p. 1093].

In agreed conclusions, the Commission expressed its concern about the impact of the global economic crisis on foreign direct investment (FDI) flows, the drastic decline of which threatened to erode development gains. It requested UNCTAD to continue strengthening its analytical research on FDI and its development implications and encouraged UNCTAD to further strengthen its research and analysis in the area of science, technology and innovation, in response to the Accra Accord. UNCTAD was also asked to assist in collecting quality data on FDI and transnational corporation activities, and the Commission called on development partners to support UNCTAD technical cooperation in that regard. The Commission called on UNCTAD to continue its role as the UN focal point for international investment agreements and to support the African Insurance Organization to strengthen the African insurance sector through advisory services and capacity-building. The Commission noted UNCTAD assistance to help countries boost administrative efficiency through e-government practices, in accordance with the Accra Accord; and requested UNCTAD to extend its support to more countries, reinforce its analytical work towards identifying relevant good practices and policies, and facilitate sharing them among UNCTAD member States.

The Commission took note of the reports of the multi-year expert meetings and requested the UNCTAD Secretary-General to ensure the greatest possible dissemination of the outcomes of the meetings, in particular to government policymakers. It encouraged the secretariat to follow up on issues identified by the expert meetings and requested UNCTAD to take into account the different needs and circumstances of countries according to the Accra Accord when implementing the Commission's conclusions. UNCTAD was asked to continue to analyse trends in international investment agreements and international investment law, and provide research and policy analysis on key and emerging issues, development implications and the impact of technical assistance and capacity-building in that area, in accordance with the Accra Accord. The Commission endorsed the conduct of voluntary peer reviews on enterprise development policies and innovation. Regarding single-year expert meetings, the Commission encouraged UNCTAD to enhance its support to sustainable development and consider climate change in its ongoing work of assisting developing countries with trade- and investment-related issues in development strategies, taking into consideration the 1992 United Nations Framework Convention on Climate Change [YUN 1992, p. 681].

TDB, at its forty-seventh executive session (Geneva, 30 June) [A/64/15 (Part III)], took note of the Commission's report and endorsed the agreed conclusions contained therein.

Commodities

The joint UNCTAD/DESA report *World Economic Situation and Prospects 2010* [Sales No. E.10.II.C.2] stated that commodity prices reached a historic peak in mid-2008 but fell sharply as a consequence of the global economic and financial crisis. Non-oil commodity prices rebounded from the second quarter of 2009, rising 20 per cent in the composite index between April and August 2009. The price index of minerals, ores and metals rose by 38 per cent between March and August 2009, but was weaker in the case of food and tropical beverages, which showed world price increases of 11 and 15 per cent, respectively.

In early January, Brent crude oil prices rose to almost $50 per barrel (pb) and subsequently fluctuated between $40 pb and $50 pb until the second half of March, when prices moved beyond the $50 pb mark with the announcement of stimulus measures by individual Governments and central banks. The crude oil price peaked at $71.55 pb in mid-June but fell back to about $59 pb in the first half of July. From August through October, however, the offsetting effects of greater optimism and continued high inventories appeared to keep crude oil prices at about $70 pb.

UNCTAD report. In response to General Assembly resolution 63/207 [YUN 2008, p. 1059], the Secretary-General transmitted to the Assembly in July [A/64/184] a UNCTAD secretariat report on world

commodity trends and prospects. The report discussed the recent boom and downturn in the commodity markets; the volatility of commodity markets
and prices; and implications of the financial crisis for
commodity trade and finance, and for commodity
exporting and importing countries. The report stated
that in 2009 commodity prices stabilized and started
slowly to recover after reaching their trough at the beginning of the year. However, many developing countries, including commodity exporters and importers,
would probably not be able to achieve the MDGs [YUN
2000, p. 51] by 2015 due to the volatile international
economic environment. UNCTAD negotiations in the
twentieth century aimed at introducing more stability
to commodity markets through internationally managed commodity buffer stocks did not succeed, and
commodity risk management techniques at the micro
level, including futures trading, also failed to resolve
the problems of instability and sometimes even aggravated them.

National and international strategies to develop
both the agricultural and minerals sectors needed to
be complementary and mutually supportive. Increasing food production in poor countries, particularly
in Africa, by raising agricultural productivity, should
be considered a priority. It was important to improve
the functioning of national and regional food markets in order to encourage increased and diversified
production by small farmers. Measures to remedy the
situation should include improving access to credit
based on secure titles to land, as well as the creation of
local and national markets. It was also important that
the role of farmers' cooperatives be reinforced so that
small and isolated farmers could be more efficient in
buying inputs, accessing finance and investing. Selective government support, in the framework of sound
national lands and strategies, could facilitate the conditions for agricultural development. Support measures could include direct financing by agricultural
development banks, the creation of research and development centres to work closely with cooperatives,
and the establishment of experimental agricultural
production centres that encouraged diversification
and value addition.

For the extractive industries, key policy issues included more efficient and transparent revenue management and fair conditions surrounding investments.
Countries with strong public-sector companies in the
oil and other mineral sectors should help those companies acquire the modern technologies and skills
needed to effectively manage the extractive industries.
Countries that were more reliant on foreign investment should help their companies attain fair conditions of cooperation with transnational corporations,
which would entail technology transfers and training
of local staff. The international community should
support fully the twin objective of making extractive

industries profitable and an engine for development
and diversification.

Low-income developing countries that were net
importers of food and other commodities needed to
receive continuous support from international financial institutions and the development community at
large to meet their basic commodity needs without
compromising their socio-economic development
programmes. The reinforcement of the UNCTAD
mandate on commodities, as stipulated in the Accra Accord [YUN 2008, p. 1057], held the possibility
of bringing together all key stakeholders of the commodity economy, thus allowing ideas agreed upon at
high-level, multi-stakeholder meetings to feed into
an intergovernmental process and national and regional commodity policies. Improving on policies
and adopting transparent and equitable rules should
permit the commodity sector to become an engine for
development and a key instrument for poverty reduction. For the more than 90 countries that depended
on primary commodities for the majority of their
exports, better policy and institutional frameworks
and public-private partnerships would eventually permit better integration in commodity supply chains,
improved possibilities for the diversification of their
economies and, hence, better prospects for their social
and economic development.

In conclusion, the report stated, it was essential
that the collective response to the crisis included
policies that would address longer-term structural issues of the commodity economy and integrate commodity policies into wider development and poverty
reduction strategies. The international community,
including UNCTAD, could contribute to that end by
making renewed efforts to build consensus. To reinforce such a process, UNCTAD was initiating a series of
multi-stakeholder commodity forums and high-level
consultations, thereby laying the ground for more
consensual approaches.

GENERAL ASSEMBLY ACTION

On 21 December [meeting 66], the General Assembly,
on the recommendation of the Second Committee
[A/64/418/Add.4], adopted **resolution 64/192** without
vote [agenda item 51 (d)].

Commodities

The General Assembly,

Recalling its resolutions 59/224 of 22 December 2004,
61/190 of 20 December 2006 and 63/207 of 19 December
2008 on commodities,

Recalling also the United Nations Millennium Declaration adopted by Heads of State and Government on 8 September 2000, the 2005 World Summit Outcome adopted
on 16 September 2005 and its resolution 60/265 of 30 June
2006 on the follow-up to the development outcome of the

2005 World Summit, including the Millennium Development Goals and the other internationally agreed development goals,

Recalling further the International Conference on Financing for Development and its outcome,

Recalling the Plan of Implementation of the World Summit on Sustainable Development ("Johannesburg Plan of Implementation"),

Recalling also the Programme of Action for the Least Developed Countries for the Decade 2001–2010 and the outcome of the high-level meeting of the sixty-first session of the General Assembly on the midterm comprehensive global review of the implementation of the Programme of Action for the Least Developed Countries for the Decade 2001–2010, held in New York on 18 and 19 September 2006, and taking note of *The Least Developed Countries Report, 2009: The State and Development Governance,*

Taking note of the Arusha Declaration and Plan of Action on African Commodities adopted by the African Union Conference of Ministers of Trade on Commodities, held in Arusha, United Republic of Tanzania, from 21 to 23 November 2005, and endorsed by the Executive Council of the African Union at its eighth ordinary session, held in Khartoum from 16 to 21 January 2006,

Taking note also of the targets set out in the Rome Declaration on World Food Security and the World Food Summit Plan of Action and the Declaration of the World Food Summit: five years later, which reaffirms the pledge to end hunger and poverty,

Welcoming the World Summit on Food Security, held in Rome from 16 to 18 November 2009, and its decision to create a Global Partnership for Agriculture, Food Security and Nutrition, the High-level Conference on World Food Security: the Challenges of Climate Change and Bioenergy, held in Rome from 3 to 5 June 2008, and the Summits of the Group of Eight held in Hokkaido, Japan, from 7 to 9 July 2008 and in L'Aquila, Italy, from 8 to 10 July 2009,

Taking note of the outcome document of the Follow-up International Conference on Financing for Development to Review the Implementation of the Monterrey Consensus, held in Doha from 29 November to 2 December 2008,

Taking note also of the Political Declaration of the High-level Meeting on Africa's Development Needs, held in New York on 22 September 2008,

Taking note further of the Accra Accord, adopted by the United Nations Conference on Trade and Development at its twelfth session, containing far-reaching recommendations on commodity issues, and of further decisions and agreed conclusions on commodities adopted by the Trade and Development Board and its subsidiary bodies in 2008 and 2009,

Recognizing that many developing countries continue to be highly dependent on primary commodities as their principal source of export revenues, employment, income generation and domestic savings, and as the driving force of investment, economic growth and social development, including poverty eradication,

Deeply concerned by recent episodes of commodity price booms and subsequent busts and by the fact that many commodity-dependent developing countries and economies in transition continue to be highly vulnerable to price fluctuations, and recognizing the need to improve the regu-

lation, functioning, and transparency of financial and commodity markets in order to address excessive commodity price volatility,

Recognizing that the present crisis has reinforced the need to comprehensively deal with the commodity problematique, while taking due account of the diversity of each country's individual situation and needs and the promotion of their sustainable development, and to strengthen the nexus between trade, food, finance, investment in sustainable agriculture, energy and industrialization,

Taking note of the United Nations Conference on Trade and Development *World Investment Report, 2009: Transnational Corporations, Agricultural Production and Development,*

Taking note also of the initiative on promoting responsible international investment in agriculture, which aims to develop relevant principles and an international framework,

Recognizing that the current economic crisis has impacted negatively on the commodity economy, as evidenced, inter alia, by the decline in demand for commodities, diminishing supply capacities owing to shrinking commodity revenues and postponement of investments, resulting in an economic slowdown in commodity-dependent economies,

Noting that the report on world commodity trends and prospects prepared by the secretariat of the United Nations Conference on Trade and Development shows that the recent sharp drop in commodity prices has been followed by a partial recovery in prices during the first months of 2009,

Stressing the importance of policies to address longer-term structural issues of the commodity economy and integrate commodity policies into wider development and poverty eradication strategies at all levels,

Taking note of all relevant voluntary initiatives aimed at improving transparency in commodity markets,

1. *Takes note* of the note by the Secretary-General transmitting the report on world commodity trends and prospects prepared by the secretariat of the United Nations Conference on Trade and Development;

2. *Underscores* the need for further efforts to address excessive commodity price volatility, in particular by assisting producers, especially small-scale producers, in managing risk;

3. *Emphasizes* the need for efforts by the developing countries that are heavily dependent on primary commodities to continue to promote a domestic policy and an institutional environment that encourage diversification and liberalization of the trade and export sectors and enhance competitiveness;

4. *Reaffirms* that each country has primary responsibility for its own economic and social development, and recognizes the importance of an effective enabling environment at the national and international levels;

5. *Calls for* a coherent set of policy actions at national, regional and international levels to address excessive price volatility and support commodity-dependent developing countries in mitigating negative impacts, in particular by facilitating value addition and enhancing their participation in commodity and related product value chains, by supporting large-scale diversification of these economies and by encouraging the use and further development of market-oriented risk management tools;

6. *Recognizes* the potential for innovation, productivity improvements and promotion of non-traditional exports in most commodity-dependent developing countries, particularly in Africa, and calls for enhanced support by the international community as well as exchanges of experience in these areas within the framework of South-South economic cooperation;

7. *Calls upon* the international community to work closely with commodity-dependent economies to identify trade-related policies and instruments as well as investment and financial policies as key elements of the development strategies of those economies;

8. *Underscores* the importance of increased investments in infrastructure as a means of promoting agricultural development and enhancing commodity diversification and trade, and urges the international community to assist commodity-dependent developing countries;

9. *Expresses concern* over the large-scale land acquisitions by, among others, transnational corporations in developing countries that incur risk to development efforts, stresses the importance of promoting responsible international investment in agriculture, and in this regard invites the United Nations Conference on Trade and Development, in cooperation with other relevant international organizations, to continue its research and analysis on this issue;

10. *Stresses* that technical assistance and capacity-building aimed at improving the commodity export competitiveness of producers is particularly important, especially in Africa, and invites the donor community to provide necessary resources for commodity-specific, financial and technical assistance, in particular for human and institutional capacity-building, as well as infrastructure development of developing countries, with a view to reducing their institutional bottlenecks and transaction costs and enhancing their commodity trade and development in accordance with national development plans;

11. *Also stresses* that the Aid for Trade Initiative should aim to help developing countries, particularly least developed countries, to build the supply-side capacity and trade-related infrastructure that they need to assist them to implement and benefit from World Trade Organization agreements and, more broadly, to expand their trade;

12. *Calls upon* the international community to take urgent measures for food security, including immediate and adequate provision of food grain in developing countries suffering from shortages, in particular least developed countries, while supporting the efforts of those countries to achieve longer-term food security and sustainable agricultural development, and notes, furthermore, that food aid should be provided in a manner that does not disrupt domestic markets and food production;

13. *Underlines* the important contribution of the commodities sector to rural development, in particular to providing rural employment and income, and to the efforts for achieving food security;

14. *Emphasizes* the importance of international measures and national strategies to improve the performance of the agricultural sector, including the functioning of markets and trading systems, to ensure a better supply-side response from producers, in particular, small farmers, in order to incentivize them to take the risks inherent in investing in increased and diversified production;

15. *Stresses* the importance of finding tools to best manage excessive price volatility, and requests the United Nations Conference on Trade and Development to carry out a study with a view to making specific recommendations on measures which could achieve more stability in commodity markets;

16. *Calls for* the conclusion of the Doha Development Round of trade negotiations of the World Trade Organization in 2010 with an ambitious, balanced and development-oriented outcome;

17. *Reaffirms its commitment* to meaningful trade liberalization and to ensure that trade plays its full part in promoting economic growth, employment and development for all;

18. *Emphasizes* that maximizing the benefits and minimizing the costs of international trade liberalization call for development-oriented and coherent policies at all levels;

19. *Recalls* the agreement to keep under regular review, by the Ministerial Conference and appropriate organs of the World Trade Organization, the impact of the results of the Uruguay Round on the least developed countries as well as on the net food-importing developing countries, with a view to fostering positive measures to enable them to achieve their development objectives, and in this regard calls for the implementation of the Marrakech Decision on Measures Concerning the Possible Negative Effects of the Reform Programme on Least Developed and Net Food-Importing Developing Countries;

20. *Welcomes* the actions taken by some individual countries since the International Conference on Financing for Development in Monterrey, Mexico, towards the goal of full duty-free and quota-free market access for all least developed countries, and calls upon other developed and developing countries, declaring themselves in a position to do so, to take steps towards this objective;

21. *Calls upon* international financial institutions and development banks to assist commodity-dependent developing countries in managing the effects of price volatility, and in this regard invites those countries to continue to implement effective economic and fiscal measures;

22. *Reaffirms* that every State has and shall freely exercise full permanent sovereignty over all its wealth, natural resources and economic activities;

23. *Recognizes* the importance of increasing efficiency and effectiveness in the management of public and private sectors revenues in developed and developing countries derived from all commodities and commodities-related industries, including final processed goods, in support of development;

24. *Recognizes* the important contributions of the Common Fund for Commodities and other international commodities organizations, and encourages them, in cooperation with the International Trade Centre UNCTAD/WTO, the United Nations Conference on Trade and Development and other relevant bodies, to continue to strengthen and study ways to establish greater stability in the commodities market as well as to enhance activities in developing countries to improve access to markets and reliability of supply, enhancing diversification and addition of value, improving the competitiveness of commodities, strengthening the market chain, improving market structures, broadening the export base and ensuring the effective participation of all stakeholders;

25. *Stresses* that the United Nations Conference on Trade and Development and its partners, in the spirit of inter-agency cooperation and multi-stakeholder partnerships and within their respective mandates, should continue to engage actively in collaborative research and analysis of the commodity problematique and related capacity and consensus-building activities with a view to providing regular analysis and policy advice relevant to the sustainable development of commodity-dependent developing countries, particularly low-income countries;

26. *Underscores* the urgent need for the provision of, and access to, trade finance to commodity-dependent developing countries, given the tightened access to all types of credit and noting debt sustainability;

27. *Stresses* the importance of the continuing substantive consideration of the sub-item entitled "Commodities", and decides to include the sub-item in the provisional agenda of its sixty-sixth session, under the item entitled "Macroeconomic policy questions";

28. *Requests* the Secretary-General, in collaboration with the secretariat of the United Nations Conference on Trade and Development, to submit to the General Assembly at its sixty-sixth session a report on the implementation of the present resolution with recommendations and on world commodity trends and prospects, including on the causes of the excessive commodity price volatility.

Individual commodities

Cocoa. As at 31 December, there were 11 signatories and 18 parties to the International Cocoa Agreement, 2001 [YUN 2001, p. 880]. Nicaragua became a party during the year.

Sugar. As at 31 December, the International Sugar Agreement, 1992 [YUN 1992, p. 625] had 22 signatories and 60 parties. Argentina and Morocco became parties during the year.

Timber. As at 31 December, there were 50 signatories and 41 parties to the International Tropical Timber Agreement, 2006 [YUN 2006, p. 1124]. During the year, Austria, Cambodia, Canada, Estonia, Germany, Ireland, Luxembourg, Mali and Slovakia signed the Agreement, and 23 States became parties.

Common Fund for Commodities

The 1980 Agreement establishing the Common Fund for Commodities [YUN 1980, p. 621], a mechanism intended to stabilize the commodities market by helping to finance buffer stocks of specific commodities, as well as commodity development activities such as research and marketing, entered into force in 1989, and the Fund became operational later that year. As at 31 December, the Agreement had 115 signatories and 117 parties. During the year, the Economic Community of West African States, the Eurasian Economic Community and the West African Economic and Monetary Union became parties.

Finance

On 21 December (**decision 64/540**), the Assembly took note of the report of the Second Committee [A/64/418] on its discussion of macroeconomic policy questions, including those related to the international financial system and development, and external debt and development.

Financial policy

The *World Economic Situation and Prospects 2010* [Sales No. E.10.II.C.2] stated that, since the intensification of the financial crisis that began in 2008 [YUN 2008, p. 1102], Governments had made available massive public funding to recapitalize banks, taking partial or full ownership of ailing financial institutions and providing guarantees on bank deposits and other financial assets. Publically guaranteed funding for financial sector rescue operations worldwide was estimated at about $20 trillion, or some 30 per cent of world gross product. Monetary and fiscal policy stances were strongly counter-cyclical in most major economies. The policies helped stabilize global financial markets, support global effective demand and alleviate the economic and social impact of the crisis, but were not sufficient to induce a self-sustained recovery process. Financial weaknesses needed to be addressed and many developing countries were not able to implement significant counter-cyclical policies on their own. Policy responses were concerted to some extent among major economies, in particular at the level of the Group of 20 (G20) nations. At their 2009 summits (London, 2 April and Pittsburgh, Pennsylvania, United States, 24–25 September), leaders promised to continue the stimulus and other extraordinary measures as long as necessary; pledged to deliver on all aid and other international development commitments and fight off protectionist tendencies; and facilitated a significant increase in resources for countries with external financing problems. The G20 provided $1.1 trillion for that purpose, including through tripling the resources available to the International Monetary Fund (IMF), facilitating additional lending by multilateral development banks and supporting trade finance.

The immediate challenge for policymakers was to determine how long the fiscal stimulus should continue, as a premature withdrawal of stimulus could result in a second recession.

Three forms of rebalancing of the global economy would have to take place over time to avoid a return to the unsustainable pattern of growth that led to the global crisis and avoid the risk of a second recession. First, pressure on Governments to hold up global demand would need to diminish through private demand. Second, the composition of aggregate demand would need to rebalance to shift greater weight to investment in support of future productivity and the transformation of energy sectors and infrastructure required to address climate change. Third, demand across countries needed to be rebalanced. Additional financial transfers to developing countries with weak fiscal capacity would be needed to complete the rebalancing process. The transfers would enable those countries to increase domestic investment in infrastructure, food production and human development so as to support growth, poverty reduction and sustainable development. They would also encourage global import demand. A successful framework for international macroeconomic policy coordination should consist of at least four components: developing a consensus on common goals through international consultations with outside mediation; addressing commitment problems by issuing multi-year schedules for policy adjustments; enhancing the context for mediation and the perceived legitimacy of the mediator; and initiating systemic reforms in the field of international monetary and financial affairs. The success of the framework would depend on progress in the broad reforms of the international financial architecture and global economic governance.

The report stated that global economic governance should be strengthened on four fronts. First, multilateral surveillance by IMF would need to be extended beyond the emphasis on exchange rates to monitor the global economy's "sustainable rebalancing" process. Second, more pervasive progress on governance reform of IMF would be needed to add legitimacy to its enhanced role in that regard and for mediating multi-annual agreements. Third, verifiable targets for desired policy outcomes should be in place to help make parties accountable. Fourth, sustainable rebalancing of the global economy would require close coordination with other areas of global governance, including those related to development financing and the multilateral trading system, as well as with the 1992 United Nations Framework Convention on Climate Change [YUN 1992, p. 681]. The report concluded by calling for urgent progress in reforming the global financial system to prevent a similar crisis from occurring again.

Communications. On 8 April [A/63/872], Portugal, in its capacity as Co-Chair of the African Partnership Forum, transmitted to the Secretary-General key messages from the Forum to the London G20 Summit related to fiscal stimulus, trade, investment, strengthened international cooperation on tax and illicit financial flows, and systemic reform of the international system.

On 23 September [A/64/373], Portugal transmitted to the Secretary-General key messages from the Forum to the Pittsburgh G20 Summit related to financial supervision and regulation, governance of international financial institutions, crisis mitigation and recovery, development resources, agriculture and food security, and global governance. The Forum called on the G20 for Africa's representation in global governance mechanisms and to maintain urgent action against the financial and economic crisis. Africa needed support from its partners to increase agricultural production in order to enhance food security for the attainment of the MDGs and sustainable growth.

Financial flows

The *World Economic Situation and Prospects 2010* reported that developing countries were expected to continue to provide net financial resources to developed countries in 2009 at a level of $568 billion, notably lower than the all-time high of $891 billion reached in 2008. The forecast reduction reflected the tentative narrowing of the global imbalances as a consequence of the global economic and financial crisis. The crisis affected net financial transfers from developing countries in all regions in 2009. Western Asia experienced the strongest decline in net resource flows, driven in particular by lower oil prices. Latin America and the Caribbean experienced lower outward investment on a net basis as the value of their export earnings declined in line with the contraction of world trade in goods. East and South Asia were the only regions where, in the aggregate, negative net transfers increased moderately in 2009. Despite a narrowing of current-account surpluses, reserve accumulation resumed at a strong pace. Net transfers from countries with economies in transition decreased from $153 billion in 2008 to $90 billion in 2009, owing mainly to the economic downturn in the Russian Federation, where the sharp decline in commodity prices and the reduction in global demand for manufactured goods in the first half of 2009 required Government intervention in the form of counter-cyclical fiscal measures.

In developing countries, the drastic downward adjustment of export sectors was imposing severe and potentially long-lasting hardships on women and the poor. Significant declines in public sector revenues in developing countries as a consequence of the fall in exports were setting off fiscal deficits and new pressures to borrow, thus increasing the prospect of a resurgence of debt-servicing defaults later. Developing countries had been attracting high and growing levels of private capital flows since 2002, but that trend reversed sharply in the second half of 2008. All components of private capital flows registered significant declines, and all cross-border capital flows, including FDI, foreign equities, debt securities and cross-border lending, experienced a steep and simultaneous fall-off. The sharp correction in cross-border lending was the biggest contributor to the contraction in capital flows, exerting severe funding pressures on developing countries.

Countries with large current-account deficits, and therefore the most dependent on foreign capital, were hardest hit by the substantial tightening of credit conditions in international markets, but even middle-income countries with current-account surplus positions were substantially affected, as a sell-off in assets triggered a marked depreciation of exchange rates in a large number of economies. The reversal continued through the first quarter of 2009, with net capital flows to developing countries shifting further downwards on an annualized basis. However, signs of stabilization had become noticeable since the second quarter in various parts of the financial market as a result of stimulus packages and other policy measures to recapitalize financial institutions.

Economic development in Africa

UNCTAD activities in favour of Africa

The UNCTAD Trade and Development Board (TDB), at its forty-seventh executive session (Geneva, 30 June) [A/64/15 (Part III)], considered the UNCTAD secretariat report on activities undertaken in favour of Africa [TD/B/EX(47)/2], which provided an overview of research and analysis undertaken by UNCTAD with regard to Africa's development and summarized specific activities, including advisory services and technical cooperation. UNCTAD supported African development through activities that enhanced governments' policymaking capacities in trade, investment, trade-supporting infrastructure, human development and institution-building, in order to ensure more effective development governance. Initiatives included efforts to: strengthen trade-facilitation and negotiation capacities through trade technical assistance; diversify production of agricultural, oil and mineral commodities; enhance service-sector technological capacities in trade, transport and the Internet; offer operational and strategic debt management support; and provide capacity-building activities for investment, enterprise development and insurance.

Although UNCTAD contributed to a broad stream of national and international policy analysis, estimating the impact of such analysis could be complex. An evaluation process was being established to solicit feedback from research and policy initiatives to ensure that the quality and utility of the work served the needs of Africa. In the field of investment, it was clear that an increasing number of African Governments had adopted more effective and predictable incentives policies, as well as regulations for the promotion of FDI. A positive indicator was the continued

demand from African countries for a number of long-standing UNCTAD technical cooperation activities, including the Automated System for Customs Data, the Debt Management and Financial Analysis Management System, support to the negotiations of the Paris Club (a group of creditor countries), and other initiatives. There was also demand for expertise in attracting FDI and increasing investment development linkages, including in the area of investment policy reviews. Important steps were taken during the year to disseminate research findings at the country level through regional workshops and the elaboration of a policymaker's handbook.

In addition, TDB considered an April UNCTAD secretariat report [TD/B/EX(47)/3] on food security in Africa and lessons learned from the 2008 food crisis [YUN 2008, p. 1343]. The report stated that food security in many African countries remained a great concern months after the crisis. Prices of staple foods remained above their long-term averages, and over 300 million Africans continued to face chronic hunger. Ensuring food security in the region would require action to increase productivity, improve rural livelihoods and address international market imbalances. Measures to improve living and production conditions of rural populations included improving farmers' access to inputs and credit, increasing agricultural research and extension services, providing essential infrastructure, social safety nets, and protecting from short-term market fluctuations. International trade in commodities should be reviewed in order to prevent a small number of investors and buyers from having a disproportionate amount of influence on the price of staple foods while the producers had none. Concluding the agricultural aspects of the Doha round of trade negotiations was essential to improving market access for African agricultural producers. The report concluded that the food crisis demonstrated the vulnerability of African countries' food security, and that action was required to avoid a repeat of the crisis.

TDB took note of the reports on UNCTAD activities in favour of Africa and on lessons learned from the food crisis there.

Strengthening regional economic integration for Africa's development

TDB, at its fifty-sixth annual session (14–25 September and 12 October) [A/64/15 (Part IV)], considered economic development in Africa. It had before it the UNCTAD report entitled *Economic Development in Africa 2009—Strengthening Regional Economic Integration for Africa's Development* [Sales No. E.09.II.D.7], which focused on economic flows aspects of integration and included analysis of emerging issues including trade in services, investment, and migration within regional integration arrangements. The report described the evolution of African regional integration efforts; analysed intraregional trade performance in goods, the direction and composition of Africa's trade flows as well as their determinants; examined the global significance and scope of FDI flows among African countries, the determinants, and the geographical and sectoral distribution of such flows; explored intraregional performance in two emerging areas of regional integration in Africa—trade in services and migration; and discussed hindrances to expanding intraregional cooperation and proposals to improve performance in those areas.

The report stated that the global financial crisis required the re-examination of current approaches to international development. It found that regional integration—when designed and implemented within a broader development strategy to promote economic diversification, structural changes and technological development—could help enhance the productive capacities of African economies, realize economies of scale, improve competitiveness and serve as a starting point for African economies' effective participation in the global economy.

On 23 September [agreed conclusions 497(LVI)], TDB acknowledged that Africa had made progress in integrating its economies over the previous 50 years and that the impetus for regional integration was now stronger than ever before, as evidenced by the constant efforts of the African Union to deepen the continent's integration agenda. However, it noted with concern that regional efforts had not generated the expected increase in intra-African trade, investment and labour mobility. The Board recognized that building and maintaining hard infrastructure—including roads, railways, ports and telecommunications—and soft infrastructure—such as improvements in the policy and regulatory environment and in customs and border procedures, as well as other trade facilitation measures—should be a priority in promoting regional economic integration. It reaffirmed that the free movement of persons across Africa was a central component of regional integration and urged regional bodies to put in place mechanisms that would ensure that labour mobility benefited both host and sending countries, in order to encourage all countries to implement existing provisions governing labour mobility, tailored to countries' specific contexts. TDB emphasized that integration could be most effectively achieved as part of a broader, long-term development strategy, and countries should commit to implementing all the provisions governing regional integration as appropriate, giving priority to dialogue at the regional level. It recognized the importance of South-South cooperation in contributing to regional cooperation, and the importance of all development partners supporting Africa's regional economic integration

agenda; and requested UNCTAD to conduct further work in that regard. UNCTAD was also requested to produce a report on the feasibility of creating a web-based network linking the various African regional economic communities and dedicated to promoting intraregional investment and trade; and was encouraged, within its mandate and as agreed in the 2008 Accra Accord [YUN 2008, p. 1042], to undertake insightful and critical analysis with respect to Africa and to widen the dissemination of its research findings.

International financial system

Report of Secretary-General. In response to General Assembly resolution 63/205 [YUN 2008, p. 1069], the Secretary-General submitted a July report [A/64/178] on the international financial system and development, which complemented his reports on the follow-up to the outcome of the International Conference on Financing for Development and on the debt crisis and development. It reviewed recent trends in international official and private capital flows to developing countries and international policy challenges arising from the financial crisis, particularly the impact of the crisis on development financing. The report highlighted the challenges that needed to be addressed by the international community in reforming the financial system in light of the weaknesses exposed by the global financial crisis.

The report stated that developing countries continued to make substantial net outward transfers of financial resources to developed countries in 2009. The structure of flows indicated that, for the most part, a disorderly unwinding of accumulated global imbalances was under way. Private capital to developing countries dropped sharply in the wake of the global financial crisis; at the same time, external financing costs rose sharply for developing countries. Total net official development assistance (ODA) from Development Assistance Committee members rose in 2008 by 10.2 per cent in real terms $119.8 billion, reaching the highest dollar figure ever recorded, and reached 0.30 per cent of the combined gross national income of donors. However, the financial crisis might lead to decreased aid volumes and undo some of the progress made towards achieving the MDGs.

The Secretary-General outlined five key areas in which progress was urgently needed: international financial regulation, multilateral surveillance, IMF lending and resources, the international system of payments and reserves and governance reforms in the Bretton Woods institutions. He stated that the global financial crisis demonstrated the necessity of introducing an international regulatory system of the globalized financial system with sufficient transparency for investors and regulators. The G20 countries stated their shared intention to reshape regulatory systems in their Declaration on Strengthening the Financial System adopted in London on 2 April.

Since the onset of the crisis, IMF had been providing large-scale financing to countries experiencing a reduction in the availability of external funding. As at May 2009, IMF lending commitments had reached a record level of $157 billion, including a sharp increase in concessional lending to low-income countries. In March, the Flexible Credit Line, a crisis-prevention instrument, was established. The special high-level meeting of the Economic and Social Council with the Bretton Woods institutions (the World Bank Group and IMF), WTO and UNCTAD (New York, 27 April) (see p. 940), reached a consensus that there was a need for effective macroeconomic coordination mechanisms that were representative of all countries' interests and that could exercise strong policy leadership. The G20 called on IMF to complete, by January 2011, the next review of quotas, including further improvement of representation for emerging and developing countries.

The report concluded that in a financially integrated world, the enduring success of regulatory reforms depended in large part on significantly enhanced international cooperation, coordination and communication among regulators. The financial crisis underscored the need to redress the deficiencies of surveillance over mature financial markets and advanced economies and to better integrate macroeconomic and financial sector surveillance. It was necessary to build an effective framework for enhanced multilateral macroeconomic and financial policy coordination against the backdrop of planned governance reform in the international financial institutions. There was room for further innovation in how official liquidity was deployed, despite recent positive changes in multilateral lending facilities. In the medium term, it was important that the quota mechanism be restored as the primary basis of expanded IMF lending. The international community should seize the opportunity to start working on the creation of a new, more stable and equitable international monetary and financial system.

GENERAL ASSEMBLY ACTION

On 21 December [meeting 66], the General Assembly, on the recommendation of the Second Committee [A/64/418/Add.2], adopted **resolution 64/190** without vote [agenda item 51 (b)].

International financial system and development

The General Assembly,

Recalling its resolutions 55/186 of 20 December 2000 and 56/181 of 21 December 2001, both entitled "Towards a strengthened and stable international financial architecture responsive to the priorities of growth and development,

especially in developing countries, and to the promotion of economic and social equity", as well as its resolutions 57/241 of 20 December 2002, 58/202 of 23 December 2003, 59/222 of 22 December 2004, 60/186 of 22 December 2005, 61/187 of 20 December 2006, 62/185 of 19 December 2007 and 63/205 of 19 December 2008,

Recalling also the United Nations Millennium Declaration and its resolution 56/210 B of 9 July 2002, in which it endorsed the Monterrey Consensus of the International Conference on Financing for Development, and the Plan of Implementation of the World Summit on Sustainable Development ("Johannesburg Plan of Implementation"),

Recalling further the 2005 World Summit Outcome,

Recalling its resolution 60/265 of 30 June 2006 on the follow-up to the development outcome of the 2005 World Summit, including the Millennium Development Goals and the other internationally agreed development goals, and its resolution 61/16 of 20 November 2006 on strengthening of the Economic and Social Council,

Recalling also the Doha Declaration on Financing for Development: outcome document of the Follow-up International Conference on Financing for Development to Review the Implementation of the Monterrey Consensus, held in Doha from 29 November to 2 December 2008,

Recalling further the Conference on the World Financial and Economic Crisis and Its Impact on Development and its outcome,

Expressing deep concern over the adverse impact of the current world financial and economic crisis on development, which not only highlighted long-standing systemic fragilities and imbalances, but has also led to an intensification of efforts to reform and strengthen the international financial system and architecture,

Recognizing the substantive discussions held and the efforts made at the national, regional and international levels in response to the world financial and economic crisis,

Taking note of the decisions taken at the 2009 annual meetings of the International Monetary Fund and the World Bank, held in Istanbul, Turkey, on 6 and 7 October 2009,

Reaffirming the purposes of the United Nations, as set forth in the Charter, including to achieve international cooperation in solving international problems of an economic, social, cultural or humanitarian character and to be a centre for harmonizing the actions of nations in the attainment of common ends, and reiterating the need to strengthen the leadership role of the United Nations in promoting development,

Recalling the commitment to work in solidarity on a coordinated and comprehensive global response to the crisis and its impact on development and to undertake actions aimed at strengthening the role of the United Nations development system in responding to the crisis and its impact on development,

Stressing the importance of commitment to ensuring sound domestic financial sectors, which make a vital contribution to national development efforts, as an important component of an international financial architecture that is supportive of development,

Recognizing the continued importance of good governance along with national ownership of policies and strategies, and recalling the commitment to promoting effective and efficient economic and financial institutions at all levels, which are key determinants of long-term economic growth and development, as well as to accelerating the collective recovery from the crisis through improved transparency, eradication of corruption and strengthened governance,

Stressing that good governance at the international level is fundamental for achieving sustainable development, reiterating in this regard the importance of promoting global economic governance by addressing the international finance, trade, technology and investment patterns that have an impact on the development prospects of developing countries in order to ensure a dynamic and enabling international economic environment, and reiterating also that, to this effect, the international community should take all necessary and appropriate measures, including ensuring support for structural and macroeconomic reform, finding a comprehensive solution to the external debt problem and increasing the market access of developing countries,

Recognizing the urgent need to enhance the coherence, governance and consistency of the international monetary, financial and trading systems and the importance of ensuring their openness, fairness and inclusiveness in order to complement national development efforts to ensure sustained economic growth and the achievement of the internationally agreed development goals, including the Millennium Development Goals,

1. *Takes note* of the report of the Secretary-General;

2. *Reaffirms* that the United Nations, on the basis of its universal membership and legitimacy, is well positioned to participate in various reform processes aimed at improving and strengthening the effective functioning of the international financial system and architecture, while recognizing that the United Nations and the international financial institutions have complementary mandates which make the coordination of their actions crucial;

3. *Recalls*, in this regard, the resolve to strengthen the coordination of the United Nations system and all other multilateral financial, trade and development institutions so as to support economic growth, poverty eradication and sustainable development worldwide, based on a clear understanding of and respect for their mandates and governance structures;

4. *Underlines* the importance of the implementation of the Outcome of the Conference on the World Financial and Economic Crisis and Its Impact on Development, and in this regard recalls the establishment of the ad hoc open-ended working group of the General Assembly to follow up on the issues considered therein;

5. *Notes* that the crisis has produced or exacerbated serious and wide-ranging yet differentiated impacts across the globe and that, since the crisis began, many States have reported negative impacts, which vary by country, region, level of development and severity, including massive reversal of private capital inflows, especially at the height of the crisis;

6. *Expresses serious concern* at the impact that the current world economic and financial crisis is having on all countries, particularly developing countries, stresses the need for actions that are commensurate with the scale, depth and urgency of the crisis to be taken, adequately financed, promptly implemented and appropriately coor-

dinated internationally, and in this regard notes the significant work under way at the national, regional and international levels to mitigate the impact of the crisis;

7. *Reaffirms* the need to further develop the comprehensive response of the United Nations development system to the world financial and economic crisis in support of national development strategies through a coordinated approach by United Nations funds and programmes, the specialized agencies and the international financial institutions at the country level;

8. *Notes* that global economic growth and a stable international financial system, inter alia, can support the ability of developing countries to pursue their national policy objectives and achieve the internationally agreed development goals, including the Millennium Development Goals, and stresses the importance of cooperative and coordinated efforts by all countries and institutions to cope with the risks of financial instability;

9. *Stresses* that this crisis has added new impetus to ongoing international discussions on the reform of the international financial system and architecture, including on issues related to mandate, scope, governance, responsiveness and development orientation, as appropriate;

10. *Notes* that major failures of regulation and supervision, plus irresponsible risk-taking by banks and other financial institutions, had created dangerous financial fragilities which contributed significantly to the current crisis, and stresses the need for greater transparency and better regulation and supervision of the international financial system by, inter alia, strengthening prudential oversight, improving risk management and reinforcing international cooperation, while noting ongoing reforms in this regard;

11. *Emphasizes* the need for global concerted efforts to restore global economic growth, particularly in developing countries, also emphasizes, in this regard, the need to take into account the human and social impact of the crisis, and underlines the need to promote a job-intensive recovery from the crisis, drawing on the decent work agenda and through the implementation of the resolution entitled "Recovering from the crisis: a Global Jobs Pact", adopted by the International Labour Conference at its ninety-eighth session;

12. *Stresses* that developing countries facing an acute and severe shortage of foreign reserves because of the fallout of the crisis can use, as a measure of last resort, temporary capital account measures, in accordance with the relevant bilateral and multilateral agreements, in order to help to mitigate the adverse impacts of the crisis;

13. *Notes* that developing countries can seek to negotiate, as a last resort, on a case-by-case basis and through existing frameworks, agreements on temporary debt standstills between debtors and creditors in order to help to mitigate the adverse impacts of the crisis and stabilize macroeconomic developments;

14. *Recalls* that countries must have the necessary flexibility to implement counter-cyclical measures and to pursue tailored and targeted responses to the crisis, and calls for a streamlining of conditionalities to ensure that they are timely, tailored and targeted and support developing countries in the face of financial, economic and development challenges;

15. *Notes*, in this regard, the recent improvement of the lending framework of the International Monetary Fund

through, inter alia, streamlined conditions and the creation of more flexible instruments such as a flexible credit line, while also noting that new and ongoing programmes should not contain unwarranted pro-cyclical conditionalities;

16. *Urges* international financial institutions to continue their efforts to mitigate the global economic impacts of the current crisis, including through the provision of financial resources to developing countries, stresses the need to assist developing countries in responding to the crisis without incurring the risk of relapsing into another debt crisis, takes note with appreciation in this regard of the additional resources that have been made available through the International Monetary Fund and the multilateral development banks, and calls for the continued provision of concessional and grant-based financing to low-income countries to enable them to respond to the crisis;

17. *Notes* recent progress on reform of the governance structures of the international financial institutions, and reaffirms the commitment to broaden and strengthen the participation of developing countries and countries with economies in transition in international economic decision-making and norm-setting, while stressing the importance to that end of continuing efforts to reform the international financial architecture, and acknowledges the need for continued discussion on the issue of the voting power of developing countries in the Bretton Woods institutions, which remains a concern;

18. *Reaffirms* the need to address the often expressed concern regarding the extent of representation of developing countries in the major standard-setting bodies, therefore welcomes, as a step in the right direction, the expansion of the membership in the Financial Stability Board and the Basel Committee on Banking Supervision, and encourages the major standard-setting bodies to further review their membership promptly while enhancing their effectiveness, with a view to expanding the representation of developing countries as appropriate;

19. *Notes* the important role played by recent allocations of special drawing rights in increasing global liquidity, recognizes the need to continue regular reviews of the role of special drawing rights, including with reference to their potential role in the international reserve system, and requests the Secretary-General to take this into account while preparing his report on the implementation of the present resolution;

20. *Also notes* the value of regional and subregional cooperation efforts in meeting the challenges of the global economic crisis, and encourages enhanced regional and subregional cooperation, for example, through regional and subregional development banks, commercial and reserve currency arrangements, and other regional initiatives, as contributions to the multilateral response to the current crisis and to improved resilience with respect to potential future crises;

21. *Invites* the international financial and banking institutions to enhance the transparency of risk-rating mechanisms, noting that sovereign risk assessments made by the private sector should maximize the use of strict, objective and transparent parameters, which can be facilitated by high-quality data and analysis, and encourages relevant development institutions, including the United Nations Conference on Trade and Development, to continue their

work on this issue, including its potential impact on the development prospects of developing countries;

22. *Invites* the multilateral and regional development banks and development funds to play a vital role in serving the development needs of developing countries and countries with economies in transition, including through coordinated action, as appropriate, and stresses that regional development banks and financial institutions add flexible financial support to national and regional development efforts, thus enhancing their ownership and overall efficiency, and in this regard calls upon the international community to ensure that multilateral and regional development banks are adequately funded;

23. *Requests* the Secretary-General to submit a report to the General Assembly at its sixty-fifth session on the implementation of the present resolution;

24. *Decides* to include in the provisional agenda of its sixty-fifth session, under the item entitled "Macroeconomic policy questions", the sub-item entitled "International financial system and development".

Debt problems of developing countries

In response to General Assembly resolution 63/206 [YUN 2008, p. 1072], the Secretary-General submitted a July report [A/64/167] on recent developments in the external debt problems of developing countries and economies in transition. The report analysed the impact of the financial and economic crisis that began in 2008 [YUN 2008, p. 1102] on external debt sustainability for countries having access to international capital markets and low-income countries, and reviewed related policy actions. It described progress in the Heavily Indebted Poor Countries (HIPC) Initiative and developments in Paris Club rescheduling; analysed new trends and modalities in multilateral financing; and discussed the implication of private external borrowing for external debt sustainability.

The Secretary-General reported that under the enhanced HIPC Initiative, as at June 2009, 35 of the 40 eligible countries qualified for debt relief. In January, Burundi was the twenty-fourth country to reach completion point under the Initiative. Côte d'Ivoire reached decision-point in March, increasing the number of decision point countries to 11. Completion-point countries received an estimated debt relief of $38 billion in end-2008 net present value terms. Six countries had rescheduled their debt with Paris Club creditors.

The report called for decisive policy action to limit the setbacks resulting from the crisis with regard to poverty and progress towards the MDGs. Some of the resources necessary to fund the proposed $1.1 trillion package agreed on in the G20 communiqué of April had yet to be identified, and the G20 did not allocate enough resources to low-income countries and small and vulnerable States. It was the duty and obligation of the international community to provide assistance and resources to help mitigate the consequences of the crisis without requiring the accumulation of unsustainable levels of debt. Low-income countries with high debt levels needed to be given alternative financing opportunities to achieve the MDGs. Switching to a system in which aid agencies were funded with an endowment would be useful in delinking aid delivery from the business cycle of donor countries and thus reduce aid procyclicality. It would also be advisable to develop aid delivery mechanisms with a built-in insurance component that would lead to an automatic increase in aid when recipient countries were hit by a negative external shock. The international community should help countries with market access develop new debt instruments and institutions that would automatically reduce or avoid amplifying debt service in the presence of negative external shocks.

A later report [A/65/155] stated that the dollar value of the total external debt of developing and transition economies stabilized at around $3.7 trillion in 2009. However, as a result of the economic crisis, the average external debt-to-export ratio of developing countries increased from 64 to 82 per cent, and their external debt-to-gross national income ratio went from 22.0 to 23.5 per cent—a substantial setback, as it reversed some of the advances achieved during the 2000–2008 period. Official lending increased substantially, with gross commitments by IMF increasing from $1.3 billion in 2007 to nearly $120 billion in 2009. About 70 per cent of the increase ($80 billion) was for the flexible credit line facility; only $3 billion was allocated to low-income countries through the Poverty Reduction and Growth Facility and the Exogenous Shock Facility. The remaining $36 billion consisted of standard standby arrangements. The World Bank also increased gross commitments from $36.5 billion in 2008 to $65 billion in 2009. Most of the increase was for the International Bank for Reconstruction and Development loans targeting middle-income countries; International Development Association commitments, which benefited low-income countries, increased only by $1 billion.

Haiti reached the decision point under the HIPC Initiative in June and rescheduled its Paris Club debt in July. On a bilateral and voluntary basis, Paris Club creditors decided to exceed the standard debt cancellation under the Initiative and wrote off an additional $152 million of Haiti's official bilateral debt, thus erasing the entire stock of eligible debt owed to the Paris Club. The Central African Republic also reached its completion point in June, leading to a Paris Club meeting in September. Following cancellations within the HIPC Initiative and additional relief granted by a number of creditors, the country's debt stock was reduced to $3.7 million. In November, the Comoros concluded an agreement with the Paris Club creditors to reschedule its debt under the Naples

terms, and exceptional treatment was applied so that payments to the creditors were decreased by 80 per cent for the period from July 2009 to June 2012.

Communication. A 9 November letter from Nicaragua to the Secretary-General [A/C.2/64/12] contained a September note by the UNCTAD secretariat on the impact of the financial and economic crisis on debt sustainability in developing countries. The note was prepared at the request of the outgoing President of the General Assembly, Miguel d'Escoto Brockmann.

GENERAL ASSEMBLY ACTION

On 21 December [meeting 66], the General Assembly, on the recommendation of the Second Committee [A/64/418/Add.3], adopted **resolution 64/191** without vote [agenda item 51 *(c)*].

External debt sustainability and development

The General Assembly,

Recalling its resolutions 58/203 of 23 December 2003, 59/223 of 22 December 2004, 60/187 of 22 December 2005, 61/188 of 20 December 2006, 62/186 of 19 December 2007 and 63/206 of 19 December 2008,

Recalling also the 2009 Conference on the World Financial and Economic Crisis and Its Impact on Development and its outcome,

Recalling further the International Conference on Financing for Development and its outcome, and the 2008 Doha Declaration on Financing for Development,

Recalling the United Nations Millennium Declaration, adopted on 8 September 2000,

Recalling also the 2005 World Summit Outcome,

Recalling further its resolution 60/265 of 30 June 2006 on the follow-up to the development outcome of the 2005 World Summit, including the Millennium Development Goals and the other internationally agreed development goals,

Recalling its resolution 57/270 B of 23 June 2003,

Recognizing the important role, on a case-by-case basis, of debt relief and debt restructuring as debt crisis prevention and management tools for mitigating the impact of the world financial and economic crisis in developing countries,

Expressing concern that some low-income countries may face increased challenges in servicing their debt,

Reaffirming that each country must take primary responsibility for its own development and that the role of national policies and development strategies, including in the area of debt management, cannot be overemphasized in the achievement of sustainable development, and recognizing that national efforts should be complemented by supportive global programmes, measures and policies aimed at expanding the development opportunities of developing countries, while taking into account national conditions and ensuring respect for national ownership, strategies and sovereignty,

Reaffirming also that the Bretton Woods institutions and other relevant organizations should continue to play an important role, given their respective mandates, in achieving and maintaining debt sustainability,

Noting, in this regard, the recent improvement of the lending framework of the International Monetary Fund, through, inter alia, streamlined conditions and the creation of more flexible instruments such as a flexible credit line, while noting also that new and ongoing programmes should not contain unwarranted procyclical conditionalities,

Emphasizing that debt sustainability is essential for underpinning growth, and underlining the importance of debt sustainability and effective debt management to the efforts to achieve national development goals, including the Millennium Development Goals,

Noting with appreciation that the Heavily Indebted Poor Countries Initiative and the Multilateral Debt Relief Initiative and bilateral donors have provided significant debt relief to twenty-six heavily indebted poor countries that have reached the completion point under the Heavily Indebted Poor Countries Initiative, and that an additional nine countries have reached the decision point under the Initiative, and expressing concern that five out of forty eligible heavily indebted poor countries have still not reached the decision point under the Initiative,

Noting that the world has been facing and confronting, in the world financial and economic crisis, the greatest economic challenge of recent times, and recognizing the international response to this crisis, which is helping to stabilize financial markets,

Recognizing that the negative impact of the world financial and economic crisis on development is still unfolding and entails the possibility of undoing the progress made towards achieving the Millennium Development Goals, and that it may threaten debt sustainability in some developing countries, inter alia, through its impact on the real economy and the increase in borrowing undertaken in order to mitigate the negative impacts of the crisis,

Welcoming the fact that the Heavily Indebted Poor Countries Initiative and the Multilateral Debt Relief Initiative have enabled heavily indebted poor countries to increase their investments in health, education and other social services consistent with national priorities, development plans and the internationally agreed development goals, including the Millennium Development Goals,

Stressing the importance of addressing the challenges of the fourteen heavily indebted poor countries that are facing difficulties in reaching the decision or completion point under the Heavily Indebted Poor Countries Initiative, and expressing concern that some heavily indebted poor countries continue to face substantial debt burdens and need to avoid rebuilding unsustainable debt burdens after reaching the completion point under the Initiative,

Acknowledging that, although the debt relief provided under the Heavily Indebted Poor Countries Initiative and the Multilateral Debt Relief Initiative has considerably reduced the debt vulnerabilities in post-completion point countries and that the vulnerabilities in those countries are on average much lower than in pre-completion point heavily indebted poor countries, some post-completion point countries remain classified as being at high risk of debt distress,

Convinced that enhanced market access for goods and services of export interest to developing countries contributes significantly to debt sustainability in those countries,

1. *Takes note* of the report of the Secretary-General entitled "Towards a durable solution to the debt problems of developing countries";

2. *Emphasizes* the special importance of a timely, effective, comprehensive and durable solution to the debt problems of developing countries, since debt financing and relief can contribute to economic growth and development;

3. *Stresses* the importance of responsible lending and borrowing, and emphasizes that creditors and debtors must share responsibility for preventing unsustainable debt situations;

4. *Reiterates* that debt sustainability depends on a confluence of many factors at the international and national levels, emphasizes that country-specific circumstances and the impact of external shocks should continue to be taken into account in debt sustainability analyses, underscores the fact that no single indicator should be used to make definitive judgements about debt sustainability, and, in this regard, while acknowledging the need to use transparent and comparable indicators, invites the International Monetary Fund and the World Bank, in their assessment of debt sustainability, to take into account fundamental changes caused by, inter alia, natural disasters, conflicts and changes in global growth prospects or in the terms of trade, especially for commodity-dependent developing countries, as well as by the impact of developments in financial markets, and to continue to provide information on this issue using existing cooperation forums, including those involving Member States;

5. *Underlines* the fact that the long-term sustainability of debt depends, inter alia, on the economic growth, mobilization of domestic resources and export prospects of debtor countries and hence on the creation of an enabling international environment conducive to development, progress in following sound macroeconomic policies, transparent and effective regulatory frameworks and success in overcoming structural development problems;

6. *Recognizes* the enormity and the multidimensional nature of the world financial and economic crisis and the significant risks it may pose to the debt sustainability of some developing countries and countries with economies in transition, and emphasizes the need for coordinated policies aimed at fostering debt financing, debt relief and debt restructuring, as appropriate;

7. *Stresses* the need to assist developing countries in responding to the crisis without incurring the risk of relapsing into another debt crisis, takes note with appreciation, in this regard, of the additional resources that have been made available through the International Monetary Fund and the multilateral development banks, and calls for the continued provision of concessional and grant-based financing to low-income countries to enable them to respond to the crisis;

8. *Notes* the provision by the International Monetary Fund of interest relief to low-income countries in the form of zero-interest payments on financing from concessional lending facilities until the end of 2011;

9. *Also notes* that developing countries can seek to negotiate, as a last resort, on a case-by-case basis and through existing frameworks, agreements on temporary debt stand-

stills between debtors and creditors in order to help mitigate the adverse impacts of the crisis and stabilize macroeconomic developments;

10. *Stresses* the importance of assisting developing countries, upon request, in managing their borrowing and in avoiding a build-up of unsustainable debt, including through capacity-building in the area of debt management and the use of grants and concessional loans, and underlines the important role of the joint Debt Sustainability Framework of the International Monetary Fund and the World Bank for low-income countries in helping to guide borrowing and lending decisions;

11. *Takes note* of the recent review of the flexibility of the Debt Sustainability Framework, urges all lenders and borrowers to make full use of debt sustainability analyses in their debt decisions in order to help maintain debt sustainability through a coordinated and cooperative approach, and encourages continued review of the Framework, with the full engagement of borrower Governments, in an open and transparent manner;

12. *Recognizes and encourages* the continued provision of assistance, including technical assistance, to enhance debt management, negotiation and renegotiation capacities, including supporting legal advice in relation to tackling external debt litigation and debt data reconciliation between creditors and debtors, in order that debt sustainability may be achieved and maintained;

13. *Takes note* of the progress made under the Heavily Indebted Poor Countries Initiative and the Multilateral Debt Relief Initiative, while expressing concern that some countries have yet to reach decision or completion points, calls for their full and timely implementation and for continued support to the remaining eligible countries in completing the Heavily Indebted Poor Countries Initiative process, and encourages all parties, both creditors and debtors, to fulfil their commitments as rapidly as possible in order to complete the debt relief process;

14. *Notes* that some low- and middle-income developing countries that are not included in existing debt relief initiatives also experience constraints on mobilizing the resources needed to achieve the internationally agreed development goals;

15. *Underlines* the fact that heavily indebted poor countries eligible for debt relief will not be able to enjoy its full benefits unless all creditors, including public and private, contribute their fair share and become involved in the international debt resolution mechanisms to ensure the debt sustainability of low-income countries;

16. *Encourages* donor countries to take steps to ensure that resources provided for debt relief under the Heavily Indebted Poor Countries Initiative and the Multilateral Debt Relief Initiative do not detract from official development assistance resources intended to be available for developing countries;

17. *Encourages* further improvement of the mutual exchange of information, on a voluntary basis, on borrowing and lending among all creditors and borrowers;

18. *Takes note* of the creation of the new International Monetary Fund lending facilities in response to the crisis and the continued review of the new lending facilities, and urges the multilateral development banks to move forward on flexible, concessional, fast-disbursing and front-loaded assistance that will substantially and quickly assist developing countries facing financing gaps in their efforts to achieve the Millennium Development Goals, bearing in mind that new lending facilities will have to consider those countries' individual absorptive capacities and debt sustainability;

19. *Welcomes and encourages* the efforts of the heavily indebted poor countries, calls upon them to continue to strengthen their domestic policies and economic management, inter alia, through poverty reduction strategies, and to create a domestic environment conducive to private-sector development, economic growth and poverty reduction, including a stable macroeconomic framework, transparent and accountable systems of public finance, a sound business climate and a predictable investment climate, and in this regard invites creditors, both private and public, that are not yet fully participating in debt relief initiatives to substantially increase their participation, including by providing comparable treatment to the extent possible to debtor countries that have concluded sustainable debt relief agreements with creditors, and invites the international financing institutions and the donor community to continue to provide adequate and sufficiently concessional financing;

20. *Stresses* that debt relief can play a key role in liberating resources that should be directed towards activities consistent with poverty eradication, sustained economic growth, economic development and the internationally agreed development goals, including the Millennium Development Goals, and in this regard urges countries to direct those resources freed through debt relief, in particular through debt cancellation and reduction, towards those objectives;

21. *Calls for* the consideration of additional measures and initiatives aimed at ensuring long-term debt sustainability through increased grant-based and other forms of concessionary financing, cancellation of 100 per cent of the eligible official multilateral and bilateral debt of heavily indebted poor countries and, where appropriate, and on a case-by-case basis, significant debt relief or restructuring for developing countries with an unsustainable debt burden that are not part of the Heavily Indebted Poor Countries Initiative;

22. *Encourages* the Paris Club, in dealing with the debt of low- and middle-income debtor countries that are not part of the Heavily Indebted Poor Countries Initiative, to take into account their medium-term debt sustainability in addition to their financing gaps, and takes note with appreciation of the Evian approach of the Paris Club in providing terms of debt relief tailored to the specific needs of debtor countries while preserving debt cancellation for heavily indebted poor countries;

23. *Stresses* the need to significantly address the debt problems of middle-income developing countries, and in this regard stresses the importance of the Evian approach of the Paris Club as a practical means of addressing this issue, and notes that the current debt sustainability framework used to analyse the debt situation of middle-income countries focuses mostly on medium-term debt dynamics;

24. *Notes* the changing composition of the sovereign debt of some countries, which has shifted increasingly from external public debt to domestic debt, notes that the levels of domestic debt could create other challenges for macroeconomic management and public debt sustainability, and

calls for reinforcing the capacity to manage the new levels of domestic debt in order to maintain overall public debt sustainability;

25. *Recognizes* that a shift has occurred from official to commercial borrowing and from external to domestic public debt, although for most low-income countries external finance is still largely official, notes that the number of creditors, both official and private, has increased significantly, and stresses the need to address the implications of these changes, including through improved data collection and analysis;

26. *Calls for* the intensification of efforts to prevent debt crises by enhancing international financial mechanisms for crisis prevention and resolution, in cooperation with the private sector, and by finding solutions that are transparent and agreeable to all;

27. *Recognizes* the roles of the United Nations and the international financial institutions in accordance with their respective mandates, and encourages them to continue to support global efforts towards sustainable development and a durable solution to the debt problem of developing countries;

28. *Invites* creditors and debtors to further explore, where appropriate, and on a mutually agreed and case-by-case basis, the use of innovative mechanisms such as debt swaps, including debt for equity in Millennium Development Goals projects;

29. *Stresses* the need to continue to take effective measures, preferably within the existing frameworks, to address the debt problems of the least developed countries, including through cancellation of the multilateral and bilateral debt owed by least developed countries to creditors, both public and private;

30. *Invites* donor countries, taking into account country-specific debt sustainability analyses, to continue their efforts to increase bilateral grants to developing countries, which could contribute to debt sustainability in the medium to long term, and recognizes the need for countries to be able to invest, inter alia, in health and education while maintaining debt sustainability;

31. *Stresses* the need to increase information-sharing, transparency and the use of objective criteria in the construction and evaluation of debt scenarios, including an assessment of domestic public and private debt, in order to ensure the achievement of development goals, recognizes that credit rating agencies also play a significant role in the provision of information, including assessment of corporate and sovereign risks, and in this regard calls for strong oversight over credit rating agencies consistent with the agreed and strengthened international code of conduct;

32. *Calls for* the consideration of enhanced approaches to sovereign debt restructuring mechanisms based on existing frameworks and principles, with the broad participation of creditors and debtors, the comparable treatment of all creditors and an important role for the Bretton Woods institutions, and in this regard, welcomes and calls upon all countries to contribute to the ongoing discussions in the International Monetary Fund and the World Bank and other forums on the need for, and feasibility of, a more structured framework for international cooperation in this area;

33. *Welcomes* the efforts of and calls upon the international community to provide flexibility, and stresses the need to continue those efforts in helping post-conflict developing countries, especially those that are heavily indebted and poor, to achieve initial reconstruction for economic and social development;

34. *Also welcomes* the efforts of and invites creditors to provide flexibility to developing countries affected by natural disasters so as to allow them to address their debt concerns, while taking into account their specific situation and needs;

35. *Further welcomes* the efforts of and calls upon the international community to support institutional capacity-building in developing countries for the management of financial assets and liabilities and to enhance sustainable debt management as an integral part of national development strategies;

36. *Invites* the United Nations Conference on Trade and Development, the International Monetary Fund and the World Bank, in cooperation with the regional commissions, development banks and other relevant multilateral financial institutions and stakeholders, to continue and intensify cooperation in respect of capacity-building activities in developing countries in the area of debt management and debt sustainability;

37. *Invites* the international community, including the United Nations system, to continue efforts to increase financial support in respect of capacity-building activities for developing countries in the area of debt management and debt sustainability, and encourages countries that have not done so to create transparent and accountable debt management systems;

38. *Calls upon* all Member States and the United Nations system, and invites the Bretton Woods institutions and the private sector, to take appropriate measures and actions for the implementation of the commitments, agreements and decisions of the major United Nations conferences and summits, in particular those related to the question of the external debt problems of developing countries;

39. *Requests* the Secretary-General to submit to the General Assembly at its sixty-fifth session a report on the implementation of the present resolution and to include in that report a comprehensive and substantive analysis of the external debt situation of developing countries;

40. *Decides* to include in the provisional agenda of its sixty-fifth session, under the item entitled "Macroeconomic policy questions", a sub-item entitled "External debt sustainability and development".

Financing for development

Follow-up to International Conference on Financing for Development and Doha Declaration

In response to a request made in the 2008 Doha Declaration on Financing for Development, endorsed by the General Assembly in resolution 63/239 [YUN 2008, p. 1077], the Secretary-General submitted, in July [A/64/189 & Corr.1], a progress report on innovative sources of development finance. The Secretary-General said that the Leading Group on Solidarity Levies to Fund Development, which was renamed the Leading Group on Innovative International Financing for Development in May, served as a federating platform for initiatives and new ideas. The new framework, which brought together countries, international organizations and NGOs, strengthened international solidarity, sought to correct the negative effects of globalization and market inefficiencies and facilitated international cooperation. The Task Force on Innovative Financing, co-chaired by the Prime Minister of the United Kingdom and the World Bank President, made recommendations at the sixth plenary meeting of the Leading Group in Paris on 29 May to raise additional funds for 100 million of the world's most vulnerable people. Meanwhile, the I-8 Group/Leading Innovative Financing for Equity was also created to bring together the most promising financing initiatives in order to share experiences; work on one common set of messages to reinforce the current initiative of the High-Level Task Force for Innovative International Finance for Health Systems and the Leading Group; prepare new initiatives; and coordinate the channelling of funds in order to achieve maximum impact. Innovative financing mechanisms helped to enhance the predictability of ODA funding and addressed market failures. The innovative financing for development framework mobilized participation in the international funding effort beyond national Governments and drew in subnational governments, private actors and citizens.

The report discussed innovative development financing mechanisms in operation, including the International Finance Facility for Immunization, which was expected to scale up spending by as much as $500 million annually up to 2015. The Advance Market Commitments scheme sought to address the shortcomings of pharmaceutical markets, especially in the poorest countries, by establishing contractual partnerships between donors and pharmaceutical firms to focus research into neglected diseases and distribute drugs at affordable prices. The Debt2Health initiative was conceived to help relieve the strain on resources of developing countries by converting portions of the debt claims into domestic resources for health. The report also outlined initiatives under development, including a currency transaction tax; carbon taxes; a plan launched by the United Nations for countries with tropical forests to issue tradable carbon credits obtained from saving and planting trees; special drawing rights (SDRs); and international tax cooperation. The Secretary-General said that innovative financing was an important element in the evolving development assistance architecture that had become highly pluralistic and eclectic. It was therefore critical to ensure transparency, accountability and effectiveness of increased resources and their use.

In response to Assembly resolution 63/208 [YUN 2008, p. 1077], the Secretary-General submitted an August report [A/64/322] on follow-up to and implementation of the Monterrey Consensus and Doha Declaration on Financing for Development. The report described recent developments in relation to the review process on financing for development and the implementation of the Consensus. Main developments were discussed under each of the six thematic chapter headings of the Consensus: mobilizing domestic financial resources for development; mobilizing international resources for development; international trade as an engine for development; increasing international financial and technical cooperation for development; external debt; and addressing systemic issues.

High-level meeting of Economic and Social Council, Bretton Woods institutions, WTO and UNCTAD. The Economic and Social Council, in accordance with **decision 2009/202** of 10 February, held a special high-level meeting with the Bretton Woods institutions, WTO and UNCTAD (New York, 27 April) under the theme "Coherence, coordination and cooperation in the context of the implementation of the Monterrey Consensus and the Doha Declaration on Financing for Development". Two sub-themes served as the focus of substantive discussions in plenary debates: addressing the impact of the global financial and economic crisis on development, including issues related to the international financial and monetary architecture and global governance structures; and strengthening the intergovernmental inclusive process to carry out the financing for development follow-up. The meeting had before it an April note by the Secretary-General [E/2009/48] on the subject.

The Council President, in her summary of the meeting [A/64/76-E/2009/60], noted that although the human cost of the global crisis was being felt in both developing and developed countries, the crisis had set back the development efforts of the poorest countries and increased the challenges they confronted. Even after the crisis had been overcome, immense developmental challenges would remain, and it was therefore critical to ensure effective follow-up to the Monterrey Consensus and Doha Declaration.

Addressing the meeting, the Secretary-General stressed the need for international cooperation. Development efforts sagged under the weight of the crisis, which had proved that the current system of global economic governance was not adequate. Faith in financial deregulation and market self-regulation had been diminished, and a new commitment to effective regulation was being seen nationally and globally. New forms of protectionism should be resisted, not only in trade but also in investment and international migration. Reform of the international economic system would require many steps and the full engagement of all countries and the United Nations.

By **decision 2009/259** of 31 July, the Economic and Social Council took note of the Council President's summary of the special high-level meeting.

ECONOMIC AND SOCIAL COUNCIL ACTION

On 31 July [meeting 45], the Economic and Social Council adopted **resolution 2009/30** [draft: E/2009/L.36] without vote [agenda item 6 *(a)*].

A strengthened and more effective intergovernmental inclusive process to carry out the financing for development follow-up

The Economic and Social Council,

Recalling the International Conference on Financing for Development, held in Monterrey, Mexico, from 18 to 22 March 2002, the Follow-up International Conference on Financing for Development to Review the Implementation of the Monterrey Consensus, held in Doha from 29 November to 2 December 2008, and all relevant General Assembly and Economic and Social Council resolutions,

Recalling also paragraph 89 of the Doha Declaration on Financing for Development, adopted in Doha on 2 December 2008, in which Heads of State and Government and High Representatives acknowledged the need for a strengthened and more effective intergovernmental inclusive process to carry out the financing for development follow-up and requested the Economic and Social Council to consider the matter at its special high-level meeting with the Bretton Woods institutions, the World Trade Organization and the United Nations Conference on Trade and Development and at its substantive session of 2009, in consultation with all relevant stakeholders, with a view to making appropriate and timely recommendations for final action by the General Assembly as early as possible in its sixty-fourth session,

Taking note of the summary by the President of the Economic and Social Council of the special high-level meeting of the Council with the Bretton Woods institutions, the World Trade Organization and the United Nations Conference on Trade and Development, held in New York on 27 April 2009,

Mindful that Member States and other stakeholders have put forward concrete proposals on the subject of strengthening the financing for development follow-up process,

Having considered the suggestions and proposals contained in the note by the Secretary-General entitled "Coherence, coordination and cooperation in the context of the implementation of the Monterrey Consensus and the Doha Declaration on Financing for Development", prepared for the special high-level meeting,

1. *Reaffirms* the importance of staying fully engaged, nationally, regionally and internationally, to ensure proper and effective follow-up to the implementation of the Monterrey Consensus and of continuing unremitting efforts to build bridges between all relevant stakeholders within the holistic agenda of the financing for development process,

as reaffirmed in the Doha Declaration on Financing for Development;

2. *Also reaffirms* the role played by the United Nations as a focal point for the financing for development follow-up process and the need to maintain that role in order to ensure the continuity and dynamism of the process, while reaffirming the need to further intensify the engagement of all stakeholders, including the United Nations system, the World Bank, the International Monetary Fund and the World Trade Organization, in the follow-up to and implementation of the commitments made in Monterrey and Doha;

3. *Reiterates* that maintaining a comprehensive and diverse multi-stakeholder follow-up process, including with civil society and the private sector, is critical, recognizes the core responsibility of all participants in the financing for development process to exercise ownership of that process and to implement their respective commitments in an integrated fashion, including through the continued engagement of all relevant ministries, in particular ministries of development, finance, trade and foreign affairs, also recognizes that an integrated treatment of financing for development issues in national development plans is important in enhancing national ownership and implementation of financing for development, and further recognizes that the international community should continue to draw upon the expertise, data and analysis available in multiple forums, while enhancing information-sharing and dialogue among the various United Nations and non-United Nations bodies that monitor progress on financing for development issues, while noting that there is substantial room to enhance the sharing of best practices;

4. *Reaffirms* the need for a strengthened and more effective intergovernmental inclusive process for carrying out the financing for development follow-up, which would review progress in the implementation of commitments, identify obstacles, challenges and emerging issues, and propose concrete recommendations and actions;

5. *Emphasizes* that the financing for development follow-up process should encompass a continuum of events, each contributing to and feeding into the next, thereby ensuring the holistic nature of the process and making better and more effective use of existing mechanisms and resources;

6. *Recommends* to the General Assembly in this regard the following modalities for a strengthened and more effective intergovernmental process for carrying out the financing for development follow-up:

(a) The special high-level meeting of the Economic and Social Council with the international financial and trade institutions could last, instead of one day, as at present, for up to two days; it should normally be held before the spring meetings of the Bretton Woods institutions and be timed appropriately, at least five weeks before those meetings, so as to meet the needs of all parties and be conducive to high-level participation; discussions at the first segment would concentrate on a topic of current interest, to be determined by the President of the Council in consultation with the participants, while the second segment would be organized under the overall theme of "Coherence, coordination and cooperation in the context of the implementation of the Monterrey Consensus and the Doha Declaration on Financing for Development" and would include a holistic

review of the Monterrey Consensus, with special emphasis on one or two topics to be determined in advance of the meeting by the President of the Council in consultation with the participants; the meeting will result in a President's summary, which should clearly identify key elements of the discussion and be formally presented to all the participants, including the major institutional stakeholders, as appropriate, in a timely manner; increased interaction and coordination at the staff level with the institutions involved prior to the holding of the Council's special high-level meeting, including the possibility of appropriate preparatory sessions, are especially encouraged; the President of the Council, in consultation with Member States, is encouraged to continue to work with the appropriate representatives of the Bretton Woods institutions, the World Trade Organization and the United Nations Conference on Trade and Development to improve, inter alia, the format of the Council's special high-level meeting;

(b) The Economic and Social Council should continue to strengthen its role in promoting coherence, coordination and cooperation in the context of the implementation of the Monterrey Consensus and the Doha Declaration on Financing for Development and as a forum for multi-stakeholder involvement; consideration of the agenda item on financing for development should be given more prominence in the work of the annual substantive session of the Council and should be allotted up to two full days within its four-week annual session; the Council should normally adopt a substantive resolution, taking into account, inter alia, the outcome of the preceding special high-level meeting;

(c) The General Assembly should give more prominence to its annual agenda item entitled "Follow-up to and implementation of the outcome of the 2002 International Conference on Financing for Development and the 2008 Review Conference"; it may also wish to reaffirm the importance of its biennial high-level dialogues on financing for development as the intergovernmental focal point for general follow-up to the 2002 International Conference on Financing for Development and the 2008 Review Conference, placing a particular emphasis on new challenges and emerging issues;

(d) The Secretariat should continue to ensure that all documents relevant to the agenda item on financing for development are made available in a timely manner, both to the Economic and Social Council and to the General Assembly; to further enhance the quality of its reports, the Secretariat should continue to make full use of all existing analytical work and relevant data, including those available from the institutional stakeholders and the specialized agencies;

(e) Participation in this strengthened process will continue to be open to all the relevant financing for development stakeholders, including specialized agencies, funds and programmes, regional commissions, other international organizations, civil society entities and business sector groups, through application of the traditional financing for development accreditation and participation modalities; prominent experts may also be invited to provide inputs to the discussions;

(f) Seminars, panel discussions and briefings may be organized as part of the preparations for and contribution to the above events in order to raise visibility, attract interest and participation and promote substantive discussions on a continuing basis; a programme of multi-stakeholder consultations, including civil society and the private sector, could be reinitiated by the Financing for Development Office of the Department of Economic and Social Affairs of the Secretariat, drawing on a broad range of financing for development-related topics, as well as a wider and more effective use of the financing for development web page as an information tool;

(g) The Department of Economic and Social Affairs, and especially the Financing for Development Office, are encouraged to maintain a regular interaction at the staff level with the World Bank, the International Monetary Fund, the World Trade Organization and the United Nations Conference on Trade and Development, in the interest of greater coherence, coordination and cooperation, each acting in accordance with its respective intergovernmental mandate, for their mutual benefit;

7. *Reiterates its appeal* to Member States and other potential donors to consider contributing generously to the Trust Fund for the Follow-up to the International Conference on Financing for Development, which would facilitate the carrying out of many of the activities outlined above;

8. *Underscores* the fact that the modalities of the financing for development follow-up process should be reviewed, as appropriate, within a time frame to be determined by the General Assembly.

GENERAL ASSEMBLY ACTION

On 21 December [meeting 66], the General Assembly, on the recommendation of the Second Committee [A/64/419 (Part II)], adopted **resolution 64/193** without vote [agenda item 52].

Follow-up to and implementation of the Monterrey Consensus and the outcome of the 2008 Review Conference (Doha Declaration on Financing for Development)

The General Assembly,

Recalling the International Conference on Financing for Development, held in Monterrey, Mexico, from 18 to 22 March 2002, and the Follow-up International Conference on Financing for Development to Review the Implementation of the Monterrey Consensus, held in Doha from 29 November to 2 December 2008, and its resolutions 56/210 B of 9 July 2002, 57/250 of 20 December 2002, 57/270 B of 23 June 2003, 57/272 and 57/273 of 20 December 2002, 58/230 of 23 December 2003, 59/225 of 22 December 2004, 60/188 of 22 December 2005, 61/191 of 20 December 2006, 62/187 of 19 December 2007 and 63/239 of 24 December 2008, as well as Economic and Social Council resolutions 2002/34 of 26 July 2002, 2003/47 of 24 July 2003, 2004/64 of 16 September 2004, 2006/45 of 28 July 2006, 2007/30 of 27 July 2007 and 2008/14 of 24 July 2008,

Recalling also the 2005 World Summit Outcome,

Recalling further the Outcome of the Conference on the World Financial and Economic Crisis and Its Impact on Development, and underlining the need for the expeditious implementation of and follow-up to the Outcome,

Taking note of Economic and Social Council resolution 2009/30 of 31 July 2009 regarding the strengthening of the intergovernmental process for carrying out the financing for development follow-up,

Taking note also of the reports of the Secretary-General on the follow-up to and implementation of the Monterrey Consensus and Doha Declaration on Financing for Development, and innovative sources of development finance,

Taking note further of the reports of the Secretary-General on the follow-up to and implementation of the outcome of the International Conference on Financing for Development and the report of the Follow-up International Conference on Financing for Development to Review the Implementation of the Monterrey Consensus,

Taking note of the special high-level meeting of the Economic and Social Council with the Bretton Woods institutions, the World Trade Organization and the United Nations Conference on Trade and Development, held in New York on 27 April 2009,

Reaffirming the Monterrey Consensus of the International Conference on Financing for Development in its entirety, its integrity and its holistic approach, recalling the resolve to take concrete action to implement the Monterrey Consensus and address the challenges of financing for development in the spirit of global partnership and solidarity in support of the achievement of the internationally agreed development goals, including the Millennium Development Goals, and also recommitting itself to staying fully engaged, nationally, regionally and internationally, so as to ensure proper and effective follow-up to and implementation of the Monterrey Consensus,

Reaffirming also that each country must take primary responsibility for its own development and that the role of national policies and development strategies cannot be overemphasized for the achievement of sustainable development, and recognizing that national efforts should be complemented by supportive global programmes, measures and policies aimed at expanding the development opportunities of developing countries, while taking into account national conditions and ensuring respect for national ownership strategies and sovereignty,

Recalling the importance of the overall commitment to just and democratic societies for development as spelled out in the Monterrey Consensus,

Deeply concerned by the adverse impacts of the global financial and economic crisis on development, including on the capacity of developing countries to mobilize resources for development, and recognizing that an effective response to the current crisis requires timely implementation of existing aid commitments,

Emphasizing that the financial and economic crisis has demonstrated the need for more effective government involvement so as to ensure an appropriate balance between the market and the public interest, and recognizing the need to better regulate financial markets,

1. *Welcomes* the holding in Doha of the Follow-up International Conference on Financing for Development to Review the Implementation of the Monterrey Consensus, which provided an opportunity to assess progress made, reaffirm goals and commitments, share best practices and lessons learned and identify obstacles and constraints encountered, actions and initiatives to overcome them and important measures for further implementation, as well as new challenges and emerging issues, in the financing for development process;

2. *Stresses* that each country has primary responsibility for its own economic and social development and that the role of national policies, domestic resources and development strategies cannot be overemphasized, and reaffirms the importance of:

(a) The implementation of the commitment to sound policies, good governance at all levels and the rule of law;

(b) The implementation of the commitment to creating an enabling environment for mobilizing domestic resources and of sound economic policies;

(c) The implementation of the commitment to enhancing the coherence and consistency of international monetary, financial and trading systems in order to complement national development efforts;

3. *Recognizes* that a dynamic, inclusive, well-functioning and socially responsible private sector is a valuable instrument for generating economic growth and reducing poverty, emphasizes the need to pursue appropriate policy and regulatory frameworks at national levels and in a manner consistent with national laws through which to encourage public and private initiatives, including at the local level, and to foster a dynamic and well-functioning business sector, while improving income growth and distribution, raising productivity, empowering women and protecting labour rights and the environment, and reiterates the importance of ensuring that the benefits of growth reach all people by empowering individuals and communities;

4. *Reiterates* the importance of investment in human capital, inter alia, in health and education, through inclusive social policies, in accordance with national strategies and priorities;

5. *Recalls* that the ongoing fight against corruption at all levels is a priority, and reaffirms the need to take urgent and decisive steps to continue to combat corruption in all of its manifestations in order to reduce obstacles to effective resource mobilization and allocation and prevent the diversion of resources away from activities that are vital for development, also recalls that this requires strong institutions at all levels, including, in particular, effective legal and judicial systems and enhanced transparency, recognizes the efforts and achievements of developing countries in this regard, takes note of the increased commitment of States that have already ratified or acceded to the United Nations Convention against Corruption, and in this regard urges all States that have not yet done so to consider ratifying or acceding to the Convention;

6. *Also recalls* the resolve of Member States to continue to undertake fiscal reforms, including tax reform, which is key to enhancing macroeconomic policies and mobilizing domestic public resources, further recalls that, while each country is responsible for its tax system, it is important to provide support to national efforts in those areas by strengthening technical assistance and enhancing international cooperation and participation in addressing international tax matters, including in the area of double taxation, and stresses that inclusive and cooperative frameworks should ensure the involvement and equal treatment of all jurisdictions;

7. *Notes* that, while foreign direct investment is a major source of financing for development, the flow of such funds to developing countries and countries with economies in transition has fallen rapidly during the crisis and remains uneven, and in this regard calls upon developed countries to continue to devise source-country measures to encourage and facilitate the flow of foreign direct investment, inter alia, through the provision of export credits and other lending instruments, risk guarantees and business development services; calls upon developing countries and countries with economies in transition to continue their efforts to create a conducive domestic environment for attracting investments by, inter alia, achieving a transparent, stable and predictable investment climate with proper contract enforcement and respect for property rights; and stresses the importance of enhancing efforts to mobilize investment from all sources in human resources and physical, environmental, institutional and social infrastructure;

8. *Reaffirms* that international trade is an engine for development and sustained economic growth and the critical role that a universal, rule-based, open, non-discriminatory and equitable multilateral trading system, as well as meaningful trade liberalization, can play in stimulating economic growth and development worldwide, thereby benefiting all countries at all stages of development;

9. *Stresses* the essential role that official development assistance plays in complementing, leveraging and sustaining financing for development in developing countries and in facilitating the achievement of development objectives, including the internationally agreed development goals, in particular the Millennium Development Goals, reiterates that official development assistance can play a catalytic role in assisting developing countries in removing constraints on sustained, inclusive and equitable growth by, inter alia, enhancing social, institutional and physical infrastructure, promoting foreign direct investment, trade and technological innovations, improving health and education, fostering gender equality, preserving the environment and eradicating poverty, and welcomes steps to improve the effectiveness and quality of aid based on the fundamental principles of national ownership, alignment, harmonization, managing for results and mutual accountability;

10. *Underlines* the fact that the fulfilment of all official development assistance commitments is crucial, including the commitments by many developed countries to achieve the target of 0.7 per cent of gross national product for official development assistance to developing countries by 2015 and to reach a level of at least 0.5 per cent of gross national product for official development assistance by 2010, as well as a target of 0.15 per cent to 0.20 per cent of gross national product for official development assistance to least developed countries, and urges developed countries that have not yet done so to fulfil their commitments for official development assistance to developing countries;

11. *Encourages* donors to work on national timetables, by the end of 2010, to increase aid levels within their respective budget allocation processes towards achieving the established official development assistance targets;

12. *Underlines* the important role of the United Nations development system in advancing development and in protecting development gains in accordance with national strategies and priorities, including progress towards achieving the internationally agreed development goals, including the Millennium Development Goals, threatened by the current economic crisis, reiterates that the United Nations should use the current economic situation as an opportunity to redouble its efforts to improve the efficiency and effectiveness of its development programmes, urges donor countries and other countries in a position to do so to substantially increase voluntary contributions to the core/regular budgets of the United Nations development system and to contribute on a multi-year basis, in a sustained and predictable manner, and notes that non-core resources represent an important supplement to the regular resource base of the United Nations development system;

13. *Recognizes* the potential of various voluntary innovative sources of financing to supplement traditional sources of financing, stresses that those funds should be disbursed in accordance with the priorities of developing countries and should not burden them unduly, and encourages the Secretary-General to organize an informal event in 2010, within existing resources, on the potential of voluntary innovative sources of development finance;

14. *Notes* the overall increase in the level of official development assistance in 2008 and that a significant part of aid flows since 2002 has comprised debt relief and humanitarian assistance;

15. *Emphasizes* the great importance of a timely, effective, comprehensive and durable solution to the debt problems of developing countries, since debt financing and relief can be an important source of capital for economic growth and development, and also emphasizes that creditors and debtors must share responsibilities for preventing unsustainable debt situations;

16. *Recognizes* that recent special drawing rights allocations helped to increase global liquidity in response to the global financial and economic crisis;

17. *Reaffirms* the need for a strengthened and more effective intergovernmental inclusive process to carry out the financing for development follow-up and to review progress in the implementation of commitments, identify obstacles, challenges and emerging issues and propose concrete recommendations and actions;

18. *Endorses*, in this regard, the recommendations of the Economic and Social Council as contained in its resolution 2009/30 of 31 July 2009;

19. *Affirms* the need to give more prominence to its annual agenda item entitled "Follow-up to and implementation of the outcome of the 2002 International Conference on Financing for Development and the 2008 Review Conference", and in this regard reiterates the need to review the modalities for the financing for development follow-up process, as appropriate;

20. *Recalls* the decision to consider the need to hold a follow-up financing for development conference by 2013;

21. *Decides* to include in the provisional agenda of its sixty-fifth session the item entitled "Follow-up to and implementation of the outcome of the 2002 International Conference on Financing for Development and the 2008 Review Conference", and requests the Secretary-General to submit, under that item, an annual analytical assessment of the state of implementation of the Monterrey Consensus and the Doha Declaration on Financing for Development, and of the present resolution, which is to be prepared in full

collaboration with the major institutional stakeholders and to include concrete proposals on the further strengthening of the financing for development follow-up process for consideration by Member States.

High-level Dialogue on Financing for Development

In response to General Assembly **decision 63/564** of 14 September, by which the Assembly decided to hold its fourth High-level Dialogue on Financing for Development at UN Headquarters in New York on 23 and 24 November, the Secretary-General issued a 30 September note [A/64/377] on the proposed organization of work of the High-level Dialogue. Three previous High-level Dialogues on Financing for Development were held in 2003 [YUN 2003, p. 988], 2005 [YUN 2005, p. 1065] and 2007 [YUN 2007, p. 992].

On 20 November 2009 (**decision 64/511**), the Assembly postponed the holding of the fourth High-level Dialogue on the understanding that the exact dates were to be determined no later than 11 December.

By resolution 64/194 of 21 December (see below), the Assembly decided to hold its fourth High-level Dialogue on 16 and 17 March 2010 in New York.

GENERAL ASSEMBLY ACTION

On 21 December [meeting 66], the General Assembly adopted **resolution 64/194** [draft: A/64/L.41] without vote [agenda item 52].

Modalities for the fourth High-level Dialogue on Financing for Development

The General Assembly,

Recalling the International Conference on Financing for Development, held in Monterrey, Mexico, from 18 to 22 March 2002, the Follow-up International Conference on Financing for Development to Review the Implementation of the Monterrey Consensus, held in Doha from 29 November to 2 December 2008, and its resolutions 56/210 B of 9 July 2002, 57/250 of 20 December 2002, 57/270 B of 23 June 2003, 57/272 and 57/273 of 20 December 2002, 58/230 of 23 December 2003, 59/225 of 22 December 2004, 60/188 of 22 December 2005, 61/191 of 20 December 2006, 62/187 of 19 December 2007 and 63/239 of 24 December 2008, as well as Economic and Social Council resolutions 2002/34 of 26 July 2002, 2003/47 of 24 July 2003, 2004/64 of 16 September 2004, 2006/45 of 28 July 2006, 2007/30 of 27 July 2007 and 2008/14 of 24 July 2008,

Recalling also its decisions 63/564 of 14 September 2009 and 64/511 of 20 November 2009,

1. *Decides* to hold its fourth High-level Dialogue on Financing for Development on 16 and 17 March 2010 at United Nations Headquarters;

2. *Takes note* of the note by the Secretary-General on the proposed organization of work of the fourth High-level Dialogue;

3. *Decides* that the overall theme of the fourth High-level Dialogue will be "The Monterrey Consensus and Doha Declaration on Financing for Development: status of implementation and tasks ahead";

4. *Stresses* the importance of the full involvement of all relevant stakeholders in the implementation of the Monterrey Consensus at all levels, and also stresses the importance of their full participation in the financing for development follow-up process, in accordance with the rules of procedure of the General Assembly, in particular the accreditation procedures and modalities of participation utilized at the Monterrey and Doha Conferences;

5. *Decides* that the modalities for the fourth High-level Dialogue will be the same as those used for the 2005 and 2007 High-level Dialogues, as described in its resolution 59/293 of 27 May 2005;

6. *Decides also* that the fourth High-level Dialogue will consist of a series of plenary and informal meetings, three interactive multi-stakeholder round tables and an informal interactive dialogue;

7. *Decides further* that the themes of the round tables and of the informal interactive dialogue will be as follows:

(a) Round table 1: The reform of the international monetary and financial system and its implications for development;

(b) Round table 2: The impact of the current financial and economic crisis on foreign direct investment and other private flows, external debt and international trade;

(c) Round table 3: The role of financial and technical development cooperation, including innovative sources of development finance, in leveraging the mobilization of domestic and international financial resources for development;

(d) Informal interactive dialogue: The link between financing for development and achieving the Millennium Development Goals: the road to the 2010 high-level event;

8. *Decides* that the fourth High-level Dialogue will result in a summary by the President of the General Assembly that will provide, as appropriate, input on financing for development to the preparatory process of the high-level plenary meeting of the Assembly in September 2010.

Response to global financial crisis

CEB consideration. The High-level Committee on Programmes (HLCP) of the United Nations System Chief Executives Board for Coordination (CEB) at its seventeenth session (Geneva, 26–27 February) [CEB/2009/4] discussed the global financial crisis and its impact on the work of the UN system. The HLCP Chairman said that the crisis required a global response, and the CEB member organizations were well placed to work together in key policy areas where coherence was crucial for results and impact. The Committee identified seven broad policy dimensions to deepen policy coherence and collaborative action: finance; trade; employment, production and aggregate demand; environment; social service, empowerment and protection of people; humanitarian, security and social stability; and development and international cooperation. The Assistant Secretary-General for Economic Development, UN Department of Economic and Social Affairs, Kwame Sundaram Jomo, identified three policy priorities: limiting the spread of the financial crisis; reflating economies proactively; and recognizing the need for regulatory reform. He stressed the importance of long-term considerations to finance growth and employment creation, as well as a broader commitment to inclusive finance. Participants stressed that initiatives such as the vulnerability fund promoted by the World Bank constituted a concrete response to the impact of the crisis on the poor and vulnerable. HLCP recommended that CEB endorse the vulnerability fund to demonstrate the commitment of the UN system to addressing the crisis in a coherent and effective manner. The Committee also supported the need for a joint World Bank-UN system approach for the development, management and implementation of the fund. It was considered vital for the UN system to be mindful of the pre-existing crises that had already been affecting vulnerable populations around the globe, and participants pointed to the need to maintain a steady focus on meeting the internationally agreed development goals, including the MDGs. HLCP concluded, among other things, that it would develop UN system joint initiatives for immediate response to the global financial crisis on the basis of a sustainable development approach. The identified initiatives were annexed to the report.

Thematic dialogue and recommendations of Commission of Experts. An interactive, thematic dialogue on the world financial and economic crisis and its impact on development was held at UN Headquarters from 25 to 27 March. Participants discussed the origins, evolution and systemic aspects of the crisis, as well as UN system responses. Following the dialogue on the crisis and its impact on development, and the observations put forward by the Member States and civil society during the dialogue, the General Assembly President, on 29 April [A/63/838], transmitted the recommendations made by the Commission of Experts of the President of the General Assembly on Reforms of the International Monetary and Financial System on 5 April. The Assembly President had convened the Commission, chaired by Professor Joseph Stiglitz, 2001 Nobel Prize winner in economics, and comprising a group of distinguished economists, policymakers and other experts, to review the workings of global financial systems and explore ways to secure a more sustainable and just global economic order. The principles and recommendations outlined in the Commission's report sought to address the need to take immediate action to revive the global economy as well as the need to resolve underlying structural problems. Among immediate measures, the Commission stated that all developed countries should take strong, coordinated actions to stimulate their economies; developing countries needed additional funding to participate effectively in a global stimulus; and

a new credit facility and new methods of disbursement were required to mobilize additional funds for developing countries. Developing countries needed more policy space, as conditions attached to support provided by international financial institutions undermined incentives for developing countries to seek support funding. The lack of coherence between policies governing trade and finance had to be rectified; crisis response had to avoid protectionism; advanced country markets had to be opened to exports from LDCs. Undertaking regulatory reforms required learning from successful policies. The domestic and global impact of government financial sector support should be coordinated, and the coordination of global economic policies needed to be improved.

The report also outlined an agenda for deeper, systemic reforms to the international system including: the introduction of a new global reserve system; reforms of the governance of the international financial institutions; the creation of a global economic coordination council; and better and more balanced surveillance of economic policies. Other measures discussed in the report related to reforming central bank policies to promote development; financial market policies; support for financial innovations to enhance risk mitigation; and the development of a mechanism for handling sovereign debt restructuring and cross-border investment disputes.

Report of Secretary-General. In response to resolution 63/277 of 7 April (see p. 955), the Secretary-General issued a June report [A/CONF.214/4] on the world financial and economic crisis and its impact on development. The report set out the origins and causes of the crisis and the mechanisms by which it was transmitted to developing countries; reviewed the impact of the crisis on development; and summarized international policy responses and those of the United Nations. It stated that although the crisis had not originated in developing countries, those countries were being severely affected by it through weaker trade, tighter global financing conditions and lower remittances. Poverty and hunger were increasing and major reversals in progress towards the MDGs were likely. There was an increased risk of accelerated environmental degradation, and social tensions were rising.

The UN system pooled its assets to assist countries and vulnerable populations to address the impact of the downturn. CEB launched nine major UN system initiatives to respond to the crisis. It committed itself to transformational change by taking action on increasing financing for the most vulnerable; providing greater food security; increasing trade; launching a green economy initiative; formulating a global jobs pact; establishing a social protection floor; taking emergency action to ensure humanitarian, security and social stability; developing technological infrastructure to facilitate the promotion of and access to innovation; and carrying out monitoring and analysis. Under the monitoring and analysis initiative, CEB also agreed to establish a UN system-wide vulnerability monitoring and alert mechanism to respond to an identified gap in information pertaining to the effects of the crisis on the world's most vulnerable populations. The UN Global Vulnerability Alert would ensure that, in times of global crisis, the fate of the poorest and most vulnerable populations was not marginalized in the international community's response.

Member States, multilateral institutions and regional bodies agreed on a range of concerted responses to the crisis. The G20 leaders, at their London Summit (2 April), announced a $1.1 trillion programme of support to restore credit, growth and jobs in the world economy; the programme would provide $50 billion to support social protection, boost trade and safeguard development in low-income countries. Member States, multilateral institutions and regional bodies had taken actions to address specific aspects of the crisis, including the implementation of unprecedented concurrent fiscal stimulus packages that amounted to $2.7 trillion; actions to create a stronger, broader and more globally consistent macro-prudential supervisory, regulatory and oversight framework in conjunction with early warning surveillance systems; strengthened international tax cooperation; more flexible terms and quicker access to balance-of-payments financing from IMF; and greater, more effective and more predictable financing for the most vulnerable.

The report recommended that the international community deploy all its resources and capacity for rapid, coordinated and effective responses and consider how to coordinate better additional fiscal stimulus measures, giving due consideration to global imbalances, destabilizing exchange-rate movements and the need to allow counter-cyclical responses by developing countries. Financial sector rescue operations should prioritize the restoration of affordable credit flows to productive sectors through more adequate bank capitalization and regulatory reforms. A larger share of the new international liquidity for emergency financing should be made available to developing countries through flexible responses to country needs that supported counter-cyclical policies. Development lending and ODA needed to be scaled up substantially to ensure reliable financing for developing countries. Protectionist trade policies had to be stopped and full access to global markets should be provided immediately to exports from LDCs to help their recovery. International tax cooperation should be strengthened and the Committee of Experts on International Cooperation in Tax Matters should be elevated to the status of an intergovernmental committee. Debt sustainability should be closely monitored, and the

reform of the Bretton Woods institutions should continue in order to increase their capacity to prevent and manage future crises. The international financial architecture should not only ensure greater financial stability but should also create the conditions for sustainable development, decent employment, more effective investment, better technology policies and financial inclusion at the national and international levels. The international community should put in place the institutions and architecture appropriate for the interrelated challenges facing the world, including development, climate change, human rights, peace and security.

Communication. In a 4 June letter [A/63/893], Syria transmitted to the Secretary-General the Damascus Declaration on responding to the international financial crisis in the United Nations Economic and Social Commission for Western Asia (ESCWA) region. The Declaration was adopted by the Regional High-level Consultative Forum on the Impacts of the International Financial Crisis on the ESCWA Member Countries: the Way Forward (Damascus, Syria, 5–7 May).

The Economic and Social Council, in **resolution 2009/5** of 24 July (see p. 1062), welcomed the adoption on 19 June by the International Labour Conference of the resolution "Recovering from the crisis: a Global Jobs Pact" and encouraged Member States to promote and make use of the Pact as a general framework within which each country could formulate a policy package specific to its situation and priorities.

Conference on the World Financial and Economic Crisis and Its Impact on Development

The Conference on the World Financial and Economic Crisis and Its Impact on Development (New York, 24–30 June) [A/CONF.214/9] was held in conformity with the 2008 Doha Declaration on Financing for Development [YUN 2008, p. 1077], which was endorsed by the Assembly in resolution 63/239 [ibid., p. 1077]; and in response to Assembly resolution 63/277 (see p. 955). The Conference was attended by 189 Member States and the European Community; Palestine and the Sovereign Military Order of Malta; 4 regional commissions; 10 UN bodies and programmes; 14 specialized agencies and related organizations; 18 intergovernmental organizations; the International Committee of the Red Cross and the Inter-Parliamentary Union; and numerous business-sector entities and NGOs. It had before it the Secretary-General's report on the crisis and its impact on development [A/CONF.214/4] (see p. 946). Four interactive round tables were held under the overall theme "Examining and overcoming the deepening world financial and economic crisis and its impact on development". The round tables considered the role of the United Nations and its Member States in the ongoing international discussions on reforming and strengthening the international financial and economic system and architecture (round table 1); coordinated and collaborative actions and appropriate measures to mitigate the impact of the crisis on development (round table 2); present and future impacts of the crisis on employment, trade, investment and development, including the achievement of the internationally agreed development goals and the MDGs (round table 3); and contributions of the UN development system in response to the crisis (round table 4). Summaries of the round-table discussions were annexed to the Conference report.

The Secretary-General, addressing the Conference on 24 June [A/CONF.214/PV.1], said that the world was struggling to overcome the worst global financial and economic crisis since the founding of the United Nations, and that the effects of climate change and extreme poverty had become starker. In a letter to leaders of the Group of Eight (G8) major industrialized countries, the Secretary-General stressed the need to commit resources to help the poorest and most vulnerable adapt to climate change and reach a deal at climate change talks to be held in Copenhagen in December (see p. 1015). He also underscored the importance of delivering on pledges of aid to achieve the MDGs. To support the economic, social and human rights of all people, the Secretary-General called for actions in three areas: mobilizing resources for better real-time data on the impact of the crisis on the poorest; honouring commitments to help women and men move from vulnerability to opportunity; and reforming international institutions for the twenty-first century.

The Conference, in resolution 1, adopted the draft outcome document, which was transmitted to the Conference by the General Assembly President in a 22 June note [A/CONF.214/3]; and recommended that the Assembly, during its resumed sixty-third (2009) session, endorse the Outcome of the Conference on the World Financial and Economic Crisis and Its Impact on Development (see below). In resolution 2, the Conference approved the report of the Credentials Committee [A/CONF.214/6].

GENERAL ASSEMBLY ACTION

On 9 July [meeting 95], the General Assembly adopted **resolution 63/303** [draft: A/63/L.75] without vote [agenda item 48].

Outcome of the Conference on the World Financial and Economic Crisis and Its Impact on Development

The General Assembly,

Noting the Conference on the World Financial and Economic Crisis and Its Impact on Development, held in New York from 24 to 30 June 2009, and the adoption by the Conference of the outcome document,

Decides to endorse the Outcome of the Conference on the World Financial and Economic Crisis and Its Impact on Development, annexed to the present resolution.

ANNEX

Outcome of the Conference on the World Financial and Economic Crisis and Its Impact on Development

We, Heads of State and Government and High Representatives, met in New York from 24 to 30 June 2009 for the Conference on the World Financial and Economic Crisis and Its Impact on Development.

1. The world is confronted with the worst financial and economic crisis since the Great Depression. The evolving crisis, which began within the world's major financial centres, has spread throughout the global economy, causing severe social, political and economic impacts. We are deeply concerned about its adverse impact on development. This crisis is negatively affecting all countries, particularly developing countries, and threatening the livelihoods, well-being and development opportunities of millions of people. The crisis has not only highlighted long-standing systemic fragilities and imbalances, but has also led to an intensification of efforts to reform and strengthen the international financial system and architecture. Our challenge is to ensure that actions and responses to the crisis are commensurate with its scale, depth and urgency, adequately financed, promptly implemented and appropriately coordinated internationally.

2. We reaffirm the purposes of the United Nations, as set forth in its Charter, including "to achieve international cooperation in solving international problems of an economic, social, cultural, or humanitarian character" and "to be a centre for harmonizing the actions of nations in the attainment of these common ends". The principles of the Charter are particularly relevant in addressing the current challenges. The United Nations, on the basis of its universal membership and legitimacy, is well positioned to participate in various reform processes aimed at improving and strengthening the effective functioning of the international financial system and architecture. This United Nations Conference is part of our collective effort towards recovery. It builds on and contributes to what already is being undertaken by diverse actors and in various forums, and is intended to support, inform and provide political impetus to future actions. This Conference also highlights the importance of the role of the United Nations in international economic issues.

3. Developing countries, which did not cause the global economic and financial crisis, are nonetheless severely affected by it. The economic and social progress achieved during recent years, in particular on internationally agreed development goals, including the Millennium Development Goals, is now being threatened in developing countries, particularly least developed countries. This progress, partially underpinned by a period of high economic growth in many countries, needs to be secured and enhanced in the face of threats posed by the crisis. Our endeavours must be guided by the need to address the human costs of the crisis: an increase in the already unacceptable number of poor and vulnerable, particularly women and children, who suffer and die of hunger, malnutrition

and preventable or curable disease; a rise in unemployment; the reduction in access to education and health services; and the current inadequacy of social protection in many countries. Women also face greater income insecurity and increased burdens of family care. These particular human costs have serious development consequences on the human security of those affected. An equitable global recovery requires the full participation of all countries in shaping appropriate responses to the crisis.

4.   Although the financial and economic crisis has affected all countries, it is important to take into account the varying impacts and challenges of the crisis on the different categories of developing countries. The crisis is further endangering the achievement of their national development objectives, as well as the internationally agreed development goals, including the Millennium Development Goals. We are particularly concerned about the impact on countries in special situations, including least developed countries, small island developing States and landlocked developing countries, and on African countries and countries emerging from conflict. We are equally concerned about the specific development challenges of middle-income countries and low-income countries with vulnerable and poor populations. For all these countries, the crisis presents unique challenges to their efforts to achieve their national development goals. Our collective responses to this crisis must be made with sensitivity to the specific needs of these different categories of developing countries, which include trade and market access, access to adequate financing and concessionary financing, capacity-building, strengthened support for sustainable development, financial and technical assistance, debt sustainability, trade facilitation measures, infrastructure development, peace and security, the Millennium Development Goals, and our previous international development commitments.

5.   Peace, stability and prosperity are indivisible. In today's globalized economy, all nations are far more closely tied together than ever before. The global reach of the crisis calls for prompt, decisive and coordinated action to address its causes, mitigate its impact and strengthen or establish the necessary mechanisms to help prevent similar crises in the future.

6.   This Conference represents a milestone in an ongoing and concerted engagement by all States Members of the United Nations to address the crisis and its impact on development. Today, we have set forth our global consensus on the responses to this crisis, prioritized required actions and defined a clear role for the United Nations. We are doing so in the interest of all nations in order to achieve a more inclusive, equitable, balanced, development-oriented and sustainable economic development to help overcome poverty and inequality.

Present state of the world economy

7.   This crisis is connected to multiple, interrelated global crises and challenges, such as increased food insecurity, volatile energy and commodity prices and climate change, as well as the lack of results so far in the multilateral trade negotiations and a loss of confidence in the international economic system. The global economic downturn is deeper than many early estimates, and the recovery is predicted to be gradual and varied. While some countries still experience positive, though much slower growth, the latest estimate of the United Nations indicates that world gross product will fall by 2.6 per cent in 2009, the first such decline since the Second World War. The crisis threatens to have calamitous human and development consequences. Millions of people all over the world are losing their jobs, their income, their savings and their homes. The World Bank estimates that more than 50 million people have already been driven into extreme poverty, particularly women and children. The Food and Agriculture Organization of the United Nations projects that the crisis will contribute to the number of hungry and undernourished people worldwide rising to a historic high of over one billion.

Impacts of the crisis

8.   The crisis has produced or exacerbated serious, wide-ranging yet differentiated impacts across the globe. Since the crisis began, many States have reported negative impacts, which vary by country, region, level of development and severity, including the following:

- Rapid increases in unemployment, poverty and hunger
- Deceleration of growth, economic contraction
- Negative effects on trade balances and balance of payments
- Dwindling levels of foreign direct investment
- Large and volatile movements in exchange rates
- Growing budget deficits, falling tax revenues and reduction of fiscal space
- Contraction of world trade
- Increased volatility and falling prices for primary commodities
- Declining remittances to developing countries
- Sharply reduced revenues from tourism
- Massive reversal of private capital inflows
- Reduced access to credit and trade financing
- Reduced public confidence in financial institutions
- Reduced ability to maintain social safety nets and provide other social services, such as health and education
- Increased infant and maternal mortality
- Collapse of housing markets.

Causes of the crisis

9.   The drivers of the financial and economic crisis are complex and multifaceted. We recognize that many of the main causes of the crisis are linked to systemic fragilities and imbalances that contributed to the inadequate functioning of the global economy. Major underlying factors in the current situation included inconsistent and insufficiently coordinated macroeconomic policies and inadequate structural reforms, which led to unsustainable global macroeconomic outcomes. These factors were made acute by major failures in financial regulation, supervision and monitoring of the financial sector, and inadequate surveillance and early warning. These regulatory failures, compounded by over-reliance on market self-regulation, overall lack of transparency, financial integrity and irresponsible behaviour, have led to excessive risk-taking, unsustainably high asset prices, irresponsible leveraging and high levels of consumption fuelled by easy credit and inflated asset prices. Financial regulators, policymakers and institutions failed to appreciate the full measure of risks in the financial system or address the extent of the growing economic vulnerabilities and their cross-border linkages. Insufficient em-

phasis on equitable human development has contributed to significant inequalities among countries and peoples. Other weaknesses of a systemic nature also contributed to the unfolding crisis, which has demonstrated the need for more effective government involvement to ensure an appropriate balance between the market and public interest.

Response to the crisis

10. We are all in this crisis together. While each country has primary responsibility for its own economic and social development, we will continue to work in solidarity on a vigorous, coordinated and comprehensive global response to the crisis in accordance with our respective abilities and responsibilities. Developed countries and emerging markets have taken the lead in restoring global growth. An immediate priority has been to stabilize the financial markets and restore confidence in them and counter falling demand and the recession. Major actions have already been taken to maintain macroeconomic stability and strengthen the international financial system. At the same time, strong and urgent actions are needed to counter the impact of the crisis on the most vulnerable populations and help to restore strong growth and recover lost ground in their progress towards our internationally agreed development goals, including the Millennium Development Goals. Therefore, an adequate share of any additional resources—both short-term liquidity and long-term development financing—will need to be made available to developing countries, especially the least developed countries. Although this crisis continues to have a significant impact on the peoples of the world, we believe that it represents an important opportunity for meaningful change. Going forward, our response must focus on creating jobs, increasing prosperity, strengthening access to health and education, correcting imbalances, designing and implementing environmentally and socially sustainable development paths and having a strong gender perspective. It must also strengthen the foundation for a fair, inclusive and sustainable globalization supported by renewed multilateralism. We are confident that we will emerge from this crisis stronger and more vigorous and more united.

The need for prompt and decisive action

11. We commit to working in solidarity on a coordinated and comprehensive global response to the crisis and to undertaking actions aimed at, inter alia:

- Restoring confidence and economic growth, and creating full and productive employment and decent work for all
- Safeguarding economic, development and social gains
- Providing adequate support for developing countries to address the human and social impacts of the crisis, in order to safeguard and build upon hard-won economic and development gains to date, including the progress being achieved towards the implementation of the Millennium Development Goals
- Ensuring long-term debt sustainability of developing countries
- Seeking to provide sufficient development resources to developing countries without unwarranted conditionalities
- Rebuilding trust in the financial sector and restoring lending
- Promoting and revitalizing open trade and investment and rejecting protectionism

- Fostering an inclusive, green and sustainable recovery, and providing continued support for sustainable development efforts by developing countries
- Strengthening the role of the United Nations development system in responding to the economic crisis and its impact on development
- Reforming and strengthening the international financial and economic system and architecture, as appropriate, to adapt to current challenges
- Fostering good governance at all levels, including in the international financial institutions and financial markets
- Addressing the human and social impacts of the crisis.

Lines of action
Make the stimulus work for all

12. In attempting to combat the immediate impacts of the crisis, there have already been a number of responses at the national, regional and international levels. While acknowledging those efforts, we encourage greater cooperation and coordination among countries' fiscal and economic actions. Support for development is an essential and integral part of the solution to the global crisis, inter alia, through actions aimed at enhancing sustained economic growth, poverty eradication and sustainable development. We encourage countries, while implementing national stimulus measures, to avoid protectionism in any form and possible adverse impacts on third countries, particularly developing countries.

13. We encourage countries in a position to do so to utilize the room for fiscal stimulus that they possess, while also ensuring long-term fiscal sustainability. We also encourage individual countries to tailor their responses to their specific circumstances and use the available scope for domestic resource mobilization.

14. While a number of developed and emerging market economies have implemented stimulus packages, the majority of the world's developing countries lack fiscal space to implement countercyclical measures to combat the effects of the crisis and spur recovery. Many also face foreign-exchange shortages. In order to adequately respond to the crisis, developing countries will need a larger share of any additional resources—both short-term liquidity and long-term development financing. We call for an examination of mechanisms to ensure that adequate resources are provided to developing countries, especially the least developed countries. We underscore that developing countries should not be unduly financially burdened by the crisis and its impacts.

15. Developing countries facing an acute and severe shortage of foreign reserves because of the fallout of the crisis, which is negatively affecting their balance-of-payment situation, should not be denied the right to use legitimate trade defence measures in accordance with relevant provisions of the World Trade Organization (wTO), and, as a last resort, impose temporary capital restrictions and seek to negotiate agreements on temporary debt standstills between debtors and creditors, in order to help mitigate the adverse impacts of the crisis and stabilize macroeconomic developments.

16. We acknowledge the G20 summit held in London on 2 April 2009, and recognize its commitment to make available an additional $1.1 trillion programme aimed

at revitalizing the world economy. A major part of these funds will be available for use by emerging markets and developing countries. A limited share ($50 billion) of these resources was targeted specifically to low-income countries. We call upon the G20 to further consider addressing the financial needs of developing countries, especially low-income countries. We also call upon all G20 countries to follow through with their commitments and to monitor the implementation of them. While recognizing the decisions taken by the G20, we are resolved to strengthen the role of the United Nations and its Member States in economic and financial affairs, including its coordinating role.

17.   Countries must have the necessary flexibility to implement countercyclical measures and to pursue tailored and targeted responses to the crisis. We call for a streamlining of conditionalities to ensure that they are timely, tailored and targeted and support developing countries in the face of financial, economic and development challenges. In this context we note the recent improvement of the lending framework of the International Monetary Fund (IMF), through inter alia, modernizing conditionality, and the creation of more flexible instruments, such as a flexible credit line, as a welcome step. New and ongoing programmes should not contain unwarranted procyclical conditionalities. We call upon the multilateral development banks to move forward on flexible, concessional, fast-disbursing and front-loaded assistance designed to substantially and quickly assist developing countries facing financing gaps. While doing so, multilateral development banks need to assure the application of agreed safeguards to ensure their financial stability.

18.   The increasing interdependence of national economies in a globalizing world and the emergence of rules-based regimes for international economic relations have meant that the space for national economic policy, that is, the scope for domestic policies, especially in the areas of trade, investment and international development, is now often framed by international disciplines and commitments and global market considerations. We recognize that these regimes, disciplines, commitments and considerations have presented challenges to many developing countries seeking to fashion a national response to the financial and economic crisis. We also recognize that many developing countries have called for opportunities to exercise greater policy flexibility within the scope of these constraints as a necessary component of recovery from the crisis and to address specific national concerns, which include, inter alia, the human and social impacts of the crisis, safeguarding progress achieved towards implementation of the Millennium Development Goals, effective use of credit and liquidity facilities, regulation of local financial markets, institutions, instruments and capital flows, and limited trade defence measures. It is for each Government to evaluate the trade-off between the benefits of accepting international rules and commitments and the constraints posed by the loss of policy space.

19.   We recognize the continued importance of good governance along with national ownership of policies and strategies. We commit ourselves to the promotion of effective and efficient economic and financial institutions at all levels—key determinants of long-term economic growth and development. We also commit ourselves to accelerating our collective recovery from the crisis through improved transparency, eradication of corruption and strengthened governance. In this regard, we urge all States that have not done so to consider ratifying or acceding to the United Nations Convention against Corruption and call upon all States parties to vigorously implement the Convention.

20.   The crisis has disparate impacts across regions, subregions and countries. These heterogeneous impacts have added complexity to our common goal of eradicating poverty, reducing inequality and promoting human development. Given the sensitivity of regional and subregional institutions to the specific needs of their constituencies, we note the value of regional and subregional cooperation efforts in meeting the challenges of the global economic crisis and we encourage enhanced regional and subregional cooperation, for example, through regional and subregional development banks, commercial and reserve currency arrangements, and other regional initiatives, as contributions to the multilateral response to the current crisis and to improved resilience to potential future crises.

Contain the effects of the crisis and improve future global resilience

21.   This crisis does not affect only the economic and financial sectors. We recognize the human and social impacts of the crisis and the inherent challenges involved in addressing them. Short-term mitigation measures should take into account long-term goals, especially those related to poverty eradication; sustainable development, including environmental protection and clean and renewable energy; food security; gender equality; health; education; and sustained economic growth, including full and productive employment and decent work for all. Strengthening existing social safety nets, establishing new ones where needed and protecting social expenditures are important for the advancement of people-centred development and addressing the human and social impacts of the crisis. We reaffirm our commitment to the timely achievement of our internationally agreed development goals, including the Millennium Development Goals.

22.   Closer cooperation and strong partnership between the United Nations development system, regional development banks and the World Bank and their scaled-up efforts can effectively address the needs of those hardest hit and ensure that their plight is not ignored. We call for the mobilization of additional resources for social protection, food security and human development through all sources of development finance, including voluntary bilateral contributions, to strengthen the foundation for early and sustained economic and social recovery in developing countries, particularly least developed countries. Such additional resources should be channelled through existing institutions such as the United Nations development system, the World Bank-proposed vulnerability fund and framework and multilateral development banks, where appropriate. These funds, including those for the United Nations development system, should be provided on a predictable basis. Furthermore, we stress the importance of the United Nations development system, given its broad field presence, in supporting the activities at the country level to mitigate the impact of the crisis in developing countries.

23.   We commit ourselves to strengthening the ability of the United Nations to fulfil its development mandate. United Nations funds and programmes and United Na-

tions agencies, in accordance with their respective mandates, have an important role to play in advancing development and in protecting development gains, in accordance with national strategies and priorities, including progress towards achieving the internationally agreed development goals, including the Millennium Development Goals, threatened by the current economic crisis. The United Nations should use the current economic situation as an opportunity to redouble its efforts to improve the efficiency and effectiveness of its development programmes in support of system-wide coherence. We recognize the unique role of the United Nations as an inclusive forum to promote a better understanding of the social and economic impact of the crisis and to fashion appropriate responses.

24. We acknowledge that the current economic crisis has the potential to increase the need for resources for humanitarian assistance in developing countries. We stress the need to take measures to ensure adequate resources for international cooperation in the provision of humanitarian assistance.

25. The crisis has severely impacted on international trade in most countries, especially developing countries. For many developing countries, these impacts include, among others, falling exports and loss of export revenue, diminishing access to trade finance, reductions in export-oriented and infrastructure investment, lower fiscal revenues and balance-of-payment problems. We undertake to resist all protectionist tendencies and rectify any protectionist measures already taken. At the same time we recognize the right of countries to fully utilize their flexibilities consistent with their WTO commitments and obligations. It is important that we contribute to the efforts of WTO and other relevant bodies to monitor and report on protectionist measures, including on how they affect developing countries.

26. We must also fully harness the potential of trade as an engine of sustained economic growth and development in our efforts to overcome this crisis. In this regard, we reaffirm our commitment to a universal, rules-based, open, non-discriminatory and equitable multilateral trading system. We reaffirm that international trade is an engine for development and sustained economic growth. We therefore reiterate our call for an early, ambitious, successful and balanced conclusion to the Doha Round that increases market access, generates increased trade flows and places the needs of developing countries at its centre. We welcome the commitment to implement duty-free and quota-free access for least developed countries, as agreed in the WTO Hong Kong Ministerial Declaration; to make operationally effective the principle of special and differential treatment for developing countries; to the parallel elimination of all forms of export subsidies; to disciplines on all export measures with equivalent effect; to substantial reductions in trade-distorting domestic support, in accordance with the mandate of the Doha Round and the WTO Hong Kong Ministerial Declaration; and to meet existing aid-for-trade pledges. We also reaffirm the need to make progress on the implementation of the WTO work programme on small economies, mandated in the Doha Ministerial Declaration.

27. Migrant workers are among the most vulnerable in the context of the current crisis. Remittances, which are significant private financial resources for households in countries of origin of migration, have been seriously affected by rising unemployment and weak earnings growth among migrant workers, particularly in advanced economies. We should resist unfair and discriminatory treatment of migrant workers and the imposition of unreasonable restrictions on labour migration in order to maximize the benefits of international migration, while complying with the relevant national legislation and applicable international instruments. We recognize the important contribution of migrant workers for both countries of origin and destination. We commit ourselves to allowing labour migration to meet labour market needs.

28. An effective response to the current economic crisis requires timely implementation of existing aid commitments. There is an urgent need for all donors to maintain and deliver on their existing bilateral and multilateral official development assistance (ODA) commitments and targets made, inter alia, in the United Nations Millennium Declaration, the Monterrey Consensus and the 2005 World Summit Outcome at the G8 summit in Gleneagles, in the Doha Declaration and at the G20 London summit. We underline that the fulfilment of all ODA commitments is crucial, including the commitments by many developed countries to achieve the target of 0.7 per cent of gross national product (GNP) for ODA to developing countries by 2015 and to reach the level of at least 0.5 per cent of GNP for ODA by 2010, as well as a target of 0.15 to 0.20 per cent of GNP for ODA to least developed countries. We recognize that many developed countries have established timetables to reach the level of at least 0.5 per cent for ODA by 2010. We encourage other donors to work on national timetables, by the end of 2010, to increase aid levels within their respective budget allocation processes towards achieving the established ODA targets. The full implementation of these commitments will substantially boost the resources available to push forward the international development agenda and to assist developing countries to mitigate and more effectively respond to the crisis in accordance with their national strategies. Donors should review and, if appropriate, increase or redirect their assistance to developing countries to enable them to mitigate and more effectively respond to the crisis in accordance with their national strategies.

29. We emphasize the importance for all development actors to continue to pursue economic and governance reforms and other steps to improve the effectiveness of aid based on the fundamental principles of national ownership, alignment, harmonization and managing for results.

30. We also encourage developing countries in a position to do so to continue to make concrete efforts to increase and make more effective their South-South cooperation initiatives, in accordance with the principles of aid effectiveness. We reiterate our support for South-South cooperation, as well as triangular cooperation, which provide much-needed additional resources for the implementation of development programmes.

31. New voluntary and innovative forms of financing can contribute to addressing our global problems. We encourage the scaling up of development finance from existing sources and the establishment, where appropriate, of new voluntary and innovative sources of financing initiatives to provide additional stable sources of development finance, which should supplement and not be a substitute for traditional sources of finance and should be disbursed in accordance with the priorities of developing countries and not unduly burden them. We reiterate our request to

the Secretary-General to produce a progress report by the sixty-fourth session of the General Assembly, taking into account all existing initiatives.

32. The crisis must not delay the necessary global response to climate change and environmental degradation, taking into account the principle of common but differentiated responsibilities and respective capabilities. We acknowledge that the response to the crisis presents an opportunity to promote green economy initiatives. In this regard, we encourage the utilization of national stimulus packages, for those countries in a position to do so, to contribute to sustainable development, sustainable long-term growth, promotion of full and productive employment and decent work for all and poverty eradication. It is important that global green initiatives and proposals be inclusive and address sustainable development and environmental challenges and opportunities, including climate change mitigation and adaptation, financing and technology transfer to developing countries and sustainable forest management. We also encourage private-sector participation in these initiatives at the national level in accordance with national development strategies and priorities. We look forward to a successful outcome of the fifteenth session of the Conference of the Parties to the United Nations Framework Convention on Climate Change, to be held in Copenhagen in December 2009, as part of our overall efforts for a green recovery from the crisis.

33. The deepening crisis threatens to increase the debt and therefore threatens the debt sustainability of developing countries. This growing pressure limits the ability of these States to enact the appropriate fiscal measures to mitigate the impact of the crisis or engage in development financing. We affirm that the appropriate measures must be taken to mitigate the negative effects of the crisis on the indebtedness of developing States and to avoid a new debt crisis. In that regard, we support making full use of the existing flexibility within the Debt Sustainability Framework.

34. We call upon States to redouble efforts to honour their commitments regarding debt relief and stress the responsibility of all debtors and creditors on the issue of debt sustainability, and emphasize the importance of equivalent treatment of all creditors. Donors and multilateral financial institutions should also increasingly consider providing grants and concessional loans as the preferred modalities of their financial support instruments to ensure debt sustainability. We will also explore enhanced approaches to the restructuring of sovereign debt based on existing frameworks and principles, broad creditors' and debtors' participation and comparable burden-sharing among creditors. We will also explore the need and feasibility of a more structured framework for international cooperation in this area.

35. We recognize that increases in global liquidity play a useful role in overcoming the financial crisis. Therefore, we strongly support and call for early implementation of the new general special drawing right (SDR) allocation of $250 billion. We also call for the urgent ratification of the fourth amendment to the IMF Articles of Agreement for a special one-time allocation of SDRs, as approved by the IMF Board of Governors in September 1997. We recognize the need for keeping under review the allocation of SDRs for development purposes. We also recognize the potential of expanded SDRs to help increase global liquidity in response to the urgent financial shortfalls caused by this crisis and to

help prevent future crises. This potential should be further studied.

36. The crisis has intensified calls by some States for reform of the current global reserve system to overcome its insufficiencies. We acknowledge the calls by many States for further study of the feasibility and advisability of a more efficient reserve system, including the possible function of SDRs in any such system and the complementary roles that could be played by various regional arrangements. We also acknowledge the importance of seeking consensus on the parameters of such a study and its implementation. We recognize the existence of new and existing regional and subregional economic and financial cooperation initiatives to address, inter alia, the liquidity shortfalls and the short-term balance-of-payment difficulties among its members.

Improved regulation and monitoring

37. The current crisis has revealed many deficiencies in national and international financial regulation and supervision. We recognize the critical need for expanding the scope of regulation and supervision and making it more effective, with respect to all major financial centres, instruments and actors, including financial institutions, credit rating agencies and hedge funds. The need for tighter and more coordinated regulation of incentives, derivatives and the trading of standardized contracts is also apparent. We reject the imposition of needlessly onerous regulatory requirements, and call for effective, credible and enforceable regulations at all levels to ensure the needed transparency and oversight of the financial system. Every relevant institution must be subject to adequate and proportionate surveillance and regulation. We underscore that each country should adequately regulate its financial markets, institutions and instruments consistent with its development priorities and circumstances, as well as its international commitments and obligations. We underscore the importance of political commitment and of capacity-building to ensure that the measures taken are fully implemented.

38. We emphasize the need to ensure that all tax jurisdictions and financial centres comply with standards of transparency and regulation. We reiterate the need to further promote international cooperation in tax matters, including within the United Nations, inter alia, by promoting double taxation agreements. Inclusive and cooperative frameworks should ensure the involvement and equal treatment of all jurisdictions. We call for consistent and non-discriminatory implementation of transparency requirements and international standards for exchange of information.

39. Illicit financial flows are estimated to amount to several times global ODA and have a harmful effect on development financing. Measures to enhance regulation and supervision of and transparency in the formal and informal financial system should include steps to curb illicit financial flows in all countries. Improving the transparency of the global financial system also deters illicit financial flows, including to international financial centres, and enhances the ability to detect illicit activities.

40. The current crisis has been compounded by an initial failure to appreciate the full scope of the risks accumulating in the financial markets and their potential to destabilize the international financial system and the global economy. We recognize the need for even-handed and effective IMF surveillance of major financial centres, interna-

tional capital flows and financial markets. In this context, we welcome the improvement of early warning systems by the relevant international institutions to provide early warning of macroeconomic and financial risks and the actions needed to address them.

41. The ongoing crisis has highlighted the extent to which our economies are integrated, the indivisibility of our collective well-being and the unsustainability of a narrow focus on short-term gains. We reaffirm the principles of sustainable development and underscore the need for a global consensus on the key values and principles that will promote sustainable, fair and equitable economic development. We believe that corporate social and environmental responsibility are important elements of such a consensus. In this regard we recognize the importance of the 10 principles of the United Nations Global Compact.

Reform of the international financial and economic system and architecture

42. This crisis has added new impetus to ongoing international discussions on the reform of the international financial system and architecture, including issues related to mandate, scope, governance, responsiveness and development orientation as appropriate. There is consensus on the need for continued reform and modernization of the international financial institutions to better enable them to respond to the current financial and economic challenges and to the needs of Member States, and to better equip them to strengthen existing monitoring, surveillance, technical assistance and coordination roles to help prevent the occurrence of similar crises in the future, in accordance with their respective mandates.

43. We stress the urgent need for further reform of the governance of the Bretton Woods institutions, on the basis of a fair and equitable representation of developing countries, in order to increase the credibility and accountability of these institutions. These reforms must reflect current realities and should enhance the perspective and voice and participation of dynamic emerging markets and developing countries, including the poorest.

44. We call for an expeditious completion of the reform process of the World Bank's governance and of an accelerated road map for further reforms on voice and participation of developing countries, with a view to reaching agreement by April 2010, based on an approach that reflects its development mandate and with the involvement of all shareholders in a transparent, consultative and inclusive process. We also call for inclusive consultations on further reforms to improve the responsiveness and adaptability of the World Bank.

45. It is imperative that the reformed World Bank emerge with the requisite technical capacities, credit facilities and financial resources needed to assist and complement the efforts of developing countries aimed at achieving their overall development needs.

46. We recognize the importance of strengthening regional development banks, taking into account the interests of all their member countries. It is also important for them to provide medium- and long-term assistance to meet the development needs of their clients. We support measures to enhance the financial and lending capacity of regional development banks. Furthermore, we recog-

nize the importance of other regional, interregional and subregional initiatives and arrangements aimed at promoting development, cooperation and solidarity among their members.

47. We recognize that it is imperative to undertake, as a matter of priority, a comprehensive and fast-tracked reform of IMF. We look forward to this accelerated progress in order to increase its credibility and accountability. We acknowledge the agreement to accelerate the implementation of the package of IMF quota and voice reforms agreed in April 2008. We strongly support completion of the next quota review, which, based on current trends, is expected to result in an increase in the quota shares of dynamic economies, particularly in the share of emerging market and developing countries as a whole, to be completed no later than January 2011, thus enhancing the legitimacy and effectiveness of the Fund.

48. We reaffirm the need to address the often expressed concern at the extent of representation of developing countries in the major standard-setting bodies. We therefore welcome, as a step in the right direction, the expansion of the membership in the Financial Stability Board and the Basel Committee on Banking Supervision and encourage the major standard-setting bodies to further review their membership promptly while enhancing their effectiveness, with a view to enhancing the representation of developing countries as appropriate.

49. We agree that the heads and senior leadership of the international financial institutions, particularly the Bretton Woods institutions, should be appointed through open, transparent and merit-based selection processes, with due regard to gender equality and geographical and regional representation.

50. The United Nations and the international financial institutions have complementary mandates that make the coordination of their actions crucial. Accordingly, we encourage continued and increasing cooperation, coordination and coherence and exchanges between the United Nations and the international financial institutions. In this regard, we believe that this Conference represents an important step to ensure increased cooperation.

The way forward

51. We have come together to raise our collective understanding of the impacts of the crisis and to contribute in the fashioning of the global response, in an inclusive manner, with actions at the national, regional and international levels.

52. We will strive to combine our short-term responses to meet the immediate impact of the financial and economic crisis, particularly on the most vulnerable countries, with medium- and long-term responses that necessarily involve the pursuit of development and the review of the global economic system. In this context, we propose the following course of action:

(a) Strengthen the capacity, effectiveness and efficiency of the United Nations; enhance the coherence and coordination of policies and actions between the United Nations, international financial institutions and relevant regional organizations;

(b) Further develop the United Nations development system's comprehensive crisis response in support of national development strategies through a coordinated approach by United Nations funds and programmes, specialized agencies and the international financial institutions at the country level. The response must continue to be led by programme countries and, in this context, address vulnerabilities caused or exacerbated by the crisis and further strengthen national ownership. It should build on steps already taken by the United Nations development system, in particular at the country level. We urge the international community to ensure adequate support to the United Nations development system's crisis response;

(c) Explore ways to strengthen international cooperation in the area of international migration and development, in order to address the challenges of the current economic and financial crisis on migration and migrants, taking into account the related work and activities of the United Nations funds and programmes, regional commissions and specialized agencies and of other international organizations, such as the International Organization for Migration.

53. We request the General Assembly and the Economic and Social Council, as well as the United Nations funds and programmes and specialized agencies, to take full advantage of their advocacy role to promote the recovery and development of the developing countries, especially the most vulnerable among them.

54. We invite the General Assembly to establish an ad hoc open-ended working group of the General Assembly to follow up on the issues contained in the present outcome document, and to submit a report on the progress of its work to the General Assembly before the end of the sixty-fourth session.

55. We encourage the President of the General Assembly to make the world financial and economic crisis and its impact on development a main theme of the general debate of the sixty-fourth session of the General Assembly.

56. We request the Economic and Social Council:

(a) To consider the promotion and enhancement of a coordinated response of the United Nations development system and specialized agencies in the follow-up to and implementation of this outcome document, in order to advance consistency and coherence in support of consensus-building around policies related to the world financial and economic crisis and its impact on development;

(b) To make recommendations to the General Assembly, in accordance with the Doha Declaration of 2 December 2008, for a strengthened and more effective and inclusive intergovernmental process to carry out the financing for development follow-up;

(c) Examine the strengthening of institutional arrangements to promote international cooperation in tax matters, including the United Nations Committee of Experts on International Cooperation in Tax Matters;

(d) Review the implementation of the agreements between the United Nations and the Bretton Woods institutions in collaboration with these institutions, focusing in particular on enhancing collaboration and cooperation between the United Nations and the Bretton Woods institutions, as well as on the opportunities for contributing to advancing their respective mandates;

(e) Consider and make recommendations to the General Assembly regarding the possible establishment of an ad hoc panel of experts on the world economic and financial crisis and its impact on development. The panel could provide independent technical expertise and analysis, which would contribute to informing international action and political decision-making and fostering constructive dialogues and exchanges among policymakers, academics, institutions and civil society.

57. We request the Secretary-General to report to the Economic and Social Council on a regular basis on the work of the High-level Task Force on the Global Food Security Crisis.

58. We invite the International Labour Organization to present the "Global Jobs Pact", adopted at the ninety-eighth session of the International Labour Conference, to the substantive session of the Economic and Social Council in July 2009, which intends to promote a job-intensive recovery from the crisis, drawing on the decent work agenda, and to shape a pattern for sustainable growth.

59. We encourage the Inter-Parliamentary Union to continue to contribute to the development of global responses to the crisis.

Preparatory process for the Conference

In April, the Assembly decided, in response to the 2008 Doha Declaration on Financing for Development [YUN 2008, p. 1077], to convene at the highest level the Conference on the World Financial and Economic Crisis and Its Impact on Development, to be held in New York in June.

GENERAL ASSEMBLY ACTION

On 7 April [meeting 79], the General Assembly adopted **resolution 63/277** [draft: A/63/L.66] without vote [agenda item 48].

Organization of a United Nations conference at the highest level on the world financial and economic crisis and its impact on development

The General Assembly,

Recalling the Monterrey Consensus of the International Conference on Financing for Development and the Doha Declaration on Financing for Development: outcome document of the Follow-up International Conference on Financing for Development to Review the Implementation of the Monterrey Consensus, as well as its resolution 63/239 of 24 December 2008, in which it endorsed the Doha Declaration which states that the United Nations will hold a conference at the highest level on the world financial and economic crisis and its impact on development, to be organized by the President of the General Assembly with the modalities to be defined by March 2009 at the latest,

Conscious of the importance of examining and overcoming the deepening world financial and economic crisis and its impact on development, concerned about the present and future impacts of the crisis on, inter alia, employment, trade, investment and development, including the achievement of the internationally agreed development goals and the Millennium Development Goals, convinced of the urgency of undertaking coordinated and collaborative actions and appropriate measures to mitigate the impact of the crisis on development, emphasizing the importance of the role of the United Nations and its Member States in the ongoing international discussions on reforming and strengthening the international financial and economic system and architecture, and stressing the contributions of the United Nations development system in the response to the crisis,

1. *Decides* that the Conference on the World Financial and Economic Crisis and Its Impact on Development:

(a) Will be convened at United Nations Headquarters from 1 to 3 June 2009;

(b) Will be held at the highest level;

(c) Will be presided over by the President of the General Assembly;

(d) Will consist of:

(i) A short opening session;

(ii) Plenary meetings;

(iii) Four interactive round tables, which will address the main issues before the Conference as outlined above;

(e) Will result in a concise outcome to be agreed by Member States;

(f) Will also result in summaries of the round-table discussions, to be included in the final report of the Conference;

2. *Invites* the Holy See, in its capacity as observer State, and Palestine, in its capacity as observer, to participate in the Conference;

3. *Invites* the United Nations funds and programmes, and the specialized agencies of the United Nations system, including the International Labour Organization and the United Nations Conference on Trade and Development, the Bretton Woods institutions, the World Trade Organization, the regional development banks, the regional commissions of the United Nations, non-governmental organizations and civil society and business sector entities to participate in the Conference and in the preparatory process of the Conference in accordance with the rules of procedure of the General Assembly and, in addition, where appropriate, the rules of procedure adopted for the Monterrey Conference and for the Doha Conference, with the practical arrangements and modalities for participation in the Conference, including the accreditation procedures for non-governmental organizations and civil society and business sector entities, to be dealt with in the note referred to in paragraph 4 below;

4. *Requests* the Secretariat, in close collaboration with the Office of the President of the General Assembly, to provide no later than 20 April 2009 a note on the organization of work of the Conference;

5. *Welcomes* the special high-level meeting in 2009 of the Economic and Social Council with the Bretton Woods institutions, the World Trade Organization and the United Nations Conference on Trade and Development, which will include a session devoted to a comprehensive discussion of the global financial and economic crisis and its impact on development, and invites the President of the Council to provide a summary of the discussion as an input to the preparatory process for the draft outcome document of the Conference;

6. *Notes with appreciation* the initiative of the President of the General Assembly in organizing the interactive, thematic dialogue on the world financial and economic crisis and its impact on development, held from 25 to 27 March 2009, as a contribution to the preparatory process;

7. *Welcomes* the initiative of the regional commissions, with the support of regional financial institutions, including regional development banks, and other relevant entities, to hold regional consultations, and invites them to provide inputs as early as possible to the preparatory process for the Conference;

8. *Requests* the Secretary-General to prepare a report, based upon the analytical work of United Nations programmes, departments and organizations, on the origins and causes of the present crisis, the mechanisms of its transmission to the developing countries, the potential impact of the crisis on development, the response of the United Nations to the crisis through its development activities and national and international policy responses to date;

9. *Requests* the President of the General Assembly, through an open, transparent and inclusive process led by the Member States, to present in a timely manner a draft text based upon all preparatory inputs to serve as the basis for an outcome document, to be agreed by the Member States;

10. *Requests* the Secretary-General to provide all appropriate assistance to the preparatory process and the Conference.

Communication. In a 4 March note [E/2009/12], Finland transmitted to the Economic and Social Council the Chairperson's summary of the forty-seventh session of the Commission for Social Development (see p. 1073) and requested that it be made available to the United Nations Conference on the World Financial and Economic Crisis and Its Impact on Development.

By **decision 63/555** of 8 May, the Assembly adopted the arrangements and organization of work of the Conference, as set out in an April Secretariat note [A/63/825]. It recommended for adoption by the Conference the provisional rules of procedure, the provisional agenda and the proposed timetable for the work of the Conference, as set out in annexes to the note.

On 26 May (**decision 63/556**), the General Assembly, on the proposal of the Assembly President, decided to postpone the Conference to 24 to 26 June.

Follow-up to Conference

GENERAL ASSEMBLY ACTION

On 31 July [meeting 102], the General Assembly adopted **resolution 63/305** [draft: A/63/L.77] without vote [agenda item 48].

**Establishment of an ad hoc open-ended working group
of the General Assembly to follow up on the issues
contained in the Outcome of the Conference on the
World Financial and Economic Crisis
and Its Impact on Development**

The General Assembly,

Recalling its resolution 63/303 of 9 July 2009, by which
it endorsed by consensus the Outcome of the Conference
on the World Financial and Economic Crisis and Its Impact
on Development,

Recognizing the depth of the current financial and economic crisis and the urgency of follow-up action,

Reaffirming that this process shall continue to be driven
by Member States,

1. *Decides* to establish immediately an ad hoc open-
ended working group of the General Assembly to follow up
on the issues contained in the Outcome of the Conference
on the World Financial and Economic Crisis and Its Impact
on Development;

2. *Requests* the Ad Hoc Open-ended Working Group
to submit a report on the progress of its work to the General
Assembly before the end of the sixty-fourth session.

Economic and Social Council action. The Economic and Social Council, in **decision 2009/258** of
31 July, requested the Secretariat to provide detailed
reports, by 15 September, on the following subjects:
the promotion and enhancement of a coordinated
response of the UN development system and the specialized agencies in the follow-up to and implementation of the outcome of the Conference on the World
Financial and Economic Crisis and Its Impact on Development; and the implementation of the agreements
between the United Nations and the Bretton Woods
institutions, focusing in particular on enhancing collaboration and cooperation between them, and on opportunities for advancing their respective mandates. It
also asked the Secretariat to report on the possible establishment of an ad hoc panel of experts on the world
economic and financial crisis and its impact on development. The panel could provide independent technical expertise and analysis, which could contribute to
informing international action and political decision-
making and to fostering constructive dialogue and exchanges among policymakers, academics, institutions
and civil society. The Council President was asked to
conduct, as soon as possible thereafter, open-ended
informal consultations involving relevant institutions.
The Council decided to review progress made in the
consideration of those issues at its resumed substantive session of 2009.

In response to Council decision 2009/258, the Secretariat submitted a 15 September note [E/2009/113]
on the possible establishment of an ad hoc panel of
experts on the world economic and financial crisis and
its impact on development to follow up on the issues
contained in the outcome of the Conference. The note
discussed past terms of reference and the experience

of previous ad hoc panels of experts. It concluded that
the Council and the Assembly should consider the
establishment of the panel. The guiding principles
should include that such a panel should provide independent technical expertise and analysis, on which
Governments, UN agencies and other international
institutions could draw in formulating policies. Duplication of efforts and overlap with terms of reference
of existing bodies should be avoided. International organizations should foster effective cooperation, and
efforts should be guided by pragmatism, specialization and division of labour.

On 16 September [E/2009/114], the Secretary-
General issued a report on the promotion and enhancement of a coordinated response of the UN
development system and the specialized agencies in
the follow-up to and implementation of the Outcome of the Conference on the World Financial and
Economic Crisis and Its Impact on Development.
The report focused on initiatives that constituted a
coordinated, UN system-wide response to the crisis.
The response, which began in 2008, was led by CEB
[YUN 2008, p. 1067]. At its spring session retreat (Paris,
4 April 2009) [CEB/2009/1], CEB issued a communiqué
in which it emphasized that the social effects of the
crisis could worsen and that responding to the crisis
required a coherent and comprehensive strategy that
rallied the knowledge, experience, strengths and capacities of the entire UN system. The Board endorsed
nine joint initiatives to assist countries and the global
community to confront the crisis. The initiatives were
related to additional financing for the most vulnerable; food security; trade; green economy; the Global
Jobs Pact; social protection, humanitarian, security
and social stability; technology and innovation; and
monitoring and analysis. The operationalization of
the joint crisis initiatives included global advocacy,
regional coordination, as well as operational activities in response to the specific needs at the country
level. On 7 July, the lead agencies of the initiatives
met in Geneva to define a common framework for
operationalizing the initiatives. Participants agreed
that the leaders of the initiatives, focusing on the crisis dimensions, would move forward with their work
in collaboration with the cooperating organizations.
The United Nations Development Group (UNDG) Advisory Group, meeting in Geneva on 14 and 15 July,
agreed that UNDG would facilitate the operationalization of the nine initiatives by consolidating the support that each agency could offer UN country teams
under each initiative and setting up a system through
which agencies could access that support.

The report concluded that the UN system had
made considerable efforts to establish mechanisms
that allowed for a coordinated response to the world
economic and financial crisis. Through CEB and other

mechanisms, the UN system would continue to enhance that response, focusing on implementation at the global, regional and country levels, in cooperation with national authorities.

On 15 September, the Secretariat submitted a note [E/2009/115] on enhancing collaboration and cooperation between the United Nations and the Bretton Woods institutions, which provided an overview of the implementation of the agreements focusing on innovative institutional arrangements for enhancing collaboration between them in the economic, social and related fields. Special attention was given to the engagement of the Bretton Woods institutions at the intergovernmental and staff levels in the financing for development process to promote coherence, coordination and cooperation. It also provided recent examples of collaboration at the operational level in support of global efforts to achieve the MDGs and to address new challenges and emerging issues, including those related to the global financial and economic crisis.

In December [E/2009/119], the President of the Economic and Social Council issued a summary on follow-up to the Outcome of the Conference on the World Financial and Economic Crisis and Its Impact on Development. In response to Council decision 2009/258, the Council President convened, on 19 October, 26 October and 10 November, respectively, open-ended, informal consultations on each of the three mandates covered by the reports.

Other issues

Competition law and policy

The Intergovernmental Group of Experts on Competition Law and Policy, at its tenth session (Geneva, 7–9 July) [TD/B/C.I/CLP/6 & Corr.1], had before it UNCTAD secretariat studies on public monopolies, concessions and competition law and policies [TD/B/C.I/CLP/2], the relationship between competition and industrial policies in promoting economic development [TD/B/C.I/CLP/3], the use of economic analysis in competition cases [TD/B/C.I/CLP/4], and capacity-building and technical assistance in the area of competition law and policy [TD/B/C.I/CLP/5]. Also before the Group of Experts was the compilation of the responses to the UNCTAD questionnaire on public monopolies, concessions and competition law and policies (part I); on the relationship between competition and industrial policies in promoting economic development (part II); on and the importance of economic analysis in competition cases (part III). The Group discussed peer reviews on competition law and policy; review of the Model Law on Competition; studies related to the 1980 Set of Multilaterally Agreed Equitable Principles and Rules for the Control of Restrictive Business Practices (known as the Set) [YUN 1980, p. 626]; and its work programme.

In agreed conclusions, the Group of Experts decided that UNCTAD should undertake further voluntary peer reviews on the competition law and policy of member States or regional groupings of States during the Sixth (2010) United Nations Conference to Review All Aspects of the Set. It underlined the importance of using economic analysis in competition cases in the enforcement of competition law, the importance of the relationship between competition and industrial policies in promoting economic development, and the need to strengthen international cooperation in those areas, particularly for the benefit of developing countries; and called on UNCTAD to promote and support cooperation between competition authorities and Governments, as directed by the 2008 Accra Accord [YUN 2008, p. 1042]. The Group requested the UNCTAD secretariat to disseminate the conclusions of the Group's discussions to all interested States, and prepare studies for the Sixth (2010) Review Conference on closer international cooperation on competition policy for the development objectives of developing countries and of LDCs. The consultations should be organized around three clusters of issues: implementation of competition law and policy (session I); review of the experience gained in the implementation of the Set, including voluntary peer reviews (session II); and the role of competition policy in promoting economic development (session III). For the consideration of the Sixth Review Conference, the UNCTAD secretariat was also asked to prepare a peer review of interested countries; reports on the items set out in the agreed conclusions, with a view to facilitating round table discussions; an updated review of capacity-building and technical assistance; a further revised and updated version of the Model Law on Competition; and further issues of the *Handbook on Competition Legislation*. The UNCTAD secretariat was asked to pursue its capacity-building and technical cooperation activities, and Member States were invited to assist UNCTAD in that regard by providing experts, training facilities or financial resources.

International standards of accounting and reporting

The Intergovernmental Working Group of Experts on International Standards of Accounting and Reporting (isar), at its twenty-sixth session (Geneva, 7–9 October) [TD/B/C.II/ISAR/54] had before it unctad secretariat reports on the 2009 reviews of corporate responsibility reporting: the largest transnational corporations and climate change-related disclosure [TD/B/C.II/ISAR/CRP.7]; the implementation status of corporate governance disclosures: an examination of reporting practices among large enterprises in 12 emerging markets [TD/B/C.II/ISAR/CRP.6]; and the reporting status of corporate responsibility indicators: case study Brazil [TD/B/C.II/ISAR/CRP.4]. Also before the Working Group were a report by the unctad secretariat and the University of Stirling on 2009 reviews of the implementation status of corporate governance disclosures: an inventory of disclosure requirements in 24 emerging markets [TD/B/C.II/ISAR/CRP.8]; a report by the secretariat and the Institute of Chartered Accountants of Pakistan on the implementation of corporate governance disclosures: case study Pakistan [TD/B/C.II/ISAR/CRP.5]; and an unctad secretariat note on the review of practical implementation issues of international financial reporting standards: impact of the financial crisis [TD/B/C.II/ISAR/53].

In its agreed conclusions, the Group of Experts noted that the financial crisis had put an unprecedented focus on accounting and reporting standards, and it reiterated the importance of a single set of high-quality global financial reporting standards for strengthening the international financial regulatory system, as highlighted by the G20 leaders in the statement issued at their Pittsburgh summit (Pittsburgh, Pennsylvania, United States, 24–25 September). Delegates called on the International Accounting Standards Board (IASB) to provide further guidance on implementation of the International Financial Reporting Standards (IFRS) in order to ensure their consistent application around the world. IsAR highlighted the need for institutional and technical capacity-building in the area of accounting and reporting faced by developing countries and countries with economies in transition. IsAR delegates agreed on the need to consider, as a result of the publication by IASB of IFRS for small and medium-sized enterprises (SMEs), withdrawing Accounting and Financial Reporting Guidelines for SMEs (SMEGA) Level 2. They requested the UNCTAD secretariat to compile feedback on practical implementation of the revised SMEGA Level 3 and conduct studies on practical implementation of IFRS for SMEs, with a view to sharing experiences.

The Group of Experts agreed on the need for further work on the capacity-building needs of member States in accounting and reporting, with a view to developing a capacity-building framework. It requested the UNCTAD secretariat to reconstitute a consultative group to propose an approach for consideration by the twenty-seventh IsAR session. The secretariat was also asked to organize workshops and seminars on those topics and further explore means of integrating discussions on those issues in future ISAR deliberations. IsAR reiterated the importance of corporate governance disclosure for promoting investment, stability and sustainable economic development, and asked UNCTAD to gather and disseminate data on corporate governance disclosure practices around the world, with a focus on providing information to policymakers, investors and other stakeholders.

The Investment, Enterprise and Development Commission, at its first session [TD/B/C.II/5], took note of the report of the twenty-fifth (2008) session of the Intergovernmental Working Group of Experts on IsAR [YUN 2008, p. 1093].

Taxation

Committee of Experts on International Cooperation in Tax Matters

The Economic and Social Council, by **decision 2009/265** of 31 July, took note of the report of the Committee of Experts on International Cooperation in Tax Matters on its fourth (2008) session [YUN 2008, p. 1095]; it decided to convene the fifth session of the Committee in Geneva from 19 to 23 October.

The fifth session of the Committee of Experts (Geneva, 19–23 October) [E/2009/45-E/C.18/2009/6] discussed the definition of permanent establishment; taxation of services, including royalties and technical fees; attribution of profits under article 7 of the United Nations Model Double Taxation Convention between Developed and Developing Countries; taxation of development projects; tax competition in corporate tax; the proposed United Nations code of conduct on cooperation in combating international tax evasion and avoidance; revision of the Manual for the Negotiation of Bilateral Tax Treaties between Developed and Developing Countries; practical issues on how treaties are developed; dispute resolution; general issues in the review of Commentaries of the United Nations Model Double Taxation Convention between Developed and Developing Countries; and transfer pricing, including a manual and checklist for developing countries.

Transport

Maritime transport

The *Review of Maritime Transport, 2009* [Sales No. E.09.II.D.11], prepared by the UNCTAD secretariat, reported that in tandem with the global economic downturn and reduced trade, growth in international seaborne trade decelerated in 2008, expanding by 3.6 per cent as compared with 4.5 per cent in 2007. UNCTAD estimated international seaborne trade at 8.17 billion tons of goods loaded, with dry cargo continuing to account for the largest share (66.3 per cent). At the beginning of 2009, the world merchant fleet had expanded by 6.7 per cent to 1.19 billion deadweight tons (dwt). For the first time, the total tonnage on dry bulk carriers exceeded the tonnage on oil tankers.

In a later report, *Review of Maritime Transport, 2010* [Sales No. E.10.II.D.4], UNCTAD stated that in

2009 international seaborne trade volumes contracted by 4.5 per cent. While no shipping segment was spared, minor dry bulks and containerized trades suffered the most severe contractions. Total goods loaded amounted to 7.8 billion tons, down from around 8.2 billion tons recorded in 2008. By the end of 2009, freight rates in all sectors had recovered from their earlier lows, although they were still significantly beneath their 2008 levels. The world fleet continued to grow by 7 per cent. Accordingly, the overall fleet productivity in 2009—measured in tons of cargo carried per deadweight ton—decreased further compared with the 2008 figures. The global average volume of cargo in tons per carrying capacity dwt decreased, and the average ship was fully loaded only 6.6 times in 2009 compared with 7.3 times in 2008. Developments in China were particularly noteworthy with regard to the supply of and demand for shipping services. Between 2008 and 2009, China overtook Germany as the third-largest shipowning country, Japan as the second-biggest shipbuilding country, and India as the busiest ship-recycling country.

Transport of dangerous goods

In response to Economic and Social Council resolution 2007/6 [YUN 2007, p. 998], the Secretary-General submitted an April report [E/2009/55] on the work during 2007–2008 of the Committee of Experts on the Transport of Dangerous Goods and on the Globally Harmonized System of Classification and Labelling of Chemicals.

The report stated that the secretariat published the fifteenth revised edition of the *Recommendations on the Transport of Dangerous Goods: Model Regulations* [Sales No. E.07.VIII.1], amendments to the fourth revised edition of the *Recommendations on the Transport of Dangerous Goods: Manual of Tests and Criteria* [Sales No. E.07.VIII.2] and the second revised edition of the *Globally Harmonized System of Classification and Labelling of Chemicals* (GHS) [Sales. No. E.07.II.E.5]. All main legal instruments and codes governing the international transport of dangerous goods by sea, air, road, rail or inland waterway were amended accordingly, with effect from 1 January 2009, and many Governments transposed the provisions of the Model Regulations into their own legislation for domestic traffic for application from 2009. Many Governments and international organizations had revised or taken steps to revise existing national and international legislation in order to implement GHS by the recommended target date of 2008 or as soon as possible thereafter.

The Committee adopted amendments to the Model Regulations and the *Manual of Tests and Criteria*, which consisted mainly of new or revised provisions that concerned listing, classification and packing of dangerous goods; transport in cryogenic receptacles; transport of fumigated freight containers; transport of radioactive material; transport of dangerous goods packed in limited quantities; metal hydride systems of storage of hydrogen; test requirements for explosives, pyrotechnic substances and lithium batteries; harmonization with GHS; and the use of electronic data interchange for documentation purposes. It also adopted amendments to GHS concerning mainly classification criteria for some physical hazards, hazards to the environment, health (chronic toxicity and respiratory and skin sensitizers) and the ozone layer. It completed the validation of the protocol on transformation/dissolution of metals and metal components in aqueous media, and issued a new set of combined hazard statements as well as guidance on the procedure of allocation of hazard statements and on the labelling of small packaging.

The Committee approved the programme of work for the 2009–2010 biennium and planned sessions for the Subcommittees of Experts on the Transport of Dangerous Goods and on the Globally Harmonized System of Classification and Labelling of Chemicals. It recommended a draft resolution for adoption by the Economic and Social Council (see below).

ECONOMIC AND SOCIAL COUNCIL ACTION

On 29 July [meeting 42], the Economic and Social Council adopted **resolution 2009/19** [draft: E/2009/55] without vote [agenda item 13 *(m)*].

Work of the Committee of Experts on the Transport of Dangerous Goods and on the Globally Harmonized System of Classification and Labelling of Chemicals

The Economic and Social Council,

Recalling its resolutions 1999/65 of 26 October 1999 and 2007/6 of 23 July 2007,

Having considered the report of the Secretary-General on the work of the Committee of Experts on the Transport of Dangerous Goods and on the Globally Harmonized System of Classification and Labelling of Chemicals during the biennium 2007–2008,

A. Work of the Committee regarding the transport of dangerous goods

Recognizing the importance of the work of the Committee of Experts on the Transport of Dangerous Goods and on the Globally Harmonized System of Classification and Labelling of Chemicals for the harmonization of codes and regulations relating to the transport of dangerous goods,

Bearing in mind the need to maintain safety standards at all times and to facilitate trade, as well as the importance of this to the various organizations responsible for modal regulations, while meeting the growing concern for the protection of life, property and the environment through the safe and secure transport of dangerous goods,

Noting the ever-increasing volume of dangerous goods being introduced into worldwide commerce and the rapid expansion of technology and innovation,

Recalling that, while the major international instruments governing the transport of dangerous goods by the various modes of transport and many national regulations are now better harmonized with the Model Regulations annexed to the Committee's recommendations on the transport of dangerous goods, further work on harmonizing these instruments is necessary to enhance safety and to facilitate trade, and recalling also that uneven progress in the updating of national inland transport legislation in some countries of the world continues to present serious challenges to international multimodal transport,

1. *Expresses its appreciation* for the work of the Committee of Experts on the Transport of Dangerous Goods and on the Globally Harmonized System of Classification and Labelling of Chemicals with respect to matters relating to the transport of dangerous goods, including their security in transport;

2. *Requests* the Secretary-General:

(a) To circulate the new and amended recommendations on the transport of dangerous goods to the Governments of Member States, the specialized agencies, the International Atomic Energy Agency and other international organizations concerned;

(b) To publish the sixteenth revised edition of the *Recommendations on the Transport of Dangerous Goods: Model Regulations* and the fifth revised edition of the *Recommendations on the Transport of Dangerous Goods: Manual of Tests and Criteria* in all the official languages of the United Nations, in the most cost-effective manner, no later than the end of 2009;

(c) To make those publications available on the website of the Economic Commission for Europe, which provides secretariat services to the Committee, and also on CD-ROM;

3. *Invites* all Governments, the regional commissions, the specialized agencies, the International Atomic Energy Agency and the other international organizations concerned to transmit to the secretariat of the Committee their views on the Committee's work, together with any comments that they may wish to make on the recommendations on the transport of dangerous goods;

4. *Invites* all interested Governments, the regional commissions, the specialized agencies and the international organizations concerned to take into account the recommendations of the Committee when developing or updating appropriate codes and regulations;

5. *Requests* the Committee to study, in consultation with the International Maritime Organization, the International Civil Aviation Organization, the regional commissions and the intergovernmental organizations concerned, the possibilities of improving the implementation of the Model Regulations on the transport of dangerous goods in all countries for the purposes of ensuring a high level of safety and eliminating technical barriers to international trade, including through the further harmonization of international agreements or conventions governing the international transport of dangerous goods;

6. *Invites* all Governments, as well as the regional commissions, the International Maritime Organization, the International Civil Aviation Organization and other organi-

zations concerned, to provide feedback to the Committee regarding differences between the provisions of national, regional or international legal instruments and those of the Model Regulations, in order to enable the Committee to develop cooperative guidelines for enhancing consistency between those requirements and reducing unnecessary impediments, to identify existing substantive and modal international, regional and national differences, with the aim of reducing such differences to the greatest extent practical and ensuring that differences, where they are necessary, do not pose impediments to the safe and efficient transport of dangerous goods, and to undertake an editorial review of the Model Regulations and various modal instruments with the aim of improving clarity, user-friendliness and ease of translation;

B. Work of the Committee regarding the Globally Harmonized System of Classification and Labelling of Chemicals

Bearing in mind that, in paragraph 23 *(c)* of the Plan of Implementation of the World Summit on Sustainable Development ("Johannesburg Plan of Implementation"), countries were encouraged to implement the Globally Harmonized System of Classification and Labelling of Chemicals as soon as possible with a view to having the system fully operational by 2008,

Bearing in mind also that the General Assembly, in its resolution 57/253 of 20 December 2002, endorsed the Johannesburg Plan of Implementation and requested the Economic and Social Council to implement the provisions of the Plan relevant to its mandate and, in particular, to promote the implementation of Agenda 21 by strengthening system-wide coordination,

Noting with satisfaction:

(a) That the Economic Commission for Europe and all United Nations programmes and specialized agencies concerned with chemical safety in the field of transport or the environment, in particular the United Nations Environment Programme, the International Maritime Organization and the International Civil Aviation Organization, either already took appropriate steps to amend their legal instruments in order to give effect to the Globally Harmonized System before the end of 2008 target date or are considering amending those instruments as soon as possible;

(b) That the International Labour Organization, the Food and Agriculture Organization of the United Nations and the World Health Organization are also taking appropriate steps to adapt their existing chemical safety recommendations, codes and guidelines to the Globally Harmonized System, in particular in the areas of occupational health and safety, pesticide management and the prevention and treatment of poisoning;

(c) That the Globally Harmonized System has already been in force in New Zealand since 2001 and in Mauritius since 2004;

(d) That a new regulation of the European Parliament and of the Council implementing the Globally Harmonized System in the States members of the European Union and the European Economic Area entered into force on 20 January 2009;

(e) That other Member States participating in the activities of the Subcommittee of Experts on the Globally Harmonized System of Classification and Labelling of

Chemicals are actively preparing revisions of national legislation applicable to chemicals with a view to implementing the Globally Harmonized System;

(f) That a number of United Nations programmes, specialized agencies and regional organizations, in particular the United Nations Institute for Training and Research, the International Labour Organization, the World Health Organization, the Economic Commission for Europe, the Asia-Pacific Economic Cooperation, the Organization for Economic Cooperation and Development and the European Commission, as well as a number of Governments, and non-governmental organizations representing the chemical industry, have organized or contributed to multiple workshops, seminars and other capacity-building activities at the international, regional, subregional and national levels in order to raise administration, health sector and industry awareness and to prepare for the implementation of the Globally Harmonized System,

Aware that effective implementation will require further cooperation between the Subcommittee of Experts and the international bodies concerned, continued efforts by the Governments of Member States, cooperation with the industry and other stakeholders, and significant support for capacity-building activities in countries with economies in transition and developing countries,

Recalling the particular significance of the United Nations Institute for Training and Research/International Labour Organization/Organization for Economic Cooperation and Development Global Partnership for Capacity-building to Implement the Globally Harmonized System of Classification and Labelling of Chemicals for building capacities at all levels,

1. *Commends* the Secretary-General for the publication of the second revised edition of the *Globally Harmonized System of Classification and Labelling of Chemicals* in the six official languages of the United Nations, in book form and on CD-ROM, and for its availability, together with that of related informational material, on the website of the Economic Commission for Europe, which provides secretariat services to the Committee of Experts on the Transport of Dangerous Goods and on the Globally Harmonized System of Classification and Labelling of Chemicals;

2. *Expresses its deep appreciation* to the Committee, the Economic Commission for Europe, United Nations programmes, specialized agencies and other organizations concerned for their fruitful cooperation and for their commitment to the implementation of the Globally Harmonized System of Classification and Labelling of Chemicals;

3. *Requests* the Secretary-General:

(a) To circulate the amendments to the second revised edition of the *Globally Harmonized System of Classification and Labelling of Chemicals* to the Governments of Member States, the specialized agencies and other international organizations concerned;

(b) To publish the third revised edition of the *Globally Harmonized System of Classification and Labelling of Chemicals* in all the official languages of the United Nations in the most cost-effective manner and no later than the end of 2009 and to make it available on CD-ROM and on the website of the Economic Commission for Europe;

(c) To continue to make information on the implementation of the Globally Harmonized System available on the website of the Economic Commission for Europe;

4. *Invites* Governments that have not yet done so to take the necessary steps, through appropriate national procedures and/or legislation, to implement the Globally Harmonized System as soon as possible;

5. *Reiterates its invitation* to the regional commissions, the United Nations programmes, the specialized agencies and other organizations concerned to promote the implementation of the Globally Harmonized System and, where relevant, to amend their respective international legal instruments addressing transport safety, workplace safety, consumer protection or the protection of the environment so as to give effect to the Globally Harmonized System through such instruments;

6. *Invites* Governments, the regional commissions, the United Nations programmes, the specialized agencies and other organizations concerned to provide feedback to the Subcommittee of Experts on the Globally Harmonized System of Classification and Labelling of Chemicals on the steps taken for the implementation of the Globally Harmonized System in all relevant sectors, through international, regional or national legal instruments, recommendations, codes and guidelines, including, when applicable, information about the transitional periods for its implementation;

7. *Encourages* Governments, the regional commissions, the United Nations programmes, the specialized agencies and other relevant international organizations and non-governmental organizations, in particular those representing industry, to strengthen their support for the implementation of the Globally Harmonized System by providing financial contributions and/or technical assistance for capacity-building activities in developing countries and countries with economies in transition;

C. Programme of work of the Committee

Taking note of the programme of work of the Committee of Experts on the Transport of Dangerous Goods and on the Globally Harmonized System of Classification and Labelling of Chemicals for the biennium 2009–2010, as contained in paragraph 46 of the report of the Secretary-General,

Noting the relatively poor level of participation of experts from developing countries and countries with economies in transition in the work of the Committee and the need to promote their wider participation in its work,

1. *Decides* to approve the programme of work of the Committee of Experts on the Transport of Dangerous Goods and on the Globally Harmonized System of Classification and Labelling of Chemicals;

2. *Stresses* the importance of the participation of experts from developing countries and countries with economies in transition in the work of the Committee, calls in that regard for voluntary contributions to facilitate such participation, including through support for travel and daily subsistence, and invites Member States and international organizations in a position to do so to contribute;

3. *Requests* the Secretary-General to submit to the Economic and Social Council in 2011 a report on the implementation of the present resolution, the recommendations on the transport of dangerous goods and the Globally Harmonized System of Classification and Labelling of Chemicals.

UNCTAD institutional and organizational questions

In 2009, the Trade and Development Board (TDB)—the governing body of UNCTAD—held the following sessions, all in Geneva: fifty-sixth annual session (14–25 September and 12 October) [A/64/15 (Part IV)], forty-sixth (27 March) [A/64/15 (Part II)], forty-seventh (30 June) [A/64/15 (Part III)] and forty-eighth (25 November) [A/65/15 (Part I)] executive sessions.

In June, TDB took note of the secretariat reports on activities undertaken by UNCTAD in favour of Africa [TD/B/EX(47)/2] (see p. 931) and food security in Africa: learning lessons from the food crisis [TD/B/EX(47)/3] [ibid.]. It took note of the report of the Trade and Development Commission on its first session [TD/B/C.I/5] endorsed the agreed conclusions contained therein; and approved the draft provisional agenda and topics for the Commission's second session. The Board also took note of the report of the Investment, Enterprise and Development Commission on its first session [TD/B/C.II/5] and the agreed conclusions contained therein (see p. 925); approved the draft provisional agenda and topics for the Commission's second session; and approved topics for single-year expert meetings for 2010. TDB further approved the holding of a second UNCTAD public symposium with civil society in 2010.

In September, TDB adopted agreed conclusions on: the review of progress in the implementation of the Programme of Action for LDCs for the Decade 2001–2010 [agreed conclusions 496(LVI)], economic development in Africa: strengthening regional economic integration for Africa's development [agreed conclusions 497(LVI)] (see p. 932), and the secretariat proposal [TD/B/56/CRP.2] to enhance the functioning of the Working Party on the Strategic Framework and the Programme Budget [agreed conclusions 501(LVI)]. It adopted a decision on the review of UNCTAD technical cooperation activities and their financing (see p. 964). In further action [agreed conclusions 499(LVI)], the Board approved the UNCTAD communications strategy [TD/B/56/9/Rev.1] and publications policy [TD/B/56/10/Rev.1]; and requested the UNCTAD secretariat to implement the strategy and policy with immediate effect and report to the Board annually on implementation through the Working Party. TDB also approved the report of the Working Party [TD/B/WP/210] on the Strategic Framework and the Programme Budget on its fifty-second (resumed) session (see p. 965) [dec. 500(LVI)].

In other action, TDB took note of the report of the ITC UNCTAD/WTO Joint Advisory Group on its forty-second session [ITC/AG(XLII)/225] (see p. 924); the UNCTAD secretariat report on progress made in the implementation of the outcomes of the major UN conferences and summits, and UNCTAD contributions [TD/B/56/8]; the secretariat report on UNCTAD assistance to the Palestinian people [TD/B/56/3] (see p. 463); and the forty-second annual report of the United Nations Commission on International Trade Law [A/64/17] (see p. 1315). The Board approved the applications of the Organization of Eastern Caribbean States and the Eurasian Development Bank to participate in UNCTAD activities as observers; and the applications of the Grain and Feed Trade Association and IQsensato to participate in UNCTAD activities in the special and general categories, respectively.

Appointment of UNCTAD Secretary-General. On 22 June [A/63/891], the UN Secretary-General proposed to extend the appointment of Supachai Panitchpakdi (Thailand) as UNCTAD Secretary-General for another four-year term of office beginning on 1 September 2009 and ending on 31 August 2013. The General Assembly confirmed the appointment on 6 July (**decision 63/424**).

Technical cooperation

In a June report [TD/B/WP/212 & Add.1,2], the UNCTAD Secretary-General reviewed technical cooperation activities in 2008. The delivery of technical cooperation increased to $38.2 million. Overall contributions to trust funds contracted by 8 per cent. Contributions by developing countries accounted for 25 per cent of the total contributions to trust funds. Expenditures on country projects increased in all the regions, and accounted for 43 per cent of total delivery.

A later report [TD/B/WP/222 & Add.1, 2] stated that in 2009, delivery of UNCTAD technical cooperation achieved its highest level amounting to $38.8 million. The Automated System for Customs Data continued to be UNCTAD's largest technical assistance activity, followed by the Debt Management and Financial Analysis System: those two programmes accounted for 47 per cent of total UNCTAD's technical cooperation delivery.

By region, $8 million (20.5 per cent of the total expenditure) was spent on technical cooperation in Asia and the Pacific; $7.3 million (18.9 per cent) in Africa; $5.3 million (13.5 per cent) in Latin America and the Caribbean; and $0.7 million (1.9 per cent) in Europe. Interregional projects accounted for $17.5 million (45.1 per cent) of the total expenditure; and LDCs accounted for $15.9 million (41 per cent).

By thematic cluster, transport and trade facilitation accounted for $14.7 million (37.8 per cent) of the total expenditure; strengthening the debt management capacity of developing countries, $5 million (13 per cent); capacity-building on trade negotiations and commercial diplomacy, $3.4 million (8.7 per cent).

Overall contributions to trust funds amounted to $29.8 million—back to the level of 2006—contracting by 12 per cent compared with the previous year due to the financial crisis. Contributions from developed countries, amounting to $13.7 million, decreased by about 13 per cent as compared with 2008, accounting for 45.7 per cent of total contributions to trust funds; nevertheless, the 2009 figure was the lowest since 2004. Contributions from developing countries increased by 16 per cent—to almost $10 million—accounting for 33.3 per cent of total contributions to trust funds. The European Commission continued to be the single largest contributor to operational activities; after two consecutive years of increase, however, its contributions decreased in 2009 to $2.6 million, accounting for 8.7 per cent of total contributions. The UN system and other international organizations contributed 2.9 million or 9.6 per cent, and the public and private sectors contributed $0.8 million or 2.6 per cent.

On 25 September [A/64/15 (Part IV), dec. 498(LVI)], TDB noted the increase in total delivery of UNCTAD technical cooperation programmes and urged donors and the UNCTAD secretariat to further enhance their assistance to LDCs. It expressed concern regarding the decrease of the funds allocated to technical assistance projects for developing countries acceding to WTO, particularly LDCs. In that regard, TDB invited donors to make contributions to the UNCTAD Trust Fund for WTO accession. It requested the UNCTAD secretariat to enhance its regional and subregional activities, and ensure that the regional dimension was given adequate attention in the delivery of technical cooperation. The secretariat was also asked to upgrade data and analytical tools on South-South flows and cooperation, and promote South-South and triangular cooperation, in accordance with the 2008 Accra Accord [YUN 2008, p. 1042]; and continue to provide information regarding requests for technical cooperation. TDB reaffirmed that the establishment of thematic trust funds should aim at enhancing the effectiveness and impact of UNCTAD technical cooperation activities without compromising the scope, content, delivery and quality of reporting, and should enhance the links between UNCTAD operational activities and analytical work. The UNCTAD secretariat was asked to report to the Working Party on progress made on the consolidation of the thematic trust funds.

Evaluation

In June, an independent team submitted an in-depth external evaluation of the UNCTAD commodities programme [TD/B/WP/213], along with supporting materials [TD/B/WP/214]. The evaluation stated that UNCTAD work on commodities had been subject to a number of external and internal challenges that had

limited its outcomes, despite a large number of activities addressing the mandate from the 2004 São Paulo Consensus [YUN 2004, p. 955], adopted at UNCTAD XI [ibid, p. 954]. Neither UNCTAD nor its external partners could adequately anticipate and warn stakeholders to deal with the swift boom and bust cycles in commodities during the evaluation period, which were caused by unprecedented events. The internal challenges in the Commodities Branch further impaired its ability to respond adequately to developments. The unpreparedness to deal swiftly with commodity issues was the result of the collective neglect of commodities on the part of donors faced with huge development aid write-offs; developing countries that were complacent during the favourable upswing phase; and insufficient attention by UNCTAD. The lack of donor support to commodities in general, and to UNCTAD commodities work in particular, lowered the profile and importance of commodities within UNCTAD, ceding importance to other streams such as trade analysis, trade negotiations and the environment. The evaluation also stated that the relevance of UNCTAD work in commodities was beyond doubt, and that, despite its internal challenges, UNCTAD attempted to analyse commodities from a development perspective and propose market-based mechanisms to deal with the challenges. In technical assistance, UNCTAD faced aggressive competition and needed to reinvent its positioning. The quality of internal and external partnerships suffered most over the previous two years, due partly to inefficient implementation and partly to poor human relationships. The Commodities Branch had been weak at marketing its offerings to donors and a lack of enthusiasm, morale and team spirit affected its performance.

Since UNCTAD XII [YUN 2008, p. 1041], the Commodities Branch had been spun off into the new Special Unit on Commodities, which reported to the Secretary-General. The evaluation, directed at the new structure and mandate, outlined recommendations which addressed the relevance, impact, sustainability and effectiveness of the Special Unit.

UNCTAD management, in its August response to the in-depth evaluation [TD/B/WP(53)/CRP.1], stated that it looked forward to implementing the recommendations contained in the evaluation report in the light of the guidance and final outcomes of the fifty-third session of the Working Party.

The Working Party, in agreed conclusions adopted at its fifty-third session in September [TD/B/WP/215], took note of the findings of the evaluation team; expressed concern at the problems and shortcomings raised by the team; and reiterated that UNCTAD had a central role to play as a leader on commodity-related development issues. It endorsed the recommendations contained in the evaluation report and encouraged the Special Unit on Commodities to increase its productivity along the lines of the recommendations, and the donor community to increase its financial support for initiatives outlined in the programme of work. The secretariat was asked to report on the implementation of all recommendations at the TDB Executive Session in 2010.

The Working Party requested the secretariat to implement, for 2010, an in-depth evaluation of UNCTAD technical cooperation activities dedicated to LDCs, landlocked developing countries, small island developing States and structurally weak, vulnerable and small economies; and for 2011, an in-depth evaluation of the UNCTAD programme on science and technology for development. It also requested that, on an exceptional basis, an independent evaluation of the UNCTAD programme of assistance to the Palestinian people be conducted by an external evaluator, and recommended that the results be considered by TDB at its fifty-eighth (2011) session.

Strategic framework and programme budget

The UNCTAD Working Party on the Strategic Framework and Programme Budget held four sessions in 2009, all in Geneva.

At its fifty-second session (Geneva, 26–30 January) [TD/B/WP/209], the Working Party considered the draft proposal of the 2010–2011 biennium work programme for UNCTAD. In its agreed conclusions, it urged the UNCTAD secretariat to strengthen its special focus on the particular needs of the LDCs, programme of assistance to the Palestinian people and technical assistance projects to developing countries acceding to WTO. It asked the UNCTAD secretariat to improve the development and use of indicators of achievement, so as to measure the implementation of UNCTAD activities more effectively, and provide an explanatory note on the programme budget documents explaining output categories and quantities and indicators of achievement.

In agreed conclusions adopted at its resumed fifty-second session (Geneva, 8–12 June) [TD/B/WP/210], the Working Party requested the UNCTAD secretariat to extend all available support so that the Working Party could fully carry out its work, including through the timely availability of documentation. The Working Party also expressed its concern that its views and recommendations expressed at its fifty-second session

were not sufficiently taken into account in the UNCTAD section of the budget fascicle [A/64/6 (Sect. 12)], and urged the competent bodies of the General Assembly to consider reflecting those views and recommendations in the approved UNCTAD budget for the 2010–2011 biennium, especially with regard to the recent establishment of the sub-account for the Special Unit on Commodities. The Working Party requested the UNCTAD secretariat to prepare for the consideration of TDB at its next regular session a comprehensive proposal to strengthen the Working Party. It also requested the UNCTAD Secretary-General to ensure that the resources provided by the Assembly for the development pillar were also used to strengthen South-South cooperation, and that the Technical Services Unit was fully staffed and had adequate resources to fulfil its additional coordination responsibilities from the Accra Accord. It further expressed concern that the resources for the Division for Africa, Least Developed Countries and Special Programmes remained inadequate, and requested the Assembly, during its sixty-fourth (2010) session, to consider that issue on a priority basis. The Working Party asked the UNCTAD Secretary-General to enhance the organization's focus on Africa, LDCs and special programmes under all subprogrammes, and to ensure that, full regard was paid to the development needs and poverty reduction of developing countries.

At its fifty-third session (7–9 September) [TD/B/WP/215], the Working Party adopted a draft decision for consideration by TDB on technical cooperation (see p. 963), and agreed conclusions on an in-depth external evaluation of UNCTAD's commodity programme (see p. 964).

At it fifty-fourth session (18–20 November) [TD/B/WP/217], the Working Party considered the draft proposed UNCTAD Biennial Programme Plan for 2012–2013 and adopted the provisional agenda for its fifty-fifth session.

TDB, at its fifty-sixth session [A/64/15 (Part IV)], approved the report of the Working Party on its fifty-second (resumed) session [TD/B/WP/210] [dec. 500(LVI)] and noted the proposal to enhance the functioning of the Working Party put forward by the UNCTAD secretariat [TD/B/56/CRP.2] [agreed conclusion 501(LVI)].

Chapter V

Regional economic and social activities

The five UN regional commissions continued in 2009 to provide technical cooperation, including advisory services, to their member States, promote programmes and projects, and provide training to enhance national capacity-building. Three of them held regular sessions during the year—the Economic Commission for Africa (ECA), the Economic Commission for Europe (ECE) and the Economic and Social Commission for Asia and the Pacific (ESCAP). The Economic Commission for Latin America and the Caribbean (ECLAC) and the Economic and Social Commission for Western Asia (ESCWA) did not meet in 2009, but were scheduled to meet in 2010. The executive secretaries of the commissions held periodic meetings to exchange views and coordinate activities and positions on major development issues.

ECA organized its annual session as part of the joint meetings of the African Union Conference of Ministers of Economy and Finance and the ECA Conference of African Ministers of Finance, Planning and Economic Development. The session met in June on the theme "Enhancing the effectiveness of fiscal policy for domestic resource mobilization" and adopted a ministerial statement on a wide range of issues. Meeting in April on the theme "Towards sustainable agriculture and food security in the Asia-Pacific region", ESCAP adopted a resolution on implementation of the Bali Outcome Document in addressing the food, fuel and financial crises. During its March/April session, ECE considered the economic situation of Europe, held three panel discussions on the topic, and adopted conclusions on economic development in the region and on climate change mitigation and adaptation.

ECLAC conducted a study on the food crisis, and summarized eight studies on climate change mitigation in the publication *Economics of climate change in Latin America and the Caribbean—Summary 2009*, which was presented at the fifteenth session of the Conference of the Parties of the United Nations Framework Convention on Climate Change. ESCWA continued to support implementation of transport agreements, such as the Integrated Transport System in the Arab Mashreq. A key development was the adoption of an agreement on the Arab railway network.

The regional commissions also addressed the economic and social effects of the global economic and financial crisis that had begun in late 2008. Within the context of their mandates, the commissions took actions to mitigate the effects of the crisis in their regions and support stabilization and economic recovery.

Regional cooperation

In 2009, the United Nations continued to strengthen cooperation among its regional commissions, between them and other UN entities, and with regional and international organizations.

On 26 March (**decision 2009/208**), the Economic and Social Council decided that the theme for the regional cooperation item of its 2009 substantive session would be "Regional perspectives on the global economic and financial crisis, including the impact on global public health". Accordingly, the Council held an interactive dialogue with the Executive Secretaries of the regional commissions on that subject on 10 July.

Meetings of Executive Secretaries. The Executive Secretaries held three regular meetings, all in New York, during the year: one in February, and two at the margins of the Economic and Social Council session in July and of their dialogue on climate change with the Second (Economic and Financial) Committee of the General Assembly in October [E/2009/15, E/2010/15]. They focused on the regional commissions' actions and efforts to support UN system-wide coherence at the regional and global levels, as well as their contributions to and perspectives on climate change, the global challenges of achieving the Millennium Development Goals (MDGs), promoting gender equality and the empowerment of women, and ongoing monitoring of the impacts of the economic and financial crisis and other prior crises, such as food and energy security. In addition, a joint side event was organized at the margin of the United Nations Climate Change Conference (Copenhagen, Denmark, 7–19 December) (see p. 1015), during which the Executive Secretaries launched the regional commissions' joint publication assessing the impacts of climate change and highlighting adaptation and mitigation policy responses in the various regions. Two other joint publications were also launched in 2009 by the regional commissions: one during the United Nations Conference on the World Financial and Economic Crisis and Its Impact on Development (24–26 June) (see p. 947), assessing the impact of the financial crisis and highlighting policy responses; and the other in December, highlighting interregional cooperation among the commissions in the area of energy efficiency.

Review and reform of the regional commissions

In a May report [E/2009/15], the Secretary-General updated actions taken by the regional commissions to implement the guidance given by the Economic and Social Council in resolution 1998/46 [YUN 1998, p. 1262] on mainstreaming the regional dimension into the work of the United Nations and enhancing the coherence of UN activities at the regional level. The report focused attention on the experience and evolution of various regional coordination mechanisms, including synergies and complementarities between the mechanisms and regional directors' teams in support of country work, as well as the interaction between the mechanism and the High-Level Committee on Programmes of the Chief Executives Board for Coordination (CEB) on enhancing policy coherence. In February, at the Committee's seventeenth session, a decision was reached on furthering the linkage between the global and regional levels allowing the work of the Committee on certain global issues with important regional dimensions to be addressed in a coherent manner at the regional level through the regional coordination mechanisms. CEB endorsed the decision at its first regular session (Paris, 4–5 April).

An addendum [E/2009/15/Add.1] contained the texts of resolutions and decisions adopted at recent meetings of the regional commissions calling for the Council's action or attention.

By **decision 2009/262** of 31 July, the Council took note of the Secretary-General's report and addendum. By the same decision, it took note of the following reports: economic situation in 2008–2009 in the Economic Commission for Europe region [E/2009/16]; overview of the economic and social conditions in Africa, 2009 [E/2009/17]; summary of the *Economic and Social Survey of Asia and the Pacific, 2009* [E/2009/18]; Latin America and the Caribbean: economic situation and outlook, 2008–2009 [E/2009/19]; and the summary of the survey of economic and social developments in the ESCWA region, 2008–2009 [E/2009/20].

The Council adopted a resolution on the Europe-Africa fixed link through the Strait of Gibraltar (see p. 971) and a decision on the venue and dates of the sixty-sixth (2010) session of ESCAP (see p. 980).

(For the summaries of economic surveys and the texts of the resolutions, see the relevant sections of this chapter.)

Global economic and financial crisis

In his May report [E/2009/15], the Secretary-General reported on regional efforts to address the worst global economic and financial crisis since the Great Depression [YUN 2008, p. 1102] that had exacerbated the effects of recent spikes in food and fuel prices with severe consequences for the poorest and most vulnerable populations, and had rapidly spread to developing countries and emerging market economies, adversely affecting export revenues, tourism, employment, capital flows and foreign direct investment and remittances. Each region was affected differently by the multiple crises and was responding according to its particular circumstances. Although growth was expected to decline in all regions due to the crisis, hardest hit was the ECE region where emerging European economies had suffered from a sudden halt in capital inflows. Annual real growth in the region was forecast to fall from -1.5 to -3.5 per cent. A consensus emerged on the need for actions at the global, regional and national levels in order to recover from the crisis and prevent the recurrence of a similar crisis in the future. To that end, the five UN regional commissions advocated a number of policy recommendations from a regional perspective, which were contained in the Secretary-General's report.

In a later report [E/2010/15], the Secretary-General provided information on the global recovery from the economic and financial crisis, including engagement by the various regions in coordinated measures and strategies. Those responses encompassed emergency meetings of the finance and planning ministers in the regions supported by some of the regional commissions; the European Recovery Plan; the establishment of the Latin American and Caribbean Summit for Integration and Development; expanding the Chiang Mai Initiative; and the recapitalization of the regional and subregional development banks in order to raise credit lines and expedite lending procedures.

There was an increased realization about the need for greater regional cooperation, coordination and coherence to increase countries' coping capabilities and regions' resiliency. The regions that, overall, had fared better during the crisis, such as Asia and the Pacific and Latin America and the Caribbean, were better integrated and coordinated at the regional level than sub-Saharan African countries and some Arab and many Eastern European countries. On the other hand, open economies and regional entities that were highly integrated into global markets, such as China, the European Union (EU), Japan and Mexico, were more severely affected by the crisis that originated in the United States because they were more exposed to the contagion channels. The report highlighted the importance of balancing the benefits of regional integration with the potential risks that it entailed through adequate regional institutional arrangements and regulations that kept pace with the evolution—in terms of liquidity, depth and sophistication—of the global and regional financial and commercial markets.

Africa

The Economic Commission for Africa (ECA) organized its 2009 annual session as part of the joint meetings of the African Union (AU) Conference of Ministers of Economy and Finance and the ECA Conference of African Ministers of Finance, Planning and Economic Development, according to Economic and Social Council resolution 2007/4 [YUN 2007, p. 1014]. ECA held its forty-second session/Second Joint Annual Meetings of the AU and ECA Conference of Ministers (Cairo, Egypt, 2–7 June) [E/2009/38-E/ECA/CM/42/5] under the theme "Enhancing the effectiveness of fiscal policy for domestic resources mobilization". It had before it an issues paper prepared by the ECA secretariat on the theme [E/ECA/COE/28/4] and the report of the twenty-eighth meeting of the Committee of Experts of the Conference of African Ministers of Finance, Planning and Economic Development [E/ECA/CM/42/2/Rev.1] (Cairo, 2–5 June). Two high-level panel discussions and a ministerial policy debate took place on the Conference's theme, and resolutions were adopted on: enhancing domestic resource mobilization [E/2009/38 (res. 862(XLII)]; the proposed programme of work and priorities for the 2010–2011 biennium [res. 863(XLII)]; repositioning of the African Institute for Economic Development and Planning [res. 864(XLII)]; the global financial and economic crises [res. 865(XLII)]; and the MDGS [res. 866(XLII)].

The session adopted a ministerial statement [E/ECA/CM/42/3], in which Ministers commended the secretariat's report on progress in Africa towards the MDGS [E/ECA/COE/28/8] and committed to strengthening their planning systems, implementing their national development plans and devolving MDG-based planning to lower tiers of government. Recognizing that the global crisis had changed the international environment in which policies were designed and implemented, the Ministers indicated that urgent actions were needed to mitigate the crisis' impact on their economies and protect vulnerable groups. They reaffirmed the commitments made at the meeting of the Committee of Ten African Ministers of Finance and Planning and Governors of Central Banks (Cape Town, South Africa, 16 January) to deepen economic reforms, strengthen regulations of financial institutions, harmonize fiscal and monetary policies, improve governance and accountability, diversify their export structure, make more judicious use of public revenue and improve debt management. Ministers also reaffirmed their commitment to advance regional integration, including in the context of the Minimum Integration Programme and the establishment of a fund for financing the Programme. Ministers also called for action to be taken related to climate change, the establishment of a mechanism for monitoring the implementation of the African Charter on Statistics, the organization by ECA of an African regional review meeting on least developed countries, support for the Aid for Trade initiative and the fast-track establishment of the African Investment Bank.

Communication. In a letter to the Security Council dated 1 October [S/2009/511], the Democratic Republic of the Congo (DRC) transmitted the communiqué of the twenty-ninth Summit of the Heads of State and Government of the Southern African Development Community (Kinshasa, DRC, 7–8 September).

Economic trends

In 2009, Africa's gross domestic product (GDP) was negatively affected by the global recession and slowed down markedly, decelerating from 4.9 per cent in 2008 to 2.4 per cent, according to the overview of the economic and social conditions in Africa [E/2010/17]. Nonetheless, some areas showed resilience compared with previous episodes of economic recession, including better management of commodity price booms and prudent fiscal approaches, particularly by the oil-producing countries. A few oil-importing countries, including Djibouti, Ethiopia, Malawi, Morocco, Rwanda, Uganda and Zambia posted GDP growth of more than 5 per cent because of a variety of country-specific factors. Consequently, the pace at which GDP grew differed across countries and subregions, with oil-exporting countries expanding more vigorously than oil-importing countries. During the year, GDP growth decelerated or declined in four of the five subregions. West Africa displaced East Africa as the fastest-growing subregion, expanding by 5.6 per cent in 2009 compared to 5.3 per cent in 2008 and mirroring the performance of Nigeria, the largest economy in the subregion that grew by 6.7 per cent, owing to expansion of oil output as well as the performance of the non-oil sector. West Africa was followed by East Africa that decelerated from 6.4 per cent growth in 2008 to 4.3 per cent in 2009; North Africa from 5.2 to 3.6 per cent; and Central Africa from 5.2 to 1.8 per cent. Growth in Southern Africa declined, falling to -1.1 per cent in 2009 owing to the -1.8 per cent contraction of the South African economy and the resulting subregional spillover effects.

The *Economic Report on Africa*, a joint publication of ECA and AU, devoted its 2009 edition to the theme "Developing African Agriculture through Regional Value Chains". The *Report* tracked Africa's economic and social performance within the global context and made policy recommendations for the management of African economies.

Activities in 2009

The ECA programme of work in 2009 was organized under ten subprogrammes: trade, finance and economic development; food security and sustainable development; governance and public administration; information, science and technology for development; economic cooperation and regional integration; gender and women in development; subregional activities for development; development planning and administration; statistics; and social development [E/ECA/COE/29/7]. In other activities, ECA continued to support the project to establish a Europe-Africa fixed link through the Strait of Gibraltar (see p. 971).

Trade, finance and economic development

In 2009, ECA continued its efforts to strengthen the capacity of member States to design and implement appropriate policies to achieve sustained economic growth for poverty reduction, in line with the priorities of the Millennium Declaration [YUN 2000, p. 49] and the New Partnership for Africa's Development (NEPAD) [YUN 2001, p. 900]. Its work under the subprogramme aimed at achieving higher and sustained economic growth through enhanced capacity for macroeconomic and sectoral policy analysis, international trade and finance.

A major accomplishment in the area of macroeconomic policy analysis was the preparation and publication of the 2009 edition of the *Economic Report on Africa*, jointly prepared with the AU Commission. ECA also contributed to the preparation of the *African Economic Outlook, 2009*, which focused on innovations in information and communication technologies in Africa. ECA and the African Development Bank (AfDB) jointly organized the African Economic Conference (Addis Ababa, Ethiopia, 11–13 November) on the theme: "Fostering development in an era of financial and economic crises". The conference provided a forum for dialogue among researchers, economists and policymakers and made recommendations on addressing the challenges facing Africa due to the global economic crisis.

On international trade, ECA, in partnership with the AU Commission and the African Trade Policy Centre, prepared an Economic Partnership Agreement (EPA) negotiation template which was later endorsed by the African ministers of trade as guidelines in negotiations with the EU towards comprehensive EPA agreements. ECA contributed to the second global review on Aid for Trade in July, which resulted in a Global Work Programme on Aid for Trade for the period 2009–2011. ECA also organized in September an expert group meeting on enhancing Africa's participation in the World Trade Organization (WTO) process. The outcome document informed the prepa-

rations for the meeting of the African Ministers of Trade in October, which in turn resulted in a communiqué that outlined Africa's common position for the Seventh WTO Ministerial Conference (Geneva, 30 November–2 December). With regard to financing for development, ECA focused on the global economic crisis, providing support to member States to cope with the crisis and undertaking a regional assessment on its impact, which served as an input to the consolidated UN report, *The Global Economic and Financial Crises: Regional Impacts, Responses and Solutions.*

In a June resolution on the global financial and economic crisis [E/2009/38 (res. 865(XLII)], the Conference of Ministers requested African countries to participate in the UN General Assembly's high-level meeting on the crisis in June; urged the AU Commission and ECA to explore debt standstill and debt restructuring arrangements; requested multilateral and regional development-finance institutions to increase the quantity and access to unconditional financing for Africa; and encouraged African governments to remove all obstacles to intra-African trade. On the MDGs [res. 866(XLII)], the Conference requested ECA and AU to promote peer learning and experience-sharing on the goals. It also mandated ECA, the AU Commission and AfDB to help Africa prepare for the 2010 UN system-wide midterm review of progress towards the MDGs.

New Partnership for Africa's Development

As the coordinator of UN agencies and organizations working in Africa in support of NEPAD, a programme for the continent's development that was initiated by African leaders in 2001 [YUN 2001, p. 900], ECA provided support for the implementation of NEPAD priorities through its analytical work and technical assistance in different areas, with particular focus on socio-economic development and political governance issues. It also collaborated with UN agencies and other partners, in particular AfDB and the regional economic communities, in supporting NEPAD infrastructure development.

(For more information on NEPAD, see p. 899.)

Food security and sustainable development

ECA continued to strengthen the capacity of States to formulate and implement policies, strategies and programmes that incorporated the synergies between agriculture and the environment with a view to fostering sustainable development in Africa. Activities in 2009 focused on promoting food security and agricultural development, enhancing capacity for land management and providing policy support in the implementation of Africa's climate change agenda. ECA, in partnership with the Food and Agriculture

Organization of the United Nations (FAO), carried out activities to follow up on the Declaration on investing in agriculture adopted at the meeting of AU heads of State and Government (Sirte, Libya, 1–3 July). The Declaration aimed at accelerating the development of strategic agricultural commodity value chains within the framework of the Comprehensive Africa Agricultural Development Programme. ECA collaborated with UN system entities and other partners in the publication of a compendium of best practices in public-private partnership in agro-industry and agribusiness in Africa, and the launching of the African Agribusiness and Agro-industries Development Initiative in 2010. ECA also convened the sixth session of the Committee on Food Security and Sustainable Development in October.

On land policy management, efforts focused on the launch of a pan-African Land Policy Framework and Guidelines, a joint initiative of the AU Commission, ECA and AfDB; the draft framework was adopted at the AU Summit in July. Consequently, the Land Policy Initiative raised the profile of African land issues at the subregional, regional and global levels, including contributing to the drafting of a new land bill in Kenya.

Climate change

In the run-up to the United Nations Climate Change Summit held in Copenhagen in December (see p. 1015), ECA organized a series of preparatory activities throughout 2009 to help inform Africa's common negotiating position and build a coalition around Africa's main concerns and expectations from the Summit and beyond. In an effort to ensure that Africa would participate effectively in the negotiations and adopt well-informed positions for Copenhagen, the ECA secretariat in May submitted a progress report on climate change and development [E/ECA/COE/28/9], which provided an update on implementation of the ClimDev–Africa programme since the 2008 conference [YUN 2008, p. 1155] and underscored issues of concern for Africa and Africa's emerging common position on the key issues under negotiation [E/ECA/COE/28/9]. Outcomes of the Summit relevant to Africa included an agreement on the continuation of the Kyoto Protocol; the need to enhance international cooperation on adaptation to reduce the vulnerability of developing countries; and the need for adequate funding for developing countries to support enhanced action. In view of its role in the follow-up to the Copenhagen commitments, in particular in supporting the negotiation of a comprehensive international climate change regime beyond the Kyoto Protocol and the development of a comprehensive framework for African climate change programmes, ECA developed a programme of work for the new African Climate Policy Centre to carry forward post-

Copenhagen work and provide African countries with technical assistance to address climate change.

ECA also helped to organize the Third African Ministerial Conference on Financing for Development (Kigali, Rwanda, 21–22 May), which focused on the theme "Climate change, an additional challenge for meeting the MDGs".

Governance and public administration

ECA's objective under the subprogramme was to improve and sustain progress towards good governance and to ensure popular participation in the governance and development process to strengthen the foundations of sustainable development. ECA provided support to the African Peer Review Mechanism process and published the second edition of the *African Governance Report*, a publication that assessed and monitored the progress of governance in Africa. The report, which covered 35 African countries, found that within the last five years Africa recorded marginal progress on governance. Gains on political governance had been mixed. While the scope for political representation and competitive electoral politics, human rights and the observance of the rule of law had improved, party and electoral systems remained weak and poorly institutionalized, with elections emerging as a conflict trigger, rather than a conflict resolution mechanism. On the other hand, economic governance, public sector management, private sector development and corporate governance had been marked by progressive policies leading to a steady growth in the economies of many countries. In other activities, ECA organized meetings and workshops on issues relevant to the development of civil society. As part of efforts to define a structured process of engagement between ECA and civil society organizations, the African Centre for Civil Society was resuscitated during the year to strengthen the capacity of civil society organizations.

Information, science and technology for development

ECA continued to strengthen the capacity of member States to formulate, implement and evaluate strategies and plans in the area of information for development. With support and assistance from ECA, seven countries (Benin, Burkina Faso, the Gambia, Ivory Coast, the Niger, Nigeria, Rwanda) made progress in the implementation of their national information and communication infrastructure plans and policies by adopting strategies for the application of information and communication technology (ICT) in various sectors. ECA also organized the first session of the Committee on Development Information, Science and Technology (Addis Ababa, 28 April–1 May) on the theme "Scientific development innovation and the knowledge economy", which was attended by more than 600 policymakers, decision makers, scientists, lawyers and journalists. In collaboration with the AU Commission, ECA organized the extraordinary Conference of AU Ministers in charge of Communications and Information Technologies (Johannesburg, South Africa, 6 November). The meeting adopted the Oliver Tambo Declaration, which committed African countries to ICT development within the framework of the African Information Society Initiative and the Global e-Policy Resource Network. The Declaration also called on ECA and AU Commission to prepare a draft regional convention and regulatory framework for cyber activities, to be adopted before the end of 2012.

Economic cooperation and regional integration

ECA continued to promote effective economic cooperation among member States and to strengthen the process of regional integration in Africa through enhanced intra-African trade and physical integration, with particular emphasis on infrastructure and natural resources development in line with the AU vision. ECA assisted African countries to develop an "African Mining Vision 2050", which was adopted by the AU at its February summit meeting. The Vision provided a framework for the promotion of transparent, equitable and optimal exploitation of mineral resources. In collaboration with AfDB, ECA and the AU Commission embarked on the preparation of the fourth edition of the *Assessment of Regional Integration in Africa*, which addressed critical challenges related to regional integration, including intra-African trade.

The sixth session of the Committee on Trade, Regional Cooperation and Integration (Addis Ababa, 13–15 October), held at ECA headquarters, considered matters pertaining to ECA activities in advancing the AU's continental agenda on economic cooperation and integration, as well as the promotion of trade within and outside Africa. The meeting also examined progress made in regional integration in Africa and reviewed developments in intra-African trade.

Transport and communications

In the area of infrastructure development, an objective of ECA was to help establish an efficient, integrated and affordable transport and communications system as a basis for Africa's physical integration, and to facilitate national and international traffic. On transport development, ECA, in collaboration with the AU Commission and *Federation Internationale de*

l'Automobile, organized a conference on road safety (Dar es Salaam, Tanzania, 7 July). Over 100 policymakers and experts from African ministries attended and recommendations to improve road safety in Africa were adopted for implementation by member States.

Europe-Africa fixed link

In response to Economic and Social Council resolution 2007/16 [YUN 2007, p. 1011], the Secretary-General submitted a May report [E/2009/63] by the Executive Secretaries of ECA and ECE on the activities carried out from 2006 to 2009 in connection with the project to establish a Europe-Africa fixed link through the Strait of Gibraltar. Under the authority of the Spanish-Moroccan Joint Committee, the work was undertaken by two engineering firms— one Spanish and the other Moroccan. The activities mainly involved the preliminary pilot project update for the tunnel option; the environmental impact, traffic forecasting and regional effects studies; the project website; an overall evaluation of the project; as well as experimental work in Malabata and Tarifa and studies of the cartography, geodesy and currents in the Strait of Gibraltar. The environmental study evaluated measures needed to counter the environmental impact of the project, while the socio-economic and traffic-forecasting studies would define the remaining variables needed to evaluate the project. A programme of future activities was under preparation as part of the overall evaluation.

ECONOMIC AND SOCIAL COUNCIL ACTION

On 28 July [meeting 39], the Economic and Social Council adopted **resolution 2009/11** [draft: E/2009/L.21] without vote [agenda item 10].

Europe-Africa fixed link through the Strait of Gibraltar

The Economic and Social Council,

Recalling its resolutions 1982/57 of 30 July 1982, 1983/62 of 29 July 1983, 1984/75 of 27 July 1984, 1985/70 of 26 July 1985, 1987/69 of 8 July 1987, 1989/119 of 28 July 1989, 1991/74 of 26 July 1991, 1993/60 of 30 July 1993, 1995/48 of 27 July 1995, 1997/48 of 22 July 1997, 1999/37 of 28 July 1999, 2001/29 of 26 July 2001, 2003/52 of 24 July 2003, 2005/34 of 26 July 2005 and 2007/16 of 26 July 2007,

Referring to resolution 912(1989), adopted by the Parliamentary Assembly of the Council of Europe on 1 February 1989 regarding measures to encourage the construction of a major traffic artery in south-western Europe and to study thoroughly the possibility of a fixed link through the Strait of Gibraltar,

Referring also to the Barcelona Declaration, adopted at the Euro-Mediterranean Ministerial Conference, held in Barcelona, Spain, on 27 and 28 November 1995, and to the work programme annexed thereto, which is aimed, inter alia, at connecting Mediterranean transport networks to the trans-European network in order to ensure their interoperability,

Referring further to the European Commission communication of 31 January 2007 related to strengthening transport cooperation with neighbouring countries, prepared on the basis of the conclusions of the November 2005 report of the High-level Group on the Extension of the Major Trans-European Transport Axes to the Neighbouring Countries and Regions, and to the conclusions of the first Euro-Mediterranean Ministerial Conference on Transport, held in Marrakech, Morocco, on 15 December 2005, as well as to the Regional Transport Action Plan for the Mediterranean Region 2007–2013, adopted by the Euro-Mediterranean Transport Forum at its eighth meeting, held in Brussels on 29 and 30 May 2007,

Referring to the final declaration adopted at the Ministerial Conference of the "Barcelona Process: Union for the Mediterranean", held in Marseille, France, on 3 and 4 November 2008, and the emphasis placed on transport projects in the Joint Declaration of the Paris Summit for the Mediterranean of 13 July 2008,

Referring also to the meeting held in Luxembourg on 8 June 2008 between the Ministers of Transport of Morocco and Spain and the Vice-President of the European Commission and Commissioner for Transport with regard to the official presentation to the European institutions of the project for a fixed link,

Taking note of the follow-up report prepared jointly by the Economic Commission for Europe and the Economic Commission for Africa in accordance with Economic and Social Council resolution 2007/16,

Noting the conclusions of the studies carried out by the Western Mediterranean Transport Group on Europe-Maghreb transport and cooperation agreements and on transport conditions for European nationals of Maghreb origin when they travel to the Western Mediterranean in the summer and the action plan for the period 2009–2011, adopted at the sixth Conference of Ministers of Transport of the Western Mediterranean, held in Rome on 20 May 2009,

Noting also the conclusions of the studies carried out by the European Commission (INFRAMED, MEDA TEN-T, REG-MED and DESTIN) for the development of an integrated transport network in the Mediterranean basin,

Taking note of the Regional Transport Action Plan, which constitutes a road map for intensifying cooperation in the Mediterranean with regard to infrastructure planning, regulatory reform and transport services, as well as the list of priority projects annexed thereto, including the fixed link through the Strait of Gibraltar,

1. *Welcomes* the cooperation on the project for the link through the Strait of Gibraltar between the Economic Commission for Africa, the Economic Commission for Europe, the Governments of Morocco and Spain, and specialized international organizations;

2. *Also welcomes* the progress made in the project studies as a result, in particular, of deep-sea drilling, which has given a decisive impetus to geological and geotechnical exploration and to the technical, economic and traffic update studies currently being finalized;

3. *Further welcomes* the organization by the International Tunnelling Association, under the auspices of the Economic Commission for Europe and the Economic Commission for Africa, of the seminar held in Madrid in January 2005 on soundings and treatments;

4. *Commends* the Economic Commission for Europe and the Economic Commission for Africa for the work done in preparing the project follow-up report requested by the Economic and Social Council in its resolution 2007/16;

5. *Renews its invitation* to the competent organizations of the United Nations system and to specialized governmental and non-governmental organizations to participate in the studies and work on the fixed link through the Strait of Gibraltar;

6. *Requests* the Executive Secretaries of the Economic Commission for Africa and the Economic Commission for Europe to continue to actively take part in the follow-up to the project and to report to the Economic and Social Council at its substantive session of 2011 on the progress made on the project studies;

7. *Requests* the Secretary-General to provide formal support and, to the extent that priorities permit, the resources necessary, from within the regular budget, to the Economic Commission for Europe and the Economic Commission for Africa, in order to enable them to carry out the activities mentioned above.

Gender and women in development

A defining aspect of ECA work under this subprogramme was supporting member States to achieve gender equality through gender mainstreaming and empowerment of women, as well as strengthening their capacity for monitoring and reporting on progress in the implementation of agreed plans and strategies for the advancement of women. ECA activities included the launch of the 2009 edition of the *African Women's Report*, which was based on the African Gender and Development Index and used both qualitative and quantitative means of data collection and analysis as a framework for measuring gender inequality; the launch of the *Guidebook* for mainstreaming gender in macroeconomic policies—a compendium of methodologies and tools that utilized time-use data, gender aware modelling and gender budgeting to measure and integrate women's unpaid work in national planning instruments and macroeconomic policies; capacity-building on gender statistics; and the operationalization of the African Women's Rights Observatory.

ECA organized the Eighth Africa Regional Conference on Women (Beijing+15) (Banjul, Gambia, 16–20 November), bringing together some 1,000 delegates to assess progress achieved, identify challenges in the implementation of the 12 critical areas of the Beijing Platform for Action [YUN 1995, p. 1170] and propose key actions for Africa to focus on during the next five years. The conference outcome document, the Banjul Declaration, formed the basis of the member States' plan of action and served as Africa's input into the global review of the Platform by the Commission on the Status of Women in March 2010. The sixth session of the Committee on Women and Development (Banjul, November) was also held to consider the new structure of the Committee, review ECA accomplishments in 2008–2009, and provide guidance on the 2010–2011 biennium work priorities.

Subregional development activities

ECA's five subregional offices (SROs), located in Central Africa (Yaounde, Cameroon), East Africa (Kigali, Rwanda), North Africa (Rabat, Morocco), Southern Africa (Lusaka, Zambia) and West Africa (Niamey, Niger), continued to promote and accelerate the process of regional integration by spearheading the delivery of ECA's operational activities targeted at the specific priorities of each subregion, within the overall framework of the implementation of NEPAD and achievement of the MDGs. A major priority of the SROs during the year was the operationalization of the multi-year programme of cooperation agreed between SROs and their respective regional economic communities. All five offices had developed extensive multi-year programmes of support and collaboration with major RECs in their subregions. The offices also organized and serviced various meetings and workshops, including the annual sessions of the Intergovernmental Committees of Experts.

Development planning and administration

The objective of the subprogramme on development planning and administration, implemented by the African Institute for Economic Development and Planning (IDEP), based in Dakar, Senegal, was to enhance national capacity to formulate and implement development policies and economic management strategies. Despite its fragile financial situation, IDEP continued to design and implement programmes that supported policymakers' priorities in the area of economic policy and to spearhead efforts in capacity-building. In April, 13 trainees from nine countries graduated from its 18-month Master of Arts degree programme in economic policy and management.

As requested by the ECA Conference of Ministers in resolution 858(XLI) in 2008 [YUN 2008, p. 1103], a report on repositioning IDEP [E/ECA/COE/28/14] was issued in May, providing information on steps taken to alleviate its financial difficulties and a plan for its repositioning. A resource mobilization campaign encouraging member States to pay their contributions had begun to yield results with several countries having paid their contributions and/or arrears. The report also outlined proposals for IDEP repositioning made by the Institute's newly appointed Director, includ-

ing initiatives in the areas of policy research, training and capacity-building, outreach and dissemination, as well as further revisions to the IDEP repositioning document and continued mobilization of resources to support the repositioning.

In a June resolution [E/2009/38 (res. 864(XLII)] on repositioning IDEP, the Conference of Ministers endorsed the vision and strategic orientation presented by the Director; urged member States to pay their contributions; and requested the Director to report on the new orientation and priorities, as well as implementation of the IDEP repositioning exercise at the Conference's 2010 session.

Statistics

The objective of ECA's work under the subprogramme was to improve the production, dissemination and use of key demographic, social, economic and environmental statistics, including the MDG indicators, in accordance with internationally agreed standards and good practices. Priority activities included promoting, coordinating and advocating for statistical activities in Africa; building a data hub at ECA for the provision of development data on Africa; implementing the 1993 System of National Accounts in Africa; supporting statistical training programmes; establishing a regional programme for population and housing censuses; and providing technical assistance in various areas of statistics.

ECA organized the fifth Africa Symposium on Statistical Development (Dakar, Senegal, 19–21 November), which adopted the Gorée Island Declaration, committing African countries to undertake a census in the 2010 round within five years and use the most effective ICT tools to collect and process census data. In order to facilitate the provision of harmonized data series, a repository of data from African countries was established under the aegis of the African Statistical Coordination Committee. The repository had data aggregated at the continental, subregional and national levels. Similarly, in collaboration with AFDB and the AU Commission through a data collection mechanism, a first-ever joint *African Statistical Yearbook* was produced in 2009. The Commission was also involved in the organization of the Forum on Statistical Training and Human Resources in Africa in June and an expert group meeting on census data processing in November, which reviewed the ECA *Handbook on Census Data Processing*. Another initiative to facilitate the exchange of technical information and best practices amongst African statistical practitioners was the publication of the *African Statistical Journal*, of which ECA was a co-editor. ECA continued to disseminate statistics-related news through its quarterly *African Statistical Newsletter*.

Social development

Eca's objective under this subprogramme was to strengthen the capacity of States to formulate policies and programmes for poverty reduction and promote social inclusion and integration to ensure equitable social services for all segments of society, in line with internationally agreed development goals, including the mdgs. To assist States in monitoring and tracking progress in implementing international and regional social development commitments, eca, together with the au Commission and the United Nation Population Fund (unfpa), organized in October the 15-year review of the implementation the International Conference on Population and Development (icpd) Programme of Action [YUN 1994, p. 955]. Also in October, eca organized the first meeting of the Committee on Human and Social Development, which drew over 130 participants from 49 African countries. The meeting emphasized the need to intensify efforts to achieve the mdgs and the icpd Programme of Action and requested eca to provide assistance to States in the design and implementation of mdg-consistent poverty reduction strategies.

Eca produced two significant reports during the year: *The African Youth Report 2009: Expanding Opportunities for and with Young People in Africa*, which drew attention to challenges faced by African youth and contributed to the development of the draft au Plan of Action for Youth Development, 2009–2018; and the *International Migration and Development in Africa: Human Rights, Regional Integration and Impacts of the Financial Crisis*, which took a critical look at the varied migration dynamics on the continent and proposed measures for enhancing the integration of international migration issues into regional and subregional development policies and frameworks. Eca also launched its hiv and aids Learning and Resource Service to provide up-to-date information on hiv/aids prevention and care.

Programme and organizational questions

Programme of work, 2010–2011

The Conference of Ministers had before it the eca proposed programme of work and priorities for the 2010–2011 biennium [E/ECA/COE/28/15]. In a June resolution [E/2009/38 (res. 863(XLII))], the Conference noted the efforts of eca to consolidate the gains resulting from its repositioning by scaling up its action towards achieving greater effectiveness and impact in programme delivery. It also endorsed the programme of work and priorities for the 2010–2011.

Construction of office facilities at ECA

In response to General Assembly resolution 63/263 [YUN 2008, p. 1545], the Secretary-General submitted an October report on construction of additional office facilities at eca headquarters in Addis Ababa [A/64/486]. The report described progress in implementing the project and two principal factors that had delayed the project: the need to pursue a revised tender process because the bids received in September 2008 were significantly higher than the approved budget; and the cancellation of the procurement process in April 2009 following the findings of the Procurement Task Force that had led to the suspension of the vendors by the Vendor Review Committee. It also outlined actions taken to address issues identified during the management review process. The estimated cost of the project remained at $14,333,100 and the revised project schedule indicated a construction completion date in December 2011, followed by an interior set-up of up to six months.

Acabq, in its December report on the project [A/64/7/Add. 12], expressed the expectation that the new arrangements put in place as the result of the reviews would enable the construction to be completed as per the revised scheduled.

On 24 December, the Assembly, in **resolution 64/245**, section VII (see p. 1407), took note of the Secretary-General's report and endorsed acabq's recommendations.

Asia and the Pacific

The Economic and Social Commission for Asia and the Pacific (escap) held its sixty-fifth session [E/2009/39] in Bangkok, Thailand, in two parts: the senior officials segment from 23 to 25 April; and the ministerial segment from 27 to 29 April, under the topic "Towards sustainable agriculture and food security in the Asia-Pacific region". In her concluding remarks at the ministerial round table, the escap Executive Secretary stated that the challenge of food security required actions to increase access to food in the short term; strengthen and develop sustainable agriculture in the medium-term; and mitigate and adapt to the effects of climate change on agricultural production in the long-term.

On 29 April, in a resolution on implementation of the Bali Outcome Document in addressing the food, fuel and financial crises [E/2009/39 (res. 65/1)], the Commission took note of the Document [E/ESCAP/65/15/Add.1], which had resulted from the December 2008 high-level regional policy dialogue on the food-fuel crisis and climate change, and invited countries of the region and international and regional organizations to consider implementation of its recommendations. Escap also requested the Executive Secretary to assist members in implementing the Document's recommendations; conduct studies and share experiences on improving food and energy security, on responding to the financial crisis, and on sustainable agriculture; convene a regional dialogue to discuss progress made in the Asian and Pacific region in addressing the economic crisis and its impact on achieving internationally agreed development goals; and report to the Commission on implementation of the resolution at its sixty-sixth (2010) session.

The Commission also discussed issues pertinent to its subsidiary structure; least developed and land-locked developing countries; management issues; work of the escap regional institutions; and activities of the Advisory Committee of Permanent Representatives and Other Representatives Designated by Members of the Commission [E/ESCAP/65/27].

Economic trends

According to the summary of the *Economic and Social Survey of Asia and the Pacific, 2010* [E/2010/18], developing economies of the region emerged in 2009 as the world's fastest growing: their annual growth rate as a whole was 4.0 per cent. The economies of China and India, growing at 8.7 per cent and 7.2 per cent, respectively, were the engines of economic growth. However, other developing economies in the region were in negative territory, contracting by 0.6 per cent. The regional impact of the global economic crisis varied across countries, reflecting each country's vulnerability to external shocks according to its dependence on export-led growth and exposure to financial and exchange-rate instabilities. Although the nature of the recovery process held issues of fundamental concern and a complex set of policy challenges remained, recovery was on the horizon and the outlook for 2010 had improved significantly with developing Asian and Pacific economies forecast to grow by 7.0 per cent.

Policy issues

Despite the economic gains achieved, some problematic policy issues faced the region, including inflation from demand and supply sides. A key threat to the sustainability of regional growth was the return of inflationary pressures as the recovery gathered steam. Consequently, a critical decision for each economy was when and how to turn off the tap of fiscal stimulus and tighten monetary policy. Other than increase in demand-side inflationary pressures, another factor behind rising prices was the return of supply-side pressure from commodity price volatility. Escap urged policymakers to be vigilant in the post-crisis phase; as oil prices had increased steadily during 2009, a return to high food prices could follow and required close monitoring.

Another policy issue was the possibility of the emergence of asset bubbles. Abundant foreign capital had been attracted to the region because of its relatively strong growth prospects. However, as the scale of inflows continued to rise, the risk would also increase that any unexpected change in interest rates, or a sudden appreciation in value of the United States dollar, could trigger an exit of capital across target countries. The issue of managing the benefits from foreign portfolio investments and minimizing attendant risks to macroeconomic stability was a huge challenge for the region.

Other areas of concern included budget deficits across the region, projections of substantial declines in import demand in the United States over the next few years that would affect Asian and Pacific countries, and the critical questions for policymakers to address in the context of when, in what sequence, and at what pace to start to withdraw stimulus programmes that had been key support for growth after the crisis. Even if advanced countries achieved substantial economic recovery, their demand for imports from the region was not expected to return to pre-crisis levels. In order to unwind global imbalances, many of the developed economies needed to restrain debt-fuelled consumption. Countries in the region needed to seek new sources of growth to rebalance their economies in favour of increased domestic and regional consumption, while policy changes needed to induce a long-term structural rebalancing of economies. Such a strategy required addressing global and regional imbalances.

At its 2009 session, the Commission considered the *Economic and Social Survey of Asia and the Pacific, 2009* [Sales No. E.09.II.F.11].

Activities in 2009
Macroeconomic policy, poverty reduction and development

The Commission had before it documents on: recent macroeconomic developments and other issues to be raised at the first session of the Committee on Macroeconomic Policy, Poverty Reduction and Inclusive Development [E/ESCAP/65/1]; addressing the financial crisis and its convergence with other threats to development [E/ESCAP/65/30]; analysis of the regional impact and policy responses to the crisis [E/ESCAP/65/30/Add.1]; and progress and challenges in achieving the mdgs [E/ESCAP/65/31].

The Commission noted the immediate and long-term impact of the global financial crisis on countries in the region in terms of employment, poverty reduction and the achievement of the mdgs. The Commission urged global coordination of macroeconomic policies to combat the crisis and called for the international community to jointly undertake measures to enhance liquidity in international money and credit markets, support cross-border capital flows to ensure investment and growth, upgrade the international financial architecture, and improve the international financial regulatory and supervisory framework. It also underlined the need for greater coordination on global financial reform and was of the view that in order to effectively tackle the crisis, trade as an engine of growth needed to be supported and protectionist pressures should be resisted.

The first session of the Committee on Macroeconomic Policy, Poverty Reduction and Inclusive Development (Bangkok, 24–26 November) [E/ESCAP/66/5] focused on the impact of the financial and economic crisis on Asian and Pacific economies and policy responses and options; implementation of the Programme of Action for the Least Developed Countries for the Decade 2001–2010; implementation of Commission resolution 65/4 on strengthening of the Centre for Alleviation of Poverty through Secondary Crops Development in Asia and the Pacific (CAPSA) (see p. 979); and programme planning and monitoring. The Committee recommended enhancing regional cooperation with regard to exchange rate policies and crisis management, as well as strengthening the intermediation of regional savings to address the region's investment and consumption needs. In that regard, the Committee requested the secretariat to take a leading role to support the development of a regional financial architecture, including a regional crisis management mechanism. It further recommended that the secretariat strengthen its efforts with regard to the sharing of experiences on the effectiveness of measures being employed to deal with the adverse impact of the crisis. In other activities, ESCAP organized the Asia-Pacific High-level Forum on ICPD at 15: Accelerating Progress towards the ICPD and MDGs (Bangkok, 16–17 September).

Trade and investment

The Commission had before it a note by the ESCAP secretariat on regional trade and investment: trends, issues and ESCAP responses [E/ESCAP/65/2] and an end-of-decade report on the implementation of Commission resolution 56/1 [YUN 2000, p. 931] on the Decade of Greater Mekong Subregion Development Cooperation, 2000–2009 [E/ESCAP/65/3]. The Commission recognized the importance of trade and investment in alleviating poverty and reviving economic growth and development and emphasized the need to keep economies open and refrain from protectionist measures and the abuse of trade remedies. In particular, the Commission recognized the role of the multilateral trading system in promoting global trade and the importance of a swift and successful conclusion of the Doha Development Agenda nego-

tiations [YUN 2001, p. 1432]. It noted the various initiatives that had been implemented for the development of the Greater Mekong Subregion and called for them to be continued.

The first session of the Committee on Trade and Investment (Bangkok, 4–6 November) [E/ESCAP/66/8] reviewed developments in trade and investment and related policy issues, and made recommendations with respect to inclusive and sustainable trade and investment. Topics addressed included: trade and investment for achieving inclusive and sustainable development beyond the crisis; developing policies for trade and investment; the role of the multilateral trading system in governing international trade; enhancing intraregional trade and investment; facilitating trade and investment; business survival and development; and programme planning and monitoring.

Transport

The Commission had before it reports on the first session of the Committee on Transport (Bangkok, 29–31 October 2008) [E/ESCAP/65/4] and on the implementation of the Regional Action Programme for Transport Development in Asia and the Pacific, phase I (2007–2011) [E/ESCAP/65/5]. At its first session, the Committee reviewed issues related to transport, including development, poverty, the environment and society, and discussed measures needed to address those issues. It also supported the celebration of the fiftieth anniversary (2009) of the Asian Highway.

The Commission noted the importance of transport in accelerating economic and social development and facilitating regional integration and expressed general support for the Committee's findings and recommendations. It also noted the outcome Declaration from the Ministerial Conference on Global Environment and Energy in Transport (Tokyo, 15–16 January); expressed satisfaction with the forthcoming entry into force of the Intergovernmental Agreement on the Trans-Asian Railway Network on 11 June; and welcomed Japan's offer to further strengthen partnerships with member countries in promoting low-carbon and low-pollution transport systems. In other activities, ESCAP convened the Expert Group Meeting on Improving Road Safety (Bangkok, 2–4 September), which noted the usefulness of compiling guidelines outlining best practices in road safety improvement in the region.

The first session of the Forum of Asian Ministers of Transport (Bangkok, 14–18 December) [E/ESCAP/66/11] endorsed, among other things, the continued implementation of the Busan Declaration on Transport Development in Asia and the Pacific and phase I of the Regional Action Programme for Transport Development (2007–2011). It also supported the development of an intergovernmental agreement on dry ports to facilitate a coordinated approach to an international integrated intermodal transport and logistics system. A major outcome of the Forum included the Bangkok Declaration on Transport Development in Asia.

Environment and development

The Commission had before it an ESCAP secretariat note entitled "Turning crisis into opportunity: greening economic recovery strategies" [E/ESCAP/65/6]; the report of the Coordinating Committee for Geoscience Programmes in East and Southeast Asia [E/ESCAP/65/INF/4]; and the report of the Mekong River Commission [E/ESCAP/65/INF/5]. The Commission noted that green recovery strategies, which included the Global Green New Deal referred to by the Secretary-General (see p. 793), had been actively promoted by UN agencies, and called on world leaders to consider a massive redirection of investment away from unsustainable production and consumption patterns into job-creating programmes that would restore the natural systems underpinning the global economy. Such strategies had been replicated by several countries in the ESCAP region.

The first session of the Committee on Environment and Development (Bangkok, 2–4 December) [E/ESCAP/66/12] discussed trends and reviewed the progress made in the field of environment and development, including progress in implementing the green growth approach, which had been adopted at the Fifth Ministerial Conference on Environment and Development in 2005 [YUN 2005, p. 1099]. It also discussed challenges in the provision of water, sanitation and energy services, as well as housing, for the poor, and the measures needed to address those issues.

Information and communications technology

The Commission had before it the report of the first session of the Committee on Information and Communications Technology (Bangkok, 19–21 November 2008) [E/ESCAP/65/7]; the summary of progress in the implementation of Commission resolutions relating to information and communications technology [E/ESCAP/65/8]; and the report of the Asian and Pacific Training Centre for Information and Communication Technology for Development [E/ESCAP/65/22]. At its first session, the Committee reviewed challenges faced by the Asia-Pacific region in developing an inclusive and development-oriented information society, as envisioned in the outcome documents of the World Summit on the Information Society [YUN 2005, p. 933], and recommended that the ESCAP secretariat establish follow-up mechanisms at the regional level to review implementation of the Summit outcomes in 2015.

The Commission recognized the important role played by ICT, including space-based technology, in supporting inclusive and sustainable economic and social development and in ensuring effective disaster management in Asia and the Pacific. It noted the progress of member States in implementing the outcomes of the World Summit and the need to strengthen regional cooperation to assist States in human resources development and capacity-building. It also recognized the importance of ICT human resources development, as well as the critical role of the Asian and Pacific Training Centre for Information and Communication Technology for Development in building an information society. The Governing Council of the Centre at its fourth session (Incheon, Republic of Korea, 13 November) recommended that the operations of the Centre continue beyond 2011.

Disaster risk reduction

The Commission had before it the report of the first session of the Committee on Disaster Risk Reduction (Bangkok, 25–27 March) [E/ESCAP/65/9]; the summary of progress in the implementation of Commission resolution 64/2 [YUN 2008, p. 1110] on regional cooperation in the implementation of the Hyogo Framework for Action 2005–2015: Building the Resilience of Nations and Communities to Disasters in Asia and the Pacific [YUN 2005, p. 1016] [E/ESCAP/65/10]; the report of the Typhoon Committee [E/ESCAP/65/INF/2]; and the report of the Panel on Tropical Cyclones [E/ESCAP/65/INF/3]. In March, the Committee on Disaster Risk Reduction reviewed the status of regional initiatives related to achieving the Hyogo Framework and made recommendations on promoting regional cooperative mechanisms and knowledge-sharing arrangements; establishing an Asia-Pacific gateway on disaster risk reduction; launching a publication on best practices and lessons learned in regional disaster risk reduction and management; enhancing partnerships and collaboration with the International Strategy for Disaster Reduction (see p. 908), other UN entities, and regional and subregional organizations to improve assistance in the area of disaster risk reduction; and building regional consensus.

The Commission recognized that the Asia-Pacific region was the most disaster-prone region in the world and noted the concern expressed over the increasing threat of natural disasters such as flooding, landslides and sinking islands as a result of climate change in the Pacific, as well as the importance of disaster risk reduction for achieving development goals in the region. On 29 April [E/2009/39 (res. 65/5)], in follow-up to Commission resolution 64/10 [YUN 2008, p. 1111] on the review of the operational details of the feasibility study for the establishment of an Asian and Pacific centre for information, communication and space technology-enabled disaster management in Iran, the Commission noted that Iran had requested additional time to provide the Commission with the supplementary information requested and invited Iran to revise its draft resolution and submit it for consideration at the Commission's sixty-sixth (2010) session.

Social development

The Commission had before it the report of the first session of the Committee on Social Development [E/ESCAP/65/11] and the summary of progress in the implementation of resolutions relating to social development issues [E/ESCAP/65/12]. During its session, the Committee considered the following: a framework for action towards an inclusive society; issues on managing emerging and persistent risks to ensure inclusive social development; and reducing disparities and exclusion. It made recommendations in a number of areas including social protection and promotion of gender equality in the region, particularly in the pursuit of the MDGs, as well as ESCAP as a regional platform for dialogue on social policy instruments to address food security challenges; ESCAP facilitating the exchange of information and developing innovative practices on disability, and providing technical assistance for creating a data collection system and formulating a feasible definition of disability; and ESCAP promoting implementation of human rights and other instruments on persons with disabilities.

On 29 April [E/2009/39 (res. 65/3)], the Commission adopted a resolution on the High-level Intergovernmental Meeting on the Final Review of the Implementation of the Asian and Pacific Decade of Disabled Persons, 2003–2012 [YUN 2003, p. 1014]. In that regard, it welcomed the offer of the Republic of Korea to host the meeting in conjunction with the Assembly of the Asia and Pacific Disability Forum and the World Congress of Rehabilitation International; and requested the ESCAP Executive Secretary to examine all offers to host the meeting and report to the Commission in 2010.

In other activities, the first meeting of the Pacific Island Forum of Disability Ministers (Rarotonga, Cook Islands, 21–23 October) endorsed the Pacific Regional Strategy on Disability 2010–2015. With regard to gender concerns, ESCAP organized, in partnership with the United Nations Development Fund for Women, the Asia-Pacific High-level Intergovernmental Meeting to Review Regional Implementation of the Beijing Platform for Action and Its Regional and Global Outcomes (Bangkok, 16–18 November). The meeting's agreed outcome, the Bangkok Declaration on Beijing+15, represented the Asia-Pacific region's input to the global review of the Beijing Platform for Action in 2010.

Statistics

The Commission had before it the report of the first session of the Committee on Statistics (Bangkok, 4–6 February) [E/ESCAP/65/13] and the annual report of the Statistical Institute for Asia and the Pacific [E/ESCAP/65/26], which reviewed the administrative and financial status of the Institute, as well as the implementation of its work programme in 2008. At its session, the Committee reviewed major issues related to statistics in the Asia-Pacific region, including statistical development, regional cooperation and capacity-building; gender statistics; economic statistics; vital statistics; statistics on measuring the progress of societies; and programme planning for the ESCAP Statistics Division. The Committee decided to establish a bureau to assist it in performing its functions between its biennial sessions. The Committee also decided to adopt a coordinating governance structure and to establish a technical advisory group to provide guidance on issues related to the development of economic statistics in the region. The Committee recommended actions in statistical development, regional technical cooperation and capacity-building; vital statistics; measuring progress of societies; and programme planning.

On 29 April [E/2009/39 (res. 65/2)], the Commission took note of the Committee's report and the annual report of the Institute, encouraged members to increase financial support to the Institute, and noting that the Institute would celebrate its fortieth anniversary in 2010, encouraged members to contribute to the preparations for the celebration. In other developments, the fifth session of the Institute's Governing Council (Phuket, Thailand, 16–17 November) endorsed the long-term workplan for the academic years 2010–2014 and the two-year workplan for the academic years 2010–2011, with the assumption that funding and partnership requirements would be met fully.

Least developed, landlocked and small island developing countries

In April, the Commission had before it the documents of the Special Body on Least Developed and Landlocked Developing Countries on the food-fuel-financial crisis and climate change: addressing threats to development [E/ESCAP/65/15]; the Bali Outcome Document [E/ESCAP/65/15/Add.1]; a secretariat note on regional cooperation for shared prosperity and social progress [E/ESCAP/65/16]; and a summary of progress in the implementation of resolutions relating to countries with special needs [E/ESCAP/65/17]. In the context of the impact on least developed, landlocked and small island developing countries, the reports addressed respectively, the sudden convergence of the food, fuel and finance crises against the backdrop of climate change; the dialogue to find strategies to address the impact of those crises; the global economic crisis; and implementation of Commission resolutions relating to countries with special needs.

The Commission noted that the impact of the food and fuel crisis varied greatly among the least developed and landlocked developing countries of the region as some countries were net exporters of food, while others, such as the least developed of the small island developing States, imported most of their food. It also noted that the food, fuel and economic crises posed significant threats to prospects of achieving MDGs in the least developed countries and landlocked developing countries. The Commission was informed about measures undertaken by countries in support of least developed and landlocked developing countries, as well as efforts by countries and the ESCAP secretariat to implement Commission resolutions relating to countries with special needs.

On 29 April [E/2009/39 (res. 65/6)] the Commission adopted a resolution on support for the establishment of an international think tank of landlocked developing countries, which endorsed Mongolia's proposal to establish such a think tank in Ulaanbaatar to enhance the analytical capability of landlocked developing countries. The Commission requested the ESCAP Executive Secretary to provide advisory and technical support for establishing the think tank in collaboration with regional and global stakeholders. It also adopted a resolution on implementation of the Bali Outcome Document in addressing the food, fuel and financial crises (see p. 974).

Agriculture and development

Ministerial round table. During its ministerial segment (27–29 April), the Commission held a ministerial round table on the session's theme, "Towards sustainable agriculture and food security in the Asia-Pacific region". Opening the segment, the Executive Secretary presented the study entitled *Sustainable Agriculture and Food Security in Asia and the Pacific* [Sales No. E.09.II.F.12]. Despite an enormous capacity for food production, the region was home to a large number of food insecure people. The root causes of food insecurity identified in the study were: poverty; low farm revenues that discouraged small- and medium-scale farmers from investing in agriculture; environmental degradation and competition for natural resources; protectionist trade policies; volatile fuel prices and speculation; and declines in investment in agricultural research and development. The study indicated that food insecurity was likely to increase if long-term trends towards increased population and prosperity continued. It identified four priority

actions at the regional level to ensure food security: developing a foundation for social protection to address food security issues, promoting sustainable agriculture, promoting food self-sufficiency, and developing and monitoring indicators on food security and socioeconomic development. The Commission also had before it a secretariat note that summarized the study's key findings [E/ESCAP/65/29].

Senior officials segment. At its senior officials segment (23–25 April), the Commission had before it secretariat notes on the United Nations Asian and Pacific Centre for Agricultural Engineering and Machinery (UNAPCAEM) [E/ESCAP/65/24] and the Centre for Alleviation of Poverty through CAPSA [E/ESCAP/65/25]. During the year, the UNAPCAEM Governing Council held its fourth (Chiang Rai, Thailand, 12–13 February) and fifth (Bangkok, 14–15 December) sessions. Meanwhile, at its fifth session (Bangkok, 4 March), the CAPSA Governing Council made recommendations for the revitalization of the Centre, including turning it into a member-driven regional centre that focused on poverty alleviation through secondary crops.

On 29 April [E/2009/39 (res. 65/4)], the Commission adopted a resolution on strengthening CAPSA, which endorsed the Governing Council's conclusions and recommendations on revitalizing the Centre, including that the Centre's primary focus would be on networking with national agricultural research centres in the region and beyond; promoting and coordinating research; highlighting and disseminating their research findings; and converting the results of primary research into relevant policy options for the region. The Commission also adopted the revised statute of the Centre, the text of which was annexed to the resolution.

Economic and technical cooperation

The Commission had before it an overview of ESCAP technical cooperation activities and extrabudgetary contributions in 2008 [E/ESCAP/65/21]. In her introduction of the report, the Executive Secretary said that in 2008, ESCAP technical cooperation work had focused on partnership-building to promote "Delivering as one" at the regional level. Key achievements included support for post-Cyclone Nargis recovery and livelihood creation; efforts to address the challenges of the food, fuel and financial crises and climate change; and work in the areas of the Asian Highway and the Trans-Asian Railway network, strengthening capacities of national statistical systems, social protection, capacity-building through the Asia-Pacific Research and Training Network on Trade, and administration of the Multi-Donor Voluntary Trust Fund on Tsunami Early Warning Arrangements in the Indian Ocean and Southeast Asia.

Total contributions received by the secretariat for technical cooperation activities in 2008 from the regular budget as well as voluntary sources amounted to $12.2 million, a decrease from $15 million in 2007. Of that amount, some $4.3 million (35 per cent) was received from the UN system and $6.7 million (55 per cent) was received from donors and participating developing countries. Other intergovernmental organizations and NGOs provided $1.2 million (10 per cent). In addition to cash contributions, some ESCAP member States and one NGO also provided, on a non-reimbursable loan basis, a total of some 156 work-months of the services of experts in various disciplines.

Science and technology

The Commission had before it a secretariat note on the Asian and Pacific Centre for Transfer of Technology [E/ESCAP/65/23], on its activities in 2008. During that period, the Centre assisted countries in the region in responding to the challenges of rapidly integrating into the new global economy by focusing on technology transfer support services for small- and medium-sized enterprises; the promotion of national innovation systems and green grass-roots innovation; and the provision of information, networking and the sharing of experiences relating to technology.

At its April 2009 session, the Commission was briefed by the head of the Centre on key achievements in 2008. The Centre had facilitated technology exchanges in the region utilizing ICT technologies through its web-based technology market and the development of an institutional cooperation mechanism on renewable energy technologies. In other activity, in accordance with Commission resolution 64/3 [YUN 2008, p. 1110] on promoting renewables for energy security and sustainable development, the Centre completed a preliminary programme of work in 2009, involving 15 member countries, entitled "Supporting the Development of an Institutional Cooperation Mechanism to Promote Renewable Energy in Asia and the Pacific". The Centre's Governing Council convened its fifth session (Bangkok, 18 December).

Programme and organizational questions
Proposed programme of work, 2010–2011

In April, the Commission endorsed ESCAP's draft work programme for the 2010–2011 biennium [E/ESCAP/65/18 & Add.1] for submission to intergovernmental review bodies at the global level and noted that it was aligned with the 2010–2011 strategic framework and responsive to the development needs and challenges facing the region. On implementation

of work programme, the Commission noted the need to ensure a balanced approach, with attention given to the needs of least developed, landlocked and small island developing countries.

ESCAP subregional offices

The Commission had before it a secretariat note on the proposed road map for the establishment of three new ESCAP subregional offices in East and North-East Asia, North and Central Asia, and South and South-West Asia [E/ESCAP/65/20], as well as a report by an independent consultant on the most feasible and strategic locations for the new offices [E/ESCAP/65/20/Add.1 & Corr.1]. The Commission noted that the independent consultant's report had recommended that the secretariat explore and consider in greater depth the "preferred" option for each subregion. The final decision in determining the most appropriate location would be conditional upon the conclusion of the relevant agreements with the prospective host Governments.

ESCAP sixty-sixth session

On 29 April, the Commission, having considered a secretariat report on the dates, venue and theme for its sixty-sixth (2010) session [E/ESCAP/65/28], decided that the next session would be held in Incheon, Republic of Korea, in April/May 2010. It also decided that the theme topic for the session would be "Addressing challenges in the achievement of the Millennium Development Goals" [E/2009/39 (dec. 65/1)].

On 28 July, the Economic and Social Council considered ESCAP's recommendation and approved to hold its sixty-sixth (2010) session in Incheon (**decision 2009/231**).

Europe

The Economic Commission for Europe (ECE) at its sixty-third session (Geneva, 30 March–1 April) [E/2009/37] organized its discussion of the economic situation in Europe around an opening segment, followed by three panel discussions on: economic integration in the wider Europe; promoting competitive knowledge-based innovative economies; and enhancing economic cohesion. Panel discussions were also held on climate change in the ECE region. The Commission adopted two conclusions, on economic development in the ECE region and on climate change mitigation and adaptation, as well as two decisions, on the work of ECE and on officers of the Commission and the Executive Committee.

The Commission considered a note by the Executive Secretary on issues calling for action by the Commission [E/ECE/1452], namely the holding in 2010 of ECE's fourth Regional Implementation Meeting for Sustainable Development; and approval of the revised Terms of Reference of the Timber Committee [ECE/TIM/2008/7]. The Commission decided to organize the fourth Regional Implementation Meeting in preparation of the eighteenth session of the Commission on Sustainable Development (Geneva, 1–2 December) and approved the revised terms of reference of the Timber Committee. The Commission also decided to amend Rules 10 and 12 of its Rules of Procedure, as well as Article 9 of its Terms of Reference.

Economic trends

A report on the economic situation in the ECE region: Europe, North America and the Commonwealth of Independent States (CIS) [E/2010/16] indicated that, of the five UN regions as defined by the regional commissions, the ECE region was the most negatively impacted by the financial crisis with real growth declining from 3.2 per cent in 2007, to 1.2 per cent in 2008, and to -3.6 per cent in 2009. Despite the severity of the financial shock, the aggressive use of monetary and fiscal policy, a relatively high level of economic cooperation among the region's Governments, and assistance from international and regional financial institutions allowed the crisis to be contained. Fifteen of the region's 56 economies were forced to turn to the International Monetary Fund for some form of assistance. The forecast was for growth of 2.3 per cent in 2010 and 2.6 per cent in 2011. However, eleven, or about 20 per cent of the region's economies, were expected to have negative growth again in 2010.

Activities in 2009

Trade

The Committee on Trade, at its third session (Geneva, 25–26 February) [ECE/TRADE/C/2009/12], considered reports of its subsidiary bodies that dealt with: trade facilitation and electronic business; regulatory cooperation and standardization policies; and commercial agricultural quality standards. In response to an ECE Executive Committee request for the 2009 annual session of the Committee on Trade to take a decision on its future: to either revitalize and maintain the Committee, or dissolve it, the Committee considered a report on its future [ECE/TRADE/C/2009/2] that summarized those two options. The Chairman reviewed the issues at stake, noting that although the future of the Committee had been questioned, there was no doubt about the usefulness of its subsidiary

bodies. During the debate, various points were raised in favour of and against the revival of the Committee. As there was no consensus, the Chairman indicated that he would transmit all the arguments in favour and against maintaining the Committee to the meeting of the ECE Executive Committee on 27 February and ask it to initiate work on possible ways forward.

In other action, the Committee on Trade endorsed: the report of the 2008 United Nations Centre for Trade Facilitation and Electronic Business (UN/CEFACT) plenary session [ECE/TRADE/C/CEFACT/2008/40] and the UN/CEFACT 2010–2011 work programme [ECE/TRADE/C/CEFACT/2008/16]; the report of the 2008 sessions of Working Party 6 (WP.6) [ECE/TRADE/C/WP.6/2008/18] and of WP.7 [ECE/TRADE/C/WP.7/2008/25]; the 2009–2010 work programme and priorities of WP.6 [ECE/TRADE/C/WP.6/2008/14/Rev.1]; and the 2010–2011 work programme of WP.7 [ECE/TRADE/C/2009/7]. The Committee approved its 2010–2011 work programme [ECE/TRADE/C/2009/10] and the renewal of the mandates and terms of reference for the Advisory Group on Market Surveillance and the Ad hoc Team of Specialists on Standardization and Regulatory Techniques [ECE/TRADE/C/2009/11]. The Committee decided to hold its fourth session from 25 to 26 February 2010.

In April, at its sixty-third session [E/2009/37], the Commission requested the ECE Executive Committee to take the necessary measures to improve efficiency of the Trade subprogramme and to take a consensus decision on the future of the Committee on Trade.

Timber

The Timber Committee, at its sixty-seventh session (Geneva, 13–16 October) [ECE/TIM/2009/9], held a policy forum on "The Forest Sector in the Green Economy" in collaboration with the FAO European Forestry Commission. The forum addressed challenges faced by the forest sector in the context of the global economic crisis and identified opportunities for its contribution to a greener economy. Participants discussed medium- and long-term development strategies, including the role and policy options of governments. The Committee took note of the Chairman's summary of the Forum's conclusions, which was annexed to the report.

The ECE/FAO Team of Specialists on Forest Products Markets and Marketing organized a green building workshop on 12 October, on "Responding to Climate Change: Wood's Place in a Global Approach to Green Building", in conjunction with the Timber Committee session. The Committee had before it a secretariat note [ECE/TIM/2009/2] which provided background information for its discussion. Following a briefing by the Chairman of the workshop, the Committee endorsed the workshop's conclusions and recommendations and requested that they be distributed widely, including to the fifteenth (2009) Conference of the Parties of the United Nations Framework Convention on Climate Change (see p. 1015) for consideration in the negotiations.

Having reviewed a secretariat note [ECE/TIM/2009/7] on its activities since the sixty-sixth (2008) session [YUN 2008, p. 1118] and the programme of work, the Committee approved the list of planned outputs for the period October 2009–December 2010. The Committee also reviewed and approved the lines of activities on forests and climate change under the joint ECE/FAO Integrated Programme of Work on Timber and Forestry, as well as the discontinuation of the forest sector country profiles and the separate collection and dissemination of forest fire statistics.

Other issues considered by the Committee included the ECE/FAO role and strategic direction in the light of the changing international environment [ECE/TIM/2009/4]; forest market developments in 2009 and prospects for 2010 [ECE/TIM/2009/5]; matters arising from ECE's sixty-third session [ECE/TIM/2009/3]; and performance evaluations [ECE/TIM/2009/8].

Transport

The seventy-first session of the Inland Transport Committee (Geneva, 24–26 February) [ECE/TRANS/206], reviewed, among other topics: ECE reform in the field of transport; implementation monitoring mechanisms of the key legal instruments in transport; gender issues; reorganization of the Transport Division and its strategy; assistance to countries with economies in transition; the Transport, Health and Environment Pan-European Programme (THE PEP) and environmental aspects of transport; review of the transport situation in ECE countries; global warming and transport; the impact of globalization on transport, logistics and trade; restrictions on the international road transport of goods; and transport security. It considered action taken by its working parties on issues such as: global road safety; intermodal transport and logistics; fuel quality standards; harmonizing navigation rules for inland water transport; transport of dangerous goods; transport of perishable foodstuffs; transport of people with reduced mobility; and rail transport security.

In its resolutions on the 2010 E-Road Traffic Census [ECE/TRANS/206 (res. 259)] and the 2010 E-Rail Traffic Census [ibid. (res. 260)], the Inland Transport Committee invited Governments to take a census in 2010 of traffic on the E-Roads and the E-rail lines on their national territory and to supply the results to the ECE secretariat by 1 November 2011 and 30 June 2012, respectively.

In other activity, the ECE Inland Transport Committee and the Committee on Trade co-organized the Joint Trade and Transport Conference on the Impact of Globalization on Transport, Logistics and Trade (Geneva, 24 February). THE PEP focused its activities on assisting States with implementing the Amsterdam Declaration adopted at the Third High-level Meeting on Transport, Health and Environment (Amsterdam, Netherlands, 22–23 January). The Declaration focused on sustainable urban transport solutions in the countries of Eastern Europe, Caucasus and Central Asia and South-Eastern Europe.

Energy

The Committee on Sustainable Energy, at its eighteenth session (Geneva, 18–20 November) [ECE/ENERGY/80], devoted its energy security dialogue to "Energy Security and the Financial Crisis" and examined the impact of the financial crisis on energy infrastructure investment and how energy companies and Governments reacted to energy security risk. It also discussed cooperation and coordination with other bodies, including the Commission's other sectoral committees; the activities of the Committee's subsidiary bodies; the regional advisory services programme in the field of energy; and the Committee's 2010–2011 work programme.

The Committee endorsed the requests for two-year mandate renewals by its Ad Hoc Group of Experts on Harmonization of Fossil Energy and Mineral Resource Terminology and Ad Hoc Group of Experts on the Supply and Use of Gas and renewed the mandate of the Energy Efficiency 21 (EE21) Steering Committee for three years. The Committee also approved the establishment of a new subsidiary body—the Group of Experts on Global EE21—with a mandate of three years.

Addressing the activities of its subsidiary bodies, the Committee expressed satisfaction with the results of the fifth three-year phase of the EE21 Project (2006–2009); endorsed the 2009–2012 Project Plan; and endorsed the request of the EE21 Steering Committee to rename the Project the "Energy Efficiency 21 Programme". It noted the progress achieved in the implementation of the work programme of the Working Party on Gas (WPG) in 2008 and 2009 and approved the WPG 2009–2012 work programme. With regard to the Ad Hoc Group of Experts on Harmonization of Fossil Energy and Mineral Resources Terminology, the Committee approved its change of name to "Expert Group on Resource Classification".

Environment

The Committee on Environmental Policy, at its sixteenth session (Geneva, 20–23 October) [ECE/CEP/155], considered the environmental performance review (EPR) of Uzbekistan and adopted related recommendations. It discussed implementation of multilateral environmental agreements and their contributions to the climate change agenda; ongoing cross-sectoral activities; and environmental indicators and monitoring, including the first meeting of the intersectoral Joint Task Force on Environmental Indicators (31 August–2 September) [ECE/CEP/2009/9]. The Committee agreed on the two themes for the Seventh Ministerial Conference "Environment for Europe" (EfE): sustainable management of water and water-related ecosystems; and greening the economy: mainstreaming the environment into economic development, which would be held in Astana, Kazakhstan, in September 2011. It also established a Steering Group to oversee the preparation of the Astana Assessment of Assessments report for the Conference. In other decisions, the Committee agreed to integrate climate change into EPRs; adopted the updated criteria for country eligibility for financial support; endorsed the environment programme performance for 2008–2009; and adopted its 2010–2011 work programme.

The Working Group on Environmental Monitoring and Assessment held its tenth session (Geneva, 3–4 September) [ECE/CEP/AC.10/2009/2]. With regard to the Astana state-of-the-environment assessment, the Working Group stressed the need to involve countries in the preparatory process in order to ensure the provision of valid, relevant and legitimate data. On the Guidelines for developing national strategies to use air quality monitoring as an environmental policy tool [ECE/CEP/2009/10] prepared by the Working Group, the Committee decided to consider their adoption at its Extended Bureau meeting in March 2010.

The Committee on Environmental Policy also convened a special session (Geneva, 27–29 January) [ECE/CEP/S/152 & Corr.1], which considered the EPR of Kyrgyzstan; approved the EfE reform plan annexed to the report; and adopted its work programme for 2009. At its April session [E/2009/37], the Commission endorsed the EfE reform plan.

Housing and land management

The Committee on Housing and Land Management, at its seventieth session (Geneva, 23–25 September) [ECE/HBP/160], held a seminar on "Climate Neutral Cities" in conjunction with the session of the Committee. The seminar explored the overlap between energy efficiency in buildings, spatial planning and urban transport to provide States with policy guidelines on those issues. The Committee welcomed ECE's decision at its sixty-third session (see p. 980) to develop an action plan on energy efficiency in housing; agreed to include climate neutrality in its work

programme under the item of urban environmental performance; and agreed to develop a study on energy efficiency in housing, identifying means and tools for adaptation and mitigation of climate change in cities.

The Committee also discussed various issues, including country profiles on the housing sector; improvement of urban environmental performance; land registration and land markets; housing modernization and management; monitoring implementation; building and construction safety; and cross-sectoral activities. The Chairperson of the Working Party on Land Administration reported on its sixth session (Geneva, 18–19 June) [ECE/HBP/WP.7/2009/9] and noted that a study with guidance on the application of fees and charges for cadastre and registration services had been issued [ECE/HBP/WP.7/2009/4]. The outcome of the first workshop on energy efficiency (Sofia, Bulgaria, 21–22 April) [ECE/HBP/2009/6] was also presented.

The Committee reviewed its 2008–2009 work programme and the draft work programme for 2010–2011, and approved the strategic framework for 2012–2013. In other activity, the International Forum on Energy Efficiency in Housing (Vienna 23–25 November) resulted in a draft action plan for energy-efficient housing in the ECE region.

Statistics

The Conference of European Statisticians, at its fifty-seventh session (Geneva, 8–10 June) [ECE/CES/76], considered the implications of the meetings of its parent bodies—the March/April session of ECE and the February session of the United Nations Statistical Commission (see p. 1257). Two seminars were convened during the session, one on "Balancing principles of professional autonomy and accountability with the mandate to produce policy relevant data", and the other on "Strategic issues in business statistics". The Conference discussed the outcomes of in-depth reviews by the Conference Bureau on housing statistics [ECE/CES/2009/4 & Add.1]; agriculture statistics [ECE/CES/2009/5]; and statistics on labour cost [ECE/CES/2009/6]; as well as the in-depth review of statistical dissemination, communication and publications [ECE/CES/2009/7].

The *Principles and Guidelines on Confidentiality Aspects of Data Integration Undertaken for Statistical or Related Research Purposes* were circulated to countries for written consultation in April, and the revised version [ECE/CES/2009/3/Rev.1] was endorsed by the Conference. The Guidelines would be reviewed by the Conference in 2011. The Conference also endorsed the *Guidelines on the Use and Dissemination of Data on International Immigration to Facilitate their Use to Improve Emigration Data of Sending Countries*, subject to amendments [ECE/CES/2009/10/Add.2.] and the *Manual on Victimization Surveys*, subject to amendments [ECE/CES/2009/12/Add.2].

The Conference considered the report of the ECE Statistical Programme on 2008 and plans for 2009 [ECE/CES/2009/44] and endorsed the plans for the rest of 2009. It also endorsed the terms of reference of the Conference steering groups, task forces, groups of experts and organizing committees created by the Conference Bureau. The topics identified for seminars during the Conference's 2010 plenary session included "the impact of the global crises on statistical systems" and "spatial statistics/role of a spatial dimension in official statistics".

In other activity, the ECE Training Workshop on Dissemination of MDG Indicators and Statistical Information for Central Asian and other CIS countries (Astana, Kazakhstan, 23–25 November) and the Joint ECE/Eurostat Work Session on Statistical Data Confidentiality (Bilbao, Spain, 2–4 December) were held.

Economic cooperation and integration

The Committee on Economic Cooperation and Integration, at its fourth session (Geneva, 28–30 September) [ECE/CECI/2009/2], organized the policy discussion segment of the session as a High-level International Conference on "Promoting innovation-based entrepreneurial opportunities in the ECE region". With regard to programme implementation, the efforts of the Teams of Specialists and networks of experts increasingly focused on capacity-building, drawing on the results of normative work, and on combining the exchange of good practices in different substantive areas with elements of training. The Committee discussed issues such as innovative development and knowledge-based competitiveness; protection of intellectual property rights and strengthening their role in innovative development; entrepreneurship and small- and medium-sized businesses development; financial intermediation in support of innovative development; best practices in public-private partnerships; fostering international economic integration in the ECE region; and capacity-building activities. It also reviewed the status of its virtual platform for exchange of information.

The Committee took note of the proposal to establish an ECE Public-Private Partnerships (PPP) Centre and invited the Team of Specialists on PPPs to further consider the proposal at its December session. It also took note of the results of the 2008–2009 biennial performance evaluation [ECE/CECI/2009/5] and of the proposals for improving its work therein, and decided that its fifth session would take place from 1 to 3 December 2010.

Programme and organizational questions
ECE reform

At its 2009 session [E/2009/37], the Commission had before it a note by the Executive Secretary on the review of ECE reform [E/ECE/1451] that presented the main achievements of the reform; work directions that required further strengthening in their implementation; and new work directions and challenges in the ECE region. It also included two pending issues to be addressed by the Commission: the review of the frequency of the Commission's sessions and its engagement, in cooperation with the Organization for Security and Cooperation in Europe (OSCE), in the development of an early warning mechanism.

The Commission expressed satisfaction with the implementation of ECE reform, welcomed the achievements of the ECE reformed work programme, and encouraged further progress, including in the three cross-sectoral issues identified in the reform: MDGs, gender issues, and private sector and non-governmental involvement. It decided to postpone the review of the effects of the biennialization of the Commission sessions until its sixty-fourth (2011) session. It also decided not to pursue the development of an early warning mechanism with OSCE.

Latin America and the Caribbean

The Economic Commission for Latin America and the Caribbean (ECLAC) did not meet in 2009. The Commission's thirty-third session was to be held in 2010.

ECLAC's 2008 and 2009 activities were described in its biennial report [E/2010/40].

Economic trends

A report on the economic situation in and outlook for Latin America and the Caribbean, 2009–2010 [E/2010/19], indicated that after six years of uninterrupted growth, GDP fell by 1.9 per cent in 2009. The impact of the international crisis and ensuing drop in growth had an adverse effect on the labour market and the estimated unemployment rate in the ECLAC region rose to 8.3 per cent. Domestic activity levels also dropped in some countries due to tighter credit conditions in the private banking sector. The heaviest contractions in economic activity occurred in Mexico and some of the Central American and Caribbean countries, while South America registered positive growth rates. Many countries implemented countercyclical policies that allowed them to partially offset the negative components of domestic demand

and speed up the recovery process, which took hold in some countries during the second quarter, and in nearly all by the third quarter of the year. Consequently, growth was projected at 4.1 per cent in 2010.

Activities in 2009

An ECLAC report on the Commission's work in 2008 and 2009 [E/2010/40] addressed activities undertaken and progress made under its 12 subprogrammes: regional integration and cooperation; production and innovation; macroeconomic policies and growth; equity and social cohesion; mainstreaming the gender perspective in regional development; population and development; public administration; sustainable development and human settlements; natural resources and infrastructure; statistics and economic projections; subregional activities in Mexico and Central America; and subregional activities in the Caribbean.

Regional integration and cooperation

The ECLAC International Trade and Integration Division continued to strengthen the Commission's role as a forum for policy discussion and the exchange of experiences, as well as a catalyst for consensus-building. The Division's efforts were oriented towards supporting and strengthening the competitiveness of the region in the global economy through research and publications as well as technical cooperation. The flagship publication, *Latin America and the Caribbean in the World Economy 2008–2009: Crisis and opportunities for regional cooperation*, was released in August. It presented a medium-term view of international economic conditions and examined the variables that were most likely to have an impact on global scenarios and affect the position of the Latin America and Caribbean economies in the world economy. A document on the international crisis and regional cooperation, published under the title "Crisis internacional y oportunidades para la cooperación regional", which was prepared for both the summit for Latin America and the Caribbean on integration and development (Costa do Sauípe, Brazil, December 2008) and the Fifth Summit of the Americas (Port of Spain, Trinidad and Tobago, April 2009), was one of the Division's most frequently consulted publications. An inventory of measures taken by ECLAC countries to address the crisis, particularly in the area of trade, was also prepared and regularly updated during the year. The Division played a pioneering role in providing assistance to several countries in organizing public-sector institutional processes, strategic national visions, and public-private partnerships and consensuses based on analysis of extraregional success stories of public-private partnerships. It also provided technical cooperation through the organization of seminars and workshops.

In other activities, ECLAC held the Twelfth Annual Conference on Global Economic Analysis "Trade Integration and Sustainable Development: Looking for an Inclusive World" (Santiago, Chile, 10–12 June), and served as a panellist at the inaugural session of the third China–Latin America Business Summit (Bogotá, Colombia, 25–26 November).

Production and innovation

The ECLAC Production, Productivity and Management Division continued efforts to strengthen the capacity of Governments to formulate and implement policies and strategies to enhance the productivity and competitiveness of their countries' production structures. It increased awareness among countries of the region by providing analyses on relevant topics, including the global economic crisis; offered medium- and long-term policy recommendations for sector development; and served as a forum for discussion and regional consensus. In collaboration with FAO and the Inter-American Institute for Cooperation on Agriculture, ECLAC published *The Outlook for Agriculture and Rural Development in the Americas: A Perspective on Latin America and the Caribbean (2009)*, which was prepared for the Fifth Ministerial Meeting on Agriculture and Rural Life in the Americas (Montego Bay, Jamaica, 28–29 October). The document provided decision-makers in the Americas with a reference report on trends in the agricultural sector and rural areas.

Through its Information Society Programme, ECLAC received technical cooperation requests from countries in the region interested in improving their national ICT programmes. Support was provided to Argentina on issues such as employment conditions in small and medium-sized enterprises and employment of women; Ecuador for the creation of clusters and local production systems; Nicaragua for formulation of its national science and technology plan, launched in December; and Uruguay for the establishment of an enterprise monitoring centre. ECLAC also signed a comprehensive technical cooperation agreement with the Government of El Salvador covering a number of areas, including innovation, science and technology, and social inclusion.

Macroeconomic policies and growth

In the context of the financial and economic crisis, the ECLAC Economic Development Division focused on providing rapid analytical and technical support to Latin American and Caribbean countries in order to assist them in assessing the impacts of the crisis and formulating policy response. The Division presented analytical studies on unemployment insurance and minimum wage and trade union issues, among other topics, through a workshop on the situation of labour market institutions in Latin America and the Caribbean (Santiago, April). The workshop analysed policy options for labour market integration and the role of such policies in a crisis context. ECLAC also contributed to the policy debate on the role of fiscal policy in the region in the context of a global crisis through the organization of three high-level meetings in Montevideo, Uruguay in May; San Salvador, El Salvador in August; and Santiago, Chile in September.

The Division continued to disseminate up-to-date information on macroeconomic policy topics and to promote information-sharing through a number of documents, including the publication *The reactions of the Governments of the Americas to the international crisis: an overview of policy measures* [LC/L.3025/Rev.6], which was updated monthly, as well as *Macroeconomic policies in times of crisis: options and perspectives* [LC/W.275]. The latter publication analysed the economic situation of the region at the onset of the global turmoil; the channels through which the crisis spread and its negative effects on the region; the relationship between macroeconomic fluctuations and fiscal policy; and the limitations of public policies as a means of containing the effects of the crisis. The *Economic Survey of Latin America and the Caribbean, 2008–2009* [LC/G.2410-P] was an important source of information and analysis relating to the economic situation in the region.

Equity and social cohesion

In 2009, as countries began to feel the effects of the global financial crisis on the social situation, the ECLAC Social Development Division focused on two areas of work: monitoring how the social impact of the crisis was affecting poverty levels, unemployment and vulnerability; and monitoring and supporting countercyclical social policies and programmes and social safety nets established in previous years. The Division contributed to a fuller understanding of the region's structural social problems through its research and dissemination activities. The 2009 edition of the publication *Social Panorama of Latin America* linked trends in poverty and income distribution with social protection systems and emphasized how those systems responded to the social impacts of the crisis; it included a section on the "care economy", with information on paid and unpaid work from a gender perspective, which highlighted inequalities and persistent imbalances in the sexual division of labour.

Several ECLAC publications focused on issues relating to social inclusion and a "sense of belonging". In November alone, three publications on topics such as the new constitutionalism in Latin America, identity and belonging, cosmopolitanism and difference, and contemporary challenges for social cohesion were released. In addition, ECLAC held an international seminar on "The Sense of Belonging in the Twenty-first Century" at its headquarters in Santiago. In other activities, a workshop on e-health was held in November, and within the framework of the 2009 Global Forum on ICT and Innovation for Education (Monterrey, Mexico, September), the Division organized a regional panel on "Learning and teaching with ICTs: challenges for Latin America". The Division also disseminated and shared information through the website of the Latin American and Caribbean Network of Social Institutions, which comprised over 1,332 institutions from 33 countries and served as a platform for knowledge-based social management.

Mainstreaming gender in regional development

The ECLAC Division for Gender Affairs continued to generate knowledge and enhance capacity for gender equality and the empowerment of women, and to contribute to gender mainstreaming in the countries of the region. The Division contributed, in particular, to raising the profile of issues on the policy agendas of the region's countries, such as the care economy and women's unpaid work, which were particularly relevant in the context of the economic and financial crisis. In response to the Quito Consensus [YUN 2007, p. 1031], a set of policy recommendations addressing the need to generate evidence and integrate a gender perspective in social protection policies, was being implemented in many countries through policy reforms, labour policies, social protection pension schemes and monetary transfers. ECLAC provided support and technical cooperation for those efforts. A high-level seminar on analysis of the impact of the economic crisis from a gender perspective (Mexico City, July) yielded new knowledge and a commitment by civil society to replicate the debate at the country level. The debate had already occurred in Colombia, the Dominican Republic and Bolivia and similar meetings were planned in other countries of Central and South America.

The Commission also convened the forty-third meeting of the Presiding Officers of the Regional Conference on Women in Latin America and the Caribbean (Port of Spain, 7–8 July) [LC/L.3177], which discussed the main regional challenges as identified by Governments in their response to a questionnaire; preparations for the eleventh (2010) session of the Regional Conference on Women in Latin America and the Caribbean in Brasilia; presentation of the website of the Gender Equality Observatory for Latin America and the Caribbean; and a progress report on the UN Secretary-General's campaign to end violence against women.

In other efforts, ECLAC promoted the adoption of a gender perspective by countries of the region, and 15 countries had integrated supplementary gender indicators into their databases and documents relating to monitoring progress towards the MDGs. Seven programmes that used those indicators to monitor Goal 3 (promote gender equality and empower women) had been established.

Population and development

The ECLAC Latin American and Caribbean Demographic Centre–Population Division was guided by mandates arising from international agreements, especially the Programme of Action of the 1994 International Conference on Population and Development [YUN 1994, p. 955] and the Madrid International Plan of Action on Ageing, 2002 [YUN 2002, p. 1194]. ECLAC provided technical cooperation services to countries of the region on a wide range of population-related topics. On the occasion of the fifteenth anniversary of the Conference, ECLAC prepared a comprehensive report and organized a regional seminar on progress in implementing the Programme of Action in the region with the support of the UNFPA (Santiago, 7 October). In addition, the Division prepared a technical guide, which helped countries of the region to evaluate progress achieved with respect to population and development policies as well as identify key challenges to the implementation of the Programme of Action and actions to be taken to achieve its goals by 2014. The Division helped to improve national capacity for conducting the 2010 round of censuses through the organization of regional workshops dealing with key census-related issues. Recommendations arising from the workshops were presented to representatives of national statistical institutes at the fifth meeting of the Statistical Conference of the Americas (Bogotá, 10–13 August).

Several activities focused on migration and ethnic issues, including support for the development and follow-up of the Plan of Action of the Ibero-American Forum on Migration and Development. The Division developed a database on indigenous peoples and Afro-descendants that included information on migration, health, employment and other variables.

Public administration

The Latin American and Caribbean Institute for Economic and Social Planning (ILPES) continued its role as the leading voice in ECLAC for development planning, performance-informed budgeting and public management in the region, at both the national and subnational levels, through its research, technical cooperation and training activities. It sought to foster a long-term balance between the State, civil society and the market economy through the art of governing for sustainable economic, social and institutional development.

ILPES/ECLAC offered comprehensive training through more than 200 international, national and e-learning courses during the 2008–2009 biennium, which benefited 4,746 trainees from 23 different countries. In other activities, the Institute provided technical cooperation services to Governments and other stakeholders from 12 ECLAC countries; conducted applied research that resulted in the publication of more than 13 documents; and supported and developed knowledge networks, including a new application on the Institute's website—Network for Interchanging and Disseminating Excellent Experiences for Achieving the MDGs—designed to increase knowledge and sharing of experiences among public officials and development experts.

The Division conducted regional, territorial and sectoral economic and social planning activities related to State modernization and public policymaking. It also provided support to countries of the region in their efforts to reform public administration and to achieve greater fiscal transparency.

Sustainable development and human settlements

The ECLAC Sustainable Development and Human Settlements Division continued to work on interrelationships between economic growth, environmental protection, urban development and social equity. It carried out technical cooperation and studies that strengthened the capacity of the countries of the region to assess their progress towards sustainable development. It also coordinated the third Regional Implementation Forum on Sustainable Development (Antigua, Guatemala, 26–27 November), at which an ECLAC document was presented to serve as the basis for discussion of the main advances, lessons learned and challenges for the region in the areas of, among others, mining, transport, chemicals and waste management.

The Division conducted eight studies on climate change mitigation, including evaluation of carbon markets and economic adaptation in the ECLAC region, which were summarized in the publication *Economics of climate change in Latin America and the Caribbean—Summary 2009* [LC/G.2425] that was presented at the fifteenth session of the Conference of the Parties of the United Nations Framework Convention on Climate Change (Copenhagen, 7–18 December) (see p. 1015). It co-organized the Meeting of Ministers and High-level Authorities of the Housing and Urban Development Sector in Latin America and the Caribbean, at which a substantive study on the housing deficit and urban management was presented.

In other efforts, the Division provided support to enable countries to cope with the estimated increase of 40 million inhabitants in urban populations over the next five years; launched a course to help design projects and programmes on human security, energy efficiency and climate change; and developed and maintained networks of technical experts, which had helped to alleviate problems stemming from frequent political changes within government institutions.

Natural resources and infrastructure

The ECLAC Natural Resources and Infrastructure Division produced analyses and research and provided technical cooperation services to Governments, civil society and academia aimed at improving public policy formulation in the management of natural resources and the provision of public utility and infrastructure services. ECLAC prepared a document on transnational infrastructure projects, which analysed investment in infrastructure in various countries and proposed a methodology for distributing the economic impacts of those investments among countries. The methodology was disseminated to 80 participants during a training course in August. In coordination with other partners, the Division prepared the document "Contribution of energy services to the MDGs and to poverty alleviation in Latin America and the Caribbean", which was released in October.

To support the Peruvian National Superintendency of Sanitation Services in the analysis of a new water law, water utilities regulation, sustainable tariff-setting, watershed conservation and institutional mechanisms for the promotion of private-sector participation in the provision of drinking water supply and sanitation services, ECLAC organized a seminar on international investment protection agreements, sustainability of infrastructure investments and regulatory and contractual measures (Lima, Peru, January), which was attended by government and sectoral representatives.

Statistics and economic projections

The ECLAC Statistics and Economic Projections Division continued its work in the systematization and dissemination of statistics and supported countries of the region in strengthening their national statistical systems and capacities in the areas of national accounts, household surveys, the production of environmental statistics and the development of indicators for measuring progress towards the MDGs. By the end of the 2008–2009 biennium, 28 countries had data available for calculating most MDG indicators, 18 more than at the end of 2007.

The Division continued to publish the *Statistical Yearbook for Latin America and the Caribbean*, which remained an important source of statistical information as evidenced by some 866,460 downloads of the document per year—a total 50 per cent higher than the target of 600,000 yearly downloads set for the biennium. In addition, the Division's website exceeded its target of 15,000 monthly visits by almost 2,500, indicating increased interest among users in the data disseminated through the website.

The fifth meeting of the ECLAC Statistical Conference of the Americas (Bogotá, 10–13 August) [LC/L.3125] held three seminars on: the development of national statistical systems: recent experiences, learning and assessment; the 2010 census round; and the use of administrative records for statistical purposes. With regard to the examination of the Conference's biennial programme of activities, the meeting discussed institution-building, human resource training, technical and methodological capacities for generating high-quality statistical information in the region, and cooperation between member countries of the Conference and international agencies. The Conference welcomed the initiative of ECLAC to remedy the shortage of experts in census information management by holding three intensive regional courses in demographic analysis for development starting in 2010 or 2011, and appealed to international agencies and organizations for securing the necessary funding.

Subregional activities

Caribbean

The ECLAC subregional headquarters for the Caribbean in Port of Spain, Trinidad and Tobago, continued to strengthen its contribution to policymaking in the subregion through the delivery of substantive research outputs, technical cooperation, and training and capacity-building support. Studies were prepared on public-private partnerships and on rising global food and oil prices and the resulting impact on Caribbean economies. A study on the food crisis, which conveyed information on the policy shifts required to mitigate the impact of higher food prices on food security, was presented to the Fifth Ministerial Meeting on Agriculture and Rural Life in the Americas (Jamaica, October).

The subregional headquarters provided a wide range of training and development activities. It helped to enhance the capacities of public officials and technical staff in the Caribbean during the 2008–2009 biennium with some 569 persons, including 263 women, benefiting from training and consultations. A training workshop on the socio-economic impact of disasters using the ECLAC methodology was convened (Jamaica, October). In addition, ECLAC held a high-level seminar on development policy in the Caribbean (Trinidad and Tobago, October) that brought together 36 high-profile experts, policymakers and academics of the subregion to explore the evolution of development thinking in the Caribbean.

The subregional headquarters continued to highlight developments in the world economy with respect to international trade, tourism, remittance flows, foreign direct investment and external financing. At the Fifth Summit of the Americas in April, presentations by the subregional headquarters during the side events—on gender mainstreaming, social exclusion, the impact of the global financial crisis and progress towards the achievement of the MDGs—helped to inform the policy debate. The subregional headquarters also initiated a review of the economics of climate change in the Caribbean, which focused on economic issues relevant to climate change, examined the economic principles of uncertainty and the precautionary approach, and addressed the key drivers behind climate change.

Mexico and Central America

In 2009, the global economic and financial crisis became the main concern for public policymakers, owing to its recessive impact on countries in the northern region of Central America and the Caribbean, which resulted from the subregion's dependence on the United States economy. The ECLAC subregional headquarters in Mexico redirected its activities to respond to the crisis. It prepared a document on confronting the crisis, which presented the causes of the crisis, the channels through which it was transmitted and its economic and social effects, together with a set of policy recommendations. The subregional headquarters reoriented reports, technical cooperation, expert meetings, projects and training activities to the new scenario; provided tools and timely inputs for policy analysis, design and implementation; and provided technical cooperation services to Governments.

In other activity, ECLAC continued to respond to Government requests for the evaluation of the socioeconomic and environmental impacts of extreme climatic events in the subregion. The subregional headquarters constructed scenarios, assessed the economic impacts of climate change for the region and discussed policy options with key stakeholders in the Central American region. The ministers of environment requested and received an interim report as input for their negotiations during the United Nations Climate Change Conference in December (see p. 1015) and for the formulation of regional and national strategies.

The subregional headquarters cooperated with beneficiaries to strengthen their understanding and analytical knowledge with regard to the development agenda and policy options. Assistance was directed to-

wards a wide range of economic and social stakeholders, including policymakers, public officials, NGOs, civil society associations, academics, researchers and experts. By the end of 2009, some 730 beneficiaries from the subregion had received services in the areas of poverty reduction and economic development and 850 beneficiaries had received services relating to trade, integration and sustainable development.

Western Asia

The Economic and Social Commission for Western Asia (ESCWA) did not meet in 2009, in accordance with its decision in 2005 [YUN 2005, p. 1120] to hold its biennial sessions in even years in order to be in harmony with the submission of the UN strategic framework. The Commission's twenty-sixth session was to be held in 2010. ESCWA 2008–2009 activities were described in its biennial report [E/ESCWA/26/5(Part I)].

Economic trends

In 2009, the ESCWA region saw a decline in growth according to the summary of the survey of economic and social developments in the ESCWA region, 2009–2010 [E/2010/20]. The region's GDP averaged 1.9 per cent, compared to 6.0 per cent in 2008. Developing countries were affected by the plunge of financial and real estate asset prices and the collapse of commodity prices, including energy, metal and food, while the shortages of liquidity at local and international money markets became a destabilizing factor for financial sectors and national economies.

The end of the credit crisis and a gradual recovery in the world demand led to a resumption of positive, forward-looking activities in developing countries, in particular China and India. Dollar liquidity had shown signs of recovery since the second quarter of 2009; the price of crude oil had stabilized; and the monetary and fiscal authorities of ESCWA member countries had successfully defended the region's banking sector. However, the economic situation remained uncertain with ongoing de-leveraging of the financial sector of several countries in the region. Several countries, mainly the region's non-oil exporters, had become more reliant on capital inflows to finance their current account deficits. The economic sentiment of the region during the fourth quarter of 2009 could be described as cautious optimism and GDP was forecast to rise to 4.6 per cent in 2010.

Activities in 2009

In 2009, ESCWA activities under its 2008–2009 work programme [E/ESCWA/26/5(Part I)] focused on seven subprogrammes: integrated management of natural resources for sustainable development; integrated social policies; economic development and integration; ICT for regional integration; statistics for evidence-based policymaking; the advancement of women; and conflict mitigation and development.

Natural resources management for sustainable development

The ESCWA Sustainable Development and Productivity Division was responsible for implementing this subprogramme, which aimed at improving the sustainable management and use of natural resources in the region, and promoting regional cooperation and harmonization in the management of water, energy and the production sectors. The submission of regional reports on agriculture, rural development, land, drought and desertification to the United Nations Commission on Sustainable Development contributed to raising awareness and building capacity on the implementation of land management policies and measures for improved rural development. Two meetings were convened, one on sustainable land management as a best practice to enhance rural development in the ESCWA region (Beirut, Lebanon, 25–27 March) and one on adopting the sustainable livelihoods approach for promoting rural development in the ESCWA region (Beirut, 21–22 December) [E/ESCWA/SDPD/2009/WG.6/10].

ESCWA worked to assist Lebanon, the Syrian Arab Republic and Yemen in adopting measures to improve water supply and sanitation in their national water policies. In addition, partnerships with NGOs and institutions resulted in the adoption of initiatives to enhance the competitiveness of small and medium-sized agricultural and manufacturing enterprises, using environmentally-sound technology. ESCWA activities also led to a number of initiatives involving the use of modern tools and techniques to enhance productivity and competitiveness in the agricultural and manufacturing sectors, focusing on *zaatar* cultivation and garment manufacturing.

Social policy

The ESCWA Social Development Division was responsible for implementing this subprogramme, which aimed at strengthening coherent and integrated national social policies that were region-specific and culturally sensitive, and encouraging community development action with a view to reducing social inequity and enhancing social stability. In the management of social policy, advocacy efforts and policy advice on integrated social and population policies, five countries either adopted measures to support the integration of social policy or pursued technical

assistance from ESCWA in that field. The advocacy and capacity development efforts of the Commission supported member countries in the formulation of national youth policies and in the preparation of national reports.

Advocacy and capacity development in the area of youth-targeted policies and programmes was received positively by 13 member countries. ESCWA implemented a regional project in which focal points were trained on the collection of youth policy-related information and the translation of the findings into national reports. ESCWA also organized, in collaboration with the Family Development Foundation in the United Arab Emirates, the expert group meeting on Reinforcing Social Equity: Integrating Youth into the Development Process (Abu Dhabi, United Arab Emirates, 29–31 March) [E/ESCWA/SDD/2009/3], which contributed to improving decision-making and guiding national efforts towards the adoption of strategies aimed at integrating youth issues into the development process. To foster regional dialogue, ESCWA organized the Arab Forum on Social Policy (Beirut, 28–29 October), which focused on the importance of integrated social policy and protection for regional development.

Economic development and integration

The ESCWA Economic Development and Globalization Division was responsible for implementing this subprogramme, which aimed at strengthening macroeconomic policymaking for short-term economic growth and sustainable economic development in member countries, negotiation of trade and investment agreements, and facilitation of trade. ESCWA contributed to the 2009 issue of the publication *World Economic Situation and Prospects* and the November issue of the *Regional Economic Forecast*, which focused on assessing the impact of the global financial crisis and food inflation. Four ESCWA national training workshops contributed to the upgrading of the negotiation skills of 90 Government officials on bilateral investment agreements and double taxation avoidance.

ESCWA continued to support the implementation of the ESCWA transport agreements. A key development was the adoption by the Arab Economic, Social and Development Summit (Kuwait, 19–20 January) of an agreement on the Arab railway network, based on the Agreement on International Railways in the Arab Mashreq. The number of countries that had adopted the Agreement on International Roads in the Arab Mashreq increased to 12 and the number of policy measures adopted by member countries in relation to implementation of the Integrated Transport System in the Arab Mashreq had increased to 40 by the end of 2009, compared with 31 in 2007. The Commission also held a workshop on setting regional and national road traffic casualty reduction targets in the ESCWA region (Abu Dhabi, 16–17 June) [E/ESCWA/EDGD/2009/4].

In other activity, ESCWA assessed trade policy trends, trade facilitation and liberalization measures and accession processes in member countries, and provided related policy advice and advocacy. The Commission provided a forum in which the Arab business community could be briefed on the latest developments concerning WTO negotiations and discuss their implications, as well as on issues concerning the global economic crisis. ESCWA also organized a workshop on Measurement of e-Commerce and External Trade Indicators (Dubai, United Arab Emirates, 30 March–1 April) [E/ESCWA/SD/2009/7], which discussed the importance of e-commerce statistics related to international merchandise trade and the preparation and publication of external trade indicators. The sixth session of the Technical Committee on Liberalization of Foreign Trade and Economic Globalization in the Countries of the ESCWA Region (Beirut, 6–7 July) [E/ESCWA/EDGD/2009/IG.2/7] was also convened.

ICT and related development issues

The ESCWA Information and Communication Technology Division was responsible for implementing this subprogramme, which aimed at narrowing the digital divide to build an inclusive development-oriented information society and knowledge-based economy. The Information Society Portal for the ESCWA Region was launched, offering a dynamic, bilingual (English/Arabic) regional e-service database. The Expert Group Meeting on Developing the Information and Communication Technologies Sector in the ESCWA region (Beirut, 11–12 March) highlighted the challenges facing the development of a self-reliant and sustainable ICT sector in the region and proposed solutions to overcome those obstacles. With regard to the Conference on Regional Follow-up to the Outcome of the World Summit on the Information Society (WSIS) (Damascus, Syria, 16–18 June) [E/ESCWA/ICTD/2009/13], the principal outcomes were the Regional Plan of Action and the Arab ICT Strategy; a roadmap for the implementation and follow-up of WSIS-related activities; and the creation of the Global Alliance for ICT and Development Regional Arab Network.

In partnership with the United Nations Educational, Scientific and Cultural Organization, ESCWA implemented a project on ICT for education in Iraq which would establish several learning centres throughout the country and was expected to increase ICT literacy of teachers and other staff. ESCWA also held the second meeting of the Technical Cooperation Knowledge-sharing Network (TC Network) (Beirut,

16–18 February) [E/ESCWA/PPTCD/2009/1/Rev.1] to follow up on implementation of the recommendations made at the preparatory meeting in 2007 and to enhance coordination among TC Network members. The TC Network website was launched during the meeting.

Statistics

The ESCWA Statistics Division was responsible for implementing this subprogramme, which aimed at improving the production and use of harmonized and comparable economic, social and sectoral statistics, including gender-disaggregated data, thereby allowing for informed and evidence-based decision-making. ESCWA assisted member countries in achieving 67 per cent implementation of the fundamental principles of official statistics. It also established a virtual library on national statistical systems, facilitated information exchange on best practice, disseminated guidelines and supported capacity-building of national statistical offices. In its role as secretariat to the Regional Task Force on Population and Housing Censuses, ESCWA hosted the fifth meeting of the Task Force (Beirut, 23–24 March).

The Regional Working Group of the ESCWA Statistical Committee (Beirut, 10 February) [E/ESCWA/SD/2009/2] discussed topics on coordinating the positions of ESCWA countries for the upcoming session of the United Nations Statistical Commission; determining the positions of the region's countries on the *Delhi Group Manual on Surveys of Informal Employment and the Informal Sector*; preparing for the Fourth Forum on Arab Statistical Capacity-Building; and following up on the World Forum on Measuring and Fostering the Progress of Societies.

In other activity, ESCWA organized the Expert Group Meeting on Poverty Measurement (Beirut, 28–29 April) [E/ESCWA/SD/2009/8], which brought together regional and international experts and concluded with a set of recommendations on statistics and poverty measurement. The Commission also held expert group meetings on energy statistics in March [E/ESCWA/SD/2009/WG.1/4] and on gender statistics in October [E/ESCWA/SD/2009/WG.2/5] and [E/ESCWA/SD/2009/WG.3/3].

Advancement of women

The ESCWA Centre for Women (ECW) was responsible for implementing the subprogramme, which aimed at increasing the focus on women and gender issues with a view to reducing the gender imbalance and empowering women. ECW organized the fourth session of the Committee on Women under the theme "Promoting Economic Participation of Arab Women", (Beirut, 21–23 October) [E/ESCWA/OES/2010/1], which discussed the ways in which member countries and regional and international organizations could contribute to creating a more supportive environment to enable women to access economic and financial resources, and be involved in economic activity. The Committee also approved the proposed programme of work for ECW for the 2010–2011 biennium and adopted a resolution on the follow-up to the implementation of the Beijing Platform for Action in the Arab region, which would be submitted to the twenty-sixth ESCWA session in 2010, and which called for the Commission to establish an index on gender and development and study the feasibility of a gender observatory for the Arab region.

ECW supported member countries in reporting to international organizations, with particular focus on the national reports required to be submitted to the Committee on the Elimination of Discrimination against Women (CEDAW) and the progress reports in follow-up to the Beijing Platform for Action. Following requests from member countries, ECW undertook several advisory missions, including training workshops on gender mainstreaming national development plans, support for report-writing for international organizations, and training on leadership and decision-making. The activities of ECW continued to raise member country awareness of the importance of internationally agreed conventions; the fact that in 2009 Qatar ratified CEDAW and Jordan lifted its reservation on the movement of persons reflected the success of those efforts. ECW also produced an in-depth study and organized an expert group meeting with participants from countries faced with ongoing conflict to identify and explore the ways in which the role of women could be strengthened in conflict resolution and peacebuilding.

Conflict mitigation and development

The ESCWA Section for Emerging and Conflict-related Issues (ECRI) was responsible for implementing the subprogramme, which aimed to increase understanding by member countries of the impact of conflict and enhance their capacity to identify, assess,

predict and respond to challenges posed by conflict with a view to reducing its impact on development. In 2009, ESCWA expanded its endeavours to strengthen State institutions in member countries. The human and institutional development interventions implemented by the Commission through ECRI work had yielded focused policy recommendations, enhancing the skills of public sector officials and contributing to supporting locally led management reform of public institutions. Within its 2008–2009 workplan, ESCWA trained 607 civil servants from member countries through its institutional development programmes, providing them with the tools needed to instigate modernization and reform strategies and processes in their respective administrations. More than 20 per cent of those trained had since become trainers, creating a cadre of experts capable of disseminating the knowledge and skills acquired. During the 2008–2009 biennium, the subprogramme had received 13 requests from member countries for technical assistance in the area of institutional development, reflecting its success in designing and implementing tailored intervention, training modules and programmes to enhance the capacity of member countries to assess and respond to the socio-economic and political challenges posed by conflict and instability in the region.

In other activities, ECRI organized the Expert Group Meeting on "Strengthening Good Governance Practices in Conflict Affected Countries: Current Priorities and Future Interventions" (Beirut, 27–28 February) [E/ESCWA/ECRI/2009/3]. The meeting brought together local, regional and international experts and representatives of ESCWA member countries to discuss issues relating to the roles of good governance, human rights, social and economic development and peacebuilding. The subprogramme also organized, in collaboration with the Heinrich Boell Foundation, a brainstorming session on the root causes of ethnic and sectarian tensions in the ESCWA region (Beirut, 26 August) [E/ESCWA/ECRI/2009/4] to discuss and solicit input and comments on a draft study entitled "Unpacking the Dynamics of Ethno-Sectarian Tensions: A Youth-Focus Group Analysis".

Chapter VI

Energy, natural resources and cartography

The conservation, development and use of energy and natural resources continued to be the focus of several UN bodies in 2009, including the Commission on Sustainable Development. The Commission continued to focus on the thematic cluster: agriculture, rural development, land, drought, desertification, and Africa. In a resolution adopted in May, the Commission reaffirmed that protecting and managing the natural resource base of economic and social development was an essential requirement for sustainable development.

Speaking before the General Assembly in November, the Director General of the International Atomic Energy Agency (IAEA) outlined the main changes in the work of IAEA over the past 12 years, including improvement of safety standards, expanded assistance to the nuclear power programmes of developing countries, and wider transfer of multilateral nuclear technology in areas such as food and agriculture, health, water resources and the environment. He expressed concern about the possibility of extremist groups having access to nuclear or radioactive materials, and stated that in addressing nuclear programme issues, the international community should let diplomacy and thorough verification take their course.

Asserting that the growth of new and renewable energy was mostly a result of more favourable policies, the Secretary-General called on States to adopt policies stimulating public and private investment and encourage public-private partnerships and international cooperation.

The Fifth World Water Forum was held in March under the theme "Bridging Divides for Water". The Forum adopted the Istanbul Declaration of Heads of States on Water, the Istanbul Ministerial Statement, the Istanbul Water Guide and the Istanbul Water Consensus. The issue of transboundary water cooperation was the focus of World Water Day (22 March) and one of the main subjects of the *UN-Water Annual Report 2009*.

The Ninth United Nations Regional Cartographic Conference for the Americas adopted resolutions on mechanisms for building spatial data infrastructures, a virtual platform/forum for sharing spatial data infrastructure best practices, and support of spatial data infrastructure in the developing countries of the Americas. The Eighteenth United Nations Regional Cartographic Conference for Asia and the Pacific adopted resolutions on regional geodesy, capacity-building in disaster management, and spatially enabled Government and society.

The twenty-fifth session of the United Nations Group of Experts on Geographical Names was held in May in Nairobi. In December, the Economic and Social Council endorsed its recommendations.

Energy and natural resources

The Commission on Sustainable Development, at its seventeenth session (New York, 16 May 2008 and 4–15 May 2009) [E/2009/29], continued to focus on the thematic cluster of agriculture, rural development, land, drought, desertification, and Africa for the 2008–2009 implementation cycle (see p. 799).

Documents before the Commission included the Secretary-General's reports on policy options and actions for expediting progress in implementation of: agriculture [E/CN.17/2009/3]; rural development [E/CN.17/2009/4]; land [E/CN.17/2009/5]; drought [E/CN.17/2009/6]; desertification [E/CN.17/2009/7]; Africa [E/CN.17/2009/8]; and interlinkages and cross-cutting issues [E/CN.17/2009/9]. Such documents addressed issues related to energy and natural resources.

Noting the growing scarcities of many natural resources and the competing claims to their use, the Commission, in its resolution [E/2009/29 (res. 17/1)], reaffirmed that eradicating poverty, changing unsustainable patterns of production and consumption, and protecting and managing the natural resources base of economic and social development were the essential requirements for sustainable development. The Commission called for local, national, regional and global actions to enhance agricultural production, productivity and sustainability by promoting sound water management and saving in agriculture. It called for actions to manage sustainably competing uses of water and land resources by supporting the implementation of sustainable and efficient water resource development and management schemes; address the challenges and opportunities posed by biofuels in view of the world's food security, energy and sustainable development needs; and promote research and development to enhance the sustainability of biofuels and other bioenergy sources, including through South-South, North-South, and triangular cooperation, and through technical cooperation and exchange of information. It further called for actions to invest in essential infrastructure and services for rural communities by improving access to reliable and affordable energy services, including renewable and alternative sources of energy.

In preparation for the seventeenth session, intersessional meetings focused on improving agricultural productivity, water use efficiency and rural livelihoods (Bangkok, 28–30 January); African agriculture in the twenty-first century: meeting the challenges, making a sustainable green revolution (Windhoek, Namibia, 9–10 February); and the role of native and desert-adapted species in slowing desertification (Kibbutz Ketura, Israel, 22–30 March).

Nuclear energy

In August [A/64/257], the Secretary-General transmitted to the General Assembly the 2008 report of IAEA. Presenting the report [A/64/PV.33] and giving his last speech to the General Assembly as the Agency's Director General on 2 November, Mohamed ElBaradei said that since he first spoke to the Assembly in 1998, the Agency had moved from being a relatively unknown technical organization to becoming a major player at the centre of issues critical to international peace and security. The Agency had gained universal respect for its independence and objectivity in nuclear verification, safety and security. It had made considerable progress in bringing the benefits of peaceful nuclear technology to developing countries, improving their access to energy, health care, food and clean water. There had been an expansion in the use of nuclear power, with scores of countries, especially developing countries, expressing interest in introducing it as part of their energy mix for poverty alleviation. As a result, IAEA had adjusted its priorities to focus more on the nuclear power programmes of the "newcomers". Nuclear safety had improved since the shock of Chernobyl in 1986; IAEA safety standards had become the global benchmark and had been adopted by the European Union (EU).

However, the Director General reported, in the past 10 years the annual budget of IAEA's technical cooperation programme had increased only slightly—from $80 million to $96 million. A significant increase in funding was required for the Agency to do more. He urged donor States to recognize the link between security and development. By helping to address the root causes of instability and insecurity, including endemic conflicts, poor governance and poverty, countries would less likely be tempted to seek nuclear or other weapons of mass destruction.

The gravest threat the world faced, according to the Director General, was that extremists could get hold of nuclear or radioactive materials. In the wake of the 9/11 attacks, IAEA initiated a comprehensive programme to combat the risk of nuclear terrorism. The nuclear security programme established by IAEA had provided $50 million in equipment, training and other assistance to member States over the past three years. However, nuclear security continued to be funded almost entirely from voluntary contributions, which came with many conditions attached and were insufficient and unpredictable. The Director General warned that the number of incidents of illicit trafficking and other unauthorized activities reported to IAEA's Illicit Trafficking Database—over 200 in 2008—remained a cause of concern and might well be only the tip of the iceberg.

IAEA had moved beyond simple verification of declared nuclear material at declared facilities to assessing information on a State's entire nuclear programme and, most importantly, verifying the absence of undeclared activities. Within the limited resources and capabilities available, the Agency had made increasing use of the advanced technology critical to verification, such as remote monitoring, environmental sampling and satellite imagery. IAEA's ability to detect possible clandestine nuclear material and activities depended on the extent to which it was given the necessary legal authority, technology and resources. Regrettably, it faced continuing shortcomings in all three areas, which, if not addressed, could put the entire non-proliferation regime at risk. Additional funding was needed for state-of-the-art technology. The Agency also needed improved and consistent access to top-quality satellite imagery.

An important lesson to be learned from both Iraq and the Democratic People's Republic of Korea, the Director General said, was that diplomacy and thorough verification must be allowed to take their course, however lengthy and tiresome the process might be. The Agency, for its part, must draw conclusions justified by the facts alone.

In the case of Iran, whose nuclear programme remained an issue before the Agency and the Security Council, the Director General reiterated that addressing the concerns of the international community was primarily a matter of confidence-building, which could only be achieved through dialogue. At the same time, Iran needed to clarify a number of questions about its nuclear programme through cooperation with the Agency.

Drawing the Assembly's attention to the growing number of States that had mastered uranium enrichment or plutonium reprocessing, the Director General warned that any of those States had the capacity to produce nuclear weapons in a short time. To address that challenge, the world needed to move from national to multinational control of the nuclear fuel cycle. He proposed to establish a low enriched uranium bank to assure States a guaranteed last-resort supply of nuclear fuel for their reactors so that they might not need their own enrichment or reprocessing capability, with the ultimate goal of the full multinationalization of uranium enrichment and plutonium reprocessing.

On 2 November [meeting 34], the General Assembly adopted **resolution 64/8** [draft: A/64/L.7 & Add.1] without vote [agenda item 85].

Report of the International Atomic Energy Agency

The General Assembly,

Having received the report of the International Atomic Energy Agency for 2008,

Taking note of the statement by the Director General of the International Atomic Energy Agency, in which he provided additional information on the main developments in the activities of the Agency during 2009,

Recognizing the importance of the work of the Agency,

Recognizing also the cooperation between the United Nations and the Agency and the Agreement governing the relationship between the United Nations and the Agency as approved by the General Conference of the Agency on 23 October 1957 and by the General Assembly in the annex to its resolution 1145(XII) of 14 November 1957,

1. *Takes note with appreciation* of the report of the International Atomic Energy Agency;

2. *Takes note* of resolutions GC(53)/RES/3 approving the appointment of Mr. Yukiya Amano as the next Director General; GC(53)/RES/4 paying tribute to Dr. Mohamed ElBaradei; GC(53)/RES/10 on measures to strengthen international cooperation in nuclear, radiation, transport and waste safety; GC(53)/RES/11 on nuclear security, including measures to protect against nuclear and radiological terrorism; GC(53)/RES/12 on strengthening the Agency's technical cooperation activities; GC(53)/RES/13 on strengthening the Agency's activities related to nuclear science, technology and applications, comprising GC(53)/RES/13 A on non-power nuclear applications and GC(53)/RES/13 B on nuclear power applications; GC(53)/RES/14 on strengthening the effectiveness and improving the efficiency of the safeguards system and application of the Model Additional Protocol; GC(53)/RES/15 on the implementation of the Agreement between the Agency and the Democratic People's Republic of Korea for the application of safeguards in connection with the Treaty on the Non-Proliferation of Nuclear Weapons; GC(53)/RES/16 on the application of Agency safeguards in the Middle East; GC(53)/RES/17 on Israeli nuclear capabilities; GC(53)/RES/18 on personnel, comprising GC(53)/RES/18 A on staffing of the Agency's secretariat and GC(53)/RES/18 B on women in the secretariat; and decisions GC(53)/DEC/11 on the amendment to article XIV.A of the Statute, GC(53)/DEC/12 on the amendment to article VI of the Statute and GC(53)/DEC/13 on prohibition of armed attack or threat of attack against nuclear installations, during operation or under construction, adopted by the General Conference of the Agency at its fifty-third regular session, held from 14 to 18 September 2009;

3. *Expresses its appreciation* for the twelve years of distinguished service by Dr. ElBaradei as Director General of the Agency, during which, in 2005, the Agency and its Director General were jointly awarded the Nobel Peace Prize, and extends its best wishes to Mr. Amano, the incoming Director General of the Agency;

4. *Reaffirms its strong support* for the indispensable role of the Agency in encouraging and assisting the development and practical application of atomic energy for peaceful uses, in technology transfer to developing countries and in nuclear safety, verification and security;

5. *Appeals* to Member States to continue to support the activities of the Agency;

6. *Requests* the Secretary-General to transmit to the Director General of the Agency the records of the sixty-fourth session of the General Assembly relating to the activities of the Agency.

New and renewable sources of energy

In response to Assembly resolution 62/197 [YUN 2007, p. 1041], the Secretary-General in August submitted a report [A/64/277] on the promotion of new and renewable sources of energy, which discussed the development, transfer and diffusion of renewable energy technologies; investment; policy options; and international cooperation.

The Secretary-General noted that world primary energy demand was projected to increase by 45 per cent from 2006 to 2030. Energy supply would continue to be based primarily on fossil fuels, with coal projected to account for more than a third of incremental global energy demand through 2030.

There had been remarkable growth of renewable energy in global markets in recent years, though the share in global energy supply remained low. Renewable energy from wind, solar, small hydro (excluding large hydro), modern biomass (including biofuels but excluding traditional biomass) and geothermal supplied 2.4 per cent of the world's final energy consumption. Wind had the largest share in renewable electric power capacity, followed by small hydro. In 2008, power capacity added from renewable energy surpassed for the first time power capacity added from conventional sources in the EU and the United States.

Besides informational, legal, regulatory, market, institutional, infrastructural, political and cultural barriers, financial barriers were the most critical constraint for the development, transfer and costs of renewable energy technologies, the Secretary-General said. Although the initial capital investment costs of renewable energy were often high, renewable technologies could offer prospects for a low-cost sustainable energy supply once they reached scale and gained operating experience, thereby lowering costs and prices.

Global investment in renewable energy generation projects reached $117 billion in 2008—a growth rate of 13 per cent compared with 2007. In fact, 2008 marked the first year that investment in new power generation capacity from renewable energy technologies was greater than investment in fossil-fuelled technologies. Most of it was invested in the wind sector (with a total financial investment of $51.8 billion), followed by the solar sector ($33.5 billion), especially in the markets of the EU, North America, China, Eastern Europe and Latin America. The price rise of crude oil in mid-July 2008 had at first positive impacts on renewable energy demand, but the roughly halving of oil prices afterwards, owing largely to the global recession, had reduced economic incentives for new investment. In the first quarter of 2009, new financial investment in the renewable energy sector decreased by 53 per cent compared with the first quarter of 2008 to $13.3 billion.

Stating that recent significant growth of renewable energy was mostly a result of more favourable policies amid increasing concerns about climate change and energy security, the Secretary-General described a number of policy tools and measures that promoted renewable energy, including feed-in laws, renewable energy quotas and portfolio standards, public competitive bidding, direct public financing and investment to promote renewable energy. The feed-in laws—enacted in some 50 countries—obliged utilities to purchase power generated from renewables at a price set by the regulatory authority, and therefore, offered producers of electricity from renewables a guaranteed feed-in tariff. The Secretary-General indicated that a possible future international policy tool could be a global feed-in tariff programme—a global fund providing guaranteed purchase prices to producers in developing countries for a 20-year period.

International financing institutions continued to play a crucial role in mobilizing financial resources for the promotion of new and renewable energy. Thirty-five per cent of the World Bank Group's total energy lending commitments of $2.7 billion in 2008 went to 95 renewable energy and energy efficiency projects in 54 countries—an 87 per cent increase compared with 2007. The UN system continued to support the promotion and expansion of new and renewable sources of energy in developing countries. UN-Energy, the inter-agency mechanism of the UN system, brought together 20 UN entities and the World Bank to promote system-wide collaboration. The Department of Economic and Social Affairs continued to promote the use of new and renewable energy resources in developing countries. Renewable energy formed the core of the energy portfolio of the United Nations Development Programme, whose energy-related project financing had risen in 2007 to $1.7 billion, about 80 per cent of which was for renewable energy project development, clean energy market creation and catalysing carbon financing.

The Secretary-General said that rising global energy demand required greater energy diversification and an increase in the share of new and renewable energy in the global energy supply. The current share of renewable energy in the global energy supply was low mainly because of the high costs of many renewable energy technologies. The cost-competitiveness of renewable energy technologies should be increased through policies that ensured research, development, deployment and transfer of those technologies, especially to developing countries. Such policies could stimulate public and private investment and encourage public-private partnerships.

GENERAL ASSEMBLY ACTION

On 21 December [meeting 66], the General Assembly, on the recommendation of the Second (Economic and Financial) Committee [A/64/420/Add.9], adopted **resolution 64/206** without vote [agenda item 53 *(i)*].

Promotion of new and renewable sources of energy

The General Assembly,

Recalling its resolutions 53/7 of 16 October 1998, 54/215 of 22 December 1999 and 55/205 of 20 December 2000, and recalling also its resolutions 56/200 of 21 December 2001, 58/210 of 23 December 2003, 60/199 of 22 December 2005 and 62/197 of 19 December 2007 on the promotion of new and renewable sources of energy,

Recalling also the 2005 World Summit Outcome,

Reiterating the principles of the Rio Declaration on Environment and Development and of Agenda 21, and recalling the recommendations and conclusions contained in the Plan of Implementation of the World Summit on Sustainable Development ("Johannesburg Plan of Implementation") concerning energy for sustainable development,

Recalling with appreciation the Interactive Thematic Dialogue of the General Assembly on "Energy efficiency, energy conservation and new and renewable sources of energy" held on 18 June 2009 and its contribution to the intergovernmental dialogue on energy issues,

Welcoming the political impetus recently given to the development of new and renewable sources of energy worldwide, including in particular in developing countries and in countries with economies in transition,

Welcoming also the offer of the Government of India to host the Delhi International Renewable Energy Conference from 27 to 29 October 2010,

Welcoming further initiatives that aim to improve access to reliable, affordable, economically viable, socially acceptable and environmentally sound energy services for sustainable development in order to contribute to the achievement of the internationally agreed development goals, including the Millennium Development Goals,

Recognizing that the development of new and renewable sources of energy plays a significant role in the diversification of the energy mix, achieving greater energy efficiency, supporting and accelerating economic growth and social development, creating employment opportunities, ensuring energy access and availability, promoting energy cooperation and rendering environmental benefits, thus contributing to achieving sustainable development and the Millennium Development Goals,

Emphasizing that the increased use and promotion of new and renewable sources of energy for sustainable development, including solar-thermal, photovoltaic, biomass, wind, hydro, tidal, ocean and geothermal forms, could make a significant contribution towards the achievement of sustainable development and the internationally agreed development goals, including the Millennium Development Goals,

Acknowledging that increased use of new and renewable sources of energy could offer increased access to modern energy services,

Noting that, in addition to increasing the efficiency of energy production and use, expanding the use of new and renewable sources of energy and advanced clean energy technology offers options that could improve global and local environmental conditions,

Recognizing that the current share of new and renewable sources of energy in the global energy supply is still low, which is due, among other factors, to the high costs of many renewable energy technologies, particularly in their development phase, and underlining the critical contribution that a rapid reduction in those costs could make to the promotion of such technologies,

Recognizing also the contributions of new and renewable sources of energy to the reduction of greenhouse gases and addressing climate change, which poses serious risks and challenges,

Noting that the global demand for energy continues to rise, while recognizing that the share of energy derived from new and renewable resources remains considerably below its significant potential despite a recent increase, and underlining in this regard the need to continue to tap new and renewable sources of energy,

Emphasizing the need to take further action to mobilize the provision of adequate financial resources, of sufficient quality and arriving in a timely manner, as well as the transfer of advanced technology to developing countries and countries with economies in transition for providing efficient and wider use of energy sources, in particular new and renewable sources of energy,

Reaffirming that each country must take primary responsibility for its own development and that the role of national policies and development strategies cannot be overemphasized in the achievement of sustainable development, and recognizing the need for the creation of an enabling environment at all levels for investment and sustained financing,

Acknowledging that the Commission on Sustainable Development and the Economic and Social Council continue to play a pivotal role as forums for the discussion of new and renewable sources of energy and sustainable development,

Welcoming efforts by Governments and institutions that have embarked on policies and programmes that seek to expand the use of new and renewable sources of energy for sustainable development, and recognizing the contributions of regional initiatives, institutions and regional economic commissions in supporting the efforts of countries, in particular developing countries and countries with economies in transition, in this respect,

Noting with appreciation the establishment of the International Renewable Energy Agency, which aims at promoting the diffusion and sustainable use of all forms of renewable energy,

Noting also with appreciation regional mechanisms and initiatives for energy cooperation and integration to encourage the use of new and renewable sources of energy such as, inter alia, the PetroCaribe Alternative Energy Source Financing Fund, the Mesoamerican integration and development project, the Caribbean Renewable Energy Development Programme, the energy initiative of the New Partnership for Africa's Development, the Mediterranean Solar Plan, the Africa-European Union Energy Partnership, the Baltic Sea Region Energy Cooperation, and the Asia-Pacific Partnership on Clean Development and Climate,

Noting with concern that millions of poor people are unable to afford to pay for modern energy services, even when those services are available, and emphasizing the need to address the challenge of access to and affordability of modern energy services for all, in particular the poor,

Emphasizing the need to promote an enabling environment for the promotion and use of new and renewable energy, including through the removal of obstacles at all levels,

1. *Takes note* of the report of the Secretary-General;

2. *Stresses* the urgent need to continue to increase the share of new and renewable sources of energy in the global energy mix;

3. *Reaffirms* the need for the full implementation of the Johannesburg Plan of Implementation, as the intergovernmental framework for sustainable development;

4. *Emphasizes* the need to improve access to reliable, affordable, economically viable, socially acceptable and environmentally sound energy services and resources for sustainable development, and takes into consideration the diversity of situations, national policies and specific needs of developing countries and countries with economies in transition;

5. *Encourages* the development of viable market-oriented strategies that could result in the most rapid reduction of the cost of new and renewable sources of energy and increase the competitiveness of those technologies, including through the adoption, as appropriate, of public policies for research, development and market deployment;

6. *Emphasizes* the need to intensify research and development in support of energy for sustainable development, which will require increased commitment on the part of Governments and all other relevant stakeholders, as appropriate, including the private sector, civil society and international organizations, to deploy financial and human resources for accelerating research efforts;

7. *Encourages* efforts by Governments aimed at creating and developing an enabling environment at all levels to ensure the promotion and use of new and renewable sources of energy;

8. *Calls upon* Governments, as well as relevant international and regional organizations and other relevant stakeholders, to combine, as appropriate, the increased use of new and renewable energy resources, more efficient use of energy, greater reliance on advanced energy technologies, including cleaner fossil fuel technologies, and the sustainable use of traditional energy resources, which could meet the growing need for energy services in the longer term to achieve sustainable development;

9. *Encourages* global, regional and national initiatives on new and renewable energies to promote access to energy, including new and renewable sources of energy, for

the poorest and to improve energy efficiency and conservation by resorting to a mix of available technologies, taking fully into account the provisions of the Johannesburg Plan of Implementation concerning energy for sustainable development;

10. *Welcomes* the efforts of some Member States to establish national voluntary new and renewable sources of energy and energy efficiency targets, and encourages others to do the same;

11. *Encourages* Member States to make greater use of effective policy tools such as voluntary national, subnational or regional goals, programmes and targets, as appropriate, to increase access to energy, energy efficiency and the share of renewable energies;

12. *Calls upon* Governments to take further action to mobilize the provision of financial resources, technology transfer, capacity-building and the diffusion of environmentally sound technologies to developing countries and countries with economies in transition, as set out in the Johannesburg Plan of Implementation;

13. *Calls upon* the international community to support the efforts of the African countries in promoting the development, production and use of new and renewable sources of energy, recognizing the special needs of Africa for reliable and affordable energy supplies and services;

14. *Also calls upon* the international community to support the least developed countries, the landlocked developing countries and the small island developing States in their efforts to develop and utilize new and renewable energy, inter alia, through financial and technical assistance and capacity-building;

15. *Reiterates its call for* all relevant funding institutions and bilateral and multilateral donors, as well as regional funding institutions and non-governmental organizations, to continue to support, as appropriate, efforts aimed at the development of the energy sector in developing countries and countries with economies in transition on the basis of environment-friendly new and renewable sources of energy of demonstrated viability, while taking fully into account the development structure of energy-based economies of developing countries, and to assist in the attainment of the levels of investment necessary to expand energy supplies, including beyond urban areas;

16. *Notes and encourages* ongoing activities related to the promotion of new and renewable sources of energy within the United Nations system, and acknowledges the role of UN-Energy in promoting system-wide collaboration in the area of energy;

17. *Encourages* the United Nations system to continue to raise awareness of the importance of energy for sustainable development, including the need for the promotion of new and renewable sources of energy and the increased role they can play in the global energy supply, particularly in the context of sustainable development and poverty eradication;

18. *Encourages* the Secretary-General to continue his efforts to promote the mobilization of financial resources, in a stable and predictable manner, and technical assistance, and to enhance the effectiveness and the full utilization of existing international funds for the effective implementation of national and regional high-priority projects in the area of new and renewable sources of energy;

19. *Stresses* that the wider use and exploration of available and additional new and renewable sources of energy require technology transfer and diffusion on a global scale, including through North-South, South-South and triangular cooperation;

20. *Requests* the Secretary-General to submit to the General Assembly at its sixty-sixth session a report on the implementation of the present resolution, taking into account, inter alia, the initiatives taken by Member States and international organizations to create an enabling environment at all levels for the promotion and use of new and renewable energy, including measures to improve access to such technologies;

21. *Decides* to include in the provisional agenda of its sixty-sixth session, under the item entitled "Sustainable development", the sub-item entitled "Promotion of new and renewable sources of energy".

Natural resources

Water resources

The Commission on Sustainable Development, in May [E/2009/29 (res. 17/1)], stressed the need to manage sustainably competing uses of water and land resources, called for policies that managed water and land resources in an integrated manner and called for action to strengthen the knowledge base and information-sharing on drought, water stress and drought risk management.

The Fifth World Water Forum (Istanbul, Turkey, 16–22 March), which coincided with the observance of World Water Day (22 March), brought together 33,058 attendees from 192 countries under the theme "Bridging Divides for Water". Discussions were held on six major themes: global changes and risk management; advancing human development and the Millennium Development Goals (MDGs); managing and protecting water resources and their supply systems to meet human and environmental needs; governance and management; finance; and education, knowledge and capacity development. Outcomes of the Forum included the adoption of: the Istanbul Declaration of Heads of States on Water, focusing on promoting water solidarity and security in their countries, as well as the tools needed to face up to climate change; the Istanbul Ministerial Statement and the Istanbul Water Guide [A/63/852]—a list of 140 recommendations which provided guidance on how to improve water security and water management; and the Istanbul Water Consensus—a commitment to prepare and implement action plans and strategies for water-related challenges in cities around the world. The Forum also put forward proposals on water-related policies, including the establishment of a permanent international "Parliamentarians' Helpdesk" to aid political cooperation on water legislation and its implementation.

On 16 March, the third edition of the *United Nations World Water Development Report*, "Water in a Changing World", was launched at the Forum. The themes addressed by the report included climate change, the MDGs, groundwater, biodiversity, water and migration, water and infrastructure and biofuels. On 22 March, World Water Day was celebrated on the theme "Shared Water–Shared Opportunities", focusing on transboundary waters. The United Nations Educational, Scientific and Cultural Organization led the activities with the support of the United Nations Economic Commission for Europe and the Food and Agriculture Organization of the United Nations.

Expressing concern that approximately 884 million people lacked access to safe drinking water and that over 2.5 billion did not have access to basic sanitation, the Human Rights Council, in its resolution 12/8 of 1 October [A/HRC/12/50], reaffirmed that international human rights instruments entailed obligations for States and parties in relation to access to safe drinking water and sanitation.

UN-Water, an inter-agency mechanism [YUN 2004, p. 1034] working to strengthen coordination and coherence among all UN bodies dealing with water-related issues, continued to address issues related to the global water crisis. Over the course of 2009, UN-Water's six operational task forces continued to focus on: sanitation; gender and water; indicators, monitoring and reporting; transboundary waters; country-level coordination; and water and climate change. The Joint Monitoring Programme (JMP) for Water Supply and Sanitation of the World Health Organization (WHO) and the United Nations Children's Fund— the UN mechanism tasked with monitoring progress towards the MDG drinking-water and sanitation target—worked to prepare its 2010 JMP report and the regional "snap shot" of drinking water and sanitation in Black Sea countries. The UN-Water Global Annual Assessment on Sanitation and Drinking-Water (GLAAS), the UN mechanism coordinated by WHO and tasked with analysing the institutional and financial capacity of countries to make progress towards the MDG water and sanitation target, established a task force to provide advice on methodology, content and style of its first comprehensive GLAAS report, to be presented in 2010.

UN-Water organized a seminar during the 2009 World Water Week (Stockholm, Sweden, 16–22 August), which focused on the theme "Managing Water in Times of Global Crises–How can the UN System Step up its Efforts?" A number of other seminars, workshops and side events were also held.

Communication. On 6 March [A/64/65], the Sudan transmitted to the Secretary-General the Muscat Declaration on Water, containing the conclusions and recommendations adopted by the first Ministerial Forum on Water of the Group of 77 (Muscat, Oman, 23–25 February).

Water Decade midterm review

In December, the General Assembly, by resolution 64/198, called for a comprehensive midterm review of the International Decade for Action "Water for Life" (2005–2015) [YUN 2003, p. 1034] through two events in 2010: a high-level interactive dialogue in March and an international conference in June in Dushanbe, Tajikistan.

GENERAL ASSEMBLY ACTION

On 21 December [meeting 66], the General Assembly, on the recommendation of the Second Committee [A/64/420/Add.1], adopted **resolution 64/198** without vote [agenda item 53 *(a)*].

Midterm comprehensive review of the implementation of the International Decade for Action, "Water for Life", 2005–2015

The General Assembly,

Recalling its resolution 55/196 of 20 December 2000, by which it proclaimed 2003 the International Year of Freshwater, its resolution 58/217 of 23 December 2003, by which it proclaimed that the International Decade for Action, "Water for Life", 2005–2015, would commence on World Water Day, 22 March 2005, and its resolution 59/228 of 22 December 2004,

Emphasizing that water is critical for sustainable development, including environmental integrity and the eradication of poverty and hunger, and is indispensable for human health and well-being,

Recalling the provisions of Agenda 21, the Programme for the Further Implementation of Agenda 21 adopted at its nineteenth special session, the Plan of Implementation of the World Summit on Sustainable Development ("Johannesburg Plan of Implementation") and the decisions of the Economic and Social Council and of the Commission on Sustainable Development at its sixth session relating to freshwater,

Reaffirming the internationally agreed development goals on water and sanitation, including those contained in the United Nations Millennium Declaration, and determined to achieve the goal to halve, by 2015, the proportion of people who are unable to reach or to afford safe drinking water, and the goals set out in the Johannesburg Plan of Implementation to halve the proportion of people without access to basic sanitation as well as to develop integrated water resources management and water efficiency plans by 2005, with support to developing countries,

Recalling Human Rights Council resolutions 7/22 of 28 March 2008 and 12/8 of 1 October 2009, on human rights and access to safe drinking water and sanitation,

Taking note of national, regional and international efforts to implement the International Decade for Action, "Water for Life", 2005–2015, and of numerous recommendations from international and regional water and water-related events, with a view to taking concrete actions to accelerate progress at all levels towards achieving the internationally agreed water-related goals contained in Agenda 21, the Programme for the Further Implementation of Agenda 21, the United Nations Millennium Declaration and the Johannesburg Plan of Implementation,

Taking note also of the holding of the Fifth World Water Forum in Istanbul, Turkey, from 16 to 22 March 2009, and noting that the Sixth World Water Forum will be held in Marseille, France, in March 2012,

1. *Takes note* of the reports of the Secretary-General;

2. *Welcomes* the activities related to the implementation of the International Decade for Action, "Water for Life", 2005–2015, undertaken by Member States, the Secretariat and the organizations of the United Nations system, inter alia, through inter-agency work, as well as contributions from major groups, and emphasizes the importance of country-level implementation of the Decade;

3. *Encourages* Member States, the Secretariat, organizations of the United Nations system through their coordination mechanism, and major groups to continue their efforts to achieve the internationally agreed water-related goals contained in Agenda 21, the Programme for the Further Implementation of Agenda 21, the United Nations Millennium Declaration and the Johannesburg Plan of Implementation;

4. *Welcomes* the work of the Commission on Sustainable Development at its twelfth, thirteenth, sixteenth and seventeenth sessions on the issues of water and sanitation, and looks forward to any relevant activities of the Commission;

5. *Welcomes* the generous offer of the Government of Tajikistan to host, in June 2010, a high-level international conference on the midterm comprehensive review of the implementation of the Decade;

6. *Invites* the President of the General Assembly to convene a high-level interactive dialogue of the sixty-fourth session of the General Assembly in New York on 22 March 2010, World Water Day, on the implementation of the Decade;

7. *Stresses* the importance of the full involvement of all relevant stakeholders, including women, children, older persons, persons with disabilities, indigenous people and other local communities, in the implementation of the Decade at all levels, including its midterm comprehensive review;

8. *Requests* the Secretary-General to prepare a note on the organization of work of the conference;

9. *Invites* the relevant United Nations bodies, the specialized agencies, the regional commissions and other organizations of the United Nations system to actively engage in the preparations for the high-level conference;

10. *Invites* the Secretary-General, in cooperation with UN-Water, to take appropriate actions to support Member States in the implementation of the second half of the Decade;

11. *Requests* the Secretary-General to report to the General Assembly at its sixty-fifth session on the implementation of the present resolution, as well as on the activities planned by the Secretary-General and other relevant organizations of the United Nations system for the Decade.

Cartography

UN Regional Cartographic Conference for the Americas

The Ninth United Nations Regional Cartographic Conference for the Americas (New York, 10–14 August) [E/CONF.99/3] was held in accordance with Economic and Social Council decision 2005/231 [YUN 2005, p. 1131]. The Conference was attended by 81 representatives of 27 countries and 16 specialized agencies and international scientific organizations. The meeting aimed at providing a regional forum where Governmental officials, planners, scientists and experts from the Americas and other regions could meet to report on efforts to develop and implement national and regional spatial data infrastructures and to address the common needs, problems and experiences in the field of surveying and mapping, cartography, remote sensing, land and geographical information systems.

The work of the Conference centred around three technical committees on: strategy, policy, economic and institutional issues and spatial data infrastructure and their development in the Americas; geospatial data collection, management and dissemination; and best practices and applications.

The Conference adopted resolutions on: workplan of the Permanent Committee on Spatial Data Infrastructure for the Americas and establishment of working groups; mechanisms for building spatial data infrastructures; new study on the status of mapping by country and region; forum for sharing spatial data infrastructure best practices; follow-up meeting on disaster risk management and spatial data infrastructure; funding issues; and support of spatial data infrastructure in the developing countries of the Americas, in particular in the Caribbean. The Conference recommended to the Council that the Tenth United Nations Regional Cartographic Conference for the Americas be convened in 2013.

UN Regional Cartographic Conference for Asia and the Pacific

The Eighteenth United Nations Regional Cartographic Conference for Asia and the Pacific (Bangkok, 26–29 October) [E/CONF.100/9] was held in accordance with Economic and Social Council decision 2007/275 [YUN 2007, p. 1044]. The theme of the Conference was "Spatial enablement and the response to climate change and the Millennium Development Goals". The meeting was attended by 149 representatives of 37 countries and 12 specialized agencies and international scientific organizations. The primary objective of the event was to provide a regional forum where Government officials, planners, scientists and experts from the Asia and Pacific region and from other regions could meet to report on efforts to develop and implement national and regional spatial data infrastructures and to address common needs, problems, experiences and best practices in the field of cartography and geographic information.

The work of the Conference centred around three technical committees on: Geographical Information System, remote sensing and geodesy for disaster management; spatial data infrastructure and spatially enabled Government; and geospatial data collection, management and dissemination.

The Conference adopted resolutions on regional geodesy; capacity-building in disaster management; data access; data integration; spatially enabled Government and society; the Annual Forum on Land Administration; and global geographic information management.

The Conference recommended to the Council that the Nineteenth United Nations Regional Cartographic Conference for Asia and the Pacific be held in 2012.

Standardization of geographical names

In accordance with Economic and Social Council decision 2008/241 [YUN 2008, p. 1140], the twenty-fifth session of the United Nations Group of Experts on Geographical Names was held in Nairobi from 5 to 12 May [E/2009/58]. The session focused on assisting Member States in the geographical information field and related cartographic areas and supporting the United Nations Conference on the Standardization of Geographical Names, whose tenth session was scheduled for 2012. The Group of Experts considered reports from its 10 working groups and 14 linguistic/geographical divisions, as well as reports from the liaison officers and international organizations. The Group proposed that the twenty-sixth session be held in the second quarter of 2011 in either Geneva or Vienna.

The Council took note of the report of the session on 29 July (**decision 2009/243**) and endorsed the proposal relating to the next session on 15 December (**decision 2009/269**).

Chapter VII

Environment and human settlements

In 2009, the United Nations and the international community continued to work towards protecting the environment through legally binding instruments and the activities of the United Nations Environment Programme (UNEP).

The twenty-fifth session of the UNEP Governing Council/Global Ministerial Environment Forum discussed the emerging policy themes of globalization and the environment and international environmental governance, and approved the 2010–2011 budget and work programme. It adopted decisions on, among other issues, the world environment situation; international environmental governance; environmental law; an intergovernmental science-policy platform on biodiversity; support to Africa in environmental management and protection; the environmental situation in Gaza; the engagement of young people in environmental issues; and chemicals management, including mercury. With regard to the latter, the Council agreed to the elaboration of a legally binding instrument on mercury to reduce risks to human health and the environment; an intergovernmental negotiating committee was to prepare that instrument, beginning its work in 2010.

In September, the Secretary-General convened a high-level summit on climate change to mobilize the political will and vision needed to reach a substantive agreed outcome at the UN climate talks in Copenhagen, Denmark. In December, the fifteenth session of the Conference of the Parties to the United Nations Framework Convention on Climate Change produced the Copenhagen Accord, which expressed the intent to constrain carbon and respond to climate change, and contained elements on which the views of Governments converged, including the long-term goal of limiting the maximum global average temperature increase to no more than 2 degrees Celsius. However, participants were not able to reach an agreement on how to achieve that goal in practical terms. During the year, the Intergovernmental Panel on Climate Change addressed preparations of its Fifth Assessment Report. Also in December, the parties to the 1979 Convention on Long-range Transboundary Air Pollution adopted amendments to the 1998 Protocol on Persistent Organic Pollutants.

In October, a special session of the ninth session of the United Nations Forum on Forests established an intergovernmental expert group to conduct an in-depth analysis of all aspects of forest financing and a facilitative process on forest financing to assist countries to mobilize funding from all sources. In April, the General Assembly designated 22 April as International Mother Earth Day and in December adopted a resolution on promoting life in harmony with nature.

The United Nations Human Settlements Programme (UN-Habitat) continued to support the implementation of the 1996 Habitat Agenda and the Millennium Development Goals. The twenty-second session of the UN-Habitat Governing Council approved the 2010–2011 work programme and budget of UN-Habitat, reviewed progress made in implementing the 2008–2013 medium-term strategic and institutional plan, and focused on affordable housing finance systems, strengthening the development of urban youth, access to basic services for all, and South-South cooperation in human settlements. The Governing Council recommended to the General Assembly that it consider convening in 2016 a third United Nations conference on housing and sustainable urban development.

Environment

UN Environment Programme

Governing Council/Ministerial Forum

The twenty-fifth session of the Governing Council/Global Ministerial Environment Forum (GC/GMEF) of the United Nations Environment Programme (UNEP) was held in Nairobi from 16 to 20 February [A/64/25]. On 20 February [A/64/25 (dec. 25/17)], the Governing Council decided to hold its eleventh special session in Bali, Indonesia, February 2010 and its twenty-sixth session in Nairobi in February 2011, and approved the provisional agendas for those sessions.

Ministerial consultations (16–19 February) on emerging policy issues focused on the themes of globalization and the environment (see p. 1009) and international environmental governance (see p. 1005). The Executive Director provided information on the ministerial consultations during the session [UNEP/GC.25/INF/37] and its two separate, but related themes: "Globalization and the Environment—Global crises: national chaos?" and "International environmental governance (IEG) and United Nations reform—IEG: help or hindrance?"

The Committee of the Whole, established by the Council/Forum on 16 February, considered policy issues, including the state of the environment; international environment governance; coordination and cooperation with the UN system and with major groups on environmental matters; the UNEP contribution as an implementing agency of the Global Environmental Facility; follow-up to and implementation of the outcomes of UN summits and major intergovernmental meetings, including Council decisions; and the budget and programme of work for the 2010–2011 biennium, the Environment Fund and other budgetary and administrative matters. The report of the Committee, along with the policy statement of UNEP Executive Director Achim Steiner and the summary presented by the Council/Forum President of the views expressed during the consultations, were annexed to the report on the proceedings of the session [UNEP/GC.25/17].

On 29 July, the Economic and Social Council took note of the Governing Council's report on its twenty-fifth session (**decision 2009/243**).

The General Assembly took note of the report in resolution 64/204 of 21 December (see below).

Subsidiary body

In 2009, the Committee of Permanent Representatives, which was open to representatives of all UN Member States and members of specialized agencies, held an extraordinary meeting on 20 January [UNEP/CPR/106/3] and regular meetings on 17 March [UNEP/CPR/107/2], 16 June [UNEP/CPR/108/2], 15 September [UNEP/CPR/109/2] and 4 December [UNEP/CPR/110/2]. The Committee discussed, among other matters, the outcome of the twenty-fifth (2009) GC/GMEF session and preparations for the eleventh special session in 2010.

The Governing Council had before it a note by the UNEP Executive Director [UNEP/GC.25/INF.4] transmitting a report on the Committee's work from December 2006 to 17 September 2008.

GENERAL ASSEMBLY ACTION

On 21 December [meeting 66], the General Assembly, on the recommendation of the Second (Economic and Financial) Committee [A/64/420/Add.7], adopted **resolution 64/204** without vote [agenda item 53 *(g)*].

Report of the Governing Council of the United Nations Environment Programme on its twenty-fifth session

The General Assembly,

Recalling its resolutions 2997(XXVII) of 15 December 1972, 53/242 of 28 July 1999, 56/193 of 21 December 2001, 57/251 of 20 December 2002, 58/209 of 23 December 2003, 59/226 of 22 December 2004, 60/189 of 22 December 2005, 61/205 of 20 December 2006, 62/195 of 19 December 2007 and 63/220 of 19 December 2008,

Recalling also the 2005 World Summit Outcome,

Taking into account Agenda 21 and the Plan of Implementation of the World Summit on Sustainable Development ("Johannesburg Plan of Implementation"),

Reaffirming the role of the United Nations Environment Programme as the leading global environmental authority and principal body within the United Nations system in the field of environment, which should take into account, within its mandate, the sustainable development needs of developing countries,

Taking note of decision 25/4 of 20 February 2009 of the Governing Council of the United Nations Environment Programme, by which the Governing Council established a consultative group of ministers or high-level representatives, with the purpose of preparing a set of options for improving international environmental governance for the consideration of the Governing Council/Global Ministerial Environment Forum at its eleventh special session, with a view to providing inputs to the General Assembly,

Taking note also of the developments in the area of global efforts in relation to chemicals management, including the Strategic Approach to International Chemicals Management, and the preparations for the negotiations on the global legally binding instrument on mercury,

Reiterating that capacity-building and technology support to developing countries in environment-related fields are important components of the work of the United Nations Environment Programme,

Taking note of the report of the United Nations Joint Inspection Unit entitled "Management review of environmental governance within the United Nations system", and the note by the Secretary-General thereon,

Taking note also of decision 25/10 of 20 February 2009 of the Governing Council of the United Nations Environment Programme on an intergovernmental science-policy platform on biodiversity and ecosystem services,

1. *Takes note* of the report of the Governing Council of the United Nations Environment Programme on its twenty-fifth session and the decisions contained therein;

2. *Welcomes* the ongoing efforts of the United Nations Environmental Programme, and encourages the further strengthening of efforts, to shift emphasis from delivery of outputs to achievement of results within its budget and programme of work, and in this regard takes note of the approval of the programme of work and the budget for the period 2010–2011;

3. *Underlines* the need to further advance and fully implement the Bali Strategic Plan for Technology Support and Capacity-building with a view to achieving its objectives in the areas of capacity-building and technology support for developing countries and countries with economies in transition, and in this regard welcomes the decision to mainstream the Bali Strategic Plan as an integral part of the United Nations Environment Programme's medium-term strategy for the period 2010–2013, invites relevant United Nations funds and programmes and the specialized agencies and multilateral environmental agreements to consider mainstreaming the Bali Strategic Plan in their overall activities, and calls upon Governments and other

stakeholders in a position to do so to provide the necessary funding and technical assistance to further advance and fully implement the Bali Strategic Plan;

4. *Requests* the United Nations Environment Programme to deepen its cooperation with related United Nations agencies, regions, subregions and existing South-South cooperation initiatives to develop joint activities and synergies of capacity in advancing South-South cooperation in support of capacity-building and technology support in the context of the Bali Strategic Plan and as reflected in the medium-term strategy for the period 2010–2013;

5. *Stresses* the importance of the implementation of the Strategic Approach to International Chemicals Management, particularly through its Quick Start Programme, and invites Governments, regional economic integration organizations, intergovernmental organizations and non-governmental organizations to engage actively and cooperate closely to support the Strategic Approach implementation activities of the United Nations Environment Programme, including by providing adequate resources;

6. *Takes note with appreciation* of the offer of the Government of Indonesia to host the eleventh special session of the Governing Council/Global Ministerial Environment Forum from 24 to 26 February 2010 in Bali, Indonesia;

7. *Welcomes* the decision of the Conference of the Parties to the Basel, Rotterdam and Stockholm conventions to hold a simultaneous extraordinary session of the Conference of the Parties on 22 and 23 February 2010 in Bali immediately before the eleventh special session of the Governing Council/Global Ministerial Environment Forum;

8. *Reaffirms* the need, while recognizing the efforts and actions taken, to strengthen the scientific base of the United Nations Environment Programme, as recommended by the intergovernmental consultation on strengthening the scientific base of the Programme, including the reinforcement of the scientific capacity of developing countries, in the area of protection of the environment, including through the provision of adequate financial resources, and in this respect emphasizes the importance of building on the experiences gained from the preparation of different global environmental assessments as well as other relevant developments in this field;

9. *Recognizes* the global challenges posed by mercury, and in this regard takes note of the decision of the Governing Council at its twenty-fifth session to convene an intergovernmental negotiating committee with the mandate to prepare a global legally binding instrument on mercury;

10. *Reiterates* the need for the United Nations Environment Programme to continue to conduct comprehensive, integrated and scientifically credible global environment assessments, in close consultation with Member States, in order to support decision-making processes at all levels, in the light of the continuing need for up-to-date, scientifically credible, policy-relevant information on environmental change worldwide, and in this regard encourages the Programme to undertake a comprehensive integrated global assessment, leading to the preparation of the fifth report in the Global Environment Outlook series, which should inform, as appropriate, the strategic directions of the Programme;

11. *Emphasizes* the need to further enhance coordination and cooperation among the relevant United Nations organizations in the promotion of the environmental dimension of sustainable development, and to enhance the cooperation between the United Nations Environment Programme and regional and subregional organizations, and welcomes the continued active participation of the Programme in the United Nations Development Group and the Environment Management Group, as well as in the United Nations "Delivering as One" exercise at the country level;

12. *Welcomes* the increased contributions to the Environment Fund, and reiterates its invitation to Governments that are in a position to do so to increase their contributions to the Environment Fund;

13. *Reiterates* the need for stable, adequate and predictable financial resources for the United Nations Environment Programme, and, in accordance with General Assembly resolution 2997(XXVII), underlines the need to consider the adequate reflection of all the administrative and management costs of the Programme in the context of the United Nations regular budget;

14. *Also reiterates* the importance of the Nairobi headquarters location of the United Nations Environment Programme, and requests the Secretary-General to keep the resource needs of the Programme and the United Nations Office at Nairobi under review so as to permit the delivery, in an effective manner, of necessary services to the Programme and to the other United Nations organs and organizations in Nairobi;

15. *Decides* to include in the provisional agenda of its sixty-fifth session, under the item entitled "Sustainable development", a sub-item entitled "Report of the Governing Council of the United Nations Environment Programme on its eleventh special session".

International environmental governance

JIU report. In February, the UNEP Governing Council had before it the report of the Joint Inspection Unit (JIU) on the management review of environmental governance within the UN system [UNEP/GC.25/INF/33]. The objective of the review was to strengthen the governance of, and programmatic and administrative support for, multilateral environmental agreements (MEAs) by UN organizations by identifying measures to promote coordination, coherence and synergies between MEAs and the UN system. The review found that the framework of international environmental governance was weakened by institutional fragmentation and specialization, as well as the lack of a holistic approach to environmental issues and sustainable development. UN system organizations had not defined clearly their responsibilities under the governance framework, which aimed at integrating environmental protection into economic and social development and mainstreaming environmental considerations in sustainable development policies. Recommendations were made for the General Assembly to: establish a clear division of labour among developmental agencies, UNEP and the MEAs outlining their respective areas and types of activities; consider upgrading the UN Strategic Framework and UNEP Medium-Term Strategy to system-wide instruments in order to allow the integration of the strategic goals of environment-related organizations into a single governance framework; and support GC/GMEF in conducting its regular review of the effectiveness of the implementation of all MEAs administered within the UN system, in accordance with the recommendations contained in the 2002 report of the Open-ended Intergovernmental Group of Ministers or Their Representatives on International Environmental Governance [YUN 2002, p. 1032], which was adopted by the Governing Council that year [ibid., p. 1033] and became known as the "Cartagena Package". In order to avoid proliferation of MEA secretariats, the Secretary-General should submit to the Assembly, through GC/GMEF, proposals for ways by which Member States could better formulate and manage multilateral environmental instruments without creating new secretariats.

The report further recommended that the Secretary-General: submit to the Assembly guidelines on the establishment of national and regional platforms on environmental protection and sustainable development policies to help Member States coordinate policies on integrated implementation of MEAs; encourage the development of joint programmes and projects by UN agencies and organizations through the establishment of a joint, system-wide planning framework based on results-based management and backed by an inventory of environmental initiatives and actors; and conduct, in consultation with MEAs and UN system organizations, a review of the adequacy and effectiveness of funding environmental activities, focusing on incremental costs, and report thereon to the General Assembly. Drawing on the Secretary-General's report on the review, the Assembly should redefine the concept of incremental cost funding applicable to the existing financial mechanisms. The Secretary-General, in consultation with MEA secretariats, should define clear delegation of authority, as well as the division of roles and responsibilities of the entities providing administrative, financial and human resources management services to conferences of the parties to MEAs. He should also increase transparency in the use of the programme support cost resources by charging them to the MEAs against the actual expenditures incurred. Those resources should be pooled in a common administrative support budget for the MEAs.

Governing Council action. In February, the UNEP Governing Council adopted a multi-part decision on the implementation of its 2002 decision [YUN 2002, p. 1032] on international environmental governance [A/64/25 (dec. 25/1)]. In the first part of the decision [dec. 25/1 I], the Council took note of the JIU

report and reaffirmed its commitment to continuing the discussion on international environmental governance with a view to adopting a General Assembly resolution on determining specific actions towards greater coherence and efficacy of the international environmental institutional framework. It also noted that the Assembly, in accordance with resolution 61/205 [YUN 2006, p. 1207], had decided to consider, if necessary, the issue of universal membership of GC/GMEF at its sixty-fourth (2009) session. The Council, having considered the 10 February report by the co-chairs of the informal consultations of the General Assembly on the institutional framework for UN environment work [UNEP/GC.25/INF/35], also decided [dec. 25/4] to establish a regionally representative consultative group of ministers or high-level representatives to present options for improving international environmental governance to the eleventh (2010) GC/GMEF special session, with a view to providing inputs to the Assembly.

Ministerial consultations. GC/GMEF held ministerial consultations from 16 to 19 February on the theme "International environmental governance and United Nations reform: international environmental governance: help or hindrance", which was presented in a discussion paper submitted by the Executive Director [UNEP/GC.25/16/Add.1]. The theme focused on international environmental governance from a country perspective, including the lack of coherence in the international environmental governance system at that level; improving coordination of multilateral environmental agreements; recurring themes; and other proposals on strengthening international environmental governance. The paper also highlighted other issues for discussion during the ministerial consultations.

Notes by Secretary-General. By a 20 May note [A/64/83-E/2009/83], the Secretary-General transmitted to the Assembly the JIU report. In June [A/64/83/Add.1-E/2009/83/Add.1], the Secretary-General transmitted his comments on the JIU report and those of the United Nations System Chief Executives Board for Coordination (CEB). Although CEB members welcomed the report and supported many of its recommendations, they also expressed concern regarding the modalities suggested for implementing the recommendations and noted that several required additional consideration.

The Economic and Social Council took note of both notes on 31 July (**decision 2009/264**).

Consultative Group meetings. The first meeting of the Consultative Group of Ministers or High-level Representatives on International Environmental Governance (Belgrade, Serbia, 27–28 June), organized in response to Governing Councils (see above), resulted in a process of reform of international environmental governance—known as the Belgrade Process—and a roadmap to guide the process.

At its second meeting (Rome, 28–29 October), the Consultative Group identified options for improving international environmental governance.

Notes by Executive Director. A December note by the UNEP Executive Director [UNEP/GCSS.XI/4] reviewed the outcome of the work of the Consultative Group of Ministers or High-level Representatives. The group identified a set of options for improving international environmental governance; considered that aspects of the objectives and functions of the international environmental governance system could be met through incremental reforms; identified a need to reassess the adequacy of the existing system by undertaking broader reforms; and suggested that the Council establish an inclusive and transparent process on broader institutional reforms for international environmental governance that involved the UN system, so as to enable a fully informed political process. Another December note [UNEP/GCSS.XI/5] contained the Executive Director's comments on the JIU report.

Bali Strategic Plan for Technology Support and Capacity-building

The Governing Council in 2005 [YUN 2005, p. 1135] adopted the Bali Strategic Plan for Technology Support and Capacity-building [YUN 2004, p. 1040], an inter-governmentally agreed framework for strengthening technology support and the capacity of Governments in developing countries and countries with economies in transition—including reinforcing UNEP's role and building on areas where it had comparative advantage and expertise—to coherently address their needs, priorities and obligations in the field of the environment.

On 20 February [A/64/25 (dec. 25/1 III)], the Governing Council noted that the Bali Strategic Plan had become an integral part of the medium-term strategy for 2010–2013 and of the implementation of the UNEP programme of work. It called on the Executive Director to advance and fully implement the Plan with a view to achieving its objectives in the areas of capacity-building and technology support for developing countries and countries with economies in transition; and requested the Executive Director to strengthen the UNEP regional offices so as to contribute to the implementation of the Plan.

UNEP activities

Monitoring and assessment

In a February note [UNEP/GC.25/INF/34], the Executive Director reviewed options for a future global environmental assessment on environmental change, as outlined in the Executive Director's 2008 report [YUN 2008, p. 1144]. The note described the con-

text of the next global environmental assessment and how it responded to strategic programmatic changes and new demands. It presented five options, with associated products and cost estimates. The options were: a global integrated environmental assessment updated to better utilize information technology; an objective expert outsourced assessment; an indicator-based approach; a targeted assessment on thematic priority areas supported by an enabling framework; and a coherent set of integrated and thematic assessments. The latter option was the preferred one: it responded best to the new UNEP strategic directions by aligning the assessment along the main themes of the Medium-term Strategy [YUN 2008, p. 1153]; it would engage all UNEP divisions in the production of the assessment; and it would provide short- and long-term perspectives on the state of the global environment related to UNEP's priority areas of focus and analysis of trade-offs under various policy responses.

The Governing Council in February [dec. 25/2 III] requested the Executive Director: to undertake a coherent set of integrated and thematic UNEP assessments, including a comprehensive integrated global assessment, the fifth report in the Global Environment Outlook series, *GEO-5*; to organize a *GEO-5* process in which the scope, objectives and process of the Global Environment Outlook were finalized and adopted at a global intergovernmental and multi-stakeholder consultation; to convene a final intergovernmental meeting to negotiate and endorse the summary for policymakers based on the scientific findings of the report; and to elaborate on the requirements for a migration to targeted assessments on thematic priority areas and to report thereon to the Governing Council at its twenty-sixth (2011) session.

The Council [dec. 25/2 I] urged Governments, UN agencies, financial institutions, the private sector and civil society to consider key environmental assessment findings in the light of the growing awareness of the complexity of those challenges and their links to human well-being and development goals. It also called on Governments to demonstrate strong leadership and to implement effective policy responses, including economic instruments and market mechanisms to regulate and manage the environment, ecosystems and their services, and to cooperate within the framework of multilateral processes aiming to reverse environmental degradation.

Regarding the international assessment landscape, the Council [dec. 25/2 II] urged Governments to improve the scientific basis of their own environmental management and decision-making and to strengthen public support for environmental action through regular assessment and reporting on the state of the national environment. It requested the Executive Director to make scientific data, metadata and standards from assessments available in an open-access electronic format; to maintain oversight of the international assessment landscape; to work with other partners in efforts to streamline and improve coherence in international environmental assessment and reporting processes; to assist in developing assessment processes that were credible, relevant and legitimate; to strengthen the capacities of countries that were experiencing challenges in meeting their environmental assessment and reporting obligations; to facilitate access to environmental assessments and reports through an online depository; and to report back to the Council on improvements through the Executive Director's report on the state of the environment.

Environment Watch strategy

Following its consideration of the revised Environment Watch strategy submitted in 2008 [YUN 2008, p. 1145], the Governing Council, in February 2009 [A/64/25 (dec. 25/1 II)], welcomed the consultative process on strengthening the UNEP scientific base and the valuable inputs made by Governments and other stakeholders. It noted that the revised strategy was consistent with the UNEP work programme and the "Delivering as one" approach. It also recognized that the important functions of the strategy included: capacity-building and technology support; assessment; early warning, monitoring and observation; data support, information-sharing and development of environmental indicators; and networking and partnerships. The Council invited countries, partners, donors and financial institutions to contribute extrabudgetary resources to meet the cost of implementing the strategy at the national level.

UNEP Year Book

The UNEP *Year Book 2009: New Science and Developments in our Changing Environment* presented work in progress on the scientific understanding of global environmental change, as well as foresight about issues on the horizon. It aimed to raise awareness of the interlinkages among environmental issues that could accelerate the rate of change and threaten human well-being. Its six chapters examined new science and developments and discussed the cumulative effects expected from the degradation of ecosystems; the release of substances harmful to ecosystems and to human health; the consequences of climate change; the continued human and economic loss resulting from disasters and conflicts; and the overexploitation of resources. The volume called for an intensified sense of urgency for responsible governance in the face of approaching critical thresholds and tipping points.

Support to Africa

In follow-up to the Executive Director's 2008 report [YUN 2008, p. 1146] on support to Africa in environmental management and protection, the Executive Director, in February 2009, submitted supplementary information [UNEP/GC.25/INF/21] on the topic, including on UNEP activities in Africa related to climate change; minimizing threats from the environmental causes and consequences of conflict and disaster; ecosystem management; environmental governance; alleviating the environmental and health impacts of harmful substances and hazardous wastes; and resource efficiency and sustainable consumption and production.

The Governing Council in February [A/64/25 (dec. 25/16)] requested the Executive Director: to continue extending implementation and institutional support to the New Partnership for Africa's Development (NEPAD), including the subregional environmental action plans; to strengthen the Africa Environment Outlook process as a tool for monitoring environmental challenges and sustainable development in Africa and as a framework for environmental reporting; to work closely with the African Union (AU), the regional economic communities, the NEPAD secretariat and other partners to enhance the strategic role of UNEP; to enhance the capacity of the UNEP regional office for Africa to lead the delivery of the UNEP programme of work in Africa; to work with the Economic Commission for Africa in providing technical support to the African climate policy centre, once established, to promote the integration of climate change into social and economic development and planning; to collaborate with African development partners and the AU to support African countries in implementing regional environmental agreements; to strengthen working relationships with the AU specialized technical committees to facilitate the integration of the environment into the AU work; to support the African Ministerial Conference on the Environment and the African Ministers' Council on Water in implementing their work programmes; to mobilize financial resources to build the capacity of African countries in assessment and reporting; and to support the use of and update the publication *Africa: Atlas of our Changing Environment* and the underlying data as a tool for policy decision-making. The Executive Director was also requested to report to the Governing Council's twenty-sixth (2011) session.

The Council also took note [dec. 25/7] of the Executive Director's 2008 report.

Water policy and strategy

The Governing Council in February [A/64/25 (dec. 25/7)] took note of the Executive Director's 2008 report [YUN 2008, p. 1147] summarizing UNEP activities related to its water policy and strategy. The Council had adopted the policy and strategy in 2007 [YUN 2007, p. 1050].

Other activities

In 2009, UNEP supported activities in more than 100 countries. Eighteen countries received support from the UNEP-United Nations Development Programme (UNDP) Poverty and Environment Initiative for integrating environmental concerns in their policies, programmes and laws. UNEP assisted 15 developing countries in assessing their renewable energy potential and more than 25 countries in identifying barriers to the uptake of clean technologies. Some 170 countries participated in the Billion Tree Campaign, planting more than 7.4 billion trees. The United Nations Reduced Emissions from Deforestation and Forest Degradation (UN-REDD) programme, a joint initiative of UNEP, UNDP and the Food and Agriculture Organization of the United Nations, provided technical and financial assistance to nine countries as they began to transform their forest sectors into the pillars of a future green economy. The programme disbursed $24 million to help participating countries to develop their REDD strategies.

Through its Finance Initiative (FI), UNEP worked with more than 180 institutions, including banks, insurers and fund managers, to understand the impact of environmental and social considerations on financial performance. The UNEP FI 2009 Global Roundtable (Cape Town, South Africa, 22–23 October) brought together more than 450 bankers, investors and insurers to discuss the future of sustainable finance and responsible investment.

UNEP supported six Indian Ocean countries in better preparing for the impacts of climate change and in improving livelihoods and environmental quality in coastal areas. It provided training on public participation in environmental impact assessment to more than 250 experts from environmental agencies, the private sector and civil society from nine countries. It also helped develop and implement biodiversity policies in Botswana, Chile, China, Costa Rica, India, Kenya, Namibia and South Africa, and worked at the regional level with the Association of Southeast Asian Nations, the Group of Latin American and Caribbean Countries and the Africa region.

Environment and sustainable development

The Commission on Sustainable Development, at its seventeenth session (New York, 4–15 May) [E/2009/29], continued to consider, for its 2008–2009 implementation cycle, the thematic cluster issues of agriculture, rural development,

land, drought, desertification and Africa. The Commission had before it reports of the Secretary-General on the review of Agenda 21 [YUN 1992, p. 672] and of the Johannesburg Plan of Implementation [YUN 2002, p. 822] with regard to agriculture [E/CN.17/2009/3], rural development [E/CN.17/2009/4], land [E/CN.17/2009/5], drought [E/CN.17/2009/6] (see p. 1031), desertification [E/CN.17/2009/7] (see p. 1032), Africa [E/CN.17/2009/8], as well as interlinkages and cross-cutting issues [E/CN.17/2009/9]. The latter report highlighted the interlocking relationships among the issues in the thematic cluster, and indicated that policies and measures aimed at one issue might have co-benefits for other issues and should be considered through an integrated approach in order to achieve long-term progress. Sustainable agriculture and natural resources management practices could increase productivity of scarce land resources and help to protect watersheds. Such interlinkages were presented in the report with a view to developing a menu of policy options and measures of optimal effectiveness.

Also before the Commission was a 30 April letter from Israel [E/CN.17/2009/17] on the seminar entitled "The Role of Native and Desert-Adapted Species for the Purpose of Slowing Desertification" (Kibbutz Ketura, Israel, 22–30 March), organized in cooperation with the UN Department of Economic and Social Affairs and designed to contribute to policies related to desertification and dryland development; and a 7 May letter from Belarus [E/CN.17/2009/18] on the initiative to declare 2009 the "Year of Our Native Land" in Belarus, with the aim of protecting and managing the natural resource base of economic and social development.

The UNEP Executive Director in December [UNEP/GCSS.XI/INF/7] summarized the contribution by UNEP to the Commission on Sustainable Development at its eighteenth (2010) session.

Small island developing States

The Governing Council in February [dec. 25/7] took note of the report of the Executive Director [YUN 2008, p. 1148] summarizing the activities undertaken by UNEP for small island developing States (SIDS).

Report of Secretary-General. In an August report [A/64/278] on follow-up to and implementation of the Mauritius Strategy for the Further Implementation of the Programme of Action for the Sustainable Development of Small Island Developing States [YUN 2005, p. 946], the Secretary-General reviewed progress made in addressing the vulnerabilities of SIDS, including the adverse effects of climate change and sea-level rise, which represented the most immediate threats to the sustainable development of SIDS. The report also gave an overview of the arrangements being made for the 2010 review of the Strategy.

(For further information on the sustainable development of SIDS, see p. 837.)

South-South cooperation

On 20 February [dec. 25/9], the Governing Council requested the Executive Director: to build on current work on South-South cooperation and to develop strategic partnerships and alliances in support of capacity-building and technology support activities using South-South cooperation arrangements; to develop and refine the strategic and operational guidelines and to develop a policy guidance for the coordinated implementation of South-South cooperation approaches across the UNEP work programme; to initiate efforts towards establishing formal cooperation arrangements with mechanisms and centres of excellence active in South-South cooperation, such as the Non-Aligned Movement Centre for South-South Technical Cooperation, to foster cooperation in the field of the environment; to strengthen the UNEP coordination mechanism and structure for South-South cooperation, including its regional presence, with a view to enhancing its role and function; to implement high-profile projects in South-South cooperation in the field of the environment; to contribute to the Secretary-General's report to the forthcoming High-level Conference on South-South Cooperation (see p. 876) and to participate in that Conference; and to report to the Council's twenty-sixth (2011) session.

(For further information on South-South cooperation, see p. 873.)

Globalization and the environment

GC/GMEF held ministerial consultations on globalization and the environment from 16 to 18 February. The Council/Forum had before it a background paper presented by the Executive Director, entitled "Globalization and the environment—global crises: national chaos?" [UNEP/GC.25/16]. It stated that over the preceding 12 months, the world had witnessed the emergence of multiple global crises related to food, fuel, freshwater and finance. The complexity of the situation was compounded by climate change, which was exacerbating the impact of each crisis. The paper identified challenges and provided information on international responses to address multiple crises, possible responses to the crises in the environmental field, and a selection of government responses to the financial crisis and the "green economy". It also presented the priority green economic sectors identified by UNEP, as well as a series of questions for discussion during the ministerial consultations.

Coordination and cooperation

The Governing Council in February [dec. 25/1 VI] welcomed the efforts of the Executive Director, in his capacity as chair of the Environment Management Group (EMG), and those of its members, in promoting cooperation across the UN system on environmental activities, including its support for the commitment made by CEB to moving the United Nations towards climate neutrality; requested the Executive Director to invite EMG to promote cooperation across the UN system to assist Member States in implementing the international environmental agenda; welcomed the UNEP efforts to engage in the "Delivering as one" initiative and in the joint UNEP-UNDP poverty and environment initiative; reaffirmed the UNEP role as the principal environmental body within the UN system; expressed its wish that cooperation between UNEP and UNDP be strengthened, including through the revised memorandum of understanding (see below) and by clearly specifying their respective roles; and requested the Executive Director to report on the implementation of the revised memorandum of understanding to the Governing Council at its next (2010) special session.

Memorandum of understanding

In response to the Governing Council's February request [dec. 25/1 VI], the Executive Director in November presented a report on the implementation of the revised memorandum of understanding between UNEP and UNDP [UNEP/GCSS.XI/3]. While UNEP and UNDP were cooperating in a number of projects and activities, there remained insufficient programmatic coherence in that cooperation, including in terms of respective agency mandates and comparative advantages. The revised memorandum, signed in December 2008 [YUN 2008, p. 1151], sought to achieve deeper cooperation between the two agencies—including via joint programming—that was consistent with the organizations' respective mandates and comparative advantages. It contained sections on administrative services, reimbursable support service arrangements and programme implementation. Areas of cooperation might include climate change, the UNDP-UNEP Poverty and Environment Initiative and other environmental endeavours, such as the implementation of Agenda 21, the Johannesburg Plan of Implementation, the Bali Strategic Plan for Technology Support and Capacity-building, the multilateral environmental agreements and other agreements to attain the Millennium Development Goals (MDGs).

The report also reviewed EMG activities to promote cooperation across the UN system on environmental activities, the UNEP contribution to UN programming guidance and its engagement with the UN system at the country level.

Environmental emergencies

In 2009, UNEP continued to assist vulnerable or crisis-affected countries and communities by providing environmental expertise for assessments and integrating environmental concerns in emergency response, post-crisis reconstruction, recovery projects, and long-term sustainable development.

During the year, UNEP established a new programme to integrate environmental issues within humanitarian operations and provided expertise in more than 12 crisis-affected locations, including Afghanistan, the Central African Republic, China, Côte d'Ivoire, the Democratic Republic of the Congo, the Gaza Strip, Haiti, Myanmar, Nigeria and Sierra Leone. The second phase of an environmental recovery programme in the Sudan focused on capacity-building and effective management of natural resources, primarily water and forests. UNEP expanded its presence in the country, establishing coordination offices in El Fasher, Juba and Nyala. Thanks to UNEP involvement, the 2009 Common Humanitarian Fund for Sudan allocated $1 million to environmental initiatives—from sustainable construction technology and drought preparedness strategies in camps for internally displaced persons to the rollout of 70,000 fuel-efficient stoves and the planting of 630,000 tree seedlings to curb deforestation. UNEP also conducted assessments of hydropolitical vulnerability and resilience along international waters in Africa, Asia, Europe, Latin America and the Caribbean, and North America.

Oil slick in Lebanon

In response to General Assembly resolution 63/211 [YUN 2008, p. 1150], the Secretary-General submitted an August report [A/64/259] reviewing progress in implementing Assembly resolutions 61/194 [YUN 2006, p. 1215], 62/188 [YUN 2007, p. 1053] and 63/211 on the oil slick on Lebanese shores that resulted from the 2006 destruction by Israel of oil storage tanks in Lebanon following the outbreak of hostilities between Israel and the paramilitary group Hizbullah [YUN 2006, p. 574]. The marine oil spill resulted in the release of some 15,000 tons of fuel oil into the Mediterranean Sea and led to the contamination of about 150 kilometres of coastline in Lebanon and the Syrian Arab Republic. Preliminary results of a comprehensive survey carried out in late 2008 of the 210-kilometre shoreline from Tyre to the northern border of Lebanon indicated that 12 sites still needed to be cleaned; many sites remained stained by the oil spill but should be left for weathering and natural effects rather than active intervention; and underwater surveys conducted in 10 sites did not reveal any underwater contamination with heavy fuel oil, with the

exception of Jbeil-Byblos beach, where a large number of tarballs were found. The findings of the survey were anticipated to be published in September 2009. Israel had yet to assume its responsibility for prompt and adequate compensation to Lebanon.

The first phase of the clean-up was completed in 2007, and involved recovering free-floating oil from the sea and confined areas; cleaning areas with potential for direct human contact or risk to public health; rehabilitating areas where oil slicks hampered economic activities; and addressing threats to environmentally or culturally important sites. Assistance for the first phase was estimated at around $18.5 million. Partners included Italy, the Fund for International Development of the Organization of Petroleum Exporting Countries, UNDP, the Swiss Agency for Development and Cooperation, the Canadian International Development Agency, the United States Agency for International Development (USAID), as well as local non-governmental organizations (NGOs). The second phase focused on the removal of fuel from rocks, wave cut platforms, cliffs and infrastructure. Clean-up work was sponsored by Japan, Norway, Spain and USAID. As at June 2008, approximately 500 cubic metres of liquid and 3,120 cubic metres of semi-solid and solid waste had been collected during both phases of clean-up operations and had been stored in containers in secure temporary storage sites, with contribution from all partners. Treatment began at two of the temporary storage sites, and was expected to be completed in the third quarter of 2009.

The Experts Working Group for Lebanon had estimated the overall cost of clean-up and rehabilitation at between $137 million and $205 million [YUN 2008, p. 1150], of which about 10 per cent of the average upper limit range had been received by Lebanon in support of its clean-up costs as at June 2008. Meanwhile, UNEP was taking steps to establish the Eastern Mediterranean Oil Spill Restoration Trust Fund. The Economic and Social Commission for Western Asia had expressed its readiness to host the Trust Fund.

The Secretary-General commended Lebanon's ongoing efforts to address the impact of the oil spill and the efforts made by the UN system in responding to the emergency. He urged Israel to assume responsibility for compensation and Member States, international organizations, international and regional financial institutions, NGOs and the private sector to continue their support for Lebanon. The international effort should be intensified as Lebanon was still engaged in oil removal, waste treatment and recovery monitoring. The Secretary-General was finalizing the mechanism under which the Eastern Mediterranean Oil Spill Restoration Trust Fund would operate.

Communication. On 28 October [A/C.2/64/10], the Syrian Arab Republic transmitted its position in respect of the Secretary-General's report.

GENERAL ASSEMBLY ACTION

On 21 December [meeting 66], the General Assembly, on the recommendation of the Second Committee [A/64/420], adopted **resolution 64/195** by recorded vote (164-8-7) [agenda item 53].

Oil slick on Lebanese shores

The General Assembly,

Recalling its resolutions 61/194 of 20 December 2006, 62/188 of 19 December 2007 and 63/211 of 19 December 2008 on the oil slick on Lebanese shores,

Reaffirming the outcome of the United Nations Conference on the Human Environment, especially principle 7 of the Declaration of the Conference, in which States were requested to take all possible steps to prevent pollution of the seas,

Emphasizing the need to protect and preserve the marine environment in accordance with international law,

Taking into account the 1992 Rio Declaration on Environment and Development, especially principle 16, in which it was stipulated that the polluter should, in principle, bear the cost of pollution, and taking into account also chapter 17 of Agenda 21,

Noting again with great concern the environmental disaster caused by the destruction by the Israeli Air Force on 15 July 2006 of the oil storage tanks in the direct vicinity of El-Jiyeh electric power plant in Lebanon, resulting in an oil slick that covered the entirety of the Lebanese coastline and extended to the Syrian coastline,

Noting again with appreciation the assistance offered by donor countries and international organizations for the clean-up operations and the early recovery and reconstruction of Lebanon through bilateral and multilateral channels, including the Athens Coordination Meeting on the response to the marine pollution incident in the Eastern Mediterranean, held on 17 August 2006, as well as the Stockholm Conference for Lebanon's Early Recovery, held on 31 August 2006,

Taking note of the fact that the Secretary-General is currently finalizing the mechanism under which the Eastern Mediterranean Oil Spill Restoration Trust Fund will operate,

1. *Takes note* of the report of the Secretary-General on the implementation of General Assembly resolution 63/211 on the oil slick on Lebanese shores;

2. *Reiterates the expression of its deep concern* about the adverse implications of the destruction by the Israeli Air Force of the oil storage tanks in the direct vicinity of the Lebanese El-Jiyeh electric power plant for the achievement of sustainable development in Lebanon;

3. *Considers* that the oil slick has heavily polluted the shores of Lebanon and partially polluted Syrian shores and consequently has had serious implications for livelihoods and the economy of Lebanon, owing to the adverse implications for natural resources, biodiversity, fisheries and tourism, and for human health, in the country;

4. *Requests* the Government of Israel to assume responsibility for prompt and adequate compensation to the Government of Lebanon and other countries directly affected by the oil slick, such as the Syrian Arab Republic whose shores have been partially polluted, for the costs of repairing the environmental damage caused by the destruction, including the restoration of the marine environment;

5. *Expresses its appreciation* for the efforts of the Government of Lebanon and those of the Member States, regional and international organizations, regional and international financial institutions, non-governmental organizations and the private sector in the initiation of clean-up and rehabilitation operations on the polluted shores, and encourages the Member States and the above-mentioned entities to continue their financial and technical support to the Government of Lebanon towards achieving the completion of clean-up and rehabilitation operations, with the aim of preserving the ecosystem of Lebanon and that of the Eastern Mediterranean Basin;

6. *Reaffirms* its decision to establish an Eastern Mediterranean Oil Spill Restoration Trust Fund, based on voluntary contributions, to provide assistance and support to the States directly adversely affected in their integrated environmentally sound management, from clean-up to safe disposal of oily waste, of this environmental disaster resulting from the destruction of the oil storage tanks at El-Jiyeh electric power plant, and requests the Secretary-General to continue working towards the hosting and operationalization of the Trust Fund and to promptly finalize the implementation of that decision before the end of the sixty-fourth session of the General Assembly;

7. *Invites* States, intergovernmental organizations, non-governmental organizations and the private sector to make voluntary financial contributions to the Trust Fund, and in this regard requests the Secretary-General to mobilize international technical and financial assistance in order to finalize the mechanism under which the Trust Fund will operate;

8. *Recognizes* the multidimensionality of the adverse impact of the oil slick, and requests the Secretary-General to submit to the General Assembly at its sixty-fifth session a report on the implementation of the present resolution under the item entitled "Sustainable development".

RECORDED VOTE ON RESOLUTION 64/195:

In favour: Afghanistan, Albania, Algeria, Andorra, Angola, Antigua and Barbuda, Argentina, Armenia, Austria, Bahamas, Bahrain, Barbados, Belarus, Belgium, Belize, Benin, Bhutan, Bolivia, Bosnia and Herzegovina, Botswana, Brazil, Brunei Darussalam, Bulgaria, Burkina Faso, Burundi, Cambodia, Cape Verde, Central African Republic, Chad, Chile, China, Comoros, Congo, Costa Rica, Côte d'Ivoire, Croatia, Cuba, Cyprus, Czech Republic, Democratic People's Republic of Korea, Denmark, Djibouti, Dominica, Dominican Republic, Ecuador, Egypt, El Salvador, Eritrea, Estonia, Ethiopia, Finland, France, Gabon, Georgia, Germany, Ghana, Greece, Grenada, Guatemala, Guinea, Guinea-Bissau, Guyana, Haiti, Hungary, Iceland, India, Indonesia, Iran, Iraq, Ireland, Italy, Jamaica, Japan, Jordan, Kazakhstan, Kenya, Kuwait, Kyrgyzstan, Lao People's Democratic Republic, Latvia, Lebanon, Lesotho, Libyan Arab Jamahiriya, Liechtenstein, Lithuania, Luxembourg, Madagascar, Malawi, Malaysia, Maldives, Mali, Malta, Mauritania, Mauritius, Mexico, Moldova, Monaco, Mongolia,

Montenegro, Morocco, Mozambique, Myanmar, Namibia, Nepal, Netherlands, New Zealand, Nicaragua, Niger, Nigeria, Norway, Oman, Pakistan, Papua New Guinea, Paraguay, Peru, Philippines, Poland, Portugal, Qatar, Republic of Korea, Romania, Russian Federation, Rwanda, Saint Lucia, Saint Vincent and the Grenadines, Samoa, San Marino, Saudi Arabia, Senegal, Serbia, Sierra Leone, Singapore, Slovakia, Slovenia, Solomon Islands, Somalia, South Africa, Spain, Sri Lanka, Sudan, Suriname, Swaziland, Sweden, Switzerland, Syrian Arab Republic, Tajikistan, Thailand, The former Yugoslav Republic of Macedonia, Timor-Leste, Togo, Trinidad and Tobago, Tunisia, Turkey, Tuvalu, Ukraine, United Arab Emirates, United Kingdom, Uruguay, Uzbekistan, Venezuela, Viet Nam, Yemen, Zambia, Zimbabwe.

Against: Australia, Canada, Israel, Marshall Islands, Micronesia, Nauru, Palau, United States.

Abstaining: Bangladesh, Cameroon, Colombia, Fiji, Liberia, Panama, Tonga.

Environmental situation in Gaza Strip

On 20 February [dec. 25/12], the Governing Council requested the Executive Director to deploy a mission of environmental experts to Gaza to assess the natural and environmental impacts on the Gaza Strip caused by the escalation of violence and hostilities (see p. 434), and to report on the findings, results and recommendations to the Council's eleventh (2010) special session.

In November, pursuant to that decision, the Executive Director submitted a report on the environmental situation in the Gaza Strip [UNEP/GCSS.XI/9] based on field work by a team of international experts deployed by UNEP. The team concluded that a wide range of environmental challenges required urgent resolve, ranging from safe disposal of large amounts of rubble, some of which was contaminated with asbestos, to sewage pollution of coastal waters. Some of the challenges had been aggravated by recent events, but their roots predated the recent hostilities. The most urgent finding concerned the state of the underground water supplies, upon which the Palestinian people—and to a large extent the people of Israel—relied for drinking and irrigation. Years of overabstraction and pollution had jeopardized the sustainability of the Gaza Strip unless the aquifer was 'rested' and improved sanitation and desalination were introduced. The report outlined options for managing the situation and leading the Gaza Strip onto a sustainable path. It also provided recommendations for remedying the damage caused by the hostilities and for addressing pre-existing, environmental degradation, including, among others, providing technical support for farmland and orchard restoration; repairing water supply and sewage systems; removing water resources from the framework of the ongoing conflict in the region; developing an alternative water supply for the Gaza Strip; establishing new sewage treatment plants; and rebuilding environmental governance.

Participation of civil society

The tenth Global Civil Society Forum (Nairobi, 14–15 February), attended by an estimated 230 participants, discussed several issues, including civil society engagement at the twenty-fifth (2009) session of the Governing Council, partnerships for implementing the 2010–2011 UNEP work programme, and the themes of the twenty-fifth session: "Globalization and the environment: global crisis: national chaos?" and "International environmental governance: help or hindrance?" Forum participants also considered the chemicals agenda and civil society statements. Civil society statements from six regions—Africa, Asia and the Pacific, Europe, Latin America and the Caribbean, North America and West Asia—were submitted to the twenty-fifth session of the Council by the Executive Director [UNEP/GC.25/INF/9]. Themes covered in the statement included climate change, disasters and conflict, globalization and the environment, and engagement with civil society.

Nearly 300 civil society organizations from 88 countries participated in the twenty-fifth session of the Governing Council. In addition to the nine major group categories included in Agenda 21, other organizations—from faith-based groups to cultural associations—were represented. Female participation increased from 40 to 46 per cent.

The Governing Council in February [dec. 25/6] took note of the final report by the Executive Director [YUN 2008, p. 1151] on the implementation of the long-term strategy on engagement and involvement of young people in environmental issues [YUN 2002, p. 1040]. It endorsed the activities of the second long-term strategy presented by the Executive Director in that report and decided to implement the strategy through the UNEP work programmes. The Council also requested the Executive Director to present a midterm progress report on the implementation of the strategy at its twenty-seventh (2013) session and to present a final report at its twenty-eighth (2015) session.

The Tunza International Children and Youth Conference on Climate Change (Daejeon, Republic of Korea, 17–23 August), organized by UNEP in cooperation with the UNEP National Committee for the Republic of Korea, brought together around 800 young people from all over the world and addressed the theme "Climate Change: Our Challenge". Participants pledged to carry out efforts to ensure that global warming remained an international priority.

General Assembly issues

The Executive Director in February provided information on issues arising from resolutions adopted by the General Assembly in 2008 that called for action by, or were of relevance to, UNEP [UNEP/GC.25/INF/3].

Administrative and budgetary matters

Environment Fund

In a January note [UNEP/GC.25/INF/5], the Executive Director provided information on the status of the Environment Fund and other sources of UNEP funding, as well as an overview of the availability of resources and their use over the 2008–2009 biennium. Total provisional resources for the biennium amounted to $441.3 million, including balances as at 1 January 2008 of $108.5 million, while total claims on resources were estimated at $382.1 million. The estimated total year-end balance of funds as at 31 December 2008 was projected to be $59.2 million. Ninety-two countries pledged $88.9 million to the Environment Fund for 2008.

In response to a 2007 Governing Council decision [YUN 2007, p. 1056], the Executive Director provided a report on the Environment Fund budgets [UNEP/GC.25/14] containing information on resources available in the 2008–2009 biennium, in the light of which a supplementary work programme and budget for 2009 were proposed. The Council was requested to approve the supplementary work programme and approve appropriations for the Environment Fund in the amount of $171 million. In February [UNEP/GC.25/14/Add.1], the Advisory Committee on Administrative and Budgetary Questions (ACABQ) stated that it had no objection to the suggested actions.

The Governing Council in February [dec. 25/15] approved the 2008–2009 supplementary work programme; approved appropriations for the Environment Fund in the amount of $171 million, including $16.9 million for the support budget and $6.9 million for the Fund programme reserve; and authorized the Executive Director to increase the financial reserve by up to $5 million in line with previous Council decisions.

Following consideration of the Executive Director's report on the proposed 2010–2011 biennial programme and support budgets [UNEP/GC.25/12], which requested appropriations for the Environment Fund in the amount of $180 million, and the related ACABQ report [UNEP/GC.25/12/Add.1], the Governing Council [dec. 25/13] approved the work programme, support budget and appropriations for the Environment Fund in the requested amount, including $18 million for the support budget and $6 million for the Fund programme reserve. It authorized the Executive Director to reallocate resources among budget lines up to a maximum of 10 per cent of the appropriation to which the resources were to be reallocated, as well as funds in excess of 10 per cent and up to 20 per cent of an appropriation, in consultation with the Committee of Permanent Representatives. The Executive

Director was also authorized to enter into forward commitments not exceeding $20 million for Environment Fund programme activities for the 2012–2013 biennium.

The Council requested the Executive Director to continue shifting emphasis from delivery of outputs to achievement of results, ensuring that UNEP managers took responsibility for achieving programme objectives and the efficient and transparent use of resources. The Executive Director was also requested: to continue consultations with Member States as he further developed the process to implement the 2010–2011 work programme and budgets; to provide Member States, through the Committee of Permanent Representatives, with a document containing additional information on internal prioritization at the expected accomplishment level within each subprogramme of the 2010–2011 work programme prior to its implementation; and to report to Governments, through the Committee of Permanent Representatives, on a half-yearly basis, and to the Governing Council at its regular and special sessions, on progress made by each of the subprogrammes and their expected accomplishments, and on the execution of UNEP budgets.

Regarding the 2012–2013 biennium, the Executive Director was requested to prepare, in consultation with the Committee of Permanent Representatives, a work programme consisting of Environment Fund programme activities, and to continue submitting prioritized, results-oriented and streamlined work programme and budgets for consideration and approval by the Governing Council at its twenty-sixth (2011) session.

Trust funds

At its February session, the Governing Council had before it a report of the Executive Director [UNEP/GC.25/13], which provided information and suggested action on the management of the trust funds and earmarked contributions that supported the UNEP work programme. As at 30 November 2008, there were 81 UNEP-administered active trust funds. For the 2008–2009 biennium, the estimated expenditure of $740.6 million included $110.8 million for trust funds directly supporting the UNEP programme of work, $168.7 million for trust funds for conventions, protocols and regional seas programmes and $461 million for special accounts and trust funds. For the 2010–2011 biennium, the projected expenditures amounted to $807.9 million, of which $162.2 million related to trust funds directly supporting the UNEP programme of work, $201.7 million to conventions and regional seas programmes and $444 million to special accounts and trust funds.

On 20 February [dec. 25/14], the Governing Council approved the establishment of 5 trust funds, the extension of 35 and the closure of 1.

Indicative scale of contributions

In response to a 2007 Governing Council decision [YUN 2007, p. 1058], which dealt with, among other issues, strengthening UNEP financing, the Executive Director provided information [UNEP/GC.25/INF/14] on the operation of the extended pilot phase of the voluntary indicative scale of contributions to the Environment Fund and other voluntary contribution options. The pilot phase of the voluntary indicative scale of contributions aimed at enhancing predictability in financing and at broadening the base of contributions was launched in 2003 [YUN 2003, p. 1047]. The main results achieved by UNEP through the introduction of the scale were: significant broadening of the donor base, as 157 Member States had pledged and paid contributions during the previous six years; greater short-term predictability of voluntary contributions to the Environment Fund, with approximately 75 per cent of Member States pledging annually in accordance with the voluntary scale; improved financial stability, as most donor countries had at least maintained the level of their voluntary payments to the Fund; and higher voluntary payments to the Fund, as the negative trends in contributions experienced during the four bienniums preceding the adoption of the scale were reversed and positive growth in contributions began immediately upon its adoption. Other factors contributing to strengthening the financial situation of UNEP included the improving strategic vision, focus and management of the organization and the good will of the donor Governments making additional voluntary payments. The Environment Fund remained vulnerable to exchange-rate fluctuations, unpredictable decreases and even non-payment and delayed payments, including by major donors. UNEP should continue building donor confidence through efficient planning, timely delivery of its programme results, improved reporting and more efficient use of funds.

On 20 February [dec. 25/1 IV], the Governing Council requested the Executive Director to notify Member States of the voluntary indicative scale of contributions that he intended to propose for the 2010–2011 biennium by 1 August of the year preceding the year in which those contributions would be paid. It also invited each Member State to inform the Executive Director as to whether it would use the proposed scale of contributions, and encouraged Governments to make their voluntary contributions to the Environment Fund in 2010–2011 in an amount equal to or greater than that suggested by the scale or on the basis of the other voluntary options.

Global Environment Facility

The Global Environment Facility (GEF) in 2009 continued to address global issues in its six areas of concern: climate change, biodiversity, persistent organic pollutants, land degradation, international waters and ozone depletion.

From June 2008 to July 2009, the two largest focal areas were biodiversity conservation and climate change mitigation and adaptation, constituting 33 per cent and 32 per cent of all GEF funds, respectively. During that period, GEF financed 234 projects for a total of $6 billion, investing $877 million in GEF resources and mobilizing an additional $5.1 billion in co-financing from development partners. Out of those 234 projects, biodiversity accounted for 84 projects, climate change for 57, persistent organic pollutants for 29, international waters for 22 and land degradation for 5. Approval was given to 37 multi-focal area projects, which took advantage of particular strengths within each focal area and aimed at creating the best synergies possible.

GEF approved 57 new investments in the climate change focal area. The total GEF allocation was approximately $235.5 million, supplemented with an additional $1.7 billion generated in co-financing from partners, including the GEF agencies, bilateral agencies, recipient countries, NGOs and the private sector. Biodiversity accounted for 34 per cent of total allocation, with $295.6 million allocated by GEF and $1.01 billion generated in co-financing. GEF approved 29 new projects in the persistent organic pollutants focal area. The total GEF allocation was approximately $73 million, supplemented by an additional $134 million generated in co-financing from partners. Twenty new projects were approved under land degradation. The total GEF grant for those projects was $91.8 million, leveraging $797.1 million in co-financing from partners. The GEF Council approved 14 new projects in the international waters focal area. The total allocation approved by the Council was $84.4 million, supplemented by an additional $1 billion generated in co-financing from partners. In addition, the GEF Council approved eight multifocal projects with strong international waters components. In the area of ozone depletion, GEF had approved during the 2007–2008 period a joint effort by UNDP, UNEP, the United Nations Industrial Development Organization (UNIDO) and the World Bank on preparing for hydrochlorofluorocarbon (HCFC) phase-out in countries with economies in transition. The project was examining ways not only to reduce HCFCs, but also how doing so would help to meet goals under the United Nations Framework Convention on Climate Change. Following that assessment and planning effort, the Russian Federation had submitted an HCFC phase-out project for funding that brought together protection of the ozone layer, climate mitigation and technology transfer. The other eligible countries in the region had developed project concepts for future GEF funding as well.

The GEF small grants programme supported 1,262 community-based projects. More than 120 countries were working with UNDP, through projects financially supported by GEF, to establish the policy, institutional and financial frameworks that would help to drive private investment flows towards environmentally sustainable solutions. The World Bank Group's GEF-funded portfolio was composed of 208 projects across all regions, with combined total GEF commitments of $1.7 billion. The GEF agencies were the Asian Development Bank, the Inter-American Development Bank, the International Fund for Agricultural Development, UNDP, UNEP, UNIDO and the World Bank.

International conventions and mechanisms

In a February note [UNEP/GC.25/INF/7], the Executive Director reviewed the status of conventions and protocols in the field of the environment, covering the period 1 February 2007–31 January 2009. The conventions and protocols that entered into force during that period were the Protocol on the Prevention of Pollution of the Mediterranean Sea by Transboundary Movements of Hazardous Wastes and their Disposal, adopted in Izmir, Turkey on 1 October 1996, which entered into force on 19 January 2008; the Amendment to the Agreement on the Conservation of Small Cetaceans of the Baltic and North Seas, adopted in Esbjerg, Denmark, on 22 August 2003, which entered into force on 3 February 2008; the Protocol for the Protection of the Mediterranean Sea against Pollution from Land-Based Sources and Activities, adopted in Syracuse, Italy, on 7 March 1996, which entered into force on 11 May 2008; and the International Convention on the Control of Harmful Anti-fouling Systems on Ships, adopted in London on 5 October 2001, which entered into force on 17 September 2008.

New conventions and protocols concluded during the reporting period included the Nairobi International Convention on the Removal of Wrecks, 2007, adopted in Nairobi on 18 May 2007; and the Protocol on Integrated Coastal Zone Management in the Mediterranean, adopted in Madrid on 21 January 2008. An appendix provided information on changes to the status of ratification for the conventions and protocols in the field of the environment.

The Governing Council in February [dec. 25/1 V] welcomed the recommendations [YUN 2008, p. 1155] of the Ad Hoc Joint Working Group on Enhancing Cooperation and Coordination Among the Basel, Rotterdam and Stockholm Conventions, and their adoption by the ninth meeting of the Conference of the Parties to the Basel Convention [ibid., p. 1173] and the fourth meeting of the Conference of the Parties to the Rotterdam Convention [ibid., p. 1170]. It requested the Executive Director, in the event of the adoption of those recommendations by the Conference of the Parties of the Stockholm Convention, to undertake relevant actions envisaged in the recommendations.

In May, the Conference of the Parties of the Stockholm Convention adopted those recommendations [UNEP/POPS/COP.4/38 (SC-4/34)].

Note by Secretary-General. In response to General Assembly resolutions 63/32 [YUN 2008, p. 1155], 63/218 [ibid., p. 1161] and 63/219 [ibid., p. 1159], the Secretary-General, in a July note [A/64/202] transmitted reports submitted by the secretariats of the United Nations Framework Convention on Climate Change (see below), the United Nations Convention to Combat Desertification in Those Countries Experiencing Serious Drought and/or Desertification, Particularly in Africa (see p. 1022) and the Convention on Biological Diversity (see p. 1018), respectively.

Climate change convention

As at 31 December, 193 States and the European Union (EU) were parties to the United Nations Framework Convention on Climate Change (UNFCCC), which was opened for signature in 1992 [YUN 1992, p. 681] and entered into force in 1994 [YUN 1994, p. 938]. Iraq and Somalia became parties during the year.

At year's end, 189 States and the EU were parties to the Kyoto Protocol to the Convention [YUN 1997, p. 1048], which entered into force in 2005 [YUN 2005, p. 1146]. Brunei Darussalam, Chad, Iraq, Kazakhstan, Turkey and Zimbabwe became parties during the year. There were 19 parties to the 2006 amendment to annex B of the Protocol [YUN 2006, p. 1220], which had not yet entered into force. Azerbaijan, Israel, Kyrgyzstan, Mauritius, Mexico, the Republic of Korea, Serbia and the Syrian Arab Republic deposited their instrument of acceptance in 2009. France deposited its instrument of acceptance in August, yet withdrew in October.

The fifteenth session of the Conference of the Parties to the UNFCCC (Copenhagen, 7–19 December) [FCCC/CP/2009/11 & Add.1] produced the Copenhagen Accord, which expressed a clear political intent to constrain carbon and respond to climate change, and contained several key elements on which the views of Governments converged, including the long-term goal of limiting the maximum global average temperature increase to no more than 2 degrees Celsius above pre-industrial levels, subject to a review in 2015. However, there was no agreement on how to achieve that goal in practical terms. The Accord also included a reference to considering limiting the temperature increase to below 1.5 degrees—a key demand made by vulnerable developing countries. Developed countries pledged to fund actions to reduce greenhouse gas emissions and to adapt to the effects of climate change in developing countries by providing $30 billion for the period 2010–2012 and to mobilize long-term finance of a further $100 billion a year by 2020. Close to 115 world leaders attended the Conference's high-level segment, making it one of the largest gatherings of world leaders ever outside UN Headquarters.

The fifth session of the Conference of the Parties serving as the meeting of the parties to the Kyoto Protocol, held concurrently with the fifteenth UNFCCC Conference session [FCCC/KP/CMP/2009/21 & Add.1], adopted decisions related to the outcome of the work of the Ad Hoc Working Group on Further Commitments for Annex I Parties under the Protocol; further guidance relating to the clean development mechanism; guidance on implementing article 6 of the Protocol; the report of the Adaptation Fund Board; the review of the Adaptation Fund; the Compliance Committee; capacity-building under the Protocol; the updated training programme for members of expert review teams participating in annual reviews under article 8 of the Protocol; administrative, financial and institutional matters; and the programme budget for the 2010–2011 biennium.

In November, the Executive Board of the Protocol's clean development mechanism issued its annual report [FCCC/KP/CMP/2009/16], covering its work from 25 October 2008 to 16 October 2009.

The Subsidiary Body for Scientific and Technological Advice (SBSTA) [FCCC/SBSTA/2009/3 & Add.1] and the Subsidiary Body for Implementation (SBI) [FCCC/SBI/2009/8 & Add.1] held their thirtieth sessions (Bonn, Germany, 1–10 June). SBSTA [FCCC/SBSTA/2009/8] and SBI [FCCC/SBI/2009/15] also held their thirty-first sessions (Copenhagen, 8–12 December).

Communication. On 12 May [A/64/81], Namibia, as President of the Inter-Parliamentary Union, transmitted to the Secretary-General a resolution adopted by the one hundred and twentieth Assembly of the Union (Addis Ababa, Ethiopia, 10 April) on climate change, sustainable development models and renewable energies.

GENERAL ASSEMBLY ACTION

On 7 December [meeting 59], the General Assembly, on the recommendation of the Second Committee [A/64/420/Add.4], adopted **resolution 64/73** without vote [agenda item 53 *(d)*].

Protection of global climate for present and future generations of humankind

The General Assembly,

Recalling its resolutions 43/53 of 6 December 1988, 54/222 of 22 December 1999, 62/86 of 10 December 2007, 63/32 of 26 November 2008 and resolutions and decisions relating to the protection of the global climate for present and future generations of mankind,

Recalling also the provisions of the United Nations Framework Convention on Climate Change, including the acknowledgement that the global nature of climate change calls for the widest possible cooperation by all countries and their participation in an effective and appropriate international response, in accordance with their common but differentiated responsibilities and respective capabilities and their social and economic conditions,

Recalling further the United Nations Millennium Declaration, in which Heads of State and Government resolved to make every effort to ensure the entry into force of the Kyoto Protocol to the United Nations Framework Convention on Climate Change and to embark on the required reduction in emissions of greenhouse gases,

Recalling the Johannesburg Declaration on Sustainable Development, the Plan of Implementation of the World Summit on Sustainable Development ("Johannesburg Plan of Implementation"), the outcome of the thirteenth session of the Conference of the Parties to the Convention and the third session of the Conference of the Parties serving as the Meeting of the Parties to the Kyoto Protocol, held in Bali, Indonesia, from 3 to 15 December 2007, the outcome of the fourteenth session of the Conference of the Parties to the Convention and the fourth session of the Conference of the Parties serving as the Meeting of the Parties to the Kyoto Protocol, held in Poznan, Poland, from 1 to 12 December 2008, and the outcomes of all previous sessions,

Reaffirming the Programme of Action for the Sustainable Development of Small Island Developing States, the Mauritius Declaration and the Mauritius Strategy for the Further Implementation of the Programme of Action for the Sustainable Development of Small Island Developing States,

Recalling the 2005 World Summit Outcome,

Remaining deeply concerned that all countries, in particular developing countries, including the least developed countries, landlocked developing countries, small island developing States and countries in Africa, face increased risks from the adverse effects of climate change, and stressing the need to address adaptation needs relating to such effects,

Noting that, to date, there are one hundred and ninety-four parties to the Convention, including one hundred and ninety-three States and one regional economic integration organization,

Noting also that, currently, the Kyoto Protocol has attracted one hundred and ninety ratifications, accessions, acceptances or approvals, including by thirty-nine parties included in annex I to the Convention,

Noting further the amendment to annex B to the Kyoto Protocol,

Noting the work of the Intergovernmental Panel on Climate Change and the need to build and enhance scientific and technological capabilities, inter alia, through continuing support to the Panel for the exchange of scientific data and information, especially in developing countries,

Noting also the significance of the scientific findings of the fourth assessment report of the Intergovernmental Panel on Climate Change, providing an integrated scientific, technical and socio-economic perspective on relevant issues and contributing positively to the discussions under the Convention and the understanding of the phenomenon of climate change, including its impacts and risks,

Reaffirming that economic and social development and poverty eradication are global priorities,

Recognizing that deep cuts in global emissions will be required to achieve the ultimate objective of the Convention,

Reaffirming its commitment to the ultimate objective of the Convention, namely, to stabilize greenhouse gas concentrations in the atmosphere at a level that prevents dangerous anthropogenic interference with the climate system, and also reaffirming that such a level should be achieved within a time frame sufficient to allow ecosystems to adapt naturally to climate change, to ensure that food production is not threatened and to enable economic development to proceed in a sustainable manner,

Reaffirming the financial obligations of developed country parties and other developed parties included in annex II under the Convention and the Kyoto Protocol,

Taking note of the initiative by the Secretary-General in convening a summit on climate change on 22 September 2009, and welcoming the determination reiterated by Member States on that occasion to urgently address the challenge of climate change,

Taking note also of the holding of World Climate Conference 3 in Geneva from 31 August to 4 September 2009 and the holding by the Government of Indonesia of the World Ocean Conference in Manado from 11 to 15 May 2009,

Taking note further of the high-level conference on "Climate Change: Technology Development and Transfer", held in New Delhi on 22 and 23 October 2009,

Acknowledging women as key actors in the efforts towards sustainable development, and recognizing that a gender perspective can contribute to efforts to address climate change,

Taking note of the note by the Secretary-General transmitting the report of the Executive Secretary of the United Nations Framework Convention on Climate Change,

1. *Stresses* the seriousness of climate change, and calls upon States to work cooperatively towards achieving the ultimate objective of the United Nations Framework Convention on Climate Change through the urgent implementation of its provisions;

2. *Notes* that States that have ratified the Kyoto Protocol to the United Nations Framework Convention on Climate Change welcome the entry into force of the Protocol on 16 February 2005, and strongly urge States that have not yet done so to ratify it in a timely manner;

3. *Takes note* of the outcome of the fourteenth session of the Conference of the Parties to the Convention and the fourth session of the Conference of the Parties serving as the Meeting of the Parties to the Kyoto Protocol, hosted by the Government of Poland from 1 to 12 December 2008;

4. *Takes note with appreciation* of the offer of the Government of Denmark to host the fifteenth session of the Conference of the Parties to the Convention and the fifth session of the Conference of Parties serving as the Meeting of the Parties to the Kyoto Protocol, to be held in Copenhagen from 7 to 18 December 2009;

5. *Notes* the ongoing parallel work of the Ad Hoc Working Group on Long-term Cooperative Action under the Convention and the Ad Hoc Working Group on Further Commitments for Annex I Parties under the Kyoto Protocol, and that the respective parties to the Convention and the Kyoto Protocol call for the completion of this work;

6. *Encourages* Member States to approach Copenhagen with ambition, optimism and determination, with a view to making the United Nations Climate Change Conference a success;

7. *Takes note with appreciation*, in this regard, of the offer of the Government of Mexico to host the sixteenth session of the Conference of the Parties to the Convention and the sixth session of the Conference of Parties serving as the Meeting of the Parties to the Kyoto Protocol, to be held in Mexico City in 2010;

8. *Urges* parties to the Convention, and invites parties to the Kyoto Protocol to the Convention, to continue to make use of the information contained in the fourth assessment report of the Intergovernmental Panel on Climate Change in their work;

9. *Recognizes* that climate change poses serious risks and challenges to all countries, particularly developing countries, especially the least developed countries, landlocked developing countries, small island developing States and countries in Africa, including those that are particularly vulnerable to the adverse effects of climate change, and calls upon States to take urgent global action to address climate change in accordance with the principles identified in the Convention, including the principle of common but differentiated responsibilities and respective capabilities, and in this regard urges all countries to fully implement their commitments under the Convention, to take effective and concrete actions and measures at all levels and to enhance international cooperation in the framework of the Convention;

10. *Reaffirms* that efforts to address climate change in a manner that enhances the sustainable development and sustained economic growth of the developing countries and the eradication of poverty should be carried out by promoting the integration of the three components of sustainable development, namely, economic development, social development and environmental protection, as interdependent and mutually reinforcing pillars, in an integrated, coordinated and balanced manner;

11. *Recognizes* the urgency of providing financial and technical resources, as well as capacity-building and access to and transfer of technology, to assist those developing countries adversely affected by climate change;

12. *Invites* the international community to fulfil the commitments made during the fourth replenishment and to secure a successful fifth replenishment of the Global Environment Facility Trust Fund, without prejudice to ongoing discussions on financial mechanisms under the Convention;

13. *Requests* the Secretary-General to make provisions for the sessions of the Conference of the Parties to the Convention and its subsidiary bodies in his proposal for the programme budget for the biennium 2010–2011;

14. *Notes* the ongoing work of the liaison group of the secretariats and offices of the relevant subsidiary bodies of the Framework Convention, the United Nations Convention to Combat Desertification in Those Countries Experiencing Serious Drought and/or Desertification, Particularly in Africa, and the Convention on Biological Diversity, and encourages close cooperation to promote complementarities among the three secretariats while respecting their independent legal status;

15. *Invites* the conferences of the parties to the multilateral environmental conventions, when setting the dates of their meetings, to take into consideration the schedule of meetings of the General Assembly and the Commission on Sustainable Development so as to ensure the adequate representation of developing countries at those meetings;

16. *Invites* the secretariat of the Framework Convention to report, through the Secretary-General, to the General Assembly at its sixty-fifth session on the work of the Conference of the Parties;

17. *Decides* to include in the provisional agenda of its sixty-fifth session the sub-item entitled "Protection of global climate for present and future generations of humankind".

Vienna Convention and Montreal Protocol

As at 31 December, 195 States and the EU were parties to the 1985 Vienna Convention for the Protection of the Ozone Layer [YUN 1985, p. 804], which entered into force in 1988 [YUN 1988, p. 810]. Andorra, San Marino and Timor-Leste became parties during the year.

Parties to the Montreal Protocol on Substances that Deplete the Ozone Layer, which was adopted in 1987 [YUN 1987, p. 686], numbered 195 States and the EU, with Andorra, San Marino and Timor-Leste becoming parties during the year. Parties to the 1990 Amendment to the Protocol [YUN 1990, p. 522] numbered 193 States and the EU, with Andorra, Brunei Darussalam, Ethiopia, San Marino and Timor-Leste becoming parties. Parties to the 1992 Amendment [YUN 1992, p. 684] numbered 190 States and the EU, with Andorra, Brunei Darussalam, Ethiopia, Myanmar, San Marino, Tajikistan and Timor-Leste becoming parties. Parties to the 1997 Amendment [YUN 1997, p. 1050] numbered 178 States and the EU, with Andorra, Brunei Darussalam, Cameroon, the Dominican Republic, Ethiopia, Malawi, Qatar, San Marino, Saint Vincent and the Grenadines, Tajikistan and Timor-Leste becoming parties. Parties to the 1999 Amendment [YUN 1999, p. 986] numbered 160 States and the EU, with Andorra, Brunei Darussalam, Cameroon, the Dominican Republic, Egypt, Ethiopia, Malawi, Qatar, San Marino, Saint Kitts and Nevis, Saint Vincent and the Grenadines, Tajikistan, Timor-Leste and Yemen becoming parties.

The twenty-first meeting of the Parties to the Montreal Protocol (Port Ghalib, Egypt, 4–8 November) [UNEP/OzL.Pro.21/8] adopted 32 decisions, including on environmentally sound alternatives to HCFCs, environmentally sound management of banks of ozone-depleting substances, methyl bromide and management and reduction of remaining uses of halons.

The Implementation Committee under the Non-Compliance Procedure held its forty-second (Geneva, 20–21 July) [UNEP/OzL.Pro.ImpCom/42/5] and forty-third meetings (Port Ghalib, 31 October–1 November) [UNEP/OzL.Pro.ImpCom/43/5].

Convention on air pollution

As at 31 December, the number of parties to the 1979 Convention on Long-range Transboundary Air Pollution [YUN 1979, p. 710], which entered into force in 1983 [YUN 1983, p. 645], remained at 50 States and the EU. Eight protocols to the Convention dealt with the programme for monitoring and evaluation of pollutants in Europe (1984); the reduction of sulphur emissions or their transboundary fluxes by at least 30 per cent (1985); the control of emissions of nitrogen oxides or their transboundary fluxes (1988); the control of volatile organic compounds or their transboundary fluxes (1991); the further reduction of sulphur emissions (1994); heavy metals (1998); persistent organic pollutants (1998); and the abatement of acidification, eutrophication and ground-level ozone (1999).

The twenty-seventh session of the Executive Body for the Convention (Geneva, 14–18 December) [ECE/EB.AIR/99 & Add.1,2] adopted amendments of: the text of and annexes I, II, III, IV, VI and VIII to the 1998 Protocol on Persistent Organic Pollutants [ECE/EB.AIR/99/Add.1 (dec. 2009/1)]; the listing of short-chain chlorinated paraffins and polychlorinated naphtalenes in annexes I and II to the Protocol [dec. 2009/2]; and the text of annexes V and VII to the Protocol [dec. 2009/3]. The amendments would enter into force for the parties which accepted them 90 days after the date on which two thirds of the parties had deposited their instruments of acceptance thereof. As at 31 December, no State had deposited its instrument of acceptance to either of the amendments.

Convention on Biological Diversity

As at 31 December, 192 States and the EU were parties to the 1992 Convention on Biological Diversity [YUN 1992, p. 683], which entered into force in 1993 [YUN 1993, p. 810]. Iraq and Somalia became parties during the year.

At year's end, the number of parties to the Cartagena Protocol on Biosafety, which was adopted in 2000 [YUN 2000, p. 973] and entered into force in 2003 [YUN 2003, p. 1051], stood at 157 States and the EU. Angola, Bosnia and Herzegovina, Comoros, Malawi and Pakistan became parties during the year.

The Subsidiary Body on Scientific, Technical and Technological Advice did not meet in 2009.

Science-policy interface

Pursuant to a request of the ad hoc international and multi-stakeholder meeting on an intergovernmental science-policy platform on biodiversity and ecosystem services [YUN 2008, p. 1159], the UNEP Executive Director in January submitted a report [UNEP/GC.25/INF/30] on the preliminary gap analysis carried out by UNEP to facilitate discussions on improving the science-policy interface for biodiversity and ecosystem services for human well-being.

The Governing Council in February [A/64/25 (dec. 25/10)] invited Governments and organizations to explore mechanisms to improve the science-policy interface for biodiversity and ecosystem services for the conservation and sustainable use of biodiversity, long-term human well-being and sustainable development. It requested the Executive Director to support those efforts by Governments and organizations; report on progress at the special session on biodiversity of the sixty-fifth (2010) session of the General Assembly; and convene a second intergovernmental and multi-stakeholder meeting in 2009 following completion of the full gap analysis on exploring mechanisms to improve the interface.

Participants at the second ad hoc intergovernmental and multi-stakeholder meeting on an intergovernmental science-policy platform on biodiversity and ecosystem services (Nairobi, 5–9 October) [UNEP/GCSS.XI/7] considered the findings of the full gap analysis on science-policy interfaces on biodiversity and ecosystem services. There was recognition that the science-policy interface could be improved by strengthening existing mechanisms, but a new mechanism could add value in areas in which strengthening was inadequate. The Chair's summary of the meeting was annexed to the report.

International Year of Biodiversity

In February, recalling General Assembly resolution 61/203 [YUN 2006, p. 1225], by which the Assembly declared 2010 the "International Year of Biodiversity", the Council [dec. 25/3] invited Governments and organizations to undertake appropriate activities to celebrate the Year and to contribute to the success of the tenth meeting (2010) of the Conference of the Parties to the Convention on Biological Diversity.

On 21 December [meeting 66], the General Assembly, on the recommendation of the Second Committee [A/64/420/Add.6], adopted **resolution 64/203** without vote [agenda item 53 (f)].

Convention on Biological Diversity

The General Assembly,

Recalling its resolutions 55/201 of 20 December 2000, 61/204 of 20 December 2006, 62/194 of 19 December 2007 and 63/219 of 19 December 2008 and other previous resolutions relating to the Convention on Biological Diversity,

Recalling also its resolution 61/203 of 20 December 2006 on the International Year of Biodiversity in 2010,

Reiterating that the Convention is the key international instrument for the conservation and sustainable use of biological resources and the fair and equitable sharing of benefits arising from the use of genetic resources,

Recognizing the potential contribution of other multilateral environmental agreements, including the biodiversity-related conventions, and of international organizations in support of the three objectives of the Convention,

Noting both the positive and the negative impacts of climate change mitigation and adaptation activities on biodiversity and relevant ecosystems,

Noting also that one hundred and ninety-two States and one regional economic integration organization have ratified the Convention and that one hundred and forty-seven States and one regional economic integration organization have ratified the Cartagena Protocol on Biosafety to the Convention on Biological Diversity,

Recognizing that the achievement of the three objectives of the Convention is important for sustainable development and poverty eradication and is a major factor underpinning the achievement of the internationally agreed development goals, including the Millennium Development Goals,

Recalling the commitments of the World Summit on Sustainable Development to pursue a more efficient and coherent implementation of the three objectives of the Convention and the achievement by 2010 of a significant reduction in the current rate of loss of biological diversity, which will require action at all levels, including the implementation of national biodiversity strategies and action plans and the provision of new and additional financial and technical resources to developing countries,

Recognizing the continuing need for greater progress in the implementation of obligations and commitments under the Convention by States parties in order to achieve its objectives, and, in this regard, emphasizing the need to comprehensively address the obstacles that impede the full implementation of the Convention at the national, regional and global levels,

Reaffirming that the fair and equitable sharing of the benefits arising out of the utilization of genetic resources is one of the three objectives of the Convention,

Recalling, in this regard, the 2005 World Summit Outcome, in which all States reaffirmed their engagement to fulfil commitments and significantly reduce the rate of loss of biodiversity by 2010 and continue ongoing efforts towards elaborating and negotiating an international regime on access to genetic resources and benefit-sharing,

Noting the need for enhanced cooperation among the Convention on Biological Diversity, the United Nations Convention to Combat Desertification in Those Countries Experiencing Serious Drought and/or Desertification, Particularly in Africa, and the United Nations Framework Convention on Climate Change (the "Rio Conventions"), while respecting their individual mandates, concerned by the negative impacts that loss of biodiversity, desertification, land degradation and climate change have on each other, and recognizing the potential benefits of complementarities in addressing these problems in a mutually supportive manner with a view to achieving the objectives of the Convention on Biological Diversity,

Acknowledging the contribution that the ongoing work of the Intergovernmental Committee on Intellectual Property and Genetic Resources, Traditional Knowledge and Folklore, of the World Intellectual Property Organization, can make in enhancing the effective implementation of the provisions of the Convention on Biological Diversity,

Noting the important contribution that South-South cooperation can make in the area of biological diversity,

Recalling its resolution 63/219, in which it decided to convene, during its sixty-fifth session in 2010, as a contribution to the International Year of Biodiversity, a high-level meeting of the General Assembly, with the participation of Heads of State and Government,

Convinced that the high-level meeting of the General Assembly on biodiversity, to be convened at its sixty-fifth session in 2010, with the participation of Heads of State, Governments and delegations, as a contribution to the International Year of Biodiversity, provides a valuable opportunity to generate awareness at the highest level of the three objectives of the Convention on Biological Diversity,

Taking note of the reports of the Millennium Ecosystem Assessment,

Noting the continuing efforts of the Life Web initiative promoted by the Government of Germany and other countries,

Noting also the initiative launched at the meeting of the environment ministers of the Group of Eight in Potsdam, Germany, in March 2007, to develop a study on the economic cost of the global loss of biodiversity,

1. *Takes note* of the report of the Executive Secretary of the Convention on Biological Diversity on the work of the Conference of the Parties to the Convention;

2. *Urges* all Member States to fulfil their commitments to significantly reduce the rate of loss of biodiversity by 2010, and emphasizes that this will require an appropriate focus on the loss of biodiversity in their relevant policies and programmes and the continued provision of new and additional financial and technical resources to developing countries, including through the Global Environment Facility;

3. *Urges* the parties to the Convention on Biological Diversity to facilitate the transfer of technology for the effective implementation of the Convention in accordance with its provisions, and in this regard takes note of the strategy for the practical implementation of the programme of work on technology transfer and scientific and technological cooperation developed by the Ad Hoc Technical Expert Group on Technology Transfer and Scientific and Tech-

nological Cooperation, as a preliminary basis for concrete activities by parties and international organizations;

4. *Takes note* of decision IX/12 of the Conference of the Parties to the Convention, on access and benefit-sharing, and the annexes thereto, by which the Conference established a road map for the negotiations set out in that decision and, inter alia:

(*a*) Reiterated its instruction to the Ad Hoc Open-ended Working Group on Access and Benefit-sharing to complete the elaboration and negotiation of the international access and benefit-sharing regime at the earliest possible time before the tenth meeting of the Conference of the Parties to the Convention, in accordance with decisions VII/19 D and VIII/4 A;

(*b*) Further instructed the Working Group to finalize the international regime and to submit for consideration and adoption by the Conference of the Parties to the Convention at its tenth meeting an instrument or instruments to effectively implement the provisions of articles 15 and 8 (*j*) of the Convention and its three objectives, without in any way prejudging or precluding any outcome regarding the nature of such instrument or instruments;

5. *Notes with appreciation*, in this regard, the progress made thus far in the Working Group, invites the Working Group to finalize the international regime, as instructed by the Conference of the Parties, emphasizes the importance of the meeting of the Working Group to be held in March 2010, and in this regard also notes with appreciation the offer of Colombia to host the meeting;

6. *Underlines* the need to strengthen the science-policy interface for biodiversity, and in this regard notes the discussions on an intergovernmental platform on biodiversity and ecosystem services and the holding of the second ad hoc intergovernmental and multi-stakeholder meeting on an intergovernmental science-policy platform on biodiversity and ecosystem services, in Nairobi from 5 to 9 October 2009;

7. *Notes* the ongoing work of the Heads of Agencies Task Force on the 2010 Biodiversity Target, of the chairpersons of the scientific advisory bodies of the biodiversity-related conventions and of the Joint Liaison Group of the secretariats and offices of the relevant subsidiary bodies of the United Nations Framework Convention on Climate Change, the United Nations Convention to Combat Desertification in Those Countries Experiencing Serious Drought and/or Desertification, Particularly in Africa, and the Convention on Biological Diversity, aimed at enhancing scientific and technical collaboration for achieving the 2010 biodiversity target;

8. *Encourages* the efforts being made to implement the seven thematic programmes of work, as established by the Conference of the Parties to the Convention on Biological Diversity, as well as the ongoing work on cross-cutting issues;

9. *Encourages* all parties to the Convention to continue to contribute to the discussions leading to an updated strategic plan for the Convention to be adopted at the tenth meeting of the Conference of the Parties, bearing in mind that this strategic plan should cover all three objectives of the Convention, and emphasizes that the revision of the strategic plan beyond 2010 is important for the enhanced implementation of the Convention;

10. *Notes* the progress made in developing a multi-year plan of action on biodiversity for development based on the framework for South-South cooperation;

11. *Reaffirms* the commitment, subject to national legislation, to respect, preserve and maintain the knowledge, innovations and practices of indigenous and local communities embodying traditional lifestyles relevant to the conservation and sustainable use of biological diversity, promote their wider application with the approval and involvement of the holders of such knowledge, innovations and practices and encourage the equitable sharing of the benefits arising from their utilization;

12. *Notes* the adoption by the Conference of the Parties at its ninth meeting of a strategy for resource mobilization in support of the achievement of the three objectives of the Convention, and, in accordance with Conference of the Parties decision IX/11 and the annexes thereto, invites parties that have not yet done so to submit, to the secretariat of the Convention, views on concrete activities and initiatives, including measurable targets and/or indicators to achieve the strategic goals contained in the strategy, and on indicators to monitor its implementation;

13. *Takes note* of decision IX/20 of the Conference of the Parties on marine and coastal biodiversity, and the annexes thereto, by which the Conference, inter alia, adopted a set of scientific criteria for identifying ecologically or biologically significant marine areas in need of protection, contained in annex I to the decision, and scientific guidance for designing representative networks of marine protected areas, contained in annex II;

14. *Stresses* the importance of private-sector engagement for the implementation of the three objectives of the Convention and in achieving biodiversity targets, and invites businesses to align their policies and practices more explicitly with the objectives of the Convention, including through partnerships;

15. *Notes* the development of the gender plan of action under the Convention, and invites parties to support the implementation of the plan by the Convention secretariat;

16. *Takes note* of decision IX/16 of the Conference of the Parties on biodiversity and climate change, and the annexes thereto, by which the Conference, inter alia, established an Ad Hoc Technical Expert Group on Biodiversity and Climate Change with a mandate to develop scientific and technical advice on biodiversity insofar as it relates to climate change;

17. *Also takes note* of the report of the Ad Hoc Technical Expert Group on Biodiversity and Climate Change, established by the Conference of the Parties in its decision IX/16 on biodiversity and climate change;

18. *Further takes note* of the ongoing work of the Joint Liaison Group of the secretariats and offices of the relevant subsidiary bodies of the United Nations Framework Convention on Climate Change, the United Nations Convention to Combat Desertification in Those Countries Experiencing Serious Drought and/or Desertification, Particularly in Africa, and the Convention on Biological Diversity, and further encourages continuing cooperation in order to promote complementarities among the secretariats while respecting their independent legal status;

19. *Encourages* developed countries parties to the Convention on Biological Diversity to contribute to the relevant trust funds of the Convention so as to enhance the full participation of the developing countries parties in all of its activities;

20. *Invites* the countries that have not yet done so to ratify or accede to the Convention;

21. *Invites* parties to the Convention that have not yet ratified or acceded to the Cartagena Protocol on Biosafety to consider doing so, reiterates the commitment of States parties to the Protocol to support its implementation, and stresses that this will require the full support of parties and of relevant international organizations, in particular with regard to the provision of assistance to developing countries in capacity-building for biosafety;

22. *Invites* countries to consider ratifying or acceding to the International Treaty on Plant Genetic Resources for Food and Agriculture;

23. *Decides*, in follow-up to its resolution 63/219, to convene the one-day high-level meeting as close as possible to the opening of the general debate of the sixty-fifth session of the General Assembly, as a contribution to the International Year of Biodiversity, and in that regard:

(*a*) Encourages all Member States to be represented at the highest possible level, including by Heads of State or Government;

(*b*) Invites heads of the United Nations funds and programmes, the specialized agencies and regional commissions, as well as heads of intergovernmental organizations and entities having observer status in the General Assembly, as well as the biodiversity-related multilateral environmental agreements, to participate, as appropriate, in the meeting, in accordance with the rules and procedures established by the General Assembly;

(*c*) Decides that the President of the General Assembly will consult with representatives of non-governmental organizations in consultative status with the Economic and Social Council, civil society organizations and the private sector, and with Member States, as appropriate, on the list of representatives of non-governmental organizations, civil society organizations and the private sector that may participate in the meeting;

(*d*) Decides that the meeting will be structured around an opening plenary meeting followed by thematic panels in the morning and the afternoon, organized within existing resources, which will address in a balanced manner the three objectives of the Convention on Biological Diversity;

(*e*) Decides also that the meeting will be chaired by the President of the General Assembly and requests the President to prepare a summary of the discussions held during the high-level meeting, for presentation at the closing plenary and for transmission, under his authority, to the tenth session of the Conference of the Parties, to be held in Nagoya, Japan, in October 2010, as a contribution to raising awareness of the three objectives of the Convention;

(*f*) Requests the Secretary-General to prepare a background paper for the high-level meeting, in consultation with Member States;

24. *Encourages* all Member States, relevant regional and international organizations, major groups and other stakeholders to support, as appropriate, the International

Year of Biodiversity in 2010, including through voluntary contributions, taking advantage of the Year to increase awareness of the importance of biodiversity for the achievement of sustainable development;

25. *Encourages* all relevant organs of the United Nations, including functional commissions and regional commissions, as well as all United Nations agencies, funds and programmes, to fully support, contribute to and participate in, as appropriate, the activities envisaged for the observance of 2010 as the International Year of Biodiversity, taking into consideration the strategy and implementation plan for the commemoration of the Year prepared by the secretariat of the Convention on Biological Diversity, including through a special event or special focus in their annual governing body meetings or high-level ministerial segments and in their annual flagship publications scheduled for 2010;

26. *Recognizes* the importance of the fifth meeting of the Conference of the Parties serving as the Meeting of the Parties to the Cartagena Protocol on Biosafety, to be held in Nagoya, Japan, from 11 to 15 October 2010, and the tenth meeting of the Conference of the Parties to the Convention on Biological Diversity, to be held in Nagoya from 18 to 29 October 2010;

27. *Invites* the secretariat of the Convention to report, through the Secretary-General, to the General Assembly at its sixty-fifth session on the work of the Conference of the Parties;

28. *Requests* the Secretary-General to include in his report to be submitted to the General Assembly at its sixty-sixth session information on the implementation of resolution 61/203 and the parts of the present resolution relevant to the commemoration of 2010 as the International Year of Biodiversity;

29. *Decides* to include in the provisional agenda of its sixty-fifth session, under the item entitled "Sustainable development", the sub-item entitled "Convention on Biological Diversity".

Convention to combat desertification

As at 31 December, the number of parties to the 1994 United Nations Convention to Combat Desertification in Those Countries Experiencing Serious Drought and/or Desertification, Particularly in Africa (UNCCD) [YUN 1994, p. 944], which entered into force in 1996 [YUN 1996, p. 958], remained at 193 States and the EU.

The eighth session of the Committee for the Review of the Implementation of the Convention (CRIC) (Buenos Aires, Argentina, 23–24 September, 30 September and 1 October) [ICCD/COP(9)/18 & Add.1], which was held concurrently with the ninth session of the Conference of the Parties to the Convention, considered, among other issues, improving the procedures for communication of information as well as the quality and format of reports to be submitted to the Conference of the Parties; and a project proposal for assistance to affected country parties in monitoring implementation of the Convention.

The ninth session of the Conference of the Parties to the Convention (Buenos Aires, 21 September–2 October) [ICCD/COP(9)/18 & Add.1 & Corr.1] adopted 36 decisions, including on: mechanisms to facilitate regional coordination of the implementation of the Convention; new terms of reference for CRIC; reshaping the operation of the Committee on Science and Technology; collaboration with the Global Environment Facility; multi-year workplans for the UNCCD institutions and subsidiary bodies; bringing the implementation of the strategy in a result-based management framework; and the adoption of a minimum set of impact indicators, which paved the way towards target-setting using the agreed indicators to effectively halt and reverse desertification, land degradation and mitigate the effects of drought.

The Conference of the Parties [ICCD/COP(9)/18/Add.1 (dec. 6/COP.9)] requested: the UNCCD secretariat and the Global Mechanism of the Convention to produce a report containing a work programme and the cost estimate involved in the context of the biennium and medium-term work programme and plan; and the Mechanism to prepare detailed regional work programmes, as well as criteria and guidelines for allocating financial resources from Mechanism funds to affected developing country parties. It also requested an evaluation of existing and potential reporting, accountability and institutional arrangements for the Mechanism, including the possibility of identifying a new institution or organization to house it, taking into account the scenarios presented in the JIU report on the Mechanism (see below) and the need to avoid duplication in the work of the secretariat and the Mechanism. The Bureau of the Conference of the Parties was requested to submit to the tenth (2011) session of the Conference of the Parties a report on the evaluation for consideration and decision on the issue of reporting, accountability and institutional arrangements for the Mechanism.

The Committee on Science and Technology held its ninth session in Buenos Aires concurrently with CRIC. The session included the UNCCD first scientific conference [ICCD/COP(9)/CST/INF.2 & ICCD/COP(9)/CST/INF.3].

JIU report. The Secretary-General in September [A/64/379] transmitted to the General Assembly the JIU report entitled "Assessment of the Global Mechanism of the United Nations Convention to Combat Desertification" [JIU/REP/2009/4]. The inspectors made recommendations for the Conference of the Parties to clearly conceptualize the intended scope of the Convention and agree on the interpretation of key issues, and for the mechanisms identified for resource mobilization to closely interact with the subsidiary bodies of the Convention, avoiding duplication of their technical and policy advisory role, fostering complementarities and focusing on their specific financial role. The inspectors reported that the Global Mechanism had not sufficiently explored the work already undertaken by other partners, in particular UNEP and its country environmental assessments. On reporting and accountability, although contributions were fully reflected in reports, the inspectors hardly found transparent breakdown information on the end use of those funds, particularly the use of the special resources for Convention finance. JIU also recommended that: the Global Mechanism and the UNCCD secretariat should submit a report to the Conference of the Parties containing a work programme and the cost estimate for their future biennium and medium-term work programme and plan, so that the Conference could exercise governance and oversight over voluntary contributions and core resources; the Mechanism should develop quantitative performance indicators by compiling data and information on the financial resources mobilized as a result of its country and regional interventions; and the Conference should guide the Mechanism in defining a work programme that avoided duplication and overlapping with the mandates of other organizations and bodies. The inspectors proposed three scenarios for enhancing coordination and effectiveness of the implementation of the Convention: improving the status quo; institutional merging of the permanent secretariat and the Global Mechanism; and converting the Global Mechanism into a desertification and land degradation fund.

GENERAL ASSEMBLY ACTION

On 21 December [meeting 66], the General Assembly, on the recommendation of the Second Committee [A/64/420/Add.5], adopted **resolution 64/202** without vote [agenda item 53 *(e)*].

Implementation of the United Nations Convention to Combat Desertification in Those Countries Experiencing Serious Drought and/or Desertification, Particularly in Africa

The General Assembly,

Recalling its resolutions 58/211 of 23 December 2003, 61/202 of 20 December 2006, 62/193 of 19 December 2007, 63/218 of 19 December 2008 and other resolutions relating to the implementation of the United Nations Convention to Combat Desertification in Those Countries Experiencing Serious Drought and/or Desertification, Particularly in Africa,

Reasserting its commitment to combating and reversing desertification and land degradation in arid, semi-arid and dry sub-humid areas, consistent with articles 1, 2 and 3 of the Convention, and to mitigating the effects of drought, eradicating extreme poverty, promoting sustainable development and food security and improving the livelihoods of vulnerable people affected by drought and/or desertifica-

tion, taking into account the ten-year strategic plan and framework to enhance the implementation of the Convention (2008–2018),

Reaffirming the universal membership of the Convention, and acknowledging that desertification, land degradation and drought are problems of a global dimension in that they affect all regions of the world,

Taking note with appreciation of the decision adopted in Sirte, Libyan Arab Jamahiriya, on 3 July 2009 by the Assembly of Heads of State and Government of the African Union at its thirteenth ordinary session, authorizing the African Union to accede to the Convention,

Reaffirming the Plan of Implementation of the World Summit on Sustainable Development ("Johannesburg Plan of Implementation"), in which the Convention is recognized as one of the tools for poverty eradication, and reiterating its resolve to eradicate extreme poverty,

Noting the need for enhanced cooperation among the United Nations Convention to Combat Desertification in Those Countries Experiencing Serious Drought and/or Desertification, Particularly in Africa, the United Nations Framework Convention on Climate Change and the Convention on Biological Diversity ("the Rio Conventions"), while respecting their individual mandates,

Welcoming the outcomes of the seventeenth session of the Commission on Sustainable Development regarding desertification, land degradation and drought,

Concerned by the increasing frequency and severity of dust/sandstorms affecting arid and semi-arid regions and their negative impact on the environment and the economy,

Concerned also by the negative impacts that desertification, land degradation, loss of biodiversity and climate change have on each other, recognizing the potential benefits of complementarities in addressing these problems in a mutually supportive manner, and recognizing also the interrelationship between climate change, loss of biodiversity and desertification and the need to intensify efforts to combat desertification and promote sustainable land management,

Recognizing the need for investment in sustainable land management in arid, semi-arid and dry sub-humid areas, and emphasizing the need for the full implementation of the ten-year strategic plan and framework,

Recognizing also the need to strengthen the scientific basis underpinning the Convention,

Recognizing further the importance given by the ten-year strategic plan and framework to the development and implementation of scientifically based and sound methods for monitoring and assessing desertification,

Expressing its deep appreciation to the Government of Argentina for hosting the ninth session of the Conference of the Parties to the Convention in Buenos Aires from 21 September to 2 October 2009,

Welcoming the offer of the Government of the Republic of Korea to host the tenth session of the Conference of the Parties to the Convention in Changwon City, Gyeongnam Province, in autumn 2011,

1. *Takes note* of the report of the Secretary-General on the implementation of the United Nations Convention to Combat Desertification in Those Countries Experiencing Serious Drought and/or Desertification, Particularly in Africa;

2. *Welcomes* the outcome of the seventeenth session of the Commission on Sustainable Development and its policy recommendations, particularly those related to the strengthening of the institutional policy framework and the implementation of practical measures to combat land degradation and desertification in arid, semi-arid and dry sub-humid areas, enhancing capacity-building, transfer of technology and financing;

3. *Recognizes* the cross-sectoral nature of desertification, land degradation and drought mitigation, and in this regard invites all relevant United Nations agencies to cooperate with the Convention in supporting an effective response to desertification and drought;

4. *Invites* Member States to continue to integrate plans and strategies related to drought, desertification and land degradation into their national development and poverty eradication strategies, as appropriate;

5. *Welcomes* the decision of the Conference of the Parties on the promotion and strengthening of relationships between the United Nations Convention to Combat Desertification and other relevant conventions and international organizations, institutions and agencies;

6. *Notes* the ongoing work of the Joint Liaison Group of the secretariats and offices of the relevant subsidiary bodies of the United Nations Framework Convention on Climate Change, the Convention on Biological Diversity and the United Nations Convention to Combat Desertification, and encourages continuing cooperation in order to promote complementarities in the work of the secretariats, while respecting their independent legal status;

7. *Encourages* actions to promote sustainable management of soil as one means for mitigating the effects of drought in arid, semi-arid and dry sub-humid areas;

8. *Invites* Member States and related organizations to cooperate in sharing information, forecasting and early warning systems related to dust/sandstorms;

9. *Takes note* of the launch of the Global Network of Dryland Research Institutes in Buenos Aires in September 2009 during the ninth session of the Conference of the Parties to the Convention, which aims to promote research, education, training and outreach relevant to the sustainable use of drylands;

10. *Expresses its appreciation* to the Committee on Science and Technology, and, in this respect, welcomes the outcome of the first United Nations Convention to Combat Desertification Scientific Conference, held in the context of the ninth session of the Conference of the Parties to the Convention;

11. *Takes note* of the report of the Joint Inspection Unit on the assessment of the Global Mechanism of the United Nations Convention to Combat Desertification as well as the decision of the Conference of the Parties at its ninth session requesting the Bureau of the ninth session, together with the Managing Director of the Global Mechanism and the Executive Secretary, and taking into account the views of other interested relevant entities such as the host countries and the International Fund for Agricultural Development, to undertake and supervise an evaluation of existing and potential reporting, accountability and institutional arrangements for the Global Mechanism and their legal and financial implications, including the possibility of identifying a new institution or organization to house the Global Mechanism, taking into account the scenarios presented in the Joint Inspection Unit assessment of the Global Mechanism and the need to avoid duplication and overlap in the work of the secretariat of the Convention and the Global Mechanism, and further requesting the Bureau to submit to the Conference of the Parties at its tenth session a report on this evaluation for consideration and decision on the issue of reporting, accountability and institutional arrangements for the Global Mechanism;

12. *Requests* all States parties to the Convention to promote awareness among local populations, particularly women, youth and civil society organizations, and to include them in, the implementation of the ten-year strategic plan and framework to enhance the implementation of the Convention (2008–2018), and encourages affected States parties and donors to take into account the issue of participation of civil society in Convention processes when setting priorities in national development strategies, in conformity, inter alia, with the comprehensive communication strategy adopted by the Conference of the Parties at its ninth session;

13. *Invites* donors to the Global Environment Facility to ensure that the Facility is adequately resourced during the next replenishment period in order to allow it to allocate sufficient and adequate resources to its six focal areas, in particular its land degradation focal area;

14. *Welcomes* the ongoing efforts of the Executive Secretary of the Convention to continue the administrative renewal and reform of the secretariat and to realign its functions in order to fully implement the relevant decisions of the Conference of the Parties and bring those functions into line with the ten-year strategic plan and framework;

15. *Decides* to include in the United Nations calendar of conferences and meetings for the biennium 2010–2011 the sessions of the Conference of the Parties and its subsidiary bodies envisaged for the biennium;

16. *Requests* the Secretary-General to make provisions for the sessions of the Conference of the Parties and its subsidiary bodies in his proposal for the programme budget for the biennium 2010–2011;

17. *Decides* to include in the provisional agenda of its sixty-fifth session the sub-item entitled "Implementation of the United Nations Convention to Combat Desertification in Those Countries Experiencing Serious Drought and/or Desertification, Particularly in Africa";

18. *Requests* the Secretary-General to submit to the General Assembly at its sixty-fifth session a report on the implementation of the present resolution, including a report on the implementation of the Convention.

United Nations Decade for Deserts and the Fight against Desertification (2010–2020)

The General Assembly, by resolution 62/195 [YUN 2007, p. 1046], declared the decade 2010–2020 as the United Nations Decade for Deserts and the Fight against Desertification. In December, the Assembly designated the UNCCD secretariat as the focal point for the Decade, in collaboration with UNEP, UNDP, the International Fund for Agricultural Development and other relevant UN entities (see below).

GENERAL ASSEMBLY ACTION

On 21 December [meeting 66], the General Assembly, on the recommendation of the Second Committee [A/64/420/Add.5], adopted **resolution 64/201** without vote [agenda item 53 (e)].

United Nations Decade for Deserts and the Fight against Desertification (2010–2020)

The General Assembly,

Recalling its resolution 58/211 of 23 December 2003, in which it declared 2006 the International Year of Deserts and Desertification,

Recalling also its resolution 62/195 of 19 December 2007, in which it decided to declare the decade 2010–2020 as the United Nations Decade for Deserts and the Fight against Desertification, based on the recommendation of the Governing Council of the United Nations Environment Programme at its twenty-fourth session,

Recalling further its resolutions 61/202 of 20 December 2006, 62/193 of 19 December 2007 and 63/218 of 19 December 2008 and other resolutions relating to the implementation of the United Nations Convention to Combat Desertification in Those Countries Experiencing Serious Drought and/or Desertification, Particularly in Africa,

Recalling the 2005 World Summit Outcome,

Deeply concerned about the deteriorating situation of desertification in all regions, particularly in Africa, and its far-reaching implications for the achievement of the internationally agreed development goals, including the Millennium Development Goals, in particular the eradication of poverty and ensuring environmental sustainability,

Responding to the call of the Conference of the Parties to the Convention at its ninth session for the implementation of the United Nations Decade for Deserts and the Fight against Desertification,

Taking into account the success of the International Year of Deserts and Desertification, 2006, in raising awareness of desertification, land degradation and drought,

Committed to raising the awareness of desertification, land degradation and drought at all levels, consistent with the ten-year strategic plan and framework to enhance the implementation of the Convention (2008–2018),

1. *Recalls* its decision to declare the decade 2010–2020 as the United Nations Decade for Deserts and the Fight against Desertification;

2. *Designates* the secretariat of the United Nations Convention to Combat Desertification in Those Countries Experiencing Serious Drought and/or Desertification, Particularly in Africa as the focal point of the Decade, in collaboration with the United Nations Environment Programme, the United Nations Development Programme, the International Fund for Agricultural Development and other relevant bodies of the United Nations, including the Department of Public Information of the Secretariat;

3. *Invites* States parties to the Convention, observers and other relevant stakeholders to organize activities to observe the Decade with the aim of raising awareness of the causes of and solutions to ongoing land degradation and desertification in the framework of the ten-year strategic plan and framework to enhance implementation of the Convention (2008–2018);

4. *Encourages* Member States and multilateral agencies in a position to do so to support the secretariat of the Convention financially and technically, with a view to supporting special initiatives in observance of the Decade as well as other observance events and activities worldwide;

5. *Requests* the Secretary-General to report to the General Assembly at its sixty-ninth session on the status of the implementation of the present resolution.

Environmental activities

The atmosphere

High-level summit. The Secretary-General convened a high-level summit on climate change (New York, 22 September) to mobilize the political will and vision needed to reach a substantive agreed outcome at the UN climate talks in Copenhagen (see p. 1015). World leaders gathered to discuss the status of climate negotiations. In his closing remarks [SG/SM/12470], the Secretary-General stated that the message from the Summit was clear that the Copenhagen deal must be comprehensive and ensure enhanced action to assist the most vulnerable and the poorest to adapt to the impacts of climate change; ambitious emission-reduction targets for industrialized countries; nationally appropriate mitigation actions by developing countries with the necessary support; significantly scaled-up financial and technological resources; and an equitable governance structure. He also indicated his intention to set up a high-level panel after the Copenhagen Conference to advise on how to better integrate climate change adaptation and mitigation into development.

Communication. On 20 October [A/C.2/64/11], Grenada, as Chair of the Alliance of Small Island States (AOSIS), transmitted the AOSIS Declaration on Climate Change, adopted by the Heads of State and Government, ministers and heads of delegations at the AOSIS Summit on Climate Change (New York, 21 September).

Intergovernmental Panel on Climate Change

The thirtieth session of the Intergovernmental Panel on Climate Change (IPCC) (Antalya, Turkey, 21–23 April) was attended by approximately 320 participants and focused mainly on the "scoping process"—identifying issues that should be prioritised for further examination in subsequent stages—for the Fifth Assessment Report (AR5), with a view to providing guidance to the climate change experts who would define the outline of the Report during its scoping meeting (Venice, Italy, 13–17 July). The Panel adopted proposals on the near-term future of IPCC and the scoping of AR5; decided to proceed with the preparation of a special report on managing the risks of extreme events and disasters; and agreed to hold expert meetings on topics such as human settlements and the detection and attribution of anthropogenic climate change. Other issues addressed included the revised rules of procedure for the election of the IPCC Bureau and the Task Force Bureau, work on new scenarios and the IPCC Peace Prize Scholarship Fund.

The thirty-first IPCC session (Bali, Indonesia, 26–29 October), attended by some 350 participants, continued to focus primarily on the scoping of AR5. During the meeting, the three IPCC working groups approved the proposed chapter outlines of the working groups' contributions to AR5, which had been developed at the Venice scoping meeting in July. The Panel accepted the outlines of the working groups' reports and considered other issues relevant to the scope of AR5. The Panel discussed progress on involving scientists from developing countries and countries with economies in transition and the use of electronic technologies. It also granted special observer status to the European Commission.

Security implications of climate change

In a 3 June General Assembly meeting [A/63/PV.85], Nauru provided an overview of the vulnerability of Pacific small island developing States (Pacific SIDS) resulting from the small size of their homelands, the volume of ocean surrounding them, and scientists' predictions that the ocean would continue to rise at an increasing rate. Urgent action was needed to address the possibility of a country submerging as a whole. While no UN Member State had ever disappeared, the international community was faced with the threat of losing many States owing to the adverse effects of climate change. On behalf of the Pacific SIDS (Fiji, Kiribati, Marshall Islands, Micronesia, Nauru, Palau, Papua New Guinea, Samoa, Solomon Islands, Tonga, Tuvalu, Vanuatu), Nauru introduced a draft resolution entitled "Climate change and its possible security implications" to the General Assembly.

GENERAL ASSEMBLY ACTION

On 3 June [meeting 85], the General Assembly adopted **resolution 63/281** [draft: A/63/L.8/Rev.1 & Add.1] without vote [agenda item 107].

Climate change and its possible security implications

The General Assembly,

Recalling its resolution 63/32 of 26 November 2008 and other resolutions relating to the protection of the global climate for present and future generations of mankind,

Recalling also Article 1 of the Charter of the United Nations, which established the purposes of the United Nations,

Recognizing the respective responsibilities of the principal organs of the United Nations, including the primary responsibility for the maintenance of international peace

and security conferred upon the Security Council and the responsibility for sustainable development issues, including climate change, conferred upon the General Assembly and the Economic and Social Council,

Noting the open debate in the Security Council on "Energy, security and climate" held on 17 April 2007,

Reaffirming that the United Nations Framework Convention on Climate Change is the key instrument for addressing climate change,

Recalling the provisions of the United Nations Framework Convention on Climate Change, including the acknowledgement that the global nature of climate change calls for the widest possible cooperation by all countries and their participation in an effective and appropriate international response, in accordance with their common but differentiated responsibilities and respective capabilities and their social and economic conditions,

Reaffirming the Programme of Action for the Sustainable Development of Small Island Developing States, the Mauritius Declaration and the Mauritius Strategy for the Further Implementation of the Programme of Action for the Sustainable Development of Small Island Developing States,

Recalling the 2005 World Summit Outcome,

Deeply concerned that the adverse impacts of climate change, including sea-level rise, could have possible security implications,

1. *Invites* the relevant organs of the United Nations, as appropriate and within their respective mandates, to intensify their efforts in considering and addressing climate change, including its possible security implications;

2. *Requests* the Secretary-General to submit a comprehensive report to the General Assembly at its sixty-fourth session on the possible security implications of climate change, based on the views of the Member States and relevant regional and international organizations.

Report of Secretary-General. Pursuant to Assembly resolution 63/281, the Secretary-General in September submitted a report on climate change and its possible security implications [A/64/350], which summarized the views of 35 Member States, 4 Member State groups and 17 regional and international organizations, including UN agencies and programmes. It identified five channels through which climate change could affect security: vulnerability; development; coping and security; statelessness; and international conflict. Threats arising from those channels were reviewed, including threats to human well-being and economic development; threats from uncoordinated coping; the threat of loss of territory and statelessness; and threats to international cooperation in managing shared resources. It also examined ways of preventing and responding to those threats and outlined the way forward. The need for a comprehensive, fair and effective deal in Copenhagen was emphasized. The report further identified emerging climate change-related threats which merited the attention and increased preparedness of the international community, including, among others, the melting of glaciers and disputes surrounding the opening of the Arctic region to resource exploitation and trade.

Terrestrial ecosystems

Rehabilitation of marshes

On 5 March [E/2009/11], Iraq requested the President of the Economic and Social Council to include a sub-item entitled "Rehabilitation of the marshes in the southern regions of Iraq" under the agenda item entitled "Economic and environmental questions: sustainable development", due to the need to draw the attention of the international community and regional stakeholders to the ongoing projects by the Government—in collaboration with UN agencies and other countries—to restore the Iraqi marshlands.

On 18 May, the Council included that supplementary sub-item in the provisional agenda of its substantive session of 2009 (**decision 2009/212**); the topic was discussed on 29 July [E/2009/SR.41].

Deforestation and forest degradation

United Nations Forum on Forests

The United Nations Forum on Forests (UNFF), at its eighth session (New York, 27 April 2007 and 20 April–1 May 2009) [E/2009/42], brought to the attention of the Economic and Social Council a draft resolution on forests in a changing environment, enhanced cooperation and cross-sectoral policy and programme coordination, regional and subregional inputs as well as two decisions. The draft resolution called for, among other things, strengthened implementation of sustainable forest management strategies into relevant programmes and processes, such as those on climate change, biodiversity and water resources management; and on countries to undertake national forest inventories and to use market-based approaches to the production and consumption of products from sustainably managed forests. The Forum recommended draft decisions on the report on its eighth session and on the dates, venue and provisional agenda for its ninth (2011) session. It also accredited observer status to one intergovernmental organization [dec. 8/1] and decided to complete consideration of agenda item 6 at its ninth (2011) session [dec. 8/2] (see below).

The Forum had before it reports of the Secretary-General on: achieving the four global objectives on forests and implementing the non-legally binding instrument on all types of forests [E/CN.18/2009/2]; regional and subregional inputs [E/CN.18/2009/3]; forests and climate change [E/CN.18/2009/4]; reversing the loss of forest cover, preventing forest degradation in all types of forests and combating desertification, including low forest cover countries [E/CN.18/2009/5]; forests and biodiversity conservation, including protected areas [E/CN.18/2009/6]; recommendations for addressing key challenges of forests in a changing en-

vironment [E/CN.18/2009/8]; finance and other means of implementation for sustainable forest management [E/CN.18/2009/9]; and enhanced cooperation and cross-sectoral policy and programme coordination [E/CN.18/2009/10]. Also before the Forum were the Chair's summary report of the meeting of the open-ended ad hoc expert group to develop proposals for the development of a voluntary global financial mechanism/portfolio approach/forest financing network (Vienna, 10–14 November 2008) [E/CN.18/2009/11]; notes by the Secretariat on: forests in a changing environment: low forest cover countries, SIDS and high and medium forest cover countries [E/CN.18/2009/7]; the multi-stakeholder dialogue [E/CN.18/2009/13]; and the United Nations Trust Fund for UNFF [E/CN.18/2009/15]; and an information document on the Collaborative Partnership on Forests Framework 2008 and 2009 [E/CN.18/2009/12].

On 29 July 2009, the Economic and Social Council took note of the report of the Forum on its eighth session, approved the provisional agenda and documentation for the ninth session (**decision 2009/242**) and decided that it would be held in New York from 24 January to 4 February 2011 (**decision 2009/241**).

Also on 29 July 2009, the Council, recalling UNFF [dec. 8/2] of 1 May, by which the Forum decided to complete the consideration at its ninth (2011) session of agenda item 6 (means of implementation for sustainable forest management), based on the bracketed draft text developed in informal consultations during its eighth (2009) session [E/CN.18/2009/WP.1], noted that the Chair of the ninth session intended to undertake informal consultations in order to reach agreement among all Member States on the substantive issues in that text and authorized the holding of a one-day special session for the purpose of adopting the agreed text (**decision 2009/240**).

At the UNFF special session of the ninth session (New York, 30 October) [E/2009/118], the Forum brought to the attention of the Economic and Social Council a resolution on means of implementation for sustainable forest management, which established an open-ended, intergovernmental ad hoc expert group to review all aspects of forest financing and a "facilitative process" on forest financing to assist countries to mobilize funding. The expert group would propose strategies to mobilize resources to support the implementation of sustainable forest management; the achievement of the global objectives on forests; and implementation of the non-legally binding instrument on all types of forests. The facilitative process would assist in mobilizing and supporting new and additional financial resources for sustainable forest management; facilitate transfer of environmentally sound technologies and capacity-building to developing countries; provide advice and share good practices; and enhance coordination, cooperation and coherence among funding sources and mechanisms.

On 15 December, the Economic and Social Council took note of the report on the UNFF special session (**decision 2009/268**).

Communications. Four documents on various 2008 activities were transmitted to UNFF by Governments, including the proceedings of the pan-European workshop "Forests in a changing environment" [E/CN.18/2009/14] from Finland; the report of the international workshop on forest governance and decentralization in Africa [E/CN.18//2009/16] from South Africa and Switzerland; the summary of the conclusions and recommendations of the international expert meeting on financing for sustainable forest management [E/CN.18/2009/17] from Suriname; and the report of the Australian-Swiss region-led initiative in support of the Forum [E/CN.18/2009/18] from Australia and Switzerland.

International Year of Forests, 2011

Pursuant to General Assembly resolution 61/193 [YUN 2006, p. 1240], the Secretary-General in August submitted a preliminary report [A/64/274] on the state of preparations for the International Year of Forests, 2011. The report highlighted initiatives and activities being organized by Governments, the United Nations and other stakeholders to celebrate the Year, and offered recommendations on the next steps, including the convening of a special, one-day high-level event of the Assembly at its sixty-sixth (2011) session in September to generate public awareness and political action towards sustainable forest management.

(For information on illicit international trafficking in forest products, see p. 1107.)

Sustainable mountain development

In response to General Assembly resolution 62/196 [YUN 2007, p. 1073], the Secretary-General submitted a report on sustainable mountain development [A/64/222] prepared by FAO, which described the status of development at the national and international levels, including an analysis of forthcoming challenges; and provided suggestions on promoting and sustaining development in mountain regions around the world within the existing policy context including that found in chapter 13 of Agenda 21 [YUN 1992, p. 672], the Johannesburg Plan of Implementation [YUN 2002, p. 822] and the MDGs.

Since the last report on the topic [YUN 2007, p. 1072], significant progress had been made on several issues—from raising awareness about the global importance of mountains to the strengthening and creation of institutional arrangements and greater col-

laborative international action to address mountain issues. However, much remained to be done, especially in the light of the often rapid and severe impact on mountain areas from climate change, soaring food prices and migration to urban areas. The Secretary-General recommended, among other things: encouraging the establishment of national committees, bodies and mechanisms to strengthen coordination and collaboration for sustainable development in mountain areas; assisting developing countries and countries with economies in transition to formulate and implement national strategies and programmes for sustainable mountain development; promoting the establishment of regional mechanisms for coordinated transboundary cooperation and strengthening existing mechanisms, such as the Alpine Convention and the Carpathian Convention; and encouraging greater engagement by civil society and the private sector in programmes related to sustainable development in mountains. He also recommended increased research efforts to gain a better understanding of the environmental, economic and social drivers of change affecting mountain regions; strengthening the role of women in planning and decision-making in mountain regions; promoting the development of high-quality products and services from mountain areas; and increasing investment and funding for sustainable development in mountain regions through innovative financial mechanisms and approaches, such as debt-for-sustainable development swaps, payment for environmental services and microfinance opportunities.

GENERAL ASSEMBLY ACTION

On 21 December [meeting 66], the General Assembly, on the recommendation of the Second Committee [A/64/420/Add.8], adopted **resolution 64/205** without vote [agenda item 53 *(h)*].

Sustainable mountain development

The General Assembly,

Recalling its resolution 53/24 of 10 November 1998, by which it proclaimed 2002 the International Year of Mountains,

Recalling also its resolutions 55/189 of 20 December 2000, 57/245 of 20 December 2002, 58/216 of 23 December 2003, 59/238 of 22 December 2004, 60/198 of 22 December 2005 and 62/196 of 19 December 2007,

Reaffirming chapter 13 of Agenda 21 and all relevant paragraphs of the Plan of Implementation of the World Summit on Sustainable Development ("Johannesburg Plan of Implementation"), in particular paragraph 42 thereof, as the overall policy frameworks for sustainable development in mountain regions,

Noting the Bishkek Mountain Platform, the outcome document of the Bishkek Global Mountain Summit, held in Bishkek from 28 October to 1 November 2002, which was the concluding event of the International Year of Mountains,

Noting also the International Partnership for Sustainable Development in Mountain Regions ("Mountain Partnership"), launched during the World Summit on Sustainable Development, with benefits from the committed support of fifty countries, sixteen intergovernmental organizations and ninety-six organizations from major groups, as an important multi-stakeholder approach to addressing the various interrelated dimensions of sustainable development in mountain regions,

Noting further the conclusions of the global meetings of the members of the Mountain Partnership, held, respectively, in Merano, Italy, in October 2003 and in Cusco, Peru, in October 2004, and the first Andean Meeting of the Andean Initiative, held in San Miguel Tucuman, Argentina, in September 2007,

Noting the outcome of the meeting of the Adelboden Group on Sustainable Agriculture and Rural Development in Mountain Regions, which met in Rome from 1 to 3 October 2007,

1. *Takes note* of the report of the Secretary-General;

2. *Notes with appreciation* that a growing network of Governments, organizations, major groups and individuals around the world recognize the importance of the sustainable development of mountain regions for poverty eradication, and recognizes the global importance of mountains as the source of most of the Earth's freshwater, as repositories of rich biological diversity and other natural resources, including timber and minerals, as providers of some sources of renewable energy, as popular destinations for recreation and tourism and as areas of important cultural diversity, knowledge and heritage, all of which generate positive, unaccounted economic benefits;

3. *Recognizes* that mountains provide sensitive indications of climate change through phenomena such as modifications of biological diversity, the retreat of mountain glaciers and changes in seasonal runoff that are having an impact on major sources of freshwater in the world, and stresses the need to undertake actions to minimize the negative effects of these phenomena and promote adaptation measures;

4. *Also recognizes* that sustainable mountain development is a key component in achieving the Millennium Development Goals in many regions of the world;

5. *Encourages* greater consideration of sustainable mountain development issues in intergovernmental discussions on climate change, biodiversity loss and combating desertification in the context of the United Nations Framework Convention on Climate Change, the Convention on Biological Diversity, the United Nations Convention to Combat Desertification in Those Countries Experiencing Serious Drought and/or Desertification, Particularly in Africa and the United Nations Forum on Forests;

6. *Notes with concern* that there remain key challenges to achieving sustainable development, eradicating poverty in mountain regions and protecting mountain ecosystems, and that populations in mountain regions are frequently among the poorest in a given country;

7. *Encourages* Governments to adopt a long-term vision and holistic approaches in their sustainable development strategies, and to promote integrated approaches to policies related to sustainable development in mountain regions;

8. *Also encourages* Governments to integrate mountain sustainable development in national, regional and global policymaking and development strategies, including through incorporating mountain-specific requirements in sustainable development policies or through specific mountain policies;

9. *Notes* that the growing demand for natural resources, including water, the consequences of erosion, deforestation and watershed degradation, the frequency and scale of natural disasters, as well as increasing outmigration, the pressures of industry, transport, tourism, mining and agriculture and the consequences of climate change and loss of biodiversity are some of the key challenges in fragile mountain ecosystems to implementing sustainable development and eradicating poverty in mountain regions, consistent with the Millennium Development Goals;

10. *Underlines* the importance of sustainable forest management, the avoidance of deforestation and the restoration of lost and degraded forest ecosystems of mountains in order to enhance the role of mountains as natural carbon and water regulators;

11. *Notes* that sustainable agriculture in mountain regions is important for the protection of the mountain environment and the promotion of the regional economy;

12. *Expresses its deep concern* at the number and scale of natural disasters and their increasing impact in recent years, which have resulted in massive loss of life and long-term negative social, economic and environmental consequences for vulnerable societies throughout the world, in particular in mountain regions, especially those in developing countries, and urges the international community to take concrete steps to support national and regional efforts to ensure the sustainable development of mountains;

13. *Encourages* Governments, the international community and other relevant stakeholders to improve the awareness, preparedness and infrastructure to reduce risks of disasters and to cope with the increasing adverse impact of disasters in mountain regions, such as flash floods, including glacial lake outburst floods, as well as landslides, debris flow and earthquakes and, in this regard, to take advantage of opportunities provided by International Mountain Day on 11 December 2009, which is dedicated to disaster risk management;

14. *Calls upon* Governments, with the collaboration of the scientific community, mountain communities and intergovernmental organizations, where appropriate, to study, with a view to promoting sustainable mountain development, the specific concerns of mountain communities, including the adverse impact of climate change on mountain environments and biological diversity, in order to elaborate sustainable adaptation strategies and subsequently implement adequate measures to cope with the adverse effects of climate change;

15. *Underlines* the fact that action at the national level is a key factor in achieving progress in sustainable mountain development, welcomes its steady increase in recent years with a multitude of events, activities and initiatives, and invites the international community to support the efforts of developing countries to develop and implement strategies and programmes, including, where required, enabling policies and laws for the sustainable development of mountains, within the framework of national development plans;

16.   *Encourages* the further establishment of committees or similar multi-stakeholder institutional arrangements and mechanisms at the national and regional levels, where appropriate, to enhance intersectoral coordination and collaboration for sustainable development in mountain regions;

17.   *Also encourages* the increased involvement of local authorities, as well as other relevant stakeholders, in particular the rural population, indigenous peoples, civil society and the private sector, in the development and implementation of programmes, land-use planning and land tenure arrangements, and activities related to sustainable development in mountains;

18.   *Underlines* the need for improved access to resources, including land, for women in mountain regions, as well as the need to strengthen the role of women in mountain regions in decision-making processes that affect their communities, cultures and environments;

19.   *Encourages* Governments and intergovernmental organizations to integrate the gender dimension, including gender-disaggregated indicators, in mountain development activities, programmes and projects;

20.   *Stresses* that indigenous cultures, traditions and knowledge, including in the field of medicine, are to be fully considered, respected and promoted in development policy and planning in mountain regions, and underlines the importance of promoting the full participation and involvement of mountain communities in decisions that affect them and of integrating indigenous knowledge, heritage and values in all development initiatives;

21.   *Underscores* the need to take into account relevant articles of the Convention on Biological Diversity;

22.   *Recalls with satisfaction* the adoption by the Conference of the Parties to the Convention on Biological Diversity of a programme of work on mountain biological diversity, the overall purpose of which is a significant reduction in the loss of mountain biological diversity by 2010 at the global, regional and national levels, and its implementation, which aims at making a significant contribution to poverty eradication in mountain regions;

23.   *Invites* States and other stakeholders to strengthen implementation of the programme of work on mountain biological diversity through renewed political commitment and the establishment of appropriate multi-stakeholder institutional arrangements and mechanisms, and in this regard notes with satisfaction the collaboration established between the secretariat of the Convention on Biological Diversity, the Mountain Partnership and the Mountain Forum to mobilize concerned Governments and other stakeholders for more effective cooperation and to assist in building capacity for implementation of the programme of work;

24.   *Recognizes* that many developing countries, as well as countries with economies in transition, need to be assisted in the formulation and implementation of national strategies and programmes for sustainable mountain development, through bilateral, multilateral and South-South cooperation, as well as through other collaborative approaches;

25.   *Emphasizes* the importance of exchange of best practices, information and appropriate environmentally sound technologies for sustainable mountain development, and encourages Member States and relevant organizations in this regard;

26.   *Notes* that funding for sustainable mountain development has become increasingly important, especially in view of the greater recognition of the global importance of mountains and the high level of extreme poverty, food insecurity and hardship mountain communities face;

27.   *Invites* Governments, the United Nations system, the international financial institutions, the Global Environment Facility, all relevant United Nations conventions and their funding mechanisms, within their respective mandates, and all relevant stakeholders from civil society and the private sector to consider providing support, including through voluntary financial contributions, to local, national and international programmes and projects for sustainable development in mountain regions, particularly in developing countries;

28.   *Underlines* the importance for sustainable mountain development of exploring a wide range of funding sources, such as public-private partnerships, increased opportunities for microfinance, including microcredit and microinsurance, small housing loans, savings, education and health accounts, and support for entrepreneurs seeking to develop small- and medium-sized businesses and, where appropriate, on a case-by-case basis, debt for sustainable development swaps;

29.   *Encourages* the further development of sustainable agricultural value chains and the improvement of access to and participation in markets for mountain farmers and agro-industry enterprises, with a view to substantially increasing the income of farmers, in particular smallholders and family farmers;

30.   *Welcomes* the growing contribution of sustainable tourism initiatives in mountain regions as a way to enhance environmental protection and socio-economic benefits to local communities and the fact that consumer demand is increasingly moving towards responsible and sustainable tourism;

31.   *Notes* that public awareness needs to be raised with respect to the positive and unaccounted economic benefits that mountains provide not only to highland communities, but also to a large portion of the world's population living in lowland areas, and underlines the importance of enhancing the sustainability of ecosystems that provide essential resources and services for human well-being and economic activity and of developing innovative means of financing for their protection;

32.   *Recognizes* that mountain ranges are usually shared among several countries, and in this context encourages transboundary cooperation approaches, where the States concerned agree, to the sustainable development of mountain ranges and information-sharing in this regard;

33.   *Notes with appreciation*, in this context, that the Convention on the Protection of the Alps promotes constructive new approaches to the integrated, sustainable development of the Alps, including through its thematic protocols on spatial planning, mountain farming, conservation of nature and landscape, mountain forests, tourism, soil protection, energy and transport, as well as the Declaration on Population and Culture, the Action Plan on Climate Change in the Alps, cooperation with other convention bodies on relevant subjects and activities in the context of the Mountain Partnership;

34. *Also notes with appreciation* the Framework Convention on the Protection and Sustainable Development of the Carpathians, adopted and signed by the seven countries of the region to provide a framework for cooperation and multisectoral policy coordination, a platform for joint strategies for sustainable development and a forum for dialogue between all involved stakeholders;

35. *Further notes with appreciation* the work of the International Centre for Integrated Mountain Development, which promotes transboundary cooperation among eight country members of the Himalaya Hindu Kush to foster action and change for overcoming the economic, social and physical vulnerability of mountain peoples;

36. *Notes with appreciation* the contribution of the Sustainable Agriculture and Rural Development in Mountain Regions project of the Food and Agriculture Organization of the United Nations and the statement of the Adelboden Group in promoting specific policies, appropriate institutions and processes for mountain regions and the positive, unaccounted economic benefits they provide;

37. *Stresses* the importance of building capacity, strengthening institutions and promoting educational programmes in order to foster sustainable mountain development at all levels and to enhance awareness of challenges to and best practices in sustainable development in mountain regions and in the nature of relationships between highland and lowland areas;

38. *Underlines* the importance of higher education in and for mountain areas in order to expand opportunities and encourage the retention of skilled people, including youth, in mountain areas, recognizes, in this context, recent and important initiatives at the regional level, such as the creation of three university campuses, in Kazakhstan, Kyrgyzstan and Tajikistan, and the creation of the Himalayan University Consortium, and encourages similar efforts in other mountain regions around the world;

39. *Encourages* the development and implementation of global, regional and national communication programmes to build on the awareness and momentum for change created by the International Year of Mountains in 2002 and the opportunity provided annually by International Mountain Day on 11 December;

40. *Encourages* Member States to collect and produce information and to establish monitoring systems on biophysical and socio-economic data devoted to mountains so as to capitalize on knowledge to support interdisciplinary research programmes and projects and to improve decision-making and planning;

41. *Encourages* all relevant entities of the United Nations system, within their respective mandates, to further enhance their constructive efforts to strengthen interagency collaboration to achieve more effective implementation of the relevant chapters of Agenda 21, including chapter 13, and paragraph 42 and other relevant paragraphs of the Johannesburg Plan of Implementation, taking into account the efforts of the Inter-Agency Group on Mountains and the need for the further involvement of the United Nations system, in particular the Food and Agriculture Organization of the United Nations, the United Nations Environment Programme, the United Nations University, the United Nations Development Programme, the United Nations Educational, Scientific and Cultural Organization

and the United Nations Children's Fund, as well as international financial institutions and other relevant international organizations;

42. *Recognizes* the efforts of the Mountain Partnership implemented in accordance with Economic and Social Council resolution 2003/61 of 25 July 2003, invites the international community and other relevant stakeholders, including civil society and the private sector, to consider participating actively in the Mountain Partnership to increase its value, and invites the Partnership secretariat to report on its activities and achievements to the Commission on Sustainable Development at its eighteenth session, in 2010, including in regard to the thematic issues of transport, chemicals, waste management, mining and a ten-year framework of programmes on sustainable consumption and production patterns;

43. *Notes with appreciation*, in this context, the efforts of the Mountain Partnership to cooperate with existing multilateral instruments relevant to mountains, such as the Convention on Biological Diversity, the United Nations Convention to Combat Desertification in Those Countries Experiencing Serious Drought and/or Desertification, Particularly in Africa, the United Nations Framework Convention on Climate Change, the International Strategy for Disaster Reduction and mountain-related regional instruments such as the Convention on the Protection of the Alps and the Framework Convention on the Protection and Sustainable Development of the Carpathians;

44. *Also notes with appreciation* the ongoing efforts to improve strategic cooperation among the institutions and initiatives dealing with mountain development, such as the Mountain Forum, the Mountain Partnership, the Mountain Research Initiative and the International Mountain Society;

45. *Requests* the Secretary-General to report to the General Assembly at its sixty-sixth session on the implementation of the present resolution under the sub-item entitled "Sustainable mountain development" of the item entitled "Sustainable development".

Drought and desertification

The Commission on Sustainable Development, at its seventeenth session (New York, 4–15 May) [E/2009/29] (see p. 799), considered a report of the Secretary-General [E/CN.17/2009/6] on policy options and actions for expediting progress in implementation in the area of drought. The report stated that policies to reduce the impacts of drought needed to be developed and adapted at all levels with the participation of all stakeholders. In addition to natural resources conservation and structural adaptation to climatic variability, policies that focused on exploiting alternative sources of water, such as rainwater harvesting, water treatment and reuse, were crucial. A more sustained impact could be ensured if policies were consistent with traditional community-based strategies for coping with drought and climate change; traditional knowledge and methods concerning soil and water conservation needed to be promoted as a cost-effective solution. Improving access by developing countries to drought-tolerant crop varieties was essential for agricultural production and food security in drought-affected regions. Reducing pastoral poverty would require Governments, NGOs and development partners to shift their focus from relief efforts to strategies aimed at resource mobilization, infrastructure development and capacity-building.

The Commission also had before it the report of the Secretary-General [E/CN.17/2009/7] on policy options and actions for expediting progress in implementation in the area of desertification. According to the report, in addition to addressing the root causes of land degradation, national policies aimed at combating desertification needed to take into account the linkages among land degradation, desertification and poverty in an integrated manner. Policies aimed at improving the productivity of land, reducing soil erosion and reversing salinization trends achieved better results if they were owned by local communities. Promoting regional cooperation in the form of sharing of information, knowledge and best practices would allow positive gains to be made. Combining implementation of land administration policies with land planning and management policies would yield quick benefits in terms of promoting sustainable land-use practices and addressing the factors causing land degradation. Improved land tenure security could encourage farmers to invest in soil and water conservation, while building partnerships might help in realizing much-needed technology transfer and capacity-building to protect the integrity of ecosystems. Community-based organizations needed to be encouraged to assume greater responsibility for natural resources management.

In May, the Commission adopted a resolution [E/2009/29 (res. 17/1)] on policy options and practical measures to expedite implementation in agriculture, rural development, land, drought, desertification and Africa, which presented, among other measures, actions to address drought and desertification.

Marine ecosystems

Oceans and seas

In response to General Assembly resolution 63/111 [YUN 2008, p. 1497], the tenth meeting of the United Nations Open-ended Informal Consultative Process on Oceans and the Law of the Sea (New York, 17–19 June) [A/64/131] focused on the implementation of the outcomes of the Consultative Process, including a review of its achievements and shortcomings in its first nine meetings. Participants discussed the mandate, objectives and role of the Process; outcomes of the Process and their implementation; format and work methods of the Process; and issues which could benefit from attention in the future work of the Process.

The Assembly took action with regard to the Consultative Process in section XIV of **resolution 64/71** of 4 December (see p. 1361).

Communication. On 28 April [A/63/839], Kazakhstan transmitted the joint statement of Heads of State-founders of the International Fund for Saving the Aral Sea (Kazakhstan, Kyrgyzstan, Tajikistan, Turkmenistan, Uzbekistan), adopted on 28 April in Almaty, Kazakhstan.

Assessment of assessments

The start-up phase of the "assessment of assessments" [YUN 2004, p. 1332] of the regular process for global reporting and assessment of the state of the marine environment, including socio-economic aspects, was completed in 2009 with the delivery of the final report to the General Assembly.

In February, the UNEP Governing Council [A/64/25 (dec. 25/2 I)], taking note of the "assessment of assessments" progress report endorsed by the Ad Hoc Steering Group for the "assessment of assessments" at its third meeting [YUN 2008, p. 1167], invited Governments and other parties to contribute financially to enable the completion of the "assessment of assessments" and its submission to the Assembly.

The Group of Experts for the start-up phase of the "assessment of assessments", selected by the Ad Hoc Steering Group in 2006 [YUN 2006, p. 1242], held its fifth and final meeting (Geneva, 19–21 March 2009) [GRAME/GOE/5/1]. The meeting focused on the finalization of the report manuscript following peer and institutional review in preparation for submission to the Ad Hoc Steering Group meeting. The process for final copy-editing, design and layout of the final outputs was agreed, including a timeline for submission to the Assembly.

The Ad Hoc Steering Group for the "assessment of assessments", established by Assembly resolution 60/30 [YUN 2005, p. 1436], held its fourth and last meeting (Paris, 15–17 April) [GRAME/AHSG/4/2]. The meeting discussed the reports presented at the fourth [YUN 2008, p. 1167] and fifth meetings of the Group of Experts, and the Secretariat reported on the peer review process and subsequent editorial process for the "assessment of assessments" report and a financial report on the resources mobilized for the execution of the start-up phase of the regular process.

In letters dated 11 May [A/64/88], the UNESCO Intergovernmental Oceanographic Commission and UNEP transmitted to the Secretary-General the report on the "assessment of assessments", to be submitted to the Assembly at its sixty-fourth (2009) session. The report would serve as a basis for discussions by the General Assembly Ad Hoc Working Group of the Whole (New York, 31 August–4 September).

The Assembly, in section XII of **resolution 64/71** of 4 December (see p. 1360), endorsed the recommendations adopted by the Ad Hoc Working Group [A/64/347], which proposed a framework for the regular process, described its first cycle and a way forward, and stressed the need for further progress to be made on the modalities for implementing the regular process prior to the Assembly's sixty-fifth (2010) session. The Assembly requested the Secretary-General to convene an informal meeting of the Ad Hoc Working Group of the Whole from 30 August to 3 September 2010 to make recommendations to the Assembly at its sixty-fifth (2010) session on the modalities for implementing the regular process, and to specify the objective and scope of its first cycle, key questions and primary target audiences, in order to ensure that assessments were relevant for decision-makers; and on the terms of reference for a voluntary trust fund that would support the operations of the first five-year cycle of the regular process. The Secretary-General was also requested to invite the Chairs of the regional groups to constitute a group of a maximum of 25 experts to make suggestions to the Working Group.

Regional Seas Programme

The eleventh Global Meeting of the Regional Seas Conventions and Action Plans (Bangkok, 5–8 October) discussed partnerships between Regional Seas Programmes and UN agencies, multilateral environmental agreements and civil society; biodiversity within ecosystem-based management; biodiversity and the Regional Seas Programmes; implementation of biodiversity targets; and strengthening the Regional Seas Alliance.

Protection against harmful products and waste

Chemical safety

As at 31 December, 130 States and the EU were parties to the 1998 Rotterdam Convention on the Prior Informed Consent Procedure for Certain Hazardous Chemicals and Pesticides in International Trade [YUN 1998, p. 997], which entered into force in 2004 [YUN 2004, p. 1063]. Costa Rica, Malawi, Serbia and Trinidad and Tobago became parties during the year.

The Chemical Review Committee, a subsidiary body of the Conference of the Parties to the Rotterdam Convention, at its fifth meeting (Rome, 23–27 March) [UNEP/FAO/RC/CRC.5/16], considered the Bureau's preliminary review of notifications and proposed priorities scheduled for review by the Committee [UNEP/FAO/RC/CRC.5/2/Rev.1]; reviewed notifications of final regulatory action to ban or severely restrict eight chemicals; and finalized the draft decision guidance documents for alachlor and aldicarb and decided to send the recommendations to

include them in Annex III of the Convention to the fifth meeting of the Conference of the Parties to the Rotterdam Convention.

International chemicals management

The UNEP Executive Director in January submitted a report [UNEP/GC.25/INF/22] providing information on the activities of the Inter-Organization Programme for the Sound Management of Chemicals [YUN 2002, p. 1063] to implement the Strategic Approach to International Chemicals Management (SAICM) [YUN 2006, p. 1246].

The UNEP Governing Council in February [dec. 25/5 I], welcoming the progress made in implementing the Strategic Approach, requested the Executive Director to strengthen support for implementation of the Approach and its secretariat, and facilitate more robust efforts in developing countries and countries with economies in transition to ensure the sound management of chemicals, in particular by ensuring that projects and programmes discussed under the Quick Start Programme [YUN 2006, p. 1246] were processed and implemented expeditiously. It urged Governments, intergovernmental organizations, NGOs and others to contribute financially and in kind to the implementation of the Strategic Approach.

The second session of the International Conference on Chemicals Management (Geneva, 11–15 May) [SAICM/ICCM.2/15] discussed various aspects related to implementation of the Strategic Approach, including the evaluation of and guidance on the implementation, review and update of the Approach; implementation of and coherence among international instruments and programmes; modalities for stakeholder reporting on progress in implementation; strengthening of national chemicals management capacities; financial and technical resources for implementation; emerging policy issues; and information exchange and scientific and technical cooperation. Delegates adopted 10 resolutions, including on rules of procedure of the Conference, regional activities and coordination, emerging policy issues, the establishment of an open-ended working group, financial and technical resources, managing perfluorinated chemicals and the transition to safer alternatives, and health aspects of the sound management of chemicals. Having established an open-ended working group as a subsidiary body, the Conference decided not to integrate the Intergovernmental Forum on Chemical Safety [YUN 1994, p. 942] into the Conference.

Lead and cadmium

In response to a 2007 Governing Council decision [YUN 2007, p. 1078], the Executive Director submitted a note [UNEP/GC.25/INF/23] containing a review of scientific information on lead; an overview of existing and future national actions, including legislation, relevant to lead; and an inventory of risk management measures. A January addendum [UNEP/GC.25/INF/23/Add.1] contained a study on the health and environmental effects of the movement of products containing lead, cadmium and mercury in Africa.

The Governing Council in February [dec. 25/5 II] took note of the study and of the key findings of the review submitted by the Executive Director, including that, because those metals had relatively short residence time in the atmosphere, they were mainly transported over local, national or regional distances. It also noted that the export of new and used products containing lead and cadmium remained a challenge for developing countries and countries with economies in transition, which lacked the capacity to manage and dispose of the substances in products in an environmentally sound manner. The Council encouraged efforts by Governments and others to reduce risks to human health and the environment of lead and cadmium throughout the life cycle of those substances and to take action to promote the use of lead and cadmium-free alternatives, for instance in toys and paint. The Council acknowledged the efforts made by Governments and others to phase out lead from gasoline, in particular through the Partnership for Clean Fuels and Vehicles [YUN 2003, p. 1070], and urged Governments in transition to phase out lead from gasoline as early as possible. The Executive Director was requested to facilitate that work in developing countries and countries with economies in transition; to address the data and information gaps identified in the UNEP reviews of scientific information on cadmium and lead; and to finalize the scientific review and report to the Governing Council at its twenty-sixth (2011) session.

Mercury

In response to a 2007 Governing Council decision [YUN 2007, p. 1078], the Executive Director in January submitted an executive summary of a 2008 report entitled "Global Atmospheric Mercury Assessment: Sources, Emissions and Transport" [UNEP/GC.25/INF/26], as well as an addendum to that report [UNEP/GC.25/INF/26/Add.1].

Also in January [UNEP/GC.25/INF/25], the Executive Director provided the report of the second meeting of the Ad Hoc Open-ended Working Group on Mercury (Nairobi, 6–10 October 2008) [YUN 2008, p. 1171].

In February 2009, the Executive Director submitted the executive summary [UNEP/GC.25/INF/28] of the report on the extent of contaminated sites, which provided information on the global study on contaminated sites. The study confirmed that it was difficult to develop robust data on the extent of contaminated sites and/or quantification of releases/pollution due to limited data available. As both the atmospheric mercury emissions and mercury inputs and distribution in the aquatic environment depended strongly on the climatic conditions and the topography of the site in question, extrapolations from a few well studied cases were associated with significant uncertainties. According to the report, total mercury emissions to the atmosphere and hydrosphere from contaminated sites were estimated to be between 150 to 300 metric tonnes per year. Releases from contaminated sites were estimated to contribute less than 5 per cent of total mercury emissions from anthropogenic sources annually. However, those secondary mercury sources would continue to emit mercury for a very long time if not managed properly or remediated. Poor management of contaminated sites might further increase the level of releases, resulting in an increased risk for local populations and ecosystems. Remediation of such sites could be expensive and decisions on when to treat were complex. Further studies were needed for the development and implementation of effective programmes to protect the populations residing in or near mercury-contaminated sites. An integrated approach for managing contaminated sites should be developed, including guidelines for characterization and remediation.

The Governing Council in February [dec. 25/5 III] agreed to further international action through the elaboration of a legally binding instrument on mercury, which could include both binding and voluntary approaches, together with interim activities, to reduce risks to human health and the environment. It requested the Executive Director to convene an intergovernmental negotiating committee with the mandate to prepare that instrument, beginning its work in 2010 with the goal of completing it prior to the Council's twenty-seventh (2013) regular session. The committee was to develop a comprehensive approach to mercury, including provisions to: specify the objectives of the instrument; reduce the supply of mercury and enhance the capacity for its environmentally sound storage; reduce its demand in products and processes; reduce its international trade; reduce its atmospheric emissions; address mercury-containing waste and remediation of contaminated sites; increase knowledge through awareness-raising and scientific information exchange; specify arrangements for capacity-building and technical and financial assistance; and address compliance. In its deliberations, the committee should consider: flexibility; approaches tailored to the characteristics of specific sectors; technical and economic availability of mercury-free alternative products and processes; the need to achieve cooperation and coordination and to avoid duplication with other international agreements and processes;

prioritization of the various sources of mercury releases for action; possible co-benefits of conventional pollutant control measures and other environmental benefits; efficient organization and streamlined secretariat arrangements; and measures to address risks to health and the environment as a consequence of anthropogenic mercury releases.

The Council requested the Executive Director to convene an ad-hoc open-ended working group, which would meet in the second half of 2009 to prepare for the work of the committee. The Executive Director would provide the necessary support to the committee, while the Chemicals Branch of the UNEP Division of Technology, Industry and Economics would serve as secretariat of the committee and the working group. To assist the committee, the Council requested the Executive Director to conduct a study on various types of mercury-emitting sources, as well as trends of mercury emissions, with a view to analysing and assessing the costs and effectiveness of alternative control technologies and measures. The Executive Director was also requested to continue work in a number of specified areas; to facilitate cooperation and coordination among the UNEP mercury programme and the Global Mercury Partnership and Governments, mercury-related activities under SAICM and its Quick Start Programme, convention secretariats, intergovernmental organizations, NGOs and the private sector; and to update the report entitled "Global Atmospheric Mercury Assessment: Sources, Emissions and Transport" for consideration by the Council's twenty-seventh (2013) session.

Pursuant to the Council's decision, the Executive Director in November submitted a progress report on mercury [UNEP/GCSS.XI/6] on the outcomes of the ad hoc open-ended working group meeting (Bangkok, 19–23 October). The meeting was attended by representatives of 101 Governments, one regional economic integration organization, six intergovernmental organizations and a number of NGOs. The working group agreed on draft rules of procedure to be recommended to the committee, in addition to work for the secretariat to undertake in preparation for the committee's first session, including compiling options for the instrument's structure and descriptions of options for substantive provisions. The negotiation process would involve five committee sessions, with the last session to be held prior to the twenty-seventh (2013) regular session of the Governing Council, followed by a diplomatic conference later in 2013, at which the text of the agreement would be opened for signature.

The report also reviewed progress under the Global Mercury Partnership. The Governing Council initiated those partnerships in 2005 [YUN 2005, p. 1162]; they were formalized in 2008 through the development of the framework for the Partnership, which established the overall goal of protecting health and the environment from the release of mercury and its compounds by minimizing and ultimately eliminating global anthropogenic mercury releases to air, water and land. The first meeting of the Global Mercury Partnership Advisory Group (Geneva, 31 March–2 April) assessed the work under way in the seven partnership areas to consider potential outputs, targets and milestones that might inform the work of the negotiating committee. The Advisory Group made recommendations based on the efforts identified in the partnership area business plans to encourage the Partnership's work.

Persistent organic pollutants

As at 31 December, 168 States and the EU were parties to the 2001 Stockholm Convention on Persistent Organic Pollutants (POPs) [YUN 2001, p. 971], which entered into force in 2004 [YUN 2004, p. 1066]. Cameroon, Indonesia, Malawi, Serbia, Tonga and Turkey became parties during the year.

At the fourth meeting of the Conference of the Parties to the Stockholm Convention (Geneva, 4–8 May) [UNEP/POPS/COP.4/38], the Convention was amended for the first time to include nine new chemicals: alpha hexachlorocyclohexane; beta hexachlorocyclohexane; hexabromodiphenyl ether and heptabromodiphenyl; tetrabromodiphenyl ether and pentabromodiphenyl; chlordecone; hexabromobiphenyl; lindane; pentachlorobenzene; and perfluorooctane sulfonic acid, its salts and perfluorooctane sulfonyl fluoride. The meeting adopted 35 decisions. It endorsed the establishment of a global alliance for the development and deployment of products, methods and strategies as alternatives to DDT for disease vector control; approved the programme activities and operational budgets for 2010 and 2011, respectively in the amounts of $5,839,267 and $5,873,643; adopted the indicative scale of contributions for the apportionment of expenses for 2010–2011; and decided to keep the working capital reserve at the level of 8.3 per cent of the annual average of the biennial operational budget. The high-level segment (7–8 May) addressed the theme "Meeting the challenges of a POPs-free future". More than 800 participants, representing approximately 149 Governments as well as UN bodies, intergovernmental organizations and NGOs, attended the meeting.

The fifth meeting of the Persistent Organic Pollutants Review Committee (Geneva, 12–16 October) [UNEP/POPS/POPRC.5/10] reviewed data on three chemicals proposed for listing in the Convention: short-chained chlorinated paraffins, hexabromocyclododecane and endosulfan.

Hazardous wastes

As at 31 December, 171 States and the EU were parties to the 1989 Basel Convention on the Control of Transboundary Movements of Hazardous Wastes and their Disposal [YUN 1989, p. 420], which entered into force in 1992 [YUN 1992, p. 685]. The 1995 amendment to the Convention [YUN 1995, p. 1333], not yet in force, had been ratified, accepted or approved by 68 parties, with Chile, Ireland, Italy and Kenya becoming parties during 2009. The number of parties to the 1999 Basel Protocol on Liability and Compensation for Damage resulting from Transboundary Movements of Hazardous Wastes and their Disposal [YUN 1999, p. 998], not yet in force, rose to 10, with Yemen becoming a party in 2009.

The first meeting of the Expanded Bureau of the ninth meeting [YUN 2008, p. 1173] of the Conference of the Parties (Geneva, 23–24 June) [UNEP/SBC/BUREAU/9/1/9] discussed enforcement of the Convention and combating illegal traffic; the 2006 Nairobi Declaration of the Environmentally Sound Management of Electrical and Electronic Waste, adopted by the Conference of the Parties at its eighth meeting; the preparation of draft technical guidelines on the environmentally sound management of mercury wastes and revised technical guidelines on used tyres; ship dismantling matters, including the International Convention for the Safe and Environmentally Sound Recycling of Ships; cooperation and coordination among the Basel, Rotterdam and Stockholm Conventions; and a way forward to attain the objectives of the Basel Convention and the Ban Amendment, namely to protect countries without adequate capacity to manage hazardous wastes in an environmentally sound manner from unwanted imports of hazardous waste, and to ensure that the transboundary movements of hazardous wastes, especially to developing countries, led to an environmentally sound management of those wastes.

The seventh session of the Basel Convention Implementation and Compliance Committee (Geneva, 25–26 June) [UNEP/CHW/CC/7/10] discussed improving national reporting by States parties, illegal traffic, organization of the work of the Committee for 2009–2011, and general issues of compliance and implementation of the Convention.

(For information on the human rights aspects of the illicit movement and dumping of toxic and dangerous products and wastes, see p. 728.)

Waste management

In February [dec. 25/8], the Governing Council welcomed the Bali Declaration on Waste Management for Human Health and Livelihood, adopted by the Conference of the Parties to the Basel Convention at its ninth meeting in June 2008 [YUN 2008, p. 1173] and requested the Executive Director to assist developing countries in strengthening national implementation of an integrated waste management approach; to support the implementation of the actions envisaged in the Bali Declaration; to strengthen support for capacity-building and technology support in the field of waste management; and to undertake demonstration and pilot projects, in cooperation with relevant actors, including UNIDO and UNDP. The Council called on Governments and other stakeholders to strengthen public-private partnership to provide additional means for assisting developing countries to implement the Basel Convention, including for the construction of facilities and infrastructure in waste management. The Council recognized the need for awareness-raising to change the attitude of waste generators, particularly industrial and municipal waste generators, consumers and the informal sector with regard to the "3Rs" concept (reduce, reuse and recycle), environmentally sound waste management and the need for final disposal of wastes in the States in which they were generated. Governments and organizations were invited to provide extrabudgetary resources in support of UNEP and the secretariat of the Basel Convention. The Executive Director was requested to report to the Council's twenty-sixth (2011) session.

Financing the chemicals and wastes agenda

In a December note on financing the chemicals and wastes agenda [UNEP/GCSS.XI/INF/8], the Executive Director recalled that the consultative process on financing options for chemicals and wastes management was launched in recognition of the need for adequate resources in that field and was first announced at the fourth meeting of the Conference of the Parties of the Stockholm Convention on Persistent Organic Pollutants (Geneva, 4–8 May) (see p. 1035) as a response to difficulties encountered in reaching agreement on a compliance mechanism owing to concerns that the available capacity and resources for such a mechanism were inadequate. The objective of the consultations would be to analyse the financing situation at the national level and devise proposals for improving it. A brainstorming meeting (Nairobi, 24–25 July) was held to initiate the process, during which participants called on UNEP to undertake a study to explore the funding and support needs of developing countries and countries with economies in transition and ways to support compliance with chemicals and waste-related multilateral environment agreements and capacity-building. UNEP prepared a preliminary study and submitted it to the second meeting of the consultative group (Bangkok, 25–26 October).

At that meeting, the consultative group provided feedback on the preliminary study and requested UNEP to revise it so that it could become a reference document that would form the basis of further discussions. The revised desk study, annexed to the note of the Executive Director, outlined the range of options for securing adequate financing.

Other matters

Environmental law

The Executive Director in February reported [UNEP/GC.25/INF/15/Add.1] on the implementation of the third Programme for the Development and Periodic Review of Environmental Law (Montevideo Programme III) [YUN 2001, p. 972] from its adoption in February 2001 to January 2009. The report highlighted UNEP activities and developments in the Programme.

In February [dec. 25/11 I], the Governing Council adopted the fourth Programme for the Development and Periodic Review of Environmental Law [YUN 2008, p. 1174] as a broad strategy for the international law community and UNEP in formulating the activities in the field of environmental law for the decade beginning in 2010. It requested the Executive Director to implement the Programme in close collaboration with States, conferences of the parties to and secretariats of multilateral environmental agreements, international organizations, non-State stakeholders and individuals. The Executive Director was also requested to undertake a midterm review of the implementation and effectiveness of the Programme no later than at the twenty-eighth (2015) session of the Governing Council and to report at the thirtieth (2019) session on the impact of the Programme.

The Council took note [dec. 25/11 II] of the draft guidelines for the development of national legislation on access to information, public participation and access to justice in environmental matters [YUN 2008, p. 1175] and requested the secretariat to carry out further work on the guidelines with a view to their adoption by the Council at its next (2010) special session. Pursuant to that request, the Executive Director in December [UNEP/GCSS.XI/8] submitted a report containing the draft guidelines, as well as the report [UNEP/GCSS.XI/INF/6] of the intergovernmental meeting held to review and further develop the draft guidelines (Nairobi, 12–13 November).

The Council took note [dec. 25/11 III] of the draft guidelines for the development of national legislation on liability, response action and compensation for damage caused by activities dangerous to the environment [YUN 2008, p. 1175] and requested the secretariat to carry out further work on the guidelines with a

view to adoption by the Council at its next (2010) special session. Pursuant to that request, the Executive Director in December [UNEP/GCSS.XI/8/Add.1] submitted a report containing the draft guidelines, as well as the report [UNEP/GCSS.XI/INF/6/Add.1] of the intergovernmental meeting held to review and further develop the draft guidelines (Nairobi, 12–13 November).

International Mother Earth Day

On 22 April [A/63/PV.80], the General Assembly considered and took action on a draft resolution entitled "International Mother Earth Day", authored by Bolivia.

GENERAL ASSEMBLY ACTION

On 22 April [meeting 80], the General Assembly adopted **resolution 63/278** [draft: A/63/L.69 & Add.1] without vote [agenda item 49 *(d)*].

International Mother Earth Day

The General Assembly,

Reaffirming Agenda 21, and the Plan of Implementation of the World Summit on Sustainable Development ("Johannesburg Plan of Implementation"),

Recalling the 2005 World Summit Outcome,

Recalling also its resolution 60/192 of 22 December 2005 proclaiming 2008 the International Year of Planet Earth,

Acknowledging that the Earth and its ecosystems are our home, and convinced that in order to achieve a just balance among the economic, social, and environmental needs of present and future generations, it is necessary to promote harmony with nature and the Earth,

Recognizing that Mother Earth is a common expression for the planet earth in a number of countries and regions, which reflects the interdependence that exists among human beings, other living species and the planet we all inhabit,

Noting that Earth Day is observed each year in many countries,

1. *Decides* to designate 22 April as International Mother Earth Day;

2. *Invites* all Member States, the organizations of the United Nations system, international, regional and subregional organizations, civil society, non-governmental organizations and relevant stakeholders to observe and raise awareness of International Mother Earth Day, as appropriate;

3. *Requests* the Secretary-General to bring the present resolution to the attention of all Member States and organizations of the United Nations system.

Harmony with nature

In December, the General Assembly, recalling resolution 37/7 [YUN 1982, p. 1024] on the 1982 World Charter for Nature, which highlighted the need for appropriate measures to protect nature and promote international cooperation in that field and presented principles of conservation by which human conduct affecting nature was to be guided, took action on the item on "harmony with nature".

GENERAL ASSEMBLY ACTION

On 21 December [meeting 66], the General Assembly, on the recommendation of the Second Committee [A/64/420], adopted **resolution 64/196** without vote [agenda item 53].

Harmony with Nature

The General Assembly,

Expressing its concern over the documented environmental degradation and the negative impact on nature resulting from human activity,

Recalling the 1982 World Charter for Nature,

Reaffirming the Rio Declaration on Environment and Development,

Reaffirming also Agenda 21 and the Programme for the Further Implementation of Agenda 21, the Johannesburg Declaration on Sustainable Development and the Plan of Implementation of the World Summit on Sustainable Development ("Johannesburg Plan of Implementation"),

Recalling the 2005 World Summit Outcome,

Reaffirming its resolution 63/278 of 22 April 2009 on the designation of International Mother Earth Day,

Convinced that humanity can and should live in harmony with nature,

1. *Invites* Member States, the relevant organizations of the United Nations system, and international, regional and subregional organizations to consider, as appropriate, the issue of promoting life in harmony with nature and to transmit to the Secretary-General their views, experiences and proposals on this issue;

2. *Invites* all Member States, the relevant organizations of the United Nations system, and international, regional and subregional organizations to make use of International Mother Earth Day, as appropriate, to promote activities and exchange opinions and views on conditions, experiences and principles for a life in harmony with nature;

3. *Decides* to include in the provisional agenda of its sixty-fifth session a sub-item entitled "Harmony with Nature", under the item entitled "Sustainable development";

4. *Requests* the Secretary-General to submit to it, at its sixty-fifth session, a report on this theme, taking into account the views and comments received in relation to the present resolution.

Human settlements

Implementation of Habitat Agenda and strengthening of UN-Habitat

In August, the Secretary-General, in response to General Assembly resolution 63/221 [YUN 2008, p. 1177], reported [A/64/260] on the implementation of

the Habitat Agenda [YUN 1996, p. 994], adopted by the 1996 United Nations Conference on Human Settlements (Habitat II) [ibid., p. 992], and on the strengthening of the United Nations Human Settlements Programme (UN-Habitat). Considerable progress had been made in implementing the 2008–2013 UN-Habitat medium-term strategic and institutional plan [YUN 2007, p. 1086], which called for several reforms and innovations. UN-Habitat launched two new initiatives: the World Urban Campaign and the Cities and Climate Change Initiative. The initiatives, together with the World Urban Forum (2010) [YUN 2008, p. 1181], would spearhead global advocacy for more sustainable urbanization and provide a coordinated approach to policy dialogue and development. Member States were invited to establish national Habitat committees to play an active role in the World Urban Campaign.

In the light of the global financial crisis, UN-Habitat organized a special meeting on affordable housing and housing finance at the Conference on the World Financial and Economic Crisis and Its Impact on Development (New York, 24–26 June) (see p. 947). Participants observed that the financial crisis had its origins in overextended housing finance systems, in particular "sub-prime mortgage instruments". While the crisis had exposed pervasive weaknesses in national and global financial systems and regulatory frameworks, it also served as a reminder that housing was both a market product and a social good. In addressing the crisis, human settlements must be at the forefront of sustainable development policy. UN-Habitat's work to improve access to sustainable financing for affordable housing and infrastructure involved promoting conducive policy frameworks, increasing financial institution activity in the sectors of affordable housing and infrastructure, creating local finance facilities for affordable housing, promoting community group access to finance and promoting local savings groups and savings instruments. In addition, the UN-Habitat experimental finance programme was modified to address the crisis and included: seeking out additional lending opportunities in Africa, Asia, Latin America and the Middle East; increasing partnerships with finance institutions; and demonstrating the benefits of well-designed investments in affordable shelter. The importance of incorporating a gender perspective and a broad spectrum of insurance mechanisms and interest rates into affordable housing plans was also highlighted.

Relationships with the private sector saw a major shift in 2008 owing to the launch of the 2008–2013 medium-term strategic and institutional plan, moving beyond corporate social responsibility to include core business practices for sustainable urbanization. UN-Habitat enhanced its advocacy and knowledge management work and started new forms of partnership at the global and country levels with financial institutions, water utility companies and the real estate sector. The first objective of such partnerships was pre-investment packaging, whereby policy reform, capacity-building and technical assistance were designed to mobilize a mix of public expenditure and private investment in housing and urban development. The second objective was to show Governments and financial institutions that business models for pro-poor housing and urban development were viable and beneficial to overall economic development.

With the support of the African Development Bank, the UN-Habitat Water for African Cities Programme was operational in 18 cities in 15 countries. UN-Habitat facilitated cooperation between banks, local authorities and urban poor organizations to mobilize and package domestic capital, public investments and community savings for slum upgrading and affordable housing; those efforts included the UN-Habitat Slum Upgrading Facility pilot programme operations in Ghana, Indonesia, Sri Lanka and the United Republic of Tanzania. Technical assistance and advisory services were provided to women's land access trusts in Ghana, Kenya, Uganda and the United Republic of Tanzania. Support was also provided for the formation of new land access trusts in Burundi, Ethiopia, Mozambique and Rwanda. The Cities and Climate Change Initiative was launched in 2009 to support government efforts to reduce the ecological footprint of cities while improving their safety and resilience to the effects of climate change. The *Global Report on Human Settlements 2009: Planning Sustainable Cities* identified innovative urban planning approaches and practices that were more responsive to the challenges of sustainable urbanization.

The report concluded that, for practically all dimensions of human settlements development and management, the global economic and financial crisis had had negative ramifications, and that the impact was particularly serious on the poor and low-income groups, whose capacity to access decent housing, secure tenure and basic urban services was impaired. It identified several areas of follow-up action, including the need for Member States to assess the effectiveness of their policies regarding pro-poor housing and urban development, and the need to integrate affordable housing and housing finance as key means of attaining internationally agreed development goals, including the MDGs [YUN 2000, p. 51]. The key recommendation, however, centred on follow-up at the global level, as well as bridging the architecture and modalities of follow-up and sustainable development. That recommendation was based on the acknowledgement that sustainable development increasingly depended on sustainable urbanization. In practical terms, sustainable development would ultimately depend on the quality of city management and planning and the effectiveness of adaptation to and mitigation of the effects of climate change. The General Assembly was thus invited to consider convening, in 2016, a UN conference on housing and sustainable urban development (Habitat III), the objective of which would be to review, formulate and adopt updated policies, strategies and approaches to address the evolving challenges of sustainable urbanization and urban development.

Coordinated implementation of Habitat Agenda

In response to a 2008 Economic and Social Council decision [YUN 2008, p. 1177], the Secretary-General submitted a May report [E/2009/80] on the coordinated implementation of the Habitat Agenda during 2008 and the first half of 2009. The report underlined the raising of international awareness of the issues and challenges associated with rapid urbanization, including their consequences for attaining the MDGs. That heightened awareness led to an increase in the scope and depth of responses to those issues at the global, regional and country levels. The implementation of the 2008–2013 medium-term strategic and institutional plan and the realization on the part of the international community of the need to focus on the consequences of rapid urbanization, which had led to collaborative arrangements and partnerships involving UN system entities as well as NGOs, had also contributed to the implementation of the Habitat Agenda.

The report listed several initiatives. The UN-Habitat Youth Empowerment Programme in the Kibera slum and the Mavoko informal settlement in Nairobi provided on-the-job training for youth through the construction of their own youth training centre. The programme aimed to equip young people with managerial and organizational skills, certification and apprenticeship experience that would allow them to find jobs in the construction industry. UN-Habitat launched the Water Operators Partnership Programme, which provided municipal water operators in Africa, Asia and Latin America and the Caribbean with a platform for exchanging strategies and applying best practices in the delivery of clean drinking water to informal settlements and slums. UN-Habitat developed its working relationships with financial institutions such as the Bank of America as part of its effort to mobilize capital for reimbursable seeding-type initiatives in Asia, Africa and Latin America. In collaboration with UNEP and the Governments of Burundi, Kenya, Rwanda, Uganda and Tanzania, a project on promoting energy efficiency in buildings in eastern Africa was being developed with Global Environment Facility funding.

The report concluded that the emerging yet robust response by Governments and partners to the coordinated implementation of the Habitat Agenda was a strong indication of the increasing internalization of the urban agenda by the world community. It called for the Economic and Social Council to adopt the following recommendations: adopt and promote sustainable urbanization as a cross-cutting issue for more effective action within the social, economic and environmental pillars of sustainable development; endorse the convening of a special General Assembly event devoted to the theme of affordable finance for housing and urban development; and recommend that the Assembly convene a third United Nations Conference on Housing and Sustainable Urban Development in 2016.

On 29 July, the Economic and Social Council, by **decision 2009/238**, took note of the report, decided to transmit it to the Assembly for consideration at its sixty-fourth (2009) session and requested the Secretary-General to report on the coordinated implementation of the Habitat Agenda to the Council in 2010.

In response to the Council's decision, the Secretary-General, by an August note [A/64/317], transmitted the report to the Assembly.

GENERAL ASSEMBLY ACTION

On 21 December [meeting 66], the General Assembly, on the recommendation of the Second Committee [A/64/421], adopted **resolution 64/207** without vote [agenda item 54].

Implementation of the outcome of the United Nations Conference on Human Settlements (Habitat II) and strengthening of the United Nations Human Settlements Programme (UN-Habitat)

The General Assembly,

Recalling its resolutions 3327(XXIX) of 16 December 1974, 32/162 of 19 December 1977, 34/115 of 14 December 1979, 56/205 and 56/206 of 21 December 2001, 57/275 of 20 December 2002, 58/226 and 58/227 of 23 December 2003, 59/239 of 22 December 2004, 60/203 of 22 December 2005, 61/206 of 20 December 2006, 62/198 of 19 December 2007 and 63/221 of 19 December 2008,

Taking note of Economic and Social Council resolutions 2002/38 of 26 July 2002 and 2003/62 of 25 July 2003 and Council decisions 2004/300 of 23 July 2004, 2005/298 of 26 July 2005, 2006/247 of 27 July 2006, 2007/249 of 26 July 2007, 2008/239 of 23 July 2008 and 2009/238 of 29 July 2009,

Recalling the goal contained in the United Nations Millennium Declaration of achieving a significant improvement in the lives of at least 100 million slum-dwellers by 2020 and the goal contained in the Plan of Implementation of the World Summit on Sustainable Development ("Johannesburg Plan of Implementation") to halve, by 2015, the proportion of people who lack access to safe drinking water and sanitation,

Recalling also the Habitat Agenda, the Declaration on Cities and Other Human Settlements in the New Millennium, the Johannesburg Plan of Implementation and the Monterrey Consensus of the International Conference on Financing for Development,

Recalling further the 2005 World Summit Outcome, which calls upon the States Members of the United Nations to achieve a significant improvement in the lives of at least 100 million slum-dwellers by 2020, recognizing the urgent need for the provision of increased resources for affordable housing and housing-related infrastructure, prioritizing slum prevention and slum upgrading, and to encourage support for the United Nations Habitat and Human Settlements Foundation and its Slum Upgrading Facility,

Recognizing the negative impact of environmental degradation, including climate change, desertification and loss of biodiversity, on human settlements,

Recognizing also that the current financial crisis could negatively affect the ability of the United Nations Human Settlements Programme (UN-Habitat) to mobilize resources and promote the use of incentives and market measures as well as the mobilization of domestic and international financial resources for supporting private sector investment in affordable housing,

Welcoming with appreciation the important contribution of UN-Habitat, within its mandate, to more cost-effective transitions between emergency relief, recovery and reconstruction, and also the decision to admit UN-Habitat to the Inter-Agency Standing Committee,

Recognizing the significance of the urban dimension of poverty eradication and the need to integrate water and sanitation and other issues within a comprehensive framework for sustainable development,

Recognizing also the importance of decentralization policies for achieving sustainable human settlements development in line with the Habitat Agenda and the internationally agreed development goals, including the Millennium Development Goals,

Welcoming the progress being made by UN-Habitat in the implementation of its medium-term strategic and institutional plan for the period 2008–2013 and its efforts, as a non-resident agency, in helping programme countries to mainstream the Habitat Agenda into their respective development frameworks,

Noting the request of the Governing Council of UN-Habitat in its resolution 22/5 of 3 April 2009 for a joint examination of the governance of UN-Habitat with a view to identifying and implementing ways to improve the transparency, accountability, efficiency and effectiveness of the functioning of the existing governance structure and to identify options for any other potential relevant changes for consideration by the Governing Council at its twenty-third session and for the Executive Director to begin work on terms of reference for this exercise,

Noting also the efforts of UN-Habitat in strengthening its collaboration with international and regional development banks and domestic financial institutions to combine public and private capital with capacity-building and policy reform activities in order to improve access by the poor to water and sanitation and affordable housing finance in support of the attainment of the internationally agreed development goals, including the Millennium Development Goals,

Welcoming the offer of the Government of Brazil and the city of Rio de Janeiro to host the fifth session of the World Urban Forum from 22 to 26 March 2010,

Reaffirming the increased importance of South-South and triangular cooperation in helping developing countries to develop capacities in order to achieve their national goals, including those related to sustainable human settlements and urban development,

Recalling its invitation to the Governing Council of UN-Habitat to keep developments in housing finance systems under review in view of the current global economic and financial crisis, and its decision to explore the possibility of convening a high-level event of the General Assembly on the subject, and acknowledging the efforts of the Governing Council at its twenty-second session in this regard,

Recognizing the continued need for increased and predictable financial contributions to the United Nations Habitat and Human Settlements Foundation to ensure timely, effective and concrete global implementation of the Habitat Agenda, the Declaration on Cities and Other Human Settlements in the New Millennium and the relevant internationally agreed development goals, including those contained in the Millennium Declaration and the Johannesburg Declaration on Sustainable Development and the Johannesburg Plan of Implementation,

Recognizing also the progress being made by UN-Habitat in the development of the Experimental Reimbursable Seeding Operations Trust Fund of the United Nations Habitat and Human Settlements Foundation, established by the Governing Council of UN-Habitat in its resolution 21/10 of 20 April 2007,

1. *Takes note* of the report of the Secretary-General on the coordinated implementation of the Habitat Agenda and the report of the Secretary-General on the implementation of the outcome of the United Nations Conference on Human Settlements (Habitat II) and strengthening of the United Nations Human Settlements Programme (UN-Habitat);

2. *Welcomes* the efforts of UN-Habitat in the continued implementation of its medium-term strategic and institutional plan for the period 2008–2013, and encourages Governments in a position to do so, and other stakeholders, to contribute to UN-Habitat so as to further strengthen its efforts in institutional reform and the pursuit of management excellence, including results-based management;

3. *Stresses* the need for Member States, taking into consideration, inter alia, the current global crisis, to assess the adequacy of their respective housing and related infrastructure policies to meet the needs of their growing urban populations and, in particular, the needs of the poor and other vulnerable groups, and requests UN-Habitat to assist Governments upon request in this regard;

4. *Encourages* Governments to promote the principles and practice of sustainable urbanization and strengthen the role and contribution of their respective local authorities in applying those principles and practices, in order to, inter alia, ensure access to basic services for all and improve the living conditions of vulnerable urban populations, slum-dwellers and the urban poor, and, as a major contribution to mitigating the causes of climate change, adapting to the effects of climate change and reducing risks and vulnerabilities in a rapidly urbanizing world, including human settlements in fragile ecosystems, and invites the international donor community to support the efforts of developing countries in this regard;

5. *Stresses* the need for the international community to support South-South cooperation, including through triangular cooperation, especially by mobilizing financial resources on a sustainable basis, providing technical assistance and encouraging city-to-city cooperation;

6. *Reiterates its call for* continued financial support to UN-Habitat through increased voluntary contributions, and invites Governments in a position to do so, and other stakeholders, to provide predictable multi-year funding and increased non-earmarked contributions to support the strategic and institutional objectives of the medium-term strategic and institutional plan for the period 2008–2013 and its Global Campaign on Sustainable Urbanization;

7. *Stresses* that the affordability of housing has become a major issue that needs to be addressed by mobilizing resources for the poor and other vulnerable groups;

8. *Invites* the international donor community and financial institutions to contribute generously to the United Nations Habitat and Human Settlements Foundation, including the Water and Sanitation Trust Fund, the Slum Upgrading Facility and the technical cooperation trust funds to enable UN-Habitat to assist developing countries in mobilizing public investment and private capital for slum upgrading, shelter and basic services;

9. *Acknowledges* the progress made in the implementation of the pilot programmes of the Experimental Reimbursable Seeding Operations Trust Fund of the United Nations Habitat and Human Settlements Foundation, and in this regard invites the international donor community and financial institutions to contribute to the Trust Fund;

10. *Encourages* UN-Habitat to continue exploring the possibility of convening a high-level special event of the General Assembly on sustainable urbanization to promote understanding of the challenges of rapid urbanization, including climate change, housing finance systems, urban planning and sustainable land management;

11. *Requests* the Secretary-General to keep the resource needs of UN-Habitat under review so as to enhance its effectiveness in supporting national policies, strategies and plans for attaining the poverty eradication, gender equality, water and sanitation and slum upgrading targets of the United Nations Millennium Declaration, the Johannesburg Plan of Implementation and the 2005 World Summit Outcome;

12. *Reiterates its encouragement* to the Economic and Social Council to include sustainable urbanization, urban poverty reduction and slum upgrading as a cross-cutting issue in the follow-up to the outcome of relevant summits and major international conferences;

13. *Emphasizes* the importance of the Nairobi headquarters location of UN-Habitat, and requests the Secretary-General to keep the resource needs of UN-Habitat and the United Nations Office at Nairobi under review so as to permit the delivery, in an effective manner, of necessary services to UN-Habitat and the other United Nations organs and organizations in Nairobi;

14.   *Takes note* of the recommendation made by the Governing Council of UN-Habitat in its resolution 22/1 of 3 April 2009 and, having considered the question of convening in 2016 a third United Nations conference on housing and sustainable urban development (Habitat III), requests the Secretary-General to prepare a report on this question, in collaboration with the Governing Council, for consideration by the General Assembly at its sixty-sixth session;

15.   *Requests* the Secretary-General to submit to the General Assembly at its sixty-fifth session a report on the implementation of the present resolution;

16.   *Decides* to include in the provisional agenda of its sixty-fifth session the item entitled "Implementation of the outcome of the United Nations Conference on Human Settlements (Habitat II) and strengthening of the United Nations Human Settlements Programme (UN-Habitat)".

UN Human Settlements Programme

Governing Council

In 2009, the Governing Council of the United Nations Human Settlements Programme (UN-Habitat) held its twenty-second session (Nairobi, 30 March–3 April) [A/64/8], which addressed the special theme "Promoting affordable housing finance systems in an urbanizing world in the face of the global financial crisis and climate change". The Council adopted 11 resolutions on various aspects of the work of UN-Habitat and one decision on future Council sessions. On 3 April, the Council adopted the report of its deliberations [HSP/GC/22/7].

The Council [res. 22/1] recommended that the General Assembly consider the question of convening in 2016 a third UN conference on housing and sustainable urban development, so as to review, update and adopt more relevant policy recommendations to address the issues of sustainable human settlements development in a rapidly urbanizing world.

Regarding affordable housing finance [res. 22/2], the Council invited member States to consider undertaking a comprehensive assessment of the state of adequate shelter, affordable housing and related infrastructure with a view to assessing the adequacy of their national housing finance systems and regulatory frameworks in meeting the basic needs of their respective populations, particularly the poor and disadvantaged segments of the population. It also encouraged member States to establish sound and conducive frameworks and mechanisms to enable extended public and private investment in slum upgrading and prevention, affordable housing and urban development. The Executive Director of UN-Habitat was requested to disseminate models and knowledge about the importance of community-based pre-investment activities; to undertake monitoring and capacity-building, particularly at the municipal level; and to work with international and regional financial institutions to

promote housing and infrastructure investments as a contributor to economic growth and as a means of reducing poverty. The Council supported exploring the possibility of convening a high-level General Assembly special event on the issue of housing finance systems in the face of the global financial crisis.

On cities and climate change [res. 22/3], the Council requested the Executive Director to continue to increase awareness of the role of cities in addressing climate change and encouraged the development in other regions of such activities as the "Climate-resilient cities in Africa" initiative. The Council invited Governments to include the issue of cities and climate change as an integral part of their national climate change strategies, including mitigation and adaptation.

To strengthen the development of urban young people [res. 22/4], the Council encouraged Governments to give priority and support to youth-led development initiatives and invited multilateral agencies, Governments, the private sector and civil society to listen to youth and develop policies on their development based on participatory processes. The Executive Director was requested to strengthen the institutional management and operations of the Opportunities Fund for Urban Youth-led Development; to evaluate the Fund's operation and to report to the Council's twenty-third (2011) session; to increase support for youth and youth-led initiatives; and to strengthen work on the engagement of young people in human settlements development.

In the area of UN-Habitat governance [res. 22/5], the Council requested the Executive Director and the Committee of Permanent Representatives to undertake an examination of the governance of the Programme with a view to identifying and implementing ways to improve the transparency, accountability, efficiency and effectiveness of the functioning of the governance structure and to identify options for any other relevant changes for consideration by the Council at its twenty-third (2011) session.

The Council approved [res. 22/7] the proposed 2010–2011 work programme and budget [HSP/GC/22/5]; approved the general-purpose budget of $66,190,500; endorsed the 2010–2011 special-purpose budget of $95,717,700; and approved an increase in the general-purpose statutory reserve from $3,279,500 to $6,619,500. It requested the Executive Director to report on the execution of the work programme against each of its expected accomplishments to Governments through the Committee of Permanent Representatives on a half-yearly basis, and also to the Governing Council.

The Council approved [res. 22/8] the guidelines on access to basic services for all [HSP/GC.22/2/Add.6 & Corr.1/Rev.1] as a valuable instrument in attaining the MDGs and invited Governments to place the issue of access to basic services for all at the centre of their national development policies, with a special emphasis on filling the gaps for the poor and marginalized groups, and to strengthen their legal and institutional frameworks for facilitating partnerships, in line with the guidelines.

The Council welcomed [res. 22/10] the invitation by the Government of Brazil to host the fifth session of the World Urban Forum in Rio de Janeiro from 22 to 26 March 2010 and requested the Executive Director to carry out a lessons-learned review of all previous Forum sessions, to be submitted to the Committee of Permanent Representatives prior to its September session, with a view to improving the planning, organization and effectiveness of future sessions.

The Council requested [res. 22/9] UN-Habitat to strengthen the integration of South-South cooperation in its activities and, to that end, to strengthen cooperation with UNDP and other organizations within and outside the UN system. It noted [res. 22/11] the progress made by UN-Habitat in implementing the special human settlements programme for the Palestinian people and called on member States and others to support the operation of that programme. It also took note [res. 22/6] of the enhancement of the Habitat Scroll of Honour awards by the establishment of complementary cash awards, including the Dubai International Award for Best Practices to Improve the Living Environment, the Sheikh Khalifa Bin Salman al Khalifa UN-Habitat Award and the Rafik Hariri Memorial Award, as a means of recognizing, rewarding and promoting best practices in human settlements, community development and leadership.

Among other documents, the Council also considered the progress report on the implementation of the 2008–2013 medium-term strategic and institutional plan for UN-Habitat [HSP/GC/22/2/Add.2]; the joint progress report of the Executive Directors of UN-Habitat and UNEP [HSP/GC/22/2/Add.4]; and the gender equality action plan [HSP/GC/22/5/Add.2].

Committee of Permanent Representatives

The Committee of Permanent Representatives, the intersessional body of the UN-Habitat Governing Council, held four regular meetings in 2009 (5 March, 11 June, 24 September, 7 December) and one extraordinary meeting (24 March). It adopted its report on its work during the intersessional period [HSP/GC/22/3 & Add.1], reviewed the regular quarterly reports on the financial status of UN-Habitat, approved the terms of reference for a governance review of UN-Habitat and elected its Bureau for the 2010–2011 biennium. In December, the co-chair of the open-ended contact group for the governance review process provided an update on the progress of the review.

UN-Habitat activities

In 2009, UN-Habitat continued to implement its work programme in line with Governing Council resolutions and the goals of the UN system and the international community. Under the medium-term strategic and institutional plan, approved by the Council in 2007 [YUN 2007, p. 1086], UN-Habitat focused on six key areas: advocacy, monitoring and partnerships; promotion of participatory planning, management and governance; promotion of pro-poor land and housing; environmentally sound basic infrastructure and services; strengthened human settlements finance systems; and excellence in management.

The agency's worldwide monitoring function was strengthened with the creation of an additional seven local units of its Global Urban Observatory, a network that collected and developed policy-oriented indicators in 133 cities around the world. To help policymakers respond to the challenge of urbanization with well-informed decisions, UN-Habitat organized capacity-building workshops on the use of census data to prepare city and slum indicators and the measurement of inequalities at the city level. UN-Habitat enhanced its role as a major source of urban data with the publication of the *Statistical Book on Human Settlements* and of *Slum levels and trends 1990–2010*, as well as a series of *Urban Inequities Surveys* and a revised edition of its *Urban Indicators Programme Training Manual*.

In March, UN-Habitat launched its Cities and Climate Change Initiative in Oslo, Norway, and deployed four pilot schemes involving the cities of Esmeraldas, Ecuador; Kampala, Uganda; Maputo, Mozambique; and Sorsogon, the Philippines. Subsequently, five other cities joined the initiative: Bobo Dioulasso, Burkina Faso; Kigali, Rwanda; Mombasa, Kenya; Saint-Louis, Senegal; and Walvis Bay, Namibia. The initiative sought to enhance the preparedness and mitigation activities of cities in developing and least developed countries. Meanwhile, the links between the agency and the private sector took on a fresh dimension in July when the first UN-Habitat International Business Forum on Better Cities was held in India's capital, New Delhi. At the three-day Forum, private-sector leaders reviewed challenges, solutions, best practices and innovation for sustainable cities with representatives of central and local government and civil society.

The UN-Habitat Urban Youth Fund granted nearly $1 million to more than 60 projects in 33 countries in its first year of operation. In seven sub-Saharan African countries, UN-Habitat developed and promoted Women Land Access Trusts, which gave women access to affordable housing finance, leading to more secure tenure. UN-Habitat promoted urban environmental governance and strategic planning in the Lake Victoria region of East Africa, seeking to reconcile urban expansion and a unique ecosystem. Lake Victoria City Development Strategies were at work in eight cities, which joined forces across borders to set up a common institutional framework and were engaged in dedicated capacity-building programmes.

In Ecuador, UN-Habitat helped to organize workshops on housing for indigenous people, attended by representatives from Bolivia, Brazil, Chile, Mexico, Nicaragua and Peru. UN-Habitat worked with Pakistan's Ministry of the Environment as well as with NGOs and UN agencies to deliver gender mainstreaming workshops on water, sanitation and hygiene programmes: participants were from federal, provincial and local governments, water and sanitation service providers, and community-based organizations. Similar training schemes took place in African cities. UN-Habitat also worked on regional training schemes in Accra, Ghana and Quito, Ecuador; the schemes enabled women to develop skills to engage with local leadership and authorities at the grassroots level, with a view to enhancing women's participation in local governance.

In the area of slum upgrading, UN-Habitat helped to establish Local Finance Facilities in Ghana, Indonesia, Sri Lanka and the United Republic of Tanzania; those sustainable, financially viable non-bank financial institutions were well positioned to reach over 10,000 households by 2014. The facilities offered credit enhancement, most commonly in the form of guarantees, to support housing and infrastructure improvement for low-income end-users. The Participatory Slum Upgrading Programme promoted participatory urban planning, management and governance in 30 countries. In Nairobi, 1,300 families were moved from shacks in a slum to modern apartments built through a partnership between the Kenyan Government and UN-Habitat. The scheme under the Kenya Slum Upgrading Programme saw residents of Kibera slums move to new high-rise flats,

for which they would be charged about $20 a month. During the year, UN-Habitat launched Phase II of the Participatory Slum Upgrading and Prevention Programme in 12 African countries. The new phase identified the steps needed for upgrading and the resources to be mobilized, and mapped out a slum-prevention policy in each country.

The Land Tool Network supported the development of innovative land tools to contribute to poverty alleviation through land reform, improved land management and security of tenure. The Network brought together international NGOs and financial institutions, research and training institutions, donors and professional bodies. It comprised 42 global partners and had 1,130 registered members from 132 countries. In Kenya, its efforts culminated in Parliament's adoption of improved land policies in December 2009.

In Madagascar, a land regularization programme was aimed at providing access to secure tenure for all. In Cape Verde, Mozambique and Rwanda, UN-Habitat helped to develop and apply enabling policies and improved regulatory frameworks. In Mozambique, it supported the massive process of land-use regularization launched in the capital, Maputo. In Colombia, the agency helped to prepare a binding policy guideline on slum upgrading that became the main reference for nine municipal integrated programmes. In Tanzania, UN-Habitat assisted authorities in Dar es Salaam in completing an upgrading plan for 50 per cent of all unplanned and un-serviced settlements in the city, and took the lead in mobilizing the necessary funding.

The three-year Settlement and Integration of Refugees Programme, which UN-Habitat completed in Serbia, provided 670 housing units, including 570 new ones, for 3,000 refugees and other vulnerable people. A new programme would bring the benefits of that experience to urban areas in Albania and Bosnia and Herzegovina. In July, UN-Habitat joined the Government of Iraq to launch a $70 million urban governance, housing, infrastructure and basic services programme.

Chapter VIII

Population

In 2009, the commemoration of the fifteenth anniversary of the landmark 1994 International Conference on Population and Development (ICPD) took place against the backdrop of financial turmoil and economic downturn. The global financial and economic crisis threatened to reverse progress achieved in eliminating poverty and derail the attainment of the Millennium Development Goals (MDGS). Estimates suggested that the crisis had left an additional 50 million people in extreme poverty. Social and economic distress further complicated redressing gender inequality and improving reproductive health and rights, which were at the centre of the ICPD agenda.

UN population activities continued to be guided by the Programme of Action adopted at the ICPD and the key actions for its implementation adopted at the twenty-first special session of the General Assembly in 1999. The Commission on Population and Development—the body responsible for monitoring, reviewing and assessing implementation of the Programme of Action—considered as its special theme "The contribution of the Programme of Action of the International Conference on Population and Development to the internationally agreed development goals, including the Millennium Development Goals". The Population Division continued to analyse and report on world demographic trends and policies and to make its findings available in publications and on the Internet. World population reached 6.8 billion in 2009, according to the Division.

The United Nations Population Fund (UNFPA) assisted countries in implementing the ICPD agenda and the MDGS through their use of population data to formulate sound policies and programmes. In 2009, UNFPA provided assistance to 155 countries, areas and territories, with emphasis on increasing the availability and quality of reproductive health services, fighting gender discrimination and gender-based violence, formulating effective population policies and intensifying HIV prevention.

Follow-up to 1994 Conference on Population and Development

Implementation of Programme of Action

Commission on Population and Development

The Commission on Population and Development, at its forty-second session (New York, 11 April 2008

and 30 March–3 April 2009) [E/2009/25] considered as its special theme "The contribution of the Programme of Action of the International Conference on Population and Development to the internationally agreed development goals, including the Millennium Development Goals". It discussed follow-up actions to the recommendations of the 1994 International Conference on Population and Development (ICPD) [YUN 1994, p. 955] and adopted a resolution [E/2009/25 (res. 2009/1)] on national, regional and international action relating to its special theme.

Documents before the Commission included the report of its Bureau on its intersessional meetings (New York, 21 October and 15 December 2008) [E/CN.9/2009/2] and the Secretary-General's reports on: world population monitoring [E/CN.9/2009/3] (see below); monitoring of population programmes [E/CN.9/2009/4] (see p. 1049); flow of financial resources for assisting in the implementation of the ICPD Programme of Action [E/CN.9/2009/5] (see p. 1046); and world demographic trends [E/CN.9/2009/6] [ibid.]. It also had before it 11 statements by non-governmental organizations (NGOS) in consultative status with the Economic and Social Council [E/CN.9/2009/NGO/1–11].

Reports of Secretary-General. The Secretary-General's report on world population monitoring, focusing on the contribution of the ICPD Programme of Action to the internationally agreed development goals, including the Millennium Development Goals (MDGS) [E/CN.9/2009/3], covered how the implementation of the core guidelines of the Programme of Action contributed to the achievement of international development goals. It found that the global population growth rate was estimated at 1.17 per cent annually and a population explosion had been averted globally due to declined fertility rates in Asia, Latin America and the Caribbean. That population explosion was still playing out in Africa and most of the least developed countries. Government policy and international commitment had made a difference in shaping population dynamics, and accelerating the implementation of the Programme of Action would contribute to achieving the internationally agreed development goals.

High fertility was associated with the persistence of poverty because low-income groups generally had much higher fertility than high-income groups. Surveys in 56 developing countries showed that women in the lowest wealth quintile had, on average, two more children than women in the upper quintile. Analyses of the impact of declining fertility on poverty reduction showed that demographic change alone accounted for a 14 per cent drop in poverty levels in the developing world during 1960–2000, and could produce an additional 14 per cent reduction during 2000–2015 if fertility decline accelerated in high-fertility countries. At the country level, higher fertility among the poor could contribute to increasing the levels of hunger and undernutrition as well as poverty. Rising food prices had increased poverty levels by about 4.5 percentage points in low-income countries between 2005 and 2007, implying that an additional 105 million people had fallen into poverty. Policies to address the effects of food price shocks needed to give priority to the immediate protection of the most vulnerable, including women and children. Longer-term policy responses needed to incorporate population policy as part of a coordinated response to promote sustainable livelihoods for all.

Much progress had been made towards achieving universal primary education, a goal established by the Programme of Action and echoed by the MDGs [YUN 2000, p. 51]. Nevertheless, at both the household and country levels, investment in the education of children was less likely to be sufficient when the number of children per family was large. Sustained high fertility resulted in rapidly increasing numbers of school-age children, translating into increased demands on education systems and families. Countries with worse education indicators tended to have higher proportions of children and high population growth rates. The level of education of women was a key determinant of fertility behaviour, as women with higher education were more likely to use contraception and have fewer children than women with fewer years of schooling.

Despite progress made in providing access to modern contraceptive methods to those who needed them, an estimated 106 million married women in developing countries had an unmet need for family planning. Satisfying that need could contribute to reducing maternal mortality, improving maternal health, reducing child mortality, promoting gender equality, combating HIV/AIDS and reducing poverty. Closely spaced births and pregnancies in adolescent and older women put children at increased risk of death. Substantial increases in domestic and external funding for family planning were necessary if reproductive health and child health were to be assured by 2015.

The relationship between population growth and increasing greenhouse gas emissions was not straightforward, and it was not possible to assess the effects of population dynamics net of other economic and technological changes, but reducing population growth could allow more time for the global population

to adapt to those changes. Moderating population growth would also make it easier to conserve water, make water accessible to more people, and expand the coverage of sanitation to meet the targets set by the MDGs.

The Secretary-General's report [E/CN.9/2009/5] on the flow of financial resources for assisting in the implementation of the ICPD Programme of Action, submitted in accordance with General Assembly resolutions 49/128 [YUN 1994, p. 963] and 50/124 [YUN 1995, p. 1094], said that donor assistance for population activities had been increasing steadily: it had reached $7.4 billion in 2006, was expected to surpass $8 billion in 2007 and might increase to $11 billion over 2009 and 2010 if donors continued to increase funding levels. Resources for population activities mobilized by developing countries, as a group, were estimated at $18.5 billion for 2007 and were expected to increase to $19.6 billion in 2008 and $20.5 billion in 2009. Those figures presupposed that developing countries would continue to increase such resources; however, given the global financial crisis, it was not certain whether countries would continue to increase funding levels for population activities.

The report presented revised cost estimates for the four components of the ICPD population package—family planning; reproductive health; sexually transmitted infections and HIV/AIDS; and basic research, data and population and development analysis—and pointed out that without political will, renewed commitment and adequate resources, it would not be possible to achieve the goals of the Conference or the Millennium Summit.

The Secretary-General's biennial report [E/CN.9/2009/6] on world demographic trends and prospects, submitted in accordance with Economic and Social Council resolution 1996/2 [YUN 1996, p. 976], said that world population was 6.8 billion and was projected to stand at 9 billion in 2045 if fertility continued to decline in developing countries. Due to varying fertility levels, high population growth was expected in several developing countries, while the population of developed countries would grow little, if at all. Eighty-six countries, including 53 developed countries, had below-replacement fertility, while 42 developing countries, many of which were least developed, had total fertility above 4.0 children per woman. In most of the world, longevity continued to increase. Life expectancy was estimated at 67.2 years globally, averaging 76.5 years in developed countries and 65.4 years in developing countries. In the least developed countries, two thirds of which were severely affected by the HIV/AIDS epidemic, life expectancy averaged 54.6 years. In the future, the population would be older and more urban. Globally, the number of persons aged 60 or over would almost triple, reaching

2 billion in 2050. In 2008, for the first time in history, the global number of urban dwellers had surpassed the number of rural inhabitants. Future population growth would be concentrated mainly in the urban areas of the developing world. By 2050, 70 per cent of the world population would likely be urban.

Commission action. The Commission brought its resolution on the contribution of the ICPD Programme of Action to the internationally agreed development goals, including the MDGs [E/2009/25 (res. 2009/1)], to the attention of the Economic and Social Council. The resolution recognized that population dynamics, development, human rights, sexual and reproductive health, reproductive rights, empowerment of young people and women and gender equality were important for achieving the goals. It also recognized that there was a dire need to increase financial resources for implementing the Programme of Action, particularly for family planning.

The Commission called on Governments, in formulating and implementing national development plans, budgets and poverty eradication strategies, to address challenges relating to the impact of population dynamics on poverty and sustainable development. It requested that the UN funds, programmes and specialized agencies continue to support countries in implementing the Programme of Action and thus contribute to eradicating poverty, promoting gender equality, improving adolescent, maternal and neonatal health, preventing HIV/AIDS and ensuring environmental sustainability. The Commission called upon the international community to assist Governments and to increase funding for family planning, and encouraged Member States to strengthen international cooperation in the area of international migration and development in order to address the negative impact of the economic crisis on migrants and the migration process.

The Commission decided that the special theme for its forty-fourth (2011) session would be "Fertility, reproductive health and development" [dec. 2009/101]. It also adopted the provisional agenda for its forty-third (2010) session.

By **decision 2009/239** of 29 July, the Economic and Social Council took note of the report of the Commission on its forty-second (2009) session and approved the provisional agenda for its forty-third (2010) session.

In preparation for its forty-third session, the Commission's Bureau held two meetings in 2009 (New York, 28 October and 9 December) [E/CN.9/2010/2].

Communications. On 2 April [E/CN.9/2009/8], Jordan, as Chairman of the Group of Arab States at the United Nations for the month of April, raised the issue of the nomination of Israel as Chair of the Commission's forty-third session. Israel replied on 7 April [E/CN.9/2009/9].

International migration and development

Global Forum Meeting. The third Global Forum on Migration and Development (Athens, Greece, 2–5 November) addressed the theme "Integrating Migration Policies into Development Strategies for the Benefit of All". It included a meeting of civil society (2–3 November), followed by an intergovernmental meeting (4–5 November). At the former, more than 300 participants from 100 countries gathered to discuss key outcomes and recommendations, which were then reported at the Government meeting. Recommendations included more flexible stay/work permits that would allow migrants to change employer and employment sector and accumulate benefits on short-term permits; more transparency in visa regimes; lower up-front costs of migration; flexible demand-driven permits; and low-cost loans to migrants and their families to start their journeys. It was suggested that Governments monitor recruiter and migration agency practices more closely and enforce laws against exploitation, discrimination and xenophobic and racist practices.

Over 530 delegates representing 142 Member States and observers and 30 international organizations gathered at the intergovernmental meeting to attend two plenary sessions and round table discussions on migration and the MDGs; migrant integration, reintegration and circulation for development; and policy and institutional coherence and partnerships. Governments agreed to pursue policy and institutional coherence on migration and development, as well as research to underpin such coherence.

On 1 October, the Philippines transmitted to the Second (Economic and Financial) Committee the report [A/C.2/64/2] of the second meeting of the Global Forum, held in Manila in 2008 [YUN 2008, p. 1185].

Eighth Meeting on International Migration and Development. In response to General Assembly resolution 58/208 [YUN 2003, p. 1087], the UN Population Division organized the Eighth Coordination Meeting on International Migration (New York, 16–17 November), which brought together some 70 representatives of UN agencies, funds and programmes, intergovernmental and regional organizations, civil society organizations and research institutes. The meeting included presentations on the global and regional impact of the economic and financial crisis on international migration, and on developments in improving the evidence base on international migration and development. Other conferences, meetings and forums on the subject included a regional workshop on international migration statistics (Cairo, Egypt, 30 June–3 July).

International Organization for Migration. In a letter dated 5 November [A/64/233], representatives from 12 Member States requested the inclusion of an additional item entitled "Cooperation between the United Nations and the International Organization for Migration" in the agenda of the resumed sixty-fourth (2010) session of the General Assembly. Annexed to the letter were an explanatory memorandum and a draft resolution. The General Committee on 24 November [A/BUR/64/SR.2] decided to defer discussion of the item to a later date.

Human Development Report. The subject of the *Human Development Report 2009*, issued by the United Nations Development Programme (UNDP), was "Overcoming barriers: Human mobility and development". The starting point of the report was that the global distribution of capabilities was extraordinarily unequal, and that was a major driver for movement of people. Migration could expand individual choices—for instance in terms of incomes, access to services and participation—but the opportunities open to people varied from those who were highly skilled to those with limited capacities and assets. Those underlying inequalities could be compounded by policy distortions.

The report investigated migration in the context of demographic changes and trends in both growth and inequality. It presented individual, family and village experiences, and explored less visible movements, such as short-term and seasonal migration. Migration had a positive impact on human development through increased household incomes and improved access to education and health services. It could empower disadvantaged groups, in particular women. At the same time, risks to human development were present where migration was a reaction to threats and denial of choice, and where regular opportunities for movement were constrained.

National and local policies played a critical role in enabling better outcomes for both those who chose to move in order to improve their circumstances and those forced to leave due to conflict or environmental degradation. Host country restrictions could raise both the costs and the risks of migration. Negative outcomes could arise where basic civic rights—like voting, schooling and health care—were denied to migrants. A human development approach could redress some of the underlying issues that eroded the potential benefits of mobility or forced migration.

United Nations Population Fund

2009 activities

Reports of Executive Director. In a report [DP/FPA/2010/17 (Part I)] to the UNDP/UNFPA Executive Board, the UNFPA Executive Director reviewed major initiatives undertaken by UNFPA in 2009 in implementing its strategic plan for 2008–2013. The report focused on outcomes in population and development, reproductive health and rights, and gender equality.

In 2009, the global financial and economic crisis threatened to reverse progress achieved in eliminating poverty and derail the achievement of the MDGs [YUN 2000, p. 51]. An estimated 50 million additional people were living in extreme poverty, and social and economic distress further complicated redressing gender inequality and improving reproductive health and rights. The crisis had exacerbated other long-term problems, including food and energy insecurity and climate change. UNFPA consistently advocated for sustained and increased investments in health and for using technology and data to reach the poor and monitor impact. The Fund coordinated with other UN agencies to design a global vulnerability alert system. It also promoted human-centred approaches for adaptation to climate change, building on community resilience and women's empowerment.

Regarding management, 91 per cent of UNFPA country offices achieved over 75 per cent of annual output targets, and 75 per cent reported that staff participated in training on results-based management. Country offices implemented 409 South-South initiatives, providing knowledge, learning and training for building national capacity. The Fund participated in 221 joint programmes with UN agencies covering reproductive health, population and development, and gender equality.

UNFPA improved stewardship of resources, particularly in the context of national execution and audit recommendations. Oversight of cash transfers to implementing partners, prudent use of biennial support budget (BSB) resources, strengthened procurement procedures, and better system controls over BSB expenditures were notable improvements. The Fund surpassed its funding targets for core and non-core resources, securing over $1 million each from 19 donors.

An addendum [DP/FPA/2010/17 (Part I, Add.1)] provided a statistical and financial review for the year. It stated that from 2008 to 2009, total UNFPA income decreased by $62.2 million, or 7.4 per cent, to $783 million due to a decline in co-financing contributions. UNFPA resources surpassed the $500 million level for the sixth sequential year, including $486.4 million in regular resource income, the highest total in the history of UNFPA. Regular resource contribution income increased by $40.6 million, or 9.5 per cent, and total expenditures increased by $98.3 million, or 14 per cent, to $800.1 million. Of that increase, $96.8 million (98.5 per cent) was attributed to increased programme activities. UNFPA closed the year in robust financial health.

The Executive Director reported on the recommendations of the Joint Inspection Unit (JIU) [DP/FPA/2010/17 (Part II)], providing a synopsis of UNFPA management responses to key recommendations of JIU. Of the eight reports issued by JIU in 2009, three were relevant to UNFPA. Those reports concerned: a more coherent UN support system to Africa [JIU/REP/2009/5]; offshoring in UN system organizations [JIU/REP/2009/6]; and the selection and conditions of service of executive heads in the UN system organizations [JIU/REP/2009/8]. The Executive Director provided information on related UNFPA policies, adding that of the 62 recommendations issued by JIU between 2006 and 2008 that were relevant to UNFPA, all had been implemented or were being pursued.

UNDP/UNFPA Executive Board. The UNFPA Executive Director reported, jointly with the Administrator of UNDP, to the Economic and Social Council on the triennial comprehensive policy review of operational activities for development of the UN system [E/2010/5].

On 3 June [E/2009/35 (dec. 2009/16)], the UNDP/UNFPA Executive Board took note of the UNFPA Executive Director's report for 2008: [DP/FPA/2009/2 (Part I & Add.1, Add.1/Corr.1, Part II)]. The Board took note of progress made in aligning UNFPA programming with the UNFPA strategic plan for 2008–2011 and requested that the Executive Director submit to the Board a midterm review of the strategic plan in 2011 and a cumulative review in 2013.

By **decision 2009/215** of 22 July, the Economic and Social Council took note of the annual report of the UNDP/UNFPA Executive Board [E/2008/35] and of the joint report of the UNDP Administrator and the UNFPA Executive Director to the Council [YUN 2008, p. 1188].

Report of Secretary-General. The Secretary-General in January submitted to the Commission on Population and Development a report on monitoring population programmes, focusing on the contribution of the ICPD Programme of Action to the internationally agreed development goals, including the MDGs [E/CN.9/2009/4]. The report, prepared by UNFPA, set out the strategic orientation of the Fund and provided examples of its global, regional and country activities aimed at achieving the MDGs.

UNFPA was engaged in policy dialogue aimed at influencing the formulation of pro-poor policies in several countries. It sought to raise awareness of the links between population dynamics and poverty, emphasizing the situation of women and young people and the positive effects that reproductive health care and family planning could have on economic and social development and poverty reduction.

UNFPA contributed to the achievement of the MDG on promoting gender equality and empowering women by addressing critical issues, including women's right to health and the right to live free from violence. The Fund was working at the global level, in collaboration with other UN agencies and in partnership with Governments and civil society organizations, to promote women's leadership and implement the Beijing Platform for Action [YUN 1995, p. 1170] and the ICPD Programme of Action.

UNFPA supported the development and implementation of national strategies and programmes aimed at promoting reproductive health in countries around the world. The Fund emphasized integrating a package of sexual and reproductive health services into the basic health services delivered at the district and local levels. UNFPA assisted countries in increasing access to maternal health services, especially skilled delivery care and emergency obstetric care. The Fund also worked with Governments through programmes in 140 countries to ensure that family planning was an integral part of national health plans and budgets, and that information and a range of family planning methods were offered in all health facilities and reached all communities.

UNFPA worked with Governments to strengthen and integrate reproductive health and HIV services. As co-sponsor of the Joint United Nations Programme on HIV/AIDS (UNAIDS), UNFPA provided support to 40 countries in developing road maps within the new Africa maternal and newborn programme, contributing to the prevention of mother-to-child transmission of HIV. The Fund also procured male condoms in 120 countries and female condoms in 50 countries and provided financial and technical support to countries enrolled in the Global Condom Initiative, including 22 in Africa, 23 in the Caribbean and 6 in Asia.

UNFPA supported research to generate and disseminate a better understanding and awareness of the different ways in which population dynamics affected environmental change. The UNFPA agenda on climate change included supporting research and advocacy for mitigating climate change; promoting sustainable cities and reducing urban vulnerability; identifying the impact of climate change on migration; and improving responses to emergency situations. The Fund devoted the *State of World Population 2009* report [Sales No. E.09.III.H.1] to the issue of environment and women to highlight the linkages between climate change and population factors.

Population, development and poverty reduction

In 2009, UNFPA programme assistance in population and development totalled $76.9 million from core resources and $38.4 million from other resources. Country offices supported policy and strategy development, data, the 2010 round of censuses, and emerging population and development issues. Population dynamics and its interlinkages with poverty were incorporated in 79 per cent of national development plans.

Among its activities, in Turkey, UNFPA supported a demographic study in collaboration with the Turkish Business Association, exploring linkages between population dynamics and social sectors. The UNFPA country office in Malawi provided technical and financial support to the youth sector, and advocacy led by young people resulted in halting a law allowing marriage at the age of 16. In the Dominican Republic, UNFPA mapped youth organizations in 14 municipalities and trained youth on policy dialogue, programme management and advocacy. UNFPA also worked with the World Bank to finalize an inter-agency resource toolkit on the inclusion of young people and their issues into poverty reduction strategies and national development plans.

Support to 2010 census operations continued to be a priority. In Africa, UNFPA made censuses one of its strategic priorities, and a needs assessment conference on census analysis was organized jointly with the United Nations Statistical Division in Senegal. In Lebanon, UNFPA organized training in methods of census analysis in collaboration with the UN Population Division, and in Peru, it supported design and implementation of new analyses of the results of the 2007 census in coordination with the National Institute of Statistics. UNFPA developed technical orientation guides and manuals on the use of census data to estimate maternal mortality and analyse gender and environment issues. UNFPA also supported national household/thematic surveys that included ICPD-related issues in Albania, Angola, Botswana, Ethiopia, Jordan, the Lao People's Democratic Republic, Panama, Papua New Guinea and Venezuela. The Fund provided technical support for the development and establishment of integrated national databases.

UNFPA collaborated with and supported the International Institute for Environment and Development to conduct case studies on urban density and sustainable development, and the Fund's flagship publication, *State of World Population 2009, Facing a changing world: women, population and climate* [Sales No. E.09.III.H.1] was dedicated to the issue of climate change and gender. UNFPA also organized an expert group meeting on population dynamics and climate change (London, 24–25 June). The Fund collaborated with the Global Migration Group in preparing fact sheets on the impact of the global financial crisis on international migration for the third Global Forum on Migration and Development, and country

offices worked on advocacy, awareness-raising, capacity-building and research to maximize the benefits and mitigate the negative impacts of international migration. UNFPA collaborated with the United Nations Programme on Ageing and the International Institute on Ageing in Malta to train policymakers on addressing challenges posed by rapid population ageing.

Reproductive health and rights

In 2009, UNFPA programme assistance in the area of reproductive health totalled $170 million from core resources and $227 million from other resources, making up 67 per cent of its development assistance. Country offices supported all five strategic plan outcomes ranging from maternal health, family planning and reproductive health commodity security to HIV/AIDS prevention and young people.

UNFPA was involved in health sector-wide approaches in 30 countries and was contributing to joint pooled funding in that area in Bangladesh, Cambodia, Ethiopia, Ghana, India, Uganda and the United Republic of Tanzania. The Fund participated in the "Health 4" initiative in 25 priority countries to coordinate efforts to accelerate progress in reproductive health and maternal and newborn survival. The UNFPA flagship Global Programme to enhance reproductive health commodity security supported 73 countries in developing sustainable approaches, up from 54 in 2008. As part of its humanitarian response, the Fund supported specialized training on reproductive health kits and the minimum initial regional and national service package.

The UNFPA maternal health thematic fund was active in 15 countries, including five of the six countries with the highest maternal mortality that accounted for nearly half of all maternal deaths worldwide—Afghanistan, Bangladesh, the Democratic Republic of the Congo, Ethiopia and Nigeria. In partnership with the International Confederation of Midwives, the midwifery programme worked in various regions, resulting in a 2 per cent increase in the contraceptive prevalence rate in Madagascar, the creation of a training coordination mechanism in Guyana, and the strengthening of clinical training of about 300 midwives in Côte d'Ivoire. The Campaign to End Fistula grew to cover 36 countries. Because of the Campaign, 4,100 women had received fistula treatment and care; the capacity of 100 health facilities in 23 countries was strengthened to manage and treat fistula; and training was conducted for more than 1,000 health care personnel in fistula prevention and management, including more than 160 doctors, 245 nurses and midwives, more than 30 social workers and paramedical staff, and more than 600 community health workers.

UNFPA initiatives in response to HIV/AIDS focused on comprehensive condom programming, women and girls, young people, HIV and sex work, and sexual and reproductive health and HIV linkages. As part of the UNFPA Global Condom Initiative, 21 countries drafted national condom strategies and worked toward developing five-year operational plans. Many countries utilized non-traditional condom distribution outlets to widen access to male and female condoms. The Fund worked with UNAIDS partners and the Australian Institute of International Health to develop a training package for UN staff on building their capacity to address HIV and sex work, injecting drug use and men having sex with men. It supported the Harvard University School of Public Health to produce a gender-based violence (GBV) and HIV study. It worked with other international and national organizations to roll out the rapid assessment tool for sexual and reproductive health and HIV linkages in five regions and 17 countries.

Gender equality and women's empowerment

Thirteen per cent of UNFPA development assistance in 2009 was in the area of gender equality, totalling $40.3 million from core resources and $39 million from other resources. UNFPA country offices supported all four strategic plan outcomes in gender equality.

UNFPA provided support to Governments for capacity building and implementation of legislative and policy reform; advocacy to incorporate gender and reproductive rights in reporting to the United Nations Committee on the Elimination of Discrimination against Women (CEDAW); and tracking progress on achievements in gender equality in relation to international conventions and platforms. In line with the Secretary-General's call to assist countries to monitor and evaluate efforts under Security Council resolution 1325(2000) [YUN 2000, p. 1113], UNFPA initiated efforts, in collaboration with the United Nations Development Fund for Women (UNIFEM) and the Office of the Special Adviser on Gender Issues and Advancement of Women, to develop and refine indicators on national action plans on Council resolutions 1325(2000) and 1820(2008) [YUN 2008, p. 1265] in several pilot countries, such as Sierra Leone and Uganda.

The UNFPA-United Nations Children's Fund (UNICEF) Joint Programme on Female Genital Mutilation/Cutting supported the implementation of a common approach for the collective abandonment of female genital mutilation/cutting in 12 countries. As a result, communities in Ethiopia, the Gambia, Guinea and Senegal abandoned the practice. To increase male involvement in support of sexual and reproductive health issues, UNFPA brought together country offices from around the globe to discuss ongoing initiatives and ways to strengthen such involvement.

A global achievement on capacity-building was the finalization of the training package and rollout of the human rights-based approach to programming within UNFPA. At the country level, UNFPA, along with other partners, supported Governments in elaborating national reports to CEDAW in the Central African Republic, China, the Dominican Republic, Jordan and Oman. Human rights intercultural approaches sought to reinforce leadership of indigenous women and preserve traditional knowledge and practices in Bolivia, Colombia, Ecuador, Mexico, Panama and Peru.

UNFPA was co-chair of the joint programme on violence against women initiative undertaken by the Inter-agency Task Force on Violence Against Women, which had been institutionalized in nine pilot countries through the development of national joint programming action plans. The Fund was also a lead member of the Secretary-General's UNiTE to End Violence against Women campaign and supported activities at all levels. UNFPA humanitarian assistance sought to strengthen coordination mechanisms for improved prevention and response to violence against women in several countries, and GBV information management systems were introduced to monitor GBV incidents in Chad, Côte d'Ivoire, Kenya, Liberia, Nepal and Uganda.

Country and intercountry programmes

UNFPA project expenditures for country, global and regional activities in 2009 totalled $347.9 million, compared with $337.2 million in 2008, according to the Executive Director's statistical and financial review [DP/FPA/2010/17 (Part I, Add.1)]. The 2009 figure included $269.3 million for country programmes (compared with $272.4 million in 2008) and $78.6 million for global and regional programmes (compared with $64.8 million in 2008). In accordance with the Executive Board's procedure for allocating resources [YUN 1996, p. 989], total expenditures in 2009 for countries most in need of assistance to realize ICPD goals amounted to $196.6 million, compared with $197.2 million in 2008.

Africa. Provisional data for UNFPA expenditures for programmes in sub-Saharan Africa gave a total of $136.2 million in 2009, compared with $141.3 million in 2008. Most of that amount went to reproductive health (46.2 per cent), followed by population and development (23.7 per cent), programme coordination and assistance (18.0 per cent) and gender equality and women's empowerment (12.1 per cent).

On 22 January [E/2009/35 (dec. 2009/8)], the UNDP/ UNFPA Executive Board, at its first regular session of 2009 (New York, 19–22 January), approved country programmes for Angola, Côte d'Ivoire, Kenya and Mauritania. On 3 June [dec. 2009/19], at its annual session (New York, 26 May–3 June), the Board took note of the draft country programme documents for Botswana and Burundi and approved the two-year extension of the country programme for Mozambique. On 11 September [dec. 2009/28], the Executive Board, at its second regular session of 2009 (New York, 8–11 September), approved the country programmes for Botswana and Burundi on a no-objection basis and took note of the draft country programme document for Uganda.

Arab States. Provisional expenditures for UNFPA programmes in the Arab States totalled $31 million in 2009, compared with $26.2 million in 2008. Most of that amount was spent on reproductive health (55.5 per cent), followed by population and development (17.7 per cent), gender equality and women's empowerment (14.8 per cent) and programme coordination and assistance (11.9 per cent).

On 3 June [dec. 2009/19], the Executive Board took note of the draft country programme document for Lebanon and of the one-year extension of the country programme for the Occupied Palestinian Territory. On 11 September [dec. 2009/28], it approved the country programme for Lebanon on a no-objection basis.

Eastern Europe and Central Asia. Provisional expenditures for UNFPA programmes in Eastern Europe and Central Asia totalled $14.9 million in 2009, compared with $15.1 million in 2008. Most of that amount was spent on reproductive health (44.3 per cent), followed by population and development (25.5 per cent), programme coordination and assistance (20.1 per cent) and gender equality and women's empowerment (10.1 per cent).

On 3 June [dec. 2009/19], the Executive Board took note of the draft country programme documents for Armenia, Bosnia and Herzegovina, Kazakhstan, Tajikistan, Turkmenistan and Uzbekistan, took note of the one-year extension of the country programme for Azerbaijan, and approved the two-year extension of the country programme for Kyrgyzstan. On 11 September [dec. 2009/28], the Board approved the country programmes for Armenia, Bosnia and Herzegovina, Kazakhstan, Tajikistan, Turkmenistan and Uzbekistan on a no-objection basis.

Asia and the Pacific. Provisional expenditures for UNFPA programmes in Asia and the Pacific amounted to $87.8 million, compared with $85 million in 2008. Most of the total went to reproductive health (66.2 per cent), followed by population and development (16.5 per cent), gender equality and women's empowerment (9.0 per cent) and programme coordination and assistance (8.3 per cent).

On 22 January [dec. 2009/8], the Executive Board approved the country programme document for Timor-Leste. On 3 June [dec. 2009/19], the Board took note of the draft country programme document for Afghanistan, approved the two-year extension of the country programme for the Philippines, and took note of the one-year extensions of the country programmes for the Democratic People's Republic of Korea and Iran. On 11 September, [dec. 2009/28], the Board approved the country programme for Afghanistan on a no-objection basis.

Latin America and the Caribbean. Provisional expenditures for UNFPA programmes in Latin America and the Caribbean totalled $34.1 million in 2009, compared with $34.3 million in 2008. Most of the total went to reproductive health (40.5 per cent), followed by population and development (27.5 per cent), gender equality and women's empowerment (17.3 per cent) and programme coordination and assistance (14.7 per cent).

On 22 January [dec. 2009/8], the Executive Board approved the country programme documents for Haiti and Venezuela. On 3 June [dec. 2009/19], the Board took note of the draft country programme document for Ecuador. On 11 September [dec. 2009/28], the Board approved the country programme for Ecuador on a no-objection basis and took note of the draft country programme document for Guatemala.

Global programme. Provisional expenditures for the UNFPA global programme totalled $43.9 million in 2009, compared with $35.3 million in 2008. Most of the total went to programme coordination and assistance (39.2 per cent), followed by reproductive health (26.2 per cent), population and development (26.0 per cent) and gender equality and women's empowerment (8.6 per cent).

Financial and management questions

Financing

UNFPA income from all sources totalled $783 million in 2009, compared with $845.2 million in 2008 [DP/FPA/2010/17 (Part I, Add.1)], comprising $469.4 million from regular resources, $288.8 million from other resources, interest income of $16.5 million and other income of $8.3 million. Expenditures totalled $800.1 million, up from $701.8 million in 2008, comprising $467.3 million related to regular resources and $332.8 million related to other resources, resulting in a net deficit of $21 million after adjustments were made for prior periods.

On 11 September [E/2009/35 (dec. 2009/26)], the Executive Board approved gross resources of $274.5 million for the 2010–2011 biennial support budget [DP/FPA/2009/10 & Corr.1]. It also noted that the estimated net resources totalled $236.3 million. The Advisory

Committee on Administrative and Budgetary Questions (ACABQ) made comments on the budget [DP/FPA/2009/11].

Other financial issues

In a report on funding commitments to UNFPA [DP/FPA/2009/3], the Executive Director analysed contributions by States and others for 2009 and future years. UNFPA considered a stable base of regular resources as critical to enable it to support countries in implementing the ICPD Programme of Action and achieving the MDGs. In line with Assembly resolution 62/208 [YUN 2007, p. 877], UNFPA recognized that non-core (co-financing) resources represented an important supplement to the Fund's regular resource base.

In 2008, UNFPA income was $800.7 million—$469.5 million in regular resources and $331.2 million in co-financing resources. UNFPA achieved a donor base of 176 donor Governments compared with 182 in 2007. The total number of multi-year pledges was 63. The Fund received donations from 13 countries belonging to the Development Assistance Committee of the Organisation for Economic Co-operation and Development and all countries in sub-Saharan Africa. The top five donor countries were the Netherlands, Sweden, Denmark, Norway and the United Kingdom.

As of 1 April 2009, the projected regular contribution from donor Governments for 2009 was estimated at $451.1 million, an increase of $22.3 million (5.2 per cent) over 2008. Ninety-seven official pledges for 2009 had been received, 42 of which were multi-year pledges.

The Executive Board took note of the report on 2 June [E/2009/35 (dec. 2009/17)] and encouraged countries to make contributions early in the year and to make multi-year pledges.

In response to Executive Board decision 2007/10 [YUN 2007, p. 1100], the Executive Director in July reported [DP/FPA/2009/12] on the revision of UNFPA financial regulations and rules. The report informed the Board of progress made in UNFPA's adoption of the International Public Sector Accounting Standards (IPSAS). UNFPA was adopting IPSAS in a phased approach and expected to be fully compliant by 2012. To allow the Fund to begin adopting IPSAS in 2010, revisions to the UNFPA Financial Regulations and Rules were necessary. In addition to the IPSAS-related changes, UNFPA proposed new regulations to achieve greater harmonization with other UN funds and programmes pertaining to sector budget support and pooled funds, retention of interest and investment revenue, and funding of financial authorizations for regular resources and trust funds. ACABQ in September [DP/FPA/2009/13] provided its comments and recommendations.

The Executive Board took note of the report on 11 September [E/2009/35 (dec. 2009/27)] and approved the revisions.

Audit reports

The Executive Director submitted to the UNDP/UNFPA Executive Board a report [DP/FPA/2009/1] on UNFPA follow-up to recommendations by the United Nations Board of Auditors for the 2006–2007 biennium [A/63/5/Add.7]. UNFPA reported that it had implemented 34 of the 58 accepted recommendations of the Board. The Fund was on track to implement the remaining 24 recommendations by their target completion dates. The Executive Board took note of the report on 22 January [E/2009/35 (dec. 2009/2)].

The Executive Director reported on the internal audit and oversight activities carried out by UNFPA in 2008 [DP/FPA/2009/5]. That included 15 audits—four in Africa, four in Latin America and the Caribbean, one in the Arab States, one in Eastern Europe and Central Asia, two in Asia and the Pacific and three at headquarters.

The Executive Board took note of the report on 3 June [E/2009/35 (dec. 2009/15)]. The Board urged the Executive Director to strengthen risk-based audit planning; adopt an internal control framework in line with internationally recognized best practices; implement enterprise risk management; fill vacant posts in the Division for Oversight Services to ensure appropriate audit coverage; and ensure that the level of resources made available to the Division was within the range recommended by JIU.

Evaluation

In response to Executive Board decision 2008/12 [YUN 2008, p. 1193], the Executive Director in March reported on the UNFPA evaluation policy [DP/FPA/2009/4]. The policy provided an overarching framework of the principles, roles and responsibilities for evaluation in UNFPA. Pursuant to Assembly resolution 62/208 [YUN 2007, p. 877], the policy focused on strengthening national evaluation capacity by using participatory and inclusive approaches and by supporting country-led evaluations. UNFPA sought to harmonize and align the policy with the evaluation efforts of UN partners through the use of common approaches and joint evaluations.

The Executive Board approved the UNFPA evaluation policy on 3 June [E/2009/35 (dec. 2009/18)]. It requested that the Executive Director submit a biennial evaluation plan in 2010 and a review of the evaluation policy in 2012.

Joint UN Programme on HIV/AIDS

A September report [DP/2009/39-DP/FPA/2009/14] presented jointly by UNFPA and UNDP focused on implementation of decisions and plans for follow-up from the recent UNAIDS Programme Coordinating Board meetings. The report focused on issues addressed during those meetings that were of particular relevance to UNFPA and UNDP, including the 2010–2011 UNAIDS unified budget and workplan; intensifying action on gender equality and AIDS; participation in One UN pilots; and HIV, forced displacement and migrant populations.

Within the framework of the 2010–2011 UNAIDS unified budget and workplan, UNFPA would focus on advancing an integrated approach to the delivery of sexual and reproductive health and HIV policies, programmes and services. UNFPA, along with UNDP, had sought to increase attention to gender equality in HIV programmes, in collaboration with UNAIDS, UNIFEM and the Global Coalition on Women and AIDS. UNFPA support contributed to an increased demand for, access to and utilization of quality prevention services for HIV and other sexually transmitted infections, especially for women, young people and other vulnerable groups. In Brazil, UNFPA, along with other UN agencies and partners, supported the Government in developing, launching and implementing the Integrated Plan to Confront the Feminization of the HIV Epidemic.

UNFPA and UNDP were committed to promoting "Delivering as one" [YUN 2006, p. 1584] and participated in joint UN teams on AIDS at the country level. The Fund had expanded HIV-focused staffing at the country level to strengthen participation in joint teams. UNFPA and UNDP also contributed to UNAIDS efforts to strengthen HIV programmes for people on the move, including migrants and populations of humanitarian concern. The Fund collaborated with the UNAIDS secretariat and the UN Department of Peacekeeping Operations to address the spread of HIV among uniformed personnel.

The Executive Board took note of the report on 11 September [E/2009/35 (dec. 2009/28)].

ECONOMIC AND SOCIAL COUNCIL ACTION

On 22 July [meeting 32], the Economic and Social Council adopted **resolution 2009/2** without vote [agenda item 3 (b)]. The draft [E/2009/L.19] was submitted by New Zealand and Norway.

Appointment of the Executive Director of the United Nations Population Fund

The Economic and Social Council

Recommends to the General Assembly the adoption of the following draft resolution:

[For text, see General Assembly resolution 64/219, below.]

GENERAL ASSEMBLY ACTION

On 21 December [meeting 66], the General Assembly, on the recommendation of the Second Committee [A/64/425], adopted **resolution 64/219** without vote [agenda item 58].

Appointment of the Executive Director of the United Nations Population Fund

The General Assembly,

Recalling its resolution 2211(XXI) of 17 December 1966, in response to which a trust fund, subsequently renamed the United Nations Population Fund, was established in 1967 by the Secretary-General,

Recalling also its resolution 3019(XXVII) of 18 December 1972, in which it placed the United Nations Population Fund under its authority as a subsidiary organ, in accordance with Article 22 of the Charter of the United Nations, taking into account the separate identity of the Fund,

1. *Notes* that, since the Administrator of the United Nations Development Programme ceased to perform the administrative role with respect to the United Nations Population Fund, no formal procedure has been established for the appointment of the Executive Director of the Fund;

2. *Decides* that the secretariat of the United Nations Population Fund shall continue to be headed by an Executive Director at the Under-Secretary-General level;

3. *Also decides* that the Executive Director of the United Nations Population Fund shall be appointed by the Secretary-General, in consultation with the Executive Board of the United Nations Development Programme/ United Nations Population Fund, for a term of four years.

UN Population Award

The 2009 United Nations Population Award was presented to Dr. Mahmoud Fahmy Fathalla (Egypt) in the individual category and to Movimiento Comunal Nicaragüense of Nicaragua in the institutional category.

The Award was established by General Assembly resolution 36/201 [YUN 1981, p. 792], to be presented annually to individuals and institutions for outstanding contributions to increasing awareness of population problems and to their solutions. In July, the Secretary-General transmitted to the Assembly the report of the UNFPA Executive Director on the Population Award [A/64/207].

Other population activities

UN Population Division

In a report on programme implementation and work progress of the UN Population Division in 2009 [E/CN.9/2010/6], the Secretary-General described the Division's activities dealing with the analysis of fertility, mortality and international migration; the preparation of world population estimates and projections; the monitoring of population policies; the analysis of the interrelations between population and development; and the monitoring and dissemination of population information. The report also highlighted the Division's substantive servicing of intergovernmental bodies, the preparation of parliamentary documentation and technical publications, the organization of expert meetings and the dissemination of results.

The Division held an expert group meeting on recent and future trends in fertility (New York, 2–4 December), which brought together experts from academic institutions, research institutes and statistical offices to examine recent trends in fertility and discuss future prospects as part of preparations for the 2010 Revision of *World Population Prospects*. To raise awareness about the implications of continued high fertility in the least developed countries, the Division produced a policy brief on the benefits of expanding access to modern family planning methods, documenting the high levels of unmet need for contraception in the least developed countries and arguing that expanding access to family planning could significantly contribute to the reduction of maternal and child mortality.

The Division was responsible for reporting on three indicators of universal access to reproductive health included in the revised framework for the achievement of the MDGs: contraceptive prevalence rate, adolescent birth rate and unmet need for family planning. The latter was monitored in collaboration with UNFPA. The Division provided updated estimates for each of the indicators, together with corresponding metadata, for the MDG database maintained by the UN Statistics Division. It also contributed to the database estimates of the contraceptive prevalence of modern methods and condom use, and of the spacing and limiting components of unmet need for family planning.

The Division convened an expert group meeting on health, mortality and development (New York, 10–12 November), which brought together experts and representatives of intergovernmental organizations to discuss health challenges and strategies to address such challenges, including the strengthening of health systems, and the estimation of adult mortality. The meeting also focused on methodological developments for estimating adult mortality. The Division continued to participate in the Inter-agency Group for Child Mortality Estimation, providing input in revising and updating the database on infant and under-five mortality estimates maintained by UNICEF. It collaborated with others in preparing the high-level plenary meeting of the Assembly to review progress towards the MDGs and other international development goals, planned for September 2010. The

Division prepared the report of the Secretary-General [A/64/263] on the scope, modalities, format and organization of the meeting.

In order to assess the gender dimensions of child mortality, the Division had been preparing revised and updated estimates of infant mortality, child mortality and under-five mortality by sex for developing countries with at least one million inhabitants in 2005. A report containing an analysis of sex differentials in child mortality was being prepared. The Division also continued to compile and document data suitable for the estimation of mortality, and was developing a database containing basic data and relevant metadata for mortality estimation.

The Division issued a report on international migration in 2006 [ESA/P/WP.209], which provided an analysis of international migration levels, trends and policies. It included international migration profiles for 228 countries and areas, data for 1995 and 2005 on total population, international migrant stock, refugees and remittances, and information on Government views and policies relating to immigration and emigration levels. The Division worked on an updated version of the report.

The Division collaborated with the Economic and Social Commission for Western Asia (ESCWA) to organize a regional workshop on international migration statistics (Cairo, 30 June–3 July), bringing together more than 50 representatives of national statistical offices and relevant ministries from ESCWA Member States, representatives from regional and international organizations, and experts from within and outside the ESCWA region. The Division also organized the Eighth Coordination Meeting on International Migration (New York, 16–17 November) (see p. 1047).

With financial support from UNICEF and the UNDP Special Unit for South-South Cooperation, the Division continued to update the United Nations Global Migration Database. The database contained the most complete set of publicly available data on the foreign or the foreign-born population enumerated by censuses or population registers and classified by sex, age and country of birth or citizenship.

The Division issued the results of the 2008 Revision of *World Population Prospects*, which showed that the world population was likely to increase from 6.8 billion in 2009 to 7 billion in 2012, and was projected to surpass 9 billion by 2050. The Division also worked toward completing the 2009 Revision of *World Urbanization Prospects* and continued developing a database to integrate all empirical data used in preparing the official population estimates and projections of the United Nations.

On population policies, the Division worked towards completion of *World Population Policies 2009*, a report that provided policy information on population growth, fertility, health and mortality, international migration and spatial distribution. To improve access to information on population policy issues, the Division was developing a relational database containing the results of all inquiries among Governments and information on population policy from other official sources. The Division also completed a report entitled *Child Adoption: Trends and Policies*, in which it discussed national legislation governing child adoption and presented data on the number of adoptions for 118 countries.

The Division, in collaboration with the Economic Commission for Latin America and the Caribbean, organized an expert group meeting on population ageing, intergenerational transfers and social protection (Santiago, Chile, 20–21 October). The meeting brought together more than 50 participants, including members of academia, representatives of international organizations and Government officials, to discuss how population ageing in Latin America and other regions was transforming the needs for economic support and social protection of different population groups. The Division also released the 2009 edition of the Population, Resources, Environment and Development Databank, which included 120 indicators on population, resources, the environment, development and policy.

The Division's work on monitoring, coordination and dissemination of population information included maintaining websites on the work of the Division, international migration and the United Nations Population Information Network. The Division continued to distribute MORTPAK for Windows, the Division's software package for demographic estimation, releasing an updated version (4.1).

The Division's programme of technical cooperation focused on building and strengthening capacity in developing countries to analyse demographic information needed to guide the formulation and implementation of population policy. The Division conducted a survey of governmental entities using or preparing demographic indicators to determine the areas most in need of capacity development. The results were being used to develop a targeted strategy for expanding the capacity of officials in developing countries to carry out demographic analysis.

Chapter IX

Social policy, crime prevention and human resources development

In 2009, the United Nations continued to promote social, cultural and human resources development, and to strengthen its crime prevention and criminal justice programme.

The Commission for Social Development, in February, considered its priority theme "Social integration". In July, the Economic and Social Council endorsed the Global Jobs Pact adopted by the International Labour Conference and invited Member States and international organizations to make full use of the Pact.

The General Assembly considered the implementation of the Copenhagen Declaration on Social Development and the Programme of Action, adopted at the 1995 World Summit for Social Development, and adopted further initiatives for social development at its twenty-fourth (2000) special session. The Assembly adopted a resolution on cooperatives in social development, discussed the follow-up to the tenth anniversary of the (1994) International Year of the Family and beyond, and proclaimed the year 2012 the International Year of Cooperatives.

With regard to persons with disabilities, UN bodies continued to monitor the implementation of the 1982 World Programme of Action concerning Disabled Persons and the 1993 Standard Rules on the Equalization of Opportunities for Persons with Disabilities. In December, the Assembly adopted a resolution on realizing the Millennium Development Goals (MDGs) for persons with disabilities and urged the UN system to integrate disability issues into its work.

In the area of cultural development, the United Nations observed the International Year of Reconciliation; and in April, more than 1,500 participants convened at the second Alliance of Civilizations Forum in Istanbul, Turkey. In other action, the Assembly adopted resolutions on interreligious and intercultural dialogue, the Alliance of Civilizations, the International Federation of Association Football World Cup in South Africa, and building a peaceful and better world through sport and the Olympic ideal. It also designated 18 July as Nelson Mandela International Day, to be observed each year beginning in 2010, and granted to the International Olympic Committee observer status in the General Assembly.

In April, the Commission on Crime Prevention and Criminal Justice held thematic discussions on economic fraud and identity-related crime and on penal reform and the reduction of prison overcrowding.

It also considered, among other subjects, preparations for the Twelfth (2010) United Nations Congress on Crime Prevention and Criminal Justice, to be held in Brazil; technical assistance for implementing the international conventions and protocols related to terrorism; international cooperation against economic fraud and identity-related crime; support for the regional programmes of the United Nations Office on Drugs and Crime; international cooperation to prevent, combat and eliminate kidnapping; improving the collection, reporting and analysis of data to enhance knowledge on trends in specific areas of crime; and supporting national and international efforts for child justice reform.

In December, the General Assembly called on Governments to criminalize trafficking in persons in all its forms; urged Member States and international organizations to develop national and regional strategies, in cooperation with the United Nations Crime Prevention and Criminal Justice Programme, to address effectively transnational organized crime; and urged Member States to strengthen international cooperation to prevent and combat terrorism.

Also in December, the Assembly stressed the need for Member States to integrate human resources development into national development strategies as a means to achieve the MDGs and promote economic and social development, and encouraged them to adopt and implement comprehensive human resources development strategies to ensure strong links between education, training and employment. The Assembly also approved amendments to the United Nations University Charter to enable the University to grant advanced academic degrees.

Social policy and cultural issues

Social development

Follow-up to the 1995 World Summit and to General Assembly special session

In response to General Assembly resolution 63/152 [YUN 2008, p. 1199], the Secretary-General submitted a July report [A/64/157] on the implementation of the Copenhagen Declaration on Social Development and the Programme of Action, adopted at the 1995

World Summit for Social Development [YUN 1995, p. 1113], and of the further initiatives for social development, adopted by the Assembly's twenty-fourth (2000) special session [YUN 2000, p. 1012]. The report provided an overview of the discussions held during the forty-seventh session of the Commission for Social Development (see p. 1063) on the priority theme of social integration, including the importance of social integration for social development and for poverty eradication and full employment and decent work for all; social groups in society that faced particular challenges to social integration, including youth and older persons; and proposed strategies to promote social integration. The overview also took into consideration the Chairperson's summary of the Commission's deliberations, as transmitted in a 4 March letter [E/2009/12] from Finland to the President of the Economic and Social Council, and the Secretary-General's report to the Commission on promoting social integration [E/CN.5/2009/2] (see p. 1063).

The report also addressed a range of issues pertinent to the impact of the global crises on social development and social integration; highlighted the social dimensions of the New Partnership for Africa's Development (NEPAD) [YUN 2001, p. 900] as described in the Secretary-General's report on the subject [E/CN.5/2009/3]; and made a series of recommendations to the Assembly.

GENERAL ASSEMBLY ACTION

On 18 December [meeting 65], the General Assembly, on the recommendation of the Third (Social, Humanitarian and Cultural) Committee [A/64/432], adopted **resolution 64/135** without vote [agenda item 61 *(a)*].

Implementation of the outcome of the World Summit for Social Development and of the twenty-fourth special session of the General Assembly

The General Assembly,

Recalling the World Summit for Social Development, held at Copenhagen from 6 to 12 March 1995, and the twenty-fourth special session of the General Assembly entitled "World Summit for Social Development and beyond: achieving social development for all in a globalizing world", held at Geneva from 26 June to 1 July 2000,

Reaffirming that the Copenhagen Declaration on Social Development and the Programme of Action and the further initiatives for social development adopted by the General Assembly at its twenty-fourth special session, as well as a continued global dialogue on social development issues, constitute the basic framework for the promotion of social development for all at the national and international levels,

Recalling the United Nations Millennium Declaration and the development goals contained therein, as well as the commitments made at major United Nations summits, conferences and special sessions, including the commitments made at the 2005 World Summit,

Recalling also its resolution 57/270 B of 23 June 2003 on the integrated and coordinated implementation of and follow-up to the outcomes of the major United Nations conferences and summits in the economic and social fields,

Recalling further its resolution 60/209 of 22 December 2005 on the implementation of the first United Nations Decade for the Eradication of Poverty (1997–2006),

Recalling its resolution 63/303 of 9 July 2009 on the Outcome of the Conference on the World Financial and Economic Crisis and Its Impact on Development,

Noting with appreciation the ministerial declaration adopted at the high-level segment of the substantive session of 2006 of the Economic and Social Council, on "Creating an environment at the national and international levels conducive to generating full and productive employment and decent work for all, and its impact on sustainable development",

Noting that the decent work agenda of the International Labour Organization, with its four strategic objectives, has an important role to play, as reaffirmed in the International Labour Organization Declaration on Social Justice for a Fair Globalization and in the Global Jobs Pact, in achieving the objective of full and productive employment and decent work for all, including its objective of social protection,

Emphasizing the need to enhance the role of the Commission for Social Development in the follow-up and review of the World Summit for Social Development and the outcome of the twenty-fourth special session of the General Assembly,

Recognizing that a people-centred approach must be at the centre of economic and social development,

Expressing deep concern that attainment of the social development objectives can be hindered by instability in global and national financial markets, as well as challenges brought about by the ongoing food and energy crises,

Recognizing the complex character of the current global food crisis as a combination of several major factors, both structural and conjunctural, also negatively affected by, inter alia, environmental degradation, drought and desertification, global climate change, natural disasters and the lack of the necessary technology, and recognizing also that a strong commitment from national Governments and the international community as a whole is required to confront the major threats to food security,

Affirming its strong support for fair globalization and the need to translate growth into eradication of poverty and commitment to strategies and policies that aim to promote full, freely chosen and productive employment and decent work for all and that these should constitute a fundamental component of relevant national and international policies as well as national development strategies, including poverty reduction strategies, and reaffirming that employment creation and decent work should be incorporated into macroeconomic policies, taking fully into account the impact and social dimension of globalization, the benefits and costs of which are often unevenly shared and distributed,

Recognizing that social inclusion is a means for achieving social integration and is crucial for fostering stable, safe, harmonious, peaceful and just societies and for improving social cohesion so as to create an environment for development and progress,

1. *Takes note* of the report of the Secretary-General;

2. *Welcomes* the reaffirmation by Governments of their will and commitment to continue implementing the Copenhagen Declaration on Social Development and the Programme of Action, in particular to eradicate poverty, promote full and productive employment and foster social integration to achieve stable, safe and just societies for all;

3. *Recognizes* that the implementation of the Copenhagen commitments and the attainment of the internationally agreed development goals, including the Millennium Development Goals, are mutually reinforcing and that the Copenhagen commitments are crucial to a coherent people-centred approach to development;

4. *Reaffirms* that the Commission for Social Development continues to have the primary responsibility for the follow-up and review of the World Summit for Social Development and the outcome of the twenty-fourth special session of the General Assembly and that it serves as the main United Nations forum for an intensified global dialogue on social development issues, and calls upon Member States, the relevant specialized agencies, funds and programmes of the United Nations system and civil society to enhance their support for its work;

5. *Expresses deep concern* that the world financial and economic crisis, the world food and energy crises, and continuing food insecurity and climate change, as well as the lack of results so far in the multilateral trade negotiations and a loss of confidence in the international economic system, have negative implications for social development, in particular for the achievement of poverty eradication, full and productive employment and decent work for all, and social integration;

6. *Recognizes* that poverty eradication, full and productive employment and decent work for all and social integration are interrelated and mutually reinforcing, and that an enabling environment therefore needs to be created so that all three objectives can be pursued simultaneously;

7. *Also recognizes* that the broad concept of social development affirmed by the World Summit for Social Development and the twenty-fourth special session of the General Assembly has been weakened in national and international policymaking and that, while poverty eradication is a central part of development policy and discourse, further attention should be given to the other commitments agreed to at the Summit, in particular those concerning employment and social integration, which have also suffered from a general disconnect between economic and social policy-making;

8. *Acknowledges* that the first United Nations Decade for the Eradication of Poverty (1997–2006), launched after the World Summit for Social Development, has provided the long-term vision for sustained and concerted efforts at the national and international levels to eradicate poverty;

9. *Recognizes* that the implementation of the commitments made by Governments during the first Decade has fallen short of expectations, and welcomes the proclamation of the Second United Nations Decade for the Eradication of Poverty (2008–2017) by the General Assembly in its resolution 62/205 of 19 December 2007 in order to support, in an efficient and coordinated manner, the internationally agreed development goals related to poverty eradication, including the Millennium Development Goals;

10. *Emphasizes* that the major United Nations conferences and summits, including the Millennium Summit and the 2005 World Summit, as well as the International Conference on Financing for Development, in its Monterrey Consensus, have reinforced the priority and urgency of poverty eradication within the United Nations development agenda;

11. *Also emphasizes* that poverty eradication policies should attack poverty by addressing its root and structural causes and manifestations, and that equity and the reduction of inequalities need to be incorporated in those policies;

12. *Stresses* that an enabling environment is a critical precondition for achieving equity and social development and that, while economic growth is essential, entrenched inequality and marginalization are an obstacle to the broad-based and sustained growth required for sustainable, inclusive, people-centred development, and recognizes the need to balance and ensure complementarity between measures to achieve growth and measures to achieve economic and social equity in order for there to be an impact on overall poverty levels;

13. *Also stresses* that stability in global financial systems and corporate social responsibility and accountability, as well as national economic policies that have an impact on other stakeholders, are essential in creating an enabling international environment to promote economic growth and social development;

14. *Recognizes* the need to promote respect for all human rights and fundamental freedoms in order to address the most pressing social needs of people living in poverty, including through the design and development of appropriate mechanisms to strengthen and consolidate democratic institutions and governance;

15. *Reaffirms* the commitment to the empowerment of women and gender equality, as well as to the mainstreaming of a gender perspective into all development efforts, recognizing that these are critical for achieving sustainable development and for efforts to combat hunger, poverty and disease and to strengthen policies and programmes that improve, ensure and broaden the full participation of women in all spheres of political, economic, social and cultural life, as equal partners, and to improve their access to all resources needed for the full exercise of all their human rights and fundamental freedoms by removing persistent barriers, including ensuring equal access to full and productive employment and decent work, as well as strengthening their economic independence;

16. *Also reaffirms* the commitment to promote opportunities for full, freely chosen and productive employment, including for the most disadvantaged, as well as decent work for all, in order to deliver social justice combined with economic efficiency, with full respect for fundamental principles and rights at work under conditions of equity, equality, security and dignity, and further reaffirms that macroeconomic policies should, inter alia, support employment creation, taking fully into account the social impact and dimension of globalization;

17. *Takes note with interest* of the adoption by the International Labour Conference on 10 June 2008 of the International Labour Organization Declaration on Social Justice for a Fair Globalization, which acknowledges the

particular role of the Organization in promoting a fair globalization and its responsibility to assist its members in their efforts, and the adoption by the International Labour Conference on 19 June 2009 of the Global Jobs Pact;

18. *Reaffirms* that there is an urgent need to create an environment at the national and international levels that is conducive to the attainment of full and productive employment and decent work for all as a foundation for sustainable development and that an environment that supports investment, growth and entrepreneurship is essential to the creation of new job opportunities, and also reaffirms that opportunities for men and women to obtain productive work in conditions of freedom, equity, security and human dignity are essential to ensuring the eradication of hunger and poverty, the improvement of economic and social well-being for all, the achievement of sustained economic growth and sustainable development of all nations and a fully inclusive and equitable globalization;

19. *Stresses* the importance of removing obstacles to the realization of the right of peoples to self-determination, in particular of peoples living under colonial or other forms of alien domination or foreign occupation, which adversely affect their social and economic development, including their exclusion from labour markets;

20. *Reaffirms* that violence, in its many manifestations, including domestic violence, particularly against women, children, older persons and persons with disabilities, and especially against persons belonging to more than one of these groups, is a growing threat to the security of individuals, families and communities everywhere; total social breakdown is an all too real contemporary experience; organized crime, illegal drugs, the illicit arms trade, trafficking in human beings, particularly women and children, ethnic and religious conflict, civil war, terrorism, all forms of extremist violence, xenophobia, and politically motivated killing and genocide present fundamental threats to societies and the global social order; they also present compelling and urgent reasons for action by Governments individually and, as appropriate, jointly to foster social cohesion while recognizing, protecting and valuing diversity;

21. *Calls upon* the organizations of the United Nations system to commit themselves to mainstreaming the goal of full and productive employment and decent work for all in their policies, programmes and activities;

22. *Requests* the United Nations funds, programmes and agencies and invites financial institutions to support efforts to mainstream the goals of full and productive employment and decent work for all in their policies, programmes and activities;

23. *Recognizes* that promoting full employment and decent work also requires investing in education, training and skills development for women and men, and girls and boys, strengthening social protection and health systems and applying international labour standards;

24. *Also recognizes* that full and productive employment and decent work for all, which encompass social protection, fundamental principles and rights at work, tripartism and social dialogue, are key elements of sustainable development for all countries and are therefore a priority objective of international cooperation;

25. *Stresses* that policies and strategies to achieve full employment and decent work for all should include ap-

propriate specific measures to promote gender equality and foster social integration for social groups such as youth, persons with disabilities and older persons, as well as migrants and indigenous peoples, on an equal basis with others;

26. *Also stresses* the need to allocate adequate resources for the elimination of all forms of discrimination against women in the workplace, including unequal access to labour market participation and wage inequalities, as well as reconciliation of work and private life for both women and men;

27. *Encourages* States to promote youth employment by, inter alia, developing and implementing action plans in collaboration with all relevant stakeholders;

28. *Also encourages* States to pursue efforts to promote the concerns of older persons and persons with disabilities and their organizations in the planning, implementation and evaluation of all development programmes and policies;

29. *Stresses* that policies and programmes designed to achieve poverty eradication, full employment and decent work for all should include specific measures to foster social integration, including by providing marginalized socioeconomic sectors and groups with equal access to opportunities and social protection;

30. *Acknowledges* the important nexus between international migration and social development, and stresses the importance of enforcing labour law effectively with regard to migrant workers' labour relations and working conditions, inter alia, those related to their remuneration and conditions of health, safety at work and the right to freedom of association;

31. *Recognizes* that, since the convening of the World Summit for Social Development in Copenhagen in 1995, advances have been made in addressing and promoting social integration, including through the adoption of the Madrid International Plan of Action on Ageing, 2002, the World Programme of Action for Youth to the Year 2000 and Beyond and the Supplement thereto, the Convention on the Rights of Persons with Disabilities, the United Nations Declaration on the Rights of Indigenous Peoples and the Beijing Declaration and Platform for Action;

32. *Also recognizes* the importance of providing social protection schemes for the formal and informal economy as instruments to achieve equity, inclusion and stability and cohesion of societies, and emphasizes the importance of supporting national efforts aimed at bringing informal workers into the formal economy;

33. *Further recognizes* that the social integration of people living in poverty should encompass addressing and meeting their basic human needs, including nutrition, health, water, sanitation, housing and access to education and employment, through integrated development strategies;

34. *Reaffirms* that social integration policies should seek to reduce inequalities, promote access to basic social services, education for all and health care, increase the participation on equal terms and integration of social groups, particularly youth, older persons and persons with disabilities, and address the challenges posed by globalization and market-driven reforms to social development in order for all people in all countries to benefit from globalization;

35. *Urges* Governments, with the cooperation of relevant entities, to develop systems of social protection and to extend or broaden, as appropriate, their effectiveness and coverage, including for workers in the informal economy, recognizing the need for social protection systems to provide social security and support labour-market participation, and invites the International Labour Organization to strengthen its social protection strategies, including assistance to countries in building social protection floors, and policies on extending social security coverage, and also urges Governments, while taking account of national circumstances, to focus on the needs of those living in, or vulnerable to, poverty and give particular consideration to universal access to basic social security systems;

36. *Requests* the United Nations system to support national efforts to achieve social development, in particular fostering social integration, at the local, national, regional and international levels, in a coherent, coordinated and results-based manner;

37. *Reaffirms* the commitment to promote the rights of indigenous peoples in the areas of education, employment, housing, sanitation, health and social security, and also notes the attention paid to those areas in the United Nations Declaration on the Rights of Indigenous Peoples;

38. *Recognizes* the need to formulate social development policies in an integral, articulated and participative manner, recognizing poverty as a multidimensional phenomenon, calls for interlinked public policies on this matter, and underlines the need for public policies to be included in a comprehensive development and well-being strategy;

39. *Acknowledges* the important role that the public sector can play as an employer and in developing an environment that enables the effective generation of full and productive employment and decent work for all;

40. *Also acknowledges* the vital role that the private sector can play in generating new investments, employment and financing for development and in advancing efforts towards full employment and decent work;

41. *Recognizes* that the majority of poor people live and work in rural areas, that priority should be given to agricultural and non-farm sectors and that steps should be taken to anticipate and offset the negative social and economic consequences of globalization and to maximize its benefits for poor people living and working in rural areas;

42. *Also recognizes* the need to give priority to investing in and further contributing to sustainable agricultural development and microenterprises, small and medium-sized enterprises and entrepreneurship cooperatives and other forms of social enterprises and the participation and entrepreneurship of women as means to promote full and productive employment and decent work for all;

43. *Reaffirms* the commitments made in respect of "Meeting the special needs of Africa" at the 2005 World Summit, underlines the call of the Economic and Social Council for enhanced coordination within the United Nations system and the ongoing efforts to harmonize the current initiatives on Africa, and requests the Commission for Social Development to continue to give due prominence in its work to the social dimensions of the New Partnership for Africa's Development;

44. *Also reaffirms* that each country has the primary responsibility for its own economic and social development and that the role of national policies and development strategies cannot be overemphasized, and underlines the importance of adopting effective measures, including new financial mechanisms, as appropriate, to support the efforts of developing countries to achieve sustained economic growth, sustainable development, poverty eradication and the strengthening of their democratic systems;

45. *Further reaffirms*, in this context, that international cooperation has an essential role in assisting developing countries, including the least developed countries, in strengthening their human, institutional and technological capacity;

46. *Stresses* that the international community shall enhance its efforts to create an enabling environment for social development and poverty eradication through increasing market access for developing countries, technology transfer on mutually agreed terms, financial aid and a comprehensive solution to the external debt problem;

47. *Also stresses* that international trade and stable financial systems can be effective tools to create favourable conditions for the development of all countries and that trade barriers and some trading practices continue to have negative effects on employment growth, particularly in developing countries;

48. *Acknowledges* that good governance and the rule of law at the national and international levels are essential for sustained economic growth, sustainable development and the eradication of poverty and hunger;

49. *Urges* developed countries that have not yet done so in accordance with their commitments to make concrete efforts towards meeting the targets of 0.7 per cent of their gross national product for official development assistance to developing countries and 0.15 to 0.2 per cent of their gross national product to least developed countries, and encourages developing countries to build on the progress achieved in ensuring that official development assistance is used effectively to help to meet development goals and targets;

50. *Urges* Member States and the international community to fulfil all their commitments to meet the demands for social development, including social services and assistance, that have arisen from the global financial and economic crisis, which particularly affects the poorest and most vulnerable;

51. *Welcomes* the contribution to the mobilization of resources for social development by the initiatives taken on a voluntary basis by groups of Member States based on innovative financing mechanisms, including those that aim to provide further drug access at affordable prices to developing countries on a sustainable and predictable basis, such as the International Drug Purchase Facility, UNITAID, as well as other initiatives, such as the International Finance Facility for Immunization and the Advance Market Commitments for Vaccines, and notes the New York Declaration of 20 September 2004, which launched the Action against Hunger and Poverty initiative and called for further attention to raise funds urgently needed to help to meet the Millennium Development Goals and to complement and ensure the long-term stability and predictability of foreign aid;

52. *Reaffirms* that social development requires the active involvement of all actors in the development process, such as civil society organizations, including workers' and employers' organizations, as well as corporations and small and medium-sized businesses, and that partnerships among all relevant actors are increasingly becoming part of national and international cooperation for social development, and also reaffirms that, within countries, partnerships among the Government, civil society and the private sector can contribute effectively to the achievement of social development goals;

53. *Underlines* the responsibility of the private sector, at both the national and the international levels, including small and large companies and transnational corporations, regarding not only the economic and financial but also the development, social, gender and environmental implications of their activities, their obligations towards their workers and their contributions to achieving sustainable development, including social development, and emphasizes the need to take concrete actions on corporate responsibility and accountability, including through the participation of all relevant stakeholders, inter alia, for the prevention or prosecution of corruption;

54. *Stresses* the importance of promoting corporate social responsibility and accountability, encourages responsible business practices, such as those promoted by the Global Compact, and invites the private sector to take into account not only the economic and financial implications but also the development, social, human rights, including rights at work, gender and environmental implications of its undertakings, and underlines the importance of the International Labour Organization Tripartite Declaration of Principles concerning Multinational Enterprises and Social Policy;

55. *Invites* the Secretary-General, the Economic and Social Council, the regional commissions, the relevant specialized agencies, funds and programmes of the United Nations system and other intergovernmental forums, within their respective mandates, to continue to integrate into their work programmes and give priority attention to the Copenhagen commitments and the Declaration on the tenth anniversary of the World Summit for Social Development, to continue to be actively involved in their follow-up and to monitor the achievement of those commitments and undertakings;

56. *Invites* the Secretary-General to submit to the General Assembly at its sixty-fifth session a comprehensive study on the impact of the converging world crises on social development, in particular for the achievement of poverty eradication, full and productive employment and decent work for all, and social integration;

57. *Invites* the Commission for Social Development to emphasize in its review of the implementation of the Copenhagen Declaration on Social Development and the Programme of Action the increased exchange of national, regional and international experiences, the focused and interactive dialogues among experts and practitioners and the sharing of best practices and lessons learned, and to address, inter alia, the potential impact of the ongoing world financial and economic crisis and the world food and energy crises on social development goals;

58. *Decides* to include in the provisional agenda of its sixty-fifth session the sub-item entitled "Implementation of the outcome of the World Summit for Social Development and of the twenty-fourth special session of the General Assembly", and requests the Secretary-General to submit a report on the question to the Assembly at that session.

Impact of global and national trends on social development

High-level segment of Economic and Social Council

The Economic and Social Council, at the high-level segment of its 2009 substantive session (Geneva, 6–9 July) [A/64/3/Rev.1], discussed the theme of "Current global and national trends and their impact on social development, including public health". The Council considered the Secretary-General's April report [E/2009/53] on the topic, which discussed global and national trends, especially in the wake of the global financial and economic crisis and fluctuations in the prices of fuel and food, and the impact of those trends on social development, focusing on: poverty and hunger; social cohesion; public spending on social protection, safety nets, education and health; job security; and food security. Special attention was also paid to the implications of the trends for public health-related goals, including the realization of the World Health Organization's "Health for All" objective. The report concluded with a number of recommendations on how to address emerging challenges.

On 9 July, the Council adopted a draft ministerial declaration on implementing the internationally agreed goals and commitments in regard to global public health (see p. 1226).

Global Jobs Pact

On 19 June, the International Labour Conference of the International Labour Organization, at its ninety-eighth session (Geneva, 3–19 June), adopted "Recovering from the crisis: A Global Jobs Pact", which called for urgent worldwide action to address the social and employment impact of the international financial and economic crisis.

In July, the Economic and Social Council considered the Global Jobs Pact and took action on it.

ECONOMIC AND SOCIAL COUNCIL ACTION

On 24 July [meeting 35], the Economic and Social Council adopted **resolution 2009/5** [draft: E/2009/L.24] without vote [agenda item 6 *(a)*].

Recovering from the crisis: a Global Jobs Pact

The Economic and Social Council,

Having regard to the depth and breadth of the economic and financial crisis affecting all countries and the ensuing employment losses and human hardship,

Recalling the outcomes of the World Summit for Social Development, the twenty-fourth special session of the General Assembly and the 2005 World Summit,

Recalling also the ministerial declaration of the high-level segment of its substantive session of 2006 and its resolutions 2007/2 of 17 July 2007 and 2008/18 of 24 July 2008,

Recalling further General Assembly resolutions 57/270 B of 23 June 2003, 59/57 of 2 December 2004, 60/265 of 30 June 2006, 61/16 of 20 November 2006, 62/208 of 19 December 2007, 63/199 of 19 December 2008 and 63/239 of 24 December 2008,

Recalling the Outcome of the Conference on the World Financial and Economic Crisis and Its Impact on Development, in which the International Labour Organization was invited to present to the Economic and Social Council at its substantive session of 2009 the Global Jobs Pact, which was adopted by the International Labour Conference at its ninety-eighth session and which is intended to promote a job-intensive recovery from the crisis and to shape a pattern for sustainable growth,

Recalling that the Global Jobs Pact, which demonstrates linkages among social progress, economic development and the response to the crisis, states that action must be guided by the decent work agenda and by commitments made by the International Labour Organization and its constituents in the International Labour Organization Declaration on Social Justice for a Fair Globalization,

1. *Welcomes* the adoption on 19 June 2009 by the International Labour Conference at its ninety-eighth session of the resolution entitled "Recovering from the crisis: a Global Jobs Pact";

2. *Encourages* Member States to promote and make full use of the Global Jobs Pact as a general framework within which each country can formulate a policy package specific to its situation and priorities, through a portfolio of appropriate policy options, which may include multisectoral development policies, technical assistance and international cooperation, joined with the effort to promote sustainable recovery from the crisis, when developing measures to promote and protect employment in recovery plans, according to its specific needs and circumstances;

3. *Requests* the United Nations funds and programmes and the specialized agencies to take into account, through their appropriate decision-making processes, the Global Jobs Pact in their policies and programmes, as well as to consider the integration of the policy contents of the Pact into the activities of the resident coordinator system and the United Nations country teams in the context of the assistance they provide for national crisis response measures, in accordance with national plans and priorities, bearing in mind the importance of national ownership and capacity-building at all levels;

4. *Invites* international financial institutions and other relevant international organizations to integrate, in accordance with their mandates, the policy contents of the Global Jobs Pact into their activities;

5. *Recognizes* that giving effect to the recommendations and policy options contained in the Global Jobs Pact requires consideration of financing and capacity-building and that least developed and developing countries and countries with economies in transition that lack the fiscal space to adopt response and recovery policies require particular support, and invites donor countries, multilateral organizations and other development partners to consider providing funding, including existing crisis resources, for the implementation of those recommendations and policy options;

6. *Requests* the Secretary-General to report to the Economic and Social Council at its substantive session of 2010 on progress made in implementing the present resolution.

Commission for Social Development

The Commission for Social Development, at its forty-seventh session (New York, 22 February 2008 and 4–13 February 2009) [E/2009/26], considered its priority theme "Social integration" (see below). Panel discussions were held on the priority theme taking into account the relationship with poverty eradication and full employment and decent work for all, as well as on the emerging issue of "The current global crises and their impact on social development and social integration". The Commission recommended for adoption by the Economic and Social Council a draft resolution on the social dimensions of NEPAD [YUN 2001, p. 900], in which the Commission would be asked to continue to give prominence to and raise awareness of the social dimensions of NEPAD and the Secretary-General would be asked to submit a report on the subject in 2010 (**resolution 2009/20**) (see p. 901). In connection with its review of plans and programmes of action pertaining to the situation of social groups, the Commission adopted and brought to the attention of the Council resolutions on policies and programmes involving youth [res. 47/1] (see p. 1185) and the first review and appraisal of the 2002 Madrid International Plan of Action on Ageing [YUN 2002, p. 1194] [res. 47/3] (see p. 1188). It also adopted a resolution on promoting full employment and decent work for all [res. 47/2] (see p. 1064) and a decision nominating five candidates for the Board of the United Nations Research Institute for Social Development (UNRISD) that required Council confirmation [ibid.].

For its consideration of the priority theme, the Commission had before it a report of the Secretary-General on promoting social integration [E/CN.5/2009/2], prepared in response to Council resolution 2008/19 [YUN 2008, p. 1208]. The report examined the importance of social integration for social development, focusing on social integration concepts, regional perspectives and the impact of social, economic and political trends on social integration. It also discussed the importance of social integration for poverty eradication, full employment and decent work for all, analysed existing strategies and made recommendations for promoting social integration at the national and international level.

On 13 February [dec. 47/102], the Commission took note of the following documents of the Secretary-General: report on promoting social integration; note transmitting the report of the Special Rapporteur on disability of the Commission for Social Development on the monitoring of the implementation of the Standard Rules on the Equalization of Opportunities for Persons with Disabilities (see p. 1069); note on the nominations of members of the UNRISD Board (see p. 1064); and the note transmitting the report of the UNRISD Board on the work of the Institute during 2007 and 2008 [ibid.].

The Commission also addressed the proposed work programme of the Division for Social Policy and Development of the Department of Economic and Social Affairs for the 2010–2011 biennium.

On 30 July, the Council took note of the Commission's report on its forty-seventh session and approved the provisional agenda and documentation for its forty-eighth (2010) session (**decision 2009/244**).

Other Commission reports. Other documents issued in 2009, to be considered during the Commission's forty-eighth (2010) session, included Secretary-General reports on: promoting social integration [E/CN.5/2010/2]; social dimensions of NEPAD [E/CN.5/2010/3]; further implementation of the Madrid International Plan of Action on Ageing, 2002 [E/CN.5/2010/4]; and mainstreaming disability in the development agenda [E/CN.5/2010/6], as well as a note by the Secretariat on policy responses on employment and the social consequences of the financial and economic crisis, including its gender dimension [E/CN.5/2010/8].

Full employment and decent work for all

In response to Economic and Social Council resolution 2008/18 [YUN 2008, p. 1205], the Secretary-General transmitted to the Commission for Social Development a report on promoting full employment and decent work for all [E/CN.5/2009/4], which focused on trends and key challenges in increasing employment and decent work in rural areas. It also highlighted the potential implications of the global crises on employment and decent work. Consequently, it examined the issue of social protection as an important instrument for reducing vulnerability, especially in the light of new challenges, and concluded with a set of policy responses for promoting employment and decent work in rural areas.

In February [E/2009/26 (res. 47/2)], the Commission took note of the Secretary-General's report; decided to keep full and productive employment and decent work for all under review; and requested the Secretary-General to include a section on implementation of Council resolution 2008/18, and on the linkage between full employment and decent work for all and social integration, and the impact of the world financial and economic crisis on full employment and decent work for all and social integration, in his report on the main theme of social integration to be submitted to the Commission's forty-eighth (2010) session.

Report on the World Social Situation

A July report [A/64/158 & Corr.1] provided the General Assembly with an overview of the world social situation 2009. It noted that although considerable progress had been made in reducing levels of absolute poverty, overall the world was not on track to meet the Millennium Development Goal of halving levels of extreme poverty by 2015 [YUN 2000, p. 52]. The number of people living on less than $1.25 a day in developing countries declined from 1.9 billion to 1.4 billion between 1981 and 2005. Improvements in overall poverty levels depended, to a large extent, on growth. Countries or regions that had experienced strong growth during the preceding two decades had managed to reduce poverty levels, particularly in urban areas, including countries such as China and India whose success had driven global poverty trends downward. However, the absolute number of poor people had gone up in several countries in sub-Saharan Africa, Latin America, the Middle East and North Africa, as well as in Central Asia. The report considered global and regional poverty trends for the period 1981–2005; described macroeconomic policies and their effect on growth and poverty reduction; examined some labour market policies and other social policies and their efficacy in reducing poverty; and made a number of policy recommendations.

On 18 December, the General Assembly took note of the overview of the world social situation 2009 (**decision 64/529**).

The full version of the report was published as *Rethinking Poverty: Report on the World Social Situation 2010* [Sales No. E.09.IV.10].

UN Research Institute for Social Development

During 2009, the United Nations Research Institute for Social Development (UNRISD) continued to carry out research under the programme designed for the period 2005–2009, which focused on social policy, poverty reduction and equity. In February [E/2009/26 (dec. 47/102)], the Commission for Social Development took note of the report [E/CN.5/2009/8] of the UNRISD Board covering 2007 and 2008 [YUN 2008, p. 1209].

UNRISD Board membership. Also in February, the Commission had before it a note by the Secretary-General on the nomination of new members of the UNRISD Board [E/CN.5/2009/7 & Corr.1]. The Commission [E/2009/26 (dec. 47/101)] nominated five candidates for the Board, which the Council confirmed by **decision 2009/245** of 30 July.

Cooperatives in social development

In response to General Assembly resolution 62/128 [YUN 2007, p. 1113], the Secretary-General submitted a July report [A/64/132 & Corr.1] on cooperatives in social development, which underscored the importance of cooperatives to socio-economic development and how agricultural and financial cooperatives contributed to long-term solutions for food security and a more resilient and inclusive financial system in the light of the food and financial crises worldwide. It described how cooperatives, as self-help organizations, generated employment and incomes and discussed how Member States and cooperative stakeholders could leverage the contributions of cooperatives for development and economic recovery. Recommendations were made for promoting the formation and growth of cooperatives, including: proclaiming an International Year of Cooperatives; ensuring an enabling environment for cooperatives with a sound legislative and regulatory framework; promoting the growth of financial cooperatives to meet the goal of inclusive finance by providing access to financial services for all; promoting the growth of agricultural cooperatives through access to finance, adoption of sustainable production techniques, investments in rural infrastructure and irrigation, strengthened marketing mechanisms, and support for the participation of women in economic activities; promoting education and training for the operation of cooperatives; and improving research and the information database on cooperatives globally to enable sound policy formulation.

GENERAL ASSEMBLY ACTION

On 18 December [meeting 65], the General Assembly, on the recommendation of the Third Committee [A/64/432], adopted **resolution 64/136** without vote [agenda item 61 *(b)*].

Cooperatives in social development

The General Assembly,

Recalling its resolutions 47/90 of 16 December 1992, 49/155 of 23 December 1994, 51/58 of 12 December 1996, 54/123 of 17 December 1999, 56/114 of 19 December 2001, 58/131 of 22 December 2003, 60/132 of 16 December 2005 and 62/128 of 18 December 2007 concerning cooperatives in social development,

Recognizing that cooperatives, in their various forms, promote the fullest possible participation in the economic and social development of all people, including women, youth, older persons, persons with disabilities and indigenous peoples, are becoming a major factor of economic and social development and contribute to the eradication of poverty,

Recognizing also the important contribution and potential of all forms of cooperatives to the follow-up to the World Summit for Social Development, the Fourth World Conference on Women and the second United Nations Conference on Human Settlements (Habitat II), including their five-year reviews, the World Food Summit, the Second World Assembly on Ageing, the International Conference on Financing for Development, the World Summit on Sustainable Development and the 2005 World Summit,

Noting with appreciation the potential role of cooperative development in the improvement of the social and economic conditions of the indigenous peoples and rural communities,

Recalling Economic and Social Council resolution 1980/67 of 25 July 1980 on international years and anniversaries,

1. *Takes note* of the report of the Secretary-General;

2. *Proclaims* the year 2012 the International Year of Cooperatives;

3. *Encourages* all Member States, as well as the United Nations and all other relevant stakeholders, to take advantage of the International Year of Cooperatives as a way of promoting cooperatives and raising awareness of their contribution to social and economic development;

4. *Draws the attention* of Member States to the recommendations contained in the report of the Secretary-General for further action to promote the growth of cooperatives as business and social enterprises that can contribute to sustainable development, eradication of poverty, and livelihoods in various economic sectors in urban and rural areas and provide support for the creation of cooperatives in new and emerging areas;

5. *Encourages* Governments to keep under review, as appropriate, the legal and administrative provisions governing the activities of cooperatives in order to enhance the growth and sustainability of cooperatives in a rapidly changing socio-economic environment by, inter alia, providing a level playing field for cooperatives vis-à-vis other business and social enterprises, including appropriate tax incentives and access to financial services and markets;

6. *Urges* Governments, relevant international organizations and the specialized agencies, in collaboration with national and international cooperative organizations, to give due consideration to the role and contribution of cooperatives in the implementation of and follow-up to the outcomes of the World Summit for Social Development, the Fourth World Conference on Women and the second United Nations Conference on Human Settlements (Habitat II), including their five-year reviews, the World Food Summit, the Second World Assembly on Ageing, the International Conference on Financing for Development, the World Summit on Sustainable Development and the 2005 World Summit by, inter alia:

(a) Utilizing and developing fully the potential and contribution of cooperatives for the attainment of social development goals, in particular the eradication of poverty, the generation of full and productive employment and the enhancement of social integration;

(b) Encouraging and facilitating the establishment and development of cooperatives, including taking measures aimed at enabling people living in poverty or belonging to vulnerable groups, including women, youth, persons with disabilities, older persons and indigenous peoples, to fully

participate, on a voluntary basis, in cooperatives and to address their social service needs;

(c) Taking appropriate measures aimed at creating a supportive and enabling environment for the development of cooperatives by, inter alia, developing an effective partnership between Governments and the cooperative movement through joint consultative councils and/or advisory bodies and by promoting and implementing better legislation, research, sharing of good practices, training, technical assistance and capacity-building of cooperatives, especially in the fields of management, auditing and marketing skills;

(d) Raising public awareness of the contribution of cooperatives to employment generation and to socio-economic development, promoting comprehensive research and statistical data-gathering on the activities, employment and overall socio-economic impact of cooperatives at the national and international levels and promoting sound national policy formulation by harmonizing statistical methodologies;

7. *Invites* Governments, in collaboration with the cooperative movement, to develop programmes aimed at enhancing capacity-building of cooperatives, including by strengthening the organizational, management and financial skills of their members, and to introduce and support programmes to improve the access of cooperatives to new technologies;

8. *Invites* Governments and international organizations, in collaboration with cooperatives and cooperative organizations, to promote, as appropriate, the growth of agricultural cooperatives through easy access to affordable finance, adoption of sustainable production techniques, investments in rural infrastructure and irrigation, strengthened marketing mechanisms and support for the participation of women in economic activities;

9. *Also invites* Governments and international organizations, in collaboration with cooperatives and cooperative organizations, to promote, as appropriate, the growth of financial cooperatives to meet the goal of inclusive finance by providing easy access to affordable financial services for all;

10. *Invites* Governments, relevant international organizations, the specialized agencies and local, national and international cooperative organizations to continue to observe the International Day of Cooperatives annually, on the first Saturday of July, as proclaimed by the General Assembly in its resolution 47/90;

11. *Requests* the Secretary-General, in cooperation with the relevant United Nations and other international organizations and national, regional and international cooperative organizations, to continue rendering support to Member States, as appropriate, in their efforts to create a supportive environment for the development of cooperatives, providing assistance for human resources development, technical advice and training and promoting an exchange of experience and best practices through, inter alia, conferences, workshops and seminars at the national and regional levels;

12. *Also requests* the Secretary-General to submit to the General Assembly at its sixty-sixth session a report on the implementation of the present resolution, including a proposal on activities to be undertaken during the International Year of Cooperatives within existing resources.

Follow-up to tenth anniversary of 1994 International Year of the Family

In response to General Assembly resolution 62/129 [YUN 2007, p. 1115], the Secretary-General submitted a July report [A/64/134] on the follow-up to the tenth anniversary of the (1994) International Year of the Family [YUN 1994, p. 1144] and beyond, observed on 6 December 2004 [YUN 2004, p. 1095]. The report discussed family policy and its relationship to social protection and intergenerational solidarity, based on information received from 19 Governments that provided information on action taken to strengthen and improve the well-being of families, and on the findings of an expert group meeting on "Family policy in a changing world: promoting social protection and intergenerational solidarity" (Doha, Qatar, 14–16 April). It also described the activities of the United Nations Programme on the Family.

The report included recommendations for Governments to: establish an institutional mechanism with sufficient organizational, fiscal and human resources capacity to promote the family as a policy priority and develop family protection measures; undertake information campaigns on family issues; improve the implementation and enforcement of laws prohibiting harmful traditional practices towards women, children, older persons and other family members; and facilitate the balancing of work and family life by promoting gender equality inside the family, family-friendly work schedules for parents and adequate childcare arrangements. It also invited Governments to stimulate public debate and consultations on family-oriented and gender- and child-sensitive social protection policies and to facilitate activities to promote intergenerational activities through the establishment of community centres for younger and older persons.

GENERAL ASSEMBLY ACTION

On 18 December [meeting 65], the General Assembly, on the recommendation of the Third Committee [A/64/432], adopted **resolution 64/133** without vote [agenda item 61].

Follow-up to the tenth anniversary of the International Year of the Family and beyond

The General Assembly,

Recalling its resolutions 44/82 of 8 December 1989, 50/142 of 21 December 1995, 52/81 of 12 December 1997, 54/124 of 17 December 1999, 56/113 of 19 December 2001, 57/164 of 18 December 2002, 58/15 of 3 December 2003, 59/111 of 6 December 2004, 59/147 of 20 December 2004, 60/133 of 16 December 2005 and 62/129 of 18 December 2007 concerning the proclamation of the International Year of the Family and the preparations for, observance of and follow-up to the tenth anniversary of the International Year of the Family,

Noting that in paragraph 5 of its resolution 59/111 and paragraph 2 of its resolution 59/147, respectively, the General Assembly underlined the need to realize the objectives of the International Year of the Family and to develop concrete measures and approaches to address national priorities in dealing with family issues,

Recognizing that the preparations for and observance of the tenth anniversary of the International Year of the Family in 2004 constituted an important opportunity to strengthen and enhance the effectiveness of efforts at all levels to carry out specific programmes within the framework of the objectives of the Year,

Aware that a major objective of the tenth anniversary of the International Year of the Family is to address the major concern of strengthening the capacity of national institutions to formulate, implement and monitor policies in respect of families,

Noting that the family-related provisions of the outcomes of the major United Nations conferences and summits of the 1990s and their follow-up processes continue to provide policy guidance on ways to strengthen family-centred components of policies and programmes as part of an integrated comprehensive approach to development,

Convinced of the necessity of ensuring an action-oriented follow-up to the tenth anniversary of the International Year of the Family beyond 2004,

Recognizing the important catalytic and supportive role of United Nations bodies, the specialized agencies and the regional commissions in ensuring an action-oriented follow-up in the field of the family, including their positive contribution to strengthening national capacities in family policymaking,

Cognizant of the need for continued inter-agency cooperation on family issues in order to generate greater awareness of this subject among the governing bodies of the United Nations system,

Convinced that civil society, including research and academic institutions, has a pivotal role in advocacy, promotion, research and policymaking in respect of family policy development and capacity-building,

Noting that, in its resolution 59/111, the General Assembly decided to celebrate the anniversary of the International Year of the Family on a ten-year basis,

Taking note with appreciation of the report of the Secretary-General,

1. *Encourages* Governments to continue to make every possible effort to realize the objectives of the International Year of the Family and to integrate a family perspective into national policymaking;

2. *Invites* Governments and regional intergovernmental entities to provide for more systematic national and regional data on family well-being and to identify and ensure support for constructive family policy developments, including the exchange of information on good policies and practices;

3. *Encourages* Member States to adopt holistic approaches to policies and programmes that confront family poverty and social exclusion, and invites Member States to stimulate public debate and consultations on family-oriented and gender- and child-sensitive social protection policies, in accordance with the objectives of the International Year of the Family;

4. *Further encourages* Member States to promote policies and programmes supporting intergenerational solidarity at the family and community levels and geared to reducing the vulnerability of younger and older generations through various social protection strategies;

5. *Urges* Member States to create a conducive environment to strengthen and support all families, recognizing that equality between women and men and respect for all the human rights and fundamental freedoms of all family members are essential to family well-being and to society at large, noting the importance of reconciliation of work and family life and recognizing the principle that both parents have common responsibilities for the upbringing and development of the child;

6. *Invites* Governments to continue to develop strategies and programmes aimed at strengthening national capacities to address national priorities relating to family issues, and encourages the United Nations Programme on the Family, within its mandate, to assist Governments in this regard, including through the provision of technical assistance to build and develop national capacities in the area of formulating, implementing and monitoring family policies;

7. *Encourages* Governments to support the United Nations Trust Fund on Family Activities to enable the Department of Economic and Social Affairs of the Secretariat to provide expanded assistance to countries, upon their request;

8. *Recommends* that United Nations agencies and bodies, intergovernmental and non-governmental organizations, research and academic institutions and the private sector play a supportive role in promoting the objectives of the International Year of the Family;

9. *Requests* the Secretary-General to submit a report to the General Assembly at its sixty-sixth session, through the Commission for Social Development at its forty-ninth session and the Economic and Social Council, on the implementation of the present resolution and on the appropriate ways and means to observe the twentieth anniversary of the International Year of the Family, in 2014;

10. *Decides* to consider the topic "Preparations for and observance of the twentieth anniversary of the International Year of the Family" at its sixty-sixth session under the sub-item entitled "Social development, including questions relating to the world social situation and to youth, ageing, disabled persons and the family".

On the same date, the Assembly adopted **resolution 64/142** (see p. 1161) on guidelines for the alternative care of children, which reaffirmed family as the fundamental group of society and the natural environment for the growth, well-being and protection of children.

Persons with disabilities

World Programme of Action concerning Disabled Persons

In response to General Assembly resolution 63/150 [YUN 2008, p. 1209], the Secretary-General submitted a July report [A/64/180] on realizing the Millennium Development Goals (MDGs) for persons with disabilities, through the implementation of the World Programme of Action concerning Disabled Persons, adopted by Assembly resolution 37/52 [YUN 1982, p. 981], and the Convention on the Rights of Persons with Disabilities, which was adopted by the Assembly in resolution 61/106 [YUN 2006, p. 785] and entered into force in 2008 [YUN 2008, p. 749]. The report discussed linkages between disability and the MDGs, analysed the situation of persons with disabilities in the context of the Goals, including information from MDG country reports, discussion of MDG monitoring and data on disability, and actions and initiatives towards the realization of the Goals for persons with disabilities by Member States, UN entities and non-governmental organizations (NGOs). An expert group meeting on Mainstreaming Disability in MDG Policies, Processes and Mechanisms: Development for All (Geneva, 14–16 April) provided input for the report.

The Secretary-General concluded that while there had been general progress towards the achievement of the MDGs, it was difficult to assess whether and how much persons with disabilities had benefited since available data showed that policies and programmes related to the MDGs had not fully addressed disability and persons with disabilities, and obtaining sufficient and appropriate data was difficult on both the conceptual and practical level. Nonetheless, the limited information that did exist indicated that, in general, persons with disabilities were much worse off than the rest of the population. He stated that the 2006 adoption of the Convention on the Rights of Persons with Disabilities and its entry into force in 2008 provided an opportunity to invigorate an overlooked issue and that accessibility should permeate all policies and activities in realizing the MDGs for persons with disabilities. International cooperation was crucial and cooperation efforts had to ensure participation of persons with disabilities as both agents and beneficiaries of development. Cooperation with the private sector was also important to make available the benefits of new technologies, especially accessible information and communications technologies for persons with disabilities.

Recommendations to the General Assembly included: encouraging Governments to develop and accelerate exchanges of information, experience and practices regarding the situation of persons with disabilities and policy approaches to particular disability issues, particularly as they related to accessibility; emphasizing that participation of persons with disabilities at all levels of policymaking and development was critical to the achievement of the MDGs for persons with disabilities and for their socio-economic advancement; encouraging Governments to use the

2010 census round to fill some of the information and data gaps regarding the living conditions of persons with disabilities; and urging Governments to carry out surveys on the situation of persons with disabilities with respect to the MDGs and specific disability-related barriers preventing their attainment.

Communication. On 29 January [A/63/699], Brazil transmitted to the Secretary-General the Santos Charter, adopted by the Meeting of Portuguese-speaking Countries for the Dissemination and Implementation of the Convention on the Rights of Persons with Disabilities and its Optional Protocol (Santos, Brazil, 10 and 14 September 2008).

GENERAL ASSEMBLY ACTION

On 18 December [meeting 65], the General Assembly, on the recommendation of the Third Committee [A/64/432], adopted **resolution 64/131** without vote [agenda item 61].

Realizing the Millennium Development Goals for persons with disabilities

The General Assembly,

Recalling the World Programme of Action concerning Disabled Persons, the Standard Rules on the Equalization of Opportunities for Persons with Disabilities and the Convention on the Rights of Persons with Disabilities, in which persons with disabilities are recognized as both development agents and beneficiaries in all aspects of development,

Recalling also its previous resolutions on the internationally agreed development goals, including the Millennium Development Goals, in which it recognized the collective responsibility of Governments to uphold the principles of human dignity, equality and equity at the global level, and stressing the duty of Member States to achieve greater justice and equality for all, in particular persons with disabilities,

Gravely concerned that persons with disabilities are often subject to multiple or aggravated forms of discrimination and can be largely invisible in the implementation, monitoring and evaluation of the Millennium Development Goals,

Noting that the entry into force of the Convention on the Rights of Persons with Disabilities, which is both a human rights treaty and a development tool, provides an opportunity to strengthen the policies related to and the implementation of the Millennium Development Goals, thereby contributing to the realization of a "society for all" in the twenty-first century,

Noting also that persons with disabilities make up an estimated 10 per cent of the world's population, of whom 80 per cent live in developing countries, and recognizing the importance of international cooperation and its promotion in support of national efforts, in particular for developing countries,

Concerned that the lack of data and information on disability and the situation of persons with disabilities at the national level contributes to the invisibility of persons with disabilities in official statistics, presenting an obstacle to achieving development planning and implementation that is inclusive of persons with disabilities,

Recognizing that the upcoming high-level plenary meeting to review the implementation of the Millennium Development Goals in 2010 is an important opportunity to enhance efforts to realize the Goals for all, in particular for persons with disabilities,

1. *Takes note* of the report of the Secretary-General on realizing the Millennium Development Goals for persons with disabilities through the implementation of the World Programme of Action concerning Disabled Persons and the Convention on the Rights of Persons with Disabilities;

2. *Urges* Member States, and invites international organizations, regional organizations, including regional integration organizations, financial institutions, the private sector and civil society, in particular organizations representing persons with disabilities, as appropriate, to promote the realization of the Millennium Development Goals for persons with disabilities, inter alia, by explicitly including disability issues and persons with disabilities in national plans and tools designed to contribute to the full realization of the Goals;

3. *Urges* the United Nations system to make a concerted effort to integrate disability issues into its work, and in this regard encourages the Inter-Agency Support Group on the Convention on the Rights of Persons with Disabilities to continue working to ensure that development programmes, including Millennium Development Goals policies, processes and mechanisms, are inclusive of and accessible to persons with disabilities;

4. *Encourages* Member States to ensure that their international cooperation, including through international development programmes, is inclusive of and accessible to persons with disabilities;

5. *Calls upon* Governments and United Nations bodies and agencies to include disability issues and persons with disabilities in reviewing progress towards achieving the Millennium Development Goals and to step up efforts to include in their assessment the extent to which persons with disabilities are able to benefit from efforts to achieve the Goals;

6. *Calls upon* Governments to enable persons with disabilities to participate as agents and beneficiaries of development, in particular in all efforts aimed at achieving the Millennium Development Goals, by ensuring that programmes and policies, namely on eradicating extreme poverty and hunger, achieving universal primary education, promoting gender equality and the empowerment of women, reducing child mortality, improving maternal health, combating HIV/AIDS, malaria and other diseases, ensuring environmental sustainability and developing a global partnership for development, are inclusive of and accessible to persons with disabilities;

7. *Emphasizes* the importance of the participation of persons with disabilities at all levels of policymaking and development, which is critical to informing policymakers on the situation of persons with disabilities, the barriers they may face and ways to overcome obstacles to the full and equal enjoyment of their rights, to the achievement of the Millennium Development Goals for all, including persons with disabilities, and to their socio-economic advancement;

8. *Encourages* international cooperation in the implementation of the Millennium Development Goals, including through global partnerships for development, which are crucial for the realization of the Goals for all, in particular for persons with disabilities;

9. *Encourages* Governments to develop and accelerate the exchange of information, guidelines and standards, best practices, legislative measures and government policies regarding the situation of persons with disabilities and disability issues, in particular as they relate to inclusion and accessibility;

10. *Calls upon* Governments to build a knowledge base of data and information about the situation of persons with disabilities that could be used to enable development policy planning, monitoring, evaluation and implementation to be disability-sensitive, in particular in the realization of the Millennium Development Goals for persons with disabilities, and in this regard:

(a) Requests the Secretary-General to disseminate widely and promote the use of the *Guidelines and Principles for the Development of Disability Statistics* and the *Principles and Recommendations for Population and Housing Censuses* and to facilitate technical assistance, within existing resources, including the provision of assistance for capacity-building of Member States, in particular to developing countries;

(b) Encourages Member States to make use of statistics, to the extent possible, to integrate a disability perspective in reviewing their progress towards realizing the Millennium Development Goals for all;

11. *Requests* the Secretary-General to submit information on the implementation of the present resolution during the sixty-fifth session of the General Assembly within the report requested by the Assembly in paragraph 13 *(b)* of its resolution 63/150 of 18 December 2008.

Standard Rules on Equalization of Opportunities for Persons with Disabilities

In response to Economic and Social Council resolution 2005/9 [YUN 2005, p. 1196], the Secretary-General submitted to the Commission for Social Development the fifth and final annual report [E/CN.5/2009/6] of the Commission's Special Rapporteur on Disability on the monitoring of the implementation of the Standard Rules on the Equalization of Opportunities for Persons with Disabilities, adopted by General Assembly resolution 48/96 [YUN 1993, p. 977]. The Rapporteur provided a summary of her main activities between 2003 and 2008 and an evaluation of the impact of that work on the rights and inclusion of persons with disabilities. Challenges facing the movement to implement the Standard Rules were also addressed. The Special Rapporteur concluded that a focus on international cooperation in policy and practice was one of the most effective ways to hasten the implementation of the Convention on the Rights of Persons with Disabilities and the Standard Rules. The effective representation of persons with disabilities in all monitoring mechanisms, especially committees of international human rights treaties, was indispensable. There was also a need to develop effective national mechanisms for offering incentives and monitoring the implementation of commitments made by Governments. Such implementation had to reach all persons with disabilities, their families and communities, and the societies in which they lived. A positive shift was needed in the attitudes towards persons with disabilities and the manner in which they were viewed should exclude both discrimination and pity and encompass a readiness to work with and involve them in all aspects of life. The Special Rapporteur recommended that the rights of persons with disabilities should become integral to all of the work of the United Nations, noting that success in including the rights of persons with disabilities in achieving the MDGs had been limited, and urged all countries to review and adopt national legislation in line with the Convention on the Rights of Persons with Disabilities, to develop programmes and plans of action, and to earmark funds for their implementation. Those countries that had not yet signed or ratified the Convention were urged to do so.

On 13 February [E/2009/26 (dec. 47/102)], the Commission took note of the Special Rapporteur's report.

Cultural development

Culture of peace

Report of UNESCO Director-General. In response to General Assembly resolution 63/113 [YUN 2008, p. 1215], the Secretary-General transmitted an August report [A/64/312] of the Director-General of the United Nations Educational, Scientific and Cultural Organization (UNESCO) on the International Decade for a Culture of Peace and Non-Violence for the Children of the World, 2001–2010, proclaimed in Assembly resolution 53/25 [YUN 1998, p. 639]. The report, which followed UNESCO's 2008 annual progress report on the Decade [YUN 2008, p. 1215], provided an overview of the activities carried out by UNESCO and other UN entities to promote and implement the Programme of Action on a Culture of Peace [YUN 1999, p. 594]. Eight actions were defined in the Programme of Action: fostering a culture of peace through education; promoting sustainable economic and social development; promoting respect for all human rights; ensuring equality between women and men; fostering democratic participation; advancing understanding, tolerance and solidarity; supporting participatory communication and the free flow of information and knowledge; and promoting international peace and security. Also addressed were the role of civil society, and communication and networking arrangements.

The Director-General encouraged UN agencies, funds and programmes to focus their programmes on the various dimensions of the culture of peace, especially at the country level. States were encouraged to: ensure that funding quality education for all was a top priority and that the financial crisis did not serve as a justification for reducing the allocation of national and international resources to education; increase investments in science and technology, especially green technologies; strengthen education for sustainable development, lifelong learning for all and equal access to learning opportunities so as to implement the principles of inclusive education; review and revise educational and cultural policies to reflect a human rights-based approach, cultural diversity, intercultural dialogue and sustainable development; strengthen efforts to remove hate messages, distortions, prejudice and negative bias from textbooks and other educational media; ensure basic knowledge and understanding of the world's main cultures, civilizations and religions; promote school environments that were child-friendly, conducive to effective learning, inclusive of all children, healthy, protective and gender-responsive; encourage the active role and participation of the learners themselves, their families and their communities; and expand access to information and communication technologies to bring the benefits of all levels and means of education to girls and women, the excluded, the poor, the marginalized and those with special needs in a lifelong perspective.

GENERAL ASSEMBLY ACTION

On 7 December [meeting 60], the General Assembly adopted **resolution 64/80** [draft: A/64/L.5 & Add.1] without vote [agenda item 49].

International Decade for a Culture of Peace and Non-Violence for the Children of the World, 2001–2010

The General Assembly,

Bearing in mind the Charter of the United Nations, including the purposes and principles contained therein, and especially the dedication to saving succeeding generations from the scourge of war,

Recalling the Constitution of the United Nations Educational, Scientific and Cultural Organization, which states that, "since wars begin in the minds of men, it is in the minds of men that the defences of peace must be constructed",

Recalling also its previous resolutions on a culture of peace, in particular resolution 52/15 of 20 November 1997 proclaiming 2000 the International Year for the Culture of Peace, resolution 53/25 of 10 November 1998 proclaiming the period 2001–2010 the International Decade for a Culture of Peace and Non-Violence for the Children of the World, and resolutions 56/5 of 5 November 2001, 57/6 of 4 November 2002, 58/11 of 10 November 2003, 59/143 of 15 December 2004, 60/3 of 20 October 2005, 61/45 of 4 December 2006, 62/89 of 17 December 2007 and 63/113 of 5 December 2008,

Reaffirming the Declaration and Programme of Action on a Culture of Peace, recognizing that they serve, inter alia, as the basis for the observance of the Decade, and convinced that the effective and successful observance of the Decade throughout the world will promote a culture of peace and non-violence that benefits humanity, in particular future generations,

Recalling the United Nations Millennium Declaration, which calls for the active promotion of a culture of peace,

Taking note of Commission on Human Rights resolution 2000/66 of 26 April 2000, entitled "Towards a culture of peace",

Taking note also of the report of the Secretary-General on the International Decade for a Culture of Peace and Non-Violence for the Children of the World, including paragraph 28 thereof, which indicates that each of the ten years of the Decade will be marked with a different priority theme related to the Programme of Action,

Noting the relevance of the World Summit on Sustainable Development, held in Johannesburg, South Africa, from 26 August to 4 September 2002, the International Conference on Financing for Development, held in Monterrey, Mexico, from 18 to 22 March 2002, the special session of the General Assembly on children, held in New York from 8 to 10 May 2002, the World Conference against Racism, Racial Discrimination, Xenophobia and Related Intolerance, held in Durban, South Africa, from 31 August to 8 September 2001, and the United Nations Decade for Human Rights Education, 1995–2004, for the International Decade for a Culture of Peace and Non-Violence for the Children of the World, 2001–2010, as well as the need to implement, as appropriate, the relevant decisions agreed upon therein,

Recognizing that all efforts made by the United Nations system in general and the international community at large for peacekeeping, peacebuilding, the prevention of conflicts, disarmament, sustainable development, the promotion of human dignity and human rights, democracy, the rule of law, good governance and gender equality at the national and international levels contribute greatly to the culture of peace,

Noting that its resolution 57/337 of 3 July 2003 on the prevention of armed conflict could contribute to the further promotion of a culture of peace,

Taking into account the "Manifesto 2000" initiative of the United Nations Educational, Scientific and Cultural Organization promoting a culture of peace, which has so far received over seventy-five million signatures of endorsement throughout the world,

Taking note with appreciation of the report of the Director-General of the United Nations Educational, Scientific and Cultural Organization on the implementation of resolution 63/113,

Taking note of the 2005 World Summit Outcome adopted at the High-level Plenary Meeting of the General Assembly,

Welcoming the designation of 2 October as the International Day of Non-Violence,

Recalling the proclamation by the United Nations Educational, Scientific and Cultural Organization of 21 February as the International Mother Language Day, which aims at promoting and preserving linguistic and cultural diversity, and multilingualism, in order to foster a culture of peace, harmony, cross-cultural dialogue and mutual understanding,

Appreciating the ongoing efforts of the Alliance of Civilizations and the Tripartite Forum on Interfaith Cooperation for Peace in promoting a culture of peace,

Welcoming the appointment of the Special Representative of the Secretary-General on Violence against Children,

1. *Reiterates* that the objective of the International Decade for a Culture of Peace and Non-Violence for the Children of the World, 2001–2010, is to strengthen further the global movement for a culture of peace following the observance of the International Year for the Culture of Peace in 2000;

2. *Invites* Member States to continue to place greater emphasis on and expand their activities promoting a culture of peace and non-violence, in particular during the Decade, at the national, regional and international levels and to ensure that peace and non-violence are fostered at all levels;

3. *Commends* the United Nations Educational, Scientific and Cultural Organization for recognizing the promotion of a culture of peace as the expression of its fundamental mandate, and encourages it, as the lead agency for the Decade, to strengthen further the activities it has undertaken for promoting a culture of peace, including the dissemination of the Declaration and Programme of Action on a Culture of Peace and related materials in various languages across the world;

4. *Commends* the relevant United Nations bodies, in particular the United Nations Children's Fund, the United Nations Development Fund for Women and the University for Peace, for their activities in further promoting a culture of peace and non-violence, including the promotion of peace education and activities related to specific areas identified in the Programme of Action, and encourages them to continue and further strengthen and expand their efforts;

5. *Encourages* the Peacebuilding Commission to continue to promote a culture of peace and non-violence for children in its activities;

6. *Encourages* the appropriate authorities to provide education, in children's schools, that includes lessons in mutual understanding, tolerance, active citizenship, human rights and the promotion of a culture of peace;

7. *Commends* civil society, including non-governmental organizations and young people, for their activities in further promoting a culture of peace and non-violence, including through their campaign to raise awareness on a culture of peace, and takes note of the progress achieved by more than seven hundred organizations in more than one hundred countries;

8. *Encourages* civil society, including non-governmental organizations, to further strengthen its efforts in furtherance of the objectives of the Decade, inter alia, by adopting its own programme of activities to complement the initiatives of Member States, the organizations of the United Nations system and other international and regional organizations;

9. *Encourages* the involvement of the mass media in education for a culture of peace and non-violence, with particular regard to children and young people, including

through the planned expansion of the Culture of Peace News Network as a global network of Internet sites in many languages;

10. *Welcomes* the efforts made by the United Nations Educational, Scientific and Cultural Organization to continue the communication and networking arrangements established during the International Year for providing an instant update of developments related to the observance of the Decade;

11. *Takes note with appreciation* of the initiative of the Special Unit for South-South Cooperation of the United Nations Development Programme, in partnership with the United Nations Human Settlements Programme and the United Nations Conference on Trade and Development, to include the theme "culture of peace" in the Creative Economy Week to be held from 19 to 24 October 2010 as part of the activities of the United Nations pavilion at the 2010 World Exposition in Shanghai, China;

12. *Invites* Member States to observe 21 September each year as the International Day of Peace, as a day of global ceasefire and non-violence, in accordance with resolution 55/282 of 7 September 2001;

13. *Invites* Member States, as well as civil society, including non-governmental organizations, to continue providing information to the Secretary-General on the observance of the Decade and the activities undertaken to promote a culture of peace and non-violence;

14. *Appreciates* the participation of Member States in the day of plenary meetings to review progress made in the implementation of the Declaration and Programme of Action and the observance of the Decade at its midpoint;

15. *Requests* the Secretary-General to explore enhancing mechanisms for the implementation of the Declaration and Programme of Action;

16. *Also requests* the Secretary-General to submit to the General Assembly at its sixty-fifth session a report on the implementation of the present resolution;

17. *Further requests* the Secretary-General to submit to the General Assembly at its sixty-fifth session a summary report on the activities carried out in the past ten years by the United Nations Educational, Scientific and Cultural Organization and other United Nations entities, Member States and civil society, including non-governmental organizations, to promote and implement the Programme of Action;

18. *Decides* to include in the provisional agenda of its sixty-fifth session the item entitled "Culture of peace".

On 24 December, the Assembly decided that the agenda item on a culture of peace would remain for consideration at its resumed sixty-fourth (2010) session (**decision 64/549**).

Interreligious and intercultural understanding

In response to General Assembly resolution 63/22 [YUN 2008, p. 1217], the Secretary-General submitted an August report [A/64/325] in which he highlighted the activities carried out by key UN entities involved in interreligious and intercultural dialogue and provided an overview of other major regional and global

initiatives taken in that field. The report, which complemented that of the UNESCO Director-General on the International Decade for a Culture of Peace and Non-Violence for the Children of the World, 2001–2010 (see p. 1070), also presented the outcome of consultations carried out by the Secretariat, in coordination with UNESCO, on the possibility of proclaiming a UN decade for interreligious and intercultural dialogue.

Communication. On 6 July [A/63/918], Kazakhstan transmitted to the Secretary-General the text of the Appeal of the Participants of the Third Congress of Leaders of World and Traditional Religions, adopted on 2 July in Astana, Kazakhstan.

International Year of Reconciliation, 2009

In 2009, the United Nations observed the International Year of Reconciliation as proclaimed by the General Assembly in 2006 in resolution 61/17 [YUN 2006, p. 53]. The Assembly had requested Governments and international and NGOs to support reconciliation processes among affected and/or divided societies and to plan and implement cultural, educational and social programmes to promote the concept of reconciliation.

On 9 November [A/64/PV.41], the Assembly President proposed that an informal thematic debate on dialogue among civilizations, religions and cultures be held in 2010.

GENERAL ASSEMBLY ACTION

On 7 December [meeting 60], the General Assembly adopted **resolution 64/81** [draft: A/64/L.15/Rev.1 & Add.1] without vote [agenda item 49].

Promotion of interreligious and intercultural dialogue, understanding and cooperation for peace

The General Assembly,

Reaffirming the purposes and principles enshrined in the Charter of the United Nations and the Universal Declaration of Human Rights, in particular the right to freedom of thought, conscience and religion,

Recalling its resolutions 56/6 of 9 November 2001, on the Global Agenda for Dialogue among Civilizations, 57/6 of 4 November 2002, on the International Decade for a Culture of Peace and Non-Violence for the Children of the World, 2001–2010, 57/337 of 3 July 2003, on the prevention of armed conflict, 58/128 of 19 December 2003, on the promotion of religious and cultural understanding, harmony and cooperation, 59/23 of 11 November 2004, on the promotion of interreligious dialogue, 61/17 of 20 November 2006, on the International Year of Reconciliation, 2009, 62/155 of 18 December 2007, on human rights and cultural diversity, 63/113 of 5 December 2008, on the International Decade for a Culture of Peace and

Non-Violence for the Children of the World, 2001–2010, and 63/181 of 18 December 2008, on the elimination of all forms of intolerance and of discrimination based on religion or belief,

Recalling also its resolution 63/22 of 13 November 2008, on the promotion of interreligious and intercultural dialogue, understanding and cooperation for peace, and the leading role played by the United Nations Educational, Scientific and Cultural Organization in the preparations for the celebration of the International Year for the Rapprochement of Cultures, in 2010,

Bearing in mind the valuable contribution that dialogue among civilizations can make to an improved awareness and understanding of the common values shared by all humankind,

Noting that interreligious and intercultural dialogue has made significant contributions to mutual understanding, the promotion of a culture of peace and tolerance and an improvement of overall relations among people from different cultural and religious backgrounds and among nations,

Recognizing that cultural diversity and the pursuit of cultural development by all peoples and nations are sources of mutual enrichment for the cultural life of humankind,

Noting the various initiatives at the national, regional and international levels for enhancing dialogue, understanding and cooperation among religions, cultures and civilizations, which are all mutually reinforcing and interrelated,

Noting also the commemoration of the International Year of Reconciliation, 2009,

Encouraging activities aimed at promoting interreligious and intercultural dialogue in order to enhance social stability, respect for diversity, and mutual respect in diverse communities, and create, at the global level, and also at the regional, national and local levels, an environment conducive to peace and mutual understanding,

Noting with appreciation the decision taken in resolution 47, adopted on 23 October 2009 by the General Conference of the United Nations Educational, Scientific and Cultural Organization at its thirty-fifth session, to approve the preliminary action plan for the celebration of the International Year for the Rapprochement of Cultures, in 2010,

Affirming the importance of sustaining the process of engaging all stakeholders in the interreligious, intercultural and intercivilizational dialogue within the appropriate initiatives at the various levels,

Recognizing the commitment of all religions to peace,

1. *Affirms* that mutual understanding and interreligious dialogue constitute important dimensions of the dialogue among civilizations and of the culture of peace;

2. *Takes note* of the report of the Secretary-General on interreligious and intercultural dialogue, understanding and cooperation for peace;

3. *Notes* the work of the United Nations Educational, Scientific and Cultural Organization on interreligious dialogue in the context of its efforts to promote dialogue among civilizations, cultures and peoples, as well as activities related to a culture of peace, and welcomes its focus on concrete action at the global, regional and subregional levels;

4. *Reaffirms* the solemn commitment of all States to fulfil their obligations to promote universal respect for, and observance and protection of, all human rights and fundamental freedoms for all in accordance with the Charter of the United Nations, the Universal Declaration of Human Rights and other instruments relating to human rights and international law, the universal nature of these rights and freedoms being beyond question;

5. *Encourages* the promotion of dialogue among the media from all cultures and civilizations, emphasizes that everyone has the right to freedom of expression, and reaffirms that the exercise of this right carries with it special duties and responsibilities and may therefore be subject to certain restrictions, but these shall be only such as are provided by law and necessary for respect of the rights or reputations of others, protection of national security or of public order, or of public health or morals;

6. *Encourages* Member States to consider, as and where appropriate, initiatives that identify areas for practical action in all sectors and levels of society for the promotion of interreligious and intercultural dialogue, tolerance, understanding and cooperation, inter alia, the ideas suggested during the High-level Dialogue on Interreligious and Intercultural Understanding and Cooperation for Peace, held on 4 and 5 October 2007, including the idea of an enhanced process of dialogue among world religions;

7. *Takes note* of the Fourth Ministerial Meeting on Interfaith Dialogue and Cooperation for Peace, held on 25 September 2009 in New York;

8. *Supports* the proposal of the President of the General Assembly to hold, at its sixty-fourth session, an informal thematic debate on dialogue among civilizations;

9. *Urges* Member States, in the context of the International Year of Reconciliation, 2009, to further promote reconciliation to help to ensure durable peace and sustained development, including through reconciliatory measures and acts of service and by encouraging forgiveness and compassion among individuals;

10. *Encourages* the United Nations Educational, Scientific and Cultural Organization, as the lead agency for the International Year for the Rapprochement of Cultures, to promote the action plan for the celebration of the Year, and encourages Member States and all organizations and institutions, including civil society organizations, working to promote the rapprochement of cultures to join in the celebration of the Year in order to demonstrate their firm commitment to intercultural dialogue, including interreligious dialogue;

11. *Invites* the Secretary-General to organize, within existing resources, a special activity to launch the celebration of the International Year for the Rapprochement of Cultures, which could include the ringing of the peace bell;

12. *Recognizes* that the Office for Economic and Social Council Support and Coordination in the Department of Economic and Social Affairs of the Secretariat plays a valuable role as focal point within the Secretariat on the issue, and encourages it to continue to interact and coordinate with the relevant entities of the United Nations system and coordinate their contribution to the intergovernmental process;

13. *Requests* the Secretary-General to report to the General Assembly at its sixty-fifth session on the implementation of the present resolution and, at its sixty-sixth

session, in coordination with the United Nations Educational, Scientific and Cultural Organization, to further solicit views of Member States on the possibility of proclaiming a United Nations decade for interreligious and intercultural dialogue and cooperation for peace, building on the information contained in the reports of the Secretary-General at the sixty-fourth and sixty-fifth sessions and the relevant initiatives to be taken in the course of 2010.

Alliance of Civilizations

In a June letter [A/63/914], the Secretary-General transmitted to the President of the General Assembly the second annual report of his High Representative for the Alliance of Civilizations, which covered the main activities carried out by the Alliance between May 2008 and May 2009, the first report having been submitted in 2008 [YUN 2008, p. 1217]. During the reporting period, the Alliance worked towards shaping its agenda for the good governance of cultural diversity at a global level, promoting national plans and regional strategies for intercultural dialogue among its member States, developing its network of partnerships and identifying the most innovative grass-roots projects across the world. Priority was also given to the cross-cultural polarization in relations between Muslim and Western societies, particularly in the Euro-Mediterranean area. The High Representative dedicated multiple efforts to addressing that issue, including political talks, consultations with a wide range of actors or analysts and initiatives with partners, namely during two major critical moments since the first Alliance of Civilizations Forum in January 2008 [ibid.]: the release of the film *Fitna* and the Gaza crisis [YUN 2008, p. 476]. Work was focused on broadening the support base of the Alliance through the Group of Friends network of member countries and international organizations; enlarging and improving cooperation and the coordination with UN agencies and specialized bodies and with other key organizations and regional processes; widening the global network of partnerships with groups that could act as forces of moderation and understanding (private sector, civil society, media organizations); and implementing the 10 main commitments made at the Madrid Forum.

At the second Alliance of Civilizations Forum (Istanbul, Turkey, 6–7 April), more than 1,500 participants convened to forge new partnerships and generate ideas aimed at building trust and cooperation among diverse communities.

GENERAL ASSEMBLY ACTION

On 10 November [meeting 42], the General Assembly adopted **resolution 64/14** [draft: A/64/L.14 & Add.1] without vote [agenda item 49].

The Alliance of Civilizations

The General Assembly,

Reaffirming the solemn commitment of all States to fulfil their obligations to promote universal respect for, and observance and protection of, all human rights and fundamental freedoms for all in accordance with the Charter of the United Nations, the Universal Declaration of Human Rights and other instruments relating to international law and human rights, and reaffirming also the universal nature of these rights and freedoms,

Recalling the 2005 World Summit Outcome, in which the Heads of State and Government welcomed the Alliance of Civilizations initiative announced by the Secretary-General on 14 July 2005 and committed themselves to promoting a culture of peace and dialogue at the local, national, regional and international levels,

Acknowledging the diversity of the world and the fact that all cultures and civilizations contribute to the enrichment of humankind, recognizing the importance of respect and understanding for religious and cultural diversity throughout the world, and encouraging tolerance, respect, dialogue and cooperation among different cultures, civilizations and peoples,

Recognizing the importance of intercultural and interreligious and intrareligious dialogue in promoting tolerance in matters related to religion or belief, and emphasizing the important role of the United Nations Educational, Scientific and Cultural Organization in this regard,

1. *Welcomes* the efforts made by the Secretary-General and his High Representative for the Alliance of Civilizations to promote greater understanding and respect among civilizations, cultures and religions, and encourages the Alliance to continue its work through a number of practical projects in the areas of youth, education, media and migrations, in collaboration with Governments, international organizations, foundations and civil society groups, as well as media and corporate leaders;

2. *Acknowledges* the results of the First Forum of the Alliance of Civilizations, held in Madrid on 15 and 16 January 2008 and of the Second Forum of the Alliance, held in Istanbul, Turkey, on 6 and 7 April 2009;

3. *Encourages* Governments, international organizations and representatives of civil society to participate in the Third Forum of the Alliance of Civilizations, which will be held in Brazil in 2010, as well as in the upcoming Forums of the Alliance, which will be hosted by Qatar in 2011 and Austria in 2012;

4. *Welcomes* the first and second reports of the High Representative to the Secretary-General on the activities of the Alliance of Civilizations, including the projects and programmes that have been launched at the Forums of the Alliance;

5. *Expresses its continuing support* for the work of the Alliance of Civilizations, recognizing the importance of its Group of Friends in this regard as well as the relevance of the national plans for the Alliance that have been approved by its member States thus far and of the activities related to the Alliance that are being developed by the international organizations that are members of the Group of Friends.

Nelson Mandela International Day

In a 24 July letter to the Secretary-General [A/63/968], Egypt, as Chair of the Coordinating Bureau of the Non-Aligned Movement, transmitted a declaration adopted by the Fifteenth Summit of the Non-Aligned Movement (Sharm el-Sheikh, Egypt, 11–16 July). It stated that the Heads of State and Government of the Non-Aligned Movement, recognizing Nelson Mandela's leading role in and support for Africa's struggle for liberation and self-determination, his values and his dedication to the service of humanity in the fields of conflict resolution, race relations, promotion and protection of human rights, reconciliation, gender equality and the rights of children and other vulnerable groups, as well as the upliftment of poor and underdeveloped communities, endorsed the observance of 18 July (Mr. Mandela's birthday) as Nelson Mandela International Day. It requested that a resolution to that effect be adopted by the General Assembly at its sixty-fourth (2009) session.

GENERAL ASSEMBLY ACTION

On 10 November [meeting 42], the General Assembly adopted **resolution 64/13** [draft: A/64/L.13 & Add.1] without vote [agenda item 49].

Nelson Mandela International Day

The General Assembly,

Recognizing the long history of Nelson Rolihlahla Mandela's leading role in and support for Africa's struggle for liberation and Africa's unity, and his outstanding contribution to the creation of a non-racial, non-sexist, democratic South Africa,

Recognizing also Nelson Mandela's values and his dedication to the service of humanity, as a humanitarian, in the fields of conflict resolution, race relations, promotion and protection of human rights, reconciliation, gender equality and the rights of children and other vulnerable groups, as well as the upliftment of poor and underdeveloped communities,

Acknowledging Nelson Mandela's contribution to the struggle for democracy internationally and the promotion of a culture of peace throughout the world,

Welcoming the international campaign initiated by the Nelson Mandela Foundation and related organizations to each year observe 18 July, his birthday, as Mandela Day,

Welcoming also the statements of support by the Secretary-General and the President of the General Assembly at its sixty-third session, on the occasion of the celebration of Mandela Day on 18 July 2009,

Recalling the worldwide participation and celebration of the inaugural Mandela Day on 18 July 2009,

Recalling also the endorsement by the Heads of State and Government of the Movement of Non-Aligned Countries of the observance of 18 July as Nelson Mandela International Day and the request that a resolution to this effect be adopted by the General Assembly at its sixty-fourth session,

1. *Decides* to designate 18 July as Nelson Mandela International Day, to be observed each year beginning in 2010;

2. *Invites* all Member States, organizations of the United Nations system and other international organizations, as well as civil society, including non-governmental organizations and individuals, to observe Nelson Mandela International Day in an appropriate manner;

3. *Requests* the Secretary-General to take the necessary measures, within existing resources, for the observance by the United Nations of Nelson Mandela International Day;

4. *Also requests* the Secretary-General to keep the General Assembly informed at its sixty-fifth session of the implementation of the present resolution within the United Nations system, and thereafter to keep the Assembly informed on an annual basis concerning the observance of Nelson Mandela International Day;

5. *Further requests* the Secretary-General to bring the present resolution to the attention of all Member States and United Nations organizations.

Sport for development and peace

Olympic Truce and ideal

The General Assembly, pursuant to resolution 62/4 [YUN 2007, p. 1124], considered the sub-item on "Building a peaceful and better world through sport and the Olympic ideal" prior to the XXI Olympic Winter Games, to be held in Vancouver, Canada in 2010.

GENERAL ASSEMBLY ACTION

On 19 October [meeting 21], the General Assembly adopted **resolution 64/4** [draft: A/64/L.2 & Add.1] without vote [agenda item 45].

Building a peaceful and better world through sport and the Olympic ideal

The General Assembly,

Recalling its resolution 62/4 of 31 October 2007, in which it decided to include in the provisional agenda of its sixty-fourth session the sub-item entitled "Building a peaceful and better world through sport and the Olympic ideal", and recalling also its prior decision to consider the sub-item every two years, in advance of each Summer and Winter Olympic Games,

Recalling also its resolution 48/11 of 25 October 1993, which, inter alia, revived the ancient Greek tradition of *ekecheiria* ("Olympic Truce") calling for a truce during the Olympic Games that would encourage a peaceful environment and ensure the safe passage and participation of athletes and relevant persons at the Games, thereby mobilizing the youth of the world to the cause of peace,

Taking into account the inclusion in the United Nations Millennium Declaration of an appeal for the observance of the Olympic Truce now and in the future and for support for the International Olympic Committee in its efforts to promote peace and human understanding through sport and the Olympic ideal,

Recognizing the valuable contribution that the appeal launched by the International Olympic Committee for an Olympic Truce could make towards advancing the purposes and principles of the Charter of the United Nations,

Recognizing also the increasingly important role of sport in achieving internationally agreed development goals, including those contained in the Millennium Declaration, and reaffirming the commitments undertaken in this regard by the Heads of State and Government gathered at the World Summit of the General Assembly, held in New York in 2005,

Recalling its resolution 63/135 of 11 December 2008, in which it recognized the value of sport as a means to promote education, health, development and peace and welcomed the establishment of a United Nations Office on Sport for Development and Peace,

Recognizing that the goal of the Olympic movement is to build a peaceful and better world by educating the youth of the world through sport, practised without discrimination of any kind and in the Olympic spirit, which is based on mutual understanding, friendship, solidarity and fair play,

Welcoming the joint endeavours of the International Olympic Committee, the International Paralympic Committee and the United Nations system in such fields as human development, poverty alleviation, humanitarian assistance, health promotion, HIV and AIDS prevention, youth education, gender equality, peacebuilding and sustainable development,

Recalling the relevant articles on leisure, recreation, sport and play of international conventions, including article 30 of the Convention on the Rights of Persons with Disabilities recognizing the right of persons with disabilities to take part on an equal basis with others in cultural life, recreation, leisure and sport,

Noting that the XXI Olympic Winter Games will take place from 12 to 28 February 2010 and the X Paralympic Winter Games will take place from 12 to 21 March 2010 in Vancouver, Canada, with the aim of upholding sport as an inspirational means to promote peace, inclusivity, indigenous participation, social and environmental responsibility and meaningful legacies for future generations,

Noting also that the inaugural Youth Olympic Games will take place from 14 to 26 August 2010, in Singapore, with the aim of inspiring the youth of the world through an integrated sport, culture and education experience to embrace, embody and express the Olympic values,

Noting with satisfaction the flying of the United Nations flag at the competition sites of the Olympic Games and the Paralympic Games,

1. *Urges* Member States to observe, within the framework of the Charter of the United Nations, the Olympic Truce, individually and collectively, during the XXI Olympic Winter Games and the X Paralympic Winter Games;

2. *Welcomes* the decisions of the International Olympic Committee and the International Paralympic Committee to mobilize international sports organizations and the National Olympic Committees and National Paralympic Committees of Member States to undertake concrete actions at the local, national, regional and world levels to promote and strengthen a culture of peace based on the spirit of the Olympic Truce, and invites those organizations

and national committees to share information and best practices, as appropriate;

3. *Calls upon* all Member States to cooperate with the International Olympic Committee and the International Paralympic Committee in their efforts to use sport as a tool to promote peace, dialogue and reconciliation in areas of conflict during the period of the Olympic Games and beyond;

4. *Requests* the Secretary-General to promote the observance of the Olympic Truce among Member States and support for human development initiatives through sport and to cooperate with the International Olympic Committee, the International Paralympic Committee and the sporting community in general in the realization of those objectives;

5. *Decides* to include in the provisional agenda of its sixty-sixth session the sub-item entitled "Building a peaceful and better world through sport and the Olympic ideal" and to consider the sub-item before the Games of the XXX Olympiad and the XIV Paralympic Games, to be held in London in 2012.

On the same date, the Assembly decided to invite the International Olympic Committee to participate in the sessions and the work of the Assembly in the capacity of observer (**resolution 64/3**) (see p. 1384).

On 24 December, the Assembly decided that the agenda item on sport for peace and development: building a peaceful and better world through sport and the Olympic ideal would remain for consideration at its resumed sixty-fourth (2010) session (**decision 64/549**).

Football World Cup event (2010)

In October, the General Assembly, in reference to the 2010 International Federation of Association Football World Cup, which would be held for the first time on the African continent, welcomed South Africa's readiness to host the event; noted the role played by the African Union in helping to start the ball rolling for the 2010 World Cup in South Africa; and supported the launch of the 1GOAL World Cup 2010 campaign, which aimed to raise global public awareness of and advocate for the importance of achieving the MDGs of universal primary education and gender parity in education by 2015.

GENERAL ASSEMBLY ACTION

On 19 October [meeting 21], the General Assembly adopted **resolution 64/5** [draft: A/64/L.3 & Add.1] without vote [agenda item 45].

2010 International Federation of Association Football World Cup in South Africa

The General Assembly,

Recalling its resolution 63/135 of 11 December 2008, in which it recognized the value of sport as a means to promote education, health, development and peace and welcomed the establishment of a United Nations Office on Sport for Development and Peace,

Recognizing the potential of sport to contribute to the achievement of the Millennium Development Goals, and noting that sport has the potential, as declared in the 2005 World Summit Outcome, to foster peace and development and to contribute to an atmosphere of tolerance and understanding,

Acknowledging the use of mass sports events to promote and support sport for development and peace initiatives,

Acknowledging also the role played by sport in Africa as an instrument for the promotion of unity, solidarity, peace and reconciliation, and the preventive campaigns against scourges, such as HIV/AIDS, affecting the youth of the continent,

Welcoming South Africa's readiness to host the historic 2010 International Federation of Association Football World Cup, which is to be held for the first time on the African continent in recognition of Africa's contribution to the advancement of world sports, and recalling the endorsement and support of the Heads of State and Government of the African Union for efforts to ensure the success of the event,

Noting with appreciation the role played by the African Union in helping to start the ball rolling for the 2010 World Cup in South Africa by rallying countries across the continent to use the great appeal of football for a broad range of development and peace activities through the International Year of African Football 2007 and the World Cup legacy programme,

1. *Emphasizes* the role of sport in the promotion of peace, solidarity, social cohesion and socio-economic development;

2. *Notes* that, given its universal popularity, football can bring people together and play a positive role in promoting development and peace;

3. *Welcomes* the historic and unique dimension of the 2010 International Federation of Association Football World Cup in South Africa, marking the first time that that major sports event will take place on the African continent;

4. *Also welcomes* the preparations by South Africa for the hosting of the 2010 World Cup, and expresses its continued support, where appropriate, to South Africa in the pursuit of ensuring the success of the tournament;

5. *Encourages* all Member States to support sport and its use as a tool to promote peace and development, including through the continued contribution to the achievement of the Millennium Development Goals and dialogue among civilizations;

6. *Firmly supports* the launch of the 1GOAL World Cup 2010 campaign, which aims to raise global public awareness of and advocate for the importance of achieving the Millennium Development Goals of universal primary education and gender parity in education by 2015;

7. *Encourages* the relevant authorities to exert every effort to ensure that the 2010 World Cup will leave a lasting legacy for peace and development in Africa;

8. *Encourages* all Member States to support, where appropriate, including through stimulating popular attendance, the 2010 World Cup, to be hosted by South Africa in June 2010.

Cultural property

Return of cultural property

In response to General Assembly resolution 61/52 [YUN 2006, p. 1285], the Secretary-General, in August [A/64/303], transmitted the UNESCO Director-General's report covering a three-year period on action taken by the organization to combat illicit trafficking in cultural property and facilitate its return and restitution to its country of origin in the case of illicit export or theft. The previous report was submitted in 2006 [YUN 2006, p. 1285]. In addition to assisting Member States in the national implementation of the relevant international standard-setting instruments, UNESCO took steps to fulfil the recommendations adopted by the Intergovernmental Committee for Promoting the Return of Cultural Property to its Countries of Origin or its Restitution in Case of Illicit Appropriation at its 2007 and 2009 sessions.

At its 2009 session (Paris, 11–13 May), the Committee invited the Director-General to assist in convening meetings between Greece and the United Kingdom with the aim of reaching a mutually acceptable solution to the issue of the Parthenon marbles. It recommended that he continue his good offices towards resolving the matter of Turkey's request that Germany return the Boğazköy sphinx and encouraged Switzerland and the United Republic of Tanzania to continue their efforts to resolve the issue of the return of the Makondé mask. On the draft rules of procedure on mediation and conciliation, the Committee decided to form a subcommittee to continue intersessional discussions on the draft text and present the results of its work at the Committee's 2010 session.

GENERAL ASSEMBLY ACTION

On 7 December [meeting 60], the General Assembly adopted **resolution 64/78** [draft A/64/L.17/Rev.1 & Add.1] without vote [agenda item 43].

Return or restitution of cultural property to the countries of origin

The General Assembly,

Reaffirming the relevant provisions of the Charter of the United Nations,

Recalling its resolutions 3026 A(XXVII) of 18 December 1972, 3148(XXVIII) of 14 December 1973, 3187(XXVIII) of 18 December 1973, 3391(XXX) of 19 November 1975, 31/40 of 30 November 1976, 32/18 of 11 November 1977, 33/50 of 14 December 1978, 34/64 of 29 November 1979, 35/127 and 35/128 of 11 December 1980, 36/64 of 27 November 1981, 38/34 of 25 November 1983, 40/19 of 21 November 1985, 42/7 of 22 October 1987, 44/18 of 6 November 1989, 46/10 of 22 October 1991, 48/15 of 2 November 1993, 50/56 of 11 December 1995, 52/24 of 25 November 1997, 54/190 of 17 December 1999, 56/97 of 14 December 2001, 58/17 of 3 December 2003 and 61/52 of 4 December 2006,

Recalling also its resolution 56/8 of 21 November 2001, in which it proclaimed 2002 the United Nations Year for Cultural Heritage,

Recalling further the Convention for the Protection of Cultural Property in the Event of Armed Conflict, adopted at The Hague on 14 May 1954, and the two Protocols thereto, adopted in 1954 and 1999,

Recalling the Convention on the Means of Prohibiting and Preventing the Illicit Import, Export and Transfer of Ownership of Cultural Property, adopted on 14 November 1970 by the General Conference of the United Nations Educational, Scientific and Cultural Organization,

Recalling also the Convention concerning the Protection of the World Cultural and Natural Heritage, adopted on 16 November 1972 by the General Conference of the United Nations Educational, Scientific and Cultural Organization,

Recalling further the Convention on Stolen or Illegally Exported Cultural Objects, adopted in Rome on 24 June 1995 by the International Institute for the Unification of Private Law,

Taking note of the adoption of the Convention on the Protection of the Underwater Cultural Heritage by the General Conference of the United Nations Educational, Scientific and Cultural Organization on 2 November 2001, and its entry into force on 2 January 2009,

Noting the adoption of the Convention for the Safeguarding of the Intangible Cultural Heritage by the General Conference of the United Nations Educational, Scientific and Cultural Organization on 17 October 2003, and its entry into force on 20 April 2006, and the Convention on the Protection and Promotion of the Diversity of Cultural Expressions by the General Conference of the United Nations Educational, Scientific and Cultural Organization on 20 October 2005, and its entry into force on 18 March 2007,

Noting also the adoption of the United Nations Convention on Jurisdictional Immunities of States and Their Property on 2 December 2004, as it might apply to cultural property,

Recalling the Medellin Declaration for Cultural Diversity and Tolerance and the Plan of Action on Cultural Cooperation, adopted at the first Meeting of the Ministers of Culture of the Movement of Non-Aligned Countries, held in Medellin, Colombia, on 4 and 5 September 1997, and the adoption by the General Conference of the United Nations Educational, Scientific and Cultural Organization on 17 October 2003 of the Declaration concerning the Intentional Destruction of Cultural Heritage,

Noting the adoption of the Universal Declaration on Cultural Diversity and the Action Plan for its implementation, adopted by the General Conference of the United Nations Educational, Scientific and Cultural Organization on 2 November 2001,

Welcoming the report of the Secretary-General submitted in cooperation with the Director-General of the United Nations Educational, Scientific and Cultural Organization,

Commending Member States, cultural and educational institutions, museums and civil society for their efforts to combat the illicit trade in cultural properties, and welcoming all initiatives for the voluntary return of cultural properties that have been illicitly appropriated,

Aware of the importance attached by some countries of origin to the return of cultural property that is of fundamental spiritual, historical and cultural value to them, so that they may constitute collections representative of their cultural heritage,

Expressing concern about the illicit traffic in cultural property and its damage to the cultural heritage of nations,

Reaffirming the necessity of international cooperation in preventing and combating all aspects of trafficking in cultural property, and noting that such cultural property is especially transferred through licit markets, such as auctions, including through the Internet,

Expressing concern about the loss, destruction, removal, theft, pillage, illicit movement or misappropriation of and any acts of vandalism or damage directed against cultural property, in particular in areas of armed conflict, including territories that are occupied, whether such conflicts are international or internal,

Recalling Security Council resolution 1483(2003), adopted on 22 May 2003, in particular paragraph 7 relating to the restitution of the cultural property of Iraq,

1. *Commends* the United Nations Educational, Scientific and Cultural Organization and the Intergovernmental Committee for Promoting the Return of Cultural Property to its Countries of Origin or its Restitution in Case of Illicit Appropriation on the work they have accomplished, in particular through the promotion of bilateral negotiations, for the return or restitution of cultural property, the preparation of inventories of movable cultural property and the implementation of the Object-ID standard related thereto, as well as for the reduction of illicit traffic in cultural property and the dissemination of information and tools to the public, institutions, Member States and others, and encourages the continuation of such endeavours;

2. *Takes note* of the hosting by the United Nations Educational, Scientific and Cultural Organization of regional training sessions and international meetings, such as the 2008 Athens International Conference on the Return of Cultural Property to its Country of Origin and the 2008 extraordinary session of the Intergovernmental Committee for Promoting the Return of Cultural Property to its Countries of Origin or its Restitution in Case of Illicit Appropriation, held in Seoul, in celebration of its thirtieth anniversary, as well as their recommendations, and the 2008 meeting of the non-governmental experts, held during the extraordinary session of the Intergovernmental Committee, under the auspices of the Republic of Korea;

3. *Calls upon* all relevant bodies, agencies, funds and programmes of the United Nations system and other relevant intergovernmental organizations to work in coordination with the United Nations Educational, Scientific and Cultural Organization, within their mandates and in cooperation with Member States, in order to continue to address the issue of return or restitution of cultural property to the countries of origin and to provide appropriate support accordingly;

4. *Reaffirms* the importance of the Convention on the Means of Prohibiting and Preventing the Illicit Import, Export and Transfer of Ownership of Cultural Property, as well as the Convention on Stolen or Illegally Exported Cultural Objects of the International Institute for the Unification of Private Law, and of their implementation, and

invites Member States that have not already done so to consider becoming parties to these Conventions;

5. *Recognizes* the importance of the Convention on the Protection of the Underwater Cultural Heritage and the Convention on the Protection and Promotion of the Diversity of Cultural Expressions, and invites Member States that have not already done so to consider becoming parties to these Conventions;

6. *Also recognizes* the importance of the United Nations Convention on Jurisdictional Immunities of States and Their Property, notes that this Convention has still not entered into force, and invites Member States that have not already done so to consider becoming parties to the Convention;

7. *Reaffirms* the importance of the principles and provisions of the Convention for the Protection of Cultural Property in the Event of Armed Conflict, and of their implementation, and invites Member States that have not already done so to consider becoming parties to the Convention;

8. *Also reaffirms* the importance of the Second Protocol to the Convention, adopted at The Hague on 26 March 1999, and of its implementation, and invites all States parties to the Convention that have not already done so to consider becoming parties to the Second Protocol;

9. *Welcomes* the most recent efforts made by the United Nations Educational, Scientific and Cultural Organization for the protection of the cultural heritage of countries in conflict, including the safe return to those countries of cultural property and other items of archaeological, historical, cultural, rare scientific and religious importance that have been illegally removed, and calls upon the international community to contribute to these efforts;

10. *Urges* Member States to introduce effective national and international measures to prevent and combat illicit trafficking in cultural property, including by publicizing legislation and offering special training for police, customs and border services;

11. *Invites* Member States, in cooperation with the United Nations Educational, Scientific and Cultural Organization, to continue to draw up systematic inventories of their cultural property, as well as to work towards the creation of a database of their national cultural legislation, in particular in electronic format;

12. *Recognizes* the advancement of the Database of National Cultural Heritage Laws of the United Nations Educational, Scientific and Cultural Organization, which includes legislation from one hundred and seventy-six Member States, and invites Member States to provide their legislation in electronic format for inclusion in the database if they have not yet done so, to provide regular updates to the database and to promote it;

13. *Applauds* the efforts of the United Nations Educational, Scientific and Cultural Organization to promote the use of identification and inventory systems, in particular the application of the Object-ID standard, and to encourage the linking of identification systems and existing databases, including the one developed by the International Criminal Police Organization (INTERPOL), to allow for the electronic transmission of information in order to reduce illicit trafficking in cultural property, and encourages the United Nations Educational, Scientific and Cultural

Organization to make further efforts in this regard in cooperation with Member States, where appropriate;

14. *Notes* that the statutes of the Intergovernmental Committee for Promoting the Return of Cultural Property to its Countries of Origin or its Restitution in Case of Illicit Appropriation include mediation and conciliation processes, and invites Member States to consider the possibility of using such processes as appropriate;

15. *Also notes* the Model Export Certificate for Cultural Objects developed by the United Nations Educational, Scientific and Cultural Organization and the World Customs Organization as a tool to combat illicit trafficking in cultural property, and invites Member States to consider adopting the model export certificate as their national export certificate, in accordance with domestic law and procedures;

16. *Notes with interest* that issues such as model legal provisions relating to state ownership of cultural property, a database of best practices in the field of return and restitution of cultural property to its countries of origin, and legal and ethical principles supporting protection of and return mechanisms for cultural property, are being considered by the Intergovernmental Committee for Promoting the Return of Cultural Property to its Countries of Origin or its Restitution in Case of Illicit Appropriation;

17. *Notes* the decision taken in resolution 41, adopted on 23 October 2009 by the General Conference of the United Nations Educational, Scientific and Cultural Organization at its thirty-fifth session, on the issue of cultural objects displaced in connection with the Second World War;

18. *Recognizes* the public awareness and increased mobilization and action in favour of heritage values that was achieved in 2002, the United Nations Year for Cultural Heritage, and calls upon the international community and the United Nations to continue to cooperate with the United Nations Educational, Scientific and Cultural Organization on the basis of that work;

19. *Welcomes* the endorsement of the International Code of Ethics for Dealers in Cultural Property by the General Conference of the United Nations Educational, Scientific and Cultural Organization on 16 November 1999, which was adopted in January 1999 by the Intergovernmental Committee for Promoting the Return of Cultural Property to its Countries of Origin or its Restitution in Case of Illicit Appropriation, and invites those who deal with trade in cultural property and their associations, where they exist, to encourage the implementation of the Code;

20. *Recognizes* the importance of the creation, by the General Conference of the United Nations Educational, Scientific and Cultural Organization, of the International Fund for the Return of Cultural Property to its Countries of Origin or its Restitution in Case of Illicit Appropriation, launched in November 2000, and encourages the United Nations Educational, Scientific and Cultural Organization to continue to promote the Fund and render it operational;

21. *Also recognizes* the importance of cooperation amongst States in the fight against illicit trafficking in cultural property, as well as its illegal removal from the countries of origin, through, inter alia, mutual legal assistance, including the prosecution of persons involved in such

activities and extradition, in accordance with the laws of cooperating States and under applicable international law;

22. *Requests* the Secretary-General to cooperate with the United Nations Educational, Scientific and Cultural Organization in its efforts to bring about the attainment of the objectives of the present resolution;

23. *Also requests* the Secretary-General, in cooperation with the Director-General of the United Nations Educational, Scientific and Cultural Organization, to submit to the General Assembly at its sixty-seventh session a report on the implementation of the present resolution;

24. *Decides* to include in the provisional agenda of its sixty-seventh session the item entitled "Return or restitution of cultural property to the countries of origin".

Crime prevention and criminal justice

Preparations for Twelfth (2010) United Nations Crime Congress

The Commission on Crime Prevention and Criminal Justice, at its eighteenth session [E/2009/30], considered a March report by the Secretary-General [E/CN.15/2009/9] on the preparations for the Twelfth United Nations Congress on Crime Prevention and Criminal Justice [YUN 2008, p. 1222], to be held in Salvador, Brazil, from 12 to 19 April 2010 with pre-congress consultations to be held on 11 April and a high-level segment to be held on 18 and 19 April. The report, prepared in response to General Assembly resolution 63/193 [ibid., p. 1223], stated that the main theme of the Congress would be "Comprehensive strategies for global challenges: crime prevention and criminal justice systems and their development in a changing world". It presented the provisional agenda and issues to be considered by workshops and indicated that as its outcome, the Congress should adopt a single declaration. The report also covered documentation, rules of procedure, and resource allocation. Four regional preparatory meetings for the Twelfth Congress were held in 2009: the Latin American and Caribbean Regional Preparatory Meeting (San Jose, Costa Rica, 25–27 May); the Western Asia Regional Preparatory Meeting (Doha, 1–3 June); the Asian and Pacific Regional Preparatory Meeting (Bangkok, Thailand, 1–3 July); and the African Regional Preparatory Meeting (Nairobi, 8–10 September).

GENERAL ASSEMBLY ACTION

On 18 December [meeting 65], the General Assembly, on the recommendation of the Third Committee [A/64/440 & Corr.1], adopted **resolution 64/180** without vote [agenda item 104].

Preparations for the Twelfth United Nations Congress on Crime Prevention and Criminal Justice

The General Assembly,

Recalling its resolution 56/119 of 19 December 2001 on the role, function, periodicity and duration of the United Nations congresses on the prevention of crime and the treatment of offenders, in which it stipulated the guidelines in accordance with which, beginning in 2005, the congresses, pursuant to paragraphs 29 and 30 of the statement of principles and programme of action of the United Nations Crime Prevention and Criminal Justice Programme, should be held,

Recalling also its resolution 60/177 of 16 December 2005 on the follow-up to the Eleventh United Nations Congress on Crime Prevention and Criminal Justice,

Recalling further its resolution 63/193 of 18 December 2008, in which it decided that the main theme of the Twelfth United Nations Congress on Crime Prevention and Criminal Justice should be "Comprehensive strategies for global challenges: crime prevention and criminal justice systems and their development in a changing world",

Recalling that, in its resolution 63/193, it requested the Commission on Crime Prevention and Criminal Justice to accord sufficient time at its eighteenth session to reviewing the progress made in the preparations for the Twelfth Congress, to finalize in good time all the necessary organizational and substantive arrangements and to make its final recommendations, through the Economic and Social Council, to the General Assembly,

Recognizing the significant contributions of the congresses in promoting the exchange of experience in research, law and policy development and the identification of emerging trends and issues in crime prevention and criminal justice among States, intergovernmental and non-governmental organizations and individual experts representing various professions and disciplines,

Recognizing also the efforts already made by the Government of Brazil to prepare for the hosting of the Twelfth Congress in Salvador from 12 to 19 April 2010,

Stressing the importance of undertaking all the preparatory activities for the Twelfth Congress in a timely and concerted manner,

1. *Takes note with appreciation* of the report of the Secretary-General;

2. *Also takes note with appreciation* of the discussion guide prepared by the Secretary-General, in cooperation with the institutes of the United Nations Crime Prevention and Criminal Justice Programme network, for the regional preparatory meetings for the Twelfth United Nations Congress on Crime Prevention and Criminal Justice;

3. *Acknowledges* the relevance of the regional preparatory meetings, which have examined the substantive items of the agenda and the workshop topics of the Twelfth Congress and made action-oriented recommendations to serve as a basis for the draft declaration to be adopted by the Twelfth Congress;

4. *Requests* the Commission on Crime Prevention and Criminal Justice to begin preparation of a draft declaration at intersessional meetings to be held well in advance of the Twelfth Congress, taking into account the recommendations of the regional preparatory meetings;

5. *Reiterates* its decision, contained in its resolution 63/193, that the high-level segment of the Twelfth Congress shall be held during the last two days of the Congress in order to allow Heads of State or Government or government ministers to focus on the main substantive agenda items of the Congress;

6. *Emphasizes* the importance of the workshops to be held during the Twelfth Congress, and invites Member States, intergovernmental and non-governmental organizations and other relevant entities to provide financial, organizational and technical support to the United Nations Office on Drugs and Crime and to the institutes of the United Nations Crime Prevention and Criminal Justice Programme network for the preparations for the workshops, including the preparation and circulation of relevant background material;

7. *Invites* donor countries to cooperate with developing countries to ensure their full participation in the workshops, and encourages States, other entities concerned and the Secretary-General to work together in order to ensure that the workshops focus on the respective issues and achieve practical results, leading to technical cooperation ideas, projects and documents related to enhancing bilateral and multilateral efforts in technical assistance activities in crime prevention and criminal justice;

8. *Reiterates its invitation* to Governments and relevant intergovernmental and non-governmental organizations to inform the Twelfth Congress about their activities aimed at the implementation of the Bangkok Declaration on Synergies and Responses: Strategic Alliances in Crime Prevention and Criminal Justice, with a view to providing guidance in the formulation of legislation, policies and programmes in the field of crime prevention and criminal justice at the national and international levels, and to that end requests the Secretary-General to compile that information and to prepare a report on the subject to be submitted to the Congress for consideration;

9. *Reiterates its request* to the Secretary-General to make available the resources necessary to ensure the participation of the least developed countries in the Twelfth Congress, in accordance with past practice;

10. *Encourages* Governments to make preparations for the Twelfth Congress at an early stage by all appropriate means, including, where appropriate, the establishment of national preparatory committees, with a view to contributing to a focused and productive discussion on the topics and to participating actively in the organization and conduct of the workshops, the submission of national position papers on the various substantive items of the agenda and the encouragement of contributions from the academic community and relevant scientific institutions;

11. *Reiterates its invitation* to Member States to be represented at the Twelfth Congress at the highest possible level, for example by Heads of State or Government or government ministers and attorneys general, and to participate actively in the high-level segment;

12. *Requests* the Secretary-General to facilitate the organization of ancillary meetings of non-governmental and professional organizations participating in the Twelfth Congress, in accordance with past practice, as well as meetings of professional and geographical interest groups, and to take appropriate measures to encourage the participation of the academic and research community in the Congress;

13. *Encourages* the relevant specialized agencies and programmes of the United Nations system and intergovernmental and non-governmental organizations, as well as other professional organizations, to cooperate with the United Nations Office on Drugs and Crime in the preparations for the Twelfth Congress;

14. *Requests* the Secretary-General to ensure, in collaboration with Member States, a wide and effective programme of public information relating to the preparations for the Twelfth Congress, to the Congress itself and to the follow-up to and implementation of its recommendations;

15. *Welcomes* the appointment by the Secretary-General of a Secretary-General and an Executive Secretary of the Twelfth Congress, to perform their functions under the rules of procedure for United Nations congresses on crime prevention and criminal justice;

16. *Requests* the Secretary-General to prepare an overview of the state of crime and criminal justice worldwide for presentation at the Twelfth Congress, in accordance with past practice;

17. *Calls upon* the Twelfth Congress to formulate concrete proposals for further follow-up and action, paying particular attention to practical arrangements relating to the effective implementation of the international legal instruments pertaining to transnational organized crime, terrorism and corruption and technical assistance activities relating thereto;

18. *Requests* the Commission on Crime Prevention and Criminal Justice at its nineteenth session to give high priority to considering the conclusions and recommendations of the Twelfth Congress, with a view to recommending, through the Economic and Social Council, appropriate follow-up by the General Assembly at its sixty-fifth session;

19. *Requests* the Secretary-General to ensure proper follow-up to the present resolution and to report thereon, through the Commission on Crime Prevention and Criminal Justice, to the General Assembly at its sixty-fifth session.

Commission on Crime Prevention and Criminal Justice

The Commission on Crime Prevention and Criminal Justice held its eighteenth session in Vienna (18 April 2008, 16–24 April 2009 and 3–4 December 2009) [E/2009/30 & Add.1]. In April 2009, it recommended to the Economic and Social Council one draft resolution for adoption by the General Assembly on technical assistance for implementing the international conventions and protocols related to terrorism (see p. 1100); and five draft resolutions for adoption by the Council related to: international cooperation in the prevention, investigation, prosecution and punishment of economic fraud and identity-related crime (see p. 1101); support for the development and implementation of the regional programmes of the United Nations Office on Drugs and Crime (UNODC) (see p. 1251); international cooperation to prevent, combat and eliminate kidnapping and to provide assistance to victims of kidnapping (see p. 1095); improving the collection, reporting and analysis of data to enhance knowledge on trends in specific areas of crime (see p. 1090); and supporting national and international efforts for child justice reform, in particular through improved coordination in technical assistance (see p. 1104). The Commission also recommended two draft decisions for adoption by the Council: one on the report of the Commission's 2009 session and the agenda of its 2010 session and the other on the appointment of members of the Board of the United Nations Interregional Crime and Justice Research Institute (see p. 1088). It also adopted five resolutions and two decisions, which it brought to the attention of the Council, including guidelines for the thematic discussions of the Commission [E/2009/30 (dec.18/1)].

In addition to thematic discussions on economic fraud and identity-related crime and on penal reform and the reduction of prison overcrowding, including the provision of legal aid in criminal justice systems, the following matters were also considered: world crime trends and responses: integration and coordination of efforts by UNODC and by Member States in the field of crime prevention and criminal justice; preparations for the Twelfth (2010) United Nations Congress on Crime Prevention and Criminal Justice; use and application of UN standards and norms in crime prevention and criminal justice; policy directives for UNODC's crime programme and the role of the Commission as its governing body, including administrative, strategic management and budgetary questions; and the provisional agenda for the Commission's nineteenth (2010) session. In December, the Commission adopted and brought to the attention of the Council a resolution on the 2010–2011 budget for the United Nations Crime Prevention and Criminal Justice Fund.

On 30 July (**decision 2009/246**), the Council took note of the Commission's report on its eighteenth session; decided that the prominent theme for the nineteenth (2010) and twentieth (2011) sessions, respectively, would be: "Protection against illicit trafficking in cultural property" and "Protecting children in a digital age: the misuse of technology in the abuse and exploitation of children"; and took note of the proposal to have "New and emerging forms of transnational organized crime, including environmental crime" as the prominent theme for the twenty-first (2012) session. It urged Member States to submit draft resolutions one month prior to the opening of each session of the Commission, and reiterated its call that draft resolutions be accompanied by such information as the intended scope, a proposed timetable for implementation, identification of resources available and other relevant information. It also approved the provisional agenda and documentation for the Commission's nineteenth (2010) session as well as a five-day duration for the nineteenth session, on an exceptional and non-precedential basis.

Commission reports for 2010 session. Documents issued in 2009, to be considered during the Commission's nineteenth (2010) session, included: report of the meeting of the Intergovernmental Expert Group to Review and Update the Model Strategies and Practical Measures on the Elimination of Violence against Women in the Field of Crime Prevention and Criminal Justice (Bangkok, 23–25 March) [E/CN.15/2010/2] and a Secretariat note on the recommendations of the expert group on protection against trafficking in cultural property [E/CN.15/2010/5].

Administrative and budgetary questions

In response to Commission on Narcotic Drugs resolution 50/14 [YUN 2007, p. 1300] and Commission on Crime Prevention and Criminal Justice resolution 16/6 [ibid., p. 1128], the UNODC Executive Director submitted to the two Commissions a January report [E/CN.7/2009/11-E/CN.15/2009/11] on implementation of the consolidated budget for the 2008–2009 biennium for UNODC, which provided information on programme performance, compared actual income and expenditure with the estimates contained in the consolidated budget as approved, explained any major deviations from the approved budget and presented revised estimates for 2008–2009. A March Secretariat report [E/CN.7/2009/10-E/CN.15/2009/10], prepared in response to Commission on Narcotic Drugs decision 51/1 [YUN 2008, p. 1371] and Commission on Crime Prevention and Criminal Justice decision 17/2 [ibid., p. 1226], presented the recommendations of the open-ended intergovernmental working group on improving the governance and financial situation of UNODC, approved at sessions held in 2008 and 2009. Secretariat notes on the report of the open-ended intergovernmental working group [E/CN.15/2009/21] and on the financial situation of UNODC [E/CN.15/2009/22] were prepared pursuant to a Commission decision [E/2009/30 (dec.18/2)].

On 24 April, the Commission adopted a resolution [E/2009/30 (res. 18/3)] on improving the governance and financial situation of UNODC, which it brought to the attention of the Economic and Social Council. The recommendations of the open-ended intergovernmental working group were annexed to the resolution.

By **decision 2009/251** of 30 July, the Council decided to establish a standing open-ended intergovernmental working group on improving the governance and financial situation of UNODC. It also decided that, starting in 2010, the Commission on Narcotic Drugs and the Commission on Crime Prevention and Criminal Justice would hold reconvened sessions on an annual basis in the second half of the year and that the annual reconvened sessions of the two Commissions would have duration of one day each and be held back to back.

At its reconvened eighteenth session (Vienna, 3–4 December) [E/2009/30/Add.1], the Commission on Crime Prevention and Criminal Justice considered the report of the Executive Director on UNODC's consolidated budget for the 2010–2011 biennium [E/CN.7/2009/13-E/CN.15/2009/23] and the related report of the Advisory Committee on Administrative and Budgetary Questions [E/CN.7/2009/14-E/CN.15/2009/24], as well as a Secretariat note on the work of the standing open-ended intergovernmental working group on improving the governance and financial situation of UNODC [E/CN.7/2009/15-E/CN.15/2009/25]. On 3 December [E/2009/30/Add.1 (res. 18/6)], the Commission approved the projected use of general-purpose funds in the 2010–2011 biennium and invited Member States to provide contributions totalling at least $4,517,200; endorsed programme support cost fund and special-purpose fund estimates totalling $152 million; and decided that the proposed consolidated 2010–2011 budget for UNODC should contain adequate provisions for the establishment of a sustainable, effective and operationally independent evaluation unit, which should brief the Member States periodically.

Crime prevention programme

At its eighteenth session, the Commission on Crime Prevention and Criminal Justice considered the UNODC Executive Director's report on the Office's 2008 activities [E/CN.7/2009/3-E/CN.15/2009/3]. The report outlined the links between, on the one hand, drug control, crime prevention, terrorism prevention and criminal justice, and, on the other, the rule of law, development, security and peace. During the period under review, UNODC supported Member States in their efforts to achieve a world safe from crime, drugs and terrorism through the three pillars of its work programme: research to increase knowledge and understanding of drug and crime issues and to expand the evidence base for policy and operational decisions; normative work to assist States in the ratification and implementation of international treaties, the development of domestic legislation on drugs, crime and terrorism, and the provision of substantive and secretariat services to treaty-based and governing bodies; and field-based technical cooperation projects.

With regard to human trafficking and smuggling of migrants, UNODC assisted States in implementing the Protocol to Prevent, Suppress and Punish Trafficking in Persons, Especially Women and Children [YUN 2000, p. 1063] and carried out technical assis-

tance projects in all regions to combat those crimes. It updated its toolkit to combat trafficking in persons and released an online version, and developed advanced training modules for combating trafficking in persons. The Vienna Forum, a key element of the Global Initiative to Fight Human Trafficking (UN.GIFT) to raise awareness about human trafficking, forge new partnerships and facilitate cooperation, was held in February 2008.

As to transitional organized crime, UNODC supported the ratification and implementation of the United Nations Convention against Transnational Organized Crime [ibid., p. 1048] and its three supplementary Protocols (Protocol to Prevent, Suppress and Punish Trafficking in Persons, Especially Women and Children [ibid., p. 1063]; Protocol against the Smuggling of Migrants by Land, Sea and Air [ibid., p. 1067]; Protocol against the Illicit Manufacturing of and Trafficking in Firearms, Their Parts and Components and Ammunition [YUN 2001, p. 1036]. UNODC offered training to prosecutors to support national authorities in addressing the increasingly sophisticated modus operandi of traffickers.

In the fight against corruption, UNODC provided numerous States with technical assistance for anti-corruption activities, supported judicial reform programmes and the development of a guide on strengthening the integrity and capacity of judicial institutions. In addition, UNODC published training manuals on alternative dispute resolution, restorative justice and judicial ethics. The joint Stolen Asset Recovery initiative of UNODC and the World Bank, launched in 2007, continued in a number of pilot countries, including Bangladesh, Haiti, Indonesia and Nigeria. On 13 October 2008, UNODC and the International Criminal Police Organization (INTERPOL) signed an agreement to establish the International Anti-Corruption Academy in Austria—the world's first educational institution dedicated to fighting corruption.

In the area of international cooperation against terrorism, the Office strengthened its technical assistance work in counter-terrorism, aiding States in ratifying and implementing the international conventions related to terrorism. In 2008, 45 States received tailor-made direct assistance; another 84 were assisted through 16 regional and subregional workshops; and more than 1,600 criminal justice authorities received training. In States having received such assistance, an estimated 469 new ratifications had occurred since 2003, including 71 in 2008. UNODC continued to work closely with the Counter-Terrorism Committee of the Security Council (see p. 70) and its Executive Directorate, and contributed to the work of the multi-agency Counter-Terrorism Implementation Task Force.

Emerging policy issues addressed by UNODC included: vulnerable transit areas along major transnational drug trafficking routes; the oversupply of heroin; a new approach to synthetic drugs; organized crime and the impact of the financial crisis; Africa's special vulnerabilities with regard to crime; identity-related crime; cybercrime; trafficking in forest products; and piracy.

The report recommended that the Commission on Narcotic Drugs, the Commission on Crime Prevention and Criminal Justice, and Member States consider supporting: the design and implementation of a new generation of UNODC regional programmes; the reconfiguring of UNODC field operations, with a view to engaging more effectively with the UN system at the field level; and the effective integration of UNODC with the UN system in post-conflict settings. In particular, UNODC would contribute to the integration of peacemaking and peacekeeping activities with efforts to develop the rule of law and to contain criminal activities. The report also made recommendations on: sustainable livelihoods; demand reduction; international drug control; transnational organized crime; human trafficking; smuggling of migrants; terrorism; scientific and forensic capacity; data collection; standards and norms; emerging policy issues; and financial support for UNODC's mandates.

Strengthening technical cooperation

In response to General Assembly resolution 63/195 [YUN 2008, p. 1228], the Secretary-General submitted a July report on implementation of the mandates of the United Nations Crime Prevention and Criminal Justice Programme, with particular reference to the technical cooperation activities of UNODC [A/64/123], which summarized the Office's work in supporting Member States to counter transnational organized crime, corruption and terrorism, and in preventing crime and reinforcing criminal justice systems. Information was also provided on efforts to strengthen the United Nations Crime Prevention and Criminal Justice Programme, with a focus on the role of the Commission on Crime Prevention and Criminal Justice as its governing body. In addition, the report described preparations for the Twelfth (2010) United Nations Congress on Crime Prevention and Criminal Justice as requested in Assembly resolution 63/193 [YUN 2008, p. 1223] and highlighted emerging policy issues and possible responses thereto. The report included recommendations aimed at enhancing the Programme's activities on: transnational organized crime; corruption; terrorism; and crime prevention and criminal justice reform in developing, transitional and post-conflict societies. It also addressed the issue of financial resources.

Follow-up to Ministerial Conference on illicit drug trafficking, transnational organized crime and terrorism

The Ministerial Conference on Illicit Drug Trafficking, Transnational Organized Crime and Terrorism as Challenges for Security and Development in the Caribbean (Santo Domingo, Dominican Republic, 17–20 February) adopted a political declaration on combating those and other serious crime in the Caribbean. The 15 signatories pledged to adopt an action plan for the Caribbean, work with international development partners towards its implementation and establish the Santo Domingo partnership monitoring mechanism as a technical assistance project facilitating periodic consultations and strategic thinking between partners at the expert and policy levels. UNODC was requested to continue providing technical assistance for the implementation of international drug control treaties, the Convention on Transnational Organized Crimes and its Protocols, and the universal anti-terrorism instruments.

In April [E/2009/30 (res.18/5)], the Commission on Crime Prevention and Criminal Justice requested UNODC to prepare a draft of the Santo Domingo partnership monitoring mechanism for approval by States that had signed the political declaration and for submission to partners active at the subregional, regional and international levels to seek support for its implementation and financing.

The Ministerial Conference on Illicit Drug Trafficking, Transnational Organized Crime and Terrorism as Challenges for Security and Development in Central America (Managua, Nicaragua, 23–24 June) also approved a political declaration and regional programme.

GENERAL ASSEMBLY ACTION

On 18 December [meeting 65], the General Assembly, on the recommendation of the Third Committee [A/64/440 & Corr.1], adopted **resolution 64/179** without vote [agenda item 104].

Strengthening the United Nations Crime Prevention and Criminal Justice Programme, in particular its technical cooperation capacity

The General Assembly,

Recalling its resolutions 46/152 of 18 December 1991, 60/1 of 16 September 2005, 60/177 of 16 December 2005, 61/252 of 22 December 2006, 63/193, 63/194 and 63/195 of 18 December 2008 and 63/226 of 19 December 2008,

Taking note with appreciation of the adoption by the Economic and Social Council of the strategy for the period 2008–2011 for the United Nations Office on Drugs and Crime, which aims, inter alia, to enhance its effectiveness and flexibility in providing technical assistance and policy services,

Reaffirming its resolutions relating to the urgent need to strengthen international cooperation and technical assistance in promoting and facilitating the ratification and implementation of the United Nations Convention against Transnational Organized Crime and the Protocols thereto, the United Nations Convention against Corruption and all the international conventions and protocols against terrorism, including those that recently entered into force,

Reaffirming also the commitments undertaken by Member States in the United Nations Global Counter-Terrorism Strategy adopted on 8 September 2006, and its review of 4 and 5 September 2008,

Emphasizing that its resolution 61/143 of 19 December 2006 on the intensification of efforts to eliminate all forms of violence against women has considerable implications for the United Nations Crime Prevention and Criminal Justice Programme and its activities,

Welcoming the outcome of the thematic discussion on aspects of violence against women that pertain directly to the Commission on Crime Prevention and Criminal Justice held by the Commission at its seventeenth session, in 2008, pursuant to Economic and Social Council decision 2007/253 of 26 July 2007,

Taking into consideration all relevant Economic and Social Council resolutions, in particular resolutions 2008/23, 2008/24 and 2008/25 of 24 July 2008, and all those relating to the strengthening of international cooperation as well as the technical assistance and advisory services of the United Nations Crime Prevention and Criminal Justice Programme of the United Nations Office on Drugs and Crime in the field of crime prevention and criminal justice, promotion and reinforcement of the rule of law and reform of criminal justice institutions, including with regard to the implementation of technical assistance,

Welcoming the outcome of the thematic discussions on economic fraud and identity-related crime and on penal reform and the reduction of prison overcrowding, including the provision of legal aid in criminal justice systems held by the Commission on Crime Prevention and Criminal Justice at its eighteenth session, in 2009, pursuant to Economic and Social Council decision 2008/245 of 24 July 2008,

Taking note of the *Global Report on Trafficking in Persons* of February 2009 of the United Nations Office on Drugs and Crime and of the joint Council of Europe/United Nations study entitled *Trafficking in organs, tissues and cells and trafficking in human beings for the purpose of the removal of organs*, launched on 13 October 2009,

Expressing its grave concern at the negative effects of transnational organized crime, including smuggling of and trafficking in human beings, narcotic drugs and small arms and light weapons, on development, peace and security and human rights, and at the increasing vulnerability of States to such crime,

Concerned by the serious challenges and threats posed by the illicit trafficking in firearms, their parts and components and ammunition, and about its links with other forms of transnational organized crime, including drug trafficking and other criminal activities, including terrorism,

Emphasizing that transnational organized crime must be addressed in full respect of the principle of the sovereignty of States and in accordance with the rule of law as part of a comprehensive response to promote durable solutions through the promotion of human rights and more equitable socio-economic conditions,

Concerned about the growing degree of penetration of criminal organizations and their proceeds into the economy,

Recognizing that actions against transnational organized crime and terrorism are a common and shared responsibility, and stressing the need to work collectively to prevent and combat transnational organized crime, corruption and terrorism in all its forms and manifestations,

Recognizing also the need to maintain a balance in the technical cooperation capacity of the United Nations Office on Drugs and Crime between all relevant priorities identified by the General Assembly and the Economic and Social Council,

Recalling that 2010 marks the tenth anniversary of the United Nations Convention against Transnational Organized Crime, and mindful of the need to ensure universal adherence to and full implementation of the Convention and the Protocols thereto,

Welcoming the adoption by the United Nations Office on Drugs and Crime of a regional approach to programming, based on continued consultations and partnerships at the national and regional levels, particularly on its implementation, and focused on ensuring that the Office responds in a sustainable and coherent manner to the priorities of Member States,

Taking note of the implementation of the Political Declaration on Combating Illicit Drug Trafficking, Organized Crime, Terrorism and Other Serious Crime in the Caribbean, adopted in Santo Domingo on 19 February 2009, as well as the outcomes of the Ministerial Conference on Illicit Drug Trafficking, Transnational Organized Crime and Terrorism as Challenges for Security and Development in Central America, held in Managua on 23 and 24 June 2009, as an example of the new regional programme approach of the United Nations Office on Drugs and Crime,

Recognizing the general progress made by the United Nations Office on Drugs and Crime in the delivery of advisory services and assistance to requesting Member States in the areas of corruption, organized crime, money-laundering, terrorism, kidnapping and trafficking in persons, including the support and protection, as appropriate, of victims, their families and witnesses, as well as drug trafficking and international cooperation, with special emphasis on extradition and mutual legal assistance,

1. *Takes note with appreciation* of the report of the Secretary-General on the progress made in the implementation of General Assembly resolution 63/195;

2. *Also takes note with appreciation* of the reports of the Secretary-General on improving the coordination of efforts against trafficking in persons, on assistance in implementing the universal conventions and protocols related to terrorism and on strengthening the United Nations Crime Prevention and Criminal Justice Programme, in particular its technical cooperation capacity;

3. *Reaffirms* the importance of the United Nations Convention against Transnational Organized Crime and the Protocols thereto as the main tools of the international community to fight transnational organized crime;

4. *Also reaffirms* the importance of the United Nations Crime Prevention and Criminal Justice Programme in promoting effective action to strengthen international cooperation in crime prevention and criminal justice, as well as of the work of the United Nations Office on Drugs and Crime in the fulfilment of its mandate in crime prevention and criminal justice, including providing to Member States, upon request and as a matter of high priority, technical cooperation, advisory services and other forms of assistance, and coordinating with and complementing the work of all relevant and competent United Nations bodies and offices;

5. *Calls upon* Member States to strengthen their efforts to cooperate, as appropriate, at the bilateral, subregional, regional and international levels to counter effectively transnational organized crime;

6. *Requests* the United Nations Office on Drugs and Crime to enhance its efforts, within existing resources and within its mandate, in providing technical assistance and advisory services for the implementation of its regional and subregional programmes in a coordinated manner with relevant Member States and regional and subregional organizations;

7. *Also requests* the United Nations Office on Drugs and Crime to finalize, as soon as possible, the Santo Domingo Pact, as well as other regional programmes, and the Managua Mechanism document for approval by the States parties in order to start their implementation with all active partners at the subregional, regional and international levels;

8. *Urges* the United Nations Office on Drugs and Crime to continue providing technical assistance to Member States to combat money-laundering and the financing of terrorism through the Global Programme against Money-Laundering, in accordance with United Nations related instruments and internationally accepted standards, including, where applicable, recommendations of relevant intergovernmental bodies, inter alia, the Financial Action Task Force on Money Laundering, and relevant initiatives of regional, interregional and multilateral organizations against money-laundering;

9. *Recognizes* the efforts made by the United Nations Office on Drugs and Crime to assist Member States in developing abilities and strengthening their capacity to prevent and combat kidnapping, and requests the Office to continue to provide technical assistance with a view to fostering international cooperation, in particular mutual legal assistance, aimed at countering effectively this growing serious crime;

10. *Urges* the United Nations Office on Drugs and Crime to increase collaboration with intergovernmental, international and regional organizations that have transnational organized crime mandates, as appropriate, in order to share best practices and to take advantage of their unique and comparative advantage;

11. *Draws attention* to the emerging policy issues identified in the report of the Secretary-General on the implementation of the mandates of the United Nations Crime Prevention and Criminal Justice Programme, with particular reference to the technical cooperation activities of the United Nations Office on Drugs and Crime, namely, piracy, cybercrime, sexual exploitation of children and urban crime, and invites the Office to explore, within its mandate, ways and means of addressing those issues, bearing in mind Economic and Social Council resolutions 2007/12 of 25 July 2007 and 2007/19 of 26 July 2007 on the strategy for the period 2008–2011 for the Office;

12. *Requests* the United Nations Office on Drugs and Crime, within its existing mandate, to strengthen the collection, analysis and dissemination of information to enhance knowledge on crime trends and support Member States in designing appropriate responses in specific areas of crime, in particular in their transnational dimension, taking into account the need to make the best possible use of existing resources;

13. *Urges* Member States and relevant international organizations to develop national and regional strategies, as appropriate, and other necessary measures, in cooperation with the United Nations Crime Prevention and Criminal Justice Programme, to address effectively transnational organized crime, including trafficking in persons, the smuggling of migrants and illicit manufacturing of and transnational trafficking in firearms, as well as corruption and terrorism;

14. *Urges* the United Nations Office on Drugs and Crime to continue to assist Member States, upon request, in combating the illicit trafficking in firearms, their parts and components and ammunition, and to support them in their efforts to address its links with other forms of transnational organized crime, through, inter alia, technical assistance;

15. *Encourages* Member States to utilize, as needed, the organized crime threat assessment handbook produced by the United Nations in order to establish an accurate and uniform assessment of domestic threat and to develop responsive and appropriate strategies to combat crime;

16. *Reaffirms* the importance of the United Nations Office on Drugs and Crime and its regional offices in building capacity at the local level in the fight against transnational organized crime and drug trafficking, and urges the Office to consider regional vulnerabilities, projects and impact in the fight against transnational organized crime, in particular in developing countries, when deciding to close and allocate offices, with a view to maintaining an effective level of support to national and regional efforts in those areas;

17. *Encourages* Member States to support the United Nations Office on Drugs and Crime in continuing to provide targeted technical assistance, within its existing mandate, to enhance the capacity of affected States, upon their request, to combat piracy by sea, including by assisting Member States in creating an effective law enforcement response and strengthening their judicial capacity;

18. *Urges* Member States that have not yet done so to consider ratifying or acceding to the United Nations Convention against Transnational Organized Crime and the Protocols thereto, the United Nations Convention against Corruption and the international conventions and protocols related to terrorism;

19. *Encourages* States parties to continue to provide full support to the Conference of the Parties to the United Nations Convention against Transnational Organized Crime and the Conference of the States Parties to the United Nations Convention against Corruption, including providing information to the conferences regarding compliance with the treaties;

20.   *Requests* the Secretary-General, within the framework of the tenth anniversary of the United Nations Convention against Transnational Organized Crime, to convene in the second quarter of 2010 a special one-day high-level meeting of the General Assembly on transnational organized crime, aimed at fostering universal adherence to the Convention and the Protocols thereto and at strengthening international cooperation;

21.   *Also requests* the Secretary-General, within the framework of the tenth anniversary of the United Nations Convention against Transnational Organized Crime, to organize a special treaty event to promote ratification or accession to the Convention and the Protocols thereto during the special one-day high-level meeting of the General Assembly referred to in paragraph 20 above;

22.   *Urges* Member States to be represented at the Twelfth United Nations Congress on Crime Prevention and Criminal Justice at the highest possible level, and encourages States to continue their preparations for the Congress with a view to making focused and productive contributions to the discussions;

23.   *Welcomes* the progress achieved by the Conference of the Parties to the United Nations Convention against Transnational Organized Crime and the Conference of the States Parties to the United Nations Convention against Corruption in the implementation of their respective mandates, and requests the Secretary-General to continue to provide the United Nations Office on Drugs and Crime with adequate resources to promote, in an effective manner, the implementation of the United Nations Convention against Transnational Organized Crime and the United Nations Convention against Corruption and to discharge its functions as the secretariat of the conferences of the parties to the conventions, in accordance with its mandate;

24.   *Also welcomes* the progress achieved by the three open-ended intergovernmental working groups on the United Nations Convention against Corruption, established by the Conference of the States Parties to the Convention, in particular the development of the terms of reference of a review mechanism, and looks forward to the relevant decisions of the Conference of the States Parties at its third session;

25.   *Reiterates its request* to the United Nations Office on Drugs and Crime to enhance its technical assistance to Member States, upon request, to strengthen international cooperation in preventing and combating terrorism through the facilitation of the ratification and implementation of the universal conventions and protocols related to terrorism, in close consultation with the Counter-Terrorism Committee and its Executive Directorate, as well as to continue to contribute to the work of the Counter-Terrorism Implementation Task Force, and invites Member States to provide the Office with appropriate resources for its mandate;

26.   *Takes note* of the report of the intergovernmental group of experts to review and update the Model Strategies and Practical Measures on the Elimination of Violence against Women in the Field of Crime Prevention and Criminal Justice, convened in accordance with Commission on Crime Prevention and Criminal Justice decision 17/1 of 18 April 2008 entitled "Strengthening crime prevention

and criminal justice responses to violence against women and girls", and looks forward to the consideration of the report of the intergovernmental group of experts by the Commission at its nineteenth session, to be held in Vienna in May 2010;

27.   *Encourages* Member States to take relevant measures, as appropriate to their national contexts, to ensure the diffusion, use and application of the United Nations standards and norms in crime prevention and criminal justice, including the consideration and, where they deem it necessary, dissemination of existing manuals and handbooks developed and published by the United Nations Office on Drugs and Crime;

28.   *Reiterates* the importance of providing the United Nations Crime Prevention and Criminal Justice Programme with sufficient, stable and predictable funding for the full implementation of its mandates, in conformity with the high priority accorded to it and in accordance with the increasing demand for its services, in particular with regard to the provision of increased assistance to developing countries, countries with economies in transition and those emerging from conflict, in the area of crime prevention and criminal justice reform;

29.   *Welcomes* resolution 18/3 of 24 April 2009 entitled "Improving the governance and financial situation of the United Nations Office on Drugs and Crime", adopted by the Commission on Crime Prevention and Criminal Justice at its eighteenth session, held in Vienna from 16 to 24 April 2009, by which the Commission adopted the recommendations of the open-ended intergovernmental working group on improving the governance and financial situation of the United Nations Office on Drugs and Crime and established a standing open-ended intergovernmental working group on governance and finance, whose mandate shall be in effect until the session of the Commission to be held in the first half of 2011;

30.   *Reiterates its request* to the Secretary-General to provide the United Nations Crime Prevention and Criminal Justice Programme with sufficient resources for the full implementation of its mandates, in conformity with its high priorities, and to provide adequate support to the Commission on Crime Prevention and Criminal Justice;

31.   *Recommends* to the Conference of the Parties to the United Nations Convention against Transnational Organized Crime, within the framework of the tenth anniversary of the Convention, to organize a high-level segment during the fifth session of the Conference of the Parties to discuss new and emerging forms of crime and ways and means of enhancing the implementation of the Convention and the Protocols thereto;

32.   *Requests* the Secretary-General to submit a report to the General Assembly at its sixty-fifth session on the implementation of the mandates of the United Nations Crime Prevention and Criminal Justice Programme, reflecting also emerging policy issues and possible responses;

33.   *Also requests* the Secretary-General to include in the report referred to in paragraph 32 above information on the status of ratifications or accessions to the United Nations Convention against Transnational Organized Crime and the Protocols thereto.

Crime Prevention and
Criminal Justice Programme network

In a February report [E/CN.15/2009/6] to the Commission on Crime Prevention and Criminal Justice, the Secretary-General summarized the activities carried out in 2008 by the institutions comprising the United Nations Crime Prevention and Criminal Justice Programme network, which included the United Nations Interregional Crime and Justice Research Institute (UNICRI); 11 regional and affiliated institutes; and the International Scientific and Professional Advisory Council.

United Nations Interregional
Crime and Justice Research Institute

In a February note [E/CN.15/2009/17], the Secretary-General drew the attention of the Commission on Crime Prevention and Criminal Justice to the need to appoint three members to the UNICRI Board of Trustees, provided background information on candidates nominated to fill the two vacant positions and recommended the reappointment of a Board member whose term was expiring.

The Commission [E/2009/30] recommended to the Economic and Social Council the adoption of a draft decision by which it would endorse the appointment of two members to the UNICRI Board of Trustees and the reappointment of a third.

By **decision 2009/247** of 30 July, the Council endorsed those appointments.

UN African crime prevention institute

In response to General Assembly resolution 63/196 [YUN 2008, p. 1232], the Secretary-General submitted a June report [A/64/121] on the United Nations African Institute for the Prevention of Crime and the Treatment of Offenders (UNAFRI). He described action taken by the Institute to deliver technical assistance to African countries in the area of crime prevention and criminal justice and provided information on UNAFRI's efforts to mobilize regional capacities and institutional collaboration as support mechanisms for practical intervention measures. The report also examined UNAFRI's governance and management, described measures taken to initiate and maintain international cooperation, funding and support, and provided information on practical measures to ensure the Institute's sustainability and on the future of the Institute as a unique promoter of socioeconomic development in Africa through crime prevention initiatives.

UNAFRI's income in 2008 totalled $593,866, a significant increase over the $344,421 received in 2007, owing to increased collections from member States

in 2008. The sources of the funds were contributions from member States (32 per cent), a UN grant (43 per cent), and other income from rental of the Institute's premises, plus interest on deposits (25 per cent). For the period January–May 2009, resources stood at $394,382.

The report concluded that the African continent experienced unique vulnerabilities imposed on it by a wide range of factors, most of which facilitated the vicious cycle of lawlessness and underdevelopment. That situation compromised efforts aimed at sustainable socioeconomic development. Given the ever-increasing sophistication of the operations of transnational organized crime, the Africa region was liable to suffer shortfalls in its planned development. An effective crime prevention agenda required a pragmatic threat assessment of existing challenges in order to design an evidence-based plan of action and a well-considered programme of activities to address specific requirements. Africa's need for skills and knowledge remained paramount in the crime prevention strategies that would strengthen national capacities to protect populations. Through action-oriented research and empirical, innovative frameworks based on the realities of African countries, the basis for streamlining measures for the prevention of crime would be established. Consequently, the management of public affairs, particularly with reference to crime prevention and criminal justice administration, would become more professional by utilizing the results of the empirical and policy-oriented research done by the Institute in conjunction with partner agencies and organizations. The report recommended that UNAFRI be considered a focal point for all professional efforts aimed at promoting the cooperation and collaboration of Governments, academics, institutions and scientific and professional organizations and experts in crime prevention and criminal justice.

GENERAL ASSEMBLY ACTION

On 18 December [meeting 65], the General Assembly, on the recommendation of the Third Committee [A/64/440 & Corr.1], adopted **resolution 64/181** without vote [agenda item 104].

United Nations African Institute for the Prevention of Crime and the Treatment of Offenders

The General Assembly,

Recalling its resolution 63/196 of 18 December 2008 and all other relevant resolutions,

Taking note of the report of the Secretary-General,

Bearing in mind that weaknesses in crime prevention lead to subsequent difficulties at the level of crime control mechanisms, and bearing in mind also the urgent need to establish effective crime prevention strategies for Africa, as well as the importance of law enforcement agencies and the judiciary at the regional and subregional levels,

Aware of the devastating impact of new and more dynamic crime trends on the national economies of African States and of the fact that crime is a major obstacle to harmonious and sustainable development in Africa,

Noting with concern that in most African countries the existing criminal justice system does not have sufficiently skilled personnel and adequate infrastructure and is therefore ill-equipped to manage the emergence of new crime trends, and acknowledging that weak laws and existing justice systems undermine efforts to facilitate the prosecution of these new crime trends,

Bearing in mind the Revised African Union Plan of Action on Drug Control and Crime Prevention (2007–2012), aimed at encouraging Member States to participate in and own the regional initiatives for effective crime prevention and good governance and strengthened justice administration,

Emphasizing the need to create necessary coalitions with all partners in the process of achieving effective crime prevention policies,

Recognizing that the United Nations African Institute for the Prevention of Crime and the Treatment of Offenders is a focal point for all professional efforts aimed at promoting the active cooperation and collaboration of Governments, academics, institutions and scientific and professional organizations and experts in crime prevention and criminal justice,

Noting that the financial situation of the Institute has greatly affected its capacity to deliver its services to African Member States in an effective and comprehensive manner,

1.   *Commends* the United Nations African Institute for the Prevention of Crime and the Treatment of Offenders for its efforts to promote and coordinate regional technical cooperation activities related to crime prevention and criminal justice systems in Africa;

2.   *Also commends* the initiative of the United Nations Office on Drugs and Crime in strengthening its working relationship with the Institute by supporting and involving the Institute in the implementation of a number of activities, including those contained in the Revised African Union Plan of Action on Drug Control and Crime Prevention (2007–2012), on strengthening the rule of law and criminal justice systems in Africa;

3.   *Reiterates* the need to strengthen further the capacity of the Institute to support national mechanisms for crime prevention and criminal justice in African countries;

4.   *Notes* the efforts of the Institute to establish contacts with organizations in those countries which are promoting crime prevention programmes and its maintenance of close links with regional and subregional political entities, such as the African Union Commission, the East African Community, the Commission of the Economic Community of West African States, the Intergovernmental Authority on Development and the Southern African Development Community;

5.   *Urges* the States members of the Institute to continue to make every possible effort to meet their obligations to the Institute;

6.   *Welcomes* the decision of the Governing Board of the Institute, at its fourth extraordinary session, held in Nairobi on 2 March 2009, to convene a conference of African ministers in November 2009 to discuss measures for improving the flow of resources to the Institute;

7.   *Also welcomes* the introduction by the Institute of a cost-sharing initiative in its execution of various programmes with Member States, partners and United Nations entities;

8.   *Urges* all Member States and non-governmental organizations and the international community to continue adopting concrete practical measures to support the Institute in the development of the requisite capacity and in the implementation of its programmes and activities aimed at strengthening crime prevention and criminal justice systems in Africa;

9.   *Urges* all States that have not already done so to consider ratifying or acceding to the United Nations Convention against Transnational Organized Crime and the Protocols thereto, as well as the United Nations Convention against Corruption;

10.   *Requests* the Secretary-General to intensify efforts to mobilize all relevant entities of the United Nations system to provide the necessary financial and technical support to the Institute to enable it to fulfil its mandate;

11.   *Also requests* the Secretary-General to continue his efforts to mobilize the financial resources necessary to maintain the Institute with the core professional staff required to enable it to function effectively in the fulfilment of its mandated obligations;

12.   *Encourages* the Institute to consider focusing on specific and general vulnerabilities of each programme country and to maximize the use of available initiatives to address crime problems with existing funds, as well as available capacity, by creating useful coalitions with regional and local institutions;

13.   *Calls upon* the United Nations Office on Drugs and Crime to continue to work closely with the Institute;

14.   *Requests* the Secretary-General to enhance the promotion of regional cooperation, coordination and collaboration in the fight against crime, especially in its transnational dimension, which cannot be dealt with adequately by national action alone;

15.   *Also requests* the Secretary-General to continue making concrete proposals, including for the provision of additional core professional staff, to strengthen the programmes and activities of the Institute and to report to the General Assembly at its sixty-fifth session on the implementation of the present resolution.

Crime data collection

In a February note on world crime trends and responses [E/CN.15/2009/13], the Secretariat submitted to the Commission on Crime Prevention and Criminal Justice a summary of UNODC's work carried out in 2008 to enhance knowledge of trends in specific crime issues, in particular international and regional trends, studies on corruption and trafficking in persons and work done towards improving the quality and quantity of information available to Member States and the international community on crime trends and the operations of criminal justice systems.

According to international homicide statistics assembled by UNODC from 198 countries and territories, the highest homicide rates were concentrated in Africa (with the exception of North Africa), and Central and South America. Those subregions fell within the higher homicide rate ranges, from 20 to more than 30 homicides per 100,000 population. By contrast, East and South-East Asia and Western and Central Europe had the lowest homicide levels, with rates lower than 3 homicides per 100,000 population. The States of the Caribbean and Eastern Europe were affected by relatively high homicide rates, which were in the range of 10 to 20 per 100,000 population. North Africa, North America and Central Asia followed, with rates of 5 to 10, while Oceania, South-West Asia, South Asia and South-Eastern Europe showed homicide rates in the range of 3 to 5. During the period 1995–2004, three of the five types of crime studied (intentional homicide, house burglary and automobile theft) decreased slightly, while two (robbery and drug-related crime) increased. Over the period 2004–2006, only drug-related crime kept increasing, while the other types of crime decreased.

New definitions and categories of crime were added to the tenth (2005–2006) United Nations Survey of Crime Trends and Operations of Criminal Justice Systems [YUN 2008, p. 1233], including drug trafficking, trafficking in persons, smuggling of migrants, participation in criminal organized groups and counterfeit currency offences. However, no clear trends could be established. A UNODC report on drug trafficking as a security threat in West Africa showed that cocaine seizures doubled every year between 2005 and 2007, suggesting that considerable quantities of cocaine from the Andean countries were transiting West Africa on their way to European markets. A report on crime and its impact on the Balkans and affected countries argued that while trends in both conventional and organized crime were decreasing, significant challenges remained. In particular, the region continued to be the primary transit zone for heroin destined for Western Europe and an important corridor for human trafficking and the smuggling of migrants.

Studies on corruption and trafficking in persons included the Global Report on Trafficking in Persons, published by UNODC and UN.GIFT [YUN 2007, p. 1141], which provided an overview of the global and regional patterns and flows of human trafficking based on information collected from 155 countries and territories for the period 2003–2007, and was the first global study on trafficking in persons based exclusively on official information provided by responding countries. UNODC developed a set of statistical tools to support countries in assessing the nature and extent of corruption in the business sector. Pilot surveys on integrity in the justice sector in Afghanistan were carried out by UNODC in partnership with the Attorney-General's office and the Supreme Court of Afghanistan in 2008.

UNODC was also developing a programme of surveys aimed at providing a comprehensive assessment of the nature, location, causes and consequences of corruption in Iraq and of the existing legal, institutional and operational anti-corruption capacities.

It was recommended that the Commission: urge Member States to support UNODC's work to meet the strategic objective of enhancing knowledge of thematic and cross-sectoral trends in specific crime issues, and note, in particular, UNODC's efforts to produce more timely and relevant data and to minimize the reporting burden and complexity for Member States through a reduced Survey to be carried out annually; encourage Member States to consider identifying national contact points for crime and criminal justice statistics with a view to facilitating the effective and timely collection, dissemination and exchange of information and efficient coordination at the national, regional and international levels; support the continuation of a standing group of experts to assist and advise UNODC and other stakeholders on the collection and analysis of crime data and information and for assisting countries to strengthen national capacity for the collection, analysis and dissemination of crime and criminal justice statistics; and encourage Member States to carry out victimization surveys within the framework of their national crime prevention programmes and programmes for the collection of crime-related information.

The Commission [E/2009/30] recommended to the Economic and Social Council for adoption a draft resolution on improving the collection, reporting and analysis of crime data.

ECONOMIC AND SOCIAL COUNCIL ACTION

On 30 July [meeting 44], the Economic and Social Council, on the recommendation of the Commission on Crime Prevention and Criminal Justice [E/2009/30], adopted **resolution 2009/25** without vote [agenda item 14 *(c)*].

Improving the collection, reporting and analysis of data to enhance knowledge of trends in specific areas of crime

The Economic and Social Council,

Convinced of the importance of relevant United Nations indicators and instruments for the collection and analysis of accurate, reliable and comparable data on all relevant aspects of specific crime issues,

Recognizing the urgent need to improve the quality, scope and completeness of data on international crime trends and specific crime issues for the purpose of developing evidence-based policies for crime prevention and the operations of criminal justice systems,

Recalling that, in its resolution 1992/22 of 30 July 1992, it reaffirmed the request of the General Assembly to the Secretary-General to take the necessary measures to enable the United Nations Crime Prevention and Criminal Justice Programme to continue and improve the surveys of crime trends and the operations of criminal justice systems carried out periodically as a means of obtaining and providing a cross-nationally updated picture of patterns and dynamics of crime in the world,

Bearing in mind the Bangkok Declaration on Synergies and Responses: Strategic Alliances in Crime Prevention and Criminal Justice, in which Member States declared their intention to improve their responses to crime and terrorism nationally and internationally by collecting and sharing information on crime and welcomed the work done by the United Nations Office on Drugs and Crime and the United Nations Crime Prevention and Criminal Justice Programme network in the area of trends in crime and justice,

Bearing in mind also the conclusions and recommendations of the open-ended expert group on crime statistics convened pursuant to Economic and Social Council resolutions 1996/11 of 23 July 1996, 1997/27 of 21 July 1997 and 2005/23 of 22 July 2005,

Noting the systems for the collection of data and information on criminal justice already in place at the regional and international levels, including the delinquency observatories, and convinced of the importance of avoiding duplication,

Underscoring the importance of improving data collection tools in order to ensure a simple and more efficient process, thus encouraging and motivating a greater number of Member States to submit the required information on time and ensuring a more representative assessment, at the international level, of all relevant aspects of specific crime issues,

Recognizing the importance of building the capacity of Member States to collect and report such information,

Recognizing also the importance of the work of the United Nations Office on Drugs and Crime in the regular collection of information through the United Nations Survey of Crime Trends and Operations of Criminal Justice Systems pursuant to General Assembly resolution 3021(XXVII) of 18 December 1972 on crime prevention and control and Economic and Social Council resolution 1984/48 of 25 May 1984 on crime prevention and criminal justice in the context of development,

1. *Invites* Member States to strengthen their efforts to review and improve data collection tools in order to obtain an objective, scientific, balanced and transparent assessment of emerging trends in specific areas of crime;

2. *Also invites* Member States to share information on the progress made and the obstacles encountered in fostering the exchange among States of information related to crime and the functioning of the criminal justice system;

3. *Requests* the United Nations Office on Drugs and Crime to establish an open-ended intergovernmental expert working group, to be convened at least once between sessions of the Commission on Crime Prevention and Criminal Justice, to prepare recommendations on the improvement of tools for the collection of relevant crime data, in particular the United Nations Survey of Crime Trends and Operations of Criminal Justice Systems, and on the improvement of the collection, collation, analysis and reporting processes, in support of the ongoing work of the Office in that area, invites Member States and other donors to provide extrabudgetary resources for that purpose in accordance with the rules and procedures of the United Nations, and notes that the working group should base its work on, inter alia, the following general considerations:

(a) The need to simplify and improve the reporting system of the Survey in order to encourage more Member States to report, in a coordinated and integrated manner, on their efforts, achievements and challenges in specific areas of crime and to provide information relating to the nature and extent of challenges posed by transnational crime;

(b) The need to avoid duplication of efforts to the extent possible by taking into account existing reporting procedures, including those of relevant regional and international bodies;

(c) The need for accurate, reliable and internationally comparable data on all relevant aspects of specific crime issues, bearing in mind the value of comparing such data with previously collected data, including from surveys on victimization, where possible;

(d) The possibility of using for the Survey a shorter, annual questionnaire containing a core set of questions;

(e) The possibility of including in such a core survey of crime trends and operations of criminal justice systems thematic modules reflecting the theme or themes of the thematic discussions of the Commission on Crime Prevention and Criminal Justice;

(f) The importance of learning from the experience acquired by the United Nations Office on Drugs and Crime through the data collection mechanisms established in respect of the United Nations Convention against Transnational Organized Crime and the Protocols thereto and the United Nations Convention against Corruption, including in relation to the use of modern technologies, where feasible;

4. *Invites* relevant international and regional organizations, upon request, to provide to the United Nations Office on Drugs and Crime information on their experiences in collecting crime-related data;

5. *Requests* the Executive Director of the United Nations Office on Drugs and Crime to submit to the Commission on Crime Prevention and Criminal Justice at its nineteenth session a report on the activities of the above-mentioned working group;

6. *Requests* the Secretary-General, in coordination with the Statistical Commission, to report to the Commission on Crime Prevention and Criminal Justice at its twentieth session on the implementation of the present resolution.

Transnational organized crime

UN Convention against transnational organized crime

In response to Economic and Social Council resolutions 2005/17 [YUN 2005, p. 1224] and 2006/24 [YUN 2006, p. 1301] and General Assembly resolution 61/181 [ibid., p. 1293], the Secretary-General submitted to the Commission on Crime Prevention and Criminal Justice a February report on international cooperation in combating transnational organized crime and corruption [E/CN.15/2009/4] (see also below, under "Corruption"). The report provided an overview of UNODC activities and complemented the reports of the Conferences of the Parties to the United Nations Convention against Transnational Organized Crime at its fourth session [YUN 2008, p. 1234] and of the Conference of the States Parties to the United Nations Convention against Corruption at its second session [ibid., p. 1239].

The Convention against Transnational Organized Crime, adopted by Assembly resolution 55/25 [YUN 2000, p. 1048], and its three supplementary Protocols (the Protocol to Prevent, Suppress and Punish Trafficking in Persons, Especially Women and Children [ibid., p. 1063]; the Protocol against the Smuggling of Migrants by Land, Sea and Air [ibid., p. 1067]; and the Protocol against the Illicit Manufacturing of and Trafficking in Firearms, Their Parts and Components and Ammunition, adopted by the Assembly in resolution 55/255 [YUN 2001, p. 1036]) continued to attract adherence. As at 31 December, 152 States were parties to the Convention, 135 were parties to the trafficking in persons Protocol, 122 were parties to the migrants Protocol and 79 were parties to the firearms Protocol. UNODC made it a priority to promote universal ratification of those instruments and provide assistance to States seeking to ratify and implement them.

The report recommended that the Commission continue to support the work of the Conferences of the Parties to the United Nations Convention against Transnational Organized Crime and of the States Parties to the United Nations Convention against Corruption. In particular, it might reiterate its call upon States to make financial contributions in support of the Conferences and related technical assistance activities and explore further ways to maintain and strengthen the political momentum necessary for the Conferences and their working groups to perform their mandated functions. The Commission might also urge Member States that had not yet done so to ratify or accede to the Organized Crime Convention and its Protocols and to the Convention against Corruption and to take every step to ensure their implementation. In particular, States might be urged to provide financial and material contributions to convene working groups and workshops for the implementation of both Conventions.

Conference of Parties to the Convention

In response to General Assembly resolution 60/175 [YUN 2005, p. 1220], the Secretary-General, by a June note [A/64/99], transmitted the report of the Conference of the Parties to the United Nations Convention against Transnational Organized Crime on its fourth session (Vienna, 8–17 October 2008) [CTOC/COP/2008/19] [YUN 2008, p. 1234].

Trafficking in persons

In response to General Assembly resolution 63/194 [YUN 2008, p. 1237], the Secretary-General transmitted a July report on improving the coordination of efforts against trafficking in persons [A/64/130], which summarized the work carried out by UNODC to implement that resolution and contained proposals on strengthening the Office's coordination capacities. The report indicated that the Secretary-General had presented a background paper to the resumed sixty-third (2009) session of the Assembly for its 13 May interactive thematic dialogue on "Taking Collective Action to End Human Trafficking". That paper summarized the views of a broad group of Member States, international organizations and civil society stakeholders on how to achieve the full and effective coordination of efforts against trafficking in persons. It also summarized responses addressing the advisability of adopting a global plan of action on preventing trafficking in persons, prosecuting traffickers and protecting and assisting victims, including the plan's potential value in ensuring efficient and coordinated action against trafficking in persons.

The main arguments presented by Member States in favour of a global plan of action included that it would foster the necessary political will and commitment at the global level; provide a comprehensive strategic framework and contribute to greater coordination of collective efforts; contribute towards and complement the implementation of international instruments and mechanisms and bridge the gaps among them; and promote international cooperation and provide an opportunity to link preventing and combating trafficking in persons to other internationally agreed goals. The plan of action would also prescribe forward-looking operational measures, targets and indicators of achievement enabling the international community to assess progress and redirect policies accordingly, as well as improve the effectiveness of national, regional and international responses.

On UNODC activities to implement resolution 63/194, the Secretary-General stated that the Office continued to hold regular consultations with Member States as a follow-up to the 2008 Vienna Forum to Fight Human Trafficking [YUN 2008, p. 1235], organized under the auspices of the United Nations Global Initiative to Fight Human Trafficking (UN.GIFT). UN.GIFT continued to operate as a technical assistance project within the mandates agreed by the relevant governing bodies. At a meeting of the Inter-Agency Cooperation Group against Trafficking in Persons (ICAT) (Vienna, 22–23 April), possible approaches to strengthening the Group's coordination efforts against trafficking in persons were discussed and the outcome was shared with Member States. ICAT agreed to publish a technical assistance toolkit containing resources and best practices recognized by all organizations and to identify opportunities for joint activities.

The Working Group on Trafficking in Persons, established by the fourth (2008) session of the Conference of the Parties to the United Nations Convention against Transnational Organized Crime [ibid., p. 1234] to advise and assist the Conference in implementing its mandate with regard to the trafficking in persons Protocol, held its first meeting (Vienna, 14–15 April) [CTOC/COP/WG.4/2009/2].

GENERAL ASSEMBLY ACTION

On 18 December [meeting 65], the General Assembly, on the recommendation of the Third Committee [A/64/440 & Corr.1], adopted **resolution 64/178** without vote [agenda item 104].

Improving the coordination of efforts against trafficking in persons

The General Assembly,

Recalling its resolution 63/194 of 18 December 2008 on improving the coordination of efforts against trafficking in persons and other relevant General Assembly resolutions on trafficking in persons and other contemporary forms of slavery,

Recalling also Economic and Social Council resolution 2008/33 of 25 July 2008 on strengthening coordination of the United Nations and other efforts in fighting trafficking in persons and previous Council resolutions on trafficking in persons,

Welcoming Human Rights Council resolution 11/3 of 17 June 2009 on trafficking in persons, especially women and children,

Recalling the United Nations Convention against Transnational Organized Crime and the Protocol to Prevent, Suppress and Punish Trafficking in Persons, Especially Women and Children, supplementing the United Nations Convention against Transnational Organized Crime, the Optional Protocol to the Convention on the Rights of the Child on the sale of children, child prostitution and child pornography and the Supplementary Convention on the Abolition of Slavery, the Slave Trade, and Institutions and Practices Similar to Slavery,

Recognizing that, in accordance with article 32 of the United Nations Convention against Transnational Organized Crime, the Conference of the Parties to the Convention is established to improve the capacity of States parties to combat transnational crime and to promote and review the implementation of the Convention, including the Protocol to Prevent, Suppress and Punish Trafficking in Persons, Especially Women and Children, by facilitating the development and exchange of relevant information, programmes and practices, and by cooperating with relevant international and regional organizations and non-government organizations, and recognizing also that each State party shall provide the Conference of the Parties with information on its programmes, plans and practices, as well as legislative and administrative measures to implement the Convention,

Taking note of the decisions of the eleventh summit of the Assembly of Heads of State and Government of the African Union, held in Sharm el-Sheikh, Egypt, on 30 June and 1 July 2008, and of the Fifteenth Summit Conference of Heads of State and Government of the Movement of Non-Aligned Countries, held in Sharm el-Sheikh from 11 to 16 July 2009, on fostering United Nations global action against human trafficking, the declaration of the European Union Ministerial Conference on the theme "Towards Global European Union Action against Trafficking in Human Beings", held in Brussels on 19 and 20 October 2009, and discussions at other subregional, regional and global forums on the need to unite and coordinate efforts in combating trafficking in persons at the international level,

Recognizing the importance of bilateral, subregional, regional and international cooperation mechanisms and initiatives, including information exchanges on good practices, of Governments and intergovernmental and non-governmental organizations to address the problem of trafficking in persons, especially women and children,

Recognizing also that broad international cooperation between Member States and relevant intergovernmental and non-governmental organizations is essential for effectively countering the threat of trafficking in persons and other contemporary forms of slavery,

Recognizing further the important role of the United Nations entities, such as the United Nations Office on Drugs and Crime, the Office of the United Nations High Commissioner for Human Rights, the United Nations Children's Fund and the International Labour Organization, the International Organization for Migration and other intergovernmental organizations in ensuring effective and comprehensive coordination in the global fight against human trafficking,

Recognizing the need to continue fostering a global partnership against trafficking in persons and other contemporary forms of slavery,

Recognizing also that trafficking in persons impairs the enjoyment of human rights, continues to pose a serious challenge to humanity and requires a concerted international response,

Taking note with appreciation of the United Nations efforts in fighting trafficking in persons, as well as the elaboration of the International Framework for Action to Implement the Trafficking in Persons Protocol, among other efforts, to assist in implementing the Protocol,

Recognizing that the current global economic crises are likely to further aggravate the problem of trafficking in persons,

Aware of the need to raise public awareness with the aim of eliminating the demand for trafficking in persons, in particular for the purpose of sexual exploitation and forced labour,

Reaffirming the commitment made by world leaders at the Millennium Summit and at the 2005 World Summit to devise, enforce and strengthen effective measures to combat and eliminate all forms of trafficking in persons to counter the demand for trafficked victims and to protect the victims,

Welcoming the report of the Special Rapporteur of the Human Rights Council on trafficking in persons, especially women and children, and the *Global Report*

on Trafficking in Persons of the United Nations Office on Drugs and Crime,

Welcoming also the report of the Secretary-General on improving the coordination of efforts against trafficking in persons and the background paper submitted by the Secretary-General on 5 May 2009 to the General Assembly at its sixty-third session,

Taking note of the outcomes of the Conference of the Parties to the United Nations Convention against Transnational Organized Crime at its fourth session, held in Vienna from 8 to 17 October 2008, in particular decision 4/4 of 17 October 2008 entitled "Trafficking in human beings", in which the Conference of the Parties underlined the need to continue to work towards a comprehensive and coordinated approach to address the problem of trafficking in persons through the appropriate national, regional and international mechanisms and acknowledged that the Protocol was the principal legally binding global instrument to combat trafficking in persons, and in this regard taking note also of the progress made by the Conference of the Parties open-ended interim Working Group on Trafficking in Persons during its meeting held in Vienna on 14 and 15 April 2009,

Taking note also of the interactive thematic dialogue of the General Assembly on the theme "Taking collective action to end human trafficking", held on 13 May 2009,

Welcoming the accession in 2008–2009 by a number of Member States to the Convention and the Protocol,

1.   *Urges* Member States that have not yet done so to consider taking measures to ratify or accede to the United Nations Convention against Transnational Organized Crime and the Protocol to Prevent, Suppress and Punish Trafficking in Persons, Especially Women and Children, supplementing the United Nations Convention against Transnational Organized Crime, and to implement fully all aspects of those instruments;

2.   *Also urges* Member States that have not yet done so to consider taking measures to ratify or accede to the Optional Protocol to the Convention on the Rights of the Child on the sale of children, child prostitution and child pornography, the Convention on the Elimination of All Forms of Discrimination against Women and the Supplementary Convention on the Abolition of Slavery, the Slave Trade, and Institutions and Practices Similar to Slavery, and to implement fully all aspects of those instruments;

3.   *Welcomes* the steps taken by human rights treaty bodies and the Special Rapporteur of the Human Rights Council on trafficking in persons, especially women and children, the Special Rapporteur of the Council on violence against women, its causes and consequences, the Special Representative of the Secretary-General on violence against children, the Special Rapporteur of the Council on the sale of children, child prostitution and child pornography and the Special Rapporteur of the Council on contemporary forms of slavery, including its causes and consequences, and United Nations agencies and other concerned intergovernmental and governmental organizations, within their existing mandates, as well as civil society, to address the serious crime of trafficking in persons, and encourages them to continue doing so and to share their knowledge and best practices as widely as possible;

4.   *Calls upon* Governments to continue their efforts to criminalize trafficking in persons in all its forms, including for labour exploitation and sexual exploitation of children, to take measures to criminalize child sex tourism, to condemn the practice of trafficking in persons, and to investigate, prosecute, condemn and penalize traffickers and intermediaries, while providing protection and assistance to the victims of trafficking with full respect for their human rights, and invites Member States to continue to support those United Nations agencies and international organizations that are actively involved in victim protection;

5.   *Encourages* all stakeholders, including the private sector, to strengthen the coordination of efforts, including through the Inter-Agency Coordination Group against Trafficking in Persons and regional and bilateral initiatives that promote cooperation and collaboration;

6.   *Recognizes* the importance of comparable data disaggregated by types of trafficking in persons, sex and age, as well as of strengthening national capacity for the gathering, analysing and reporting of such data, and welcomes the efforts of the Inter-Agency Coordination Group, drawing on the comparative advantages of the respective agencies, to share information, experiences and good practices on anti-trafficking activities of the partner agencies with Governments, other international and regional organizations, non-governmental organizations and other relevant bodies;

7.   *Acknowledges* the important work on data collection and analysis conducted by the United Nations Office on Drugs and Crime under its Global Programme against Trafficking in Human Beings, by the International Organization for Migration through its global Counter-Trafficking Module database and by the International Labour Organization;

8.   *Takes note with appreciation* of the decision of the President of the sixty-third session of the General Assembly to appoint the co-facilitators to start consultations and consideration by Member States of a United Nations global plan of action on preventing trafficking in persons, prosecuting traffickers and protecting and assisting victims of trafficking, and stresses the need for the consultations to be held in an open, inclusive and transparent manner, taking into account all the views expressed by Member States;

9.   *Reiterates its request* to the Secretary-General to provide the United Nations Crime Prevention and Criminal Justice Programme with sufficient resources for the full implementation of its mandates on combating trafficking in persons, in conformity with its high priorities, and to provide adequate support to the Commission on Crime Prevention and Criminal Justice, and invites Member States to provide voluntary contributions to the United Nations Office on Drugs and Crime for the purpose of providing assistance to Member States upon request;

10.   *Requests* the Secretary-General to invite, as appropriate, regional organizations to share information on challenges experienced and best practices in coordinating efforts to prevent and combat trafficking in persons;

11.   *Also requests* the Secretary-General to submit to the Conference of the Parties to the United Nations Convention against Transnational Organized Crime and to the General Assembly at its sixty-fifth session a report on the implementation of the present resolution.

Communications. In a 21 April note [A/63/829] to the General Assembly, Bahrain, Belarus, Egypt, Nicaragua and the Philippines underscored the need to initiate consultations in the Assembly on the global plan of action and proposed a debate on the topic.

By a 6 May letter [A/63/845], Bahrain transmitted to the Assembly the Manama Declaration on Human Trafficking, which was adopted at the International Conference entitled "Human Trafficking at the Crossroads" (Manama, Bahrain, 1–3 March).

By a 12 August note [A/64/290], the Secretary-General transmitted to the Assembly the report of the Special Rapporteur on trafficking in persons, especially women and children (see p. 734).

Kidnapping

At its April session [E/2009/30], the Commission on Crime Prevention and Criminal Justice recommended to the Economic and Social Council for adoption a draft resolution on international cooperation to prevent, combat and eliminate kidnapping and to provide assistance to victims of kidnapping.

ECONOMIC AND SOCIAL COUNCIL ACTION

On 30 July [meeting 44], the Economic and Social Council, on the recommendation of the Commission on Crime Prevention and Criminal Justice [E/2009/30], adopted **resolution 2009/24** without vote [agenda item 14 *(c)*].

International cooperation to prevent, combat and eliminate kidnapping and to provide assistance to victims of kidnapping

The Economic and Social Council,

Concerned about the increase in the number of kidnappings in various countries around the world and about the harmful effects of that crime both on victims and on their families, and determined to support measures to assist and protect victims of kidnapping and their families and to promote their recovery,

Reiterating that kidnapping under any circumstances and for any purpose constitutes a serious crime and a violation of individual freedom that undermines human rights and may have a negative impact on the economies, development and security of States,

Concerned about the growing tendency of organized criminal groups and, in certain circumstances, terrorist groups to resort to kidnapping, especially for the purpose of extortion, with a view to consolidating their criminal operations and undertaking other illegal activities, such as trafficking in firearms or drugs, money-laundering and trafficking in persons,

Convinced that any linkage between various illegal activities involving kidnapping poses an additional threat to quality of life and hinders economic and social development,

Convinced also that the United Nations Convention against Transnational Organized Crime, the applicable provisions of the relevant terrorism conventions and the applicable provisions of other relevant multilateral and bilateral agreements provide the legal framework necessary for international cooperation to prevent, combat and eliminate kidnapping and that, in order to achieve that objective, it is necessary to create opportunities for dialogue among States and for the exchange of experiences and best practices in combating kidnapping,

Recalling General Assembly resolution 59/154 of 20 December 2004, entitled "International cooperation in the prevention, combating and elimination of kidnapping and in providing assistance to victims", in which the Assembly requested the United Nations Office on Drugs and Crime to prepare a handbook, for use by competent authorities, of proven and promising practices in the fight against kidnapping,

Acknowledging the financial and technical contributions made by Member States to the preparation of that handbook,

Recalling General Assembly resolution 61/179 of 20 December 2006, in which the Assembly noted with satisfaction the publication of an operational manual against kidnapping prepared pursuant to its resolution 59/154 and invited Member States to consider the possibility of using the manual in their national efforts to combat kidnapping,

1. *Vigorously condemns and rejects once again* the offence of kidnapping under any circumstances and for any purpose;

2. *Encourages* Member States to continue to foster international cooperation, especially extradition, mutual legal assistance, collaboration between law enforcement authorities and the exchange and joint analysis of information, with a view to preventing, combating and eliminating kidnapping, including by denying kidnappers the benefit of substantive concessions;

3. *Calls upon* Member States that have not yet done so, in furtherance of the fight against kidnapping, to establish kidnapping as a predicate offence for money-laundering and to engage in international cooperation and mutual assistance in, inter alia, the tracing, detection, freezing and confiscation of proceeds of kidnapping;

4. *Calls upon* Member States, consistent with their obligations as parties to the relevant international conventions, to fully implement the provisions of those conventions, in accordance with the fundamental principles of their legal systems, by permitting extradition when any one of the bases for jurisdiction provided for in any one of those conventions is asserted by a requesting State;

5. *Encourages* Member States to take such measures as they deem appropriate, including measures to raise awareness, to ensure that judges, judicial officials, prosecutors and others in the criminal justice system are aware of the obligations of parties to the relevant international conventions and understand the utility of those conventions as a vital tool for assisting States in the administration of justice, particularly in the prosecution of kidnapping cases;

6. *Also encourages* Member States to take measures intended to provide adequate assistance and protection to victims of kidnapping and their families, including measures addressing their rights and legal interests;

7. *Invites* Member States to consider using the operational manual against kidnapping prepared pursuant to General Assembly resolution 59/154 in their national efforts to combat kidnapping, and requests the United Nations Office on Drugs and Crime, within its mandate, to continue to provide Member States, upon request, with technical assistance and advice in implementing the manual;

8. *Requests* the United Nations Office on Drugs and Crime, in coordination with other relevant entities, to provide technical assistance to Member States, upon request, to enable them to strengthen their capacity to combat kidnapping, including by:

(a) Providing training for judges, judicial officials, prosecutors and law enforcement officials to promote their understanding of processes and mechanisms available for disbanding criminal organizations, including training in the use of special investigative techniques for the rescue of kidnapped persons, bearing in mind the particular need to safeguard and protect victims of kidnapping;

(b) Reviewing trends and enhancing understanding of the problem in order to create a basis for developing policies and strategies against kidnapping;

(c) Organizing practical courses or workshops for the exchange of experiences and best practices in combating kidnapping, in collaboration with international or regional organizations;

9. *Invites* Member States and other donors to contribute resources for the above-mentioned purposes;

10. *Requests* the Executive Director of the United Nations Office on Drugs and Crime to report to the Commission on Crime Prevention and Criminal Justice at its nineteenth session on the implementation of the present resolution.

Strategies for crime prevention

Corruption

United Nations Convention against Corruption

In response to Economic and Social Council resolutions 2005/17 [YUN 2005, p. 1224] and 2006/24 [YUN 2006, p. 1301] and General Assembly resolution 61/181 [ibid., p. 1293], the Secretary-General submitted to the Commission on Crime Prevention and Criminal Justice a February report on international cooperation in combating transnational organized crime and corruption [E/CN.15/2009/4] (see also above, under "Transnational organized crime"). The report described UNODC activities to promote ratification and implementation of the United Nations Convention against Corruption, adopted by Assembly resolution 58/4 [YUN 2003, p. 1127], and complemented the report of the Conference of the Parties to the Convention against Corruption on its third session (see below).

The report recommended that the Commission: continue to support the work of the Conference of the States Parties to the United Nations Convention against Corruption; call on States to make financial

contributions in support of the Conference and related technical assistance activities; explore ways to maintain and strengthen the political momentum necessary for the Conference and its working groups to perform their mandated functions; urge States that had not yet done so to ratify or accede to the Convention and to ensure its implementation; and urge States to provide financial and material contributions for the convening of working groups and workshops for the Convention's implementation.

As at 31 December, 143 States were parties to the Convention.

Conference of States Parties to the Convention

The Conference of the States Parties to the United Nations Convention against Corruption, at its third session (Doha, 9–13 November) [CAC/COSP/2009/15], adopted four resolutions on: the Mechanism for the Review of Implementation of the Convention, including terms of reference for the mechanism; preventive measures; asset recovery; and technical assistance to implement the Convention. It also adopted a decision in which it welcomed Morocco's offer to host the fourth (2011) session of the Conference and Panama's offer to host the fifth (2013) session.

Assets of illicit origin

In response to General Assembly resolution 63/226 [YUN 2008, p. 1239], the Secretary-General submitted a July report on preventing and combating corrupt practices and transfer of assets of illicit origin and returning such assets, in particular to the countries of origin, consistent with the United Nations Convention against Corruption [A/64/122]. The report provided information on the preparations for the third session of the Conference of the States Parties to the United Nations Convention against Corruption (see above), and described measures taken by States to prevent and combat corruption and to work for the prompt return of assets. It also provided an overview of international action being taken against corruption and for asset recovery, reviewed UNODC work carried out individually and in partnership with other institutions, and presented information on matters related to resources.

The report recommended that the Assembly: encourage Member States to ratify or accede to the Convention and support its implementation; provide support for the establishment and operation of the mechanism for the review of implementation; make use of the comprehensive self-assessment tool that was expected to be approved by the Conference of the States Parties at its third session (see above); and encourage Member States to invest energy, time and resources in the implementation of the asset recovery provisions of the Convention and identify the best possible ways forward. With regard to the steadily growing number of States parties, the report concluded that the number of countries that might require technical assistance to enable them to meet their obligations under the Convention would also grow. While UNODC and other providers of technical assistance were making significant efforts in that area, those efforts were by no means commensurate with the challenges facing developing countries and countries emerging from conflict when seeking to align their legal and institutional framework with the requirements of the Convention, and even less so when trying to build the necessary professional skills and capacities to ensure implementation. Consequently, as the number of States parties continued to rise, expectations towards UNODC would increase exponentially. To meet those expectations, increased financial and human resources would be required to enable the Office to promote the implementation of the Convention and to discharge its functions as the secretariat of the Conference of the States Parties and of the review mechanism. The report recommended that the Assembly consider UNODC's needs and explore ways to address them in the context of the 2010–2011 biennium and subsequent bienniums.

GENERAL ASSEMBLY ACTION

On 24 December [meeting 68], the General Assembly, on the recommendation of the Second (Economic and Financial) Committee [A/64/422/Add.2], adopted **resolution 64/237** without vote [agenda item 55 *(b)*].

Preventing and combating corrupt practices and transfer of assets of illicit origin and returning such assets, in particular to the countries of origin, consistent with the United Nations Convention against Corruption

The General Assembly,

Recalling its resolutions 54/205 of 22 December 1999, 55/61 of 4 December 2000, 55/188 of 20 December 2000, 56/186 of 21 December 2001 and 57/244 of 20 December 2002, and recalling also its resolutions 58/205 of 23 December 2003, 59/242 of 22 December 2004, 60/207 of 22 December 2005, 61/209 of 20 December 2006, 62/202 of 19 December 2007 and 63/226 of 19 December 2008,

Welcoming the entry into force on 14 December 2005 of the United Nations Convention against Corruption,

Recognizing that fighting corruption at all levels is a priority and that corruption is a serious barrier to effective resource mobilization and allocation and diverts resources away from activities that are vital for poverty eradication, the fight against hunger, and economic and sustainable development,

Recognizing also that supportive domestic legal systems are essential in preventing and combating corrupt practices and transfer of assets of illicit origin and returning such assets,

Recalling that the fight against all forms of corruption requires strong institutions at all levels, including at the local level, able to undertake efficient preventive and law enforcement measures consistent with the Convention, in particular chapters II and III,

Acknowledging the important progress made towards the implementation of chapter V of the Convention, but recognizing that States parties continue to face challenges in asset recovery owing to, inter alia, differences in legal systems, the complexity of multijurisdictional investigations and prosecutions, lack of familiarity with mutual legal assistance procedures of other States and difficulties in identifying the flow of proceeds of corruption, and noting the particular challenges posed in recovering the proceeds of corruption in cases involving individuals who are, or have been, entrusted with prominent public functions and their family members and close associates,

Reiterating its concern about the seriousness of problems and threats posed by corruption to the stability and security of societies, undermining the institutions and the values of democracy, ethical values and justice and jeopardizing sustainable development and the rule of law, in particular when an inadequate national and international response leads to impunity,

Convinced that corruption is no longer a local matter but a transnational phenomenon that affects all societies and economies, making international cooperation to prevent and control it essential,

Convinced also that a stable and transparent environment for national and international commercial transactions in all countries is essential for the mobilization of investment, finance, technology, skills and other important resources, and recognizing that effective efforts at all levels to prevent and combat corruption in all its forms in all countries are essential elements of an improved national and international business environment,

Mindful of the very important role that the private sector can play in fostering economic growth and development and of the active involvement of the United Nations system in facilitating the constructive participation and orderly interaction of the private sector in the development process by embracing universal principles and norms, such as honesty, transparency and accountability,

Recognizing the concern about the laundering and the transfer of assets of illicit origin derived from corruption, and stressing the need to address this concern consistent with the Convention,

Determined to prevent, detect and deter, in a more effective manner, international transfers of illicitly acquired assets and to strengthen international cooperation through the commitment of Member States to effective national and international action,

Concerned about the links between corruption in all its forms, including bribery, corruption-related money-laundering and the transfer of assets of illicit origin, and other forms of crime, in particular organized crime and economic crime,

Noting the particular concern of developing countries and countries with economies in transition regarding the return of assets of illicit origin derived from corruption, in particular to countries from which they originated, consistent with the principles of the Convention, in particular chapter V, so as to enable countries to design and fund development projects in accordance with their national priorities, in view of the importance that such assets can have to their sustainable development,

1. *Takes note* of the report of the Secretary-General;

2. *Welcomes* the significant number of Member States that have already ratified or acceded to the United Nations Convention against Corruption, and in this regard urges all Member States and competent regional economic integration organizations, within the limits of their competence, that have not yet done so to consider ratifying or acceding to the Convention as a matter of priority, and calls upon all States parties to fully implement the Convention as soon as possible;

3. *Expresses concern* about the magnitude of corruption at all levels, including the scale of the transfer of assets of illicit origin derived from corruption, and in this regard reiterates its commitment to preventing and combating corrupt practices at all levels, consistent with the Convention;

4. *Urges* Member States to combat and penalize corruption in all its forms as well as the laundering of proceeds of corruption, to prevent the transfer of illicitly acquired assets, and to work for the prompt return of such assets through asset recovery consistent with the principles of the Convention, particularly chapter V;

5. *Condemns* corruption in all its forms, including bribery, as well as the laundering of proceeds of corruption and other forms of economic crime;

6. *Welcomes* the conclusion of the third session of the Conference of the States Parties to the United Nations Convention against Corruption, held in Doha from 9 to 13 November 2009, and requests the Secretary-General to transmit to the General Assembly a report on the third session of the Conference of the States Parties to the Convention;

7. *Stresses* the need for transparency in financial institutions, invites Member States to work on the identification and tracing of financial flows linked to corruption, the freezing or seizing of assets derived from corruption and the return of such assets, consistent with the Convention, and encourages the promotion of human and institutional capacity-building in that regard;

8. *Welcomes* the successful outcome of the third session of the Conference of the States Parties to the Convention, especially the establishment by consensus of a review mechanism for the implementation of the Convention, and calls upon States parties to fully implement the outcomes of the Conference;

9. *Calls*, in particular, for the rapid and effective implementation of the mechanism for the review of implementation of the Convention by all States parties, and, where appropriate, relevant stakeholders, in accordance with the terms of reference of the mechanism;

10. *Takes note with appreciation* of the work of the Open-ended Intergovernmental Working Groups on Asset Recovery, Technical Assistance and Review of the Implementation of the United Nations Convention against Corruption and the open-ended dialogue with international organizations, including the Institutional Integrity Initiative, and calls upon States parties to the Convention to support the work of the newly established Implementation

Review Group, including its work on technical assistance, and the newly established Open-ended Intergovernmental Working Group on Prevention of Corruption, as well as the continuing work of the Open-ended Intergovernmental Working Group on Asset Recovery;

11. *Also takes note with appreciation* of the decision of the Conference of the States Parties to the Convention to accept the offer by the Governments of Morocco and Panama to host its fourth and fifth sessions in 2011 and 2013, respectively;

12. *Welcomes* the efforts of Member States that have enacted laws and taken other positive measures in the fight against corruption in all its forms, including in accordance with the Convention, and in this regard encourages Member States that have not yet done so to enact such laws and to implement effective measures at the national level and, in accordance with domestic laws and policies, at the local level, to prevent and combat corruption;

13. *Affirms* the need for Member States, consistent with the Convention, to take measures to prevent the transfer abroad and laundering of assets derived from corruption, including to prevent the financial institutions in both countries of origin and destination from being used to transfer or receive illicit funds, as well as to assist in their recovery and to return such assets to the requesting State, consistent with the Convention;

14. *Urges* all Member States, consistent with the Convention, to abide by the principles of proper management of public affairs and public property, fairness, responsibility and equality before the law and the need to safeguard integrity and to foster a culture of transparency, accountability and rejection of corruption;

15. *Stresses* the importance of mutual legal assistance, and encourages Member States to enhance international cooperation, consistent with the Convention;

16. *Calls for* further international cooperation, inter alia, through the United Nations system, in support of national, subregional and regional efforts to prevent and combat corrupt practices and the transfer of assets of illicit origin, consistent with the principles of the Convention, and in this regard encourages close cooperation between anti-corruption agencies, law enforcement agencies and financial intelligence units;

17. *Requests* the Secretary-General to continue to provide the United Nations Office on Drugs and Crime with the resources necessary to enable it to promote, in an effective manner, the implementation of the Convention and to discharge its functions as the secretariat of the Conference of the States Parties to the Convention, and also requests the Secretary-General to ensure that the new mechanism for the review of implementation of the Convention is adequately funded, in line with the resolution adopted by the Conference of the States Parties;

18. *Reiterates its call upon* the private sector, at both the international and the national levels, including small and large companies and transnational corporations, to remain fully engaged in the fight against corruption, notes in this context the role that the Global Compact can play in fighting corruption and promoting transparency, and emphasizes the need for all relevant stakeholders, including within the United Nations system, as appropriate, to continue to promote corporate responsibility and accountability;

19. *Takes note* of the holding of the sixth Global Forum on Fighting Corruption and Safeguarding Integrity on the theme "Strength in unity: public-private partnership to fight corruption" in Doha on 7 and 8 November 2009;

20. *Requests* the international community to provide, inter alia, technical assistance to support national efforts to strengthen human and institutional capacity aimed at preventing and combating corrupt practices and the transfer of assets of illicit origin as well as for asset recovery in accordance with chapter V of the Convention, consistent with the principles of the Convention, and to support national efforts in formulating strategies for mainstreaming and promoting transparency and integrity in both the public and private sectors;

21. *Takes note with appreciation* of the Stolen Asset Recovery Initiative of the United Nations Office on Drugs and Crime and the World Bank, takes note of its cooperation with relevant partners, including the International Centre for Asset Recovery, and encourages coordination among existing initiatives;

22. *Takes note* of the partnership between the United Nations Office on Drugs and Crime, the International Criminal Police Organization and the Government of Austria, with the support of the European Anti-Fraud Agency to establish the International Anti-Corruption Academy to serve as a centre of excellence for education, training and academic research in the field of anti-corruption, including in the area of asset recovery;

23. *Requests* the Secretary-General to submit to the General Assembly, at its sixty-fifth session, a report on preventing and combating corrupt practices and transfer of assets of illicit origin and returning such assets, in particular to the countries of origin, consistent with the Convention;

24. *Decides* to include in the provisional agenda of its sixty-fifth session, under the item entitled "Globalization and interdependence", the sub-item entitled "Preventing and combating corrupt practices and transfer of assets of illicit origin and returning such assets, in particular to the countries of origin, consistent with the United Nations Convention against Corruption".

Terrorism

In a January report to the Commission on Crime Prevention and Criminal Justice on assistance in implementing the international conventions and protocols related to terrorism [E/CN.15/2009/5], the Secretary-General reviewed progress made by UNODC in 2008 in delivering technical assistance on legal and related capacity-building in the area of counter-terrorism, in particular by its Terrorism Prevention Branch. The report identified the challenges ahead and emphasized the need for enhanced governmental support to meet them.

During 2008, direct technical assistance was provided to 45 countries and 16 thematic regional and subregional meetings attended by 117 countries were organized, two of them at the ministerial level. A number of technical assistance tools including a checklist of the offences set out in the international

legal instruments, were developed. In cooperation with other UNODC entities and partner organizations, the Branch organized and participated in several specialized activities that addressed complex aspects of legal assistance work, including strengthening international cooperation in criminal matters pertaining to counter-terrorism; suppressing the financing of terrorism; preventing nuclear terrorism; and enhancing a criminal justice response to terrorism based on the rule of law. Delivery of technical assistance was fostered through enhanced coordination and partnerships with other entities and organizations active in the counter-terrorism field and included: cooperation with Security Council bodies dealing with counter-terrorism; participation in the Counter-Terrorism Implementation Task Force; partnerships with other organizations; and cooperation with recipient and donor countries. The report on a comprehensive evaluation of the Global Project on Strengthening the Legal Regime against Terrorism during the period from 1 January 2003 to June 2007 was issued in 2008 and included nine recommendations on the future work of the Global Project. Meanwhile, between 2003 and 2008, the Branch had assisted Member States in completing some 469 new ratifications. In addition, at least 62 countries assisted by the Branch had taken steps to incorporate the provisions of the international legal instruments into national legislation: 23 countries had passed new anti-terrorism legislation and at least another 39 countries had new anti-terrorism legislation in progress. Approximately 7,700 national criminal justice officials were provided with specialized training on the international legal instruments, with approximately 1,600 trained in 2008.

The Secretary-General concluded that the scope of legal and related capacity-building technical assistance in the area of counter-terrorism provided by UNODC had consistently expanded since 2003. A key challenge was to ensure sustained services and adequate follow-up to the initial assistance provided and thus achieve a long-term impact. Assistance in the areas of ratification and legislative incorporation needed to be reinforced. Efforts were also needed to build and transfer specialized legal knowledge and expertise to help strengthen the capacity of national criminal justice systems to apply the legal regime against terrorism in conformity with the rule of law. Innovative training delivery methods needed to be pursued, such as online and computer-based training courses. The Secretary-General recommended that the Commission provide further guidance on the reinforcement of UNODC's technical assistance work on counter-terrorism issues, covering both specialized services for strengthening the legal regime against terrorism and services for addressing the cross-cutting issues of crime, drug and terrorism prevention; provide further guidance concerning UNODC involvement in the work of the Counter-Terrorism Implementation Task Force; invite relevant organizations to enhance their cooperation with the Office on counter-terrorism issues; and invite Member States to increase the level of resources for implementing UNODC technical assistance activities in the area of terrorism prevention.

ECONOMIC AND SOCIAL COUNCIL ACTION

On 30 July [meeting 44], the Economic and Social Council, on the recommendation of the Commission on Crime Prevention and Criminal Justice [E/2009/30], adopted **resolution 2009/21** without vote [agenda item 14 *(c)*].

Technical assistance for implementing the international conventions and protocols related to terrorism

The Economic and Social Council
Recommends to the General Assembly the adoption of the following draft resolution:

[For text, see General Assembly **resolution 64/177** below.]

GENERAL ASSEMBLY ACTION

On 18 December [meeting 65], the General Assembly, on the recommendation of the Third Committee [A/64/440 & Corr.1], adopted **resolution 64/177** without vote [agenda item 104].

Technical assistance for implementing the international conventions and protocols related to terrorism

The General Assembly,
Reaffirming all General Assembly and Security Council resolutions related to technical assistance in countering terrorism,

Stressing again the need to strengthen international, regional and subregional cooperation to effectively prevent and combat terrorism, in particular by enhancing the national capacity of States through the provision of technical assistance,

Reaffirming the commitments undertaken by Member States, and recalling all aspects of the United Nations Global Counter-Terrorism Strategy, adopted by the General Assembly in its resolution 60/288 of 8 September 2006,

Recalling its resolution 62/272 of 5 September 2008, in which it called upon Member States, the United Nations and other appropriate international, regional and subregional organizations to step up their efforts to implement the Strategy in an integrated manner and in all its aspects, and reaffirmed the need to enhance international cooperation in countering terrorism,

Recalling also its resolution 63/195 of 18 December 2008, in which it requested the United Nations Office on Drugs and Crime to enhance its technical assistance to Member States, upon request, to strengthen international cooperation in preventing and combating terrorism,

1. *Commends* the United Nations Office on Drugs and Crime, including its Terrorism Prevention Branch, for providing, in close consultation with the Counter-Terrorism Committee and its Executive Directorate, technical assistance to States, upon request, to facilitate the implementation of the international conventions and protocols related to terrorism and relevant United Nations resolutions, and requests the Office, within its mandate, to continue to enhance its efforts in that regard, in close coordination with the Counter-Terrorism Committee and the Counter-Terrorism Implementation Task Force;

2. *Urges* Member States that have not yet done so to consider becoming parties without delay to the existing international conventions and protocols related to terrorism, and requests the United Nations Office on Drugs and Crime, within its mandate, to reinforce the provision of technical assistance to Member States, upon request, for the ratification and legislative incorporation of those international legal instruments and for the building of capacity to implement them;

3. *Urges* Member States to strengthen, to the greatest extent possible, international cooperation in order to prevent and combat terrorism, including, when appropriate, by entering into bilateral and multilateral treaties on extradition and mutual legal assistance, within the framework of the international conventions and protocols related to terrorism and relevant United Nations resolutions and in accordance with international law, including the Charter of the United Nations, and to ensure adequate training of all relevant personnel in executing international cooperation, and requests the United Nations Office on Drugs and Crime, within its mandate, to provide technical assistance to Member States, upon request, to that end;

4. *Recognizes* the importance of the development and maintenance of fair and effective criminal justice systems, in accordance with applicable international law, as a fundamental basis of any strategy to counter terrorism, and requests the United Nations Office on Drugs and Crime, whenever appropriate, to take into account in its technical assistance programme to counter terrorism the elements necessary for building national capacity in order to strengthen criminal justice systems and the rule of law;

5. *Requests* the United Nations Office on Drugs and Crime, within its mandate, to intensify its efforts to continue to systematically develop specialized legal knowledge in the area of counter-terrorism and pertinent thematic areas of relevance to the mandates of the Office and to provide, upon request, technical assistance for building the capacity of Member States to ratify and implement the international conventions and protocols related to terrorism, especially through the preparation of technical tools and publications and the training of criminal justice officials, and requests the Office to report to the Commission on Crime Prevention and Criminal Justice at its nineteenth and twentieth sessions on the activities of the Office in that regard;

6. *Also requests* the United Nations Office on Drugs and Crime, within its mandate and in coordination with the Counter-Terrorism Committee and its Executive Directorate and the Counter-Terrorism Implementation Task Force, to continue to work with international organizations and relevant entities of the United Nations system, as well

as with regional and subregional organizations and arrangements, in the delivery of technical assistance, whenever appropriate;

7. *Expresses its appreciation* to all Member States that have supported the technical assistance activities of the United Nations Office on Drugs and Crime, including through financial contributions, and invites all Member States to consider making additional voluntary financial contributions, as well as providing in-kind support, especially in view of the need for enhanced and effective delivery of technical assistance to assist Member States with the implementation of relevant provisions of the United Nations Global Counter-Terrorism Strategy;

8. *Requests* the Secretary-General to provide the United Nations Office on Drugs and Crime with sufficient resources to carry out activities within its mandate, including in the area of counter-terrorism, and, in the context of the strategy for the period 2008–2011 for the Office, to assist Member States, upon request, in the implementation of the relevant elements of the United Nations Global Counter-Terrorism Strategy;

9. *Also requests* the Secretary-General to submit to the General Assembly at its sixty-fifth session a report on the implementation of the present resolution.

Economic fraud and identity-related crime

In response to Economic and Social Council resolution 2007/20 [YUN 2007, p. 1139], the Secretary-General submitted to the Commission on Crime Prevention and Criminal Justice a February report [E/CN.15/2009/2 & Corr.1] on international cooperation in the prevention, investigation, prosecution and punishment of economic fraud and identity-related crime, which provided an overview and an analysis of the replies received from 22 Member States on their efforts to implement that resolution and their domestic policies and measures in the areas of prevention, investigation, prosecution and punishment of economic fraud and identity-related crime. The report highlighted the need to develop comprehensive, multifaceted and coherent strategies aimed at: improving legislative responses; enhancing the law enforcement and investigative capacity of competent institutions; strengthening international cooperation to combat economic fraud and identity-related crime; developing and implementing effective preventive policies; developing partnerships and synergies between the public and private sectors; and further promoting training and technical assistance activities. The Secretary-General recommended that the Commission suggest ways to enhance and enrich the debate at the international level.

In March, the Secretariat submitted to the Commission a note [E/CN.15/2009/15] on "Economic fraud and identity-related crime" and on "Penal reform and the reduction of prison overcrowding, including the provision of legal aid in criminal justice systems" to guide the thematic discussions of the two topics at its

eighteenth session. The guide posed a series of questions for discussion by the Commission, outlined some issues for shaping the discussion and further elaborated on the relevant sub-themes. The thematic discussion on economic fraud and identity-related crime took place on 17 April and also had before it the report of the third meeting of the core group of experts on identity-related crime (Vienna, 20–22 January) [E/CN.15/2009/CRP.12].

ECONOMIC AND SOCIAL COUNCIL ACTION

On 30 July [meeting 44], the Economic and Social Council, on the recommendation of the Commission on Crime Prevention and Criminal Justice [E/2009/30], adopted **resolution 2009/22** without vote [agenda item 14 *(c)*].

International cooperation in the prevention, investigation, prosecution and punishment of economic fraud and identity-related crime

The Economic and Social Council,

Concerned about the serious threats posed by economic fraud and identity-related crime and by other illicit activities that those forms of crime support,

Concerned also about the exploitation of new information, communications and commercial technologies by perpetrators of economic fraud and identity-related crime and about the threats that such exploitation poses to commerce and to those technologies and their users,

Concerned further about the short- and long-term impact of economic fraud and identity-related crime,

Convinced of the need to have in place appropriate and effective domestic powers to detect and investigate, prosecute and punish economic fraud and identity-related crime, as well as mechanisms for promoting international cooperation to prevent and combat such forms of crime, and recognizing the close relationship between identity-related crime and information and communications technologies,

Convinced also of the need to develop comprehensive, multifaceted and coherent strategies and measures to counter such forms of crime, including both reactive and preventive measures,

Convinced further of the importance of partnerships and synergies among public and private sector entities and civil society in developing such strategies and measures,

Convinced of the need to explore the development of appropriate and timely support and services for victims of economic fraud and identity-related crime,

Bearing in mind the need to respect the human rights of persons that relate to their identity and the need to protect identities and related documents and information from inappropriate disclosure and criminal misuse, consistent with national and international human rights obligations, including individual privacy rights,

Bearing in mind also the conclusions and recommendations of the Intergovernmental Expert Group to Prepare a Study on Fraud and the Criminal Misuse and Falsification of Identity, convened pursuant to Economic and Social Council resolution 2004/26 of 21 July 2004,

Recalling that, in its resolution 2004/26, it requested the Intergovernmental Expert Group to use the information gained by the study for the purpose of developing useful practices, guidelines or other materials in the prevention, investigation and prosecution of fraud and the criminal misuse and falsification of identity,

Reaffirming the importance of the United Nations Convention against Transnational Organized Crime and the Protocols thereto and of the United Nations Convention against Corruption in terms of preventing and combating economic fraud and identity-related crime,

Recalling the Council of Europe Convention on Cybercrime, currently the only international treaty specifically addressing computer-related fraud, computer-related forgery and other forms of cybercrime that may contribute to the perpetration of economic fraud, identity-related crime, money-laundering and other related illicit activities,

Recalling also that, in its resolution 2007/20 of 26 July 2007, it requested the United Nations Office on Drugs and Crime to provide, upon request and subject to the availability of extrabudgetary resources, legal expertise or other forms of technical assistance to Member States reviewing or updating their laws dealing with transnational fraud and identity-related crime, in order to ensure that appropriate legislative responses to such offences were in place,

1. *Takes note* of the report of the Secretary-General, which contains information on the efforts of reporting Member States to implement Economic and Social Council resolution 2007/20 and on their strategies for responding to the problems posed by such forms of crime;

2. *Also takes note* of the thematic discussion of the Commission on Crime Prevention and Criminal Justice at its eighteenth session on the theme "Economic fraud and identity-related crime";

3. *Acknowledges* the efforts of the United Nations Office on Drugs and Crime to establish, in consultation with the United Nations Commission on International Trade Law, a core group of experts on identity-related crime and to bring together, on a regular basis, representatives of Governments, private sector entities, international and regional organizations and academia to pool experience, to develop strategies, to facilitate further research and to agree on practical action against identity-related crime;

4. *Takes note* of the work done by the Core Group of Experts on Identity-related Crime at its meetings held in Courmayeur, Italy, on 29 and 30 November 2007 and in Vienna on 2 and 3 June 2008 and from 20 to 22 January 2009;

5. *Welcomes* the initiative of the International Criminal Police Organization (INTERPOL), the United Nations Office on Drugs and Crime and the Government of Austria, with the support of the European Anti-fraud Office and other partners, to work collaboratively towards the establishment of an international anti-corruption academy, and looks forward to the academy becoming fully operational in the shortest possible time and contributing to capacity-building in the area of countering economic fraud and identity-related crime, as well as corruption;

6. *Encourages* Member States, taking into account the recommendations of the Intergovernmental Expert Group to Prepare a Study on Fraud and the Criminal Misuse and

Falsification of Identity, convened pursuant to Economic and Social Council resolution 2004/26:

(a) To combat economic fraud and identity-related crime by ensuring adequate investigative powers and, where appropriate, by reviewing and updating the relevant laws;

(b) To develop and maintain adequate law enforcement and investigative capacity to keep abreast of and deal with new developments in the exploitation of information, communications and commercial technologies in economic fraud and identity-related crime, including websites and other online forums used to facilitate trafficking in identity information or documents, such as passports, driving licences and national identity cards;

(c) To consider, where appropriate, the establishment of new offences and the updating of existing offences in response to the evolution of economic fraud and identity-related crime, bearing in mind the advantages of common approaches to criminalization, where feasible, in facilitating efficient and effective international cooperation;

(d) To strengthen international cooperation to prevent and combat economic fraud and identity-related crime, in particular by making full use of the relevant international legal instruments;

(e) To develop an approach for the collection of comparable data on the nature and extent of identity-related crime, including, where feasible, from the victim's perspective, that would allow the sharing of data among appropriate law enforcement entities and provide a central source of data at the national level on the nature and extent of identity-related crime, taking due account of national law;

(f) To study, at the national level, the specific short- and long-term impact of economic fraud and identity-related crime on society and on victims of such forms of crime and to develop strategies or programmes to combat those forms of crime;

(g) To adopt useful practices and efficient mechanisms for supporting and protecting victims of economic fraud and identity-related crime and, to that effect, to enable effective cooperation among public and private sector entities through computer emergency response teams or other mechanisms providing an emergency response capability to public and private organizations requiring technical support and advice during periods of electronic attack or other network security incidents;

7. *Requests* the United Nations Office on Drugs and Crime, in consultation with Member States and taking into account relevant intergovernmental organizations and, in accordance with the rules and procedures of the Economic and Social Council, experts from academic institutions, relevant non-governmental organizations and the private sector, to collect, develop and disseminate:

(a) Material and guidelines on the typology of identity-related crime and on relevant criminalization issues to assist Member States, upon request, in establishing new identity-based criminal offences and in modernizing existing offences, taking into account the relevant work of other intergovernmental organizations engaged in related matters;

(b) Technical assistance material for training, such as manuals, compilations of useful practices or guidelines and scientific, forensic or other reference material for law enforcement officials and prosecution authorities, in order

to enhance their expertise and capacity in preventing and combating economic fraud and identity-related crime;

(c) A set of useful practices and guidelines to assist Member States in establishing the impact of such crimes on victims;

(d) A set of material and best practices on public-private partnerships to prevent economic fraud and identity-related crime;

8. *Also requests* the United Nations Office on Drugs and Crime to provide, upon request, technical assistance, including legal expertise, to Member States reviewing or updating their laws dealing with economic fraud and identity-related crime, in order to ensure that appropriate legislative responses are in place;

9. *Further requests* the United Nations Office on Drugs and Crime to make available to the Conference of the Parties to the United Nations Convention against Transnational Organized Crime at its fifth session and to the Conference of the States Parties to the United Nations Convention against Corruption at its third session the text of the present resolution and the outcome of the thematic discussion on the theme "Economic fraud and identity-related crime" held at the eighteenth session of the Commission on Crime Prevention and Criminal Justice, with a view to promoting the full use of the relevant provisions of those instruments to prevent and combat identity-related crime;

10. *Requests* the United Nations Office on Drugs and Crime to continue its efforts, in consultation with the United Nations Commission on International Trade Law, to promote mutual understanding and the exchange of views among public and private sector entities on issues related to economic fraud and identity-related crime, with the aim of facilitating cooperation among various stakeholders from both sectors through the continuation of the work of the Core Group of Experts on Identity-related Crime, the composition of which should respect the principle of equitable geographical distribution, and to report to the Commission on Crime Prevention and Criminal Justice on the outcome of its work on a regular basis;

11. *Invites* Member States and other donors to provide extrabudgetary resources to support the work set out in paragraphs 7 and 10 of the present resolution;

12. *Requests* the Secretary-General to report to the Commission on Crime Prevention and Criminal Justice at its twentieth session on the implementation of the present resolution.

Sexual exploitation of children

In response to Commission on Crime Prevention and Criminal Justice resolution 16/2 [YUN 2007, p. 1141], the UNODC Executive Director submitted a February report [E/CN.15/2009/14] on effective crime prevention and criminal justice responses to combat sexual exploitation of children, based on information received from Governments on their efforts to implement that resolution. It also provided an overview of the main activities of UNODC to assist countries in combating the sexual exploitation of children. Issues covered included: crime prevention responses; the legal definition of "child"; crimi-

nalization, prosecution and punishment of sexual exploitation of children; combating recidivism by promoting appropriate forms of treatment; prosecution of offences committed in other countries; mutual legal assistance and extradition; humanitarian crises; awareness-raising; technical assistance; protection and support of victims; cooperation in investigations and information campaigns; coordination, collaboration and support among governmental and non-governmental organizations; the private sector; and information and communications technology and Internet service providers.

The replies received from 31 Member States indicated that most of them had adopted national legislation in conformity with international instruments governing the rights of the child, as well as measures to promote the investigation and prosecution of offences, international judicial cooperation, awareness-raising, protection of child victims and witnesses and collaboration with civil society. However, as the use of information and communications technology in child sexual exploitation was a relatively new phenomenon, few countries indicated that adequate or specific legislative and other measures were in place. An increasingly large proportion of child sexual abuse websites were of a commercial nature, generating significant proceeds for organized criminal groups. It was recommended, therefore, that States ensure the coverage of those offences under the Organized Crime Convention. The report also recommended that the Commission provide guidance to Member States on what was required in terms of legislation, conditions for successful national and international law enforcement and promotion of the involvement of the private sector, in particular Internet service providers, in the prevention and detection of sexual exploitation of children; consider the advisability of calling for the development of model strategies and measures towards the prevention of and adequate criminal justice responses to combat sexual exploitation of children; and invite Member States and other donors to provide contributions to enable UNODC to fulfil its mandate.

UN standards and norms

The Commission on Crime Prevention and Criminal Justice had before it a February report [E/CN.15/2009/16] on the use and application of UN standards and norms in crime prevention and criminal justice, which provided information on the implementation of Economic and Social Council resolution 2006/20 [YUN 2006, p. 1306], based on replies received from Member States, UN system entities and international, regional and national organizations. Issues addressed included: legislative measures; assistance to victims; information provided to the general public and to victims; victims in the criminal justice process; informal mechanisms for the resolution of disputes; protection; restitution and compensation; research and education and prevention campaigns; international standards and cooperation; and technical assistance.

Replies received from 28 Member States indicated that they had implemented, at least in part, the measures contained in the Declaration of Basic Principles of Justice for Victims of Crime and Abuse of Power, adopted by the General Assembly in resolution 40/34 [YUN 1985, p. 742]. Approaches to implementing the recommendations contained in the Declaration varied widely and difficulties encountered in implementing legislative measures differed significantly from country to country, ranging from a lack of awareness of available services to cultural restraints to differences in the judicial process. Some States needed UN technical assistance, but were unaware of opportunities to receive such assistance through UN agencies. The report recommended that the Commission invite Member States that needed assistance to strengthen and improve their national mechanisms to assist and protect victims to request such assistance from relevant UN agencies and offices, in particular from UNODC; encourage Member States to use UNODC tools and handbooks on victim assistance and protection; invite Member States to provide resources, including financial resources, to UNODC in support of its activities to assist States; and request UNODC to continue to provide advisory services and technical assistance to Member States in the area of victim assistance and protection.

Child justice reform

In response to Economic and Social Council resolution 2007/23 [YUN 2007, p. 1144], the Secretary-General submitted to the Commission on Crime Prevention and Criminal Justice a March report on support of national efforts for child justice reform, in particular through technical assistance and improved UN system-wide coordination [E/CN.15/2009/12]. The report contained information provided by 31 Member States and members of the Interagency Panel on Juvenile Justice, including UNODC. The report described encouraging trends towards the reduction of pretrial detention and detention for children and the growing use of prevention, diversion, restorative justice and alternatives to imprisonment, while underscoring that much progress remained to be made. It described progress in the coordination and joint provision by the UN system and NGOs of technical assistance to Member States.

The Secretary-General recommended that the Commission: welcome the measures adopted by

States to reduce the use of detention for children and the development by several States of programmes for diversion, restorative justice and alternatives to imprisonment and encourage other States to adopt similar measures; welcome the provision by the Interagency Panel on Juvenile Justice and its members of technical assistance to Member States and the issuance of the Secretary-General's 2008 guidance note on the UN approach to justice for children; invite Member States to provide resources to the Interagency Panel secretariat and its members so that they could continue to provide high-level technical assistance to Member States; encourage the Interagency Panel, its secretariat and its members to continue to provide technical assistance to Member States in implementing international standards and the Secretary-General's guidance note, in particular through joint programming; and invite Member States and other donors to provide resources to UNODC for the purpose of providing technical assistance in the area of child justice reform to Member States, particularly those that referred to technical assistance needs in response to Council resolution 2007/23.

ECONOMIC AND SOCIAL COUNCIL ACTION

On 30 July [meeting 44], the Economic and Social Council, on the recommendation of the Commission on Crime Prevention and Criminal Justice [E/2009/30], adopted **resolution 2009/26** without vote [agenda item 14 *(c)*].

Supporting national and international efforts for child justice reform, in particular through improved coordination in technical assistance

The Economic and Social Council,

Recalling the Universal Declaration of Human Rights, which states, in its article 25, that children are entitled to special care and assistance,

Recalling also the Convention on the Rights of the Child, in particular its article 37, in which States parties to the Convention agreed to ensure, inter alia, that the deprivation of liberty of persons below the age of eighteen years should be used only as a measure of last resort, and recalling also article 40 of the Convention,

Recalling further the numerous other United Nations standards and norms in the area of child justice, such as the United Nations Standard Minimum Rules for the Administration of Juvenile Justice (The Beijing Rules), the United Nations Rules for the Protection of Juveniles Deprived of their Liberty, the United Nations Guidelines for the Prevention of Juvenile Delinquency (The Riyadh Guidelines) and the Guidelines on Justice in Matters involving Child Victims and Witnesses of Crime,

Recalling General Assembly resolutions 62/158 of 18 December 2007 and 63/241 of 24 December 2008, Commission on Human Rights resolution 2004/43 of 19 April 2004 and Human Rights Council resolutions 7/29 of 28 March 2008 and 10/2 of 25 March 2009,

Noting the adoption by the Committee on the Rights of the Child of General Comment No. 10 (2007) on children's rights in juvenile justice,

Noting also the guidance note of the Secretary-General on the United Nations approach to justice for children, of September 2008, and the report of the independent expert for the United Nations study on violence against children, in particular the recommendations contained therein concerning children in care and justice systems,

Recalling its resolution 1997/30 of 21 July 1997, in which it welcomed the Guidelines for Action on Children in the Criminal Justice System, contained in the annex thereto, and invited the Secretary-General to consider establishing a coordination panel on technical advice and assistance in juvenile justice,

Recalling also its resolution 2007/23 of 26 July 2007 concerning child justice reform,

Welcoming the report of the Secretary-General on the support of national efforts for child justice reform, in particular through technical assistance and improved United Nations system-wide coordination,

Noting that, according to that report, some States have reported on the implementation of effective measures to reduce the use of pretrial detention and imprisonment for juveniles in conflict with the law, while many States still use deprivation of liberty as a rule rather than an exception,

Noting also the increased specialization of institutions and professionals and the provision of appropriate training and retraining in this area and the development of programmes for diversion, restorative justice and alternatives to imprisonment reported by Member States, and encouraging other States to adopt such programmes,

Acknowledging with satisfaction the work of the Interagency Panel on Juvenile Justice and its members, the Department of Peacekeeping Operations of the Secretariat, the Office of the United Nations High Commissioner for Human Rights, the United Nations Office on Drugs and Crime, the United Nations Children's Fund, the United Nations Development Programme, the United Nations Interregional Crime and Justice Research Institute, the Committee on the Rights of the Child and a number of non-governmental organizations, in particular the coordination of the provision of technical advice and assistance in the area of child justice and the active participation of civil society in that work,

Bearing in mind that the United Nations approach to justice for children contained in the guidance note of the Secretary-General of September 2008 aims at ensuring full application of United Nations standards and norms for all children who come into contact with justice and related systems as victims, witnesses or alleged offenders or in other circumstances where judicial intervention is needed,

1. *Urges* Member States to pay particular attention to or increase the attention paid to the issue of child justice and to take into consideration applicable international instruments and, as appropriate, applicable United Nations standards and norms for the treatment of children in conflict with the law, in particular juveniles deprived of their liberty, and child victims and witnesses of crimes, taking into account also the age, gender, social circumstances and development needs of such children;

2. *Invites* Member States to adopt, where appropriate, comprehensive national action plans on crime prevention and child justice reform dealing, in particular, with preventing child involvement in crime, ensuring access to legal assistance, especially for those children with scarce resources, and reducing the use and the duration of juvenile detention, especially at the pretrial stages, including through the use of diversion, restorative justice and alternatives to detention, the reintegration of children in conflict with the law into their communities and child-sensitive procedures for all children in contact with the justice system;

3. *Invites* Member States and their relevant institutions to adopt, where appropriate, a comprehensive approach to child justice reform, including through policy reform, legal reform, the establishment of data collection and information management systems, the strengthening of institutional capacity, including with regard to social workers and providers of legal assistance, awareness-building and monitoring, and the establishment of child-sensitive procedures and institutions;

4. *Encourages* Member States, where appropriate, to conduct scientific research in relation to children in conflict with the law, in such areas as their social environment and other risk factors, and to take measures for their social rehabilitation and integration into society;

5. *Invites* Member States, as appropriate, to make use of the technical assistance tools developed by the Interagency Panel on Juvenile Justice and its members and to seek technical advice and assistance in the area of child justice from the members of the Panel in order to design, implement and monitor comprehensive child justice policies;

6. *Encourages* Member States and international funding agencies to provide adequate resources to the secretariat of the Panel and its members so that they may continue to provide enhanced technical assistance, upon request, to Member States, in particular those having expressed a need for technical assistance pursuant to Council resolution 2007/23;

7. *Invites* the members of the Panel to continue providing assistance to Member States, upon request and subject to the availability of resources, in the area of child justice, including by following up on the recommendations of the United Nations study on violence against children and by setting up national data collection and criminal justice information systems with regard to children in conflict with the law, using as a guide the *Manual for the Measurement of Juvenile Justice Indicators*;

8. *Encourages* the members of the Panel to further increase their cooperation, to share information and to pool their capacities and resources in order to increase the effectiveness of programme implementation, including through joint programming, when appropriate, and the development of common tools and awareness-raising;

9. *Requests* the Secretary-General to report to the Commission on Crime Prevention and Criminal Justice at its twentieth session on the implementation of the present resolution.

Women in detention and in custodial and non-custodial settings

The Commission on Crime Prevention and Criminal Justice, in an April resolution [E/2009/30 (res. 18/1)] on supplementary rules specific to the treatment of women in detention and in custodial and non-custodial settings, took note of the expert round-table meeting on the development of rules for the treatment of women prisoners and non-custodial measures for women offenders (Bangkok, 2–6 February); requested UNODC to provide technical assistance and advisory services to Member States to develop legislation, procedures, policies and practices for women in prison; and requested the UNODC Executive Director to convene in 2009 an open-ended intergovernmental expert group meeting to develop supplementary rules specific to the treatment of women in detention and in custodial and non-custodial settings.

Access to legal aid, particularly in Africa

In response to Economic and Social Council resolution 2007/24 [YUN 2007, p. 1145], the Secretary-General submitted a February report [E/CN.15/2009/8] to the Commission on Crime Prevention and Criminal Justice on international cooperation for the improvement of access to legal aid in criminal justice systems, particularly in Africa. The report provided information received from 14 Member States on efforts to implement the resolution and UNODC activities in that area.

To promote access to legal aid in criminal justice systems, particularly in Africa, UNODC initiated several programmes and activities to provide technical assistance to Member States; pursued partnerships with UN agencies and NGOs in developing tools and guidelines and for delivering technical assistance programmes; and increased its engagement in a number of post-conflict countries in the area of criminal justice reform by contributing to the development of rule-of-law assistance programmes. In that regard, the Office worked with the Department of Peacekeeping Operations in Afghanistan, Burundi, the Democratic Republic of the Congo, Guinea-Bissau, Haiti, Iraq, Sierra Leone, Somalia, the Sudan and Timor-Leste in building up their criminal justice institutions, focusing on juvenile justice reform, penitentiary reform, alternatives to imprisonment and police oversight and integrity. UNODC also developed regional programmes highlighting penal reform and access to legal aid through a new generation of technical cooperation programmes in response to the needs and requests of Member States.

The report concluded that the theme of legal aid was a key element of the criminal justice system and access to aid needed to be addressed from the point of view of the suspect and defendant, as well as from that of the victim. The Secretary-General recommended that the Commission invite Member States to strengthen and improve access to justice for their citizens, particularly the most vulnerable ones; encourage Member States to involve civil society organizations in implementing criminal justice reform; invite Member States to provide extrabudgetary resources to support the development and implementation of UNODC technical cooperation activities; and invite Member States to provide funding for the organization of the open-ended intergovernmental meeting of experts to study ways and means of strengthening access to legal aid in the criminal justice system, as well as the possibility of developing an instrument for improving access to legal aid.

Thematic discussion. At its eighteenth session [E/2009/30], the Commission on Crime Prevention and Criminal Justice held a thematic discussion on penal reform and the reduction of prison overcrowding, including the provision of legal aid in criminal justice systems. The Commission had before it a secretariat note [E/CN.15/2009/15] as a guide on the topic. The discussion, which took place on 20 and 21 April, was guided by six subthemes: respect for human rights in penal establishments; pretrial detention and the principle of a fair trial; case management in penal establishments; reducing prison overcrowding; restorative justice; and alternatives to imprisonment, and social reintegration.

Other crime prevention and criminal justice issues

Third World Summit of Attorneys General, Prosecutors General and Chief Prosecutors

On 7 April [E/CN.15/2009/18], Romania transmitted to UNODC the outcome of the Third World Summit of Attorneys General, Prosecutors General and Chief Prosecutors (Bucharest, Romania, 24–25 March) and requested that it be made available as an official document at the eighteenth (2009) session of the Commission on Crime Prevention and Criminal Justice.

In April [E/2009/30 (res.18/4)], the Commission took note of the conclusions and recommendations of the Third Word Summit and welcomed the decision of Romania to establish in Bucharest a secretariat to service the World Summit of Attorneys General, Prosecutors General and Chief Prosecutors. It also requested UNODC to assist the Government of Chile—as host to the Fourth World Summit (2011)—in the preparations for the Summit and invited Member States and other donors to provide extrabudgetary contributions for those purposes.

Trafficking in forest products

In response to Economic and Social Council resolution 2008/25 [YUN 2008, p. 1165], the UNODC Executive Director submitted to the Commission on Crime Prevention and Criminal Justice a February report [E/CN.15/2009/7] on international cooperation in preventing and combating illicit international trafficking in forest products, including timber, wildlife and other forest biological resources, which provided an overview and brief analysis of replies received from 18 Member States on their efforts to implement that resolution and to combat illicit trafficking in forest products, harvested in contravention of national laws. It also reviewed initiatives undertaken by international organizations, partnerships and law enforcement mechanisms, and the mandates and roles of the main relevant organizations. Reporting Member States highlighted different aspects of the problem and stressed the importance of streamlining efforts to better target criminal activities. The need to focus attention on more concerted counteraction was also reflected in the conclusions of the 2008 meeting of the Open-ended Expert Group on International Cooperation in Preventing and Combating Illicit International Trafficking in Forest Products, including Timber, Wildlife and Other Forest Biological Resources [YUN 2008, p. 1165].

The report recommended that the Commission provide more in-depth guidance on ways and means to further specify the bridging role that UNODC could play between the security and developmental aspects of illicit international trafficking in forest products and environmental crime in general, as well as on how the Office could best make available its expertise on identifying criminal justice needs and providing legal advisory and technical assistance services.

Civilian private security services

The Commission on Crime Prevention and Criminal Justice, in a resolution on civilian private security services: their role, oversight and contribution to crime prevention and community safety [E/2009/30 (res. 18/2)], decided to establish an ad hoc open-ended intergovernmental expert group to study the role of civilian private security services and their contribution to crime prevention and community safety, and to consider issues relating to their oversight by competent State authorities. It also requested UNODC to report on implementation of the resolution at the Commission's twentieth (2011) session.

Human resources development

In response to General Assembly resolution 62/207 [YUN 2007, p. 1148], the Secretary-General submitted an August report [A/64/329] on human resources development, which provided an overview of human resources development strategies, including progress and challenges in their implementation and lessons learned. The report drew examples from countries with and without comprehensive national human resources development strategies and highlighted the implications of adopted human resources development strategies for the economic and social development of those countries. The report urged countries to adopt such strategies as a means to achieve the MDGs and to promote economic and social development. It focused on the role of the international community, the UN system and other entities, including the private sector, in promoting human resources development. The report also described the critical role of human resources development in mitigating the worst effects of the global economic crisis and building a foundation for sustainable recovery. Recommendations included: integrating human resources development into national development frameworks to ensure that human resources development implications were taken into account by all national development stakeholders; continually revising human resources development strategies and adjusting them to national development objectives to ensure a strong link between education, training and employment; promoting multidepartmental approaches and mechanisms to allow Governments to identify human resources needs in the medium and long term for various sectors of the economy and translate those needs into national human resources development policy targets and related funding and investment allocations; and establishing tripartite systems of employers, unions and Governments to facilitate the integration of economic, labour market and human resources policies and objectives.

GENERAL ASSEMBLY ACTION

On 21 December [meeting 66], the General Assembly, on the recommendation of the Second Committee [A/64/424/Add.3], adopted **resolution 64/218** without vote [agenda item 57 *(c)*].

Human resources development

The General Assembly,

Recalling its resolutions 52/196 of 18 December 1997, 54/211 of 22 December 1999, 56/189 of 21 December 2001, 58/207 of 23 December 2003, 60/211 of 22 December 2005 and 62/207 of 19 December 2007,

Stressing that human resources development is key to the efforts to achieve the internationally agreed development goals, including the Millennium Development Goals, and to expand opportunities for people, in particular for the most vulnerable groups of the population,

Stressing also that health and education are at the core of human resources development,

Welcoming the considerable efforts made over the years, yet recognizing that many countries continue to face formidable challenges in developing a sufficient pool of human resources capable of meeting national economic and social needs and that the formulation and implementation of effective human resources strategies often require resources and capacities not always available in developing countries,

Recognizing that the adverse impacts of the global financial and economic crisis will further diminish the ability of many countries, especially developing countries, to cope with and address human resources development challenges and to formulate and implement effective strategies for poverty eradication and sustainable development,

Stressing that human resources development is even more critical in the current global financial and economic crisis in order to mitigate the worst effects of the crisis and set the basis for future and sustainable recovery,

Acknowledging the important nexus between international migration and development and the need to deal with the challenges and opportunities that migration presents to countries of origin, transition and destination, recognizing that migration brings benefits as well as challenges to the global community, and stressing that the brain drain continues to be a severe problem in many developing and transitioning countries, undermining efforts in the area of human resources development,

Reaffirming that gender equality is of fundamental importance for achieving sustained economic growth, poverty eradication and sustainable development, in accordance with the relevant General Assembly resolutions and United Nations conferences, and that investing in the development of women and girls has a multiplier effect, in particular on productivity, efficiency and sustained economic growth, in all sectors of the economy, especially in key areas such as agriculture, industry and services,

Recognizing that education is the key to promoting the development of human potential, equality and understanding among peoples, as well as to sustaining economic growth and eradicating poverty, and recognizing also that, to achieve those ends, it is essential that quality education be available to all, including indigenous peoples, girls and women, rural inhabitants and persons with disabilities,

Stressing that Governments have the primary responsibility for defining and implementing appropriate policies for human resources development and the need for greater support from the international community for the national efforts of developing countries,

1. *Takes note* of the report of the Secretary-General;

2. *Stresses* the need for Member States to emphasize and integrate human resources development into national development strategies, including national development policies and strategies to eradicate poverty and achieve the Millennium Development Goals, in order to ensure that human resources development implications are taken into account by all national development stakeholders;

3. *Encourages* Member States to adopt and implement comprehensive human resources development strategies premised on national development objectives that ensure a strong link between education, training and employment, help to maintain a productive and competitive workforce and are responsive to the needs of the economy;

4. *Stresses* that investment in human resources development should be an integral part of national development policies and strategies, and in this regard calls for the adoption of policies to facilitate investment focused on infrastructure and capacity development, including education, health and science and technology, including information and communications technology;

5. *Encourages* Member States to continue to strengthen social protection systems and to adopt policies that strengthen existing safety nets, protect vulnerable groups and boost domestic consumption and production especially to cushion the effect of the crisis and prevent people from falling into poverty, acknowledges in this regard that many developing countries lack the necessary financial resources and capacity to implement such countercyclical measures, and recognizes the need for continued mobilization of additional domestic and international resources, as appropriate;

6. *Emphasizes* the need for Member States to adopt cross-sectoral approaches and mechanisms to identify human resources development needs in the medium and long term for all sectors of the economy and to formulate and implement policies and programmes to address those needs;

7. *Calls upon* the international community to assist developing countries in the implementation of national human resources development strategies, and encourages the international community to provide financial resources, capacity-building, technical assistance and transfer of technology, as appropriate and on mutually agreed terms;

8. *Calls upon* the international community, including the entities of the United Nations system, to support the efforts of developing countries to address the adverse effects of HIV/AIDS, malaria, tuberculosis and other infectious diseases on their human resources, in particular in Africa;

9. *Stresses* that sustainable development is dependent, inter alia, on healthy human resources, calls upon Member States to continue their efforts to strengthen national health systems, urges the further strengthening of international cooperation in the area of health, inter alia, through the exchange of best practices in the areas of health system strengthening, access to medicines, training of health personnel, transfer of technology and production of affordable, safe, effective and good-quality medicine, and in this regard stresses that international cooperation and assistance, in particular external funding, need to become more predictable and to be better aligned with national priorities and channelled to recipient countries in ways that strengthen national health systems;

10. *Encourages* efforts by Member States and the international community to promote a balanced, coherent and comprehensive approach to international migration and development, in particular by building partnerships and ensuring coordinated action to develop capacities, including for the management of migration, and in this regard reiterates the need to consider how the migration of highly skilled persons and those with advanced education affects the development efforts of developing countries;

11. *Calls for* steps to integrate gender perspectives into human resources development, including through policies, strategies and targeted actions aimed at promoting women's capacities and access to productive activities, and in this regard emphasizes the need to ensure the full participation of women in the formulation and implementation of such policies, strategies and actions;

12. *Stresses* the important contributions of the public and private sectors, respectively, in meeting national training and education needs to support the efficient functioning of enterprises and matching the needs of a rapidly changing economy, and encourages the integration of those contributions, including through the greater use of public-private partnerships and incentives;

13. *Calls for* actions at the national, regional and international levels that will give high priority to improving and expanding literacy, as well as science proficiency, including by providing tertiary, technical-vocational and adult education, and stresses the need to ensure that, by 2015, children everywhere, boys and girls alike, will be able to complete a full course of primary schooling and will have equal access to all levels of education;

14. *Requests* the Secretary-General to submit to the General Assembly at its sixty-sixth session a report that reviews lessons learned from the global financial and economic crisis on the requirements for human resources development to help countries to prevent and overcome the negative effects of crises and progress towards a more sustainable path of development;

15. *Decides* to include in the provisional agenda of its sixty-sixth session, under the item entitled "Eradication of poverty and other development issues", the sub-item entitled "Human resources development".

UN research and training institutes

UN Institute for Training and Research

In response to General Assembly resolution 62/210 [YUN 2007, p. 1150], the Secretary-General submitted an April report [E/2009/57] to the Economic and Social Council on the United Nations Institute for Training and Research (UNITAR), which had undertaken a major strategic reform over the preceding two years and was excelling in programmatic achievement. The reform was pinned on four priorities: strengthening institutional capacity for training and research; enhancing human capital; building and strengthening strategic partnerships; and rationalizing the organizational structure. He summarized areas of achievement in the Institute's efforts to: deliver integrated approaches to learning; provide a privileged platform for strategic policy thinking; strengthen its capacity-development activities and approaches through innovative training methodologies; establish in-roads in the area of global governance training and support; and ensure the gradual introduction of results-based management tools in all of its areas of activity. From a financial perspective, UNITAR had doubled its income over five years. The revised budget for 2008–2009 was 57 per cent higher than the actual expenditures of the prior period and 95 per cent of the 2008–2009 budget was secured through special purpose grants. Globally, the Institute's ability to deliver on its mandate was positive, with the exception of core diplomatic training.

ECONOMIC AND SOCIAL COUNCIL ACTION

On 30 July [meeting 44], the Economic and Social Council adopted **resolution 2009/27** [draft: E/2009/L.37, as orally revised] without vote [agenda item 15].

United Nations Institute for Training and Research

The Economic and Social Council,

Recalling its resolution 2008/35 of 25 July 2008,

Reiterating that training and capacity-development activities should be accorded a more visible and larger role in support of the management of international affairs and in the execution of the economic and social development programmes of the United Nations system,

Taking note of the report of the Secretary-General,

Acknowledging the progress made by the United Nations Institute for Training and Research through the implementation of its strategic reforms and the achievements in strengthening institutional capacity for training and research, enhancing human capital, building strategic partnerships and rationalizing its organizational structure,

Acknowledging also the programmatic achievements and the leadership role that the Institute is playing in the area of training in such diverse fields as the environment, local development and international migration and development and in the area of research in such fields as knowledge systems,

Encouraged by the role of the Institute as a convener of high-level policy discussions and by the recent partnership efforts with the United Nations System Staff College and the United Nations Office at Geneva,

Noting the solid overall financial situation of the Institute and the budget increase that was approved by the Board of Trustees of the Institute in January 2009, and expressing its appreciation to the Governments, foundations, academic institutions and private institutions that have made or pledged financial or other contributions to the Institute,

1. *Notes* as areas for continued progress by the United Nations Institute for Training and Research the establishment of results-based management across the work of the Institute, the establishment of quality standards and certification and the expanded use of technology-enhanced learning tools;

2. *Takes note* of the recommendation of the Secretary-General, contained in paragraph 67 of his report, concerning the important role that the Institute can play in laying the groundwork for more efficient training and research service provision within the United Nations system;

3. *Requests* the Secretary-General to report to the Economic and Social Council at its substantive session of 2011 on the implementation of the present resolution.

UNITAR financing

In response to the Secretary-General's 2008 report on financing of the core diplomatic training activities of UNITAR [YUN 2008, p. 1246], in a March 2009 report [A/63/744], the Advisory Committee on Administrative and Budgetary Questions (ACABQ) recommended approval, on an exceptional basis for the 2010–2011 biennium, of an annual $600,000 subvention, or a total of $1.2 million for the biennium, on the understanding that the Institute would intensify its efforts to raise funds for the programme and undertake a prioritization exercise. It recommended against the Secretary-General's proposal to amend the UNITAR statute to include a subvention from the regular budget. The Committee also requested UNITAR to report in the Institute's 2012–2013 proposed programme budget on results achieved with regard to fund-raising for core diplomatic training activities, the prioritization exercise and possible cost-sharing arrangements for training services provided to UN agencies, funds and programmes.

On 7 April, the General Assembly decided to defer consideration of the ACABQ report until the first part of its resumed sixty-fourth (2010) session (**decision 63/550 B**).

United Nations University

The Council of the United Nations University (UNU), at its fifty-fifth session (Bonn, Germany, 1–5 December 2008) [E/2009/84], considered the UNU Rector's annual "State of the University" report; adopted the draft UNU Strategic Plan: 2009–2012; adopted a proposal to begin to award accredited graduate degrees and to establish a quality assurance and accreditation mechanism; authorized the establishment of a review and evaluation panel to assess UNU activity over the previous three decades; adopted the draft statute for establishment of the UNU Institute for Sustainability and Peace in Tokyo; and deliberated on a range of issues relating to the financial and administrative management of the University in the 2008–2009 biennium.

During 2008, UNU carried out research projects and activities in the areas of: sustainable development; environmental resources management; environmental governance; water resources; environmental change and human vulnerabilities; human health; information technology; peace and security; regional integration and governance; and justice and accountability. UNU's training and capacity development efforts focused on building individual, group and institutional capabilities for self-sustained learning, for the generation of new knowledge and technology, for the accumulation of knowledge, and for the implementation of development activities. In 2008, UNU held 94 specialized training courses, organized 14 online learning courses, awarded 237 fellowships and offered 125 internship opportunities. It also organized or co-organized more than 400 public events and conducted public outreach activities, including 11 sessions of the UNU Global Seminar series, which were held worldwide and were attended by almost 600 participants.

On 31 July, the Economic and Social Council took note of the report of the UNU Council on the work of the University (**decision 2009/266**).

Amendment to UNU Charter

In a 16 November letter [A/64/234] to the General Assembly, the Secretary-General requested the Assembly to consider an amendment to the UNU Charter in order for the University to grant advanced academic degrees, as approved by the UNU Council at its fifty-fifth session in December 2008 (see above).

On 21 December 2009, the Assembly approved amendments to the UNU Charter by resolution 64/255.

GENERAL ASSEMBLY ACTION

On 21 December [meeting 66], the General Assembly, on the recommendation of the Second Committee [A/64/430], adopted **resolution 64/225** without vote [agenda item 170].

**Amendments to the Charter of
the United Nations University**

The General Assembly,

Recalling its resolutions 2951(XXVII) of 11 December 1972, by which it decided to establish the United Nations University, and 3081(XXVIII) of 6 December 1973, by which it adopted the Charter of the United Nations University, and taking note of the resolutions adopted since then on the progress of the University,

Taking note of the decision on the United Nations University adopted by the Executive Board of the United Nations Educational, Scientific and Cultural Organization at its one hundred and eighty-second session, held in Paris in September 2009,

Taking note also of the proposal adopted by the Council of the United Nations University at its fifty-fifth session, in December 2008, for the United Nations University to build upon its existing joint graduate programmes and to develop and implement its own postgraduate degree programmes as a part of the United Nations University strategic plan 2009–2012,

Taking note further of the proposal of the Secretary-General to amend the Charter of the United Nations University in accordance with article XII thereof, made after consultation with the United Nations Educational, Scientific and Cultural Organization and the Council of the United Nations University,

1. *Approves* the following amendments to the Charter of the United Nations University:

(a) A new paragraph 8 shall be added to article I, to read as follows:

"8. The University shall grant and confer master's degrees and doctorates, diplomas, certificates and other academic distinctions under conditions laid down for that purpose in the statutes by the Council";

(b) A new paragraph 2 bis shall be added to article IX, to read as follows:

"2 bis. The costs of the postgraduate degree programmes of the University as referred to in article I,
paragraph 8, above may also be met from tuition fees
and related charges";

2. *Invites* the Council of the United Nations University to adopt such statutes as may be necessary to implement
these amendments.

University for Peace

In response to General Assembly resolution
61/108 [YUN 2006, p. 1325], the Secretary-General
submitted an August report [A/64/281] on the University for Peace, which summarized the activities
and development of the Costa Rica-based University during the preceding three years and described
the challenges it faced as a result of its rapid growth
and lack of reliable funding. The report covered five
major areas: the University for Peace 2007–2009;
accreditation and external evaluation; future development strategy (2009–2010); practical challenges;
and the resource base. Substantial progress had been
made towards building high-quality programmes
of education and training, developing relationships
with other institutions to reach as many interested
students as possible, public relations efforts, and the
University's determination to be self-sustaining on
the basis of its earned income. The report also described the specific needs of the institution, principally the expansion and modernization of campus
facilities, the regularization of the international staff
under the UN salary and retirement system and the
establishment of regular funding and an endowment to stabilize the institution. The report concluded that the University had made major progress
towards the two main objectives of its mandate from
the Assembly: to build a high-quality academic programme of education, training and research on critical issues of peace and security; and to extend the
programme into different regions of the world from
its headquarters in Costa Rica. The continued success of the University was dependent on the political
and financial support of Member States.

GENERAL ASSEMBLY ACTION

On 10 December [meeting 62], the General Assembly,
on the recommendation of the Fourth (Special Political and Decolonization) Committee [A/64/401],
adopted **resolution 64/83** without vote [agenda item 27].

University for Peace

The General Assembly,

Recalling its resolution 61/108 of 14 December 2006,
in which it recalled that, in its resolution 34/111 of 14 December 1979, it had approved the idea of establishing the
University for Peace as a specialized international centre
for higher education, research and the dissemination of

knowledge specifically aimed at training and education
for peace and its universal promotion within the United
Nations system, as well as all preceding resolutions on
this item,

Recalling also that, in its resolution 35/55 of 5 December
1980, it approved the establishment of the University for
Peace in conformity with the International Agreement for
the Establishment of the University for Peace, contained in
the annex to that resolution,

Noting that as the University approaches its thirtieth
anniversary year, it continues to experience extraordinary
growth and development in the exercise of the mandate
given to it by the General Assembly,

Noting with appreciation the vigorous actions taken by
the Secretary-General, in consultation with the Director-
General of the United Nations Educational, Scientific and
Cultural Organization and with the encouragement and
support of the Government of Costa Rica, to revitalize the
University,

Recognizing the extraordinary progress the University
has made in developing and carrying out programmes on
critical subjects related to peace and security and in expanding its educational, training and research programmes
to Africa, Asia and the Pacific, Central Asia and Latin
America and the Caribbean,

Noting that the University has become a recognized
leader in education, training and research on issues related
to peace and conflict and that it is focusing its efforts on
strengthening the three main components of its activities,
namely, face-to-face teaching and research, expanding its
presence and programmes in all regions of the world and
distance learning to reach students who cannot come to
its campus,

Noting also that the University places special emphasis
on the areas of conflict prevention, peacekeeping, peacebuilding and the peaceful settlement of disputes and that
it has launched programmes in the areas of democratic
consensus-building and training of academic experts in the
techniques of peaceful settlement of conflicts,

Noting further that in 1991 the Secretary-General, with
the assistance of the United Nations Development Programme, established the Trust Fund for Peace consisting of
voluntary contributions in order to provide the University
with the means necessary to extend its sphere of activity
to the whole world, taking full advantage of its potential
capacity for education, research and support of the United
Nations and to carry out its mandate of promoting peace
in the world,

Considering the importance of promoting education for
peace that fosters respect for the values inherent in peace
and universal co-existence among people, including respect
for the life, dignity and integrity of human beings, as well
as friendship and solidarity among peoples irrespective of
their nationality, race, sex, religion or culture,

1. *Welcomes* the report of the Secretary-General submitted pursuant to General Assembly resolution 61/108,
outlining the extraordinary progress made by the University for Peace in building exemplary programmes on critical
subjects related to peace and security;

2. *Requests* the Secretary-General, in view of the important mandate given to the University and its potential
role in developing new concepts and approaches to security

through education, training and research in order to respond effectively to emerging threats to peace, to consider ways to further strengthen cooperation between the United Nations and the University;

3. *Also requests* the Secretary-General to continue using the services of the University as part of his conflict resolution and peacebuilding efforts through the training of staff, especially those concerned with peacekeeping and peacebuilding, in order to strengthen their capacities in this area, and in the promotion of the Declaration and the Programme of Action on a Culture of Peace;

4. *Invites* the University to further strengthen and broaden the outreach of its programmes and activities for cooperation with and capacity-building for Member States in the areas of conflict prevention, conflict resolution and peacebuilding;

5. *Invites* Member States that have not already done so to accede to the International Agreement for the Establishment of the University for Peace, thereby demonstrating their support for an educational institution devoted to the promotion of a universal culture of peace;

6. *Requests* the Secretary-General to consider either reviving the existing Trust Fund for Peace or alternatively establishing a new trust fund for peace to facilitate receipt of voluntary contributions for the University;

7. *Encourages* Member States, intergovernmental bodies, non-governmental organizations and interested individuals to contribute to the programmes, the trust fund, when established for the University, or the core budget of the University to enable it to continue to perform its valuable work;

8. *Decides* to include in the provisional agenda of its sixty-seventh session the item entitled "University for Peace", and requests the Secretary-General to submit to the General Assembly at that session a report on the work of the University.

Staff College

In response to General Assembly resolution 60/214 [YUN 2005, p. 1527], the Secretary-General, in May [E/2009/77], transmitted to the Economic and Social Council the fourth report of the Director of the United Nations System Staff College, covering the period from 1 July 2007 to 30 April 2009. The report showed the progress made towards the College's main goal of becoming a centre of excellence for learning and training in the UN system by fostering the implementation of knowledge-sharing mechanisms and improving system-wide coherence.

From 2007 to 2008, there was a notable increase in the number of staff trained, with the figure doubling from 4,032 to 8,032. Learning and training activities were delivered in more than 50 countries, encompassing the entire management of the UN system. During the reporting period, the College introduced the online course "Welcome to the UN: a UN System Induction Course", which was being continually updated and developed and was aimed at supporting common staff orientation in the system. In March, the College de-

ployed an enhanced version of the course, which was offered to UN colleagues across the system in English, French and Spanish. Furthermore, in moving towards the concept of results-based management, a detailed programme strategy and priorities for 2009, together with a results-based budget, were presented for the first time to the Board of Governors in December 2008. As part of the College's overall strategy, more partnerships were initiated both inside and outside the system. The College joined with a number of UN organizations and departments, including UNITAR, the Development Operations Coordination Office, the United Nations Department of Safety and Security, the United Nations Evaluation Group and the United Nations Office of the Special Adviser on Gender Issues and the Advancement of Women, to find better ways of improving system-wide coherence. The College continued to strengthen its reputation as a centre of excellence by increasing academic partnerships through the signing of institutional agreements and the use of world-renowned academic experts to design and deliver its activities. The report also presented proposed changes to the statute of the College relating to the composition of the Board of Governors and the functions of the Expert Technical Review Panel, which were annexed to the report.

ECONOMIC AND SOCIAL COUNCIL ACTION

On 27 July [meeting 38], the Economic and Social Council adopted **resolution 2009/10** [draft: E/2009/L.27] without vote [agenda item 15].

United Nations System Staff College in Turin, Italy

The Economic and Social Council,

Recalling General Assembly resolutions 54/228 of 22 December 1999, 55/207 of 20 December 2000, 55/258 of 14 June 2001 and 55/278 of 12 July 2001,

Recalling also General Assembly resolution 60/214 of 22 December 2005, in which the Assembly decided that the biennial reports on the activities of the United Nations System Staff College would be submitted to the Economic and Social Council rather than to the Assembly,

Reaffirming the role of the Staff College as an institution for system-wide knowledge management, training and continuous learning for the staff of the United Nations system, in particular in the areas of economic and social development, peace and security, and internal management,

Having considered the note by the Secretary-General transmitting the biennial report of the Director of the Staff College on the work, activities and accomplishments of the College, pursuant to paragraph 8 of resolution 60/214,

1. *Takes note* of the note by the Secretary-General and the report of the Director of the United Nations System Staff College transmitted therewith;

2. *Approves* the proposed changes to the statute of the Staff College, as contained in the enclosure appended to annex I of the report, in particular paragraph 3 of article IV of

the proposed revised statute, and notes that those changes have no budgetary implications;

3.　*Welcomes* the progress made by the Staff College, in the light of the strategic reforms introduced by its Director and endorsed by its Board of Governors;

4.　*Acknowledges* the introduction of strategic reforms to the governance structure of the Staff College, as endorsed by its Board of Governors and by the United Nations System Chief Executives Board for Coordination.

International Year of Languages

In response to General Assembly resolution 61/266 [YUN 2007, p. 1515] on multilingualism, the Secretary-General, by a March note [A/63/752], transmitted the final report of the unesco Director-General on the impact of the activities carried out during the International Year of Languages (2008). The report provided comprehensive information on the activities developed for the International Year and completed the information provided by unesco in its 2008 interim report [YUN 2008, p. 1249].

The report concluded that the important mobilization raised by the International Year, with its restricted time frame and resources, proved that languages and multilingualism were vital items on the international agenda, at both the governmental and the non-governmental level. Civil society demon-strated unexpected vitality and responsiveness during the International Year and, in many cases, was able to act more quickly than institutions and Governments, with innovative views that revealed new transdisciplinary areas of action. The goals pursued by the different actors of the International Year were diverse and sometimes contradictory; thus, the shared interest for languages did not necessarily imply a shared vision. Accurate measurement of the sustainable effects of the International Year, notably for implementation of national language policies in all relevant domains (education, culture, media and administration) would require an in-depth assessment throughout 2009, 2010 and 2011. To that end, a series of monitoring tools should be created, based on consolidated methodologies. Fund-raising and research would be a key factor in that regard. The unesco Atlas of the World's Languages in Danger of Disappearing was a tool that would serve as a source of inspiration for the development of international monitoring instruments.

By **resolution 63/306** of 9 September (see p. 1468), the Assembly welcomed the activities of unesco, Member States, the UN system and all other participating bodies aimed at fostering respect for and the promotion and protection of all languages, in particular endangered ones, linguistic diversity and multilingualism.

Chapter X

Women

In 2009, United Nations efforts to advance the status of women worldwide continued to be guided by the Beijing Declaration and Platform for Action, adopted at the Fourth (1995) World Conference on Women, and the outcome of the General Assembly's twenty-third (2000) special session (Beijing+5), which reviewed progress in their implementation.

The Assembly, following a series of meetings among representatives of Member States and relevant UN bodies, adopted a September resolution in which it supported the consolidation of the Office of the Special Adviser on Gender Issues and Advancement of Women, the Division for the Advancement of Women, the United Nations Development Fund for Women (UNIFEM) and the International Research and Training Institute for the Advancement of Women (INSTRAW) into a composite entity, to be led by an Under-Secretary-General. The aim of the strengthened organizational architecture, which was part of the UN reform agenda, was to provide the UN system with a single driver and voice on gender equality.

The Commission on the Status of Women, at its March session, adopted conclusions on the equal sharing of responsibilities between women and men, which included caregiving in the context of HIV/AIDS, and a summary on gender perspectives on global public health. Both were transmitted to the Economic and Social Council for adoption and as input into its annual ministerial review. The Commission recommended to the Council for adoption draft resolutions on the future operation of INSTRAW; the situation of and assistance to Palestinian women; the future organization and methods of work of the Commission; and the Commission's Working Group on Communications on the Status of Women, all of which the Council adopted in July, along with a resolution on mainstreaming a gender perspective into all UN system policies and programmes. The Commission adopted and brought to the Council's attention resolutions on women, the girl child and HIV and AIDS, and on preparations for its 2010 session, during which there would be a review of the Fourth World Conference and Beijing+5.

The Assembly adopted resolutions on: eliminating violence against women; the Convention on the Elimination of All Forms of Discrimination against Women; violence against women migrant workers; improvement of the situation of women in rural areas; the girl child; and women in development. The Coun-

cil and the Assembly both decided that a meeting would be held in 2010 to commemorate the fifteenth anniversary of the adoption of the Beijing Declaration and Platform for Action.

UNIFEM continued its work on strengthening women's economic security and rights; ending violence against women; reducing the prevalence of HIV/AIDS among girls and women; and advancing gender justice in democratic governance, including in conflict-affected and post-conflict countries. In June, the UNIFEM strategic plan, 2008–2011, including its integrated financial resources framework, was extended to 2013.

Two resolutions adopted by the Security Council in September and October addressed issues of women, peace and security and focused on the impact of armed conflict on women and girls, including: the use of sexual violence; the needs of women and girls in post-conflict situations; and the underrepresentation of women in peace processes. In the September resolution, the Council requested the Secretary-General to appoint a Special Representative on sexual violence in conflict.

Follow-up to the Fourth World Conference on Women and Beijing+5

During 2009, the Commission on the Status of Women, the Economic and Social Council and the General Assembly considered follow-up to the 1995 Fourth World Conference on Women, particularly the implementation of the Beijing Declaration and Platform for Action [YUN 1995, p. 1170], and the political declaration and further actions and initiatives to implement both instruments adopted at the twenty-third (2000) special session of the Assembly (Beijing+5) by resolution S/23-2 [YUN 2000, p. 1084]. The Declaration had reaffirmed the commitment of Governments to the goals and objectives of the Fourth World Conference and to the implementation of the 12 critical areas of concern outlined in the Platform for Action: women and poverty; education and training of women; women and health; violence against women; women and armed conflict; women and the economy; women in power and decision-making; institutional mechanisms for the advancement of women; the human rights of women; women and the media; women and the environment; and the girl child. The issue of mainstreaming a gender perspective into UN policies and programmes continued to be addressed (see p. 1144).

Report of Secretary-General. In response to General Assembly resolution 63/159 [YUN 2008, p. 1251], the Secretary-General, in an August report [A/64/218], described measures taken and progress achieved in the follow-up to the implementation of the Beijing Declaration and Platform for Action and the outcome of the twenty-third special session of the Assembly. The report provided an overview of steps taken by intergovernmental bodies to promote gender perspectives in their work, including advances made during the sixty-third (2008) session of the Assembly and the 2008 substantive session of the Economic and Social Council and in the work of their subsidiary bodies, especially at the 2008 session of the Commission on the Status of Women. It also assessed, in response to Council resolution 2006/9 [YUN 2006, p. 1356], the impact of the Commission's input into discussions within the UN system.

The Secretary-General noted that the Assembly, the Council and their subsidiary bodies considered a number of issues during the year to strengthen the global policy framework on gender equality, but the issue most consistently addressed across agenda items was violence against women, including trafficking in women and girls. Other areas that received attention were decent work, and peace, security and humanitarian assistance. While many Assembly reports and resolutions expressed commitments to gender equality goals, fewer contained specific data and recommendations to guide and monitor implementation. Gender equality and the empowerment of women were also addressed at several high-level meetings and events, as well as in the work of Assembly subsidiary bodies, such as the Peacebuilding Commission and the Human Rights Council. An estimated 30 per cent of resolutions analysed in preparation for the report (as at mid-June 2009) included some references to gender-equality issues. As in previous years, outcomes of the Assembly's Second (Economic and Financial) and Third (Social, Humanitarian and Cultural) Committees and the plenary contained more information on gender perspectives than those of the other Assembly Committees.

At its 2008 high-level segment and annual ministerial review, the Economic and Social Council discussed several issues of relevance to the implementation of the Beijing Platform for Action. The Ministerial Declaration of the Council's high-level segment on "Implementing the internationally agreed goals and commitments in regard to sustainable development" [YUN 2008, p. 903] reaffirmed commit-

ments to promoting gender equality and the empowerment of women. Most of the Council's functional commissions, in addition to the Commission on the Status of Women, addressed gender perspectives in their deliberations and outcomes to some extent.

The Secretary-General concluded that there was a need to improve the mainstreaming of gender equality in policy development, programme planning and monitoring and reporting, including through improved use of sex-disaggregated data, gender-sensitive indicators and gender-responsive budgeting. He stated that concerns were raised about the limited progress made on Millennium Development Goal (MDG) 5 (improving maternal health) and observed that progress on promoting gender equality and empowering women depended on the extent to which the actions taken to achieve the other MDGs were designed to promote the equality of women and men. In 2010, several reviews and intergovernmental events would assess progress towards achieving the MDGs and provide opportunities to address implementation gaps and challenges regarding the Beijing Declaration and Platform for Action, the outcome of the twenty-third special session of the Assembly, and other initiatives on women (see below). The Secretary-General suggested that the Assembly might wish to encourage Member States, UN entities, international and regional organizations and other actors to use the opportunities provided by intergovernmental bodies in 2010 to accelerate progress towards gender equality and the empowerment of women.

Review of the Fourth World Conference and Beijing+5 (2010)

Commission action. On 13 March, the Commission on the Status of Women adopted a resolution [E/2009/27 (res. 53/1)] on preparations for its fifty-fourth (2010) session, in which it decided to review in 2010 the implementation of the Beijing Declaration and Platform for Action [YUN 1995, p. 1170] and the outcome of the twenty-third special session of the General Assembly, entitled "Women 2000: gender equality, development and peace for the twenty-first century" [YUN 2000, p. 1082]. It requested the Commission's Bureau to hold informal consultations with the Commission's member States and observer States on the modalities of the review in order to agree on its format and outcome. It also decided to commemorate the fifteenth anniversary of the adoption of the Beijing Declaration and Platform for Action during its fifty-fourth session in March 2010.

Commemoration of fifteenth anniversary. On 28 July, the Council recommended to the Assembly the adoption of a draft decision on holding a commemorative meeting during the 2010 session of the Commission on the Status of Women to mark the fifteenth anniversary of the adoption of the Beijing Declaration and Platform for Action (**decision 2009/233**). On 18 December, the Assembly took that action (**decision 64/530**).

NGO participation. On 28 July, the Council decided, on an exceptional basis, to invite the non-governmental organizations (NGOs) that were accredited either to the Fourth World Conference on Women or the twenty-third special session of the Assembly to attend the Commission's 2010 session (**decision 2009/234**). The Council urged relevant UN system bodies to assist NGOs, particularly those from developing and least developed countries and countries with economies in transition, which did not have the resources to participate.

High-level round table. In December, a discussion guide [E/CN.6/2010/3] was issued for the forthcoming high-level round table on "Implementation of the Beijing Declaration and Platform for Action and the outcome of the twenty-third special session of the Assembly and its contribution to shaping a gender perspective towards the full realization of the MDGs".

GENERAL ASSEMBLY ACTION

On 18 December [meeting 65], the General Assembly, on the recommendation of the Third Committee [A/64/433], adopted **resolution 64/141** without vote [agenda item 62 *(b)*].

Follow-up to the Fourth World Conference on Women and full implementation of the Beijing Declaration and Platform for Action and the outcome of the twenty-third special session of the General Assembly

The General Assembly,

Recalling its previous resolutions on the question, including resolution 63/159 of 18 December 2008,

Deeply convinced that the Beijing Declaration and Platform for Action and the outcome of the twenty-third special session of the General Assembly entitled "Women 2000: gender equality, development and peace for the twenty-first century" are important contributions to the achievement of gender equality and the empowerment of women, and must be translated into effective action by all States, the United Nations system and other organizations concerned,

Reaffirming the commitments to gender equality and the advancement of women made at the Millennium Summit, the 2005 World Summit and other major United Nations summits, conferences and special sessions, and reaffirming also that their full, effective and accelerated implementation is integral to achieving the internationally agreed development goals, including the Millennium Development Goals,

Welcoming progress made towards achieving gender equality, but stressing that challenges and obstacles remain in the implementation of the Beijing Declaration and Platform for Action and the outcome of the twenty-third special session,

Recognizing that the responsibility for the implementation of the Beijing Declaration and Platform for Action and the outcome of the twenty-third special session rests primarily at the national level and that strengthened efforts are necessary in this respect, and reiterating that enhanced international cooperation is essential for full, effective and accelerated implementation,

Noting that the Commission on the Status of Women will undertake, at its fifty-fourth session, a review of the implementation of the Beijing Declaration and Platform for Action and the outcome of the twenty-third special session, emphasizing the sharing of experiences and good practices, with a view to overcoming remaining obstacles and new challenges, including those related to the Millennium Development Goals,

Taking into consideration the theme of the annual ministerial review to be held by the Economic and Social Council in 2010, "Implementing the internationally agreed goals and commitments in regard to gender equality and empowerment of women",

Welcoming the work of the Commission on the Status of Women in reviewing the implementation of the Beijing Declaration and Platform for Action, and noting with appreciation all its agreed conclusions, including the latest, on the equal sharing of responsibilities between women and men, including caregiving in the context of HIV/AIDS, adopted by the Commission at its fifty-third session,

Reaffirming that gender mainstreaming is a globally accepted strategy for promoting the empowerment of women and achieving gender equality by transforming structures of inequality, and reaffirming also the commitment to actively promote the mainstreaming of a gender perspective in the design, implementation, monitoring and evaluation of policies and programmes in all political, economic and social spheres, as well as the commitment to strengthen the capabilities of the United Nations system in the area of gender equality,

Taking note with appreciation of the report of the Secretary-General on mainstreaming a gender perspective into all policies and programmes in the United Nations system, and stressing the importance of the continued integration of a gender perspective in the work and activities of the Human Rights Council,

Reaffirming the commitments in regard to gender equality and the empowerment of women in the Doha Declaration on Financing for Development: outcome document of the Follow-up International Conference on Financing for Development to Review the Implementation of the Monterrey Consensus,

Bearing in mind the challenges and obstacles to changing discriminatory attitudes and gender stereotypes, and stressing that challenges and obstacles remain in the implementation of international standards and norms to address the inequality between men and women,

Reaffirming the Declaration of Commitment on HIV/AIDS and the Political Declaration on HIV/AIDS adopted at the High-level Meeting on HIV/AIDS, held from 31 May to 2 June 2006, which, inter alia, acknowledged the feminization of the pandemic,

Expressing serious concern that the urgent goal of 50/50 gender balance in the United Nations system, especially at senior and policymaking levels, with full respect for the principle of equitable geographical distribution, in conformity with Article 101, paragraph 3, of the Charter of the United Nations, remains unmet, and that the representation of women in the United Nations system has remained almost static, with negligible improvement in some parts of the system, and in some cases has even decreased, as reflected in the report of the Secretary-General on the improvement of the status of women in the United Nations system,

Reaffirming the important role of women in the prevention and resolution of conflicts and in peacebuilding,

Recalling Security Council resolutions 1325(2000) of 31 October 2000 and 1820(2008) of 19 June 2008 on women and peace and security, and welcoming the adoption of Council resolution 1882(2009) of 4 August 2009 on children and armed conflict and Council resolutions 1888(2009) of 30 September 2009 and 1889(2009) of 5 October 2009 on women and peace and security,

Welcoming its resolution 63/311 of 14 September 2009, in particular the provisions on strengthening the institutional arrangements for support of gender equality and the empowerment of women, reaffirming its strong support expressed therein for the consolidation of the Office of the Special Adviser on Gender Issues and Advancement of Women, the Division for the Advancement of Women, the United Nations Development Fund for Women and the International Research and Training Institute for the Advancement of Women into a composite entity, taking into account the existing mandates, which would be led by an Under-Secretary-General, and looking forward to the full implementation of resolution 63/311,

1. *Takes note with appreciation* of the report of the Secretary-General on the measures taken and progress achieved in follow-up to the implementation of the Beijing Declaration and Platform for Action and the outcome of the twenty-third special session of the General Assembly;

2. *Reaffirms* the Beijing Declaration and Platform for Action adopted at the Fourth World Conference on Women, the outcome of the twenty-third special session of the General Assembly, and the declaration adopted on the occasion of the ten-year review and appraisal of the implementation of the Beijing Declaration and Platform for Action at the forty-ninth session of the Commission on the Status of Women, and also reaffirms its commitment to their full, effective and accelerated implementation;

3. *Also reaffirms* the primary and essential role of the General Assembly and the Economic and Social Council, as well as the catalytic role of the Commission on the Status of Women, in promoting gender equality and the empowerment of women based on the full implementation of the Beijing Declaration and Platform for Action and the outcome of the twenty-third special session, and in promoting and monitoring gender mainstreaming within the United Nations system;

4. *Recognizes* that the implementation of the Beijing Declaration and Platform for Action and the fulfilment of the obligations of States parties under the Convention on the Elimination of All Forms of Discrimination against Women are mutually reinforcing in respect of achieving gender equality and the empowerment of women, and in this regard welcomes the contributions of the Committee on the Elimination of Discrimination against Women to promoting the implementation of the Platform for Action and the outcome of the twenty-third special session, and invites States parties to the Convention to include information on measures taken to enhance implementation at the national level in their reports to the Committee under article 18 of the Convention;

5. *Calls upon* States parties to comply fully with their obligations under the Convention on the Elimination of All Forms of Discrimination against Women and the Optional Protocol thereto and to take into consideration the concluding observations as well as the general recommendations of the Committee, urges States parties to consider limiting the extent of any reservations that they lodge to the Convention, to formulate any reservations as precisely and narrowly as possible, and to regularly review such reservations with a view to withdrawing them so as to ensure that no reservation is incompatible with the object and purpose of the Convention, also urges all Member States that have not yet ratified or acceded to the Convention to consider doing so, and calls upon those Member States that have not yet done so to consider signing and ratifying or acceding to the Optional Protocol;

6. *Welcomes* the opportunities provided in intergovernmental bodies in 2010 to accelerate progress in the achievement of gender equality, the empowerment of women and gender balance, including the fifteen-year review of the implementation of the Beijing Declaration and Platform for Action and the review of the outcome of the twenty-third special session at the fifty-fourth session of the Commission on the Status of Women, the annual ministerial review to be held by the Economic and Social Council on the theme "Implementing the internationally agreed goals and commitments in regard to gender equality and empowerment of women", the high-level plenary meeting of the General Assembly on the Millennium Development Goals, and the tenth anniversary of the adoption of Security Council resolution 1325(2000);

7. *Encourages* Member States, United Nations entities, international and regional organizations and other relevant actors to fully utilize the opportunities provided in intergovernmental bodies in 2010, including intergovernmental consultations, with a view to ensuring prompt progress as set forth in resolution 63/311, including strengthening the institutional arrangements for the support of gender equality and the empowerment of women, so as to accelerate progress in the achievement of gender equality and the empowerment of women based on the full and effective implementation of the Beijing Declaration and Platform for Action and the outcome of the twenty-third special session;

8. *Underlines* the significance of the fifty-fourth session of the Commission on the Status of Women, at which the Commission will undertake the fifteen-year review of the implementation of the Beijing Declaration and Platform for Action and the review of the outcome of the twenty-third special session, emphasizing the sharing of experiences and good practices, with a view to overcoming remaining obstacles and new challenges, including those

related to the full realization of all Millennium Development Goals, including Goal 3;

9. *Encourages* all actors, inter alia, Governments, the United Nations system, other international organizations and civil society, to continue to support the work of the Commission on the Status of Women in fulfilling its central role in the follow-up to and review of the implementation of the Beijing Declaration and Platform for Action and the outcome of the twenty-third special session, and, as applicable, to carry out its recommendations, and welcomes in this regard the revised programme and methods of work of the Commission adopted at its fifty-third session, which continue to focus attention on the sharing of experiences, lessons learned and good practices in overcoming challenges to full implementation at the national and international levels as well as to the evaluation of progress in the implementation of priority themes;

10. *Encourages* participation at a high political level in the fifty-fourth session of the Commission on the Status of Women and the 2010 annual ministerial review of the Economic and Social Council;

11. *Invites* States and requests relevant bodies of the United Nations system to publicize the forthcoming sessions of the Commission on the Status of Women and the Economic and Social Council, including through consultation with civil society;

12. *Calls upon* Governments and the organs and relevant funds, programmes and specialized agencies of the United Nations system, within their respective mandates, and other international and regional organizations, including financial institutions, and all relevant actors of civil society, including non-governmental organizations, to intensify action to achieve the full and effective implementation of the Beijing Declaration and Platform for Action and the outcome of the twenty-third special session;

13. *Reaffirms* that States have an obligation to exercise due diligence to prevent violence against women and girls, provide protection to the victims and investigate, prosecute and punish the perpetrators of violence against women and girls, and that failure to do so violates and impairs or nullifies the enjoyment of their human rights and fundamental freedoms, calls upon Governments to elaborate and implement laws and strategies to eliminate violence against women and girls, encourages and supports men and boys in taking an active part in the prevention and elimination of all forms of violence, encourages increased understanding among men and boys of how violence harms girls, boys, women and men and undermines gender equality, encourages all actors to speak out against any violence against women, and in this regard welcomes the Secretary-General's campaign "UNiTE to End Violence against Women" and the United Nations Development Fund for Women social mobilization and advocacy platform "Say NO to violence against women";

14. *Reiterates its call* to the United Nations system, including the main organs, their main committees and subsidiary bodies, new functions such as the annual ministerial review and the Development Cooperation Forum of the Economic and Social Council, and the funds, programmes and specialized agencies, to increase efforts to fully mainstream a gender perspective into all issues under their consideration and within their mandates, as well as in all United Nations summits, conferences and special sessions and in their follow-up processes, including the fifteenth session of the Conference of the Parties to the United Nations Framework Convention on Climate Change, held in Copenhagen from 7 to 18 December 2009, and to give attention to gender equality and the empowerment of women in preparations for such events, and in this regard looks forward to efficient and effective support for these efforts by the consolidated gender entity upon its establishment;

15. *Requests* that the entities of the United Nations system systematically incorporate the outcomes of the Commission on the Status of Women into their work within their mandates, inter alia, to ensure effective support for the efforts of Member States towards the achievement of gender equality and the empowerment of women;

16. *Strongly encourages* Governments to continue to support the role and contribution of civil society, in particular non-governmental organizations and women's organizations, in the implementation of the Beijing Declaration and Platform for Action and the outcome of the twenty-third special session;

17. *Requests* that reports of the Secretary-General submitted to the General Assembly and the Economic and Social Council and their subsidiary bodies systematically address gender perspectives through qualitative gender analysis, sex- and age-disaggregated data and, where available, quantitative data, in particular through concrete conclusions and recommendations for further action on gender equality and the empowerment of women, in order to facilitate gender-sensitive policy development;

18. *Calls upon* all parts of the United Nations system to continue to play an active role in ensuring the full, effective and accelerated implementation of the Beijing Declaration and Platform for Action and the outcome of the twenty-third special session, through, inter alia, the maintenance of gender specialists in all entities of the United Nations system, as well as by ensuring that all personnel, especially in the field, receive training and appropriate follow-up, including tools, guidance and support, for accelerated gender mainstreaming, and reaffirms the need to strengthen the capabilities of the United Nations system in the area of gender;

19. *Requests* the Secretary-General to review and redouble his efforts to make progress towards achieving the goal of 50/50 gender balance at all levels in the Secretariat and throughout the United Nations system, with full respect for the principle of equitable geographical distribution, in conformity with Article 101, paragraph 3, of the Charter of the United Nations, considering, in particular, women from developing and least developed countries, from countries with economies in transition and from unrepresented or largely underrepresented Member States, and to ensure managerial and departmental accountability with respect to gender balance targets, and strongly encourages Member States to identify and regularly submit more women candidates for appointment to positions in the United Nations system, especially at more senior and policymaking levels, including in peacekeeping operations;

20. *Calls upon* the United Nations system to continue its efforts towards achieving the goal of gender balance, including with the active support of gender focal points, and requests the Secretary-General to provide an oral re-

port to the Commission on the Status of Women at its fifty-fourth session, to report to the General Assembly on a biennial basis, beginning at its sixty-fifth session, under the item entitled "Advancement of women", and to include in his report on human resources management information on the status of women in the United Nations system, including on progress made and obstacles encountered in achieving gender balance, recommendations for accelerating progress, and up-to-date statistics, including the number and percentage of women and their functions and nationalities throughout the United Nations system, and information on the responsibility and accountability of the Office of Human Resources Management of the Secretariat and the secretariat of the United Nations System Chief Executives Board for Coordination for promoting gender balance;

21. *Encourages* increased efforts by Governments and the United Nations system to enhance accountability for the implementation of commitments to gender equality and the empowerment of women at the international, regional and national levels, including by improved monitoring and reporting on progress in relation to policies, strategies, resource allocations and programmes, and by achieving gender balance;

22. *Reaffirms* that Governments bear the primary responsibility for the achievement of gender equality and the empowerment of women and that international cooperation has an essential role in assisting developing countries in progressing towards the full implementation of the Beijing Declaration and Platform for Action;

23. *Requests* the Secretary-General to continue to report annually to the General Assembly under the item entitled "Advancement of women", as well as to the Commission on the Status of Women and the Economic and Social Council, on the follow-up to and progress made in the implementation of the Beijing Declaration and Platform for Action and the outcome of the twenty-third special session, with an assessment of progress in gender mainstreaming, including information on key achievements, lessons learned and good practices, and recommendations on further measures to enhance implementation, taking into account the discussions and outcome of the fifty-fourth session of the Commission in respect of the fifteen-year review of the Beijing Declaration and Platform for Action and the review of the outcome of the twenty-third special session.

Critical areas of concern

Women and poverty

Women in development

World survey. In response to General Assembly resolution 59/248 [YUN 2004, p. 1166], the Secretary-General, in June, submitted the sixth *World Survey on the Role of Women in Development* [A/64/93], a report presented to the Assembly at five-year intervals. As decided by the Assembly in resolution 60/210 [YUN 2005, p. 1262], the theme of the *Survey* was "Women's control over economic resources and access to financial resources, including microfinance".

The *Survey* observed that for many developing countries, the ongoing global economic and financial crisis would exacerbate the hardships associated with the food and fuel crises of 2007–2008. The gender equality implications and social and economic costs of those crises were likely to jeopardize the achievement of internationally agreed development goals, including the MDGs. The *Survey* noted that gender equality perspectives had been largely ignored in macroeconomic analyses, and most equality-enhancing measures had been undertaken at the micro level. Many of those measures, such as the promotion of microfinance and cash transfers, had not addressed the underlying constraints on women's access to and control over economic and financial resources. There was growing evidence that women brought critical perspectives and skills to public life, which made policy and budgetary decision-making more responsive to the needs and priorities of all groups. Efforts were required to promote women's participation in economic decision-making bodies in all areas at the highest levels. Women's unequal access to and control over resources, and their continued responsibility for unpaid domestic and care work, curtailed their productivity and restricted their capacity to respond to new economic opportunities and participate fully in public life.

The *Survey* recommended that Member States should implement the commitments contained in the Beijing Platform for Action, the outcome of the twenty-third special session of the Assembly, and the MDGs. States parties to the Convention on the Elimination of All Forms of Discrimination against Women [YUN 1979, p. 895] should implement their obligations under the Convention. With regard to the macroeconomic environment, the *Survey* suggested strengthening efforts to implement gender mainstreaming in relation to economic and financial resources, including through gender analysis, gender-impact assessment and gender-responsive budgeting. Recommendations also included implementing gender-sensitive, employment-centred growth strategies, and strengthening the impact of development assistance that targeted gender equality and women's empowerment. On employment, the *Survey* recommended: the adoption and enforcement of the International Labour Organization's principles of decent work in both formal and informal sectors; the undertaking of a gender analysis of national labour laws; the adoption and/or review of gender-sensitive legislation and policies; the enforcement of minimum-wage regulations; promotion of the recognition that care work should be shared among the State, the private sector, civil society and households; and development of the provision of public care services for children, the elderly, the sick and the disabled. As to land, housing and other productive resources, the *Survey* recommended the adoption and/or review of legislation and policies to ensure women's equal access to and control over land, housing and other property. Further recommendations in that regard addressed measures to: strengthen investment to increase the productivity of women in rural areas and to provide water and sanitation to rural areas and urban slums; recognize and protect women's access to communal resources; ensure women's participation in decision-making on forest and water management; promote equal access for women and girls to information and communications technology; and ensure that women's critical role in food security was recognized. On financial services, the *Survey* recommended: promoting gender mainstreaming in all financial policies; strengthening the capacity of microcredit institutions to reach poor women; and ensuring that the mandates of financial providers included a commitment to gender equality. With regard to social protection, the *Survey* recommended improved gender-responsive social protection schemes and increases in the share of public expenditure allocated to social security to address vulnerabilities related to childhood, old age, ill health, disability, unemployment and poverty, taking into account the needs of women related to the unequal sharing of unpaid work. For each of the issues covered, the *Survey* recommended improving the collection and use of data, statistics and research on women's needs.

In an earlier note [E/CN.6/2009/14], the Secretary-General transmitted to the Commission on the Status of Women information regarding the preparation of the 2009 *Survey*.

In resolution 64/217 (see below), the Assembly took action on the *Survey*.

Integrating a gender perspective into national development strategies

In response to Assembly resolution 62/206 [YUN 2007, p. 1178], the Secretary-General submitted a July report [A/64/162 & Corr.1] on progress in integrating the specific priorities and needs of women in development, including in the formulation of national development strategies. Contributions from 34 Member States and a number of UN entities were used as a basis for the report.

The Secretary-General concluded that while progress had been made on integrating women in development in some areas, such as the targets for MDG 3 on education, employment and political participation, the gains were slow and uneven across regions, and the priorities and needs of women were not systematically incorporated into national development policies and strategies. The food crisis posed new challenges for women in development in many parts of the world and the financial and economic crisis was expected

to have disproportionate impacts on women, particularly with regard to employment. Despite initiatives to integrate gender perspectives into employment, entrepreneurship and social protection as part of national development strategies, gender inequalities persisted. Strengthened efforts to fully implement gender mainstreaming and increase resource allocation, including through gender-responsive budgeting, were needed in all areas. It was also necessary for responses to the financial and economic crisis, including social protection measures and employment creation, to be gender responsive to ensure that gains made in the promotion of gender equality and the empowerment of women were not reversed. Adequate levels of national resource allocations and official development assistance for gender equality and women's empowerment, including in productive sectors, should be maintained throughout the crisis and its aftermath.

In addition to recommending that the share of development assistance targeting gender equality and women's empowerment be increased, the Secretary-General suggested that a gender perspective be integrated into the design, implementation, monitoring and reporting of all national development policies, strategies and plans. Further recommendations included: the incorporation of gender perspectives into local, national, regional and international responses to the financial and economic crisis; the development of methodologies and tools for systematic gender-responsive budgeting across all sectors; the adoption, implementation and evaluation of gender-sensitive legislation and policies that promoted balance between paid work and family responsibilities; the development and implementation of programmes aimed at promoting women's entrepreneurship; and the establishment and funding of gender-sensitive labour market policies. The Secretary-General further recommended strengthening the capacity of national statistical offices in order to undertake the collection of reliable, comparable and gender-sensitive statistics to identify the needs and priorities of women and girls in all areas of development.

Communication. In a 2 February letter to the Secretary-General [A/63/704], Cuba, as Chair of the Coordinating Bureau of the Non-Aligned Movement (NAM), transmitted the text of the Guatemala Declaration and Programme of Action, adopted by the Second Ministerial Meeting of NAM on the Advancement of Women Towards the Achievement of the MDGs (Guatemala City, 21–24 January).

GENERAL ASSEMBLY ACTION

On 21 December [meeting 66], the General Assembly, on the recommendation of the Second Committee [A/64/424/Add.2], adopted **resolution 64/217** without vote [agenda item 57 *(b)*].

Women in development

The General Assembly,

Recalling its resolutions 52/195 of 18 December 1997, 54/210 of 22 December 1999, 56/188 of 21 December 2001, 58/206 of 23 December 2003, 59/248 of 22 December 2004, 60/210 of 22 December 2005 and 62/206 of 19 December 2007 and all its other resolutions on the integration of women in development, and the relevant resolutions and agreed conclusions adopted by the Commission on the Status of Women, including the Declaration adopted at its forty-ninth session,

Reaffirming the Beijing Declaration and Platform for Action and the outcome of the twenty-third special session of the General Assembly, entitled "Women 2000: gender equality, development and peace for the twenty-first century",

Reaffirming also the commitments to gender equality and the advancement of women made at the Millennium Summit, the 2005 World Summit and other major United Nations summits, conferences and special sessions, and reaffirming further that their full, effective and accelerated implementation are integral to achieving the internationally agreed development goals, including the Millennium Development Goals,

Reaffirming further the United Nations Millennium Declaration, which affirms that the equal rights and opportunities of women and men must be assured, and calls for, inter alia, the promotion of gender equality and the empowerment of women as being effective in and essential to eradicating poverty and hunger, combating diseases and stimulating development that is truly sustainable,

Recalling the outcomes of the International Conference on Financing for Development and the World Summit on Sustainable Development, the Doha Declaration on Financing for Development and the Outcome of the Conference on the World Financial and Economic Crisis and Its Impact on Development,

Taking note with appreciation of the discussion on women in development in the Commission on the Status of Women at its fiftieth session, and recalling its agreed conclusions on "Enhanced participation of women in development: an enabling environment for achieving gender equality and the advancement of women, taking into account, inter alia, the fields of education, health and work",

Recognizing that access to basic affordable health care, preventive health information and the highest standard of health, including in the areas of sexual and reproductive health, is critical to women's economic advancement, that lack of economic empowerment and independence increases women's vulnerability to a range of negative consequences, including the risk of contracting HIV/AIDS, and that the neglect of the full enjoyment of human rights by women severely limits their opportunities in public and private life, including the opportunity for education and economic and political empowerment,

Reaffirming that gender equality is of fundamental importance for achieving sustained and inclusive economic growth, poverty eradication and sustainable development, in accordance with the relevant General Assembly resolutions and United Nations conferences, and that investing in the development of women and girls has a multiplier effect,

in particular on productivity, efficiency and sustained and inclusive economic growth, in all sectors of the economy, especially in key areas such as agriculture, industry and services,

Reaffirming also the significant contribution that women make to the economy, that women are key contributors to the economy and to combating poverty and inequalities through both remunerated and unremunerated work at home, in the community and in the workplace and that the empowerment of women is a critical factor in the eradication of poverty,

Recognizing that the difficult socio-economic conditions that exist in many developing countries, in particular the least developed countries, have contributed to the feminization of poverty,

Expressing deep concern over the disproportionate negative impact on women of the multiple interrelated and mutually exacerbating current global crises, in particular the world financial and economic crisis, the volatile energy prices, the food crisis and the challenges posed by climate change,

Noting that gender biases in labour markets and women's lack of control over their own labour and earned income are also major factors in women's vulnerability to poverty and, together with women's disproportionate responsibilities for domestic work, result in a lack of economic autonomy and influence in economic decision-making within households and in society at all levels,

Recognizing that population and development issues, education and training, health, nutrition, the environment, water supply, sanitation, housing, communications, science and technology and decent employment opportunities are important elements for effective poverty eradication and the advancement and empowerment of women,

Welcoming its resolution 63/311 of 14 September 2009, in particular the provisions on strengthening the institutional arrangements for support of gender equality and the empowerment of women, reaffirming its strong support expressed therein for the consolidation of the Office of the Special Adviser on Gender Issues and Advancement of Women, the Division for the Advancement of Women, the United Nations Development Fund for Women and the International Research and Training Institute for the Advancement of Women into a composite entity, taking into account the existing mandates, to be led by an Under-Secretary-General, and looking forward to the full implementation of resolution 63/311,

Recognizing, in this context, the importance of respect for all human rights, including the right to development, and of a national and international environment that promotes, inter alia, justice, gender equality, equity, civil and political participation and civil, political, economic, social and cultural rights and fundamental freedoms for the advancement and empowerment of women,

Reaffirming the need to eliminate gender disparities in primary and secondary education by the earliest possible date and at all levels by 2015, and reaffirming that equal access to education and training at all levels, in particular in business, trade, administration, information and communications technology and other new technologies, and fulfilment of the need to eliminate gender inequalities at all levels, are essential for gender equality, the empowerment of women and poverty eradication and to allow women's full and equal contribution to, and equal opportunity to benefit from, development,

Recognizing that poverty eradication and the achievement and preservation of peace are mutually reinforcing, and recognizing also that peace is inextricably linked to equality between women and men and to development,

Aware that, while globalization and liberalization processes have created employment opportunities for women in many countries, they have also made some women, especially in developing countries and in particular in the least developed countries, more vulnerable to problems caused by increased economic volatility, including in the agricultural sector, and that special support, particularly for women who are small-scale farmers, and empowerment are necessary to enable them to take advantage of the opportunities arising from agricultural market liberalization,

Recognizing that enhanced trade opportunities for developing countries, including through trade liberalization, will improve the economic condition of their societies, including women, which is of particular importance in rural communities,

Expressing its concern that, while women represent an important and growing proportion of business owners, their contribution to economic and social development is constrained by, inter alia, the denial and lack of equal rights and their lack of access to legal aid, education, training, information, support services and credit facilities including salaries, and control over land, capital, technology and other areas of production,

Expressing its concern also regarding the underrepresentation of women in political and economic decision-making, and stressing the importance of mainstreaming a gender perspective in the formulation, implementation and evaluation of all policies and programmes, including in conflict prevention and fragile situations and in post-conflict peace-building,

Noting the importance of the organizations and bodies of the United Nations system, in particular its funds and programmes, and the specialized agencies, in facilitating the advancement of women in development,

1. *Takes note* of the reports of the Secretary-General;

2. *Calls upon* Member States, the United Nations system and other international and regional organizations, within their respective mandates, and all sectors of civil society, including non-governmental organizations, as well as all women and men, to fully commit themselves and to intensify their contributions to the implementation of the Beijing Declaration and Platform for Action and the outcome of the twenty-third special session of the General Assembly;

3. *Recognizes* the mutually reinforcing links between gender equality and poverty eradication and the achievement of all of the Millennium Development Goals, as well as the need to elaborate and implement, where appropriate, in consultation with civil society, comprehensive gender-sensitive poverty eradication strategies that address social, structural and macroeconomic issues;

4. *Emphasizes* the need to link policies on economic and social development to ensure that all people, including those in poor and vulnerable groups, benefit from inclusive economic growth and development, in accordance with

the goals of the Monterrey Consensus of the International Conference on Financing for Development;

5. *Urges* Member States, non-governmental organizations and the United Nations system to accelerate further efforts to increase the number of women in decision-making and to build their capacity as agents of change, and to empower women to participate actively and effectively in the development, implementation and evaluation of national development and/or poverty eradication policies, strategies and programmes, including, where appropriate, programme-based approaches;

6. *Stresses* the importance of the adoption by Member States, international organizations, including the United Nations, the private sector, non-governmental organizations, trade unions and other stakeholders of appropriate measures to identify and address the negative impacts of the economic and financial crisis on women and girls and of maintaining adequate levels of funding for the achievement of gender equality and the empowerment of women;

7. *Also stresses* the importance of the creation by Member States, international organizations, including the United Nations, the private sector, non-governmental organizations, trade unions and other stakeholders of a favourable and conducive national and international environment in all areas of life for the effective integration of women in development, and of their undertaking and disseminating a gender analysis of policies and programmes related to macroeconomic stability, structural reform, taxation, investments, including foreign direct investment, and all relevant sectors of the economy;

8. *Urges* the donor community, Member States, international organizations, including the United Nations, the private sector, non-governmental organizations, trade unions and other stakeholders to strengthen the focus and impact of development assistance targeting gender equality and the empowerment of women and girls through gender mainstreaming, the funding of targeted activities and enhanced dialogue between donors and partners, and to also strengthen the mechanisms needed to effectively measure the resources allocated to incorporating gender perspectives in all areas of development assistance;

9. *Urges* Member States, non-governmental organizations and the United Nations system to accelerate further their efforts to increase the number of women in economic decision-making bodies, including at the highest levels in the relevant government ministries, international organizations, corporate boards and the banking sector, as well as to improve the collection, compilation, dissemination and use of data on women's participation in economic decision-making bodies;

10. *Urges* Member States to incorporate a gender perspective, commensurate with gender equality goals, into the design, implementation, monitoring and reporting of national development strategies, and to encourage the involvement of men and boys in the promotion of gender equality, and in this regard calls upon the United Nations system to support national efforts to develop methodologies and tools and to promote capacity-building and evaluation;

11. *Calls upon* Member States to integrate a gender perspective into the design, implementation, monitoring, evaluation and reporting of national environmental policies, and to strengthen mechanisms and provide adequate

resources to ensure women's full and equal participation in decision-making at all levels on environmental issues, in particular on strategies related to the impact of climate change on the lives of women and girls;

12. *Encourages* Member States to ensure inclusive and more effective participation of national mechanisms for gender equality and women's empowerment in formulating national development strategies, including strategies aimed at eradicating poverty and reducing inequalities, and calls upon the United Nations system to support national efforts in this regard;

13. *Calls upon* Member States to continue to increase women's representation and participation in government decision-making at all levels in development policy areas in order to ensure that the priorities, needs and contributions of women are taken into consideration by, inter alia, providing access to training, developing measures to reconcile family and professional responsibilities and eliminating gender stereotyping in appointments and promotions;

14. *Expresses deep concern* about the pervasiveness of violence against women and girls, reiterates the need to further intensify efforts to prevent and eliminate all forms of violence against women and girls, and recognizes that violence against women and girls is one of the obstacles to the achievement of the objectives of equality, development and peace and that women's poverty and the lack of political, social and economic empowerment, as well as their marginalization, may result from their exclusion from social policies for and benefits of sustainable development and can place them at increased risk of violence;

15. *Recognizes* the need to strengthen the capacity of Governments to incorporate a gender perspective into policies and decision-making, and encourages all Governments, international organizations, including the United Nations system, and other relevant stakeholders to assist and support the efforts of developing countries in integrating a gender perspective into all aspects of policymaking, including through the provision of technical assistance and financial resources;

16. *Encourages* Governments, the private sector, nongovernmental organizations and other actors of civil society to promote and protect the rights of women workers, to take action to remove structural and legal barriers as well as stereotypic attitudes towards gender equality at work and to initiate positive steps to promote equal pay for equal work or work of equal value;

17. *Urges* Governments to develop and adequately resource active labour-market policies on full and productive employment and decent work for all, including the full participation of women and men in both rural and urban areas;

18. *Calls upon* Governments to strengthen efforts to protect the rights of, and ensure decent work conditions for, domestic workers, including migrant women, in relation to, inter alia, working hours, conditions and wages, access to health-care services and other social and economic benefits;

19. *Encourages* Member States to adopt and/or review and to fully implement gender-sensitive legislation and policies that reduce, through specifically targeted measures, horizontal and vertical occupational segregation and gender-based wage gaps;

20. *Urges* all Member States to undertake a gender analysis of national labour laws and standards and to establish gender-sensitive policies and guidelines for employment practices, including for transnational corporations, with particular attention to export-processing zones, building in this regard on multilateral instruments, including the Convention on the Elimination of All Forms of Discrimination against Women and Conventions of the International Labour Organization;

21. *Also urges* all Member States to take all appropriate measures to eliminate discrimination against women with regard to their access to financial services, including bank loans, bank accounts, mortgages and other forms of financial credit, giving special attention to poor, uneducated women, to support women's access to legal assistance and to encourage the financial sector to mainstream gender perspectives in their policies and programmes;

22. *Recognizes* the role of microfinance, including microcredit, in the eradication of poverty, the empowerment of women and the generation of employment, notes in this regard the importance of sound national financial systems, and encourages the strengthening of existing and emerging microcredit institutions and their capacities, including through the support of international financial institutions;

23. *Urges* Governments to ensure that microfinance programmes focus on developing savings products that are safe, convenient and accessible to women in their efforts and support women's efforts to retain control over their savings;

24. *Urges* all Governments to eliminate discrimination against women in the field of education and ensure their equal access to all levels of education;

25. *Stresses* the importance of developing national strategies for the promotion of sustainable and productive entrepreneurial activities that will generate income among disadvantaged women and women living in poverty;

26. *Urges* Member States to encourage women entrepreneurs, including through education, vocational training and training of women in business, administration and information and communications technology, and invites business associations to assist national efforts in this regard;

27. *Encourages* Governments to create a climate that is conducive to increasing the number of women entrepreneurs and the size of their businesses by giving them greater access to financial instruments, providing training and advisory services, facilitating networking and information-sharing and increasing their participation in advisory boards and other forums so as to enable them to contribute to the formulation and review of policies and programmes being developed by financial institutions;

28. *Calls upon* Governments to promote, inter alia, through legislation and family-friendly and gender-sensitive work environments, the facilitation of breastfeeding for working mothers and the provision of the necessary care for working women's children and other dependants and to consider promoting policies and programmes, as appropriate, to enable men and women to reconcile their work, social and family responsibilities;

29. *Encourages* Member States to adopt and implement legislation and policies to promote the reconciliation of work and family responsibilities, including through increased flexibility in working arrangements such as part-time work, and to ensure that both women and men have access to maternity, paternity, parental and other forms

of leave and are not discriminated against when availing themselves of such benefits;

30. *Urges* Member States to adopt and review legislation and policies to ensure women's equal access to and control over land, housing and other property, including through inheritance, land reform programmes and land markets, and to take measures to implement those laws and policies;

31. *Urges* Governments to take measures to facilitate equitable access to land and property rights by providing training designed to make the judicial, legislative and administrative system more responsive to gender equality issues, to provide legal aid for women seeking to claim their rights, to support the efforts of women's groups and networks and to carry out awareness campaigns to draw attention to the need for women's equal rights to land and property;

32. *Recognizes* the need to empower women, particularly poor women, economically and politically, and in this regard encourages Governments, with the support of their development partners, to invest in appropriate infrastructure and other projects, including the provision of water and sanitation to rural areas and urban slums to increase health and well-being, relieve the workloads of women and girls and release their time and energy for other productive activities, including entrepreneurship;

33. *Also recognizes* the role of agriculture in development, and stresses the importance of reviewing agricultural policies and strategies to ensure that women's critical role in food security is recognized and addressed as an integral part of both short- and long-term responses to the food crisis;

34. *Expresses its concern* at the overall expansion and feminization of the HIV/AIDS pandemic and the fact that women and girls bear a disproportionate share of the burden imposed by HIV/AIDS, that they are more easily infected, that they play a key role in care and that they have become more vulnerable to violence, stigmatization and discrimination, poverty and marginalization from their families and communities as a result of HIV/AIDS, and calls upon Governments and the international community to intensify efforts towards achieving the goal of universal access to comprehensive HIV prevention programmes, treatment, care and support by 2010 and of having halted and begun to reverse the spread of HIV/AIDS by 2015;

35. *Reaffirms* the commitment to achieve universal access to reproductive health by 2015, as set out at the International Conference on Population and Development, by integrating this goal into strategies to attain the internationally agreed development goals, including those contained in the United Nations Millennium Declaration aimed at reducing maternal mortality, improving maternal health, reducing child mortality, promoting gender equality, combating HIV/AIDS and eradicating poverty;

36. *Recognizes* that there is a need for all donors to maintain and deliver on their existing bilateral and multilateral official development assistance commitments and targets, and that the full implementation of these commitments will substantially boost resources available to push forward the international development agenda;

37. *Expresses deep concern* that maternal health remains one area constrained by some of the largest health inequities in the world, and over the uneven progress in improving child and maternal health, and in this context calls upon States to renew their commitment to preventing and eliminating child and maternal mortality and morbidity;

38. *Encourages* the international community, the United Nations system, the private sector and civil society to continue to provide the necessary financial resources to assist national Governments in their efforts to meet the development targets and benchmarks agreed upon at the World Summit for Social Development, the Fourth World Conference on Women, the International Conference on Population and Development, the Millennium Summit, the International Conference on Financing for Development, the World Summit on Sustainable Development, the Second World Assembly on Ageing, the twenty-third and twenty-fourth special sessions of the General Assembly and other relevant United Nations conferences and summits;

39. *Urges* multilateral donors, and invites international financial institutions, within their respective mandates, and regional development banks to review and implement policies that support national efforts to ensure that a higher proportion of resources reaches women, in particular in rural and remote areas;

40. *Stresses* the importance of collecting and exchanging all relevant information needed on the role of women in development, including data on international migration, as well as the need to develop statistics disaggregated by age and sex, and in that regard encourages developed countries and relevant entities of the United Nations to provide support and assistance to developing countries, upon their request, with respect to establishing, developing and strengthening their databases and information systems;

41. *Recognizes* the critical role and contribution of rural women, including indigenous women, and their traditional knowledge, in enhancing agricultural and rural development, improving food security and eradicating rural poverty;

42. *Calls upon* all organizations of the United Nations system, within their organizational mandates, to mainstream a gender perspective and to pursue gender equality in their country programmes, planning instruments and sector-wide programmes and to articulate specific country-level goals and targets in this domain in accordance with national development strategies;

43. *Calls upon* the organizations of the United Nations development system, within their organizational mandates, to further improve their institutional accountability mechanisms and to include intergovernmentally agreed gender-equality results and gender-sensitive indicators in their strategic frameworks;

44. *Calls upon* the United Nations system to integrate gender mainstreaming into all its programmes and policies, including in the integrated follow-up to United Nations conferences, in accordance with agreed conclusions 1997/2 on gender mainstreaming adopted by the Economic and Social Council at its substantive session of 1997;

45. *Requests* the Secretary-General to submit to the General Assembly at its sixty-sixth session a report on the progress made in the implementation of the present resolution, including on integrating a gender perspective into national development strategies;

46. *Also requests* the Secretary-General to update the *2009 World Survey on the Role of Women in Development*

for consideration by the General Assembly at its sixty-ninth session, noting that the survey should continue to focus on selective emerging development themes that have an impact on the role of women in the economy at the national, regional and international levels;

47. *Decides* to include in the provisional agenda of its sixty-sixth session the sub-item entitled "Women in development".

Women in rural areas

In response to General Assembly resolution 62/136 [YUN 2007, p. 1182], the Secretary-General submitted a July report [A/64/190] on the improvement of the situation of women in rural areas. The report, based on information received from 28 Member States and a number of UN entities, summarized action taken to address different aspects of the empowerment of rural women, such as: including rural women in intergovernmental processes; promoting the participation of rural women in decision-making; strengthening the economic empowerment of rural women; providing health-care services; eliminating violence against women in rural areas; and meeting the needs of vulnerable rural women, such as those with disabilities, indigenous women, and older rural women.

The Secretary-General concluded that the persistent inequalities and discrimination faced by rural women posed significant challenges to the achievement of internationally agreed development goals, including the MDGs. The adverse impacts of multiple global crises affected rural women, particularly poor women, disproportionately. There was growing recognition that rural women, including indigenous women, could be critical agents in crisis response, but little had been done to mobilize and empower them to contribute effectively. Improving the situation of rural women required the promotion of non-agricultural employment and full access to productive resources. Other elements included strengthening the responsiveness of public health systems to the needs of rural women and enhanced measures to prevent violence against women. Recommendations included: promoting rural women's participation in decision-making; strengthening efforts to protect the rights of and ensure decent work conditions for rural women workers; promoting the rights of women and girls with disabilities in rural areas; and strengthening measures to accelerate progress towards the achievement of MDG 5 on maternal health.

GENERAL ASSEMBLY ACTION

On 18 December [meeting 65], the General Assembly, on the recommendation of the Third Committee [A/64/433], adopted **resolution 64/140** without vote [agenda item 62 *(a)*].

Improvement of the situation of women in rural areas

The General Assembly,

Recalling its resolutions 56/129 of 19 December 2001, 58/146 of 22 December 2003, 60/138 of 16 December 2005 and 62/136 of 18 December 2007,

Recalling also the importance attached to the problems of rural women in the Nairobi Forward-looking Strategies for the Advancement of Women, the Beijing Declaration and Platform for Action adopted by the Fourth World Conference on Women and the outcome documents of the twenty-third special session of the General Assembly entitled "Women 2000: gender equality, development and peace for the twenty-first century", including the review and appraisal of the implementation of the outcomes, and in the Convention on the Elimination of All Forms of Discrimination against Women,

Recalling further the United Nations Millennium Declaration, in which Member States resolved, inter alia, to promote gender equality and the empowerment of women as effective ways to combat poverty, hunger and disease and to stimulate development that is truly sustainable, and the 2005 World Summit Outcome, in which they also resolved to promote gender equality and eliminate pervasive gender discrimination by taking all the necessary resolute action,

Welcoming the declaration adopted by the Commission on the Status of Women at its forty-ninth session in the context of the review and appraisal of the implementation of the Beijing Declaration and Platform for Action and the outcome of the twenty-third special session of the General Assembly,

Noting the attention paid to the improvement of the situation of indigenous women in rural areas in the United Nations Declaration on the Rights of Indigenous Peoples,

Recognizing the work of relevant United Nations agencies, funds and programmes, especially the United Nations Educational, Scientific and Cultural Organization, in promoting education for all, giving particular attention to girls and women in rural areas,

Welcoming the Monterrey Consensus of the International Conference on Financing for Development, as well as the Johannesburg Declaration on Sustainable Development and the Plan of Implementation of the World Summit on Sustainable Development ("Johannesburg Plan of Implementation"), in which Governments were called upon to mainstream the gender perspective into development at all levels and in all sectors, and recalling the Follow-up International Conference on Financing for Development to Review the Implementation of the Monterrey Consensus, held in Doha from 29 November to 2 December 2008,

Welcoming also the ministerial declaration of the high-level segment of the substantive session of 2003 of the Economic and Social Council, adopted on 2 July 2003, which stressed the need for rural development to become an integral part of national and international development policies and of activities and programmes of the United Nations system, and called for an enhanced role for rural women at all levels of rural development, including decision-making,

Recalling the World Summit on the Information Society, held in Geneva in 2003 and Tunis in 2005, as well as the Tunis Agenda for the Information Society, adopted by the World Summit in 2005, which reaffirmed the commitment to building capacity in information and communications technology for all and confidence in the use of information and communications technology by all, including women, indigenous peoples and remote and rural communities,

Recognizing the critical role and contribution of rural women, including indigenous women, in enhancing agricultural and rural development, improving food security and eradicating rural poverty,

Reiterating that eradicating poverty is the greatest global challenge facing the world today, and an indispensable requirement for sustainable development, in particular for developing countries, while recognizing that rural areas of developing countries continue to be home to the vast majority of the world's poor people,

Recognizing the contributions of older rural women to the family and the community, especially in cases where they are left behind by migrating adults or as a result of other socio-economic factors to assume childcare, household and agricultural responsibility,

Reiterating the call for fair globalization and the need to translate growth into eradication of poverty, including for rural women, and in this regard applauding the resolve to make the goals of full and productive employment and decent work for all, including for rural women, a central objective of relevant national and international policies as well as national development strategies, including poverty eradication strategies,

Recognizing the urgent need to take appropriate measures aimed at further improving the situation of women in rural areas,

1. *Takes note* of the report of the Secretary-General;

2. *Urges* Member States, in collaboration with the organizations of the United Nations and civil society, as appropriate, to continue their efforts to implement the outcome of and to ensure an integrated and coordinated follow-up to the United Nations conferences and summits, including their reviews, and to attach greater importance to the improvement of the situation of rural women, including indigenous women, in their national, regional and global development strategies by, inter alia:

(a) Creating an enabling environment for improving the situation of rural women and ensuring systematic attention to their needs, priorities and contributions, including through enhanced cooperation and a gender perspective, and their full participation in the development, implementation and follow-up of macroeconomic policies, including development policies and programmes and poverty eradication strategies, including poverty reduction strategy papers where they exist, based on internationally agreed development goals, including the Millennium Development Goals;

(b) Pursuing the political and socio-economic empowerment of rural women and supporting their full and equal participation in decision-making at all levels, including through affirmative action, where appropriate, and support for women's organizations, labour unions or other associations and civil society groups promoting rural women's rights;

(c) Promoting consultation with and the participation of rural women, including indigenous women and women

with disabilities, through their organizations and networks, in the design, development and implementation of gender equality and rural development programmes and strategies;

(d) Ensuring that the perspectives of rural women are taken into account and that they participate in the design, implementation, follow-up and evaluation of policies and activities related to emergencies, including natural disasters, humanitarian assistance, peacebuilding and post-conflict reconstruction, and taking appropriate measures to eliminate all forms of discrimination against rural women in this regard;

(e) Integrating a gender perspective into the design, implementation, follow-up and evaluation of development policies and programmes, including budget policies, paying increased attention to the needs of rural women so as to ensure that they benefit from policies and programmes adopted in all spheres and that the disproportionate number of rural women living in poverty is reduced;

(f) Investing in and strengthening efforts to meet the basic needs of rural women through improved availability, access to and use of critical rural infrastructure, such as energy and transport, capacity-building and human resources development measures and the provision of a safe and reliable water supply and sanitation, nutritional programmes, affordable housing programmes, education and literacy programmes, and health and social support measures, including in the areas of sexual and reproductive health and HIV/AIDS prevention, treatment, care and support services;

(g) Strengthening measures, including resource generation, to accelerate progress towards the achievement of Millennium Development Goal 5 on improving maternal health by addressing the specific health needs of rural women and taking concrete measures to enhance and provide access to the highest attainable standards of health for women in rural areas, as well as quality, affordable and universally accessible primary health care and support services, including in such areas of sexual and reproductive health as prenatal and post-natal health care, emergency obstetric care, family planning information and increasing knowledge, awareness and support for the prevention of sexually transmitted diseases, including HIV/AIDS;

(h) Designing and implementing national policies that promote and protect the enjoyment by rural women and girls of all human rights and fundamental freedoms and creating an environment that does not tolerate violations of their rights, including domestic violence, sexual violence and all other forms of gender-based violence;

(i) Ensuring that the rights of older women in rural areas are taken into account with regard to their equal access to basic social services, appropriate social protection/social security measures, equal access to and control of economic resources, and empowerment of older women through access to financial and infrastructure services, with special focus on support to older women, including indigenous women, who often have access to few resources and are more vulnerable;

(j) Promoting the rights of women and girls with disabilities in rural areas, including by ensuring access on an equal basis to productive employment and decent work, economic and financial resources and disability-sensitive infrastructure and services, in particular in relation to health and education, as well as by ensuring that their priorities and needs are fully incorporated into policies and programmes, inter alia, through their participation in decision-making processes;

(k) Developing specific assistance programmes and advisory services to promote economic skills of rural women in banking, modern trading and financial procedures and providing microcredit and other financial and business services to a greater number of women in rural areas, in particular female-headed households, for their economic empowerment;

(l) Mobilizing resources, including at the national level and through official development assistance, for increasing women's access to existing savings and credit schemes, as well as targeted programmes that provide women with capital, knowledge and tools that enhance their economic capacities;

(m) Integrating increased employment opportunities for rural women into all international and national development strategies and poverty eradication strategies, including by expanding non-agricultural employment opportunities, improving working conditions and increasing access to productive resources;

(n) Taking steps towards ensuring that women's unpaid work and contributions to on-farm and off-farm production, including income generated in the informal sector, are recognized and supporting remunerative non-agricultural employment of rural women, improving working conditions and increasing access to productive resources;

(o) Promoting programmes to enable rural women and men to reconcile their work and family responsibilities and to encourage men to share, equally with women, household and childcare responsibilities;

(p) Considering the adoption, where appropriate, of national legislation to protect the knowledge, innovations and practices of women in indigenous and local communities relating to traditional medicines, biodiversity and indigenous technologies;

(q) Addressing the lack of timely, reliable and sex-disaggregated data, including by intensifying efforts to include women's unpaid work in official statistics, and developing a systematic and comparative research base on rural women that will inform policy and programme decisions;

(r) Designing, revising and implementing laws to ensure that rural women are accorded full and equal rights to own and lease land and other property, including through the right to inheritance, and undertaking administrative reforms and all necessary measures to give women the same right as men to credit, capital, appropriate technologies and access to markets and information;

(s) Supporting a gender-sensitive education system that considers the specific needs of rural women in order to eliminate gender stereotypes and discriminatory tendencies affecting them;

(t) Developing the capacity of personnel working in the areas of national development strategies, rural development, agricultural development, poverty eradication and implementation of the Millennium Development Goals to identify and address the challenges and constraints facing rural women, including through training programmes and the development and dissemination of methodologies

and tools, while acknowledging the technical assistance of relevant United Nations organizations;

3. *Strongly encourages* Member States, United Nations entities and all other relevant stakeholders to take measures to identify and address any negative impact of the current global crises on women in rural areas, including legislation, policies and programmes that strengthen gender equality and the empowerment of women;

4. *Invites* the Commission on the Status of Women to continue to pay due attention to the situation of rural women in the consideration of its priority themes;

5. *Requests* the relevant organizations and bodies of the United Nations system, in particular those dealing with issues of development, to address and support the empowerment of rural women and their specific needs in their programmes and strategies;

6. *Stresses* the need to identify the best practices for ensuring that rural women have access to and full participation in the area of information and communications technology, to address the priorities and needs of rural women and girls as active users of information and to ensure their participation in developing and implementing global, regional and national information and communications technology strategies;

7. *Encourages* Member States, the United Nations and relevant organizations of its system to ensure that the needs of rural women are mainstreamed into the integrated process of follow-up to the major conferences and summits in the economic and social fields, in particular the Millennium Summit, the World Summit on Sustainable Development, the International Conference on Financing for Development and the Follow-up International Conference on Financing for Development to Review the Implementation of the Monterrey Consensus, the 2005 review and appraisal of the progress achieved in implementing all the commitments made in the Beijing Declaration and Platform for Action and the outcome of the twenty-third special session of the General Assembly, and the 2005 World Summit;

8. *Calls upon* Member States to take into consideration the concluding observations and recommendations of the Committee on the Elimination of Discrimination against Women concerning their reports to the Committee when formulating policies and designing programmes focused on the improvement of the situation of rural women, including those to be developed and implemented in cooperation with relevant international organizations;

9. *Invites* Governments, relevant international organizations and the specialized agencies to continue to observe the International Day of Rural Women annually, on 15 October, as proclaimed in its resolution 62/136;

10. *Requests* the Secretary-General to report to the General Assembly at its sixty-sixth session on the implementation of the present resolution.

Women's health

Women, the girl child and HIV/AIDS

In response to Commission on the Status of Women resolution 52/4 [YUN 2008, p. 1255], the

Secretary-General submitted a report [E/CN.6/2009/6] on women, the girl child and HIV/AIDS, which described action taken by Member States and UN entities towards implementing that resolution. The Secretary-General noted that gender inequality was a key driver of the HIV/AIDS pandemic. Women and adolescent girls were especially vulnerable to HIV/AIDS owing to biological conditions, economic and social inequalities and culturally accepted gender roles that placed them in a subordinate position in relation to men regarding sexual decision-making. Their frequent exposure to sexual violence—both inside and outside the home, and during armed conflict—also put women at an increased risk of contracting HIV. Factors such as poverty, illiteracy and gender-based power imbalances within families and communities restricted access for women to preventive care, drugs and treatment. In addition, women and girls bore the disproportionate burden of caring for those infected and affected by HIV/AIDS.

HIV/AIDS continued to impact women and girls in increasing numbers. Globally, the percentage of women among people living with HIV had remained stable (at 50 per cent) in recent years. However, women accounted for nearly 60 per cent of HIV infections in sub-Saharan Africa and women's share of infections had been increasing in a number of other regions, particularly in Asia, Eastern Europe and Latin America. Although in 14 out of 17 African countries with survey data the percentage of young pregnant women (aged 15–24) living with HIV had declined since 2000–2001, among young people in Africa HIV prevalence was notably higher among women than men. Young women represented about two-thirds of all new cases among people aged 15 to 24 in developing countries, which made them the most affected group in the world. Studies suggested the risk of infection was three times higher in women who had experienced gender-based violence than among those who had not. The fear of violence prevented women from accessing HIV/AIDS information, being tested, disclosing their HIV status, accessing services and receiving treatment, even when they knew they were infected. Certain behaviours, such as unprotected sex, increased the risk of infection, while other factors could reduce the ability of the individual to avoid HIV risk. These included lack of knowledge and skills regarding protection and lack of access to services due to discrimination, sociocultural norms, and distance and cost.

The Secretary-General concluded that progress in achieving universal access to prevention programmes, treatment, care and support by 2010, in line with the commitments on HIV/AIDS made at the 2005 World Summit Outcome [YUN 2005, p. 55], required that existing HIV/AIDS policies, strategies and resource allocation be reviewed and adapted to ensure they contributed to empowering women and reducing their vulnerability. Efforts were needed to expand access to services, such as education and information, sexual and reproductive health, antenatal care, prevention of mother-to-child transmission and antiretroviral therapy and microbicides. Recommendations included: increasing investment in female-controlled prevention methods, such as the female condom; increasing the participation and influence of women in HIV/AIDS decision-making bodies; and ensuring that women living with HIV continued to receive treatment after the risk of transmission to their children had ended. Governments needed to strengthen laws, public awareness campaigns and other measures to eliminate violence against women and girls, including harmful traditional practices, abuse and rape, and trafficking, which aggravated the conditions underlying women's vulnerability to HIV/AIDS.

Commission action. In a March resolution [E/2009/27 (res. 53/2)], the Commission on the Status of Women requested Governments to provide equal access for women and men throughout their life cycle to social services related to health care, especially for women and girls living with or affected by HIV/AIDS, including treatment for opportunistic infections and other HIV-related diseases. It also requested the Secretariat and co-sponsors of the Joint United Nations Programme on HIV/AIDS (UNAIDS) and other UN agencies responding to the HIV/AIDS pandemic to mainstream a gender and human rights perspective throughout their HIV- and AIDS-related operations, and to ensure that programmes and policies were developed to address the specific needs of women and girls. The Secretary-General was requested to invite Member States to work in partnership with the Global Coalition on Women and HIV/AIDS, convened by UNAIDS and its partners, to mobilize and support a range of national actors to ensure that national HIV and AIDS programmes were better able to respond to the needs and vulnerabilities of women and girls. Governments were called on to intensify efforts to eliminate all forms of discrimination against women and girls in relation to HIV/AIDS; to integrate HIV prevention, voluntary counselling and voluntary testing of HIV into other health services; and to integrate, along with the international donor community, a gender perspective in all matters of international assistance, and to take measures to ensure that resources concomitant with the impact of HIV/AIDS on women and girls were made available. In the process of the review of the MDGs, it was recommended that gender-equality perspectives be included throughout the deliberations and that attention be paid to the situation of women and girls infected or affected by HIV and AIDS.

Sharing of caregiving responsibilities and HIV/AIDS

In response to Economic and Social Council resolution 2006/9 [YUN 2006, p. 1356] and Assembly resolution 63/159 [YUN 2008, p. 1251], the Secretary-General submitted to the Commission on the Status of Women a report [E/CN.6/2009/4] on progress in mainstreaming a gender perspective into the development, implementation and evaluation of national policies and programmes, with a particular focus on the equal sharing of responsibilities between women and men, including in the context of HIV/AIDS. Based on information from 28 Member States and on data from UN entities and other sources, the report was intended to be read in conjunction with the Secretary-General's report [E/CN.6/2009/2] on the equal sharing of responsibilities between women and men, including caregiving in the context of HIV/AIDS, which was the priority theme of the Commission's session (see below).

The report's recommendations included that: States should ensure that comprehensive, multidisciplinary and gender-sensitive national policies and strategies on labour and social protection are in place, with measurable goals and timetables, monitoring and accountability measures, and mechanisms to ensure coordination with key stakeholders in the private sector and civil society; provisions for parental leave, policies on flexible working hours and other social protection measures, such as health insurance, pensions, and child and family allowances, should be extended to all sectors, including the informal sector; Member States and other actors should strengthen efforts to protect the rights and regulate the working conditions of domestic workers; men should be engaged in caregiving at the household level and in paid care work; and gender stereotypes should be challenged, particularly the stereotypical perceptions of the male breadwinner and female caretaker. In addition, the value and cost of care to households and society at large should be recognized and incorporated into national economic and social policies, strategies and budgets, as well as in international development cooperation policies and programmes.

Commission action. On 3 March [E/2009/27], the Commission on the Status of Women held a panel discussion on "Capacity-building for mainstreaming a gender perspective into national policies and programmes to support the equal sharing of responsibilities between women and men, including caregiving in the context of HIV/AIDS". On 13 March [dec. 53/101], the Commission took note of the Secretary-General's report on the subject.

Report of Secretary-General. Also in response to Council resolution 2006/9, the Secretary-General submitted to the Commission a report [E/CN.6/2009/2]

that analysed the situation in relation to the session's priority theme "The equal sharing of responsibilities between women and men, including caregiving in the context of HIV/AIDS", and proposed recommendations for consideration by the Commission.

The Secretary-General noted that the nature of caregiving was affected by factors such as household size and number and age of children. There were significant differences between developed and developing countries in the availability of infrastructure and services supporting caregiving. Changes in demographics in rapidly ageing societies and in the context of HIV/AIDS had increased the need for care and expanded the focus of care from children to the elderly and to adults of prime working age. The HIV/AIDS pandemic had drawn attention to both the importance of care work and the weaknesses of public policies and institutions created to address the care needs created by the disease. Data and information on home-based care were scarce, but most research showed that women and girls disproportionately assumed the responsibilities for HIV/AIDS-related care. As the unequal sharing of responsibilities had implications for a range of policy areas, including health, social welfare, family, education and the labour market, addressing the issue required a complex set of policy responses.

The Secretary-General suggested a number of actions that the Commission might consider recommending to Governments, the United Nations, the private sector and other stakeholders. They included: taking measures to eliminate discrimination against women in relation to marriage, family law, inheritance and property; promoting recognition of the fact that care work should be shared between women and men, as well as among the State, the private sector, civil society and households; adopting and reviewing gender-sensitive policies for the purpose of improving the rights, social protection and working conditions of paid and unpaid caregivers; strengthening the collection of sex- and age-disaggregated data to inform policymaking and measure progress in responsibility-sharing; and integrating gender perspectives into national HIV/AIDS policies and programmes and improving public health services to alleviate the demands on women and girls.

On 13 March [E/2009/27 (dec. 53/101)], the Commission took note of the Secretary-General's report.

Commission action. In March [E/2009/27], the Commission on the Status of Women held parallel high-level round tables on the theme "The equal sharing of responsibilities between women and men, including caregiving in the context of HIV/AIDS", as well as panel discussions on key policy initiatives. The round tables had before them a discussion guide [E.CN.6/2009/12] prepared by the Commission's Bureau. On 13 March, the Commission adopted agreed conclusions on the equal sharing of responsibilities between women and men, including caregiving in the context of HIV/AIDS, which made recommendations for actions to be taken by Governments, UN system entities, international and regional organizations, civil society, the private sector, employer organizations, trade unions and the media. In accordance with resolution 2008/29 [YUN 2008, p. 1528], the Commission transmitted its agreed conclusions to the Council for adoption and as input into the annual ministerial review.

Gender in global public health

Note by Secretariat. In preparation for the Economic and Social Council's 2009 annual ministerial review on "Implementing the internationally agreed goals and commitments in regard to global public health" (see p. 1226), the Secretariat submitted a note [E/CN.6/2009/13] to the Commission on the Status of Women to assist it in providing input for the review. The note presented an overview of recommendations for actions to incorporate gender perspectives into global public health.

Commission action. In March [E/2009/27], the Commission convened an interactive expert panel on the theme "Gender perspectives on global public health: implementing the internationally agreed development goals, including the MDGs" and transmitted the summary of the panel discussion to the Council, in accordance with resolution 2008/29, and as an input into its 2009 annual ministerial review (see p. 1226).

Violence against women

In response to General Assembly resolution 63/155 [YUN 2008, p. 1260], the Secretary-General submitted a July report [A/64/151] on the intensification of efforts to eliminate all forms of violence against women, based on information received from 38 UN entities, the International Organization for Migration (IOM), and the results of six inter-agency initiatives. Efforts to achieve greater coordination and collaboration within the UN system included: the Secretary-General's campaign "UNiTE to End Violence against Women", 2008–2015; the Inter-Agency Network on Women and Gender Equality Task Force on Violence against Women; the United Nations Action against Sexual Violence in Conflict initiative; the United Nations Trust Fund in Support of Actions to Eliminate Violence against Women; the Inter-agency Cooperation Group against Trafficking in Persons; the Global Initiative to Fight Human Trafficking; and coordination at the regional level. Also discussed were initiatives on violence against women by UN entities in support of

national efforts, including those that expanded the knowledge base and strengthened data collection and analysis; promoted awareness-raising, advocacy and training; implemented training and capacity-building measures, including the development of tools; and supported legislative and policy development and access to services for victims/survivors.

The report noted that a framework for action had been elaborated for the UNiTE campaign, which provided an umbrella for activities by stakeholders at all levels and identified five key outcomes to be achieved in all countries by 2015. The Inter-Agency Network on Women and Gender Equality Task Force on Violence against Women, co-chaired by the United Nations Population Fund (UNFPA) and the UN Division for the Advancement of Women (DAW), achieved notable results with the joint programming pilot initiative that had taken place in 10 countries. The United Nations Action against Sexual Violence in Conflict initiative continued to build the knowledge base on sexual violence in conflict-related situations. The Department of Peacekeeping Operations (DPKO) led research missions to countries with a UN peacekeeping presence in order to finalize the *Analytical Inventory of Responses by Peacekeeping Personnel to War-Related Violence against Women*, which would catalogue good practices in protecting women from sexual violence and inform the training of peacekeepers. UN country teams were invited for the first time to apply for funding through the United Nations Trust Fund in Support of Actions to Eliminate Violence against Women, which was managed by UNIFEM and aimed to contribute to the goals of the UNiTE campaign. In response to the growing demand for financial support, which continued to exceed available resources, the Trust Fund set an annual target of $100 million by 2015. In March 2009, the Secretary-General's database on violence against women was launched; it provided the first global publicly accessible "one-stop shop" for information on measures by Member States to address violence against women. At its 2009 session, the Statistical Commission approved an interim set of indicators to assist States in assessing the scope, prevalence and incidence of violence against women (see p. 1262).

The report concluded that key inter-agency initiatives had resulted in better coordinated support for national action on violence against women. It was noted that the database on violence against women had resulted in an increase in attention to issues such as female genital mutilation, the links between HIV/AIDS and violence against women, and violence against women in humanitarian and conflict situations. Other areas required increased attention, however. There was, for example, a need to increase knowledge about the impact of measures taken and results achieved.

The Special Rapporteur on violence against women, its causes and consequences submitted to the Human Rights Council her third report, which was on the political economy of women's human rights [A/HRC/11/6] (see p. 733).

UNIFEM activities. In response to General Assembly resolution 50/166 [YUN 1995, p. 1188], the Secretary-General transmitted the report [A/HRC/13/71-E/CN.6/2010/8] of UNIFEM on its 2009 activities to eliminate violence against women, including management of the United Nations Trust Fund in Support of Actions to Eliminate Violence against Women. By the end of 2009, the Trust Fund had supported 304 initiatives in 121 countries and territories with expenditures of more than $50 million. The report noted that the Fund was uniquely positioned to support countries in translating commitments into real change in the lives of women and girls on the ground, in line with the Secretary-General's UNiTE campaign. The report summarized the Fund's progress in implementing its strategy for 2005–2008, under which it continued to operate in 2009. The strategy's five pillars were: impact; involvement; efficiency; knowledge management and capacity development; and resource mobilization.

In 2009, the Fund had a portfolio of 81 active grants, covering 76 countries and territories, with a total value of nearly $30 million. The Latin America and the Caribbean region had the largest portfolio (24 per cent), followed closely by Africa, and Asia and the Pacific (23 per cent each). Central and Eastern Europe and the Commonwealth of Independent States, and Arab States had the smallest portfolios (15 and 8 per cent, respectively), while cross-regional programmes accounted for 7 per cent. A total of 1,643 concept notes were received requesting $857 million, reflecting increases of 53 per cent in the number of applications and 63 per cent in the funds requested in just one year. The majority of new grantees included women's organizations and other NGOs (71 per cent), followed by UN country teams (19 per cent) and governmental organizations (10 per cent). In 2009, the Fund made significant progress in establishing a new grantee reporting system designed to capture results, learning and knowledge, and analyse trends across the entire grant-making portfolio. The comprehensive database reporting system would be launched in 2010. The Fund advanced a new fund-raising strategy in 2009, guided by the drive to reach the target of $100 million annually by 2015, a benchmark set in the UNiTE campaign, and also launched an urgent web-based Alert to draw attention to the need to end violence against women and girls in the context of the global financial crisis, with an appeal for individual online donations made possible through a site hosted by the United Nations Foundation.

With regard to its future work, UNIFEM would continue efforts to bridge the implementation and accountability gap by supporting intensified country-level action through technical assistance; capacity development; broadened advocacy and awareness-raising initiatives; strengthened partnerships within and outside the UN system; improved monitoring and evaluation of programmes; and the provision of new learning and knowledge-sharing opportunities and products through its online global virtual knowledge centre on ending violence against women and girls, aimed at developing the capacity of country-level practitioners.

Communication. In a 9 March letter to the Secretary-General [A/63/755], Qatar transmitted the recommendations of the Colloquium on the impact of violence against women on the family (Doha, Qatar, 19–20 November 2008).

GENERAL ASSEMBLY ACTION

On 18 December [meeting 65], the General Assembly, on the recommendation of the Third Committee [A/64/433], adopted **resolution 64/137** without vote [agenda item 62 *(a)*].

Intensification of efforts to eliminate all forms of violence against women

The General Assembly,

Recalling its resolutions 61/143 of 19 December 2006, 62/133 of 18 December 2007 and 63/155 of 18 December 2008, and all its previous resolutions on the elimination of violence against women,

Reaffirming the strong support expressed in its resolution 63/311 of 14 September 2009 for the consolidation of the Office of the Special Adviser on Gender Issues and Advancement of Women, the Division for the Advancement of Women, the United Nations Development Fund for Women and the International Research and Training Institute for the Advancement of Women into a composite entity, taking into account the existing mandates, which would be led by an Under-Secretary-General,

Reaffirming also the obligation of all States to promote and protect all human rights and fundamental freedoms, and reaffirming further that discrimination on the basis of sex is contrary to the Charter of the United Nations, the Convention on the Elimination of All Forms of Discrimination against Women and other international human rights instruments, and that its elimination is an integral part of efforts towards the elimination of all forms of violence against women,

Reaffirming further the Declaration on the Elimination of Violence against Women, the Beijing Declaration and Platform for Action, the outcome of the twenty-third special session of the General Assembly entitled "Women 2000: gender equality, development and peace for the twenty-first century", and the declaration adopted at the forty-ninth session of the Commission on the Status of Women,

Reaffirming the international commitments in the field of social development and to gender equality and the advancement of women made at the World Conference on Human Rights, the International Conference on Population and Development, the World Summit for Social Development and the World Conference against Racism, Racial Discrimination, Xenophobia and Related Intolerance, as well as those made in the United Nations Millennium Declaration and at the 2005 World Summit,

Recalling Security Council resolutions 1325(2000) of 31 October 2000 and 1820(2008) of 19 June 2008 on women and peace and security, and welcoming the adoption of Council resolution 1882(2009) of 4 August 2009 on children and armed conflict and Council resolutions 1888(2009) of 30 September 2009 and 1889(2009) of 5 October 2009 on women and peace and security,

Welcoming Human Rights Council resolution 11/2 of 17 June 2009,

Recognizing that women's poverty and lack of empowerment, as well as their marginalization resulting from their exclusion from social policies and from the benefits of sustainable development, can place them at increased risk of violence, and that violence against women impedes the social and economic development of communities and States, as well as the achievement of the internationally agreed development goals, including the Millennium Development Goals,

Deeply concerned about the pervasiveness of violence against women and girls in all its different forms and manifestations worldwide, and reiterating the need to intensify efforts to prevent and eliminate all forms of violence against women and girls throughout the world,

Stressing that States have the obligation to promote and protect all human rights and fundamental freedoms for all, including women and girls, and must exercise due diligence to prevent and investigate acts of violence against women and girls and punish the perpetrators, to eliminate impunity and to provide protection to the victims, and that failure to do so violates and impairs or nullifies the enjoyment of their human rights and fundamental freedoms,

Expressing its appreciation for the high number of activities undertaken by the United Nations bodies, entities, funds and programmes and the specialized agencies, including by the Special Rapporteur of the Human Rights Council on violence against women, its causes and consequences, to eliminate all forms of violence against women, and welcoming the recent appointment of the Special Representative of the Secretary-General on violence against children,

1.   *Takes note with appreciation* of the report of the Secretary-General, submitted pursuant to General Assembly resolution 63/155;

2.   *Calls upon* the international community, including the United Nations system and, as appropriate, regional and subregional organizations, to support national efforts to promote the empowerment of women and gender equality in order to enhance national efforts to eliminate violence against women and girls, including, upon request, in the development and implementation of national action plans on the elimination of violence against women and girls, through, inter alia, official development assistance and

other appropriate assistance, such as facilitating the sharing of guidelines, methodologies and best practices, and taking into account national priorities;

3.   *Calls upon* all United Nations bodies, entities, funds and programmes and the specialized agencies and invites the Bretton Woods institutions to intensify their efforts at all levels to eliminate all forms of violence against women and girls and to better coordinate their work, inter alia, through the Task Force on Violence against Women of the Inter-Agency Network on Women and Gender Equality, and looks forward to the results of the ongoing work of the Task Force on composing a manual on joint programming, with a view to increasing effective support for national efforts to eliminate all forms of violence against women;

4.   *Expresses its appreciation* for the progress achieved in the Secretary-General's 2008–2015 campaign "UNiTE to End Violence against Women", through the development of a framework for action outlining five key outcomes to be achieved by 2015, supported, inter alia, by the United Nations Development Fund for Women social mobilization and advocacy platform "Say NO to violence against women", the United Nations inter-agency initiative "Stop Rape Now: United Nations Action against Sexual Violence in Conflict" and the regional components of the campaign, stresses the need to accelerate implementation of concrete follow-up activities by the United Nations system to end all forms of violence against women, in close consultation with existing system-wide activities on violence against women, requests the Secretary-General to report on the basis of the results of his campaign, and encourages Member States to join forces in addressing the global pandemic of all forms of violence against women;

5.   *Calls upon* the inter-agency Programme Appraisal Committee of the United Nations Trust Fund in Support of Actions to Eliminate Violence against Women, in consultation with the Inter-Agency Network on Women and Gender Equality, to include in its next strategy for the Trust Fund ways and means to further enhance its effectiveness as a system-wide funding mechanism for preventing and redressing all forms of violence against women and girls and to give due consideration, inter alia, to the findings and recommendations of the external evaluation of the Trust Fund once finalized;

6.   *Notes with concern* the growing gap between available funding in the United Nations Trust Fund in Support of Actions to Eliminate Violence against Women and the funds required to meet the increasing demand, and urges States and other stakeholders, where possible, to significantly increase their voluntary contributions to the Trust Fund in order to meet the annual target of 100 million United States dollars by 2015 as set by the Secretary-General's campaign "UNiTE to End Violence against Women", while expressing its appreciation for the contributions already made by States, the private sector and other donors to the Trust Fund;

7.   *Stresses* that, within the United Nations system, adequate resources should be assigned to those bodies, specialized agencies, funds and programmes responsible for the promotion of gender equality and women's rights and to efforts throughout the United Nations system to eliminate violence against women and girls, calls upon

the United Nations system to make the necessary support and resources available in order to allow the Task Force on Violence against Women to undertake a resource flow analysis to assess the resources available for this work and elaborate recommendations for their most effective and efficient use, and also calls upon the United Nations system to respond swiftly to those recommendations once they have been issued;

8. *Welcomes* the establishment of the Secretary-General's database on violence against women, expresses its appreciation to all the States that have provided the database with information regarding, inter alia, their national policies and legal frameworks aimed at eliminating violence against women and supporting victims of such violence, strongly encourages all States to regularly provide updated information for the database, and calls upon all relevant entities of the United Nations system to continue to support States, at their request, in the compilation and regular updating of pertinent information and to raise awareness of the database among all relevant stakeholders, including civil society;

9. *Also welcomes* the adoption of an interim set of indicators to measure violence against women by the Statistical Commission at its fortieth session, and looks forward to the results of the ongoing work of the Commission on this topic;

10. *Requests* the Secretary-General to present an oral report to the Commission on the Status of Women at its fifty-fourth session, and thereafter to the General Assembly at its sixty-fifth session, with information provided by the United Nations bodies, funds and programmes and the specialized agencies, on recent follow-up activities to implement resolution 63/155 and the present resolution, including on the United Nations Trust Fund in Support of Actions to Eliminate Violence against Women, and urges United Nations bodies, entities, funds and programmes and the specialized agencies to contribute promptly to that report.

Crime prevention and criminal justice responses to violence

The intergovernmental expert group to review and update the Model Strategies and Practical Measures on the Elimination of Violence against Women in the Field of Crime Prevention and Criminal Justice (Bangkok, 23–25 March) [E/CN.15/2010/2], convened in response to Commission on Crime Prevention and Criminal Justice decision 17/1 [YUN 2008, p. 1264], considered current developments and research on the matter. It also discussed the suggestions of 26 Member States with regard to potential changes and improvements to the Model Strategies and Practical Measures. Annexed to the report of the meeting was the text of the updated Model Strategies and Practical Measures. The expert group recommended to the Commission on Crime Prevention and Criminal Justice, for adoption at its 2010 session, a draft resolution on strengthening crime prevention and criminal justice responses to violence against women.

Violence against women migrant workers

In response to General Assembly resolution 62/132 [YUN 2007, p. 1162], the Secretary-General submitted a July report [A/64/152] on violence against women migrant workers, which provided information on measures taken by 28 Member States with regard to adherence to international instruments; legislation and the justice system; policies; prevention measures and training; protection and assistance; data collection and research; and bilateral, regional, international and other cooperation. The report also reviewed activities undertaken by entities of the UN system and IOM to address the issue, particularly with regard to global legal and policy development and initiatives in support of national efforts.

The report noted an increase in the number of States parties to the United Nations Convention against Transnational Organized Crime, adopted by the Assembly in resolution 55/25 [YUN 2000, p. 1048], and its Protocol to Prevent, Suppress and Punish Trafficking in Persons, Especially Women and Children [ibid., p. 1063]. The number of States parties to the International Convention on the Protection of the Rights of All Migrant Workers and Members of Their Families, adopted by the Assembly in resolution 45/158 [YUN 1990, p. 594], also continued to increase. States indicated their adherence to regional instruments addressing violence against women and their adoption of a range of laws to protect women migrant workers from discrimination and violence and punish perpetrators.

Within the UN system, a number of conferences and meetings addressed issues related to women migrant workers. For example, the Durban Review Conference (see p. 657) to evaluate progress towards goals set by the World Conference against Racism, Racial Discrimination, Xenophobia and Related Intolerance [YUN 2001, p. 615] addressed the situation of women domestic workers. At its 2010 session, the International Labour Conference would consider the issue of decent work for domestic workers with a view to setting international labour standards, including those that would help prevent violence against women migrant domestic workers. IOM's capacity-building activities for policymakers included a focus on the promotion of gender-sensitive migration policies and provided guidance on how countries of origin and destination could include gender analysis in their migration policies. UNIFEM supported the drafting of laws to promote and protect the rights of women migrant workers in a number of countries and organized or supported conferences and meetings among Government representatives and other stakeholders to raise awareness and exchange good practices. UNFPA initiated a project that aimed to prevent reproductive rights abuses and gender-based violence among migrant women along the borders of 10 countries in Latin America and the Caribbean.

The report concluded that violence against women migrant workers persisted, and women continued to be subjected to violence and have their rights violated at every stage of the migration cycle. Many of the efforts reported related to the development of laws and policies on gender equality, rather than specific measures to address violence against women migrant workers. While acknowledging that States had made efforts to collect data on gender and migration, specific data on violence against women migrant workers were needed, including on the different forms of violence, perpetrators and the context in which such violence took place.

GENERAL ASSEMBLY ACTION

On 18 December [meeting 65], the General Assembly, on the recommendation of the Third Committee [A/64/433], adopted **resolution 64/139** without vote [agenda item 62 *(a)*].

Violence against women migrant workers

The General Assembly,

Recalling all of its previous resolutions on violence against women migrant workers and those adopted by the Commission on the Status of Women, the Commission on Human Rights and the Commission on Crime Prevention and Criminal Justice, and the Declaration on the Elimination of Violence against Women,

Reaffirming the provisions concerning women migrant workers contained in the outcome documents of the World Conference on Human Rights, the International Conference on Population and Development, the Fourth World Conference on Women and the World Summit for Social Development and their reviews,

Noting with appreciation the various activities initiated by entities of the United Nations system, such as the Regional Programme on Empowering Women Migrant Workers in Asia of the United Nations Development Fund for Women, the high-level panel discussion on the gender dimensions of international migration held by the Commission on the Status of Women at its fiftieth session, the discussions held by the Commission at its fifty-third session, during which it recognized the particular situation of women migrant domestic workers of all ages, and the general discussion on migrant domestic workers held by the Committee on the Protection of the Rights of All Migrant Workers and Members of Their Families at its eleventh session, and noting the contribution of the International Labour Organization through the development of the Multilateral Framework on Labour Migration, as well as other activities through which the plight of women migrant workers continues to be assessed and alleviated,

Recalling the discussions during the High-level Dialogue on International Migration and Development, held on 14 and 15 September 2006, which recognized, inter alia, the need for special protection for migrant women,

Taking note with appreciation of the United Nations Development Programme *Human Development Report 2009: Overcoming Barriers—Human Mobility and Development*, which discussed, inter alia, the need to protect women migrant workers from abuse, exploitation and violence,

Noting the decision of the Governing Body of the International Labour Office to include discussion of the issue of decent work for domestic workers in the agenda for the ninety-ninth session of the International Labour Conference in June 2010,

Recognizing the increasing participation of women in international migration, driven in large part by socio-economic factors, and that this feminization of migration requires greater gender sensitivity in all policies and efforts related to the subject of international migration,

Stressing the shared responsibility of all stakeholders, in particular countries of origin, transit and destination, relevant regional and international organizations, the private sector and civil society, in promoting an environment that prevents and addresses violence against women migrant workers, and in this regard recognizing the importance of joint and collaborative approaches and strategies at the national, bilateral, regional and international levels,

Recognizing that women migrant workers are important contributors to social and economic development, and underlining the value and dignity of their labour, including the labour of domestic workers,

Acknowledging the contribution that women migrant workers make to development through the economic benefits that accrue to both the country of origin and the country of destination,

Recognizing the particular vulnerability of women and their children at all stages of the migration process, extending from the moment of deciding to migrate, and including transit, engagement in formal and informal employment, and integration into the host society, as well as during their return to their countries of origin,

Expressing deep concern at the continuing reports of grave abuses and violence committed against migrant women and girls, including gender-based violence, in particular sexual violence, trafficking, domestic and family violence, racist and xenophobic acts, abusive labour practices and exploitative conditions of work,

Recognizing that the intersection of, inter alia, gender, age, class and ethnic discrimination and stereotypes can compound the discrimination faced by women migrant workers,

Reaffirming the commitment to protect and promote the human rights of all women, including, without discrimination, indigenous women who migrate for work, and in this regard noting the attention paid in the United Nations Declaration on the Rights of Indigenous Peoples to the elimination of all forms of violence and discrimination against indigenous women, as appropriate,

Concerned that many migrant women who are employed in the informal economy and in less skilled work are especially vulnerable to abuse and exploitation, underlining in this regard the obligation of States to protect the human rights of migrants so as to prevent abuse and exploitation, and observing with concern that many women migrant workers take on jobs for which they may be overqualified and in which, at the same time, they may be more vulnerable because of poor pay and inadequate social protection,

Emphasizing the need for objective, comprehensive and broad-based information, including sex- and age-disaggregated data and statistics, and gender-sensitive indicators for research and analysis, and a wide exchange of experience and lessons learned by individual Member States and civil society in the formulation of policies and concrete strategies to address the problem of violence against women migrant workers,

Realizing that the movement of a significant number of women migrant workers may be facilitated and made possible by means of fraudulent or irregular documentation and sham marriages with the object of migration, that this may be facilitated through, inter alia, the Internet, and that those women migrant workers are more vulnerable to abuse and exploitation,

Recognizing the importance of exploring the link between migration and trafficking in order to further efforts towards protecting women migrant workers from violence, discrimination, exploitation and abuse,

Encouraged by some measures adopted by some countries of destination to alleviate the plight of women migrant workers residing in their areas of jurisdiction, such as the establishment of protection mechanisms for migrant workers, facilitating their access to mechanisms for reporting complaints, or providing assistance during legal proceedings,

Underlining the important role of relevant United Nations treaty bodies in monitoring the implementation of human rights conventions and the relevant special procedures, within their respective mandates, in addressing the problem of violence against women migrant workers and in protecting and promoting their human rights and welfare,

1. *Takes note with appreciation* of the report of the Secretary-General;

2. *Encourages* Member States to consider signing and ratifying or acceding to relevant International Labour Organization conventions and to consider signing and ratifying or acceding to the International Convention on the Protection of the Rights of All Migrant Workers and Members of Their Families, the Protocol to Prevent, Suppress and Punish Trafficking in Persons, Especially Women and Children, supplementing the United Nations Convention against Transnational Organized Crime, and the Protocol against the Smuggling of Migrants by Land, Sea and Air, supplementing the United Nations Convention against Transnational Organized Crime, as well as all human rights treaties that contribute to the protection of the rights of women migrant workers;

3. *Takes note* of the report of the Special Rapporteur of the Human Rights Council on violence against women, its causes and consequences entitled "Political economy of women's human rights", submitted to the Council at its eleventh session, in particular her elaboration in that report of the current issues of the exploitation and violence that women migrants face in the context of the current global economic trends and crises;

4. *Encourages* all United Nations special rapporteurs on human rights whose mandates touch on the issues of violence against women migrant workers to improve the collection of information on and analysis of the current challenges facing women migrant workers, and also encourages Governments to cooperate with the special rapporteurs in this regard;

5. *Calls upon* all Governments to incorporate a human rights and gender perspective in legislation and policies on international migration and on labour and employment, consistent with their human rights obligations and commitments under human rights instruments, for the prevention of and protection of migrant women against violence and discrimination, exploitation and abuse, and to take effective measures to ensure that such migration and labour policies do not reinforce discrimination and bias against women;

6. *Calls upon* Governments to adopt or strengthen measures to protect the human rights of women migrant workers, regardless of their immigration status, including in policies that regulate the recruitment and deployment of women migrant workers, and to consider expanding dialogue among States on devising innovative methods to promote legal channels of migration, inter alia, in order to deter illegal migration;

7. *Urges* Governments to enhance bilateral, regional, interregional and international cooperation to address violence against women migrant workers, fully respecting international law, including international human rights law, as well as to strengthen efforts in reducing the vulnerability of women migrant workers, including by fostering sustainable development alternatives to migration in countries of origin;

8. *Also urges* Governments to take into account the best interests of the child, by adopting or strengthening measures to promote and protect the human rights of migrant girls, including unaccompanied girls, regardless of their immigration status, so as to prevent labour and economic exploitation, discrimination, sexual harassment, violence and sexual abuse in the workplace, including in domestic work;

9. *Further urges* Governments, in cooperation with international organizations, civil society, including non-governmental organizations, and the private sector, to strengthen the focus on and funding support for the prevention of violence against women migrant workers, in particular by promoting the access of women to meaningful and gender-sensitive information and education on, inter alia, the costs and benefits of migration, rights and benefits to which they are entitled in the countries of origin and employment, overall conditions in countries of employment and procedures for legal migration, as well as to ensure that laws and policies governing recruiters, employers and intermediaries promote adherence to and respect for the human rights of migrant workers, particularly women;

10. *Encourages* all States to remove obstacles that may prevent the transparent, safe, unrestricted and expeditious transfer of remittances of migrants to their countries of origin or to any other countries, in conformity with applicable legislation, and to consider, as appropriate, measures to solve other problems that may impede women migrant workers' access to and management of their economic resources;

11. *Calls upon* Governments to recognize the right of women migrant workers, regardless of immigration status, to have access to emergency health care and in this regard to ensure that women migrant workers are not discriminated against on the grounds of pregnancy and childbirth;

12. *Urges* States that have not yet done so to adopt and implement legislation and policies that protect all women

migrant domestic workers, and to grant women migrant workers in domestic service access to transparent mechanisms for bringing complaints against employers, while stressing that such instruments should not punish women migrant workers, and calls upon States to promptly investigate and punish all violations;

13. *Calls upon* Governments, in cooperation with international organizations, non-governmental organizations, the private sector and other stakeholders, to provide women migrant workers who are victims of violence with the full range of immediate assistance and protection, such as access to counselling, legal and consular assistance and temporary shelter, as well as mechanisms to allow the views and concerns of victims to be presented and considered at appropriate stages of proceedings, including other measures that will allow victims to be present during the judicial process, to the extent possible, as well as to establish reintegration and rehabilitation schemes for returning women migrant workers;

14. *Also calls upon* Governments, in particular those of the countries of origin and destination, to put in place penal and criminal sanctions in order to punish perpetrators of violence against women migrant workers and intermediaries, and redress and justice mechanisms that victims can access effectively, as well as to ensure that migrant women victims of violence do not suffer from re-victimization, including by authorities;

15. *Urges* all States to adopt effective measures to put an end to the arbitrary arrest and detention of women migrant workers and to take action to prevent and punish any form of illegal deprivation of the liberty of women migrant workers by individuals or groups;

16. *Encourages* Governments to formulate and implement training programmes for their law enforcers, immigration officers and border officials, diplomatic and consular officials, prosecutors and service providers, with a view to sensitizing those public-sector workers to the issue of violence against women migrant workers and imparting to them the necessary skills and attitude to ensure the delivery of proper, professional and gender-sensitive interventions;

17. *Calls upon* States, in accordance with the provisions of article 36 of the Vienna Convention on Consular Relations, to ensure that, if a woman migrant worker is arrested or committed to prison or custody pending trial, or is detained in any other manner, competent authorities respect her freedom to communicate with and have access to the consular officials of the country of her nationality, and in this regard to inform without delay, if that woman migrant worker so requests, the consular post of her State of nationality;

18. *Invites* Governments, the United Nations system and other concerned intergovernmental and nongovernmental organizations to cooperate towards a better understanding of the issues concerning women and international migration, and to improve the collection, dissemination and analysis of sex- and age-disaggregated data and information in order to assist in the formulation of migration and labour policies that are, inter alia, gender-sensitive and that protect human rights, as well as to aid in policy assessment;

19. *Encourages* concerned Governments, in particular those of the countries of origin, transit and destination, to avail themselves of the expertise of the United Nations, including the Statistics Division of the Department of Economic and Social Affairs of the Secretariat, the United Nations Development Fund for Women and the International Research and Training Institute for the Advancement of Women, to develop appropriate national data-collection and analysis methodologies that will generate comparable data and tracking and reporting systems on violence against women migrant workers;

20. *Notes with appreciation* the elaboration and adoption by the Committee on the Elimination of Discrimination against Women of general recommendation No. 26, on women migrant workers, and calls upon States parties to the Convention on the Elimination of All Forms of Discrimination against Women to consider the recommendation;

21. *Requests* the Secretary-General to report to the General Assembly at its sixty-sixth session on the problem of violence against women migrant workers and on the implementation of the present resolution, taking into account updated information from the organizations of the United Nations system, in particular the International Labour Organization, the United Nations Development Programme, the United Nations Development Fund for Women, the International Research and Training Institute for the Advancement of Women and the United Nations Office on Drugs and Crime, as well as the reports of special rapporteurs that refer to the situation of women migrant workers and other relevant sources, such as the International Organization for Migration, including non-governmental organizations.

Women and armed conflict

Sexual violence and armed conflict

In response to Security Council resolution 1820(2008) [YUN 2008, p. 1265], the Secretary-General submitted a July report [S/2009/362] on the implementation of that resolution. The report determined that conflict environments, characterized by a breakdown in the rule of law and a climate of impunity, created the conditions whereby parties, State and non-State alike, emboldened by their weapons, power and status, enjoyed free reign to inflict sexual violence, with far-reaching implications for efforts to consolidate peace and secure development. Sexual violence prolonged conflict by creating a cycle of attack and counter-attack, fuelling insecurity and fear, which were among the causes of displacement, internally and across borders. It also restricted the ability of women to exercise their rights on the basis of equality with men and to participate in conflict resolution and peacebuilding. All countries that were transitioning to peace from conflicts in which sexual violence was a defining feature indicated that rape and other forms of sexual violence were major factors undermining early recovery and peacebuilding.

Addressing specific conflicts in which sexual violence was used to attack civilians and communities, including by targeting women and girls, the Secretary-General observed that commonalities had emerged that shed light on the nature and patterns of violations and the identity/affiliation and intent of their perpetrators. Examples were cited from conflicts in Afghanistan, Chad, the Democratic Republic of the Congo (DRC), Côte d'Ivoire, Haiti, Myanmar, Nepal, Rwanda, Sierra Leone, the Sudan, Uganda and the former Yugoslavia. Factors contributing to and exacerbating sexual violence included the absence of adequate measures to: prevent sexual violence and protect civilians; combat impunity for sexual violence; and address continuing discrimination against women and girls, in law and practice. The Secretary-General therefore proposed action in the areas of prevention and protection, impunity and assistance to victims that warranted renewed commitment from States and other parties to conflict in order to prevent and respond to sexual violence. In discussing UN efforts, he said that the Organization had to lead by example and drew attention to the development by DPKO of gender guidelines for military personnel in peacekeeping operations to facilitate the implementation of relevant Council resolutions.

The Secretary-General concluded that in bringing together available data, the report showed a disturbing picture of the use of sexual violence against civilians in armed conflicts and their aftermath. He stated that the continued leadership of the Council would be critical to significant progress on combating sexual violence, and made a series of recommendations for the Council's consideration. These included urging the Council to establish a commission of inquiry to investigate and report on violations of international humanitarian and human rights law and recommend to the Council the most effective mechanisms for ensuring accountability. He also requested a follow-up report to include a proposal for an appropriate Council mechanism or procedure to consider and act on information regarding measures taken by parties to armed conflict towards complying with their obligations under international law, and on the perpetrators of sexual violence.

SECURITY COUNCIL ACTION

On 30 September [meeting 6195], the Security Council unanimously adopted **resolution 1888(2009)**. The draft [S/2009/489] was submitted by 68 Member States.

The Security Council,

Reaffirming its commitment to the continuing and full implementation of resolutions 1325(2000) of 31 October 2000, 1612(2005) of 26 July 2005, 1674(2006) of 28 April 2006, 1820(2008) of 19 June 2008 and 1882(2009) of 4 August 2009 and all relevant statements by its President,

Welcoming the report of the Secretary-General of 15 July 2009, but remaining deeply concerned over the lack of progress on the issue of sexual violence in situations of armed conflict, in particular against women and children, notably against girls, and noting, as documented in the report of the Secretary-General, that sexual violence occurs in armed conflicts throughout the world,

Reiterating its deep concern that, despite its repeated condemnation of violence against women and children, including all forms of sexual violence in situations of armed conflict, and despite its calls addressed to all parties to armed conflict for the cessation of such acts with immediate effect, such acts continue to occur, and in some situations have become systematic or widespread,

Recalling the commitments contained in the Beijing Declaration and Platform for Action as well as those contained in the outcome documents of the twenty-third special session of the General Assembly entitled "Women 2000: gender equality, development and peace for the twenty-first century", in particular those concerning women and armed conflict,

Reaffirming the obligations of States parties to the Convention on the Elimination of All Forms of Discrimination against Women and the Optional Protocol thereto, and the Convention on the Rights of the Child and the Optional Protocols thereto, and urging States that have not yet done so to consider ratifying or acceding to them,

Recalling that international humanitarian law affords general protection to women and children as part of the civilian population during armed conflicts and special protection due to the fact that they can be placed particularly at risk,

Recalling also the responsibilities of States to end impunity and to prosecute those responsible for genocide, crimes against humanity, war crimes and other egregious crimes perpetrated against civilians, and in this regard noting with concern that only limited numbers of perpetrators of sexual violence have been brought to justice, while recognizing that in conflict and in post-conflict situations national justice systems may be significantly weakened,

Reaffirming that ending impunity is essential if a society in conflict or recovering from conflict is to come to terms with past abuses committed against civilians affected by armed conflict and to prevent such abuses in the future, drawing attention to the full range of justice and reconciliation mechanisms to be considered, including national, international and "mixed" criminal courts and tribunals and truth and reconciliation commissions, and noting that such mechanisms can promote not only individual responsibility for serious crimes but also peace, truth, reconciliation and the rights of the victims,

Recalling the inclusion of a range of sexual violence offences in the Rome Statute of the International Criminal Court and the statutes of the ad hoc international criminal tribunals,

Stressing the necessity for all States and non-State parties to conflicts to comply fully with their obligations under applicable international law, including the prohibition on all forms of sexual violence,

Recognizing the need for civilian and military leaders, consistent with the principle of command responsibility, to demonstrate commitment and political will to prevent sexual violence and to combat impunity and enforce accountability, and that inaction can send a message that the incidence of sexual violence in conflicts is tolerated,

Emphasizing the importance of addressing sexual violence issues from the outset of peace processes and mediation efforts, in order to protect populations at risk and promote full stability, in particular in the areas of pre-ceasefire humanitarian access and human rights agreements, ceasefires and ceasefire monitoring, disarmament, demobilization and reintegration and security sector reform arrangements, justice and reparations, and post-conflict recovery and development,

Noting with concern the underrepresentation of women in formal peace processes, the lack of mediators and ceasefire monitors with proper training in dealing with sexual violence and the lack of women as chief or lead peace mediators in United Nations-sponsored peace talks,

Recognizing that the promotion and empowerment of women and support for women's organizations and networks are essential in the consolidation of peace to promote the equal and full participation of women, and encouraging Member States, donors and civil society, including non-governmental organizations, to provide support in this respect,

Welcoming the inclusion of women in peacekeeping missions in civil, military and police functions, and recognizing that women and children affected by armed conflict may feel more secure working with and reporting abuse to women in peacekeeping missions and that the presence of women peacekeepers may encourage local women to participate in the national armed and security forces, thereby helping to build a security sector that is accessible and responsive to all, especially women,

Welcoming also the efforts of the Department of Peacekeeping Operations of the Secretariat to develop gender guidelines for military personnel in peacekeeping operations to facilitate the implementation of resolutions 1325(2000) and 1820(2008), and operational guidance to assist civilian, military and police components of peacekeeping missions to effectively implement resolution 1820(2008),

Having considered the report of the Secretary-General of 15 July 2009, and stressing that the present resolution does not seek to make any legal determination as to whether situations that are referred to in the report of the Secretary-General are or are not armed conflicts in the context of the Geneva Conventions of 1949 and the Additional Protocols thereto, of 1977, nor does it prejudge the legal status of the non-State parties involved in those situations,

Recalling its decision, in resolution 1882(2009), to expand the list of parties in situations of armed conflict engaged in the recruitment or use of children in violation of international law annexed to the annual report of the Secretary-General on children and armed conflict to also include those parties to armed conflict that engage, in contravention of applicable international law, in patterns of killing and maiming of children and/or rape and other sexual violence against children in situations of armed conflict,

Noting the role currently assigned to the Office of the Special Adviser on Gender Issues and Advancement of Women to monitor the implementation of resolution

1325(2000) and to promote gender mainstreaming within the United Nations system, the empowerment of women and gender equality, and expressing the importance of effective coordination within the United Nations system in these areas,

Recognizing that States bear the primary responsibility to respect and ensure the human rights of their citizens, as well as all individuals within their territory, as provided for by relevant international law,

Reaffirming that parties to armed conflict bear the primary responsibility to take all feasible steps to ensure the protection of affected civilians,

Reiterating its primary responsibility for the maintenance of international peace and security and, in this connection, its commitment to continue to address the widespread impact of armed conflict on civilians, including with regard to sexual violence,

1.   *Reaffirms* that sexual violence, when used or commissioned as a tactic of war in order to deliberately target civilians or as a part of a widespread or systematic attack against civilian populations, can significantly exacerbate situations of armed conflict and may impede the restoration of international peace and security, affirms in this regard that effective steps to prevent and respond to such acts of sexual violence can significantly contribute to the maintenance of international peace and security, and expresses its readiness, when considering situations on the agenda of the Security Council, to take, where necessary, appropriate steps to address widespread or systematic sexual violence in situations of armed conflict;

2.   *Reiterates its demand* for the complete cessation by all parties to armed conflict of all acts of sexual violence with immediate effect;

3.   *Demands* that all parties to armed conflict immediately take appropriate measures to protect civilians, including women and children, from all forms of sexual violence, including measures such as enforcing appropriate military disciplinary measures and upholding the principle of command responsibility, training troops on the categorical prohibition of all forms of sexual violence against civilians, debunking myths that fuel sexual violence and vetting candidates for national armies and security forces to ensure the exclusion of those associated with serious violations of international humanitarian and human rights law, including sexual violence;

4.   *Requests* that the Secretary-General appoint a Special Representative to provide coherent and strategic leadership, to work effectively to strengthen existing United Nations coordination mechanisms and to engage in advocacy efforts, inter alia, with Governments, including military and judicial representatives, as well as with all parties to armed conflict and civil society, in order to address, both at the headquarters and at the country levels, sexual violence in armed conflict, while promoting cooperation and coordination of efforts among all relevant stakeholders, primarily through the inter-agency initiative "United Nations Action against Sexual Violence in Conflict";

5.   *Encourages* the entities constituting United Nations Action against Sexual Violence in Conflict, as well as other relevant parts of the United Nations system, to support the work of the Special Representative of the Secretary-General mentioned in paragraph 4 above and to continue

and enhance cooperation and information-sharing among all relevant stakeholders in order to reinforce coordination and avoid overlap at the headquarters and country levels and improve system-wide response;

6. *Urges* States to undertake comprehensive legal and judicial reforms, as appropriate, in conformity with international law, without delay and with a view to bringing perpetrators of sexual violence in conflicts to justice and to ensuring that survivors have access to justice, are treated with dignity throughout the justice process and are protected and receive redress for their suffering;

7. *Urges* all parties to conflict to ensure that all reports of sexual violence committed by civilians or by military personnel are thoroughly investigated and the alleged perpetrators brought to justice, and that civilian superiors and military commanders, in accordance with international humanitarian law, use their authority and powers to prevent sexual violence, including by combating impunity;

8. *Calls upon* the Secretary-General to identify and take the appropriate measures to deploy rapidly a team of experts to situations of particular concern with respect to sexual violence in armed conflict, working through the United Nations presence on the ground and with the consent of the host Government, to assist national authorities to strengthen the rule of law, and recommends making use of existing human resources within the United Nations system and voluntary contributions, drawing upon requisite expertise, as appropriate, in the rule of law, civilian and military judicial systems, mediation, criminal investigation, security sector reform, witness protection, fair trial standards and public outreach to, inter alia:

(*a*) Work closely with national legal and judicial officials and other personnel in the civilian and military justice systems of the relevant Governments to address impunity, including by the strengthening of national capacity, and drawing attention to the full range of justice mechanisms to be considered;

(*b*) Identify gaps in national response and encourage a holistic national approach to address sexual violence in armed conflict, including by enhancing criminal accountability responsiveness to victims and judicial capacity;

(*c*) Make recommendations to coordinate domestic and international efforts and resources to reinforce the ability of the Government to address sexual violence in armed conflict;

(*d*) Work with the United Nations mission, country team and the Special Representative of the Secretary-General mentioned in paragraph 4 above, as appropriate, towards the full implementation of the measures called for in resolution 1820(2008);

9. *Encourages* States, relevant United Nations entities and civil society, as appropriate, to provide assistance, in close cooperation with national authorities, to build national capacity in the judicial and law enforcement systems in situations of particular concern with respect to sexual violence in armed conflict;

10. *Reiterates its intention*, when adopting or renewing targeted sanctions in situations of armed conflict, to consider including, where appropriate, designation criteria pertaining to acts of rape and other forms of sexual violence; and calls upon all peacekeeping and other relevant United Nations missions and United Nations bodies, in particu-

lar the Security Council Working Group on Children and Armed Conflict, to share with relevant Security Council sanctions committees, including through relevant monitoring groups and groups of experts of sanctions committees, all pertinent information about sexual violence;

11. *Expresses its intention* to ensure that resolutions to establish or renew peacekeeping mandates contain provisions, as appropriate, on the prevention of, and response to, sexual violence, with corresponding reporting requirements to the Council;

12. *Decides* to include specific provisions, as appropriate, for the protection of women and children from rape and other sexual violence in the mandates of United Nations peacekeeping operations, including, on a case-by-case basis, the identification of women's protection advisers among gender advisers and human rights protection units, and requests the Secretary-General to ensure that the need for, and the number and roles of, women's protection advisers is systematically assessed during the preparation of each United Nations peacekeeping operation;

13. *Encourages* States, with the support of the international community, to increase access to health care, psychosocial support, legal assistance and socio-economic reintegration services for victims of sexual violence, in particular in rural areas;

14. *Expresses its intention* to make better use of periodical field visits to conflict areas, through the organization of interactive meetings with the local women and women's organizations in the field about the concerns and needs of women in areas of armed conflict;

15. *Encourages* leaders at the national and local levels, including traditional leaders where they exist and religious leaders, to play a more active role in sensitizing communities on sexual violence to avoid marginalization and stigmatization of victims, to assist with their social reintegration and to combat a culture of impunity for these crimes;

16. *Urges* the Secretary-General, Member States and the heads of regional organizations to take measures to increase the representation of women in mediation processes and decision-making processes with regard to conflict resolution and peacebuilding;

17. *Urges* that issues of sexual violence be included in all United Nations-sponsored peace negotiation agendas, and also urges the inclusion of sexual violence issues from the outset of peace processes in such situations, in particular in the areas of pre-ceasefire humanitarian access and human rights agreements, ceasefires and ceasefire monitoring, disarmament, demobilization and reintegration and security sector reform arrangements, vetting of armed and security forces, justice and reparations and recovery/development;

18. *Reaffirms* the role of the Peacebuilding Commission in promoting inclusive gender-based approaches to reducing instability in post-conflict situations, noting the important role of women in rebuilding society, and urges the Commission to encourage all parties in the countries on its agenda to incorporate and implement measures to reduce sexual violence in post-conflict strategies;

19. *Encourages* Member States to deploy greater numbers of female military and police personnel to United Nations peacekeeping operations and to provide all military

and police personnel with adequate training to carry out their responsibilities;

20. *Requests* the Secretary-General to ensure that technical support is provided to troop- and police-contributing countries in order to include guidance for military and police personnel on addressing sexual violence in predeployment and induction training;

21. *Also requests* the Secretary-General to continue and strengthen efforts to implement the policy of zero tolerance of sexual exploitation and abuse in United Nations peacekeeping operations, and urges troop- and police-contributing countries to take appropriate preventative action, including predeployment and in-theatre awareness training, and other action to ensure full accountability in cases of such conduct involving their personnel;

22. *Further requests* the Secretary-General to continue to direct all relevant United Nations entities to take specific measures to ensure systematic mainstreaming of gender issues within their respective institutions, including by ensuring the allocation of adequate financial and human resources within all relevant offices and departments and on the ground, as well as to strengthen, within their respective mandates, their cooperation and coordination when addressing the issue of sexual violence in armed conflict;

23. *Urges* relevant Special Representatives of the Secretary-General and the Emergency Relief Coordinator, with strategic and technical support from the United Nations Action against Sexual Violence in Conflict network, to work with Member States to develop joint Government–United Nations comprehensive strategies to combat sexual violence, in consultation with all relevant stakeholders, and to regularly provide updates on this in their standard reporting to Headquarters;

24. *Requests* the Secretary-General to ensure more systematic reporting on the incidence of trends, emerging patterns of attack and early warning indicators of the use of sexual violence in armed conflict in all relevant reports to the Council, and encourages the Special Representatives of the Secretary-General, the Emergency Relief Coordinator, the United Nations High Commissioner for Human Rights, the Special Rapporteur on violence against women, its causes and consequences and the Chair(s) of United Nations Action against Sexual Violence in Conflict to provide to the Council, in coordination with the Special Representative mentioned in paragraph 4 above, additional briefings and documentation on sexual violence in armed conflict;

25. *Also requests* the Secretary-General to include, where appropriate, in his regular reports on individual peacekeeping operations, information on steps taken to implement measures to protect civilians, particularly women and children, against sexual violence;

26. *Further requests* the Secretary-General, taking into account the proposals contained in his report as well as any other relevant elements, to devise urgently and preferably within three months specific proposals on ways to ensure monitoring and reporting in a more effective and efficient way within the existing United Nations system on the protection of women and children from rape and other sexual violence in armed conflict and post-conflict situations, utilizing expertise from the United Nations system

and the contributions of national Governments, regional organizations, non-governmental organizations in their advisory capacity and various civil society actors, in order to provide timely, objective, accurate and reliable information on gaps in the response by United Nations entities, for consideration in taking appropriate action;

27. *Requests* the Secretary-General to continue to submit annual reports to the Council on the implementation of resolution 1820(2008) and to submit by September 2010 his next report, on the implementation of the present resolution and resolution 1820(2008), to include, inter alia:

(*a*) A detailed coordination and strategy plan on the timely and ethical collection of information;

(*b*) Updates on efforts by United Nations mission focal points on sexual violence to work closely with the Resident Coordinator/Humanitarian Coordinator, the United Nations country team and, where appropriate, the Special Representative mentioned in paragraph 4 above and/or the team of experts mentioned in paragraph 8 above to address sexual violence;

(*c*) Information regarding parties to armed conflict that are credibly suspected of committing patterns of rape or other forms of sexual violence in situations that are on the agenda of the Council;

28. *Decides* to review, taking into account the process established by General Assembly resolution 63/311 of 14 September 2009 regarding a United Nations composite gender entity, the mandates of the Special Representative requested in paragraph 4 above and the team of experts requested in paragraph 8 above, within two years, and as appropriate thereafter;

29. *Decides also* to remain actively seized of the matter.

Women, peace and security

In response to a Security Council request contained in presidential statement S/PRST/2008/39 [YUN 2008, p. 1264] for a report on the implementation of resolution 1325(2000) [YUN 2000, p. 1113], the Secretary-General submitted a September report [S/2009/465 & Corr.1] on women, peace and security. He also reviewed progress made by key actors towards implementing resolution 1325(2000). The report drew on information provided by UN entities and reports of the Secretary-General to the Council.

Although much had been done in response to resolution 1325(2000), which called for the adoption of a gender perspective that would take into account the special needs of women during conflict prevention, conflict resolution and peacebuilding, progress in its implementation was found to be limited. The Secretary-General had responded to the call in resolution 1325(2000) to increase the number of women in senior peacekeeping positions, with three women serving as Head of Mission and six serving as Deputy to the Head of Mission. There was also a need for a dedicated monitoring mechanism and a system to review progress and feedback of lessons learned from implementation of the resolution.

The Secretary-General proposed specific actions, including that Member States condemn violations of the rights of women and girls during armed conflict and take swift action in prosecuting those who committed gender-based violence in the context of armed conflict, and use all provisions under international law to address those crimes. Member States should also ensure the representation of women at all decision-making levels in accordance with resolution 1325(2000) and all actors involved in conflict prevention, conflict resolution and peacebuilding must make efforts to collect data on all aspects of the resolution. The Council should require that all country reports provide specific information on the impact of armed conflict on women and girls and use the commemoration of the tenth (2010) anniversary of resolution 1325(2000) to organize a high-level ministerial event to direct the attention of the international community towards implementing the resolution fully.

Communication. On 5 October [meeting 6196], the Council held an open debate on women and peace and security, and had before it a concept paper [S/2009/490] submitted by Viet Nam.

SECURITY COUNCIL ACTION

On 5 October [meeting 6196], the Security Council unanimously adopted **resolution 1889(2009)**. The draft [S/2009/500] was submitted by 21 Member States.

The Security Council,

Reaffirming its commitment to the continuing and full implementation, in a mutually reinforcing manner, of resolutions 1325(2000) of 31 October 2000, 1612(2005) of 26 July 2005, 1674(2006) of 28 April 2006, 1820(2008) of 19 June 2008, 1882(2009) of 4 August 2009 and 1888(2009) of 30 September 2009 and all relevant statements by its President,

Guided by the purposes and principles of the Charter of the United Nations, and bearing in mind the primary responsibility of the Security Council under the Charter for the maintenance of international peace and security,

Recalling the resolve, expressed in the 2005 World Summit Outcome, to eliminate all forms of violence against women and girls and the obligations of States parties to the Convention on the Elimination of All Forms of Discrimination Against Women and the Optional Protocol thereto, and the Convention on the Rights of the Child and the Optional Protocols thereto, recalling also the commitments contained in the Beijing Declaration and Platform for Action as well as those contained in the outcome documents of the twenty-third special session of the General Assembly entitled "Women 2000: gender equality, development and peace for the twenty-first century", in particular those concerning women and armed conflict,

Having considered the report of the Secretary-General of 16 September 2009, and stressing that the present resolution does not seek to make any legal determination as to whether situations that are referred to in the report of the Secretary-General are or are not armed conflicts in the context of the Geneva Conventions of 1949 and the Additional Protocols thereto, of 1977, nor does it prejudge the legal status of the non-State parties involved in those situations,

Welcoming the efforts of Member States in implementing resolution 1325(2000) at the national level, including the development of national action plans, and encouraging Member States to continue to pursue such implementation,

Reiterating the need for the full, equal and effective participation of women at all stages of peace processes, given their vital role in the prevention and resolution of conflict and in peacebuilding, reaffirming the key role that women can play in re-establishing the fabric of recovering society, and stressing the need for their involvement in the development and implementation of post-conflict strategies in order to take into account their perspectives and needs,

Expressing deep concern about the underrepresentation of women at all stages of peace processes, in particular the very low numbers of women in formal roles in mediation processes, and stressing the need to ensure that women are appropriately appointed at decision-making levels, as high-level mediators, and in the composition of the mediators' teams,

Remaining deeply concerned about the persistent obstacles to women's full involvement in the prevention and resolution of conflicts and participation in post-conflict public life, as a result of violence and intimidation, lack of security and lack of rule of law, cultural discrimination and stigmatization, including the rise of extremist or fanatical views on women, and socio-economic factors, including the lack of access to education, and in this respect recognizing that the marginalization of women can delay or undermine the achievement of durable peace, security and reconciliation,

Recognizing the particular needs of women and girls in post-conflict situations, including physical security, health services, including reproductive and mental health, ways to ensure their livelihoods, land and property rights, employment, as well as their participation in decision-making and post-conflict planning, particularly at early stages of post-conflict peacebuilding,

Noting that despite progress, obstacles to strengthening the participation of women in conflict prevention, conflict resolution and peacebuilding remain, expressing concern that the capacity of women to engage in public decision-making and economic recovery often does not receive adequate recognition or financing in post-conflict situations, and underlining that funding for early recovery needs of women is vital to increase the empowerment of women, which can contribute to effective post-conflict peacebuilding,

Noting also that women in situations of armed conflict and post-conflict situations continue to be considered often as victims and not as actors in addressing and resolving situations of armed conflict, and stressing the need to focus not only on the protection of women but also on their empowerment in peacebuilding,

Recognizing that an understanding of the impact of situations of armed conflict on women and girls, including as refugees and internally displaced persons, adequate and rapid response to their particular needs and effective institutional arrangements to guarantee their protection and full participation in the peace process, particularly at early stages of post-conflict peacebuilding, can significantly contribute to the maintenance and promotion of international peace and security,

Welcoming the United Nations initiative to develop a system similar to that pioneered by the United Nations Development Programme to allow decision-makers to track gender-related allocations in United Nations Development Group Multi-Donor Trust Funds,

Welcoming also the efforts of the Secretary-General to appoint more women to senior United Nations positions, particularly in field missions, as a tangible step towards providing United Nations leadership on implementation of resolution 1325(2000),

Welcoming further the upcoming establishment of a United Nations steering committee to enhance visibility and strengthen coordination within the United Nations system regarding the preparations for the tenth anniversary of resolution 1325(2000),

Encouraging relevant actors to organize events during the period 2009–2010 at the global, regional and national levels to increase awareness about resolution 1325(2000), including ministerial events, to renew commitments to "Women and peace and security" and to identify ways to address remaining and new challenges in implementing resolution 1325(2000) in the future,

1.   *Urges* Member States and international and regional organizations to take further measures to improve the participation of women during all stages of peace processes, particularly in conflict resolution, post-conflict planning and peacebuilding, including by enhancing their engagement in political and economic decision-making at early stages of recovery processes, by, inter alia, promoting women's leadership and capacity to engage in aid management and planning, supporting women's organizations and countering negative societal attitudes about the capacity of women to participate equally;

2.   *Reiterates its call* for all parties to armed conflicts to respect fully international law applicable to the rights and protection of women and girls;

3.   *Strongly condemns* all violations of applicable international law committed against women and girls in situations of armed conflict and post-conflict situations, demands that all parties to conflicts cease such acts with immediate effect, and emphasizes the responsibility of all States to put an end to impunity and to prosecute those responsible for all forms of violence committed against women and girls in armed conflicts, including rape and other sexual violence;

4.   *Calls upon* the Secretary-General to develop a strategy, including through appropriate training, to increase the number of women appointed to pursue good offices on his behalf, particularly as Special Representatives and Special Envoys, and to take measures to increase the participation of women in United Nations political, peacebuilding and peacekeeping missions;

5.   *Requests* the Secretary-General to ensure that all country reports to the Security Council provide information on the impact of situations of armed conflict on women and girls, their particular needs in post-conflict situations and obstacles to meeting those needs;

6.   *Also requests* the Secretary-General to ensure that relevant United Nations bodies, in cooperation with Member States and civil society, collect data on, analyse and systematically assess the particular needs of women and girls in post-conflict situations, including information on their needs for physical security and participation in decision-making and post-conflict planning, in order to improve system-wide response to those needs;

7.   *Expresses its intention*, when establishing and renewing the mandates of United Nations missions, to include provisions on the promotion of gender equality and the empowerment of women in post-conflict situations, requests the Secretary-General to continue, as appropriate, to appoint gender advisers and/or women's protection advisers to United Nations missions, and asks them, in cooperation with United Nations country teams, to render technical assistance and improved coordination efforts to address recovery needs of women and girls in post-conflict situations;

8.   *Urges* Member States to ensure gender mainstreaming in all post-conflict peacebuilding and recovery processes and sectors;

9.   *Urges* Member States, United Nations bodies, donors and civil society to ensure that the empowerment of women is taken into account during post-conflict needs assessments and planning and factored into subsequent funding disbursements and programme activities, including by developing transparent analysis and tracking of funds allocated for addressing the needs of women in the post-conflict phase;

10.   *Encourages* Member States in post-conflict situations, in consultation with civil society, including women's organizations, to specify in detail the needs and priorities of women and girls and to design concrete strategies, in accordance with their legal systems, to address those needs and priorities, which cover, inter alia, support for greater physical security and better socio-economic conditions, through education, income-generating activities, access to basic services, in particular health services, including sexual and reproductive health and reproductive rights and mental health, gender-responsive law enforcement and access to justice, as well as enhancing capacity to engage in public decision-making at all levels;

11.   *Urges* Member States, United Nations bodies and civil society, including non-governmental organizations, to take all feasible measures to ensure women and girls' equal access to education in post-conflict situations, given the vital role of education in the promotion of women's participation in post-conflict decision-making;

12.   *Calls upon* all parties to armed conflicts to respect the civilian and humanitarian character of refugee camps and settlements and ensure the protection of all civilians inhabiting such camps, in particular women and girls, from all forms of violence, including rape and other sexual violence, and to ensure full, unimpeded and secure humanitarian access to them;

13.   *Calls upon* all those involved in the planning for disarmament, demobilization and reintegration to take into account the particular needs of women and girls associated with armed forces and armed groups and their children, and provide for their full access to these programmes;

14. *Encourages* the Peacebuilding Commission and the Peacebuilding Support Office to continue to ensure systematic attention to and mobilization of resources for advancing gender equality and the empowerment of women as an integral part of post-conflict peacebuilding, and to encourage the full participation of women in this process;

15. *Requests* the Secretary-General, in his agenda for action to improve the peacebuilding efforts of the United Nations, to take account of the need to improve the participation of women in political and economic decision-making from the earliest stages of the peacebuilding process;

16. *Also requests* the Secretary-General to ensure full transparency, cooperation and coordination of efforts between the Special Representative of the Secretary-General for Children and Armed Conflict and the Special Representative of the Secretary-General on sexual violence and armed conflict whose appointment has been requested in resolution 1888(2009);

17. *Further requests* the Secretary-General to submit to the Council within six months, for consideration, a set of indicators for use at the global level to track implementation of resolution 1325(2000), which could serve as a common basis for reporting by relevant United Nations entities, other international and regional organizations and Member States on the implementation of resolution 1325(2000) in 2010 and beyond;

18. *Requests* the Secretary-General, in the report requested in the statement by the President of the Security Council of 23 October 2007, to also include a review of progress in the implementation of resolution 1325(2000), an assessment of the processes by which the Council receives, analyses and takes action on information pertinent to resolution 1325(2000), recommendations on further measures to improve coordination across the United Nations system and with Member States and civil society to deliver implementation, and data on the participation of women in United Nations missions;

19. *Also requests* the Secretary-General to submit a report to the Council within twelve months on addressing women's participation and inclusion in peacebuilding and planning in the aftermath of conflict, taking into consideration the views of the Peacebuilding Commission and including, inter alia:

(a) An analysis of the particular needs of women and girls in post-conflict situations;

(b) Challenges to the participation of women in conflict resolution and peacebuilding and gender mainstreaming in all early post-conflict planning, financing and recovery processes;

(c) Measures to support national capacity in planning for and financing responses to the needs of women and girls in post-conflict situations;

(d) Recommendations for improving international and national responses to the needs of women and girls in post-conflict situations, including the development of effective financial and institutional arrangements to guarantee the full and equal participation of women in the peacebuilding process;

20. *Decides* to remain actively seized of the matter.

Communications. In identical letters of 6 October to the Secretary-General and the Security Council President [A/64/483-S/2009/512], Malta stated that it supported the overall thrust of resolution 1889(2009), but wished to register its reservations about the reference in paragraph 10 to "health services, including sexual and reproductive health and reproductive rights", for reasons related to the question of abortion.

Women in power and decision-making

Mainstreaming gender into national policies and programmes

In accordance with Economic and Social Council resolution 2006/9 [YUN 2006, p. 1356], the Commission on the Status of Women considered progress on mainstreaming a gender perspective in the development, implementation and evaluation of national policies and programmes. At its March session [E/2009/27], the Commission's priority theme was "The equal sharing of responsibilities between women and men, including caregiving in the context of HIV/AIDS" (see p. 1129).

2010 ECOSOC thematic discussion

On 20 April, the Economic and Social Council decided that "Current global and national trends and challenges and their impact on gender equality and empowerment of women" would be the topic for the thematic discussion of the high-level segment of its 2010 substantive session (**decision 2009/210**).

Institutional mechanisms for the advancement of women

Inter-Agency Network. The United Nations Inter-Agency Network on Women and Gender Equality (IANWGE), at its eighth annual session (New York, 24–26 February) [IANWGE/2009/Report], discussed matters for consideration by the High-Level Committees on Programme and on Management of the United Nations System Chief Executives Board for Coordination, including: UN reform; preparations for the fifteenth anniversaries of the Fourth World Conference on Women (Beijing Conference) [YUN 1995, p. 1170] and the United Nations Conference on Population and Development (Cairo Conference) [YUN 1994, p. 955]; the outcome of the Follow-up International Conference on Financing for Development to Review Implementation of the Monterrey Consensus [YUN 2008, p. 1076] in the context of economic crises and their gender impacts; review and appraisal of the system-wide implementation of the Economic and Social Council agreed conclusions

1997/2 [YUN 1997, p. 1186] on mainstreaming a gender perspective into all polices and programmes of the UN system; and operationalization of the system-wide policy and strategy on gender mainstreaming. The session heard oral briefings on those topics by representatives of UN entities. Presentations on new and emerging issues dealt with the gender impact of the food crisis and gender aspects of climate change, among other matters.

IANWGE decided to develop a system-wide strategy on capacity development on gender mainstreaming in order to improve the understanding of gender issues by UN system staff and harmonize system-wide interventions on gender mainstreaming. It would also contribute to the fifteen-year review of the implementation of the Beijing Declaration and Platform for Action and the outcomes of the twenty-third special session of the General Assembly. Further, the Network closed the Task Force on Gender Mainstreaming in Results-Based Management Systems and set up a new task force on the gender impacts of the financial and economic crises. It also decided to intensify its work in preparation for a system-wide action plan of activities, events and initiatives for the fifteenth anniversaries of the Beijing Conference and the Cairo Conference and intensify preparatory work towards the commemoration of the tenth anniversary of Security Council resolution 1325(2000) on women and peace and security [YUN 2000, p. 1113].

Report of Secretary-General. In response to Economic and Social Council resolution 2008/34 [YUN 2008, p. 1269], the Secretary-General submitted a May report [E/2009/71] on mainstreaming a gender perspective into all UN system policies and programmes. The report was based on the responses of 38 UN entities to an IANWGE-approved questionnaire. It also updated information on actions taken to implement paragraph 4 of Council resolution 2006/36 [YUN 2006, p. 1350] and paragraph 19 of Council resolution 2006/9 [ibid., p. 1356].

A persistent area of weakness with regard to accountability was the slow development of a common tool for assessing progress and gaps, which made it difficult to compare and evaluate progress throughout the system. Although the Secretariat had instituted a criterion of "respect for diversity/gender" as part of the performance indicators for all staff, it was not consistently applied. As to financial and human resources for gender mainstreaming, entities reported that budgetary restraints and lack of funding hindered their abilities to meet goals on integrating gender perspectives. Most entities reported using results-based management frameworks to improve gender mainstreaming and narrow the gap between policy and practice. They were also increasingly setting concrete targets to be monitored at the country level and using sex-disaggregated data and gender-sensitive indicators in materials disseminated to policymakers and the public. In the context of unifying evaluation methodologies, several entities reported their participation in working groups of the United Nations Evaluation Group, which was preparing an overview of institutional practices regarding management response to evaluation in order to standardize approaches towards mainstreaming a gender perspective in evaluations. However, the efforts of individual entities suggested a variety of approaches without an emerging unified approach to the development of methodologies, and that constrained the ability of the UN system to make progress in closing gaps in gender mainstreaming. On the implementation of resolution 2006/36, the report found that an effective programme on gender equality had yet to be established, although the commitment to gender mainstreaming training had evolved, including in core competence development programmes. Progress was also made towards developing gender mainstreaming training for different categories of staff, including management, and on making such training mandatory for all staff. The report stated that a gender scorecard was being developed through consultation between the Office of the Special Adviser on Gender Issues and Advancement of Women (OSAGI), the Department of Management and the Office of Human Resources Management (OHRM). In addition, OHRM was working with OSAGI to develop revised gender balance targets for the 2009–2010 human resources action plans.

Recommendations included: strengthening of the monitoring, reporting and evaluation of progress, and identifying gaps by using common methods and indicators; increasing the use of electronic means to provide capacity development for managers and staff, including mandatory staff training; ensuring that all field offices and headquarters had gender focal points and specialists; ensuring operationalization of the system-wide policy and strategy on gender mainstreaming; using existing training institutions to assist entities in developing unified training modules on gender mainstreaming; and using all avenues, including the Secretary-General's campaign to end violence against women, to strengthen inter-agency collaboration for gender mainstreaming.

ECONOMIC AND SOCIAL COUNCIL ACTION

On 28 July [meeting 40], the Economic and Social Council adopted **resolution 2009/12** [draft: E/2009/L.20] without vote [agenda item 7 *(e)*].

Mainstreaming a gender perspective into all policies and programmes in the United Nations system

The Economic and Social Council,

Reaffirming its agreed conclusions 1997/2 of 18 July 1997 on mainstreaming a gender perspective into all policies and programmes in the United Nations system, and recalling its resolutions 2001/41 of 26 July 2001, 2002/23 of 24 July 2002, 2003/49 of 24 July 2003, 2004/4 of 7 July 2004, 2005/31 of 26 July 2005, 2006/36 of 27 July 2006, 2007/33 of 27 July 2007 and 2008/34 of 25 July 2008,

Reaffirming also the commitment made at the 2005 World Summit to actively promote the mainstreaming of a gender perspective in the design, implementation, monitoring and evaluation of policies and programmes in all political, economic and social spheres and to strengthen the capabilities of the United Nations system in the area of gender,

Reaffirming further that gender mainstreaming is a globally accepted strategy for achieving gender equality and constitutes a critical strategy in the implementation of the Beijing Platform for Action and the outcomes of the twenty-third special session of the General Assembly,

Bearing in mind the fifteenth anniversary of the adoption of the Beijing Declaration and Platform for Action,

Taking into consideration the theme for the 2010 annual ministerial review of the Economic and Social Council, "Implementing the internationally agreed goals and commitments in regard to gender equality and empowerment of women",

1. *Takes note with appreciation* of the report of the Secretary-General and the recommendations contained therein, and calls for further and continued efforts to mainstream a gender perspective into all policies and programmes of the United Nations in accordance with all relevant Economic and Social Council resolutions;

2. *Requests* the Inter-Agency Network on Women and Gender Equality to continue to provide practical support in gender mainstreaming to its members;

3. *Requests* the Secretary-General to submit to the Economic and Social Council at its substantive session of 2010 a detailed report on progress made by United Nations entities in mainstreaming a gender perspective in the design, implementation, monitoring and evaluation of all policies and programmes and in capacity development, including through mandatory training for all staff and personnel and specific training for senior managers, as a critical means of raising their awareness, knowledge, commitment and competencies, as well as with regard to collaborative efforts to ensure effective gender mainstreaming in the United Nations system.

Strengthening of
UN gender equality architecture

During 2009, United Nations efforts towards strengthening the gender architecture of the Organization continued. The Co-Chairs of the High-level Panel on UN System-wide Coherence (see p. 1367) convened six meetings on gender between March and June, at which Member State delegations and representatives of UN bodies discussed ways to advance the work on gender architecture reform that had been undertaken by the General Assembly.

Institutional options papers. By a 13 March letter, the General Assembly President transmitted to Member States a document entitled "Further Details on Institutional Options for Strengthening the Institutional Arrangements for Support to Gender Equality and the Empowerment of Women", which was prepared by the Secretary-General in response to Assembly resolution 62/277 [YUN 2008, p. 1516]. The document described the four potential approaches to strengthening the UN gender equality architecture. The first option—the status quo—received limited coverage, as analysis confirmed it would be the least effective in eliminating fragmentation or providing a single driver and voice for the UN system on gender equality. The second option would involve the establishment of a fund/programme by the Assembly that would be separately administered and funded. It would partially consolidate the existing four gender-focused entities: OSAGI, DAW, UNIFEM and the International Research and Training Institute for the Advancement of Women (INSTRAW), with the exception of those staff resources that provided support to intergovernmental bodies. The third option envisioned a UN Secretariat department on gender equality and women's empowerment that would consolidate the four gender-focused entities. The fourth option—the composite entity—would combine Headquarters policy and normative support functions currently performed by departments with the country-level operational and technical support characteristic of Funds and Programmes. The last option received particular attention as many Member States had expressed interest in it during informal consultations.

The document concluded that the composite entity had the greatest potential to consolidate the strengths and experiences of the four existing gender-specific entities and create synergy between operational work and normative and policy development functions. It would bring together the normative inputs of the Commission on the Status of Women and other intergovernmental bodies with a strengthened operational component overseen by an Executive Board dedicated to gender equality and women's empowerment. It would also ensure a link between the consideration of gender mainstreaming in the intergovernmental sphere and in operational activities.

By a 4 June letter, the Assembly President transmitted to Member States a document entitled "Consolidated response regarding questions raised following discussions of the paper 'Further Details on Institutional Options for Strengthening the Institutional Arrangements for Support to Gender Equality and the Empowerment of Women'", which was prepared by the Secretary-General in response to questions raised by Member States at a working-level interactive meeting on 15 April. The document further addressed the proposed structure, governance, staffing and funding for a new gender-specific entity and the relationships between it and intergovernmental bodies.

Reports of Co-Chairs. By a 19 June letter, the Co-Chairs on system-wide coherence transmitted to Member States an executive summary that reflected the state of discussions on strengthening the institutional arrangements for the support of gender equality and the empowerment of women. The summary noted that the establishment of a composite entity remained the most promising option for the United Nations to meet its mandate in that regard. The proposed entity would have the same flexibility as other UN operational entities to provide an effective response to countries' requests. It would service all countries, while establishing a strategic and cost-effective field presence as its resources grew. After considering the views of Member States, the Co-Chairs recommended that the Assembly take action at its sixty-third session in 2009. They recognized, however, that two areas required further discussion: the funding sources for the new entity from UN regular resources and voluntary sources; and the intergovernmental oversight mechanisms for the new gender entity. In that context, the Co-Chairs would hold meetings in order to find common ground for the establishment of the new entity.

In a 7 August letter, the Co-Chairs again recommended that the Assembly decide at its sixty-third session on the establishment of a composite gender entity that built on the existing four entities, while consolidating them into one that would perform the functions outlined in the relevant reports of the Secretary-General. Regarding the intergovernmental oversight mechanisms for the proposed new entity, there was general consensus that the Assembly and the Economic and Social Council, including the Commission on the Status of Women, would remain the overarching normative and policymaking bodies. As regards the intergovernmental oversight mechanism for operational activities, the Co-Chairs sensed an emerging recognition that a decision on an executive board to oversee the entity's organizational work in a manner similar to that established in Assembly resolution 48/162 [YUN 1993, p. 1118] was important in order to achieve appropriate oversight and guidance during the entity's transitional period. Should the Assembly decide to create the composite entity, a transitional arrangement was envisaged to ensure the necessary leadership and preparatory work throughout the establishment process. During such a period, the existing entities would continue to carry out their mandates.

In **resolution 63/311** (see p. 1368), the Assembly strongly supported the consolidation of OSAGI, DAW, UNIFEM and INSTRAW into a composite entity, taking into account the existing mandates. It also supported that the entity would be led by an Under-Secretary-General, who would report directly to the Secretary-General. It requested the Secretary-General to produce, for the Assembly's consideration at its sixty-fourth session, a proposal specifying the mission statement, funding, and organizational arrangements of the composite entity so that intergovernmental negotiations could commence.

Women and human rights

Division for the Advancement of Women and OHCHR activities

During the year, cooperation continued between DAW and the Office of the United Nations High Commissioner for Human Rights (OHCHR) with the goal of achieving equality between women and men and promoting and protecting women's human rights. In December, the Secretary-General transmitted a report [A/HRC/13/70-E/CN.6/2010/7] on implementation of the 2009 joint worplan of DAW and OHCHR, which summarized the major activities carried out and presented the 2010 joint workplan.

Palestinian women

In accordance with Economic and Social Council resolution 2008/11 [YUN 2008, p. 514], a report of the Secretary-General [E/CN.6/2009/5] reviewed the situation of and assistance to Palestinian women from October 2007 to September 2008 (see p. 473).

On 28 July, the Council took action on the situation of and assistance to Palestinian women in **resolution 2009/14** (see p. 474).

The girl child

In response to General Assembly resolution 62/140 [YUN 2007, p. 1173], the Secretary-General submitted an August report [A/64/315] on the girl child, which reviewed international obligations and commitments with respect to the girl child, stemming from human rights treaties and international conferences, as well as legal and policy developments. The report addressed progress and challenges with respect to discrimination against the girl child in the areas of: poverty and the impact of crises; preventing abuse, exploitation and violence; protecting girls in conflict situations and humanitarian crises; promoting girls' education; promoting human rights education; improving water, sanitation and hygiene; combating HIV/AIDS; girls' participation in policy and practice; improving the health status of the girl child; and UN collaboration in support of the girl child. The report also described efforts to support the abandonment of female genital mutilation.

The Assembly took note of the Secretary-General's report on 18 December (**decision 64/532**).

On 18 December [meeting 65], the General Assembly, on the recommendation of the Third Committee [A/64/435 & Corr.1], adopted **resolution 64/145** without vote [agenda item 65 *(a)*].

The girl child

The General Assembly,

Recalling its resolution 62/140 of 18 December 2007 and all relevant resolutions, including the agreed conclusions of the Commission on the Status of Women, in particular those relevant to the girl child,

Reaffirming the equal rights of women and men as enshrined in the Charter of the United Nations,

Recalling all human rights and other instruments relevant to the rights of the child, in particular the girl child, including the Convention on the Rights of the Child, the Convention on the Elimination of All Forms of Discrimination against Women, the Convention on the Rights of Persons with Disabilities and the Optional Protocols thereto,

Welcoming the entry into force of the Convention on the Rights of Persons with Disabilities and the specific attention paid therein to the fact that women and girls with disabilities are subject to multiple discrimination, including in education and schooling,

Reaffirming the internationally agreed development goals, including the Millennium Development Goals, as well as the commitments relevant to the girl child made at the 2005 World Summit,

Recalling the Convention on Consent to Marriage, Minimum Age for Marriage and Registration of Marriages,

Reaffirming the outcome document of the twenty-seventh special session of the General Assembly on children, entitled "A world fit for children", the Declaration of Commitment on HIV/AIDS adopted at the twenty-sixth special session of the General Assembly on HIV/AIDS, entitled "Global Crisis–Global Action", and the Political Declaration on HIV/AIDS of 2006,

Reaffirming also all other relevant outcomes of major United Nations summits and conferences relevant to the girl child, as well as their five- and ten-year reviews, including the Beijing Declaration and Platform for Action adopted at the Fourth World Conference on Women, the outcome of the twenty-third special session of the General Assembly entitled "Women 2000: gender equality, development and peace for the twenty-first century", the Programme of Action of the International Conference on Population and Development, the Programme of Action of the World Summit for Social Development and the declaration adopted by the Commission on the Status of Women at its forty-ninth session in 2005, as well as the agreed conclusions adopted by the Commission at its fifty-first session, at which it considered "The elimination of all forms of discrimination and violence against the girl child" as its priority theme,

Looking forward to the fifteen-year review of the implementation of the Beijing Platform for Action and the review of the outcome of the twenty-third special session of the General Assembly, emphasizing the sharing of experiences and good practices, with a view to overcoming remaining obstacles and new challenges, including those related to the Millennium Development Goals, which will take place during the fifty-fourth session of the Commission on the Status of Women, in 2010,

Reaffirming the Dakar Framework for Action, adopted at the World Education Forum in 2000,

Welcoming the appointment of the Special Representative of the Secretary-General on violence against children, the creation of the new post of Special Representative of the Secretary-General on sexual violence in conflict and the launch of the Secretary-General's 2008–2015 campaign "UNiTE to End Violence against Women",

Recognizing that chronic poverty remains the single biggest obstacle to meeting the needs of and promoting and protecting the rights of children and that urgent national and international action is therefore required to eliminate it, and noting that the burden of the global financial and economic crisis, the energy crisis, the food crisis and the continuing food insecurity as a result of various factors is felt directly by households, especially those depending on income from the informal sector, and particularly by women and girls,

Recognizing also that girl children are often at greater risk of being exposed to and encountering various forms of discrimination and violence, which continue to hinder efforts towards the achievement of the Millennium Development Goals, and reaffirming the need to achieve gender equality to ensure a just and equitable world for girls, including through partnering with men and boys, as an important strategy for advancing the rights of the girl child,

Recognizing further that progress has been made in the passage of national legislation that affirms the equality of girls and boys and that corresponding measures have not been taken to effectively implement such legislation, and recognizing the continuing existence of discrimination against women and girls throughout the world and that addressing this situation will require additional efforts to strengthen policy implementation, including through international cooperation,

Recognizing that the empowerment of girls is key in breaking the cycle of discrimination and violence and in promoting and protecting the full and effective enjoyment of their human rights, and further recognizing that empowering girls requires the active support and engagement of their parents, legal guardians, families, boys and men, as well as the wider community,

Deeply concerned about all forms of violence against children, in particular about phenomena that disproportionately affect girls, such as commercial sexual exploitation and child pornography, child and forced marriage, rape and domestic violence, and, in addition, about the corresponding lack of accountability and impunity, which reflect discriminatory norms reinforcing the lower status of girls in society,

Deeply concerned also about discrimination against the girl child and the violation of the rights of the girl child, which often result in less access for girls to education, and to quality education, nutrition and physical and mental health care, in girls enjoying fewer of the rights, opportunities and benefits of childhood and adolescence than boys, and in leaving them more vulnerable than boys to the consequences of unprotected and premature sexual relations and often being subjected to various forms of cultural, social, sexual and economic exploitation and violence, abuse, rape, incest, honour-related crimes and harmful traditional practices, such as female infanticide, child and forced marriages, prenatal sex selection and female genital mutilation,

Deeply concerned further that female genital mutilation violates and impairs the full enjoyment of the human rights of women and girls and that it is an irreparable and irreversible harmful practice that affects between 100 million and 140 million women and girls alive today, and that each year over 3 million girls are at risk of undergoing the harmful procedure,

Deeply concerned that the goal of ending female genital mutilation by 2010, set out in the document entitled "A world fit for children", will go unmet,

Deeply concerned also that, in situations of poverty, war and armed conflict, girl children are among those most affected and furthermore become the victims of sexual violence, abuse and exploitation and sexually transmitted infections and diseases, including HIV and AIDS, which have a serious impact on the quality of their lives and leave them open to further discrimination, violence and neglect, thus limiting their potential for full development,

Emphasizing that increased access to education, including in the areas of sexual and reproductive health, for young people, especially girls, dramatically lowers their vulnerability to preventable diseases, in particular HIV infection and sexually transmitted diseases,

Concerned by the increasing number of child-headed households, in particular those headed by orphaned girls, including those orphaned by the HIV and AIDS pandemic,

Deeply concerned that early childbearing and limited access to sexual and reproductive health care, including in the area of emergency obstetric care, causes high levels of obstetric fistula and maternal mortality and morbidity,

Convinced that racism, racial discrimination, xenophobia and related intolerance reveal themselves in a differentiated manner for women and girls and can be among the factors leading to a deterioration in their living conditions, poverty, violence, multiple forms of discrimination and limitation or denial of their human rights,

Recognizing that early childbearing continues to be an impediment to the improvement of the educational and social status of girls in all parts of the world and that, overall, child and forced marriages and early motherhood can severely curtail their educational opportunities and are likely to have a long-term, adverse impact on their employment opportunities and on their and their children's quality of life,

Noting with concern that in some areas of the world men outnumber women as a result, in part, of harmful attitudes and practices, such as female genital mutilation, son preference, which results in female infanticide and prenatal sex selection, early marriage, including child marriage, violence against women, sexual exploitation, sexual abuse and discrimination against girls in food allocation and in other practices related to health and well-being, resulting in fewer girls than boys surviving into adulthood,

Taking note with appreciation of the adoption of the Rio de Janeiro Declaration and Call for Action to Prevent and Stop Sexual Exploitation of Children and Adolescents, which is the outcome document of the Third World Congress against Sexual Exploitation of Children and Adolescents, held in Rio de Janeiro, Brazil, from 25 to 28 November 2008,

1. *Stresses* the need for full and urgent implementation of the rights of the girl child as provided to her under human rights instruments, and urges States to consider signing and ratifying or acceding to the Convention on the Rights of the Child, the Convention on the Elimination of All Forms of Discrimination against Women, the Convention on the Rights of Persons with Disabilities and the Optional Protocols thereto as a matter of priority;

2. *Urges* all States that have not yet signed and ratified or acceded to the Minimum Age Convention, 1973 (No. 138) and the Worst Forms of Child Labour Convention, 1999 (No. 182), of the International Labour Organization to consider doing so;

3. *Urges* all Governments and the United Nations system to strengthen efforts bilaterally and with international organizations and private sector donors in order to achieve the goals of the World Education Forum, in particular that of eliminating gender disparities in primary and secondary education by 2005, which have not been fully met, and to implement the United Nations Girls' Education Initiative as a means of reaching this goal, and calls for the implementation of and reaffirms the commitments contained in the Education for All goals and the Millennium Development Goals, particularly those related to gender and education;

4. *Calls upon* all States to place enhanced emphasis on quality education for the girl child, including catch-up and literacy education for those who did not receive formal education, to promote access to skills and entrepreneurial training for young women and to tackle male and female stereotypes in order to ensure that young women entering the labour market have opportunities to obtain full and productive employment and decent work;

5. *Calls upon* States and the international community to recognize the right to education on the basis of equal opportunity and non-discrimination by making primary education compulsory and available free to all children, ensuring that all children have access to education of good quality, as well as making secondary education generally available and accessible to all, in particular through the progressive introduction of free education, bearing in mind that special measures to ensure equal access, including affirmative action, contribute to achieving equal opportunity and combating exclusion, and ensuring school attendance, in particular for girls and children from low-income families;

6. *Stresses* the importance of a substantive assessment of the implementation of the Beijing Platform for Action with a life cycle perspective so as to identify gaps and obstacles in the implementation process and to develop further actions for the achievement of the goals of the Platform for Action;

7. *Calls upon* all States and international and nongovernmental organizations, individually and collectively, to implement further the Beijing Platform for Action, in particular the strategic objectives relating to the girl child, and the further actions and initiatives to implement the Beijing Declaration and Platform for Action, and to mobilize all necessary resources and support in order to achieve the goals and strategic objectives and actions set out in the Beijing Declaration and Platform for Action;

8. *Calls upon* all States to take measures to address the obstacles that continue to affect the achievement of the goals set forth in the Beijing Platform for Action, as contained in paragraph 33 of the further actions and initiatives, where appropriate, including the strengthening of national mechanisms to implement policies and programmes for the girl child and, in some cases, to enhance coordination among responsible institutions for the realization of the human rights of girls, as indicated in the further actions and initiatives;

9. *Urges* States to strengthen efforts to urgently eradicate all forms of discrimination against women and girls, and, where applicable, to remain dedicated to the implementation of the Convention on the Elimination of All Forms of Discrimination against Women and the Optional Protocol thereto;

10. *Also urges* States to fulfil the pledges that they made at the Fourth World Conference on Women and at the twenty-third special session of the General Assembly to modify or abolish remaining laws that discriminate against women and girls;

11. *Further urges* States to improve the situation of girl children living in poverty, deprived of nutrition, water and sanitation facilities, with limited or no access to basic physical and mental health-care services, shelter, education, participation and protection, taking into account that, while a severe lack of goods and services hurts every human being, it is most threatening and harmful to the girl child, leaving her unable to enjoy her rights, to reach her full potential and to participate as a full member of society;

12. *Urges* States to ensure that the applicable requirements of the International Labour Organization for the employment of girls and boys are respected and effectively enforced and that girls who are employed have equal access to decent work, and equal payment and remuneration, are protected from economic exploitation, discrimination, sexual harassment, violence and abuse in the workplace, are aware of their rights and have access to formal and non-formal education, skills development and vocational training, and further urges States to develop gender-sensitive measures, including national action plans, where appropriate, to eliminate the worst forms of child labour, including commercial sexual exploitation, slavery-like practices, forced and bonded labour, trafficking and hazardous forms of child labour;

13. *Calls upon* States to take all measures necessary to ensure the right of girls to the enjoyment of the highest attainable standard of health, including sexual and reproductive health, and to develop sustainable health systems and social services;

14. *Urges* all States to promote gender equality and equal access to basic social services, such as education, nutrition, birth registration, health care, including sexual and reproductive health, vaccinations and protection from diseases representing the major causes of mortality, and to mainstream a gender perspective in all development policies and programmes, including those relating to children as well as those specific to the girl child;

15. *Calls upon* States to take appropriate measures to address the root factors of child and forced marriages, including by undertaking educational activities to raise awareness regarding the negative aspects of such practices, and to strengthen existing legislation and policies with a view to providing better promotion and protection of the rights of the child, in particular the girl child;

16. *Urges* all States to enact and strictly enforce laws to ensure that marriage is only entered into with the free and full consent of the intending spouses, and, in addition, to enact and strictly enforce laws concerning the minimum legal age of consent and the minimum age for marriage and raise the minimum age for marriage where necessary, and to develop and implement comprehensive policies, plans of action and programmes for the survival, protection, development and advancement of the girl child in order to promote and protect the full enjoyment of her human rights and to ensure equal opportunities for girls, including by making such plans an integral part of her total development process;

17. *Calls upon* States, with the support of international organizations and civil society, including non-governmental organizations, to generate social support for the enforcement of laws on the minimum legal age for marriage, in particular by providing educational opportunities for girls;

18. *Also calls upon* States, with the support of international organizations, civil society and non-governmental organizations, as appropriate, to develop policies and programmes, giving priority to formal and informal education programmes that support girls and enable them to acquire knowledge, develop self-esteem and take responsibility for their own lives, and to place special focus on programmes to educate women and men, especially parents, about the importance of girls' physical and mental health and well-being, including the elimination of discrimination against girls in child and forced marriages;

19. *Urges* all States to enact and enforce legislation to protect girls from all forms of violence and exploitation, including female infanticide and prenatal sex selection, female genital mutilation, rape, domestic violence, incest, sexual abuse, sexual exploitation, child prostitution and child pornography, trafficking and forced migration, forced labour, and forced marriage, as well as marriage under legal age, and to develop age-appropriate safe and confidential programmes and medical, social and psychological support services to assist girls who are subjected to violence and discrimination;

20. *Urges* States to complement punitive measures with educational activities designed to promote a process of consensus towards the abandonment of harmful practices such as female genital mutilation and to provide appropriate services for those affected by the practices;

21. *Calls upon* all States to enact and enforce the necessary legislative or other measures, in cooperation with relevant stakeholders, to prevent the distribution over the Internet of child pornography, including depictions of child sexual abuse, ensuring that adequate mechanisms are in place to enable reporting and removal of such material and that its creators, distributors and collectors are prosecuted as appropriate;

22. *Urges* States to formulate comprehensive, multidisciplinary and coordinated national plans, programmes or strategies to eliminate all forms of discrimination and violence against women and girls, which should be widely disseminated and should provide targets and timetables for implementation, as well as effective domestic enforce-

ment procedures through the establishment of monitoring mechanisms involving all parties concerned, including consultations with women's organizations, giving attention to the recommendations relating to the girl child of the Special Rapporteurs of the Human Rights Council on violence against women, its causes and consequences, and on trafficking in persons, especially women and children, of the Secretary-General in his in-depth study on all forms of violence against women and of the independent expert in his study on violence against children;

23. *Also urges* States to ensure that the right of children to express themselves and to participate in all matters affecting them, in accordance with their age and maturity, is fully and equally enjoyed by girls;

24. *Further urges* States to involve girls, including girls with special needs, and their representative organizations, in decision-making processes, as appropriate, and to include them as full and active partners in identifying their own needs and in developing, planning, implementing and assessing policies and programmes to meet those needs;

25. *Recognizes* that a considerable number of girl children are particularly vulnerable, including orphans, children living on the street, internally displaced and refugee children, children affected by trafficking and sexual and economic exploitation, children living with HIV and AIDS, and children who are incarcerated who live without parental support, and therefore urges States, with the support of the international community, where relevant, to take appropriate measures to address the needs of such children by implementing national policies and strategies to build and strengthen governmental, community and family capacities to provide a supportive environment for such children, including by providing appropriate counselling and psychosocial support, and ensuring their enrolment in school and access to shelter, good nutrition and health and social services on an equal basis with other children;

26. *Encourages* States to promote actions, including through bilateral and multilateral technical cooperation and financial assistance, for the social reintegration of children in difficult situations, in particular girls, considering, inter alia, views, skills and capacities that those children have developed in the conditions in which they lived and, where appropriate, with their meaningful participation;

27. *Urges* all States and the international community to respect, promote and protect the rights of the girl child, taking into account the particular vulnerabilities of the girl child in pre-conflict, conflict and post-conflict situations, and further urges States to take special measures for the protection of girls, in particular to protect them from sexually transmitted infections, including HIV infection, gender-based violence, including rape, sexual abuse and sexual exploitation, torture, abduction and forced labour, paying special attention to refugee and displaced girls, and to take into account their special needs in the delivery of humanitarian assistance and disarmament, demobilization, rehabilitation assistance and reintegration processes;

28. *Deplores* all cases of sexual exploitation and abuse of women and children, especially girls, in humanitarian crises, including those cases involving humanitarian workers and peacekeepers, and urges States to take effective measures to address gender-based violence in humanitarian emergencies and to make all possible efforts to ensure

that their laws and institutions are adequate to prevent, promptly investigate and prosecute acts of gender-based violence;

29. *Also deplores* all acts of sexual exploitation, abuse of and trafficking in women and children by military, police and civilian personnel involved in United Nations operations, welcomes the efforts undertaken by United Nations agencies and peacekeeping operations to implement a zero-tolerance policy in this regard, and requests the Secretary-General and personnel-contributing countries to continue to take all appropriate action necessary to combat these abuses by such personnel, including through the full implementation without delay of those measures adopted in the relevant General Assembly resolutions based on recommendations of the Special Committee on Peacekeeping Operations;

30. *Calls upon* Member States to devise, enforce and strengthen effective child- and youth-sensitive measures to combat, eliminate and prosecute all forms of trafficking in women and girls, including for sexual and economic exploitation, as part of a comprehensive anti-trafficking strategy within wider efforts to eliminate all forms of violence against women and girls, including by taking effective measures against the criminalization of girls who are victims of exploitation and ensuring that girls who have been exploited receive access to the necessary psychosocial support;

31. *Calls upon* Governments, civil society, including the media, and non-governmental organizations to promote human rights education and full respect for and the enjoyment of the human rights of the girl child, inter alia, through the translation, production and dissemination of age-appropriate and gender-sensitive information material on those rights to all sectors of society, in particular to children;

32. *Requests* the Secretary-General, as Chairman of the United Nations System Chief Executives Board for Coordination, to ensure that all organizations and bodies of the United Nations system, individually and collectively, in particular the United Nations Children's Fund, the United Nations Educational, Scientific and Cultural Organization, the World Food Programme, the United Nations Population Fund, the United Nations Development Fund for Women, the World Health Organization, the United Nations Development Programme, the Office of the United Nations High Commissioner for Refugees and the International Labour Organization, take into account the rights and the particular needs of the girl child in country programmes of cooperation in accordance with national priorities, including through the United Nations Development Assistance Framework;

33. *Requests* all human rights treaty bodies and the human rights mechanisms of the Human Rights Council, including the special procedures, to adopt regularly and systematically a gender perspective in the implementation of their mandates and to include in their reports information on the qualitative analysis of violations of the human rights of women and girls, and encourages the strengthening of cooperation and coordination in that regard;

34. *Requests* States to ensure that, in all policies and programmes designed to provide comprehensive HIV and AIDS prevention, treatment, care and support, particular

attention and support is given to the girl child at risk, infected with or affected by HIV, including pregnant girls and young and adolescent mothers, as part of the global effort to scale up significantly towards achieving the goal of universal access to comprehensive prevention, treatment, care and support by 2010;

35. *Invites* States to promote initiatives aimed at reducing the prices of antiretroviral drugs, especially second-line drugs, available to the girl child, including bilateral and private sector initiatives as well as initiatives on a voluntary basis taken by groups of States, including those based on innovative financing mechanisms that contribute to the mobilization of resources for social development, including those that aim to provide further access to drugs at affordable prices to developing countries on a sustainable and predictable basis, and in this regard takes note of the International Drug Purchase Facility, UNITAID;

36. *Calls upon* all States to integrate food and nutritional support with the goal that children, especially girl children, have access at all times to sufficient, safe and nutritious food to meet their dietary needs and food preferences, for an active and healthy life, as part of a comprehensive response to HIV and AIDS and other communicable diseases;

37. *Urges* States and the international community to increase resources at all levels, particularly in the education and health sectors, to enable young people, especially girls, to gain the knowledge, attitudes and skills that they need to prevent HIV infection and early pregnancy and to enjoy the highest attainable standard of physical and mental health, including sexual and reproductive health;

38. *Stresses* the need to strengthen the commitment of States and the United Nations system in their responsibility to mainstream the promotion and protection of the rights of the child, in particular the girl child, in the development agenda at the national and international levels;

39. *Urges* States, the international community, the relevant United Nations entities, civil society and international financial institutions to continue to actively support, through the allocation of increased financial resources, targeted innovative programmes that address ending female genital mutilation and developing and providing education programmes, such as the United Nations Population Fund-United Nations Children's Fund joint programme on accelerating the abandonment of female genital mutilation, and sensitization workshops on the dire consequences of this harmful practice for the health of the girl, and to provide training programmes for those who perform the harmful procedure so that they may adopt an alternative profession;

40. *Welcomes* the commitment of ten United Nations agencies, in their joint statement of 27 February 2008, to continue working towards the elimination of female genital mutilation, by, inter alia, providing technical and financial assistance, and stresses that a common coordinated approach that promotes positive social change at the community, national and international levels could lead to female genital mutilation being abandoned within a generation, with some of the main achievements being obtained by 2015, in line with the Millennium Development Goals;

41. *Calls upon* States to strengthen the capacity of national health systems, and in this regard calls upon the international community to assist national efforts, including by allocation of adequate resources in order to provide essential services needed to prevent obstetric fistula and to treat those cases that occur by providing the continuum of services, including family planning, prenatal and post-natal care, skilled birth attendance, emergency obstetric care and post-partum care, to adolescent girls, including those living in poverty and in underserved rural areas where obstetric fistula is most common;

42. *Calls upon* States and the international community to create an environment in which the well-being of the girl child is ensured, inter alia, by cooperating, supporting and participating in global efforts for poverty eradication at the global, regional and country levels, recognizing that strengthened availability and effective allocation of resources are required at all levels, in order to ensure that all the internationally agreed development and poverty eradication goals, including those set out in the United Nations Millennium Declaration, are realized within their time framework, and reaffirming that investment in children, particularly girls, and the realization of their rights are among the most effective ways to eradicate poverty;

43. *Requests* the Secretary-General to submit a report to the General Assembly at its sixty-sixth session on the implementation of the present resolution, including an emphasis on ending child and forced marriages, using information provided by Member States, the organizations and bodies of the United Nations system and non-governmental organizations with a view to assessing the impact of the present resolution on the well-being of the girl child.

UN machinery

Convention on the elimination of discrimination against women

As at 31 December, 187 States were parties to the 1979 Convention on the Elimination of All Forms of Discrimination against Women, adopted by the General Assembly in resolution 34/180 [YUN 1979, p. 895]. Qatar acceded on 29 April. At year's end, 55 States had accepted the amendment to article 20, paragraph 1, of the Convention in respect of the meeting time of the Committee on the Elimination of Discrimination against Women, which was adopted by States parties in 1995 [YUN 1995, p. 1178]. The amendment would enter into force when accepted by a two-thirds majority of States parties.

The Optional Protocol to the Convention, adopted by the Assembly in resolution 54/4 [YUN 1999, p. 1100] and which entered into force in 2000 [YUN 2000, p. 1123], had 99 States parties as at 31 December.

In accordance with Assembly resolution 62/218 [YUN 2007, p. 1191], the Secretary-General submitted a September report [A/64/342] on the status of the Convention covering the period from 15 August 2007 to 24 August 2009.

CEDAW

In 2009, the Committee on the Elimination of Discrimination against Women (CEDAW), established in 1982 [YUN 1982, p. 1149] to monitor compliance with the 1979 Convention, held two regular sessions [A/64/38 & A/65/38].

At its forty-third session (Geneva, 19 January– 6 February), CEDAW reviewed the initial or periodic reports of Armenia, Cameroon, Dominica, Germany, Guatemala, Haiti, the Libyan Arab Jamahiriya and Rwanda on measures taken to implement the Convention. CEDAW considered a Secretariat report on ways and means of expediting its work [CEDAW/C/2009/I/4] and a report of the Secretary-General on the status of submission of reports by States parties under article 18 of the Convention [CEDAW/C/2009/I/2]. The Secretary-General also transmitted a report by the International Labour Organization (ILO) on the implementation of the Convention in areas falling within the scope of its activities [CEDAW/C/2009/I/3/ Add.4]. The Committee elected its Chairperson for the next (2009–2010) period from the African Group, on the understanding that the next regional group in the rotation would be the Latin American and Caribbean Group, for the period 2011–2012. Thereafter, in electing the Chairperson, due consideration would be given to the principle of rotation among the regional groups in the following order: Western European and Others Group; Asian Group; Eastern European Group; African Group; and Latin American and Caribbean Group [A/64/38 (dec. 43/I)]. The Committee adopted a statement on the international financial crisis and its consequences for the human rights of women and girls [dec. 43/II], in which it called for gender perspectives to be taken into account in relation to the impacts of the crisis on both a long- and short-term basis. The Committee also adopted a statement on the situation in Gaza [dec. 43/III], in which it expressed concern about the January military engagement between Israel and Hamas that resulted in heavy civilian casualties, and called on the parties to implement the ceasefire and to involve women in the decision-making process on the promotion and maintenance of peace and security.

At its forty-fourth session (New York, 20 July– 7 August), CEDAW reviewed the initial or periodic reports of Azerbaijan, Bhutan, Denmark, Guinea-Bissau, Japan, Lao People's Democratic Republic, Liberia, Spain, Switzerland, Timor-Leste and Tuvalu. The Committee considered a report on the status of submission of reports by States parties under article 18 of the Convention [CEDAW/C/2009/II/2]. It also had before it a Secretariat report on ways and means of expediting the work of the Committee [CEDAW/C/2009/ II/4] and an ILO report on the implementation of the

Convention in areas falling within the scope of its activities [CEDAW/C/2009/II/3/Add.4]. The Committee decided that experts from States parties might advise their Governments during the reporting process, including in the preparation of the report under article 18 of the Convention, but that they should not lead or write the report. Experts who received invitations to participate in events in their personal capacities might respond without seeking authorization from the Chair; they should, however, indicate in any statements that their views did not necessarily reflect the views of the Committee [A/65/38 (dec. 44/I)]. As gender equality was essential to the initiation, implementation, monitoring and evaluation of climate change policies, CEDAW called on States parties to include it as an overarching guiding principle in the agreement expected at the fifteenth Conference of the Parties to the United Nations Framework Convention on Climate Change in December [dec. 44/II].

In view of the celebration, in 2009, of the thirtieth anniversary of the adoption of the Convention and the tenth anniversary of the adoption of its Optional Protocol by the Assembly, the Committee urged States that had not yet acceded to or ratified the Convention and/or its Optional Protocol to do so. It encouraged all States parties to the instruments to celebrate the anniversaries at the national level [dec. 44/III].

In other action, the Committee endorsed the report of the Working Group on Communications under the Optional Protocol on its fifteenth session (annexed to the report); took action on communications 12/2007 and 13/2007; decided to revise its model communication form; and adopted a fact sheet on the submission of individual communications under the Protocol. In accordance with its 2008 decision [YUN 2008, p. 1278] to introduce a follow-up procedure whereby it would request further information from individual States parties on steps taken to implement recommendations contained in CEDAW's concluding observations, the Committee appointed a rapporteur on follow-up to concluding observations, and an alternate, as well as a framework of the mandate of the follow-up rapporteur. The Committee also decided that the Secretariat should systematically remind States parties whose reports were five years or more overdue to submit their reports as soon as possible. Failing receipt of a response from the States parties concerned, the Secretariat was to inform the Committee at its forty-fifth (2010) session.

On 2 October, the Human Rights Council adopted a resolution on the elimination of discrimination against women (see p. 733).

On 18 December, by **decision 64/531**, the Assembly took note of the report of CEDAW on its forty-second and forty-third sessions.

On 18 December [meeting 65], the General Assembly, on the recommendation of the Third Committee [A/64/433], adopted **resolution 64/138** without vote [agenda item 62 *(a)*].

Convention on the Elimination of All Forms of Discrimination against Women

The General Assembly,

Recalling its resolution 62/218 of 22 December 2007 and its previous resolutions on the elimination of discrimination against women,

Bearing in mind that one of the purposes of the United Nations, as stated in Articles 1 and 55 of the Charter, is to promote universal respect for human rights and fundamental freedoms for all without distinction of any kind, including distinction as to sex,

Reiterating the need to intensify efforts to eliminate all forms of discrimination against women throughout the world,

Affirming that women and men should participate equally in social, economic and political development, should contribute equally to such development and should share equally in improved conditions of life,

Recalling the Vienna Declaration and Programme of Action adopted by the World Conference on Human Rights on 25 June 1993, in which the Conference reaffirmed that the human rights of women and the girl child were an inalienable, integral and indivisible part of universal human rights,

Acknowledging the need for a comprehensive and integrated approach to the promotion and protection of the human rights of women, which includes the integration of the human rights of women into the mainstream of United Nations activities system-wide,

Reaffirming the Beijing Declaration and Platform for Action and the outcome documents of the twenty-third special session of the General Assembly entitled "Women 2000: gender equality, development and peace for the twenty-first century", in particular those paragraphs concerning the Convention on the Elimination of All Forms of Discrimination against Women and the Optional Protocol thereto,

Welcoming the declaration of the Commission on the Status of Women on the occasion of the tenth anniversary of the Fourth World Conference on Women, in which the Commission recognized that the implementation of the Beijing Declaration and Platform for Action and the fulfilment of the obligations under the Convention are mutually reinforcing in respect of achieving gender equality and the empowerment of women,

Welcoming also the decision of the Commission to commemorate the fifteenth anniversary of the adoption of the Beijing Declaration and Platform for Action in conjunction with the fifty-fourth session of the Commission, to be held from 1 to 12 March 2010,

Recalling that, in the United Nations Millennium Declaration, Heads of State and Government resolved to implement the Convention, and recalling also that the 2005 World Summit Outcome reaffirmed that gender equality and the promotion and protection of the full enjoyment of all human rights and fundamental freedoms for all are essential to advance development and peace and security,

Recognizing that the equal enjoyment by women of all human rights and fundamental freedoms will promote the realization of the rights of the child, bearing in mind the special needs of girls, and acknowledging the mutual reinforcement of the implementation of the Convention on the Elimination of All Forms of Discrimination against Women and the Convention on the Rights of the Child and the Optional Protocols thereto,

Noting that 18 December 2009 marks the thirtieth anniversary of the adoption by the General Assembly of the Convention on the Elimination of All Forms of Discrimination against Women,

Noting also that 6 October 2009 marked the tenth anniversary of the adoption by the General Assembly of the Optional Protocol to the Convention,

Bearing in mind the recommendation of the Committee on the Elimination of Discrimination against Women that national reports should contain information on the implementation of the Beijing Platform for Action, in accordance with paragraph 323 of the Platform,

Having considered the reports of the Committee on its fortieth and forty-first and forty-second and forty-third sessions,

Noting with appreciation the elaboration and adoption by the Committee at its forty-second session of general recommendation No. 26, on women migrant workers,

Expressing deep concern at the great number of reports that are still overdue, in particular initial reports, which constitutes an obstacle to the full implementation of the Convention,

1. *Welcomes* the report of the Secretary-General on the status of the Convention on the Elimination of All Forms of Discrimination against Women;

2. *Also welcomes* the growing number of States parties to the Convention, which now stands at one hundred and eighty-six, while expressing disappointment that universal ratification of the Convention was not achieved by 2000, and urges all States that have not yet ratified or acceded to the Convention to do so;

3. *Further welcomes* the growing number of States parties to the Optional Protocol to the Convention, which now stands at ninety-nine, and urges other States parties to the Convention to consider signing and ratifying or acceding to the Optional Protocol;

4. *Urges* States parties to comply fully with their obligations under the Convention and the Optional Protocol thereto and to take into consideration the concluding observations as well as the general recommendations of the Committee on the Elimination of Discrimination against Women;

5. *Encourages* all relevant entities of the United Nations system, within their mandates, as well as Governments and intergovernmental and non-governmental organizations, in particular women's organizations, as appropriate, to strengthen assistance to States parties, upon their request, in implementing the Convention;

6. *Notes* that some States parties have modified their reservations, expresses satisfaction that some reservations have been withdrawn, and urges States parties to limit the extent of any reservations that they lodge to the Convention, to formulate any such reservations as precisely and as narrowly as possible, to ensure that no reservations are

incompatible with the object and purpose of the Convention, to review their reservations regularly with a view to withdrawing them and to withdraw reservations that are contrary to the object and purpose of the Convention;

7. *Welcomes* the adoption by the Committee of Convention-specific reporting guidelines, which must be applied in conjunction with the harmonized reporting guidelines on a common core document;

8. *Recalls* the great number of overdue reports, in particular initial reports, and urges States parties to the Convention to make every possible effort to submit their reports on the implementation of the Convention in a timely manner, in accordance with article 18 thereof;

9. *Also recalls* its resolution 50/202 of 22 December 1995, in which it took note with approval of the amendment to article 20, paragraph 1, of the Convention, which has yet to enter into force, and urges States parties to the Convention that have not yet done so to accept the amendment;

10. *Strongly urges* States parties to the Convention to take appropriate measures so that acceptance of the amendment to article 20, paragraph 1, of the Convention by a two-thirds majority of States parties can be reached as soon as possible and the amendment can enter into force;

11. *Expresses its appreciation* for the efforts made by the Committee to improve the efficiency of its working methods, and welcomes the decision of the Committee to introduce a procedure to enhance the follow-up of its recommendations;

12. *Welcomes* the gradual alleviation of the backlog of reports awaiting consideration by the Committee;

13. *Continues to encourage* the Secretariat to extend further technical assistance to States parties, upon their request, to strengthen their capacity in the preparation of reports, in particular initial reports, and urges Governments to contribute to those efforts;

14. *Invites* States parties to make use of the technical assistance provided by the Secretariat to facilitate the preparation of reports, in particular initial reports;

15. *Encourages* the continued participation of members of the Committee in inter-committee meetings and meetings of persons chairing the human rights treaty bodies, including those on methods of work relating to the State reporting system;

16. *Encourages* the Committee, within its mandate, to continue to contribute to the efforts to strengthen cooperation and coordination between the treaty bodies, and welcomes as a positive example the joint working group of the Committee on the Elimination of Discrimination against Women and the Committee on the Rights of the Child, and in this regard invites the Committee on the Elimination of Discrimination against Women to consider other informal cooperative initiatives maximizing existing resources;

17. *Requests* the Secretary-General, in accordance with General Assembly resolution 54/4 of 6 October 1999, to provide the resources, including staff and facilities, necessary for the effective functioning of the Committee within its full mandate, including as set out in the Optional Protocol to the Convention;

18. *Urges* Governments, organizations and bodies of the United Nations system and intergovernmental and non-governmental organizations to disseminate the Convention and the Optional Protocol thereto;

19. *Encourages* States parties to disseminate the concluding observations adopted in relation to the consideration of their reports, as well as the general recommendations of the Committee;

20. *Encourages* States parties and all relevant entities of the United Nations system to continue to build women's knowledge and understanding of and capacity to utilize human rights instruments, in particular the Convention and the Optional Protocol thereto;

21. *Urges* the specialized agencies, at the invitation of the Committee, to submit reports on the implementation of the Convention in areas falling within the scope of their activities;

22. *Welcomes* the contribution of non-governmental organizations, and national human rights institutions, where they exist, to the work of the Committee;

23. *Invites* the Chair of the Committee on the Elimination of Discrimination against Women to address and to engage in an interactive dialogue with the General Assembly at its sixty-fifth and sixty-sixth sessions under the item on the advancement of women;

24. *Requests* the Secretary-General to submit to the General Assembly at its sixty-sixth session a report on the status of the Convention on the Elimination of All Forms of Discrimination against Women and the implementation of the present resolution.

Commission on the Status of Women

The Commission on the Status of Women, at its fifty-third session (New York, 2–13 March) [E/2009/27], recommended to the Economic and Social Council the adoption of draft resolutions on: the future operation of INSTRAW (see p. 1159); the situation of and assistance to Palestinian women (see p. 474); the future organization and methods of work of the Commission (see p. 1155); and the Working Group on Communications on the Status of Women of the Commission on the Status of Women (see p. 1157); as well as a draft decision on the report of the Commission's fifty-third session and the provisional agenda and documentation for its fifty-fourth (2010) session. The Commission adopted and brought to the Council's attention resolutions on women, the girl child and HIV and AIDS (see p. 1128) and on preparations for the Commission's 2010 session, during which there would be a review of the implementation of the Beijing Declaration and Platform for Action and the outcomes of the twenty-third special session of the General Assembly (see p. 1115). Also adopted and brought to the Council's attention were agreed conclusions on the equal sharing of responsibilities between women and men, including caregiving in the context of HIV/AIDS (see p. 1130), which was also the priority theme of the session; a summary of the discussions of an expert panel on gender perspectives on global public health in the context of implementing the internationally agreed development goals [ibid.]; and a decision by which the Commission took note of several documents, including the UNIFEM report on its activities to eliminate violence against women [A/HRC/10/43-E/CN.6/2009/10] and the Secretary-General's report on the joint workplan of DAW and OHCHR [A/HRC/10/42-E/CN.6/2009/7].

By **decision 2009/232** of 28 July, the Economic and Social Council took note of the Commission's report on its fifty-third session and approved the provisional agenda for its fifty-fourth (2010) session.

Communication. In a 19 November letter [E/CN.6/2010/9] to the Commission Chairperson, the Economic and Social Council President summarized the outcome of its 2009 substantive session and attached a list of resolutions adopted by the Council calling for action by the functional commissions.

Other reports. Other documents issued in 2009, to be addressed during the Commission's 2010 session, included reports of the Secretary-General on ending female genital mutilation [E/CN.6/2010/6]; the release of women and children taken hostage, including those subsequently imprisoned, in armed conflicts [E/CN.6/2010/5]; and the situation of and assistance to Palestinian women [E/CN.6/2010/4].

Future organization and working methods

In accordance with Economic and Social Council resolutions 1998/46 [YUN 1998, p. 1262] and 2006/9 [YUN 2006, p. 1356], the Secretary-General submitted a report [E/CN.6/2009/3 & Corr.1], which provided an overview of the Commission's working methods during the period 2007–2009, including in the context of the strengthening of the Council, and a proposed multi-year programme of work for 2010–2014. There was greater emphasis on implementation at the national level, including through interactive events, which increased the exchange of ideas, experiences, lessons learned and good practices on progress made and on constraints and challenges. The Commission's inputs into the Council's annual ministerial review provided overviews of policy recommendations on the promotion of gender equality in relation to the themes addressed each year.

The report noted that the Commission might wish to continue to provide those inputs and to organize an interactive expert panel on the theme of the Council's ministerial review at each of its annual sessions. For example, the Commission could make a significant contribution to the Council's work in 2010 on the theme: "Implementing the internationally agreed development goals and commitments in regard to gender equality and the empowerment of women".

With regard to the 2010 review and appraisal of implementation of the Beijing Declaration and Platform for Action and the outcome of the twenty-third special session of the General Assembly (2000), a questionnaire had been developed to solicit informa-

tion from Member States. The results would be submitted to the Commission in 2010.

As to the multi-year programme of work for 2010–2014, the report proposed priority themes to be discussed by the Commission in each of those years. In March, the Commission recommended a draft resolution on the subject for adoption by the Council, which approved the multi-year programme in resolution 2009/15 (see below).

ECONOMIC AND SOCIAL COUNCIL ACTION

On 28 July [meeting 40], the Economic and Social Council, on the recommendation of the Commission on the Status of Women [E/2009/27], adopted **resolution 2009/15** without vote [agenda item 14 *(a)*].

Future organization and methods of work of the Commission on the Status of Women

The Economic and Social Council,

Recalling its resolution 1998/46 of 31 July 1998, annex II of which contains the recommendation that the functional commissions responsible for follow-up to the major United Nations conferences adopt a multi-year thematic programme in their working methods,

Recalling also its request, in its resolution 2008/29 of 24 July 2008, that the functional commissions, the regional commissions and other relevant subsidiary bodies of the Council, in accordance with their mandates, as appropriate, contribute to the annual ministerial review and to the Development Cooperation Forum, in the context of their respective annual workplans, taking into account their specificities,

Recalling further that, in its resolutions 1987/24 of 26 May 1987, 1990/15 of 24 May 1990, 1996/6 of 22 July 1996, 2001/4 of 24 July 2001 and 2006/9 of 25 July 2006, the Council adopted multi-year programmes of work for a focused and thematic approach for the Commission on the Status of Women,

Recalling that, in its resolution 2006/9, the Council decided that the Commission, at its fifty-third session, should review the functioning of its revised methods of work, in the light of the outcome of the discussions on the strengthening of the Council, in order to ensure the effective functioning of the Commission,

Recalling also that, in its resolution 2006/9, the Council decided that the Commission, at its fifty-third session, would also discuss the possibility of conducting in 2010 a review and appraisal of the Beijing Declaration and Platform for Action and the outcomes of the twenty-third special session of the General Assembly,

Reaffirming the primary responsibility of the Commission for follow-up to the Fourth World Conference on Women and the outcomes of the twenty-third special session of the General Assembly,

Recognizing that the organization of work of the Commission should contribute to advancing the implementation of the Beijing Declaration and Platform for Action and the outcomes of the twenty-third special session of the General Assembly,

Recognizing also that the implementation of the Beijing Declaration and Platform for Action and the outcomes of the twenty-third special session of the General Assembly and the fulfilment of the obligations under the Convention on the Elimination of All Forms of Discrimination against Women are mutually reinforcing in achieving gender equality and the empowerment of women,

Reaffirming that gender mainstreaming constitutes a critical strategy in the implementation of the Beijing Declaration and Platform for Action and the outcomes of the twenty-third special session of the General Assembly, and underlining the catalytic role of the Commission in promoting gender mainstreaming,

Recognizing the importance of non-governmental organizations in advancing the implementation of the Beijing Declaration and Platform for Action and, in this respect, the work of the Commission,

Noting with appreciation the continuation of the annual parliamentary meetings organized by the Inter-Parliamentary Union, as well as the programme of side events held during the sessions of the Commission,

A. Methods of work of the Commission on the Status of Women

1. *Decides* that, following the review of the functioning of its revised methods of work, the Commission on the Status of Women should, from its fifty-fourth session onwards, maintain its current working methods, adopted by the Economic and Social Council in its resolution 2006/9, and should continue to keep its working methods under review;

B. Themes for the period 2010–2014

2. *Also decides* that:

(a) In 2010, at its fifty-fourth session, the Commission will review the implementation of the Beijing Declaration and Platform for Action and the outcomes of the twenty-third special session of the General Assembly, as well as its contribution to shaping a gender perspective towards the full realization of the Millennium Development Goals;

(b) In 2011, at its fifty-fifth session, the priority theme will be "Access and participation of women and girls to education, training, science and technology, including for the promotion of women's equal access to full employment and decent work" and progress in the implementation of the agreed conclusions from the fifty-first session on the elimination of all forms of discrimination and violence against the girl child will be evaluated;

(c) In 2012, at its fifty-sixth session, the priority theme will be "The empowerment of rural women and their role in poverty and hunger eradication, development and current challenges" and progress in the implementation of the agreed conclusions from the fifty-second session on financing for gender equality and the empowerment of women will be evaluated;

(d) In 2013, at its fifty-seventh session, the priority theme will be "Elimination and prevention of all forms of violence against women and girls" and progress in the implementation of the agreed conclusions from the fifty-third session on the equal sharing of responsibilities between women and men, including caregiving in the context of HIV/AIDS, will be evaluated;

(e) In 2014, at its fifty-eighth session, the priority theme will be "Challenges and achievements in the im-plementation of the Millennium Development Goals for women and girls" and progress in the implementation of the agreed conclusions from the fifty-fifth session on access and participation of women and girls to education, training, science and technology, including for the promotion of women's equal access to full employment and decent work, will be evaluated;

3. *Further decides* that, at its fifty-seventh session, in 2013, the Commission will discuss the possibility of conducting in 2015 a review and appraisal of the Beijing Declaration and Platform for Action and the outcomes of the twenty-third special session of the General Assembly and will decide on priority themes for future sessions.

Communications on the status of women

In accordance with decision 52/101 of the Commission on the Status of Women [YUN 2008, p. 1278], the Secretary-General submitted a report [E/CN.6/2009/8] on the future work of the Working Group on Communications on the Status of Women, which compiled additional or updated views of eight Member States and the European Union received since the preparation of the previous report on the subject [YUN 2004, p. 1170].

Working Group. At a closed meeting in March [E/2009/27], the Commission considered the report of the Working Group on Communications on the Status of Women [E/CN.6/2009/CRP.3], established in 1993 [YUN 1993, p. 1050], which had considered 21 confidential communications received by DAW. No non-confidential communications were received. The Group noted that Governments had replied to nine of the 21 confidential communications, and one Government replied to a communication that was on the list from the previous year. The Group observed that communications received most frequently concerned: sexual violence, including rape and gang rape, and failure by the State to prevent such violations, provide adequate protection, care and compensation to victims and bring perpetrators to justice; other forms of violence, with a lack of due diligence by States to investigate, prosecute and punish perpetrators or provide protection and support for victims and their families; abuse of power by the police, impunity, humiliation and lack of due process; inhumane treatment and inadequate conditions in mental facilities and in detention; the impact on women and girls of ongoing situations of violence, insecurity and unmet basic needs, as well as the exclusion of women from decision-making processes; serious and systematic violations of the human rights of women and girls, including torture, killings and abductions, with a lack of due diligence by States to investigate, prosecute and punish the perpetrators and provide protection and support for victims and their families; attacks, murders, harassment, death threats, arbitrary arrests and detentions, and disproportionate penalties and restrictions on the rights to freedom of expression and movement of women human rights defenders and their families by State and non-State actors as a means of pressuring them to stop their work, as well as failure by the State to prevent such violations, provide protection and care to victims, bring perpetrators to justice and provide compensation; violations of the right to health, including reproductive health, of women, especially low-income and marginalized women in rural areas and women displaced by conflict; stereotypical attitudes and discriminatory policies towards women, including non-remunerated caregivers; and denial of visas for visits of spouses of foreign male inmates.

During its consideration of communications, the Working Group expressed its concern about violence against women and girls and the climate of impunity and abuse of power. The failure of States to exercise due diligence to prevent all forms of violence against women and girls and violations of the right of women to health, including reproductive health, were also of concern. However, the Working Group was encouraged to note that some Governments had carried out investigations into the allegations and had taken general measures, including enacting new legislation, conducting legal reforms, introducing health policies and gender-budgeting initiatives, improving health care, making efforts to increase women's participation in political life and in key sectors of the economy, and improving awareness-raising activities to promote gender equality and the advancement of women.

ECONOMIC AND SOCIAL COUNCIL ACTION

On 28 July [meeting 40], the Economic and Social Council, on the recommendation of the Commission on the Status of Women [E/2009/27], adopted **resolution 2009/16** without vote [agenda item 14 *(a)*].

Working Group on Communications on the Status of Women of the Commission on the Status of Women

The Economic and Social Council,

Recalling the mandate of the Commission on the Status of Women as set out by the Economic and Social Council in its resolutions 76(V) of 5 August 1947, 304 I(XI) of 14 and 17 July 1950, 1983/27 of 26 May 1983, 1990/8 of 24 May 1990, 1992/19 of 30 July 1992 and 1993/11 of 27 July 1993, as well as in its decision 2002/235 of 24 July 2002 on the communications procedure,

1. *Decides,* in order to make the communications procedure of the Commission on the Status of Women more effective and efficient, that the Commission, starting at its fifty-fourth session, should appoint the members of the Working Group on Communications on the Status of Women for a two-year period;

2. *Reiterates* its decision to continue to raise awareness of the existing mandate of the communications mechanism of the Commission, as appropriate;

3. *Decides* to remain seized of the matter, as necessary.

UN Development Fund for Women (UNIFEM)

During 2009 [A/65/218], the United Nations Development Fund for Women (UNIFEM) continued to work with Governments, civil society and UN organizations on the four key areas of its development results framework: strengthening women's economic security and rights; ending violence against women; reducing the prevalence of HIV/AIDS among girls and women; and advancing gender justice in democratic governance, including in conflict-affected and post-conflict countries. UNIFEM responded to requests for technical and programming support in 98 countries in 2009, compared with 82 in 2008. Since UNIFEM would be consolidated into the composite United Nations Entity for Gender Equality and the Empowerment of Women (UN-Women), the year 2009 would be the last to be reported on in fulfilment of the mandate set out in General Assembly resolution 39/125 [YUN 1984, p. 893]. However, UNIFEM would continue reporting on its strategic plan for 2008–2013, as authorized by the Executive Board of the United Nations Development Programme (UNDP)/UNFPA in decision 2007/35 [YUN 2007, p. 1195] and extended in decision 2009/13 (see p. 1158), until it was replaced by a new plan.

With regard to enhancing women's economic security and rights, UNIFEM worked to: incorporate national commitments to gender equality in 15 national or regional poverty-reduction frameworks; support efforts towards the adoption of 20 laws or policies advancing women's economic capacities and rights in 13 countries (compared with 15 in 2008); support expanded access to legal assistance for women in five countries (seven in 2008); and support the institutionalization of gender-responsive budgeting in 27 countries (32 in 2008). On ending violence against women, UNIFEM supported efforts to: end impunity for violations of women's rights, which resulted in justice system reforms in six countries (four in 2008); secure the approval of 16 laws (eight in 2008) and five policies (seven in 2008) relating to multiple forms of violence against women; and advocate for the inclusion of commitments to end such violence in national development strategies in three countries (five in 2008). UNIFEM supported Governments in developing the capacities of decision makers in justice systems by ensuring that women survivors of violence could access legal assistance under 15 country/territory programmes (11 in 2008). In 31 countries (11 in 2008), it supported the tracking of the prevalence of gender-based violence and the availability of services for survivors. UNIFEM supported HIV-positive women's networks and groups in calling for Government action in 12 countries (five in 2008), and assisted partners to strengthen service delivery to women infected or affected by HIV through mainstream institutions in nine countries and throughout the Caribbean region. As to advancing gender justice in democratic governance, UNIFEM worked with partners to incorporate commitments on gender equality and women's empowerment into humanitarian relief strategies in three countries and to support the passage of 33 laws or policies strengthening women's participation in democratic governance (27 in 2008). In 71 countries (58 in 2008), UNIFEM supported initiatives to develop the capacity of advocates to press for the implementation of national commitments to gender equality.

The Fund's management results framework tracked performance across four areas: policy advice and catalytic programming; UN coordination and reform; accountability, risk and oversight; and administrative, human and financial capacities. UNIFEM produced guidance for the United Nations and other partners to strengthen knowledge and practice to advance gender equality and women's empowerment. Highlights in 2009 included guidance notes for mediators in five key areas of peace negotiations that contributed to discussions relevant to Security Council resolutions 1888(2009) (see p. 1137) and 1889(2009) (see p. 1141); guidance on integrating gender-responsive budgeting in the aid effectiveness agenda; the launch of a virtual knowledge centre on ending violence against women; and an accountability checklist for national AIDS planning. UNIFEM participated in eight "Delivering as one" pilot programmes and was engaged in 95 joint programmes (72 in 2008) with other parts of the UN system. It participated in or led gender theme groups in 69 countries, as well as 75 other coordination mechanisms at the global, regional and country levels.

In 2009, UNIFEM contributions increased by 14 per cent to $138 million, compared with $121 million in 2008. Core contributions increased to $62 million, an increase of 21 per cent over the 2008 total of $51 million, while non-core contributions (excluding special trust funds managed by UNIFEM) increased by $6 million, or 8 per cent, to reach $76 million. The number of countries contributing to the Fund's regular and other resources increased from 80 in 2008 to 102 in 2009. The number of multi-year pledges more than doubled over the year, from 11 to 24. For the first time, the United Nations Trust Fund in Support of Actions to Eliminate Violence against Women disbursed grants to UN country teams, in addition to Governments and NGOs. The Fund for Gender Equality made its first grant of $9.99 million in 2009.

In July [A/64/164 & Corr.1], the Secretary-General transmitted to the Assembly a report on UNIFEM activities in 2008 [YUN 2008, p. 1279], of which the Assembly took note on 18 December in **decision 64/531**. On 24 December, the Assembly decided that the agenda item on the advancement of women would remain for consideration during its sixty-fourth (2010) session (**decision 64/549**).

UNDP/UNFPA Board action. In June, the UNDP/UNFPA Executive Board [E/2009/35 (dec. 2009/13)] took note of the annual report of the UNIFEM Executive Director [DP/2009/21 & Corr.1/Rev.1], which covered 2008. It extended the UNIFEM strategic plan, 2008–2011, including the integrated financial resources framework, to 2013. The Executive Board requested UNIFEM to include in its annual reports qualitative and quantitative information on progress and challenges toward achieving the goals and outcomes of its strategic plan, using the indicators defined in the plan. It requested the Executive Director to submit to the Executive Board's 2011 session a midterm review of the extended strategic plan, 2008–2013, including the integrated financial resources framework and the relevant UNIFEM global and regional programmes. The Executive Director was further asked to submit to the Executive Board, at its first regular session in 2013, a cumulative review of the extended strategic plan, 2008–2013, prior to the submission of the draft UNIFEM strategic plan, 2014–2017, at the 2013 annual session, and ahead of its formal submission at the second 2013 regular session.

In July, the Consultative Committee on UNIFEM transmitted to the Executive Board a document [DP/2009/38] containing information on UNIFEM's criteria for regular resources allocation and proposing options for future programming resources distribution. The document analysed two options for the development and application of resource allocation criteria and methodology. The first was to devise UNIFEM-specific criteria and methodology, while the second was to adopt criteria and methodology from a sister agency and adjust it for gender, in line with UNIFEM's mandate. The criteria and methodology used by UNDP and UNFPA were reviewed for that purpose and the document suggested the adoption of the UNDP approach with a methodology to adjust for gender. The Executive Board took note of the document in September [dec. 2009/28].

In November [dec. 2009/30], the Board approved a UNIFEM interim budget allocation for January 2010 in the amount of $1.2 million, pending final approval of the biennial support budget for 2010–2011. It agreed that the interim budget allocation would be part of and not incremental to the biennial support budget for 2010–2011.

International Research and Training Institute (INSTRAW)

The Executive Board of INSTRAW, at its sixth session (New York, 23 April) [E/2009/62], considered: the election of Executive Board officers; the directorship of the Institute; progress made during the Management Support Services consultancy to strengthen INSTRAW;

implementation of the programme of work for the period 1 October 2008 to 31 March 2009; and the workplan and operational budget for 2009. Pending the appointment of a Director, it was explained to the Board that the Secretary-General had recommended the immediate appointment of an interim Director to fill the position on a short-term basis, while an internal recruitment process would be initiated for a longer-term interim Director. Regarding communications between INSTRAW and UN Headquarters and other entities, it was reported that the lack of staff presence in New York presented an obstacle to advancing the Institute's agenda, particularly in terms of discussions on UN gender equality architecture reform. The Board approved the reallocation of savings from 2008 and 2009 towards budget lines for consultants' fees and travel and general temporary assistance.

On 30 July, the Economic and Social Council took note of the report of the INSTRAW Executive Board (**decision 2009/256**).

Future of INSTRAW

In response to Commission on the Status of Women resolution 52/3 [YUN 2008, p. 1281], the Secretary-General submitted a report on strengthening INSTRAW [E/CN.6/2009/11]. In March [E/2009/27], the Commission recommended to the Economic and Social Council the adoption of a resolution on the future operation of INSTRAW.

In accordance with General Assembly resolution 63/157 [YUN 2008, p. 1281], the Secretary-General, by a May note [A/64/79-E/2009/74], transmitted to the Council and the Assembly his report on strengthening INSTRAW, which had been considered by the Commission. The report summarized the Institute's efforts, in line with its strategic framework for 2008–2011, to expand its training and research activities.

The report concluded that the Institute had consolidated its research and training programmes and enhanced its knowledge management capacity to ensure that research results impacted policy and programme development and implementation. It had improved its collaboration with UN entities in the area of research, and strengthened its training and capacity-building programmes, as well as enhanced its formulation of policy recommendations for Member States and civil society. Voluntary contributions to INSTRAW's regular operations had increased, allowing it to operate on the basis of resources received through those contributions. Multi-year funding agreements were negotiated to ensure a more stable financial base. The report noted that the Institute should intensify its efforts to build on that progress, enhance its visibility, and impact UN system work on gender equality and women's empowerment.

On 30 July (**decision 2009/256**), the Council took note of the Secretary-General's report, as did the Assembly on 18 December (**decision 64/531**).

ECONOMIC AND SOCIAL COUNCIL ACTION

On 28 July [meeting 40], the Economic and Social Council, on the recommendation of the Commission on the Status of Women [E/2009/27], adopted **resolution 2009/13** without vote [agenda item 14 *(a)*].

Future operation of the International Research and Training Institute for the Advancement of Women

The Economic and Social Council,

Recalling all previous resolutions on the situation of the International Research and Training Institute for the Advancement of Women, in particular General Assembly resolution 63/157 of 18 December 2008,

Taking into account Commission on the Status of Women resolution 52/3 of 7 March 2008 on the strengthening of the Institute,

Welcoming the contributions of the Institute to the achievement of the Millennium Development Goals and the implementation of the Convention on the Elimination of All Forms of Discrimination against Women, the Beijing Declaration and Platform for Action, and the outcomes of the twenty-third special session of the General Assembly,

Acknowledging the contributions of the Institute in promoting gender equality and the empowerment of women in the areas of security, international migration, in particular remittances and development, and governance and political participation,

Recognizing the contribution of the Institute to the ongoing efforts in gender mainstreaming through its research and training outputs involving national gender machineries, academic institutes, regional intergovernmental organizations, non-governmental organizations and the private sector,

1. *Takes note* of the report of the Secretary-General on strengthening the International Research and Training Institute for the Advancement of Women;

2. *Requests* the Institute, within its mandate, to continue to assist countries in promoting and supporting the political participation and economic and social advancement of women through training programmes;

3. *Stresses* the critical importance of voluntary financial contributions by Member States to the United Nations Trust Fund for the International Research and Training Institute for the Advancement of Women to enable it to carry out its mandate, and invites Member States to make voluntary contributions to the Trust Fund;

4. *Calls for* the diversification of funding resources, and in this regard invites Member States to continue to provide assistance and support to the Institute through voluntary contributions and substantive involvement in its projects and activities;

5. *Looks forward* to the enhanced implementation of the strategic plan of the Institute under the leadership of its new Director, and in this regard urges the Secretary-General to appoint its new Director as a matter of priority.

Children, youth and ageing persons

As the only UN development and humanitarian agency wholly dedicated to children, the United Nations Children's Fund (UNICEF) assisted more than 150 countries and territories in 2009, the year of the twentieth anniversary of the Convention on the Rights of the Child. The Convention continued to guide UNICEF's mission for children, resulting in advances in child survival, development, protection and participation.

UNICEF continued to focus on five main areas: young child survival and development; basic education and gender equality; HIV/AIDS and children; child protection from violence, exploitation and abuse; and policy advocacy and partnerships for children's rights. In 2009, UNICEF cooperated with 155 countries and responded to emergencies in more than 79 countries. The General Assembly, in December, welcomed the Guidelines for the Alternative Care of Children.

Progress and constraints with respect to the well-being of youth and their role in society were recorded in implementing the 1995 World Programme of Action for Youth to the Year 2000 and Beyond. In December, the Assembly proclaimed the year commencing on 12 August 2010 as the International Year of Youth.

The United Nations continued to implement the 2002 Madrid International Plan of Action on Ageing. In February, the Secretary-General reported on the strategic implementation framework for the Plan, identifying policy priorities and measures for international cooperation to support national implementation activities. In July, the Secretary-General reported on the follow-up to the 2002 Second World Assembly on Ageing, focusing on the promotion and protection of the human rights of older persons. In December, the General Assembly called on Member States to design more effective prevention strategies, laws and policies to address cases of neglect, abuse and violence against older persons.

Children

Follow-up to 2002 General Assembly special session on children

In response to General Assembly resolution 58/282 [YUN 2004, p. 1175], the Secretary-General, in his seventh report [A/64/285] on the follow-up to the Assembly's twenty-seventh (2002) special session on children [YUN 2002, p. 1168], reviewed progress achieved in realizing the commitments set out in the Declaration and Plan of Action contained in the session's final document, "A world fit for children", adopted in resolution S-27/2 [ibid., p. 1169]. The report highlighted progress in the four major areas of the Plan of Action: promoting healthy lives; providing quality education; protecting against abuse, exploitation and violence; and combating HIV/AIDS.

Within the area of health, deaths in children under five declined, but progress remained geographically uneven. Fifty-one per cent of child deaths were attributed to five diseases: pneumonia, diarrhoea, malaria, measles and AIDS. Immunization coverage fell in countries dealing with emergencies and economic crises, and significant acceleration of immunization would be required to meet the "world fit for children" target of 90 per cent coverage against diphtheria, polio and tetanus by 2010. Nutrition promotion efforts focused on expanding malnutrition treatment programmes, and the global use of therapeutic foods grew by 63 per cent over 2007. The Secretary-General reported that the average rate of reduction in underweight prevalence was 1.4 per cent, and was insufficient to meet the Millennium Development Goal (MDG) related to child nutrition.

Regarding education, gender disparities declined at the primary school level, with about two-thirds of countries achieving parity; however, only 37 per cent of countries had achieved parity at the secondary level since the special session. National education plans that included measures to reduce gender disparities increased from 58 in 2005 to 87 in 2008. Secondary school expansion was too slow to meet demand, and scaling up second-chance and catch-up programmes would be required to close the gap. Educational quality, higher investment in basic education and education in emergency, reconstruction and post-emergency situations were also areas requiring further efforts.

Several improvements were made in the area of child exploitation since the special session. In December 2008, the International Conference of Labour Statisticians approved the inclusion of household chores in the statistical definition of child labour, addressing girls' absence in child labour monitoring. Efforts through the UN accountability mechanisms and through the ministerial follow-up forum to the

2007 Paris Principles on children in armed groups led to the release of children from several armed groups. A joint programme of the United Nations Population Fund (UNFPA) and UNICEF on accelerating the abandonment of female genital mutilation/cutting within a generation (2008–2012) brought stakeholders together to achieve that goal.

Children younger than 15 years of age constituted about 14 per cent of new global HIV infections, 14 per cent of AIDS deaths and 6 per cent of the people living with HIV in 2008. About 90 per cent of the estimated 2.1 million children living with HIV were in sub-Saharan Africa. There was an increased focus on preventing mother-to-child transmission of HIV, and advocacy, communication and resource mobilization efforts were supporting the scaling up of early infant HIV diagnosis. Further efforts for education in HIV prevention would need to focus on out-of-school adolescents and other excluded children and youth. Health systems, detection, reporting and follow-up were additional areas for improvement.

The Secretary-General warned that the effects of climate change would have negative consequences for children and future generations, and said that improving safety nets and social protections for families were necessary steps to bridge the gaps in access to basic services.

General Assembly action. The General Assembly, by **resolution 64/80** (see p. 1070), encouraged efforts to promote a culture of peace in the framework of the International Decade for a Culture of Peace and Non-Violence for the Children of the World, 2001–2010 [YUN 2001, p. 609]. By **resolution 64/146** (see p. 637), the Assembly recognized the right of children to be heard on all matters affecting them. It also called on States to adopt arrangements for children's participation in all settings, to ensure the equal participation of girls and to address, in their response to the global financial and economic crisis, any impact on children's enjoyment of their rights.

Guidelines for the Alternative Care of Children

In early 2004, UNICEF and the International Reference Centre for the Rights of Children Deprived of their Family launched an initiative to prepare draft UN guidelines for the protection and alternative care of children without parental care. At its thirty-seventh session in 2004, the Committee on the Rights of the Child adopted a decision on children without parental care, recommending the establishment of a working group to prepare such guidelines. A working group was formed and its draft guidelines were reviewed at a meeting of intergovernmental experts (Brasilia, Brazil, 9–11 August 2006). In June 2009 [A/64/53 (res.

11/7)], the Human Rights Council welcomed the accomplishment of the Guidelines for the Alternative Care of Children, the text of which was annexed to the resolution, and submitted them to the General Assembly for adoption in 2009, the twentieth anniversary of the Convention on the Rights of the Child [YUN 1989, p. 560].

GENERAL ASSEMBLY ACTION

On 18 December [meeting 65], the General Assembly, on the recommendation of the Third (Social, Humanitarian and Cultural) Committee [A/64/434], adopted **resolution 64/142** without vote [agenda item 64].

Guidelines for the Alternative Care of Children

The General Assembly,

Reaffirming the Universal Declaration of Human Rights and the Convention on the Rights of the Child, and celebrating the twentieth anniversary of the Convention in 2009,

Reaffirming also all previous resolutions on the rights of the child of the Human Rights Council, the Commission on Human Rights and the General Assembly, the most recent being Council resolutions 7/29 of 28 March 2008, 9/13 of 24 September 2008 and 10/8 of 26 March 2009 and Assembly resolution 63/241 of 24 December 2008,

Considering that the Guidelines for the Alternative Care of Children, the text of which is annexed to the present resolution, set out desirable orientations for policy and practice with the intention of enhancing the implementation of the Convention on the Rights of the Child and of relevant provisions of other international instruments regarding the protection and well-being of children deprived of parental care or who are at risk of being so,

1. *Welcomes* the Guidelines for the Alternative Care of Children, as contained in the annex to the present resolution, as a set of orientations to help to inform policy and practice;

2. *Encourages* States to take the Guidelines into account and to bring them to the attention of the relevant executive, legislative and judiciary bodies of government, human rights defenders and lawyers, the media and the public in general;

3. *Requests* the Secretary-General, within existing resources, to take steps to disseminate the Guidelines in all the official languages of the United Nations, including by transmitting them to all Member States, regional commissions and relevant intergovernmental and non-governmental organizations.

ANNEX

Guidelines for the Alternative Care of Children

I. Purpose

1. The present Guidelines are intended to enhance the implementation of the Convention on the Rights of the Child and of relevant provisions of other international instruments regarding the protection and well-being of children who are deprived of parental care or who are at risk of being so.

2. Against the background of these international instruments and taking account of the developing body of knowledge and experience in this sphere, the Guidelines set out desirable orientations for policy and practice. They are designed for wide dissemination among all sectors directly or indirectly concerned with issues relating to alternative care, and seek in particular:

(a) To support efforts to keep children in, or return them to, the care of their family or, failing this, to find another appropriate and permanent solution, including adoption and *kafala* of Islamic law;

(b) To ensure that, while such permanent solutions are being sought, or in cases where they are not possible or are not in the best interests of the child, the most suitable forms of alternative care are identified and provided, under conditions that promote the child's full and harmonious development;

(c) To assist and encourage Governments to better implement their responsibilities and obligations in these respects, bearing in mind the economic, social and cultural conditions prevailing in each State; and

(d) To guide policies, decisions and activities of all concerned with social protection and child welfare in both the public and the private sectors, including civil society.

II. General principles and perspectives
A. The child and the family

3. The family being the fundamental group of society and the natural environment for the growth, well-being and protection of children, efforts should primarily be directed to enabling the child to remain in or return to the care of his/her parents, or when appropriate, other close family members. The State should ensure that families have access to forms of support in the caregiving role.

4. Every child and young person should live in a supportive, protective and caring environment that promotes his/her full potential. Children with inadequate or no parental care are at special risk of being denied such a nurturing environment.

5. Where the child's own family is unable, even with appropriate support, to provide adequate care for the child, or abandons or relinquishes the child, the State is responsible for protecting the rights of the child and ensuring appropriate alternative care, with or through competent local authorities and duly authorized civil society organizations. It is the role of the State, through its competent authorities, to ensure the supervision of the safety, well-being and development of any child placed in alternative care and the regular review of the appropriateness of the care arrangement provided.

6. All decisions, initiatives and approaches falling within the scope of the present Guidelines should be made on a case-by-case basis, with a view, notably, to ensuring the child's safety and security, and must be grounded in the best interests and rights of the child concerned, in conformity with the principle of non-discrimination and taking due account of the gender perspective. They should respect fully the child's right to be consulted and to have his/her views duly taken into account in accordance with his/her evolving capacities, and on the basis of his/her access to all necessary information. Every effort should be made to enable such consultation and information provision to be carried out in the child's preferred language.

7. In applying the present Guidelines, determination of the best interests of the child shall be designed to identify courses of action for children deprived of parental care, or at risk of being so, that are best suited to satisfying their needs and rights, taking into account the full and personal development of their rights in their family, social and cultural environment and their status as subjects of rights, both at the time of the determination and in the longer term. The determination process should take account of, inter alia, the right of the child to be heard and to have his/her views taken into account in accordance with his/her age and maturity.

8. States should develop and implement comprehensive child welfare and protection policies within the framework of their overall social and human development policy, with attention to the improvement of existing alternative care provision, reflecting the principles contained in the present Guidelines.

9. As part of efforts to prevent the separation of children from their parents, States should seek to ensure appropriate and culturally sensitive measures:

(a) To support family caregiving environments whose capacities are limited by factors such as disability, drug and alcohol misuse, discrimination against families with indigenous or minority backgrounds, and living in armed conflict regions or under foreign occupation;

(b) To provide appropriate care and protection for vulnerable children, such as child victims of abuse and exploitation, abandoned children, children living on the street, children born out of wedlock, unaccompanied and separated children, internally displaced and refugee children, children of migrant workers, children of asylum-seekers, or children living with or affected by HIV/AIDS and other serious illnesses.

10. Special efforts should be made to tackle discrimination on the basis of any status of the child or parents, including poverty, ethnicity, religion, sex, mental and physical disability, HIV/AIDS or other serious illnesses, whether physical or mental, birth out of wedlock, and socioeconomic stigma, and all other statuses and circumstances that can give rise to relinquishment, abandonment and/or removal of a child.

B. Alternative care

11. All decisions concerning alternative care should take full account of the desirability, in principle, of maintaining the child as close as possible to his/her habitual place of residence, in order to facilitate contact and potential reintegration with his/her family and to minimize disruption of his/her educational, cultural and social life.

12. Decisions regarding children in alternative care, including those in informal care, should have due regard for the importance of ensuring children a stable home and of meeting their basic need for safe and continuous attachment to their caregivers, with permanency generally being a key goal.

13. Children must be treated with dignity and respect at all times and must benefit from effective protection from abuse, neglect and all forms of exploitation, whether on the part of care providers, peers or third parties, in whatever care setting they may find themselves.

14. Removal of a child from the care of the family should be seen as a measure of last resort and should, whenever possible, be temporary and for the shortest possible duration. Removal decisions should be regularly reviewed and the child's return to parental care, once the original causes of removal have been resolved or have disappeared, should be in the best interests of the child, in keeping with the assessment foreseen in paragraph 49 below.

15. Financial and material poverty, or conditions directly and uniquely imputable to such poverty, should never be the only justification for the removal of a child from parental care, for receiving a child into alternative care, or for preventing his/her reintegration, but should be seen as a signal for the need to provide appropriate support to the family.

16. Attention must be paid to promoting and safeguarding all other rights of special pertinence to the situation of children without parental care, including, but not limited to, access to education, health and other basic services, the right to identity, freedom of religion or belief, language and protection of property and inheritance rights.

17. Siblings with existing bonds should in principle not be separated by placements in alternative care unless there is a clear risk of abuse or other justification in the best interests of the child. In any case, every effort should be made to enable siblings to maintain contact with each other, unless this is against their wishes or interests.

18. Recognizing that, in most countries, the majority of children without parental care are looked after informally by relatives or others, States should seek to devise appropriate means, consistent with the present Guidelines, to ensure their welfare and protection while in such informal care arrangements, with due respect for cultural, economic, gender and religious differences and practices that do not conflict with the rights and best interests of the child.

19. No child should be without the support and protection of a legal guardian or other recognized responsible adult or competent public body at any time.

20. The provision of alternative care should never be undertaken with a prime purpose of furthering the political, religious or economic goals of the providers.

21. The use of residential care should be limited to cases where such a setting is specifically appropriate, necessary and constructive for the individual child concerned and in his/her best interests.

22. In accordance with the predominant opinion of experts, alternative care for young children, especially those under the age of 3 years, should be provided in family-based settings. Exceptions to this principle may be warranted in order to prevent the separation of siblings and in cases where the placement is of an emergency nature or is for a predetermined and very limited duration, with planned family reintegration or other appropriate long-term care solution as its outcome.

23. While recognizing that residential care facilities and family-based care complement each other in meeting the needs of children, where large residential care facilities (institutions) remain, alternatives should be developed in the context of an overall deinstitutionalization strategy, with precise goals and objectives, which will allow for their progressive elimination. To this end, States should establish care standards to ensure the quality and conditions that are conducive to the child's development, such as individualized and small-group care, and should evaluate existing facilities against these standards. Decisions regarding the establishment of, or permission to establish, new residential care facilities, whether public or private, should take full account of this deinstitutionalization objective and strategy.

Measures to promote application

24. States should, to the maximum extent of their available resources and, where appropriate, within the framework of development cooperation, allocate human and financial resources to ensure the optimal and progressive implementation of the present Guidelines throughout their respective territories in a timely manner. States should facilitate active cooperation among all relevant authorities and the mainstreaming of child and family welfare issues within all ministries directly or indirectly concerned.

25. States are responsible for determining any need for, and requesting, international cooperation in implementing the present Guidelines. Such requests should be given due consideration and should receive a favourable response wherever possible and appropriate. The enhanced implementation of the present Guidelines should figure in development cooperation programmes. When providing assistance to a State, foreign entities should abstain from any initiative inconsistent with the Guidelines.

26. Nothing in the present Guidelines should be interpreted as encouraging or condoning lower standards than those that may exist in given States, including in their legislation. Similarly, competent authorities, professional organizations and others are encouraged to develop national or professionally specific guidelines that build upon the letter and spirit of the present Guidelines.

III. Scope of the Guidelines

27. The present Guidelines apply to the appropriate use and conditions of alternative formal care for all persons under the age of 18 years, unless, under the law applicable to the child, majority is attained earlier. Only where indicated do the Guidelines also apply to informal care settings, having due regard for both the important role played by the extended family and the community and the obligations of States for all children not in the care of their parents or legal and customary caregivers, as set out in the Convention on the Rights of the Child.

28. Principles in the present Guidelines are also applicable, as appropriate, to young persons already in alternative care and who need continuing care or support for a transitional period after reaching the age of majority under applicable law.

29. For the purposes of the present Guidelines, and subject, notably, to the exceptions listed in paragraph 30 below, the following definitions shall apply:

(a) Children without parental care: all children not in the overnight care of at least one of their parents, for whatever reason and under whatever circumstances. Children without parental care who are outside their country of habitual residence or victims of emergency situations may be designated as:

    (i) "Unaccompanied" if they are not cared for by another relative or an adult who by law or custom is responsible for doing so; or

(ii) "Separated" if they are separated from a previous legal or customary primary caregiver, but who may nevertheless be accompanied by another relative;

(b) Alternative care may take the form of:

(i) Informal care: any private arrangement provided in a family environment, whereby the child is looked after on an ongoing or indefinite basis by relatives or friends (informal kinship care) or by others in their individual capacity, at the initiative of the child, his/her parents or other person without this arrangement having been ordered by an administrative or judicial authority or a duly accredited body;

(ii) Formal care: all care provided in a family environment which has been ordered by a competent administrative body or judicial authority, and all care provided in a residential environment, including in private facilities, whether or not as a result of administrative or judicial measures;

(c) With respect to the environment where it is provided, alternative care may be:

(i) Kinship care: family-based care within the child's extended family or with close friends of the family known to the child, whether formal or informal in nature;

(ii) Foster care: situations where children are placed by a competent authority for the purpose of alternative care in the domestic environment of a family other than the children's own family that has been selected, qualified, approved and supervised for providing such care;

(iii) Other forms of family-based or family-like care placements;

(iv) Residential care: care provided in any non-family-based group setting, such as places of safety for emergency care, transit centres in emergency situations, and all other short- and long-term residential care facilities, including group homes;

(v) Supervised independent living arrangements for children;

(d) With respect to those responsible for alternative care:

(i) Agencies are the public or private bodies and services that organize alternative care for children;

(ii) Facilities are the individual public or private establishments that provide residential care for children.

30. The scope of alternative care as foreseen in the present Guidelines does not extend, however, to:

(a) Persons under the age of 18 years who are deprived of their liberty by decision of a judicial or administrative authority as a result of being alleged as, accused of or recognized as having infringed the law, and whose situation is covered by the United Nations Standard Minimum Rules for the Administration of Juvenile Justice and the United Nations Rules for the Protection of Juveniles Deprived of Their Liberty;

(b) Care by adoptive parents from the moment the child concerned is effectively placed in their custody pursuant to a final adoption order, as of which moment, for the purposes of the present Guidelines, the child is considered to be in parental care. The Guidelines are, however, applicable to pre-adoption or probationary placement of a child with the prospective adoptive parents, as far as they are compatible with requirements governing such placements as stipulated in other relevant international instruments;

(c) Informal arrangements whereby a child voluntarily stays with relatives or friends for recreational purposes and reasons not connected with the parents' general inability or unwillingness to provide adequate care.

31. Competent authorities and others concerned are also encouraged to make use of the present Guidelines, as applicable, at boarding schools, hospitals, centres for children with mental and physical disabilities or other special needs, camps, the workplace and other places which may be responsible for the care of children.

IV. Preventing the need for alternative care

A. Promoting parental care

32. States should pursue policies that ensure support for families in meeting their responsibilities towards the child and promote the right of the child to have a relationship with both parents. These policies should address the root causes of child abandonment, relinquishment and separation of the child from his/her family by ensuring, inter alia, the right to birth registration, and access to adequate housing and to basic health, education and social welfare services, as well as by promoting measures to combat poverty, discrimination, marginalization, stigmatization, violence, child maltreatment and sexual abuse, and substance abuse.

33. States should develop and implement consistent and mutually reinforcing family-oriented policies designed to promote and strengthen parents' ability to care for their children.

34. States should implement effective measures to prevent child abandonment, relinquishment and separation of the child from his/her family. Social policies and programmes should, inter alia, empower families with attitudes, skills, capacities and tools to enable them to provide adequately for the protection, care and development of their children. The complementary capacities of the State and civil society, including non-governmental and community-based organizations, religious leaders and the media should be engaged to this end. These social protection measures should include:

(a) Family strengthening services, such as parenting courses and sessions, the promotion of positive parent-child relationships, conflict resolution skills, opportunities for employment and income generation and, where required, social assistance;

(b) Supportive social services, such as day care, mediation and conciliation services, substance abuse treatment, financial assistance, and services for parents and children with disabilities. Such services, preferably of an integrated and non-intrusive nature, should be directly accessible at the community level and should actively involve the participation of families as partners, combining their resources with those of the community and the carer;

(c) Youth policies aiming at empowering youth to face positively the challenges of everyday life, including when they decide to leave the parental home, and preparing future parents to make informed decisions regarding their sexual and reproductive health and to fulfil their responsibilities in this respect.

35. Various complementary methods and techniques should be used for family support, varying throughout the process of support, such as home visits, group meetings with other families, case conferences and securing commitments by the family concerned. They should be directed towards both facilitating intrafamilial relationships and promoting the family's integration within its community.

36. Special attention should be paid, in accordance with local laws, to the provision and promotion of support and care services for single and adolescent parents and their children, whether or not born out of wedlock. States should ensure that adolescent parents retain all rights inherent to their status both as parents and as children, including access to all appropriate services for their own development, allowances to which parents are entitled, and their inheritance rights. Measures should be adopted to ensure the protection of pregnant adolescents and to guarantee that they do not interrupt their studies. Efforts should also be made to reduce the stigma attached to single and adolescent parenthood.

37. Support and services should be available to siblings who have lost their parents or caregivers and choose to remain together in their household, to the extent that the eldest sibling is both willing and deemed capable of acting as the household head. States should ensure, including through the appointment of a legal guardian, a recognized responsible adult or, where appropriate, a public body legally mandated to act as guardian, as stipulated in paragraph 19 above, that such households benefit from mandatory protection from all forms of exploitation and abuse, and supervision and support on the part of the local community and its competent services, such as social workers, with particular concern for the children's health, housing, education and inheritance rights. Special attention should be given to ensuring that the head of such a household retains all rights inherent to his/her child status, including access to education and leisure, in addition to his/her rights as a household head.

38. States should ensure opportunities for day care, including all-day schooling, and respite care which would enable parents better to cope with their overall responsibilities towards the family, including additional responsibilities inherent in caring for children with special needs.

Preventing family separation

39. Proper criteria based on sound professional principles should be developed and consistently applied for assessing the child's and the family's situation, including the family's actual and potential capacity to care for the child, in cases where the competent authority or agency has reasonable grounds to believe that the well-being of the child is at risk.

40. Decisions regarding removal or reintegration should be based on this assessment and should be made by suitably qualified and trained professionals, on behalf of or authorized by a competent authority, in full consultation with all concerned and bearing in mind the need to plan for the child's future.

41. States are encouraged to adopt measures for the integral protection and guarantee of rights during pregnancy, birth and the breastfeeding period, in order to ensure conditions of dignity and equality for the adequate develop-

ment of the pregnancy and the care of the child. Therefore, support programmes should be provided to future mothers and fathers, particularly adolescent parents, who have difficulty exercising their parental responsibilities. Such programmes should aim at empowering mothers and fathers to exercise their parental responsibilities in conditions of dignity and at avoiding their being induced to surrender their child because of their vulnerability.

42. When a child is relinquished or abandoned, States should ensure that this may take place in conditions of confidentiality and safety for the child, respecting his/her right to access information on his/her origins where appropriate and possible under the law of the State.

43. States should formulate clear policies to address situations where a child has been abandoned anonymously, which indicate whether and how family tracing should be undertaken and reunification or placement within the extended family pursued. Policies should also allow for timely decision-making on the child's eligibility for permanent family placement and for arranging such placements expeditiously.

44. When a public or private agency or facility is approached by a parent or legal guardian wishing to relinquish a child permanently, the State should ensure that the family receives counselling and social support to encourage and enable them to continue to care for the child. If this fails, a social worker or other appropriate professional assessment should be undertaken to determine whether there are other family members who wish to take permanent responsibility for the child, and whether such arrangements would be in the best interests of the child. Where such arrangements are not possible or are not in the best interests of the child, efforts should be made to find a permanent family placement within a reasonable period.

45. When a public or private agency or facility is approached by a parent or caregiver wishing to place a child in care for a short or indefinite period, the State should ensure the availability of counselling and social support to encourage and enable him or her to continue to care for the child. A child should be admitted to alternative care only when such efforts have been exhausted and acceptable and justified reasons for entry into care exist.

46. Specific training should be provided to teachers and others working with children in order to help them to identify situations of abuse, neglect, exploitation or risk of abandonment and to refer such situations to competent bodies.

47. Any decision to remove a child against the will of his/her parents must be made by competent authorities, in accordance with applicable law and procedures and subject to judicial review, the parents being assured the right of appeal and access to appropriate legal representation.

48. When the child's sole or main carer may be the subject of deprivation of liberty as a result of preventive detention or sentencing decisions, non-custodial remand measures and sentences should be taken in appropriate cases wherever possible, the best interests of the child being given due consideration. States should take into account the best interests of the child when deciding whether to remove children born in prison and children living in prison with a parent. The removal of such children should be treated in the same way as other instances where separa-

tion is considered. Best efforts should be made to ensure that children remaining in custody with their parent benefit from adequate care and protection, while guaranteeing their own status as free individuals and access to activities in the community.

B. Promoting family reintegration

49.   In order to prepare and support the child and the family for his/her possible return to the family, his/her situation should be assessed by a duly designated individual or team with access to multidisciplinary advice, in consultation with the different actors involved (the child, the family, the alternative caregiver), so as to decide whether the reintegration of the child in the family is possible and in the best interests of the child, which steps this would involve and under whose supervision.

50.   The aims of the reintegration and the family's and alternative caregiver's principal tasks in this respect should be set out in writing and agreed on by all concerned.

51.   Regular and appropriate contact between the child and his/her family specifically for the purpose of reintegration should be developed, supported and monitored by the competent body.

52.   Once decided, the reintegration of the child in his/her family should be designed as a gradual and supervised process, accompanied by follow-up and support measures that take account of the child's age, needs and evolving capacities, as well as the cause of the separation.

V. Framework of care provision

53.   In order to meet the specific psychoemotional, social and other needs of each child without parental care, States should take all necessary measures to ensure that the legislative, policy and financial conditions exist to provide for adequate alternative care options, with priority to family- and community-based solutions.

54.   States should ensure the availability of a range of alternative care options, consistent with the general principles of the present Guidelines, for emergency, short-term and long-term care.

55.   States should ensure that all entities and individuals engaged in the provision of alternative care for children receive due authorization to do so from a competent authority and are subject to regular monitoring and review by the latter in keeping with the present Guidelines. To this end, these authorities should develop appropriate criteria for assessing the professional and ethical fitness of care providers and for their accreditation, monitoring and supervision.

56.   With regard to informal care arrangements for the child, whether within the extended family, with friends or with other parties, States should, where appropriate, encourage such carers to notify the competent authorities accordingly so that they and the child may receive any necessary financial and other support that would promote the child's welfare and protection. Where possible and appropriate, States should encourage and enable informal caregivers, with the consent of the child and parents concerned, to formalize the care arrangement after a suitable lapse of time, to the extent that the arrangement has proved to be in the best interests of the child to date and is expected to continue in the foreseeable future.

VI. Determination of the most appropriate form of care

57.   Decision-making on alternative care in the best interests of the child should take place through a judicial, administrative or other adequate and recognized procedure, with legal safeguards, including, where appropriate, legal representation on behalf of children in any legal proceedings. It should be based on rigorous assessment, planning and review, through established structures and mechanisms, and should be carried out on a case-by-case basis, by suitably qualified professionals in a multidisciplinary team, wherever possible. It should involve full consultation at all stages with the child, according to his/her evolving capacities, and with his/her parents or legal guardians. To this end, all concerned should be provided with the necessary information on which to base their opinion. States should make every effort to provide adequate resources and channels for the training and recognition of the professionals responsible for determining the best form of care so as to facilitate compliance with these provisions.

58.   Assessment should be carried out expeditiously, thoroughly and carefully. It should take into account the child's immediate safety and well-being, as well as his/her longer-term care and development, and should cover the child's personal and developmental characteristics, ethnic, cultural, linguistic and religious background, family and social environment, medical history and any special needs.

59.   The resulting initial and review reports should be used as essential tools for planning decisions from the time of their acceptance by the competent authorities onwards, with a view to, inter alia, avoiding undue disruption and contradictory decisions.

60.   Frequent changes in care setting are detrimental to the child's development and ability to form attachments, and should be avoided. Short-term placements should aim at enabling an appropriate permanent solution to be arranged. Permanency for the child should be secured without undue delay through reintegration in his/her nuclear or extended family or, if this is not possible, in an alternative stable family setting or, where paragraph 21 above applies, in stable and appropriate residential care.

61.   Planning for care provision and permanency should be carried out from the earliest possible time, ideally before the child enters care, taking into account the immediate and longer-term advantages and disadvantages of each option considered, and should comprise short- and long-term propositions.

62.   Planning for care provision and permanency should be based on, notably, the nature and quality of the child's attachment to his/her family, the family's capacity to safeguard the child's well-being and harmonious development, the child's need or desire to feel part of a family, the desirability of the child remaining within his/her community and country, the child's cultural, linguistic and religious background, and the child's relationships with siblings, with a view to avoiding their separation.

63.   The plan should clearly state, inter alia, the goals of the placement and the measures to achieve them.

64.   The child and his/her parents or legal guardians should be fully informed about the alternative care options available, the implications of each option and their rights and obligations in the matter.

65. The preparation, enforcement and evaluation of a protective measure for a child should be carried out, to the greatest extent possible, with the participation of his/her parents or legal guardians and potential foster carers and caregivers, with respect to his/her particular needs, convictions and special wishes. At the request of the child, parents or legal guardians, other important persons in the child's life may also be consulted in any decision-making process, at the discretion of the competent authority.

66. States should ensure that any child who has been placed in alternative care by a properly constituted court, tribunal or administrative or other competent body, as well as his/her parents or others with parental responsibility, are given the opportunity to make representations on the placement decision before a court, are informed of their rights to make such representations and are assisted in doing so.

67. States should ensure the right of any child who has been placed in temporary care to regular and thorough review—preferably at least every three months—of the appropriateness of his/her care and treatment, taking into account, notably, his/her personal development and any changing needs, developments in his/her family environment, and the adequacy and necessity of the current placement in these circumstances. The review should be carried out by duly qualified and authorized persons, and should fully involve the child and all relevant persons in the child's life.

68. The child should be prepared for all changes of care settings resulting from the planning and review processes.

VII. Provision of alternative care

A. Policies

69. It is a responsibility of the State or appropriate level of government to ensure the development and implementation of coordinated policies regarding formal and informal care for all children who are without parental care. Such policies should be based on sound information and statistical data. They should define a process for determining who has responsibility for a child, taking into account the role of the child's parents or principal caregivers in his/her protection, care and development. Presumptive responsibility, unless shown to be otherwise, is with the child's parents or principal caregivers.

70. All State entities involved in the referral of, and assistance to, children without parental care, in cooperation with civil society, should adopt policies and procedures which favour information-sharing and networking between agencies and individuals in order to ensure effective care, aftercare and protection for these children. The location and/or design of the agency responsible for the oversight of alternative care should be established so as to maximize its accessibility to those who require the services provided.

71. Special attention should be paid to the quality of alternative care provision, both in residential and in family-based care, in particular with regard to the professional skills, selection, training and supervision of carers. Their role and functions should be clearly defined and clarified with respect to those of the child's parents or legal guardians.

72. In each country, the competent authorities should draw up a document setting out the rights of children in alternative care in keeping with the present Guidelines.

Children in alternative care should be enabled to understand fully the rules, regulations and objectives of the care setting and their rights and obligations therein.

73. All alternative care provision should be based on a written statement of the provider's aims and objectives in providing the service and the nature of the provider's responsibilities to the child that reflects the standards set by the Convention on the Rights of the Child, the present Guidelines and applicable law. All providers should be appropriately qualified or approved in accordance with legal requirements to provide alternative care services.

74. A regulatory framework should be established to ensure a standard process for the referral or admission of a child to an alternative care setting.

75. Cultural and religious practices regarding the provision of alternative care, including those related to gender perspectives, should be respected and promoted to the extent that they can be shown to be consistent with the rights and best interests of the children. The process of considering whether such practices should be promoted should be carried out in a broadly participatory way, involving the cultural and religious leaders concerned, professionals and those caring for children without parental care, parents and other relevant stakeholders, as well as the children themselves.

1. Informal care

76. With a view to ensuring that appropriate conditions of care are met in informal care provided by individuals or families, States should recognize the role played by this type of care and take adequate measures to support its optimal provision on the basis of an assessment of which particular settings may require special assistance or oversight.

77. Competent authorities should, where appropriate, encourage informal carers to notify the care arrangement and should seek to ensure their access to all available services and benefits likely to assist them in discharging their duty to care for and protect the child.

78. The State should recognize the de facto responsibility of informal carers for the child.

79. States should devise special and appropriate measures designed to protect children in informal care from abuse, neglect, child labour and all other forms of exploitation, with particular attention to informal care provided by non-relatives, or by relatives previously unknown to the children or living far from the children's habitual place of residence.

2. General conditions applying to all forms of formal alternative care arrangements

80. The transfer of a child into alternative care should be carried out with the utmost sensitivity and in a child-friendly manner, in particular involving specially trained and, in principle, non-uniformed personnel.

81. When a child is placed in alternative care, contact with his/her family, as well as with other persons close to him or her, such as friends, neighbours and previous carers, should be encouraged and facilitated, in keeping with the child's protection and best interests. The child should have access to information on the situation of his/her family members in the absence of contact with them.

82.   States should pay special attention to ensuring that children in alternative care because of parental imprisonment or prolonged hospitalization have the opportunity to maintain contact with their parents and receive any necessary counselling and support in that regard.

83.   Carers should ensure that children receive adequate amounts of wholesome and nutritious food in accordance with local dietary habits and relevant dietary standards, as well as with the children's religious beliefs. Appropriate nutritional supplementation should also be provided when necessary.

84.   Carers should promote the health of the children for whom they are responsible and make arrangements to ensure that medical care, counselling and support are made available as required.

85.   Children should have access to formal, non-formal and vocational education in accordance with their rights, to the maximum extent possible in educational facilities in the local community.

86.   Carers should ensure that the right of every child, including children with disabilities, living with or affected by HIV/AIDS or having any other special needs, to develop through play and leisure activities is respected and that opportunities for such activities are created within and outside the care setting. Contact with the children and others in the local community should be encouraged and facilitated.

87.   The specific safety, health, nutritional, developmental and other needs of babies and young children, including those with special needs, should be catered for in all care settings, including ensuring their ongoing attachment to a specific carer.

88.   Children should be allowed to satisfy the needs of their religious and spiritual life, including by receiving visits from a qualified representative of their religion, and to freely decide whether or not to participate in religious services, religious education or counselling. The child's own religious background should be respected, and no child should be encouraged or persuaded to change his/her religion or belief during a care placement.

89.   All adults responsible for children should respect and promote the right to privacy, including appropriate facilities for hygiene and sanitary needs, respecting gender differences and interaction, and adequate, secure and accessible storage space for personal possessions.

90.   Carers should understand the importance of their role in developing positive, safe and nurturing relationships with children, and should be able to do so.

91.   Accommodation in all alternative care settings should meet the requirements of health and safety.

92.   States must ensure through their competent authorities that accommodation provided to children in alternative care, and their supervision in such placements, enable them to be effectively protected against abuse. Particular attention needs to be paid to the age, maturity and degree of vulnerability of each child in determining his/her living arrangements. Measures aimed at protecting children in care should be in conformity with the law and should not involve unreasonable constraints on their liberty and conduct in comparison with children of similar age in their community.

93.   All alternative care settings should provide adequate protection to children from abduction, trafficking, sale and all other forms of exploitation. Any consequent constraints on their liberty and conduct should be no more than are strictly necessary to ensure their effective protection from such acts.

94.   All carers should promote and encourage children and young people to develop and exercise informed choices, taking account of acceptable risks and the child's age, and according to his/her evolving capacities.

95.   States, agencies and facilities, schools and other community services should take appropriate measures to ensure that children in alternative care are not stigmatized during or after their placement. This should include efforts to minimize the identification of children as being looked after in an alternative care setting.

96.   All disciplinary measures and behaviour management constituting torture, cruel, inhuman or degrading treatment, including closed or solitary confinement or any other forms of physical or psychological violence that are likely to compromise the physical or mental health of the child, must be strictly prohibited in conformity with international human rights law. States must take all necessary measures to prevent such practices and ensure that they are punishable by law. Restriction of contact with members of the child's family and other persons of special importance to the child should never be used as a sanction.

97.   Use of force and restraints of whatever nature should not be authorized unless strictly necessary for safeguarding the child's or others' physical or psychological integrity, in conformity with the law and in a reasonable and proportionate manner and with respect for the fundamental rights of the child. Restraint by means of drugs and medication should be based on therapeutic needs and should never be employed without evaluation and prescription by a specialist.

98.   Children in care should be offered access to a person of trust in whom they may confide in total confidentiality. This person should be designated by the competent authority with the agreement of the child concerned. The child should be informed that legal or ethical standards may require breaching confidentiality under certain circumstances.

99.   Children in care should have access to a known, effective and impartial mechanism whereby they can notify complaints or concerns regarding their treatment or conditions of placement. Such mechanisms should include initial consultation, feedback, implementation and further consultation. Young people with previous care experience should be involved in this process, due weight being given to their opinions. This process should be conducted by competent persons trained to work with children and young people.

100.   To promote the child's sense of self-identity, a life story book comprising appropriate information, pictures, personal objects and mementoes regarding each step of the child's life should be maintained with the child's participation and made available to the child throughout his/her life.

B.   Legal responsibility for the child

101.   In situations where the child's parents are absent or are incapable of making day-to-day decisions in the best interests of the child, and the child's placement in alternative care has been ordered or authorized by a competent

administrative body or judicial authority, a designated individual or competent entity should be vested with the legal right and responsibility to make such decisions in the place of parents, in full consultation with the child. States should ensure that a mechanism is in place for designating such an individual or entity.

102. Such legal responsibility should be attributed by the competent authorities and be supervised directly by them or through formally accredited entities, including non-governmental organizations. Accountability for the actions of the individual or entity concerned should lie with the designating body.

103. Persons exercising such legal responsibility should be reputable individuals with relevant knowledge of children's issues, an ability to work directly with children and an understanding of any special and cultural needs of the children to be entrusted to them. They should receive appropriate training and professional support in this regard. They should be in a position to make independent and impartial decisions that are in the best interests of the children concerned and that promote and safeguard each child's welfare.

104. The role and specific responsibilities of the designated person or entity should include:

(a) Ensuring that the rights of the child are protected and, in particular, that the child has appropriate care, accommodation, health-care provision, developmental opportunities, psychosocial support, education and language support;

(b) Ensuring that the child has access to legal and other representation where necessary, consulting with the child so that the child's views are taken into account by decision-making authorities, and advising and keeping the child informed of his/her rights;

(c) Contributing to the identification of a stable solution in the best interests of the child;

(d) Providing a link between the child and various organizations that may provide services to the child;

(e) Assisting the child in family tracing;

(f) Ensuring that, if repatriation or family reunification is carried out, it is done in the best interests of the child;

(g) Helping the child to keep in touch with his/her family, when appropriate.

1. Agencies and facilities responsible for formal care

105. Legislation should stipulate that all agencies and facilities must be registered and authorized to operate by social welfare services or another competent authority, and that failure to comply with such legislation constitutes an offence punishable by law. Authorization should be granted and be regularly reviewed by the competent authorities on the basis of standard criteria covering, at a minimum, the agency's or facility's objectives, functioning, staff recruitment and qualifications, conditions of care and financial resources and management.

106. All agencies and facilities should have written policy and practice statements, consistent with the present Guidelines, setting out clearly their aims, policies, methods and the standards applied for the recruitment, monitoring, supervision and evaluation of qualified and suitable carers to ensure that those aims are met.

107. All agencies and facilities should develop a staff code of conduct, consistent with the present Guidelines, that defines the role of each professional and of the carers in particular and includes clear reporting procedures on allegations of misconduct by any team member.

108. The forms of financing care provision should never be such as to encourage a child's unnecessary placement or prolonged stay in care arrangements organized or provided by an agency or facility.

109. Comprehensive and up-to-date records should be maintained regarding the administration of alternative care services, including detailed files on all children in their care, staff employed and financial transactions.

110. The records on children in care should be complete, up to date, confidential and secure, and should include information on their admission and departure and the form, content and details of the care placement of each child, together with any appropriate identity documents and other personal information. Information on the child's family should be included in the child's file as well as in the reports based on regular evaluations. This record should follow the child throughout the alternative care period and be consulted by duly authorized professionals responsible for his/her current care.

111. The above-mentioned records could be made available to the child, as well as to the parents or guardians, within the limits of the child's right to privacy and confidentiality, as appropriate. Appropriate counselling should be provided before, during and after consultation of the record.

112. All alternative care services should have a clear policy on maintaining the confidentiality of information pertaining to each child, which all carers are aware of and adhere to.

113. As a matter of good practice, all agencies and facilities should systematically ensure that, prior to employment, carers and other staff in direct contact with children undergo an appropriate and comprehensive assessment of their suitability to work with children.

114. Conditions of work, including remuneration, for carers employed by agencies and facilities should be such as to maximize motivation, job satisfaction and continuity, and hence their disposition to fulfil their role in the most appropriate and effective manner.

115. Training should be provided to all carers on the rights of children without parental care and on the specific vulnerability of children, in particularly difficult situations, such as emergency placements or placements outside their area of habitual residence. Cultural, social, gender and religious sensitization should also be assured. States should also provide adequate resources and channels for the recognition of these professionals in order to favour the implementation of these provisions.

116. Training in dealing appropriately with challenging behaviour, including conflict resolution techniques and means to prevent acts of harm or self-harm, should be provided to all care staff employed by agencies and facilities.

117. Agencies and facilities should ensure that, wherever appropriate, carers are prepared to respond to children with special needs, notably those living with HIV/AIDS or other chronic physical or mental illnesses, and children with physical or mental disabilities.

2. Foster care

118.   The competent authority or agency should devise a system, and should train concerned staff accordingly, to assess and match the needs of the child with the abilities and resources of potential foster carers and to prepare all concerned for the placement.

119.   A pool of accredited foster carers should be identified in each locality who can provide children with care and protection while maintaining ties to family, community and cultural group.

120.   Special preparation, support and counselling services for foster carers should be developed and made available to carers at regular intervals, before, during and after the placement.

121.   Carers should have, within fostering agencies and other systems involved with children without parental care, the opportunity to make their voice heard and to influence policy.

122.   Encouragement should be given to the establishment of associations of foster carers that can provide important mutual support and contribute to practice and policy development.

C.   Residential care

123.   Facilities providing residential care should be small and be organized around the rights and needs of the child, in a setting as close as possible to a family or small group situation. Their objective should generally be to provide temporary care and to contribute actively to the child's family reintegration or, if this is not possible, to secure his/her stable care in an alternative family setting, including through adoption or *kafala* of Islamic law, where appropriate.

124.   Measures should be taken so that, where necessary and appropriate, a child solely in need of protection and alternative care may be accommodated separately from children who are subject to the criminal justice system.

125.   The competent national or local authority should establish rigorous screening procedures to ensure that only appropriate admissions to such facilities are made.

126.   States should ensure that there are sufficient carers in residential care settings to allow individualized attention and to give the child, where appropriate, the opportunity to bond with a specific carer. Carers should also be deployed within the care setting in such a way as to implement effectively its aims and objectives and ensure child protection.

127.   Laws, policies and regulations should prohibit the recruitment and solicitation of children for placement in residential care by agencies, facilities or individuals.

D.   Inspection and monitoring

128.   Agencies, facilities and professionals involved in care provision should be accountable to a specific public authority, which should ensure, inter alia, frequent inspections comprising both scheduled and unannounced visits, involving discussion with and observation of the staff and the children.

129.   To the extent possible and appropriate, inspection functions should include a component of training and capacity-building for care providers.

130.   States should be encouraged to ensure that an independent monitoring mechanism is in place, with due consideration for the principles relating to the status of national institutions for the promotion and protection of human rights (the Paris Principles). The monitoring mechanism should be easily accessible to children, parents and those responsible for children without parental care. The functions of the monitoring mechanism should include:

(a)   Consulting in conditions of privacy with children in all forms of alternative care, visiting the care settings in which they live and undertaking investigations into any alleged situation of violation of children's rights in those settings, on complaint or on its own initiative;

(b)   Recommending relevant policies to appropriate authorities with the aim of improving the treatment of children deprived of parental care and ensuring that it is in keeping with the preponderance of research findings on child protection, health, development and care;

(c)   Submitting proposals and observations concerning draft legislation;

(d)   Contributing independently to the reporting process under the Convention on the Rights of the Child, including to periodic State party reports to the Committee on the Rights of the Child with regard to the implementation of the present Guidelines.

E.   Support for aftercare

131.   Agencies and facilities should have a clear policy and should carry out agreed procedures relating to the planned and unplanned conclusion of their work with children to ensure appropriate aftercare and/or follow-up. Throughout the period of care, they should systematically aim at preparing children to assume self-reliance and to integrate fully in the community, notably through the acquisition of social and life skills, which are fostered by participation in the life of the local community.

132.   The process of transition from care to aftercare should take into consideration children's gender, age, maturity and particular circumstances and include counselling and support, notably to avoid exploitation. Children leaving care should be encouraged to take part in the planning of aftercare life. Children with special needs, such as disabilities, should benefit from an appropriate support system, ensuring, inter alia, avoidance of unnecessary institutionalization. Both the public and the private sectors should be encouraged, including through incentives, to employ children from different care services, particularly children with special needs.

133.   Special efforts should be made to allocate to each child, whenever possible, a specialized person who can facilitate his/her independence when leaving care.

134.   Aftercare should be prepared as early as possible in the placement and, in any case, well before the child leaves the care setting.

135.   Ongoing educational and vocational training opportunities should be imparted as part of life skills education to young people leaving care in order to help them to become financially independent and generate their own income.

136.   Access to social, legal and health services, together with appropriate financial support, should also be provided to young people leaving care and during aftercare.

VIII. Care provision for children outside their country of habitual residence

A. Placement of a child for care abroad

137. The present Guidelines should apply to all public and private entities and all persons involved in arrangements for a child to be sent for care to a country other than his/her country of habitual residence, whether for medical treatment, temporary hosting, respite care or any other reason.

138. States concerned should ensure that a designated body has responsibility for determining specific standards to be met regarding, in particular, the criteria for selecting carers in the host country and the quality of care and follow-up, as well as for supervising and monitoring the operation of such schemes.

139. To ensure appropriate international cooperation and child protection in such situations, States are encouraged to ratify or accede to the Hague Convention on Jurisdiction, Applicable Law, Recognition, Enforcement and Cooperation in respect of Parental Responsibility and Measures for the Protection of Children, of 19 October 1996.

B. Provision of care for a child already abroad

140. The present Guidelines, as well as other relevant international provisions, should apply to all public and private entities and all persons involved in arrangements for a child needing care while in a country other than his/her country of habitual residence, for whatever reason.

141. Unaccompanied or separated children already abroad should, in principle, enjoy the same level of protection and care as national children in the country concerned.

142. In determining appropriate care provision, the diversity and disparity of unaccompanied or separated children (such as ethnic and migratory background or cultural and religious diversity) should be taken into consideration on a case-by-case basis.

143. Unaccompanied or separated children, including those who arrive irregularly in a country, should not, in principle, be deprived of their liberty solely for having breached any law governing access to and stay within the territory.

144. Child victims of trafficking should neither be detained in police custody nor subjected to penalties for their involvement under compulsion in unlawful activities.

145. As soon as an unaccompanied child is identified, States are strongly encouraged to appoint a guardian or, where necessary, representation by an organization responsible for his/her care and well-being to accompany the child throughout the status determination and decision-making process.

146. As soon as an unaccompanied or separated child is taken into care, all reasonable efforts should be made to trace his/her family and re-establish family ties, when this is in the best interests of the child and would not endanger those involved.

147. In order to assist in planning the future of an unaccompanied or separated child in a manner that best protects his/her rights, relevant State and social service authorities should make all reasonable efforts to procure documentation and information in order to conduct an assessment of the child's risk and social and family conditions in his/her country of habitual residence.

148. Unaccompanied or separated children must not be returned to their country of habitual residence:

(*a*) If, following the risk and security assessment, there are reasons to believe that the child's safety and security are in danger;

(*b*) Unless, prior to the return, a suitable caregiver, such as a parent, other relative, other adult caretaker, a Government agency or an authorized agency or facility in the country of origin, has agreed and is able to take responsibility for the child and provide him or her with appropriate care and protection;

(*c*) If, for other reasons, it is not in the best interests of the child, according to the assessment of the competent authorities.

149. With the above aims in mind, cooperation among States, regions, local authorities and civil society associations should be promoted, strengthened and enhanced.

150. The effective involvement of consular services or, failing that, legal representatives of the country of origin should be foreseen, when this is in the best interests of the child and would not endanger the child or his/her family.

151. Those responsible for the welfare of an unaccompanied or separated child should facilitate regular communication between the child and his/her family, except where this is against the child's wishes or is demonstrably not in his/her best interests.

152. Placement with a view to adoption or *kafala* of Islamic law should not be considered a suitable initial option for an unaccompanied or separated child. States are encouraged to consider this option only after efforts to determine the location of his/her parents, extended family or habitual carers have been exhausted.

IX. Care in emergency situations

A. Application of the Guidelines

153. The present Guidelines should continue to apply in situations of emergency arising from natural and man-made disasters, including international and non-international armed conflicts, as well as foreign occupation. Individuals and organizations wishing to work on behalf of children without parental care in emergency situations are strongly encouraged to operate in accordance with the Guidelines.

154. In such circumstances, the State or de facto authorities in the region concerned, the international community and all local, national, foreign and international agencies providing or intending to provide child-focused services should pay special attention:

(*a*) To ensure that all entities and persons involved in responding to unaccompanied or separated children are sufficiently experienced, trained, resourceful and equipped to do so in an appropriate manner;

(*b*) To develop, as necessary, temporary and long-term family-based care;

(*c*) To use residential care only as a temporary measure until family-based care can be developed;

(*d*) To prohibit the establishment of new residential facilities structured to provide simultaneous care to large groups of children on a permanent or long-term basis;

(*e*) To prevent the cross-border displacement of children, except under the circumstances described in paragraph 160 below;

(f) To make cooperation with family tracing and reintegration efforts mandatory.

Preventing separation

155. Organizations and authorities should make every effort to prevent the separation of children from their parents or primary caregivers, unless the best interests of the child so require, and ensure that their actions do not inadvertently encourage family separation by providing services and benefits to children alone rather than to families.

156. Separation initiated by the child's parents or other primary caregivers should be prevented by:

(a) Ensuring that all households have access to basic food and medical supplies and other services, including education;

(b) Limiting the development of residential care options and restricting their use to those situations where it is absolutely necessary.

B. Care arrangements

157. Communities should be assisted in playing an active role in monitoring and responding to care and protection issues facing children in their local context.

158. Care within a child's own community, including fostering, should be encouraged, as it provides continuity in socialization and development.

159. As unaccompanied or separated children may be at heightened risk of abuse and exploitation, monitoring and specific support to carers should be foreseen to ensure their protection.

160. Children in emergency situations should not be moved to a country other than that of their habitual residence for alternative care except temporarily for compelling health, medical or safety reasons. In that case, this should be as close as possible to their home, they should be accompanied by a parent or caregiver known to them, and a clear return plan should be established.

161. Should family reintegration prove impossible within an appropriate period or be deemed contrary to the best interests of the child, stable and definitive solutions, such as adoption or *kafala* of Islamic law, should be envisaged; failing this, other long-term options should be considered, such as foster care or appropriate residential care, including group homes and other supervised living arrangements.

C. Tracing and family reintegration

162. Identifying, registering and documenting unaccompanied or separated children are priorities in any emergency and should be carried out as quickly as possible.

163. Registration activities should be conducted by or under the direct supervision of State authorities and explicitly mandated entities with responsibility for and experience in this task.

164. The confidential nature of the information collected should be respected and systems put in place for safe forwarding and storage of information. Information should only be shared among duly mandated agencies for the purpose of tracing, family reintegration and care.

165. All those engaged in tracing family members or primary legal or customary caregivers should operate within a coordinated system, using standardized forms and mutually compatible procedures, wherever possible. They should ensure that the child and others concerned would not be endangered by their actions.

166. The validity of relationships and the confirmation of the willingness of the child and family members to be reunited must be verified for every child. No action should be taken that may hinder eventual family reintegration, such as adoption, change of name or movement to places far from the family's likely location, until all tracing efforts have been exhausted.

167. Appropriate records of any placement of a child should be made and kept in a safe and secure manner so that reunification can be facilitated in the future.

United Nations Children's Fund

In 2009, UNICEF remained committed to achieving the MDGs [YUN 2000, p. 51] and the goals set out by the Assembly's twenty-seventh (2002) special session on children [YUN 2002, p. 1168] in its document "A world fit for children", [ibid., p. 1169]. UNICEF's work was also guided by the 1989 Convention on the Rights of the Child, adopted by the Assembly in resolution 44/25 [YUN 1989, p. 560], and its Optional Protocols. Its mission was to defend children's rights, help meet their basic needs and increase their opportunities to flourish; rally political will and resources to invest in children's well-being; respond to emergencies to protect children; promote equal rights for women and girls and support their full participation in developing their communities; and work towards the human development goals adopted by the world community. In line with its 2006–2009 medium-term strategic plan (MTSP) [YUN 2005, p. 1284], UNICEF continued to focus its work on five priorities—young child survival and development; basic education and gender equality; HIV/AIDS and children; child protection from violence, exploitation and abuse; and policy advocacy and partnerships for children's rights.

The annual UNICEF flagship publication, *The State of the World's Children 2009* [Sales No. E.09.XX.1], focused on maternal and newborn health, underscoring the need to establish comprehensive care for mothers, newborns and children. Africa and Asia were a key focus for the report, which complemented the previous year's issue on child survival [YUN 2008, p. 1285]. The report noted that the causes of maternal and newborn death were well understood, and most were preventable or treatable through access to basic health-care services. Examining global data on maternal health-care coverage and gender issues, the report outlined interventions needed for improving maternal and newborn health, including improving water, sanitation, and hygiene (WASH) facilities and practices; strengthening the quality of health-care systems; and creating an environment supportive of women's rights.

In 2009, UNICEF cooperated with 155 countries, areas and territories: 44 in sub-Saharan Africa, 35 in Latin America and the Caribbean, 35 in Asia, 20 in the Middle East and North Africa, and 21 in Central and Eastern Europe and the Commonwealth of Independent States (CIS).

Total expenditures were $3,298 million in 2009, a 6 per cent increase from 2008, and programme assistance expenditures rose by 5 per cent, to $2,943 million. Expenditures on programme support were $201 million, a 20 per cent increase over 2008, and management and administration expenditures were $120 million, a 43 per cent increase over 2008. The bulk of UNICEF support continued to go to initiatives for child survival and development and towards sub-Saharan Africa and Asia, where most of the world's poorest people lived. Resources were predicted to remain constrained through 2010. UNICEF operations in 2009 were described in the *UNICEF Annual Report 2009*, the UNICEF annual report to the Economic and Social Council [E/2010/6] and the annual report of the Executive Director on progress and achievements against the Fund's extended 2006–2013 MTSP [E/ICEF/2010/9 & Corr.1].

The UNICEF Executive Board held its first regular session of 2009 (4–6 February), the annual session (8–10 June) and the second regular session (14–16 September), all in New York [E/2009/34/Rev.1], during which it adopted 21 decisions.

By **decision 2009/215** of 22 July, the Economic and Social Council took note of the Board's report on its first, second and annual sessions of 2008 [E/2008/34/Rev.1]; the annual report of UNICEF covering the year 2008 [E/2009/6]; the Board's report on its first regular session of 2009 and the joint meeting of the Executive Boards of UNICEF, the United Nations Development Programme (UNDP)/UNFPA and the World Food Programme (WFP) [E/2009/34/Rev.1]; and the extract from the Board's report on its 2009 annual session [E/2009/L.11].

On 16 September, the Executive Board adopted the programme of work for its 2010 sessions [E/2009/34/Rev.1 (dec. 2009/13)].

Programme policies

In her annual report to the Economic and Social Council, covering 2009 [E/2010/6], the UNICEF Executive Director provided updates on funding for operational activities for development; partnerships and collaborative relationships with other organizations; contributions to national capacity development and development effectiveness; South-South cooperation and development of national capacities; gender equality and women's empowerment within the organization; and the transition from relief to development.

The report also described progress made to improve the functioning of the UN development system and to evaluate operational activities.

Medium-term strategic plan (2006–2013)

On 6 February [dec. 2009/5], the Executive Board decided to extend the MTSP by two years, until the end of 2013, in order to align UNICEF's planning cycle with the quadrennial comprehensive policy review of operational activities for development of the UN system outlined in resolution 63/232 [YUN 2008, p. 962]. The Board requested that UNICEF prepare its next strategic plan, to start in 2014, taking into account the recommendations of the comprehensive policy review to be held in 2012 and the end-of-cycle review of the MTSP.

The Executive Director, in her annual report on the progress and achievements against the MTSP (2006–2013) [E/ICEF/2010/9 & Corr.1], focused on the urgency of achieving the MDGs and the actions needed to address areas for growth outlined in the midterm review of the MTSP [YUN 2008, p. 1285]. The report detailed the status and trends in the five areas: young child survival and development; basic education and gender equality; HIV/AIDS and children; child protection from violence, exploitation and abuse; and policy advocacy and partnerships for children's rights. The report also focused on emergency preparedness, response and recovery.

In the area of child survival and development, data showed that inequalities remained between the richest and poorest populations in not only the least developed countries but in many middle-income countries as well. Scaling up actions to address the major killers of children—pneumonia, diarrhoea, malaria, measles and HIV/AIDS—was a priority. Rising food costs led to the reorientation of the United Nations Standing Committee on Nutrition and a continuing emphasis on sustaining improvements in nutrition.

Addressing the needs of the whole life cycle of children's education and prioritizing funding and staffing for early childhood development (ECD) programming were ongoing goals for UNICEF, as was improving planning and coordination for emergency preparedness and response. Integrating HIV prevention into both emergency response and sexual and gender-based violence prevention initiatives was an area for improvement. Strengthening linkages between formal and informal child protection systems was a challenge requiring further research.

UNICEF's efforts in promoting evidence-based analysis and policy engagement through building national capacities and ownership yielded promising results. Responding to economic shocks and post-crisis adjustments was a priority. The "Recovery with a Human Face" approach was used to prevent countries from regressing on the realization of children's rights during economic recovery and to ensure that the recovery benefited the most excluded children and families by increasing and protecting national pro-poor expenditures and assessing different social policy options. The Executive Director called for greater attention to youth issues and, in partnership with the International Labour Organization, Bretton Woods agencies and others, to policies for providing young people with skills to gain employment. UNICEF's focus on humanitarian action and post-crisis recovery, guided by the Core Commitments for Children (CCCs), aided more than 79 countries in responding to crises.

On 10 June [dec. 2009/7], the Board called on UNICEF to strengthen the Executive Director's annual report by providing a more in-depth analysis on the challenges and opportunities of implementing the MTSP, and requested that the Executive Director provide information on the actions UNICEF would take to address those challenges in future reports. It also called on UNICEF to continue to improve performance on mainstreaming gender equality.

Medium-term financial plan (2009–2012)

In September, the Executive Board considered the planned financial estimates for the period 2009–2012 [E/ICEF/2009/AB/L.5]. The UNICEF secretariat recommended that the Board approve the framework of planned financial estimates for 2009–2012. UNICEF also recommended approval of the preparation of programme expenditure submissions to the Board of up to $798 million from regular resources in 2010, subject to the availability of resources and the continued validity of those planned financial estimates. The Board was requested to suspend the annual transfer of $30 million to the after-service health insurance reserve for 2009 and 2010 in view of the impact of the global economic downturn.

The Board approved those recommendations on 16 September [dec. 2009/21], and requested that UNICEF continue making annual transfers to the after-service health insurance reserve if end-of-year unexpended balances for regular resources so permitted.

Global strategy for collaborative relationships and partnerships

In March, UNICEF issued a report containing its strategic framework for partnerships and collaborative relationships [E/ICEF/2009/10], as well as a document mapping the organization's engagements with partners [E/ICEF/2009/11 & Corr.1], as outlined in a 2008 preliminary concept note [YUN 2008, p. 1287]. The added value of engaging in partnerships and collaborative relationships included stronger advocacy for

children's rights, transformative potential, greater aid effectiveness, innovations for children, a strengthened knowledge base, and additional resources for children and UNICEF-supported programmes.

Despite the results achieved, several challenges remained in managing partnerships and collaborative relationships. Many engagements remained ad hoc, without an organization-wide, coherent understanding of the function of such relationships, and with inconsistencies in approaches to engagements across country offices, National Committees, regional offices and headquarters. Businesses and civil society organizations identified the administrative burden of working with UNICEF as a significant obstacle to doing business. Furthermore, UNICEF lacked specialized monitoring and evaluation tools for partnerships and collaborative relationships, and frequently did not properly factor transaction costs into its analysis of potential engagements.

To address those challenges and strengthen its business relationships, UNICEF intended to develop a more strategic approach to its involvement in global programme partnerships, strengthen partnerships with civil society organizations, and utilize the full potential of business partnerships and collaborative relationships while mitigating risks. It also planned to strengthen its cooperation with knowledge partners and the media, and to increase the use of informal collaborative relationships.

On 10 June [dec. 2009/9], the Board endorsed the UNICEF strategic framework for partnerships and collaborative relationships. It stressed the importance of adequate monitoring and evaluation mechanisms for strategic partnerships, and encouraged partners to be involved in those processes. The Board asked that UNICEF take into account lessons learned in implementation and submit to the Board in 2012 a revised version of the framework widened to include all relevant actors, including multilateral organizations.

Evaluation system

In accordance with UNICEF's evaluation policy and Executive Board decisions [YUN 2008, p. 1287 and 1288], UNICEF in July submitted an annual report on its evaluation function and major evaluations [E/ICEF/2009/19 & Corr.1]. The report reviewed the implementation of the evaluation policy and summarized major country, regional and global evaluations conducted in the past year.

An Executive Directive on the Evaluation Function, issued in March, provided operational guidance for implementing the evaluation policy: it emphasized clear accountability for evaluation at different levels of the organization; a strong leadership role for the Evaluation Office in the evaluation function; and the importance of management attention at all stages of the evaluation process. In response to the Directive, regional offices used multiple means to educate stakeholders on their accountabilities and developed or revised evaluation strategies to determine the highest priority needs and effective regional responses. UNICEF predicted that fast progress and improvement was likely in the areas of accountability and leadership, staff capacity, planning and prioritization, and quality assurance. Additional efforts were needed to improve human and financial resources and management response.

UNICEF conducted several major evaluations and provided recommendations on a variety of regional and country-level programmes aligned with every focus area outlined in the MTSP.

The Board on 16 September took note of the report [dec. 2009/18]. It called on UNICEF to continue conducting evaluations of operations at the country level in close consultation with Governments, and to assist Governments in developing their national evaluation capacities. The Board requested that UNICEF report in 2010 on concrete steps taken to address the deficiencies in prioritization of evaluations and research activities at the field level as well as management responses to all evaluations.

Gender policy

In response to a 2008 Executive Board decision [YUN 2008, p. 1288], UNICEF reported to the Board [E/ICEF/2009/4] on the follow-up to recommendations made on the evaluation of gender policy implementation in UNICEF. The report included actions and time frames for completion. UNICEF was updating its gender policy through a consultative process based on review of literature, research and a network of experts. It was also carrying out organizational improvements, strengthening its staffing capacity for addressing gender equality, boosting gender equality training and improving capacity to programme for gender equality results.

On 6 February [dec. 2009/3], the Executive Board took note of the evaluation of gender policy implementation and the management response outlined in the report. It welcomed the strengthening of gender analysis in the results framework of the MTSP and the creation of a gender task force. It encouraged ongoing improvements in the establishment of and reporting on gender equality results in programmes, including the integration of sex-disaggregated indicators to support monitoring of implementation, and urged continued effort in the area of leadership to improve the integration of gender equality into programming. The Board requested that UNICEF consult it when updating the gender equality policy, clarify expected results for effectiveness and impact, measure progress in implementation of the management response, and report on progress to the Board in 2010.

Emergency assistance

In 2009, UNICEF responded to emergencies in more than 79 countries. The internal Emergency Programme Fund released more than $123 million in 2008–2009 to assist 44 country offices with implementing the CCCs, with $40.3 million given in 2009. That amount significantly exceeded allocations from previous years, mainly due to the number and severity of crises that affected all regions. The 36 countries covered in UNICEF's Humanitarian Action Report also received assistance, and UNICEF received $94 million in grants for rapid response and underfunded crises.

UNICEF continued as a leading organization for addressing humanitarian crises and providing emergency assistance worldwide. It served as co-chair for the Sub-Working Group on Preparedness of the Inter-Agency Standing Committee (IASC); through that position, it piloted the Harmonized Emergency Risk Management initiative in four countries, streamlining risk-based planning processes into regular office planning. It also launched in April an updated early warning action system—an online tool to support and monitor UNICEF emergency preparedness. UNICEF was the global lead for the IASC nutrition and WASH clusters, and co-lead for the education cluster together with the Save the Children Alliance. It was the focal point agency, along with UNFPA, for the child protection and gender-based violence "areas of responsibility" under the protection cluster, as well as the chair of the cross-cutting Mental Health and Psychosocial Reference Group. UNICEF also played a strong role in the health and logistics clusters and the Cluster Working Group on Early Recovery.

A changing humanitarian context meant that UNICEF needed to adapt its approach based on new evidence and emerging threats. The effects of climate change and the growing influence of the policy and security environment on humanitarian action, as well as UNICEF's role as cluster lead, meant that UNICEF needed to do more to support capacity development and harmonize efforts across development and humanitarian contexts. The revised CCCs in humanitarian action reflected the changing environment. Other challenges that affected UNICEF's work included constrained humanitarian access in countries in which Governments limited NGO activities, and the role of armed forces in delivering relief and development aid in certain situations, which blurred the line between armed forces and humanitarian actors.

UNICEF programmes by region

In 2009 [E/ICEF/2010/9 & Corr.1], UNICEF programme assistance expenditure totalled $2,943 million, of which $1,603.0 million (54.5 per cent) went to programmes in sub-Saharan Africa; $810.1 million

(27.5 per cent) to Asia; $147.9 million (5.0 per cent) to the Middle East and North Africa; $147.4 million (5.0 per cent) to the Americas and the Caribbean; $144.2 million (4.9 per cent) to interregional programmes; and $90.6 million (3.1 per cent) to Central and Eastern Europe and CIS.

Programme expenditures were highest in countries with low incomes and high and very high under-five mortality rates. The 47 low-income countries—defined as those with a per capita gross national income of $935 or less—had a total child population in 2008 of 439 million, or 22 per cent of all children worldwide; they received 50 per cent of programme expenditures. Countries with high and very high under-five mortality rates accounted for 57 per cent of total assistance.

In September [E/2009/34/Rev.1], the Executive Board had before it the summaries of the midterm reviews of country programmes in Eastern and Southern Africa [E/ICEF/2009/P/L.20], West and Central Africa [E/ICEF/2009/P/L.21 & Corr.1], Latin America and the Caribbean [E/ICEF/2009/P/L.22], East Asia and the Pacific [E/ICEF/2009/P/L.23], South Asia [E/ICEF/2009/P/L.24], Central and Eastern Europe and CIS [E/ICEF/2009/P/L.25] and the Middle East and North Africa [E/ICEF/2009/P/L.26]. The reports reviewed progress made, resources used, constraints faced, and adjustments made in country programmes.

Field visits

Executive Board members visited Kenya (28 February–7 March) [E/ICEF/2009/12] to gain a first-hand understanding of UNICEF work at the country level and demonstrate concrete examples of UNICEF cooperation with the Government and other partners, including the UN country team. The delegation noted key issues facing children and women during its meetings with UNICEF country and regional offices, the UN country team, senior Government officials, representatives from the private sector, and during visits to the Ayany primary school and North Eastern Province. The delegation also noted serious child protection challenges, including corporal punishment, children working as sex workers, children living on the streets, children victims of sexual abuse, the practice of female genital mutilation/cutting and evidence that Kenya was a fast-growing source, transit and destination country for human trafficking. It appreciated the cooperation between UNICEF and governmental institutions in developing and implementing key policies affecting children, such as education support, water sector reforms, the development of a child health policy, the introduction of sector budgeting and the establishment of social protection mechanisms for the most vulnerable children. The delegation noted the importance of strengthening the capacity of national duty-bearers.

In a visit to Nepal (30 March–8 April) [E/ICEF/2009/13], Executive Board members observed UNICEF's field operations in order to understand how its country programme contributed to achieving national development priorities and to witness concrete examples of how UNICEF cooperated with the Government and other partners. The delegation noted the serious likelihood that Nepal would not meet the MDG on eradicating extreme poverty and hunger by 2015 [YUN 2000, p. 51], and that UNICEF could help Nepal achieve the MDGs by facilitating financial and technical support to underfunded sectors such as health and nutrition. Nepal's gross domestic product grew the least compared with other South Asian countries, which created difficulties in the social policy context. Significant progress was achieved in providing universal primary education, but challenges remained in access to services, caste, quality of education and drop-out rates. Conflicts, a rising prevalence of HIV/AIDS, and low health, nutrition and sanitation indicators were also concerns. The delegation found that capacity-building was one of the key factors for enhancing development at the district and village levels, and that enabling people to identify and decide how to achieve further improvement was a crucial element of UNICEF's engagements.

UNICEF programmes by sector

In 2009, UNICEF programme assistance expenditures, linked to the five organizational priorities established in 2005 under the 2006–2009 MTSP [YUN 2005, p. 1284], totalled $2,943 million [E/ICEF/2010/9 & Corr.1], a 5 per cent increase over 2008. The largest share of expenditure, $1,365.7 million (46.4 per cent), went to young child survival and development, followed by basic education and gender equality ($628.9 million, or 21.4 per cent), policy advocacy and partnerships for children's rights ($401 million, or 13.6 per cent), child protection from violence, exploitation and abuse ($342.3 million, or 11.6 per cent) and HIV/AIDS and children ($188.5 million, or 6.4 per cent). Some $16.8 million (0.6 per cent) was expended in other areas. Programme support costs amounted to an additional $198 million.

Programme expenditure on young child survival and development saw a slight decrease in overall programme assistance compared with 2008, leading to a 4 per cent fall in its overall share, partly due to a decrease in emergency-related expenditures. Overall shares in other expenditure areas remained stable, except for policy advocacy and partnerships for children's rights, which increased significantly, reflecting the greater emphasis of UNICEF in supporting analysis and advocacy, as well as responses to economic shocks affecting children.

Young child survival and development

In 2009, UNICEF and its partners helped to raise the priority of child nutrition within the national development agendas of several countries. In Sri Lanka, the Government launched a comprehensive integrated nutrition programme; in Rwanda, UNICEF supported the first-ever national nutrition summit. Community-based child nutrition programmes expanded, notably in Ethiopia and Madagascar, and mobile telephone-based child malnutrition monitoring and mapping initiatives helped to improve reporting in countries such as Mauritania and Senegal. By 2009, 58 countries had adopted legislation or decrees mandating that flour be fortified with at least iron or folic acid, up from 33 in 2003. The use of home-based micronutrient supplementation expanded as well, with pilot projects launched in several countries in Asia and elsewhere. Improvements in the policy environment for universal salt iodization were reported in several countries, including Pakistan and the Russian Federation. More than 90 per cent of households in 36 countries used iodized salt in 2009, compared with 21 countries in 2002. A global shortage of ready-to-use therapeutic food (RUTF) was avoided due to improvements in forecasting, stock prepositioning and production capacity. Total RUTF procured by UNICEF rose from 2,500 metric tons in 2006 to 7,850 metric tons in 2009. Community-based and outreach therapeutic feeding programmes were expanded in Afghanistan and Ethiopia, and more than 70 countries had national legislation or regulatory provisions in force to protect breastfeeding based on the International Code on the Marketing of Breast Milk Substitutes. UNICEF distributed more than 574 million vitamin A capsules in 74 countries in 2009, and 54 countries had national policies that promoted the use of zinc in treating childhood diarrhoea.

UNICEF's efforts to reduce child mortality and improve maternal health continued through public health campaigns and the distribution of vaccines. Some 176 million children in 57 countries were reached through measles campaigns in 2008 and 2009, and an increased number of UNICEF country offices promoted the Reach Every District strategy to reduce disparities in immunization coverage. UNICEF procured 2.95 billion doses of measles vaccines on behalf of 82 countries, along with 346 million auto-disable syringes. The Fund remained a core partner of the Global Polio Eradication Initiative, supplying 2 billion doses of oral polio vaccine in 2009. The number of confirmed wild polio virus cases was 1,606, down slightly from 1,651 in 2008. Globally, 162 countries had introduced *haemophillus influenzae* type B (Hib) vaccine by the end of the year, and *rotavirus* vaccine was recommended for universal use, with priority given to countries with high diarrhoea

mortality. UNICEF provided support to 19 countries to implement campaigns and assess progress towards maternal and neonatal tetanus elimination, and Turkey became the thirteenth country to eliminate it since 2000, with 45 countries still remaining.

UNICEF in 2009 supported WASH programmes in 99 countries, including in 57 of 60 priority countries. Programmes addressed the development of national capacities and policy environment, together with appropriate support to the implementation of water supply and sanitation programmes. Data on household water treatment and safe storage (HWTS) from 67 countries showed that an estimated 33 per cent of households reported treating drinking water at home. Given the fact that rural households, especially in Africa, were less likely to practice HWTS, UNICEF made it a programme priority. The success of the first Global Handwashing Day in 2008, which drew attention to the importance of handwashing with soap, was repeated in 2009, with over 200 million children and 600,000 schools participating.

UNICEF remained a key member of the Roll Back Malaria partnership and the largest provider of insecticide-treated nets, procuring nearly 43 million nets for 49 countries in 2009, a 62 per cent increase over 2008. It also procured over 8.25 million malaria rapid diagnostic test kits globally, directly contributing to significant declines in case prevalence and mortality rates. New partnerships with the World Health Organization and the Office of the United Nations Secretary-General's Special Envoy for Malaria led to initiatives aimed at ensuring that malaria would cease to be a public health problem by 2015.

Through its health-related emergency response interventions, UNICEF provided an estimated 2,900 emergency health kits to 28 countries, 14.5 million doses of meningitis vaccine to six countries, and 122 million doses of measles vaccine to emergency-affected countries. UNICEF field office estimates indicated that specific emergency interventions in 2009 reached a large number of beneficiaries: 17.3 million from health interventions in 39 reporting countries; 6.5 million from WASH interventions in 41 countries; and 775,000 ECD interventions in 21 countries. An ECD kit was launched in 2009 and was used in 45 countries as a tool to restore normalcy for young children in emergency and post-crisis situations.

Basic education and gender equality

UNICEF made progress in supporting national capacity to improve children's developmental readiness to start primary school on time, especially for marginalized children. UNICEF provided support to revise or develop new national ECD policies in 23 countries, which were translated into a range of school-readiness initiatives, including the preparation of early childhood educators, school-readiness monitoring and parental education. Some 43 countries adopted the UNICEF-led Early Learning and Development Standards approach, which provided quality standards to monitor school and developmental readiness of young children. Based on the evaluation of UNICEF's "Getting Ready for School: A Child-to-Child Approach" pilot programme [YUN 2008, p. 1292], the six countries involved were putting plans in place to integrate school-readiness policies and practices within their education systems. Efforts of UNICEF and its partners to strengthen national capacity resulted in substantial increases in enrolment in early learning centres in several countries, including Ethiopia, Nepal and Uganda.

UNICEF assisted programmes to reduce gender and other disparities in access and completion of quality basic education. Through the School Fee Abolition Initiative, UNICEF strengthened the policy dialogue on financial barriers to education and furthered school fee abolition. It also promoted pilot initiatives that addressed disparities in access to education for ethnic minorities, orphans, vulnerable children, and children of nomads and internally displaced persons, and supported initiatives to reduce gender disparities in education.

More than half of UNICEF education programme assistance in 2009 focused on improving the quality of education. The Child-Friendly Schools (CFS) principles were incorporated into national policies in China and India, and India passed the landmark Right of Children to Free and Compulsory Education Act. Capacity development activities for the CFS approaches were supported in 63 countries, and the manual was expanded to include modules on climate change and environmental education, WASH in schools, and education management information systems.

An estimated 5.4 million children in 41 countries were reached in 2009 through emergency interventions in education. UNICEF contributed to increased enrolment in emergency and post-emergency countries through support to comprehensive back-to-school programmes, including in Burundi, the Democratic Republic of the Congo, the Sudan, Uganda and Afghanistan, where enrolment rates of girls and boys continued to rise despite the ongoing conflict. In West and Central Africa, increasing attention was paid to integrating HIV/AIDS in education initiatives. In the Americas and Eastern Europe, UNICEF continued to support sector activities aimed at HIV prevention and mitigation.

HIV/AIDS

HIV/AIDS continued to be a major threat to the rights, lives and well-being of children and adolescents. Globally, there were 430,000 new infections among children under the age of 15 in 2008, and over 4.9 million young people aged 15–24 years were living with HIV. Four years into the global *Unite for Children, Unite against AIDS* campaign [YUN 2005, p. 1290], several examples of global commitments to achieving the *Unite for Children* goals had emerged. The Global Fund to Fight AIDS, Tuberculosis and Malaria authorized a review of portfolios to increase support for more efficacious regimens for preventing mother-to-child transmission (PMTCT), and children and families were central to the nine priority areas of the UNAIDS Outcome Framework 2009–2011. However, the economic slowdown affected the likelihood of newly diagnosed individuals starting or maintaining antiretroviral treatment. To mitigate the effects of the downturn, the International Health Partnership, the Global Fund and the World Bank planned to focus their efforts in the next biennium on strengthening health systems and scaling up AIDS responses.

UNICEF support to PMTCT and paediatric HIV-reduction programmes expanded to 111 countries in 2009. Some 45 per cent of pregnant women living with HIV in low- and middle-income countries received antiretroviral regimens for PMTCT in 2008, compared with 24 per cent in 2006. On average, in low-income and middle-income countries, 32 per cent of infants born to HIV-positive mothers were given antiretroviral prophylaxis for PMTCT at birth in 2008, up from 20 per cent in 2007. Couples testing grew to over 90 per cent in some facilities in Rwanda in 2008, and as a result of the Laços Sul-Sul initiative—a South-South cooperation agreement on HIV/AIDS between Brazil and seven other countries—paediatric infection rates dropped tenfold in Paraguay from 2005 to 2008.

UNICEF continued as the co-chair of the UNAIDS outcome areas on social protection and the chair of the inter-agency task team on children affected by HIV/AIDS, providing leadership on integrating the HIV response into a national social protection and welfare response. National cash transfer programmes for caretakers of orphans and vulnerable children expanded in eastern and southern Africa, a new programme was launched in Lesotho and a pilot programme started in Zambia. Overall, UNICEF supported initiatives that directly supported children affected by AIDS in 29 countries.

By the end of 2009, 87 programme countries had integrated HIV/AIDS education into national secondary school curricula, up from 56 in 2005. The first-ever *International Technical Guidance on Sexuality Education* was issued in December. UNICEF increased support to peer-based awareness-raising programmes that focused on reaching the most at-risk adolescents in several countries, including Kenya and the Philippines.

UNAIDS programme coordination

At its second regular session in September [E/2009/34/ Rev.1], the Executive Board considered an oral report on the follow-up to the UNAIDS Programme Coordinating Board meetings. Issues important to UNICEF at the twenty-second, twenty-third, and twenty-fourth meetings included strengthened collaboration with the Global Fund to Fight AIDS, Tuberculosis and Malaria; gender sensitivity in AIDS responses; HIV prevention among injecting drug users; the 2010–2011 unified budget and workplan and 2008–2009 reports; and the UNAIDS second independent evaluation. Delegations requested regular updates at future Executive Board sessions on follow-up to the recommendations of the 2008 Global Partners Forum on Children Affected by AIDS.

Child protection from violence, exploitation and abuse

In 2009, notable progress was made in developing and improving national child protection systems. Approximately 19 countries began to map and assess their child protection systems, and UNICEF provided technical assistance to 114 Governments for policy development and strengthening direct care support. UNICEF also supported national institutions in 125 countries in the area of justice for children, focusing on policy advocacy and legal reforms for juvenile justice legislation and alternatives to deprivation of liberty. The Fund contributed to national efforts in 68 countries to combat child trafficking, focusing on policy advocacy and support for legal frameworks, and it co-authored the International Framework for Action to Implement the Trafficking in Persons Protocol. UNICEF also supported birth registration activities in over 65 countries, although challenges with low levels of registration remained, exacerbated by high mobility and migration.

The number of programme countries that implemented gender-sensitive programmes addressing social conventions and norms that contributed to violence, exploitation and abuse increased from 55 in 2008 to 66 in 2009. In partnership with UNFPA, the NGO Tostan, religious leaders and women's organizations, UNICEF supported programmes to end female genital mutilation/cutting in 20 countries, with results including advocacy breakthroughs in Burkina Faso, awareness-raising campaigns in the Sudan and community abandonment of the practice in Egypt and Senegal. Government and civil society capacities to combat child labour were strengthened in the areas of training, technical assistance and reintegration. UNICEF-supported partners created new opportunities for 1,786 child mine workers in Burkina Faso, and UNICEF sponsored studies and surveys and helped to develop new national plans and legislative instruments in Argentina, Ghana and Rwanda.

UNICEF continued its involvement in protecting children from the impact of armed conflict and natural disasters. It provided direct assistance and helped to coordinate large-scale child protection interventions in Gaza, Indonesia, Sri Lanka and Zimbabwe. In the 36 programme countries reporting specific emergency child protection interventions in 2009, 1.53 million children were reached. With UNICEF support, 49 programme countries incorporated child protection into national emergency preparedness and response planning, and the Fund expanded its emergency response capacity-building programme on child protection to 41 countries, compared with 29 in 2008. It also continued to support the disarmament, demobilization and reintegration (DDR) of child soldiers in a number of countries, including Burundi, the Central African Republic, the Philippines and the Democratic Republic of the Congo, where 6,630 children were reintegrated into communities through a mixed system of transit centres and foster families. A child DDR programme was launched in the Darfur region of the Sudan after a two-year delay.

In September, UNICEF released the *Progress for Children* report [Sales No.: E.09.XX.14], the first comprehensive global resource for child protection statistics. Indicators were developed on juvenile justice and formal care; training was provided on psychosocial monitoring and evaluation; and "macro-monitoring" methodologies for armed conflict situations were being piloted in collaboration with leading research institutions. Approximately 250 evaluations and studies were conducted on child protection, and the number of countries conducting gender analysis of key child protection issues rose to 43 from 35 in 2008.

Policy advocacy and partnerships for children's rights

UNICEF provided support to data collection and analysis of the situation of children and women in 73 countries, compared with 58 in 2005. The fourth round of the Multiple Indicator Cluster Survey was launched, with 26 countries participating. The round included new data collection modules on early childhood development, early childbearing and handwashing. An evaluation highlighted the role of the UNICEF-supported DevInfo—a database for compiling, analysing and disseminating data on human development—in establishing national repositories of human development data. The technology was upgraded to DevInfo 6.0, introducing new data presentation methods, enhanced web collaboration and extended mapping capabilities. It was adopted by 20 partner agencies and 132 national statistical offices. UNICEF also collaborated with Columbia University to develop Rapid SMS, a system that used text messages to collect data from field locations. The system was piloted by Malawi to monitor undernutrition.

In-depth research and policy analysis continued to be central to developing an evidence base for protecting children's rights. UNICEF issued a special edition of its flagship publication, *The State of the World's Children: Celebrating 20 Years of the Convention on the Rights of the Child* [Sales No.: E.10.XX.1], and continued supporting situation analyses and thematic studies related to children and women. The UNICEF Innocenti Research Centre generated knowledge and research on social and economic policies and the implementation of international standards to protect children, producing publications on child well-being, early childhood education, implementation of the Convention on the Rights of the Child, violence against girls and child trafficking. The Global Study on Child Poverty and Disparities continued, with 48 countries participating and six national reports completed.

The UNICEF regional offices and networks took forward the organization's policy advocacy agenda in response to rapidly changing conditions. Almost two-thirds of UNICEF offices provided advice to Governments on regulatory, legal, institutional or financial reform in areas such as juvenile justice, public finance transparency and social protection. UNICEF supported 124 social protection programmes in 65 countries, assisting national partners to ensure that stable social protection schemes replaced temporary responses to the economic shocks.

The number of programme countries in which opinion polls or other tools were used to gauge children's views continued to rise, with 31 countries utilizing such tools. Significant achievements in support of child participation were the adoption of the General comment on Article 12 (Right to be Heard) by the Committee on the Rights of the Child (see p. 636) and the adoption of resolution 64/146 by the General Assembly on child participation (see p. 637).

Operational and administrative matters

UNICEF finances

In 2009, UNICEF income totalled $3,256 million, a 4 per cent decrease from 2008, which was primarily due to decreased contributions to other resources, both regular and emergency, reflecting the negative impact of the global economic downturn on development assistance. Total income exceeded the financial plan for 2009 by $332 million. UNICEF derived its incomes mainly from Governments, which contributed $1,955 million (60 per cent), and from private sector sources, which contributed $916 million (28.1 per cent). The balance came from inter-organizational arrangements, with contributions of $296 million (9 per cent), and other sources, with contributions of $89 million (2.7 per cent).

Budget appropriations

On 6 February [dec. 2009/1], the Board approved recommendations for additional regular resources in the amount of $32,103,455 for 30 approved country programmes whose regular resources planning levels, based on the modified allocation system and estimated global levels of programmable regular resources, were higher than the levels originally approved by the Board [E/ICEF/2009/P/L.1 & Corr.1].

In April [E/ICEF/2009/P/L.18], UNICEF recommended increasing the other resources ceilings for 29 country programmes previously approved by the Board, as the contributions to other resources for those programmes had exceeded or were expected to exceed the planning levels originally approved by the Board. The Fund recommended that the Board approve $416,819,500 in other resources for the remaining periods of those programmes, subject to the availability of other resources contributions. The Executive Board approved that request on 10 June [dec. 2009/12], decided to delegate authority to increase other resources ceilings for approved country programmes to the Executive Director, and requested the Executive Board to be informed on an annual basis.

Also on 10 June [dec. 2009/10], the Board approved the aggregate indicative budget for 16 country programmes, amounting to the following totals for regular and other resources, respectively, by region: Eastern and Southern Africa, $53,075,000 and $65,000,000; the Americas and the Caribbean, $3,750,000 and $16,250,000; Central and Eastern Europe and CIS, $60,876,000 and $99,746,000; South Asia, $157,668,000 and $243,536,000; and the Middle East and North Africa, $3,750,000 and $16,500,000.

According to a July report [E/ICEF/2009/AB/L.9], $3,835,512 from regular resources would be used to cover overexpenditures for completed projects financed from other resources for which no additional support had been forthcoming. The report noted that the allocation of regular resources for that amount would allow UNICEF to finalize the accounting for other resources for the period to 31 December 2007.

The Executive Board, at its second regular session in September [dec. 2009/14], approved the aggregate indicative budget for three country programmes, amounting to the following totals of regular and other resources, respectively, by region: Eastern and Southern Africa, $106,440,000 and $134,890,295; and the Americas and the Caribbean, $7,980,000 and $66,250,000.

Also in September [dec. 2009/16], the Board approved a regular resources programme budget [E/ICEF/2009/P/L.31] of $31,450,000 for advocacy and programme development during the 2010–2011 biennium for headquarters and regional offices. A budget ceiling of $496,225,000 for other resources was approved, subject to the availability of specific-purpose contributions. Other resources in excess of the indicated amounts for specific programme areas and regions could be received, provided that the total amount of funds received were within the approved limit.

In September [dec. 2009/17], the Board approved recommendations of $186,303,485 in additional regular resources to fund, for 2010, the approved country programmes of 29 countries whose regular resources planning levels, based on the modified allocation system and estimated global levels of regular resources available for programmes, were higher than the levels originally approved by the Board [E/ICEF/2009/P/L.30].

Also in September [dec. 2009/20], the Board took note of the functions, management results, indicators and resource requirements in the report on the biennial support budget [E/ICEF/2009/AB/L.4], including the outcome of the midterm review of the MTSP [E/ICEF/2008/19]. It took note of the recommendations of the Advisory Committee on Administrative and Budgetary Questions (ACABQ) [E/ICEF/2009/AB/L.8], approved gross resources in the amount of $975.0 million, representing the total biennial support budget for 2010–2011, and noted that the income estimates of $246.6 million would be used to offset the gross appropriation, resulting in an estimated net appropriation of $728.4 million. The Board requested that UNICEF improve the indicators of the biennial support budget, making them more specific and measurable, and submit an update of the results matrix by the first regular session of 2010. The Executive Director was requested to improve the budgeting method in collaboration with UNDP and UNFPA, with a view to submitting a single, integrated budget for each organization beginning in 2014, and to submit joint reports on steps taken and progress achieved at its second regular session in 2011 and at the annual session in 2012. The Executive Board also requested a joint report on improved results focus and enhanced linkages within the management results of the strategic plan and on further harmonized budget methodologies by the second regular session of 2010.

Audits

On 6 February [dec. 2009/4], the Executive Board took note of the 2008 Board of Auditors report on UNICEF [YUN 2008, p. 1296], the Secretary-General's report on the implementation of the recommendations of the Board of Auditors on the financial statements of the UN funds and programmes for the financial period ended 31 December 2007, the related ACABQ

report, and resolution 63/246 A [ibid., p. 1560]. The Board noted that 14 recommendations of the Board of Auditors for the biennium ended in 2005 had not been fully implemented, and took note of the 42 recommendations for the biennium ended in 2007. It requested that the UNICEF Executive Director continue to implement the recommendations and requested that UNICEF provide a report to the Board's second regular session of 2009 on the strategic implications of the recommendations for the UNICEF management and strategy, as well as an update on the implementation of the main recommendations. UNICEF was asked to include a summary of financial results per biennium, versus those originally budgeted in the annual report of the Executive Director, on a biennial basis. The Board expressed concern about the increase in total year-end unexpended funds for programme activities and requested that UNICEF submit a report, including recommendations, to its second regular session in September.

Pursuant to the Board's decision, UNICEF submitted a progress report on steps taken to implement the recommendations of the Board of Auditors on the UNICEF accounts for the biennium 2006–2007 [E/ICEF/2009/AB/L.10] at the Executive Board's second regular session in September. As of 30 April, 9 of the 13 main recommendations were fully implemented, with the remaining 4 under implementation; 34 of the 42 total recommendations were fully implemented, with the remaining 8 under implementation. The report also provided information about the total year-end unexpended funds for programme activities, including recommendations and efforts undertaken to address the issue.

In its annual report [E/ICEF/2009/AB/L.6 & Corr.1], the Office of Internal Audit (OIA) stated it had completed, in 2008, 25 field office audits and 10 headquarters, thematic and systems audits. OIA issued 327 risk observations to country offices, including 55 high-risk observations in the areas of programme management (45 per cent), financial controls (20 per cent), supply assistance (15 per cent) and the management of cash transfers to implementing partners (13 per cent). The proportion of the risks observed due to inadequate oversight by country office managers of the functioning of internal controls increased from 36 per cent in 2007 to 53 per cent in 2008. The proportion of risks due to human errors and lack of resources substantially decreased. Inadequate monitoring of the functioning of internal controls and planning was a prominent underlying cause for weaknesses in programme management and supply assistance. Weaknesses in financial controls were mainly caused by inadequate monitoring of controls, human errors and inadequate guidance.

On 16 September [dec. 2009/19], the Executive Board took note of the OIA annual report and the UNICEF management response [E/ICEF/2009/AB/L.7], noting with concern that 33 per cent of the previously implemented recommendations were not sustained. The Board requested that the UNICEF management address the follow-up and implementation of internal audit observations and recommendations, especially in high-risk areas. It called on UNICEF to address systematic weaknesses within the organization, and requested that UNICEF report on its progress in implementing improvement initiatives, in conjunction with the annual report on internal audit, at the second regular session of 2010.

Also on 10 June [dec. 2009/8], the Board took note of the report on the UNICEF accountability system [E/ICEF/2009/15], welcoming the integration of UNICEF oversight mechanisms, risk management and internal controls within the accountability system. The Board authorized the Executive Director to make UNICEF internal audit reports available to Member States for review, and requested that the Executive Director include a report on the implementation of the decision, including information on any requests to make internal audit reports available, in the Executive Director's annual report to the Board starting in 2010.

Resource mobilization

UNICEF continued to collaborate with Governments to mobilize regular and other resources. By the tenth pledging event in February, 41 countries had committed $291 million for 2009 regular resources. By year's end, 102 Governments had contributed to UNICEF resources, down from 109 in 2008. In all, contributions from Government and intergovernmental sources decreased by 4 per cent over 2008 levels, while contributions from inter-organizational arrangements (also originating from Government donors) increased by 16 per cent. Private sector contributions, comprising income from private sector fundraising and contributions from NGOs, decreased by 7 per cent. The United States remained the largest donor ($299 million), followed by Norway ($199 million), the Netherlands ($191 million), the United Kingdom ($182 million) and Sweden ($171 million).

Overall thematic funding decreased by 14 per cent compared with 2008, mainly due to a steep fall in thematic humanitarian funding. Thematic funding for the five MTSP areas increased by 13 per cent over 2008, from $203 million to $230 million. In addition to 22 Governments and 30 National Committees, the European Commission and private donors also provided thematic funding. Child protection received a boost in funding from major Government donors.

Income from public sector donors accounted for nearly 88 per cent of total humanitarian funding, enabling UNICEF to request funding for 65 emergency situations. The European Commission increased its humanitarian contribution by nearly 44 per cent over 2008, while the United States was the largest contributor for overall emergency funding among Government donors. Contributions from Belgium and the German National Committee showed rapid growth.

UNICEF continued to expand its participation in United Nations coherence and inter-organizational partnership arrangements through pooled funds and multi-donor trust funds (MDTFs). Income from pooled funds and MDTFs increased by 16 per cent, from $256 million in 2008 to $296 million in 2009: of that, $156 million were allocated for humanitarian assistance and $140 million for development programmes.

Private Fundraising and Partnerships

In February, the Executive Board had before it a report on the 2009 Private Fundraising and Partnerships (PFP) workplan and proposed budget [E/ICEF/2009/AB/L.1 & Corr.1,2], according to which PFP would generate a projected sum of $682.3 million in net consolidated income, of which $349.4 million would be for regular resources and $332.9 million for other resources. That would be achieved with expenditures of $121.9 million. For 2008, the total net consolidated income was $813.2 million, an increase of $99.3 million (13.9 per cent) compared with 2007 [E/ICEF/2009/AB/L.2]. The net operating income from private fundraising activities related to regular resources was $315.9 million in 2008, compared with $343.3 million in 2007, a decrease of $27.4 million (8 per cent).

On 6 February [dec. 2009/6], the Executive Board approved budgeted expenditures of $121.9 million for the 2009 PFP workplan. It authorized UNICEF to increase expenditures up to $125.5 million should the proceeds from fundraising or card and gift sales increase, and to reduce expenditures accordingly should net proceeds decrease. The Board authorized UNICEF to redeploy resources among budget lines up to a maximum of 10 per cent of the approved amounts, and, when necessary, to spend an additional amount between Board sessions up to the amount caused by currency fluctuations to implement the 2009 workplan. The Board also renewed investment funds, with $20.5 million established for 2009. It authorized UNICEF to incur expenditures in the 2009 fiscal period related to the cost of goods delivered (production and purchase of raw materials, cards and other products) for the 2009 fiscal year up to $30.7 million, as indicated in the PFP medium-term plan. It approved an interim one-month allocation of $12 million for January 2010, to be absorbed in the annual 2010 PFP budget, and also approved the PFP medium-term plan for 2010–2013.

Extensions of country programmes

A report issued in April [E/ICEF/2009/P/L.19] recommended that the Executive Board adopt simplified approval procedures for extensions of ongoing country programmes, harmonized with those of UNDP and UNFPA. The Board adopted the modified procedures on 10 June [dec. 2009/11], under which, the Executive Director would approve the first one-year extension for ongoing country programmes and would inform the Executive Board. Requests for two-year or second one-year extensions of such programmes would continue to be submitted to the Board for approval.

In accordance with that decision, the UNICEF secretariat at the second regular session in September informed the Board [E/ICEF/2009/P/L.32] of the one-year extensions of country and area programmes approved by the Executive Director for Azerbaijan, Chile, the Democratic People's Republic of Korea, Iran, Palestinian children and women, Serbia, Somalia and Uruguay. On 16 September [dec. 2009/15], the Board took note of the one-year extensions of the country and area programmes approved by the Executive Director, and approved the two-year extensions for the Philippines and Mozambique.

Joint programming

The joint meeting of the Executive Boards of UNICEF, UNDP/UNFPA and WFP (New York, 23–26 January) discussed population growth and rapid urbanization as they related to nutrition and food insecurity issues. Introducing a background paper and discussion on behalf of the four participating organizations, the WFP Deputy Executive Director noted the rapid growth of urban areas and the "new face" of poverty, hunger and food insecurity confronting the people living in them. He stressed that Government responses and initiatives needed to be supported by coordinated action among UN organizations, and that there was a need to mobilize a wide coalition of actors, engaging Governments and city administrators and reaching out to civil society organizations that dealt with urban poverty.

Recommendations made by delegations to address the issue included: increasing the purchasing power of the poorest people; including other partners such as the United Nations Human Settlements Programme (UN-Habitat) and the private sector; basing programme planning and interventions on vulnerability assessments; engaging all stakeholders among the urban poor, especially women; and supporting Government responses and initiatives while ensuring adequate policy preparations. Many delegations cautioned against neglecting rural areas in addressing food security concerns. The panellists responded that engaging with the poor in urban areas was more difficult than in rural areas because community and kinship ties were not as strong. Additional challenges faced by the urban poor included mobility, lack of a voice and the difficulty of organizing communities.

The UNICEF Executive Director introduced a background paper on unstable food prices and the linkage to food and nutrition security. She highlighted the challenges created by unstable food prices, especially their role in increasing vulnerabilities in developing countries, as the deteriorating nutritional status of the poor was likely to be exacerbated by the global economic crisis. Several delegations expressed concern that the MDG on eradicating extreme poverty and hunger would not be achieved due to the decreased purchasing power of the poor. Delegations supported the Comprehensive Framework for Action [YUN 2008, p. 1343], a joint strategy and action plan on the global food crisis, and emphasized the importance of a coordinated UN response. A number of delegations recommended an integrated multisectoral response to unstable food prices, as well as a greater focus on women's empowerment. The panellists indicated that the instability and likelihood of worsening conditions should also be seen as an opportunity to address deep-seated problems. The United Nations could play a strong role in building national capacities, providing technical assistance and promoting partnerships.

The joint meeting also discussed harmonization of business practices among the UN funds and programmes. The UNFPA Executive Director introduced a background paper and led a discussion focusing on global progress made with respect to the harmonization of business practices. She noted the clear division of labour between the UN system, which sought system-wide solutions through the United Nations System Chief Executives Board for Coordination and its High-level Committee on Management (HLCM), and the United Nations Development Group (UNDG) in its work in support of countries. UNDG passed on to HLCM lessons learned and issues that needed the attention of the entire UN system.

Regarding support to national capacity development, the UNDP Administrator stressed the importance of a coordinated UN system in contributing to increased economic activity, the fair distribution of wealth, sustainable environmental management and the engagement of more people in democratic processes. States had an essential role in ensuring economic and social development, stability and peace, and investing in the capacities of leadership and State institutions was necessary for that purpose. The Executive Board asked for continued dialogue on the issue of reinforcing national capacity development and the role of the UN system in that regard.

JIU reports

In February, the Executive Board considered a secretariat note [E/ICEF/2009/6] on reports of the Joint Inspection Unit (JIU) of relevance to UNICEF. The note provided information on reports prepared by JIU between October 2007 and September 2008. The document presented action taken and views held by UNICEF on the issues raised by the inspectors. During that period, JIU issued two reports of interest to UNICEF, on knowledge management in the UN system [JIU/REP/2007/6] and on progress made by the UN system organizations in achieving the MDG on combating HIV/AIDS [JIU/REP/2007/12]. The Board discussed the note at its first regular session.

Youth

World Programme of Action for Youth

In 2009, UN policies and programmes on youth continued to focus on efforts to implement the 1995 World Programme of Action for Youth to the Year 2000 and Beyond, adopted by the General Assembly in resolution 50/81 [YUN 1995, p. 1211]. The Programme of Action identified 10 priority issues for youth: education, employment, hunger and poverty, health, environment, drug abuse, juvenile delinquency, leisure-time activities, girls and young women, and participation in society and decision-making. In resolution 60/2 [YUN 2005, p. 1296], the Assembly added five priority issues: globalization, the increased use of information and communication technology (ICT), HIV/AIDS, the increased participation of young people in armed conflict as both victims and perpetrators, and the growing importance of intergenerational relations in an ageing global society. The World Youth Report 2005 [ibid., p. 1295] grouped the 15 priority areas into three clusters—youth in the global economy, youth in civil society, and youth and their well-being, which the Assembly took note of in resolution 60/2.

Report of Secretary-General. In response to General Assembly resolution 62/126 [YUN 2007, p. 1221], the Secretary-General submitted a report [A/64/61-E/2009/3] on the progress achieved and constraints faced by young people in relation to their role in, and contributions to, civil society, as well as the progress and challenges faced in ensuring their well-being. The Secretary-General proposed goals and targets for monitoring the progress of youth in those areas. The report was based on the findings of a 2008 inter-agency expert group meeting on the subject [YUN 2008, p. 1299], and was built around two of the clusters of the World Programme of Action for Youth—youth and their well-being and youth in civil society. It identified goals and targets in the areas of health, HIV/AIDS, drug abuse, juvenile delinquency, girls and young women, armed conflict, environment, leisure-time activities, full and effective participation of youth in the life of society and in decision-making, intergenerational issues, and ICT.

Regarding youth and their well-being, all world regions had made progress in improving the health of young people, especially in the area of reproductive health. Government and international efforts to improve knowledge, practices and services in reproductive health contributed to lowering unwanted fertility and maternal mortality among young women. Furthermore, in 14 of 17 African countries with adequate survey data, the percentage of young pregnant women living with HIV had declined since 2000–2001. Despite progress, HIV/AIDS continued to place young people's well-being at risk, with youth aged 15 to 24 years accounting for 45 per cent of all new infections worldwide. Unintentional injury was the leading killer of young people in nearly every region of the world, followed by homicide, war and interpersonal violence. HIV/AIDS, drug use, violence associated with armed conflict and juvenile delinquency were areas of concern. While amphetamine use was slowing among youth in North America and cannabis use had stabilized or declined in Western Europe and North America, rising levels of drug consumption among youth in the transition countries of Central and Eastern Europe and in rapidly expanding urban areas raised concern over the links between drug abuse and criminal behaviour. Children and adolescents who became delinquent were increasingly viewed as victims, and the majority of youth involved in crime were victims of neglect, abuse, exploitation, poverty and other forms of marginalization. Progress was made in integrating the needs of girls and young women in all areas of the World Programme of Action for Youth, with gains registered in female enrolment in primary education, literacy rates, participation in paid, non-agricultural employment and wage gaps. While there had been improvements in the post-conflict reintegration of young people into society, UNICEF reported that an estimated 300,000 children and youth under the age of 18 were still participating in armed conflict, most as members of non-State armed groups.

As to youth and civil society, young people were active in major UN initiatives on the environment, participating in global meetings on climate change and annual sessions of the Commission on Sustainable Development. While there were many positive examples of youth participation in volunteer activities and decision-making, too often youth participation in adult-organized or political activities was tokenistic or symbolic, and shaped by the expectations of adults. Demographic shifts and changes in family structure created new challenges for intergenerational cohesion, with societies facing a growing divide between younger and older generations together with increased interdependence between younger and older persons. ICT was causing rapid transformations in young people's lives, increasing social networking among youth and helping to address their health needs.

The Secretary-General suggested that the Assembly might wish to consider: adopting the proposed goals and targets to assist Governments, civil society and other stakeholders to monitor progress in young people's well-being and their engagement with civil society; encouraging regular data collection at the national and international levels to facilitate the monitoring of the goals and targets set in the report; encouraging Governments to work with youth-led organizations; urging countries to learn from each other to achieve the proposed goals and targets through the sharing of good practices; and emphasizing the need for the international community, Governments and the private sector to support youth-led organizations to broaden their membership and strengthen their capacity to participate in development activities. An annex to the report set out the proposed goals and targets.

The Economic and Social Council took note of the report by **decision 2009/256** of 30 July.

Commission for Social Development action. The Commission for Social Development, at its forty-seventh session (4–13 February) (see p. 1063) adopted a resolution [E/2009/26 (res. 47/1)] on policies and programmes involving youth and brought it to the attention of the Economic and Social Council. The resolution, among other things, urged Member States to work with youth-led organizations and other stakeholders, such as the private sector, to implement the World Programme of Action for Youth; called upon Member States to develop effective national youth policies as an integral aspect of their national development agendas; and called upon them to create effective channels of cooperation and information exchange among young people, their Governments and other decision makers and to support the establishment and functioning of independent national youth councils or equivalent bodies, including junior parliaments.

GENERAL ASSEMBLY ACTION

On 18 December [meeting 65], the General Assembly, on the recommendations of the Third Committee [A/64/432], adopted **resolution 64/130** without vote [agenda item 61 *(b)*].

Policies and programmes involving youth

The General Assembly,

Recalling the World Programme of Action for Youth, adopted by the General Assembly in its resolutions 50/81 of 14 December 1995 and 62/126 of 18 December 2007,

Recalling also that, in its resolution 62/126, the General Assembly requested the Secretary-General to report to the Assembly at its sixty-fourth session, through the Commission for Social Development at its forty-seventh session, on the implementation of eleven of the fifteen priority areas of the World Programme of Action for Youth, namely armed conflict, drug abuse, environment, girls and young women, health, HIV/AIDS, information and communications tech-

nology, intergenerational issues, juvenile delinquency, leisure-time activities and youth participation in society and decision-making,

Emphasizing that all fifteen priority areas of the World Programme of Action for Youth are interrelated,

Stressing the important role of effective sectoral and cross-sectoral national youth policies, reflecting youth in all its diversity, as well as of international cooperation in promoting the achievement of the internationally agreed development goals, including the Millennium Development Goals,

Taking note of the report of the Africa Commission entitled "Realizing the potential of Africa's youth", which addresses ways to create employment for young people through growth led by the private sector and improved competitiveness of African economies,

Welcoming the fifth World Youth Congress, to be held in Istanbul, Turkey, European Capital of Culture 2010, from 31 July to 13 August 2010, and also welcoming the initiative of the Government of Mexico to host a World Youth Conference, in Mexico City from 24 to 27 August 2010, which will focus on the issue of youth and development in the context of the Millennium Development Goals,

Welcoming also the youth-related initiatives of the Alliance of Civilizations, such as Silatech, a youth employment initiative launched by Qatar, the annual League of Arab States Youth Forum, whose third forum, on the theme "Youth and migration: a human-rights based approach", was held in Assilah, Morocco, from 14 to 20 November 2009, and the inaugural Youth Olympic Games, to be held in Singapore from 14 to 26 August 2010, the aim of which is to inspire young people around the world to embrace, embody and express the Olympic values of excellence, friendship and respect, welcoming further the declaration of 2010 as the International Year for the Rapprochement of Cultures, and in this regard stressing the importance of increasing international youth interaction,

Recognizing the special vulnerability of young people in the current financial and economic crisis, in particular with regard to youth unemployment and precarious working conditions,

Emphasizing that all human beings are born free and equal in dignity and rights, are endowed with reason and conscience and should act towards one another in a spirit of brotherhood, and in this regard underlining the particular vulnerability of young people to all forms and manifestations of racism, racial discrimination, xenophobia and related intolerance, and also to various extremist political parties, movements and groups that are based on neo-Nazi, neo-fascist and other violent ideologies,

1. *Reaffirms* the World Programme of Action for Youth;

2. *Takes note with appreciation* of the report of the Secretary-General entitled "Implementation of the World Programme of Action for Youth: progress and constraints with respect to the well-being of youth and their role in civil society";

3. *Stresses* that young people are often among the main victims of armed conflict, expresses its deep concern at the violations of international humanitarian law that undermine the protection of the human rights of civilians in armed conflict, calls upon Member States, in accordance

with the World Programme of Action for Youth, to take concrete measures to further protect and assist young women and men in these situations, bearing in mind that armed and other types of conflict and terrorism and hostage-taking still persist in many parts of the world and that aggression, foreign occupation and ethnic and other types of conflict are an ongoing reality affecting young persons in nearly every region, from which they need to be protected, and also calls upon Member States to recognize young women and men as important actors in conflict prevention, peacebuilding and post-conflict processes;

4. *Urges* Member States to strengthen or establish, in collaboration with young people and youth-led organizations, youth-friendly substance abuse prevention programmes and affordable treatment and rehabilitation programmes, in accordance with existing anti-drug conventions and other instruments of the United Nations, in order to address the vulnerability of young people to substance abuse and to avoid the marginalization of young people with a substance abuse problem;

5. *Emphasizes* that the deterioration of the natural environment, including the impacts of climate change and loss of biodiversity, is one of the principal concerns of young people worldwide and has direct implications for the well-being and empowerment of youth both now and in the future, and therefore urges Member States:

(a) To promote environmental awareness and protection among youth, inter alia, by supporting programmes for non-formal education implemented by youth-led organizations, in accordance with the goals of the United Nations Decade of Education for Sustainable Development;

(b) To strengthen the participation of young people, as important actors in the protection, preservation and improvement of the environment at the local, national and international levels, as envisioned in Agenda 21;

(c) To ensure the involvement of young people in the renewable and sustainable energy sectors, through access to adequate education and training, the promotion of youth employment and entrepreneurship opportunities and cooperation initiatives in these sectors;

6. *Reaffirms* the Convention on the Elimination of All Forms of Discrimination against Women, the Beijing Platform for Action and the outcome of the twenty-third special session of the General Assembly, urges Member States to take measures, including the involvement of boys and young men, to promote gender equality in all aspects of society and to eliminate violence against girls and young women as a matter of priority, and notes the importance of promoting women leaders in the public and private sectors as role models for young women and girls;

7. *Calls upon* Member States to work to ensure that young people enjoy the highest attainable standard of physical and mental health by providing youth with access to sustainable health systems and social services without discrimination and by paying special attention to, and raising awareness of, nutrition, including eating disorders and obesity, to the effects of non-communicable and communicable diseases and to sexual and reproductive health, as well as to measures to prevent sexually transmitted diseases, including HIV/AIDS;

8. *Reaffirms* the Declaration of Commitment on HIV/AIDS and the Political Declaration on HIV/AIDS, and urges Member States to fulfil their commitments on the provision of universal access to prevention, treatment, care and support in order to halt and reverse the spread of HIV/AIDS by 2015, engage young people in the AIDS response, ensure education and employment opportunities to reduce vulnerability to HIV, provide youth-friendly health services, including voluntary and confidential counselling and testing, continue efforts to eliminate the stigma of, and discrimination against, young people living with HIV, and ensure that HIV/AIDS policies and programmes are reviewed so that they contribute to reducing the particular vulnerability of young women and girls to HIV;

9. *Stresses* the potential of information and communications technology to improve the quality of life of young people, and calls upon Member States, with the support of the United Nations system, donors, the private sector and civil society, to ensure universal, non-discriminatory, equitable, safe and affordable access to information and communications technology, especially in schools and public places, and to remove the barriers to bridging the digital divide, including through transfer of technology and international cooperation, as well as to promote the development of locally relevant content and implement measures to equip young people with the knowledge and skills to use information and communications technology appropriately and safely;

10. *Recognizes* the importance of strengthening intergenerational partnerships and solidarity among generations, and in this regard calls upon Member States to promote opportunities for voluntary, constructive and regular interaction between young people and older generations in the family, the workplace and society at large;

11. *Urges* Member States to develop policies and programmes to reduce youth violence and youth involvement in crime and ensure that judicial systems and rehabilitation services are safe, fair, age-appropriate and in accordance with the relevant international human rights instruments and promote the well-being of youth by:

(a) Promoting systematic and comprehensive prevention measures regarding youth violence;

(b) Providing non-discriminatory access to education, opportunities for decent employment and leisure programmes that improve the competencies and self-esteem of young people in detention;

(c) Promoting, where appropriate, the physical and legal separation of juvenile from adult judicial and penal systems;

(d) Promoting alternatives to detention and institutionalization, such as social and community service;

(e) Providing to young people after they leave juvenile detention support services that ensure their full rehabilitation and reintegration into society;

12. *Recognizes* that leisure time is an important aspect of youth well-being and health as well as of crime and violence prevention, and in this regard calls upon Member States to protect the right of all young people, particularly girls and young women, to rest and leisure and to enhance opportunities for the exercise of this right in a positive way;

13. *Also recognizes* that the implementation of the World Programme of Action for Youth and the achievement of the internationally agreed development goals, including the Millennium Development Goals, require the full and effective participation of young people and youth-led organizations, and therefore encourages Member States

to ensure the full and effective participation of youth in the life of society and in decision-making processes by:

(a) Creating effective channels of cooperation and information exchange among young people, their national Governments and other decision makers;

(b) Encouraging and promoting youth-led organizations and the important role they play in supporting young people's civic engagement, capacity-building and providing non-formal education through financial and technical support and promotion of their activities;

(c) Supporting, including through State and local governments, the establishment and functioning of independent national youth councils or equivalent bodies;

(d) Strengthening the participation and inclusion of young persons with disabilities in decision-making processes on an equal basis with others;

(e) Providing young people who are disconnected or socially and economically excluded with opportunities to participate in decision-making processes to ensure their full involvement in society;

14. *Calls upon* Member States to consider using the goals and targets proposed in the reports of the Secretary-General at the national level as a means of facilitating the monitoring of progress towards the implementation of the World Programme of Action for Youth;

15. *Requests* the Secretary-General to intensify efforts to further develop and propose a set of possible indicators linked to the World Programme of Action for Youth and the proposed goals and targets, in order to assist States in assessing the situation of youth, with a view to allowing it to be considered by the Commission for Social Development and by the Statistical Commission at the earliest opportunity;

16. *Recognizes* the positive contribution that youth representatives make to the General Assembly and other United Nations bodies and their role in serving as an important channel of communication between young people and the United Nations, and in this regard requests the Secretary-General to support adequately the United Nations Programme on Youth of the Department of Economic and Social Affairs of the Secretariat so that it can continue to facilitate their effective participation in meetings;

17. *Urges* Member States to consider including youth representatives in their delegations at all relevant discussions in the General Assembly, the Economic and Social Council and its functional commissions and relevant United Nations conferences, as appropriate, bearing in mind the principles of gender balance and non-discrimination, and emphasizes that such youth representatives should be selected through a transparent process that ensures that they have a suitable mandate to represent young people in their countries;

18. *Recognizes* the need for a greater geographical balance of youth representation, and encourages Member States and intergovernmental and non-governmental organizations to contribute to the United Nations Youth Fund in order to facilitate the participation of youth representatives from developing countries;

19. *Welcomes* the recent increased collaboration among United Nations entities in the area of youth development, and calls upon the United Nations Programme on Youth to continue to act as the focal point within the United Nations system for promoting further collaboration.

International Year of Youth, 2010

At a General Assembly plenary meeting on 28 September [A/64/PV.11], the Minister for Foreign Affairs of Tunisia, Abdelwaheb Abdallah, on behalf of the President of Tunisia, Zine El Abidine Ben Ali, called on the Assembly to adopt a resolution declaring 2010 as the International Year of Youth and calling for the convening of a world youth conference in 2010. The initiative, Mr. Abdallah said, already enjoyed the support of Arab, African and Islamic regional organizations as well as the Non-Aligned Movement. On 7 October, the Sudan, on behalf of the members of the Group of 77 and China, introduced in the Third Committee a draft resolution on the topic.

GENERAL ASSEMBLY ACTION

On 18 December [meeting 65], the General Assembly, on the recommendations of the Third Committee [A/64/432], adopted **resolution 64/134** without vote [agenda item 61 *(b)*].

Proclamation of 2010 as the International Year of Youth: Dialogue and Mutual Understanding

The General Assembly,

Bearing in mind the Charter of the United Nations and the principles contained therein,

Considering that it is necessary to disseminate among young people the ideals of peace, respect for human rights and fundamental freedoms, solidarity and dedication to the objectives of progress and development,

Recalling the provisions of the Declaration on the Promotion among Youth of the Ideals of Peace, Mutual Respect and Understanding between Peoples, proclaimed by the General Assembly in its resolution 2037(XX) of 7 December 1965,

Recalling also its resolutions 50/81 of 14 December 1995 and 62/126 of 18 December 2007, by which it adopted the World Programme of Action for Youth to the Year 2000 and Beyond and the Supplement thereto,

Bearing in mind that the ways in which the challenges and potential of young people are addressed will influence current social and economic conditions and the well-being and livelihood of future generations,

Bearing in mind also that 2010 will mark the twenty-fifth anniversary of the 1985 International Youth Year: Participation, Development, Peace, and stressing the importance of commemorating this anniversary,

Convinced that young people should be encouraged to devote their energy, enthusiasm and creativity to economic, social and cultural development and the promotion of mutual understanding,

Welcoming the fifth World Youth Congress, to be held in Istanbul, Turkey, European Capital of Culture 2010, from 31 July to 13 August 2010, and the initiative of the Government of Mexico to host a World Youth Conference, in Mexico City from 24 to 27 August 2010, both of which will focus on the issue of youth and development in the context of the Millennium Development Goals, as well as the inaugural Youth Olympic Games, to be held in Singapore from 14 to 26 August 2010, the aim of which is to inspire young people around the world to embrace, embody and express the Olympic values of excellence, friendship and respect,

1. *Decides* to proclaim the year commencing on 12 August 2010 the International Year of Youth: Dialogue and Mutual Understanding;

2. *Invites* all Member States, the specialized agencies, funds and programmes of the United Nations system and youth organizations to take advantage of the Year to build on the synergies among the activities to be carried out at the national, regional and international levels during the Year and to promote actions at all levels aimed at disseminating among young people the ideals of peace, freedom, progress, solidarity and dedication to the objectives and goals of progress and development, including the Millennium Development Goals;

3. *Decides* to organize under the auspices of the United Nations a world youth conference as the highlight of the Year, and invites the President of the General Assembly to conduct open-ended informal consultations with Member States with a view to determining the modalities of the conference, which is to be funded by voluntary contributions;

4. *Requests* Member States, international and, where appropriate, regional organizations, and all relevant stakeholders, including the private sector and civil society, to support all activities related to the Year, including by means of voluntary contributions;

5. *Requests* the Secretary-General to submit to the General Assembly at its sixty-sixth session a report on the implementation of the present resolution.

Ageing persons

Follow-up to the Second World Assembly on Ageing (2002)

Report of Secretary-General. In response to resolution 46/1 of the Commission for Social Development [YUN 2008, p. 1300], the Secretary-General reported [E/CN.5/2009/5] to the Commission's forty-seventh session (4–13 February) on a strategic implementation framework for the Madrid International Plan of Action on Ageing, 2002 [YUN 2002, p. 1194] through the year 2012. The report outlined the purpose, objectives and content of the framework, as well as key priority areas for further action, approaches to implementation, essential tools for the process and international cooperation.

The strategic implementation framework was a promotional document intended to assist Member States as they focused their efforts on implementing the Plan of Action through the remainder of its first decade, to 2012. Determining key priority areas would vary by country, but all countries were likely to share common priorities: emphasizing the link between ageing and development; establishing or maintaining sustainable systems of social protection to guard against poverty

in old age; ensuring the participation of older persons in labour markets; meeting the growing demand for quality and accessible health care for older persons; creating age-friendly environments; and guaranteeing the rights and participation of older persons in society. To advance the achievement of key priorities on ageing, Member States needed to focus on empowerment and participation, awareness-raising and strengthened national capacity on ageing. The Secretary-General suggested employing a number of tools concerning older persons; devising evidence-based policies; integrating policies on ageing in all national policies; utilizing participatory approaches to policy planning, design, implementation and monitoring; and using indicators to measure progress in policy implementation. Well-coordinated and enhanced international cooperation would be necessary to fully implement the Plan of Action in developing countries and countries in transition.

The Secretary-General recommended that the Commission encourage Member States to consult the strategic framework for future implementation of the Madrid Plan when developing national strategies and policies on ageing, also referring to the UN Secretariat's *Guide to the National Implementation of the Madrid International Plan of Action on Ageing*. He further recommended that the Commission call upon Member States to adopt legislative measures to guarantee the basic rights of older persons; undertake awareness-raising activities; review their national capacity for policy development concerning older persons and demographic ageing; and promote the development of regional and subregional networks of experts and practitioners to increase the potential for policy action on ageing. He also suggested that the Commission appoint a special rapporteur to examine the rights of older persons.

Commission for Social Development action. On 13 February, the Commission adopted a resolution [E/2009/26 (res. 47/3)] on the first review and appraisal of the Madrid International Plan of Action on Ageing [YUN 2008, p. 1300] and brought it to the attention of the Economic and Social Council. The Commission called upon Member States to continue their efforts to implement the Plan of Action; strengthen their networks of national focal points on ageing; work with the regional commissions to exchange best practices and undertake awareness-raising activities; and reach out to older persons and the organizations that represented them to provide them with information and solicit their feedback. The Commission requested that the Secretary-General report on the implementation of the resolution at its forty-eighth (2010) session.

Report of Secretary-General. In response to General Assembly resolution 63/151 [YUN 2008, p. 1301], the Secretary-General in July submitted a report [A/64/127] on the follow-up to the Second World Assembly on Ageing [YUN 2002, p. 1193], which focused on the promotion and protection of human rights as they pertained to older persons in the context of the implementation of international legal and policy instruments as well as national action.

The report noted that the world was ageing at an increasing pace, owing to declines in fertility and rising longevity. In the more developed regions, the population aged 60 and over was expected to increase by more than 50 per cent over the following four decades, from 264 million in 2009 to 416 million in 2050. In the developing world, the 60 and over population was projected to triple, from 473 million in 2009 to 1.6 billion in 2050. Those demographic changes were expected to cause major challenges for development. Human rights instruments lacked the capacity to effectively protect the rights of older persons, who in all parts of the world continued to face barriers in their participation as equal members of society. Discrimination, violence, abuse and neglect were all infringements on the rights of older persons.

An analysis of the submissions by Member States for the review and appraisal of the Plan of Action provided insight into the extent to which the rights of older persons were being addressed through national legislation. Of the 62 national contributions, 52 (84 per cent) raised the issue of the rights of older persons in some manner, with the most common reference found in country constitutions. Reference to discrimination of older persons was made in 37 of the 62 submissions (60 per cent), with the most frequently mentioned areas of concern being employment, accessibility of quality health care and long-term care, patients' rights, accessible and affordable transportation, pensions and social security, and the right to information and participation in decisions that affected older persons' lives. Nineteen submissions (31 per cent) raised the issue of abuse or neglect. Some countries had set up special authorities to determine if the rights of older persons had been violated, and many States reported efforts to raise awareness and increase the ability of older persons to demand their rights.

At an expert group meeting on the rights of older persons, convened by the UN Department of Economic and Social Affairs (Bonn, Germany, 5–7 May), professionals from academia, government and civil society organizations gathered to explore how human rights of older persons could be assured and how the Plan of Action could be better implemented. The meeting recommended, among other things: providing easily accessible and free identity documentation to older persons; supporting older persons' associations; providing paralegal support and legal aid to older persons; initiating nationwide reviews on neglect, abuse and violence against older persons; in-

corporating a gender perspective in policy actions on ageing; increasing the visibility of older persons' rights among policymakers; and establishing national ombudsmen and human rights commissions on issues relevant to older persons. The possibility of drafting an international convention on the rights of older persons was discussed, as well as of appointing a special rapporteur to offer assistance and advice to Member States on the rights of older persons.

Based on the recommendations from the expert group meeting, the Secretary-General recommended that Member States: ensure that older persons had better access to information about their rights; develop their capacity for monitoring and enforcing the rights of older persons; strengthen the gender perspective in policy actions on ageing and eliminate discrimination on the basis of age and gender; address the issues of neglect, abuse and violence against older persons by initiating nationwide reviews; and consider how to improve international norms and standards pertaining to older persons.

GENERAL ASSEMBLY ACTION

On 18 December [meeting 65], the General Assembly, on the recommendation of the Third Committee [A/64/432], adopted **resolution 64/132** without vote [agenda item 61 *(c)*].

Follow-up to the Second World Assembly on Ageing

The General Assembly,

Recalling its resolution 57/167 of 18 December 2002, in which it endorsed the Political Declaration and the Madrid International Plan of Action on Ageing, 2002, its resolution 58/134 of 22 December 2003, in which it took note, inter alia, of the road map for the implementation of the Madrid Plan of Action, and its resolutions 60/135 of 16 December 2005, 61/142 of 19 December 2006, 62/130 of 18 December 2007 and 63/151 of 18 December 2008,

Recognizing that, in many parts of the world, awareness of the Madrid Plan of Action remains limited or nonexistent, which limits the scope of implementation efforts,

Taking note of the report of the Secretary-General,

1. *Encourages* Governments to pay greater attention to building capacity to eradicate poverty among older persons, in particular older women, by mainstreaming ageing issues into poverty eradication strategies and national development plans, and to include both ageing-specific policies and ageing-mainstreaming efforts in their national strategies;

2. *Encourages* Member States to strengthen their efforts to develop national capacity to address their national implementation priorities identified during the review and appraisal of the Madrid International Plan of Action on Ageing, 2002, and invites Member States that have not done so to consider a step-by-step approach to developing capacity that includes the setting of national priorities, the strengthening of institutional mechanisms, research, data collection and analysis and the training of necessary personnel in the field of ageing;

3. *Also encourages* Member States to overcome obstacles to the implementation of the Madrid Plan of Action

by devising strategies that take into account the entirety of the human life-course and foster intergenerational solidarity in order to increase the likelihood of greater success in the years ahead;

4. *Further encourages* Member States to place particular emphasis on choosing national priorities that are realistic, feasible and have the greatest likelihood of being achieved in the years ahead and to develop targets and indicators to measure progress in the implementation process;

5. *Recommends* that Member States increase awareness-raising of the Madrid Plan of Action, including by strengthening networks of national focal points on ageing, working with the regional commissions and enlisting the help of the Department of Public Information of the Secretariat to seek increased attention to ageing issues;

6. *Encourages* Governments that have not done so to designate focal points for handling follow-up of national plans of action on ageing;

7. *Invites* Governments to conduct their ageing-related policies through inclusive and participatory consultations with relevant stakeholders and social development partners, in the interest of developing effective policies creating national policy ownership and consensus-building;

8. *Calls upon* Governments to ensure, as appropriate, conditions that enable families and communities to provide care and protection to persons as they age and to evaluate improvement in the health status of older persons, including on a gender-specific basis, and to reduce disability and mortality;

9. *Encourages* Governments to continue their efforts to implement the Madrid Plan of Action and to mainstream the concerns of older persons into their policy agendas, bearing in mind the crucial importance of family intergenerational interdependence, solidarity and reciprocity for social development and the realization of all human rights for older persons, and to prevent age discrimination and provide social integration;

10. *Invites* Member States to ensure that older persons have access to information about their rights so as to enable them to participate fully and justly in their societies and to claim full enjoyment of all human rights;

11. *Calls upon* Member States to develop their national capacity for monitoring and enforcing the rights of older persons, in consultation with all sectors of society, including organizations of older persons through, inter alia, national institutions for the promotion and protection of human rights where applicable;

12. *Also calls upon* Member States to strengthen and incorporate a gender perspective into all policy actions on ageing, as well as to eliminate and address discrimination on the basis of age and gender, and recommends that Member States engage with all sectors of society, including women's groups and organizations of older persons, in changing negative stereotypes about older persons, in particular older women, and promote positive images of older persons;

13. *Further calls upon* Member States to address the well-being and adequate health care of older persons, as well as any cases of neglect, abuse and violence against older persons, by designing more effective prevention strategies and stronger laws and policies to address these problems and their underlying factors;

14. *Encourages* Member States to consider how best the international framework of norms and standards can ensure the full enjoyment of the rights of older persons, including, as appropriate, the possibility of instituting new policies, instruments or measures to further improve the situation of older persons;

15. *Calls upon* Member States to take concrete measures to further protect and assist older persons in emergency situations, in accordance with the Madrid Plan of Action;

16. *Stresses* that, in order to complement national development efforts, enhanced international cooperation is essential to support developing countries in implementing the Madrid Plan of Action, while recognizing the importance of assistance and the provision of financial assistance;

17. *Encourages* the international community to enhance international cooperation to support national efforts to eradicate poverty, in keeping with internationally agreed goals, in order to achieve sustainable social and economic support for older persons;

18. *Also encourages* the international community to support national efforts to forge stronger partnerships with civil society, including organizations of older persons, academia, research foundations, community-based organizations, including caregivers, and the private sector, in an effort to help to build capacity on ageing issues;

19. *Encourages* the international community and the relevant agencies of the United Nations system, within their respective mandates, to support national efforts to provide funding for research and data-collection initiatives on ageing in order to better understand the challenges and opportunities presented by population ageing and to provide policymakers with more accurate and more specific information on gender and ageing;

20. *Recommends* that Member States reaffirm the role of United Nations focal points on ageing, increase technical cooperation efforts, expand the role of the regional commissions on ageing issues and provide added resources for those efforts, facilitate the coordination of national and international nongovernmental organizations on ageing and enhance cooperation with academia on a research agenda on ageing;

21. *Reiterates* the need for additional capacity-building at the national level in order to promote and facilitate further implementation of the Madrid Plan of Action, as well as the result of its first review and appraisal cycle, and in that connection encourages Governments to support the United Nations Trust Fund for Ageing to enable the Department of Economic and Social Affairs of the Secretariat to provide expanded assistance to countries, upon their request;

22. *Recommends* that ongoing efforts to achieve the internationally agreed development goals, including those contained in the United Nations Millennium Declaration, take into account the situation of older persons;

23. *Requests* the Secretary-General to submit to the General Assembly at its sixty-fifth session a report on the implementation of the present resolution, and also requests the Secretary-General to submit to the Assembly at its sixty-fifth session, taking into consideration the discussions and conclusions of the Commission for Social Development at its forty-eighth session, a comprehensive report on the current status of the social situation, well-being, development and rights of older persons at the national and regional levels.

Chapter XII

Refugees and displaced persons

In 2009, the number of people of concern to the United Nations High Commissioner for Refugees (UNHCR) increased to 36.5 million (from 34.4 million in 2008), including 10.4 million refugees, 5.5 million of whom were living in a protracted situation. The number of internally displaced persons (IDPs) as a result of conflict reached an estimated 27.1 million, with an unprecedented 15.6 million of them receiving UNHCR protection and assistance. The latter figure constituted an increase of more than 1.2 million compared to the 2008 total of 14.4 million. The number of stateless persons identified by UNHCR remained at 6.6 million, although the actual number was estimated to be closer to 12 million. Humanitarian crises and political tensions not only uprooted millions, but also prevented the return of refugees and IDPs. Consequently, the number of returned refugees (251,000) in 2009 was the lowest in two decades. In contrast, the number of returned IDPs (2.2 million) was the highest in more than a decade. There were more than 922,000 claims for asylum or refugee status submitted to Governments or UNHCR offices in 159 countries or territories, representing a 5 per cent increase over the previous year (875,300).

UNHCR exercised its protection mandate effectively in some regions, but it was hampered by constraints in others. Strife in the Central African Republic, the Democratic Republic of the Congo, Somalia and the Sudan caused massive internal displacement and drove hundreds of thousands of refugees into neighbouring States. The crisis in Somalia alone produced 1.5 million IDPs and caused 560,000 persons to seek refuge in other countries. In response to those and other emergencies in Africa, UNHCR was present in 33 countries. On a positive note, UNHCR began reviewing the situation of refugees from Angola, Burundi, Liberia and Rwanda with a view to closing those chapters of displacement. The General Assembly took action on assistance to refugees, returnees and displaced persons in Africa through resolution 64/129, adopted in December.

In response to the high rate of displacement in Colombia, UNHCR supported the Government in narrowing protection gaps, focusing on local-level implementation of policies supporting the rights of IDPs. Following the movement of some 3 million people in Pakistan during the year, UNHCR mounted an emergency response focusing on the establishment of camps, registration, the distribution of non-food items and protection monitoring. UNHCR confronted the humanitarian situation faced by persons of concern in Iraq by expanding its field presence and accessing most areas through national staff. In Yemen, where conflict led to the displacement of 250,000 people, UNHCR responded by setting up an emergency coordination system. In Europe, where nearly 80 per cent of asylum applications in the industrialized world were received, UNHCR worked in 48 countries and territories.

In its pursuit of durable solutions in all regions, UNHCR supported initiatives for resettlement and voluntary repatriation. The Office also facilitated local integration by implementing shelter, livelihoods, income-generation and community development programmes to benefit former refugees. In response to shrinking humanitarian space, increased pressure on asylum space in more prosperous States, a surge of refoulement and a spate of involuntary returns, UNHCR worked to narrow the gap between law and practice in the area of refugee protection. To ensure that refugees and asylum-seekers received documentation in a timely manner, the Office worked with Governments on strengthening refugee status determination procedures. UNHCR, as well as the Assembly through resolution 64/127, also encouraged States to work with the United Nations in identifying stateless populations on their territories and review their legislation with a view to eliminating gaps that could cause or perpetuate statelessness.

With regard to structural and management change, UNHCR reform focused on regionalization and decentralization, human resources and organizational development. Five key initiatives were implemented in the area of results-based management: the results framework; the results-based management systems tool, *Focus*; the global needs assessment; the revised budget structure; and the global management accountability framework. UNHCR also undertook initiatives aimed at enhancing staff safety and security, including establishing a high-level Security Steering Committee under the chairmanship of the High Commissioner to conduct regular reviews of high-risk operations in critical locations. International financial support for UNHCR's activities in 2009 was unprecedented, with income exceeding $1.7 billion including, for the first time, more than $50 million from the private sector.

In September, UNHCR issued a new urban refugee policy, and, in that context, the third High Commissioner's Dialogue on Protection Challenges (Geneva, 8–10 December) focused on "Challenges for Persons of Concern in Urban Settings". In December, the Executive Committee adopted a conclusion on protracted refugee situations and a decision endorsing revised Financial Rules for Voluntary Funds Administered by the High Commissioner for Refugees.

Office of the United Nations High Commissioner for Refugees

Programme policy

Executive Committee action. At its sixtieth session (Geneva, 28 September–2 October) [A/64/12/Add.1], the Executive Committee of the UNHCR Programme adopted decisions on the programme of work of the Standing Committee in 2010 and observer participation in the Standing Committee's 2009–2010 meetings. It also adopted general decisions on administrative, financial and programme matters, including that it would meet by 31 December 2009 to adopt revised Financial Rules for Voluntary Funds Administered by the High Commissioner for Refugees and to ensure consistency between those rules and the Biennial Programme Budget for 2010–2011 (see p. 1199). Negotiations on a draft conclusion on protracted refugee situations were inconclusive, but they would be pursued by Member States in order to reach consensus by the end of the year, so that a conclusion on the issue could be adopted by the Executive Committee at an extraordinary meeting in December.

In his opening statement to the Committee [A/AC.96/SR.628], the High Commissioner discussed reform measures within UNHCR, as well as the main challenges and global trends affecting its work. He noted that upon his election in 2005, UNHCR staff and headquarters costs were consuming an ever greater proportion of total expenditure, endangering the Office's sustainability. In response, comprehensive reform decisions were taken, including on management and human resources, and on decentralization and regionalization. Reviews had been conducted at headquarters and in the field. Subsequent implementation of reforms had enhanced the Office's emergency response capacity. In 2006, the High Commissioner noted, the Office's total expenditure had been $1.1 billion, while in 2009 it was expected to reach approximately $1.7 billion. Activities had increased by more than 50 per cent without increasing the number of staff worldwide. Between 2006 and 2008, the proportion of total expenditure dedicated to headquar-

ters was reduced from nearly 14 per cent to approximately 10 per cent, and staff costs were reduced from 41 per cent to 34 per cent. Savings generated through reform had allowed resources to be allocated to special projects aimed at addressing malaria, malnutrition, reproductive health, sexual and gender violence and new programmes for anaemia and water and sanitation. A new and systematic approach to assessing beneficiary needs and a new results-based framework were also being introduced. On decentralization and regionalization, authority for decisions was moved as close as possible to the point of delivery. At headquarters, the reconfiguration of support services had been decided and implemented. A new Division for Programme Support and Management was created to ensure that the global needs assessment initiative and results-based management were incorporated in all operational activities.

Turning to the challenges faced by UNHCR, the High Commissioner took account of five global "megatrends": population growth, urbanization, climate change, migration, and food, water and energy insecurity. Increasingly interlinked and self-reinforcing, those megatrends increased displacement and, in conjunction with the global recession, caused crises to multiply and deepen. In the current environment, he continued, UNHCR faced four main challenges. The first—shrinking humanitarian space—had created a worsening security environment, in response to which UNHCR had established a permanent Security Steering Committee (SSC) to decide on a range of enhanced security measures; local SSCs had likewise been established. The second challenge was shrinking asylum space, as some countries in the developed world were limiting access to their territory for asylum-seekers. On that issue, he said, a common approach was needed, and a truly "European asylum space" had to be created. He attributed the third challenge—the increasing difficulty of achieving durable solutions—to the increasing complexity of contemporary forms of conflict. The fourth challenge was urban refugees, a category that included all persons of concern to UNHCR in urban settings, including refugees, asylum-seekers, returnees, internally displaced persons (IDPs) and the stateless, all of whom increasingly resided in or migrated to cities. The challenge presented by that issue was the subject of the third High Commissioner's Dialogue on Protection Challenges, to be held in December.

The High Commissioner expressed gratitude to developing countries that hosted large numbers of refugees, without whose contribution four fifths of UNHCR's work would be not possible. In that context, the influx of Somali refugees into Kenya was the most compelling emergency currently facing UNHCR. In the previous 21 months, more than 100,000 Somalis had arrived in the Dadaab camps, fleeing the fighting in their country. However, the camps were highly congested and inadequate, and he renewed his appeal to the Government of Kenya to make additional land available for the establishment of a fourth camp.

UNHCR effectiveness, he noted, also depended on its strategic partnerships with non-governmental organizations (NGOs), including national NGOs, which, pursuant to the UNHCR commitment to increasing the proportion of funds implemented through partners, had been allocated an additional $100 million the previous year. Partnerships with the private sector and with the United Nations and other key agencies also continued to be strengthened. For example, given the centrality of climate change to its work, UNHCR had participated in the preparations for the UN global conference on climate change, to be held in Copenhagen in December.

On 8 December, the UNHCR Executive Committee held an extraordinary meeting [A/AC.96/1080] of its sixty-first session, at which it adopted a conclusion on protracted refugee situations. That conclusion recommended further action to address and facilitate durable solutions, with a view to burden- and responsibility-sharing, including through the provision of financial assistance and other forms of support where voluntary repatriation was foreseeable and where local integration was feasible. It recommended a more effective and strategic use of resettlement, and the mobilization of support for rehabilitating refugee-impacted areas in the host country from which refugees had returned. States were called upon to provide resettlement places and to explore more flexible approaches to bridge gaps which might exist between the resettlement criteria they used and the needs of and situation of refugees in protracted situations. The Committee requested that UNHCR enhance its awareness-raising measures, including among refugees, through the organization of regular campaigns and local and regional workshops on durable solutions. It also urged States, UNHCR and humanitarian and development partners to pursue partnerships and coordination in implementing durable solutions, and to develop new opportunities for partnership, including through implementation of the "Delivering as one" objectives; increased information exchange with the United Nations Peacebuilding Commission; and partnerships with other actors such as financial institutions, the Inter-Agency Standing Committee, the United Nations Development Group, regional bodies, parliaments, local governments, mayors, business leaders, the media and diaspora communities.

At the same meeting, the Executive Committee adopted a decision endorsing revised Financial Rules for Voluntary Funds Administered by the High Commissioner for Refugees [A/AC.96/503/Rev.9] and requesting the High Commissioner to promulgate the revised rules effective 1 January 2010.

On 18 December [meeting 65], the General Assembly, on the recommendation of the Third (Social, Humanitarian and Cultural) Committee [A/64/431], adopted **resolution 64/127** without vote [agenda item 41].

Office of the United Nations High Commissioner for Refugees

The General Assembly,

Having considered the report of the United Nations High Commissioner for Refugees on the activities of his Office and the report of the Executive Committee of the Programme of the United Nations High Commissioner for Refugees on the work of its sixtieth session and the decisions contained therein,

Recalling its previous annual resolutions on the work of the Office of the United Nations High Commissioner for Refugees since its establishment by the General Assembly,

Expressing its appreciation for the leadership shown by the High Commissioner, commending the staff and implementing partners of the Office of the High Commissioner for the competent, courageous and dedicated manner in which they discharge their responsibilities, and underlining its strong condemnation of all forms of violence to which humanitarian personnel and United Nations and associated personnel are increasingly exposed,

1. *Endorses* the report of the Executive Committee of the Programme of the United Nations High Commissioner for Refugees on the work of its sixtieth session;

2. *Welcomes* the important work undertaken by the Office of the United Nations High Commissioner for Refugees and its Executive Committee in the course of the year, which is aimed at strengthening the international protection regime and at assisting Governments in meeting their protection responsibilities;

3. *Reaffirms* the 1951 Convention relating to the Status of Refugees and the 1967 Protocol thereto as the foundation of the international refugee protection regime, recognizes the importance of their full and effective application by States parties and the values they embody, notes with satisfaction that one hundred and forty-seven States are now parties to one instrument or to both, encourages States not parties to consider acceding to those instruments, underlines, in particular, the importance of full respect for the principle of non-refoulement, and recognizes that a number of States not parties to the international refugee instruments have shown a generous approach to hosting refugees;

4. *Notes* that sixty-five States are now parties to the 1954 Convention relating to the Status of Stateless Persons and that thirty-seven States are parties to the 1961 Convention on the Reduction of Statelessness, encourages States that have not done so to give consideration to acceding to those instruments, notes the work of the High Commissioner in regard to identifying stateless persons, preventing and reducing statelessness and protecting stateless persons, and urges the Office of the High Commissioner to continue to work in this area in accordance with relevant General Assembly resolutions and Executive Committee conclusions;

5. *Takes note* of the sixtieth anniversary of the Geneva Conventions and the fortieth anniversary of the Organization of African Unity Convention governing the specific

aspects of refugee problems in Africa, commemorated in 2009;

6. *Re-emphasizes* that the protection of refugees is primarily the responsibility of States, whose full and effective cooperation, action and political resolve are required to enable the Office of the High Commissioner to fulfil its mandated functions, and strongly emphasizes, in this context, the importance of active international solidarity and burden- and responsibility-sharing;

7. *Also re-emphasizes* that prevention and reduction of statelessness are primarily the responsibility of States, in appropriate cooperation with the international community;

8. *Further re-emphasizes* that protection of and assistance to internally displaced persons are primarily the responsibility of States, in appropriate cooperation with the international community;

9. *Encourages* the Office of the High Commissioner to pursue its efforts to strengthen its capacity to respond adequately to emergencies and thereby ensure a more predictable response to inter-agency commitments in case of emergency;

10. *Takes note* of the current activities of the Office of the High Commissioner related to protection of and assistance to internally displaced persons, including in the context of inter-agency arrangements in this field, emphasizes that such activities should be consistent with relevant General Assembly resolutions and should not undermine the mandate of the Office for refugees and the institution of asylum, and encourages the High Commissioner to continue his dialogue with States on the role of his Office in this regard;

11. *Encourages* the Office of the High Commissioner to work in partnership and in full cooperation with relevant national authorities, United Nations offices and agencies, international and intergovernmental organizations, regional organizations and non-governmental organizations to contribute to the continued development of humanitarian response capacities at all levels, and recalls the role of the Office as the cluster lead for protection, camp coordination and management, and emergency shelter in complex emergencies;

12. *Also encourages* the Office of the High Commissioner, among other relevant United Nations and other relevant intergovernmental organizations and humanitarian and development actors, to continue to work with the Office for the Coordination of Humanitarian Affairs of the Secretariat to enhance the coordination, effectiveness and efficiency of humanitarian assistance, as stated in General Assembly resolution 63/139 of 11 December 2008 on the strengthening of the coordination of emergency humanitarian assistance of the United Nations;

13. *Further encourages* the Office of the High Commissioner to engage in and implement in full the objectives of the Delivering as One initiative;

14. *Notes with appreciation* the ongoing implementation of the process of structural and management change undertaken by the Office of the High Commissioner, and encourages the Office to complete the implementation of the reforms process, including the implementation of a results-based management and accountability framework and strategy, as well as human resources reform, and to focus on continuous improvement to enable a more efficient

response to the needs of beneficiaries and ensure the effective and transparent use of its resources;

15. *Strongly condemns* attacks on refugees, asylum-seekers and internally displaced persons as well as acts that pose a threat to their personal security and well-being, and calls upon all States concerned and, where applicable, parties involved in an armed conflict to take all necessary measures to ensure respect for human rights and international humanitarian law;

16. *Expresses deep concern* about the increasing number of attacks against humanitarian aid workers and convoys and, in particular, the loss of life of humanitarian personnel working in the most difficult and challenging conditions in order to assist those in need;

17. *Emphasizes* the need for States to ensure that perpetrators of attacks committed on their territory against humanitarian personnel and United Nations and associated personnel do not operate with impunity, and that the perpetrators of such acts are promptly brought to justice as provided for by national laws and obligations under international law;

18. *Deplores* the refoulement and unlawful expulsion of refugees and asylum-seekers, and calls upon all States concerned to ensure respect for the relevant principles of refugee protection and human rights;

19. *Emphasizes* that international protection of refugees is a dynamic and action-oriented function that is at the core of the mandate of the Office of the High Commissioner and that it includes, in cooperation with States and other partners, the promotion and facilitation of, inter alia, the admission, reception and treatment of refugees in accordance with internationally agreed standards and the ensuring of durable, protection-oriented solutions, bearing in mind the particular needs of vulnerable groups and paying special attention to those with specific needs, and notes in this context that the delivery of international protection is a staff-intensive service that requires adequate staff with the appropriate expertise, especially at the field level;

20. *Affirms* the importance of age, gender and diversity mainstreaming in analysing protection needs and in ensuring the participation of refugees and other persons of concern to the Office of the High Commissioner, as appropriate, in the planning and implementation of programmes of the Office and State policies, and also affirms the importance of according priority to addressing discrimination, gender inequality and the problem of sexual and gender-based violence, recognizing the importance of addressing the protection needs of women and children in particular;

21. *Strongly reaffirms* the fundamental importance and the purely humanitarian and non-political character of the function of the Office of the High Commissioner of providing international protection to refugees and seeking permanent solutions to refugee problems, and recalls that those solutions include voluntary repatriation and, where appropriate and feasible, local integration and resettlement in a third country, while reaffirming that voluntary repatriation, supported, as necessary, by rehabilitation and development assistance to facilitate sustainable reintegration, remains the preferred solution;

22. *Expresses concern* about the particular difficulties faced by the millions of refugees in protracted situations,

and emphasizes the need to redouble international efforts and cooperation to find practical and comprehensive approaches to resolving their plight and to realize durable solutions for them, consistent with international law and relevant General Assembly resolutions;

23. *Recognizes* the importance of achieving durable solutions to refugee problems and, in particular, the need to address in this process the root causes of refugee movements in order to avert new flows of refugees;

24. *Welcomes* the initiative of the High Commissioner to convene, in Geneva on 9 and 10 December 2009, the third Dialogue on Protection Challenges, on the theme "Challenges for persons of concern to the Office of the United Nations High Commissioner for Refugees in urban settings";

25. *Recalls* the important role of effective partnerships and coordination in meeting the needs of refugees and in finding durable solutions to their situations, welcomes the efforts under way, in cooperation with countries hosting refugees and countries of origin, including their respective local communities, relevant United Nations agencies, international and intergovernmental organizations, regional organizations, as appropriate, non-governmental organizations and development actors, to promote a framework for durable solutions, particularly in protracted refugee situations, which includes an approach to sustainable and timely return which encompasses repatriation, reintegration, rehabilitation and reconstruction activities, and encourages States, in cooperation with relevant United Nations agencies, international and intergovernmental organizations, regional organizations, non-governmental organizations and development actors, to support, inter alia, through the allocation of funds, the implementation of such a framework to facilitate an effective transition from relief to development;

26. *Recognizes* that no solution to displacement can be durable unless it is sustainable, and therefore encourages the Office of the High Commissioner to support the sustainability of return and reintegration;

27. *Welcomes* the progress that has been achieved in increasing the number of refugees resettled and the number of States offering opportunities for resettlement, and the contribution that those States make to durable solutions for refugees, and invites interested States, the Office of the High Commissioner and other relevant partners to make use of the Multilateral Framework of Understandings on Resettlement, where appropriate and feasible;

28. *Notes with appreciation* the activities undertaken by States to strengthen the regional initiatives that facilitate cooperative policies and approaches on refugees, and encourages States to continue their efforts to address, in a comprehensive manner, the needs of the people who require international protection in their respective regions, including the support provided for host communities that receive large numbers of persons who require international protection;

29. *Notes* the importance of States and the Office of the High Commissioner discussing and clarifying the role of the Office in mixed migratory flows, in order to better address protection needs in the context of mixed migratory flows, including by safeguarding access to asylum for those in need of international protection, and notes the readiness of the High Commissioner, consistent with his mandate, to assist States in fulfilling their protection responsibilities in this regard;

30. *Emphasizes* the obligation of all States to accept the return of their nationals, calls upon States to facilitate the return of their nationals who have been determined not to be in need of international protection, and affirms the need for the return of persons to be undertaken in a safe and humane manner and with full respect for their human rights and dignity, irrespective of the status of the persons concerned;

31. *Expresses deep concern* about the challenges posed by climate change and environmental degradation to the protection activities of the Office of the High Commissioner and the assistance it provides to vulnerable populations of concern across the globe, particularly in the least developed countries, and urges the Office to continue to address such challenges in its work, within its mandate, in consultation with national authorities and in cooperation with competent agencies in its operations;

32. *Notes* the important number of displaced in and from Iraq and its serious impact on the social and economic situation of countries in the region, and calls upon the international community to act in a targeted and coordinated manner to provide protection and increased assistance to the persons displaced to enable the countries in the region to strengthen their capacity to respond to the needs in partnership with the Office of the High Commissioner, other United Nations agencies, the International Red Cross and Red Crescent Movement and non-governmental organizations;

33. *Urges* all States and relevant non-governmental and other organizations, in conjunction with the Office of the High Commissioner, in a spirit of international solidarity and burden- and responsibility-sharing, to cooperate and to mobilize resources with a view to enhancing the capacity of and reducing the heavy burden borne by host countries, in particular those that have received large numbers of refugees and asylum-seekers, and calls upon the Office to continue to play its catalytic role in mobilizing assistance from the international community to address the root causes as well as the economic, environmental and social impact of large-scale refugee populations in developing countries, in particular the least developed countries, and countries with economies in transition;

34. *Expresses deep concern* about the existing and potential challenges posed by the world financial and economic crisis to the activities of the Office of the High Commissioner;

35. *Calls upon* the Office of the High Commissioner to further explore ways and means to broaden its donor base, so as to achieve greater burden-sharing by reinforcing cooperation with governmental donors, non-governmental donors and the private sector;

36. *Recognizes* that adequate and timely resources are essential for the Office of the High Commissioner to continue to fulfil the mandate conferred upon it through its statute and by subsequent General Assembly resolutions on refugees and other persons of concern, recalls its resolutions 58/153 of 22 December 2003, 58/270 of 23 December 2003, 59/170 of 20 December 2004, 60/129 of 16 December 2005, 61/137 of 19 December 2006, 62/124

of 18 December 2007 and 63/148 of 18 December 2008 concerning, inter alia, the implementation of paragraph 20 of the statute of the Office, and urges Governments and other donors to respond promptly to annual and supplementary appeals issued by the Office for requirements under its programmes;

37. *Requests* the High Commissioner to report on his activities to the General Assembly at its sixty-fifth session.

Strengthening UNHCR

Oral report of UNHCR. In response to General Assembly resolution 58/153 [YUN 2003, p. 1226] on strengthening UNHCR capacity to carry out its mandate, a UNHCR representative on 30 July provided an oral report to the Economic and Social Council [E/2009/SR.43]. Speaking in the context of UNHCR's cooperation with UN agencies, international organizations and NGOs, the representative said that as conflicts became more complex, effective partnerships in favour of humanitarian action were more important than ever. Notably, the Office had worked over the past year with the Inter-Agency Standing Committee (IASC) to develop new policies for furthering humanitarian reform, had taken the lead in providing and coordinating protection and shelter for IDPs, and had been involved in IASC project to improve the humanitarian coordinator system. Within the IASC framework, UNHCR was spearheading efforts, together with the United Nations Office for the Coordination of Humanitarian Affairs, to achieve conceptual clarity and identify good practices in relation to humanitarian space. UNHCR had also been participating in the IASC informal task force concerned with identifying the humanitarian consequences of climate change.

UNHCR was involved in five of the eight pilot countries under the "Delivering as one" initiative [YUN 2006, p. 1060]. With a view to increasing UN system coherence at the country level, the Office worked to ensure that the development needs of refugee-hosting and return areas were reflected in the common country assessments and the United Nations Development Assistance Frameworks. The representative further noted that UNHCR had been involved in efforts to increase efficiency in delivering life-saving humanitarian assistance in challenging environments. UNHCR welcomed measures to enable front-line agencies to continue essential programme delivery by integrating improved security into operational planning. Protecting persons from sexual exploitation and abuse remained a top priority. To that end, the High Commissioner had, in 2009, designated the UNHCR's newly established Ethics Office as the focal point to represent UNHCR on the IASC Task Force on Protection from Sexual Exploitation and Abuse in Humanitarian Crises.

UNHCR had continued to strengthen bilateral cooperation with key partners on a range of operational issues, including the World Food Programme (WFP) on the 2008 global food crisis; the Office of the High Commissioner for Human Rights through its eight treaty monitoring bodies and special procedures process; the United Nations Human Rights Council and the Council of Europe on the subject of statelessness; the United Nations Children's Fund (UNICEF) on child protection; the United Nations Relief and Works Agency for Palestine Refugees in the Near East (see p. 466) on providing assistance to Gaza Strip populations; and the International Committee of the Red Cross on providing assistance to IDPs and ensuring the inclusion of refugees and IDPs in national HIV plans and programmes. UNHCR, said the representative, had signed more than 1,000 agreements with NGOs, covering all sectors of assistance.

On 30 July, the Economic and Social Council took note of the UNHCR oral report (**decision 2009/256**).

Partnerships and coordination

In 2009 [A/65/12], UNHCR continued to participate in cooperative initiatives to reform the UN system and improve the global humanitarian response capacity, particularly in the area of inter-agency cooperation. It remained committed to improving the coherence of humanitarian action, notably through the cluster approach to situations of internal displacement and the "Delivering as one" initiative. UNHCR had almost 700 national partners and nearly 190 international partners worldwide during the year. It worked closely with IASC on strengthening the humanitarian coordinator system, preserving humanitarian space and addressing the humanitarian consequences of climate change. In November, the Office hosted the fourth meeting of the Inter-agency Support Group for the Convention on the Rights of Persons with Disabilities, highlighting the need to include non-citizens in national assistance programmes for persons with disabilities.

With global food security continuing to deteriorate, UNHCR and WFP collaborated to cover the food and nutrition needs of more than 2 million refugees and 10 million IDPs in 26 countries. Cooperation with the International Organization for Migration (IOM) increased substantially in 2009, particularly in the areas of mixed migration and human trafficking. NGOs—the single largest group of UNHCR partners—continued to play an essential role in meeting the needs of populations of concern to the Office. In 2009, 27 per cent of UNHCR's total expenditure was channelled through 672 NGOs (159 international and 513 national). In June, some 180 NGO representatives attended the UNHCR-NGO annual consultations, providing input into the Office's new urban refugee policy. UNHCR also developed partnerships with Governments and organizations at the regional level. In the Middle East, the Office and the Organization of the Islamic Conference published a joint study to generate a better understanding of the compatibility between concepts of international refugee law and Islamic sharia law. In Europe, UNHCR supported the development of a common European asylum system to harmonize European Union legal standards with international norms. In Africa, UNHCR established its representation to the African Union and the Economic Commission for Africa.

In 2009, UNHCR focused on reinforcing its corporate partnerships, which brought in financial support, expertise, goods and media space, as well as its relationships with major charitable organizations, which generated important contributions and material support and played a critical role in terms of advocacy.

Evaluation activities

In a July report [A/AC.96/1071], UNHCR described the activities of its Policy Development and Evaluation Service (PDES), which focused its work on refugee protection and solutions; return and reintegration; international migration and refugee protection; protracted refugee situations; urban displacement; strengthening the dissemination and utilization of its outputs; humanitarian and UN reform; accountability to beneficiaries; supply chain management; and external relations.

On urban displacement, PDES, in preparation for the 2009 meeting of the High Commissioner's Dialogue on Protection Challenges (see p. 1203), worked with the Division of Operational Support to develop a concept note and establish a work programme on the issue. That included a major review of UNHCR's response to the Iraqi refugee situation in urban areas of Jordan, Lebanon and the Syrian Arab Republic. The conclusions from that review assisted the Service in drafting the new UNHCR Policy on Refugee Protection and Solutions in Urban Areas, released in September. On refugee protection and solutions, PDES worked with the Division of International Protection to ensure that the findings and recommendations of an independent evaluation of UNHCR's role in preventing and responding to sexual and gender-based violence were used in the formulation of a three-year organizational strategy on that issue. The Service also initiated a global independent review of the implementation of UNHCR's age, gender and diversity mainstreaming initiative, and completed studies on public health equity in refugee situations in different regions of the world, and on the refugee protection implications of witchcraft accusations. With regard to return and re-

integration, PDES completed evaluations of the UNHCR return and reintegration programmes in Angola and southern Sudan, which fed into the policy development process on reintegration issues and were used as a basis for country-level planning. On international migration and refugee protection, PDES commenced a series of reviews of UNHCR's role in mixed migration situations, beginning with the Spanish Canary Islands and Italy. In association with the Division of International Protection, the Service undertook a follow-up to the evaluation of UNHCR's role in relation to human trafficking.

In 2009, PDES examined the way its outputs were disseminated within UNHCR, in order to ensure that they were brought to the attention of relevant stakeholders within the Office and that they were utilized for policymaking, planning and programming. On humanitarian and UN reform, PDES, in association with other headquarters entities, prepared a review of the humanitarian space challenges encountered by UNHCR. The Service also made a presentation on the issue to an IASC task force meeting in June. Regarding its accountability to beneficiaries, PDES played a key role in UNHCR's involvement in the peer review on accountability to disaster-affected populations— an initiative of the Steering Committee for Humanitarian Response, an alliance of nine major international humanitarian organizations and networks. On supply chain management, PDES commissioned an independent evaluation entitled "Assuring effective supply chain management to support UNHCR's beneficiaries", which contributed to the UNHCR structural and management change process and was instrumental in establishing the new Division of Emergency and Supply Management. Regarding external relations, between October 2008 and July 2009, PDES published 12 papers in the series "New Issues in Refugee Research". Other publications from the Service included an article on the relationship between environmental factors and human mobility for the United Nations Population Fund's 2009 *State of the World Population* report, on which it collaborated with IOM.

Inspections

In 2009 [A/65/12], the UNHCR Inspector General established a "road map" to strengthen the capacity of his office and to implement the recommendations made by the independent panel review of the Inspector General's Office (IGO) conducted in 2008 by the European Anti-Fraud Office [YUN 2008, p. 1309]. The establishment, in January, of an on-line IGO complaints mechanism to facilitate the reporting of possible misconduct by UNHCR personnel led to a sharp increase in the number of complaints compared to previous periods. The predominant types of situations investigated were harassment, abuse of authority and discrimination. An ad hoc inquiry carried out in October was related to the attacks that led to the death of three UNHCR staff members in Pakistan. A report [A/AC.96/1070] covering IGO activities in the first half of 2009 was transmitted to the UNHCR Executive Committee in July. Between January and June, IGO logged 467 complaints; there were 86 ongoing investigations, comprising 50 cases from 2009, 33 from 2008 and 3 from 2007. A later report [A/AC.96/1089] outlined IGO activities undertaken in the second half of 2009, including 74 investigations opened from July to December.

OIOS activities. The audit service of the United Nations Office of Internal Oversight Services (OIOS), which provided the internal audit function for UNHCR, conducted 27 audits in 2009. In July, OIOS submitted to the UNHCR Executive Committee a report [A/AC.96/1069] on its internal audit of UNHCR for the period from 1 July 2008 to 30 June 2009, which reviewed the Office's activities in the areas of risk assessment, work planning, cooperation and coordination, and response to management concerns and advisory services. The report also covered the status of the implementation rate of OIOS recommendations, and key findings with regard to programme and project management, as well as financial, supply chain, information technology and human resources management. OIOS issued 21 reports during the period, generating 264 recommendations to improve processes and procedures, as well as governance, management oversight, accountability and risk management mechanisms. A later OIOS report [A/AC.96/1088] submitted to the Executive Committee provided an overview of its internal audit of UNHCR for the period from 1 July 2009 to 30 June 2010. In addition to the topics noted above, the report also covered organization and staffing, strategic management and governance, and safety and security.

Enlargement of the Executive Committee

On 30 July, the Economic and Social Council, by **decision 2009/252**, noted Slovenia's request [E/2009/47] for enlarging the membership of the UNHCR Executive Committee and recommended that the General Assembly take a decision at its sixty-fourth (2009) session on the question of enlarging the membership from 78 to 79 States.

GENERAL ASSEMBLY ACTION

On 18 December [meeting 65], the General Assembly, on the recommendation of the Third Committee [A/64/431], adopted **resolution 64/128** without vote [agenda item 41].

Enlargement of the Executive Committee of the Programme of the United Nations High Commissioner for Refugees

The General Assembly,

Taking note of Economic and Social Council decision 2009/252 of 30 July 2009 concerning the enlargement of the Executive Committee of the Programme of the United Nations High Commissioner for Refugees,

Taking note also of the request regarding the enlargement of the Executive Committee contained in the letter dated 10 March 2009 from the Permanent Representative of Slovenia to the United Nations addressed to the Secretary-General,

1. *Decides* to increase the number of members of the Executive Committee of the Programme of the United Nations High Commissioner for Refugees from seventy-eight to seventy-nine States;

2. *Requests* the Economic and Social Council to elect the additional member at its resumed organizational session for 2010.

Financial and administrative questions

The UNHCR revised annual programme budget for 2009 was set at $1,265.5 million in 2008 [YUN 2008, p. 1310]. Total funds available for 2009 amounted to $1,956.9 million, including a carry-over from 2008 of $157.4 million. Income and adjustments totalled $1,799.5 million, comprising $1,086.1 million from the annual budget, $46 million from the UN regular budget, $10.5 million from the Junior Professional Officer (JPO) programme and $656.9 million from the supplementary programme budget. Expenditures totalled $1,754.5 million, of which Africa accounted for $661.2 million; the Middle East and North Africa $312.9 million; Asia and the Pacific $301.6 million; Europe $132.4 million; and the Americas $54.0 million.

In an October decision [A/64/12/Add.1], the Executive Committee noted that the "New or additional activities—mandate-related" reserve appropriation level of $75 million for 2009 might prove insufficient and authorized UNHCR to increase the 2009 appropriation to $90 million. It also approved the revised annual programme budget for 2009, which amounted to $1,280.5 million. Those provisions, it noted, together with those of $10 million for JPOs and the needs under Supplementary Programmes of $934.8 million, brought total requirements in 2009 to $2,225.3 million. The Committee authorized the High Commissioner, within those total appropriations, to effect adjustments in regional programmes, global programmes and headquarters budgets.

The Committee also approved the 2010–2011 Biennial Programme Budget (see p. 1199), which amounted to $2,778.5 million in 2010 and $2,565.4 million in 2011, including the UN regular budget contribution, an operational reserve of $196.8 million in 2010 and $182.6 million in 2011 and $20 million for the "New and additional activities—mandate-related" reserve in both 2010 and 2011 respectively. It noted that those provisions, together with the $12.0 million for JPOs in both 2010 and 2011, brought total requirements for 2010 to $3,007.3 million and for 2011 to $2,780 million. The Committee authorized the High Commissioner, within those total appropriations, to effect adjustments in regional programmes, global programmes and headquarters budgets. The Committee requested the High Commissioner, within the resources available, to respond flexibly and efficiently to the needs indicated for the 2010–2011 biennial programme budget. The Committee also authorized the High Commissioner, in case of new emergency needs that could not be fully met from the operational reserve, to create supplementary budgets and issue special appeals.

Biennial Programme Budget 2010–2011.
In a September report [A/AC.96/1068], the High Commissioner reviewed general budgetary issues, including trends in funding and expenditure, mid-year resources and expenditure in 2008 and 2009, and proposed budgetary requirements for the 2010–2011 biennium. The report also described UNHCR's new budget structure, approved by the Standing Committee in 2008 and taking effect beginning with the 2010–2011 biennium. The four pillars of the new budget structure were: the global refugee programme; the global stateless programme; the global reintegration projects; and the global IDP projects. The purpose of the breakdown was not to prioritize one component or population over another, but to provide clarity and transparency in terms of how the UNHCR budget structure would address the different categories of populations of concern. The introduction of the new budget structure and the comprehensive results-based management framework, as well as the implementation of the International Public Sector Accounting Standards (IPSAS), required that a revision to the Financial Rules would come into effect on 1 January 2010 (see p. 1193).

In October [A/AC.96/1068/Add.1], the Advisory Committee on Administrative and Budgetary Questions (ACABQ) responded to the report of the High Commissioner, as well as to documents relating to UNHCR accounts for the year ended 31 December 2008 (see below). ACABQ noted that the proposed budget for 2010–2011 was not only presented in a new budget structure, but was also based on an assessment of needs rather than on the expected availability of funds. To ACABQ, the new budget structure raised a number of issues, such as the means of prioritization and its impact on the ability of the High Commissioner to respond to emerging situations. Another concern was related to the funding and earmarking of UNHCR activities. In the Advisory Committee's view, given the funding gap UNHCR had experienced, and because the budget structure might lead to further earmarking by donors, the new division of resources might not guarantee sufficient funding for all four pillars. UNHCR was therefore encouraged to further its efforts on fundraising and donor relations to ensure that all needs groups were covered. With respect to presentation of the budget, ACABQ noted that the link between resource requirements and the various initiatives undertaken with respect to the structural and management change process was not clearly explained. Furthermore, limited attention was given to providing justification for the allocation of resources and posts. ACABQ recommended that future budgets provide fuller explanations for changes in post and non-post resources. The Advisory Committee welcomed the progress made by UNHCR in the structural and management change process, including results-based management, the reduction of headquarters personnel, the strengthening of the field and the relocation of administrative functions to Budapest, Hungary; it noted, however, that the proposed programme budget did not offer much information regarding concrete efficiency gains realized through those initiatives. It expected that UNHCR would continue to monitor and assess the implementation of those initiatives and inform the Executive Committee accordingly.

Accounts (2008)

The audited financial statements of voluntary funds administered by UNHCR for the year ending 31 December 2008 [A/64/5/Add.5] showed a total expenditure of $1,628 million and total income of $1,652 million in 2008, with a negative reserve balance of $130.1 million.

The Board of Auditors found instances of obligations raised, for a total amount of $1.4 million, which did not relate to the 2008 financial year, indicating that checks had not been implemented with sufficient accuracy to completely rule out the risk of overstatement of expenditure. It also found that: no funding had been found for the after-service health insurance benefits and end-of-service and post-retirement liabilities; limited progress had been made regarding the transition to IPSAS; bank accounts remained inactive without being closed and petty cash accounts were subject to negative balances resulting from erroneous conversions of local currencies or errors in accounting records; although UNHCR had continued to clean up its non-expendable property database, anomalies remained which suggested incomplete clean-up; there was a discrepancy between the value of non-expendable property disclosed in the financial statements and the value calculated by the Board on the basis of data communicated by UNHCR; the value of expendable property held at the end of the year was not disclosed in financial statements, although the value of said stock was significant; there was a deterioration in the rate of receipt for subproject reports from implementing partners; as at 29 June 2009, audit certificates accounting for 50.5 per cent of the total amount of $498.6 million due for 2008 had not been received; and excluding projects for which extension of the liquidation period had been approved, the compliance rate was 58.1 per cent ($224 million out of $385.7 million). The Board also reported that the total accrued liabilities for after-service health insurance benefits, estimated by actuarial valuation, amounted to $307.8 million as at 31 December 2008; in accordance with the request of the General Assembly in its resolution 61/264 [YUN 2007, p. 1502], the Board validated the calculation of those liabilities by the actuaries. The Board made a number of recommendations based on its audit.

In September, [A/AC.96/1067/Add.1], UNHCR described measures taken or proposed in response to the Board's recommendations.

In an October report [A/64/469], ACABQ trusted that UNHCR would make every effort to implement the Board's recommendations, which covered areas such as after-service health liabilities, progress towards IPSAS implementation, write-offs, ex gratia payments, internal audit activities, cases of fraud and presumptive fraud, expendable property, programme and project management, and the management of cash, non-expendable property and human resources. ACABQ noted that, as at 29 June, of the total amount of $498.6 million that required audit certification, certificates covering $252 million, or 50.5 per cent, had not been received by UNHCR, although the audit reports were generally due by 30 April. With regard to the non-receipt of those certificates, the Committee emphasized that audit certificates were an important internal control mechanism and believed that the absence of an audit trail for such a large sum could lead to a heightened risk of exposure to potential fraud. While acknowledging the difficult environment in which UNHCR often operated, the Committee nevertheless urged UNHCR to take measures to address the substantive concerns raised by the Board. On the subject of progress towards IPSAS implementation, the Committee noted that the Board of Auditors was preparing a paper that would clarify the requirements to be met prior to implementing IPSAS, to be shared among a number of organizations that had encountered difficulties in that regard. The Committee noted the Board's willingness to review UNHCR revisions to its Financial Rules in relation to the adoption of IPSAS, and, in that regard, recommended that UNHCR submit to the Board its proposed revisions when available.

The Executive Committee, in an October decision [A/64/12/Add.1], requested that it be kept regularly informed on measures taken to address the recommendations made by the Board of Auditors and ACABQ.

On 22 December, the General Assembly took action on the financial reports and audited financial statements, and reports of the Board of Auditors (**resolution 64/227**) (see p. 1415).

Management and administrative change

In 2009, UNHCR remained engaged in its process of structural and management change, which was launched in 2006 [YUN 2006, p. 1392]. A UNHCR report [A/64/12] covering the first half of 2009 noted that reform efforts for that period focused on organizational development management, human resources, results-based management, regionalization and decentralization. The outposting of several administrative and support functions from Geneva to the Global Service Centre in Budapest was one of the most visible reforms, and one that yielded considerable savings which allowed UNHCR to dedicate more resources to its beneficiaries. Another change, which resulted from an external review of UNHCR's supply chain performance, was the relocation of supply management to Budapest. To strengthen its capacity to deliver goods and services to populations of concern, UNHCR also adopted an integrated supply chain concept, uniting procurement and logistics, as well as improving its fleet, warehouse and asset management. With regard to human resources, a number of initiatives took place during the reporting period in the areas of career management, assignments and promotion, and staff well-being and staff relations. Those included the launch of a new performance appraisal management system; the creation of an Ethics Office; the establishment of a Staff/Management Consultative Council; and the transformation of the Staff Development Section into the Global Learning Centre in Budapest, through which UNHCR created a unified learning structure with a Governance Board on Learning and a learning-management system. UNHCR also pursued efforts to ensure the implementation of policy on gender equity, issues of disability and staff, and HIV in the workplace.

On results-based management, UNHCR embarked on five key initiatives: the results framework; the results-based management systems tool, *Focus*; the global needs assessment (GNA); the revised budget structure; and the global management accountability framework. The results framework, a protection-based framework providing a standardized description of the results the Office wanted to achieve, was implemented in 2009. Analogously, the software *Focus*, developed by UNHCR in order to plan, budget and report on its programmes according to the results framework, was rolled out to all operations during the year. The GNA (see below), designed to better express the needs of persons of concern to the Office and present plans, activities and the resource levels required to meet those needs, was also globally introduced in 2009. UNHCR tested a draft global management accountability framework during the year. That framework, which would map accountability, responsibilities and authorities across the organization, was expected to foster stronger organizational accountability towards populations of concern. On regionalization and decentralization, UNHCR pursued efforts to empower and capacitate field operations in Europe and the Americas. For Europe, the Director of the Bureau was relocated to Brussels, Belgium, and for the Americas, the Deputy Director was relocated to Panama.

A later UNHCR report [A/65/12] covering 2009 noted that internal reforms continued to pay dividends. With the same number of staff worldwide, but 30 per cent fewer at headquarters in Geneva, UNHCR had increased its activities by more than 60 per cent since reforms were launched in 2006. Staffing costs in 2009 decreased to 28 per cent of total costs, while headquarters costs were again reduced, down to 9.5 per cent of total costs. The percentage of expenditure managed through implementing partners had increased to 35.9 per cent, reflecting an improvement in the expertise and flexibility that UNHCR was able to mobilize. The Office continued to implement the Headquarters Review, under which the Division for Programme Support and Management had integrated the programme management, analysis and support functions to enhance the quality of operations. Furthermore, the Division of International Protection was restructured into three pillars covering legal and protection policy, operational support to protection activities, and comprehensive solutions, while the Division of Information Services and Technology was being reorganized to decentralize technical support from Geneva to six regional platforms. Reforms to human resources continued throughout the year, including new procedures for assignments of international staff. Guidelines aimed at systematizing the use of additional workforce personnel were developed in conjunction with the United Nations Volunteers programme, the United Nations Office for Project Services, and NGOs with which the Office had standby arrangements.

Standing Committee

The UNHCR Standing Committee held three meetings in 2009 (3–5 March [A/AC.96/1065]; 23–25 June [A/AC.96/1073]; and 15–16 September [A/AC.96/1074]). It considered issues relating to UNHCR programme

budgets and funding; international protection; regional activities and global programmes; programme/protection policy; coordination; management, financial control, administrative oversight and human resources; governance; and consultations. The work of the Committee was summarized in a 30 September note by the Secretariat [A/AC.96/1075].

In October [A/64/12/Add.1], the Executive Committee called upon its members to ensure that debate at the Executive Committee and its Standing Committee was substantive and interactive, yielding practical guidance and clear advice to the High Commissioner, in keeping with the Committee's statutory functions. It called on UNHCR to be explicit and analytical in its reports and presentations to the Committee and to submit documentation in a timely manner. It further requested the Standing Committee to report on its work in 2010. The Executive Committee also approved applications by States and intergovernmental and international organizations to participate as observers in Standing Committee meetings.

Global needs assessment

At its June meeting [A/AC.96/1073], the Standing Committee discussed the global needs assessment (GNA) [EC/60/SC/CRP.14] and the progress made by UNHCR in shifting from a resource-based approach to one based on a realistic assessment of needs. The GNA, introduced globally in 2009, was designed to map overall needs more comprehensively, and to present the plans, activities and level of resources required to meet those needs. As part of the GNA, all operations would record the findings of their respective needs assessment and design their plans in UNHCR's new software planning application, *Focus*, using the common results framework, both of which were also implemented in 2009. Operations would also plan for the populations represented in the budget structure. With assessments, plans and budgets structured in a common manner and accessible in *Focus*, it would be possible to consolidate information provided at a country and regional level to present a global view in the GNA. In early 2009, over 1,200 staff at headquarters and in the field were introduced to the GNA and trained on how to use the new software. At the meeting, the Deputy High Commissioner and the Director of the UNHCR Office for Organizational Development Management responded to requests from delegations for clarification about GNA resource allocation and prioritization criteria; the need to consult and collaborate with other agencies undertaking similar needs assessment exercises; and on how UNHCR would monitor field plans to ensure flexibility to incorporate needs during the year and avoid mid-year budgetary capping.

Staff safety

At the June meeting of the Standing Committee [A/AC.96/1073], the Director of the UNHCR Division of Operational Services presented an update on staff safety and security issues, including refugee security [EC/60/SC/CRP.13], which described efforts to implement the recommendations of the UNHCR Security Policy and Policy Implementation Review, as well as new initiatives in support of the security of beneficiaries and other security-related activities. He drew attention to the dramatic increase in the number of security incidents against humanitarian workers—up by more than 350 per cent in the past three years—and noted that steps taken in response included risk mitigation strategies and training. However, many issues related to humanitarian space had yet to be addressed and he foresaw the need to be prepared to meet the rising cost of security measures while finding new ways of operating. The Office's response to safety and security was welcomed at the meeting, as was the shift from a "when to leave" to a "how to stay" approach. The move from fixed security levels to security management based on local risk assessments was also deemed positive, in line with comments about the importance of balancing security measures with the needs of beneficiaries. UNHCR was asked to clarify the proposal for a centralized fund for security and the criteria used for risk evaluation, and there were calls for greater emphasis on reporting on security for beneficiaries. The Director urged States to help communicate the message that humanitarian workers were neutral parties and to support mechanisms for staff safety and security. He acknowledged that greater reference to the matter of refugee security could be made; nevertheless, he wished to avoid giving the impression that the two were separate issues. The Chief of the Field Safety Section commented on the central funding mechanism. The cost-share arrangement for the United Nations Department of Safety and Security placed a heavy burden on organizations like UNHCR, at both central and local levels. UNHCR believed that additional support ought to be made available through the UN regular budget to equip field staff with adequate security resources. Progress on improving the security management system had been achieved through inter-agency fora, although more training was needed to equip field managers to be able to conduct security risk assessments.

High Commissioner's report. In his annual report covering 2009 [A/65/12], the High Commissioner said that UNHCR had undertaken a number of initiatives aimed at enhancing security management. Those included a strengthened Field Safety Section in the newly created Division of Emergency, Security and Supply; better support to staff and managers in the field; a more systematic approach to the provision of physical security for persons of concern, in conjunction with the Division of International Protection; the identification and hiring of qualified field safety advisors; enhanced security analysis with an emphasis on helping decision-makers judge threats, risks and vulnerabilities more accurately; and multiplied opportunities for security specialists, managers and staff to undergo specialized security training. In addition, a high-level Security Steering Committee under the chairmanship of the High Commissioner was instituted in 2009 to conduct regular reviews of high-risk operations in critical locations.

Refugee protection and assistance

Protection issues

In his annual report covering 2009 [A/65/12], the High Commissioner said that insecurity, continuing human rights violations by State and non-State actors and weak State structures—often compounded by dire social conditions and food, water and economic crises—complicated protection responses and solutions to displacement. The report described the main challenges faced by States and UNHCR in protecting and assisting persons of concern, such as protecting asylum-seekers and refugees at sea; providing basic needs and essential services for persons of concern; protecting older persons of concern and those living with disabilities; resolving protracted refugee solutions and achieving durable solutions; protecting and assisting trafficked persons who wished to seek asylum; strengthening emergency preparedness and response capacities; applying environmental management projects, approaches and tools; addressing global resettlement needs; assisting with the local integration of refugees; and responding to the movement of unaccompanied and separated children across borders. Also discussed was the challenge of ensuring the human rights of stateless persons. In that context, a progress report [EC/60/SC/CRP.10] issued in May covered UNHCR activities on statelessness from 2005 to 2009.

The High Commissioner noted the issue of shrinking humanitarian space in developing regions, as well as increased pressure on the asylum space available in the world's more prosperous States, including a surge in refoulement during the reporting period. A spate of involuntary returns in 2009, notably in the Mediterranean, the Great Lakes region, the Horn of Africa and South-East Asia, reflected the increasingly hostile environment for refugees and asylum-seekers. Due to a growing determination to uphold traditional notions of State sovereignty, the year was characterized by greater restrictions and fewer rights, with a clear trend towards introducing laws to deter and criminalize asylum-seekers who arrived irregularly or overstayed their visas. As a result, UNHCR intensified efforts to narrow the gap between law and practice in the area of refugee protection and find new, creative approaches to assist displaced populations around the world. While it recognized the legitimate interest of States to manage immigration and control the entry, stay and removal of migrants, UNHCR stressed the need for mechanisms that were responsive to those seeking international protection, including alternatives to detention.

Ongoing conflicts in many countries caused significant internal and cross-border displacement. Major conflicts such as those in Afghanistan and Somalia showed no signs of resolution, while conflicts which appeared to have ended or almost ended experienced resurgences. As a result, the number of people returning home voluntarily in 2009 was the lowest in 20 years. Furthermore, the increasing number of refugees residing in urban areas continued to grow, and millions more who fled their homes due to conflict and became internally displaced also lived in urban areas. In September, UNHCR issued a new urban refugee policy which provided field guidance on handling the specific challenges encountered in urban settings. The third High Commissioner's Dialogue on Protection Challenges (Geneva, 8–10 December) focused on the theme of "Challenges for Persons of Concern in Urban Settings" and emphasized the importance of strong and innovative partnerships in that context, including at the local level. Subsequently, seven "pilot sites" were selected for monitoring during the course of 2010, in order to look at the implementation of the urban refugee policy, examine the challenges encountered, and identify good practices that might be replicated elsewhere.

In March [A/AC.96/1065], the Director of the Division of International Protection briefed the Standing Committee on the second meeting of the High Commissioner's Dialogue on Protection Challenges [YUN 2008, p. 1312], which focused on protracted refugee situations.

In a June note on international protection [A/AC.96/1066], the High Commissioner examined developments from May 2008 to May 2009 in the areas of protecting persons of concern in emergencies; improving access to international protection; ensuring refugee protection within mixed migration movements; strengthening implementation of the 1951 Convention relating to the Status of Refugees [YUN 1951, p. 520]; preventing and responding to statelessness; and securing durable solutions for persons of concern. The High Commissioner said that continuing or new emergencies during the reporting period had caused massive displacement. Humanitarian space was reduced due to the changing nature of armed conflict; greater reliance by States on sovereignty arguments; side effects of peacekeeping where there was no peace to keep; restrictions on access; attacks on humanitarian staff; and growing difficulties related to access to asylum. Nevertheless, a majority of States continued to uphold their obligations and millions of refugees were able to find asylum, at least temporarily, and eventually a durable solution. The Office sought to support initiatives to strengthen refugee protection in the context of mixed migratory flows through the implementation of its 10-Point Plan of Action on refugee protection and mixed migration [YUN 2006, p. 1386]. Patterns of conflict became more complex, as did contemporary forms of displacement. It was increasingly evident that displacement would likely be further impacted by environmental factors, such as population growth, declining resources and inequality of access to them, ecological damage and climate change, and demographic and urbanization trends. The legal implications of displacement driven by forces other than persecution, human rights violations and war had yet to be assessed, and varying root causes of displacement created differing response needs. In any case, however, the concept of asylum would have to be safeguarded and the international protection regime strengthened and made flexible enough to respond to new challenges.

In December [A/AC.96/1080], the Executive Committee adopted a conclusion on protracted refugee situations that called upon States and other actors to take action in addressing the root causes of those situations; ensure that people were not compelled to flee their countries of origin in the first place to find safety elsewhere; and resolve the protracted refugee situations which persisted. It recommended actions to address and facilitate durable solutions, in the form of voluntary repatriation, local integration or resettlement in third countries.

International instruments

In 2009, the number of parties to both the 1951 Convention relating to the Status of Refugees [YUN 1951, p. 520] and its 1967 Protocol [YUN 1967, p. 477] remained at 144; the number of States parties to one or both instruments remained at 149. With the ratification of Liechtenstein and the accession of Malawi, the number of States parties to the 1954 Convention relating to the Status of Stateless Persons [YUN 1954, p. 416] increased to 65. With the accession of Hungary and Liechtenstein, the number of States parties to the 1961 Convention on the Reduction of Statelessness [YUN 1961, p. 533] increased to 37.

Assistance measures

In 2009, the global population of concern to UNHCR was 36.5 million, an increase from 34.4 million in 2008. That figure included some 10.4 million refugees, which represented a decrease from the 10.5 million refugees counted in 2008. The number of stateless persons identified by UNHCR remained at 6.6 million, although the actual number was estimated to be closer to 12 million. The number of people displaced within their own country as a result of conflict reached an estimated 27.1 million, with an unprecedented 15.6 million of them benefiting from UNHCR protection and assistance. The latter figure constituted an increase of more than 1.2 million compared to the previous year (14.4 million).

While mature conflicts remained unresolved, new and renewed conflicts emerged during the reporting period, all of which caused internal and cross-border displacement. In September, as refugees were repatriating in significant numbers from Zambia back to Katanga Province of the Democratic Republic of the Congo (DRC), armed conflict erupted in Equateur Province of the DRC, adding to the displacement in eastern areas of the country. Ongoing conflicts in the Central African Republic (CAR), Somalia and the Sudan also generated major displacement. On a positive note, UNHCR began to review the situation of refugees from Angola, Burundi, Liberia and Rwanda with a view to bringing closure to those chapters of displacement. During the first half of 2009, tensions in Pakistan, particularly in the province of Khyber-Pakhtunkhwa and the Federally Administered Tribal Areas, caused massive internal population displacement. UNHCR assisted many of the estimated 2 million people displaced in those areas, as well as with the return of nearly 150,000 Afghan refugees from Pakistan and Iran. In Yemen, renewed tensions in the north led to fighting that displaced an estimated 250,000 persons. In Latin America, Colombia and its neighbours continued to experience an elevated rate of new displacement. In Colombia, UNHCR and the Government agreed on a plan for 2010–2011 that built upon the State's efforts to protect, assist and find solutions for displaced persons. In Ecuador, a registration initiative supported by UNHCR resulted in the provision of identity documents to 26,000 Colombians who were subsequently granted refugee status by the host Government.

During 2009, more than 922,000 individual claims for asylum or refugee status were submitted to Governments or UNHCR offices in 159 countries or territories, representing a 5 per cent increase compared to the previous year (875,300). That was partly the result of a persistently high number of asylum applications in South Africa. The majority of applications came from asylum-seekers originating in Afghanistan, Colombia, Ethiopia, Myanmar and Zimbabwe. In Europe, applicants from Afghanistan, Iraq and Somalia made up the largest groups. While challenges to asylum space grew, there were some encouraging developments, including preparations to establish a European Asylum Support Office, in which UNHCR had been involved.

Some 5.5 million refugees lived in a protracted situation at the end of 2009. In an effort to alleviate the burdens on countries hosting large numbers of refugees for prolonged periods, UNHCR, together with Governments and the international community, worked to create space for development programmes, reduce dependency and increase possibilities for self-sufficiency.

Humanitarian crises, conflicts and prevailing political situations not only uprooted millions, but prevented the return of refugees. The number of voluntarily returned refugees (251,000) had steadily decreased since 2004, with the 2009 figure being the lowest in two decades. Of the repatriation movements that did take place, the main countries of return included Afghanistan (57,600), the DRC (44,300), Iraq (38,000), the Sudan (33,100), Burundi (32,400) and Rwanda (20,600). The organized repatriation of Mauritanian refugees from Senegal ended in December. During the latter half of 2009, UNHCR secured, in principle, agreement for the expansion of the Confidence Building Measures programme for Western Sahara, which would entail the use of road transport for family visits. In another positive development, the number of returned IDPs in 2009 (2.2 million) was the highest in more than a decade. Regarding local integration—another durable solution pursued by UNHCR—achievements in 2009 remained difficult to measure in quantitative terms, although 162,000 Burundian refugees living in exile since 1972 in the United Republic of Tanzania were granted citizenship, and the United States granted citizenship to some 55,000 refugees during the year. UNHCR was also informed of refugees being granted citizenship in Armenia, Belgium, Ireland and the Russian Federation. As far as resettlement, UNHCR estimated the global need in 2009 at about 747,000 persons, including some 200,000 persons for whom resettlement was a pressing need. As part of its efforts to promote the strategic use of resettlement, UNHCR ensured that at least 10 per cent of its overall submissions to resettlement countries were for women and girls at risk.

Refugees and the environment

During 2009, UNHCR continued to implement its environmental policy and activities, based on the four principles outlined in the 2005 revision [YUN 2005, p. 1310] of its Environmental Guidelines: prevention, integrated approach, cost-effectiveness, and local participation. At its June meeting [A/AC.96/1073], the

Standing Committee adopted a decision on addressing environmental issues in operations for persons of concern to UNHCR. That decision encouraged UNHCR, together with relevant partners, to extend the scope of its assessment and monitoring of environmental activities and to develop strategies for disaster risk reduction in refugee and IDP hosting and returnee areas. It also called on UNHCR to allocate adequate resources for addressing environmental issues identified through its comprehensive needs assessment.

UNHCR worked throughout the year to apply and support a range of environmental management projects, approaches and tools. Those included developing community environmental management plans in camps, such as those in Chad, Ethiopia, Kenya, Rwanda, the United Republic of Tanzania and Uganda, as well as undertaking environmental impact assessments, notably in Bangladesh, the DRC, Kenya and Rwanda. UNHCR also implemented reforestation projects; organized environmental management training for staff, implementing partners and governmental counterparts; and promoted the use of alternative energy, environmentally-friendly shelters and green technologies.

Refugees and HIV/AIDS

During 2009, in line with its Strategic Plan for HIV and AIDS (2008–2012), UNHCR continued to advocate for access of people of concern to national HIV prevention and treatment programmes. By the end of the year, approximately 87 per cent of refugees in need of antiretroviral treatment had access to it, and 75 per cent of pregnant women had access to prevention of mother-to-child transmission programmes. The Office strengthened the inclusion of young people in anti-HIV programmes and, to improve access to HIV testing, worked with the World Health Organization and the Joint United Nations Programme on HIV/AIDS to publish guidelines on *Provider-initiated HIV testing and counselling for refugees and IDPs in health facilities.*

Refugee women

At the June meeting of the Standing Committee [A/AC.96/1073], the Director of the Division of International Protection presented a document [EC/60/SC/CRP.11] which reviewed UNHCR's work with displaced women and girls and the development of the age, gender and diversity mainstreaming (AGDM) strategy, which was developed in 2004 [YUN 2004, p. 1205]. The document explained how the cycle of empowerment—from education to participation and self-reliance—would provide the most effective response to concerns about the protection of women and girls. It concluded that systematic policies and programmes

to empower women and girls through participatory, rights- and community-based approaches should receive increased attention as a strategy to enhance their protection. At the meeting, delegates inquired about the linkages and integration of the AGDM strategy in the results-based management system and called for more disaggregated data, demographic analyses, and involvement of men and boys in prevention of and response to sexual and gender-based violence. They expressed concern regarding the lack of provision of sanitary materials, which had broad implications for the dignity of women and girls, including the risk of affecting the retention of girls in school. They also requested a report on progress in implementing commitments to women as well as to children, and how that would be included in the budget for the next biennium. The Director responded that with the introduction of the global accountability framework and the *Focus* software, it would be possible to gather indicators related to sexual and gender-based violence and empowerment. He acknowledged that data gathered from communities should be operationalized and implemented, including in budgetary allocations, and, with regard to sanitary materials, a policy on ensuring sustainability of supplies would have to be considered.

During 2009, UNHCR continued to strengthen the implementation of AGDM. An evaluation of the approach during the year led the Office to introduce new measures designed to boost accountability for AGDM, including by expanding staff and partners' capacity and prioritizing AGDM efforts in terms of resource allocation. The evaluation also noted fundamental changes in the way UNHCR staff operated in promoting gender equality, taking into consideration vulnerable groups and contributing to a better understanding of the protection dimensions of assistance. In July a seminar organized by the Office and the United Nations Committee on the Elimination of All Forms of Discrimination Against Women examined ways in which the international treaty on women's human rights—the Convention on the Elimination of All Forms of Discrimination against Women—could be applied to help protect women of concern to UNHCR. The Office issued French and Spanish versions of the *Handbook for the Protection of Women and Girls*, as well as CD-ROMs in Arabic, French and Spanish. UNHCR also produced four community-based films on economic self-reliance, education, gender equality and sexual and gender-based violence.

Refugee children

In 2009, UNHCR continued to emphasize education, nutrition and protection from violence in addressing the needs of refugee children. The movement of unaccompanied and separated children across borders was a worrying trend, and one that often involved detention and the lack of access to asylum procedures and proper reception facilities. Responding to the situation of unaccompanied and separated children in mixed migration flows necessitated inter-agency cooperation and partnerships with Governments in countries of origin, transit and destination. In that connection, UNHCR, UNICEF and IOM established a working group to enhance responses to child protection challenges in mixed migration. Access to education was not widely available to refugees, with low rates of enrolment at both the primary and secondary levels. Though progress had been achieved, there was a need to improve enrolment in both camp and urban settings. In 2009, operations in 11 countries began receiving technical support and assistance to improve enrolment and establish safe schools and learning environments. Cooperation with UNICEF and the United Nations Educational, Scientific and Cultural Organization was reinforced through joint missions and activities in the field. The Office also worked to implement the 2007 Executive Committee conclusion on children at risk [YUN 2007, p. 1234], which called for non-discriminatory access of children to child protection systems. In cooperation with its partners, UNHCR developed draft guidelines on child protection systems in emergencies, which sought to improve child protection programming in different operations. In 2009, the guidelines were tested in Ecuador, Ethiopia, Nepal and Yemen.

Regional activities

Africa

In 2009, the total population of concern to UNHCR in Africa, excluding North Africa, remained at 10.2 million. The total comprised some 2.1 million refugees, 6.5 million IDPs, 420,000 asylum-seekers, 984,000 returned refugees and IDPs, as well as 274,000 other persons of concern. UNHCR's total expenditure for Africa was $661.2 million.

Report of Secretary-General. In response to General Assembly resolution 63/149 [YUN 2008, p. 1319], the Secretary-General in August submitted a report [A/64/330] on UN assistance to refugees, returnees and displaced persons in Africa, updating information contained in his 2008 report [YUN 2008, p. 1316].

In East Africa and the Horn of Africa, recurrent droughts, floods, conflict, insecurity and violence, as well as soaring food prices were the main challenges. The Sudan remained the focus of the largest humanitarian operation in Africa and the second largest refugee-producing country on the continent. Somalia was the largest refugee-producing country in Africa; although tens of thousands of IDPs returned home in the first four months of 2009, recent fighting

in Mogadishu had more than reversed those returns. In May, militias raided the UNICEF compound in Jowhar, destroying vaccines and therapeutic food supplies to prevent and treat acute malnutrition.

In Central Africa and the Great Lakes region, the political situation remained essentially stable in most countries, despite some instances of rioting over price hikes in food and fuel in Cameroon, the Congo, Gabon, Rwanda and the United Republic of Tanzania. However, the Central Africa Republic, Chad and the DRC continued to experience turmoil.

In the southern African country of Zimbabwe, election-related violence, continuing political uncertainty, a rapidly deteriorating economic situation, hyperinflation and the near total collapse of basic social services posed enormous challenges for the population. The formation of an inclusive Government in February 2009 gave rise to cautious optimism. Humanitarian organizations were able to provide limited legal and medical assistance, as well as food and non-food items, to various affected communities.

The Secretary-General concluded that to find durable solutions for refugees and IDPs, Governments, humanitarian and development organizations and civil society needed to collectively promote environments capable of sustaining return or integration. Special attention had to be paid to access, without discrimination, to basic public services, legal and personal documentation, and livelihood opportunities. In addition, mechanisms to deal with land and property restitution needed to be put in place. The needs of host populations should also be taken into account when devising a return programme. He recommended that States respect the principle of the non-refoulement of refugees and ensure the proper reception and timely registration of refugees in line with international and regional instruments; host countries receive support in their efforts to create environments enabling refugees to become self-reliant; and UN organizations continue to support efforts of African States in developing a binding regional convention for the protection of internally displaced people.

UNHCR report. According to UNHCR *Global Report 2009*, ongoing or new emergencies in sub-Saharan Africa caused considerable displacement in 2009, both within countries and across borders. Although overall refugee numbers remained stable, the number of IDPs increased slightly. Strife in the CAR drove some 125,000 refugees into neighbouring States, while another 197,000 were internally displaced. In the DRC, hostilities in the east propelled fresh displacement, while a new inter-ethnic conflict in Equateur province uprooted 60,000 people within the country and caused another 102,000 to seek asylum in the Congo and 18,000 in the CAR. The crisis in Somalia, aggravated by renewed fighting in May, uprooted some 1.5 million people within the country and drove 560,000 more to seek refuge in neighbouring States. In response to those and other emergencies, UNHCR was present in 33 African countries and, for the most part, was able to discharge its mandated responsibilities.

With regard to voluntary repatriation, assisted voluntary returns to Liberia and Togo were concluded. On the other hand, the voluntary repatriation operations to return to Burundi, the DRC and Southern Sudan slowed significantly. Initiatives for local integration, another durable solution pursued by UNHCR, were moving ahead. UNHCR provided support for the local integration of the 155,000 Burundian refugees naturalized by Tanzania during the year. Shelter, livelihoods, income-generation and community development programmes benefited former refugees and local communities in Côte d'Ivoire, Guinea, Liberia, Nigeria and Sierra Leone, also facilitating local integration. With regard to resettlement, UNHCR increased its referrals from Africa as part of its strategy to find solutions for refugees, particularly those in protracted situations. In 2009, more than 28,000 cases involving refugees in 36 asylum countries were submitted for resettlement to 14 different countries.

In the DRC, where more than 15,000 cases of sexual and gender-based violence were registered in 2009, UNHCR implemented the protection and prevention pillars of the Comprehensive Strategy on Combating Sexual Violence, which covered a range of actions to stem sexual and gender-based violence and assist victims in receiving justice. For example, to help counter the culture of impunity, UNHCR arranged for the temporary deployment of judges of the High Court to Katanga to rule on cases of sexual violence that involved girls between the ages of 6 and 15 years. In Liberia, the Office worked with the Ministry of Justice to prevent and respond to sexual violence. With regard to national refugee status determination, UNHCR worked with government authorities towards ensuring that refugees and asylum-seekers received documentation in a timely manner. In Senegal, 62 per cent of refugees and asylum-seekers were in possession of refugee identity cards. Another major development was the commencement of the verification process of refugees in camps in eastern Chad. In Côte d'Ivoire, where UNHCR estimated that 1 million people were at risk of statelessness, the Office worked to reduce that risk by providing legal and technical advice to people of concern; strengthening the capacity of local institutions to provide civil-status documentation; and conducting sensitization campaigns.

UNHCR promoted livelihood activities to improve the living conditions of people of concern and, where possible, reduce dependence on humanitarian aid. The Office's self-reliance strategy in eastern Sudan included agricultural and livelihoods projects, as well as vocational training and access to microcredit. In Somalia, UNHCR used livelihoods activities for IDPs, particularly women, as a practical protection tool. In Rwanda, UNHCR distributed essential non-food items and firewood in all camps and transit centres. Efforts to increase refugees' access to education continued. In eastern Chad, all camps provided primary education, with an average enrolment rate of 80 per cent. The attendance rates for girls increased to 50 per cent for those in younger years, although they decreased in the higher grades. There was modest progress in reducing malnutrition and anaemia rates in the refugee camps in Ethiopia and Zambia. Advocacy for the inclusion of refugees and returnees in national health plans and services, particularly with regard to HIV/AIDS services, malaria control and reproductive health, was a priority. By the end of 2009, refugees in Angola, Burundi, Cameroon, the DRC, Ethiopia, Kenya, Malawi, Namibia, Rwanda, South Africa, Uganda, Tanzania and Zambia had access to a range of services, including anti-retroviral therapy and testing.

By subregion, UNHCR assisted 5.0 million persons in East Africa and the Horn of Africa, which received $2.9 million in agency expenditures. In Central Africa and the Great Lakes region, $291.1 million was spent on 3.9 million persons of concern, while some $42.4 million was spent on programmes assisting 486,090 persons in need in Southern Africa. In West Africa, $54.7 million was spent on 850,980 persons of concern.

AU Convention. On 22 October, a special summit of the African Union (AU) held in Kampala, Uganda adopted the AU Convention for the Protection and Assistance of Internally Displaced Persons in Africa (Kampala Convention), which would enter into force when ratified by 15 member States. The new Convention, which was the first legally binding instrument on internal displacement with a continent-wide scope, provided a comprehensive framework for the protection and assistance of IDPs during and after displacement. Noted in the Convention were the specific roles of international organizations and agencies within the framework of the UN inter-agency collaborative approach to IDPs, especially the protection expertise of UNHCR. The Secretary-General stated that while the Convention applied to AU member States, its importance as a standard and model extended well beyond Africa.

GENERAL ASSEMBLY ACTION

On 18 December [meeting 65], the General Assembly, on the recommendation of the Third Committee [A/64/431], adopted **resolution 64/129** without vote [agenda item 41].

Assistance to refugees, returnees and displaced persons in Africa

The General Assembly,

Recalling the Organization of African Unity Convention governing the specific aspects of refugee problems in Africa of 1969 and the African Charter on Human and Peoples' Rights,

Reaffirming that the 1951 Convention relating to the Status of Refugees, together with the 1967 Protocol thereto, as complemented by the Organization of African Unity Convention of 1969, remains the foundation of the international refugee protection regime in Africa,

Recognizing the particular vulnerability of women and children among refugees and other persons of concern, including exposure to discrimination and sexual and physical abuse,

Gravely concerned by the deteriorating conditions in some of the refugee camps in Africa,

Recognizing that refugees, internally displaced persons and, in particular, women and children are at an increased risk of exposure to HIV/AIDS, malaria and other infectious diseases,

Welcoming the adoption of the African Union Convention for the Protection and Assistance of Internally Displaced Persons in Africa, which marks a significant step towards strengthening the national and regional normative framework for the protection of and assistance to internally displaced persons,

Noting with appreciation the Pact on Security, Stability and Development in the Great Lakes Region and its instruments, in particular two of the protocols to the Pact which are relevant to the protection of displaced persons, namely, the Protocol on the Protection of and Assistance to Internally Displaced Persons and the Protocol on the Property Rights of Returning Persons,

Recognizing that host States have the primary responsibility for the protection of and assistance to refugees on their territory, and the need to redouble efforts to develop and implement comprehensive durable solution strategies, in appropriate cooperation with the international community, and burden- and responsibility-sharing,

Emphasizing that States have the primary responsibility to provide protection and assistance to internally displaced persons within their jurisdiction, as well as to address the root causes of the displacement problem in appropriate cooperation with the international community,

1. *Takes note* of the reports of the Secretary-General and the United Nations High Commissioner for Refugees;

2. *Calls upon* African Member States that have not yet signed or ratified the African Union Convention for the Protection and Assistance of Internally Displaced Persons in Africa to consider doing so as early as possible in order to ensure its early entry into force and implementation;

3. *Takes note* of the fortieth anniversary, on 10 September 2009, of the Organization of African Unity Convention governing the specific aspects of refugee problems in Africa of 1969;

4. *Notes* the need for African Member States to address resolutely root causes of all forms of forced displacement in Africa and to foster peace, stability and prosperity throughout the African continent so as to forestall flows of refugees;

5. *Notes with great concern* that, despite all of the efforts made so far by the United Nations, the African Union and others, the situation of refugees and displaced persons in Africa remains precarious, and calls upon States and other parties to armed conflict to observe scrupulously the letter and spirit of international humanitarian law, bearing in mind that armed conflict is one of the principal causes of forced displacement in Africa;

6. *Welcomes* decision EX.CL/Dec.494(XV) on the situation of refugees, returnees and displaced persons in Africa, adopted by the Executive Council of the African Union at its fifteenth ordinary session, held in Sirte, Libyan Arab Jamahiriya, from 28 to 30 June 2009;

7. *Expresses its appreciation* for the leadership shown by the Office of the United Nations High Commissioner for Refugees, and commends the Office for its ongoing efforts, with the support of the international community, to assist African countries of asylum, including by providing support to vulnerable local host communities, and to respond to the protection and assistance needs of refugees, returnees and displaced persons in Africa;

8. *Notes with appreciation* the initiatives taken by the African Union, the Subcommittee on Refugees, Returnees and Internally Displaced Persons of its Permanent Representatives Committee, and the African Commission on Human and Peoples' Rights, in particular the role of its Special Rapporteur on Refugees, Asylum-Seekers, Migrants and Internally Displaced Persons in Africa, to ensure the protection of and assistance to refugees, returnees and displaced persons in Africa;

9. *Acknowledges* the important contribution of the age, gender and diversity mainstreaming strategy in identifying, through a participatory approach, the protection risks faced by the different members of the refugee community, in particular the non-discriminatory treatment and protection of refugee women and refugee children and minority groups of refugees;

10. *Affirms* that children, because of their age, social status and physical and mental development, are often more vulnerable than adults in situations of forced displacement, recognizes that forced displacement, return to post-conflict situations, integration in new societies, protracted situations of displacement and statelessness can increase child-protection risks, taking into account the particular vulnerability of refugee children to forcible exposure to the risks of physical and psychological injury, exploitation and death in connection with armed conflict, and acknowledges that wider environmental factors and individual risk factors, particularly when combined, may generate different protection needs;

11. *Recognizes* that no solution to displacement can be durable unless it is sustainable, and therefore encourages the Office of the High Commissioner to support the sustainability of return and reintegration;

12. *Also recognizes* the importance of early registration and effective registration systems and censuses as a tool of protection and as a means to the quantification and assessment of needs for the provision and distribution of humanitarian assistance and to implement appropriate durable solutions;

13. *Recalls* the conclusion on registration of refugees and asylum-seekers adopted by the Executive Committee

of the Programme of the United Nations High Commissioner for Refugees at its fifty-second session, notes the many forms of harassment faced by refugees and asylum-seekers who remain without any form of documentation attesting to their status, recalls the responsibility of States to register refugees on their territories and, as appropriate, the responsibility of the Office of the High Commissioner or mandated international bodies to do so, reiterates in this context the central role that early and effective registration and documentation can play, guided by protection considerations, in enhancing protection and supporting efforts to find durable solutions, and calls upon the Office, as appropriate, to help States to conduct this procedure should they be unable to register refugees on their territory;

14. *Calls upon* the international community, including States and the Office of the High Commissioner and other relevant United Nations organizations, within their respective mandates, to take concrete action to meet the protection and assistance needs of refugees, returnees and displaced persons and to contribute generously to projects and programmes aimed at alleviating their plight, facilitating durable solutions for refugees and displaced persons and supporting vulnerable local host communities;

15. *Reaffirms* the importance of timely and adequate assistance and protection for refugees, returnees and displaced persons, also reaffirms that assistance and protection are mutually reinforcing and that inadequate material assistance and food shortages undermine protection, notes the importance of a rights- and community-based approach in engaging constructively with individual refugees, returnees and displaced persons and their communities so as to achieve fair and equitable access to food and other forms of material assistance, and expresses concern in regard to situations in which minimum standards of assistance are not met, including those in which adequate needs assessments have yet to be undertaken;

16. *Also reaffirms* that respect by States for their protection responsibilities towards refugees is strengthened by international solidarity involving all members of the international community and that the refugee protection regime is enhanced through committed international cooperation in a spirit of solidarity and burden- and responsibility-sharing among all States;

17. *Further reaffirms* that host States have the primary responsibility to ensure the civilian and humanitarian character of asylum, calls upon States, in cooperation with international organizations, within their mandates, to take all necessary measures to ensure respect for the principles of refugee protection and, in particular, to ensure that the civilian and humanitarian nature of refugee camps is not compromised by the presence or the activities of armed elements or used for purposes that are incompatible with their civilian character, and encourages the High Commissioner to continue efforts, in consultation with States and other relevant actors, to ensure the civilian and humanitarian character of camps;

18. *Condemns* all acts that pose a threat to the personal security and well-being of refugees and asylum-seekers, such as refoulement, unlawful expulsion and physical attacks, calls upon States of refuge, in cooperation with international organizations, where appropriate, to take all necessary measures to ensure respect for the principles of refugee

protection, including the humane treatment of asylum-seekers, notes with interest that the High Commissioner has continued to take steps to encourage the development of measures to better ensure the civilian and humanitarian character of asylum, and encourages the High Commissioner to continue those efforts, in consultation with States and other relevant actors;

19. *Deplores* the continuing violence and insecurity which constitute an ongoing threat to the safety and security of staff members of the Office of the High Commissioner and other humanitarian organizations and an obstacle to the effective fulfilment of the mandate of the Office and the ability of its implementing partners and other humanitarian personnel to discharge their respective humanitarian functions, urges States, parties to conflict and all other relevant actors to take all necessary measures to protect activities related to humanitarian assistance, prevent attacks on and kidnapping of national and international humanitarian workers and ensure the safety and security of the personnel and property of the Office and that of all humanitarian organizations discharging functions mandated by the Office, and calls upon States to investigate fully any crime committed against humanitarian personnel and bring to justice the persons responsible for such crimes;

20. *Calls upon* the Office of the High Commissioner, the African Union, subregional organizations and all African States, in conjunction with agencies of the United Nations system, intergovernmental and non-governmental organizations and the international community, to strengthen and revitalize existing partnerships and forge new ones in support of the protection system for refugees, asylum-seekers and internally displaced persons;

21. *Calls upon* the Office of the High Commissioner, the international community and other entities concerned to intensify their support to African Governments through appropriate capacity-building activities, including training of relevant officers, disseminating information about refugee instruments and principles, providing financial, technical and advisory services to accelerate the enactment or amendment and implementation of legislation relating to refugees, strengthening emergency response and enhancing capacities for the coordination of humanitarian activities, in particular those Governments that have received large numbers of refugees and asylum-seekers;

22. *Reaffirms* the right of return and the principle of voluntary repatriation, appeals to countries of origin and countries of asylum to create conditions that are conducive to voluntary repatriation, and recognizes that, while voluntary repatriation remains the pre-eminent solution, local integration and third-country resettlement, where appropriate and feasible, are also viable options for dealing with the situation of African refugees who, owing to prevailing circumstances in their respective countries of origin, are unable to return home;

23. *Also reaffirms* that voluntary repatriation should not necessarily be conditioned on the accomplishment of political solutions in the country of origin in order not to impede the exercise of the refugees' right to return, recognizes that the voluntary repatriation and reintegration process is normally guided by the conditions in the country of origin, in particular that voluntary repatriation can be accomplished in conditions of safety and dignity, and urges

the High Commissioner to promote sustainable return through the development of durable and lasting solutions, particularly in protracted refugee situations;

24. *Calls upon* the international donor community to provide financial and material assistance that allows for the implementation of community-based development programmes that benefit both refugees and host communities, as appropriate, in agreement with host countries and consistent with humanitarian objectives;

25. *Appeals* to the international community to respond positively, in the spirit of solidarity and burden- and responsibility-sharing, to the third-country resettlement needs of African refugees, notes in this regard the importance of using resettlement strategically, as part of situation-specific comprehensive responses to refugee situations, and to this end encourages States, the Office of the High Commissioner and other relevant partners to make full use of the Multilateral Framework of Understandings on Resettlement, where appropriate;

26. *Calls upon* the international donor community to provide material and financial assistance for the implementation of programmes intended for the rehabilitation of the environment and infrastructure affected by refugees in countries of asylum as well as internally displaced persons, where appropriate;

27. *Urges* the international community, in the spirit of international solidarity and burden-sharing, to continue to fund generously the refugee programmes of the Office of the High Commissioner and, taking into account the substantially increased needs of programmes in Africa, inter alia, as a result of repatriation possibilities, to ensure that Africa receives a fair and equitable share of the resources designated for refugees;

28. *Encourages* the Office of the High Commissioner and interested States to identify protracted refugee situations which might lend themselves to resolution through the development of specific, multilateral, comprehensive and practical approaches to resolving such refugee situations, including improvement of international burden- and responsibility-sharing and realization of durable solutions, within a multilateral context;

29. *Expresses grave concern* about the plight of internally displaced persons in Africa, notes the efforts of African States in strengthening the regional mechanisms for the protection of and assistance to internally displaced persons, calls upon States to take concrete action to pre-empt internal displacement and to meet the protection and assistance needs of internally displaced persons, recalls in that regard the Guiding Principles on Internal Displacement, takes note of the current activities of the Office of the High Commissioner related to the protection of and assistance to internally displaced persons, including in the context of inter-agency arrangements in this field, emphasizes that such activities should be consistent with relevant General Assembly resolutions and should not undermine the refugee mandate of the Office and the institution of asylum, and encourages the High Commissioner to continue his dialogue with States on the role of his Office in this regard;

30. *Invites* the Representative of the Secretary-General on the human rights of internally displaced persons to continue his ongoing dialogue with Member States and the intergovernmental and non-governmental organizations

concerned, in accordance with his mandate, and to include information thereon in his reports to the Human Rights Council and the General Assembly;

31. *Requests* the Secretary-General to submit a comprehensive report on assistance to refugees, returnees and displaced persons in Africa to the General Assembly at its sixty-fifth session, taking fully into account the efforts expended by countries of asylum, under the item entitled "Report of the United Nations High Commissioner for Refugees, questions relating to refugees, returnees and displaced persons and humanitarian questions".

Report of Secretary-General. In a later report [A/65/324], the Secretary-General stated that the refugee population in Africa decreased by 1.5 per cent in 2009 compared with 2008, mainly owing to the naturalization of refugees from Burundi in the United Republic of Tanzania and successful voluntary repatriation operations to Angola, Burundi, the DRC, Rwanda and Southern Sudan. Nonetheless, renewed armed conflict and human rights violations in the DRC and Somalia led to new refugee outflows of some 277,000 people, as well as to more internal displacement. At the end of 2009, an estimated 11.6 million people were internally displaced by conflict in 21 countries in sub-Saharan Africa, representing more than 40 per cent of the world's IDPs. That figure included more than 2.1 million newly displaced persons, with a similar number returning home during 2009.

In East Africa and the Horn of Africa, some 32,000 Southern Sudanese refugees returned to their areas of origin in 2009. Security and humanitarian conditions in southern and central Somalia steadily deteriorated during the year and 132,000 refugees and asylum-seekers fled abroad, mainly to Kenya, Yemen, Ethiopia and Djibouti.

The Central Africa and the Great Lakes region suffered economic hardship and conflict, creating new displacement within countries and across borders. In the DRC, insecurity prevailed in many areas. Military operations and human rights violations by armed groups displaced more than 1 million people, offsetting the 1 million returns of IDPs in North and South Kivu registered in 2009. Access to displaced populations remained challenging because of insecurity, the remoteness of many areas and high transportation costs. The outbreak of violence in the north-western Equateur Province in November caused the internal displacement of 60,000 people. Some 125,000 refugees from the DRC crossed the border into the Congo and the CAR. UNHCR responded rapidly to the humanitarian and protection needs of the refugees, as did the host communities. In Burundi, the construction of "peace villages" that integrated IDPs, landless returnees and vulnerable people with different ethnic backgrounds was an innovative contribution towards closing the chapter of displacement in that country.

South Africa remained the main destination for asylum-seekers worldwide, receiving 222,000 asylum claims in 2009, the majority of which came from Zimbabwe. However, despite South Africa's protection-oriented refugee legislation, with a national unemployment rate of more than 24 per cent, as well as income disparities, rapid urbanization and lack of basic services, sporadic xenophobic violence continued to occur in the country. The Government, UN organizations, NGOs and civil society worked together to prevent intolerance of foreigners, including through awareness-raising, community engagement and increased police vigilance. In Zimbabwe, lack of access to basic services remained a major problem for millions, including an unknown number of IDPs. In response, a joint assessment by the United Nations and the Government, initiated in August, helped to gauge the needs of IDP communities.

Although voluntary repatriation had been the most typical durable solution for millions of displaced people in Africa, the pace of returns slowed significantly. In 2009, some 137,000 refugees returned voluntarily to their places of origin, the lowest number in a decade. Many more internally displaced persons returned home, with nearly 1 million returning in the DRC, 400,000 in Uganda and 280,000 in the Sudan.

The Americas

Developments in North America and the Caribbean included new parole guidelines in the United States that treated asylum-seekers more favourably and repeal of the inclusion of HIV on the list of medical conditions that barred refugees and other immigrants from entering the country. In the United States, UNHCR used various means to pursue its objective of ensuring that international standards of protection were met for all people of concern. Those included advocating for continued improvement of the asylum system as well as efforts to address statelessness issues. UNHCR regularly engaged with the Government and also trained government adjudicators, immigration attorneys and NGOs. In 2009, the United States accepted some 61,000 people referred by UNHCR. In Canada, UNHCR worked to ensure that asylum-seekers were allowed into the country and had access to its refugee status determination (RSD) procedures. During the year, Canada resettled some 6,500 refugees referred by UNHCR. In the Caribbean, UNHCR provided humanitarian assistance and legal aid to asylum-seekers and refugees through its implementing partners and a network of Honorary Liaisons. The Office registered asylum-seekers and determined their status in non-signatory States as well as a number of signatory States that did not have refugee legislation or national asylum procedures.

In Latin America, displacement continued to occur at a high rate in Colombia, with more than 3 million Colombians displaced within the country and hundreds of thousands of people experiencing refugee-like conditions outside of it. In response, UNHCR reinforced its capacity to support the Government in its efforts to narrow protection gaps, focusing on the implementation at the local level of national policies to protect the rights of IDPs and addressing the plight of groups with specific protection needs. UNHCR's protection delivery capacity was strengthened through the opening of new offices on the Pacific coast and in the south-eastern provinces, as well as through the consolidation of inter-agency coordination mechanisms. The protection of civilians was at the core of that strategy, which was implemented in the 87 districts most affected by displacement. The Office also worked with countries hosting Colombian people of concern. The enhanced registration carried out by the Government of Ecuador with UNHCR's support resulted in the registration and documentation of more than 23,000 refugees. UNHCR also provided technical assistance to help identify any cases not warranting international protection. In Venezuela, an agreement between UNHCR and the Government strengthened the RSD system in order to address the backlog of asylum claims.

The Regional Conference on Refugee Protection and International Migration (San José, Costa Rica, 19–20 November), organized by UNHCR and IOM, was an opportunity to identify the main protection challenges in the context of mixed migration, with the aim of finding responses to them. As more than 70 per cent of people of concern in Latin America resided in urban centres, UNHCR worked to promote solutions focusing on refugees in urban settings. In the framework of the Mexico Plan of Action [YUN 2004, p. 1210], the Cities of Solidarity initiative had developed from a mere concept to a platform that convened refugees, asylum-seekers, host communities and local authorities in an effort to integrate people of concern as they became accustomed to the dynamics of urban centres. More than 25 local governments were engaged in welcoming and assisting spontaneous or resettled refugees. Under the Solidarity Resettlement programme, 121 Colombian refugees who were living temporarily in Ecuador and Costa Rica were resettled in several cities of the Southern Cone, bringing the total of those benefiting from the programme since 2004 to almost 1,000. Furthermore, in 2009, Uruguay accepted its first group for resettlement under the programme, composed of some 15 refugees.

As part of the decentralization process, as of July, headquarters functions of the Bureau of the Americas were divided between Geneva and Panama. The Bureau in Panama was liaising with the UN Regional Director's Team and—with the support of a legal and technical regional hub—was providing support to UNHCR's operations in Latin America. That office also developed a regional emergency preparedness and response capacity in Latin America.

In 2009, total UNHCR expenditure in the Americas was $54.0 million for a population of concern of 4.3 million.

Asia and the Pacific

The working environment in the region was characterized by the dramatic expansion of major humanitarian situations in the first half of 2009. UNHCR played a prominent role in providing emergency assistance and protection to affected civilians, as well as in subsequent return and reintegration efforts. There was increased emphasis on working with local partners who were able to reach communities in areas where access was difficult. UNHCR also faced challenges in ensuring respect for the principle of non-refoulement and safeguarding access to individuals of concern. The fragility of protection environments for asylum-seekers in the region was highlighted by an increase in detention, as well as deportations towards the end of the year. UNHCR worked to help States manage migratory movements in a systematic manner while ensuring protection for those who needed it.

UNHCR and its partners mounted a swift emergency response following the mass population movement of some 3 million people within Pakistan. The focus was on the rapid establishment of camps, registration, the distribution of non-food items and protection monitoring. When returns began, UNHCR assisted the Government with transport, distributed non-food items in return areas and set up temporary shelters and social services centres. In the aftermath of typhoons that hit the Philippines, UNHCR assumed leadership of the protection cluster in order to support the national authorities in meeting the needs of vulnerable people. In Sri Lanka, UNHCR responded to the needs of more than 280,000 IDPs in the space of a few weeks. UNHCR's advocacy was particularly important in expanding humanitarian space and protection for IDPs, including obtaining freedom of movement for them in the camps. By the end of the year, some 156,000 Sri Lankans had returned to their areas of origin through a Government-led return process. Another 29,000 were released into host-family and community care. UNHCR also helped some 54,000 registered Afghans to return to their country in 2009. That effort was in line with Afghanistan's National Development Strategy, which sought to ensure that returns were voluntary and gradual, given the country's limited absorption capacity. In that context, UNHCR also engaged with the Governments of Pakistan and Iran regarding the continued temporary legal stay of Afghans in both countries. Between

them, the two countries hosted some 2.7 million Afghans, the largest population of registered refugees in the world. Another UNHCR protection effort involved cooperating with the Government of Thailand to revitalize the national screening mechanism for asylum-seekers from Myanmar. A pilot pre-screening exercise resulted in more than 11,000 interviews of unregistered persons. In Malaysia, significant progress was made in registering asylum-seekers and securing their release from detention. Nearly 40,000 people were registered, many through an innovative mobile registration programme.

Countries in the region took steps towards affirming and developing an international protection regime benefiting people of concern: Cambodia assumed full responsibility for processing and adjudicating national refugee cases, and Kazakhstan adopted national refugee legislation. In that regard, the Office continued to advocate for the preservation of asylum and protection space. In Kyrgyzstan, UNHCR initiated a strategy for preventing and reducing statelessness; in Nepal, it worked with members of the Constituent Assembly and others to ensure that the new Constitution met international standards regarding access to citizenship; in Tajikistan, it helped the relevant government ministry to respond to the protection and assistance needs of Afghan asylum-seekers; in Turkmenistan, it helped the Government to assume responsibility for RSD. A steady increase of new arrivals in Indonesia required UNHCR to strengthen cooperation with the authorities; the Office conducted emergency RSD and resettlement processing to assist the Government when a boat carrying Sri Lankan asylum-seekers was rescued at sea en route to Australia.

Efforts towards realizing the social and economic well-being of people of concern included the launch by the Government of Pakistan of the Refugee-Affected and Hosting Areas initiative, with the support of UNHCR and the United Nations Development Programme in the context of the "Delivering as one" initiative. UNHCR also began to implement some 16 projects in Pakistan, focusing on health, education, water and sanitation and community services. In Sri Lanka, 93 small-scale and quick-impact projects promoted stability and helped build confidence among populations in the east of the country. UNHCR also provided shelter grants to almost 25,200 IDP families, facilitating their reintegration upon return to the north. In Bangladesh, constructive government policies and UNHCR initiatives resulted in improved living conditions for 28,300 refugees from Myanmar living in two camps.

With regard to attaining durable solutions, UNHCR made progress towards resolving protracted refugee situations, including in Nepal, where more than 25,500 refugees departed for resettlement countries in 2009, reducing the population in camps by 16 per cent. Malaysia and Thailand saw more than 30,000 resettlement submissions and more than 24,000 departures during the year. In Viet Nam, steps were taken to reduce statelessness through the naturalization of former Cambodian refugees, particularly those residing in camps who had previously been assisted by UNHCR. UNHCR also welcomed Japan's first resettlement programme and supported it by identifying refugees from Myanmar in Thailand who would be resettled over the following three years.

In addition, UNHCR offices in the region supported Governments and NGO partners to promote age, gender and diversity considerations in programme planning, implementation and evaluation. In Thailand and Malaysia, UNHCR led best interest determinations (BID) processes to identify the most appropriate durable solutions for unaccompanied and separated children. More than 450 BID cases were completed in Thailand in 2009, and over 800 in Malaysia. In China, the first age, gender and diversity mainstreaming assessment saw the participation of both Government authorities and refugees. In Afghanistan, UNHCR led the creation of a gender-based violence prevention and response sub-cluster. The Office strengthened a protection project to provide legal, psycho-social and material assistance to victims of sexual and gender-based violence, in cooperation with the United Nations Development Fund for Women and a national network of safe houses for women and girls.

In 2009, UNHCR spent $301.6 million on activities in Asia and the Pacific for a population of concern of 13.0 million.

Middle East and North Africa

Despite the impact of the global financial crisis on their already overburdened social services and infrastructure, many countries in the region continued to allow large numbers of refugees and others of concern to take refuge on their soil. In most countries, the absence of national asylum systems and administrative procedures to deal with refugees and asylum-seekers constituted the biggest hurdle for UNHCR in its bid to protect persons of concern. RSD in the region was conducted solely by UNHCR. The legal vacuum in relation to asylum-seekers and refugees was particularly apparent in the sphere of livelihoods, as refugees and asylum-seekers were not given the right to work.

In Iraq, UNHCR expanded its presence in Baghdad, Basra, Erbil, Kirkuk and Mosul, and despite security restrictions, was able to reach most areas of the country through national staff. UNHCR protected and assisted some 35,000 refugees in Iraq, focusing on emergency assistance and documentation. More than 1,200 community assessments were conducted to monitor protection. Some 1,900 mobile-team visits were made to villages, collective centres, camps and communities in order to provide legal assistance, assess needs and maintain contact with local authorities. UNHCR operated 14 protection and assistance committees and 35 mobile teams with 130 Iraqi staff. More than 12,900 individuals, of whom 40 per cent were women, benefited from PAC services. The flow of IDPs returning to their places of origin in Iraq continued in 2009, with an estimated 167,000 doing so during the year. Some 38,000 Iraqi refugees, including 2,500 UNHCR-assisted, also returned home. However, resettlement remained the main durable solution for vulnerable Iraqi refugees in countries neighbouring Iraq. UNHCR submitted 36,000 Iraqi refugees for resettlement and recorded some 23,000 departures. Elsewhere, the Office registered and provided documentation to some 50,000 Iraqi refugees in Egypt, Iran, Jordan, Lebanon, the Syrian Arab Republic, Turkey and the Gulf States. The total number of registered Iraqi refugees in those countries at the end of 2009 stood at 230,000, of whom 35 per cent had special needs.

In Yemen, the conflict between the Government and the Al Houthi group in the north of the country escalated in August, leading to massive displacement. Five governorates—Sa'ada, Amran, AlJawf, Hajjah and Sana'a—were affected by the fighting, which displaced some 250,000 people by year's end. In response, the United Nations and NGO communities set up an emergency coordination system. UNHCR helped the Government to assist the displaced by coordinating protection, camp management and shelter sectors in the governorates where it had access. Meanwhile, mixed migration from the Horn of Africa to Yemen continued unabated, with more than 77,800 people arriving in the country in 2009, a 55 per cent increase from the previous year. Many planned onward travel to the Gulf States, but more than 41,700 arrivals were transported to reception centres in Mayfa'a, Ahwar and Kharaz camps, where they were registered and provided with food, health care, shelter and non-food items. Another 13,000 people, mainly Ethiopians, who arrived at the transit centre in Bab al Mandab on the Red Sea, were assisted and then transported to Kharaz camp. A profiling exercise of the refugees in the Basateen and Kharaz camps was completed in 2009; the establishment of a database using the Heightened Risk Identification Tool helped to identify resettlement cases. A similar profiling exercise began in Sana'a during the year.

The Office assisted in the resettlement of many Palestinians who had been stranded in camps on the Jordanian and Syrian borders. It also supported the Government of Iraq in re-registering approximately 11,300 Palestinian refugees and 500 refugees of other nationalities in Baghdad and Mosul. Some 1,850 individuals were referred for resettlement, including 1,300 Palestinian refugees from Al Waleed camp.

More than 270 Palestinians and 130 Sudanese from Darfur were evacuated to Romania and Slovakia prior to their resettlement in third countries. An important achievement in 2009 was the closure of Al Tanf camp, which was located on the Iraqi/Syrian border and hosted Palestinian refugees. The majority of the camp's residents were resettled, while some 170 of the remaining refugees were transferred to Al-Hol camp in Syria.

UNHCR expanded its financial aid programme in Jordan, Lebanon and Syria by providing refugees in those countries with automated banking cards, which helped some 15,000 families receive assistance by the end of 2009. In Mauritania, over 19,000 Mauritanian refugees returned home from Senegal between 2008 and the end of 2009. In 2009 alone, more than 12,000 people returned home in 49 convoys. UNHCR expanded its relations with the Gulf States and reinforced links with intergovernmental organizations and civil society. Notably, cooperation with Governments from the Cooperation Council for the Arab States of the Gulf and regional NGOs led to a strong donor response. UNHCR fielded several protection missions to Bahrain, Oman and Qatar, during which some 130 people were interviewed. Of those, 94 were submitted for resettlement. Authorities in the United Arab Emirates approached UNHCR to intervene in several cases related to prospective asylum-seekers, arrangements for resettlement, or to conduct RSD. In January, a training workshop on statelessness was organized in Bahrain for UNHCR staff in the region. UNHCR also cooperated with the Naif Arab University for Security Sciences and the Organization of Islamic Conference to publish _The Right to Asylum between Islamic Shari'ah and International Refugee Law: a Comparative Study._

In 2009, UNHCR spent $312.9 million on activities in the Middle East and North Africa for a population of concern of 4.8 million.

Europe

UNHCR worked in 48 European countries and territories in contexts involving mature and developing asylum systems, return and reintegration, protracted refugee situations, internal displacement and statelessness. Nearly 80 per cent of asylum applications in the industrialized world were lodged in Europe, representing more than 291,000 people in 2009. In many countries, political attention was focused on the control of irregular migration, making refugee protection particularly challenging.

Asylum claims in Central Europe increased to nearly 20,000, while the number of asylum-seekers in the Baltic States remained low. In Turkey, a key entry point to Europe, UNHCR received applications from more than 7,800 persons. In South-Eastern Europe

the number of applications, although low, increased slightly, whereas in Eastern Europe, 7,500 persons sought asylum, a decrease of 8 per cent from 2008.

UNHCR worked to preserve asylum space in Europe by monitoring borders, training border guards and cooperating with the European Union (EU) borders agency, Frontex. Formal border-monitoring agreements involving governmental and in some cases non-governmental partners were implemented in Belarus, Bulgaria, Hungary, Moldova, Poland, Romania, Slovenia and Ukraine. The Office also instituted a new presence in north-western France and counselling services in reception facilities in Italy and Greece. UNHCR advised States on the drafting of legislation and consolidation of institutional frameworks on asylum. New laws or by-laws on which UNHCR was consulted were adopted in Albania, Armenia, Belarus, Croatia, Greece, Moldova, Montenegro, the Russian Federation, Spain and the former Yugoslav Republic of Macedonia. To contribute to the development of a Common European Asylum System, UNHCR implemented the Asylum Quality Assurance and Evaluation Mechanism in eight Western and Central European countries. Judicial engagement was another part of the strategy to support asylum processes in Europe. UNHCR submitted its views to national courts in numerous cases, seeking to ensure respect for principles of international refugee law. The Office intervened as a third party before the European Court of Human Rights on several occasions and issued statements relating to requests for preliminary rulings pending before the European Court of Justice. Particular attention was devoted to the situation of unaccompanied and separated children applying for asylum in Europe. More than 15,000 such children, of whom 40 per cent were Afghans, applied for asylum in 27 countries. UNHCR worked to reinforce cooperation with key child protection partners, both from the UN system and the world of NGOs. In a number of countries, UNHCR led the development of standard operating procedures in sexual and gender-based violence to assist governmental and non-governmental partners engaged with asylum-seekers, refugees and IDPs.

With regard to facilitating durable solutions, UNHCR promoted greater engagement by European countries and the EU in refugee resettlement. In 2009, UNHCR assisted with the resettlement in Europe of more than 8,180 refugees. Of those, 25 per cent were Iraqis resettled in Germany under a special initiative. Annual resettlement programmes were present in 12 European countries, including the Czech Republic and Romania, which had their first resettlement intakes during the year. In Turkey, UNHCR conducted RSD and sought resettlement for refugees in the absence of locally available durable solutions. Some 6,000 refugees were resettled from Turkey in 2009. A number of new initiatives, such as the Emergency Transit Centre in

Romania, which operated through national authorities and IOM, as well as a second facility in Slovakia, also aided refugee resettlement.

UNHCR advocated for the integration of those displaced persons who were unable or unwilling to return home. In that regard, it welcomed the adoption by Montenegro and the former Yugoslav Republic of Macedonia of national action plans that opened prospects for the sustainable integration of populations of concern. Progress was made on local integration in Belarus, Georgia, Moldova and Ukraine, resulting in better housing, education, vocational training and national social protection schemes for people of concern. Thousands of IDPs in countries such as Azerbaijan, Bosnia and Herzegovina, Georgia, the Russian Federation and Serbia received legal assistance, and very vulnerable persons were provided with material assistance. UNHCR also redoubled its efforts to provide legal counsel to asylum-seekers, refugees and stateless people in Eastern Europe. Working with partners, more than 50,000 legal consultations were provided. There was a reinvigorated effort to close the chapter on displacement originating from conflicts in the former Yugoslavia in the 1990s. UNHCR supported regional dialogue to resolve outstanding issues and continued to help persons of concern find decent living conditions. As a result, 13 collective centres were closed in Serbia alone.

Other developments included public information campaigns that contributed to a better understanding of the situation of refugees and the work of UNHCR. In mid-2009, UNHCR and IOM launched "Not Just Numbers", an educational kit on asylum and migration. Also in mid-2009, the Office of the Director of the Bureau for Europe moved to Brussels and merged with the former Liaison Office to the EU, while the Deputy Director and staff covering Eastern and South-Eastern Europe remained in Geneva.

In 2009, UNHCR spent $134.5 million on activities in Europe for a population of concern of 4.1 million. More than 43 per cent of that amount ($58.3 million) was spent on 1.3 million persons of concern in Eastern Europe, while $38.3 million was for 572,260 persons of concern in South-Eastern Europe.

Chapter XIII

Health, food and nutrition

In 2009, the United Nations continued to promote health and food security, coordinate food aid and support research in nutrition.

At the end of the year, about 33.3 million people were living with HIV/AIDS and an estimated 2.6 million people had become newly infected with the virus. Deaths due to AIDS-related illnesses were estimated at 1.8 million. The Joint United Nations Programme on HIV/AIDS (UNAIDS) issued the *2009 AIDS Epidemic Update*, which documented regional progress in implementing the 2001 Declaration of Commitment on HIV/AIDS.

The Intergovernmental Negotiating Body on a Protocol on Illicit Trade in Tobacco Products held its third session from 28 June to 5 July. The World Health Organization (WHO) released a summary report on global progress in implementing the Framework Convention on Tobacco Control, as well as its annual *Report on the Global Tobacco Epidemic*, on the theme "Implementing Smoke-free Environments".

A WHO report to the General Assembly on the Decade to Roll Back Malaria in Developing Countries, Particularly in Africa (2001–2010) noted that the 2010 target for malaria control and elimination was already being achieved by five African countries, with several other countries approaching the goal of reducing malaria morbidity and mortality by 50 per cent or more by the end of 2010.

The Economic and Social Council at its high-level segment discussed the theme of "Current global and national trends and their impact on social development, including public health." Its annual ministerial review resulted in a declaration with objectives on HIV/AIDS, emerging health threats and epidemics, malaria, tobacco use and road safety.

The first global high-level conference on road safety was held in November in Moscow. In a ministerial declaration, participants set ambitious yet feasible national targets to reduce road traffic casualties.

The World Food Programme (WFP) provided life-saving food and nutrition assistance for 101.8 million people affected by conflict, storms, droughts, displacement, financial crises and other shocks that left them without food; 84 million of those beneficiaries were women and children. The Food and Agriculture Organization of the United Nations (FAO) continued to implement the Plan of Action adopted at the 1996 World Food Summit and the Declaration of the 2002 World Food Summit, which called on the international community to halve the number of undernourished people by 2015. World leaders convened at FAO headquarters in November for the World Summit on Food Security, pledging renewed commitment to eradicate hunger.

Health

AIDS prevention and control

Implementation of the Declaration of Commitment on HIV/AIDS

Report of Secretary-General. In May, the Secretary-General reported [A/63/812] to the General Assembly on progress made in implementing the 2001 Declaration of Commitment on HIV/AIDS [YUN 2001, p. 1126] and the 2006 Political Declaration on HIV/AIDS [YUN 2006, p. 1411].

Reports from 147 countries demonstrated important progress in the response to the HIV epidemic, including in access to antiretroviral therapy and the prevention of mother-to-child transmission. In only five years, antiretroviral coverage in resource-limited settings had increased tenfold, resulting in the first decline in the annual number of AIDS deaths since the epidemic was first recognized in the early 1980s. However, considerable challenges remained, including significant access gaps for key HIV-related services. The pace of new infections continued to outstrip the expansion of treatment programmes, and commitment to HIV prevention remained inadequate.

Many countries had indicated that they were at risk of falling short of achieving their universal access goals for 2010. The global economic downturn rendered even more acute the challenges of meeting global AIDS commitments. The HIV pandemic was affecting different populations and geographic settings in different ways. While women accounted for 60 per cent or more of new HIV infections in sub-Saharan Africa, men represented the majority of people living with HIV in other regions. Adolescents and young adults were the most likely age groups to become infected.

Key recommendations included the need for stakeholders to reaffirm their commitment to move toward universal access to HIV prevention, treatment, care and support by 2010. National prevention strategies needed to address national and local needs, taking into account the dynamics of national epidemics and evidence of effective interventions. Financing from all sources would have to increase to $25 billion by 2010 in order to achieve national universal access targets, and relevant laws and law enforcement would need to be improved as a means of preventing discrimination against people living with HIV and populations vulnerable to infection. The Secretary-General concluded that all stakeholders must fully commit to maximum transparency and accountability in the global response to HIV/AIDS, including regular reporting on national and global commitments.

The Assembly took note of the report on 9 September (**decision 63/560**).

JIU review

In May [A/63/152/Add.1], the Secretary-General transmitted to the General Assembly his comments, and those of the United Nations System Chief Executives Board for Coordination (CEB), on the report of the Joint Inspection Unit (JIU) on the review of the progress made by the UN system in achieving Millennium Development Goal (MDG) 6, Target 7, to combat HIV/AIDS [YUN 2008, p. 1330]. The report focused on the role and involvement of the UNAIDS secretariat, the 10 UNAIDS co-sponsors and other stakeholders in achieving the goal to halt, and begin to reverse, the spread of HIV/AIDS by 2015.

CEB members welcomed the report's wide-ranging review of a complex subject. UN system organizations commended JIU for recognizing the commitment and dedication of those working to address challenges posed by the HIV/AIDS pandemic. It was noted that achieving the MDGs depended principally on actions by Member States and that many of the recommendations contained in the report went beyond what organizations could achieve by themselves. In addition, some of the recommendations conflicted with the governance structures and mandates of the various co-sponsors, and therefore would be difficult to implement. The organizations indicated that JIU could have strengthened several of its recommendations by including examples of areas in which co-sponsor activities could improve. Although they supported the call for innovative ideas in the fight against HIV/AIDS, they stressed that there would be greater merit in the further alignment of existing mechanisms and the scaling up of demonstrated best practices. The organizations urged caution in considering the creation of additional funding mechanisms, as that would most likely cause more confusion and greater transaction costs. UN system agencies noted the report's call for continuing support for the development of an HIV

vaccine. While acknowledging that the development of a safe and effective HIV vaccine was a key component of a comprehensive response to the epidemic, they maintained that a vaccine would represent just one component of a complete package of prevention interventions, and advocated for the sustained implementation of such a package along with continuous work on mitigating the socio-economic factors contributing to increased transmission of HIV.

The General Assembly took note of the JIU report and the Secretary-General's and CEB comments on 9 September (**decision 63/560**). On 24 December, the General Assembly decided that the item on the implementation of the Declaration of Commitment on HIV/AIDS and the Political Declaration on HIV/AIDS would remain for consideration during its resumed sixty-fourth (2010) session (**decision 64/549**).

Joint UN Programme on HIV/AIDS

UNAIDS continued to serve as the main advocate for global action on HIV/AIDS. In 2009, UNAIDS had ten co-sponsors: the International Labour Organization; the United Nations Development Programme (UNDP); the United Nations Educational, Scientific and Cultural Organization; the United Nations Children's Fund (UNICEF); the Office of the United Nations High Commissioner for Refugees; the United Nations Office on Drugs and Crime (UNODC); WHO; WFP; the United Nations Population Fund (UNFPA); and the World Bank.

Report of Executive Director. In response to Economic and Social Council resolution 2007/32 [YUN 2007, p. 1265], the Secretary-General in May transmitted the report [E/2009/70] of the UNAIDS Executive Director, which provided an update on the AIDS epidemic and described results achieved by UNAIDS since the previous report to the Council [YUN 2007, p. 1263].

The Executive Director stated that tangible results had been achieved in the global response to AIDS, demonstrating that a collective and comprehensive commitment to addressing AIDS could produce positive outcomes. However, a continued and unwavering sense of urgency was required to address the long-term impact of AIDS. Improved modelling methods and expanded surveillance programmes had led to adjusted and generally lower estimates for global HIV incidence, prevalence and mortality. Expanded coverage of antiretroviral treatment, as well as access to mother-to-child transmission prevention services in low and middle-income countries, illustrated that universal access to treatment might be ambitious but ultimately achievable. At the country level, the Joint Programme consolidated its support to the national response by working in joint UN teams on AIDS. All partners continued to support the "Three Ones" principles [YUN 2004, p. 1219] for coordination of national AIDS responses—one national strategic framework, one coordinating authority and one monitoring and evaluation system. Achieving universal access to HIV prevention, treatment, care and support remained the core priority for UNAIDS. Methods and systems to help countries understand the epidemic continued to improve, owing to the work of the Joint Programme and its reference groups. As a result, more information was available about the diversity of national epidemics, which in turn could inform prevention strategies and coverage of HIV programming.

While many aspects of the epidemic were evolving over time, certain key elements appeared resistant to change, and without fundamental reforms in attitudes, beliefs and laws, the marginalization of people living with HIV and at-risk populations would continue to negate the efforts of those contributing to the AIDS response. A number of actions were proposed to the Council, including acknowledging the drivers of the epidemic, the importance of prevention, the gains made in terms of access to treatment, and the critical importance of people living with HIV to all aspects of national AIDS responses, global advocacy efforts and the work of the UN system.

AIDS epidemic update

According to the 2009 *AIDS Epidemic Update* [UNAIDS/09.36E/JC1700E], issued in November by UNAIDS and WHO, new HIV infections had been reduced by 17 per cent over the past eight years. Since 2001, when the United Nations Declaration of Commitment on HIV/AIDS was signed, the number of new infections in sub-Saharan Africa was approximately 15 per cent lower, which was about 400,000 fewer infections in 2008. In East Asia new HIV infections declined by nearly 25 per cent and in South and South East Asia by 10 per cent in the same period. In Eastern Europe, after a dramatic increase in new infections among injecting drug users, the epidemic had levelled off considerably. However, in some countries there were signs that new HIV infections were rising again.

According to the report, an estimated 33.4 million people were living with HIV worldwide, 2.7 million people were newly infected in 2008 and 2 million people died of AIDS-related illness in 2008. People were living longer due to the beneficial effects of antiretroviral therapy. The number of AIDS-related deaths had declined by over 10 per cent over the past five years as more people had gained access to the life-saving treatment.

UNAIDS activities

In 2009, the UNAIDS secretariat supported HIV prevention reviews in more than 30 countries, help-

ing countries analyse their prevention programmes to ensure that they met the needs of those most vulnerable to HIV infection. The UNAIDS Caribbean team supported Guyana in carrying out an HIV prevention mapping exercise that led to the development of the country's HIV prevention action plan.

WHO held a consultation involving more than 100 leading experts to review the scientific data available on the use of antiretroviral therapy for HIV prevention, taking into consideration human rights and public health implications. The meeting resulted in recommendations for future research.

At the global consultation in Tunisia organized by the UNAIDS secretariat on 'positive prevention', participants adopted the term 'positive health, dignity and prevention' to link the issues of HIV treatment, prevention, care and support within a human rights framework. As a result of the meeting, the United States Government's prevention strategy for 2010–2011 incorporated 'positive health, dignity and prevention' values and principles.

The UNFPA-led Global Condom Initiative expanded to include over 70 countries worldwide. As a result, access to female condoms dramatically increased, reaching a record number of 50 million in 2009. Partnership with several agencies helped to maximize access to male and female condoms through the public, civil society, social marketing and private sectors. Efforts were made to reach populations in remote and rural areas.

As a result of UNAIDS' advocacy to eliminate mother-to-child HIV transmission, the Global Fund to Fight AIDS, Tuberculosis and Malaria launched an initiative to ensure that at least 80 per cent of transmission prevention programmes supported by the Global Fund would provide combination regimens by December 2010. The Global Fund worked closely with the UNAIDS secretariat, UNICEF and WHO to accelerate the scale-up of transmission prevention programmes and to extend coverage to at least 60 per cent of women in need globally.

More than 4 million people in low- and middle-income countries were receiving antiretroviral therapy at the end of 2008, representing a 36 per cent increase in one year and a ten-fold increase over five years. Other gains included expanded HIV testing and counselling and improved access to services to prevent HIV transmission from mother to child.

To make HIV treatment more affordable, WHO supported efforts to reduce the cost of HIV medicines and diagnostics. WHO published a report entitled *Transaction prices for antiretroviral medicines and HIV diagnostics from 2004 to October 2009*, which facilitated price reduction negotiations and access to cheaper products. During 2008 and 2009, WHO and UNDP assisted 75 countries to amend patent legislation to facilitate greater use of generic antiretroviral drugs.

In 2009, UNAIDS made the integration of tuberculosis and HIV services a programme-wide priority. The UNAIDS secretariat supported a series of workshops in Dakar and Bali to encourage countries to develop integrated tuberculosis/HIV plans.

Civil society groups in more than 40 countries benefited from capacity-building support by UNODC to reduce stigma and discrimination towards people using drugs. Advocacy, policy guidance and technical support facilitated the inclusion of people using drugs in Nepal's national HIV strategy, as well as the integration of gender-sensitive harm reduction services in the HIV strategy of India. In the Russian Federation, more than 150 police officers received harm reduction training in five regions.

In 2008 and 2009, UNAIDS strengthened its efforts to support people living with HIV through expanded employment opportunities. Pilot projects were supported in 17 countries to create employment opportunities through microfinance initiatives, and networks of people living with HIV and other stakeholders in 17 countries received technical support for the development of social protection schemes and income-generating initiatives. Seven countries in Africa and Asia received guidance and support to extend social security schemes to people living with HIV.

Technical guides and frameworks. In February, WHO, UNODC and UNAIDS issued a *Technical Guide for Countries to Set Targets for Universal Access to HIV Prevention, Treatment and Care for Injecting Drug Users.* The document provided technical guidance on setting ambitious but achievable national targets for attaining universal access to HIV/AIDS prevention, treatment and care in that area.

In May, UNAIDS issued the *Joint Action for Results: UNAIDS Outcome Framework 2009–2011* to optimize partnerships between the UNAIDS secretariat and the 10 co-sponsoring UN organizations. The *Framework* would guide future investment and hold the secretariat and the co-sponsors accountable for making their resources work for results.

The *UNAIDS Action Framework: Universal Access for Men who have Sex with Men and Transgender People*, issued in May, aimed at fostering and facilitating universal access to appropriate HIV prevention, care, treatment and support in that area.

In August, UNAIDS issued the *UNAIDS Action Framework: Addressing Women, Girls, Gender Equality and HIV*, which focused on the critical need to scale up policies and programming in that area.

Programme Coordinating Board. The report [DP/2009/39-DP/FPA/2009/14] on the implementation of the recommendations of the UNAIDS Programme Coordinating Board (PCB) focused on implementation of decisions from the twenty-third PCB meeting, held in December 2008, and plans for follow-up on

the decisions of the twenty-fourth PCB meeting held in June 2009. Key issues addressed at the meetings included: the 2010–2011 UNAIDS unified budget and workplan (UBW); intensifying action on gender equality and AIDS; partnerships between UNAIDS and the Global Fund to Fight AIDS, Tuberculosis and Malaria; progress in the second independent evaluation of UNAIDS; UNAIDS participation in One UN pilots; and HIV, forced displacement and migrant populations.

The UBW, which was endorsed by PCB in June, united in a single framework the activities of the 10 UNAIDS co-sponsors and the UNAIDS secretariat. The 2010–2011 UBW prioritized progress towards the goal of universal access to HIV prevention, treatment, care and support, as well as contributing to the achievement of the MDGs. In addition, a UBW performance monitoring framework was designed to monitor and assess results and to increase accountability.

PCB noted that gender inequality and unequal power relations between women and men continued to be major drivers of HIV transmission. UNDP coordinated an inter-agency process, working with UNFPA, UNAIDS and UNIFEM to develop a UNAIDS action framework for addressing women, girls, gender equality and HIV. In parallel to supporting inter-agency collaboration, UNDP focused on several key areas to ensure that national AIDS programmes addressed critical gender issues. UNFPA support contributed to increased demand for quality HIV prevention services, especially for women and other vulnerable groups. UNFPA supported a global symposium on engaging men and boys in achieving gender equality (Rio de Janeiro, Brazil, 29 March–3 April) and published and disseminated advocacy tools, action briefs and guidance documents.

The twenty-third PCB meeting included a thematic segment focusing on the relationship between UNAIDS and the Global Fund to Fight AIDS, Tuberculosis and Malaria. Following the thematic segment, PCB requested that the UNAIDS secretariat and co-sponsors work with the Global Fund to advance mutual goals, including support for implementing Global Fund HIV grants and assistance to countries to reduce duplication between national AIDS coordinating authorities and Global Fund country coordinating mechanisms.

Progress reports for the second independent evaluation of UNAIDS, which assessed the effectiveness of UNAIDS at global, regional and country levels, were presented to PCB in December 2008 and June 2009. The evaluation addressed the evolving role of UNAIDS, the administration of UNAIDS as a joint programme, "Delivering as one", strengthening health systems, working with civil society, human rights and gender dimensions, and technical support.

The thematic segment of the twenty-fourth PCB meeting in June focused on the vulnerability of migrants and displaced persons to HIV. The segment encompassed four areas: mobility and labour; economic drivers and pull factors for mobility; forced displacement and humanitarian situations; and HIV-related travel restrictions. PCB requested that the UNAIDS secretariat and co-sponsors ensure that their staff facilitate the incorporation of mobile populations into regional and national AIDS strategies, and support Governments in harmonizing laws and policies on HIV testing to ensure adherence to internationally accepted standards.

At its meeting in June 2007, PCB examined a report on UNAIDS participation in One UN country pilots, which highlighted the experience and challenges of the UNAIDS model in informing UN reform efforts. PCB requested that the UNAIDS secretariat and co-sponsors strengthen their capacity for effective involvement in the "Delivering as one" agenda.

ECONOMIC AND SOCIAL COUNCIL ACTION

On 24 July [meeting 36], the Economic and Social Council adopted **resolution 2009/6** [draft: E/2009/L.23] without vote [agenda item 7 *(g)*].

Joint United Nations Programme on HIV/AIDS (UNAIDS)

The Economic and Social Council,

Recalling its resolution 2007/32 of 27 July 2007,

Welcoming the report of the Executive Director of the Joint United Nations Programme on HIV/AIDS (UNAIDS), and expressing its appreciation for the concerted efforts of the secretariat of the Joint Programme and its co-sponsoring agencies in fighting HIV/AIDS,

Recalling the goals and targets set forth in the Declaration of Commitment on HIV/AIDS, adopted by the General Assembly at its twenty-sixth special session, held in 2001, the 2005 World Summit Outcome and the Political Declaration on HIV/AIDS, adopted by the Assembly at its High-level Meeting on HIV/AIDS, held in 2006, as well as the HIV/AIDS-related goals contained in the United Nations Millennium Declaration of 2000,

Recognizing that HIV/AIDS constitutes a global emergency, poses one of the most formidable challenges to the development, progress and stability of individual societies and the world at large and requires an exceptional and comprehensive global response, while acknowledging the need to maximize synergies between the AIDS response and the broader health and development agendas in a timely manner,

Expressing serious concern about the continued global spread of HIV/AIDS, which exacerbates poverty and gender inequalities and poses a major public-health challenge and a threat to economic and social development and to food security in heavily affected regions,

Expressing serious concern also about the lack of progress, twenty-eight years into the HIV/AIDS pandemic, in developing effective prevention technologies, including an HIV vaccine, and recognizing that ensuring sustained financial and political support for research and development over the long term will be a critical factor in finding effective prevention technologies,

Acknowledging the adverse impact of the global economic and financial crisis on funding for the AIDS response and the need to mitigate its impact on the gap that already exists between available resources and the human, technical and financial resources necessary to combat HIV/AIDS,

Recognizing the contribution of new, voluntary and innovative financing approaches and initiatives, such as the International Drug Purchase Facility, UNITAID, as well as the need to support and strengthen existing financial mechanisms, including the Global Fund to Fight AIDS, Tuberculosis and Malaria, and relevant United Nations organizations, through the provision of funds in a sustained manner in order to address the funding gap and thereby to ensure an effective and successful response to the HIV/AIDS pandemic,

Reaffirming the importance of global coordination efforts to scale up sustainable, intensified and comprehensive HIV/AIDS responses, in a comprehensive and inclusive partnership, as called for in the Political Declaration on HIV/AIDS, with people living with HIV, vulnerable groups, most affected communities, civil society and the private sector, within the framework of the "Three Ones" principles,

1. *Urges* the Joint United Nations Programme on HIV/AIDS (UNAIDS) and other relevant organizations and bodies of the United Nations system to intensify their support to Governments, with a view to achieving the goals contained in the United Nations Millennium Declaration and the goals and targets contained in the Declaration of Commitment on HIV/AIDS, the 2005 World Summit Outcome and the Political Declaration on HIV/AIDS;

2. *Commends* the support provided by the Joint Programme to the process of achieving universal access to prevention, treatment, care and support by 2010, in particular its assistance to countries in setting their national targets for universal access;

3. *Welcomes* the submission by Member States of a total of one hundred and forty-seven country progress reports in 2008 as part of the reporting process set out in the Declaration of Commitment on HIV/AIDS, which provided the most comprehensive overview to date of the response at the country level, and encourages all Member States to provide full support for the next round of reports, due on 31 March 2010;

4. *Acknowledges* the insidious and persistent drivers of the epidemic, in particular stigma, discrimination, gender inequality, socio-economic inequality and lack of respect for human rights, also acknowledges that in some cases food insecurity and displacements, for example, can lead to increased vulnerability, and encourages intensified analysis and advocacy by the Joint Programme to ensure that underlying obstacles to universal access are understood and appropriately addressed at all levels and in all settings, including through services to underserved and vulnerable populations;

5. *Emphasizes* the importance of comprehensive, evidence-informed HIV prevention programmes as an essential element of national, regional and international responses, through which actions and policies are tailored to the local profile of the epidemic, and commits to further intensifying efforts in this regard;

6. *Welcomes* the publication entitled "Joint Action for Results: UNAIDS Outcome Framework 2009–2011", for moving towards the goal of universal access, including the recognition by the Joint Programme of the need to improve the effectiveness of efforts to prevent the sexual transmission of HIV, the elimination of vertical transmission from mother to child and the importance of linking HIV and sexual and reproductive health;

7. *Recognizes* the need to link the AIDS response more closely with the overall response to achieving the Millennium Development Goals, particularly those related to health;

8. *Acknowledges* the need to address the underlying obstacles to the achievement of the goal of universal access to prevention, treatment, care and support, including the gap in available human, technical and financial resources, as well as inadequately functioning health systems, in order to ensure an effective and successful response to HIV/AIDS;

9. *Reaffirms* the right to use, to the full, the provisions contained in the World Trade Organization Agreement on Trade-related Aspects of Intellectual Property Rights (TRIPS Agreement), the Doha Declaration on the TRIPS Agreement and Public Health, the decision of the General Council of the World Trade Organization of 30 August 2003 on the implementation of paragraph 6 of the Doha Declaration on the TRIPS Agreement and Public Health, and, when formal acceptance procedures have been completed, the amendments to article 31 of the TRIPS Agreement, adopted by the General Council of the World Trade Organization in its decision of 6 December 2005, which provide flexibilities for the protection of public health, and, in particular, to promote access to medicines for all, and also calls for a broad and timely acceptance of the amendment to article 31 of the TRIPS Agreement;

10. *Recalls* the Global Strategy and Plan of Action on Public Health, Innovation and Intellectual Property, adopted by the World Health Assembly, and urges States, the relevant international organizations and other relevant stakeholders to actively support its wide implementation;

11. *Urges* Governments to prioritize and expand access to the prevention and treatment of HIV-related opportunistic infections, to promote access to and the effective use of safe and effective antiretroviral drugs of assured quality, at affordable prices, and to support both biomedical and socio-economic research on new products to prevent HIV infection, including those controlled by women, diagnostics, medicines and other treatment commodities and technologies related to HIV;

12. *Urges* Governments, donors and other stakeholders to continue to provide financial and political support for research and the development of an effective HIV vaccine;

13. *Encourages* the strengthening of the United Nations response to AIDS at the country level, the UNAIDS technical support division of labour and the concept of a joint United Nations team and programme on AIDS, with the aim of harmonizing technical support, strengthening programmatic coherence and improving the collective accountability of the United Nations system at the country level;

14. *Encourages* the Joint Programme to fully participate in the process of reforming the operational activities of the United Nations, including in the context of progress

made in increasing coherence in the delivery of development assistance by the United Nations, in particular in the pilot programme countries, within the framework of the role of the Joint Programme as the coordinator of responses to HIV/AIDS;

15. *Urges* Governments, donors and other stakeholders, including the Joint Programme, to promote coherence in the support provided to and the alignment with national HIV/AIDS response strategies in a transparent, accountable and effective manner, within the framework of the "Three Ones" principles;

16. *Acknowledges* the critical importance of people living with HIV to all aspects of national AIDS responses, global advocacy efforts and the work of the United Nations system on AIDS, and encourages increased support for the capacity of civil society to carry out programme implementation and advocacy, directed towards the goal of ensuring universal access to prevention, treatment, care and support;

17. *Encourages* improved collaboration between the Joint Programme and the Global Fund to Fight AIDS, Tuberculosis and Malaria, aimed at strengthening the meaningful participation of African States through the pilot initiative, which is to be monitored and potentially extended to other regions, and in the Programme Coordinating Board of the Joint Programme and the Board of the Global Fund;

18. *Welcomes* the *Report of the International Task Team on HIV-related Travel Restrictions: Findings and Recommendations—December 2008,* and further encourages all countries to eliminate HIV-specific restrictions on entry, stay and residence and to ensure that people living with HIV are no longer excluded, detained or deported on the basis of their HIV status;

19. *Recognizes* the need for the Joint Programme to significantly expand and strengthen its work with national Governments and to work with all groups of civil society in order to address the gap in access to services for injecting drug users in all settings, including prisons, to develop comprehensive models of appropriate service delivery for injecting drug users, to tackle the issues of stigmatization and discrimination and to support increased capacity and resources for the provision of a comprehensive package of services for injecting drug users, including harm reduction programmes in relation to HIV, as elaborated in the *WHO, UNODC, UNAIDS Technical Guide for Countries to Set Targets for Universal Access to HIV Prevention, Treatment and Care for Injecting Drug Users,* in accordance with relevant national circumstances;

20. *Welcomes* the promulgation of the *UNAIDS Action Framework: Universal Access for Men Who Have Sex with Men and Transgender People* and the follow-up action that is already under way, and calls upon the Joint Programme and other partners to support further action and to strengthen partnerships to address the political, social, legal and economic barriers to universal access, as part of the agreed Unified Budget and Workplan priorities;

21. *Recognizes* the interrelated nature of the health- and gender-related Millennium Development Goals, and welcomes the progress made by the Joint Programme in assisting countries in accelerating action on women, girls and gender equality within the context of AIDS, including the appointment of an advisory working group, under the

leadership of the Executive Director, to develop, implement and monitor an operational plan for the strengthened inter-agency strategy on the subject (the UNAIDS Action Framework: Addressing Women, Girls, Gender Equality and HIV);

22. *Looks forward* to the consideration by the Programme Coordinating Board of the Joint Programme at its twenty-fifth meeting, to be held in Geneva from 8 to 10 December 2009, of a report on the anticipated impact that the global financial and economic crisis will have on the ability of countries to meet their universal access targets, to include recommendations and mitigation strategies;

23. *Calls upon* the Joint Programme to provide a critical, constructive, inclusive and transparent response to the second independent evaluation of UNAIDS, to be presented to the Programme Coordinating Board of the Joint Programme at its twenty-fifth meeting;

24. *Requests* the Secretary-General to transmit to the Economic and Social Council, at its substantive session of 2011, a report prepared by the Executive Director of the Joint Programme, in collaboration with its co-sponsors and other relevant organizations and bodies of the United Nations system, on progress made in implementing a coordinated response by the United Nations system to the HIV/AIDS pandemic.

Non-communicable diseases

During 2009, the impact of the global economic crisis on progress towards achieving the health-related MDGs, including universal access to HIV prevention, treatment and care, remained a concern. At the Commonwealth Heads of Government meeting (Trinidad and Tobago, 27–29 November), attended by representatives from 49 countries, the "Statement on Commonwealth Action to Combat Non-Communicable Diseases (NCDs)" was adopted. Government Heads noted that international cooperation was critical in addressing the phenomenon of NCDs and called for the consideration of a summit to be held in September 2011, under the auspices of the UN General Assembly, in order to develop strategic responses to those diseases and their repercussions.

Tobacco

The WHO Framework Convention on Tobacco Control, adopted by the World Health Assembly in 2003 [YUN 2003, p. 1251], entered into force in 2005. At the end of 2009, 168 States and the European Union were parties to the Convention. In December, WHO released a summary report on global progress in implementing the Convention [FCTC/2009.1].

WHO's *Report on the Global Tobacco Epidemic, 2009* focused on implementing smoke-free environments around the world. The report indicated that tobacco use continued to kill more than 5 million people worldwide each year, mostly in low- and middle-income countries. It also documented many gains

in tobacco control over the previous year. Seventeen countries had comprehensive smoke-free laws. Seven countries had adopted such laws in 2008, including some countries that progressed from minimal or no protection to full protection in public places. However, only 9 per cent of countries mandated smoke-free bars and restaurants, and 65 countries reported no implementation of any smoke-free policies.

Intergovernmental Negotiating Body on a Protocol on Illicit Trade in Tobacco Products. The third session of the Intergovernmental Negotiating Body on a Protocol on Illicit Trade in Tobacco Products (Geneva, 28 June–5 July) [FCTC/COP/INB-IT/3/REC/1 & 2] was attended by representatives of 136 States parties, 13 States non-parties, two intergovernmental organizations and seven non-governmental organizations (NGOs). Participants agreed [FCTC/COP/INB-IT/3(1)] on a negotiating text that would form the basis for further negotiations.

Smoke-free UN premises. In response to Assembly resolution 63/8 [YUN 2008, p. 1334], the Secretary-General in August transmitted a report on smoke-free UN premises [A/64/335], prepared by WHO in consultation with the Department of Management at Headquarters, offices away from Headquarters and regional commissions. The Secretary-General had received positive feedback on smoke-free measures from representatives of Member States as well as staff members; however, it would take personal commitment and a sense of responsibility for oneself and the well-being of others to fully implement the smoking ban. He called on staff, delegations and visitors to the United Nations to respect their own health and that of others and to refrain from smoking on the premises.

Malaria

Roll Back Malaria initiative

In August, the Secretary-General transmitted a report [A/64/302], prepared by WHO pursuant to General Assembly resolution 63/234 [YUN 2008, p. 1335], on the Decade to Roll Back Malaria in Developing Countries, Particularly in Africa (2001–2010), which was proclaimed by the Assembly in resolution 55/284 [YUN 2001, p. 1139]. The report was based on data collected for the *World Malaria Report 2009*, which would be published in October. It highlighted progress made and strategies needed to meet malaria-related goals by 2010.

While funding for malaria control had increased as a result of coordinated global advocacy efforts, most countries were likely to need universal coverage with insecticide-treated nets and other interventions in order to reach the 2010 targets. Major potential threats to malaria control and elimination were parasite resistance to medicines and mosquito resistance to pyrethroid insecticides. The regular monitoring of the efficacy of medicines and insecticides needed to become a routine component of malaria programmes. Diagnostic facilities for malaria needed to be scaled up and integrated into the management of the sick child. The quality of commodities and services was an increasingly critical issue as scale-up intensified. Access to malaria treatment was an important issue, in addition to timely malaria surveillance systems.

Intervention coverage was increasing in Africa and globally, and an impact was confirmed in those countries with prior low-to-moderate malaria transmission and higher intervention coverage. Initial evidence from Sao Tome and Principe, Zambia and the islands of Zanzibar pointed to a substantially higher reduction in child mortality than previously estimated— a greater than 40 per cent reduction in all-cause inpatient child deaths if malaria inpatient child deaths were reduced by 90 per cent. That indicated that aggressive malaria control could be the leading edge for many African countries to reach, by 2015, the target of a two-thirds reduction in child mortality, as set forth in the MDGs. The Secretary-General concluded that nearly all of the 1 million malaria deaths each year could be prevented with the universal application of existing tools.

GENERAL ASSEMBLY ACTION

On 7 December [meeting 60], the General Assembly adopted **resolution 64/79** [draft: A/64/L.28 & Add.1] without vote [agenda item 47].

2001–2010: Decade to Roll Back Malaria in Developing Countries, Particularly in Africa

The General Assembly,

Recalling that the period 2001–2010 has been proclaimed the Decade to Roll Back Malaria in Developing Countries, Particularly in Africa, by the General Assembly, and that combating HIV/AIDS, malaria, tuberculosis and other diseases is included in the internationally agreed development goals, including the Millennium Development Goals,

Recalling also its resolution 63/234 of 22 December 2008 and all previous resolutions concerning the struggle against malaria in developing countries, particularly in Africa,

Recalling further World Health Assembly resolution 60.18 of 23 May 2007 urging a broad range of national and international actions to scale up malaria control programmes and resolution 61.18 of 24 May 2008 on monitoring of the achievement of the health-related Millennium Development Goals,

Bearing in mind the relevant resolutions of the Economic and Social Council relating to the struggle against malaria and diarrhoeal diseases, in particular resolution 1998/36 of 30 July 1998,

Taking note of the declarations and decisions on health issues adopted by the Organization of African Unity, in particular the declaration and plan of action on the "Roll Back Malaria" initiative adopted at the Extraordinary Summit of Heads of State and Government of the Organization of African Unity, held in Abuja on 24 and 25 April 2000, as well as decision AHG/Dec.155(XXXVI) concerning the implementation of that declaration and plan of action, adopted by the Assembly of Heads of State and Government of the Organization of African Unity at its thirty-sixth ordinary session, held in Lomé from 10 to 12 July 2000,

Also taking note of the Maputo Declaration on Malaria, HIV/AIDS, Tuberculosis and Other Related Infectious Diseases, adopted by the Assembly of the African Union at its second ordinary session, held in Maputo from 10 to 12 July 2003, and the Abuja call for accelerated action towards universal access to HIV and AIDS, tuberculosis and malaria services in Africa, issued by the Heads of State and Government of the African Union at the special summit of the African Union on HIV and AIDS, tuberculosis and malaria, held in Abuja, from 2 to 4 May 2006,

Recognizing the linkages in efforts being made to reach the targets set at the Abuja Summit in 2000 as necessary and important for the attainment of the "Roll Back Malaria" goal and the targets of the Millennium Development Goals by 2010 and 2015, respectively, and welcoming in this regard the commitment of Member States to respond to the specific needs of Africa,

Also recognizing that malaria-related ill health and deaths throughout the world can be substantially reduced with political commitment and commensurate resources if the public is educated and sensitized about malaria and appropriate health services are made available, particularly in countries where the disease is endemic,

Acknowledging the progress made in parts of Africa in reversing the malaria epidemic through political engagement and sustainable national malaria control programmes, and recognizing the challenges of making the most effective use of available resources as well as rapid and accurate diagnoses,

Expressing concern about the continued morbidity, mortality and debility attributed to malaria, and recalling that more efforts are needed if the malaria targets for 2010 and the malaria and Millennium Development Goal targets for 2015 are to be reached on time,

Emphasizing the importance of strengthening health systems to effectively support malaria control and elimination,

Commending the efforts of the World Health Organization, the United Nations Children's Fund, the Roll Back Malaria Partnership, the Global Fund to Fight AIDS, Tuberculosis and Malaria, the World Bank and other partners to fight malaria over the years,

Taking note with appreciation of the Roll Back Malaria Global Strategic Plan 2005–2015 and the Global Malaria Action Plan developed by the Roll Back Malaria Partnership,

1. *Welcomes* the report prepared by the World Health Organization, and calls for support for the recommendations contained therein;

2. *Encourages* Member States, relevant organizations of the United Nations system, international institutions, non-governmental organizations, the private sector and civil society to continue to observe World Malaria Day and to collaborate in the observance of the final year of the Decade to Roll Back Malaria in Developing Countries,

Particularly in Africa, in order to raise public awareness of and knowledge about the prevention, control and treatment of malaria as well as the importance of meeting the Millennium Development Goals;

3. *Encourages* the Special Envoy of the Secretary-General for Malaria to continue raising the issue in collaboration with other United Nations organizations already working on those issues on the international political and development agendas and to work with national and global leaders to help to secure the political will, the partnerships and the funds to drastically reduce malaria deaths by 2010 through increased access to protection and treatment, especially in Africa;

4. *Welcomes* the launch on 23 September 2009 in New York of the African Leaders Malaria Alliance to provide political leadership at the highest level in the fight against malaria in Africa;

5. *Also welcomes* the United Against Malaria campaign which aims at uniting football stars and teams, governmental and non-governmental organizations, foundations and corporations in the fight against malaria ahead of the 2010 International Federation of Association Football World Cup event, to be held in South Africa;

6. *Further welcomes* the increased funding for malaria interventions and for research and development of preventive and control tools from the international community, through funding from multilateral and bilateral sources and from the private sector, as well as by making predictable financing available through appropriate and effective aid modalities and in-country health financing mechanisms aligned with national priorities, which are key to strengthening health systems and promoting universal and equitable access to high-quality malaria prevention and treatment services;

7. *Urges* the international community, together with United Nations agencies and private organizations and foundations, to support the implementation of the Global Malaria Action Plan, including through support for programmes and activities at the country level in order to achieve internationally agreed targets on malaria;

8. *Calls upon* the international community to continue to support the secretariat of the Roll Back Malaria Partnership and partner organizations, including the World Health Organization, the World Bank and the United Nations Children's Fund, as vital complementary sources of support for the efforts of malaria-endemic countries to combat the disease;

9. *Appeals* to the international community to work in a spirit of cooperation towards effective, increased, harmonized and sustained bilateral and multilateral assistance to combat malaria, including support for the Global Fund to Fight AIDS, Tuberculosis and Malaria, in order to assist States, in particular malaria-endemic countries, to implement sound national plans, in particular health plans and sanitation plans, including malaria control strategies and integrated management of childhood illnesses, in a sustained and equitable way that, inter alia, contributes to health system development;

10. *Appeals* to the malaria partners to resolve the financial and delivery bottlenecks that are responsible for stockouts of long-lasting insecticide-treated nets, artemisinin-based combination therapies and rapid diagnostic tests at the national level, whenever they occur, including through the strengthening of malaria programme management at the country level;

11. *Welcomes* the contribution to the mobilization of additional and predictable resources for development by voluntary innovative financing initiatives taken by groups of Member States, and in this regard notes the International Drug Purchase Facility, UNITAID, the International Finance Facility for Immunization, the Affordable Medicines Facility for Malaria, the Global Alliance for Vaccines and Immunization, the advance market commitment initiatives and the work of the High-level Task Force on Innovative International Financing for Health Systems;

12. *Urges* malaria-endemic countries to work towards financial sustainability, to increase, to the extent possible, domestic resource allocation to malaria control and to create favourable conditions for working with the private sector in order to improve access to good-quality malaria services;

13. *Urges* Member States to assess and respond to the needs for integrated human resources at all levels of the health system, in order to achieve the targets of the Abuja Declaration on Roll Back Malaria in Africa and the internationally agreed development goals, including the Millennium Development Goals, to take actions, as appropriate, to effectively govern the recruitment, training and retention of skilled health personnel, and to give particular focus to the availability of skilled personnel at all levels to meet technical and operational needs as increased funding for malaria control programmes becomes available;

14. *Calls upon* the international community, inter alia, by helping to meet the financial needs of the Global Fund to Fight AIDS, Tuberculosis and Malaria and through country-led initiatives with adequate international support, to intensify access to affordable, safe and effective antimalarial combination treatments, intermittent preventive treatment in pregnancies, adequate diagnostic facilities, long-lasting insecticide-treated mosquito nets, including, where appropriate, through the free distribution of such nets and, where appropriate, to insecticides for indoor residual spraying for malaria control, taking into account relevant international rules, including the Stockholm Convention on Persistent Organic Pollutants standards and guidelines;

15. *Requests* relevant international organizations, in particular the World Health Organization and the United Nations Children's Fund, to assist efforts of national Governments to provide universal access to malaria control interventions especially to address at-risk young children and pregnant women in malaria-endemic countries, particularly in Africa, as rapidly as possible, with due regard to ensuring proper use of those interventions, including long-lasting insecticide nets, and sustainability through full community participation and implementation through the health system;

16. *Calls upon* Member States, in particular malaria-endemic countries, with the support of the international community, to establish and/or strengthen national policies and operational plans, with a view to scaling up efforts to achieve internationally agreed malaria targets for 2010 and 2015, in accordance with the technical recommendations of the World Health Organization;

17. *Encourages* all African countries that have not yet done so to implement the recommendations of the Abuja Summit in 2000 to reduce or waive taxes and tariffs for nets and other products needed for malaria control, both to reduce the price of the products to consumers and to stimulate free trade in those products;

18. *Calls upon* United Nations agencies and their partners to continue to provide the technical support necessary to build and enhance the capacity of Member States to implement the Global Malaria Action Plan and meet the internationally agreed goals, including the Millennium Development Goals;

19. *Expresses its concern* about the increase in resistant strains of malaria in several regions of the world, and calls upon Member States, with support from the World Health Organization and other partners, to strengthen surveillance systems for drug and insecticide resistance and upon the World Health Organization to coordinate a global network for the monitoring of drug and insecticide resistance and to ensure that drug and insecticide testing is fully operational in order to enhance the use of current insecticide- and artemisinin-based combination therapies;

20. *Urges* all Member States experiencing resistance to conventional monotherapies to replace them with combination therapies, as recommended by the World Health Organization, and to develop the necessary financial, legislative and regulatory mechanisms in order to introduce artemisinin combination therapies at affordable prices and to prohibit the marketing of oral artemisinin monotherapies, in a timely manner;

21. *Recognizes* the importance of the development of safe and cost-effective vaccines and new medicines to prevent and treat malaria and the need for further and accelerated research, including into safe, effective and high-quality traditional therapies, using rigorous standards, including by providing support to the Special Programme for Research and Training in Tropical Diseases and through effective global partnerships, such as the various malaria vaccine initiatives and the Medicines for Malaria Venture, where necessary stimulated by new incentives to secure their development and through effective and timely support towards pre-qualification of new antimalarials and their combinations;

22. *Calls upon* the international community, including through existing partnerships, to increase investment in and efforts towards the research and development of new, safe and affordable malaria-related medicines, products and technologies, such as vaccines, rapid diagnostic tests, insecticides and delivery modes, to prevent and treat malaria, especially for at-risk children and pregnant women, in order to enhance effectiveness and delay the onset of resistance;

23. *Calls upon* malaria-endemic countries to assure favourable conditions for research institutions, including allocation of adequate resources and development of national policies and legal frameworks, where appropriate, with a view to, inter alia, informing policy formulation and strategic interventions on malaria;

24. *Reaffirms* the right to use, to the fullest extent, the provisions contained in the World Trade Organization Agreement on Trade-Related Aspects of Intellectual Property Rights (TRIPS Agreement), the Doha Declaration on the TRIPS Agreement and Public Health, the decision of the World Trade Organization's General Council of 30 August 2003 and amendments to article 31 of the Agreement, which provide flexibilities for the protection of public health, and in particular to promote access to medicines for all, including the production, under compulsory licensing, of generic drugs in the prevention and treatment of malaria, and resolves to assist developing countries in this regard;

25. *Calls upon* the international community to support ways to expand access to and the affordability of key products, such as vector control measures, including indoor residual spraying, long-lasting insecticide-treated nets and artemisinin-based combination therapy for populations at risk of exposure to resistant strains of falciparum malaria in malaria-endemic countries, particularly in Africa, including through additional funds and innovative mechanisms, inter alia, for the financing and scaling up of artemisinin production and procurement, as appropriate, to meet the increased need;

26. *Welcomes* the increased level of public-private partnerships for malaria control and prevention, including the financial and in-kind contributions of private sector partners and companies operating in Africa, as well as the increased engagement of non-governmental service providers;

27. *Encourages* the producers of long-lasting insecticide-treated nets to accelerate technology transfer to developing countries, and invites the World Bank and regional development funds to consider supporting malaria-endemic countries in establishing factories to scale up production of long-lasting insecticide-treated nets;

28. *Calls upon* the international community and malaria-endemic countries, in accordance with existing guidelines and recommendations of the World Health Organization and the requirements of the Stockholm Convention, to increase capacity for the safe, effective and judicious use of indoor residual spraying and other forms of vector control and for quality control measures to ensure conformity with international rules, standards and guidelines;

29. *Urges* the international community to become fully knowledgeable about World Health Organization technical policies and strategies and the provisions in the Stockholm Convention related to the use of DDT, including for indoor residual spraying, long-lasting insecticide-treated nets and case management, intermittent preventive treatment for pregnant women and monitoring of in vivo resistance studies to artemisinin-based combination therapy treatment, so that projects support those policies, strategies and provisions;

30. *Requests* the World Health Organization, the United Nations Children's Fund and donor agencies to provide support to those countries which choose to use DDT for indoor residual spraying so as to ensure that it is implemented in accordance with international rules, standards and guidelines, and to provide all possible support to malaria-endemic countries to manage the intervention effectively and prevent the contamination, in particular, of agricultural products with DDT and other insecticides used for indoor residual spraying;

31. *Encourages* the World Health Organization and its member States, with the support of the parties to the Stockholm Convention, to continue to explore possible alternatives to DDT as a vector control agent;

32. *Calls upon* malaria-endemic countries to encourage regional and intersectoral collaboration, both public and private, at all levels, especially in education, health, agriculture, economic development and the environment, to advance malaria control objectives;

33. *Calls upon* the international community to support the strengthening of health systems and national pharmaceutical policies, to monitor and fight against the trade in counterfeit antimalarial medicines and prevent their distribution and use, and to support coordinated efforts, inter alia, by providing technical assistance to improve surveillance, monitoring and evaluation systems and their alignment with national plans and systems so as to better track and report changes in coverage, the need for scaling up recommended interventions and the subsequent reductions in the burden of malaria;

34. *Urges* Member States, the international community and all relevant actors, including the private sector, to promote the coordinated implementation and enhance the quality of malaria-related activities, including via the Roll Back Malaria Partnership, in accordance with national policies and operational plans that are consistent with the technical recommendations of the World Health Organization and recent efforts and initiatives, including, where appropriate, the Paris Declaration on Aid Effectiveness and the Accra Agenda for Action, adopted during the Third High-level Forum on Aid Effectiveness, held in Accra from 2 to 4 September 2008;

35. *Notes* that the 2010 High-level Plenary Meeting of the sixty-fifth session of the General Assembly will provide an opportunity to review progress in achieving the Millennium Development Goals, and requests the Secretary-General, in close collaboration with the Director-General of the World Health Organization and in consultation with Member States, to submit to the Assembly at its sixty-fifth session a report on progress towards achieving the internationally agreed targets for 2010 and an evaluation of the implementation of the first Decade to Roll Back Malaria in Developing Countries, Particularly in Africa, including recommendations for further actions.

Global public health

High-level segment of Economic and Social Council

The Economic and Social Council, at the high-level segment of its 2009 substantive session (Geneva, 6–9 July) [A/64/3/Rev.1], discussed the theme of "Current global and national trends and their impact on social development, including public health", in accordance with its decision 2008/257 [YUN 2008, p. 1339].

The Council had before it an April report by the Secretary-General on the topic [E/2009/53] that focused on the effect of current global and national trends on poverty and hunger; social cohesion; public spending on social areas, such as social protection, safety nets, education and health; job security; and food security, along with implications for public health, including health spending and household health-seeking behaviour. The world economy was in

the most severe financial and economic crisis since the Great Depression. Unemployment rates were rising in many countries, straining national budgets and putting pressure on household disposable incomes. In many developing countries, that constituted a major setback in efforts to achieve the MDGs, in particular the goal of eradicating extreme poverty and hunger [YUN 2000, p. 51]. The Secretary-General outlined nine joint initiatives taken by CEB to assist countries and the global community to overcome the crisis, and recommended a range of short-term and medium-to-long-term measures at the global and national levels for managing the impact of current trends.

The Council also had before it the reports of the regional preparatory ministerial meetings for the annual ministerial review held in Beijing [E/2009/104], Accra [E/2009/106], Montego Bay [E/2009/109], Doha [E/2009/102] and Colombo [E/2009/88], as well as reports submitted by several NGOs [E/2009/NGO/1-32].

Parallel to its thematic discussion on 9 July, the Council held round tables on "Social trends and emerging challenges and their impact on public health: renewing our commitment to the vulnerable in a time of crisis" and "Trends in aid and aid effectiveness in the health sector".

On 10 July, the Council held a dialogue with the Executive Secretaries of the regional commissions on the theme "Regional perspectives on the global economic and financial crisis, including the impact on global public health". The Council had selected that theme for the item on regional cooperation on 26 March (**decision 2009/208**).

Annual ministerial review. On 7 and 8 July, the Council held its annual ministerial review on the theme "Implementing the internationally agreed goals and commitments in regard to global public health", in accordance with its decision 2007/272 [YUN 2007, p. 1425]. The Council also heard voluntary national presentations on the theme of the review by Japan [E/2009/86], Jamaica [A/2009/93], China [E/2009/94], Mali [E/2009/95], Bolivia [E/2009/96], the Sudan [E/2009/97] and Sri Lanka [E/2009/111].

The Council had before it a May report [E/2009/81] by the Secretary-General that reviewed the state of global health and how it was affected by food insecurity, climate change, conflict, and the recent economic crisis. The report also examined development cooperation for health, of inequities in health and access to health services, and partnerships for health. Underscoring that political leadership at the highest levels could make the greatest difference in galvanizing global and national efforts to promote and protect health, reduce inequities in health outcomes and access to services, and achieve the MDGs, the Secretary-General highlighted priority actions and recommendations to achieve the health-related MDGs and to ensure progress in universal health coverage, health system strengthening, and aid delivery and effectiveness.

The Council also had before it a Secretariat note [E/2009/101] summarizing the joint panel discussion held during the twelfth session (Geneva, 25–29 May) of the Commission on Science and Technology for Development on the theme "Delivering innovation in global public health", submitted in response to its resolution 2008/29 [YUN 2008, p. 1528].

Ministerial declaration. On 9 July, the Council adopted the ministerial declaration of its 2009 high-level segment, entitled "Implementing the internationally agreed goals and commitments in regard to global public health" [A/64/3/Rev.1]. It reaffirmed those commitments; recognized the link between health and poverty; stressed the need for a combination of good public-health policies and for international cooperation to meet emerging threats and epidemics, as well as the need to strengthen health information systems; stressed the need to scale up efforts towards meeting the HIV/AIDS-related goals; reaffirmed the importance of the Framework Convention on Tobacco Control; expressed concern at the continued increase in road traffic fatalities and injuries worldwide; noted with concern the lack of health workers and their imbalanced distribution throughout the world; and reaffirmed the values and principles of primary health care.

Global health and foreign policy

WHO report. Pursuant to General Assembly resolution 63/33 [YUN 2008, p. 1339], the Secretary-General in September transmitted to the General Assembly a report [A/64/365] on global health and foreign policy, prepared in collaboration with the WHO Director-General and after consultations with Member States. The report examined the links between health, poverty alleviation and development, as well as the role of health in relation to foreign policy, including controlling emerging infectious diseases such as the recent influenza A(H1N1) pandemic.

Recommendations for Member States included identifying priority global health issues that required foreign policy action; strengthening the political and institutional foundations for foreign policy action on global health; increasing the quantity and quality of health information; heightening the involvement of diplomatic forums in improving foreign policy efforts on global health; and training more diplomats and health officials in global health diplomacy.

GENERAL ASSEMBLY ACTION

On 10 December [meeting 62], the General Assembly adopted **resolution 64/108** [draft: A/64/L.16 & Add.1] without vote [agenda item 123].

Global health and foreign policy

The General Assembly,

Recalling its resolution 63/33 of 26 November 2008, entitled "Global health and foreign policy",

Recalling also the outcomes of the major United Nations conferences and summits in the economic, social and related fields, especially those related to global health,

Recalling further that achieving the health-related Millennium Development Goals is essential to socio-economic development, concerned by the relatively slow progress in achieving them, and mindful that special consideration should be given to the situation in sub-Saharan Africa,

Noting the adoption by the World Health Assembly on 24 May 2008 of its resolution 61.18, by which it initiated its annual monitoring of the achievement of the health-related Millennium Development Goals,

Recalling its resolutions 58/3 of 27 October 2003, 59/27 of 23 November 2004 and 60/35 of 30 November 2005, all entitled "Enhancing capacity-building in global public health", the resolutions of the World Health Assembly, in particular resolution 60.28 of 23 May 2007 and resolution 62.10 of 22 May 2009, both entitled "Pandemic influenza preparedness: sharing of influenza viruses and access to vaccines and other benefits", and resolution 62.16 of 22 May 2009, entitled "Global strategy and plan of action on public health, innovation and intellectual property",

Noting the contribution of the High-level Forum on Advancing Global Health in the Face of Crisis, which took place at United Nations Headquarters on 15 June 2009 and engaged multisectoral high representatives from around the world in the global health debate on protecting vulnerable populations, building resilient health systems and enhancing coherence towards multi-stakeholder strategic partnerships,

Welcoming the outcome of the annual ministerial review held by the Economic and Social Council in 2009, on the theme "Implementing the internationally agreed goals and commitments in regard to global public health",

Recognizing the leading role of the World Health Organization as the primary specialized agency for health, including its roles and functions with regard to health policy in accordance with its mandate,

Noting the role and contribution of the Foreign Policy and Global Health Initiative in promoting synergy between foreign policy and global health, as well as the contribution of the Oslo Ministerial Declaration entitled "Global health: a pressing foreign policy issue of our time" to placing health as a foreign policy issue on the international agenda,

Noting also the outcome of the Thirty-fourth Summit of the Group of Eight, held in Tōyako, Hokkaidō, Japan, from 7 to 9 July 2008, which highlighted the principles for action on global health to achieve all the health-related Millennium Development Goals,

Emphasizing that the United Nations system has an important responsibility to assist Governments in the follow-up to and full implementation of agreements and commitments reached at the major United Nations conferences and summits, especially those focusing on health-related areas,

Underscoring the fact that global health is also a long-term objective which is local, national, regional and international in scope and requires sustained attention, commitment and closer international cooperation beyond emergency,

Reaffirming the commitment to strengthening health systems that deliver equitable health outcomes as the basis for a comprehensive approach, which requires appropriate attention to, inter alia, health financing, the health workforce, the procurement and distribution of medicines and vaccines, infrastructure, information systems, service delivery and political will in leadership and governance,

Appreciating the contribution made by civil society, including non-governmental organizations and the private sector, on issues related to foreign policy and global health,

Welcoming the ongoing partnerships between a variety of stakeholders at the local, national, regional and global levels aimed at addressing the multifaceted determinants of global health and the commitments and initiatives to accelerate progress on the health-related Millennium Development Goals, including those announced at the high-level event on the Millennium Development Goals, held at United Nations Headquarters on 25 September 2008, and at the corresponding follow-up high-level event held on 23 September 2009,

Noting with concern that for millions of people throughout the world, the right of everyone to the enjoyment of the highest attainable standard of physical and mental health, including access to medicines, still remains a distant goal and that, in many cases, especially for those living in poverty, this goal is becoming increasingly remote,

1. *Notes with appreciation* the report of the Secretary-General and the recommendations contained therein;

2. *Recognizes* the close relationship between foreign policy and global health and their interdependence, and in that regard also recognizes that global challenges require concerted and sustained efforts by the international community;

3. *Stresses* the importance of achieving the health-related Millennium Development Goals;

4. *Welcomes* the ministerial declaration adopted during the annual ministerial review held by the Economic and Social Council in 2009 which focused on the theme "Implementing the internationally agreed goals and commitments in regard to global public health", and in that regard calls for enhanced coordination within the United Nations system;

I

Control of emerging infectious diseases and foreign policy

5. *Welcomes* the international coordinated actions in response to the recent influenza A (H1N1) pandemic as a good example of synergies between global health and foreign policy;

6. *Emphasizes* the need for further international cooperation to meet emerging, new and unforeseen threats and epidemics, such as the recent influenza A (H1N1) pandemic, and the H5N1 and other influenza viruses with human pandemic potential, and acknowledges the growing health problem of antimicrobial resistance;

7. *Recognizes* the need for a fair, transparent, equitable and efficient framework for the sharing of the H5N1 and other influenza viruses with human pandemic potential, and for the sharing of benefits, including access to and

distribution of affordable vaccines, diagnostics and treatments, to those in need, especially in developing countries, in a timely manner;

8. *Acknowledges with serious concern* that current global influenza vaccine production capacity remains insufficient to meet anticipated need in pandemic situations, particularly in developing countries, and that some countries cannot develop, produce, afford or access needed vaccines and other benefits, and acknowledges also in this regard the interlinkage with production capacity of seasonal influenza vaccines and the ability to ensure their effective use;

9. *Calls for* the strengthening of surveillance and response capacity at the national, regional and international levels through the full implementation of the International Health Regulations;

10. *Stresses* the importance of finalizing any remaining elements of the Pandemic Influenza Preparedness Framework for the sharing of influenza viruses and access to vaccines and other benefits;

11. *Acknowledges* that communication with the public must be improved in order to increase awareness of the steps in basic hygiene that citizens can and should take in order to lessen their risk of contracting and transmitting influenza;

II

Human resources for health and foreign policy

12. *Notes with concern* the lack of health workers, as well as their uneven distribution within countries and throughout the world, in particular the shortage in sub-Saharan Africa, which undermines the health systems of developing countries;

13. *Emphasizes* the need for countries to review policies, including recruitment policies and retention policies that exacerbate this problem;

14. *Underlines* the importance of national and international actions, including the development of health workforce plans, which are necessary to increase universal access to health services, including in remote and rural areas, taking into account the challenges facing developing countries in the retention of skilled health personnel, and in this regard encourages the finalization of a World Health Organization code of practice on the international recruitment of health personnel;

15. *Urges* Member States to affirm their commitment to the training of more health workers by promoting training in accredited institutions of a full spectrum of high-quality professionals, as well as community health workers, public health workers and para-professionals, in particular through international cooperation programmes including South-South cooperation, North-South cooperation and triangular cooperation;

III

Follow-up actions

16. *Urges* Member States to consider health issues in the formulation of foreign policy;

17. *Encourages* Member States, the United Nations system, academic institutions and networks to increase their capacity for the training of diplomats and health officials, in particular those from developing countries, on global health and foreign policy, by developing best practices and

guidelines for training and open-source information, and educational and training resources for this purpose;

18. *Requests* the Secretary-General, in close collaboration with the Director-General of the World Health Organization, with the participation of relevant programmes, funds and specialized agencies of the United Nations system, and in consultation with Member States, to submit a report to the General Assembly at its sixty-fifth session, under the item entitled "Global health and foreign policy", which, inter alia:

(a) Examines ways in which foreign and health policy coordination and coherence can be strengthened at the national, regional and international levels;

(b) Identifies institutional linkages;

(c) Makes concrete recommendations, with a specific focus on making foreign policy contribute better to creating a global policy environment supportive of global health, as a contribution to the High-level Plenary Meeting of the General Assembly to be held in September 2010.

On 24 December, the General Assembly decided that the item on global health and foreign policy would remain for consideration during its resumed sixty-fourth (2010) session (**decision 64/549**).

Follow-up to International Year of Sanitation

Report of Secretary-General. Pursuant to General Assembly resolution 61/192, which proclaimed 2008 the International Year of Sanitation [YUN 2006, p. 1419], the Secretary-General reported in July [A/64/169] that not only did the Year provide an opportunity to put the issue of sanitation in the spotlight, it galvanized the efforts and thinking of the international community to work more effectively and coherently. Advocacy efforts during the Year attracted widespread interest and inspired wide-ranging actions and partnerships. That momentum was expected to continue well beyond the Year with the key message that sanitation mattered and was an important development issue. However, efforts would need to approach the issue in a broader context and encompass all its aspects, including provision of basic sanitation services, sewerage, and wastewater treatment and reuse.

In terms of the three main expected results— awareness-raising, political buy-in and contribution to achieving the MDG target on sanitation—the activities of the Year in many ways exceeded expectations. The global momentum created by the launch and various media- and organization-specific events had slowly translated into activities and activism that were expected to continue well after the end of the Year. The Year had provided the structure, guidance and support to design and launch national and regional events targeted at politicians, decision-makers and the general public. It had prompted action by international organizations, development banks, Governments, NGOs, the private sector, sanitation experts and

practitioners, artists and private citizens. The strong partnerships forged during the Year should be maintained, the Secretary-General said. Governments should design and implement strong, gender-sensitive national policies and programmes. Low-cost sanitation and wastewater treatment and reuse technologies should be transferred and disseminated. Low-income countries should focus public spending on basic, low-cost sanitation facilities, leveraging household and community investments. Microcredit programmes should be expanded to include housing improvements such as water supply and sanitation. Public-private partnerships should play a role in financing and developing sanitation infrastructure. Efforts to mobilize large-scale private sector investment for urban sewerage and wastewater treatment systems in developing countries should be encouraged.

Road safety

WHO report. In August, the Secretary-General transmitted to the General Assembly a report [A/64/266] on improving global road safety, prepared by WHO in consultation with partners of the United Nations Road Safety Collaboration. The report indicated that, since the previous report [YUN 2007, p. 1271], many actions had been taken at the local, national and international levels. Existing programmes were maintained and had gained momentum, and new initiatives had emerged, including the first International Conference on Road Safety at Work, the first global status report on road safety, the first global project on setting road traffic casualty reduction targets, and the first meeting of road safety NGOs. That signified the increasing recognition by Member States and other stakeholders that action for road safety was urgent.

The report recommended that more action plans and strategies be developed, and that Member States monitor progress in road safety and continue strengthening dialogue on road traffic injury prevention. Member States were also encouraged to participate in the global ministerial conference on road safety (see below) and to support efforts to establish a decade of action for road safety for the 10 years leading to 2020.

On 24 December, the Assembly decided that the item on the global road safety crisis would remain for consideration during its resumed sixty-fourth (2010) session (**decision 64/549**).

Global ministerial conference on road safety

The first Global Ministerial Conference on Road Safety (Moscow, 19–20 November) brought together Ministers and representatives of Governments, international governmental organizations, NGOs and private bodies. On 2 December, the Russian Federation transmitted to the General Assembly the Moscow Declaration adopted at the Conference [A/64/540]. The Declaration emphasized the need for global sustained action on road safety, while acknowledging the work of the United Nations and other stakeholders in implementing road safety initiatives. Participants resolved to implement recommendations of the *World Report on Road Traffic Injury Prevention* [YUN 2004, p. 1223]; set national road traffic casualty reduction targets; promote harmonization of road safety and vehicle safety regulations; implement safer and more sustainable transportation, including alternative forms of transportation; improve national data collection and comparability at the international level; and invite the Assembly to declare the decade 2011–2020 as the Decade of Action for Road Safety.

Food and agriculture

Food aid

World Food Programme

At its 2009 substantive session in July, the Economic and Social Council had before it two reports pertaining to the World Food Programme (WFP): the annual report of WFP for 2008 [E/2009/14] and the report of the WFP Executive Board on its first and second regular sessions and annual session of 2008 [E/2009/36]. The Council took note of those reports on 22 July (**decision 2009/215**).

The WFP Executive Board, at its 2009 sessions [E/2010/36]—first regular session (9–11 February), annual session (8–12 June) and second regular session (9–12 November)—all of which were held in Rome, decided on organizational and programme matters and approved several projects. In November, the Board approved the biennial programme of work of the Executive Board for 2010–2011 [WFP/2009/EB.2/19].

WFP activities

According to its Annual Performance Report for 2009 [WFP/EB.A/2010/4], WFP distributed 4.6 million metric tons of food aid, two thirds of which was channelled through humanitarian interventions. A total of 101.8 million hungry people—including 84 million women and children—were assisted in 75 countries during the year.

In 2009, the first implementation year of the new Strategic Plan [YUN 2008, p. 1342], WFP began the transition from a focus on food aid to providing hunger solutions. In addition to reinforcing its core focus

on emergency response, WFP launched new initiatives that included improved approaches to tackling malnutrition; operationalizing Purchase for Progress (P4P), a programme seeking to improve market opportunities for smallholder farmers; and the use of cash transfers and vouchers to address food needs and protect markets.

World hunger reached a historic high in 2009, with 1.02 billion people being undernourished as a result of the combined effects of the food, fuel and financial crises exacerbating vulnerability caused by disasters, conflict and poverty. There were unprecedented attacks on WFP staff and other humanitarian workers; in October, a suicide bomber killed five WFP staff members and seriously injured four others at WFP's Islamabad office. Truck drivers delivering WFP food to insecure regions were also vulnerable; five were killed in Afghanistan, the Occupied Palestinian Territory and the Sudan. Altogether, nine staff members and six contractors were killed in acts of violence in 2009; despite the threats, WFP staff continued to risk their lives each day to ensure that assistance reached the most vulnerable people.

Administrative and financial matters

In 2009, WFP scaled up food distribution as a result of the increase in operational activity and a decline in food prices from 2008 levels. Interim procedures to achieve full cost recovery were implemented. The Programme continued to pursue savings through administrative collaboration with the Rome-based agencies and climate-neutral initiatives. WFP spent $173 million in extrabudgetary funding for grants and trust funds in support of quality improvement and capacity development, primarily at the field level. WFP's corporate online platform for operational information, EPWeb, was overhauled in 2009 and site traffic increased by 22 per cent. WFP purchased 2.6 million metric tons of food in 2009, 80 per cent of which was sourced from 75 developing countries. That amounted to an 8 per cent decrease in quantity due to carry-over stocks from 2008.

Resources and financing

Contribution revenue for the year was $4.2 billion—$3.4 billion in cash and $760 million in kind. Contributions covered only 65 per cent of total estimated needs of $6.5 billion in 2009. Private-sector partnerships raised $145 million in cash and in kind. Contributions came from 79 donors. The United States was again the largest contributor, providing $1,757 million to the Programme. Expenditures amounted to $4.2 billion, $535 million more than in 2008, reflecting the increased operational activity.

JIU review

In December, the Joint Inspection Unit (JIU) submitted a review of management and administration in WFP [JIU/REP/2009/7], with the objective of identifying areas for improvement in governance, executive management, administration, strategic planning, budgeting, human resources management and oversight. The inspectors held interviews with WFP officials and representatives of other international organizations, NGOs and Member States, in particular members of the WFP Executive Board.

The review indicated that WFP played a primary role in achieving the MDGs, especially the goal to eradicate extreme poverty and hunger. The inspectors made 12 recommendations—nine directed to the Executive Director and three addressed to the Executive Board.

Food security

Food and Agriculture Organization

In 2009, the Food and Agriculture Organization of the United Nations (FAO) continued to address the world food crisis. FAO released two annual reports: the 2009 *State of Food Insecurity in the World*, with the theme "Economic crises—impacts and lessons learned", and the 2009 *State of Food and Agriculture*, with the theme "Livestock in the Balance".

The Committee on World Food Security, at its thirty-fifth session (Rome, Italy, 14–17 October) [C 2009/21-Rev.1], considered the impact of the economic crisis on food security and how various stakeholders were addressing the crisis at the national level.

On 4 December, the General Assembly adopted **resolution 64/72** on sustainable fisheries (see p. 1331), which welcomed the work carried out by FAO and its Committee on Fisheries, encouraged strengthened collaboration between FAO and the International Maritime Organization to combat illegal, unreported and unregulated fishing, and requested FAO to report to the Secretary-General on priorities for cooperation and coordination.

High-Level Meeting on Food Security

The High-Level Meeting on Food Security for All (Madrid, Spain, 26–27 January), a follow-up to the 2008 High-Level Conference on World Food Security [YUN 2008, p. 1343], was attended by more than 126 countries, 62 of which were represented at the ministerial level, in addition to international organizations, donor agencies and NGOs. The high-level meeting was held in order to address the effects of the volatility of food prices on the most vulnerable populations and to accelerate progress towards the eradication of extreme poverty and hunger.

On 18 February [A/63/732-E/2009/8], Spain transmitted to the Secretary-General the Madrid Declaration, which summarized the work done during the meeting, including agreements on short-, medium- and long-term food security measures, and reaffirmed the objectives of the 1996 World Food Summit [YUN 1996, p. 1129] and commitment to the MDGs. Participants reaffirmed that States had a primary responsibility to respect, fulfil and promote the right to access to adequate food, especially for children, women and other vulnerable groups. Participants expressed their determination to ensure access to adequate food for all in a sustainable manner, to improve nutrition, to stimulate food production, to strengthen social protection systems and to increase investment in all areas related to food security.

World Summit on Food Security

Sixty Heads of State and Government and 191 ministers from 182 countries and the European Community attended the World Summit on Food Security (Rome, 16–18 November). The Summit resulted in a declaration [WSFS 2009/2] that outlined strategic objectives, commitments and actions. The attending Heads of State and Government pledged to ensure national, regional and global action to eradicate extreme poverty and hunger; join efforts and expertise to work in the Global Partnership for Agriculture, Food Security and Nutrition; reverse the decline in domestic and international funding for agriculture, food security and rural development in developing countries; and proactively face the challenges of climate change to food security and the need for adaptation of, and mitigation in, agriculture. Countries also agreed to invest in country-owned plans; strive for a comprehensive twin-track approach to food security consisting of direct action to immediately tackle hunger for the most vulnerable and medium- and long-term agricultural, food security, nutrition and rural development programmes; improve governance of global food issues in partnership with stakeholders from the public and private sector; improve the efficiency, responsiveness, coordination and effectiveness of multilateral institutions; and ensure sustained and substantial commitment to investment in agriculture, food security and nutrition.

Agriculture development and food security

Communication. On 20 February [A/63/740], Namibia transmitted to the Secretary-General the Windhoek High-level Ministerial Declaration on African Agriculture in the Twenty-first Century: Meeting the Challenges, Making a Sustainable Green Revolution, adopted at a high-level meeting for the Africa region on that theme (Windhoek, Namibia, 9–10 February).

Report of Secretary-General. Pursuant to General Assembly resolution 63/235 [YUN 2008, p. 1343], the Secretary-General on 3 August submitted a report [A/64/221] that addressed agriculture development and food security within the context of national and international development policies.

The Secretary-General underlined that the food crisis of 2008 had drawn welcome attention to the long-existing problem of hunger and food insecurity. The global policy community had produced a range of analyses and agreements that provided a way forward towards an effective response to the crisis, including the strategic framework advanced initially under the Comprehensive Framework for Action [YUN 2008, p. 1343] and developed more fully by the Commission on Sustainable Development at its seventeenth session (see p. 799). The strategic framework included two components—the immediate component of improving the situation of households affected by the crisis and the longer-term component of building resilience against future shocks and ensuring the ability to sustain food security. The Secretary-General concluded that this agenda required concerted support from the international community. The review of the situation suggested that countries were making efforts to implement such a strategy, albeit with varying degrees of commitment and success, and still at some distance from the vision of an integrated strategy.

Special Representative on food security. On 29 October [SG/A/1203], the Secretary-General nominated David Nabarro (United Kingdom) as his Special Representative on Food Security and Nutrition. Dr. Nabarro was the coordinator of the High-Level Task Force on the Global Food Security Crisis [YUN 2008, p. 1343], which the Secretary-General had chaired since April 2008. As Special Representative, he would assist the Secretary-General as he encouraged and supported country-led actions for food security. The General Assembly welcomed that appointment by resolution 64/224 (see below).

GENERAL ASSEMBLY ACTION

On 21 December [meeting 66], the General Assembly, on the recommendation of the Second (Economic and Financial) Committee [A/64/427], adopted **resolution 64/224** without vote [agenda item 60].

Agriculture development and food security

The General Assembly,

Welcoming the establishment of the agenda item and the discussions that have been undertaken on agriculture development and food security in the General Assembly,

Welcoming also the convening of the World Summit on Food Security in Rome from 16 to 18 November 2009,

Recalling the Rio Declaration on Environment and Development, Agenda 21, the Programme for the Further Implementation of Agenda 21, the Johannesburg Declaration on Sustainable Development and the Plan of Implementation of the World Summit on Sustainable Development ("Johannesburg Plan of Implementation"), the Monterrey Consensus of the International Conference on Financing for Development, the 2005 World Summit Outcome and the Doha Declaration on Financing for Development: outcome document of the Follow-up International Conference on Financing for Development to Review the Implementation of the Monterrey Consensus,

Reaffirming the goal set out in paragraph 19 of the United Nations Millennium Declaration, to halve, by 2015, the proportion of the world's people whose income is less than one dollar a day and the proportion of people who suffer from hunger,

Recalling the Rome Declaration on World Food Security and the World Food Summit Plan of Action, the Declaration of the World Food Summit: five years later, including the goal of achieving food security for all through an ongoing effort to eradicate hunger in all countries, with an immediate view to reducing by half the number of undernourished people by no later than 2015, as well as the commitment to achieving the Millennium Development Goals,

Welcoming the outcome of the seventeenth session of the Commission on Sustainable Development on the thematic cluster of issues on agriculture, rural development, land, drought, desertification and Africa,

Recognizing that agriculture plays a crucial role in addressing the needs of a growing global population and is inextricably linked to poverty eradication, especially in developing countries, and stressing that integrated and sustainable agriculture and rural development approaches are therefore essential to achieving enhanced food security and food safety in an environmentally sustainable way,

Expressing concern that the number of people suffering from hunger and poverty now exceeds one billion, which is an unacceptable blight on the lives, livelihoods and dignity of one sixth of the world's population, mostly in developing countries, and noting that the effects of long-standing underinvestment in food security, agriculture, and rural development have recently been further exacerbated by the food, financial and economic crises, among other factors,

Striving for a world free from hunger in which countries implement the Voluntary Guidelines to Support the Progressive Realization of the Right to Adequate Food in the Context of National Food Security, adopted by the Council of the Food and Agriculture Organization of the United Nations in November 2004, and supporting the practical application of the guidelines based on the principles of participation, transparency and accountability,

Recognizing the importance of an enabling international and national environment to increase and sustain investment in the agriculture sector of developing countries and to create a more level playing field in agriculture through greater market access, substantial reduction of trade-distorting domestic support, and the parallel elimination of all forms of export subsidies and disciplines on all export measures with equivalent effect in accordance with the mandate from the Doha Work Programme of the World Trade Organization,

Emphasizing the urgent need to increase efforts at the national, regional and international levels to address food security and agriculture development as an integral part of the international development agenda,

Recognizing the need to foster strategic coordination for agriculture development and food security involving all actors at the national, regional and global levels to improve governance, promote better allocation of resources, avoid duplication of efforts and identify response gaps,

Recognizing also that a sense of urgency and a commitment to solving the global food crisis have served as catalysts for strengthening international coordination and governance for food security, through the Global Partnership for Agriculture, Food Security and Nutrition, of which the Committee on World Food Security is a central component, and reiterating that it is essential to enhance global governance, building on existing institutions and fostering effective partnerships,

Remaining deeply concerned at the high volatility of global food prices, including for basic food commodities, owing to, inter alia, structural and systemic problems,

Remaining deeply concerned also that the global financial and economic crisis, climate change and the food crisis pose a serious challenge to the fight against poverty and hunger, as well as to the efforts of developing countries to attain food security and achieve the objective of reducing by half the number of undernourished people by no later than 2015 as well as the other internationally agreed development goals, including the Millennium Development Goals, and reiterating that the global food crisis has multiple and complex causes and that its consequences require a comprehensive and coordinated response, including the adoption of political, economic, social, financial and technical solutions in the short, medium and long term by national Governments and the international community,

Recognizing the work undertaken by relevant international bodies and organizations, including the Food and Agriculture Organization of the United Nations, the International Fund for Agricultural Development and the World Food Programme, on agriculture development and enhancing food security,

Acknowledging the work undertaken by the High-level Task Force on the Global Food Security Crisis,

Welcoming the recent appointment of the Special Representative of the Secretary-General on Food Security and Nutrition,

Taking note of the work to be undertaken, including by the Food and Agriculture Organization of the United Nations and the International Fund for Agricultural Development, on the follow-up to the International Conference on Agrarian Reform and Rural Development, in view of its relevance to food security,

Noting the convening of the World Grain Forum on 6 and 7 June 2009 in St. Petersburg, Russian Federation,

Emphasizing that the United Nations can play an effective role in building a global consensus in addressing agriculture development and food security,

1. *Takes note* of the report of the Secretary-General;

2. *Welcomes* the adoption of the Declaration of the World Summit on Food Security, and notes the Five Rome Principles for Sustainable Global Food Security contained in the Declaration;

3. *Stresses* that food security is central to poverty eradication, public health and sustainable economic growth, and the need for a comprehensive twin-track approach to food security that consists of direct action to immediately tackle hunger for the most vulnerable and medium- and long-

term sustainable agricultural, food security, nutrition, and rural development programmes to eliminate the root causes of hunger and poverty, including through the progressive realization of the right to food;

4. *Also stresses* that achieving food security for all has as its core element the strengthening and revitalizing of the agricultural sector in developing countries, where it has been identified as a priority by Governments, including through enhanced international support, an enabling environment at all levels and the empowerment of small-scale farmers, indigenous peoples and other rural communities, and stresses the need for the involvement of women, in particular in decision-making;

5. *Underlines* the importance of enhancing synergies between agriculture, food security and development policies and strategies at both the national and international levels, including by prioritizing and mainstreaming agriculture and food security into development policies;

6. *Encourages* efforts at all levels to create a strong enabling environment for enhancing agricultural production, productivity and sustainability, developing strong agricultural value chains and improving farmers' and agro-industry access to and participation in markets;

7. *Welcomes* the strengthening of cooperation between the Food and Agriculture Organization of the United Nations, the International Fund for Agricultural Development, the World Food Programme and all other relevant entities of the United Nations system and other intergovernmental organizations, the international financial institutions and international trade, financial and economic institutions, in accordance with their respective mandates, in order to increase their effectiveness, as well as the strengthening of cooperation with non-governmental organizations and the private sector in promoting and strengthening efforts towards agriculture development and food security;

8. *Expresses its support* for initiatives and actions to strengthen governance for agriculture development and food security and for the Global Partnership for Agriculture, Food Security and Nutrition, which will strive to achieve strategic coordination of efforts at the national, regional and global levels, building on existing structures, ensuring inclusiveness of participation and promoting a genuine bottom-up approach based on field-level experiences and developments;

9. *Welcomes* the efforts of the Committee on World Food Security, as a platform for discussion and coordination to strengthen collaborative action, to ensure that the voices of all relevant stakeholders, particularly those most affected by food insecurity, are heard, supports the important roles of the Committee, particularly in areas of coordination at the global level, policy convergence and facilitated support and advice to countries and regions, and affirms that, within the context of the implementation plan laid down in the reform of the Committee, it will gradually take on additional roles, such as promoting coordination at the national and regional levels, promoting accountability and sharing best practices at all levels, and developing a global strategic framework for food security and nutrition;

10. *Underlines* the need for sustained funding and increased targeted investment to enhance world food production, and calls for new and additional financial resources from all sources to achieve sustainable agriculture development and food security;

11.   *Stresses* the urgent need to increase the share of official development assistance devoted to agriculture and food security based on country-led requests, and encourages international financial institutions and regional development banks to do likewise;

12.   *Calls for* actions at the national, regional and international levels to intensify public and private investment in the agriculture sector, including through public-private partnerships;

13.   *Encourages* international, regional and national efforts to strengthen the capacity of developing countries, in particular their small-scale producers, to enhance the productivity of food crops, and to promote sustainable practices in pre-harvest and post-harvest agricultural activities;

14.   *Underlines* the importance of the conservation of, access to, and fair and equitable sharing of the benefits arising from the use of genetic resources, in accordance with national law and international agreements;

15.   *Reaffirms* the need to mobilize the resources needed to increase productivity, including the review, approval and adoption of biotechnology and other new technologies and innovations that are safe, effective and environmentally sustainable;

16.   *Promotes* research for food and agriculture, including research to adapt to and mitigate climate change, and access to research results and technologies at national, regional and international levels, including through the international research centres of the Consultative Group on International Agricultural Research, as well as other relevant international and regional research organizations;

17.   *Recognizes* that appropriate, affordable and sustainable agriculture technology can play an important role in helping developing countries to eradicate poverty and hunger and achieve global food security, and calls upon the international community to make greater efforts to promote the development and transfer of appropriate technologies and know-how on mutually agreed terms to developing countries;

18.   *Stresses* the importance of strengthening North-South, as well as South-South and triangular cooperation, and enhancing support from the United Nations development system in promoting cooperation in agriculture development and food security;

19.   *Encourages* efforts at all levels to establish and strengthen social protection measures and programmes, including national social safety nets and protection programmes for the needy and vulnerable, such as food and cash for work, cash transfer and voucher programmes, school feeding programmes and mother-and-child nutrition programmes;

20.   *Stresses* that a universal, rules-based, open, non-discriminatory and equitable multilateral trading system will promote agriculture and rural development in developing countries and contribute to world food security, and urges national, regional and international strategies to promote the participation of farmers, especially smallholders and women, in community, domestic, regional and international markets;

21.   *Underlines* the importance of the provision of, and the unhindered access to, safe emergency food and humanitarian assistance and support for the most vulnerable populations, recognizes the value of local purchase of food supplies, which supports local markets, and stresses the need to remove food export restrictions or extraordinary

taxes for food purchased for non-commercial humanitarian purposes, and the benefits of consultation and notification of any such new restrictions;

22.   *Urges* Member States and international organizations to pursue policies and strategies that improve the functioning of domestic, regional and international markets and ensure equitable access for all, especially smallholders and women farmers from developing countries, notes the importance of non-trade-distorting special measures that are consistent with World Trade Organization rules aimed at creating incentives for smallholder farmers in developing countries to enable them to increase their productivity and compete on a more equal footing on world markets, and urges Member States to refrain from taking measures that are inconsistent with the rules of the World Trade Organization and that have adverse impacts on global, regional and national food security;

23.   *Recognizes* the urgency of, and reaffirms its commitment to, reaching a successful and timely conclusion by 2010 to the Doha Round of World Trade Organization negotiations with an ambitious, comprehensive and balanced outcome as a key action to improve food security;

24.   *Also recognizes* the need for Africa to embark on a green revolution to help boost agricultural productivity, food production and regional food security, welcomes the strong leadership taken by African countries in undertaking initiatives to address the challenges of sustainable agricultural development and to achieve food security, such as the Comprehensive Africa Agriculture Development Programme of the New Partnership for Africa's Development, that can provide a framework through which support for agriculture and food security can be coordinated, and calls upon the international community to support Africa in the implementation of the various programmes under the New Partnership for Africa's Development;

25.   *Reaffirms* the commitment to a crucial, decisive shift towards increased short-, medium- and long-term national and international investment in agriculture in developing countries, welcomes the commitment made by African leaders in the Maputo Declaration on Agriculture and Food Security in Africa to raise the share of agriculture and rural development in their budget expenditures to at least 10 per cent, and encourages other geographical regions to adopt similar quantitative, time-bound commitments;

26.   *Notes*, in this regard, the adoption of the Windhoek High-level Ministerial Declaration on African Agriculture in the Twenty-first Century: Meeting the Challenges, Making a Sustainable Green Revolution, on 10 February 2009;

27.   *Notes* the challenges faced by indigenous peoples in the context of food security, and in this regard calls upon States to take special actions to combat the root causes of the disproportionately high level of hunger and malnutrition among indigenous peoples;

28.   *Reiterates* the importance of developing countries determining their own food security strategies, that food security is a national responsibility, and that any plans for addressing food security challenges and eradication of poverty in relation to food security must be nationally articulated, designed, owned and led, and built on consultation with all key stakeholders, and urges Member States to make food security a high priority and reflect this in their national programmes and budgets;

29. *Acknowledges*, in this regard, national and regional efforts by developing countries to implement long-term policies and measures that contribute to food security and agricultural development, such as the food security fund of some Latin American and Caribbean countries, the Latin American and the Caribbean without Hunger 2025 initiative, adopted at the twenty-ninth Food and Agriculture Organization of the United Nations Regional Conference for Latin America and the Caribbean, held in Caracas from 24 to 28 April 2006, the Presidential Summit on Sovereignty and Food Security: Foods for Life, held in Managua on 7 May 2008, the Sirte Declaration on Investing in Agriculture for Economic Growth and Food Security, adopted at the thirteenth ordinary session of the Assembly of the African Union in Sirte, Libyan Arab Jamahiriya, on 3 July 2009, the Emergency Programme for Arab Food Security launched at the Arab Economic and Social Development Summit, held in Kuwait on 19 and 20 January 2009, the South Asian Association for Regional Cooperation Food Security Reserve, and the Integrated Food Security Framework and Strategic Plan of Action on Food Security of the Association of Southeast Asian Nations;

30. *Underlines* the importance of the initiatives and commitments undertaken by the international community to enhance development of the agricultural sector and food security in developing countries, and of their full realization and implementation in a timely and reliable manner;

31. *Welcomes*, in that regard, the commitments made at the Group of Eight Summit held in L'Aquila, Italy, from 8 to 10 July 2009, to act with the scale and urgency needed to achieve sustainable global food security, and welcomes the commitments made by the countries represented at L'Aquila towards a goal of mobilizing 20 billion United States dollars over three years through this coordinated, comprehensive strategy focused on sustainable agriculture development;

32. *Invites* all members of the international community, including international and regional financial institutions, and urges relevant bodies within the United Nations system, to cooperate actively in a coordinated manner in the implementation of the outcome of the World Summit on Food Security adopted in Rome in November 2009;

33. *Requests* the Secretary-General to ensure that a coordinated follow-up at the field level to the World Summit on Food Security is undertaken in the context of the resident coordinator system, taking into account the coordinated follow-up to United Nations major international conferences;

34. *Invites* the Chairperson of the Committee on World Food Security to report, as part of the Committee's report to the General Assembly at its sixty-fifth session, through the Economic and Social Council, on the implementation of the reform of and on progress made towards achieving the vision of the Committee;

35. *Requests* the Secretary-General to report to the General Assembly at its sixty-fifth session on developments related to issues highlighted in the present resolution and the progress of the implementation of the outcome of the World Summit on Food Security;

36. *Decides* to include in the provisional agenda of its sixty-fifth session the item entitled "Agriculture development and food security", to be allocated to the Second Committee.

International Year of Natural Fibres, 2009

In 2009, in response to General Assembly resolution 61/189 [YUN 2006, p. 1428], the United Nations observed the International Year of Natural Fibres, which aimed to focus attention on the role of natural fibres in contributing to food security and poverty alleviation. Activities during the year, many of which were coordinated by FAO, promoted and raised awareness of the importance of familiar natural resources that were often taken for granted. The virtues of fibres such as cotton, flax, sisal and hemp, as well as wool, alpaca, camel hair and angora were celebrated.

Nutrition

Standing Committee on Nutrition

The United Nations System Standing Committee on Nutrition (SCN) held two meetings in 2009: one in Bangkok on 10 October and another in Brussels from 23 to 25 November. The Bangkok meeting involved technical discussions on policy and programming, while the Brussels meeting—hosted by the European Commission in cooperation with Save the Children, the Institute of Development Studies and the Institut de Recherche pour le Développement—covered policy coherence and nutrition architecture during a time of increasing global attention to nutrition.

In 2009, SCN released three reports on nutrition information in crisis situations. The reports highlighted the challenges presented by high levels of food insecurity exacerbated by conflict and increases in food prices.

UNU activities

The United Nations University (UNU), through its Food and Nutrition Programme for Human and Social Development (Ithaca, New York, United States), continued to carry out global research projects, to develop institutional capacity in developing countries in the areas of food and nutrition and to provide technical advisory services for the UN system.

UNU continued its involvement with the *Food and Nutrition Bulletin*, a peer-reviewed, academic journal published quarterly by the Nevin Scrimshaw International Nutrition Foundation in association with UNU that explored critical nutrition issues and potential solutions in developing countries, including undernutrition, malnutrition, nutrient bioavailability and food safety. In 2009, topics addressed by the journal included WHO growth standards, school feeding programmes, anaemia in low-income countries and the framing of nutrition concerns in the humanitarian appeals process.

Chapter XIV

International drug control

In 2009, the United Nations, through the Commission on Narcotic Drugs, the International Narcotics Control Board (INCB) and the United Nations Office on Drugs and Crime (UNODC), continued to strengthen international cooperation in countering the world drug problem. UNODC put the estimated number of problem drug users worldwide at between 15 and 39 million in 2009.

The Commission on Narcotic Drugs—the main UN policymaking body dealing with drug control—held its fifty-second session in March, during which it recommended one draft resolution for adoption by the Economic and Social Council and adopted 13 resolutions on topics such as alternative development, regional cooperation, female drug couriers, money laundering and evaluation of drug analysis laboratories. At the high-level segment of its fifty-second session, the Commission adopted the Political Declaration and Plan of Action on International Cooperation towards an Integrated and Balanced Strategy to Counter the World Drug Problem.

INCB reviewed the issue of primary prevention, a crucial area of demand reduction, and discussed the challenges facing the international community in applying the three major international drug control conventions, how Governments were responding to them and what action they should take. The Board continued to oversee the implementation of the conventions, analyse the drug situation worldwide and draw the attention of Governments to weaknesses in national control and treaty compliance, making suggestions and recommendations for improvements at the national and international levels.

UNODC provided technical assistance, legal advice and research to the main UN policymaking bodies in drug control, and assisted Member States in developing domestic legislation on drugs and in implementing the international drug control conventions. During the year, activities were carried out in the areas of sustainable livelihoods, with particular emphasis on illicit drug crop monitoring, illicit crop cultivation and poverty eradication; supply reduction; drug demand reduction, treatment and rehabilitation; follow-up to the outcome of the high-level segment of the Commission's fifty-second session; and strengthening cooperation between UNODC and other UN entities for the promotion of human rights in the implementation of the international treaties.

In July, the Economic and Social Council expressed its support for the development and implementation of the regional programmes of UNODC. In December, the Security Council called for stronger international cooperation to combat drug trafficking in Africa. Also in December, the General Assembly, in a resolution on international cooperation against the world drug problem, recognized that sustainable crop control strategies targeting the illicit cultivation of crops used for producing narcotic drugs and psychotropic substances required international cooperation based on the principle of shared responsibility; such strategies should include alternative development programmes and eradication and law enforcement measures. The Assembly recognized the role played by developing countries with extensive expertise in alternative development in promoting best practices, and stressed the need to respond to the challenges posed by the links between drug trafficking, corruption and other forms of organized crime.

The centennial of the convening of the first multinational initiative in drug control—the 1909 International Opium Commission—was commemorated in February in Shanghai, China.

Cooperation against the world drug problem

Commission on Narcotic Drugs. On 18 March [E/2009/28], the Commission on Narcotic Drugs, at its fifty-second session, considered the follow-up to the Assembly's twentieth special session on countering the world drug problem [YUN 1998, p. 1135]. It was noted that, although progress had been made since 1998, much remained to be done. Speakers referred to the emergence of new trends in the manufacture of synthetic drugs, drew attention to the use of latest-generation technologies to cultivate cannabis plant rich in tetrahydrocannabinol and to the spread of cannabis seeds, and noted the need to improve data collection and research. They emphasized that demand reduction measures were an essential part of drug control policy, and recognized the role of communities in demand reduction efforts. States were urged to increase the control of precursor chemicals, and the importance of conducting controlled deliveries was stressed. Noting the commitment and political will of Afghanistan, speakers called on the international community to increase assistance to that State, and emphasized the need to strengthen cooperation at the local, bilateral, subregional, regional and international levels, the exchange of information, and cooperation between the public and private sectors. Several speakers reported on changes made to their national drug control legislation to bring it in line with the international drug control conventions, and highlighted the importance of providing training to health and law enforcement personnel to tackle the drug situation.

High-level segment. The high-level segment of the fifty-second session of the Commission on Narcotic Drugs was held on 11 and 12 March [E/2009/28]. The theme for the general debate was "Review of the progress achieved and the difficulties encountered by Member States in meeting the goals and targets set out in the Political Declaration adopted by the General Assembly at its twentieth special session: challenges for the future". The themes for the round-table discussions were: current and emerging challenges, new trends and patterns of the world drug problem and possible improvements to the evaluation system; strengthening international cooperation in countering the world drug problem using shared responsibility as a basis for an integrated, comprehensive, balanced and sustainable approach in the fight against drugs through domestic and international policies; demand reduction, treatment and preventive policies and practices; and countering illicit drug traffic and supply, and alternative development. On 12 March, the participating ministers and Government representatives adopted the Political Declaration and Plan of Action on International Cooperation towards an Integrated and Balanced Strategy to Counter the World Drug Problem, which set out demand and supply reduction measures including in the areas of control of precursors and amphetamine-type stimulants, international cooperation on the eradication of illicit drug crops and on alternative development, countering money-laundering and promoting judicial cooperation.

On 20 March [E/2009/28 (res. 52/12)], the Commission invited States to strengthen their efforts to review and improve data collection tools in order to attain an objective, scientific, balanced and transparent assessment of the progress made and the obstacles encountered in implementing the Political Declaration and Plan of Action, and of all other aspects of the world drug situation. The Commission decided to convene an open-ended intergovernmental expert group to review the data collection tools and the collection, analysis and reporting processes; the expert group was to submit a revised set of data collection tools and mechanisms to the Commission's fifty-third (2010) session.

In response to General Assembly resolutions 56/124 [YUN 2001, p. 1144] and 63/197 [YUN 2008, p. 1348], the Commission in June submitted a report [A/64/92-E/2009/98] on progress achieved in meeting the goals and targets set out in the Political Declaration adopted by the Assembly's twentieth special session [YUN 1998, p. 1135]. The report reviewed the biennial reports to the Commission, the ministerial and high-level segments of the sessions of the Commission, and the outcome of the high-level segment of the Commission's fifty-second session. The Economic and Social Council took note of the report on 30 July (**decision 2009/256**).

Report of Secretary-General. In response to General Assembly resolution 63/197 [YUN 2008, p. 1348], the Secretary-General issued a June report on international cooperation against the world drug problem [A/64/120]. The report reviewed the world drug situation and the implementation of mandates relating to international drug control by the Commission on Narcotic Drugs and by UNODC. The Secretary-General stated that illicit drugs continued to pose a health danger to humanity, as drug use was one of the top 20 risk factors to health worldwide. He noted that health was at the centre of drug control, and drug dependence should be recognized as a disease to be treated by using non-discriminatory approaches and interventions. The report concluded that development was essential for reducing the world's supply of illicit drugs, and alternative development remained a cornerstone of supply reduction strategies. It also noted that the development community had yet to fully recognize the importance of directly addressing small farmers within the context of poverty reduction and food security.

GENERAL ASSEMBLY ACTION

On 18 December [meeting 65], the General Assembly, on the recommendation of the Third (Social, Humanitarian and Cultural) Committee [A/64/441], adopted **resolution 64/182** without vote [agenda item 105].

International cooperation against the world drug problem

The General Assembly,

Reaffirming the Political Declaration adopted by the General Assembly at its twentieth special session, the Declaration on the Guiding Principles of Drug Demand Reduction, the Action Plan on International Cooperation on the Eradication of Illicit Drug Crops and on Alternative Development, the Action Plan for the Implementation of the Declaration on the Guiding Principles of Drug Demand Reduction and the joint ministerial statement adopted at the ministerial segment of the forty-sixth session of the Commission on Narcotic Drugs,

Recalling the United Nations Millennium Declaration, the provisions of the 2005 World Summit Outcome addressing the world drug problem, the Political Declaration on HIV/AIDS and other relevant United Nations resolutions, including General Assembly resolution 63/197 of 18 December 2008 and those on regional and international cooperation to prevent the diversion and smuggling of precursors,

Gravely concerned that, despite continuing increased efforts by States, relevant organizations, civil society and non-governmental organizations, the world drug problem continues to constitute a serious threat to public health and safety and the well-being of humanity, in particular children and young people and their families, and to the national security and sovereignty of States, and that it undermines socio-economic and political stability and sustainable development,

Welcoming the outcome of the high-level segment of the fifty-second session of the Commission on Narcotic Drugs, and in that regard recalling resolution 63/197, in which the General Assembly decided to consider the results of the high-level segment at a plenary meeting of the Assembly at its sixty-fourth session,

Recalling resolutions adopted by the Commission on Narcotic Drugs at its fifty-second session, in particular resolutions 52/2, 52/3, 52/4 and 52/10 of 20 March 2009, and noting the outcomes of all the round-table discussions of the high-level segment of that session,

Reaffirming that countering the world drug problem in all its aspects requires a political commitment to reducing supply, as an integral component of a balanced and comprehensive drug control strategy, in accordance with the principles enshrined in the Political Declaration adopted by the General Assembly at its twentieth special session and the measures to enhance international cooperation to counter the drug problem, including the Action Plan on International Cooperation on the Eradication of Illicit Drug Crops and on Alternative Development, also adopted at that session,

Reaffirming equally that reducing illicit drug use and its consequences requires a political commitment to efforts to reduce demand, which must be demonstrated by sustained widespread demand reduction initiatives that integrate a comprehensive public health approach spanning the spectrum of prevention, education, early intervention, treatment, recovery support, rehabilitation and reintegration efforts, in accordance with the Declaration on the Guiding Principles of Drug Demand Reduction, adopted by the General Assembly at its twentieth special session,

Recognizing that international cooperation in demand reduction and supply reduction has shown that positive results can be achieved through sustained and collective efforts, and expressing its appreciation for the initiatives in this regard,

Reaffirming that the world drug problem remains a common and shared responsibility that requires effective and increased international cooperation and demands an integrated, multidisciplinary, mutually reinforcing and balanced approach to supply and demand reduction strategies,

1. *Adopts* the Political Declaration and Plan of Action on International Cooperation towards an Integrated and Balanced Strategy to Counter the World Drug Problem, as adopted at the high-level segment of the fifty-second session of the Commission on Narcotic Drugs, and calls upon States to take the measures necessary to fully implement the actions set out therein, with a view to attaining in a timely manner their goals and targets;

2. *Reaffirms* that countering the world drug problem is a common and shared responsibility that must be addressed in a multilateral setting, requires an integrated and balanced approach and must be carried out in full conformity with the purposes and principles of the Charter of the United Nations and other provisions of international law, the Universal Declaration of Human Rights, and the Vienna Declaration and Programme of Action on human rights, and, in particular, with full respect for the sovereignty and territorial integrity of States, for the principle of non-intervention in the internal affairs of States and for all human rights and fundamental freedoms, and on the basis of the principles of equal rights and mutual respect;

3. *Undertakes* to promote bilateral, regional and international cooperation, including through intelligence-sharing and cross-border cooperation, aimed at countering the world drug problem more effectively, in particular by encouraging and supporting such cooperation by those States most directly affected by illicit crop cultivation and the illicit production, manufacture, transit, trafficking, distribution and abuse of narcotic drugs and psychotropic substances;

4. *Reiterates* the commitment of Member States to promoting, developing, reviewing or strengthening effective, comprehensive, integrated drug demand reduction programmes, based on scientific evidence and covering a range of measures, including primary prevention, early intervention, treatment, care, rehabilitation, social reintegration and related support services, aimed at promoting health and social well-being among individuals, families and communities and reducing the adverse consequences of drug abuse for individuals and society as a whole, taking into account the particular challenges posed by high-risk drug users, in full compliance with the three international drug control conventions and in accordance with national legislation, and commits Member States to investing increased resources in ensuring access to those interventions on a non-discriminatory basis, including in detention facilities, bearing in mind that those interventions should also consider vulnerabilities that undermine human development, such as poverty and social marginalization;

5. *Notes with great concern* the adverse consequences of drug abuse for individuals and society as a whole, reaffirms the commitment of all Member States to tackling those problems in the context of comprehensive, complementary and multisectoral drug demand reduction strategies, in particular such strategies targeting youth, also notes with great concern the alarming rise in the incidence of HIV/AIDS and other blood-borne diseases among injecting drug users, reaffirms the commitment of all Member States to working towards the goal of universal access to comprehensive prevention programmes and treatment, care and related support services, in full compliance with the international drug control conventions and in accordance with national legislation, taking into account all relevant General Assembly resolutions and, when applicable, the *WHO, UNODC, UNAIDS Technical Guide for Countries to Set Targets for Universal Access to HIV Prevention, Treatment and Care for Injecting Drug Users*, and requests the United Nations Office on Drugs and Crime to carry out its mandate in

this area in close cooperation with relevant organizations and programmes of the United Nations system, such as the World Health Organization, the United Nations Development Programme and the Joint United Nations Programme on HIV/AIDS (UNAIDS);

6. *Acknowledges* the continuing efforts made and progress achieved in countering the world drug problem, notes with great concern the unprecedented surge in the illicit production of and trafficking in opium, the continuing illicit manufacture of and trafficking in cocaine, the increasing illicit production of and trafficking in cannabis and the increasing diversion of precursors, as well as the related distribution and use of illicit drugs, and stresses the need to strengthen and intensify joint efforts at the national, regional and international levels to tackle those global challenges in a more comprehensive manner, in accordance with the principle of common and shared responsibility, including by means of enhanced and better coordinated technical and financial assistance;

7. *Recognizes* that:

(a) Sustainable crop control strategies targeting the illicit cultivation of crops used for the production of narcotic drugs and psychotropic substances require international cooperation based on the principle of shared responsibility and an integrated and balanced approach, taking into account the rule of law and, where appropriate, security concerns, with full respect for the sovereignty and territorial integrity of States, the principle of non-intervention in the internal affairs of States and all human rights and fundamental freedoms;

(b) Such crop control strategies include, inter alia, alternative development and, where appropriate, preventive alternative development programmes, eradication and law enforcement measures;

(c) Such crop control strategies should be in full conformity with article 14 of the United Nations Convention against Illicit Traffic in Narcotic Drugs and Psychotropic Substances of 1988 and appropriately coordinated and phased in accordance with national policies in order to achieve the sustainable eradication of illicit crops, noting furthermore the need for Member States to undertake to increase long-term investment in such strategies, coordinated with other development measures, in order to contribute to the sustainability of social and economic development and poverty eradication in affected rural areas, taking due account of the traditional licit uses of crops where there is historical evidence of such use and giving due consideration to the protection of the environment;

8. *Also recognizes* the significant role played by developing countries with extensive expertise in alternative development in promoting best practices and lessons learned from such programmes, and invites them to continue sharing those best practices with States affected by illicit crop cultivation, including those emerging from conflict, with a view to using them, where appropriate, in accordance with the national specificities of each State;

9. *Stresses* the urgent need to respond to the serious challenges posed by the increasing links between drug trafficking, corruption and other forms of organized crime, including trafficking in human beings, trafficking in firearms, cybercrime and, in some cases, terrorism and money-laundering, including money-laundering in con-

nection with the financing of terrorism, and to the significant challenges faced by law enforcement and judicial authorities in responding to the ever-changing means used by transnational criminal organizations to avoid detection and prosecution;

10. *Reaffirms* the importance of the United Nations Office on Drugs and Crime and its regional offices in building capacity at the local level in the fight against transnational organized crime and drug trafficking, and urges the Office to consider regional vulnerabilities, projects and impact in the fight against drug trafficking, in particular in developing countries, when deciding to close and allocate offices, with a view to maintaining an effective level of support to national and regional efforts in combating the world drug problem;

11. *Urges* the United Nations Office on Drugs and Crime to increase collaboration with intergovernmental, international and relevant regional organizations involved in combating the world drug problem, as appropriate, in order to share best practices and to maximize the benefits from their unique comparative advantage;

12. *Recognizes* the need to collect relevant data and information regarding international cooperation for countering the world drug problem at the national, bilateral, subregional, regional and international levels, and urges all Member States to support dialogue through the Commission on Narcotic Drugs in order to address this issue;

13. *Requests* the United Nations Office on Drugs and Crime, upon request, to continue providing technical assistance to Member States so as to enhance capacity in countering the world drug problem, including by carrying out training programmes to develop indicators and instruments for the collection and analysis of accurate, reliable and comparable data on all relevant aspects of the world drug problem and, where appropriate, the enhancement or development of new national indicators and instruments;

14. *Urges* all Governments to provide the fullest possible financial and political support to the United Nations Office on Drugs and Crime by widening its donor base and increasing voluntary contributions, in particular general-purpose contributions, so as to enable it to continue, expand, improve and strengthen its operational and technical cooperation activities, within its mandates, in particular with a view to the full implementation of the Political Declaration adopted by the General Assembly at its twentieth special session and the Political Declaration and Plan of Action on International Cooperation towards an Integrated and Balanced Strategy to Counter the World Drug Problem adopted at the high-level segment of the fifty-second session of the Commission on Narcotic Drugs, as well as, where appropriate, relevant resolutions adopted by the Commission at that session, and recommends that a sufficient share of the regular budget of the United Nations continue to be allocated to the Office to enable it to carry out its mandates in a consistent and stable manner;

15. *Encourages* the Commission on Narcotic Drugs, as the principal policymaking organ of the United Nations on matters of international drug control and as the governing body of the drug programme of the United Nations Office on Drugs and Crime, and the International Narcotics Control Board to strengthen their useful work on the control of precursors and other chemicals used in the illicit manufacture of narcotic drugs and psychotropic substances;

16. *Urges* States that have not done so to consider ratifying or acceding to, and States parties to implement, as a matter of priority, all the provisions of the Single Convention on Narcotic Drugs of 1961 as amended by the 1972 Protocol, the Convention on Psychotropic Substances of 1971, the United Nations Convention against Illicit Traffic in Narcotic Drugs and Psychotropic Substances of 1988, the United Nations Convention against Transnational Organized Crime and the Protocols thereto and the United Nations Convention against Corruption;

17. *Urges* all Member States to implement the Action Plan for the Implementation of the Declaration on the Guiding Principles of Drug Demand Reduction and to strengthen their national efforts to counter the abuse of illicit drugs in their populations, in particular among children and young people;

18. *Takes note* of the outcome of the high-level segment of the fifty-second session of the Commission on Narcotic Drugs, the *World Drug Report 2009* of the United Nations Office on Drugs and Crime and the most recent report of the International Narcotics Control Board, and calls upon States to strengthen international and regional cooperation to counter the threat to the international community caused by the illicit production of and trafficking in drugs, as well as other aspects of the world drug problem, and to continue to take concerted measures, such as within the framework of the Paris Pact and other relevant international initiatives;

19. *Notes* that the International Narcotics Control Board needs sufficient resources to carry out all its mandates, reaffirms the importance of its work, encourages it to continue to carry out its work in accordance with its mandates, urges Member States to commit themselves in a common effort to assigning, where possible, adequate and sufficient budgetary resources to the Board, in accordance with Economic and Social Council resolution 1996/20 of 23 July 1996, emphasizes the need to maintain its capacity, inter alia, through the provision of appropriate means by the Secretary-General and adequate technical support from the United Nations Office on Drugs and Crime, and calls for enhanced cooperation and understanding between Member States and the Board to enable it to implement all its mandates under the international drug control conventions;

20. *Welcomes* the important role played by civil society, in particular non-governmental organizations, in addressing the world drug problem, notes with appreciation their important contribution to the review process, and also notes that representatives of affected populations and civil society entities, where appropriate, should be enabled to play a participatory role in the formulation and implementation of drug demand and supply reduction policy;

21. *Recommends* that the Economic and Social Council devote one of its high-level segments to a theme related to the world drug problem, and also recommends that the General Assembly hold a special session to address the world drug problem;

22. *Encourages* the meetings of Heads of National Drug Law Enforcement Agencies and of the Subcommission on Illicit Drug Traffic and Related Matters in the Near and Middle East of the Commission on Narcotic Drugs to continue to contribute to the strengthening of regional and international cooperation, and in this regard acknowledges the discussions that took place at the nineteenth meeting of Heads of National Drug Law Enforcement Agencies, Latin America and the Caribbean, held on Isla Margarita, Bolivarian Republic of Venezuela, from 28 September to 2 October 2009, on how to improve cooperation among the States of Latin America and the Caribbean and the States of West Africa in combating drug trafficking;

23. *Welcomes* the ongoing efforts to strengthen regional cooperation in combating illicit trafficking in drugs and the diversion of precursor chemicals undertaken by the members of the Commonwealth of Independent States, the Shanghai Cooperation Organization, the Economic Cooperation Organization, the Collective Security Treaty Organization, the Eurasian Group on Combating Money-Laundering and Financing of Terrorism and other relevant subregional and regional organizations, including the adoption of the plan of action on combating terrorism, illicit drug trafficking and organized crime at the special conference held under the auspices of the Shanghai Cooperation Organization in Moscow on 27 March 2009 and the efforts undertaken within the framework of the permanent counter-narcotics mechanism "Channel";

24. *Acknowledges* other ongoing regional efforts to combat illicit trafficking in drugs, such as those of the Association of Southeast Asian Nations Senior Officials on Drug Matters, who adopted the Association workplan on combating illicit drug production, trafficking and use (2009–2015) at their thirtieth meeting, held in Phnom Penh from 29 September to 20 October 2009, with the aim of achieving a drug-free South-East Asia by 2015;

25. *Calls upon* the relevant United Nations agencies and entities and other international organizations, and invites international financial institutions, including regional development banks, to mainstream drug control issues into their programmes, and calls upon the United Nations Office on Drugs and Crime to maintain its leading role by providing relevant information and technical assistance;

26. *Takes note* of the report of the Secretary-General, and requests the Secretary-General to submit to the General Assembly at its sixty-fifth session a report on the implementation of the present resolution.

Conventions

International efforts to control narcotic drugs were governed by three global conventions: the 1961 Single Convention on Narcotic Drugs [YUN 1961, p. 382], which, with some exceptions of detail, replaced earlier narcotics treaties and was amended by the 1972 Protocol [YUN 1972, p. 397] to strengthen the role of the International Narcotics Control Board (INCB); the 1971 Convention on Psychotropic Substances [YUN 1971, p. 380]; and the 1988 United Nations Convention against Illicit Traffic in Narcotic Drugs and Psychotropic Substances [YUN 1988, p. 690].

As at 31 December, 185 States were parties to the 1961 Convention, as amended by the 1972 Protocol. Afghanistan and Chad continued to be parties to the Convention in its unamended form only. The Lao

People's Democratic Republic acceded to the Protocol in March.

The number of parties to the 1971 Convention remained at 183 as at 31 December.

At year's end, 183 States and the European Union (EU) were parties to the 1988 Convention, with Namibia acceding in 2009.

Commission action. In March [E/2009/28], the Commission on Narcotic Drugs reviewed implementation of the international drug control treaties. It had before it the INCB report covering its 2008 activities [YUN 2008, p. 1354]; the INCB report on follow-up to the General Assembly twentieth special session [YUN 2008, p. 1348]; the 2008 INCB technical report on the implementation of Article 12 of the 1988 Convention, dealing with precursors and chemicals frequently used in the illicit manufacture of narcotic drugs and psychotropic substances [E/INCB/2008/4]; and the report of the Competent National Authorities under the Treaties [ST/NAR.3/2008/1].

INCB action. In its report covering 2009 [E/INCB/2009/1, Sales No. E.10.XI.1], INCB requested those States that were not parties to one or more of the international drug control treaties to accede to them without delay. It also called on Governments to ensure that the provisions of the treaties were implemented and that national drug control laws and policies were consistent with them, and to furnish all statistical reports required under the treaties. Governments were called upon to establish annual estimates of requirements for narcotic drugs at the levels that were adequate to ensure access to narcotic drugs for medical treatment and to prevent diversion into illicit channels. The Board requested Governments not to authorize imports of psychotropic substances in quantities exceeding their assessments of annual medical and scientific requirements and to introduce the requirement of import and export authorizations for substances in Schedules III and IV of the 1971 Convention. It further requested Governments to furnish information on the results of investigations concerning seizures and intercepted shipments of precursors and to review estimates of their annual requirements for selected precursors.

In 2009, the Board reviewed the drug control situation in Bolivia, Colombia, Mauritania and Morocco, as well as measures taken by those countries to implement the international treaties. During the year, it sent missions to Angola, Australia, Finland, the Holy See, Hungary, Ireland, Jordan, Malta, Spain, the Sudan and the Syrian Arab Republic.

Proposed amendment to Convention

On 15 May [E/2009/78], the Secretary-General transmitted to the Economic and Social Council a proposal from Bolivia to amend article 49, paragraphs 1 (c) and 2 (e), of the Single Convention on Narcotic Drugs of 1961, as amended by the 1972 Protocol. The proposal was aimed at deleting a provision on abolishing coca leaf chewing, an ancestral practice of the Andean indigenous peoples.

By **decision 2009/250** of 30 July, the Council decided, with reference to article 47, paragraph 1, of the 1961 Convention, as amended by the 1972 Protocol, to initiate the procedures established in paragraph 1 (b) of that article, which stated that the parties should be asked whether they accepted the proposed amendment and also asked to submit to the Council any comments on the proposal.

On 9 October [E/2009/116], the Secretary-General transmitted to the Council a 28 August note from Egypt to the Office of Legal Affairs, which stated that Egypt had rejected the proposed amendment. A 1960 law prohibited cultivation of coca leaf in Egypt due to its negative effects on health.

Centennial of the convening of the International Opium Commission

On 26 February [E/INCB/2009/1], the centennial of the convening of the 1909 International Opium Commission—the first multinational initiative in drug control—was commemorated in Shanghai, China. More than 100 delegates from around the world participated in the event, including delegates from the 13 countries—Austria, China, France, Germany, Iran, Italy, Japan, the Netherlands, Portugal, the Russian Federation, Thailand, the United Kingdom and the United States—that had been represented in the 1909 Commission. The Shanghai Declaration [E/INCB/2009/1, annex IV], adopted at the event, reaffirmed the political commitment to a comprehensive, balanced and mutually reinforcing approach to supply and demand reduction. It also reaffirmed that international drug control cooperation should be in full conformity with the purposes and principles of the UN Charter and urged States to fully implement the international treaties and fulfil other international drug control obligations.

The Board expressed appreciation to China for organizing and hosting the event to mark the beginning of a century of multilateral drug control.

International Narcotics Control Board

The 13-member International Narcotics Control Board (INCB) held its ninety-fourth (2–6 February), ninety-fifth (11–22 May) and ninety-sixth (27 October–13 November) sessions, all in Vienna.

In accordance with the tasks assigned to it under the international conventions, the Board monitored the implementation of the international drug control treaties and maintained a permanent dialogue with Governments. The information received from Governments was used to identify the enforcement of treaty provisions requiring them to limit to medical and scientific purposes the licit manufacture of, trade in and distribution and use of narcotic drugs and psychotropic substances. The Board, which was requested by the treaties to report annually on the drug control situation worldwide, noted weaknesses in national control and treaty compliance and made recommendations for improvements at the national and international levels.

The Board's 2009 report [E/INCB/2009/1, Sales No. E.10.XI.1] focused on primary prevention, a crucial area of demand reduction, which encompassed measures to prevent and reduce drug abuse in populations that were either not abusing or not seriously involved with drugs. Primary prevention promoted the non-use of drugs and was aimed at preventing or delaying their first use and the transition to more serious use among occasional users. The Board stated that strategies might address whole populations (universal prevention) or more vulnerable population groups (selective prevention), and activities should be integrated into public health, health promotion and child and youth development programmes. The Board recommended that partnerships with civil society should be forged at the local, national and international levels to ensure the most efficient use of scarce resources and to increase effectiveness in reducing the prevalence of abuse. Efforts to prevent drug use should be based on the best possible available data, and a primary prevention strategy aimed at preventing the transition of occasional use into serious involvement with drugs should include the collection of information on the frequency of use, the amount of drugs used and the factors linked to making such a transition. To ensure the implementation of effective primary prevention, the Board called on Governments to: establish a clear focal point and accountability for primary prevention; integrate primary prevention into national drug control strategy and use a public health framework; build capacity for and ensure collaboration among all Government sectors pursuing similar prevention aims; encourage groups with a stake in prevention to work together; and improve the understanding of drug use and the factors that influence it. Governments were also encouraged to build and disseminate knowledge of best practices; increase their commitment to the evaluation of primary prevention; and develop the primary prevention workforce. The Board recommended that UNODC collaborate with others to develop standards against which Governments could measure their primary prevention efforts, and also collaborate with the United Nations Children's Fund, the International Labour Organization, the United Nations Educational, Scientific and Cultural Organization, the World Health Organization (WHO), non-governmental organizations (NGOs) and the private sector to develop, promote and disseminate resources to help Governments strengthen the quality of their primary prevention work.

The INCB report was supplemented by three technical reports: Narcotic Drugs: Estimated World Requirements for 2010; Statistics for 2008 [E/INCB/2009/2]; Psychotropic Substances: Statistics for 2008 [E/INCB/2009/3]; and Precursors and Chemicals Frequently Used in the Illicit Manufacture of Narcotic Drugs and Psychotropic Substances [E/INCB/2009/4].

By **decision 2009/249** of 30 July, the Economic and Social Council took note of the INCB report for 2008 [YUN 2008, p. 1354].

World drug situation

In its 2009 report [E/INCB/2009/1, Sales No. E.10.XI.1], INCB presented a regional analysis of world drug abuse trends and control efforts to keep Governments aware of situations that might endanger the objectives of international drug control treaties.

Africa

Most African States continued to lack proper systems for monitoring drug abuse and were therefore unable to gather data on its extent and patterns. The only systematic monitoring took place in South Africa. Furthermore, in most countries, national health care systems were not able to meet the needs relating to the treatment and rehabilitation of drug-dependent persons.

Cannabis was the most problematic illicit drug in Africa: it was used by an estimated 8 per cent of the population, and its widespread abuse by children was of particular concern. Its production, trafficking and abuse were reported in practically all countries. Cannabis herb continued to be the most abused drug in most countries and was illicitly produced in all subregions. While it was usually trafficked within Africa for local consumption, a proportion was smuggled into other regions, mostly Europe. The production of cannabis resin was concentrated in North Africa, mainly in Morocco, and most of the resin was smuggled into Europe and into or through North African and sub-Saharan countries. In 2008, Morocco seized more resin than any other African country; however, the area under cannabis cultivation in that country had been significantly reduced, from 134,000 hectares in 2003 to 60,000 in 2008, and the amount of illicitly produced resin fell from 3,070 tons to 877 tons. Eradication measures in Morocco were supplemented by alternative livelihood programmes in rural areas in the northern provinces and local awareness-raising campaigns.

Cocaine abuse appeared to have risen, particularly along emerging cocaine trafficking routes in West and Southern Africa. There were no reports of coca bush cultivation or cocaine manufacture. Since 2005, however, West Africa had increasingly been used as a transit area for consignments from South America into Europe and North America. The cocaine seized in Africa originated mainly in Colombia and Peru and, in many cases, was smuggled through Brazil and Venezuela. Since 2008, there had been a decline in cocaine seizures in West Africa, however, the smuggling of cocaine through the subregion continued. Some cocaine was smuggled into countries in Southern Africa, notably South Africa, to be abused locally or smuggled into other countries. Cocaine from South America was also smuggled through the United Arab Emirates into Zimbabwe. Mozambique emerged as an area where cocaine entered into Africa to be smuggled through South Africa into Europe.

Opium poppy cultivation was limited and confined to Algeria and the Sinai peninsula in Egypt. The opium produced was abused locally. Heroin trafficking and abuse increased across the continent. Heroin was the most abused drug by problem drug abusers in Kenya, Mauritius, Nigeria, the United Republic of Tanzania and Zambia, with Rwanda and Seychelles also reporting an increase. In South Africa and other countries in the region, drug abuse by injection was still limited. Heroin continued to enter Africa mainly through East African countries as countries of both destination and transit. Its smuggling to the islands of the Indian Ocean increased, particularly to Mauritius. While heroin seizures in West Africa remained very small, organized crime networks based in the subregion played a key role in supplying heroin to countries throughout the world. Côte d'Ivoire was a significant transit country.

Between 1.4 million and 4 million persons in Africa had abused amphetamine-type stimulants (ATS) at least once in 2009. Nigeria and South Africa reported their highest annual prevalence rates. Methaqualone and methamphetamine abuse remained of concern in South Africa, and the abuse of over-the-counter and prescription medicines, such as slimming tablets, phenobarbital, analgesics and benzodiazepines, continued to be a problem in many countries. The illicit manufacture of psychotropic substances, notably methaqualone (Mandrax), methamphetamine, methcathinone and methylenedioxymethamphetamine (MDMA), commonly known as ecstasy, remained limited to South Africa and some countries in Southern and East Africa, where they were also abused.

Africa, in particular South Africa, continued to be used for the diversion of precursor chemicals, notably ephedrine and pseudoephedrine, often in the form of pharmaceutical preparations, mainly for use in illicit methamphetamine manufacture in Central and North America. However, their diversion in Africa was decreasing. In addition, Africa was used for the diversion of acetic anhydride, used in the illicit manufacture of heroin, into illicit channels. There was also concern regarding the threat posed by transnational organized criminal groups involved in the manufacture of and trafficking in ATS and psychotropic substances.

Khat, which was not under international control, continued to be cultivated in East Africa and in parts of the Arabian peninsula, and was commonly chewed as a stimulant. Only some countries in East Africa prohibited it.

As to regional cooperation, under the African Union (AU) Plan of Action on Drug Control and Crime Prevention, the AU Commission strengthened its cooperation in drug control and crime prevention with relevant international organizations. Progress was made by members of the Economic Community of West African States (ECOWAS), which adopted a subregional action plan on drug trafficking, organized crime and drug abuse in 2008 and, at the mid-year summit meeting of ECOWAS Heads of State and Government (Abuja, Nigeria, 23 June), endorsed an operational plan to combat drug trafficking and related organized crime. UNODC and WHO launched the international network of drug dependence treatment and rehabilitation resource centres (Treatnet) to improve the quality of treatment for drug-dependent persons; participants included Cape Verde, Côte d'Ivoire, Kenya, Mozambique, Nigeria, Sierra Leone, the United Republic of Tanzania and Zambia. Capacity-building initiatives were launched in Algeria, Egypt and Morocco to provide a comprehensive response to drug abuse and HIV/AIDS. In East Africa, an opiate substitution programme was implemented in Mauritius, while treatment for abusers was provided in Kenya, Seychelles and Uganda. A programme for opioid substitution therapy was launched in Morocco.

At the national level, Ethiopia adopted a national drug control master plan; Kenya introduced a drug control component in its system for the performance appraisal of civil servants; and a number of countries established or were in the process of establishing national programmes to combat trafficking, abuse and associated transnational organized crime. In 2009, Lesotho and Nigeria conducted successful operations to combat the problem of counterfeit medical products.

Commission action. On 20 March [E/2009/28 (res. 52/3)], the Commission on Narcotic Drugs, noting the increasing use of East Africa as a transit area for heroin consignments destined for international markets, invited States and international organizations to support those East African States most affected by drug trafficking, in particular Ethiopia and Kenya. International financial institutions and other potential donors were urged to provide financial assistance.

The Commission [E/2009/28 (res. 52/4)] also called on States, especially the main countries of origin, transit and destination of illicit consignments, in particular of cocaine, smuggled through West Africa, to reduce the supply of their trafficking and demand, and encouraged States and multilateral organizations to collaborate with West African States. It invited States, donors, organizations and NGOs to provide financial and material assistance to the ECOWAS Commission and ECOWAS member States to counter drug trafficking and abuse through the Regional Response Action Plan.

The Security Council, in presidential statement **S/PRST/2009/32** of 8 September (see p. 115), discussed drug trafficking as a threat to international security in Africa.

Americas

Central America and the Caribbean

The region of Central America and the Caribbean continued to be used as a major trans-shipment area for consignments of drugs originating in South America and destined for North America and Europe. Drug trafficking had become a major security threat. Jamaica, where the most abused drug was cannabis, followed by cocaine, continued to be a major cannabis producer and exporter in the Caribbean. However, cannabis plants were also cultivated in other Caribbean countries, such as the Dominican Republic and Saint Vincent and the Grenadines, where the cannabis produced was destined mostly for local markets. Cultivation and trafficking decreased in Cuba, Costa Rica and Guatemala. Cannabis was the most commonly abused drug in Guatemala, followed by cocaine and psychotropic substances. In El Salvador, the second most abused drug after cannabis in 2008 was the benzodiazepines group. While cultivation decreased slightly in Honduras, cocaine trafficking by air increased.

Cocaine continued to be trafficked in large quantities in Nicaragua, where drug availability and abuse was increasing. The Dominican Republic remained a major trans-shipment area for cocaine from Colombia; however, Belize, Haiti and Jamaica were increasingly used as trans-shipment areas for South American cocaine consignments bound for North America and Europe. Cocaine was also trafficked in other Caribbean countries, but on a smaller scale.

In Guatemala, levels of opium poppy cultivation and heroin trafficking were significant. While cannabis cultivation and trafficking diminished and cocaine trafficking remained at the same level, there was a rising trend in opium and heroin trafficking. In the Dominican Republic in 2008, there was a significant increase in the number of cases involving trafficking in heroin of Colombian origin bound for the United States.

Despite new regulations banning ephedrine and pseudoephedrine in several countries, the region continued to be used as a trans-shipment area for the smuggling of precursor chemicals into Mexico, where the illicit manufacture of ATS continued. MDMA primarily from the Netherlands continued to be trafficked in the Caribbean. Trafficking in pseudoephedrine and ephedrine was reported in Belize, the Dominican Republic, El Salvador, Guatemala and Honduras.

As to regional cooperation, the Ministerial Conference on Illicit Drug Trafficking, Transnational Organized Crime and Terrorism as Challenges for Security and Development in the Caribbean (Santo Domingo, Dominican Republic, 17–20 February), organized by UNODC, adopted the Political Declaration on Combating Illicit Trafficking, Organized Crime, Terrorism and Other Serious Crime in the Caribbean. The Inter-American Drug Abuse Control Commission (CICAD) continued to organize regional cooperation activities in Costa Rica, the Dominican Republic, Guatemala and Panama. In March, a meeting on standards of care at treatment and rehabilitation facilities for abusers was held in Montego Bay, Jamaica, under the auspices of CICAD and the Caribbean Community. Also in March, the EU launched the project "Prevention of the diversion of drug precursors in the Latin American and Caribbean region" to strengthen the capacity of national authorities responsible for precursor control and to improve communication and cooperation between countries.

At the national level, Costa Rica launched a drug control plan for 2008–2012, establishing a national policy on abuse prevention; Guatemala imposed a ban on pseudoephedrine and launched a programme to prevent drug abuse and gang activity among schoolchildren; and Honduras issued a regulation prohibiting pseudoephedrine.

Follow-up to Ministerial Conference in the Caribbean

Commission action. On 20 March [E/2009/28 (res. 52/11)], the Commission on Narcotic Drugs encouraged the implementation of the Political Declaration on Combating Illicit Drug Trafficking, Organized Crime, Terrorism and Other Serious Crime in the Caribbean. It supported the implementation of the action plan for the Caribbean and the establishment of the Santo Domingo partnership monitoring mechanism; requested UNODC to facilitate mobilization of the resources necessary for their implementation; and urged States to provide voluntary contributions and technical assistance.

North America

The United States continued to be the world's largest market for illicit drugs and a major destination of their consignments. Except for cannabis and methamphetamine, illicit drugs were not produced domestically but were largely smuggled into the country. One matter of concern was the high prevalence of abuse of prescription drugs containing controlled substances. In addition to being used as a major transit area for illicit consignments, Mexico experienced increasing problems related to the abuse of cocaine and other drugs. Canada remained one of the primary countries supplying MDMA to North America and other regions; it was also a source of high-potency cannabis. Trafficking organizations based in Mexico predominated in illicit production, trafficking and distribution in North America: they expanded their control to cover the entire supply chain, shipping drugs from South America and distributing them in the United States.

In the United States, the declining trend in the abuse of cannabis and other illicit drugs among youth continued. Illicit cultivation of cannabis rose in 2008, and the quantity of eradicated plants increased by 14 per cent. The potency of the cannabis seized continued to increase: the average tetrahydrocannabinol content exceeded 10 per cent, the highest level ever recorded in that country. In Mexico, less cannabis herb was seized in 2008, and its illicit production declined to 22,275 tons, most of which was destined for the United States. The area of illicitly cultivated cannabis eradicated in Mexico dropped; however, the quantity of cannabis seized along the south-west border of the United States indicated a sustained flow from Mexico.

In the United States, cocaine abuse (including "crack") declined in 2008, and the quantity of cocaine seized decreased from 97 to 50 tons, the lowest level since 1999. Mexico seized 60 per cent less cocaine in 2008 than in 2007. Nevertheless, the estimated quantity of cocaine shipped from South America to the United States remained significant. Mexico's role as a transit country for cocaine destined for Canada increased in 2008, and drug abuse spread throughout the country.

In the United States, heroin abuse was stable at a relatively low level. Most of the heroin found on the illicit market originated in Colombia and Mexico. Mexico eradicated 13,095 hectares of opium poppy in 2008, an increase over 2007. In Canada, 70 per cent of the heroin found in 2008 originated in South-West Asia.

In the United States, the number of persons abusing prescription drugs declined in 2008, but still remained greater than the number of persons abusing cocaine, heroin, hallucinogens and/or inhalants. The number of first-time abusers of prescription drugs continued to be high, with an increase in the number of deaths due to overdose. Internet pharmacies in 2008 continued to be the main channel used for the illicit distribution of pharmaceutical preparations in the United States. However, their number dropped by 15 per cent from 2007, owing to increased efforts by law enforcement agencies.

The abuse of methamphetamine declined further in the United States, and its illicit manufacture decreased following the introduction of regulations to increase domestic control over the sale of pharmaceutical preparations containing its precursors. The number of methamphetamine laboratories dismantled dropped by more than 70 per cent from 2004 to 2008. In Mexico, new control measures contributed to a decrease in the illicit manufacture of methamphetamine and to a reduction in the quantity smuggled into the United States in 2007 and 2008. However, data on seizures in the United States suggested that its illicit manufacture was increasing in some areas. Canada continued to be the primary source of MDMA found in the United States and a major supplier of its growing illicit markets in other regions, in particular in Asia and the Pacific. The high level of ATS manufacture in Canada was fuelled by the acquisition of bulk quantities of precursor chemicals by organized criminal groups.

Regional efforts to counter drug trafficking intensified. The Merida Initiative, a multi-year security programme involving Mexico, the United States and countries in Central America, was a major element in those efforts. Cooperation between Canada and the United States continued and included joint operations and training activities and the exchange of intelligence. At the national level, the United States in 2009 expanded the National Southwest Border Counternarcotics Strategy, aimed at reducing the flow of illicit drugs by enhancing drug control capabilities. In the United States, 38 states had prescription drug monitoring programmes in 2008, compared with 15 in 2001, aiming at preventing the diversion and abuse of prescription drugs. The United States Congress in September 2008 passed the Ryan Haight Online Pharmacy Consumer Protection Act of 2008, prohibiting the delivery, distribution or dispensing of prescription drugs over the Internet without a valid prescription. Canada continued to implement its National Anti-Drug Strategy.

South America

South America continued to be the sole source of illicitly manufactured cocaine, smuggled primarily into North America and Europe. In 2008, its potential manufacture in the region had been the lowest since 2003. That decline could be attributed to a significant decrease in the total area under coca bush cultivation in Colombia in 2008. In Bolivia and Peru, the area under cultivation increased for the third consecutive year. The estimated prevalence of cannabis abuse among the general population in South America in the past 12 months was 3.4 per cent. It was the highest in Argentina and Venezuela, exceeding 7 per cent of the adult population. Paraguay remained one of the major producers in South America; cannabis plants were also cultivated in Colombia, where cannabis continued to be the most abused drug. In 2008, seizures of cannabis herb increased in Bolivia, Chile, Ecuador, Paraguay and Peru, and decreased in Brazil and Venezuela. The primary drugs of abuse among persons treated for drug problems in South America were cocaine-type drugs (accounting for 52 per cent of cases), followed by cannabis (33 per cent). The demand for treatment for abuse of ATS and opiates was significantly lower.

The abuse of illicit drugs continued to increase in several countries. The estimated annual prevalence of cocaine abuse in South America among persons aged 15–64 was 0.9 per cent, approximately double the world prevalence rate. Although Colombia was one of the world's main producers, prevalence of its abuse in 2008 was 0.7 per cent, slightly less than the rate for the region as a whole. In 2008, cocaine abuse increased in Chile, Ecuador, Paraguay, Uruguay and Venezuela and remained stable in Peru. The total area under illicit coca bush cultivation in the region decreased in 2008 to 167,600 hectares, 8 per cent less than in 2007. Colombia accounted for 48.3 per cent, followed by Peru (33.5 per cent) and Bolivia (18.2 per cent). Colombia saw a major decline in 2008: the area under cultivation decreased by 18 per cent, to 81,000 hectares. Cocaine manufacture in Colombia declined by 28 per cent, to 430 tons, a reduction not fully offset by increased manufacture in Bolivia and Peru. As a result, the potential global manufacture decreased from 994 tons in 2007 to 845 tons in 2008. Colombia's share of global manufacture fell to 51 per cent, the lowest in a decade. In 2008, all three of the main countries producing coca leaf, as well as Argentina, Brazil and Ecuador, reported a significant increase in the quantity of cocaine seized compared with 2007. Almost all countries in the region were affected by drug trafficking. Cocaine smuggled into North America typically originated in Colombia and entered the United States from Mexico after having passed through South America and Central America and the Caribbean.

In 2007, over 99 per cent of coca-processing laboratories were located in the three main countries cultivating coca bush. A small number of clandestine laboratories were dismantled in Argentina, Brazil, Chile, Ecuador and Venezuela. The spreading of laboratories beyond the main cocaine-producing countries resulted in increased abuse of coca paste, in particular among adolescents and young people in Argentina and Brazil. The number of clandestine laboratories dismantled in Colombia in 2008 was 36 per cent greater than in 2007. In Colombia, traditional use of coca leaf was marginal and illegal: virtually all of the coca leaves produced were destined for cocaine manufacture. About 40 per cent of coca bush growers sold the coca leaves without any further processing at the farm, while the remaining 60 per cent of growers processed the leaves into coca paste or cocaine base to increase their profits. The last step, the processing of the cocaine base into cocaine hydrochloride, was carried out by traffickers in clandestine laboratories.

The annual prevalence of the abuse of opiates and MDMA in South America was 0.3 and 0.2 per cent respectively, one of the lowest rates of all regions. As a result of continued eradication efforts, the area under illicit opium poppy cultivation in Colombia declined to 400 hectares in 2008. Potential manufacture of heroin in Colombia was 1.3 tons, 43 per cent less than in 2007.

Europe was one of the main sources of MDMA seized in South America. However, in 2008 and 2009, MDMA laboratories were dismantled in Argentina and Brazil. In 2007 and 2008, seizures of potassium permanganate, the key precursor used in the illicit manufacture of cocaine hydrochloride, were reported in Argentina, Brazil, Chile, Colombia, Ecuador and Peru. From 2007 to 2009, seizures of ephedrine and pseudoephedrine were made in Argentina, Chile, Paraguay and Venezuela. The diverted substances were destined primarily for clandestine methamphetamine laboratories in North America, in particular Mexico.

Regionally, the Eleventh High-level Specialized Dialogue on Drugs between the Andean Community and the European Union (Quito, Ecuador, May) adopted the Quito Declaration, reaffirming the importance of cooperation in combating illicit drugs, including in alternative development and preventive alternative development. Nationally, Colombia in November 2008 launched its national plan for the reduction of drug consumption for 2009–2010, and in 2009 took further measures to ensure the availability of opioids for medical use. Ecuador in November 2008 strengthened control measures on substances listed in the international drug control treaties, and in 2009 adopted its national plan for the comprehensive prevention and control of drugs for 2009–2012. In June, Venezuela approved its national drug control plan for 2008–2013.

Asia

East and South-East Asia

In 2008, the area under illicit opium poppy cultivation in East and South-East Asia increased by 3.3 per cent compared with 2007. In addition, there was a significant increase in methamphetamine trafficking and MDMA illicit manufacture, and, for the first time in recent years, the illicit manufacture of gamma-hydroxybutyric acid (GHB) was reported.

The illicit cultivation of cannabis continued throughout the region. In 2008, Japan, Mongolia and the Republic of Korea seized the largest quantity of cannabis in recent years. The Philippines continued to seize significant amounts, and Viet Nam reported that a new, more potent strain of cannabis was emerging on the illicit market. Cannabis was the most abused drug in Mongolia and Thailand, and remained the second most abused drug in the Philippines and the Republic of Korea.

In 2008, illicit opium poppy cultivation increased in the Lao People's Democratic Republic, Myanmar, Thailand and Viet Nam, and opium seizures were reported in China, Myanmar, Thailand and Viet Nam. The Hong Kong Special Administrative Region of China and Thailand composed trans-shipment areas for heroin trafficking from Asia and Africa to East Asia and Oceania. The decreasing trend in heroin seizures continued in China; however, heroin remained the most abused drug in China, Malaysia and Viet Nam. In the Lao People's Democratic Republic, opium abuse decreased but the relapse of opium addicts continued.

The illicit manufacture of ATS remained a problem. During 2008 and the first half of 2009, laboratories involved in methamphetamine manufacture continued to be dismantled in China, and many countries reported seizures of methamphetamine and MDMA. Methamphetamine was the most abused drug in Japan, the Philippines and the Republic of Korea. Japan reported a significant increase in methamphetamine and MDMA abuse in 2008, and significant quantities of precursor chemicals continued to be seized in the region, mainly in China, the Philippines, the Republic of Korea and Thailand. The illicit manufacture, trafficking and abuse of ketamine became major problems in many countries.

As to regional cooperation, countries in the region continued to cooperate through joint drug control investigations. The thirtieth meeting of the Association of Southeast Asian Nations (ASEAN) Senior Officials on Drug Matters (Phnom Penh, Cambodia, 29 September–20 October) endorsed the action-oriented ASEAN Work Plan on Combating Illicit Drug Production, Trafficking and Use, 2009–2015. The eighth meetings of the ASEAN and China Cooperative Operations in Response to Dangerous Drugs (ACCORD) Task Force on Civic Awareness and of the ACCORD Task Force on Demand Reduction (Jakarta, Indonesia, 5–6 August) discussed progress made by ACCORD member States.

At the national level, China established a drug control intelligence and forensic centre to implement its Narcotics Control Law, which entered into force in 2008. Also in 2008 China placed hydroxylamine, a precursor for ketamine, under national control; introduced a new requirement for drug regulatory agencies to impose further controls on compound pharmaceutical preparations containing ephedrine; and strengthened control measures for compound oral solutions containing codeine. In 2008, the Philippine Drug Enforcement Agency joined forces with a telecommunications provider to launch a pilot project to combat illegal drug-related activities, and signed a memorandum of understanding with chemical and pharmaceutical companies to prevent the diversion of precursor chemicals; the Republic of Korea revised its Act on the Control of Narcotic Drugs and added two substances to the list of substances under national control; and Singapore strengthened its efforts to prevent the abuse of inhalants, particularly among youth.

South Asia

Trafficking in cannabis herb and resin remained widespread throughout South Asia. India regularly eradicated opium poppy illicit cultivation and conducted awareness campaigns among villagers. An increasing proportion of the heroin seized in India originated in Afghanistan and was abused locally or smuggled out of the country. Heroin smuggling into Maldives contributed to an increase in its abuse. Sri Lanka in 2008 reported seizures of heroin originated in India and Pakistan. Although India produced and exported large quantities of opium derived from licit cultivation, access to morphine for the treatment of pain remained limited.

Trafficking in ATS increased in South Asia, as evidenced by their continued seizures in the region. Several seizures of methamphetamine were made in India in 2008, and methaqualone continued to be illicitly manufactured. India also became one of the main sources of drugs sold through illegal Internet pharmacies.

The widespread abuse of pharmaceutical preparations, smuggled from India and containing narcotic drugs such as codeine, was a problem in Bangladesh, which also reported seizures of pharmaceutical preparations containing buprenorphine, widely abused by injection. Pharmaceutical preparations containing benzodiazepines were among the most abused drugs in Bhutan. In India, pharmaceutical preparations containing dextropropoxyphene were often used by abusers by injection as an alternative to heroin. The abuse of pharmaceutical preparations containing psychotropic substances in Nepal was facilitated by its open border with India. India continued to report seizures of acetic anhydride. As one of the world's largest manufacturers of ephedrine and pseudoephedrine, India was a main source of those precursor chemicals. Bangladesh, like India, was a significant source of preparations containing pseudoephedrine. India reported increasing ketamine seizures.

Most countries in South Asia lacked data on abuse prevalence, and information on its patterns was often based on rapid situation assessments, the habits of patients in treatment and rehabilitation centres, and the habits of persons arrested on drug-related charges.

As to regional cooperation, representatives of Bangladesh, Bhutan, India and Sri Lanka attended the thirty-second Meeting of Heads of National Drug Law Enforcement Agencies, Asia and the Pacific (Bangkok, Thailand, 10–13 February). At the national level, the Bhutan Narcotic Control Agency in January released three advocacy tools to prevent and reduce drug abuse and raise public awareness of its risks. In December 2008, India passed a law amending its Drugs and Cosmetics Act of 1940, increasing penalties for the manufacture of counterfeit drugs.

West and Central Asia

Many countries in West Asia reported positive developments in drug control in 2009 as a result of national and multilateral efforts by Governments and the allocation of increased resources to fight the scourge of Afghan opiates. However, in 2009, Afghanistan remained by far the world's largest illicit producer of heroin and other opiates and was becoming a major producer of illicitly cultivated cannabis. After peaking in 2007, opium poppy cultivation decreased by 22 per cent, to 123,000 hectares in 2009, and the Afghan provinces free from cultivation increased from 18 to 20. However, due to the record opium poppy yield of 56 kilograms per hectare in 2009 (an increase of 15 per cent over 2008), opium production fell by only 10 per cent, to 6,900 tons. The prices of fresh and dry poppies fell by a third, causing the farm-gate value of opium production to fall by 40 per cent in 2009, to $438 million. The number of people involved in opium production dropped from 2.4 to 1.6 million.

The abuse of opiates continued in Afghanistan and its neighbouring countries. Iran, Pakistan, the Russian Federation and countries in Central Asia and the Caucasus and on the Arabian peninsula remained particularly vulnerable to large-scale trafficking and abuse. Iran had the world's highest rate of abuse of opiates: more than 2 million people, resulting in a prevalence rate of 2.8 per cent. In Central Asia, drug abuse reached alarming proportions due to the sharp increase in the use of opiates, and heroin was the most abused drug. Abuse remained a concern in the Southern Caucasus: in Azerbaijan, the drugs of choice were opioids and cannabis. While there were very little data on the Middle East, heroin abuse increased. In 2008, the number of male abusers increased in Lebanon, where the prevalent drugs remained cannabis herb and cannabis resin ("hashish"). In Israel, 60 per cent of the 20,000 problematic drug users abused opioids by injection.

Significant seizures were made in Afghanistan, though they were small in comparison with the scale of drug production. More than half of Afghan opiates were smuggled through Iran, which continued to seize more opiates than any other country, and one third through Pakistan, which continued to be a major transit area. Turkey reported an increase in the heroin seized, and approximately 121 tons of heroin and 293 tons of opium transited through Central Asia in 2008. In Central Asia, Tajikistan continued to seize the largest quantities of opiates (53 per cent in 2008) and large seizures were reported by Kazakhstan, Turkmenistan and Uzbekistan. The quantities of heroin, opium and cocaine smuggled through the Southern Caucasus increased. The Afghan opiates entered Azerbaijan from Iran and Central Asia en route to Georgia, the Russian Federation and Western Europe. The Middle East became a market for drugs, such as cocaine, which had not previously been abused in the subregion, and Jordan continued to be a transit area.

Cannabis resin production increased in Afghanistan, and the amount seized in Pakistan increased by 33 per cent in 2007–2008. Cannabis continued to be the drug most seized in Central Asia, where, in addition to the fact that its plants grew wild in Kazakhstan and Kyrgyzstan, more shipments of Afghan cannabis herb and resin were discovered. Lebanon reported a small increase in cannabis cultivation in 2008 and growing drug abuse, particularly among young persons.

Trafficking in and abuse of ATS continued to increase in West Asia, particularly in the eastern Mediterranean and on the Arabian peninsula. In Turkey, seizures of ecstasy and Captagon tablets decreased. Counterfeit Captagon continued to be seized in Jordan, Saudi Arabia, the Syrian Arab Republic and the United Arab Emirates. Trafficking in and abuse of counterfeit Captagon continued in the countries on the Arabian peninsula. In 2008, most of the amphetamine seized worldwide was seized in the Middle East (73 per cent), followed by Western Europe (19 per cent). In Iraq, pharmaceutical preparations containing diazepam (Valium) were the most abused drug. In Jordan, benzodiazepine abuse was reported.

With regard to regional cooperation, Afghanistan, Iran and Pakistan were increasingly cooperating through the Triangular Initiative, aimed at combating the smuggling of opiates out of Afghanistan, enhancing joint interdiction operations and strengthening efforts to counter the illicit trade in precursor chemicals used in processing opium in Afghanistan and neighbouring countries. To plan for full deployment of border liaison officers in common border areas, Iran hosted the International Conference of Drug Liaison Officers (28–29 April); its purpose was to reach agreement on a comprehensive cross-border communication plan and on cooperation to stop precursor chemicals from entering Afghanistan. At international summits, emphasis was placed on adopting a regional approach to combating Afghanistan's drug industry. In March, the Special Conference on Afghanistan was convened in Moscow under the auspices of the Shanghai Cooperation Organization; and representatives of 73 countries and 20 international organizations attended an international conference on Afghanistan in The Hague. Countries in Central Asia increased their cooperation and carried out regional projects and international operations under the auspices of the Commonwealth of Independent States (CIS), the Collective Security Treaty Organization (CSTO) and the Shanghai Cooperation Organization. Joint measures taken by countries in the Middle East to combat trafficking continued, and cooperation in controlled deliveries and the sharing of information on trafficking, especially between Turkey and other countries in West Asia, proved effective.

At the national level, Iran in 2008 increased its resources allocated for drug control, strengthened its capacity for prevention and treatment, and strengthened border control. In May, Azerbaijan, Kazakhstan, Kyrgyzstan, Tajikistan and Turkmenistan ratified the framework agreement on the establishment of the Central Asia Regional Information and Coordination Centre (CARICC); the Russian Federation ratified the agreement in September. With those ratifications, CARICC began the transition from its pilot phase to full-fledged functionality as a regional focal point to prevent and combat trans-border trafficking. In May, Kazakhstan adopted a new programme against drug abuse and drug trafficking for 2009–2011.

Communication. On 31 March [A/63/805-S/2009/177], the Russian Federation transmitted the Declaration, Statement and Plan of Action of the member States of the Shanghai Cooperation Organization and Afghanistan on combating terrorism, illicit drug trafficking and organized crime, adopted at the Special Conference on Afghanistan (Moscow, 27 March).

Afghanistan

In response to Commission on Narcotic Drugs resolution 51/1 [YUN 2008, p. 1366], the UNODC Executive Director submitted a January report [E/CN.7/2009/8] on follow-up to the Second Ministerial Conference on Drug Trafficking Routes from Afghanistan [YUN 2006, p. 1450]. The report reviewed progress made on the outcomes of three Paris Pact expert round tables, and stated that the Paris Pact recommendations [YUN 2003, p. 1263] had been translated into action-oriented plans and goals, including the Rainbow Strategy, resulting in significant seizures of precursor chemicals in 2008.

On 5 January [E/CN.7/2009/7], the Executive Director submitted a report on provision of international assistance to the most affected States neighbouring Afghanistan, based on information available to UNODC at the end of 2008, including reports voluntarily submitted by States and data and other information contained in the Automated Donor Assistance Mechanism, an Internet-based tool for coordinating technical assistance in the field of counter-narcotics. The report provided information on Afghanistan and on cooperation among Afghanistan, Iran, Pakistan and other Central Asian countries.

Commission action. On 20 March [E/2009/28 (res. 52/2)], the Commission requested the international community, in particular countries of destination, to provide technical assistance and support to the States most affected by the transit of illicit drugs in order to promote their capacities to counter their flow. It urged States and UNODC to provide assistance and support for implementing the initiatives of Afghanistan, Iran and Pakistan, including the Triangular Initiative; and called on international organizations, financial institutions and donors to support and provide technical and financial assistance to the most affected transit States and to Afghanistan.

Europe

While cannabis resin remained the most abused drug in Europe, cannabis herb abuse increased. The abuse of cocaine was concentrated in a few countries in Western Europe, while it was low in most other European countries. Declining or stable abuse was reported in Austria, Germany, Spain, Switzerland and the United Kingdom, whereas an increase was reported in France and Ireland. Heroin abuse was stable in most countries. In the Russian Federation, the abuse of heroin and other opiates predominated, and in 2008 the abuse of opiates increased in most Eastern European countries, particularly in Albania, Belarus, Croatia, Moldova and the Russian Federation, as well as in countries along the Balkan route. The abuse of amphetamines and MDMA stabilized or decreased, and methamphetamine abuse continued to be limited in Eastern Europe.

In 2009, cannabis plants were illicitly cultivated in many European countries, such as Albania, Bulgaria and Serbia. Cannabis cultivation, both outdoors and indoors, intensified in Germany. In Switzerland, there was a reduction in the area under cultivation and in the number of facilities producing cannabis on a smaller scale. European cultivation sites were the source of a growing proportion of the cannabis herb found in Europe; however, with its large market for cannabis, Europe was the only region into which significant quantities of cannabis herb were smuggled from other regions, such as Africa or Asia. In Eastern and Central Europe, trafficking in cannabis herb continued; most of it originated in Albania, Moldova, Montenegro, Serbia, the former Yugoslav Republic of Macedonia and Ukraine. Western Europe remained the world's largest market for cannabis resin. Spain accounted for more than 70 per cent of its seizures in Western and Central Europe and for the largest amount worldwide. Trafficking in resin, though limited in Eastern Europe, was slightly more widespread in the Russian Federation. The main sources of resin found in Western Europe were Morocco and countries in South-West Asia, notably Afghanistan.

Europe continued to account for all cocaine seizures occurring outside the Americas. However, seizures decreased substantially in 2008. Most of the cocaine entering Western Europe was smuggled out of Venezuela; Central and West Africa continued to be used as storage and transit areas. The smuggling of cocaine through Eastern Europe increased in recent years. While "crack" cocaine continued to be of marginal importance in Western Europe, its seizure increased in Germany.

The increase in heroin seizures in Europe in 2007 and 2008 was attributed to South-Eastern and Eastern Europe, used as transit areas for opiates destined for Western and Central Europe. France, Germany, Italy, Norway and the United Kingdom were the main countries of destination. The illicit market for opiates continued to expand in Eastern Europe, particularly in the Russian Federation and Ukraine. Almost all of the heroin in Eastern Europe originated in Afghanistan; Turkey continued to be the starting point for the Balkan route, used for smuggling heroin into Europe. In addition, heroin continued to be smuggled along the "silk route" through Central Asia into the Russian Federation, where it was abused or smuggled further into other CIS member States. In 2008, heroin accounted for 92 per cent of all the seizures of opiates in Eastern and Central Europe. In Western Europe, the amount of opium seized was significantly lower than the amount of heroin.

The quantity of amphetamine seized in Eastern Europe increased significantly in 2008, with Poland accounting for more than 77 per cent. Seizures of amphetamine and methamphetamine increased in Germany. MDMA seizures declined in Western Europe. The majority of the seized MDMA with a known origin or transit route was from the Netherlands, and the second source continued to be Belgium. The illicit manufacture of methamphetamine took place mainly in Central and Eastern Europe, above all in the Czech Republic and the Russian Federation. Bosnia and Herzegovina, Bulgaria, Montenegro and Serbia were emerging countries for amphetamine manufacture. Khat was often smuggled into Europe via the Netherlands and the United Kingdom.

With regard to regional cooperation, CSTO and the Federal Drug Control Service of the Russian Federation in November 2008 conducted the second phase of the operation Channel 2008, with the participation of Armenia, Belarus, Kazakhstan, Kyrgyzstan, the Russian Federation, Tajikistan and Uzbekistan, to build a system of enhanced collective security to prevent trafficking from Afghanistan and the entry of precursor chemicals into Central Asia and Afghanistan. At the national level, a series of referendums was held in Switzerland in November 2008 to decide on the national drug control policy. Voters decided in favour of offering prescribed heroin to abusers on a permanent basis but rejected the decriminalization of cannabis. Spain in January 2009 adopted its national drug control strategy for 2009–2016. In March, Serbia adopted the National Palliative Care Strategy, which focused on the use of opioids for pain relief.

Oceania

In Australia, abuse by injection remained low. Methamphetamine and amphetamine were the drugs most commonly injected, followed by heroin. Demand for MDMA increased: 36 per cent of the total amount seized globally in 2008 was destined for Australia, where widespread use and stable prices underpinned its demand. In New Zealand, the abuse of cannabis declined, and the drug most commonly injected was heroin. Despite low demand for cocaine in New Zealand, its abuse increased; the annual prevalence rate of MDMA abuse also increased. The country's rate of amphetamine and methamphetamine abuse was among the highest in the world. On account of its ready availability and low cost, cannabis was the most abused drug in the majority of the countries in Oceania other than Australia and New Zealand.

Illicit cannabis cultivation continued in the region, not only in Australia and New Zealand, but also in Fiji, Papua New Guinea, Samoa and Tonga. Cannabis remained the drug most commonly seized.

It was produced domestically, with a very small proportion smuggled from other regions. The quantity of cocaine seized in the region increased, with Australia accounting for 99 per cent of seizures. Cocaine smuggling from Canada continued, and the drug was increasingly smuggled through China. South-West and South-East Asia remained major sources of the heroin smuggled into Australia.

Combating the illicit manufacture of ATS remained a priority in Oceania. Domestic clandestine manufacture remained the main source in Australia, and most of the methamphetamine seized in New Zealand was manufactured in the country. Although ATS were supplied primarily by domestic manufacturers, they were increasingly smuggled from North America and South-East Asia. The quantity of precursors seized in the region was increasing, and trafficking in ephedrine and pseudoephedrine as raw materials continued in Australia and New Zealand. East and South-East Asia remained the major source. While MDMA illicit manufacture continued in Australia, the quantity of its seized precursors decreased. An increasing quantity of gamma-butyrolactone, a precursor of GHB, was seized in Oceania, and seizures of GHB and ketamine continued in Australia.

As to regional cooperation, Australia and New Zealand continued to provide support for capacity-building initiatives in the region, and regional conferences continued to bring countries together to address drug control issues. The annual meeting of the Regional Security Committee of the Pacific Islands Forum (Fiji, June) addressed the need for closer regional cooperation in Oceania. At the national level, Australia in April launched a campaign against illicit drugs to reduce the abuse of methamphetamines, MDMA and cannabis among youth. In February, the New Zealand police launched its "Illicit Drug Strategy to 2010" to reduce the supply of and demand for drugs, particularly cannabis and methamphetamine. In October, New Zealand announced a new national action plan to tackle the problem of methamphetamine.

UN action to combat drug abuse

UN Office on Drugs and Crime

The United Nations Office on Drugs and Crime (UNODC) addressed the interrelated issues of drug control, crime prevention and international terrorism in the context of sustainable development and human security (see also PART THREE, Chapter IX). The Organization's drug programme continued to be implemented in accordance with General Assembly resolution 45/179 [YUN 1990, p. 874]. The Office was responsible for coordinating all UN drug control activities and was the repository of technical expertise in international drug control for the UN Secretariat. It acted on behalf of the Secretary-General in fulfilling his responsibilities under the terms of international treaties and resolutions relating to drug control, and provided services to the Assembly, the Economic and Social Council, and committees and conferences dealing with drug control matters.

The UNODC Executive Director described the Office's 2009 activities in a report to the Commission on Narcotic Drugs and to the Commission on Crime Prevention and Criminal Justice [E/CN.7/2010/3-E/CN.15/2010/3]. Activities were carried out in the areas of sustainable livelihoods, with particular emphasis on illicit drug crop monitoring and illicit crop cultivation and poverty eradication; supply reduction; drug demand reduction, treatment and rehabilitation; follow-up to the outcome of the high-level segment of the fifty-second session of the Commission on Narcotic Drugs; and strengthening cooperation between UNODC and other UN entities for the promotion of human rights in the implementation of the international treaties. The report also considered emerging issues such as: the evolving threat of Afghan opiates and the work of UNODC in the region; new trafficking routes for cocaine; ATS production in West Africa; and international support provided to West Africa.

During the year, the Office published: *World Drug Report 2009* [Sales No. E.09.XI.12]; *Afghanistan Opium Survey 2009*; *Opium Poppy Cultivation in South-East Asia: Lao People's Democratic Republic, Myanmar*; *Patterns and Trends of ATS and Other Drugs in East and South-East Asia (and neighbouring regions)*; and *100 Years of Drug Control*.

ECONOMIC AND SOCIAL COUNCIL ACTION

On 30 July [meeting 44], the Economic and Social Council, on the recommendation of the Commission on Narcotic Drugs [E/2009/28], adopted **resolution 2009/23** without vote [agenda item 14 *(c)*].

Support for the development and implementation of the regional programmes of the United Nations Office on Drugs and Crime

The Economic and Social Council,

Recalling General Assembly resolutions 63/195 of 18 December 2008, entitled "Strengthening the United Nations Crime Prevention and Criminal Justice Programme, in particular its technical cooperation capacity", and 63/197 of 18 December 2008, entitled "International cooperation against the world drug problem",

Recalling also the strategy for the period 2008–2011 for the United Nations Office on Drugs and Crime, which provides a clear framework for the work of the Office,

1. *Welcomes* the adoption by the United Nations Office on Drugs and Crime of a regional approach to programming based on consultation and partnership at the national

and regional levels and focused on ensuring that the Office responds in a sustainable and coherent manner to the priorities of Member States;

2. *Notes* the activities of the United Nations Office on Drugs and Crime aimed at achieving a stronger working relationship with other entities of the United Nations system, including the Department of Peacekeeping Operations of the Secretariat, the United Nations Development Programme and the World Bank;

3. *Welcomes* the outcomes of the recent ministerial and expert meetings held for the subregions of East Africa, West Africa, East Asia and the Pacific and the Caribbean, at which programmes were discussed and agreement was reached on the way forward;

4. *Looks forward* to receiving the outcomes of the subregional meetings for Central America and South-Eastern Europe that will be held in the near future;

5. *Encourages* Member States from other subregions to engage with the United Nations Office on Drugs and Crime in the preparation of similar subregional programmes;

6. *Expresses its appreciation* to Governments that have hosted regional conferences and expert group meetings and to Governments that have provided financial support to make those conferences and meetings possible;

7. *Requests* the United Nations Office on Drugs and Crime to continue to make every effort to ensure an effective consultation process for the regional programmes and to ensure that such programmes are distributed as widely as possible;

8. *Also requests* the United Nations Office on Drugs and Crime to enhance, in a coordinated manner, its efforts to provide technical assistance and advisory services for the implementation of regional programmes;

9. *Encourages* all Member States, where appropriate, to draw upon the regional programmes of the United Nations Office on Drugs and Crime and the technical assistance activities outlined therein in the development of national legislation, procedures, policies and strategies for strengthening criminal justice systems and related institutions;

10. *Invites* all Member States, as well as subregional and regional institutions, to mainstream measures to counter organized crime, corruption and illicit drug trafficking into their national and regional development strategies, in accordance with the relevant international conventions, and to make every effort to allocate resources for the implementation of those measures;

11. *Encourages* bilateral and multilateral aid agencies and financial institutions to support the implementation of the regional programmes of the United Nations Office on Drugs and Crime;

12. *Invites* relevant entities of the United Nations system, including the Department of Peacekeeping Operations, the United Nations Development Programme and the World Bank, as well as other international agencies and organizations, to continue coordinating with the United Nations Office on Drugs and Crime in order to support the implementation of the regional programmes of the Office and to integrate crime prevention and drug control measures into their development programmes;

13. *Requests* the Executive Director of the United Nations Office on Drugs and Crime to give high priority to the implementation of the regional programmes of the

Office and to report to the Commission on Narcotic Drugs and the Commission on Crime Prevention and Criminal Justice at their sessions to be held in the first half of 2011 on progress made on such implementation.

Administrative and budgetary matters

In January [E/CN.7/2009/11-E/CN.15/2009/11], the Executive Director presented a report on the implementation of the UNODC consolidated budget for the 2008–2009 biennium [YUN 2007, p. 1300]. The report informed States about programme performance, compared actual income and expenditure with the estimates contained in the consolidated budget as approved, explained major deviations from the approved budget and presented revised estimates for the biennium. It concluded that lower-than-anticipated general-purpose income and higher costs demonstrated that decisive action was needed to reduce general-purpose fund expenditure by at least $2 million in 2009. Cost-saving measures would affect the ability of UNODC to continue to deliver on its expanding mandates. A detailed review of critical functions was under way with a view to restructuring and streamlining the work of UNODC at headquarters and in the field.

A March Secretariat report [E/CN.7/2009/10-E/CN.15/2009/10] stated that, at its final meeting on 9 March, the open-ended intergovernmental working group on improving the governance and financial situation of UNODC [YUN 2008, p. 1371] approved recommendations for submission to the Commission on Narcotic Drugs and the Commission on Crime Prevention and Criminal Justice on: creating a standing, open-ended working group on governance and finance; improving the governing role and functioning of the Commissions; evaluation; measures to improve the UNODC funding situation; and a workplan to further improve the UNODC efficiency and funding situation.

Commission action. On 20 March [E/2009/28 (res. 52/13], the Commission adopted a resolution on improving the governance and financial situation of UNODC. Noting the financial challenges facing UNODC, in particular the shortfall in general-purpose funding, the Commission adopted the recommendations of the working group, contained in the annex to the resolution. It established a standing open-ended intergovernmental working group on governance and finance, whose mandate should be in effect until the Commission's session to be held in the first half of 2011, at which time the Commission should review the functioning of the working group and consider extending its mandate. The Commission emphasized that the working group should be a forum for dialogue among States and between States and the Secretariat on the development of UNODC programmes. It recommended that the General Assembly, as part of the budget process for the 2010–2011 biennium, should reallocate available resources in such a way that reconvened sessions of the Commission on Narcotic Drugs and the Commission on Crime Prevention and Criminal Justice could be held back to back in the second half of each year, in order to consider the reports of and recommendations proposed by the working group. The Commission also decided that the working group should hold at least two formal meetings, one in the third quarter of 2009 and one in the first quarter of 2010.

By **decision 2009/251** of 30 July, the Economic and Social Council established a standing open-ended intergovernmental working group on improving the governance and financial situation of UNODC, whose mandate should be in effect until the sessions of the Commission on Narcotic Drugs and the Commission on Crime Prevention and Criminal Justice to be held in the first half of 2011, at which time the Commissions would review the functioning of the working group and consider extending its mandate. Starting in 2010, the two Commissions would hold reconvened sessions on an annual basis in the second half of the year; their annual reconvened sessions would have a duration of one day each, unless the respective Commission decided otherwise in the preceding year, and would be held back to back.

A November Secretariat note [E/CN.7/2009/15-E/CN.15/2009/25] provided information on the activities of the working group in October and November.

In a September report [E/CN.7/2009/13-E/CN.15/2009/23], the Executive Director submitted the UNODC consolidated budget for the 2010–2011 biennium to the Commission on Narcotic Drugs and the Commission on Crime Prevention and Criminal Justice. In December [E/CN.7/2009/14-E/CN.15/2009/24], the Advisory Committee on Administrative and Budgetary Questions submitted its comments and recommendation on that report.

At its reconvened fifty-second session in December [E/2009/28/Add.1 (res. 52/14)], the Commission on Narcotic Drugs approved the projected use of general-purpose funds in the 2010–2011 biennium and invited States to provide contributions totalling at least $17,241,800. It also invited States to provide additional general-purpose contributions to the Fund of the United Nations International Drug Control Programme and the United Nations Crime Prevention and Criminal Justice Fund, totalling $9,570,800, to enable UNODC to restore and strengthen the functions and activities discontinued in 2008–2009 as a result of the decline in its general-purpose income. The Commission decided that the UNODC proposed consolidated budget for 2010–2011 should contain adequate provisions for establishing an independent evaluation unit.

Commission on Narcotic Drugs

At its fifty-second session (Vienna, 11–20 March), the Commission on Narcotic Drugs recommended one resolution and two decisions for adoption by the Economic and Social Council. It also adopted 13 resolutions, which it brought to the attention of the Council. The Commission held a reconvened fifty-second session (Vienna, 1–2 December), at which it adopted one resolution and brought it to the attention of the Council.

Following the closure of its reconvened fifty-second session on 2 December, the Commission opened its fifty-third session to elect the new chairperson and other bureau members.

By **decision 2009/248** of 30 July, the Council took note of the Commission's report on its fifty-second session [E/2009/28] and approved the provisional agenda and documentation for the fifty-third (2010) session.

Pursuant to Commission resolution 51/14 [YUN 2008, p. 1372], the Executive Director in January submitted a report [E/CN.7/2009/9] on promoting coordination and alignment of decisions between the Commission on Narcotic Drugs and the Programme Coordinating Board of the Joint United Nations Programme on HIV/AIDS (UNAIDS).

Drug demand reduction and drug abuse

The Commission on Narcotic Drugs had before it a January report by the Secretariat [E/CN.7/2009/2] that reviewed the global and regional situation with respect to illicit drug use from 1998 to 2008. Available information suggested that the abuse of opioids and cocaine was stabilizing or decreasing in countries where it was in general high. The prevalence of heroin by injection remained high in Central Asia and Eastern Europe. The abuse of ATS stabilized, and in some areas decreased, in the large markets of Western and Central Europe, North America and Oceania. However, increases in ATS abuse were registered in parts of East and South-East Asia, the Near and Middle East and parts of Africa and Latin America. Cannabis abuse remained globally widespread; it stabilized or declined among young people in countries with more established cannabis markets in Western Europe, North America and parts of Oceania, but increased in many developing countries. Although there had been improvements in the quality and reliability of data since 1998, up-to-date information was not available in many countries, and the lack of sustainable drug information systems hindered the monitoring of emerging epidemics and the implementation of evidence-based responses.

Misuse of substances to facilitate sexual assault

On 20 March [E/2009/28 (res. 52/8)], the Commission urged States to address the emerging problem of the use of substances to facilitate sexual assault ("date rape"), which affected many States, by enhancing public awareness. The Commission urged States to consider imposing stricter controls on those substances or taking measures aimed at discouraging their use for committing drug-facilitated sexual assault, including with regard to substances not under international control. The Commission invited industries concerned to cooperate in developing formulations with safety features, such as dyes and flavourings, to alert potential victims to the contamination of their drinks, without affecting the bioavailability of the active ingredients in legitimate drugs. States were urged to share information on emerging trends in the use of drugs to commit such offences.

Illicit cultivation, manufacture and trafficking

A December report by the Secretariat [E/CN.7/2010/4] reviewed the latest trends in illicit drug production and trafficking worldwide, focusing on seizure statistics for 2007–2008 and on cultivation and production for 2008–2009.

Cannabis continued to be the most widely produced, trafficked and consumed plant-based drug. In 2008, cannabis resin seizures rose by one quarter to reach record levels, partly due to seizures in South-West Asia, which reflected the growing cannabis cultivation in Afghanistan. Morocco reported a reduction in cannabis cultivation but remained a source for cannabis resin. Global seizures of cannabis herb sustained the increasing trend of recent years, with significant increases in South America, Africa, Asia and Europe.

The illicit market for opiates continued to be centred around Afghanistan, where a dominant share of the world's opium poppy cultivation and opium production, as well as a substantial portion of global heroin manufacture, were located. For the second consecutive year, opium poppy cultivation in Afghanistan fell by one fifth in 2009, while opium production fell less markedly. Global opiate seizures continued to increase, with the exception of morphine. In 2008, Iran registered the largest seizures worldwide of opium, morphine and heroin.

In 2008, coca bush cultivation remained concentrated in Colombia, Peru and Bolivia. The area under cultivation fell in Colombia, which nevertheless continued to account for one half of global cultivation. Global cocaine seizures remained stable but exhibited a shift towards the source countries, with South America accounting for 61 per cent of the total in 2008. Africa's role as a transit area for cocaine trafficking increased.

Seizures of ATS remained stable in 2008, with the exception of MDMA (ecstasy): its global seizures had fallen to the lowest level since 1999, partly due to reduced levels in the Netherlands and Australia. Manufacture of ATS continued in areas where it was well-established, notably East and South-East Asia, Europe, North America and Oceania, but also showed signs of spreading to vulnerable countries with little or no previous history of reported manufacture, notably countries in Latin America.

Use of cannabis seeds for illicit purposes

On 20 March [E/2009/28 (res. 52/5)], the Commission urged Member States to take measures against the illicit cultivation of cannabis plant, in compliance with the 1961 Convention, and to consider not allowing trade in cannabis seeds for illicit purposes. It requested UNODC to share information regarding the health risks posed by cannabis with the WHO Expert Committee on Drug Dependence, and requested INCB to gather from States regulatory information on cannabis seeds, including on their sale through the Internet, and to share that information with States. The Commission also requested UNODC to conduct a global survey on cannabis seeds and to report to the Commission at its fifty-third (2010) session.

Involvement of women and girls in trafficking

On 20 March [E/2009/28 (res. 52/1)], the Commission addressed the involvement of women and girls in drug trafficking as couriers, in drug abuse and illicit cultivation, and in the illicit manufacture, processing, smuggling, distribution and sale of narcotic drugs and psychotropic substances. It requested UNODC to carry out scientific research and analysis based on information and statistical data received from States, and stressed the importance of collecting and analysing data disaggregated by sex and age and of conducting research on gender issues relating to drug trafficking, especially the use of women and girls as couriers. The Commission encouraged States to provide additional reporting on and analysis of data, and requested UNODC to ensure that gender issues were given attention in future reports. It urged States to implement programmes aimed at preventing women and girls from being used as couriers and requested UNODC to assist States in developing such programmes and implementing alternative development policies. States were encouraged to establish programmes of financial assistance to support income-generating projects for the educational, economic and social development and the rehabilitation of women and girls involved in drug trafficking.

Measures against laundering of assets

On 20 March [E/2009/28 (res. 52/9)], the Commission urged States parties to the 1988 Convention to apply fully its provisions, in particular with regard to the laundering of assets derived from drug trafficking, and invited States that had not yet done so to ratify or accede to it. It also invited States parties to the United Nations Convention against Transnational Organized Crime [YUN 2000, p. 1048] and the United Nations Convention against Corruption [YUN 2003, p. 1127] to apply their provisions, in particular with a view to countering money-laundering, and invited States that had not yet done so to ratify or accede to them. It urged States to strengthen cooperation for combating the laundering of assets derived from drug trafficking, and to enhance international judicial cooperation in detecting and prosecuting those involved in money-laundering. It also invited States to review and strengthen their national legislation against the laundering of assets, to review the criminal and administrative penalties and to expand the predicate offences to the crime of money-laundering. States were urged to establish or strengthen national institutions specializing in financial intelligence; promote the sharing of information between law enforcement authorities; make use of available state-of-the-art technologies and techniques; complement national and international measures against the laundering of assets; establish transparent mechanisms to distribute confiscated funds; and ensure that banking secrecy laws did not impede criminal investigations. UNODC was requested to provide technical assistance and training and to cooperate with specialized bodies. States and other donors were invited to provide extrabudgetary contributions and to promote the involvement of the private sector.

Alternative development

On 20 March [E/2009/28 (res. 52/6)], the Commission acknowledged that alternative development was an important component in generating and promoting sustainable economic alternatives to illicit drug cultivation and was one of the key components of policies and programmes for reducing illicit drug production. The Commission recognized the role played by developing countries with extensive expertise in alternative development, and the importance of promoting a set of best practices and lessons learned and of sharing them with States affected by illicit cultivation or facing the risks of illicit cultivation. It urged Governments, multilateral agencies and international and regional financial institutions to increase and sustain their support of alternative development programmes and to strengthen technical assistance and cooperation, including South-South cooperation, and

called upon States to consider measures enabling the products of those programmes to have easier access to markets. The Commission requested UNODC to continue promoting best practices and lessons learned, including by organizing an international conference on the topic in 2010.

Evaluation of drug analysis laboratories

On 20 March [E/2009/28 (res. 52/7)], the Commission recommended that UNODC continue to support the analytical work of drug analysis laboratories and the training of experts, and to evaluate the performance of those laboratories through its quality assurance programme. It invited States to consider a certification process coordinated by UNODC, and urged States and subregional, regional and international entities to contribute to UNODC work by providing expertise for the development of cooperative networks among laboratories and scientists and by exploring innovative ways to ensure the exchange of expertise and information worldwide.

Regional cooperation

In 2009, two Secretariat reports described action taken by regional subsidiary bodies of the Commission on Narcotic Drugs during the year. Following a review of drug trafficking trends and regional and subregional cooperation, each body addressed drug law enforcement issues of priority in its region and made recommendations. A February report [E/CN.7/2009/5/Add.1] reviewed the thirty-second meeting of Heads of National Drug Law Enforcement Agencies (HONLEA), Asia and the Pacific (Bangkok, 10–13 February) [UNODC/HONLAP/32/5], which made recommendations on changing trends in trafficking in heroin; recovering the proceeds of crime; and precursor control and the impact on the manufacture of ATS.

A November report [E/CN.7/2010/5] reviewed action taken by five subsidiary bodies in 2009. The eighth meeting of HONLEA, Europe (Vienna, 16–18 June) [UNODC/HONEURO/8/5] made recommendations on the influence of the Internet and other electronic media on drug trafficking; information as the key to dismantling trafficking groups; and drug trafficking in Europe: trends, strategies and effective responses. The thirty-third meeting of HONLEA, Asia and the Pacific (Denpasar, Indonesia, 6–9 October) [UNODC/HONLAP/33/5] made recommendations on illicit drug trafficking: emerging trends across the region; measures to counter the manufacture of ATS in the region; and removing the profit from drug trafficking. The nineteenth meeting of HONLEA, Africa (Windhoek, Namibia, 12–16 October) [UNODC/HONLAF/19/5] made recommendations on developing effective drug law enforcement intelligence-led operational responses; national responses in support of regional efforts and initiatives in the fight against illicit drug trafficking; the impact of the Internet and other electronic media on drug trafficking; and forensic services in Africa. The forty-fourth session of the Subcommission on Illicit Drug Traffic and Related Matters in the Near and Middle East (Vienna, 16–19 November) [UNODC/SUBCOM/44/5] made recommendations on combating the challenge of illicit opiate trafficking in the region; the use of the Internet in trafficking in narcotic drugs, psychotropic substances and precursor chemicals; and ATS.

On 20 March [E/2009/28 (res. 52/10)], the Commission on Narcotic Drugs invited Venezuela, as host of the nineteenth meeting of HONLEA, Latin America and the Caribbean, to revise the agenda of that meeting in order to ensure that particular focus was placed on cooperation among the bodies involved in tackling drug trafficking between Latin American and Caribbean States and African States, in particular West African States. It invited the States concerned to participate in the meeting and to provide resources through UNODC to ensure the participation of senior officials of drug law enforcement agencies from West African States, particularly from those affected by trafficking.

Pursuant to that request, the nineteenth meeting of HONLEA, Latin America and the Caribbean (Isla Margarita, Venezuela, 28 September–2 October) [UNODC/HONLAC/19/5] held a roundtable discussion on the topic and recommended measures to strengthen cooperation among the bodies involved in tackling drug trafficking between Latin America and the Caribbean and West Africa. The meeting also made recommendations on improving the effectiveness of controlled deliveries among States and effective border management at sea container terminals.

Chapter XV

Statistics

The United Nations continued its statistical work programme in 2009, mainly through the Statistical Commission and the United Nations Statistics Division. In February, the Commission adopted the *System of National Accounts, 2008*, volume 2, which, combined with volume 1, provided the international statistical standard for national accounts. It also adopted the proposed set of indicators on violence against women as an interim set and first step; recognized that official statistics had an important role to play in closing data gaps related to climate change; and approved its multi-year programme of work for 2009–2012.

The Commission reviewed the work of groups of countries and international organizations in various areas of economic, social, demographic and environmental statistics, and made recommendations and suggestions.

Work of Statistical Commission

In accordance with Economic and Social Council decision 2008/238 [YUN 2008, p. 1380], the Statistical Commission held its fortieth session in New York from 24 to 27 February [E/2009/24] and brought to the attention of the Council 15 decisions adopted during the session. Welcoming the programme review on climate change and official statistics prepared by the Australian Bureau of Statistics, it noted that climate change was a new area of official statistics and that work in that field should be approached with caution, as countries were at different levels of statistical development. The Commission expressed its support for the revision of the System of Environmental-Economic Accounting. Noting that there were differing views regarding the proposed expansion of the mandate of the Committee of Experts on Environmental-Economic Accounting to include environment and climate change statistics, the Commission requested the Committee to review its mandate, terms of reference and governance structure to reflect the focus of its work on environmental-economic accounting and its role in environment and climate change statistics.

The Commission congratulated the member organizations of the Intersecretariat Working Group on National Accounts for bringing the multi-year project of updating the *System of National Accounts, 1993* [YUN 1993, p. 1112] to conclusion; adopted the *System of National Accounts, 2008*, volume 2; and encouraged Member States and regional and subregional organizations to implement it. It expressed support for the development of a strategic plan to improve agricultural and rural statistics based on the recommendations set out in the report of the Working Group on Agricultural Statistics. It also endorsed the strategy of the United Nations Statistics Division to prepare international recommendations for energy statistics that would provide a foundation for the long-term development of official energy statistics.

The Commission emphasized the importance of developing a substantive inventory of social statistics to identify methodological gaps and to facilitate sharing of best practices. It expressed appreciation for the efforts of the Intersecretariat Working Group on Health Statistics in developing the framework for health statistics, and encouraged it to finalize the framework. The Commission further endorsed the establishment of an expert group on the revision and implementation of the International Standard Classification of Education and agreed, in principle, with the establishment of an intersecretariat working group on education statistics to improve coordination. It agreed with the priority issues listed in the report of the International Labour Organization (ILO) on labour statistics, as well as the road map put forward. In particular, the Commission agreed with the need to address the issues of the changing structure of the labour force, including ageing and the definition and measurement of employment and unemployment.

On gender statistics, the Commission adopted the proposed set of indicators on violence against women as an interim set and first step, and recognizing the substantial cultural differences on the issue, urged the Friends of the Chair to expand its composition to ensure that different perspectives and sensitivities were taken into consideration. With regard to the International Comparison Programme, the Commission endorsed the proposed governance structure and work programme for the 2011 round.

The Commission congratulated the Economic and Social Commission for Asia and the Pacific (ESCAP) for holding the first session of the re-established Committee on Statistics, and requested that ESCAP establish an informal mechanism for donor coordination for statistical development in the region. Taking note of the report of the Secretary-General on the indicators for monitoring the Millennium Development

Goals (MDGs), the Commission requested the Inter-Agency and Expert Group on Millennium Development Goals Indicators and the Statistics Division to continue improving the indicators through methodological and technical refinement.

On 29 July, the Economic and Social Council took note of the Commission's report, decided that the forty-first session would be held in New York from 23 to 26 February 2010, and approved the provisional agenda and documentation for the session (**decision 2009/237**).

Economic statistics

National accounts

In accordance with a request of the Statistical Commission at its thirty-ninth session [YUN 2008, p. 1380], the Secretary-General transmitted to the Commission the report of the Intersecretariat Working Group on National Accounts (ISWGNA) [E/CN.3/2009/8], which requested the Commission to adopt the draft of volume 2 of the *System of National Accounts, 2008*. ISWGNA comprised the Statistical Office of the European Communities (Eurostat), the International Monetary Fund (IMF), the Organization for Economic Cooperation and Development (OECD), the United Nations and the World Bank.

The report reviewed progress made since the thirty-ninth session of the Commission and outlined future work, which would end with the publication of the complete, updated System of National Accounts (SNA). It proposed a strategy for implementing the updated SNA, which aimed to support sound macroeconomic management and evidence-based policy formulation through the sustained compilation and reporting of national accounts and related source data by national, regional and international statistical systems. The report also summarized the deliberations of a high-level forum (Washington, D.C., 17–18 November 2008) that discussed possible future developments of the SNA and related procedures, taking into consideration the rapid changes in the global economy, changes in economic theory and emerging policy needs.

The Commission on 27 February [E/2009/24 (dec. 40/105)] congratulated the member organizations of ISWGNA for bringing the multi-year project of updating the 1993 SNA to conclusion. It adopted volume 2 of the 2008 SNA and encouraged Member States and regional and subregional organizations to implement the standard and support all aspects of the implementation of the updated SNA, including the national and international reporting of national accounts statistics. It requested the secretariat and the members of ISWGNA to finalize the 2008 SNA, to proceed with its publication in all six UN official languages and to promote its dissemination. It endorsed the proposed implementation strategy for the 2008 SNA, empha-

sizing the advocacy element of the implementation strategy and the importance of a global communication strategy. It requested the Working Group to report, in 2010, on progress with the implementation programme and the research agenda of the 2008 SNA.

International Comparison Programme

The Commission considered the Secretary-General's note [E/CN.3/2009/14] transmitting the World Bank report on the International Comparison Programme (ICP), which outlined the proposed governance structure and work programme for the ICP 2011 round. To maintain the momentum of the successful completion of the ICP 2005 round [YUN 2005, p. 1369], the Statistical Commission, at its thirty-ninth session [YUN 2008, p. 1381], had requested that preparations for the next ICP round begin immediately, with a target year for data collection of 2011. The report set out proposals for developing and strengthening the governance structure of the ICP 2011 round, based on the success of the 2005 round and taking into account recommendations made by the Friends of the Chair evaluation. It also proposed a work programme with actions required in seven key areas: putting the governance structure in place; establishing the Global Office; completing the activities under the 2005 round; expanding advocacy and outreach to data users; financing the 2011 round; establishing regional offices; and addressing technical issues.

The Commission on 27 February [dec. 40/111] took note of the increasing use of purchasing power parity data from the 2005 round by academics, researchers and international organizations and their feedback for improving data quality for the 2011 round. It endorsed the proposed governance structure and work programme for the 2011 round; drew attention to expediting the research programme with a focus on data quality assessment, ring comparison and compilation software; encouraged the development of advocacy strategies; welcomed the plan for holding an ICP data users conference in 2010; urged that the Programme's new Executive Board be established as soon as possible; requested that the subcommittee of the interim Executive Board in charge of handling operational matters for the 2011 round continue its work; and requested that a status report on the start of the 2011 round be submitted to the Commission at its forty-first (2010) session.

Other economic statistics

Energy statistics

The Secretary-General transmitted to the Statistical Commission the report of the 24-member Intersecretariat Working Group on Energy Statistics

[E/CN.3/2009/6], which described the activities of the Working Group in 2007–2008, including progress on harmonizing definitions of energy products and flows, as well as planned future activities.

The Secretary-General also transmitted to the Commission the report of the 26-member Oslo Group on Energy Statistics [E/CN.3/2009/5], which described the activities of the Oslo Group in 2007–2008, including the main findings of the second (New Delhi, India, 5–7 February 2007) and third (Vienna, 4–6 February 2008) meetings, the launching of the new interactive website, the drafting of the revised and updated international recommendations for energy statistics, and future activities.

Report of Secretary-General. At the request of the Commission at its thirty-seventh session [YUN 2006, p. 1468], the Secretary-General submitted a report entitled "Towards international recommendations for energy statistics" [E/CN.3/2009/4], which elaborated the need for preparing and updating the international recommendations for energy statistics; outlined the strategy of the Statistics Division for organizing the revision and updating process; described actions undertaken; and summarized its action plan for 2009–2011.

The Commission on 27 February [dec. 40/103] welcomed the report of the Secretary-General and expressed its appreciation for the work accomplished by the Statistics Division, the Oslo Group on Energy Statistics, the Intersecretariat Working Group on Energy Statistics and other stakeholders. It endorsed the strategy of the Statistics Division to prepare international recommendations for energy statistics, and emphasized that the revised recommendations should provide a firm foundation for the long-term development of official energy statistics and contain the necessary guidance on the underlying concepts, definition and classifications as well as on data compilation and dissemination. It stressed the importance of close cooperation of international, supranational and regional organizations in developing the recommendations, in order to avoid overlapping of activities and to ensure consistency of concepts and methodologies. It stressed the importance of involving countries in preparing the recommendations, and encouraged countries to participate in the drafting process by providing their contributions.

Price statistics

The Statistical Commission had before it the Secretary-General's note transmitting the report of the Intersecretariat Working Group on Price Statistics [E/CN.3/2009/20]. The Group comprised representatives from the Economic Commission for Europe (ECE), ILO, IMF, OECD, Eurostat and the World Bank. The report described activities of the Group since the

thirty-eighth session of the Statistical Commission in 2007 [YUN 2007, p. 1315]. In particular, the *Producer Price Index Manual* was available in English in hard copy and online from the IMF web page; an *Export and Import Price Index Manual* was being drafted under the lead of IMF; work began on producing the *Supplementary Handbook: Practical Guide to Compiling Consumer Price Indices*; and Eurostat agreed to lead the work on a *Handbook on House Price Indices*. To strengthen the coordination of international work on price statistics, mutual representation had been established between the joint ECE/ILO meeting on Consumer Price Indices, the Ottawa Group and the Intersecretariat Working Group on Price Statistics.

The Commission took note of the Secretary-General's note on 26 February [E/2009/24].

Environment statistics

The Secretary-General transmitted to the Statistical Commission the report of the Committee of Experts on Environmental-Economic Accounting [E/CN.3/2009/7]. The report elaborated on the mandate and governance structure of the Committee of Experts, as discussed at its third meeting (June 2008), in response to a request from the Bureau of the Conference of European Statisticians and the outcome of the Conference on Climate Change and Official Statistics (April 2008). It summarized the Committee's progress in revising the System of Environmental-Economic Accounting (SEEA), in particular on advances in energy and material flow accounts; on coordinating the various groups working within its mandate on the development of environment, energy and related statistics; and on promoting and implementing environmental-economic accounting and related statistics. The report also provided an update on the drafting of the international recommendations for water statistics.

The Commission on 27 February [dec. 40/104] expressed its support for the revision of SEEA, confirmed that the revision was the highest priority of the Committee, and recognized the urgency to complete the SEEA handbook. The Commission noted that there were differing views regarding the proposed expansion of the mandate of the Committee to include environment and climate change statistics, and requested the Committee to review its mandate, terms of reference and governance structure to reflect the focus of its work on environmental-economic accounting and its role in environment and climate change statistics; considered the establishment of an advisory group on environmental-economic accounting and environment statistics not necessary at that stage, agreed that the Committee would need to receive advice on substantive issues, and recommended that technical panels be convened on an ad hoc basis; and requested the Committee to submit the revised mandate, governance and terms of reference to the Bureau of the Commission for review and to the Commission for further consideration at its forty-first (2010) session.

Climate change statistics

In accordance with a request of the Statistical Commission at its thirty-ninth session, the Secretary-General transmitted the report of the Australian Bureau of Statistics on Climate Change and Official Statistics [E/CN.3/2009/2], which contained a programme review of climate change and official statistics. The report explored the areas where official statistics could provide input and added value to the analysis of the environmental, social and economic aspects of climate change and the related adaptation and mitigation measures. It also made recommendations to strengthen the role of official statistics in climate change policy- and decision-making, including integrating the climate change dimension in official statistics, strengthening the role of official statistics in the compilation of national greenhouse gas emission inventories, and developing statistics on measures of mitigation, adaptation and their supporting mechanisms.

Welcoming the report, the Commission on 27 February [dec. 40/101] recognized that official statistics played an important role in closing data gaps related to climate change; acknowledged that climate change was a new area of official statistics, and that countries were at different levels of statistical development and had different national governance arrangements with respect to the production of climate change statistics; noted that current negotiations under the United Nations Framework Convention on Climate Change (UNFCCC) were of paramount importance and that any potential interference with those processes should be avoided; agreed on the need to understand the data needs of various stakeholders, including UNFCCC and the Intergovernmental Panel on Climate Change, and to engage them in identifying areas where the official statistical community could make the best contribution; recognized that many of the statistics produced by national statistical systems could be used for calculating emissions and measuring and analysing climate change; emphasized the importance of coordination among national stakeholders for producing high-quality statistics; noted the differing views regarding the proposed expansion of the mandate of the Committee of Experts on Environmental-Economic Accounting to cover the area of climate change-related statistics; and requested the Committee to prepare new terms of reference and a priority list of its work programme, including statistics related to climate change, for further consultation with the Bureau

prior to a decision by the Commission at its forty-first (2010) session.

Agricultural statistics

The Statistical Commission had before it the report of the Working Group on Agricultural Statistics, led by Eurostat, on global initiatives to improve agricultural and rural statistics [E/CN.3/2009/3 & Corr.1]. The Working Group comprised the World Bank, the Food and Agriculture Organization of the United Nations (FAO) and the United States Department of Agriculture. The report outlined a proposed strategic plan to improve national and international agricultural and rural statistics, which was discussed at an expert group meeting (Washington, D.C., 22–23 October 2008). The plan provided for the establishment of a core set of agricultural statistics, methodologies to measure them, and ways to support international and national organizations in developing those statistics.

The Commission on 27 February [dec. 40/102] endorsed the development of a strategic plan based on the recommendations and road map set out in the report. It agreed that the main lines of action should be: to identify a minimum set of indicators reflecting core agricultural statistical needs and emerging requirements; to provide a blueprint for a better integration of agricultural statistics in the national statistical system; to advocate for national statistical organizations and ministries of agriculture to obtain funding to meet agreed international requirements; to establish a basis for statistical capacity-building by identifying a set of methodological tools; and to establish coordination of donor efforts to improve agricultural and rural statistics. It also agreed with the creation of a Friends of the Chair group to steer the process, with FAO and the Statistics Division serving as secretariat; it requested the group to report back to the Commission at its forty-first (2010) session on progress in developing the strategic plan.

Business registers

The Secretary-General transmitted to the Statistical Commission the report of the Wiesbaden Group on Business Registers (formerly Round Table on Business Survey Frames) [E/CN.3/2009/18], which described the twenty-first meeting of the Wiesbaden Group (Paris, 24–27 November 2008). The meeting, entitled "The Central Place of Business Register Systems in Response to Globalization Needs", provided a rich list of priority actions for the coming years. The Steering Group of the Wiesbaden Group would formulate a multi-year programme. The next Wiesbaden meeting would be held from 27 to 30 September 2010 in Estonia.

The Commission took note of the Secretary-General's submission on 26 February [E/2009/24].

Demographic and social statistics

Population and housing censuses

The Statistical Commission had before it the Secretary-General's report on population and housing censuses [E/CN.3/2009/17], which reviewed activities completed with regard to implementing the 2010 World Programme on Population and Housing Censuses, including the conduct of an expert group meeting and training workshops; the dissemination of the second revision of the *Principles and Recommendations for Population and Housing Censuses*; the development of a website to serve as a census knowledge base; and the development of a software package, CensusInfo, to help countries disseminate census data. It also contained information on future activities related to the 2010 World Programme.

The Commission took note of the report on 26 February [E/2009/24].

Health statistics

The Statistical Commission had before it a report of the Intersecretariat Working Group on Health Statistics [E/CN.3/2009/10], which proposed to continue developing the framework for health statistics proposed in 2007 and to convene an expert group to review and evaluate the framework once the initial draft was complete. The framework would outline the content of health statistics and the relationship between content and the most common sources of health data. The Statistical Commission, at its thirty-ninth session, had expressed support for that proposal [YUN 2008, p. 1386]. A preliminary draft of the framework, prepared by the Intersecretariat Working Group, was annexed to the report.

The Commission on 27 February [dec. 40/107] encouraged the Working Group to finalize the framework of health statistics and urged the Working Group to ensure that the framework: was easy to use and identified priority areas; enhanced the comparability of health statistics and internationally comparable indicators; was of practical utility; was synchronized with international standards; was developed in coordination with all stakeholders; and took into account the different circumstances in different countries. It welcomed the offer of support of the World Health Organization (WHO) in developing the framework, especially its work on compiling the registry of health indicators; and requested the Statistics Division and other organizations to provide support.

Education statistics

The Statistical Commission had before it the report of the Task Force on Education Statistics

[E/CN.3/2009/11], convened by the Institute for Statistics of the United Nations Educational, Scientific and Cultural Organization (UNESCO), which reviewed the main measurement frameworks employed in the field of education for data collection at the international, regional or national levels and how they affected the production and use of statistics. The review also examined coordination mechanisms among agencies with respect to different stages of the statistical production and dissemination cycle. The Task Force recommended that the UNESCO Institute for Statistics create an expert group on the International Standard Classification of Education Programmes for reaching consensus on developing methodology, updating definitions, providing country support and developing procedures for mapping educational attainment data to the International Standard Classification. It also proposed the creation of an intersecretariat working group on education statistics to improve coordination mechanisms for data collection, production and dissemination.

The Commission on 27 February [dec. 40/108], endorsed the establishment of an expert group on the revision and implementation of the International Standard Classification of Education. It also agreed, in principle, with the establishment of an intersecretariat working group on education statistics, led by the UNESCO Institute for Statistics, to improve coordination mechanisms, promote the development of international standards and minimize duplicative efforts among international agencies. The Commission requested that the UNESCO Institute for Statistics clarify the mandate of the group and explore working modalities so that the existing coordination mechanisms were fully embedded into the scope of the intersecretariat working group.

Social statistics

The Statistical Commission considered the Secretary-General's report on social statistics [E/CN.3/2009/9], which included the conclusions and recommendations of the Expert Group Meeting on the Scope and Content of Social Statistics (New York, 9–12 September 2008). The Commission was invited to review and adopt the recommendations regarding the production of an exhaustive inventory of: international methodological standards and guidelines in each area of social statistics; the availability of social statistics at the global level, including measures of quality; and ongoing statistical and methodological activities in social statistics at the international, regional, subregional and national levels.

The Commission on 27 February [dec. 40/106] endorsed the recommendations of the Expert Group; recognized that the content, scope and profile of social statistics varied from country to country, making the harmonization of those statistics a particular challenge; emphasized the importance of developing a substantive inventory of social statistics to identify methodological gaps and to facilitate sharing of best practices; and urged the Statistics Division to undertake the development of the inventory on a priority basis and to release components as they became available. The Division was requested to: develop an information technology platform to ensure continuous and effective dissemination of information; interact with international and regional stakeholders; explore the best mechanism for meeting the needs of developing countries in sharing experiences and for providing training on social statistics; and report periodically to the Commission on progress made.

Employment statistics

The Statistical Commission had before it the report of ILO [E/CN.3/2009/12] on labour statistics and on the outcomes of the eighteenth International Conference of Labour Statisticians (ICLS) (Geneva, 24 November–5 December 2008), which described the priorities for future development work in international labour statistics that had been identified by ILO and through the ICLS mechanism. The report laid out the main issues relating to future work items in labour statistics for the global statistical system and plans for implementation over the period 2009–2014; stressed the need for cooperation between national statistical offices and international agencies, including ILO, to move towards achieving those goals; outlined the recommendations of the eighteenth ICLS on its organization, frequency and duration; and discussed the provision of support to national statistical systems for the production of employment statistics.

The Commission on 27 February [dec. 40/109] took note of the resolutions on working time and child labour adopted by the eighteenth ICLS and the recommendations made by the Conference to the ILO Governing Body regarding the organization, frequency and duration of the Conference. It agreed with the priority issues as listed in the ILO report, as well as the road map put forward. In particular, it agreed with the need to address the changing structure of the labour force, including ageing, and the definition and measurement of employment and unemployment, including underutilization of labour and work on the measurement of productivity. It stressed the need to assist countries in improving their employment statistics, especially in view of the current global economic circumstances, and took note of the ILO plans for a technical cooperation programme in that area; welcomed the offer of the United Kingdom to take the lead on work to extend the labour statistics framework; endorsed the proposal that dedicated working groups take up specific priority issues and that ILO provide overall coordination; and invited ILO to submit a progress report to the Commission's forty-first (2010) session.

Gender statistics

The Statistical Commission had before it the report of the Friends of the Chair on indicators on violence against women [E/CN.3/2009/13], which discussed the development of a set of such indicators, including their criteria; concepts, definitions and classifications; and sources of statistics. Categories included physical violence, sexual violence, intimate partner violence and harmful practices, such as female genital mutilation/cutting and marriage under the age of 18. The Friends of the Chair recommended a set of six indicators as a starting point for initiating further work on identifying the most appropriate measurements.

The Commission on 27 February [dec. 40/110] adopted the proposed set of indicators as an interim set and first step, and requested the Friends of the Chair to continue their work and report back to the Commission. It recognized the substantial cultural differences on the issue of violence against women and urged the Friends of the Chair to expand their membership to ensure that different perspectives and sensitivities were taken into consideration. It requested the Statistics Division and other stakeholders, including WHO, the United Nations Office on Drugs and Crime and the regional commissions, to draw upon and further elaborate existing methodological guidelines for measuring violence against women. It requested the Statistics Division to begin a trial compilation of national statistics based on the interim set of indicators to determine their feasibility and relevance.

Human settlement statistics

The Statistical Commission had before it the report of the United Nations Human Settlements Programme (UN-Habitat) on human settlements statistics [E/CN.3/2009/25], which was prepared in response to a 2008 request of the Statistical Commission for information on the status of such statistics. The report outlined the activities undertaken by UN-Habitat in monitoring the implementation of the MDG target on slum dwellers, including the convening of a peer review meeting on slum estimation (New York, 3–6 April 2008). The report discussed the findings and recommendations of the meeting regarding the definition of a slum dweller, data gaps, projection methodologies and the work of UN-Habitat on developing international comparability in its statistics.

The Commission took note of the report on 26 February [E/2009/24].

Other statistical activities

Information and communications technology statistics

The Secretary-General transmitted to the Statistical Commission the report of the Partnership on Measuring Information and Communication Technologies (ICT) for Development [E/CN.3/2009/19], which reviewed progress made by the Partnership since the thirty-eighth session of the Commission [YUN 2007, p. 1319] and presented a revised core list of ICT indicators, annexed to the report, including new indicators on measuring ICT in education. The members of the Partnership were: International Telecommunication Union; OECD; United Nations Conference on Trade and Development; UNESCO Institute for Statistics; Economic Commission for Latin America and the Caribbean; Economic and Social Commission for Western Asia; ESCAP; Economic Commission for Africa; Eurostat; and World Bank.

The report noted that the core list of ICT indicators had been further revised; the Partnership Task Group on Education had held wide consultations on a set of education indicators to be included in the core list; the Task Group on e-Government had met in May 2008 to discuss progress on work to measure ICT in government and the preparation of a draft list of indicators; and a new Task Group on Impacts had been established, with the aim of examining how the social and economic impacts of ICT could be measured and what the data requirements were. The Task Group on Capacity-building had established a work programme on technical assistance and capacity-building for developing economies; a comprehensive statistical report, *The Global Information Society: a Statistical View*, had been prepared and issued in May 2008; and the Task Group on Database Development had agreed to include the core indicators collected by members of the Partnership in the newly established UN data portal maintained by the Statistics Division. The report stated that the proposed revisions of the core list of ICT indicators were submitted in 2008; an important improvement to the 2005 core list was the addition of eight new indicators on measuring ICT in education, developed by the UNESCO Institute for Statistics. The members of the Partnership would continue to work together to improve internationally comparable ICT statistics globally, in particular in developing countries.

The Commission took note of the report on 26 February [E/2009/24].

Regional statistical development

The Secretary-General transmitted to the Statistical Commission a report of ESCAP on regional statistics development in Asia and the Pacific [E/CN.3/2009/15], which reviewed progress in statistics development among countries in the region, including key trends in the institutional and technical capacity development of national statistical systems; identified the main challenges and opportunities for statistical capacity-building; and highlighted the role of bilateral and multilateral statistics development partners.

The Commission on 27 February [dec. 40/112] congratulated the region for holding the first session of the re-established Committee on Statistics. It noted the willingness of countries to assist the ESCAP secretariat in steering statistical development in the region, and urged the secretariat to strengthen and coordinate the work on statistical capacity-building; requested that ESCAP establish an informal mechanism for donor coordination for statistical development in the region; took note of the contributions that had been made in the region by the Development Account projects of the UN Department of Economic and Social Affairs; and welcomed the new interregional component in recent projects, which allowed the sharing of expertise across regions.

Standards for data dissemination and exchange

The Secretary-General transmitted to the Statistical Commission the report of the Task Force to Establish Standards on Data and Metadata Exchange [E/CN.3/2009/24], which reviewed activities related to the Statistical Data and Metadata Exchange (SDMX) initiative and discussed future activities. The goal of the SDMX initiative was to foster standards and guidelines allowing national and international organizations to gain efficiencies and avoid duplication of work in the area of data and metadata exchange through the use of modern technology. The SDMX initiative strengthened its framework of standards and guidelines by working with the International Organization for Standardization to approve version 2 of the SDMX Technical Standards. The SDMX Sponsors Committee approved the first set of SDMX content-oriented guidelines to be released on the SDMX website. An action plan involving capacity-building and outreach to encourage awareness-building and implementations was being developed and implemented. The report concluded that the SDMX technical standards and guidelines were facilitating improvements in the exchange and sharing of statistical data and metadata through a widening range of implementations in subject-matter domains. It further concluded that subject-matter domain activities involving SDMX were taking shape and could be monitored via the SDMX website, including developments in national accounts, balance of payments, commodity trade, external debt, education, food and agriculture, health, labour and MDG indicators.

The Commission took note of the Secretary-General's submission on 26 February [E/2009/24].

Statistical capacity-building

The Secretary-General transmitted to the Statistical Commission the report of the Partnership in Statistics for Development in the Twenty-First Century (PARIS 21) on statistical capacity-building [E/CN.3/2009/23], which outlined the Partnership's efforts to promote the use of better statistics, particularly through support to countries in the design, implementation and monitoring of national strategies for the development of statistics. It described progress made in areas such as regional programmes; advocacy and the development of statistical advocacy tools; promotion of donor collaboration; development of a methodology for national strategies; and satellite programmes. It also presented plans to organize in 2009 the fourth Forum on Statistical Capacity-building for Arab Countries in Cairo, Egypt, and support to the fourth Africa Symposium on Statistical Development in Luanda, Angola.

Report of Secretary-General. The Commission also had before it the report of the Secretary-General on statistical capacity-building [E/CN.3/2009/22], which described the strategy and implementation of capacity-building activities of the Statistics Division and the coordination of such activities among international agencies. The report described the Division's three programmatic subject domains (national statistical systems; population censuses and social statistics; and national accounts, basic economic statistics, environment statistics, and environmental-economic accounting frameworks), supplemented by capacity-building related to MDG indicators. It reviewed the Division's capacity-building activities in 2006–2008 and outlined progress made in coordination in that area through the Committee for the Coordination of Statistical Activities.

The Commission took note of both reports on 26 February [E/2009/24].

Follow-up to UN conferences and summits

The Statistical Commission considered the Secretary-General's report [E/CN.3/2009/16 & Corr.1] on indicators for monitoring the MDGs, which described the progress made by the Inter-Agency and Expert Group on Millennium Development Goals Indicators and the Statistics Division during 2008 in implementing the recommendations contained in Economic and Social Council resolution 2006/6 [YUN 2006, p. 1472] and the requests made by the Sta-

tistical Commission, at its thirty-ninth session, to improve data and indicators to monitor the MDGs as well as to improve capacity-building in countries for producing the indicators [YUN 2008, p. 1388]. The report reviewed progress in improving the coverage, transparency and reporting on all indicators as presented in the database on all MDGs; in reviewing the data and indicators in order to develop a mechanism for monitoring progress towards all goals; and in coordinating data gathering and compilation at the global level and preparation of the yearly analysis and progress reports on the MDGs.

The Commission on 27 February [dec. 40/113] welcomed the many new initiatives announced by member States to improve national and subnational MDG monitoring. Recognizing that the population and housing census was an important source of data for producing the MDG indicators, the Commission urged countries that had not yet done so to undertake their 2010 round of the census. It requested the Inter-Agency and Expert Group to: continue improving data development and reporting on data availability for indicators to monitor progress towards all MDGs; increase their support to countries in developing their statistical capacity to monitor the MDGs; further improve the MDG indicators through methodological and technical refinement; explain and resolve discrepancies between national and international data sets; address the issue of improving national coordination of MDG monitoring at its next meeting and develop a strategy to address the requests by many member countries for support; and widely distribute the manual of indicators in all official languages and provide further training on subnational data production and analysis for MDG monitoring.

Coordination and integration of statistical programmes

The Statistical Commission had before it the Secretary-General's report on the work of the 37-member Committee for the Coordination of Statistical Activities [E/CN.3/2009/21], which summarized the conclusions of the eleventh and twelfth sessions of the Committee (New York, 25 February 2008 and Tunis, Tunisia, 11–12 September 2008). Subjects discussed included: revised terms of reference of the Committee; the 2008 Rome conference on data quality for international organizations; coordination of statistical capacity-building activities; use of population estimates by international organizations; modalities of data sharing among international organizations; and further involvement of national and international agencies in the SDMX. At the twelfth session of the Committee, the Statistics Division announced the proposal for observing a World Statistics

Day on 20 October 2010 and invited the Committee members to support the initiative.

The Commission took note of the report on 26 February [E/2009/24].

Follow-up to Economic and Social Council policy decisions

The Statistical Commission had before it a note by the Secretary-General on policy decisions of the Economic and Social Council adopted in 2008 that were relevant to the Commission's work [E/CN.3/2009/26]. The note covered actions related to the follow-up to major UN conferences and summits; the multi-year programme of work for annual ministerial reviews of the Council; integrating gender perspectives; strengthening national capacity in statistics; the 2010 World Population and Housing Census Programme; and the assessment of progress made in the implementation of and follow-up to the outcomes of the World Summit on the Information Society.

The Commission took note of the Secretary-General's submission on 26 February [E/2009/24].

Programme and institutional questions

The Commission on 27 February took note of the Statistics Division's draft programme of work for the biennium 2010–2011 [E/CN.3/2009/27] and approved the Division's multi-year programme of work for 2009–2012 [E/CN.3/2009/28], as orally amended. It also approved the provisional agenda and documentation for its forty-first (2010) session, as orally revised, to be held in New York from 23 to 26 February 2010.

PART FOUR

Legal questions

Chapter I

International Court of Justice

In 2009, the International Court of Justice (ICJ) delivered three Judgments, made seven Orders, and had 18 contentious cases and one advisory procedure pending before it. Addressing the General Assembly on 29 October, the ICJ President, Judge Hisashi Owada, noted that during the period from 1 August 2008 to 31 July 2009, the cases before the Court had involved States from nearly all continents—Asia, Europe, North America, Central America and Africa. The universal character of the Court was reflected in the wide range of subjects addressed in those cases, including territorial and maritime delimitation, diplomatic protection, human rights, the status of individuals, international humanitarian law and environmental issues.

Judicial work of the Court

During 2009, the Court delivered its Judgment on the merits in the cases concerning *Maritime Delimitation in the Black Sea (Romania v. Ukraine), Request for Interpretation of the Judgment of 31 March 2004 in the Case concerning* Avena and Other Mexican Nationals (Mexico v. United States) *(Mexico v. United States),* and *Dispute regarding Navigational and Related Rights (Costa Rica v. Nicaragua).*

During the year, the Court was seized of three new cases: *Questions relating to the Obligation to Prosecute or Extradite (Belgium v. Senegal); Certain Questions concerning Diplomatic Relations (Honduras v. Brazil);* and *Jurisdiction and Enforcement of Judgments in Civil and Commercial Matters (Belgium v. Switzerland).*

The Court held public hearings in the cases concerning *Dispute regarding Navigational and Related Rights (Costa Rica v. Nicaragua), Questions relating to the Obligation to Prosecute or Extradite (Belgium v. Senegal)* and *Pulp Mills on the River Uruguay (Argentina v. Uruguay),* as well as on the request for an advisory opinion on the question of the *Accordance with International Law of the Unilateral Declaration of Independence by the Provisional Institutions of Self-Government of Kosovo.*

The Court issued an Order on a request for the indication of provisional measures submitted by Belgium in the case concerning *Questions relating to the Obligation to Prosecute or Extradite (Belgium v. Senegal).* The Court or its President made Orders on the conduct of the proceedings in the cases concerning *Application*

of the Convention on the Prevention and Punishment of the Crime of Genocide (Croatia v. Serbia), Certain Criminal Proceedings in France (Congo v. France), Application of the International Convention on the Elimination of All Forms of Racial Discrimination (Georgia v. Russian Federation), Application of the Interim Accord of 13 September 1995 (The former Yugoslav Republic of Macedonia v. Greece), Jurisdictional Immunities of the State (Germany v. Italy), and *Questions relating to the Obligation to Prosecute or Extradite (Belgium v. Senegal).*

In the cases concerning *Ahmadou Sadio Diallo (Guinea v. Democratic Republic of the Congo), Territorial and Maritime Dispute (Nicaragua v. Colombia), Maritime Dispute (Peru v. Chile)* and *Aerial Herbicide Spraying (Ecuador v. Colombia),* pleadings were submitted within the fixed time limits. While there were no new developments in the cases concerning *Gabcikovo-Nagymaros Project (Hungary/Slovakia)* [YUN 1998, p. 1186] and *Armed Activities on the Territory of the Congo (Democratic Republic of the Congo v. Uganda)* [YUN 1999, p. 1209], in both cases the Parties kept the Court informed of progress made in their respective negotiations.

In other developments, the Court revised Practice Directions III and VI and adopted new Practice Direction XIII. ICJ activities in 2009 were covered in two reports to the General Assembly, for the periods 1 August 2008 to 31 July 2009 [A/64/4] and 1 August 2009 to 31 July 2010 [A/65/4]. On 29 October, the Assembly took note of the 2008–2009 report (**decision 64/508**).

Contentious proceedings

Application of the Convention on the Prevention and Punishment of the Crime of Genocide (Croatia v. Serbia)

On 2 July 1999 [YUN 1999, p. 1210], Croatia instituted proceedings before the Court against Serbia, then known as the Federal Republic of Yugoslavia, for alleged violations of the 1948 Convention on the Prevention and Punishment of the Crime of Genocide [YUN 1948–49, p. 959] committed between 1991 and 1995. In its Application, Croatia contended that by "directly controlling the activity of its armed forces, intelligence agents, and various paramilitary detachments, on the territory of … Croatia, in the Knin region, eastern and western Slovenia, and Dalmatia", Serbia was liable for "ethnic cleansing" of Croatian citizens. It requested the Court to adjudge and declare that Serbia had "breached its legal obligations" to Croatia under the Genocide Convention and that it had "an obligation to pay to … Croatia … reparations for damages to persons and property, as well as to the Croatian economy and environment caused by the foregoing violations of international law in a sum to be determined by the Court".

By an Order of 14 September 1999, the Court fixed 14 March 2000 and 14 September 2000 as the respective time limits for the filing of a Memorial by Croatia and a Counter-Memorial by Serbia. Those limits were twice extended by Orders made during 2000 [YUN 2000, p. 1219]. Croatia filed its Memorial within the time limit. On 11 September 2002 [YUN 2002, p. 1268], within the extended time limit for filing its Counter-Memorial, Serbia filed certain preliminary objections on jurisdiction and admissibility. The proceedings on the merits were suspended, in accordance with Article 79 of the Rules of the Court.

On 25 April 2003, within the time limit fixed by an Order of the Court of 14 November 2002 [ibid.], Croatia filed a written statement of its observations and submissions on Serbia's preliminary objections [YUN 2003, p. 1304].

At the conclusion of public hearings on the preliminary objections on jurisdiction and admissibility held from 26 to 30 May 2008, the Parties presented final submissions to the Court [YUN 2008, p. 1395]. In its Judgment rendered on 18 November 2008 [ibid.], the Court found that, subject to its statement concerning the second preliminary objection raised by Serbia, it had jurisdiction, on the basis of the Genocide Convention, to entertain Croatia's application, adding that Serbia's second preliminary objection did not possess an exclusively preliminary character. It also rejected the first and third preliminary objections submitted by Serbia.

By an Order of 20 January 2009, the President of the Court fixed 22 March 2010 as the time limit for the filing of the Counter-Memorial of Serbia.

Certain Criminal Proceedings in France (Republic of the Congo v. France)

On 9 December 2002 [YUN 2002, p. 1263], the Congo filed an Application instituting proceedings against France seeking the annulment of the investigation and prosecution measures taken by the French judicial authorities further to a complaint for crimes against humanity and torture filed by various associations against the President of the Congo, Denis Sassou Nguesso, the Congolese Minister of the Interior, Pierre Oba, and other individuals including General Norbert Dabira, Inspector-General of the Congolese

armed forces. The Application further stated that, in connection with the proceedings, an investigating judge of the Meaux (France) Tribunal de grande instance had issued a warrant for the President of the Congo to be examined as witness.

The Congo contended that, by "attributing to itself universal jurisdiction in criminal matters and by arrogating to itself the power to prosecute and try the Minister of the Interior of a foreign State for crimes allegedly committed by him in connection with the exercise of his powers for the maintenance of public order in his country", France had violated "the principle that a State may not, in breach of the principle of sovereign equality among all Members of the United Nations … exercise its authority on the territory of another State". It further submitted that, in issuing a warrant instructing police officers to examine the President of the Congo as witness in the case, France had violated "the criminal immunity of a foreign Head of State, an international customary rule recognized by the jurisprudence of the Court".

In its Application, the Congo indicated that it sought to found the jurisdiction of the Court, pursuant to Article 38, paragraph 5, of the Rules of Court, "on the consent of the French Republic, which w[ould] certainly be given". In accordance with that provision, the Application by the Congo was transmitted to the French Government and no further action was taken in the proceedings at that stage.

By a letter of 8 April 2003 [YUN 2003, p. 1308], France stated that it "consent[ed] to the jurisdiction of the Court to entertain the Application pursuant to Article 38, paragraph 5", which made it possible to enter the case in the Court's List and to open the proceedings. France added that its consent to the Court's jurisdiction applied strictly within the limits "of the claims formulated by the Republic of the Congo" and that "Article 2 of the Treaty of Co-operation signed on 1 January 1974 by the French Republic and the People's Republic of the Congo, to which the latter refers in its Application, d[id] not constitute a basis of jurisdiction for the Court in the present case".

The Application of the Congo was accompanied by a request for the indication of a provisional measure "seek[ing] an order for the immediate suspension of the proceedings being conducted by the investigating judge of the Meaux Tribunal de grande instance".

Public hearings were held from 28 to 29 April 2003 on the request for the indication of a provisional measure. In its Order of 17 June 2003 [ibid.], the Court declared that the circumstances, as they presented themselves to it, were not such as to require the exercise of its power under Article 41 of the Statute to indicate provisional measures. The Memorial of the Congo and the Counter-Memorial of France were filed within the time limits fixed by the Order of 11 July 2003.

By an Order of 17 June 2004 [YUN 2004, p. 1270], the Court, taking account of the agreement of the Parties and of the particular circumstances of the case, authorized the submission of a reply by the Congo and a rejoinder by France, and fixed the time limits for the filing of those pleadings. Following four successive requests for extensions to the time limit for filing the reply [YUN 2005, p. 1384], the President of the Court fixed the time limits for the filing of the reply by the Congo and the rejoinder by France as 11 July 2006 and 11 August 2008, respectively. Those pleadings were filed within those time limits.

By an Order of 16 November 2009, the Court, citing Article 101 of the Rules of Court and taking account of the agreement of the Parties and the exceptional circumstances of the case, authorized the submission of an additional pleading by the Congo, followed by an additional pleading by France. It fixed 16 February 2010 and 17 May 2010 as the respective time limits for the filing of those pleadings.

Maritime Delimitation in the Black Sea (Romania v. Ukraine)

On 16 September 2004 [YUN 2004, p. 1271], Romania filed an Application instituting proceedings against Ukraine in respect of a dispute concerning the establishment of a single maritime boundary between the two States in the Black Sea, thereby delimiting the continental shelf and the exclusive economic zones appertaining to them. Romania requested the Court to draw, in accordance with international law, and specifically the criteria laid down in article 4 of the Additional Agreement to the June 1997 Treaty on Relations of Co-operation and Good Neighbourliness between Romania and Ukraine, a single maritime boundary between the continental shelf and the exclusive economic zone of the two States in the Black Sea.

All pleadings by Orders of 19 November 2004 [YUN 2004, p. 1272], 30 June 2006 [YUN 2006, p. 1480] and 8 June 2007 [YUN 2007, p. 1331] were filed within the time limits set. Public hearings were held from 2 to 19 September 2008 [YUN 2008, p. 1397].

The Court rendered its Judgment on 3 February 2009. It decided unanimously that "starting from Point 1, as agreed by the Parties in Article 1 of the 2003 State Border Régime Treaty, the line of the single maritime boundary delimiting the continental shelf and the exclusive economic zones of Romania and Ukraine in the Black Sea shall follow the 12-nautical-mile arc of the territorial sea of Ukraine around Serpents' Island until Point 2 (with co-ordinates 45°03' 18.5" N and 30° 09' 24.6" E) where the arc intersects with the line equidistant from Romania's and Ukraine's adjacent coasts. From Point 2 the boundary line shall follow the equidistance line

through Point 3 (with co-ordinates 44° 46' 38.7" N and 30° 58' 37.3" E) and Point 4 (with co-ordinates 44° 44' 13.4" N and 31° 10' 27.7" E) until it reaches Point 5 (with co-ordinates 44° 02' 53.0" N and 31° 24' 35.0" E). From Point 5 the maritime boundary line shall continue along the line equidistant from the opposite coasts of Romania and Ukraine in a southerly direction starting at a geodetic azimuth of 185° 23' 54.5" until it reaches the area where the rights of third States may be affected."

Dispute regarding Navigational and Related Rights (Costa Rica v. Nicaragua)

On 29 September 2005 [YUN 2005, p. 1385], Costa Rica filed an Application instituting proceedings against Nicaragua in a dispute concerning the navigational and related rights of Costa Rica on the San Juan River. Costa Rica stated in its Application that it sought "the cessation of [the] Nicaraguan conduct which prevent[ed] the free and full exercise and enjoyment of the rights that Costa Rica possess[ed] on the San Juan River, and which also prevent[ed] Costa Rica from fulfilling its responsibilities" under certain agreements between itself and Nicaragua. It stated that Nicaragua had, in particular since the late 1990s, imposed restrictions on the navigation of Costa Rican boats and their passengers on the San Juan River, in violation of article VI of the Treaty of Limits, signed in 1858 between the two Parties, which granted Nicaragua sovereignty over the waters of the river, while recognizing important rights to Costa Rica.

Costa Rica and Nicaragua filed their respective pleadings within the time limits set by Orders of 29 November 2005 [ibid.] and of 9 October 2007 [YUN 2007, p. 1332]. Public hearings were held from 2 to 12 March 2009.

The Court rendered its Judgment on 13 July 2009. On Costa Rica's navigational rights on the San Juan River under the 1858 Treaty, in that part where navigation was common, the Court found unanimously that Costa Rica had the right of free navigation on the river for purposes of commerce, and that the right included the transport of passengers and tourists. By 9 votes to 5, it found that persons travelling on the river on board Costa Rican vessels exercising Costa Rica's right of free navigation were not required to obtain Nicaraguan visas; and found, unanimously, that such persons were not required to purchase Nicaraguan tourist cards.

By 13 votes to 1, the Court found that the inhabitants of the Costa Rican bank of the San Juan River had the right to navigate on the river between the riparian communities for the purposes of the essential needs of everyday life which required expeditious transportation. By 12 votes to 2, it found that Costa

Rica had the right of navigation on the river with official vessels used solely, in specific situations, to provide essential services for the inhabitants of the riparian areas where expeditious transportation was a condition for meeting the inhabitants' requirements. The Court found unanimously that Costa Rica did not have the right of navigation on the San Juan River with vessels carrying out police functions, or for the purposes of the exchange of personnel of the police border posts along the right bank of the river and of the resupply of those posts with official equipment, including service arms and ammunition.

On Nicaragua's right to regulate navigation on the San Juan River, in that part where navigation was common, the Court found unanimously that Nicaragua had the right to: require Costa Rican vessels and their passengers to stop at the first and last Nicaraguan post on their route along the river; require persons travelling on the river to carry a passport or an identity document; issue departure clearance certificates to Costa Rican vessels exercising Costa Rica's right of free navigation, but not to request the payment of a charge for the issuance of such certificates; impose timetables for navigation on vessels navigating on the river; and require Costa Rican vessels fitted with masts or turrets to display the Nicaraguan flag. On subsistence fishing, the Court, by 13 votes to 1, found that fishing by the inhabitants of the Costa Rican bank of the San Juan River for subsistence purposes from that bank was to be respected by Nicaragua as a customary right.

On Nicaragua's compliance with its international obligations under the 1858 Treaty, the Court, by 9 votes to 5, found that Nicaragua was not acting in accordance with its obligations when it required persons travelling on the San Juan River on board Costa Rican vessels exercising Costa Rica's right of free navigation to obtain Nicaraguan visas; and it found, unanimously, that Nicaragua was not acting in accordance with its obligations when it required such persons to purchase Nicaraguan tourist cards, or when it required the operators of vessels exercising Costa Rica's right of free navigation to pay charges for departure clearance certificates. The Court unanimously rejected all other submissions presented by Costa Rica and Nicaragua.

Pulp Mills on the River Uruguay (Argentina v. Uruguay)

On 4 May 2006 [YUN 2006, p. 1481] Argentina filed an Application instituting proceedings against Uruguay for alleged breaches by Uruguay of obligations incumbent upon it under the Statute of the River Uruguay, a treaty signed between the two States on 26 February 1975 for the purpose of establishing the joint machinery necessary for the optimum and rational utilization of that part of the river which constituted their joint boundary. In its Application, Argentina charged Uruguay with having unilaterally authorized the construction of two pulp mills on the River Uruguay without complying with the obligatory prior notification and consultation procedures under the Statute. Argentina claimed that the mills posed a threat to the river, and were likely to impair the quality the river's waters and cause significant transboundary damage to Argentina.

Following public hearings in June and December 2006 [YUN 2006, p. 1482] on requests for the indication of provisional measures, Argentina and Uruguay filed their pleadings within the time limits fixed by Orders of 13 July 2006 [ibid.] and 14 September 2007 [YUN 2007, p. 1333].

By letters dated 16 June and 17 June 2009, respectively, Uruguay and Argentina notified the Court that they had come to an agreement on producing new documents pursuant to Article 56 of the Rules of the Court, which were filed, following authorization from the Court on 23 June, within the agreed time limit. On 15 July, each of the Parties submitted comments on the new documents provided by the other Party, as well as documents in support of its comments. Public hearings were held between 14 September and 2 October.

Interpretation of the Judgment of 31 March 2004 in the Case concerning Avena and Other Mexican Nationals (Mexico v. United States)

On 5 June 2008 [YUN 2008, p. 1400], Mexico filed a request for interpretation of the Judgment delivered on 31 March 2004 [YUN 2004, p. 1270] by the Court in the case concerning *Avena and Other Mexican Nationals (Mexico v. United States)* [YUN 2003, p. 1306].

Public hearings were held on 19 and 20 June 2008 [YUN 2008, p. 1400] and by an Order of 16 July 2008, the Court indicated provisional measures: the United States should take all measures necessary to ensure that José Ernesto Medellín Rojas, César Roberto Fierro Reyna, Rubén Ramírez Cárdenas, Humberto Leal García and Roberto Moreno Ramos were not executed pending judgment on the request for interpretation submitted by Mexico, unless and until those five Mexican nationals received review and reconsideration consistent with paragraphs 138 to 141 of the Court's Judgment delivered on 31 March 2004 in the case concerning *Avena and Other Mexican Nationals (Mexico v. United States)*.

On 28 August 2008 [ibid.], Mexico, informing the Court of the execution on 5 August 2008 of José Ernesto Medellín Rojas in the State of Texas, United States, and referring to Article 98, paragraph 4 of the Rules of Court, requested the Court to afford Mexico the opportunity of furnishing further written explanations for elaborating on the merits of the request for interpretation in the light of the written observations which the United States was due to file, and for amending its pleading to state a claim based on the violation of the Order of 16 July 2008. On 2 September 2008, the Court authorized Mexico and the United States to furnish further written explanations, which were filed within the fixed time limit.

The Court delivered its Judgment on 19 January 2009. By 11 votes to 1, it found that the matters claimed by Mexico to be in issue between the Parties, requiring an interpretation under Article 60 of the Statute, were not matters which had been decided by the Court in its Judgment of 31 March 2004 in the case concerning *Avena and Other Mexican Nationals (Mexico v. United States)*, including paragraph 153(9), and thus could not give rise to the interpretation requested by Mexico. The Court unanimously found that the United States had breached the obligation incumbent upon it under the Order indicating provisional measures of 16 July 2008, in the case of José Ernesto Medellín Rojas. By 11 votes to 1, it reaffirmed the continuing binding character of the obligations of the United States under paragraph 153(9) of the *Avena* Judgment and took note of the undertakings given by the United States in those proceedings; it declined, in those circumstances, the request of Mexico for the Court to order the United States to provide guarantees of non-repetition; and rejected all further submissions of Mexico.

Application of the International Convention on the Elimination of All Forms of Racial Discrimination (Georgia v. Russian Federation)

On 12 August 2008 [YUN 2008, p. 1401], Georgia instituted proceedings against the Russian Federation on the grounds of "its actions on and around the territory of Georgia" in breach of the International Convention on the Elimination of All Forms of Racial Discrimination [YUN 1965, p. 433]. In its Application, Georgia also sought to ensure that the individual rights under the Convention of all persons on the territory of Georgia were fully respected and protected.

Georgia claimed that the "Russian Federation, through its State organs, State agents, and other persons and entities exercising governmental authority, and through the South Ossetian and Abkhaz separatist forces and other agents acting on the instructions of, and under the direction and control of the Russian Federation, is responsible for serious violations of its fundamental obligations under [the Convention], including articles 2, 3, 4, 5 and 6" and that the Russian Federation had "violated its obligations under [the Convention] during three distinct phases of its interventions in South Ossetia and Abkhazia", in the period from 1990 to August 2008. Georgia requested the Court to order the Russian Federation to take all steps necessary to comply with its obligations under [the Convention].

On 15 August 2008, having considered the gravity of the situation, the President of the Court urgently called upon the Parties "to act in such a way as will enable any order the Court may take on the request for provisional measures to have its appropriate effects".

Public hearings were held from 8 to 10 October 2008 and on 15 October, the Court handed down its Order. The Court, reminding the Parties of their duty to comply with their obligations under the Convention, indicated provisional measures, adopted by 8 votes to 7. Both Parties, within South Ossetia and Abkhazia and adjacent areas in Georgia, should: refrain from any act of racial discrimination against persons, groups or institutions; abstain from sponsoring, defending or supporting racial discrimination by any persons or organizations; do all in their power to ensure, without distinction as to national or ethnic origin: security of persons, the right of persons to freedom of movement and residence within the border of the State, and the protection of the property of displaced persons and of refugees; and do all in their power to ensure that public authorities and public institutions under their control or influence did not engage in acts of racial discrimination against persons, groups or institutions. It further indicated that both Parties should facilitate humanitarian assistance in support of the rights to which the local population were entitled under the Convention; refrain from any action which might prejudice the rights of the other Party in respect of whatever judgment the Court might render, or which might aggravate or extend the dispute before the Court or make it more difficult to resolve; and inform the Court as to their compliance with the provisional measures.

By an Order of 2 December 2008 [YUN 2008, p. 1402], the President fixed 2 September 2009 as the time limit for the filing of a Memorial by Georgia and 2 July 2010 as the time limit for the filing of a Counter-Memorial by the Russian Federation. The Memorial of Georgia was filed within that time limit.

On 1 December 2009, within the time limit set in Article 79, paragraph 1, of the Rules of Court, the Russian Federation filed preliminary objections in respect of jurisdiction. Pursuant to Article 79, paragraph 5, of the Rules of Court, the proceedings on the merits were then suspended. By an Order of 11 December 2009, the Court fixed 1 April 2010 as the time limit for the filing by Georgia of a written statement containing its observations and submissions on the preliminary objections in respect of jurisdiction raised by the Russian Federation.

Application of the Interim Accord of 13 September 1995 (The former Yugoslav Republic of Macedonia v. Greece)

On 17 November 2008 [YUN 2008, p. 1402], the former Yugoslav Republic of Macedonia (FYROM) instituted proceedings against Greece for what it described as "a flagrant violation of [Greece's] obligations under article 11" of the Interim Accord signed by the Parties on 13 September 1995. In its Application, FYROM requested the Court to protect its rights under the Interim Accord and to ensure that it was allowed to exercise its rights as an independent State acting in accordance with international law, including the right to pursue membership of international organizations. It contended that Greece violated its rights under the Accord by objecting, in April 2008, to its application to join the North Atlantic Treaty Organization (NATO). FYROM contended, in particular, that Greece vetoed its application to join NATO because Greece desired "to resolve the difference between the Parties concerning the constitutional name of the Applicant as an essential precondition" for such membership.

By an Order of 20 January 2009, the Court fixed 20 July 2009 as the time limit for the filing of a Memorial by FYROM and 20 January 2010 as the time limit for the filing of a Counter-Memorial by Greece. The Memorial of FYROM was filed within the prescribed time limit.

Jurisdictional Immunities of the State (Germany v. Italy)

On 23 December 2008 [YUN 2008, p. 1402], Germany instituted proceedings against Italy, alleging that "through its judicial practice ... Italy has infringed and continues to infringe its obligations towards Germany under international law".

In its Application, Germany contended that in recent years Italian judicial bodies had repeatedly disregarded the jurisdictional immunity of Germany as a sovereign State. After the judgment of the Corte di Cassazione of 11 March 2004 in the *Ferrini* case had been rendered, where that court "declared that Italy held jurisdiction with regard to a claim ... brought by a person who during World War II had been deported to Germany to perform forced labour in the armaments industry", numerous other proceedings were instituted against Germany before Italian courts by persons who had also suffered injury as a consequence of the armed conflict. Germany was concerned "that hundreds of additional cases may be brought against it".

Germany concluded its Application by requesting the Court to adjudge and declare, among others, that Italy: failed to respect its jurisdictional immunity under international law, by allowing civil claims to be brought against Germany based on violations of international humanitarian law by the German Reich during World War II; violated its jurisdictional immunity by taking measures of constraint against Villa Vigoni, a German State property used for government non-commercial purposes; and had to take any and all steps to ensure that all decisions of Italian courts and other judicial authorities infringing Germany's sovereign immunity became unenforceable, and that in the future Italian courts would not entertain legal actions against Germany founded on the occurrences described in its first request (see above).

By an Order of 29 April 2009, the Court fixed 23 June and 23 December as the time limits, respectively for the filing of a Memorial by Germany and a Counter-Memorial by Italy. Those pleadings were filed within the fixed time limits.

In its Counter-Memorial, Italy made a counterclaim, and in accordance with Article 80 of the Rules of the Court, asked the Court to adjudge and declare that, considering the existence under international law of an obligation of reparation owed to the victims of war crimes and crimes against humanity perpetrated by the III Reich: Germany had violated that obligation with regard to Italian victims of such crimes by denying them effective reparation; Germany's international responsibility was engaged for that conduct; and Germany must cease its wrongful conduct and offer reparation to those victims, by means of its choosing, as well as through the conclusion of agreements with Italy.

Questions relating to the Obligation to Prosecute or Extradite (Belgium v. Senegal)

On 19 February 2009, Belgium instituted proceedings against Senegal, on the grounds that a dispute existed between them regarding Senegal's compliance with its obligation to prosecute the former President of Chad, Hissène Habré, or to extradite him to Belgium for criminal proceedings. Belgium also submitted a request for the indication of provisional measures, in order to protect its rights pending the Court's Judgment on the merits.

In its Application, Belgium maintained that Senegal, where Mr. Habré had been living in exile since 1990, had taken no action on Belgium's repeated requests to see the former President prosecuted in Senegal—failing his extradition to Belgium—for acts characterized as including crimes of torture and crimes against humanity. The Applicant recalled that, following a complaint filed on 25 January 2000 by seven individuals and the NGO Association of Victims of Political Repression and Crime, Mr. Habré was indicted in Dakar on 3 February 2000 for complicity in crimes against humanity, acts of torture and barbarity, and placed under house arrest. The *Chambre d'accusation* of the Dakar Court of Appeal dismissed that indictment on 4 July 2000 after finding that "crimes against humanity" did not form part of Senegalese criminal law.

Belgium further indicated that "between 30 November 2000 and 11 December 2001, a Belgian national of Chadian origin and Chadian nationals" filed similar complaints in the Belgian courts. Since the end of 2001, Belgium's legal authorities had requested numerous investigative measures of Senegal and, in September 2005, issued an international arrest warrant against Mr. Habré, on which the Senegalese courts did not see fit to take action. At the end of 2005, according to the Applicant, Senegal passed the case on to the African Union. Belgium added that in February 2007, Senegal decided to amend its penal code and code of criminal procedure to include "the offences of genocide, war crimes and crimes against humanity". However, it pointed out that Senegal had cited financial difficulties which prevented it from bringing Mr. Habré to trial.

Belgium contended that under conventional international law, Senegal's failure to prosecute Mr. Habré, if he was not extradited to Belgium to answer for the acts of torture that were alleged against him, violated the 1984 Convention against Torture and Other Cruel, Inhuman or Degrading Treatment or Punishment [YUN 1984, p. 813]. It added that, under customary international law, Senegal's failure to prosecute Mr. Habré or extradite him to Belgium violated the general obligation to punish crimes against international humanitarian law.

To found the Court's jurisdiction, Belgium, in its Application, first invoked the unilateral declarations recognizing the compulsory jurisdiction of the Court made by the Parties pursuant to Article 36, paragraph 2, of the Statute of the Court, on 17 June 1958 (Belgium) and 2 December 1985 (Senegal). Moreover, Belgium indicated that the two States had been parties to the Convention against Torture since 21 August 1986 (Senegal) and 25 June 1999 (Belgium). Article 30 of that Convention provided that any dispute between two States parties concerning the interpretation or application of the Convention which it had not been possible to settle through negotiation or arbitration might be submitted to the ICJ by one of the States. Belgium contended that negotiations between the two States had continued unsuccessfully since 2005, and that it had reached the conclusion on 20 June 2006 that those negotiations had failed.

At the end of its Application, Belgium requested the Court to adjudge and declare that: the Court had jurisdiction to entertain the dispute; Belgium's claim was admissible; Senegal was obliged to bring criminal proceedings against Mr. Habré for acts including crimes of torture and crimes against humanity which

were alleged against him as perpetrator, co-perpetrator or accomplice; and failing the prosecution of Mr. Habré, Senegal was obliged to extradite him to Belgium to answer for those crimes before the Belgian courts.

Belgium's Application was accompanied by a request for the indication of provisional measures. It explained therein that while Mr. Habré was under house arrest in Dakar, Senegal might lift his house arrest if it failed to find the budget necessary to hold his trial. In such an event, it would be easy for Mr. Habré to leave Senegal and avoid prosecution, which would cause irreparable prejudice to the rights conferred on Belgium by international law and violate the obligations which Senegal must fulfil.

Public hearings were held from 6 to 8 April 2009 to hear the oral observations of the Parties on the request for the indication of provisional measures submitted by Belgium. At the close of the hearings, Belgium asked the Court to indicate the following provisional measures—that "Senegal is requested to take all the steps within its power to keep Mr. Hissène Habré under the control and surveillance of the Senegalese authorities so that the rules of international law with which Belgium requests compliance may be correctly applied". Senegal asked the Court to reject the provisional measures requested by Belgium.

On 28 May, the Court gave its decision on the request for the indication of provisional measures submitted by Belgium. By 13 votes to 1, it found that the circumstances, as presented to the Court, were not such as to require the exercise of its power under Article 41 of the Statute to indicate provisional measures.

By an Order of 9 July 2009, the Court fixed 9 July 2010 and 11 July 2011 as the time limits, respectively, for the filing of a Memorial by Belgium and a Counter-Memorial by Senegal.

Certain Questions concerning Diplomatic Relations (Honduras v. Brazil)

On 28 October 2009, the Ambassador of Honduras to the Netherlands, Julio Rendón Barnica, appointed through a letter of 24 October from Carlos López Contreras, Minister for Foreign Affairs in the Government headed by Roberto Micheletti, instituted proceedings against Brazil in relation to a "dispute between [the two States] relating to legal questions concerning diplomatic relations and associated with the principle of non-intervention in matters which are essentially within the domestic jurisdiction of any State, a principle incorporated in the Charter of the United Nations". It was alleged therein that Brazil had "breached its obligations under Article 2(7) of the Charter and those under the 1961 Vienna Convention on Diplomatic Relations" [YUN 1961, p. 512].

At the end of the Application the Court was requested "to adjudge and declare that Brazil does not have the right to allow the premises of its Mission in Tegucigalpa to be used to promote manifestly illegal activities by Honduran citizens who have been staying within it for some time now and that it shall cease to do so". An original copy of the Application was sent to the Brazilian Government on 28 October 2009, and the UN Secretary-General was informed about the filing of the Application.

By a letter dated 28 October 2009, Patricia Isabel Rodas Baca, Minister for Foreign Affairs in the Government headed by José Manuel Zelaya Rosales, informed the Court that the Ambassador of Honduras to the Netherlands was not the legitimate representative of Honduras before the Court and that "Ambassador Eduardo Enrique Reina was being appointed as the sole legitimate representative of the Government of Honduras to the ICJ". A copy of the communication was sent on 3 November to Brazil, as well as to the UN Secretary-General.

The Court decided that, given the circumstances, no other action would be taken in the case until further notice.

(See also PART ONE, Chapter III.)

Jurisdiction and Enforcement of Judgments in Civil and Commercial Matters (Belgium v. Switzerland)

On 21 December 2009, Belgium initiated proceedings against Switzerland in respect of a dispute concerning "the interpretation and application of the Lugano Convention of 16 September 1988 on jurisdiction and the enforcement of judgments in civil and commercial matters ... and the application of the rules of general international law that govern the exercise of State authority, in particular in the judicial domain, [and relating to] the decision by Swiss courts not to recognize a decision by Belgian courts and not to stay proceedings later initiated in Switzerland on the subject of the same dispute".

In its Application, Belgium stated that the dispute "has arisen out of the pursuit of parallel judicial proceedings in Belgium and Switzerland" in respect of the civil and commercial dispute between the "main shareholders in Sabena, the former Belgian airline now in bankruptcy". The Swiss shareholders in question were SAirGroup (formerly Swissair) and its subsidiary SAirLines, and the Belgian shareholders were the Belgian State and three companies in which it held the shares. Belgium affirmed that "in connection with the Swiss companies' acquisition of equity in Sabena in 1995 and with their partnership with the Belgian shareholders, contracts were entered into, between 1995 and 2001, for among other things, the

financing and joint management of Sabena". That set of contracts "provided for exclusive jurisdiction on the part of the Brussels courts in the event of dispute and for the application of Belgian law".

Belgium also stated that, "on 3 July 2001, taking the position that the Swiss shareholders had breached their contractual commitments and non-contractual duties, causing [the Belgian shareholders] injury", the Belgian shareholders sued the Swiss shareholders in the commercial court of Brussels, seeking damages to compensate for the lost investments and for the expenses incurred "as a result of the defaults by the Swiss shareholders". After finding jurisdiction in the matter, that court "found various instances of wrongdoing on the part of the Swiss shareholders, but rejected the claims for damages brought by the Belgian shareholders". Both Parties appealed against that decision to the Court of Appeal of Brussels, which in 2005 by partial judgment upheld the Belgian courts' jurisdiction over the dispute on the basis of the Lugano Convention. The proceedings on the merits were pending before that court.

Belgium stated that in various proceedings concerning the application for a debt-restructuring moratorium submitted by the Swiss companies to the Zurich courts, the Belgian shareholders had sought to declare their debt claims against them. It was asserted that the Swiss courts had refused to recognize the future Belgian decisions on the civil liability of the Swiss shareholders or to stay their proceedings pending the outcome of the Belgian proceedings. According to Belgium, those refusals violated provisions of the Lugano Convention and "the rules of general international law that govern the exercise of State authority, in particular in the judicial domain".

Concluding its Application, Belgium requested the Court to adjudge and declare that: it had jurisdiction to entertain the dispute between Belgium and Switzerland concerning the interpretation and application of the Lugano Convention and of the rules of general international law governing the exercise by States of their authority, in particular in the judicial domain; Belgium's claim was admissible; Switzerland, by virtue of the decision of its courts to hold that the future decision in Belgium on the contractual and non-contractual liability of SAirGroup and SAirLines to the Belgian State and Zephyr-Fin, SFP and SFI (since merged, having become SFPI) would not be recognized in Switzerland in the SAirGroup and SAirLines debt-scheduling proceedings, was breaching the Lugano Convention; Switzerland, by refusing to stay the proceedings pursuant to its municipal law in the disputes between, on the one hand, the Belgian State and SFPI, and on the other, the estates of SAirGroup and SAirLines, companies in debt-restructuring liquidation, specifically on the ground that the future decision in Belgium on the contractual and non-contractual liability of SAirGroup and SAirLines to the Belgian State and SFPI would not be recognized in Switzerland in the SAirGroup and SAirLines debt-scheduling proceedings, was breaching the rule of general international law that all State authority, especially in the judicial domain, must be exercised reasonably; Switzerland, by virtue of the refusal by its judicial authorities to stay those proceedings in those disputes, pending the conclusion of the proceedings taking place in the Belgian courts concerning the contractual and non-contractual liability of SAirGroup and SAirLines to the first cited parties, was violating the Lugano Convention; Switzerland's international responsibility had been engaged; Switzerland must take all appropriate steps to enable the decision by the Belgian courts on the contractual and non-contractual liability of SAirGroup and SAirLines to the Belgian State and SFPI to be recognized in Switzerland in accordance with the Lugano Convention for purposes of the debt-scheduling proceedings for SAirLines and SAirGroup; and Switzerland must take all appropriate steps to ensure that the Swiss courts stay their proceedings in the disputes between, on the one hand, the Belgian State and SFPI and, on the other, the estates of SAirGroup and SAirLines, pending the conclusion of the proceedings in the Belgian courts concerning the contractual and non-contractual liability of SAirGroup and SAirLines to the first cited parties.

Advisory proceedings

Accordance with International Law of the Unilateral Declaration of Independence by the Provisional Institutions of Self-Government of Kosovo

In response to General Assembly resolution 63/3 of 8 October 2008 [YUN 2008, p. 1404], which referred to Article 65 of the ICJ Statute and requested the Court to render an advisory opinion on the question of whether the unilateral declaration of independence by the Provisional Institutions of Self-Government of Kosovo of 17 February 2008 [ibid., p. 437] was in accordance with international law, the Court, by an Order of 17 October 2008 [ibid., p. 1403], decided that the United Nations and its Member States, as well as the authors of the unilateral declaration of independence, were considered likely to be able to furnish information on the question. The Court fixed 17 April 2009 as the time limit within which written statements on the question could be presented to it and 17 July 2009 as the time limit within which States and organizations having presented written statements could submit written comments on the other statements.

Written statements were filed within the time limit fixed by the Court for that purpose by: Albania, Argentina, Austria, Azerbaijan, Bolivia, Brazil, China, Cyprus, the Czech Republic, Denmark, Egypt, Estonia, Finland, France, Germany, Iran, Ireland, Japan, Latvia, the Libyan Arab Jamahiriya, Luxembourg, Maldives, the Netherlands, Norway, Poland, Romania, the Russian Federation, Serbia, Sierra Leone, Slovakia, Slovenia, Spain, Switzerland, the United Kingdom and the United States. Venezuela filed a written statement on 24 April 2009; the Court agreed to the filing of that written statement after the expiry of the time limit. The authors of the unilateral declaration of independence also filed a written contribution within the time limit fixed by the Court. Written comments on the other written statements were filed within the time limit by 14 Member States; the authors of the unilateral declaration of independence filed a written contribution within the same time limit.

Public hearings were held from 1 to 11 December. Twenty-eight States, as well as the authors of the unilateral declaration of independence, participated in the oral proceedings before the Court. At the end of the hearings, the Court began its deliberation.

The General Assembly on 14 September decided to include the item entitled "Request for an advisory opinion of ICJ on whether the unilateral declaration of independence of Kosovo is in accordance with international law" in the draft agenda of its sixty-fourth (2009) session (**decision 63/570**).

Other questions

Functioning and organization of the Court

Rules of the Court

In the ongoing review of its procedures and working methods, the Court took further measures to increase its productivity. The Court amended Practice Direction III, requiring the parties not only to "append to their pleadings only strictly selected documents", but also to keep written proceedings as concise as possible, in a manner compatible with the full presentation of their positions. It also amended Practice Direction VI, reiterating the need to keep oral proceedings as brief as possible, in compliance with Article 60, paragraph 1, of the Rules of the Court, and requesting parties to focus, in the first round of oral proceedings, "on those points which have been raised by one party at the stage of written proceedings but which have not so far been adequately addressed by the other, as well as on those which each party wishes to emphasize by way of winding up its arguments". The Court adopted new Practice Direction XIII, giving guidance to the parties as to how their views with regard to questions of procedure could be ascertained under Article 31 of the Rules.

Trust Fund to Assist States in the Settlement of Disputes

In August [A/64/308], the Secretary-General reported on the activities and status of the Trust Fund to Assist States in the Settlement of Disputes through icj since the submission of his 2008 report [YUN 2008, p. 1405]. The Fund, established in 1989 [YUN 1989, p. 818], provided financial assistance to States for expenses incurred in connection with a dispute submitted to icj by way of a special agreement, an application of its Statute, or the execution of a Judgment of the Court.

During the period under review (1 July 2008–30 June 2009), the Fund did not receive any applications for financial assistance from States. Two States contributed to the Fund, which as at 30 June had a balance of some $2.7 million. Noting that the Fund had a decreasing level of resources since its inception, and that the number of contributions to the Fund remained low, the Secretary-General urged States and other entities to consider making substantial contributions to the Fund and to contribute on a regular basis.

Chapter II

International tribunals and court

In 2009, the international tribunals for the former Yugoslavia and for Rwanda worked towards the completion of their mandates.

The International Tribunal for the Prosecution of Persons Responsible for Serious Violations of International Humanitarian Law Committed in the Territory of the Former Yugoslavia since 1991 continued to expedite its proceedings, in keeping with its completion strategy. During the year, the Tribunal rendered two Trial Chambers judgements and three Appeals Chamber judgements. As at 3 December, the nine remaining trials were expected to be completed by September 2012 and all appeals by February 2014.

The International Criminal Tribunal for the Prosecution of Persons Responsible for Genocide and Other Serious Violations of International Humanitarian Law Committed in the Territory of Rwanda and Rwandan Citizens Responsible for Genocide and Other Such Violations Committed in the Territory of Neighbouring States between 1 January and 31 December 1994 (ICTR) continued to work towards its completion strategy, despite an unprecedented workload. In 2009, it rendered five Trial and two Appeals Chamber judgements and commenced 10 new trials. Two fugitives were arrested, yet 11 remained at large.

The International Criminal Court, in its sixth year of functioning, continued its proceedings with respect to situations of concern in four countries. A warrant of arrest was delivered against Omar Hassan Ahmad Al-Bashir, the President of the Sudan, for crimes against humanity and war crimes. Eight warrants of arrest were outstanding at year's end. In November, the Prosecutor requested authorization to open an investigation into the situation in Kenya, where over 355,000 civilians had allegedly been forcibly displaced, injured, raped or killed as part of a widespread and systematic attack.

International Tribunal for the Former Yugoslavia

In 2009, the International Tribunal for the Former Yugoslavia (ICTY), established by Security Council resolution 827(1993) [YUN 1993, p. 440] and based in The Hague, continued efforts to implement its

completion strategy [YUN 2002, p. 1275], which was endorsed by Council resolution 1503(2003) [YUN 2003, p. 1330]. The Tribunal focused on expediting its proceedings and the completion of all trials and appeals. During the year, ICTY also adopted or amended rules of procedure in order to enhance the efficiency of proceedings, based on recommendations made by a working group. The Office of the Prosecutor continued to seek the cooperation of the States of the former Yugoslavia and other States to fulfil its mandate, strengthen relations with its regional counterparts, and support the furtherance of the rule of law in the region. Meanwhile, the Registry continued to play a crucial role in the provision of administrative and judicial support.

On 26 October, Judge Patrick Robinson (Jamaica) and Judge O-Gon Kwon (Republic of Korea) were re-elected to the positions of President and Vice-President of the Tribunal, respectively. The Registrar, John Hocking, and the Prosecutor, Serge Brammertz, continued to fulfil their duties at the Tribunal. The Security Council adopted two resolutions—1877(2009) and 1900(2009)—addressing, among other issues, the appointment of judges, extension of their terms of office, their redeployment between Tribunals, and the maximum number of judges serving at the Tribunal (see pp. 1282–1285).

ICTY President Robinson informed the Council on 3 December [meeting 6228] that of the 161 persons indicted by the Tribunal, only a single accused remained in the pre-trial stage, 24 accused were on trial in nine cases and another 13 accused had appeals pending. Five trials were expected to be completed during the course of 2010, three in the first half of 2011, and the remaining case—that of Radovan Karadžić—in August or September 2012. It was anticipated that all appeals would be completed in 2013, except for the Karadžić appeal, which was estimated to finish in February 2014. The Council, in resolution 1900(2009), requested that the ICTY President submit an updated trial and appeals schedule.

The activities of ICTY were covered in two reports to the Security Council and the General Assembly, for the periods 1 August 2008 to 31 July 2009 [A/64/205-S/2009/394] and 1 August 2009 to 31 July 2010 [A/65/205-S/2010/413]. On 8 October, the Assembly took note of the 2008/2009 report (**decision 64/506**).

The Chambers

During the year, the Tribunal's three Trial Chambers continued to function at full capacity, running up to eight trials simultaneously and rendering two judgements involving eight accused, while the Appeals Chamber rendered three judgements on the merits involving four accused. Judicial activities included first-instance and appeals proceedings against judgements, interlocutory decisions, State requests for review, and contempt cases. As at 31 July, ICTY had 27 judges from 25 countries, comprising 13 permanent judges; two ICTR permanent judges serving in the Appeals Chamber; and 12 ad litem (short-term) judges.

New arrests and indictments

In 2009, no new arrests or indictments were issued by the Prosecutor, except for those for contempt of the Tribunal. Vojislav Šešelj was charged with contempt of court on 21 January (see below) and Zuhdija Tabaković was charged on 17 November (see p. 1281). Meanwhile, two fugitives—Ratko Mladić and Goran Hadžić—remained at large. The Office of the Prosecutor closely followed the work of the Serbian authorities to locate them and was regularly briefed on their activities. Serbia's National Security Council and Action Team in charge of tracking the fugitives led complex and widespread search operations against the two accused and their support networks.

Ongoing cases and trials

In the case against Vojislav Šešelj, who was charged with crimes against humanity and violations of the laws or customs of war allegedly committed in Croatia, Bosnia and Herzegovina and Vojvodina (Serbia) between August 1991 and September 1993 [YUN 2003, p. 1311; YUN 2004, p. 1277], the trial started on 27 November 2006 in his absence [YUN 2006, p. 1490] and began anew on 7 November 2007 [YUN 2007, p. 1337]. On 21 January 2009, Trial Chamber II issued an order in lieu of indictment charging Mr. Šešelj with contempt for having disclosed, in a book authored by him, confidential information in violation of orders granting protective measures to three witnesses, as well as excerpts of one of their written statements. On 11 February, Trial Chamber III, at the prosecution's request, adjourned the hearing of certain prosecution witnesses, finding that hearing them at that time would jeopardize the integrity of proceedings and the security of the witnesses. Also on that date, an amicus curiae Prosecutor was assigned by the Acting Registrar. At his initial appearance on the contempt charges on 6 March, Mr. Šešelj pleaded not guilty. The trial was held on 29 May and in the

judgement rendered on 24 July, he was convicted of contempt of the Tribunal and sentenced to 15 months of imprisonment. The primary trial of Mr. Šešelj resumed on 23 November.

The trial of Vlastimir Đorđević, a former senior Serbian police official charged with deportation, inhumane acts (forcible transfer), murder and persecutions in Kosovo [YUN 2003, p. 1312] and arrested on 17 June 2007 [YUN 2007, p. 1337], commenced on 27 January 2009. Originally, Mr. Đorđević's case was part of the Milutinović et al. case [YUN 2005, p. 1390], yet was severed from that of the others when the Milutinović case began with Mr. Đorđević still at large [YUN 2006, p. 1487]. The prosecution closed its case on 28 October and the defence case opened on 30 November.

On 26 February, in the case against Milan Milutinović, Nikola Šainović, Dragoljub Ojdanić, Nebojša Pavković, Vladimir Lazarević and Sreten Lukić, (Milutinović et al. case) [YUN 2006, p. 1487], who were charged with crimes against humanity and violations of the laws or customs of war allegedly committed in Kosovo in 1999, the Trial Chamber issued its judgement, acquitting Mr. Milutinović on all counts and convicting the others on some or all of the charges. Messrs. Šainović, Pavković and Lukić were each sentenced to 22 years of imprisonment. Messrs. Ojdanić and Lazarević were each sentenced to 15 years of imprisonment. On 27 May, notices of appeal were filed for all of the accused except Milutinović.

Momčilo Krajišnik, a member of the Bosnian Serb leadership during the war, was sentenced in 2006 to 27 years in prison for persecutions, extermination, murder, deportation and forced transfer of non-Serb civilians [YUN 2006, p. 1489]. On 17 March 2009, the Appeals Chamber granted a number of grounds and subgrounds of Mr. Krajišnik's appeal, quashed a number of convictions, dismissed the remaining grounds of appeal, and reduced his sentence to 20 years in prison.

Following the refusal of Dragan Jokić to testify in the case of Popović et al. [YUN 2005, p. 1390], on 1 November 2007, the Trial Chamber issued an order in lieu of indictment on contempt and initiated contempt proceedings against him. On 27 March 2009, Mr. Jokić was found guilty of contempt of the Tribunal and sentenced to four months of imprisonment. On 25 June, the Appeals Chamber dismissed all grounds of a 14 April confidential appeal and affirmed Mr. Jokić's sentence; a public redacted version of the judgement was filed on 3 July.

In the case against Jadranko Prlić, Bruno Stojić, Slobodan Praljak, Milivoj Petković, Valentin Ćorić and Berislav Pušić, who were charged with grave breaches of the 1949 Geneva Conventions, crimes against humanity and violations of the laws or customs of war allegedly committed against Serbs and

Muslims in the Croatian-held part of Bosnia and Herzegovina between November 1991 and April 1994 [YUN 2006, p. 1487], the trial was in the defence stage. As at 31 July 2009, Messrs. Prlić and Stojić had ended their cases, while Mr. Praljak had begun to present his case on 5 May.

Following the trial of Mile Mrkšić, Miroslav Radić and Veselin Šljivančanin [YUN 2006, p. 1490], indicted in 1997 for alleged involvement in the execution of some 200 Croatians and non-Serbs removed from Vukovar hospital in 1991 [YUN 1997, p. 1322], on 27 September 2007, the Tribunal sentenced Messrs. Mrkšić and Šljivančanin, former senior officers of the Yugoslav People's Army (JNA), to 20 years of imprisonment and five years of imprisonment, respectively, for their role in the crimes at Ovčara [YUN 2007, p. 1336]. Mr. Radić, a former JNA captain, was acquitted of all charges. On 5 May 2009, the Appeals Chamber dismissed all grounds of appeal from Messrs. Mrkšić and Šljivančanin. It affirmed Mr. Mrkšić's sentence of 20 years of imprisonment and granted the prosecution's appeal in part, increasing Mr. Šljivančanin's sentence from five to 17 years of imprisonment.

In the trial of Rasim Delić, charged on the basis of his superior command responsibility with violations of the laws or customs of war allegedly committed in Bosnia and Herzegovina between July 1993 and December 1995 [YUN 2005, p. 1388], judgement was rendered on 15 September 2008, sentencing him to three years of imprisonment. Following the filing of appeal briefs, on 11 May 2009, Mr. Delić was granted provisional release pending the hearing of his appeal.

In the case against Milan Lukić, the former leader of a paramilitary group called the "White Eagles" or "Avengers" and his cousin Sredoje Lukić, charged with murdering some 70 Bosnian Muslim women, children and elderly in a house in Višegrad, and beating Bosnian Muslim men at a detention camp in Višegrad [YUN 2007, p. 1337], the trial commenced on 9 July 2008 [YUN 2008, p. 1408] and the evidence was completed on 19 May 2009. On 20 July, judgement was delivered, sentencing Milan Lukić to life imprisonment and Sredoje Lukić to 30 years of imprisonment. On 2 November, the prosecution and the defence of Sredoje Lukić filed their appeal briefs. On 17 November, Zuhdija Tabaković, a potential witness in the case of Messrs. Lukić and Lukić, was charged with contempt of the Tribunal for allegedly providing a false statement in exchange for payment. At his initial appearance on the contempt charges on 22 December, Mr. Tabaković pleaded not guilty.

On 2 June, the trial of Jovica Stanišić and Franko Simatović recommenced [YUN 2003, p. 1311]. The Trial Chamber in May 2006 [YUN 2006, p. 1487] charged Mr. Stanišić, former head of the State Security Service (DB) of the Ministry of Internal Affairs of the

Republic of Serbia, and Mr. Simatović, commander of the DB Special Operations Unit, with four counts of crimes against humanity and one count of violation of the laws or customs of war. The trial began on 28 April 2008, but due to the health condition of Mr. Stanišić, the Appeals Chamber adjourned the proceedings on 16 May [YUN 2008, p. 1408].

The trial of Florence Hartmann, charged with contempt of the Tribunal for disclosing two confidential decisions of the Appeals Chamber in her book *Paix et châtiment*, and in an article "Vital genocide documents concealed", published by the Bosnian Institute, began on 15 June 2009. Closing arguments were heard on 3 July and in the judgement, issued on 14 September, Ms. Hartmann was convicted and sentenced to pay a fine of €7,000. An appeal brief was filed on 9 October and refiled on 23 November.

Dragomir Milošević, a former Bosnian Serb Army General, was convicted on 21 December 2007 of a range of crimes committed against civilians during the final months of the 1992–1995 siege of Sarajevo and was sentenced to 33 years of imprisonment [YUN 2007, p. 1338]. Following a hearing on 21 July 2009, the Appeals Chamber, on 12 November, granted Mr. Milošević's appeal in part and reduced his sentence to 29 years of imprisonment. The prosecution's sole ground of appeal, requesting that Mr. Milošević be sentenced to life imprisonment, was dismissed in its entirety.

In the trial of Astrit Haraqija and Bajrush Morina, charged with contempt of the Tribunal for alleged intimidation and interference with a protected witness, judgement was rendered on 17 December 2008. Messrs. Haraqija and Morina were sentenced to five and three months of imprisonment, respectively. On 23 July 2009, the Appeals Chamber found that the Trial Chamber had given too much weight to untested evidence when it concluded that Mr. Haraqija had influence over Mr. Morina and instructed him to commit the crime of contempt. The Appeals Chamber reversed the conviction of Mr. Haraqija, yet affirmed the sentence of three months of imprisonment for Mr. Morina.

In the case against Mićo Stanišić and Stojan Župljanin, charged with 10 counts of crimes against humanity and violations of the laws or customs of war allegedly committed from April to December 1992 in Bosnia and Herzegovina, the trial commenced on 14 September 2009. According to the joinder indictment filed on 29 September 2008 [YUN 2008, p. 1409], Messrs. Stanišić and Župljanin participated in a joint criminal enterprise as co-perpetrators and were charged with persecutions, extermination, murder, torture, inhumane acts (including forcible transfer) and deportation; and murder, torture, and cruel treatment.

The trial of Radovan Karadžić, former President of Republika Srpska and Supreme Commander of its armed forces, commenced on 26 October 2009. Mr. Karadžić was charged under 11 counts with genocide, crimes against humanity, and violations of the laws or customs of war allegedly committed in Bosnia and Herzegovina between 1992 and 1995. Following his arrest and transfer to the Tribunal on 30 July 2008 [YUN 2008, p. 1407], pleas of not guilty were entered on his behalf to all charges.

In the trial of Ramush Haradinaj, Idriz Balaj and Lahi Brahimaj, charged with crimes against humanity and violations of the laws or customs of war allegedly committed in Kosovo in 1998, judgement was delivered on 3 April 2008 [YUN 2008, p. 1407]. Mr. Brahimaj was sentenced to six years of imprisonment, while Messrs. Haradinaj and Balaj were acquitted. Appeals from judgement were filed before the Appeals Chamber with the prosecution requesting a reversal of the decision to acquit Messrs. Haradinaj, Balaj and Brahimaj on certain counts in the indictment. The appeal hearing was held on 28 October 2009.

In the case against Ljube Boškoski and Johan Tarčulovski, charged with violations of the laws or customs of war allegedly committed against ethnic Albanians in the former Yugoslav Republic of Macedonia in August 2001 [YUN 2005, p. 1388], Mr. Boškoski was acquitted on all counts and Mr. Tarčulovski was sentenced to 12 years of imprisonment in the judgement delivered on 10 July 2008 [YUN 2008, p. 1408]. Appeals were filed on both judgements and the appeal hearing took place on 29 October 2009.

Judges of the Court

Extension of terms of office

In a May assessment report [S/2009/252] to the Security Council, the ICTY President indicated that the Tribunal would not be in a position to complete all its work in 2010, with two cases anticipated to be completed in 2011 and early 2012. He noted that the extension of the terms of office of the Tribunal's trial and ad litem judges until 31 December 2009, and its current appeal judges until 31 December 2010, by Council resolution 1837(2008) [YUN 2008, p. 1411], was not sufficient. Consequently, a request would be made to the Council to remedy the situation.

On 19 June [S/2009/333], the Secretary-General transmitted to the Council letters from the ICTY and ICTR Presidents relating to the ability of the Tribunals to implement their completion strategies. In his letter dated 27 May (Annex I), the ICTY President requested that the Council extend the term of office of ICTY judges; authorize ICTY to exceed temporarily the statutory maximum number of ad litem judges serving at the Tribunal; and expand the membership of

the Appeals Chamber through the redeployment of four permanent judges from the Trial Chambers to the Appeals Chamber.

SECURITY COUNCIL ACTION

On 7 July [meeting 6155], the Security Council unanimously adopted **resolution 1877(2009)**. The draft [S/2009/339] was submitted by Austria.

The Security Council,

Taking note of the letter dated 19 June 2009 from the Secretary-General to the President of the Security Council attaching the letter dated 27 May 2009 from the President of the International Tribunal for the Former Yugoslavia ("the International Tribunal") and the letter dated 29 May 2009 from the President of the International Criminal Tribunal for Rwanda,

Recalling its resolutions 827(1993) of 25 May 1993, 1581(2005) of 18 January 2005, 1597(2005) of 20 April 2005, 1613(2005) of 26 July 2005, 1629(2005) of 30 September 2005, 1660(2006) of 28 February 2006, 1668(2006) of 10 April 2006, 1800(2008) of 20 February 2008, 1837(2008) of 29 September 2008 and 1849(2008) of 12 December 2008,

Recalling in particular its resolutions 1503(2003) of 28 August 2003 and 1534(2004) of 26 March 2004, in which the Council calls upon the International Tribunal to take all possible measures to complete investigations by the end of 2004, to complete all trial activities at first instance by the end of 2008 and to complete all work in 2010,

Taking note of the assessment by the International Tribunal in its completion strategy report that the International Tribunal will not be in a position to complete all its work in 2010,

Having considered the proposals submitted by the President of the International Tribunal,

Expressing its determination to support the efforts made by the International Tribunal towards the completion of its work at the earliest date,

Recalling that in its resolution 1837(2008), the Council extended the term of office of the permanent judges of the International Tribunal, including permanent judges Liu Daqun (China), Theodor Meron (United States of America) and Fausto Pocar (Italy), who are members of the Appeals Chamber, until 31 December 2010, or until the completion of the cases to which they are assigned if sooner,

Expressing its expectation that the extension of the term of office of judges will enhance the effectiveness of judicial proceedings and contribute towards the implementation of the completion strategy of the International Tribunal,

Noting that permanent judges Iain Bonomy (United Kingdom of Great Britain and Northern Ireland), Mohamed Shahabuddeen (Guyana) and Christine Van Den Wyngaert (Belgium) have resigned from the International Tribunal,

Convinced of the advisability of allowing the Secretary-General to appoint an ad litem judge additional to the twelve ad litem judges authorized by the statute of the International Tribunal, as a temporary measure, to enable the International Tribunal to assign a reserve judge to one of the trials, and taking note of the assurance by the President of the International Tribunal that this temporary measure will be within existing resources,

Convinced also of the need to enlarge the membership of the Appeals Chamber in view of the anticipated increase in the workload of the Appeals Chamber upon completion of the trial proceedings,

Stressing the need to ensure that none of the Appeals Chamber judges is assigned to any case to which he or she was assigned at the pretrial or trial stage,

Urging the International Tribunal to take all possible measures to complete its work expeditiously,

Acting under Chapter VII of the Charter of the United Nations,

1. *Decides* to review the extension of the term of office of the permanent judges at the International Tribunal, who are members of the Appeals Chamber, by 31 December 2009, in the light of the progress of the International Tribunal in the implementation of the completion strategy;

2. *Decides also* to extend the term of office of the following permanent judges at the International Tribunal until 31 December 2010, or until the completion of the cases to which they are assigned if sooner:

—Mr. Carmel A. Agius (Malta)
—Mr. Jean-Claude Antonetti (France)
—Mr. Christoph Flügge (Germany)
—Mr. O-gon Kwon (Republic of Korea)
—Mr. Bakone Melema Moloto (South Africa)
—Mr. Alphonsus Martinus Maria Orie (Netherlands)
—Mr. Kevin Horace Parker (Australia)
—Mr. Patrick Lipton Robinson (Jamaica)

3. *Decides further* that the term of office of the permanent judges appointed to replace Mr. Iain Bonomy (United Kingdom of Great Britain and Northern Ireland), Mr. Mohamed Shahabuddeen (Guyana) and Ms. Christine Van Den Wyngaert (Belgium) shall extend until 31 December 2010, or until the completion of the cases to which they will be assigned if sooner;

4. *Decides* to extend the term of office of the following ad litem judges, currently serving at the International Tribunal, until 31 December 2010, or until the completion of the cases to which they are assigned if sooner:

—Mr. Melville Baird (Trinidad and Tobago)
—Mr. Pedro David (Argentina)
—Ms. Elizabeth Gwaunza (Zimbabwe)
—Mr. Frederik Harhoff (Denmark)
—Mr. Uldis Kinis (Latvia)
—Ms. Flavia Lattanzi (Italy)
—Mr. Antoine Mindua (Democratic Republic of the Congo)
—Ms. Michèle Picard (France)
—Mr. Árpád Prandler (Hungary)
—Mr. Stefan Trechsel (Switzerland)

5. *Decides also* to extend the term of office of the following ad litem judges, who are not currently appointed to serve at the International Tribunal, until 31 December 2010, or until the completion of any cases to which they may be assigned if sooner:

—Mr. Frans Bauduin (Netherlands)
—Sir Burton Hall (Bahamas)

—Mr. Raimo Lahti (Finland)
—Mr. Jawdat Naboty (Syrian Arab Republic)
—Ms. Chioma Egondu Nwosu-Iheme (Nigeria)
—Ms. Prisca Matimba Nyambe (Zambia)
—Mr. Brynmor Pollard (Guyana)
—Ms. Vonimbolana Rasoazanany (Madagascar)
—Tan Sri Dato' Lamin bin Haji Mohd Yunus (Malaysia)

6. *Decides further* to allow ad litem judges Harhoff, Lattanzi, Mindua, Prandler and Trechsel to serve in the International Tribunal beyond the cumulative period of service provided for under article 13 ter, paragraph 2, of the statute of the International Tribunal;

7. *Decides* that, upon the request of the President of the International Tribunal, the Secretary-General may appoint additional ad litem judges in order to complete existing trials or conduct additional trials, notwithstanding the fact that the total number of ad litem judges serving at the International Tribunal will from time to time temporarily exceed the maximum of twelve provided for in article 12, paragraph 1, of the statute, to a maximum of thirteen at any one time, returning to a maximum of twelve by 31 December 2009;

8. *Decides also* to amend article 14, paragraphs 3 and 4, of the statute and to replace those paragraphs with the provisions set out in the annex to the present resolution;

9. *Decides further* to remain seized of the matter.

ANNEX

Article 14

Officers and members of the Chambers

3. After consultation with the permanent judges of the International Tribunal, the President shall assign four of the permanent judges elected or appointed in accordance with article 13 bis of the Statute to the Appeals Chamber and nine to the Trial Chambers. Notwithstanding the provisions of article 12, paragraph 1, and article 12, paragraph 3, the President may assign to the Appeals Chamber up to four additional permanent judges serving in the Trial Chambers, on the completion of the cases to which each judge is assigned. The term of office of each judge redeployed to the Appeals Chamber shall be the same as the term of office of the judges serving in the Appeals Chamber.

4. Two of the permanent judges of the International Criminal Tribunal for Rwanda elected or appointed in accordance with article 12 bis of the Statute of that Tribunal shall be assigned by the President of that Tribunal, in consultation with the President of the International Tribunal, to be members of the Appeals Chamber and permanent judges of the International Tribunal. Notwithstanding the provisions of article 12, paragraph 1, and article 12, paragraph 3, up to four additional permanent judges serving in the Trial Chambers of the International Criminal Tribunal for Rwanda may be assigned to the Appeals Chamber by the President of that Tribunal, on the completion of the cases to which each judge is assigned. The term of office of each judge redeployed to the Appeals Chamber shall be the same as the term of office of the judges serving in the Appeals Chamber.

In a letter dated 8 July [A/63/957], the Security Council President transmitted the text of resolution 1877(2009) to the General Assembly President. On 9 September, the Assembly endorsed the actions taken by the Council in operative paragraphs 1 through 8 of that resolution (**decision 63/426**).

Appointment of new judges

By a letter of 22 July [S/2009/386], the Secretary-General referred to the resignations of Judges Mohamed Shahabuddeen (Guyana), Iain Bonomy (United Kingdom) and Christine Van Den Wyngaert (Belgium), effective 10 May, 31 August and 1 September respectively. The Governments of Belgium and the United Kingdom had nominated Guy Delvoie and Howard Morrison to replace Judges Wyngaert and Bonomy, respectively. The Government of Guyana, indicating that it was not in a position to nominate a candidate to replace Judge Shahabuddeen, had requested that the other States of the region be asked for possible nominees. Consequently, the Government of the Bahamas nominated Sir Burton Hall, an ad litem judge at the International Tribunal not yet assigned to any cases. As the three candidates met the qualifications prescribed in the Tribunal's Statute, the Secretary-General expressed his intent to appoint them as permanent judges of the International Tribunal, which the Security Council supported on 27 July [S/2009/387].

On 7 August, the Secretary-General informed the Council [S/2009/410] and General Assembly [A/63/946] Presidents that he had appointed Mr. Delvoie, Mr. Morrison and Sir Burton Hall as ICTY permanent judges, effective 1 September 2009, 31 August 2009 and 7 August 2009, respectively, until 31 December 2010, or until the completion of the cases to which they would be assigned if sooner.

On 9 September, the Assembly decided to include the agenda item on ICTY in the draft agenda of its sixty-fourth (2009) session and to consider it directly in plenary meeting (**decision 63/562**).

Ad litem judges

By identical letters of 28 October to the Security Council [S/2009/570] and General Assembly [A/64/510] Presidents, the Secretary-General transmitted a 29 September letter from the ICTY President, requesting the extension of the terms of office of two ad litem judges, Judges Kimberly Prost (Canada) and Ole Bjørn Støle (Norway), until the end of March 2010, to enable them to complete the judgment in the case of the *Prosecutor v. Popović et al.* [YUN 2008, p. 1408]. Their terms of office were set to expire on 31 December 2009. He also sought the appointment of ad litem Judge Prisca Matimba Nyambe (Zambia) effective 1 December in order to commence the Zdravko Tolimir trial [ibid., p. 1409].

SECURITY COUNCIL ACTION

On 16 December [meeting 6242], the Security Council unanimously adopted **resolution 1900(2009)**. The draft [S/2009/644] was submitted by Austria.

The Security Council,

Taking note of the letter dated 28 October 2009 from the Secretary-General to the President of the Security Council, attaching the letter dated 29 September 2009 from the President of the International Tribunal for the Former Yugoslavia ("the International Tribunal"),

Recalling its resolutions 827(1993) of 25 May 1993, 1581(2005) of 18 January 2005, 1597(2005) of 20 April 2005, 1613(2005) of 26 July 2005, 1629(2005) of 30 September 2005, 1660(2006) of 28 February 2006, 1668(2006) of 10 April 2006, 1800(2008) of 20 February 2008, 1837(2008) of 29 September 2008, 1849(2008) of 12 December 2008 and 1877(2009) of 7 July 2009,

Recalling in particular its resolutions 1503(2003) of 28 August 2003 and 1534(2004) of 26 March 2004, in which the Council called upon the International Tribunal to take all possible measures to complete investigations by the end of 2004, to complete all trial activities at first instance by the end of 2008 and to complete all work in 2010,

Taking note of the assessment of the International Tribunal in its completion strategy report that the International Tribunal will not be in a position to complete all its work in 2010,

Recalling that, in resolution 1877(2009), the Council extended the term of office of permanent judges and ad litem judges until 31 December 2010, or until the completion of the cases to which they are assigned, if sooner, and decided to review the extension of the term of office of the permanent judges at the International Tribunal, who are members of the Appeals Chamber, by 31 December 2009, in the light of the progress of the International Tribunal in the implementation of the completion strategy,

Convinced of the advisability of allowing the total number of ad litem judges serving at the International Tribunal to temporarily exceed the maximum of twelve provided for in article 12, paragraph 1, of the statute of the International Tribunal,

Urging the International Tribunal to take all possible measures to complete its work expeditiously,

Acting under Chapter VII of the Charter of the United Nations,

1. *Underlines its intention* to extend, by 30 June 2010, the terms of office of all trial judges at the International Tribunal based on the International Tribunal's projected trial schedule and the terms of office of all appeals judges until 31 December 2012, or until the completion of the cases to which they are assigned, if sooner, and requests the President of the International Tribunal to submit to the Security Council an updated trial and appeals schedule, including information on the judges for whom extension of the terms of office or redeployment to the Appeals Chamber will be sought;

2. *Decides* that, notwithstanding the expiry of their terms of office on 31 December 2009, Judges Kimberly Prost (Canada) and Ole Bjørn Støle (Norway) shall complete the *Popović* case, which they began before the expiry of their terms of office, and takes note of the intention of the International Tribunal to complete the case before the end of March 2010;

3. *Also decides*, in this regard, that the total number of ad litem judges serving at the International Tribunal may temporarily exceed the maximum of twelve provided for in article 12, paragraph 1, of the statute of the International Tribunal, to a maximum of thirteen at any one time, returning to a maximum of twelve by 31 March 2010;

4. *Further decides* to allow ad litem Judges Prost and Støle to serve at the International Tribunal beyond the cumulative period of service provided for under article 13 ter, paragraph 2, of the statute of the International Tribunal;

5. *Decides* to remain seized of the matter.

By a letter dated 22 December [A/64/591], the Council President transmitted the text of resolution 1900(2009) to the General Assembly President. On 23 December, the Assembly endorsed the actions taken in operative paragraphs 1 through 4 of that resolution (**decision 64/416**).

Office of the Prosecutor

In 2009, the Office of the Prosecutor made significant progress towards the completion of the trial programme. It also continued to seek the full cooperation of the States of the former Yugoslavia and other States to fulfil its mandate. Two fugitives—Ratko Mladić and Goran Hadžić—remained at large. On 15 October, the Office of the Prosecutor severed the Mladić indictment from the Karadžić indictment, and streamlined it. The Office also completed the transfer of all investigative dossiers to regional authorities late in the year. Seventeen case files with investigative material on 43 suspects were transferred to the prosecutors' offices in Bosnia and Herzegovina, Croatia and Serbia. Serge Brammertz and Norman Farrell continued their duties as Prosecutor and Deputy Prosecutor, respectively [YUN 2008, p. 1412].

As at 31 July, the Office was prosecuting 21 accused in seven trials. Meanwhile, appellate work had remained constant. During the year, the prosecution had filed appeals against five of the six accused in the first multiple-accused judgement. In addition, briefs were filed in four cases, one oral hearing was held on 21 July and hearings in two other briefed cases were held in October. By year's end, only one case remained at the pre-trial stage.

On international cooperation, developments at the political level and the new leadership at the operational level led to an improvement in Serbia's cooperation with the Office of the Prosecutor. Serbia had complied with the majority of requests for assistance and by July nearly all requests for access to documents and archives had been addressed. The Office closely followed the work of the Serbian authorities to locate the two fugitives (Mladić and Hadžić), and was regularly briefed on their activities. The Serbian authorities continued to facilitate the appearance of witnesses before the Tribunal, including serving summonses on individuals.

Croatia responded adequately to the majority of requests for assistance, and the Office received adequate assistance from the Office of the Croatian Prosecutor. However, the Office faced difficulties in securing Croatia's cooperation in the Gotovina et al. trial [YUN 2008, p. 1407], including the prosecution's long-standing request for military documents relating to Operation Storm in 1995 that remained outstanding. In October, the Croatian Government created an inter-agency task force to examine concerns communicated by the Prosecutor's Office about identified shortcomings in the administrative investigation concerning the missing military documents and to locate, or account for, those records.

The authorities of Bosnia and Herzegovina responded adequately to requests for assistance regarding documents and access to government archives and to facilitate the appearance of witnesses before the Tribunal. However, the Office remained concerned that Radovan Stanković, indicted by the Tribunal for crimes against humanity and war crimes, remained at large. The Tribunal had transferred Mr. Stanković to Bosnia and Herzegovina in May 2005, where he escaped from prison while serving a 20-year sentence in Foča. The Prosecutor's Office encouraged Bosnia and Herzegovina authorities, as well as neighbouring States, to take all necessary measures to apprehend him.

The Registry

The Registry continued to provide operational support to the Chambers and the Office of the Prosecutor and to manage the administration of the Tribunal. It also managed the Detention Unit, the Victims and Witness Section, the legal aid office and the interpretation and translation service. In an effort to downsize the Tribunal's staff and its legacy, the Registrar merged sections and redistributed functions within the Registry to streamline their operations and increase efficiency, in line with the completion strategy [YUN 2002, p. 1275]. The Deputy Registrar, John Hocking, served as Acting Registrar from 1 January 2009 until his appointment as Registrar, effective 15 May.

Between August 2008 and July 2009, the Court Management and Support Services Section supported up to eight trials, as well as numerous pretrial, contempt and appeals hearings. It was also involved in establishing the Court Records Database, and worked closely with the Tribunal's Archive Section on a project to digitize the audio-visual archives of all court proceedings. The Victims and Witnesses Section facilitated 727 witnesses travelling to The Hague to give evidence, while its Protection Unit coordinated professional responses to an increased number of threats to witnesses. The Office for Legal Aid and Detention Matters serviced over 500 defence team members in cases in pretrial, trial and appellate proceedings. The Detention Unit continued to operate at a high level of activity, serving the judicial process on a daily basis for accused in the trial phase and providing secure custodial care for all detained persons.

The Communications Service, which fell under the Registrar's supervision, managed major public events, such as the beginning of the Radovan Karadžić trial, that aroused interest on the part of the media, academics and members of the general public. The Tribunal's outreach programme, which marked its tenth anniversary, continued to raise awareness of the Tribunal's work. The website of the Tribunal was further developed as an information and legacy tool through the inclusion of new features and the translation of material into Bosnian/Croatian/Serbian and French.

Financing

2008–2009 biennium

Report of Secretary-General. The second performance report on the ICTY budget for the 2008–2009 biennium [A/64/512], submitted in response to General Assembly resolution 63/255 [YUN 2008, p. 1414], reflected an increase of $12,655,400 gross ($3,623,900 net) as compared with the revised appropriation for that biennium of $376,232,900 gross ($342,067,000 net). The Assembly was requested to approve the final appropriation of $388,888,300 gross ($345,690,900 net) for 2008–2009 to the ICTY Special Account.

ACABQ report. In December [A/64/555], the Advisory Committee on Administrative and Budgetary Questions (ACABQ) recommended approval of the final appropriation.

2010–2011 biennium

In October [A/64/476], the Secretary-General submitted ICTY resource requirements for the 2010–2011 biennium, which before recosting amounted to $301,895,900 gross ($279,847,400 net) and reflected a decrease in real terms of $62,219,600 net or 18.2 per cent, compared to the revised appropriation for 2008–2009. ACABQ, in December, recommended approval of those requirements, subject to its observations and recommendations [A/64/555].

In December [A/64/570], the Secretary-General submitted revised estimates to the ICTY proposed budget for 2010–2011, which included the effect of changes in rates of exchange and inflation, and after recosting amounted to $290,923,100 gross. ACABQ found no technical basis for objecting to the Secretary-General's revised estimates and transmitted them to the Assembly for consideration [A/64/7/Add.19].

On 24 December [meeting 68], the General Assembly, on the recommendation of the Fifth (Administrative and Budgetary) Committee [A/64/593], adopted **resolution 64/240** without vote [agenda item 144].

Financing of the International Tribunal for the Prosecution of Persons Responsible for Serious Violations of International Humanitarian Law Committed in the Territory of the Former Yugoslavia since 1991

The General Assembly,

I

Second performance report on the budget of the International Tribunal for the Former Yugoslavia for the biennium 2008–2009

Having considered the second performance report of the Secretary-General on the budget, for the biennium 2008–2009, of the International Tribunal for the Prosecution of Persons Responsible for Serious Violations of International Humanitarian Law Committed in the Territory of the Former Yugoslavia since 1991 and the related report of the Advisory Committee on Administrative and Budgetary Questions,

Recalling its resolution 47/235 of 14 September 1993 on the financing of the International Tribunal for the Former Yugoslavia and its subsequent resolutions thereon, the latest of which were resolutions 62/230 of 22 December 2007 and 63/255 of 24 December 2008,

1. *Takes note* of the second performance report of the Secretary-General on the budget, for the biennium 2008–2009, of the International Tribunal for the Prosecution of Persons Responsible for Serious Violations of International Humanitarian Law Committed in the Territory of the Former Yugoslavia since 1991 and the related report of the Advisory Committee on Administrative and Budgetary Questions;

2. *Endorses* the conclusions and recommendations contained in section IV.B of the report of the Advisory Committee on Administrative and Budgetary Questions;

3. *Resolves* that, for the biennium 2008–2009, the amount of 376,232,900 United States dollars gross (342,067,000 dollars net) approved in its resolution 63/255 for the financing of the International Tribunal for the Former Yugoslavia shall be adjusted by the amount of 12,655,400 dollars gross (3,623,900 dollars net), for a total amount of 388,888,300 dollars gross (345,690,900 dollars net);

II

Budget of the International Tribunal for the Former Yugoslavia for the biennium 2010–2011

Having considered the reports of the Secretary-General on the financing of the International Tribunal for the Former Yugoslavia for the biennium 2010–2011 and on the revised estimates arising from the effects of changes in rates of exchange and inflation,

Having also considered the related report of the Advisory Committee on Administrative and Budgetary Questions,

1. *Takes note* of the reports of the Secretary-General on the financing of the International Tribunal for the Former Yugoslavia for the biennium 2010–2011 and on the revised estimates arising from the effects of changes in rates of exchange and inflation;

2. *Endorses* the conclusions and recommendations contained in the related report of the Advisory Committee on Administrative and Budgetary Questions, subject to the provisions of the present resolution;

3. *Welcomes* the work of the Tribunal to ensure the expeditious completion of its mandate and, with regard to the current budget, the commensurate reduction in the financing of the Tribunal;

4. *Stresses* the importance of transparency in the presentation of staffing changes;

5. *Emphasizes* that redeployment should not be used to transfer posts to different functional areas;

6. *Takes note* of paragraphs 49 *(a)* to *(d)* of the report of the Advisory Committee on Administrative and Budgetary Questions, and decides not to accept the redeployment and reclassification of staff as set out in paragraphs 72 to 74 of the report of the Secretary-General on the financing of the Tribunal for the biennium 2010–2011;

7. *Decides* to establish the following posts:

(a) One P-5 Chief of the Immediate Office of the Registrar;

(b) One P-4 Legal Officer for the Immediate Office of the Registrar;

(c) One P-3 Legal Officer for the Immediate Office of the Registrar;

(d) One P-4 Head of the Press and Information Office;

(e) One P-3 Registry Liaison Officer in Zagreb;

8. *Emphasizes* that general temporary assistance positions shall be provided to replace posts while their functions are required;

9. *Requests* that future budget proposals of the International Criminal Tribunal for Rwanda and the International Tribunal for the Former Yugoslavia be harmonized to facilitate better comparative analysis, particularly with respect to their completion strategies;

10. *Decides* to appropriate to the Special Account for the International Tribunal for the Prosecution of Persons Responsible for Serious Violations of International Humanitarian Law Committed in the Territory of the Former Yugoslavia since 1991 a total amount of 290,285,500 dollars gross (268,265,300 dollars net) for the biennium 2010–2011, as detailed in the annex to the present resolution;

11. *Also decides* that the financing of the appropriation for the biennium 2010–2011 under the Special Account shall take into account the estimated income of 277,500 dollars for the biennium, which shall be set off against the aggregate amount of the appropriation;

12. *Further decides* that the total assessment for 2010 under the Special Account, amounting to 157,659,400 dollars, shall consist of:

(a) 145,004,000 dollars, being half of the estimated appropriation approved for the biennium 2010–2011, after taking into account 138,750 dollars, which is half of the estimated income for the biennium of 277,500 dollars;

(b) 12,655,400 dollars, being the increase in the final appropriation for the biennium 2008–2009 approved by the General Assembly in paragraph 3 of section I above;

13. *Decides* to apportion the amount of 78,829,700 dollars gross (68,808,900 dollars net) among Member States in accordance with the scale of assessments applicable to the regular budget of the United Nations for 2010;

14. *Also decides* to apportion the amount of 78,829,700 dollars gross (68,808,900 dollars net) among Member States in accordance with the scale of assessments applicable to peacekeeping operations for 2010;

15. *Further decides* that, in accordance with the provisions of its resolution 973(X) of 15 December 1955, there shall be set off against the apportionment among Member States, as provided for in paragraphs 13 and 14 above, their respective share in the Tax Equalization Fund of the estimated staff assessment income of 20,041,600 dollars approved for the International Tribunal for the Former Yugoslavia for 2010.

ANNEX

Financing for the biennium 2010–2011 of the International Tribunal for the Prosecution of Persons Responsible for Serious Violations of International Humanitarian Law Committed in the Territory of the Former Yugoslavia since 1991

	Gross	Net
	(United States dollars)	
Estimated appropriation for the biennium 2010–2011	294,311,100	272,744,600
Revised estimates: effect of changes in rates of exchange and inflation	16,783,000	16,239,800
Recommendations of the Advisory Committee on Administrative and Budgetary Questions	(20,171,000)	(20,171,000)
Recommendations of the Fifth Committee	(637,600)	(548,100)
Estimated initial appropriation for the biennium 2010–2011	290,285,500	268,265,300
Less:		
Estimated income for the biennium 2010–2011	(277,500)	(277,500)
TOTAL assessment for 2010	**157,659,400**	**137,617,800**
Comprising:		
(a) Requirements representing half of the estimated appropriation for the biennium 2010–2011, after taking into account 138,750 dollars, which is half of the estimated income for the biennium 2010–2011 of 277,500 dollars	145,004,000	133,993,900
(b) Requirements arising from the final appropriation for the biennium 2008–2009	12,655,400	3,623,900
Of which:		
Contributions assessed on Member States in accordance with the scale of assessments applicable to the regular budget of the United Nations for 2010	78,829,700	68,808,900
Contributions assessed on Member States in accordance with the scale of assessments applicable to peacekeeping operations of the United Nations for 2010	78,829,700	68,808,900

On 24 December, the General Assembly decided that the agenda item on ICTY financing would remain for consideration during its resumed sixty-fourth (2010) session (**decision 64/549**).

International Tribunal for Rwanda

In 2009, the International Criminal Tribunal for Rwanda (ICTR), established by Security Council resolution 955(1994) [YUN 1994, p. 299] and based in Arusha, United Republic of Tanzania, delivered five Trial Chambers judgements and two Appeals Chamber judgements. The accelerated efforts of the Office of the Prosecutor resulted in the arrest of two fugitives, who made their initial appearance before the Tribunal. ICTR continued to explore innovative measures to expedite trials, requesting the Council to authorize a judge to engage in another professional occupation in his home country and work part-time while drafting his final judgement; and two judges of the same nationality to serve at the Tribunal simultaneously (see p. 1291). The Council also permitted, as a temporary measure, an increase in the number of ad litem judges from nine to twelve and extended the term of office of judges [ibid.].

In May [S/2009/247] and November [S/2009/587] the ICTR President reported on progress made in implementing the completion strategy. Addressing the Security Council on 3 December [meeting 6228], he said that of the 10 new trials that began during the year, judgements had been delivered in two; the entire evidence had been heard in three; and the defence phase would be completed by year's end or in the first half of 2010 in the remaining five. The four ongoing multi-accused cases continued to pose the greatest challenge to the Tribunal. Judgement drafting in those cases was expected to be completed during 2010, but progress was continuously challenged by parallel assignments of the judges and their legal staff to support other cases. On the 11 fugitives remaining at large, he said that the time for their arrest was long overdue and called upon Member States, particularly those where there was significant evidence that fugitives were hiding in their territory, such as Kenya, to fully cooperate with the Tribunal.

The activities of ICTR were covered in two reports to the Security Council and the General Assembly, for the periods of 1 July 2008 to 30 June 2009 [A/64/206-S/2009/396] and 1 July 2009 to 30 June 2010 [A/65/188-S/2010/408]. On 8 October, the Assembly took note of the 2008/2009 report (**decision 64/505**).

The Chambers

The ICTR Chambers were composed of 14 permanent judges and 11 ad litem judges at the end of June. Seven permanent judges sat in the three Trial Chambers, while seven permanent judges sat in the Appeals Chamber. Each Trial Chamber could be divided into sections of three judges. Since the adoption of Security Council resolution 1855(2008) [YUN 2008, p. 1419], the sections could be composed of ad litem judges exclusively, which also meant that they were competent to preside over a case. The Appeals Chamber was common with ICTY, and was composed of seven judges.

New arrests

Grégoire Ndahimana, a former *bourgmestre,* was arrested on 10 August in the Democratic Republic of the Congo (DRC) and made his initial appearance on 28 September, when he pleaded not guilty to all counts in the indictment. The Chamber began pre-trial proceedings in the case. It was also handling pre-trial matters in the case of Ildephonse Nizeyimana, former second-in-command in charge of intelligence and military operations at the École des sous-officiers during 1994. Mr. Nizeyimana was arrested on 5 October in Uganda and made his initial appearance on 14 October, when he pleaded not guilty to all counts in the indictment.

Ongoing cases and trials

The case of Ildephonse Hategekimana, former commander of Ngoma Military Camp, opened on 26 January following the Trial and Appeals Chambers' rejection of the requested referral of the case to Rwanda for trial in late 2008 [YUN 2008, p. 1417]. The trial commenced on 8 March 2009 and closed on 6 October. Over the course of 43 trial days, the prosecution and the defence called 20 witnesses each. A site visit to Rwanda involving the Chambers and both parties was conducted between 2 and 6 November.

François Karera, former préfet of Kigali-Rural, convicted and sentenced to life imprisonment in December 2007 [YUN 2007, p. 1344], filed his notice of appeal on 14 January 2008 [YUN 2008, p. 1417]. On 2 February 2009, the Appeals Chamber upheld the convictions for instigating and committing genocide and extermination, and instigating, committing, ordering, and aiding and abetting murder. It also affirmed the sentence imposed.

The contempt trial of Léonidas Nshogoza, a former defence investigator in the *Kamuhanda* trial, commenced on 9 February and the evidence was concluded on 31 March. The Chamber heard testimony from five prosecution witnesses and 11 defence witnesses. On 2 July, the Chamber convicted Mr. Nshogoza on one count of contempt of the Tribunal and acquitted him on three other counts in the indictment. He was sentenced to 10 months of imprisonment, but since he was entitled to credit for time served at the UN Detention Facility in Arusha since 8 February 2008, the Chamber ordered his immediate release.

In the case of Augustin Ngirabatware, former Minister of Planning, following his initial appearance before the Court on 10 October 2008 [YUN 2008, p. 1416], at which he pleaded not guilty to all counts in the indictment, a further appearance took place on 9 February 2009. On 12 March, after concluding that sufficient evidence existed to initiate contempt proceedings against an individual for allegedly disclosing confidential information and threatening, intimidating and otherwise interfering with a prosecution witness, the Chamber issued an order in lieu of an indictment. The case opened on 23 September and over the course of 46 trial days, the Chamber heard the evidence of 17 prosecution witnesses.

The trial of Hormisdas Nsengimana, the priest and former rector of the *Collège Christ-Roi* in Nyanza (Butare prefecture), began on 22 June 2007 [YUN 2007, p. 1343]. The Chamber called 43 witnesses during 42 trial days, including the defence case that began on 2 June 2008 [YUN 2008, p. 1416], and heard closing arguments on 12 and 13 February 2009. On 17 November, the Chamber rendered a judgement acquitting Mr. Nsengimana on all counts: genocide and murder and extermination as crimes against humanity.

The trial of Colonel Tharcisse Renzaho, former prefect of Kigali-ville, charged with six counts of genocide, complicity in genocide, crimes against humanity (murder, rape) and violations of the Geneva Conventions and Additional Protocol II, began on 8 January 2007 [YUN 2007, p. 1343]. During the trial, the parties called 53 witnesses over the course of 49 trial days, with closing arguments heard on 14 and 15 February 2008 [YUN 2008, p. 1416]. In the judgement delivered on 14 July 2009, Mr. Renzaho was sentenced to life imprisonment for genocide, crimes against humanity and war crimes.

In the Ndindiliyimana et al. ("Military II") case [YUN 2006, p. 1497]—against Augustin Ndindiliyimana, former Chief of Staff of the Gendarmerie; Augustin Bizimungu, former Chief of Staff of the Army; François-Xavier Nzuwonemeye, former Commander of the Reconnaissance Battalion; and Innocent Sagahutu, former Second-in-Command of the Reconnaissance Battalion—the proceedings were adjourned on 4 December 2008 [YUN 2008, p. 1417]. On 16 February 2009, the Chamber heard the evidence of four recall and additional witnesses as a remedy for the prosecution's violation of its obligation to disclose exculpatory material under rule 68 of the Rules of Procedure and Evidence. On 31 March, the parties filed their final closing briefs, and from 13 to 17 April, the Chamber and the parties conducted a site visit to Rwanda. The Chamber heard closing arguments on 24, 25 and 26 June.

In the Nyiramasuhuko et al. trial ("Butare" case), which closed on 2 December 2008 [YUN 2008, p. 1417],

pursuant to defence requests, the Chamber recalled four prosecution witnesses on 23 and 24 February 2009. The case opened in 2001 [YUN 2001, p. 1208] and involved six persons charged with genocide, crimes against humanity and serious violations of the Geneva Conventions: Pauline Nyiramasuhuko, former Rwandan Minister for Family and Women Affairs; her son and alleged former leader of an Interahamwe militia in Butare, Arsène Shalom Ntahobali; Sylvain Nsabimana, former prefect of Butare; Alphonse Nteziryayo, former Commanding Officer of the Military Police and former prefect of Butare; Joseph Kanyabashi, former Mayor of Ngoma; and Elie Ndayambaje, former Mayor of Muganza. They were accused of committing killings in a calculated, cold-blooded and methodical manner and playing a prominent role in the commission of the crimes in Butare, a religious and academic centre in Rwanda [YUN 2007, p. 1343]. Oral closing arguments were heard from 20 to 30 April 2009, and following a 30 October order by the Chamber, a new amicus curiae report for alleged false testimony and contempt of court in relation to three witnesses was filed.

On 27 February, the Chamber delivered its judgement in the case of Emmanuel Rukundo, a former military chaplain [YUN 2001, p. 1207]. He was convicted of genocide and crimes against humanity (extermination and murder) based on his participation in the killing of and the causing of serious bodily harm to Tutsi in April and May 1994 in Kabgayi, Gitarama prefecture. Mr. Rukundo was also found guilty, by a majority of the Chamber, of causing serious mental harm for the sexual assault of a young Tutsi woman. Considering Mr. Rukundo's stature in society as a priest as an aggravating circumstance, the Chamber sentenced the accused to 25 years of imprisonment. Over 67 trial days, the Chamber heard 50 witnesses, including Mr. Rukundo. The judgement was under appeal.

Since February, the Chamber had been overseeing the trial readiness in the case of Callixte Nzabonimana, former Minister of Youth [YUN 2008, p. 1416]. The trial opened on 9 November.

On 3 March, in the trial of Karemera et al.—against Édouard Karemera, Matthieu Ngirumpatse and Joseph Nzirorera—which was stayed from August 2008 until March 2009 due to the ill-health of the second accused [YUN 2008, p. 1416], the Chamber ordered the severance of Mr. Ngirumpatse from the case, finding that he would be unfit to stand trial for an indeterminate period of time, yet stayed its decision pending the Appeals Chamber ruling. Mr. Ngirumpatse consented to the proceedings continuing in his absence, and Mr. Karemera concluded his defence on 28 May. On 19 June, the Appeals Chamber reversed the Chamber's decision on severance and remanded the matter to the Trial Chamber, which ordered a further stay of proceedings. Joseph Nzirorera, former National Secretary of the Mouvement républicain national pour le développement et la démocratie, began his defence at the end of October.

On 20 March, a pretrial conference was held in the case of Yussuf Munyakazi, a businessman and former leader of a militia group in Cyangugu prefecture [YUN 2004, p. 1286]. The trial opened on 22 April; the Chamber heard 11 prosecution and 20 defence witnesses over the course of 19 trial days. The parties filed their written closing briefs on 16 December.

On 26 March, the Chamber handled a status conference for the trial of Jean-Baptiste Gatete, a businessman and former Mayor of Murambi commune (Byumba prefecture) [YUN 2002, p. 1285]. The trial began on 20 October; the prosecution concluded its case on 16 November, with 22 witnesses having been presented.

In the case of Lieutenant-Colonel Ephrem Setako, former Director of the Judicial Affairs Division of the Ministry of Defence, the trial began on 25 August 2008 [YUN 2008, p. 1416], the prosecution completed its case on 22 April 2009 and the Defence finished its case on 26 June. Over the course of 60 trial days, 56 witnesses gave evidence. The closing arguments were heard on 5 November.

The trial of Dominique Ntawukulilyayo, former sub-prefect in the Butare prefecture [YUN 2008, p. 1416], commenced on 6 May. The prosecution called 12 witnesses over 12 trial days and the Chamber heard 23 defence witnesses over 21 trial days. The evidence phase of the case closed on 17 December.

Following the Appeals Chamber judgement of 29 August 2008, in which it ordered a retrial of Tharcisse Muvunyi, former Lieutenant-Colonel, École des sous-officiers in Butare, for an alleged speech he gave in May 1994 at the Gikore Trade Centre [YUN 2008, p. 1418], the prosecution commenced its case on 17 June. It concerned one allegation of the indictment—namely incitement to commit genocide. The Chamber heard 13 witnesses over nine trial days. Closing arguments were presented on 2 October.

On 22 June, the Chamber delivered the judgement in the case of Callixte Kalimanzira, the former chef de cabinet of the Ministry of the Interior [YUN 2005, p. 1397]. The trial began on 5 May 2008 [YUN 2008, p. 1416] and the Chamber heard 66 witnesses, including Mr. Kalimanzira, over 37 trial days, with closing arguments on 20 April 2009. The Chamber found Mr. Kalimanzira guilty of genocide and direct and public incitement to commit genocide; it sentenced him to 30 years of imprisonment.

The trial against Gaspard Kanyarukiga, a former businessman arrested and transferred to the Tribunal on charges of genocide, complicity in genocide, conspiracy to commit genocide and extermination as a crime against humanity in July 2004 [YUN 2004, p. 1286], commenced on 31 August.

The trial of Michel Bagaragaza, the former Director-General of the Government office that controlled the Rwandan tea industry [YUN 2007, p. 1345], was to have begun on 31 August. However, the parties filed a joint motion for the consideration of a guilty plea for complicity in genocide, which the Chamber accepted on 17 September, granting the prosecution's motion to amend the indictment, and dropping all other charges against Mr. Bagaragaza. On 3 and 4 November, the Chamber heard one character witness, admitted written evidence and heard the parties' closing arguments. On 5 November, the Chamber rendered its judgement, sentencing Mr. Bagaragaza to eight years of imprisonment.

In the trial of Protais Zigiranyirazo, a businessman and brother-in-law of the late Rwandan President, Juvénal Habyarimana, the Chamber found him guilty of having participated in a joint criminal enterprise with the common purpose of committing genocide and extermination of Tutsi, as well as aiding and abetting genocide, and sentenced him to 20 years of imprisonment on 18 December 2008 [YUN 2008, p. 1417]. On 28 September 2009, the Appeals Chamber heard the parties, and in its judgement on 16 November, having found serious legal and factual errors in the assessment of his alibi, reversed Mr. Zigiranyirazo's convictions and entered a verdict of acquittal.

In the trial of Siméon Nchamihigo, former Deputy Prosecutor of Cyangugu, the Chamber convicted him in September 2008 [YUN 2008, p. 1416] of genocide and extermination, murder and other inhumane acts as crimes against humanity based on his participation in the killing of Tutsi in April 1994 at various places in Cyangugu. He was sentenced to life imprisonment. The Appeals Chamber heard the parties on 29 September 2009.

The hearing of the appeal in the case of Simon Bikindi, a singer and composer of popular music [YUN 2002, p. 1285], took place on 30 September. Mr. Bikindi was convicted of direct and public incitement to commit genocide and sentenced to 15 years of imprisonment in December 2008 [YUN 2008, p. 1417].

Judges of the Court

Extension of terms of office and ad litem judges

In a 14 May assessment report [S/2009/247] to the Security Council, the ICTR President indicated that the Tribunal would not be in a position to complete all its work in 2010, with judgement deliveries expected at the end of 2010 in one case and in mid-2010 in three multi-accused cases. He also reported that the existing number of judges, not all of whom were available to assume new cases, had turned out to be insufficient to form benches for all ten new cases. Consequently, requests to the Council were being prepared to address the need for a higher number of ad litem judges and for a mechanism to add additional judges to the roster, as well as to extend the mandate of judges.

The Secretary-General transmitted a 29 May letter [A/63/942] from the ICTR President, requesting that the General Assembly expand the membership of the Appeals Chamber by authorizing the President to redeploy four permanent judges from the Trial Chambers to the Appeals Chamber; extend the term of office of ICTR judges; allow one judge to engage in another professional occupation in his home country and work part-time while drafting his final judgement; and reconsider the entitlements of ad litem judges. The ICTR President further requested, in a letter dated 15 June [A/63/941], that the Assembly permit the Tribunal to recruit an additional ad litem judge from among the former ICTY permanent judges or the ICTY ad litem judges who had not been assigned to any case.

On 19 June [S/2009/333], the Secretary-General transmitted to the Council letters from the ICTR and ICTY Presidents relating to the ability of the Tribunals to implement their completion strategies, including the ICTR President's 29 May letter. On 26 June, the ICTR President's 15 June letter [S/2009/334] was transmitted to the Council.

In a 1 July letter [A/63/940] transmitted to the Assembly, the ICTR President stated that the Russian Federation intended to replace Judge Sergei Aleckseevich Egorov when he resigned from the Tribunal, and requested that, though replaced, Judge Egorov be permitted to continue to serve at the Tribunal until the completion of the cases to which he was assigned. As the Tribunal would then have two permanent judges from the Russian Federation serving at the same time, he also requested that the Assembly allow derogation from the statutory prohibition against two judges of the same nationality serving at the same time. The Secretary-General also transmitted the ICTR President's 1 July letter to the Council [S/2009/336] for its consideration.

SECURITY COUNCIL ACTION

On 7 July [meeting 6156], the Security Council unanimously adopted **resolution 1878(2009)**. The draft [S/2009/340] was submitted by Austria.

The Security Council,

Taking note of the letter dated 19 June 2009 from the Secretary-General to the President of the Security Council attaching the letter dated 29 May 2009 from the President of the International Criminal Tribunal for Rwanda ("the International Tribunal") and the letter dated 27 May 2009 from the President of the International Tribunal for the Former Yugoslavia, the letter dated 26 June 2009 from the Secretary-General to the President of the Security Council attaching the letter dated 15 June 2009 from the President of the International Tribunal and the letter dated 7 July 2009 from the Secretary-General to the President of the Security Council attaching the letter dated 1 July 2009 from the President of the International Tribunal,

Recalling its resolutions 955(1994) of 8 November 1994, 1165(1998) of 30 April 1998, 1329(2000) of 30 November 2000, 1411(2002) of 17 May 2002, 1431(2002) of 14 August 2002, 1717(2006) of 13 October 2006, 1824(2008) of 18 July 2008 and 1855(2008) of 19 December 2008,

Recalling in particular its resolutions 1503(2003) of 28 August 2003 and 1534(2004) of 26 March 2004, in which the Council called upon the International Tribunal to take all possible measures to complete investigations by the end of 2004, to complete all trial activities at first instance by the end of 2008 and to complete all work in 2010,

Taking note of the assessment by the International Tribunal in its completion strategy report that the International Tribunal will not be in a position to complete all its work in 2010,

Having considered the proposals submitted by the President of the International Tribunal,

Expressing its determination to support the efforts made by the International Tribunal towards the completion of its work at the earliest date,

Recalling that in its resolution 1824(2008), the Council extended the term of office of permanent judges Mehmet Güney (Turkey) and Andrésia Vaz (Senegal), who are members of the Appeals Chamber, until 31 December 2010, or until the completion of the cases before the Appeals Chamber if sooner,

Expressing its expectation that the extension of the term of office of judges will enhance the effectiveness of judicial proceedings and contribute towards the implementation of the completion strategy of the International Tribunal,

Noting that permanent judge Sergei Alekseevich Egorov (Russian Federation) intends to resign from the International Tribunal,

Convinced of the need to enlarge the membership of the Appeals Chamber in view of the anticipated increase in the workload of the Appeals Chamber upon completion of the trial proceedings,

Stressing the need to ensure that none of the Appeals Chamber judges is assigned to any case to which he or she was assigned at the pretrial or trial stage,

Noting the concerns expressed by the President of the International Tribunal about the terms and conditions of service of ad litem judges in the light of their duration of service and share of the workload of the International Tribunal,

Urging the International Tribunal to take all possible measures to complete its work expeditiously,

Acting under Chapter VII of the Charter of the United Nations,

1. *Decides* to review the extension of the term of office of the permanent judges at the International Tribunal, who are members of the Appeals Chamber, by 31 December 2009, in the light of the progress of the International Tribunal in the implementation of the completion strategy;

2. *Decides also* to extend the term of office of the following permanent judges at the International Tribunal, who are members of the Trial Chambers, until 31 Decem-

ber 2010, or until the completion of the cases to which they are assigned if sooner:

— Sir Charles Michael Dennis Byron (Saint Kitts and Nevis)
— Mr. Joseph Asoka Nihal de Silva (Sri Lanka)
— Ms. Khalida Rachid Khan (Pakistan)
— Ms. Arlette Ramaroson (Madagascar)
— Mr. William H. Sekule (United Republic of Tanzania)

3. *Decides further* that the term of office of the permanent judge appointed to replace Mr. Sergei Alekseevich Egorov (Russian Federation) shall extend until 31 December 2010, or until the completion of the cases to which he or she will be assigned if sooner;

4. *Decides* to extend the term of office of the following ad litem judges, currently serving at the International Tribunal, until 31 December 2010, or until the completion of the cases to which they are assigned if sooner:

— Mr. Aydin Sefa Akay (Turkey)
— Ms. Florence Rita Arrey (Cameroon)
— Ms. Solomy Balungi Bossa (Uganda)
— Ms. Taghreed Hikmat (Jordan)
— Mr. Vagn Joensen (Denmark)
— Mr. Gberdao Gustave Kam (Burkina Faso)
— Mr. Joseph Edward Chiondo Masanche (United Republic of Tanzania)
— Mr. Lee Gacuiga Muthoga (Kenya)
— Mr. Seon Ki Park (Republic of Korea)
— Mr. Mparany Mamy Richard Rajohnson (Madagascar)
— Mr. Emile Francis Short (Ghana)

5. *Decides also* to allow ad litem judge Joensen to serve at the International Tribunal beyond the cumulative period of service provided for under article 12 ter, paragraph 2, of the statute of the International Tribunal;

6. *Decides further*, in the light of the exceptional circumstances, that, notwithstanding article 12 bis, paragraph 3, of the statute of the International Tribunal, Judge Joseph Asoka Nihal de Silva and Judge Emile Francis Short may work part-time and engage in another judicial occupation or occupation of equivalent independent status in their home countries during the remainder of their terms of office until the completion of the cases to which they are assigned; takes note of the intention of the International Tribunal to complete the cases by mid-2010; and underscores that this exceptional authorization shall not be considered as establishing a precedent. The President of the International Tribunal shall have the responsibility to ensure that this arrangement is compatible with the independence and impartiality of the judges, does not give rise to conflicts of interest and does not delay the delivery of the judgement;

7. *Decides* that, notwithstanding article 11, paragraph 1, of the statute of the International Tribunal, and on an exceptional basis, Judge Egorov, once replaced as a member of the International Tribunal, shall complete the cases which he began before his resignation; and takes note of the intention of the International Tribunal to complete the cases by the end of 2009;

8. *Decides also* to amend article 13, paragraph 3, of the statute of the International Tribunal as set out in the annex to the present resolution;

9. *Decides further* to remain seized of the matter.

ANNEX

Article 13

Officers and members of the Chambers

3. After consultation with the permanent judges of the International Tribunal for Rwanda, the President shall assign two of the permanent judges elected or appointed in accordance with article 12 bis of the present Statute to be members of the Appeals Chamber of the International Tribunal for the Former Yugoslavia and eight to the Trial Chambers of the International Tribunal for Rwanda. Notwithstanding the provisions of article 11, paragraph 1, and article 11, paragraph 3, the President may assign to the Appeals Chamber up to four additional permanent judges serving in the Trial Chambers, on the completion of the cases to which each judge is assigned. The term of office of each judge redeployed to the Appeals Chamber shall be the same as the term of office of the judges serving in the Appeals Chamber.

On 8 July [A/63/956], the Council President transmitted the text of resolution 1878(2009) to the General Assembly President. On 9 September, the Assembly endorsed the actions taken by the Council in operative paragraphs 1 through 8 of that resolution (**decision 63/425**).

Appointment of new judge. In a 31 July letter [S/2009/403], the Secretary-General informed the Security Council President that Judge Sergei Alekseevich Egorov (Russian Federation) had resigned and that the Russian Federation had nominated Professor Bakhtiyar Tuzmukhamedov to replace him. He expressed the view that Professor Tuzmukhamedov met the qualifications prescribed in the statute of the Tribunal. Citing Council resolution 1878(2009), he also stated that, on an exceptional basis, Judge Egorov, once replaced, would complete the cases he began before his resignation. On 4 August, the Council supported the Secretary-General's intention to appoint Professor Tuzmukhamedov as a permanent judge of the Tribunal [S/2009/404].

On 18 August [S/2009/425], the Secretary-General informed the Council President that he had appointed Professor Tuzmukhamedov as a permanent judge of the ICTR, effective 18 August 2009 until 31 December 2010, or until the completion of the cases to which he would be assigned, if sooner. On the same date [A/63/947], he also informed the Assembly President of the appointment.

On 9 September, the Assembly decided to include the item relating to the ICTR in the draft agenda of its sixty-fourth (2009) session and to consider it directly in plenary meeting (**decision 63/561**).

Letters from ICTR President. The Secretary-General transmitted a 15 October letter [S/2009/571] from the ICTR President requesting that the Council permit the Tribunal to exceed the maximum number of ad litem judges allowed by its statue by extending, to 31 December 2010, the authorization granted in Council resolution 1855(2008) [YUN 2008, p. 1419]. In a 6 November letter [S/2009/601] transmitted by the Secretary-General, he further requested that the Council authorize Judge Erik Møse to serve at the Tribunal beyond the 31 December 2009 expiry of his term of office so that he might complete the *Setako* case.

On 23 November [A/64/513], the Secretary-General transmitted to the General Assembly two letters from the ICTR President, noting that the Council, as the Tribunal's parent organ, and the Assembly, as the organ that elected its judges, would have to decide on those requests.

SECURITY COUNCIL ACTION

On 16 December [meeting 6243], the Security Council unanimously adopted **resolution 1901(2009)**. The draft [S/2009/645] was submitted by Austria.

The Security Council,

Taking note of the letters dated 2 and 23 November 2009 from the Secretary-General to the President of the Security Council attaching letters dated 15 October and 6 November 2009, respectively, from the President of the International Criminal Tribunal for Rwanda ("the International Tribunal"),

Recalling its resolutions 955(1994) of 8 November 1994, 1165(1998) of 30 April 1998, 1329(2000) of 30 November 2000, 1411(2002) of 17 May 2002, 1431(2002) of 14 August 2002, 1717(2006) of 13 October 2006, 1824(2008) of 18 July 2008, 1855(2008) of 19 December 2008 and 1878(2009) of 7 July 2009,

Recalling in particular its resolutions 1503(2003) of 28 August 2003 and 1534(2004) of 26 March 2004, in which the Council called upon the International Tribunal to take all possible measures to complete investigations by the end of 2004, to complete all trial activities at first instance by the end of 2008 and to complete all work in 2010,

Taking note of the assessment by the International Tribunal in its completion strategy report that the International Tribunal will not be in a position to complete all its work in 2010,

Recalling that, in resolution 1878(2009), the Council extended the term of office of permanent judges and ad litem judges, who are members of the Trial Chambers, until 31 December 2010, or until the completion of the cases to which they are assigned, if sooner, and decided to review the extension of the term of office of the permanent judges at the International Tribunal, who are members of the Appeals Chamber, by 31 December 2009, in the light of the progress of the International Tribunal in the implementation of its completion strategy,

Convinced of the advisability of extending the authorization granted to the Secretary-General in resolution 1855(2008) to appoint ad litem judges additional to the nine ad litem judges authorized by the statute of the International Tribunal, as a temporary measure to enable the International Tribunal to complete trials and conduct additional trials as soon as possible in order to meet the goals of the completion strategy,

Urging the International Tribunal to take all possible measures to complete its work expeditiously,

Acting under Chapter VII of the Charter of the United Nations,

1. *Underlines its intention* to extend, by 30 June 2010, the terms of office of all trial judges at the International Tribunal based on the International Tribunal's projected trial schedule and the terms of office of all appeals judges until 31 December 2012, or until the completion of the cases to which they are assigned, if sooner, and requests the President of the International Tribunal to submit to the Security Council an updated trial and appeals schedule, including information on the judges for whom extension of the terms of office or redeployment to the Appeals Chamber will be sought;

2. *Decides* that, in order for the International Tribunal to complete existing trials or conduct additional trials, the total number of ad litem judges serving at the International Tribunal may from time to time temporarily exceed the maximum of nine provided for in article 11, paragraph 1, of the statute of the International Tribunal, to a maximum of twelve at any one time, returning to a maximum of nine by 31 December 2010;

3. *Decides also* that, notwithstanding the expiry of his term of office on 31 December 2009, Judge Erik Møse shall complete the *Setako* case, which he began before the expiry of his term of office, and takes note of the intention of the International Tribunal to complete the case before the end of February 2010;

4. *Decides further* to remain seized of the matter.

On 22 December [A/64/590], the Council President transmitted the text of resolution 1901(2009) to the General Assembly President. On 23 December, the Assembly endorsed the actions taken by the Council in operative paragraphs 1 through 3 of that resolution (**decision 64/415**).

Office of the Prosecutor

The Office of the Prosecutor accelerated efforts to ensure the arrest of the remaining 13 fugitives, many of whom were in the conflict zones of the Great Lakes region. The Prosecutor continued to finalize preparation of the cases against the fugitives, with a view to the eventual transfer of 9 of the 13 fugitives to national jurisdictions for trial. The Office also continued to respond to requests for mutual legal assistance from national jurisdictions conducting investigations, with a view to the prosecution or extradition of Rwandan fugitives appearing on the INTERPOL wanted list.

During the second half of 2009, the efforts of the tracking team resulted in the arrest of two fugitives, Grégoire Ndahimana and Ildephonse Nizeyimana, and cooperation with Member States in the region made possible their transfer to the Tribunal for trial. In November, the Prosecutor hosted the annual Colloquium of Prosecutors of the International Criminal Tribunals in Kigali, which was attended by the prosecutors and senior staff of all the international tribunals and representatives of civil society organizations.

The Registry

The Registry continued to support the judicial process by servicing the Tribunal's other organs and the defence, as well as by seeking support from States, international organizations and other stakeholders in the conduct of proceedings. It maintained high-level diplomatic contacts with States and international organizations, and reported a significant increase in judicial cooperation with Member States. The Registry's Press and Public Affairs Unit continued to improve the internal circulation of Tribunal-related media reports. It also processed numerous local and international media enquiries and broadcast several trial proceedings via satellite for use by media professionals. Through the Outreach Programme, the Tribunal inaugurated six provincial information centres strategically located throughout Rwanda. The Court Management Section provided support services to the Chambers and other stakeholders in the judicial process, including support for site visits in Rwanda, depositions and video-link hearings from various countries. The Defence Council and Detention Management Section provided administrative support to the various defence teams and detainees in Arusha.

Between August 2008 and July 2009, the Witness and Victims Support Section ensured the timely availability of 311 witnesses, who were brought from 32 countries in support of the trials of 16 accused persons.

Financing

2008–2009 biennium

In November [A/64/538], the Secretary-General submitted, in response to General Assembly resolution 63/254 [YUN 2008, p. 1420], the second performance report on the ICTR budget for the 2008–2009 biennium, which reflected a decrease in requirements of $840,600 gross ($3,224,500 net) as compared to the revised appropriation of $305,378,600 gross ($282,597,100 net) [ibid.] for the biennium. The General Assembly was requested to revise the appropriation for 2008–2009 to the Special Account for ICTR to $304,538,000 gross ($279,372,600 net).

ACABQ, in December [A/64/555], recommended approval of the final appropriation as proposed by the Secretary-General.

2010–2011 biennium

In October [A/64/478], the Secretary-General presented resource requirements for the ICTR budget for the 2010–2011 biennium, which before recosting, amounted to $244,085,700 gross ($226,618,500

net), reflecting a decrease in real terms of $61,292,900 gross or 20.1 per cent ($55,978,600 net or 19.8 per cent), compared to the revised appropriation for the 2008–2009 biennium.

ACABQ, on 4 December [A/64/555], recommended approval of those resource requirements, subject to its observations and recommendations.

In November [A/64/532], the Secretary-General presented revised estimates to the proposed programme budget for the 2010–2011 biennium, which included measures identified for strengthening security and incorporated the related resource proposals in the ICTR budget.

ACABQ, on 11 December [A/64/7/Add.15 & Corr.1], recommended that the PACT II security enhancements for ICTR should be reviewed and prioritized during 2010–2011, taking into account the lessons learned in the initial implementation at other duty stations, and the revised requirements should be submitted in the context of the budget proposals for the 2012–2013 biennium.

On 14 December [A/64/570], the Secretary-General submitted revised estimates for the ICTR proposed budget for 2010–2011, which included the effect of changes in rates of exchange and inflation, and after recosting, amounted to $244,615,400 gross. ACABQ found no technical basis for objecting to the Secretary-General's revised estimates and transmitted them to the Assembly for consideration [A/64/7/Add.19].

GENERAL ASSEMBLY ACTION

On 24 December [meeting 68], the General Assembly, on the recommendation of the Fifth Committee [A/64/592], adopted **resolution 64/239** without vote [agenda item 143].

Financing of the International Criminal Tribunal for the Prosecution of Persons Responsible for Genocide and Other Serious Violations of International Humanitarian Law Committed in the Territory of Rwanda and Rwandan Citizens Responsible for Genocide and Other Such Violations Committed in the Territory of Neighbouring States between 1 January and 31 December 1994

The General Assembly,

I

Second performance report on the budget of the International Criminal Tribunal for Rwanda for the biennium 2008–2009

Having considered the second performance report of the Secretary-General on the budget, for the biennium 2008–2009, of the International Criminal Tribunal for the Prosecution of Persons Responsible for Genocide and Other Serious Violations of International Humanitarian Law Committed in the Territory of Rwanda and Rwandan Citizens Responsible for Genocide and Other Such Violations Committed in the Territory of Neighbouring States between 1 January and 31 December 1994, and the related report of the Advisory Committee on Administrative and Budgetary Questions,

Recalling its resolution 49/251 of 20 July 1995 on the financing of the International Criminal Tribunal for Rwanda and its subsequent resolutions thereon, the latest of which were resolutions 62/229 of 22 December 2007 and 63/254 of 24 December 2008,

1. *Takes note* of the second performance report of the Secretary-General on the budget, for the biennium 2008–2009, of the International Criminal Tribunal for the Prosecution of Persons Responsible for Genocide and Other Serious Violations of International Humanitarian Law Committed in the Territory of Rwanda and Rwandan Citizens Responsible for Genocide and Other Such Violations Committed in the Territory of Neighbouring States between 1 January and 31 December 1994 and the related report of the Advisory Committee on Administrative and Budgetary Questions;

2. *Endorses* the conclusions and recommendations contained in section III.B of the report of the Advisory Committee on Administrative and Budgetary Questions;

3. *Resolves* that, for the biennium 2008–2009, the amount of 305,378,600 United States dollars gross (282,597,100 dollars net) approved in its resolution 63/254 for the financing of the International Criminal Tribunal for Rwanda shall be adjusted by the amount of 840,600 dollars gross (3,224,500 dollars net), for a total amount of 304,538,000 dollars gross (279,372,600 dollars net);

II

Budget of the International Criminal Tribunal for Rwanda for the biennium 2010–2011

Having considered the reports of the Secretary-General on the financing of the International Criminal Tribunal for Rwanda for the biennium 2010–2011 and on the revised estimates arising from the effects of changes in rates of exchange and inflation,

Having also considered the related report of the Advisory Committee on Administrative and Budgetary Questions,

1. *Takes note* of the reports of the Secretary-General on the financing of the International Criminal Tribunal for Rwanda for the biennium 2010–2011, and on the revised estimates arising from the effects of changes in rates of exchange and inflation;

2. *Endorses* the conclusions and recommendations contained in the report of the Advisory Committee on Administrative and Budgetary Questions, subject to the provisions of the present resolution;

3. *Welcomes* the arrest of two further indictees, requests the Tribunal to proceed with their prosecutions from available resources, and requests the Secretary-General, in this respect, to report to the General Assembly on the financial implications of these prosecutions at its next session;

4. *Also welcomes* the work of the Tribunal to ensure the expeditious completion of its mandate and, with regard to the current budget, the commensurate reduction in the cost of the Tribunal;

5. *Recognizes* the critical importance of retaining highly skilled and experienced staff members with relevant institutional memory in order to successfully complete the trials and meet the targets set out in the completion strategy of the Tribunal;

6. *Reaffirms* paragraph 5 of its resolution 63/256 of 24 December 2008, and requests the Secretary-General to utilize his existing authority under the existing contractual framework to offer contracts to staff, taking into account the needs of the Tribunal;

7. *Requests* the Secretary-General to explore the possibility of employing at the United Nations, should their services be required, staff who remain with the Tribunal until the completion of its mandate;

8. *Recognizes* the importance of ensuring that the Tribunal retains the courtroom capacity needed for the expeditious completion of all trials, and in this regard, decides that the fourth courtroom shall be funded during the biennium from within the 2010–2011 budget;

9. *Notes* that the Tribunal relies on ad litem judges in the implementation of its completion strategy;

10. *Also notes* that the Secretary-General is conducting a review of conditions of service of ad litem judges at the Tribunal, and anticipates addressing the review at the first part of the resumed sixty-fourth session;

11. *Requests* that future budget proposals of the International Criminal Tribunal for Rwanda and the International Tribunal for the Former Yugoslavia be harmonized to facilitate better comparative analysis, particularly with respect to their completion strategies;

12. *Decides* to appropriate to the Special Account for the International Criminal Tribunal for the Prosecution of Persons Responsible for Genocide and Other Serious Violations of International Humanitarian Law Committed in the Territory of Rwanda and Rwandan Citizens Responsible for Genocide and Other Such Violations Committed in the Territory of Neighbouring States between 1 January and 31 December 1994 a total amount of 245,295,800 dollars gross (227,246,500 dollars net) for the biennium 2010–2011, as detailed in the annex to the present resolution;

13. *Also decides* that the total assessment for 2010 under the Special Account amounting to 121,807,300 dollars shall consist of:

   (*a*) 122,647,900 dollars, being half of the estimated appropriation approved for the biennium 2010–2011;

   (*b*) 840,600 dollars, being the decrease in the final appropriation for the biennium 2008–2009 approved by the General Assembly in paragraph 3 of section I above;

14. *Further decides* to apportion the amount of 60,903,650 dollars gross (55,199,375 dollars net) among Member States in accordance with the scale of assessments applicable to the regular budget of the United Nations for 2010;

15. *Decides* to apportion the amount of 60,903,650 dollars gross (55,199,375 dollars net) among Member States in accordance with the scale of assessments applicable to peacekeeping operations for 2010;

16. *Also decides* that, in accordance with the provisions of its resolution 973(X) of 15 December 1955, there shall be set off against the apportionment among Member States, as provided for in paragraphs 14 and 15 above, their respective share in the Tax Equalization Fund of the estimated staff assessment income of 11,408,550 dollars approved for the International Criminal Tribunal for Rwanda for 2010.

ANNEX

Financing for the biennium 2010–2011 of the International Criminal Tribunal for the Prosecution of Persons Responsible for Genocide and Other Serious Violations of International Humanitarian Law Committed in the Territory of Rwanda and Rwandan Citizens Responsible for Genocide and Other Such Violations Committed in the Territory of Neighbouring States between 1 January and 31 December 1994

	Gross	*Net*
	(United States dollars)	
Estimated appropriation for the biennium 2010–2011	257,849,900	239,988,300
Revised estimates: effects of changes in rates of exchange and inflation	5,186,500	5,066,200
Recommendations of the Advisory Committee on Administrative and Budgetary Questions	(18,421,000)	(18,421,000)
Proposals under the standardized access control project (A/64/532) less the reduction recommended by the Advisory Committee on Administrative and Budgetary Questions	680,400	613,000
Recommendations of the Fifth Committee	—	—
Estimated initial appropriation for the biennium 2010–2011	245,295,800	227,246,500
TOTAL assessment for 2010	**121,807,300**	**110,398,750**
Comprising:		
(a) Requirements representing half of the estimated appropriation for the biennium 2010–2011	122,647,900	113,623,250
(b) Requirements arising from the final appropriation for the biennium 2008–2009	(840,600)	(3,224,500)
Of which:		
Contributions assessed on Member States in accordance with the scale of assessments applicable to the regular budget of the United Nations for 2010	60,903,650	55,199,375
Contributions assessed on Member States in accordance with the scale of assessments applicable to peacekeeping operations of the United Nations for 2010	60,903,650	55,199,375

On 24 December, the Assembly decided that the agenda item on ICTR financing would remain for consideration during its resumed sixty-fourth (2010) session (**decision 64/549**).

Functioning of the Tribunals

Implementation of completion strategies

ICTY

In response to Security Council resolution 1534(2004) [YUN 2004, p. 1292], the ICTY President reported in May [S/2009/252] and November [S/2009/589] on progress made in implementing the ICTY completion strategy. The Tribunal adopted concrete measures to enhance the efficiency of proceedings, including those identified by the Working Groups on Speeding up Appeals and Trials, which were reconstituted in 2008 [YUN 2008, p. 1423] to assess the effectiveness of measures implemented and to identify innovations to enhance the efficient conduct of trials and appeals.

As at 15 November, out of the 161 accused indicted by the Tribunal, only one remained in the pretrial stage awaiting the commencement of trial, 24 were being tried and another 13 had appeals pending. However, two accused, Ratko Mladić and Goran Hadžić, were still at large. All other cases had been completed. Eight cases were at the trial stage and one was at the judgement drafting stage. Five of those nine cases would be completed during the course of 2010, three during the first half of 2011 and the remaining case, that of Radovan Karadžić, was estimated to be completed by September 2012. While there had been slippage in the trial schedule resulting from factors not within the Tribunal's control, it was expected to have minimal impact on the completion of all appeals by mid-2013, provided a significant redeployment of trial resources was made to the Appeals Chamber during 2010 and 2011. Those changes would enable the Tribunal to form three Appeals Chamber benches to deal with an anticipated total of 24 appeal cases. Each appellate Judge would be assigned six or seven appeals. Thirteen appeals would be completed in 2011, eight in 2012, two during the first half of 2013 and the remaining appeal, that of Mr. Karadžić, by February 2014.

As the Tribunal neared the end of its mandate, the issue of staff retention remained a concern, with highly qualified and essential staff continuing to leave the Tribunal at alarming rates for more secure employment. The ICTR President urged the Security Council to formulate and support meaningful staff retention measures.

ICTR

In response to Security Council resolution 1534(2004) [YUN 2004, p. 1292], the ICTR President submitted reports in May [S/2009/247] and November [S/2009/587] that assessed progress made in implementing the ICTR completion strategy. That strategy called for completing investigations by the end of 2004, all trial activities at first instance by the end of 2008, and all of its work in 2010.

Between May and November 2009, four judgements in single-accused cases were delivered, including one contempt of court case and a sentencing judgement for a guilty plea. Six cases concerning 17 accused, including one retrial, were in the judgement drafting phase, with at least two more judgements to be delivered by December. The presentation of evidence in two cases had been completed and closing arguments were forthcoming at the beginning of 2010. Six trials involving eight accused were ongoing. The evidence phase of all first instance trials was projected to be finalized before mid-2010, with the exception of the trial in Karemera et al. The Appeals Chamber was seized of eight appeals from judgement.

The judicial calendar remained an essential element in the Tribunal's efforts to comply with its completion strategy. In the ongoing pre-closure and downsizing phase, it was the basis of planning for all three organs of the Tribunal concerning the scope of budget requests and contract extensions. Between May and November, 10 different sections of the Trial Chambers used the four Tribunal courtrooms in 12 different cases. On the management of proceedings, the Tribunal achieved significant results, and in a majority of cases, the Chambers were able to adhere to the time standards set out in previous reports. The projected average duration of four weeks for the presentation of prosecution and defence evidence was met in a number of cases, and certain cases took significantly less time.

The Office of the Prosecutor, in addition to continuing with ongoing trial and appellate work and preparations in pending cases, had also started preparation for the trials of the two indictees arrested during the year. It was also in the process of preparing the cases of the three top fugitives for preservation of the evidence. Efforts at tracking the remaining 11 fugitives in the DRC and neighbouring countries had been intensified. The Office also awaited a response to its latest communication with the Kenyan Government on the movement of Félicien Kabuga, who had allegedly left Kenya. Several requests from the Prosecutor to Kenyan authorities on the alleged departure had remained unanswered as at 9 November. The increasing workload of its Appeals and Legal Advisory Division was another area of the Office's focus, as it was expected that every judgement passed by the Trial Chamber, except for those in which the indictee pleaded guilty, would be challenged on appeal by the defence, and in some cases appeals would also be filed by the Office.

Establishment of ad hoc mechanism

Report of Secretary-General. In a 21 May report [S/2009/258], submitted pursuant to Security Council presidential statement S/PRST/2008/47 [YUN 2008, p. 1424], the Secretary-General explored administrative and budgetary aspects of possible locations for the ICTY and ICTR archives and the seat of the residual mechanism(s), including the availability of suitable premises for the conduct of judicial proceedings by the mechanism(s), with particular emphasis on locations where the United Nations had a presence.

Discussion in the Security Council Informal Working Group on the International Tribunals (see below) was ongoing, and there were many key areas where further decisions were needed. Consequently, the report identified the key areas where it fell to the Council to make decisions, in particular on which

potential residual functions were to be transferred to the mechanism(s); presented rough estimates of the staffing requirements and costs on the basis of illustrative examples of a possible mechanism or mechanisms; and provided information regarding the feasibility and costs of 14 potential locations for the mechanism(s) and/or archives with UN offices, or offices of other international organizations. The report set out a series of recommendations to the Council. It was suggested that when agreement was reached among Working Group members on further key issues, a report be requested from the Secretary-General on the establishment and location of the residual mechanism(s) and the location of the archives.

The recommendations to the Council included requesting that the Tribunals, as part of their completion strategies, intensify their efforts to: refer further cases to national jurisdictions, and strengthen the capacity of the affected countries; consider ways to review witness protection orders and decisions with a view to withdrawing or varying those that were no longer necessary; implement an approved records retention policy in order to identify archives for permanent preservation; prepare all digital records for future migration into the recordkeeping systems of the institution designated to receive them; prepare all hard-copy archives and inventories for transfer to that institution; develop a regime to govern the management of, and access to, the Tribunals' archives; develop and implement an information security strategy that included the appropriate (de)classification of all records and archives; review all agreements with States and other international bodies, and contracts with private entities, to determine whether there were any that should not continue after the closure of the Tribunals; and examine the feasibility of establishing information centres in the affected countries to give access to the public records.

In a 28 September letter [S/2009/496] to the Secretary-General, Council members welcomed the recommendations of the Tribunals and requested that the Secretary-General write to the ICTY and ICTR Presidents to ensure that those tasks were carried out. The Council emphasized the request for the Tribunals to report on ways to review witness protection orders and decisions with a view to withdrawing or varying unnecessary ones, as well as on concrete steps to be taken by the Tribunals towards that end.

Working Group report. On 30 December [S/2009/687], the Chairman of the Security Council Informal Working Group on the International Tribunals submitted a summary of its activities in 2009. The Working Group was established in 2000 on an informal basis to consider matters relating to the United Nations and UN-assisted tribunals—particularly the ICTY and the ICTR. During the first half of the year, the Working Group met nearly every week to discuss the establishment of the residual mechanism, including its location, structure and organization, commencement date and residual functions, and fugitives to be tried by the mechanism. From July to September, the Working Group considered the Secretary-General's report, and then resumed its negotiations on a draft resolution on the establishment of an international residual mechanism prepared by the Working Group chair with assistance from the Office of Legal Affairs. The Group completed its first reading of the draft resolution in December and would resume its negotiations in early 2010.

In other activities, the Working Group considered requests by the ICTR and ICTY Presidents, including the extension of the terms of office of judges, redeployment of judges to the Appeals Chamber and the appointment of additional ad litem judges. The Group's recommendations led to the adoption of Security Council resolutions addressing those issues.

International Criminal Court

In 2009, the International Criminal Court (ICC), established by the Rome Statute [YUN 1998, p. 1209] as a permanent institution with jurisdiction over persons accused of the most serious crimes of international concern (genocide, crimes against humanity, war crimes and the crime of aggression), carried out investigations in the Central African Republic, the DRC, Darfur (the Sudan) and Uganda. Reports covering ICC activities during the year were submitted to the General Assembly [A/64/356; A/65/313]. As at 31 December, 110 countries had ratified the Rome Statute.

In March, an arrest warrant was issued against Omar Hassan Ahmad Al-Bashir, the President of the Sudan, for crimes against humanity and war crimes. By year's end, there were eight arrest warrants outstanding, including Mr. Al-Bashir's. Seven had been outstanding for two years and five had been outstanding for three or more years.

The Office of the Prosecutor received and analysed 4,870 communications related to purported crimes between 1 August 2008 and 30 June 2009. Of those, some 3,823 related to the situation in South Ossetia, Georgia. The remaining 1,047 communications did not provide any basis for the Office to take further action. Six situations under analysis by the Office had been made public: Afghanistan, Colombia, Côte d'Ivoire, Georgia, Kenya and Palestine.

GENERAL ASSEMBLY ACTION

On 2 November [meeting 34], the General Assembly adopted **resolution 64/9** [draft: A/64/L.9 & Add.1] without vote [agenda item 75].

Report of the International Criminal Court

The General Assembly,

Recalling its resolution 63/21 of 11 November 2008, and all its previous relevant resolutions,

Recalling also that the Rome Statute of the International Criminal Court reaffirms the purposes and principles of the Charter of the United Nations,

Reiterating the historic significance of the adoption of the Rome Statute,

Emphasizing that justice, especially transitional justice in conflict and post-conflict societies, is a fundamental building block of sustainable peace,

Convinced that ending impunity is essential if a society in conflict or recovering from conflict is to come to terms with past abuses committed against civilians affected by armed conflict and to prevent such abuses in the future,

Noting with satisfaction the fact that the International Criminal Court has achieved considerable progress in its analyses, investigations and judicial proceedings in various situations and cases which were referred to it by States parties to the Rome Statute and by the Security Council, in accordance with the Rome Statute,

Recalling that effective and comprehensive cooperation and assistance in all aspects of its mandate by States, the United Nations and other international and regional organizations remains essential for the International Criminal Court to carry out its activities,

Expressing its appreciation to the Secretary-General for providing effective and efficient assistance to the International Criminal Court in accordance with the Relationship Agreement between the United Nations and the International Criminal Court ("Relationship Agreement"),

Acknowledging the Relationship Agreement as approved by the General Assembly in its resolution 58/318 of 13 September 2004, including paragraph 3 of the resolution with respect to the payment in full of expenses accruing to the United Nations as a result of the implementation of the Relationship Agreement, which provides a framework for continued cooperation between the International Criminal Court and the United Nations, which could include the facilitation by the United Nations of the Court's field activities, and encouraging the conclusion of supplementary arrangements and agreements, as necessary,

Welcoming the continuous support given by civil society to the International Criminal Court,

Recognizing the role of the International Criminal Court in a multilateral system that aims to end impunity, establish the rule of law, promote and encourage respect for human rights and achieve sustainable peace, in accordance with international law and the purposes and principles of the Charter,

Expressing its appreciation to the International Criminal Court for providing assistance to the Special Court for Sierra Leone,

1.   *Welcomes* the report of the International Criminal Court for 2008/09;

2.   *Welcomes* the States that have become parties to the Rome Statute of the International Criminal Court in the past year, and calls upon all States in all regions of the world that are not yet parties to the Rome Statute to consider ratifying or acceding to it without delay;

3. *Welcomes* the States parties as well as States not parties to the Rome Statute that have become parties to the Agreement on the Privileges and Immunities of the International Criminal Court, and calls upon all States that have not yet done so to consider becoming parties to that Agreement;

4. *Calls upon* States parties to the Rome Statute that have not yet done so to adopt national legislation to implement obligations emanating from the Rome Statute and to cooperate with the International Criminal Court in the exercise of its functions, and recalls the provision of technical assistance by States parties in this respect;

5. *Welcomes* the cooperation and assistance provided thus far to the International Criminal Court by States parties as well as States not parties, the United Nations and other international and regional organizations, and calls upon those States that are under an obligation to cooperate to provide such cooperation and assistance in the future, in particular with regard to arrest and surrender, the provision of evidence, the protection and relocation of victims and witnesses and the enforcement of sentences;

6. *Emphasizes* the importance of cooperation with States that are not parties to the Rome Statute;

7. *Invites* regional organizations to consider concluding cooperation agreements with the International Criminal Court;

8. *Recalls* that, by virtue of article 12, paragraph 3, of the Rome Statute, a State which is not a party to the Statute may, by declaration lodged with the Registrar of the International Criminal Court, accept the exercise of jurisdiction by the Court with respect to specific crimes that are mentioned in paragraph 2 of that article;

9. *Encourages* all States parties to take the interests, the need for assistance and the mandate of the International Criminal Court into account when relevant matters are being discussed in the United Nations;

10. *Emphasizes* the importance of the full implementation of the Relationship Agreement between the United Nations and the International Criminal Court, which forms a framework for close cooperation between the two organizations and for consultation on matters of mutual interest pursuant to the provisions of the Relationship Agreement and in conformity with the respective provisions of the Charter of the United Nations and the Rome Statute, as well as the need for the Secretary-General to inform the General Assembly at its sixty-fifth session of the expenses incurred and reimbursements received by the United Nations in connection with assistance provided to the International Criminal Court;

11. *Expresses its appreciation* for the work undertaken by the International Criminal Court liaison office to United Nations Headquarters, and encourages the Secretary-General to continue to work closely with that office;

12. *Encourages* States to contribute to the Trust Fund established for the benefit of victims of crimes within the jurisdiction of the International Criminal Court and the families of such victims, and acknowledges with appreciation contributions made to that Trust Fund thus far;

13. *Notes* that the Special Working Group on the Crime of Aggression, which was open to all States on an equal footing, has concluded its mandate and has elaborated proposals for a provision on the crime of aggression, in accordance with article 123 of the Rome Statute;

14. *Notes* that the Assembly of States Parties to the Rome Statute decided at its seventh session, while recalling that, according to article 112, paragraph 6, of the Rome Statute, the Assembly of States Parties shall meet at the seat of the International Criminal Court or at the United Nations Headquarters, to hold its eighth session in The Hague, looks forward to the eighth session, which is to be held from 18 to 26 November 2009, and requests the Secretary-General to provide the necessary services and facilities in accordance with the Relationship Agreement and resolution 58/318;

15. *Notes* the convening by the Secretary-General of the Review Conference, which will begin on 31 May 2010 in Kampala, and which may provide an opportunity to address issues, in addition to those related to the possible definition of the crime of aggression, that have been identified by States, including States that are not parties to the Rome Statute;

16. *Encourages* the widest possible participation of States in the Assembly of States Parties and particularly in the Review Conference, invites States to contribute to the Trust Fund for the participation of the least developed countries, and acknowledges with appreciation contributions made to that Trust Fund thus far;

17. *Invites* the International Criminal Court to submit, in accordance with article 6 of the Relationship Agreement, a report on its activities for 2009/10, for consideration by the General Assembly at its sixty-fifth session.

Report of Secretary-General. Pursuant to General Assembly resolution 63/21 [YUN 2008, p. 1426], the Secretary-General submitted a report [A/64/363] on expenses incurred and reimbursement received by the United Nations in connection with assistance to ICC.

Assembly of States Parties

The Assembly of States Parties to the Rome Statute of the International Criminal Court adopted one decision at its resumed seventh session (New York, 19–23 January and 9–13 February) [ICC-ASP/7/20/Add.1] and seven resolutions at its eighth session (The Hague, 18–26 November) [ICC-ASP/8/20].

Following a 13 February decision [ICC-ASP/7/Dec.1], in which the Assembly requested that its Bureau continue consideration of the establishment of an independent oversight mechanism, the Assembly, in a 26 November resolution [ICC-ASP/8/Res.1], decided to establish an independent oversight mechanism with a budget of €341,600 to cover its start-up and continuing maintenance costs. By another resolution, the Assembly requested that its Bureau appoint a new facilitator of the Assembly for cooperation, for a two-year period [ICC-ASP/8/Res.2].

On strengthening ICC and the Assembly [ICC-ASP/8/Res.3], the Assembly decided to keep the status of ratifications to the Rome Statue under review, and to monitor legislation implementation, with a view to facilitating the provision of technical assistance that States parties or those wishing to become States parties to the Statute might wish to request from other States parties or institutions. It also decided to establish a liaison office for the Court at AU headquarters in Addis Ababa, Ethiopia. Also on 26 November, the Assembly adopted resolutions on family visits for indigent detainees [ICC-ASP/8/Res.4]; permanent premises for the Court [ICC-ASP/8/Res.5]; and the Review Conference of States Parties to the Rome Statue [ICC-ASP/8/Res.6], which would be held in Kampala, Uganda, from 31 May to 11 June 2010, for a period of ten working days.

On financing, the Assembly approved the Court's 2010 programme budget [ICC-ASP/8/Res.7], with appropriations totalling €103,623,300. It resolved that the Working Capital Fund for 2010 would be established in the amount of €7,405,983, and authorized the Registrar to make advances from the Fund.

The Chambers

The judicial activities of the Court were conducted by the Chambers, which consisted of 18 judges, organized in three divisions: the Appeals Division, the Trial Division and the Pre-Trial Division. The Presidency constituted three Pre-Trial Chambers: Pre-Trial Chamber I—the DRC and Darfur (the Sudan); Pre-Trial Chamber II—Uganda; and Pre-Trial Chamber III—the Central African Republic.

In March, Pre-Trial Chamber I issued a warrant of arrest against Omar Hassan Ahmad Al-Bashir, the President of the Sudan (see below). Pre-Trial Chamber II confirmed charges of war crimes and charges of crimes against humanity against Jean-Pierre Bemba Gombo in June. In September, the Appeals Chamber upheld the decision rendered by Pre-Trial Chamber II in March, which had ruled that the case against four accused (alleged members of the Lord's Resistance Army) was admissible before the Court. Two trials commenced during the year.

New arrests, warrants and summonses

During the year, there were no new arrests by the Court. One arrest warrant was issued in the situation in Darfur (the Sudan). Eight arrest warrants were outstanding at year's end: one in the situation in the DRC, three in the situation in Darfur and four in the situation in Uganda. Seven had been outstanding for two years and five had been outstanding for three or more years. The Court also issued two summonses, both in the situation in Darfur.

On 4 March, Pre-Trial Chamber I, issued a first warrant of arrest against President Al-Bashir, for five counts of crimes against humanity (murder, extermination, forcible transfer, torture and rape) and two counts of war crimes (attacking civilians and pillaging). The prosecution appealed a decision rejecting the additional counts of genocide.

On 7 May, Pre-Trial Chamber I issued a summons to appear for Bahr Idriss Abu Garda for crimes allegedly committed against AU peacekeepers in Haskanita, Darfur on 29 September 2007. Mr. Abu Garda made his initial appearance voluntarily on 18 May 2009. The hearing took place from 19 to 30 October. A total of 87 victims were authorized to participate through their legal representatives in the confirmation of charges proceedings.

On 27 August, in the case against Abdallah Banda Abakaer Nourain (Commander-in-Chief of the Justice and Equality Movement) and Saleh Mohammed Jerbo Jamus (former Chief-of-Staff of the Sudan Liberation Army-Unity), Pre-Trial Chamber I issued an under-seal summons to appear against the two alleged rebel leaders. The prosecution alleged that both men participated as co-perpetrators or indirect co-perpetrators to an attack on the Haskanita military group site on 29 September 2007.

On 4 December [meeting 6230], during the presentation of his tenth report to the Security Council on the status of the investigation into the situation in Darfur, the Prosecutor highlighted the lack of cooperation by the Government of the Sudan, the continuation of the alleged crimes on the ground and the need to execute the outstanding arrest warrants.

Communications. On 16 March [S/2009/148], a resolution adopted by the League of Arab States Council at its extraordinary session (Cairo, Egypt, 4 March), expressing concern regarding the ICC issuance of an arrest warrant for President Al-Bashir, was transmitted to the Security Council President.

On 8 July [A/63/926], Botswana transmitted to the Secretary-General a press release issued by the Government of Botswana indicating that it did not agree with the AU Summit decision (Sirte, Libyan Arab Jamahiriya, 3 July) to denounce the ICC and refuse to extradite President Al-Bashir.

Ongoing cases and trials

A hearing that began on 12 January to confirm eight charges against Jean-Pierre Bemba Gombo (the situation in the Central African Republic), was adjourned on 3 March by Pre-Trial Chamber III, requesting the Prosecutor to consider amending the charges. On 15 June, Pre-Trial Chamber II confirmed three charges of war crimes (murder, rape and pillage) and two charges of crimes against humanity (murder and rape) against Mr. Bemba in his capacity as a military commander, but not as originally charged as a co-perpetrator. On 22 June, the Prosecutor sought leave to appeal the decision of the Chamber that declined to confirm the charge of torture as a war crime or as a crime against humanity. On 18 September, the Presidency referred the case to Trial Chamber III. The trial was scheduled to start in April 2010.

On 26 January, the Court commenced the trial against Thomas Lubanga Dyilo, the alleged leader of the Union des patriots congolais and Commander-in-Chief of its military wing, charged with having committed war crimes in the DRC, specifically the enlisting, conscripting and use of children under the age of 15 to participate actively in hostilities. The prosecution concluded the presentation of its evidence on 14 July, having tendered 119 items of evidence. On the same date, Trial Chamber I issued a decision giving notice to the parties that the legal characterization of facts might be subject to changes in accordance with regulations of the Court, which both the defence and the prosecution appealed. On 8 December, the Appeals Chamber reversed the Trial Chamber decision, determining that the Chamber had erred.

In the case against Joseph Kony, Vincent Otti, Okot Odhiambo and Dominic Ongwen, the arrest warrants for the four alleged members of the Lord's Resistance Army (LRA) in the situation in Uganda had been outstanding since July 2005 [YUN 2005, p. 1404]. Following the initiation of proceedings on the admissibility of the case by Pre-Trial Chamber II in October 2008, the Chamber, on 10 March 2009, issued its decision on admissibility, reaffirming that it was the Court that had the responsibility for determining whether or not a case was inadmissible. On 16 September, the Appeals Chamber upheld the Chamber's decision, which had ruled that the case against the four accused was admissible before the Court. Mr. Kony, alleged LRA Commander-in-Chief, was charged with 33 counts, including 12 counts of crimes against humanity and Mr. Otti, alleged Vice-Chair and Second-in-Command of LRA, was charged with 11 counts of crimes against humanity and 21 counts of war crimes. Mr. Odhiambo, alleged Deputy Army Commander and LRA Brigade Commander, was charged with 2 counts of crimes against humanity and 8 counts of war crimes. Mr. Ongwen, alleged LRA Brigade Commander, was charged with 3 counts of crimes against humanity and 4 counts of war crimes. None of the four accused had been arrested as at 31 December 2009.

In the case against Germain Katanga and Mathieu Ngudjolo Chui, two former leaders of armed groups active in the Ituri region of the DRC, Pre-Trial Chamber I confirmed 7 charges of war crimes (wilful killing, using children to participate actively in hostilities, sexual slavery, rape, attacking civilians, pillaging and destroying the enemy's property) and 3 charges of crimes against humanity (murder, sexual slavery and rape) for each of the accused in September 2008 [YUN 2008, p. 1428]. Mr. Katanga challenged the admissibility of the case against him, arguing that he had previously been subject to legal proceedings for the same crimes in the DRC. Following the holding of a public hearing on the issue, Trial Chamber II dismissed Mr. Katanga's challenge on 12 June, finding that the national authorities had not opened any investigation into the attack for which he was being prosecuted. The trial of Messrs. Katanga and Ngudjolo Chui for crimes allegedly committed in an attack on the Bogoro village on 24 February 2003, started on 24 November with the presentation of prosecution evidence.

Office of the Prosecutor

Investigations

Throughout the year, the Office of the Prosecutor continued investigations into four situations: the Central African Republic, the DRC, Darfur (the Sudan) and Uganda. During the year ending 31 July, the Office conducted 34 missions to eight countries for trial preparations and investigations related to the ongoing cases in the situation in the DRC and a third case focusing on alleged crimes committed in the North and South Kivu provinces. From 8 to 11 July, the Prosecutor visited Bunia and the Ituri district in the DRC.

The Office conducted investigative activities on the situation in Uganda, including eight missions to six countries, collecting information on crimes allegedly being committed by LRA in the DRC, the Sudan and the Central African Republic. According to the information received, the incidence of alleged crimes rose sharply from September 2008. The Office received reports of particularly savage attacks taking place in December 2008 and January 2009, with the killing and abduction of several hundred people in a series of raids on towns and villages across a broad area of the DRC and southern Sudan. The Office continued efforts to galvanize support for the arrests of suspects sought by the Court.

The Office carried out 49 missions to six countries in relation to the situation in the Central African Republic, gathering evidence with a view to establishing responsibility for the crimes committed in 2002 and 2003, including through forensic activities such as exhumation and autopsy, with the cooperation of the Government.

On the situation in Darfur, the Office conducted 30 missions to 13 countries. On the execution of arrest warrants, the tracking team worked for six months with a variety of actors to locate and facilitate the voluntary surrender of the alleged perpetrators. In his briefing to the Security Council on 3 December [meeting 6228], the Prosecutor reported that the Government of the Sudan continued to not comply with its legal obligation under Council resolution 1593(2005) to enforce the judicial decisions of the Court. He emphasized that the execution of arrest warrants required concrete decision-making.

On 26 November, the Prosecutor requested authorization from Pre-Trial Chamber II to open an investigation into the situation in Kenya, noting that 1,220 persons had been killed, thousands raped (both reported and unreported), 350,000 forcibly displaced and 3,561 injured as part of a widespread and systematic attack against civilians.

The Registry

The ICC Registry provided judicial and administrative support to all organs of the Court and carried out its specific responsibilities concerning victims, witnesses, defence and outreach. On the instruction of Pre-Trial Chamber I, the Registrar transmitted requests for cooperation to all States parties to the Rome Statute, and to all Security Council members not party to it, for the arrest and surrender of President Al-Bashir. The Chamber also directed the Registrar to transmit requests for cooperation to any other State as might be necessary to ensure Mr. Al-Bashir's arrest.

In the case of Mr. Bemba, the Registrar on 24 September rejected a second application for the payment of legal aid to Mr. Bemba, who alleged that he was unable to pay the fees because his properties and assets had been frozen or seized by the Court. On 19 November, Trial Chamber III ordered the Registrar to advance funding in a sum equivalent to the amount of legal aid payable by the Court retrospectively to March and ongoing until a material change in the circumstances. The Registrar was asked to search for, freeze and realize Mr. Bemba's assets to fund that advance.

International cooperation

ICC continued to rely on cooperation with and assistance from States, international organizations and civil society. UN cooperation remained essential to the Court institutionally and in the different situations and cases. UN logistical support facilitated the Court's work in the field. Peacekeeping missions assisted the Court in areas such as transportation, provision of information, communication support and the use of UN facilities. ICC benefited from the expertise provided by UN offices, for example, in the area of witness protection. The Office of Legal Affairs played the leading role in facilitating cooperation, in particular with respect to the testimony of UN officials before the Court, the provision of information and the mainstreaming of the Court throughout the UN system.

The Court made numerous requests to States parties, other States and international organizations for cooperation or assistance. It also continued to develop its structural arrangements for cooperation, especially with respect to investigative activities, witness protection, sentence enforcement, and the provisional release of accused persons pending trial. Efforts continued to finalize a memorandum of understanding between the AU and the Court, as well as on a possible cooperation agreement with the Organization of American States. The Court met regularly with representatives of States, international organizations and civil society to update them on the Court's work and discuss items of mutual interest.

Chapter III

International legal questions

In 2009, the International Law Commission continued to examine topics relating to the progressive development and codification of international law. It adopted 32 draft guidelines on reservations to treaties and the procedure for formulating interpretive declarations, and adopted on first reading a set of 66 draft articles on the responsibility of international organizations. It established working groups on shared natural resources to consider the issue of oil and gas, and on the obligation to extradite or prosecute (*aut dedere aut judicare*).

The Ad Hoc Committee established by the General Assembly continued to elaborate a draft comprehensive convention on international terrorism, and, in July, recommended that the Sixth (Legal) Committee of the Assembly establish a working group with a view to finalizing the draft convention. Also in July, the Secretary-General reported on measures taken by States, UN system entities and intergovernmental organizations to implement the 1994 General Assembly Declaration on Measures to Eliminate International Terrorism. In December, the Assembly condemned all acts, methods and practices of terrorism as criminal and unjustifiable, and called on States to implement the United Nations Global Counter-Terrorism Strategy at the international, regional, subregional and national levels without delay.

The United Nations Commission on International Trade Law adopted its Practice Guide on Cross-Border Insolvency Cooperation. In December, the Assembly recommended that the Practice Guide be given due consideration by judges, insolvency practitioners and other stakeholders involved in cross-border insolvency proceedings. The Commission commended use of the 2007 revision of the International Chamber of Commerce Uniform Customs and Practice for Documentary Credits in transactions involving the establishment of a documentary credit, and continued its work on public procurement, arbitration and conciliation, security interests and economic commerce. In October, the United Nations Audiovisual Library of International Law received the 2009 Best Website Award from the International Association of Law Librarians.

The Special Committee on the Charter of the United Nations and on the Strengthening of the Role of the Organization continued to consider, among other subjects, proposals relating to the maintenance of international peace and security, with a view to strengthening the Organization, and the implementation of Charter provisions on assistance to third States affected by the application of sanctions under Chapter VII.

The Committee on Relations with the Host Country addressed a number of issues raised by permanent missions to the United Nations, including transportation and parking issues, acceleration of immigration and customs procedures, and travel regulations.

Legal aspects of international political relations

International Law Commission

The 34-member International Law Commission (ILC) held its sixty-first session in Geneva in two parts (4 May–5 June; 6 July–7 August) [A/64/10]. During the second part, the International Law Seminar held its forty-fifth session, which was attended by 27 participants from all the regions of the world. They observed ILC meetings, attended specially arranged lectures and participated in working groups on specific topics.

On the topic of reservations to treaties, ILC considered the fourteenth report of the Special Rapporteur dealing, in particular, with the procedure for the formulation of interpretative declarations, and with the permissibility of reactions to reservations, interpretative declarations and reactions to interpretative declarations. It referred two draft guidelines to the Drafting Committee on the form and communication of interpretative declarations, and seven draft guidelines on the permissibility of reactions to reservations and interpretative declarations. The Commission also adopted 32 draft guidelines, together with commentaries thereto. On the responsibility of international organizations, ILC considered the seventh report of the Special Rapporteur, which contained a review of comments from Governments and international organizations on the draft articles the Commission had adopted provisionally, along with proposed amendments. ILC adopted on first reading a set of 66 draft articles, together with commentaries, and decided to transmit the draft articles, through the Secretary-General, to Governments and international organizations, with a request for their comments and observations by 1 January 2011.

On the expulsion of aliens, the Commission considered the Special Rapporteur's fifth report on the protection of the human rights of persons who had been or were being expelled. Following a revised version of the draft articles contained in the report, the Commission decided to postpone consideration of those articles until its next (2010) session. On the protection of persons in the event of disasters, the Commission had before it the second report of the Special Rapporteur, which focused on the scope of the topic *ratione materiae, ratione personae* and *ratione temporis*, the definition of disaster, and the principles of solidarity and cooperation. Ilc referred three draft articles to its Drafting Committee. Subsequently, some draft articles were split into a total of five draft articles, which were provisionally adopted by the Drafting Committee. The Commission took note of their adoption. On the immunity of State officials from foreign criminal jurisdiction, ilc did not consider the topic during its 2009 session.

Ilc established a working group on shared natural resources, which recommended, and the Commission endorsed, that a decision on any future work on oil and gas be deferred until 2010, and that the 2007 questionnaire on oil and gas be recirculated to Governments. On the obligation to extradite or prosecute (*aut dedere aut judicare*), the Commission established an open-ended Working Group, which elaborated a general framework of issues that might need to be addressed by the Special Rapporteur. It also established two study groups: one on the most-favoured-nation clause, which agreed on a road map for future work; and the other on treaties over time, which agreed on a course of action to begin consideration of the topic. The Commission established a planning group to consider its programme, procedures and working methods, which decided to reconstitute the Working Group on the Long-term programme of work. Lucius Caflisch (Switzerland) was appointed as Special Rapporteur on of the topic "Effects of armed conflicts on treaties". The Commission referenced the report of the Secretary-General on assistance to special rapporteurs and expressed the hope that the General Assembly would consider the matter. Ilc decided that its sixty-second session would be held in Geneva from 3 May to 4 June and 5 July to 6 August 2010.

Topical summary report. Pursuant to Assembly resolution 63/123 [YUN 2008, p. 1431], the Secretariat prepared a topical summary [A/CN.4/606 & Add.1] of the debate held on the report of the Commission at the Assembly's sixty-third (2008) session.

Assistance to special rapporteurs. Pursuant to Assembly resolution 63/123, the Secretary-General submitted an August report [A/64/283] on assistance provided to ilc special rapporteurs, which also contained information on the practical needs and challenges encountered in their work.

On 16 December [meeting 64], the General Assembly, on the recommendation of the Sixth (Legal) Committee [A/64/449], adopted **resolution 64/114** without vote [agenda item 81].

Report of the International Law Commission on the work of its sixty-first session

The General Assembly,

Having considered the report of the International Law Commission on the work of its sixty-first session,

Emphasizing the importance of furthering the progressive development and codification of international law as a means of implementing the purposes and principles set forth in the Charter of the United Nations and in the Declaration on Principles of International Law concerning Friendly Relations and Cooperation among States in accordance with the Charter of the United Nations,

Recognizing the desirability of referring legal and drafting questions to the Sixth Committee, including topics that might be submitted to the International Law Commission for closer examination, and of enabling the Sixth Committee and the Commission to enhance further their contribution to the progressive development and codification of international law,

Recalling the need to keep under review those topics of international law which, given their new or renewed interest for the international community, may be suitable for the progressive development and codification of international law and therefore may be included in the future programme of work of the International Law Commission,

Reaffirming the importance to the successful work of the International Law Commission of the information provided by Member States concerning their views and practice,

Recognizing the importance of the work of the special rapporteurs of the International Law Commission,

Recalling the role of Member States in submitting proposals for the consideration of the International Law Commission,

Welcoming the holding of the International Law Seminar, and noting with appreciation the voluntary contributions made to the United Nations Trust Fund for the International Law Seminar,

Acknowledging the importance of facilitating the timely publication of the *Yearbook of the International Law Commission* and of eliminating the backlog,

Stressing the usefulness of focusing and structuring the debate on the report of the International Law Commission in the Sixth Committee in such a manner that conditions are provided for concentrated attention to each of the main topics dealt with in the report and for discussions on specific topics,

Wishing to enhance further, in the context of the revitalization of the debate on the report of the International Law Commission, the interaction between the Sixth Committee as a body of governmental representatives and the Commission as a body of independent legal experts, with a view to improving the dialogue between the two bodies,

Welcoming initiatives to hold interactive debates, panel discussions and question time in the Sixth Committee, as envisaged in resolution 58/316 of 1 July 2004 on further measures for the revitalization of the work of the General Assembly,

1. *Takes note* of the report of the International Law Commission on the work of its sixty-first session, and recommends that the Commission continue its work on the topics in its current programme, taking into account the comments and observations of Governments, whether submitted in writing or expressed orally in debates in the Sixth Committee;

2. *Expresses its appreciation* to the International Law Commission for the work accomplished at its sixty-first session, in particular for the completion, on first reading, of the draft articles on the topic "Responsibility of international organizations";

3. *Draws the attention* of Governments to the importance for the International Law Commission of having their views on the various aspects of the topics on the agenda of the Commission, in particular on all the specific issues identified in chapter III of its report, regarding:

(a) Responsibility of international organizations;

(b) Expulsion of aliens;

(c) Shared natural resources;

4. *Invites* Governments, within the context of paragraph 3 above, to provide information to the International Law Commission regarding practice in respect of the topic "Expulsion of aliens";

5. *Draws the attention* of Governments to the importance for the International Law Commission of having their comments and observations by 1 January 2011 on the draft articles and commentaries on the topic "Responsibility of international organizations" adopted on first reading by the Commission at its sixty-first session;

6. *Takes note* of the report of the Secretary-General on assistance to special rapporteurs of the International Law Commission and of paragraphs 240 to 242 of the report of the International Law Commission, and requests the Secretary-General to submit to the General Assembly at its sixty-fifth session options regarding additional support for the work of special rapporteurs;

7. *Invites* the International Law Commission to continue taking measures to enhance its efficiency and productivity and to consider making proposals to that end;

8. *Encourages* the International Law Commission to continue taking cost-saving measures at its future sessions, without prejudice to the efficiency and effectiveness of its work;

9. *Takes note* of paragraph 244 of the report of the International Law Commission, and decides that the next session of the Commission shall be held at the United Nations Office at Geneva from 3 May to 4 June and from 5 July to 6 August 2010;

10. *Welcomes* the enhanced dialogue between the International Law Commission and the Sixth Committee at the sixty-fourth session of the General Assembly, stresses the desirability of further enhancing the dialogue between the two bodies, and in this context encourages, inter alia, the continued practice of informal consultations in the form of discussions between the members of the Sixth

Committee and the members of the Commission attending the sixty-fifth session of the Assembly;

11. *Encourages* delegations, during the debate on the report of the International Law Commission, to adhere as far as possible to the structured work programme agreed to by the Sixth Committee and to consider presenting concise and focused statements;

12. *Encourages* Member States to consider being represented at the level of legal adviser during the first week in which the report of the International Law Commission is discussed in the Sixth Committee (International Law Week) to enable high-level discussions on issues of international law;

13. *Requests* the International Law Commission to continue to pay special attention to indicating in its annual report, for each topic, any specific issues on which expressions of views by Governments, either in the Sixth Committee or in written form, would be of particular interest in providing effective guidance for the Commission in its further work;

14. *Takes note* of paragraphs 243 and 245 to 249 of the report of the International Law Commission with regard to cooperation and interaction with other bodies, and encourages the Commission to continue the implementation of article 16, paragraph *(e)*, article 25 and article 26, paragraphs 1 and 2, of its statute in order to further strengthen cooperation between the Commission and other bodies concerned with international law, having in mind the usefulness of such cooperation;

15. *Notes* that consulting with national organizations and individual experts concerned with international law may assist Governments in considering whether to make comments and observations on drafts submitted by the International Law Commission and in formulating their comments and observations;

16. *Reaffirms* its previous decisions concerning the indispensable role of the Codification Division of the Office of Legal Affairs of the Secretariat in providing assistance to the International Law Commission, including in the preparation of memorandums and studies on topics on the agenda of the Commission;

17. *Approves* the conclusions reached by the International Law Commission in paragraph 232 of its report, and reaffirms its previous decisions concerning the documentation and summary records of the Commission;

18. *Takes note* of paragraph 233 of the report of the International Law Commission, and stresses the need to expedite the preparation of the summary records of the Commission;

19. *Also takes note* of paragraph 234 of the report of the International Law Commission and, without prejudice to the importance of ensuring necessary allocations in the regular budget, acknowledges the establishment by the Secretary-General of a trust fund to accept voluntary contributions so as to address the backlog relating to the *Yearbook of the International Law Commission*, and invites voluntary contributions to that end;

20. *Welcomes* the continuous efforts of the Codification Division to maintain and improve the website relating to the work of the International Law Commission;

21. *Expresses the hope* that the International Law Seminar will continue to be held in connection with the

sessions of the International Law Commission and that an increasing number of participants, in particular from developing countries, will be given the opportunity to attend the Seminar, and appeals to States to continue to make urgently needed voluntary contributions to the United Nations Trust Fund for the International Law Seminar;

22. *Requests* the Secretary-General to provide the International Law Seminar with adequate services, including interpretation, as required, and encourages him to continue considering ways to improve the structure and content of the Seminar;

23. *Also requests* the Secretary-General to forward to the International Law Commission, for its attention, the records of the debate on the report of the Commission at the sixty-fourth session of the General Assembly, together with such written statements as delegations may circulate in conjunction with their oral statements, and to prepare and distribute a topical summary of the debate, following established practice;

24. *Requests* the Secretariat to circulate to States, as soon as possible after the conclusion of the session of the International Law Commission, chapter II of its report containing a summary of the work of that session, chapter III containing the specific issues on which the views of Governments would be of particular interest to the Commission and the draft articles adopted on either first or second reading by the Commission;

25. *Encourages* the International Law Commission to continue considering ways in which specific issues on which the views of Governments would be of particular interest to the Commission could be framed so as to help Governments to have a better appreciation of the issues on which responses are required;

26. *Recommends* that the debate on the report of the International Law Commission at the sixty-fifth session of the General Assembly commence on 25 October 2010.

Shared natural resources

The Commission [A/64/10] reconvened the Working Group on shared natural resources, chaired by Enrique Candioti (Argentina). The Group had before it a working paper on oil and gas [A/CN.4/608] prepared by Chusei Yamada (Japan), the Special Rapporteur on that topic before he resigned in March [A/CN.4/613]. The Group also had before it comments and observations received from Governments on oil and gas [A/CN.4/607 & Corr.1 & Add.1]. The focus of the Working Group was on the feasibility of any future work by the Commission on aspects of the topic relating to transboundary oil and gas resources. The Working Group entrusted Shinya Murase (Japan) [A/CN.4/613/Add.1] with the responsibility of preparing a study, with the assistance of the Secretariat, to be submitted to the Working Group on Shared Natural Resources that might be reconvened at the Commission's 2010 session. In addition, the Group recommended, and ILC endorsed, that a decision on any future work on oil and gas be deferred until 2010,

and that in the interim, the 2007 questionnaire on oil and gas be recirculated to Governments [YUN 2007, p. 1362], while also encouraging them to provide comments and information on any matter concerning the issue, including whether or not the Commission should address the subject.

Responsibility of international organizations

ILC [A/64/10] considered the seventh report on responsibility of international organizations [A/CN.4/610] by Special Rapporteur Giorgio Gaja (Italy), which contained a review of comments made by Governments and international organizations on the draft articles provisionally adopted by the Commission and proposed amendments thereto. Some of the amendments related to the general structure of the draft articles, yet most of them concerned the part dealing with the internationally wrongful act of an international organization. The report also addressed outstanding issues, such as the general provisions of the draft articles and the place of the chapter concerning the responsibility of the State in connection with the act of an international organization; and contained four new draft articles: draft articles 61-64. The Commission also had before it the comments received from international organizations [A/CN.4/609].

Following its consideration, the Commission adopted on first reading a set of 66 draft articles, together with commentaries thereto, on responsibility of international organizations and decided to transmit them, through the Secretary-General, to Governments and international organizations for comments and observations, to be submitted to the Secretary-General by 1 January 2011.

Expulsion of aliens

ILC [A/64/10] had before it the fifth report on the expulsion of aliens [A/CN.4/611 & Corr.1] by Special Rapporteur Maurice Kamto (Cameroon), and the comments and information received from Governments [A/CN.4/604]. The report continued the study of the rules of international law limiting the right of expulsion and dealt with the limits relating to the requirement of respect for fundamental rights. On 15 May 2009, the Special Rapporteur presented to the Commission a revised and restructured version of draft articles 8 to 14, taking into account the plenary debate. He also submitted a set of revised and restructured draft articles on protection of the human rights of persons who had been or were being expelled [A/CN.4/617]; and a new draft workplan with a view to restructuring the draft articles [A/CN.4/618].

During its discussions, some Commission members were of the view that a fair balance must be maintained between the right of States to expel aliens and the need to respect human rights, taking into account also the situation in the receiving State. Some felt that it was not necessary to address all human rights obligations of the expelling State, but only those that were closely related to expulsion. Reservations were expressed as to the approach taken by the Special Rapporteur, which consisted of drawing up a list of fundamental, or inviolable, rights that must be respected in the case of persons subject to expulsion. Members proposed the expansion of the list of rights set out in the draft articles and the inclusion of draft articles governing other questions, including a provision stipulating that unreasonably prolonged expulsion procedures might constitute inhuman or degrading treatment. It was also proposed that the draft articles should state that the proclamation of a state of emergency did not permit any derogation from the rights they recognized. The Commission decided to postpone its consideration of the revised draft articles to its sixty-second (2010) session.

Extradition

The Commission [A/64/10] had before it the comments and information received from Governments [A/CN.4/612] on the obligation to extradite or prosecute (*aut dedere aut judicare*), submitted pursuant to General Assembly resolution 62/66 [YUN 2007, p. 1357]. On 27 May, ILC established an open-ended Working Group on the topic, which held meetings on 28 May, and 29 and 30 July. The Working Group agreed that its mandate would be to draw up a general framework for consideration of the topic, with the aim of specifying the issues to be addressed and establishing an order of priority.

Following discussions in the Working Group, the Chairman introduced a proposed general framework, which aimed to facilitate the work of the Special Rapporteur in the preparation of future reports. The list of questions and issues to be addressed included the legal bases of the obligation to extradite or prosecute; material scope of the obligation to extradite or prosecute; content of the obligation to extradite or prosecute; relationship between the obligation to extradite or prosecute and other principles; conditions for the triggering of the obligation to extradite or prosecute; implementation of the obligation to extradite or prosecute; and the relationship between the obligation to extradite or prosecute and the surrender of the alleged offender to a competent international criminal tribunal (the "third alternative"). The Special Rapporteur would determine the exact order of the questions to be considered, as well as the structure of, and linkage between, his planned draft articles on the various aspects of the topic.

Protection of persons in the event of disasters

The Commission [A/64/10] considered the second report on the protection of persons in the event of disasters [A/CN.4/615 & Corr.1] by Special Rapporteur Eduardo Valencia-Ospina (Colombia), analysing the scope of the topic *ratione materiae*, *ratione personae* and *ratione temporis*, and issues relating to the definition of "disaster" for purposes of the topic, as well as undertaking a consideration of the basic duty to cooperate. The report further contained proposals for draft articles 1 (Scope), 2 (Definition of disaster) and 3 (Duty to cooperate). The Commission also had before it a Secretariat memorandum [YUN 2008, p. 1438] as well as written replies submitted by the United Nations Office for the Coordination of Humanitarian Affairs and the International Federation of the Red Cross and Red Crescent Societies to the questions addressed to them by the Commission in 2008.

ILC referred draft articles 1 to 3 to the Drafting Committee, on the understanding that if no agreement was possible on draft article 3, it could be referred back to the plenary with a view to establishing a working group to discuss the draft article. On 31 July, the Commission took note of draft articles 1 to 5, as provisionally adopted by the Drafting Committee [A/CN.4/L.758]. The Commission decided that it should be represented at the sixty-fourth (2009) session of the Assembly by its Chairman, Ernest Petrič, and on 7 August, requested that Special Rapporteur Valencia-Ospina also attend the Assembly's session.

Most-favoured-nation clause

On 29 May, the Commission [A/64/10] established a study group on the most-favoured-nation (MFN) clause, which held two meetings on 3 June and 20 July. The Group considered a framework that would serve as a road map for future work, in the light of issues highlighted in the syllabus on the topic. It also made a preliminary assessment of the 1978 draft articles [YUN 1978, p. 945] with a view to reviewing the developments that had taken place since their adoption. The Group agreed on a work schedule for the preparation of papers to shed additional light on questions concerning, in particular, the scope of MFN clauses and their interpretation and application. Eight topics were identified for research and the preparation of related papers: a catalogue of MFN provisions; the 1978 ILC draft articles; the relationship between MFN and national treatment; MFN in the General Agreement on Tariffs and Trade and the World Trade Organization; United Nations Conference on Trade and Development work on MFN; Organization for Economic Co-operation and Development work on MFN; the *Maffezini* problem under investment treaties; and regional economic integration agreements and free trade agreements. The Study Group also assigned primary responsibility to its members for the preparation of the papers.

Treaties over time

On 29 May, the Commission established a study group on treaties over time [A/64/10], which held two meetings on 7 and 28 July. Its discussions focused on the identification of the issues to be covered, the working methods of the group and the possible outcome of the Commission's work on the topic. Several members underlined that the final product should present practical guidance for States. The study group agreed that work should start on subsequent agreement and practice on the basis of successive reports to be prepared by the Chairman, as addressed in the jurisprudence of the International Court of Justice, and other international courts and tribunals of general or ad hoc jurisdiction. Contributions by other members of the study group were encouraged, as well as contributions on other issues falling within the broader scope of the topic.

International State relations and international law

Jurisdictional immunities of States and their properties

The General Assembly, by resolution 59/38 [YUN 2004, p. 1304], adopted the Convention on Jurisdictional Immunities of States and Their Property. The Convention was opened for signature from 17 January 2005 until 17 January 2007 at UN Headquarters. As at 31 December 2009, the Convention had 28 signatories and seven States parties. The Convention would enter into force when ratified by 30 parties.

International terrorism

Convention on international terrorism

Ad Hoc Committee. In accordance with General Assembly resolution 62/71 [YUN 2007, p. 1366], the Ad Hoc Committee established by Assembly resolution 51/210 [YUN 1996, p. 1208] held its thirteenth session (New York, 29 June–2 July) [A/64/37] to continue, within the framework of a working group of the Sixth Committee, the elaboration of a draft comprehensive convention on international terrorism.

The Ad Hoc Committee held informal consultations and contacts on the draft comprehensive convention, and informal consultations on the question of convening a high-level conference under UN auspices to formulate a joint organized response of the international community to terrorism in all its forms and manifestations. Delegations reiterated the importance of an early conclusion to the draft convention and stressed the necessity for the international community to coordinate its actions to combat terrorism at the regional and international levels. Discussions focused on the scope and application of the convention, the need for the Convention to include a clear legal definition of terrorism, and the possibility of removing the word "comprehensive" from the title of the convention to attenuate some of the concerns. Following a 2 July statement of the Coordinator on the results of the bilateral contacts and informal meetings concerning outstanding issues during the session, delegations affirmed their commitment to remaining engaged in the negotiating process and to reaching agreement on the draft convention by consensus.

On the proposed convening of a high-level conference, Egypt, as sponsor delegation, recalled the importance of holding such a conference [YUN 2006, p. 1515], which had been endorsed by the Movement of Non-Aligned Countries, the Organization of the Islamic Conference, the African Union and the League of Arab States. The conference would consider the question of terrorism in all its aspects, especially its definition and any link to education, human rights and the rule of law. While underscoring that the holding of the conference should not be tied to the conclusion of the convention, it was stressed that such a conference could assist the process, as it would contribute to fleshing out and resolving the outstanding issues.

At the conclusion of its session, on 2 July, the Ad Hoc Committee recommended that the Sixth Committee, at the Assembly's sixty-fourth (2009) session, establish a working group with a view to finalizing the draft comprehensive convention and continue to discuss the agenda item on the question of convening a high-level conference.

Measures to eliminate international terrorism

In accordance with Assembly resolution 50/53 [YUN 1995, p. 1330], the Secretary-General, in July [A/64/161], issued his annual report on measures taken by 26 States, five UN system entities and five intergovernmental organizations to implement the 1994 Declaration on Measures to Eliminate International Terrorism, approved by Assembly resolution 49/60 [YUN 1994, p. 1293] and Security Council resolution 1269(1999) [YUN 1999, p. 1240]. It listed 30 international instruments pertaining to terrorism, indicating the status of State participation in each, and provided information on workshops and training courses on combating terrorism by four UN bodies and five international organizations. A September addendum [A/64/161/Add.1] summarized information submitted by one additional State.

In other action, the Commission on Crime Prevention and Criminal Justice, at its eighteenth session (16–24 April) [E/2009/30], recommended to the Economic and Social Council a resolution entitled "Technical assistance for implementing the international conventions and protocols relating to terrorism", which the Council adopted on 30 July as **resolution 2009/21** (see p. 1100).

GENERAL ASSEMBLY ACTION

On 16 December [meeting 64], the General Assembly, on the recommendation of the Sixth Committee [A/64/453], adopted **resolution 64/118** without vote [agenda item 106].

Measures to eliminate international terrorism

The General Assembly,

Guided by the purposes and principles of the Charter of the United Nations,

Reaffirming, in all its aspects, the United Nations Global Counter-Terrorism Strategy adopted on 8 September 2006, enhancing the overall framework for the efforts of the international community to effectively counter the scourge of terrorism in all its forms and manifestations, and recalling the first biennial review of the Strategy, on 4 and 5 September 2008, and the debates that were held on that occasion,

Recalling the Declaration on the Occasion of the Fiftieth Anniversary of the United Nations,

Recalling also the United Nations Millennium Declaration,

Recalling further the 2005 World Summit Outcome, and reaffirming in particular the section on terrorism,

Recalling the Declaration on Measures to Eliminate International Terrorism, contained in the annex to General Assembly resolution 49/60 of 9 December 1994, and the Declaration to Supplement the 1994 Declaration on Measures to Eliminate International Terrorism, contained in the annex to Assembly resolution 51/210 of 17 December 1996,

Recalling also all General Assembly resolutions on measures to eliminate international terrorism and Security Council resolutions on threats to international peace and security caused by terrorist acts,

Convinced of the importance of the consideration of measures to eliminate international terrorism by the General Assembly as the universal organ having competence to do so,

Deeply disturbed by the persistence of terrorist acts, which have been carried out worldwide,

Reaffirming its strong condemnation of the heinous acts of terrorism that have caused enormous loss of human life, destruction and damage, including those which prompted the adoption of General Assembly resolution 56/1 of 12 September 2001, as well as Security Council resolutions 1368(2001) of 12 September 2001, 1373(2001) of 28 September 2001 and 1377(2001) of 12 November 2001, and those that have occurred since,

Recalling the strong condemnation of the atrocious and deliberate attack against the headquarters of the United Nations Assistance Mission for Iraq in Baghdad on 19 August 2003 in General Assembly resolution 57/338 of 15 September 2003 and Security Council resolution 1502(2003) of 26 August 2003,

Affirming that States must ensure that any measure taken to combat terrorism complies with all their obligations under international law and must adopt such measures in accordance with international law, in particular international human rights, refugee and humanitarian law,

Stressing the need to strengthen further international cooperation among States and among international organizations and agencies, regional organizations and arrangements and the United Nations in order to prevent, combat and eliminate terrorism in all its forms and manifestations, wherever and by whomsoever committed, in accordance with the principles of the Charter, international law and the relevant international conventions,

Noting the role of the Security Council Committee established pursuant to resolution 1373(2001) concerning counter-terrorism in monitoring the implementation of that resolution, including the taking of the necessary financial, legal and technical measures by States and the ratification or acceptance of the relevant international conventions and protocols,

Mindful of the need to enhance the role of the United Nations and the relevant specialized agencies in combating international terrorism and of the proposals of the Secretary-General to enhance the role of the Organization in this respect,

Mindful also of the essential need to strengthen international, regional and subregional cooperation aimed at enhancing the national capacity of States to prevent and suppress effectively international terrorism in all its forms and manifestations,

Reiterating its call upon States to review urgently the scope of the existing international legal provisions on the prevention, repression and elimination of terrorism in all its forms and manifestations, with the aim of ensuring that there is a comprehensive legal framework covering all aspects of the matter,

Emphasizing that tolerance and dialogue among civilizations and the enhancement of interfaith and intercultural understanding are among the most important elements in promoting cooperation and success in combating terrorism, and welcoming the various initiatives to this end,

Reaffirming that no terrorist act can be justified in any circumstances,

Recalling Security Council resolution 1624(2005) of 14 September 2005, and bearing in mind that States must ensure that any measure taken to combat terrorism complies with their obligations under international law, in particular international human rights, refugee and humanitarian law,

Taking note of recent developments and initiatives at the international, regional and subregional levels to prevent and suppress international terrorism, including those of the African Union, the ASEAN Regional Forum, the Asia-Pacific Economic Cooperation, the Association of Southeast Asian Nations, the Bali Counter-Terrorism Process, the Central American Integration System, the Collective Security Treaty Organization, the Common Market for Eastern and Southern Africa, the Cooperation Council for the Arab States of the Gulf, the Council of Europe, the East African Community, the Economic Community of West

African States, the Euro-Mediterranean Partnership, the European Free Trade Association, the European Union, the Group of Eight, the Intergovernmental Authority on Development, the International Civil Aviation Organization, the International Maritime Organization, the League of Arab States, the Movement of Non-Aligned Countries, the North Atlantic Treaty Organization, the Organization for Economic Cooperation and Development, the Organization for Security and Cooperation in Europe, the Organization of American States, the Organization of the Islamic Conference, the Pacific Islands Forum, the Shanghai Cooperation Organization, the Southern African Development Community and the World Customs Organization,

Noting regional efforts to prevent, combat and eliminate terrorism in all its forms and manifestations, wherever and by whomsoever committed, including through the elaboration of, and adherence to, regional conventions,

Recalling its decision in resolutions 54/110 of 9 December 1999, 55/158 of 12 December 2000, 56/88 of 12 December 2001, 57/27 of 19 November 2002, 58/81 of 9 December 2003, 59/46 of 2 December 2004, 60/43 of 8 December 2005, 61/40 of 4 December 2006, 62/71 of 6 December 2007 and 63/129 of 11 December 2008 that the Ad Hoc Committee established by General Assembly resolution 51/210 should address, and keep on its agenda, the question of convening a high-level conference under the auspices of the United Nations to formulate a joint organized response of the international community to terrorism in all its forms and manifestations,

Recalling also the Final Document of the Fifteenth Summit Conference of Heads of State and Government of the Movement of Non-Aligned Countries, adopted in Sharm el-Sheikh, Egypt, on 16 July 2009, which reiterated the collective position of the Non-Aligned Movement on terrorism and reaffirmed its previous initiative calling for an international summit conference under the auspices of the United Nations to formulate a joint organized response of the international community to terrorism in all its forms and manifestations, as well as other relevant initiatives,

Aware of its resolutions 57/219 of 18 December 2002, 58/187 of 22 December 2003, 59/191 of 20 December 2004, 60/158 of 16 December 2005, 61/171 of 19 December 2006, 62/159 of 18 December 2007 and 63/185 of 18 December 2008,

Having examined the report of the Secretary-General, the report of the Ad Hoc Committee established by General Assembly resolution 51/210 and the oral report of the Chairperson of the Working Group established by the Sixth Committee at the sixty-fourth session of the Assembly,

1. *Strongly condemns* all acts, methods and practices of terrorism in all its forms and manifestations as criminal and unjustifiable, wherever and by whomsoever committed;

2. *Calls upon* all Member States, the United Nations and other appropriate international, regional and subregional organizations to implement the United Nations Global Counter-Terrorism Strategy, as well as the resolution relating to the first biennial review of the Strategy, in all its aspects at the international, regional, subregional and national levels without delay, including by mobilizing resources and expertise;

3. *Recalls* the pivotal role of the General Assembly in following up the implementation and the updating of the Strategy, and in this regard also recalls its invitation to the Secretary-General to contribute to the future deliberations of the Assembly, and requests the Secretary-General when doing so to provide information on relevant activities within the Secretariat to ensure overall coordination and coherence in the counter-terrorism efforts of the United Nations system;

4. *Reiterates* that criminal acts intended or calculated to provoke a state of terror in the general public, a group of persons or particular persons for political purposes are in any circumstances unjustifiable, whatever the considerations of a political, philosophical, ideological, racial, ethnic, religious or other nature that may be invoked to justify them;

5. *Reiterates its call upon* all States to adopt further measures in accordance with the Charter of the United Nations and the relevant provisions of international law, including international standards of human rights, to prevent terrorism and to strengthen international cooperation in combating terrorism and, to that end, to consider in particular the implementation of the measures set out in paragraphs 3 *(a)* to *(f)* of General Assembly resolution 51/210;

6. *Also reiterates its call upon* all States, with the aim of enhancing the efficient implementation of relevant legal instruments, to intensify, as and where appropriate, the exchange of information on facts related to terrorism and, in so doing, to avoid the dissemination of inaccurate or unverified information;

7. *Reiterates its call upon* States to refrain from financing, encouraging, providing training for or otherwise supporting terrorist activities;

8. *Urges* States to ensure that their nationals or other persons and entities within their territory that wilfully provide or collect funds for the benefit of persons or entities who commit, or attempt to commit, facilitate or participate in the commission of terrorist acts are punished by penalties consistent with the grave nature of such acts;

9. *Reminds* States of their obligations under relevant international conventions and protocols and Security Council resolutions, including Council resolution 1373(2001), to ensure that perpetrators of terrorist acts are brought to justice;

10. *Reaffirms* that international cooperation as well as actions by States to combat terrorism should be conducted in conformity with the principles of the Charter, international law and relevant international conventions;

11. *Recalls* the adoption of the International Convention for the Suppression of Acts of Nuclear Terrorism, the Amendment to the Convention on the Physical Protection of Nuclear Material, the Protocol of 2005 to the Convention for the Suppression of Unlawful Acts against the Safety of Maritime Navigation and the Protocol of 2005 to the Protocol for the Suppression of Unlawful Acts against the Safety of Fixed Platforms Located on the Continental Shelf, and urges all States to consider, as a matter of priority, becoming parties to these instruments;

12. *Urges* all States that have not yet done so to consider, as a matter of priority and in accordance with Security Council resolution 1373(2001) and Council resolution 1566(2004) of 8 October 2004, becoming parties to the

relevant conventions and protocols as referred to in paragraph 6 of General Assembly resolution 51/210, as well as the International Convention for the Suppression of Terrorist Bombings, the International Convention for the Suppression of the Financing of Terrorism, the International Convention for the Suppression of Acts of Nuclear Terrorism and the Amendment to the Convention on the Physical Protection of Nuclear Material, and calls upon all States to enact, as appropriate, the domestic legislation necessary to implement the provisions of those conventions and protocols, to ensure that the jurisdiction of their courts enables them to bring to trial the perpetrators of terrorist acts and to cooperate with and provide support and assistance to other States and relevant international and regional organizations to that end;

13. *Urges* States to cooperate with the Secretary-General and with one another, as well as with interested intergovernmental organizations, with a view to ensuring, where appropriate within existing mandates, that technical and other expert advice is provided to those States requiring and requesting assistance in becoming parties to and implementing the conventions and protocols referred to in paragraph 12 above;

14. *Notes with appreciation and satisfaction* that, consistent with the call contained in paragraphs 11 and 12 of General Assembly resolution 63/129, a number of States became parties to the relevant conventions and protocols referred to therein, thereby realizing the objective of wider acceptance and implementation of those conventions;

15. *Reaffirms* the Declaration on Measures to Eliminate International Terrorism and the Declaration to Supplement the 1994 Declaration on Measures to Eliminate International Terrorism, and calls upon all States to implement them;

16. *Calls upon* all States to cooperate to prevent and suppress terrorist acts;

17. *Urges* all States and the Secretary-General, in their efforts to prevent international terrorism, to make the best use of the existing institutions of the United Nations;

18. *Requests* the Terrorism Prevention Branch of the United Nations Office on Drugs and Crime in Vienna to continue its efforts to enhance, through its mandate, the capabilities of the United Nations in the prevention of terrorism, and recognizes, in the context of the United Nations Global Counter-Terrorism Strategy and Security Council resolution 1373(2001), its role in assisting States in becoming parties to and implementing the relevant international conventions and protocols relating to terrorism, including the most recent among them, and in strengthening international cooperation mechanisms in criminal matters related to terrorism, including through national capacity-building;

19. *Welcomes* the current efforts by the Secretariat to prepare the third edition of the publication *International Instruments related to the Prevention and Suppression of International Terrorism* in all official languages;

20. *Invites* regional intergovernmental organizations to submit to the Secretary-General information on the measures they have adopted at the regional level to eliminate international terrorism, as well as on intergovernmental meetings held by those organizations;

21. *Notes* the progress made in the elaboration of the draft comprehensive convention on international terrorism during the meetings of the Ad Hoc Committee established by General Assembly resolution 51/210 and of the Working Group established by the Sixth Committee during the sixty-fourth session of the Assembly, and welcomes continuing efforts to that end;

22. *Decides* that the Ad Hoc Committee shall, on an expedited basis, continue to elaborate the draft comprehensive convention on international terrorism and shall continue to discuss the item included in its agenda by General Assembly resolution 54/110 concerning the question of convening a high-level conference under the auspices of the United Nations;

23. *Also decides* that the Ad Hoc Committee shall meet from 12 to 16 April 2010 in order to fulfil the mandate referred to in paragraph 22 above;

24. *Requests* the Secretary-General to continue to provide the Ad Hoc Committee with the facilities necessary for the performance of its work;

25. *Requests* the Ad Hoc Committee to report to the General Assembly at its sixty-fourth session in the event of the completion of the draft comprehensive convention on international terrorism;

26. *Also requests* the Ad Hoc Committee to report to the General Assembly at its sixty-fifth session on progress made in the implementation of its mandate;

27. *Decides* to include in the provisional agenda of its sixty-fifth session the item entitled "Measures to eliminate international terrorism".

On 24 December, the Assembly decided that the agenda item on measures to eliminate international terrorism would remain for consideration during its resumed sixty-fourth (2010) session (**decision 64/549**).

Principle of universal jurisdiction

In letters dated 21 January [A/63/237] and 29 June [A/63/237/Rev.1], the United Republic of Tanzania, on behalf of the Group of African States, requested that the General Assembly include in the agenda of its resumed sixty-third (2009) session additional items entitled "Abuse of the principle of universal jurisdiction" and "The scope and application of the principle of universal jurisdiction", respectively. Annexed to the latter communication was an explanatory memorandum in support of the request and a draft decision [A/63/L.100] to be adopted at the conclusion of general plenary discussions.

On 14 September, the Assembly decided to include in the draft agenda of its sixty-fourth (2009) session the item entitled "The scope and application of the principle of universal jurisdiction", and recommended that it be considered by the Sixth Committee (**decision 63/568**), which considered the item on 20 and 21 October and on 12 November [A/64/452].

On 16 December [meeting 64], the General Assembly, on the recommendation of the Sixth Committee [A/64/452], adopted **resolution 64/117** without vote [agenda item 84].

The scope and application of the principle of universal jurisdiction

The General Assembly,

Reaffirming its commitment to the purposes and principles of the Charter of the United Nations, to international law and to an international order based on the rule of law, which is essential for peaceful coexistence and cooperation among States,

1. *Requests* the Secretary-General to invite Member States to submit, before 30 April 2010, information and observations on the scope and application of the principle of universal jurisdiction, including information on the relevant applicable international treaties, their domestic legal rules and judicial practice, and to prepare and submit to the General Assembly, at its sixty-fifth session, a report based on such information and observations;

2. *Decides* that the Sixth Committee shall continue its consideration of the scope and application of the principle of universal jurisdiction, without prejudice to the consideration of related issues in other forums of the United Nations;

3. *Decides* to include in the provisional agenda of its sixty-fifth session the item entitled "The scope and application of the principle of universal jurisdiction".

Diplomatic relations

Protection of diplomatic and consular missions and representatives

As at 31 December, the States parties to the following conventions relating to the protection of diplomatic and consular relations numbered: 186 States parties to the 1961 Vienna Convention on Diplomatic Relations [YUN 1961, p. 512], 51 parties to the Optional Protocol concerning the acquisition of nationality [ibid., p. 516] and 66 parties to the Optional Protocol concerning the compulsory settlement of disputes [ibid.].

The 1963 Vienna Convention on Consular Relations [YUN 1963, p. 510] had 172 parties, the Optional Protocol concerning acquisition of nationality [ibid., p. 512] had 39, and the Optional Protocol concerning the compulsory settlement of disputes [ibid.] had 48.

Parties to the 1973 Convention on the Prevention and Punishment of Crimes against Internationally Protected Persons, including Diplomatic Agents [YUN 1973, p. 775] numbered 173.

Treaties and agreements

Reservations to treaties

ILC, at its sixty-first session [A/64/10], considered the fourteenth report of Special Rapporteur Alain Pellet (France) on the procedure for the formulation of interpretative declarations, and with the permissibility of reactions to reservations, interpretative declarations and reactions to interpretative declarations [A/CN.4/614 & Corr.1 & Add.1,2]. The Commission also had before it a memorandum by the Secretariat on reservations to treaties in the context of succession of States [A/CN.4/616]. The Commission referred to the Drafting Committee two draft guidelines on the form and communication of interpretative declarations, and seven draft guidelines on the permissibility of reactions to reservations and on the permissibility of interpretative declarations and reactions thereto. ILC also adopted 32 draft guidelines, together with commentaries, on the basis of the draft guidelines contained in the Special Rapporteur's tenth [YUN 2005, p. 1422; YUN 2006, p. 1523], twelfth [YUN 2007, p. 1371], thirteenth [YUN 2008, p. 1447] and fourteenth reports.

The Commission provisionally adopted draft guidelines 2.8.1 (Tacit acceptance of reservations), 2.8.2 (Unanimous acceptance of reservations), 2.8.3 (Express acceptance of a reservation), 2.8.4 (Written form of express acceptance), 2.8.5 (Procedure for formulating express acceptance), 2.8.6 (Non-requirement of confirmation of an acceptance made prior to formal confirmation of a reservation), 2.8.7 (Acceptance of a reservation to the constituent instrument of an international organization), 2.8.8 (Organ competent to accept a reservation to a constituent instrument), 2.8.9 (Modalities of the acceptance of a reservation to a constituent instrument), 2.8.10 (Acceptance of a reservation to a constituent instrument that has not yet entered into force), 2.8.11 (Reaction by a member of an international organization to a reservation to its constituent instrument), 2.8.12 (Final nature of acceptance of a reservation), 2.4.0 (Form of interpretative declarations), 2.4.3 *bis* (Communication of interpretative declarations), 2.9.1 (Approval of an interpretative declaration), 2.9.2 (Opposition to an interpretative declaration), 2.9.3 (Recharacterization of an interpretative declaration), 2.9.4 (Freedom to formulate approval, opposition or recharacterization), 2.9.5 (Form of approval, opposition and recharacterization), 2.9.6 (Statement of reasons for approval, opposition and recharacterization), 2.9.7 (Formulation and communication of approval, opposition or recharacterization), 2.9.8 (Non-presumption of approval or opposition), 2.9.9 (Silence with respect to an interpretative declaration), 2.9.10 (Reactions to conditional interpretative declarations), 3.2 (Assessment of the permissibility of reservations),

3.2.1 (Competence of the treaty monitoring bodies to assess the permissibility of reservations), 3.2.2 (Specification of the competence of treaty monitoring bodies to assess the permissibility of reservations), 3.2.3 (Cooperation of States and international organizations with treaty monitoring bodies), 3.2.4 (Bodies competent to assess the permissibility of reservations in the event of the establishment of a treaty monitoring body), 3.2.5 (Competence of dispute settlement bodies to assess the permissibility of reservations), 3.3 (Consequences of the non-permissibility of a reservation), and 3.3.1 (Non-permissibility of reservations and international responsibility. The Commission also adopted the commentaries to the draft guidelines provisionally adopted.

Treaties involving international organizations

The 1986 Vienna Convention on the Law of Treaties between States and International Organizations or between International Organizations [YUN 1986, p. 1006], which had not yet entered into force, had 41 parties.

UN registration and publication of treaties

During 2009, a total of 1,900 treaties were received and 765 subsequent actions were registered or filed and recorded with the Secretariat. In addition, 941 treaty actions (signatures, ratifications, acceptances, approvals, accessions and other formalities) for which the Secretary-General performed depositary functions were received. Twelve issues of the *Monthly Statement of Treaties and International Agreements* were published.

In addition, 31 volumes of the *United Nations Treaty Series* (UNTS) were published, incorporating the texts of treaties registered or filed and recorded and related subsequent actions in the original languages, with translations into English and French where necessary. The United Nations Treaty Collection on the Internet, which contained published UNTS volumes up to January 2007, the *League of Nations Treaty Series*, the *Treaty Handbook, Multilateral Treaties Deposited with the Secretary-General*, the *Summary of Practice of the Secretary-General as Depositary of Multilateral Treaties*, the Treaty Event booklets, and information on capacity-building training and a range of materials on treaty law and practice, generated over 200,000 page views per month.

The 2009 Treaty Event: Towards Universal Participation and Implementation (New York, 23–25 and 28–29 September) resulted in 103 treaty actions undertaken by 64 States with respect to 34 treaties deposited with the Secretary-General. The Treaty Event's theme focused attention on the goal of moving towards universal participation and implementation, as well as on targeted areas such as human rights and statelessness, the environment, sustainable development and climate change, terrorism, organized crime and penal matters, disarmament, privileges and immunities, the safety of UN and associated personnel, and transport.

In addition, a special treaty event took place on 20 April in Vienna during the eighteenth session of the Commission on Crime Prevention and Criminal Justice, which promoted the universal counter-terrorism and crime conventions, as well as the Convention on the Safety of United Nations and Associated Personnel and its Optional Protocol.

Advice and capacity-building in treaty law and practice

Advice and assistance on treaty law and practice were provided to Member States, specialized agencies, regional commissions, other UN bodies and other entities such as international organizations. Two seminars on treaty law and practice were conducted at UN Headquarters for legal advisers from Member States and other officials. One regional capacity-building workshop on treaty law and practice and the implementation of treaty obligations was held in Kingstown, St. Vincent and the Grenadines. It was hosted by the Caribbean Community and attended by 86 participants from 14 countries.

Multilateral treaties

The *United Nations Treaty Series* and the regularly updated status of multilateral treaties deposited with the Secretary-General were available on the Internet at the UN Treaty Collection website (*http://treaties.un.org*).

Multilateral treaties deposited with the Secretary-General

At the end of 2009, the Secretary-General performed depositary functions for 544 multilateral treaties.

The following multilateral treaties deposited with the Secretary-General came into force in 2009:

Protocol on Combined Transport on Inland Waterways to the European Agreement on Important International Combined Transport Lines and Related Installations (AGTC) *of 1991*, adopted on 17 January 1997

Protocol on Pollutant Release and Transfer Registers to the Convention on Access to Information, Public Participation in Decision-Making and Access to Justice in Environmental Matters, adopted on 21 May 2003

Intergovernmental Agreement on the Trans-Asian Railway Network, adopted on 12 April 2006

Other international legal questions

Rule of law at the national and international levels

In August, pursuant to General Assembly resolution 63/128 [YUN 2008, p. 1450], the Secretary-General submitted the first annual report [A/64/298] on strengthening and coordinating UN rule of law activities, which illustrated key achievements of UN support to Member States over the preceding year, identified areas in need of further concerted action and highlighted implementation of the recommendations made in his 2008 report [YUN 2008, p. 1449]. Efforts to ensure the overall coordination and coherence of UN engagement by the Rule of Law Coordination and Resource Group, supported by the Rule of Law Unit [ibid.], continued to drive the Organization towards more strategic and effective rule of law assistance.

UN rule of law programming extended to over 120 States worldwide. In at least 50 countries, a minimum of three UN entities were carrying out rule of law activities. Five or more UN entities were working on the rule of law in over 30 countries, 22 of which hosted UN peace operations. The first annual system-wide meeting held in June was attended by 27 UN system entities. The Secretary-General observed that his previous recommendations remained critical. In addition, under the Deputy Secretary-General's leadership, the Coordination and Resource Group and the Rule of Law Unit would: support donor efforts to establish a policy platform to address challenges in rule of law assistance; consult with regional stakeholders on means for collaboration on rule of law issues; convene UN entities to explore enhancing rule of law activities that protect economic and social rights; and enhance rule of law activities aimed at strengthening States' capacity to end impunity.

GENERAL ASSEMBLY ACTION

On 16 December [meeting 64], the General Assembly, on the recommendation of the Sixth Committee [A/64/451], adopted **resolution 64/116** without vote [agenda item 83].

The rule of law at the national and international levels

The General Assembly,

Recalling its resolution 63/128 of 11 December 2008,

Reaffirming its commitment to the purposes and principles of the Charter of the United Nations and international law, which are indispensable foundations of a more peaceful, prosperous and just world, and reiterating its determination to foster strict respect for them and to establish a just and lasting peace all over the world,

Reaffirming that human rights, the rule of law and democracy are interlinked and mutually reinforcing and that they belong to the universal and indivisible core values and principles of the United Nations,

Reaffirming also the need for universal adherence to and implementation of the rule of law at both the national and international levels and its solemn commitment to an international order based on the rule of law and international law, which, together with the principles of justice, is essential for peaceful coexistence and cooperation among States,

Convinced that the advancement of the rule of law at the national and international levels is essential for the realization of sustained economic growth, sustainable development, the eradication of poverty and hunger and the protection of all human rights and fundamental freedoms, and acknowledging that collective security depends on effective cooperation, in accordance with the Charter and international law, against transnational threats,

Reaffirming the duty of all States to refrain in their international relations from the threat or use of force in any manner inconsistent with the purposes and principles of the United Nations and to settle their international disputes by peaceful means in such a manner that international peace and security, and justice are not endangered, in accordance with Chapter VI of the Charter, and calling upon States that have not yet done so to consider accepting the jurisdiction of the International Court of Justice in accordance with its Statute,

Convinced that the promotion of and respect for the rule of law at the national and international levels, as well as justice and good governance, should guide the activities of the United Nations and of its Member States,

Recalling paragraph 134 *(e)* of the 2005 World Summit Outcome,

1. *Takes note* of the annual report of the Secretary-General on strengthening and coordinating United Nations rule of law activities;

2. *Reaffirms* the role of the General Assembly in encouraging the progressive development of international law and its codification, and reaffirms further that States shall abide by all their obligations under international law;

3. *Stresses* the importance of adherence to the rule of law at the national level, and the need to strengthen support to Member States, upon their request, in the domestic implementation of their respective international obligations through enhanced technical assistance and capacity-building, based on greater coordination and coherence within the United Nations system and among donors, and calls for greater evaluation of the effectiveness of such activities;

4. *Calls upon* the United Nations system to systematically address, as appropriate, aspects of the rule of law in relevant activities, recognizing the importance of the rule of law to virtually all areas of United Nations engagement;

5. *Expresses full support* for the overall coordination and coherence role of the Rule of Law Coordination and Resource Group within the United Nations system within existing mandates, supported by the Rule of Law Unit in the Executive Office of the Secretary-General, under the leadership of the Deputy Secretary-General;

6. *Requests* the Secretary-General to submit his next annual report on United Nations rule of law activities, in accordance with paragraph 5 of resolution 63/128, taking note of paragraph 97 of the report;

7. *Welcomes* the dialogue initiated by the Rule of Law Coordination and Resource Group and the Rule of Law Unit with Member States on the topic "Promoting the rule of law at the international level", and calls for the continuation of this dialogue with a view to fostering the rule of law at the international level;

8. *Encourages* the Secretary-General and the United Nations system to accord high priority to rule of law activities;

9. *Invites* the International Court of Justice, the United Nations Commission on International Trade Law and the International Law Commission to continue to comment, in their respective reports to the General Assembly, on their current roles in promoting the rule of law;

10. *Invites* the Rule of Law Coordination and Resource Group and the Rule of Law Unit to continue to interact with Member States on a regular basis, in particular in informal briefings;

11. *Stresses* the need to provide the Rule of Law Unit with the necessary funding and staff in order to enable it to carry out its tasks in an effective and sustainable manner and urges the Secretary-General and Member States to continue to support the functioning of the Unit;

12. *Decides* to include in the provisional agenda of its sixty-fifth session the item entitled "The rule of law at the national and international levels", invites Member States to focus their comments in the upcoming Sixth Committee debate on the sub-topic "Laws and practices of Member States in implementing international law", without prejudice to the consideration of the item as a whole, and invites the Secretary-General to provide information on this sub-topic in his report, after seeking the views of Member States.

International economic law

In 2009, legal aspects of international economic law continued to be considered by the United Nations Commission on International Trade Law (UNCITRAL) and by the Sixth Committee of the General Assembly.

International trade law

At its forty-second session (New York, 29 June–17 July), the Commission adopted the UNCITRAL Practice Guide on Cross-Border Insolvency Cooperation (the Practice Guide) and authorized the Secretariat to edit and finalize its text. On the 2007 revision of the International Chamber of Commerce Uniform Customs and Practice for Documentary Credits (UCP 600), UNCITRAL adopted a decision commending its use, as appropriate, in transactions involving the establishment of a documentary credit.

The Commission considered the status of the conventions and model laws emanating from its work and the status of the 1958 New York Convention on the Recognition and Enforcement of Foreign Arbitral Awards (the New York Convention) [YUN 1958, p. 391], on the basis of a Secretariat note [A/CN.9/674], and updated the information available on the UNCITRAL

website. The Commission also had before it a bibliography of writings relating to its work [A/CN.9/673]. UNCITRAL continued its work on public procurement, arbitration and conciliation, insolvency law, security interests, transport law, electronic commerce and commercial fraud. It also reviewed the implementation of the New York Convention, the work on the collection and dissemination of case law on UNCITRAL texts, and training and technical assistance activities.

The report [A/64/17] of the session described actions taken on those topics. (For details, see below, pp. 1317–1320.)

GENERAL ASSEMBLY ACTION

On 16 December [meeting 64], the General Assembly, on the recommendation of the Sixth Committee [A/64/447], adopted **resolution 64/111** without vote [agenda item 79].

Report of the United Nations Commission on International Trade Law on the work of its forty-second session

The General Assembly,

Recalling its resolution 2205(XXI) of 17 December 1966, by which it established the United Nations Commission on International Trade Law with a mandate to further the progressive harmonization and unification of the law of international trade and in that respect to bear in mind the interests of all peoples, in particular those of developing countries, in the extensive development of international trade,

Reaffirming its belief that the progressive modernization and harmonization of international trade law, in reducing or removing legal obstacles to the flow of international trade, especially those affecting developing countries, would contribute significantly to universal economic cooperation among all States on a basis of equality, equity, common interest and respect for the rule of law, to the elimination of discrimination in international trade and, thereby, to peace, stability and the well-being of all peoples,

Having considered the report of the Commission on the work of its forty-second session,

Reiterating its concern that activities undertaken by other bodies in the field of international trade law without adequate coordination with the Commission might lead to undesirable duplication of efforts and would not be in keeping with the aim of promoting efficiency, consistency and coherence in the unification and harmonization of international trade law,

Reaffirming the mandate of the Commission, as the core legal body within the United Nations system in the field of international trade law, to coordinate legal activities in this field, in particular to avoid duplication of efforts, including among organizations formulating rules of international trade, and to promote efficiency, consistency and coherence in the modernization and harmonization of international trade law, and to continue, through its secretariat, to maintain close cooperation with other international organs and organizations, including regional organizations, active in the field of international trade law,

1.   _Takes note with appreciation_ of the report of the United Nations Commission on International Trade Law on the work of its forty-second session;

2.   _Commends_ the Commission for the completion and adoption of its Practice Guide on Cross-Border Insolvency Cooperation;

3.   _Welcomes_ the progress made by the Commission in its work on a revision of its Model Law on Procurement of Goods, Construction and Services through the consideration of chapter I of the draft revised model law, and encourages the Commission to complete its work on the revised model law as soon as possible;

4.   _Also welcomes_ the progress made by the Commission in its work on a revision of its Arbitration Rules, on the preparation of a draft legislative guide on the treatment of enterprise groups in insolvency and on the preparation of a supplement to its Legislative Guide on Secured Transactions dealing with security rights in intellectual property, and endorses the decision of the Commission to undertake further work in the area of arbitration, electronic commerce, transport law and commercial fraud and to consider at its forty-third session proposals for future work in the areas of insolvency and security interests, as set out in its report;

5.   _Further welcomes_ the decision of the Commission to request the Secretariat to hold, resources permitting, an international colloquium on electronic commerce and another international colloquium on security interests;

6.   _Notes with appreciation_ the decision of the Commission with regard to the publication of its Legislative Guide on Secured Transactions, of a commentary on the United Nations Convention on the Assignment of Receivables in International Trade and of a text discussing the interrelationship of various texts on security interests prepared by the Commission, the International Institute for the Unification of Private Law and the Hague Conference on Private International Law;

7.   _Also notes with appreciation_ the decision of the Commission to commend the use of the 2007 revision of the Uniform Customs and Practice for Documentary Credits, published by the International Chamber of Commerce, as appropriate, in transactions involving the establishment of a documentary credit;

8.   _Welcomes_ the progress made in the ongoing project of the Commission on monitoring the implementation of the Convention on the Recognition and Enforcement of Foreign Arbitral Awards, done at New York on 10 June 1958, and the preparation of a draft guide to enactment of the Convention to promote a uniform interpretation and application of the Convention;

9.   _Endorses_ the efforts and initiatives of the Commission, as the core legal body within the United Nations system in the field of international trade law, aimed at increasing coordination of, and cooperation on, legal activities of international and regional organizations active in the field of international trade law, as well as promoting the rule of law at the national and international levels in this field, and in this regard appeals to relevant international and regional organizations to coordinate their legal activities with those of the Commission, to avoid duplication of efforts and to promote efficiency, consistency and coherence in the modernization and harmonization of international trade law;

10.   _Reaffirms_ the importance, in particular for developing countries, of the work of the Commission concerned with technical assistance and cooperation in the field of international trade law reform and development, and in this connection:

(a)   Welcomes the initiatives of the Commission towards expanding, through its secretariat, its technical assistance and cooperation programme, and in that respect encourages the Secretary-General to seek partnerships with State and non-State actors to increase awareness about the work of the Commission and to facilitate the effective implementation of legal standards resulting from its work;

(b)   Expresses its appreciation to the Commission for carrying out technical assistance and cooperation activities, including at the country, subregional and regional levels, and for providing assistance with legislative drafting in the field of international trade law, and draws the attention of the Secretary-General to the limited resources that are made available in this field;

(c)   Expresses its appreciation to the Governments whose contributions enabled the technical assistance and cooperation activities to take place, and appeals to Governments, the relevant bodies of the United Nations system, organizations, institutions and individuals to make voluntary contributions to the United Nations Commission on International Trade Law Trust Fund for Symposia and, where appropriate, to the financing of special projects and otherwise to assist the secretariat of the Commission in carrying out technical assistance activities, in particular in developing countries;

(d)   Reiterates its appeal to the United Nations Development Programme and other bodies responsible for development assistance, such as the World Bank and regional development banks, as well as to Governments in their bilateral aid programmes, to support the technical assistance programme of the Commission and to cooperate and coordinate their activities with those of the Commission, in the light of the relevance and importance of the work and programmes of the Commission for promotion of the rule of law at the national and international levels and for the implementation of the United Nations development agenda, including the achievement of the Millennium Development Goals;

(e)   Notes the request by the Commission that the Secretariat explore the possibility of establishing a presence in regions or specific countries by, for example, having dedicated staff in United Nations field offices, collaborating with such existing field offices or establishing Commission country offices with a view to facilitating the provision of technical assistance with respect to the use and adoption of Commission texts;

11.   _Expresses its appreciation_ to the Government whose contribution to the trust fund established to provide travel assistance to developing countries that are members of the Commission, at their request and in consultation with the Secretary-General, enabled renewal of the provision of that assistance, and appeals to Governments, the relevant bodies of the United Nations system, organizations, institutions and individuals to make voluntary contributions to the trust fund in order to increase expert representation from developing countries at sessions of the Commission and its working groups, necessary to build local expertise and capacities in the field of international trade law in those coun-

tries to facilitate the development of international trade and the promotion of foreign investment;

12. *Decides*, in order to ensure full participation by all Member States in the sessions of the Commission and its working groups, to continue, in the competent Main Committee during the sixty-fourth session of the General Assembly, its consideration of granting travel assistance to the least developed countries that are members of the Commission, at their request and in consultation with the Secretary-General;

13. *Welcomes*, in the light of the recent increase in membership of the Commission and the number of topics being dealt with by the Commission, the comprehensive review undertaken by the Commission of its working methods, which was started at its fortieth session, with the aim of continuing consideration of the matter during its next sessions and with a view to ensuring the high quality of the work of the Commission and international acceptability of its instruments, and in this regard recalls its previous resolutions related to this matter;

14. *Also welcomes* the discussion by the Commission of its role in promoting the rule of law at the national and international levels, in particular the conviction of the Commission that the implementation and effective use of modern private law standards on international trade are essential for advancing good governance, sustained economic development and the eradication of poverty and hunger and that promotion of the rule of law in commercial relations should be an integral part of the broader agenda of the United Nations to promote the rule of law at the national and international levels, including through the Rule of Law Coordination and Resource Group, supported by the Rule of Law Unit in the Executive Office of the Secretary-General, and the fact that the Commission is looking forward to being part of strengthened and coordinated activities of the Organization and sees its role, in particular, as providing assistance to States that seek to promote the rule of law in the area of international and domestic trade and investment;

15. *Further welcomes* the consideration by the Commission of the proposed strategic framework for the period 2010–2011 and its review of the proposed biennial programme plan for the progressive harmonization, modernization and unification of the law of international trade (subprogramme 5), and takes note that, while the Commission noted with satisfaction that the objectives and expected accomplishments of the Secretariat and the overall strategy for subprogramme 5 were in line with its general policy, the Commission also expressed concern that the resources allotted to the Secretariat under subprogramme 5 were insufficient for it to meet, in particular, the increased demand for technical assistance from developing countries and countries with economies in transition to meet their urgent need for law reform in the field of commercial law and urged the Secretary-General to take steps to ensure that the comparatively small amount of additional resources necessary to meet a demand so crucial to development are made available promptly;

16. *Recalls* its resolutions on partnerships between the United Nations and non-State actors, in particular the private sector, and its resolutions in which it encouraged the Commission to further explore different approaches to the use of partnerships with non-State actors in the implementation of its mandate, in particular in the area of technical assistance, in accordance with the applicable principles and guidelines and in cooperation and coordination with other relevant offices of the Secretariat, including the Global Compact Office;

17. *Reiterates its request* to the Secretary-General, in conformity with its resolutions on documentation-related matters, which, in particular, emphasize that any reduction in the length of documents should not adversely affect either the quality of the presentation or the substance of the documents, to bear in mind the particular characteristics of the mandate and work of the Commission in implementing page limits with respect to the documentation of the Commission;

18. *Requests* the Secretary-General to continue providing summary records of the meetings of the Commission, including committees of the whole established by the Commission for the duration of its annual session, relating to the formulation of normative texts;

19. *Recalls* its resolution approving the establishment of the *Yearbook of the United Nations Commission on International Trade Law*, with the aim of making the work of the Commission more widely known and readily available, expresses its concern regarding the timeliness of the publication of the *Yearbook*, and requests the Secretary-General to explore options to facilitate the timely publication of the *Yearbook*;

20. *Stresses* the importance of bringing into effect the conventions emanating from the work of the Commission for the global unification and harmonization of international trade law, and to this end urges States that have not yet done so to consider signing, ratifying or acceding to those conventions;

21. *Welcomes* the preparation of digests of case law relating to the texts of the Commission, such as a digest of case law relating to the United Nations Convention on Contracts for the International Sale of Goods and a digest of case law relating to the Model Law on International Commercial Arbitration of the United Nations Commission on International Trade Law, with the aim of assisting in the dissemination of information on those texts and promoting their use, enactment and uniform interpretation.

Procurement

UNCITRAL [A/64/17] took note of the reports of Working Group I (Procurement) on its fourteenth (Vienna, 8–12 September 2008) [A/CN.9/664], fifteenth (New York, 2–6 February 2009) [A/CN.9/668] and sixteenth (New York, 26–29 May) [A/CN.9/672] sessions relating to the revision of the UNCITRAL Model Law on Procurement of Goods, Constructions and Services, in response to the Commission's 2004 request [YUN 2004, p. 1356]. At those sessions, the Working Group considered issues such as general aspects of electronic procurement, electronic reverse auctions, framework agreements and suppliers' lists. On the evaluation and comparison of tenders, the Working Group formulated a single set of requirements on evaluation criteria that would replace several inconsistent, incomplete provisions in the 1994

Model Procurement Law [YUN 1994, p. 1328], and recommended a requirement to use the most competitive procurement method available.

UNCITRAL approved the holding of a seventeenth session of the Working Group (Vienna, 7–11 December). It also adopted the report of the Committee of the Whole on its consideration of the draft revised model law, which concluded that the revised model law was not ready for adoption at the Commission's current session.

International commercial arbitration

UNCITRAL [A/64/17] considered the reports of Working Group II (Arbitration and Conciliation) on its forty-ninth (Vienna, 15–19 September 2008) [A/CN.9/665] and fiftieth (New York, 9–13 February 2009) [A/CN.9/669] sessions relating to revision of the UNCITRAL Arbitration Rules and commended the Group on progress made. It also approved the holding of a fifty-first Working Group session (Vienna, 14–18 September).

On the proposal to expand the role of the Secretary-General of the Permanent Court of Arbitration at The Hague under the UNCITRAL Arbitration Rules, which was discussed at the Working Group's forty-ninth session, UNCITRAL had before it a 7 April Secretariat note on designating and appointing authorities [A/CN.9/677]. After discussion, the Commission agreed that the existing mechanism, as designed under the 1976 version of the Rules [YUN 1976, p. 823], should not be changed. The Commission, noting that the Working Group had asked for sufficient time to complete its work on the UNCITRAL Arbitration Rules, agreed that the time required for meeting the high standard of UNCITRAL should be taken and hoped that the work on the revised Rules in their generic form would be completed so that their final review and adoption would take place at the Commission's forty-third (2010) session. UNCITRAL also recalled its earlier decision that the question of transparency in treaty-based investor-State arbitration should be addressed immediately after completion of the revised UNCITRAL Arbitration Rules.

Following an oral report on progress, the Commission requested the Secretariat to pursue the preparation of a guide to enactment and use in relation to the entire UNCITRAL Model Law on International Commercial Arbitration, as amended in 2006 [YUN 2006, p. 1528].

Implementation of the 1958 New York Convention

Under the ongoing project, approved by UNCITRAL in 1995 [YUN 1995, p. 1364], aimed at monitoring the legislative implementation of the 1958 New York Convention [YUN 1958, p. 391], UNCITRAL, at its forty-second session [A/64/17], noted that a draft guide to the enactment of the Convention was being planned for preparation, and that information collected during the project would be published on the UNCITRAL website. It also noted that technical assistance activities would be designed and implemented in coordination with other international organizations to address specific issues identified during the project. Recalling that the International Chamber of Commerce Commission on Arbitration had created a task force to examine the national rules of procedure for recognizing and enforcing foreign arbitral awards on a country-by-country basis, UNCITRAL commended the Secretariat for maintaining close collaboration between the two institutions, expressed the wish that more opportunities for joint activities with the Chamber would be identified, and encouraged the Secretariat to develop new joint initiatives.

Transport law

UNCITRAL [A/64/17] considered future work in the area of transport law: commentary on the United Nations Convention on Contracts for the International Carriage of Goods Wholly or Partly by Sea. It had before it a Secretariat note [A/CN.9/679] suggesting possible models of commentary or note that should accompany the publication of the Convention. After discussion, the Commission agreed that the Secretariat should prepare an introductory note to describe how the Convention had come into being, which would be published as an introduction to the index to the legislative history of the text, rather than as an attachment to the text of the Convention.

Insolvency law

UNCITRAL [A/64/17] noted the substantial progress of Working Group V (Insolvency Law) on consideration of the treatment of enterprise groups in insolvency, as reflected in the reports of its thirty-fifth (Vienna, 17–21 November 2008) [A/CN.9/666] and thirty-sixth (New York, 18–22 May 2009) [A/CN.9/671] sessions. It also noted that the Working Group had adopted in substance recommendations on the domestic treatment of enterprise groups; reached agreement on its approach to the international treatment of such groups; and agreed that the text resulting from the work on enterprise groups should form part III of the UNCITRAL Legislative Guide on Insolvency Law and adopt the same format, i.e. recommendations and commentary. UNCITRAL also approved the holding of a thirty-seventh session of the Working Group (Vienna, 9–13 November).

The Commission heard a report on the Eighth Multinational Judicial Colloquium (Vancouver, Canada, 20–21 June), organized by UNCITRAL, the International Association of Insolvency Practitioners and the World Bank, and noted that a report of the colloquium would be prepared and made available on the respective websites of the three organizations.

The Commission also adopted the UNCITRAL Practice Guide on Cross-Border Insolvency Cooperation (the Practice Guide) contained in working paper [A/CN.9/WG.V/WP.86], authorized the Secretariat to edit and finalize the text and requested the Secretary-General to publish, including electronically, the Practice Guide and to transmit it to Governments.

GENERAL ASSEMBLY ACTION

On 16 December [meeting 64], the General Assembly, on the recommendation of the Sixth Committee [A/64/447], adopted **resolution 64/112** without vote [agenda item 79].

Practice Guide on Cross-Border Insolvency Cooperation of the United Nations Commission on International Trade Law

The General Assembly,

Noting that increased trade and investment leads to a greater incidence of cases where business is conducted on a global basis and where enterprises and individuals have assets and interests in more than one State,

Noting also that, where the subjects of insolvency proceedings are debtors with assets in more than one State or are members of an enterprise group with business operations and assets in more than one State, there is generally an urgent need for cross-border cooperation in, and coordination of, the supervision and administration of the assets and affairs of those debtors,

Recognizing that cooperation and coordination in cross-border insolvency cases has the potential to significantly improve the chances for rescuing financially troubled individuals and enterprise groups,

Acknowledging that familiarity with cross-border cooperation and coordination and the means by which it might be implemented in practice is not widespread and that the availability of readily accessible information on current practice with respect to cross-border coordination and cooperation has the potential to facilitate and promote that cooperation and coordination and to avoid unnecessary delay and costs,

Noting with satisfaction the completion and the adoption on 1 July 2009 of the Practice Guide on Cross-Border Insolvency Cooperation by the United Nations Commission on International Trade Law at its forty-second session,

Noting that the preparation of the Practice Guide was the subject of deliberations and consultation with Governments, judges and other professionals active in the field of cross-border insolvency,

1. *Expresses its appreciation* to the United Nations Commission on International Trade Law for the completion and adoption of its Practice Guide on Cross-Border Insolvency Cooperation;

2. *Requests* the Secretary-General to publish, including electronically, the text of the Practice Guide and to transmit it to Governments with the request that the text be made available to relevant authorities so that it becomes widely known and available;

3. *Recommends* that the Practice Guide be given due consideration, as appropriate, by judges, insolvency practitioners and other stakeholders involved in cross-border insolvency proceedings;

4. *Recommends also* that all States continue to consider implementation of the Model Law on Cross-Border Insolvency of the United Nations Commission on International Trade Law.

Electronic commerce

UNCITRAL [A/64/17] considered future work in the area of electronic commerce and had before it a Secretariat note [A/CN.9/678], which provided an update on work related to policy considerations and legal issues in the implementation and operation of single window facilities. It also reported on the activities of the World Customs Organization (WCO)-UNCITRAL Joint Legal Task Force on Coordinated Border Management incorporating the International Single Window. The Commission requested the Secretariat to remain engaged in the WCO-UNCITRAL Joint Legal Task Force; report periodically on its achievements; and convene a working group session should the progress of work warrant it. In that connection, it authorized Working Group IV (Electronic Commerce) to hold its forty-fifth session in New York from 17 to 21 May 2010.

The Commission also had before it further proposals for future work on electronic commerce [A/CN.9/681 & Add.1,2], [A/CN.9/682]. The Commission requested the Secretariat to prepare studies on the basis of the proposals, with a view to reconsidering the matter at a future session, and to hold colloquiums on the same issues, resources permitting.

Commercial fraud

UNCITRAL [A/64/17] considered future work in the area of commercial fraud and was informed that the eighteenth session of the Commission on Crime Prevention and Criminal Justice (see p. 1081) had considered a number of texts on the issue of economic fraud. Those included, among others, a report of the Secretary-General on international cooperation in the prevention, investigation, prosecution and punishment of economic fraud and identity-related crime [E/CN.15/2009/2 & Corr.1]; and a Secretariat note [E/CN.15/2009/15], which contained a section on economic fraud and identity-related crime. UNCITRAL was advised of relevant themes raised at that session, as well as the conclusions reached after the thematic discussions on economic crime and identity-related crime. Collaboration between UNCITRAL and the United Nations Office on Drugs and Crime was also discussed. One delegation proposed that the Commission's work in the area of commercial fraud be extended to include financial fraud, of which the Commission took note.

Security interests

UNCITRAL [A/64/17] considered the report of Working Group VI (Security Interests) on its fourteenth (Vienna, 20–24 October 2008) [A/CN.9/667] and fifteenth (New York, 27 April–1 May 2009) [A/CN.9/670] sessions and noted that the Working Group had made significant progress, completing the reading of two versions of the annex (supplement) to the *UNCITRAL Legislative Guide on Secured Transactions* [YUN 2007, p. 1378] relating to security rights in intellectual property. Emphasizing the importance of the supplement, the Commission expressed appreciation to Working Group VI and the Secretariat for their work, noting that the Working Group had agreed it should be able to complete its work on the draft supplement in time for final approval and adoption at the Commission's forty-third (2010) session.

UNCITRAL requested that the Secretariat expedite publication of the *Legislative Guide* as a whole and in part (the terminology and recommendations as a separate publication). The Secretariat was also asked to raise awareness regarding the *Legislative Guide* and to promote implementation of its recommendations by States by holding seminars, organizing briefing missions, preparing articles for publication, drafting or reviewing draft legislation, and cooperating with other organizations active in the field of secured transactions law reform.

Case law on UNCITRAL texts

UNCITRAL [A/64/17] noted the continuing work under the established system for the collection and dissemination of case law on UNCITRAL texts (CLOUT), consisting of the preparation of case-law abstracts. As at 8 April, 83 issues of CLOUT abstracts had been prepared for publication, dealing with 851 cases. It was widely agreed that CLOUT continued to be an important tool for promoting broader use and better understanding of the legal standards developed by the Commission. UNCITRAL noted the need to enhance the completeness of the collection of case law both from countries that already participated in the CLOUT system, and from countries that were underrepresented. It also noted that work was commencing on a revised edition of the digest of case law on the United Nations Sales Convention [YUN 2002, p. 1345] for possible publication in 2010.

The Commission expressed appreciation to the national correspondents and other contributors for their work in developing the CLOUT system. The term of current national correspondents would expire in 2012, at which time States would be asked to reconfirm the appointment of their national correspondents and every five years thereafter.

Training and technical assistance

UNCITRAL [A/64/17] had before it a Secretariat note [A/CN.9/675 & Add.1] describing technical cooperation and assistance activities undertaken since 2008 [YUN 2008, p. 1475]. The Commission requested the Secretariat to explore the possibility of establishing a presence in regions or specific countries by having dedicated staff in UN field offices, collaboration with such existing field offices, or establishing UNCITRAL country offices. Noting that funds available in the UNCITRAL Trust Fund for Symposia were limited, the Commission reiterated its appeal to States, international organizations and other entities to consider making contributions to the Trust Fund, in order to facilitate planning and enable the Secretariat to meet the increasing requests from developing countries and countries with economies in transition for technical assistance and cooperation activities.

UNCITRAL also co-sponsored the sixteenth Willem C. Vis International Commercial Arbitration Moot (Vienna, 2–9 April) to disseminate information about uniform law texts and teaching of international trade law.

Future work

UNCITRAL [A/64/17] considered the working methods of the Commission and had before it a Secretariat note [A/CN.9/676] containing a first draft of a reference document. As requested by the Commission at its forty-first (2008) session, the draft reference document had been circulated for comments by States and international organizations [YUN 2008, p. 1475], and comments received by the Secretariat had been compiled in documents [A/CN.9/676/Add.1-9]. The Commission also had before it a proposal by France [A/CN.9/680] for revisions to be made to the reference.

The Commission generally agreed that the documents provided a sound basis for formulating a set of guidelines as a reference for the chairpersons, delegates and secretariat of UNCITRAL. The subsequent discussion was based on the Secretariat note containing the first draft of reference document. After informal consultations, possible revisions to paragraphs 11, 12 and 14 were made available for consideration by the Commission. The text of revised paragraphs 14(c) to (e), 37, 39, 41 and 43 were prepared by the Secretariat, yet not considered by the Commission for lack of time.

UNCITRAL approved the holding of its forty-third session in New York from 21 June to 9 July 2010. It also approved the schedule of meetings for its working groups up to and after its forty-third (2010) session.

International organizations and international law

Strengthening the role of the United Nations

Special Committee on United Nations Charter

In accordance with General Assembly resolution 63/127 [YUN 2008, p. 1476], the Special Committee on the Charter of the United Nations and on the Strengthening of the Role of the Organization, at its sixty-fourth session (New York, 17–25 February) [A/64/33], continued to consider proposals relating to: the maintenance of international peace and security; the peaceful settlement of disputes between States; the improvement of the Committee's working methods; and the status of the publications *Repertory of Practice of United Nations Organs* and *Repertoire of the Practice of the Security Council*.

On the maintenance of international peace and security, the Committee continued its consideration of the further revised working paper submitted by the Russian Federation [YUN 2008, p. 1475] entitled "Basic conditions and standard criteria for the introduction and implementation of sanctions imposed by the United Nations," which was submitted to the Committee in 2004 [YUN 2004, p. 1342] and revised in 2005 [YUN 2005, p. 1445]. A revised working paper submitted by the Libyan Arab Jamahiriya on the strengthening of certain principles concerning the application of sanctions [YUN 2002, p. 1329] was also discussed. While some delegations expressed support for its salient points, in particular the provision of possible payment of compensation to target and/or third States for damage caused by sanctions found to have been unlawfully imposed, others expressed doubt concerning the proposal's relevance in view of ongoing work on the Russian Federation's proposal on a similar issue. The Special Committee continued its consideration of implementation of the Charter provisions relating to assistance to third States affected by sanctions, and was briefed by representatives of the Department of Political Affairs and the Department of Economic and Social Affairs on developments on the matter.

A further revised working paper entitled "Strengthening of the role of the Organization and enhancing its effectiveness" [A/AC.182/L.93/Rev.1], introduced by Cuba, was discussed. The sponsor noted that the issues addressed in the working paper were highly relevant in the light of the persistence of international tensions that threatened international peace and security, and invited delegations to examine it. The delegation of Libya also requested that a revised proposal it had submitted on strengthening the UN role in the maintenance of international peace and security [YUN 1998, p. 1233] be kept on the agenda of the Special Committee and be transmitted to the Sixth Committee.

On the revised working paper submitted by Belarus and the Russian Federation in 2005 [YUN 2005, p. 1446], which recommended that an advisory opinion be requested from the International Court of Justice (ICJ) as to the legal consequences of a State's resort to the use of force without prior Security Council authorization, except in the exercise of the right to self-defence. The Special Committee heard a statement by the representative of Belarus, who said that the goal of the proposal was to achieve a uniform interpretation and application of the Charter provisions establishing the conditions for the resort to the use of armed force for the purpose of stopping aggression and restoring international peace and security. The Special Committee decided to keep the proposal on its agenda.

Delegations reaffirmed that the peaceful settlement of disputes was one of the basic principles of international law under the UN Charter and the most effective and efficient tool for maintaining international peace and security. While a concern was expressed on the role of the Council regarding unilateral use of force under the pretext of self-defence, States were reminded of their obligation to settle international disputes by peaceful means. The role of ICJ in adjudicating disputes among States was also emphasized.

Delegations commended ongoing Secretariat efforts to reduce the backlog in preparation of the *Repertory of Practice of United Nations Organs* and *Repertoire of the Practice of the Security Council*, including the enhanced cooperation with academic institutions and progress made towards making both publications available on the Internet. The *Repertory* website continued to be updated regularly and the thirteenth supplement to the *Repertoire* had been completed; its advance version was accessible in its entirety on the *Repertoire* website. The Committee made recommendations for the General Assembly to commend the Secretary-General for progress made on both publications and call on him to continue efforts to update the two publications and make them available in all their respective language versions, as well as to reiterate its call for voluntary contributions to the trust funds for updating the *Repertoire* and eliminating the backlog of the *Repertory*.

On the identification of new subjects, Mexico, on behalf of the Rio Group, recalled the proposal by the Group entitled "Consideration of the legal aspects of the reform of the United Nations" reproduced in the Committee's 2008 report [YUN 2008, p. 1476]. Following discussion, the Special Committee decided to remove that proposal from its agenda.

Report of Secretary-General. In response to General Assembly resolution 63/127, the Secretary-General submitted a July report [A/64/125] outlining the progress made in updating the *Repertory of Practice of United Nations Organs* and *Repertoire of the Practice of the Security Council.*

With respect to the *Repertory,* the Secretary-General concluded that the Assembly might wish to note the progress made in the preparation of *Repertory* studies and their posting on the Internet in English, French and Spanish; consider the recommendations of the Special Committee—including the increased use of the UN internship programme and expanded cooperation with academic institutions for the preparation of the studies and the sponsoring, on a voluntary basis, and with no cost to the United Nations, of associate experts to assist in updating the publication; express appreciation for the contribution received to the trust fund for the elimination of the backlog of the *Repertory*; note the progress made towards the elimination of the backlog through use of the trust fund; and encourage States to make additional contributions to it.

With regard to the *Repertoire,* the Secretary-General concluded that the Assembly might wish to note the progress made towards its updating and its posting in electronic form in all language versions on the UN website; call for voluntary contributions to the trust fund for updating the *Repertoire*; and note the support of Germany, Italy and Norway for sponsoring associate experts, and encourage other States to consider providing such assistance.

GENERAL ASSEMBLY ACTION

On 16 December [meeting 64], the General Assembly, on the recommendation of the Sixth Committee [A/64/450], adopted **resolution 64/115** without vote [agenda item 82].

Report of the Special Committee on the Charter of the United Nations and on the Strengthening of the Role of the Organization

The General Assembly,

Recalling its resolution 3499(XXX) of 15 December 1975, by which it established the Special Committee on the Charter of the United Nations and on the Strengthening of the Role of the Organization, and its relevant resolutions adopted at subsequent sessions,

Recalling also its resolution 47/233 of 17 August 1993 on the revitalization of the work of the General Assembly,

Recalling further its resolution 47/62 of 11 December 1992 on the question of equitable representation on and increase in the membership of the Security Council,

Taking note of the report of the Open-ended Working Group on the Question of Equitable Representation on and

Increase in the Membership of the Security Council and Other Matters related to the Security Council,

Recalling the elements relevant to the work of the Special Committee contained in its resolution 47/120 B of 20 September 1993,

Recalling also its resolution 51/241 of 31 July 1997 on the strengthening of the United Nations system and its resolution 51/242 of 15 September 1997, entitled "Supplement to an Agenda for Peace", by which it adopted the texts on coordination and the question of sanctions imposed by the United Nations, which are annexed to that resolution,

Concerned about the special economic problems confronting certain States arising from the carrying out of preventive or enforcement measures taken by the Security Council against other States, and taking into account the obligation of Members of the United Nations under Article 49 of the Charter of the United Nations to join in affording mutual assistance in carrying out the measures decided upon by the Council,

Recalling the right of third States confronted with special economic problems of that nature to consult the Security Council with regard to a solution of those problems, in accordance with Article 50 of the Charter,

Recalling also that the International Court of Justice is the principal judicial organ of the United Nations, and reaffirming its authority and independence,

Mindful of the adoption of the revised working papers on the working methods of the Special Committee,

Taking note of the report of the Secretary-General on the *Repertory of Practice of United Nations Organs* and the *Repertoire of the Practice of the Security Council,*

Taking note also of paragraphs 106 to 110, 176 and 177 of the 2005 World Summit Outcome,

Mindful of the decision of the Special Committee in which it expressed its readiness to engage, as appropriate, in the implementation of any decisions that might be taken at the High-level Plenary Meeting of the sixtieth session of the General Assembly in September 2005 that concerned the Charter and any amendments thereto,

Recalling the provisions of its resolutions 50/51 of 11 December 1995, 51/208 of 17 December 1996, 52/162 of 15 December 1997, 53/107 of 8 December 1998, 54/107 of 9 December 1999, 55/157 of 12 December 2000, 56/87 of 12 December 2001, 57/25 of 19 November 2002, 58/80 of 9 December 2003 and 59/45 of 2 December 2004,

Recalling also its resolution 63/127 of 11 December 2008,

Having considered the report of the Special Committee on the work of its session held in 2009,

Noting with appreciation the work done by the Special Committee to encourage States to focus on the need to prevent and to settle peacefully their disputes which are likely to endanger the maintenance of international peace and security,

1. *Takes note* of the report of the Special Committee on the Charter of the United Nations and on the Strengthening of the Role of the Organization;

2. *Takes note also* of the document entitled "Introduction and implementation of sanctions imposed by the United Nations" as set out in the annex to the present resolution;

3. *Decides* that the Special Committee shall hold its next session from 1 to 9 March 2010;

4. *Requests* the Special Committee, at its session in 2010, in accordance with paragraph 5 of General Assembly resolution 50/52 of 11 December 1995:

(a) To continue its consideration of all proposals concerning the question of the maintenance of international peace and security in all its aspects in order to strengthen the role of the United Nations, and, in this context, to consider other proposals relating to the maintenance of international peace and security already submitted or which may be submitted to the Special Committee at its session in 2010;

(b) To continue to consider, on a priority basis and in an appropriate substantive manner and framework, the question of the implementation of the provisions of the Charter of the United Nations related to assistance to third States affected by the application of sanctions under Chapter VII of the Charter based on all of the related reports of the Secretary-General and the proposals submitted on the question;

(c) To keep on its agenda the question of the peaceful settlement of disputes between States;

(d) To consider, as appropriate, any proposal referred to it by the General Assembly in the implementation of the decisions of the High-level Plenary Meeting of the sixtieth session of the Assembly in September 2005 that concern the Charter and any amendments thereto;

(e) To continue to consider, on a priority basis, ways and means of improving its working methods and enhancing its efficiency with a view to identifying widely acceptable measures for future implementation;

5. *Invites* the Special Committee at its session in 2010 to continue to identify new subjects for consideration in its future work with a view to contributing to the revitalization of the work of the United Nations;

6. *Notes* the readiness of the Special Committee to provide, within its mandate, such assistance as may be sought at the request of other subsidiary bodies of the General Assembly in relation to any issues before them;

7. *Requests* the Special Committee to submit a report on its work to the General Assembly at its sixty-fifth session;

8. *Recognizes* the important role of the International Court of Justice, the principal judicial organ of the United Nations, in adjudicating disputes among States and the value of its work, as well as the importance of having recourse to the Court in the peaceful settlement of disputes, takes note, consistent with Article 96 of the Charter, of the Court's advisory jurisdiction that may be requested by the General Assembly, the Security Council or other authorized organs of the United Nations and the specialized agencies, and requests the Secretary-General to distribute, in due course, the advisory opinions requested by the principal organs of the United Nations as official documents of the United Nations;

9. *Commends* the Secretary-General for the progress made in the preparation of studies of the *Repertory of Practice of United Nations Organs*, including the increased use of the internship programme of the United Nations and further expanded cooperation with academic institutions for this purpose, as well as the progress made towards updating the *Repertoire of the Practice of the Security Council*;

10. *Notes with appreciation* the contributions made by Member States to the trust fund for the updating of the *Repertoire*, as well as the trust fund for the elimination of the backlog in the *Repertory*;

11. *Reiterates its call for* voluntary contributions to the trust fund for the updating of the *Repertoire*; voluntary contributions to the trust fund for the elimination of the backlog in the *Repertory* so as to further support the Secretariat in carrying out the effective elimination of that backlog; as well as the sponsoring, on a voluntary basis, and with no cost to the United Nations, of associate experts to assist in the updating of the two publications;

12. *Calls upon* the Secretary-General to continue his efforts towards updating the two publications and making them available electronically in all their respective language versions;

13. *Reiterates* the responsibility of the Secretary-General for the quality of the *Repertory* and the *Repertoire*, and with regard to the *Repertoire*, calls upon the Secretary-General to continue to follow the modalities outlined in paragraphs 102 to 106 of the report of the Secretary-General of 18 September 1952;

14. *Requests* the Secretary-General to submit a report on both the *Repertory* and the *Repertoire* to the General Assembly at its sixty-fifth session;

15. *Also requests* the Secretary-General to brief the Special Committee at its next session on the information referred to in paragraph 11 of his report on the implementation of the provisions of the Charter of the United Nations related to assistance to third States affected by the application of sanctions;

16. *Further requests* the Secretary-General to submit a report on the implementation of the provisions of the Charter of the United Nations related to assistance to third States affected by the application of sanctions to the General Assembly at its sixty-fifth session, under the item entitled "Report of the Special Committee on the Charter of the United Nations and on the Strengthening of the Role of the Organization";

17. *Decides* to include in the provisional agenda of its sixty-fifth session the item entitled "Report of the Special Committee on the Charter of the United Nations and on the Strengthening of the Role of the Organization".

ANNEX
Introduction and implementation of sanctions imposed by the United Nations

I. General issues

1. Sanctions remain an important tool under the Charter of the United Nations in efforts to maintain international peace and security without recourse to the use of force. Sanctions should be carefully targeted in support of clear and legitimate objectives under the Charter and be implemented in ways that balance effectiveness to achieve the desired results against possible adverse consequences, including socio-economic and humanitarian consequences, for populations and third States.

2. The purpose of sanctions is to modify the behaviour of the target State, party, individual or entity threatening international peace and security and not to punish or otherwise exact retribution. Sanctions regimes should be commensurate with these objectives.

3.   Sanctions may be resorted to by the Security Council when it determines the existence of any threat to the peace, breach of the peace, or act of aggression. The Security Council should be guided by the approach taken in annex II to General Assembly resolution 51/242, where it is indicated that sanctions should be resorted to only with the utmost caution, when other peaceful options provided by the Charter are inadequate. The reasons that necessitate the imposition of sanctions should be identified and stated in advance.

4.   The Security Council should introduce sanctions in conformity with the provisions of the Charter, taking into account other applicable rules of international law, in particular all of those related to human rights and fundamental freedoms.

5.   Best practices and guidelines adopted by the Security Council and the General Assembly in the field of sanctions, in particular those contained in the 2005 World Summit Outcome, General Assembly resolution 51/242 and Security Council resolutions 1730(2006), 1735(2006) and 1822(2008), should be taken into account in the elaboration and implementation of sanctions regimes. The best practices and methods contained in the report of the Informal Working Group of the Security Council on General Issues of Sanctions (S/2006/997), as taken note of in Security Council resolution 1732(2006), might also be considered for these purposes.

6.   Sanctions should be implemented and monitored effectively with clear benchmarks and should, as appropriate, have an expiration date or be periodically reviewed with a view to lifting them or not, or to adjusting them, taking into account the humanitarian situation and depending on the fulfilment by the target State and other parties of the requirements of the Security Council. Sanctions should remain in place for as limited a period as necessary to achieve their objectives and be lifted once their objectives have been achieved.

7.   Sanctions regimes with regard to individuals and entities should ensure that the decision to list such individuals and entities is based on fair and clear procedures, including, as appropriate, a detailed statement of case provided by Member States, and that regular reviews of names on the list are conducted; ensure, to the degree possible, maximum specificity in identifying individuals and entities to be targeted; and ensure also that fair and clear procedures for de-listing exist early in sanctions regimes. Listed individuals and entities should be notified of the decision and of as much detail as possible in the publicly releasable portion of the statement of case. There should be an appropriate mechanism for handling individuals' or entities' requests for de-listing.

II.   Unintended side effects of sanctions

8.   Sanctions should avoid to the extent possible adverse humanitarian effects or unintended consequences for individuals and entities not targeted or third States. Targeted sanctions are a way of achieving this.

9.   An objective assessment of the short-term and long-term socio-economic and humanitarian consequences of sanctions should be conducted by the Security Council and its sanctions committees with the assistance of the Secretariat at the stage of their preparation, as appropriate, and in the course of their implementation. In this regard, the methodology for the assessment of the humanitarian implications of sanctions reflected in the *Sanctions Assessment Handbook* (2004) might be useful.

10.   Information on the humanitarian consequences of the introduction and implementation of sanctions, including those which have a bearing on the basic living conditions of the civilian population of the target State, on its socio-economic development and on third States which have suffered or may suffer as a result of their implementation, may be useful for the Security Council and its sanctions committees to consider.

11.   To the maximum extent possible, situations in which the consequences of the introduction of sanctions would inflict considerable material and financial harm on third States or in which the civilian population in the target State or third States would experience considerable adverse consequences should be avoided.

12.   Humanitarian and other exemptions should be made available in a consistent manner to all targeted measures such as arms embargoes, travel restrictions, aviation bans and financial sanctions, and considered in accordance with fair and clear procedures.

13.   Efforts should be made to ensure that sanctions regimes do not hinder an adequate supply of humanitarian assistance from reaching the civilian population. Targeted States and parties should cooperate to this end. Essential humanitarian assistance should be considered for exemption by the relevant United Nations bodies, including the sanctions committees.

14.   The principles of neutrality, independence, transparency, impartiality and non-discrimination should guide the provision of humanitarian and medical assistance and other forms of humanitarian support for all sectors and groups of the civilian population.

15.   Humanitarian and medical assistance and other forms of humanitarian support for all sectors and groups of the civilian population should not be provided without the consent of the recipient State or a request on its part.

16.   In emergency situations and cases of force majeure (natural disasters, threat of famine, mass disturbances resulting in the disorganization of the country's Government), consideration should be given to the suspension of sanctions in order to prevent a humanitarian disaster. A decision on this must be taken in each specific case.

17.   Decisions on sanctions should be in accordance with the purposes and principles set out in the Charter of the United Nations. Sanctions regimes should be designed to avoid unintended consequences in the target State or third States which may lead to violations of human rights and fundamental freedoms.

III.   Implementation

18.   Sanctions should be implemented in good faith by all States.

19.   Monitoring and compliance are first and foremost the responsibility of individual Member States. Member States should endeavour to prevent or correct activities in violation of the sanctions measures within their jurisdiction. In this regard the provisions of the report of the Informal Working Group of the Security Council on General Issues of Sanctions (S/2006/997) should be taken into account, as appropriate.

20. International monitoring by the Security Council or by one of its subsidiary organs of compliance with sanctions measures, in accordance with relevant Security Council resolutions, can contribute to the effectiveness of United Nations sanctions. States that may require assistance in the implementation and monitoring of sanctions may seek the assistance of the United Nations or relevant regional organizations and donors.

21. States and relevant international and regional organizations with the capacity to do so should be encouraged to offer appropriate technical and financial assistance to other States to enhance their capacity to implement sanctions effectively.

22. States should be encouraged to cooperate in exchanging information about the legislative, administrative and practical implementation of sanctions.

Charter provisions relating to sanctions

Special Committee consideration. During the Special Committee's consideration of the implementation of the Charter provisions related to assistance to third States affected by sanctions [A/64/33], delegations reaffirmed the use of sanctions as an important tool in the maintenance and restoration of international peace and security, and that they should be designed to minimize any adverse impact on civilian populations and third States. Several delegations recalled the provisions of Assembly resolutions addressing the topic, noted the work accomplished by the Council's Informal Working Group on General Issues of Sanctions and expressed the view that the Council had effectively addressed the question of the effects of sanctions. The more precise methods adopted by the Council and its committees had been increasingly successful in avoiding unintended effects, and the Special Committee should avoid duplication of work and conclude its consideration of the topic. Other delegations said that the issue of assistance to third States affected by sanctions should be given special consideration by the Special Committee—as even targeted sanctions could have a significant impact on third States—and that certain assessment mechanisms and other practical measures appeared necessary. A call was made for the establishment of a ready-to-function mechanism relating to assistance to third States affected by sanctions, as well as the development of a methodology for assessing the impact of sanctions on third States and exploring measures to assist those affected. On the need to establish a specific fund to minimize the losses incurred as a consequence of sanctions, some delegations questioned it, while others held that calls for special funds or multilateral assistance in such cases deserved in-depth consideration.

The further revised working paper by the Russian Federation entitled "Basic conditions and standard criteria for the introduction and implementation of sanctions imposed by the United Nations" [YUN 2007, p. 1382] was also discussed. Several delegations supported further consideration by the Committee of the proposal and encouraged it to conclude its deliberations. Other delegations stressed that important issues remained to be discussed. The Special Committee continued its work on the working document entitled "Introduction and implementation of sanctions imposed by the United Nations", annexed to the report, and decided to submit it to the Assembly for consideration with a view to its adoption.

Report of Secretary-General. In response to General Assembly resolution 63/127 [YUN 2008, p. 1476], the Secretary-General submitted an August report [A/64/225] highlighting Secretariat arrangements related to assistance to third States affected by the application of sanctions; recent developments concerning the activities of the Assembly and the Economic and Social Council in the area of assistance to such States; and operational changes due to the shift in focus in the Security Council and its sanctions committees' towards targeted sanctions.

UN Programme for the teaching and study of international law

In response to General Assembly resolution 62/62 [YUN 2007, p. 1383], the Secretary-General submitted an October report [A/64/495] on the United Nations Programme of Assistance in the Teaching, Study, Dissemination and Wider Appreciation of International Law, which covered activities during the 2008–2009 biennium.

Activities during 2009 included the holding of the forty-fifth session of the International Law Seminar (Geneva, 6–24 July) and the convening of the International Law Fellowship Programme (The Hague, 6 July–14 August), in which fellows—nine men and seven women—from 16 countries participated. In addition, lectures, seminars and study visits were organized by the United Nations Office of Legal Affairs (OLA) and the United Nations Institute for Training and Research. The Department of Public Information, in consultation with OLA, launched the new international law web page, as approved by the United Nations Legal Counsel.

The OLA Codification Division also organized regional courses in international law, and was responsible for the United Nations Audiovisual Library of International Law, which was created in response to the increasing demand for international law training and in October received the 2009 Best Website Award from the International Association of Law Librarians at its annual meeting in Turkey. The Division also maintained 19 websites relating to the codification and progressive development of international law, the Programme of Assistance and various legal publications, four of which were created during the reporting period: the *United Nations Reports of International Arbitral Awards*; the *United Nations Juridical Yearbook*, including legal opinions since 1963; the UN diplomatic conferences containing the *travaux préparatoires* of legal instruments adopted on the basis of drafts prepared by ILC; and the UN legal publications portal, featuring a global keyword, sentence and full-text seach capability. The Division contributed published UN legal opinions to the Global Legal Information Network—a public database of laws, regulations, judicial decisions and other legal sources contributed by governmental agencies and international organizations, which aimed to address the need of governmental organs, during the law-making process, to have knowledge of the laws and regulations of other jurisdictions. The Office's Treaty Section expanded its technical assistance and training programme on participation in multilateral treaties, registration of treaties, depositary practices and final clauses. Another programme included the Hamilton Shirley Amerasinghe Memorial Fellowship on the Law of the Sea (see p. 1363), awarded annually by OLA, which provided successful fellows, subject to the availability of new voluntary contributions, with facilities for postgraduate study and research in that area.

The report also described the legal publications issued during the year, provided guidelines and recommendations for the execution of the 2010–2011 Programme of Assistance and outlined the administrative and financial implications of UN participation in the Programme for the 2008–2009 and 2010–2011 bienniums.

The Advisory Committee on the Programme held its forty-third and forty-fourth sessions on 6 November 2008 and 16 October 2009, respectively.

GENERAL ASSEMBLY ACTION

On 16 December [meeting 64], the General Assembly, on the recommendation of the Sixth Committee [A/64/448], adopted **resolution 64/113** without vote [agenda item 80].

United Nations Programme of Assistance in the Teaching, Study, Dissemination and Wider Appreciation of International Law

The General Assembly,

Recalling its resolution 2099(XX) of 20 December 1965, in which it established the United Nations Programme of Assistance in the Teaching, Study, Dissemination and Wider Appreciation of International Law to contribute towards a better knowledge of international law as a means of strengthening international peace and security and of promoting friendly relations and cooperation among States,

Recognizing that the Programme of Assistance is a core activity of the United Nations and that the Programme

has provided the foundation for the efforts of the United Nations to promote a better knowledge of international law for more than four decades,

Recognizing also that the increasing demand for international law training and dissemination activities creates new challenges for the Programme of Assistance,

Taking note with appreciation of the report of the Secretary-General on the implementation of the Programme of Assistance and the views of the Advisory Committee on the Programme of Assistance, which are contained in that report,

Considering that international law should occupy an appropriate place in the teaching of legal disciplines at all universities,

Convinced that States, international and regional organizations, universities and institutions should be encouraged to give further support to the Programme of Assistance and increase their activities to promote the teaching, study, dissemination and wider appreciation of international law, in particular those activities which are of special benefit to persons from developing countries,

Reaffirming that in the conduct of the Programme of Assistance it would be desirable to use as far as possible the resources and facilities made available by Member States, international and regional organizations, universities, institutions and others,

Reaffirming also the hope that, in appointing lecturers for the seminars to be held within the framework of the fellowship programmes in international law, account would be taken of the need to secure the representation of major legal systems and balance among various geographical regions,

1. *Approves* the guidelines and recommendations contained in section III of the report of the Secretary-General, in particular those designed to achieve the best possible results in the administration of the United Nations Programme of Assistance in the Teaching, Study, Dissemination and Wider Appreciation of International Law within a policy of maximum financial restraint;

2. *Authorizes* the Secretary-General to carry out in 2010 and 2011 the activities specified in his report, including the provision of:

(a) A number of fellowships to be determined in the light of the overall resources for the Programme of Assistance and to be awarded to qualified candidates from developing countries to attend the International Law Fellowship Programme in The Hague in 2010 and 2011;

(b) A number of fellowships to be determined in the light of the overall resources for the Programme of Assistance and to be awarded to qualified candidates from developing countries to attend regional courses in international law in 2010 and 2011;

and to finance the above activities from provisions in the regular budget, when appropriate, as well as from voluntary financial contributions for these fellowships, which would be received as a result of the requests set out in paragraphs 19 to 21 below;

3. *Also authorizes* the Secretary-General to award a minimum of one scholarship in both 2010 and 2011 under the Hamilton Shirley Amerasinghe Memorial Fellowship on the Law of the Sea, subject to the availability of new voluntary contributions made specifically for this fellowship;

4. *Expresses its appreciation* to the Secretary-General for his efforts to strengthen, expand and enhance the international law training and dissemination activities within the framework of the Programme of Assistance in 2008 and 2009;

5. *Requests* the Secretary-General to consider admitting, for participation in the various components of the Programme of Assistance, candidates from countries willing to bear the entire cost of such participation;

6. *Also requests* the Secretary-General to continue to provide the necessary resources to the programme budget for the Programme of Assistance for the next and the future bienniums with a view to ensuring the continued effectiveness of the Programme of Assistance;

7. *Recognizes* the importance of the United Nations legal publications prepared by the Office of Legal Affairs of the Secretariat, and strongly encourages their continued publication;

8. *Welcomes* the efforts undertaken by the Office of Legal Affairs to bring up to date the United Nations legal publications, and, in particular, commends the Codification Division for its desktop publishing initiative, which has greatly enhanced the timely issuance of its legal publications;

9. *Welcomes* the creation by the Codification Division of the new websites for the *United Nations Juridical Yearbook*, the United Nations diplomatic conferences, and the United Nations legal publications portal, as well as the expansion of the website on the *Summaries of Judgments, Advisory Opinions and Orders of the International Court of Justice*;

10. *Encourages* the Office of Legal Affairs to continue to maintain and expand its websites listed in annex I to the report of the Secretary-General as an invaluable tool for the dissemination of international law materials as well as for advanced legal research;

11. *Recognizes* the importance of the United Nations Audiovisual Library of International Law as a major contribution to the teaching and dissemination of international law around the world, and urges States to make voluntary contributions to enable the Codification Division to continue and further develop the Library;

12. *Commends* the Codification Division on the 2009 Best Website Award granted to the United Nations Audiovisual Library of International Law by the International Association of Law Libraries at its annual meeting, held in Turkey in October 2009;

13. *Requests* the Secretary-General to provide relevant information to the Advisory Committee on the Programme of Assistance, to facilitate its consideration of the matter referred to in paragraph 89 of his report;

14. *Encourages* the use of the internship programme for the preparation of materials for the United Nations Audiovisual Library of International Law;

15. *Welcomes* the training and technical assistance activities in international law undertaken by the Office of Legal Affairs in the framework of the Programme of Assistance, as described in the report of the Secretary-General, and encourages the continuation of such activities within available resources;

16. *Expresses its appreciation* to the United Nations Institute for Training and Research for its participation in the Programme of Assistance through the activities described in the report of the Secretary-General;

17. *Also expresses its appreciation* to The Hague Academy of International Law for the valuable contribution it continues to make to the Programme of Assistance, which has enabled candidates under the International Law Fellowship Programme to attend and participate in the Fellowship Programme in conjunction with the Academy courses;

18. *Notes with appreciation* the contributions of The Hague Academy to the teaching, study, dissemination and wider appreciation of international law, and calls upon Member States and interested organizations to give favourable consideration to the appeal of the Academy for a continuation of support and a possible increase in their financial contributions, to enable the Academy to carry out its activities, particularly those relating to the summer courses, regional courses and programmes of the Centre for Studies and Research in International Law and International Relations;

19. *Requests* the Secretary-General to continue to publicize the Programme of Assistance and periodically to invite Member States, universities, philanthropic foundations and other interested national and international institutions and organizations, as well as individuals, to make voluntary contributions towards the financing of the Programme of Assistance or otherwise to assist in its implementation and possible expansion;

20. *Reiterates its request* to Member States and to interested organizations and individuals to make voluntary contributions, inter alia, for the International Law Fellowship Programme and the United Nations Audiovisual Library of International Law, and expresses its appreciation to those Member States, institutions and individuals that have made voluntary contributions for this purpose;

21. *Urges* in particular all Governments to make voluntary contributions for regional courses in international law, as an important complement to the International Law Fellowship Programme, organized by the Codification Division of the Office of Legal Affairs, thus alleviating the burden on prospective host countries and making it possible to resume the organization of regional courses;

22. *Requests* the Secretary-General to report to the General Assembly at its sixty-fifth session on the implementation of the Programme of Assistance during 2010 and, following consultations with the Advisory Committee on the Programme of Assistance, to submit recommendations regarding the execution of the Programme of Assistance in subsequent years;

23. *Decides* to include in the provisional agenda of its sixty-fifth session the item entitled "United Nations Programme of Assistance in the Teaching, Study, Dissemination and Wider Appreciation of International Law".

Host country relations

At four meetings held in New York (12 March, 16 June, 2 October and 2 November), the Committee on Relations with the Host Country considered the following aspects of relations between the UN diplomatic community and the United States, the host country: transportation, including the use of motor vehicles, parking and related matters; acceleration of immigration and customs procedures; and host country travel regulations.

The recommendations and conclusions on those items, approved by the Committee at its 2 November meeting, were incorporated in its report [A/64/26]. The Committee expressed appreciation for the host country's efforts to maintain appropriate conditions for delegations and missions accredited to the United Nations and anticipated that all issues raised at its meetings would be duly settled in accordance with international law.

Noting the importance of the observance of privileges and immunities, the Committee emphasized the need to solve, through negotiations, problems that might arise in that regard for the normal functioning of accredited delegations and missions. It urged the host country to continue to take appropriate action, such as the training of police, security, customs and border control officers, with a view to maintaining respect for diplomatic privileges and immunities. In case of violations, the Committee urged the host country to ensure that such cases were properly investigated and remedied, in accordance with applicable law. Considering that the security of missions and the safety of their personnel were indispensable for their effective functioning, the Committee appreciated the host country's efforts to that end and anticipated that the host country would continue to take all measures necessary to prevent any interference with the missions' functioning.

Noting the problems experienced by some missions in connection with the implementation of the Parking Programme for Diplomatic Vehicles, in force since 2002 [YUN 2002, p. 1338], the Committee decided to remain seized of the matter, with a view to ensuring its proper implementation in a manner that was fair, non-discriminatory, effective and therefore consistent with international law. It also requested that the host country continue to bring to the attention of New York City officials reports about other problems experienced by permanent missions or their staff, in order to improve the conditions for their functioning and to promote compliance with international norms concerning diplomatic privileges and immunities.

The Committee anticipated that the host country would enhance its efforts to ensure the issuance, in a timely manner, of entry visas to representatives of Member States to travel to New York on official UN business, and noted that a number of delegations had requested shortening the time frame applied by the host country for issuance of entry visas since the existing time frame posed difficulties for the full-fledged participation of Member States in UN meetings.

On host country travel regulations for personnel of certain missions and staff members of the Secretariat of certain nationalities, the Committee urged the host country to remove the remaining restrictions. It also stressed the importance of permanent missions, their personnel and Secretariat personnel meeting their financial obligations.

The Committee reiterated its appreciation to the representative of the United States Mission in charge of host country affairs and to the Host Country Affairs Section of the United States Mission to the United Nations, as well as to those local entities, in particular the New York City Commission for the United Nations, Consular Corps and Protocol, that contributed to its efforts to help accommodate the needs, interests and requirements of the diplomatic community and to promote mutual understanding between the diplomatic community and the people of the City of New York.

Communications. The Committee had before it a letter from Venezuela to the Secretary-General regarding a delay in the processing of a visa application by the host country [A/AC.154/387], as well as the response from the United States as host country [A/AC.154/388].

GENERAL ASSEMBLY ACTION

On 16 December [meeting 64], the General Assembly, on the recommendation of the Sixth Committee [A/64/455], adopted **resolution 64/120** without vote [agenda item 164].

Report of the Committee on Relations with the Host Country

The General Assembly,

Having considered the report of the Committee on Relations with the Host Country,

Recalling Article 105 of the Charter of the United Nations, the Convention on the Privileges and Immunities of the United Nations, the Agreement between the United Nations and the United States of America regarding the Headquarters of the United Nations and the responsibilities of the host country,

Recalling also that, in accordance with paragraph 7 of General Assembly resolution 2819(XXVI) of 15 December 1971, the Committee should consider, and advise the host country on, issues arising in connection with the implementation of the Agreement between the United Nations and the United States of America regarding the Headquarters of the United Nations,

Recognizing that effective measures should continue to be taken by the competent authorities of the host country, in particular to prevent any acts violating the security of missions and the safety of their personnel,

1. *Endorses* the recommendations and conclusions of the Committee on Relations with the Host Country contained in paragraph 25 of its report;

2. *Considers* that the maintenance of appropriate conditions for the normal work of the delegations and the missions accredited to the United Nations and the observance of their privileges and immunities, which is an issue of great importance, are in the interest of the United Nations and all Member States, and requests the host country to continue to solve, through negotiations, problems that might arise and to take all measures necessary to prevent any interference with the functioning of missions; and urges the host country to continue to take appropriate action, such as training of police, security, customs and border control officers, with a view to maintaining respect for diplomatic privileges and immunities and if violations occur to ensure that such cases are properly investigated and remedied, in accordance with applicable law;

3. *Notes* the problems experienced by some permanent missions in connection with the implementation of the Parking Programme for Diplomatic Vehicles and shall remain seized of the matter, with a view to continuing to maintain the proper implementation of the Parking Programme in a manner that is fair, non-discriminatory, effective and therefore consistent with international law;

4. *Requests* the host country to consider removing the remaining travel restrictions imposed by it on staff of certain missions and staff members of the Secretariat of certain nationalities, and, in this regard, notes the positions of affected States, as reflected in the report of the Committee, of the Secretary-General and of the host country;

5. *Notes* that the Committee anticipates that the host country will enhance its efforts to ensure the issuance of entry visas, in a timely manner, to representatives of Member States, pursuant to article IV, section 11, of the Agreement between the United Nations and the United States of America regarding the Headquarters of the United Nations to travel to New York on United Nations business; and

notes that the Committee anticipates that the host country will enhance efforts, including visa issuance, to facilitate the participation of representatives of Member States in other United Nations meetings as appropriate;

6. *Notes also* that a number of delegations have requested shortening the time frame applied by the host country for issuance of entry visas to representatives of Member States, since this time frame poses difficulties for the full-fledged participation of Member States in United Nations meetings;

7. *Expresses its appreciation* for the efforts made by the host country, and hopes that the issues raised at the meetings of the Committee will continue to be resolved in a spirit of cooperation and in accordance with international law;

8. *Affirms* the importance of the Committee being in a position to fulfil its mandate and meet on short notice to deal with urgent and important matters concerning the relations between the United Nations and the host country, and in that connection requests the Secretariat and the Committee on Conferences to accord priority to requests from the Committee on Relations with the Host Country for conference-servicing facilities for meetings of that Committee that must be held while the General Assembly and its Main Committees are meeting, without prejudice to the requirements of those bodies and on an "as available" basis;

9. *Requests* the Secretary-General to remain actively engaged in all aspects of the relations of the United Nations with the host country;

10. *Requests* the Committee to continue its work in conformity with General Assembly resolution 2819(XXVI);

11. *Decides* to include in the provisional agenda of its sixty-fifth session the item entitled "Report of the Committee on Relations with the Host Country".

Chapter IV

Law of the sea

In 2009, the United Nations continued to promote universal acceptance of the 1982 United Nations Convention on the Law of the Sea and its two implementing Agreements, one on the conservation and management of straddling fish stocks and highly migratory fish stocks and the other on the privileges and immunities of the International Tribunal for the Law of the Sea.

The three institutions created by the Convention—the International Seabed Authority, the International Tribunal for the Law of the Sea and the Commission on the Limits of the Continental Shelf—held sessions during the year.

UN Convention on the Law of the Sea

Signatures and ratifications

In 2009, Chad, the Dominican Republic and Switzerland ratified or acceded to the United Nations Convention on the Law of the Sea, bringing the number of parties to 160. The Convention, which was adopted by the Third United Nations Conference on the Law of the Sea in 1982 [YUN 1982, p. 178], entered into force on 16 November 1994 [YUN 1994, p. 1301].

Meeting of States Parties

The nineteenth Meeting of States Parties to the Convention (New York, 22–26 June) [SPLOS/203] discussed the 2008 activities of the International Tribunal for the Law of the Sea [YUN 2008, p. 1495], took action on a number of Tribunal-related financial and administrative issues, including the surrender and deduction of €784,136 of the cash surplus for the 2007–2008 financial period from the assessed contributions of the States parties for 2010, and adopted a decision on adjustment of the remuneration of members of the Tribunal and their pension [SPLOS/200]. Also discussed were the activities of the International Seabed Authority (see p. 1344) and the Commission on the Limits of the Continental Shelf (see p. 1345) during the previous 12 months, the arrangement for the allocation of seats on the Commission and the Tribunal [SPLOS/201], as well as the Secretary-General's report [A/64/66] submitted under article 319 of the Convention (see p. 1346). The Meeting also adopted an agreed outcome on the Commission's workload.

Special Meeting of States Parties. As a vacancy had occurred in the International Tribunal for the Law of the Sea—owing to the death of Judge Choon-Ho Park (Republic of Korea) in 2008—a Special Meeting of States Parties to the Convention was convened (New York, 6 March) [SPLOS/190] to elect one member of the Tribunal. The Meeting had before it the list of candidates nominated by States Parties [SPLOS/186] and their curricula vitae [SPLOS/187]. Following the balloting, Jin-Hyun Paik (Republic of Korea) was elected for the remainder of his predecessor's nine-year term, which would end on 30 September 2014.

Agreement relating to the Implementation of Part XI of the Convention

During 2009, the number of parties to the 1994 Agreement relating to the Implementation of Part XI of the Convention (governing exploitation of seabed resources beyond national jurisdiction), adopted by General Assembly resolution 48/263 [YUN 1994, p. 1301], reached 138, with Chad, the Dominican Republic and Switzerland becoming parties. The Agreement, which entered into force on 28 July 1996 [YUN 1996, p. 1215], sought to address certain difficulties with the seabed mining provisions contained in Part XI of the Convention, which had been raised primarily by the industrialized countries. The Agreement was to be interpreted and applied together with the Convention as a single instrument, and, in the event of any inconsistency between the Agreement and Part XI of the Convention, the provisions of the Agreement would prevail. Any ratification of or accession to the Convention after 28 July 1994 represented consent to be bound by the Agreement also. Parties to the Convention prior to the Agreement's adoption had to deposit a separate instrument of ratification of or accession to the Agreement.

Agreement relating to conservation and management of straddling fish stocks and highly migratory fish stocks

As at 31 December, the number of parties to the 1995 Agreement for the Implementation of the Provisions of the United Nations Convention on the Law of the Sea of 10 December 1982 relating to the Conservation and Management of Straddling Fish Stocks and Highly Migratory Fish Stocks [YUN 1995, p. 1334] reached 77, with Indonesia, Nigeria and Tuvalu becoming parties. Referred to as the Fish Stocks Agreement, it entered into force on 11 December 2001 [YUN 2001, p. 1232].

Report of the Secretary-General. In response to General Assembly resolution 61/105 [YUN 2006, p. 1543], the Secretary-General submitted an August report [A/64/305] on the status of implementation of the Fish Stocks Agreement, which included actions taken by States and regional fisheries management organizations and arrangements to sustainably manage fisheries, regulate bottom fisheries and protect vulnerable marine ecosystems. The report described the vulnerable ecosystems and the impacts of bottom fishing on them, as well as initiatives by States to establish new regional fisheries management organizations and arrangements in the north-west and south Pacific with the competence to regulate bottom fisheries, as well as interim measures adopted by States pending the establishment of those organizations or arrangements.

The Secretary-General observed that the international community had initiated a wide range of protective measures to address the impacts of bottom fishing on vulnerable marine ecosystems; yet implementation of the resolution had been uneven. Further efforts were needed, including the adoption and implementation of conservation and management measures to address the negative impacts of bottom fishing activities; the development of support tools such as a global database on vulnerable marine ecosystems, as many countries lacked the capacity to identify potentially harmful fishing activities; and increased cooperation and coordination on data collection and sharing, and for capacity-building and the transfer of appropriate technology to developing States.

GENERAL ASSEMBLY ACTION

On 4 December [meeting 58], the General Assembly adopted **resolution 64/72** [draft: A/64/L.29 & Add.1] without vote [agenda item 76 *(b)*].

Sustainable fisheries, including through the 1995 Agreement for the Implementation of the Provisions of the United Nations Convention on the Law of the Sea of 10 December 1982 relating to the Conservation and Management of Straddling Fish Stocks and Highly Migratory Fish Stocks, and related instruments

The General Assembly,

Reaffirming its annual resolutions on sustainable fisheries, including resolution 63/112 of 5 December 2008, and other relevant resolutions,

Recalling the relevant provisions of the United Nations Convention on the Law of the Sea ("the Convention"), and bearing in mind the relationship between the Convention and the 1995 Agreement for the Implementation of the

Provisions of the United Nations Convention on the Law of the Sea of 10 December 1982 relating to the Conservation and Management of Straddling Fish Stocks and Highly Migratory Fish Stocks ("the Agreement"),

Welcoming the recent ratifications of and accessions to the Agreement and the fact that a growing number of States, and entities referred to in the Convention and in article 1, paragraph 2 *(b)*, of the Agreement, as well as subregional and regional fisheries management organizations and arrangements, have taken measures, as appropriate, towards the implementation of the provisions of the Agreement,

Welcoming also the work of the Food and Agriculture Organization of the United Nations and its Committee on Fisheries and the 2005 Rome Declaration on Illegal, Unreported and Unregulated Fishing, adopted on 12 March 2005, and recognizing that the Code of Conduct for Responsible Fisheries of the Food and Agriculture Organization of the United Nations ("the Code") and its associated international plans of action set out principles and global standards of behaviour for responsible practices for conservation of fisheries resources and the management and development of fisheries,

Welcoming further the outcomes, including the decisions and recommendations, of the twenty-eighth session of the Committee on Fisheries of the Food and Agriculture Organization of the United Nations, held from 2 to 6 March 2009,

Noting with concern that effective management of marine capture fisheries has been made difficult in some areas by unreliable information and data caused by, inter alia, unreported and misreported fish catch and fishing effort and that this lack of accurate data contributes to overfishing in some areas,

Recognizing the significant contribution of sustainable fisheries to food security, income, wealth and poverty alleviation for present and future generations,

Recognizing also the urgent need for action at all levels to ensure the long-term sustainable use and management of fisheries resources through the wide application of the precautionary approach and ecosystem approaches,

Expressing concern over the current and projected adverse effects of climate change on food security and the sustainability of fisheries, and noting in that regard the work of the Intergovernmental Panel on Climate Change, the Food and Agriculture Organization of the United Nations and the United Nations Environment Programme,

Deploring the fact that fish stocks, including straddling fish stocks and highly migratory fish stocks, in many parts of the world are overfished or subject to sparsely regulated and heavy fishing efforts, as a result of, inter alia, illegal, unreported and unregulated fishing, inadequate flag State control and enforcement, including monitoring, control and surveillance measures, inadequate regulatory measures, harmful fisheries subsidies and overcapacity, as well as inadequate port State control, as highlighted in the report of the Food and Agriculture Organization of the United Nations, *The State of World Fisheries and Aquaculture 2008*,

Concerned that a limited number of States have taken measures to implement, individually and through regional fisheries management organizations and arrangements, the International Plan of Action for the Management of Fishing Capacity adopted by the Food and Agriculture Organization of the United Nations,

Recalling the International Plan of Action to Prevent, Deter and Eliminate Illegal, Unreported and Unregulated Fishing, adopted by the Food and Agriculture Organization of the United Nations,

Particularly concerned that illegal, unreported and unregulated fishing constitutes a serious threat to fish stocks and marine habitats and ecosystems, to the detriment of sustainable fisheries as well as the food security and the economies of many States, particularly developing States,

Concerned that some operators increasingly take advantage of the globalization of fishery markets to trade fishery products stemming from illegal, unreported and unregulated fishing and make economic profits from those operations, which constitutes an incentive for them to pursue their activities,

Recognizing that effective deterrence and combating of illegal, unreported and unregulated fishing has significant financial and other resource implications,

Recognizing also the duty provided in the Convention, the Agreement to Promote Compliance with International Conservation and Management Measures by Fishing Vessels on the High Seas ("the Compliance Agreement"), the Agreement and the Code for flag States to exercise effective control over fishing vessels flying their flag, and vessels flying their flag which provide support to fishing vessels, to ensure that the activities of such fishing and support vessels do not undermine the effectiveness of conservation and management measures taken in accordance with international law and adopted at the national, subregional, regional or global levels,

Recalling paragraph 46 of its resolution 63/112, and welcoming in this regard the convening by the Food and Agriculture Organization of the United Nations of the Expert Consultation on Flag State Performance, held in Rome from 23 to 26 June 2009,

Noting the obligation of all States, in accordance with international law, as reflected in the relevant provisions of the Convention, to cooperate in the conservation and management of living marine resources, and recognizing the importance of coordination and cooperation at the global, regional, subregional as well as national levels in the areas, inter alia, of marine scientific research, data collection, information-sharing, capacity-building and training for the conservation, management and sustainable development of marine living resources,

Acknowledging the importance of ocean data buoy systems moored in areas beyond national jurisdiction to sustainable development, promoting safety at sea and limiting human vulnerability to natural disasters, due to their use in weather and marine forecasts, fisheries management, tsunami forecasts and climate prediction, and expressing concern that most damage to ocean data buoys, such as moored buoys and tsunameters, frequently results from actions taken by some fishing operations which render the buoys inoperable,

Recognizing the need for States, individually and through regional fisheries management organizations and arrangements, to continue to develop and implement, consistent with international law, effective port State measures to combat overfishing and illegal, unreported and unregu-

lated fishing, the critical need for cooperation with developing States to build their capacity, and the importance of cooperation between the Food and Agriculture Organization of the United Nations and the International Maritime Organization in this regard,

Welcoming, in this regard, the approval by the Conference of the Food and Agriculture Organization of the United Nations of the Agreement on Port State Measures to Prevent, Deter and Eliminate Illegal, Unreported and Unregulated Fishing and its opening for signature on 22 November 2009,

Concerned that marine pollution from all sources, including vessels and, in particular, land-based sources, constitutes a serious threat to human health and safety, endangers fish stocks, marine biodiversity and marine and coastal habitats and has significant costs to local and national economies,

Recognizing that marine debris is a global transboundary pollution problem and that, due to the many different types and sources of marine debris, different approaches to their prevention and removal are necessary,

Noting that the contribution of sustainable aquaculture to global fish supplies continues to respond to opportunities in developing countries to enhance local food security and poverty alleviation and, together with the efforts of other aquaculture producing countries, will make a significant contribution to meeting future demands in fish consumption, bearing in mind article 9 of the Code,

Calling attention to the circumstances affecting fisheries in many developing States, in particular African States and small island developing States, and recognizing the urgent need for capacity-building, including the transfer of marine technology and in particular fisheries-related technology, to enhance the ability of such States to meet their obligations and exercise their rights under international instruments, in order to realize the benefits from fisheries resources,

Recognizing the need for appropriate measures to minimize by-catch, waste, discards, including high-grading, loss of fishing gear and other factors which adversely affect fish stocks and may also have undesirable effects on the economies and food security of small island developing States, other developing coastal States, and subsistence fishing communities,

Recognizing also the need to further integrate ecosystem approaches into fisheries conservation and management and, more generally, the importance of applying ecosystem approaches to the management of human activities in the ocean, and noting in this regard the Reykjavik Declaration on Responsible Fisheries in the Marine Ecosystem, the work of the Food and Agriculture Organization of the United Nations related to guidelines for the implementation of the ecosystem approach to fisheries management and the importance of this approach to relevant provisions of the Agreement and the Code, as well as decision VII/11 and other relevant decisions of the Conference of the Parties to the Convention on Biological Diversity,

Recognizing further the economic and cultural importance of sharks in many countries, the biological importance of sharks in the marine ecosystem as key predatory species, the vulnerability of certain shark species to overexploitation, the fact that some are threatened with extinction, the need for measures to promote the long-term conservation, management and sustainable use of shark populations and fisheries, and the relevance of the International Plan of Action for the Conservation and Management of Sharks, adopted by the Food and Agriculture Organization of the United Nations in 1999, in providing guidance on the development of such measures,

Reaffirming its support for the initiative of the Food and Agriculture Organization of the United Nations and relevant subregional and regional fisheries management organizations and arrangements on the conservation and management of sharks, and noting with concern that basic data on shark stocks and harvests continue to be lacking, that only a small number of countries have implemented the International Plan of Action for the Conservation and Management of Sharks, and that not all regional fisheries management organizations and arrangements have adopted conservation and management measures for directed shark fisheries and for the regulation of by-catch of sharks from other fisheries,

Expressing concern that, despite the adoption of General Assembly resolution 46/215 of 20 December 1991, the practice of large-scale pelagic drift-net fishing still exists and remains a threat to marine living resources,

Expressing concern also over reports of continued losses of seabirds, particularly albatrosses and petrels, as well as other marine species, including sharks, fin-fish species and marine turtles, as a result of incidental mortality in fishing operations, particularly longline fishing, and other activities, while recognizing considerable efforts by States and through various regional fisheries management organizations and arrangements to reduce by-catch in longline fishing,

I

Achieving sustainable fisheries

1. *Reaffirms* the importance it attaches to the long-term conservation, management and sustainable use of the marine living resources of the world's oceans and seas and the obligations of States to cooperate to this end, in accordance with international law, as reflected in the relevant provisions of the Convention, in particular the provisions on cooperation set out in Part V and Part VII, section 2, of the Convention, and where applicable, the Agreement;

2. *Encourages* States to give due priority to the implementation of the Plan of Implementation of the World Summit on Sustainable Development ("Johannesburg Plan of Implementation") in relation to achieving sustainable fisheries, especially restoring depleted stocks to levels that can produce maximum sustainable yield on an urgent basis and, where possible, not later than 2015;

3. *Urges* States, either directly or through appropriate subregional, regional or global organizations or arrangements, to intensify efforts to assess and address, as appropriate, the impacts of global climate change on the sustainability of fish stocks and the habitats that support them;

4. *Emphasizes* the obligations of flag States to discharge their responsibilities, in accordance with the Convention and the Agreement, to ensure compliance by vessels flying their flag with the conservation and management measures adopted and in force with respect to fisheries resources on the high seas;

5. *Calls upon* all States that have not done so, in order to achieve the goal of universal participation, to become parties to the Convention, which sets out the legal framework within which all activities in the oceans and seas must be carried out, taking into account the relationship between the Convention and the Agreement;

6. *Calls upon* all States, directly or through regional fisheries management organizations and arrangements, to apply widely, in accordance with international law and the Code, the precautionary approach and ecosystem approaches to the conservation, management and exploitation of fish stocks, and also calls upon States parties to the Agreement to implement fully the provisions of article 6 of the Agreement as a matter of priority;

7. *Encourages* States to increase their reliance on scientific advice in developing, adopting and implementing conservation and management measures, and to increase their efforts to promote science for conservation and management measures, including through international cooperation, that apply, in accordance with international law, the precautionary approach and ecosystem approaches to fisheries management, enhancing understanding of ecosystem approaches, in order to ensure the long-term conservation and sustainable use of marine living resources, and in this regard encourages the implementation of the Strategy for Improving Information on Status and Trends of Capture Fisheries of the Food and Agriculture Organization of the United Nations as a framework for the improvement and understanding of fishery status and trends;

8. *Calls upon* all States, directly or through regional fisheries management organizations and arrangements, to apply stock-specific precautionary reference points, as described in Annex II to the Agreement and in the Code, to ensure that populations of harvested stocks, and, where necessary, associated or dependent species, are maintained at, or restored to, sustainable levels, and to use these reference points for triggering conservation and management action;

9. *Encourages* States to apply the precautionary approach and ecosystem approaches in adopting and implementing conservation and management measures addressing, inter alia, by-catch, pollution and overfishing, and protecting habitats of specific concern, taking into account existing guidelines developed by the Food and Agriculture Organization of the United Nations;

10. *Also encourages* States to enhance or develop observer programmes individually or through regional fisheries management organizations or arrangements in order to improve data collection on, inter alia, target and by-catch species, which could also assist monitoring, control and surveillance tools, and to take into account standards, forms of cooperation and other existing structures for such programmes as described in article 25 of the Agreement and article 5 of the Code;

11. *Calls upon* States and regional fisheries management organizations and arrangements to collect and, where appropriate, report to the Food and Agriculture Organization of the United Nations required catch and effort data, and fishery-related information, in a complete, accurate and timely way, including for straddling fish stocks and highly migratory fish stocks within and beyond areas under national jurisdiction, discrete high seas fish stocks,

and by-catch and discards; and, where they do not exist, to establish processes to strengthen data collection and reporting by members of regional fisheries management organizations and arrangements, including through regular reviews of member compliance with such obligations, and, when such obligations are not met, require the member concerned to rectify the problem, including through the preparation of plans of action with timelines;

12. *Invites* States and regional fisheries management organizations and arrangements to cooperate with the Food and Agriculture Organization of the United Nations in the implementation and further development of the Fisheries Resources Monitoring System initiative;

13. *Reaffirms* paragraph 10 of resolution 61/105 of 8 December 2006, and calls upon States, including through regional fisheries management organizations or arrangements, to urgently adopt measures to fully implement the International Plan of Action for the Conservation and Management of Sharks for directed and non-directed shark fisheries, based on the best available scientific information, through, inter alia, limits on catch or fishing effort, by requiring that vessels flying their flag collect and regularly report data on shark catches, including species-specific data, discards and landings, undertaking, including through international cooperation, comprehensive stock assessments of sharks, reducing shark by-catch and by-catch mortality, and, where scientific information is uncertain or inadequate, not increasing fishing effort in directed shark fisheries until measures have been established to ensure the long-term conservation, management and sustainable use of shark stocks and to prevent further declines of vulnerable or threatened shark stocks;

14. *Calls upon* States to take immediate and concerted action to improve the implementation of and compliance with existing regional fisheries management organization or arrangement and national measures that regulate shark fisheries, in particular those measures which prohibit or restrict fisheries conducted solely for the purpose of harvesting shark fins, and, where necessary, to consider taking other measures, as appropriate, such as requiring that all sharks be landed with each fin naturally attached;

15. *Calls upon* regional fisheries management organizations with the competence to regulate highly migratory species to strengthen or establish precautionary, science-based conservation and management measures, as appropriate, for sharks taken in fisheries within their convention areas consistent with the International Plan of Action for the Conservation and Management of Sharks, taking into account the Course of Actions adopted at the second joint meeting of tuna regional fisheries management organizations and arrangements, held in San Sebastian, Spain, from 29 June to 3 July 2009;

16. *Reiterates its request* to the Food and Agriculture Organization of the United Nations to prepare a report containing a comprehensive analysis of the implementation of the International Plan of Action for the Conservation and Management of Sharks, as well as progress in implementing paragraph 11 of General Assembly resolution 62/177 of 18 December 2007;

17. *Urges* States to eliminate barriers to trade in fish and fisheries products which are not consistent with their rights and obligations under the World Trade Organization

agreements, taking into account the importance of the trade in fish and fisheries products, particularly for developing countries;

18. *Urges* States and relevant international and national organizations to provide for the participation of small-scale fishery stakeholders in related policy development and fisheries management strategies in order to achieve long-term sustainability for such fisheries, consistent with the duty to ensure the proper conservation and management of fisheries resources;

II

Implementation of the 1995 Agreement for the Implementation of the Provisions of the United Nations Convention on the Law of the Sea of 10 December 1982 relating to the Conservation and Management of Straddling Fish Stocks and Highly Migratory Fish Stocks

19. *Calls upon* all States, and entities referred to in the Convention and in article 1, paragraph 2 *(b)*, of the Agreement, that have not done so to ratify or accede to the Agreement and in the interim to consider applying it provisionally;

20. *Calls upon* States parties to the Agreement to effectively implement, as a matter of priority, the provisions of the Agreement through their domestic legislation and through regional fisheries management organizations and arrangements in which they participate;

21. *Emphasizes* the importance of those provisions of the Agreement relating to bilateral, subregional and regional cooperation in enforcement, and urges continued efforts in this regard;

22. *Urges* States parties to the Agreement, in accordance with article 21, paragraph 4, thereof to inform, either directly or through the relevant subregional or regional fisheries management organization or arrangement, all States whose vessels fish on the high seas in the same subregion or region of the form of identification issued by those States parties to officials duly authorized to carry out boarding and inspection functions in accordance with articles 21 and 22 of the Agreement;

23. *Also urges* States parties to the Agreement, in accordance with article 21, paragraph 4, thereof, to designate an appropriate authority to receive notifications pursuant to article 21 and to give due publicity to such designation through the relevant subregional or regional fisheries management organization or arrangement;

24. *Invites* regional fisheries management organizations and arrangements which have not yet done so to adopt procedures for high seas boarding and inspection that are consistent with articles 21 and 22 of the Agreement;

25. *Calls upon* States, individually and, as appropriate, through subregional and regional fisheries management organizations and arrangements with competence over discrete high seas fish stocks, to adopt the necessary measures to ensure the long-term conservation, management and sustainable use of such stocks in accordance with the Convention and consistent with the Code and the general principles set forth in the Agreement;

26. *Invites* States to assist developing States in enhancing their participation in regional fisheries management organizations or arrangements, including by facilitating

access to fisheries for straddling fish stocks and highly migratory fish stocks, in accordance with article 25, paragraph 1 *(b)*, of the Agreement, taking into account the need to ensure that such access benefits the developing States concerned and their nationals;

27. *Invites* States and international financial institutions and organizations of the United Nations system to provide assistance according to Part VII of the Agreement, including, if appropriate, the development of special financial mechanisms or instruments to assist developing States, in particular the least developed among them and small island developing States, to enable them to develop their national capacity to exploit fishery resources, including developing their domestically flagged fishing fleet, value-added processing and the expansion of their economic base in the fishing industry, consistent with the duty to ensure the proper conservation and management of fisheries resources;

28. *Notes with appreciation* the contributions made by States to the Assistance Fund established under Part VII of the Agreement, and encourages States, intergovernmental organizations, international financial institutions, national institutions and non-governmental organizations, as well as natural and juridical persons, to make further voluntary financial contributions to the Fund;

29. *Notes with satisfaction* that the Food and Agriculture Organization of the United Nations and the Division for Ocean Affairs and the Law of the Sea of the Office of Legal Affairs of the Secretariat ("the Division") have taken measures to publicize the availability of assistance through the Assistance Fund, and encourages the Organization and the Division to continue their efforts in this regard;

30. *Encourages* accelerated progress by States, individually and, as appropriate, through subregional and regional fisheries management organizations and arrangements, regarding the recommendations of the Review Conference on the Agreement, held in New York from 22 to 26 May 2006, and the identification of emerging priorities;

31. *Recalls* paragraph 31 of resolution 63/112 concerning the request to the Secretary-General to resume the Review Conference, convened pursuant to article 36 of the Agreement, which will be held in New York from 24 to 28 May 2010;

32. *Encourages* wide participation in the resumed Review Conference, in accordance with article 36 of the Agreement;

33. *Takes note* of the report of the eighth round of informal consultations of States parties to the Agreement, and requests that the Secretary-General, in preparing, in cooperation with the Food and Agriculture Organization of the United Nations, the updated comprehensive report referred to in paragraph 32 of resolution 63/112, take into account the specific guidance proposed by the eighth round of informal consultations regarding that report;

34. *Recalls* paragraph 6 of resolution 56/13 of 28 November 2001, and requests the Secretary-General to convene in March 2010 a ninth round of informal consultations of States parties to the Agreement for a duration of two days, to serve primarily as a preparatory meeting for the resumed Review Conference;

35. *Requests* the Secretary-General to prepare a draft provisional agenda and draft organization of work for the resumed Review Conference and to circulate them at the same time as the provisional agenda of the ninth round of informal consultations of States parties to the Agreement, sixty days in advance of these consultations;

36. *Also requests* the Secretary-General to invite States, and entities referred to in the Convention and in article 1, paragraph 2 *(b)*, of the Agreement, not parties to the Agreement, as well as the United Nations Development Programme, the Food and Agriculture Organization of the United Nations and other specialized agencies, the Commission on Sustainable Development, the World Bank, the Global Environment Facility and other relevant international financial institutions, subregional and regional fisheries management organizations and arrangements, other fisheries bodies, other relevant intergovernmental bodies and relevant non-governmental organizations, in accordance with past practice, to attend the ninth round of informal consultations of States parties to the Agreement as observers;

37. *Reaffirms its request* that the Food and Agriculture Organization of the United Nations initiate arrangements with States for the collection and dissemination of data on fishing in the high seas by vessels flying their flag at the subregional and regional levels where no such arrangements exist;

38. *Reaffirms its request* that the Food and Agriculture Organization of the United Nations revise its global fisheries statistics database to provide information on straddling fish stocks, highly migratory fish stocks and discrete high seas fish stocks on the basis of where the catch is taken;

III
Related fisheries instruments

39. *Emphasizes* the importance of the effective implementation of the provisions of the Compliance Agreement, and urges continued efforts in this regard;

40. *Calls upon* all States and other entities referred to in article X, paragraph 1, of the Compliance Agreement that have not yet become parties to that Agreement to do so as a matter of priority and, in the interim, to consider applying it provisionally;

41. *Urges* States and subregional and regional fisheries management organizations and arrangements to implement and promote the application of the Code within their areas of competence;

42. *Urges* States to develop and implement, as a matter of priority, national and, as appropriate, regional plans of action to put into effect the international plans of action of the Food and Agriculture Organization of the United Nations;

43. *Encourages* the development of best practice guidelines for safety at sea in connection with marine fisheries by the competent international organizations;

IV
Illegal, unreported and unregulated fishing

44. *Emphasizes once again its serious concern* that illegal, unreported and unregulated fishing remains one of the greatest threats to marine ecosystems and continues to have serious and major implications for the conservation and management of ocean resources, and renews its call upon

States to comply fully with all existing obligations and to combat such fishing and urgently to take all necessary steps to implement the International Plan of Action to Prevent, Deter and Eliminate Illegal, Unreported and Unregulated Fishing of the Food and Agriculture Organization of the United Nations;

45. _Urges_ States to exercise effective control over their nationals, including beneficial owners, and vessels flying their flag, in order to prevent and deter them from engaging in illegal, unreported and unregulated fishing activities or supporting vessels engaging in illegal, unreported and unregulated fishing activities, including those vessels listed by regional fisheries management organizations or arrangements as engaged in those activities, and to facilitate mutual assistance to ensure that such actions can be investigated and proper sanctions imposed;

46. _Also urges_ States to take effective measures, at the national, subregional, regional and global levels, to deter the activities, including illegal, unreported and unregulated fishing, of any vessel which undermines conservation and management measures that have been adopted by subregional and regional fisheries management organizations and arrangements in accordance with international law;

47. _Calls upon_ States not to permit vessels flying their flag to engage in fishing on the high seas or in areas under the national jurisdiction of other States, unless duly authorized by the authorities of the States concerned and in accordance with the conditions set out in the authorization, and to take specific measures, including deterring the reflagging of vessels by their nationals, in accordance with the relevant provisions of the Convention, the Agreement and the Compliance Agreement, to control fishing operations by vessels flying their flag;

48. _Urges_ States, individually and collectively through regional fisheries management organizations and arrangements, to develop appropriate processes to assess the performance of States with respect to implementing the obligations regarding fishing vessels flying their flag set out in relevant international instruments;

49. _Encourages_ the Food and Agriculture Organization of the United Nations to continue its work on flag State performance, including the possible convening of a technical consultation;

50. _Reaffirms_ the need to strengthen, where necessary, the international legal framework for intergovernmental cooperation, in particular at the subregional and regional levels, in the management of fish stocks and in combating illegal, unreported and unregulated fishing, in a manner consistent with international law, and for States and entities referred to in the Convention and in article 1, paragraph 2 _(b)_, of the Agreement to collaborate in efforts to address these types of fishing activities;

51. _Urges_ regional fisheries management organizations and arrangements to further coordinate measures for combating illegal, unreported and unregulated fishing activities, such as through the development of a common list of vessels identified as engaged in illegal, unreported and unregulated fishing or the mutual recognition of the illegal, unreported and unregulated vessel lists established by each organization or arrangement;

52. _Reaffirms its call upon_ States to take all necessary measures consistent with international law, without prejudice to a State's sovereignty over ports in its territory and to reasons of force majeure or distress, including the prohibition of vessels from accessing their ports followed by a report to the flag State concerned, when there is clear evidence that they are or have been engaged in or have supported illegal, unreported and unregulated fishing, or when they refuse to give information either on the origin of the catch or on the authorization under which the catch has been made;

53. _Urges_ enhanced action consistent with international law, including cooperation and coordination, to eliminate illegal, unreported and unregulated fishing by vessels flying "flags of convenience", to require that a "genuine link" be established between States and fishing vessels flying their flags, and to clarify the role of the "genuine link" in relation to the duty of States to exercise effective control over such vessels, and calls upon States to implement the 2005 Rome Declaration on Illegal, Unreported and Unregulated Fishing as a matter of priority;

54. _Recognizes_ the need for enhanced port State measures to combat illegal, unreported and unregulated fishing, and urges States to cooperate, in particular at the regional level and through subregional and regional fisheries management organizations and arrangements, to adopt all necessary port measures, consistent with international law taking into account article 23 of the Agreement, and to further promote the development and application of standards at the regional level;

55. _Encourages_, in this regard, States to consider signing and ratifying, accepting, approving or acceding to the Agreement on Port State Measures to Prevent, Deter and Eliminate Illegal, Unreported and Unregulated Fishing of the Food and Agriculture Organization of the United Nations with a view to its early entry into force;

56. _Encourages_ strengthened collaboration between the Food and Agriculture Organization of the United Nations and the International Maritime Organization, taking into account the respective competencies, mandates and experience of the two organizations, to combat illegal, unreported and unregulated fishing, particularly in improving the implementation of flag State responsibilities and port State measures;

57. _Encourages_ States, with respect to vessels flying their flag, and port States, to make every effort to share data on landings and catch quotas, and in this regard encourages regional fisheries management organizations or arrangements to consider developing open databases containing such data for the purpose of enhancing the effectiveness of fisheries management;

58. _Calls upon_ States to take all necessary measures to ensure that vessels flying their flag do not engage in transshipment of fish caught by fishing vessels engaged in illegal, unreported and unregulated fishing;

59. _Urges_ States, individually and through regional fisheries management organizations and arrangements, to adopt and implement internationally agreed market-related measures in accordance with international law, including principles, rights and obligations established in World Trade Organization agreements, as called for in the International Plan of Action to Prevent, Deter and Eliminate Illegal, Unreported and Unregulated Fishing;

60. *Encourages* information-sharing regarding emerging market- and trade-related measures by States and other relevant actors with appropriate international forums, given the potential implications of these measures for all States, consistent with the established plan of work of the Committee on Fisheries of the Food and Agriculture Organization of the United Nations, and taking into account the Technical Guidelines for Responsible Fish Trade of the Food and Agriculture Organization of the United Nations;

61. *Notes* the concerns about possible connections between international organized crime and illegal fishing in certain regions of the world, and encourages States, including through the appropriate international forums and organizations, to study the causes and methods of and contributing factors to illegal fishing to increase knowledge and understanding of those possible connections, and to make the findings publicly available, bearing in mind the distinct legal regimes and remedies under international law applicable to illegal fishing and international organized crime;

V

Monitoring, control and surveillance and compliance and enforcement

62. *Calls upon* States, in accordance with international law, to strengthen implementation of or, where they do not exist, adopt comprehensive monitoring, control and surveillance measures and compliance and enforcement schemes individually and within those regional fisheries management organizations or arrangements in which they participate, in order to provide an appropriate framework for promoting compliance with agreed conservation and management measures, and further urges enhanced co-ordination among all relevant States and regional fisheries management organizations and arrangements in these efforts;

63. *Encourages* further work by competent international organizations, including the Food and Agriculture Organization of the United Nations and subregional and regional fisheries management organizations and arrangements, to develop guidelines on flag State control of fishing vessels;

64. *Urges* States, individually and through relevant regional fisheries management organizations and arrangements, to establish mandatory vessel monitoring, control and surveillance systems, in particular to require that vessel monitoring systems be carried by all vessels fishing on the high seas as soon as practicable, recalling that paragraph 62 of resolution 63/112 urged that large-scale fishing vessels be required to carry vessel monitoring systems no later than December 2008, and to share information on fisheries enforcement matters;

65. *Calls upon* States, individually and through regional fisheries management organizations or arrangements, to strengthen or establish, consistent with national and international law, positive or negative lists of vessels fishing within the areas covered by relevant regional fisheries management organizations and arrangements in order to promote compliance with conservation and management measures and to identify products from illegal, unreported and unregulated catches, and encourages improved coordi-

nation among all States and regional fisheries management organizations and arrangements in sharing and using this information, taking into account the forms of cooperation with developing States as set out in article 25 of the Agreement;

66. *Welcomes* the decision of the Committee on Fisheries at its twenty-eighth session that the Food and Agriculture Organization of the United Nations should develop a comprehensive global record of fishing vessels, refrigerated transport vessels, and supply vessels;

67. *Requests* States and relevant international bodies to develop, in accordance with international law, more effective measures to trace fish and fishery products to enable importing States to identify fish or fishery products caught in a manner that undermines international conservation and management measures agreed in accordance with international law, taking into account the special requirements of developing States and the forms of cooperation with developing States as set out in article 25 of the Agreement, and at the same time to recognize the importance of market access, in accordance with provisions 11.2.4, 11.2.5 and 11.2.6 of the Code, for fish and fishery products caught in a manner that is in conformity with such international measures;

68. *Requests* States to take the necessary measures, consistent with international law, to help to prevent fish and fishery products caught in a manner that undermines applicable conservation and management measures adopted in accordance with international law from entering international trade;

69. *Welcomes* the decision of the Committee on Fisheries at its twenty-eighth session that the Food and Agriculture Organization of the United Nations should develop best practice guidelines for catch documentation schemes and for traceability for consideration by the Sub-Committee on Fish Trade at its next session;

70. *Encourages* States to establish and undertake cooperative surveillance and enforcement activities in accordance with international law to strengthen and enhance efforts to ensure compliance with conservation and management measures, and prevent and deter illegal, unreported and unregulated fishing;

71. *Urges* States, directly and through regional fisheries management organizations or arrangements, to develop and adopt effective monitoring, control and surveillance measures for trans-shipment, as appropriate, in particular at-sea trans-shipment, in order to, inter alia, monitor compliance, collect and verify fisheries data, and to prevent and suppress illegal, unreported and unregulated fishing activities, in accordance with international law; and, in parallel, to encourage and support the Food and Agriculture Organization of the United Nations in studying the current practices of trans-shipment and produce a set of guidelines for this purpose;

72. *Expresses its appreciation* for financial contributions from States to improve the capacity of the existing voluntary International Monitoring, Control and Surveillance Network for Fisheries-Related Activities, and encourages States to join and actively participate in the Network and to consider supporting, when appropriate, its transformation in accordance with international law into an international unit with dedicated resources to further assist Network

members, taking into account the forms of cooperation with developing States as set out in article 25 of the Agreement;

VI
Fishing overcapacity

73. *Calls upon* States to commit themselves to urgently reducing the capacity of the world's fishing fleets to levels commensurate with the sustainability of fish stocks, through the establishment of target levels and plans or other appropriate mechanisms for ongoing capacity assessment, while avoiding the transfer of fishing capacity to other fisheries or areas in a manner that undermines the sustainable management of fish stocks, including, inter alia, those areas where fish stocks are overexploited or in a depleted condition, and recognizing in this context the legitimate rights of developing States to develop their fisheries for straddling fish stocks and highly migratory fish stocks consistent with article 25 of the Agreement, article 5 of the Code, and paragraph 10 of the International Plan of Action for the Management of Fishing Capacity;

74. *Reiterates its call upon* States, individually and through regional fisheries management organizations and arrangements, to ensure that the urgent actions required in the International Plan of Action for the Management of Fishing Capacity are undertaken expeditiously and that its implementation is facilitated without delay;

75. *Invites* the Food and Agriculture Organization of the United Nations to report on the state of progress in the implementation of the International Plan of Action for the Management of Fishing Capacity, as provided for in paragraph 48 of the Plan of Action;

76. *Notes* that the second joint meeting of the five regional fisheries management organizations with competence to regulate highly migratory species, held in San Sebastian, Spain, from 29 June to 3 July 2009, agreed, in its Course of Actions, that global fishing capacity for tunas had to be addressed urgently and, inter alia, in a way which recognized the legitimate rights of developing States, in particular small island developing States, to participate in and benefit from such fisheries;

77. *Encourages* those States which are cooperating to establish subregional and regional fisheries management organizations and arrangements, taking into account the best scientific information available as well as the precautionary approach, to exercise voluntary restraint of fishing effort levels in those areas that will come under the regulation of the future organizations and arrangements until adequate regional conservation and management measures are adopted and implemented, taking into account the need to ensure the long-term conservation, management and sustainable use of the relevant fish stocks and to prevent significant adverse impacts on vulnerable marine ecosystems;

78. *Urges* States to eliminate subsidies that contribute to overfishing and overcapacity and to illegal, unreported and unregulated fishing, including through completion of World Trade Organization negotiations on fisheries subsidies in accordance with the 2001 Doha Ministerial Declaration and the 2005 Hong Kong Ministerial Declaration to strengthen disciplines on fisheries subsidies, taking into account the importance of the fisheries sector, including small-scale and artisanal fisheries, to developing countries;

VII
Large-scale pelagic drift-net fishing

79. *Reaffirms* the importance it attaches to continued compliance with its resolution 46/215 and other subsequent resolutions on large-scale pelagic drift-net fishing, and urges States and entities referred to in the Convention and in article 1, paragraph 2 *(b)*, of the Agreement to enforce fully the measures recommended in those resolutions in order to eliminate the use of large-scale pelagic drift nets in all seas and oceans, which means that efforts to implement resolution 46/215 should not result in the transfer to other parts of the world of drift nets that contravene the resolution;

VIII
Fisheries by-catch and discards

80. *Urges* States, subregional and regional fisheries management organizations and arrangements and other relevant international organizations that have not done so to take action, including with consideration of the interests of developing coastal States and, as appropriate, subsistence fishing communities, to reduce or eliminate by-catch, catch by lost or abandoned gear, fish discards and post-harvest losses, including juvenile fish, consistent with international law and relevant international instruments, including the Code, and in particular to consider measures including, as appropriate, technical measures related to fish size, mesh size or gear, discards, closed seasons and areas and zones reserved for selected fisheries, particularly artisanal fisheries, the establishment of mechanisms for communicating information on areas of high concentration of juvenile fish, taking into account the importance of ensuring the confidentiality of such information, and support for studies and research that will reduce or eliminate by-catch of juvenile fish, and to ensure that these measures are implemented so as to optimize their effectiveness;

81. *Welcomes* the support of the Committee on Fisheries at its twenty-eighth session for the development of international guidelines on by-catch management and the reduction of discards, and the convening by the Food and Agriculture Organization of the United Nations of an expert consultation to be followed by a technical consultation to develop such international guidelines;

82. *Encourages* States and entities referred to in the Convention and in article 1, paragraph 2 *(b)*, of the Agreement to give due consideration to participation, as appropriate, in subregional and regional instruments and organizations with mandates to conserve non-target species taken incidentally in fishing operations;

83. *Encourages* States to strengthen, if necessary, the capacity of those subregional and regional fisheries management organizations and arrangements in which they participate to ensure the adequate conservation of non-target species taken incidentally in fishing operations, taking into consideration best practices for non-target species management, and to expedite their ongoing efforts in this regard;

84. *Requests* States and regional fisheries management organizations and arrangements to urgently implement, as appropriate, the measures recommended in the 2004 Guidelines to Reduce Sea Turtle Mortality in Fishing Operations and the International Plan of Action for

Reducing Incidental Catch of Seabirds in Longline Fisheries of the Food and Agriculture Organization of the United Nations in order to prevent the decline of sea turtles and seabird populations by minimizing by-catch and increasing post-release survival in their fisheries, including through research and development of gear and bait alternatives, promoting the use of available by-catch mitigation technology, and establishing and strengthening data-collection programmes to obtain standardized information to develop reliable estimates of the by-catch of these species;

85. *Welcomes* the decision of the Committee on Fisheries at its twenty-eighth session that the Food and Agriculture Organization of the United Nations should publish the best practices technical guidelines for the implementation of the International Plan of Action for Reducing Incidental Catch of Seabirds in Longline Fisheries;

86. *Notes* measures for the protection of seabirds, including those adopted at the Third Session of the Meeting of Parties to the Agreement on the Conservation of Albatrosses and Petrels, held in Bergen, Norway, from 27 April to 1 May 2009, in relation to albatrosses and petrels;

IX

Subregional and regional cooperation

87. *Urges* coastal States and States fishing on the high seas, in accordance with the Convention, the Agreement and other relevant instruments, to pursue cooperation in relation to straddling fish stocks and highly migratory fish stocks, either directly or through appropriate subregional or regional fisheries management organizations or arrangements, to ensure the effective conservation and management of such stocks;

88. *Urges* States fishing for straddling fish stocks and highly migratory fish stocks on the high seas, and relevant coastal States, where a subregional or regional fisheries management organization or arrangement has the competence to establish conservation and management measures for such stocks, to give effect to their duty to cooperate by becoming members of such an organization or participants in such an arrangement, or by agreeing to apply the conservation and management measures established by such an organization or arrangement, or to otherwise ensure that no vessel flying their flag is authorized to access the fisheries resources to which regional fisheries management organizations and arrangements or conservation and management measures established by such organizations or arrangements apply;

89. *Invites*, in this regard, subregional and regional fisheries management organizations and arrangements to ensure that all States having a real interest in the fisheries concerned may become members of such organizations or participants in such arrangements, in accordance with the Convention, the Agreement and the Code;

90. *Encourages* relevant coastal States and States fishing on the high seas for a straddling fish stock or a highly migratory fish stock, where there is no subregional or regional fisheries management organization or arrangement to establish conservation and management measures for such stocks, to cooperate to establish such an organization or enter into another appropriate arrangement to ensure the conservation and management of such stocks, and to participate in the work of the organization or arrangement;

91. *Urges* all signatory States and other States whose vessels fish within the area of the Convention on the Conservation and Management of Fishery Resources in the South-East Atlantic Ocean for fishery resources covered by that Convention to become parties to that Convention as a matter of priority and, in the interim, to ensure that vessels flying their flags fully comply with the measures adopted;

92. *Encourages* signatory States and States having a real interest to become parties to the South Indian Ocean Fisheries Agreement, and urges those States to agree on and implement interim measures, including measures in accordance with paragraphs 80 and 83 to 87 of resolution 61/105 and paragraphs 117, 119, 120, 122 and 123 of the present resolution, to ensure the conservation and management of the fisheries resources and their marine ecosystems and habitats in the area to which that Agreement applies until such time as that Agreement enters into force;

93. *Takes note* of recent efforts at the regional level to promote responsible fishing practices, including combating illegal, unreported and unregulated fishing;

94. *Welcomes with satisfaction* the adoption of the Convention on the Conservation and Management of High Seas Fishery Resources in the South Pacific Ocean in Auckland, New Zealand, on 14 November 2009, encourages the States and the regional economic integration organization and the entities referred to in article 1, paragraph 2 *(b)*, of that Convention that participated in its negotiation, to sign it when it is opened for signature on 1 February 2010, and to implement fully the voluntary interim measures that have been adopted to give effect to paragraphs 80 and 83 to 87 of resolution 61/105 and to voluntarily restrain fishing effort and catches to avoid overexploitation of certain pelagic fisheries resources in the area to which that Convention will apply until it has entered into force and conservation and management measures have been adopted;

95. *Notes with satisfaction* the progress of negotiations to establish a subregional and regional fisheries management organization in the North Pacific, urges States having a real interest to participate in and expedite such negotiations, and to apply provisions of the Convention and the Agreement to their work, and encourages those participants to implement fully interim measures adopted in accordance with paragraphs 80 and 83 to 87 of resolution 61/105 and paragraphs 117, 119, 120, 122 and 123 of the present resolution;

96. *Takes note* of the ongoing efforts of the members of the Indian Ocean Tuna Commission to strengthen the functioning of the Commission so that it can more effectively discharge its mandate, and invites the Food and Agriculture Organization of the United Nations to continue to provide members of the Commission with the necessary assistance to this end;

97. *Urges* further efforts by regional fisheries management organizations and arrangements, as a matter of priority, in accordance with international law, to strengthen and modernize their mandates and the measures adopted by such organizations or arrangements, and to implement modern approaches to fisheries management, as reflected in the Agreement and other relevant international instruments, relying on the best scientific information available and application of the precautionary approach and incorporating an ecosystem approach to fisheries management and

biodiversity considerations, where these aspects are lacking, to ensure that they effectively contribute to long-term conservation and management and sustainable use of marine living resources;

98. *Calls upon* regional fisheries management organizations with the competence to conserve and manage highly migratory fish stocks that have not yet adopted effective conservation and management measures in line with the best scientific information available to conserve and manage stocks falling under their mandate to do so urgently;

99. *Urges* States to strengthen and enhance cooperation among existing and developing regional fisheries management organizations and arrangements in which they participate, including increased communication and further coordination of measures, such as through the holding of joint consultations, and to strengthen integration, coordination and cooperation by such regional fisheries management organizations and arrangements with other relevant fisheries organizations, regional seas arrangements and other relevant international organizations;

100. *Welcomes* the second joint meeting of the five regional fisheries management organizations with competence to manage highly migratory species, and urges those regional fisheries management organizations to take immediate measures towards implementing the Course of Actions adopted at that meeting;

101. *Urges* regional fisheries management organizations and arrangements to improve transparency and to ensure that their decision-making processes are fair and transparent, rely on the best scientific information available, incorporate the precautionary approach and ecosystem approaches, address participatory rights, including through, inter alia, the development of transparent criteria for allocating fishing opportunities which reflect, where appropriate, the relevant provisions of the Agreement, taking due account, inter alia, of the status of the relevant stocks and the respective interests in the fishery;

102. *Welcomes* the fact that a number of regional fisheries management organizations and arrangements have completed performance reviews, and encourages the implementation, as appropriate, of the recommendations of their respective reviews as a matter of priority;

103. *Urges* States, through their participation in regional fisheries management organizations and arrangements that have not done so, to undertake, on an urgent basis, performance reviews of those regional fisheries management organizations and arrangements, initiated either by the organization or arrangement itself or with external partners, including in cooperation with the Food and Agriculture Organization of the United Nations, using transparent criteria based on the provisions of the Agreement and other relevant instruments, and taking into account the best practices of regional fisheries management organizations or arrangements and, as appropriate, any set of criteria developed by States or other regional fisheries management organizations or arrangements, and encourages that such performance reviews include some element of independent evaluation and propose means for improving the functioning of the regional fisheries management organization or arrangement, as appropriate;

104. *Encourages* regional fisheries management organizations and arrangements to make the results of those performance reviews publicly available and to discuss the results jointly;

105. *Urges* States to cooperate, taking into account those performance reviews, to develop best practice guidelines for regional fisheries management organizations and arrangements and to apply, to the extent possible, those guidelines to organizations and arrangements in which they participate;

106. *Encourages* the development of regional guidelines for States to use in establishing sanctions for noncompliance by vessels flying their flag and by their nationals, to be applied in accordance with national law, that are adequate in severity for effectively securing compliance, deterring further violations and depriving offenders of the benefits deriving from their illegal activities, as well as in evaluating their systems of sanctions to ensure that they are effective in securing compliance and deterring violations;

X

Responsible fisheries in the marine ecosystem

107. *Encourages* States to apply by 2010 the ecosystem approach, in accordance with paragraph 30 *(d)* of the Johannesburg Plan of Implementation;

108. *Also encourages* States, individually or through regional fisheries management organizations and arrangements and other relevant international organizations, to work to ensure that fisheries and other ecosystem data collection is performed in a coordinated and integrated manner, facilitating incorporation into global observation initiatives, where appropriate;

109. *Calls upon* States and regional fisheries management organizations or arrangements, working in cooperation with other relevant organizations, including the Food and Agriculture Organization of the United Nations, the Intergovernmental Oceanographic Commission and the World Meteorological Organization, to adopt, as appropriate, measures to protect ocean data buoy systems moored in areas beyond national jurisdiction from actions that impair their operation;

110. *Encourages* States to increase scientific research in accordance with international law on the marine ecosystem;

111. *Calls upon* States, the Food and Agriculture Organization of the United Nations and other specialized agencies, subregional and regional fisheries management organizations and arrangements, where appropriate, and other appropriate intergovernmental bodies, to cooperate in achieving sustainable aquaculture, including through information exchange, developing equivalent standards on such issues as aquatic animal health and human health and safety concerns, assessing the potential positive and negative impacts of aquaculture, including socio-economic, on the marine and coastal environment, including biodiversity, and adopting relevant methods and techniques to minimize and mitigate adverse effects, and in this regard encourages the implementation of the 2007 Strategy and Outline Plan for Improving Information on Status and Trends of Aquaculture of the Food and Agriculture Organization of the United Nations, as a framework for the improvement and understanding of aquaculture status and trends;

112. *Expresses its appreciation* to the Secretary-General for the report on the actions taken by States and regional

fisheries management organizations and arrangements to give effect to paragraphs 83 to 90 of resolution 61/105;

113. *Calls upon* States to take action immediately, individually and through regional fisheries management organizations and arrangements, and consistent with the precautionary approach and ecosystem approaches, to implement the 2008 International Guidelines for the Management of Deep-sea Fisheries in the High Seas of the Food and Agriculture Organization of the United Nations ("the Guidelines") in order to sustainably manage fish stocks and protect vulnerable marine ecosystems, including seamounts, hydrothermal vents and cold water corals, from destructive fishing practices, recognizing the immense importance and value of deep sea ecosystems and the biodiversity they contain;

114. *Reaffirms* the importance of paragraphs 80 to 91 of resolution 61/105 addressing the impacts of bottom fishing on vulnerable marine ecosystems and the long-term sustainability of deep sea fish stocks and the actions called for in that resolution, and emphasizes the need for full implementation by all States and relevant regional fisheries management organizations or arrangements of their commitments under those paragraphs on an urgent basis;

115. *Recalls* that nothing in the paragraphs of resolution 61/105 and the present resolution addressing the impacts of bottom fishing on vulnerable marine ecosystems prejudices the sovereign rights of coastal States over their continental shelf or the exercise of the jurisdiction of coastal States with respect to their continental shelf under international law as reflected in the Convention, in particular article 77;

116. *Welcomes* the important progress made by States, regional fisheries management organizations or arrangements and those States participating in negotiations to establish a regional fisheries management organization or arrangement competent to regulate bottom fisheries to implement paragraphs 80 and 83 to 87 of resolution 61/105 and address the impacts of bottom fishing on vulnerable marine ecosystems;

117. *Also welcomes* the substantial work of the Food and Agriculture Organization of the United Nations related to the management of deep sea fisheries in the high seas and the protection of vulnerable marine ecosystems, in particular the development and adoption of the Guidelines, and urges States and regional fisheries management organizations or arrangements to ensure that their actions in sustainably managing deep sea fisheries and implementing paragraphs 80 and 83 to 87 of resolution 61/105 and paragraphs 119, 120 and 122 to 124 of the present resolution are consistent with the Guidelines;

118. *Notes with concern* that, despite the progress made, the urgent actions called for in paragraphs 80 and 83 to 87 of resolution 61/105 have not been sufficiently implemented in all cases;

119. *Considers* that, on the basis of the review carried out in accordance with paragraph 91 of resolution 61/105, further actions in accordance with the precautionary approach, ecosystem approaches and international law are needed to strengthen the implementation of paragraphs 80 and 83 to 87 of resolution 61/105, and in this regard calls upon regional fisheries management organizations or arrangements with the competence to regulate bottom fisheries, States participating in negotiations to establish such organizations or arrangements, and flag States to take the following urgent actions in areas beyond national jurisdiction:

(a) Conduct the assessments called for in paragraph 83 *(a)* of resolution 61/105, consistent with the Guidelines, and ensure that vessels do not engage in bottom fishing until such assessments have been carried out;

(b) Conduct further marine scientific research and use the best scientific and technical information available to identify where vulnerable marine ecosystems are known to occur or are likely to occur and adopt conservation and management measures to prevent significant adverse impacts on such ecosystems consistent with the Guidelines, or close such areas to bottom fishing until conservation and management measures have been established, as called for in paragraph 83 *(c)* of resolution 61/105;

(c) Establish and implement appropriate protocols for the implementation of paragraph 83 *(d)* of resolution 61/105, including definitions of what constitutes evidence of an encounter with a vulnerable marine ecosystem, in particular threshold levels and indicator species, based on the best available scientific information and consistent with the Guidelines, and taking into account any other conservation and management measures to prevent significant adverse impacts on vulnerable marine ecosystems, including those based on the results of assessments carried out pursuant to paragraph 83 *(a)* of resolution 61/105 and paragraph 119 *(a)* of the present resolution;

(d) Adopt conservation and management measures, including monitoring, control and surveillance measures, on the basis of stock assessments and the best available scientific information, to ensure the long-term sustainability of deep sea fish stocks and non-target species, and the rebuilding of depleted stocks, consistent with the Guidelines; and, where scientific information is uncertain, unreliable, or inadequate, ensure that conservation and management measures are established consistent with the precautionary approach, including measures to ensure that fishing effort, fishing capacity and catch limits, as appropriate, are at levels commensurate with the long-term sustainability of such stocks;

120. *Calls upon* flag States, members of regional fisheries management organizations or arrangements with the competence to regulate bottom fisheries and States participating in negotiations to establish such organizations or arrangements to adopt and implement measures in accordance with paragraphs 83, 85 and 86 of resolution 61/105, paragraph 119 of the present resolution, and international law, and consistent with the Guidelines, and not to authorize bottom fishing activities until such measures have been adopted and implemented;

121. *Recognizes* the special circumstances and requirements of developing States and the specific challenges they may face in giving full effect to certain technical aspects of the Guidelines, and that implementation by such States of paragraphs 83 to 87 of resolution 61/105, paragraph 119 of the present resolution and the Guidelines should proceed in a manner that gives full consideration to section 6 of the Guidelines on special requirements of developing countries;

122. *Calls upon* States and regional fisheries management organizations or arrangements to enhance efforts to

cooperate to collect and exchange scientific and technical data and information related to the implementation of the measures called for in the relevant paragraphs of resolution 61/105 and the present resolution to manage deep sea fisheries in areas beyond national jurisdiction and to protect vulnerable marine ecosystems from significant adverse impacts of bottom fishing by, inter alia:

(a) Exchanging best practices and developing, where appropriate, regional standards for use by States engaged in bottom fisheries in areas beyond national jurisdiction and regional fisheries management organizations or arrangements with a view to examining current scientific and technical protocols and promoting consistent implementation of best practices across fisheries and regions, including assistance to developing States in accomplishing these objectives;

(b) Making publicly available, consistent with domestic law, assessments of whether individual bottom fishing activities would have significant adverse impacts on vulnerable marine ecosystems and the measures adopted in accordance with paragraphs 83, 85 and 86, as appropriate, of resolution 61/105, and promoting the inclusion of this information on the websites of regional fisheries management organizations or arrangements;

(c) Submission by flag States to the Food and Agriculture Organization of the United Nations of a list of those vessels flying their flag authorized to conduct bottom fisheries in areas beyond national jurisdiction, and the measures they have adopted to give effect to the relevant paragraphs of resolution 61/105 and the present resolution;

(d) Sharing information on vessels that are engaged in bottom fishing operations in areas beyond national jurisdiction where the flag State responsible for such vessels cannot be determined;

123. *Encourages* States and regional fisheries management organizations or arrangements to develop or strengthen data collection standards, procedures and protocols and research programmes for identification of vulnerable marine ecosystems, assessment of impacts on such ecosystems, and assessment of fishing activities on target and non-target species, consistent with the Guidelines and in accordance with the Convention, including Part XIII thereof;

124. *Calls upon* relevant States to cooperate and make efforts to establish, as appropriate, regional fisheries management organizations or arrangements competent to regulate bottom fisheries in areas beyond national jurisdiction where there are no such organizations or arrangements;

125. *Expresses its appreciation* to the Food and Agriculture Organization of the United Nations for its important work to provide expert technical advice on the management of deep sea fisheries in areas beyond national jurisdiction and the protection of vulnerable marine ecosystems from the impacts of fishing, and encourages the Organization in its further work related to the implementation of the Guidelines;

126. *Welcomes* the programme proposal for deep sea fisheries in the high seas on ensuring sustainable use of marine resources and protection of vulnerable marine ecosystems of the Food and Agriculture Organization of the United Nations, including the development of support tools and a database on vulnerable marine ecosystems, and

invites States to support the programme so that its elements may be finalized as a matter of priority;

127. *Invites* the Food and Agriculture Organization of the United Nations, working with other relevant international governmental organizations, to consider means to support flag States and regional fisheries management organizations or arrangements in their implementation of paragraphs 83 to 87 of resolution 61/105, paragraphs 119 to 122 of the present resolution and the Guidelines;

128. *Requests* the Secretary-General to convene, within existing resources, within the time made available for the informal consultations on the sustainable fisheries resolution and without prejudice to future arrangements, a two-day workshop in 2011 in order to discuss implementation of paragraphs 80 and 83 to 87 of resolution 61/105 and paragraphs 117 and 119 to 127 of the present resolution, and invite States, the Food and Agriculture Organization of the United Nations and other relevant specialized agencies, funds and programmes, subregional and regional fisheries management organizations and arrangements, other fisheries bodies, other relevant intergovernmental bodies, and relevant non-governmental organizations and stakeholders, in accordance with United Nations practice, to attend the workshop;

129. *Decides* to conduct a further review in 2011 of the actions taken by States and regional fisheries management organizations and arrangements in response to paragraphs 80 and 83 to 87 of resolution 61/105 and paragraphs 117 and 119 to 127 of the present resolution, with a view to ensuring effective implementation of the measures and to make further recommendations, where necessary, and taking into account the discussions during the workshop referred to in paragraph 128 above;

130. *Requests* the Secretary-General, in cooperation with the Food and Agriculture Organization of the United Nations, to include in his report on fisheries to the General Assembly at its sixty-sixth session a section on the actions taken by States and regional fisheries management organizations and arrangements in response to paragraphs 80 and 83 to 87 of resolution 61/105 and paragraphs 117 and 119 to 127 of the present resolution, and invites States and regional fisheries management organizations and arrangements to consider making such information publicly available;

131. *Encourages* accelerated progress to establish criteria on the objectives and management of marine protected areas for fisheries purposes, and in this regard welcomes the proposed work of the Food and Agriculture Organization of the United Nations to develop technical guidelines in accordance with the Convention and the Code on the design, implementation and testing of marine protected areas for such purposes, and urges coordination and cooperation among all relevant international organizations and bodies;

132. *Urges* all States to implement the 1995 Global Programme of Action for the Protection of the Marine Environment from Land-based Activities and to accelerate activity to safeguard the marine ecosystem, including fish stocks, against pollution and physical degradation;

133. *Reaffirms* the importance it attaches to paragraphs 77 to 81 of resolution 60/31 concerning the issue of lost, abandoned or discarded fishing gear and related marine debris and the adverse impacts such debris and derelict fish-

ing gear have on, inter alia, fish stocks, habitats and other marine species, and urges accelerated progress by States and regional fisheries management organizations and arrangements in implementing those paragraphs of the resolution;

XI

Capacity-building

134. *Reiterates* the crucial importance of cooperation by States directly or, as appropriate, through the relevant subregional and regional organizations, and by other international organizations, including the Food and Agriculture Organization of the United Nations through its FishCode programme, including through financial and/or technical assistance, in accordance with the Agreement, the Compliance Agreement, the Code and its associated international plans of action, to increase the capacity of developing States to achieve the goals and implement the actions called for in the present resolution;

135. *Welcomes* the work of the Food and Agriculture Organization of the United Nations in developing guidance on the strategies and measures required for the creation of an enabling environment for small-scale fisheries, including the development of a code of conduct and guidelines for enhancing the contribution of small-scale fisheries to poverty alleviation and food security that include adequate provisions with regard to financial measures and capacity-building, including transfer of technology, and encourages studies for creating possible alternative livelihoods for coastal communities;

136. *Encourages* increased capacity-building and technical assistance by States, international financial institutions and relevant intergovernmental organizations and bodies for fishers, in particular small-scale fishers, in developing countries, and in particular small island developing States, consistent with environmental sustainability;

137. *Encourages* the international community to enhance the opportunities for sustainable development in developing countries, in particular the least developed countries, small island developing States and coastal African States, by encouraging greater participation of those States in authorized fisheries activities being undertaken within areas under their national jurisdiction, in accordance with the Convention, by distant-water fishing nations in order to achieve better economic returns for developing countries from their fisheries resources within areas under their national jurisdiction and an enhanced role in regional fisheries management, as well as by enhancing the ability of developing countries to develop their own fisheries, as well as to participate in high seas fisheries, including access to such fisheries, in conformity with international law, in particular the Convention and the Agreement, and taking into account article 5 of the Code;

138. *Requests* distant-water fishing nations, when negotiating access agreements and arrangements with developing coastal States, to do so on an equitable and sustainable basis, including by giving greater attention to fish processing and fish-processing facilities within the national jurisdiction of the developing coastal State to assist the realization of the benefits from the development of fisheries resources, and also the transfer of technology and assistance for monitoring, control and surveillance and compliance and enforcement within areas under the national jurisdic-

tion of the developing coastal State providing fisheries access, taking into account the forms of cooperation set out in article 25 of the Agreement and article 5 of the Code;

139. *Encourages* States, individually and through regional fisheries management organizations and arrangements, to provide greater assistance and to promote coherence in such assistance for developing States in designing, establishing and implementing relevant agreements, instruments and tools for the conservation and sustainable management of fish stocks, including in designing and strengthening their domestic regulatory fisheries policies and those of regional fisheries management organizations or arrangements in their regions, and the enhancement of research and scientific capabilities through existing funds, such as the Assistance Fund under Part VII of the Agreement, bilateral assistance, regional fisheries management organizations and arrangements assistance funds, the FishCode programme, the World Bank's global programme on fisheries and the Global Environment Facility;

140. *Encourages* States to provide technical and financial support to developing countries to address their special requirements and challenges in implementing the Guidelines;

141. *Calls upon* States to promote, through continuing dialogue and the assistance and cooperation provided in accordance with articles 24 to 26 of the Agreement, further ratification of or accession to the Agreement by seeking to address, inter alia, the issue of lack of capacity and resources that might stand in the way of developing States becoming parties;

142. *Notes with appreciation* the compilation prepared by the Secretariat of the needs of developing States for capacity-building and assistance in the conservation and management of straddling fish stocks and highly migratory fish stocks and the sources of available assistance for developing States to address such needs;

143. *Encourages* States, regional fisheries management organizations and arrangements and other relevant bodies to assist developing States in the implementation of the actions called for in paragraphs 80 and 83 to 87 of resolution 61/105 and paragraphs 113 and 119 to 124 of the present resolution;

XII

Cooperation within the United Nations system

144. *Requests* the relevant parts of the United Nations system, international financial institutions and donor agencies to support increased enforcement and compliance capabilities for regional fisheries management organizations and their member States;

145. *Invites* the Food and Agriculture Organization of the United Nations to continue its cooperative arrangements with United Nations agencies on the implementation of the international plans of action and to report to the Secretary-General, for inclusion in his annual report on sustainable fisheries, on priorities for cooperation and coordination in this work;

XIII

Sixty-fifth session of the General Assembly

146. *Requests* the Secretary-General to bring the present resolution to the attention of all States, relevant inter-

governmental organizations, the organizations and bodies of the United Nations system, subregional and regional fisheries management organizations and relevant non-governmental organizations, and to invite them to provide the Secretary-General with information relevant to the implementation of the present resolution;

147. *Also requests* the Secretary-General to submit to the General Assembly at its sixty-seventh session a report on "Sustainable fisheries, including through the 1995 Agreement for the Implementation of the Provisions of the United Nations Convention on the Law of the Sea of 10 December 1982 relating to the Conservation and Management of Straddling Fish Stocks and Highly Migratory Fish Stocks, and related instruments", taking into account information provided by States, relevant specialized agencies, in particular the Food and Agriculture Organization of the United Nations, and other appropriate organs, organizations and programmes of the United Nations system, subregional and regional organizations and arrangements for the conservation and management of straddling fish stocks and highly migratory fish stocks, as well as other relevant intergovernmental bodies and non-governmental organizations, and consisting, inter alia, of elements provided in relevant paragraphs in the present resolution;

148. *Decides* to include in the provisional agenda of its sixty-fifth session, under the item entitled "Oceans and the law of the sea", the sub-item entitled "Sustainable fisheries, including through the 1995 Agreement for the Implementation of the Provisions of the United Nations Convention on the Law of the Sea of 10 December 1982 relating to the Conservation and Management of Straddling Fish Stocks and Highly Migratory Fish Stocks, and related instruments".

Institutions created by the Convention

International Seabed Authority

Through the International Seabed Authority, established by the United Nations Convention on the Law of the Sea and the 1994 Implementation Agreement [YUN 1994, p. 1301], States organized and conducted exploration of the resources of the seabed and ocean floor and subsoil beyond the limits of national jurisdiction. In 2009, the Authority, which had 160 members as at 31 December, held its fifteenth session (Kingston, Jamaica, 25 May–5 June) [ISBA/15/A/1]. Its subsidiary bodies, namely, the Assembly, the Council, the Legal and Technical Commission and the Finance Committee, also met during the session.

The Assembly considered the annual report of the Authority's Secretary-General [ISBA/15/A/2], which reviewed the Authority's work since the fourteenth session and provided a brief overview of the present status of and prospects for deep seabed mining. The depth of the global recession had a severe impact on metal markets, as well as on the prospects for seabed mining and future development of land-based mines. A fall in demand for metals had led to sharp falls in prices and expectations were for a prolonged and se-

vere downturn in the mining industry. On the other hand, prospects for the offshore oil and gas industry were more positive, with a leading energy business analyst forecasting that the deepwater oil and gas sector would continue its growth trend. In other developments, the first training opportunities under the International Seabed Authority Endowment Fund for Marine Scientific Research in the Area, established in 2006 [YUN 2006, p. 1554], became available in 2009. The Authority continued to develop a geological model of polymetallic nodule deposits in the Clarion-Clipperton fracture zone (East Pacific Ocean), and work on developing a model for the Central Indian Ocean basin would continue throughout 2010.

It was anticipated that consideration of the implementation by the Authority of article 82 of the Convention would assume greater importance in the Authority's future work. Article 82 required States or individual operators to contribute a proportion of the revenues they generated from exploiting the non-living resources of the outer continental shelf—the part of the continental shelf that extends beyond 200 nautical miles from the baselines of the territorial sea—for the benefit of the international community as a whole. Although the Authority was responsible for collecting and distributing those revenues, it remained one of the few provisions of the Convention for which few, if any, steps towards its implementation had been taken. On the future potential of seabed resources, the Authority's Secretary-General observed that despite setbacks from the global economic downturn, there remained considerable public- and private-sector interest in exploration work to better understand and characterize the mineral resources of the deep seabed.

The Legal and Technical Commission reported to the Council on its work during the fifteenth session [ISBA/15/C/5], in which it discussed the annual reports submitted by contractors; two applications for approval of work plans for exploration; a proposal for a network of areas of particular environmental interest in the Clarion-Clipperton fracture zone; recommendations for the guidance of contractors; draft regulations on prospecting and exploration for cobalt-rich ferromanganese crusts in the Area (the seabed and ocean floor and subsoil beyond the limits of national jurisdiction); and an update on progress on the geological model for the Clarion-Clipperton fracture zone. In May, it adopted recommendations for the guidance of contractors on reporting actual and direct exploration expenditures [ISBA/15/LTC/7].

The Finance Committee held four meetings during the session, on 26 and 27 May [ISBA/15/A/5-ISBA/15/C/6]. It took note of the balance of the Endowment Fund as at 20 May at $2,915,057 and of the Voluntary Trust Fund at $16,871. After considering three bids, it recommended that Pricewaterhouse-

Coopers be appointed for two years to audit the 2009 and 2010 financial statements of the Authority, which the Assembly endorsed on 4 June [ISBA/15/A/8].

As at 31 December, the 1998 Protocol on the Privileges and Immunities of the International Seabed Authority [YUN 1998, p. 1226], which entered into force in 2003 [YUN 2003, p. 1353], had 28 signatories and 31 parties.

International Tribunal for the Law of the Sea

The International Tribunal for the Law of the Sea held its twenty-seventh (9–20 March) and twenty-eighth (21 September–2 October) sessions, both in Hamburg, Germany [SPLOS/204].

In the *Case concerning the Conservation and Sustainable Exploitation of Swordfish Stocks in the South-Eastern Pacific Ocean (Chile/European Union)*, by communications of 13 October and 25 November, respectively, the European Community and Chile informed the Special Chamber that they were committed to the signature, ratification or approval, and implementation of and compliance with the "Understanding" agreed between the Parties' negotiators in October 2008 [YUN 2008, p. 1495], and would request the discontinuance of their case. In response to a 30 November request from the Special Chamber, the parties provided additional information in a 15 December joint communication outlining the terms of their settlement. The European Commission, on 7 December, informed the Special Chamber President that since the entry into force on 1 December of the Treaty of Lisbon, the European Union (EU) had replaced and succeeded the European Community. The Agent of Chile expressed no objection to treating the EU as a party to the case in place of the European Community. On 16 December, the Special Chamber, placed on record the discontinuance of the proceedings initiated on 20 December 2000 by Chile and the EU, ordering that the matter be removed from the list of cases.

On 14 December, proceedings were instituted before the Tribunal in relation to the *Dispute concerning delimitation of the maritime boundary between Bangladesh and Myanmar in the Bay of Bengal (Bangladesh/Myanmar)*, which had initially been submitted to an arbitral tribunal to be constituted under annex VII to the Convention, through a notification dated 8 October, made by Bangladesh to Myanmar. In declarations dated 4 November and 12 December, respectively, Myanmar and Bangladesh accepted the Tribunal's jurisdiction for settlement of the dispute. Those declarations were brought to the attention of the Tribunal's President by a 13 December letter from Bangladesh, in which the Tribunal was invited to exercise jurisdiction over the dispute. Consequently, the dispute relating to the delimitation of the maritime boundary

in the Bay of Bengal was entered in the list of cases of the Tribunal as Case No. 16.

As at 31 December, the Agreement on the Privileges and Immunities of the International Tribunal for the Law of the Sea, which was adopted by the seventh Meeting of States Parties to the Convention in 1997 [YUN 1997, p. 1361] and entered into force in 2001 [YUN 2001, p. 1235], had 21 signatories and 38 parties.

Commission on the Limits of the Continental Shelf

In 2009, the Commission on the Limits of the Continental Shelf, established in 1997 [YUN 1997, p. 1362], held its twenty-third (2 March–9 April) [CLCS/62] and twenty-fourth (10 August–11 September) [CLCS/64] sessions, both in New York. Among other things, it examined submissions by States regarding the establishment of the outer limits of the continental shelf beyond 200 nautical miles.

At its twenty-third session, the Commission adopted recommendations on the limits of the continental shelf related to a joint submission made by France, Ireland, Spain and the United Kingdom in 2006 [YUN 2006, p. 1555] in respect of the area of the Celtic Sea and the Bay of Biscay; a submission by Norway [ibid.] regarding areas in the Arctic Ocean, the Barents Sea and the Norwegian Sea; and a submission by Mexico in 2007 in respect of the Western Polygon in the Gulf of Mexico. Its draft final recommendations regarding a 2007 submission by France [YUN 2007, p. 1401] were being reviewed by the French delegation. The Commission also began consideration of the 2008 submissions by Barbados, Indonesia, Japan and the United Kingdom [YUN 2008, p. 1496], as well as the joint submission by Mauritius and Seychelles.

At its twenty-fourth session, the Commission adopted recommendations on the limits of the continental shelf in regard to the submission made by France in respect of the areas of French Guiana and New Caledonia. It continued to consider the submissions made by Barbados, Indonesia, Japan and the United Kingdom. On the Hatton Rockall Area, as submissions were made by Ireland and the United Kingdom, and both Denmark and Iceland had also expressed interest in the continental shelf in the Area, the Commission deferred consideration of the submissions and related notes verbales until such time as those submissions were next in line for consideration as queued in the order in which they were received. The Commission decided that the joint submission by Mauritius and Seychelles would be addressed through the establishment of a subcommission, but did not establish one during the session. It also decided that the submissions made by the Cook Islands, Côte d'Ivoire, Denmark (regarding the area north of the

Faroe Islands), Ghana, Kenya, Mauritius (in the region of Rodrigues Island), Nigeria, the Philippines, Seychelles, Suriname, and Uruguay would be addressed by way of a subcommission to be established at a future session.

The Commission also decided to defer consideration of submissions by Argentina, Fiji, Myanmar, Viet Nam (in respect of the North Area), and a joint submission by Malaysia and Viet Nam, along with related notes verbales from Bangladesh, India, Kenya and Sri Lanka.

Other developments related to the Convention

In response to General Assembly resolution 63/111 [YUN 2008, p. 1497], the Secretary-General submitted a March report on oceans and the law of the sea [A/64/66], which provided information on the establishment of the United Nations Open-ended Informal Consultative Process on Oceans and the Law of the Sea; an overview of its functioning and outcomes; follow-up on the outcomes; and summaries of views presented on the achievements and shortcomings of the Consultative Process.

An August addendum [A/64/66/Add.1] reviewed developments surrounding international shipping activities, maritime space, people at sea, maritime security, marine science and technology, marine living resources, marine biological diversity, protection of the marine environment and climate change and oceans. The report also provided information on the settlement of disputes, international coordination and cooperation and capacity-building activities. A July addendum [A/64/66/Add.2], submitted to assist the Ad Hoc Open-ended Informal Working Group in studying issues related to the conservation and sustainable use of marine biological diversity beyond areas of national jurisdiction, and in preparing the agenda of its third (2010) meeting, contained information on activities undertaken by relevant organizations since the previous report in 2007 [YUN 2007, p. 1401].

Marine environment: Global Marine Assessment

The fourth meeting [GRAME/AHSG/4/2] of the Ad Hoc Steering Group for the "assessment of assessments" of the regular process for the global reporting and assessment of the state of the marine environment, including socio-economic aspects, was held at the Intergovernmental Oceanographic Commission of the United Nations Educational, Scientific and Cultural Organization (UNESCO) headquarters (Paris, 15–17 April). The meeting was convened pursuant to General Assembly resolution 60/30 [YUN 2005, p. 1436], by which the Assembly established the Ad Hoc Steering Group and invited

the United Nations Environment Programme (UNEP) and the Intergovernmental Oceanographic Commission of UNESCO to jointly lead the process of, among other things, preparing a report on the results of the "assessment of assessments" for the Assembly.

Assessment of assessments report. On 11 May, in response to Assembly resolution 60/30, UNEP and the Intergovernmental Oceanographic Commission of UNESCO transmitted the report [A/64/88] on the "assessment of assessments", which contained a report on the outcomes of the fourth meeting of the Ad Hoc Steering Group and the findings of the "assessment of assessments", including options on a framework for a regular process. The report was prepared by a Group of Experts established in 2006 [YUN 2006, p. 1557], which comprised 34 recognized experts in relevant fields, 15 international institutions and 29 Governments. More than 1,200 comments were received, all of which were considered and addressed by the authors. The "assessment of assessments" report was finalized and signed at the fifth meeting of the Group of Experts (Geneva, 19–21 March).

Ad Hoc Working Group report. On 10 September, the Ad Hoc Working Group of the Whole, established pursuant to Assembly resolution 63/111 to recommend a course of action on the regular process for global reporting and assessment of the state of the marine environment, submitted a report [A/64/347] on the work of the Group. Its recommendations, which were annexed to the report, envisaged a first cycle of the process, from 2010 to 2014. The first phase of the cycle (2010–2012) would be devoted to the development of the strategy and timetable for the production of an integrated assessment of the world's oceans and seas. The second phase of the first cycle (2013–2014) would produce an integrated assessment of the oceans, including agreed priority cross-cutting thematic issues such as food security, and establish a baseline for future global assessments. Following the completion of each phase of the five-year cycle, the Assembly would be provided with a report on the results of the work undertaken. The length, scope, objectives and guiding principles of future cycles of the regular process would be determined by the Assembly following the completion of the first five-year cycle.

United Nations Open-ended Informal Consultative Process

In response to General Assembly resolutions 63/111 [YUN 2008, p. 1497], the tenth meeting of the United Nations Open-ended Informal Consultative Process on Oceans and the Law of the Sea (New York, 17–19 June) [A/64/131] focused on the implementation of the outcomes of the Consultative Process, including a review of its achievements and shortcomings in its first nine meetings. It also drew attention to issues where further efforts were needed, such as illegal, unreported and unregulated fishing, including as it might relate to international organized crime; piracy and armed robbery; maritime safety and security; oceans and climate change; climate change as it related to security and survival; preservation of the marine environment; protection of living resources; safety of navigation and the production of nautical charts; sustainable use of ocean resources; the impact of unfair subsidies on the fishing industry of developing States; cooperation and coordination among flag States, coastal States and port States in implementing the Convention; and conservation as it related to marine life and environment.

In April, Nigeria submitted a contribution [A/AC.259/18] to the tenth meeting, finding that the meeting's topic, including a review of the achievements and shortcomings of the Consultative Process, was apt and timely, and suggesting areas for discussion at the meeting, such as the need for capacity-building and assistance to developing States.

GENERAL ASSEMBLY ACTION

On 4 December [meeting 58], the General Assembly adopted **resolution 64/71** [draft: A/64/L.18 & Add.1] by recorded vote (120-1-3) [agenda item 76 *(a)*].

Oceans and the law of the sea

The General Assembly,

Recalling its annual resolutions on the law of the sea and on oceans and the law of the sea, including resolution 63/111 of 5 December 2008, and other relevant resolutions concerning the United Nations Convention on the Law of the Sea ("the Convention"),

Having considered the report of the Secretary-General, and also the reports on the work of the United Nations Open-ended Informal Consultative Process on Oceans and the Law of the Sea ("the Consultative Process") at its tenth meeting, on the nineteenth Meeting of States Parties to the Convention, and the report entitled "Regular process for global reporting and assessment of the state of the marine environment, including socio-economic aspects: the 'assessment of assessments'",

Emphasizing the pre-eminent contribution provided by the Convention to the strengthening of peace, security, cooperation and friendly relations among all nations in conformity with the principles of justice and equal rights and to the promotion of the economic and social advancement of all peoples of the world, in accordance with the purposes and principles of the United Nations as set forth in the Charter of the United Nations, as well as to the sustainable development of the oceans and seas,

Emphasizing also the universal and unified character of the Convention, and reaffirming that the Convention sets out the legal framework within which all activities in the oceans and seas must be carried out and is of strategic importance as the basis for national, regional and global action and cooperation in the marine sector, and that its integrity needs to be maintained, as recognized also by the United Nations Conference on Environment and Development in chapter 17 of Agenda 21,

Recognizing the important contribution of sustainable development and management of the resources and uses of the oceans and seas to the achievement of international development goals, including those contained in the United Nations Millennium Declaration,

Conscious that the problems of ocean space are closely interrelated and need to be considered as a whole through an integrated, interdisciplinary and intersectoral approach, and reaffirming the need to improve cooperation and coordination at the national, regional and global levels, in accordance with the Convention, to support and supplement the efforts of each State in promoting the implementation and observance of the Convention, and the integrated management and sustainable development of the oceans and seas,

Reiterating the essential need for cooperation, including through capacity-building and transfer of marine technology, to ensure that all States, especially developing countries, in particular the least developed countries and small island developing States, as well as coastal African States, are able both to implement the Convention and to benefit from the sustainable development of the oceans and seas, as well as to participate fully in global and regional forums and processes dealing with oceans and law of the sea issues,

Emphasizing the need to strengthen the ability of competent international organizations to contribute, at the global, regional, subregional and bilateral levels, through cooperation programmes with Governments, to the development of national capacity in marine science and the sustainable management of the oceans and their resources,

Recalling that marine science is important for eradicating poverty, contributing to food security, conserving the world's marine environment and resources, helping to understand, predict and respond to natural events and promoting the sustainable development of the oceans and seas, by improving knowledge, through sustained research efforts and the evaluation of monitoring results, and applying such knowledge to management and decision-making,

Reiterating its deep concern at the serious adverse impacts on the marine environment and biodiversity, in particular on vulnerable marine ecosystems, including corals, hydrothermal vents and seamounts, of certain human activities,

Emphasizing the need for the safe and environmentally sound recycling of ships,

Expressing deep concern at the adverse economic, social and environmental impacts of the physical alteration and destruction of marine habitats that may result from land-based and coastal development activities, in particular those land reclamation activities that are carried out in a manner that has a detrimental impact on the marine environment,

Reiterating its serious concern at the current and projected adverse effects of climate change on the marine environment and marine biodiversity, and emphasizing the urgency of addressing this issue,

Expressing concern that climate change continues to increase the severity and incidence of coral bleaching throughout tropical seas and weakens the ability of reefs to withstand ocean acidification, which could have serious and irreversible negative effects on marine organisms, particularly corals, as well as to withstand other pressures, including overfishing and pollution,

Reiterating its deep concern at the vulnerability of the environment and the fragile ecosystems of the polar regions, including the Arctic Ocean and the Arctic ice cap, particularly affected by the projected adverse effects of climate change,

Recognizing that there is a need for a more integrated approach and to further study and promote measures for enhanced cooperation, coordination and collaboration relating to the conservation and sustainable use of marine biodiversity beyond areas of national jurisdiction,

Recognizing also that the realization of the benefits of the Convention could be enhanced by international cooperation, technical assistance and advanced scientific knowledge, as well as by funding and capacity-building,

Recognizing further that hydrographic surveys and nautical charting are critical to the safety of navigation and life at sea, environmental protection, including the protection of vulnerable marine ecosystems, and the economics of the global shipping industry, and encouraging further efforts towards electronic charting, which not only provides significantly increased benefits for safe navigation and management of ship movement, but also provides data and information that can be used for sustainable fisheries activities and other sectoral uses of the marine environment, the delimitation of maritime boundaries and environmental protection,

Emphasizing that underwater archaeological, cultural and historical heritage, including shipwrecks and watercrafts, holds essential information on the history of humankind and that such heritage is a resource that needs to be protected and preserved,

Noting with concern the continuing problem of transnational organized crime committed at sea, including illicit traffic in narcotic drugs and psychotropic substances, the smuggling of migrants and trafficking in persons, and threats to maritime safety and security, including piracy, armed robbery at sea, smuggling and terrorist acts against shipping, offshore installations and other maritime interests, and noting the deplorable loss of life and adverse impact on international trade, energy security and the global economy resulting from such activities,

Noting the importance of the delineation of the outer limits of the continental shelf beyond 200 nautical miles and that it is in the broader interest of the international community that coastal States with a continental shelf beyond 200 nautical miles submit information on the outer limits of the continental shelf beyond 200 nautical miles to the Commission on the Limits of the Continental Shelf ("the Commission"), and welcoming the submissions to the Commission by a considerable number of States Parties on the outer limits of their continental shelf beyond 200 nautical miles, that the Commission has continued to fulfil its role, including of making recommendations to coastal States, and that the summaries of recommendations have been made publicly available,

Noting also that many coastal States Parties have submitted preliminary information indicative of the outer limits of the continental shelf beyond 200 nautical miles, as provided for in the decision of the eighteenth Meeting of States Parties to the Convention regarding the workload of the Commission and the ability of States, particularly developing States, to fulfil the requirements of article 4 of annex II to the Convention, as well as the decision contained in SPLOS/72, paragraph *(a)*,

Noting further that some coastal States may continue to face particular challenges in relation to preparing and presenting submissions to the Commission,

Noting that financial and technical assistance may be sought by developing countries for activities in relation to preparing and presenting submissions to the Commission, including through the voluntary trust fund established by resolution 55/7 of 30 October 2000 for the purpose of facilitating the preparation of submissions to the Commission for developing States, in particular the least developed countries and small island developing States, and compliance with article 76 of the Convention, as well as other accessible international assistance,

Recognizing the importance of the trust funds established by resolution 55/7 in facilitating the participation of members of the Commission from developing States in the meetings of the Commission and in fulfilling the requirements of article 4 of annex II to the Convention, while noting with appreciation the recent contributions made to them,

Reaffirming the importance of the work of the Commission for coastal States and for the international community,

Recognizing the significant workload of the Commission in view of the large number of submissions already received and a number of submissions yet to be received, which places additional demands and challenges on its members and the secretariat as provided by the Secretary-General of the United Nations through the Division for Ocean Affairs and the Law of the Sea of the Office of Legal Affairs of the Secretariat ("the Division"),

Noting with concern the projected timetable of the work of the Commission on the submissions already received by it and those yet to be received and, in this regard, the consequences of the duration of the sessions of the Commission and the meetings of its subcommissions,

Recognizing significant inequities and difficulties for States arising out of the projected timetable, including with respect to retaining expertise, when there is a considerable delay between preparation of submissions and their consideration by the Commission,

Recognizing also the need to take action to ensure that the Commission can perform its functions under the Convention expeditiously, efficiently and effectively, and maintain its high level of quality and expertise,

Welcoming the agreed outcome reflected in the report of the nineteenth Meeting of States Parties to the Convention regarding the workload of the Commission, and noting in particular the decision of the Meeting to continue to address the issues related to the workload of the Commission as a matter of priority, as well as the decision that its bureau would facilitate an informal working group to continue consideration of the issues related to the workload of the Commission,

Recalling its decision, in resolutions 57/141 of 12 December 2002 and 58/240 of 23 December 2003, to establish a regular process under the United Nations for global reporting and assessment of the state of the marine environment, including socio-economic aspects, both current and foreseeable, building on existing regional assessments, as recommended by the World Summit on Sustainable Development, and noting the need for cooperation among all States to this end,

Recalling also the launching of the start-up phase, the "assessment of assessments", and noting the work carried out by the Group of Experts established pursuant to resolution 60/30 of 29 November 2005 under the guidance of the Ad Hoc Steering Group for the "assessment of assessments" and with the assistance of the lead agencies, the United Nations Environment Programme and the Intergovernmental Oceanographic Commission of the United Nations Educational, Scientific and Cultural Organization, and the support provided by other organizations and experts,

Recognizing the importance and the contribution of the work of the Consultative Process established by resolution 54/33 of 24 November 1999 to facilitate the annual review of developments in ocean affairs by the General Assembly,

Noting the responsibilities of the Secretary-General under the Convention and related resolutions of the General Assembly, in particular resolutions 49/28 of 6 December 1994, 52/26 of 26 November 1997 and 54/33, and in this context the substantial increase in activities of the Division, in particular in view of the growing number of requests to the Division for additional outputs and servicing of meetings, its increasing capacity-building activities, the need for enhanced support and assistance to the Commission and the role of the Division in inter-agency coordination and cooperation,

Reaffirming the importance of the work of the International Seabed Authority ("the Authority") in accordance with the Convention and the Agreement relating to the Implementation of Part XI of the United Nations Convention on the Law of the Sea of 10 December 1982 ("the Part XI Agreement"),

Reaffirming also the importance of the work of the International Tribunal for the Law of the Sea ("the Tribunal") in accordance with the Convention,

I

Implementation of the Convention and related agreements and instruments

1. *Reaffirms* its annual resolutions on the law of the sea and on oceans and the law of the sea, including resolution 63/111, and other relevant resolutions concerning the Convention;

2. *Also reaffirms* the unified character of the Convention and the vital importance of preserving its integrity;

3. *Calls upon* all States that have not done so, in order to achieve the goal of universal participation, to become parties to the Convention and the Part XI Agreement;

4. *Calls upon* States that have not done so, in order to achieve the goal of universal participation, to become parties to the Agreement for the Implementation of the Provisions of the United Nations Convention on the Law of the Sea of 10 December 1982 relating to the Conservation and Management of Straddling Fish Stocks and Highly Migratory Fish Stocks ("the Fish Stocks Agreement");

5. *Calls upon* States to harmonize their national legislation with the provisions of the Convention and, where

applicable, relevant agreements and instruments, to ensure the consistent application of those provisions and to ensure also that any declarations or statements that they have made or make when signing, ratifying or acceding to the Convention do not purport to exclude or to modify the legal effect of the provisions of the Convention in their application to the State concerned and to withdraw any such declarations or statements;

6. *Calls upon* States Parties to the Convention that have not yet done so to deposit with the Secretary-General charts or lists of geographical coordinates, as provided for in the Convention;

7. *Urges* all States to cooperate, directly or through competent international bodies, in taking measures to protect and preserve objects of an archaeological and historical nature found at sea, in conformity with the Convention, and calls upon States to work together on such diverse challenges and opportunities as the appropriate relationship between salvage law and scientific management and conservation of underwater cultural heritage, increasing technological abilities to discover and reach underwater sites, looting and growing underwater tourism;

8. *Notes* the entry into force of the 2001 Convention on the Protection of the Underwater Cultural Heritage on 2 January 2009, and notes in particular the rules annexed thereto, which address the relationship between salvage law and scientific principles of management, conservation and protection of underwater cultural heritage among Parties, their nationals and vessels flying their flag;

II

Capacity-building

9. *Calls upon* donor agencies and international financial institutions to keep their programmes systematically under review to ensure the availability in all States, particularly in developing States, of the economic, legal, navigational, scientific and technical skills necessary for the full implementation of the Convention and the objectives of the present resolution, as well as the sustainable development of the oceans and seas nationally, regionally and globally, and in so doing to bear in mind the interests and needs of landlocked developing States;

10. *Encourages* intensified efforts to build capacity for developing countries, in particular for the least developed countries and small island developing States, as well as coastal African States, to improve hydrographic services and the production of nautical charts, including electronic charts, as well as the mobilization of resources and building of capacity with support from international financial institutions and the donor community;

11. *Calls upon* States and international financial institutions, including through bilateral, regional and global cooperation programmes and technical partnerships, to continue to strengthen capacity-building activities, in particular in developing countries, in the field of marine scientific research by, inter alia, training personnel to develop and enhance relevant expertise, providing the necessary equipment, facilities and vessels and transferring environmentally sound technologies;

12. *Also calls upon* States and international financial institutions, including through bilateral, regional and global cooperation programmes and technical partner-

ships, to strengthen capacity-building activities in developing countries, in particular least developed countries and small island developing States, to develop their maritime administration and appropriate legal frameworks to establish or enhance the necessary infrastructure, legislative and enforcement capabilities to promote effective compliance with, and implementation and enforcement of, their responsibilities under international law;

13. *Recognizes* the importance of the work of the International Maritime Law Institute of the International Maritime Organization as a centre of education and training of Government legal advisers, mainly from developing States, notes that the number of its graduates in 115 States confirms its effective capacity-building role in the field of international law, congratulates the Institute on the celebration of its twentieth anniversary, and urges States, intergovernmental organizations and financial institutions to make voluntary financial contributions to the budget of the Institute;

14. *Also recognizes* the importance of the World Maritime University of the International Maritime Organization as a centre for maritime education and research, confirms its effective capacity-building role in the field of maritime transportation, policy, administration, management, safety, security and environmental protection, as well as its role in the international exchange and transfer of knowledge, notes that almost 2,900 persons from 157 countries have graduated from the University since it was founded in 1983, welcomes the increasing number of students, and urges States, intergovernmental organizations and other bodies to make voluntary financial contributions to the University;

15. *Welcomes* ongoing activities for capacity-building so as to address maritime security and safety needs and the protection of the marine environment of developing States, and encourages States and international financial institutions to provide additional funding for capacity-building programmes, including for transfer of technology, including through the International Maritime Organization and other competent international organizations;

16. *Recognizes* the considerable need to provide sustained capacity-building assistance, including on financial and technical aspects, by relevant international organizations and donors to developing States, with a view to further strengthening their capacity to take effective measures against the multiple facets of international criminal activities at sea, in line with the relevant international instruments, including the United Nations Convention against Transnational Organized Crime and the Protocols thereto;

17. *Also recognizes* the need to build the capacity of developing States to raise awareness of, and support the implementation of, improved waste management practices, noting the particular vulnerability of small island developing States to the impact of marine pollution from land-based sources and marine debris;

18. *Further recognizes* the importance of assisting developing States, in particular the least developed countries and small island developing States, as well as coastal African States, in implementing the Convention, and urges States, intergovernmental organizations and agencies, national institutions, non-governmental organizations and international financial institutions, as well as natural and

juridical persons, to make voluntary financial or other contributions to the trust funds, as referred to in resolution 57/141, established for this purpose;

19. *Encourages* States to use the Criteria and Guidelines on the Transfer of Marine Technology adopted by the Assembly of the Intergovernmental Oceanographic Commission of the United Nations Educational, Scientific and Cultural Organization, and recalls the important role of the secretariat of that Commission in the implementation and promotion of the Criteria and Guidelines;

20. *Calls upon* States to continue to assist developing States, and especially the least developed countries and small island developing States, as well as coastal African States, at the bilateral and, where appropriate, multilateral levels, in the preparation of submissions to the Commission regarding the establishment of the outer limits of the continental shelf beyond 200 nautical miles, including the assessment of the nature and extent of the continental shelf of a coastal State, and recalls that coastal States can make requests to the Commission for scientific and technical advice in the preparation of data for their submissions, in accordance with article 3 of annex II to the Convention;

21. *Calls upon* the Division to continue to disseminate information on relevant procedures related to the trust fund established for the purpose of facilitating the preparation of submissions to the Commission and to continue its dialogue with potential beneficiaries with a view to providing financial support to developing countries for activities to facilitate their submissions in accordance with the requirements of article 76 of the Convention and with the rules of procedure and the Scientific and Technical Guidelines of the Commission;

22. *Requests* the Secretary-General, in cooperation with States and relevant international organizations and institutions, to continue to support training and other activities to assist developing States in the preparation and presentation of their submissions to the Commission;

23. *Notes with appreciation* the regional workshop of the Tribunal, held in Cape Town, South Africa, from 7 to 9 October 2009, on the role of the Tribunal in the settlement of disputes relating to the law of the sea;

24. *Invites* Member States and others in a position to do so to support the capacity-building activities of the Division, including, in particular, the training and other activities to assist developing States in the preparation of their submissions to the Commission, and invites Member States and others in a position to do so to contribute to the trust fund established by the Secretary-General for the Office of Legal Affairs to support the promotion of international law;

25. *Recognizes* the important contribution of the Hamilton Shirley Amerasinghe Memorial Fellowship on the Law of the Sea to the capacity-building of developing countries and the promotion of the law of the sea, reiterates its serious concern regarding the continued lack of resources, which has prevented the implementation of the twenty-second and subsequent awards, advises the Secretary-General to continue to finance the Fellowship from resources made available through an appropriate Office of Legal Affairs trust fund, reiterates its urgent appeal to Member States and others in a position to do so to contribute generously to the further development of the Fellowship to ensure that it is awarded every year, and requests the Secretary-General

to include the Fellowship on the list of trust funds for the United Nations Pledging Conference for Development Activities;

26. *Also recognizes* the contribution that the United Nations-Nippon Foundation of Japan Fellowship Programme, which has awarded 50 fellowships to individuals from 44 Member States since 2005 and in April 2009 launched a fellowship alumni programme with an inaugural meeting of the Asia-Pacific alumni at the Foundation's headquarters in Tokyo, has made to human resources development for developing coastal States Parties and non-Parties to the Convention in the field of ocean affairs and the law of the sea or related disciplines;

III
Meeting of States Parties

27. *Welcomes* the report of the nineteenth Meeting of States Parties to the Convention;

28. *Requests* the Secretary-General to convene the twentieth Meeting of States Parties to the Convention, in New York from 14 to 18 June 2010, and to provide the services required;

IV
Peaceful settlement of disputes

29. *Notes with satisfaction* the continued and significant contribution of the Tribunal to the settlement of disputes by peaceful means in accordance with Part XV of the Convention, and underlines the important role and authority of the Tribunal concerning the interpretation or application of the Convention and the Part XI Agreement;

30. *Equally pays tribute* to the important and long-standing role of the International Court of Justice with regard to the peaceful settlement of disputes concerning the law of the sea;

31. *Notes* that States Parties to an international agreement related to the purposes of the Convention may submit to, inter alia, the Tribunal or the International Court of Justice any dispute concerning the interpretation or application of that agreement submitted in accordance with that agreement, and notes also the possibility, provided for in the statutes of the Tribunal and the Court, to submit disputes to a chamber;

32. *Encourages* States Parties to the Convention that have not yet done so to consider making a written declaration choosing from the means set out in article 287 of the Convention for the settlement of disputes concerning the interpretation or application of the Convention and the Part XI Agreement, bearing in mind the comprehensive character of the dispute settlement mechanism provided for in Part XV of the Convention;

V
The Area

33. *Notes* the progress made by the Authority in its deliberations, urges the finalization at its sixteenth session of the regulations for prospecting and exploration for polymetallic sulphides, encourages progress on the regulations for prospecting and exploration for cobalt-rich ferromanganese crusts in the Area, and reiterates the importance of the ongoing elaboration by the Authority, pursuant to article 145

of the Convention, of rules, regulations and procedures to ensure the effective protection of the marine environment, for, inter alia, the protection and conservation of the natural resources of the Area, and for the prevention of damage to the flora and fauna of the marine environment from harmful effects that may arise from activities in the Area;

34. *Also notes* the importance of the responsibilities entrusted to the Authority by articles 143 and 145 of the Convention, which refer to marine scientific research and protection of the marine environment, respectively;

VI
Effective functioning of the Authority and the Tribunal

35. *Appeals* to all States Parties to the Convention to pay their assessed contributions to the Authority and to the Tribunal in full and on time, and also appeals to States Parties in arrears with their contributions to fulfil their obligations without delay;

36. *Urges* all States Parties to the Convention to attend the sessions of the Authority, and calls upon the Authority to continue to pursue all options, including making concrete recommendations on the issue of dates, in order to improve attendance in Kingston and to ensure global participation;

37. *Calls upon* States that have not done so to consider ratifying or acceding to the Agreement on the Privileges and Immunities of the Tribunal and to the Protocol on the Privileges and Immunities of the Authority;

38. *Emphasizes* the importance of the Tribunal's rules and staff regulations in promoting the recruitment of a geographically representative staff in the Professional and higher categories, and welcomes the actions taken by the Tribunal in observance of those rules and regulations;

VII
The continental shelf and the work of the Commission

39. *Recalls* that, in accordance with article 76, paragraph 8, of the Convention, information on the limits of the continental shelf beyond 200 nautical miles from the baselines from which the breadth of the territorial sea is measured shall be submitted by the coastal State to the Commission set up under annex II to the Convention on the basis of equitable geographical representation, that the Commission shall make recommendations to coastal States on matters related to the establishment of the outer limits of their continental shelf, and that the limits of the shelf established by a coastal State on the basis of these recommendations shall be final and binding;

40. *Also recalls* that, in accordance with article 77, paragraph 3, of the Convention, the rights of the coastal State over the continental shelf do not depend on occupation, effective or notional, or on any express proclamation;

41. *Notes with satisfaction* that a considerable number of States Parties to the Convention have submitted information to the Commission regarding the establishment of the outer limits of the continental shelf beyond 200 nautical miles, in conformity with article 76 of the Convention and article 4 of annex II to the Convention, taking into account the decision of the eleventh Meeting of States Parties to the Convention contained in SPLOS/72, paragraph *(a)*;

42. *Also notes with satisfaction* that a considerable number of States Parties to the Convention have submitted to the Secretary-General, pursuant to the decision of the eighteenth Meeting of States Parties to the Convention, preliminary information indicative of the outer limits of the continental shelf beyond 200 nautical miles and a description of the status of preparation and intended date of submission in accordance with the requirements of article 76 of the Convention and with the rules of procedure and the Scientific and Technical Guidelines of the Commission;

43. *Further notes with satisfaction* the progress in the work of the Commission and that it is giving current consideration to a number of submissions that have been made regarding the establishment of the outer limits of the continental shelf beyond 200 nautical miles;

44. *Notes with satisfaction* that the Commission, taking into account the decision of the eighteenth Meeting of States Parties to the Convention, has compiled lists of websites of organizations, data/information portals and data holders where general information and publicly available scientific and technical data can be accessed that may be relevant to the preparation of submissions, and has made this information available on its website;

45. *Takes note* of the recommendations made by the Commission on the submissions of a number of States, and welcomes the fact that summaries of recommendations are being made publicly available;

46. *Notes* that consideration by the Commission of submissions by coastal States in accordance with article 76 of and annex II to the Convention is without prejudice to the application of other parts of the Convention by States Parties;

47. *Notes with concern* that the heavy workload of the Commission, owing to the considerable number of submissions, places additional demands on and challenges before its members and the secretariat as provided by the Division, and in that regard emphasizes the need to ensure that the Commission can perform its functions expeditiously, efficiently and effectively and maintain its high level of quality and expertise;

48. *Takes note* of the decision of the nineteenth Meeting of States Parties to the Convention, as reflected in the report of the Meeting, to continue to address, as a matter of priority, issues related to the workload of the Commission, including funding for its members attending the sessions of the Commission and the meetings of the subcommissions, and, in particular, the decision that the bureau of the Meeting will facilitate an informal working group to continue consideration of the issues;

49. *Reiterates* the duty of States under the Convention, whose experts are serving on the Commission, to defray the expenses of the experts they have nominated while in performance of Commission duties, and calls upon these States to do their utmost to ensure the full participation of those experts in the work of the Commission, including the meetings of subcommissions, in accordance with the Convention;

50. *Requests* the Secretary-General to continue to take appropriate measures, within overall existing resource levels, to further strengthen the capacity of the Division, serving as the secretariat of the Commission, including in the context of the proposed programme budget for the biennium 2010–2011, in order to ensure enhanced support and assistance to the Commission and its subcommissions in their consideration of submissions, as required by paragraph 9 of annex III to the rules of procedure of the Commission, in particular its human resources, taking into account the need for simultaneous work on several submissions;

51. *Urges* the Secretary-General to continue to provide all necessary secretariat services to the Commission in accordance with article 2, paragraph 5, of annex II to the Convention;

52. *Encourages* States to participate actively and contribute constructively to the ongoing work of the informal working group considering the issues related to the workload of the Commission, so that the Meeting of States Parties to the Convention may consider ways and means, including short-, medium- and long-term measures, to ensure that the Commission can perform its functions under the Convention expeditiously, efficiently and effectively and maintain its high level of quality and expertise;

53. *Requests* the Secretary-General to consider the comments of the informal working group, which are invited as soon as possible before mid-February 2010, in the context of the update of the document entitled "Issues related to the workload of the Commission on the Limits of the Continental Shelf";

54. *Encourages* States to make additional contributions to the voluntary trust fund established by resolution 55/7 for the purpose of facilitating the preparation of submissions to the Commission and to the voluntary trust fund also established by that resolution for the purpose of defraying the cost of participation of the members of the Commission from developing States in the meetings of the Commission;

55. *Approves* the convening by the Secretary-General of the twenty-fifth and twenty-sixth sessions of the Commission, in New York from 15 March to 23 April 2010 and from 2 to 27 August 2010, respectively, with full conference services for the plenary parts of these sessions, and requests the Secretary-General to make every effort to meet these requirements within overall existing resources, on the understanding that the following periods will be used for the technical examinations of submissions at the Geographic Information System laboratories and other technical facilities of the Division: 15 March to 1 April 2010; 19 to 23 April 2010; and 2 to 13 August 2010;

56. *Expresses its firm conviction* about the importance of the work of the Commission, carried out in accordance with the Convention, including with respect to the participation of coastal States in relevant proceedings concerning their submissions, and recognizes the continued need for active interaction between coastal States and the Commission;

57. *Encourages* States to continue exchanging views in order to increase understanding of issues, including expenditures involved, arising from the application of article 76 of the Convention, thus facilitating the preparation of submissions by States, in particular developing States, to the Commission;

58. *Notes* the number of submissions yet to be considered by the Commission, and in this regard stresses the urgent need for States Parties to the Convention to take

appropriate and prompt steps that will allow the Commission to consider the increased number of submissions in a timely, efficient and effective manner;

59. *Requests* the Secretary-General, in cooperation with Member States, to continue supporting workshops or symposiums on scientific and technical aspects of the establishment of the outer limits of the continental shelf beyond 200 nautical miles, taking into account the need to strengthen capacity-building for developing countries in preparing their submissions;

VIII

Maritime safety and security and flag State implementation

60. *Encourages* States to ratify or accede to international agreements addressing the safety and security of navigation, as well as maritime labour, and to adopt the necessary measures consistent with the Convention and other relevant international instruments aimed at implementing and enforcing the rules contained in those agreements, and emphasizes the need for capacity-building for and assistance to developing States;

61. *Recognizes* that the legal regimes governing maritime safety and maritime security may have common and mutually reinforcing objectives that may be interrelated and could benefit from synergies, and encourages States to take this into account in their implementation;

62. *Emphasizes* that safety and security measures should be implemented with minimal negative effects on seafarers and fishers, especially in relation to their working conditions;

63. *Invites* States that have not yet done so to ratify or accede to the Maritime Labour Convention, 2006, the Work in Fishing Convention, 2007 (No. 188) and the Seafarers' Identity Documents Convention (Revised), 2003 (No. 185) of the International Labour Organization and to effectively implement those Conventions, and emphasizes the need to provide to States, at their request, technical cooperation and assistance in that regard;

64. *Emphasizes* the need for further efforts to promote a culture of safety and security in the shipping industry and to address the shortage of adequately trained personnel, notes the importance of the process in the International Maritime Organization to review the International Convention on Standards of Training, Certification and Watchkeeping for Seafarers, 1978, and urges the establishment of more centres to provide the required education and training;

65. *Welcomes* ongoing cooperation between the Food and Agriculture Organization of the United Nations, the International Maritime Organization and the International Labour Organization relating to the safety of fishers and fishing vessels, underlines the urgent need for continued work in that area, and takes note of discussions in the Food and Agriculture Organization of the United Nations on the merit of an international plan of action in this area;

66. *Encourages* continued cooperation between the parties to the Basel Convention on the Control of Transboundary Movements of Hazardous Wastes and their Disposal and the International Maritime Organization on regulations on the prevention of pollution from ships;

67. *Calls upon* States to participate in the diplomatic conference to be convened by the International Maritime Organization in 2010 on a protocol to the International Convention on Liability and Compensation for Damage in Connection with the Carriage of Hazardous and Noxious Substances by Sea, 1996;

68. *Recalls* that all actions taken to combat threats to maritime security must be in accordance with international law, including the principles embodied in the Charter and the Convention;

69. *Recognizes* the crucial role of international cooperation at the global, regional, subregional and bilateral levels in combating, in accordance with international law, threats to maritime security, including piracy, armed robbery at sea, terrorist acts against shipping, offshore installations and other maritime interests, through bilateral and multilateral instruments and mechanisms aimed at monitoring, preventing and responding to such threats, the enhanced sharing of information among States relevant to the detection, prevention and suppression of such threats, and the prosecution of offenders with due regard to national legislation, and the need for sustained capacity-building to support such objectives;

70. *Notes* that piracy affects the entire range of vessels engaged in maritime activities;

71. *Emphasizes* the importance of promptly reporting incidents to enable accurate information on the scope of the problem of piracy and armed robbery against ships and, in the case of armed robbery against ships, by affected vessels to the coastal State, underlines the importance of effective information-sharing with States potentially affected by incidents of piracy and armed robbery against ships, and takes note of the important role of the International Maritime Organization;

72. *Calls upon* States to take appropriate steps under their national law to facilitate the apprehension and prosecution of those who are alleged to have committed acts of piracy;

73. *Urges* all States, in cooperation with the International Maritime Organization, to actively combat piracy and armed robbery at sea by adopting measures, including those relating to assistance with capacity-building through training of seafarers, port staff and enforcement personnel in the prevention, reporting and investigation of incidents, bringing the alleged perpetrators to justice, in accordance with international law, and by adopting national legislation, as well as providing enforcement vessels and equipment and guarding against fraudulent ship registration;

74. *Invites* all States, the International Maritime Organization and the International Labour Organization to consider possible solutions for the seafarers and fishers who are victims of pirates;

75. *Takes note* of the ongoing cooperation between the International Maritime Organization, the United Nations Office on Drugs and Crime and the Division with respect to the compilation of national legislation on piracy;

76. *Welcomes* the significant decrease in the number of attacks by pirates and armed robbers in the Asian region through increased national, bilateral and trilateral initiatives as well as regional cooperative mechanisms, and calls upon other States to give immediate attention to adopting,

concluding and implementing cooperation agreements at the regional level on combating piracy and armed robbery against ships;

77. *Expresses serious concern* regarding continued increases in incidents of piracy and armed robbery at sea off the coast of Somalia, expresses alarm in particular at the hijacking of vessels, supports the recent efforts to address this problem at the global and regional levels, notes the adoption by the Security Council of resolutions 1816(2008) of 2 June 2008, 1838(2008) of 7 October 2008, 1846(2008) of 2 December 2008 and 1851(2008) of 16 December 2008 and also notes that the authorization in resolution 1816(2008) and the provisions in resolutions 1838(2008), 1846(2008) and 1851(2008) apply only to the situation in Somalia and do not affect the rights, obligations or responsibilities of Member States under international law, including any rights or obligations under the Convention, with respect to any other situation, and underscores, in particular, the fact that they are not to be considered as establishing customary international law;

78. *Notes* the establishment of the Contact Group on Piracy off the Coast of Somalia on 14 January 2009, following the adoption of Security Council resolution 1851(2008), and the ongoing efforts within the Contact Group, and commends contributions of all States in the efforts to fight piracy off the coast of Somalia;

79. *Recognizes* the importance of a comprehensive and sustainable settlement of the situation in Somalia and the primary role of the Transitional Federal Government in rooting out piracy and armed robbery against ships, and further re-emphasizes the need, in particular, to assist Somalia and States in the region in strengthening capacity to fight piracy and armed robbery against ships off the coast of Somalia and bring to justice those involved in piracy and armed robbery at sea;

80. *Notes* the approval by the International Maritime Organization of revised recommendations to Governments for preventing and suppressing piracy and armed robbery against ships, revised guidance to shipowners and ship operators, shipmasters and crews on preventing and suppressing acts of piracy and armed robbery against ships and the Code of Practice for the Investigation of the Crimes of Piracy and Armed Robbery Against Ships, as well as the endorsement of Best Management Practices to Deter Piracy in the Gulf of Aden and off the Coast of Somalia;

81. *Invites* the Assembly of the International Maritime Organization to consider adopting a resolution on commitments to best management practices to avoid, deter or delay acts of piracy;

82. *Welcomes* the adoption on 29 January 2009 of the Code of Conduct concerning the Repression of Piracy and Armed Robbery against Ships in the Western Indian Ocean and the Gulf of Aden (Djibouti Code of Conduct) under the auspices of the International Maritime Organization, the establishment of the International Maritime Organization Djibouti Code Trust Fund, a multi-donor trust fund initiated by Japan, and the ongoing activities for the implementation of the Code of Conduct;

83. *Urges* States to ensure the full implementation of resolution A.1002(25) of the International Maritime Organization on acts of piracy and armed robbery against ships in waters off the coast of Somalia;

84. *Calls upon* States that have not yet done so to become parties to the Convention for the Suppression of Unlawful Acts against the Safety of Maritime Navigation and the Protocol for the Suppression of Unlawful Acts against the Safety of Fixed Platforms Located on the Continental Shelf, invites States to consider becoming parties to the 2005 Protocols amending those instruments, and urges States Parties to take appropriate measures to ensure the effective implementation of those instruments through the adoption of legislation, where appropriate;

85. *Calls upon* States to effectively implement the International Ship and Port Facility Security Code and the amendments to the International Convention for the Safety of Life at Sea, and to work with the International Maritime Organization to promote safe and secure shipping while ensuring freedom of navigation;

86. *Urges* all States, in cooperation with the International Maritime Organization, to improve the protection of offshore installations by adopting measures related to the prevention, reporting and investigation of acts of violence against installations, in accordance with international law, and by implementing such measures through national legislation to ensure proper and adequate enforcement;

87. *Emphasizes* the progress in regional cooperation, including the efforts of littoral States, on the enhancement of safety, security and environmental protection in the Straits of Malacca and Singapore, and the effective functioning of the Cooperative Mechanism on safety of navigation and environmental protection to promote dialogue and facilitate close cooperation between the littoral States, user States, shipping industry and other stakeholders in line with article 43 of the Convention, and notes with appreciation the convening of the second Cooperation Forum and second Project Coordination Committee meeting, in Singapore from 14 to 16 October 2009, and the fourth Aids to Navigation Fund Committee Meeting, in Malaysia on 19 and 20 October 2009, the three events being key pillars of the Cooperative Mechanism, and the important role of the Information Sharing Centre of the Regional Cooperation Agreement on Combating Piracy and Armed Robbery against Ships in Asia, based in Singapore, and calls upon States to give immediate attention to adopting, concluding and implementing cooperation agreements at the regional level;

88. *Recognizes* that some transnational organized criminal activities threaten legitimate uses of the oceans and endanger the lives of people at sea;

89. *Notes* that transnational organized criminal activities are diverse and may be interrelated in some cases and that criminal organizations are adaptive and take advantage of the vulnerabilities of States, in particular coastal and small island developing States in transit areas, and calls upon States and relevant intergovernmental organizations to increase cooperation and coordination at all levels to detect and suppress the smuggling of migrants and trafficking in persons, in accordance with international law;

90. *Recognizes* the importance of enhancing international cooperation at all levels to fight transnational organized criminal activities, including illicit traffic in narcotic drugs and psychotropic substances, within the scope of the United Nations instruments against illicit drug trafficking, as well as the smuggling of migrants and trafficking in per-

sons and criminal activities at sea falling within the scope of the United Nations Convention against Transnational Organized Crime;

91. *Calls upon* States that have not yet done so to become parties to the Protocol against the Smuggling of Migrants by Land, Sea and Air, supplementing the United Nations Convention against Transnational Organized Crime, and the Protocol to Prevent, Suppress and Punish Trafficking in Persons, Especially Women and Children, supplementing the United Nations Convention against Transnational Organized Crime, and to take appropriate measures to ensure their effective implementation;

92. *Calls upon* States to ensure freedom of navigation, the safety of navigation and the rights of transit passage, archipelagic sea lanes passage and innocent passage in accordance with international law, in particular the Convention;

93. *Welcomes* the work of the International Maritime Organization relating to the protection of shipping lanes of strategic importance and significance, and in particular in enhancing safety, security and environmental protection in straits used for international navigation, and calls upon the International Maritime Organization, States bordering straits and user States to continue their cooperation to keep such straits safe, secure and environmentally protected and open to international navigation at all times, consistent with international law, in particular the Convention;

94. *Calls upon* user States and States bordering straits used for international navigation to continue to cooperate by agreement on matters relating to navigational safety, including safety aids for navigation, and the prevention, reduction and control of pollution from ships, and welcomes developments in this regard;

95. *Calls upon* States that have accepted the amendments to regulation XI-1/6 of the International Convention for the Safety of Life at Sea, 1974, to implement the Code of International Standards and Recommended Practices for a Safety Investigation into a Marine Casualty or Marine Incident, which will take effect on 1 January 2010;

96. *Calls upon* States to consider becoming members of the International Hydrographic Organization, and urges all States to work with that Organization to increase the coverage of hydrographic information on a global basis to enhance capacity-building and technical assistance and to promote safe navigation, especially in areas used for international navigation, in ports and where there are vulnerable or protected marine areas;

97. *Encourages* States to continue their efforts in the implementation of all areas of the Action Plan for the Safety of Transport of Radioactive Material, approved by the Board of Governors of the International Atomic Energy Agency in March 2004;

98. *Notes* that cessation of the transport of radioactive materials through the regions of small island developing States is an ultimate desired goal of small island developing States and some other countries, and recognizes the right of freedom of navigation in accordance with international law; that States should maintain dialogue and consultation, in particular under the auspices of the International Atomic Energy Agency and the International Maritime Organization, with the aim of improved mutual understanding, confidence-building and enhanced communication in relation to the safe maritime transport of radioactive

materials; that States involved in the transport of such materials are urged to continue to engage in dialogue with small island developing States and other States to address their concerns; and that these concerns include the further development and strengthening, within the appropriate forums, of international regulatory regimes to enhance safety, disclosure, liability, security and compensation in relation to such transport;

99. *Acknowledges*, in the context of paragraph 98 above, the potential environmental and economic impacts of maritime incidents and accidents on coastal States, in particular those related to the transport of radioactive materials, and emphasizes the importance of effective liability regimes in that regard;

100. *Encourages* States to draw up plans and to establish procedures to implement the Guidelines on Places of Refuge for Ships in Need of Assistance;

101. *Invites* States that have not yet done so to consider becoming parties to the Nairobi International Convention on the Removal of Wrecks, 2007;

102. *Requests* States to take appropriate measures with regard to ships flying their flag or of their registry to address hazards that may be caused by wrecks and drifting or sunken cargo to navigation or the marine environment;

103. *Calls upon* States to ensure that masters on ships flying their flag take the steps required by relevant instruments to provide assistance to persons in distress at sea, and urges States to cooperate and to take all necessary measures to ensure the effective implementation of the amendments to the International Convention on Maritime Search and Rescue and to the International Convention for the Safety of Life at Sea relating to the delivery of persons rescued at sea to a place of safety, as well as of the associated Guidelines on the Treatment of Persons Rescued at Sea;

104. *Recognizes* that all States must fulfil their search and rescue responsibilities and the ongoing need for the International Maritime Organization and other relevant organizations to assist, in particular, developing States both to increase their search and rescue capabilities, including through the establishment of additional rescue coordination centres and regional subcentres, and to take effective action to address, to the extent feasible, the issue of unseaworthy ships and small craft within their national jurisdiction;

105. *Welcomes* the ongoing work of the International Maritime Organization in relation to disembarkation of persons rescued at sea, and notes in this regard the need to implement all relevant international instruments;

106. *Calls upon* States to continue to cooperate in developing comprehensive approaches to international migration and development, including through dialogue on all their aspects;

107. *Reaffirms* that flag, port and coastal States all bear responsibility for ensuring the effective implementation and enforcement of international instruments relating to maritime security and safety, in accordance with international law, in particular the Convention, and that flag States have primary responsibility that requires further strengthening, including through increased transparency of ownership of vessels;

108. *Urges* flag States without an effective maritime administration and appropriate legal frameworks to

establish or enhance the necessary infrastructure, legislative and enforcement capabilities to ensure effective compliance with, and implementation and enforcement of, their responsibilities under international law, in particular the Convention, and, until such action is taken, to consider declining the granting of the right to fly their flag to new vessels, suspending their registry or not opening a registry, and calls upon flag and port States to take all measures consistent with international law necessary to prevent the operation of substandard vessels;

109. *Recognizes* that international shipping rules and standards adopted by the International Maritime Organization in respect of maritime safety, efficiency of navigation and the prevention and control of marine pollution, complemented by best practices of the shipping industry, have led to a significant reduction in maritime accidents and pollution incidents, and encourages all States to participate in the Voluntary International Maritime Organization Member State Audit Scheme;

110. *Also recognizes* that maritime safety can also be improved through effective port State control, the strengthening of regional arrangements and increased coordination and cooperation among them, and increased information-sharing, including among safety and security sectors;

111. *Encourages* flag States to take appropriate measures sufficient to achieve or maintain recognition by intergovernmental arrangements that recognize satisfactory flag State performance, including, as appropriate, satisfactory port State control examination results on a sustained basis, with a view to improving quality shipping and furthering flag State implementation of relevant instruments under the International Maritime Organization as well as relevant goals and objectives of the present resolution;

IX

Marine environment and marine resources

112. *Emphasizes once again* the importance of the implementation of Part XII of the Convention in order to protect and preserve the marine environment and its living marine resources against pollution and physical degradation, and calls upon all States to cooperate and take measures consistent with the Convention, directly or through competent international organizations, for the protection and preservation of the marine environment;

113. *Notes* the work of the Intergovernmental Panel on Climate Change, including its findings on the acidification of oceans, and in this regard encourages States and competent international organizations and other relevant institutions, individually and in cooperation, to urgently pursue further research on ocean acidification, especially programmes of observation and measurement, noting in particular paragraph 4 of decision IX/20 adopted at the ninth meeting of the Conference of the Parties to the Convention on Biological Diversity, held in Bonn, Germany, from 19 to 30 May 2008, and to increase national, regional and international efforts to address levels of ocean acidity and the negative impact of such acidity on vulnerable marine ecosystems, particularly coral reefs;

114. *Encourages* States, individually or in collaboration with relevant international organizations and bodies, to enhance their scientific activity to better understand the effects of climate change on the marine environment and

marine biodiversity and develop ways and means of adaptation;

115. *Encourages* States that have not yet done so to ratify or accede to international agreements addressing the protection and preservation of the marine environment and its living marine resources against the introduction of harmful aquatic organisms and pathogens and marine pollution from all sources, including the dumping of wastes and other matter, and other forms of physical degradation, as well as agreements that provide for preparedness for, response to and cooperation on pollution incidents and that include provisions on liability and compensation for damage resulting from marine pollution, and to adopt the necessary measures consistent with international law, including the Convention, aimed at implementing and enforcing the rules contained in those agreements;

116. *Encourages* States, directly or through competent international organizations, to consider the further development, as appropriate and consistent with international law, including the Convention, of environmental impact assessment processes covering planned activities under their jurisdiction or control that may cause substantial pollution of, or significant and harmful changes to, the marine environment;

117. *Encourages* States to become parties to regional seas conventions addressing the protection and preservation of the marine environment;

118. *Also encourages* States, in accordance with international law, including the Convention and other relevant instruments, either bilaterally or regionally, to jointly develop and promote contingency plans for responding to pollution incidents, as well as other incidents that are likely to have significant adverse effects on the marine environment and biodiversity;

119. *Recognizes* the importance of improving understanding of the impact of climate change on the ocean, and expresses appreciation to the Government of Indonesia for holding the World Ocean Conference in Manado, Indonesia, from 11 to 15 May 2009, at which the Manado Ocean Declaration was adopted;

120. *Welcomes* the activities of the United Nations Environment Programme relating to marine debris carried out in cooperation with relevant United Nations bodies and organizations, and encourages States to further develop partnerships with industry and civil society to raise awareness of the extent of the impact of marine debris on the health and productivity of the marine environment and consequent economic loss;

121. *Urges* States to integrate the issue of marine debris into national strategies dealing with waste management in the coastal zone, ports and maritime industries, including recycling, reuse, reduction and disposal, and to encourage the development of appropriate economic incentives to address this issue, including the development of cost recovery systems that provide an incentive to use port reception facilities and discourage ships from discharging marine debris at sea, and encourages States to cooperate regionally and subregionally to develop and implement joint prevention and recovery programmes for marine debris;

122. *Notes* the work of the International Maritime Organization to prevent pollution by garbage from ships, including the current review by the Marine Environment

Protection Committee of the provisions of annex V to the International Convention for the Prevention of Pollution from Ships, 1973, as modified by the Protocol of 1978 relating thereto, on the prevention of pollution by garbage from ships, and encourages States and relevant international organizations to contribute to this work through participation in the relevant processes of the Committee;

123.   *Encourages* States that have not done so to become parties to the Protocol of 1997 (Annex VI-Regulations for the Prevention of Air Pollution from Ships) to the International Convention for the Prevention of Pollution from Ships, 1973, as modified by the Protocol of 1978 relating thereto, and the 1996 Protocol to the Convention on the Prevention of Marine Pollution by Dumping of Wastes and Other Matter, 1972 ("the London Protocol"), and furthermore to ratify or accede to the International Convention for the Control and Management of Ships' Ballast Water and Sediments, 2004, thereby facilitating its early entry into force;

124.   *Takes note* of the adoption of amendments to the Protocol of 1997 to the International Convention for the Prevention of Pollution from Ships, 1973, as modified by the Protocol of 1978 relating thereto, to reduce harmful emissions from ships;

125.   *Notes* the ongoing work of the International Maritime Organization in accordance with its resolution on International Maritime Organization policies and practices related to the reduction of greenhouse gas emissions from ships;

126.   *Urges* States to cooperate in correcting the shortfall in port waste reception facilities in accordance with the action plan to address the inadequacy of port waste reception facilities developed by the International Maritime Organization;

127.   *Recognizes* that most of the pollution load of the oceans emanates from land-based activities and affects the most productive areas of the marine environment, and calls upon States as a matter of priority to implement the Global Programme of Action for the Protection of the Marine Environment from Land-based Activities and to take all appropriate measures to fulfil the commitments of the international community embodied in the Beijing Declaration on Furthering the Implementation of the Global Programme of Action;

128.   *Expresses its concern* regarding the spreading of hypoxic dead zones in oceans as a result of eutrophication fuelled by riverine run-off of fertilizers, sewage outfall and reactive nitrogen resulting from the burning of fossil fuels and resulting in serious consequences for ecosystem functioning, and calls upon States to enhance their efforts to reduce eutrophication and, to this effect, to continue to cooperate within the framework of relevant international organizations, in particular the Global Programme of Action;

129.   *Calls upon* all States to ensure that urban and coastal development projects and related land-reclamation activities are carried out in a responsible manner that protects the marine habitat and environment and mitigates the negative consequences of such activities;

130.   *Notes* the agreement of the twenty-fifth session of the United Nations Environment Programme Governing Council/Global Ministerial Environment Forum, held in Nairobi from 16 to 20 February 2009, on a process and timetable for the negotiation of a global legally binding instrument on mercury to reduce the risks to human health and the environment arising from worldwide emissions and discharges of mercury;

131.   *Welcomes* the continued work of States, the United Nations Environment Programme and regional organizations in the implementation of the Global Programme of Action, and encourages increased emphasis on the link between freshwater, the coastal zone and marine resources in the implementation of international development goals, including those contained in the United Nations Millennium Declaration, and of the time-bound targets in the Plan of Implementation of the World Summit on Sustainable Development ("Johannesburg Plan of Implementation"), in particular the target on sanitation, and the Monterrey Consensus of the International Conference on Financing for Development;

132.   *Recalls* the resolution of the thirtieth Consultative Meeting of Contracting Parties to the Convention on the Prevention of Marine Pollution by Dumping of Wastes and Other Matter, 1972 ("the London Convention") and the third Meeting of Contracting Parties to the London Protocol, held from 27 to 31 October 2008, on the regulation of ocean fertilization, in which the Contracting Parties agreed, inter alia, that the scope of the London Convention and Protocol includes ocean fertilization activities and that, given the present state of knowledge, ocean fertilization activities other than for legitimate scientific research should not be allowed, and that scientific research proposals should be assessed on a case-by-case basis using an assessment framework to be developed by the scientific groups under the London Convention and Protocol, and also agreed that, to this end, such other activities should be considered as contrary to the aims of the London Convention and Protocol and should not currently qualify for any exemption from the definition of dumping in article III, paragraph 1*(b)*, of the London Convention and article 1, paragraph 4.2, of the London Protocol;

133.   *Also recalls* decision IX/16 C adopted at the ninth meeting of the Conference of the Parties to the Convention on Biological Diversity, in which the Conference of the Parties, inter alia, bearing in mind the ongoing scientific and legal analysis occurring under the auspices of the London Convention and Protocol, requested parties and urged other Governments, in accordance with the precautionary approach, to ensure that ocean fertilization activities were not carried out until there was an adequate scientific basis on which to justify such activities, including an assessment of associated risks, and that a global, transparent and effective control and regulatory mechanism was in place for those activities, with the exception of small-scale scientific research studies within coastal waters, and stated that such studies should be authorized only if justified by the need to gather specific scientific data, should be subject to a thorough prior assessment of the potential impacts of the research studies on the marine environment, should be strictly controlled and should not be used for generating and selling carbon offsets or for any other commercial purposes;

134.   *Reaffirms* paragraph 119 of resolution 61/222 of 20 December 2006 regarding ecosystem approaches and oceans, including the proposed elements of an ecosystem approach, means to achieve implementation of an ecosys-

tem approach and requirements for improved application of an ecosystem approach, and in this regard:

(a) Notes that continued environmental degradation in many parts of the world and increasing competing demands require an urgent response and the setting of priorities for management actions aimed at conserving ecosystem integrity;

(b) Notes that ecosystem approaches to ocean management should be focused on managing human activities in order to maintain and, where needed, restore ecosystem health to sustain goods and environmental services, provide social and economic benefits for food security, sustain livelihoods in support of international development goals, including those contained in the Millennium Declaration, and conserve marine biodiversity;

(c) Recalls that States should be guided in the application of ecosystem approaches by a number of existing instruments, in particular the Convention, which sets out the legal framework for all activities in the oceans and seas, and its implementing Agreements, as well as other commitments, such as those contained in the Convention on Biological Diversity and the World Summit on Sustainable Development call for the application of an ecosystem approach by 2010;

(d) Encourages States to cooperate and coordinate their efforts and take, individually or jointly, as appropriate, all measures, in conformity with international law, including the Convention and other applicable instruments, to address impacts on marine ecosystems within and beyond areas of national jurisdiction, taking into account the integrity of the ecosystems concerned;

135. *Invites* competent organizations and bodies that have not yet done so to examine the possibility of incorporating ecosystem approaches into their mandates in order to address impacts on marine ecosystems;

136. *Invites* States, in particular those States with advanced technology and marine capabilities, to explore prospects for improving cooperation with, and assistance to, developing States, in particular least developed countries and small island developing States, as well as coastal African States, with a view to better integrating into national policies and programmes sustainable and effective development in the marine sector;

137. *Encourages* the competent international organizations, the United Nations Development Programme, the World Bank and other funding agencies to consider expanding their programmes within their respective fields of competence for assistance to developing countries and to coordinate their efforts, including in the allocation and application of Global Environment Facility funding;

138. *Notes* the information provided in the study prepared by the Secretariat in relation to the assistance available to and measures that may be taken by developing States, in particular the least developed countries and small island developing States, as well as coastal African States, to realize the benefits of sustainable and effective development of marine resources and uses of the oceans, as provided by States and competent international organizations and global and regional funding agencies, and urges them to provide further information for the annual report of the Secretary-General and for incorporation on the website of the Division;

139. *Takes note* of the adoption by the International Conference on the Safe and Environmentally Sound Recycling of Ships, held in Hong Kong, China, from 11 to 15 May 2009, of the Hong Kong International Convention for the Safe and Environmentally Sound Recycling of Ships, 2009, and six resolutions related thereto, and encourages States to ratify or accede to this Convention to facilitate its early entry into force;

140. *Also takes note* of the role of the Basel Convention in protecting the marine environment against the adverse effects which may result from such wastes;

X

Marine biodiversity

141. *Reaffirms* its role relating to the conservation and sustainable use of marine biological diversity beyond areas of national jurisdiction, notes the work of States and relevant intergovernmental organizations and bodies on those issues, and invites them to contribute to its consideration of these issues within the areas of their respective competence;

142. *Notes* the discussion on the relevant legal regime on marine genetic resources in areas beyond national jurisdiction in accordance with the Convention, and calls upon States to further consider this issue in the context of the mandate of the Ad Hoc Open-ended Informal Working Group to study issues relating to the conservation and sustainable use of marine biological diversity beyond areas of national jurisdiction ("the Ad Hoc Open-ended Informal Working Group"), with a view to making further progress on this issue;

143. *Recognizes* the abundance and diversity of marine genetic resources and their value in terms of the benefits, goods and services they can provide;

144. *Also recognizes* the importance of research on marine genetic resources for the purpose of enhancing the scientific understanding, potential use and application, and enhanced management of marine ecosystems;

145. *Encourages* States and international organizations, including through bilateral, regional and global cooperation programmes and partnerships, to continue in a sustainable and comprehensive way to support, promote and strengthen capacity-building activities, in particular in developing countries, in the field of marine scientific research, taking into account, in particular, the need to create greater taxonomic capabilities;

146. *Reaffirms its request* to the Secretary-General to convene a meeting of the Ad Hoc Open-ended Informal Working Group in accordance with paragraphs 127 to 130 of resolution 63/111, to take place from 1 to 5 February 2010, to provide recommendations to the General Assembly;

147. *Takes note* of the report of the Secretary-General relating to the conservation and sustainable use of marine biological diversity beyond areas of national jurisdiction, prepared in response to the request contained in paragraph 128 of resolution 63/111;

148. *Invites* States to further consider, at the upcoming meeting of the Ad Hoc Open-ended Informal Working Group, in the context of its mandate, issues of marine protected areas and environmental impact assessment processes;

149. *Notes* the work under the Jakarta Mandate on Marine and Coastal Biological Diversity and the Convention on Biological Diversity elaborated programme of work on marine and coastal biological diversity, as well as the relevant decisions adopted at the ninth meeting of the Conference of the Parties to the Convention on Biological Diversity;

150. *Reaffirms* the need for States, individually or through competent international organizations, to urgently consider ways to integrate and improve, based on the best available scientific information and the precautionary approach and in accordance with the Convention and related agreements and instruments, the management of risks to the marine biodiversity of seamounts, cold water corals, hydrothermal vents and certain other underwater features;

151. *Calls upon* States and international organizations to urgently take further action to address, in accordance with international law, destructive practices that have adverse impacts on marine biodiversity and ecosystems, including seamounts, hydrothermal vents and cold water corals;

152. *Calls upon* States to strengthen, in a manner consistent with international law, in particular the Convention, the conservation and management of marine biodiversity and ecosystems and national policies in relation to marine protected areas;

153. *Reaffirms* the need for States to continue and intensify their efforts, directly and through competent international organizations, to develop and facilitate the use of diverse approaches and tools for conserving and managing vulnerable marine ecosystems, including the possible establishment of marine protected areas, consistent with international law, as reflected in the Convention, and based on the best scientific information available, and the development of representative networks of any such marine protected areas by 2012;

154. *Notes* the work of States, relevant intergovernmental organizations and bodies, including the Convention on Biological Diversity, in the assessment of scientific information on, and compilation of ecological criteria for the identification of, marine areas that require protection, in light of the objective of the World Summit on Sustainable Development to develop and facilitate the use of diverse approaches and tools, such as the establishment of marine protected areas consistent with international law, as reflected in the Convention, and based on scientific information, including representative networks, by 2012, and notes with satisfaction that the Conference of the Parties to the Convention on Biological Diversity at its ninth meeting adopted scientific criteria for identifying ecologically or biologically significant marine areas in need of protection in open-ocean waters and deep-sea habitats and the scientific guidance for selecting areas to establish representative networks of marine protected areas, including in open-ocean waters and deep-sea habitats, and took note of the four initial steps to be considered in the development of representative networks of marine protected areas;

155. *Also notes* the work of the expert workshop of the Convention on Biological Diversity on scientific and technical guidance on the use of biogeographic classification systems and identification of marine areas beyond national jurisdiction in need of protection, held in Ottawa from 29 September to 2 October 2009;

156. *Encourages* States to foster progress in the implementation of the 2012 target for the establishment of marine protected areas, including representative networks, and calls upon States to further consider options to identify and protect ecologically or biologically significant areas, consistent with international law and on the basis of the best available scientific information;

157. *Acknowledges* the Micronesia Challenge, the Eastern Tropical Pacific Seascape project, the Caribbean Challenge and the Coral Triangle Initiative, which in particular seek to create and link domestic marine protected areas to better facilitate ecosystem approaches, and reaffirms the need for further international cooperation, coordination and collaboration in support of such initiatives;

158. *Reiterates its support* for the International Coral Reef Initiative, takes note of the International Coral Reef Initiative General Meeting, held in Phuket, Thailand, from 20 to 23 April 2009, and supports the work under the Jakarta Mandate on Marine and Coastal Biological Diversity and the elaborated programme of work on marine and coastal biological diversity related to coral reefs;

159. *Encourages* States and relevant international institutions to improve efforts to address coral bleaching by, inter alia, improving monitoring to predict and identify bleaching events, supporting and strengthening action taken during such events and improving strategies to manage reefs to support their natural resilience and enhance their ability to withstand other pressures, including ocean acidification;

160. *Encourages* States to cooperate, directly or through competent international bodies, in exchanging information in the event of accidents involving vessels on coral reefs and in promoting the development of economic assessment techniques for both restoration and non-use values of coral reef systems;

161. *Emphasizes* the need to mainstream sustainable coral reef management and integrated watershed management into national development strategies, as well as into the activities of relevant United Nations agencies and programmes, international financial institutions and the donor community;

162. *Encourages* further research, studies and consideration of the impacts of ocean noise on marine living resources, and requests the Division to continue to compile the peer-reviewed scientific studies it receives from Member States and intergovernmental organizations pursuant to paragraph 107 of resolution 61/222 and, as appropriate, to make them, or references and links to them, available on its website;

163. *Welcomes* 2010 as the International Year of Biodiversity;

XI

Marine science

164. *Calls upon* States, individually or in collaboration with each other or with relevant international organizations and bodies, to continue to strive to improve understanding and knowledge of the oceans and the deep sea, including, in particular, the extent and vulnerability of deep sea biodiversity and ecosystems, by increasing their marine scientific research activities in accordance with the Convention;

165. *Notes* the contribution of the Census of Marine Life to marine biodiversity research, and encourages participation in the initiative;

166. *Takes note with appreciation* of the work of the Intergovernmental Oceanographic Commission of the United Nations Educational, Scientific and Cultural Organization, with the advice of the Advisory Body of Experts on the Law of the Sea, on the development of procedures for the implementation of Parts XIII and XIV of the Convention, and notes further the resolutions adopted by the Oceanographic Commission in this regard;

167. *Encourages* the Advisory Body of Experts to continue its work, in cooperation with the Division, on the practice of Member States related to marine scientific research and transfer of marine technology within the framework of the Convention;

168. *Notes with appreciation* the work carried out by the Group of Experts at its meeting held in New York from 20 to 24 April 2009, to assist the Division in the revision of the publication entitled *Marine Scientific Research: A guide to the implementation of the relevant provisions of the United Nations Convention on the Law of the Sea*, and further notes that, consistent with such work, the revised version is scheduled to be issued as a publication of the United Nations in 2010;

169. *Stresses* the importance of increasing the scientific understanding of the oceans-atmosphere interface, including through participation in ocean observing programmes and geographic information systems, such as the Global Ocean Observing System, sponsored by the Intergovernmental Oceanographic Commission, the United Nations Environment Programme, the World Meteorological Organization and the International Council for Science, particularly considering their role in monitoring and forecasting climate change and variability and in the establishment and operation of tsunami warning systems;

170. *Takes note with appreciation* of the progress made by the Intergovernmental Oceanographic Commission and Member States towards the establishment of regional and national tsunami warning and mitigation systems, welcomes the continued collaboration of the United Nations and other intergovernmental organizations in this effort, and encourages Member States to establish and sustain their national warning and mitigation systems, within a global, ocean-related multi-hazard approach, as necessary, to reduce loss of life and damage to national economies and strengthen the resilience of coastal communities to natural disasters;

171. *Takes note* of resolution XXV-13 on the global coordination of early warning and mitigation systems for tsunamis and other sea-level-related hazards, adopted by the Assembly of the Intergovernmental Oceanographic Commission at its twenty-fifth session, held in Paris from 16 to 25 June 2009;

172. *Expresses its concern* at the intentional or unintentional damage to platforms used for ocean observation and marine scientific research, such as moored buoys and tsunameters, and urges States to take necessary action and to cooperate in relevant organizations, including the Food and Agriculture Organization of the United Nations, the Intergovernmental Oceanographic Commission and the World Meteorological Organization, to address such damage;

XII

Regular Process for Global Reporting and Assessment of the State of the Marine Environment, including Socio-economic Aspects

173. *Reiterates* the need to strengthen the regular scientific assessment of the state of the marine environment in order to enhance the scientific basis for policymaking;

174. *Notes with appreciation* the report on the "assessment of assessments" of the Group of Experts established pursuant to resolution 60/30, and acknowledges the support of the United Nations Environment Programme and the Intergovernmental Oceanographic Commission, the lead agencies of the "assessment of assessments";

175. *Takes note* of the report on the results of the "assessment of assessments" submitted by the lead agencies pursuant to resolution 60/30, which also includes, in accordance with resolution 63/111, the report of the fourth meeting of the Ad Hoc Steering Group for the "assessment of assessments", held in Paris from 15 to 17 April 2009;

176. *Welcomes* the meeting of the Ad Hoc Working Group of the Whole to recommend a course of action to the General Assembly at its sixty-fourth session based on the outcomes of the fourth meeting of the Ad Hoc Steering Group, convened in New York from 31 August to 4 September 2009 in accordance with paragraph 157 of resolution 63/111;

177. *Endorses* the recommendations adopted by the Ad Hoc Working Group of the Whole that propose a framework for the Regular Process, describe its first cycle and a way forward and stress the need for further progress to be made on the modalities for the implementation of the Regular Process prior to the sixty-fifth session of the General Assembly;

178. *Requests* the Secretary-General to convene an informal meeting of the Ad Hoc Working Group of the Whole from 30 August to 3 September 2010 to further consider and make recommendations to the General Assembly at its sixty-fifth session on the modalities for the implementation of the Regular Process, including the key features, institutional arrangements and financing, and to specify the objective and scope of its first cycle, key questions to be answered and primary target audiences, in order to ensure that assessments are relevant for decision-makers, as well as on the terms of reference for the voluntary trust fund and the scholarship fund referred to in paragraph 183 below;

179. *Invites* States, as a means to facilitate decisions on the first cycle of the Regular Process, to submit their views to the Secretary-General on the fundamental building blocks of the Regular Process, and requests the Secretary-General to present these views to the General Assembly at its sixty-fifth session in the context of his annual report on oceans and the law of the sea;

180. *Requests* the Secretary-General to invite the Chairs of the regional groups to constitute a group of experts, ensuring adequate expertise and geographical distribution, comprised of a maximum of 25 experts and no more than 5 experts per regional group, for a period up to and including the informal meeting of the Ad Hoc Working Group of the Whole referred to in paragraph 178 above;

181. *Requests* the group of experts to respond and make suggestions on the issues listed in paragraph 60 of the report on the results of the "assessment of assessments" at the

next meeting of the Ad Hoc Working Group of the Whole, including the possibility of conducting preparatory work, as appropriate, and subject to the availability of funds, taking into account the views and observations submitted by States;

182. *Requests* the Division to provide support for the Regular Process as noted in paragraphs 178 to 181 and 183 of the present resolution using existing resources or resources from the voluntary trust fund, in cooperation, as appropriate, with relevant United Nations specialized agencies and programmes;

183. *Requests* the Secretary-General to establish a voluntary trust fund for the purpose of supporting the operations of the first five-year cycle of the Regular Process, including for the provision of assistance to the experts referred to in paragraph 180 above from developing countries, in particular least developed countries, small island developing States and landlocked developing States, attending the meeting of the Ad Hoc Working Group of the Whole in 2010, as well as a special scholarship fund to support training programmes for developing countries, and encourages Member States, international financial institutions, donor agencies, intergovernmental organizations, non-governmental organizations and natural and juridical persons to contribute to the funds;

XIII

Regional cooperation

184. *Notes* that there have been a number of initiatives at the regional level, in various regions, to further the implementation of the Convention, takes note in that context of the Caribbean-focused Assistance Fund, which is intended to facilitate, mainly through technical assistance, the voluntary undertaking of maritime delimitation negotiations between Caribbean States, takes note once again of the Fund for Peace: Peaceful Settlement of Territorial Disputes, established by the General Assembly of the Organization of American States in 2000 as a primary mechanism, given its broader regional scope, for the prevention and resolution of pending territorial, land border and maritime boundary disputes, and calls upon States and others in a position to do so to contribute to these funds;

XIV

Open-ended Informal Consultative Process on Oceans and the Law of the Sea

185. *Welcomes* the report on the work of the Consultative Process at its tenth meeting, which focused on the implementation of the outcomes of the Consultative Process, including a review of its achievements and shortcomings in its first nine meetings;

186. *Recognizes* the role of the Consultative Process as a unique forum for comprehensive discussions on issues related to oceans and the law of the sea, consistent with the framework provided by the Convention and chapter 17 of Agenda 21, and that the perspective of the three pillars of sustainable development should be further enhanced in the examination of the selected topics;

187. *Welcomes* the work of the Consultative Process and its contribution to improving coordination and cooperation between States and strengthening the annual debate of the General Assembly on oceans and the law of the sea

by effectively drawing attention to key issues and current trends;

188. *Also welcomes* efforts to improve and focus the work of the Consultative Process, and in that respect recognizes the primary role of the Consultative Process in integrating knowledge, the exchange of opinions among multiple stakeholders and coordination among competent agencies, and enhancing awareness of topics, including emerging issues, while promoting the three pillars of sustainable development, and recommends that the Consultative Process devise a transparent, objective and inclusive process for the selection of topics and panellists so as to facilitate the work of the General Assembly during informal consultations concerning the annual resolution on oceans and the law of the sea;

189. *Recalls* the need to strengthen and improve the efficiency of the Consultative Process, and encourages States, intergovernmental organizations and programmes to provide guidance to the Co-Chairs to this effect, particularly before and during the preparatory meeting for the Consultative Process, and recalls its decision in this regard, in resolution 63/111, that the eleventh meeting of the Consultative Process shall be based on the decisions taken by the General Assembly at its sixty-fourth session;

190. *Requests* the Secretary-General to convene, in accordance with paragraphs 2 and 3 of resolution 54/33, the eleventh meeting of the Consultative Process, in New York from 21 to 25 June 2010, to provide it with the necessary facilities for the performance of its work and to arrange for support to be provided by the Division, in cooperation with other relevant parts of the Secretariat, as appropriate;

191. *Expresses its serious concern* regarding the lack of resources available in the voluntary trust fund established by resolution 55/7 for the purpose of assisting developing countries, in particular least developed countries, small island developing States and landlocked developing States, in attending the meetings of the Consultative Process, and urges States to make additional contributions to the trust fund;

192. *Decides* that those representatives from developing countries who are invited by the Co-Chairs, in consultation with Governments, to make presentations during the meetings of the Consultative Process shall receive priority consideration in the disbursement of funds from the voluntary trust fund established by resolution 55/7 in order to cover the costs of their travel, and shall also be eligible to receive daily subsistence allowance subject to the availability of funds after the travel costs of all other eligible representatives from those countries mentioned in paragraph 191 above have been covered;

193. *Also decides* that, in its deliberations on the report of the Secretary-General on oceans and the law of the sea, the Consultative Process at its eleventh meeting will focus its discussions on capacity-building in ocean affairs and the law of the sea, including marine science;

XV

Coordination and cooperation

194. *Encourages* States to work closely with and through international organizations, funds and programmes, as well as the specialized agencies of the United Nations system and relevant international conventions, to

identify emerging areas of focus for improved coordination and cooperation and how best to address these issues;

195. *Encourages* bodies established by the Convention to strengthen coordination and cooperation, as appropriate, in fulfilling their respective mandates;

196. *Requests* the Secretary-General to bring the present resolution to the attention of heads of intergovernmental organizations, the specialized agencies, funds and programmes of the United Nations engaged in activities relating to ocean affairs and the law of the sea, as well as funding institutions, and underlines the importance of their constructive and timely input for the report of the Secretary-General on oceans and the law of the sea and of their participation in relevant meetings and processes;

197. *Welcomes* the work done by the secretariats of relevant United Nations specialized agencies, programmes, funds and bodies and the secretariats of related organizations and conventions to enhance inter-agency coordination and cooperation on ocean issues, including through UN-Oceans, the inter-agency coordination mechanism on ocean and coastal issues within the United Nations system;

198. *Encourages* continued updates to Member States by UN-Oceans regarding its priorities and initiatives, in particular with respect to the proposed participation in UN-Oceans;

XVI

Activities of the Division for Ocean Affairs and the Law of the Sea

199. *Expresses its appreciation* to the Secretary-General for the annual comprehensive report on oceans and the law of the sea, prepared by the Division, as well as for the other activities of the Division, which reflect the high standard of assistance provided to Member States by the Division;

200. *Notes with satisfaction* the first observance by the United Nations of World Oceans Day on 8 June 2009, and invites the Division to continue to promote and facilitate international cooperation on the law of the sea and ocean affairs in the context of the future observance of World Oceans Day, as well as through its participation in other events such as the World Expo, to be held in Shanghai, China, in 2010, and in Yeosu, Republic of Korea, in 2012, and the European Maritime Day to be celebrated in Gijón, Spain, from 19 to 21 May 2010;

201. *Requests* the Secretary-General to continue to carry out the responsibilities and functions entrusted to him in the Convention and by the related resolutions of the General Assembly, including resolutions 49/28 and 52/26, and to ensure the allocation of appropriate resources to the Division for the performance of its activities under the approved budget for the Organization;

XVII

Sixty-fifth session of the General Assembly

202. *Requests* the Secretary-General to prepare a comprehensive report, in its current extensive format and in accordance with established practice, for the consideration of the General Assembly at its sixty-fifth session, on developments and issues relating to ocean affairs and the law of the sea, including the implementation of the present resolution, in accordance with resolutions 49/28, 52/26 and 54/33, and to make the section of the report related to the topic that is the focus of the eleventh meeting of the Consultative Process available at least six weeks in advance of the meeting of the Consultative Process;

203. *Emphasizes* the critical role of the annual comprehensive report of the Secretary-General, which integrates information on developments relating to the implementation of the Convention and the work of the Organization, its specialized agencies and other institutions in the field of ocean affairs and the law of the sea at the global and regional levels, and as a result constitutes the basis for the annual consideration and review of developments relating to ocean affairs and the law of the sea by the General Assembly as the global institution having the competence to undertake such a review;

204. *Notes* that the report referred to in paragraph 202 above will also be submitted to States Parties pursuant to article 319 of the Convention regarding issues of a general nature that have arisen with respect to the Convention;

205. *Also notes* the desire to further improve the efficiency of, and effective participation of delegations in, the informal consultations concerning the annual General Assembly resolution on oceans and the law of the sea and the resolution on sustainable fisheries, decides that the period of the informal consultations on both resolutions should not exceed a maximum of four weeks in total and that the consultations should be scheduled in such a way that the Division has sufficient time to produce the report referred to in paragraph 202 above, and invites States to submit text proposals for inclusion in the resolutions to the coordinators of the informal consultations at the earliest possible date;

206. *Decides* to include in the provisional agenda of its sixty-fifth session the item entitled "Oceans and the law of the sea".

RECORDED VOTE ON RESOLUTION 64/71:

In favour: Albania, Algeria, Andorra, Argentina, Armenia, Australia, Austria, Bahamas, Bahrain, Bangladesh, Belgium, Benin, Bolivia, Botswana, Brazil, Brunei Darussalam, Cameroon, Canada, Cape Verde, Chile, China, Congo, Costa Rica, Cuba, Cyprus, Czech Republic, Democratic People's Republic of Korea, Denmark, Djibouti, Dominican Republic, Egypt, Estonia, Fiji, Finland, France, Georgia, Germany, Ghana, Greece, Guatemala, Guinea-Bissau, Iceland, India, Indonesia, Ireland, Italy, Japan, Jordan, Kazakhstan, Kuwait, Lao People's Democratic Republic, Latvia, Liechtenstein, Lithuania, Luxembourg, Madagascar, Malaysia, Maldives, Mali, Malta, Marshall Islands, Mauritania, Mauritius, Mexico, Micronesia, Moldova, Monaco, Mongolia, Morocco, Mozambique, Myanmar, Nauru, Netherlands, New Zealand, Nigeria, Norway, Oman, Pakistan, Palau, Panama, Papua New Guinea, Peru, Philippines, Poland, Portugal, Qatar, Republic of Korea, Romania, Russian Federation, Samoa, San Marino, Saudi Arabia, Senegal, Seychelles, Singapore, Slovakia, Slovenia, Solomon Islands, South Africa, Spain, Sri Lanka, Sudan, Suriname, Sweden, Thailand, The former Yugoslav Republic of Macedonia, Togo, Trinidad and Tobago, Uganda, Ukraine, United Arab Emirates, United Kingdom, United Republic of Tanzania, United States, Uruguay, Viet Nam, Yemen, Zambia, Zimbabwe.

Against: Turkey.

Abstaining: Colombia, El Salvador, Venezuela.

Division for Ocean Affairs and the Law of the Sea

During 2009, the Division for Ocean Affairs and the Law of the Sea of the Office of Legal Affairs continued to fulfil its role as the substantive unit of the UN Secretariat responsible for reviewing and monitoring all developments related to the law of the sea and ocean affairs, as well as for the implementation of the United Nations Convention on the Law of the Sea and related General Assembly resolutions.

The Division, in cooperation with intergovernmental bodies and host Governments, continued its capacity-building efforts through the organization of training courses. Two training courses were held: one by the Train-Sea-Coast/Black Sea Course Development Unit on "Nutrient pollution from agriculture and nutrient loads reduction" (Antalya, Turkey, 2–6 February) and another by the Benguela Current Course Development Unit on marine pollution control (Cape Town, South Africa, 23–27 February). The Division also organized, in cooperation with the Department of Public Information, events at UN Headquarters in New York on the occasion of the first observance of World Oceans Day (8 June), under the theme "Our Oceans, Our Responsibility".

The Hamilton Shirley Amerasinghe Memorial Fellowship on the Law of the Sea, established in 1981 [YUN 1981, pp. 130 & 139], was not awarded to any candidate owing to insufficient funds.

PART FIVE

Institutional, administrative and budgetary questions

Chapter I

United Nations restructuring and institutional matters

In 2009, the General Assembly continued consideration of efforts to further enhance system-wide coherence and support progress toward reaching internationally agreed development goals, including the Millennium Development Goals (MDGs), focusing on the priority areas of: the United Nations "Delivering as one" at the country level; governance and funding of UN operational activities for development; and reform of the gender architecture within the Organization. In September, the Assembly adopted a resolution on system-wide coherence, expressing strong support for consolidating the Office of the Special Adviser on Gender Issues and Advancement of Women, the Division for the Advancement of Women, the United Nations Development Fund for Women and the United Nations International Research and Training Institute for the Advancement of Women into a composite entity led by an Under-Secretary-General. The Assembly also asked the Secretary-General to make proposals for the further improvement of the governance of operational activities for development, and to arrange for an independent evaluation of the "Delivering as one" programme. In October, an intergovernmental meeting of the eight "Delivering as one" pilot countries reviewed progress and lessons learned and made proposals for moving forward. The Assembly also agreed to convene in 2010 a high-level meeting on accelerating progress towards achieving the MDGs.

The Ad Hoc Working Group on the Revitalization of the General Assembly continued to identify ways to further enhance the Assembly's role, authority, effectiveness and efficiency. The Assembly continued to focus on administrative and institutional matters. It resumed its sixty-third session, and opened its sixty-fourth session on 15 September. The Assembly resumed the tenth emergency special session on illegal Israeli actions in occupied East Jerusalem and the rest of the Occupied Palestinian Territory; held a conference at the highest level on the world financial and economic crisis and its impact on development; and held a commemorative meeting to mark the fifteenth anniversary of the International Conference on Population and Development.

The Security Council held 194 formal meetings to deal with regional conflicts, peacekeeping operations and other issues related to the maintenance of international peace and security.

In addition to its organizational and substantive sessions, the Economic and Social Council held a special high-level meeting with the Bretton Woods institutions (the World Bank Group and the International Monetary Fund), the World Trade Organization and the United Nations Conference on Trade and Development.

Restructuring issues

Programme of reform

UN system-wide coherence

In 2009, the General Assembly continued consultations on system-wide coherence through 13 informal consultations and interactive meetings, led by the Co-Chairs of the System-wide Coherence process (Namibia and Spain), including a plenary of informal consultation held on 22 June and meetings with regional groupings and individuals. Those consultations addressed the strengthening of institutional arrangements for gender equality and the empowerment of women; strengthening governance of operational activities for development of the UN system for enhanced system-wide coherence, including the "Delivering as one" programme; and improving the funding system of UN operational activities for development. The consultations were supported by discussion documents prepared by the Secretary-General. The Co-Chairs reported periodically on the results of those consultations for the Assembly's consideration.

Delivering as one. On 8 June, the Chair of the United Nations Development Group (UNDG), Helen Clark, briefed the General Assembly on UN development system efforts to increase coherence, effectiveness and efficiency, particularly through the "Delivering as one" pilots (Albania, Cape Verde, Mozambique, Pakistan, Rwanda, United Republic of Tanzania, Uruguay, Viet Nam). She stated that the important results reported by pilot countries included increased guidance by the Governments of those countries to the UN development system; greater alignment of the work of the UN country teams in those countries with national priorities and development strategies; and greater emphasis on strengthening national capacity. Common budgetary frameworks and country funds had significantly improved the transparency of the United Nations, enhancing inter-agency collaboration and facilitating greater coherence in monitoring and financial reporting obligations. The pooled "One Fund" mechanism had helped to harmonize resource mobilization and reporting and reduce transaction costs; and many pilot countries had embarked on and made progress in harmonizing and simplifying business practices in procurement, information and communication technologies and human resources, which should enhance the effectiveness and efficiency of UN country teams' operations. However, many challenges remained, such as accelerating the harmonization of business practices, identifying and measuring transaction costs and efficiencies, ensuring funding predictability, and addressing the call by pilot countries for the development of a single results report. UNDG would support countries wishing to conduct country-level evaluations in advance of the independent evaluation to take place.

Institutional arrangements for gender issues. In response to General Assembly resolution 62/277 [YUN 2008, p. 1516], the Deputy Secretary-General, on behalf of the Secretary-General, submitted on 5 March a discussion note on "Further details on institutional options for strengthening the institutional arrangements for support to gender equality and the empowerment of women". The note provided detailed modalities on the options set out in a 2008 paper on the subject [ibid., p. 1271], focusing in particular on the composite entity option for strengthening the institutional arrangements through consolidation of the four gender-specific entities, namely, the Office of the Special Adviser on Gender Issues and Advancement of Women, the Division for the Advancement of Women, the United Nations Development Fund for Women and the United Nations International Research and Training Institute for the Advancement of Women. The paper concluded that the composite entity had the greatest potential to address the identified gaps and challenges.

On 3 June, additional information was provided on the proposed new entity, including its organizational structure, governance, staffing, funding and the relationships between the entity and intergovernmental bodies.

In their 7 August summary of consultations on UN system-wide coherence, the Co-Chairs of the System-wide Coherence process said that the new entity would, in particular, provide support to UN intergovernmental bodies, advance gender mainstreaming throughout the UN system, provide a link between the normative functions and operational activities, and carry out operational activities more effectively and on a larger scale, with a view to strengthening the impact of its support to Member States. It would be led by an Under-Secretary-General, and supported by funding from the UN regular budget for core functions and voluntary contributions for operational activities.

(For more details, see PART THREE, Chapter II and Chapter X.)

On 14 September [meeting 105], the General Assembly adopted **resolution 63/311** [draft: A/63/L.103] without vote [agenda item 107].

System-wide coherence

The General Assembly,

Recalling the 2005 World Summit Outcome,

Recalling also its resolution 62/208 of 19 December 2007 on the triennial comprehensive policy review of operational activities for development of the United Nations system,

Recalling further its resolution 62/277 of 15 September 2008 on system-wide coherence,

Recalling the Convention on the Elimination of All Forms of Discrimination against Women, the Beijing Declaration and Platform for Action, and the outcome of the twenty-third special session of the General Assembly,

Reaffirming the importance of the comprehensive policy review of operational activities for development of the United Nations system, through which the General Assembly establishes key system-wide policy orientations for the development cooperation and country-level modalities of the United Nations system,

Recalling the role of the Economic and Social Council in providing coordination and guidance to the United Nations system to ensure that those policy orientations are implemented on a system-wide basis in accordance with resolution 62/208 and other relevant resolutions,

Having considered the discussion notes on "Further details on institutional options for strengthening the institutional arrangements for support of gender equality and the empowerment of women" of 5 March 2009, on "Strengthening governance of operational activities for development of the United Nations system for enhanced system-wide coherence" of 15 April 2009 and on "Strengthening the system-wide funding architecture of operational activities of the United Nations for development" of 3 May 2009, which the Deputy Secretary-General, on behalf of the Secretary-General, provided to the President of the General Assembly in response to a request from Member States,

Strengthening the institutional arrangements for support of gender equality and the empowerment of women

1. *Strongly supports* the consolidation of the Office of the Special Adviser on Gender Issues and Advancement of Women, the Division for the Advancement of Women, the United Nations Development Fund for Women and the United Nations International Research and Training Institute for the Advancement of Women, into a composite entity, taking into account the existing mandates;

2. *Supports* that the composite entity shall be led by an Under-Secretary-General, who will report directly to the Secretary-General, to be appointed by the Secretary-General, in consultation with Member States, on the basis of equitable geographical representation and gender balance;

3. *Requests* the Secretary-General to produce, for the consideration of the General Assembly at its sixty-fourth session, a comprehensive proposal specifying, inter alia, the mission statement of the composite entity, the organizational arrangements, including an organizational chart, funding and

the executive board to oversee its operational activities in order to commence intergovernmental negotiations;

Strengthening governance of operational activities for development of the United Nations system for enhanced system-wide coherence

4. *Reaffirms* that the strengthening of the governance of operational activities for development of the United Nations system should focus on enhancing existing intergovernmental bodies with the purpose of making the United Nations development system more efficient and effective in its support to developing countries for the achievement of the internationally agreed development goals;

5. *Underscores* that the governance of operational activities for development should be transparent and inclusive and should support national ownership and national development strategies;

6. *Requests* the Secretary-General, in consultation with the United Nations System Chief Executives Board for Coordination, to propose to the General Assembly, at its sixty-fourth session, actionable proposals for the further improvement of the governance of the operational activities for development;

7. *Also requests* the Secretary-General, in consultation with the members of United Nations System Chief Executives Board for Coordination and the United Nations Development Group, to propose to the General Assembly, at its sixty-fourth session, modalities for the submission and approval of common country programmes on a voluntary basis, bearing in mind the importance of national ownership and effective intergovernmental oversight of the development process;

8. *Reaffirms* the importance of strengthening evaluation as a United Nations system function and the guidance contained to this effect in its resolution 62/208, and in this regard requests the Secretary-General, in consultation with the members of the United Nations System Chief Executives Board for Coordination, to propose to the General Assembly, at its sixty-fourth session, modalities for the establishment of an independent system-wide evaluation mechanism to assess system-wide efficiency, effectiveness and performance, bearing in mind the evaluation functions carried out by respective United Nations organizations, the Joint Inspection Unit and the United Nations Evaluation Group;

9. *Urges* the United Nations System Chief Executives Board for Coordination and the United Nations Development Group to enhance the transparency of their activities through regular briefings to the General Assembly and through regular reports and effective interaction with the Economic and Social Council and relevant intergovernmental bodies;

10. *Encourages* continued and increased cooperation, coordination and coherence and exchanges between the United Nations and the Bretton Woods institutions, and requests the Secretary-General, in consultation with the United Nations System Chief Executives Board for Coordination, to regularly apprise the General Assembly of progress made in this regard as part of the triennial and quadrennial comprehensive policy review reporting process;

Improving the funding system of operational activities for development of the United Nations system for enhanced system-wide coherence

11. *Emphasizes* that increasing financial contributions to the United Nations development system is key to achieving the internationally agreed development goals, including the Millennium Development Goals, and in this regard recognizes the mutually reinforcing links between the increased effectiveness, efficiency and coherence of the United Nations development system, achieving concrete results in assisting developing countries in eradicating poverty and achieving sustained economic growth and sustainable development through operational activities for development and the overall resourcing of the United Nations development system;

12. *Stresses* that core resources, because of their untied nature, continue to be the bedrock of the operational activities for development of the United Nations system;

13. *Notes with concern* the continuing imbalance between core and non-core resources received by the operational activities for development of the United Nations system and the potential negative impact of non-core funding on the coordination and effectiveness of operational activities for development at the country level, while recognizing that thematic trust funds, multi-donor trust funds and other voluntary non-earmarked funding mechanisms linked to organization-specific funding frameworks and strategies, as established by the respective governing bodies, constitute some of the funding modalities that are complementary to regular budgets;

14. *Urges* donor countries and other countries in a position to do so to substantially increase their voluntary contributions to the core/regular budgets of the United Nations development system, in particular its funds, programmes and specialized agencies, to contribute on a multiyear basis, in a sustained and predictable manner, and to undertake voluntary commitments to provide a greater share of system-wide contributions to operational activities for development as core/regular resources;

15. *Requests* the Secretary-General to include in his comprehensive statistical analysis of the financing of operational activities for development further analysis and actionable proposals on the current situation and perspectives in respect of core and non-core funding for the United Nations development system, notably the implications of various forms of non-core funding, in terms of predictability, country ownership and the implementation of intergovernmental mandates;

16. *Also requests* the Secretary-General to create a central repository of information on operational activities for development, including disaggregated statistics on all funding sources and expenditures, building on his comprehensive statistical analysis of the financing of operational activities for development, and to ensure appropriate and user-friendly online access and regular updating of the information contained therein;

"Delivering as one"

17. *Acknowledges* the interim assessments of the progress made and the challenges remaining in efforts to increase coherence in country-level programming, including in the "programme country pilots";

18. *Encourages* the Secretary-General to support "programme country pilot" countries to undertake expeditiously their own country-led evaluations with the participation of relevant stakeholders and with the technical support of the United Nations Evaluation Group;

19. *Requests* the Secretary-General to urgently undertake arrangements for an independent evaluation of lessons learned from the above efforts, as requested in resolution 62/208, and to inform the General Assembly of the modalities and terms of reference of this independent evaluation at its sixty-fourth session;

20. *Underscores* that the independent evaluation should be guided by the principles contained in resolution 62/208 with regard to national ownership and leadership and be conducted in the context of system-wide norms and standards, that it should be based on an inclusive, transparent, objective and independent approach, and that its outcome should be submitted to the General Assembly at its sixty-sixth session;

Harmonization of business practices

21. *Calls upon* the Secretary-General, in cooperation with the members of the United Nations System Chief Executives Board for Coordination, to continue progress in the simplification and harmonization of business practices within the United Nations development system, and requests the Secretary-General, in consultation with the System Chief Executives Board, to regularly inform the Economic and Social Council about progress being made and challenges encountered in this regard and to refer any matter requiring an intergovernmental decision to the relevant intergovernmental bodies;

The way forward

22. *Decides* to continue the intergovernmental work of the General Assembly on system-wide coherence on the issues addressed in the present resolution during the sixty-fourth session, with a view to achieving further substantive action in all areas, and resolves, at the conclusion of its entire process on system-wide coherence, to review and take stock of all its prior actions and deliberations in a single resolution or decision.

Intergovernmental meeting. On 3 December, Rwanda transmitted to the Secretary-General the Statement of Outcome and Way Forward adopted at the Intergovernmental Meeting of the programme country pilots on "Delivering as one" (Kigali, Rwanda, 19–21 October) [A/64/578-E/2010/3]. Representatives of the eight "Delivering as one" pilot countries, as well as of those countries that had voluntarily adopted the "Delivering as one" approach (Benin, Bhutan, Comoros, Kiribati, Malawi, Papua New Guinea), exchanged views on their experiences and lessons learned since the 2008 seminar in Maputo, Mozambique [YUN 2008, p. 1515], and on how to move the process forward while implementing the recommendations contained in Assembly resolution 62/208 [YUN 2007, p. 877]. Participants found that the "Delivering as one" approach had provided benefits for achieving better development results through increased national leadership and ownership. Pro-

gramme pilot countries and countries voluntarily adopting the approach had increased access to UN system mandates and resources, and their Governments were able to determine which of those best responded to national needs and priorities. Institutional frameworks for steering the process and the coordinating role of the Governments had been strengthened, bringing greater coherence in UN support for addressing national priorities and thus allowing the United Nations to become a more effective partner.

Major constraints to full implementation of the initiative included the lack of predictability and timeliness of funding, the lack of harmonization and simplification of business practices, high transaction costs, the low level of use of national operational capacities and the slow progress of the co-location of UN organizations. Participants welcomed the initiative to conduct country-led evaluations of their "Delivering as one" approach in seven of the eight programme countries. They agreed on a set of common parameters and institutional arrangements to ensure the independence, quality and credibility of the evaluations. They also requested the Assembly to organize the independent evaluations of lessons learned from the "Delivering as one" programme in accordance with resolution 63/311 (see p. 1368). Addressing the way forward, participants reaffirmed that there was no going back to the way of doing business prior to the "Delivering as one" initiative; underscored that the approach should continue to be guided by the principle of national ownership and leadership; and called upon agency headquarters, governing bodies, the Assembly and Member States to continue to support the reform process. They also called upon donors to support Governments of pilot countries and countries voluntarily adopting the approach in sustaining efforts to mobilize timely, predictable, unearmarked and multi-year financial support for the initiative through the country funds. They further agreed that all country-led evaluations should be completed by 1 July 2010, as an input to the following meeting to be held in Hanoi, Viet Nam.

Report of Secretary-General. In a December report [A/64/589] on follow-up to General Assembly resolution 63/311, the Secretary-General made proposals for improving the functioning of the governing bodies to ensure that the tiers of governance engaged in operational activities for development functioned as an integrated system, with clear roles and well-defined lines of responsibilities and accountability. The proposals provided the basis for further consultations among Member States and governing bodies on the challenges and opportunities that would be created by strengthening the governance of UN operational activities for development (see p. 853).

The Secretary-General also addressed the purpose, timing and scope of the independent evaluation of lessons learned from the "Delivering as one" programme country pilots. He stated that the purpose of the evaluation was to feed into the Assembly's quadrennial comprehensive policy review and contribute to consultations on system-wide coherence. The evaluation should be completed by the end of 2011. The Secretary-General proposed two options for conducting the evaluation: identifying an existing evaluation function that had the mandate to deliver an exercise of that nature; or setting up an ad hoc arrangement through the establishment of an evaluation management group.

Comprehensive accountability architecture

At its resumed sixty-third session, the General Assembly had before it the Secretary-General's report on the accountability framework, enterprise risk management and internal control framework, and results-based management framework [YUN 2008, p. 1519]; the related report of the Advisory Committee on Administrative and Budgetary Questions [ibid., p. 1520]; the related section of the report of the Independent Audit Advisory Committee on its activities for the period from 1 January to 31 July 2008 [ibid., p. 1562]; the report of the Office of Internal Oversight Services on the review of results-based management in the United Nations [ibid., p. 1520]; the report of the Joint Inspection Unit on results-based management in the United Nations in the context of the reform process [YUN 2006, p. 1652]; and the Secretary-General's comments thereon [YUN 2008, p. 1520].

GENERAL ASSEMBLY ACTION

On 7 April [meeting 79], the General Assembly, on the recommendation of the Fifth (Administrative and Budgetary) Committee [A/63/649/Add.1], adopted **resolution 63/276** without vote [agenda item 117].

Accountability framework, enterprise risk management and internal control framework, and results-based management framework

The General Assembly,

Recalling its resolutions 59/272 of 23 December 2004 and 60/254 of 8 May 2006, section I of its resolution 60/260 of 8 May 2006, its resolution 60/283 of 7 July 2006, paragraph 4 of its resolution 61/245 of 22 December 2006, paragraph 22 of its resolution 62/236 of 22 December 2007 and paragraphs 15 and 16 of its resolution 62/250 of 20 June 2008,

Recalling also its resolutions 55/231 of 23 December 2000, 56/253 of 24 December 2001, 57/290 B of 18 June 2003 and 59/296 of 22 June 2005 and paragraph 2 of its resolution 60/257 of 8 May 2006,

Aware of the significant flaws in terms of internal monitoring, inspection and accountability regarding, for example, the management of the United Nations oil-for-food programme,

Noting that since its sixtieth session, the General Assembly has included in its agenda the item entitled "Follow-up to the recommendations on administrative management and internal oversight of the Independent Inquiry Committee into the United Nations Oil-for-Food Programme",

Having considered the report of the Secretary-General on the accountability framework, enterprise risk management and internal control framework, and results-based management framework, and the related report of the Advisory Committee on Administrative and Budgetary Questions, as well as the related section of the report of the Independent Audit Advisory Committee on its activities for the period from 1 January to 31 July 2008,

Having also considered the report of the Office of Internal Oversight Services on the review of results-based management in the United Nations, and the report of the Joint Inspection Unit on results-based management in the United Nations in the context of the reform process and the comments of the Secretary-General thereon,

1. *Takes note* of the report of the Secretary-General on the accountability framework, enterprise risk management and internal control framework, and results-based management framework, and the related section of the report of the Independent Audit Advisory Committee on its activities for the period from 1 January to 31 July 2008;

2. *Also takes note* of the report of the Office of Internal Oversight Services on the review of results-based management in the United Nations, and the report of the Joint Inspection Unit on results-based management in the United Nations in the context of the reform process and the comments of the Secretary-General thereon;

3. *Endorses* the conclusions and recommendations contained in the report of the Advisory Committee on Administrative and Budgetary Questions, subject to the provisions of the present resolution;

4. *Reaffirms its commitment* to strengthening accountability in the Secretariat and the accountability of the Secretary-General to Member States and the achievement of results, and emphasizes the importance of establishing real, effective and efficient mechanisms that foster institutional and personal accountability;

5. *Stresses* that accountability is a central pillar of effective and efficient management that requires attention at the highest level;

6. *Reaffirms* paragraph 2 of its resolution 60/257, in which it endorsed the benchmarking framework for the implementation of results-based management in the United Nations, and that the implementation of any proposal on the accountability of the Secretariat to Member States shall in no way call into question the sole prerogative of Member States in respect of defining the roles and responsibilities of the intergovernmental bodies and oversight bodies for results-based management, including all aspects of programme planning, budgeting, monitoring and evaluation;

7. *Strongly urges* the Secretary-General to respect the sole prerogative of Member States regarding the application of the proposed actions included in paragraph 86 of his report, in particular principle 4, and requests him to refrain from redefining the roles and responsibilities of the intergovernmental bodies and oversight bodies for results-based management, including all aspects of programme planning, budgeting, monitoring and evaluation;

8. *Decides* not to endorse the proposed accountability framework;

9. *Requests* the Secretary-General to submit to the General Assembly, for consideration at the first part of its resumed sixty-fourth session, in consultation with the respective oversight bodies, drawing on the expertise of relevant United Nations entities and taking fully into account all relevant resolutions on accountability, a comprehensive report including, inter alia:

(*a*) A clear definition of accountability and proposals on accountability mechanisms, including clear parameters for their application and the instruments for their rigorous enforcement, without exceptions at any level, and a clear definition of roles and responsibilities;

(*b*) Clear and specific measures to ensure the access of Member States to timely and reliable information on results achieved and resources used by the United Nations Secretariat, as well as its performance including on measures to improve performance reporting;

(*c*) Concrete measures to ensure the timely implementation of the recommendations of the oversight bodies;

(*d*) Measures to strengthen personal accountability within the Secretariat and institutional accountability towards Member States on the results achieved and resources used;

(*e*) Measures to ensure transparency in the selection and appointment process of senior managers, including at the Assistant Secretary-General and Under-Secretary-General levels;

(*f*) Concrete proposals on the reform of the performance appraisal system, taking fully into account the views of staff, as well as on sanctions for under-performance and rewards for outstanding performance to be applied for staff and senior management, including at the Assistant Secretary-General and Under-Secretary-General levels;

(*g*) A clear definition of responsibilities resulting from the delegation of authority, and clear guidelines for programme managers for exercising that authority and actions to improve the system of the delegation of authority, including, inter alia, through systematic reporting mechanisms on how the delegated authority is exercised;

(*h*) Measures taken to implement the results-based management framework, including measures taken by the Secretary-General to strengthen the senior management's leadership and commitment to promoting and supporting a culture of results in the United Nations, as well as a common understanding of results-based management and its implications;

(*i*) Scope, parameters and time frame for the application of a reliable results-based management information system, including detailed information on its compatibility with existing and projected information management systems;

(*j*) A proposed detailed plan and road map for the implementation of the enterprise risk management and internal control framework;

(*k*) An explanation of how the measures to strengthen the Secretariat's accountability mechanisms would address the significant flaws in terms of internal monitoring, inspection and accountability regarding the management of the United Nations oil-for-food programme;

10. *Approves*, under the programme budget for the biennium 2008–2009, the creation of one position at the P-4 level under section 28A, Office of the Under-Secretary-General for Management, to be financed under general temporary assistance for nine months, the primary objective being the preparation of the report referred to in paragraph 9 above, and to be reported in the context of the second performance report on the programme budget;

11. *Also approves*, under the programme budget for the biennium 2008–2009, the redeployment of two posts (one P-4 and one General Service (Principal-level)) from section 29, Internal oversight, to section 28A, Office of the Under-Secretary-General for Management, as well as the amount of 24,000 United States dollars in non-post resources;

12. *Takes note* of paragraph 38 of the report of the Advisory Committee on Administrative and Budgetary Questions with regard to the pilot project referred to in paragraph 104 (*b*) of the report of the Secretary-General;

13. *Requests* the Secretary-General to submit a report, to be considered by the Fifth Committee at the first part of the resumed sixty-fourth session of the General Assembly, on the modalities to be applied regarding the sharing of information contained in consultants' reports on management-related issues;

14. *Decides* that the consultants' reports referred to in paragraph 13 above are to be made available by the Secretary-General, upon the request of Member States, subject to approval by the General Assembly of the modalities to be applied;

15. *Notes* the existing practice of informal sharing of consultants' reports, and decides that the Secretary-General is to continue this practice, pending a decision on the report mentioned in paragraph 13 above;

16. *Requests* the Secretary-General to entrust the Office of Internal Oversight Services with carrying out a review of the practices of the Secretariat in this regard;

17. *Invites* the Sixth Committee to consider the legal aspects of the report of the Secretary-General entitled "Information-sharing practices between the United Nations and national law enforcement authorities, as well as referrals of possible criminal cases related to United Nations staff, United Nations officials and experts on mission", without prejudice to the role of the Fifth Committee as the Main Committee of the General Assembly responsible for administrative and budgetary matters.

Strengthening of UN system

In 2009, the General Assembly continued its consideration of the agenda item on strengthening the United Nations system. It had before it reports of the Secretary-General on peacebuilding in the immediate aftermath of conflict [A/63/881] (see p. 43), and on implementation of Assembly resolution 61/257 on strengthening the capacity of the Organization to advance the disarmament agenda [YUN 2008, p. 559].

By **decision 64/549** of 24 December, the Assembly decided that the items on strengthening the United Nations system and on United Nations reform: measures and proposals would remain for consideration during its resumed sixty-fourth (2010) session.

Institutional matters

Intergovernmental machinery

Revitalization of the work of the General Assembly

In accordance with General Assembly resolution 58/316 [YUN 2004, p. 1374], the Secretary-General in July submitted a report [A/63/915] on the revitalization of the work of the Assembly, which outlined the draft programme of work of the plenary and five of the six Assembly's Main Committees for its sixty-fourth (2009) session. An addendum [A/63/915/Add.1] contained the status of documentation for that session, as at 3 August 2009.

Ad Hoc Working Group report. Pursuant to Assembly resolution 62/276 [YUN 2008, p. 1522], the Ad Hoc Working Group on the Revitalization of the Assembly in September submitted a report [A/63/959] summarizing its activities and presenting recommendations for further progress. The Working Group held eight meetings and conducted its work programme through a general discussion and exchange of views on all issues related to revitalization, thematic meetings and briefings. The three thematic meetings focused on: the implementation of Assembly resolutions and its agenda; operational and technical issues, including information on the Assembly's voting system in the framework of the capital master plan; its role and relationship to the other principal organs of the Organization and its visibility and public outreach capacity; its role and responsibility in appointing UN Secretaries-General; and strengthening the institutional memory of the Office of the President of the General Assembly and enhancing its functions and relationship with the Secretariat. Member States also heard briefings on voting/balloting and documentation, as well as the views of the United Nations Correspondents Association on ways in which coverage of the Assembly and its work could be facilitated.

GENERAL ASSEMBLY ACTION

On 14 September [meeting 105], the General Assembly adopted **resolution 63/309** [A/63/959] without vote [agenda item 110].

Revitalization of the work of the General Assembly

The General Assembly,

Reaffirming its previous resolutions relating to the revitalization of its work, including resolutions 46/77 of 12 December 1991, 47/233 of 17 August 1993, 48/264 of 29 July 1994, 51/241 of 31 July 1997, 52/163 of 15 December 1997, 55/14 of 3 November 2000, 55/285 of 7 September 2001, 56/509 of 8 July 2002, 57/300 of 20 December 2002, 57/301 of 13 March 2003, 58/126 of 19 December 2003, 58/316 of 1 July 2004, 59/313 of 12 September 2005, 60/286 of 8 September 2006, 61/292 of 2 August 2007 and 62/276 of 15 September 2008,

Stressing the importance of implementing resolutions on the revitalization of its work,

Recalling the role of the General Assembly in addressing issues of peace and security, in accordance with the Charter of the United Nations,

Recognizing the need to further enhance the role, authority, effectiveness and efficiency of the General Assembly,

Recalling paragraph 18 of the annex to its resolution 60/286 on the selection of the Secretary-General,

Noting the role of the Office of the President of the General Assembly and the importance of providing adequate resources for its substantive work,

Noting also the current practice of balloting observed by the General Assembly,

1.   *Welcomes* the report of the Ad Hoc Working Group on the Revitalization of the General Assembly;

2.   *Decides* to establish, at its sixty-fourth session, an ad hoc working group on the revitalization of the General Assembly, open to all Member States:

(*a*)   To identify further ways to enhance the role, authority, effectiveness and efficiency of the Assembly, inter alia, by building on previous resolutions;

(*b*)   To submit a report thereon to the Assembly at its sixty-fourth session;

Selection of the Secretary-General

3.   *Affirms its commitment* to continuing, in the Ad Hoc Working Group at the sixty-fourth session, its consideration of the revitalization of the role of the General Assembly in the selection and appointment of the Secretary-General in accordance with Article 97 of the Charter;

Role and authority of the General Assembly

4.   *Welcomes* the holding of interactive thematic debates on current issues of critical importance to the international community in the General Assembly, and invites the President of the Assembly to continue with this practice in consultation with Member States;

5.   *Notes* the importance of strengthening the institutional memory of the Office of the President of the General Assembly, and invites the President at the sixty-fourth session to submit his views to the Ad Hoc Working Group at the sixty-fourth session for its consideration;

Working methods

6.   *Requests* the President of the General Assembly at its sixty-fourth session, in consultation with Member States, to make proposals for the further biennialization, triennialization, clustering and elimination of items on the agenda of the Assembly, taking into account the relevant recommendations of the Ad Hoc Working Group, including the introduction of a sunset clause;

7.   *Calls upon* Member States to respond to the annual review of the Meetings and Publishing Division of the Department for General Assembly and Conference Management on the distribution of printed documents to Missions, bearing in mind the cost savings, as well as the reduced environmental impact, which may accrue from this exercise, in order to improve the quality and distribution of those documents;

8.   *Invites* the Committee on Information at its thirty-second session to consider the sections on media and visibility in the report of the Ad Hoc Working Group, in particular those that call for less rigid restrictions and better access to people and information, and requests the Committee on Information to consider recommending measures for the operationalization and implementation of aspects thereof in its report to the Assembly through the Special Political and Decolonization Committee (Fourth Committee) at its sixty-fifth session;

9.   *Decides* that the Ad Hoc Working Group, during the sixty-fourth session, shall further consider options for more time-effective, efficient and secure balloting, reiterating the need to ascertain the credibility, reliability and confidentiality of the balloting process.

On 21 December, the Assembly decided that, in order to rationalize further its methods of work for subsequent sessions, the Second (Economic and Financial) Committee should elect its Rapporteur on the basis of experience and personal competence, as well as rotation among the regional groups as follows: African States, Asian States, Eastern European States, Latin American and Caribbean States and Western European and Other States (**decision 64/544**).

On 24 December, the Assembly decided that the item on the revitalization of its work would remain for consideration during its resumed sixty-fourth (2010) session (**decision 64/549**).

Review of Security Council membership and related matters

The Open-ended Working Group on the Question of Equitable Representation on and Increase in the Membership of the Security Council and Other Matters related to the Security Council in September submitted a report on its work [A/63/47], carried out during seven formal meetings held between November 2008 and September 2009. At its second meeting, the Working Group addressed the framework and modalities in preparation for the intergovernmental negotiations. At its third, fourth and fifth meetings, the Working Group continued to address framework and modalities issues. The results of those consultations were discussed at its sixth meeting and presented to an informal plenary of the Assembly on 29 January. At its seventh meeting in September, the Working Group adopted its draft report to the Assembly.

The Assembly took note of the Working Group's report on 14 September (**decision 63/565 A**). It decided to immediately continue intergovernmental negotiations on Security Council reform in informal plenary at its sixty-fourth (2009) session, building on the progress achieved during its sixty-third session and the positions and proposals of Member States, while noting the initiative and efforts of the Assembly President and the Working Group Chairperson in the process of a comprehensive reform of the Council (**decision 63/565 B**).

On 24 December, the Assembly decided that the item on equitable representation on and increase in the membership of the Security Council and related matters would remain for consideration during its resumed sixty-fourth (2010) session (**decision 64/549**).

Institutional machinery

General Assembly

The General Assembly met throughout 2009; it resumed and concluded its sixty-third session and held the major part of its sixty-fourth session. The sixty-third session was resumed in plenary meetings on 20 February; 2 and 31 March; 7, 22 and 24 April; 8, 12 and 26 May; 3, 10, 16–17 and 29–30 June; 6, 9, 21, 23–24, 28 and 31 July; 11 August; and 9 and 14 September. The sixty-fourth session opened on 15 September and continued until its suspension on 24 December.

The Assembly held the tenth emergency special session on Illegal Israeli actions in Occupied East Jerusalem and the rest of the Occupied Palestinian Territory (15–16 January) (see p. 435); interactive thematic dialogues on: access to education in emergency, post-conflict and transition situations caused by man-made conflicts or natural disasters (18 March); the world financial and economic crisis and its impact on development (25–27 March) (see p. 792); the global food crisis and the right to food (6 April) (see p. 718); taking collective action to end human trafficking (13 May) (see p. 1092); and energy efficiency, energy conservation and new and renewable sources of energy (18 June) (see p. 996). It also held a conference at the highest level on the world financial and economic crisis and its impact on development (24–26 June) (see p. 792).

On 24 September, the Assembly held a high-level meeting to commemorate the work of the United Nations Relief and Works Agency for Palestine Refugees in the Near East on the occasion of its sixtieth anniversary. On 12 and 13 October, the Assembly held a commemorative meeting to mark the fifteenth anniversary of the International Conference on Population and Development.

Organization of Assembly sessions

2009 session

On 20 February, the General Assembly, on the proposal of its President, decided that the general debate of the sixty-fourth (2009) session would be held from Wednesday 23 to Saturday 26 September, and from

Monday 28 to Wednesday 30 September, and that those arrangements would in no way create a precedent for future sessions (**decision 63/553**).

By **decision 64/502** of 18 September, the Assembly adopted a number of provisions concerning the organization of the sixty-fourth session [A/64/250].

By **decision 64/501** of 15 September and 27 October, the Assembly authorized a number of subsidiary bodies to meet in New York during the main part of that session.

2010 session

High-level plenary meeting on Millennium Declaration

GENERAL ASSEMBLY ACTION

On 9 July [meeting 95], the General Assembly adopted **resolution 63/302** [draft: A/63/L.76] without vote [agenda items 44 and 107].

2010 high-level plenary meeting of the General Assembly

The General Assembly,

Recalling its resolution 55/2 of 8 September 2000, by which it adopted the United Nations Millennium Declaration, and resolution 60/1 of 16 September 2005, by which it adopted the 2005 World Summit Outcome,

1.   *Decides* to convene in 2010, at the commencement of the sixty-fifth session of the General Assembly, a high-level plenary meeting of the Assembly, on dates to be decided, with the participation of Heads of State and Government, and encourages all Member States to be represented at that level;

2.   *Also decides* to hold consultations on the scope, modalities, format and organization of the high-level plenary meeting of the Assembly with a view to concluding consultations before the end of 2009 and, in this regard, requests the Secretary-General to submit a report to the Assembly at the beginning of its sixty-fourth session.

Report of Secretary-General. In response to resolution 63/302 (see above), the Secretary General, in August [A/64/263], laid out his proposals for the scope, format and organization of the high-level plenary meeting of the Assembly's sixty-fifth session and proposed that the Assembly hold interactive round-table meetings, as well as informal interactive hearings with civil society organizations as part of the preparatory activities.

On 21 December [meeting 66], the General Assembly adopted **resolution 64/184** [draft: A/64/L.36] without vote [agenda items 48 and 114].

Organization of the High-level Plenary Meeting of the sixty-fifth session of the General Assembly

The General Assembly,

Recalling its resolutions 55/2 of 8 September 2000 and 60/1 of 16 September 2005, by which it adopted the United Nations Millennium Declaration and the 2005 World Summit Outcome, respectively,

Recalling also its resolution 63/302 of 9 July 2009, by which it decided to convene in 2010, at the commencement of the sixty-fifth session of the General Assembly, a high-level plenary meeting of the Assembly,

Taking note of the report of the Secretary-General entitled "Scope, modalities, format and organization of the high-level plenary meeting of the sixty-fifth session of the General Assembly" requested in resolution 63/302,

Convinced that the High-level Plenary Meeting will be a significant opportunity to galvanize commitment, rally support and spur collective action in order to reach the Millennium Development Goals by 2015,

1.   *Decides* that the High-level Plenary Meeting of the sixty-fifth session of the General Assembly shall be held from Monday, 20 September 2010, to Wednesday, 22 September 2010, in New York;

2.   *Also decides* to hold the general debate at its sixty-fifth session from Thursday, 23 September 2010, on the understanding that these arrangements shall in no way create a precedent for the general debate at future sessions;

3.   *Further decides* that the High-level Plenary Meeting shall focus on accelerating progress towards the achievement of all the Millennium Development Goals by 2015, taking into account the progress made with regard to the internationally agreed development goals, through a comprehensive review of successes, best practices and lessons learned, obstacles and gaps, challenges and opportunities, leading to concrete strategies for action, and requests the Secretary-General to submit a comprehensive report in this regard in March 2010;

4.   *Decides* that the above-mentioned report, together with the *Millennium Development Goals Report 2009* and the 2009 report of the Millennium Development Goals Gap Task Force, shall serve as an input for the consultations leading to the High-level Plenary Meeting;

5.   *Reiterates* that the High-level Plenary Meeting will be held with the participation of Heads of State or Government, and encourages all Member States to be represented at that level;

6.   *Decides* that the High-level Plenary Meeting shall be composed of six plenary meetings, on the basis of two meetings a day, and six interactive round-table sessions to be held in concurrence with plenary meetings;

7.   *Invites* the President of the General Assembly at its sixty-fourth session and the President of the Assembly at its sixty-fifth session to jointly preside over the High-level Plenary Meeting;

8.   *Decides* that the Holy See, in its capacity as observer State, and Palestine, in its capacity as observer, shall participate in the High-level Plenary Meeting;

9.   *Also decides* that the plenary meetings shall be organized in accordance with the modalities set forth in annex I to the present resolution and that the list of speakers for the plenary meetings shall be established in accordance with the procedure set forth in that annex;

10.   *Emphasizes* that the deliberations of the Economic and Social Council, in particular during its 2010 substantive session, including the Development Cooperation Forum and the annual ministerial review, could provide a valuable contribution to the preparations for the High-level Plenary Meeting;

11.   *Decides* that the six round-table sessions shall be organized in accordance with the modalities set forth in annex II to the present resolution;

12.   *Invites* the United Nations funds and programmes and the specialized agencies of the United Nations system, as well as the Bretton Woods institutions, the World Trade Organization, the regional development banks, the regional commissions of the United Nations, non-governmental organizations and civil society organizations and the private sector, to participate in the High-level Plenary Meeting, including in the round tables and in the preparatory process for the Meeting, according to the modalities specified in the annexes to the present resolution, and encourages them to consider initiatives in support of the preparatory process and the Meeting;

13.   *Invites* the regional commissions, with the support of the regional development banks and other relevant entities, to hold regional consultations, as appropriate, during the first half of 2010, which will serve to provide inputs to the preparations for the High-level Plenary Meeting as well as the Meeting itself;

14.   *Invites* the Inter-Parliamentary Union, as part of the preparatory process for the third World Conference of Speakers of Parliament, to develop and submit a contribution to the High-level Plenary Meeting;

15.   *Requests* the President of the General Assembly to organize, in consultation with representatives of non-governmental organizations in consultative status with the Economic and Social Council, civil society organizations and the private sector, two days of informal interactive hearings no later than June 2010 with non-governmental organizations, civil society organizations and the private sector to provide an input to the preparatory process for the High-level Plenary Meeting;

16.   *Decides* that the President of the General Assembly shall preside over the informal interactive hearings with representatives of non-governmental organizations, civil society organizations and the private sector, and that the hearings shall be organized in accordance with the modalities set forth in annex III to the present resolution, and requests the President of the Assembly to prepare a summary of the hearings, to be issued as an Assembly document prior to the High-level Plenary Meeting;

17.   *Encourages* Member States to actively participate in the hearings at the ambassadorial level to facilitate interaction between the Member States and the representatives of non-governmental organizations, civil society organizations and the private sector;

18.   *Requests* the Secretary-General to establish a trust fund to enhance the participation in the hearings of representatives of non-governmental organizations and civil society organizations from developing countries, and calls upon Member States and others to support the trust fund generously and speedily;

19.   *Requests* the President of the General Assembly to continue to hold open, inclusive, timely and transparent consultations with all Member States, with a view to reaching the broadest possible agreement on all major issues relating to the High-level Plenary Meeting, including the adoption of a concise and action-oriented outcome to be agreed by Member States;

20.   *Strongly urges* all Member States to actively engage in the process of formal and informal consultations leading to the High-level Plenary Meeting with a view to reaching a successful outcome of the Meeting.

ANNEX I

Organization of the plenary meetings and establishment of the list of speakers for the High-level Plenary Meeting of the General Assembly

1.   The High-level Plenary Meeting will consist of a total of six meetings, on the basis of two meetings a day, as follows:

> Monday, 20 September 2010, from 9 a.m. to 1 p.m. and from 3 p.m. to 9 p.m.
> Tuesday, 21 September 2010, from 9 a.m. to 1 p.m. and from 3 p.m. to 9 p.m.
> Wednesday, 22 September 2010, from 9 a.m. to 1 p.m. and from 3 p.m. to 6 p.m.

2.   The podium in the General Assembly Hall will have three seats to accommodate the two Co-Chairs and the Secretary-General.

3.   At the opening plenary meeting, on Monday morning, 20 September 2010, the initial speakers will be the two Co-Chairs, the Secretary-General, the head of the delegation of the host country of the Organization, the President of the Economic and Social Council, the President of the World Bank, the Managing Director of the International Monetary Fund, the Director-General of the World Trade Organization, the Secretary-General of the United Nations Conference on Trade and Development and the Administrator of the United Nations Development Programme, as the Chair of the United Nations Development Group.

4.   The list of speakers for the High-level Plenary Meeting will therefore be established on the basis of six meetings. The morning meeting on Monday, 20 September 2010, following the opening of the Meeting will have 20 speaking slots. The morning meetings on Tuesday, 21 September 2010, and Wednesday, 22 September 2010, will each have 30 speaking slots. The afternoon meetings on Monday, 20 September 2010, and Tuesday, 21 September 2010, will each have 50 speaking slots. The afternoon meeting on Wednesday, 22 September 2010, will have 20 speaking slots, since the last hour will be devoted to the closing of the High-level Plenary Meeting.

5.   The list of speakers for the High-level Plenary Meeting will be established initially as follows:

(a)   The representative of the Secretary-General will draw one name from a first box containing the names of all Member States that will be represented by Heads of State, Heads of Government, vice-presidents, crown princes/princesses, and of the Holy See, in its capacity as observer State, and Palestine, in its capacity as observer, should they be represented by their highest-ranking officials. This procedure will be repeated until all names have been drawn from the box, thus establishing the order in which participants will be invited to choose their meetings and select their speaking slots. The representative of the Secretary-General will then draw from a second box the names of those not contained in the first box in accordance with the same procedure;

(b)   Six boxes will be prepared, each one representing a meeting and each one containing numbers corresponding to speaking slots at that meeting;

(c) Once the name of a Member State, the Holy See, in its capacity as observer State, or Palestine, in its capacity as observer, has been drawn by the representative of the Secretary-General, that Member State, the Holy See, in its capacity as observer State, or Palestine, in its capacity as observer, will be invited first to choose a meeting and then to draw from the appropriate box the number indicating the speaking slot in the meeting.

6. The initial list of speakers for the High-level Plenary Meeting as outlined in paragraph 5 above will be established at a meeting to be scheduled in the month of May 2010.

7. Subsequently, when each category of speakers is organized following the order resulting from the selection process outlined in paragraph 5 above, the list of speakers for each meeting will be rearranged in accordance with the established practice of the General Assembly:

(a) Heads of State will thus be accorded first priority, followed by Heads of Government; vice-presidents, crown princes/princesses; the highest-ranking official of the Holy See, in its capacity as observer State, and of Palestine, in its capacity as observer; ministers; and permanent representatives;

(b) In the event that the level at which a statement is to be made is subsequently changed, the speaker will be moved to the next available speaking slot in the appropriate category at the same meeting;

(c) Participants may arrange to exchange their speaking slots in accordance with the established practice of the General Assembly;

(d) Speakers who are not present when their speaking turn comes will be automatically moved to the next available speaking slot within their category.

8. In order to accommodate all speakers at the High-level Plenary Meeting, statements will be limited to five minutes, on the understanding that this will not preclude the distribution of more extensive texts.

9. Without prejudice to other organizations which have observer status in the General Assembly, a representative of each of the following may also be included in the list of speakers for the plenary meetings of the High-level Plenary Meeting:

League of Arab States
African Union
European Union
Organization of the Islamic Conference
World Conference of Speakers of Parliament of the Inter-Parliamentary Union.

10. Other than for Member States, the list of speakers for the plenary meetings of the High-level Plenary Meeting will be closed on Monday, 2 August 2010.

11. The arrangements set out above shall in no way create a precedent.

Annex II

Organization of the interactive round-table sessions for the High-level Plenary Meeting of the General Assembly

1. The High-level Plenary Meeting will hold six interactive round-table sessions, as follows:

Monday, 20 September 2010, from 10 a.m. to 1 p.m. and from 3 p.m. to 6 p.m.

Tuesday, 21 September 2010, from 10 a.m. to 1 p.m. and from 3 p.m. to 6 p.m.

Wednesday, 22 September 2010, from 10 a.m. to 1 p.m. and from 2 p.m. to 5 p.m.

2. The six round-table sessions will have at least 50 seats each and will be co-chaired by two Heads of State or Government.

3. The Chairs of the six round-table sessions will be from the African States, the Asian States, the Eastern European States, the Latin American and Caribbean States and the Western European and Other States. Those 12 Chairs will be selected by their respective regional groups in consultation with the President of the General Assembly.

4. Following the selection of Chairs of the round-table sessions, the participation of the members of each group will be determined on a first-come, first-served basis, ensuring that equitable geographical distribution is maintained, allowing for some flexibility. Member States are encouraged to be represented at the round tables at the level of Head of State or Government.

5. The six round-table sessions will have the overarching objective of "Making it happen by 2015", and each one will focus on one theme, as follows:

Round table 1—Addressing the challenge of poverty, hunger and gender equality

Round table 2—Meeting the goals of health and education

Round table 3—Promoting sustainable development

Round table 4—Addressing emerging issues and evolving approaches

Round table 5—Addressing the special needs of the most vulnerable

Round table 6—Widening and strengthening partnerships

6. Each Head of State or Government or head of delegation attending the round-table sessions may be accompanied by one adviser.

7. The composition of the six round-table sessions will be subject to the principle of equitable geographical distribution. Thus, for each regional group, the distribution of its members for participation in each round-table session will be as follows:

(a) African States: ten Member States;

(b) Asian States: ten Member States;

(c) Eastern European States: five Member States;

(d) Latin American and Caribbean States: seven Member States;

(e) Western European and other States: six Member States;

(f) Other organizations with observer status in the General Assembly: two representatives, in addition to those mentioned in paragraph 9 of annex I to the present resolution;

(g) Entities of the United Nations system: four representatives;

(h) Civil society and non-governmental organizations: four representatives;

(i) Private sector: four representatives.

8. A Member State that is not a member of any of the regional groups may participate in a round-table session to be determined in consultation with the President of the

General Assembly. The Holy See, in its capacity as observer State, and Palestine, in its capacity as observer, as well as the organizations listed in paragraph 9 of annex I to the present resolution, may also participate in different round-table sessions to be determined also in consultation with the President of the Assembly.

9. The list of participants in each round-table session will be made available prior to the meeting.

10. The round-table sessions will be closed to the media and the general public. Accredited delegates and observers will be able to follow the proceedings of the round-table sessions via a closed-circuit television in the overflow room.

11. Summaries of the deliberations of the six round-table sessions will be presented orally by the Chairs of the round-table sessions or their representatives during the concluding plenary meeting of the High-level Plenary Meeting.

ANNEX III

Organization of the informal interactive hearings

1. The President of the General Assembly will preside over the informal interactive hearings to be held no later than June 2010. The hearings shall consist of a brief opening plenary meeting followed by four sequential sessions of the hearings on the basis of two sessions a day, from 10 a.m. to 1 p.m., and from 3 p.m. to 6 p.m. Each session will consist of presentations by invited participants from non-governmental organizations in consultative status with the Economic and Social Council, civil society organizations and the private sector and an exchange of views with Member States.

2. The hearings will be attended by representatives of non-governmental organizations in consultative status with the Economic and Social Council, civil society organizations, the private sector, Member States and observers.

3. The President of the General Assembly will determine the list of invited participants and the exact format and organization of the hearings, in consultation with Member States and representatives of non-governmental organizations in consultative status with the Economic and Social Council, civil society organizations and the private sector.

4. The themes for the hearings will be based on the comprehensive report of the Secretary-General.

5. The President of the General Assembly will consult with representatives of non-governmental organizations in consultative status with the Economic and Social Council, civil society organizations and the private sector, and with Member States, as appropriate, on the list of representatives of non-governmental organizations, civil society organizations and the private sector that may participate in the plenary meetings of the High-level Plenary Meeting of September 2010.

ANNEX IV

Other participants

1. On the understanding that the principle of precedence will be strictly applied, to allow participation at the level of Heads of State or Government, the Secretary-General, the head of the delegation of the host country of the Organization, the President of the Economic and Social Council, the President of the World Bank, the Managing Director of the International Monetary Fund, the Director-General of the World Trade Organization, the Secretary-

General of the United Nations Conference on Trade and Development and the Administrator of the United Nations Development Programme, as the Chair of the United Nations Development Group, will be invited to make a statement in the plenary meeting.

2. The President of the General Assembly will consult with representatives of non-governmental organizations in consultative status with the Economic and Social Council, civil society organizations and the private sector, and with Member States, as appropriate, on the list of representatives of non-governmental organizations, civil society organizations and the private sector that may participate in the plenary meetings and the round tables of the High-level Plenary Meeting of September 2010.

3. Representatives of non-governmental organizations in consultative status with the Economic and Social Council, civil society organizations and the private sector, one from each grouping, selected during the informal interactive hearings, may also be included in the list of speakers for the plenary meetings of the High-level Plenary Meeting, in consultation with the President of the General Assembly.

4. In addition, interested non-governmental organizations that are not in consultative status with the Economic and Social Council and private sector representatives may apply to the General Assembly for accreditation following the established accreditation procedure.

5. The arrangements set out above shall in no way create a precedent.

Credentials

The Credentials Committee, at its meeting of 8 and 11 December [A/64/571], had before it a memorandum by the Secretary-General, which indicated that 141 Member States had submitted the formal credentials of their representatives. Information concerning the representatives of 51 other Member States had also been communicated. The representative of Zambia expressed concern over the acceptance of the credentials of Guinea and Madagascar in the light of the situation in those countries. The Committee sought information from the Assistant Secretary-General for Legal Affairs on communications received from those two Member States. The Chairperson proposed that the Committee defer consideration of the credentials submitted by Guinea and Madagascar, and accept those of the remaining Member States. The Committee adopted the proposal on the understanding that the representatives of both Guinea and Madagascar would continue to have the right to participate provisionally in the sixty-fourth session with all rights and privileges until the Credentials Committee was able to review the matter and make a final recommendation to the General Assembly. Should there be a formal objection during the sixty-fourth session to the participation of either country, that objection could be referred to the Credentials Committee for consideration.

The Committee adopted a resolution accepting the credentials received, and recommended a draft resolution to the Assembly for adoption. On 16 December, the Assembly, by **resolution 64/126**, approved the Committee's report.

Agenda

During the resumed sixty-third (2009) session, the General Assembly, by **decision 63/503 B**, decided to include additional items on the agenda of the session and decided on those items to be considered directly in plenary and those on which consideration would be reopened. The Assembly, by decisions on 7 April (**decision 63/550 B**) and 30 June (**decision 63/550 C**) decided on those items to be deferred until the second part of its resumed sixty-third (2009) session, its sixty-fourth (2009) session and the first part of its resumed sixty-fourth (2010) session. On 9 September, the Assembly deferred until its sixty-fourth (2009) session consideration of the item on the question of the Comorian island of Mayotte (**decision 63/559**).

At its sixty-fourth session, the Assembly, by **decision 64/503** of 18 September, on the recommendation of the General Committee [A/64/250], adopted the agenda [A/64/251] and the allocation of agenda items [A/64/252] for its sixty-fourth session. The Assembly deferred consideration of, and included in the provisional agenda of its sixty-fifth (2010) session, the item "Question of the Malagasy islands of Glorieuses, Juan de Nova, Europa and Bassas da India". By the same decision, it included additional items in the agenda on observer status for the Parliamentary Assembly of the Mediterranean in the General Assembly; United Nations University; observer status in the General Assembly for the Council of Presidents of the General Assembly; and question of the Comorian island of Mayotte. The Assembly also decided to consider in plenary the agenda item "South-South cooperation for development". The Assembly on 24 December decided to retain 84 items for consideration during its resumed sixty-fourth (2010) session (**decision 64/549**).

By **decision 64/524** of 10 December, the Assembly deferred consideration of the agenda item "Implementation of the resolutions of the United Nations" and included it in the provisional agenda of its sixty-fifth (2010) session. By **decision 64/548 A** of 24 December, the Assembly deferred until its resumed sixty-fourth session (2010) consideration of the items on the review of the efficiency of the administrative and financial functioning of the United Nations; proposed programme budget for the biennium 2010–2011; and review of the implementation of General Assembly resolutions 48/218 B, 54/244 and 59/272. It deferred until its sixty-fifth (2010) session consideration of reports on the review of the efficiency of the administrative and financial functioning of the United Nations, and on human resources management.

First, Second, Third, Fourth and Sixth Committees

The General Assembly, on 2 December, approved the proposed programme of work and timetable of the First (Disarmament and International Security) Committee for the sixty-fifth (2010) session (**decision 64/517**), and on 10 December, the programme of work and timetable of the Fourth (Special Political and Decolonization) Committee (**decision 64/522**). The Assembly noted, on 16 December, that the Sixth (Legal) Committee had decided to adopt the provisional programme of work for the Assembly's sixty-fifth session (**decision 64/525**). On 18 and 21 December, respectively, it approved the programme of work for the Third (Social, Humanitarian and Cultural) Committee (**decision 64/538**), and the programme of work of the Second Committee (**decision 64/543**).

Security Council

The Security Council held 194 formal meetings in 2009, adopted 48 resolutions and issued 35 presidential statements. It considered 46 agenda items (see APPENDIX IV). The President made 35 statements to the press on behalf of Council members. Monthly assessments on the Council's work in 2009 were issued by the successive Council Presidents [S/2009/107, S/2009/138, S/2009/229, S/2009/353, S/2009/363, S/2009/412, S/2009/447, S/2009/557, S/2010/315, S/2009/625, S/2009/653, S/2010/387]. In a 3 September note [A/64/300], the Secretary-General, in accordance with Article 12, paragraph 2 of the UN Charter, and with the consent of the Council, notified the General Assembly of 81 matters relative to the maintenance of peace and security that were being dealt with by the Council since his previous annual notification [YUN 2008, p. 1525]. Items with which the Council had ceased to deal had been deleted and were recorded in document [S/2009/10/Add.9]. The Assembly took note of the Secretary-General's note on 12 November (**decision 64/509**).

On 13 November, the Assembly took note of the Council's report for the period of 1 August 2008 to 31 July 2009 [A/64/2] (**decision 64/510**). It decided, on 24 December, that the item on the Council's report would remain for consideration during its resumed sixty-fourth (2010) session (**decision 64/549**).

Membership

The General Assembly continued to examine the question of expanding the Council membership. It considered the report of the Open-ended Working Group on the Question of Equitable Representation on and Increase in the Membership of the Security Council and Other Matters related to the Security Council [A/63/47]. (For details and related Assembly decisions, see p. 1374.)

Economic and Social Council

The Economic and Social Council held its organizational session for 2009 on 15 January, 10 February, 26 March and 20 April; a resumed organizational session on 18 May; its special high-level meeting with the Bretton Woods institutions (the World Bank Group and the International Monetary Fund), the World Trade Organization (WTO) and the United Nations Conference on Trade and Development (UNCTAD) on 27 April; its substantive session in Geneva from 6 to 31 July; and its resumed substantive session on 8 October and 15 December in New York. The Council's work for 2009 was covered in its report to the General Assembly [A/64/3 & Add.1].

On 15 January, the Council elected its Bureau (a President and four Vice-Presidents) for 2009 (see APPENDIX III) and adopted the agenda of its organizational session [E/2009/2 & Corr.1; E/2009/2/Add.1 & Corr.1,2 & Add.2].

On 10 February, the Council approved the provisional agenda of its 2009 substantive session (**decision 2009/203**) and decided on the working arrangements for that session (**decision 2009/205**). On 6 July, it adopted the agenda [E/2009/100 & Corr.1], and approved the programme of work of that session [E/2009/L.8], and approved the requests for hearings from non-governmental organizations (NGOs) [E/2009/107] (**decision 2009/213**).

On 24 July, the Council approved the provisional calendar of conferences and meetings for 2010 and 2011 in the economic, social and related fields (**decision 2009/218**).

The General Assembly, by **decision 64/549** of 24 December, decided that the report of the Economic and Social Council would remain for consideration during its resumed sixty-fourth (2010) session.

Sessions and segments

During 2009, the Economic and Social Council adopted 35 resolutions and 69 decisions [E/2009/99]. By **decision 2009/205** of 10 February, the Council decided that the high-level segment would be held from 6 to 9 July; the dialogue with the Executive Secretaries of the regional commissions would be held on 10 July; the coordination segment from 10 to 14 July; the operational activities segment from 15 to 17 July; the humanitarian affairs segment from 20 to 22 July; and the general segment from 23 to 30 July. It also decided to conclude its work on 31 July. On the same date, the Council decided that the special high-level meeting with the Bretton Woods institutions, WTO and UNCTAD would be held in New York on 27 April (**decision 2009/202**).

2009 and 2010 sessions

On 10 February, the Council decided that the work of the operational activities segment of its 2009 substantive session should be devoted to the progress on and implementation of General Assembly resolution 62/208 [YUN 2007, p. 877] on the triennial comprehensive policy review of operational activities for development of the United Nations system; and Assembly resolution 63/232 [YUN 2008, p. 962] on the operational activities for development of the United Nations system (**decision 2009/206**).

On 26 March (**decision 2009/207**), the Council decided that the theme for the humanitarian affairs segment of its 2009 substantive session would be "Strengthening of the coordination of humanitarian assistance: present challenges and their impact on the future"; and that it would convene two panels on: respecting and implementing guiding principles of humanitarian assistance at the operational level: assisting the affected populations; and addressing the impact of current global challenges and trends on the effective delivery of humanitarian assistance. On the same date, it decided that the theme for the item on regional cooperation would be "Regional perspectives on the global economic and financial crisis, including the impact on global public health" (**decision 2009/208**).

On 20 April, the Council decided that the theme for its 2010 thematic discussion of the high-level segment would be "Current global and national trends and challenges and their impact on gender equality and empowerment of women" (**decision 2009/210**).

On 18 May, the Council included in the provisional agenda of its 2009 substantive session an item entitled "Economic and environmental questions: sustainable development", and a supplementary sub-item entitled "Rehabilitation of the marshes in the southern regions of Iraq" (**decision 2009/212**).

Work programme

On 10 February, the Economic and Social Council, having considered its proposed basic programme of work for 2009 and 2010 [E/2009/1], took note of the list of questions for inclusion in its programme of work for 2010 (**decision 2009/204**).

Coordination, monitoring and cooperation

Institutional mechanisms

CEB activities

According to its annual overview report for 2009–2010 [E/2010/69], the United Nations System Chief Executives Board for Coordination (CEB) continued to focus on the global financial and economic crisis. Together with the international community, CEB monitored the development of the crisis, its effect on society and its impact on the achievement of the Millennium Development Goals (MDGs) [YUN 2000, p. 51]. The Joint Crisis Initiatives, launched by CEB [YUN 2008, p. 1527] as an immediate response to the global crisis, enhanced the UN system's role in dealing with the crisis and its impact on development. CEB also intensified its efforts for a coordinated and effective UN system delivery on climate change, and led efforts to simplify and harmonize business practices. In addition, it took steps to improve the safety and security of UN staff members. A new package of United Nations Development Assistance Framework guidance was developed to offer UN country teams greater flexibility, allowing for closer alignment with national planning processes. Work continued to strengthen the resident coordinator system and implement the management and accountability system for the UN development and resident coordinator systems. CEB also addressed several other cross-cutting issues, including the UN system's contribution to the Economic and Social Council, system-wide coherence (see p. 1367), collaboration with the Joint Inspection Unit, the Second United Nations Decade for the Eradication of Poverty (2008–2017) (see p. 809), science and technology (see p. 813), and the International Public Sector Accounting Standards (see p. 1416).

CEB held two regular sessions in 2009: the first in Paris (4 April) [CEB/2009/1] and the second in New York (30 October) [CEB/2009/2]. Its principal subsidiary bodies met as follows: the High-level Committee on Management, seventeenth (Rome, Italy, 24–25 February) [CEB/2009/3], and eighteenth (New York, 29–30 September) [CEB/2009/6] sessions; and the High-level Committee on Programmes, seventeenth (Geneva, 26–27 February) [CEB/2009/4], and eighteenth (New York, 17–18 September) [CEB/2009/5] sessions.

CEB report

CPC consideration. The Committee for Programme and Coordination (CPC) [A/64/16] considered the CEB annual overview report for 2008/09 [YUN 2008, p. 1527]. CPC recommended that the General Assembly bring to the Secretary-General's attention the need to continue to enhance CEB's system-wide coordination activity. It requested CEB to: ensure that support for Africa and the New Partnership for Africa's Development (NEPAD) [YUN 2001, p. 899] remained a UN system priority; enhance the UN role in dealing with the world financial and economic crisis and its impact on development; and invite executive heads to closely monitor the development and social effects of the crisis and its impact on the achievement of the

MDGs and of progress in reducing poverty and hunger in developing countries. The Secretary-General should initiate a comprehensive evaluation of the management and accountability system of the UN development and resident coordinator systems, including the "functional firewall" for the resident coordinator system, and report on the results to the Economic and Social Council in 2012. He should also report to the Council on the results of the joint review by CEB and the Department of Economic and Social Affairs on options for enhancing the UN system's contribution to the Council's work. CPC encouraged CEB to use a balanced approach in setting UN system priorities in implementing the decisions of Member States, and encouraged more frequent and substantive dialogue between CEB and the Member States to enhance the Board's transparency and accountability. CPC reiterated its recommendations [YUN 2008, p. 1527] that any criteria and methodology for the comprehensive evaluation of the eight "Delivering as one" pilot projects (see p. 1367) should first be considered and approved by the General Assembly and that UN support to the projects should not prejudice the outcome of the intergovernmental deliberations on system-wide coherence by the Assembly.

On 24 July, the Economic and Social Council took note of the CEB annual overview report for 2008/09 (**decision 2009/217**).

Programme coordination

The Committee for Programme and Coordination held its organizational meeting (30 April) and its forty-ninth session (8 June–1 July) in New York [A/64/16].

CPC considered questions related to the 2008–2009 programme budget and the 2010–2011 proposed programme budget and strategic framework. It considered strengthening the role of evaluation and the application of evaluation findings on programme design, delivery and policy (see p. 1418); the evaluation of UN support for least developed countries, landlocked developing countries, small island developing States and Africa [ibid.]; the triennial review of the implementation of the Committee's recommendations made at its forty-sixth session on: the in-depth evaluation of political affairs [ibid.] and the thematic evaluation of knowledge management networks in the pursuit of the goals of the Millennium Declaration [ibid.]; and the thematic evaluations of lessons learned: protocols and practices [ibid.] and of UN coordinating bodies [ibid.]. In addition to its review of CEB's annual report for 2008/09 [ibid.], CPC considered the UN system support for NEPAD [ibid.], as well as the improvement of its working methods and procedures.

On 24 July, the Economic and Social Council took note of the CPC report on its forty-ninth session (**decision 2009/217**).

Other coordination matters

Follow-up to international conferences

In response to Economic and Social Council resolution 2008/29 [YUN 2008, p. 1528], the Secretary-General in June submitted a report [A/64/87-E/2009/89] on the Council's role in the integrated and coordinated implementation of the outcomes of and follow-up to major UN conferences and summits, which illustrated how the annual ministerial review had provided substantive coherence to the follow-up to conferences. The report also described how the Council's biennial Development Cooperation Forum [YUN 2008, p. 902] had helped to advance the implementation of internationally agreed development goals, and how the General Assembly's annual specific meeting on development provided similar substantive coherence for the Assembly's work and that of its relevant Committees. It therefore suggested that the integrated and coordinated follow-up could be enhanced by reorienting its focus away from process-related coordination to substantive coherence. To facilitate the reorientation of the integrated follow-up to conferences, it proposed that the Secretary-General prepare a quadrennial report, the first of which should be submitted to the Council and the Assembly in 2015. The report should assess progress in the integrated and coordinated implementation of the outcomes of major UN conferences and summits, enable the Assembly and the Council to determine areas in which additional oversight and guidance were needed, and assess how follow-up mechanisms had contributed to the follow-up, as well as the effectiveness of the UN system in providing policy advice in support of national policies.

The Economic and Social Council took note of the report on 31 July (**decision 2009/259**).

ECONOMIC AND SOCIAL COUNCIL ACTION

On 31 July [meeting 45], the Economic and Social Council adopted **resolution 2009/29** [draft: E/2009/L.32] without vote [agenda items 4, 6 & 8].

Role of the Economic and Social Council in the integrated and coordinated implementation of and follow-up to the outcomes of the major United Nations conferences and summits, in the light of relevant General Assembly resolutions, including resolution 61/16

The Economic and Social Council,

Recalling General Assembly resolutions 45/264 of 13 May 1991, 48/162 of 20 December 1993, 50/227 of 24 May 1996, 52/12 B of 19 December 1997, 57/270 B of 23 June 2003, 60/265 of 30 June 2006 and 61/16 of 20 November 2006,

Noting the current segment structure of its substantive session, and bearing in mind the role of the coordination segment, as outlined in relevant resolutions,

Recalling its agreed conclusions 1995/1 of 28 July 1995 and 2002/1 of 26 July 2002 and its relevant resolutions and decisions on the integrated and coordinated implementation of and follow-up to the outcomes of the major United Nations conferences and summits, in the light of relevant General Assembly resolutions, including resolution 61/16,

Recognizing the important role of the annual ministerial review and the Development Cooperation Forum in strengthening the Economic and Social Council and in promoting the integrated and coordinated implementation of and follow-up to the outcomes of major United Nations conferences and summits,

1.	*Takes note* of the report of the Secretary-General;

2.	*Underscores* the need to implement General Assembly resolution 57/270 B as well as subsequent resolutions relevant to the integrated and coordinated implementation of and follow-up to the outcomes of the major United Nations conferences and summits in the economic and social fields;

3.	*Reaffirms* its role as the central mechanism for system-wide coordination as well as its role in promoting the integrated and coordinated implementation of and follow-up to the outcomes of the major United Nations conferences in the economic, social and related fields, in accordance with the Charter of the United Nations and relevant General Assembly resolutions, in particular resolutions 50/227, 57/270 B and 61/16;

4.	*Stresses* the need for the United Nations system, including the United Nations funds and programmes and the specialized agencies, to support, in accordance with their respective mandates, the integrated and coordinated implementation of and follow-up to the outcomes of the major United Nations conferences and summits;

5.	*Recognizes* the strengthened cooperation between the Economic and Social Council and the Bretton Woods institutions, the World Trade Organization and the United Nations Conference on Trade and Development, and emphasizes that the interaction should be further improved;

6.	*Reiterates* the invitation extended to the organizations of the United Nations system, including the Bretton Woods institutions and the World Trade Organization, to contribute, within their respective mandates, to the work of the Economic and Social Council, as appropriate, including to the integrated and coordinated implementation of and follow-up to the outcomes of the major United Nations conferences and summits, in accordance with relevant General Assembly resolutions, including resolution 61/16;

7.	*Reaffirms* the important contribution of civil society to the implementation of conference outcomes, and emphasizes that the contribution of non-governmental organizations and the private sector to the work of the Economic and Social Council should be further encouraged and improved, in accordance with the rules and procedures of the Council;

8.	*Recognizes* the need for a more effective consideration of the issue of the integrated and coordinated implementation of and follow-up to the outcomes of the major United Nations conferences and summits, in the light of relevant General Assembly resolutions, including resolution 61/16, at the substantive session of the Economic and Social Council, and in this regard decides to review the programme of work for the substantive session of the Council so as to avoid duplication and overlap between the coordination and general segments;

9. *Decides* to further review the periodicity of the report of the Secretary-General on the role of the Economic and Social Council in the integrated and coordinated implementation of and follow-up to the outcomes of the major United Nations conferences and summits, in the light of relevant General Assembly resolutions, including resolution 61/16, for consideration and decision at the substantive session of 2010 of the Council;

10. *Requests* the Secretary-General to prepare, taking into account the views of Member States, a report on the role of the Economic and Social Council in the integrated and coordinated implementation of and follow-up to the outcomes of the major United Nations conferences and summits, in the light of relevant General Assembly resolutions, including resolution 61/16, which should also include recommendations on the periodicity of future reports, and to submit the report for consideration by the Economic and Social Council at its substantive session of 2010.

On 24 December, the Assembly decided that the agenda item on the integrated and coordinated implementation of and follow-up to the outcomes of the major UN conferences and summits in the economic, social and related fields would remain for consideration during its resumed sixty-fourth (2010) session (**decision 64/549**).

UN and other organizations

Cooperation with organizations

African Union

In 2009, the African Union continued its cooperation with the United Nations. The General Assembly, in **resolution 63/310** of 14 September (see p. 106), invited the Secretary-General to request all relevant UN agencies, funds and programmes to intensify their efforts to support cooperation with the African Union.

Cooperation between the United Nations and the International Organization for Migration

On 5 November [A/64/233], Azerbaijan, Benin, Colombia, Costa Rica, Haiti, Kyrgyzstan, Mexico, the Philippines, Portugal, Slovenia, Timor-Leste and the United Republic of Tanzania requested the inclusion in the agenda of the General Assembly's sixty-fourth session of an item entitled "Cooperation between the United Nations and the International Organization for Migration (IOM)". Those Member States noted that the Assembly had granted IOM observer status in 1992 and that the United Nations and IOM had signed a cooperative agreement in 1996. While the Assembly in its resolution 51/148 [YUN 1996, p. 1354] had noted the conclusion of the agreement, it did not establish systematic and periodic reporting on IOM/UN cooperation. Those Member States were therefore requesting that the Secretary-General include reporting on

that cooperation in his biennial report on cooperation between the United Nations and other regional organizations.

Collective Security Treaty Organization

On 14 July [A/64/191], the Russian Federation, on behalf of Armenia, Belarus, Kazakhstan, Kyrgyzstan, Tajikistan and Uzbekistan, requested the inclusion in the agenda of the General Assembly's sixty-fourth session of a supplementary item on "Cooperation between the United Nations and the Collective Security Treaty Organization". The Organization, which had observer status with the Assembly since 2004, had established contacts with the Department of Political Affairs, the United Nations Office for Drugs and Crime and the Security Council Counter-Terrorism Committee. A resolution on cooperation between the two organizations would permit the strengthening of interaction between them, expand their mutual capabilities and promote the safeguarding of peace, security and cooperation at the regional and global levels.

On 24 December, by **decision 64/549**, the Assembly decided that the agenda item on cooperation between the United Nations and the Collective Security Treaty Organization would remain for consideration during its resumed sixty-fourth (2010) session.

Shanghai Cooperation Organization

On 20 November 2008 [A/64/141], China, Kazakhstan, Kyrgyzstan, the Russian Federation, Tajikistan and Uzbekistan requested the inclusion in the agenda of the General Assembly's sixty-fourth session of an item entitled "Cooperation between the United Nations and the Shanghai Cooperation Organization (SCO)". In an explanatory memorandum annexed to the request, the Members stated that SCO, established in 2001, had enjoyed observer status with the Assembly since 2004 and cooperated closely with the UN system on most of its major areas of activity. To enhance the practical component of that cooperation and ensure its synergy for addressing common tasks in the socio-economic field, it was necessary to make relations between SCO and the United Nations more systematic.

GENERAL ASSEMBLY ACTION

On 18 December [meeting 65], the General Assembly adopted **resolution 64/183** [draft: A/64/L.34 & Add.1] without vote [agenda item 124].

Cooperation between the United Nations and the Shanghai Cooperation Organization

The General Assembly,

Recalling that one of the objectives of the United Nations is to achieve cooperation in maintaining international peace and security and solving international problems of an economic, social, cultural or humanitarian character,

Recalling also the Articles of the Charter of the United Nations that encourage activities on the basis of regional cooperation to promote the goals and objectives of the United Nations,

Recalling further its resolution 59/48 of 2 December 2004, by which it granted observer status to the Shanghai Cooperation Organization,

Taking into consideration the fact that countries with economies in transition are among the members of the Shanghai Cooperation Organization, and in this regard recalling its resolution 61/210 of 20 December 2006, in which it proposed that the United Nations system enhance dialogue with regional and subregional cooperation organizations whose membership includes countries with economies in transition and increase support provided to them,

Noting with satisfaction that the declaration on the establishment of the Shanghai Cooperation Organization confirms the commitment of its member States to the principles of the Charter,

Noting that the Shanghai Cooperation Organization has become an essential forum for addressing security in the region in all its dimensions,

Convinced that strengthening cooperation between the United Nations and other organizations of the United Nations system and the Shanghai Cooperation Organization helps to promote the goals and objectives of the United Nations,

1. *Takes note* of the activities of the Shanghai Cooperation Organization aimed at strengthening peace, security and stability in the region, countering terrorism, separatism and extremism, drug trafficking and other types of criminal activity of a transnational character and promoting regional cooperation in various areas such as trade and economic development, energy, transportation, agriculture and agro-industry, the regulation of migration, banking and finances, information and telecommunications, science and new technology, customs, education, public health, environmental protection and reducing the danger of natural disasters, as well as in other related areas;

2. *Emphasizes* the importance of strengthening dialogue, cooperation and coordination between the United Nations system and the Shanghai Cooperation Organization, and proposes that the Secretary-General, for this purpose, hold regular consultations with the Secretary-General of the Shanghai Cooperation Organization through the existing inter-agency forums and formats, including the annual consultations between the Secretary-General of the United Nations and the heads of regional organizations;

3. *Proposes* that the specialized agencies, organizations, programmes and funds of the United Nations system cooperate with the Shanghai Cooperation Organization with a view to jointly implementing programmes to achieve their goals, and in this regard recommends that the heads of such entities commence consultations with the Secretary-General of the United Nations;

4. *Requests* the Secretary-General to submit to the General Assembly at its sixty-fifth session a report on the implementation of the present resolution;

5. *Decides* to include in the provisional agenda of its sixty-fifth session the sub-item entitled "Cooperation between the United Nations and the Shanghai Cooperation Organization".

Participation in UN work

Observer status

International Olympic Committee

On 14 July [A/64/145], Italy requested the inclusion in the agenda of the General Assembly's sixty-fourth session of an item on observer status for the International Olympic Committee (IOC) in the General Assembly. An explanatory memorandum recalled UN support, through Assembly resolutions since 1993, for IOC and the Olympic Movement and their contribution to the UN mission to promote mutual understanding, solidarity and peaceful dialogue among communities. IOC had worked with the United Nations, Governments and the international community in using sport to transform the lives of millions of people, especially young citizens across the globe, delivering education and services to the vulnerable, supporting environmental campaigns and providing a vehicle for the UN peacekeeping missions. The cornerstone of IOC social responsibility was to support the United Nations for the achievement of the MDGs [YUN 2000, p. 51]. As part of its reasons for seeking observer status, IOC identified six areas where sport could make an impact: eradicate extreme poverty; achieve universal primary education; promote gender equality and women's issues; combat HIV/AIDS, malaria and other diseases; ensure environmental sustainability; and develop a global partnership for development. IOC provided support through national programmes or through UN agencies in all those areas, and intended to maintain that momentum and support the United Nations in pursuing its mandate, as well as in intensifying its communication and collaborative action with the Organization.

GENERAL ASSEMBLY ACTION

On 19 October [meeting 21], the General Assembly, on the recommendation of the Sixth Committee [A/64/458 & Corr.1], adopted **resolution 64/3** without vote [agenda item 167].

Observer status for the International Olympic Committee in the General Assembly

The General Assembly,

Wishing to promote cooperation between the United Nations and the International Olympic Committee,

1. *Decides* to invite the International Olympic Committee to participate in the sessions and the work of the General Assembly in the capacity of observer;

2. *Requests* the Secretary-General to take the necessary action to implement the present resolution.

International Humanitarian Fact-Finding Commission

On 1 July [A/64/142], Switzerland requested the inclusion in the provisional agenda of the General Assembly's sixty-fourth session of an item on observer status for the International Humanitarian Fact-Finding Commission (IHFFC) in the General Assembly. An explanatory memorandum annexed to the request stated that IHFFC, established in 1991 under the Protocol additional to the 1949 Geneva Convention relating to the protection of victims of armed conflict, was a permanent international body, headquartered in Berne, Switzerland, whose main purpose was to investigate allegations of grave breaches and serious violations of international humanitarian law. Having observer status in the Assembly would enhance IHFFC presence in fora and bodies where the solutions to conflicts were discussed, and enable it to better perform the functions assigned to it by international humanitarian law.

GENERAL ASSEMBLY ACTION

On 16 December [meeting 64], the General Assembly, on the recommendation of the Sixth Committee [A/64/456], adopted **resolution 64/121** without vote [agenda item 165].

Observer status for the International Humanitarian Fact-Finding Commission in the General Assembly

The General Assembly,

Wishing to promote cooperation between the United Nations and the International Humanitarian Fact-Finding Commission,

1. *Decides* to invite the International Humanitarian Fact-Finding Commission to participate in the sessions and the work of the General Assembly in the capacity of observer;

2. *Requests* the Secretary-General to take the necessary action to implement the present resolution.

Global Fund to Fight AIDS, Tuberculosis and Malaria

On 14 July [A/64/144], the United Republic of Tanzania requested the inclusion in the provisional agenda of the General Assembly's sixty-fourth session of an item on observer status in the Assembly for the Global Fund to Fight AIDS, Tuberculosis and Malaria [YUN 2002, p. 1217]. An explanatory memorandum stated that the Fund was established in 2002 to finance a response to the epidemic. The Fund's participation as an observer in the Assembly's proceedings would strengthen cooperation between the United Nations and the Fund and facilitate the Fund's work in its mission to reduce the impact of HIV/AIDS, tuberculosis and malaria.

GENERAL ASSEMBLY ACTION

On 16 December [meeting 64], the General Assembly, on the recommendation of the Sixth Committee [A/64/457], adopted **resolution 64/122** without vote [agenda item 166].

Observer status for the Global Fund to Fight AIDS, Tuberculosis and Malaria in the General Assembly

The General Assembly,

Wishing to promote cooperation between the United Nations and the Global Fund to Fight AIDS, Tuberculosis and Malaria,

1. *Decides* to invite the Global Fund to Fight AIDS, Tuberculosis and Malaria to participate in the sessions and the work of the General Assembly in the capacity of observer;

2. *Requests* the Secretary-General to take the necessary action to implement the present resolution.

International Conference on the Great Lakes Region of Africa

On 6 August [A/64/193], Kenya, in its capacity as Chair of the International Conference on the Great Lakes Region of Africa, requested the inclusion in the agenda of the General Assembly's sixty-fourth session of an item on observer status in the Assembly for the International Conference on the Great Lakes Region of Africa. An explanatory memorandum stated that the intergovernmental organization's main objective was to provide a comprehensive framework for cooperation and collaboration to end violence and resolve intractable conflicts in the Great Lakes Region of Africa. It sought to collaborate with the United Nations and observer status would strengthen and enhance its scope of interactions.

GENERAL ASSEMBLY ACTION

On 16 December [meeting 64], the General Assembly, on the recommendation of the Sixth Committee [A/64/459], adopted **resolution 64/123** without vote [agenda item 168].

Observer status for the International Conference on the Great Lakes Region of Africa in the General Assembly

The General Assembly,

Wishing to promote cooperation between the United Nations and the International Conference on the Great Lakes Region of Africa,

1. *Decides* to invite the International Conference on the Great Lakes Region of Africa to participate in the sessions and the work of the General Assembly in the capacity of observer;

2. *Requests* the Secretary-General to take the necessary action to implement the present resolution.

Parliamentary Assembly of the Mediterranean

On 7 October [A/64/232], France and Malta requested the inclusion in the agenda of the General Assembly's sixty-fourth session of an item on observer status for the Parliamentary Assembly of the Mediterranean (PAM) in the Assembly. An explanatory memorandum stated that PAM, established in 2006, had as its main objective to bring together all 25 littoral States of the Mediterranean on an equal footing under a unique forum of their own. Since its inception, it had successfully cooperated with the United Nations. Strengthened cooperation between the United Nations and PAM could play a role in achieving desired results in the region. It proposed that the Assembly invite PAM to participate in its work and that of its subsidiary organs, as well as in international conferences convened under UN auspices.

GENERAL ASSEMBLY ACTION

On 16 December [meeting 64], the General Assembly, on the recommendation of the Sixth Committee [A/64/567], adopted **resolution 64/124** without vote [agenda item 169].

Observer status for the Parliamentary Assembly of the Mediterranean in the General Assembly

The General Assembly,

Wishing to promote cooperation between the United Nations and the Parliamentary Assembly of the Mediterranean,

1. *Decides* to invite the Parliamentary Assembly of the Mediterranean to participate in the sessions and the work of the General Assembly in the capacity of observer;

2. *Requests* the Secretary-General to take the necessary action to implement the present resolution.

Council of Presidents of the General Assembly

On 12 November [A/64/235], Saint Lucia, Saudi Arabia and Ukraine requested the inclusion in the agenda of the General Assembly's sixty-fourth session of an item on observer status in the Assembly for the Council of Presidents of the General Assembly. An explanatory memorandum stated that the Council of Presidents of the General Assembly, which consisted of former Assembly Presidents, was established in 1997 as a mechanism to coordinate their collective diplomatic and international experience, with the aim of supporting the work of the United Nations. Observer status would promote consultation and cooperation between the Council and the principal UN system organs and serve as a focal point for the continuing supportive involvement of the Council of Presidents in the work and objectives of the Assembly.

The Sixth Committee considered the item on 9 and 14 December [A/64/568]. At the latter meeting, Saudi Arabia, on behalf of the sponsoring countries, withdrew the draft resolution [A/C.6/64/L.20].

The Assembly took note of the report of the Sixth Committee [A/64/568] on 16 December (**decision 64/528**).

Intergovernmental Renewable Energy Organization

On 15 September [A/64/231], Honduras requested the inclusion in the agenda of General Assembly's sixty-fourth session of an item on observer status for the Intergovernmental Renewable Energy Organization (IREO). An explanatory memorandum stated that IREO was established to contribute to the achievement of the MDGs. Its work was directly related to those MDGs addressing issues of environmental sustainability and creating a global partnership.

Non-governmental organizations

Committee on NGOs

The Committee on Non-Governmental Organizations held its regular 2009 session (19–28 January and 2 February) [E/2009/32 (Part I) & Corr.1] and its resumed session (18–27 May) [E/2009/32 (Part II)] in New York. In January, the Committee considered 153 applications for consultative status with the Economic and Social Council, including applications deferred from its 1999–2008 sessions. It recommended 64 applications for consultative status, deferred consideration of 82, suspended consideration of one, took note of the withdrawal of two and closed consideration of four. It did not recommend one request deferred from previous sessions. The Committee also had before it four requests for reclassification of consultative status, of which it recommended three and deferred one. It took note of 95 quadrennial reports, deferred consideration of one and heard 14 NGO representatives. The Committee recommended four draft decisions for action by the Council.

The Committee also considered the strengthening of the NGO section of the Department of Economic and Social Affairs of the UN Secretariat; reviewed its working methods relating to the implementation of Council resolution 1996/31 [YUN 1996, p. 1360], including the process of accreditation of NGO representatives, and Council decision 1995/304 [YUN 1995, p. 1445]; and discussed the general voluntary trust fund in support of the United Nations Non-Governmental Organizations Informal Regional Network (UN-NGO-IRENE).

On 27 July, the Economic and Social Council granted consultative status to 64 organizations, reclassified three from the roster to special consultative status, noted that the Committee had taken note of

94 quadrennial reports, closed consideration of four requests for consultative status, and noted the withdrawal by two organizations of their applications for consultative status (**decision 2009/221**).

On the same day, the Council took note of the Committee's decision to submit, at its resumed session, a list of NGOs that had failed to submit their quadrennial reports for two or more consecutive periods, for suspension of their consultative status (**decision 2009/222**).

On 19 January, the Committee heard a complaint by Algeria concerning the Arab Commission for Human Rights, an organization with special consultative status with the Council. On 28 January, by a roll-call vote of 18 in favour, with one abstention, the Committee recommended suspension of the consultative status of that NGO for one year, and requested that it submit a list of its members and associates by 1 April 2010, prior to consideration of the reinstatement of its status. On 27 July, the Council endorsed the Committee's recommendation (**decision 2009/223**).

The Committee also decided not to grant consultative status to the NGO Associação Brasileira de Gays, Lésbicas e Transgêneros. However, on 27 July, the Council decided to grant special consultative status to that organization by a roll-call vote of 25 to 12, with 13 abstentions (**decision 2009/224**).

On the same date, the Council took note of the Committee's report on its 2009 regular session (**decision 2009/225**).

At its resumed session in May, the Committee considered 142 applications for consultative status with the Council, including 82 applications deferred from its 1999–2009 sessions. It recommended granting consultative status to 36 NGOs, not granting consultative status to one and reclassifying the status of one. It further recommended that consideration of four applications be closed, one suspended and 101 deferred, including 62 for which the receipt of responses to questions posed by the Committee was pending. The Committee reviewed 123 quadrennial reports, 14 of which had been deferred from previous sessions, and took note of 110. It recommended the suspension of consultative status of 94 organizations for one year, in accordance with Council resolution 2008/4 [YUN 2008, p. 1540]. The Committee interacted with representatives of 19 NGOs and recommended five draft decisions for action by the Council.

The Committee also considered the strengthening of the NGO Branch of the Department of Economic and Social Affairs and reviewed its working methods relating to the implementation of Council resolution 1996/31, including the process of accreditation of NGO representatives, and Council decision 1995/304; and considered the implementation of resolution 2006/46 [YUN 2006, p. 1001] and decision 2008/217 [YUN 2008, p. 927].

On 27 July, the Council granted consultative status to 36 organizations, reclassified one from special to general consultative status, and noted that the Committee had taken note of 110 quadrennial reports and that it had decided to suspend its consideration of the application submitted by the Ethiopian Human Rights Council. It further decided to close consideration of four requests for consultative status, which included the rejection of proposed amendments to the draft decision [E/2009/L.29] related to the Dynamic Christian World Mission Foundation by a roll-call vote of 23 to 22, with 3 abstentions (**decision 2009/226**).

On the application of the NGO Democracy Coalition Project, the Committee had recommended that the Council not to grant consultative status to that NGO. However, on 27 July, the Council decided to grant special consultative status to that organization by a roll-call vote of 30 to 9, with 8 abstentions (**decision 2009/227**).

On the same day, on the recommendation of the Committee, the Council decided, in accordance with its resolution 2008/4, to suspend immediately, for one year, the consultative status of 94 organizations with outstanding quadrennial reports, and requested the Secretary-General to advise them accordingly (**decision 2009/228**).

The Council took note of the Committee's report on its resumed 2009 session (**decision 2009/230**); decided that the Committee's 2010 regular session would be held from 25 January to 3 February and the resumed session from 26 May to 4 June 2010; and approved the provisional agenda for that session (**decision 2009/229**).

Chapter II

United Nations financing and programming

During 2009, the financial situation of the United Nations was generally mixed, showing some improvement in the last quarter. By year's end, aggregate assessments had decreased to $9 billion, compared with $10.1 billion in 2008. Total unpaid assessments were lower, with $335 million for the regular budget and $1.9 billion for peacekeeping operations, down from $417 million and $2.9 billion in 2008. Cash balances were higher for all categories, except peacekeeping, with $520 million available for the regular budget, while debt owed to Member States was $775 million. The number of Member States paying their regular budget assessments in full dropped to 136.

In December, the General Assembly adopted final budget appropriations for the 2008–2009 biennium, decreasing the amount of $4,885,155,400 approved in 2008 and in April and June 2009 to $4,799,914,500 and decreasing income estimates by $7,478,600, to $550,377,100. It also adopted revised budget appropriations for the 2010–2011 biennium totalling $5,156,029,100.

The Committee on Contributions continued to review the methodology for preparing the scale of assessments of Member States' contributions to the UN budget and to encourage the payment of arrears through the multi-year payment process. Also in December, the Assembly adopted the scale of assessments for 2010–2012.

Financial situation

The overall UN financial situation in 2009 was mixed. In October [A/64/497], the Secretary-General reported that unpaid assessed contributions were concentrated among a few Member States and that cash balances at the end of the year were projected to be higher than at the end of 2008 for all categories except peacekeeping. The final outcome for 2009 would depend on payments made by those States in the last months of the year. As at 13 October, aggregate assessments stood at $8.7 billion (compared with $9.1 billion in 2008). That amount included assessments for the regular budget ($2.5 billion), the two international tribunals ($348 million), peacekeeping ($5.5 billion) and a fixed amount for the capital master plan (CMP) ($341 million). Meanwhile, reimbursements had fallen behind the normal quarterly

reimbursement process for seven missions. Debt to Member States providing troops and equipment to peacekeeping operations at the end of 2009 was expected to be some $944 million.

As at 13 October, unpaid assessments for the regular budget, peacekeeping and the tribunals totalled $3 billion, which included $2.1 billion for peacekeeping (compared to $2.9 billion at 24 October 2008); $830 million for the regular budget ($74 million more than in 2008); and $63 million for the tribunals ($10 million more than in 2008). Member States that had paid their regular budget assessments in full as at 13 October 2009 numbered 120, which was 13 fewer than at 24 October 2008.

In his end-of-year review of the financial situation [A/64/497/Add.1], the Secretary-General noted that the performance of the four main indicators of the Organization's financial health reflected improvement compared to 31 December 2008: aggregate assessments were lower at $9 billion (compared with $10.1 billion in 2008), mainly due to a $1.8 billion decrease for peacekeeping operations (from $7.6 billion to $5.8 billion), while unpaid assessments were lower for all categories except the international tribunals, with $335 million for the regular budget, down from $417 million in 2008, and $1.9 billion for peacekeeping operations, down from $2.9 billion in 2008. Outstanding assessments for the two tribunals rose from $26 million to $37 million. Cash balances were higher for all categories except peacekeeping, with $520 million available for the regular budget; and the debt owed to Member States was $775 million. The number of Member States paying their regular budget assessments in full was 136, ten less than in 2008.

On 24 December, the General Assembly decided that the agenda item on improving the financial situation of the United Nations would remain for consideration at its resumed sixty-fourth (2010) session (**decision 64/549**).

UN budget

Budget for 2008–2009
Final appropriations

In 2009, the General Assembly adopted final budget appropriations for the 2008–2009 biennium, decreasing the amount of $4,885,155,400 approved in resolutions 63/264 A [YUN 2008, p. 1543], 63/268 (see p. 1391) and 63/283 (see p. 1393) by $85,240,900 to $4,799,914,500, and decreasing income estimates by $7,478,600 to $550,377,100.

Report of Secretary-General. In his second performance report on the 2008–2009 programme budget [A/64/545], the Secretary-General provided estimates of the anticipated final expenditures and income for the biennium, based on actual expenditures for the first 21 months, projections for the last three months, changes in inflation and exchange rates, and cost-of-living adjustments.

The anticipated final level of expenditures and income represented a net decrease of $85.4 million, reflecting projected additional requirements of $36.9 million due to changes in exchange rates ($22.9 million), commitments ($6.6 million) entered into under the provisions of Assembly resolution 60/249 [YUN 2005, p. 1498] and a decrease in income ($7.4 million); and reduced requirements of $122.3 million due to changes in inflation ($27.9 million) and variations in post costs and adjustments to other objects of expenditure ($94.4 million).

The projected expenditure for the biennium was estimated at $4,792.4 million gross—a decrease of $92.8 million compared with the revised appropriation of $4,885.2 million approved in 2008 and in April and June 2009. The projected income was estimated at $550.5 million—a decrease of $7.4 million compared with the revised income estimate of $557.9 million.

The Advisory Committee on Administrative and Budgetary Questions (ACABQ), in December [A/64/574], commended the Secretary-General for submitting the report earlier than in the past to ensure its availability to Member States in time for their consideration of the 2010–2011 proposed programme budget. It also indicated that the report would have been a more useful accountability and monitoring tool if it had contained a greater degree of analysis of data and subsequent trends over past bienniums.

GENERAL ASSEMBLY ACTION

On 24 December [meeting 68], the General Assembly, on the recommendation of the Fifth (Administrative and Budgetary) Committee [A/64/594], adopted **resolution 64/242 A** and **B** without vote [agenda item 131].

Programme budget for the biennium 2008–2009

A

FINAL BUDGET APPROPRIATIONS FOR THE BIENNIUM 2008–2009

The General Assembly

1. *Takes note* of the second performance report of the Secretary-General on the programme budget for the biennium 2008–2009, and endorses the observations and recommendations contained in the related report of the Advisory Committee on Administrative and Budgetary Questions;

2. *Resolves* that, for the biennium 2008–2009:

(a) The amount of 4,885,155,400 United States dollars appropriated by it in its resolutions 63/264 A of 24 December 2008, 63/268 of 7 April 2009 and 63/283 of 30 June 2009 shall be decreased by 85,240,900 dollars, as follows:

Section	Amount approved in resolutions 63/264 A, 63/268 and 63/283	Increase/ (decrease)	Final appropriation
	(United States dollars)		
Part I. Overall policymaking, direction and coordination			
1. Overall policymaking, direction and coordination	94,562,100	(2,588,700)	91,973,400
2. General Assembly and Economic and Social Council affairs and conference management	662,261,100	3,252,500	665,513,600
Subtotal	756,823,200	663,800	757,487,000
Part II. Political affairs			
3. Political affairs	980,078,600	(4,059,100)	976,019,500
4. Disarmament	22,459,700	(191,900)	22,267,800
5. Peacekeeping operations	105,788,500	(4,855,900)	100,932,600
6. Peaceful uses of outer space	7,642,300	354,400	7,996,700
Subtotal	1,115,969,100	(8,752,500)	1,107,216,600
Part III. International justice and law			
7. International Court of Justice	45,127,700	822,600	45,950,300
8. Legal affairs	47,708,200	(312,500)	47,395,700
Subtotal	92,835,900	510,100	93,346,000
Part IV. International cooperation for development			
9. Economic and social affairs	165,534,400	(6,362,100)	159,172,300
10. Least developed countries, landlocked developing countries and small island developing States	5,862,900	(749,500)	5,113,400
11. United Nations support for the New Partnership for Africa's Development	12,208,100	(3,445,200)	8,762,900
12. Trade and development	133,094,600	(4,661,800)	128,432,800
13. International Trade Centre UNCTAD/WTO	30,873,700	(60,600)	30,813,100
14. Environment	14,059,800	(161,800)	13,898,000
15. Human settlements	20,801,600	323,700	21,125,300
16. International drug control, crime and terrorism prevention and criminal justice	37,575,900	1,876,400	39,452,300
Subtotal	420,011,000	(13,240,900)	406,770,100

Section		Amount approved in resolutions 63/264 A, 63/268 and 63/283	Increase/ (decrease)	Final appropriation
		(United States dollars)		
Part V. Regional cooperation for development				
17. Economic and social development in Africa		128,642,100	(16,390,500)	112,251,600
18. Economic and social development in Asia and the Pacific		92,415,800	(1,679,500)	90,736,300
19. Economic development in Europe		64,726,300	(1,836,300)	62,890,000
20. Economic and social development in Latin America and the Caribbean		103,159,300	842,300	104,001,600
21. Economic and social development in Western Asia		64,718,700	(4,712,500)	60,006,200
22. Regular programme of technical cooperation		54,832,500	(3,298,000)	51,534,500
	Subtotal	**508,494,700**	**(27,074,500)**	**481,420,200**
Part VI. Human rights and humanitarian affairs				
23. Human rights		127,353,200	(8,965,900)	118,387,300
24. International protection, durable solutions and assistance to refugees		80,005,500	—	80,005,500
25. Palestine refugees		45,070,100	(5,076,700)	39,993,400
26. Humanitarian assistance		29,861,800	(522,500)	29,339,300
	Subtotal	**282,290,600**	**(14,565,100)**	**267,725,500**
Part VII. Public information				
27. Public information		189,374,600	(843,400)	188,531,200
	Subtotal	**189,374,600**	**(843,400)**	**188,531,200**
Part VIII. Common support services				
28A. Office of the Under-Secretary-General for Management		15,593,900	2,139,100	17,733,000
28B. Office of Programme Planning, Budget and Accounts		40,645,700	(6,382,600)	34,263,100
28C. Office of Human Resources Management		73,048,700	484,100	73,532,800
28D. Office of Central Support Services		211,088,400	(562,300)	210,526,100
28E. Administration, Geneva		122,047,100	2,138,700	124,185,800
28F. Administration, Vienna		39,652,400	706,800	40,359,200
28G. Administration, Nairobi		27,642,200	1,015,500	28,657,700
36. Office of Information and Communications Technology		37,031,600	5,618,200	42,649,800
	Subtotal	**566,750,000**	**5,157,500**	**571,907,500**
Part IX. Internal oversight				
29. Internal oversight		37,482,700	(1,715,800)	35,766,900
	Subtotal	**37,482,700**	**(1,715,800)**	**35,766,900**
Part X. Jointly financed administrative activities and special expenses				
30. Jointly financed administrative activities		12,455,400	(916,800)	11,538,600
31. Special expenses		100,372,700	2,565,300	102,938,000
	Subtotal	**112,828,100**	**1,648,500**	**114,476,600**
Part XI. Capital expenditures				
32. Construction, alteration, improvement and major maintenance		62,199,400	(510,400)	61,689,000
	Subtotal	**62,199,400**	**(510,400)**	**61,689,000**
Part XII. Safety and security				
33. Safety and security		207,925,900	(7,349,400)	200,576,500
	Subtotal	**207,925,900**	**(7,349,400)**	**200,576,500**
Part XIII. Development Account				
34. Development Account		18,651,300	7,500,000	26,151,300
	Subtotal	**18,651,300**	**7,500,000**	**26,151,300**
Part XIV. Staff assessment				
35. Staff assessment		513,518,900	(26,668,800)	486,850,100
	Subtotal	**513,518,900**	**(26,668,800)**	**486,850,100**
	Total	**4,885,155,400**	**(85,240,900)**	**4,799,914,500**

(b) The Secretary-General shall be authorized to transfer credits between sections of the budget, with the concurrence of the Advisory Committee on Administrative and Budgetary Questions;

(c) In addition to the appropriations approved under subparagraph *(a)* above, an amount of 75,000 dollars shall be appropriated for each year of the biennium 2008–2009 from the accumulated income of the Library Endowment Fund for the purchase of books, periodicals, maps and library equipment and for such other expenses of the Library at the Palais des Nations in Geneva as are in accordance with the objects and provisions of the endowment;

(d) To increase the provision under section 34 (Development Account) by the amount of 7.5 million dollars.

B

**FINAL INCOME ESTIMATES
FOR THE BIENNIUM 2008–2009**

The General Assembly

Resolves that, for the biennium 2008–2009:

(a) The estimates of income of 557,855,700 United States dollars approved by it in its resolutions 63/264 B of 24 December 2008, 63/268 of 7 April 2009 and 63/283 of 30 June 2009 shall be decreased by 7,478,600 dollars, as follows:

	Amount approved in resolutions 63/264 B, 63/268 and 63/283	Increase/ (decrease)	Final estimate
	(United States dollars)		
Income section			
1. Income from staff assessment	518,124,800	(27,165,000)	490,959,800
Subtotal	518,124,800	(27,165,000)	490,959,800
2. General income	37,751,000	15,427,300	53,178,300
3. Services to the public	1,979,900	4,259,100	6,239,000
Subtotal	39,730,900	19,686,400	59,417,300
TOTAL	557,855,700	(7,478,600)	550,377,100

(b) The income from staff assessment shall be credited to the Tax Equalization Fund in accordance with the provisions of General Assembly resolution 973(X) of 15 December 1955;

(c) Direct expenses of the United Nations Postal Administration, services to visitors, catering and related services, garage operations, television services and the sale of publications not provided for under the budget appropriations shall be charged against the income derived from those activities.

Also on 24 December, the Assembly, by **decision 64/549**, decided that the agenda item on the programme budget for the 2008–2009 biennium would remain for consideration during its resumed sixty-fourth (2010) session.

Questions relating to the 2008–2009 programme budget

The Fifth Committee considered special subjects related to the 2008–2009 programme budget concerning estimates in respect of special political missions, good offices and other political initiatives authorized by the General Assembly and/or the Security Council (see below). Other subjects considered included the United Nations Postal Administration (UNPA) (see p. 1393), standards of accommodation for air travel (see p. 1472) and business continuity management (see p. 1437). In addition, on 20 April the Secretary-General submitted a consolidated report on the changes to the biennial programme plan as reflected in the proposed 2008–2009 programme budget [A/64/73 & Corr.1].

Revised estimates in respect of matters of which the Security Council was seized

In March [A/63/346/Add.6], the Secretary-General submitted additional resource requirements for the period 1 January to 31 December 2009 for four special political missions: the United Nations Representative on the International Advisory and Monitoring Board (IAMB) of the Development Fund for Iraq, the United Nations International Independent Investigation Commission (UNIIIC), the United Nations Political Office for Somalia (UNPOS), and the United Nations Mission in Nepal (UNMIN), totalling $15,051,600.

ACABQ, in March [A/63/779], recommended that the General Assembly approve the resources requested for the United Nations IAMB Representative, UNIIIC and UNMIN, subject to the Committee's observations and recommendations; and defer action on the UNPOS proposed budget, with the exception of the establishment of four additional temporary security staff posts, pending submission by the Secretary-General of an updated proposal.

In May [A/63/346/Add.7], the Secretary-General submitted a proposed revised UNPOS budget in the amount of $16,004,100, which ACABQ, in a June report [A/63/868], recommended that the Assembly approve, subject to its recommendations.

On 7 April [meeting 79], the General Assembly, on the recommendation of the Fifth Committee [A/63/648/Add.5], adopted **resolution 63/268** without vote [agenda item 118].

Special subjects relating to the programme budget for the biennium 2008–2009

The General Assembly,

I

United Nations Postal Administration

Recalling section XIV of its resolution 62/238 of 22 December 2007,

Having considered the report of the Secretary-General on the contingent liability reserve for the United Nations Postal Administration and the related report of the Advisory Committee on Administrative and Budgetary Questions,

1. *Takes note* of the report of the Secretary-General on the contingent liability reserve for the United Nations Postal Administration;

2. *Endorses* the conclusions and recommendations contained in the related report of the Advisory Committee on Administrative and Budgetary Questions subject to the provisions of the present resolution;

3. *Takes note* of paragraph 8 of the report of the Advisory Committee;

4. *Decides* not to create a reserve for contingent liabilities for postal services;

II

Standards of accommodation for air travel

Recalling its resolution 42/214 of 21 December 1987, section IV, paragraph 14, of its resolution 53/214 of 18 December 1998, section IV of its resolution 60/255 of 8 May 2006 and section XV of its resolution 62/238 of 22 December 2007, and its decision 57/589 of 18 June 2003,

Having considered the report of the Secretary-General on standards of accommodation for air travel and the related report of the Advisory Committee on Administrative and Budgetary Questions,

1.   *Takes note* of the report of the Secretary-General on standards of accommodation for air travel;

2.   *Endorses* the conclusions and recommendations contained in the related report of the Advisory Committee on Administrative and Budgetary Questions;

3.   *Requests* the Secretary-General to explore all possible options, including the use of mileage points accumulated from official travel, for reducing the cost of air travel, and to present his conclusions thereon in the context of the comprehensive report referred to in paragraph 7 of the report of the Advisory Committee;

III

Business continuity management

Recalling section VII of its resolution 62/238,

Recalling also its resolution 63/262 of 24 December 2008,

Having considered the report of the Secretary-General on the revised estimates under sections 3, 17, 18, 20, 21, 27, 28C to G, 33 and 35 of the programme budget for the biennium 2008–2009 related to business continuity management and the related report of the Advisory Committee on Administrative and Budgetary Questions,

Recognizing the multiplicity of risks currently facing the United Nations and its increasing dependency on information and communications technology systems,

Noting the complementarities and the close linkages between disaster recovery for information and communications technology and business continuity management,

Emphasizing the importance of close coordination of business continuity management policies among all United Nations entities, and of systematically sharing and exploiting lessons learned and best practices on a system-wide basis,

1.   *Takes note* of the report of the Secretary-General;

2.   *Also takes note* of the work undertaken and progress achieved so far by the Secretary-General on business continuity management in response to the business risks faced by the United Nations;

3.   *Further takes note* of the establishment by the Secretary-General of the Senior Emergency Policy Team and the Crisis Operations Group;

4.   *Endorses* the conclusions and recommendations contained in the report of the Advisory Committee on Administrative and Budgetary Questions, subject to the provisions of the present resolution;

5.   *Reaffirms* paragraphs 6 and 12 of section IV of its resolution 63/262, and stresses the need for a comprehensive, unified and multi-hazard approach to business continuity;

6.   *Notes* that the proposals of the Secretary-General on business continuity overlap and duplicate proposals contained in other reports, in particular on information and communications technology;

7.   *Requests* the Secretary-General to further develop and justify the approach as set out in his report, including by clarifying the relationship with other initiatives, in particular on information and communications technology, and the roles of the various actors in the process, with a view to avoiding a piecemeal approach to business continuity;

8.   *Also requests* the Secretary-General to ensure that all departments and offices of the United Nations Secretariat, offices away from Headquarters and the regional commissions have business continuity plans in place and that the respective heads of departments and offices of the United Nations Secretariat and of the offices away from Headquarters and regional commissions are held accountable for their implementation;

9.   *Further requests* the Secretary-General to ensure that lessons learned within the Secretariat for human influenza pandemic preparedness are taken into account as the work on business continuity management is implemented;

10.   *Requests* the Secretary-General to ensure a coordinated approach to business continuity management between the United Nations Secretariat, offices away from Headquarters and the regional commissions, including systematic support, appropriate coordination structures and regular consultations between the business continuity management focal points in New York and in other duty stations;

11.   *Stresses* the need to draw upon the experiences of other United Nations entities in formulating the business continuity strategy;

12.   *Also stresses* the importance of cooperation with host country authorities both at Headquarters and at all other duty stations;

13.   *Requests* the Secretary-General to strive for economies of scale through coordination among organizations within the United Nations system on relevant issues, including the use of backup centres for information and communications technology, the use of consultants, the procurement of specialized equipment and medical supplies and training;

14.   *Also requests* the Secretary-General to take all steps necessary to ensure that medical supplies and materials, including vaccines and antibiotics, are procured in compliance with the relevant provisions of General Assembly resolution 62/269 of 20 June 2008, in particular, among others, paragraph 20 thereof;

15.   *Takes note* of paragraphs 14 to 16 and 19 to 21 of the report of the Advisory Committee on Administrative and Budgetary Questions;

16.   *Requests* the Secretary-General to submit a fully justified proposal for post and non-post resources in relation to the work currently under way on business continuity management in the context of the proposed programme budget for the biennium 2010–2011;

17.   *Also requests* the Secretary-General to report in the context of the proposed programme budget for the biennium 2012–2013 on progress made;

IV

Estimates in respect of special political missions, good offices and other political initiatives authorized by the General Assembly and/or the Security Council

Recalling its resolution 62/237 A of 22 December 2007, section V of its resolution 62/238 of 22 December 2007, section III of its resolution 62/245 of 3 April 2008 and section XI of its resolution 63/263 of 24 December 2008,

Having considered the report of the Secretary-General on the estimates in respect of special political missions, good offices and other political initiatives authorized by the General Assembly and/or the Security Council and the related report of the Advisory Committee on Administrative and Budgetary Questions,

1. *Takes note* of the report of the Secretary-General;

2. *Endorses* the conclusions and recommendations contained in the report of the Advisory Committee on Administrative and Budgetary Questions, subject to the provisions of the present resolution;

3. *Takes note* of the revised narrative and logical framework for the budget of the Special Envoy of the Secretary-General for the implementation of Security Council resolution 1559(2004) for the period 1 January to 31 December 2009, and of paragraphs 28 and 29 *(e)* of the related report of the Advisory Committee;

4. *Approves* the revised budgets totalling 26,848,900 United States dollars for the United Nations Representative on the International Advisory and Monitoring Board of the Development Fund for Iraq, the United Nations International Independent Investigation Commission and the United Nations Mission in Nepal presented in the report of the Secretary-General;

5. *Takes note* of the balance of 17,973,900 dollars of the appropriations for these missions for the biennium 2008–2009 based on actual expenditures incurred in 2008;

6. *Decides* to appropriate, after taking into account the unencumbered balance of 17,973,900 dollars for the three missions mentioned in paragraph 4 above, under the procedure provided for in paragraph 11 of annex I to resolution 41/213 of 19 December 1986, an amount of 8,875,000 dollars under section 3, Political affairs, of the programme budget for the biennium 2008–2009;

7. *Also decides* to appropriate an amount of 1,663,100 dollars under section 35, Staff assessment, to be offset by a corresponding amount under income section 1, Income from staff assessment, of the programme budget for the biennium 2008–2009;

8. *Requests* the Secretary-General to submit a revised budget proposal for the United Nations Political Office for Somalia for 2009 for consideration by the General Assembly during the second part of its resumed sixty-third session.

On 30 June [meeting 93], the General Assembly, on the recommendation of the Fifth Committee [A/63/648/Add.6], adopted **resolution 63/283** without vote [agenda item 118].

Estimates in respect of special political missions, good offices and other political initiatives authorized by the General Assembly and/or the Security Council

The General Assembly,

Recalling its resolution 62/237 A of 22 December 2007, section V of its resolution 62/238 of 22 December 2007, section III of its resolution 62/245 of 3 April 2008, section XI of its resolution 63/263 of 24 December 2008 and section IV of its resolution 63/268 of 7 April 2009,

Having considered the report of the Secretary-General on the estimates in respect of special political missions, good offices and other political initiatives authorized by the General Assembly and/or the Security Council and the related report of the Advisory Committee on Administrative and Budgetary Questions,

1. *Takes note* of the report of the Secretary-General;

2. *Endorses* the conclusions and recommendations of the Advisory Committee on Administrative and Budgetary Questions, subject to the provisions of the present resolution;

3. *Decides* to establish one Legal Affairs Officer position (P-4), one Senior Security Sector Reform Officer position (P-5) and one Human Rights Officer position (P-4);

4. *Approves* the revised budget for the United Nations Political Office for Somalia for 2009 in the amount of 16,178,500 United States dollars gross (15,262,300 dollars net);

5. *Takes note* of the balance of 6,641,400 dollars under the appropriation for the biennium 2008–2009 based on actual expenditures incurred in 2008;

6. *Decides* to appropriate, after taking into account the unencumbered balance of 6,641,400 dollars, under the procedure provided for in paragraph 11 of annex I to General Assembly resolution 41/213 of 19 December 1986, an amount of 8,620,900 dollars under section 3, Political affairs, of the programme budget for the biennium 2008–2009;

7. *Also decides* to appropriate an amount of 916,200 dollars under section 35, Staff assessment, to be offset by a corresponding amount under income section 1, Income from staff assessment, of the programme budget for the biennium 2008–2009.

Revised estimates resulting from Human Rights Council action

In May [A/63/853], the Secretary-General submitted revised estimated requirements relating to the 2008–2009 programme budget, totalling $1,821,500, arising from resolution S-9/1 adopted by the Human Rights Council at its ninth special session held in 2009 (see p. 780). Of that amount, $650,600 would be met from extrabudgetary resources, while $266,900 would be met from resources already appropriated under the programme budget. For the remaining balance, the General Assembly was requested to authorize the Secretary-General to enter into commitments totalling $904,000 under the programme budget for the 2008–2009 biennium. In October, ACABQ recommended approval of the additional requirements [A/64/7/Add.3].

The Assembly, in resolution 64/245 of 24 December (section V) (see p. 1407), endorsed the conclusions and recommendations in the ACABQ report.

Reserve for United Nations Postal Administration

In 2009, the General Assembly considered the Secretary-General's 2008 report [YUN 2008, p. 1552] on the contingent liability reserve for UNPA, as well as the related ACABQ report [ibid.], wherein the Committee had noted the Secretary-General's recommendation against the establishment of a reserve.

On 7 April, by resolution 63/268 (see p. 1391), the Assembly endorsed the conclusions and recommendations of ACABQ and decided not to create a reserve for contingent liabilities for postal services.

Budget for 2010–2011

Introducing the proposed programme budget for the 2010–2011 biennium [A/64/6 & Corr.1] before the Fifth Committee on 29 October, the Secretary-General said that the proposed budget, which amounted to approximately $4.9 billion before recosting, represented a 0.5 per cent increase ($22.4 million) over the 2008–2009 programme budget, and was in accordance with the figure endorsed by the General Assembly in resolution 63/266 [YUN 2008, p. 1555]. Adjustment to the staffing table would result in a net decrease of 24 posts. Priorities for the 2010–2011 biennium included: promotion of sustained economic growth and sustainable development; maintenance of international peace and security; development of Africa; promotion of human rights; coordination of humanitarian assistance; promotion of justice and international law; disarmament; and drug control, crime prevention and combating international terrorism. In conjunction with the reallocation of resources and the implementation of efficiency measures, the programme budget also reflected continued focus on the implementation of the Regulations and Rules Governing Programme Planning [ST/SGB/2000/8] and on the issues of categorization and quantification of outputs. Based on a review of outputs delivered in 2008–2009, some 4,541 would be discontinued in 2010–2011. Other areas to be addressed included administrative and financial arrangements at the United Nations Office at Nairobi; the provision of training with a view to strengthening the Organization's human resources capacity, developing mechanisms to encourage and support mobility and expand staff training and leadership development; activities related to monitoring and evaluation; and information technology.

The Secretary-General expressed his commitment to management reform and greater transparency, accountability and efficiency. On budget flexibility and the Assembly's authorization of limited discretion, on an experimental basis, for the previous two bienniums, he intended to propose the continuation of that arrangement, in view of its successful implementation and the lessons drawn from it. In addition, consultations between the Secretariat and some Member States had led to general agreement that the existing process no longer met the Organization's needs and

that the matter should be addressed. His three top priorities included ending real or perceived micromanagement and creating an environment of trust; consolidating the number of budget fascicles, which exceeded 40, even though 20 would suffice; and establishing an alternative funding arrangement for special political missions. Another matter to be addressed was the systemic underinvestment in information and communications technology (ICT) projects, which had resulted in the Secretariat falling far behind other organizations in overall effectiveness and efficiency.

The Committee for Programme and Coordination (CPC) considered the proposed programme budget at its 2009 session (8 June–2 July) [A/64/16], including the strategic framework for the 2010–2011 period [A/63/6/Rev.1] and the Secretary-General's consolidated report on the changes to the biennial programme plan as reflected in the proposed 2010–2011 programme budget [A/64/74]. CPC recommended that the Assembly: approve the changes to the biennial programme, subject to certain modifications; further review the logical framework for the ICT Office to more accurately reflect the terms of Assembly resolution 63/262 [YUN 2008, p. 1592]; and consider the logical framework for the enterprise resource planning system.

Limited budgetary discretion

In response to General Assembly resolution 60/283 [YUN 2006, p. 1580], the Secretary-General submitted a December report [A/64/562] on limited budgetary discretion, which described its application, on an experimental basis, during the 2006–2007 and 2008–2009 bienniums. That discretion authorized the Secretary-General to enter into commitments up to $20 million in each biennium to meet the evolving needs of the Organization. The Secretary-General reported that use of the limited budgetary discretion had centred on organizational management requirements such as influenza pandemic preparedness, fire code compliance and the start-up of the enterprise resource planning system, and that those activities had a positive impact on all sections of the budget. He recommended that the Assembly continue the limited discretionary provision as an established procedure, with some modifications.

In December [A/64/7/Add.18], ACABQ stated that the Secretary-General's report lacked sufficient justification and/or explanation to support his request and indicated that of the four criteria requested by the Assembly: utilization of the experiment to date; implications for the human resources management policies and UN rules and regulations; impact on programme delivery and organizational priorities; and criteria used to define the Organization's evolving needs, only one—utilization of the discretionary provision—had been fully addressed. Nonetheless, the Committee did not object to the continuation of the limited discretionary provision for the 2010–2011 biennium. It recommended that the Secretary-General submit a report to the Assembly at its sixty-sixth (2012) session that fully addressed all the requests in resolution 60/283.

On 24 December, the Assembly deferred consideration of the reports of the Secretary-General and ACABQ on limited budgetary discretion until its resumed sixty-fourth (2010) session (**decision 64/548 A**).

GENERAL ASSEMBLY ACTION

On 24 December [meeting 68], the General Assembly, on the recommendation of the Fifth Committee [A/64/548/Add.1], adopted **resolution 64/243** without vote [agenda item 132].

Questions relating to the proposed programme budget for the biennium 2010–2011

The General Assembly,

Recalling its resolutions 58/270 of 23 December 2003, 60/246 of 23 December 2005, 61/263 of 4 April 2007, 62/236 of 22 December 2007 and 63/262 of 24 December 2008,

Reaffirming its resolutions 41/213 of 19 December 1986, 42/211 of 21 December 1987, 45/248 B, section VI, of 21 December 1990, 55/231 of 23 December 2000, 56/253 of 24 December 2001, 58/269 and 58/270 of 23 December 2003, 59/276, section XI, of 23 December 2004, 60/247 A to C of 23 December 2005, 60/283 of 7 July 2006, 62/237 A to C of 22 December 2007 and 63/266 of 24 December 2008,

Reaffirming also the respective mandates of the Advisory Committee on Administrative and Budgetary Questions and the Committee for Programme and Coordination in the consideration of the proposed programme budget,

Reaffirming further the role of the General Assembly, through the Fifth Committee, in carrying out a thorough analysis and approval of posts and financial resources, as well as of human resources policies,

Having considered the proposed programme budget for the biennium 2010–2011, the report of the Secretary-General on the enterprise content management and customer relationship management systems and proposal for a unified disaster recovery and business continuity plan, the first progress report of the Secretary-General on the enterprise resource planning project, the second progress report of the Secretary-General on the adoption of International Public Sector Accounting Standards by the United Nations, the report of the Secretary-General on revised estimates relating to business continuity management, the sixth progress report of the Secretary-General on the implementation of projects financed from the Development Account, the report of the Secretary-General entitled "Conditions of service and compensation for officials, other than Secretariat officials, serving the General Assembly: full-time members of the International Civil Service Commission and the Chairman of the Advisory Committee on

Administrative and Budgetary Questions", the reports of the Secretary-General on safety and security issues, the letter dated 10 December 2009 from the President of the General Assembly addressed to the Chairman of the Fifth Committee, the report of the Secretary-General on limited budgetary discretion and the related reports of the Advisory Committee on Administrative and Budgetary Questions,

Having also considered chapter II, section A, of the report of the Committee for Programme and Coordination on its forty-ninth session, the consolidated report of the Secretary-General on the changes to the biennial programme plan as reflected in the programme budget for 2008–2009 and the consolidated report of the Secretary-General on the changes to the biennial programme plan as reflected in the proposed programme budget for the biennium 2010–2011,

Having further considered the report of the Independent Audit Advisory Committee on the proposed programme budget for internal oversight for the biennium 2010–2011, the report of the Office of Internal Oversight Services on the audit of human resources management at the Office of the United Nations High Commissioner for Human Rights, the report of the Office of Internal Oversight Services on the efficiency of the implementation of the mandate of the Office of the United Nations High Commissioner for Human Rights and the related note by the Secretary-General, the report of the Office of Internal Oversight Services on the audit of conference services put at the disposal of the Human Rights Council in 2009 and the report of the Office of Internal Oversight Services on the comprehensive management audit of the Department of Safety and Security,

Having considered the reports of the Joint Inspection Unit on the review of management of Internet websites in the United Nations system organizations, the review of information and communication technology hosting services in the United Nations system organizations, liaison offices in the United Nations system and a common payroll for United Nations system organizations, as well as the notes by the Secretary-General transmitting his comments and those of the United Nations System Chief Executives Board for Coordination thereon,

Recognizing the detrimental effect of the withholding of assessed contributions on the administrative and financial functioning of the United Nations and its ability to implement mandates and programmes,

1. *Stresses* that all Member States should fulfil their financial obligations as set out in the Charter of the United Nations on time, in full and without conditions;

2. *Reaffirms* that the Fifth Committee is the appropriate Main Committee of the General Assembly entrusted with responsibilities for administrative and budgetary matters, and reaffirms the role of the Fifth Committee in carrying out a thorough analysis and approving human and financial resources and policies, with a view to ensuring full, effective and efficient implementation of all mandated programmes and activities and the implementation of policies in this regard;

3. *Also reaffirms* rule 153 of its rules of procedure;

4. *Further reaffirms* the Regulations and Rules Governing Programme Planning, the Programme Aspects of the Budget, the Monitoring of Implementation and the Methods of Evaluation;

5. *Reaffirms* the Financial Regulations and Rules of the United Nations;

6. *Endorses* the conclusions and recommendations of the Committee for Programme and Coordination as contained in chapter II, section A, of its report;

7. *Also endorses* the conclusions and recommendations contained in the first report of the Advisory Committee on Administrative and Budgetary Questions on the proposed programme budget for the biennium 2010–2011, subject to the provisions of the present resolution;

Policy/cross-cutting issues

8. *Reaffirms* the established budgetary procedures and methodologies, based on its resolutions 41/213 and 42/211;

9. *Also reaffirms* paragraph 21 of its resolution 51/221 B of 18 December 1996, in which it decided that no changes to the budget methodology, to established budgetary procedures and practices or to the financial regulations could be implemented without prior review and approval by the General Assembly, through the Advisory Committee on Administrative and Budgetary Questions, in accordance with agreed budgetary procedures;

10. *Stresses* the need for Member States to participate fully in the budget preparation process, from its early stages and throughout the process;

11. *Emphasizes* the importance of providing the consistent and timely information necessary to enable Member States to make well-informed decisions;

12. *Reiterates* the priorities of the Organization for the biennium 2010–2011 as outlined in General Assembly resolution 63/266;

13. *Also reiterates* that the allocation of resources should reflect fully the priorities established in the biennial programme plan;

14. *Notes with concern* that the allocation of resources in the proposed programme budget does not track precisely the priorities of the Organization, as adopted in resolution 63/266, and stresses the need to correct imbalances in the allocation of resources among the three pillars of the Organization;

15. *Recalls* paragraph 10 of the report of the Advisory Committee on Administrative and Budgetary Questions, stresses the need to present the budget in a comprehensive and holistic manner, and requests the Secretary-General, for all future proposed programme budgets, to take the steps necessary to ensure the fullest possible picture of the requirements of the Organization for the full biennium;

16. *Urges* the Secretary-General to ensure that a complete and timely budget is presented to Member States in the future;

17. *Notes* the practice of incremental budgeting where only new requirements are justified, and requests the Secretary-General to ensure that whenever new proposals lead to requests for additional resources, sufficient efforts are made to meet the new requirements using existing resources;

18. *Also notes* the efforts of the Secretary-General to meet the emerging needs of the Organization by redeploying existing posts and non-post resources, in accordance with the established rules and procedures and relevant resolutions of the General Assembly;

19. *Reaffirms its request* to the Secretary-General, in future budget submissions, to propose measures to offset budget increases, wherever possible, without undermining the implementation of mandated programmes and activities;

20. *Requests* the Secretary-General to intensify efforts to ensure that direct and quantifiable objectives, expected accomplishments and indicators of achievement are included in future proposed programme budgets that are directly and clearly linked to the objectives of the programme and to report thereon to the General Assembly at its sixty-fifth session through the Committee for Programme and Coordination;

21. *Recalls* paragraph 29 of the report of the Advisory Committee on Administrative and Budgetary Questions, and stresses that the proposed programme budget for the biennium 2012–2013 should provide a clear picture of the reform measures that have been taken, their budgetary implications and the efficiency gains derived from their implementation as well as an assessment of progress in accomplishing the objectives;

22. *Also recalls* paragraph 21 of the report of the Advisory Committee on Administrative and Budgetary Questions, notes that cost accounting is more suitably applied to the support services of the Organization and may not be suitable for use in its substantive work, and requests the Secretary-General to develop an effective methodology for measuring and conducting comparisons over time of the costs of support services in the budget and to report thereon to the General Assembly at its sixty-fifth session;

23. *Reaffirms* the role of the Committee for Programme and Coordination as the main subsidiary organ of the General Assembly and the Economic and Social Council for planning, programming and coordination;

24. *Notes* chapter I, section A, of the report of the Advisory Committee on Administrative and Budgetary Questions, and in this context reiterates that the Committee for Programme and Coordination is the sole subsidiary organ of the General Assembly for planning, programming and coordination;

25. *Emphasizes* the importance of continuous efforts to reduce administrative costs as a proportion of the regular budget with a view to maximizing the resources available for programmatic purposes;

26. *Recalls* paragraph 14 of the report of the Advisory Committee on Administrative and Budgetary Questions, stresses that results-based budgeting and results-based management are mutually supportive management tools and that improved implementation of results-based budgeting enhances both management and accountability in the Secretariat, and encourages the Secretary-General to continue his efforts in this regard;

27. *Also recalls* paragraph 1 of its resolution 63/247 of 24 December 2008, in which it approved the recommendations of the Committee for Programme and Coordination, and requests the Secretary-General to further improve the results-based budgeting framework and the qualitative aspects of indicators of achievement, as recommended by the Committee for Programme and Coordination;

28. *Reaffirms* paragraph 28 of resolution 55/231, and stresses the importance of adequate training to ensure the full implementation of results-based budgeting;

29. *Requests* the Secretary-General to ensure that, in presenting the programme budget, expected accomplishments and, where possible, indicators of achievement are included to measure achievements in the implementation of the programmes of the Organization and not those of individual Member States;

Human resources, vacancy rates and staffing

30. *Takes note* of paragraph 44 of the report of the Advisory Committee on Administrative and Budgetary Questions, stresses that, for budgetary purposes, a post is defined as vacant only if no person is charged against the post, and notes that the enterprise resource planning system should assist in providing comprehensive information on vacancies;

31. *Stresses* the importance of having a comprehensive succession plan for the Organization, including, inter alia, for the language services, and in this regard requests the Secretary-General to formulate a strategy on succession planning for all departments of the Secretariat and to report thereon to the General Assembly at its sixty-fifth session;

32. *Requests* the Secretary-General to examine the continuing need for posts that fall vacant owing to retirements in the biennium 2010–2011 and to report thereon in the context of the second performance report on the programme budget for the biennium;

33. *Reaffirms* the role of the General Assembly with regard to the structure of the Secretariat, including the creation, conversion, suppression and redeployment of posts, and requests the Secretary-General to continue to provide the Assembly with comprehensive information on all decisions involving established and temporary high-level posts, including equivalent positions financed from the regular budget and from extrabudgetary resources;

34. *Also reaffirms* Article 101, paragraph 3, of the Charter, further reaffirms sections IX and X of its resolution 63/250 of 24 December 2008, and requests the Secretary-General to recruit staff to fill the posts approved in the budget for the biennium 2010–2011 with a view to improving geographical representation and gender balance in the Secretariat, with due regard to the principle of equitable geographical distribution;

35. *Regrets* the slow pace of recruitment in the Organization, and requests the Secretary-General to fill vacancies expeditiously, in accordance with relevant resolutions of the General Assembly and existing provisions governing recruitment in the United Nations;

36. *Reaffirms* that the vacancy rate is a tool for budgetary calculations and should not be used to achieve budgetary savings;

37. *Decides* that a vacancy rate of 9.6 per cent for Professional staff, 4 per cent for General Service staff, 14.0 per cent for Professional field security staff and 14.7 per cent for General Service field security staff, respectively, shall be used as a basis for the calculation of the budget for the biennium 2010–2011;

Extrabudgetary resources

38. *Welcomes* the efforts by donors to continue to support priorities approved by the General Assembly;

39. *Stresses* that all extrabudgetary posts must be administered and managed with the same rigour as regular budget posts;

40. *Also stresses* that extrabudgetary resources shall be used in consistency with the policies, aims and activities of the Organization, and requests the Secretary-General to provide information on the financial and human resource implications of the use of extrabudgetary resources in the Organization in his next proposed programme budget;

41. *Requests* the Secretary-General to include, in future budget submissions, clear and specific information on extrabudgetary resources, in order to make a distinction between voluntary and assessed contributions, and programme support costs;

Consultants

42. *Recalls* paragraphs IV.8 and IV.41 of the report of the Advisory Committee on Administrative and Budgetary Questions, and requests the Secretary-General to select consultants and experts, as well as staff charged against general temporary assistance, on as wide a geographical basis as possible, in accordance with Article 101, paragraph 3, of the Charter and the provisions of General Assembly resolution 53/221 of 7 April 1999;

43. *Requests* the Secretary-General to ensure that, in future programme budget proposals, requests for consultants and experts are clearly and separately identified in the programme narratives;

Training

44. *Reiterates its request* to the Secretary-General to allocate the approved resources for training on the basis of need and in an equitable manner, throughout the Secretariat, including for duty stations and regional commissions, and in this context stresses that equal training opportunities should be available for all staff, in accordance with their functions and categories;

45. *Stresses* that workshops, seminars and training courses should take advantage of the diverse sources of training opportunities available throughout the regions of the world;

Conference services and publications

46. *Emphasizes* the importance of ensuring that there is no discriminatory treatment among the principal organs of the United Nations and the Main Committees and subsidiary bodies, and that they are provided with adequate and quality conference services and support;

Non-post resources

47. *Decides* to reduce non-post resources by 2 per cent, other than under sections 35 (Development Account) and 28D (Office of Central Support Services) of the proposed programme budget;

48. *Also decides* to reduce by 7 per cent the overall requirements for consultants and experts in the biennium 2010–2011;

49. *Further decides* to reduce the overall requirements for external printing by one million United States dollars;

Recosting

50. *Acknowledges* the current challenges caused by the global financial crisis;

51. *Decides* not to assess in 2010 half of the amount for recosting pending review of the issue in the context of the first performance report on the programme budget for the biennium 2010–2011;

52. *Requests* the Secretary-General, in the context of the first performance report, to report on options for protecting the United Nations against fluctuations in exchange rates and inflation, drawing on the experience of other organizations of the United Nations system, as set out in section V of the second performance report of the Secretary-General on the programme budget for the biennium 2008–2009;

PART I

Overall policymaking, direction and coordination

Section 1

Overall policymaking, direction and coordination

53. *Decides* to establish a dedicated post of Director-General of the United Nations Office at Nairobi at the level of Under-Secretary-General;

54. *Recalls* paragraph I.18 of the report of the Advisory Committee on Administrative and Budgetary Questions, and decides to authorize the Advisory Committee to meet for an additional four weeks per biennium for a total of seventy-eight weeks, on an experimental basis;

55. *Notes* the ongoing management review of the secretariat of the Advisory Committee on Administrative and Budgetary Questions;

56. *Encourages* the Advisory Committee on Administrative and Budgetary Questions, within its own mandate, to review its working methods and to inform the General Assembly of the results of the review;

57. *Recalls* paragraph 46 of its resolution 62/228 of 22 December 2007, and decides to establish a post of Legal Research Officer at the P-4 level for the Registry of the United Nations Dispute Tribunal in New York;

Section 2

General Assembly and Economic and Social Council affairs and conference management

58. *Recalls* that all documents should be translated in conformity with relevant resolutions of the General Assembly;

59. *Requests* the Secretary-General to ensure that all duty stations are given equal treatment in respect of the application of modern technologies;

60. *Emphasizes* the paramount importance of the equality of the six official languages of the United Nations;

61. *Requests* the Secretary-General to continue his efforts to ensure the highest quality of interpretation and translation services in all official languages;

62. *Also requests* the Secretary-General to improve the on-time submission of documents and to institute measures for the accountability of the author departments for the late submission of documents;

63. *Takes note* of the report of the Office of Internal Oversight Services on the audit of conference services put at the disposal of the Human Rights Council in 2009;

64. *Notes with concern* the circumstances that led to insufficient conference services for the Human Rights Council in 2009, and requests the Secretary-General to ensure that the Council, as well as other entities served by the Conference Services Division at the United Nations Office at Geneva, are provided with all conference services necessary to support their activities;

65. *Requests* the Secretary-General to report on ways to better address the needs of the Organization through enhancing the efficiency of services provided by the Department for General Assembly and Conference Management of the Secretariat;

66. *Notes* that the Working Group on the Universal Periodic Review of the Human Rights Council should endeavour to apply in its reports the word limits established in the annex to the Human Rights Council President's statement 9/295, and requests the Secretary-General to report on any additional requirements in the context of the second performance report on the programme budget for the biennium 2010–2011;

67. *Stresses* the need for programme managers, and duty stations resourced through section 2 of the programme budget, to be cost-effective and efficient in the use of services from the Department for General Assembly and Conference Management, particularly with respect to the effective functioning of the global management of conference services, and requests the Secretary-General to develop mechanisms that would enhance accountability in this regard;

68. *Requests* the Secretary-General to undertake a comprehensive review of printing and publishing and translation services, including, inter alia, full costing of in- and out-of-house printing, publishing and translation and an analysis of the Department for General Assembly and Conference Management costing methodologies, with due consideration to quality and confidentiality, and without prejudice to the quality of all language services and with respect for the specificities of the six official languages, and to submit a report thereon to the General Assembly at its sixty-sixth session, to be considered in the context of the proposed programme budget for the biennium 2012–2013;

69. *Recalls* paragraph I.83 of the report of the Advisory Committee on Administrative and Budgetary Questions, and stresses that particular attention should be given to the provision of remote access to terminology and reference resources to all translators, editors and verbatim reporters working off site;

PART II

Political affairs

Section 4

Disarmament

70. *Requests* the Secretary-General to continue to provide the United Nations regional centres for peace and disarmament with the necessary resources to discharge their mandates;

Section 5

Peacekeeping operations

71. *Also requests* the Secretary-General to make further concrete efforts to ensure proper representation of troop-contributing countries in the Department of Peacekeeping Operations and the Department of Field Support of the Secretariat, taking into account their contribution to United Nations peacekeeping;

PART III

International justice and law

Section 7

International Court of Justice

72. *Takes note* of paragraph III.4 of the report of the Advisory Committee on Administrative and Budgetary Questions, and decides to increase the pool of Law Clerks by six P-2 posts;

Section 8

Legal affairs

73. *Decides* not to abolish the one General Service (Other level) post in the Division for Ocean Affairs and the Law of the Sea;

PART IV

International cooperation for development

74. *Requests* the Secretary-General to intensify his efforts to mobilize adequate resources from all sources to support the mandates related to sections 10 and 11 of the programme budget during the biennium 2010–2011;

75. *Reaffirms* its resolutions 57/7 of 4 November 2002 and 57/300 of 20 December 2002, by which it established the Office of the Special Adviser on Africa, and its resolution 56/227 of 24 December 2001, by which it established the Office of the High Representative for the Least Developed Countries, Landlocked Developing Countries and Small Island Developing States;

76. *Also reaffirms* the relevant provisions of its resolutions 62/236 of 22 December 2007 and 63/260 of 24 December 2008 and, in this regard, requests the Secretary-General to implement the provisions pertaining to the Office of the Special Adviser on Africa and the Office of the High Representative for the Least Developed Countries, Landlocked Developing Countries and Small Island Developing States in those resolutions accordingly, in full and without delay;

Section 9

Economic and social affairs

77. *Decides* to establish one P-5 post and one P-4 post to provide programme support to the Development Account;

Section 10

Least developed countries, landlocked developing countries and small island developing States

78. *Recalls* paragraph 75 of its resolution 62/236, and requests a detailed description of the new donor strategy of the Office of the High Representative for the Least Developed Countries, Landlocked Developing Countries and Small Island Developing States in the proposed programme budget for the biennium 2012–2013;

79. *Emphasizes* the crucial importance of the Office of the High Representative for the Least Developed Countries, Landlocked Developing Countries and Small Island Developing States, established as the follow-up mechanism to ensure the timely and effective implementation of the Programme of Action for the Least Developed Countries for the Decade 2001–2010, the Almaty Programme of Action: Addressing the Special Needs of Landlocked Developing Countries within a New Global Framework for Transit Transport Cooperation for Landlocked and Transit Developing Countries, and the Mauritius Strategy for the Further Implementation of the Programme of Action for the Sustainable Development of Small Island Developing States;

Section 11

United Nations support for the New Partnership for Africa's Development

80. *Recalls* that the development of Africa is an established priority of the United Nations, and reaffirms its commitment to address the special needs of Africa;

81. *Also recalls* General Assembly resolution 57/300 and other resolutions calling for the strengthening of mechanisms to support the New Partnership for Africa's Development;

Section 12

Trade and development

82. *Encourages* the Secretary-General to broaden the efforts of the United Nations Conference on Trade and Development in supporting the strengthening of regional economic integration in Africa by providing, within the allocation to the Conference, technical assistance and capacity-building in the areas of trade, customs and infrastructure, including the strengthening of statistical capacity;

Section 16

International drug control, crime and terrorism prevention and criminal justice

83. *Expresses its appreciation* to the United Nations Office on Drugs and Crime for having successfully drawn the attention of the international community to the security problem in West Africa related to illicit trafficking and transnational organized crime, requests the Secretary-General to provide an effective level of support to the joint United Nations Office on Drugs and Crime/Department of Peacekeeping Operations/Department of Political Affairs/United Nations Office for West Africa/International Criminal Police Organization programme concept known as the West Africa Coast Initiative, and recommends that a sufficient share of the regular budget continue to be allocated to the United Nations Office on Drugs and Crime to enable it to carry out its mandate in a consistent and stable manner;

84. *Welcomes* the initiative of the Secretary-General to open a programme office of the United Nations Office on Drugs and Crime in Barbados to collaborate with the Caribbean Community in such areas as corruption, drug

trafficking, international judicial cooperation and the promotion of firearms control, and looks forward to its establishment;

85. *Expresses concern* at the overall financial situation of the United Nations Office on Drugs and Crime, and requests the Secretary-General to submit proposals in his proposed programme budget for the biennium 2012–2013 to ensure that the Office has sufficient resources to carry out its mandate;

PART V

Regional cooperation for development

86. *Emphasizes* the important contribution that the regional commissions are making towards the implementation of the development agenda and other mandates given to them arising from the outcome of the Millennium Summit, the Conference on the World Financial and Economic Crisis and Its Impact on Development and other major United Nations conferences and summits in the economic, social and related fields;

87. *Requests* the Secretary-General to ensure that the resource requirements of the commissions are allocated in such a way as to enable them to fully implement their mandates and contribute to the implementation of the development priorities and mandates of the Organization;

Section 17

Economic and social development in Africa

88. *Recalls* paragraph V.28 of the report of the Advisory Committee on Administrative and Budgetary Questions, expresses concern at the negative impact of post reductions on programme implementation, and decides to review the staffing requirements of the Economic Commission for Africa from all sources of funding;

89. *Recognizes* that the repositioning of the Economic Commission for Africa is a crucial element of reform shaping the work of the Commission, and notes that the repositioning will enhance the role of the Commission in strengthening coordination and collaboration among United Nations agencies and other agencies;

PART VI

Human rights and humanitarian affairs

Section 23

Human rights

90. *Encourages* Member States participating in the Junior Professional Officer programme to increase sponsorship of Junior Professional Officers from developing countries;

91. *Requests* the Secretary-General, in proposing posts for the Office of the United Nations High Commissioner for Human Rights, to ensure that they conform to relevant legislative mandates, including those of the Human Rights Council;

92. *Also requests* the Secretary-General to assess the impact of the doubling of regular budgetary resources over the last two bienniums on all activities of the Office of the United Nations High Commissioner for Human Rights

and to report thereon to the General Assembly at its sixty-sixth session;

93. *Recalls* paragraph 100 of its resolution 62/236, in which it decided to use the revised estimates for the biennium 2004–2005 as the basis for the agreed doubling of resources of the Office of the United Nations High Commissioner for Human Rights;

94. *Takes note* of the report of the Office of Internal Oversight Services and the related note of the Secretary-General, and requests the Secretary-General to ensure the full implementation of the recommendations contained therein, including those concerning the activities of the Office of the United Nations High Commissioner for Human Rights in the field, and to report thereon to the General Assembly at its sixty-fifth session;

95. *Stresses* that the establishment of any future regional offices of the Office of the United Nations High Commissioner for Human Rights requires thorough consultations with all Member States concerned, in accordance with all relevant legislative mandates;

Section 25

Palestine refugees

96. *Reaffirms* its resolution 3331B(XXIX) of 17 December 1974, stating that expenses for salaries of international staff in the service of the United Nations Relief and Works Agency for Palestine Refugees in the Near East, which would otherwise be a charge on voluntary contributions, should be financed by the regular budget of the United Nations for the duration of the Agency's mandate;

97. *Notes with concern* the significant reduction in the total resources for the United Nations Relief and Works Agency for Palestine Refugees in the Near East over the past ten years while the overall workload and responsibilities of the Agency have continued to increase;

98. *Also notes with concern* the acute cash crisis of the United Nations Relief and Works Agency for Palestine Refugees in the Near East, and requests the Secretary-General to propose a possible funding mechanism to address this issue;

99. *Notes with appreciation* the valuable work done by the United Nations Relief and Works Agency for Palestine Refugees in the Near East, and decides to approve the establishment of the following posts for the Agency: one D-2 for Director of Human Resources; one D-1 for Spokesperson; one P-5 for Ombudsperson; one P-5 for the Deputy Director, Relief and Social Services and Senior Poverty Adviser; one P-5 Senior Investigator; one P-4 Health Policy Planning Officer; one P-4 Monitoring and Evaluation Officer; one P-4 Field Programme Support Officer (Lebanon); one P-4 for the Special Assistant to the Deputy Commissioner-General; one P-3 Human Resources Officer; and one P-3 Monitoring and Evaluation Officer;

PART VII

Public information

Section 27

Public information

100. *Notes with concern* that the review requested in paragraph 120 of its resolution 62/236 has not been carried

out, and requests the Secretary-General to undertake the requested review as a matter of priority and to include the results of the review in the first performance report on the programme budget for the biennium 2010–2011;

101. *Recalls* paragraph VII.19 of the report of the Advisory Committee on Administrative and Budgetary Questions, and encourages the Secretary-General to ensure intensive collaboration with the Department of Peacekeeping Operations and the Department of Field Support to promote a positive image of the peacekeeping activities of the Organization and to support the public information components of peacekeeping missions;

102. *Stresses* the importance of the Department of Public Information of the Secretariat addressing effectively and in a timely manner any allegations of misconduct against peacekeepers, as well as other allegations against the Secretariat;

103. *Decides* to reclassify one P-2 post (Chinese web writer) to the P-3 level and one P-2 post (Russian web writer) to the P-3 level, with a view to ensuring the same level of support in those languages as in the other four official languages;

104. *Stresses* the importance of publishing United Nations information materials and translating important documents into languages other than United Nations official languages, with a view to reaching the widest possible spectrum of audiences and extending the United Nations message to all the corners of the world in order to strengthen international support for the activities of the Organization;

105. *Requests* the Secretary-General to promote public awareness of and to mobilize support for the work of the United Nations at the local level through all possible means of communication, including publications, the broadcasting of news and the network of United Nations information centres, bearing in mind that information in local languages has the strongest impact on local populations;

106. *Recognizes* the vital role of the United Nations information centres in promoting awareness about the United Nations, and requests the Secretary-General to continue to make efforts to mobilize resources for the effective functioning of United Nations information centres in developing countries;

107. *Requests* the Secretary-General to establish a United Nations information centre in Luanda to address the special needs of Portuguese-speaking African countries, and, in this context, welcomes the offer made by the Government of Angola to provide rent-free premises;

108. *Also requests* the Secretary-General to continue to expand the scope of press releases in addition to the existing languages in order to widen the United Nations message, assuring their comprehensiveness and up-to-date nature and ensuring their accuracy;

PART VIII

Common support services

109. *Endorses* the conclusions and recommendations contained in the reports of the Advisory Committee on Administrative and Budgetary Questions, subject to the provisions of the present resolution;

110. *Reaffirms* the importance of including the participation of the most knowledgeable staff of the Organization

in the implementation of the enterprise resource planning, enterprise content management, customer relationship management and disaster recovery and business continuity programmes and of developing in-house expertise and knowledge in the implementation of these programmes in order to support the systems after deployment;

Section 28A

Office of the Under-Secretary-General for Management

Enterprise resource planning project

111. *Recognizes* the considerable operational and financial risks involved in the implementation of the enterprise resource planning system, and stresses the need for the Secretary-General to ensure full accountability and clear lines of responsibility for the project;

112. *Reaffirms* that the enterprise resource planning system will serve as the backbone for implementation by the United Nations of the International Public Sector Accounting Standards;

113. *Endorses* the proposal of the Secretary-General to deploy the enterprise resource planning project through the "pilot first" option, and, in this context, requests the Secretary-General to present options for lowering the cost of the project;

114. *Approves* 24,192,200 dollars for the enterprise resource planning system, to be funded from the regular budget for the biennium 2010–2011, including 11,775,900 dollars under section 28A, and authorizes the Secretary-General to enter into commitments in the amount of 12,416,300 dollars, taking due consideration of the lower-cost options referred to in paragraph 113 above;

115. *Authorizes* the Secretary-General to enter into commitments in a total amount not to exceed 28,516,500 dollars under the support account for peacekeeping operations for the period from 1 July 2009 to 30 June 2010 in respect of the support account share of the enterprise resource planning system and to report on the expenditures incurred, with justifications for the utilization of resources, in the context of the performance report on the support account for the period from 1 July 2009 to 30 June 2010;

116. *Notes* that future remaining requirements for the enterprise resource planning system will be included in subsequent budget proposals for the regular budget and the support account for peacekeeping operations for the financial periods until 2013;

117. *Requests* the Secretary-General to continue to ensure that the General Assembly is kept informed, on an annual basis, of the progress of the enterprise resource planning project, including milestones and deliverables, progress made, outstanding activities and utilization of resources, and to provide information on the resources that could be redistributed to the enterprise resource planning project as a result of the merging of any elements of other enterprise systems with the enterprise resource planning system;

Section 28C

Office of Human Resources Management

118. *Recalls* paragraph 51 of the report of the Advisory Committee on Administrative and Budgetary Questions,

and requests the Secretary-General not to take measures on geographic mobility until the consideration by the General Assembly of the proposals contained in the report requested in section VII of its resolution 63/250;

Section 28D

Office of Central Support Services

Business continuity management

119.   *Also recalls* section III of its resolution 63/268 of 7 April 2009;

120.   *Notes* the work undertaken and progress achieved so far by the Secretary-General in business continuity management in response to the business risks faced by the United Nations;

121.   *Decides* to appropriate an amount of 2.2 million dollars for business continuity management, and requests the Secretary-General to submit a fully justified proposal for post and non-post resources in relation to the work currently under way on business continuity management in the context of the proposed programme budget for the biennium 2012–2013;

122.   *Requests* the Secretary-General, when developing comprehensive administrative and technical procedures and management and construction project guidelines for the implementation of future construction and major maintenance projects, to ensure that its relevant resolutions are strictly abided by, in particular the ones on procurement, and to draw upon the relevant lessons learned in the planning and implementation of the capital master plan;

Section 28G

Administration, Nairobi

123.   *Recalls* paragraph 101 of its resolution 52/220 of 22 December 1997;

124.   *Reiterates its request* to the Secretary-General to continue to bring the financial arrangements of the United Nations Office at Nairobi into line with those of similar United Nations administrative offices;

Section 29

Office of Information and Communications Technology

125.   *Recognizes* the benefits of the implementation of the customer relationship management and enterprise content management systems, and reiterates its request to the Secretary-General to continue to implement these applications throughout the Organization as appropriate;

126.   *Decides* not to appropriate resources for the enterprise content management and customer relationship management systems, and requests the Secretary-General to submit a fully justified proposal for post and non-post resources in the context of the proposed programme budget for the biennium 2012–2013;

127.   *Decides* to approve resources in the amount of 1.5 million dollars for the development of a unified disaster recovery plan and for maintaining the Brindisi enterprise data centre;

PART IX

Internal oversight

Section 30

Internal oversight

128.   *Requests* the Secretary-General to ensure that the Office of Internal Oversight Services designs and implements a plan to complete a risk analysis in preparation for its 2012–2013 biennium budget request;

129.   *Also requests* the Secretary-General to ensure that the Office of Internal Oversight Services prepares a workplan for investigations;

130.   *Reaffirms* its resolution 63/287 of 30 June 2009, and takes note of paragraphs IX.21 and IX.23 of the report of the Advisory Committee on Administrative and Budgetary Questions;

PART X

Jointly financed administrative activities and special expenses

131.   *Recalls* paragraph X.17 of the report of the Advisory Committee on Administrative and Budgetary Questions, in which the Advisory Committee expressed concern that the United Nations System Chief Executives Board for Coordination might be taking on substantive functions that its member organizations were carrying out rather than continuing its focus on system-wide coordination;

132.   *Decides* to reclassify one P-5 post to the D-1 level and to establish one P-4 post for the secretariat of the Chief Executives Board;

PART XI

Capital expenditures

133.   *Endorses* the conclusions and recommendations contained in the report of the Advisory Committee on Administrative and Budgetary Questions, subject to the provisions of the present resolution;

134.   *Recalls* paragraph XI.9 of the report of the Advisory Committee on Administrative and Budgetary Questions, and decides to reduce provisions under section 33 by 10 million dollars;

135.   *Stresses* the importance of a sound project management framework for the strategic heritage plan, with clearly assigned roles and responsibilities of all entities involved at Headquarters and at the United Nations Office at Geneva, and requests the Secretary-General to include in his progress report to the General Assembly at its sixty-fifth session detailed information on the strategic heritage plan;

136.   *Recalls* paragraph XI.11 of the report of the Advisory Committee on Administrative and Budgetary Questions, and stresses that the renovation phase of the strategic heritage plan shall not start before the General Assembly has taken a decision on this matter and the capital master plan has been completed;

137.   *Requests* the Secretary-General to submit a report on the outcome of the conceptual engineering study of the strategic heritage plan, including an estimate of the overall costs and timeline of the project, to the General Assembly at its sixty-fifth session;

138. *Calls upon* the Secretary-General to ensure that the conceptual engineering study for the strategic heritage plan identifies all viable alternatives in the most cost-effective and efficient manner;

PART XII
Safety and security

139. *Endorses* the conclusions and recommendations contained in the reports of the Advisory Committee on Administrative and Budgetary Questions;

PART XIII
Development Account
Section 35
Development Account

140. *Decides* to appropriate an additional 5 million dollars for the Development Account;

Income section 3
Services to the public

141. *Takes note* of paragraphs IS3.16 and IS3.17 of the report of the Advisory Committee on Administrative and Budgetary Questions, and stresses that the United Nations is a non-profit organization;

Limited budgetary discretion

142. *Recalls* section III of its resolution 60/283, and decides to extend its provisions until 30 April 2010, pending a decision at the first part of the resumed sixty-fourth session of the General Assembly.

ANNEX
Staffing table for the biennium 2010–2011

Category	Number of posts
Professional and above	
Deputy Secretary-General	1
Under-Secretary-General	31
Assistant Secretary-General	27
D-2	100
D-1	276
P-5	830
P-4/3	2,742
P-2/1	536
Subtotal	**4,543**
General Service	
Principal level	276
Other level	2,735
Subtotal	**3,011**
Other	
Security Service	320
Local level	2,020
Field Service	147
National Officer	70
Trades and Crafts	170
Subtotal	**2,727**
TOTAL	**10,281**

Appropriations

In his proposed programme budget for the 2010–2011 biennium [A/64/6], the Secretary-General recommended expenditures of $5,059.3 million, general income of $31.6 million, and staff assessment income of $531.8 million (an increase of $16.3 million), resulting in a net budget estimate of $4,495.9 million, or a 4.3 per cent real growth over the 2008–2009 budget.

Extrabudgetary resources for the 2010–2011 biennium were estimated at $9,441.9 million, comprising $1,047.6 million for support activities, $1,610.4 million for substantive activities and $6,783.9 million for operational activities.

ACABQ, in its first report on the proposed 2010–2011 programme budget [A/64/7], agreed with the overall budget proposed by the Secretary-General; made recommendations regarding posts and other objects of expenditure; and pointed to areas where economies could be achieved. On the effective use of resources, including the emphasis on results and the demand of Member States for accountability, the Committee recommended the provision of specific guidelines and objectives for achieving greater productivity and efficiency.

In December [A/64/576], the Secretary-General recommended revised estimates to reflect the latest data on actual inflation experience, the outcome of salary surveys, the movement of post adjustment indices in 2009, and the effect of the evolution of operational rates of exchange in 2009 on the proposed 2010–2011 programme budget. The recosted level of expenditure amounted to $5,143.5 million, while income was revised to $563.2 million.

Also in December [A/64/570], the Secretary-General recommended revised estimates in the amount of $244.6 million for the International Criminal Tribunal for Rwanda and $290.9 million for the International Tribunal for the Former Yugoslavia.

ACABQ, in its twentieth report on the 2010–2011 programme budget [A/64/7/Add.19], found no technical basis for objecting to the Secretary-General's revised estimates in the two reports and transmitted them to the Fifth Committee.

GENERAL ASSEMBLY ACTION

On 24 December [meeting 68], the General Assembly, on the recommendation of the Fifth Committee [A/64/548/Add.1], adopted **resolutions 64/244 A** to **C** without vote [agenda item 132].

Programme budget for the biennium 2010–2011

A

BUDGET APPROPRIATIONS
FOR THE BIENNIUM 2010–2011

The General Assembly
Resolves that, for the biennium 2010–2011:

1. Appropriations totalling 5,156,029,100 United States dollars are hereby approved for the following purposes:

Section			Amount (United States dollars)
	Part I. Overall policymaking, direction and coordination		
1.	Overall policymaking, direction and coordination		100,847,600
2.	General Assembly and Economic and Social Council affairs and conference management		676,592,200
		Subtotal	**777,439,800**
	Part II. Political affairs		
3.	Political affairs		1,109,991,000
4.	Disarmament		22,299,100
5.	Peacekeeping operations		107,710,900
6.	Peaceful uses of outer space		8,437,400
		Subtotal	**1,248,438,400**
	Part III. International justice and law		
7.	International Court of Justice		51,010,200
8.	Legal affairs		45,845,000
		Subtotal	**96,855,200**
	Part IV. International cooperation for development		
9.	Economic and social affairs		166,217,100
10.	Least developed countries, landlocked developing countries and small island developing States		7,422,500
11.	United Nations support for the New Partnership for Africa's Development		12,786,400
12.	Trade and development		140,432,100
13.	International Trade Centre UNCTAD/WTO		30,541,400
14.	Environment		14,406,200
15.	Human settlements		21,510,400
16.	International drug control, crime and terrorism prevention and criminal justice		40,995,600
		Subtotal	**434,311,700**
	Part V. Regional cooperation for development		
17.	Economic and social development in Africa		132,697,100
18.	Economic and social development in Asia and the Pacific		93,919,300
19.	Economic development in Europe		67,876,000
20.	Economic and social development in Latin America and the Caribbean		111,654,000
21.	Economic and social development in Western Asia		66,602,800
22.	Regular programme of technical cooperation		53,706,900
		Subtotal	**526,456,100**
	Part VI. Human rights and humanitarian affairs		
23.	Human rights		142,743,800
24.	International protection, durable solutions and assistance to refugees		80,544,200
25.	Palestine refugees		48,744,700
26.	Humanitarian assistance		29,904,900
		Subtotal	**301,937,600**
	Part VII. Public information		
27.	Public information		186,707,400
		Subtotal	**186,707,400**
	Part VIII. Common support services		
28.	Management and support services		505,808,500
29.	Office of Information and Communications Technology		72,160,600
		Subtotal	**577,969,100**
	Part IX. Internal oversight		
30.	Internal oversight		39,438,800
		Subtotal	**39,438,800**
	Part X. Jointly financed administrative activities and special expenses		
31.	Jointly financed administrative activities		12,109,800
32.	Special expenses		113,138,400
		Subtotal	**125,248,200**
	Part XI. Capital expenditures		
33.	Construction, alteration, improvement and major maintenance		61,265,500
		Subtotal	**61,265,500**
	Part XII. Safety and security		
34.	Safety and security		239,288,500
		Subtotal	**239,288,500**
	Part XIII. Development Account		
35.	Development Account		23,651,300
		Subtotal	**23,651,300**
	Part XIV. Staff assessment		
36.	Staff assessment		517,021,500
		Subtotal	**517,021,500**
		TOTAL	**5,156,029,100**

2. The Secretary-General shall be authorized to transfer credits between sections of the budget with the concurrence of the Advisory Committee on Administrative and Budgetary Questions;

3. In addition to the appropriations approved under paragraph 1 above, an amount of 75,000 dollars shall be appropriated for each year of the biennium 2010–2011 from the accumulated income of the Library Endowment Fund for the purchase of books, periodicals, maps and library equipment and for such other expenses of the library at the Palais des Nations in Geneva as are in accordance with the objects and provisions of the endowment.

B

INCOME ESTIMATES FOR THE BIENNIUM 2010–2011

The General Assembly

Resolves that, for the biennium 2010–2011:

1. Estimates of income other than assessments on Member States totalling 554,171,800 United States dollars are approved as follows:

Income section	Amount (United States dollars)
1. Income from staff assessment	521,183,700
2. General income	31,176,500
3. Services to the public	1,811,600
TOTAL	**554,171,800**

2. The income from staff assessment shall be credited to the Tax Equalization Fund in accordance with the provisions of General Assembly resolution 973(X) of 15 December 1955;

3. Direct expenses of the United Nations Postal Administration, services to visitors, the sale of statistical products, catering operations and related services, garage operations, television services and the sale of publications not provided for under the budget appropriations shall be charged against the income derived from those activities.

C

FINANCING OF APPROPRIATIONS FOR THE YEAR 2010

The General Assembly

Resolves that, for the year 2010:

1. Budget appropriations consisting of 2,578,014,550 United States dollars, being half of the appropriation of 5,156,029,100 dollars approved for the biennium 2010–2011 by the General Assembly in paragraph 1 of resolution A above, minus 67,745,000 dollars, being the net decrease in revised appropriations for the biennium 2008–2009 approved by the Assembly in its resolutions 63/268 of 7 April 2009, 63/283 of 30 June 2009 and 64/242 A of 24 December 2009, offset by the amount of 45 million dollars not assessed pursuant to section XII of its resolution 63/263 of 24 December 2008, shall be financed in accordance with regulations 3.1 and 3.2 of the Financial Regulations and Rules of the United Nations, as follows:

(a) 177,278,350 dollars, consisting of 16,494,050 dollars, being half of the estimated income other than staff assessment income approved for the biennium 2010–2011 under resolution B above, plus 19,686,400 dollars, being

the increase in income other than staff assessment income for the biennium 2008–2009 approved by the Assembly in its resolution 64/242 B of 24 December 2009, plus 141,097,900 dollars, being the unutilized surplus of the final appropriations for the biennium 2006–2007 as at 31 December 2007;

(b) 2,350,606,850 dollars, being the assessment on Member States in accordance with its resolution 64/248 of 24 December 2009 on the scale of assessments for the apportionment of the expenses of the United Nations;

(c) 27,384,350 dollars, being half of the recosting amount for the year 2010, which will not be assessed on Member States in 2010, in accordance with paragraph 51 of its resolution 64/243 of 24 December 2009;

2. There shall be set off against the assessment on Member States, in accordance with the provisions of General Assembly resolution 973(X) of 15 December 1955, their respective share in the Tax Equalization Fund in the total amount of 236,006,150 dollars, consisting of:

(a) 260,591,850 dollars, being half of the estimated staff assessment income approved for the biennium 2010–2011 in resolution B above;

(b) 2,579,300 dollars, being the increase in income from staff assessment for the biennium 2008–2009 approved by the Assembly in its resolutions 63/268 and 63/283;

(c) Offset by 27,165,000 dollars, being the decrease in income from staff assessment for the biennium 2008–2009 approved by the Assembly in its resolution 64/242 B.

Also on 24 December, the Assembly decided that the item on the 2010–2011 proposed programme budget would remain for consideration during its resumed sixty-fourth (2010) session (**decision 64/549**).

Other questions relating to the programme budget

The Fifth Committee considered a number of special subjects relating to the 2010–2011 programme budget, among them, revised estimates resulting from resolutions and decisions adopted by the Economic and Social Council at its substantive session of 2009; revised estimates resulting from resolutions and decisions adopted by the Human Rights Council; estimates in respect of special political missions, good offices and other political initiatives authorized by the General Assembly and/or the Security Council; the effect of changes in rates of exchange and inflation; the contingency fund; unforeseen and extraordinary expenses; and the Working Capital Fund (see sections below).

Other subjects concerned the International Trade Centre UNCTAD/WTO (United Nations Conference on Trade and Development/World Trade Organization) (see p. 923); administrative expenses of the United Nations Joint Staff Pension Fund (see p. 1471); a request for a subvention to the United Nations Institute for Disarmament Research (see p. 563); and construction of additional office facilities at the Economic Commission for Africa in Addis Ababa and the United Nations Office at Nairobi (see p. 1451). The Committtee also considered administrative and financial implications of the decisions and recommendations contained in the 2009 report of the International Civil Service Commission (ICSC) (see p. 1452); after-service health insurance: medical and dental reserve funds (see p. 1456); along with the gross budgets for the Joint Inspection Unit, ICSC and the UN Department of Safety and Security.

GENERAL ASSEMBLY ACTION

On 24 December [meeting 68], the General Assembly, on the recommendation of the Fifth Committee [A/64/548/Add.1], adopted **resolution 64/245** without vote [agenda item 132].

Special subjects relating to the proposed programme budget for the biennium 2010–2011

The General Assembly,

I

International Trade Centre UNCTAD/WTO

Having considered the programme budget proposals for the International Trade Centre UNCTAD/WTO for the biennium 2010–2011 and the related report of the Advisory Committee on Administrative and Budgetary Questions,

1. *Endorses* the conclusions and recommendations contained in the report of the Advisory Committee on Administrative and Budgetary Questions;

2. *Decides* to approve resources in the amount of 29,459,792 United States dollars (at the exchange rate of 1.2 Swiss francs to 1 dollar) proposed for the biennium 2010–2011 under section 13 (International Trade Centre UNCTAD/WTO) of the proposed programme budget for the biennium 2010–2011;

II

Administrative expenses of the United Nations Joint Staff Pension Fund

Recalling its resolutions 55/224 of 23 December 2000, 57/286 of 20 December 2002, 59/269 of 23 December 2004, 61/240 of 22 December 2006, 62/241 of 22 December 2007 and 63/252 of 24 December 2008,

Having considered the report of the United Nations Joint Staff Pension Board on the administrative expenses of the United Nations Joint Staff Pension Fund, the report of the Secretary-General on the administrative and financial implications arising from the report of the Board and the related report of the Advisory Committee on Administrative and Budgetary Questions,

1. *Concurs* with the recommendations contained in the report of the Advisory Committee on Administrative and Budgetary Questions, subject to the provisions of the present resolution;

2. *Emphasizes* the importance of providing the information necessary to enable Member States to make well-informed decisions;

3. *Decides* to establish five out of the requested fourteen additional posts in the secretariat of the Fund as follows: one P-4 Risk Management Officer, one P-4 Senior Benefits Officer, two General Service (Principal level) Senior Benefits Assistants and one D-1 Chief Finance Officer;

4. *Approves* expenses, chargeable directly to the Fund, totalling 154,749,100 dollars net for the biennium 2010–2011 and a revised estimate of 109,757,800 dollars net for the biennium 2008–2009 for the administration of the Fund;

5. *Also approves* the additional amount of 1,438,800 dollars above the level of resources set out in section 1 (Overall policymaking, direction and coordination) of the proposed programme budget for the biennium 2010–2011 as the United Nations share of the cost of the administrative expenses of the central secretariat of the Fund;

6. *Reaffirms* the need for a strategic approach to the human resources requirements for the Fund;

7. *Urges* the Fund administration to continue to make every possible effort to fill the existing vacancies in the staffing table as soon as feasible;

8. *Requests* the Secretary-General, as fiduciary for the investment of the assets of the Fund, to continue to diversify its investments between developed and developing markets, wherever this serves the interests of the participants and the beneficiaries of the Fund, and also requests the Secretary-General to ensure that, under the current volatile market conditions, decisions concerning the investments of the Fund in any country should be implemented very cautiously, fully taking into account the four main criteria for investment, namely, safety, profitability, liquidity and convertibility;

9. *Also requests* the Secretary-General to keep under review the Investment Management Division, in order to ensure that the long-term objectives of the Fund are met and to report back to the General Assembly in the context of the biennial report on the Fund;

III

Request for a subvention to the United Nations Institute for Disarmament Research

Recalling section IV of its resolution 60/248 of 23 December 2005,

Having considered the note by the Secretary-General on the request for a subvention to the United Nations Institute for Disarmament Research resulting from the recommendations of the Board of Trustees of the Institute on the work programme of the Institute for 2010–2011 and the related report of the Advisory Committee on Administrative and Budgetary Questions,

1. *Takes note* of the note by the Secretary-General;

2. *Endorses* the conclusions and recommendations contained in the report of the Advisory Committee on Administrative and Budgetary Questions;

3. *Approves* the request for a subvention to the Institute of 558,200 dollars for the biennium 2010–2011 from the regular budget of the United Nations, on the understanding that no additional provision would be required under section 4 (Disarmament) of the programme budget for the biennium 2010–2011;

IV

Revised estimates resulting from resolutions and decisions adopted by the Economic and Social Council at its substantive session of 2009

Having considered the report of the Secretary-General on revised estimates resulting from resolutions and decisions adopted by the Economic and Social Council at its substantive session of 2009 and the related report of the Advisory Committee on Administrative and Budgetary Questions,

1. *Takes note* of the report of the Secretary-General;

2. *Endorses* the conclusions and recommendations contained in the report of the Advisory Committee on Administrative and Budgetary Questions;

V

Revised estimates resulting from resolution S-9/1 adopted by the Human Rights Council at its ninth special session and from resolutions and decisions adopted by the Council at its tenth and eleventh sessions in 2009

Having considered the reports of the Secretary-General on revised estimates resulting from resolution S-9/1 adopted by the Human Rights Council at its ninth special session and on revised estimates resulting from resolutions and decisions adopted by the Council at its tenth and eleventh sessions in 2009 and the related report of the Advisory Committee on Administrative and Budgetary Questions,

1. *Takes note* of the reports of the Secretary-General;

2. *Endorses* the conclusions and recommendations contained in the report of the Advisory Committee on Administrative and Budgetary Questions;

VI

Estimates in respect of special political missions, good offices and other political initiatives authorized by the General Assembly and/or the Security Council

Having considered the reports of the Secretary-General on the estimates in respect of special political missions, good offices and other political initiatives authorized by the General Assembly and/or the Security Council, the related report of the Advisory Committee on Administrative and Budgetary Questions, the letter dated 10 December 2009 from the President of the Assembly to the Chair of the Fifth Committee, the oral statement by the Chair of the Advisory Committee on Administrative and Budgetary Questions and the report of the Office of Internal Oversight Services on the follow-up audit of the management of special political missions by the Department of Political Affairs,

1. *Takes note* of the reports of the Secretary-General and the letter dated 10 December 2009 from the President of the General Assembly to the Chair of the Fifth Committee;

2. *Also takes note* of the report of the Office of Internal Oversight Services on the follow-up audit of the management of special political missions by the Department of Political Affairs;

3. *Endorses* the conclusions and recommendations contained in the report of the Advisory Committee on Administrative and Budgetary Questions and in the oral statement

by the Chair of the Advisory Committee, subject to the provisions of the present resolution;

4. *Expresses deep concern* with regard to the recurrent late submission of the reports on the matter under consideration, which hinders their proper examination by the General Assembly, and requests the Secretary-General and the Advisory Committee on Administrative and Budgetary Questions to submit their reports in a timely manner;

5. *Reaffirms* the need to ensure adequate levels of safety and security for United Nations personnel and associated humanitarian personnel;

6. *Takes note* of paragraphs 20, 73, 74, 79, 83, 89, 94, 111 and 113 of the report of the Advisory Committee on Administrative and Budgetary Questions;

7. *Reaffirms* paragraph 12 of General Assembly resolution 63/291 of 30 June 2009, and requests the Secretary-General to continue the current funding arrangements for the activities of the Office of the Special Envoy of the Secretary-General for the Great Lakes Region through 30 June 2010;

8. *Takes note* of paragraph 38 of the report of the Advisory Committee on Administrative and Budgetary Questions, and decides to approve 200,000 dollars for consultancy resources for the Special Adviser to the Secretary-General on Cyprus;

9. *Also takes note* of paragraph 96 of the report of the Advisory Committee on Administrative and Budgetary Questions, and decides to approve the fifteen positions for the United Nations Political Office for Somalia as proposed by the Secretary-General;

10. *Further takes note* of paragraph 107 of the report of the Advisory Committee on Administrative and Budgetary Questions;

11. *Requests* the Secretary-General to submit updated detailed comprehensive financial requirements for the construction of the United Nations integrated compound in Baghdad to the General Assembly for consideration at the main part of its sixty-fifth session;

12. *Approves* the budgets totalling 569,526,500 dollars for the twenty-six special political missions authorized by the General Assembly and/or the Security Council, which are presented in table 1 of the report of the Secretary-General;

13. *Also approves* a charge totalling 569,526,500 dollars net against the provision for special political missions requested in section 3 (Political affairs) of the proposed programme budget for the biennium 2010–2011;

14. *Decides* that the overall provision for special political missions requested in section 3 of the proposed programme budget for the biennium 2010–2011 should be one billion dollars;

VII

Construction of additional office facilities at the Economic Commission for Africa in Addis Ababa and the United Nations Office at Nairobi

Having considered the report of the Secretary-General on construction of additional office facilities at the Economic Commission for Africa in Addis Ababa and the United Nations Office at Nairobi and the related report of the Advisory Committee on Administrative and Budgetary Questions,

1. *Takes note* of the report of the Secretary-General;

2. *Endorses* the conclusions and recommendations contained in the report of the Advisory Committee on Administrative and Budgetary Questions;

3. *Recalls* paragraph 4 of the report of the Advisory Committee on Administrative and Budgetary Questions and stresses that the use of vacancy management for meeting requirements of additional post-related project costs at the Economic Commission for Africa should not unduly undermine the original purpose of the post;

VIII

Administrative and financial implications of the decisions and recommendations contained in the report of the International Civil Service Commission for 2009

Having considered the statement submitted by the Secretary-General in accordance with rule 153 of the rules of procedure of the General Assembly on the administrative and financial implications of the decisions and recommendations contained in the report of the International Civil Service Commission for 2009 and the related report of the Advisory Committee on Administrative and Budgetary Questions,

1. *Recalls* General Assembly resolution 64/231 of 22 December 2009;

2. *Takes note* of the statement submitted by the Secretary-General;

3. *Endorses* the conclusions and recommendations contained in the report of the Advisory Committee on Administrative and Budgetary Questions;

IX

Effects of changes in rates of exchange and inflation

Having considered the report of the Secretary-General on the revised estimates resulting from changes in rates of exchange and inflation and the related report of the Advisory Committee on Administrative and Budgetary Questions,

Takes note of the revised estimates arising from recosting due to changes in the rates of exchange and inflation;

X

Contingency fund

Notes that a balance of 31,331,900 dollars remains in the contingency fund;

XI

After-service health insurance: medical and dental reserve funds

Having considered the report of the Secretary-General on liabilities and proposed funding for after-service health insurance benefits and the related report of the Advisory Committee on Administrative and Budgetary Questions,

Decides to revert to the issue of the 83.1 million dollars from the medical and dental reserve funds included in the proposal of the Secretary-General on the funding of after-service health insurance liabilities, and requests the Secretary-General to provide the General Assembly at its sixty-fifth session with information on the composition of these reserve funds;

XII

Joint Inspection Unit

Approves the gross budget for the Joint Inspection Unit for the biennium 2010–2011 in the amount of 13,075,300 dollars;

XIII

International Civil Service Commission

Also approves the gross budget for the International Civil Service Commission for the biennium 2010–2011 in the amount of 17,755,900 dollars;

XIV

Gross jointly financed budget of the Department of Safety and Security

Further approves the gross jointly financed budget of the Department of Safety and Security for the biennium 2010–2011 in the amount of 242,040,500 dollars, broken down as follows:

(a) Field Security Operations: 212,381,300 dollars;

(b) Security and Safety Services at the United Nations Office at Vienna: 29,659,200 dollars.

Revised estimates resulting from Economic and Social Council action

In a 9 September report [A/64/344], the Secretary-General submitted estimates of $167,800 additional to the resources initially proposed in the 2010–2011 programme budget, of which all could be absorbed, resulting from Economic and Social Council **resolution 2009/4** (see p. 904) and **decisions 2009/251** (see pp. 1082 & 1253), **2009/253** (see p. 749) and **2009/254** (see p. ibid.).

In October [A/64/7/Add.1], ACABQ stated that it had no objection to the recommendations proposed in the Secretary-General's report.

Revised estimates resulting from Human Rights Council action

In an 18 September report [A/64/353], the Secretary-General submitted revised estimated requirements relating to the proposed 2010–2011 programme budget, totalling $3,659,000, arising from resolutions and decisions adopted by the Human Rights Council at its tenth and eleventh sessions held in 2009. Of that amount, $824,700 had been included in the budget as relating to activities of a "perennial nature", while the balance of $2,834,300 would be accommodated, to the extent possible, within the requirements proposed for the 2010–2011 biennium.

In October [A/64/7/Add.3], ACABQ recommended that the Assembly take note of the Secretary-General's report.

Revised estimates in respect of matters of which the Security Council was seized

In October [A/64/349], as a result of action taken or expected to be taken by the General Assembly and/or the Security Council, the Secretary-General submitted the proposed resource requirements for the period up to 31 December 2010 for 27 special political missions, which were estimated at $599,526,500 net ($637,320,600 gross). Five addenda [A/64/349/Add.1–5] to the report were issued.

ACABQ, in its fourteenth report on the 2010–2011 proposed programme budget [A/64/7/Add.13], recommended that the Assembly approve the resources requested by the Secretary-General, subject to the Committee's observations and recommendations.

Contingency fund

The contingency fund, established by General Assembly resolution 41/213 [YUN 1986, p. 1024], accommodated additional expenditures relating to each biennium that derived from legislative mandates not provided for in the proposed programme budget or from revised estimates. Guidelines for its use were annexed to Assembly resolution 42/211 [YUN 1987, p. 1098].

The Fifth Committee considered the Secretary-General's December report [A/C.5/64/14] containing a consolidated statement of all programme budget implications and revised estimates falling under the guidelines for the use of the fund. The consolidated amount of $5,201,000 would be within the approved level of the fund; an available balance of $31,331,900 would remain in the fund.

Unforeseen and extraordinary expenses

Under the terms of General Assembly resolution 62/239 [YUN 2007, p. 1459], the Secretary-General was authorized, with the prior concurrence of ACABQ, to enter into commitments to meet unforeseen and extraordinary expenses arising either during or subsequent to the 2008–2009 biennium, without reverting to the Assembly for approval.

GENERAL ASSEMBLY ACTION

On 24 December [meeting 68], the General Assembly, on the recommendation of the Fifth Committee [A/64/548/Add.1], adopted **resolution 64/246** without vote [agenda item 132].

Unforeseen and extraordinary expenses for the biennium 2010–2011

The General Assembly

1. *Authorizes* the Secretary-General, with the prior concurrence of the Advisory Committee on Administra-

tive and Budgetary Questions and subject to the Financial Regulations and Rules of the United Nations and the provisions of paragraph 3 below, to enter into commitments in the biennium 2010–2011 to meet unforeseen and extraordinary expenses arising either during or subsequent to the biennium, provided that the concurrence of the Advisory Committee shall not be necessary for:

(a) Such commitments not exceeding a total of 8 million United States dollars in any one year of the biennium 2010–2011 as the Secretary-General certifies relate to the maintenance of peace and security;

(b) Such commitments as the President of the International Court of Justice certifies relate to expenses occasioned by:

(i) The designation of ad hoc judges (Statute of the International Court of Justice, Article 31), not exceeding a total of 200,000 dollars;

(ii) The calling of witnesses and the appointment of experts (Statute, Article 50) and the appointment of assessors (Statute, Article 30), not exceeding a total of 50,000 dollars;

(iii) The maintenance in office for the completion of cases of judges who have not been re-elected (Statute, Article 13, paragraph 3), not exceeding a total of 40,000 dollars;

(iv) The payment of pensions and travel and removal expenses of retiring judges and travel and removal expenses and installation grants of members of the Court (Statute, Article 32, paragraph 7), not exceeding a total of 410,000 dollars;

(v) The work of the Court or its Chambers away from The Hague (Statute, Article 22), not exceeding a total of 25,000 dollars;

(c) Such commitments not exceeding a total of 1 million dollars in the biennium 2010–2011 as the Secretary-General certifies are required for security measures pursuant to section XI, paragraph 6, of General Assembly resolution 59/276 of 23 December 2004;

2. *Resolves* that the Secretary-General shall report to the Advisory Committee on Administrative and Budgetary Questions and to the General Assembly at its sixty-fifth and sixty-sixth sessions all commitments made under the provisions of the present resolution, together with the circumstances relating thereto, and shall submit supplementary estimates to the Assembly in respect of such commitments;

3. *Decides* that, for the biennium 2010–2011, if a decision of the Security Council results in the need for the Secretary-General to enter into commitments relating to the maintenance of peace and security in an amount exceeding 10 million dollars in respect of the decision, that matter shall be brought to the General Assembly, or, if the Assembly is suspended or not in session, a resumed or special session of the Assembly shall be convened by the Secretary-General to consider the matter.

Working capital fund

In December, the General Assembly established the Working Capital Fund for the 2010–2011 biennium at $150 million, the same level as for the 2008–2009 biennium [YUN 2007, p. 1458]. As in the past, the Fund was to be used to finance appropriations, pending the receipt of assessed contributions, to pay for unforeseen and extraordinary expenses, as well as for miscellaneous self-liquidating purchases and advance insurance premiums, and to enable the Tax Equalization Fund to meet current commitments pending the accumulation of credits.

GENERAL ASSEMBLY ACTION

On 24 December [meeting 68], the General Assembly, on the recommendation of the Fifth Committee [A/64/548/Add.1], adopted **resolution 64/247** without vote [agenda item 132].

Working Capital Fund for the biennium 2010–2011

The General Assembly

Resolves that:

1. The Working Capital Fund shall be established for the biennium 2010–2011 in the amount of 150 million United States dollars;

2. Member States shall make advances to the Working Capital Fund in accordance with the scale of assessments adopted by the General Assembly for contributions of Member States to the budget for the year 2010;

3. There shall be set off against this allocation of advances:

(a) Credits to Member States resulting from transfers made in 1959 and 1960 from the surplus account to the Working Capital Fund in an adjusted amount of 1,025,092 dollars;

(b) Cash advances paid by Member States to the Working Capital Fund for the biennium 2008–2009 in accordance with General Assembly resolution 62/240 of 22 December 2007;

4. Should the credits and advances paid by any Member State to the Working Capital Fund for the biennium 2008–2009 exceed the amount of that Member State's advance under the provisions of paragraph 2 above, the excess shall be set off against the amount of the contributions payable by the Member State in respect of the biennium 2010–2011;

5. The Secretary-General is authorized to advance from the Working Capital Fund:

(a) Such sums as may be necessary to finance budgetary appropriations pending the receipt of contributions; sums so advanced shall be reimbursed as soon as receipts from contributions are available for that purpose;

(b) Such sums as may be necessary to finance commitments that may be duly authorized under the provisions of the resolutions adopted by the General Assembly, in particular resolution 64/246 of 24 December 2009 relating to unforeseen and extraordinary expenses; the Secretary-General shall make provision in the budget estimates for reimbursing the Working Capital Fund;

(c) Such sums as may be necessary to continue the revolving fund to finance miscellaneous self-liquidating purchases and activities, which, together with net sums outstanding for the same purpose, do not exceed 200,000 dollars; advances in excess of 200,000 dollars may be made with the prior concurrence of the Advisory Committee on Administrative and Budgetary Questions;

(d) With the prior concurrence of the Advisory Committee on Administrative and Budgetary Questions, such sums as may be required to finance payments of advance insurance premiums where the period of insurance extends beyond the end of the biennium in which payment is made; the Secretary-General shall make provision in the budget estimates of each biennium, during the life of the related policies, to cover the charges applicable to each biennium;

(e) Such sums as may be necessary to enable the Tax Equalization Fund to meet current commitments pending the accumulation of credits; such advances shall be repaid as soon as credits are available in the Tax Equalization Fund;

6. Should the provision in paragraph 1 above prove inadequate to meet the purposes normally related to the Working Capital Fund, the Secretary-General is authorized to utilize, in the biennium 2010–2011, cash from special funds and accounts in his custody, under the conditions approved by the General Assembly in its resolution 1341(XIII) of 13 December 1958, or the proceeds of loans authorized by the Assembly.

Contributions

According to the Secretary-General's report on improving the financial situation of the United Nations [A/64/497/Add.1], unpaid assessed contributions to the UN budget at the end of 2009 totalled $335 million (compared with $417 million in 2008); outstanding peacekeeping arrears totalled $1,900 million (compared with $2,900 million in 2008); and total unpaid assessments to the international tribunals increased to $37 million (compared with $26 million in 2008).

The number of Member States paying their regular budget assessment in full decreased to 136 (compared with 146 at the end of 2008).

Assessments

The Committee on Contributions, at its sixty-ninth session (New York, 1–26 June) [A/64/11], considered a number of issues related to the payment of assessments, including a review of the methodology for preparing the scale of assessments for the period 2010–2012, multi-year payment plans and the application of Article 19 of the Charter. The Committee decided to hold its seventieth session from 7 to 25 June 2010. On its working methods, the Committee welcomed the establishment of a restricted website to assist its intersessional work and to facilitate the dissemination of documents and other information for the Committee's review. It also noted that a computer would be useful in the conference room during its deliberations for ease of reference for information required.

The General Assembly took action on the Committee's recommendations in October and December (see below).

Application of Article 19

Committee on Contributions. The Committee on Contributions [A/64/11] reviewed requests for exemption under Article 19, whereby a Member would lose its vote in the General Assembly if the amount of its arrears should equal or exceed the amount of contributions due from it for the preceding two full years. The Committee noted the Members' written and oral presentations and evaluated them against their payment records and economic and political circumstances.

Having reviewed requests from six Member States, the Committee determined that the failure of the Central African Republic, the Comoros, Guinea-Bissau, Liberia, Sao Tome and Principe and Somalia to pay the full minimum amount of their arrears necessary to avoid the application of Article 19 was due to conditions beyond their control and recommended that they be allowed to vote until the end of the sixty-fourth session of the Assembly. The Committee urged the Central African Republic, which had not made a contribution in the previous decade, and Sao Tome and Principe, which had made no payment since 2002, to consider the multi-year payment plan system, and to at least pay amounts equivalent to their current annual assessments. The Committee expressed its appreciation for the efforts of Guinea-Bissau to address its arrears by making an $80,000 payment in 2008, which was approximately 10 per cent of its outstanding contributions. Noting the regular payments made by Liberia under its payment plan over the previous four years, with each of those annual payments totalling more than three times its annual assessment, thereby contributing to reducing its arrears, the Committee encouraged Liberia to continue those efforts.

Reports of Secretary-General. During the year, the Secretary-General reported to the Assembly on payments made by certain Member States to reduce their level of arrears below that specified in Article 19, so that they could vote in the Assembly. As at 4 February [A/63/725], 13 Member States were below the gross amount assessed for the preceding two full years (2007–2008). By a series of letters from February to August [A/63/725/Add.1–6], that number was reduced to six and remained at that number through 4 September [A/64/345].

GENERAL ASSEMBLY ACTION

On 8 October [meeting 16], the General Assembly, on the recommendation of the Fifth Committee [A/64/482], adopted **resolution 64/2** without vote [agenda item 136].

Scale of assessments for the apportionment of the expenses of the United Nations requests under Article 19 of the Charter

The General Assembly,

Having considered chapter V of the report of the Committee on Contributions on its sixty-ninth session,

Reaffirming the obligation of Member States under Article 17 of the Charter of the United Nations to bear the expenses of the Organization as apportioned by the General Assembly,

1. *Reaffirms* its role in accordance with the provisions of Article 19 of the Charter of the United Nations and the advisory role of the Committee on Contributions in accordance with rule 160 of the rules of procedure of the General Assembly;

2. *Also reaffirms* its resolution 54/237 C of 23 December 1999;

3. *Requests* the Secretary-General to continue to bring to the attention of Member States the deadline specified in resolution 54/237 C, including through an early announcement in the *Journal of the United Nations* and through direct communication;

4. *Urges* all Member States requesting exemption under Article 19 of the Charter to submit as much information as possible in support of their requests and to consider submitting such information in advance of the deadline specified in resolution 54/237 C so as to enable the collation of any additional detailed information that may be necessary;

5. *Agrees* that the failure of the Central African Republic, the Comoros, Guinea-Bissau, Liberia, Sao Tome and Principe and Somalia to pay the full minimum amount necessary to avoid the application of Article 19 of the Charter was due to conditions beyond their control;

6. *Decides* that the Central African Republic, the Comoros, Guinea-Bissau, Liberia, Sao Tome and Principe and Somalia shall be permitted to vote in the General Assembly until the end of its sixty-fourth session.

Multi-year payment plans

Pursuant to General Assembly resolutions 57/4 B [YUN 2002, p. 1385] and 61/237 [YUN 2006, p. 1626], the Secretary-General submitted a March report [A/64/68] on multi-year payment plans, which provided information on the payment plans/schedules submitted by Liberia, Sao Tome and Principe and Tajikistan, and on the status of their implementation as at 31 December 2008. Under the plans, each year a Member State would pay for the current year's assessments and a part of its arrears, so as to eliminate the arrears within six years. However, some of the plans had durations between 8 and 11 years. In 2008, although Liberia had not submitted a revised multi-year payment plan, it continued to make payments during the year, while Sao Tome and Principe fell short of the amount foreseen in its plan. Tajikistan continued to significantly exceed the payments foreseen in its schedule for the period 2000–2008 [YUN 2008, p. 1558]. The Secretary-

General recommended that the Assembly encourage Member States with significant arrears to consider submitting a multi-year payment plan.

On 7 April, the General Assembly deferred consideration of the agenda item on reports of the Secretary-General on multi-year payment plans until its sixty-fourth (2009) session (**decision 63/550 B**).

The Committee on Contributions [A/64/11] noted that Tajikistan had paid its arrears and completed its multi-year payment plan during the first half of 2009, ahead of its schedule. Recalling the successful implementation of the plans of four other States in prior years, the Committee concluded that the system of multi-year payment plans continued to be a viable means to assist Member States in reducing their unpaid assessed contributions and in demonstrating their commitment to meeting their financial obligations. The Committee noted that no new multi-year payment plans had been submitted.

Other matters related to payment of assessed contributions

The General Assembly also considered the recommendations of the Committee on Contributions on the methodology for future scales of assessments, the scale of assessments for the period 2010–2012, and the assessment of non-member States (see below).

GENERAL ASSEMBLY ACTION

On 24 December [meeting 68], the General Assembly, on the recommendation of the Fifth Committee [A/64/482/Add.1], adopted **resolution 64/248** without vote [agenda item 136].

Scale of assessments for the apportionment of the expenses of the United Nations

The General Assembly,

Recalling its previous resolutions and decisions on the scale of assessments for the apportionment of the expenses of the United Nations, including its resolutions 55/5 B and C of 23 December 2000, 57/4 B of 20 December 2002, 58/1 B of 23 December 2003 and 61/237 of 22 December 2006,

Reaffirming Article 17 of the Charter of the United Nations and rule 160 of its rules of procedure,

Recalling paragraphs 5 and 6 of its resolution 58/1 B,

Having considered the reports of the Committee on Contributions on its sixty-seventh, sixty-eighth and sixty-ninth sessions as well as the reports of the Secretary-General on multi-year payment plans,

1. *Reaffirms* that the determination of the scale of assessments for the apportionment of expenses of the United Nations shall remain the prerogative of the General Assembly;

2. *Also reaffirms* the fundamental principle that the expenses of the Organization shall be apportioned broadly according to the capacity to pay;

3. *Further reaffirms* the obligation of all Member States to bear the expenses of the United Nations, as apportioned by the General Assembly, in conformity with Article 17, paragraph 2, of the Charter of the United Nations;

4. *Reaffirms* that the Committee on Contributions as a technical body is required to prepare the scale of assessments strictly on the basis of reliable, verifiable and comparable data;

5. *Decides* that the scale of assessments for the period 2010–2012 shall be based on the following elements and criteria:

(a) Estimates of gross national income;

(b) Average statistical base periods of three and six years;

(c) Conversion rates based on market exchange rates, except where that would cause excessive fluctuations and distortions in the income of some Member States, when price-adjusted rates of exchange or other appropriate conversion rates should be employed, taking due account of its resolution 46/221 B of 20 December 1991;

(d) The debt-burden approach employed in the scale of assessments for the period 2007–2009;

(e) A low per capita income adjustment of 80 per cent, with a threshold per capita income limit of the average per capita gross national income of all Member States for the statistical base periods;

(f) A minimum assessment rate of 0.001 per cent;

(g) A maximum assessment rate for the least developed countries of 0.01 per cent;

(h) A maximum assessment rate of 22 per cent;

6. *Resolves* that the scale of assessments for the contributions of Member States to the regular budget of the United Nations for 2010, 2011 and 2012 shall be as follows:

Member State	Percentage
Afghanistan	0.004
Albania	0.010
Algeria	0.128
Andorra	0.007
Angola	0.010
Antigua and Barbuda	0.002
Argentina	0.287
Armenia	0.005
Australia	1.933
Austria	0.851
Azerbaijan	0.015
Bahamas	0.018
Bahrain	0.039
Bangladesh	0.010
Barbados	0.008
Belarus	0.042
Belgium	1.075
Belize	0.001
Benin	0.003
Bhutan	0.001
Bolivia	0.007
Bosnia and Herzegovina	0.014
Botswana	0.018
Brazil	1.611
Brunei Darussalam	0.028
Bulgaria	0.038
Burkina Faso	0.003
Burundi	0.001
Cambodia	0.003
Cameroon	0.011
Canada	3.207
Cape Verde	0.001
Central African Republic	0.001

Member State	Percentage	Member State	Percentage
Chad	0.002	Mongolia	0.002
Chile	0.236	Montenegro	0.004
China	3.189	Morocco	0.058
Colombia	0.144	Mozambique	0.003
Comoros	0.001	Myanmar	0.006
Congo	0.003	Namibia	0.008
Costa Rica	0.034	Nauru	0.001
Côte d'Ivoire	0.010	Nepal	0.006
Croatia	0.097	Netherlands	1.855
Cuba	0.071	New Zealand	0.273
Cyprus	0.046	Nicaragua	0.003
Czech Republic	0.349	Niger	0.002
Democratic People's Republic of Korea	0.007	Nigeria	0.078
Democratic Republic of the Congo	0.003	Norway	0.871
Denmark	0.736	Oman	0.086
Djibouti	0.001	Pakistan	0.082
Dominica	0.001	Palau	0.001
Dominican Republic	0.042	Panama	0.022
Ecuador	0.040	Papua New Guinea	0.002
Egypt	0.094	Paraguay	0.007
El Salvador	0.019	Peru	0.090
Equatorial Guinea	0.008	Philippines	0.090
Eritrea	0.001	Poland	0.828
Estonia	0.040	Portugal	0.511
Ethiopia	0.008	Qatar	0.135
Fiji	0.004	Republic of Korea	2.260
Finland	0.566	Romania	0.177
France	6.123	Russian Federation	1.602
Gabon	0.014	Rwanda	0.001
Gambia	0.001	Saint Kitts and Nevis	0.001
Georgia	0.006	Saint Lucia	0.001
Germany	8.018	Saint Vincent and the Grenadines	0.001
Ghana	0.006	Samoa	0.001
Greece	0.691	San Marino	0.003
Grenada	0.001	Sao Tome and Principe	0.001
Guatemala	0.028	Saudi Arabia	0.830
Guinea	0.002	Senegal	0.006
Guinea-Bissau	0.001	Serbia	0.037
Guyana	0.001	Seychelles	0.002
Haiti	0.003	Sierra Leone	0.001
Honduras	0.008	Singapore	0.335
Hungary	0.291	Slovakia	0.142
Iceland	0.042	Slovenia	0.103
India	0.534	Solomon Islands	0.001
Indonesia	0.238	Somalia	0.001
Iran	0.233	South Africa	0.385
Iraq	0.020	Spain	3.177
Ireland	0.498	Sri Lanka	0.019
Israel	0.384	Sudan	0.010
Italy	4.999	Suriname	0.003
Jamaica	0.014	Swaziland	0.003
Japan	12.530	Sweden	1.064
Jordan	0.014	Switzerland	1.130
Kazakhstan	0.076	Syrian Arab Republic	0.025
Kenya	0.012	Tajikistan	0.002
Kiribati	0.001	Thailand	0.209
Kuwait	0.263	The former Yugoslav Republic of Macedonia	0.007
Kyrgyzstan	0.001	Timor-Leste	0.001
Lao People's Democratic Republic	0.001	Togo	0.001
Latvia	0.038	Tonga	0.001
Lebanon	0.033	Trinidad and Tobago	0.044
Lesotho	0.001	Tunisia	0.030
Liberia	0.001	Turkey	0.617
Libyan Arab Jamahiriya	0.129	Turkmenistan	0.026
Liechtenstein	0.009	Tuvalu	0.001
Lithuania	0.065	Uganda	0.006
Luxembourg	0.090	Ukraine	0.087
Madagascar	0.003	United Arab Emirates	0.391
Malawi	0.001	United Kingdom	6.604
Malaysia	0.253	United Republic of Tanzania	0.008
Maldives	0.001	United States	22.000
Mali	0.003	Uruguay	0.027
Malta	0.017	Uzbekistan	0.010
Marshall Islands	0.001	Vanuatu	0.001
Mauritania	0.001	Venezuela	0.314
Mauritius	0.011	Viet Nam	0.033
Mexico	2.356	Yemen	0.010
Micronesia	0.001	Zambia	0.004
Moldova	0.002	Zimbabwe	0.003
Monaco	0.003	**TOTAL**	**100.000**

7. *Recognizes* that the current methodology can be enhanced bearing in mind the principle of capacity to pay;

8. *Also recognizes* the need to study the methodology in depth and in an effective and expeditious manner, taking into account views expressed by Member States;

9. *Decides* to review, at its earliest opportunity, all elements of the methodology of the scale of assessments with a view to a decision before the end of its sixty-sixth session to take effect, if agreed, for the 2013–2015 scale period;

10. *Requests* the Committee on Contributions, in accordance with its mandate and the rules of procedure of the General Assembly, to make recommendations, in the light of the review referred to in paragraph 9 above, and report thereon to the Assembly at the main part of its sixty-fifth session;

11. *Recognizes* the concern expressed by Member States with regard to conversion rates, and requests the Committee on Contributions to review further criteria to be used to identify cases where market rates of exchange should be replaced with price-adjusted rates of exchange or other appropriate conversion rates for preparing the scale of assessments and to report thereon to the Assembly at its sixty-fifth session in the context of the report to be submitted pursuant to paragraph 10 above;

12. *Resolves* that:

(a) Notwithstanding the terms of financial regulation 3.9, the Secretary-General shall be empowered to accept, at his discretion and after consultation with the Chairman of the Committee on Contributions, a portion of the contributions of Member States for the calendar years 2010, 2011 and 2012 in currencies other than the United States dollar;

(b) In accordance with financial regulation 3.8, the Holy See, which is not a member of the United Nations but which participates in certain of its activities, shall be called upon to contribute towards the expenses of the Organization for 2010, 2011 and 2012 on the basis of a notional assessment rate of 0.001 per cent, which represents the basis for the calculation of the flat annual fees to be charged to the Holy See in accordance with General Assembly resolution 44/197 B of 21 December 1989;

13. *Takes note* of the reports of the Secretary-General on multi-year payment plans and of the related conclusions and recommendations of the Committee on Contributions;

14. *Reaffirms* paragraph 1 of its resolution 57/4 B;

15. *Takes note with appreciation* of the considerable efforts undertaken by those Member States that fully implemented their multi-year payment plans;

16. *Encourages* Member States in arrears with their assessed contributions to the United Nations to consider submitting multi-year payment plans, and in this context requests the Committee on Contributions to make recommendations with a view to mitigating large scale-to-scale increases for those Member States that have fulfilled their multi-year payment plans and to report thereon to the Assembly at its sixty-fifth session in the context of the report to be submitted pursuant to paragraph 10 above.

On 24 December, the Assembly decided that the item on the scale of assessments for the apportionment of UN expenses would remain for consideration during its resumed sixty-fourth (2010) session (**decision 64/549**).

Scale methodology

Pursuant to General Assembly resolution 58/1 B [YUN 2003, p. 1424], the Committee on Contributions [A/64/11] continued to review the different elements of the methodology for preparing future scales of assessments, focusing on elements relating to income measure; conversion rates; base period; debt-burden adjustment; low per capita income adjustment; minimum (floor) and maximum (ceiling) assessment rates; annual recalculation; and large scale-to-scale increases in rates of assessments. In the absence of guidance from the Assembly, the Committee decided to review the scale of assessments for the period 2010–2012.

With regard to income measure, the Committee recommended that the scale continue to be based on the most current, comprehensive and comparable gross national income (GNI) data and encouraged States to submit the required statistical information under the 1993 System of National Accounts [YUN 1993, p. 1112] in the first quarter of each year. It also reaffirmed its recommendation for the use of conversion rates based on market exchange rates, except where it would cause excessive fluctuations and distortions in GNI, and agreed that there were advantages in using the same base period for as long as possible. In other recommendations, the Committee decided to further consider the debt-burden adjustment and low per capita income at future sessions; conduct a detailed study on annual recalculation at its next session; and continue its analysis of the merits and possible necessity of measures dealing with large scale-to-scale changes in the assessment rates of Member States. The Committee also adjusted the conversion rate of Iraq and decided to use UN operational rates of exchange for the Democratic People's Republic of Korea, Myanmar and the Syrian Arab Republic.

Scale of assessments for 2010–2012

The General Assembly decided to conduct its review of the scale of assessments for the period 2010–2012 on the basis of the elements of the methodology for the scale of assessments for the period 2001–2003, as set out in its resolution 55/5 B [YUN 2000, p. 1311] (see above). Meanwhile, in order to identify the impact of the inclusion of new GNI data in calculations for the 2010–2012 scale, the Committee on Contributions considered the application of new data to the methodology used in preparing the current scale and, for information, included the results in the report on its sixty-ninth (2009) session [A/64/11].

Assessment of non-member States

The Committee on Contributions [A/64/11] considered the assessment for one non-member State (the Holy See). It recommended continuation of the simplified methodology for assessing non-member States endorsed by the General Assembly in resolution 58/1 B [YUN 2003, p. 1424]; that the flat annual fee percentage of the Holy See remain fixed at 50 per cent; and that the notional rate of assessment for the Holy See for the period 2010–2012 be fixed at 0.001 per cent.

Accounts and auditing

The General Assembly, at its resumed sixty-third (2009) session, considered the report of the Board of Auditors on UN peacekeeping operations for the period 1 July 2007 to 30 June 2008 [A/63/5 (Vol. II)] and the related ACABQ report [A/63/746], together with the Secretary-General's report on the implementation of the Board's recommendations [A/63/784].

On 30 June, the Assembly, in **resolution 63/246 B**, endorsed the Board's report (see p. 89).

Board of Auditors reports. The Assembly, at its sixty-fourth session, had before it the reports of the Board of Auditors on the financial report and audited financial statements of the voluntary funds administered by the United Nations High Commissioner for Refugees [A/64/5/Add.5] (see p. 1199) and on the capital master plan [A/64/5 (Vol. V)] (see p. 1447) for the year ended 31 December 2008, as well as the Secretary-General's June note [A/64/98], submitted pursuant to resolution 52/212 B [YUN 2002, p. 1288], transmitting the report of the Board of Auditors on the implementation of its recommendations relating to the 2006–2007 biennium and covering the accounts of 15 organizations. The comments and recommendations of ACABQ on those reports were contained in the Committee's reports of 1 [A/64/469] and 28 October [A/64/7/Add.5].

On 22 December, the Assembly, in **resolution 64/228** (see p. 1447), took note of the Board's report on the capital master plan and endorsed the conclusions and recommendations of ACABQ.

GENERAL ASSEMBLY ACTION

On 22 December [meeting 67], the General Assembly, on the recommendation of the Fifth Committee [A/64/547], adopted **resolution 64/227** without vote [agenda item 129].

Financial reports and audited financial statements, and reports of the Board of Auditors

The General Assembly,

Recalling its resolutions 52/212 B of 31 March 1998, 57/278 A of 20 December 2002, 60/234 A and B of 23

December 2005 and 30 June 2006, 62/223 A and B of 22 December 2007 and 20 June 2008, and 63/246 A and B of 24 December 2008 and 30 June 2009,

Having considered the financial report and audited financial statements and the report of the Board of Auditors on the voluntary funds administered by the United Nations High Commissioner for Refugees for the year ended 31 December 2008, the note by the Secretary-General transmitting to the General Assembly the letter dated 10 July 2009 from the Chairman of the Board of Auditors transmitting the report of the Board on the implementation of its recommendations relating to the biennium 2006–2007, and the related report of the Advisory Committee on Administrative and Budgetary Questions,

1. *Accepts* the financial report and audited financial statements and the report and audit opinion of the Board of Auditors on the voluntary funds administered by the United Nations High Commissioner for Refugees for the year ended 31 December 2008;

2. *Endorses* the recommendations of the Board of Auditors contained in its report on the voluntary funds administered by the United Nations High Commissioner for Refugees for the year ended 31 December 2008;

3. *Notes* the concerns as contained in the qualified audit opinion of the Board of Auditors on the financial statements of the voluntary funds administered by the United Nations High Commissioner for Refugees for the year ended 31 December 2008, after its modified opinion on the financial statements for the year ended 31 December 2007, notes also the measures taken by the Office of the United Nations High Commissioner for Refugees to address the seriousness of its financial problems, and encourages the High Commissioner to implement all the recommendations of the Board and to report to the relevant governing bodies on progress made in this regard;

4. *Commends* the Board of Auditors for the quality of its report and the streamlined format thereof;

5. *Takes note* of the note by the Secretary-General transmitting to the General Assembly the letter dated 10 July 2009 from the Chairman of the Board of Auditors transmitting the report of the Board on the implementation of its recommendations relating to the biennium 2006–2007;

6. *Endorses* the conclusions and recommendations contained in the report of the Advisory Committee on Administrative and Budgetary Questions, subject to the provisions of the present resolution;

7. *Commends* the Board of Auditors for its identification of common reasons for the lack of full implementation of the recommendations, as well as good practices in relation to the implementation and follow-up of its reports;

8. *Requests* the Secretary-General and the executive heads of the funds and programmes of the United Nations to ensure full implementation of all the recommendations of the Board of Auditors and the related recommendations of the Advisory Committee on Administrative and Budgetary Questions in a prompt and timely manner and to continue to hold programme managers accountable for the non-implementation of recommendations;

9. *Reiterates its request* to the Secretary-General to provide in his reports on the implementation of the recom-

mendations of the Board of Auditors on the accounts of the United Nations as well as on the financial statements of its funds and programmes a full explanation for the delays in the implementation of the recommendations of the Board, in particular those not yet fully implemented that are two or more years old;

10. *Also reiterates its request* to the Secretary-General to indicate in future reports an expected time frame for the implementation of the recommendations of the Board of Auditors, as well as the priorities, benchmarks and deadlines, and measures to hold office holders accountable;

11. *Takes note* of paragraph 16 of the report of the Advisory Committee on Administrative and Budgetary Questions.

Financial management practices

International Public Sector Accounting Standards

In September, the Secretary-General submitted the second progress report [A/64/355] on the adoption of the International Public Sector Accounting Standards (IPSAS) by the United Nations, which provided an update on IPSAS implementation since the first progress report in 2008 [YUN 2008, p. 1561] and covered the period from 1 April 2008 to 31 July 2009. The General Assembly adopted IPSAS in 2006 by resolution 60/283 [YUN 2006, p. 1580].

The Secretary-General indicated that the major areas of achievement for the system-wide IPSAS Project Team had been the development of further accounting guidance papers, input into new standards, communication of IPSAS information, and the development of IPSAS training courses. Another main development was the decision of the High-Level Committee on Management to approve project continuance for the period 2010–2011. On implementation of IPSAS, all UN system organizations continued to make progress, and while some organizations had to push out their implementation dates to 2011, 2012 and, in the case of the United Nations, to 2014, 10 organizations reported that their target date remained 2010. A major accomplishment was the implementation of IPSAS, effective 1 January 2008, by the World Food Programme (WFP), which issued in May 2009 its first set of IPSAS-compliant financial statements for the year ended 31 December 2008. Those statements received an unqualified audit opinion from the external auditor.

On UN adoption of IPSAS, the target date for the first full set of IPSAS-compliant UN financial statements had been adjusted to 31 December 2014, subject to the successful and on-time implementation of the Umoja Project. The Secretary-General submitted a separate progress report on the enterprise resource planning (ERP) project (see p. 1439)—referred to as the Umoja Project—that recommended, inter alia, the most appropriate ERP implementation strategy for the Organization. Meanwhile, governance structure had been strengthened to provide more robust guidance, such as the expansion of the UN IPSAS Steering Committee membership to include representation from the field and all major stakeholders. On the IPSAS requirement for the presentation of consolidated financial statements for reporting entities and their controlled entities, the IPSAS Implementation Project Team initiated a project to consider further whether there was a requirement for the United Nations to present such statements under IPSAS; the issue of consolidation under IPSAS for the United Nations remained under examination, with further consultations required with the Office of Legal Affairs and the funds and programmes.

In a November report [A/64/531], ACABQ indicated that the WFP transition to IPSAS—becoming the first adopter within the UN system—was a milestone and emphasized the role of the Steering Committee and project team in drawing lessons learned from the experience of early adopters and in disseminating information to the other UN system entities, as well as in supporting participating organizations through all phases of their projects, providing guidance on implementation requirements and project planning, and monitoring implementation progress. ACABQ also emphasized the need to keep the training plan under review and to adjust requirements so as to ensure the efficient utilization of resources; requested the Secretary-General to ensure coordination between the ERP project and the IPSAS project teams; and encouraged the Secretary-General to pursue his examination of the IPSAS requirement for consolidated statements and its applicability to the UN system.

Review of UN administrative and financial functioning

In 2009, the General Assembly continued its consideration of the efficiency of the administrative and financial functioning of the United Nations. In that connection, the Secretary-General issued reports on UN procurement activities (see p. 1419). He also issued reports on the review of the practice of the Secretariat on the sharing of information contained in the reports of consultants on management-related issues, and the Independent Audit Advisory Committee (see p. 1423).

On 24 December, the Assembly decided that the agenda item on the review of the efficiency of UN administrative and financial functioning would remain for consideration during its resumed sixty-fourth (2010) session (**decision 64/549**).

Independent Audit Advisory Committee

Pursuant to General Assembly resolution 61/275 [YUN 2007, p. 1471], the Secretary-General submitted an August report [A/64/288] on the activities of the Independent Audit Advisory Committee, established in 2007 to serve in an expert advisory capacity and assist the Assembly in fulfilling its oversight responsibilities [ibid., p. 1471]. The report covered the period from 1 August 2008 to 31 July 2009, in which the Committee held four sessions, and summarized developments since its first annual report in 2008 [YUN 2008, p. 1562]. It also contained an overview of the Committee's sessions, the status of its recommendations and workplan for 2010, as well as the Committee's comments on the status of the recommendations of UN oversight bodies; the Office of Internal Oversight Services (OIOS) workplan and budget for 2009; risk management and internal control framework; and cooperation and access. Annexed to the report were recommendations of the Committee on the effectiveness, efficiency and impact of the audit activities and other oversight functions of the OIOS for consideration by the Assembly in its review of OIOS functions and reporting procedures.

During the reporting period, the Committee submitted three reports to the General Assembly, including on: the budget for OIOS under the support account for peacekeeping operations for the period from 1 July 2009 to 30 June 2010 [A/63/703]; the OIOS proposed programme budget for the 2010–2011 biennium [A/64/86]; and vacant posts in OIOS [A/63/737], bringing the total number of reports submitted to the Assembly to six. The Committee made 29 recommendations in its reports, two of which would be considered by the Assembly at its sixty-fourth session. Of the remaining 27 recommendations, 13 had been implemented, another 13 were in the process of being implemented and one was not commented on by the Assembly. Some of the recommendations related to: improving cooperation between OIOS and the Board of Auditors and the Joint Inspection Unit; the need for modification of the risk-based approach of OIOS to work planning for internal audit; the reorganization of the OIOS Investigations Division; the need for OIOS to focus on the value it delivers to the Organization; the need for a definition of key oversight terms; and the immediate and urgent action required to fill vacant posts in OIOS. The Committee's workplan presented the key focus area for each of its 2010 (ninth to twelfth) sessions.

Programme planning

On 2, 10, 16, 18 and 21 December, the General Assembly took note, respectively, of the reports of the First (Disarmament and International Security)

Committee [A/64/400] (**decision 64/518**), Fourth (Special Political and Decolonization) Committee [A/64/415] (**decision 64/523**), Sixth (Legal) Committee [A/64/462] (**decision 64/526**), Third (Social, Humanitarian and Cultural) Committee [A/64/443] (**decision 64/539**); and Second (Economic and Financial) Committee [A/64/429] (**decision 64/545**).

GENERAL ASSEMBLY ACTION

On 22 December [meeting 67], the General Assembly, on the recommendation of the Fifth Committee [A/64/549], adopted **resolution 64/229** without vote [agenda item 133].

Programme planning

The General Assembly,

Recalling its resolutions 37/234 of 21 December 1982, 38/227 A of 20 December 1983, 41/213 of 19 December 1986, 55/234 of 23 December 2000, 57/282 of 20 December 2002, 58/268 and 58/269 of 23 December 2003, 59/275 of 23 December 2004, 60/257 of 8 May 2006, 61/235 of 22 December 2006, 62/224 of 22 December 2007 and 63/247 of 24 December 2008,

Recalling also the terms of reference of the Committee for Programme and Coordination, as outlined in the annex to Economic and Social Council resolution 2008(LX) of 14 May 1976,

Having considered the report of the Committee for Programme and Coordination on the work of its forty-ninth session,

1. *Reaffirms* the role of the Committee for Programme and Coordination as the main subsidiary organ of the General Assembly and the Economic and Social Council for planning, programming and coordination;

2. *Re-emphasizes* the role of the plenary and the Main Committees of the General Assembly in reviewing and taking action on the appropriate recommendations of the Committee for Programme and Coordination relevant to their work, in accordance with regulation 4.10 of the Regulations and Rules Governing Programme Planning, the Programme Aspects of the Budget, the Monitoring of Implementation and the Methods of Evaluation;

3. *Stresses* that setting the priorities of the United Nations is the prerogative of the Member States, as reflected in legislative mandates;

4. *Also stresses* the need for Member States to participate fully in the budget preparation process, from its early stages and throughout the process;

5. *Endorses* the conclusions and recommendations of the Committee for Programme and Coordination on evaluation, on the annual overview report of the United Nations System Chief Executives Board for Coordination for 2008/09, on United Nations system support for the New Partnership for Africa's Development and on improving the working methods and procedures of the Committee within the framework of its mandate.

On 24 December, the Assembly decided that the item on programme planning would remain for consideration during its resumed sixty-fourth (2010) session (**decision 64/549**).

Programme performance

Evaluation

OIOS reports to CPC. The Secretary-General transmitted to the Committee for Programme and Coordination the OIOS evaluation reports on strengthening the role of evaluation and the application of evaluation findings on programme design, delivery and policy directives [A/64/63 & Corr.1]; the evaluation of UN support for least developed countries, landlocked developing countries, small island developing States and Africa [E/AC.51/2009/2]; the triennial review of the implementation of recommendations made by CPC at its forty-sixth session on the in-depth evalua-

tion of political affairs [E/AC.51/2009/3]; the triennial review of the implementation of recommendations made by CPC at its forty-sixth session on the thematic evaluation of knowledge management networks in the pursuit of the goals of the Millennium Declaration [E/AC.51/2009/4]; the thematic evaluation of lessons learned: protocols and practices [E/AC.51/2009/5]; and the thematic evaluation of UN coordinating bodies [E/AC.51/2009/6].

CPC comments and recommendations on those reports were contained in the report on its 2009 session [A/64/16].

By **decision 2009/217** of 24 July, the Economic and Social Council took note of the CPC report.

Chapter III

Administrative and staff matters

During 2009, the General Assembly continued to review the administrative functioning of the Organization and matters related to United Nations staff. In April, the General Assembly, by resolution 63/269, reaffirmed the need for a global operational framework to enable the United Nations to respond to emergency situations that might impair operations of critical elements of its information and communications technology infrastructure and facilities, and encouraged the Secretary-General to take a unified approach to disaster recovery and business continuity. In October, the Secretary-General presented a framework for a unified approach to disaster recovery and business continuity, highlighting the guiding principles of a strategy for an Organization-wide plan. Also in October, the Secretary-General submitted his first progress report on the enterprise resource planning project (Umoja), cornerstone of reform to the administrative and peacekeeping support functions of the United Nations. In addition, he presented a proposal for risk mitigation measures to protect data and the information and communications systems of the Secretariat during construction work of the capital master plan. The Assembly also adopted resolutions on the capital master plan, the report of the work of the Joint Inspection Unit for 2008 and programme of work for 2009, the timely submission of documents, the pattern of conferences, and the report of the Office of Internal Oversight Services on its activities, as well as on the need to harmonize and improve UN informatics systems for optimal utilization and accessibility by all States.

Attacks against the safety and security of UN personnel continued: 27 civilian staff members lost their lives as a result of acts of violence between 1 July 2008 and 30 June 2009. Increased challenges to the UN security management system worldwide compelled an extensive review of operating procedures, driven by the need to expand and sustain operations, particularly in conflict or post-conflict areas. Following the report of the Independent Panel on Safety and Security of United Nations Personnel and Premises Worldwide, the High-Level Committee on Management, at the request of the Secretary-General, undertook a detailed review of the report's recommendations.

During the year, the Assembly, through the International Civil Service Commission, continued to review the conditions of service of staff of the UN common system and adopted the Commission's rec-

ommendations relating to post adjustment, review of separation payments, and considerations related to reviewing the job evaluation standards for the General Service and related categories.

The Secretary-General also reported on: human resources development; human resources challenges within the UN development system at the country level; liabilities and proposed funding for after-service health insurance benefits; an audit of human resources management at the Office of the United Nations High Commissioner for Human Rights; implementation of continuing appointments; provisional staff rules; amendments to the Staff Regulations; safety and security of humanitarian and UN personnel; activities of the Ethics Office; staff composition of the Secretariat; protection from sexual exploitation and abuse; travel and related matters; and the United Nations Joint Staff Pension Fund.

In July, the new system of administration of justice at the United Nations came into effect, under which the following bodies were abolished as of 1 July: Joint Appeals Board; Joint Disciplinary Committees; United Nations Administrative Tribunal; Panels of Counsel; and Panels on Discrimination and Other Grievances. The Assembly also took action on the Secretary-General's reports on the activities of the Office of the Ombudsman and Mediation Services; approval of the rules of procedure of the United Nations Dispute Tribunal and the United Nations Appeals Tribunal; criminal behaviour and disciplinary action; and criminal accountability of UN officials and experts on mission.

Administrative matters

Managerial reform and oversight

Procurement

In a comprehensive report on UN procurement activities [A/64/284] issued in August, the Secretary-General provided information on the implementation of the procurement reform agenda proposed in 2006 [YUN 2006, p. 1644], focusing on strengthening internal controls, optimizing the procurement process and establishing a strategic procurement function. He said that the restructuring of the Procurement Division had been implemented, creating the Procurement

Operations Service and the Integrated Support Service, with a view to strengthening internal controls. A pilot independent bid protest system was operationalized, allowing unsuccessful bidders to file challenges and request review of award decisions; and a Senior Vendor Review Committee, chaired by the Director of the Ethics Office, was created to advise the Organization on proposed sanction in cases of fraud or unethical behaviour. Steps were also taken to safeguard the independence of the Headquarters Committee on Contracts; to revise the United Nations General Conditions of Contract, especially relating to subcontractors; and to update the vendor database and implement a new, streamlined vendor registration process. A contract for the new Enterprise Resource Planning software was negotiated to provide a unified database across the Organization, as well as tools to strengthen internal controls. The report also discussed additional governance issues such as ethics, integrity and conflict of interest, staff management and training, as well as the optimization of the procurement process including partnership in procurement activities with other UN organizations, implementation of the best value for money principle, and contract management. The report noted the high workload and low staffing of the Procurement Division, which increased the potential for a deficient acquisition process and risks associated with the procurement function.

On strategic procurement management, the Secretary-General reported that out of the $3.2 billion spent in 2008 for goods and services for Headquarters and peacekeeping missions, 46 per cent was spent on vendors in developing countries and countries with economies in transition, an increase of 48 per cent over 2007. He highlighted initiatives taken by the Procurement Division and field missions to promote the participation of vendors in those countries, including the signing of a cooperation agreement with the World Chambers Federation of the International Chamber of Commerce on 4 June; the development in the United Nations Global Marketplace of a local vendor database; the proposal to grant local vendors with limited or no Internet access free access to peacekeeping mission Internet facilities to register as vendors; and consideration of supplier financing to alleviate finance-related challenges. The policy on security instruments was redesigned to accommodate small businesses so as to avoid any restrictions on access to UN procurement opportunities; and the number of business seminars conducted in developing countries and countries with economies in transition had increased.

The Secretary-General, while stressing that a modern procurement function must develop three critical pillars—information technology support, expert staff, and a policy and training framework—noted that the Secretariat procurement function was not adequately equipped with the necessary resources. In order for the Division to cope with the increasing volume, complexity and tempo of peacekeeping activities, the Secretary-General called upon Member States to recognize that procurement was indispensable to the smooth and effective implementation of the activities of the Organization and required their full support.

In an August addendum on procurement governance arrangements within the United Nations [A/64/284/Add.1], submitted pursuant to General Assembly resolution 59/288 [YUN 2005, p. 1471] and 61/246 [YUN 2006, p. 1645], the Secretary-General outlined the regulatory framework within which the UN procurement functions were performed, as well as the internal control framework, and proposed an updated and streamlined governance arrangement between the Department of Management and the Department of Field Support for the performance of the procurement function. Under the proposed arrangement, the Procurement Division and its Department of Field Support clients would be co-located to improve coordination between the procurement officers in the Department of Management and the logisticians in the Department of Field Support. The Procurement Division would also increase its participation in technical assessment teams in peacekeeping missions, and its staff at Headquarters would participate in short-term staff exchanges in the field missions. Department of Field Support staff would participate in the Headquarters Committee on Contracts. To improve the quality and timeliness of procurement services to missions, the Department of Field Support intended to create a regional procurement office to respond to urgent requirements in field operations. The department was pursuing the option of Entebbe, Uganda, as a suitable location to establish the shared-services model and outposted procurement office on a pilot basis. The arrangement would optimize the procurement process for peacekeeping operations while maintaining adequate control mechanisms. The proposal was accompanied by an action plan, consisting of an implementation plan for the short term, to be completed by the end of 2009, and one for the medium term, to be completed by the end of 2011.

In another August addendum on sustainable procurement [A/64/284/Add.2], issued in response to resolution 62/269 [YUN 2008, p. 1568], the Secretary-General reported on the content and criteria for the concept of sustainable procurement and its possible impact on the diversification of the origin of vendors and international competition, including for developing countries and countries with economies in transition. The Secretary-General described sustainable procurement as an acquisition process for meeting the requirements for goods and services so as to achieve value for money on a whole-life basis in terms of generating benefits not only to the Organization, but also to society and the economy, while minimizing its impact on the environment. The concept of sustainable procurement fitted well within the principles guiding the UN procurement function, namely, best value for money; fairness, integrity and transparency; effective international competition; and the interest of the Organization. It would be implemented in phases, at a pace determined by the degree of maturity of the supply market, the development of a policy framework, staff training and the readiness of the United Nations to fully embrace the concept.

Regarding the impact on the diversification of the origin of vendors and on international competition, the Secretary-General stated that due to the volume of the Secretariat's procurement, the United Nations could play a role in shaping the business culture of its suppliers through ethical and socially responsible management of the procurement function. By seeking the most appropriate solutions for particular requirements, UN procurement could help to open up new opportunities for all its vendors by allowing them to offer new and innovative solutions to meeting UN requirements. Competition would not be limited to those vendors offering high-tech solutions, but would include the whole spectrum of vendors, including those offering low-tech solutions that best fitted the requisitioner's need.

The Secretary-General emphasized that sustainable procurement was an enabler and a fundamental tenet for sustainable development programmes. A gradual implementation of sustainable procurement would formalize values, principles and provisions existing in the Organization and in commercial markets where the UN Secretariat operated, and would facilitate an evolution of the procurement function towards a more inclusive and responsible buying approach.

OIOS report. The Office of Internal Oversight Services (OIOS) in September reported [A/64/369] on its audit of the activities of the Procurement Division for the period 2006–2008. The audit covered areas of strategy, governance, the procurement process and information resources in order to assess whether the related systems and internal controls were adequately designed and implemented in a manner that ensured the efficient and effective use of resources. It also reviewed the status of procurement reform carried out since 1995. The audit concluded that a more clearly defined governance structure, a comprehensive strategy and reliable management information systems were needed for the effective management and oversight of UN procurement.

The audit found that, although the Division had made progress in implementing the stated reform activities, not all of the activities deemed as procurement reform could be considered real reform. More-

over, critical reforms still needed to be implemented, including the procurement governance structure, the bid protest system, the Enterprise Resource Planning system and the ethics guidelines. The delegation of authority to the Procurement Division for high-value procurement needed to be reviewed for short-term logistics and transportation contracts, and the compensatory control to review them on an ex post facto basis was not established. While the annual procurement increased from $2.1 billion in 2006 to $3.3 billion in 2008, no comprehensive procurement strategy involving senior management was documented. Due to the lack of a formal and comprehensive strategy, procurement actions appeared to be ad hoc and at times ineffective and not in the best interests of the Organization. The Division lacked an information and communications technology infrastructure to support its operations and control environment. Various control weaknesses were identified, such as limited validation controls and unreliable data fields, exposing the Organization to system vulnerabilities and risks of unreliable data. As a result, OIOS could not monitor, query and analyse procurement data in a systematic manner to identify potential risks and cases of non-compliance with United Nations Regulations and Rules. At the conclusion of the audit, OIOS made 39 recommendations, 25 of which were to mitigate high-risk areas. The Department of Management rejected 19 recommendations, including 13 addressing high-risk areas. OIOS reiterated the rejected recommendations and requested the Department to reconsider them.

ACABQ report. In its comments [A/64/501] on the Secretary-General's report (see p. 1419), the Advisory Committee on Administrative and Budgetary Questions (ACABQ) in October said that the report did not provide a basis for assessing improvements in the procurement function or the adequacy of the internal control. It requested that, in future reports, the Secretary-General provide data and other evidence to substantiate the statements on the progress achieved, including performance indicators, and present the totality of procurement volume of the entire Secretariat, including for offices away from Headquarters, tribunals and regional commissions. The Committee stressed that the implementation of delegated authority should be regularly monitored and offices equipped to evaluate and manage the associated risk. It recommended elaborating the proposal for establishing regional procurement offices, explaining how the objectives and the benefits would be realized, and recommended improving the functioning of the end-to-end supply chain at the Secretariat. ACABQ noted the launching of the pilot project establishing an independent award review board and requested the Secretary-General to clarify its terms of reference and authority and provide statistics on the cases reviewed.

Noting that the Senior Vendor Review Committee, established in June, was chaired by the Director of the Ethics Office, the Committee expressed concern with the potential proliferation of new structures, and requested the Secretary-General to address whether future procurement activities could be accommodated from within existing ones. It expressed reservations about the chairing of the Committee by the Director of the Ethics Office.

The involvement of the Headquarters Committee on Contracts in the procurement process, especially when reviewing cases for field missions, should be clarified and the Committee's composition and administrative arrangements reviewed. The Secretary-General should report on the experience gained in implementing the delegation of procurement authority, including information on action taken to strengthen monitoring, oversight and accountability. ACABQ welcomed the proactive approach taken to increase procurement opportunities for vendors from developing countries and countries with economies in transition, and encouraged the Secretary-General to continue efforts in that regard. It recommended using business seminars effectively to generate awareness about opportunities and the procedural requirements for participation in UN procurement activities. With regard to sustainable procurement, ACABQ stated that its implementation should be explored with caution, consistent with best market practices and UN procurement principles. However, it should not become a new challenge to the participation of developing countries and countries with economies in transition in UN procurement activities.

By **decision 64/548 A** of 24 December, the General Assembly deferred until its sixty-fifth (2010) session consideration of the Secretary-General's reports on UN procurement activities, procurement governance arrangements within the United Nations and sustainable procurement; the ACABQ report thereon; and the OIOS report on the audit of procurement management in the Secretariat (see above).

Oversight

Internal oversight

By **decision 63/550 C** of 30 June, the General Assembly deferred until its sixty-fourth (2009) session consideration of the report on the activities of OIOS in 2007 [YUN 2008, p. 1573], the note by the Secretary-General transmitting his comments thereon [A/62/281 (Part II)/Add.1] and the OIOS report on peacekeeping operations (see p. 78).

OIOS activities. In August, the Under-Secretary-General for OIOS, Inga-Britt Ahlenius, transmitted the OIOS annual report [A/64/326 (Part I) & Corr.1] covering activities from 1 July 2008 to 30 June 2009,

except for the results of OIOS peacekeeping oversight activities that would be reported to the Assembly separately. The report covered initiatives aimed at improving OIOS operations and quality of work; oversight findings by risk category; and mandated reporting on oversight activities concerning the capital master plan and the United Nations Compensation Commission. During the reporting period, OIOS issued 390 oversight reports, including 12 reports to the General Assembly and 59 closure reports. The reports included 1,941 recommendations to improve internal controls, accountability mechanisms and organizational efficiency and effectiveness. Of those recommendations, 635 were classified as critical to the Organization. The financial implications of OIOS recommendations issued during the period amounted to approximately $49 million. The financial implications of similar recommendations that were satisfactorily implemented during the period totalled approximately $32 million.

The Under-Secretary-General stressed that transparency was the primary condition for accountability and reiterated the importance of resolution 59/272 [YUN 2004, p. 1370], stating that increased transparency would not be fully achieved without increased public access to other types of UN documentation. Assignments conducted during the reporting period underscored the need for the Organization to develop an accountability framework, including a formal internal control framework, to ensure that risks were managed consistently and systematically through focused control processes across the Organization.

An addendum [A/64/326 (Part I)/Add.1] provided an assessment of the implementation of OIOS recommendations and an analysis of those not fully implemented.

In September [A/64/326 (Part I)/Add.2], the Secretary-General submitted his comments on Part I of the OIOS annual report and the related addendum.

In addition to the report on its own activities, OIOS issued, in 2009, reports to the Assembly on: peacekeeping operations [A/63/302 (Part II)]; audit of the use of extraordinary measures for the African Union-United Nations Hybrid Operations in Darfur [A/63/668]; programme evaluation of the performance and the achievement of results by the United Nations Operation in Côte d'Ivoire [A/63/713]; audit of the Secretariat structure for managing and sustaining peacekeeping operations [A/63/837]; strengthening the role of evaluation and the application of evaluation findings on programme design, delivery and policy directives [A/64/63 & Corr.1]; evaluation of UN support for the least developed countries, landlocked developing countries, small island developing States and Africa [E/AC.51/2009/2]; triennial review of the implementation of recommendations made by the Committee for Programme and Coordination (CPC) at its forty-sixth session on the in-depth evaluation of political affairs [E/AC.51/2009/3]; triennial review of the implementation of recommendations made by CPC at its forty-sixth session on the thematic evaluation of knowledge management networks in the pursuit of the goals of the United Nations Millennium Declaration [E/AC.51/2009/4]; thematic evaluation of lessons learned: protocols and practices [E/AC.51/2009/5]; thematic evaluation of UN coordinating bodies [E/AC.51/2009/6]; evaluation of the integrated global management initiative of the Department for General Assembly and Conference Management (DGACM) [A/64/166]; audit of human resources management of the Office of the United Nations High Commissioner for Human Rights (OHCHR) [A/64/201]; efficiency of the implementation of the mandate of OHCHR [A/64/203 & Corr.1]; follow-up audit of the management of special political missions by the Department of Political Affairs [A/64/294]; audit of procurement management in the Secretariat [A/64/369]; audit of conference services put at the disposal of the Human Rights Council in 2009 [A/64/511]; and review of the Secretariat practice regarding the sharing of information contained in reports of consultants on management-related issues [A/64/587].

Independent Audit Advisory Committee. The Independent Audit Advisory Committee, in its second annual report [A/64/288], reviewed its activities from 1 August 2008 to 31 July 2009, the status of its recommendations and plans for 2010, as well as comments on the effectiveness, efficiency and impact of its audit activities and other oversight functions for consideration by the General Assembly. The Committee made 29 recommendations during the reporting period, 13 of which had been implemented and 13 were being implemented. Among its significant recommendations were suggestions for improving cooperation between OIOS and the Board of Auditors and the Joint Inspection Unit; modification of OIOS risk-based approach to work planning for internal audit, involving the revision of the risk assessment framework; the reorganization of the OIOS Investigations Division; definition of key oversight terms; and urgent action to fill vacant posts in OIOS. The Advisory Committee proposed a definition of the role and operational independence of OIOS, and defined what constituted impairment to its independence. It advised that the Under-Secretary-General for Internal Oversight should provide assurance of that independence in the annual report and disclose any details of impairment. The Advisory Committee also recommended that OIOS should prepare an internal oversight charter, which would serve as its terms of reference. In terms of transparency and fa-

cilitating Member States' access to internal oversight reports, the Advisory Committee recommended that the implementation of Assembly resolution 59/272 [YUN 2004, p. 1370] on making internal oversight reports available to Member States should be reviewed and/or revised.

The General Assembly, on 24 December, deferred consideration of the Advisory Committee's report until the first part of its resumed sixty-fourth (2010) session (**decision 64/548 A**).

OIOS vacant posts

In February, the Independent Audit Advisory Committee submitted a report on vacant posts in OIOS [A/63/737]. The Committee noted that OIOS had vacancies for over 27 per cent of its authorized posts and that the Assembly, in resolution 63/265 [YUN 2008, p. 1574], had expressed concern over the number of vacancies in the OIOS Investigations Division since the beginning of 2008, and had requested the Secretary-General to make every effort to fill them. Of particular concern to the Committee was the fact that all three Director-level positions within OIOS were vacant, and that the high vacancy rate could adversely affect OIOS capacity to accomplish its programme of work and to cover certain risks in the Organization. Taking into account the Assembly's concern, the Committee advised that all possibilities with the UN regulations and rules be explored, including the judicious use of temporary staff to minimize the adverse impact of vacant posts on the completion of the OIOS programme of work. It noted the disagreement between management and OIOS regarding recruitment and selection processes for posts at the director level, particularly that of the Director of the Investigations Division. The Committee agreed to bring the matter to the attention of the Assembly and urged that immediate action be taken to have the vacant posts filled.

The General Assembly, on 7 April, deferred consideration of the Committee's report until the second part of its resumed sixty-third (2009) session (**decision 63/550 B**).

In August [A/64/288], the Independent Advisory Committee was informed that the vacancy rate had improved to 22 per cent. A recommendation concerning the post of Director of Investigations had been submitted for the Secretary-General's approval and candidates for the Director of Internal Audit Division and Director of the Inspection and Evaluation Division were under consideration. The Committee said that it would continue to monitor implementation by OIOS of the recommendations relating to the filling of vacancies.

GENERAL ASSEMBLY ACTION

On 22 December [meeting 67], the General Assembly, on the recommendation of the Fifth (Administrative and Budgetary) Committee [A/64/551], adopted **resolution 64/232** without vote [agenda item 140].

Report of the Office of Internal Oversight Services on its activities

The General Assembly,

Recalling its resolutions 48/218 B of 29 July 1994, 54/244 of 23 December 1999, 59/272 of 23 December 2004, 60/259 of 8 May 2006, 61/275 of 29 June 2007, 63/265 of 24 December 2008, 63/276 of 7 April 2009 and 63/287 of 30 June 2009,

Having considered the report of the Office of Internal Oversight Services on its activities for the period from 1 July 2008 to 30 June 2009 and the related note by the Secretary-General, as well as chapter III of the annual report of the Independent Audit Advisory Committee,

1. *Reaffirms* its primary role in the consideration of and action taken on reports submitted to it;

2. *Also reaffirms* its oversight role and the role of the Fifth Committee in administrative and budgetary matters;

3. *Further reaffirms* the independence and the separate and distinct roles of the internal and external oversight mechanisms;

4. *Recalls* that the Office of Internal Oversight Services shall exercise operational independence under the authority of the Secretary-General relating to the performance of its internal oversight functions, in accordance with the relevant resolutions;

5. *Encourages* United Nations internal and external oversight bodies to enhance the level of their cooperation with one another, such as joint work planning sessions, without prejudice to the independence of each;

6. *Emphasizes* the importance to effective internal oversight of good cooperation at all levels between management and the Office of Internal Oversight Services;

7. *Notes with appreciation* the work of the Independent Audit Advisory Committee;

8. *Recalls* that in its resolution 61/275 it approved the terms of reference of the Independent Audit Advisory Committee;

9. *Takes note* of the report of the Office of Internal Oversight Services on its activities for the period from 1 July 2008 to 30 June 2009 and the related note by the Secretary-General;

10. *Also takes note* of chapter III of the annual report of the Independent Audit Advisory Committee in respect of the Office of Internal Oversight Services;

11. *Stresses* that all reports of the Office of Internal Oversight Services shall continue to be submitted in accordance with the format prescribed in section IV, paragraphs 7 and 8, of General Assembly resolution 63/248 of 24 December 2008;

12. *Requests* the Secretary-General to address recurring recommendations of the Office of Internal Oversight Services dealing with issues that are systemic in nature;

13. *Also requests* the Secretary-General to ensure the full implementation of the accepted recommendations of the Office of Internal Oversight Services in a prompt and timely manner and to provide detailed justifications in cases where recommendations of the Office are not accepted;

14. *Further requests* the Secretary-General to ensure that all relevant resolutions, including resolutions of a cross-cutting nature, are brought to the attention of relevant managers, and that the Office of Internal Oversight Services also takes those resolutions into account in the conduct of its activities;

15. *Requests* the Secretary-General to ensure that all relevant resolutions pertaining to the work of the Office of Internal Oversight Services are brought to the attention of the relevant managers;

16. *Expresses deep concern* at the recommendations of the Office of Internal Oversight Services referred to in paragraph 37 of its report, and reiterates that the Office shall not propose to the General Assembly any change in the legislative decisions and mandates approved by intergovernmental legislative bodies;

17. *Urges* the Secretary-General to ensure that the Office of Internal Oversight Services conducts its activities in accordance with its mandate as contained in resolutions 48/218 B, 54/244 and 59/272 and in the present resolution;

18. *Reiterates its requests* to the Secretary-General to make every effort to fill vacancies in the Office of Internal Oversight Services as a matter of priority, in accordance with the existing relevant provisions governing recruitment in the United Nations;

19. *Notes* that the five-year non-renewable term of the Under-Secretary-General for Internal Oversight Services will expire in July 2010, and in this regard urges the Secretary-General to ensure that timely arrangements are made to find a successor in full conformity with the provisions of paragraph 5 *(b)* of resolution 48/218 B.

On 24 December, the Assembly decided that the items on the appointment of the Under-Secretary-General for Internal Oversight Services and the report on OIOS activities would remain for consideration during its resumed sixty-fourth (2010) session (**decision 64/549**).

External oversight

Joint Inspection Unit

At its resumed sixty-third session, the General Assembly had before it the annual report of the Joint Inspection Unit (JIU) for 2008 and its programme of work for 2009 [YUN 2008, p. 1579].

Note of Secretary-General. In response to Assembly resolution 62/246 [YUN 2008, p. 1578], the Secretary-General in February [A/63/731] outlined steps taken to support JIU. He said that, as a matter of practice, system-wide JIU reports were circulated for comment upon receipt and all participating organizations were requested to respond with their comments. Regarding the provision of support to JIU by the secretariats of participating organizations, additional efforts were taken to enhance the dialogue between the secretariats of JIU and the United Nations System Chief Executives Board for Coordination (CEB). In particular, the CEB High-level Committee on Management, at its sixteenth session [YUN 2008, p. 1527], considered ways to enhance collaboration with JIU, including by encouraging its members to review communication procedures within their respective organizations to ensure a better information flow. Furthermore, CEB, at JIU's request, implemented an extensive consultation process for providing inputs to JIU's 2009 programme of work. A closer informal working relationship between the two secretariats resulted in an increased responses rate and more involvement by organizations in the preparation of reports. The Secretary-General undertook to pursue a closer working relationship with JIU and to encourage all organizations to respond quickly and in a spirit of cooperation to its requests.

GENERAL ASSEMBLY ACTION

On 7 April [meeting 79], the General Assembly, on the recommendation of the Fifth Committee [A/63/786], adopted **resolution 63/272** without vote [agenda item 124].

Report of the Joint Inspection Unit for 2008 and programme of work for 2009

The General Assembly,

Reaffirming its previous resolutions on the Joint Inspection Unit, in particular resolutions 31/192 of 22 December 1976, 50/233 of 7 June 1996, 54/16 of 29 October 1999, 55/230 of 23 December 2000, 56/245 of 24 December 2001, 57/284 A and B of 20 December 2002, 58/286 of 8 April 2004, 59/267 of 23 December 2004, 60/258 of 8 May 2006, 61/238 of 22 December 2006, 61/260 of 4 April 2007, 62/226 of 22 December 2007 and 62/246 of 3 April 2008,

Reiterating that the impact of the Unit on the cost-effectiveness of activities within the United Nations system is a shared responsibility of the Member States, the Unit and the secretariats of the participating organizations,

Reaffirming the commitment by the Unit, the legislative organs and the secretariats of the participating organizations to implement a system of follow-up to the recommendations of the Unit, as set out in resolution 54/16,

Reaffirming also the statute of the Unit and the unique role of the Unit as the only external and independent system-wide inspection, evaluation and investigation body,

Having considered the report of the Joint Inspection Unit for 2008 and programme of work for 2009 and the note by the Secretary-General on the report of the Unit for 2008,

1. *Recalls* its resolutions 61/260, 62/226 and 62/246;

2. *Takes note with appreciation* of the report of the Joint Inspection Unit for 2008 and programme of work for 2009;

3. *Takes note* of the note by the Secretary-General;

4. *Affirms* that oversight is a shared responsibility of Member States, the organizations and the internal and external oversight bodies;

5. *Welcomes* progress in the reform process of the Unit and its improved collaboration with participating organizations and other oversight bodies, and invites the Unit to report to the General Assembly at its sixty-fourth session on measures taken in this regard;

6. *Acknowledges* the Unit's undertaking to apply results-based management in its work;

7. *Requests* the Unit, in line with its mandate, to continue to focus its work and reports on system-wide issues of interest and relevance to the participating organizations and the States Members of the United Nations and to provide advice on ways to ensure the avoidance of duplication and more efficient and effective use of resources in implementing the mandates of the Organization;

8. *Reiterates its request* to the executive heads of the participating organizations to fully comply with the statutory procedures for consideration of the reports of the Unit and, in particular, to submit their comments and to distribute reports in time for their consideration by legislative organs;

9. *Reiterates its request* to the Secretary-General and the other executive heads of the participating organizations to fully assist the Unit with the timely provision of all information requested by it;

10. *Reiterates its invitation* to the legislative organs of the participating organizations to take concrete action on the recommendations of the Unit;

11. *Requests* the Secretary-General, in his capacity as Chairman of the United Nations System Chief Executives Board for Coordination, to expedite the implementation of the present resolution, including through the expected provision of support to the Unit by the secretariats of the participating organizations in the preparation of its reports, notes and confidential letters, and the consideration of and action on the Unit's recommendations in the light of pertinent resolutions of the General Assembly, and to report to the Assembly on an annual basis on the results achieved;

12. *Notes with appreciation* the ongoing efforts of the Unit to report on the impacts of its recommendations, as illustrated in chapter I, section E, of its annual report, and in this context requests the Unit, in coordination with participating organizations, to provide information on the improvement of the presentation of those impacts and their financial implications, wherever possible, in future annual reports;

13. *Invites* the Unit, in this context, to include in its annual report information on its experience in the implementation of the follow-up system by the participating organizations, and in this regard requests the Unit to continue working towards implementation of a web-based follow-up system to monitor the status of recommendations and receive updates from individual organizations;

14. *Recalls* paragraph 17 of its resolution 62/246, and encourages the Secretary-General, in his capacity as Chairman of the Chief Executives Board, to continue enhancing the dialogue of the Board with the Unit, including, where appropriate, through the invitation to participate in the meetings of its Committees and networks;

15. *Welcomes* the coordination of the Unit with the Board of Auditors and the Office of Internal Oversight Services of the Secretariat, and encourages those bodies to continue sharing experiences, knowledge, best practices and lessons learned with other United Nations audit and oversight bodies as well as with the Independent Audit Advisory Committee;

16. *Requests* the Secretary-General to expedite the appointment of the Executive Secretary of the Joint Inspection Unit after consultation with the Unit and the Chief Executives Board, in full accordance with article 19 of the statute of the Unit as well as the relevant provisions of the resolutions of the General Assembly regarding staff selection;

17. *Acknowledges* the undertaking by the Unit of a medium- and long-term strategy approach for 2010–2019, as contained in annex III to its report, stresses the need for the Unit to continuously update and improve its medium- and long-term strategy for 2010–2019, taking into account the dynamics and challenges of the environment in which it undertakes its activities, and decides to consider any resources associated with the implementation of the medium- and long-term strategy approach in the context of future programme budgets;

18. *Encourages* the Unit to keep the General Assembly informed, if necessary, about any difficulty or delay in obtaining visas for the official travel of the inspectors, as well as members of its secretariat.

JIU activities. In its annual report to the Assembly [A/64/34], JIU reviewed its activities in 2009, during which it issued reports on: management review of environmental governance within the UN system [JIU/REP/2008/3]; review of management and administration in the World Tourism Organization [JIU/REP/2009/1]; second follow-up to the management review of OHCHR [JIU/REP/2009/2]; effectiveness of the International Telecommunications Union regional presence [JIU/REP/2009/3]; assessment of the Global Mechanism of the United Nations Convention to Combat Desertification [JIU/REP/2009/4]; towards more coherent UN system support to Africa [JIU/REP/2009/5]; offshoring in UN system organizations [JIU/REP/2009/6]; review of management and administration in the World Food Programme [JIU/REP/2009/7]; selection and conditions of service of executive heads in UN system organizations [JIU/REP/2009/8]; and role of the special representatives of the Secretary-General and resident coordinators: a benchmarking framework for coherence and integration within the UN system [JIU/REP/2009/9]. It also issued notes on corporate sponsoring in the UN system: principles and guidelines [JIU/NOTE/2009/1]; internships in the UN system [JIU/NOTE/2009/2]; as well as management letters on disbursement of travel advances by travellers cheques at the United Nations Office at Geneva [JIU/ML/2009/1]; and membership criteria for inclusion in International Organizations of Geneva Joint Airlines Negotiating Group [JIU/ML/2009/2].

During the year, JIU continued to improve its working methods to achieve greater efficiency. It reviewed its internal working procedures in all key areas to streamline its operation and administrative arrangements. It also acted upon the self-evaluation undertaken in 2008 by its secretariat [YUN 2008, p. 1579], which confirmed an increased appreciation for JIU's work and indicated some early results of its reform efforts, but also revealed a number of areas for improvement, such as follow-up to recommendations, quality control, documentation management, knowledge-sharing and human resources. The Unit's management was strengthened with the arrival of the new Executive Secretary in August and the subsequent realignment of the work of the secretariat to allow for a more coherent grouping of tasks in preparing and implementing the annual plan of work. JIU worked on 21 ongoing assignments, 11 of which were completed—eight carried over from previous work programmes and three from the current one. JIU enhanced its dialogue with participating organizations in line with its revised policy and guidelines adopted in 2008 [ibid.], and the designated focal point inspectors solicited interviews with officials of participating organizations to discuss ways to improve mutual relations.

At the end of 2009, JIU had received information from all but four participating organizations to its request to provide information on recommendations issued from 2006 to 2008. The response rate was unchanged from the previous year. For the 183 recommendations contained in single-organization reports issued between 2006 and 2008, the overall acceptance rate of 64 per cent remained unchanged as compared to the previous reporting period (2005–2007). No information was provided for 13 per cent of the recommendations, 14 per cent were rejected and 11 per cent were under consideration. For the 283 recommendations contained in the system-wide reports, the low overall acceptance rate of 49 per cent was due to the fact that no information had been provided for 40 per cent of them; only 3 per cent were rejected, while 8 per cent were under consideration. As to implementation of accepted recommendations in single-organization reports, the overall rate improved, with 49 per cent of recommendations implemented and 32 per cent in progress, against 33 and 40 per cent, respectively, in the previous period. Implementation rate for system-wide reports also improved, with 50 per cent of the recommendations implemented and 33 per cent in progress, compared to 43 per cent and 36 per cent, respectively, during the preceding reporting period.

Throughout the year, JIU continued its increasingly active interactions with other oversight and coordinating bodies, including the Board of Auditors, OIOS and the Internal Audit Advisory Committee.

The report highlighted the fact that the Assembly, in its resolution 63/272 (see p. 1425), acknowledged JIU's undertaking to apply results-based management in its medium- and long-term strategic framework. However, no additional resources were obtained in the approved programme budget for 2010–2011, and JIU would therefore adjust its work programme for the next biennium accordingly. The report also contained the JIU work programme for 2010.

On 24 December, the Assembly decided that the item on JIU would remain for consideration during its resumed sixty-fourth (2010) session (**decision 64/549**).

Oil-for-food programme

On 14 September (**decision 63/566**), the Assembly deferred consideration of the item entitled "Follow-up to the recommendations on administrative management and internal oversight of the Independent Inquiry Committee into the United Nations Oil-for-Food Programme" [YUN 2005, p. 1475] and included it in the agenda of its sixty-fourth (2009) session.

On 24 December (**decision 64/549**), the Assembly decided that the item would remain for consideration during its resumed sixty-fourth (2010) session.

Other administrative matters

Conference management

Committee on Conferences

The Committee on Conferences held an organizational meeting on 7 April and its substantive session from 8 to 14 September [A/64/32 & Add.1]. It reviewed the draft biennial calendar of conferences and meetings for 2010 and 2011 [A/AC.172/2009/CRP.1] and examined requests for changes to the approved calendar of conferences and meetings for 2009 [A/63/119/Add.1]. The Committee also considered meetings management and improved utilization of conference-serving resources and facilities; the impact of the capital master plan (CMP) on meetings held at Headquarters; progress in integrated global management; and matters related to documentation, publication, translation and interpretation. (The Committee's deliberations and recommendations on those matters are detailed in the sections below.)

The Committee recommended that the General Assembly authorize its subsidiary bodies, listed in letters of 8 September [A/64/348] and 26 October [A/64/348/Add.1] from the Committee Chairman, to meet in New York during the main part of the Assembly's sixty-fourth session. It also approved requests for changes to the approved calendar for 2009.

The Assembly, by **decision 64/501** of 15 September, authorized those subsidiary organs to meet as recommended.

Use of conference services

In July [A/64/136], the Secretary-General submitted a report on issues related to conference management, including the integrated global management of conference services, evaluation by Member States of the quality of conference services, meetings management, document management and matters related to translation and interpretation (see sections below).

The report also provided information on the utilization of conference-servicing resources and facilities. The overall utilization factor in 2008 at the four duty stations—Geneva, Nairobi, New York and Vienna—was 85 per cent, an improvement of 2 percentage points over 2007.

The Committee on Conferences [A/64/32], in September, noted the increase in overall utilization, especially in New York, where the utilization factor improved by four percentage points in 2008 (83 per cent) over 2007 (79 per cent). The Chairperson reported on consultations held with two intergovernmental bodies that had underutilized their conference resources and suggested reducing the impact of foreseeable cancellations by: providing at least one-week advance notice to the conference planners; starting meetings in a timely manner, even without a quorum; reducing meetings blocks to two hours when it was anticipated that less time would be required; and reducing the number of meetings with conference services but maintaining the established entitlements to conference services.

Use of regional conference facilities

Nairobi and Addis Ababa

The United Nations Office at Nairobi [A/64/136] confirmed that, in 2008, all meetings of the Nairobi-based bodies were held in Nairobi. At the conference centre of the Economic Commission for Africa (ECA) in Addis Ababa, Ethiopia, the utilization rate increased to 76 per cent in 2008, compared to 70 per cent in 2007 and 60 per cent in 2006, mostly due to the promotional efforts by the centre's management. The centre's marketing activities included participation in high-profile international conventions and exhibitions. The centre also initiated the process of contracting specialized assistance in business development. Over the past few years, the centre had faced new challenges, as the local conference industry had become increasingly competitive. As a result, the increase in the centre's utilization rate might not realistically be sustainable.

In September [A/64/32], the Committee on Conferences requested an update on minimum operating security standards at ECA in 2009, progress in the utilization rate, measures taken by ECA to address the challenges of competition in the local conference market, and elaboration on the efforts in marketing and specialized assistance in business development.

Impact of CMP on conference services

In July [A/64/136], the Secretary-General, reporting on the impact of the implementation of CMP (see p. 1442) on meetings held at Headquarters, stated that the accelerated strategy IV [YUN 2008, p. 1589], which would compress the total period for the renovation of the Headquarters complex from seven to five years, was being implemented. One of the challenges facing DGACM was the relocation of most of the staff servicing meetings in the conference rooms to 300 East 42nd Street, as they would have to travel constantly from their off-site locations to the Conference building and back. He also outlined the arrangements for ensuring the ongoing provision of a full range of technical support to staff located in temporary swing space, and pointed out that, as neither storage space to facilitate prompt access to stock items nor office space to accommodate rotational support staff had been made available to any of the new locations, the ability of the Help Desk and the Stock and Inventory Group to provide the required services would be tested. The Secretary-General suggested that the General Assembly emphasize the importance of adequate resources for all temporary arrangements, including move support, information technology and space, as well as design features and appropriate amenities, so that staff of the Department could continue to provide services without interruption during the CMP process.

In September [A/64/32], the Committee on Conferences requested clarification of the financial implications of the moves into swing spaces, including the budget impact of the additional information technology needs. Concern was expressed about the availability of a medium-sized conference room for informal consultations of the Fifth Committee during the next phase of the renovation of the Conference building. The Committee requested more information on plans to mitigate risks and respond to contingencies.

In October [A/64/484], ACABQ, noting the challenges facing the Department, with more than a dozen mission-critical systems expected to operate during the construction period, stressed the importance of ensuring that proper support was provided throughout CMP to ensure uninterrupted service.

Integrated global management

OIOS report. In response to General Assembly resolution 63/248 [YUN 2008, p. 1580], OIOS reported, in July [A/64/166], on the evaluation of the integrated global management initiative of DGACM. OIOS found that, although the Department had implemented a wide range of operational activities, there had been no precise or consistent articulation of the initiative's objectives, assumptions about causality or implementation risks. Likewise, no measurable goals and targets had been set in explicit reference to it. While the integrated global management had allowed duty stations to collaborate and share information, that information-sharing had highlighted the differences among them rather than bring about any alignment of practices. The initiative was implemented on two tracks: the preparation of the compendium of conference services administrative policies, practices and procedures, and the establishment in 2006 [YUN 2006, p. 1658] of the integrated conference management system and the information technology governance board to oversee the development of three information technology systems. OIOS found that, after the first version of the compendium was published, the focus of the initiative became the global information technology projects, one shortcoming of which was that they did not start with a clear commitment to the standardization of work processes. The projects had also become the focus of much of the efforts related to integrated global management in DGACM, but they had failed to spearhead the work of process reform and alignment at all duty stations. Moreover, although the Under-Secretary-General for the Department had budgetary responsibility for all four duty stations, in practice there was little room to allocate funds across duty stations and outside New York. With regard to financial savings, at the aggregate level none were evident. Neither total costs nor total volume of conference-service delivery had significantly changed. While recognizing that technology could provide many benefits to DGACM and its work and be a useful tool for implementing integrated global management, OIOS warned against assuming that technology would result in reform. To make integrated global management of UN conference management a reality, clear management authority was needed. The dual reporting line tension needed to be resolved. OIOS concluded that the integrated global management was still a work in progress, and its major anticipated organization-wide benefits had not materialized.

OIOS recommended that DGACM should: prepare a renewed articulation of the overarching objective, limitations and operational parameters of integrated global management, as well as a comprehensive and detailed strategy; review, in collaboration with the Office of Programme Planning, Budget and Accounts (OPPBA), the relevance, feasibility and implications of the future budgeting and expenditure management practices of the Organization; articulate, in collaboration with OPPBA, the Department of Public Information (DPI) and other relevant Secretariat officials, the merits of either moving library services at Geneva and/or Vienna from DGACM to DPI or, alternatively, placing them under the authority of the DGACM Under-Secretary-General; and consider, after due cost-benefit analysis, interim information technology arrangements that would reduce both the resources spent and the proliferation of silo applications and utilize any existing applications to achieve efficiencies and cost savings.

Report of Secretary-General. In his July report on the pattern of conferences [A/64/136], the Secretary-General stated that progress had been made in the implementation of the integrated global management. The Under-Secretary-General was directly exercising his authority in matters relating to the overall management of resources across all duty stations, and had initiated discussions of expenditures at all duty stations, as well as additional management and strategic discussion with conference managers at the four duty stations. The report contained a performance matrix for 2008, which provided indicators for human resources, finance, meetings management and timeliness of documentation, as well as productivity measures for the language services.

Concerning the OIOS evaluation, the Secretary-General stated that, while DGACM was largely in agreement with its findings and recommendations, it did not share its pessimistic tone and tenor, and recalled the numerous achievements of integrated global management, including the development and implementation of a common roster for contractual translation; the entry into force of the compendium of policies and practices; global waiver management; the global document slotting system; staff exchanges; workload sharing; and progress in implementing the three technology projects. However, he noted that information technology project 3 (document planning and management) had encountered challenges owing to the disparity of working methods and systems used in the various duty stations, which had slowed progress, requiring further designing and implementation in 2010.

Committee on Conferences consideration. The Committee on Conferences [A/64/32] said that it was yet to be convinced that the achievements, while commendable, would not have taken place without integrated global management. There was a need to define the objectives of the integrated global management, as well as to have a clear picture of associated costs and

savings. The Committee raised the question of how to reconcile the specificities of the individual duty stations with the objective of harmonizing working procedures between duty stations. It was also unclear why workload sharing had not been applied to the situation of Human Rights Council documentation in Geneva, and more explanation was needed as to why the Office at Vienna had taken the lead in information technology project 2 on meetings planning and management, when the meeting services function was concentrated mainly in New York and Geneva. Ways to ensure greater precision of data on integrated global management needed to be explored.

ACABQ report. In October [A/64/484], ACABQ reiterated its recommendation that DGACM methodologies for the collection and analysis of costing information be further developed in order to better assess efficiency and cost-effectiveness. It also recommended that the Secretary-General include in his next report on the pattern of conferences steps taken to implement the OIOS findings and recommendations that had been accepted by DGACM. It expressed disappointment that information technology project 3 would have to start again from the beginning and urged DGACM, in designing and implementing the next iteration of that project, to cooperate closely with the Office of Information and Communications Technology to ensure that the selected platform fully met the needs of all conference-servicing duty stations and that it was compatible with other applications Organization-wide.

Documentation

Timely submission

Report of Secretary-General. In a February report on action taken to improve the timely submission of documents for the Fifth Committee [A/63/735], prepared in response to General Assembly resolution 63/248 [YUN 2008, p. 1580], the Secretary-General said that to prevent a recurrence of the situation in which an unprecedented number of documents were submitted late for the second resumed session of the Fifth Committee during the Assembly's sixty-second session, a number of actions had been taken, including the establishment in August 2008 of an interdepartmental task force comprising all Secretariat entities involved in the drafting and processing of documents for the second resumed session of the Fifth Committee during the Assembly's sixty-third session, close interaction among all Secretariat author entities, as well as capacity planning in DGACM. The report summarized lessons learned and provided recommendations for the next steps, including the institutionalization of the task force as a standing mechanism to handle the documentation of the Fifth Committee at its successive sessions.

In April [A/63/32/Add.1], the Committee on Conference welcomed the progress achieved by the task force, looked forward to further concerted efforts by the task force aimed at ensuring the timely availability of documents, and requested the Secretary-General to include in his comprehensive report further information on the arrangements to handle the documentation of the Fifth Committee at its successive sessions.

Also in April [A/63/746], ACABQ welcomed the efforts made to improve the documentation process for the peacekeeping session. It regretted that the full documentation packages for a number of peacekeeping missions, particularly some of the larger ones, were either submitted late or were not submitted at all during the Committee's session.

GENERAL ASSEMBLY ACTION

On 30 June [meeting 93], the General Assembly, on the recommendation of the Fifth Committee [A/63/638/Add.1], adopted **resolution 63/284** without vote [agenda item 121].

Timely submission of documents

The General Assembly,

Recalling section IV, paragraph 12, of its resolution 63/248 of 24 December 2008,

Having considered the report of the Secretary-General on action taken to improve the timely submission of documents for the Fifth Committee and the related reports of the Committee on Conferences and the Advisory Committee on Administrative and Budgetary Questions,

1. *Takes note* of the report of the Secretary-General on action taken to improve the timely submission of documents for the Fifth Committee;

2. *Welcomes* the report of the Committee on Conferences;

3. *Reiterates* the importance of the timely issuance of documents for the Fifth Committee;

4. *Welcomes* the progress achieved so far by the task force concerning the timely issuance of documents for the Fifth Committee on peacekeeping financing;

5. *Notes with concern* the lack of conference services being provided to the Human Rights Council, and requests the Secretary-General to ensure that the Council, as a subsidiary body of the General Assembly, is provided with all necessary conference services to support its activities, including the universal periodic review;

6. *Requests* the Secretary-General to entrust the Office of Internal Oversight Services with a review of the circumstances that led to insufficient conference services being put at the disposal of the Human Rights Council in 2009 and to submit its recommendations to the General Assembly at the main part of its sixty-fourth session in order to avoid similar situations;

7. *Also requests* the Secretary-General to maintain the support to major groups participating in the 2009 substantive session of the Economic and Social Council, to be held in Geneva.

Report of Secretary-General. In annex VII to his July report on the pattern of conferences [A/64/136], the Secretary-General provided an update of submission compliance for documents slotted as at 30 June. As of that date, 71 per cent of pre-session documents had been submitted on time, on a par with 2008, and up from 61 per cent in 2007. At the same time, the overall issuance compliance had increased to 73 per cent, up from 72 per cent in 2008 and 66 per cent in 2007. He said that further improvement was contingent upon more timely submission of documents, adequate intervals between the adoption of new mandates by intergovernmental bodies and the time of consideration of the relevant documents, and the length of budgetary and performance reports, which were exempt from waivers. He pointed out that the latter reports had often proven to be disruptive to documentation processing, particularly given the urgency required for their processing, and thereby affecting the timely issuance of other documents already in the pipeline.

Regarding the challenges associated with the continuing development of the activities of the Human Rights Council, the Secretary-General drew attention to the issue of word and page limits of documentation for the universal periodic review sessions of the Council (see p. 624) and the legal opinion of the Office of Legal Affairs on the subject. He invited the Assembly to ensure that the Council's requirements for document submission were brought in line with relevant Assembly resolutions.

The Committee on Conferences [A/64/32] in September expressed concern about the servicing of the Human Rights Council and its periodic review mechanism. Some members felt that that legal opinion by the Office of Legal Affairs ran counter to the Assembly's rules. It was suggested that a coordination mechanism between the Council and DGACM be established to enable it to follow up on the submission of documents and ensure that additional resources be provided.

On documentation for the second resumed session of the Fifth Committee, the Committee expressed appreciation for the progress made by DGACM in speeding up the issuance of those documents and the work of the interdepartmental task force. It was suggested that the task force be institutionalized as a standing mechanism for coordination among author departments on document management issues, regular meetings be held between the Chairs of the Fifth Committee and ACABQ as part of a multipronged approach to finding a solution to the problem of the late issuance of documents, and the Committee on Conferences consider adjusting the dates on which the Fifth Committee met during the first and second parts of the Assembly's resumed session to provide adequate time for consideration of documents.

In October [A/64/484], ACABQ stressed that the timely submission of documentation was key to the effective implementation of DGACM's mandate and urged all author departments to comply with submission deadlines and page-limit requirements. The Committee reaffirmed its support for proposals to address the additional requirements generated by the activities of the Human Rights Council and its subsidiary bodies. However, given its concerns about the adequacy of the additional capacity proposed, the Committee reiterated its recommendation that the Assembly request the Secretary-General to monitor the situation closely and to report on developments that might have financial implications.

In October [A/64/511], OIOS, in its report on the audit of conference services put at the disposal of the Human Rights Council in 2009, prepared pursuant to Assembly resolution 63/284 (see p. 1430), concluded that insufficient resources were put at the disposal of the Division of Conference Management to provide conference services to the Council. A combination of factors indicated that the processes for determining resource requirements for conference services on an "as required" basis needed to be reviewed. The Division's permanent capacity should be increased to provide flexibility in dealing with its workload. The Division should establish collaborative arrangements with the Office of the High Commissioner for Human Rights through the designation of focal points, regular meetings and outreach activities.

Translation and interpretation

In July [A/64/136], the Secretary-General stated that, given the high vacancy rate in language services and the severe depletion of rosters, it might be necessary to temporarily increase the capacity of the Examinations and Tests Section to ensure that the examination needs of DGACM were met. An unprecedented 13 language examinations were scheduled for 2009, including multiple examinations in the same language for different professions. It was anticipated that all duty stations would benefit from other initiatives, such as the university outreach programme and enhanced training programmes for serving language staff. However, the anticipated high number of retirements in the coming years made the issue of raising, or waiving, the mandatory age of separation for language staff worthy of consideration. Also being envisaged was the revamping of the language examination format and methods to take advantage of new technologies and modalities. An expert panel could be set up to evaluate the additional resources and investment required to implement such ideas. As to freelance interpreters, for which the demand had risen, especially in New York, recruitment was affected by the limited availability of interpreters, the uncompeti-

tive rate of remuneration in North America, and fierce competition among international organizations and duty stations. To fill current and future vacancies at the United Nations Office at Nairobi, the Division of Conference Services in Nairobi intended to classify some interpreter and translator posts at a higher level. To seek a long-term solution to the high vacancy rates in the language services in Nairobi, the services of a consultant were engaged to explore the possibilities of providing enhanced training programmes to potential professional translators and interpreters on the African continent.

In September [A/64/32], the Committee on Conferences stated that the demographic transition in the language services was a broader issue that required more than a focus on a specific part of the Secretariat workforce. Rather than raising or waiving the age of separation, efforts should be focused on finding ways to bring new staff members on board more quickly. The increase in resources required to expand the capacity of the Examination and Tests Section needed to be further elaborated. Measures were also needed to address the competition for freelance interpreters through action with the International Civil Service Commission to raise rates in New York. It would be important to have clear time frames for reductions in vacancy rates.

In October [A/64/484], ACABQ stated that the financial and administrative implications of raising or waiving the age of separation for one category of staff should be thoroughly explored, including from the perspective of equality of treatment, before a formal proposal was made. It welcomed the proactive approach to staffing in Nairobi and requested that information on its impact be included in the Secretary-General's next report. It also stressed the importance of robust workload planning to ensure that adequate numbers of freelance interpreters who could perform to the required standard were recruited sufficiently in advance.

Interpretation for regional and other groupings

In July [A/64/136], the Secretary-General reported that, in 2008, in the four duty stations, 77 per cent of requests for meetings with interpretation from regional and other major groupings of Member States were accommodated, compared with 84 per cent in 2007, a decrease of 7 percentage points. In New York, 83 per cent of requests were met, a decrease of 4 percentage points over 2007. The Secretary-General said that it was worth noting that over the past three years demand for interpretation services for meetings of those groupings had decreased. The "strategic reserve" of interpretation and other conference services had a positive effect on the provision of services to the meetings of bodies entitled to meet "as required", and DGACM would continue that practice.

The Committee on Conferences [A/64/32] expressed concern at the decrease in demand for interpretation services for meetings of regional and other groupings, along with a decline in the services provided. It highlighted the fact that 50 per cent of the requests for services by the Group of African States in New York had not been met; the figure for the Group of Latin American and Caribbean States in Geneva was even lower. Concern was also expressed that regional groups might have given up asking for services because their requests had been denied so often. To correct the situation, the Committee asked for a more detailed breakdown of requests from regional groups, information on how the strategic reserve could best be used to meet requests, as well as analysis of the reasons for denied requests for services from certain groups.

GENERAL ASSEMBLY ACTION

On 22 December [meeting 67], the General Assembly, on the recommendation of the Fifth Committee [A/64/580], adopted **resolution 64/230** without vote [agenda item 135].

Pattern of conferences

The General Assembly,

Recalling its relevant resolutions, including resolutions 40/243 of 18 December 1985, 41/213 of 19 December 1986, 43/222 A to E of 21 December 1988, 51/211 A to E of 18 December 1996, 52/214 of 22 December 1997, 53/208 A to E of 18 December 1998, 54/248 of 23 December 1999, 55/222 of 23 December 2000, 56/242 of 24 December 2001, 56/254 D of 27 March 2002, 56/262 of 15 February 2002, 56/287 of 27 June 2002, 57/283 A of 20 December 2002, 57/283 B of 15 April 2003, 58/250 of 23 December 2003, 59/265 of 23 December 2004, 60/236 A of 23 December 2005, 60/236 B of 8 May 2006, 61/236 of 22 December 2006, 62/225 of 22 December 2007, 63/248 of 24 December 2008 and 63/284 of 30 June 2009,

Reaffirming its resolution 42/207 C of 11 December 1987, in which it requested the Secretary-General to ensure the equal treatment of the official languages of the United Nations,

Having considered the report of the Committee on Conferences for 2009, the relevant reports of the Secretary-General and the report of the Office of Internal Oversight Services on the evaluation of the integrated global management initiative of the Department for General Assembly and Conference Management,

Having also considered the report of the Advisory Committee on Administrative and Budgetary Questions,

Reaffirming the provisions relating to conference services in its resolutions on multilingualism, in particular resolution 63/306 of 9 September 2009,

Bearing in mind its resolutions 60/251 of 15 March 2006 and 62/219 of 22 December 2007, Human Rights Council resolutions 5/1 of 18 June 2007 and 8/1 of 18 June 2008 and decision 9/103 of 24 September 2008 and the Council President's statements 8/1 of 9 April 2008 and 9/2 of 24 September 2008,

Stressing that the Working Group on the Universal Periodic Review of the Human Rights Council adopted reports on the review of thirty-two Member States at its fourth and fifth sessions,

Noting that thirteen of the reports adopted at the fourth session of the Working Group were not issued as documents of the United Nations in the six official languages prior to their consideration and adoption by the Council at its eleventh session and that the processing and issuance of two of the reports adopted by the Working Group at its fifth session remain delayed,

Recalling the importance of multilingualism in the work of the United Nations and the need to issue all of the reports of the Working Group in all official languages of the Organization,

I

Calendar of conferences and meetings

1. *Welcomes* the report of the Committee on Conferences for 2009;

2. *Approves* the draft biennial calendar of conferences and meetings of the United Nations for 2010 and 2011, as submitted by the Committee on Conferences, taking into account the observations of the Committee and subject to the provisions of the present resolution;

3. *Requests* the Secretary-General to examine the feasibility and the implications of all options and proposals to adjust the calendar of conferences and meetings and other options aimed at addressing the problem of timely availability and consideration of documentation for the Fifth Committee and to report thereon to the General Assembly at its sixty-fifth session through the Committee on Conferences;

4. *Authorizes* the Committee on Conferences to make any adjustments to the calendar of conferences and meetings for 2010 and 2011 that may become necessary as a result of actions and decisions taken by the General Assembly at its sixty-fourth session;

5. *Notes with satisfaction* that the Secretariat has taken into account the arrangements referred to in General Assembly resolutions 53/208 A, 54/248, 55/222, 56/242, 57/283 B, 58/250, 59/265, 60/236 A, 61/236, 62/225 and 63/248 concerning Orthodox Good Friday and the official holidays of Eid al-Fitr and Eid al-Adha, and requests all intergovernmental bodies to observe those decisions when planning their meetings;

6. *Requests* the Secretary-General to ensure that any modification to the calendar of conferences and meetings is implemented strictly in accordance with the mandate of the Committee on Conferences and other relevant resolutions of the General Assembly;

7. *Notes* that accurate, timely and consistent information provided to the Fifth Committee during its informal consultations facilitates the decision-making process in the Committee;

II

A. Utilization of conference-servicing resources

1. *Reaffirms* the practice that, in the use of conference rooms, priority must be given to the meetings of Member States;

2. *Notes* that the overall utilization factor at the four main duty stations in 2008 was 85 per cent as compared

with 83 per cent in 2007 and 2006, which is above the established benchmark of 80 per cent;

3. *Welcomes* the steps taken by those bodies that have adjusted their programmes of work in order to achieve the optimum utilization of conference-servicing resources, and requests the Committee on Conferences to continue consultations with the secretariats and bureaux of bodies that underutilize their conference-servicing resources;

4. *Recognizes* that late starts and unplanned early endings seriously affect the bodies' utilization factor owing to the amount of time lost, and invites the secretariats and bureaux of bodies to pay adequate attention to avoiding late starts and unplanned early endings;

5. *Notes* that the percentage of meetings held by the bodies entitled to meet "as required" that were provided with interpretation services in New York in 2008 was 90 per cent, as compared with 88 per cent in 2007, and requests the Secretary-General to continue to report on the provision of conference services to these bodies through the Committee on Conferences;

6. *Recognizes* the importance of meetings of regional and other major groupings of Member States for the smooth functioning of the sessions of intergovernmental bodies, requests the Secretary-General to ensure that, as far as possible, all requests for conference services for the meetings of regional and other major groupings of Member States are met, and requests the Secretariat to inform the requesters as early as possible about the availability of conference services, including interpretation, as well as about any changes that might occur before the meeting;

7. *Regrets* that the percentage of meetings held by regional and other major groupings of Member States that were provided with interpretation services at the four main duty stations was 77 per cent in 2008 as compared to 84 per cent in 2007, and requests the Secretary-General to continue to employ innovative means to address the difficulties experienced by Member States owing to the lack of conference services for some meetings of regional and other major groupings of Member States and to report thereon to the General Assembly through the Committee on Conferences;

8. *Once again urges* intergovernmental bodies to spare no effort at the planning stage to take into account the meetings of regional and other major groupings of Member States, to make provision for such meetings in their programmes of work and to notify conference services, well in advance, of any cancellations so that unutilized conference-servicing resources may, to the extent possible, be reassigned to meetings of regional and other major groupings of Member States;

9. *Notes with satisfaction* that, in accordance with several resolutions of the General Assembly, including resolution 63/248, section II.A, paragraph 9, in conformity with the headquarters rule, all meetings of Nairobi-based United Nations bodies were held in Nairobi in 2008, and requests the Secretary-General to report thereon to the Assembly at its sixty-fifth session through the Committee on Conferences;

10. *Notes with appreciation* ongoing promotional efforts and initiatives undertaken by the management of the conference centre of the Economic Commission for Africa, which led to a continued upward trend in utilization of the premises in 2008;

11. *Requests* the Secretary-General to continue to explore means to increase the utilization of the conference centre of the Economic Commission for Africa, bearing in mind the headquarters minimum operating security standards, and to report thereon to the General Assembly at its sixty-fifth session;

12. *Calls upon* the Secretary-General and Member States to adhere to the guidelines and procedures contained in the administrative instruction for the authorization of the use of United Nations premises for meetings, conferences, special events and exhibits;

13. *Emphasizes* that such meetings, conferences, special events and exhibits must be consistent with the purposes and principles of the United Nations;

B. Impact of the capital master plan, strategy IV (phased approach), on meetings held at Headquarters during its implementation

1. *Requests* the Secretary-General to ensure that the implementation of the capital master plan, including the temporary relocation of conference-servicing staff to a swing space, will not compromise the quality of conference services provided to Member States in the six official languages and the equal treatment of the language services, which should be provided with equally favourable working conditions and resources, with a view to receiving the maximum quality of services;

2. *Requests* all meeting requesters and organizers to liaise closely with the Department for General Assembly and Conference Management of the Secretariat on all matters related to the scheduling of meetings to allow maximum predictability in coordinating activities at Headquarters during the construction period;

3. *Requests* the Committee on Conferences to keep the matter under constant review, and requests the Secretary-General to report regularly to the Committee on matters pertaining to the calendar of conferences and meetings of the United Nations during the construction period;

4. *Requests* the Secretary-General to continue to provide adequate information technology support for conference services, within the existing resources of the Department for General Assembly and Conference Management, in order to ensure their seamless operation throughout the implementation of the capital master plan;

5. *Notes* that, for the duration of the implementation of the capital master plan, a part of the conference-servicing staff and information technology resources of the Department for General Assembly and Conference Management has been temporarily relocated to a swing space, and requests the Secretary-General to continue to provide adequate support, within the existing resources of the Department, to ensure continued maintenance of the information technology facilities of the Department, implementation of the global information technology initiative and delivery of quality conference services;

6. *Requests* the Secretary-General to consult Member States on initiatives that affect the utilization of conference services and conference facilities;

III
Integrated global management

1. *Notes* the progress achieved in the implementation of the global information technology project, aimed at

integrating, across duty stations, information technology into meetings management and documentation-processing systems, and the global approach to harmonizing standards and information technology and sharing good practices and technological achievements among conference services at the four main duty stations;

2. *Also notes* the initiatives undertaken in the context of integrated global management aimed at streamlining procedures, achieving economies of scale and improving the quality of conference services, and in this regard stresses the importance of ensuring equal treatment of conference-servicing staff as well as the principle of equal grade for equal work at the four main duty stations;

3. *Emphasizes* that the major goals of the Department for General Assembly and Conference Management are to provide high-quality documents in a timely manner in all official languages in accordance with established regulations, as well as high-quality conference services to Member States at all duty stations, and to achieve those aims as efficiently and cost-effectively as possible, in accordance with the relevant resolutions of the General Assembly;

4. *Requests* the Secretary-General to ensure that all language services are given equal treatment and are provided with equally favourable working conditions and resources, with a view to achieving the maximum quality of services, with full respect for the specificities of the six official languages and taking into account their respective workloads;

5. *Reiterates* the need for the Secretary-General to ensure the compatibility of technologies used in all duty stations and to ensure that they are user-friendly in all official languages;

6. *Requests* the Secretary-General to complete the task of uploading all important older United Nations documents onto the United Nations website in all six official languages on a priority basis, so that these archives are also available to Member States through that medium;

7. *Reiterates* that the satisfaction of Member States is a key performance indicator in conference management and conference services;

8. *Requests* the Secretary-General to continue to ensure that measures taken by the Department for General Assembly and Conference Management to seek the evaluation by Member States of the quality of the conference services provided to them, as a key performance indicator of the Department, provide equal opportunities to Member States to present their evaluations in the six official languages of the United Nations and are in full compliance with relevant resolutions of the General Assembly, and requests the Secretary-General to report to the General Assembly, through the Committee on Conferences, on progress made in this regard;

9. *Also requests* the Secretary-General to continue to explore best practices and techniques in client satisfaction evaluations and to report on a regular basis to the General Assembly on the results achieved;

10. *Welcomes* the efforts made by the Department for General Assembly and Conference Management to seek the evaluation by Member States of the quality of the conference services provided to them, and requests the Secretary-General to continue to explore innovative ways to systematically capture and analyse feedback from Member

States and committee Chairs and secretaries on the quality of conference services and to report thereon to the General Assembly through the Committee on Conferences;

11. *Requests* the Secretary-General to keep the General Assembly apprised of progress made in integrated global management;

12. *Notes with concern* that the Secretary-General did not include in his report on the pattern of conferences information about the financial savings achieved through implementation of the integrated global management projects as requested in section III, paragraph 4, of its resolution 63/248, and requests the Secretary-General to redouble his efforts to include this information in his next report on the pattern of conferences;

13. *Takes note* of the recommendations provided by the Office of Internal Oversight Services in its report, and requests the Secretary-General to ensure their full implementation and to report thereon to the General Assembly at its sixty-fifth session through the Committee on Conferences;

IV
Documentation and publication-related matters

1. *Decides* that all the reports adopted by the Working Group on the Universal Periodic Review of the Human Rights Council at its fourth and fifth sessions and the additional information submitted by the States under review before the adoption of the outcome by the Council shall be issued as documents in all official languages of the United Nations, and requests the Secretary-General to undertake the necessary measures to that effect;

2. *Also decides* that all reports adopted by the Working Group shall be issued as documents in all official languages of the United Nations in a timely manner before their consideration by the Council, in accordance with General Assembly resolutions 36/117 A of 10 December 1981, 51/211 A to E, 52/214, 53/208 A to E and 59/265, and requests the Secretary-General to ensure the support necessary to that effect;

3. *Emphasizes* the paramount importance of the equality of the six official languages of the United Nations;

4. *Reiterates* the importance of the timely issuance of documents for the Fifth Committee;

5. *Stresses* that matters related to conference management, including documentation, fall within the purview of the Fifth Committee;

6. *Reiterates with concern* its request to the Secretary-General to ensure that the rules concerning the simultaneous distribution of documents in all six official languages are strictly respected as regards both the distribution of printed copies and the posting of parliamentary documentation on the Official Document System and the United Nations website, in keeping with section III, paragraph 5, of its resolution 55/222;

7. *Reaffirms* that the Fifth Committee is the appropriate Main Committee of the General Assembly entrusted with responsibilities for administrative and budgetary matters;

8. *Also reaffirms* its decision in section III, paragraph 9, of its resolution 59/265 that the issuance of documents in all six official languages on planning, budgetary and administrative matters requiring urgent consideration by the General Assembly shall be accorded priority;

9. *Reiterates its request* to the Secretary-General to direct all departments of the Secretariat to include the following elements in their reports:

(a) Summary of the report;

(b) Consolidated conclusions, recommendations and other proposed actions;

(c) Relevant background information;

10. *Reiterates its request* that all documents submitted to legislative organs by the Secretariat and intergovernmental and expert bodies for consideration and action have conclusions and recommendations in bold print;

11. *Recognizes* the work done by the task force chaired by the Department for General Assembly and Conference Management in positively addressing the problem of issuance of documents for the Fifth Committee;

12. *Welcomes* the continued efforts of the task force to shepherd the submission of documents by the author departments of the Secretariat;

13. *Expresses deep concern* at the unprecedented high level of late submission of documentation, which, in turn, has a negative impact on the functioning of intergovernmental bodies, and urges author departments to fully adhere to deadlines in meeting the goal of 90 per cent submission compliance;

14. *Decides* to review, at its sixty-sixth session, the work of the task force and to consider, where necessary, additional measures to ensure compliance with submission deadlines by author departments if the goal of 90 per cent compliance is not met;

15. *Acknowledges* that a multipronged approach is required to find a solution to the perennial difficulties of the late issuance of documents for the Fifth Committee;

16. *Encourages* the Chairs of the Fifth Committee and the Advisory Committee on Administrative and Budgetary Questions to promote cooperation between the two bodies in the sphere of documentation;

V
Translation and interpretation-related matters

1. *Requests* the Secretary-General to redouble his efforts to ensure the highest quality of interpretation and translation services in all six official languages;

2. *Also requests* the Secretary-General to continue to seek evaluation by Member States of the quality of the conference services provided to them, including through the language-specific informational meetings held twice a year, and to ensure that such measures provide equal opportunities to Member States to present their evaluations in the six official languages of the United Nations and that they are in full compliance with the relevant resolutions of the General Assembly;

3. *Reiterates its request* that the Secretary-General ensure that the terminology used in the translation and interpretation services reflects the latest linguistic norms and terminology of the official languages in order to ensure the highest quality;

4. *Reaffirms* section V, paragraph 3, of its resolution 61/236, section V, paragraph 3, of its resolution 62/225 and section V, paragraph 5, of its resolution 63/248, and reiterates its request that the Secretary-General, when recruiting temporary assistance in the language services, ensure

that all language services are given equal treatment and are provided with equally favourable working conditions and resources, with a view to achieving maximum quality of their services, with full respect for the specificities of each of the six official languages and taking into account their respective workloads;

5. *Notes with appreciation* the measures taken by the Secretariat to fill current and future vacancies at the United Nations Office at Nairobi and the information contained in paragraphs 87 to 89 of the report of the Secretary-General on the pattern of conferences, and requests the Secretary-General to consider further measures aimed at decreasing the vacancy rates in Nairobi and to report thereon to the General Assembly at its sixty-fifth session;

6. *Acknowledges* the measures undertaken by the Secretary-General, in accordance with its resolutions, to address the issue of the replacement of retiring staff in the language services, and requests the Secretary-General to maintain and intensify those efforts, including the strengthening of cooperation with institutions that train language specialists, in order to meet the need in the six official languages of the United Nations;

7. *Requests* the Secretary-General to hold competitive examinations for the recruitment of language staff sufficiently in advance in order to fill current and future vacancies in language services in a timely manner, and to inform the General Assembly at its sixty-fifth session of efforts in this regard;

8. *Also requests* the Secretary-General to continue to improve the accuracy of translation of documents into the six official languages, giving particular significance to the quality of translation;

9. *Further requests* the Secretary-General to take the steps necessary to enhance translation quality in all six official languages, in particular for contractual translation, and to report thereon to the General Assembly at its sixty-fifth session;

10. *Requests* the Secretary-General to provide, at all duty stations, adequate staff at the appropriate level, with a view to ensuring appropriate quality control for external translation, with due consideration of the principle of equal grade for equal work;

11. *Takes note* of the information on the impact of freelance recruitment on the quality of interpretation at all duty stations contained in paragraphs 81 to 86 of the report of the Secretary-General, and requests the Secretary-General to report on the issue to the General Assembly at its sixty-fifth session through the Committee on Conferences;

12. *Requests* the Secretary-General to report to the General Assembly at its sixty-fifth session on the experience, lessons learned and best practices of the main duty stations in performing quality control of contractual translations, including on requirements relating to the number and appropriate level of the staff needed to carry out this function.

On 24 December, the Assembly decided that the item "Pattern of conferences" would remain for consideration during its resumed sixty-fourth (2010) session (**decision 64/549**).

UN information systems

Information and communication technology

In October [A/64/477], the Secretary-General, reported on the enterprise content management (ECM) and customer relationship management (CRM) systems and a proposal for a unified disaster recovery and business continuity plan, submitted in response to General Assembly resolution 63/262 [YUN 2008, p. 1592]. The report provided the context for the implementation of the ECM and CRM systems, and highlighted their synergies with each other, as well as their relationship to the enterprise resource planning project (Umoja) (see respective sections below). The goals, rationale and benefits of each project were presented together with plans for phased implementation throughout the UN Secretariat, including offices away from Headquarters, regional commissions, peacekeeping and political missions and other field missions. The report also responded to the Assembly's request, in the same resolution, for a report on data storage and business continuity services, drawing on the experience of other UN entities and global developments in information and communications technology (ICT). It presented a framework for a unified approach to disaster recovery and business continuity for ICT, highlighted the principles to guide the refinement of the strategy for an Organization-wide disaster recovery and business continuity plan, and proposed an action plan outlining the processes, timelines and resource requirements for delivery of a comprehensive plan to address the Secretariat's requirements as a whole.

JIU reports. In June [A/64/96], the Secretary-General transmitted to the General Assembly a JIU report entitled "Review of information and communication technology (ICT) hosting services in the UN system organizations", which provided the governing bodies and executive heads of the UN system organizations with a comparative study of the main ICT hosting services, and identified best practices used by the UN system organizations. On 19 June [A/64/95], the Secretary-General transmitted another JIU report entitled "Review of management of Internet websites in the UN system organizations", which provided the governing bodies and executive heads of the UN system organizations with an assessment on the effectiveness and efficiency of the use of Internet websites as a communication tool for information dissemination.

Enterprise content management

In March [E/AC.51/2009/4], OIOS submitted a report on the triennial review of the implementation of recommendations made by the Committee for Programme and Coordination (CPC) at its forty-sixth session [YUN 2006, p. 1596] on the thematic evaluation of knowledge management networks in pursuit of the goals of the Millennium Declaration [YUN 2000, p. 50]. OIOS concluded that neither a UN system-wide nor a Secretariat-wide knowledge management strategy had been developed. However, the Organization's information and communication strategy [YUN 2008, p. 1589] addressed knowledge management issues, and the Office of Information and Communications Technology had within it a Knowledge Management Service that was sufficiently structured to act as a dedicated unit for knowledge management. The new Working Group on Knowledge Management, established in 2008, planned to develop a Secretariat knowledge management strategy during 2009. A WikiSeek Task Force was also established, which undertook a feasibility study to assess ways in which wikis—web pages that allowed anyone who accesses them to contribute to their content—could be used to enhance availability of knowledge on operations and work processes.

CPC, at its forty-ninth session in June [A/64/16], recommended that the General Assembly note the work done by the Working Group on Knowledge Management and request the Secretary-General to ensure that the placement of the Knowledge Management Service in the Office of Information and Communications Technology did not result in an overemphasis on technology at the expense of other equally important components of knowledge management.

In October [A/64/477], the Secretary-General, responding to the Assembly's request that he and the Secretariat enhance the technological infrastructure for the management of content, and take advantage of information technology developments to improve the dissemination of information, stated that the multiplicity of information systems in duty stations across the Secretariat had led to a patchwork of fragmented, support-intensive, home-grown systems that were inefficient and unsustainable. Too often, efforts were duplicated and departments and offices used different approaches and technologies to manage information and content, resulting in information silos and inconsistent policies on information management, which made it difficult for UN stakeholders and staff to find the information needed. Critical component of the knowledge management programme included: providing the appropriate information technology tools, with ECM as the core system to support the management of content and information; changing cumbersome processes; and eliminating silos and championing collaboration. The Knowledge Management Service would plan and coordinate the approach for the deployment of ECM, in cooperation with departments and offices. ECM modules would be made available to all duty stations and field missions. As part of the Secretariat's ICT strategy, ECM would be implemented in a manner that integrated with CRM and the enterprise resource planning system. That was intended to lead to better and consolidated access to the UN body of information and knowledge; improved management of organizational records, legacy knowledge capture and Internet presence; and the standardization and simplification of information creation and management.

ECM would be deployed over a five-year period. Each project would be implemented in incremental phases. Following a foundational phase for governance and technical infrastructure requirements, two phases were planned for 2010–2011. Phase I, to be conducted in 2010, would focus on initiatives providing value for all Secretariat stakeholders; Phase II would be conducted in 2011 to expand knowledge management capabilities throughout the Secretariat. The estimated cost of ECM implementation under the 2010–2011 programme budget was $14,548,300.

In November [A/64/7/Add.9], ACABQ emphasized the need for effective monitoring of the timeline and deliverables of the ECM programme. It recommended that the Secretary-General provide information on the implementation plan, progress achieved and outstanding activities, and elaborate on the efficiency gains expected in the context of the proposed 2012–2013 programme budget. On funding requirements, since little information was provided on the overall costs over the five-year span of the implementation of ECM, ACABQ requested that additional data on resources be provided. As for the resource requirements for the biennium 2010–2011, it stated that that every effort should be made to draw upon the experience and skills available in house and to reassess requirements as the various ECM implementation activities progressed. It recommended approval of 7 of the 11 positions proposed for the Knowledge Management Service and a reduction of $1 million in the proposed $8,066,400 for contractual services.

Customer relationship management

The Secretary-General reported in October [A/64/477] that CRM at the Secretariat was a key element of the resource management programme of the ICT strategy. The initiative sought to implement service-delivery and workflow-based applications to improve the handling of day-to-day services and the effective management of UN resources related to service management. Its primary objective was to improve the quality and cost-effectiveness of services provided to end-users through the creation of an Organization-wide common service management framework. The goal was to implement the framework by providing an integrated platform for managing the service delivery life cycle based on standardized business processes. The main CRM project was iNeed, an enterprise solution using the Oracle Siebel technology platform, which would replace the legacy systems used to manage service requests, in-

cident tracking and inventories of technology and facility assets. The funding requirement for CRM in 2010–2011 was estimated at $4,433,000.

In November [A/67/Add.9], ACABQ pointed out that a quantitative analysis of the activities automated with the implementation of CRM should be carried out so as to provide an objective basis for measuring the efficiencies actually realized. In view of the imminent implementation of the first phase of CRM by the end of 2009, ACABQ recommended that the Secretary-General ensure that mechanisms were in place for gathering the necessary data before the systems were deployed. ACABQ was supportive of the Secretary-General's intention to build internal capacity for managing and supporting the deployment of CRM and to reduce the Organization's reliance on external vendors. It recommended making further efforts to utilize in-house capacity and reducing the requirements for contractual services by $500,000.

Information and communications technology, disaster recovery and business continuity

In response to section IV of Assembly resolution 63/262 [YUN 2008, p. 1595], the Secretary-General in February submitted a report [A/63/743] on ICT, disaster recovery and business continuity for the UN: arrangements for the secondary data centre at Headquarters, in which he presented a new proposal for a secondary data centre, including cost-sharing arrangements, and addressed the Assembly's request to consolidate systems in central data centres in order to strengthen disaster recovery and business continuity. A new secondary date centre was necessary, as the current one, located in the DC2 building, because of inadequate infrastructure facilities, could not assume the function of primary data centre during the relocation of the primary centre to the North Lawn facility under the capital master plan. The Secretary-General therefore proposed leasing a commercial data centre facility, from 1 July 2009 to 31 December 2011, enter into a service delivery agreement with the International Computing Centre to install new ICT equipment in that facility, and migrate all systems from the secondary data centre in the DC2 building to the leased facility by 1 November 2009, in time to provide a reliable backup during the relocation of the primary data centre from the Secretariat building to the North Lawn. The Secretary-General stated that the option of leasing a commercial data centre facility also allowed for flexibility in adjusting to changes in scope and offered a viable solution for the secondary data centre for UN Headquarters in the short term. The costs for the new secondary data centre, estimated at $25,737,500, would be shared between the regular programme budget and the peacekeeping support account. The Secretary-General said that a proposal for a permanent solution for the secondary data centre for UN Headquarters would be submitted during the 2012–2013 biennium.

In March [A/63/774], ACABQ said that the sequence of events demonstrated continued deficiencies in the planning and management of the project. Other options should have been considered since 2008 [YUN 2008, p. 1591], when the Long Island City option was abandoned. The Committee considered the proposal to be lacking in analysis and information, especially on the financial implications. More importantly, it was not convinced that the proposal was the most cost-effective or the most workable. The proposal did not provide the necessary assurance that its implementation would sufficiently mitigate risks. Under the circumstances and given the time constraints, the Committee had no prudent alternative but to recommend approval of the Secretary-General's proposal to establish the new secondary data centre, and that the Assembly note the estimate of $25,737,500 for the project, as well as the Secretariat's strategy of entering into a service delivery agreement with the International Computing Centre.

GENERAL ASSEMBLY ACTION

On 7 April [meeting 79], the General Assembly, on the recommendation of the Fifth Committee [A/63/648/Add.5], adopted **resolution 63/269** without vote [agenda item 118].

Information and communications technology, disaster recovery and business continuity for the United Nations: arrangements for the secondary data centre at Headquarters

The General Assembly,

Recalling its resolution 63/262 of 24 December 2008,

Having considered the report of the Secretary-General entitled "Information and communications technology, disaster recovery and business continuity for the United Nations: arrangements for the secondary data centre at Headquarters" and the related report of the Advisory Committee on Administrative and Budgetary Questions,

1. *Takes note* of the report of the Secretary-General;

2. *Reaffirms* the need for a global operational framework to enable the United Nations to respond effectively to emergency situations that may impair operations of critical elements of its information and communications technology infrastructure and facilities;

3. *Encourages* the Secretary-General to take a unified approach to disaster recovery and business continuity, utilizing all available infrastructure, in order to achieve economies of scale and cost efficiencies;

4. *Requests* the Secretary-General to ensure that the United Nations uses enterprise data centres rather than local data centres as far as possible;

5. *Notes with concern* the continued deficiencies in the planning and management of the project;

6. *Regrets* that the proposal of the Secretary-General did not provide the necessary assurances that its implementation would sufficiently mitigate risks, including risks related to the physical security of data, during the relocation of the primary data centre to the North Lawn at Headquarters;

7. *Requests* the Secretary-General, when utilizing the services of the International Computing Centre, to ensure compliance with all regulations and rules regarding procurement, in order to guarantee the cost-effectiveness of the services provided by the Centre;

8. *Endorses* the conclusions and recommendations contained in the report of the Advisory Committee on Administrative and Budgetary Questions, subject to the provisions of the present resolution;

9. *Reiterates its request* to the Secretary-General, expressed in section IV, paragraph 7, of its resolution 63/262, to ensure that the leased space is fully utilized if it is not possible to terminate the lease;

10. *Notes with concern* that the delays caused by the lack of reliable disaster recovery and business continuity services for Headquarters may lead to further cost escalation, including in respect of the capital master plan, and risk to data;

11. *Decides* that any further proposal for risk mitigation measures to protect data and the information and communications systems of the Secretariat during the construction work of the capital master plan, if necessary, shall be reported in the context of the annual progress report on the capital master plan;

12. *Requests* the Secretary-General to absorb 5,096,880 United States dollars within the approved budget of the capital master plan, and decides that 2,031,860 dollars shall be financed from the resources to be approved for the support account for peacekeeping operations for the period from 1 July 2009 to 30 June 2010 in order to pursue the most reliable and cost-effective risk mitigation measures during the migration of the primary data centre to the North Lawn;

13. *Also requests* the Secretary-General to carry out a classification of critical/non-critical systems of the Secretariat and to provide to the General Assembly an inventory of systems classified according to their degree of criticality at the time of its consideration of the proposal for a permanent secondary data centre;

14. *Further requests* the Secretary-General to ensure that the level of protection proposed has been subject to a thorough cost-benefit analysis;

15. *Recalls* paragraph 12 of section IV of resolution 63/262, and requests the Secretary-General to submit to the General Assembly no later than at the main part of its sixty-fifth session a unified disaster recovery and business continuity plan, including a permanent solution for Headquarters.

Also on 7 April, the Assembly, having considered the Secretary-General's report on revised estimates in the 2008–2009 programme budget related to business continuity management [YUN 2008, p. 1551] and the ACABQ comments thereon [ibid., p. 1552], took note, in section III of **resolution 63/268** (see p. 1391), of the progress in business continuity management and endorsed the ACABQ recommendations and conclusions. It requested the Secretary-General to further develop and justify the approach set out in his report, including clarifying the relationship with other initiatives, with a view to avoiding a piecemeal approach. He should submit a fully justified proposal for post and non-post resources in the 2010–2011 budget.

In his October report [A/64/477], the Secretary-General proposed an ICT framework and principles for a programme of work for developing a unified approach to disaster recovery and business continuity for UN Headquarters, offices away from Headquarters, regional commissions, peacekeeping and political missions and international tribunals. He also proposed a high-level strategy and action plan, with related resource requirements. The strategy would be implemented jointly by the Business Continuity Management Unit in the Department of Management and the Office of Information and Communications Technology. For the purposes of site recovery, the Secretary-General proposed establishing two enterprise data centres, one at Brindisi, Italy, and the other to be determined. Full implementation of a unified disaster recovery and business continuity plan was scheduled for late 2011. Project expenditures for 2010–2011 were estimated at $3,392,300. Comprehensive plans on disaster recovery and business continuity would be submitted for consideration in the context of the proposed 2012–2013 programme budget.

In October [A/64/472], the Secretary-General issued another report on revised estimates related to business continuity management, in which he described the progress made in relation to business continuity and pandemic preparedness activities, clarified the relationship with other initiatives and proposed a programme of work and related resource requirements for the implementation of business continuity management-related activities in all offices of the UN Secretariat, including offices away from Headquarters and regional commissions. The requirements related to activities pertaining to business continuity management and pandemic preparedness which were not included in other reports for 2010–2011. The General Assembly was requested to approve the establishment of 17 new posts and an amount of $9,786,800 for the 2010–2011 biennium.

In November [A/64/7/Add.8], ACABQ reiterated the importance of a coordinated approach to ensure the overall effectiveness of the business continuity objectives. ACABQ recommended acceptance of eight of the 17 posts requested on a temporary basis for the 2010–2011 biennium. It was of the opinion the business continuity capacity should be evaluated and a progress report submitted, indicating achievements and how the tasks, responsibilities and operationalization had been incorporated into organizational and management structures. It recommended that operational

costs to support the posts be adjusted, and non-post requirements be reduced by $663,500.

Also in November [A/64/7/Add.9], ACABQ emphasized the need to ensure that disaster recovery requirements were based on objective needs and that the most cost-effective solutions were fully explored. It encouraged the Secretary-General to explore all possibilities for consolidating and using the most reliable and cost-effective solution for data storage, business continuity services and hosting of enterprise systems, as requested by Assembly resolution 63/262 [YUN 2008, p. 1592], to report to the Assembly on the results of his review and to provide justification as to the cost-effectiveness of the sites selected for hosting the enterprise data centres. It recommended that the Assembly approve the Secretary-General's proposals related to the unified disaster recovery and business continuity plan, including revised estimates of $19,421,900 gross ($18,904,100 net) for the 2010–2011 biennium. It noted that a comprehensive plan would be submitted in the context of the 2012–2013 programme budget.

On 24 December, the Assembly, in **resolution 64/243** (see p. 1395), noted the progress achieved by the Secretary-General in business continuity management in response to the business risks faced by the Organization. It appropriated $2.2 million for the initiative and requested him to submit fully justified proposals for post and non-post resources in the 2012–2013 programme budget.

Enterprise resource planning system

As requested by Assembly resolution 63/262 [YUN 2008, p. 1592], the Secretary-General in October submitted his first progress report [A/64/380] on the enterprise resource planning (ERP) project known as "Umoja" (Swahili for "unity"). The Assembly, in resolution 60/283 [YUN 2006, p. 1580], decided to replace the Integrated Management Information System with a next-generation ERP or comparable system. In 2008, the Assembly, in resolution 63/262, approved the Secretary-General's proposal [YUN 2008, p. 1591] for the phased implementation of an ERP solution at Headquarters and other duty stations, and financial resources amounting to $20 million for its implementation. The system was intended to renew the way the Organization managed its human, financial and material resources, allowing staff to work in a truly coordinated manner, and ensuring the more effective use of funds in the longer term. The Secretary-General estimated that, if fully funded, Umoja could deliver some $134 million to $224 million in annual capacity improvements and cost recovery, and significant qualitative benefits, such as increased operational effectiveness and timeliness, improved accountability, adoption of international best practices and standards, enhanced transparency and higher client satisfaction. Umoja was in the second of its four phases, namely the design phase, developing future business processes in detail. As at 31 July, key outputs delivered included: a comparative analysis of implementation strategies and scenarios; a comprehensive analysis of benefits; and other deliverables that supported the ongoing design of a "business blueprint" of the future resource management solution. Responding to Member States' requests for options for a reduced ERP planning package at lower cost, the Secretary-General recommended the "pilot first" option, which would minimize the number of deployment phases to three and involve a smaller-scale initial deployment to allow the system to be tested operationally in a contained environment. The "pilot first" option was the fastest and least expensive path to benefit realization. The design phase would be completed in the second quarter of 2010, followed immediately by the build phase and the development and execution of a comprehensive training programme. The complete solution would be ready by the end of 2011, and deployed to the entire Organization by the end of 2013. The Secretary-General stressed the importance of Umoja in improving the efficiency and effectiveness of the UN administrative, programme, and peacekeeping support activities. He requested the Assembly to endorse the proposals and approach described in the report, and approve the overall cost of the ERP project to be completed during the 2008–2013 period, estimated at $323,137,900 gross (315,792,300 net).

In November [A/64/7/Add.9], ACABQ, while recommending acceptance of the Secretary-General's proposals, noted that a significant portion was based on estimates, since contracts for the systems integration services had not been concluded. It recommended that the Secretary-General make every effort to reduce the overall project costs, exercise prudence in the utilization of resources, and provide, in future annual progress reports, full details on cost-containment efforts, project expenditures and justifications for the utilization of resources. The Committee recommended that the Assembly note the proposals and approach described in the Secretary-General's report, as well as the overall cost of the ERP project at a total project budget estimate of $315,792,300 gross.

On 24 December, the Assembly, in **resolution 64/243** (see p. 1395), endorsed the Secretary-General's "pilot first" option for deploying ERP and requested him to present options for lowering the project's overall cost. It approved $24,192,200 for ERP, to be funded from the regular budget for 2010–2011; authorized the Secretary-General to enter into commitments in the amount of $12,416,300; authorized him to enter into commitments in a total amount not to exceed $28,516,500 under the support account for

peacekeeping operations for the period from 1 July 2009 to 30 June 2010 in respect of the support account share of ERP; and requested him to report on the expenditures incurred.

Information and communications in UN system organizations

Management of Internet websites in UN system organizations

JIU report. In June [A/64/95], the Secretary-General transmitted a JIU report entitled "Review of the management of Internet websites in the United Nations system organizations". The objective of the review was to provide governing bodies and executive heads of UN system organizations with an assessment of the effectiveness and efficiency of the use of Internet websites as a communication tool for information dissemination. The report stressed the importance of issues such as content management system, accessibilities and multilingualism, and discussed the main challenges faced by those organizations in managing their websites.

JIU found that the level of staffing and training funds for website management were insufficient, considering the importance and impact the websites had on the mandate of the organizations. Without commensurate funding and qualified staffing, a website would soon lose its effectiveness and value. UN system organizations were also facing challenges in unifying their web presence through streamlined content and the application of a consistent online virtual branding. Awareness should be raised by the organizations to Member States that the web must continue to develop, and would require substantial and sustained investment in human resources and training. The report noted that the all those challenges stemmed from the decentralized structure of UN system organizations' websites in terms of content generation and management, due to the absence of an overall web governance structure, organizational web strategy integrated with business communication strategy (branding), standardized guidelines, policies and technology.

JIU recommended, among other measures, that UN system governing bodies should: establish an ad hoc committee dealing with the implementation of multilingualism on their corporate websites, review its report on measures and financial implications to achieve language parity on their websites and take appropriate action; and request the executive heads to report to the next session on the implementation of the recommendations made by JIU.

In October [A/64/95/Add.1], the Secretary-General transmitted his comments and those of CEB on the JIU report. Agencies generally agreed with the recommendations and suggested that future studies consider the application and utility of the Web beyond institutional outreach.

Review of ICT hosting services in UN system organizations

JIU report. In June [A/64/96], the Secretary-General transmitted a JIU report entitled "Review of information and communication technology (ICT) hosting services in the United Nations system organizations". The objective of the review was to provide a comparative study of the main ICT hosting services and identify best practices used by the UN system organizations, with a view to reducing costs and enhancing efficiency and effectiveness.

JIU noted that an ICT hosting decision should be based on three factors: the organizational situation and business demands; ICT governance and ICT strategy; and cost-benefits analysis of each ICT service considered. The selection process should incorporate a strengths, weakness, opportunities and threats analysis. UN system organizations encountered various difficulties in carrying out cost-benefits analysis in selecting an ICT hosting service. They also differed on the costing methodology applied and cost elements considered. Thus, they should implement consistent and comparable cost-benefits analysis in order to be accountable to the resources provided by Member States. It further noted that ICT hosting services should be selected through effective ICT governance. For that to take place, a competent ICT manager should be held responsible and accountable for a well-managed and strategic ICT operation, including hosted ICT services. The executive heads of UN system organizations should ensure that ICT managers were appointed at a senior level with sufficient access to the strategic decision-making process in the organization so that the ICT strategy and operation was aligned with the business strategy. The report also considered the joint governance structure of the Atlas project, a PeopleSoft enterprise resource planning system [YUN 2004, p. 1082], as a best practice for implementing a common ICT system, and viewed the lead agency and cluster model as best practice in joint ICT initiatives. Through that model, one UN system organization would take the lead to implement a new ICT initiative, build the business case and achieve benefits which would become attractive and feasible for other organizations to join later, thereby formulating a cluster of organizations sharing the same system/application.

In October [A/64/96/Add.1], the Secretary-General transmitted his comments and those of CEB on the JIU report. Agencies generally agreed with the recommendations.

International cooperation in informatics

In response to Economic and Social Council resolution 2007/14 [YUN 2007, p. 1486], the Secretary-General in March submitted a report [E/2009/21] on international cooperation in the field of informatics. The continuing cooperation of the Ad Hoc Open-ended Working Group on Informatics and the UN Secretariat resulted in practical technology enhancements that facilitated the work of Member States, UN observers and accredited non-governmental organizations (NGOs). The Secretariat and the Working Group shared responsibility for creating and maintaining web pages. The Secretariat maintained Wi-Fi connectivity and dedicated Internet access points for delegates throughout the public areas and conference rooms of the New York campus; supported 792 e-mail accounts; handled 1,920 work orders in 2008 related to technical support for the permanent missions; and provided website services for many permanent missions. The Secretariat and the Working Group created a prototype website called CandiWeb in support of elections processes, and implemented a portal pilot that improved and consolidated web access to information resources and services for delegates at UN Headquarters. Relevant information previously only accessible on the Secretariat's Intranet was made available to Member States on that portal. In 2008, over 217 mission staff participated in training or coaching programmes provided by the Dag Hammarskjöld Library. The Secretariat also enhanced and upgraded its electronic meetings planning and resource allocation (e-Meets) and electronic documents control systems, and developed in-house technical solutions for presenting meeting data on electronic panels/displays. Idle time during the door displays were utilized for showing UN photos and movies from DPI's digital library. The United Nations Institute for Training and Research continued to broaden and streamline the use of instructional technology.

ECONOMIC AND SOCIAL COUNCIL ACTION

On 27 July [meeting 38], the Economic and Social Council adopted **resolution 2009/9** [draft: E/2009/L.30] without vote [agenda item 7 *(c)*].

The need to harmonize and improve United Nations informatics systems for optimal utilization and accessibility by all States

The Economic and Social Council,

Welcoming the report of the Secretary-General on international cooperation in the field of informatics and the initiatives of the Ad Hoc Open-ended Working Group on Informatics,

Recognizing the interest of Member States in taking full advantage of information and communications technologies for the acceleration of economic and social development,

Recalling its previous resolutions on the need to harmonize and improve United Nations informatics systems for optimal utilization and accessibility by all States, with due regard to all the official languages,

Welcoming the intensification of efforts by the Office of Information and Communications Technology of the Secretariat to provide interconnectivity and unhindered Internet access to all permanent and observer missions at the United Nations,

1. *Reiterates once again* the high priority that it attaches to easy, economical, uncomplicated and unhindered access for States Members of the United Nations and Observers, as well as non-governmental organizations accredited to the United Nations, to the computerized databases and information systems and services of the United Nations, provided the unhindered access of non-governmental organizations to such databases, systems and services does not prejudice the access of Member States or impose an additional financial burden for their use;

2. *Requests* the President of the Economic and Social Council to convene the Ad Hoc Open-ended Working Group on Informatics for one more year to enable it to carry out, from within existing resources, the due fulfilment of the provisions of the Council resolutions on this item, to facilitate the successful implementation of the initiatives being taken by the Secretary-General with regard to the use of information technology and to continue the implementation of measures required to achieve its objectives, and in that regard requests the Working Group to continue its efforts to act as a bridge between the evolving needs of Member States and the actions of the Secretariat and, in addition, to consider its future role, status and mandate and to develop findings in that regard;

3. *Expresses its appreciation* to the Secretariat for the continuing cooperation that it extends to the Working Group in the endeavour to further improve the information technology services available to all permanent and observer missions at the United Nations and, in particular, for the implementation of a Member State web portal to consolidate and simplify secure access by authorized representatives of Member States to relevant information, for the continued upgrading and stabilizing of e-mail services for delegates and for the continued assistance in the hosting of many mission websites, a cooperative effort of the Secretariat and the diplomatic community coordinated by the Working Group;

4. *Also expresses its appreciation* to the Working Group and the Secretariat for their efforts in providing training and support and in raising awareness in the area of United Nations informatics systems for optimal utilization and accessibility by all States;

5. *Requests* the Secretary-General to extend his full cooperation to the Working Group and to give priority to implementing its recommendations and guidance, particularly with regard to the upgrading of web-based services, including through the replacement of the CandiWeb elections and candidatures site;

6. *Also requests* the Secretary-General to report to the Economic and Social Council at its substantive session of 2010 on action taken in follow-up to the present resolution, including the findings of the Working Group and an assessment of its work and mandate.

UN premises and property

Capital master plan

Implementation of CMP

ACABQ report. In February [A/63/736], ACABQ transmitted its comments and recommendations on the reports of the Secretary-General on the sixth annual progress report on the implementation of the capital master plan (CMP) [YUN 2008, p. 1597] and on associated costs related to CMP [ibid., p. 1598]; the report of the Board of Auditors on the CMP for the year ended 31 December 2007 [ibid.]; and the Secretary-General's report on the implementation of those recommendations [ibid.]. Commenting on those reports, ACABQ urged the Secretary-General to take all necessary steps to avoid any further slippages in the relocation schedule, as such delays would be extremely costly. He should continue to pursue the value engineering exercise and include in his seventh annual progress report (see p. 1446) a detailed description of the value engineering initiatives under way and a breakdown of the potential savings to be realized through each initiative. ACABQ also made comments and recommendations on additional issues, including sustainability, safety and security, procurement, donations and parking. It expressed concerns about the way in which the request for additional resources to meet the associated costs had been presented in the Secretary-General's report on associated costs related to CMP, in which a number of the requirements listed did not relate directly to CMP but rather to ongoing capital improvements, and should not be considered as associated costs. The Committee considered that it was too early to take any decision on the estimated resource requirements for the next two bienniums (2010–2011 and 2012–2013). Accordingly, the Committee did not recommend approval at that time of the overall level of associated costs, estimated at $185,997,400 gross ($176,569,000 net). However, it recommended approval of a total amount of $30,272,400 net ($31,768,700 gross) for the 2008–2009 biennium.

GENERAL ASSEMBLY ACTION

On 7 April [meeting 79], the General Assembly, on the recommendation of the Fifth Committee [A/63/648/Add.5], adopted **resolution 63/270** without vote [agenda item 118].

Capital master plan

The General Assembly,

Recalling its resolutions 54/249 of 23 December 1999, 55/238 of 23 December 2000, 56/234 and 56/236 of 24 December 2001, 56/286 of 27 June 2002, section II of its resolution 57/292 of 20 December 2002, its resolution 59/295 of 22 June 2005, section II of its resolution 60/248 of 23 December 2005, its resolutions 60/256 of 8 May 2006, 60/282 of 30 June 2006, 61/251 of 22 December 2006, 62/87 of 10 December 2007 and section II.B of its resolution 63/248 of 24 December 2008, and its decision 58/566 of 8 April 2004,

Recognizing the importance of ensuring that persons with disabilities have access to the physical environment on an equal basis with others,

Having considered the sixth annual progress report of the Secretary-General on the implementation of the capital master plan, the report of the Secretary-General on associated costs related to the capital master plan, the report of the Board of Auditors on the capital master plan for the year ended 31 December 2007, the report of the Secretary-General on the implementation of the recommendations of the Board of Auditors on the capital master plan, section IV.A of the annual report of the Office of Internal Oversight Services for the period from 1 July 2007 to 30 June 2008, the report of the Office of Internal Oversight Services on the comprehensive audit of the capital master plan and the related report of the Advisory Committee on Administrative and Budgetary Questions,

1. *Takes note* of the sixth annual progress report of the Secretary-General on the implementation of the capital master plan, the report of the Secretary-General on associated costs related to the capital master plan, the report of the Board of Auditors on the capital master plan for the year ended 31 December 2007, the report of the Secretary-General on the implementation of the recommendations of the Board of Auditors on the capital master plan, section IV.A of the annual report of the Office of Internal Oversight Services for the period from 1 July 2007 to 30 June 2008 and the report of the Office of Internal Oversight Services on the comprehensive audit of the capital master plan;

2. *Endorses* the conclusions and recommendations contained in the report of the Advisory Committee on Administrative and Budgetary Questions, subject to the provisions of the present resolution;

3. *Accepts* the report of the Board of Auditors on the capital master plan for the year ended December 2007;

4. *Approves* the recommendations of the Board of Auditors contained in its report;

5. *Reiterates its serious concern* at the hazards, risks and deficiencies of the United Nations Headquarters building in its current condition, which endanger the safety, health and well-being of staff, delegations, visitors and tourists;

6. *Stresses* the special role of the host country Government with regard to support for United Nations Headquarters, in New York;

7. *Notes* the benefits, including economic ones, accruing to host countries from the presence of the United Nations, and the costs incurred;

8. *Recalls* the current practices of host Governments with regard to support for United Nations headquarters and United Nations bodies located in their territories;

9. *Takes note* of paragraph 21 of the sixth annual progress report of the Secretary-General, and recalls paragraph 23 of the report of the Advisory Committee on Administrative and Budgetary Questions, and stresses that any arrangement with the host country shall safeguard the integrity of the relevant body of international law, including the Headquarters Agreement between the United Nations and the host country and the Convention on the Privileges and Immunities of the United Nations;

I
Sixth annual progress report
Financial management

1. *Requests* the Secretary-General to ensure by all means that project costs are brought back within the approved budget;

2. *Reiterates its request* that the Secretary-General make every effort to avoid budget increases through sound project management practices and to ensure that the capital master plan is completed within the budget as approved in its resolution 61/251;

Value engineering

3. *Welcomes* the success of value engineering activities in identifying over 100 million United States dollars in potential cost savings;

4. *Requests* the Secretary-General to include detailed information on the following in his seventh annual progress report:

(a) Value engineering activities, as well as costs and fees;

(b) The advantages that could potentially be realized as a result of the prevailing market conditions;

(c) A cost-benefit analysis of any additional sustainability options;

5. *Encourages* the Secretary-General to continue finding efficiency gains and cost reductions throughout the implementation of the capital master plan;

6. *Emphasizes* that the value engineering exercise shall not undermine the quality, durability and sustainability of the materials used, the original design of Headquarters or the commitment of the project to the highest standards of safety, health and well-being of staff and delegations, in particular with regard to the handling of asbestos;

Schedule

7. *Notes* the delay in the process of relocating Secretariat staff to office swing space, and requests the Secretary-General to ensure that the current schedule is adhered to as a matter of urgency;

8. *Recalls* paragraph 14 of the report of the Advisory Committee on Administrative and Budgetary Questions, and urges the Secretary-General to take all steps necessary to avoid any further slippage in the relocation schedule in order to prevent costly delays, including those which may disrupt the work of the General Assembly;

Sustainability

9. *Welcomes* the implementation of projects relating to sustainability approved by the General Assembly, and notes that those projects are being pursued within existing resources;

10. *Requests* the Secretary-General to continue to consider cost-beneficial ways of improving energy efficiency and lowering energy consumption and to report thereon in his seventh annual progress report;

11. *Recalls* paragraph 10 of its resolution 61/251 and paragraph 37 of its resolution 62/87, and reaffirms that any scope options in addition to those already approved by

the General Assembly shall be submitted by the Secretary-General to the Assembly for its consideration and approval;

Procurement

12. *Reaffirms* its resolution 62/269 of 20 June 2008, and requests the Secretary-General to comply fully with the relevant provisions contained therein;

13. *Recalls* paragraph 33 of its resolution 62/269, and stresses that, until a decision is taken by the General Assembly on the issue of environmentally friendly and sustainable procurement, the Secretary-General shall not use any criteria that unduly restrict the ability of vendors to participate in procurement processes owing to environmental friendliness or sustainability requirements;

14. *Notes* the lack of diversification in the origin of vendors subcontracted by the construction manager of the capital master plan and also notes that no procurement contract has been awarded to vendors from developing countries or countries with economies in transition;

15. *Reiterates its requests* to the Secretary-General in its resolutions 61/276 of 29 June 2007 and 62/269 to continue to explore additional innovative ways to promote procurement from developing countries and countries with economies in transition and to identify obstacles preventing their participation in United Nations procurement contracts and to report on concrete measures taken in this regard;

16. *Reaffirms* paragraph 18 of its resolution 62/87 on procurement opportunities for developing countries and countries with economies in transition, as well as paragraph 28 of its resolution 62/269 relating to bidding by joint ventures, and reiterates its request to the Secretary-General to submit a report in this regard for consideration by the General Assembly at its sixty-fourth session;

17. *Requests* the Secretary-General to ensure that the construction manager, in consultation with the Procurement Division of the Department of Management of the Secretariat, prepares and implements an action plan to promote procurement opportunities for contractors and vendors from developing countries and countries with economies in transition, and to include detailed information on the action plan and its implementation in his forthcoming annual progress reports;

18. *Reaffirms* paragraphs 19 to 23 of its resolution 62/87, and requests the Secretary-General to continue to report on their implementation in the annual progress reports on the capital master plan;

19. *Requests* the Secretary-General to review all expression of interest notices and invitations to bid issued by the construction manager in order to ensure that their contents fully comply with the relevant resolutions of the General Assembly and do not unduly restrict the diversification of the origin of vendors;

20. *Notes* that some measures taken to avoid delays in the capital master plan procurement process, in particular the ex post facto review of contracts, risk having a negative impact in terms of internal controls, and requests the Secretary-General to ensure that the procurement processes are in full compliance with the Financial Regulations and Rules of the United Nations;

21. *Also notes* that the Office of Internal Oversight Services is engaged in the preparation of a comprehensive report on all aspects of the procurement process related to the capital master plan, and in this regard requests the Secretary-General to entrust the Office to include in its report factors that may restrict the diversification of the origin of vendors, including the current subcontracting process, local regulations, labour laws and sustainability options, as well as information on vendors' compliance with existing rules and regulations of the United Nations and general conditions of contract, and to report thereon to the General Assembly at its sixty-fourth session;

Health and safety

22. *Reaffirms* its commitment to the safety, security, health and well-being of staff, delegations, visitors and tourists at the United Nations, and requests the Secretary-General to ensure that concrete safeguards for the achievement of those objectives are in place and are part of the standard operating procedures throughout the implementation of the capital master plan;

23. *Requests* the Secretary-General to ensure, in particular, strict compliance with the highest applicable standards for the handling of asbestos, and to report to the General Assembly on measures taken in this regard in the context of the forthcoming annual reports and the regular briefings on the implementation of the capital master plan;

24. *Reaffirms* its resolution 63/8 of 3 November 2008, and in this regard requests the Secretary-General to designate sheltered smoking areas in order to make the renovated United Nations Headquarters premises smoke-free;

Donations

25. *Decides* not to endorse the donation policy related to the capital master plan, and requests the Secretary-General to make new proposals in this regard that allow all Member States, without distinction or conditions, to make donations, in full conformity with the international and intergovernmental character of the Organization as well as the Financial Regulations and Rules of the United Nations and without prejudice to the scope, specifications and design of the project, and to report thereon to the General Assembly;

26. *Stresses* that the donations shall be used, where possible, to offset approved estimated costs of the project, as well as associated costs approved by the General Assembly;

27. *Requests* the Secretary-General to develop a gift registry accessible by all staff members in the Secretariat for declaring gifts received from governmental and non-governmental sources;

28. *Also requests* the Secretary-General to promulgate an administrative issuance on policies and procedures addressing the acceptance, reporting, recording, storing and disposing of gifts to the Organization in the context of relocations related to the capital master plan;

29. *Reaffirms* paragraphs 44 and 45 of its resolution 62/87, and requests the Secretary-General to fully ensure the appropriate handling of works of art, masterpieces and other gifts throughout all stages of construction work;

Parking

30. *Reaffirms* paragraph 10 of its resolution 61/251, by which it approved the capital master plan and its budget, including the resources for additional scope options, in particular the structural strengthening of various components of the existing structure to provide greater blast resistance;

31. *Also reaffirms* paragraph 37 of its resolution 62/87, in which it decided that any scope options in addition to those already approved by the General Assembly should be submitted by the Secretary-General to the Assembly for its consideration and approval;

32. *Further reaffirms* that the General Assembly has the sole prerogative of deciding on any changes to the capital master plan project, budget and implementation strategy, as approved in its resolutions;

33. *Notes with concern* the existing difficulties with regard to the availability of parking at the United Nations, and requests the Secretary-General to ensure that the total number of parking spaces available to Member States will not diminish upon the completion of the capital master plan;

Accessibility

34. *Recalls* paragraph 5 of its resolutions 61/106 of 13 December 2006 and paragraph 5 of its resolution 62/170 of 18 December 2007;

35. *Requests* the Secretary-General to provide specific information in his next annual report about the measures taken to eliminate physical, communication or technical barriers to persons with disabilities at United Nations Headquarters in the framework of the capital master plan;

36. *Also requests* the Secretary-General to ensure that measures to be taken in the context of the capital master plan with a view to applying host city building, fire and safety codes do not violate the provisions of the Convention on the Rights of Persons with Disabilities, especially those related to accessibility, and also requests the Secretary-General to report on this subject in future annual progress reports;

Oversight

37. *Reaffirms* paragraphs 16 and 17 of its resolution 62/87, and stresses the importance of ensuring effective oversight and audit coverage of the implementation of the capital master plan;

38. *Requests* the Secretary-General to develop adequate and effective tools to permanently monitor essential elements of progress made in the context of the implementation of the capital master plan, including a summary scoreboard to describe the development of the project at any given time, and to include detailed information on such tools in forthcoming annual progress reports;

Advisory board

39. *Regrets* that the advisory board requested in its resolutions 57/292, 61/251 and 62/87 has not yet been established;

40. *Decides* that the advisory board shall be established no later than 31 December 2009, as originally intended, within its current mandate and in accordance with the provisions of paragraph 26 of General Assembly resolution 62/87;

41. *Also decides* that if the advisory board has not been established by 31 December 2009, the General Assembly will appoint five members, one from each regional group, for a non-renewable term of four years, and in that event will request the Secretary-General to seek candidatures from Member States;

Seventh annual progress report

42. *Requests* the Secretary-General to continue to report on the status of the project, the schedule, the projected completion cost, the status of contributions, the working capital reserve, the status of the advisory board and the letter of credit in his seventh annual progress report;

II

Associated costs

1. *Recalls* paragraph 34 of the report of the Advisory Committee on Administrative and Budgetary Questions, and notes with concern that a number of the requirements set out in the report of the Secretary-General on associated costs do not relate directly to the capital master plan, but rather are investment costs and long-term commitments;

2. *Decides* that the approved associated costs for the capital master plan will be financed from within the approved budget of the capital master plan unless otherwise specified by the General Assembly;

3. *Decides* not to approve the overall level of associated costs at this time, bearing in mind opportunities for further cost reductions posed by the present economic circumstances as well as savings realized by the Secretary-General;

4. *Expresses its regret* that the Secretary-General has entered into commitments for the financial period 2008–2009 for associated costs absent the formal approval of the Assembly, which is inconsistent with the Financial Regulations and Rules of the United Nations, and further expresses its concern that the Secretary-General has not complied with paragraph 43 of its resolution 62/87;

5. *Recalls* paragraph 60 of the report of the Advisory Committee on Administrative and Budgetary Questions, and decides not to suspend the provisions for the application of credits under regulations 3.2 *(d)*, 5.3 and 5.4 of the Financial Regulations and Rules of the United Nations;

6. *Also recalls* section II.B of its resolution 63/248, and regrets that the Secretary-General did not consult Member States on the need to upgrade the broadcast facility, even though the upgrade was conceived long before the conception of the capital master plan;

7. *Requests* the Secretary-General to utilize the existing furniture where possible in a cost-effective manner;

8. *Also requests* the Secretary-General to reduce the projected costs of furniture for the new facilities of the United Nations;

9. *Recalls* paragraph 50 of the report of the Advisory Committee on Administrative and Budgetary Questions, and requests the Secretary-General to make every effort to absorb the associated costs for the biennium 2008–2009 from within the overall budget approved for the capital master plan in a total amount of 30,272,400 dollars (net), broken down as follows:

(a) 995,300 dollars for the Department for General Assembly and Conference Management;

(b) 3,823,100 dollars for the Department of Public Information;

(c) 11,720,100 dollars for the Office of Central Support Services;

(d) 1,636,000 dollars for the Office of Information and Communications Technology;

(e) 7,576,300 dollars for the Department of Safety and Security;

(f) 4,521,600 dollars for construction, alteration, improvement and major maintenance activities at Headquarters;

(g) 1,496,300 dollars for staff assessment requirements, to be offset by the equivalent amount of income from staff assessment;

and to report the related expenditures in financial statements of the Organization in accordance with established procedures;

10. *Requests* the Secretary-General to submit to the General Assembly, for its decision at the main part of its sixty-fourth session, in the context of his seventh annual progress report on the implementation of the capital master plan, proposals for financing the associated costs required for the year 2010 from within the approved budget for the capital master plan;

11. *Recalls* section II.B of its resolution 63/248, and requests the Secretary-General to continue to provide adequate information technology support for conference services, within the existing resources of the Department for General Assembly and Conference Management, in order to ensure their seamless operation throughout the implementation of the capital master plan.

Report of Secretary-General. In response to General Assembly resolution 57/292 [YUN 2002, p. 1375], the Secretary-General in September submitted his seventh annual progress report on CMP [A/64/346], which outlined activities undertaken since his previous report [YUN 2008, p. 1597]. He said that significant progress had been achieved during the first year of the construction phase of the project, including the completion of the design and construction documents for 80 per cent of the entire project; the award to the construction manager of approximately $746.7 million in guaranteed maximum price contracts for construction work; the initiation of the construction of the temporary North Lawn building and all the other swing spaces; asbestos abatement and swing space construction work in the Dag Hammarskjöld Library building and off-site buildings; and the commencement of work to modernize the infrastructure systems and basements on campus. The Secretary-General said that off-site swing space fit-out would be completed in the autumn of 2009 to temporarily house Secretariat departments and offices during the renovation and modernization. The relocation of staff to swing spaces commenced in the spring of 2009 in order to prepare for the start of construction in the Secretariat and Conference buildings in late 2009 and early 2010. The project remained on schedule for completion in 2013. Continuous value engineering, as well as the current economic climate, had helped the CMP procurement process to maintain the budget goals established in the sixth annual progress report.

The Secretary-General recommended that the Assembly take note of the progress made; appropriate the remaining balance of $689.9 million towards the construction phases; and request the Secretary-General to continue reporting on the status of the project, the schedule, the projected cost to complete, the status of contributions and the working capital reserve.

Associated costs

In an addendum to his seventh report on CMP [A/64/346/Add.2], the Secretary-General, as requested by the Assembly in resolution 63/270 (see p. 1442), provided information on the status of expenditures of the associated costs for the biennium 2008–2009 and estimated requirements for 2010. He recommended that the Assembly approve the continued funding of associated costs for 2010 from within the approved CMP budget, as well as the total associated costs for that year in the amount of $50,114,100.

In October [A/64/7/Add.5], ACABQ reiterated that the associated costs should not be investment costs or long-term commitments. It recommended approval of associated costs for 2010 in the amount of $45,841,700.

Risk mitigation measures

Responding to resolution 63/269 (see p. 1438), the Secretary-General in September submitted a report [A/64/346/Add.1] on the proposal for risk mitigation measures to protect data and the information and communications systems of the Secretariat during construction work of CMP, in which he provided an update on the project for implementing a new secondary data centre, including the resources required for the 2010–2011 biennium. The Secretariat had engaged a consulting company experienced in data centre relocation to provide expert advice in planning the relocation of both the primary and the secondary data centres, had identified a suitable data facility in New Jersey and had entered into a 30-month lease. However, the proposal to engage the services of the International Computing Centre to provide ICT equipment and services was deemed technically unacceptable as the Centre was unable to meet the Secretariat's schedule for completing the secondary data centre migration. The Secretariat had therefore set up an in-house dedicated project team to ensure proper execution. The new secondary data centre was expected to be operational in time to mitigate the risks during the migration of the primary data centre. With regard to resource requirements, as a result of the decision not to engage the Centre, the Secretariat was required to purchase and/or lease all the equipment directly, resulting in total revised resource requirements of $21,697,500.

In October [A/64/7/Add.5], ACABQ expressed concern about the risks posed to the project and urged the Secretary-General to continue monitoring the situation and ensuring that the activities related to the migration and running of the secondary data centre were completed within the CMP time frame. The Committee recommended that Secretary-General review the procedures in place and make the necessary adjustments, and report on the measures taken in the context of the annual report on procurement activities.

Review of CMP

Report of Board of Auditors. A July report of the Board of Auditors on CMP for the year ended 31 December 2008 [A/64/5 (Vol. V)] reviewed the financial transactions and programme management for 2008, as well as the actions taken to implement the nine recommendations it had made in its previous report [YUN 2008, p. 1598]. It found that six recommendations had been implemented; one was under implementation; and two, including the long-outstanding recommendation concerning the establishment of an advisory board, had not been implemented.

Expenditure for 2008 amounted to $229.6 million, an increase of 395 per cent over the 2007 expenditure of $46.4 million, representing more that twice the amount of aggregate expenditure for the previous financial years of $113.9. The excess of income over expenditure was $139 million in 2008, providing the CMP fund with a significant interest income of $27.7 million. Total assets of $1.379 billion were significantly higher than total liabilities of $477.9 million as at 31 December 2008, indicating that the project was still in its early stages.

The most recent estimate of the total cost of the project amounted to $1.967 billion, which was $90.7 million higher than the budget of $1.877 billion approved by the General Assembly, but lower than $1.974 billion and $2.067 billion presented in the sixth and fifth progress report of the Secretary-General, respectively. The reduction in the project cost estimate was due to a large reduction in the budget for contingencies (including price escalation). The Board stated that the budget approved by the Assembly for CMP could be adequate only if the specifications of the project were not further modified and the economic situation did not significantly change. However, the associated costs were unlikely to be absorbed within the overall approved budget. On procurement and contract management, the Board expressed concern about the inadequate level of internal control over amendments to contracts, as well as the non-adherence to the requirements of the Procurement Manual relating to the review and recommendation process. The Board made 11 main recommendations related both to the management of the project and to financial issues.

Report of Secretary-General. In September [A/64/368 & Corr.1], in accordance with General Assembly resolution 48/216 B [YUN 1993, p. 1207], the Secretary-General provided additional information on the implementation of the recommendations contained in the report of the Board of Auditors (see above). Of the 18 recommendations, the implementation of six was in progress, and nine recommendations had been implemented. The report also provided information on the status of implementation of the recommendations of the Board relating to prior periods.

OIOS report. In August [A/64/326 (Part I)], OIOS, reporting on the comprehensive audit of CMP, conducted in response to General Assembly resolution 62/87 [YUN 2007, p. 1488], stated that 90 risks were identified in four main risk types: delays, funding, project complexity and decision-making. More than half of the risks identified were considered high level. The audit of the provision of alternative offices, storage and other facilities indicated that: the majority of UN Secretariat departments and offices had not complied with policies on record keeping and management of UN archives; there were no digitization guidelines covering taxonomy and metadata standards, retention and disposition, information security and accessibility of digital records; and there were delays in finalizing guaranteed maximum price contracts, which contributed to the postponing of scheduled staff moves to swing spaces for three months. An audit of the CMP value engineering process concluded that the CMP Office followed a suitable process for identifying value engineering savings, resulting in a nearly $100 million reduction of the projected budget shortfall at the time of the audit. The audit also found that the Office had embedded value engineering into its culture and was applying it in a manner that had not compromised project objectives. Audits of CMP's project budgeting and financial control processes and the security provisions applied to staff, site and assets were also conducted.

GENERAL ASSEMBLY ACTION

On 22 December [meeting 67], the General Assembly, on the recommendation of the Fifth Committee [A/64/548], adopted **resolution 64/228** without vote [agenda item 132].

Capital master plan

The General Assembly,

Recalling its resolutions 54/249 of 23 December 1999, 55/238 of 23 December 2000, 56/234 and 56/236 of 24 December 2001 and 56/286 of 27 June 2002, section II of its resolution 57/292 of 20 December 2002, its resolution 59/295 of 22 June 2005, section II of its resolution 60/248 of 23 December 2005, its resolutions 60/256 of 8 May 2006, 60/282 of 30 June 2006, 61/251 of 22 December

2006 and 62/87 of 10 December 2007, section II.B of its resolution 63/248 of 24 December 2008 and its resolution 63/270 of 7 April 2009, and its decision 58/566 of 8 April 2004,

Recognizing the importance of ensuring that persons with disabilities have access to the physical environment on an equal basis with others,

Having considered the seventh annual progress report of the Secretary-General on the implementation of the capital master plan, the report of the Secretary-General on the proposal for risk mitigation measures to protect data and the information and communications systems of the Secretariat during the construction work of the capital master plan, the report of the Secretary-General on proposals for financing the associated costs required for the year 2010 from within the approved budget for the capital master plan, the report of the Board of Auditors on the capital master plan for the year ended 31 December 2008, the report of the Secretary-General on the implementation of the recommendations of the Board of Auditors contained in its report on the capital master plan for the year ended 31 December 2008, section IV.A of the annual report of the Office of Internal Oversight Services for the period from 1 July 2008 to 30 June 2009 and the related report of the Advisory Committee on Administrative and Budgetary Questions,

1. *Reiterates its serious concern* at the hazards, risks and deficiencies of the United Nations Headquarters building in its current condition, which endanger the safety, health and well-being of staff, delegations, visitors and tourists;

2. *Reaffirms* that the General Assembly has the sole prerogative of deciding on any changes to the capital master plan project, budget and implementation strategy, as approved in its resolutions;

3. *Stresses* the special role of the host country Government with regard to support for United Nations Headquarters, in New York;

4. *Notes* the benefits, including economic ones, accruing to host countries from the presence of the United Nations, and the costs incurred;

5. *Recalls* the current practices of Governments of host countries with regard to support for United Nations headquarters and United Nations bodies located in their territories, and takes note of paragraph 46 of the seventh annual progress report of the Secretary-General on the implementation of the capital master plan;

6. *Takes note* of the seventh annual progress report of the Secretary-General, the report of the Secretary-General on the proposal for risk mitigation measures to protect data and the information and communications systems of the Secretariat during the construction work of the capital master plan, the report of the Secretary-General on proposals for financing the associated costs required for the year 2010 from within the approved budget for the capital master plan, the report of the Board of Auditors on the capital master plan for the year ended 31 December 2008, the report of the Secretary-General on the implementation of the recommendations of the Board of Auditors contained in its report on the capital master plan and section IV.A of the annual report of the Office of Internal Oversight Services for the period from 1 July 2008 to 30 June 2009;

7. *Endorses* the conclusions and recommendations contained in the report of the Advisory Committee on Administrative and Budgetary Questions, subject to the provisions of the present resolution;

8. *Accepts* the report of the Board of Auditors on the capital master plan for the year ended 31 December 2008;

9. *Approves* the recommendations of the Board of Auditors contained in its report;

10. *Notes with concern* the findings of the Board of Auditors as contained in its report, emphasizes the importance of the full implementation of the recommendations of the Board, and requests the Secretary-General to provide, in his eighth annual progress report, the steps taken and the progress achieved towards the full implementation of those recommendations;

I
Seventh annual progress report
Financial management

1. *Requests* the Secretary-General to ensure by all means that project costs are brought back within the approved budget;

2. *Reiterates its request* that the Secretary-General make every effort to avoid budget increases through sound project management practices and to ensure that the capital master plan is completed within the budget as approved in its resolution 61/251;

3. *Expresses concern* about the merging of the provision for contingencies with that for forward pricing escalation, contrary to the outline of the budget as presented in the fifth annual progress report of the Secretary-General, and approved in its resolution 61/251;

4. *Requests* the Secretary-General to distinguish between the provision for contingencies and that for forward pricing escalation as was done in the previous presentation of the cost estimate for the project;

Value engineering

5. *Encourages* the Secretary-General to pursue the value engineering exercise so as to maximize savings and the cost-effective use of resources to complete the project within or below its approved budget, while ensuring, inter alia, that the quality, functionality and scope of the project are not compromised, that materials are used as originally intended and that the integrity of the architectural design of the complex is preserved;

6. *Requests* the Secretary-General to include in his eighth annual progress report detailed information on the following:

(a) Further clarification of the definition of value engineering;

(b) Detailed description of the value engineering activities, as well as the related costs and fees;

(c) The advantages that could potentially be realized as a result of the prevailing market conditions;

(d) A cost-benefit analysis of any additional sustainability options;

(e) Breakdown of the estimated cost savings to be realized through each value engineering initiative;

7. *Encourages* the Secretary-General to continue finding efficiency gains and cost reductions throughout the implementation of the capital master plan;

8. *Emphasizes* that the value engineering exercise shall not undermine the quality, durability and sustainability of

the materials used, the original design of Headquarters or the commitment of the project to the highest standards for the safety, health and well-being of staff and delegations, in particular with regard to the handling of asbestos;

Schedule

9. *Expresses concern* that the completion date for the capital master plan has slipped from mid-2013 to late 2013, as a consequence of the delay in the construction of the temporary North Lawn building, and takes note, in this regard, of the accelerated schedule developed by the Secretary-General, which allows for the completion of the capital master plan on time;

10. *Notes with concern* the delay in relocating Secretariat staff to office swing space, and requests the Secretary-General to ensure that the relocation of staff is undertaken in accordance with the relevant schedules to avoid any further delay;

11. *Requests* the Secretary-General to provide more comprehensive and specific information in future progress reports with respect to project delays and accountability for them, including the range of their cost implications and other potential consequences for the execution of the project, as well as actions to be taken to effectively manage and mitigate the delays or cost risk;

12. *Expresses its regret* that security concerns and space requirements were not duly considered at an earlier stage of the capital master plan and that the decision to maintain the Security Council within the main complex of buildings had not been part of the initial planning and has thus resulted in delays, significant changes in project design and additional costs;

Procurement

13. *Reaffirms* paragraphs 12 to 21 of section I of its resolution 63/270, and requests the Secretary-General to continue to report on their implementation in his annual progress reports on the capital master plan;

14. *Requests* the Secretary-General to fully address in a satisfactory manner the concerns raised by the Board of Auditors and the Headquarters Committee on Contracts regarding procurement and contract management, and further requests the Secretary-General to consider ways and means to increase significantly the level of internal control over amendments to contracts relating to the capital master plan;

15. *Also requests* the Secretary-General to report in his eighth annual progress report on the steps taken to ensure that all previous and future amendments to contracts relating to procurement for the capital master plan are in line with the United Nations Procurement Manual, and on the efforts undertaken to involve the Headquarters Committee on Contracts in the adjudication process prior to the signing or amendment of contracts relating to the project that are within the scope of the authority of that Committee in a manner which will not impede the expeditious progress of the project;

16. *Reiterates* that contracts relating to procurement for the capital master plan should continue to stipulate that the United Nations will not be responsible for delays, damage or loss on the part of the contractor;

17. *Expresses concern* at the risk to internal controls posed by the absence of a review of contractual amendments;

18. *Notes* that some measures taken to avoid delays in the capital master plan procurement process, in particular the ex post facto review of contracts, risk having a negative impact in terms of internal controls;

19. *Requests* the Secretary-General to ensure that the procurement process is in full compliance with the Financial Regulations and Rules of the United Nations;

20. *Decides* to keep the issue of oversight of contractual amendments under review;

21. *Notes with concern* that the seventh annual progress report of the Secretary-General did not contain adequate information on concrete steps taken to promote procurement opportunities for contractors and vendors from developing countries and countries with economies in transition relating to the capital master plan, reiterates its request to the Secretary-General to continue exploring ways to increase procurement opportunities for vendors from developing countries and countries with economies in transition, and reaffirms in this context the relevant provisions of its resolutions 54/14 of 29 October 1999, 55/247 of 12 April 2001, 57/279 of 20 December 2002, 59/288 of 13 April 2005, 60/1 of 16 September 2005, 61/246 of 22 December 2006 and 62/269 of 20 June 2008;

22. *Requests* the Advisory Committee on Administrative and Budgetary Questions, in accordance with regulations 7.6 and 7.7 of the Financial Regulations and Rules of the United Nations, to request the Board of Auditors to include in its next report on the capital master plan information on the factors that restrict the diversification of the origin of vendors and progress achieved in increasing the procurement opportunities for vendors from developing countries and countries with economies in transition relating to the capital master plan;

23. *Reiterates its request* to the Secretary-General to ensure that the construction manager, in consultation with the Procurement Division of the Department of Management of the Secretariat, prepares and implements an action plan to promote procurement opportunities for contractors and vendors from developing countries and countries with economies in transition, and to include detailed information on the action plan and its implementation in his forthcoming annual progress reports;

Health and safety

24. *Reaffirms its commitment* to the safety, security, health and well-being of staff, delegations, visitors and tourists at the United Nations, and requests the Secretary-General to ensure that concrete safeguards for the achievement of those objectives are in place and are part of the standard operating procedures throughout the implementation of the capital master plan;

25. *Requests* the Secretary-General to continue to ensure, in particular, strict compliance with the highest applicable standards for the handling of asbestos, and to continue to report to the General Assembly on measures taken in this regard in the context of the forthcoming annual reports and the regular briefings on the implementation of the capital master plan;

26. *Reaffirms* its resolution 63/8 of 3 November 2008, and requests the Secretary-General, in this regard, to designate sheltered smoking areas in order to make the renovated United Nations Headquarters premises smoke-free;

Donations

27. *Also reaffirms* the relevant provisions of its resolutions, in particular resolution 63/270, relating to donations for the capital master plan, and reiterates that the donation policy should not be restrictive and that it should be in full conformity with the international and intergovernmental character of the Organization as well as with the Financial Regulations and Rules of the United Nations and without prejudice to the scope, specifications and design of the project;

28. *Requests* the Secretary-General to continue to accept in-kind donations of Member States in the implementation of the capital master plan, in full conformity with the international and intergovernmental character of the Organization as well as with the Financial Regulations and Rules of the United Nations and without prejudice to the scope, specifications and design of the project;

29. *Also requests* the Secretary-General to ensure that works of art, masterpieces and other gifts are handled appropriately during all the stages of the capital master plan, and further requests him to cooperate with those Member States that wish to take care of their gifts of works of art, masterpieces and other items during the renovation period;

Parking

30. *Recalls* paragraphs 30 to 33 of section I of its resolution 63/270, expresses concern about the issue of the availability of parking spaces to the Member States in the garage of the United Nations complex, and the limitations imposed on Member States in this regard, including those related to night-time parking, reiterates its request that the total number of parking spaces available to the Member States before the implementation of the capital master plan be retained upon its completion and that every effort be made to maintain that number during the implementation of the capital master plan, and looks forward, in this context, to information on the review of the options in the forthcoming annual progress report;

Accessibility

31. *Requests* the Secretary-General to continue providing specific information, in his next annual report, about the measures taken to eliminate physical, communication or technical barriers to persons with disabilities at United Nations Headquarters in the framework of the capital master plan, in particular regarding improvement in the accessibility of interpretation booths;

32. *Also requests* the Secretary-General to ensure that measures to be taken in the context of the capital master plan with a view to applying host city building, fire and safety codes do not violate the provisions of the Convention on the Rights of Persons with Disabilities, especially those relating to accessibility, and also reiterates its request to the Secretary-General to report on this subject in future annual progress reports;

Oversight

33. *Reaffirms* paragraphs 37 and 38 of section I of its resolution 63/270, stresses the importance of ensuring effective oversight and audit coverage of the implementation of the capital master plan, and reiterates its request to the Secretary-General to develop adequate and effective tools to permanently monitor essential elements of progress made in the context of the implementation of the capital master

plan, including a summary scoreboard to describe the development of the project at any given time, and to include detailed information on such tools in forthcoming annual progress reports;

34. *Requests* the Board of Auditors and all other relevant oversight bodies to continue to report to the General Assembly annually on the capital master plan;

Advisory board

35. *Takes note* of paragraph 39 of the seventh annual progress report of the Secretary-General, and emphasizes that an independent, impartial advisory board for the capital master plan reflecting a wide geographical representation should be established, in accordance with General Assembly resolutions 57/292, 61/251, 62/87 and 63/270, no later than 31 December 2009;

Eighth annual progress report

36. *Requests* the Secretary-General to continue to report on the status of the project, the schedule, the projected completion cost, the status of contributions, the working capital reserve, the status of the advisory board and the letter of credit in his eighth annual progress report, as well as to include therein the information requested in the present resolution;

II

Risk mitigation measures to protect data and the information and communications systems of the Secretariat

1. *Recalls* its resolution 63/269 of 7 April 2009, and notes with concern that the Secretary-General did not move forward with arrangements with the International Computing Centre to lease services for the transfer of the secondary data centre, and urges the Secretary-General to continue to closely monitor the situation to ensure that the activities related to the migration and running of the secondary data centre are completed in accordance with the time frame of the capital master plan;

2. *Requests* the Secretary-General to continue to take advantage of the current economic climate in order to negotiate the most cost-effective lease and services possible and to report thereon to the General Assembly in the context of the eighth annual progress report;

3. *Also requests* the Secretary-General to absorb 11,644,530 United States dollars for the biennium 2010–2011 within the approved budget for the capital master plan, and decides that the Secretary-General shall include 1,254,190 dollars in the proposed requirements for the support account for peacekeeping operations for the period from 1 July 2010 to 30 June 2011 and 941,640 dollars in the proposed requirements for the support account for peacekeeping operations for the period from 1 July 2011 to 30 June 2012;

III

Associated costs

1. *Recalls* paragraph 79 of the report of the Advisory Committee on Administrative and Budgetary Questions, and notes with concern that there is a lack of adequate planning and coordination of the associated costs for the various departments and offices involved with the capital master plan;

2. *Also recalls* paragraphs 80 and 81 of the report of the Advisory Committee on Administrative and Budgetary Questions, encourages the Secretary-General to make every effort to ensure close coordination of activities across departments involved in the capital master plan to ensure that the project is completed on time and within the approved budget, and stresses the importance of designating a focal point in this regard;

3. *Notes with concern* that a number of the requirements set out in the report of the Secretary-General on proposals for financing the associated costs required for the year 2010 from within the approved budget for the capital master plan did not relate directly to the capital master plan but rather to ongoing capital improvements, investment costs and long-term commitments;

4. *Requests* the Secretary-General to closely review the requirements for additional safety and security related to the capital master plan and to seek all possible means for maximizing efficiencies, including through intensified use of host country support capacity, so as to reduce the requirements for temporary Security Officer positions;

5. *Also requests* the Secretary-General to provide an assessment of the extent to which more intensive recourse to technological systems could reduce requirements for round-the-clock services of a temporary security contingent to provide security coverage during the construction phase of the capital master plan project, in order to allow a better understanding of the potential for achieving further efficiency gains;

6. *Decides* that the approved associated costs for the capital master plan will be financed from within the approved budget for the capital master plan unless otherwise specified by the General Assembly;

7. *Also decides* not to approve the overall level of associated costs at this time, bearing in mind opportunities for further cost reductions posed by the present economic circumstances as well as savings realized by the Secretary-General;

8. *Recalls* paragraph 83 of the report of the Advisory Committee on Administrative and Budgetary Questions, and requests the Secretary-General to make every effort to absorb the associated costs for 2010 from within the overall budget approved for the capital master plan in a total amount of 42,069,695 dollars (net), broken down as follows:

(*a*) 645,600 dollars for the Department for General Assembly and Conference Management;

(*b*) 27,032,220 dollars for the Department of Public Information;

(*c*) 6,009,500 dollars for the Office of Central Support Services;

(*d*) 2,174,645 dollars for construction, alteration, improvement and major maintenance activities at Headquarters;

(*e*) 5,595,930 dollars for the Department of Safety and Security;

(*f*) 611,800 dollars for the Office of Information and Communications Technology;

9. *Requests* the Secretary-General to submit to the General Assembly, for its decision at the main part of its sixty-fifth session, in the context of his eighth annual progress report, proposals for financing the associated costs required for the year 2011 from within the approved budget for the capital master plan.

Additional office/conference facilities

Addis Ababa. In accordance with General Assembly resolution 63/263 [YUN 2008, p. 1546], the Secretary-General submitted, in October [A/64/486], his annual report on construction of additional office facilities at the Economic Commission for Africa (ECA) in Addis Ababa and the United Nations Office at Nairobi (UNON).

On progress in the construction in Addis Ababa, the Secretary-General reported that, as a result of negotiations with the host country, a voucher system had been worked out for the waiver of value added tax on related construction purchases, and renewed initiatives had been taken to finalize the construction of the alternate public access roads. A management review by the Department of Management of the Secretariat in February 2009 to address the Assembly's concerns, as reflected in resolution 63/263 found that the local project management team needed strengthening and the local architect should be made fully responsible for the building design. Subsequently, based on the findings of a report of the Procurement Task Force, the vendors involved in the construction tender were suspended and the tender cancelled. The Headquarters Procurement Division conducted another management review in March and made recommendations for advancing the construction project as a matter of priority. The project was scheduled to be completed in December 2011, within the approved cost estimate of $14,333,100, followed by an interior set-up of up to six months.

The Secretary-General said that action had been taken to strengthen the project's local leadership and management capacity. The local architect had been engaged to assume legal responsibility for the project design and to provide guidance on the tender process. Those measures would contribute to ensuring the implementation of the project within its revised time frame.

Nairobi. In February, a management review of the additional office facilities construction project at UNON, undertaken to address the Assembly's concerns expressed in resolution 63/263, concluded that the project was on schedule but there had been a failure to maintain appropriate communication between the additional office facilities project team and senior UNON management. Recommendations were made both to strengthen the local project management team and to form a senior-level management working group to provide independent technical advice to the UNON Director-General. The construction contract was signed on 3 April for $17,431,493, which was $231,493 greater than the initial estimate of $17,200,000. The increase would be funded from within the approved contingency. The total approved cost estimate of $25,252,200 would cover the full cost based on the signed contracts. Construction began on 4 May as scheduled and was expected to be completed by the end of 2010, in keeping with the original schedule.

In December [A/64/7/Add.12], ACABQ stated that it expected the new arrangements put in place at ECA as the result of the management reviews would enable the construction to be completed as scheduled. It welcomed the resolution of the issue of the value added tax normally levied on purchases related to the construction of new office facilities, as well as the progress made in implementing the UNON project. It emphasized that, in carrying out the construction projects at ECA and UNON, the lessons learned in the planning and implementation of CMP should be drawn upon.

The General Assembly, in section VII of **resolution 64/245** of 24 December (see p. 1407), endorsed ACABQ's conclusions and recommendations.

Integrated headquarters facility for UNAMI

In an October addendum [A/64/349/Add.5] on the estimates in respect of special political missions, good offices and other political initiatives authorized by the General Assembly and/or the Security Council, the Secretary-General provided an update on the status of the construction project related to the planned integrated headquarters compound in Baghdad.

The Secretary-General said that following a review of the planning assumptions, it had been determined that the best approach would be to build an integrated compound that included a single hardened structure for common areas and a series of smaller "pre-engineered buildings" for office and living accommodation. Steps were taken to identify an architectural consultancy firm for the design phase. Proposals were invited from potential bidders, which were due on 20 November. In response to concerns expressed over issues of proper management and oversight, a high-level advisory group was set up to serve as the principal interdepartmental committee to provide oversight, support and guidance to the project managers of the construction project and to monitor developments. In addition, a dedicated project manager was being recruited. The Government of Iraq had decided to allocate $25 million as a contribution towards the building of the new United Nations Assistance Mission for Iraq (UNAMI) headquarters in Baghdad; a trust fund was established to receive that contribution.

The Secretary-General explained that, in view of uncertainties and new developments in Iraq, which had led to repeated reviews of all planning requirements to respond to the changing conditions on the ground, the submission of the comprehensive report requested by the Assembly would be postponed to the resumed part of the sixty-fourth session (2010). As no obligations had been made in 2009 against the commitment authority of up to $5 million for UNAMI approved by the Assembly in resolution 63/263 [YUN 2008, p. 1546], the Secretary-General proposed that a similar commitment authority be provided for the 2010–2011 biennium.

ACABQ, in December [A/64/7/Add.13], recommended that the Assembly approve commitment authority for UNAMI of up to $5 million under the proposed 2010–2011 programme budget, to undertake design work in connection with the construction of the UN integrated compound in Baghdad.

By section VI of **resolution 64/245** of 24 December (see p. 1407), the Assembly endorsed that recommendation and requested the Secretary-General to submit updated comprehensive financial requirements for the construction of the compound for consideration at the main part of its sixty-fifth (2010) session.

Staff matters

Conditions of service

International Civil Service Commission

The International Civil Service Commission (ICSC), a 15-member body established in 1974 by General Assembly resolution 3357(XXIX) [YUN 1974, p. 875] to regulate and coordinate the conditions of service and the salaries and allowances of the UN common system, held its sixty-eighth (New York, 23 March–3 April) and sixty-ninth (Montréal, Canada, 29 June–10 July) sessions, at which it considered, in addition to organizational matters, the conditions of service applicable to Professional and General Service categories of staff and for locally recruited staff. The deliberations, recommendations and decisions of ICSC on those matters were detailed in its annual report to the Assembly [A/64/30 & Corr.2] (see sections below on specific issues).

In a statement of 17 September [A/64/358], the Secretary-General estimated the administrative and financial implications of ICSC decisions and recommendations for the 2010–2011 proposed programme budget and the proposed budgets of the International Criminal Tribunal for Rwanda (ICTR) and the International Tribunal for the Former Yugoslavia (ICTY) to be $2,593,600, $280,700 and $112,600, respectively, with regard to end-of-service severance pay for staff under fixed-term appointments and separation payments for staff in the Professional and higher categories. That would be reflected in the recosting of the corresponding 2010–2011 proposed budget.

On 9 October [A/64/7/Add.2], ACABQ stated that it had no objection to the Secretary-General's approach.

The Assembly, in section VIII of **resolution 64/245** of 24 December (see p. 1408), took note of the Secretary-General's statement and endorsed the ACABQ conclusions and recommendations.

Remuneration issues

In keeping with General Assembly resolutions 47/216 [YUN 1992, p. 1055] and 55/223 [YUN 2000, p. 1331], ICSC reviewed the relationship between the net remuneration of UN staff in the Professional and higher categories (grades P-1 to D-2) in New York, and that of the current comparator, the United States federal civil service employees in comparable positions in Washington, D.C. (referred to as the "margin"). In its 2009 report to the Assembly [A/64/30 & Corr.2], ICSC reported that the net remuneration margin for the period from 1 January to 31 December 2009 was estimated at 113.8. It drew the Assembly's attention to the fact that the average margin level for the past five years (2005–2009) had been below the desirable midpoint of 115, and currently stood at 113.6.

ICSC recommended to the Assembly that the base/floor salary scale for the Professional and higher categories be adjusted by 3.04 per cent through the standard consolidation procedure of increasing base salary and commensurately reducing post adjustment levels, with effect from 1 January 2010. The proposed base/floor salary scale resulting from that adjustment was shown in annex IV to the ICSC report.

Post adjustment

ICSC [A/64/30 & Corr.2] reviewed the operation of the post adjustment system, designed to measure cost-of-living movements through periodic place-to-place surveys at all duty stations. It considered the report of the Advisory Committee on Post Adjustment Questions (ACPAQ) at its thirty-first session (Vienna, 26 January–2 February), which contained recommendations on a wide range of methodological issues pertaining to the next round of cost-of-living surveys, scheduled to take place in 2010.

Based on the ACPAQ recommendations, ICSC requested that suggestions and proposals from organizations and staff federations concerning the list of items and their specifications to be used in the 2010 round of surveys be submitted by the end of July 2009 to the secretariat. The secretariat was requested to finalize the list of items and specifications, as well as procedures and guidelines governing data collection in the 2010 round of surveys, and present them for review and final recommendations by ACPAQ at its next ses-

sion. ICSC approved ACPAQ recommendations regarding the modus operandi for implementing the new approach to cost-of-living measurement based on real-time price comparisons with New York, for use in the 2010 round of cost-of-living surveys. The secretariat was requested to study the effects of modifications to the post adjustment classification with a view to aligning the review of the post adjustment classifications of all duty stations to that of New York. The secretariat was also requested to study the impact of shortening survey rounds for Group I duty stations (countries with convertible currencies and where out-of-area expenditures reported by staff members accounted for less than 25 per cent of the total expenditures), with due consideration of the costs and benefits, and present its findings for review and a final recommendation by ACPAQ at its next session.

Review of separation payments

ICSC [A/64/30 & Corr.2] concluded its review of separation payments, including termination indemnity, repatriation grant, death grant and end-of-service grant. The issues reviewed were: variations in termination indemnity schedules across organizations and contract types; the possible introduction of an end-of-service grant for staff on fixed-term contracts; cross-organizational variations in eligibility for repatriation grant; inconsistency of the name "repatriation grant" with the scope of the grant; and cross-organizational variations in the eligibility for death grant of surviving secondary dependants of a deceased staff member. It also considered a number of revisions to the separation payment arrangements.

ICSC recommended that the Assembly invite the governing bodies of the common system organizations to harmonize their termination indemnity schedules with that of the United Nations, pursuant to Assembly resolution 63/271 (see p. 1464); introduce end-of-service severance pay for fixed-term staff separating from the organization upon the expiration of contract after 10 or more years of continuous service in those organizations which had introduced the new contractual framework, as defined by ICSC in its 2005 annual report [YUN 2005, p. 1516]; reaffirm that the repatriation grant should not be payable to staff living in their home country and working abroad or to staff with permanent resident status at the last duty station; reiterate its call to the governing bodies of the common system organizations to align their provisions regarding repatriation grant eligibility and death grant eligibility with those of the United Nations; and reiterate that the death grant should not be payable to secondary dependants. ICSC also decided to monitor the introduction of end-of-service severance pay as an integral part of the new contractual arrangements.

Mandatory age of separation

Icsc [A/64/30 & Corr.2] considered the issue of changing the mandatory age of separation for staff members, in the context of a document prepared by the ceb Human Resources Network on the subject, in response to a jiu recommendation [YUN 2007, p. 1474] and the General Assembly's request, in resolution 63/250 [YUN 2008, p. 1616], that the Secretary-General and icsc explore that possibility, taking into account such issues as the rejuvenation of the secretariat, vacancy rates and the actuarial implications of that course of action for the Pension Fund. The Human Resources Network proposed that the age of separation for current staff be set at 62 by 1 January 2012, and that staff eligible to retire at 60 retain that right or remain in service until 62. It also agreed to review the raising of the mandatory age of separation to 65, once the United Nations Joint Staff Pension Fund had completed its actuarial study in 2010, and to examine innovative and flexible modalities in applying the mandatory age of separation.

Icsc noted that the issue involved a much wider scope of study which would integrate various human resources policy and pension aspects, such as geographical distribution; gender balance; rejuvenation of the workforce; career development; planning for the succession of retiring staff members; the actuarial situation of the Pension Fund; and the financial situation of the organizations. It requested its secretariat, in cooperation with the organizations and the Pension Fund, to prepare a report on the possibility of changing the mandatory age of separation, and decided to revert to the issue at its seventy-second session in 2011.

Senior Management Network

In accordance with General Assembly resolution 61/239 [YUN 2006, p. 1677], icsc, in August [A/64/30 & Corr.2], considered the status of the Senior Management Network (smn) (formerly Senior Management Service), the Organization's instrument for building managerial capacity throughout the common system in order to improve performance. Icsc continued to receive regular updates from ceb on progress made towards the development of smn. The ceb Human Resources Network reported to icsc that the first cohort of the newly redesigned programme, entitled "United Nations Leaders Programme: Developing Strategic Leaders", had been rolled out by the United Nations System Staff College in May. It was anticipated that the training programme would provide an opportunity for senior managers to network in a structured and continuous manner, resulting in a network of senior managers across the UN system. Thus, smn aims and objectives were expected to be achieved through the process of the Leaders Programme. The

Human Resources Network believed that, in the light of those new developments and in support of the bottom-up approach to developing a network, it would be more appropriate and effective if a senior managers' network were to develop in that manner. It therefore concluded that direct ceb involvement in managing a separate network was no longer required.

Icsc members noted that the smn original objectives had not been met and that it had never been adequately funded or resourced, much less given the priority it deserved. Members saw the shift of focus towards a common system leadership programme as a positive development. Icsc decided to report to the Assembly that ceb had decided to discontinue further work on smn.

Standards of conduct for the international civil service

The updated standards of conduct for the international civil service, developed to promote a common system of values and ethics essential to the international civil service, articulating the basic values and ethical standards of the United Nations, were adopted in 2001 by icsc [YUN 2001, p. 1342], which recommended them to the General Assembly and to legislative organs of the organizations of the common system. All organizations, except the United Nations Office for Project Services, the Office of the High Commissioner for Refugees and the International Fund for Agricultural Development, had implemented the standards as recommended by icsc. However, organizations had identified gaps and ethical challenges not addressed by the standards, including conflict of interest, post-employment restrictions, accountability, protection of whistleblowers from retaliation, abuse of authority, disclosure of information and negligence in the management of assets and resources.

Icsc noted that the principles and guidelines set out in the standards of conduct were still relevant and, although some updating might be necessary, no major revision was needed. Taking into consideration the fact that some organizations had identified gaps in the standards, icsc requested its secretariat to undertake with organizations and representatives of staff federations an initial review of the standards to ensure that they continued to meet the needs of the organizations and to define areas for updating.

Job evaluation standards
for General Service and related categories

At its fifty-seventh session [YUN 2003, p. 1431], icsc endorsed new job evaluation standards for the Professional and higher categories, and requested its secretariat to research proposals to reform the job evaluation system for staff in the General Service and related categories, in consultation with organizations and staff federations' representatives. At its 2009 session [A/64/30 & Corr.2], ICSC was informed that a job evaluation system had been developed based on the same conceptual framework and underlying principles of the standard promulgated for the Professional and higher categories [YUN 2003, p. 1445]. The proposed new system consisted of a master standard, which would be the primary job classification tool, and the grade level descriptors, which would provide linkages to competency development and performance management. The supporting elements (a glossary, guidelines and benchmark post descriptions) were soon to be completed. Like the Professional standard, the proposed General Service standard operated from an automated platform and had similar factors, adapted to better reflect its work. The detailed definitions of the factors for the master standard and the grade-level descriptors were annexed to the ICSC report. Further fine-tuning of the system would continue, and the secretariat would work with organizations to support its implementation. ICSC was asked to approve the new job evaluation system for the General Service and related categories for promulgation in January 2010.

ICSC confirmed that the following elements of the standard should be completed: guidelines in the use of the standard; a glossary; refinement of the grade level descriptors; and training within the organizations. ICSC approved the new job evaluation system for the General Service and related categories, consisting of a master standard and grade level descriptors; the new definition of General Service work as set out in annex VIII of its report; and the changes to the common classification of occupational groups. It requested its secretariat to finalize the work on the new job description format, a glossary and guidelines in the use of the system, as well as benchmark post descriptions, and to present the final elements at its seventieth (2010) session for final promulgation of the standard.

GENERAL ASSEMBLY ACTION

On 22 December [meeting 67], the General Assembly, on the recommendation of the Fifth Committee [A/64/581], adopted **resolution 64/231** without vote [agenda item 139].

United Nations common system: report of the International Civil Service Commission for 2009

The General Assembly,

Recalling its resolutions 44/198 of 21 December 1989, 51/216 of 18 December 1996, 52/216 of 22 December 1997, 53/209 of 18 December 1998, 55/223 of 23 December 2000, 56/244 of 24 December 2001, 57/285 of 20 December 2002, 58/251 of 23 December 2003, 59/268 of 23 December 2004, 60/248 of 23 December 2005, 61/239

of 22 December 2006, 62/227 of 22 December 2007 and 63/251 of 24 December 2008,

Having considered the report of the International Civil Service Commission for 2009,

Reaffirming its commitment to a single, unified United Nations common system as the cornerstone for the regulation and coordination of the conditions of service of the common system,

Reaffirming the statute of the Commission and the central role of the Commission and the General Assembly in the regulation and coordination of the conditions of service of the common system,

1. *Takes note with appreciation* of the work of the International Civil Service Commission;

2. *Takes note* of the report of the Commission for 2009;

A. Conditions of service of staff in the Professional and higher categories

1. Evolution of the margin

Recalling section I.B of its resolution 51/216 and the standing mandate from the General Assembly, in which the Commission is requested to continue its review of the relationship between the net remuneration of United Nations staff in the Professional and higher categories in New York and that of the comparator civil service (the United States federal civil service) employees in comparable positions in Washington, D.C. (referred to as "the margin"),

1. *Notes* that the margin between net remuneration of the United Nations staff in grades P-1 to D-2 in New York and that of officials in comparable positions in the United States federal civil service in Washington, D.C., for the period from 1 January to 31 December 2009 is estimated at 113.8 and that the average margin level for the past five years (2005–2009) stands at 113.6;

2. *Reaffirms* that the range of 110 to 120 for the margin between the net remuneration of officials in the Professional and higher categories of the United Nations in New York and officials in comparable positions in the comparator civil service should continue to apply, on the understanding that the margin would be maintained at a level around the desirable midpoint of 115 over a period of time;

2. Base/floor salary scale

Recalling its resolution 44/198, by which it established a floor net salary level for staff in the Professional and higher categories by reference to the corresponding base net salary levels of officials in comparable positions serving at the base city of the comparator civil service (the United States federal civil service),

Approves, with effect from 1 January 2010, as recommended by the Commission in paragraph 66 of its report, the revised base/floor scale of gross and net salaries for staff in the Professional and higher categories contained in annex IV to the report;

3. Gender balance and geographical distribution

1. *Notes with disappointment* the insufficient progress made with regard to the representation of women in the organizations of the United Nations common system, and in particular their significant underrepresentation at senior levels;

2. *Notes* the decisions of the Commission contained in paragraph 88 of its report;

3. *Invites* the Commission to continue to monitor future progress in achieving gender balance, including the aspect of regional representation if it deems it appropriate, and to make recommendations on practical steps that should be taken to improve the representation of women in the organizations of the common system;

4. *Welcomes* the decision of the Commission to encourage the organizations of the common system to promote and implement innovative approaches, such as outreach initiatives, to attract, develop and retain the most talented men and women;

5. *Requests* the Commission to review measures taken by organizations participating in the common system concerning the implementation of paragraph 3 of Article 101 of the Charter of the United Nations and to report its findings, as appropriate;

6. *Encourages* the Commission to consider further issues relating to the retention of female staff;

B. Conditions of service applicable to both categories of staff

1. Separation payments

1. *Takes note* of the recommendation of the Commission to introduce end-of-service severance pay in the organizations of the common system for fixed-term staff involuntarily separating from the Organization upon the expiration of their contract after ten or more years of continuous service;

2. *Decides* to revert to the question of the proposed end-of-service severance pay at its sixty-fifth session;

3. *Takes note* of the recommendation of the Commission for governing bodies of the organizations of the common system to harmonize their termination indemnity schedule with that of the United Nations, and requests the Commission to review the application of the termination indemnity and to report thereon to the General Assembly at its sixty-fifth session;

4. *Reaffirms* that the repatriation grant should not be payable to staff living in their home country and working abroad or to staff with permanent resident status at the last duty station, and reiterates its call to the governing bodies of the organizations of the common system to align their provisions regarding repatriation grant eligibility with those applicable in the United Nations;

5. *Reiterates* that the death grant should not be payable to secondary dependants, and reiterates its call to the governing bodies of the organizations of the common system to align their provisions regarding the death grant with those applicable in the United Nations;

2. Mandatory age of separation

1. *Notes* paragraphs 17 and 20 of the report of the Commission, and requests the Commission to report to the General Assembly at its sixty-sixth session on the results of the comprehensive analysis of the possibility of changing the mandatory age of separation, including the implications in the areas of human resources policies and pensions;

2. *Requests* the Commission to report to the General Assembly at its sixty-sixth session with advice and recom-

mendations on succession planning within the organizations of the common system;

C. Other matters
1. Senior Management Network

1. *Notes* the decision of the United Nations System Chief Executives Board for Coordination to discontinue work on the Senior Management Network;

2. *Requests* the Commission to monitor the adequacy and effectiveness of measures aimed at improving management capacity and performance within the common system and to report to the General Assembly on these matters, as appropriate;

2. General Service salary survey methodologies

Also requests the Commission, when reviewing the General Service salary survey methodologies under the Fleming principle, in accordance with the programme of work of the Commission for 2010–2011, to give higher consideration to the local national civil service among the retained employers, taking into account that the United Nations is a civil service organization.

On 24 December, the Assembly decided that the agenda item on the United Nations common system would remain for consideration during its resumed sixty-fourth (2010) session (**decision 64/549**).

Other remuneration issues

Conditions of service and compensation for non-Secretariat officials

ACABQ report. In February [A/63/726], ACABQ considered the 2008 report of the Secretary-General on conditions of service and compensation for officials, other than Secretariat officials, serving the General Assembly: full-time members of ICSC and the ACABQ Chairman [YUN 2008, p. 1604]. Upon inquiry, it was informed that the three officials were not entitled to the following conditions of service applicable to senior Secretariat officials: dependency allowance, rental subsidy, representation allowance, commutation of accrued annual leave upon separation and repatriation grant. It recommended that the Assembly take note of the Secretary-General's report.

By **decision 63/550 B** of 7 April, the Assembly deferred until its sixty-fourth (2009) session consideration of the Secretary-General's 2008 report and the related ACABQ report.

After-service health insurance benefits

In response to Assembly resolution 61/264 [YUN 2007, p. 1502], the Secretary-General, in September [A/64/366], provided additional information on liabilities and proposed funding for after-service health insurance benefits of the United Nations. The valuation of after-service health insurance liabilities, as at 31 December 2007, stood at $2,430.9 million from all funding sources, compared with $2,072.8 million as at 31 December 2005. Related pay-as-you-go costs for current retirees in the 2010–2011 biennium amounted to $130.4 million, compared with $102.2 million for 2008–2009, and was projected to increase to over $600 million by the 2036–2037 biennium, with the current $2.4 billion unfunded accrued liability increasing to over $11 billion by 31 December 2037. The Secretary-General stated that the current pay-as-you-go financing arrangement was not sustainable, given the anticipated accelerated growth in after-service health insurance expenditure. He therefore presented an alternative funding strategy involving a one-time infusion of $425 million, based on a transfer of $290 million from unencumbered balances and miscellaneous income under peacekeeping operations for the 2008–2009 biennium, with suspension of the appropriate financial regulation; and the a transfer of $135 million from extrabudgetary funds. In addition, the proposal involved systematic and ongoing funding under the special expense section of the regular budget and the support account for peacekeeping operations, as well as a charge of 9.6 per cent, 2.6 per cent and 1.0 per cent, respectively, to be applied against the net salary costs of the regular budget, extrabudgetary funds and peacekeeping operations chargeable as common staff costs. The proposal was intended to attain an initial funding goal of about 70 per cent on accrued after-service health insurance liabilities after 30 years.

ACABQ report. In October [A/64/7/Add.4], ACABQ stated that establishing a reserve fund or continuing the current pay-as-you-go approach to finance after-service health insurance liabilities was a policy matter for the General Assembly. That notwithstanding, it agreed with the proposal to continue biennial appropriations under the regular and peacekeeping budgets and to establish biennial appropriations to cover after-service health insurance benefits for those who retired from service under extrabudgetary funds. The Secretary-General should provide the Assembly with information on potential investment strategies for an after-service health insurance reserve fund, in particular the administrative costs. With respect to the initial funding of $290 million from the transfer of unencumbered balances from peacekeeping budgets for the 2008–2009 financial period through the suspension of financial regulation 5.3, ACABQ reiterated its recommendation that the transfer of such balances to entirely alternate uses represented an inappropriate financial management practice and recommended against the suspension of the financial regulation. Regarding the proposals for funding of current and future after-service health insurance liabilities for ICTY and ICTR, ACABQ was of the view that the United Nations should have a consistent approach towards the funding of those liabilities and recom-

mended that appropriations be made to cover the cost of current after-service health insurance participants who retired from the Tribunals. Recognizing that the Tribunals had limited mandates, the Assembly would need to address the Tribunals' long-term after-service health insurance liabilities in the context of the final performance reports. The Assembly might also wish to review the scope and coverage of existing after-service health insurance plans, as well as the contribution levels by the Organization and the participants.

GENERAL ASSEMBLY ACTION

On 24 December [meeting 68], the General Assembly, on the recommendation of the Fifth Committee [A/64/594], adopted **resolution 64/241** without vote [agenda item 131].

After-service health insurance

The General Assembly,

Recalling its resolution 58/249 A of 23 December 2003, section III of its resolution 60/255 of 8 May 2006 and its resolutions 60/283 of 7 July 2006 and 61/264 of 4 April 2007,

Having considered the report of the Secretary-General on liabilities and proposed funding for after-service health insurance benefits and the related report of the Advisory Committee on Administrative and Budgetary Questions,

Having also considered the report of the Joint Inspection Unit on United Nations system staff medical coverage and the comments of the Secretary-General and those of the United Nations System Chief Executives Board for Coordination thereon,

1. *Takes note* of the report of the Secretary-General on liabilities and proposed funding for after-service health insurance benefits;

2. *Also takes note* of the conclusions and recommendations contained in the report of the Advisory Committee on Administrative and Budgetary Questions;

3. *Requests* the Secretary-General to submit to the General Assembly at its sixty-seventh session, for its priority consideration, a report on managing after-service health insurance liabilities, bearing in mind that the "pay-as-you-go" principle is also one of the viable options, and to include in that report information on and an analysis of the following issues, inter alia;

(a) Scope and coverage of existing after-service health insurance plans;

(b) Administration costs related to alternative financial options;

(c) Arrangements for ensuring accurate funding from the different sources of funding;

(d) Options for contribution levels to after-service health insurance plans by its participants and by the United Nations;

(e) Comprehensive long-term strategies for financing after-service health insurance liabilities;

(f) Further measures to reduce the United Nations costs related to health-care plans;

(g) After-service health insurance plans for retired public sector employees offered by their respective Governments;

(h) The financial and legal implications of changing, for current retirees and active staff members: (i) the scope and coverage of the after-service health insurance plans and (ii) the contribution levels;

4. *Also requests* the Secretary-General to continue to validate the accrued liabilities with the figures audited by the Board of Auditors and to include this information and the outcome of the validation in the report requested in paragraph 3 above.

Staff safety and security

ACABQ report. In March [A/63/769], ACABQ, in its observations and recommendation on the Secretary-General's report on a strengthened and unified security management system for the United Nations [YUN 2008, p. 1611], was of the view that the question of strengthening UN security arrangements should be dealt with in an integrated manner, and recommended that a comprehensive report on a UN safety and security policy framework be submitted to the General Assembly early in the main part of the sixty-fourth (2009) session to permit consideration of the report in conjunction with the proposed 2010–2011 programme budget. The report should take into account the outcome of the management review of the Department of Safety and Security. As to the standardized access control project (PACT) (see p. 1462), the Committee recommended additional funding for phase I in the amount of $1.9 million and requested that the Secretary-General provide cost estimates for phase II directly to the Assembly. It also made recommendations on posts and equipment.

The General Assembly, by **decision 63/550 C** of 30 June, deferred until its sixty-fourth (2009) session consideration of the Secretary-General's report on a strengthened and unified security management system for the United Nations [YUN 2008, p. 1611] and the ACABQ report thereon (see above); his report on measures taken to ensure the effective implementation of the arrangements in place for the sharing of costs for safety and security across the UN system [A/62/641]; and the OIOS report on a comprehensive management audit of the Department of Safety and Security [YUN 2008, p. 1573].

Report of Secretary-General. In response to General Assembly resolution 63/138 [YUN 2008, p. 1611], the Secretary-General, in August [A/64/336], submitted a report on the safety and security of humanitarian personnel and protection of UN personnel, covering the period from 1 July 2008 to 30 June 2009. He noted that staff security remained precarious and personnel continued to be subjected to such threats as armed conflicts, terrorism, hostage-taking, kidnapping, banditry, harassment and intimidation. Abduc-

tion and hostage-taking, whether politically, economically or criminally motivated, continued unabated, compelling in some cases a large-scale and protracted hostage incident management response requiring extraordinary investment of time and resources. United Nations and humanitarian personnel continued to face deteriorating security conditions in many locations, hindering their ability to deliver lifesaving programmes, and were subjected to collateral damage during situations of open conflict. They were increasingly the targets of attacks by extremists, armed groups and disenfranchised elements, a situation further exacerbated by a disinformation campaign by extremists urging violence against humanitarians.

Increased challenges to the UN security management system worldwide, such as the 9 June killing of two UN international staff members during a suicide bomb attack on the Pearl Continental Hotel in Peshawar, Pakistan, compelled an extensive review of operating procedures. A reinforced common framework for security risk management and a new, threat-focused concept for a security level system would aim to maintain an effective UN presence even in situations of extreme insecurity. However, resources and new strategic tools were required to keep pace with evolving security situations.

During the reporting period, 27 UN civilian staff members lost their lives as a result of acts of violence, 11 in Africa, 7 in the Middle East, 5 in the Americas, and 4 in Asia and the Pacific. Locally recruited personnel accounted for the majority of casualties and victims; of the 27 deaths, 25 were nationally recruited staff. Violent incidents also continued unabated: there were 273 recorded cases of attacks, 505 incidents of harassment and intimidation, 654 robberies, 258 physical assaults, and 131 cases of hijacking. There were 208 reported cases of arrest by State actors and 50 cases of detention by non-State actors. In addition, there were 89 cases of forced entry and/or occupations of UN offices and 628 residential break-ins. The greatest number of security incidents and threats occurred in Africa, the Middle East and Asia.

As part of measures taken to enhance security, the Department of Safety and Security (DSS) had redoubled efforts to improve liaison with host country security elements to gain more timely and effective information to enable UN programmes to continue in difficult security environments. The Secretary-General requested the CEB High-Level Committee on Management to review the recommendations contained in the report of the Independent Panel on Safety and Security of United Nations Personnel and Premises Worldwide [YUN 2008, p. 1611], and to prepare recommendations and options for a more effective UN system-wide security management system. In response, a steering committee was established, chaired by the Under-Secretary-General for Field

Support, with the participation of DSS and representatives at the highest level of CEB member organizations.

In line with the new approach and vision, DSS promoted three key principles: "how to stay", "no programme without security" and "no security without resources", reflecting a shift in security culture throughout the UN system by, among other measures, mainstreaming security management, enhancing critical incident stress management, improving information security management, and adopting a framework for threat and risk analysis. CEB adopted a statement [CEB/2009/1] urging Member States to uphold their host Government responsibilities, support core resource needs for the UN security management system and provide appropriate and sustainable funding. It also made recommendations as part of a comprehensive plan for a strengthened and enhanced system-wide security management system, including the establishment of the Executive Group on Security to facilitate rapid decision-making and the development of a UN policy and guidelines for estate safety and security.

The Secretary-General encouraged the UN system at the highest level to address the CEB recommendations as priorities, working closely with host Governments and local communities, and reaffirmed the responsibility of Member States as host Governments and as providers of financial resources. He added that DSS would intensify its efforts to implement and maintain a modern and flexible information management capacity in support of its analytical and operational requirements, and would introduce flexible methods to enable operations based on security risk assessments.

Terrorist attack in Afghanistan. On 29 October, following a terrorist attack in Kabul the previous day, in which several UN staff members were killed, the Security Council, in presidential statement **S/PRST/2009/28** (see p. 67), stressed the need to ensure the security of UN staff, expressed support for the measures taken by the Secretary-General in that regard and looked forward to his further detailed proposals.

GENERAL ASSEMBLY ACTION

On 7 December [meeting 60], the General Assembly adopted **resolution 64/77** [draft: A/64/L.33 & Add.1] without vote [agenda item 70 *(a)*].

Safety and security of humanitarian personnel and protection of United Nations personnel

The General Assembly,

Reaffirming its resolution 46/182 of 19 December 1991 on the strengthening of the coordination of humanitarian emergency assistance of the United Nations,

Recalling all relevant resolutions on safety and security of humanitarian personnel and protection of United Nations

personnel, including its resolution 63/138 of 11 December 2008, as well as Security Council resolution 1502(2003) of 26 August 2003 and relevant statements by the President of the Council,

Recalling also all Security Council resolutions and presidential statements and reports of the Secretary-General to the Council on the protection of civilians in armed conflict,

Recalling further all relevant provisions of international law, including international humanitarian law and human rights law, as well as all relevant treaties,

Reaffirming the need to promote and ensure respect for the principles and rules of international law, including international humanitarian law,

Reaffirming also the principles of neutrality, humanity, impartiality and independence for the provision of humanitarian assistance,

Recalling that primary responsibility under international law for the security and protection of humanitarian personnel and United Nations and associated personnel lies with the Government hosting a United Nations operation conducted under the Charter of the United Nations or its agreements with relevant organizations,

Expressing its appreciation to those Governments which respect the internationally agreed principles on the protection of humanitarian and United Nations personnel, while expressing concern over the lack of respect for these principles in some areas,

Urging all parties involved in armed conflicts, in compliance with international humanitarian law, in particular their obligations under the Geneva Conventions of 12 August 1949 and the obligations applicable to them under the Additional Protocols thereto of 8 June 1977, to ensure the security and protection of all humanitarian personnel and United Nations and associated personnel,

Welcoming the fact that the number of States parties to the Convention on the Safety of United Nations and Associated Personnel, which entered into force on 15 January 1999, has continued to rise, the number now having reached eighty-eight, mindful of the need to promote the universality of the Convention, and recalling with appreciation the adoption of the Optional Protocol to the Convention on the Safety of United Nations and Associated Personnel, which expands the scope of legal protection under the Convention,

Deeply concerned by the dangers and security risks faced by humanitarian personnel and United Nations and associated personnel at the field level, as they operate in increasingly complex contexts, as well as the continuous erosion, in many cases, of respect for the principles and rules of international law, in particular international humanitarian law,

Stressing the importance of fully respecting the obligations relating to the use of vehicles and premises of humanitarian personnel and United Nations and associated personnel as defined by relevant international instruments, as well as the obligations relating to distinctive emblems recognized in the Geneva Conventions,

Commending the courage and commitment of those who take part in humanitarian operations, often at great personal risk, especially locally recruited staff,

Expressing profound regret at the deaths of and violent acts against international and national humanitarian personnel and United Nations and associated personnel involved in the provision of humanitarian assistance, and strongly deploring the rising toll of casualties among such personnel in complex humanitarian emergencies, in particular in armed conflicts and in post-conflict situations,

Expressing deep concern at the deep and long-lasting impacts of attacks and threats against humanitarian personnel and United Nations and associated personnel,

Strongly condemning acts of murder and other forms of violence, rape and sexual assault and all forms of violence committed in particular against women and children, and intimidation, armed robbery, abduction, hostage-taking, kidnapping, harassment and illegal arrest and detention to which those participating in humanitarian operations are increasingly exposed, as well as attacks on humanitarian convoys and acts of destruction and looting of property,

Expressing deep concern that the occurrence of attacks and threats against humanitarian personnel and United Nations and associated personnel is a factor that increasingly restricts the provision of assistance and protection to populations in need,

Recalling the report entitled "Towards a Culture of Security and Accountability" of the Independent Panel on Safety and Security of United Nations Personnel and Premises Worldwide and its recommendations, including on accountability,

Affirming the need for States to ensure that perpetrators of attacks committed on their territory against humanitarian personnel and United Nations and associated personnel do not operate with impunity, and that the perpetrators of such acts are brought to justice, as provided for by national laws and obligations under international law,

Recalling the inclusion of attacks intentionally directed against personnel involved in a humanitarian assistance or peacekeeping mission in accordance with the Charter as a war crime in the Rome Statute of the International Criminal Court, and noting the role that the Court can play in appropriate cases in bringing to justice those responsible for serious violations of international humanitarian law,

Reaffirming the need to ensure adequate levels of safety and security for United Nations personnel and associated humanitarian personnel, including locally recruited staff, which constitutes an underlying duty of the Organization, and mindful of the need to promote and enhance security consciousness within the organizational culture of the United Nations and a culture of accountability at all levels, as well as to continue to promote awareness of and sensitivity to national and local cultures and laws,

Noting the importance of reinforcing the close collaboration between the United Nations and the host country on contingency planning, information exchange and risk assessment in the context of good mutual cooperation on issues relating to the security of United Nations and associated personnel,

1. *Welcomes* the report of the Secretary-General;

2. *Urges* all States to make every effort to ensure the full and effective implementation of the relevant principles and rules of international law, including international humanitarian law, human rights law and refugee law related to the safety and security of humanitarian personnel and United Nations personnel;

3. *Strongly urges* all States to take the necessary measures to ensure the safety and security of humanitarian personnel and United Nations and associated personnel and to respect and ensure respect for the inviolability of United Nations premises, which are essential to the continuation and successful implementation of United Nations operations;

4. *Calls upon* all Governments and parties in complex humanitarian emergencies, in particular in armed conflicts and in post-conflict situations, in countries in which humanitarian personnel are operating, in conformity with the relevant provisions of international law and national laws, to cooperate fully with the United Nations and other humanitarian agencies and organizations and to ensure the safe and unhindered access of humanitarian personnel and delivery of supplies and equipment, in order to allow those personnel to perform efficiently their task of assisting the affected civilian population, including refugees and internally displaced persons;

5. *Calls upon* all States to consider becoming parties to and to respect fully their obligations under the relevant international instruments;

6. *Also calls upon* all States to consider becoming parties to the Rome Statute of the International Criminal Court;

7. *Further calls upon* all States to consider becoming parties to the Optional Protocol to the Convention on the Safety of United Nations and Associated Personnel as soon as possible so as to ensure its rapid entry into force, and urges States parties to put in place appropriate national legislation, as necessary, to enable its effective implementation;

8. *Calls upon* all States, all parties involved in armed conflict and all humanitarian actors to respect the principles of neutrality, humanity, impartiality and independence for the provision of humanitarian assistance;

9. *Expresses deep concern* over the recent dramatic escalation of threats and deliberate targeting of, and the disturbing trend of politically or criminally motivated attacks against, the safety and security of humanitarian personnel and United Nations and associated personnel;

10. *Strongly condemns* all threats and acts of violence against humanitarian personnel and United Nations and associated personnel, reaffirms the need to hold accountable those responsible for such acts, strongly urges all States to take stronger action to ensure that any such acts committed on their territory are investigated fully and to ensure that the perpetrators of such acts are brought to justice in accordance with national laws and obligations under international law, and urges States to end impunity for such acts;

11. *Calls upon* all States to comply fully with their obligations under international humanitarian law, including as provided by the Geneva Convention relative to the Protection of Civilian Persons in Time of War of 12 August 1949, in order to respect and protect all humanitarian personnel in territories subject to their jurisdiction;

12. *Also calls upon* all States to provide adequate and prompt information in the event of the arrest or detention of humanitarian personnel or United Nations and associated personnel, so as to afford them the necessary medical assistance and to allow independent medical teams to visit and examine the health of those detained, and urges them to take the necessary measures to ensure the speedy release of those who have been arrested or detained in violation of the relevant conventions referred to in the present resolution and applicable international humanitarian law;

13. *Calls upon* all other parties involved in armed conflict to refrain from abducting humanitarian personnel or United Nations and associated personnel or detaining them in violation of the relevant conventions referred to in the present resolution and applicable international humanitarian law, and speedily to release, without harm or requirement of concession, any abductee or detainee;

14. *Requests* the Secretary-General to take the necessary measures to promote full respect for the human rights, privileges and immunities of United Nations and other personnel carrying out activities in fulfilment of the mandate of a United Nations operation, and also requests the Secretary-General to seek the inclusion, in negotiations of headquarters and other mission agreements concerning United Nations and associated personnel, of the applicable conditions contained in the Convention on the Privileges and Immunities of the United Nations, the Convention on the Privileges and Immunities of the Specialized Agencies and the Convention on the Safety of United Nations and Associated Personnel;

15. *Recommends* that the Secretary-General continue to seek the inclusion of, and that host countries include, key provisions of the Convention on the Safety of United Nations and Associated Personnel, among others, those regarding the prevention of attacks against members of the operation, the establishment of such attacks as crimes punishable by law and the prosecution or extradition of offenders, in future as well as, if necessary, in existing status-of-forces, status-of-mission, host country and other related agreements negotiated between the United Nations and those countries, mindful of the importance of the timely conclusion of such agreements, and encourages further efforts in this regard;

16. *Reaffirms* the obligation of all humanitarian personnel and United Nations and associated personnel to respect and, where required, observe the national laws of the country in which they are operating, in accordance with international law and the Charter of the United Nations;

17. *Stresses* the importance of ensuring that humanitarian personnel and United Nations and associated personnel remain sensitive to national and local customs and traditions in their countries of assignment and communicate clearly their purpose and objectives to local populations;

18. *Requests* the Secretary-General to continue to take the necessary measures to ensure that United Nations and other personnel carrying out activities in fulfilment of the mandate of a United Nations operation are properly informed about and operate in conformity with the minimum operating security standards and relevant codes of conduct and are properly informed about the conditions under which they are called upon to operate and the standards that they are required to meet, including those contained in relevant national laws and international law, and that adequate training in security, human rights law and international humanitarian law is provided so as to enhance their security and effectiveness in accomplishing their functions, and reaffirms the necessity for all other humanitarian organizations to provide their personnel with similar support;

19. *Also requests* the Secretary-General to continue, in coordination with Member States, to take the necessary measures to ensure that all United Nations premises and assets, including staff residences, are compliant with the United Nations minimum operating security standards and other relevant United Nations security standards;

20. *Welcomes* the ongoing efforts of the Secretary-General, stresses the need to ensure that all United Nations staff members receive adequate security training, including training to enhance cultural awareness, prior to their deployment to the field, as well as the need to attach a high priority to stress management training and related counselling services for United Nations staff throughout the system, and reaffirms the necessity for all other humanitarian organizations to provide their personnel with similar support;

21. *Also welcomes* the ongoing efforts of the Secretary-General to further enhance the security management system of the United Nations, and in this regard invites the United Nations and, as appropriate, other humanitarian organizations, working closely with host States, to further strengthen the analysis of threats to their safety and security in order to manage security risks by facilitating informed decisions on the maintenance of an effective presence in the field, inter alia, to fulfil their humanitarian mandate;

22. *Requests* the Secretary-General, inter alia, through the Inter-Agency Security Management Network, to continue to promote increased cooperation and collaboration among United Nations departments, organizations, funds and programmes and affiliated international organizations, including between their headquarters and field offices, in the planning and implementation of measures aimed at improving staff security, training and awareness, and calls upon all relevant United Nations departments, organizations, funds and programmes and affiliated international organizations to support those efforts;

23. *Calls upon* all relevant actors to make every effort in their public statements to support a favourable environment for the safety and security of humanitarian personnel and United Nations and associated personnel;

24. *Emphasizes* the need to pay particular attention to the safety and security of locally recruited humanitarian personnel, who are particularly vulnerable to attacks and who account for the majority of casualties, including in cases of kidnapping, harassment, banditry and intimidation, requests the Secretary-General to keep under review the relevant United Nations safety and security policy, operational and administrative arrangements related to locally recruited personnel, and calls upon humanitarian organizations to ensure that their staff are adequately informed about and trained in the relevant security measures, plans and initiatives of their respective organizations, which should be in line with applicable national laws and international law;

25. *Takes note* of the ongoing efforts by the Secretary-General in addressing the recommendations of the Independent Panel on Safety and Security of United Nations Personnel and Premises Worldwide, including on accountability, and looks forward to a progress report on measures to follow up on the recommendations of the Independent Panel and on the independent process on the issue of accountability, to be included in the report of the Secretary-General on safety and security to be submitted to the General Assembly at its sixty-fifth session;

26. *Requests* the Department of Safety and Security of the Secretariat to continue to improve and implement an effective, modern and flexible information management capacity in support of analytical and operational requirements, including information on the range and scope of security incidents involving humanitarian personnel and United Nations and associated personnel, including attacks against them, in order to reduce the risks arising in the context of United Nations-related operations;

27. *Welcomes* the work of the Secretary-General in enhancing security collaboration with host Governments, including efforts to support United Nations designated officials with regard to collaboration with host Government authorities on staff safety and security;

28. *Stresses* that the effective functioning of security operations at the country level requires a unified capacity for policy, standards, coordination, communication, compliance and threat and risk assessment, and notes the benefits thereof to United Nations and associated personnel, including those achieved by the Department of Safety and Security since its establishment;

29. *Recognizes* the steps taken by the Secretary-General thus far, as well as the need for continued efforts to enhance coordination and cooperation, both at the headquarters and at the field levels, between the United Nations and other humanitarian and non-governmental organizations on matters relating to the safety and security of humanitarian personnel and United Nations and associated personnel, with a view to addressing mutual security concerns in the field, taking into account relevant national and local initiatives in this regard, inter alia, those derived from the "Saving Lives Together" framework, encourages collaborative initiatives to address security training needs, invites Member States to consider increasing support to those initiatives, and requests the Secretary-General to report on steps taken in this regard;

30. *Underlines* the urgent need to allocate adequate and predictable resources to the safety and security of United Nations personnel, through regular and extrabudgetary resources, including through the consolidated appeals process, and encourages all States to contribute to the Trust Fund for Security of Staff Members of the United Nations System, inter alia, with a view to reinforcing the efforts of the Department of Safety and Security to meet its mandate and responsibilities;

31. *Also underlines* the need for better coordination between the United Nations and host Governments, in accordance with the relevant provisions of international law and national laws, on the use and deployment of essential equipment required to provide for the safety and security of United Nations personnel and associated personnel working in the delivery of humanitarian assistance by United Nations organizations;

32. *Recalls* the essential role of telecommunication resources in facilitating the safety of humanitarian personnel and United Nations and associated personnel, calls upon States to consider acceding to or ratifying the Tampere Convention on the Provision of Telecommunication Resources for Disaster Mitigation and Relief Operations of 18 June 1998, which entered into force on 8 January 2005, and urges them to facilitate and expedite, consistent with their national laws and international obligations applicable to them, the use of communications equipment in such operations, inter alia, by limiting and, whenever possible, expeditiously lifting the restrictions placed on the use of communications equipment by United Nations and associated personnel;

33. *Requests* the Secretary-General to submit to the General Assembly at its sixty-fifth session a comprehensive and updated report on the safety and security of humanitarian personnel and protection of United Nations personnel and on the implementation of the present resolution.

Standardized access control project

In November [A/64/532], in response to General Assembly resolution 61/263 [YUN 2007, p. 1493], the Secretary-General outlined revised estimates of resource requirements for strengthening security for other departments and entities not covered in budget estimates for 2010–2011 [A/64/6 (Sect. 34) & Add.1]. The revised estimates related to the implementation of the standardized access control project initiated in 2006 [YUN 2006, p. 1674]. The Secretary-General reported that at Headquarters, Geneva, Vienna, Nairobi, the regional commissions for Latin America and the Caribbean and Asia and the Pacific, and ICTR, the first phase of the project (PACT I) had been completed. At the Economic Commission for Africa, 75 per cent of the project had been completed, and was expected to be completed by 30 June 2010. The first phase of the project was not implemented at the Economic Commission for Western Asia owing to an absence of qualified bidders. Both phases of the project there would be conducted as one initiative. At the International Tribunal for the Former Yugoslavia, the closed-circuit television portion of PACT II had been completed. However, in the light of other delays and the establishment of a closing date for the Tribunal, it was decided not to continue with the project.

Implementation of PACT II was expected to begin by 1 January 2010 and be completed by December 2011. The second phase would ensure compliance with access control requirements through protection beyond the perimeter layer by incorporating multiple internal layers of protection, including doors, windows, roofs, conference and meeting rooms, critical infrastructure rooms, elevator cars, lobby controls, archival and storage areas and parking garages. Elements from the second phase would be integrated with the elements of the first phase through the use of the standardized security operating system. The second phase would also provide for an enterprise network where limited real-time and forensic video from the duty stations would be centrally accessible, and would provide for interoperability of access cards among offices.

The estimated cost of the project for the 2010–2011 biennium was $43,633,000 gross ($42,759,400 net). The delayed impact of the proposals for the 2012–2013 biennium was estimated at $2,341,800.

In December [A/64/7/Add.15 & Corr.1], ACABQ recommended that the estimates be adjusted to take into account its recommendations and be submitted to the Assembly. It also recommended that the Assembly approve the additional resources requested subject to its recommendations.

On 24 December, the Assembly, by **resolution 64/243** (see p. 1395), endorsed ACABQ's recommendations.

Other staff matters

Personnel policies

Human resources management

By **decision 63/550 C** of 30 June, the General Assembly deferred consideration of the Secretary-General's reports on National Professional Officers [YUN 2008, p. 1626] and special measures for protection from sexual exploitation and sexual abuse [A/63/720] until its sixty-fourth (2009) session.

At that session, the Assembly had before it for consideration the Secretary-General's reports on human resources development [A/64/329]; human resources challenges within the United Nations development system at the country level [E/2009/75]; implementation of continuing appointments [A/64/267]; provisional staff rules [A/64/230]; amendments to the staff regulations [A/63/694] and a related ACABQ report [A/63/754]; an audit of human resources management at the Office of the United Nations High Commissioner for Human Rights [A/64/201]; junior professional/associate expert/associate professional officer programmes [A/64/82-E/2009/82]; review of the management of Internet websites in the United Nations system organizations [A/64/95 & Add.1]; review of information and communication technology hosting services in the United Nations system organizations [A/64/96 & Add.1]; activities of the Ethics Office [A/64/316]; composition of the Secretariat [A/64/352]; the practice of the Secretary-General in disciplinary matters and possible criminal behaviour, 1 July 2008 to 30 June 2009 [A/64/269]; special measures for protection from sexual exploitation and abuse [A/63/720]; and an ACABQ report on human resources management [A/64/518].

On 24 December, the Assembly decided that the item on human resources management would remain for consideration during its resumed sixty-fourth (2010) session (**decision 64/549**).

Human resources challenges within UN development system

Report of Secretary-General. In May [E/2009/75], the Secretary-General submitted a report on human resources challenges within the UN development system at the country level, in response to General Assembly resolution 62/208 [YUN 2007, p. 877]. Prepared in collaboration with UN system organizations and ICSC, the report focused on how the UN system could best meet the demands of programme countries at the country level, while recognizing the differences and unique requirements in various country situations. It outlined challenges related to the recruitment and career management of UN system staff, including issues affecting resident coordinators and other UN staff at the country level, and those associated with dealing with multiple human resources policies and procedures across the UN system. The report noted the CEB plan of action for the harmonization of business practices and the ongoing reform of UN contractual status as steps in the right direction. It also addressed staff security, planning for the succession of retiring staff members and equal representation of women. Recommendations were put forward for the consideration of the Economic and Social Council (see p. 846 for more details).

Staff regulations and rules

Amendments to staff regulations

In response to General Assembly resolution 63/250 [YUN 2008, p. 1616], the Secretary-General in January transmitted a report [A/63/694] containing the proposed amendments to the staff regulations that would implement a streamlined system of contracts (temporary, fixed-term and continuing) [YUN 2008, p. 1622]. Following review by the Assembly and its decision on the proposed amendments to staff regulations, the Secretary-General would prepare and provisionally promulgate the new set of Staff Rules (see p. 1466), effective 1 July 2009, and would present the full text of the provisional new Staff Rules to the Assembly for its consideration. Annexed to the report were explanations of the proposed amendments to the staff regulations and the full text of the amended staff regulations to implement a streamlined system of contracts. The Assembly was requested to approve the amended staff regulations, to be effective 1 July 2009.

ACABQ report. In March [A/63/754], ACABQ said that the Secretary-General's report would have benefited from the inclusion of a more detailed introduction to the context of the proposed amendments and to the drafting and approval process, as well as an overview of the transitional arrangements and any additional steps that might be required. He should also have provided a more detailed commentary on the amendments, including the legislative basis for the wording and/or the justification for the proposed changes, together with an account of the staff-management consultative process and its outcomes.

Information should have been provided on the arrangements to be made for current staff members who, once the streamlined system of contracts entered into force on 1 July 2009, were found to meet the requirements for conversion to continuing appointments but whose contracts expired before 1 January 2010. ACABQ pointed out that under current staff regulations, termination "in the interest of the good administration of the Organization" was permitted only if the action was not contested by the staff member concerned. However, if the proposed amendments to the staff regulations were adopted, terminations of staff members holding continuing appointments in the interest of the good administration of the Organization could occur without the consent of the staff member concerned, which would represent a change to the current staff regulations. Clarification of the basis for that proposed change should be provided to the Assembly.

GENERAL ASSEMBLY ACTION

On 7 April [meeting 79], the General Assembly adopted **resolution 63/271** [A/63/639/Add.1] without vote [agenda item 123)].

Amendments to the Staff Regulations

The General Assembly,

Recalling its resolutions 59/266 of 23 December 2004, 61/244 of 22 December 2006, 62/248 of 3 April 2008 and 63/250 of 24 December 2008,

Having considered the report of the Secretary-General on amendments to the Staff Regulations and the related report of the Advisory Committee on Administrative and Budgetary Questions,

1. *Takes note* of the report of the Secretary-General;

2. *Endorses* the conclusions and recommendations contained in the report of the Advisory Committee on Administrative and Budgetary Questions, subject to the provisions of the present resolution;

3. *Approves* the amendments to the Staff Regulations as contained in the report of the Secretary-General, subject to the provisions of the present resolution and the modified amendments contained in the annex hereto;

4. *Reaffirms* section II of its resolution 63/250;

5. *Stresses* that staff regulation 4.5 *(b)* does not prejudice the possibility of renewal of a temporary appointment, taking fully into account the provisions of paragraph 7 of section II of its resolution 63/250;

6. *Also stresses* that staff regulation 4.4 shall not preclude consideration of external candidates in filling vacant positions under conditions defined by the Secretary-General in accordance with Article 101, paragraph 3, of the

Charter of the United Nations and the relevant provisions of the resolutions of the General Assembly;

7. *Emphasizes* that the change of the term "personnel" to the term "human resources" in the "Scope and purpose" of the Staff Regulations, as well as in regulations 8.1 *(a)* and 8.2, is strictly to harmonize the language of the Staff Regulations with the current terminology in effect at the United Nations;

8. *Reaffirms* that staff members recruited through the national competitive examinations and language competitive examinations who hold probationary appointments as at 30 June 2009 will be considered for conversion to permanent appointments upon successful completion of their probationary appointments on or after 1 July 2009;

9. *Emphasizes* that nothing in the regulations approved in the present resolution and the annex to it precludes persons with disabilities from being considered for employment under any type of contract in full compliance with the Charter, in particular Article 101, paragraph 3;

10. *Recalls* paragraph 4 of section II of its resolution 63/250, and stresses that the implementation of the part of the new staff regulation 4.5 concerning conversion to continuing appointments shall require further decisions by the General Assembly on the criteria for eligibility;

11. *Also recalls* paragraph 2 of section I of its resolution 63/250, and stresses the importance of a meaningful and constructive dialogue between staff and management to overcome differences;

12. *Requests* the Secretary-General to report to it at its sixty-fourth session on the full implications of converting all currently eligible staff to permanent appointments, including the financial impact and the effects on workforce management;

13. *Also requests* the Secretary-General to submit a report to the General Assembly at its sixty-fifth session regarding the status of the review of staff members eligible for consideration as at 30 June 2009 for a permanent appointment;

14. *Further requests* the Secretary-General to ensure that the Staff Rules and related administrative issuances derived from the Staff Regulations comply with the provisions of its relevant resolutions;

15. *Requests* the Secretary-General to report to the General Assembly at the main part of its sixty-fourth session on the provisional new Staff Rules.

ANNEX

Modified amendments to the Staff Regulations
Regulation 4.5

...

(c) A fixed-term appointment does not carry any expectancy, legal or otherwise, of renewal or conversion, irrespective of the length of service;

Regulation 9.3

(a) The Secretary-General may, giving the reasons therefor, terminate the appointment of a staff member who holds a temporary, fixed-term or continuing appointment in accordance with the terms of his or her appointment or for any of the following reasons:

...

(vi) In the interest of the good administration of the Organization and in accordance with the standards of the Charter, provided that the action is not contested by the staff member concerned;

(b) In addition, in the case of a staff member holding a continuing appointment, the Secretary-General may terminate the appointment without the consent of the staff member if, in the opinion of the Secretary-General, such action would be in the interest of the good administration of the Organization, to be interpreted principally as a change or termination of a mandate, and in accordance with the standards of the Charter;

...

(d) The Secretary-General may, where the circumstances warrant and he or she considers it justified, pay to a staff member terminated, provided that the termination is not contested, a termination indemnity payment not more than 50 per cent higher than that which would otherwise be payable under the Staff Regulations.

ANNEX I
Salary scales and related provisions

...

6. The Secretary-General shall fix the salary scales for staff members in the General Service and related categories, normally on the basis of the best prevailing conditions of employment in the locality of the United Nations Office concerned, provided that the Secretary-General may, where he or she deems it appropriate, establish rules and salary limits for payment of a non-resident allowance to General Service staff members recruited from outside the local area. The gross pensionable remuneration of such staff shall be determined in accordance with the methodology specified in article 54 *(a)* of the Regulations of the United Nations Joint Staff Pension Fund and are shown in the salary scales applicable to such staff.

ANNEX II
Letters of appointment

...

(viii)   That a fixed-term appointment does not carry any expectancy, legal or otherwise, of renewal or conversion, irrespective of the length of service;

Implementation of continuing appointments

Report of Secretary-General. As requested by the General Assembly in resolution 63/250 [YUN 2008, p. 1616], the Secretary-General in August submitted a report [A/64/267] on the implementation of continuing appointments, part of the new contractual arrangements approved by the Assembly in resolution 63/250, in order to facilitate the Assembly's review of the issue with a view to its implementation by 1 January 2010. The report included proposals for granting and terminating continuing appointments, including eligibility criteria and the role of the performance appraisal system; financial and management implications, including the possible establishment of a ceiling (the established cap on the number of staff who would be eligible to have their fixed-term appointments converted to continuing ones or would be granted a continuing appointment); and implications

of the implementation of continuing appointments for the system of geographical ranges, for Junior Professional Officers and for successful candidates from competitive examinations. According to the proposal, a continuing appointment would be granted to staff with a minimum of five years of continuous service, provided there was a continuing need for that service and the staff member met the highest standards of efficiency and was not subject to any disciplinary measure during the five years prior to the time of review. Staff members previously appointed under the 100, 200 or 300 series or appointed since 1 July 2009 under the new Staff Rules would be eligible for such appointment. Staff holding appointments limited to service in a particular office would not be excluded from consideration. Implementation of continuing appointments would not impact Junior Professional Officers, who would continue to be considered external candidates. The criterion for continuing need would be based on the Organization's need for the particular functions performed by the staff member at the time of review, as well as the staff member's qualifications, experience and training. In the case of UN peacekeeping operations, continuing needs would be identified through workforce planning to project baseline staffing requirements needed for ongoing functions and skills required in all missions and transferable among missions. A Secretary-General's bulletin outlined the criteria for a one-time review of all fixed-term appointments to determine eligibility for permanent appointment. The system was expected to be implemented as of 1 January 2010.

ACABQ report. In November [A/64/518], ACABQ stated that the Secretary-General's proposals did not respond fully to the Assembly's request, and identified areas for further clarification and/or explanation, including on the sequencing of the central review process and the review of eligibility for consideration for continuing appointments. ACABQ was not convinced that locally recruited mission staff should be eligible for continuing appointments, since individual peacekeeping operations were, by their very nature, temporary. Local staff employed by those operations should continue to be hired on contracts of a finite duration.

Noting the large percentage of the non-field mission staff who would be eligible for permanent appointment and the absence of an estimate of the actual number who might eventually be awarded continuing appointments, ACABQ recommended that the Secretary-General take measures to improve the security of tenure of mission staff by, for instance, offering them appointments of a duration that reflected mission operational requirements. He should also explain how he intended to achieve a judicious mix of career and fixed-term appointments.

ACABQ considered that in the absence of Organization-wide data on the types of functions for which there was a continuing need and on the populations required in the major occupational groups, it would be difficult to have a basis on which to award continuing appointments. It recommended that the Secretary-General make use of the strategic workforce planning techniques to provide a clearer picture of ongoing functions, as well as an estimate of how many staff members in the major occupational groups would be required on a continuing basis to ensure the effective implementation of the Organization's mandates. He should also address the relationship between mobility and continuing appointment, and clarify how the joint review bodies would be able to take an organization-wide view or have enough knowledge to assess future requirements and staff potential.

The General Assembly on 24 December deferred consideration of the Secretary-General's proposals and the related ACABQ report until its sixty-fifth (2010) session (**decision 64/548 A**).

Provisional staff rules

Pursuant to staff regulation 12.3, the Secretary-General in August [A/64/230] provided information on the new Staff Rules [ST/SGB/2009/7] that he provisionally promulgated on 1 July 2009 in order to implement the new contractual arrangements approved by General Assembly resolution 63/250 [YUN 2008, p. 1616]. Consistent with Staff Regulation 12.4, the provisional Staff Rules would enter into force on 1 January 2010, taking into account any modifications and/or deletions by the General Assembly. The report provided information relative to the legal framework and legislative basis for the Staff Rules and the drafting and approval process of the new Rules, including staff-management consultations.

The Assembly was requested to take note of the new Staff Rules; request the Secretary-General to amend Staff Rules staff rules 4.14 and 4.15 (j) on the basis of the Assembly's consideration of his report on continuing appointments and to report on the new Staff Rules at its sixty-fifth (2010) session; and reconsider the requirement to renounce permanent resident status as it applied to all internationally recruited staff members and, if it agreed to remove that requirement, decide to delete staff rule 1.5 (c).

ACABQ report. In November [A/64/518], ACABQ recommended that the Assembly request the Secretary-General to amend staff rules 4.14 and 4.15 (j) on the basis of its consideration of his report on continuing appointments and to report on the new Staff Rules at its sixty-fifth session. Information as well as data on the financial impact of removing the requirement to renounce permanent resident status should be provided to the Assembly at the time of its consideration of that question. Believing that it was unreasonable to expect serving staff members to make a choice between renouncing their permanent resident status and continuing their employment with the Organization, ACABQ recommended that measures be taken to ensure that those individuals were not disadvantaged by the new contractual regime, that the Assembly reconsider that requirement and, in the event that there was agreement to remove it, that provisional staff rule 1.5 (c) be deleted. It further recommended that the Assembly take note of the provisional Staff Rules.

On 22 December, the Assembly decided that the Staff Rules, as referred to in the Secretary-General's report, would remain provisional pending their further consideration at its resumed sixty-fourth (2010) session (**decision 64/546**).

Recruitment and staffing

Junior professional/Associate expert/Associate professional officer programmes

JIU report. In May [A/64/82-E/2009/82], the Secretary-General transmitted a JIU report entitled "Junior Professional Officer/Associate Expert/Associate Professional Officer Programmes in United Nations system organizations". JIU found that those programmes, begun nearly five decades ago, had evolved, enlarging their volume and scope, and were widespread across UN system organizations, embracing almost 1,000 Junior Professional Officers/Associate Experts/Associate Professional Officers (JPOs/AEs/APOs) at any given moment. Overall donor contribution to the programmes was about $100 million per year. The programmes had successfully served the original objectives to: provide additional resources for the UN development activity; enhance the source of potential future experts and officials for the UN system and for donors' bilateral development programmes; and offer on-the-job training for young professionals. The difficulties encountered stemmed from the contradictions between the outdated legislative basis and the evolved practice, from the absence of clear and transparent priority setting and from the lack of coherent strategies and monitoring.

The report noted that the number of JPOs/AEs/APOs coming from developing countries was low, and that in most cases the programmes were open only to donor country nationals. There were serious political and professional arguments regarding the need to remedy that situation, and measures were needed to enhance the sponsoring of candidates from developing countries. System-wide attention was needed to strengthen the follow-up of the careers of former JPOs/AEs/APOs and to improve cooperation among the recruitment services to make better use across the system of JPOs after their assignment.

The evolution of the programmes had resulted in more harmonized conditions of service, the application of standardized eligibility criteria, job descriptions, and supervision and appraisal of the individual JPOS/AES/APOS. More attention was needed from human resources management to monitor and control the implementation of the programmes, especially at the beginning and concluding phases of the term of assignment. JIU recommended that the Economic and Social Council redefine the objectives, guidelines and financing of the programmes to reflect current realities.

In June [A/64/82/Add.1-E/2009/82/Add.1], the Secretary-General submitted his comments and those of CEB on the report.

The Economic and Social Council took note of the report on 31 July (**decision 2009/260**).

National Professional Officers

On 30 June, the General Assembly deferred consideration of the Secretary-General's report on National Professional Officers [YUN 2008, p. 1626] to its sixty-fourth (2010) session (**decision 63/550 C**).

Staff composition

In a September annual report on the UN Secretariat's staff composition [A/64/352], the Secretary-General updated information on the demographic characteristics of the Secretariat's staff and on the system of desirable ranges for geographical distribution. The report, covering the period from 1 July 2008 to 30 June 2009, reviewed the global population of Secretariat staff, as well as staff with contracts of one year or more, staff appointed under the 100 series of Staff Rules and those in posts subject to geographical distribution. It also included information on all staff with valid contracts irrespective of the funding source, type of engagement, duration of contract, level or duty station.

The global number of Secretariat staff as at 30 June 2009 totalled 39,978. Of that number, 34,268 held contracts of one year or longer. The number of staff in the Professional and higher categories was 10,839 (27.1 per cent), and was 28,424 (71.1 per cent) in the General Service and related categories. Staff in field missions administered by the Department of Field Support (DFS) numbered 21,746 (54.4 per cent of the global Secretariat workforce). Up to 26,538 (66.46 per cent) of the global Secretariat staff were men, while women accounted for 13,440 (33.6 per cent). Of the local staff in field missions administered by DFS, 82.6 per cent were men. Nationals of all 192 Member States were represented in the Secretariat. In posts subject to geographical distribution, 177 States were represented: 15 States were unrepresented, one

fewer than in June 2008, 30 were underrepresented and 22 overrepresented, as against 24 and 21, respectively, the previous year. The remaining 125 States were within range. Appointments to posts subject to geographical distribution totalled 186.

The report provided information on the demographic profile of Secretariat staff, including the breakdown of staff by department or office, gender, age, and length of service, and movements of staff, covering recruitment, promotion, transfer, separation, turnover and forecasts of anticipated retirements between 2009 and 2013. In addition, the report reviewed the geographical representation of staff at the senior and policymaking levels, the implementation status of human resources action plans and the level of underrepresentation of Member States.

ACABQ report. In November [A/64/518], ACABQ took note of the Secretary-General's report and said that it intended to comment in more detail on the information contained therein, as well as on information to be submitted as part of the 2010 report. In the interim, it urged the Secretary-General to intensify efforts to achieve the geographical distribution and gender balance targets set by the Assembly.

The General Assembly on 24 December deferred consideration of the Secretary-General's report until its sixty-fifth (2010) session (**decision 64/548 A**).

Ethics Office

In response to General Assembly resolutions 60/254 [YUN 2006, p. 1633] and 63/250 [YUN 2008, p. 1616], the Secretary-General in August submitted a report [A/64/316] on the activities of the Ethics Office from 1 August 2008 to 31 July 2009. During that period, the Office continued to develop ethical standards; ensure annual training on ethics issues to enhance awareness of ethics, integrity and accountability, in collaboration with the Office of Human Resources Management (OHRM); provide confidential ethics advice and guidance to individual staff, staff groups and other departments and offices; administer the financial disclosure programme in order to maintain and enhance public trust in the integrity of the Organization; and protect staff against retaliation for reporting misconduct and for cooperating with audits or investigations, in collaboration with the Office of Internal Oversight Services (OIOS).

The Office responded to 434 staff requests for its services: 73 per cent related to ethics advice, 15 per cent to protection against retaliation for reporting misconduct, 6 per cent to standard-setting and policy support, 3 per cent to alerts to the Office, 1 per cent to general information, 1 per cent for Ethics Committee review and 1 per cent to training. New York accounted for 55 per cent of the requests; Offices in Geneva,

Vienna and Nairobi together, 14 per cent; UN bodies and agencies, 11 per cent; peacekeeping operations and tribunals, 9 per cent; outside sources, 5 per cent; regional commissions, 5 per cent; and Member States, 1 per cent. Requests were received from staff at different levels across the Secretariat, with the Professional levels accounting for 63 per cent, and the General Service and related categories, 10 per cent. Concerning financial disclosure, of the 3,118 staff members required to file a financial disclosure or declaration of interest statement in 2007, 3,092, or 99.16 per cent, complied with their obligation. The remaining 0.83 per cent (25 staff members) were referred to OHRM for follow-up action, while one case was referred to the United Nations High Commissioner for Refugees (UNHCR). The Ethics Office received 64 requests for protection against retaliation, 29 of which warranted a preliminary review. Of the 35 remaining complaints, 7 were determined to fall outside the scope of the mandate, and 28 led to the provision of advice and guidance to the staff members concerned.

The Secretary-General noted that after more than three years in operation, the Ethics Office continued to assert its relevance and role in fostering a culture of ethics, integrity and accountability within the Organization, while fulfilling its growing mandated responsibilities and overcoming budgetary and staff constraints. The Office had proved itself to be a useful mechanism to ensure a coherent application of ethics standards and enhance synergy within the United Nations, as demonstrated in the process of developing the system-wide Code of Ethics for United Nations personnel and harmonizing ethics-related policies and practices.

The Secretary-General also submitted the draft system-wide Code of Ethics for United Nations Personnel (annexed to the report) to the Assembly for consideration and endorsement. The Code included the 12 core values and principles to guide the conduct and behaviour of UN personnel.

ACABQ report. In November [A/64/518], ACABQ reiterated its earlier recommendations that information on reasons for failure to comply with the provisions of the financial disclosure programme be included in future reports on the activities of the Ethics Office. It noted that the arrangements for addressing circumstances in which OIOS declined to investigate cases referred by the Ethics Office should be clarified. ACABQ said that it was not clear what value the voluntary Code of Ethics would add to the Staff Regulations and Rules, which provided the legal framework governing staff conduct. Furthermore, the work to be undertaken by ICSC could have a bearing on a code of ethics for the United Nations. It therefore recommended that the Assembly revert to the issue once the ICSC review had been completed.

By **decision 64/548 A** of 24 December, the General Assembly deferred consideration of the Secretary-General's report on the activities of the Ethics Office until its sixty-fifth (2010) session.

Multilingualism

The General Assembly in September had before it the Secretary-General's report on multilingualism [YUN 2008, p. 1630] and the final report by the United Nations Educational, Scientific and Cultural Organization (UNESCO) [A/63/752] on the impact of its activities during the International Year of Languages (2008). The Assembly proclaimed the International Year by resolution 61/266 [YUN 2007, p. 1515] and invited UNESCO to serve as the lead agency for the Year.

GENERAL ASSEMBLY ACTION

On 9 September [meeting 104], the General Assembly adopted **resolution 63/306** [draft: A/63/L.70/Rev.1 & Add.1] without vote [agenda item 113].

Multilingualism

The General Assembly,

Recognizing that the United Nations pursues multilingualism as a means of promoting, protecting and preserving diversity of languages and cultures globally,

Recognizing also that genuine multilingualism promotes unity in diversity and international understanding, and recognizing the importance of the capacity to communicate to the peoples of the world in their own languages, including in formats accessible to persons with disabilities,

Stressing the need for strict observance of the resolutions and rules establishing language arrangements for the different bodies and organs of the United Nations,

Emphasizing the importance of multilingualism in the activities of the United Nations, including those linked to public relations and information,

Recalling its resolution 47/135 of 18 December 1992, by which it adopted the Declaration on the Rights of Persons Belonging to National or Ethnic, Religious and Linguistic Minorities, and the International Covenant on Civil and Political Rights, in particular article 27 thereof, concerning the rights of persons belonging to ethnic, religious or linguistic minorities,

Recalling also its resolutions 2(I) of 1 February 1946, 2480 B(XXIII) of 21 December 1968, 42/207 C of 11 December 1987, 50/11 of 2 November 1995, 52/23 of 25 November 1997, 54/64 of 6 December 1999, 56/262 of 15 February 2002, 59/309 of 22 June 2005, 61/244 of 22 December 2006, 61/266 of 16 May 2007, 63/100 B of 5 December 2008, 63/248 of 24 December 2008 and 63/280 of 8 May 2009,

1. *Takes note* of the report of the Secretary-General and the note by which the Secretary-General transmitted the final report on the impact of the activities carried out by the United Nations Educational, Scientific and Cultural Organization during the International Year of Languages (2008);

2.   *Also takes note* of the appointment of a new Coordinator for Multilingualism, and calls upon the Secretary-General to continue to develop the informal network of focal points in order to support the Coordinator;

3.   *Emphasizes* the paramount importance of the equality of the six official languages of the United Nations;

4.   *Underlines* the need for full implementation of the resolutions establishing language arrangements for the official languages of the United Nations and the working languages of the Secretariat;

5.   *Requests* the Secretary-General to ensure that all language services are given equal treatment and are provided with equally favourable working conditions and resources, with a view to achieving maximum quality of those services, with full respect for the specificities of the six official languages and taking into account their respective workloads;

6.   *Reiterates its request* to the Secretary-General to complete the task of uploading all important older United Nations documents onto the United Nations website in all six official languages on a priority basis, so that those archives are also available to Member States through that medium;

7.   *Reiterates* that all content-providing offices in the Secretariat should continue their efforts to translate into all official languages all English-language materials and databases posted on the United Nations website in the most practical, efficient and cost-effective manner;

8.   *Requests* the Secretary-General to continue to ensure, through the provision of documentation services and meeting and publishing services under conference management, including high-quality translation and interpretation, effective multilingual communication among representatives of Member States in intergovernmental organs and members of expert bodies of the United Nations equally in all the official languages of the United Nations;

9.   *Stresses* the importance of providing United Nations information, technical assistance and training materials, whenever possible, in the local languages of the beneficiary countries;

10.   *Recalls* its resolution 63/248, in which it reaffirmed the provisions relating to conference services in its resolutions on multilingualism;

11.   *Acknowledges* the measures undertaken by the Secretary-General, in accordance with its resolutions, to address the issue of the replacement of retiring staff in the language services, and requests the Secretary-General to maintain and intensify those efforts, including through the strengthening of cooperation with institutions that train language specialists to meet the need in the six official languages of the United Nations;

12.   *Notes with satisfaction* the willingness of the Secretariat to encourage staff members, in meetings with interpretation services, to use any of the six official languages of which they have a command;

13.   *Reiterates with concern* its request to the Secretary-General to ensure that the rules concerning the simultaneous distribution of documents in all six official languages are strictly respected as regards both the distribution of printed copies and the posting of parliamentary documentation on the Official Document System and the United Nations website, in keeping with section III, paragraph 5, of its resolution 55/222 of 23 December 2000;

14.   *Emphasizes* the importance of:

(a)   Making appropriate use of all the official languages of the United Nations in all the activities of the Department of Public Information of the Secretariat, with the aim of eliminating the disparity between the use of English and the use of the five other official languages;

(b)   Ensuring the full and equitable treatment of all the official languages of the United Nations in all the activities of the Department of Public Information;

and, in this regard, reaffirms its request to the Secretary-General to ensure that the Department has appropriate staffing capacity in all the official languages of the United Nations to undertake all its activities;

15.   *Requests* the Secretary-General to continue his efforts to ensure that, in accordance with their income-generating nature, guided tours at United Nations Headquarters are consistently available, in particular, in all six official languages of the United Nations;

16.   *Encourages* the Secretary-General to continue his efforts to develop and maintain multilingual United Nations websites, from within existing resources, including efforts to keep the Secretary-General's web page up to date in all the official languages of the United Nations;

17.   *Reaffirms* the need to achieve full parity among the six official languages on United Nations websites;

18.   *Also reaffirms* that the United Nations website is an essential tool for Member States, the media, educational institutions, the general public and non-governmental organizations, and reiterates the continued need for efforts by the Department of Public Information to maintain and improve it;

19.   *Further reaffirms* its request to the Secretary-General to ensure, while maintaining an up-to-date and accurate website, the adequate distribution of financial and human resources within the Department of Public Information allocated to the United Nations website among all official languages, taking into consideration the specificity of each official language, on a continuous basis;

20.   *Notes with concern* that the multilingual development and enrichment of the United Nations website in several official languages has improved at a much slower rate than expected, and, in this regard, requests the Department of Public Information, in coordination with content-providing offices, to improve the actions taken to achieve parity among the six official languages on the United Nations website, in particular by expediting the filling of current vacant posts in some sections;

21.   *Requests* the Department of Public Information, in cooperation with the Office of Information and Communications Technology of the Secretariat, to continue its efforts to ensure that technological infrastructures and supportive applications fully support Latin, non-Latin and bidirectional scripts in order to enhance the equality of all official languages on the United Nations website;

22.   *Welcomes* the cooperative arrangements undertaken by the Department of Public Information with academic institutions in order to increase the number of web pages available in some official languages, and requests the Secretary-General, in coordination with content-providing offices, to extend these cooperative arrangements, in a cost-effective manner, to all the official languages of the United

Nations, bearing in mind the necessity of adherence to United Nations standards and guidelines;

23. *Notes with satisfaction* the official launch of iSeek in Geneva in the two working languages of the Secretariat, and encourages the Secretariat to continue its efforts to implement iSeek at all duty stations as well as to develop and implement cost-neutral measures to provide Member States with secure access to the information currently accessible only on the Intranet of the Secretariat;

24. *Notes with appreciation* the work carried out by the United Nations information centres, including the United Nations Regional Information Centre, in favour of the publication of United Nations information materials and the translation of important documents into languages other than the official languages of the United Nations, with a view to reaching the widest possible audience and extending the United Nations message to all corners of the world in order to strengthen international support for the activities of the Organization, and encourages United Nations information centres to continue their multilingual activities in the interactive and proactive aspects of their work, especially by arranging seminars and debates to further the spread of information and the understanding and exchange of views regarding United Nations activities at the local level;

25. *Recalls* its resolution 61/244, in which it reaffirmed the need to respect the equality of the two working languages of the Secretariat, reaffirmed the use of additional working languages in specific duty stations as mandated, and, in that regard, requested the Secretary-General to ensure that vacancy announcements specified the need for either of the working languages of the Secretariat, unless the functions of the post required a specific working language;

26. *Also recalls* section II, paragraph 17, of its resolution 61/244, in which it acknowledged that the interaction of the United Nations with the local population in the field was essential and that language skills constituted an important element of the selection and training processes, and therefore affirmed that a good command of the official language(s) spoken in the country of residence should be taken into account as an additional asset during those processes;

27. *Takes note* of section II.E.2 of the report of the Secretary-General, requests the Secretary-General to continue his ongoing efforts in this regard, and further recalls its resolution 63/280 without prejudice to Article 101 of the Charter of the United Nations;

28. *Stresses* that the employment of staff shall continue to be carried out in strict accordance with Article 101 of the Charter and in line with the relevant provisions of General Assembly resolutions;

29. *Also stresses* that the promotion of staff in the Professional and higher categories shall be carried out in strict accordance with Article 101 of the Charter and in line with the provisions of resolution 2480 B(XXIII) and the relevant provisions of resolution 55/258 of 14 June 2001;

30. *Encourages* United Nations staff members to continue actively to use existing training facilities to acquire and enhance their proficiency in one or more of the official languages of the United Nations;

31. *Recalls* that linguistic diversity is an important element of cultural diversity, and takes note of the entry into force, on 18 March 2007, of the Convention on the Protection and Promotion of the Diversity of Cultural Expressions;

32. *Also recalls* paragraph 25 *(a)* of its resolution 61/266, and welcomes the activities of the United Nations Educational, Scientific and Cultural Organization, Member States, the United Nations system and all other participating bodies aimed at fostering respect for and the promotion of all languages, in particular endangered ones, linguistic diversity and multilingualism;

33. *Requests* the Secretary-General to submit to the General Assembly at its sixty-fifth session a comprehensive report on the full implementation of its resolutions on multilingualism;

34. *Decides* to include in the provisional agenda of its sixty-fifth session the item entitled "Multilingualism".

Protection from sexual exploitation and abuse

Report of Secretary-General. Pursuant to Assembly resolution 57/306 [YUN 2003, p. 1237], the Secretary-General in February submitted a report on special measures for protection from sexual exploitation and abuse [A/63/720] that presented data on allegations of sexual exploitation and abuse in the UN system in 2008 and described progress in the enforcement of UN standards of conduct. Information on allegations was received from all of the 43 UN entities from which information was sought. Eight entities reported receiving allegations, whereas 35 entities reported receiving no allegations. The number of alleged cases totalled 111, compared with 159 in 2007. Twenty-eight involved personnel of UN entities other than the Department of Peacekeeping Operations (DPKO) and DFS: UNHCR reported 13 cases, United Nations Volunteers seven, the World Food Programme five, the United Nations Relief and Works Agency for Palestine Refugees in the Near East one, the United Nations Development Programme (UNDP) one, and the International Criminal Tribunal for Rwanda one. Fifteen cases were deemed unsubstantiated or were closed, 17 were substantiated and 10 were under investigation; five staff members were summarily dismissed and one was referred for disciplinary action.

The majority of the allegations, 83, related to peacekeeping personnel, with the highest number (40) reported in the United Nations Organization Mission in the Democratic Republic of the Congo. Ten cases were deemed unsubstantiated, 4 were deemed substantiated and referred to the relevant office and 66 were deemed substantiated and forwarded to the Member State.

The Task Force on Protection from Sexual Exploitation in May 2008 brought together some 50 experts on protection from sexual exploitation and abuse from around the world, including NGOs, UN personnel and victim advocates, to address challenges to efforts to eliminate that scourge. Participants agreed on the way forward, which included efforts under four pillars: engagement with and support of local populations; prevention; response systems, including victim assistance; and management and coordination. The meeting produced a compilation of good practices and lessons learned and a collection of tools for inclusion in an on-line tools repository. Other activities included the establishment of a mechanism for managerial compliance, including minimum operating standards for protection from sexual exploitation and abuse.

The amendments on sexual exploitation and abuse to the model memorandum of understanding (MOU) between the United Nations and troop-contributing countries were endorsed by the Assembly in resolution 61/267 B [YUN 2007, p. 69]. DPKO/DFS informed the permanent missions of 50 Member States in July 2008 that the provisions of the revised MOU had become an integral part of all signed MOUs and that those provisions were also included in newly signed MOUs.

The Secretary-General concluded that the United Nations continued efforts to enhance the framework for preventing and addressing sexual exploitation and abuse, including progress in achieving awareness-raising, and improving report mechanisms and policies and strategic collaboration with non-governmental partners. The Task Force meeting in May 2008 represented an important step towards the establishment of a unified and streamlined approach to addressing allegations of sexual exploitation and abuse, and served to coordinate best practices and policies on how to eliminate it. Increasing training programmes for focal points and senior managers at the country level was of pivotal importance for achieving increased awareness of the issue among UN staff and related personnel. The revised MOU between the United Nations and troop-contributing countries was another milestone in advancing the comprehensive strategy to address the problem. The number of allegations of sexual exploitation and abuse reported in 2008 showed a marked decline, with significant reductions in the number of cases reported, particularly involving DPKO/DFS. However, there had been a sharp increase in the number of reported allegations of rape and sexual abuse of minors, which was of serious concern. That situation would be monitored closely.

The Secretary-General recognized the continuing challenges to improve reporting mechanisms, investigative procedures, strengthening of community outreach and awareness-training and remained committed to addressing them in a proactive and diligent manner. He further recognized the valuable support of Member States in assisting the Organization to ensure that the zero tolerance policy was applied equally to all troop contingents, and urged Member States

to assist the Organization in changing the organizational culture so as to deter all acts of sexual exploitation and abuse.

The General Assembly on 30 June deferred consideration of the Secretary-General's report to its sixty-fourth (2010) session (**decision 63/550 C**).

UN Joint Staff Pension Fund

As at 31 December, the United Nations Joint Staff Pension Fund (UNJSPF) had 117,580 active participants as compared to 112,804 at the end of 2008 [YUN 2008, p. 1632]. The number of periodic payments in awards increased from 59,945 to 61,841: 21,292 full retirement benefits; 13,881 early retirement benefits; 6,926 deferred retirement benefits; 10,319 widows' and widowers' benefits; 1,175 disability benefits; 8,208 child benefits; and 40 secondary dependants' benefits. The payroll for benefits in payment for the year ending 31 December 2009 increased by 17.9 per cent over the prior year to $3.2 billion. The total expenditure for benefits, administration and investment costs of $3.9 billion exceeded by $161 million contribution income, which increased from $3.1 billion to $3.7 billion (approximately 18.6 per cent).

The Fund was administered by the 33-member United Nations Joint Staff Pension Board (UNJSPB), which held its fifty-sixth session (Vienna, 13–17 July 2009) [JSPB/56/R.33].

Administrative and financial matters

A report by the UNJSPB [A/64/291] issued in August contained the 2008–2009 revised budget for UNJSPF, which indicated a reduction in appropriations amounting to $21,709,300. It also contained proposed budget estimates for 2010–2011 which amounted to $179,131,200 (before recosting). The report provided for 214 continuing posts, 23 new established posts and 18 temporary posts. The Board proposed that it be authorized by the Assembly to supplement contributions to the Emergency Fund for 2010–2011 by an amount not exceeding $200,000.

Report of Secretary-General. In September [A/C.5/64/2], the Secretary-General, reporting on the administrative and financial implications arising from the UNJSPB report (see above), noted that additional appropriation required under the regular budget for the 2010–2011 biennium, arising from the Board's recommendations, was estimated at $1,865,500 after recosting. The Assembly's approval of those recommendations would result in overall requirements estimated at $22,238,300 at 2010–2011 rates. Of the total requirements for 2010–2011, the cost to the regular budget would amount to $14,188,000, and the balance of $8,050,300 would be reimbursed to the

United Nations by UNDP, UNFPA and the United Nations Children's Fund (UNICEF). Accordingly, the additional appropriation of $1,865,500 under section 1, Overall policymaking, direction and coordination, of the 2010–2011 proposed programme budget would represent a charge against the contingency fund.

ACABQ report. In November [A/64/7/Add.6], ACABQ did not object to the Pension Board's recommendations with respect to the proposed staffing of the Fund for the 2010–2011 biennium, but emphasized restraint in future budgets when proposing staffing requirements. It recommended that the impact of Board's decision to establish a full in-house investment management function be carefully monitored and that the Secretary-General keep the issue under review to ensure that the Fund's long-term investment objectives were met. Noting the Secretary-General's continued efforts to diversify the Fund's investments among developed and emerging markets, it stressed that investments decisions should be based on the four main criteria for investment, namely, safety, profitability, liquidity and convertibility. ACABQ also recommended that the Secretary-General keep the issue of cost-sharing arrangements under review, and that the Assembly approve the Pension Board's recommendations contained in its 2009 report and an additional appropriation of $1,865,500 under the regular budget for the 2010–2011 biennium, arising from the Board's recommendations.

The General Assembly on 24 December, in section II of **resolution 64/245** (see p. 1406), endorsed the recommendations of ACABQ. It requested the Secretary-General to ensure that, under the current volatile market conditions, investment decisions in any country were implemented cautiously, in accordance with the main investment criteria, and to report to the Assembly.

Travel-related matters

ACABQ report. In February [A/63/715], ACABQ examined the Secretary-General's biennial report on standards of accommodation for air travel [YUN 2008, p. 1635]. It considered the purely statistical presentation in the report of limited use and recommended that future reports contain an analysis of the reasons for the increases and/or decreases in the number of exceptions authorized by the Secretary-General, taking into account issues such as industry trends and security requirements.

Endorsing the conclusions and recommendations of ACABQ, the General Assembly, in section II of **resolution 63/268** (see p. 1391) of 7 April, requested the Secretary-General to explore all possible options, including the use of mileage points accumulated from official travel, for reducing the cost of air travel, and to present his conclusions thereon in the context of the comprehensive report it had requested [YUN 2007, p. 1523] on harmonizing standards of air travel for the UN common system.

Administration of justice

Joint Appeals Board

In response to General Assembly resolution 55/258 [YUN 2001, p. 1337], the Secretary-General in August submitted a report [A/64/292] on the outcome of the work of the Joint Appeals Board (JAB) in New York, Geneva, Vienna and Nairobi for 2007 and 2008 and between January and June 2009, statistics on the disposition of cases, and information on the work of the Panel of Counsel.

The Secretary-General reported that 194 appeals and suspension-of-action cases were filed with JAB in those duty stations in 2008, compared to 177 the previous year. Of that number, JAB disposed of 189 cases, compared to 181 in 2007. Regarding disciplinary cases, which were accorded priority, 102 such cases (a threefold increase) were referred to the New York Joint Disciplinary Committee, which disposed of 71 of those cases; the Geneva Committee received 6 new cases (in addition to 3 cases at the beginning of 2008) and disposed of 9; the Nairobi Committee did not receive any disciplinary cases in 2008; and no cases were submitted to the Vienna Committee. In 2008, the Secretary-General accepted fully or partially 109 (or 81 per cent) of the unanimous JAB recommendations, compared to 88 in 2007, and rejected 25 (19 per cent), compared to 20 (12 per cent) in 2007. In 2008, 384 cases were brought to the Panel of Counsel in New York, compared with 339 in 2007, an increase of 13.27 per cent. Of those cases, 286 (74.48 per cent) went through the formal appeals process and 98 (25.52 per cent) were dealt with informally.

ACABQ report. In October [A/64/508], ACABQ recommended that information concerning monetary compensation, provided about the New York Joint Appeals Board between 1 January 2007 and 30 June 2009, should also be provided about the Joint Appeals Boards in Geneva, Nairobi and Vienna. Furthermore, an analysis of monetary compensation awarded and indirect costs associated with an appeal, such as staff time, should be provided in the next report on the administration of justice. Such an analysis should include identification of those aspects of staff administration that gave rise to a large number of appeals, and should compare data from the old system with data from the new system.

Office of Ombudsman and Mediation Services

In accordance with General Assembly resolution 59/283 [YUN 2005, p. 1529], the Secretary-General submitted, in August [A/64/314], the first joint report for the entities covered by the integrated Office of the Ombudsman, renamed the Office of the United Nations Ombudsman and Mediation Services, on its activities in 2008. The report reviewed the operations of the integrated Office covering the Secretariat, the funds and programmes and UNHCR as part of the new system of administration of justice, including consolidated statistical information and systemic and cross-cutting issues brought to the attention of the Office, together with related recommendations. The report reflected the realignment of the different reporting cycles of the Secretariat, funds and programmes and UNHCR so that the report of the activities of the new consolidated Office could be produced.

In 2008, 787 new cases were opened. The most important issues raised by staff related to promotion or career (27 per cent of all cases), followed by inter-personal issues, entitlements, standards of conduct, separation/termination and conditions of service. Promotion and career-related issues and evaluative relationships continued to represent the highest number of cases in all locations. The Office performed a wide variety of services for staff members, including listening, providing and receiving information, identifying and reframing issues, helping visitors to develop and evaluate a range of responsible options, undertaking informal fact-finding, and engaging in informal third-party intervention or mediation. In addition, the Office helped staff to identify the appropriate UN office or unit to which they could bring their issue for resolution. It continued to identify, analyse and report on broad systemic issues and to make recommendations to improve policies, procedures, systems or structures that could address and prevent issues from recurring.

The Secretary-General noted that the Office had a global view of the systemic issues in the Secretariat, the funds and programmes and UNHCR. It had introduced regular case and systemic issue debriefings to facilitate the detection of any organization-wide procedures, practices or rules that could generate common concerns among staff. Additionally, the Office was creating a uniform case categorization process that ensured consistency and enhanced analysis of root causes and trends. Regional branch offices would facilitate access to ombudsman services for people serving outside headquarters, and provide information on systemic issues from the field perspective. Drawing on new opportunities generated by its expanded reach, the Office would help foster positive systemic change and encourage the adoption of common practices and policies system-wide. The Office would continue efforts to ensure consistency in its practices and principles through the development of an internal Ombudsman Practices Manual, the dissemination of its revised terms of reference, the standard operating procedures for the Mediation Division and the development of a common case information form and integrated case database system. It would focus on building conflict management capability through learning activities for managers and through selecting, training and strengthening the Respectful Workplace Advisers in field offices.

ACABQ report. In October [A/64/508], ACABQ emphasized the importance of interaction between the Office of the Ombudsman and Mediation Services and other parts of the Secretariat, such as OHRM, to ensure that systemic issues were adequately addressed. In that connection, it reiterated its view that the Secretary-General should report regularly to the Assembly on actions to address the findings of the Ombudsman on systemic issues.

Criminal behaviour and disciplinary action

In July [A/64/183 & Add.1], the Secretary-General submitted a report on the criminal accountability of UN officials and experts on mission (see p. 95), which the General Assembly acted on in **resolution 64/110** of 16 December [ibid.].

In response to Assembly resolution 59/287 [YUN 2005, p. 1475], the Secretary-General in September transmitted a report [A/64/269] on disciplinary matters and possible criminal behaviour, covering the period from 1 July 2008 to 30 June 2009. The report provided information to Member States on the disciplinary and/or legal action taken by the Secretary-General in cases of established misconduct and/or criminal behaviour by staff members. It reviewed the administrative machinery in disciplinary matters and summarized cases for which a disciplinary measure was imposed by the Secretary-General, which mostly related to abuse of authority/harassment; fraud/misrepresentation; theft/misappropriation; sexual exploitation and abuse; computer-related misconduct; and other matters. During the reporting period, 301 cases were completed, resulting in 16 summary dismissals, 15 disciplinary measures after waiver of referral to the Joint Disciplinary Committee, 19 disciplinary measures after a Joint Disciplinary Committee review and 91 administrative measures. In 160 cases, no disciplinary or administrative action was taken.

By **decision 64/548 A** of 24 December, the General Assembly deferred consideration of the Secretary-General's report on disciplinary matters and possible criminal behaviour until its sixty-fifth (2010) session.

UN Administrative Tribunal

In its annual note to the General Assembly [A/INF/64/7], the seven-member United Nations Administrative Tribunal reported, through the Secretary-General, that it had delivered 66 judgements in 2009, relating to cases brought by staff against the Secretary-General or the executive heads of other UN bodies concerning disputes involving terms of appointment and other issues. It also drew the Assembly's attention to cases that merited special attention. The Tribunal met in plenary in New York on 23 November and held two panel sessions (Geneva, 29 June–31 July; New York, 26 October–25 November).

New system of administration of justice

Report of Ad Hoc Committee. The Ad Hoc Committee on the Administration of Justice at the United Nations convened, in response to General Assembly decision 63/531 [YUN 2008, p. 1647], its second session (New York, 20–24 April) [A/64/55]. At that session the Ad Hoc Committee continued its work on the outstanding legal aspects of the item "Administration of justice at the United Nations", focusing on the scope of the new system, as well as other legal aspects, including legal assistance to staff and whether staff associations could file applications before the United Nations Dispute Tribunal. It recommended that a working group of the Sixth (Legal) Committee of the General Assembly be established to continue the discussion on the outstanding legal aspects of the administration of justice at the United Nations.

Transitional arrangements. On 24 June, the Secretary-General issued a bulletin on transitional measures related to the introduction of a new system of the administration of justice [ST/SGB/2009/11], which indicated that, pursuant to Assembly resolutions 62/228 [YUN 2007, p. 1528] and 63/253 [YUN 2008, p. 1637], a new system of administration of justice would be implemented in the United Nations as of 1 July 2009. As of that date, a new unit, the Management Evaluation Unit, would be created in the Office of the Under-Secretary-General for Management, and the United Nations Dispute Tribunal would be established as the first tier of the system of justice. As of that date, the Joint Appeals Board, the Joint Disciplinary Committees, the Panels of Counsel and all Panels on Discrimination and Other Grievances would be abolished. The United Nations Administrative Tribunal would be abolished on 31 December. The Panels of Counsel would be succeeded by the Office of Staff Legal Assistance. The Secretary-General outlined interim arrangements for handling pending cases.

Communication. On 20 October [A/C.5/64/3], the General Assembly President transmitted to the Fifth Committee Chairman the comments of the Sixth Committee, to assist it in its consideration of the agenda item entitled "Administration of justice at the United Nations." According to the Sixth Committee, for the Assembly to be able to consider the scope of the new system of the administration of justice at its sixty-fifth (2010) session, the Secretary-General should be requested to provide more information, including on the exact terms of reference of the Office of the Ombudsman and Mediation Services concerning access by non-staff personnel; a description of the new procedure for management evaluation; an update of the exact number of persons working for the UN system under different types of contracts; and a compilation of the standard contract and rules. He should also analyse and compare the advantages and disadvantages of the options to remedies available to different categories of non-staff personnel.

By **decision 64/527** of 16 December, the Assembly decided that the consideration of the outstanding legal aspects of the item on the administration of justice at the United Nations would continue during its sixty-fifth (2010) session in the framework of a working group of the Sixth Committee. The Assembly also decided to include the item in the provisional agenda of that session.

GENERAL ASSEMBLY ACTION

On 22 December [meeting 67], the General Assembly, on the recommendation of the Sixth Committee, adopted **resolution 64/233** [A/64/582] without vote [agenda item 142].

Administration of justice at the United Nations

The General Assembly,

Recalling section XI of its resolution 55/258 of 14 June 2001 and its resolutions 57/307 of 15 April 2003, 59/266 of 23 December 2004, 59/283 of 13 April 2005, 61/261 of 4 April 2007, 62/228 of 22 December 2007 and 63/253 of 24 December 2008, and its decision 63/531 of 11 December 2008,

Reaffirming the goal of gender parity within the United Nations system, with due regard to the principle of geographical representation, in conformity with Article 101 of the Charter of the United Nations,

Having considered the reports of the Secretary-General on the outcome of the work of the Joint Appeals Board during 2007 and 2008 and between January and June 2009 and statistics on the disposition of cases and work of the Panel of Counsel and on the activities of the Office of the United Nations Ombudsman and Mediation Services, the related report of the Advisory Committee on Administrative and Budgetary Questions and the letter dated 20 October 2009 from the President of the General Assembly to the Chairman of the Fifth Committee,

1. *Takes note* of the reports of the Secretary-General on the outcome of the work of the Joint Appeals Board during 2007 and 2008 and between January and June 2009 and statistics on the disposition of cases and work of the Panel of Counsel and on the activities of the Office of the United Nations Ombudsman and Mediation Services;

2. *Reaffirms* its resolutions 61/261, 62/228 and 63/253 on the establishment of the new system of administration of justice;

3. *Expresses its appreciation* to staff members who have participated in the system of administration of justice, including the joint disciplinary committees, the joint appeals boards and the panels of counsel;

4. *Also expresses its appreciation* to the members and staff of the United Nations Administrative Tribunal for their work;

5. *Endorses* the conclusions and recommendations contained in the report of the Advisory Committee on Administrative and Budgetary Questions, subject to the provisions of the present resolution;

6. *Takes note* of paragraph 12 of the report of the Advisory Committee on Administrative and Budgetary Questions;

7. *Requests* the Secretary-General to report to the General Assembly at its sixty-fifth session on the status of the judges of the United Nations Appeals Tribunal and their entitlements, including travel and daily subsistence allowance;

8. *Also requests* the Secretary-General to include, inter alia, the following information in his report to be submitted to General Assembly at its sixty-fifth session pursuant to paragraph 59 of resolution 63/253:

(a) The exact terms of reference of the Office of the United Nations Ombudsman and Mediation Services concerning access by non-staff personnel;

(b) An update concerning the exact number of persons other than staff personnel working for the United Nations and the funds and programmes under different types of contracts, including individual contractors, consultants, personnel under service contracts, personnel under special service agreements and daily paid workers;

(c) A description of the new procedure for management evaluation, including the types of work-related administrative decisions for which it is required, and of the procedure normally followed in other cases where non-staff personnel submit a complaint concerning a violation of contract that does not qualify for management evaluation;

(d) A compilation of the standard contracts and rules, including dispute settlement clauses, that govern the relations between the Organization and the various categories of non-staff personnel;

(e) An analysis of monetary compensation awarded, as well as indirect costs associated with an appeal, such as staff time, including identification of those aspects of staff administration which give rise to large numbers of appeals, as well as comparative data from the old and the new system;

(f) Measures in place to provide for accountability of officials for causing financial loss to the Organization under the new system for administration of justice, including

recovery action, as well as actions taken to enforce such accountability;

9. *Further requests* the Secretary-General, with regard to remedies available to the different categories of non-staff personnel, to analyse and compare the respective advantages and disadvantages, including the financial implications, of the options set out below, bearing in mind the status quo concerning dispute settlement mechanisms for non-staff personnel, including the United Nations Commission on International Trade Law arbitration clause, in his report to be submitted to the General Assembly at its sixty-fifth session pursuant to paragraph 59 of resolution 63/253:

(a) Establishment of an expedited special arbitration procedure, conducted under the auspices of local, national or regional arbitration associations, for claims under 25,000 United States dollars submitted by personal service contractors;

(b) Establishment of an internal standing body that would make binding decisions on disputes submitted by non-staff personnel, not subject to appeal and using streamlined procedures, as proposed by the Secretary-General in paragraphs 51 to 56 of his report on the administration of justice;

(c) Establishment of a simplified procedure for non-staff personnel before the United Nations Dispute Tribunal, which would make binding decisions not subject to appeal and using streamlined procedures;

(d) Granting of access to the United Nations Dispute Tribunal and the United Nations Appeals Tribunal, under their current rules of procedure, to non-staff personnel;

10. *Reaffirms* that the informal resolution of conflict is a crucial element of the system of administration of justice, and emphasizes that all possible use should be made of the informal system in order to avoid unnecessary litigation;

11. *Takes note* of section IV, on systemic issues, of the report of the Secretary-General on the activities of the Office of the United Nations Ombudsman and Mediation Services, and emphasizes that the role of the Ombudsman is to report on broad systemic issues that he or she identifies, as well as issues that are brought to his or her attention, in order to promote greater harmony in the workplace;

12. *Emphasizes* the importance of interaction between the Office of the United Nations Ombudsman and Mediation Services and other parts of the Secretariat, such as the Office of Human Resources Management, to ensure that systemic issues are adequately addressed, and requests the Secretary-General to report regularly to the General Assembly on actions taken to address the findings of the Ombudsman on systemic issues;

13. *Welcomes* the submission of the first joint report for the entities covered by the integrated Office of the Ombudsman, and requests the Secretary-General to submit to the General Assembly such a report at its sixty-fifth session and thereafter on a regular basis;

14. *Recalls* paragraphs 48 and 49 of resolution 63/253, and requests the Secretary-General to ensure that the best possible use is made of the three ad litem judges in order to reduce the existing backlog of cases before the United Nations Dispute Tribunal;

15. *Requests* the Secretary-General to create a comprehensive website and an electronic filing system for the new system of administration of justice as soon as possible, taking into account the role of the Office of Information and Communications Technology, and also requests the Secretary-General to include information on the progress made in that regard in his report to be submitted pursuant to paragraph 59 of resolution 63/253;

16. *Invites* the Sixth Committee to consider the legal aspects of the reports to be submitted by the Secretary-General, without prejudice to the role of the Fifth Committee as the Main Committee entrusted with responsibilities for administrative and budgetary matters.

By **decision 64/549** of 24 December, the Assembly decided that the item on the administration of justice at the United Nations would remain for consideration during its resumed sixty-fourth (2010) session.

United Nations Dispute Tribunal and United Nations Appeals Tribunal

Appointment of judges

On the basis of memoranda by the Secretary-General [A/63/700 & Add.1; A/63/701], the General Assembly, by **decision 63/417 A** of 2 March and **decision 63/417 B** of 31 March, appointed three full-time judges, two part-time judges and three ad litem judges to the United Nations Dispute Tribunal, and by **decision 63/418** of 2 March appointed seven judges to the United Nations Appeals Tribunal.

By **decision 64/549** of 24 December, the Assembly decided that the item on the election of three ad litem judges for the United Nations Dispute Tribunal would remain for consideration in its resumed sixty-fourth (2010) session.

Approval of rules of procedure

As requested in General Assembly resolution 63/253 [YUN 2008, p. 1637], by which the statutes of the United Nations Dispute Tribunal and the United Nations Appeals Tribunal were adopted, the Secretary-General in August submitted to the Assembly the rules of procedure of the respective Tribunals [A/64/229], which were established by the judges of the Tribunals on 26 June.

GENERAL ASSEMBLY ACTION

On 16 December [meeting 64], the General Assembly, on the recommendation of the Sixth Committee [A/64/454], adopted **resolution 64/119** without vote [agenda item 142].

Administration of justice at the United Nations

The General Assembly,

Recalling its resolution 63/253 of 24 December 2008, by which it adopted the statutes of the United Nations Dispute

Tribunal and the United Nations Appeals Tribunal, as set out in annexes I and II to that resolution,

Recalling also article 7, paragraph 1, of the statute of the United Nations Dispute Tribunal and article 6, paragraph 1, of the statute of the United Nations Appeals Tribunal, by virtue of which, subject to the provisions of the respective statutes, each Tribunal shall establish its own rules of procedure, which shall be subject to approval by the General Assembly,

Recalling further its request that the Secretary-General submit, for approval, the rules of procedure of the Tribunals as soon as possible but no later than at its sixty-fourth session, and its decision that until then the Tribunals may apply the rules of procedure on a provisional basis,

Having considered the report of the Secretary-General on approval of the rules of procedure of the United Nations Dispute Tribunal and the United Nations Appeals Tribunal, containing the rules of procedure established by the respective Tribunals on 26 June 2009,

Approves the rules of procedure of the United Nations Dispute Tribunal and the United Nations Appeals Tribunal, as set out in annexes I and II to the present resolution.

ANNEX I

Rules of procedure of the United Nations Dispute Tribunal

Article 1

Election of the President

1. The Dispute Tribunal shall elect a President from among the full-time judges, for a renewable term of one year, to direct the work of the Tribunal and of the Registries, in accordance with the statute of the Dispute Tribunal.

2. Until otherwise decided by the Dispute Tribunal:

(a) The election shall occur at a plenary meeting every year and the President shall take up his or her duties upon election;

(b) The retiring President shall remain in office until his or her successor is elected;

(c) If the President should cease to be a judge of the Dispute Tribunal, should resign his or her office before the expiration of the normal term or is unable to act, an election shall be held for the purpose of appointing a successor for the unexpired portion of the term;

(d) Elections shall be by majority vote. Any judge who cannot attend for that purpose is entitled to vote by correspondence.

Article 2

Plenary meeting

1. The Dispute Tribunal shall normally hold a plenary meeting once a year to deal with questions affecting the administration or operation of the Dispute Tribunal.

2. Three judges shall constitute a quorum for plenary meetings of the Dispute Tribunal.

Article 3

Commencement of office

Unless otherwise decided by the General Assembly, the term of office of the judges of the Dispute Tribunal shall commence on the first day of July following their appointment by the General Assembly.

Article 4
Venue

The judges of the Dispute Tribunal shall exercise their functions in New York, Geneva and Nairobi respectively. However, the Dispute Tribunal may decide to hold sessions at other duty stations as required.

Article 5
Consideration by a panel

1. Except in cases falling under article 5.2 below, cases shall be considered by a single judge.

2. As provided for in its statute, the Dispute Tribunal may refer any case to a panel of three judges for a decision.

3. If a case is examined by a panel of three judges, the decision shall be taken by majority vote. Any concurring, separate or dissenting opinion shall be recorded in the judgement.

Article 6
Filing of cases

1. An application shall be filed at a Registry of the Dispute Tribunal, taking into account geographical proximity and any other relevant material considerations.

2. The Dispute Tribunal shall assign cases to the appropriate Registry. A party may apply for a change of venue.

Article 7
Time limits for filing applications

1. Applications shall be submitted to the Dispute Tribunal through the Registrar within:

(a) 90 calendar days of the receipt by the applicant of the management evaluation, as appropriate;

(b) 90 calendar days of the relevant deadline for the communication of a response to a management evaluation, namely, 30 calendar days for disputes arising at Headquarters and 45 calendar days for disputes arising at other offices; or

(c) 90 calendar days of the receipt by the applicant of the administrative decision in cases where a management evaluation of the contested decision is not required.

2. Any person making claims on behalf of an incapacitated or deceased staff member of the United Nations, including the Secretariat and separately administered funds and programmes, shall have one calendar year to submit an application.

3. Where the parties have sought mediation of their dispute, the application shall be receivable if filed within 90 calendar days after mediation has broken down.

4. Where an application is filed to enforce the implementation of an agreement reached through mediation, the application shall be receivable if filed within 90 calendar days of the last day for implementation as specified in the mediation agreement or, when the mediation agreement is silent on the matter, after 30 calendar days from the date of the signing of the agreement.

5. In exceptional cases, an applicant may submit a written request to the Dispute Tribunal seeking suspension, waiver or extension of the time limits referred to in article 7.1 above. Such request shall succinctly set out the exceptional circumstances that, in the view of the applicant, justify the request. The request shall not exceed two pages in length.

6. In accordance with article 8.4 of the statute of the Dispute Tribunal, no application shall be receivable if filed more than three years after the applicant's receipt of the contested administrative decision.

Article 8
Applications

1. An application may be submitted on an application form to be prescribed by the Registrar.

2. The application should include the following information:

(a) The applicant's full name, date of birth and nationality;

(b) The applicant's employment status (including United Nations index number and department, office and section) or relationship to the staff member if the applicant is relying on the staff member's rights;

(c) Name of the applicant's legal representative (with authorization attached);

(d) The address to which documents should be sent;

(e) When and where the contested decision, if any, was taken (with the contested decision attached);

(f) Action and remedies sought;

(g) Any supporting documentation (annexed and numbered, including, if translated, an indication thereof).

3. The signed original application form and the annexes thereto shall be submitted together. The documents may be transmitted electronically.

4. After ascertaining that the requirements of the present article have been complied with, the Registrar shall transmit a copy of the application to the respondent and to any other party a judge considers appropriate. If the formal requirements of the article are not fulfilled, the Registrar may require the applicant to comply with the requirements of the article within a specified period of time. Once the corrections have been properly made, the Registrar shall transmit a copy of the application to the respondent.

Article 9
Summary judgement

A party may move for summary judgement when there is no dispute as to the material facts of the case and a party is entitled to judgement as a matter of law. The Dispute Tribunal may determine, on its own initiative, that summary judgement is appropriate.

Article 10
Reply

1. The respondent's reply shall be submitted within 30 calendar days of the date of receipt of the application by the respondent. The signed original reply and the annexes thereto shall be submitted together. The document may be transmitted electronically. A respondent who has not submitted a reply within the requisite period shall not be entitled to take part in the proceedings, except with the permission of the Dispute Tribunal.

2.   After ascertaining that the requirements of the present article have been complied with, the Registrar shall transmit a copy of the response to the applicant and to any other party a judge considers appropriate. If the formal requirements of the article are not fulfilled, the Registrar may require the respondent to comply with the requirements of the article within a specified period of time. Once the corrections have been properly made, the Registrar shall transmit a copy of the reply to the applicant.

Article 11
Joining of a party

The Dispute Tribunal may at any time, either on the application of a party or on its own initiative, join another party if it appears to the Dispute Tribunal that that party has a legitimate interest in the outcome of the proceedings.

Article 12
Representation

1.   A party may present his or her case to the Dispute Tribunal in person, or may designate counsel from the Office of Staff Legal Assistance or counsel authorized to practice law in a national jurisdiction.

2.   A party may also be represented by a staff member or a former staff member of the United Nations or one of the specialized agencies.

Article 13
Suspension of action during a management evaluation

1.   The Dispute Tribunal shall order a suspension of action on an application filed by an individual requesting the Dispute Tribunal to suspend, during the pendency of the management evaluation, the implementation of a contested administrative decision that is the subject of an ongoing management evaluation, where the decision appears prima facie to be unlawful, in cases of particular urgency and where its implementation would cause irreparable damage.

2.   The Registrar shall transmit the application to the respondent.

3.   The Dispute Tribunal shall consider an application for interim measures within five working days of the service of the application on the respondent.

4.   The decision of the Dispute Tribunal on such an application shall not be subject to appeal.

Article 14
Suspension of action during the proceedings

1.   At any time during the proceedings, the Dispute Tribunal may order interim measures to provide temporary relief where the contested administrative decision appears prima facie to be unlawful, in cases of particular urgency and where its implementation would cause irreparable damage. This temporary relief may include an order to suspend the implementation of the contested administrative decision, except in cases of appointment, promotion or termination.

2.   The Registrar shall transmit the application to the respondent.

3.   The Dispute Tribunal shall consider an application for interim measures within five working days of the service of the application on the respondent.

4.   The decision of the Dispute Tribunal on such an application shall not be subject to appeal.

Article 15
Referral to mediation

1.   At any time during the proceedings, including at the hearing, the Dispute Tribunal may propose to the parties that the case be referred for mediation and suspend the proceedings.

2.   Where the judge proposes and the parties consent to mediation, the Dispute Tribunal shall send the case to the Mediation Division in the Office of the Ombudsman for consideration.

3.   Where parties on their own initiative decide to seek mediation, they shall promptly inform the Registry in writing.

4.   Upon referral of a case to the Mediation Division, the concerned Registry shall forward the case file to the Mediation Division. The proceedings will be suspended during mediation.

5.   The time limit for mediation normally shall not exceed three months. However, after consultation with the parties, where the Mediation Division considers it appropriate, it will notify the Registry that the informal efforts will require additional time.

6.   It shall be the responsibility of the Mediation Division to apprise the Dispute Tribunal of the outcome of the mediation in a timely manner.

7.   All documents prepared for and oral statements made during any informal conflict-resolution process or mediation are absolutely privileged and confidential and shall never be disclosed to the Dispute Tribunal. No mention shall be made of any mediation efforts in documents or written pleadings submitted to the Dispute Tribunal or in any oral arguments made before the Dispute Tribunal.

Article 16
Hearing

1.   The judge hearing a case may hold oral hearings.

2.   A hearing shall normally be held following an appeal against an administrative decision imposing a disciplinary measure.

3.   The Registrar shall notify the parties of the date and time of a hearing in advance and confirm the names of witnesses or expert witnesses for the hearing of a particular case.

4.   The parties or their duly designated representatives must be present at the hearing either in person or, where unavailable, by video link, telephone or other electronic means.

5.   If the Dispute Tribunal requires the physical presence of a party or any other person at the hearing, the necessary costs associated with the travel and accommodation of the party or other person shall be borne by the Organization.

6. The oral proceedings shall be held in public unless the judge hearing the case decides, at his or her own initiative or at the request of one of the parties, that exceptional circumstances require that the oral proceedings be closed. If appropriate in the circumstances, the oral hearing may be held by video link, telephone or other electronic means.

Article 17
Oral evidence

1. The parties may call witnesses and experts to testify. The opposing party may cross-examine witnesses and experts. The Dispute Tribunal may examine witnesses and experts called by either party and may call any other witnesses or experts it deems necessary. The Dispute Tribunal may make an order requiring the presence of any person or the production of any document.

2. The Dispute Tribunal may, if it considers it appropriate in the interest of justice to do so, proceed to determine a case in the absence of a party.

3. Each witness shall make the following declaration before giving his or her statement: "I solemnly declare upon my honour and conscience that I will speak the truth, the whole truth and nothing but the truth."

4. Each expert shall make the following declaration before giving his or her statement: "I solemnly declare upon my honour and conscience that my statement will be in accordance with my sincere belief."

5. Any party may object to the testimony of a given witness or expert, stating reasons for such objection. The Dispute Tribunal shall decide on the matter. Its decision shall be final.

6. The Dispute Tribunal shall decide whether the personal appearance of a witness or expert is required at oral proceedings and determine the appropriate means for satisfying the requirement for personal appearance. Evidence may be taken by video link, telephone or other electronic means.

Article 18
Evidence

1. The Dispute Tribunal shall determine the admissibility of any evidence.

2. The Dispute Tribunal may order the production of evidence for either party at any time and may require any person to disclose any document or provide any information that appears to the Dispute Tribunal to be necessary for a fair and expeditious disposal of the proceedings.

3. A party wishing to submit evidence that is in the possession of the opposing party or of any other entity may, in the initial application or at any stage of the proceedings, request the Dispute Tribunal to order the production of the evidence.

4. The Dispute Tribunal may, at the request of either party, impose measures to preserve the confidentiality of evidence, where warranted by security interests or other exceptional circumstances.

5. The Dispute Tribunal may exclude evidence which it considers irrelevant, frivolous or lacking in probative value. The Dispute Tribunal may also limit oral testimony as it deems appropriate.

Article 19
Case management

The Dispute Tribunal may at any time, either on an application of a party or on its own initiative, issue any order or give any direction which appears to a judge to be appropriate for the fair and expeditious disposal of the case and to do justice to the parties.

Article 20
Remand of case for the institution or correction of the required procedure

Prior to a determination of the merits of a case, should the Dispute Tribunal find that a relevant procedure prescribed in the Staff Regulations and Rules or applicable administrative issuances has not been observed, the Tribunal may, with the concurrence of the Secretary-General, remand the case for the institution or correction of the required procedure, which, in any case, should not take longer than three months. In such cases, the Dispute Tribunal may order the payment of compensation to the applicant for such loss as may have been caused by the procedural delay. The compensation is not to exceed the equivalent of three months' net base salary.

Article 21
Registry

1. The Dispute Tribunal shall be supported by Registries, which shall provide all necessary administrative and support services to it.

2. The Registries shall be established in New York, Geneva and Nairobi. Each Registry shall be headed by a Registrar appointed by the Secretary-General and such other staff as is necessary.

3. The Registrars shall discharge the duties set out in the rules of procedure and shall support the work of the Dispute Tribunal at the direction of the President or the judge at each location. In particular, the Registrars shall:

(*a*) Transmit all documents and make all notifications required in the rules of procedure or required by the President in connection with proceedings before the Dispute Tribunal;

(*b*) Establish for each case a master Registry file, which shall record all actions taken in connection with the preparation of the case for hearing, the dates thereof and the dates on which any document or notification forming part of the procedure is received in or dispatched from his or her office;

(*c*) Perform any other duties that are required by the President or the judge for the efficient functioning of the Dispute Tribunal.

4. A Registrar, if unable to act, shall be replaced by an official appointed by the Secretary-General.

Article 22
Intervention by persons not party to the case

1. Any person for whom recourse to the Dispute Tribunal is available under article 2.4 of the statute may apply, on an application form to be prescribed by the Registrar, to intervene in a case at any stage thereof on the grounds that he or she has a right that may be affected by the judgement to be issued by the Dispute Tribunal.

2. After ascertaining that the requirements of the present article have been complied with, the Registrar shall transmit a copy of the application for intervention to the applicant and to the respondent.

3. The Dispute Tribunal shall decide on the admissibility of the application for intervention. Such decision shall be final and shall be communicated to the intervener and the parties by the Registrar.

4. The Dispute Tribunal shall establish the modalities of the intervention. If admissible, the Dispute Tribunal shall decide which documents, if any, relating to the proceedings are to be transmitted to the intervener by the Registrar and shall fix a time by which any written submissions must be submitted by the intervener. It shall also decide whether the intervener shall be permitted to participate in any oral proceedings.

Article 23
Intervention procedure

An application for intervention shall be submitted on a prescribed form, the signed original of which shall be submitted to the Registrar. It may be transmitted electronically.

Article 24
Friend-of-the-court briefs

1. A staff association may submit a signed application to file a friend-of-the-court brief on a form to be prescribed by the Registrar, which may be transmitted electronically. The Registrar shall forward a copy of the application to the parties, who shall have three days to file any objections, which shall be submitted on a prescribed form.

2. The President or the judge hearing the case may grant the application if it considers that the filing of the brief would assist the Dispute Tribunal in its deliberations. The decision will be communicated to the applicant and the parties by the Registrar.

Article 25
Judgements

1. Judgements shall be issued in writing and shall state the reasons, facts and law on which they are based.

2. When a case is decided by a panel of three judges, a judge may append a separate, dissenting or concurring opinion.

3. Judgements shall be drawn up in any official language of the United Nations, two signed originals of which shall be deposited in the archives of the United Nations.

4. The Registrars shall transmit a copy of the judgement to each party. An individual applicant or respondent shall receive a copy of the judgement in the language in which the original application was submitted, unless he or she requests a copy in another official language of the United Nations.

5. The Registrars shall send to all judges of the Dispute Tribunal copies of all the judgements of the Dispute Tribunal.

Article 26
Publication of judgements

1. The Registrars shall arrange for publication of the judgements of the Dispute Tribunal on the website of the Dispute Tribunal after they are delivered.

2. The judgements of the Dispute Tribunal shall protect personal data and shall be available at the Registry of the Dispute Tribunal.

Article 27
Conflict of interest

1. The term "conflict of interest" means any factor that may impair or reasonably give the appearance of impairing the ability of a judge to independently and impartially adjudicate a case assigned to him or her.

2. A conflict of interest arises where a case assigned to a judge involves any of the following:

(a) A person with whom the judge has a personal, familiar or professional relationship;

(b) A matter in which the judge has previously served in another capacity, including as an adviser, counsel, expert or witness;

(c) Any other circumstances that would make it appear to a reasonable and impartial observer that the judge's participation in the adjudication of the matter would be inappropriate.

Article 28
Recusal

1. A judge of the Dispute Tribunal who has or appears to have a conflict of interest as defined in article 27 of the rules of procedure shall recuse himself or herself from the case and shall so inform the President.

2. A party may make a reasoned request for the recusal of a judge on the grounds of a conflict of interest to the President of the Dispute Tribunal, who, after seeking comments from the judge, shall decide on the request and shall inform the party of the decision in writing. A request for recusal of the President shall be referred to a three-judge panel for decision.

3. The Registrar shall communicate the decision to the parties concerned.

Article 29
Revision of judgements

1. Either party may apply to the Dispute Tribunal for a revision of a judgement on the basis of the discovery of a decisive fact that was, at the time the judgement was rendered, unknown to the Dispute Tribunal and to the party applying for revision, always provided that such ignorance was not due to negligence.

2. An application for revision must be made within 30 calendar days of the discovery of the fact and within one year of the date of the judgement.

3. The application for revision will be sent to the other party, who has 30 days after receipt to submit comments to the Registrar.

Article 30
Interpretation of judgements

Either party may apply to the Dispute Tribunal for an interpretation of the meaning or scope of a judgement, provided that it is not under consideration by the Appeals Tribunal. The application for interpretation shall be sent to the other party, who shall have 30 days to submit comments on the application. The Dispute Tribunal will decide whether to admit the application for interpretation and, if it does so, shall issue its interpretation.

Article 31
Correction of judgements

Clerical or arithmetical mistakes, or errors arising from any accidental slip or omission, may at any time be corrected by the Dispute Tribunal, either on its own initiative or on the application by any of the parties on a prescribed form.

Article 32
Execution of judgements

1. Judgements of the Dispute Tribunal shall be binding on the parties, but are subject to appeal in accordance with the statute of the Appeals Tribunal. In the absence of such appeal, it shall be executable following the expiry of the time provided for appeal in the statute of the Appeals Tribunal.

2. Once a judgement is executable under article 11.3 of the statute of the Dispute Tribunal, either party may apply to the Dispute Tribunal for an order for execution of the judgement if the judgement requires execution within a certain period of time and such execution has not been carried out.

Article 33
Titles

The titles of the articles in the rules of procedure are for reference purposes only and do not constitute an interpretation of the article concerned.

Article 34
Calculation of time limits

The time limits prescribed in the rules of procedure:

(a) Refer to calendar days and shall not include the day of the event from which the period runs;

(b) Shall include the next working day of the Registry when the last day of the period is not a working day;

(c) Shall be deemed to have been met if the documents in question were dispatched by reasonable means on the last day of the period.

Article 35
Waiver of time limits

Subject to article 8.3 of the statute of the Dispute Tribunal, the President, or the judge or panel hearing a case, may shorten or extend a time limit fixed by the rules of procedure or waive any rule when the interests of justice so require.

Article 36
Procedural matters not covered in the rules of procedure

1. All matters that are not expressly provided for in the rules of procedure shall be dealt with by decision of the Dispute Tribunal on the particular case, by virtue of the powers conferred on it by article 7 of its statute.

2. The Dispute Tribunal may issue practice directions related to the implementation of the rules of procedure.

Article 37
Amendment of the rules of procedure

1. The Dispute Tribunal in plenary meeting may adopt amendments to the rules of procedure, which shall be submitted to the General Assembly for approval.

2. The amendments shall operate provisionally until approved by the General Assembly or until they are amended or withdrawn by the Dispute Tribunal in accordance with a decision of the General Assembly.

3. The President, after consultation with the judges of the Dispute Tribunal, may instruct the Registrars to revise any forms from time to time in the light of experience, provided that such modifications are consistent with the rules of procedure.

Article 38
Entry into force

1. The rules of procedure shall enter into force on the first day of the month following their approval by the General Assembly.

2. The rules of procedure shall operate provisionally from the date of their adoption by the Dispute Tribunal until their entry into force.

ANNEX II
Rules of procedure of the United Nations Appeals Tribunal

Article 1
Election of the President and Vice-Presidents

1. The Appeals Tribunal shall elect a President, a First Vice-President and a Second Vice-President.

2. Until otherwise decided by the Appeals Tribunal:

(a) The election shall occur at a plenary meeting during the Appeals Tribunal's last session each year. The President and Vice-Presidents shall hold office for one year and shall take up their duties upon election;

(b) The retiring President and Vice-Presidents shall remain in office until their successors are elected;

(c) If a President or a Vice-President should cease to be a judge of the Appeals Tribunal or should resign his or her office before the expiration of the normal term, an election shall be held for the purpose of appointing a successor for the unexpired portion of the term;

(d) Elections shall be by majority vote. Any judge who cannot attend for that purpose is entitled to vote by correspondence.

Article 2
Functions of the President and Vice-Presidents

1. The President shall direct the work of the Appeals Tribunal and of the Registry, shall represent the Appeals Tribunal in all administrative matters and shall preside at the meetings of the Appeals Tribunal.

2. If the President is unable to act, he or she shall designate one of the Vice-Presidents to act as President. In the absence of any such designation by the President, the First Vice-President or, in the event of the latter's incapacity, the Second Vice-President shall act as President.

3. The President of the Appeals Tribunal may, within seven calendar days of a written request by the President of the Dispute Tribunal, authorize the referral of a case to a panel of three judges of the Dispute Tribunal, when necessary, by reason of the particular complexity or importance of the case.

Article 3
Composition of the Appeals Tribunal for its sessions

1. Unless otherwise decided by the General Assembly, the term of office of the judges of the Appeals Tribunal shall commence on the first day of July following their appointment by the General Assembly.

2. No member of the Appeals Tribunal can be dismissed by the General Assembly unless the other members unanimously agree that he or she is unsuited for further service.

Article 4
Panels

1. The President shall normally designate a panel of three judges to hear a case or a group of cases.

2. When the President or any two judges sitting on a particular case consider that the case so warrants, the case shall be heard by the whole Appeals Tribunal.

Article 5
Ordinary and extraordinary sessions

1. The Appeals Tribunal shall exercise its functions in New York and shall hold ordinary sessions for the purpose of hearing cases. The Appeals Tribunal shall normally hold two ordinary sessions per calendar year and may decide to hold sessions in Geneva or Nairobi, as required by its caseload.

2. Extraordinary sessions for the consideration of cases may be convened by the President when, in his or her opinion, the number or urgency of the cases requires such sessions. Notice of an extraordinary session shall be given to the members of the Tribunal at least 30 days before the opening date of the session.

3. The President shall decide the date and venue of ordinary and extraordinary sessions after consultation with the Registrar.

Article 6
Plenary meetings

1. The Appeals Tribunal shall normally hold four plenary meetings a year, at the beginning and at the end of each of the regular sessions, to deal with questions affecting the administration or operation of the Appeals Tribunal. It shall elect its officers at a plenary meeting, normally the last one in the calendar year.

2. Four judges shall constitute a quorum for plenary meetings of the Appeals Tribunal.

Article 7
Time limits for filing appeals

1. Appeals instituting proceedings shall be submitted to the Appeals Tribunal through the Registrar within:

(a) 45 calendar days of the receipt by a party appealing a judgement of the Dispute Tribunal;

(b) 90 calendar days of the date of receipt by a party appealing a decision of the Standing Committee acting on behalf of the United Nations Joint Staff Pension Board; or

(c) A time limit fixed by the Appeals Tribunal under article 7.2 of the rules of procedure.

2. In exceptional cases, an appellant may submit a written request to the Appeals Tribunal seeking suspension, waiver or extension of the time limits referred to in article 7.1. The written request shall succinctly set out the exceptional reasons that, in the view of the appellant, justify the request. The written request shall not exceed two pages.

3. In accordance with article 7.4 of the statute of the Appeals Tribunal, no application shall be receivable if filed more than one year after the judgement of the Dispute Tribunal.

Article 8
Appeals

1. Appeals shall be submitted on a prescribed form.

2. The appeal form shall be accompanied by:

(a) A brief that explains the legal basis of any of the five grounds for appeal set out in article 2.1 of the statute of the Appeals Tribunal that is relied upon or, in the case of an appeal against a decision of the Standing Committee acting on behalf of the United Nations Joint Staff Pension Board, a brief containing pleas and an explanatory statement. The brief shall not exceed 15 pages;

(b) A copy of each document referred to by the appellant in the appeal, accompanied by a translation into one of the official languages of the United Nations if the original language is not one of the official languages; such documents shall be identified by the word "Annex" at the top of the first page of each document followed by sequential arabic numerals.

3. The signed original appeal form and the annexes thereto shall be submitted together to the Registrar. The documents may be transmitted electronically.

4. After ascertaining that the appeal complies with the requirements of the present article, the Registrar shall transmit a copy of the appeal to the respondent. If the formal requirements of the article are not fulfilled, the Registrar may require the appellant to conform the appeal to the requirements of the article within a specified time. Once the corrections have been properly made, the Registrar shall transmit a copy of the appeal to the respondent.

5. The President may direct the Registrar to inform an appellant that his or her appeal is not receivable because it is not an appeal against either a decision of the Dispute Tribunal or of the Standing Committee acting on behalf of the United Nations Joint Staff Pension Board, as the case may be.

6. The filing of an appeal shall suspend the execution of the judgement contested.

Article 9
Answers

1. The respondent's answer shall be submitted on a prescribed form.

2. The answer form shall be accompanied by:

(a) A brief, which shall not exceed 15 pages, setting out legal arguments in support of the answer;

(b) A copy of each document referred to by the respondent in the answer, accompanied by a translation into one of the official languages of the United Nations if the original language is not one of the official languages; such documents shall be identified by the word "Annex" at the top of the first page of each document and an arabic numeral which follows in sequence the numbering of the annexes to the appeal form referred to in article 8.2 *(b)*.

3. The signed original answer form and the annexes thereto shall be submitted together to the Registrar within 45 days of the date on which the respondent received the appeal transmitted by the Registrar. The documents may be transmitted electronically.

4. Within 15 days of notice of the appeal, a party answering the appeal may serve a notice of cross-appeal with the Appeals Tribunal stating the relief sought and the grounds of the cross-appeal. The cross-appeal may not add new claims.

5. After ascertaining that the answer complies with the requirements of the present article, the Registrar shall transmit a copy of the answer to the appellant. If the formal requirements of the article are not fulfilled, the Registrar may require the respondent to conform the answer to the requirements of the present article within a specified time. Once the corrections have been properly made, the Registrar shall transmit a copy of the answer to the appellant. If the corrections are not submitted within the established time limit, including any extension granted by the Appeals Tribunal, the preliminary proceedings will be considered closed and the Appeals Tribunal will adjudicate the matter on the basis of the appeal lodged by the appellant.

Article 10
Additional documentary evidence, including written testimony

1. A party may seek to submit to the Appeals Tribunal, with an appeal or an answer, documentary evidence, including written testimony, in addition to that contained in the written record. In exceptional circumstances and where the Appeals Tribunal determines that the facts are likely to be established with such additional documentary evidence, it may receive the additional evidence from a party. On its own volition, the Tribunal may order the production of evidence if it is in the interest of justice and the efficient and expeditious resolution of the case, provided that the Appeals Tribunal shall not receive additional written evidence if it was known to the party seeking to submit the evidence and should have been presented to the Dispute Tribunal.

2. In all other cases where additional findings of fact are needed, the Appeals Tribunal may remand the case to the Dispute Tribunal for further fact-finding. Where the Appeals Tribunal remands a case to the Dispute Tribunal, it may order that the case be considered by a different judge of the Dispute Tribunal.

Article 11
Docket of cases

1. When the President considers the documentation of a case to be sufficiently complete, he or she shall instruct the Registrar to place the case on the docket of cases ready for adjudication by the Appeals Tribunal. The docket for the session shall be communicated to the parties.

2. As soon as the date of opening of the session at which a case listed for hearing has been fixed, the Registrar shall notify the parties thereof.

3. Any request for the adjournment of a case that is listed on the docket shall be decided by the President or, when the Appeals Tribunal is in session, by the judges hearing the case.

Article 12
Working languages

The working languages of the Appeals Tribunal shall be English and French.

Article 13
Representation

1. A party may present his or her case before the Appeals Tribunal in person or may designate counsel from the Office of Staff Legal Assistance or counsel authorized to practice law in a national jurisdiction.

2. A party may also be represented by a staff member or a former staff member of the United Nations or one of the specialized agencies.

Article 14
Waiver of rules concerning written pleadings

Subject to article 7.4 of the statute of the Appeals Tribunal and provided that the waiver does not affect the substance of the case before the Appeals Tribunal, the President may waive the requirements of any article of the rules of procedure dealing with written proceedings.

Article 15
Exclusion of all documents and statements made during mediation

1. Except in cases concerning enforcement of a settlement agreement, all documents prepared for and oral statements made during any informal conflict-resolution process or mediation are absolutely privileged and confidential and shall never be disclosed to the Appeals Tribunal. No mention shall be made of any mediation efforts in documents or written pleadings submitted to the Appeals Tribunal or in any oral arguments made before the Appeals Tribunal.

2. Subject to the provisions of paragraph 1 above, if a document relating to the mediation process is submitted to the Appeals Tribunal, the Registrar shall return that document to the submitting party. If such information is part of the brief or any other written pleadings submitted to the Appeals Tribunal by a party, all pleadings shall be returned to that party for resubmission to the Appeals Tribunal in compliance with paragraph 1 above.

3. Subject to article 7.4 of the statute of the Appeals Tribunal, the President may fix one non-renewable time limit not exceeding five days for the resubmission of the written pleadings if the initial period for the submission of such pleadings has expired.

Article 16
Intervention by persons not party to the case

1. Any person for whom recourse to the Appeals Tribunal is available under article 6.2 (*f*) of the statute may apply to intervene in a case at any stage thereof on the grounds that his or her rights may have been affected by the judgement of the Dispute Tribunal and might, therefore, be affected by the judgement of the Appeals Tribunal.

2. After ascertaining that the requirements of the present article have been complied with, the Registrar shall transmit a copy of the application for intervention to the appellant and to the respondent.

3. The President or, when the Tribunal is in session, the presiding judge of the panel of the Appeals Tribunal hearing the case shall rule on the admissibility of every application for intervention. Such decision shall be final and shall be communicated to the intervener and the parties by the Registrar.

4. An application for intervention shall be submitted on a prescribed form, the signed original of which shall be submitted to the Registrar. It may be transmitted electronically.

Article 17
Friend-of-the-court briefs

1. A person or organization for whom recourse to the Appeals Tribunal is available and staff associations may submit a signed application to file a friend-of-the-court brief, which may be transmitted electronically. The Registrar shall forward a copy of the application to the parties, who shall have three days to file any objections on a prescribed form.

2. The President or the panel hearing the case may grant the application if it considers that the filing of the brief would assist the Appeals Tribunal in its deliberations. The decision will be communicated to the applicant and the parties by the Registrar.

Article 18
Oral proceedings

1. The judges hearing a case may hold oral hearings on the written application of a party or on their own initiative if such hearings would assist in the expeditious and fair disposal of the case.

2. The oral proceedings shall be held in public unless the judges hearing the case decide, on their own initiative or at the request of one of the parties, that exceptional circumstances require that the oral proceedings be closed. If appropriate in the circumstances, the oral hearing may be held by electronic means.

Article 19
Adoption and issuance of judgements

1. Judgements shall be adopted by majority vote. All deliberations shall be kept confidential.

2. Judgements shall be issued in writing and shall state the reasons, facts and law on which they are based.

3. A judge may append a separate, dissenting or concurring opinion.

4. Judgements shall be drawn up in any official language of the United Nations, two signed originals of which shall be deposited in the archives of the United Nations.

5. The Registrar shall transmit a copy of the judgement to each party. An individual appellant or respondent shall receive a copy of the judgement in the language of the appeal or answer, as the case may be, unless a copy is requested in another official language of the United Nations.

6. The Registrar shall send to all judges of the Appeals Tribunal copies of all the decisions of the Appeals Tribunal.

Article 20
Publication of judgements

1. The Registrar shall arrange for publication of the judgements of the Appeals Tribunal on the website of the Appeals Tribunal after they are delivered.

2. The published judgements will normally include the names of the parties.

Article 21
Registry

1. The Appeals Tribunal shall be supported by a Registry, which shall provide all necessary administrative and support services to it.

2. The Registry shall be established in New York and shall be headed by a Registrar appointed by the Secretary-General and such staff as is necessary.

3. The Registrar shall discharge the duties set out in the rules of procedure and shall support the work of the Appeals Tribunal at the direction of the President. In particular, the Registrar shall:

(a) Transmit all documents and make all notifications required in the rules of procedure or required by the President or a panel hearing a case in connection with proceedings before the Appeals Tribunal;

(b) Establish for each case a master Registry file, which shall record all actions taken in connection with the preparation of the case for hearing, the dates thereof and the dates on which any document or notification forming part of the procedure is received in or dispatched from his or her office;

(c) Perform any other duties that are required by the President for the efficient functioning of the Appeals Tribunal and the efficient disposal of its caseload.

4. The Registrar, if unable to act, shall be replaced by an official appointed by the Secretary-General.

Article 22
Conflict of interest

1. The term "conflict of interest" means any factor that may impair or reasonably give the appearance of impairing the ability of a judge to independently and impartially adjudicate a case assigned to him or her.

2. A conflict of interest arises where a case assigned to a judge involves any of the following:

(a) A person with whom the judge has a personal, familiar or professional relationship;

(b) A matter in which the judge has previously served in another capacity, including as an adviser, counsel, expert or witness;

(c) Any other circumstances that would make it appear to a reasonable and impartial observer that the judge's participation in the adjudication of the matter would be inappropriate.

Article 23
Recusal

1. A judge of the Appeals Tribunal who has or appears to have a conflict of interest as defined in article 22 of the rules of procedure shall recuse himself or herself from the case and shall so inform the President.

2. A party may make a reasoned request for the recusal of a judge on the grounds of conflict of interest to the President or the Appeals Tribunal, which, after seeking comments from the judge, shall decide on the request and shall inform the party of the decision in writing.

3. A decision by a judge to recuse himself or herself, or a decision by the President or the Appeals Tribunal to recuse a judge, shall be communicated to the parties concerned by the Registrar.

Article 24
Revision of judgements

Either party may apply to the Appeals Tribunal, on a prescribed form, for a revision of a judgement on the basis of the discovery of a decisive fact that was, at the time the judgement was rendered, unknown to the Appeals Tribunal and to the party applying for revision, always provided that such ignorance was not due to negligence. The application for revision will be sent to the other party, who has 30 days to submit comments to the Registrar on a prescribed form. The application for revision must be made within 30 calendar days of the discovery of the fact and within one year of the date of the judgement.

Article 25
Interpretation of judgements

Either party may apply to the Appeals Tribunal for an interpretation of the meaning or scope of a judgement on a prescribed form. The application for interpretation shall be sent to the other party, who shall have 30 days to submit comments on the application on a prescribed form. The Appeals Tribunal will decide whether to admit the application for interpretation and, if it does so, shall issue its interpretation.

Article 26
Correction of judgements

Clerical or arithmetical mistakes, or errors arising from any accidental slip or omission, may at any time be corrected by the Appeals Tribunal, either on its own initiative or on the application by any of the parties on a prescribed form.

Article 27
Execution of judgements

Where a judgement requires execution within a certain period of time and such execution has not been carried out, either party may apply to the Appeals Tribunal for an order for execution of the judgement.

Article 28
Titles

The titles to the articles in the rules of procedure are for reference purposes only and do not constitute an interpretation of the article concerned.

Article 29
Calculation of time limits

The time limits prescribed in the rules of procedure:

(a) Refer to calendar days, but shall not include the day of the event from which the period runs;

(b) Shall include the next working day of the Registry when the last day of the period is not a working day;

(c) Shall be deemed to have been met if the documents in question were dispatched by reasonable means on the last day of the period.

Article 30
Waiver of time limits

Subject to article 7.4 of the statute of the Appeals Tribunal, the President or the panel hearing a case may shorten or extend a time limit fixed by the rules of procedure or waive any rule when the interests of justice so require.

Article 31
Procedural matters not covered in the rules of procedure

1. All matters that are not expressly provided for in the rules of procedure shall be dealt with by decision of the Appeals Tribunal on the particular case, by virtue of the powers conferred on it by article 6 of its statute.

2. The Appeals Tribunal may issue practice directions related to the implementation of the rules of procedure.

Article 32
Amendment of the rules of procedure

1. The Appeals Tribunal in plenary meeting may adopt amendments to the rules of procedure, which shall be submitted to the General Assembly for approval.

2. The amendments shall operate provisionally until approved by the General Assembly.

3. The President, after consultation with the judges of the Appeals Tribunal, may instruct the Registrar to revise any forms from time to time in the light of experience, provided that such modifications are consistent with the rules of procedure.

Article 33
Entry into force

1. The rules of procedure shall enter into force on the first day of the month following their approval by the General Assembly.

2. The rules of procedure shall operate provisionally from the date of their adoption by the Appeals Tribunal until their entry into force.

Appendices

Roster of the United Nations

(There were 192 Member States as at 31 December 2009.)

Member State	Date of admission	Member State	Date of admission	Member State	Date of admission
Afghanistan	19 Nov. 1946	Democratic Republic of the Congo[4]	20 Sep. 1960	Latvia	17 Sep. 1991
Albania	14 Dec. 1955			Lebanon	24 Oct. 1945
Algeria	8 Oct. 1962	Denmark	24 Oct. 1945	Lesotho	17 Oct. 1966
Andorra	28 July 1993	Djibouti	20 Sep. 1977	Liberia	2 Nov. 1945
Angola	1 Dec. 1976	Dominica	18 Dec. 1978	Libyan Arab Jamahiriya	14 Dec. 1955
Antigua and Barbuda	11 Nov. 1981	Dominican Republic	24 Oct. 1945	Liechtenstein	18 Sep. 1990
Argentina	24 Oct. 1945	Ecuador	21 Dec. 1945	Lithuania	17 Sep. 1991
Armenia	2 Mar. 1992	Egypt[5]	24 Oct. 1945	Luxembourg	24 Oct. 1945
Australia	1 Nov. 1945	El Salvador	24 Oct. 1945	Madagascar	20 Sep. 1960
Austria	14 Dec. 1955	Equatorial Guinea	12 Nov. 1968	Malawi	1 Dec. 1964
Azerbaijan	2 Mar. 1992	Eritrea	28 May 1993	Malaysia[8]	17 Sep. 1957
Bahamas	18 Sep. 1973	Estonia	17 Sep. 1991	Maldives	21 Sep. 1965
Bahrain	21 Sep. 1971	Ethiopia	13 Nov. 1945	Mali	28 Sep. 1960
Bangladesh	17 Sep. 1974	Fiji	13 Oct. 1970	Malta	1 Dec. 1964
Barbados	9 Dec. 1966	Finland	14 Dec. 1955	Marshall Islands	17 Sep. 1991
Belarus[1]	24 Oct. 1945	France	24 Oct. 1945	Mauritania	27 Oct. 1961
Belgium	27 Dec. 1945	Gabon	20 Sep. 1960	Mauritius	24 Apr. 1968
Belize	25 Sep. 1981	Gambia	21 Sep. 1965	Mexico	7 Nov. 1945
Benin	20 Sep. 1960	Georgia	31 July 1992	Micronesia (Federated States of)	17 Sep. 1991
Bhutan	21 Sep. 1971	Germany[6]	18 Sep. 1973		
Bolivia	14 Nov. 1945	Ghana	8 Mar. 1957	Monaco	28 May 1993
Bosnia and Herzegovina[2]	22 May 1992	Greece	25 Oct. 1945	Mongolia	27 Oct. 1961
Botswana	17 Oct. 1966	Grenada	17 Sep. 1974	Montenegro[2]	28 June 2006
Brazil	24 Oct. 1945	Guatemala	21 Nov. 1945	Morocco	12 Nov. 1956
Brunei Darussalam	21 Sep. 1984	Guinea	12 Dec. 1958	Mozambique	16 Sep. 1975
Bulgaria	14 Dec. 1955	Guinea-Bissau	17 Sep. 1974	Myanmar	19 Apr. 1948
Burkina Faso	20 Sep. 1960	Guyana	20 Sep. 1966	Namibia	23 Apr. 1990
Burundi	18 Sep. 1962	Haiti	24 Oct. 1945	Nauru	14 Sep. 1999
Cambodia	14 Dec. 1955	Honduras	17 Dec. 1945	Nepal	14 Dec. 1955
Cameroon	20 Sep. 1960	Hungary	14 Dec. 1955	Netherlands	10 Dec. 1945
Canada	9 Nov. 1945	Iceland	19 Nov. 1946	New Zealand	24 Oct. 1945
Cape Verde	16 Sep. 1975	India	30 Oct. 1945	Nicaragua	24 Oct. 1945
Central African Republic	20 Sep. 1960	Indonesia[7]	28 Sep. 1950	Niger	20 Sep. 1960
		Iran (Islamic Republic of)	24 Oct. 1945	Nigeria	7 Oct. 1960
Chad	20 Sep. 1960	Iraq	21 Dec. 1945	Norway	27 Nov. 1945
Chile	24 Oct. 1945	Ireland	14 Dec. 1955	Oman	7 Oct. 1971
China	24 Oct. 1945	Israel	11 May 1949	Pakistan	30 Sep. 1947
Colombia	5 Nov. 1945	Italy	14 Dec. 1955	Palau	15 Dec. 1994
Comoros	12 Nov. 1975	Jamaica	18 Sep. 1962	Panama	13 Nov. 1945
Congo	20 Sep. 1960	Japan	18 Dec. 1956	Papua New Guinea	10 Oct. 1975
Costa Rica	2 Nov. 1945	Jordan	14 Dec. 1955	Paraguay	24 Oct. 1945
Côte d'Ivoire	20 Sep. 1960	Kazakhstan	2 Mar. 1992	Peru	31 Oct. 1945
Croatia[2]	22 May 1992	Kenya	16 Dec. 1963	Philippines	24 Oct. 1945
Cuba	24 Oct. 1945	Kiribati	14 Sep. 1999	Poland	24 Oct. 1945
Cyprus	20 Sep. 1960	Kuwait	14 May 1963	Portugal	14 Dec. 1955
Czech Republic[3]	19 Jan. 1993	Kyrgyzstan	2 Mar. 1992	Qatar	21 Sep. 1971
Democratic People's Republic of Korea	17 Sep. 1991	Lao People's Democratic Republic	14 Dec. 1955	Republic of Korea	17 Sep. 1991

Member State	Date of admission	Member State	Date of admission	Member State	Date of admission
Republic of Moldova	2 Mar. 1992	Somalia	20 Sep. 1960	Turkmenistan	2 Mar. 1992
Romania	14 Dec. 1955	South Africa	7 Nov. 1945	Tuvalu	5 Sep. 2000
Russian Federation[9]	24 Oct. 1945	Spain	14 Dec. 1955	Uganda	25 Oct. 1962
Rwanda	18 Sep. 1962	Sri Lanka	14 Dec. 1955	Ukraine	24 Oct. 1945
Saint Kitts and Nevis	23 Sep. 1983	Sudan	12 Nov. 1956	United Arab Emirates	9 Dec. 1971
Saint Lucia	18 Sep. 1979	Suriname	4 Dec. 1975	United Kingdom of Great Britain and Northern Ireland	24 Oct. 1945
Saint Vincent and the Grenadines	16 Sep. 1980	Swaziland	24 Sep. 1968		
		Sweden	19 Nov. 1946		
Samoa	15 Dec. 1976	Switzerland	10 Sep. 2002	United Republic of Tanzania[10]	14 Dec. 1961
San Marino	2 Mar. 1992	Syrian Arab Republic[5]	24 Oct. 1945	United States of America	24 Oct. 1945
Sao Tome and Principe	16 Sep. 1975	Tajikistan	2 Mar. 1992		
Saudi Arabia	24 Oct. 1945	Thailand	16 Dec. 1946	Uruguay	18 Dec. 1945
Senegal	28 Sep. 1960	The former Yugoslav Republic of Macedonia[2]	8 Apr. 1993	Uzbekistan	2 Mar. 1992
Serbia[2]	1 Nov. 2000			Vanuatu	15 Sep. 1981
Seychelles	21 Sep. 1976	Timor-Leste	27 Sep. 2002	Venezuela (Bolivarian Republic of)	15 Nov. 1945
Sierra Leone	27 Sep. 1961	Togo	20 Sep. 1960		
Singapore[8]	21 Sep. 1965	Tonga	14 Sep. 1999	Viet Nam	20 Sep. 1977
Slovakia[3]	19 Jan. 1993	Trinidad and Tobago	18 Sep. 1962	Yemen[11]	30 Sep. 1947
Slovenia[2]	22 May 1992	Tunisia	12 Nov. 1956	Zambia	1 Dec. 1964
Solomon Islands	19 Sep. 1978	Turkey	24 Oct. 1945	Zimbabwe	25 Aug. 1980

NOTES

[1] On 19 September 1991, the Byelorussian Soviet Socialist Republic informed the United Nations that it had changed its name to Belarus.

[2] The Socialist Federal Republic of Yugoslavia was an original Member of the United Nations, the Charter having been signed on its behalf on 26 June 1945 and ratified 19 October 1945, until its dissolution following the establishment and subsequent admission, as new Members, of Bosnia and Herzegovina, the Republic of Croatia, the Republic of Slovenia, The former Yugoslav Republic of Macedonia, and the Federal Republic of Yugoslavia. The Republic of Bosnia and Herzegovina, the Republic of Croatia and the Republic of Slovenia were admitted as Members of the United Nations on 22 May 1992. On 8 April 1993, the General Assembly decided to admit as a Member of the United Nations the state provisionally referred to for all purposes within the United Nations as "The former Yugoslav Republic of Macedonia", pending settlement of the difference that had arisen over its name. The Federal Republic of Yugoslavia was admitted as a Member of the United Nations on 1 November 2000. On 12 February 2003, it informed the United Nations that it had changed its name to Serbia and Montenegro, effective 4 February 2003. In a letter dated 3 June 2006, the President of the Republic of Serbia informed the Secretary-General that the membership of Serbia and Montenegro was being continued by the Republic of Serbia following Montenegro's declaration of independence from Serbia on 3 June 2006. On 28 June 2006, Montenegro was accepted as a United Nations Member State by the General Assembly.

[3] Czechoslovakia, an original Member of the United Nations from 24 October 1945, changed its name to the Czech and Slovak Federal Republic on 20 April 1990. It was dissolved on 1 January 1993 and succeeded by the Czech Republic and Slovakia, both of which became Members of the United Nations on 19 January 1993.

[4] The Republic of Zaire informed the United Nations that, effective 17 May 1997, it had changed its name to the Democratic Republic of the Congo.

[5] Egypt and Syria, both of which became Members of the United Nations on 24 October 1945, joined together—following a plebiscite held in those countries on 21 February 1958—to form the United Arab Republic. On 13 October 1961, Syria, having resumed its status as an independent State, also resumed its separate membership in the United Nations; it changed its name to the Syrian Arab Republic on 14 September 1971. The United Arab Republic continued as a Member of the United Nations and reverted to the name Egypt on 2 September 1971.

[6] Through accession of the German Democratic Republic to the Federal Republic of Germany on 3 October 1990, the two German States (both of which had become Members of the United Nations on 18 September 1973) united to form one sovereign State. As from that date, the Federal Republic of Germany has acted in the United Nations under the designation Germany.

[7] On 20 January 1965, Indonesia informed the Secretary-General that it had decided to withdraw from the United Nations. On 19 September 1966, it notified the Secretary-General of its decision to resume participation in the activities of the United Nations. On 28 September 1966, the General Assembly took note of that decision, and the President invited the representatives of Indonesia to take their seats in the Assembly.

[8] On 16 September 1963, Sabah (North Borneo), Sarawak and Singapore joined with the Federation of Malaya (which became a Member of the United Nations on 17 September 1957) to form Malaysia. On 9 August 1965, Singapore became an independent State; on 21 September 1965, it became a Member of the United Nations.

[9] The Union of Soviet Socialist Republics was an original Member of the United Nations from 24 October 1945. On 24 December 1991, the President of the Russian Federation informed the Secretary-General that the membership of the USSR in all United Nations organs was being continued by the Russian Federation.

[10] Tanganyika was admitted to the United Nations on 14 December 1961, Zanzibar on 16 December 1963. Following ratification, on 26 April 1964, of the Articles of Union between Tanganyika and Zanzibar, the two States became represented as a single Member: the United Republic of Tanganyika and Zanzibar; it changed its name to the United Republic of Tanzania on 1 November 1964.

[11] Yemen was admitted to the United Nations on 30 September 1947, Democratic Yemen on 14 December 1967. On 22 May 1990, the two countries merged and were thereafter represented as one Member of the United Nations under the designation Yemen.

Charter of the United Nations and Statute of the International Court of Justice

Charter of the United Nations

NOTE: The Charter of the United Nations was signed on 26 June 1945, in San Francisco, at the conclusion of the United Nations Conference on International Organization, and came into force on 24 October 1945. The Statute of the International Court of Justice is an integral part of the Charter.

Amendments to Articles 23, 27 and 61 of the Charter were adopted by the General Assembly on 17 December 1963 and came into force on 31 August 1965. A further amendment to Article 61 was adopted by the General Assembly on 20 December 1971 and came into force on 24 September 1973. An amendment to Article 109, adopted by the General Assembly on 20 December 1965, came into force on 12 June 1968.

The amendment to Article 23 enlarges the membership of the Security Council from 11 to 15. The amended Article 27 provides that decisions of the Security Council on procedural matters shall be made by an affirmative vote of nine members (formerly seven) and on all other matters by an affirmative vote of nine members (formerly seven), including the concurring votes of the five permanent members of the Security Council.

The amendment to Article 61, which entered into force on 31 August 1965, enlarges the membership of the Economic and Social Council from 18 to 27. The subsequent amendment to that Article, which entered into force on 24 September 1973, further increases the membership of the Council from 27 to 54.

The amendment to Article 109, which relates to the first paragraph of that Article, provides that a General Conference of Member States for the purpose of reviewing the Charter may be held at a date and place to be fixed by a two-thirds vote of the members of the General Assembly and by a vote of any nine members (formerly seven) of the Security Council. Paragraph 3 of Article 109, which deals with the consideration of a possible review conference during the tenth regular session of the General Assembly, has been retained in its original form in its reference to a "vote of any seven members of the Security Council", the paragraph having been acted upon in 1955 by the General Assembly, at its tenth regular session, and by the Security Council.

WE THE PEOPLES OF THE UNITED NATIONS
DETERMINED

to save succeeding generations from the scourge of war, which twice in our lifetime has brought untold sorrow to mankind, and

to reaffirm faith in fundamental human rights, in the dignity and worth of the human person, in the equal rights of men and women and of nations large and small, and

to establish conditions under which justice and respect for the obligations arising from treaties and other sources of international law can be maintained, and

to promote social progress and better standards of life in larger freedom,

AND FOR THESE ENDS

to practice tolerance and live together in peace with one another as good neighbours, and

to unite our strength to maintain international peace and security, and

to ensure, by the acceptance of principles and the institution of methods, that armed force shall not be used, save in the common interest, and

to employ international machinery for the promotion of the economic and social advancement of all peoples,

HAVE RESOLVED TO COMBINE OUR EFFORTS
TO ACCOMPLISH THESE AIMS

Accordingly, our respective Governments, through representatives assembled in the city of San Francisco, who have exhibited their full powers found to be in good and due form, have agreed to the present Charter of the United Nations and do hereby establish an international organization to be known as the United Nations.

Chapter I

PURPOSES AND PRINCIPLES

Article 1

The Purposes of the United Nations are:

1. To maintain international peace and security, and to that end: to take effective collective measures for the prevention and removal of threats to the peace, and for the suppression of acts of aggression or other breaches of the peace, and to bring about by peaceful means, and in conformity with the principles of justice and international law, adjustment or settlement of international disputes or situations which might lead to a breach of the peace;

2. To develop friendly relations among nations based on respect for the principle of equal rights and self-determination of peoples, and to take other appropriate measures to strengthen universal peace;

3. To achieve international co-operation in solving international problems of an economic, social, cultural or humanitarian character, and in promoting and encouraging respect for human rights and for fundamental freedoms for all without distinction as to race, sex, language or religion; and

4. To be a centre for harmonizing the actions of nations in the attainment of these common ends.

Article 2

The Organization and its Members, in pursuit of the Purposes stated in Article 1, shall act in accordance with the following Principles:

1. The Organization is based on the principle of the sovereign equality of all its Members.

2. All Members, in order to ensure to all of them the rights and benefits resulting from membership, shall fulfil in good faith the obligations assumed by them in accordance with the present Charter.

3. All Members shall settle their international disputes by peaceful means in such a manner that international peace and security, and justice, are not endangered.

4. All Members shall refrain in their international relations from the threat or use of force against the territorial integrity or political independence of any state, or in any other manner inconsistent with the Purposes of the United Nations.

5. All Members shall give the United Nations every assistance in any action it takes in accordance with the present Charter, and shall refrain from giving assistance to any state against which the United Nations is taking preventive or enforcement action.

6. The Organization shall ensure that states which are not Members of the United Nations act in accordance with these Principles so far as may be necessary for the maintenance of international peace and security.

7. Nothing contained in the present Charter shall authorize the United Nations to intervene in matters which are essentially within the domestic jurisdiction of any state or shall require the Members to submit such matters to settlement under the present Charter; but this principle shall not prejudice the application of enforcement measures under Chapter VII.

Chapter II
MEMBERSHIP

Article 3

The original Members of the United Nations shall be the states which, having participated in the United Nations Conference on International Organization at San Francisco or having previously signed the Declaration by United Nations of 1 January 1942, sign the present Charter and ratify it in accordance with Article 110.

Article 4

1. Membership in the United Nations is open to all other peace-loving states which accept the obligations contained in the present Charter and, in the judgment of the Organization, are able and willing to carry out these obligations.

2. The admission of any such state to membership in the United Nations will be effected by a decision of the General Assembly upon the recommendation of the Security Council.

Article 5

A Member of the United Nations against which preventive or enforcement action has been taken by the Security Council may be suspended from the exercise of the rights and privileges of membership by the General Assembly upon the recommendation of the Security Council. The exercise of these rights and privileges may be restored by the Security Council.

Article 6

A Member of the United Nations which has persistently violated the Principles contained in the present Charter may be expelled from the Organization by the General Assembly upon the recommendation of the Security Council.

Chapter III
ORGANS

Article 7

1. There are established as the principal organs of the United Nations: a General Assembly, a Security Council, an Economic and Social Council, a Trusteeship Council, an International Court of Justice, and a Secretariat.

2. Such subsidiary organs as may be found necessary may be established in accordance with the present Charter.

Article 8

The United Nations shall place no restrictions on the eligibility of men and women to participate in any capacity and under conditions of equality in its principal and subsidiary organs.

Chapter IV
THE GENERAL ASSEMBLY

Composition

Article 9

1. The General Assembly shall consist of all the Members of the United Nations.

2. Each Member shall have not more than five representatives in the General Assembly.

Functions and Powers

Article 10

The General Assembly may discuss any questions or any matters within the scope of the present Charter or relating to the powers and functions of any organs provided for in the present Charter, and, except as provided in Article 12, may make recommendations to the Members of the United Nations or to the Security Council or both on any such questions or matters.

Article 11

1. The General Assembly may consider the general principles of co-operation in the maintenance of international peace and security, including the principles governing disarmament and the regulation of armaments, and may make recommendations with regard to such principles to the Members or to the Security Council or to both.

2. The General Assembly may discuss any questions relating to the maintenance of international peace and security brought before it by any Member of the United Nations, or by the Security Council, or by a state which is not a Member of the United Nations in accordance with Article 35, paragraph 2, and, except as provided in Article 12, may make recommendations with regard to any such questions to the state or states concerned or to the Security Council or to both. Any such question on which action is necessary shall be referred to the Security Council by the General Assembly either before or after discussion.

3. The General Assembly may call the attention of the Security Council to situations which are likely to endanger international peace and security.

4. The powers of the General Assembly set forth in this Article shall not limit the general scope of Article 10.

Article 12

1.   While the Security Council is exercising in respect of any dispute or situation the functions assigned to it in the present Charter, the General Assembly shall not make any recommendation with regard to that dispute or situation unless the Security Council so requests.

2.   The Secretary-General, with the consent of the Security Council, shall notify the General Assembly at each session of any matters relative to the maintenance of international peace and security which are being dealt with by the Security Council and shall similarly notify the General Assembly, or the Members of the United Nations if the General Assembly is not in session, immediately the Security Council ceases to deal with such matters.

Article 13

1.   The General Assembly shall initiate studies and make recommendations for the purpose of:

   a. promoting international co-operation in the political field and encouraging the progressive development of international law and its codification;
   b. promoting international co-operation in the economic, social, cultural, educational and health fields, and assisting in the realization of human rights and fundamental freedoms for all without distinction as to race, sex, language or religion.

2.   The further responsibilities, functions and powers of the General Assembly with respect to matters mentioned in paragraph 1 (b) above are set forth in Chapters IX and X.

Article 14

Subject to the provisions of Article 12, the General Assembly may recommend measures for the peaceful adjustment of any situation, regardless of origin, which it deems likely to impair the general welfare or friendly relations among nations, including situations resulting from a violation of the provisions of the present Charter setting forth the Purposes and Principles of the United Nations.

Article 15

1.   The General Assembly shall receive and consider annual and special reports from the Security Council; these reports shall include an account of the measures that the Security Council has decided upon or taken to maintain international peace and security.

2.   The General Assembly shall receive and consider reports from the other organs of the United Nations.

Article 16

The General Assembly shall perform such functions with respect to the international trusteeship system as are assigned to it under Chapters XII and XIII, including the approval of the trusteeship agreements for areas not designated as strategic.

Article 17

1.   The General Assembly shall consider and approve the budget of the Organization.

2.   The expenses of the Organization shall be borne by the Members as apportioned by the General Assembly.

3.   The General Assembly shall consider and approve any financial and budgetary arrangements with specialized agencies referred to in Article 57 and shall examine the administrative budgets of such specialized agencies with a view to making recommendations to the agencies concerned.

Voting

Article 18

1.   Each member of the General Assembly shall have one vote.

2.   Decisions of the General Assembly on important questions shall be made by a two-thirds majority of the members present and voting. These questions shall include: recommendations with respect to the maintenance of international peace and security, the election of the non-permanent members of the Security Council, the election of the members of the Economic and Social Council, the election of members of the Trusteeship Council in accordance with paragraph 1 (c) of Article 86, the admission of new Members to the United Nations, the suspension of the rights and privileges of membership, the expulsion of Members, questions relating to the operation of the trusteeship system, and budgetary questions.

3.   Decisions on other questions, including the determination of additional categories of questions to be decided by a two thirds majority, shall be made by a majority of the members present and voting.

Article 19

A Member of the United Nations which is in arrears in the payment of its financial contributions to the Organization shall have no vote in the General Assembly if the amount of its arrears equals or exceeds the amount of the contributions due from it for the preceding two full years. The General Assembly may, nevertheless, permit such a Member to vote if it is satisfied that the failure to pay is due to conditions beyond the control of the Member.

Procedure

Article 20

The General Assembly shall meet in regular annual sessions and in such special sessions as occasion may require. Special sessions shall be convoked by the Secretary-General at the request of the Security Council or of a majority of the Members of the United Nations.

Article 21

The General Assembly shall adopt its own rules of procedure. It shall elect its President for each session.

Article 22

The General Assembly may establish such subsidiary organs as it deems necessary for the performance of its functions.

Chapter V

THE SECURITY COUNCIL

Composition

Article 23[1]

1.   The Security Council shall consist of fifteen Members of the United Nations. The Republic of China, France, the Union of Soviet Socialist Republics, the United Kingdom of Great Britain and Northern Ireland and the United States of America shall be permanent members of the Security Council. The General Assembly shall elect ten other Members of the United Nations to be non-permanent members of the Security Council, due regard being specially paid, in the first instance to the contribution of Members of the United Nations to the maintenance of international peace and security and to the other purposes of the Organization, and also to equitable geographical distribution.

2. The non-permanent members of the Security Council shall be elected for a term of two years. In the first election of the non-permanent members after the increase of the membership of the Security Council from eleven to fifteen, two of the four additional members shall be chosen for a term of one year. A retiring member shall not be eligible for immediate re-election.

3. Each member of the Security Council shall have one representative.

Functions and Powers

Article 24

1. In order to ensure prompt and effective action by the United Nations, its Members confer on the Security Council primary responsibility for the maintenance of international peace and security, and agree that in carrying out its duties under this responsibility the Security Council acts on their behalf.

2. In discharging these duties the Security Council shall act in accordance with the Purposes and Principles of the United Nations. The specific powers granted to the Security Council for the discharge of these duties are laid down in Chapters VI, VII, VIII and XII.

3. The Security Council shall submit annual and, when necessary, special reports to the General Assembly for its consideration.

Article 25

The Members of the United Nations agree to accept and carry out the decisions of the Security Council in accordance with the present Charter.

Article 26

In order to promote the establishment and maintenance of international peace and security with the least diversion for armaments of the world's human and economic resources, the Security Council shall be responsible for formulating, with the assistance of the Military Staff Committee referred to in Article 47, plans to be submitted to the Members of the United Nations for the establishment of a system for the regulation of armaments.

Voting

Article 27[2]

1. Each member of the Security Council shall have one vote.

2. Decisions of the Security Council on procedural matters shall be made by an affirmative vote of nine members.

3. Decisions of the Security Council on all other matters shall be made by an affirmative vote of nine members including the concurring votes of the permanent members; provided that, in decisions under Chapter VI, and under paragraph 3 of Article 52, a party to a dispute shall abstain from voting.

Procedure

Article 28

1. The Security Council shall be so organized as to be able to function continuously. Each member of the Security Council shall for this purpose be represented at all times at the seat of the Organization.

2. The Security Council shall hold periodic meetings at which each of its members may, if it so desires, be represented by a member of the government or by some other specially designated representative.

3. The Security Council may hold meetings at such places other than the seat of the Organization as in its judgment will best facilitate its work.

Article 29

The Security Council may establish such subsidiary organs as it deems necessary for the performance of its functions.

Article 30

The Security Council shall adopt its own rules of procedure, including the method of selecting its President.

Article 31

Any Member of the United Nations which is not a member of the Security Council may participate, without vote, in the discussion of any question brought before the Security Council whenever the latter considers that the interests of that Member are specially affected.

Article 32

Any Member of the United Nations which is not a member of the Security Council or any state which is not a Member of the United Nations, if it is a party to a dispute under consideration by the Security Council, shall be invited to participate, without vote, in the discussion relating to the dispute. The Security Council shall lay down such conditions as it deems just for the participation of a state which is not a Member of the United Nations.

Chapter VI
PACIFIC SETTLEMENT
OF DISPUTES

Article 33

1. The parties to any dispute, the continuance of which is likely to endanger the maintenance of international peace and security, shall, first of all, seek a solution by negotiation, enquiry, mediation, conciliation, arbitration, judicial settlement, resort to regional agencies or arrangements, or other peaceful means of their own choice.

2. The Security Council shall, when it deems necessary, call upon the parties to settle their dispute by such means.

Article 34

The Security Council may investigate any dispute, or any situation which might lead to international friction or give rise to a dispute, in order to determine whether the continuance of the dispute or situation is likely to endanger the maintenance of international peace and security.

Article 35

1. Any Member of the United Nations may bring any dispute, or any situation of the nature referred to in Article 34, to the attention of the Security Council or of the General Assembly.

2. A state which is not a Member of the United Nations may bring to the attention of the Security Council or of the General Assembly any dispute to which it is a party if it accepts in advance, for the purposes of the dispute, the obligations of pacific settlement provided in the present Charter.

3. The proceedings of the General Assembly in respect of matters brought to its attention under this Article will be subject to the provisions of Articles 11 and 12.

Article 36

1. The Security Council may, at any stage of a dispute of the nature referred to in Article 33 or of a situation of like nature, recommend appropriate procedures or methods of adjustment.

2. The Security Council should take into consideration any procedures for the settlement of the dispute which have already been adopted by the parties.

3. In making recommendations under this Article the Security Council should also take into consideration that legal disputes should as a general rule be referred by the parties to the International Court of Justice in accordance with the provisions of the Statute of the Court.

Article 37

1. Should the parties to a dispute of the nature referred to in Article 33 fail to settle it by the means indicated in that Article, they shall refer it to the Security Council.

2. If the Security Council deems that the continuance of the dispute is in fact likely to endanger the maintenance of international peace and security, it shall decide whether to take action under Article 36 or to recommend such terms of settlement as it may consider appropriate.

Article 38

Without prejudice to the provisions of Articles 33 to 37, the Security Council may, if all the parties to any dispute so request, make recommendations to the parties with a view to a pacific settlement of the dispute.

Chapter VII

ACTION WITH RESPECT TO THREATS TO THE PEACE, BREACHES OF THE PEACE, AND ACTS OF AGGRESSION

Article 39

The Security Council shall determine the existence of any threat to the peace, breach of the peace, or act of aggression and shall make recommendations, or decide what measures shall be taken in accordance with Articles 41 and 42, to maintain or restore international peace and security.

Article 40

In order to prevent an aggravation of the situation, the Security Council may, before making the recommendations or deciding upon the measures provided for in Article 39, call upon the parties concerned to comply with such provisional measures as it deems necessary or desirable. Such provisional measures shall be without prejudice to the rights, claims or position of the parties concerned. The Security Council shall duly take account of failure to comply with such provisional measures.

Article 41

The Security Council may decide what measures not involving the use of armed force are to be employed to give effect to its decisions, and it may call upon the Members of the United Nations to apply such measures. These may include complete or partial interruption of economic relations and of rail, sea, air, postal, telegraphic, radio and other means of communication, and the severance of diplomatic relations.

Article 42

Should the Security Council consider that measures provided for in Article 41 would be inadequate or have proved to be inadequate, it may take such action by air, sea or land forces as may be necessary to maintain or restore international peace and security. Such action may include demonstrations, blockade, and other operations by air, sea, or land forces of Members of the United Nations.

Article 43

1. All Members of the United Nations, in order to contribute to the maintenance of international peace and security, undertake to make available to the Security Council, on its call and in accordance with a special agreement or agreements, armed forces, assistance and facilities, including rights of passage, necessary for the purpose of maintaining international peace and security.

2. Such agreement or agreements shall govern the numbers and types of forces, their degree of readiness and general location, and the nature of the facilities and assistance to be provided.

3. The agreement or agreements shall be negotiated as soon as possible on the initiative of the Security Council. They shall be concluded between the Security Council and Members or between the Security Council and groups of Members and shall be subject to ratification by the signatory states in accordance with their respective constitutional processes.

Article 44

When the Security Council has decided to use force it shall, before calling upon a Member not represented on it to provide armed forces in fulfilment of the obligations assumed under Article 43, invite that Member, if the Member so desires, to participate in the decisions of the Security Council concerning the employment of contingents of that Member's armed forces.

Article 45

In order to enable the United Nations to take urgent military measures, Members shall hold immediately available national airforce contingents for combined international enforcement action. The strength and degree of readiness of these contingents and plans for their combined action shall be determined, within the limits laid down in the special agreement or agreements referred to in Article 43, by the Security Council with the assistance of the Military Staff Committee.

Article 46

Plans for the application of armed force shall be made by the Security Council with the assistance of the Military Staff Committee.

Article 47

1. There shall be established a Military Staff Committee to advise and assist the Security Council on all questions relating to the Security Council's military requirements for the maintenance of international peace and security, the employment and command of forces placed at its disposal, the regulation of armaments, and possible disarmament.

2. The Military Staff Committee shall consist of the Chiefs of Staff of the permanent members of the Security Council or their representatives. Any Member of the United Nations not permanently represented on the Committee shall be invited by the Committee to be associated with it when the efficient discharge of the Committee's responsibilities requires the participation of that Member in its work.

3. The Military Staff Committee shall be responsible under the Security Council for the strategic direction of any armed forces placed at the disposal of the Security Council. Questions relating to the command of such forces shall be worked out subsequently.

4. The Military Staff Committee, with the authorization of the Security Council and after consultation with appropriate regional agencies, may establish regional sub-committees.

Article 48

1. The action required to carry out the decisions of the Security Council for the maintenance of international peace and security shall be taken by all the Members of the United Nations or by some of them, as the Security Council may determine.

2. Such decisions shall be carried out by the Members of the United Nations directly and through their action in the appropriate international agencies of which they are members.

Article 49

The Members of the United Nations shall join in affording mutual assistance in carrying out the measures decided upon by the Security Council.

Article 50

If preventive or enforcement measures against any state are taken by the Security Council, any other state, whether a Member of the United Nations or not, which finds itself confronted with special economic problems arising from the carrying out of those measures shall have the right to consult the Security Council with regard to a solution of those problems.

Article 51

Nothing in the present Charter shall impair the inherent right of individual or collective self-defence if an armed attack occurs against a Member of the United Nations, until the Security Council has taken measures necessary to maintain international peace and security. Measures taken by Members in the exercise of this right of self-defence shall be immediately reported to the Security Council and shall not in any way affect the authority and responsibility of the Security Council under the present Charter to take at any time such action as it deems necessary in order to maintain or restore international peace and security.

Chapter VIII
REGIONAL ARRANGEMENTS

Article 52

1. Nothing in the present Charter precludes the existence of regional arrangements or agencies for dealing with such matters relating to the maintenance of international peace and security as are appropriate for regional action, provided that such arrangements or agencies and their activities are consistent with the Purposes and Principles of the United Nations.

2. The Members of the United Nations entering into such arrangements or constituting such agencies shall make every effort to achieve pacific settlement of local disputes through such regional arrangements or by such regional agencies before referring them to the Security Council.

3. The Security Council shall encourage the development of pacific settlement of local disputes through such regional arrangements or by such regional agencies either on the initiative of the states concerned or by reference from the Security Council.

4. This Article in no way impairs the application of Articles 34 and 35.

Article 53

1. The Security Council shall, where appropriate, utilize such regional arrangements or agencies for enforcement action

under its authority. But no enforcement action shall be taken under regional arrangements or by regional agencies without the authorization of the Security Council, with the exception of measures against any enemy state, as defined in paragraph 2 of this Article, provided for pursuant to Article 107 or in regional arrangements directed against renewal of aggressive policy on the part of any such state, until such time as the Organization may, on request of the Governments concerned, be charged with the responsibility for preventing further aggression by such a state.

2. The term enemy state as used in paragraph 1 of this Article applies to any state which during the Second World War has been an enemy of any signatory of the present Charter.

Article 54

The Security Council shall at all times be kept fully informed of activities undertaken or in contemplation under regional arrangements or by regional agencies for the maintenance of international peace and security.

Chapter IX
INTERNATIONAL ECONOMIC AND SOCIAL CO-OPERATION

Article 55

With a view to the creation of conditions of stability and well-being which are necessary for peaceful and friendly relations among nations based on respect for the principle of equal rights and self-determination of peoples, the United Nations shall promote:

a. higher standards of living, full employment, and conditions of economic and social progress and development;
b. solutions of international economic, social, health, and related problems; and international cultural and educational co-operation; and
c. universal respect for, and observance of, human rights and fundamental freedoms for all without distinction as to race, sex, language, or religion.

Article 56

All Members pledge themselves to take joint and separate action in co-operation with the Organization for the achievement of the purposes set forth in Article 55.

Article 57

1. The various specialized agencies, established by intergovernmental agreement and having wide international responsibilities, as defined in their basic instruments, in economic, social, cultural, educational, health, and related fields, shall be brought into relationship with the United Nations in accordance with the provisions of Article 63.

2. Such agencies thus brought into relationship with the United Nations are hereinafter referred to as specialized agencies.

Article 58

The Organization shall make recommendations for the coordination of the policies and activities of the specialized agencies.

Article 59

The Organization shall, where appropriate, initiate negotiations among the states concerned for the creation of any new specialized agencies required for the accomplishment of the purposes set forth in Article 55.

Article 60

Responsibility for the discharge of the functions of the Organization set forth in this Chapter shall be vested in the General Assembly and, under the authority of the General Assembly, in the Economic and Social Council, which shall have for this purpose the powers set forth in Chapter X.

Chapter X

THE ECONOMIC AND SOCIAL COUNCIL

Composition

Article 61[3]

1. The Economic and Social Council shall consist of fifty-four Members of the United Nations elected by the General Assembly.

2. Subject to the provisions of paragraph 3, eighteen members of the Economic and Social Council shall be elected each year for a term of three years. A retiring member shall be eligible for immediate re-election.

3. At the first election after the increase in the membership of the Economic and Social Council from twenty-seven to fifty-four members, in addition to the members elected in place of the nine members whose term of office expires at the end of that year, twenty-seven additional members shall be elected. Of these twenty-seven additional members, the term of office of nine members so elected shall expire at the end of one year, and of nine other members at the end of two years, in accordance with arrangements made by the General Assembly.

4. Each member of the Economic and Social Council shall have one representative.

Functions and Powers

Article 62

1. The Economic and Social Council may make or initiate studies and reports with respect to international economic, social, cultural, educational, health, and related matters and may make recommendations with respect to any such matters to the General Assembly, to the Members of the United Nations, and to the specialized agencies concerned.

2. It may make recommendations for the purpose of promoting respect for, and observance of, human rights and fundamental freedoms for all.

3. It may prepare draft conventions for submission to the General Assembly, with respect to matters falling within its competence.

4. It may call, in accordance with the rules prescribed by the United Nations, international conferences on matters falling within its competence.

Article 63

1. The Economic and Social Council may enter into agreements with any of the agencies referred to in Article 57, defining the terms on which the agency concerned shall be brought into relationship with the United Nations. Such agreements shall be subject to approval by the General Assembly.

2. It may co-ordinate the activities of the specialized agencies through consultation with and recommendations to such agencies and through recommendations to the General Assembly and to the Members of the United Nations.

Article 64

1. The Economic and Social Council may take appropriate steps to obtain regular reports from the specialized agencies. It may make arrangements with the Members of the United Nations and with the specialized agencies to obtain reports on the steps taken to give effect to its own recommendations and to recommendations on matters falling within its competence made by the General Assembly.

2. It may communicate its observations on these reports to the General Assembly.

Article 65

The Economic and Social Council may furnish information to the Security Council and shall assist the Security Council upon its request.

Article 66

1. The Economic and Social Council shall perform such functions as fall within its competence in connection with the carrying out of the recommendations of the General Assembly.

2. It may, with the approval of the General Assembly, perform services at the request of Members of the United Nations and at the request of specialized agencies.

3. It shall perform such other functions as are specified elsewhere in the present Charter or as may be assigned to it by the General Assembly.

Voting

Article 67

1. Each member of the Economic and Social Council shall have one vote.

2. Decisions of the Economic and Social Council shall be made by a majority of the members present and voting.

Procedure

Article 68

The Economic and Social Council shall set up commissions in economic and social fields and for the promotion of human rights, and such other commissions as may be required for the performance of its functions.

Article 69

The Economic and Social Council shall invite any Member of the United Nations to participate, without vote, in its deliberations on any matter of particular concern to that Member.

Article 70

The Economic and Social Council may make arrangements for representatives of the specialized agencies to participate, without vote, in its deliberations and in those of the commissions established by it, and for its representatives to participate in the deliberations of the specialized agencies.

Article 71

The Economic and Social Council may make suitable arrangements for consultation with non-governmental organizations which are concerned with matters within its competence. Such arrangements may be made with international organizations and, where appropriate, with national organizations after consultation with the Member of the United Nations concerned.

Article 72

1. The Economic and Social Council shall adopt its own rules of procedure, including the method of selecting its President.

2. The Economic and Social Council shall meet as required in accordance with its rules, which shall include provision for the convening of meetings on the request of a majority of its members.

Chapter XI

DECLARATION REGARDING NON-SELF-GOVERNING TERRITORIES

Article 73

Members of the United Nations which have or assume responsibilities for the administration of territories whose peoples have not yet attained a full measure of self-government recognize the principle that the interests of the inhabitants of these territories are paramount, and accept as a sacred trust the obligation to promote to the utmost, within the system of international peace and security established by the present Charter, the well-being of the inhabitants of these territories and, to this end:

a. to ensure, with due respect for the culture of the peoples concerned, their political, economic, social, and educational advancement, their just treatment, and their protection against abuses;

b. to develop self-government, to take due account of the political aspirations of the peoples, and to assist them in the progressive development of their free political institutions, according to the particular circumstances of each territory and its peoples and their varying stages of advancement;

c. to further international peace and security;

d. to promote constructive measures of development, to encourage research, and to co-operate with one another and, when and where appropriate, with specialized international bodies with a view to the practical achievement of the social, economic, and scientific purposes set forth in this Article; and

e. to transmit regularly to the Secretary-General for information purposes, subject to such limitation as security and constitutional considerations may require, statistical and other information of a technical nature relating to economic, social, and educational conditions in the territories for which they are respectively responsible other than those territories to which Chapters XII and XIII apply.

Article 74

Members of the United Nations also agree that their policy in respect of the territories to which this Chapter applies, no less than in respect of their metropolitan areas, must be based on the general principle of good-neighbourliness, due account being taken of the interests and well-being of the rest of the world, in social, economic, and commercial matters.

Chapter XII

INTERNATIONAL TRUSTEESHIP SYSTEM

Article 75

The United Nations shall establish under its authority an international trusteeship system for the administration and supervision of such territories as may be placed thereunder by subsequent individual agreements. These territories are hereinafter referred to as trust territories.

Article 76

The basic objectives of the trusteeship system, in accordance with the Purposes of the United Nations laid down in Article 1 of the present Charter, shall be:

a. to further international peace and security;

b. to promote the political, economic, social, and educational advancement of the inhabitants of the trust territories, and their progressive development towards self-government or independence as may be appropriate to the particular circumstances of each territory and its peoples and the freely expressed wishes of the peoples concerned, and as may be provided by the terms of each trusteeship agreement;

c. to encourage respect for human rights and for fundamental freedoms for all without distinction as to race, sex, language, or religion, and to encourage recognition of the interdependence of the peoples of the world; and

d. to ensure equal treatment in social, economic, and commercial matters for all Members of the United Nations and their nationals, and also equal treatment for the latter in the administration of justice, without prejudice to the attainment of the foregoing objectives and subject to the provisions of Article 80.

Article 77

1. The trusteeship system shall apply to such territories in the following categories as may be placed thereunder by means of trusteeship agreements:

a. territories now held under mandate;

b. territories which may be detached from enemy states as a result of the Second World War; and

c. territories voluntarily placed under the system by states responsible for their administration.

2. It will be a matter for subsequent agreement as to which territories in the foregoing categories will be brought under the trusteeship system and upon what terms.

Article 78

The trusteeship system shall not apply to territories which have become Members of the United Nations, relationship among which shall be based on respect for the principle of sovereign equality.

Article 79

The terms of trusteeship for each territory to be placed under the trusteeship system, including any alteration or amendment, shall be agreed upon by the states directly concerned, including the mandatory power in the case of territories held under mandate by a Member of the United Nations, and shall be approved as provided for in Articles 83 and 85.

Article 80

1. Except as may be agreed upon in individual trusteeship agreements, made under Articles 77, 79 and 81, placing each territory under the trusteeship system, and until such agreements have been concluded, nothing in this Chapter shall be construed in or of itself to alter in any manner the rights whatsoever of any states or any peoples or the terms of existing international instruments to which Members of the United Nations may respectively be parties.

2. Paragraph 1 of this Article shall not be interpreted as giving grounds for delay or postponement of the negotiation and conclusion of agreements for placing mandated and other territories under the trusteeship system as provided for in Article 77.

Article 81

The trusteeship agreement shall in each case include the terms under which the trust territory will be administered and designate the authority which will exercise the administration of the trust territory. Such authority, hereinafter called the administering authority, may be one or more states or the Organization itself.

Article 82

There may be designated, in any trusteeship agreement, a strategic area or areas which may include part or all of the trust territory to which the agreement applies, without prejudice to any special agreement or agreements made under Article 43.

Article 83

1. All functions of the United Nations relating to strategic areas, including the approval of the terms of the trusteeship agreements and of their alteration or amendment, shall be exercised by the Security Council.

2. The basic objectives set forth in Article 76 shall be applicable to the people of each strategic area.

3. The Security Council shall, subject to the provisions of the trusteeship agreements and without prejudice to security considerations, avail itself of the assistance of the Trusteeship Council to perform those functions of the United Nations under the trusteeship system relating to political, economic, social, and educational matters in the strategic areas.

Article 84

It shall be the duty of the administering authority to ensure that the trust territory shall play its part in the maintenance of international peace and security. To this end the administering authority may make use of volunteer forces, facilities, and assistance from the trust territory in carrying out the obligations towards the Security Council undertaken in this regard by the administering authority, as well as for local defence and the maintenance of law and order within the trust territory.

Article 85

1. The functions of the United Nations with regard to trusteeship agreements for all areas not designated as strategic, including the approval of the terms of the trusteeship agreements and of their alteration or amendment, shall be exercised by the General Assembly.

2. The Trusteeship Council, operating under the authority of the General Assembly, shall assist the General Assembly in carrying out these functions.

Chapter XIII
THE TRUSTEESHIP COUNCIL

Composition

Article 86

1. The Trusteeship Council shall consist of the following Members of the United Nations:
   a. those Members administering trust territories;
   b. such of those Members mentioned by name in Article 23 as are not administering trust territories; and
   c. as many other Members elected for three-year terms by the General Assembly as may be necessary to ensure that the total number of members of the Trusteeship Council is equally divided between those Members of the United Nations which administer trust territories and those which do not.

2. Each member of the Trusteeship Council shall designate one specially qualified person to represent it therein.

Functions and Powers

Article 87

The General Assembly and, under its authority, the Trusteeship Council, in carrying out their functions, may:
   a. consider reports submitted by the administering authority;
   b. accept petitions and examine them in consultation with the administering authority;
   c. provide for periodic visits to the respective trust territories at times agreed upon with the administering authority; and
   d. take these and other actions in conformity with the terms of the trusteeship agreements.

Article 88

The Trusteeship Council shall formulate a questionnaire on the political, economic, social, and educational advancement of the inhabitants of each trust territory, and the administering authority for each trust territory within the competence of the General Assembly shall make an annual report to the General Assembly upon the basis of such questionnaire.

Voting

Article 89

1. Each member of the Trusteeship Council shall have one vote.

2. Decisions of the Trusteeship Council shall be made by a majority of the members present and voting.

Procedure

Article 90

1. The Trusteeship Council shall adopt its own rules of procedure, including the method of selecting its President.

2. The Trusteeship Council shall meet as required in accordance with its rules, which shall include provision for the convening of meetings on the request of a majority of its members.

Article 91

The Trusteeship Council shall, when appropriate, avail itself of the assistance of the Economic and Social Council and of the specialized agencies in regard to matters with which they are respectively concerned.

Chapter XIV
THE INTERNATIONAL COURT OF JUSTICE

Article 92

The International Court of Justice shall be the principal judicial organ of the United Nations. It shall function in accordance with the annexed Statute, which is based upon the Statute of the Permanent Court of International Justice and forms an integral part of the present Charter.

Article 93

1. All Members of the United Nations are *ipso facto* parties to the Statute of the International Court of Justice.

2. A state which is not a Member of the United Nations may become a party to the Statute of the International Court of Justice on conditions to be determined in each case by the General Assembly upon the recommendation of the Security Council.

Article 94

1. Each Member of the United Nations undertakes to comply with the decision of the International Court of Justice in any case to which it is a party.

2. If any party to a case fails to perform the obligations incumbent upon it under a judgment rendered by the Court, the other party may have recourse to the Security Council, which may, if it deems necessary, make recommendations or decide upon measures to be taken to give effect to the judgment.

Article 95

Nothing in the present Charter shall prevent Members of the United Nations from entrusting the solution of their differences to other tribunals by virtue of agreements already in existence or which may be concluded in the future.

Article 96

1. The General Assembly or the Security Council may request the International Court of Justice to give an advisory opinion on any legal question.

2. Other organs of the United Nations and specialized agencies, which may at any time be so authorized by the General Assembly, may also request advisory opinions of the Court on legal questions arising within the scope of their activities.

Chapter XV
THE SECRETARIAT

Article 97

The Secretariat shall comprise a Secretary-General and such staff as the Organization may require. The Secretary-General shall be appointed by the General Assembly upon the recommendation of the Security Council. He shall be the chief administrative officer of the Organization.

Article 98

The Secretary-General shall act in that capacity in all meetings of the General Assembly, of the Security Council, of the Economic and Social Council, and of the Trusteeship Council, and shall perform such other functions as are entrusted to him by these organs. The Secretary-General shall make an annual report to the General Assembly on the work of the Organization.

Article 99

The Secretary-General may bring to the attention of the Security Council any matter which in his opinion may threaten the maintenance of international peace and security.

Article 100

1. In the performance of their duties the Secretary-General and the staff shall not seek or receive instructions from any government or from any other authority external to the Organization. They shall refrain from any action which might reflect on their position as international officials responsible only to the Organization.

2. Each Member of the United Nations undertakes to respect the exclusively international character of the responsibilities of the Secretary-General and the staff and not to seek to influence them in the discharge of their responsibilities.

Article 101

1. The staff shall be appointed by the Secretary-General under regulations established by the General Assembly.

2. Appropriate staffs shall be permanently assigned to the Economic and Social Council, the Trusteeship Council, and, as required, to other organs of the United Nations. These staffs shall form a part of the Secretariat.

3. The paramount consideration in the employment of the staff and in the determination of the conditions of service shall be the necessity of securing the highest standards of efficiency, competence, and integrity. Due regard shall be paid to the importance of recruiting the staff on as wide a geographical basis as possible.

Chapter XVI
MISCELLANEOUS PROVISIONS

Article 102

1. Every treaty and every international agreement entered into by any Member of the United Nations after the present Charter comes into force shall as soon as possible be registered with the Secretariat and published by it.

2. No party to any such treaty or international agreement which has not been registered in accordance with the provisions of paragraph 1 of this Article may invoke that treaty or agreement before any organ of the United Nations.

Article 103

In the event of a conflict between the obligations of the Members of the United Nations under the present Charter and their obligations under any other international agreement, their obligations under the present Charter shall prevail.

Article 104

The Organization shall enjoy in the territory of each of its Members such legal capacity as may be necessary for the exercise of its functions and the fulfilment of its purposes.

Article 105

1. The Organization shall enjoy in the territory of each of its Members such privileges and immunities as are necessary for the fulfilment of its purposes.

2. Representatives of the Members of the United Nations and officials of the Organization shall similarly enjoy such privileges and immunities as are necessary for the independent exercise of their functions in connection with the Organization.

3. The General Assembly may make recommendations with a view to determining the details of the application of paragraphs 1 and 2 of this Article or may propose conventions to the Members of the United Nations for this purpose.

Chapter XVII
TRANSITIONAL SECURITY ARRANGEMENTS

Article 106

Pending the coming into force of such special agreements referred to in Article 43 as in the opinion of the Security Council enable it to begin the exercise of its responsibilities under Article 42, the parties to the Four-Nation Declaration, signed at Moscow, 30 October 1943, and France, shall, in accordance with the provisions of paragraph 5 of that Declaration, consult with one another and as occasion requires with other Members of the United Nations with a view to such joint action on behalf of the Organization as may be necessary for the purpose of maintaining international peace and security.

Article 107

Nothing in the present Charter shall invalidate or preclude ¹ action, in relation to any state which during the Second World War has been an enemy of any signatory to the present Charter, taken or authorized as a result of that war by the Governments having responsibility for such action.

Chapter XVIII
AMENDMENTS

Article 108

Amendments to the present Charter shall come into force for all Members of the United Nations when they have been adopted by a vote of two thirds of the members of the General Assembly and ratified in accordance with their respective constitutional processes by two thirds of the Members of the United Nations, including all the permanent members of the Security Council.

Article 109⁴

1.   A General Conference of the Members of the United Nations for the purpose of reviewing the present Charter may be held at a date and place to be fixed by a two-thirds vote of the members of the General Assembly and by a vote of any nine members of the Security Council. Each Member of the United Nations shall have one vote in the conference.

2.   Any alteration of the present Charter recommended by a two-thirds vote of the conference shall take effect when ratified in accordance with their respective constitutional processes by two thirds of the Members of the United Nations including all the permanent members of the Security Council.

3.   If such a conference has not been held before the tenth annual session of the General Assembly following the coming into force of the present Charter, the proposal to call such a conference shall be placed on the agenda of that session of the General Assembly, and the conference shall be held if so decided by a majority vote of the members of the General Assembly and by a vote of any seven members of the Security Council.

Chapter XIX
RATIFICATION AND SIGNATURE

Article 110

1.   The present Charter shall be ratified by the signatory states in accordance with their respective constitutional processes.

2.   The ratifications shall be deposited with the Government of the United States of America, which shall notify all the signatory states of each deposit as well as the Secretary-General of the Organization when he has been appointed.

3.   The present Charter shall come into force upon the deposit of ratifications by the Republic of China, France, the Union of Soviet Socialist Republics, the United Kingdom of Great Britain and Northern Ireland and the United States of America, and by a majority of the other signatory states. A protocol of the ratifications deposited shall thereupon be drawn up by the Government of the United States of America which shall communicate copies thereof to all the signatory states.

4.   The states signatory to the present Charter which ratify it after it has come into force will become original Members of the United Nations on the date of the deposit of their respective ratifications.

Article 111

The present Charter, of which the Chinese, French, Russian, English, and Spanish texts are equally authentic, shall remain deposited in the archives of the Government of the United States of America. Duly certified copies thereof shall be transmitted by that Government to the Governments of the other signatory states.

IN FAITH WHEREOF the representatives of the Governments of the United Nations have signed the present Charter.

DONE at the city of San Francisco the twenty-sixth day of June, one thousand nine hundred and forty-five.

NOTES

¹Amended text of Article 23, which came into force on 31 August 1965. The text of Article 23 before it was amended read as follows:
1.   The Security Council shall consist of eleven Members of the United Nations. The Republic of China, France, the Union of Soviet Socialist Republics, the United Kingdom of Great Britain and Northern Ireland and the United States of America shall be permanent members of the Security Council. The General Assembly shall elect six other Members of the United Nations to be non-permanent members of the Security Council, due regard being specially paid in the first instance to the contributions of Members of the United Nations to the maintenance of international peace and security and to the other purposes of the Organization, and also to equitable geographical distribution.
2.   The non-permanent members of the Security Council shall be elected for a term of two years. In the first election of the non-permanent members, however, three shall be chosen for a term of one year. A retiring member shall not be eligible for immediate re-election.
3.   Each member of the Security Council shall have one representative.

²Amended text of Article 27, which came into force on 31 August 1965. The text of Article 27 before it was amended read as follows:
1.   Each member of the Security Council shall have one vote.
2.   Decisions of the Security Council on procedural matters shall be made by an affirmative vote of seven members.

3. Decisions of the Security Council on all other matters shall be made by an affirmative vote of seven members including the concurring votes of the permanent members; provided that, in decisions under Chapter VI, and under paragraph 3 of Article 52, a party to a dispute shall abstain from voting.

[3] Amended text of Article 61, which came into force on 24 September 1973. The text of Article 61 as previously amended on 31 August 1965 read as follows:

1. The Economic and Social Council shall consist of twenty-seven Members of the United Nations elected by the General Assembly.
2. Subject to the provisions of paragraph 3, nine members of the Economic and Social Council shall be elected each year for a term of three years. A retiring member shall be eligible for immediate re-election.
3. At the first election after the increase in the membership of the Economic and Social Council from eighteen to twenty-seven members, in addition to the members elected in place of the six members whose term of office expires at the end of that year, nine additional members shall be elected. Of these nine additional members, the term of office of three members so elected shall expire at the end of one year, and of three other members at the end of two years, in accordance with arrangements made by the General Assembly.
4. Each member of the Economic and Social Council shall have one representative.

[4] Amended text of Article 109, which came into force on 12 June 1968. The text of Article 109 before it was amended read as follows:

1. A General Conference of the Members of the United Nations for the purpose of reviewing the present Charter may be held at a date and place to be fixed by a two-thirds vote of the members of the General Assembly and by a vote of any seven members of the Security Council. Each Member of the United Nations shall have one vote in the conference.
2. Any alteration of the present Charter recommended by a two-thirds vote of the conference shall take effect when ratified in accordance with their respective constitutional processes by two thirds of the Members of the United Nations including all the permanent members of the Security Council.
3. If such a conference has not been held before the tenth annual session of the General Assembly following the coming into force of the present Charter, the proposal to call such a conference shall be placed on the agenda of that session of the General Assembly, and the conference shall be held if so decided by a majority vote of the members of the General Assembly and by a vote of any seven members of the Security Council.

Statute of the International Court of Justice

Article 1

The International Court of Justice established by the Charter of the United Nations as the principal judicial organ of the United Nations shall be constituted and shall function in accordance with the provisions of the present Statute.

Chapter I

ORGANIZATION OF THE COURT

Article 2

The Court shall be composed of a body of independent judges, elected regardless of their nationality from among persons of high moral character, who possess the qualifications required in their respective countries for appointment to the highest judicial offices, or are jurisconsults of recognized competence in international law.

Article 3

1. The Court shall consist of fifteen members, no two of whom may be nationals of the same state.

2. A person who for the purposes of membership in the Court could be regarded as a national of more than one state shall be deemed to be a national of the one in which he ordinarily exercises civil and political rights.

Article 4

1. The members of the Court shall be elected by the General Assembly and by the Security Council from a list of persons nominated by the national groups in the Permanent Court of Arbitration, in accordance with the following provisions.

2. In the case of Members of the United Nations not represented in the Permanent Court of Arbitration, candidates shall be nominated by national groups appointed for this purpose by their governments under the same conditions as those prescribed for members of the Permanent Court of Arbitration by Article 44 of the Convention of The Hague of 1907 for the pacific settlement of international disputes.

3. The conditions under which a state which is a party to the present Statute but is not a Member of the United Nations may participate in electing the members of the Court shall, in the absence of a special agreement, be laid down by the General Assembly upon recommendation of the Security Council.

Article 5

1. At least three months before the date of the election, the Secretary-General of the United Nations shall address a written request to the members of the Permanent Court of Arbitration belonging to the states which are parties to the present Statute, and to the members of the national groups appointed under Article 4, paragraph 2, inviting them to undertake, within a given time, by national groups, the nomination of persons in a position to accept the duties of a member of the Court.

2. No group may nominate more than four persons, not more than two of whom shall be of their own nationality. In no case may the number of candidates nominated by a group be more than double the number of seats to be filled.

Article 6

Before making these nominations, each national group is recommended to consult its highest court of justice, its legal faculties and schools of law, and its national academies and national sections of international academies devoted to the study of law.

Article 7

1. The Secretary-General shall prepare a list in alphabetical order of all the persons thus nominated. Save as provided in Article 12, paragraph 2, these shall be the only persons eligible.

2. The Secretary-General shall submit this list to the General Assembly and to the Security Council.

Article 8

The General Assembly and the Security Council shall proceed independently of one another to elect the members of the Court.

Article 9

At every election, the electors shall bear in mind not only that the persons to be elected should individually possess the qualifications required, but also that in the body as a whole the representation of the main forms of civilization and of the principal legal systems of the world should be assured.

Article 10

1. Those candidates who obtain an absolute majority of votes in the General Assembly and in the Security Council shall be considered as elected.

2. Any vote of the Security Council, whether for the election of judges or for the appointment of members of the conference envisaged in Article 12, shall be taken without any distinction between permanent and non-permanent members of the Security Council.

3. In the event of more than one national of the same state obtaining an absolute majority of the votes both of the General Assembly and of the Security Council, the eldest of these only shall be considered as elected.

Article 11

If, after the first meeting held for the purpose of the election, one or more seats remain to be filled, a second and, if necessary, a third meeting shall take place.

Article 12

1. If, after the third meeting, one or more seats still remain unfilled, a joint conference consisting of six members, three appointed by the General Assembly and three by the Security Council, may be formed at any time at the request of either the General Assembly or the Security Council, for the purpose of choosing by the vote of an absolute majority one name for each seat still vacant, to submit to the General Assembly and the Security Council for their respective acceptance.

2. If the joint conference is unanimously agreed upon any person who fulfils the required conditions, he may be included in its list, even though he was not included in the list of nominations referred to in Article 7.

3. If the joint conference is satisfied that it will not be successful in procuring an election, those members of the Court who have already been elected shall, within a period to be fixed by the Security Council, proceed to fill the vacant seats by selection from among those candidates who have obtained votes either in the General Assembly or in the Security Council.

4. In the event of an equality of votes among the judges, the eldest judge shall have a casting vote.

Article 13

1. The members of the Court shall be elected for nine years and may be re-elected; provided, however, that of the judges elected at the first election, the terms of five judges shall expire at the end of three years and the terms of five more judges shall expire at the end of six years.

2. The judges whose terms are to expire at the end of the above-mentioned initial periods of three and six years shall be chosen by lot to be drawn by the Secretary-General immediately after the first election has been completed.

3. The members of the Court shall continue to discharge their duties until their places have been filled. Though replaced, they shall finish any cases which they may have begun.

4. In the case of the resignation of a member of the Court, the resignation shall be addressed to the President of the Court for transmission to the Secretary-General. This last notification makes the place vacant.

Article 14

Vacancies shall be filled by the same method as that laid down for the first election, subject to the following provision: the Secretary-General shall, within one month of the occurrence of the vacancy, proceed to issue the invitations provided for in Article 5, and the date of the election shall be fixed by the Security Council.

Article 15

A member of the Court elected to replace a member whose term of office has not expired shall hold office for the remainder of his predecessor's term.

Article 16

1. No member of the Court may exercise any political or administrative function, or engage in any other occupation of a professional nature.

2. Any doubt on this point shall be settled by the decision of the Court.

Article 17

1. No member of the Court may act as agent, counsel, or advocate in any case.

2. No member may participate in the decision of any case in which he has previously taken part as agent, counsel, or advocate for one of the parties, or as a member of a national or international court, or of a commission of enquiry, or in any other capacity.

3. Any doubt on this point shall be settled by the decision of the Court.

Article 18

1. No member of the Court can be dismissed unless, in the unanimous opinion of the other members, he has ceased to fulfil the required conditions.

2. Formal notification thereof shall be made to the Secretary-General by the Registrar.

3. This notification makes the place vacant.

Article 19

The members of the Court, when engaged on the business of the Court, shall enjoy diplomatic privileges and immunities.

Article 20

Every member of the Court shall, before taking up his duties, make a solemn declaration in open court that he will exercise his powers impartially and conscientiously.

Article 21

1. The Court shall elect its President and Vice-President for three years; they may be re-elected.

2. The Court shall appoint its Registrar and may provide for the appointment of such other officers as may be necessary.

Article 22

1. The seat of the Court shall be established at The Hague. This, however, shall not prevent the Court from sitting and exercising its functions elsewhere whenever the Court considers it desirable.

2. The President and the Registrar shall reside at the seat of the Court.

Article 23

1. The Court shall remain permanently in session, except during the judicial vacations, the dates and duration of which shall be fixed by the Court.

2. Members of the Court are entitled to periodic leave, the dates and duration of which shall be fixed by the Court, having in mind the distance between The Hague and the home of each judge.

3. Members of the Court shall be bound, unless they are on leave or prevented from attending by illness or other serious reasons duly explained to the President, to hold themselves permanently at the disposal of the Court.

Article 24

1. If, for some special reason, a member of the Court considers that he should not take part in the decision of a particular case, he shall so inform the President.

2. If the President considers that for some special reason one of the members of the Court should not sit in a particular case, he shall give him notice accordingly.

3. If in any such case the member of the Court and the President disagree, the matter shall be settled by the decision of the Court.

Article 25

1. The full Court shall sit except when it is expressly provided otherwise in the present Statute.

2. Subject to the condition that the number of judges available to constitute the Court is not thereby reduced below eleven, the Rules of the Court may provide for allowing one or more judges, according to circumstances and in rotation, to be dispensed from sitting.

3. A quorum of nine judges shall suffice to constitute the Court.

Article 26

1. The Court may from time to time form one or more chambers, composed of three or more judges as the Court may determine, for dealing with particular categories of cases; for example, labour cases and cases relating to transit and communications.

2. The Court may at any time form a chamber for dealing with a particular case. The number of judges to constitute such a chamber shall be determined by the Court with the approval of the parties.

3. Cases shall be heard and determined by the chambers provided for in this Article if the parties so request.

Article 27

A judgment given by any of the chambers provided for in Articles 26 and 29 shall be considered as rendered by the Court.

Article 28

The chambers provided for in Articles 26 and 29 may, with the consent of the parties, sit and exercise their functions elsewhere than at The Hague.

Article 29

With a view to the speedy dispatch of business, the Court shall form annually a chamber composed of five judges which, at the request of the parties, may hear and determine cases by summary procedure. In addition, two judges shall be selected for the purpose of replacing judges who find it impossible to sit.

Article 30

1. The Court shall frame rules for carrying out its functions. In particular, it shall lay down rules of procedure.

2. The Rules of the Court may provide for assessors to sit with the Court or with any of its chambers, without the right to vote.

Article 31

1. Judges of the nationality of each of the parties shall retain their right to sit in the case before the Court.

2. If the Court includes upon the Bench a judge of the nationality of one of the parties, any other party may choose a person to sit as judge. Such person shall be chosen preferably from among those persons who have been nominated as candidates as provided in Articles 4 and 5.

3. If the Court includes upon the Bench no judge of the nationality of the parties, each of these parties may proceed to choose a judge as provided in paragraph 2 of this Article.

4. The provisions of this Article shall apply to the case of Articles 26 and 29. In such cases, the President shall request one or, if necessary, two of the members of the Court forming the chamber to give place to the members of the Court of the nationality of the parties concerned, and, failing such, or if they are unable to be present, to the judges specially chosen by the parties.

5. Should there be several parties in the same interest, they shall, for the purpose of the preceding provisions, be reckoned as one party only. Any doubt upon this point shall be settled by the decision of the Court.

6. Judges chosen as laid down in paragraphs 2, 3 and 4 of this Article shall fulfil the conditions required by Articles 2, 17 (paragraph 2), 20, and 24 of the present Statute. They shall take part in the decision on terms of complete equality with their colleagues.

Article 32

1. Each member of the Court shall receive an annual salary.

2. The President shall receive a special annual allowance.

3. The Vice-President shall receive a special allowance for every day on which he acts as President.

4. The judges chosen under Article 31, other than members of the Court, shall receive compensation for each day on which they exercise their functions.

5. These salaries, allowances, and compensation shall be fixed by the General Assembly. They may not be decreased during the term of office.

6. The salary of the Registrar shall be fixed by the General Assembly on the proposal of the Court.

7. Regulations made by the General Assembly shall fix the conditions under which retirement pensions may be given to members of the Court and to the Registrar, and the conditions under which members of the Court and the Registrar shall have their travelling expenses refunded.

8. The above salaries, allowances, and compensation shall be free of all taxation.

Article 33

The expenses of the Court shall be borne by the United Nations in such a manner as shall be decided by the General Assembly.

Chapter II
COMPETENCE OF THE COURT

Article 34

1. Only states may be parties in cases before the Court.

2. The Court, subject to and in conformity with its Rules, may request of public international organizations information relevant to cases before it, and shall receive such information presented by such organizations on their own initiative.

3. Whenever the construction of the constituent instrument of a public international organization or of an international convention adopted thereunder is in question in a case before the Court, the Registrar shall so notify the public international organization concerned and shall communicate to it copies of all the written proceedings.

Article 35

1. The Court shall be open to the states parties to the present Statute.

2. The conditions under which the Court shall be open to other states shall, subject to the special provisions contained in treaties in force, be laid down by the Security Council, but in no case shall such conditions place the parties in a position of inequality before the Court.

3. When a state which is not a Member of the United Nations is a party to a case, the Court shall fix the amount which that party is to contribute towards the expenses of the Court. This provision shall not apply if such state is bearing a share of the expenses of the Court.

Article 36

1. The jurisdiction of the Court comprises all cases which the parties refer to it and all matters specially provided for in the Charter of the United Nations or in treaties and conventions in force.

2. The states parties to the present Statute may at any time declare that they recognize as compulsory *ipso facto* and without special agreement, in relation to any other state accepting the same obligation, the jurisdiction of the Court in all legal disputes concerning:

a. the interpretation of a treaty;

b. any question of international law;

c. the existence of any fact which, if established, would constitute a breach of an international obligation;

d. the nature or extent of the reparation to be made for the breach of an international obligation.

3. The declarations referred to above may be made unconditionally or on condition of reciprocity on the part of several or certain states, or for a certain time.

4. Such declarations shall be deposited with the Secretary-General of the United Nations, who shall transmit copies thereof to the parties to the Statute and to the Registrar of the Court.

5. Declarations made under Article 36 of the Statute of the Permanent Court of International Justice and which are still in force shall be deemed, as between the parties to the present Statute, to be acceptances of the compulsory jurisdiction of the Inter-

national Court of Justice for the period which they still have to run and in accordance with their terms.

6.   In the event of a dispute as to whether the Court has jurisdiction, the matter shall be settled by the decision of the Court.

Article 37

Whenever a treaty or convention in force provides for reference of a matter to a tribunal to have been instituted by the League of Nations, or to the Permanent Court of International Justice, the matter shall, as between the parties to the present Statute, be referred to the International Court of Justice.

Article 38

1.   The Court, whose function is to decide in accordance with international law such disputes as are submitted to it, shall apply:

   a.   international conventions, whether general or particular, establishing rules expressly recognized by the contesting states;
   b.   international custom, as evidence of a general practice accepted as law;
   c.   the general principles of law recognized by civilized nations;
   d.   subject to the provisions of Article 59, judicial decisions and the teachings of the most highly qualified publicists of the various nations, as subsidiary means for the determination of rules of law.

2.   This provision shall not prejudice the power of the Court to decide a case *ex aequo et bono*, if the parties agree thereto.

Chapter III
PROCEDURE

Article 39

1.   The official languages of the Court shall be French and English. If the parties agree that the case shall be conducted in French, the judgment shall be delivered in French. If the parties agree that the case shall be conducted in English, the judgment shall be delivered in English.

2.   In the absence of an agreement as to which language shall be employed, each party may, in the pleadings, use the language which it prefers; the decision of the Court shall be given in French and English. In this case the Court shall at the same time determine which of the two texts shall be considered as authoritative.

3.   The Court shall, at the request of any party, authorize a language other than French or English to be used by that party.

Article 40

1.   Cases are brought before the Court, as the case may be, either by the notification of the special agreement or by a written application addressed to the Registrar. In either case the subject of the dispute and the parties shall be indicated.

2.   The Registrar shall forthwith communicate the application to all concerned.

3.   He shall also notify the Members of the United Nations through the Secretary-General, and also any other states entitled to appear before the Court.

Article 41

1.   The Court shall have the power to indicate, if it considers that circumstances so require, any provisional measures which ought to be taken to preserve the respective rights of either party.

2.   Pending the final decision, notice of the measures suggested shall forthwith be given to the parties and to the Security Council.

Article 42

1.   The parties shall be represented by agents.

2.   They may have the assistance of counsel or advocates before the Court.

3.   The agents, counsel, and advocates of parties before the Court shall enjoy the privileges and immunities necessary to the independent exercise of their duties.

Article 43

1.   The procedure shall consist of two parts: written and oral.

2.   The written proceedings shall consist of the communication to the Court and to the parties of memorials, counter-memorials and, if necessary, replies; also all papers and documents in support.

3.   These communications shall be made through the Registrar, in the order and within the time fixed by the Court.

4.   A certified copy of every document produced by one party shall be communicated to the other party.

5.   The oral proceedings shall consist of the hearing by the Court of witnesses, experts, agents, counsel, and advocates.

Article 44

1.   For the service of all notices upon persons other than the agents, counsel, and advocates, the Court shall apply direct to the government of the state upon whose territory the notice has to be served.

2.   The same provision shall apply whenever steps are to be taken to procure evidence on the spot.

Article 45

The hearing shall be under the control of the President or, if he is unable to preside, of the Vice-President; if neither is able to preside, the senior judge present shall preside.

Article 46

The hearing in Court shall be public, unless the Court shall decide otherwise, or unless the parties demand that the public be not admitted.

Article 47

1.   Minutes shall be made at each hearing and signed by the Registrar and the President.

2.   These minutes alone shall be authentic.

Article 48

The Court shall make orders for the conduct of the case, shall decide the form and time in which each party must conclude its arguments, and make all arrangements connected with the taking of evidence.

Article 49

The Court may, even before the hearing begins, call upon the agents to produce any document or to supply any explanations. Formal note shall be taken of any refusal.

Article 50

The Court may, at any time, entrust any individual, body, bureau, commission, or other organization that it may select, with the task of carrying out an enquiry or giving an expert opinion.

Article 51

During the hearing any relevant questions are to be put to the witnesses and experts under the conditions laid down by the Court in the rules of procedure referred to in Article 30.

Article 52

After the Court has received the proofs and evidence within the time specified for the purpose, it may refuse to accept any further oral or written evidence that one party may desire to present unless the other side consents.

Article 53

1. Whenever one of the parties does not appear before the Court, or fails to defend its case, the other party may call upon the Court to decide in favour of its claim.

2. The Court must, before doing so, satisfy itself, not only that it has jurisdiction in accordance with Articles 36 and 37, but also that the claim is well founded in fact and law.

Article 54

1. When, subject to the control of the Court, the agents, counsel, and advocates have completed their presentation of the case, the President shall declare the hearing closed.

2. The Court shall withdraw to consider the judgment.

3. The deliberations of the Court shall take place in private and remain secret.

Article 55

1. All questions shall be decided by a majority of the judges present.

2. In the event of an equality of votes, the President or the judge who acts in his place shall have a casting vote.

Article 56

1. The judgment shall state the reasons on which it is based.

2. It shall contain the names of the judges who have taken part in the decision.

Article 57

If the judgment does not represent in whole or in part the unanimous opinion of the judges, any judge shall be entitled to deliver a separate opinion.

Article 58

The judgment shall be signed by the President and by the Registrar. It shall be read in open court, due notice having been given to the agents.

Article 59

The decision of the Court has no binding force except between the parties and in respect of that particular case.

Article 60

The judgment is final and without appeal. In the event of dispute as to the meaning or scope of the judgment, the Court shall construe it upon the request of any party.

Article 61

1. An application for revision of a judgment may be made only when it is based upon the discovery of some fact of such a nature as to be a decisive factor, which fact was, when the judgment was given, unknown to the Court and also the party claiming revision, always provided that such ignorance was not due to negligence.

2. The proceedings for revision shall be opened by a judgment of the Court expressly recording the existence of the new fact, recognizing that it has such a character as to lay the case open to revision, and declaring the application admissible on this ground.

3. The Court may require previous compliance with the terms of the judgment before it admits proceedings in revision.

4. The application for revision must be made at latest within six months of the discovery of the new fact.

5. No application for revision may be made after the lapse of ten years from the date of the judgment.

Article 62

1. Should a state consider that it has an interest of a legal nature which may be affected by the decision in the case, it may submit a request to the Court to be permitted to intervene.

2. It shall be for the Court to decide upon this request.

Article 63

1. Whenever the construction of a convention to which states other than those concerned in the case are parties is in question, the Registrar shall notify all such states forthwith.

2. Every state so notified has the right to intervene in the proceedings; but if it uses this right, the construction given by the judgment will be equally binding upon it.

Article 64

Unless otherwise decided by the Court, each party shall bear its own costs.

Chapter IV

ADVISORY OPINIONS

Article 65

1. The Court may give an advisory opinion on any legal question at the request of whatever body may be authorized by or in accordance with the Charter of the United Nations to make such a request.

2. Questions upon which the advisory opinion of the Court is asked shall be laid before the Court by means of a written request containing an exact statement of the question upon which an opinion is required, and accompanied by all documents likely to throw light upon the question.

Article 66

1. The Registrar shall forthwith give notice of the request for an advisory opinion to all states entitled to appear before the Court.

2. The Registrar shall also, by means of a special and direct communication, notify any state entitled to appear before the Court or international organization considered by the Court, or, should it not be sitting, by the President, as likely to be able to furnish information on the question, that the Court will be prepared to receive, within a time limit to be fixed by the President, written statements, or to hear, at a public sitting to be held for the purpose, oral statements relating to the question.

3. Should any such state entitled to appear before the Court have failed to receive the special communication referred to in paragraph 2 of this Article, such state may express a desire to submit a written statement or to be heard; and the Court will decide.

4. States and organizations having presented written or oral statements or both shall be permitted to comment on the statements made by other states or organizations in the form, to the extent, and within the time limits which the Court, or, should

it not be sitting, the President, shall decide in each particular case. Accordingly, the Registrar shall in due time communicate any such written statements to states and organizations having submitted similar statements.

Article 67

The Court shall deliver its advisory opinions in open court, notice having been given to the Secretary-General and to the representatives of Members of the United Nations, of other states and of international organizations immediately concerned.

Article 68

In the exercise of its advisory functions the Court shall further be guided by the provisions of the present Statute which apply in contentious cases to the extent to which it recognizes them to be applicable.

Chapter V
AMENDMENT

Article 69

Amendments to the present Statute shall be effected by the same procedure as is provided by the Charter of the United Nations for amendments to that Charter, subject however to any provisions which the General Assembly upon recommendation of the Security Council may adopt concerning the participation of states which are parties to the present Statute but are not Members of the United Nations.

Article 70

The Court shall have power to propose such amendments to the present Statute as it may deem necessary, through written communications to the Secretary-General, for consideration in conformity with the provisions of Article 69.

Structure of the United Nations

General Assembly

The General Assembly is composed of all the Members of the United Nations.

SESSIONS
Resumed sixty-third session: 20 February–14 September 2009
Sixty-fourth session: 15 September–24 December 2009 (suspended)
Resumed tenth emergency special session: 15–16 January 2009

OFFICERS
Resumed sixty-third session
President: Miguel d'Escoto Brockmann (Nicaragua)
Vice-Presidents: Afghanistan, Bolivia, Cameroon, China, Egypt, France, Jamaica, Kyrgyzstan, Moldova, Mongolia, Myanmar, Namibia, Niger, Portugal, Russian Federation, Rwanda, Solomon Islands, Spain, Togo, United Kingdom, United States

Sixty-fourth session
President: Ali Abdussalam Treki (Libya) [1]
Vice-Presidents: [2] Barbados, Belgium, Cameroon, China, El Salvador, Finland, France, Ghana, Guinea-Bissau, India, Kazakhstan, Maldives, Nepal, Russian Federation, Slovenia, South Africa, Sudan, Turkmenistan, Venezuela, United Kingdom, United States

The Assembly has four types of committees: (1) Main Committees; (2) procedural committees; (3) standing committees; (4) subsidiary and ad hoc bodies. In addition, it convenes conferences to deal with specific subjects.

Main Committees

By resolution 47/233, the General Assembly rationalized its Committee structure as follows:
Disarmament and International Security Committee (First Committee);
Special Political and Decolonization Committee (Fourth Committee);
Economic and Financial Committee (Second Committee);
Social, Humanitarian and Cultural Committee (Third Committee);
Administrative and Budgetary Committee (Fifth Committee);
Legal Committee (Sixth Committee).

The General Assembly may constitute other committees, on which all Members of the United Nations have the right to be represented.

OFFICERS OF THE MAIN COMMITTEES
Resumed sixty-third session

Fourth Committee [3]

Chairperson: Jorge Argüello (Argentina)
Vice-Chairpersons: Emr Elsherbini (Egypt), Alexandru Cujba (Moldova), Elmer Cato (Philippines)
Rapporteur: Paula Parviainen (Finland)

Fifth Committee [3]

Chairperson: Gabor Brodi (Hungary)
Vice-Chairpersons: Olivio Fermin (Dominican Republic), Mohamed Yousif Ibrahim Abdelmannan (Sudan), Henric Rasbrant (Sweden)
Rapporteur: Patrick Chuasoto (Philippines)

Sixty-fourth session

First Committee

Chairperson: José Luis Cancela (Uruguay) [4]
Vice-Chairpersons: Hossam Aly (Egypt), Hilario G. Davide, Jr. (Philippines), Florian Laudi (Germany)
Rapporteur: Tetyana Pokhval'ona (Ukraine)

Fourth Committee

Chairperson: Nassir Abdulaziz Al-Nasser (Qatar) [4]
Vice-Chairpersons: Ridas Petkus (Lithuania), Heidi Schroderus-Fox (Finland), Reniery Valladares (Honduras)
Rapporteur: Khalid Mohammed Osman Sidahmed Mohammed Ali (Sudan)

Second Committee

Chairperson: In-kook Park (Republic of Korea) [4]
Vice-Chairpersons: Mohamed Cherif Diallo (Guinea), Carlos Enrique García González (El Salvador), Dragan Mićić (Serbia)
Rapporteur: Denise McQuade (Ireland)

Third Committee

Chairperson: Normans Penke (Latvia) [4]
Vice-Chairpersons: Fiyola Hoosen (South Africa), Zahid Rastam (Malaysia), Edgard Pérez (Peru)
Rapporteur: Nicola Hill (New Zealand)

Fifth Committee

Chairperson: Peter Maurer (Switzerland) [4]
Vice-Chairpersons: Danilo Rosales Diaz (Nicaragua), Babou Sène (Senegal), Sirithon Wairatpanij (Thailand)
Rapporteur: Yuliana Zhivkova Georgieva (Bulgaria)

Sixth Committee

Chairperson: Mourad Benmehidi (Algeria) [4]
Vice-Chairpersons: Esmaeil Baghaei Hamaneh (Iran), Andris Stastoli (Albania), Marcelo Böhlke (Brazil)
Rapporteur: Jean-Cédric Janssens de Bisthoven (Belgium)

Procedural committees

General Committee

The General Committee consists of the President of the General Assembly, as Chairperson, the 21 Vice-Presidents and the Chairpersons of the six Main Committees.

Credentials Committee

The Credentials Committee consists of nine members appointed by the General Assembly on the proposal of the President.
Resumed sixty-third and tenth emergency special sessions [5]
Botswana, China, Cyprus, Luxembourg, Mexico, Mozambique, Russian Federation, Saint Kitts and Nevis, United States
Sixty-fourth session [6]
Brazil, China, Jamaica, Philippines, Russian Federation, Spain, Tanzania, United States, Zambia

Standing committees

The two standing committees consist of experts appointed in their individual capacity for three-year terms.

Advisory Committee on Administrative and Budgetary Questions (ACABQ)

Chairperson: Susan McLurg (United States)
To serve until 31 December 2009: Andrzej T. Abraszewski (Poland), Collen V. Kelapile (Botswana), Stafford Neil (Jamaica), Mohammad Mustafa Tal (Jordan), Nonye Udo (Nigeria)
To serve until 31 December 2010: Jorge Flores Callejas (Honduras), Imtiaz Hussain (Pakistan), Misako Kaji (Japan) (until July), Akira Sugiyama (Japan) (from July), Jerry Kramer (Canada), Peter Maddens (Belgium), Nagesh Singh (India)

To serve until 31 December 2011: Aïcha Afifi (Morocco), Renata Archini (Italy), Vladimir A. Iosifov (Russian Federation), Susan M. McLurg (United States), Alejandro Torres Lépori (Argentina)

On 19 November 2009 (decision 64/408), the General Assembly appointed the following for a three-year term beginning on 1 January 2010 to fill vacancies occurring on 31 December 2009: Jasminka Dinić (Croatia), Collen V. Kelapile (Botswana), Stafford O. Neil (Jamaica), Mohammad Mustafa Tal (Jordan) and Nonye Udo (Nigeria).

Committee on Contributions

To serve until 31 December 2009: Kenshiro Akimoto (Japan), Meshal Al-Mansour (Kuwait), Petru Dumitriu (Romania), Ihor V. Humenny (Ukraine), Gobona Susan Mapitse (Botswana), Lisa P. Spratt (United States)

To serve until 31 December 2010: Joseph Acakpo-Satchivi (Benin), Abdelmalek Bouheddou (Algeria), Gordon Eckersley (Australia), Bernardo Greiver del Hoyo (Uruguay), Luis Mariano Hermosillo Sosa (Mexico), Eduardo Manuel da Fonseca Fernandes Ramos (Portugal)

To serve until 31 December 2011: Vyacheslav A. Logutov (Russian Federation), Richard Moon (United Kingdom), Hae-yun Park (Republic of Korea), Thomas Thomma (Germany), Courtney H. Williams (Jamaica), Wu Gang (China)

On 26 May 2009 (decision 63/408 B), the General Assembly appointed Gönke Roscher (Germany) to serve until 31 December 2011 as a result of the resignation of Thomas Thomma.

On 19 November 2009 (decision 64/409), the General Assembly appointed the following for a three-year term beginning on 1 January 2010 to fill the vacancies occurring on 31 December 2009: Andrzej T. Abraszewski (Poland), Meshal Al-Mansour (Kuwait), Elmi Ahmed Dualeh (Somalia), Ihor V. Humenny (Ukraine), Lisa Spratt (United States) and Shigeki Sumi (Japan).

Subsidiary and ad hoc bodies

The following is a list of subsidiary and ad hoc bodies functioning in 2009, including the number of members, dates of meetings/sessions in 2009, document numbers of reports (which generally provide specific information on membership), and relevant decision numbers pertaining to elections.

Ad Hoc Committee on the Administration of Justice at the United Nations

Session: Second, New York, 20–24 April
Chairperson: Ganeson Sivagurunathan (Malaysia)
Membership: Open to all States Members of the United Nations or members of the specialized agencies or of IAEA
Report: A/64/55

Ad Hoc Committee on Criminal Accountability of United Nations Officials and Experts on Mission

Session: did not meet in 2009
Membership: Open to all States Members of the United Nations or members of the specialized agencies or of IAEA

Ad Hoc Committee established by General Assembly resolution 51/210 of 17 December 1996

Session: Thirteenth, New York, 29 June–2 July
Chairperson: Rohan Perera (Sri Lanka)
Membership: Open to all States Members of the United Nations or members of the specialized agencies or of IAEA
Report: A/64/37

Ad Hoc Committee on the Indian Ocean

Meeting: Four hundred and fifty-third, New York, 24 July
Chairperson: H.M.G.S. Palihakkara (Sri Lanka)
Membership: 43
Report: A/64/29

Advisory Board on Disarmament Matters

Sessions: Fifty-first, New York, 18–20 February; Fifty-second, Geneva, 1–3 July
Chairperson: Carolina Hernandez (Philippines)

Membership: 14 (plus 1 ex-officio member), fifty-first session; 15 (plus 1 ex-officio member), fifty-second session
Report: A/64/286

Advisory Committee on the United Nations Programme of Assistance in the Teaching, Study, Dissemination and Wider Appreciation of International Law

Session: Forty-fourth, New York, 16 October
Chairperson: Leslie K. Christian (Ghana)
Membership: 25
Report: A/64/495

Board of Auditors

Sessions: Sixty-third regular session, New York, 9–10 July; thirty-ninth special session, Bonn, Germany, 9 December
Chairperson: Terence Nombembe (South Africa)
Membership: 3
Decision: GA 64/411

Committee on Conferences

Sessions: New York, 7 April (organizational), 8–14 September (substantive)
Chairperson: Barbara Kaudel (Austria)
Membership: 21
Report: A/64/32
Decision: GA 63/405 B, 64/407

Committee on the Exercise of the Inalienable Rights of the Palestinian People

Meetings: Throughout the year
Chairperson: Paul Badji (Senegal)
Membership: 23
Report: A/64/35

Committee on Information

Session: Thirty-first, New York, 4–15 May
Chairperson: Antonio Pedro Monteiro Lima (Cape Verde)
Membership: 113
Report: A/64/21
Decision: GA 64/520

Committee on the Peaceful Uses of Outer Space

Session: Fifty-second, Vienna, 3–12 June
Chairperson: Ciro Arévalo Yepes (Colombia)
Membership: 69
Report: A/64/20

Committee for Programme and Coordination (CPC)

Sessions: Forty-ninth, New York, 30 April (organizational), 8 June–1 July (substantive)
Chairperson: Hendrik Ockert van der Westhuizen (South Africa)
Membership: 34
Report: A/64/16
Decisions: ESC 2009/201 C & D; GA 63/414 B, 64/404

Committee on Relations with the Host Country

Meetings: New York, 12 March, 16 June, 2 October and 2 November
Chairperson: Minas Hadjimichael (Cyprus)
Membership: 19 (including the United States as host country)
Report: A/64/26

Committee for the United Nations Population Award

Chairperson: Hamidon Ali (Malaysia)
Membership: 10 (plus the Secretary-General and the UNFPA Executive Director as ex-officio members)
Report: A/64/207
Decision: 2009/201 C & D

Disarmament Commission

Sessions: New York, 15 January (organizational); 13 April–1 May (substantive)
Chairperson: Andrzej Towpik (Poland)
Membership: All UN Members
Report: A/64/42

High-level Committee on South-South Cooperation

Session: Did not meet in 2009
President: Macharia Kamau (Kenya)
Membership: All States participating in UNDP

Human Rights Council

Sessions: Ninth special, 9 and 12 January; tenth special, 20 and 23 February; eleventh special, 26–27 May; twelfth special, 15–16 October; tenth regular, 2–27 March; eleventh regular, 2–18 June; twelfth regular, 14 September–2 October, all in Geneva
President: Martin I. Uhomoibhi (Nigeria) (until June); Alex Van Meeuwen (Belgium) (from June)
Membership: 47
Reports: A/64/53, A/64/53/Add.1, A/65/53
Decision: GA 63/420

Independent Audit Advisory Committee

Sessions: Fifth, 20–22 February; sixth, 13–15 April; seventh, 30 June–2 July, all in New York; eighth, Geneva, 2–4 December
Chairperson: David M. Walker (United States)
Membership: 5
Reports: A/64/288, A/65/329

International Civil Service Commission (ICSC)

Sessions: Sixty-eighth, New York, 23 March–3 April; sixty-ninth, Montreal, 29 June–10 July
Chairperson: Kingston P. Rhodes (Sierra Leone)
Membership: 15
Report: A/64/30
Decision: GA 64/412

ADVISORY COMMITTEE ON POST ADJUSTMENT QUESTIONS

Session: Thirty-first, Vienna, 26 January–2 February
Chairperson: Wolfgang Stöckl (Germany)
Membership: 6

International Law Commission

Session: Sixty-first, Geneva, 4 May–5 June; 6 July–7 August
Chairperson: Ernest Petrič (Slovenia)
Membership: 34
Report: A/64/10

Investments Committee

Chairperson: William J. McDonough (United States)
Membership: 9
Decision: GA 64/410

Joint Advisory Group on the International Trade Centre UNCTAD/WTO

Session: Forty-third, Geneva, 14–15 December
Chairperson: Dennis Francis (Trinidad and Tobago)
Membership: Open to all States members of UNCTAD and all members of WTO
Report: ITC/AG(XLIII)/232

Joint Inspection Unit (JIU)

Chairpersons: Even Fontaine Ortiz (Cuba) (January–May); Gérard Biraud (France) (June–December)
Membership: 11
Report: A/64/34
Decision: GA 63/416

Office of the United Nations High Commissioner for Refugees (UNHCR)

EXECUTIVE COMMITTEE OF THE HIGH COMMISSIONER'S PROGRAMME

Session: Sixtieth, Geneva, 28 September–2 October
Chairperson: Alberto J. Dumont (Argentina)
Membership: 78
Report: A/64/12/Add.1
Decisions: ESC 2009/201 C, ESC 2009/252
High Commissioner: António Manuel de Oliveira Guterres

Panel of External Auditors

Session: Fiftieth, Bonn, Germany, 7–8 December
Membership: Members of the UN Board of Auditors and the appointed external auditors of the specialized agencies and IAEA

Special Committee on the Charter of the United Nations and on the Strengthening of the Role of the Organization

Meeting: New York, 17–25 February
Chairperson: Emmanuel Bichet (Switzerland)
Membership: Open to all States Members of the United Nations
Report: A/64/33

Special Committee to Investigate Israeli Practices Affecting the Human Rights of the Palestinian People and Other Arabs of the Occupied Territories

Meetings: Cairo, Egypt, 3–7 August; Amman, Jordan, 7–11 August; Damascus, Syrian Arab Republic, 11–13 August
Chairpersons: Samantha Jayasuriya (Sri Lanka), Hamidon Ali (Malaysia) (Acting)
Membership: 3
Report: A/64/339

Special Committee on Peacekeeping Operations

Meetings: New York, 23 February–20 March
Chairperson: U. Joy Ogwu (Nigeria)
Membership: 144
Report: A/63/19

Special Committee on the Situation with regard to the Implementation of the Declaration on the Granting of Independence to Colonial Countries and Peoples

Session: New York, 27 February and 6 April (first part); 8–9, 15–19 and 23 June (second part)
Chairperson: R. M. Marty M. Natalegawa (Indonesia)
Membership: 28
Report: A/64/23

United Nations Administrative Tribunal

Sessions: Sixtieth plenary, New York, 23 November; regular, Geneva, 29 June–31 July; regular, New York, 26 October–25 November
Presidents: Spyridon Flogaitis (Greece), Geneva session; Dayendra Sena Wijewardane (Sri Lanka), New York session
Membership: 7
Report: A/INF/64/7

United Nations Capital Development Fund (UNCDF)

EXECUTIVE BOARD

The UNDP/UNFPA Executive Board acts as the Executive Board of the Fund.
Managing Director: Helen Clark (UNDP Administrator)

United Nations Commission on International Trade Law (UNCITRAL)

Session: Forty-second, Vienna, 29 June–17 July
Chairperson: Soo-Geun Oh (Republic of Korea)
Membership: 60
Report: A/64/17
Decision: GA 64/405

United Nations Conciliation Commission for Palestine

Membership: 3
Report: A/64/174

United Nations Conference on Trade and Development (UNCTAD)

Session: Did not meet in 2009
Membership: Open to all States Members of the United Nations or members of the specialized agencies or of IAEA
Secretary-General of UNCTAD: Supachai Panitchpakdi

Security Council

The Security Council consists of 15 Member States of the United Nations (five permanent members and ten non-permanent members), in accordance with the provisions of Article 23 of the United Nations Charter as amended in 1965.

MEMBERS
Permanent members: China, France, Russian Federation, United Kingdom, United States
Non-permanent members: Austria, Burkina Faso, Costa Rica, Croatia, Japan, Libya, Mexico, Turkey, Uganda, Viet Nam

On 15 October 2009 (decision 64/402), the General Assembly elected Bosnia and Herzegovina, Brazil, Gabon, Lebanon and Nigeria for a two-year term beginning on 1 January 2010, to replace Burkina Faso, Costa Rica, Croatia, Libya and Viet Nam, whose terms of office were to expire on 31 December 2009.

PRESIDENT
The presidency of the Council rotates monthly, according to the English alphabetical listing of its Member States. The following served as President during 2009:

Month	Member	Representative
January	France	Jean-Maurice Ripert
February	Japan	Yukio Takasu
March	Libya	Abdurrahman Mohamed Shalgham
April	Mexico	Claude Heller
May	Russian Federation	Vitaly I. Churkin
June	Turkey	Baki İlkin
July	Uganda	Ruhakana Rugunda
August	United Kingdom	John Sawers
September	United States	Susan Rice
October	Viet Nam	Le Luong Minh
November	Austria	Thomas Mayr-Harting
December	Burkina Faso	Michel Kafando

Military Staff Committee

The Military Staff Committee consists of the chiefs of staff of the permanent members of the Security Council or their representatives. It meets fortnightly.

Standing committees

Each of the three standing committees of the Security Council is composed of representatives of all Council members:
Committee of Experts (to examine the provisional rules of procedure of the Council and any other matters entrusted to it by the Council);
Committee on the Admission of New Members;
Committee on Council Meetings Away from Headquarters.

Subsidiary bodies

Counter-Terrorism Committee (CTC)

Chairperson: Neven Jurica (Croatia) (until September); Ranko Vilović (Croatia) (from September)
Membership: 15

United Nations Compensation Commission

Governing Council

Sessions: Sixty-seventh and sixty-eigth, Geneva, 28–29 April and 10–12 November
President: Christian Strohal (Austria)
Membership: 15
Reports: S/2009/226, S/2009/594

1540 Committee

Chairman: Jorge Urbina (Costa Rica)
Membership: 15

International Tribunal for the former Yugoslavia (ICTY)

President: Judge Patrick Lipton Robinson (Jamaica)
Under-Secretary-General, Prosecutor: Serge Brammertz
Assistant Secretary-General, Registrar: John Hocking

International Criminal Tribunal for Rwanda (ICTR)

President: Judge Dennis Byron (Saint Kitts and Nevis)
Under-Secretary-General, Prosecutor: Hassan Bubacar Jallow

Advisory Subsidiary body

United Nations Peacebuilding Commission (PBC) [9]

Organizational Committee

Session: Third, New York, 7 January–29 June
Chairperson: Heraldo Muñoz (Chile)
Membership: 31
Report: A/64/341-S/2009/444
Decision: GA 64/414

Peacekeeping operations

United Nations Truce Supervision Organization (UNTSO)

Head of Mission, Chief of Staff: Major General Robert Mood

United Nations Military Observer Group in India and Pakistan (UNMOGIP)

Chief Military Observer: Major General Kim Moon Hwa

United Nations Peacekeeping Force in Cyprus (UNFICYP)

Special Representative of the Secretary-General and Head of Mission: Tayé-Brook Zerihoun
Force Commander: Rear Admiral Mario Sánchez Debernardi

United Nations Disengagement Observer Force (UNDOF)

Head of Mission and Force Commander: Major General Wolfgang Jilke

United Nations Interim Force in Lebanon (UNIFIL)

Force Commander: Major General Claudio Graziano

United Nations Mission for the Referendum in Western Sahara (MINURSO)

Special Representative of the Secretary-General and Head of Mission: Julian Harston (until March); Hany Abdel-Aziz (from October)
Force Commander: Major General Zhao Jingmin

United Nations Observer Mission in Georgia (UNOMIG) [10]

Special Representative of the Secretary-General and Head of Mission: Johan Verbeke
Deputy Special Representative of the Secretary-General: Ivo Petrov
Chief Military Observer: Major General Anwar Hussain

United Nations Interim Administration Mission in Kosovo (UNMIK)

Special Representative of the Secretary-General: Lamberto Zannier
OSCE Head of Mission in Kosovo: Werner Wnendt

Deputy Special Representative of the Secretary-General: Robert E. Sorenson
Police Commissioner: Mustafa Tekinbas

United Nations Organization Mission in the Democratic Republic of the Congo (MONUC)

Special Representative of the Secretary-General and Head of Mission: Alan Doss
Deputy Special Representative for Recovery and Governance: Ross Mountain
Force Commander: Lieutenant-General Babacar Gaye
Police Commissioner: Sudesh Kumar

United Nations Mission in Liberia (UNMIL)

Special Representative of the Secretary-General and Head of Mission: Ellen Margrethe Løj
Deputy Special Representative: Jordan Ryan (until June); Moustapha Soumaré (from June)
Deputy Special Representative for Rule of Law: Henrietta Joy Abena Nyarko Mensa-Bonsu
Force Commander: Lieutenant General A. T. M. Zahirul Alam (until October); Lieutenant General Sikander Afzal (from October)
Police Commissioner: Henrik Stiernblad

United Nations Operation in Côte d'Ivoire (UNOCI)

Special Representative of the Secretary-General and Head of Mission: Choi Young-jin
Principal Deputy Special Representative: Abou Moussa
Deputy Special Representative: Georg Charpentier
Force Commander: Major-General Fernand Marcel Amoussou

United Nations Stabilization Mission in Haiti (MINUSTAH)

Special Representative of the Secretary-General and Head of Mission: Hédi Annabi
Principal Deputy Special Representative: Luiz Carlos da Costa
Deputy Special Representative: Joel Boutroue (until November); Kim Bolduc (from November)
Force Commander: Major-General Carlos Alberto Dos Santos Cruz (until April); Major General Floriano Peixoto Vieira Neto (from April)
Police Commissioner: Mamadou Mountaga Diallo

United Nations Mission in Sudan (UNMIS)

Special Representative of the Secretary-General and Head of Mission: Ashraf Jehangir Qazi
Deputy Special Representative: Ameerah Haq (until December)
Force Commander: Major General Paban Jung Thapa
Police Commissioner: Rajesh Dewan

United Nations Integrated Mission in Timor-Leste (UNMIT)

Special Representative of the Secretary-General and Head of Mission: Atul Khare
Deputy Special Representative for Governance Support, Development and Humanitarian Coordination: Finn Reske-Nielsen
Deputy Special Representative for Security Sector Support and Rule of Law: Takahisa Kawakami
Police Commissioner: Luis Carrilho (from February)

African Union-United Nations Hybrid Operation in Darfur (UNAMID)

AU-UN Joint Special Representative for Darfur and Head of Mission: Rodolphe Adada (until July); Henry K. Anyidodho (a.i., from July)
Deputy Joint Special Representative for Operations and Management: Hocine Medili (until September); Mohamed Yonis (from September)
Force Commander: General Martin Agwai (until September); Lieutenant General Patrick Nyamvumba (from September)
Police Commissioner: Major-General Michael Fryer

United Nations Mission in the Central African Republic and Chad (MINURCAT)

Special Representative of the Secretary-General and Head of Mission: Victor da Silva Angelo
Deputy Special Representative of the Secretary-General: Rima Salah

Force Commander: Major-General Elhadji Mouhamedou Kandji (from March)
Police Commissioners: Major-General Gerardo Christian Chaumont (until December); Mamadou Mountaga Diallo (from December)

Political, peacebuilding and other missions

United Nations Political Office for Somalia (UNPOS)

Special Representative of the Secretary-General and Head of UNPOS: Ahmedou Ould-Abdallah
Deputy Special Representative of the Secretary-General for Somalia: Charles Petrie

United Nations Peacebuilding Support Office in Guinea-Bissau (UNOGBIS)

Special Representative of the Secretary-General and Head of UNOGBIS: Joseph Mutaboba (from February)

Office of the United Nations Special Coordinator for the Middle East (UNSCO)

Special Coordinator for the Middle East Peace Process and Personal Representative of the Secretary-General to the Palestine Liberation Organization and the Palestinian Authority: Robert H. Serry
Deputy Special Coordinator for the Middle East Peace Process: Maxwell Gaylard

United Nations Peacebuilding Office in the Central African Republic (BONUCA) [11]

Special Representative of the Secretary-General and Head of BONUCA: François Lonseny Fall (until June); Sahle-Work Zewde (from June)

Office of the United Nations Special Coordinator of the Secretary-General for Lebanon (UNSCOL)

Special Coordinator of the Secretary-General for Lebanon: Michael C. Williams
Deputy Special Coordinator: Marta Ruedas

Office of the Special Representative of the Secretary-General for West Africa (UNOWA)

Special Representative of the Secretary-General: Said Djinnit

United Nations Assistance Mission in Afghanistan (UNAMA)

Special Representative of the Secretary-General and Head of Mission: Kai Eide
Deputy Special Representative: Christopher Alexander (until March); Peter Galbraith (until September)

United Nations Assistance Mission for Iraq (UNAMI)

Special Representative of the Secretary-General for Iraq: Staffan de Mistura (until June); Ad Melkert (from July)
Deputy Special Representative for Political, Electoral and Constitutional Support: Andrew Gilmour
Deputy Special Representative for Humanitarian, Reconstruction and Development Affairs: David Shearer (until October); Christine McNab (from October)

United Nations Integrated Peacebuilding Office in Sierra Leone (UNIPSIL)

Executive Representative of the Secretary-General: Michael von der Schulenburg

United Nations Integrated Office in Burundi (BINUB)

Executive Representative of the Secretary-General and Head of BINUB: Youssef Mahmoud

United Nations Mission in Nepal (UNMIN)

Special Representative of the Secretary-General in Nepal and Head of Mission: Ian Martin (until February); Karin Landgren (from February)

Deputy Special Representative: Karin Landgren (until February)

United Nations Regional Centre for Preventive Diplomacy for Central Asia (UNRCCA)

Special Representative of the Secretary-General: Miroslav Jenča

Economic and Social Council

The Economic and Social Council consists of 54 Member States of the United Nations, elected by the General Assembly, each for a three-year term, in accordance with the provisions of Article 61 of the United Nations Charter as amended in 1965 and 1973.

MEMBERS

To serve until 31 December 2009: Algeria, Barbados, Belarus, Bolivia, Canada, Cape Verde, El Salvador, Indonesia, Iraq, Kazakhstan, Luxembourg, Malawi, Netherlands, Philippines, Romania, Somalia, Sudan, United States

To serve until 31 December 2010: Brazil, Cameroon, China, Congo, Iceland, Malaysia, Moldova, Mozambique, New Zealand, Niger, Pakistan, Poland, Republic of Korea, Russian Federation, Saint Lucia, Sweden, United Kingdom, Uruguay

To serve until 31 December 2011: Côte d'Ivoire, Estonia, France, Germany, Greece, Guatemala, Guinea-Bissau, India, Japan, Liechtenstein, Mauritius, Morocco, Namibia, Peru, Portugal, Saint Kitts and Nevis, Saudi Arabia, Venezuela

On 26 October 2009 (decision 64/403), the General Assembly elected Australia, Finland, Malta and Turkey for the remaining term of office of New Zealand, Sweden, Greece and Portugal, respectively, beginning on 1 January 2010. At the same meeting, the General Assembly elected the following for a three-year term of office beginning on 1 January 2010 to fill vacancies occurring on 31 December 2009: Argentina, Bahamas, Bangladesh, Belgium, Canada, Chile, Comoros, Egypt, Ghana, Iraq, Italy, Mongolia, Philippines, Rwanda, Slovakia, Ukraine, United States and Zambia.

SESSIONS

Organizational session: New York, 15 January, 10 February, 26 March and 20 April

Resumed organizational session: New York, 18–19 May

Special high-level meeting with the Bretton Woods institutions, the World Trade Organization and UNCTAD: New York, 27 April

Substantive session: Geneva, 6–31 July

OFFICERS

President: Sylvie Lucas (Luxembourg)

Vice-Presidents: Carmen María Gallardo Hernández (El Salvador), Tiina Intelmann (Estonia), Hamidon Ali (Malaysia), Somduth Soborun (Mauritius)

Subsidiary and other related organs

SUBSIDIARY ORGANS

The Economic and Social Council may, at each session, set up committees or working groups, of the whole or of limited membership, and refer to them any item on the agenda for study and report.

Other subsidiary organs reporting to the Council consist of functional commissions, regional commissions, standing committees, expert bodies and ad hoc bodies.

The inter-agency United Nations System Chief Executives Board for Coordination also reports to the Council.

Functional commissions

Commission on Crime Prevention and Criminal Justice

Sessions: Eighteenth, Vienna, 16–24 April (regular); 3–4 December (resumed)

Chairperson: Cosmin Dinescu (Romania)

Membership: 40

Reports: E/2009/30, E/2009/30/Add.1

Decision: ESC 2009/201 C

Commission on Narcotic Drugs

Session: Fifty-second, Vienna, 11–20 March

Chairperson: Selma Ashipala-Musavyi (Namibia)

Membership: 53

Reports: E/2009/28, E/2009/28/Add.1

Decision: ESC 2009/201 C

Commission on Population and Development

Sessions: Forty-second, New York, 30 March–3 April; forty-third, New York, 3 April

Chairman: Elena Zúñiga (Mexico)

Membership: 47

Reports: E/2009/25, E/2010/25

Decision: ESC 2009/201 C & D

Commission on Science and Technology for Development

Session: Twelfth, Geneva, 25–29 May

Chairman: Juan Eduardo Eguiguren (Chile)

Membership: 43

Report: E/2009/31

Decision: ESC 2009/201 C & D

Commission for Social Development

Session: Forty-seventh, New York, 4–13 February

Chairperson: Kirsti Lintonen (Finland)

Membership: 46

Report: E/2009/26

Decision: ESC 2009/201 C

Commission on the Status of Women

Session: Fifty-third, New York, 2–13 March

Chairperson: Olivier Belle (Belgium)

Membership: 45

Report: E/2009/27

Decision: ESC 2009/201 C

Commission on Sustainable Development

Session: Seventeenth, New York, 4–15 May

Chairperson: Gerda Verburg (Netherlands)

Membership: 53

Report: E/2009/29

Decision: ESC 2009/201 C

Statistical Commission

Session: Fortieth, New York, 24–27 February

Chairman: Pali Lehohla (South Africa)

Membership: 24

Report: E/2009/24

Decision: ESC 2009/201 C

United Nations Forum on Forests

Session: Eighth, New York, 20 April–1 May

Chairperson: Boen Purnama (Indonesia)

Membership: Open to all States Members of the United Nations and members of the specialized agencies

Report: E/2009/42

Regional commissions

Economic Commission for Africa (ECA)

Session: Forty-second session of the Commission/Second Joint Annual Meetings of the African Union

Conference of Ministers of Economy and Finance and the ECA Conference of African Ministers of Finance, Planning and Economic Development, Cairo, 2–7 June
Chairperson: Youssef Boutros-Ghali (Egypt)
Membership: 53
Report: E/2009/38

Economic Commission for Europe (ECE)

Session: Sixty-third, Geneva, 30 March–1 April
Chairperson: Alex Van Meeuwen (Belgium)
Membership: 56
Report: E/2009/37

Economic Commission for Latin America and the Caribbean (ECLAC)

Session: Did not meet in 2009
Membership: 44 members, 8 associate members

Economic and Social Commission for Asia and the Pacific (ESCAP)

Session: Sixty-fifth, Bangkok, Thailand, 23–29 April
Chairperson: Kasit Piromya (Thailand)
Membership: 53 members, 9 associate members
Report: E/2009/39

Economic and Social Commission for Western Asia (ESCWA)

Session: Did not meet in 2009
Membership: 17

Standing committees

Committee on Non-Governmental Organizations

Sessions: New York, 19–28 January and 2 February (regular), 18–27 May (resumed)
Chairperson: Hassan Hamid Hassan (Sudan)
Membership: 19
Reports: E/2009/32 (Part I), E/2009/32 (Part II)

Committee for Programme and Coordination (CPC)

Sessions: Forty-ninth, New York, 30 April (organizational), 8 June–2 July (substantive)
Chairman: Hendrik Ockert van der Westhuizen (South Africa)
Membership: 34
Report: A/64/16
Decision: ESC 2009/201 C & D

Expert bodies

Committee of Experts on International Cooperation in Tax Matters

Session: Fifth, Geneva, 19–23 October
Chairperson: Armando Lara Yaffar (Mexico)
Membership: 25
Report: E/2009/45
Decision: ESC 2009/201 D

Committee for Development Policy

Session: Eleventh, New York, 9–13 March
Chairperson: Ricardo Ffrench-Davis (Chile)
Membership: 24
Report: E/2009/33
Decision: ESC 2009/201 A & D

Committee on Economic, Social and Cultural Rights

Sessions: Forty-second and forty-third, Geneva, 4–22 May and 2–20 November
Chairperson: Jaime Marchan-Romero (Ecuador)
Membership: 18
Report: E/2010/22

Committee of Experts on Public Administration

Session: Eighth, New York, 30 March–3 April
Chairperson: Jocelyne Bourgon (Canada)
Membership: 24
Report: E/2009/44
Decision: ESC 2009/201 C

Committee of Experts on the Transport of Dangerous Goods and on the Globally Harmonized System of Classification and Labelling of Chemicals

Session: Did not meet in 2009
Membership: 37
Decision: ESC 2009/201 C

Permanent Forum on Indigenous Issues

Session: Eighth, New York, 18–29 May
Chairperson: Victoria Tauli-Corpuz (Philippines)
Membership: 16
Report: E/2009/43

United Nations Group of Experts on Geographical Names

Session: Twenty-fifth, Nairobi, Kenya, 5–12 May
Chairperson: Helen Kerfoot (Canada)
Membership: Representatives of the 23 geographical/linguistic divisions of the Group of Experts
Report: E/2009/58

Ad hoc body

United Nations System Chief Executives Board for Coordination (CEB)

Sessions: First, Paris, 4 April; second, New York, 30 October
Chairman: Secretary-General Ban Ki-moon
Membership: 28
Reports: CEB/2009/1, CEB/2009/2

Other related bodies

International Research and Training Institute for the Advancement of Women (INSTRAW)

Executive Board
Sessions: Sixth, New York, 23 April (regular); 18–19 May (resumed)
President: Marie Yvette L. Banzon-Abalos (Philippines) (Acting)
Membership: 10 (plus 5 ex-officio members)
Reports: E/2009/62, E/2009/0/Add.7
Director of INSTRAW: Carmen Moreno

Joint United Nations Programme on Human Immunodeficiency Virus/Acquired Immunodeficiency Syndrome (UNAIDS)

Programme Coordinating Board
Meetings: Twenty-forth, Geneva, 22–24 June; twenty-fifth, Geneva, 8–10 December
Chairperson: Tedros Adhanom Ghebreuesus (Ethiopia)
Membership: 22
Reports: UNAIDS/PCB(24)/09.15, UNAIDS/PCB(25)/09.29
Executive Director of UNAIDS: Michel Sidibé

United Nations Children's Fund (UNICEF)

Executive Board
Sessions: First and second regular, 4–6 February and 8–11 September; annual, 8–10 June, all in New York
President: Oumar Daou (Mali)
Membership: 36
Report: E/2009/34/Rev.1
Decision: ESC 2009/201 C
Executive Director of UNICEF: Ann M. Veneman

United Nations Development Programme (UNDP)/ United Nations Population Fund (UNFPA)

Executive Board
Sessions: First and second regular, 19–22 January and 14–16 September; annual, 26 May–3 June, all in New York
President: Mohammad Khazaee (Iran)
Membership: 36
Report: E/2009/35
Decision: ESC 2009/201 C

Administrators of UNDP: Kemal Dervis (until February), Helen Clark (from April)
Associate Administrator: Ad Melkert
Executive Director of UNFPA: Thoraya Ahmed Obaid

UNITED NATIONS VOLUNTEERS (UNV)
Report: DP/2010/28

United Nations Research Institute for Social Development (UNRISD)

BOARD

Session: Forty-seventh, Geneva, 10–11 November
Chairperson: Lourdes Arizpe (Mexico)
Membership: 11
Report: Board/09/3
Director of UNRISD: Thandika Mkandawire (until April); Sarah Cook (from November)

United Nations Interregional Crime and Justice Research Institute (UNICRI)

BOARD OF TRUSTEES

Membership: 7 (plus 4 ex-officio members)
Decision: ESC 2009/247
Director of UNICRI: Sandro Calvani

World Food Programme (WFP)

EXECUTIVE BOARD

Sessions: First and second regular, Rome, 9–11 February and 9–12 November; annual, Rome, 8–12 June
President: Vladimir V. Kuznetsov (Russian Federation)
Membership: 36
Report: E/2010/36
Decision: ESC 2009/201 C & D
Executive Director of WFP: Josette Sheeran

Trusteeship Council

The Trusteeship Council suspended operation on 1 November 1994 following the independence of Palau, the last remaining United Nations trust territory, on 1 October 1994. The General Assembly, in resolution 60/1 of 16 September 2005, considering that the Council no longer met and had no remaining functions, decided that Chapter XIII of the United Nations Charter and references to the Council in Chapter XII should be deleted.

International Court of Justice

Judges of the Court

The International Court of Justice consists of 15 Judges elected for nine-year terms by the General Assembly and the Security Council.

The following were the Judges of the Court serving in 2009, listed in the order of precedence:

Judge	Country of nationality	End of term
Hisashi Owada, *President*	Japan	2012
Peter Tomka, *Vice-President*	Slovakia	2012
Shi Jiuyong	China	2012
Abdul G. Koroma	Sierra Leone	2012
Awn Shawkat Al-Khasawneh	Jordan	2018
Thomas Buergenthal	United States	2015
Bruno Simma	Germany	2012
Ronny Abraham	France	2018
Kenneth Keith	New Zealand	2015
Bernardo Sepúlveda Amor	Mexico	2015
Mohamed Bennouna	Morocco	2015
Leonid Skotnikov	Russian Federation	2015
Antônio Augusto Cançado Trindade	Brazil	2018
Abdulqawi Ahmed Yusuf	Somalia	2018
Christopher Greenwood	United Kingdom	2018

Registrar: Philippe Couvreur
Deputy Registrar: Thérèse de Saint Phalle

Chamber of Summary Procedure

Members: Hisashi Owada (ex officio), Peter Tomka (ex officio), Abdul G. Koroma, Thomas Buergenthal, Bruno Simma
Substitute members: Bernardo Sepúlveda Amor, Leonid Skotnikov

Parties to the Court's Statute

All Members of the United Nations are ipso facto parties to the Statute of the International Court of Justice.

States accepting the compulsory jurisdiction of the Court

Declarations made by the following States, several with reservations, accepting the Court's compulsory jurisdic-

tion (or made under the Statute of the Permanent Court of International Justice and deemed to be an acceptance of the jurisdiction of the International Court), were in force at the end of 2009:

Australia, Austria, Barbados, Belgium, Botswana, Bulgaria, Cambodia, Cameroon, Canada, Costa Rica, Côte d'Ivoire, Cyprus, Democratic Republic of the Congo, Denmark, Djibouti, Dominican Republic, Egypt, Estonia, Finland, Gambia, Georgia, Germany, Greece, Guinea, Guinea-Bissau, Haiti, Honduras, Hungary, India, Japan, Kenya, Lesotho, Liberia, Liechtenstein, Luxembourg, Madagascar, Malawi, Malta, Mauritius, Mexico, Nauru, Netherlands, New Zealand, Nicaragua, Nigeria, Norway, Pakistan, Panama, Paraguay, Peru, Philippines, Poland, Portugal, Senegal, Serbia and Montenegro, Slovakia, Somalia, Spain, Sudan, Suriname, Swaziland, Sweden, Switzerland, Togo, Uganda, United Kingdom, and Uruguay.

United Nations organs and specialized and related agencies authorized to request advisory opinions from the Court

Authorized by the United Nations Charter to request opinions on any legal question: General Assembly, Security Council
Authorized by the General Assembly in accordance with the Charter to request opinions on legal questions arising within the scope of their activities: Economic and Social Council, Trusteeship Council, Interim Committee of the General Assembly, ILO, FAO, UNESCO, ICAO, WHO, World Bank, IFC, IDA, IMF, ITU, WMO, IMO, WIPO, IFAD, UNIDO, IAEA

Committees of the Court

BUDGETARY AND ADMINISTRATIVE COMMITTEE
Members: Hisashi Owada (Chairperson) (ex officio), Peter Tomka (ex officio), Kenneth Keith, Bernardo Sepúlveda Amor, Mohamed Bennouna, Abdulqawi Ahmed Yusuf, Christopher Greenwood
LIBRARY COMMITTEE
Members: Thomas Buergenthal (Chairperson), Bruno Simma, Ronny Abraham, Mohamed Bennouna, Antônio Augusto Cançado Trindade
RULES COMMITTEE
Members: Awn Shawkat Al-Khasawneh (Chairperson), Ronny Abraham, Kenneth Keith, Leonid Skotnikov, Antônio Augusto Cançado Trindade, Christopher Greenwood

Other United Nations-related bodies

The following bodies are not subsidiary to any principal organ of the United Nations but were established by an international treaty instrument or arrangement sponsored by the United Nations and are thus related to the Organization and its work.

These bodies, often referred to as "Treaty organs", are serviced by the United Nations Secretariat and may be financed in part or wholly from the Organization's regular budget, as authorized by the General Assembly, to which most of them report annually.

Committee on the Elimination of Discrimination against Women (CEDAW)

Sessions: Forty-third, Geneva, 19 January–6 February; forty-fourth, New York, 20 July–7 August
Chairperson: Naéla Gabr (Egypt)
Membership: 22
Reports: A/64/38, A/65/38

Committee on the Elimination of Racial Discrimination (CERD)

Sessions: Seventy-fourth and seventy-fifth, Geneva, 16 February–6 March and 3–28 August
Chairperson: Fatimata-Binta Victoire Dah (Burkina Faso)
Membership: 18
Report: A/64/18

Committee on the Protection of the Rights of All Migrant Workers and Members of Their Families

Sessions: Tenth and eleventh, Geneva, 20 April–1 May and 12–16 October
Chairperson: Abdelhamid El Jamri (Morocco)
Membership: 10
Reports: A/64/48, A/65/48

Committee on the Rights of the Child

Sessions: Fiftieth, fifty-first, and fifty-second, all in Geneva, 12–30 January, 25 May–12 June, 14 September–2 October
Chairperson: Yanghee Lee (Republic of Korea)
Membership: 18
Report: A/65/41

Committee against Torture

Sessions: Forty-second and forty-third, Geneva, 27 April–15 May and 2–20 November
Chairperson: Claudio Grossman (Chile)
Membership: 10
Reports: A/64/44, A/65/44

Conference on Disarmament

Meetings: Geneva, 19 January–27 March, 18 May–3 July, 3 August–18 September
President: Viet Nam, Zimbabwe, Algeria, Argentina, Australia and Austria (successively)
Membership: 65
Report: A/64/27

Human Rights Committee

Sessions: Ninety-fifth, New York, 16 March–3 April; ninety-sixth and ninety-seventh, Geneva, 13–31 July and 12–30 October
Chairperson: Yuji Iwasawa (Japan)
Membership: 18
Reports: A/64/40 (Vol. I), A/65/40 (Vol. I)

International Narcotics Control Board (INCB)

Sessions: Ninety-forth, ninety-fifth and ninety-sixth, Vienna, 2–6 February, 11–23 May and 27 October–13 November
President: Hamid Ghodse (Iran)
Membership: 13
Reports: E/INCB/2008/W.12/Add.2/Rev.1, E/INCB/2009/W.1
Decision: ESC 2009/201 E

Principal members of the United Nations Secretariat [12]

Secretariat

Secretary-General: Ban Ki-moon
Deputy Secretary-General: Asha-Rose Migiro

Executive Office of the Secretary-General

Under-Secretary-General, Chef de Cabinet: Vijay Nambiar
Assistant Secretary-General, Deputy Chef de Cabinet: Kim Won-soo
Assistant Secretary-General for Policy Planning: Robert Orr

Office of Internal Oversight Services

Under-Secretary-General: Inga-Britt Ahlenius

Office of Legal Affairs

Under-Secretary-General, Legal Counsel: Patricia O'Brien
Assistant Secretary-General: Peter Taksøe-Jensen

Department of Political Affairs

Under-Secretary-General: B. Lynn Pascoe
Assistant Secretary-General: Haile Menkerios; Oscar Fernandez-Taranco (from July)

Office for Disarmament Affairs

Under-Secretary-General, High Representative: Sergio de Queiroz Duarte

Department of Peacekeeping Operations

Under-Secretary-General: Alain Le Roy
Assistant Secretaries-General: Edmond Mulet, Dmitry Titov
Assistant Secretary-General, Military Adviser: Lieutenant General Chikadibia Obiakor

Department of Field Support

Under-Secretary General: Susana Malcorra
Assistant Secretary-General: Jane Holl Lute (until April); Anthony Banbury (from April)

Office for the Coordination of Humanitarian Affairs

Under-Secretary-General for Humanitarian Affairs, Emergency Relief Coordinator: John Holmes
Assistant Secretary-General, Deputy Emergency Relief Coordinator: Catherine Bragg

Department of Economic and Social Affairs

Under-Secretary-General: Sha Zukang
Assistant Secretary-General, Special Adviser on Gender Issues and Advancement of Women: Rachel Mayanja
Assistant Secretary-General for Economic Development: Jomo Kwame Sundaram
Assistant Secretary-General for Policy Coordination and Inter-Agency Affairs: Thomas Stelzer

Department for General Assembly and Conference Management

Under-Secretary-General: Muhammad Shaaban
Assistant Secretary-General: Yohannes Mengesha (until May); Franz Baumann (from May)

Department of Public Information

Under-Secretary-General for Communications and Public Information: Kiyotaka Akasaka

Department of Safety and Security

Under-Secretary-General: David Veness (until May), Gregory B. Starr (from May)

Department of Management

Under-Secretary-General: Angela Kane
OFFICE OF PROGRAMME PLANNING, BUDGET AND ACCOUNTS
Assistant Secretary-General, Controller: Jun Yamazaki
OFFICE OF HUMAN RESOURCES MANAGEMENT
Assistant Secretary-General: Catherine Pollard
OFFICE OF CENTRAL SUPPORT SERVICES
Assistant Secretary-General: Warren Sach
CAPITAL MASTER PLAN PROJECT
Assistant Secretary-General, Executive Director: Michael Adlerstein

Office of Information and Communications Technology

Assistant Secretary-General, Chief Information Technology Officer: Choi Soon-Hong

Office of the United Nations Ombudsman

Assistant Secretary-General, Ombudsman: Johnston Barkat

Peacebuilding Support Office

Assistant Secretary-General: Jane Holl Lute (until August); Judy Cheng-Hopkins (from August)

United Nations Joint Staff Pension Fund

Assistant Secretary-General, Chief Executive Officer: Bernard G. Cochemé

Economic Commission for Africa

Under-Secretary-General, Executive Secretary: Abdoulie Janneh

Economic Commission for Europe

Under-Secretary-General, Executive Secretary: Ján Kubiš

Economic Commission for Latin America and the Caribbean

Under-Secretary-General, Executive Secretary: Alicia Bárcena

Economic and Social Commission for Asia and the Pacific

Under-Secretary-General, Executive Secretary: Noeleen Heyzer

Economic and Social Commission for Western Asia

Under-Secretary-General, Executive Secretary: Bader Al-Dafa

United Nations Office at Geneva

Under-Secretary-General, Director-General of the United Nations Office at Geneva: Sergei Ordzhonikidze

United Nations Office at Vienna

Under-Secretary-General, Director-General of the United Nations Office at Vienna and Executive Director of the United Nations Office on Drugs and Crime: Antonio Maria Costa

United Nations Office at Nairobi

Under-Secretary-General and Director-General of the United Nations Office at Nairobi: Anna Tibaijuka

International Court of Justice Registry

Assistant Secretary-General, Registrar: Philippe Couvreur

Secretariats of subsidiary organs, special representatives and other related bodies

Counter-Terrorism Committee Executive Directorate

Assistant Secretary-General, Executive Director: Michael Smith

International Civil Service Commission

Under-Secretary-General, Chairman: Kingston Papie Rhodes
Assistant Secretary-General, Vice-Chairman: Wolfgang Stöckl

International Trade Centre UNCTAD/WTO

Executive Director: Patricia Francis

Joint United Nations Programme on HIV/AIDS

Under-Secretary-General, Executive Director: Michel Sidibé
Assistant Secretary-General, Deputy Executive Director: Paul De Lay
Assistant Secretary-General, Deputy Executive Director: Jan Beagle (from September)
Assistant Secretary-General, Special Envoy for HIV/AIDS in Africa: Elizabeth Mataka
Assistant Secretary-General, Special Envoy for HIV/AIDS in Asia and the Pacific: Nafis Sadik
Assistant Secretary-General, Special Envoy for HIV/AIDS in the Caribbean: George Alleyne

Office of the Administrations of Justice

Executive Director: Andrei Terekhov

Office of the High Representative for the Least Developed Countries, Landlocked Developing Countries and Small Island Developing States

Under-Secretary-General, High Representative: Cheick Sidi Diarra

Office of the Secretary-General's Special Envoy for Malaria

Assistant Secretary-General, Special Envoy: Ray Chambers

Office of the Special Adviser to the Secretary-General on Africa

Under-Secretary-General, Special Adviser: Cheick Sidi Diarra

Office of the Special Adviser to the Secretary-General on the International Compact with Iraq and Other Issues

Under-Secretary-General, Special Adviser: Ibrahim Gambari

Office of the Special Adviser of the Secretary-General for Myanmar

Under-Secretary-General, Special Adviser: Ibrahim Gambari

Office of the Special Representative of the Secretary-General for Children and Armed Conflict

Under-Secretary-General, Special Representative: Radhika Coomaraswamy

Office of the Special Adviser of the Secretary-General on the Prevention of Genocide

Under-Secretary-General, Special Adviser: Francis Deng

Office of the Special Representative of the Secretary-General for West Africa

Under-Secretary-General, Special Representative: Said Djinnit

Office of the United Nations High Commissioner for Refugees

Under-Secretary-General, High Commissioner: António Manuel de Oliveira Guterres
Assistant Secretary-General, Deputy High Commissioner: L. Craig Johnstone
Assistant Secretary-General, Assistant High Commissioner (Protection): Erika Feller
Assistant Secretary-General, Assistant High Commissioner (Operations): Janet Lim

Office of the United Nations High Commissioner for Human Rights

Under-Secretary-General, High Commissioner: Navanethem Pillay
Assistant Secretary-General, Deputy High Commissioner: Kyung-wha Kang

Office of the United Nations Special Coordinator for the Middle East

Under-Secretary-General, Special Coordinator for the Middle East Peace Process and Personal Representative of the Secretary-General to the Palestine Liberation Organization and the Palestinian Authority: Robert H. Serry

Office of the Special Representative of the Secretary-General for Violence against Children

Assistant Secretary-General, Special Representative: Marta Santos Pais

Personal Envoy of the Secretary-General for the Greece-FYROM Talks

Under-Secretary-General, Personal Envoy: Matthew Nimetz

Personal Envoy of the Secretary-General for Western Sahara

Under-Secretary-General, Personal Envoy: Christopher Ross

Secretary-General's High-level Coordinator for compliance by Iraq with its obligations regarding the repatriation or return of all Kuwaiti and third country nationals or their remains, as well as the return of all Kuwaiti property, including archives seized by Iraq

Under-Secretary-General, High-Level Coordinator: Gennady P. Tarasov

Senior UN System Coordinator for Avian and Human Influenza

Assistant Secretary-General, Senior UN System Coordinator: David Nabarro

Special Advisers to the Secretary-General

Special Advisers: Joseph V. Reed, Iqbal Riza

Special Adviser to the Secretary-General on Cyprus

Under-Secretary-General, Special Adviser: Alexander Downer

Special Adviser to the Secretary-General on Innovative Financing for Development

Under-Secretary-General, Special Adviser: Philippe Douste-Blazy

Special Adviser of the Secretary-General for Internet Governance

Special Adviser: Nitin Desai

Special Adviser to the Secretary-General on Latin American Issues

Under-Secretary-General, Special Adviser: Diego Cordovez

Special Adviser to the Secretary-General and Mediator in the border dispute between Equatorial Guinea and Gabon

Under-Secretary-General, Special Adviser: Nicolas Michel

Special Envoy of the Secretary-General for the implementation of Security Council resolution 1559/2004

Under-Secretary-General, Special Envoy: Terje Roed-Larsen

Special Representative of the Secretary-General on Food Security and Nutrition

Special Representative: David Nabarro

Special Representative of the Secretary-General on Migration

Under-Secretary-General, Special Representative: Peter Sutherland

Special Representative of Secretary-General on the Issue of Human Rights, Transnational Corporations and other Business Enterprises

Special Adviser: John Ruggie

Special Representative of the Secretary-General for the Sudan

Under-Secretary-General, Special Representative: Ashraf Jehangir Qazi
Assistant Secretary-General, Principal Deputy Special Representative: Tayé-Brook Zerihoun (until April 2008); Jasbir Singh Lidder (from December)

Special Court for Sierra Leone

Assistant Secretary General, Registrar: Herman von Hebel (until June); Binta Mansaray (from June)

Special Tribunal for Lebanon

Assistant Secretary General, Registrar: Robin Vincent (until August); David Tolbert (from August)

Staff-Management Coordination Committee

Assistant Secretary-General, President: Dieter Goethel

United Nations Alliance of Civilizations

Under-Secretary-General, High Representative: Jorge Sampaio

United Nations Children's Fund

Under-Secretary-General, Executive Director: Ann M. Veneman
Assistant Secretaries-General, Deputy Executive Directors: Hilde Johnson, Omar Abdi, Saad Houry

United Nations Compensation Commission

Assistant Secretary-General, Executive Secretary: Mojtaba Kazazi

United Nations Conference on Trade and Development

Under-Secretary-General: Supachai Panitchpakdi
Deputy-Secretary-General: Petko Draganov

United Nations Convention on Biological Diversity

Assistant Secretary General, Executive Secretary: Ahmed Djoghlaf

United Nations Convention to Combat Desertification

Assistant Secretary General, Executive Secretary: Luc Gnacadja

United Nations Development Programme

Administrator: Kemal Dervis (until February); Helen Clark (from April)
Under-Secretary-General, Associate Administrator: Ad Melkert
Assistant Administrator and Director, Bureau for Crisis Prevention and Recovery: Kathleen Cravero (until February); Jordan Ryan (from February)
Assistant Administrator and Director, Bureau for Resources and Strategic Partnerships: Bruce Jenks
Assistant Administrator and Director, Bureau of Management: Akiko Yuge
Assistant Administrator and Director, Bureau for Development Policy: Olav Kjørven
Assistant Administrator and Regional Director, UNDP Africa: Tegegnework Gettu (from February)
Assistant Administrator and Regional Director, UNDP Arab States: Amat Al Aleem Ali Alsoswa
Assistant Administrator and Regional Director, UNDP Asia and the Pacific: Ajay Chhibber
Assistant Administrator and Regional Director, UNDP Europe and the Commonwealth of Independent States: Kori Udovicki
Assistant Administrator and Regional Director, UNDP Latin America and the Caribbean: Rebeca Grynspan

United Nations Environment Programme

Under-Secretary-General, Executive Director: Achim Steiner
Assistant Secretary-General, Deputy Executive Director: Angela Cropper
Assistant Secretary-General, Executive Secretary United Nations Framework Convention on Climate Change: Yvo de Boer

United Nations Global Compact

Executive Director: Georg Kell

United Nations Human Settlements Programme

Under-Secretary-General, Executive Director: Anna Kajumulo Tibaijuka

Assistant Secretary General, Deputy Executive Director: Inga Björk-Klevby

United Nations Institute for Training and Research

Assistant Secretary-General, Executive Director: Carlos Lopes

United Nations International School

Assistant Secretary General, Special Representative: Sylvia Fuhrman

United Nations Office for Disaster Risk Reduction

Assistant Secretary-General, Special Representative: Margareta Wahlström

United Nations Office for Project Services

Assistant Secretary-General, Executive Director: Jan Mattsson

United Nations Office for Partnerships

Executive Director: Amir Dossal

United Nations Office of the Special Envoy to Haiti

Special Envoy: William J. Clinton
Deputy Special Envoy: Paul Farmer

United Nations Office on Sport for Development and Peace

Under-Secretary-General, Special Adviser: Wilfried Lemke

United Nations Millennium Project

Under-Secretary-General, Senior Adviser to the Secretary-General on the Millennium Goals, Director UN Millennium Project: Jeffrey Sachs

United Nations Population Fund

Under-Secretary-General, Executive Director: Thoraya Ahmed Obaid
Assistant Secretary-General, Deputy Executive Director (Management): Mari Simonen
Assistant Secretary-General, Deputy Executive Director (Programme): Purnima Mane

United Nations Relief and Works Agency for Palestine Refugees in the Near East

Under-Secretary-General, Commissioner-General: Karen Koning AbuZayd
Assistant Secretary-General, Deputy Commissioner-General: Filippo Grandi

United Nations University

Under-Secretary-General, Rector: Konrad Osterwalder

World Food Programme

Executive Director: Josette Sheeran
Assistant Secretary-General, Deputy Executive Director: Amir Mahmoud Abdulla
Assistant Secretary-General, Deputy Executive Director for Hunger Solutions: Sheila Sisulu

---

NOTES

[1] Elected on 10 June 2009 (decision 63/421).

[2] Elected on 10 June 2009 (decision 63/423).

[3] One of the Main Committees that met during the resumed session.

[4] Elected by the Committees; announced by the Assembly President on 10 June 2009 (decision 63/422).

[5] On 15 January 2009, the General Assembly decided that the Credentials Committee for the resumed tenth emergency special session would have the same composition as that for the sixty-third session (decision ES-10/101 H).

[6] Appointed on 15 September 2009 (decision 64/401).

[7] Established in 2008 at UNCTAD XII, the Investment, Enterprise and Development Commission combines the mandate of the previous Commission on Investment, Technology and Related Financial Issues with responsibility for enterprise and information and communication technology issues from the previous Commission on Enterprise, Business Facilitation and Development.

[8] Established in 2008 at UNCTAD XII, the Trade and Development Commission combines the mandate of the previous Commission on Trade in Goods and Services, and Commodities, with responsibility for transport and trade logistics issues from the previous Commission on Enterprise, Business Facilitation and Development.

[9] Also an advisory subsidiary body of the General Assembly.

[10] Mandate ended on 15 June 2009.

[11] Mandate ended on 31 December 2009, and BONUCA was succeeded on 1 Janury 2010 by the United Nations Integrated Peacebuilding Office in the Central African Republic (BINUCA).

[12] As at 30 June 2009, staff internationally and locally recruited in the United Nations Secretariat, including staff on an appointment of less than one year, numbered 39,978 under contract with the Secretariat under the 100, 200 or 300 series of the Staff Rules. Of these, 11,554 were in the Professional and higher categories, 28,424 in the General Service and related categories, and 21,746 in field missions administered by the Department of Field Support.

Agendas of United Nations principal organs in 2009

This appendix lists the items on the agendas of the General Assembly, the Security Council and the Economic and Social Council during 2009. For the Assembly, the column headed "*Allocation*" indicates the assignment of each item to plenary meetings or committees.

General Assembly

**Agenda items considered at the resumed sixty-third session
(20 February–14 September 2009) [decision 63/552, A/63/49 (Vol. II)]**

Item No.	Title	Allocation
9.	Report of the Security Council.	Plenary
12.	Prevention of armed conflict.	Plenary
13.	Protracted conflicts in the GUAM area and their implications for international peace, security and development.	Plenary
14.	Zone of peace and cooperation of the South Atlantic.	Plenary
15.	The situation in the Middle East.	Plenary
16.	Question of Palestine.	Plenary
18.	The situation in the occupied territories of Azerbaijan.	Plenary
21.	Question of Cyprus.	Plenary
22.	Armed aggression against the Democratic Republic of the Congo.	Plenary
23.	Question of the Falkland Islands (Malvinas).	Plenary
24.	The situation of democracy and human rights in Haiti.	Plenary
25.	Armed Israeli aggression against the Iraqi nuclear installations and its grave consequences for the established international system concerning the peaceful uses of nuclear energy, the non-proliferation of nuclear weapons and international peace and security.	Plenary
26.	Consequences of the Iraqi occupation of and aggression against Kuwait.	Plenary
31.	Comprehensive review of the whole question of peacekeeping operations in all their aspects.	Plenary
40.	Report of the Economic and Social Council.	Plenary
41.	Implementation of the Declaration of Commitment on HIV/AIDS and the Political Declaration on HIV/AIDS.	Plenary
44.	Integrated and coordinated implementation of and follow-up to the outcomes of the major United Nations conferences and summits in the economic, social and related fields.	Plenary
45.	Culture of peace.	Plenary
48.	Follow-up to and implementation of the outcome of the 2002 International Conference on Financing for Development and the preparation of the 2008 Review Conference.	Plenary
49.	Sustainable development: (d) Protection of global climate for present and future generations of mankind.	Plenary
57.	New Partnership for Africa's Development: progress in implementation and international support.	Plenary
59.	Holocaust remembrance.	Plenary
71.	Request for an advisory opinion of the International Court of Justice on whether the unilateral declaration of independence of Kosovo is in accordance with international law.	Plenary
79.	The rule of law at the national and international levels.	Plenary
89.	General and complete disarmament.	Plenary
99.	Measures to eliminate international terrorism.	Plenary
100.	Report of the Secretary-General on the work of the Organization.	Plenary
103.	Elections to fill vacancies in principal organs: (c) Election of five members of the International Court of Justice.	Plenary
104.	Elections to fill vacancies in subsidiary organs and other elections: (a) Election of twenty members of the Committee for Programme and Coordination; (c) Election of eighteen members of the Human Rights Council.	Plenary
105.	Appointments to fill vacancies in subsidiary organs and other appointments: (d) Appointment of members of the United Nations Administrative Tribunal; (g) Appointment of members of the Committee on Conferences; (h) Appointment of a member of the Joint Inspection Unit; (i) Confirmation of the appointment of the Administrator of the United Nations Development Programme; (j) Confirmation of the appointment of the Secretary-General of the United Nations Conference on Trade and Development; (k) Appointment of the judges of the United Nations Dispute Tribunal; (l) Appointment of the judges of the United Nations Appeals Tribunal.	Plenary
106.	Admission of new Members to the United Nations.	Plenary
107.	Follow-up to the outcome of the Millennium Summit.	Plenary

Item No.	Title	Allocation
110.	Revitalization of the work of the General Assembly.	Plenary
111.	Question of equitable representation on and increase in the membership of the Security Council and related matters.	Plenary
112.	Strengthening of the United Nations system.	Plenary
113.	Multilingualism.	Plenary
114.	Cooperation between the United Nations and regional and other organizations:	Plenary
	(a) Cooperation between the United Nations and the African Union;	
	(h) Cooperation between the United Nations and the Economic Community of Central African States;	
	(p) Cooperation between the United Nations and the Organization for Security and Cooperation in Europe;	
	(q) Cooperation between the United Nations and the Organization of American States;	
	(u) Cooperation between the United Nations and the Southern African Development Community.	
115.	Follow-up to the recommendations on administrative management and internal oversight of the Independent Inquiry Committee into the United Nations Oil-for-Food Programme.	Plenary
116.	Financial reports and audited financial statements, and reports of the Board of Auditors.	Plenary
117.	Review of the efficiency of the administrative and financial functioning of the United Nations.	Plenary
118.	Programme budget for the biennium 2008–2009.	Plenary
119.	Programme planning.	Plenary
120.	Improving the financial situation of the United Nations.	
121.	Pattern of conferences.	Plenary
122.	Scale of assessments for the apportionment of the expenses of the United Nations.	Plenary
123.	Human resources management.	Plenary
124.	Joint Inspection Unit.	Plenary
125.	United Nations common system.	Plenary
126.	United Nations pension system.	Plenary
127.	Administrative and budgetary coordination of the United Nations with the specialized agencies and the International Atomic Energy Agency.	Plenary
128.	Report on the activities of the Office of Internal Oversight Services.	Plenary
129.	Administration of justice at the United Nations.	
130.	Financing of the International Criminal Tribunal for the Prosecution of Persons Responsible for Genocide and Other Serious Violations of International Humanitarian Law Committed in the Territory of Rwanda and Rwandan Citizens Responsible for Genocide and Other Such Violations Committed in the Territory of Neighbouring States between 1 January and 31 December 1994.	Plenary
131.	Financing of the International Tribunal for the Prosecution of Persons Responsible for Serious Violations of International Humanitarian Law Committed in the Territory of the Former Yugoslavia since 1991.	Plenary
132.	Administrative and budgetary aspects of the financing of the United Nations peacekeeping operations.	Plenary
133.	Financing of the United Nations Operation in Burundi.	Plenary
134.	Financing of the United Nations Operation in Côte d'Ivoire.	Plenary
135.	Financing of the United Nations Peacekeeping Force in Cyprus.	Plenary
136.	Financing of the United Nations Organization Mission in the Democratic Republic of the Congo.	Plenary
137.	Financing of the United Nations Mission in East Timor.	Plenary
138.	Financing of the United Nations Integrated Mission in Timor-Leste.	Plenary
139.	Financing of the United Nations Mission in Ethiopia and Eritrea.	Plenary
140.	Financing of the United Nations Observer Mission in Georgia.	Plenary
141.	Financing of the United Nations Stabilization Mission in Haiti.	Plenary
142.	Financing of the United Nations Interim Administration Mission in Kosovo.	Plenary
143.	Financing of the United Nations Mission in Liberia.	Plenary
144.	Financing of the United Nations peacekeeping forces in the Middle East.	Plenary
145.	Financing of the United Nations Mission in Sierra Leone.	Plenary
146.	Financing of the United Nations Mission in the Sudan.	Plenary
147.	Financing of the United Nations Mission for the Referendum in Western Sahara.	Plenary
148.	Financing of the African Union-United Nations Hybrid Operation in Darfur.	Plenary
149.	Financing of the United Nations Mission in the Central African Republic and Chad.	Plenary
152.	Observer status for the Agency for International Trade Information and Cooperation in the General Assembly.	Plenary
154.	Judges of the International Tribunal for the Prosecution of Persons Responsible for Serious Violations of International Humanitarian Law Committed in the Territory of the Former Yugoslavia since 1991.	Plenary
157.	Financing of activities arising from Security Council resolution 1863(2009)[1].	5th
158.	The scope and application of the principle of universal jurisdiction[1].	Plenary
159.	International Criminal Tribunal for the Prosecution of Persons Responsible for Genocide and Other Serious Violations of International Humanitarian Law Committed in the Territory of Rwanda and Rwandan Citizens Responsible for Genocide and Other Such Violations Committed in the Territory of Neighbouring States between 1 January and 31 December 1994[1].	Plenary
160.	International Tribunal for the Prosecution of Persons Responsible for Serious Violations of International Humanitarian Law Committed in the Territory of the Former Yugoslavia since 1991[1].	Plenary

Agenda of the sixty-fourth session, first part
(15 September–24 December 2009) [A/64/49 (Vol. I), Annex I]

Item No.	Title	Allocation
1.	Opening of the session by the President of the General Assembly.	Plenary
2.	Minute of silent prayer or meditation.	Plenary
3.	Credentials of representatives to the sixty-fourth session of the General Assembly:	Plenary
	(a) Appointment of the members of the Credentials Committee;	
	(b) Report of the Credentials Committee.	
4.	Election of the President of the General Assembly.	Plenary
5.	Election of the officers of the Main Committees.	1st, 4th, 2nd, 3rd, 5th, 6th
6.	Election of the Vice-Presidents of the General Assembly.	Plenary
7.	Organization of work, adoption of the agenda and allocation of items: reports of the General Committee.	Plenary
8.	General debate.	Plenary

A. Maintenance of international peace and security

9.	Report of the Security Council.	Plenary
10.	Report of the Peacebuilding Commission.	Plenary
11.	Support by the United Nations system of the efforts of Governments to promote and consolidate new or restored democracies.	Plenary
12.	The role of diamonds in fuelling conflict.	Plenary
13.	Prevention of armed conflict.	Plenary
14.	Protracted conflicts in the GUAM area and their implications for international peace, security and development.	Plenary
15.	The situation in the Middle East.	Plenary
16.	Question of Palestine.	Plenary
17.	The situation in Afghanistan.	Plenary
18.	The situation in the occupied territories of Azerbaijan.	Plenary
19.	Necessity of ending the economic, commercial and financial embargo imposed by the United States of America against Cuba.	Plenary
20.	The situation in Central America: progress in fashioning a region of peace, freedom, democracy and development.	Plenary
21.	Question of Cyprus.	Plenary
22.	Armed aggression against the Democratic Republic of the Congo.	Plenary
23.	Question of the Falkland Islands (Malvinas).	Plenary
24.	The situation of democracy and human rights in Haiti.	Plenary
25.	Armed Israeli aggression against the Iraqi nuclear installations and its grave consequences for the established international system concerning the peaceful uses of nuclear energy, the non-proliferation of nuclear weapons and international peace and security.	Plenary
26.	Consequences of the Iraqi occupation of and aggression against Kuwait.	Plenary
27.	University for Peace.	4th
28.	Assistance in mine action.	4th
29.	Effects of atomic radiation.	4th
30.	International cooperation in the peaceful uses of outer space.	4th
31.	United Nations Relief and Works Agency for Palestine Refugees in the Near East.	4th
32.	Report of the Special Committee to Investigate Israeli Practices Affecting the Human Rights of the Palestinian People and Other Arabs of the Occupied Territories.	4th
33.	Comprehensive review of the whole question of peacekeeping operations in all their aspects.	
34.	Questions relating to information.	4th
35.	Information from Non-Self-Governing Territories transmitted under Article 73 e of the Charter of the United Nations.	4th
36.	Economic and other activities which affect the interests of the peoples of the Non-Self-Governing Territories.	4th
37.	Implementation of the Declaration on the Granting of Independence to Colonial Countries and Peoples by the specialized agencies and the international institutions associated with the United Nations.	4th
38.	Offers by Member States of study and training facilities for inhabitants of Non-Self-Governing Territories.	4th
39.	Implementation of the Declaration on the Granting of Independence to Colonial Countries and Peoples.	4th
40.	Permanent sovereignty of the Palestinian people in the Occupied Palestinian Territory, including East Jerusalem, and of the Arab population in the occupied Syrian Golan over their natural resources.	2nd
41.	Report of the United Nations High Commissioner for Refugees, questions relating to refugees, returnees and displaced persons and humanitarian questions.	3rd
172.	Question of the Comorian island of Mayotte.	Plenary

Item No.	*Title*	*Allocation*

B. Promotion of sustained economic growth and sustainable development in accordance with the relevant resolutions of the General Assembly and recent United Nations conferences

42.	Report of the Economic and Social Council.	Plenary
43.	Return or restitution of cultural property to the countries of origin.	Plenary
44.	Implementation of the Declaration of Commitment on HIV/AIDS and the Political Declaration on HIV/AIDS.	Plenary
45.	Sport for peace and development: building a peaceful and better world through sport and the Olympic ideal.	Plenary
46.	Global road safety crisis.	Plenary
47.	2001–2010: Decade to Roll Back Malaria in Developing Countries, Particularly in Africa.	Plenary
48.	Integrated and coordinated implementation of and follow-up to the outcomes of the major United Nations conferences and summits in the economic, social and related fields.	Plenary
49.	Culture of peace.	Plenary
50.	Information and communication technologies for development.	2nd
51.	Macroeconomic policy questions:	2nd
	(a) International trade and development;	
	(b) International financial system and development;	
	(c) External debt and development: towards a durable solution to the debt problems of developing countries;	
	(d) Commodities.	
52.	Follow-up to and implementation of the outcome of the 2002 International Conference on Financing for Development and the 2008 Review Conference.	Plenary, 2nd
53.	Sustainable development:	2nd
	(a) Implementation of Agenda 21, the Programme for the Further Implementation of Agenda 21 and the outcomes of the World Summit on Sustainable Development;	
	(b) Follow-up to and implementation of the Mauritius Strategy for the Further Implementation of the Programme of Action for the Sustainable Development of Small Island Developing States;	
	(c) International Strategy for Disaster Reduction;	
	(d) Protection of global climate for present and future generations;	
	(e) Implementation of the United Nations Convention to Combat Desertification in Those Countries Experiencing Serious Drought and/or Desertification, Particularly in Africa;	
	(f) Convention on Biological Diversity;	
	(g) Report of the Governing Council of the United Nations Environment Programme on its twenty-fifth session;	
	(h) Sustainable mountain development;	
	(i) Promotion of new and renewable sources of energy.	
54.	Implementation of the outcome of the United Nations Conference on Human Settlements (Habitat II) and strengthening of the United Nations Human Settlements Programme (UN-Habitat).	2nd
55.	Globalization and interdependence:	2nd
	(a) Role of the United Nations in promoting development in the context of globalization and interdependence;	
	(b) Preventing and combating corrupt practices and transfer of assets of illicit origin and returning such assets, in particular to the countries of origin, consistent with the United Nations Convention against Corruption;	
	(c) Science and technology for development.	
56.	Groups of countries in special situations:	2nd
	(a) Third United Nations Conference on the Least Developed Countries;	
	(b) Specific actions related to the particular needs and problems of landlocked developing countries: outcome of the International Ministerial Conference of Landlocked and Transit Developing Countries and Donor Countries and International Financial and Development Institutions on Transit Transport Cooperation.	
57.	Eradication of poverty and other development issues:	2nd
	(a) Implementation of the second United Nations Decade for the Eradication of Poverty (2008–2017);	
	(b) Women in development;	
	(c) Human resources development.	
58.	Operational activities for development:	2nd
	(a) Operational activities for development of the United Nations system;	
	(b) South-South cooperation for development.	
59.	Towards global partnerships.	2nd
60.	Agriculture development and food security.	2nd
61.	Social development:	3rd
	(a) Implementation of the outcome of the World Summit for Social Development and of the twenty-fourth special session of the General Assembly;	

Item No.	Title	Allocation
	(b) Social development, including questions relating to the world social situation and to youth, ageing, disabled persons and the family;	
	(c) Follow-up to the International Year of Older Persons: Second World Assembly on Ageing.	
62.	Advancement of women:	3rd
	(a) Advancement of women;	
	(b) Implementation of the outcome of the Fourth World Conference on Women and of the twenty-third special session of the General Assembly.	
170.	United Nations University.	2nd

C. Development of Africa

63.	New Partnership for Africa's Development: progress in implementation and international support:	Plenary
	(a) New Partnership for Africa's Development: progress in implementation and international support;	
	(b) Causes of conflict and the promotion of durable peace and sustainable development in Africa.	

D. Promotion of human rights

64.	Report of the Human Rights Council.	Plenary, 3rd
65.	Promotion and protection of the rights of children:	3rd
	(a) Promotion and protection of the rights of children;	
	(b) Follow-up to the outcome of the special session on children.	
66.	Indigenous issues:	3rd
	(a) Indigenous issues;	
	(b) Second International Decade of the World's Indigenous People.	
67.	Elimination of racism, racial discrimination, xenophobia and related intolerance:	3rd
	(a) Elimination of racism, racial discrimination, xenophobia and related intolerance;	
	(b) Comprehensive implementation of and follow-up to the Durban Declaration and Programme of Action.	
68.	Right of peoples to self-determination.	3rd
69.	Promotion and protection of human rights:	Plenary, 3rd
	(a) Implementation of human rights instruments;	
	(b) Human rights questions, including alternative approaches for improving the effective enjoyment of human rights and fundamental freedoms;	
	(c) Human rights situations and reports of special rapporteurs and representatives;	
	(d) Comprehensive implementation of and follow-up to the Vienna Declaration and Programme of Action.	

E. Effective coordination of humanitarian assistance efforts

70.	Strengthening of the coordination of humanitarian and disaster relief assistance of the United Nations, including special economic assistance:	Plenary
	(a) Strengthening of the coordination of emergency humanitarian assistance of the United Nations;	
	(b) Assistance to the Palestinian people.	
71.	Assistance to survivors of the 1994 genocide in Rwanda, particularly orphans, widows and victims of sexual violence.	Plenary

F. Promotion of justice and international law

72.	Report of the International Court of Justice.	Plenary
73.	Report of the International Criminal Tribunal for the Prosecution of Persons Responsible for Genocide and Other Serious Violations of International Humanitarian Law Committed in the Territory of Rwanda and Rwandan Citizens Responsible for Genocide and Other Such Violations Committed in the Territory of Neighbouring States between 1 January and 31 December 1994.	Plenary
74.	Report of the International Tribunal for the Prosecution of Persons Responsible for Serious Violations of International Humanitarian Law Committed in the Territory of the Former Yugoslavia since 1991.	Plenary
75.	Report of the International Criminal Court.	Plenary
76.	Oceans and the law of the sea:	Plenary
	(a) Oceans and the law of the sea;	
	(b) Sustainable fisheries, including through the 1995 Agreement for the Implementation of the Provisions of the United Nations Convention on the Law of the Sea of 10 December 1982 relating to the Conservation and Management of Straddling Fish Stocks and Highly Migratory Fish Stocks, and related instruments.	
77.	Request for an advisory opinion of the International Court of Justice on whether the unilateral declaration of independence of Kosovo is in accordance with international law.	Plenary
78.	Criminal accountability of United Nations officials and experts on mission.	6th
79.	Report of the United Nations Commission on International Trade Law on the work of its forty-second session.	6th
80.	United Nations Programme of Assistance in the Teaching, Study, Dissemination and Wider Appreciation of International Law.	6th

Item No.	Title	Allocation
81.	Report of the International Law Commission on the work of its sixty-first session.	6th
82.	Report of the Special Committee on the Charter of the United Nations and on the Strengthening of the Role of the Organization.	6th
83.	The rule of law at the national and international levels.	6th
84.	The scope and application of the principle of universal jurisdiction.	6th

G. Disarmament

85.	Report of the International Atomic Energy Agency.	Plenary
86.	Reduction of military budgets:	1st
	(a) Reduction of military budgets;	
	(b) Objective information on military matters, including transparency of military expenditures.	
87.	Implementation of the Declaration of the Indian Ocean as a Zone of Peace.	1st
88.	African Nuclear-Weapon-Free Zone Treaty.	1st
89.	Verification in all its aspects, including the role of the United Nations in the field of verification.	1st
90.	Review of the implementation of the Declaration on the Strengthening of International Security.	1st
91.	Developments in the field of information and telecommunications in the context of international security.	1st
92.	Establishment of a nuclear-weapon-free zone in the region of the Middle East.	1st
93.	Conclusion of effective international arrangements to assure non-nuclear weapon States against the use or threat of use of nuclear weapons.	1st
94.	Prevention of an arms race in outer space.	1st
95.	Role of science and technology in the context of international security and disarmament.	1st
96.	General and complete disarmament:	1st

(a) Notification of nuclear tests;
(b) Follow-up to nuclear disarmament obligations agreed to at the 1995 and 2000 Review Conferences of the Parties to the Treaty on the Non-Proliferation of Nuclear Weapons;
(c) Treaty on the South-East Asia Nuclear-Weapon-Free Zone (Bangkok Treaty);
(d) Prohibition of the dumping of radioactive wastes;
(e) Preventing the acquisition by terrorists of radioactive materials and sources;
(f) Regional disarmament;
(g) Conventional arms control at the regional and subregional levels;
(h) Confidence-building measures in the regional and subregional context;
(i) Nuclear disarmament;
(j) Reducing nuclear danger;
(k) Implementation of the Convention on the Prohibition of the Development, Production, Stockpiling and Use of Chemical Weapons and on Their Destruction;
(l) Follow-up to the advisory opinion of the International Court of Justice on the *Legality of the Threat or Use of Nuclear Weapons*;
(m) Promotion of multilateralism in the area of disarmament and non-proliferation;
(n) Observance of environmental norms in the drafting and implementation of agreements on disarmament and arms control;
(o) Relationship between disarmament and development;
(p) Towards a nuclear-weapon-free world: accelerating the implementation of nuclear disarmament commitments;
(q) Measures to prevent terrorists from acquiring weapons of mass destruction;
(r) Problems arising from the accumulation of conventional ammunition stockpiles in surplus;
(s) The Hague Code of Conduct against Ballistic Missile Proliferation;
(t) Nuclear-weapon-free southern hemisphere and adjacent areas;
(u) Assistance to States for curbing the illicit traffic in small arms and light weapons and collecting them;
(v) Transparency and confidence-building measures in outer space activities;
(w) Transparency in armaments;
(x) The illicit trade in small arms and light weapons in all its aspects;
(y) Renewed determination towards the total elimination of nuclear weapons;
(z) Towards an arms trade treaty: establishing common international standards for the import, export and transfer of conventional arms;
(aa) Convening of the fourth special session of the General Assembly devoted to disarmament;
(bb) United Nations conference to identify appropriate ways of eliminating nuclear dangers in the context of nuclear disarmament.

97.	Review and implementation of the Concluding Document of the Twelfth Special Session of the General Assembly:	1st

(a) United Nations Regional Centre for Peace, Disarmament and Development in Latin America and the Caribbean;
(b) Convention on the Prohibition of the Use of Nuclear Weapons;
(c) United Nations regional centres for peace and disarmament;

Item No.	Title	Allocation
	(d) United Nations Regional Centre for Peace and Disarmament in Asia and the Pacific;	
	(e) Regional confidence-building measures: activities of the United Nations Standing Advisory Committee on Security Questions in Central Africa;	
	(f) United Nations Regional Centre for Peace and Disarmament in Africa.	
98.	Review of the implementation of the recommendations and decisions adopted by the General Assembly at its tenth special session:	1st
	(a) Report of the Conference on Disarmament;	
	(b) Report of the Disarmament Commission.	
99.	The risk of nuclear proliferation in the Middle East.	1st
100.	Convention on Prohibitions or Restrictions on the Use of Certain Conventional Weapons Which May Be Deemed to Be Excessively Injurious or to Have Indiscriminate Effects.	1st
101.	Strengthening of security and cooperation in the Mediterranean region.	1st
102.	Comprehensive Nuclear-Test-Ban Treaty.	1st
103.	Convention on the Prohibition of the Development, Production and Stockpiling of Bacteriological (Biological) and Toxin Weapons and on Their Destruction.	1st

H. Drug control, crime prevention and combating international terrorism in all its forms and manifestations

104.	Crime prevention and criminal justice.	3rd
105.	International drug control.	Plenary, 3rd
106.	Measures to eliminate international terrorism.	6th

I. Organizational, administrative and other matters

107.	Report of the Secretary-General on the work of the Organization.	Plenary
108.	Report of the Secretary-General on the Peacebuilding Fund.	Plenary
109.	Notification by the Secretary-General under Article 12, paragraph 2, of the Charter of the United Nations.	Plenary
110.	Elections to fill vacancies in principal organs:	Plenary
	(a) Election of five non-permanent members of the Security Council;	
	(b) Election of eighteen members of the Economic and Social Council.	
111.	Elections to fill vacancies in subsidiary organs and other elections:	Plenary
	(a) Election of seven members of the Committee for Programme and Coordination;	
	(b) Election of the United Nations High Commissioner for Refugees;	
	(c) Election of thirty members of the United Nations Commission on International Trade Law;	
	(d) Election of the Executive Director of the United Nations Environment Programme;	
	(e) Election of twenty-nine members of the Governing Council of the United Nations Environment Programme;	
	(f) Election of the Executive Director of the United Nations Human Settlements Programme;	
	(g) Election of two members of the Organizational Committee of the Peacebuilding Commission;	
	(h) Election of fourteen members of the Human Rights Council.	
112.	Appointments to fill vacancies in subsidiary organs and other appointments:	Plenary, 5th
	(a) Appointment of members of the Advisory Committee on Administrative and Budgetary Questions;	
	(b) Appointment of members of the Committee on Contributions;	
	(c) Confirmation of the appointment of members of the Investments Committee;	
	(d) Appointment of a member of the Board of Auditors;	
	(e) Appointment of members of the International Civil Service Commission;	
	(i) Appointment of members of the Commission;	
	(ii) Designation of the Vice-Chairman of the Commission;	
	(f) Appointment of members of the Committee on Conferences;	
	(g) Appointment of members of the Joint Inspection Unit;	
	(h) Appointment of members of the Consultative Committee of the United Nations Development Fund for Women;	
	(i) Appointment of the Under-Secretary-General for Internal Oversight Services;	
	(j) Appointment of three ad litem judges of the United Nations Dispute Tribunal.	
113.	Admission of new Members to the United Nations.	Plenary
114.	Follow-up to the outcome of the Millennium Summit.	Plenary
115.	The United Nations Global Counter-Terrorism Strategy.	Plenary
116.	Follow-up to the commemoration of the two-hundredth anniversary of the abolition of the transatlantic slave trade.	Plenary
117.	Implementation of the resolutions of the United Nations.	Plenary
118.	Revitalization of the work of the General Assembly.	Plenary, 1st, 4th, 2nd, 3rd, 5th, 6th
119.	Question of equitable representation on and increase in the membership of the Security Council and related matters.	Plenary

Item No.	*Title*	*Allocation*
120.	Strengthening of the United Nations system.	Plenary
121.	United Nations reform: measures and proposals.	Plenary
122.	Follow-up to the recommendations on administrative management and internal oversight of the Independent Inquiry Committee into the United Nations Oil-for-Food Programme.	Plenary
123.	Global health and foreign policy.	Plenary
124.	Cooperation between the United Nations and the Shanghai Cooperation Organization.	Plenary
125.	Cooperation between the United Nations and the Collective Security Treaty Organization.	Plenary
126.	Sixty-fifth anniversary of the end of the Second World War.	Plenary
127.	International Criminal Tribunal for the Prosecution of Persons Responsible for Genocide and Other Serious Violations of International Humanitarian Law Committed in the Territory of Rwanda and Rwandan Citizens Responsible for Genocide and Other Such Violations Committed in the Territory of Neighbouring States between 1 January and 31 December 1994.	Plenary
128.	International Tribunal for the Prosecution of Persons Responsible for Serious Violations of International Humanitarian Law Committed in the Territory of the Former Yugoslavia since 1991.	Plenary
129.	Financial reports and audited financial statements, and reports of the Board of Auditors: (a) United Nations peacekeeping operations; (b) Voluntary funds administered by the United Nations High Commissioner for Refugees; (c) Capital master plan.	5th
130.	Review of the efficiency of the administrative and financial functioning of the United Nations.	5th
131.	Programme budget for the biennium 2008–2009.	5th
132.	Proposed programme budget for the biennium 2010–2011.	5th
133.	Programme planning.	Plenary, 1st, 4th, 2nd, 3rd, 5th, 6th
134.	Improving the financial situation of the United Nations.	5th
135.	Pattern of conferences.	5th
136.	Scale of assessments for the apportionment of the expenses of the United Nations.	5th
137.	Human resources management.	5th
138.	Joint Inspection Unit.	5th
139.	United Nations common system.	5th
140.	Report on the activities of the Office of Internal Oversight Services.	5th
141.	Review of the implementation of General Assembly resolutions 48/218 B, 54/244 and 59/272.	5th
142.	Administration of justice at the United Nations.	5th, 6th
143.	Financing of the International Criminal Tribunal for the Prosecution of Persons Responsible for Genocide and Other Serious Violations of International Humanitarian Law Committed in the Territory of Rwanda and Rwandan Citizens Responsible for Genocide and Other Such Violations Committed in the Territory of Neighbouring States between 1 January and 31 December 1994.	5th
144.	Financing of the International Tribunal for the Prosecution of Persons Responsible for Serious Violations of International Humanitarian Law Committed in the Territory of the Former Yugoslavia since 1991.	5th
145.	Scale of assessments for the apportionment of the expenses of United Nations peacekeeping operations.	5th
146.	Administrative and budgetary aspects of the financing of the United Nations peacekeeping operations.	5th
147.	Financing of the United Nations Operation in Burundi.	5th
148.	Financing of the United Nations Operation in Côte d'Ivoire.	5th
149.	Financing of the United Nations Peacekeeping Force in Cyprus.	5th
150.	Financing of the United Nations Organization Mission in the Democratic Republic of the Congo.	5th
151.	Financing of the United Nations Mission in East Timor.	5th
152.	Financing of the United Nations Integrated Mission in Timor-Leste.	5th
153.	Financing of the United Nations Mission in Ethiopia and Eritrea.	5th
154.	Financing of the United Nations Observer Mission in Georgia.	5th
155.	Financing of the United Nations Stabilization Mission in Haiti.	5th
156.	Financing of the United Nations Interim Administration Mission in Kosovo.	5th
157.	Financing of the United Nations Mission in Liberia.	5th
158.	Financing of the United Nations peacekeeping forces in the Middle East: (a) United Nations Disengagement Observer Force; (b) United Nations Interim Force in Lebanon.	5th
159.	Financing of the United Nations Mission in the Sudan.	5th
160.	Financing of the United Nations Mission for the Referendum in Western Sahara.	5th
161.	Financing of the African Union-United Nations Hybrid Operation in Darfur.	5th
162.	Financing of the United Nations Mission in the Central African Republic and Chad.	5th
163.	Financing of the activities arising from Security Council resolution 1863(2009).	5th
164.	Report of the Committee on Relations with the Host Country.	6th
165.	Observer status for the International Humanitarian Fact-Finding Commission in the General Assembly.	6th
166.	Observer status for the Global Fund to Fight AIDS, Tuberculosis and Malaria in the General Assembly.	6th

Item No.	Title	Allocation
167.	Observer status for the International Olympic Committee in the General Assembly.	6th
168.	Observer status for the International Conference on the Great Lakes Region of Africa in the General Assembly.	6th
169.	Observer status for the Parliamentary Assembly of the Mediterranean in the General Assembly.	6th
171.	Observer status in the General Assembly for the Council of Presidents of the General Assembly.	6th

Security Council

Questions considered during 2009

Title

The situation in the Middle East, including the Palestinian question.

The situation in the Middle East.

The situation in Cyprus.

The situation concerning Western Sahara.

The situation in Timor-Leste.

United Nations peacekeeping operations.

The situation in Liberia.

The situation in Somalia.

The situation in Bosnia and Herzegovina.

Security Council resolutions 1160(1998), 1199(1998), 1203(1998), 1239(1999) and 1244(1999).

International Tribunal for the Prosecution of Persons Responsible for Serious Violations of International Humanitarian Law Committed in the Territory of the Former Yugoslavia since 1991.

International Criminal Tribunal for the Prosecution of Persons Responsible for Genocide and Other Serious Violations of International Humanitarian Law Committed in the Territory of Rwanda and Rwandan Citizens Responsible for Genocide and Other Such Violations Committed in the Territory of Neighbouring States between 1 January 1994 and 31 December 1994.

The situation in Georgia.

The question concerning Haiti.

The situation in Burundi.

The situation in Afghanistan.

The situation in Sierra Leone.

The situation in the Great Lakes region.

The situation concerning the Democratic Republic of the Congo.

The situation in the Central African Republic.

Children and armed conflict.

The situation in Guinea-Bissau.

Protection of civilians in armed conflict.

Women and peace and security.

Briefing by the President of the International Court of Justice.

Briefing by the United Nations High Commissioner for Refugees.

Briefing by the Chairperson-in-Office of the Organization for Security and Cooperation in Europe.

Meeting of the Security Council with the troop-contributing countries [UNFICYP, UNDOF, UNIFIL, MINURSO, UNOMIG, MONUC, UNMIL, UNOCI, MINUSTAH, UNMIS, UNMIT, UNAMID, MINURCAT].

Threats to international peace and security caused by terrorist acts.

Briefings by Chairmen of subsidiary bodies of the Security Council.

The situation in Côte d'Ivoire.

Security Council mission.

Non-proliferation of weapons of mass destruction.

The promotion and strengthening of the rule of law in the maintenance of international peace and security.

Central African region.

Reports of the Secretary-General on the Sudan.

Post-conflict peacebuilding.

The situation concerning Iraq.

Non-proliferation.

The situation in Chad and the Sudan.

Peace consolidation in West Africa: United Nations Office for West Africa and Guinea.

The situation in Myanmar.

Non-proliferation/Democratic People's Republic of Korea.

Letter dated 22 November 2006 from the Secretary-General addressed to the President of the Security Council.

Title

Maintenance of international peace and security, including mediation and settlement of disputes; strengthening collective security through general regulation and reduction of armaments; respect for international humanitarian law; nuclear non-proliferation and nuclear disarmament; intercultural dialogue for peace and security; and optimizing the use of preventive diplomacy tools: prospects and challenges in Africa.

The situation in Chad, the Central African Republic and the subregion.

Peace and security in Africa, [general issues, as well as Djibouti and Eritrea, Zimbabwe, Mauritania, and drug trafficking as a threat to international security].

Cooperation between the United Nations and regional and subregional organizations in maintaining international peace and security.

Implementation of the note by the President of the Security Council.

Other matters considered during 2009

Items relating to Security Council documentation and working methods and procedure.

Annual report of the Security Council to the General Assembly.

International Court of Justice [election of members].

Economic and Social Council

Agenda of the organizational and resumed organizational session for 2009
(15 January, 10 February, 26 March, 20 April and 18 May)

Item No.   *Title*

1.   Election of the Bureau.

2.   Adoption of the agenda and other organizational matters.

3.   Basic programme of work of the Council.

4.   Elections, nominations, confirmations and appointments.

Agenda of the substantive and resumed substantive sessions of 2009
(6–31 July, 8 October and 15 December)

Item No.   *Title*

1.   Adoption of the agenda and other organizational matters.

High-level segment

2.   High-level segment:
     (a) High-level policy dialogue with international financial and trade institutions;
     (b) Annual ministerial review: Implementing the internationally agreed goals and commitments in regard to global public health;
     (c) Thematic discussion: Current global and national trends and their impact on social development, including public health.

Operational activities segment

3.   Operational activities of the United Nations for international development cooperation:
     (a) Follow-up to policy recommendations of the General Assembly and the Council;
     (b) Reports of the Executive Boards of the United Nations Development Programme/United Nations Population Fund, the United Nations Children's Fund and the World Food Programme;
     (c) South-South cooperation for development.

Coordination segment

4.   The role of the United Nations system in implementing the ministerial declaration of the high-level segment of the substantive session of 2008 of the Council.

Humanitarian affairs segment

5.   Special economic, humanitarian and disaster relief assistance.

General segment

6.   Implementation of and follow-up to major United Nations conferences and summits:
     (a) Follow-up to the International Conference on Financing for Development;
     (b) Review and coordination of the implementation of the Programme of Action for the Least Developed Countries for the Decade 2001–2010.

Item No.   *Title*

7. Coordination, programme and other questions:
    - (a) Reports of coordination bodies;
    - (b) Proposed programme budget for the biennium 2010–2011;
    - (c) International cooperation in the field of informatics;
    - (d) Long-term programme of support for Haiti;
    - (e) Mainstreaming a gender perspective into all policies and programmes in the United Nations system;
    - (f) African countries emerging from conflict;
    - (g) Joint United Nations Programme on HIV/AIDS (UNAIDS);
    - (h) Calendar of conferences and meetings in the economic, social and related fields.
8. Implementation of General Assembly resolutions 50/227, 52/12 B, 57/270 B and 60/265.
9. Implementation of the Declaration on the Granting of Independence to Colonial Countries and Peoples by the specialized agencies and the international institutions associated with the United Nations.
10. Regional cooperation.
11. Economic and social repercussions of the Israeli occupation on the living conditions of the Palestinian people in the Occupied Palestinian Territory, including East Jerusalem, and the Arab population in the occupied Syrian Golan.
12. Non-governmental organizations.
13. Economic and environmental questions:
    - (a) Sustainable development:
        - (i) Rehabilitation of the marshes in the southern regions of Iraq;
    - (b) Science and technology for development;
    - (c) Statistics;
    - (d) Human settlements;
    - (e) Environment;
    - (f) Population and development;
    - (g) Public administration and development;
    - (h) International cooperation in tax matters;
    - (i) United Nations Forum on Forests;
    - (j) Assistance to third States affected by the application of sanctions;
    - (k) Cartography;
    - (l) Women and development;
    - (m) Transport of dangerous goods.
14. Social and human rights questions:
    - (a) Advancement of women;
    - (b) Social development;
    - (c) Crime prevention and criminal justice;
    - (d) Narcotic drugs;
    - (e) United Nations High Commissioner for Refugees;
    - (f) Comprehensive implementation of the Durban Declaration and Programme of Action;
    - (g) Human rights;
    - (h) Permanent Forum on Indigenous Issues.
15. United Nations research and training institutes.

NOTE

[1] Item added at the resumed session.

United Nations information centres and services

(as at December 2012)

ACCRA. United Nations Information
Centre
Gamal Abdel Nasser/Liberia Roads
(P.O. Box GP 2339)
Accra, Ghana
Serving: Ghana, Sierra Leone

ALGIERS. United Nations Information
Centre
41 Rue Mohamed Khoudi, El Biar
El Biar, 16030 El Biar, Alger
(Boite postale 444, Hydra-Alger)
Algiers, Algeria
Serving: Algeria

ANKARA. United Nations Information
Centre
Birlik Mahallesi, 415. Cadde No. 11
06610 Cankaya
Ankara, Turkey
Serving: Turkey

ANTANANARIVO. United Nations
Information Centre
22 Rue Rainitovo, Antasahavola
(Boite postale 1348)
Antananarivo, Madagascar
Serving: Madagascar

ASUNCION. United Nations Information
Centre
Avda. Mariscal Lopez esq.
Guillermo Saravi
Edificio Naciones Unidas
(Casilla de Correo 1107)
Asuncion, Paraguay
Serving: Paraguay

BANGKOK. United Nations Information
Service, Economic and Social Commission
for Asia and the Pacific
United Nations Building
Rajdamnern Nok Avenue
Bangkok 10200, Thailand
Serving: Cambodia, Lao People's
Democratic Republic, Malaysia,
Singapore, Thailand, Viet Nam,
ESCAP

BEIRUT. United Nations Information
Centre/United Nations Information
Service, Economic and Social Commission
for Western Asia
ESCWA UN House, Riad El-Solh Square
(P.O. Box 11-8575-4656)
Beirut, Lebanon
Serving: Jordan, Kuwait, Lebanon,
Syrian Arab Republic, ESCWA

BOGOTA. United Nations Information
Centre
Calle 100 No. 8A-55, Piso 10
Edificio World Trade Center—Torre "C"
(Apartado Aereo 058964)
Bogota 2, Colombia
Serving: Colombia, Ecuador, Venezuela

BRAZZAVILLE. United Nations Information
Centre
Avenue Foch, Case ortf 15
(Boite postale 13210)
Brazzaville, Congo
Serving: Congo

BRUSSELS. Regional United Nations
Information Centre
Residence Palace
Rue de la Loi/Wetstraat 155
Quartier Rubens, Block C2
1040 Brussels, Belgium
Serving: Andorra, Belgium, Cyprus,
Denmark, Finland, France,
Germany, Greece, Holy See,
Iceland, Ireland, Italy,
Luxembourg, Malta, Monaco,
Netherlands, Norway,
Portugal, San Marino, Spain,
Sweden, United Kingdom,
European Union

BUENOS AIRES. United Nations Information
Centre
Junin 1940, 1er piso
1113 Buenos Aires, Argentina
Serving: Argentina, Uruguay

BUJUMBURA. United Nations Information
Centre
117 Avenue de la Revolution
(Boite postale 2160)
Bujumbura, Burundi
Serving: Burundi

CAIRO. United Nations Information
Centre
1 Osiris Street, Garden City
(P.O. Box 262)
Cairo, Egypt
Serving: Egypt, Saudi Arabia

CANBERRA. United Nations Information Centre
Level 1 Barton,
7 National Circuit
(P.O. Box 5366, Kingston, ACT 2604)
Canberra ACT 2600, Australia
Serving: Australia, Fiji, Kiribati, Nauru,
New Zealand, Samoa, Tonga,
Tuvalu, Vanuatu

COLOMBO. United Nations Information
Centre
202/204 Bauddhaloka Mawatha
(P.O. Box 1505, Colombo)
Colombo 7, Sri Lanka
Serving: Sri Lanka

DAKAR. United Nations Information
Centre
Immeuble Soumex—3ème Etage,
Mamelles-Almadies
(Boite postale 154)
Dakar, Senegal
Serving: Cape Verde, Côte d'Ivoire, Gambia,
Guinea-Bissau, Mauritania,
Senegal

DAR ES SALAAM. United Nations
Information Centre
Kings Way/Mafinga Street
Plot 134-140, Kinondoni
(P.O. Box 9224)
Dar es Salaam, United Republic of Tanzania
Serving: United Republic of Tanzania

DHAKA. United Nations Information
Centre
IDB Bhaban (8th floor)
Sher-e-Banglanagar
(G.P.O. Box 3658, Dhaka-1000)
Dhaka-1207, Bangladesh
Serving: Bangladesh

GENEVA. United Nations Information
Service
United Nations Office at Geneva
Palais des Nations
1211 Geneva 10, Switzerland
Serving: Switzerland

HARARE. United Nations Information
Centre
Sanders House (2nd floor)
Cnr. First Street/Jason Moyo Avenue
(P.O. Box 4408)
Harare, Zimbabwe
Serving: Zimbabwe

ISLAMABAD. United Nations Information
Centre
Level 2, Serena Business Complex
Sector G-5/1
Khayaban-e-Suhrawardy
(P.O. Box 1107)
Islamabad, Pakistan
Serving: Pakistan

JAKARTA. United Nations Information Centre
Menara Thamrin Building (floor 3A)
Jalan MH Thamrin, Kav. 3
Jakarta 10250, Indonesia

Serving: Indonesia

KATHMANDU. United Nations Information Centre
Harihar Bhavan Pulchowk
(P.O. Box 107, UN House)
Kathmandu, Nepal

Serving: Nepal

KHARTOUM. United Nations Information Centre
United Nations Compound House #7, Blk 5
Gamma'a Avenue
(P.O. Box 1992)
Khartoum, Sudan

Serving: Somalia, Sudan

LAGOS. United Nations Information Centre
17 Alfred Rewane (ex Kingsway) Road, Ikoyi
(P.O. Box 1068)
Lagos, Nigeria

Serving: Nigeria

LA PAZ. United Nations Information Centre
Calle 14 esq. S. Bustamante
Edificio Metrobol II, Calacoto
(Apartado Postal 9072)
La Paz, Bolivia

Serving: Bolivia

LIMA. United Nations Information Centre
Lord Cochrane 130
San Isidro (L-27)
(P.O. Box 14-0199)
Lima, Peru

Serving: Peru

LOME. United Nations Information Centre
468, Angle rue Atime
Avenue de la Liberation
(Boite postale 911)
Lome, Togo

Serving: Benin, Togo

LUSAKA. United Nations Information Centre
Revenue House (Ground floor)
Cnr. Great North and Kalambo Roads
(P.O. Box 32905, Lusaka 10101)
Lusaka, Zambia

Serving: Botswana, Malawi, Swaziland, Zambia

MANAMA. United Nations Information Centre
United Nations House
Bldg. 69, Road 1901, Block 319
(P.O. Box 26004, Manama)
Manama, Bahrain

Serving: Bahrain, Qatar, United Arab Emirates

MANILA. United Nations Information Centre
GC Corporate Plaza
(ex Jaka II Building) (5th floor)
150 Legaspi Street, Legaspi Village
(P.O. Box 7285 ADC (DAPO),
1300 Domestic Road Pasay City)
Makati City, 1229 Metro Manila, Philippines

Serving: Papua New Guinea, Philippines, Solomon Islands

MASERU. United Nations Information Centre
United Nations Road
UN House
(P.O. Box 301, Maseru 100)
Maseru, Lesotho

Serving: Lesotho

MEXICO CITY. United Nations Information Centre
Montes Urales 440 (3rd floor)
Colonia Lomas de Chapultepec
Mexico City, D.F. 11000, Mexico

Serving: Cuba, Dominican Republic, Mexico

MOSCOW. United Nations Information Centre
4/16 Glazovsky Pereulok
Moscow 119002,
Russian Federation

Serving: Russian Federation

NAIROBI. United Nations Information Centre
United Nations Office, Gigiri
(P.O. Box 67578-00200)
Nairobi, Kenya

Serving: Kenya, Seychelles, Uganda

NEW DELHI. United Nations Information Centre
55 Lodi Estate
New Delhi 110 003, India

Serving: Bhutan, India

OUAGADOUGOU. United Nations Information Centre
14 Avenue de la Grande Chancellerie
Secteur no. 4
(Boite postale 135 Ouagadougou 01)
Ouagadougou, Burkina Faso

Serving: Burkina Faso, Chad, Mali, Niger

PANAMA CITY. United Nations Information Centre
UN House Bldg 128 (1st floor)
Ciudad del Saber, Clayton
(P.O. Box 0819-01082)
Panama City, Panama

Serving: Panama

PORT OF SPAIN. United Nations Information Centre
Bretton Hall (2nd floor)
16 Victoria Avenue
(P.O. Box 130)
Port of Spain, Trinidad and Tobago, W.I.

Serving: Antigua and Barbuda, Aruba, Bahamas, Barbados, Belize, Dominica, Grenada, Guyana, Jamaica, Netherlands Antilles, Saint Kitts and Nevis, Saint Lucia, Saint Vincent and the Grenadines, Suriname, Trinidad and Tobago

PRAGUE. United Nations Information Centre
nam. Kinskych 6
15000 Prague 5,
Czech Republic

Serving: Czech Republic

PRETORIA. United Nations Information Centre
Metro Park Building
351 Schoeman Street
(P.O. Box 12677), Tramshed
Pretoria, South Africa 0126

Serving: South Africa

RABAT. United Nations Information Centre
6 Angle Avenue Tarik Ibn Ziyad et rue Roudana
(Boite postale 601, Casier ONU, Rabat-Chellah)
Rabat, Morocco

Serving: Morocco

RIO DE JANEIRO. United Nations Information Centre
Palacio Itamaraty
Av. Marechal Floriano 196
20080-002 Rio de Janeiro RJ, Brazil

Serving: Brazil

SANA'A. United Nations Information Centre
Street 5, Off Albawnya Area
Handhel Zone, beside Handhal Mosque
(P.O. Box 237)
Sana'a, Yemen

Serving: Yemen

SANTIAGO. United Nations Information Service,
Economic Commission for Latin America and the Caribbean
Edificio Naciones Unidas
Avenida Dag Hammarskjold 3477
Vitacura (Casilla 179-D)
Santiago, Chile

Serving: Chile, ECLAC

TEHRAN. United Nations Information Centre
No. 8, Shahrzad Blvd. Darrous
(P.O. Box 15875-4557, Tehran)
Tehran, Iran

Serving: Iran

TOKYO. United Nations Information Centre
UNU Building (8th floor)
53-70 Jingumae 5-Chome, Shibuya-Ku
Tokyo 150-0001, Japan

Serving: Japan

TRIPOLI. United Nations Information Centre
Khair Aldeen Baybers Street
Hay El-Andalous
(P.O. Box 286, Hay El-Andalous)
Tripoli, Libyan Arab Jamahiriya
  Serving: Libyan Arab Jamahiriya

TUNIS. United Nations Information Centre
41 Bis, Av. Louis Braille, Cite El Khadra
(Boite postale 863)
1003 Tunis, Tunisia
  Serving: Tunisia

VIENNA. United Nations Information Service
United Nations Office at Vienna
Vienna International Centre
Wagramer Strasse 5
(P.O. Box 500, A-1400 Vienna)
A-1220 Vienna, Austria
  Serving: Austria, Hungary, Slovakia,
        Slovenia

WARSAW. United Nations Information Centre
Al. Niepodleglosci 186
(UN Centre P.O. Box 1, 02-514 Warsaw 12)
00-608 Warszawa, Poland
  Serving: Poland

WASHINGTON, D.C. United Nations Information Centre
1775 K Street, N.W., Suite 400
Washington, D.C. 20006
United States
  Serving: United States

WINDHOEK. United Nations Information Centre
United Nations House
38–44 Stein Street, Klein
(Private Bag 13351)
Windhoek, Namibia
  Serving: Namibia

YANGON. United Nations Information Centre
6 Natmauk Road,
Tamwe Township
(P.O. Box 230)
Yangon, Myanmar
  Serving: Myanmar

YAOUNDE. United Nations Information Centre
Immeuble Tchinda,
Rue 2044,
Derriere camp SIC TSINGA
(Boite postale 836)
Yaounde, Cameroon
  Serving: Cameroon, Central African
        Republic, Gabon

NOTE: For the most current information on UNICS, please visit the website: **unic.un.org**.

Intergovernmental organizations related to the United Nations

International Atomic Energy Agency (IAEA)
Vienna International Centre
Wagramer Strasse, 5
P.O. Box 100
1400 Vienna, Austria
  Telephone: (431) 2600-0
  Fax: (431) 2600-7
  E-mail: official.mail@iaea.org
  Internet: www.iaea.org
Director General: Yukiya Amano (Japan)

IAEA Office at the United Nations
1 United Nations Plaza, Room 1155
New York, NY 10017, U.S.A.
  Telephone: (1) (212) 963-6010/6011
  Fax: (1) (917) 367-4046
  E-mail: iaeany@un.org

International Labour Organization (ILO)
4 route des Morillons
CH-1211 Geneva 22, Switzerland
  Telephone: (41) (22) 799-6111
  Fax: (41) (22) 798-8685
  E-mail: ilo@ilo.org
  Internet: www.ilo.org
Director General: Juan Somavia (Chile)

ILO Office at the United Nations
220 East 42nd Street, Suite 3101
New York, NY 10017, U.S.A.
  Telephone: (1) (212) 697-0150
  Fax: (1) (212) 697-5218
  E-mail: newyork@ilo.org

Food and Agriculture Organization of the United Nations (FAO)
Viale delle Terme di Caracalla
00153 Rome, Italy
  Telephone: (39) (06) 57051
  Fax: (39) (06) 570 53152
  E-mail: fao-hq@fao.org
  Internet: www.fao.org
Director General: Jacques Diouf (Senegal)

FAO Office at the United Nations
1 United Nations Plaza, Room 1125
New York, NY 10017, U.S.A.
  Telephone: (1) (212) 963-6036
  Fax: (1) (212) 963-5425
  E-mail: FAO-LON@fao.org

United Nations Educational, Scientific and Cultural Organization (UNESCO)
UNESCO House
7 place de Fontenoy
75352 Paris 07-SP, France
  Telephone: (33) (1) 45-68-10-00
  Fax: (33) (1) 45-67-16-90
  E-mail: info@unesco.org
  Internet: www.unesco.org
Director General: Irina Bokova (Bulgaria)

UNESCO Office at the United Nations
2 United Nations Plaza, Room 900
New York, NY 10017, U.S.A.
  Telephone: (1) (212) 963-5995
  Fax: (1) (212) 963-8014
  E-mail: newyork@unesco.org

World Health Organization (WHO)
Avenue Appia, 20
1211 Geneva 27, Switzerland
  Telephone: (41) (22) 791-2111
  Fax: (41) (22) 791-3111
  E-mail: info@who.int
  Internet: www.who.int
Director General: Dr. Margaret Chan (China)

WHO Office at the United Nations
1 Dag Hammarskjold Plaza,
885 Second Avenue, 26th floor
New York, NY 10017, U.S.A.
  Telephone: (1) (646) 626-6060
  Fax: (1) (646) 626-6080
  E-mail: wun@whoun.org

World Bank Group (IBRD, IDA, IFC, MIGA and ICSID)
1818 H Street, NW
Washington, D.C. 20433, U.S.A.
  Telephone: (1) (202) 473-1000
  Fax: (1) (202) 477-6391
  Internet: www.worldbank.org
President: Robert B. Zoellick (United States)

The World Bank Mission to the United Nations
1 Dag Hammarskjold Plaza
885 Second Avenue, 26th floor
New York, NY 10017, U.S.A.
  Telephone: (1) (212) 355-5112
  Fax: (1) (212) 355-4523

International Monetary Fund (IMF)
700 19th Street, NW
Washington, D.C. 20431, U.S.A.
  Telephone: (1) (202) 623-7000
  Fax: (1) (202) 623-4661
  E-mail: publicaffairs@imf.org
  Internet: www.imf.org
Managing Director: Dominique Strauss-Kahn (France)

IMF Office at the United Nations
1 Dag Hammarskjold Plaza
885 Second Avenue, 26th floor
  New York, NY 10017, U.S.A.
  Telephone: (1) (212) 317-4720
  Fax: (1) (212) 317-4733

International Civil Aviation Organization (ICAO)
999 University Street
Montreal, Quebec H3C 5H7, Canada
  Telephone: (1) (514) 954-8219
  Fax: (1) (514) 954-6077
  E-mail: icaohq@icao.int
  Internet: www.icao.int
Secretary-General: Raymond Benjamin (France)

Universal Postal Union (UPU)
Weltpost Strasse, 4
Case Postale 3000
3000 Berne 15, Switzerland
  Telephone: (41) (31) 350-3111
  Fax: (41) (31) 350-3110
  E-mail: info@upu.int
  Internet: www.upu.int
Director General: Edouard Dayan (France)

International Telecommunication Union (ITU)
Place des Nations
1211, Geneva 20, Switzerland
  Telephone: (41) (22) 730-5111
  Fax: (41) (22) 733-7256
  E-mail: itumail@itu.int
  Internet: www.itu.int
Secretary-General: Hamadoun Toure (Mali)

World Meteorological Organization (WMO)
7 bis, avenue de la Paix
Case postale 2300
CH-1211 Geneva 2, Switzerland
Telephone: (41) (22) 730-8111
Fax: (41) (22) 730-8181
E-mail: wmo@wmo.int
Internet: www.wmo.int
President: Alexander Bedritsky (Russia)
Secretary-General: Michel Jarraud (France)

WMO
Office at the United Nations
866 United Nations Plaza, Room A-302
New York, NY 10017, U.S.A.
Telephone: (1) (917) 367-9867
Fax: (1) (917) 367-9868
E-mail: zbatjargal@wmo.int

International Maritime Organization (IMO)
4, Albert Embankment
London SE1 7SR
United Kingdom
Telephone: (44) (207) 735-7611
Fax: (44) (207) 587-3210
E-mail: info@imo.org
Internet: www.imo.org
Director General: Efthimios E. Mitropoulos (Greece)

World Intellectual Property Organization (WIPO)
34, chemin des Colombettes
P.O. Box 18
CH-1211 Geneva 20, Switzerland
Telephone: (41) (22) 338-9111
Fax: (41) (22) 733-5428
E-mail: wipo.mail@wipo.int
Internet: www.wipo.int
Director General: Francis Gurry (Australia)

WIPO Office at the United Nations
2 United Nations Plaza, Room 2525
New York, NY 10017, U.S.A.
Telephone: (1) (212) 963-6813
Fax: (1) (212) 963-4801
E-mail: wipo@un.org

International Fund for Agricultural Development (IFAD)
Via Paolo di Dono, 44
00142 Rome, Italy
Telephone: (39) (06) 54591
Fax: (39) (06) 504-3463
E-mail: ifad@ifad.org
Internet: www.ifad.org
President: Kanayo F. Nwanze (Nigeria)

IFAD Office at the United Nations
2 United Nations Plaza, Rooms 1128-29
New York, NY 10017, U.S.A.
Telephone: (1) (212) 963-0546
Fax: (1) (212) 963-2787
E-mail: ifad@un.org

United Nations Industrial Development Organization (UNIDO)
Vienna International Centre
Wagramer Strasse, 5
P.O. Box 300
A-1400 Vienna
Austria
Telephone: (43) (1) 26026-0
Fax: (43) (1) 269-2669
E-mail: unido@unido.org
Internet: www.unido.org
Director General: Kandeh K. Yumkella (Sierra Leone)

UNIDO Office at Geneva
Palais des Nations
Le Bocage, Pavillion 1
Rooms 77-82
Avenue de la Paix 8-14
CH-1211 Geneva 10
Switzerland
Telephone: (41) (22) 917-1423
Fax: (41) (22) 917-0059
E-mail: office.geneva@unido.org

UNIDO Office in New York
1 United Nations Plaza, Room 1118
New York, NY 10017, U.S.A.
Telephone: (1) (212) 963-6890/6885
Fax: (1) (212) 963-7904
E-mail: office.newyork@unido.org

World Trade Organization (WTO)
Centre William Rappard
Rue de Lausanne, 154
CH-1211 Geneva 21, Switzerland
Telephone: (41) (22) 739-5111
Fax: (41) (22) 731-4206
E-mail: enquiries@wto.org
Internet: www.wto.org
Director General: Pascal Lamy (France)

World Tourism Organization (UNWTO)
Capitan Haya, 42
28020 Madrid, Spain
Telephone: (34) (91) 567-8100
Fax: (34) (91) 571-3733
E-mail: omt@unwto.org
Internet: www.unwto.org
Secretary-General: Taleb Rifai (Jordan)
UNWTO maintains a regional support office for Asia and the Pacific in Osaka, Japan.

NOTE: For more information on liaison, regional, subregional and country offices maintained by any of these organizations, please visit their respective websites.

Indices

Subject index

BOLD CAPITAL LETTERS are used for main subject entries (e.g. **DEVELOPMENT**) and chapter topics (e.g. **DISARMAMENT**), as well as country names (e.g. **TIMOR-LESTE**), region names (e.g. **AFRICA**) and principal UN organs (e.g. **GENERAL ASSEMBLY**).

CAPITAL LETTERS are used to highlight major issues (e.g. POVERTY), as well as the names of territories (e.g. MONTSERRAT), subregions (e.g. CENTRAL AMERICA), specialized agencies (e.g. WORLD HEALTH ORGANIZATION) and regional commissions (e.g. ECONOMIC COMMISSION FOR EUROPE).

Regular text is used for single and cross-reference entries (e.g. anti-personnel mines, malaria, terrorism).

An asterisk (*) preceding a page number or range of page numbers indicates the presence of a text, reproduced in full, of a General Assembly, Security Council or Economic and Social Council resolution or decision, or a Security Council presidential statement.

United Nations bodies are listed alphabetically and may also appear under related entries.

A

Abkhazia *see* Georgia
ACABQ *see* Advisory Committee on Administrative and Budgetary Questions
accounts and auditing, UN *1415–1417
administration, UN *see* institutional, administrative and budgetary questions
Advisory Committee on Administrative and Budgetary Questions (ACABQ)
  capital master plan 1442
  conferences 1429
  managerial reform and oversight 1421–1422
  staff matters *1456–1458, *1463–1468, 1472–1473
advisory proceedings
  International Court of Justice (ICJ) 1277

AFGHANISTAN
  Food and Agriculture Organization of the United Nations *339
  HIV/AIDS 763
  human rights 762–763
  political and security questions *334–362
  sanctions *353–362
  situation in Afghanistan *334–353
  terrorism 67

AFRICA
  African Union *103–106, *109–112
  African Union-United Nations Hybrid Operation in Darfur *105
  Burundi *137–145
    human rights 751–752
    Cameroon–Nigeria 226–228
  Central Africa and Great Lakes region *116–166
    Burundi *137–145
    Central African Republic *146–153
    Chad and Central African Republic *153–163
    Democratic Republic of the Congo *118–137
    Great Lakes region *116–118

    Rwanda *165–166
    Uganda *163–165
  Central African Republic *146–153
  Chad and Central African Republic *153–163
  Chad–Sudan *268–270
  Côte d'Ivoire *170–191
  Democratic Republic of the Congo *110, 111, *118–137
    human rights 752–754
  Djibouti and Eritrea *297–302
  economic and social questions *968–974
    economic trends 968
    programme and organizational questions 974
  economic recovery and development *899–904
  economic trends 968
  Eritrea–Ethiopia *302–304
  European Union 969
    Food and Agriculture Organization of the United Nations 970
  Great Lakes region *116–118 *see also* Central Africa and Great Lakes region
  Guinea *228–231
  Guinea-Bissau *215–226
  HIV/AIDS *108, *114, *116, 165, *166, *899–901
  Horn of Africa *232–304
    Chad–Sudan *268–270
    Djibouti and Eritrea *297–302
    Eritrea–Ethiopia *302–304
    Somalia *270–297
    Sudan *232–268
  human rights 751–758
    Burundi 751–752
    Democratic Republic of the Congo 752–754
    Liberia 754–755
    Office for the Coordination of Humanitarian Affairs 752
    Sierra Leone 755–756
    Somalia 756–757
    Sudan 757–758

International Maritime Organization 103
International Year for People of African Descent *655
Liberia *191–206
    human rights 754–755
Madagascar *310–311
Mauritania 232
Mauritius–United Kingdom/France 311
New Partnership for Africa's Development 103, *112
North Africa *304–310
    Western Sahara *304–310
Office for the Coordination of Humanitarian Affairs 752
Office of the Special Adviser on Africa 112
Office of the Special Representative of the Secretary-
    General for West Africa 168–170
Office of the United Nations High Commissioner for
    Human Rights 756
political and security questions *100–311
programme and organizational questions 974
promotion of peace in *103–116
    African Union *103–106, *109–112
    African Union-United Nations Hybrid Operation
        in Darfur *105
    Democratic Republic of the Congo *110, 111
    HIV/AIDS *108, *114
    International Maritime Organization 103
    least developed country *112
    New Partnership for Africa's Development 103, *112
    United Nations Mission in Liberia 111, *112
    United Nations Mission in the Sudan *105
regional issues, West Africa *166–170
Rwanda *165–166
Sierra Leone *206–215
    human rights 755–756
Somalia *270–297
    human rights 756–757
special economic assistance *899–904
Sudan *232–268
    Chad–Sudan *268–270
    human rights 757–758
Uganda *163–165
United Nations Mission in Liberia 111, *112
United Nations Mission in the Sudan *105
United Nations Office on Drugs and Crime *116
West Africa *166–232
    Cameroon–Nigeria 226–228
    Côte d'Ivoire *170–191
    Guinea *228–231
    Guinea-Bissau *215–226
    Liberia *191–206
    Mauritania 232
    regional issues *166–170
    Sierra Leone *206–215
Western Sahara *304–310
World Trade Organization 969
see also African Union; disarmament; Economic
    Commission for Africa; Economic Community of
    West African States; human rights; humanitarian
    assistance; West Africa; *specific country names*
African Union (AU)
    Burundi *137–140
    Central African Republic 148
    Chad–Sudan *269
    Democratic Republic of the Congo 124
    Eritrea–Ethiopia *303
    Great Lakes region 117
    Guinea *228–231
    Guinea-Bissau *218–219, 224
    Haiti *322, *324, 326
    Horn of Africa 297, *299, *302
    human rights 756–758
    humanitarian and special economic assistance *899
    International Criminal Court 1300
    international drug control 1243
    operational activities for development 866
    peacekeeping operations 72, 77, 100
    promotion and maintenance of international peace
        and security *39
    promotion of peace in Africa *103–106, *109–112
    refugees and displaced persons *1207
    regional economic and social activities *968–971,
        973–974
    Somalia *277, *279–281, 283–284, 286, *293
    special economic assistance *900
    Sudan 250–253, *255, 259, 261–262, 265, *268
    UN Environment Programme 1007
    West Africa *167, 169–170, 232
    Western Sahara *310
African Union-United Nations Hybrid Operation
    in Darfur (UNAMID) *79, 82, 102
        human rights 757–758
        political and security questions *155, *235, 243, 246,
            *249–260, 262, *264, *266, *268
        promotion of peace in Africa *105
AGEING PERSONS
    economic and social questions *1188–1190
    Second World Assembly on Ageing (2002), follow-up
        to the *1188–1190
agendas of United Nations principal organs in 2009 1523
AGRICULTURE
    aid *see* humanitarian assistance
    International Maritime Organization 1231
    Joint Inspection Unit 1231
    see also nutrition
AIDS *see* HIV/AIDS
AMERICAN SAMOA *594–595
AMERICAS
    Bolivia, human rights 758–759
    Central America *312–318
        Guatemala *312–314
        Honduras *314–318
    Colombia *329
        human rights 759–760
    cooperation between the UN and regional organiza-
        tions *331
        Cuba–El Salvador *329–330
        Cuba–United States *330–331
        El Salvador–Cuba *329–330
        Guatemala *312–314
            human rights 760
        Haiti *318–329
            human rights 761
            MINUSTAH *326–329
            political and security situation *318–325
            programme of support for Haiti *325–326

Honduras *314–318
    human rights 761–762
human rights 758–762
    Bolivia 758–759
    Colombia 759–760
    Guatemala 760
    Haiti 761
    Honduras 761–762
Office of the United Nations High Commissioner for
    Human Rights 758–763
political and security questions *312–331
    Central America *312–318
    Colombia *329
    cooperation between the UN and regional
        organizations *331
    Cuba–El Salvador *329–330
    Cuba–United States *330–331
    Guatemala *312–314
    Haiti *318–329
        MINUSTAH *326–329
        political and security situation *318–325
        programme of support for Haiti *325–326
    Honduras *314–318
    MINUSTAH *326–329
    United States–Cuba *330–331
    see also Caribbean; Central America; Economic
        Commission for Latin America and the Caribbean;
        specific country names
ANGUILLA *595
anti-personnel mines
    disarmament *553–555
    humanitarian assistance, mine clearance *891–893
ARMENIA
    Organization for Security and Cooperation in Europe
        422
    political and security questions *421–422
arms trade treaty
    disarmament *544–545
    arms embargo *131–135, *184–188, 191, *199–203,
        *262–264, *277, *287–291, *296–302, 353–354, 482,
        484, 529 *see also* sanctions
ASIA AND THE PACIFIC
    Afghanistan
        human rights 762–763
        sanctions *353–362
        situation in Afghanistan *334–353
    Cambodia, human rights 763–764
    Democratic People's Republic of Korea, human rights
        *764–768
    drugs *see* drug abuse and control
    economic and social questions 974–980
        economic trends 975
        programme and organizational questions 980
    economic trends 975
    human rights 762
        Afghanistan 762–763
        Cambodia 763–764
        Democratic People's Republic of Korea *764–768
        Iran *768–771
        Myanmar *771–776
        Nepal 777
        Sri Lanka 777–778

India, Benazir Bhutto assassination inquiry, with
    Pakistan 398–399
International Atomic Energy Agency 333
Iran
    human rights *768–771
    IAEA reports 394–396
Iraq
    International Advisory and Monitoring Board
        *372–375
    situation in Iraq *362
    UN Assistance Mission for Iraq *362–372
Iraq–Kuwait
    Kuwaiti property and missing persons 375–376
    UN Compensation Commission and Fund 376
Myanmar, human rights *771–776
Nepal, human rights 777
Office of the United Nations High Commissioner for
    Human Rights *768, 777–778
Pakistan, Benazir Bhutto assassination inquiry, with
    India 398–399
political and security questions
    Afghanistan *334–362
    Benazir Bhutto assassination inquiry 398–399
    Democratic People's Republic of Korea *383–387
    financing of UN operations, Timor-Leste
        *381–383
    IAEA reports 394–396
    India–Pakistan 398–399
    International Advisory and Monitoring Board,
        Iraq *372–375
    Iran 394–396
    Iraq *362–375
    Iraq–Kuwait 375–376
    Myanmar 396–397
    Nepal *388–393
    the Philippines 399
    Kuwaiti property and missing persons 375–376
    sanctions, Afghanistan *353–362
    situation in Afghanistan *334–353
    situation in Iraq *362
    Sri Lanka 397–398
    Timor-Leste *376–383
    UN Assistance Mission for Iraq *362–372
    UN Compensation Commission and Fund,
        Iraq–Kuwait 376
    UN Integrated Mission in Timor-Leste *377–381
    United Arab Emirates–Iran 399
programme and organizational questions 980
Sri Lanka, human rights 777–778
Timor-Leste
    financing of UN operations *381–383
    United Nations Integrated Mission in Timor-Leste
        *377–381
see also Economic and Social Commission for Asia
    and the Pacific; Economic and Social Commission
    for Western Asia; landlocked developing countries;
    specific country names
assassination
    Benazir Bhutto assassination inquiry 398–399
    Guinea-Bissau 102, 216–218, 224
assessments, UN *1410–1415

assistance
  African economic recovery and development *899–904
  disaster assistance *912–915
  refugees and displaced persons 1204–1206
  special economic assistance *899–907
  see also disasters and disaster response; humanitarian
    assistance
atomic radiation
  effects of *607–609
AU *see* African Union
aviation 75, 169, *1324
  see also International Civil Aviation Organization (ICAO)
AZERBAIJAN
  Organization for Security and Cooperation in Europe
    422
  political and security questions *421–422

B

bacteriological (biological) weapons
  disarmament *540–541
  Food and Agriculture Organization of the United
    Nations *541
BERMUDA *595
BINUB *see* United Nations Integrated Office in Burundi
biological weapons
  disarmament *540–541
  Food and Agriculture Organization of the United
    Nations *541
BOLIVIA
  human rights 758–759
BONUCA *see* United Nations Peacebuilding Support
  Office in the Central African Republic
BOSNIA AND HERZEGOVINA
  Brcko District *404–407
  European Union *400–402, *407–408
  implementation of Peace Agreement *401–404
  International Court of Justice 408
  International Monetary Fund 403
  political and security questions *400–408
    Brcko District *404–407
    European Union missions in Bosnia and Herzego-
      vina *407–408
    implementation of Peace Agreement *401–404
Bretton Woods Institutions *see* International Monetary
  Fund
BRITISH VIRGIN ISLANDS *596
budget, UN *see* institutional, administrative and
  budgetary questions
BURUNDI
  African Union *137–140
  human rights 751–752
  Office of the United Nations High Commissioner for
    Human Rights 751
  political and security questions *137–145
  United Nations Development Programme *138–140

C

CAMBODIA
  human rights 763–764
CAMEROON
  CAMEROON–NIGERIA MIXED COMMISSION 226–228
  International Court of Justice 227

CARIBBEAN *see* Caribbean Community; Economic
  Commission for Latin America and the Caribbean;
  Latin America and the Caribbean; *specific country names*
Caribbean Community (CARICOM)
  Cuba *331
  Haiti 326
  Honduras *315
CARICOM *see* Caribbean Community
CARTOGRAPHY *1000–1001
CAYMAN ISLANDS *596
CDP *see* Committee for Development Policy
CEB *see* United Nations System Chief Executives Board
  for Coordination
CEDAW *see* Committee on the Elimination of Discrimina-
  tion against Women
CENTRAL AFRICA AND GREAT LAKES REGION
  Burundi *137–145
  Central African Republic *146–153
  Chad and Central African Republic *153–163
  Democratic Republic of the Congo *118–137
  Great Lakes region *116–118
  political and security questions *116–166
    Burundi *137–145
    Central African Republic *146–153
    Chad and Central African Republic *153–163
    Democratic Republic of the Congo *118–137
    Great Lakes region *116–118
    Rwanda *165–166
    Uganda *163–165
  Rwanda *165–166
  Uganda *163–165
  United Nations Children's Fund 153
  see also specific country names
Central Africa Standing Advisory Committee
  disarmament *567–568
CENTRAL AFRICAN REPUBLIC
  African Union 148
  Economic Commission for Europe 152
  political and security questions *146–153
  United Nations Development Programme 149, 152
  see also Chad
CENTRAL AMERICA
  Guatemala *312–314
  Honduras *314–318
  political and security questions *312–318
    Guatemala *312–314
    Honduras *314–318
  see also Economic Commission for Latin America and
    the Caribbean; *specific country names*
CHAD
  European Union *157, 159
  political and security questions *153–163
  and Sudan
    African Union *269
    Department of Peacekeeping Operations *269
    political and security questions *268–270
  see also Central African Republic
Charter of the United Nations 1492
CHEMICALS 728, *960–963
chemical weapons
  disarmament *542–543
  European Union *543
  weapons of mass destruction *542–543
  see also disarmament

CHILDREN *1160–1188
  2002 General Assembly Special Session on Children,
    follow-up to *1160–1161
  and armed conflict *131, 144, 153, 164, *184, 246, 291,
    329, 350, 397–399, *736–742
  Commonwealth of Independent States 1176, 1180
  Convention on the Rights of the Child *636–641
  economic and social questions *1160–1188
  Guidelines for Alternative Care of Children *1161–1172
  HIV/AIDS *1160–1162
  Joint Inspection Unit 1183
  Joint United Nations Programme on HIV/AIDS 1178–
    1179
  Millennium Development Goals 1160, 1176, 1183–
    1184
  United Nations Development Programme 1173, 1181,
    1183
  United Nations Human Settlements Programme
    (UN-Habitat) 1183
  World Food Programme 1173, 1183
  World Health Organization 1177
  see also United Nations Children's Fund (UNICEF);
    youth; specific country names
CIS see Commonwealth of Independent States
CIVIL AND POLITICAL RIGHTS see human rights
CLIMATE CHANGE see environment
cluster munitions
  disarmament *553
COLOMBIA
  human rights 759–760
  political and security questions *329
colonies and colonialism see decolonization;
  Non-Self-Governing Territories (NSGTs)
Commission for Social Development see New Partnership
  for Africa's Development (NEPAD)
Commission on Crime Prevention and Criminal Justice
  *1081–1083
  United Nations Office on Drugs and Crime *1081–1084
Commission on Narcotic Drugs 1253–1256
Commission on the Status of Women *1154–1157
  Office of the United Nations High Commissioner for
    Human Rights *1155
commissions see main part of the title
Committee for Development Policy *828–829
Committee on the Elimination of Discrimination against
  Women *1152–1154
Committee for Programme and Coordination (CPC)
  administrative and staff matters 1436
  coordination, monitoring and cooperation 1381
  humanitarian and special economic assistance *899
  special economic assistance *900
  UN budget 1394
  UN financing and programming 1418
committees see main part of the title
commodities, international trade *925–929
  least developed country *927
  United Nations Conference on Trade and Development
    *926, *928
  World Trade Organization *928
Commonwealth of Independent States (CIS) 34
  children 1176, 1180
  Europe, regional economic and social activities 981

Georgia 415
  international drug control 1249–1250
  operational activities for development 873
  regional economic and social activities 984
  UNICEF 1173
Comprehensive Nuclear-Test-Ban Treaty (CTBT) *512–516
  and Treaty on the Non-Proliferation of Nuclear
    Weapons *514–516
conference see specific conferences by main part of title
conference management *1427–1436
  Advisory Committee on Administrative and Budgetary
    Questions *1428–1431
  Office of Internal Oversight Services 1428–1429, 1431
conflict diamonds *39–42
contentious proceedings
  International Court of Justice (ICJ) 1269–1277
contributions, UN *1410–1415
Convention on elimination of discrimination against
  women (CEDAW) *635, *1151–1154
conventional weapons
  anti-personnel mines *553–555
  arms trade treaty, towards an *544–545
  cluster munitions *553
  Convention on Excessively Injurious Conventional
    Weapons and Protocols *550–553
  disarmament *544–559
    anti-personnel mines *553–555
    cluster munitions *553
    practical disarmament *555
    small arms *545–550
    towards an arms trade treaty *544–545
    transparency *555–559
  practical disarmament *555
  small arms *545–550
  transparency *555–559
  see also disarmament
Convention on elimination of discrimination against
  women *635, *1151–1154
  environment *1015–1025
  Excessively Injurious Conventional Weapons and
    Protocols *550–553
  international drug control *1240–1242
  on Migrant Workers *641–642
  on the Rights of the Child *636–641
  UN Convention on the Law of the Sea *1330–1363
  see also human rights
conventions see main part of the title
cooperation
  disaster response, international cooperation *907–908
  economic see development
  HIV/AIDS *1384–1385
  technical see development
  UN, cooperation with other organizations *1383–1384
coordination, monitoring and cooperation
  Committee for Programme and Coordination 1381
  International Committee of the Red Cross *883–884,
    *886–887
  New Partnership for Africa's Development 1381
  Office of the United Nations High Commissioner for
    Refugees *883

United Nations System Chief Executives Board for Coordination 1380

CÔTE D'IVOIRE
Department of Peacekeeping Operations *189
Economic Community of West African States *188
HIV/AIDS 174, *176, *181, 184
International Monetary Fund *175
Office of Internal Oversight Services *188–189
Office of the United Nations High Commissioner for Refugees *176
political and security questions *170–191
United Nations Development Programme *176, *180–181, 184
see also United Nations Operation in Côte d'Ivoire (UNOCI)
Counter-Terrorism Committee 70
covenants *see* human rights
CPC *see* Committee for Programme and Coordination
CRIME PREVENTION AND CRIMINAL JUSTICE *1080–1107
Commission on Crime Prevention and Criminal Justice *1081–1083
crime prevention programme *1083–1091
preparations for Twelfth (2010) United Nations Crime Congress *1080–1081
strategies for crime prevention *1096–1103
United Nations Office on Drugs and Crime *1097, *1099–1100, *1103
transnational organized crime *1091–1096
UN Office on Drugs and Crime *1251–1253
UN standards and norms *1103–1106
United Nations Office on Drugs and Crime *1097, *1099–1100, *1103–1104, 1106, *1107
UNODC *see* United Nations Office on Drugs and Crime
see also international drug control; terrorism
crime prevention programme
United Nations Office on Drugs and Crime *1089–1090
CTBT *see* Comprehensive Nuclear-Test-Ban Treaty (CTBT)
CTC *see* Counter-Terrorism Committee
CUBA
Caribbean Community *331
El Salvador, political and security questions *329–330
HIV/AIDS *331
political and security questions
El Salvador *329–330
United States *330–331
United States, political and security questions *330–331
cultural development *1070–1080
HIV/AIDS *1076–1077
United Nations Educational, Scientific and Cultural Organization *1072, *1077
cultural issues *see* social policy and cultural issues
cultural rights
human rights *724–726
CYPRUS
developments *423–431
European Union *423, 424
HIV/AIDS *426, *428
human rights 778
political and security questions *422–431

D

dangerous goods, transport of *960–962
International Civil Aviation Organization *961
International Maritime Organization *961
Darfur *see* Sudan
Decade for the Eradication of Colonialism *576–58
decolonization *576–599
Decade for the Eradication of Colonialism *576–58
Joint United Nations Programme on HIV/AIDS *585
Non-Self-Governing Territory *576–596
Puerto Rico *588
territories under review *588–599
United Nations Development Programme *579
see also Non-Self-Governing Territories (NSGTs)
democracies and democratic procedure
and human rights *685–689
Office of the United Nations High Commissioner for Human Rights 685
support for democracies *573–575
Non-Self-Governing Territory 573
DEMOCRATIC PEOPLE'S REPUBLIC OF KOREA (DPRK)
disarmament 503, *504, *527, 529–530
human rights 764, *764–768
Office of the United Nations High Commissioner for Human Rights *765
operational activities for development 856
political and security questions *383–387
Treaty on the Non-Proliferation of Nuclear Weapons *384–385
World Food Programme *765
World Health Organization *766
DEMOCRATIC REPUBLIC OF THE CONGO (DRC)
African Union 124
Department of Peacekeeping Operations 119, 125
disarmament *567
European Union 124
human rights *739, *742, 752–754
humanitarian activities 894
International Criminal Court 1300
international tribunals and courts 1288, 1297, *1298
Office of Internal Oversight Services *135
Office of the United Nations High Commissioner for Human Rights 753
peacekeeping operations 100
political and security questions *116–137, *163–165
promotion of peace in Africa *110, 111
refugees and displaced persons *1204–1207, *1210, 1211
regional economic and social activities 968
United Nations Children's Fund 131
United Nations Development Programme 125, 131
vulnerable groups *739, *742
women *1137
see also United Nations Organization Mission in the Democratic Republic of the Congo (MONUC)
demographic and social statistics 1261–1262
Department of Peacekeeping Operations (DPKO) 45, 71–72, *74–77
administrative and staff matters *1470, 1471
Chad–Sudan *269
Côte d'Ivoire *189
Democratic Republic of the Congo 119, 125

financial and administrative aspects *93–95, 98–99
Liberia 192
promotion and maintenance of international peace and security *38
Somalia *274, 281, 284
Sudan 259, 265
women 1130, *1137
DEVELOPING COUNTRIES
development, cooperation *873–880
LDCs *see* least developed countries
see also landlocked developing countries; least developed countries (LDCs); small island developing States
DEVELOPMENT
African Union 866
Committee for Development Policy *828–829
Commonwealth of Independent States 873
cooperation, economic
among developing countries *873–880
international economic *792–799
Democratic People's Republic of Korea 856
developing countries, cooperation among *873–880
Development Account 867–868
Economic and Social Commission for Western Asia 792
eradication of poverty *808–813
Executive Board, UNDP/UNFPA 854–856
financial and administrative matters, technical cooperation 862–867
Food and Agriculture Organization of the United Nations 854
groups of countries in special situations *831–843
HIV/AIDS 854
human rights, right to development *703–716
International Civil Service Commission 846
international economic relations *792–828
international financing for development *939–958
International Fund for Agricultural Development 854
international migration and 1047–1048
Joint Inspection Unit 844, *851–852, 862
Joint United Nations Programme on HIV/AIDS 854
landlocked developing countries *840–843
least developed countries *791–793, 828, *829, *831–838
least developed country 869, 881
Millennium Development Goals 856–858, 868
New Partnership for Africa's Development *831
Office of Internal Oversight Services *831
official development assistance *847
operational activities for *844–881
African Union 866
Commonwealth of Independent States 873
cooperation among developing countries *873–880
Democratic People's Republic of Korea 856
developing countries, cooperation among *873–880
Development Account 867–868
economic and technical cooperation among developing countries *873–880
economic cooperation among developing countries *873–880
Executive Board, UNDP/UNFPA 854–856
financial and administrative matters, technical cooperation 862–867

Food and Agriculture Organization of the United Nations 854
HIV/AIDS 854
International Civil Service Commission 846
International Fund for Agricultural Development 854
Joint Inspection Unit 844, *851–852, 862
Joint United Nations Programme on HIV/AIDS 854
Millennium Development Goals 856–858, 868
official development assistance *847
Organisation for Economic Co-operation and Development *847, 863
system-wide activities *844–854
technical cooperation *854–881
UN activities 868
UN Capital Development Fund *880–881
UN Office for Partnerships 868–869
UN Office for Project Services 869–873
UN Volunteers 873
UNDP 854–867
UNDP/UNFPA Executive Board 854–856
United Nations Children's Fund 854–855, 863–864
United Nations Conference on Trade and Development 854
United Nations Development Programme 844–846, 854–872, *880, 881
United Nations Environment Programme 854–855
United Nations Industrial Development Organization 854
United Nations Office for Project Services 844, 855, 865–866
United Nations Population Fund 844, 854–857, 863–866, 869–872, *880
United Nations System Chief Executives Board for Coordination *847, *851–854
World Health Organization 854
Organisation for Economic Co-operation and Development *847, 863
policy *791–843
Committee for Development Policy *828–829
development and international economic cooperation *792–799
eradication of poverty *808–813
groups of countries in special situations *831–843
international economic relations *792–828
landlocked developing countries *840–843
least developed countries *832–836
public administration and *828–831
science and technology for development *813–827
small island developing States *837–840
sustainable development *799–808
trends, economic and social *827–828
population, international migration and 1047–1048
public administration and *828–831
science and technology for development *813–827
small island developing States *837–840
sustainable development *799–808
system-wide activities *844–854
technical cooperation *854–881
among developing countries *873–880
trends, economic and social *827–828
UN activities 868

UN Capital Development Fund *880–881
UN Office for Partnerships 868–869
UN Office for Project Services 869–873
UN Volunteers 873
UNDP 854–867 *see also* United Nations Development Programme
UNDP/UNFPA Executive Board 854–856
United Nations Children's Fund 854–855, 863–864
United Nations Conference on Trade and Development 828, 854
United Nations Development Programme 828, 844–846, 854–872, *880, 881
United Nations Environment Programme 854–855
United Nations Industrial Development Organization 854
United Nations Office for Project Services 844, 855, 865–866
United Nations Population Fund 844, 854–857, 863–866, 869–872, *880
United Nations System Chief Executives Board for Coordination *847, *851–854
World Health Organization 854
see also developing countries; least developed countries; sustainable development; United Nations Conference on Trade and Development (UNCTAD); United Nations Development Programme; United Nations Office for Project Services (UNOPS); *specific country names*
Development Account 867–868
diamonds, conflict *39–42
diplomatic relations
   international legal questions *1312
   Middle East peace process *433–434
disabled persons *see* persons with disabilities
disappearance of persons
   International Convention for protection from enforced disappearance *643–644
DISARMAMENT *495–572
   advisory opinion of ICJ, nuclear disarmament *516–517
   anti-personnel mines *553–555
   arms trade treaty *544–545
   bacteriological (biological) weapons *540–541
   Central Africa Standing Advisory Committee *567–568
   centres for peace and disarmament, regional *568–572
   chemical weapons *542–543
   cluster munitions *553
   Comprehensive Nuclear-Test-Ban Treaty *512–516
   Convention on Excessively Injurious Conventional Weapons and Protocols *550–553
   conventional weapons *544–559
      anti-personnel mines *553–555
      arms trade treaty, towards an *544–545
      cluster munitions *553
      Convention on Excessively Injurious Conventional Weapons and Protocols *550–553
      practical disarmament *555
      small arms *545–550
      transparency *555–559
   Democratic People's Republic of Korea 503, *504, *527, 529–530
   Democratic Republic of the Congo *567
   European Union 528, *540, *543, *560, *569

ICJ advisory opinion, nuclear disarmament *516–517
International Atomic Energy Agency 503, *504, *518, *527
International Committee of the Red Cross *540, *552, *555
mines *553–555
multilateralism *523–527
NGO conference, with Department of Public Information 564
non-proliferation issues *518–540
   International Atomic Energy Agency *527–532
   multilateralism in disarmament and non-proliferation *523–527
   nuclear-weapon-free zones *533–540
   radioactive waste *532–533
   treaty *518–520
   weapons of mass destruction *520–523
nuclear disarmament *502–518
   advisory opinion of International Court of Justice *516–517
   Comprehensive Nuclear-Test-Ban Treaty *512–516
   prohibition of use of nuclear weapons *517–518
nuclear-weapon-free zones, non-proliferation *533–540
observance of environmental norms *562–563
practical disarmament *555
prevention of an arms race in outer space *560–562
prohibition of use of nuclear weapons *517–518
radioactive waste, non-proliferation *532–533
regional disarmament *564–572
   Central Africa Standing Advisory Committee *567–568
   regional centres for peace and disarmament *568–572
science and technology and disarmament *563
small arms *545–550
studies, research and training *563–564
transparency *555–559
Treaty on the Non-Proliferation of Nuclear Weapons 495, 503, *505–507, *509–511, *518–520, 529, *531–532, *540
UN machinery *495–499
UN role in disarmament *499–502
weapons of mass destruction 496, 502, *543, *548
   non-proliferation *520–523
World Health Organization 528, *540
see also terrorism
DISASTERS AND DISASTER RESPONSE *907–915
   disaster assistance *912–915
   disaster reduction *908–912
   International Committee of the Red Cross *910
   international cooperation *907–908
   Office for the Coordination of Humanitarian Affairs *912
   United Nations Development Programme *909
   see also earthquakes; hurricanes; Office of the United Nations High Commissioner for Refugees (UNHCR); refugees
discrimination *see* human rights
displaced persons *see* refugees and displaced persons
Division for Ocean Affairs and the Law of the Sea 1363
DJIBOUTI
   political and security questions *297–302
DPKO *see* Department of Peacekeeping Operations

DPRK *see* Democratic People's Republic of Korea; Democratic People's Republic of Korea
DRC *see* Democratic Republic of the Congo
DRUG ABUSE AND CONTROL
   Commission on Narcotic Drugs 1253–1256
   conventions, international drug control *1240–1242
   cooperation against world drug problem *1236–1240
   international drug control *1236–1256
      African Union 1243
      Commission on Narcotic Drugs 1253–1256
      Commonwealth of Independent States 1249–1250
      conventions *1240–1242
         International Narcotics Control Board 1241–1242
      cooperation against world drug problem *1236–1240
      economic and social questions *1236–1256
      Economic Community of West African States 1243–1244
      European Union 1241
      HIV/AIDS *1238–1239, 1243, 1253
      International Narcotics Control Board 1241–1242
      Joint United Nations Programme on HIV/AIDS *1238–1239, 1253
      UN action to combat drug abuse *1251–1256
         Commission on Narcotic Drugs 1253–1256
      UN Office on Drugs and Crime *1236–1238, 1242–1245, 1249, *1251–1256
      world drug situation *1242–1251
      World Health Organization *1239, 1242
   International Narcotics Control Board 1241–1242
   UN action to combat drug abuse *1251–1256
   UN Office on Drugs and Crime *1236–1238, 1242–1245, 1249, *1251–1256
   world drug situation *1242–1251
   see also United Nations Office on Drugs and Crime

E

earthquakes *742, *1029
   disaster response 907
   humanitarian affairs 882
   Indonesia *913
EAST TIMOR *see* Timor-Leste
ECA *see* Economic Commission for Africa
ECE *see* Economic Commission for Europe; Economic Commission For Europe
ECLAC *see* Economic Commission for Latin America and the Caribbean
economic, social and cultural rights *see* human rights
ECONOMIC AND SOCIAL COMMISSION FOR ASIA AND THE PACIFIC (ESCAP) 974–980
   regional cooperation 966–967
   Statistical Commission 1257
   statistics 1263
ECONOMIC AND SOCIAL COMMISSION FOR WESTERN ASIA (ESCWA)
   development policy and international economic cooperation 792
   international finance 947
   Middle East Peace Process *452
   population 1055
   regional cooperation 966–967
   regional economic and social activities 989–992

ECONOMIC AND SOCIAL COUNCIL
   institutional, administrative and budgetary questions 1380
   see also economic and social questions
ECONOMIC AND SOCIAL QUESTIONS *789–1265
   1994 Conference on Population and Development, follow-up to 1045–1047
   2002 General Assembly Special Session on Children, follow-up to *1160–1161
   Africa *968–974
      economic trends 968
      programme and organizational questions 974
   African economic recovery and development *899–904
   ageing persons *1188–1190
      Second World Assembly on Ageing (2002), follow-up to the *1188–1190
   AIDS prevention and control *1216–1222
   Asia and the Pacific 974–980
      economic trends 975
      programme and organizational questions 980
   assistance measures, refugees and displaced persons 1204–1206
   cartography *1000–1001
   children *1160–1188
      2002 General Assembly Special Session on Children, follow-up to *1160–1161
      Guidelines for Alternative Care of Children *1161–1172
      United Nations Children's Fund *1172–1184
   Commission on Crime Prevention and Criminal Justice *1081–1083
   Commission on Narcotic Drugs 1253–1256
   Commission on the Status of Women *1154–1157
   Committee for Development Policy *828–829
   commodities, international trade *925–929
   Convention on elimination of discrimination against women *1151–1154
   conventions, international drug control *1240–1242
   cooperation
      among developing countries *873–880
      against world drug problem *1236–1240
   crime prevention and criminal justice *1080–1107
      Commission on Crime Prevention and Criminal Justice *1081–1083
      crime prevention programme *1083–1091
      preparations for Twelfth (2010) United Nations Crime Congress *1080–1081
      strategies for crime prevention *1096–1103
      transnational organized crime *1091–1096
      UN standards and norms *1103–1106
   cultural development *1070–1080
   dangerous goods, international transport of *960–962
   demographic and social statistics 1261–1262
   Department of Economic and Social Affairs 868
   developing countries, cooperation among *873–880
   Development Account 867–868
   development and international economic cooperation *792–799
   development policy *791–843
   disaster response *907–915
      disaster assistance *912–915
      disaster reduction *908–912

economic and social trends *827–828
economic and technical cooperation among developing countries *873–880
economic cooperation among developing countries
   *873–880
economic statistics 1258–1260
economic trends
   Africa 968
   Asia and the Pacific 975
   Latin America and the Caribbean 984–985
   Western Asia 989
energy and natural resources *993–1000
environment *1002–1038
   activities, environmental *1025–1038
   Global Environment Facility 1014–1015
   international conventions and mechanisms *1015–
     1025
   United Nations Environment Programme *1002–
     1014
eradication of poverty *808–813
Europe 980–984
   economic trends 981
   housing and land management 983–984
   programme and organizational questions 984
Executive Board, UNDP/UNFPA 854–856
financial and administrative matters
   international finance *929–959
   Office of the United Nations High Commissioner
     for Refugees *1198–1202
   technical cooperation 862–867
follow-up to 1994 Conference on Population and
   Development 1045–1047
food and agriculture *1230–1235
   food aid 1230–1231
   food security *1231–1235
Fourth World Conference on Women and Beijing+5,
   follow-up to *1114–1151
Global Environment Facility 1014–1015
global public health *1226–1229
global trade activity, international trade 916–917
groups of countries in special situations, development
   policy *831–843
Guidelines for Alternative Care of Children *1161–1172
Habitat Agenda, implementation of *1038–1042
health *1216–1230
   AIDS prevention and control *1216–1222
   global public health *1226–1229
   malaria *1222–1226
   non-communicable diseases *1222
   road safety *1229–1230
   tobacco *1222
housing and land management 983–984
human resources development *1107–1113
   International Year of Languages *1113
   UN research and training institutes *1109–1113
human settlements *1038–1044
   implementation of Habitat Agenda and strength-
     ening of UN-Habitat *1038–1042
   UN Human Settlements Programme *1042–1044
humanitarian assistance *882–899
   coordination *882–888

mine clearance *891–893
resource mobilization *888–890
White Helmets *890–891
international conventions and mechanisms, environment *1015–1025
international cooperation, disaster response *907–908
international drug control *1236–1256
   Commission on Narcotic Drugs 1253–1256
   conventions *1240–1242
   cooperation against world drug problem *1236–
     1240
   International Narcotics Control Board 1241–1242
   UN action to combat drug abuse *1251–1256
   UN Office on Drugs and Crime *1251–1253
   world drug situation *1242–1251
international economic relations, development policy
   *792–828
   development and international economic coop-
     eration *792–799
   economic and social trends *827–828
   eradication of poverty *808–813
   science and technology for development *813–827
   sustainable development *799–808
international finance *929–959
   financial policy *929–939
   financing for development *939–958
international migration and development, population
   1047–1048
International Narcotics Control Board 1241–1242
International Research and Training Institute for
   the Advancement of Women (INSTRAW) *1158–1159
international trade *916–929
   commodities *925–929
   global trade activity 916–917
   multilateral trading system *917–922
   trade policy *922–923
   trade promotion and facilitation 923–925
international transport *959–962
   maritime transport *959–960
   transport of dangerous goods *960–962
International Year of Languages *1113
land management 983–984
landlocked developing countries, development policy
   *840–843
Latin America and the Caribbean 984–989
   economic trends 984–985
least developed countries *832–836, *875, *878, *880
malaria *1222–1226
maritime transport, international *959–960
Millennium Development Goals *874
mine clearance, humanitarian assistance *891–893
multilateral trading system, international trade *917–
   922
natural resources *993–1000
non-communicable diseases *1222
nutrition *1235
   Standing Committee on Nutrition *1235
   UN University activities *1235
Office of the United Nations High Commissioner for
   Refugees *1192–1202
operational activities for development *844–881
   developing countries, cooperation among *873–880

Development Account 867–868
Executive Board, UNDP/UNFPA 854–856
financial and administrative matters, technical cooperation 862–867
system-wide activities *844–854
technical cooperation *854–881
UN activities 868
UN Capital Development Fund *880–881
UN Office for Partnerships 868–869
UN Office for Project Services 869–873
UN Volunteers 873
UNDP 854–867
UNDP/UNFPA Executive Board 854–856
persons with disabilities, social policy and cultural issues *1067–1070
policy, international finance *929–939
population *1045–1056
follow-up to 1994 Conference on Population and Development 1045–1047
implementation of Programme of Action 1045–1047
international migration and development 1047–1048
United Nations Population Fund *1048–1054
poverty, eradication of *808–813
preparations for Twelfth (2010) United Nations Crime Congress *1080–1081
programme and organizational questions
Africa 974
Asia and the Pacific 980
Europe 984
programme policy, Office of the United Nations High Commissioner for Refugees *1192–1198
protection issues, refugees and displaced persons 1202–1203
public administration and development policy *828–831
Committee for Development Policy *828–829
refugees and displaced persons *1191–1215
assistance measures 1204–1206
financial and administrative questions, Office of the United Nations High Commissioner for Refugees *1198–1202
Office of the United Nations High Commissioner for Refugees *1192–1202
programme policy, Office of the United Nations High Commissioner for Refugees *1192–1198
protection issues 1202–1203
regional activities *1206–1215
regional economic and social activities *966–992
Asia and the Pacific 974–980
cooperation, regional 966–967
economic trends 968, 975, 981, 984–985, 989
Europe 980–984
housing and land management 983–984
Latin America and the Caribbean 984–989
programme and organizational questions 974, 980, 984
refugees and displaced persons *1206–1215
Western Asia 989–992
research and training institutes, UN *1109–1113
resource mobilization, humanitarian assistance *888–890

road safety *1229–1230
science and technology for development *813–827
Second World Assembly on Ageing (2002), follow-up to the *1188–1190
small island developing States, development policy *837–840
social policy and cultural issues *1057–1080
cultural development *1070–1080
persons with disabilities *1067–1070
social development *1057–1067
social statistics 1261–1262
special economic assistance *899–907
special situation countries, development policy *831–843
Standing Committee on Nutrition *1235
statistics 1257–1265
demographic and social statistics 1261–1262
economic statistics 1258–1260
work of Statistical Commission 1257–1265
strategies for crime prevention *1096–1103
sustainable development *799–808
system-wide activities, development *844–854
technical cooperation, development *854–881
among developing countries *873–880
technology for development *813–827
tobacco *1222
trade, international *916–929
trade policy, international trade *922–923
transnational organized crime *1091–1096
transport, international *959–962
Twelfth (2010) United Nations Crime Congress, preparations for *1080–1081
UN action to combat drug abuse *1251–1256
UN activities, development 868
UN Capital Development Fund *880–881
UN Crime Congress, preparations for Twelfth (2010) *1080–1081
UN Development Fund for Women (UNIFEM) *1157–1158
UN Environment Programme *1002–1014
UN-Habitat, strengthening of *1038–1042
UN Human Settlements Programme *1042–1044
UN machinery, women *1151–1159
UN Office for Partnerships, development 868–869
UN Office for Project Services, development 869–873
UN Office on Drugs and Crime *1251–1253
UN Population Fund *1048–1054
UN research and training institutes *1109–1113
UN Volunteers, development 873
UNCTAD institutional and organizational questions 963–965
UNDP, development 854–867
technical cooperation 856–862
UNDP/UNFPA Executive Board 854–856
United Nations Children's Fund *1172–1184
UN University activities, nutrition *1235
Western Asia 989–992
economic trends 989
White Helmets *890–891
women *1114–1159
Commission on the Status of Women *1154–1157

Convention on the elimination of discrimination against women *1151–1154

critical areas of concern *1119–1151

follow-up to Fourth World Conference on Women and Beijing+5 *1114–1151

Fourth World Conference on Women and Beijing+5, follow-up to *1114–1151

International Research and Training Institute for the Advancement of Women (INSTRAW) *1158–1159

UN Development Fund for Women (UNIFEM) *1157–1158

UN machinery *1151–1159

world drug situation *1242–1251

youth *1184–1188

see also development; international economic relations; statistics; *specific topics and social issues*

ECONOMIC COMMISSION FOR AFRICA (ECA)

administrative and staff matters 1427–1428, *1451, 1452

regional cooperation 966

regional economic and social activities *968–974

ECONOMIC COMMISSION FOR EUROPE (ECE)

administrative and staff matters 1427–1428, *1451

Central African Republic 152

regional cooperation 966

regional economic and social activities *968–974

ECONOMIC COMMISSION FOR LATIN AMERICA AND THE CARIBBEAN (ECLAC)

regional cooperation 966

regional economic and social activities 984–989

Economic Community of West African States (ECOWAS) *167–170, 228

Côte d'Ivoire *188

Guinea *229–231

Guinea-Bissau *222, 224

international drug control 1243–1244

Liberia 193, *201

political and security questions

Guinea-Bissau *216, *218–219, *221

economic cooperation, international *see* development

economic law

international economic law *1315–1321

economic statistics 1258–1260

economic trends

Africa 968

Asia and the Pacific 975

Latin America and the Caribbean 984–985

Western Asia 989

ecosystems *see* environment

ECOWAS *see* Economic Community of West African States

EDUCATION

human rights

education on *653–655

right to education *726–727

Office of the United Nations High Commissioner for Human Rights *654

see also research and training

EL SALVADOR

Cuba, political and security questions *329–330

political and security questions, Cuba *329–330

elderly persons *see* ageing persons

ENERGY

economic and social questions *993–1000

European Union *994–996

Millennium Development Goals *999

Treaty on the Non-Proliferation of Nuclear Weapons *995

weapons of mass destruction 994

World Health Organization *999

ENVIRONMENT

activities, environmental *1025–1038

economic and social questions *1002–1038

European Union 1015, *1018–1019, *1022, 1033, 1035–1036

Food and Agriculture Organization of the United Nations *1028, 1033

Global Environment Facility 1014–1015

HIV/AIDS 729

human rights, environmental and scientific concerns 727–729

international conventions and mechanisms *1015–1025

International Fund for Agricultural Development 1015, *1024

Joint Inspection Unit *1022–1023

Office of the United Nations High Commissioner for Human Rights 728

United Nations Development Programme 1014–1015, *1024, 1036

United Nations Educational, Scientific and Cultural Organization 1032

United Nations Environment Programme *1002–1014, *1018–1019, *1023–1024, *1032–1037

United Nations Industrial Development Organization 1014–1015, 1036

World Health Organization 729

World Intellectual Property Organization *1020

see also sustainable development; United Nations Environment Programme

ERITREA

African Union *303

Djibouti, political and security questions with *297–302

Ethiopia, political and security questions with *302–304

political and security questions

with Djibouti *297–302

with Ethiopia *302–304

ESCAP *see* Economic and Social Commission for Asia and the Pacific

ESCWA *see* Economic and Social Commission for Western Asia

ETHIOPIA

African Union *303

political and security questions, with Eritrea *302–304

EU *see* European Union

EULEX

political and security questions *412

EUROPE AND THE MEDITERRANEAN

Armenia and Azerbaijan *421–422

Bosnia and Herzegovina *400–408

Brcko District *404–407

European Union missions in Bosnia and Herzegovina *407–408

Implementation of Peace Agreement *401–404

Brcko District *404–407

Commonwealth of Independent States 981
cooperation with the Organization for Security and Cooperation in Europe *432
Cyprus *422–431
    human rights 778
    political and security developments *423–431
developments, political and security
    Cyprus *423–431
    Kosovo *408–412
economic and social questions 980–984
    economic trends 981
    housing and land management 983–984
    land management 983–984
    programme and organizational questions 984
economic trends 981
EULEX *412
European Union missions in Bosnia and Herzegovina *407–408
Food and Agriculture Organization of the United Nations 981–982
Georgia *414–421
    human rights *778–780
    situation in Abkhazia *415–419
    UN Observer Mission in Georgia *419–421
housing and land management 983–984
human rights *778–780
    Cyprus 778
    Georgia *778–780
implementation of Peace Agreement, Bosnia and Herzegovina *401–404
Kosovo *408–414
    EULEX *412
    Political and security developments *408–412
    UNMIK *412–414
Macedonia, the former Yugoslav Republic of *414
observer status *432
Office of the United Nations High Commissioner for Human Rights *780
Organization for Democracy and Economic Development-GUAM 422
Organization for Security and Cooperation in Europe *432
political and security questions *400–432
    Armenia and Azerbaijan *421–422
    Bosnia and Herzegovina *400–408
    Brcko District *404–407
    cooperation with the Organization for Security and Cooperation in Europe *432
    Cyprus *422–431
    developments, Cyprus *423–431
    developments, Kosovo *408–412
    EULEX *412
    European Union missions in Bosnia and Herzegovina *407–408
    The former Yugoslav Republic of Macedonia *414
    Georgia *414–421
    implementation of Peace Agreement, Bosnia and Herzegovina *401–404
    Kosovo *408–414
    observer status *432
    Organization for Democracy and Economic Development-GUAM 422

strengthening of security and cooperation in the Mediterranean *431–432
UN Observer Mission in Georgia *419–421
UNMIK *412–414
programme and organizational questions 984
strengthening of security and cooperation in the Mediterranean *431–432
UN Observer Mission in Georgia *419–421
UNMIK *412–414
weapons of mass destruction *432
see also Economic Commission for Europe; European Union; *specific country names*
EUROPEAN UNION (EU)
Abkhazia 417–418
Africa, regional economic and social activities 969
Bosnia and Herzegovina *400–402, 408
Chad and Central African Republic *157, 159
chemical weapons *543
Cyprus *423, 424
Democratic Republic of the Congo 124
disarmament 528, *540, *543, *560, *569
energy and natural resources *994–996
environment 1015
environment, international conventions and mechanisms *1018–1019, *1022
environmental activities 1033, 1035–1036
Georgia 415, 417–418
Guinea 231
Guinea-Bissau *216, *218–219, *222, 224
international drug control 1241
Kosovo *412
missions in Bosnia and Herzegovina *407–408
peacekeeping operations 72, 80
refugees and displaced persons 1214–1215
regional centres for peace and disarmament *569
regional cooperation 967
Somalia 288
UN Convention on the Law of the Sea 1345
West Africa 228
Western Sahara *305

F

FAO *see* Food and Agriculture Organization of the United Nations
financial and administrative matters
    Department of Peacekeeping Operations *93–95, 98–99
    development
        International Monetary Fund 947, *951, *953–954
        technical cooperation 862–867
    International Monetary Fund 932, *933, *936, 947, *951, *953–954
    management practices, UN *1416
    Timor-Leste, financing of UN operations *381–383
    UN financial situation 1388
    UN financing and programming *1388–1418
    United Nations Integrated Mission in Timor-Leste 83
    United Nations Interim Administration Mission in Kosovo 83, *88
    United Nations Mission for the Referendum in Western Sahara 83, *88
    United Nations Mission in Liberia 83, *88

United Nations Mission in the Central African Republic and Chad 83
United Nations Mission in the Sudan 83, *88
United Nations Observer Mission in Georgia 83
United Nations Operation in Côte d'Ivoire 83, *88
United Nations Organization Mission in the Democratic Republic of the Congo *88, 100
United Nations Peacekeeping Force in Cyprus 83
United Nations Stabilization Force in Haiti 83, *88
see also international finance; international trade; international transport; legal questions
FOOD *1230–1235
and agriculture *1230–1235
aid *see* humanitarian assistance
economic and social questions *1230–1235
food aid 1230–1231
food security *1231–1235
human rights, right to food *718–723
International Fund for Agricultural Development *1233
International Maritime Organization 1231
Joint Inspection Unit 1231
see also Food and Agriculture Organization of the United Nations; nutrition; World Food Programme
FOOD AND AGRICULTURE ORGANIZATION OF THE UNITED NATIONS (FAO) 1231, *1235
Afghanistan *339
Africa, regional economic and social activities 970
bacteriological (biological) and chemical weapons *541
environmental activities *1028, 1033
Europe, regional economic and social activities 981–982
food security *1235
health 1216
Iraq 366
Latin America and the Caribbean, regional economic and social activities 985
operational activities for development 854
statistics 1260
UNDP operational activities 859
THE FORMER YUGOSLAVIA
International Tribunal for the Former Yugoslavia *1279–1287
Chambers *1280–1285
financing *1286–1287
Office of Prosecutor *1285
Registry *1285–1286
see also International Tribunal for the Former Yugoslavia
Fourth World Conference on Women and Beijing+5, follow-up to *1114–1151
FRANCE
Mauritius, political and security questions, with United Kingdom 311

G

gender issues *see* women
GENERAL ASSEMBLY
institutional, administrative and budgetary questions *1374–1379
genocide
Convention against genocide *644–645

GEORGIA
Commonwealth of Independent States 415
European Union 415, 417–418
human rights *778–780
Organization for Security and Cooperation in Europe 415, 417–418
political and security questions *414–421
situation in Abkhazia *415–419
UN Observer Mission in Georgia *419–421
UN Observer Mission in Georgia *419–421
United Nations Observer Mission in Georgia 418, *419
Global Environment Facility 1014–1015
global public health *1226–1229
HIV/AIDS *1227
global trade activity
United Nations Conference on Trade and Development *916–918
World Trade Organization 916
GREAT LAKES REGION
African Union 117
political and security questions *116–118
see also Central Africa and Great Lakes region
GUAM *596–597
see also Organization for Democracy and Economic Development
GUATEMALA
human rights 760
political and security questions *312–314
Guidelines for Alternative Care of Children *1161–1172
HIV/AIDS *1168–1169, *1172
United Nations Population Fund *1161
GUINEA
African Union *228–231
Economic Community of West African States *229–231
European Union 231
political and security questions *228–231
GUINEA-BISSAU
African Union *218–219, 224
Economic Community of West African States *222, 224
European Union *216, *218–219, *222, 224
International Monetary Fund *216, *219, *222, 224–225
political and security questions *215–226
United Nations Development Programme *218, *221
United Nations Office on Drugs and Crime *219, *222

H

HAITI
African Union *322, *324, 326
Caribbean Community 326
HIV/AIDS *327
human rights 761
Millennium Development Goals *327
Office of the United Nations High Commissioner for Human Rights 326
Organization of American States 319, *322–323
political and security questions *318–329
MINUSTAH *326–329
programme of support for *325–326
United Nations Children's Fund 326
United Nations Development Programme 326, *327
World Health Organization *327
see also United Nations Stabilization Force in Haiti

HEALTH *1216–1230
  AIDS prevention and control *1216–1222
  economic and social questions *1216–1230
  Food and Agriculture Organization of the United Nations 1216
  global public health *1226–1229
  human rights, right to health 729–731
  Joint Inspection Unit 1217
  malaria *1222–1226
  Millennium Development Goals 1217, *1229
  non-communicable diseases *1222
  road safety *1229–1230
  tobacco *1222
  United Nations Children's Fund 1217–1218
  United Nations Development Programme 1217–1219
  United Nations Office on Drugs and Crime 1217, 1219, *1221
  United Nations Population Fund 1217–1219
  United Nations System Chief Executives Board for Coordination 1217, *1226
  World Food Programme 1216–1217
  see also HIV/AIDS; Joint United Nations Programme on HIV/AIDS (UNAIDS)
Herzegovina *see* Bosnia and Herzegovina
highway safety *1229–1230
HIV/AIDS
  Afghanistan 763
  Africa *116, 165, *166
  African economic recovery and development *899–901
  Brcko District *405
  children, youth and ageing persons *1160–1162
  Convention on the Rights of the Child *637–638
  cooperation, UN and other organizations *1384–1385
  Côte d'Ivoire 174, *176, *181, 184
  Cuba *331
  cultural development *1076–1077
  Cyprus *426, *428
  economic and social questions *1216–1222
  environmental and scientific concerns 729
  global public health *1227
  Guidelines for the Alternative Care of Children *1168–1169, *1172
  Haiti *327
  human resources development *1108
  human rights *707, 729–730, 763, *776
  humanitarian activities 896
  international drug control *1238–1239, 1243, 1253
  international economic relations *797, 813
  Liberia 199
  multilateral trading system *920
  Myanmar *776
  operational activities for development 854
  Palestine 463
  peacekeeping operations 75, 98
  persons with disabilities *1069
  political and security questions 5, 10, 13, 16, 26, 28
  population 1045–1047, 1049–1051, *1054
  prevention and control *1216–1223
  promotion of international peace and security *63
  promotion of peace in Africa *108, *114
  public information *612, *614

  refugees and displaced persons *1196, 1200, 1205, *1207–1208, 1211
  regional economic and social activities 974
  right to food *722
  right to health 730
  UNAIDS *see* Joint United Nations Programme on HIV/AIDS
  UNDP operational activities 857–858
  United Nations Children's Fund 1174, 1176, 1178–1179
  women 1114, *1116, *1121, *1124, *1126–1130, *1143, *1146–1148, *1150–1151, *1154, *1156–1157
  youth *1184–1185
HONDURAS
  Caribbean Community *315
  human rights 761–762
  Organization of American States *314–318
  political and security questions *314–318
HORN OF AFRICA *232–304
  African Union 297, *299, *302
  Chad–Sudan *268–270
  Djibouti and Eritrea *297–302
  Eritrea–Ethiopia *302–304
  political and security questions *232–304
    Chad–Sudan *268–270
    Djibouti and Eritrea *297–302
    Eritrea–Ethiopia *302–304
    Somalia *270–297
    Sudan *232–268
  Somalia *270–297
  Sudan *232–268
  see also specific country names
host country relations
  international legal questions *1327–1329
housing
  human rights, right to adequate housing *723–724
human immunodeficiency virus/acquired immuno-deficiency syndrome (HIV/AIDS) *see* HIV/AIDS
HUMAN RESOURCES DEVELOPMENT *1107–1113
  HIV/AIDS *1108
  International Year of Languages *1113
  UN research and training institutes *1109–1113
HUMAN RIGHTS *621–788
  1993 World Conference, follow-up to *655
  action to promote human rights, strengthening *647–653
  adequate housing, right to *723–724
  Afghanistan 762–763
  Africa 751–758
    Burundi 751–752
    Democratic Republic of the Congo 752–754
    Liberia 754–755
    Sierra Leone 755–756
    Somalia 756–757
    Sudan 757–758
  African Descent, International Year for People of *655
  African Union 756–758
  African Union-United Nations Hybrid Operation in Darfur 757–758
  Americas 758–762
    Bolivia 758–759
    Colombia 759–760

Guatemala 760
Haiti 761
Honduras 761–762
Asia 762
    Afghanistan 762–763
    Cambodia 763–764
    Democratic People's Republic of Korea *764–768
    Iran *768–771
    Myanmar *771–776
    Nepal 777
    Sri Lanka 777–778
Bolivia 758–759
Burundi 751–752
Cambodia 763–764
the Child, Convention on the Rights of *636–641
civil and political rights *657–702
    Covenant on Civil and Political Rights and Optional
        Protocols 632
    democracy and human rights *685–689
    discrimination against minorities *672–673
    human rights defenders *666–668
    migrants, protection of *668–672
    minorities, discrimination against *672–673
    racism and racial discrimination *657–665
    religious intolerance *673–680
    reprisals for cooperation with human rights bodies
        *668
    rule of law, democracy and human rights *685–689
    self-determination, right to *680–684
Colombia 759–760
conventions
    on elimination of discrimination against women
        *635, *1151–1154
    against genocide *644–645
    International Convention for protection from
        enforced disappearance *643–644
    on migrant workers *641–642
    against racial discrimination 631–632
    on Rights of Persons with Disabilities *642–643
    on the Rights of the Child *636–641
    against torture *635–636
country situations *750–788
Covenant on Civil and Political Rights and Optional
    Protocols 632
Covenant on Economic, Social and Cultural Rights
    and Optional Protocol *632–635
cultural rights *724–726
Cyprus 778
defenders *666–668
democracy and human rights *685–689
Democratic People's Republic of Korea *764–768
Democratic Republic of the Congo *739, *742, 752–754
development, right to *703–716
Disabled Persons, Convention on Rights of *642–643
disappearance, enforced, International Convention for
    protection from *643–644
discrimination against minorities *672–673
discrimination against women and Optional Protocol,
    Convention on elimination of *635
economic, social and cultural rights *702–749
    Covenant on Economic, Social and Cultural Rights
        and Optional Protocol *632–635
    cultural rights *724–726

development, right to *703–716
education, right to *726–727
environmental and scientific concerns 727–729
extreme poverty 717–718
food, right to *718–723
health, right to 729–731
housing, right to adequate *723–724
Human Rights Council special session 702–703
poverty, extreme 717–718
realizing economic, social and cultural rights 702
scientific concerns 727–729
slavery and related issues *731–733
Social Forum *716–717
vulnerable groups *733–749
education *653–655
education, right to *726–727
elimination of discrimination against women and
    Optional Protocol, Convention on *635
enforced disappearance, International Convention for
    protection from *643–644
environmental and scientific concerns 727–729
Europe and the Mediterranean *778–780
    Cyprus 778
    Georgia *778–780
extreme poverty 717–718
follow-up to 1993 World Conference *655
food, right to *718–723
    HIV/AIDS *722
    International Labour Organization 719
general aspects *645–647
genocide, Convention against *644–645
Georgia *778–780
Guatemala 760
Haiti 761
health, right to 729–731
    HIV/AIDS 730
    Office of the United Nations High Commissioner
        for Human Rights 730
HIV/AIDS *707, *722, 729–730, 763, *776
Honduras 761–762
housing, right to adequate *723–724
Human Rights Council *623–627
    special session 702–703
human rights defenders *666–668
human rights education *653–655
human rights instruments *630–647
instruments *630–647
International Committee of the Red Cross *644, *698,
    *744, *786
International Convention for protection from enforced
    disappearance *643–644
International Labour Organization 719, *746
International Maritime Organization 728
International Year for People of African Descent *655
Iran *768–771
Israel, territories occupied by *780–788
Liberia 754–755
Middle East *780–788
    territories occupied by Israel *780–788
migrant workers, Convention on *641–642
migrants, protection of *668–672
Millennium Development Goals 703

minorities, discrimination against *672–673
    Office of the United Nations High Commissioner
       for Human Rights *672–674
Myanmar *771–776
Nepal 777
Non-Self-Governing Territory 631
Office of the United Nations High Commissioner for
    Human Rights *624, 627–631, *642–643, *649–651,
    690, 702–703, 727, 730
Organization of American States *746
Palestinian Authority *689, 781, 787
Persons with Disabilities, Convention on Rights of
    *642–643
poverty, extreme 717–718
promotion of human rights *623–655
    general aspects *645–647
    human rights education *653–655
    human rights instruments *630–647
    Office of the United Nations High Commissioner
       for Human Rights *624, 627–631, *642–643
    strengthening action to promote human rights
       *647–653
    UN machinery *623–630
protection of human rights *656–749
    adequate housing, right to *723–724
    civil and political rights *657–702
    cultural rights *724–726
    democracy and human rights *685–689
    development, right to *703–716
    discrimination against minorities *672–673
    economic, social and cultural rights *702–749
    education, right to *726–727
    environmental and scientific concerns 727–729
    extreme poverty 717–718
    food, right to *718–723
    health, right to 729–731
    Human Rights Council special session 702–703
    human rights defenders *666–668
    migrants, protection of *668–672
    minorities, discrimination against *672–673
    poverty, extreme 717–718
    racism and racial discrimination *657–665
    realizing economic, social and cultural rights 702
    religious intolerance *673–680
    reprisals for cooperation with human rights
       bodies *668
    rule of law, democracy and human rights *685–689
    scientific concerns 727–729
    self-determination, right to *680–684
    slavery and related issues *731–733
    Social Forum *716–717
    special procedures 656–657
    vulnerable groups *733–749
racial discrimination, Convention against 631–632
racism and racial discrimination *657–665
realizing economic, social and cultural rights 702
religious intolerance *673–680
reprisals for cooperation with human rights bodies *668
Rights of Persons with Disabilities, Convention on
    *642–643
Rights of the Child, Convention on the *636–641
rule of law, democracy and human rights *685–689

scientific concerns 727–729
self-determination, right to *680–684
Sierra Leone 755–756
slavery and related issues *731–733
Social Forum *716–717
Somalia 756–757
special procedures 656–657
Sri Lanka 777–778
strengthening action to promote human rights
    *647–653
    Office of the United Nations High Commissioner
       for Human Rights *649–651
Sudan 757–758
territories occupied by Israel *780–788
torture, Convention against *635–636
UN machinery *623–630
    Human Rights Council *623–627
    Office of the High Commissioner for Human Rights
       627–630
United Nations Children's Fund 735, *739
United Nations Development Programme 673
United Nations Educational, Scientific and Cultural
    Organization *724
United Nations Integrated Peacebuilding Office
    in Sierra Leone 755
United Nations Mission in the Sudan 758
United Nations Organization Mission in the
    Democratic Republic of the Congo 752–753
United Nations Peacekeeping Force in Cyprus 778
United Nations Relief and Works Agency for Palestine
    Refugees in the Near East *780, 781, 784
United Nations Stabilization Force in Haiti 761
vulnerable groups *733–749
women, Convention on elimination of discrimination
    against *635
World Food Programme 764
World Health Organization 729
see also Office of the United Nations High Commis-
    sioner for Human Rights (OHCHR); racism and racial
    discrimination; torture and cruel treatment; specific
    rights
Human Rights Council *623–627
    special sessions 702–703, 777–778, 780
human rights defenders
    Office of the United Nations High Commissioner for
       Human Rights *668
HUMAN SETTLEMENTS *1038–1044
    implementation of Habitat Agenda and strengthen-
       ing of UN-Habitat *1038–1042
    UN Human Settlements Programme *1042–1044
    United Nations Development Programme 1014
    United Nations Environment Programme 1039
    United Nations Industrial Development Organization
       1014
HUMANITARIAN ASSISTANCE *882–899
    African Union *899
    Committee for Programme and Coordination *899
    coordination *882–888
    Democratic Republic of the Congo 894
    HIV/AIDS 896
    internally displaced persons 894–895, 897–898
    mine clearance *891–893

New Partnership for Africa's Development *899
Office of the United Nations High Commissioner for Refugees *893, 897
resource mobilization *888–890
White Helmets *890–891
World Health Organization *891
see also Disasters and disaster response; New Partnership for Africa's Development (NEPAD); Office for the Coordination of Humanitarian Affairs; refugees and displaced persons
hurricanes *907
El Salvador *912
Haiti 318, *320, *323, 326–327, *905
humanitarian affairs 9
Ida *912–913
non-self-governing territories *579, *581–582

I

IAEA see International Atomic Energy Agency
IAMB see International Advisory and Monitoring Board for Iraq
ICAO see International Civil Aviation Organization
ICC see International Criminal Court
ICJ see International Court of Justice (ICJ)
ICRC see International Committee of the Red Cross
ICSC see International Civil Service Commission
ICTR see International Criminal Tribunal for Rwanda
ICTY see International Tribunal for the Former Yugoslavia
IDPs see internally displaced persons
IFAD see International Fund for Agricultural Development
ILO see International Labour Organization
IMF see International Monetary Fund
IMO see International Maritime Organization
INCB see International Narcotics Control Board
INDIA
  political and security questions, with Pakistan 398–399
INDIAN OCEAN
  political and security questions *575–576
indigenous peoples 746–749
  Permanent Forum on Indigenous Issues 749
INDONESIA
  earthquakes *913
  terrorism 69
INFORMATION
  Department of Public Information activities 617–619
  HIV/AIDS, public information *612, *614
  international security, political and security questions *609–619
  Joint Inspection Unit 1440, *1441
  least developed country, public information *614
  UN information centres and services 1534
  UN information systems *1436–1442
  United Nations System Chief Executives Board for Coordination 1440, *1441
INSTITUTIONAL, ADMINISTRATIVE AND BUDGETARY QUESTIONS *1365–1485
  2008–2009 budget *1388–1394
  2010–2011 budget *1394–1410
  accounts and auditing *1415–1417
  administration of justice, UN staff *1472–1485

administrative matters *1419–1427
assessments *1410–1415
budget, UN *1388–1410
Committee for Programme and Coordination 1394, 1418, 1436
conditions of service, UN staff *1452–1458
conference management *1427–1436
contributions *1410–1415
cooperation with organizations *1383–1384
coordination, monitoring and cooperation *1380–1383
Department of Peacekeeping Operations *1470, 1471
Economic and Social Council 1380
Economic Commission for Africa 1427–1428, *1451, 1452
Economic Commission for Europe 1427–1428, *1451
financial management practices *1416
financial situation 1388
financing and programming *1388–1418
  Committee for Programme and Coordination 1418
  Office of Internal Oversight Services *1417, 1418
  World Food Programme *1416
General Assembly *1374–1379
information systems, UN *1436–1442
institutional matters *1373–1374
intergovernmental machinery *1373–1374
International Civil Service Commission *1406, *1452–1456, 1463, *1468
International Criminal Tribunal for Rwanda 1452, *1457
International Fund for Agricultural Development 1454
International Tribunal for the Former Yugoslavia 1452, *1457
Joint Inspection Unit *1371, *1424–1427, 1436
managerial reform and oversight *1419–1427
  Joint Inspection Unit *1424–1427
  United Nations System Chief Executives Board for Coordination *1425
monitoring *1380–1383
Office of Internal Oversight Services *1371, *1417, 1418, *1421–1424, *1426, 1436
Office of the United Nations High Commissioner for Human Rights 1423
Office of the United Nations High Commissioner for Refugees *1468, *1470, 1473
participation in UN work *1384–1387
premises and property, UN *1442–1452
programme performance 1418
programme planning *1417–1418
restructuring issues *1367–1373
  Joint Inspection Unit *1371
  Office of Internal Oversight Services *1371
review of UN administrative and financial functioning *1416–1417
Security Council 1379
staff matters *1452–1485
  administration of justice *1472–1485
  conditions of service *1452–1458
  safety and security, UN staff *1458–1463
travel-related matters, UN staff 1472
UN and other organizations *1383–1387
UN information systems *1436–1442
UN Joint Staff Pension Fund 1471–1472
UN machinery *1374–1381

UN premises and property *1442–1452
United Nations Assistance Mission for Iraq 1452
United Nations Children's Fund 1472
United Nations Conference on Trade and Development 1380, *1389, *1404–1406
United Nations Development Programme *1470, 1472
United Nations Educational, Scientific and Cultural Organization *1468
United Nations information centres and services 1534
United Nations Organization Mission in the Democratic Republic of the Congo *1470
United Nations Population Fund 1472
United Nations Relief and Works Agency for Palestine Refugees in the Near East *1470
United Nations System Chief Executives Board for Coordination 1380, *1425
World Food Programme *1416, *1470
World Trade Organization 1380, *1389, *1404–1406
INSTRAW see International Research and Training Institute for the Advancement of Women
instruments, human rights *630–647
intergovernmental machinery *1373–1374
intergovernmental organizations related to United Nations 1537
internally displaced persons (IDPs) 1199, 1205
　humanitarian activities 894–895, 897–898
　refugees and displaced persons 1211–1212
　Somalia 285, *291
　Sudan 240, 243, 245, *249, 250, *252–255, *257, 258
International Advisory and Monitoring Board for Iraq *372–375
INTERNATIONAL ATOMIC ENERGY AGENCY (IAEA) *509, 993–994, *998
　Asia and the Pacific 333
　disarmament 503, *504, *518, *527
　Iran 394–396
　non-proliferation 521, *522, 528, *529–532
　non-proliferation of weapons *527–532
　reports of 394–396
　special economic assistance *905
International Civil Aviation Organization (ICAO)
　dangerous goods, transport of *961
　international State relations and international law *1310
International Civil Service Commission (ICSC)
　administrative and staff matters *1452–1456, 1463, *1468
　operational activities for development 846
　peacekeeping operations *87
　UN budget *1406
International Committee of the Red Cross (ICRC)
　coordination of humanitarian assistance *883–884, *886–887
　disarmament *540, *552, *555
　disaster reduction *910
　human rights *644, *698, *744, *786
　international finance 947
　International Law Commission 1307
　Middle East Peace Process *440, *444, *452
　Myanmar *776
　promotion of international peace and security *61, *63
　refugees and displaced persons *1195–1196

Syrian Arab Republic *491
territories occupied by Israel *786
vulnerable groups *744
Western Sahara *308
International Convention for protection from enforced disappearance *643–644
INTERNATIONAL COURT OF JUSTICE (ICJ) 1269–1278, 1321
　advisory proceedings 1277
　Bosnia and Herzegovina 408
　Cameroon–Nigeria 227
　contentious proceedings 1269–1277
　functioning of the Court 1277–1278
　judicial work of the Court 1269–1277
　Kosovo 410
　Middle East Peace Process *447, 448, *458
　nuclear disarmament, advisory opinion *516–517
　organization of the Court 1277–1278
　Palestine 463
　Statute of the International Court of Justice 1492
　territories occupied by Israel 782, *786, 787
　Trust Fund to Assist States in Settlement of Disputes 1278
　West Africa 226
INTERNATIONAL CRIMINAL COURT (ICC) 29, *1298–1302
　African Union 1300
　Chambers 1300–1302
　Democratic Republic of the Congo 1300
　Sudan 233, *234, 253–254, 261–262
INTERNATIONAL CRIMINAL TRIBUNAL FOR RWANDA (ICTR) *1282
　administrative and staff matters 1452, *1457
　Chambers *1288–1293
　financing *1294–1296
　Office of Prosecutor *1293
　Registry *1294
INTERNATIONAL ECONOMIC RELATIONS
　cooperation, development and *792–799
　development policy *792–828
　economic and social trends *827–828
　eradication of poverty *808–813
　HIV/AIDS *797, 813
　international economic law *1315–1321
　Millennium Development Goals 813
　science and technology for development *813–827
　sustainable development *799–808
　United Nations Conference on Trade and Development *827
　see also sustainable development
INTERNATIONAL FINANCE *929–959
　Economic and Social Commission for Western Asia 947
　financial policy *929–939
　financing for development *939–958
　LDCs *939, *944, *948–952
　official development assistance 932, 940, 947, *952–953
　United Nations Conference on Trade and Development *931–933, *936, 940, *958
　United Nations System Chief Executives Board for Coordination *945–947, *957

World Trade Organization *933, 940, *950, *952
see also development; International Monetary Fund; United Nations Conference on Trade and Development (UNCTAD)
INTERNATIONAL FUND FOR AGRICULTURAL DEVELOPMENT (IFAD) *1025
    administrative and staff matters 1454
    environment 1015
    environment, international conventions and mechanisms *1024
    food security *1233
    operational activities for development 854
    sustainable development *808
INTERNATIONAL LABOUR ORGANIZATION (ILO)
    human rights *746
    right to food 719
    statistics 1259, 1262
    vulnerable groups *746
    women 1152
INTERNATIONAL LAW *1303–1329
    diplomatic relations *1312
    host country relations *1327–1329
    international economic law *1315–1321
    International Law Commission (ILC) *1303–1308
    international organizations and international law *1321–1327
    International State relations and international law *1308–1312
    legal aspects of international political relations *1303–1313
    rule of law at national and international levels *1314–1315
    treaties and agreements *1312–1313
    see also treaties and agreements
international legal questions *see* legal questions
International Maritime Organization (IMO)
    dangerous goods, transport of *961
    food and agriculture 1231
    human rights 728
    international State relations and international law *1310
    promotion of peace in Africa 103
    Somalia 286, 288, *290–291
    UN Convention on the Law of the Sea *1332, *1336, *1350, *1353–1357
International Monetary Fund (IMF)
    Bosnia and Herzegovina 403
    Côte d'Ivoire *175
    financial policy 932, *933, *936
    financing for development 947, *951, *953–954
    Guinea-Bissau *216, *219, *222, 224–225
    international trade, finance and transport *929, 930
    Sierra Leone 207
    statistics 1258–1259
    Sudan 239
    West Africa *167
International Narcotics Control Board (INCB) 1241–1242
INTERNATIONAL PEACE AND SECURITY *37–99
    conflict prevention *39–43
    general aspects of *573–575
    information and telecommunications in *609–610
    international terrorism *66–71
    maintenance of 37, *38–39

Office of the United Nations High Commissioner for Refugees *69
    peacemaking and peacebuilding *43–49
    promotion of *37–66
        Department of Peacekeeping Operations *38
    protection issues *50–63
    regional aspects of *575–576
    special political missions *63–66
    telecommunications in *609–610
    terrorism *66–71
    threats to *66–71
    World Food Programme *69
    see also peacebuilding; peacekeeping operations; peacekeeping operations; terrorism
International Research and Training Institute for the Advancement of Women (INSTRAW) *1158–1159
International State relations
    International Civil Aviation Organization *1310
    and international law *1308–1312
    International Maritime Organization *1310
    Organization of American States *1310
International Telecommunication Union (ITU)
    science and technology for development *816, *820–824, *826
    statistics 1263
international terrorism *see* terrorism
INTERNATIONAL TRADE *916–929
    commodities *925–929
    global trade activity 916–917
    International Monetary Fund *929, 930
    multilateral trading system *917–922
    trade policy *922–923
    trade promotion and facilitation 923–925
    World Trade Organization 924
    see also United Nations Conference on Trade and Development (UNCTAD); World Trade Organization (WTO)
INTERNATIONAL TRANSPORT *959–962
    dangerous goods, transport of *960–962
    maritime transport *959–960
    United Nations Conference on Trade and Development 959
INTERNATIONAL TRIBUNAL FOR THE FORMER YUGOSLAVIA (ICTY) *1279–1288, *1291, *1296–1298
    administrative and staff matters 1452, *1457
    Chambers *1280–1285
    financing *1286–1287
    Office of Prosecutor *1285
    Registry *1285–1286
INTERNATIONAL TRIBUNALS AND COURTS *1279–1302
    Chambers *1280–1285, *1288–1293, 1300–1302
    Democratic Republic of the Congo 1288, 1297, *1298
    financing *1286–1287, *1294–1296
    functioning of the Tribunals *1296–1298
    implementation of completion strategies *1296–1298
    International Criminal Court *1298–1302
    International Criminal Tribunal for Rwanda *1288–1296
    International Tribunal for the Former Yugoslavia *1279–1287
    see also International Criminal Court (ICC); International Criminal Tribunal for Rwanda (ICTR); International Tribunal for the Former Yugoslavia (ICTY)

International Year for People of African Descent *655
International Year of Languages *1113
   United Nations Educational, Scientific and Cultural
      Organization *1113
IRAN
   human rights *768–771
   International Atomic Energy Agency 394–396
   Office of the United Nations High Commissioner for
      Human Rights *769
   political and security questions 394–396
   terrorism 69–70
IRAQ
   Food and Agriculture Organization of the United
      Nations 366
   International Advisory and Monitoring Board *372–375
   Kuwait, political and security questions with 375–376
   Office of Internal Oversight Services 376
   Office of the United Nations High Commissioner
      for Refugees 363, 366
   political and security situation *362–375
   terrorism 69
   UN Assistance Mission for Iraq *362–372
   UN Compensation Commission and Fund 376
   United Nations Office on Drugs and Crime 366
   World Food Programme *364–365
   World Health Organization *365
islands *see* small island developing states
ISRAEL
   human rights, occupied territories *780–788
   International Court of Justice 782, *786, 787
   see also Middle East; Palestine
ITU *see* International Telecommunication Union

J

Joint Inspection Unit (JIU)
   administrative matters 1436
   children 1183
   environment, international conventions and mech-
      anisms *1022–1023
   food and agriculture 1231
   health 1217
   managerial reform and oversight *1424–1427
   Office of the High Commissioner for Human Rights
      629–630
   operational activities for development 844, *851–852,
      862
   population 1049, 1053
   staff matters 1466–1467
   staff matters, conditions of service 1454
   UN Environment Programme *1004–1006
   UN information systems 1440, *1441
   UN restructuring issues *1371
Joint United Nations Programme on HIV/AIDS (UNAIDS)
   *1216–1222
   children 1178–1179
   decolonization *585
   international drug control *1238–1239, 1253
   operational activities for development 854
   population 1049, 1051, *1054
   refugees and displaced persons 1205
   women 1128
justice, administration of *1472–1485

K

Kimberley Process *39–42
KOSOVO
   EULEX *412
   European Union *412
   International Court of Justice 410
   Organization for Security and Cooperation in Europe
      408–411
   political and security situation *408–412
   UNMIK *412–414
KUWAIT
   Office of Internal Oversight Services 376
   political and security questions, with Iraq 375–376
   Kuwaiti property and missing persons 375–376
   UN Compensation Commission and Fund 376

L

LANDLOCKED DEVELOPING COUNTRIES
   development policy *840–843
   official development assistance *840
LATIN AMERICA AND THE CARIBBEAN
   economic and social questions 984–989
      economic trends 984–985
   Food and Agriculture Organization of the United
      Nations 985
   see also Americas; Caribbean; Central America;
      Economic Commission for Latin America and
      the Caribbean; *specific country names*
LAW OF THE SEA *1330–1363
   Division for Ocean Affairs and the Law of the Sea 1363
   UN Convention on the Law of the Sea *1330–1363
      institutions created by the Convention *1344–1346
   see also landlocked developing countries; small island
      developing States
LDCs *see* Least Developed Countries
LEAST DEVELOPED COUNTRIES (LDCs) 832–836
   administrative and staff matters 1422
   children 1173
   commodities, international trade of *927
   coordination, monitoring and cooperation 1381
   economic and technical cooperation among develop-
      ing countries *875, *878, *880
   eradication of poverty *809–810, *812
   global trade activity 916
   human rights 631
   International Criminal Court *1299
   international economic law *1317
   landlocked developing countries *842–844
   legal questions *1317
   MDGs 18–34
   multilateral trading system *918–921
   official development assistance 832
   operational activities for development 869, 881
   peacekeeping operations *90
   population 1046, 1055
   promotion of peace in Africa *112
   public information *614
   refugees and displaced persons *1195
   right to food *720

science and technology for development *819, *822, *824–825

social policy and cultural issues *1061, *1063

UN budget *1389, *1399, *1404

UN Convention on the Law of the Sea *1335, *1343, *1347–1350, *1358, *1361

UN financing and programming *1412, 1418

UNDP operational activities 857

United Nations Conference on Trade and Development 832, *835

women *1116, *1118, *1121–1122

LEBANON

Middle East peacekeeping operations *476–488

see also Middle East

LEGAL QUESTIONS *1267–1363

diplomatic relations, international legal questions *1312

Division for Ocean Affairs and the Law of the Sea 1363

financing

International Criminal Tribunal for Rwanda *1294–1296

International Tribunal for the Former Yugoslavia *1286–1287

host country relations, international legal questions *1327–1329

International Court of Justice 1269–1278

International Criminal Court *1298–1302

Chambers 1300–1302

international economic law *1315–1321

International Law Commission *1303–1308

international legal questions *1303–1329

international organizations and international law *1321–1327

International State relations and international law *1308–1312

international tribunals and court *1279–1302

Chambers *1280–1285, *1288–1293, 1300–1302

functioning of the Tribunals *1296–1298

implementation of completion strategies *1296–1298

International Criminal Court *1298–1302

Office of the Prosecutor *1285, *1293

Registry *1285–1286, *1294

Law of the Sea *1330–1363

Division for Ocean Affairs and the Law of the Sea 1363

legal aspects of international political relations *1303–1313

Office of the Prosecutor

International Criminal Tribunal for Rwanda *1293

International Tribunal for the Former Yugoslavia *1285

Organization of American States 1302

Registry

International Criminal Tribunal for Rwanda *1294

International Tribunal for the Former Yugoslavia *1285–1286

rule of law at national and international levels *1314–1315

treaties and agreements, international legal questions *1312–1313

UN Convention on the Law of the Sea *1330–1363

Legal Subcommittee

peaceful uses of outer space *606–607

LIBERIA

Department of Peacekeeping Operations 192

Economic Community of West African States 193, *201

HIV/AIDS 199

human rights 754–755

political and security questions *191–206

United Nations Development Programme 193, 195

M

MACEDONIA *see* the former Yugoslav Republic of Macedonia

MADAGASCAR

political and security questions *310–311

malaria *1222–1226

management, UN *see* Institutional, Administrative and Budgetary Questions

maritime law *see* law of the sea

maritime transport

international *959–960

MAURITANIA

political and security situation 232

MAURITIUS

political and security questions, with United Kingdom and France 311

MDGs *see* Millennium Development Goals

Mediterranean region *see* Europe and the Mediterranean

MIDDLE EAST

diplomatic efforts, peace process *433–434

human rights *780–788

Israel, territories occupied by *780–788

Lebanon, peacekeeping operations *476–488

Occupied Palestinian Territory, peace process *434–458

Office of the United Nations High Commissioner for Human Rights *780

Palestine, political and security issues related to *458–476

assistance to Palestinians *462–466

UNRWA *466–476

peacekeeping operations *476–494

Lebanon *476–488

Syrian Arab Republic *488–494

political and security questions *433–494

diplomatic efforts, peace process *433–434

Lebanon, peacekeeping operations *476–488

Palestine, issues related to *458–476

peace process *433–458

peacekeeping operations *476–494

Syrian Arab Republic, peacekeeping operations *488–494

United Nations Disengagement Observer Force *476, 488

United Nations Truce Supervision Organization *476

UNRWA *466–476

see also Palestine; *specific country names*

MIDDLE EAST PEACE PROCESS *433–458

diplomatic efforts *433–434

Economic and Social Commission for Western Asia *452

Gaza, crisis in 434–439
International Committee of the Red Cross *440, *444, *452
International Court of Justice *447, 448, *458
Occupied Palestinian Territory *434–458
Office for the Coordination of Humanitarian Affairs *444, *447
Office of the United Nations High Commissioner for Human Rights *444, *447, *451
Palestinian Authority *435, *437–443, *447, *453–455, *460, *462–465
Special Committee on Israeli Practices 488
Special Committee to Investigate Israeli Practices Affecting Human Rights *447–452
United Nations Disengagement Observer Force 433
United Nations Interim Force in Lebanon 433
migrant workers
Convention on migrant workers *641–642
migrants
human rights, protection *668–672
Office of the United Nations High Commissioner for Human Rights 669
see also refugees and displaced persons
MILLENNIUM DEVELOPMENT GOALS (MDGs) 34
children 1176, 1183–1184
children, youth and ageing persons 1160
economic and technical cooperation among developing countries *874
energy and natural resources *999
Haiti *327
health, food and nutrition 1217, *1229
human rights 703
international economic relations 813
operational activities for development 856–858, 868
peaceful uses of outer space 603–604
persons with disabilities *1068
population 1049, 1055
regional cooperation 968
regional economic and social activities 973–974, 988
statistics 1262, 1264
women 1115, *1120, *1125
youth 1184
mines see anti-personnel mines
minorities
human rights, discrimination against *672–673
MINURCAT see United Nations Mission in the Central African Republic and Chad
MINURSO see United Nations Mission for the Referendum in Western Sahara
MINUSTAH see United Nations Stabilization Force in Haiti
monitoring
institutional, administrative and budgetary questions *1380–1383
MONTSERRAT *597
MONUC see United Nations Organization Mission in the Democratic Republic of the Congo
multilateral trading system
HIV/AIDS *920
LDCs *918–921
World Intellectual Property Organization *920–921
World Trade Organization *918

multilateralism
disarmament *523–527
munitions see disarmament; weapons
MYANMAR
HIV/AIDS *776
human rights *771–776
International Committee of the Red Cross *776
Office of the United Nations High Commissioner for Refugees 773

N

NATO see North Atlantic Treaty Organization
NATURAL RESOURCES
economic and social questions *998–1000
NEPAD see New Partnership for Africa's Development
NEPAL
human rights 777
United Nations Children's Fund 393
United Nations Development Programme 393
United Nations Mission in Nepal 66, 388–393
United Nations Population Fund 393
World Food Programme 393
New Partnership for Africa's Development (NEPAD)
coordination, monitoring and cooperation 1381
development policy and public administration *831
humanitarian and special economic assistance *899
promotion of peace in Africa 103, *112
regional economic and social activities 969, 973
social policy and cultural issues *1058, *1063, 1064
special economic assistance *900–901, *903
UN Environment Programme 1007
NGO see non-governmental organization
NIGERIA
Cameroon–Nigeria Mixed Commission 226–228
non-communicable diseases *1222
non-governmental organizations (NGOs)
Asia and the Pacific, regional economic and social activities 980
Chad and Central African Republic 158, 160
children 1175, 1179
cooperation, UN and other organizations *1386, 1387
disarmament *564
health, food and nutrition *1226
human rights *647, *666, *724, 731
humanitarian assistance *888, 889
legal questions 1274
population 1045
refugees and displaced persons *1196, 1213
resource mobilization, humanitarian assistance 889
Somalia 283
Sudan 238, 254, 259
Western Sahara *308
women *1116
non-proliferation issues *518–540
International Atomic Energy Agency 521, *522, *527–532
multilateralism in disarmament and non-proliferation *523–527
nuclear-weapon-free zones *533–540
radioactive waste *532–533
treaty *518–520
weapons of mass destruction *520–525, *527

Non-Proliferation of Nuclear Weapons (NPT), Treaty on the *518–520, *525–527
  and Comprehensive Nuclear-Test-Ban Treaty *514–516
  Democratic People's Republic of Korea *384–385
  disarmament 495, 503, *505–507, *509–511, 529, *531–532, *540
  energy and natural resources *995
  non-proliferation treaty *519–520
  political and security questions 14, 43
  UN role in disarmament *501, 502
Non-Self-Governing Territories (NSGTs)
  decolonization *576–596
  human rights 631
  support for democracies 573
  territories under review *599
  see also decolonization
NORTH AFRICA
  political and security questions *304–310
  Western Sahara *304–310
  see also specific country names
North Atlantic Treaty Organization 286, 332, 400, 1274
NPT *see* Non-Proliferation of Nuclear Weapons, Treaty on the
NSGTs *see* Non-Self-Governing Territories
nuclear and radiological terrorism 71
nuclear disarmament *502–518
  advisory opinion of International Court of Justice *516–517
  Comprehensive Nuclear-Test-Ban Treaty *512–516
  prohibition of use of nuclear weapons *517–518
  weapons of mass destruction *504, *506, *508
nuclear-weapon-free zones
  non-proliferation *533–540
  Organization of American States *537
  Treaty on the Non-Proliferation of Nuclear Weapons *534–538
  weapons of mass destruction *536, *538–539
nutrition *1235
  economic and social questions *1235
  Standing Committee on Nutrition *1235
  UN University (UNU) activities *1235
  see also food; humanitarian assistance

O

OAS *see* Organization of American States
OCCUPIED PALESTINIAN TERRITORY
  Middle East peacekeeping operations *434–458
  see also Israel, Middle East, Middle East peace process; Palestine
oceans and seas *see* law of the sea
OCHA *see* Office for the Coordination of Humanitarian Affairs
ODA *see* official development assistance
OECD *see* Organisation for Economic Co-operation and Development
office *see under main part of title*
Office for the Coordination of Humanitarian Affairs (OCHA) 882, *885
  Africa, human rights 752
  disaster response *912
  Middle East Peace Process *444, *447

Office of Internal Oversight Services (OIOS) 64
  administrative matters 1436
  conference management 1428–1429, 1431
  Côte d'Ivoire *188–189
  Democratic Republic of the Congo *135
  development policy and public administration *831
  Iraq–Kuwait 376
  managerial reform and oversight *1421–1424, *1426
  Office of the High Commissioner for Human Rights 629
  peacekeeping operations 76, 78, *84, 94
  promotion of international peace and security *63
  refugees and displaced persons *1198
  staff matters *1458, 1467, *1468
  Sudan *266
  UN financing and programming *1417, 1418
  UN premises and property *1447
  UN restructuring issues *1371
Office of the United Nations High Commissioner for Human Rights (OHCHR) 627–630
  administrative and staff matters 1423
  Africa 756
  Americas 758–763
  Asia *768, 777–778
  Burundi 751
  civil and political rights 690, 702
  Commission on the Status of Women *1155
  democracy 685
  Democratic People's Republic of Korea *765
  discrimination against minorities *672–674
  DRC 753
  economic, social and cultural rights 703, 727
  education *654
  environmental and scientific concerns 728
  Europe and the Mediterranean *780
  Haiti 326
  human rights defenders *668
  Iran *769
  Joint Inspection Unit 629–630
  Middle East *780
  Middle East Peace Process *444, *447, *451
  migrants 669
  Office of Internal Oversight Services 629
  promotion of human rights *624, 627–631, *642–643
  racism and racial discrimination 658, *660
  right to health 730
  rule of law, democracy and human rights *687, *689
  strengthening action to promote human rights *649–651
  territories occupied by Israel 781
  vulnerable groups 734–735, 748, 750
  women 1146
Office of the United Nations High Commissioner for Refugees (UNHCR) *1191–1207, *1210–1215
  administrative and staff matters *1468, *1470, 1473
  coordination of humanitarian assistance *883
  Côte d'Ivoire *176
  financial and administrative questions *1198–1202
  humanitarian activities 897
  humanitarian assistance *893
  Iraq 363, 366
  Myanmar 773

programme policy *1192–1198
threats to international peace and security *69
Western Sahara *305
official development assistance (ODA) 32–33
international finance 932, 940, 947, *952–953
landlocked developing countries *840
least developed countries 832
operational activities for development *847
small island developing states *840
special economic assistance *900
OHCHR see Office of the United Nations High Commissioner for Human Rights
ONUB see United Nations Operation in Burundi
OIOS see Office of Internal Oversight Services
Organisation for Economic Co-operation and Development (OECD) 32–33
operational activities for development *847, 863
statistics 1258–1259, 1263
Organization for Democracy and Economic Development-GUAM 422
Organization for Security and Cooperation in Europe (OSCE)
Abkhazia 417–418
Armenia and Azerbaijan 422
Georgia 415, 417–418
Kosovo 408–411
Mediterranean, strengthening of security and cooperation in *432
regional economic and social activities 984
Organization of American States (OAS) 17
Haiti 319, *322–323
Honduras *314–318
human rights *746
international State relations and international law *1310
legal questions 1302
nuclear-weapon-free zones *537
special economic assistance *905
UN Convention on the Law of the Sea *1361
vulnerable groups *746
organized crime, transnational *1091–1096
OSCE see Organization for Security and Cooperation in Europe
OUTER SPACE
implementation of UNISPACE III recommendations *602–603
Legal Subcommittee *606–607
Millennium Development Goals 603–604
peaceful uses of *599–607
Scientific and Technical Subcommittee 603–606

P

PAKISTAN 398–399
Benazir Bhutto assassination inquiry 398–399
political and security questions, with India 398–399
terrorism 70
PALESTINE
assistance to Palestinians *462–466
HIV/AIDS 463
International Court of Justice 463
Occupied Palestinian Territory, peace process *434–458
political and security situation *458–476

refugees, UNRWA *466–476
United Nations Children's Fund 463
United Nations Conference on Trade and Development 463, *464
United Nations Relief and Works Agency for Palestine Refugees in the Near East (UNRWA) *466–476
World Health Organization 463
see also Israel; Middle East
Palestinian Authority
human rights *689, 781, 787
Middle East Peace Process *435, *437–443, *447, *453–455, *460, *462–465
promotion of international peace and security 65
peace process see Middle East peace process
PEACEBUILDING 43–49
PEACEBUILDING COMMISSION *45–49
Peacebuilding Fund *49
PEACEKEEPING OPERATIONS *71–99
African Union 72, 77, 100
comprehensive review *78–79
Democratic Republic of the Congo 100
European Union 72, 80
financial and administrative aspects of *82–99
general aspects *74–78
HIV/AIDS 75, 98
International Civil Service Commission *87
Lebanon *476–488
Middle East *476–494
Office of Internal Oversight Services 76, 78, *84, 94
operations in 2009 *79–80
roster of 2009 operations 80–82
Syrian Arab Republic *488–494
United Nations Development Programme *49
women in 77
see also specific country names
persons with disabilities
Convention on Rights of Disabled Persons *642–643
HIV/AIDS *1069
Millennium Development Goals *1068
social policy and cultural issues *1067–1070
piracy 286–291, *289–291
PITCAIRN *597–598
POLITICAL AND SECURITY QUESTIONS *37–619
Africa *100–311
African Union-United Nations Hybrid Operation in Darfur *155, *235, 243, 246, *249–260, 262, *264, *266, *268
Americas *312–331
Asia and the Pacific *332–399
atomic radiation, effects of *607–609
decolonization *576–599
Decade for the Eradication of Colonialism *576–58
Puerto Rico *588
territories under review *588–599
democracies, support for *573–575
Democratic Republic of the Congo *116–120, 122–124, *126, 131, *132, *135, *163–165
disarmament *495–572
Europe and the Mediterranean *400–432
general aspects of international security *573–575
HIV/AIDS 5, 10, 13, 16, 26, 28
Indian Ocean *575–576

information in international security *609–619
international peace and security *37–99
　general aspects of *573–575
　information and telecommunications in *609–610
　regional aspects of *575–576
Middle East *433–494
outer space, peaceful uses of *599–607
　implementation of UNISPACE III recommendations
　　*602–603
　Legal Subcommittee *606–607
　Scientific and Technical Subcommittee 603–606
peacekeeping operations *71–99
political missions, special 63–66
promotion of peace and security
　Africa *103–116
　international *37–66
Puerto Rico, decolonization *588
regional aspects of international peace and security
　*575–576
support for democracies *573–575
telecommunications in international security *609–610
territories under review for decolonization *588–599
Treaty on the Non-Proliferation of Nuclear Weapons
　14, 43
UN public information *610–619
UNISPACE III recommendations, implementation of
　*602–603
see also Africa; Americas; Asia and the Pacific; Information; International peace and security; outer space
political missions, special 63–66
　political missions and offices, roster of 64–66
　see also specific mission names
pollution *see* environment
POPULATION *1045–1056
development, international migration and 1047–1048
follow-up to 1994 Conference on Population and
　Development 1045–1047
HIV/AIDS 1045–1047, 1049–1051, *1054
implementation of Programme of Action 1045–1047
international migration and development 1047–1048
Joint Inspection Unit 1049, 1053
Joint United Nations Programme on HIV/AIDS 1049,
　1051, *1054
Millennium Development Goals 1049, 1055
United Nations Children's Fund 1051, 1055
United Nations Development Programme 1048–1049,
　*1053–1055
United Nations Population Fund 1045, *1048–1054
see also United Nations Population Fund (UNFPA)
POVERTY
eradication of *808–813
　United Nations System Chief Executives Board for
　　Coordination *809
human rights, extreme poverty 717–718
programme and organizational questions
　Africa 974
　Asia and the Pacific 980
　Europe 984
programme planning and performance, UN *1417–1418
protection issues
　refugees and displaced persons 1202–1203

public administration
　Committee for Development Policy *828–829
　and development policy *828–831
public information *see* information
PUERTO RICO
　decolonization *588

R

racism and racial discrimination *657–665
Convention against racial discrimination 631–632
Office of the United Nations High Commissioner for
　Human Rights 658, *660
see also human rights
radiation
atomic, effects of *607–609
waste, non-proliferation of weapons *532–533
REFUGEES AND DISPLACED PERSONS *1191–1215
African Union *1207
assistance measures 1204–1206
Democratic Republic of the Congo *1204–1207, *1210, 1211
economic and social questions *1191–1215
European Union 1214–1215
HIV/AIDS *1196, 1200, 1205, *1207–1208, 1211
internally displaced persons 1211–1212
International Committee of the Red Cross *1195–1196
Joint United Nations Programme on HIV/AIDS 1205
Office of Internal Oversight Services *1198
Office of the United Nations High Commissioner for
　Refugees *1192–1202
　financial and administrative questions *1198–1202
　programme policy *1192–1198
protection issues 1202–1203
regional activities *1206–1215
United Nations Children's Fund *1196, 1206
United Nations Educational, Scientific and Cultural
　Organization 1203
World Food Programme *1196
World Health Organization 1205
see also internally displaced persons (IDPs); Office of
　the United Nations High Commissioner for Refugees
　(UNHCR)
regional centres for peace and disarmament
European Union *569
regional disarmament *564–572
Central Africa Standing Advisory Committee *567–568
regional centres for peace and disarmament *568–572
REGIONAL ECONOMIC AND SOCIAL ACTIVITIES
　*966–992
African Union *968–971, 973–974
Asia and the Pacific 974–980
Commonwealth of Independent States 984
cooperation, regional 966–967
Democratic Republic of the Congo 968
Economic and Social Commission for Asia and the
　Pacific 966–967
Economic and Social Commission for Western Asia
　966–967, 989–992
Economic Commission for Africa 966, *968–974
Economic Commission for Europe 966, *968–974
Economic Commission for Latin America and the
　Caribbean 966, 984–989
economic trends 968, 975, 981, 984–985, 989
Europe 980–984

European Union 967
HIV/AIDS 974
housing and land management 983–984
Latin America and the Caribbean 984–989
Millennium Development Goals 968, 973–974, 988
New Partnership for Africa's Development 969, 973
Organization for Security and Cooperation in Europe 984
programme and organizational questions 974, 980, 984
refugees and displaced persons *1206–1215
United Nations System Chief Executives Board for Coordination 967
Western Asia 989–992
see also specific regions and regional commissions
religious intolerance, human rights *673–680
research and training
  disarmament studies, research and training *563–564
  human resources development, UN research and training institutes *1109–1113
  International Research and Training Institute for the Advancement of Women (INSTRAW) *1158–1159
  UN research and training institutes *1109–1113
  women, International Research and Training Institute for the Advancement of Women (INSTRAW) *1158–1159
restructuring issues
  United Nations *1367–1373
rights *see* human rights
road safety *1229–1230
Roster of the United Nations 1489
rule of law
  human rights and *685–689
  at national and international levels *1314–1315
  Office of the United Nations High Commissioner for Human Rights *687, *689
RWANDA
  International Criminal Tribunal for Rwanda *1288–1296
    Chambers *1288–1293
    financing *1294–1296
    Office of Prosecutor *1293
    Registry *1294
  political and security questions *165–166
  see also International Criminal Tribunal for Rwanda (ICTR)

S

safety
  road safety *1229–1230
  UN staff, safety and security *1458–1463
SAINT HELENA *598
sanctions
  Afghanistan *353–362
  Côte d'Ivoire *184–188
  Democratic People's Republic of Korea 384, 387
  Djibouti and Eritrea *299–302
  Iran 395–396
  Liberia *199–204
  Sierra Leone 212–213
  Somalia 296–297
  strengthening the role of the United Nations *321–325
  Sudan *262–265
    extension of Panel of Experts *263–264
    report of Panel of Experts 264
    report of Sanctions Committee 265
  third States affected by 907

science and technology for development *813–827
  and disarmament *563
  human rights and 727–729
  International Telecommunication Union *816, *820–824, *826
  United Nations Conference on Trade and Development *816, *822
  World Health Organization *822, *824–825
  World Intellectual Property Organization *822
  World Meteorological Organization *822
  World Trade Organization *822
Scientific and Technical Subcommittee
  peaceful uses of outer space 603–606
SCN *see* United Nations System Standing Committee on Nutrition
SECRETARIAT, UN *see* United Nations
SECURITY COUNCIL
  institutional, administrative and budgetary questions 1379
self-determination
  human rights *680–684
SIERRA LEONE
  human rights 755–756
  International Monetary Fund 207
  political and security questions *206–215
  United Nations Development Programme 209, *211, 213
  World Health Organization 208
slavery and related issues
  human rights *731–733
  transatlantic slave trade 731–733
small arms
  disarmament *545–550
small island developing States
  development policy *837–840
  official development assistance *840
Social Forum *716–717
SOCIAL POLICY AND CULTURAL ISSUES *1057–1080
  Commission for Social Development 1063–1064
  cultural development *1070–1080
  New Partnership for Africa's Development *1058, *1063, 1064
  persons with disabilities *1067–1070
  social development *1057–1067
  see also crime prevention and criminal justice; human resources; persons with disabilities
social statistics 1261–1262
SOMALIA
  African Union *277, *279–281, 283–284, 286, *293
  Department of Peacekeeping Operations *274, 281, 284
  European Union 288
  human rights 756–757
  internally displaced persons 285, *291
  International Maritime Organization 286, 288, *290–291
  political and security questions *270–297
  terrorism 70
  United Nations Children's Fund 281
  United Nations Development Programme *274, 281
  World Food Programme 275, 283, 288

SOUTHERN AFRICA *see specific country names*
space *see* outer space
special economic assistance *899–907
    African economic recovery and development
        *899–904
    African Union *900
    Committee for Programme and Coordination *900
    International Atomic Energy Agency *905
    New Partnership for Africa's Development *900–901,
        *903
    official development assistance *900
    Organization of American States *905
SRI LANKA
human rights 777–778
staff of United Nations *1452–1485
    administration of justice *1472–1485
    conditions of service *1452–1458
        Joint Inspection Unit 1454
        United Nations System Chief Executives Board for
            Coordination 1454
    Joint Inspection Unit 1466–1467
    Office of Internal Oversight Services *1458, 1467, *1468
    safety and security of staff *1458–1463
        United Nations System Chief Executives Board for
            Coordination *1459
    travel-related matters 1472
    UN Joint Staff Pension Fund 1471–1472
    United Nations System Chief Executives Board for
        Coordination *1458, 1463, 1467
    see also institutional, administrative and budgetary
        questions
Statistical Commission 1257–1265
STATISTICS 1257–1265
    demographic and social statistics 1261–1262
    Economic and Social Commission for Asia and the
        Pacific 1263
    economic statistics 1258–1260
    Food and Agriculture Organization of the United
        Nations 1260
    International Labour Organization 1259, 1262
    International Monetary Fund 1258–1259
    International Telecommunication Union 1263
    Millennium Development Goals 1262, 1264
    Organisation for Economic Co-operation and Develop-
        ment 1258–1259, 1263
    other statistical activities 1263–1265
    Statistical Commission, work of 1257–1265
    United Nations Educational, Scientific and Cultural
        Organization 1261, 1263
    United Nations Human Settlements Programme
        (UN-Habitat) 1262
    World Health Organization 1261
Statute of the International Court of Justice 1492
structure of the United Nations 1510
SUDAN
    African Union 250–253, *255, 259, 261–262, 265, *268
    Department of Peacekeeping Operations 259, 265
    human rights 757–758
    internally displaced persons 240, 243, 245, *249, 250,
        *252–255, *257, 258
    International Criminal Court 233, *234, 253–254, 261–262
    International Monetary Fund 239

Office of Internal Oversight Services *266
political and security questions *232–268
United Nations Children's Fund 240, 258
United Nations Development Programme 239–240,
    243–244
sustainable development *799–808
    International Fund for Agricultural Development
        *808
    United Nations System Chief Executives Board for
        Coordination 801
SYRIAN ARAB REPUBLIC
    International Committee of the Red Cross *491
    peacekeeping operations *488–494
    United Nations Children's Fund *491
    United Nations Disengagement Observer Force
        *491–492
    United Nations Truce Supervision Organization *491

T

technical cooperation *see* development
technology *see* science and technology
telecommunications
    international security *609–610
terrorism *609–701
    Afghanistan *67
    Counter-Terrorism Committee 70
    Indonesia 69
    Iran 69–70
    Iraq 69
    measures to eliminate 70
    nuclear and radiological terrorism 71
    Pakistan 70
    Somalia 70
THE FORMER YUGOSLAV REPUBLIC OF MACEDONIA
    political and security questions *414
TIMOR-LESTE
    financing of UN operations *381–383
    political and security questions *376–383
        financing of UN operations *381–383
    UN Integrated Mission in Timor-Leste *377–381
    United Nations Development Programme 380
tobacco *1222
torture and cruel treatment
    Convention against torture *635–636
trade *see* international trade
training *see* research and training
transnational organized crime
    United Nations Office on Drugs and Crime 1092, *1096
transparency
    disarmament *555–559
    weapons of mass destruction *557
transportation
    road safety *1229–1230
    transport of dangerous goods *961–962
travel-related matters, UN staff 1472
TREATIES AND AGREEMENTS
    international legal questions *1312–1313
    non-proliferation of weapons *518–520
    see also specific name of treaty or agreement
Trust Fund to Assist States in Settlement of Disputes 1278
TURKS AND CAICOS ISLANDS *598–599

U

UGANDA
political and security questions *163–165
UN-Habitat *see* United Nations Human Settlements Programme
UNAIDS *see* Joint United Nations Programme on HIV/AIDS
UNAMA *see* United Nations Assistance Mission in Afghanistan
UNAMI *see* United Nations Assistance Mission for Iraq
UNAMID *see* African Union-United Nations Hybrid Operation in Darfur
UNCDF *see* United Nations Capital Development Fund
UNCTAD *see* United Nations Conference on Trade and Development
UNDOF *see* United Nations Disengagement Observer Force
UNDP *see* United Nations Development Programme
UNDP/UNFPA
Executive Board 854–856
UNEP *see* United Nations Environment Programme
UNESCO *see* United Nations Educational, Scientific and Cultural Organization
UNFICYP *see* United Nations Peacekeeping Force in Cyprus
UNFPA *see* United Nations Population Fund
UNHCR *see* Office of the United Nations High Commissioner for Refugees
UNICEF *see* United Nations Children's Fund
UNIDO *see* United Nations Industrial Development Organization
UNIFEM *see* United Nations Development Fund for Women
UNIFIL *see* United Nations Interim Force in Lebanon
UNIPSIL *see* United Nations Integrated Peacebuilding Office in Sierra Leone
UNISPACE III recommendations, implementation of *602–603
UNITED KINGDOM
and Mauritius 311
UNITED NATIONS
action to combat drug abuse *1251–1256
agendas of United Nations principal organs in 2009 1523
budget *see* institutional, administrative and budgetary questions
Charter of the United Nations and Statute of the International Court of Justice 1492
information centres and services 1534
intergovernmental organizations related to 1537
Office of Internal Oversight Services *1447
Population Fund Executive Board (UNDP/UNFPA) *see* United Nations Development Programme
premises and property *1442–1452
  Advisory Committee on Administrative and Budgetary Questions *1446, 1452
  Office of Internal Oversight Services *1447
public information, political and security questions *610–619
role in disarmament, Treaty on the Non-Proliferation of Nuclear Weapons *501, 502
Roster 1489

Statute of the International Court of Justice 1504
structure 1510
see also Economic and Social Council; General Assembly; Institutional, Administrative and Budgetary Questions; Office of Internal Oversight Services; Security Council; staff of United Nations; United Nations System Chief Executives Board for Coordination
United Nations Assistance Mission for Iraq (UNAMI) 64–65, 332, *362–372
administrative and staff matters 1452
United Nations Assistance Mission in Afghanistan (UNAMA) 64–65, *67
political and security questions 332, 334, *335, *339–342, 350–351
United Nations Capital Development Fund *880–881
United Nations Children's Fund (UNICEF) 1160, *1161, *1172–1184
administrative and staff matters 1472
Central Africa and Great Lakes region 153
Commonwealth of Independent States 1173
Democratic Republic of the Congo 131
Haiti 326
health 1217–1218
HIV/AIDS 1174, 1176, 1178–1179
human rights 735, *739
Iraq *365, 366, 369
Nepal 393
operational activities for development 854–855, 863–864
Palestine 463
population 1051, 1055
refugees and displaced persons *1196, 1206
Somalia 281
Sudan 240, 258
Syrian Arab Republic *491
United Nations Population Fund 11, *173, *721, 1175, 1179, 1181, 1183
vulnerable groups 735, *739
United Nations Compensation Commission and Fund Iraq–Kuwait 376
United Nations Conference on Trade and Development (UNCTAD) 813, *922
commodities, international trade of *926, *928
development policy and international economic cooperation 828
global trade activity *916–918
institutional and organizational questions 963–965
international economic relations *827
international finance *931–933, *936, 940, *958
international trade, finance and transport 959
least developed countries 832, *835
operational activities for development 854
Palestine 463, *464
science and technology for development *816, *822
UN budget *1389, *1404–1406
UN institutional matters 1380
World Trade Organization 963–965
United Nations Convention on the Law of the Sea *1330–1363
European Union 1345

International Maritime Organization *1332, *1336, *1350, *1353–1357
Organization of American States *1361
United Nations Educational, Scientific and Cultural Organization 1346
United Nations Environment Programme 1346
World Meteorological Organization *1340, *1360
United Nations Crime Congress, Twelfth (2010) *1080–1081
United Nations Development Fund for Women (UNIFEM) *1157–1158
United Nations Development Programme (UNDP) 854–867, 1043
  administrative and staff matters *1470, 1472
  Burundi *138–140
  Central African Republic 149, 152
  children 1173, 1181, 1183
  Côte d'Ivoire *176, *180–181, 184
  decolonization *579
  Democratic Republic of the Congo 125, 131
  development policy and international economic cooperation 828
  disaster reduction *909
  environment 1015, 1036
    and human settlements 1014
    international conventions and mechanisms *1024
  Guinea-Bissau *218, *221
  Haiti 326, *327
  health 1217–1219
  human rights 673
  Iraq 366, 369
  Liberia 193, 195
  Nepal 393
  operational activities 844–846, 854–872, *880, 881
  peacemaking and peacebuilding *49
  population 1048–1049, *1053–1055
  promotion of international peace and security 43
  Sierra Leone 209, *211, 213
  Somalia *274, 281
  Sudan 239–240, 243–244
  Timor-Leste 380
  UN Environment Programme 1008–1010
  West Africa 232
  women *1157, 1158
United Nations Disengagement Observer Force (UNDOF) 80
  Middle East *476, 488
  Middle East Peace Process 433
  Syrian Arab Republic *491–492
United Nations Educational, Scientific and Cultural Organization (UNESCO) 22–23, *1070
  administrative and staff matters *1468
  cultural development *1072, *1077
  environmental activities 1032
  human rights *724
  International Year of Languages *1113
  refugees and displaced persons 1203
  statistics 1261, 1263
  UN Convention on the Law of the Sea 1346
United Nations Environment Programme (UNEP) *1002–1015, 1043

African Union 1007
environment, international conventions and mechanisms *1018–1019, *1023–1024
environmental activities *1032–1037
human settlements 1039
Joint Inspection Unit *1004–1006
New Partnership for Africa's Development 1007
UN Convention on the Law of the Sea 1346
United Nations Development Programme 1008–1010
United Nations Human Settlements Programme (UN-Habitat) 1002
United Nations System Chief Executives Board for Coordination 1005, 1009
United Nations General Assembly *see* General Assembly
United Nations Human Settlements Programme (UN-Habitat) *1038–1044
  children 1183
  statistics 1262
  strengthening of *1038–1042
  UN Environment Programme 1002
United Nations Industrial Development Organization (UNIDO)
  environment and human settlements 1014
  operational activities for development 854
  UNDP cooperation agreement 861
United Nations information systems *1436–1442
  Joint Inspection Unit 1440, *1441
  United Nations System Chief Executives Board for Coordination 1440, *1441
United Nations Institute for Disarmament Research (UNIDIR) 502, 563
United Nations Institute for Training and Research (UNITAR) *1109–1110
United Nations Integrated Mission in Timor-Leste (UNMIT) 80, 82, *377–381
  financial and administrative aspects 83
  political and security questions 333, 376, *377, *379–381, *383
United Nations Integrated Office in Burundi (BINUB) 64, *66, *137–140, *142, *145
United Nations Integrated Peacebuilding Office in Sierra Leone (UNIPSIL) 48, 64, *66, *206–213
  human rights 755
United Nations Interim Administration Mission in Kosovo (UNMIK) 80–82, *412–414
  financial and administrative aspects 83, *88
  political and security questions *408–412, *414
United Nations Interim Force in Lebanon (UNIFIL) 80
  Middle East peace process 433
  political and security questions *476, 477, 479–482, *484–485
United Nations Joint Staff Pension Fund 1471–1472
United Nations machinery
  agendas of United Nations principal organs in 2009 1523
  disarmament *495–499
  human rights *623–630
  institutional, administrative and budgetary questions *1374–1381
  women *1151–1159
United Nations Mission for the Referendum in Western Sahara (MINURSO) *79, 81, 103

financial and administrative aspects 83, *88
political and security questions *304–305, *308, *310
United Nations Mission in Liberia (UNMIL) 78, *79, 81–82
financial and administrative aspects 83, *88
political and security questions *176, *188, *191–201, *203–204, *206
promotion of peace in Africa 111, *112
United Nations Mission in the Central African Republic and Chad (MINURCAT) *79, 82, 101
financial and administrative aspects 83
political and security questions 153, *157–161, 164, *269
United Nations Mission in the Sudan (UNMIS) 78, *79, 81
financial and administrative aspects 83, *88
human rights 758
political and security questions *232–234, *237–247, *249, 258
promotion of peace in Africa *105
United Nations Observer Mission in Georgia (UNOMIG) 80–81, *414–416, *419–421
Abkhazia 418, *419
financial and administrative aspects 83
United Nations Office for Partnerships 868–869
United Nations Office for Project Services (UNOPS) 869–873
operational activities for development 844, 855, 865–866
United Nations Office on Drugs and Crime (UNODC) 70, *1251–1253
Africa *116
Commission on Crime Prevention and Criminal Justice *1081–1084
crime prevention and criminal justice *1104, 1106, *1107
crime prevention programme *1089–1090
Guinea-Bissau *219, *222
health 1217, 1219, *1221
international drug control *1236–1238, 1242–1245, 1249, *1251–1256
Iraq 366
strategies for crime prevention *1097, *1099–1100, *1103
transnational organized crime 1092, *1096
West Africa 169
United Nations Operation in Burundi (ONUB) 145
United Nations Operation in Côte d'Ivoire (UNOCI) 80–81, 101
financial and administrative aspects 83, *88
political and security questions 170, *171, *173–177, *180–181, *183–186, *188–189, *191
United Nations Organization Mission in the Democratic Republic of the Congo (MONUC) 78, *79, 81–82
administrative and staff matters *1470
financial and administrative aspects *88, 100
human rights 752–753
political and security questions *117–126, *130, 131, *135, *137
United Nations Peacebuilding Support Office in Guinea-Bissau (UNOGBIS) 64–65, 102
political and security questions *221–222, 224–226
United Nations Peacebuilding Support Office in the Central African Republic (BONUCA) 64–65, *146–151
United Nations Peacekeeping Force in Cyprus (UNFICYP) 80
financial and administrative aspects 83

human rights 778
political and security questions *423, *425, *427, *429, *431
United Nations Population Fund (UNFPA) *1048–1055
administrative and staff matters 1472
Guidelines for the Alternative Care of Children *1161
health 1217–1219
Nepal 393
operational activities for development 844, 854–857, 863–866, 869–872, *880
population 1045
UNDP operational activities 859, 861
United Nations Children's Fund *1172, 1173, 1175, 1179, 1181, 1183
women 1130, *1133, *1157, 1158
United Nations Relief and Works Agency for Palestine Refugees in the Near East (UNRWA) *436, 439, 463, *466–476, 482
administrative and staff matters *1470
human rights *780, 781, 784
United Nations Research Institute for Social Development (UNRISD) 1064
United Nations research and training institutes *1109–1113
United Nations Security Council see Security Council
United Nations Stabilization Force in Haiti (MINUSTAH) 80–81, *318–322, *326–329
financial and administrative aspects 83, *88
human rights 761
United Nations Standing Committee on Nutrition (SCN) *1235
United Nations Statistical Commission see statistics
United Nations System Chief Executives Board for Coordination (CEB) 12, 16
coordination, monitoring and cooperation 1381
eradication of poverty *809
health 1217, *1226
international finance *945–947, *957
managerial reform and oversight *1425
operational activities for development *847, *851–854
regional economic and social activities 967
staff matters 1454, *1458, 1463, 1467
staff safety and security *1459
sustainable development 801
UN Environment Programme 1005, 1009
UN information systems 1440, *1441
UN institutional matters 1380
United Nations System Staff College *1112–1113
United Nations Truce Supervision Organization (UNTSO) 80
Middle East *476
Syrian Arab Republic *491
United Nations University (UNU) *1110–1111
United Nations Volunteers 873
UNITED STATES
and Cuba *330–331
UNITED STATES VIRGIN ISLANDS *599
University for Peace *1111–1112
UNMIK see United Nations Interim Administration Mission in Kosovo
UNMIL see United Nations Mission in Liberia
UNMIS see United Nations Mission in the Sudan

UNMIT *see* United Nations Integrated Mission in Timor-Leste

UNOCI *see* United Nations Operation in Côte d'Ivoire (UNOCI)

UNODC *see* United Nations Office on Drugs and Crime

UNOGBIS *see* United Nations Peacebuilding Support Office in Guinea-Bissau

UNOMIG *see* United Nations Observer Mission in Georgia

UNOPS *see* United Nations Office for Project Services

UNRWA *see* United Nations Relief and Works Agency for Palestine Refugees in the Near East (UNRWA)

UNTSO *see* United Nations Truce Supervision Organization

V

vulnerable groups
Democratic Republic of the Congo *739, *742
human rights *733–749
International Committee of the Red Cross *744
International Labour Organization *746
Office of the United Nations High Commissioner for Human Rights 734–735, 748, 750
Organization of American States *746
United Nations Children's Fund 735, *739

W

weapons *see* disarmament
weapons of mass destruction (WMDs) 13, 70
bacteriological (biological) and chemical weapons *542
chemical weapons *543
disarmament 496, 502, *543, *548
energy and natural resources 994
Europe *432
non-proliferation *520–525, *527
nuclear disarmament *504, *506, *508
nuclear-weapon-free zones *536, *538–539
small arms *548
transparency, conventional weapons *557
see also disarmament; terrorism
WEST AFRICA
African Union *167, 169–170, 232
Cameroon–Nigeria 226–228
Côte d'Ivoire *170–191
European Union 228
Guinea *228–231
Guinea-Bissau *215–226
International Court of Justice 226
International Monetary Fund *167
Liberia *191–206
Mauritania 232
political and security questions *166–232
regional issues *166–170
Sierra Leone *206–215
United Nations Development Programme 232
United Nations Office on Drugs and Crime 169
see also Cameroon; Côte d'Ivoire; Guinea-Bissau; Mauritania; Sierra Leone
West African Economic and Monetary Union, Benin and Senegal *see* Economic Community of West African States; *specific country names*

WESTERN ASIA
economic and social questions 989–992
economic trends 989
economic trends 989
World Trade Organization 991
see also Economic and Social Commission for Western Asia
WESTERN SAHARA
African Union *310
European Union *305
International Committee of the Red Cross *308
Office of the United Nations High Commissioner for Refugees *305
political and security questions *304–310
WFP *see* World Food Programme
White Helmets *890–891
WHO *see* World Health Organization; *see also* health; HIV/AIDS
WIPO *see* World Intellectual Property Organization
WMDs *see* weapons of mass destruction
WMO *see* World Meteorological Organization
WOMEN
Commission on the Status of Women *1154–1157
Convention on elimination of discrimination against women *635, *1151–1154
critical areas of concern *1119–1151
Democratic Republic of the Congo *1137
Department of Peacekeeping Operations 1130, *1137
economic and social questions *1114–1159
follow-up to Fourth World Conference on Women and Beijing+5 *1114–1151
HIV/AIDS 1114, *1116, *1121, *1124, *1126–1130, *1143, *1146–1148, *1150–1151, *1154, *1156–1157
International Labour Organization 1152
International Research and Training Institute for the Advancement of Women (INSTRAW) *1158–1159
Joint United Nations Programme on HIV/AIDS 1128
Millennium Development Goals 1115, *1120, *1125
Office of the United Nations High Commissioner for Human Rights 1146
peacekeeping 77
UN Development Fund for Women (UNIFEM) *1157–1158
UN machinery *1151–1159
United Nations Development Programme *1157, 1158
United Nations Population Fund 1130, *1133, *1157, 1158
World Conference on Women and Beijing+5, Fourth follow-up to *1114–1151
World Food Programme (WFP) 1230–1231
administrative and staff matters *1470
children 1173, 1183
Democratic People's Republic of Korea *765
health 1216–1217
human rights 764
Iraq *364–365
Nepal 393
refugees and displaced persons *1196
resource mobilization 889, *890
Somalia 275, 283, 288
threats to international peace and security *69
UN financing and programming *1416
see also food

WORLD HEALTH ORGANIZATION (WHO) 1216, *1223–1229
    children 1177
    Democratic People's Republic of Korea *766
    disarmament 528, *540
    energy and natural resources *999
    environmental and scientific concerns 729
    Haiti *327
    human rights 729
    humanitarian assistance *891
    international drug control *1239, 1242
    Iraq *365
    operational activities for development 854
    Palestine 463
    refugees and displaced persons 1205
    science and technology for development *822, *824–825
    Sierra Leone 208
    statistics 1261
    transport of dangerous goods *961–962
    Western Sahara *305
    women *1150
    see also HIV/AIDS
World Intellectual Property Organization (WIPO)
    environment, international conventions and mechanisms *1020
    multilateral trading system *920–921
    science and technology for development *822

World Meteorological Organization (WMO)
    science and technology for development *822
    UN Convention on the Law of the Sea *1340, *1360
World Trade Organization (WTO) 923
    Africa, regional economic and social activities 969
    commodities, international trade of *928
    global trade activity 916
    international finance *933, 940, *950, *952
    multilateral trading system *918
    promotion and facilitation of trade 924
    science and technology for development *822
    UN budget *1389, *1404–1406
    UN institutional matters 1380
    UNCTAD institutional and organizational questions 963–965
    Western Asia, regional economic and social activities 991
WTO *see* World Trade Organization

Y

YOUTH
    economic and social questions *1184–1188
    HIV/AIDS *1184–1185
    Millennium Development Goals 1184
    see also children; United Nations Children's Fund (UNICEF)

Index of resolutions and decisions

(For dates of sessions please refer to Appendix III.)

General Assembly

Sixty-third session

Resolution No.	Page
63/246 B	89
63/257 B	303
63/258 B	266
63/267	899
63/268	1391
63/269	1438
63/270	1442
63/271	1464
63/272	1425
63/273 A	247
63/273 B	247
63/274 A	161
63/274 B	161
63/275 A	293
63/275 B	294
63/276	1371
63/277	955
63/278	1037
63/279	905
63/280	79
63/281	1026
63/282	49
63/283	1393
63/284	1430
63/285	92
63/286	92
63/287	84
63/288	145
63/289	189
63/290	429
63/291	135
63/292	382
63/293	419
63/294	327
63/295	412
63/296	204
63/297	492
63/298	485
63/299	214
63/300	308
63/301	315
63/302	1375
63/303	948
63/304	112
63/305	956
63/306	1468
63/307	779
63/308	50
63/309	1373
63/310	106
63/311	1368

Decision No.	Page
63/405 B	1511
63/408 B	1511
63/414 B	1511
63/416	1512
63/417 A	1476
63/417 B	1476
63/418	1476
63/419	855
63/420	624, 1512
63/421	1522
63/422	1522
63/423	1522
63/424	963
63/425	1292
63/426	1284
63/503 B	1379
63/550 B	1110, 1379, 1412, 1423, 1456
63/550 C	76, 78, 83, 88, 98, 1379, 1422, 1458, 1463, 1467, 1471
63/553	1375
63/554	303
63/555	956
63/556	956
63/557	88
63/558	467
63/559	1379
63/560	1217
63/561	1292
63/562	1284
63/563	39
63/564	945
63/565 A	1374
63/565 B	1374
63/566	1427
63/567	381
63/568	1311
63/569	422
63/570	411, 1277
63/571	43

Sixty-fourth session

Resolution No.	Page
64/1	875
64/2	1411
64/3	1384
64/4	1075
64/5	1076
64/6	330
64/7	314
64/8	995
64/9	1298
64/10	785
64/11	342
64/12	574

Resolution No.	Page
64/13	1075
64/14	1074
64/15	732
64/16	459
64/17	460
64/18	461
64/19	440
64/20	446
64/21	489
64/22	558
64/23	575
64/24	534
64/25	609
64/26	537
64/27	511
64/28	560
64/29	510
64/30	548
64/31	519
64/32	500
64/33	562
64/34	523
64/35	518
64/36	553
64/37	504
64/38	522
64/39	536
64/40	558
64/41	564
64/42	565
64/43	566
64/44	539
64/45	533
64/46	542
64/47	505
64/48	544
64/49	562
64/50	546
64/51	549
64/52	535
64/53	507
64/54	556
64/55	516
64/56	554
64/57	514
64/58	568
64/59	517
64/60	571
64/61	567
64/62	569
64/63	570
64/64	498
64/65	497
64/66	531
64/67	552
64/68	431

Resolution No.	Page
64/69	513
64/70	541
64/71	1347
64/72	1331
64/73	1016
64/74	912
64/75	890
64/76	886
64/77	1459
64/78	1077
64/79	1223
64/80	1070
64/81	1072
64/82	654
64/83	1111
64/84	891
64/85	607
64/86	599
64/87	468
64/88	472
64/89	469
64/90	475
64/91	451
64/92	457
64/93	444
64/94	449
64/95	490
64/96 A	610
64/96 B	610
64/97	586
64/98	583
64/99	581
64/100	587
64/101	307
64/102	589
64/103	590
64/104 A	592
64/104 B	592
64/105	585
64/106	577
64/107	295
64/108	1227
64/109	40
64/110	95
64/111	1315
64/112	1319
64/113	1326
64/114	1304
64/115	1322
64/116	1314
64/117	1312
64/118	1309
64/119	1476
64/120	1328
64/121	1385
64/122	1385
64/123	1385

General Assembly

Sixty-fourth session (cont.)

Resolution No.	Page
64/124	1386
64/125	464
64/126	1379
64/127	1193
64/128	1198
64/129	1207
64/130	1185
64/131	1068
64/132	1189
64/133	1066
64/134	1187
64/135	1058
64/136	1065
64/137	1131
64/138	1153
64/139	1134
64/140	1125
64/141	1116
64/142	1161
64/143	623
64/144	624
64/145	1147
64/146	637
64/147	663
64/148	660
64/149	680
64/150	681
64/151	683
64/152	633
64/153	693
64/154	642
64/155	687
64/156	674
64/157	708
64/158	648
64/159	720
64/160	711
64/161	651
64/162	743
64/163	666
64/164	678
64/165	650
64/166	670
64/167	643
64/168	698
64/169	655
64/170	714
64/171	647
64/172	704
64/173	646
64/174	724
64/175	766
64/176	769
64/177	1100
64/178	1093
64/179	1084
64/180	1080
64/181	1088
64/182	1237
64/183	1383
64/184	1375

Resolution No.	Page
64/185	455
64/186	818
64/187	818
64/188	918
64/189	921
64/190	933
64/191	936
64/192	926
64/193	942
64/194	945
64/195	1011
64/196	1038
64/197	807
64/198	999
64/199	838
64/200	909
64/201	1025
64/202	1023
64/203	1019
64/204	1003
64/205	1028
64/206	996
64/207	1040
64/208	795
64/209	794
64/210	793
64/211	825
64/212	816
64/213	835
64/214	841
64/215	811
64/216	809
64/217	1120
64/218	1107
64/219	1054
64/220	852
64/221	874
64/222	877
64/223	796
64/224	1232
64/225	1110
64/226	166
64/227	1415
64/228	1447
64/229	1417
64/230	1432
64/231	1455
64/232	1424
64/233	1474
64/234	420
64/235	66
64/236	802
64/237	1097
64/238	774
64/239	1294
64/240	1286
64/241	1457
64/242 A	1389
64/242 B	1389
64/243	1395
64/244 A	1403
64/244 B	1403
64/244 C	1403
64/245	1406

Resolution No.	Page
64/246	1409
64/247	1410
64/248	1412
64/249	90

Decision No.	Page
64/401	1522
64/402	1514
64/403	1516
64/404	1511
64/405	1512
64/406	1513
64/407	1511
64/408	1511
64/409	1511
64/410	1512
64/411	1511
64/412	1512
64/413	1513
64/414	1514
64/415	1293
64/416	1285
64/501	1375, 1427
64/502	1375
64/503	1379
64/504	3
64/505	1288
64/506	1279
64/507	788
64/508	1269
64/509	1379
64/510	1379
64/511	945
64/512	559
64/513	42
64/514	563
64/515	497
64/516	523
64/517	1379
64/518	1417
64/519	79
64/520	610, 1511
64/521	589
64/522	1379
64/523	1417
64/524	1379
64/525	1379
64/526	1417
64/527	1474
64/528	1386
64/529	1064
64/530	1116
64/531	1152, 1158, 1159
64/532	735, 1146
64/533	747
64/534	657
64/535	658
64/536	628, 636, 645, 647, 669, 686, 691, 693, 698, 713, 714, 717, 724, 727, 729
64/537	655
64/538	1379
64/539	1417

Decision No.	Page
64/540	792, 916, 929
64/541	793
64/542	831
64/543	1379
64/544	1374
64/545	1417
64/546	1466
64/547	868
64/548 A	1379, 1395, 1422, 1423, 1466, 1467, 1468, 1473
64/549	39, 91, 137, 145, 163, 191, 206, 249, 268, 304, 310, 312, 329, 376, 381, 383, 411, 414, 421, 422, 425, 431, 443, 476, 496, 588, 609, 624, 805, 901, 908, 1072, 1076, 1158, 1217, 1229, 1287, 1296, 1311, 1372, 1374, 1379, 1380, 1383, 1388, 1391, 1405, 1414, 1416, 1417, 1424, 1427, 1435, 1456, 1463, 1476

Tenth emergency special session

Resolution No.	Page
ES-10/18	435

Decision No.	Page
ES-10/101 H	1522
ES-10/202	435

Security Council

Resolution No.	Page
1860(2009)	434
1861(2009)	154
1862(2009)	298
1863(2009)	271
1864(2009)	388
1865(2009)	171
1866(2009)	416
1867(2009)	377
1868(2009)	335
1869(2009)	401
1870(2009)	234
1871(2009)	305
1872(2009)	277
1873(2009)	425
1874(2009)	384
1875(2009)	491
1876(2009)	219
1877(2009)	1282
1878(2009)	1291
1879(2009)	391
1880(2009)	177
1881(2009)	255
1882(2009)	739
1883(2009)	367

Security Council *(cont.)*

Resolution No.	Page
1884(2009)	483
1885(2009)	197
1886(2009)	210
1887(2009)	525
1888(2009)	1137
1889(2009)	1141
1890(2009)	352
1891(2009)	263
1892(2009)	322
1893(2009)	186
1894(2009)	60
1895(2009)	405
1896(2009)	132
1897(2009)	289
1898(2009)	427
1899(2009)	492
1900(2009)	1284
1901(2009)	1293
1902(2009)	140
1903(2009)	201
1904(2009)	355
1905(2009)	372
1906(2009)	126
1907(2009)	299

Economic and Social Council

Organizational session, 2009

Decision No.	Page
2009/201 A	1517
2009/201 B	1513
2009/202	940, 1380
2009/203	1380
2009/204	1380
2009/205	1380
2009/206	844, 1380
2009/207	882, 1380
2009/208	966, 1226, 1380
2009/209	882
2009/210	1143, 1380
2009/211	326, 904

Resumed organizational session, 2009

Decision No.	Page
2009/201 C	1511, 1512, 1513, 1516, 1517, 1518
2009/212	1027, 1380

Substantive session, 2009

Resolution No.	Page
2009/1	847
2009/2	1054
2009/3	883
2009/4	904
2009/5	1062
2009/6	1220
2009/7	822
2009/8	814
2009/9	1441
2009/10	1112
2009/11	971
2009/12	1144
2009/13	1159
2009/14	474
2009/15	1155
2009/16	1157
2009/17	837
2009/18	830
2009/19	960
2009/20	901
2009/21	1100
2009/22	1101
2009/23	1251
2009/24	1095
2009/25	1090
2009/26	1104
2009/27	1109
2009/28	805
2009/29	1382
2009/30	941
2009/31	833
2009/32	904
2009/33	579
2009/34	453
2009/35	829

Decision No.	Page
2009/201 D	1511, 1516, 1517, 1518
2009/213	1380
2009/214	847
2009/215	852, 853, 855, 1049, 1173, 1230
2009/216	876
2009/217	1381, 1418
2009/218	1380
2009/219	813
2009/220	821
2009/221	1387
2009/222	1387
2009/223	1387
2009/224	1387
2009/225	1387
2009/226	1387
2009/227	1387
2009/228	1387
2009/229	1387
2009/230	1387
2009/231	980
2009/232	1155
2009/233	1116
2009/234	1116
2009/235	801
2009/236	801
2009/237	1258
2009/238	1040
2009/239	1047
2009/240	1027
2009/241	1027
2009/242	1027
2009/243	1001, 1003
2009/244	1064

Decision No.	Page
2009/245	1064
2009/246	1082
2009/247	1088
2009/248	1253
2009/249	1242
2009/250	1241
2009/251	1082, 1253, 1408
2009/252	1198, 1512
2009/253	749, 1408
2009/254	749, 1408
2009/255	749
2009/256	633, 702, 749, 1159, 1185, 1196, 1237
2009/257	805, 822
2009/258	957, 958
2009/259	941, 1382
2009/260	1467
2009/261	463
2009/262	967
2009/263	453
2009/264	811, 1005
2009/265	959
2009/266	1110

Resumed substantive session, 2009

Decision No.	Page
2009/201 E	1519
2009/201 F	47
2009/267	326, 904
2009/268	1028
2009/269	1001

Index of Security Council presidential statements

Number	Subject	Date	Page
S/PRST/2009/1	Protection of civilians in armed conflict	14 January	51, 59
S/PRST/2009/2	The situation in Guinea-Bissau	3 March	216
S/PRST/2009/3	Peace and security in Africa	18 March	39, 105, 106
S/PRST/2009/4	The question concerning Haiti	6 April	320
S/PRST/2009/5	The situation in the Central African Republic	7 April	146, 148, 151
S/PRST/2009/6	The situation in Guinea-Bissau	9 April	217
S/PRST/2009/7	Non-proliferation/Democratic People's Republic of Korea	13 April	384, 529
S/PRST/2009/8	Maintenance of international peace and security: mediation and settlement of disputes	21 April	38
S/PRST/2009/9	Children and armed conflict	29 April	131, 144, 153, 737
S/PRST/2009/10	The situation in Cyprus	30 April	423
S/PRST/2009/11	Peace and security in Africa	5 May	104, 167
S/PRST/2009/12	Letter dated 22 November 2006 from the Secretary-General addressed to the President of the Security Council	5 May	390
S/PRST/2009/13	The situation in Chad, the Central African Republic and the subregion	8 May	269
S/PRST/2009/14	The situation in the Middle East, including the Palestinian question	11 May	437
S/PRST/2009/15	The situation in Somalia	15 May	277
S/PRST/2009/16	The situation in Côte d'Ivoire	29 May	175
S/PRST/2009/17	The situation concerning Iraq	18 June	365
S/PRST/2009/18	The situation in the Middle East	23 June	492
S/PRST/2009/19	The situation in Somalia	9 July	279
S/PRST/2009/20	Peace consolidation in West Africa	10 July	167
S/PRST/2009/21	The situation in Afghanistan	15 July	340
S/PRST/2009/22	Threats to international peace and security caused by terrorist acts	17 July	68
S/PRST/2009/23	Post-conflict peacebuilding	22 July	44
S/PRST/2009/24	United Nations peacekeeping operations	5 August	73
S/PRST/2009/25	The situation in Côte d'Ivoire	29 September	181
S/PRST/2009/26	Peace and security in Africa	26 October	39, 109
S/PRST/2009/27	Peace consolidation in West Africa	28 October	229
S/PRST/2009/28	The situation in Afghanistan	29 October	67, 342, 1459
S/PRST/2009/29	The situation in Guinea-Bissau	5 November	222
S/PRST/2009/30	The situation concerning Iraq	16 November	68, 370
S/PRST/2009/31	The situation in Somalia	3 December	69, 284
S/PRST/2009/32	Peace and security in Africa	8 December	115, 1244
S/PRST/2009/33	The situation in Côte d'Ivoire	8 December	182
S/PRST/2009/34	The situation in the Middle East	16 December	492
S/PRST/2009/35	The situation in the Central African Republic	21 December	150

Recent volumes of the *Yearbook of the United Nations* may be obtained through bookstores worldwide, as well as ordered from:

United Nations Publications
300 East 42nd Street
9th Floor
New York, New York 10017
United States of America

e-mail: **publications@un.org**
website: **un.org/publications**

All volumes of the *Yearbook of the United Nations* from the 1946–47 edition (Vol. 1) to the 2008 edition (Vol. 62) can be accessed in full online on the *Yearbook* website: **unyearbook.un.org**.